THE NEW INTERNATIONAL
WEBSTER'S
COMPREHENSIVE
DICTIONARY
OF THE ENGLISH LANGUAGE

DELUXE ENCYCLOPEDIC EDITION

TRIDENT PRESS INTERNATIONAL
1996 EDITION

THE NEW
INTERNATIONAL
WEBSTER'S COMPREHENSIVE DICTIONARY
OF THE ENGLISH LANGUAGE
Deluxe Encyclopedic Edition

1996 Edition published by Trident Press International, and distributed exclusively by Trident Promotional Corporation, 801 12th Avenue South, Suite 302, Naples, Florida 33940.

The New International Webster's Comprehensive Dictionary of the English Language
is also published as the
Webster Comprehensive International Dictionary of the English Language
which is also published as
Funk & Wagnalls New International Dictionary of the English Language
and
Webster Comprehensive Dictionary
and was previously published as
Funk & Wagnalls New Comprehensive International Dictionary of the English Language

ISBN 1888777001 DELUXE
ISBN 1888777028 GILDED
ISBN 1888777052 STANDARD
R-7

TABLE OF CONTENTS

Editorial Advisory Board	ii
Editors and Consultants	iii
Introduction—Definition and Semantic Change	iv
Usage Levels and Labels	vi
Synonyms and Antonyms	vii
The Pronunciations—The Etymologies	viii
Perspective on the English Language	ix
Canadian English	xii
Australian English	xiv
Explanatory Notes	xvi
Table of English Spellings	
—Spelling: Plurals and Participles	xix
Pronunciation Key	
—Abbreviations Used in This Work	xx
Dictionary of the English Language	1
Encyclopedic Supplements	1467

Abbreviations	1469	Glossary of Biological Terms	1703
Gazetteer	1488	Glossary of Physics Terms	1708
Grammar and Usage Handbook	1515	African American History	1713
The Library Research Paper	1529	African American Biographies	1725
Greek and Latin Elements in English	1542	Chemical Elements	1731
Foreign Words and Phrases	1557	Periodic Table of Elements	1734
Given Names	1573	Metrics Glossary	
Business Law	1585	Units of Measurement—Conversion	
Business Math	1594	Factors	1738
Business Letter Writing	1617	Tables of Weights and Measures	1743
Wills and Estate Planning	1650	Special Signs and Symbols	1746
Where To Write for Vital Records	1656	Medical Glossary	1750
Perpetual Calendar	1670	Generic Drugs	1785
Glossary of Computer Terms	1673	Biographies	1794
Word Processing Glossary	1678	Quotations Dictionary	1846
Spanish Glossary	1684	Spelling Dictionary	1896
German Glossary	1694		

Editorial Advisory Board

Introduction

The New International Webster's Comprehensive Dictionary is the latest in a long and distinguished series. It is backed by three quarters of a century of experience in dictionary-making and, like its predecessors, is designed to serve the practical and professional needs of all who speak or use the English language. No resource of lexicographical skill has been spared to fulfill this purpose.

Throughout their work, the editors, with the valued cooperation of many of the nation's eminent leaders in education, industry, the arts, sciences, and professions, have been guided by the following objectives:

To PRESENT the fundamental facts and characteristics of the language accurately, fully, and interestingly. The definitions, and the wealth of additional material here presented, are the result of years of scholarly research into the many facets of word–meaning and usage, combined with an editorial awareness of the wide–ranging developments of our expanding world. Details of syllabication, spelling, pronunciation, morphological forms, and grammatical usage have been included without stint. Etymologies, or short word–histories, are provided for the interesting insight they give into the richness and versatility of the English vocabulary. Particular attention is given to the word builders — the indispensable prefixes, suffixes, and combining forms in which English is so rich and which are constantly at work supplying new words to the language. An innovation in dictionary practice — the inclusion of hundreds of homophones and collateral adjectives under their appropriate entries — has been effected to highlight two of the more interesting and valuable, but seldom considered, features of the language.

To PRESENT adequately the significant contributions to English made in the United States, with requisite definitions, usage notes, and discriminative comment. Similar treatment is accorded to such areas of speech as slang, dialects, colloquialisms, and various forms of English as modified or influenced by Scottish, Irish, Canadian, Australian, and other sources — all of these being properly labeled for ready identification.

To SECURE the widest possible coverage of both the established word stock of English and of the rapidly expanding vocabularies of the arts, sciences, trades, and professions. In the first group, selection has depended upon the overriding factors of usage, word–frequency counts, and sound historical judgment, reinforced by the consensus of the many authorities consulted in the course of preparation. In the second, choice of entries has been determined by a conscientious and extensive review of the appropriate sources in every technical field.

These, then, have been the major, but by no means the only, objectives of the editors and their many specialist consultants. A fuller discussion of the what, how, why, and wherefore of the contents of this book is given in the following pages of the Introduction and in the Explanatory Notes at page xvi.

Definition & Semantic Change

DEFINITIONS in this dictionary are adapted to the nature of the word. Any effort to tailor all words to fit a rigid pattern of definition would result in distortion rather than clarification of meaning. Instead of following a standard formula for defining, the editors have constantly kept in mind the need to study the meanings of words in phrases, compounds, and sentences and the processes of meaning–change which words have undergone and are still undergoing. This semantic approach enables the definer to stress variety rather than uniformity. It leads to a frank acceptance of the policy of different techniques of defining for different types of words. Our basic aim has been to formulate a definition that can substitute for the word itself in the context in which the user reads or hears it. The context, too, is often shown, in the form of illustrative phrases and sentences following many of the definitions. Pictures are used at points where a visual aid tells a fuller story about an object or process than words can.

Either the most relevant or the most general meaning is given first, depending on the sequence which will best convey to the user the interrelations between the various meanings of the entry. Historical order is not usually followed, for it is of more practical value to the user to start with the word as it is today. Where the current sense of a word is more meaningful in the light of its history, however, the original sense is given first. (Note, for example, the flow of semantic development in the entry **scapegoat** in the vocabulary section.)

A different approach in defining is needed for words that are far removed from concrete, picturable things, and that deal with concepts or abstract ideas of a complex nature. Terms dealing with theology, politics, economics, psychology, and sociology are often packed with different meanings for different people. It is desirable to give space and time coordinates, so that the meaning of the word at different times and places is thrown into strong relief; its various interpretations and applications are then more readily evident if the coverage is detailed and complete. Every user will thus find the particular reference he is looking for. For examples of the application of this pattern of defining, see the entries **dean** and **fusion**.

The user will often find in this, as in most dictionaries, definitions or parts of definitions that are introduced by such qualifying words as "specifically," "figuratively," "loosely," and the like. (See **disinterested, gale, seasoning.**) He will also find following others such limiting or warning signs after a colon as "in derogatory use," "a term of contempt," "a genteelism," or "used ironically." (See **smart** or **canicular.**) These added qualifying notes indicate that the word or phrase in question has acquired certain overtones of meaning that are conveyed either by the intonation of the voice, or by the habitual association of the word with a certain kind of situation. Its literal or primary meaning is thus specialized, bettered, worsened, or figuratively extended, as the case may be.

Specialization and Generalization   Many words that now have very general meanings started life as the names of specific things. At one time the nineteen animals chiefly hunted

as game were each blessed with an individual term for the tail, but, as the general word *tail* came into vogue, most of these special names disappeared. The *brush* of the fox, however, still survives.

Often the processes of specialization and generalization of meaning work like a shuttle service. A word will shift from a specific to a general sense and then back again in the course of centuries of use. The word *gear,* for example, in early Middle English meant habits or manners. By 1500 it acquired a more generalized sense: property or equipment, comprising clothing, arms, armor, harness, or any tool or apparatus — a fairly comprehensive coverage. Then, with the increasing use of machinery in the Renaissance period, *gear* came to mean "an arrangement of fixed and moving parts in a machine for any special purpose." Finally, in modern mechanics, *gear* is now further specialized to mean "a wheel having teeth that fit into another wheel of the same kind, usually of a different size, to make the second wheel turn at a different speed from the first."

Radiation   One of the most interesting ways in which words extend meaning is by radiation. In this case the word does not change its basic meaning, but it radiates out from this central core of meaning a variety of extended senses. Take the word *action,* for example. Its primary meaning is "doing." In an extended sense it may mean (1) an acting; a state of activity (*thought* vs. *action*), (2) the natural or usual motion of an organ (the *action* of the heart), (3) the movements of a mechanism (the valve *action* in an engine), (4) a thing done; a deed (the *actions* of a fool), (5) the sequence of events in a play, (6) a military or naval battle, (7) a legal proceeding (a court *action*), (8) attitude or position expressing some kind of emotion (the *action* of a painting). In all of these senses of *action,* the primary notion of "doing" is the underlying factor. According to dictionary convention, the meanings are given in sequence, but they may be envisaged as radiating from the central sense.

Transference   This is another way in which words change meaning or enlarge in scope. It applies particularly to words involving feeling attitudes or value judgments. A kind of projection occurs whereby an emotion in the speaker is transferred to the objects or persons represented. If a poet speaks of "the cruel, crawling foam," a moment's reflection will tell us that the foam is not cruel, nor does it crawl. Rather, the speaker has projected his own very human feeling as to the cruelty of the sea, and imagines that the movement of the foam is an encroaching one. The attributing of human emotions and motivation to inanimate objects is an example of a semantic process whereby a word may be greatly extended in use.

Melioration and Deterioration   Here are two additional processes by which words reflect attitudes either complimentary or contemptuous. For example, the social standing of a word seems to depend very closely on the status of the class, group, or profession which it describes. Since the rise of the city-state in ancient Greece and Rome, and the predominance of urban culture as the supposed center of civilization, words that have to do with the city usually have a favorable aura; thus the word *urbane* — a variant of *urban* — has to do not merely with a person who lives in a city, but one who supposedly has polish, manners, tact, and a pleasing manner. This process of elevation in the status of a word is called melioration.

In contrast, words associated with farming and the farmer have shown a tendency to come down in the world. Deterioration of meaning has set in again and again. To be sure, in any agrarian society where farming is the basic occupation, words associated with the lord of the manor, or even

with a country squire who has sizable land holdings, usually give evidence of the high esteem with which landowners are held in the community. Serfs who worked on a villa or manorial estate in the late Roman Imperial period, or in the early Middle Ages, were described by the word *villanus* meaning "one attached to the villa or manor." Such a person was considered part of the property of the lord, and went with the villa when it was sold. When these "villeins," as they were called in early medieval France, went to visit in a nearby city, they were at once recognized as coming from the country. They often got into rows and quarrels, and were considered to have rough and uncouth manners. The name by which they were known was "villain" in Norman French, and the word passed into English, where it later acquired something close to its modern sense of a rascally person of evil intentions. Finally, the word took on the meaning of arch scoundrel, wicked opponent of the hero.

Genteelisms   A genteelism constitutes a special case of deterioration. The word itself is a case in point, for genteelism originally meant the possession of qualities expected in well-bred and well-mannered persons, and was thus synonymous with gentility. But it went downhill as changing economic conditions made it increasingly difficult for many people in this group to maintain their standards of living. The novelists, noting the prevalence of "shabby genteel" characters in run-down urban areas and suburbs, associated them with an unsuccessful effort to maintain status, so that the word *genteelism* itself acquired rather a contemptuous or ironic flavor, as have *genteel* and *gentility.* (See these entries in the vocabulary section.)

Adulteration   Adulteration of meaning occurs when a word is corrupted in sense by adroit manipulation of the context in which it appears, so that by association it takes on a flavor and feeling which subtly and gradually shift it from its primary sense. It can then be used as a clever weapon in propaganda in whatever direction the manipulator wants it to go. This fate has overtaken the word *semantics* itself. It is necessarily concerned with the processes of meaning shift, and the transition to a loose sense of "verbal shiftiness" or "verbal trickery" is one that is easily made. This process very nearly negates the proper meaning of the word and makes suspect the integrity and rigor of semantic analysis.

Euphemisms   Polite substitutes for words that have an unpleasant or somehow embarrassing connotation are called euphemisms. Euphemistic replacement is, by its nature, a continual process, for the euphemism loses its power to conceal once it becomes too closely connected with the thing it represents. Thus, each age has its own euphemisms. The Victorian era is considered to have seen the height of verbal prudishness, and today we smile at conventions which made shocking such words as *leg* and *shirt* when used in the presence of ladies. With the reaction against Victorianism and the revolt against convention that marked the Jazz Age, blunt speaking became the fashion and the old euphemisms were rapidly discarded. Today, one finds in wide use words which would have been considered gross or obscene fifty years ago. The modern tendency is indeed toward the use of straightforward language, but the essence of the euphemistic process is still preserved in such commonly encountered substitutions as *rest-room, criminal assault,* and *social disease.*

Hyperbole   The tendency to exaggeration in speech and writing has remained a constant throughout most periods of the language. Particularly has this been true of the United States, beginning with the time of the tall tale of the frontier. This tendency flourished richly in the field of slang, but it

was very far from being confined to that area. Some once strong adjectives have, in informal speech, lost most of their original potency (see the definitions labeled *Colloq.* under **awful** and **terrible**), and many adjectives of size, such as *colossal, gigantic,* and *mammoth,* have been considerably reduced in stature. The constant caution in the use of superlatives finally had its effect upon many of these terms, and today the understatement is esteemed in principle if not always in practice by American speakers and writers.

Figurative extension   The use of a word in a figurative sense is perhaps the commonest way of extending meaning. When in the mid–thirties the study of allergies came into fashion in medicine, the adjective *allergic,* with a precise technical meaning, soon came into use in the sense of "adversely sensitive to," but it was picked up by around 1940 as at first a slang translation for "antipathetic." It became fashionable to say, "I'm allergic to crooners — or boring lectures" or any other pet aversion that the speaker harbored. This figurative sense is now accepted as having good colloquial standing.

This process has left many deposits in the language. The *flag* symbolizes the power of a country, just as the Roman *eagles,* the standard of the Roman legions, came to stand for the legions themselves, and by further extension, for the power of the Roman Empire. This type of figure of speech is called a metonomy, or sign for the thing signified. Next to metaphor, a comparison made without the use of the word *like* or *as,* it is one of the commonest devices for giving a figurative meaning to an individual word.

Usage Levels and Labels

IN THIS DICTIONARY the most important label is one that is not here. As the best style is the absence of it, so the "best" words in our language are those needing no label that make up general–purpose English. A writer who is a general practitioner will usually stick to this level of standard English.

Colloquialisms   The words or phrases labeled *Colloq.* in this dictionary belong to the informal, comfortable language of everyday social life. The line between standard English and colloquial is hard to draw because expressions labeled *Colloq.* are usually understood just as well as if they were standard words, and the company they keep means that, unlike slang, they are in good repute among cultivated speakers. They would not be usable in full–dress, formal discourse but neither would they lower the tone to the level of slang.

Slang   Slang consists either of words in themselves substandard and in bad repute or of standard words and phrases that are used in something less than a reputable sense. Slang may be highly colorful and bold, but very often it is derogatory or irreverent. As one of its basic characteristics is its daring newness, ninety–five percent of it is ephemeral.

Dialect   The label *Dial.* (for *Dialectal*) in this dictionary indicates a word or usage that occurs in a local or regional dialect: a type of language that deviates from the standard language in vocabulary and often also in idiom, pronunciation, morphology, and syntactical construction. Sometimes words that are peculiar to a particular dialect are understood in other areas, but they are still felt as belonging to a distinctive type of local speech. A dialect that exists as an enclave within a country that uses an entirely different language is a *patois,* as, for example, the French Canadian spoken in Quebec, and its

The process of adapting proper names — historical or mythological personification — for the purpose of describing qualities or conditions, is also a way in which new meaning is brought into play. One who admires himself inordinately is called a *Narcissus,* a man of great wisdom is a *Solomon,* one of prodigious strength is a *Hercules,* and a woman of great beauty is called a *Venus.*

The various methods used to extend the meanings of words exhibit the long poetic tradition of our language. Words are constantly acquiring new figurative senses, and the lexicographer must continually consider whether or not to add the new meanings to his treatment of the words in question. If the extended meaning is not self–evident, it must be supplied. The word *extrapolation* is a case in point. In the last ten years this mathematical term, which means extending a graph or table by projecting values beyond the point for which data are known, has acquired a quite natural figurative sense: projection of known scientific data into the realm of conjecture; in short, something close to legitimate scientific prophecy. The user of a dictionary, if he finds only the technical mathematical sense, may not be able to infer the figurative meaning in which he finds "extrapolation" in a magazine or newspaper. Here, and in many similar cases, the dictionary must include the figurative sense (see **extrapolation,** definition 2). Since this process has been going on in the language for nearly a millennium, constantly reinforcing and interplaying with the several other processes of meaning–change, it is not surprising that English is perhaps the richest of all languages in words with multiple meanings.

offshoot, the Cajun dialect of the descendants of the Acadians, who came down from Nova Scotia to Louisiana.

Americanisms   American English came fully of age between the two World Wars and acquired its official chronicler in H. L. Mencken, who produced, in 1919, a book called *The American Language,* later much revised and supplemented. Initially, Mencken made too large claims for the American variety of English, basing his case for an American language on distinctive differences, and deemphasizing the total pattern of basic similarity between the language of this country and that of England. In this dictionary the label *U.S.* indicates words, phrases, and usages current in the United States and usually, though not always, originating here. In this way an attempt has been made to meet the needs of foreign users and those in other parts of the English–speaking world who want to be at home with American literature and its idioms. Often this has meant applying to the label *U.S.* the further label *Slang* or *Colloq.*

Briticisms   The label *Brit.* (for *British*) in this dictionary denotes words, idioms, phrases, verb forms, and usages current in Great Britain (often also in other parts of the Commonwealth) but not in the United States. How it is that a monkey wrench is a *spanner* in England, a windshield is a *windscreen,* a baby carriage a *perambulator* ("pram"), suspenders *braces,* and a motor truck a *lorry*; and why a "close call" or "close shave" should be " a near thing" in British English, is anybody's guess. Sometimes the distinction between British and American usage involves a grammatical form. Such is the case with *gotten,* quite obsolete in standard British speech, but widely used in this country as a past participle of *get* when a completed action is expressed ("I've *gotten* much accomplished today").

Gotten is accordingly labeled *U.S.* in this book when it appears as one of the inflected forms in the entry **get,** and a short discussion of American and British usage is given under the main entry **gotten.**

Scottish   There is a certain condescension in labeling words in Burns's poems and the novels of Sir Walter Scott by what is in effect a dialect label: *Scot.* (for *Scottish*). Such a label, however, is the fashion and it is used here with the note that the language of the Court of Scotland was in a sense merged with the Queen's English of Elizabeth I when the son of Mary Stuart, James VI of Scotland, became James I of England and launched the Authorized Version of the Bible known by his name.

Australian, Canadian, etc.   In the overseas members of the Commonwealth new words have come into the English language just as they have in the United States. Local fauna and flora, the objects and processes peculiar to each area, have required new terms. In Australia, particularly, there have been additions in the way of riming slang, words from the language of the aborigines, and some modifications of British usage — the whole resulting in what may be properly called Australian English. To a lesser degree, Canadian English may also be differentiated. In all such cases, however, the departure from the English current in Great Britain is far less than in the case of the United States.

Archaic, Obsolete, Rare, or Poetic   Words go out of fashion or fall into disuse, rapidly in the case of slang, at a more leisurely pace for cliches and informal words, while the jargons of pseudo–science, outmoded science, or mannered literary criticism decay more slowly, but none the less surely. When, therefore, an unusual word turns up in prose meant for the general reader, it is natural to ask about its status. If the word happens to be encased in a well–known quotation, it is likely to be labeled *Archaic* by the lexicographer. In "I'll make a ghost of him that lets me," the use of *let* in the sense of "hinder" is thus labeled *Archaic,* meaning that it is known and understood in our older literature, ranging from Elizabethan writing down through the works of Milton and Dryden but ordinarily not usable in present everyday writing or speaking. So in effect the label *Archaic* means "current from around 1500 until 1700," and hence turning up in quotations from that period but no longer used much, if at all, in writing subsequent to that stretch of about two hundred years.

Another group of words is labeled *Obs.* (for *Obsolete*). This is a more final verdict. It means that a word has gone so far out of use that it is quite forgotten. It has somehow failed to meet the test of survival, even to the extent of leading the somewhat ghostly life of an archaic word. Some such words

Synonyms   Full advantage is taken of the dual nature of the English language, by giving not only the long literary synonyms that derive mainly from classical and Romance sources but also the short, sinewy words which come into play with such force in speech, and which, aptly used in writing, make the discourse sound like a man speaking, not like a book. However, the user will not find in the synonymies in this work any undue stress on the notion, first given currency by Herbert Spencer, that the so–called Saxon element in the language should be favored over the classical, for many of the short, pithy, highly expressive words in the language are from

died very early in the history of the language, failing to make their way from Old English to Middle English, and, while they had some slight and sporadic use in occasional writings, they did not really become established. One such word is *wanhope,* a native compound replaced by the Old French borrowing *despair*

The lexicographer also has to take into account a borderline area of words that, once current, are now in the process of becoming obsolete. The best solution in the way of a label for these waifs and strays is *Rare.* More often the dictionary must be content to say of such locutions "Formerly," or "In the early —th century," or some such phrasing which will indicate a definite period when the objects to which they referred were in active use, without labeling the word itself as obsolete — for often the word survives the object.

Lastly, there are the words that are closely associated with poetry — at least with traditional old–fashioned poetry — but which are felt as out of place in prose, even in that "other music of prose" which Landor described as producing a poetic effect without being avowedly poetic in form, diction, or outward aspect. The label *Poetic* is employed to suggest to the user of this dictionary that if he is writing traditional verse the word may do well enough, but that if he is writing prose discretion is indicated.

Field Labels   An important part of the lexicographer's task is not only the correct defining of the words in a dictionary but also the assignment of many of the definitions to specific areas of knowledge. In a great many cases this can be done by so phrasing the definition that the reader can immediately see the bearing of the word in any one of a large number of special areas, ranging from Aeronautics and Architecture to Theology and Zoology. Where this procedure can be applied simply and without loss of clarity, it has been used in this dictionary; but, for the further assistance of both layman and specialist, some sixty special fields of knowledge have been represented by appropriate labels for the purpose of indicating that a term, or a particular sense of it, has a restricted or specialized meaning within the designated area.

Conspicuous in this group of labels are those that pertain to the sciences, in both their fundamental and applied aspects. It is here that the language is being expanded with hundreds of new terms or of new meanings attached to old, often venerable words. Such terms as *automation, cybernetics, motivation research, nucleonics, information theory,* and hundreds of others in the physical, biological, medical, and social sciences have been given particular attention in the preparation of this dictionary. The editors have utilized all dependable sources of information and checked their findings with those of carefully chosen authorities in specified fields.

Synonyms and Antonyms

Greek and Latin, either directly or through Romance channels. The view taken throughout in treating synonyms is that each member of a group of related words has equal validity and usefulness in its own context, regardless of its origin. The only criterion by which they have been considered is the suitability of the word to the context.

Thus, we might speak of a thief as having *stolen* a wallet, but a child *filches* candy from a store, and a soldier *pilfers* army supplies. Similarly, a valuable document is *purloined,* while funds are *embezzled.* Bandits may *rob* all whom they meet, but they *plunder* the countryside.

The synonymy under the entry for **steal** will enable the reader to see why the above distinctions were made and to judge for himself the extent to which the words can be interchanged without complete loss either of sense or of shading. A great many ample synonymies such as these will be found throughout the vocabulary section of this book.

Antonyms   In further pursuit of a sharper sense of word meaning, the reader may then look at the antonyms, which are listed immediately following most synonym entries. Words that are opposed or contrasted in meaning furnish, oddly enough, a valuable extension of the definitions of the words involved. To be sure, it is definition by contraries, but teachers who understand the art of testing know that the surest proof of a student's knowledge of the meaning of a word is his ability to give its antonym.

As the synonymies show, a key word in English may have a dozen synonyms that approximate it or overlap with it in meaning; but there are few words that have more than one exact antonym, as *black* has *white*, and *wet* has *dry*. The juxtaposition of the synonyms and the antonyms for a given word makes it possible for the user to carry out for himself a further refinement of interpretation. The user can check whether the antonyms given negate one or more of the synonyms as well as the key word.

The Pronunciations

THE PRONUNCIATIONS in this dictionary have been compiled by editors trained in phonetics and acquainted with the facts of the spoken language. There is, however, no single authority on pronunciation in this country, and no standard dialect. In the case of major regional variations in speech, the editors have recorded first the patterns of pronunciation of the largest region, that of the great midwestern section that was formerly called "General American." Work on a linguistic atlas for the United States has indicated that the large speech areas are far from homogeneous, but the method of recording used in this book is suited to the purposes of a dictionary where the aim is to provide reference rather than extensive linguistic data. It is not intended, of course, that if you are in a speech community where words like *forest* and *orange* are pronounced with the vowel of *stop*, or where *four* and *explore* are pronounced with the vowel of *stone*, you are to change your speech pattern to that of the first pronunciation here recorded, that is (fôr′ist) and (fôr). It has not been possible or practicable to record the speech of all dialect areas in this country. (Not recorded, for example, is the speech of those parts of the country where *r* is not pronounced when in final or pre–consonantal position, as in *car, better*, and *part*.) You may not, then, find your particular dialect recorded, but your mode of speech, if it is normal for your area, is right for you.

There are, of course, other variations in pronunciation apart from those of regional speech patterns. Whether you say (ab′də·mən) or (ab·dō′mən), (ser′ə·brəl) or (sə·rē′brəl) is purely a matter of personal choice; both variants are recorded. It is sometimes impossible to determine the most frequent pronunciation in such cases, and a second or third variant shown is to be regarded as equally acceptable.

Although the words in a dictionary must be pronounced in isolation, the editors have attempted to record them as they would be uttered in the flow of speech. In accordance with this policy, the symbol (ə). called *schwa*, was borrowed from the International Phonetic Alphabet to record the unstressed neutral vowel heard in the first syllable of *about* and in the second syllables of *comma, barren*, and *lemon*.

Some variant pronunciations are restricted to particular fields or professions, such as the medical or military. These have been labeled in this book as follows:

ob·lique (ə·blēk′, *in military usage* ə·blīk′)

Foreign pronunciations, when pertinent, are duly recorded and labeled, although an established Anglicization is always shown first:

a·dieu (ə·dōō′, ə·dyōō′; *Fr.* å·dyœ′)

It sometimes occurs that a word will differ in its pronunciation depending on its use as a noun, verb, etc., or in some particular sense. The differing pronunciation is ordinarily shown immediately before the particular use or uses to which it applies, as follows:

> **en·sign** (en′sīn) *n.* **1** A distinguished flag or banner; especially, a national standard or naval flag. **2** (en′sən) In the U.S. Navy or Coast Guard, a commissioned officer of the lowest grade, ranking with a second lieutenant in the U.S. Army, Air Force, or Marine Corps.

The Key   The system used for the recording of pronunciation in this book is one which has been determined to be the simplest, most meaningful, and accurate one for the purposes of dictionary transcription. It utilizes, with a few exceptions, the letters of the alphabet, combined with certain standard diacritical marks, such as the macron for the so–called "long vowels" (ā), (ē), (ī), (ō), (yōō). The conventional breve for the "short vowels" (a), (e), (i), (o), (u), has been eliminated from this key in all but one case, as these symbols are generally understood to be "short" when unmarked. The breve is retained in the one symbol (ŏŏ), the vowel in *book*, to avoid confusion with the vowel in *pool*. The elimination of the breve in all other cases, and the use of the one symbol (ə) for the unstressed neutral vowel however spelled, has resulted in a key for this dictionary in which only twelve characters, excluding the special symbols for foreign sounds, require special marking.

The Etymologies

THE ETYMOLOGIES in this dictionary present a concise history of the word with reference to origin, form changes, and semantic development. Native words that existed in the earliest period of the language are shown in their Old English form:

bedridden . . . [OE *bedrida* < *bed* bed + *rida* rider]

For borrowings, the immediate source is indicated first, followed by as many intermediate forms and languages as are necessary to show significant changes, and the word is then traced back to its earliest recorded forms or components in Latin, Greek, etc.:

diameter . . . [<OF *diametre* <L *diametrus* <Gk. *diametros* <*dia-* through + *metron* measure]

Where the ultimate language of origin cannot be determined, and the general provenance is known, a linguistic family is cited as the source:

garden . . . [<AF *gardin* <Gmc.]

or a geographical area is indicated:

banana . . . [<Sp. < native African name]

In the case of words of obscure origin, it has sometimes been possible to cite likely cognates in related languages:

gloat . . . [Cf. ON *glotta* grin]
groom . . . [ME *grom.* Cf. OF *gromet* a servant.]

Otherwise, such words are marked "origin uncertain" or "origin unknown," and the Middle English form is cited where one exists:

boy . . . [ME *boi*; origin unknown]

Of special interest to the student of words are the many other informative facts also given in the etymologies. Pairs or sets of words which have entered English through different intermediate languages or dialects, but can be traced back to the same ultimate source word, have been marked as "doublets." The etymologies of such words will show a common form, indicating the point at which the divergence of form and meaning first occurred and the necessary intermediate forms needed to show clearly the development of the modern words.

zero . . . [<F *zéro* <Ital. *zero* <Arabic *sifr.* Doublet of CIPHER.]
cipher . . . [<OF *cyfre* <Arabic *sifr.* Doublet of ZERO.]

A similar situation occurs when two or more words may be traced to the same primitive root; the divergence in meaning is much earlier than in the case of doublets, and so these words have no common recorded form. Such cognates are indicated by the phrase "Akin to . . .".

language . . . [<OF *langage* < *langue* tongue <L *lingua* tongue, language. Akin to TONGUE.]
tongue . . . [OE *tunge.* Akin to LANGUAGE.]

Another class of words may be derived from variants or different stems of the same recorded word in an ancient language, as Old English or Latin. This type of relationship is shown by the phrase "Related to . . ." in the etymologies.

hale[2] . . . [OE *hāl.* Related to WHOLE.]
whole . . . [OE (Northumbrian) *hol,* var. of *hāl.* Related to HALE[2].]

The use of numerous cross-references has made it possible to present a large amount of information in a small space and without unnecessary repetition. The etymologies of many compound words, such as *acrophobia, hydrophone, transoceanic* may be found under the main entries for each of their components, where complete histories are given: *acro-, -phobia; hydro-, -phone; trans-, -oceanic.* In other compound words where the identity of the components may be obscure, the break-down is made in the form of cross-references to the source of additional information.

morphology . . . [<MORPHO- + -LOGY]
azine . . . [<AZ- + -INE[2]]

Etymologies of special interest, connecting words with important people, places, or events, are recorded with additional notes explaining the historic background of the word. (See **gerrymander, buncombe.**)

Many etymologies provide interesting insights into the cultural and social history of other times and places which still influence our thoughts and speech.

Usage

by Albert H. Marckwardt

Every society places its stamp of approval upon certain forms or modes of social behavior and looks askance upon deviations from them. In our culture, applause for a fine musical performance would be considered out of place at a church service, but entirely appropriate and in fact praiseworthy in a concert hall. The particular mode of behavior which is accorded such prestige may vary according to geography and social class. The English and European continentals recognize one manner of manipulating a knife and fork to convey food to the mouth; Americans employ a quite different technique. The American way seems needlessly awkward to the European; the European way seems crude to the Americans. When they entertain at dinner, upper middle-class Americans are likely to eat by candlelight and to have flowers on the table. This is regarded as ostentatious, or at best superfluous, in working-class circles.

The use of language is one of many kinds of social behavior. Here, as in other matters, certain forms of speech and writing have acquired prestige, whereas others are looked upon with disfavor. Moreover, differentiations on the basis of geography and social class are readily apparent. The past tense of the verb *eat (et),* used by many speakers of British English of unquestioned social standing, would be considered rustic or uneducated by most Americans; conversely, the Americanism *donate* has not yet gained thorough acceptance in Britain.

"Bring them crates over here," is a sentence calculated to produce co-operation and a speedy result when addressed to a group of factory workmen; the substitution of *those containers* in that particular social context would produce suspicion, resentment, and probably not the desired result.

Standard English

That form of the English language which has acquired prestige from its use by those educated persons who are carrying on the affairs of the English-speaking community (whether narrowly or broadly conceived) is known as Standard English. In short, the standard language is that which possesses social utility and social prestige. History bears out this observation with remarkable fidelity. All we know of the earliest stage of our language, that which we refer to as Old English, spoken on the island between the mid-fifth century incursions of Germanic-speaking Angles, Saxons, and Jutes and the mid-11th century Norman Conquest, was that there were decided regional differences, resulting in four major dialects. During the first two of these six centuries the center of power was clearly in the kingdom of Northumbria, and that dialect constituted

the standard. At the time of the powerful King Offa, political and cultural influence shifted southward, and the dialect of Mercia acquired prestige. From the mid-ninth century onward, the West Saxon dynasty assumed political leadership; King Alfred fathered a cultural renaissance and a major educational program; and this time the standard moved westward, remaining there through the period of religious reform, also centered in the same area. Thus it is that most of the Old English literature which has come down to us is in West Saxon. Even the early selections originally written in other dialects were finally recopied in the prestige dialect.

The development of the language during the Middle English period (1050–1475) bears out the same principle. By the time the English language had recovered from its temporary subjugation to Norman French, London was firmly established as the political, economic, and cultural center of the island. It is interesting to observe that by the end of the 14th century the dialect of London was used by many of the major literary figures irrespective of where they were born. Chaucer, a native Londoner, employed it in his poetry, which is possibly no surprise, but so too did Gower, born in Kent, and Wycliffe, who hailed from Lincolnshire. One acute observer has pointed out that Standard English had its origin in the kind of language employed in the courts of law and the governmental offices at Westminster, that it was essentially administrative English. This is another telling bit of evidence of the close relationship between the standard language and the bases of influence.

The emergence of the London dialect as a standard for the entire country first won formal recognition in Puttenham's *The Arte of English Poesie* (1589) in which the language of London and of the shires within a radius of sixty miles, "and not much beyond," was recommended as a model for aspiring writers to follow. This was accompanied by the statement that educated gentlemen in the outlying portions of England had adopted London English as a standard and were speaking it as well as people living in the capital.

It was just at this point in time that the English language entered on its worldwide career. It was transported first across the Atlantic to the American mainland and the Caribbean islands. The spread to the Asian subcontinent followed in the 18th century; to Australia and South Africa in the 19th. At the outset the colonies were generally willing and eager to follow the standard of the mother country, even though it was at times less than ideally suited to all aspects of the local situation, but as they acquired more and more independence, economic and cultural as well as political, new national forms of the language tended to emerge and to develop their own standard norms.

Today English is spoken as a native language by vast numbers of people—approximately 300,000,000—distributed over four continents of the globe. The standard reveals a considerable amount of variation from one country to another, and even in one part of some countries as compared with another. Thus, Standard West Indian English differs from both Standard British and Standard American English, and Standard South African differs from all of these. Standard Canadian English is distinct from Standard Australian. It is even possible to speak of standard forms of English in areas where it is not the native language, notably India and the Philippines. In the United Kingdom itself there is a standard form of Scots and a standard Northern English, both of which differ from the Received Standard of the London area.

The Role of the Dictionary

Ideally a dictionary is an accurate record of a language as it is employed by those who speak and write it. But as we have already seen, the English language, even in terms of just its present use, to say nothing of its past, exists on such a vast scale that no single work is likely to do justice to it in its entirety. Inevitably the task has had to be broken up into smaller segments. Some dictionaries deal with pronunciation only, at times even confined to a particular country—England or America. Others confine themselves to particular segments of the language: dialect, slang, or one or another technical vocabulary. More ambitious is the attempt by the historical dictionary to include within the bounds of a single work evidence of both the present and earlier stages of the language, although sometimes a dictionary may be confined to just one early period—Old or Middle English, for example. There are dictionaries which concentrate on the language as it is, and has been, used in England, in Scotland, in the United States, and in Canada. Consequently, in the face of this inescapable specialization and division of labor, a dictionary which purports to be general in its purpose must of necessity exercise a high degree of selective reporting on those aspects of the language which will best serve the needs of those who consult it.

The editors of this dictionary have assumed that it will be used principally in the United States, by persons who are familiar with American English. Only rarely have they felt it necessary to identify features of the language which are characteristic of this country. For example, the past participial form *gotten* is identified in a note as an American usage, and the peculiarly American use of *integrate* as used in "to integrate schools" bears the label *U.S.* The editors have taken on the responsibility of identifying usages peculiar to Britain, Canada, or Australia, indicating these with the appropriate label. Any item not so identified is in current use in the United States. In this connection it should be realized that despite all that has been said here about differences throughout the world, the unity of the English language in the many countries in which it is spoken far outweighs the diversity.

The obligation of the dictionary to record the state of the language or some segment of it as accurately as possible has already been mentioned. This may properly be termed a descriptive function, and it reflects the way in which the editors approach their task. But the nonprofessional, the layman who consults the dictionary, does so from other motives. Either he is seeking information on some particular facet of the language about which he knows nothing—the most obvious instance being the meaning of a word he has not previously encountered —or to discover which of several possible uses of the language, relative to spelling, pronunciation, word division, word meaning, or grammatical form, has acquired a sufficient degree of prestige and propriety to justify his employment of it. In short, his view of the dictionary function is essentially prescriptive. He hopes to be told what to say and to write, or more accurately perhaps, how to say and how to write.

In the light of all that has been said up to this point, these two concepts, the descriptive and the prescriptive, should not be in conflict with each other. It has already been pointed out that the standard language *is* the language of the socially and culturally dominant group within a speech community. There can be no other source upon which to base it. Accordingly, if the dictionary records that language accurately and faithfully, it should constitute a reliable guide and preceptor.

Unfortunately, the problem is not so simple as it seems on the surface. For a number of reasons too complicated to explain here, many people, Americans in particular, are reluctant to accept this simple and straightforward view of the matter. For one thing, experience has taught them that some persons of position and influence have little feeling for or command of the niceties of the language, and accordingly they are led to question the reliability and usefulness of an accurate exercise of the descriptive technique. Second, they are committed to a rigid and monolithic view of what constitutes the standard language and expect to find a single answer as to what is linguistically approved or appropriate, irrespective of the circumstances in which it may occur. The facts of the case are quite at variance with this assumption. Again, language like any form of social behavior varies in response to the demands of the particular social situation. Many of us would not hesitate to pick up a chicken drumstick with our fingers at a picnic but would feel constrained to use a knife and fork at a formal dinner. Neither form of behavior is superior or inferior to the other; it is a question of adaptation to the circumstances. Differences in regional standards prevail as well. In some parts of the country, for the host at a cocktail party to employ a bartender smacks of ostentation, whereas a hired caterer is accepted as the norm. Elsewhere just the reverse set of values prevails.

Varieties of Usage

It is precisely for this reason that dictionaries find it necessary to employ various kinds of labels to indicate the sphere of usage in which a particu-

ar word or expression is or is not acceptable. Those labels which are most often misunderstood have to do with the degree of formality which characterizes the communication. No dictionary has found it possible to recognize more than a dichotomy here, namely a formal and an informal type of speech. Clearly, each one of us in the course of a day's use of the language communicates much more in an informal manner than in a formal. The differences are pervasive, including pronunciation and structure as well as vocabulary. To take just a few obvious instances: the clipped form *dorm* is a frequent informal equivalent for *dormitory;* the phrase *all in* often serves for *exhausted, catch on* for *understand,* to cover at least three of the four major parts of speech. There is a whole battery of adverbs such as *consequently* and *accordingly* which may find *so* as their normal equivalent in less formal discourse. The same distinction extends to such phrase structures as *at all events* and *needless to say.* In the negative-interrogative form of the verb, *isn't he, can't he, won't he* are the informal expressions corresponding to *is he not, can he not, will he not,* a consideration affecting both syntax and pronunciation.

Actually we are faced with more than a dichotomy here. Some observers recognize at least four distinct linguistic styles, including the formal (*This is not the man whom we seek*), the consultative (*This is not the man we're looking for*), the casual (*He's not our man*) and the intimate (*'Fraid you picked a lemon*). It is beyond the bounds of practicality or serviceability for the dictionary to recognize more than two broad types of situation, the formal and the informal. Moreover, in terms of the expectations of most of the people who consult a dictionary, it is more to the point to label the justifiably informal than it would be to signalize the formal. Generally the length and stylistic aura of a word will identify it as being primarily confined to formal use.

Distinctions drawn on the basis of formality often cut across differences in the mode of communication, speech or writing. Much, but not all, of our speech activity in the course of a day is informal. Some of our writing at least is more likely to be formal, although many personal letters, memoranda, the private writing contained in diaries and journals, may well fall into the informal category.

The point is that these are matters of the function of language, not of acceptability or correctness. A person whose informal speech may be characterized as "talking like a book" or "talking as if he had swallowed the dictionary," has simply failed to sort out the styles properly. One may rest assured that whatever a dictionary labels as *informal* is not less correct than an unlabeled item but that it is appropriate to an informal situation or purpose. Dictionaries usually do not affix a label to those words appropriate only for formal use on the ground that the social penalties for excessive formality of speech, though very real, seem somehow less onerous than those for misplaced informality.

Slang

Somewhat akin to informality, but differing from it in several important respects, is the use of language we have come to call slang. Slang is difficult to define, partly because the term itself has changed in meaning over the centuries. Originally it referred to thieves' argot, and today the term is still applied to the special terminology of certain occupations and other groups, including oil drillers, baseball players, rock or jazz musicians, college students, shoe salesmen, tramps, drug addicts, and prison inmates, but it has also taken on a much broader application. It includes clipped forms like *benny* and *frag,* echoic terms like *slurp,* meaningless tag phrases of the class of *twenty-three skidoo* from the early years of the century, *so's your old man, and how, you better believe it,* all of which have had their fleeting currency, only to be replaced by what will undoubtedly be the equally temporary *got to* (*He's got to be the best ball player in the league*) and the interjection *Wow!* which appears to be the stock in trade of the younger generation and the mindless consumer pictured on television commercials.

Not included in the concept of slang are dialect, localisms, profanity, and the so-called four-letter words once taboo in polite society, now increasingly accepted. It is also important to recognize that most slang is colloquial in nature in that it occurs in speech much more frequently than in writing; on the other hand, it would be a grave error

to think of all colloquial or informal language as slang. Nor is slang to be confused with nonstandard language; it is at times consciously employed for a particular effect by persons of unquestioned cultivation.

Dictionaries are far from uniform in what they label as slang; even the special dictionaries of slang include many entries which do not at all fit the concept as it has been set forth here. The label *slang* after a word or a particular meaning of a word is an indication of its general unsuitability for formal communication; it suggests moreover that when used informally, it may have something of a slight shock value in a serious context; at the very least it will call attention to itself. This would be true, for example, of *boss* used adjectivally in the sense of "great, wonderful," of *bug off* for "go away!" and of *bug out,* "to escape, run away." Each country where English is a native language has its own variety of slang. *Wizard* is often used in England as a blanket term of approval; *dinkum* is confined to Australia. Both are relatively unknown in the United States. In this dictionary, slang terms found in other English-speaking countries will be labeled as to their place of origin. If an item is simply characterized as *slang* with no additional qualifying term, it may be assumed to be current in this country.

Regional Variation

In no English-speaking country is the language uniform over the entire area. In certain fields of the vocabulary, terminology differs from one part of the country to the other. This is especially true of words having to do with the more homelike and intimate aspects of life: the physical environment, the home, foods and cooking, the farm and farm operations, the fauna and flora. The literary term *earthworm* is called an *angleworm* in certain regions and a *fishworm* or *fishing worm* in others, and in addition there are several terms which have a much more restricted currency: *eaceworm, angle dog,* and *dewworm. Skillet* and *spider,* though now somewhat old-fashioned, are still used for *frying pan* or *fry pan* in some areas. Limited access highways have developed a highly varied terminology: *turnpike, freeway, expressway, parkway,* to mention only a few.

It is impossible in a general dictionary such as this to include all such variants, nor would it be helpful to label as *Regional* every term limited to extensive regions. Nevertheless, in terms of its function as an accurate recorder of the language, the dictionary must inform its users when a term, limited geographically, differs from a more commonly preferred synonym. There is a problem here in that dialect research in this country is still going on and that reliable information about the regional incidence of many terms is not yet readily available. In general the policy of this dictionary will be to indicate that a word is regional when that is known to be the case and when the word is not likely to be familiar to others outside the region of its use, but there will be no attempt to delimit the precise areas of its occurrence.

Nonstandard English

The very fact that a painstaking attempt has been made to clarify the concept of Standard English should be evidence in itself that there are features of the language which do not meet these requirements. Most of the aberrations are matters of grammatical form: *hisself* instead of *himself, hisn* instead of *his, growed* instead of *grew* or *grown, anyways* instead of *anyway,* and so on. Occasionally these are matters which pertain wholly to the vocabulary, like *irregardless,* or to the pronunciation, as with the dropping of the first *r* in *secretary* and *library.*

At one time it was the custom for dictionaries to employ the label *illiterate* for such deviations from standard usage. For several reasons the term is far from satisfactory. The percentage of actual illiterates in the United States is relatively small, even if so-called functional illiteracy is to be used as a criterion. The type of expressions so labeled often extended to many persons who had experienced some schooling. Because of these and other considerations dictionaries have recently tended to use *nonstandard* as the preferred designation for deviations from the linguistic norm which tend to be matters of social rather than regional dialect. It is rare, of course, for anyone to consult the dictionary

for the meanings of words so labeled. The principal service that the dictionary performs is to indicate their status.

Usage Notes

It must be recognized, however, that there is no immediately definable hard-and-fast line separating the standard from the nonstandard. There is, indeed, a gray area, a zone of disputed items about which there may be considerable difference of opinion, even among authorities of equal experience and eminence. In connection with some of the locutions falling within this zone of uncertainty, not only must the extent of use by speakers of the standard language be considered but also the attitude toward the word or construction in question. For example, there can be no doubt that many react with aversion to the terms *lady doctor* and *cleaning lady*. They regard *lady* here as an example of false gentility, and much prefer *woman* to signify gender. Logical or illogical, informed or uninformed, this fairly widespread feeling is part of the total record, the total history of the word, and as such, it is the function of the dictionary to take note of that fact. Clearly no single label would suffice in this instance; an explanation of some sort is called for. This dictionary, along with many other reference works on language, copes with problems such as this through the device of a usage note, which, although necessarily brief and concise, does explain the nature of the problem that has arisen in connection with this particular word.

Further issues about usage may arise from mistaken grammatical analysis on the one hand, or the failure to distinguish what is current in informal as opposed to the formal standard language on the other. An instance of the latter is the use of *like* as a conjunction introducing a subordinate clause ("He didn't work like his father worked.") Reliable measures of the incidence of this construction indicate that it has a high frequency in informal English but that it occurs only rarely in the formal written language. But again there are some who are reluctant to accept it. Labeling the construction *informal* would probably satisfy the purely factual requirements of the situation, but it would fail to warn the reader of the dictionary that his use of the construction might give offense in some quarters. Again a brief statement is more helpful than a single unmodified categorization.

As one compares the usage notes in various dictionaries, he is likely to find a wide divergence of attitude and philosophy, ranging from a fairly broad permissiveness to a nervous reluctance to admit any deviation from the most rigid adherence to approved formal usage of a century ago. It is the considered opinion of the editors of this work that neither of these extremes is well calculated to serve the needs of those who look to the dictionary for help in matters of this kind.

Language changes from century to century and from generation to generation. To the extent that these changes have affected the usage of Standard English it is the responsibility of the dictionary to acknowledge them. There is often a discrepancy, as well, between what is in actual fact current as Standard English and what many opinionated or ill-informed persons believe that usage to be. The responsibility of the dictionary here is to set the record straight, to report and interpret the facts as accurately as possible. At the same time the dictionary must be equally perceptive in distinguishing, for the person who consults it, between standard usage which is acceptable beyond a shadow of doubt and that about which there is some qualification or question. Unfortunately, there is a great lack of awareness on the part of the general public about the services which dictionaries do perform with respect to matters of usage. As dictionaries improve in their faithfulness to fact and the nicety of their discrimination, it is reasonably certain that readers will take fuller advantage of the service which only a carefully and conscientiously edited dictionary is capable of offering.

The English of Canada, Australia, and New Zealand

by H. Rex Wilson

As the language of the greatest colonizing nation in modern times, English has spread to widely separated parts of the world and has evolved on its own as the first language of the dominant peoples of several now-independent nations. The largest of these is the United States, but just as inhabitants of both sides of the Atlantic recognize the difference between American English and that of the Old Country, so Canadians, Australians, and New Zealanders are conscious of respectable varieties of English within their boundaries which differ in various degrees and ways from the language used by the residents of Great Britain or the United States.

Canadian English

Scholarly interest in Canadian English has developed real strength only since World War II, although the bibliography of writings on the English spoken in Canada goes back over a hundred years. This literature is disproportionately loaded with alarm and indignation over the unfortunate spread of "Americanisms." Because Canada evolved by gradual stages from a group of colonies to an independent nation, the long-held British connection has led to false linguistic expectations on the part of some Englishmen and Canadians, and even of a few residents of the United States. To the majority of visitors from the U.S. who come from the states just south of the border from New York and on westward, Canadians speak "just like us." And indeed even the most exacting students of Canadian English would have to admit that superficially this remark is justified.

Origins

In its origins Canadian English is predominantly American. It descends directly from the language of pre-Revolutionary War settlers on the seaboard and immediate hinterland of the present United States. In the uprootings, both forced and voluntary, which followed the Revolution, Canada received an English-speaking population drawn almost entirely from the old American colonies. It is estimated that by 1830 eighty percent of the English-speaking population of Canada could be traced back to the United States. Upon the language of this majority the relative handful of governors, administrators, military officers and clergy of English origin could not be expected to make any substantial impression, although as members of a highly prestigious group they were bound to have some effect.

Some time before the settlement of the American colonies, some groups in England began to lose the *r*-sound between a vowel and a following consonant (as in *art*). This sort of pronunciation and the one which retained the older *r* were rivals both in England and in some of the settlement areas of the U.S. The "*r*-droppers" prevailed in eastern New England and in the coastal South, but the *r*-sound was retained throughout the rest of the colonies, and it was largely from these areas

that the basic post-Revolutionary population of Canada was drawn. Meanwhile, the *r*-dropping became the dominant speech fashion in England. These easily-noted features are the main ones which cause superficial observers from England to identify Canadian speakers as "American" and U.S. visitors to find that Canadians talk "just like us."

But subsequent settlement, independent patterns of pronunciation, the distinctive experience of the physical environment, contact with other linguistic groups, and the prestige of the colonial administration have imposed upon Canadian English features which set it off from other types of English.

Pronunciation

The first difference in language that most people notice when they meet someone from another speech area is in pronunciation. Strangers have accents. But this is just what Canadians seem to lack when they are first heard by many residents of the U.S., and even visitors from the South and Southwest will find Canadian speech little different from that of the "Yankees." The origins of Canadian English just mentioned will help account for this.

Sooner or later the visitor to Canada will notice that Canadians say *oot* and *aboot* for *out* and *about*, but if he asks about it Canadians will deny it. And, strictly speaking, they are right. However, what has been heard is something different from the vowel in *down* and *mountain*. This tendency to have a different vowel before sounds like *t* and *s* than before sounds like *d, z, n* is very widespread. In the verb *house* (where the vowel is followed by a *z* sound) the vowel sound will be the same as the one in *down*, and although it may sound different in various places in Canada the range of difference will be about the same as in the U.S. But the vowel sound of the noun *house* (where the vowel is followed by an *s* sound) is different. This pronunciation varies quite a bit from place to place and even in the pronunciations of one speaker, but the general characteristic of most Canadian speech is to have a difference between the vowels in these different situations, and Americans are left with the impression that Canadians say *oot* and *aboot*.

The pronunciation of vowels varying on the basis of the following sound is not unique and can be found in scattered parts of the United States. In these areas and in Canada the vowels of *write* and *ride* show a similar pattern.

The pronunciation of a few individual words may also catch the visitor's ear. The words *either* and *neither* have first syllables which rhyme with *eye* with far greater frequency than is found in the United States. Some longer words, such as *controversy,* may have the main stress on the second rather than the first syllable, reflecting the prestige of British pronunciation supported by private schools set up on the British model and by returning Canadians who have studied at British universities. Although not unknown before World War II, the British pronunciation of *schedule* (shed′yŏŏl) has gained ground in recent years, apparently under the influence of the Canadian Broadcasting Corporation.

The pronunciation of the word *clerk* like that of the family name *Clark,* once a striking feature of Ontario speech, has now died out except in official usage *(County Clerk)* and in the Presbyterian Church *(Clerk of Session).*

Regional accents are not prominent in Canada, probably because of a large amount of movement within the country and relatively few isolated homogeneous settlements of native speakers of English. The island provinces of Newfoundland and Prince Edward Island are notable exceptions, while the imprint of New England continues to set parts of Nova Scotia and New Brunswick off from Ontario and from the Scottish-settled areas of Nova Scotia. Some areas originally settled by non-English-speakers have produced distinctive varieties of English as the result of earlier bilingualism.

Spelling Differences

For the most part, differences in spelling between England and the United States are traceable to Noah Webster, America's first great lex-

icographer. Canadians understandably did not come under the influence of Webster's spelling reforms in the early 19th century, and British spelling conventions have persisted. Words like *traveller* and *jeweller* continued to have double *l,* and *-our* spellings persisted in words like *honour* and *flavour.* The noun *practice* continued to be set off from the verb *practise.* Today these spellings are no longer insisted upon in most school systems, although consistency in usage by the individual is expected. This "loss of standards," especially in the *-our* spellings, can still raise furious condemnation in the editorial pages of some newspapers in Canada. In their own style these pages and the advertisements in the paper may tend to be conservative, while the news columns tend toward "American" spellings.

The spellings *tyre* and *kerb(stone)* are as strange to Canadians as to Americans and must be explained in Canadian dictionaries as *Brit.* for *tire* and *curb(stone).* The spelling *gaol* for *jail* was once common in newspapers but began disappearing even before World War II.

Vocabulary

The words which a nation uses to conduct its business are great reflectors of its discovery of its environment and its historical development. In 1967 a group of scholars under Professor Walter S. Avis produced *A Dictionary of Canadianisms on Historical Principles* which provides a comprehensive view of the growing and changing vocabulary of Canadian life. This vocabulary has been drawn from many sources, and much of it belongs to experiences shared with settlers of the northern states in the common development of North America. It is not surprising, therefore, that many words reflecting this early experience have passed out of use or are found only in writings referring to specific historical periods.

An American would be puzzled, to say the least, by a reference to an alligator in the forests of Ontario. In the movement of logs by water the lumber industry was greatly helped by *alligators,* amphibious paddle-wheel scows, equipped with a winching arrangement for travel overland.

An equally puzzling term, but in this case a contemporary one, might be found in the statement, "We went to separate schools together." In many parts of Canada religious groups have the legal right to set up their own schools supported by public funds. These are usually referred to as *separate schools,* and a statement such as the one mentioned may be made without suspicion of humorous intent or mental deficiency.

In the Arctic (usually pronounced *Artic*) the term *white-out* has been formed on the model of *black-out* to describe a condition where reflected light from snow or haze or fine blowing snow obscures the horizon and features of the landscape.

Canadian coiners of words have sometimes shown a fine sense of irony as in the now obsolete *Nova Scotia nightingale* for a "singing" marsh frog, and *CPR strawberries* for prunes, which were a prominent item of diet during the building of the Canadian Pacific Railway. On the whole, Canadians have not been distinguished in coining regional names. Most are obviously derivative, like Winipegger or Newfie (Newfoundlander), but Maritimers may be called *Bluenoses* (from Nova Scotia), *Herringchokers* (from New Brunswick) and *Spud Islanders* (a reference to the importance of the potato in the economy of Prince Edward Island).

The *Dictionary of Canadianisms* shows a surprising number of words which have long been accepted in the United States but apparently first gained currency in Canada. In recent times the most striking exports have been in the vocabulary of lacrosse and hockey. *Lacrosse* is of Canadian French origin from a fancied resemblance between the stick used in the game and a Bishop's crozier. While U.S. fans are familiar with the whole standard terminology of hockey, including the penitential seat known as the *penalty box,* they may not know the journalistic coinage *sin bin.*

Because of an administrative history different from that of the United States, Canadian government offers a large number of distinctive terms of British origin. The title *Prime Minister* is, of course, widely

used in other countries, but the names of some other positions may be surprising and even a little quaint, such as the term *Reeve* for the council chairman of a village, township, or municipal district council in Ontario and the West. In Ontario the County Council composed of Reeves and Deputy Reeves is presided over by a *Warden.* The familiar title *Sheriff* in Canada signifies a court officer and not a man charged with general law enforcement and peacekeeping duties. A Lieutenant- (pronounced *leftenant*) Governor is not a person who acts for a Governor but the official and ceremonial head of the government of a Province, representing the Crown.

Since colonial times Canadian English has imported virtually its whole technological vocabulary from the United States. Visitors from England have problems in discussing automobile maintenance until they have learned the American words for parts of their motor cars. Canadian railroading, established in large part by American engineers, uses the terminology they brought augmented by later imports. The term *sleeper* for a railway tie held its own until the 1920's at least, but now is rarely heard and one Canadian dictionary labels it *British.*

Canada made its first contribution to the jet age in 1854 by the invention and naming of kerosene in Nova Scotia. Oddly, in Ontario a term of apparent Pennsylvania origin, *coal oil,* is preferred. So widely accepted has *kerosene* become in the U.S. that it has even raised objections in New Zealand as an "Americanism" displacing the British *paraffin (oil).*

Canadians have borrowed words from languages with which they have had contact. *Woodchuck,* although it looks and sounds English, is derived from an Algonquian word which was first imitated by English speakers as *wejack.* The Canada jay has a name that goes one step further. A Cree name was first imitated as *Whisky John* and then familiarized to *whiskyjack.*

Naturally the long French sojourn in Canada before English settlement has left its marks and, as far as place names go, this extends beyond the border of Canada. The word *portage* is classically representative of the early years, and it has never been displaced by *carry* or *carrying place.* In politics the old terms *Bleu* (or *Parti Bleu,* Conservative) and *Rouge* (or *Parti Rouge,* Liberal) may occasionally appear in English newspaper accounts of politics in Quebec. Sometimes these are Anglicized to *Blue* and *Red.*

Influenced by the special economics of printing in a bilingual country, no passenger train of the Canadian National Railways has "left" its station for many years, although most have "departed" fairly close to schedule. The abbreviations *Arr.* and *Dep.* in the timetable require no translation. Similarly, the two telegraph companies in the country have settled on *telecommunications* in their names.

In its modest space program Canada has named its first communications satellite *Alouette* (French, lark) and a more recent one *anik* (Eskimo, brother).

The English of Australia and New Zealand

The English of Australia and New Zealand is much more satisfyingly exotic to the American ear than that of Canada. The first impression is that the language of these countries is very much like British English, and, although extended observation will show that these dialects do have some very distinctive characteristics of their own, the initial impression is justified by history. The time of separation from the mother country is much shorter for both of these countries; there are still members of the older generation who refer to England as "Home" although not born there themselves. Australia did not begin to receive English-speaking settlers until after the American Revolution, and New Zealand not until about fifty years later. Further, the origin of the population was much more predominantly English in the formative years of Australian and New Zealand society than it was in North America in a similar period, with a much lower proportion of Scots and Irish. Apparently the majority of the settlers were from the south rather than the north of England. Australian and New Zealand speakers tend to be "*r*-droppers."

Australian English

Australian English became well known to United States servicemen during the Second World War. Although the song "Waltzing Matilda" with its baffling vocabulary had made its way across the Pacific some time before, wartime contacts first made Americans aware of the peculiarities of Australian pronunciation, and a considerable collection of teasing jokes developed—such as the one about the USAAF Major who was brought unconscious to an Australian hospital in Port Moresby, New Guinea. Regaining consciousness and feeling more dead than alive, he asked a nursing sister:

"Was I brought here to die?"

"Oh, no, sir," she replied, "You were brought here yesterday."

Like most such jokes this exploits the so-called Cockney feature in which the vowel of *day* as pronounced by most Americans and Canadians is replaced by the vowel of *die.* Australians themselves seem to enjoy humor based on their speech peculiarities, as is evidenced by the success of a slim volume called *Let Stalk Strine* by Afferbeck Lauder, who claims to be Professor of Strine Studies at the University of Sinny. (The title and author are stated, appropriately, in Strine and are translated as follows: *Let's Talk Australian* by Alphabetical Order, Professor of Australian Studies at the University of Sydney.)

The form of language on which this book is based is what is usually called "Broad" Australian, a term also used in New Zealand. Australians and New Zealanders often modify their speech toward the standard British "Received Pronunciation" (RP), although the tendency seems stronger in New Zealand than in Australia. Accordingly it is not unusual to find an Australian Ph.D. at a North American university happily doin' what comes naturally as far as pronunciation is concerned, although his professional writing would show no marked difference, beyond personal style, from that of his colleagues who speak other dialects of English.

English speakers did not originally come voluntarily to Australia. English law had provided "transportation" as a punishment as early as the reign of Queen Elizabeth, and a substantial amount of the labor on early American plantations was performed by convicts shipped out from England. After the American Revolution attention turned to Australia as a place to send these undesirables. These "unwilling emigrants" were a very mixed group, and included many who had been convicted of such crimes as petty theft or poaching, or had been imprisoned for debt. Such constructive skills as they brought with them were chiefly those most useful in an urban setting. The unskilled often learned trades to supplement these. Their language was that of the city, so that Australian rural vocabulary had to be supplied from new sources, thus distinguishing the agricultural and cattle-raising vocabulary from that of the Old Country (although some technical terms, like *drover* for a cattle herder, have had currency in England, Australia, and America).

Australians have been, almost from the beginning, very mobile. Originally the population was confined between the sea and the Great Dividing Range on the east coast, but in 1813 a pass was found through the range, and free settlers, who had begun to arrive in 1793, began moving into the rest of the continent. As cattle and sheep raising and mining developed, convict labor was assigned to free settlers on contract, so that even they became mobile—often more so than the free settler who held land. Under varying special arrangements some convicts were free to move about within certain territorial limits and make their own working contracts with employers. As a result, Australia appears to have few dialect differences, except in local borrowings from the languages of the native peoples and the distribution of the vowel of *bat* and that of *father* in certain words.

Pronunciation   The most obvious difference between Australian and most American English, after *r*-dropping, is the apparent *day/die* confusion. When an Australian pronounces *day* he does not quite rhyme it with an American's pronunciation of *die,* but it is close enough to cause confusion to the American, at least on first meeting. This parallels roughly the initial impression that Canadians say *oot* for *out.* A characteristic less apparent to Americans, unless they come from New Eng-

land, lies in the vowels of *path, grass, contrast* which have the sound of the vowel in *bat* rather than of *father* in the areas of oldest settlement, but may be found with the vowel of *father* in the state of South Australia, and there *dance* may also be found with this pronunciation.

Whenever a vowel in any English dialect becomes too much like another, the speakers of that dialect tend to shift the second one to keep distinctions between words which otherwise would come to sound too nearly alike. Thus, other vowels in Australian English also seem displaced to the American ear. The distinction between *day* and *die* is maintained by a vowel in *die* which approaches that of *boy* in American speech, and *boy* in turn has a vowel which is difficult for "foreigners" to hear and impossible to represent without using phonetic notation.

Vocabulary   Once a jolly swagman camped by a billabong,
Under the shade of a coolibah tree;
And he sang as he watched and waited
    till his billy boiled,
"You'll come a-waltzing matilda with me."

This verse and several equally incomprehensible ones following it are well known to participants in American community sings. Much of the diction is now rather old-fashioned in Australia. The *a-waltzing* is quite common to many older varieties of English and certainly is not typical of today's Australian speech. *Waltzing matilda* is probably preserved only because of this song. *Matilda* is not capitalized, nor is "she" surrounded by commas—although more than one tank and possibly some aircraft received "her" name in World War II. The *swagman*, roughly equivalent to the older American *bindlestiff*, an itinerant who carried his belongings rolled up in a bundle or *swag (bindle)*, is gone from the scene. Carrying the swag or *matilda* was known as *waltzing matilda*. The *billabong* is a name given by native people to a blind channel of a river, roughly equivalent to a bayou; *coolibah* is a native tree name. The *billy* is a cylindrical metal cooking pot assumed to be derived from the native word *billa* (water, as in *billabong*).

In the vocabulary of daily use Australians unexpectedly use the word *station* for what animal raisers in the United States would call a ranch, and they have adapted words of international currency to special uses, such as calling a shopping cart a *jeep*.

Among the borrowings from the native languages the word *kangaroo* appeared in print in the reports of Captain James Cook before actual settlement had begun. It has been borrowed for the American coinage *kangaroo court* which in turn has been reborrowed into Australian English. The word *boomerang* has developed many figurative meanings throughout the English-speaking world, starting, apparently, with Oliver Wendell Holmes' use of it in 1845.

New Zealand English

New Zealand English shares some features with Australian, partly through exchange of population and partly through being settled from the same general area of England. Although from a distance the two countries seem close together, New Zealand is not a group of islands off the Australian coast, as it has sometimes been described. The Tasman Sea which separates them is 1,200 miles wide. Nevertheless, some of the earliest settlers of New Zealand were escaped convicts from Australia. In the period before organized settlement began in 1839 there were also deserters from ships, particularly whaling vessels, so that there may have been a small contribution to the population from New England.

Pronunciation   Some of the vowel features of Australian English which have been discussed are reflected in New Zealand speech. The vowels in words of the type *dance, path,* and *grass* have the vowel of *father* (as in South Australia) rather than that of *bat*. Greek compounds ending in *-graph,* however, have the vowel of *bat*.

The vowels of *day, die,* and *boy* follow the Australian pattern, and some speakers even have a vowel for *die* which could sound like a short "o" to visitors, who might look in vain on a map for a place called Crosschurch, not knowing that the mapmakers spell it *Christchurch*.

The most striking feature of New Zealand pronunciation is the shift of short vowels so that *bet* might sound like *bit* (and a parade might be described as a *precision*). The vowel of *bat* meanwhile gets close to that of *bet* so that the main mountain range of the country, the Southern Alps, would seem to rhyme with *helps*.

Vocabulary   Except for borrowings from the native languages and obvious recent imports, it is often very difficult to tell which of the items of the New Zealand vocabulary that it shares with Australia are the products of these islands. Because of its slightly earlier settlement and its role as the source of some of the early New Zealand population, Australia is usually assumed to be the source of the common vocabulary, but scholars in that part of the world are engaged in sorting these words out. As yet neither Australia nor New Zealand possesses the equivalent of the *Dictionary of Americanisms* or the *Dictionary of Canadianisms,* but an absorbing collection of essays on the English of the two countries and related territories has been published in Australia under the title *English Transported*, edited by W. S. Ramson. One of its important themes is the need for such works.

Whatever their origin, some terms have a specific New Zealand meaning. To an Australian the term *bush* may merely mean undeveloped scrub country, but to the New Zealander it is dense forest.

Recent American influence is easier to trace. The adoption of the term *cent* in both Australian and New Zealand as a unit of decimal coinage reflects this, although the term *dollar* was long known as a slang name for five shillings.

Borrowings from the native population, particularly for the names of plants and animals, have been very important. The *kiwi*, a flightless bird, has given its name not only as a term for New Zealander, but for nonflying personnel in air forces and airlines outside of New Zealand, especially former American stewardesses who have been assigned to ground duties.

The interplay of English and the native language (Maori) has been beset by some interesting pronunciation problems, particularly in the matter of the type of "r" used by each. One apparent borrowing from Maori, *taipo,* meaning *devil,* has been reinterpreted as a possible Maori borrowing from English *tripod,* for the support for the land-surveyor's theodolite which the Maori saw as a "land-stealing devil." On their side, English speakers have had their problems pronouncing some Maori words, particularly in interpreting "r"s as "d"s. Thus to find a burr referred to as a *biddybid* might seem to a visitor like a too-cute joke, but actually this is a distortion of the Maori word *piripiri*.

New Zealanders seem to share some words with other parts of the English-speaking world but with surprisingly different meanings. The term *section* for a city building lot might give a western American farmer an exaggerated idea of the spaciousness of New Zealand real estate developments. An Englishman, to whom *lay-by* is a recess at the roadside suitable for parking, would be startled to find that this refers to a purchase plan known in America as *layaway*.

Do We Speak the Same Language?

Not even the most extreme differences in the dialects of English justify calling any two of them different languages, and yet the ways in which we use what are apparently the same words can seem a barrier rather than an aid to understanding. Not only would the New Zealand use of *section* surprise a North American wheat farmer, but his use of *block* for a large tract of land in a rural area seems to carry confusion to extremes.

The Australian use of *jeep* as the name for a shopping cart is merely whimsical to the American, and if he were a trotting fan he would be surprised a few years ago to learn that mothers in Dunedin, New Zealand, wheeled their young children about in *sulkies*.

Sometimes we sort out sets of words in peculiar ways. The American *checks* his *baggage*, the Englishman *registers* his *luggage*, the New Zealander *checks* his *luggage*. The American gets his *mail* from the *mailman* or *letter carrier*, the Canadian may be served by a *mailman* or

postman who brings his *mail*, and the New Zealander gets his *mail* or *letters* from a *postman*.

The quality of a meaning may be very different, too. In the north of England *homely* is complimentary, and in Australia a *squatter* or a descendant of one has a certain prestige. Early settlement of the interior was rather haphazard and settlers merely occupied land, having their titles regularized later. In the history of the United States the nearest equivalent is *homesteader*, which is in distinct contrast with the American use of the term *squatter*.

Even a word so closely associated with Old England as *tea* is highly unreliable. To most Americans it is either a beverage or an afternoon social event (at which, in some regions, only coffee is served). In England it can be a daily or twice-daily occurrence and range, in the latter part of the day, from a light meal to a rather heavy one in the form known as Scottish High Tea. In Australia and the Maritime Provinces of Canada *tea* is apt to be another name for *supper*. And in New Zealand *supper* is a bedtime snack.

Explanatory Notes

See pronunciation key on page xx.

Car·bo·run·dum (kär'bə·run'dəm) *n.* An abrasive of silicon carbide: a trade name.

-cidal *combining form* Killing; able to kill: *homicidal*. [< L *caedere* kill]

Col·o·ra·do (kol'ə·rä'dō, -rad'ō) A western State of the United States; 103,967 square miles; capital, Denver; entered the Union Aug. 1, 1876: nicknamed *Centennial State*: abbr. *Colo.*

com– *prefix* With; together: *combine, compare*. Also: *co–* before *gn, h,* and vowels; *col–* before *l,* as in *collide; con–* before *c, d, f, g, j, n, q, s, t, v,* as in *concur, confluence, connect, conspire; cor–* before *r,* as in *correspond*. [< L *com– < cum* with]

craal (kräl) See KRAAL.

crab¹ (krab) *n.* **1** Any of various species of ten-footed crustaceans of the suborder *Brachyura* in the order *Decapoda*, characterized by a small abdomen folded under the body, a flattened carapace, and short antennae. They can walk in any direction without turning, but usually move sideways. **2** The hermit crab. **3** The horseshoe crab. **4** A crab louse, *Phthirus pubis*. **5** *Aeron.* The lateral slant in an airplane needed to maintain a flight line in a cross-wind. **6** A form of windlass. **7** *pl.* The lowest throw of a pair of dice. **— to catch a crab** In rowing, to sink an oar blade too deeply; also, to miss the water entirely or skim the surface in making a stroke, and thus fall backward. **—** *v.* **crabbed, crab·bing** *v.i.* **1** To take or fish for crabs. **2** *U.S. Colloq.* To back out: to *crab* out of an agreement. **3** *Naut.* To drift sideways, as a ship. **—** *v.t.* **4** *Aeron.* To head (an airplane) across a contrary wind so as to compensate for drift. [OE *crabba*. Akin to CRAB³.]

crab² (krab) *n.* **1** A crab apple. **2** A crab-apple tree. **3** An ill-tempered, surly, or querulous person. **—** *v.* **crabbed, crab·bing** *v.i.* **1** *Colloq.* To disparage; belittle; complain about. **2** *Colloq.* To ruin or spoil: He *crabbed* the entire act. **3** *Obs.* To make surly or sour; irritate. **4** *Brit. Dial.* To cudgel or beat, as with a crabstick. **—** *v.i.* **5** To be ill-tempered. [? < Scand. Cf. dial. Sw. *scrabba* wild apple.]

crab³ (krab) *v.i.* **crabbed, crab·bing** To seize each other fiercely, as hawks when fighting; claw. [< MDu. *crabben* scratch. Akin to CRAB¹.]

Crab A constellation and sign of the Zodiac; Cancer.

crab angle The angle between the direction of movement of an airplane, rocket, or guided missile and the direction in which the nose points, resembling . . .

crab apple A kind of small, sour apple: also called *crab*.

deep-seat·ed (dēp'sē'tid) *adj.* So far in as to be ineradicable or almost ineradicable: said of emotions, diseases, etc.

Deep South The southernmost parts of Alabama, Georgia, Louisiana, and Mississippi, conventionally regarded as typifying Southern culture and traditions.

deer (dir) *n. pl.* **deer 1** A ruminant (family *Cervidae*) having deciduous antlers, usually in the male only, as the moose, elk, and reindeer. Popularly, *deer* is used mainly of the smaller species. [◆ Collateral adjective: *cervine*.] See FALLOW DEER, VENISON. **2** A deerlike animal. **3** Formerly, any quadruped; a wild animal. [◆ Homophone: *dear*.] [OE *dēor* beast]

deer·fly (dir'flī') *n. pl.* **·flies** A bloodsucking fly (genus *Chrysops*), similar to a horsefly but smaller and with banded wings. For illustration see INSECTS (injurious).

di·eth·y·lene glycol (dī·eth'ə·lēn) *Chem.* An organic compound, $O(CH_2CH_2OH)_2$, used as an anti-freeze mixture and as an agent in many chemical processes for the ....

di·eth·yl·stil·bes·trol (dī·eth'əl·stil·bes'trōl) *n. Biochem.* Stilbestrol.

di·e·ti·tian (dī'ə·tish'ən) *n.* One skilled in the principles of dietetics and in their practical application in health and disease. Also **di·e·tet·ist** (dī'ə·tet'ist), **di·e·ti'cian.**

Dieu vous garde (dyœ' vōō' gàrd') *French* God protect you.

Diez (dēts), **Friedrich Christian,** 1794–1876, German philologist.

dif·fer (dif'ər) *v.i.* **1** To be unlike in quality, degree, form, etc.: often with *from.* **2** To disagree; dissent: often with *with.* **3** To quarrel: sometimes with *over* or *about.* [< OF *differer* < L *differre* < *dis–* apart + *ferre* carry. Doublet of DEFER¹.]

dif·fer·ence (dif'ər·əns, dif'rəns) *n.* **1** The state or quality of being other or unlike, or that in which two things are unlike; .... **8** *Her.* A device in blazons to distinguish persons bearing the same arms. **—** *v.t.* **·enced, ·enc·ing 1** To make or mark as different; distinguish; discriminate. **2** *Her.* To add a mark of difference to.

Synonyms (noun): contrariety, contrast, disagreement, discrepancy, discrimination, disparity, dissimilarity, dissimilitude, distinction, divergence, diversity, inconsistency, inequality, unlikeness, variation. A *difference* is in the things compared; .... *Diversity* involves more than two objects; *variation* is a *difference* in the condition or action of the same object at different times. *Antonyms*: agreement, consonance, harmony, identity, likeness, resemblance, sameness, similarity, uniformity, unity.

dif·fer·ent (dif'ər·ənt, dif'rənt) *adj.* **1** Not the same; distinct; other: A *different* clerk is there now. **2** Marked by a difference; completely or partly unlike; dissimilar. **3** Unusual. See synonyms under CONTRARY. [< F *différent* < L *differens, -entis,* ppr. of *differre*. See DIFFER.] **— dif·fer·ent·ly** *adv.* **— dif·fer·ent·ness** *n.* ◆ **different from, than, to** In American usage, *from* is established as the idiomatic preposition to follow *different*; when, however, a clause follows the connective, *than* is gaining increasing acceptance: a result *different than* (= *from that which* or *from what*) had been expected. This last is established British usage, which also accepts *to* ....

–dom *suffix of nouns* **1** State or condition of being: *freedom*. **2** Rank of; domain of: *kingdom*. **3** The totality of those having a certain rank, state or condition: *Christendom*. [< OE *–dōm < dōm* state]

Margin labels (left): Syllabication · Pronunciation · Trade name · Combining form · Geographic entry · Abbreviation · Prefix · Cross-reference · Part of speech · Taxonomic classification · Idiomatic phrase · Usage label · Field label · Homograph · Illustrative example · Inflected forms · Phrasal entry · Variant · Hyphenation

Margin labels (right): Collateral adjective · Homophone · Inflected form · Chemical formula · Cross-reference · Variants · Foreign language label · Biographic entry · Usage notes · Definition numbers · Synonyms · Antonyms · Illustrative example · Run-on entries · Usage note · Suffix · Etymology

Syllabication Division of words into syllables — as an indication of the points at which a word may be broken at the end of a line — is indicated by a centered dot (·) in the main bold-faced entries, as **ad·jec·ti·val.** In the secondary entries (run-on derivatives and variant forms) the centered dot is eliminated wherever the primary and secondary syllable stresses are marked, as in **ad′jec·ti′val·ly.** In hyphened compounds the hyphen takes the place of a centered dot. Phrasal entries of two or more words are not syllabified when each element is entered elsewhere, as in **caballine fountain.**

Pronunciations The pronunciation is shown in parentheses immediately following the bold-faced entry, as **di·chot·o·my** (dī·kot′ə·mē). When more than one pronunciation is recorded, the first given is usually the most widely used wherever it has been possible to determine extent of usage; often, however, usage may be almost equally divided. The order of the pronunciations is not intended to be an indication of preference; all pronunciations shown are valid for educated American speech.

The syllabication of the pronunciations follows, in general, the syllabic breaks heard in speech, rather than the conventional division of the bold-faced entry, as **bod·ing** (bō′ding), **grat·er** (grā′tər), **ju·di·cial** (jo͞o·dish′əl), **an·es·the·tize** (ə·nes′thə·tīz).

When a variant pronunciation differs merely in part from the first pronunciation recorded, only the differing syllable or syllables are shown, provided that there is no possibility of misinterpretation, as **eq·ua·bil·i·ty** (ek′wə·bil′ə·tē, ē′kwə-). Phrasal entries (those which consist of two or more words) are not pronounced if the individual elements are separately entered in proper alphabetic place.

Parts of speech These are shown in italics following the pronunciation for main entries, and are abbreviated as follows: *n.* (noun), *v.* (verb), *pron.* (pronoun), *adj.* (adjective), *adv.* (adverb), *prep.* (preposition), *conj.* (conjunction), *interj.* (interjection). When more than one part of speech is entered under a main entry, the additional designations are run in and preceded by a bold-faced dash, as **cor·ner** (kôr′nər) *n.* . . . — *v.t.* . . . — *v.i.* . . . — *adj.* . . .

Verbs used transitively are identified as *v.t.*, those intransitively as *v.i.*; those used both transitively and intransitively in all senses are designated *v.t. & v.i.*

Inflected forms These include the past tense, past participle, and present participle of verbs, the plural of nouns, and the comparative and superlative of adjectives and adverbs. The inflected forms are entered wherever there is some irregularity in spelling or form. They are shown in boldface type, with syllabication, immediately after the part of speech designation. Only the syllable affected is shown, provided there is no ambiguity possible, as **com·pute** (kəm·pyo͞ot′) *v.t.* **·put·ed, ·put·ing.** An inflected form that requires pronunciation or is alphabetically distant from the main entry may also be separately entered and pronounced in its proper vocabulary place.

Principal parts of verbs The order in which the principal parts are shown is past tense, past participle, and present participle, as **come** (kum) *v.* **came, come, com·ing.** Where the past tense and past participle are identical, only two forms are entered, as **bake** (bāk) *v.* **baked, bak·ing.** When alternative forms are given, the first form indicated is usually the one preferred, as **grov·el** (gruv′əl, grov′-) *v.i.* **grov·eled** or **grov·elled, grov·el·ing** or **grov·el·ling.** Variant forms not in the standard vocabulary are shown in parentheses and labeled, as **drink** (dringk) *v.* **drank** (*Obs.* **drunk**), **drunk** (*Obs.* **drunk·en**), **drink·ing.** Principal parts entirely regular in formation — those that add *-ed* and *-ing* directly to the infinitive without spelling modification — are not shown.

Plural of nouns Irregular forms are here preceded by the designation *pl.*, as **a·lum·nus** (ə·lum′nəs) *n. pl.* **·ni** (-nī); **co·dex** (kō′deks) *n. pl.* **co·di·ces** (kō′də·sēz, kod′ə-); **deer** (dir) *n. pl.* **deer.** When alternative plurals are given, the first shown is the preferred form, as **buf·fa·lo** (buf′ə·lō) *n. pl.* **·loes** or **·los; chrys·a·lis** (kris′ə·lis) *n. pl.* **chrys·a·lis·es** or **chry·sal·i·des** (kri·sal′ə·dēz). Words that have different plural forms for specific senses are shown as follows:

an·ten·na (an·ten′ə) *n. pl.* **an·ten·nae** (an·ten′ē) *for def.* **1, an·ten·nas** *for def.* **2. 1** *Entomol.* One of the paired, lateral, movable, jointed appendages on the head of an insect or other arthropod. **2** *Telecom.* A system of wires upheld in a vertical or horizontal position by a mast or tower, for transmitting or receiving electromagnetic waves in wireless telegraphy, telephony, and radio. . . . .

Comparison of adjectives and adverbs The comparatives and superlatives of adjectives and adverbs are shown immediately after the part of speech when there is some spelling modification or a complete change of form, as **mer·ry** (mer′ē) *adj.* **·ri·er, ·ri·est; bad**[1] (bad) *adj.* **worse, worst; well**[2] (wel) *adv.* **bet·ter, best.**

Definition numbers In entries for words having several senses, the order in which the definitions appear is, wherever possible, that of frequency of use, rather than semantic evolution. Each such definition is distinguished by a bold-faced number, the numbering starting anew after each part-of-speech designation when it is followed by more than one sense. Closely related meanings, especially those within a specific field or area of study, are defined under the same number and set apart by small bold-faced letters.

bol·ster (bōl′stər) *n.* **1** A long, narrow pillow as wide as a bed. **2** A pad used as a support or . . . . **3** Anything shaped like . . . . **4** *Archit.* **a** The lateral part of the volute of an Ionic capital. **b** A crosspiece of an arch centering . . . . **5** *Mech.* A steel block . . . . — *v.t.* **1** To support with a pillow. **2** To prop up . . . . **3** To furnish with padding. . . .

Restrictive labels Entries or particular senses of words and terms having restricted application are variously labeled according to: (1) usage level, as *Slang, Colloq.* (colloquial), *Dial.* (dialectal), *Poetic*, etc.; (2) localization, as *U.S.* (United States), *Brit.* (British), *Austral.* (Australian), *Scot.* (Scottish English), etc.; (3) field or subject, as *Astron.* (astronomy), *Geom.* (geometry), *Mining* (mining), *Naut.* (nautical), *Surg.* (surgery), etc.; (4) language of origin, as *Afrikaans, French, German, Latin*, etc.

These labels serve as a guide in the ready identification of special aspects of a word or term as a whole or of one or more of its parts. The usage labels qualify a word in terms of its relationship to standard English; the localized area designations identify the geographical region of the English-speaking world in which a word has originated or where it has particular application; the subject labels indicate that a word or definition has a specialized use in some field of work or study; and the foreign language labels reflect the fact that a word or phrase, although used in English speech and writing, has not yet undergone the process of Anglicization of pronunciation, meaning, or usage, and is still felt to be foreign (these foreign terms are usually italicized in writing).

Restrictive labels that apply to only one sense of a word are entered after the definition number, as:

beat (bēt) *v.* . . . . **9** *Music* To mark or measure with or as with a baton: to *beat* time. . . . . **13** *Colloq.* To baffle; perplex: It *beats* me. **14** *Slang* To defraud; swindle. . . . . **20** *Physics* To alternate in intensity so as to pulsate . . . . **24** *Naut.* To work against contrary winds or currents by tacking.

Labels entered immediately after the part of speech designation apply to all the senses for that part of speech; those shown directly after the pronunciation and before the first part-of-speech designation refer to the entire entry, as:

hal·i·dom (hal′ə·dəm) *n. Archaic* **1** Holiness. **2** A holy relic. **3** A holy place; sanctuary. . . .
grouch (grouch) *U.S. Colloq. v.i.* To grumble; be surly or discontented. — *n.* **1** A discontented, grumbling person. **2** A grumbling, sulky mood. . . . .

A complete list of the label abbreviations used in this dictionary will be found on page xx.

Variant forms In the case of words having more than one approved spelling (as *esthetic, aesthetic; center, centre*), the main entry is made under what is considered to be the form in more general use in the United States. The alternate form is cross-referred when it is not within close range of the alphabetic position of the main entry, and is also shown in italic type at the end of the main entry or after all the definitions for a particular part of speech to which it applies. Variant forms that do not require cross-reference are shown in the same position in the main entry but in boldface type with syllabication, stress marks, and, when necessary, pronunciation. A variant that applies to but one of several senses of a word is attached with a colon to the definition to which it pertains.

bach·e·lor (bach′ə·lər, bach′lər) *n.* . . . . **3** A young knight serving under another's banner: also **bach′e·lor-at-arms′.** . . . . **5** A young male fur seal kept from the breeding grounds by the older males: also called *holluschick.* . . . .

Forms that have some restricted usage are labeled accordingly, as **hon·or** . . . Also *Brit.* **hon′our.**

Phrasal entries Numerous phrases are entered and defined in the vocabulary section of this book in alphabetic place according to the first word of the phrase, as **bird of paradise, earth inductor, free verse, right of search.** In many other instances, however, it has been more expedient to enter and define such phrases under the main element. Thus, *Old English* and *Middle English* are run in as subordinate entries under **English,** preceded by a heavy dash; *alternating current, direct current,* and *eddy current* are entered and defined under **current.** All such entries are cross-referred in alphabetic place.

In some entries, particularly those for plants and animals, varying combinations of the word being defined are given within the main entry in boldface type and not entered in alphabetic place, as **leop·ard** · · · **2** Any similar cat, such as the **American leopard** or jaguar, the **hunting leopard** or cheetah, the **snow leopard** or ounce.

Encyclopedic entries A similar device has been employed where it has been advisable to bring together in one place as much logically related information as possible. Certain groups of terms are fully treated in an alphabetic boldface listing under the primary word common to each group. This treatment points up significant relationships between terms, facilitates comparison and selection of the term desired, and allows for the presentation of a range of information ordinarily characteristic of encyclopedias. For example, the entry for **time** contains a listing, with full definitions, of the various classifications from *astronomical time* through *zone time.* Similar listings have been included under the following entries: *angle, calendar, court, cross, current* (*ocean currents*), *diamond, fraction, glass, law, number, school, spaniel,* and *terrier.* All terms so entered are separately cross-referred.

Idiomatic phrases Often a main-entry word, when in conjunction with various prepositions, adverbs, adjectives, etc., will form a phrase distinct in sense from the meaning of the combined elements. Such idiomatic phrases are shown in smaller boldface type within the entry for the principal word in the phrase; they are preceded by a heavy dash, and follow all the definitions for the particular part of speech involved. Thus, under the verb **carry** will be found subordinate entries for the phrases *carry arms, carry away, carry off, carry on,* etc.; under the entry for the noun **hand** such phrases as *at first hand, by hand, to have one's hands full,*

add,āce,câre,pälm; end,ēven; it,īce; odd,ōpen,ôrder; to͝ok,po͞ol; up,bûrn; ə = a in *above,* e in *sicken,* i in *clarity,* o in *melon,* u in *focus;* yo͞o = u in *fuse;* oi,oil; ou,pout; ch,check; g,go; ng,ring; th,thin; t͟h,this; zh,vision. Foreign sounds à,œ,ü,kh,ṅ; and ◆: see page xx. < from; + plus; ? possibly.

to lend a hand, etc., are set apart and defined in detail.

Collateral adjectives Because of the grafting of Norman French and late Renaissance Latin idioms on early English we find a good many English nouns which have adjectives closely connected with them in sense but not in form, such as *brachial* with *arm, cervical* with *neck, lacustrine* with *lake, hibernal* with *winter, diurnal* with *day, reticular* with *net*, and the like. Such adjectives which, through a collateral line of meaning, have come to express certain special adjectival senses, are, of course, listed in their regular alphabetic place, but, as a convenience for those who do not know or cannot recall them, a large number of such functionally related adjectives have been entered with their associated nouns, attached to the particular meaning of the noun to which they apply, in the form ◆ Collateral adjective: *brachial*.

Homophones Words identical in sound but different in spelling and meaning, such as the groups *altar / alter, filter / philter, hail / hale, principal / principle, right / rite / write*, and several hundred others, often lead to confusion in the writing of English. A large number of these have been listed just before the etymology of every relevant entry, in the form ◆ Homophone: *altar*. No entries have been made for such groups as *horse / hoarse, burrow / burro* which, because of variant pronunciations, are homophonic for some speakers but not for others.

Etymologies The etymologies are shown in brackets after the definitions and before the run–on derivatives. The following examples show the manner of entry and the use of cross–references: (1) **spe·cial** . . . [<OF *especial* <L *specialis* < *species* kind, species]; the etymology is to be read: derived from (<) the Old French (OF) word *especial* from the Latin (L) word *specialis* which in turn is from Latin *species* meaning "kind, species"; (2) **arroyo** . . . [<Sp.]; here the reading is to be: derived from (<) a Spanish (Sp.) word of the same form and meaning; (3) **has·sle** . . . [? <HAGGLE + TUSSLE]; this etymology is to be read: perhaps (?) derived from (<) a blending of "haggle" and (+) "tussle," the small capital letters indicating that the etymologies of these words will be found under their main entries; (4) **de·cep·tion** . . . [<L *deceptio, -onis* < *decipere*. See DECEIVE.]; (5) **bul·wark** . . . [<MHG *bolwerc*. Akin to BOULEVARD.]; (6) **a·dult** . . . [<L *adultus*, pp. of *adolescere* grow up < *ad-* + *alescere* grow. Related to ADOLESCENT.]; (7) **jour·nal** . . . [<OF <L *diurnalis*. Doublet of DIURNAL.]

Cross–references In (4), "See" directs attention to the etymology under "deceive" for further information; in (5), "Akin to" points to the fact that "boulevard" and "bulwark" are cognate words; in (6), "Related to" indicates that these words derive from different recorded stems of the same word; in (7), "Doublet of" marks the fact that "journal" and "diurnal" are ultimately derived from the same Latin word, but have come into English by different paths, in this case, the former through Old French and the latter directly from Latin.

For the complete list of the abbreviations which are used in the etymologies in this work, see page xx.

Run–on entries Words that are actually or ostensibly derived from other words by the addition or replacement of a suffix, and whose sense can be inferred from the meaning of the main word, are run on, in smaller boldface type, at the end of the appropriate main entries. The run–on entries are preceded by a heavy dash and followed by a part–of–speech designation. They are syllabified and stressed, and, when necessary, a full or partial pronunciation is indicated, as **in·sip·id** (in·sip′id) *adj.* . . . **— in·si·pid·i·ty** (in′si·pid′ə·tē), **in·sip′id·ness** *n.* **— in·sip′id·ly** *adv.*

Usage notes Points of grammar and idiom, when an integral part of definition, are included, following a colon, after the particular sense of a word to which they apply, as **anx·ious** . . . **3** Intent; eagerly desirous; solicitous: with *for* or the infinitive with *to*: *anxious* for success; *anxious* to succeed . . .

More extensive notes consisting of supplementary information on grammar, accepted usage, the relative status of variant forms, etc., are entered at the end of the relevant entries and prefaced with the symbol ◆. (See **any-one, Asiatic, can, have.**)

Synonyms and antonyms Extended discussions of the differentiation in shades of meaning within a group of related words, or in some cases simple lists of synonyms, are given at the end of relevant entries in paragraphed form after the run–on derivatives. Lists of antonyms are often added as well to point up further distinctions in meaning.

Alphabetization All entries in this dictionary (general vocabulary, affixes, geographical and biographical entries, foreign words and phrases, etc.) are in one alphabetic list, with the exception of an extended list of abbreviations given, for the sake of ready reference, in one section at the back of the book. Thus, the entry for **ampere** (the electrical unit) immediately precedes that for **André Marie Ampère**, for whom it was named; the entry for **Bridge of Sighs** precedes **Bridgeport** and follows **bridgehead**; the prefix **pro–** is entered immediately after the word **pro** (a professional) and before the word **proa** (a sailing vessel).

Hyphens The hyphen used in the spelling of hyphemes (hyphened words) in this dictionary is printed with extra length to distinguish it as a spelling characteristic, as **cap–a–pie, battle–scarred.** This lengthened hyphen is also used in the entries for prefixes, suffixes, and combining forms, as **un–, –less, hydro–.** The standard hyphen is utilized at the ends of lines to indicate syllabic breaks in words ordinarily written solid, as *com-prehensive*, while the lengthened hyphen is retained for the end–of–line breaks in hyphemes.

Homographs These words, which are identical in spelling but differ in meaning and origin (and often in pronunciation), are separately entered and differentiated by the following superior figure, as **bushel**[1] (measure), **bushel**[2] (mend); **pink**[1] (color), **pink**[2] (stab), **pink**[3] (sailing vessel), **pink**[4] (fade). The numbering also serves to simplify cross–reference to such words.

Cross–references Cross–references are directions to see another entry for additional information. They direct the reader from a variant spelling, inflected form, subentry, etc., to a main entry. The entry to be sought is generally indicated in small capital letters, as **car·a·cul** . . . See KARAKUL; **aes·thete** . . . , **aes·thet·ic** . . . See ESTHETE, etc.; **cor·po·ra** . . . Plural of CORPUS; **Old English** See under ENGLISH.

Sometimes a cross–reference is made to a homograph entry or to a particular definition or part of speech of the main entry, as

flied (flīd) Past tense and past participle of FLY[1] (def. 7).

taps (taps) See TAP[2] (*n.* def. 3).

Some entries are defined by citing another form, as

se·pi·o·lite . . . *n.* Meerschaum.

This is a type of cross–reference. Complete information will be found under the word or term used in the definition.

See the note on **Etymologies**, for the system of cross–referring there used.

Prefixes, suffixes, and combining forms These are entered and defined in regular alphabetic order. The prefix is followed by the lengthened hyphen, the suffix preceded by it, as **anti–** *prefix*; **–ical** *suffix*.

Similarly, the combining form is followed or preceded by the lengthened hyphen depending on its position in combination, as **proto–** *combining form*; **–cide** *combining form*.

Word lists The meaning of many combinations of words (hyphemes, solidemes, and two–word phrases) is easily deduced by combining the senses of their component parts. Such self–explaining compounds have been entered in list form under the first element — that is, under prefixes (**bi–, co–, non–, re–**, etc.) combining forms (**auto–, counter–, mid–**, etc.), and words (**corn, heart, man, peace**, etc.). These lists serve to indicate the preferred form of a compound — whether written solid, with a hyphen, or as a two–word phrase. The listings are not intended to be all–inclusive; most of the prefixes and combining forms so entered combine freely in English in the formation of new compounds based on existing forms.

Chemical formulas As an integral part of the definitions of the large number of chemical substances listed in this dictionary, the reader will find the formulas which, in the chemist's shorthand, indicate what constituents enter into a compound, and in what proportions. These formulas, though usually of the simple empirical type, help to prevent confusion in the identification of hundreds of the substances used in medicine, industry, and the arts, and are particularly useful in recognizing distinctions between the two broad fields of inorganic and organic chemicals.

Taxonomic classification Essential technical information regarding the many plants and animals described under their common names is provided by the listing, usually in italic type enclosed in parentheses, of one or more of the principal taxonomic categories — phylum or division, class, order, family, genus, and species — by which they are correctly identified in botanical and zoological usage. This information, checked against the latest and most reliable sources, is especially useful in showing relationships between seemingly very different types and in discriminating within and between deceptively similar groups, such as toads and frogs, spruce and hemlock, and moths and butterflies.

Trade names Of the thousands of words used to identify trademarked or proprietary articles, drugs, processes, and services, a generous number have been entered and defined in this book because of their wide public acceptance. In every such case the word is entered as though it were a proper name: that is, with an initial capital letter, and the added notation, "a trade name" or — chiefly for the pharmaceutical products — "a proprietary name (or brand) . . ." This technique is employed to alert the reader to the commercial status of a word and, by implication, to caution him against employing it in a generic sense that might involve him in legal difficulties with those claiming a prescriptive or legal right to its use. This treatment of proprietary names is in no sense to be interpreted as establishing a formal status within the meaning of any of the various statutes involving the protection and use of trade names, registered or otherwise.

Illustrations, maps, and tables The illustrations in this book — all of them carefully prepared line drawings — have been selected with the emphasis on their explanatory value rather than their pictorial or decorative effect. They often include informative captions, and are intended to supplement the definitions.

A certain number of geographic entries are accompanied by small, precise spot maps which show at a glance just how a given place, region, lake, island, or other feature is related to its immediate surroundings — as under *Congo* (river system), *English Channel, Holy Roman Empire, Suez.*

For a selected group of entries supplementary information has been provided in the form of charts and tables, as for foreign alphabets (see **alphabet**), the geological time scale (see **geology**), chemical elements (see **periodic table**), the major wars of history (see **war**), constellations, clouds, the endocrine glands, etc.

Abbreviations The abbreviations used in the body of this book (in labeling within entries, in etymologies, etc.) will be found listed on page xx. Where abbreviations of main-entry words are entered, they are shown at the end of the entry, as Abbr. *B.A., A.B.* (Bachelor of Arts); Abbr. *AWOL, awol, A.W.O.L., a.w.o.l.* (absent without leave); Abbr. *Dan.* (Danish). Biblical references are to the King James Bible and indicate book, chapter, and verse, in that order, as *Matt.* v 3–12. An extended list of standard abbreviations will be found at the end of the dictionary, following the vocabulary section.

TABLE OF ENGLISH SPELLINGS

FOLLOWING is a list of words exemplifying the possible spellings for the sounds of English. The sounds represented by these spellings are shown in the pronunciation symbols used in this dictionary, followed by their equivalents in the International Phonetic Alphabet.

a	æ	c*a*t, pl*ai*d, c*a*lf, l*au*gh
ā	eɪ,e	m*a*te, b*ai*t, g*ao*l, g*au*ge, p*a*y, st*ea*k, sk*ei*n, w*ei*gh, pr*e*y
â(r)	ɛ,ɛr	d*a*re, f*ai*r, pr*a*yer, wh*e*re, b*ea*r, th*ei*r
ä	ɑ	d*a*rt, *a*h, c*a*lf, l*au*gh, s*e*rgeant, h*ea*rt
b	b	*b*oy, ru*bb*er
ch	tʃ	*ch*ip, ba*tch*, righ*t*eous, bas*ti*on, struc*t*ure
d	d	*d*ay, la*dd*er, calle*d*
e	ɛ	m*a*ny, a*e*sthete, s*ai*d, s*a*ys, b*e*t, st*ea*dy, h*ei*fer, l*eo*pard, fr*ie*nd, f*oe*tid
ē	i	C*ae*sar, qu*ay*, sc*e*ne, m*ea*t, s*ee*, s*ei*ze, p*eo*ple, k*e*y, rav*i*ne, gr*ie*f, ph*oe*be
f	f	*f*ake, co*ff*in, cou*gh*, hal*f*, *ph*ase
g	g	*g*ate, be*gg*ar, *gh*oul, *g*uard, va*gue*
h	h	*h*ot, *wh*om
hw	hw,ʍ	*wh*ale
i	ɪ	pr*e*tty, b*ee*n, t*i*n, s*ie*ve, w*o*men, b*u*sy, g*ui*lt, l*y*nch
ī	aɪ	*ai*sle, *a*ye, sl*ei*ght, *e*ye, d*i*me, p*ie*, s*igh*, g*ui*le, b*u*y, tr*y*, l*y*e
j	dʒ	*e*dge, sol*di*er, mo*d*ulate, ra*ge*, exa*gg*erate, *j*oy
k	k	*c*an, a*c*cost, sa*cch*arine, *ch*ord, ta*ck*, a*c*quit, *k*ing, ta*lk*, li*qu*or
l	l	*l*et, ga*ll*
m	m	dra*chm*, phle*gm*, pa*lm*, *m*ake, li*mb*, gra*mm*ar, conde*mn*
n	n	*gn*ome, *kn*ow, *mn*emonic, *n*ote, ba*nn*er, *pn*eumatic
ng	ŋ	si*nk*, ri*ng*, meri*ng*ue
o	ɑ,ɒ	w*a*tch, p*o*t
ō	ou,o	b*eau*, y*eo*man, s*ew*, *o*ver, s*oa*p, r*oe*, *oh*, br*oo*ch, s*ou*l, th*ough*, gr*ow*
ô	ɔ	b*a*ll, b*a*lk, f*au*lt, d*aw*n, c*o*rd, br*oa*d, *ough*t
oi	ɔɪ	p*oi*son, t*oy*
ou	aʊ	*ou*t, b*ough*, c*ow*
ōō	u	r*heu*m, dr*ew*, m*o*ve, can*oe*, m*oo*d, gr*ou*p, *th*r*ough*, fl*u*ke, s*ue*, fr*ui*t
ōō	ʊ	w*o*lf, f*oo*t, c*ou*ld, p*u*ll
p	p	ma*p*, ha*pp*en
r	r	*r*ose, *rh*ubarb, ma*rr*y, dia*rrh*ea, w*r*iggle
s	s	*c*ite, di*c*e, *ps*yche, *s*aw, *sc*ene, *sch*ism, ma*ss*
sh	ʃ	o*c*ean, *ch*ivalry, vi*ci*ous, *p*s*h*aw, *s*ure, *sch*ist, pre*sci*ence, nau*s*eous, *sh*all, pen*s*ion, ti*ss*ue, fi*ss*ion, po*ti*on
t	t	walk*ed*, though*t*, *phth*isic, *p*tarmigan, *t*one, *Th*omas, bu*tt*er
th	θ	*th*ick
th	ð	*th*is, ba*th*e
u	ʌ	s*o*me, d*oe*s, bl*oo*d, y*ou*ng, s*u*n
yōō	ju,ɪu	b*eau*ty, *eu*logy, q*ueue*, p*ew*, *ew*e, ad*ieu*, v*iew*, f*u*se, c*ue*, y*ou*th, *yu*le
û(r)	ɝr,ɝ	y*ear*n, f*er*n, *err*, g*ir*l, w*or*m, j*our*nal, b*ur*n, g*uer*don, m*yr*tle
v	v	o*f*, Ste*ph*en, *v*ise, fli*vv*er
w	w	*ch*oir, q*u*ilt, *w*ill
y	j	*o*nion, hallelu*j*ah, *y*et
z	z	wa*s*, di*s*cern, sci*ss*ors, *x*ylophone, *z*oo, mu*zz*le
zh	ʒ	rou*g*e, plea*s*ure, inci*s*ion, sei*z*ure, gla*z*ier
ə	ə	*a*bove, fount*ai*n, dark*e*n, clar*i*ty, parl*ia*ment, cann*o*n, porp*oi*se, vic*iou*s, loc*u*s
ər	ər,ɚ	mort*ar*, broth*er*, elix*ir*, don*or*, glam*our*, aug*ur*, nat*ure*, zeph*yr*

SPELLING:
Plurals and Participles

BASICALLY, plurals in English are formed by the addition of -*s* or -*es* (depending on the preceding sound) to the complete word; past participles are formed by the addition of -*ed*, and present participles by adding -*ing*. There are, however, many exceptions. In this book, all such exceptions (the "irregular" inflected forms) are indicated within the entry, in boldface immediately following the part-of-speech label.

fly (flī) *n.* *pl.* **flies** . . .
sheep (shēp) *n.* *pl.* **sheep** . . .
cal·ci·fy (kal′sə-fī) *v.t.* & *v.i.* **·fied, ·fy·ing** . . .
go (gō) *v.i.* **went, gone, go·ing** . . .

Some rules for the spelling of these forms (with the exception of nouns which form their plurals by some internal change and the so-called strong verbs) are listed below:

PLURALS

1. Nouns ending in *y* preceded by a consonant change *y* to *i* and add -*es*.

baby babies   story stories

2. Nouns ending in *y* preceded by a vowel add -*s* without change.

chimney chimneys   valley valleys

Note, however, that *money* may have either form in the plural — *moneys, monies.*

3. Some nouns ending in *f* or *fe* change this to *v* and add -*es*.

knife knives   shelf shelves
BUT: roof roofs   safe safes

Note: Some words may have alternate plural forms.

scarf   scarfs or scarves

4. Most words ending in *o* form a plural in -*os*.

cameo cameos   folio folios   halo halos

A few words ending in *o* (*echo, hero, Negro,* etc.) form the plural only in -*oes* (*echoes, heroes, Negroes*), but many others in this category have alternative plurals in both forms.

buffalo   buffalos or buffaloes
mosquito   mosquitos or mosquitoes
volcano   volcanoes or volcanos

PAST AND PRESENT PARTICIPLES

1. The final consonant is doubled for monosyllables or words accented on the final syllable when they end in a *single* consonant preceded by a *single* vowel.

control, controlled, controlling
hop, hopped, hopping
occur, occurred, occurring
quit, quitted, quitting (*Note*: a u following q *is not to be counted as an additional vowel.*)
BUT: help, helped, helping (*two consonants*)
seed, seeded, seeding (*two vowels*)

Some words *not* accented on the final syllable have a variant participial form with a doubled consonant; the single consonant form is preferred in the United States.

travel, traveled or travelled, traveling or travelling
worship, worshiped or worshipped, worshiping or worshipping

2. Words ending in silent or mute *e* drop the *e* before -*ed* and -*ing*, unless it is needed to avoid confusion with another word.

change, changed, changing   love, loved, loving
singe, singed, singeing   dye, dyed, dyeing

3. Verbs ending in *ie* usually change this to *y* before adding -*ing*.

die, died, dying   lie, lied, lying

4. Verbs ending in *c* add a *k* before -*ed* and -*ing*.

mimic, mimicked, mimicking
picnic, picnicked, picnicking

PRONUNCIATION KEY

The primary stress mark (′) is placed after the syllable bearing the heavier stress or accent; the secondary stress mark (′) follows a syllable having a somewhat lighter stress, as in **com·men·da·tion** (kom′ən·dā′shən).

a	add, map	f	fit, half	n	nice, tin	p	pit, stop	u	up, done	ə the schwa, an un-
ā	ace, rate	g	go, log	ng	ring, song	r	run, poor	û(r)	urn, term	stressed vowel
â(r)	care, air	h	hope, hate			s	see, pass	yōō	use, few	representing the
ä	palm, father	i	it, give	o	odd, hot	sh	sure, rush			sound of
		ī	ice, write	ō	open, so	t	talk, sit	v	vain, eve	*a* in *above*
b	bat, rub			ô	order, jaw	th	thin, both	w	win, away	*e* in *sicken*
ch	check, catch	j	joy, ledge	oi	oil, boy	th	this, bathe	y	yet, yearn	*i* in *clarity*
d	dog, rod	k	cool, take	ou	out, now			z	zest, muse	*o* in *melon*
e	end, pet	l	look, rule	ōō	pool, food			zh	vision, pleasure	*u* in *focus*
ē	even, tree	m	move, seem	ōō	took, full					

FOREIGN SOUNDS

à as in French *ami, patte.* This is a vowel midway in quality between (a) and (ä).

œ as in French *peu,* German *schön.* Round the lips for (ō) and pronounce (ā).

ü as in French *vue,* German *grün.* Round the lips for (ōō) and pronounce (ē).

kh as in German *ach,* Scottish, *loch.* Pronounce a strongly aspirated (h) with the tongue in position for (k) as in *cool* or *keep.*

n This symbol indicates that the preceding vowel is nasal. The nasal vowels in French are œṅ (*brun*), aṅ (*main*), äṅ (*chambre*), ôṅ (*dont*). This symbol indicates that a preceding (l) or (r) is voiceless, as in French *débâcle* (dā·bä′kl′) or *fiacre* (fyà′kr′), or that a preceding (y) is pronounced consonantly in a separate syllable followed by a slight schwa sound, as in French *fille* (fē′y′).

Note on the accentuation of foreign words:

Many languages do not employ stress in the manner of English; only an approximation can be given of the actual situation in such languages. As it is not possible to reproduce the tones of Chinese in a work of this kind, Chinese names have been here recorded with primary stress on each syllable and may be so pronounced. Japanese and Korean have been shown without stress and may be pronounced with a level accent throughout. French words are shown conventionally with a primary stress on the last syllable; however, this stress tends to be evenly divided among the syllables (except for those that are completely unstressed), with slightly more force and higher pitch on the last syllable.

ABBREVIATIONS USED IN THIS WORK

abbr.	abbreviation(s)	Ezek.	Ezekiel	Mech.	Mechanics	Philos.	Philosophy
A.D.	year of our Lord	F, Fr.	French	Med.	Medicine, Me-	Phonet.	Phonetics
adj.	adjective	fem.	feminine		dieval	Phot.	Photography
adv.	adverb	freq.	frequentative	Med. Gk.	Medieval Greek	Physiol.	Physiology
Aeron.	Aeronautics	G, Ger.	German		(600–1500)	pl.	plural
AF	Anglo-French	Gal.	Galatians	Med. L	Medieval Latin	pp.	past participle
Agric.	Agriculture	Gen.	Genesis		(600–1500)	ppr.	present participle
Alg.	Algebra	Geog.	Geography	Metall.	Metallurgy	prep.	preposition
alter.	alteration	Geol.	Geology	Meteorol.	Meteorology	prob.	probably
Am. Ind.	American Indian	Geom.	Geometry	MF	Middle French	pron.	pronoun
Anat.	Anatomy	Gk.	Greek (Homer—		(1400–1600)	Prov.	Proverbs
Anthropol.	Anthropology		A.D. 200)	MHG	Middle High	Ps., Psa.	Psalms
appar.	apparently	Gmc.	Germanic		German (1100	Psychoanal.	Psychoanalysis
Archeol.	Archeology	Govt.	Government		–1450)	Psychol.	Psychology
Archit.	Architecture	Gram.	Grammar	Mic.	Micah	pt.	preterit
assoc.	association	Hab.	Habakkuk	Mil.	Military	ref.	reference
Astron.	Astronomy	Hag.	Haggai	MLG	Middle Low	Rev.	Revelation
aug.	augmentative	Heb.	Hebrews		German (1100	Rom.	Romans
Austral.	Australian	Her.	Heraldry		–1450)	Sam., Saml.	Samuel
Bacteriol.	Bacteriology	HG	High German			Scand.	Scandinavian
B.C.	Before Christ	Hind.	Hindustani	n.	noun	Scot.	Scottish
Biochem.	Biochemistry	Hos.	Hosea	Nah.	Nahum	SE	Southeast
Biol.	Biology	Icel.	Icelandic	Naut.	Nautical	sing.	singular
Bot.	Botany	Illit.	Illiterate	Nav.	Naval	Skt.	Sanskrit
Brit.	British	imit.	imitative	N. Am. Ind.	North American	Sociol.	Sociology
c.	century	infl.	influence, influ-		Indian	S. of Sol.	Song of Solomon
Can.	Canadian		enced	NE	Northeast	S. Am. Ind.	South American
cf.	compare	intens.	intensive	Neh.	Nehemiah		Indian
Chem.	Chemistry	interj.	interjection	neut.	neuter	Sp.	Spanish
Chron.	Chronicles	Is., Isa.	Isaiah	NL	New Latin (after	Stat.	Statistics
Col.	Colossians	Ital.	Italian		1500)	superl.	superlative
Colloq.	Colloquial	Jas.	James	Norw.	Norwegian	Surg.	Surgery
compar.	comparative	Jer.	Jeremiah	Num., Numb.	Numbers	Sw.	Swedish
conj.	conjunction	Jon.	Jonah	NW	Northwest	SW	Southwest
Cor.	Corinthians	Josh.	Joshua	O	Old	Technol.	Technology
Dan.	Daniel, Danish	Judg.	Judges	Ob., Obad.	Obadiah	Telecom.	Telecommunica-
def.	definition	L, Lat.	Latin (Classical,	Obs.	Obsolete		tion
Dent.	Dentistry		80 B.C.–A.D. 200)	OE	Old English (be-	Theol.	Theology
Deut.	Deuteronomy	Lam.	Lamentations		fore 1150)	Thess.	Thessalonians
Dial.	Dialect, Dialectal	Lev., Levit.	Leviticus	OF	Old French (be-	Tim.	Timothy
dim.	diminutive	LG	Low German		fore 1400)	Tit.	Titus
Du.	Dutch	LGk.	Late Greek (200–	OHG	Old High Ger-	trans.	translation
E	English		600)		man (before	Trig.	Trigonometry
Eccl.	Ecclesiastical	Ling.	Linguistics		1100)	ult.	ultimate, ulti-
Eccles.	Ecclesiastes	lit.	literally	ON	Old Norse (be-		mately
Ecclus.	Ecclesiasticus	LL	Late Latin (200–		fore 1500)	U.S.	United States
Ecol.	Ecology		600)	orig.	original, origi-	v.	verb
Econ.	Economics	M	Middle		nally	var.	variant
Electr.	Electricity	Mal.	Malachi	Ornithol.	Ornithology	v.i.	verb intransitive
Engin.	Engineering	masc.	masculine	OS	Old Saxon (be-	v.t.	verb transitive
Entomol.	Entomology	Math.	Mathematics		fore 1100)	WGmc.	West Germanic
Eph.	Ephesians	Matt.	Matthew	Paleontol.	Paleontology	Zech.	Zechariah
esp.	especially	MDu.	Middle Dutch	Pet.	Peter	Zeph.	Zephaniah
Esth.	Esther	ME	Middle English	Pg.	Portuguese	Zool.	Zoology
Ex., Exod.	Exodus		(1150–1500)	Phil.	Philippians		
				Philem.	Philemon		

◆ Usage note; Homophone; Collateral adjective   < from   + plus   ? possibly

THE NEW INTERNATIONAL
WEBSTER'S
COMPREHENSIVE
DICTIONARY
OF THE ENGLISH LANGUAGE
Deluxe Encyclopedic Edition

a, A (ā) *n. pl.* **a's, A's** or **As, aes** (āz) **1** The first letter of the English alphabet: from Phoenician *aleph*, through the Hebrew *aleph*, Greek *alpha*, and Roman *A*. **2** Any sound of the letter *a*. See ALPHABET. — *symbol* **1** Primacy in class or order: grade *A* beef. **2** A substitute for the numeral 1: section *A*. **3** *Music* **a** One of a series of tones, the sixth in the natural diatonic scale of C, or the first note in the related minor scale. **b** A standard for tuning instruments: the pitch of this tone. **c** The written note representing this tone. **d** The scale built upon A. **3** *Chem.* Argon (symbol A).

a[1] (ə, *stressed* ā) *indefinite article* or *adj.* In each; to each; for each: twice a year; one dollar *a* bushel: equivalent to *per.* ◆ **a, per** *A* is preferred to *per*, except where *per* is required in business and statistical writing. [OE *an, on* in, on, at; orig. a prep.]

a[2] (ə, *stressed* ā) *indefinite article* or *adj.* One; any; some; each: before a vowel, *an.* See AN, ARTICLE.

Special uses: before plural nouns with *few, great many*, or *good many*; with *on, at,* or *of*, denoting oneness, sameness: birds of *a* feather; before proper names referring to the qualities or character of an individual: He is a Hercules in strength [Reduced form of AN used before consonant sounds]

◆ **a, an** *A* is used before a word beginning with a consonant sound, now including *h* when pronounced: *a* history, *a* hotel (*Brit.* often *an* hotel). Before an unaccented syllable beginning with *h* some writers prefer the older usage: *an* historical novel, *an* hysterical cry. *An* is used before a word beginning with a vowel sound, including one which is pronounced though not written: *an* X-ray, *an* n–dimensional figure.

a[3] (ə, ā) *v. Brit. Dial.* Have.

a[4] (ā, ô, ə) *pron. Brit. Dial.* He, she, it, they: an unstressed form.

a–[1] *prefix* On; in; at: *aboard, asleep, agog, agoing.* [OE *an, on* in, on, at]

a–[2] *prefix* Used as an intensive or without added meaning: *arise, abide.* [OE *ā–*]

a–[3] *prefix* Of; from: *athirst, akin, anew.* [OE *of* off, of]

a–[4] *prefix* **1** Without; not: *achromatic.* **2** Apart from; unconcerned with: *amoral.* See note under ALPHA PRIVATIVE. [Reduced form of AN– used before consonant sounds]

a–[5] Reduced var. of AB– before *m, p,* and *v.*

a–[6] Reduced var. of AD– before *sc, sp,* and *st.*

a·a (ä′ä′) *n.* A brittle, scoriaceous substance consisting of sand, earth, stones, and melted lava, cooled and broken up. [<Hawaiian]

Aa (ä) Any of several small rivers of Europe, especially, two in Latvia, both emptying into the Gulf of Riga, and two in NW Germany.

Aa·chen (ä′kən, *Ger.* ä′khən) A city in western Germany on the Belgian border; capital of Charlemagne's empire: French *Aix–la–Chapelle.*

aal (äl) *n.* **1** An East Indian shrub (*Morinda royoc*), the root of which yields a red dye. **2** The dye. Also called *Indian mulberry.* [<Hind.]

Aa·land Islands (ō′län) A Finnish archipelago at the entrance of the Gulf of Bothnia; 551 square miles; chief town, Mariehamn:

also *Åland Islands. Finnish* **Ah·ve·nan·maa** (ä′ve·nän·mä′).

Aal·borg (ôl′bôr) A port in northern Denmark: also *Ålborg.*

a·a·li·i (ä′ä·lē′ē) *n.* A small tropical tree (*Dodonaea viscosa*), native in Australia, Hawaii, Jamaica, and Madagascar, valued for its dark, hard, and durable timber. [<Hawaiian]

Aar (är) The longest river that is entirely in Switzerland, flowing 183 miles to the Rhine. Also **Aa·re** (ä′rə).

Aa·rau (ä′rou) A city in north central Switzerland.

aard·vark (ärd′-värk′) *n.* A burrowing, ant–eating African mammal (genus *Orycteropus*) about the size of the pig, with long protrusile, sticky tongue to which the ants adhere, and strong, digging forefeet; an ant bear. [<Afrikaans <Du. *aarde* earth + *vark* pig]

AARDVARK
(4 to 5 1/2 feet from nose to tail; tail 2 to 2 1/2 feet)

aard·wolf (ärd′wŏŏlf′) *n.* A hyenalike, nocturnal, carnivorous mammal (*Proteles cristata*) of southern and eastern Africa, living chiefly on carrion and termites. [<Afrikaans <Du. *aarde* earth + *wolf* wolf]

Aar·hus (ôr′hŏŏs) A port in eastern Jutland, the second largest city in Denmark.

Aar·on (âr′ən, ar′ən) A masculine personal name. [<Hebrew *Aharōn* ? enlightener] — **Aaron** The first Jewish high priest; brother of Moses. *Ex.* iv 14.

Aa·ron·ic (â·ron′ik) *adj.* Of or pertaining to Aaron, the high priest, or his descendants; hence, of or pertaining to a high priest; pontifical. Also **Aa·ron′i·cal.**

Aaron's rod **1** The rod cast by Aaron before Pharaoh, which became a serpent (*Ex.* vii 9–15), and later blossomed (*Num.* xvii 8). **2** *Archit.* A rod–shaped molding, ornamented with sprouting leaves or with a single serpent twined about it. **3** A plant that flowers on long stems, as the mullein.

aas·vo·gel (äs′fō′gəl) *n.* A vulture. [<Afrikaans]

Ab (ab, äb) A Hebrew month. The 9th day of Ab is a fast day to commemorate the destruction of Jerusalem and the Temple, 586 B.C. and A.D. 70. The 15th day is a secular festival. See CALENDAR (Hebrew).

ab–[1] *prefix* Off; from; away: *absolve, abduet, abrogate.* Also: *a–* before *m, p, v,* as in *avocation; abs–* before *c, t,* as in *abscess, abstract.* [<L <*ab* from]

ab–[2] Assimilated var. of AD–.

a·ba (ä′bə) *n.* A sleeveless garment of camel's– or goat's–hair cloth worn in Arabia, Syria, etc.; also, the cloth. [<Arabic *'abā*′]

ab·a·ca (ab′ə·kä, ä′bä·kä′) *n.* **1** A banana plant (*Musa textilis*) of the Philippine Islands. **2** The inner fiber of this plant, used for cordage. Also **ab′a·ka.** [<Tagalog]

ab·a·cis·cus (ab′ə·sis′kəs) *n.* **1** A square tile in a mosaic floor or pavement. **2** *Obs.* An abacus. [<L <Gk. *abakiskos,* dim. of *abax* a slab]

ab·a·cist (ab′ə·sist) *n.* One who uses an abacus.

a·back (ə·bak′) *adv.* So as to be pressed backward, as sails; backward; aloof. — **taken aback 1** *Naut.* Caught by a sudden change of wind so as to reverse the sails. **2** Disconcerted, as by a sudden check. [OE *on bæc* to or on the back]

a·ba·cus (ab′ə·kəs) *n. pl.* **cus·es** or **·ci** (-sī) **1** An ancient calculating device with counters sliding on wires or in grooves. **2** *Archit.* A slab forming the top of a capital. For illustration see CAPITAL. [<L <Gk. *abax* counting table]

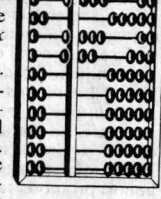

ABACUS (*def. 1*)

A·ba·dan (ä′bä·dän′, ab′ə·dan′) Chief town on **Abadan Island** in the Shatt–al–Arab delta of SW Iran: oil refining and shipping center.

A·bad·don (ə·bad′ən) In the Old Testament: **1** The bottomless pit; hell; the place of destruction. **2** The angel of the bottomless pit; Apollyon. [<Hebrew *ăbaddōn* destruction]

a·baft (ə·baft′, ə·bäft′) *adv. Naut.* Toward the stern; back; behind. — *prep.* Further aft than; astern of: *abaft* the mainmast. [OE *on beæftan* <*on* on, at + *be* about + *æftan,* adv., behind, back]

ab·a·lo·ne (ab′ə·lō′nē) *n.* A shellfish (genus *Haliotis*) having a perforated ear–shaped shell lined with mother–of–pearl, which is used for inlaying, making buttons, beads, etc. Its meat is used for food. [<Sp.]

ab·am·pere (ab·am′pir) *n.* The cgs electromagnetic unit of current, equal to 10 absolute amperes. [<AB(SOLUTE) + AMPERE]

a·ban·don (ə·ban′dən) *v.t.* **1** To give up wholly; desert; forsake, as an effort or attempt. **2** To surrender or give over: with *to*: He abandoned his share to his partner. **3** To yield (oneself) without restraint, as to a feeling or pastime. — *n.* **1** Utter surrender to one's feelings or natural impulses. **2** Freedom. [<OF *abandoner* <*a bandon* under one's own control] — **a·ban′don·a·ble** *adj.* — **a·ban′don·er** *n.* — **a·ban′don·ment** *n.*

Synonyms (verb): abdicate, abjure, cease, cede, desert, discontinue, forgo, forsake, forswear, leave, quit, recant, relinquish, renounce, repudiate, resign, retract, surrender, vacate. *Abandon* denotes the complete and final giving up, letting go, or withdrawal from persons or things of any kind; *abdicate* and *resign* apply to office, authority, or power; *cede* to territorial possessions; *surrender* especially to military force, and more generally to any demand, claim, passion, etc. *Quit* carries an idea of suddenness or abruptness not necessarily implied in *abandon*, and may not have the same suggestion of finality. *Relinquish* commonly implies reluctance; the creditor *relinquishes* his claim. *Abandon* implies previous association with responsibility for or control of; *forsake* implies previous association with inclination or attachment; a man may *abandon* or *forsake* home or friends; he *abandons* an enterprise. *Forsake*, like *abandon*, may be used either in the favorable or unfavorable sense; *desert* is commonly unfavorable, except when used of localities; as, "The *Deserted* Village"; a soldier *deserts* his post. While a monarch *abdicates*,

a president or other elected or appointed officer *resigns*. See also RENOUNCE. *Antonyms*: adopt, advocate, assert, cherish, claim, court, defend, favor, haunt, hold, keep, maintain, occupy, prosecute, protect, pursue, retain, seek, support, undertake, uphold, vindicate.

a·ban·doned (ə·ban′dənd) *adj.* **1** Deserted; left behind; forsaken. **2** Unrestrained; without moderation. **3** Given over to dissolute practices; profligate; shameless. See synonyms under ADDICTED, BAD.

a·ban·don·ee (ə·ban′də·nē′) *n. Law* A person to whom something is abandoned, as an insurance underwriter to whom the salvage of a wrecked vessel is abandoned.

à bas (á bä′) *French* Down with: an expression indicating disapproval of a person or thing: opposed to *vive*.

a·base (ə·bās′) *v.t.* **a·based, a·bas·ing 1** To lower in position, rank, prestige, or estimation; cast down; humble. **2** *Obs.* To reduce in value, as coin; debase. [< OF *abaissier* < *a* to + *baissier* to lower < L *ad-* + LL *bassus* low] —**a·bas·ed·ly** (ə·bā′sid·lē) *adv.* —**a·bas′ed·ness** *n.* —**a·bas′er** *n.* —**a·base′ment** *n.*

Synonyms: debase, degrade, depress, discredit, disgrace, dishonor, humble, humiliate, lower, reduce, sink. *Abase* generally refers to outward conditions, *debase* to quality or character: The coinage is *debased* by excess of alloy, the man by vice. *Humble* refers chiefly to the feelings, *humiliate* to outward conditions. To *disgrace* is chiefly applied to deserved moral odium: he *disgraced* himself by his conduct. To *dishonor* a person is to deprive him of honor that should or might be given. To *discredit* one is to injure his reputation. *Degrade* may refer to station, but is now chiefly used of character: drunkenness is a *degrading* vice. *Antonyms*: advance, aggrandize, dignify, elevate, exalt, honor, promote, raise, uplift.

a·bash (ə·bash′) *v.t.* To deprive of self-possession; disconcert; make ashamed or confused. [< OF *esbaïss-*, stem of *esbaïr* astonish] —**a·bash·ed·ly** (ə·bash′id·lē) *adv.* —**a·bash′ment** *n.*

Synonyms: bewilder, chagrin, confound, confuse, daunt, discompose, disconcert, dishearten, embarrass, humble, humiliate, mortify, overawe, shame. Any sense of inferiority *abashes*, with or without the sense of wrong. The poor are *abashed* at the splendor of wealth, the ignorant at the learning of the scholar. To *confuse* is to bring into a state of mental bewilderment; to *confound* is to overwhelm the mental faculties; to *daunt* is to subject to a certain degree of fear. Confusion generally refers to the intellect, embarrassment to the feelings. A witness may be *embarrassed* by annoying remarks or questions so as to become *confused* in statements. To *mortify* a person is to bring upon him a painful sense of humiliation: The parent is *mortified* by the child's rudeness, the child *abashed* at the parent's reproof. The *embarrassed* speaker finds it difficult to proceed. The mob is *overawed* by the military, the hypocrite *shamed* by exposure. See EMBARRASS. Compare CHAGRIN. *Antonyms*: animate, assure, buoy, cheer, embolden, encourage, inspirit, rally, uphold.

ab·a·tage (ab′ə·täj′) *n. Mil.* **1** Demolition; destruction, especially by high explosives. **2** The anchoring of a piece of artillery. [< F *abattage* < *abattre* demolish, knock down]

a·bate (ə·bāt′) *v.* **a·bat·ed, a·bat·ing** *v.t.* **1** To make less; reduce in size, number, degree, amount, importance, speed, or force. **2** To deduct, as part of a payment. **3** *Law* To do away with; annul. —*v.i.* **4** To become less, as in strength or degree. **5** *Law* To fail; become void. [< OF *abatre* beat down < *a-* to (< L *ad-*) + *batre* beat < L *batuere*] —**a·bat·a·ble** (ə·bā′tə·bəl) *adj.* —**a·bat′er** (ə·bā′tər) *n.*

Synonyms: decline, decrease, diminish, ebb, lessen, lower, mitigate, moderate, reduce, relax, subside. See ABOLISH, ALLAY, ALLEVIATE. *Antonyms*: aggravate, augment, enhance, increase, intensify.

a·bate·ment (ə·bāt′mənt) *n.* **1** An abating or the amount abated. **2** *Law* A doing away with; annulment.

ab·a·tis (ab′ə·tis, ab′ə·tē′) *n. Mil.* An obstruction of felled trees or bent saplings pointed in the direction of expected enemy attack, often interwoven with barbed wire. Also **ab′at·tis**. [< *abattre* to fell]

a·ba·tor (ə·bā′tər) *n. Law* **1** One who removes a nuisance. **2** One who unlawfully seizes an inheritance in the place of the rightful heir. **3** The agent or cause in effecting an abatement. [< AF < *abatre*. See ABATE.]

A battery *Electr.* A battery that supplies the power for the filaments of a vacuum tube.

ab·at·toir (ab′ə·twär′) *n.* A slaughter house. [< F]

ab·ax·i·al (ab·ak′sē·əl) *adj.* Situated or facing away from the axis. [< AB-[1] + AXIAL]

abb (ab) *n.* In weaving, the warp or the yarn for it. [OE *āweb*]

Ab·ba (ab′ə) *n.* **1** Father: a title used with the names of patriarchs and bishops in the Syrian, the Coptic, and the Ethiopian churches. **2** God: a form of address used in the New Testament: *Mark* xiv 36. [< Aramaic]

ab·ba·cy (ab′ə·sē) *n. pl.* **·cies** The office, term of office, dignity, or jurisdiction of an abbot. [< LL *abbatia* < L *abbas* ABBOT]

Ab·bas (ä′bäs), 566–652, the uncle of Mohammed.

Ab·bas·side (ə·bas′īd, ab′ə·sīd) *n.* Any of the caliphs of the dynasty ruling at Baghdad, 749–1258, and claiming descent from Abbas. — *adj.* Of or pertaining to this dynasty. Also **Ab·bas·sid** (ə·bas′id, ab′ə·sid).

ab·ba·tial (ə·bā′shəl) *adj.* Of or pertaining to an abbot or an abbey. Also **ab·bat·i·cal** (ə·bat′i·kəl).

ab·bé (ab′ā, *Fr.* á·bā′) *n.* **1** A title of respect in France given to a priest or any person entitled to wear ecclesiastical dress. **2** An abbot. [< F]

Ab·bé (á·bā′), Lake A salt lake on the Ethiopian-French Somaliland border.

ab·bess (ab′is) *n.* A woman superior of a community of nuns connected with an abbey. [< OF *abbesse* < LL *abbatissa* < L *abbas* ABBOT]

Ab·be·ville (ab′ə·vil, *Fr.* äb·vēl′) A town in northern France.

Ab·be·vil·li·an (ab′ə·vil′ē·ən) *adj. Anthropol.* Designating a culture stage of the Lower Paleolithic period, represented by crude handaxes of the core type: with the Clactonian it comprises most of the stage formerly known as the Chellean. [from *Abbeville*, France, where artifacts were found]

ab·bey (ab′ē) *n. pl.* **ab·beys 1** The monastic establishment of a society of monks under the jurisdiction of an abbot or of nuns under an abbess. **2** The buildings of such a society; its monastery or convent. **3** The church attached to a monastery or convent. See synonyms under CLOISTER. [< OF *abaie* < LL *abbatia* < L *abbas* ABBOT]

Ab·bey (ab′ē), **Edwin Austin**, 1852–1911, U.S. artist.

Abbey Theatre A repertory theater in Dublin, associated since 1904 with the Irish literary revival.

ab·bot (ab′ət) *n.* The superior of a community of monks connected with an abbey. [OE *abbod* < L < Gk. *abbas* < Aramaic *abba* father] —**ab′bot·cy**, **ab′bot·ship** *n.*

Abbot of Misrule The leader of festivities in medieval Christian revels.

Ab·bott (ab′ət), **Jacob**, 1803–79, U.S. clergyman and author of juvenile literature. —**Lyman**, 1835–1922, son of Jacob, U.S. clergyman, editor, and author.

Ab·bots·ford (ab′əts·fərd) An estate on the Tweed in SE Scotland: residence of Sir Walter Scott.

ab·bre·vi·ate (ə·brē′vē·āt) *v.t.* **·at·ed, ·at·ing 1** To condense or make briefer. **2** To shorten, as a word or expression, especially by omission or contraction: Mistress is *abbreviated* to Mrs. [< L *abbreviatus*, pp. of *abbreviare* < *ad-* to + *breviare* shorten < *brevis* short. Doublet of ABRIDGE.] —**ab·bre′vi·a′tor** *n.*

Synonyms: abridge, compress, condense, contract, curtail, epitomize, prune, reduce, shorten. Compare ABBREVIATION, ABRIDGMENT. *Antonyms*: amplify, enlarge, expand, extend, lengthen.

ab·bre·vi·a·tion (ə·brē′vē·ā′shən) *n.* **1** A shortened form or contraction, as of a word or phrase; abridgment. **2** A making shorter or the state of being shortened. **3** *Music* A notation indicating repeated notes, chords, etc., by a single symbol.

Synonyms: abridgment, abstract, compendium, condensation, contraction, curtailment, epitome, reduction, shortening, summary. An *abbreviation* is a shortening by any method; a *contraction* is a *reduction* of size by the drawing together of the parts. A *contraction* of a word is made by omitting certain letters or syllables and bringing together the first and last letters or elements; a *contraction* is an *abbreviation*, but an *abbreviation* is not necessarily a *contraction*. *Rec't* for receipt, *mdse.* for merchandise, and *Dr.* for debtor are *contractions* and also *abbreviations*; *Am.* for American is an *abbreviation*, but not a *contraction*. *Abbreviation* and *contraction* are used of words and phrases, *abridgment* of books, paragraphs, sentences, etc. See ABRIDGMENT. *Antonyms*: amplification, dilation, dilution, elongation, enlargement, expansion, expatiation, explication, extension, prolongation.

ABBREVIATION (*def. 3*)

Ab·by (ab′ē) Diminutive of ABIGAIL.

ABC (ā′bē·sē′) *pl.* **ABC's 1** The alphabet: usually plural. **2** The rudiments, elements, or basic facts (of a subject). **3** *Obs.* A primer.

ab·cou·lomb (ab′kōō·lom′) *n.* The cgs electromagnetic unit of charge, equal to 10 absolute coulombs. [< AB(SOLUTE) + COULOMB]

ABC powers A former diplomatic grouping, consisting of Argentina, Brazil, Chile.

Abd- A word element meaning "servant," "slave," used as a prefix before names for the Deity to form proper names in Semitic languages; as, *Abdallah* servant of God.

Ab·dal·lah·ibn·Ya·sin (äb′däl·lä′ib′ən·yä·sēn′), died c. 1058, Arab scholar; founder of the Almoravides. Also **Ab·dul·lah·ibn·Ya·sin** (äb′dōōl·lä′-).

Abd-el-Ka·der (äb′del·kä′dir), 1807?–83, Algerian tribal emir. Also **Abd′-el-Ka′dir.**

Abd-er Rah·man Khan (äb′dər rə·män′ khän′), 1830?–1901, amir of Afghanistan 1880–1901.

ab·di·cate (ab′də·kāt) *v.* **·cat·ed, ·cat·ing** *v.t.* To give up formally; renounce, as claims to or possession of a throne, power, or rights. —*v.i.* To renounce a throne, power, or rights: His subjects forced the king to *abdicate*. See synonyms under ABANDON. [< L *abdicatus*, pp. of *abdicare* renounce < *ab-* away + *dicare* proclaim] —**ab·di·ca·ble** (ab′di·kə·bəl) *adj.* —**ab′di·ca′tion** *n.* —**ab′di·ca′tive** *adj.* —**ab′di·ca′tor** *n.*

Ab·di·el (ab′dē·əl) A masculine personal name. [< Hebrew, servant of God]
—**Abdiel** An angel who opposed Satan's revolt, in Milton's *Paradise Lost*.

ab·do·men (ab′də·mən, ab·dō′mən) *n.* **1** In mammals, the visceral cavity between the diaphragm and the pelvic floor; the belly: in human anatomy often restricted to the cavity above the true pelvis. **2** In vertebrates other than mammals, the region or cavity that contains the viscera. **3** *Entomol.* The hindmost of the main divisions of the arthropod body. [< L]

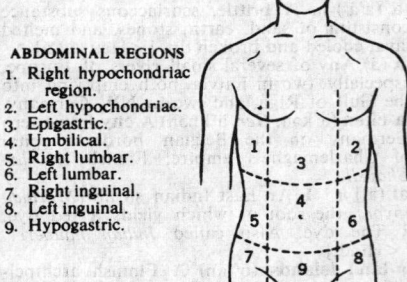

ABDOMINAL REGIONS
1. Right hypochondriac region.
2. Left hypochondriac.
3. Epigastric.
4. Umbilical.
5. Right lumbar.
6. Left lumbar.
7. Right inguinal.
8. Left inguinal.
9. Hypogastric.

ab·dom·i·nal (ab·dom′ə·nəl) *adj.* Of, pertaining to, or situated on or in the abdomen. —**ab·dom′i·nal·ly** *adv.*

ab·dom·i·nous (ab·dom′ə·nəs) *adj.* Big-bellied.

ab·duce (ab·do͞os′, -dyo͞os′) *v.t. Physiol.* To draw or lead away, as by muscular action. [< L *abducere.* See ABDUCT.] **—ab·du′cent** *adj.*

ab·duct (ab·dukt′) *v.t.* **1** To carry away wrongfully, as by force or fraud; kidnap. **2** *Physiol.* To draw aside or away from the original position. [< L *abductus,* pp. of *abducere* < *ab-* away + *ducere* lead] **—ab·duc′tion** *n.* **—ab·duc′tor** *n.*

Ab·dul-A·ziz (äb′do͝ol·ä·zēz′), 1830–76, Turkish sultan 1861–76.

Ab·dul Ba·ha (äb′do͝ol bä·hä′), 1844–1921, Persian leader. Also **Ab·bas Ef·fen·di** (äb·bäs′e·e·fen′dē).

Ab·dul-Ha·mid II (äb′do͝ol·hä·mēd′), 1842–1918, sultan of Turkey 1876–1909.

Ab·dul ibn-Hu·sein (äb′do͝ol ib′ən·hoo·sīn′), 1882–1951, ruler of Transjordania, amir 1921–46; king 1946–51; assassinated.

Ab·dul-Me·jid (äb′do͝ol·me·jēd′), 1823–61, Turkish sultan 1839–61. Also **Ab′dul-Me·djid′.**

Ab·dul-Wah·hab (äb′do͝ol·wä·hôb′), 1691–1787, Mohammedan reformer; founder of Wahabiism.

Abd-ur-Rah·man (äb′do͞or·rä′män), died 788, founder of the Ommiad Moslem dynasty in Spain in 756.

Abe (āb) Diminutive of ABRAHAM or ABRAM.

a·beam (ə·bēm′) *adj. & adv.* At right angles to the line of a vessel's keel; opposite the waist of a ship.

a·be·ce·dar·i·an (ā′bē·sē·dâr′ē·ən) *adj.* **1** Pertaining to or formed by the alphabet; alphabetically arranged. **2** Pertaining to a learner of the alphabet; rudimentary; ignorant. *—n.* **1** A teacher of the alphabet or one who is learning it. **2** A novice; beginner. Also **a·be·ce·da·ry** (ā′bē·sē′dar·ē). [< Med.L *abecedarius*]

A·bé·ché (á·bā·shā′) A market town of eastern Chad Colony, French Equatorial Africa: Arabic *Abeshr.* Also **A·bé·cher** (á·bā·shā′).

a·bed (ə·bed′) *adv.* In bed; on a bed; to bed.

A·bed·ne·go (ə·bed′ni·gō) Babylonian captive. *Dan.* iii. See SHADRACH.

A·bel (ā′bəl) A masculine personal name. [< L < Gk. *Abel* < Hebrew *Hebel,* lit., breath] **—Abel** Second son of Adam. *Gen.* iv 2.

A·bel (ā′bəl), **John Jacob,** 1857–1938, U.S. pharmacologist.

Ab·e·lard (ab′ə·lärd), **Pierre,** 1079–1142, French scholastic philosopher; husband of Héloïse. Also **Ab′ai·lard.**

a·bele (ə·bēl′, ā′bəl) *n.* The white poplar (*Populus alba*). [< Du. *abeel* < OF *abel* < LL *albellus,* dim. of L *albus* white]

a·bel·i·a (ə·be′lē·ə,-lyə) *n.* A shrub having small glossy leaves and bell-like flowers ranging from pink to white.

a·bel·mosk (ā′bəl·mosk) *n.* An Indian and North African shrub (*Hibiscus abelmoschus*) of the mallow family, having evergreen leaves, and yielding fragrant seeds used in perfumery. [< NL *abelmoschus* < Arabic *abu-al-misk* father (source) of musk]

Ab·er·corn (ab′ər·kôrn), **James Albert,** 1869–1953, third duke of Abercorn, governor of Northern Ireland 1922–45.

Ab·er·crom·bie (ab′ər·krom′bē, -krum′bē), **James,** 1706–81, British general.

Ab·er·deen (ab′ər·dēn′) A county in NE Scotland; 1,972 square miles; county town, Aberdeen. Also **Ab′er·deen′shire.**

Ab·er·deen (ab′ər·dēn) A town in NE Maryland near Chesapeake Bay: site of **Aberdeen Proving Ground,** a U.S. Army reservation.

Aberdeen An·gus (ang′gəs) A breed of hornless black cattle of Scottish origin.

ab·er·rance (ab·er′əns) *n.* A wandering from the right way; deviation from the path of rectitude. Also **ab·er′ran·cy.**

ab·er·rant (ab·er′ənt) *adj.* **1** Straying from the right way or usual course; wandering. **2** Varying from type; abnormal; exceptional. [< L *aberrans, -antis,* ppr. of *aberrare* < *ab-* from + *errare* wander]

ab·er·ra·tion (ab′ə·rā′shən) *n.* **1** Deviation from a right, customary, prescribed, or natural course or condition; wandering; error. **2** Partial mental derangement. **3** *Optics* The failure of a lens or mirror to bring all light rays to the same focus: called **chromatic aberration** when due to different refrangibility of light of different colors, and **spherical aberration** when due to the form of lens or mirror. **4** *Astron.* An apparent displacement of a heavenly body, due to the effect of relative motion upon the light coming from it. **5** An abnormal structure; a deviation from a standard type: a chromosomal *aberration.* [< L *aberratio, -onis* < *aberrare.* See ABERRANT.]

Ab·er·yst·with (ab′ə·rist′with) A port in Cardiganshire, Wales.

A·beshr (a·besh′ər) Arabic name for ABÉCHÉ.

a·bet (ə·bet′) *v.t.* **a·bet·ted, a·bet·ting** To encourage and support, especially wrong-doing or a wrongdoer; instigate; countenance. [< OF *abeter* incite, arouse < *a-* to (< L *ad-*) + *beter* tease, bait < ON *beita* cause to bite] **—a·bet′ment, a·bet′·tal** *n.*

Synonyms: aid, assist, countenance, embolden, encourage, help, incite, instigate, promote, sanction, support, uphold. *Abet* and *instigate* are used almost without exception in a bad sense; one may *incite* either to good or evil. One *incites* or *instigates* to the doing of something not yet done, or to increased activity or further advance in the doing of it; one *abets* by giving sympathy, countenance, or substantial aid to the doing of that which is already projected or in process of commission. See AID. *Antonyms:* baffle, confound, counteract, denounce, deter, disapprove, disconcert, discourage, dissuade, frustrate, hinder, impede, obstruct.

a·bet·tor (ə·bet′ər) *n.* One who abets. See synonyms under ACCESSORY. Also **a·bet′ter.**

a·bey·ance (ə·bā′əns) *n.* **1** Suspension or temporary inaction. **2** *Law* An undetermined condition, as of an estate awaiting an owner. Also **a·bey′an·cy.** [< AF *abeiance* < OF *beer* gape < LL *badare*] **—a·bey′ant** *adj.*

ab·far·ad (ab·far′əd, -ad) *n.* The cgs electromagnetic unit of capacitance, equal to 1 abcoulomb per abvolt, or 1,000,000,000 farads. [< AB(SOLUTE) + FARAD]

Ab·ha (ab·hä′) The chief town of Asir, Saudi Arabia.

ab·hen·ry (ab·hen′rē) *n.* The cgs electromagnetic unit of inductance, equal to 10^{-9} henry. [< AB(SOLUTE) + HENRY]

ab·he·sive (ab·hē′siv) *adj.* Not sticking to another material.

ab·hom·i·na·ble (ab·hom′ə·nə·bəl) *adj. Obs.* Abominable: a spelling commonly used until the 17th century.

ab·hor (ab·hôr′) *v.t.* **ab·horred, ab·hor·ring** To regard with repugnance; feel horror of; detest; loathe. [< L *abhorrere* < *ab-* from + *horrere* shrink] **—ab·hor′rer** *n.*

Synonyms: abominate, despise, detest, dislike, hate, loathe, scorn, shun. *Abhor* is stronger than *despise,* implying a shuddering recoil, especially a moral recoil. *Detest* expresses indignation, with something of contempt. *Loathe* implies disgust, physical or moral. We *abhor* a traitor, *despise* a coward, *detest* a liar. We *dislike* an uncivil person. We *abhor* cruelty, *hate* tyranny. Compare ABOMINATION. *Antonyms:* admire, approve, covet, crave, desire, enjoy, esteem, like, love, relish.

ab·hor·rence (ab·hôr′əns, -hor′-) *n.* The act of abhorring, or that which is abhorred. See synonyms under ABOMINATION, ANTIPATHY, HATRED.

ab·hor·rent (ab·hôr′ənt, -hor′-) *adj.* **1** Detestable or horrible: with *to.* **2** Feeling abhorrence. **—ab·hor′rent·ly** *adv.*

A·bib (ā·bib′, *Hebrew* ä·vēv′) See NISAN.

a·bi·dal (ə·bīd′l) *n.* **1** Abidance. **2** Abode.

a·bi·dance (ə·bīd′ns) *n.* **1** An abiding; dwelling. **2** Continuance; adherence to or an abiding by (rules, methods, etc.).

a·bide (ə·bīd′) *v.* **a·bode** or **a·bid·ed, a·bid·ing** *v.i.* **1** To continue in a place; stay. **2** To have one's abode; dwell; reside. **3** To continue in some condition or state; remain faithful or unchanging. *—v.t.* **4** To look for; wait for: to *abide* the event. **5** To await expectantly or defiantly. **6** To endure; put up with. **—to abide by 1** To behave in accordance with; be faithful to, as a promise or rule. **2** To accept the consequences of; submit to. [OE *abidan*] **—a·bid′er** *n.* **—a·bid′ing** *adj.* **—a·bid′ing·ly** *adv.*

Synonyms: anticipate, await, bear, bide, continue, dwell, endure, expect, inhabit, live, lodge, remain, reside, rest, sojourn, stand, stay, stop, tarry, tolerate, wait, watch. To *abide* is to remain continuously without limit of time unless expressed by the text. *Lodge, sojourn, stay, tarry,* and *wait,* always imply a limited time; *lodge,* to pass the night; *sojourn,* to *remain* temporarily; *live, dwell, reside,* to have a permanent home. *Reside* is a word of more dignity than *live or dwell. Stop,* in the sense of *stay* or *sojourn,* is colloquial. Compare ENDURE, REST. *Antonyms:* abandon, avoid, depart, forfeit, forfend, journey, migrate, move, proceed, reject, resist, shun.

Ab·i·djan (ab′i·jän′) A port in west Africa, capital of the Ivory Coast Republic.

A·bi·el (ā′bē·el, ə·bī′el) A masculine personal name. [< Hebrew, father of strength] **—Abiel** One of David's thirty mighty men. I *Chron.* xi 32.

ab·i·et·ic acid (ab′ē·et′ik) *Chem.* An acid, $C_{20}H_{30}O_2$, isolated from pine rosin in the form of a slightly yellow crystalline powder; it is used in lacquers, varnishes, soaps, and driers. [< L *abies* fir]

Ab·i·gail (ab′ə·gāl) A feminine personal name. [< Hebrew, my father's joy] **—Abigail** The wife of Nabal and afterward of David. I *Sam.* xxv 14.

ab·i·gail (ab′ə·gāl) *n.* A lady's maid: from a character in Beaumont and Fletcher's *The Scornful Lady.*

A·bi·hu (ə·bī′hyo͞o) Second son of Aaron. *Lev.* x 1.

A·bi·jah (ə·bī′jə) King of Judah. I *Kings* xiv 1. [< Hebrew, whose father is Jehovah]

a·bil·i·ty (ə·bil′ə·tē) *n. pl.* **·ties 1** The state of being able; physical, mental, legal, or financial power to do. **2** *pl.* Talents. **3** *Psychol.* That which a person can actually do on the basis of present development and training. [< OF *ablete* < L *habilitas* < *habilis.* See ABLE.]

Synonyms: aptitude, capability, capacity, cleverness, competence, competency, dexterity, efficiency, expertness, faculty, power, qualification, readiness, skill, talent. *Ability* includes every form of *power. Capacity* is power to receive. *Dexterity* and *skill* are readiness and facility in action, having a special end, and are largely acquired. *Efficiency* brings all one's *ability* to bear promptly on the thing to be done. Compare POWER. *Antonyms:* awkwardness, imbecility, inability, incapacity, incompetency, inefficiency, stupidity.

A·bim·e·lech (ə·bim′ə·lek) Son of Gideon; king of Shechem. *Judges* viii 31.

ab in·con·ve·ni·en·ti (ab in′kən·vē′nē·en′tē) *Latin* From the inconvenience involved: a legal phrase signifying that an argument based on such grounds carries much weight.

Ab·in·ger (ab′in·jər) A village SW of London, England: site of British magnetic observation station, moved there from Greenwich in 1923.

ab in·i·ti·o (ab i·nish′ē·ō) *Latin* From the beginning.

ab in·tra (ab in′trə) *Latin* From within.

ab·i·o·gen·e·sis (ab′ē·ō·jen′ə·sis) *n.* The springing up of living from non-living matter; especially, the old doctrine of the generation of new organisms from putrid and decomposing organic matter; spontaneous generation. Compare BIOGENESIS. [< A-[4] + BIO- + GENESIS] **—ab·i·o·ge·net·ic** (ab′ē·ō·jə·net′ik) or **·i·cal** *adj.* **—ab·i·og·e·nist** (ab′ē·oj′ə·nist) *n.*

ab·i·o·sis (ab′ē·ō′sis) *n.* Absence of life; a lifeless state. [< Gk. *abios* lifeless] **—ab·i·ot·ic** (ab′ē·ot′ik) *adj.*

ab·i·ot·ro·phy (ab′ē·ot′rə·fē) *n.* Premature or abnormal degeneration or wasting away of the body. [< A-[4] + BIO- + -TROPHY]

ab·ir·ri·tant (ab·ir′ə·tənt) *n.* A soothing agent; a medicine that eases irritation. *—adj.* Relieving irritation; soothing.

ab·ir·ri·tate (ab·ir′ə·tāt) *v.t.* **·tat·ed, ·tat·ing** To diminish sensibility in; relieve irritation in. **—ab·ir′ri·ta′tion** *n.*

A·bi·shai (ä·bē′shī) A Jewish general. II *Sam.* xxiii 18.

ab·ject (ab′jekt, ab·jekt′) *adj.* Sunk to a low condition; groveling; mean; despicable; also, downcast in spirit; servile. See synonyms under PITIFUL. [< L *abjectus,* pp. of *abjicere* throw away < *ab-* away + *jacere* throw] **—ab·jec′tive** *adj.* **—ab′ject·ly** *adv.* **—ab′ject·ness, ab·jec′tion** *n.*

ab·ju·ra·tion (ab′jo͞o·rā′shən) *n.* The act of ab-

juring or state of being abjured; repudiation.

ab·jure (ab·jŏŏr′) *v.t.* **ab·jured, ab·jur·ing 1** To renounce under oath; forswear. **2** To retract or recant, as an opinion; repudiate; abandon. See synonyms under ABANDON, RENOUNCE. [< L *abjurare* deny on oath < *ab-* away + *jurare* swear] —**ab·jur·a·to·ry** (ab·jŏŏr′a·tôr′ē, -tō′rē) *adj.* —**ab·jur′er** *n.*

Ab·khaz Autonomous Soviet Socialist Republic (ab·kaz′) An administrative division of NW Georgian S.S.R., between the Black Sea and the Greater Caucasus; 3,300 square miles; capital, Sukhumi. Also **Ab·kha·zia, Ab·kha·sia** (ab·kā′zhə).

ab·lac·ta·tion (ab′lak·tā′shən) *n.* The act or process of weaning from the breast. [< L *ablactatus,* pp. of *ablactare* wean < *ab-* away + *lactare* suckle < *lac* milk]

ab·late (ab·lāt′) *v.t.* **·lat·ed, ·lat·ing 1** To remove, as by cutting away, eroding, etc. **2** To undergo ablation.

ab·la·tion (ab·lā′shən) *n.* **1** The surgical removal of tissues or organs from the body. **2** *Geol.* The wearing away of rocks. **3** *Aerospace* The disintegration of part of the nose cone on a missile or spacecraft when it reenters the atmosphere. [< L *ablatio, -onis* a carrying away < *ablatus,* pp. of *auferre* < *ab-* away + *ferre* carry]

ab·la·ti·tious (ab′lə·tish′əs) *adj.* Tending to lessen or take away; diminishing. [< L *ablatus* carried away. See ABLATION.]

ab·la·tive (ab′lə·tiv) *adj.* **1** *Gram.* Pertaining to a grammatical case expressing separation or instrumentality. **2** *Obs.* Subtractive. —*n. Gram.* **1** A case of Latin and Sanskrit nouns, denoting *from, with, in, by,* etc. **2** A word in this case. [< L *ablativus* < *ablatus* carried away. See ABLATION.]

ablative absolute In Latin grammar, the construction in the ablative case of a noun and participle, a noun and an adjective, or two nouns, constituting an adverbial phrase which stands apart in syntax from the rest of the sentence; as, *sole oriente,* nox fugit (*the sun rising,* night flees).

ab·laut (äb′lout, ab′-; *Ger.* äp′lout) *n.* The change of one root vowel into another to show a variation of tense, part of speech, or meaning, as in *swim, swam, swum.* Compare UMLAUT. [< G < *ab* off + *laut* sound]

a·blaze (ə·blāz′) *adj.* & *adv.* On fire; in a blaze; hence, in a glow of excitement; zealous; ardent.

a·ble (ā′bəl) *adj.* **a·bler** (ā′blər), **a·blest** (ā′blist) **1** Having adequate power; competent; qualified. **2** Having superior abilities; capable. See synonyms under ADEQUATE, CLEVER, COMPETENT, GOOD, SAGACIOUS. [< OF *hable* able < L *habilis* manageable, suitable, fit < *habere* have, hold]

-able *suffix* **1** Given to; tending to; like to: *peaceable, changeable.* **2** Fit to; able to; capable of; worthy of: *eatable, salable, solvable.* Also spelled *-ble, -ible. -ible* is used to form words from Latin verbs of the third and fourth conjugations (ending in *-ere, -ire*) as *edible* from *edere, audible* from *audire.* The *-able* ending, originally used to form adjectives from Latin verbs of the first conjugation, as *disputable, estimable,* etc., is now extended in English to form adjectives from native verbs, nouns, and phrases, as *answerable, plowable, get-at-able,* etc. [< F < L *-abilis,-ibilis, -bilis*]

a·ble-bod·ied (ā′bəl·bod′ēd) *adj.* Having a sound strong body; competent for physical service; robust.

able-bodied seaman An experienced and skilled seaman, receiving higher pay than an ordinary seaman: usually abbreviated *A.B.*

ab·le·gate (ab′li·gāt) *n.* A special papal envoy charged with various missions, as the bearing of the official insignia to newly appointed cardinals. [< L *ablegatus,* pp. of *ablegare* < *ab-* away + *legare* dispatch]

a·blins (ā′blinz) *adv. Scot.* Perhaps: also spelled *aiblins.*

a·bloom (ə·blŏŏm′) *adj.* & *adv.* Blooming; in blossom.

ab·lu·ent (ab′lŏŏ·ənt) *adj.* Cleansing. —*n.* A cleansing agent; a detergent. [< L *abluens, -entis,* ppr. of *abluere* < *ab-* away + *luere* wash]

a·blush (ə·blush′) *adj.* Blushing.

ab·lu·tion (ab·lŏŏ′shən) *n.* **1** A washing or cleansing, especially of the body; a bath. **2** A ceremonial or symbolic washing; especially, in the Roman Catholic Church, the wine and water used to remove any trace of the eucharistic elements from the chalice and the priest's fingers after communion. **3** The washing of the hands of the priest before, during, and after the celebration of the Mass. **4** In the Greek Church, the public washing of persons seven days after their baptism. **5** Any liquid used in washing or cleansing. [< L *ablutio, -onis* < *abluere* wash away. See ABLUENT.] —**ab·lu′tion·ar′y** *adj.*

a·bly (ā′blē) *adv.* With ability; capably.

-ably *suffix* Like; in the manner of: *peaceably:* used to form adverbs from adjectives ending in *-able.*

ab·mho (ab′mō) *n.* The cgs electromagnetic unit of conductance, equal to a current in a conductor of one abampere when the potential difference between the ends of the conductor is one abvolt. [< AB(SOLUTE) + MHO]

ab·ne·gate (ab′nə·gāt) *v.t.* **·gat·ed, ·gat·ing** To deny to oneself, as a right or privilege; renounce. [< L *abnegatus,* pp. of *abnegare* < *ab-* away + *negare* deny] —**ab′ne·ga′tor** *n.*

ab·ne·ga·tion (ab′nə·gā′shən) *n.* Renunciation: denial; self-denial.

Ab·ner (ab′nər) A masculine personal name. [< Hebrew, father of light]
—**Abner** A Jewish general; slain by Joab. I *Sam.* xiv 50.

ab·net (ab′net) *n.* A long girdle or sash, usually of linen, worn around the body by ancient Jewish priests. [< Hebrew]

ab·nor·mal (ab·nôr′məl) *adj.* Not according to rule; different from the usual or average; hence, unnatural; irregular. See synonyms under IRREGULAR. [Earlier *anormal* < F < Med.L *anormalus,* alter. of *anomalus* < Gk. *anōmalos* irregular; re-formed on Latin *ab* away, from] —**ab·nor′mal·ly** *adv.*

ab·nor·mal·i·ty (ab′nôr·mal′ə·tē) *n. pl.* **·ties 1** Irregularity. **2** That which is abnormal.

ab·nor·mi·ty (ab·nôr′mə·tē) *n. pl.* **·ties** An irregularity; malformation; a monstrosity. [< L *abnormitas, -tatis* < *abnormis* irregular < *ab-* from + *norma* rule]

ab·o (ab′ō) *n. pl.* **·bos** *Austral.* An Australian aborigine. [Short for *aboriginal*]

A·bo (ō′bŏŏ) Swedish name for TURKU.

a·board (ə·bôrd′, ə·bōrd′) *adv.* **1** On board; into, in, or on a conveyance. **2** Alongside; on one side. —**all aboard!** Get on board or in!: a warning to passengers that their conveyance is about to start. —*prep.* **1** On board of; upon or within, as a conveyance: *aboard* the train. **2** Across or alongside of.

a·bode[1] (ə·bōd′) *n.* **1** A place of abiding; dwelling; home. **2** The state or act of abiding; sojourn; stay. See synonyms under HOME, HOUSE. —*v.* Past tense and past participle of ABIDE. [OE *abad*]

a·bode[2] (ə·bōd′) *Obs. v.t.* & *v.i.* **a·bod·ed, a·bod·ing** To forebode; be ominous. —*n.* An omen. Also *Obs.* **a·bode′ment** *n.* [ME *abeden* announce, OE *abeodan*]

ab·ohm (ab·ōm′) *n.* The cgs electromagnetic unit of resistance, equal to one millionth of an ohm. [< AB(SOLUTE) + OHM]

a·boi·deau (à·bwä·dō′) *n. pl.* **·deaus** -dōz′) or **·deaux** (-dō′) *Canadian* A sluicegate in the dikes along the Bay of Fundy; also, a dike with sluicegates. Also **a·boi·teau′.** [< dial F (Canadian)]

a·bol·ish (ə·bol′ish) *v.t.* To do away with; put an end to; annul; destroy. [< F *aboliss-,* stem of *abolir* < L *abolescere* decay, vanish, inceptive of *abolere* destroy] —**a·bol′ish·a·ble** *adj.* —**a·bol′·ish·er** *n.* —**a·bol′ish·ment** *n.*

Synonyms: abate, abrogate, annihilate, annul, destroy, end, eradicate, exterminate, extirpate, nullify, obliterate, overthrow, prohibit, remove, repeal, reverse, revoke, subvert, supplant, suppress, terminate. *Abolish* is now used only of institutions, customs, and conditions, especially those wide-spread and long-existing; as, to *abolish* poverty. A building that is burned to the ground is said to be *destroyed* by fire. *Annihilate* signifies to put absolutely out of existence. Matter is never *annihilated,* but only changes its form. *Abolish* is not said of laws. There we use *repeal, abrogate, nullify,* etc.; *repeal* by the enacting body, *nullify* by revolutionary proceedings; a later statute *abrogates,* without formally *repealing,* any earlier law with which it conflicts. An appellate court may *reverse* or set aside the decision of an inferior court. *Overthrow* may be used in either a good or a bad sense; *suppress* is commonly in a good, *subvert* always in a bad sense; as to *subvert* our liberties; to *suppress* a rebellion. The law *prohibits* what may never have existed; it *abolishes* an existing evil. We *abate* a nuisance, *terminate* a controversy. Compare CANCEL, DEMOLISH, EXTERMINATE. *Antonyms:* authorize, cherish, confirm, continue, enact, establish, institute, introduce, legalize, promote, reinstate, renew, repair, restore, revive, support, sustain.

ab·o·li·tion (ab′ə·lish′ən) *n.* The act of abolishing; extinction; the state or fact of being abolished; specifically, the abolishing of slavery in the United States. [< L *abolitio, -onis* < *abolere* destroy] —**ab′o·li′tion·al** *adj.*

ab·o·li·tion·ar·y (ab′ə·lish′ən·er′ē) *adj.* Destructive; subversive.

ab·o·li·tion·ism (ab′ə·lish′ən·iz′əm) *n.* The principles of those who opposed slavery in the United States. —**ab′o·li′tion·ist** *n.*

a·bol·la (ə·bol′ə) *n. pl.* **a·bol·lae** (-ē) A Roman cloak. [< L]

a·bo·ma (ə·bō′mə) *n.* The ringed boa or one of other large South American snakes of the family *Boidae.* [< Pg.]

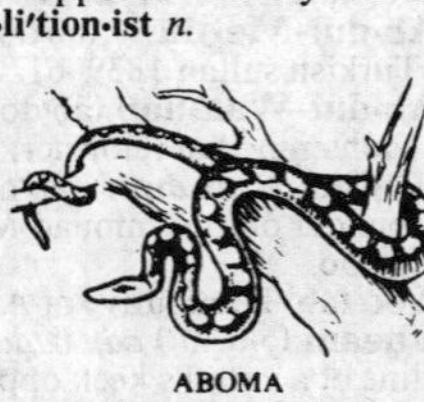

ABOMA
(Length to 11 feet)

ab·o·ma·sum (ab′ə·mā′səm) *n. pl.* **·sa** (-sə) The fourth or true digestive stomach of a ruminant. [< NL < L *ab-* away from + *omasum* bullock's tripe]

A-bomb (ā′bom′) See ATOMIC BOMB under BOMB.

a·bom·i·na·ble (ə·bom′ə·nə·bəl) *adj.* Very hateful; loathsome; detestable; horrible. See synonyms under BAD, CRIMINAL. [< OF < L *abominabilis* < *abominari.* See ABOMINATE.] —**a·bom′i·na·bly** *adv.*

abominable snowman A legendary humanoid creature supposed to inhabit the Himalayas and reported to leave giant footprints in the snow. Also called *yeti.*

a·bom·i·nate (ə·bom′ə·nāt) *v.t.* **·nat·ed, ·nat·ing 1** To regard with horror or loathing; abhor. **2** To dislike strongly. See synonyms under ABHOR. [< L *abominatus,* pp. of *abominari* abhor as an ill omen < *ab-* off + *omen* omen] —**a·bom′i·na′tor** *n.*

a·bom·i·na·tion (ə·bom′ə·nā′shən) *n.* **1** Strong aversion or loathing; extreme disgust and hatred. **2** Anything that excites disgust, hatred, or loathing; any detestable act or practice; anything vile or shamefully wicked.

Synonyms: abhorrence, abuse, annoyance, aversion, crime, curse, detestation, disgust, evil, execration, hatred, horror, iniquity, nuisance, offense, plague, shame, villainy, wickedness. *Abomination* was originally applied to anything held in religious or ceremonial *aversion* or *abhorrence.* The word is now oftener applied to the object of such *aversion* or *abhorrence* than to the state of mind that so regards it; in common use *abomination* signifies something loathed, or that deserves to be. A toad is to many an object of *disgust;* a foul sewer is an *abomination. Antonyms:* affection, appreciation, approval, benefit, blessing, delight, desire, enjoyment, esteem, gratification, joy.

à bon droit (á′ bôn′ drwá′) *French* With justice; rightfully.

à bon mar·ché (á′ bôn′ már·shā′) *French* At a good bargain; inexpensively.

a·boon (ə·bŏŏn′) *adv.* & *prep. Scot.* & *Brit. Dial.* Above.

ab·o·ral (ab·ôr′əl, -ō′rəl) *adj. Zool.* Pertaining to or situated away from the mouth. —**ab·o′ral·ly** *adv.*

ab·o·rig·i·nal (ab′ə·rij′ə·nəl) *adj.* **1** Of or pertaining to the aborigines. **2** Native to the soil; indigenous; primitive. —*n.* **1** *pl.* **·nes** (-nēz) *Austral.* An Australian aborigine. **2** An original inhabitant. —**ab′o·rig′i·nal·ly** *adv.*

ab o·rig·i·ne (ab ō·rij′ə·nē) *Latin* From the origin.

ab·o·rig·i·ne (ab′ə·rij′ə·nē) *n.* **1** One of the original native inhabitants of a country. **2** *pl.* Flora and fauna indigenous to a geographical area. [< L *aborigines* earliest inhabitants < *ab origine* from the beginning]

a·born·ing (ə·bôr′ning) *adv.* While being born or produced: to die *aborning.*

a·bort (ə·bôrt′) *v.i.* **1** To bring forth young prematurely; miscarry. **2** *Biol.* To fail of com-

plete development. 3 *Mil.* To fail to carry out a mission. —*v.t.* 4 To cause to have a miscarriage. 5 To bring to a premature or unsuccessful conclusion. [< L *abortus,* pp. of *aboriri* miscarry < *ab-* off, away + *oriri* arise, be born]

a·bor·ti·cide (ə·bôr′tə·sīd) *n.* 1 The intentional destruction of the fetus in the womb. 2 An agent for killing the fetus. [< L *abortus* (see ABORT) + -CIDE]

a·bor·ti·fa·cient (ə·bôr′tə·fā′shənt) *adj.* Causing abortion. —*n.* Anything used to cause abortion. [< L *abortus* (see ABORT) + *-i-* + -FACIENT]

a·bor·tion (ə·bôr′shən) *n.* 1 The expulsion of a fetus prematurely, when non-viable; miscarriage. 2 A miscarriage produced artificially. 3 The defective result of a premature birth; a monstrosity. 4 *Biol.* Partial or complete arrest of development, as of an embryo. 5 Failure of anything to progress or develop normally or as expected. [< L *abortio, -onis* < *aboriri.* See ABORT.] — **a·bor′tion·al** *adj.*

a·bor·tion·ist (ə·bôr′shən·ist) *n.* One who causes abortion.

a·bor·tive (ə·bôr′tiv) *adj.* 1 Brought forth or born prematurely. 2 Imperfectly developed. 3 Rudimentary, as an organ or stamen. 4 Coming to naught; failing, as an effort. 5 Causing abortion. 6 *Med.* Shortened in its course: an *abortive* fever. See synonyms under USELESS, VAIN. — **a·bor′tive·ly** *adv.* —**a·bor′tive·ness** *n.*

a·bor·tus (ə·bôr′təs) *n. pl.* **·tus·es** An aborted fetus, or any product of an abortion.

A·bou·kir (ä′bōō·kir′, ə·bōō′kər) See ABUKIR.

a·bou·li·a (ə·bōō′lē·ə), **a·bou·lic** (ə·bōō′lik) See ABULIA, etc.

a·bound (ə·bound′) *v.i.* 1 To be in abundance; be plentiful. 2 To have plenty of; be rich in: with *in*: The book *abounds* in humorous incidents. 3 To be full of; teem: with *with*: The lakes *abound* with fish. See synonyms under FLOW. Compare AMPLE. [< OF *abunder* < L *abundare* overflow < *ab-* from + *undare* flow in waves < *unda* wave]

a·bout (ə·bout′) *adv.* 1 Around the outside; on every side: Blessings compass thee *about.* 2 Almost: *about* finished; approximately: in *about* an hour. 3 Around, in revolution or rotation: turn and turn *about.* 4 In any direction; toward any, every, or the opposite side: to look or move *about.* 5 Here and there, as without direction: to wander *about.* —*prep.* 1 On the outside or on every side of; encircling: walls *about* the city. 2 Here and there in; to and fro upon: lambs running *about* the fields. 3 Somewhere near or within; on some side of: Stay *about* the house today. 4 Attached to as an attribute: an aura of sanctity *about* him. 5 Approximating to; not far from, as in quantity or time: leaving *about* midnight; troops numbering *about* four thousand. 6 Engaged in; concerned with: Go on *about* your business; He goes *about* his work skilfully. 7 In reference to; concerning: a book *about* Napoleon. 8 In possession of; at hand: I do not have the money *about* me. See synonyms under AT. [OE *onbūtan, ābūtan*]

a·bout-face (ə·bout′fās′) *n.* 1 *Mil.* A drill movement and command for pivoting about to face in exactly the opposite direction. 2 Any turning around or reversal, as of opinion or point of view, especially if sudden. —*v.i.* (ə·bout′fās′) **-faced, -fac·ing** 1 To perform an about-face. 2 To change one's opinions, ways, etc.

about-ship (ə·bout′ship′) *v.i.* **-shipped, -ship·ping** *Naut.* To change a ship's course by going on the opposite tack.

a·bove (ə·buv′) *adv.* 1 Vertically up or in a higher place; overhead; on the upper side. 2 Superior in rank or position. 3 In a previous or an earlier place: in the paragraph *above.* 4 In heaven. —*adj.* Given, said, placed, etc., in what is above; preceding. —*n.* That which precedes or is just before; something above. —*prep.* 1 Vertically over; higher than; rising beyond: books piled *above* one another; mountains towering *above* the plain. 2 *Geog.* Farther north than: *above* the fortieth parallel. 3 Exceeding a specific period; more than: a show lasting *above* three hours. 4 More than; in excess of: He ran *above* 500 yards. 5 Surpassing in volume, clearness, or intensity: a voice heard *above* the din. 6 Surpassing in authority, quality, or power: a moral law *above* the civil law. 6 Beyond the reach or influence of: conduct *above* suspicion. [OE *abufen*]

Above may appear as a combining form in hyphemes or solidemes, or as the first element in two-word phrases:

above all	**above measure**
above-cited	**above-mentioned**
above deck	**above-named**
above-given	**above-quoted**
aboveground	**above-said**
above-listed	**above-written**

Synonyms (prep.): on, over, upon. *Above* is the most inclusive of these prepositions. It can ordinarily be substituted for *on, upon,* or *over;* as, the boards were piled one *on* or *upon* another (one *above* another), the hawk flies *over* the wood (*above* the wood). But it will be seen that while *above* is more inclusive it is less definite; the boards laid one *on* another are in contact, but when laid one *above* another, they may not touch. *Over* often contains an intimation of extension or motion across, while *above* may simply imply greater elevation. If we say, the mountain towers *above* the plain, we think only of its height; but if we say, the mountain towers *over* the plain, we think of the plain as in the shadow of the mountain and dominated by it. So we say the mountain is 7,000 feet *above* the sea, where it would be impossible to say 7,000 feet *over* the sea. *Upon* is practically identical with *on,* preference being generally for euphonic reasons. *Antonyms*: see BENEATH.

a·bove·board (ə·buv′bôrd′, -bōrd′) *adj. & adv.* In open sight; hence, without concealment, fraud, or trickery; honest. See synonyms under CANDID.

a·bove·ground (ə·buv′ground′) *adj. & adv.* 1 Above the surface of the ground: *aboveground* nuclear testing. 2 In the open; not secret. 3 Not buried; alive.

a·bove·men·tioned (ə·buv′men′shənd) *adj.* mentioned before: the *abovementioned* data.

ab o·vo (ab ō′vō) *Latin* From the beginning; literally, from the egg.

ab·ra·ca·dab·ra (ab′rə·kə·dab′rə) *n.* A cabalistic word written in triangular form, anciently used as a preventive or curative charm; a spell; hence, any jargon of conjuring or nonsensical words. [< L]

a·brade (ə·brād′) *v.t.* **a·brad·ed, a·brad·ing** To rub or wear off by friction; scrape away. [< L *abradere* < *ab-* away + *radere* scrape] — **a·bra′dant** *adj. & n.* —**a·brad′er** *n.*

A·bra·ham (ā′brə·ham; *Dan., Du., Ger., Sw.* ä′brä·häm) A masculine personal name. Also *Fr.* **A·bra·ham,** (å·brå·åm′), *Ital.* **A·bra·ha·mo** (ä′brä·ä′mō), *Lat.* **A·bra·ha·mus** (ä′brə·hä′·məs), *Pg.* **A·bra·hão** (ä′brä·oun′), *Sp.* **A·bra·han** (ä′brä·än′). [< Hebrew, ? father of a multitude (of nations)]
—**Abraham** The progenitor of the Hebrews; first called Abram.

Abraham, Plains of The plateau in the SW part of the city of Quebec, Canada: battlefield where the British defeated the French in 1759, establishing British control of Canada.

Abraham Lincoln National Historical Park A park in Hodgenville, central Kentucky, containing the house in which Lincoln supposedly was born.

A·bram (ā′brəm; *Fr.* ȧ·brän′; *Sp.* ä·bräm′) A masculine personal name. Also *Ital.* **A·bra·mo** (ä·brä′mō), *Lat.* **A·bra·mus** (ä·brä′məs). [< Hebrew, ? exalted father]
—**Abram** Abraham, before God changed his name. *Gen.* xvii 5.

a·bran·chi·al (ə·brang′kē·əl, ā-) *adj.* Without gills. Also **a·bran·chi·ate** (ə·brang′kē·it, -āt, ā-), **a·bran·chi·ous** (ə·brang′kē·əs, ā-). [< A-[4] without + Gk. *branchia* gills]

a·bra·sion (ə·brā′zhən) *n.* 1 The act or result of abrading. 2 *Geol.* A wearing away, as of rocks by glaciers. 3 An abraded place. See synonyms under FRICTION. [< L *abrasio, -onis* < *abradere.* See ABRADE.]

a·bra·sive (ə·brā′siv, -ziv) *adj.* Abrading or tending to abrade. —*n.* An abrading substance.

ab·re·act (ab′rē·akt′) *v.t. Psychoanal.* To produce abreaction. [< *abreaction*]

ab·re·ac·tion (ab′rē·ak′shən) *n. Psychoanal.* The releasing of pent-up emotion or disagreeable memories by reliving them through words, feelings, or actions: a form of catharsis. [< AB-[1] from + REACTION, after G *abreagierung*]

ab·re·ac·tive (ab′rē·ak′tiv) *adj.* Pertaining to or causing abreaction.

a·bread (ə·brēd′) *adv. Scot.* Abroad. Also **a·breed′.**

a·breast (ə·brest′) *adv.* Side by side and equally advanced. —**abreast of** (or **with**) Side by side with; not behind or ahead of.

a·bri (ə·brē′, *Fr.* å·brē′) *n. pl.* **a·bris** (ə·brēz′, *Fr.* å·brē′) A refuge or shelter; specifically, a dugout or an air-raid shelter. [< F]

a·bridge (ə·brij′) *v.t.* **a·bridged, a·bridg·ing** 1 To give the substance of in fewer words; condense; epitomize. 2 To shorten, as in time. 3 To curtail or lessen, as rights. 4 To deprive; stint, as a person of privileges: with *of.* See synonyms under ABBREVIATE, RESTRAIN, RETRENCH. [< OF *abregier* < L *abbreviare.* Doublet of ABBREVIATE.]

a·bridg·ment (ə·brij′mənt) *n.* 1 The act of abridging; the state of being abridged. 2 Something that has been abridged; an epitome or abstract. 3 *Obs.* That which causes time to pass quickly. Also **a·bridge′ment.**

Synonyms: abbreviation, abstract, analysis, compend, compendium, conspectus, digest, epitome, outline, *précis,* summary, synopsis. An *abridgment* gives the most important portions of a work substantially as they stand. An *outline* or *synopsis* is a kind of sketch closely following the plan. An *abstract, digest* or *précis* is an independent statement of what a book or an article contains, the *abstract* closely following the main heads, the *digest* or *précis* giving the substance with careful consideration of all. An *analysis* draws out the chief thoughts or arguments, expressed or implied. An *epitome, compend,* or *compendium* is a condensed view of a subject, whether derived from a previous publication or not. See ABBREVIATION. *Antonyms:* amplification, expansion, paraphrase.

a·brim (ə·brim′) *adj.* Brimming: eyes *abrim* with tears.

a·broach (ə·brōch′) *adj. & adv.* In a condition to let out the liquor; on tap; in circulation; astir. [< A-[1] on + BROACH]

a·broad (ə·brôd′) *adv.* 1 Out of one's home or abode; out of doors. 2 Out of one's own country; in or into foreign lands. 3 Broadly; widely; at large; in circulation. 4 Wide of the mark; astray. [ME *abroad.* See A-[1] and BROAD.]

ab·ro·gate (ab′rə·gāt) *v.t.* **·gat·ed, ·gat·ing** To annul by authority, as a law; abolish; repeal. See synonyms under ABOLISH, ANNUL, CANCEL. [< L *abrogatus,* pp. of *abrogare* < *ab-* away + *rogare* ask, propose] —**ab·ro·ga·ble** (ab′rə·gə·bəl) *adj.* —**ab′ro·ga′tive** *adj.* —**ab′ro·ga′tor** *n.*

ab·ro·ga·tion (ab′rə·gā′shən) *n.* The act or process of abrogating; authoritative repeal.

a·brupt (ə·brupt′) *adj.* 1 Beginning, ending, or changing suddenly; broken off. 2 Unceremonious; sudden, as a departure. 3 Changing subject suddenly; unconnected, as style. 4 Steep, as a cliff. See synonyms under BLUFF[2], STEEP[1]. [< L *abruptus,* pp. of *abrumpere* < *ab-* off + *rumpere* break] —**a·brup′tion** *n.* **a·brupt′ly** *adv.* —**a·brupt′ness** *n.*

A·bruz·zi (ä·brōōt′tsē), **Duke of the,** Prince Luigi of Savoy-Aosta, 1873–1933, Italian naval officer and explorer.

A·bruz·zi (ä·brōōt′tsē) A region of central Italy on the Adriatic, including the most rugged part of the Apennines.

abs- Var. of AB-.

Ab·sa·lom (ab′sə·ləm) A masculine personal name. [< Hebrew, the father is peace] —**Absalom** The favorite and rebellious son of David. II *Sam.* xiii–xix.

ab·scess (ab′ses) *n.* A collection of pus in a body cavity formed by tissue disintegration; it may be caused by bacteria and is often accompanied by painful inflammation. —*v.i.* to form an abscess. [< L *abscessus* < *abscedere* go away < *ab-* away + *cedere* go;

with ref. to the flowing of humors into the area] **—ab′scessed** *adj.*

ab·scind (ab·sind′) *v.t.* To cut off. [< L *absindere* < *ab-* off + *scindere* cut]

ab·scis·sa (ab·sis′ə) *n. pl.* **ab·scis·sas** or **ab·scis·sae** (-ē) The distance of any point from the vertical Y-axis of ordinates in a two-dimensional system of reference, measured on a line parallel to the horizontal X-axis of abscissas. [< L *(linea) abscissa* (line) cut off, fem. of *abscissus*, pp. of *abscindere*. See ABSCIND.]

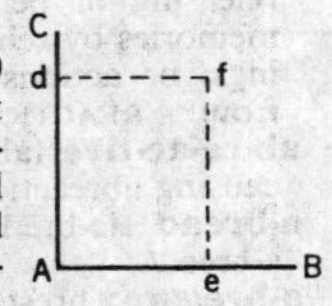

ABSCISSA
AB: X-axis. AC: Y-axis. *df* or *Ae*: abscissa of point *f*.

ab·scis·sion (ab·sizh′ən, sish′ən) *n.* **1** The act of cutting off or the state of being cut off or removed. **2** *Bot.* The shedding of parts of a plant by the action of certain cells located in the branch or bark; also, the freeing of a fungus spore through breakdown of a portion of its stalk. **3** In rhetoric, an abrupt breaking off for effect, as in the middle of a sentence. Compare APOSIOPESIS. [< L *abscissio, -onis* < *abscindere.* See ABSCIND.]

ab·sciss layer (ab′sis) *Bot.* A layer of cells formed in autumn at the base of the petiole, permitting the leaf to fall. Also **abscission layer.**

ab·scond (ab·skond′) *v.i.* To depart suddenly and secretly; to escape and hide oneself. See synonyms under ESCAPE. [< L *abscondere* < *ab-* away + *condere* store] **—ab·scon′dence** *n.* **—ab·scond′er** *n.*

ab·scond·ee (ab·skon′dē) *n.* One who absconds; absconder.

ab·sence (ab′səns) *n.* **1** The state, fact, or time of not being present. **2** Lack; want. **3** Mental abstraction; lack of attention. See synonyms under WANT. [< F < L *absentia* < *absens.* See ABSENT.]

ab·sent (ab′sənt) *adj.* **1** Not present. **2** Lacking; missing; nonexistent: In some fishes the ribs are *absent.* **3** Inattentive; absent-minded. See synonyms under INATTENTIVE. *—v.t.* (ab·sent′) To take or keep (oneself) away; not be present. [< L *absens, -entis,* ppr. of *abesse* < *ab-* away + *esse* be] **—ab·sen·ta·tion** (ab′sən·tā′shən) *n.* **—ab·sent′er** *n.* **—ab′sent·ly** *adv.* **—ab′sent·ness** *n.*

ab·sen·tee (ab′sən·tē′) *n.* One who is absent, as from a job. *—adj.* **1** Relating to one who is temporarily absent: an *absentee* voter. **2** Nonresident: an *absentee* landlord. **—ab′·sen·tee′ism** *n.*

ab·sen·te re·o (ab·sen′tē rē′ō) *Law Latin* In the absence of the defendant.

ab·sent-mind·ed (ab′sənt·mīn′did) *adj.* Lacking in attention to immediate demands or business because of preoccupation. See synonyms under ABSTRACTED. **—ab′sent-mind′ed·ly** *adv.* **—ab′sent-mind′ed·ness** *n.*

absent without leave Absent from a military duty or post without permission from the proper authority, but not intending to desert. Abbr. *AWOL, awol, A.W.O.L., a.w.o.l.*

ab·sinthe (ab′sinth) *n.* **1** Wormwood or absinthium. **2** A green, bitter, alcoholic liqueur having the flavor of licorice, made from oils of wormwood and other aromatics. Also **ab′sinth.** [< F < L *absinthium* wormwood < Gk. *apsinthion*] **—ab·sin′thi·al, ab·sin′thi·an** *adj.*

ab·sin·thi·um (ab·sin′thē·əm) *n.* **1** Common wormwood; the aromatic bitter herb *Artemisia absinthium.* **2** The dried leaves and flowers of this herb, used in medicine as a gastric tonic and cardiac stimulant. [< L. See ABSINTHE.]

ab·so·lute (ab′sə·lo͞ot) *adj.* **1** Free from restriction or relation; unlimited; independent; unconditional: an *absolute* monarchy. **2** Complete; perfect. **3** Unadulterated; pure. **4** Postive; entire; total; unquestionable. **5** *Gram.* **a** Free from the usual relations of syntax or construction with other words in the sentence, as *It being late* in *It being late, we started home.* **b** Of a transitive verb, having no object expressed and, hence, functioning as intransitive, as *He writes well.* **c** Of an adjective standing without a noun, as *Only the brave deserve the fair.* **6** *Physics* Not dependent on any arbitrary standard; non-relative; specifically determined or measured only by the fundamental notions of space, mass, and time: *absolute* measurement; also, relating to the absolute-temperature scale: 15° *absolute.* *—n.* That which is absolute or perfect. **—the Absolute** The ultimate basis of all thought, reasoning, or being; God. [< L *absolutus,* pp. of *absolvere.* See ABSOLVE.] **—ab′so·lute′ness** *n.*

Synonyms (adj.): arbitrary, autocratic, despotic, infinite, perfect, pure, supreme, tyrannical, unconditional, unequivocal. As used of human authorities, *absolute* signifies free from limitation by other authority and *supreme* exalted over all other; as, an *absolute* monarch, the *supreme* court. As *absolute* power in human hands is usually abused, the unfavorable meaning of the word predominates. *Autocratic* power is *absolute* power self-established and self-maintained. *Despotic* is commonly applied to a masterful or severe use of power, which is expressed more decidedly by *tyrannical. Arbitrary* may be used in good sense; as, the pronunciation of proper names is *arbitrary;* but the bad sense is the prevailing one; as, an *arbitrary* proceeding, *arbitrary* power. Compare ARBITRARY, FLAT[1], IMPERIOUS, INFINITE, PERFECT. *Antonyms:* accountable, conditional, conditioned, constitutional, limited, responsible, restrained.

absolute alcohol Ethyl alcohol containing not more than 1 percent alcohol.

ab·so·lute·ly (ab′sə·lo͞ot′lē, *emphatic* ab′sə·lo͞ot′lē) *adv.* **1** Completely; unconditionally. **2** *Colloq.* Positively. **3** *Gram.* So as not to take an object: to use a verb *absolutely.*

absolute magnitude A measure of the intrinsic as distinguished from the apparent brightness of a star. It is equal to the luminosity a star would have if located at the standard distance of 10 parsecs from the sun.

absolute music See under MUSIC.

absolute pitch 1 The pitch of a musical tone determined by the number of its vibrations per second in relation to the frequency of a basic or standard tone (usually middle C). **2** The inherent ability to discriminate very minute differences in pitch. Also called *perfect pitch.*

absolute temperature Temperature reckoned from absolute zero.

absolute zero That temperature at which a body would be wholly deprived of heat, and at which a perfect gas would exert no pressure: equivalent to about −273°C., −459°F., or −219° Réaumur.

ab·so·lu·tion (ab′sə·lo͞o′shən) *n.* **1** An absolving, or a being absolved; forgiveness. **2** In the Roman Catholic Church, the act of a priest in pronouncing the remission of sin, its eternal punishment, or the canonical penalties attached to it; the act of releasing from censure without the sacrament of penance; or a solemn rite performed at the end of a requiem mass. **3** In other churches, the declaration or imploring of God's forgiveness by a priest or minister; also, the forgiveness itself. [< L *absolutio, -onis* < *absolvere.* See ABSOLVE.]

ab·so·lu·tism (ab′sə·lo͞o·tiz′əm) *n.* **1** The doctrine or practice of unlimited authority and control; despotism; predestination. **2** Absoluteness; positiveness. **—ab′so·lu′tist** *n.* **—ab′so·lu·tis′tic** *adj.*

ab·sol·u·to·ry (ab·sol′yə·tôr′ē, -tō′rē) *adj.* Having power to absolve; absolving. [< L *absolutorius* < *absolvere.* See ABSOLVE.]

ab·solve (ab·solv′, -zolv′) *v.t.* **ab·solved, ab·solv·ing 1** To pronounce free from the penalties or consequences of an action: His excuses do not *absolve* him from blame. **2** To acquit, as of guilt or complicity. **3** To release from an obligation, liability, or promise. **4** *Eccl.* To grant a remission of sin, its punishment, or the canonical penance attached to it; pardon. [< L *absolvere* < *ab-* from + *solvere* loose. Doublet of ASSOIL.] **—ab·solv′a·ble** *adj.* **—ab·sol′vent** *adj. & n.* **—ab·solv′er** *n.*

Synonyms: acquit, clear, discharge, exculpate, exempt, exonerate, forgive, free, justify, liberate, pardon, release. To *absolve,* in the strict sense, is to *set free* from any bond. One may be *absolved* from a promise by a breach of faith on the part of one to whom the promise was made. To *absolve* from sins is formally to remit their condemnation and penalty. To *acquit* of sin or crime is to *free* from the accusation of it; the innocent are rightfully *acquitted;* the guilty may be mercifully *absolved.* Compare JUSTIFY, PARDON. *Antonyms*: accuse, bind, charge, compel, condemn, convict, impeach, inculpate, obligate, oblige.

ab·so·nant (ab′sə·nənt) *adj.* Discordant; unreasonable. [< AB-[1] + L *sonans.* See SONANT.]

ab·sorb (ab·sôrb′, -zôrb′) *v.t.* **1** To drink in or suck up, as through or into pores: A sponge *absorbs* water. **2** To engross completely; occupy wholly: Study *absorbs* him. **3** *Physics, Chem.* To take up or in by chemical or molecular action, as gases, heat, liquid, light, etc.: distinguished from *adsorb.* **4** To assimilate, as in the processes of nutrition and growth. **5** To take in and incorporate so as to swallow up identity or individuality: The city *absorbs* the suburbs. **6** To receive the force or action of; intercept: A spring *absorbs* a jar or jolt. **7** To take up entirely by purchase or use, as an issue of bonds or the output of a factory. [< L *absorbere* < *ab-* from + *sorbere* suck in] **—ab·sorb′a·bil′i·ty** *n.* **—ab·sorb′a·ble** *adj.* **—ab·sorb′ing** *adj.* **—ab·sorb′ing·ly** *adv.*

Synonyms: consume, engross, exhaust, imbibe, swallow. A fluid that is *absorbed* is taken up into the mass of the *absorbing* body, with which it may or may not permanently combine. A substance is *consumed* which is appropriated by some other substance, being, or agency, so that it ceases to exist or to be recognized as existing in its original condition; fuel is *consumed* in the fire, food in the body; *consume* also means to buy and use up, as an individual or the public *consumes* coal. A great talker *engrosses* his listeners. A credulous person *swallows* the most preposterous statement. A busy student is *absorbed* in a subject that takes his whole attention. *Antonyms*: disgorge, disperse, dissipate, distract, eject, emit, exude, radiate.

ab·sorbed (ab·sôrbd′, -zôrbd′) *adj.* **1** Deeply engrossed; rapt. **2** Sucked up or sunken in, as paint on a porous surface. See synonyms under ABSTRACTED. **—ab·sorb·ed·ly** (ab·sôr′·bid·lē, -zôr′-) *adv.* **—ab·sorb′ed·ness** *n.*

ab·sor·be·fa·cient (ab·sôr′bə·fā′shənt, -zôr′-) *adj.* Causing absorption or drying up. *—n.* A substance causing or promoting absorption. [< L *absorbere* (see ABSORB) + -FACIENT]

ab·sor·bent (ab·sôr′bənt, -zôr′-) *adj.* Absorbing or tending to absorb. *—n.* A substance, duct, etc., that absorbs. [< L *absorbens, -entis,* ppr. of *absorbere.* See ABSORB.] **—ab·sor′·ben·cy** *n.*

ab·sorb·er (ab·sôr′bər, -zôr′-) *n.* **1** One who or that which absorbs. **2** *Mech.* A part, as in a caloric engine, having the function of absorbing heat and giving it out later; a regenerator. **3** In an automobile spring, a device for absorbing the shock or jar of a machine in motion; a shock absorber.

ab·sorp·tance (ab·sôrp′təns, -zôrp′-) *n.* The ratio of the light absorbed by a body to the light that enters it.

ab·sorp·tion (ab·sôrp′shən, -zôrp′-) *n.* **1** The act of absorbing or the condition of being absorbed. **2** *Physics* **a** The process by which a liquid or gas is taken into the interstices of a porous substance and held there. **b** The transformation of any emission as it passes through a material substance. **3** Engrossment of the mind; preoccupation. **4** Assimilation, as by incorporation or by the digestive process. **—ab·sorp′tive** *adj.* **—ab·sorp′tive·ness, ab′·sorp·tiv′i·ty** *n.* [< L *absorptio, -onis* < *absorbere.* See ABSORB.]

absorption spectrum A spectrum which, by characteristic dark lines, indicates the presence of a substance absorbing certain wavelengths of a continuous spectrum: distinguished from *emission spectrum.*

abs·que hoc (abz′kwē hok′) *Latin* Without this.

ab·stain (ab·stān′) *v.i.* To keep oneself back; refrain voluntarily: with *from.* See synonyms under CEASE, REFRAIN[1]. [< F *abstenir* < L *abstinere* < *ab-* from + *tenere* hold]

ab·stain·er (ab·stā′nər) *n.* One who abstains; especially, a teetotaler.

ab·ste·mi·ous (ab·stē′mē·əs) *adj.* **1** Eating and drinking sparingly. **2** Characterized by or spent in abstinence; avoiding excess; self-denying; temperate. See synonyms under SOBER. < L *abstemius* temperate < *ab-* from + root of *temetum* intoxicating drink] **—ab·ste′mi·ous·ly** *adv.* **—ab·ste′mi·ous·ness** *n.*

ab·sten·tion (ab·sten′shən) *n.* A refraining or abstaining. [<L *abstentio, -onis* <*abstinere.* See ABSTAIN.] —**ab·sten′tious** *adj.*

ab·sterge (ab·stûrj′) *v.t.* **·sterged, ·sterg·ing 1** To wipe away; cleanse. **2** To purge. [<L *abstergere* <*ab-* away +*tergere* wipe] —**ab·ster·sion** (ab·stûr′shən, -zhən) *n.* —**ab·ster·sive** (ab·stûr′siv) *adj.*

ab·ster·gent (ab·stûr′jənt) *adj.* Cleansing. —*n.* A cleansing substance.

ab·sti·nence (ab′stə·nəns) *n.* The act or practice of abstaining; forbearing voluntarily, especially from intoxicating drinks; self–denial. [<F <L *abstinentia* <*abstinere.* See ABSTAIN.]
Synonyms: abstemiousness, continence, fasting, frugality, moderation, self–control, self–denial, self–restraint, sobriety, temperance. *Abstinence* from food commonly signifies going without; *abstemiousness,* partaking moderately; *abstinence* may be for a single occasion, *abstemiousness* is habitual *moderation. Self–denial* is giving up what one wishes; *abstinence* may be refraining from what one does not desire. *Fasting* is *abstinence* from food for a limited time, and generally for religious reasons. *Sobriety* and *temperance* signify moderate indulgence. Total *abstinence* has come to signify the entire abstaining from intoxicating liquors. *Antonyms:* drunkenness, excess, gluttony, greed, intemperance, intoxication, reveling, revelry, self–indulgence sensuality, wantonness.

ab·sti·nent (ab′stə·nənt) *adj.* Abstemious. See synonyms under SOBER. —**ab′sti·nent·ly** *adv.*

ab·stract (ab·strakt′, ab′strakt) *adj.* **1** Considered apart from the concrete; general, as opposed to particular. **2** Theoretical; ideal, as opposed to practical. **3** Considered or expressed without reference to particular example, as numbers, attributes, or qualities: 8 is an *abstract* number; Redness and valor are *abstract* nouns. **4** Withdrawn from contemplation of present objects; abstracted. **5** *Philos.* Dissociated from closely applied perceptions or ideas: *abstract* truth. **6** In art, generalized or universal, as opposed to concrete, specific, or representational; tending away from the realistic or literal.
—*n.* (ab′·strakt) **1** A summary or epitome. **2** *Law* A compendium. **3** *Logic* An abstract idea or term. **4** *Gram.* An abstract noun. See under NOUN. **5** In pharmacy, the preparation of a drug in powder form. See synonyms under ABBREVIATION, ABRIDGMENT.
—**in the abstract** Apart from concrete relation or embodiment; in its general reference or meaning; abstractly. —*v.t.* (ab·strakt′) **1** To take away; remove. **2** To take away secretly; purloin. **3** To withdraw or disengage (the attention, interest, etc.). **4** To consider apart from particular or material instances; form a general notion of: to *abstract* the idea of humanity from a crowd of men. **5** (ab′strakt) To make an abstract of, as a book or treatise; summarize; abridge. [<L *abstractus,* pp. of *abstrahere* <*ab-* away + *trahere* draw] —**ab·stract′er** *n.* —**ab·stract′ly** *adv.* —**ab·stract′ness** *n.*
Synonyms (verb): detach, disengage, divide, draw, purloin, remove, separate, steal, withdraw. The central idea of *withdrawing* makes *abstract* in common speech a euphemism for *purloin, steal.* In mental processes, we *separate* some one element from all that does not necessarily belong to it, *abstract* it, and view it alone. The mind is *abstracted* when it is *withdrawn* from all other subjects and concentrated upon one. *Antonyms:* add, increase, insert, interpose, restore, unite.

ab·stract·ed (ab·strak′tid) *adj.* **1** Absent–minded. **2** Separated from all else; apart; abstruse. —**ab·stract′ed·ly** *adv.* —**ab·stract′ed·ness** *n.*
Synonyms: absent, absent–minded, absorbed, heedless, inattentive, oblivious, preoccupied. As regards mental action, *absorbed, abstracted,* and *preoccupied* refer to the cause, *absent* or *absent–minded* to the effect. The man *absorbed* in one thing will appear *absent* in others. The *absent–minded* man is *oblivious* of ordinary matters, because his thoughts are elsewhere. One who is *preoccupied* is intensely busy in thought; one may be *absent–minded* simply through inattention, with fitful and aimless wandering of thought. Compare ABSTRACT. *Antonyms:* alert, attentive, ready.

abstract idea A mental representation or concept that isolates and generalizes an aspect or quality of an object or of a group of experiences, from which relationships may be or are perceived.

ab·strac·tion (ab·strak′shən) *n.* **1** State of being abstracted; an abstracting. **2** An abstract idea; a theory. **3** Separation; removal; theft. **4** Absence of mind; preoccupation. **5** Seclusion of life, as by a hermit; withdrawal from worldly objects. **6** The quality that makes a work of art generalized or universal, as distinguished from literal or concrete, present in varying degrees in widely differing art forms. **7** An art form or a work of art in which the qualities are either predominantly or totally abstract: opposed to *naturalism, realism.* Compare NON–OBJECTIVE ART. [<L *abstractio, -onis* <*abstractus.* See ABSTRACT.]

ab·strac·tive (ab·strak′tiv) *adj.* Of, pertaining to, or tending to abstraction; having the power of abstraction; epitomizing. —**ab·strac′tive·ly** *adv.* —**ab·strac′tive·ness** *n.*

abstract of title A document containing a brief and orderly statement of the original grant and subsequent conveyances and encumbrances relating to the title and ownership of real estate.

ab·stric·tion (ab·strik′shən) *n. Bot.* A process of spore–formation in certain fungi, in which the sporophore becomes constricted by septa at the place of division. [<AB-[1] + L *strictio, -onis* a binding <*stringere* bind]

ab·struse (ab·strōōs′) *adj.* **1** Hard to understand. **2** *Obs.* Hidden; concealed. See synonyms under COMPLEX, MYSTERIOUS, OBSCURE. [<L *abstrusus,* pp. of *abstrudere* < *ab-* away + *trudere* thrust] —**ab·struse′ly** *adv.* —**ab·struse′ness** *n.*

ab·surd (ab·sûrd′, -zûrd′) *adj.* Opposed to manifest reason or truth; irrational; preposterous; ridiculous. —*n.* a literary and philosophical term suggesting the illogicality or pointlessness of the human condition from an existential point of view. [<F *absurde* <L *absurdus* out of tune, incongruous, senseless <*ab-* completely + *surdus* deaf] —**ab·surd′·ly** *adv.* —**ab·surd′ness** *n.*
Synonyms: anomalous, foolish, incorrect, irrational, ludicrous, mistaken, monstrous, nonsensical, paradoxical, preposterous, ridiculous, senseless, stupid, unreasonable, wild. That is *absurd* which is contrary to the first principles of reasoning; as, that a part should be greater than the whole is *absurd.* A *paradoxical* statement appears at first thought contradictory or *absurd,* while it may be really true. Anything is *irrational* when clearly contrary to sound reason, *foolish* when contrary to practical good sense, *unreasonable* when there seems a perverse bias or an intent to go wrong. *Monstrous* and *preposterous* refer to what is overwhelmingly *absurd.* The *ridiculous* or the *nonsensical* is worthy only to be laughed at. Compare INCONGRUOUS. *Antonyms:* consistent, demonstrable, established, incontestable, incontrovertible, indisputable, indubitable, logical, rational, reasonable, sagacious, sensible, sound, substantial, true, undeniable, unquestionable, wise.

ab·surd·i·ty (ab·sûr′də·tē, -zûr′-) *n. pl.* **·ties 1** The quality of being absurd. **2** Something absurd.

A·bu–Bek·r (ə·bōō′·bek′ər), 573–634, first Moslem caliph of Mecca and Mohammed's successor.

A·bu·kir (ä′bōō·kir′, ə·bōō′kər) A village in northern Egypt on the western limit of **Abukir Bay** on the Mediterranean, site of the Battle of the Nile, 1798, where the British defeated the Napoleonic naval forces: also *Aboukir.*

a·bu·li·a (ə·bōō′lē·ə, ə·byōō′-) *n. Psychiatry* A form of mental derangement in which the will power is lost or impaired: also *aboulia.* [<*NL* <*Gk. aboulia* <*a-* without+ *boulē* will] —**a·bu′lic** *adj.*

A·bul Ka·sim (ə·bŏŏl′ kä′sim), died 1013? Arab surgeon and medical encyclopedist. Also *Albucasis.*

a·bun·dance (ə·bun′dəns) *n.* A plentiful supply; a great quantity or number; copiousness; plenty. See synonyms under COMFORT. [<OF <L *abundantia* <*abundans.* See ABUNDANT.]

a·bun·dant (ə·bun′dənt) *adj.* Affording a plentiful supply; abounding; ample; copious. See synonyms under AMPLE. [<OF <L *abundans, -antis,* ppr. of *abundare.* See ABOUND.] —**a·bun′dant·ly** *adv.*

ab ur·be con·di·ta (ab ûr′bē kon′di·tə) *Latin* From the founding of the city (of Rome, about 753 B.C.). Abbr. *A.U.C.*

a·buse (ə·byōōz′) *v.t.* **a·bused, a·bus·ing 1** use improperly or injuriously; misuse. **2** To hurt by treating wrongly; injure: to *abuse* friendship. **3** To speak in coarse or bad terms of; revile; malign. **4** *Obs.* To deceive.
—*n.* (ə·byōōs′) **1** Improper or injurious use; perversion; misuse. **2** Ill–treatment; cruel treatment; injury. **3** Vicious conduct, practice, or act. **4** Vituperation; slander. See synonyms under ABOMINATION, OUTRAGE. [<F *abuser* <L *abusus,* pp. of *abuti* misuse < *ab-* away + *uti* use] —**a·bus′er** *n.*
Synonyms (verb): damage, defame, defile, harm, ill–treat, ill–use, injure, malign, maltreat, misemploy, misuse, molest, oppress, persecute, pervert, pollute, prostitute, ravish, reproach, revile, ruin, slander, victimize, vilify, violate, vituperate, wrong. *Abuse* covers all unreasonable or improper use or treatment by word or act. A tenant does not *abuse* rented property by reasonable wear, even if that may *damage* the property and *injure* its sale; he may *abuse* it by needless defacement or neglect. *Defame, malign, revile, slander, vilify,* and *vituperate* are used always in a bad sense. One may be justly *reproached.* To *persecute* one is to *ill–treat* him for opinion's sake, commonly for religious belief; to *oppress* is generally for political or pecuniary motives. *Misemploy, misuse,* and *pervert* are commonly applied to objects rather than to persons. Compare POLLUTE. *Antonyms:* applaud, benefit, cherish, conserve, consider, eulogize, extol, favor, laud, panegyrize, praise, protect, respect, shield, sustain, uphold, vindicate.

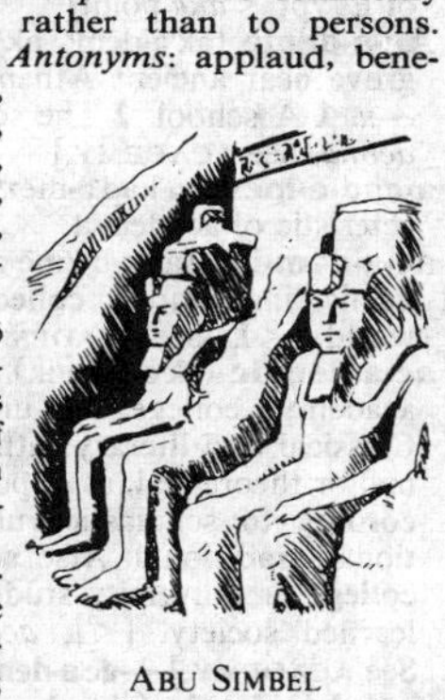

ABU SIMBEL
Colossal statues of Rameses II.

A·bu Sim·bel (ä′bōō sim′bel) Site of ancient rock temples on the west bank of the Nile in southern Egypt: also *Ipsambul.*

a·bu·sive (ə·byōō′·siv) *adj.* **1** Of the nature of or characterized by abuse; harsh; vituperative. **2** Using wrongly or improperly; misapplying. —**a·bu′sive·ly** *adv.* —**a·bu′sive·ness** *n.*

a·but (ə·but′) *v.* **a·but·ted, a·but·ting** *v.i.* To touch, join, or cause to adjoin or touch at the end or side; border: with *on, upon,* or *against.* —*v.t.* To border on; end at: This building *abuts* the park. See synonyms under ADJACENT. [<OF *abouter* border on (<*a-* to + *bout* end); infl. by OF *abuter* touch with an end (<*a-* to + *but* end)] —**a·but′ter** *n.* —**a·but′ting** *adj.*

a·bu·ti·lon (ə·byōō′tə·lon) *n.* Any plant of a genus (*Abutilon*) of the mallow family having single bell–shaped flowers: some cultivated varieties are called *flowering maple.* [<NL< Arabic *aubūtīlūn*]

a·but·ment (ə·but′mənt) *n.* **1** The act of abutting. **2** That which abuts, or the place which is abutted upon. **3** A supporting or buttressing structure, as at the end of a bridge or wall; also, that part of an arch that takes the thrust or strain. For illustration see ARCH. **4** *Mil.* The block at the rear end of a gun which receives the rearward pressure of explosion or detonation.

a·but·tal (ə·but′l) *n.* **1** An abutting or abutment. **2** An abutting part; a boundary.

ab·volt (ab·vōlt′) *n.* The cgs electromagnetic unit of electromotive force, equal to one one–hundred–millionth of a volt. [<AB(SOLUTE) + VOLT]

a·by (ə·bī′) *v.t.* **a·bought** *Obs.* **1** To pay the

penalty for. 2 To endure; suffer, as a fate. Also **a·bye′**. [OE *ābycgan* pay for]

A·by·dos (ə·bī′dos) 1 An ancient city of Asia Minor opposite Sestos at the narrowest point of the Hellespont. 2 The site of a group of ancient temples in central Egypt.

a·bysm (ə·biz′əm) n. An abyss; an unfathomable depth. [< OF *abisme* < L *abyssus* ABYSS]

a·bys·mal (ə·biz′məl) adj. Unfathomable; hence, extreme: an *abysmal* ignorance. —**a·bys′mal·ly** adv.

a·byss (ə·bis′) n. 1 A bottomless gulf. 2 Hell. 3 Any vast depth; hence, a great moral or intellectual depth: an *abyss* of degradation and humiliation. 4 The lowest depths of the sea. [< L *abyssus* < Gk. *abyssos* < *a-* without + *byssos* bottom]

a·bys·sal (ə·bis′əl) adj. 1 Pertaining to an abyss. 2 Designating those ocean depths beyond the continental shelf. Also **a·bys′sic**. (ə·bis′ik).

Ab·ys·sin·i·a (ab′ə·sin′ē·ə) Ethiopia. —**Ab′·ys·sin·i·an** adj. & n.

Abyssinian cat Any of a breed of medium-sized cats with long, tapering tails, small paws, and short, silky hair with dark-colored tips.

ac- Assimilated var. of AD-.

-ac suffix 1 Having; affected by: *demoniac*. 2 Pertaining to; of: *cardiac*. [< Gk. *-akos* or L *-acus* or F *-aque*]

Ac Chem. Actinium (symbol Ac).

a·ca·cia (ə·kā′shə) n. 1 Any of a large genus (*Acacia*) of flowering trees and shrubs of the bean family found in the tropics and warm temperate regions, especially the green wattle acacia (*A. decurrens*) of Australia. 2 The common locust tree. 3 Gum arabic or gummy exudation of certain acacias. [< L < Gk. *akakia* a thorny tree of Egypt < *akē* point]

Ac·a·deme (ak′ə·dēm′, ak′ə·dēm) The garden or grove near ancient Athens where Plato taught. —n. 1 A school. 2 The scholarly life. [< L *academia*. See ACADEMY.]

a·cad·e·mese (ə·kad′ə·mēz′) n. The jargon characteristic of academia.

ac·a·dem·i·a (ak′ə·dē′mē·ə) n. Often cap. Academic institutions collectively; the academic world. [< L. See ACADEMY.]

ac·a·dem·ic (ak′ə·dem′ik) adj. 1 Pertaining to an academy, college, or university; scholarly. 2 Classical and literary rather than technical; formal or theoretical, as opposed to practical. 3 According to scholastic rules or usage; conventional; traditional. Also **ac′a·dem′i·cal**. —n. 1 A college or university student. 2 A member of a learned society. [< L *academicus* < *academia*. See ACADEMY.] —**ac′a·dem′i·cal·ly** adv.

ac·a·dem·i·cals (ak′ə·dem′i·kəlz) n. pl. The prescribed dress of an academy, college, etc.; cap and gown.

a·cad·e·mi·cian (ə·kad′ə·mish′ən, ak′ə·də-) n. A member of an academy of art, science, or literature.

ac·a·dem·i·cism (ak′ə·dem′ə·siz′əm) n. 1 The state or quality of being academic in style or procedure. 2 Pedantic formalism, as in art or literature. Also **a·cad·e·mism** (ə·kad′ə·miz′əm).

a·cad·e·my (ə·kad′ə·mē) n. pl. **·mies** 1 A school, especially one intermediate between a common school and a college. 2 A learned society for the advancement of arts or sciences. [< F *académie* < L *academia* < Gk. *akadēmeia* the grove of *Akadēmos* where Plato taught] —**ac′a·dem′ic** adj. & n.

Academy Award One of the awards made annually by the Academy of Motion Picture Arts and Sciences.

A·ca·di·a (ə·kā′dē·ə) 1 A former name for the Atlantic coast region of North America, including Nova Scotia, settled originally by the French. 2 A parish in southern Louisiana settled by deported Acadians.

A·ca·di·an (ə·kā′dē·ən) adj. Of or pertaining to Acadia. —n. One of the early French settlers of Acadia, or a descendant. See CAJUN.

Acadia National Park A rocky, mountainous area mainly on Mount Desert Island off the southern coast of Maine; 44 square miles.

ac·a·jou (ak′ə·zhoo) n. 1 A tropical American wood (genus *Cedrela*), valued for fine furniture and interior trim. 2 The cashew tree or its fruits; also the gum which exudes from its bark. 3 French mahogany; also, the color of the fin-

ished wood. [< F. See CASHEW.]

ac·a·leph (ak′ə·lef) n. A jellyfish. Also **ac·a·lephe** (ak′ə·lēf). [< Gk. *akalēphē* nettle] —**ac·a·le·phan** (ak′ə·lē′fən) adj. & n. —**ac·a·le·phoid** (ak′ə·lē′foid) adj.

a·can·thine (ə·kan′thin) adj. 1 Pertaining to or like an acanthus. 2 Decorated with the acanthus leaf.

acantho- combining form Thorn or thorny; spine, point, prickle: *acanthocephalan*. Also, before vowels, **acanth-**, as in *acanthoid*. [< Gk. *akantha* thorn]

a·can·tho·ceph·a·lan (ə·kan′thō·sef′ə·lən) n. Any of a phylum (*Acanthocephala*) of worms parasitic when adult in the intestines of fishes and other vertebrates, having a proboscis covered with hooks. Also **a·can′tho·ceph′a·lid**. [< ACANTHO- + Gk. *kephalē* head]

a·can·thoid (ə·kan′thoid) adj. Spiny.

ac·an·thop·ter·yg·i·an (ak′an·thop′tə·rij′ē·ən) n. Any of a superorder (*Acanthopterygii*) of teleost fishes, including most fishes having spines in the fins, as the mackerel, bass, etc. [< ACANTHO- + Gk. *pterygion* fin]

a·can·thus (ə·kan′thəs) n. pl. **·thus·es** or **·thi** (-thī) 1 Any plant of the genus *Acanthus* having large spinous leaves: common in the Mediterranean region. 2 A conventionalized architectural and decorative representation of its leaf, characteristic of the Corinthian capital. Also **acanthus leaf**. [< L < Gk. *akanthos* < *akē* thorn]

ACANTHUS (def. 2)

a cap·pel·la (ä′ kə·pel′ə, Ital. ä′ käp·pel′lä) Music 1 In chapel or church style, i.e., sung without instrumental accompaniment. 2 In church time, i.e., with four half notes in each bar. [< Ital. < L *ad* according to + *cappella* chapel]

a ca·pric·cio (ä′ kä·prēt′chō) Music At the performer's pleasure as to tempo and expression; capriciously. [< Ital.]

A·ca·pul·co (ä′kä·pool′kō) A port and resort city of SW Mexico on the Pacific.

ac·a·ri·a·sis (ak′ə·rī′ə·sis) n. An itch caused by mites.

a·car·i·cide (ə·kar′ə·sīd, ak′ə·rə-) n. Miticide. [< ACARID + -CIDE]

ac·a·rid (ak′ə·rid) n. Any of an order (*Acarina*) of arachnids, including the mites and ticks. —adj. Of or pertaining to the acarids. [Gk. *akari* mite]

Ac·ar·na·ni·a (ak′är·nā′nē·ə) A region on the Ionian Sea, comprising a nome of modern Greece; 2,137 square miles.

ac·a·roid (ak′ə·roid) adj. Of or like the acarids; mitelike. [< Gk. *akari* mite, + -OID]

acaroid gum A yellow, fragrant, alcohol-soluble resin from Australian grasstrees. Also **acaroid resin**.

a·car·pel·ous (ā·kär′pəl·əs) adj. Bot. Having no carpels. Also **a·car′pel·lous**.

a·car·pous (ā·kär′pəs) adj. Bot. Not bearing fruit. [< A-⁴ without + Gk. *karpos* fruit]

ac·a·rus ak′ər·əs) n. pl. **·a·ri** (-ə·rī) Any of the numerous mites of the genus *Acarus*. [< Gk. *akari* mite]

a·cat·a·lec·tic (ā·kat′ə·lek′tik) adj. Metrically complete; not catalectic; having the required number of feet or of syllables, especially in the last foot. —n. A full or metrically complete verse.

a·cat·a·lep·si·a (ə·kat′ə·lep′sē·ə) n. Impairment of the reasoning faculty; abnormal inability to comprehend. [< NL]

a·cat·a·lep·sy (ə·kat′ə·lep′sē) n. Philos. The incomprehensibility of all things; specifically, among the Skeptics, the doctrine that all human knowledge is only probable and that all positive judgment should be suspended. [< Gk. *akatalēpsia* < *a-* not + *kata-* thoroughly + *lēpsis* a seizing. See CATALEPSY.]

a·cau·date (ā·kô′dāt) adj. Zool. Having no tail; tailless. Also **a·cau′dal**. [< A-⁴ not + CAUDATE]

ac·au·les·cence (ak′ô·les′əns) n. Bot. Absence, real or apparent, of the stem. —**ac′au·les′cent**, adj.

a·caus·al (ā kôz′əl) adj. not causal; not having

to do with cause and effect.

Ac·cad (ak′ad, ä′käd), **Ac·ca·di·an** (ə·kā′dē·ən, ə·kä′-) See AKKAD, etc.

ac·cede (ak·sēd′) v.i. **ac·ced·ed**, **ac·ced·ing** 1 To give one's consent or adherence; agree; assent: with *to*. 2 To come into or enter upon an office or dignity: with *to*. See synonyms under AGREE, ASSENT. [< L *accedere* < *ad-* to + *cedere* yield, go]

ac·ced·ence (ak·sē′dəns) n. The act of acceding; agreeing to.

ac·cel·er·an·do (ak·sel′ə·ran′dō; Ital. ät·che·le·rän′dō) adj. & adv. Music With gradual quickening of the time. [< Ital.]

ac·cel·er·ant (ak·sel′ər·ənt) adj. Accelerating; hastening. —n. That which accelerates.

ac·cel·er·ate (ak·sel′ə·rāt) v. **·at·ed**, **·at·ing** v.t. 1 To cause to act or move faster; increase the speed of. 2 Physics To increase the rate of change of (the linear or angular velocity of a body). 3 To hasten the natural or usual course of: to *accelerate* combustion. 4 To cause to happen ahead of time. —v.i. 5 To move or become faster; to increase in speed. See synonyms under QUICKEN. [< L *acceleratus*, pp. of *accelerare* < *ad-* to + *celer* quick] —**ac·cel·er·a·ble** (ak·sel′ər·ə·bəl) adj.

ac·cel·er·a·tion (ak·sel′ə·rā′shən) n. 1 The act of accelerating, or the process of being accelerated; a quickening, as of progress, action, functional activity, etc. 2 The rate at which the speed of a body increases. 3 Physics The rate at which the velocity of a body increases per unit of time: used also of decrease of velocity, which is expressed as a **negative acceleration**.

acceleration of gravity An increase in the velocity of a body due to the force of gravity. At sea level it is about 32.17 feet per second per second.

ac·cel·er·a·tive (ak·sel′ə·rā′tiv) adj. Of, pertaining to, or causing acceleration; tending to accelerate. Also **ac·cel′er·a·to·ry**.

ac·cel·er·a·tor (ak·sel′ə·rā′tər) n. 1 One who or that which accelerates. 2 Phot. Any chemical or device for hastening the appearance or development of the picture on an exposed sensitized plate or print. 3 Mech. A device for increasing the speed of a machine. 4 Chem. A substance or agent which quickens the speed of a chemical reaction; a catalyst. 5 Physiol. A muscle or nerve which acts to increase the speed of a function. 6 Physics Any of various devices for accelerating the velocity of subatomic particles by subjecting them to the force of a synchronized electromagnetic field, as a cyclotron or synchrotron.

ac·cel·er·o·graph (ak·sel′ər·ə·graf′, -gräf′) n. A device for measuring the pressures developed by the combustion of an explosive in an enclosed or nearly enclosed space. [< ACCELER(ATE) + -O- + -GRAPH]

ac·cel·er·om·e·ter (ak·sel′ə·rom′ə·tər) n. An instrument designed to measure and record the acceleration of an aircraft.

ac·cent (ak′sent) n. 1 A stress of voice on a particular syllable in pronouncing a word. 2 A mark used to indicate such stress: known as **primary** (noting the chief stress) and **secondary** (noting weaker stress on some other syllable or syllables) accents. In ə·brēvē·ā′·shən, the primary accent is on the fourth syllable, and the secondary accent is on the second syllable. 3 One of three marks, used chiefly in the Romance languages, to indicate the quality of a vowel or diphthong: acute (′), grave (`), and circumflex (^) accents. 4 Music Stress of voice or instrument. 5 A modulation of the voice; mode of utterance; pronounciation. 6 pl. Speech. 7 Math. A mark or marks to distinguish the value or order of similar symbols: a′ (a prime), a″ (a second), a‴ (a third), etc.; also to denote minutes and seconds in geometry, trigonometry, etc.: ′ = minutes, ″ = seconds. 8 In mensuration, a similar mark or marks to denote feet and inches, as ′ = feet; ″ = inches. 9 In prosody, the stress determining the rhythm of poetry; ictus. —v.t. (ak′sent, ak·sent′) 1 To speak or pronounce with an accent; stress. 2 To write or print with a mark indicating accent or stress. 3 To call attention to; accentuate. [< L *accentus*, lit., song added to speech (a trans. of Gk. *prosōidia* PROSODY) < *ad-* to + *cantus* a singing < *canere* sing]

ac·cen·tu·al (ak·sen′choo·əl) adj. Of, pertaining to, having, or made by accent. —**ac·cen′tu·al·ly** adv.

ac·cen·tu·ate (ak·sen′chōō·āt) *v.t.* ·**at·ed**, ·**at·ing** **1** To strengthen or heighten the effect of; emphasize. **2** To speak or pronounce with an accent. **3** To write or print with a mark indicating accent. [< Med.L *accentuatus*, pp. of *accentuare* < L *accentus* ACCENT] —**ac·cen′tu·a′tion** *n.*

ac·cept (ak·sept′) *v.t.* **1** To take when offered; receive with favor or willingness, as a gift. **2** To give an affirmative answer to: to *accept* an invitation, an offer of marriage, etc. **3** To agree to; admit: to *accept* an apology. **4** To take with good grace; submit to: to *accept* the inevitable. **5** To agree to pay, as a draft. **6** To believe in: to *accept* Christianity. **7** *Law* To acknowledge as valid or received: He *accepted* the subpoena. — *v.i.* **8** To agree or promise to fulfil an engagement; receive favorably. See synonyms under ACKNOWLEDGE, AGREE, ASSENT, ASSUME, CONFESS, RATIFY. [< L *acceptare*, freq. of *accipere* take < *ad-* to + *capere* take] —**ac·cept′er** *n.*

ac·cept·a·ble (ak·sep′tə·bəl) *adj.* **1** That is worthy of being accepted or capable of acceptance; pleasing; welcome. **2** Tolerable; detrimental, though not judged to require corrective measures: *acceptable* air pollution. See synonyms under AGREEABLE, DELIGHTFUL. —**ac·cept′a·ble·ness, ac·cept′a·bil′i·ty** *n.* —**ac·cept′a·bly** *adv.*

ac·cep·tance (ak·sep′təns) *n.* **1** The act of accepting; state of being accepted or acceptable; also, consent to receive. **2** An agreement to pay a bill of exchange, draft, order, or the like, according to its terms; also, the paper itself when endorsed accepted." **3** *Law* Any form or act by which one positively or constructively acknowledges the validity or sufficiency of an act done by another, agrees to the terms of a contract, or the like. Also **ac·cep·tan·cy.**

ac·cep·tant (ak·sep′tənt) *adj.* Ready or willing to accept; receptive.

ac·cep·ta·tion (ak′sep·tā′shən) *n.* **1** The accepted meaning of a word or expression; general interpretation. **2** The state of being accepted or acceptable.

ac·cept·ed (ak·sep′tid) *adj.* Commonly recognized, believed, or approved; popular.

ac·cep·tor (ak·sep′tər) *n. Law* One who has given his acceptance on a check or draft.

ac·cess (ak′ses) *n.* **1** The act, opportunity, or means of approaching; admittance; approach; passage; path. **2** Increase; addition; accession: an *access* of territory. **3** An attack, as of disease; a fit of passion or zeal; outburst. **4** *Eccl.* Approach to God: *access* by faith (*Rom.* v 2): used especially in the titles of certain prayers. See synonyms under ENTRANCE, INCREASE. [< L *accessus* an approach < *accedere.* See ACCEDE].

ac·ces·sa·ry (ak·ses′ər·ē) *adj., n. pl.* ·**ries** *Law* Accessory. ◆ **accessary, accessory** The earlier form is *accessary* (see -ARY¹), now retained primarily in legal usage. Later, the adjective was refashioned to *accessory* (on analogy with *promissory, amatory, illusory,* etc.), which also influenced the form of the noun. The two spellings are now practically interchangeable, although *accessory* is supplanting the other in both common and legal usage.

ac·ces·si·ble (ak·ses′ə·bəl) *adj.* **1** Easy of access. **2** That can be approached. **3** Attainable; that can be obtained. **4** Open to the influence of: with *to:* His heart is *accessible* to pity. See synonyms under FRIENDLY. —**ac·ces′si·bil′i·ty** *n.* —**ac·ces′si·bly** *adv.*

ac·ces·sion (ak·sesh′ən) *n.* **1** One who or that which is added; addition. **2** Attainment, as of office; succession to a throne; induction or elevation. **3** Access; admittance; approach: the *accession* of light. **4** Assent; agreement; consent. **5** *Law* The acquisition of property of a concomitant nature by virtue of the ownership of the principal, to which it is accessory as an incident. **6** A beginning, increase, or paroxysm, of disease, anger, folly, etc. See ACCESS. —*v.t.* To record, as additions to a library or museum. [< L *accessio, -onis* < *accedere.* See ACCEDE.] —**ac·ces′sion·al** *adj.*

Synonyms (noun): addition, arrival augmentation, enlargement, extension, inauguration, increase, influx. See ENTRANCE.

ac·ces·so·ri·al (ak′sə·sôr′ē·əl, -sō′rē·əl) *adj.* Pertaining to an accessory.

ac·ces·so·ry (ak·ses′ər·ē) *n. pl.* ·**ries 1** A person or thing that aids subordinately; an adjunct; appurtenance; accompaniment. **2** *pl.* Such items of apparel as complete an outfit, as gloves, a scarf, hat, or handbag. **3** *Law* A person who, even if not present, is concerned, either before or after, in the perpetration of a felony below the crime of treason. See also note under ACCESSARY. — *adj.* **1** Aiding the principal design, or assisting subordinately the chief agent, as in the commission of a crime. **2** Contributory; supplemental; additional: *accessory* nerves. Also *accessary.* [< L *accessorius* < *accessus,* pp. of *accedere.* See ACCEDE.] —**ac·ces′so·ri·ly** *adv.* —**ac·ces′so·ri·ness** *n.*

Synonyms (noun): abetter or abettor, accomplice, ally, assistant, associate, attendant, coadjutor, colleague, companion, confederate, follower, helper, henchman, participator, partner, retainer. *Colleague* is used always in a good sense, *associate* and *coadjutor* generally so; *ally, assistant, associate, attendant, companion, helper,* either in a good or a bad sense; *abettor, accessory, accomplice, confederate,* almost always in a bad sense. In law, an *abettor* (the general legal spelling) is always present, either actively or constructively, at the commission of the crime; an *accessory* never. An *accomplice* is usually a principal; an *accessory* never. If present, though only to stand outside and keep watch against surprise, one is an *abettor,* and not an *accessory.* At common law, an *accessory* implies a principal, and cannot be convicted until after the conviction of the principal; the *accomplice* or *abettor* can be convicted as a principal. *Accomplice* and *abettor* have nearly the same meaning, but the former is the popular, the latter the legal term. Compare APPENDAGE, AUXILIARY. *Antonyms:* adversary, antagonist, betrayer, chief, commander, enemy, foe, hinderer, instigator, leader, opponent, principal, rival.

accessory after the fact A person who, knowing a felony to have been committed, comforts, conceals, or assists the felon.

accessory before the fact One who instigates, aids, or encourages another to commit a felony, but is not present at its perpetration.

accessory fruit Pseudocarp.

access time *Electronics* **1** The time required for a unit of information to be released from the memory or storage element of an electronic computer. **2** The time required for the effective storage of such information in the computer.

ac·ciac·ca·tu·ra (ät·chäk′kä·tōō′rä) *n. Music* **1** A short clear appoggiatura. **2** In old organ music, a grace note in which the principal note is sustained while the note below is struck for an instant only. [< Ital. < *acciaccare* crush]

ac·ci·dence (ak′sə·dəns) *n.* **1** *Gram.* That part of grammar that treats of the accidents or inflections of words. **2** A book dealing with the rudiments of grammar. **3** The rudiments or elements of any art or science. [< *accidents,* pl. of ACCIDENT (def. 3)]

ac·ci·dent (ak′sə·dənt) *n.* **1** Anything that happens by chance; anything occurring unexpectedly, undesignedly, or without known or assignable cause; a contingency; especially, any unpleasant or unfortunate occurrence involving injury, loss, suffering, or death; a casualty; mishap. **2** Any non-essential circumstance or attribute. **3** *Gram.* An inflection, as of case, gender, number, etc. **4** *Logic* Any feature, element, or accompaniment of an object not essential to the conception of it. [< L *accidens, -entis,* ppr. of *accidere* happen < *ad-* upon + *cadere* fall]

Synonyms: adventure, calamity, casualty, chance, contingency, disaster, fortuity, hap, happening, hazard, incident, misadventure, misfortune, mishap, possibility. An *accident* is that which happens without anyone's direct intention; a *chance* that which happens without any known cause. An *incident* is viewed as occurring in the regular course of things, but subordinate to the main purpose, or aside from the main design. *Fortune* and *chance* are nearly equivalent, but *chance* can be used of human ef-

fort and endeavor as *fortune* cannot be; we say there is one *chance* in a thousand"; as personified, we speak of fickle *Fortune,* blind *Chance.* Since the unintended is often the undesirable, *accident* tends to signify some *calamity* or *disaster,* but we may speak of a fortunate or happy *accident.* An *adventure* is that which may turn out ill, a *misadventure* that which does turn out ill. A slight disturbing *accident* is a *mishap.* Compare CATASTROPHE, EVENT, HAZARD. *Antonyms:* appointment, calculation, certainty, decree, fate, foreordination, intention, law, necessity, ordainment, ordinance, plan, preparation, provision, purpose.

ac·ci·den·tal (ak′sə·den′təl) *adj.* **1** Happening or coming by chance or without design; casual; fortuitous; taking place unexpectedly, unintentionally, or out of the usual course. **2** Non-essential; subordinate; incidental: said of any attribute or feature not entering into the very nature of a thing. **3** *Music* Pertaining to or indicating a sharp, natural, flat, etc., elsewhere than in the signature. —*n.* **1** A casual, incidental, or non-essential feature or property. **2** *Music* A sharp, flat, or natural elsewhere than in the signature. There are five *accidentals* or signs of chromatic alteration to show that the notes to which they are applied have to be raised or lowered a semitone or a tone: the sharp, double-sharp, flat, double-flat, and the natural. —**ac′ci·den′tal·ness** *n.*

Synonyms (adj.): chance, uncontemplated, undesigned, unexpected, unforeseen, unintended, unpremediated. See INCIDENTAL. *Antonyms:* calculated, contemplated, deliberate, designed, intended, planned, preconcerted, purposed, studied.

ac·ci·den·tal·ism (ak′sə·den′təl·iz′əm) *n.* **1** An accidental condition or effect. **2** *Med.* A theory that ignores the causes of disease and deals only with symptoms. **3** *Philos.* The theory that events occur by accident or without cause. —**ac′ci·den′tal·ist** *n.*

ac·ci·den·tal·ly (ak′sə·den′təl·ē) *adv.* **1** By accident or chance; unintentionally; casually. **2** As an accidental or subsidiary feature or effect; incidentally.

ac·ci·dent·ed (ak′sə·den′tid) *adj.* Marked by undulations in the surface: an *accidented* field.

ac·ci·die (ak′sə·dē) See ACEDIA.

ac·cip·i·ter ak·sip′ə·tər) *n.* **1** Any of the birds of prey belonging to the genus *Accipiter,* characterized by short rounded wings and a long tail, as a goshawk. **2** Any member of the family Accipitridae, as an eagle, hawk, or kite. [< L *accipiter* hawk]

ac·cip·i·trine (ak·sip′ə·trin, -trīn) *adj.* **1** Belonging to birds of prey; of or pertaining to a family of hawks (*Accipitridae*); like a hawk. **2** Raptorial.

ac·claim (ə·klām′) *v.t.* **1** To proclaim by acclamation; hail as: to *acclaim* him victor. **2** To shout approval of; show enthusiasm for. **3** To shout; call out: *acclaim* one's sorrow. —*v.i.* **4** To applaud; shout approval. —*n.* Applause; pronouncement. See synonyms under APPLAUSE. [< L *acclamare* < *ad-* to + *clamare* shout] —**ac·claim′a·ble** *adj.* —**ac·claim′er** *n.*

ac·cla·ma·tion (ak′lə·mā′shən) *n.* **1** The act of acclaiming; that which is expressed in the act; a shout, as of applause. **2** A loud and general viva-voce vote of approval, as in public assembly. **3** In the Roman Catholic Church, the elevation to an ecclesiastical dignity by the unanimous voice of the electors, without voting: one of the ways of electing a pope. **4** *Music* The responsive chant in antiphonal singing. **5** *Archeol.* A short inscription containing a wish or injunction, found on tombs, amulets, etc.; also, a representation, in sculpture or on a medal, of persons expressing joy or approval. See synonyms under APPLAUSE. [< L *acclamatio, -onis* < *acclamare.* See ACCLAIM.]

ac·clam·a·to·ry (ə·klam′ə·tôr′ē, -tō′rē) *adj.* Relating to or expressing joy and acclamation.

ac·cli·mate (ə·klī′mit, ak′lə·māt) *v.t. & v.i.* ·**mat·ed**, ·**mat·ing** To adapt or become adapted

to a foreign climate or new environment: said of persons, plants, or animals; acclimatize. [<F *acclimater* < *à* to (<L *ad-*) + *climat* CLIMATE] — **ac·cli·ma·ta·ble** (ə·klī′mə·tə·bəl) *adj.* — **ac·cli·ma·tion** (ak′lə·mā′shən), **ac·cli·ma·ta·tion** (ə·klī′mə·tā′shən) *n.*

ac·cli·ma·tize (ə·klī′mə·tīz) *v.t.* & *v.i.* **·tized, ·tiz·ing** Acclimate. — **ac·cli′ma·tiz′a·ble** *adj.* — **ac·cli′ma·ti·za′tion** *n.* — **ac·cli′ma·tiz′er** *n.*

ac·cliv·i·ty (ə·kliv′ə·tē) *n. pl.* **·ties** An upward slope: opposed to *declivity.* See synonyms under HEIGHT. [<L *acclivitas, -tatis* steepness <*ad-* to + *clivus* hill]

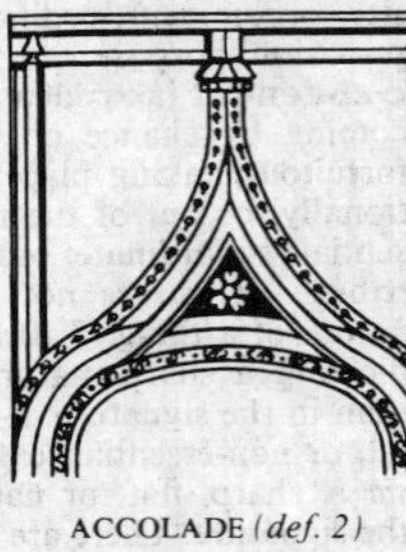

ACCOLADE (*def. 2*)

ac·cli·vous (ə·klī′vəs) *adj.* Sloping upward. Also **ac·cliv·i·tous** (ə·kliv′ə·təs).

ac·co·lade (ak′ə·lād′, -läd′) *n.* **1** *Music* A vertical brace or heavy bar. **2** *Archit.* A curved ornamental molding. **3** The salutation, at first an embrace, later a light blow with a sword, in conferring knighthood; hence, an honor conferred. [<F <Ital. *accollata* < *accollare* embrace about the neck <L *ad* to + *collum* neck]

ac·com·mo·date (ə·kom′ə·dāt) *v.* **·dat·ed, ·dat·ing** *v.t.* **1** To do a favor for; oblige; help. **2** To provide for; give lodging to. **3** To be suitable for; to contain comfortably: The hall *accommodates* large numbers. **4** To adapt or modify; adjust: He *accommodated* his needs to our capacity to fulfil them. **5** To reconcile or settle, as conflicting opinions. — *v.i.* **6** To be or become adjusted or conformed, as the eye to distance. [<L *accommodatus,* pp. of *accommodare* < *ad-* to + *commodare* make fit, suit < *com-* with + *modus* measure] — **ac·com′mo·da′tive** *adj.* — **ac·com′mo·da′tive·ness** *n.*

Synonyms: adapt, adjust, entertain, fit, furnish, harmonize, lodge, oblige, receive, reconcile, serve, suit, supply. See ADAPT, ADJUST.

ac·com·mo·dat·ing (ə·kom′ə·dā′ting) *adj.* Disposed to accommodate; obliging. — **ac·com′mo·dat′ing·ly** *adv.*

ac·com·mo·da·tion (ə·kom′ə·dā′shən) *n.* **1** The act of accommodating, or the state of being accommodated; adjustment; adaptation. **2** A convenience; entertainment; specifically, lodging, board, etc. **3** A loan or other help or favor; specifically, an accommodation bill. **4** Obligingness. **5** An accommodation train. **6** The adjustment of the eye to vision at different distances.

accommodation bill or **note** A note given, or bill of exchange accepted not for value received but as an accommodation or favor in the course of business.

accommodation ladder A ladder or stairway hung at the side of a ship.

accommodation train A railway train that stops at all or at most of the stations.

ac·com·pa·ni·ment (ə·kum′pə·ni·mənt, ə·kump′ni-) *n.* **1** Anything that accompanies. **2** *Music* A subordinate part, vocal or instrumental, accompanying, enriching, or supporting a leading part. See synonyms under APPENDAGE, CIRCUMSTANCE.

ac·com·pa·nist (ə·kum′pə·nist, ə·kump′nist) *n.* A musician who plays or sings the accompaniment.

ac·com·pa·ny (ə·kum′pə·nē) *v.t.* **·nied, ·ny·ing 1** To go with; attend; escort. **2** To be or occur with; coexist with: Weakness often *accompanies* disease. **3** To supplement with: He *accompanied* his insults with blows. **4** To play a musical accompaniment to or for. See synonyms under FOLLOW. [<F *accompagner* < *à* to + *compagne* COMPANION] — **ac·com′pa·ni·er** *n.*

ac·com·plice (ə·kom′plis) *n.* **1** An associate in wrong or crime, whether as principal or accessory. **2** *Obs.* One who cooperates; an associate. See synonyms under ABETTOR, ACCESSORY. [< *a,* indefinite article + F *complice* accomplice <LL *complex* accomplice. See COMPLEX.]

ac·com·plish (ə·kom′plish) *v.t.* **1** To bring to pass; perform; effect. **2** To bring to completion; finish. **3** *Obs.* To make complete; perfect, as in external acquirements or mental polish. [<OF *acompliss-,* stem of *acomplir* <LL *accomplere* <L *ad-* to + *complere* fill up, complete] — **ac·com′plish·a·ble** *adj.* — **ac·com′plish·er** *n.*

Synonyms: achieve, complete, consummate, discharge, do, effect, execute, finish, fulfil, perform, realize. *Perform* and *accomplish* both imply working toward the end; but *perform* always allows a possibility of not attaining, while *accomplish* carries the thought of full completion. See ATTAIN, EFFECT.

ac·com·plished (ə·kom′plisht) *adj.* **1** Proficient; polite; polished; having accomplishments. **2** Completed; consummated. See synonyms under POLITE.

ac·com·plish·ment (ə·kom′plish·mənt) *n.* **1** An accomplishment; fulfilment; performance; completion. **2** An acquirement or attainment that tends to perfect or equip in character, manners, or person. See synonyms under ACT, ATTAINMENT, END.

ac·cord (ə·kôrd′) *v.t.* **1** To render as due; grant; concede: to *accord* merited honor. **2** To bring into agreement; make harmonize or correspond, as opinions. **3** To reconcile; literally, to bring heart to heart, as former enemies. — *v.i.* **4** To agree; harmonize: Those colors *accord* well together. See synonyms under AGREE, ASSENT. — *n.* **1** Harmony, especially of sounds; agreement. **2** Spontaneous impulse; choice: of one's own *accord.* **3** A settlement of any difference; reconciliation; specifically, an agreement between governments. See synonyms under HARMONY. [<OF *acorder* <LL *accordare* be of one mind, agree <L *ad-* to + *cor* heart] — **ac·cord′a·ble** *adj.* — **ac·cord′er** *n.*

ac·cord·ance (ə·kôr′dəns) *n.* Agreement; conformity. See synonyms under HARMONY.

ac·cord·ant (ə·kôr′dənt) *adj.* Consonant; agreeing; corresponding. — **ac·cord′ant·ly** *adv.*

ac·cord·ing (ə·kôr′ding) *adj.* Being in accordance or agreement; harmonizing. — *adv.* Agreeably; conformably; just.

according as 1 In proportion as, in accordance with. **2** Depending on whether.

ac·cord·ing·ly (ə·kôr′ding·lē) *adv.* In a conformable manner; suitably; consequently. See synonyms under CONSEQUENTLY, HENCE, THEREFORE, WHEREFORE.

according to 1 In accordance with; in conformity with. **2** As stated or believed by; on the authority of. **3** In proportion to.

ac·cor·di·on (ə·kôr′dē·ən) *n.* A portable free-reed musical wind-instrument with from 5 to 50 keys, the air for which is furnished by a bellows alternately pulled apart and pressed together by the performer. [<Ital. *accordare* accord, harmonize] — **ac·cor′di·on·ist** *n.*

accordion pleating Pleating which resembles the folds of the bellows part of an accordion.

ac·cost (ə·kôst′, ə·kost′) *v.t.* **1** To speak to first; address; greet. **2** To approach for sexual purposes; proposition. See synonyms under ADDRESS. — *n.* Manner or act of addressing; greeting. [<F *accoster* <LL *accostare* be side to side <L *ad-* to + *costa* rib]

ac·couche·ment (ə·ko͞osh′mənt, *Fr.* à·ko͞osh·mäṅ′) *n.* Delivery in childbed; confinement. [<F *accoucher* put to bed, give birth < *à* to (<L *ad-*) + *coucher* put to bed. See COUCH.]

ac·cou·cheur (à·ko͞o·shœr′) *n. French* A professional obstetrician; a male physician who practices obstetrics.

ac·cou·cheuse (à·ko͞o·shœz′) *n. French* A midwife.

ac·count (ə·kount′) *v.t.* **1** To hold to be; consider; estimate. — *v.i.* **2** To provide a reckoning, as of funds paid or received: with *to* or *with* (someone) *for* (something). **3** To give a rational explanation; refer to some cause or natural law: with *for.* **4** To be responsible; answer: with *for.* **5** To cause death, capture, or incapacitation: with *for.* See synonyms under CALCULATE. — *n.* **1** A record of a transaction; reckoning; computation. **2** Any narrative, statement, report, or description; notice; explanation. **3** The act or time of rendering a reckoning; judgment. **4** Consideration, as of value; importance; concern; estimation; esteem. **5** A record of debits and credits, receipts and expenditures; any methodical enumeration, score, or reckoning: to render an *account,* charge to one's *account,* an *account* at a bank. See synonyms under HISTORY, REASON, REPORT. — **on account of** Because of; for the sake of. [<OF *aconter* <LL *accomptare* <L *ad-* to + *computare* COUNT]

ac·count·a·ble (ə·koun′tə·bəl) *adj.* **1** Liable to be called to account; responsible. **2** Capable of being accounted for or explained. — **ac·count′a·bil′i·ty** *n.* — **ac·count′a·bly** *adv.*

ac·count·an·cy (ə·koun′tən·sē) *n.* The work, art, or business of an accountant.

ac·count·ant (ə·koun′tənt) *n.* **1** One whose business is to keep or examine books, as of a mercantile or banking house or in a public office. **2** One who keeps, examines, or is skilled in accounts. **3** One who is accountable or responsible. — **certified public accountant** In the United States, a public accountant who has been granted a certificate of proficiency by a State examining body, and is allowed to use the designation C.P.A. — **chartered accountant** In Great Britain, a member of an Institute of Chartered Accountants. — **public accountant** An accountant whose services, for a compensation, are available to the public.

ac·count·ing (ə·koun′ting) *n.* The art or system of recording, classifying, and summarizing commercial transactions in monetary terms. Compare BOOKKEEPING.

account rendered An account or bill presented by the creditor for examination by the debtor, to be paid if correct.

account stated An account presented by the creditor and assented to as correct by the debtor.

ac·cou·ter (ə·ko͞o′tər) *v.t.* **·tered** or **·tred** (-tərd), **·ter·ing** or **·tring** To furnish with dress or trappings; equip, as for military service. Also **ac·cou′tre.** [<F *accoutrer,* ult. origin uncertain]

ac·cou·ter·ment (ə·ko͞o′tər·mənt) *n.* **1** Equipment; apparel; dress; trappings: chiefly used in plural; also, the act of accoutering. **2** *Mil.* The equipment of a soldier other than arms and dress. Also **ac·cou′tre·ment.** See synonyms under CAPARISON.

Ac·cra (ak′rə) A port on the Gulf of Guinea, capital of Ghana: also *Akkra.*

ac·cred·it (ə·kred′it) *v.t.* **1** To furnish or send with credentials, as an ambassador; authorize. **2** To vouch for officially; certify as fulfilling requirements. **3** To enter on the credit side of the ledger; give credit for. **4** To attribute to: with *with*: He *accredited* his foes with as much wit as his friends. **5** To accept as true; believe. **6** To confer acceptance or favor on: His actions do not tend to *accredit* his words. [<F *accréditer* < *à* to (<L *ad-*) + *crédit* CREDIT]

ac·cred·i·ta·tion (ə·kred′ə·tā′shən) *n.* *U.S.* The grant to an academic institution, by an accrediting body, of status indicating valuation of its course credits and degrees as in accord with the standards set by the accrediting body.

ac·cre·men·ti·tion (ak′rə·men·tish′ən) *n. Biol.* Growth by division of cells; accretion. — **ac′cre·men·ti′tious** *adj.*

ac·cresce (ə·kres′) *v.i.* **·cresced, ·cresc·ing** *Obs.* **1** To accrue. **2** To increase. [<L *accrescere* < *ad-* to + *crescere* grow]

ac·cres·cence (ə·kres′əns) *n.* Gradual growth; an accretion. Also **ac·cres′cen·cy.**

ac·cres·cent (ə·kres′ənt) *adj.* **1** *Bot.* Continuing to grow after flowering: said of a calyx or other part of the flower. **2** Growing continuously; expanding with age.

ac·crete (ə·krēt′) *v.* **ac·cret·ed, ac·cret·ing** *v.i.* **1** To grow together or be united by adhesion: with *to.* **2** To increase by a series of additions. — *v.t.* **3** To cause to grow together or be added: with *to*: The student should *accrete* discretion to his other qualities of mind. — *adj.* **1** Formed or marked by accretions. **2** *Bot.* Grown together: said of parts normally separate. [<L *accretus,* pp. of *accrescere.* See ACCRESCE.]

ac·cre·tion (ə·krē′shən) *n.* **1** Growth or formation by external additions; increase by adhesion or inclusion; an accumulation or external addition; matter added. **2** *Pathol.* Abnormal adhesion or growing together. **3** *Law* Increase, as of land along the seashore or a river, by deposit of alluvium. **4** Increase by natural growth. **5** *Geol.* The enlargement of rock masses and inorganic bodies by the addition of new material. — **ac·cre′tive** *adj.*

ac·croach (ə·krōch′) *v.t. Rare* To usurp, as

royal prerogatives. [< OF *accrocher* < *a* to + *croc* hook]

ac·cru·al (ə·kro͞o′əl) *n.* **1** The act of accruing; increase. **2** The amount of increase. Also **ac·crue′ment.**

accrual basis The keeping of accounts in such manner as to show accrued earned income and accrued expense without regard to actual paid income and actual disbursements: opposed to *cash basis.*

ac·crue (ə·kro͞o′) *v.i.* **·crued, ·cru·ing 1** To come as a natural result or increment, as by growth: with *to.* **2** To arise as an addition, accession, or advantage; accumulate, as the interest on money: with *from.* **3** *Law* To become established as a permanent right. —*n.* A loop or false mesh in network which increases the number of meshes in a given row. [< obs. n. *accrue* an accession < F *accrû,* pp. of *accroître* increase < L *accrescere.* See ACCRESCE.]

ac·cu·ba·tion (ak′yo͞o·bā′shən) *n. Archaic* The act or position of reclining, as the ancient Romans at meals. [< L *accubatio, -onis* < *accubare* lie near to < *ad-* to + *cubare* lie down]

ac·cul·tur·a·tion (ə·kul′chə·rā′shən) *n. Sociol.* The modification of culture traits induced by contacts between peoples having different ways of life; culture change.

ac·cum·bent (ə·kum′bənt) *adj.* **1** Lying down; recumbent. **2** *Bot.* Lying against something, as a cotyledon against a radicle. [< L *accumbens, -entis,* ppr. of *accumbere* lie down] **—ac·cum′ben·cy** *n.*

ac·cu·mu·late (ə·kyo͞om′yə·lāt) *v.* **·lat·ed, ·lat·ing** *v.t.* **1** To heap or pile up; amass; collect. —*v.i.* **2** To become greater in quantity or number; increase. [< L *accumulatus,* pp. of *accumulare* < *ad-* to + *cumulare* heap < *cumulus* a heap] **—ac·cu·mu·la·ble** (ə·kyo͞om′·yə·lə·bəl) *adj.*

ac·cu·mu·la·tion (ə·kyo͞om′yə·lā′shən) *n.* **1** An amassing; increase; a collected mass. **2** A surplus accumulated in excess of all liabilities and credited to the active capital of a corporation. **3** *Geol.* The underground movement of oil and gas into porous rock formations, where large reserves may collect.

ac·cu·mu·la·tive (ə·kyo͞om′yə·lā′tiv) *adj.* Serving or tending to accumulate; characterized by accumulation; given to amassing; cumulative; collective. **—ac·cu′mu·la′tive·ly** *adv.* **—ac·cu′mu·la′tive·ness** *n.*

ac·cu·mu·la·tor (ə·kyo͞om′yə·lā′tər) *n.* **1** A person or thing that accumulates. **2** A power-storing hydraulic apparatus. **3** *Electr.* A storage battery or cell utilizing the energy of reversible chemical reactions. **4** A Leyden jar, or a condenser. **5** A resilient insert in a trace or in a chain or rope used in dredging, to prevent parting by too sudden strain.

ac·cu·ra·cy (ak′yər·ə·sē) *n.* The quality of being accurate; exactness; precision; correctness.

ac·cu·rate (ak′yər·it) *adj.* Conforming exactly to truth or to a standard; without error; precise; exact; correct. See synonyms under CORRECT, JUST, PARTICULAR, PRECISE. [< L *accuratus* done with care, pp. of *accurare* take care of < *ad-* to + *cura* care] **—ac′cu·rate·ly** *adv.* **—ac′cu·rate·ness** *n.*

ac·curs·ed (ə·kûr′sid, ə·kûrst′) *adj.* **1** Doomed to, deserving, or causing a curse. **2** Cursed; detestable; miserable. Also **ac·curst′.** **—ac·curs′ed·ly** *adv.* **—ac·curs′ed·ness** *n.*

ac·cu·sa·tion (ak′yo͞o·zā′shən) *n.* **1** A charge of crime or misconduct; an indictment. **2** The act of accusing; arraignment. **3** The crime or act with which one is charged. Also **ac·cu·sal** (ə·kyo͞o′zəl). **—ac·cu·sa·to·ry** (ə·kyo͞o′zə·tôr′ē, -tō′rē) *adj.*

ac·cu·sa·tive (ə·kyo͞o′zə·tiv) *Gram. adj.* Denoting, in inflected languages, the relation of the direct object of a verb or preposition, or the goal toward which an action is directed; objective. Also **ac·cu·sa·ti·val** (ə·kyo͞o′zə·tī′vəl). —*n.* **1** The case of Latin and Greek nouns corresponding to the English objective. **2** A word in this case. [< L *accusativus,* trans. of Gk. *(ptōsis) aitiatikē* (the case) of accusing or pertaining to that which is caused < *aitiatos* produced by a cause] **—ac·cu′sa·tive·ly** *adv.*

ac·cu·sa·to·ri·al (ə·kyo͞o′zə·tôr′ē·əl, -tō′rē·əl) *adj.* Pertaining to an accuser.

ac·cuse (ə·kyo͞oz′) *v.* **ac·cused, ac·cus·ing** *v.t.* **1** To charge with fault or error; blame; censure. **2** To bring charges against, as of a crime or an offense: with *of.* —*v.i.* **3** To make accusation; utter charges. See synonyms under ARRAIGN, BLAME. [< OF *acuser* < L *accusare* call to account < *ad-* to + *causa* cause, lawsuit] **—ac·cus′er** *n.* **—ac·cus′ing·ly** *adv.*

ac·cused (ə·kyo͞ozd′) *n. Law* The defendant or defendants in a criminal case: The judge ordered the *accused* to be brought before him.

ac·cus·tom (ə·kus′təm) *v.t.* To make familiar by use; habituate or inure, as oneself: with *to.* [< OF *acostumer* < *a-* to (< L *ad-*) + *costume* CUSTOM]

ac·cus·tomed (ə·kus′təmd) *adj.* **1** Habitual; usual: his *accustomed* haunts. **2** Used; in the habit: with the infinitive or *to:* He is *accustomed* to rising early. See synonyms under ADDICTED, HABITUAL, USUAL.

ac·cus·tom·ize (ə·kus′təm·īz) *v.t. & v.i.* **·ized, ·iz·ing** To adapt or become adapted to the conditions and requirements of a new environment. **—ac·cus′tom·i·za′tion** *n.*

ACD An anticoagulant solution of acid, citrate, and dextrose, used to prolong the period during which whole blood can be stored for use in transfusions.

ace (ās) *n.* **1** A single spot, as on a playing card or die; a card or side of a die so marked. **2** A very small amount, distance, or degree; a unit; particle. **3** Something excellent or first-rate; hence, one who excels in any field. **4** A military aviator who has destroyed five or more enemy aircraft. **5** In tennis and similar games, a point won by a single stroke, as upon the service. — **within an ace** Within a hair's breadth; on the very point or verge. —*v.t.* **aced** (āst), **ac·ing 1** To score a point against in a single stroke, as upon the service in tennis. **2** *Slang* To get the better of, as by a timely move or act. [< OF *as* < L *as* unity, unit]

-acea *suffix Zool.* Used in forming names of classes and orders of animals: *Crustacea* (class), *Cetacea* (order). [< L, neut. pl. of *-aceus*]

-aceae *suffix Bot.* Used in forming names of families of plants: *Vitaceae,* the vine family. [< L, fem. pl. of *-aceus*]

-acean *suffix* **1** Forming adjectives equivalent to those in -ACEOUS. **2** Forming singular nouns to collective plurals in *-acea: crustacean.* [< L *-aceus* + -AN]

a·ce·di·a (ə·sē′dē·ə) *n.* **1** Listlessness; mental depression. **2** Sloth, the fourth of the seven deadly sins. Also *accidie.* [< LL < Gk. *akēdia* < *a-* without + *kēdos* care]

A·cel·da·ma (ə·sel′də·mə) The field of blood; the potter's field, near Jerusalem; hence, any place of bloody or murderous associations. *Matt.* xxvii 8 and *Acts* i 18. [< L < Gk. *Akeldama* < Aramaic *hakal damā* the field of blood]

a·cel·lu·lar (ā′sel′yə·lər) *adj.* Lacking cells; not composed of cells.

a·cen·tric (ā·sen′trik) *adj.* Without a center; not in, or directed from, a center. —*n. Genetics* A fragment of a chromosome without a centromere.

-aceous *suffix* Of the nature of; belonging or pertaining to; like: *cretaceous* chalky: *herbaceous* herblike: used in botany and zoology to form adjectives corresponding to nouns in *-acea, -aceae.* [< L *-aceus* of the nature of]

a·ceph·a·lous (ā·sef′ə·ləs) *adj.* **1** Headless. **2** *Zool.* Without a clearly defined head, as certain mollusks. **3** Having no ruler. **4** Lacking proper beginning, as a line of verse. [< L *acephalus* < Gk. *akephalos* headless < *a-* without + *kephalē* head]

a·ce·qui·a (ä·sā′kē·ə) *n. SW U.S.* A canal for irrigation. [< Sp.]

ac·e·rate (as′ə·rāt) *adj. Bot.* Acerose. Also **ac′e·rat′ed.**

a·cerb (ə·sûrb′) *adj.* Sour and astringent; harsh; sharp. See synonyms under BITTER. [< L *acerbus* < *acer* sharp] Also **a·cerb′ic.**

ac·er·bate (as′ər·bāt) *v.t.* **·bat·ed, ·bat·ing 1** To make sour; embitter. **2** To irritate; exasperate.

a·cer·bi·ty (ə·sûr′bə·tē) *n. pl.* **·ties 1** Sourness, bitterness, or astringency of flavor, as that of unripe fruit. **2** Severity, as of temper, etc.; harshness; sharpness. See synonyms under ACRIMONY. Also **a·cer·bi·tude** (ə·sûr′bə·to͞od, -tyo͞od) [< F *acerbité* < L *acerbitas, -tatis* < *acerbus* sharp]

a·cer·ic (a·ser′ik) *adj.* Pertaining to the maple. [< NL *acericus* < L *acer* maple]

ac·e·rose[1] (as′ə·rōs) *adj. Bot.* Needle-shaped, like pine leaves. [< L *acerosus* ACEROSE[2]; later erroneously derived from L *acus* needle]

ac·e·rose[2] (as′ə·rōs) *adj.* Like chaff. [< L *acerosus* < *acus* chaff]

a·cer·vate (ə·sûr′vit, -vāt, as′ər·vāt) *adj. Bot.* Massed or heaped together; growing compactly in clusters. [< L *acervatus,* pp. of *acervare* heap up < *acervus* heap] **—a·cer′vate·ly** *adv.*

a·cer·vu·lus (ə·sûr′vyo͞o·ləs) *n. pl.* **·li** (·lī) *Bot.* An open, saucer-shaped, non-sexual, spore-producing fruit body, appearing in some parasitic, imperfectly known fungi. [< NL, dim. of L *acervus* heap]

a·ces·cent (ə·ses′ənt) *adj.* Becoming or tending to become sour; slightly sour. —*n.* That which is slightly sour. [< L *acescens, -entis,* ppr. of *acescere* become sour]

acet- Var. of ACETO-.

ac·e·tab·u·lum (as′ə·tab′yə·ləm) *n. pl.* **·la** (·lə) **1** *Anat.* The socket in the hip in which the head of the femur rests and revolves. **2** A sucker, as on a tapeworm, leech, or other invertebrate. **3** Any of the depressions in an insect's exoskeleton into which a leg fits. [< L, a small vinegar cup < *acetum* vinegar]

ac·e·tal (as′ə·tal) *n.* **1** A volatile, flammable liquid, $CH_3CH(OC_2H_5)_2$, used as a solvent and in perfumery. **2** Any of a class of compounds formed from alcohol and aldehydes.

ac·et·al·de·hyde (as′ə·tal′də·hīd) *n.* A flammable, colorless, fuming liquid, used chiefly in organic synthesis.

ac·et·am·ide (as′ə·tam′īd, -id; ə·set′ə·mīd, -mid) *n.* The amide of acetic acid; a white crystalline compound, C_2H_5NO, formed by heating acetic ether with ammonia.

ac·e·ta·min·o·phen (as′ə·tə·min′ə·fən) *n.* A synthetic crystalline compound, $C_8H_9NO_2$, used in chemical synthesis and in medicine as an analgesic and antipyretic drug.

ac·et·an·i·lide (as′ə·tan′ə·līd, -lid) *n.* An acetyl derivative of aniline, C_8H_9ON, consisting of white shining crystalline scales, and used as a sedative and antipyretic.

ac·e·tate (as′ə·tāt) *n.* **1** A salt or ester of acetic acid. **2** A fiber formed of partially hydrolyzed cellulose acetate, used in the textile industry. Also called *acetate rayon.*

acetate rayon Acetate.

a·ce·tic (ə·sē′tik, ə·set′ik) *adj.* Pertaining to or like vinegar; sour. [< L *acetum* vinegar]

acetic acid A colorless, pungent liquid or deliquescent crystalline solid acid, $C_2H_4O_2$, used industrially and constituting in dilute solution the chief component of vinegar.

acetic anhydride A pungent liquid, $(CH_3CO)_2O$, that combines with water to form acetic acid, used in the manufacture of acetyl compounds.

a·cet·i·fy (ə·set′ə·fī) *v.* **·fied, ·fy·ing** *v.t.* To convert into acid or vinegar. —*v.i.* To become acid or vinegar. **—a·cet′i·fi·ca′tion** *n.* **—a·cet′i·fi′er** *n.*

aceto- *combining form* Of, pertaining to, or from acetic acid or acetyl. Also, before vowels, *acet.* [< L *acetum* vinegar]

ac·e·to·a·ce·tic acid (as′ə·to·ə·sē′tik) A colorless product of fat metabolism, CH_3COCH_2COOH, present in abnormal amounts in the urine of diabetics.

ac·e·tone (as′ə·tōn) *n.* A colorless, volatile, flammable liquid ketone, CH_3COCH_3, used mainly as a solvent. [< ACET- + -ONE] **—ac·e·ton·ic** (as′ə·ton′ik) *adj.*

acetone body Ketone body.

ac·e·to·phe·net·i·din (as′ə·tō·fə·net′ə·din) *n.*

add,āce,câre,pälm; end,ēven; it,īce; odd,ōpen,ôrder; to͝ok,po͞ol; up,bûrn; ə = a in *above,* e in *sicken,* i in *clarity,* o in *melon,* u in *focus*; yo͞o = u in *fuse,* oi,oil; ou,pout; ch,check; g,go; ng,ring; th,thin; t͟h,this; zh,vision. Foreign sounds á,œ,ü,kh,ṅ; and ◆: see page xx. < from; + plus; ? possibly.

A white, crystalline, phenol derivative $C_{10}H_{13}NO_2$, used as an analgesic and anti-pyretic drug. Also called *phenacetin.*

ac·e·to·phe·none (as′ə·tō·fē′nōn) *n.* Transparent crystals or a colorless liquid, C_8H_8O, obtained by distilling calcium acetate and calcium benzoate, used as a hypnotic. [< ACETO- + PHEN(YL) + -ONE]

ac·e·tous (as′ə·təs) *adj.* **1** Of, pertaining to, or producing vinegar or acetic acid. **2** Tasting like vinegar; sour. See synonyms under BITTER. Also **ac·e·tose** (as′ə·tōs). **—ac·e·tos·i·ty** (as′ə·tos′ə·tē) *n.*

a·ce·tum (ə·sē′təm) *n.* Vinegar. [< L]

ac·e·tyl (as′ə·til) *n.* The univalent radical, CH_3CO, of acetic acid. [< ACET- + -YL] — **ac′e·tyl′ic** *adj.*

a·cet·y·late (ə·set′ə·lāt) *v.t.* **·lat·ed, ·lat·ing** *Chem.* To introduce an acetyl group into (the molecule of an organic compound), as by treatment with acetic anhydride. **—a·cet′y·la′tion** *n.*

ac·e·tyl·cho·line (as′ə·til·kō′lēn, -kol′in) *n.* A compound, $C_7H_{17}O_3N$, released at certain nerve endings where it facilitates transmission of autonomous nerve impulses, and also present in many tissues and species of organisms, including ergot, from which it is obtained for medical uses.

ac·e·tyl·cho·lin·es·ter·ase (as′ə·təl·kō′lə·nes′·tə·rās, -kol′ə-) *n.* An enzyme that inactivates acetylcholine.

a·cet·y·lene (ə·set′ə·lēn) *n.* A colorless flammable, gaseous hydrocarbon, C_2H_2, obtainable by the action of water on calcium carbide, and used in organic syntheses and as a fuel for welding, cutting metals, etc. [< ACETYL + -ENE]

acetylene series The series of alkynes, of which the simplest member is acetylene.

ac·e·tyl·sal·i·cyl·ic acid (as′ə·til·sal′ə·sil′ik, ə·sē′təl-) Aspirin.

A·chae·a (ə·kē′ə) A district of the northern Peloponnesus, comprising a nome of modern Greece. Also **A·chæ′a, A·cha·ia** (ə·kā′ə, ə·kī′ə).

A·chae·an (əkē′ən) *adj.* Pertaining to Achaea, its people, or their culture. —*n.* **1** A member of one of the four major tribes of ancient Greece. The Achaeans migrated into Greece about 1300 B.C. **2** A Greek. Also **A·chæ′an, A·cha′ian.**

A·cha·tes (ə·kā′tēz) In Vergil's *Aeneid,* the faithful friend of Aeneas; hence, any loyal companion.

ache (āk) *v.i.* **ached** (ākt), **ach·ing 1** To suffer dull, continued pain; be in pain or distress. **2** *Colloq.* To yearn; be eager; followed by *for* or the infinitive. [Orig. *ake,* OE *acan;* present spelling due to infl. of the n.] —*n.* A local, dull, and protracted pain. See synonyms under AGONY. [OE *æce* < the v.; pron. before 1700 (ăch), present pron. due to infl. of the v.] **—ach′er** *n.* **—ach′ing** *adj. & n.* **—ach′ing·ly** *adv.*

a·chene (ā·kēn′) *n. Bot.* A small, dry, indehiscent pericarp containing one seed, as in the dandelion, buttercup, etc.: also spelled *akene.* Also **a·che·ni·um** (ā·kē′·nē·əm) *pl.* **·ni·a** (-nē·ə). [< NL *achenium* < A-[4] not + Gk. *chainein* gape, recoil] **—a·che′·ni·al** *adj.*

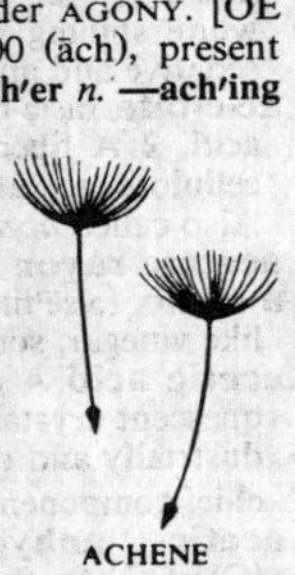

ACHENE
(Of dandelion:
actual size)

A·cher·nar (ā′kər·när) One of the 20 brightest stars, 0.60 magnitude; Alpha in the constellation Eridanus. See STAR. [< Arabic *ākhir al-nahr* end of the river]

Ach·e·ron (ak′ə·ron) **1** In Greek and Roman mythology, the river of woe, one of the five rivers surrounding Hades, across which Charon ferried the dead. **2** Hades.

Ach·e·son (ach′ə·sən), **Dean Gooderham,** 1893–1971, lawyer and statesman; U.S. secretary of state 1949–53.

A·cheu·le·an (ə·shōō′lē·ən) *adj. Anthropol.* Describing a culture stage following the second glacial epoch of the Pleistocene and noted chiefly for a superior working of stone implements and weapons. Also **A·cheu′li·an.** [from *St. Acheul,* France, where artifacts were found]

à che·val (á shə·vál′) *French* On horseback; astride.

a·chieve (ə·chēv′), *v.* **a·chieved, a·chiev·ing** *v.t.* **1** To accomplish; finish successfully. **2** To win or attain, as by effort, skill, or perseverance; He *achieved* a position of eminence. —*v.i.* **3** To accomplish something; to attain an object. See synonyms under ACCOMPLISH, ATTAIN, EFFECT, GAIN, GET, SUCCEED. [< OF *achever* < *a chief (venir)* (come) to a head, finish < LL *ad caput (venire)*] **—a·chiev′a·ble** *adj.* **—a·chiev′er** *n.*

a·chieve·ment (ə·chēv′mənt) *n.* **1** An achieving or accomplishing attainment. **2** A thing achieved; a noteworthy and successful action or a distinguished feat. **3** *Her.* An escutcheon. See synonyms under ACT, CAREER, END, VICTORY, WORK.

achievement age *Psychol.* A measure of performance on an achievement test, expressed in terms of an empirically determined average age for the same performance.

achievement quotient *Psychol.* A number expressing the ratio of the achievement age to the chronological age. Abbr. *A.Q.*

achievement test *Psychol.* A test for measuring an individual's progress in the mastery of a subject to be learned. Compare INTELLIGENCE TEST.

Ach·il·le·an (ak′ə·lē′ən) *adj.* Of or like Achilles; all but invulnerable; wrathful; valiant; swift.

A·chil·les (ə·kil′ēz) In the *Iliad,* the son of Peleus and Thetis, foremost Greek hero of the Trojan War who killed Hector and was killed by the arrow Paris shot into his right heel, the only vulnerable spot on his body.

Achilles' heel A vulnerable point.

Achilles' tendon The large tendon for the superficial muscles of the calf of the leg, attached to the bone of the heel.

A·chit·o·phel (ə·kit′ə·fel) In Dryden's satire *Absalom and Achitophel,* a caricature of Lord Shaftesbury: in allusion to a counselor of King David who joined with Absalom in rebelling against him. II *Sam.* xv–xvii. Also spelled *Ahithophel.*

ach·la·myd·e·ous (ak′lə·mid′ē·əs) *adj. Bot.* Lacking both calyx and corolla. [< A-[4] without + Gk. *chlamys, chlamydos* cloak]

a·chlor·hy·dri·a (ā′klôr·hī′drē·ə) *n.* Absence of hydrochloric acid in the gastric juice. — **a′chlor·hy·dric** *adj.*

a·chon·dro·pla·si·a (ə·kon′drō·plā′zhē·ə) *n.* A genetic disease characterized by failure in development of the long bones, resulting in a form of dwarfism. Also **a·chon·dro·plas·ty** [< NL < A-[4] not + Gk. *chondros* cartilage + -PLASIA] — **a·chon·dro·plas·tic** *adj.*

ach·ro·mat·ic (ak′rə·mat′ik) *adj.* **1** *Optics* Free from color or iridescence; transmitting light without showing or separating it into its constituent colors, as a lens. **2** *Biol.* Resisting the usual staining agents; also, containing achromatin. **3** *Music* Unmodulated; without accidentals. [< Gk. *achrōmatos* < *a-* without + *chrōma* color] **—ach′ro·mat′i·cal·ly** *adv.* **—a·chro·ma·tism** (ə·krō′mə·tiz′əm), **a·chro·ma·tic·i·ty** (ə·krō′mə·tis′ə·əté) *n.*

a·chro·ma·tin (ə·krō′mə·tin) *n.* The substance in the cell nucleus which does not readily take color from basic stains.

a·chro·ma·tize (ə·krō′mə·tīz) *v.t.* **·tized, ·tiz·ing** To make achromatic.

a·chro·ma·top·si·a (ə·krō′mə·top′sē·ə) *n.* Total lack of color vision. [< Gk. *achrōmatos* without color + *opsis* sight]

a·chro·ma·tous (ə·krō′mə·təs) *adj.* Having less than the normal color; colorless.

a·chro·mic (ə·krō′mik) *adj.* Colorless. Also **a·chro′mous.**

a·cic·u·la (ə·sik′yə·lə) *n. pl.* **·lae** (-lē) **1** A slender needlelike process; a bristle or prickle, as on a plant or animal. **2** A needle-shaped body, as some crystals. [< L, dim. of *acus* needle] — **a·cic′u·lar, a·cic′u·late** (-lit, -lāt), **a·cic′u·lat′ed** *adj.*

ac·id (as′id) *adj.* **1** Sharp and biting to the taste, as vinegar; sour. **2** Pertaining to, yielding, like, or reacting like, an acid. **3** Acidic. **4** Sharp-tempered; biting. —*n.* **1** Any sour substance. **2a** Any of a class of compounds that in aqueous solution turns blue litmus red and reacts with bases and with certain metals to form salts. **b** A compound that dissociates in water to yield hydrogen ions. **c** A compound that dissociates in a solvent to produce the positive ion of the solvent. **d** A molecule or ion that can attach itself to another molecule or ion by a covalent bond with an unshared pair of electrons. See synonyms under BITTER. [< L *acidus* sharp, sour] — **ac′id·ly** *adv.* **—ac′id·ness** *n.*

ac·id–fast (as′id·fast′, -fäst′) *adj.* Not readily decolorized by acids when stained: said of bacteria, epithelial tissue, etc.

ac·id–form·ing (as′id·fôr′ming) *adj.* Pertaining to or designating foods which in metabolism yield a large acid residue.

ac·id·head (as′id·hed′) *n. Slang.* One who uses or is addicted to LSD.

a·cid·ic (ə·sid′ik) *adj.* **1** Acid; having properties of an acid. **2** Forming an acid as a result of a chemical or metabolic process; acid-forming.

a·cid·i·fy (ə·sid′ə·fī) *v.* **·fied, ·fy·ing** *v.t.* **1** To render acid. **2** To change into an acid. —*v.i.* **3** To become acid. **—a·cid′i·fi′a·ble** *adj.* **—a·cid′i·fi·ca′tion** *n.* **—a·cid′i·fi′er** *n.*

ac·i·dim·e·ter (as′i·dim′ə·tər) *n.* Any apparatus or device for estimating or measuring the amount of acid in a sample. See HYDROMETER. **—ac·i·di·met·ric** (as′i·di·met′rik), **ac′i·di·met′ri·cal** *adj.* **—ac′i·dim′e·try** *n.*

a·cid·i·ty (ə·sid′ə·tē) *n.* **1** The state or quality of being acid. **2** Degree of acid strength. **3** Hyperacidity.

a·cid·o·phil (a·sid′ə·fil) *n.* Any acidophilic substance, organism, or tissue. Also **a·cid·o·phile.**

ac·i·doph·i·lic (as′ə·dof′ə·lik) *adj.* **1** Having an affinity for acid stains. **2** Having a preference for an acid environment.

ac·i·doph·i·lus milk (as′ə·dof′ə·ləs) Milk that has been fermented by certain bacteria *(Lactobacillus acidophilus)* to improve its qualities as an intestinal tonic.

ac·i·do·sis (as′ə·dō′sis) *n.* An abnormal condition of depleted alkaline reserves in the blood and other body fluids. **—as·i·dot·ic** *adj.*

acid rain Atmospheric precipitation with a pH of 5.6 or lower due to dissolved air pollutants such as oxides of nitrogen and sulfur.

acid rock A kind of rock-and-roll music with sound and lyrics which suggest drug-taking or psychedelic experiences.

acid test A definite test of value, quality, truth, virtue, etc.: from the alchemists' method of testing metals after attempting transmutation to gold.

a·cid·u·late (ə·sij′ōō·lāt) *v.t.* **·lat·ed, ·lat·ing** To make somewhat acid or sour. **—a·cid′u·la′·tion** *n.*

a·cid·u·lous (ə·sij′ōō·ləs) *adj.* Slightly acid; subacid; sour. Also **a·cid′u·lent.** See synonyms under BITTER. [< L *acidulus* slightly sour, dim. of *acidus* sour]

ac·i·er·ate (as′ē·ə·rāt) *v.t.* **·at·ed, ·at·ing** To turn into steel. [< F *acier* steel] **—ac′i·er·a′tion** *n.*

ac·i·form (as′ə·fôrm) *adj.* Needle-shaped. [< L *acus* needle + -FORM]

ac·i·nac·i·form (as′ə·nas′ə·fôrm, ə·sin′ə·sə-) *adj. Bot.* Scimitar-shaped; having one edge thick and slightly concave, the other thin and convex: said of a leaf. [< L *acinaces* scimitar (< Gk. *akinakēs*) + -FORM]

ac·i·nar (as′ə·nər) *adj.* Pertaining to, constituting an acinus.

a·cin·i·form (ə·sin′ə·fôrm) *adj.* **1** Having a clustered structure like a bunch of grapes. **2** Like a grape. [< L *acinus* grape + -FORM]

ac·i·nose (as′ə·nōs) *adj. Geol.* Consisting of minute granular concretions, as certain ores.

ac·i·nous (as′ə·nəs) *adj.* Composed of small racemose lobules or acini.

ac·i·nus (as′ə·nəs) *n. pl.* **·ni** (-nī) **1** *Bot.* One of the drupelets of an aggregate baccate fruit, as a raspberry; also, a grape seed. **2** A berry, as a grape, growing in bunches; a bunch of such berries. **3** *Anat.* The terminal division of the secreting portion of a racemose gland. [< L, ape]

-acious *suffix of adjectives* Abounding in; characterized by; given to: *pugnacious, vivacious.* [< L *-ax, -acis* + -OUS]

-acity *suffix* Quality or state of: *tenacity, pugnacity*: used to form abstract nouns corresponding to adjectives in *-acious.* [< L *-acitas, -acitatis*]

ack-ack (ak′ak′) *n. Slang* Anti-aircraft fire. [British radio operator's code for *A.A.* (anti-aircraft)]

Ack·ia Battleground National Monument (ak′yə) A site near Tupelo in NE Mississippi where Chickasaw Indians and English forces defeated French troops and Choctaw Indians in 1736; established 1938.

ac·knowl·edge (ak-nol′ij) v. **·edged, ·edg·ing** v.t. **1** To own or admit as true; confess: He *acknowledged* his ignorance. **2** To recognize as or avow to be: The savages *acknowledged* the idol as their god. **3** To declare or admit the authority of, as a claim or right. **4** *Law* To assent to the validity of; certify: He *acknowledged* the service of a writ. **5** To own or admit as implying obligation or incurring responsibility: He *acknowledged* his debts to all his creditors. **6** To show appreciation of; thank for: She *acknowledged* the favor graciously. **7** To report and respond to the receipt or arrival of: His secretary *acknowledged* our letter. —v.i. **8** In card games, to respond to a partner's bid so as to indicate a weak hand. [Earlier *acknowledge* <obs. *aknow* admit, confess (OE *oncnāwan*) + *knowledge*, v., admit] —**ac·knowl′edge·a·ble** *adj.* —**ac·knowl′edg·er** *n.*

Synonyms: accept, admit, avow, certify, concede, confess, endorse, grant, own, profess, recognize. See AVOW, CONFESS. *Antonyms:* deny, disavow, disclaim, disown, repudiate.

ac·knowl·edg·ment (ak-nol′ij-mənt) *n.* **1** The act of acknowledging; avowal; confession; recognition; report or admission of receipt. **2** *Law* A formal declaration before competent authority, or the official certificate of such declaration. Also *Brit.* **ac·knowl′edge·ment.** See synonyms under APOLOGY.

a·clas·tic (ā-klas′tic) *adj. Physics* Not refracting. [<GK. *aklastos* unbroken + -IC]

a·cline (ā′klīn) *n. Geol.* A rock bed without any dips or folds, lying in a horizontal position.

a·clin·ic (ā-klin′ik) *adj.* Having no inclination or dip: said of the magnetic equator, where the compass needle does not dip. [<Gk. *aklinēs* <a- not + *klinein* bend]

ac·me (ak′mē) *n.* The highest point, or summit; perfection; climax. [<Gk. *akmē* point]

ac·ne (ak′nē) *n.* A chronic skin affliction seen chiefly in adolescents and characterized by inflammation of the sebaceous glands and hair follicles and the development of blackheads and pimples on the face, chest, and back. —**ac·need** *adj.* [? Alter. of Gk. *akmē* point]

ac·node (ak′nōd) *n. Math.* A point outside a curve whose coordinates satisfy the equation of the curve; a conjugate point. [<L *acus* needle + NODE]

a·cock (ə-kok′) *adj.* **1** In cocked fashion or position. **2** Alert; vigilant. —*adv.* In a cocked manner or position: He set his hat *acock.*

a·coe·lo·mate (ā-sē′lə-māt, -mit) *adj.* Lacking either a true or false body cavity, as the flatworms. —*n.* Flatworm.

a·cold (ə-kōld′) *adj. Obs.* Cold; chilly.

ac·o·lyte (ak′ə-līt) *n.* **1** An attendant or assistant. **2** *Eccl.* An attendant for subordinate duties on the ministers officiating at a sacred rite; especially, a member of the highest of the four minor orders of the Roman Catholic Church. [<Med. L *acolitus* <Gk. *ako- louthos* follower, attendant]

à compte (á kôńt′) *French* On account; in part payment.

A·con·ca·gua (ä′kôn·kä′gwä) An extinct volcano in west central Argentina; 22,834 feet; highest peak in the Western Hemisphere.

ACOLYTE *(def. 2)*

ac·o·nite (ak′ə-nīt) *n.* **1** The monkshood or any of the generally poisonous plants of the genus *Aconitum.* Also **aco·ni′tum. 2** A very toxic drug obtained from the root of *Aconitum napellus.* [<F *aconit* <L *aconitum* <Gk. *akoniton*]

a·corn (ā′kôrn, ā′kərn) *n.* **1** The fruit of the oak, a one-seeded nut, fixed in a woody cup. **2** *Aeron.*

A special type of fitting used to prevent

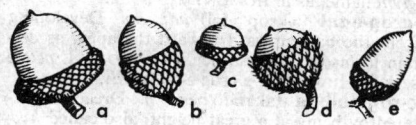

ACORNS
a. Red oak. *b.* Scarlet oak. *c.* Pin oak.
d. Black oak. *e.* White oak.

abrasion of intersecting wires in the cross-bracing of an aircraft. [OE *æcern*]

acorn squash A variety of winter squash of acornlike shape having a dark green, ridged rind and yellow flesh.

acorn tube A small thermionic radio tube for use at high frequencies. Also *Brit.* **acorn valve.**

à corps per·du (á kôr per·dü′) *French* Headlong; impetuously; literally, with lost body.

a·cot·y·le·don (ā′kot·ə·lē′dən) *n. Bot.* A plant without cotyledons or seed lobes. [<A.⁴ without + COTYLEDON] —**a′cot·y·le′do·nous** *adj.*

a·cou·me·ter (ə·kōō′mi·tər, ə·kou′-) *n.* An instrument for testing the delicacy of the sense of hearing. [<Gk. *akouein* hear + -METER]

a·cous·ma (ə·kōōs′mə) *n. Psychiatry* An auditory hallucination. [<Gk. *akousma* a thing heard]

a·cous·tic (ə·kōōs′tik, ə·kous′-) *adj.* **1** Pertaining to the act or sense of hearing, the science of sound, or the sound heard. **2** Designed to deaden, enhance, or otherwise modify sound. **3** Having no electronic amplification, as a musical instrument. Also **a·cous′ti·cal.** [<F *acoustique* <Gk. *akoustikos* pertaining to hearing <*akouein* hear] —**a·cous′ti·cal·ly** *adv.*

acoustic distortion The discrepancy between the acoustic values of sounds as transmitted over a telecommunication system and as received by the listener.

acoustic phonetics See under PHONETICS.

a·cous·tics (ə·kōōs′tiks, ə·kous′-) *n.* **1** That branch of physics which treats of the phenomena and laws of sound: construed as singular. **2** The sound-producing qualities of an auditorium: construed as plural. See -ICS.

acoustic saturation The auditory effectiveness of one source of sound as compared with other sources: used in determining the instrumental composition of an orchestra or band playing under specified conditions.

acoustic wind A theoretical wind of constant velocity whose effects on a sound wave are assumed to be identical to the actual winds of varying velocities.

à cou·vert (á kōō·vâr′) *French* Under cover; sheltered.

ac·quaint (ə·kwānt′) *v.t.* **1** To make familiar or conversant with: with *with: Acquaint* yourself with the court routine. **2** To cause to know; inform: with *with:* He *acquainted* his son with the circumstances of his birth. [<OF *acointer* <LL *adcognitare* make known <L *ad-* to + *cognitus,* pp. of *cognoscere* know <*com-* with + *gnoscere* come to know]

ac·quain·tance (ə·kwān′təns) *n.* **1** Knowledge of any person or thing. **2** A person or persons with whom one is acquainted. —**ac·quain′tance·ship** *n.*

Synonyms: association, companionship, experience, familiarity, fellowship, friendship, intimacy, knowledge. *Acquaintance* between persons is mutual, assuming that each knows the other. *Acquaintance* is less than *familiarity* or *intimacy;* it does not involve *friendship,* for one may be well acquainted with an enemy. *Fellowship* involves not merely *acquaintance* and *companionship,* but sympathy as well. Compare FRIENDSHIP, LOVE. As regards studies, pursuits, etc., *acquaintance* is less than *familiarity,* which supposes minute *knowledge* of particulars, arising often from long *experience* or *association. Antonyms:* ignorance, ignoring, inexperience, unfamiliarity.

ac·quaint·ed (ə·kwān′tid) *adj.* Having acquaintance; having personal knowledge of: with *with.*

ac·quest (ə·kwest′) *n.* **1** An act of acquiring; also, the thing acquired. **2** *Law* Property acquired by means other than inheritance, as by gift or purchase. [<MF <LL *acquistum* for L *acquisitum* <*acquirere.* See ACQUIRE.]

ac·qui·esce (ak′wē·es′) *v.i.* **·esced** (-est′), **esc·ing** To consent or concur tacitly; assent; comply; with *in* (formerly with *to*): The candidate *acquiesced* in all his party's plans. See synonyms under AGREE, ASSENT. [<MF *acquiescer* <L *acquiescere* <*ad-* to + *quiescere* rest] —**ac·qui·es′cent** *adj.* —**ac·qui·esc′ing·ly** *adv.*

ac·qui·es·cence (ak′wē·es′əns) *n.* Quiet submission; passive consent: with *in* (formerly with *to*). Also **ac′qui·es′cen·cy.**

ac·quire (ə·kwīr′) *v.t.* **·quired, ·quir·ing 1** To obtain or receive by one's endeavor or purchase. **2** To get as one's own; gain. See synonyms under ATTAIN, GAIN, GET, LEARN. [<L *acquirere* <*ad-* to + *quaerere* seek] —**ac·quir′a·ble** *adj.* —**ac·quir′er** *n.*

acquired character or **characteristic** A structural or functional modification of an organism considered as a result of the activities of the organism or from the postnatal influences of the environment: distinguished from *inherited character.*

acquired immunodeficiency syndrome A virulent disease of irregular distribution and unknown cause in which a deficient immune system is manifested in infections by any of various pathogens and/or in certain forms of cancer. Also **AIDS.**

ac·quire·ment (ə·kwīr′mənt) *n.* **1** The act of acquiring. **2** An acquired power or attainment. See synonyms under ATTAINMENT.

ac·qui·si·tion (ak′wə·zish′ən) *n.* **1** The act of acquiring. **2** Anything gained or won; a power or possession. See synonyms under ATTAINMENT. [<L *acquisitio, -onis* <*acquirere.* See ACQUIRE.]

ac·quis·i·tive (ə·kwiz′ə·tiv) *adj.* Able or inclined to acquire, as money or property. —**ac·quis′i·tive·ly** *adv.* —**ac·quis′i·tive·ness** *n.*

ac·quit (ə·kwit′) *v.t.* **ac·quit·ted, ac·quit·ting 1** To free or clear, as from an accusation; declare innocent; exonerate. **2** To relieve, as of an obligation; absolve: Your generosity *acquits* you of all further duties toward me. **3** To repay or return, as a favor; discharge, as a debt. **4** To conduct (oneself); perform one's part: He *acquitted* himself like a man. See synonyms under ABSOLVE, JUSTIFY, PARDON. [<OF *aquiter* <L *ad-* to + *quietare* settle, quiet] —**ac·quit′ter** *n.*

ac·quit·tal (ə·kwit′l) *n.* **1** The act of acquitting, or the state of being acquitted or found innocent of a charge or accusation. **2** The performance of a duty. Also **ac·quit′ment.**

ac·quit·tance (ə·kwit′ns) *n.* Release or discharge, as from indebtedness; satisfaction of indebtedness or obligation; a receipt; an acquittal.

a·cra·si·a (ə·krā′zhē·ə) *n.* Extreme lack of self-control. [<Med.L <Gk. *akrasia* bad mixture <*akratos* unmixed (of drinks), intemperate]

a·cre (ā′kər) *n.* **1** A measure of land, commonly 160 square rods; also 43,560 square feet, 4,840 square yards, or 0.404 hectare. The Scottish acre contains about 6,150 square yards and the Irish acre, 7,840. **2** A field. **3** *pl.* Lands. —**God's acre** A churchyard or burial ground. [OE *æcer* field]

A·cre (ā′kər, ä′kər) A town NE of Haifa, Israel, on the **Bay of Acre** of the eastern Mediterranean: Old Testament *Accho;* New Testament *Ptolemais:* called **Saint Jean d'A·cre** (sań zhäń dä′kr′) during the Crusades.

A·cre (ä′kri) A federal territory in western Brazil; 59,139 square miles; capital, Rio Branco.

a·cre·age (ā′kər·ij) *n.* Area in acres; acres collectively.

a·cred (ā′kərd) *adj.* Comprising or owning many acres of land.

a·cre-foot (ā′kər·fŏŏt′) *n.* The amount of

water required to cover one level acre to a depth of 1 foot; 43,560 cubic feet: used by irrigation engineers.

a·cre-inch (ā′kər-inch′) *n.* One twelfth of an acre-foot, or 3,630 cubic feet.

ac·rid (ak′rid) *adj.* Of a cutting, burning taste or odor; pungent. See synonyms under BITTER. [< L *acer, acris;* infl. by *acid*] **—ac′rid·ly** *adv.* **—ac′rid·ness** *n.*

ac·ri·dine (ak′rə·dēn, -din) *n.* A crystalline compound, $C_{13}H_9N$, obtained from coal tar and used in the synthesis of an important series of dyes and antiseptics. [< ACRID + -INE]

a·crid·i·ty (ə·krid′ə·tē) *n.* The quality of being acrid; acrimony of speech or temper.

ac·ri·fla·vine (ak′rə·flā′vēn, -vin) *n.* An odorless brownish-red, granular compound, $C_{14}H_{14}N_3Cl$, derived from acridine; used as an antiseptic and disinfectant.

Ac·ri·lan (ak′rə·lan) *n.* A synthetic fiber consisting of a copolymer of acrylonitrile and vinyl acetate: a trade name.

ac·ri·mo·ni·ous (ak′rə·mō′nē·əs) *adj.* Full of bitterness; sarcastic; caustic; sharp. See synonyms under BITTER, MOROSE. **—ac′ri·mo′ni·ous·ly** *adv.* **—ac′ri·mo′ni·ous·ness** *n.*

ac·ri·mo·ny (ak′rə·mō′nē) *n. pl.* **·nies** Sharpness or bitterness of speech or temper; acridity. [< L *acrimonia* < *acer* sharp]

acro- *combining form* **1** At the top; highest; topped with; at the tip or end of: *acrogen.* **2** *Med.* Pertaining to the extremities: *acromegaly.* [< Gk. *akros* at the top or end]

ac·ro·bat (ak′rə·bat) *n.* **1** One who is skilled in feats requiring muscular coordination, as in tight-rope walking, tumbling, trapeze performing, etc.; a gymnast. **2** One who makes surprising political or other changes. [< F *acrobate* < Gk. *akrobatos* walking on tiptoe < *akros* tip + *bainein* walk, go] **—ac′ro·bat′ic** or **·i·cal** *adj.* **—ac′ro·bat′i·cal·ly** *adv.*

ac·ro·car·pous (ak′rō·kär′pəs) *adj. Bot.* Bearing fruit at the end of a stem, as some mosses.

ac·ro·cen·tric (ak′ro·sen′trik) *adj.* Having the centromere located close to one end: said of a chromosome.

ac·ro·dont (ak′rə·dont) *adj.* Having rootless teeth firmly ankylosed at the base with the bony edge of the jaw. *—n.* An acrodont creature.

ac·ro·drome (ak′rə·drōm) *adj. Bot.* Running to the point: said of leaves in which the nerves in running through the blade all point to or reach the apex. Also **a·crod·ro·mous** (ə·krod′rə·məs).

ac·ro·gen (ak′rə·jən) *n. Bot.* An organism growing at the apex only, as ferns, mosses, etc. [< ACRO- + -GEN]

ac·ro·gen·ic (ak′rə·jen′ik) *adj. Bot.* Growing at the apex, as certain cryptogams and zoophytes; also, of or pertaining to an acrogen. Also **a·crog·e·nous** (ə·kroj′ə·nəs). **—a·crog′e·nous·ly** *adv.*

a·cro·le·in (ə·krō′lē·in) *n.* A volatile colorless liquid C_3H_4O, intensely irritating to the nose and eyes, and obtained variously, as by dehydrating glycerol or destructively distilling fats: used as a tear gas. [< ACR(ID) + L *olere* smell + -IN]

ac·ro·lith (ak′rə·lith) *n.* A statue with stone head and extremities, the trunk being usually of wood and draped. [< ACRO- + -LITH[1]] **—a·crol·i·than** (ə·krol′ə·thən), **ac′ro·lith′ic** *adj.*

ac·ro·log·ic (ak′rə·loj′ik) *adj.* Relating to or based on initials. [< ACRO- + Gk. *logos* word]

ac·ro·meg·a·ly (ak′rō·meg′ə·lē) *n.* A chronic disorder due to oversecretion of pituitary growth hormone, characterized by enlargement of the face, extremities, and viscera, including both soft and bony tissue. [< F *acromégalie* < Gk. *akros* ACRO- + *megas, megalon* big] **—ac·ro·me·gal·ic** (ak′rō·mi·gal′ik) *adj.*

a·cro·mi·on (ə·krō′mē·ən) *n. pl.* **·mi·a** (-mē·ə) *Anat.* The projecting prolongation of the scapula or shoulder blade forming the point of the shoulder. Also **acromial process.** [< NL < Gk. *akrōmion* < *akros* at the tip + *ōmos* shoulder] **—a·cro′mi·al** *adj.*

ac·ro·nym (ak′rə·nim) *n.* A word formed by the combining of initial letters *(Eniac, Unesco)* or syllables and letters (*radar* and *sonar*) of a series of words or a compound term. [< ACRO- + *-nym* name, as in HOMONYM]

a·crop·e·tal (ə·krop′ə·təl) *adj. Bot.* Developing from the base upward toward the apex, as certain forms of inflorescence. [< ACRO- + L *petere* seek, go toward] **—a·crop′e·tal·ly** *adv.*

ac·ro·pho·bi·a (ak′rə·fō′bē·ə) *n.* Dread stimulated by being at a great height: also called *hypsophobia.*

a·crop·o·lis (ə·krop′ə·lis) *n.* The citadel of an ancient Greek city, especially **the Acropolis,** that of Athens. [< Gk. *akropolis* < *akros* top, highest part + *polis* city]

ac·ro·some (ak′rə·som) *n.* A tiny structure at the front of a sperm cell. [< ACRO- + Gk. *soma* body]

ac·ro·spire (ak′rə·spīr) *n. Bot.* The first sprout from a germinating seed of grain. [< ACRO- + Gk. *speira* anything twisted]

a·cross (ə·krôs′, ə·kros′) *adv.* **1** From one side to the other. **2** On or at the other side. **3** Crosswise; crossed, as arms. *—prep.* **1** On or from the other side of; beyond; over: the music from *across* the street. **2** Through or over the surface of: riding *across* the field; A tree fell *across* the road. [< A-[1] on, in + CROSS]

a·cros·tic (ə·krôs′tik, ə·kros′-) *n.* A poem or other composition in which initial or other letters, taken in order, form a word or phrase. [< L *acrostichis* < Gk. *akrostichis* < *akros* end + *stichos* line of verse] **—a·cros′ti·cal·ly** *adv.*

ac·ry·late (ak′rə·lāt) *n.* A slat of acrylic acid.

acrylate resin Acrylic resin.

a·cryl·ic (ə·kril′ik) *adj.* Designating an acid, $C_3H_4O_2$, having a sharp, acrid odor, prepared from acrolein or from certain derivatives of propionic acid, used in making commercial transparent resins and plastics. *—n.* **1** A paint having a base of acrylic resin. **2** A painting made with such a paint. **3** Acrylic resin. **4** Acrylic fiber. [< ACR(OLEIN) + -YL + -IC]

acrylic adic A colorless, corrosive, easily polymerized liquid, $C_3H_4O_2$, used in the manufacture of acrylic resins.

acrylic fiber Any of various synthetic fibers made by polymerizing acnylonitrile, often combined with a copolymer.

acrylic resin Any of numerous tough, transparent, thermoplastic resins made by polymerizing acrylic acid or its derivatives, used to fashion various molded objects and as a component of protective coatings, adhesives, etc.

ac·ry·lo·ni·trile (ak′rə·lō·nī′trəl, -tril) *n.* A colorless, liquid compound, CH_2CHCN, used in the manufacture of synthetic rubber and fiber.

act (akt) *v.t.* **1** To play the part of; impersonate, as in a drama: She *acted* Juliet well. **2** To perform on the stage, as a play: The company *acted* most of Shakespeare's works. **3** To perform as if on a stage; feign the character of: Don't *act* the martyr. **4** To behave as suitable to: *Act* your age. **5** *Obs.* To actuate. *—v.i.* **5** To behave or conduct oneself: He knows how to *act* in society. **6** To carry out a purpose or function; perform: The brake refused to *act.* **7** To carry out a purpose or function in a particular way: with *as:* The test *acted* as a check. **8** To put forth power; produce an effect: often with *on:* The poison *acted* on his stomach at once. **9** To serve temporarily or as a substitute, as in some office or capacity: with *for:* The corporal *acted* for his commanding officer. **10** To perform on or as on the stage: She *acts* for a living. **11** To pretend; play a part so as to appear: She concealed her real feelings and *acted* friendly. **12** To serve for theatrical performance or use: This scene *acts* well. **—to act on** (or **upon**) To order one's conduct in accordance with; obey: to *act on* someone's advice. **—to act up** *Colloq.* To behave mischievously; appear troublesome. [< L *actus,* pp. of *agere* do, infl. in development by the n.] *—n.* **1** The exertion of power, bodily or mental; something done; a deed. **2** A section of a drama; the largest division of a play or opera. **3** An enactment or edict; a formal transaction, as of a legislative body. **4** A formal written statement. **5** The performance of a natural function or process. [< L *actus* a doing, and *actum* a thing done < *agere* do]

Synonyms (noun): accomplishment, achievement, action, consummation, deed, doing, effect, execution, exercise, exertion, exploit, feat, motion, movement, operation, performance, proceeding, transaction, work. *Act* is single, individual, momentary; *action* a complex of *acts,* or a process, state, or habit of exerting power. *Act* and *deed* are both used for the thing done, but *act* refers to the power put forth, *deed* to the result accomplished. *Deed* is commonly used of great, notable, and impressive *acts,* as are *achievement, exploit,* and *feat.* A *feat* exhibits strength, skill, personal power, whether mental or physical; as, a *feat* of arms, a *feat* of memory. *Achievement* is the doing of something great and noteworthy; an *exploit* is brilliant, but its effect may be transient; an *achievement* is solid, and its effect enduring. See EXERCISE, MOTION. *Antonyms:* cessation, deliberation, endurance, immobility, inaction, inactivity, inertia, passion (in philosophic sense), quiescence, quiet, repose, rest, suffering, suspension.

ac·ta (ak′tə) *n.* Acts; especially, proceedings or minutes of proceedings kept on record in a court. [< L, pl. of *actum* a thing done]

act·a·ble (ak′tə·bəl) *adj.* That can be acted, as a role in a play. **—act′a·bil′i·ty** *n.*

Ac·tae·on (ak·tē′ən) In Greek mythology, a hunter who surprised Diana bathing and was turned by her into a stag and killed by his own dogs. Also **Ac·tæ′on.**

Ac·te (ak′tē) See AKTI.

ACTH A hormone that is secreted by the anterior lobe of the pituitary gland and that stimulates the secretion of cortisone and other hormones by the cortex of the adrenal glands. [< *a(dreno)c(ortico)t(ropic) h(ormone)*]

Ac·ti·an (ak′shē·ən) *adj.* Of or relating to Actium in Greece.

actin- Var. of ACTINO-.

ac·tin (ak′tin) *n.* A protein component of muscle fibrils that interacts with myosin in muscular contraction.

ac·ti·nal (ak′tə·nəl, ak·tī′-) *adj. Zool.* **1** Bearing tentacles or rays. **2** Of or pertaining to the tentacle-bearing oral region of certain radially symmetrical animals, as the sea anemone.

act·ing (ak′ting) *adj.* **1** Operating or officiating, especially in place of another: *acting* secretary. **2** Functioning; in working order. **3** Containing directions for actors: the *acting* script. *—n.* **1** Performance, especially of a part in a play. **2** Pretense or simulation.

ac·tin·i·a (ak·tin′ē·ə) *n. pl.* **·i·ae** (-i·ē) or **·i·as** A sea anemone. [< NL < Gk. *aktis, aktinos* ray] **—ac·tin′i·an** *adj. & n.*

ac·tin·ic (ak·tin′ik) *adj.* **1** Pertaining to actinism. **2** Potent to effect chemical changes by radiant energy. **—ac·tin′i·cal·ly** *adv.*

actinic rays Radiation in the violet and ultraviolet part of the spectrum capable of effecting chemical changes, as in photography.

ac·ti·nide series (ak′ti·nīd) *Chem.* A transition series of radioactive elements arranged within the periodic table on the analogy of the lanthanide or rare-earth series: it begins with actinium, atomic number 89, and continues to lawrencium, atomic number 103.

ac·tin·i·form (ak·tin′ə·fôrm) *adj.* Having a radiate form, as actinia.

ac·tin·ism (ak′tin·iz′əm) *n.* **1** The property of electromagnetic radiation, especially in the violet and ultra-violet range, of effecting chemical change. **2** The production of such change. [< ACTIN(O)- + -ISM]

ac·tin·i·um (ak·tin′ē·əm) *n.* A short-lived radioactive element (symbol Ac, atomic number 89), occurring naturally in uranium and radium ores and produced synthetically in nuclear reactors, the most stable isotope having an atomic mass of 227 and a half-life of 21.6 years. See PERIODIC TABLE.

actinium series The succession of radioactive elements resulting from the stepwise disintegration of uranium of mass number 235 to the stable isotope of lead of mass number 207.

actino- *combining form* **1** Pertaining to a radiate structure or the presence of tentacles: *actinozoan.* **2** Pertaining to the action of light or other electromagnetic radiation: *actinograph.* Also **actin-, actini-.** [< Gk. *aktis, aktinos* ray]

ac·tin·o·graph (ak·tin′ə·graf, -gräf) *n.* A recording actinometer.

ac·ti·noid (ak′ti·noid) *adj.* Having the form of rays; radiate, as a starfish. [< ACTIN(O)- + -OID]

ac·ti·o·lite (ak·tin′ə·līt) *n.* A variety of amphibole.

ac·ti·nol·o·gy (ak′ti·nol′ə·jē) *n.* The science of the chemical action of light.

ac·tin·o·mere (ak·tin′ə·mir) See ANTIMERE.

ac·ti·nom·e·ter (ak′ti·nom′ə·tər) *n.* 1 An instrument for measuring the heat intensity of the sun's rays and for determining the actinic effect of light rays. 2 An instrument for determining the power of radiation by its chemical effect on gases, acids, etc. —**ac·ti·no·met·ric** (ak′ti·nō·met′rik) or **·ri·cal** *adj.* —**ac′ti·nom′e·try** *n.*

ac·ti·no·mor·phic (ak′ti·nō·môr′fik) *adj. Biol.* Exhibiting radial symmetry in structure. Also **ac′ti·no·mor′phous.** —**ac′ti·no·mor′phy** *n.*

ac·ti·no·my·cete (ak′ti·nō·mī·sēt′) *n.* Any of an order (Actinomycetales) of filamentous or rod-shaped bacteria, including many animal and plant pathogens as well as saprophytes in soil, water, and decaying organic matter. —**ac·ti·no·my·cet·ous** *adj.*

ac·ti·no·my·co·sis (ak′ti·nō·mī·kō′sis) *n.* An infectious disease of cattle, hogs, and occasionally humans, caused by an actinomycete (*Actinomyces bovis*) and characterized by tumors about the jaws and neck: also called *lumpy jaw.* —**ac′ti·no·my·cot′ic** (-kot′ik) *adj.*

ac·ti·non (ak′ti·non) *n.* An isotope of radon emanating from actinium, having mass number 219 and a half-life of nearly four seconds.

ac·tin·o·ther·a·py (ak·tin·ō·ther′ə·pē) *n.* Radiotherapy.

ac·tin·o·u·ra·ni·um (ak·tin·ō·yŏŏq·rā′nē·əm) *n.* The uranium isotope of mass 238.

ac·ti·no·zo·an (ak′ti·nə·zō′ən) *n.* An anthozoan. [< ACTINO- + Gk. *zōon* life] —**ac′ti·no·zo′an** *adj.*

ac·tion (ak′shən) *n.* 1 The putting forth or exerting of power; an acting, doing, or working; operation; activity. 2 The performance by any organ of its proper function: The *action* of the heart was normal. 3 The movement of the parts or mechanism of something: the *action* of the engine. 4 The result of putting forth power; the thing done; especially, any act of volition; deed: the rational *actions* of men. 5 In literature, the connected series of events on which the interest depends. 6 A military conflict; battle: a general *action.* 7 *Rel.* A devotional exercise or religious function. 8 *Law* The lawful demand of one's right through judicial proceedings; a judicial proceeding for the enforcement of rights, the redress of wrongs, or the punishment of public offenses. 9 In sculpture or painting, gesture or attitude represented as expressing passion or sentiment. 10 *Physics* A magnitude describing the condition of any dynamic system, expressible as twice the mean kinetic energy of the system during a given interval, multiplied by the duration of the interval. 11 *Slang* Lively or exciting social activity; excitement: where the *action* is. 12 *Slang* Money wagered; betting. See synonyms under ACT, BATTLE, BEHAVIOR, EXERCISE, MOTION, OPERATION, TRANSACTION, WORK. [< F < L *actio, -onis* < *agere* do]

ac·tion·a·ble (ak′shən·ə·bəl) *adj.* Affording ground for prosecution, as a trespass or a libel. —**ac′tion·a·bly** *adv.*

Ac·ti·um (ak′tē·əm, ak′shē·əm) An ancient Greek town and promontory in NW Acarnania: site of the naval victory of Octavian (later, Augustus Caesar) over Mark Antony, 31 B.C.

ac·ti·vate (ak′tə·vāt) *v.t.* **·vat·ed, ·vat·ing** 1 To make active. 2 To put into or make capable of action, as a military unit. 3 To make radioactive. 4 To promote or hasten chemical reactivity, as by heat or other agency. 5 To purify sewage by aeration or other means of facilitating bacterial action. —**ac′ti·va′tion** *n.*

activated carbon Amorphous carbon specially prepared in finely divided or porous form and highly adsorptive owing to the very large surface area per unit volume. Also **activated charcoal.**

activation analysis A method of chemical analysis by the identification of characteristic radioactive disintegration patterns following neutron bombardment of the sample.

ac·ti·va·tor (ak′tə·vā′tər) *n.* 1 *Biochem.* A substance that renders active an enzyme that is secreted in an inactive form. 2 *Chem.* A catalyst.

ac·tive (ak′tiv) *adj.* 1 Abounding in action; agile; lively; quick; brisk; busy. 2 *Gram.* **a** Designating a voice of the verb which indicates that the subject of the sentence is performing the action, as *fires* is in the active voice in *The soldier fires the gun*: opposed to *passive* **b** Describing verbs expressing action as distinguished from being and state, as *run, hit, jump.* 3 Being in or pertaining to a state of action: opposed to *quiescent, extinct,* or *latent*: an *active* volcano. 4 Causing or promoting action, or manifested in action; practical. 5 Bearing interest; also, consisting of cash or of property easily exchanged for cash. 6 Radioactive. —*n. Gram.* The active voice. [< F *actif,* fem. *active* < L *activus* < *agere* do] —**ac′tive·ly** *adv.* —**ac′tive·ness** *n.*

Synonyms: agile, alert, brisk, bustling, busy, diligent, energetic, expeditious, industrious, lively, mobile, nimble, prompt, quick, ready, restless, sprightly, spry, supple, vigorous. *Active* refers to both quickness and constancy of action; in the former sense it is allied with *agile, alert, brisk,* etc.; in the latter, with *busy, diligent, industrious.* The *active* enjoy employment, the *busy* are actually employed, the *diligent* and the *industrious* are habitually *busy.* The *restless* are *active* from inability to keep quiet; their activity may be without purpose, or out of all proportion to the purpose contemplated. The *officious* are undesirably *active* in the affairs of others. Compare ALERT, ALIVE, BUSY, MEDDLESOME. *Antonyms*: dull, heavy, idle, inactive, indolent, inert, lazy, quiescent, quiet, slow, sluggish, stupid.

active account One against which many checks are drawn and deposited.

active component *Electr.* The component of an alternating current that is in phase with the electromotive force.

active duty 1 Full military or naval status with full pay and allowances. 2 Service or action in the field or at sea in time of war. Also **active service.**

active euthanasia Euthanasia (def. 2).

active immunity Resistance to a disease due to antibodies produced by the body in response to exposure to or inoculation with a pathogenic antigen.

active list 1 A list of officers of the regular United States military establishment who are in a permanent legal active status entitling them to promotion by seniority. 2 Officers of other components of the United States Army on active duty.

active transport Movement of a substance across a cell membrane in a direction contrary to diffusion, from a lower to a higher concentration.

ac·tiv·i·ty (ak·tiv′ə·tē) *n. pl.* **·ties** 1 The state or quality of being active; action; vigorous movement; active force or operation. 2 *Mech.* Mechanical work done in a unit of time. 3 *Physics* **a** The degree of emission from a radioactive substance in terms of observed effects. **b** The excitability of a gas subject to ionization. 4 *Optics* Capacity of a substance to rotate the plane of polarized light to left or right, measured by a polariscope. See synonyms under EXERCISE.

Act of Congress A bill which has passed both houses of the United States Congress and has become law either with or without the approval of the President, in accordance with the provisions of the Constitution.

act of God *Law* An inevitable event occurring by reason of the operations of nature unmixed with human agency or human negligence.

act of war An act of armed aggression by a nation without a formal declaration of war.

ac·to·my·o·sin (ak′tə·mī′ə·sin) *n.* A protein complex of actin and myosin forming the principal contractile constituent of muscle.

Ac·ton (ak′tən), **Lord,** John Emerich Edward Dalberg-Acton, 1834–1902, English historian.

ac·tor (ak′tər) *n.* 1 One who acts; specifically, a player on the stage, motion pictures, etc. 2 Any doer. See synonyms under AGENT, CAUSE. [< L, a doer < *agere* do]

ac·tress (ak′tris) *n.* A woman who acts, as on the stage, in television, motion pictures, etc.

Acts of the Apostles The fifth book of the New Testament. Also **Acts.**

ac·tu·al (ak′chŏŏ·əl) *adj.* 1 Existing in fact; real. 2 Being in existence or action now; existent; present. See synonyms under SURE. —*n.* 1 Something real or actually existing; a reality. 2 In finance, actual assets or receipts. 3 A drama based on actual persons or events; especially, such a story adapted to television presentation. [< F *actuel* < LL *actualis* < L *actus* a doing. See ACT.]

ac·tu·al·i·ty (ak′chŏŏ·al′ə·tē) *n. pl.* **·ties** 1 The quality of being actual; reality; realism. 2 A documentary film or broadcast.

ac·tu·al·ize (ak′chŏŏ·əl·īz) *v.t.* **·ized, ·iz·ing** 1 To make real; realize in action, as a possibility. 2 To make seem real; describe or represent realistically. —**ac′tu·al·i·za′tion** *n.*

ac·tu·al·ly (ak′chŏŏ·əl·ē) *adv.* In act or fact; as a matter of fact; in reality; really; truly.

ac·tu·ar·y (ak′chŏŏ·er′ē) *n. pl.* **·ar·ies** One who specializes in the mathematics of insurance, mortality rates, and the like; especially, the official statistician of an insurance company, who calculates and states risks, premiums, etc. [< L *actuarius* clerk < *actus.* See ACT.] —**ac·tu·ar·i·al** (ak′chŏŏ·âr′ē·əl) *adj.* —**ac′tu·ar′i·al·ly** *adv.*

ac·tu·ate (ak′chŏŏ·āt) *v.t.* **·at·ed, ·at·ing** 1 To move to action; impel, as a mechanism. 2 To incite or influence, as the will: He was *actuated* by motives of kindness. [< Med.L *actuatus,* pp. of *actuare* < L *actus* a doing. See ACT.] —**ac′tu·a′tion** *n.*

Synonyms: activate, compel, dispose, draw, drive, excite, impel, incite, incline, induce, influence, lead, move, persuade, prompt, stir, urge. One is *urged* from without, *actuated* or *impelled* from within. See INFLUENCE. *Antonyms*: deter, dissuade, hinder, restrain.

ac·tu·a·tor (ak′chŏŏ·ā′tər) *n.* 1 One who or that which actuates. 2 The mechanism which releases the trigger of an automatic weapon.

acu- *combining form* Needle; point. [< L *acus*]

ac·u·ate (ak′yŏŏ·it, -āt) *adj.* Pointed; sharp.

a·cu·i·ty (ə·kyŏŏ′ə·tē) *n.* Acuteness; sharpness. [< MF *acuité* < Med.L *acuitas* < L *acus* needle]

a·cu·le·ate (ə·kyŏŏ′lē·it, -āt) *adj.* 1 Armed with a sting. 2 *Bot.* Provided with prickles; prickly. [< L *aculeatus* < *aculeus,* dim. of *acus* needle]

a·cu·le·o·late (ə·kyŏŏ′lē·ə·lit) *adj. Bot.* Provided with very tiny prickles.

a·cu·men (ə·kyŏŏ′mən) *n.* Quickness of insight or discernment; keenness of intellect. [< L, point, sharpness (of the mind) < *acuere* sharpen]

Synonyms: acuteness, cleverness, discernment, insight, keenness, perception, perspicacity, sagacity, sharpness, shrewdness. *Sharpness, acuteness,* and *insight,* however keen, and *perception,* however deep, fall short of the meaning of *acumen,* which belongs to an astute and discriminating mind. *Cleverness* is a practical aptitude for study or learning. *Perspicacity* is the power to see clearly and quickly through that which is difficult or involved. Compare SAGACIOUS. *Antonyms*: dullness, obtuseness, stupidity.

a·cu·mi·nate (ə·kyŏŏ′mə·nāt) *v.t.* **·nat·ed, ·nat·ing** To sharpen; make pointed. —*adj.* (ə·kyŏŏ′mə·nit, -nāt) Ending in a long tapering point, as a leaf, feather, fin, etc. Compare ACUTE, and see illustration under LEAF. [< L *acuminatus,* pp. of *acuminare* point < *acumen.* See ACUMEN.] —**a·cu′mi·na′tion** *n.*

a·cu·mi·nous (ə·kyŏŏ′mə·nəs) *adj.* Having acumen.

ac·u·punc·ture (ak′yŏō·pungk′chər) *n.* A traditional Chinese treatment for pain or disease in which numerous long, fine needles are inserted at predetermined points on the body. [< ACU- + PUNCTURE]

ac·u·punc·tur·ist (ak′yŏō·pungk′chər·ist) *n.* One who practices acupuncture.

a·cush·la (ä·kŏōsh′lə) *n.* Dear one; darling. [< Irish *ac* oh + *cuisle* pulse of the heart]

a·cute (ə·kyŏōt′) *adj.* **1** Keenly discerning or sensitive: an *acute* thinker. **2** Keenly discerning or sensitive: *acute* hearing. **3** Affecting keenly; poignant; intense. **4** Of rapid onset and short duration: an *acute* illness. **5** *Music* Shrill; high. **6** Threatening; critical: an *acute* shortage of water. [< L *acutus*, pp. of *acuere* sharpen] —**a·cute′ly** *adv.* —**a·cute′ness** *n.*
Synonyms: astute, cunning, discerning, intelligent, keen, penetrating, perspicacious, piercing, pointed, sagacious, sharp, shrewd, subtile, subtle. See ASTUTE, SAGACIOUS. *Antonyms:* blunt, chronic, dull, grave, heavy, obtuse, stolid, stupid.

acute accent See under ACCENT.

acute angle See under ANGLE.

-acy *suffix of nouns* Forming nouns of quality, state or condition from adjectives in *-acious*, and nouns and adjectives in *-ate: fallacy, celibacy, curacy.* [< F *-atie* < L *-acia, -atia* < Gk. *-ateia*; or directly < L or < Gk.]

a·cy·clic (ə·sī′klik, ə·sik′lik) *adj.* **1** *Bot.* Arranged in spirals rather than whorls. **2** *Chem.* Having atoms in the molecule connected in an open chain rather than a ring.

ac·yl (as′əl) *n.* A radical derived from an organic acid by removal of the hydroxyl (OH) group.

ad¹ (ad) *n. Colloq.* An advertisement.

ad² (ad) *prep. Latin* To; toward; as to.

ad- *prefix* To; toward; near: *adhere, advert, adrenal*; often, in English, without perceptible force. Also: *a-* before *sc, sp, st*, as in *ascribe*; *ab-* before *b*, as in *abbreviate*; *ac-* before *c, q*, as in *acquire*; *af-* before *f*, as in *afferent*; *ag-* before *g*, as in *agglutinate*; *al-* before *l*, as in *allude*; *an-* before *n*, as in *annex*; *ap-* before *p*, as in *append*; *ar-* before *r*, as in *arrive*; *as-* before *s*, as in *associate*; *at-* before *t*, as in *attract*. [< L *ad-* < *ad* to]

-ad¹ *suffix* Of or pertaining to; used to form: **1** Collective numerals: *triad*. **2** Names of poems: *Iliad, Dunciad*. **3** *Bot.* Names of some plants: *cycad*. [< Gk. *-as, -ados*]

-ad² *suffix of adverbs Anat., Zool.* To; toward; in the direction of: *dorsad*, toward the back. [< L *ad* to, toward]

A·da (ā′də) A feminine personal name. [< Hebrew, beauty]

A·da·ba·zar (ä′dä·bä·zär′) See ADAPAZARI.

a·dac·tyl·i·a (ä′dak·til′ē·ə) *n.* Congenital absence of fingers or toes. Also **adactyly**[< NL < Gk. *a-* without + *daktylos* finger] —**a·dac·ty·lous** (ə·dak′tə·ləs) *adj.*

ad·age (ad′ij) *n.* A saying that has obtained credit or force by long use; a proverb. [< F < L *adagium* < *ad-* to + root of *aio* I say]
Synonyms: aphorism, apothegm, axiom, byword, dictum, maxim, motto, precept, proverb, saw, saying. See PROVERB.

a·da·gio (ə·dä′jō, -zhē·ō) *Music adj.* Slow: faster than *largo* but slower than *andante*. —*n.* A musical composition, movement, etc. in adagio time. —*adv.* Slowly. [< Ital. *adagio*, lit., at ease]

adagio dance A ballet dance in slow tempo.

A·dak (ā′dak) One of the Aleutian Islands in the central Andreanof group.

A·dal·bert (ä′däl·bert) German form of ALBERT.

A·da·li·a (ä·dä′lē·ä) See ANTALYA.

Ad·a·line (ad′ə·līn) See ADELINE.

Ad·am (ad′əm) A masculine personal name. [< Hebrew, man]
—**Adam** The first man, progenitor of the human race, *Gen.* ii 7. Hence, mankind collectively. —**the old Adam** Unregenerate or depraved human nature. —**A·dam·ic** (ə·dam′ik) *adj.*

Ad·am (ad′əm) Of or pertaining to a neoclassic style of architecture, furniture, etc., originated in England by the **Adam** brothers, **Robert**, 1728–92, and **James**, 1730–94.

Ad·am-and-Eve (ad′əm·ənd·ēv′) *n.* The putty-

root.

ad·a·mant (ad′ə·mant, -mənt) *n.* **1** A very hard imaginary mineral. **2** Formerly, the diamond or lodestone. **3** *Archaic* Exceeding hardness; impenetrability. —*adj.* Immovable; unyielding. [< OF *adamaunt* < L *adamas, -antis* the hardest metal (hence, unyielding) < Gk. *adamas* < *a-* not + *damaein* conquer. Doublet of DIAMOND.]

ad·a·man·tine (ad′ə·man′tin, -tēn, -tīn) *adj.* **1** Made of or like adamant; of impenetrable hardness. **2** Having a diamondlike luster. Also **ad·a·man·te·an** (ad′ə·man·tē′ən).

Ad·am·ite (ad′əm·īt) *adj.* Descended from Adam. —*n.* **1** A descendant of Adam; a human being. **2** One who goes naked in imitation of Adam. —**Ad·am·it·ic** (ad′əm·it′ik) or **·i·cal** *adj.*

A·da·mo (ä·dä′mō) Italian form of ADAM.

Ad·ams (ad′əmz) A prominent Massachusetts family, including **John**, 1735–1826, second president of the United States 1797–1801; his son **John Quincy**, 1767–1848, sixth president of the United States 1825–29; **Charles Francis**, 1807–86, son of John Quincy, diplomat; **Henry Brooks**, 1838–1918, son of Charles Francis, author; **Samuel**, 1722–1803, cousin of John, patriot, signer of Declaration of Independence. —**Franklin Pierce**, ("F.P.A"), 1881–1960, U.S. journalist. —**James Truslow**, 1878–1949, U.S. historian. —**John Couch**, 1819–92, English astronomer. —**Maude**, stage name of Maude Kiskadden, 1872–1953, U.S. actress.

Ad·ams (ad′əmz), **Mount 1** A peak of the White Mountains in New Hampshire; 5,805 feet. **2** A peak of the Cascade Range in Washington; 12,307 feet.

Adam's ale Water.

Adam's apple *Anat.* The prominence made by the thyroid cartilage on the front of the human throat, conspicuous in males.

ad·ams·ite (ad′əmz·īt) *n.* A yellow, crystalline, arsenical compound, $(C_6H_4)_2NHAsCl$, used dispersed in air as a poison gas causing skin, eye, and lung irritation and nausea. [after Major Roger *Adams*, born 1889, American discoverer]

Ad·am's-nee·dle (ad′əmz·nēd′l) *n.* Any of various species of yucca.

A·dan (ä·dän′) Spanish form of ADAM.

A·da·na (ä′dä·nä) A city in southern Turkey on the Seyhan River.

A·dão (ä·doun′) Portuguese form of ADAM.

A·da·pa·za·ri (ä·dä·pä·zä′ri) A town in NW Turkey: also Adabazar.

a·dapt (ə·dapt′) *v.t.* **1** To make suitable, as by remodeling: with *for*: to *adapt* a novel for the theater. **2** To modify (oneself) to conform to a situation or environment. —*v.i.* **3** To become adjusted to a circumstance or environment: with *to*: Some plants *adapt* well to high altitudes. [< F *adapter* < L *adaptare* < *ad-* to + *aptare* fit]
Synonyms: accommodate, adjust, arrange, attune, conform, fashion, fit, harmonize, prepare, proportion, set, suit. *Fit* and *adapt* refer to the bringing about of agreement; *fit* applies especially to original purpose; as, the key is *fitted* to the lock; *adapt* often applies to the securing of agreement by partial change; a novel is *adapted* for the stage by changing it from the narrative to the dramatic form. *Adjust* refers chiefly to relative position; the parts of a typewriter, already *fitted* and *adapted* to each other, must be *adjusted* for perfect alinement. To *suit* is to make one thing or person in all respects agreeable to another. *Conform* implies external agreement, as of a glacier to a rock surface, or of dissenters to an established church. *Accommodate* implies some concession or yielding to secure harmony; as, to *accommodate* oneself to circumstances. *Arrange* refers to position and order, commonly of detached objects; as, to *arrange* the furniture of a room, or the heads of a discourse. See ACCOMMODATE. Compare SET.

a·dapt·a·ble (ə·dapt′ə·bəl) *adj.* Capable of being adapted. —**a·dapt′a·bil·i·ty, a·dapt′a·ble·ness** *n.*

ad·ap·ta·tion (ad′əp·tā′shən) *n.* **1** The act of adapting or fitting one thing to another; the state of being suited or fitted. **2** The process of adapting or adjusting to new conditions. **3** Anything adapted. **4** *Biol.* An advantageous conformation of an organism to changes in its

environment. **5** *Physiol.* The change in the response of an organ of sense due to prolonged or repeated stimulation. —**ad′ap·ta′tion·al** *adj.* —**ad′ap·ta′tion·al·ly** *adv.*

a·dapt·er (ə·dap′tər) *n.* **1** A person or thing that adapts. **2** *Mech.* Any device that serves to connect or fit together two parts of an apparatus, or to permit the use of an apparatus for a purpose for which it was not intended. **3** A device for converting available electric current to a form required to power a given device. Also **a·dap′tor**.

a·dap·tive (ə·dap′tiv) *adj.* Capable of, pertaining to, fit for, or manifesting adaptation. —**a·dap′tive·ly** *adv.* —**a·dap′tive·ness** *n.*

adaptive radiation An evolutionary process by which a single relatively unspecialized type of organism gives rise to a variety of specialized forms by adaptation to different environmental conditions.

a·dap·to·me·ter (ə·dap′tə·mē′tər) *n.* Any of various instruments for measuring individual physiologic adaptation to sensory stimuli.

A·dar (ə·där′, ä′där) A Hebrew month. See CALENDAR (Hebrew).

ad ar·bit·ri·um (ad är·bit′rē·əm) *Latin* At will; arbitrarily.

ad·ax·i·al (ad·ak′sē·əl) *adj.* Toward or beside the axis of an organism or an organ.

a·days (ə·dāz′) *adv.* By day; on each day; during the day: now only in *nowadays*.

add (ad) *v.t.* **1** To join or unite, so as to increase the importance, size, quantity or number: to *add* more weight to his load; *add* insult to injury. **2** To find the sum of, as a column of figures; unite in a total. **3** To say or write further. —*v.i.* **4** To produce an increase in: with *to*: His new duties *added* to his worries. **5** To perform the arithmetical process of addition. —**to add up 1** To accumulate to a total. **2** *Colloq.* To make sense. [< L *addere* < *ad-* to + *dare* give] —**add′·i·bil·i·ty, add′i·bil·i·ty** *n.* —**add′a·ble, add′i·ble** *adj.*
Synonyms: adjoin, affix, amplify, annex, append, attach, augment, enlarge, extend, increase, subjoin. To *add* is to *increase* by *adjoining* or *uniting*: in distinction from *multiply*, which is to *increase* by repeating. To *augment* a thing is to *increase* it by any means, but this word chiefly indicates an extension of volume. We may *enlarge* a house, a farm, or an empire, *extend* influence or dominion, *augment* a stream, power, or influence, *attach* or *annex* a building to one that it *adjoins*, or *annex* a territory, *affix* a seal or a signature, *attach* a condition to a promise. A speaker may *amplify* a discourse by a fuller treatment throughout than was originally planned, or he may *append* or *subjoin* certain remarks without change of what has gone before. *Antonyms:* abstract, deduct, diminish, dissever, lessen, reduce, remove, subtract, withdraw.

Ad·dams (ad′əmz), **Jane**, 1860–1935, U.S. social worker.

ad·dax (ad′aks) *n.* A North African and Arabian antelope (*Addax nasomaculata*) with shaggy hair on the throat and forehead, long and twisted horns, a white spot on the face, and a whitish body. [< L < native African word]

ADDAX
(3 feet high at shoulder; 3 to 4 feet long)

ad·dend (ad′end, ə·dend′) *n. Math.* A quantity or number which is to be united in one sum with another quantity or number called the *augend*. [See ADDENDUM]

ad·den·dum (ə·den′dəm) *n. pl.* **-da** (-də) **1** A thing added, or to be added. **2** *Mech.* The radial distance between the pitch circle and the outer ends of the teeth on a geared wheel; also, the part of a tooth outside the pitch circle. See synonyms under APPENDAGE,

INCREASE. [< L, neut. gerundive of *addere* add]

ad·der[1] (ad′ər) *n.* **1** A viper, especially the common European viper *(Vipera berus),* about two feet long, of a brownish color variegated with black. **2** One of various other snakes, as the harmless puff adder of the United States. [OE *nædre* (*a nadder* in ME becoming *an adder*)]

add·er[2] (ad′ər) *n.* **1** A person or thing that adds. **2** An adding machine.

ad·ders·mouth (ad′ərz·mouth′) *n.* Any of various delicate terrestrial orchids (genus *Malaxis*), having small greenish flowers.

ad·der's-tongue (ad′ərz·tung′) *n.* **1** A cosmopolitan fern (genus *Ophio-glossum*), so named from the form of its spore-bearing spike. **2** Any of various flowering plants, as the dog's-tooth violet.

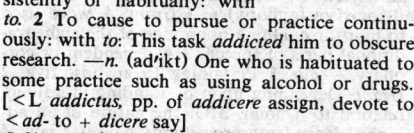

ADDER'S-TONGUE (*def. 2*)

ad·dict (ə·dikt′) *v.t.* **1** To apply or devote (oneself) persistently or habitually: with *to.* **2** To cause to pursue or practice continuously: with *to*: This task *addicted* him to obscure research. —*n.* (ad′ikt) One who is habituated to some practice such as using alcohol or drugs. [< L *addictus,* pp. of *addicere* assign, devote to < *ad-* to + *dicere* say]

ad·dict·ed (ə·dik′tid) *adj.* Accustomed; inclined to the pursuit, practice, or taking of anything: *addicted* to drugs.

Synonyms: abandoned, accustomed, attached, devoted, disposed, given, habituated, inclined, predisposed, prone, wedded. One is *addicted* to that which he has allowed to gain a strong, habitual, and enduring hold upon action, inclination, or involuntary tendency. A man may be *accustomed* to labor, *attached* to his profession, *devoted* to his religion, *given* to study or to gluttony (in the bad sense). One *inclined* to luxury may become *habituated* to poverty. One is *wedded* to that which has become a second nature, as to science or to art. *Prone* is used only in a bad sense, and generally of natural tendencies; as, our hearts are *prone* to evil. *Abandoned* tells of acquired viciousness to which one has surrendered himself. *Addicted* is used in a good or, more frequently, a bad sense; *devoted,* chiefly in the good sense; as, a mother's *devoted* affection. *Antonyms*: averse, disinclined, indisposed, unaccustomed.

ad·dic·tion (ə·dik′shən) *n.* **1** Habitual inclination; bent. **2** A condition of compulsive psychological or physiological dependence on a drug.

ad·dic·tive (ə·dik′tiv) *adj.* Of, pertaining to, or causing addiction; habit-forming.

adding machine A keyboard machine that automatically adds a series of numbers recorded by the operator.

Ad·dis A·ba·ba (ä′dis ä′bə·bä, ad′is ab′ə·bə) The capital of Ethiopia. Also **A′dis A′ba·ba.**

Ad·di·son (ad′ə·sən), **Joseph,** 1672–1719, English essayist and poet.

Ad·di·so·ni·an (ad′ə·sō′nē·ən) *adj.* Of or pertaining to Joseph Addison; especially, like his literary style, characterized by clarity, urbanity, etc.

Addison's disease A syndrome resulting from insufficient hormonal secretion by the adrenal cortex, characterized by brownish pigmentation of the skin, anemia, and prostration. [after Thomas *Addison,* 1793–1860, English physician]

ad·dit·a·ment (ə·dit′ə·mənt) *n.* A thing added; addition. Also **ad·dit′i·ment.** [< L *additamentum*]

ad·di·tion (ə·dish′ən) *n.* **1** The act of adding, or that which is added; an increase; annex; accession. **2** *Music* A dot at the right of a musical note, lengthening it one half. **3** *Law* A title or mark of designation attached to a man's name. **4** *Her.* Augmentation. **5** *Math.* The uniting of two or more arithmetical or algebraic quantities in one sum, indicated by the plus sign (+). See synonyms under ACCESSION, APPENDAGE, INCREASE. [< F < L *additio, -onis* < *addere.* See ADD.]

ad·di·tion·al (ə·dish′ən·əl) *adj.* Being in addition, supplementary. —*n.* An addition. —**ad·di′tion·al·ly** *adv.*

additional tax A surtax.

additions and betterments Improvements that enhance the value of railroad property.

ad·di·tive (ad′ə·tiv) *n.* An extra ingredient added in small quantity to a product for the purpose of altering or improving some characteristic, such as stability, flavor, performance, cost, or the like. —*adj.* That is to be added; serving or tending to increase. [< L *additivus* < *addere.* See ADD.] —**ad′di·tive·ly** *adv.*

ad·dle (ad′l) *v.* **ad·dled, ad·dling** *v.i.* **1** To become spoiled, as eggs. **2** To become muddled or mixed up, as a discourse. —*v.t.* **3** To cause to spoil. **4** To cause to become confused. —*adj.* **1** Spoiled, as eggs; rotten. **2** Confused; mixed up, as discourse: now generally in compounds: *addlepated.* [OE *adela* liquid filth]

ad·dle-brained (ad′l·brānd′) *adj.* Confused; mixed up. Also **ad′dle-head′ed, ad′dle-pat′ed, ad′dle-wit′ted.**

add·on (ad′on′, -ôn′) —*n.* An additional or added sum, quantity, or item. —*adj.* Additional; accessory: *add-on* units for air conditioning.

ad·dress (ə·dres′) *v.t.* **ad·dressed, ad·dress·ing** **1** To speak to; accost: He *addressed* the bystanders fiercely. **2** To deliver a set discourse to: The president *addressed* the council every third week. **3** To direct, as spoken or written words, to the attention of: with *to*: He *addressed* his prayers to his God. **4** To devote the energy or force of (oneself): with *to*: He *addressed* himself to the task. **5** To superscribe or mark with a destination, as a letter. **6** To consign, as a cargo to a merchant. **7** To aim or direct, as a ball by a golf club. **8** To pay court to, as a lover; woo. —*n.* (ə·dres′, *esp. for* **2** *and* **3** ad′res) **1** A set or formal discourse; a speaking to or accosting; an appeal; application; petition. **2** The writing on an envelope, etc. directing something to a person or place. **3** The name, place, residence, etc. of a person. **4** Consignment, as of a vessel or cargo. **5** The manner of a person; delivery; bearing. **6** *Chiefly pl.* Any courteous or devoted attention; wooing. **7** Skilful conduct or action; adroitness; tact. **8** *Electronics* A particular location in the memory or storage element of a computer, as indicated by a number or other symbol. **9** *Obs.* Preparation or that which is prepared. [< OF *adresser* < VL *addrictiare, addirectiare* < L *ad-* to + *directus* straight] —**ad·dress·er, ad·dress·or** *n.*

Synonyms (verb): accost, apostrophize, appeal, approach, court, greet, hail, inscribe, salute, woo. To *accost* is to speak first to; *greet* is not so distinctly limited; to *salute* is to *greet* with special token of respect; to *hail* is to *greet* in a loud-voiced and commonly hearty and joyous way. *Address* is slightly more formal than *accost* or *greet,* though it may often be interchanged with them. One may *address* another at considerable length in a speech or in writing; he *accosts* orally and briefly. *Antonyms*: avoid, cut, elude, ignore, overlook, pass, shun.

Synonyms (noun): adroitness, courtesy, dexterity, discretion, ingenuity, manners, politeness, readiness, speech, tact. *Address,* as here considered, is a general power to direct to the matter in hand whatever qualities are most needed for it at the moment. It includes *adroitness* and *discretion* to know what to do or say and what to avoid; *ingenuity* to devise; *readiness* to speak or act; the *dexterity* that comes of practice; and *tact,* which is the power of fine touch as applied to human character and feeling. *Courtesy* and *politeness* are indispensable elements of good *address.* Compare SPEECH. *Antonyms*: awkwardness, boorishness, clownishness, clumsiness, fatuity, folly, rudeness, stupidity, unmannerliness, unwisdom.

ad·dress·ee (ad′res·ē′, ə·dres′ē′) *n.* One who is addressed.

Ad·dres·so·graph (ə·dres′ə·graf, -gräf) *n.* A machine for printing addresses from stencils: a trade name.

ad·duce (ə·do͞os′, ə·dyo͞os′) *v.t.* **ad·duced, ad·duc·ing** To bring forward for proof or consideration, as an example; cite; allege. See synonyms under ALLEGE. [< L *adducere* < *ad-* to + *ducere* lead] —**ad·duce′a·ble, ad·duc′i·ble** *adj.*

ad·du·cent (ə·do͞o′sənt, ə·dyo͞o′-) *adj.* Drawing together; adducting.

ad·duct (ə·dukt′) *v.t. Physiol.* To draw toward the axis: said of muscles. [< L *adductus,* pp. of *adducere.* See ADDUCE.] —**ad·duc′tion** *n.*

ad·duc·tive (ə·duk′tiv) *adj.* **1** Adducing. **2** Tending to adduct.

ad·duc·tor (ə·duk′tər) *n.* An adducting muscle.

Ad·dy (ad′ē) Diminutive of ADELINE.

-ade[1] *suffix of nouns* **1** Act or action: *cannonade.* **2** A person or group concerned in an action or process: *cavalcade.* **3** Product of an action or process: *lemonade.* [< F *-ade* < Provençal, Pg., or Sp. *-ada* or Ital. *-ata* < L *-ata,* fem. pp. ending]

-ade[2] *suffix of nouns* Relating to; pertaining to: *decade.* The more common English form of this suffix is *-ad.* See -AD[1]. [< F *-ade* < Gk. *-as, -ados*]

Ade (ād), **George,** 1866–1944, U.S. humorist.

a·deem (ə·dēm′) *v.t.* **1** To take away. **2** *Law* To revoke, as the bequest of a legacy. [< L *adimere* < *ad-* to (oneself) + *emere* take]

Ad·e·la (ad′ə·lə) A feminine personal name. Also *Fr.* **A·dèle** (à·del′), *Ger.* **A·de·le** (ä·dā′lə). See ADELINE.

Ad·e·laide (ad′ə·lād) A feminine personal name. Also *Fr.* **A·dé·la·ïde** (à·dā·là·ēd′), *Ger.* **A·del·heid** (ä′del·hīt), *Ital.* **A·de·la·i·da** (ä′dā·lä′ī·dä). See ADELINE. [< OHG, nobility]—**Adelaide, Queen,** 1792–1849, wife of William IV of England.

Ad·e·laide (ad′ə·lād) The capital of South Australia.

A·dé·lie Coast (ad′ə·lē, *Fr.* à·dà·lē′) A region on the coast of Wilkes Land, Antarctica, under French sovereignty; 150,000 square miles. *French* **Terre A·dé·lie** (târ à·dā·lē′).

Ad·e·line (ad′ə·līn; *Dan.* ä′di·lē′ni, *Fr.* àd·lēn′, *Ger.* ä′de·lē′nə) A feminine personal name. Also **Ad·e·li·cia** (ad′ə·lish′ə), **Ad·e·li·na** (ad′ə·lī′nə, *Du.* ä′di·lē′nə). [< OHG, of noble birth]

a·del·phous (ə·del′fəs) *adj. Bot.* Having stamens with clustered or coalescent filaments: used mainly as a suffix. [< Gk. *adelphos* brother]

a·demp·tion (ə·demp′shən) *n. Law* Disposal by a testator in his lifetime of specific property bequeathed in his will so that the bequest is adeemed. [< L *ademptio, -onis* < *adimere.* See ADEEM.]

A·den (äd′n, ād′n) A former British colony at the sw tip of the Arabian peninsula, now a part of South Yemen; principal city **Aden,** pop. about 100,000.

Aden, Gulf of A western inlet of the Arabian Sea, between South Yemen and Somalia.

Ad·en·au·er (ad′ən·ou′ər, *Ger.* ä′dən·ou′ər), **Konrad,** 1876–1967, German statesman; first chancellor of the West German republic 1949–63.

A·den·i (ä′den·ē) *n. pl.* **A·den·is** A native or inhabitant of Aden. —*adj.* Of or pertaining to Aden. Also **A·den·ese** (ä′dən·ēz′, -ēs′, ä′dən-).

ad·e·nine (ad′ə·nin, -nēn, -nīn) *n.* A purine base, $C_5H_5N_5$, occurring as a constituent of DNA and RNA and of various nucleotides essential in cellular metabolism. [< ADEN(O)- + -INE[2]]

adeno- *combining form* Gland: *adenology.* Also, before vowels, **aden-.** [< Gk. *adēn* gland]

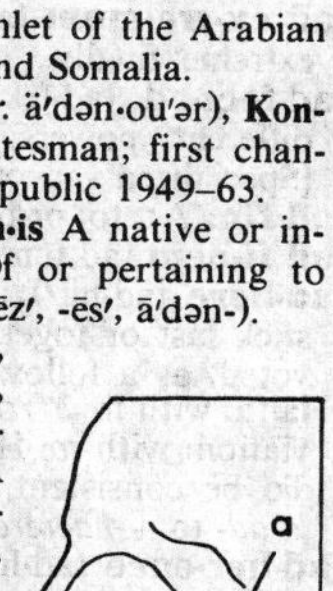

ADENOIDS (*a*)

ad·e·no·hy·poph·y·sis (ad′ə·nō·hī·pof′ə·sis) *n. pl.* **·y·ses** (-ə·sēz) The anterior and principal hormone-secreting lobe of the pituitary gland. —**ad·e·no·hy·po·phys·e·al** (ad′ə·nō·hī·pō·fiz′ē·əl) *adj.*

ad·e·noid (ad′ə·noid) *adj.* Of or like a gland; glandular: also **ad′e·noi′dal.** —*n. Usually pl.* An enlarged mass of lymphoid tissue in the nasopharynx, in severe cases obstructing breathing and speech. [< ADEN(O)- + -OID]

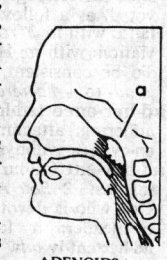

ad·e·no·ma (ad′ə·nō′mə) *n. pl.* **-ma·ta** (-mə·tə) or **-mas** *Pathol.* A usually benign tumor of glandular origin or structure. [< ADEN(O)- + -OMA] **—ad·e·nom·a·tous** (ad′ə·nom′ə·təs) *adj.*

a·den·o·sine (ə·den′ə·sēn, -sin) *n.* A nucleoside, $C_{10}H_{13}N_5O_4$, composed of adenosine and ribose.

adenosine diphosphate A compound of adenosine and two phosphate groups resulting from the hydrolysis of adenosine triphosphate. Symbol ADP.

adenosine monophosphate Any of several isomers of a coenzyme consisting of adenosine with an attached phosphate group and playing a major part in energy transfer and hormonal action in living cells. Also called *adenylic acid.* Symbol AMP.

adenosine triphosphate The major energy-carrying molecule in cellular metabolism, consisting of an adenosine nucleotide with three phosphate groups attached by bonds that release large amounts of energy when the compound is hydrolyzed. Symbol ATP.

ad·e·no·vi·rus (ad′ə·nō·vī′rəs) *n.* Any of a group of viruses found in humans and other mammals and producing infections chiefly of the respiratory system.

Aden Protectorate Formerly, a group of Arab tribal districts on the southern coast of the Arabian Peninsula comprising a British protectorate, now a part of South Yemen.

ad·e·nyl·ic acid (ad′ə·nil′ik) Adenosine monophosphate.

a·dept (ə·dept′) *adj.* Highly skilful; proficient. **—ad·ept** (ad′ept, ə·dept′) *n.* **1** One fully skilled in any art; an expert. **2** *Archaic* An alchemist who professed to have discovered how to convert base metals into gold. [< L *adeptus* having attained, pp. of *adipisci* attain < *ad-* to + *apisci* get] **—a·dept′ly** *adv.* **—a·dept′ness** *n.*

ad·e·quate (ad′ə·kwit) *adj.* **1** Equal to what is required; suitable to the case or occasion; fully sufficient. **2** Equal in size, extent, value, etc. [< L *adaequatus,* pp. of *adaequare* < *ad-* to + *aequus* equal] **—ad·e·qua·cy** (ad′ə·kwə·sē), **ad′e·quate·ness** *n.* **—ad′e·quate·ly** *adv.*

Synonyms: commensurate, enough, equal, fit, fitting, plentiful, satisfactory, sufficient. *Adequate, commensurate, enough,* and *sufficient* signify *equal* to some given occasion or work. *Commensurate* is the more precise and learned word, signifying that which exactly measures the matter in question. Work is *satisfactory* if it satisfies those for whom it is done, while it may be very poor work judged by some higher standard. Compare AMPLE, COMPETENT. *Antonyms*: inadequate, insufficient, unequal, unfit, unsatisfactory.

A·der·nò (ä·der·nō′) Former name of ADRANO.

ad ex·tre·mum (ad eks·trē′məm) *Latin* To the extreme; finally.

ad·fect·ed (ad·fek′tid) *adj. Math.* Containing different powers of an unknown quantity. [Specialized var. of AFFECTED]

ad fin. At, to, or toward the end (L *ad finem*).

ad fi·nem (ad fī′nem) *Latin* To the end.

ad·here (ad·hir′) *v.i.* **ad·hered, ad·her·ing 1** To stick fast or together. **2** To be attached or devoted, as a follower or disciple, to a party or faith: with *to.* **3** To follow closely or without deviation: with *to*: He *adhered* to the plan. **4** *Obs.* To be consistent, as an alibi. [< L *adhaerere* < *ad-* to + *haerere* stick]

ad·her·ence (ad·hir′əns) *n.* The act or state of adhering; attachment; adhesion. Also **ad·her′·en·cy.** See synonyms under ATTACHMENT.

ad·her·ent (ad·hir′ənt) *adj.* **1** Clinging or sticking fast. **2** *Bot.* Adnate; grown together. —*n.* One who is devoted or attached, as to a cause or leader; a follower: also **ad·her′er.** **—ad·her′ent·ly** *adv.*

Synonyms (noun): aid, aider, ally, backer, disciple, follower, partisan, supporter. An *adherent* is one who is devoted or attached to a person, party, principle, cause, creed, or the like. *Allies* may differ on every point except the specific ground of union. *Allies* are regarded as equals; *adherents* and *disciples* are followers. *Partisan* has the narrow sense of adhesion to a party. One may be an *adherent* or *supporter* of a party and not a *partisan. Backer* usually indicates a financial *supporter.* Compare ACCESSORY. *Antonyms*: adversary, antagonist, betrayer, deserter, enemy, hater, opponent, renegade, traitor.

ad·he·sion (ad·hē′zhən) *n.* **1** The act of adhering; the state of being attached; adherence. **2** Assent; concurrence. **3** Close connection, as of ideas. **4** *Physics* The binding force exerted by molecules of unlike substances when brought in contact, as wood and glue. **5** The union of normally separate tissues in the body by proliferating fibrous tissue. See synonyms under ATTACHMENT. [< F *adhésion* < L *adhaesio, -onis* < *adhaerere.* See ADHERE.]

ad·he·sive (ad·hē′siv) *adj.* **1** Having the quality of adhering; tending or causing to adhere; sticky; clinging. **2** Prepared to adhere; gummed. —*n.* A substance that causes adhesion. **—ad·he′sive·ly** *adv.* **—ad·he′sive·ness** *n.*

Synonyms (adj.): cohesive, glutinous, gummy, sticking, sticky, viscid, viscous. *Adhesive* is the scientific, *sticky* the popular word. That which is *adhesive* tends to join itself to the surface of any other body with which it is placed in contact; *cohesive* expresses the tendency of particles of the same substance to hold together. *Antonyms*: free, inadhesive, loose, separable.

adhesive tape A piece or strip of fabric coated with adhesive material, used for bandages, dressings, etc.

ad·hib·it (ad·hib′it) *v.t.* **1** To let in; admit, as to a court of law. **2** To affix; fasten, as a label. **3** To apply; administer, as a medicine. [< L *adhibitus,* pp. of *adhibere* hold towards, apply to < *ad-* to + *habere* have, hold] **—ad·hi·bi·tion** (ad′hi·bish′ən) *n.*

ad hoc (ad hok′) *Latin* With respect to this (particular thing); up to this time.

ad hoc committee A committee formed for a specific purpose in a specific situation.

ad hom·i·nem (ad hom′ə·nem) *Latin* To the man; to one's individual passions and prejudices.

ad·i·a·bat·ic (ad′ē·ə·bat′ik, ā′dē·ə-) *adj. Physics* Pertaining to a closed thermodynamic system in which changes are effected without gain or loss of heat, as in the insulated cylinder of an engine. [< Gk. *adiabatos* impassable < *a-* not + *dia-* through + *bainein* go]

ad·i·aph·o·rous (ad′ē·af′ər·əs) *adj.* Not included under the essential tenets or principles of religion and morality. [< Gk. *adiaphoros* < *a-* not + *diaphoros* different < *dia-* through + *pherein* carry]

ad·i·a·ther·man·cy (ad′ē·ə·thûr′mən·sē) *n. Physics* The quality of being impervious to radiant heat. [< Gk. *a-* not + *dia* through + *thermē* heat]

a·dieu (ə·dōō′, ə·dyōō′; *Fr.* à·dyœ′) *n. pl.* **a·dieus,** *Fr.* **a·dieux** (à·dyœ′) A farewell. —*interj.* Good-by; farewell: literally, "to God (I commend you)." See synonyms under FAREWELL. [< F *à* to + *dieu* God]

A·di·ge (ä′dē·jā) A river of northern Italy, flowing 220 miles to the Adriatic.

ad in·fi·ni·tum (ad in′fə·nī′təm) To infinity; hence, limitlessly. [< L]

ad in·ter·im (ad in′tər·im) Meanwhile; in the meantime. [< L]

a·di·os (ä′dē·ōs′, ad′ē·ōs′; *Sp.* ä·dyōs′) *interj.* Farewell; good-by: literally, "to God (I commend you)." [< Sp. < *a* to + *dios* God]

ad·i·po·cere (ad′ə·pō·sir′) *n.* A waxy substance formed in decomposing human or animal corpses under moist and airless conditions. [< F *adipocire* < L *adeps, adipis* fat + *cera* wax] **—ad·i·poc·er·ous** (ad′ə·pos′ər·əs) *adj.*

ad·i·pose (ad′ə·pōs) *adj.* Of or pertaining to fat; fatty. See synonyms under CORPULENT. [< NL *adiposus* < L *adeps* fat] **—ad′i·pose′ness, ad·i·pos·i·ty** (ad′ə·pos′ə·tē) *n.*

adipose tissue A type of connective tissue containing many cells specialized for storing fat.

Ad·i·ron·dack Mountains (ad′ə·ron′dak) A mountain range in NE New York; highest peak, 5,344 feet. Also **Ad′i·ron′dacks.**

ad·it (ad′it) *n.* **1** An approach; entrance; passage. **2** A nearly horizontal entrance to a mine. **3** Access; admission. See synonyms under ENTRANCE. [< L *aditus,* pp. of *adire* approach < *ad-* to + *ire* go]

ad·ja·cen·cy (ə·jā′sən·sē) *n. pl.* **·cies** That which is contiguous or adjacent; contiguity. Also **ad·ja′cence.**

ad·ja·cent (ə·jā′sənt) *adj.* Lying near or close at hand; adjoining, contiguous. [< L *adjacens, -entis,* ppr. of *adjacere* < *ad-* near + *jacere* lie] **—ad·ja′cent·ly** *adv.*

Synonyms: abutting, adjoining, attached, beside, bordering, close, conterminous, contiguous, near, neighboring, next, nigh. *Adjacent* farms may not be connected; if *adjoining,* they meet at the boundary line. *Conterminous* would imply that their dimensions were exactly equal on the side where they adjoin. *Contiguous* may be used for either *adjacent* or *adjoining. Near* is a relative word, places being called *near* upon the railroad which would elsewhere be deemed remote. *Neighboring* always implies such proximity that the inhabitants may be neighbors. *Next* views some object as the nearest of several or many. *Antonyms*: detached, disconnected, disjoined, distant, remote, separate.

adjacent angle See under ANGLE.

ad·jec·ti·val (aj′ik·tī′vəl, aj′ik·ti·vəl) *adj.* **1** Pertaining to or like an adjective. **2** Used as an adjective. —*n.* A word or group of words used as an adjective. **—ad′jec·ti′val·ly** *adv.*

ad·jec·tive (aj′ik·tiv) *n.* **1** *Gram.* A word used to limit or qualify a noun: one of the eight traditional parts of speech. **2** A dependent or corollary. —*adj.* **1** Pertaining to an adjective. **2** *Gram.* Depending upon or standing in adjunct relation to a noun. **3** Of the nature of an adjunct; dependent; procedural: *adjective* law. **4** *Chem.* Requiring the use of a mordant, as in dyeing. [< L *adjectivus* that is added < *adjicere* add to < *ad-* to + *jacere* throw] **—ad′jec·tive·ly** *adv.*

ad·join (ə·join′) *v.t.* **1** To be next to; border upon. **2** *Obs.* To join to; append; unite: with *to.* —*v.i.* **3** To lie close together; be in contact. See synonyms under ADD. [< OF *ajoindre* < L *adjungere* < *ad-* to + *jungere* join]

ad·join·ing (ə·joi′ning) *adj.* Lying next; bordering; contiguous. See synonyms under ADJACENT.

ad·journ (ə·jûrn′) *v.t.* **1** To put off to another day or place, as a meeting or session; postpone. **2** To put off to the next session, as the decision of a council. —*v.i.* **3** To postpone or suspend proceedings for a specified time: The court *adjourned* for three days. **4** *Colloq.* To move or go to another place: Shall we *adjourn* to the porch? See synonyms under PROCRASTINATE, POSTPONE. [< OF *ajorner, ajurner* < LL *adjurnare* set a day < L *ad-* to + *diurnus* daily < *dies* day]

ad·journ·ment (ə·jûrn′mənt) *n.* The act of adjourning, or the period for which anything is adjourned; postponement.

ad·judge (ə·juj′) *v.t.* **1** To determine or decide judicially, as a case. **2** To pronounce or order by law: His testimony was *adjudged* perjury. **3** To condemn or sentence: with *to*: The defendant was *adjudged* to imprisonment. **4** To award by law, as damages. **5** *Obs.* To regard or consider. [< OF *ajugier* < L *adjudicare* < *ad-* to + *judicare* judge. Doublet of ADJUDICATE.]

ad·ju·di·cate (ə·jōō′də·kāt) *v.* **·cat·ed, ·cat·ing** *v.t.* To determine judicially, as a case; adjudge. —*v.i.* To act as a judge. [< L *adjudicatus,* pp. of *adjudicare.* Doublet of ADJUDGE.] **—ad·ju′di·ca′tor** *n.*

ad·ju·di·ca·tion (ə·jōō′də·kā′shən) *n.* The act or process of adjudicating or adjudging; judicial decision.

ad·junct (aj′ungkt) *adj.* Joined subordinately; auxiliary. —*n.* **1** Something connected subordinately; an auxiliary. **2** A person associated with another person in an auxiliary or subordinate relation; a helper; associate; assistant. **3** *Gram.* A word or words added to define, limit, qualify, or modify other words. **4** *Logic* Any non-essential quality of a thing, as distinguished from its essence or substance. See synonyms under APPENDAGE, HELP. [< L *adjunctus,* pp. of *adjungere.* See ADJOIN.]

ad·junc·tive (ə·jungk′tiv) *adj.* Constituting or contributing to form an adjunct. **—ad·junc′tive·ly** *adv.*

ad·ju·ra·tion (aj′ōō·rā′shən) *n.* The act of adjuring; a solemn oath.

ad·jur·a·to·ry (ə·jōōr′ə·tôr′ē, -tō′rē) *adj.* Of, pertaining to, or containing an adjuration or command.

ad·jure (ə·jōōr′) *v.t.* **ad·jured, ad·jur·ing 1** To

charge or entreat solemnly, as under oath or penalty. 2 To appeal to earnestly. [< L *adjurare* < *ad-* to + *jurare* swear] **—ad·jur′er, ad·ju′ror** *n.*

ad·just (ə·just′) *v.t.* 1 To arrange so as to fit or match; make correspond, as to a standard. 2 To harmonize or compose, as differences. 3 To arrange in order; systematize. 4 To regulate or make accurate, as a compass. 5 To make allowance for elevation and deflection, as of a gun in firing. 6 To determine an amount to be paid, as in settling an insurance claim. *—v.i.* 7 To adapt oneself; conform, as to a new environment. See synonyms under ACCOMMODATE, ADAPT, PREPARE, REGULATE, SET, SETTLE. [< OF *ajouster* < L *ad-* to + *juxta* near; refashioned on F *juste* right < L *justus*] **—ad·just′a·ble** *adj.* **—ad·just′er, ad·jus′tor** *n.* **—ad·jus′tive** *adj.*

ad·just·ment (ə·just′mənt) *n.* 1 The act, process, means, or result of adjusting; regulation; arrangement; settlement. 2 *Mech.* **a** An instrument or means whereby something may be adjusted; that which regulates; as, the *adjustments* of a watch, telescope, or microscope. **b** A device, as a screw or wedge, for raising or adjusting a part so as to take up wear or lost motion. 4 The determining of the just amount of insurance payable for losses, as in fire or shipping; also, of the just amount payable for the failure of an article to fulfil a guarantee made of its reasonable wear and use.

ad·ju·tage (aj′ə·tij) *n.* 1 *Mech.* A tube or nozzle for the discharge of liquid, so shaped as to offer the least friction. 2 A spout or tube, as of a fountain. [< F *ajutage*, var. of *ajoutage* < *ajouter* add, join to]

ad·ju·tant (aj′ə·tənt) *n.* 1 *Mil.* A military staff officer who issues the administrative orders of a command. 2 Any of various large storks of the genus *Leptoptilus.* Also called **adjutant bird,** *marabou.* [< L *adjutans, -antis,* ppr. of *adjutare* assist, freq. of *adjuvare.* See AID.] **—ad′ju·tan·cy, ad′ju·tant·ship** *n.*

adjutant general The adjutant of a division or larger military unit. **—The Adjutant General** The officer, holding the rank of major general, in charge of the administrative branch of the United States Army.

ad·ju·vant (aj′ə·vənt) *adj.* Assisting; helpful. *—n.* 1 A helper. 2 Any substance that heightens the action of an antigen or a drug. [< L *adjuvans, -antis,* ppr. of *adjuvare.* See AID.]

Ad·ler (äd′lər), **Alfred,** 1870–1937, Austrian psychiatrist.

Ad·ler (ad′lər), **Cyrus,** 1863–1940, U.S. educator and reformer.
—**Felix,** 1851–1933, U.S. educator; founder of the Ethical Culture Society.

ad·lib (ad′lib′) *v.t.* & *v.i.* **·libbed, ·lib·bing** *Colloq.* To improvise, as words, gestures, or music not called for in the original script or score. *—adj.* Made up on the spot: *adlib* comments. *—adv.* On the spur of the moment: to dictate *adlib.* [< AD LIBITUM]

ad lib·i·tum (ad lib′ə·təm) *Latin* 1 At will; as one pleases. 2 *Music* Freely: a direction indicating that a section or passage may be omitted or varied as the performer wishes.

ad li·tem (ad lī′təm) *Latin* For the particular suit or action.

ad·man (ad′man′) *n. U.S. Colloq.* An advertising man.

ad·meas·ure (ad·mezh′ər) *v.t.* **·ured, ·ur·ing** To assign a share of or to; apportion. [< OF *amesurer* < LL *admensurare* < *ad-* to + *mensurare* MEASURE] **—ad·meas′ur·er** *n.*

ad·meas·ure·ment (ad·mezh′ər·mənt) *n.* 1 An admeasuring. 2 Measure; size; dimensions. Also **ad·men·su·ra·tion** (ad·men′shə·rā′shən).

Ad·me·tus (ad·mē′təs) In Greek mythology, a king of Thessaly, husband of Alcestis.

ad·min·i·cle (ad·min′i·kəl) *n.* 1 Anything that helps or supports; an auxiliary. 2 *Law* Corroborative or explanatory evidence. [< L *adminiculum* a prop, orig., a support for the hand < *ad-* to + *manus* hand] **—ad·mi·nic·u·lar** (ad′mə·nik′yə·lər) *adj.* **—ad′mi·nic′u·la′tion** *n.*

ad·mi·nic·u·late (ad′mə·nik′yə·lāt) *v.t.* **·lat·ed, ·lat·ing** *Law* To furnish corroborative evidence.

ad·min·is·ter (ad·min′is·tər) *v.t.* 1 To have the charge or direction of; manage. 2 To supply or provide with; apply, as medicine or treatment. 3 To inflict; mete out; dispense, as punishment or the sacraments. 4 *Law* To settle by testamentary or official appointment; act as executor of, as an estate. 5 To tender, as an oath. *—v.i.* 6 To contribute toward an end; minister: with *to.* 7 To carry out the functions of an administrator. See synonyms under EXECUTE. [< OF *aministrer* (F *administrer*) < L *administrare* minister to < *ad-* to + *ministrare* serve] **—ad·min·is·te·ri·al** (ad·min′is·tir′ē·əl) *adj.* **—ad·min·is·tra·ble** (ad·min′is·trə·bəl) *adj.*

ad·min·is·trant (ad·min′is·trənt) *adj.* Managing affairs; executive. *—n.* One who administers.

ad·min·is·trate (ad·min′is·trāt) *v.t.* **·trat·ed, ·trat·ing** To administer.

ad·min·is·tra·tion (ad·min′is·trā′shən) *n.* 1 The act of administering, or the state of being administered; management of public affairs. 2 The government as existing, or the persons collectively who compose it, especially its executive department; also, the official tenure of such government. 3 *Law* The legal management and settlement of the estate of a deceased person, as by an executor, or of a minor, lunatic, or one otherwise incompetent, as by a trustee or administrator.

ad·min·is·tra·tive (ad·min′is·trā′tiv) *adj.* Pertaining to administration; executive. **—ad·min′is·tra′tive·ly** *adv.*

ad·min·is·tra·tor (ad·min′is·trā′tər) *n.* 1 One who administers something. 2 *Law* One commissioned by a competent court to administer upon the personal property of a deceased person. [< L] **—ad·min′is·tra′tor·ship** *n.*

ad·min·is·tra·trix (ad·min′is·trā′triks) *n. pl.* **·tra·trix·es** or **·tra·tri·ces** (-trā′trə·sēz, -trə·trī′sēz) A woman administrator. Also **ad·min′is·tra′tress.**

ad·mi·ra·ble (ad′mər·ə·bəl) *adj.* 1 Worthy of admiration; excellent. 2 Wonderful; praiseworthy. See synonyms under EXCELLENT, GOOD. [< F < L *admirabilis* < *admirari.* See ADMIRE.] **—ad′mi·ra·ble·ness, ad′mi·ra·bil′i·ty** *n.* **—ad′mi·ra·bly** *adv.*

ad·mi·ral (ad′mər·əl) *n.* 1 A naval officer of the highest rank, in the United States Navy equivalent in rank to a general in the United States Army; also, loosely, a rear admiral in the United States Navy, and a rear admiral or vice admiral in other navies. 2 The flagship of a fleet. 3 Any of various showy butterflies of Europe and North America, such as the red admiral (*Vanessa atalanta*), and the white admiral (*Limenitis sybilla*). **—rear admiral** A naval officer ranking next below a vice admiral: in the United States Navy, equivalent in rank to a major general. **—vice admiral** A naval officer ranking next below an admiral: in the United States Navy, equivalent in rank to a lieutenant general. See table under GRADE. [< OF *amiral, admiral* < Arabic *amīr-al* commander of the (as in *amīr-al-bahr* commander of the sea); influenced by L *admirabilis* admirable]

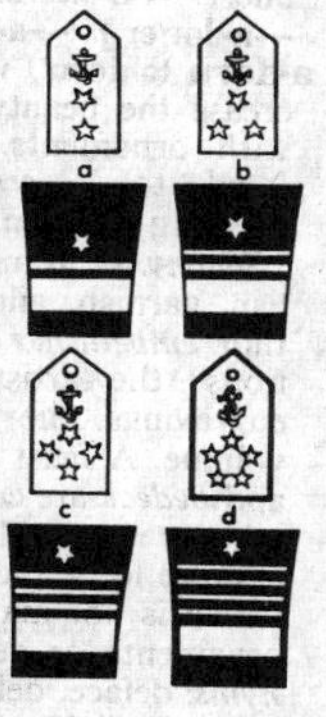

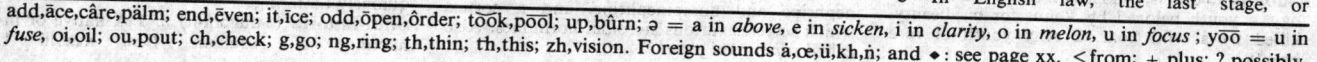

INSIGNIA—U.S.N.
a. Rear Admiral.
b. Vice Admiral.
c. Admiral.
d. Admiral of the Fleet.

Admiral of the Fleet 1 The highest rank in the United States Navy, above admiral and corresponding to General of the Army. 2 Any officer entitled to hold that rank. Also, as a form of address, *Fleet Admiral.*

ad·mi·ral·ship (ad′mər·əl·ship′) *n.* The office or rank of an admiral.

Ad·mi·ral·ty (ad′mər·əl·tē) *n. pl.* **·ties** A department of the British government having supreme charge of naval affairs; the Board of Admiralty; also the building in London which houses the Board of Admiralty.

ad·mi·ral·ty (ad′mər·əl·tē) *n.* 1 The office or functions of an admiral. 2 The branch of jurisprudence or of the judiciary that takes cognizance of maritime affairs, civil and criminal.

Admiralty Island An island of the Alexander Archipelago of SE Alaska; 1,664 square miles.

Admiralty Islands An island group in the Bismarck Archipelago; 800 square miles; capital, Lorengau, on Manus. Also **Admiralties.**

admiralty law The code or system of law and procedure relating to maritime affairs; maritime law.

Admiralty Range The mountains on the north coast of Victoria Land, Antarctica.

ad·mi·ra·tion (ad′mə·rā′shən) *n.* 1 Wonder combined with approbation in view of anything rare, great, excellent, beautiful, sublime; hence, pleased and gratified observation and contemplation. 2 That which is admired or excites pleased approval; anything marvelous or prodigious. 3 *Obs.* Wonder. See synonyms under AMAZEMENT.

ad·mire (ad·mīr′) *v.* **ad·mired, ad·mir·ing** *v.t.* 1 To regard with wonder, pleasure, and approbation. 2 To have respect or esteem for. 3 *Obs.* To wonder or marvel at. *—v.i.* 4 To feel or express admiration. 5 *U.S. Dial.* To wish or desire: with *to*: I would *admire* to go to your party. [< L *admirari* < *ad-* at + *mirari* wonder] **—ad·mir′er** *n.* **—ad·mir′ing** *adj.* **—ad·mir′ing·ly** *adv.*

Synonyms: adore, applaud, approve, enjoy, esteem, extol, honor, love, respect, revere, venerate. We *admire* beauty in nature and art, *enjoy* books or society. We *approve* what is excellent, *applaud* heroic deeds, *esteem* the good, *love* our friends. We *honor* and *respect* noble character wherever found; we *revere* and *venerate* it in the aged. We *extol* or *adore* the goodness, majesty, and power of God. *Antonyms*: abhor, abominate, contemn, despise, detest, dislike, execrate, hate, ridicule, scorn.

ad·mis·si·ble (ad·mis′ə·bəl) *adj.* 1 Such as may be admitted; allowable, as proof. 2 Worthy of being considered, as an idea. **—ad·mis′si·bil′i·ty, ad·mis′si·ble·ness** *n.* **—ad·mis′si·bly** *adv.*

ad·mis·sion (ad·mish′ən) *n.* 1 The act of admitting, or the state of being admitted; entrance. 2 A conceding, or that which is conceded; acknowledging or confessing: an *admission* of guilt. 3 The price charged or paid to be admitted; entrance fee. 4 *Rel.* A formal act, by ecclesiastical authority, admitting a candidate to a benefice or church. 5 *Mech.* **a** Entrance of steam or other motive fluid into a cylinder. **b** The point in the stroke or rotation at which such entrance takes place. **c** The period between entrance of motive force and expansion or exhaust thereof. See synonyms under BELIEF, ENTRANCE[1]. [< L *admissio, -onis* < *admissus,* pp. of *admittere.* See ADMIT.]

Admission Day A legal holiday to commemorate the admission of a State into the Union.

ad·mis·sive (ad·mis′iv) *adj.* Characterized by, tending to, implying, or granting admission. Also **ad·mis·so·ry** (ad·mis′ər·ē).

ad·mit (ad·mit′) *v.* **ad·mit·ted, ad·mit·ting** *v.t.* 1 To allow to enter; grant entrance to: to *admit* visitors to a house. 2 To be the means or channel of admission to; let in: This key will *admit* you. 3 To have room for; contain: The port *admits* only two ships at once. 4 To leave room for; permit: His impatience *admits* no delay. 5 To concede or grant, as the truth of an argument. 6 To acknowledge or avow: He *admitted* his part in the conspiracy. 7 To allow to join or become associated with; consider as entitled to the privileges of: to *admit* a person to the bar as an attorney. *—v.i.* 8 To give scope or warrant: with *of*: This problem *admits* of several solutions. 9 To afford entrance; open on: with *to*: This gate *admits* to the garden. [< L *admittere* < *ad-* to + *mittere* send, let go] **—ad·mit′ta·ble, ad·mit′ti·ble** *adj.*

ad·mit·tance (ad·mit′ns) *n.* 1 The act of admitting, or the state or fact of being admitted; entrance; right or permission to enter; actual entrance; admission. 2 *Electr.* The reciprocal of the impedance of an alternating-current circuit. 3 In English law, the last stage, or

perfection, of copyhold assurances of title. See synonyms under ACCESS, ENTRANCE[1].

ad·mit·ta·tur (ad'mi·tā'tər) n. A certificate of admission granted by some colleges. [< L, let him be admitted]

ad·mit·ted (ad·mit'id) adj. Accepted as valid or true; acknowledged; conceded. See synonyms under AUTHENTIC.

ad·mit·ted·ly (ad·mit'id·lē) adv. Confessedly.

ad·mix (ad·miks') v.t. **ad·mixed** or **ad·mixt**, **ad·mix·ing** To mingle or mix with something else. [Back formation from ME admixt mixed with < L admixtus, pp. of admiscere < ad- to + miscere mix]

ad·mix·ture (ad·miks'chər) n. **1** That which is formed by admixing; a mixture. **2** The ingredient added to the principal substance in forming a mixture. **3** The act of mingling or mixing, or the state of being mixed. See synonyms under ALLOY. [< L admixtus, pp. of admiscere mix with. See ADMIX.]

ad·mon·ish (ad·mon'ish) v.t. **1** To advise of a fault; administer mild reproof to. **2** To caution against danger or error; warn, as of something to be avoided: The gallows admonished the citizens against a life of crime. **3** To charge authoritatively; exhort; urge: He admonished me to follow him. [< OF amonester < LL admonestare < L admonere < ad- to + monere warn] —**ad·mon'ish·er** n.

ad·mo·ni·tion (ad'mə·nish'ən) n. The act of admonishing; gentle reproof. Also **ad·mon'ish·ment**. [< L admonitio, -onis < admonere. See ADMONISH.]

ad·mon·i·tor (ad·mon'ə·tər) n. One who admonishes; a monitor. [< L]

ad·mon·i·to·ry (ad·mon'ə·tôr'ē, -tō'rē) adj. Giving admonition. Also **ad·mon'i·tive**.

ad·nate (ad'nāt) adj. Biol. Grown together; fused: said esp. of unlike parts not typically joined, as the calyx and ovary of a flower. [< L adnatus, pp. of adnasci. See ADNASCENT.] —**ad·na'tion** n.

ad nau·se·am (ad nô'shē·am, -sē-) Latin To the degree of disgust; so as to nauseate or produce disgust.

ad·nex·a (ad·nek'sə) n. pl. Anat. The structures accessory to a main organ or part, as the eyelids and lacrimal glands that serve the eyeball. —**ad·nex'al** adj.

ad·noun (ad'noun') n. Gram. An adjective; especially, an adjective used as a noun. [< AD- + NOUN; modeled on adverb] —**ad·nom·i·nal** (ad·nom'ə·nəl) adj.

a·do (ə·dōō') n. Unnecessary activity; bustle; fuss; trouble. [ME at do, northern dial. form for the infinitive to do]

a·do·be (ə·dō'bē) n. **1** A sun-dried brick or a structure of such material. **2** The mixed earth or sandy, calcareous clay of which such bricks are made. **3** A brick of clay material with which pulverized ore may be combined. **4** U.S. Dial. A Mexican silver dollar. —adj. Composed of adobe: often used figuratively to denote things made in Mexico. [< Sp. < Arabic at-tub brick]

adobe flat Geol. A smooth, gently sloping, and usually narrow plain composed of clay deposited by an ephemeral stream.

ad·o·les·cence (ad'ə·les'əns) n. **1** The process of growing up. **2** The state or period of growth from the onset of puberty to the stage of adult development. Also **ad'o·les'cen·cy**.

ad·o·les·cent (ad'ə·les'ənt) adj. **1** Approaching adult development. **2** Characteristic of or pertaining to youth. —n. A person in the period of adolescence. [< L adolescens, -entis, ppr. of adolescere grow up. See ADULT.]

Ad·olph (ad'olf, ā'dolf) A masculine personal name. Also Dan., Du., Ger. **A·dolf** (ä'dôlf), Fr. **A·dolphe** (à·dôlf'), Ital., Sp. **A·dol·fo** (ä·dôl'fō), Pg. **A·dol·pho** (ä·dôl'fō), Lat. **A·dol·phus** (ə·dol'fəs). [< OHG, noble wolf]

A·do·na·i (ä'dō·nā'ī, -nī') In the Old Testament, Lord: a name for God. [< Hebrew, my Lord]

A·don·ic (ə·don'ik) adj. **1** Pertaining to Adonis. **2** In prosody, designating a verse consisting of a dactyl and a spondee, supposedly first used in laments for Adonis. —n. An Adonic verse.

A·don·is (ə·don'is, ə·dō'nis) **1** In Greek mythology, a youth beloved by Venus for his beauty: killed by a wild boar. **2** Any youth of rare beauty.

a·dopt (ə·dopt') v.t. **1** To take into a new relationship; accept and treat as a member of one's family. **2** To take into one's family or as one's child by legal measures. **3** To take and follow as one's own, as a course of action. **4** To take up from someone else and use as one's own, as a phrase, practice, or creed. **5** To vote to accept, as a motion or committee report See synonyms under EMBRACE. [< F adopter < L adoptare < ad- to + optare choose] —**a·dopt'er** n.

a·dopt·ee (ə·dop'tē') n. One who is adopted.

a·dop·tion (ə·dop'shən) n. **1** The act of adopting, or the condition of being adopted. **2** The legal act whereby an adult person takes a minor into the relation of a child. **3** The acceptance of a word unchanged in form from a foreign language. **4** The receiving into a clan or tribe of one from outside, and treating him as one of the same blood.

A·dop·tion·ist (ə·dop'shən·ist) n. One of a Spanish sect (8th century) maintaining that Christ was the son of God by adoption only. Also **A·dop'tian·ist**. —**A·dop'tion·ism** n.

a·dop·tive (ə·dop'tiv) adj. Pertaining or tending to adoption; characterized by adoption. —**a·dop'tive·ly** adv.

a·dor·a·ble (ə·dôr'ə·bəl, ə·dōr'-) adj. **1** Worthy of adoration. **2** Worthy of or calling forth devoted affection or attachment. —**a·dor·a·bil'i·ty**, **a·dor'a·ble·ness** n. —**a·dor'a·bly** adv.

ad·o·ra·tion (ad'ə·rā'shən) n. **1** The act of adoring; worship of God or reverence of the divine. **2** An emotion composed of profound admiration, utmost love, and devotion. **3** Formerly, a method of electing a pope by an act of homage from two thirds of the cardinals present, now, the homage given by the cardinals after his election. **4** A representation of homage to or worship of a person or object, especially of a divine person, as the infant Jesus. See synonyms under PRAYER, REVERENCE, VENERATION. [< F < L adoratio, -onis < adorare. See ADORE.]

a·dore (ə·dôr', ə·dōr') v. **a·dored**, **a·dor·ing** v.t. **1** To render divine honor to; worship as divine. **2** To love or honor with intense devotion. **3** Colloq. To like especially. —v.i. **4** To worship. See synonyms under ADMIRE, PRAISE, VENERATE. [< F adorer < L adorare < ad- to + orare speak, pray] —**a·dor'er** n. —**a·dor'ing** adj.

a·dorn (ə·dôrn') v.t. **1** To be an ornament to; increase the beauty of. **2** To furnish or decorate with ornaments. [< F adorner < L adornare < ad- to + ornare furnish, deck out] —**a·dorn'ing** adj. & n. —**a·dorn'ment** n.

Synonyms: beautify, bedeck, decorate, embellish, garnish, gild, illustrate, ornament. An author embellishes his narrative with fine descriptions, the artist illustrates it with beautiful engravings, the binder glids and decorates the volume. A feast is garnished with flowers. Deck and bedeck are commonly said of apparel. To ornament is to add outward embellishment. Adorn is more lofty and spiritual, referring to a beauty which is not material and cannot be put on by ornaments or decorations. See GARNISH. Antonyms: deface, deform, disfigure, mar, spoil.

A·do·wa (ä'dō·wä) See ADUWA.

a·down (ə·doun') adv. & prep. Archaic & Poetic Downward; down. [OE of dune off the hill]

ADP Symbol for adenosine diphosphate.

ad pa·tres (ad pā'trēz) Latin Dead; literally, to his fathers.

ad·press (ad·pres') v.t. To press close to. [< L adpressus, pp. of adprimere < ad- to + premere press]

ad quem (ad kwem') Latin At or to which.

A·dras·tus (ə·dras'təs) In Greek legend, a king of Argos who led the Seven against Thebes, of whom he was the only survivor. See SEVEN AGAINST THEBES.

ad ref·er·en·dum (ad ref'ə·ren'dəm) Latin For further consideration.

ad rem (ad rem') Latin To the point; direct; pertinent.

ad·re·nal (ə·drē'nəl) adj. **1** Near the kidneys. **2** Of or from the adrenal glands. —n. Either of the adrenal glands. [< AD- + L renes kidneys]

adrenal gland Either of the two endocrine glands located on the upper end of each kidney and consisting of a medulla, which secretes epinephrine and norepinephrine, and a cortex, which secretes various steroidal hormones. Also called suprarenal gland.

ad·ren·a·lin (ə·dren'ə·lin) n. **1** Brit. Epinephrine. **2** An internal stimulant popularly adduced as the initiator of energetic reactions to danger, challenge, etc. Also **ad·ren·a·line**.

Ad·ren·a·lin (ə·dren'ə·lin) Proprietary name for a pharmaceutical preparation of epinephrine.

ad·ren·er·gic (ad'rə·nėr'gik) adj. **1** Having chemical activity similar to that of epinephrine or related substances. **2** Stimulating the release of epinephrine or similar hormones.

ad·re·no·cor·ti·cal (ə·drē'nō·kôr'tə·kəl) adj. Pertaining to or secreted by the cortex of the adrenal gland.

ad·re·no·cor·ti·co·tro·pic (ə·drē'nō·kôr'ti·kō·trō'pik) adj. Acting upon the cortex of the adrenal gland. Also **adrenocorticotrophic**.

adrenocorticotropic hormone ACTH.

A·dri·an (ā'drē·ən) **1** A masculine personal name. Also Fr. **A·dri·en** (à·drē·aṅ'), Ital. **A·dri·a·no** (ä'drē·ä'nō), Lat. **A·dri·a·nus** (ä'drē·ä'nəs). **2** Appellation of six popes. [< L] —Adrian See HADRIAN.
—Adrian IV, 1100?–59, real name Nicholas Breakspear, pope 1154–59; the only English pope.

A·dri·a·no·ple (ā'drē·ə·nō'pəl) A city of European Turkey: ancient Uskudama and Hadrianopolis: also Edirne.

A·dri·at·ic (ā'drē·at'ik) adj. Of or pertaining to the Adriatic Sea or to the inhabitants of its coastal regions.

Adriatic race See DINARIC RACE.

Adriatic Sea An arm of the Mediterranean Sea, east of Italy; 500 miles long.

a·drift (ə·drift') adv. & adj. In a drifting state; drifting.

a·droit (ə·droit') adj. Skilful in emergencies; dexterous; expert. See synonyms under CLEVER. [< F à to (< L ad-) + droit right < L directus] —**a·droit'ly** adv. —**a·droit'ness** n.

à droite (à drwàt') French To, toward, or on the right.

ad·sci·ti·tious (ad'sə·tish'əs) adj. Supplemental; adventitious; added from without; not essential. [< L adscitus, pp. of adsciscere admit, accept < ad- to + sciscere acknowledge]

ad·script (ad'skript) adj. Written after: distinguished from subscript. [< L adscriptus, pp. of adscribere, ascribere. See ASCRIBE.] —**ad·scrip'tion** n.

ad·sorb (ad·sôrb', -zôrb') v.t. Chem. To condense and hold by adsorption: distinguished from absorb. [< AD- + L sorbere suck in] —**ad·sor'bent** n.

ad·sor·bate (ad·sôr'bāt, -zôr'-) n. A substance which has been or is being adsorbed.

ad·sorp·tion (ad·sôrp'shən, -zôrp'-) n. The retention of molecules or ions of a gas or liquid on the surface of a different substance. [< ADSORB; modeled on absorption] —**ad·sorp'tive** adj.

ad·su·ki bean (ad·sōō'kē, -zōō'-) **1** A leguminous plant (Phaseolus angularis) widely cultivated in the orient. **2** The edible seed of this plant. Also **adzuki bean**. [< Japanese adzuki]

ad·sum (ad'sum) Latin I am present: an answer to a roll call.

ad sum·mum (ad sum'əm) Latin To the highest point or amount.

ad·u·la·res·cence (aj'ə·lə·res'əns) n. The peculiar sheen of the ordinary moonstone. [< ADULARIA + -ESCENCE]

ad·u·lar·i·a (aj'ə·lâr'ē·ə) n. Mineral. A transparent or translucent form of orthoclase; moonstone. [from Mt. Adula, in Switzerland]

ad·u·late (aj'ə·lāt) v.t. **·lat·ed**, **·lat·ing** To flatter servilely; praise extravagantly. [< L adulatus, pp. of adulari fawn] —**ad'u·la'tor** n.

ad·u·la·tion (aj'ə·lā'shən) n. Servile flattery; extravagant and hypocritical praise; fulsome compliment.

ad·u·la·to·ry (aj'ə·lə·tôr'ē, -tō'rē) adj. Obsequiously flattering.

A·dul·lam·ite (ə·dul'əm·it) n. **1** A native or inhabitant of Adullam. Gen. xxxviii 1.

2 In English history, a seceder (1866) from the Liberal party. Compare I *Sam.* xxii 1, 2.

a·dult (ə·dult′, ad′ult) *n.* **1** A person who has attained the age of maturity or legal majority. **2** *Biol.* A fully developed animal or plant. —*adj.* **1** Grown-up; full-grown: an *adult* person. **2** Of or for grown-up persons: *adult* behavior, *adult* education. [< L *adultus,* pp. of *adolescere* grow up < *ad-* to + *alescere* grow. Related to ADOLESCENT.] **—a·dult′ness** *n.*

a·dul·ter·ant (ə·dul′tər·ənt) *n.* An adulterating substance. See synonyms under ALLOY.

a·dul·ter·ate (ə·dul′tər·āt) *v.t.* **·at·ed, ·at·ing** To make impure or inferior by admixture of other or baser ingredients; corrupt. —*adj.* (ə·dul′tər·it) **1** Adulterated; corrupted; debased; spurious. **2** Adulterous. [< L *adulteratus,* pp. of *adulterare* corrupt < *ad-* to + *alter* other, different] — **a·dul′ter·a′tion** *n.* **—a·dul′ter·a′tor** *n.*

a·dul·ter·ine (ə·dul′tər·in, -īn) *adj.* **1** Originating in, or pertaining to, adultery: *adulterine* children. **2** Unauthorized; spurious.

a·dul·ter·ous (ə·dul′tər·əs) *adj.* Of, pertaining to, or given to adultery; illicit. **—a·dul′·ter·ous·ly** *adv.*

a·dul·ter·y (ə·dul′tər·ē) *n. pl.* **·ter·ies 1** The sexual intercourse of two persons, either of whom is married to a third person; unchastity; unfaithfulness. **2** Any lewdness or unchastity of act or thought, as in violation of the divine commandments. *Matt.* v 27, 28. **3** *Eccl.* A marriage not approved by ecclesiastical authority. [< L *adulterium*] **—a·dul′ter·er** *n.* **—a·dul′ter·ess** *n. fem.*

a·dult·hood (ə·dult′hŏŏd) *n.* The state of being an adult.

ad·um·bral (ad·um′brəl) *adj.* Overshadowing; shady.

ad·um·brant (ad·um′brənt) *adj.* Dimly shadowing.

ad·um·brate (ad·um′brāt) *v.t.* **·brat·ed, ·brat·ing 1** To represent the mere shadow of; to outline sketchily. **2** To foreshadow; prefigure. **3** To shade or overshadow; darken. [< L *adumbratus,* pp. of *adumbrare* < *ad-* to + *umbrare* shade < *umbra* shade]

ad·um·bra·tion (ad′əm·brā′shən) *n.* **1** A slight sketch. **2** A foreshadowing. **3** An overshadowing; obscuration.

ad·um·bra·tive (ad·um′brə·tiv) *adj.* Faintly indicative.

a·dust (ə·dust′) *adj.* **1** Burning; hot; seared. **2** Browned; sunburnt. **3** Parched and dry; formerly said of the body or blood. **4** Melancholy; gloomy. [< L *adustus,* pp. of *adurere* burn up < *ad-* to + *urere* burn]

A·du·wa (ä′dŏŏ·wä) A town in Eritrea: also *Adowa. Italian* **A·du·a** (ä′dŏŏ·ä).

ad va·lo·rem (ad və·lôr′əm, -lō′rəm) According or in proportion to the value: *Ad valorem* duties are based on a percentage of the value of the goods imported. [< L]

ad·vance (ad·vans′, -väns′) *v.* **ad·vanced, ad·vanc·ing** *v.t.* **1** To cause to go forward or upward; move forward in position or place. **2** To put in a better or more advantageous situation. **3** To further; promote: to *advance* the progress of science. **4** To make occur earlier; accelerate. **5** To offer; propose: to *advance* a suggestion. **6** To raise in rate or price: to *advance* a discount to five per cent. **7** To pay, as money or interest, before legally due. **8** To lend: Can you *advance* me some money? **9** *Law* To provide, as financial support, for children, especially before the distribution of an estate. —*v.i.* **10** To move or go forward: The armies *advance* on all fronts. **11** To make progress; rise or improve: The stock market *advanced* three points. See synonyms under ACCELERATE, AMEND, FLOURISH, INCREASE, PROMOTE, SERVE. —*adj.* Of, pertaining to, or being an advance; being before in time or place: an *advance* payment. —*n.* **1** The act of advancing, or the state of being advanced; forward movement; progress; improvement; also, an increase or rise, as of prices. **2** One who or that which is at the head; the foremost part. **3** Anything supplied or paid beforehand; also, the act of so supplying or paying. **4** An act of personal approach; overture; proposal: His *advances* were rejected. **5** The place at the front, or in the lead. **6** *Naut.* The distance made by a vessel in the line of a previous course after putting down the helm, as for a tack: distinguished from *transfer.* **7** In fencing, a swift, short step forward with the right foot, promptly followed by the left, in such a manner as to enable the fencer to retain his balance and be in readiness for parry, etc. See synonyms under PROGRESS. [ME *avancen* < OF *avancier* < L *ab-* away + *ante* before; the initial *a-* was later altered to *ad-* as if from L *ad-* to, toward] **—in advance 1** In front. **2** Before due; beforehand. **—ad·vanc′er** *n.*

ad·vanced (ad·vanst′, -vänst′) *adj.* **1** Being ranged at the front, or in advance of others, as in progress or thought: *advanced* ideas. **2** Having arrived at a somewhat late or forward stage, as of life, time, etc.: an *advanced* age.

Advanced Flying School A special school of the United States Air Force in which the pilots and crews of military aircraft are instructed and trained.

advanced standing Credit allowed a student by one college for courses taken at another.

advance guard A detachment of troops marching ahead of the main body to insure its security and progress, and to locate the main body of enemy troops.

ad·vance·ment (ad·vans′mənt, -väns′-) *n.* **1** The act of advancing, or the state of being advanced; progression; furtherance; promotion; preferment; uplift: the *advancement* of knowledge. **2** A payment of money before it is due.

advance post One of the positions of a detachment of troops in advance of the main body, occupied for its security, from which information about the enemy is sent back to headquarters.

advance signal A signal, in the block system, indicating that a train may pass a block even when the entire block is not clear.

ad·vanc·ing (ad·vans′ing, -väns′-) *adj.* Forward-moving; increasing; progressive. **—ad·vanc′ing·ly** *adv.*

ad·van·tage (ad·van′tij, -vän′-) *n.* **1** Anything favorable to success; superiority; favoring circumstance. **2** Gain or benefit; profit. See synonyms under PROFIT, RIGHT, UTILITY, VICTORY. **—to advantage** So as to reveal the best of or bring about the best results. —*v.t.* **·taged, ·tag·ing** To give advantage or profit to; be a benefit or service to. [< OF *avantage* < *avant* before < L *ab ante* from before. See ADVANCE.]

ad·van·ta·geous (ad′vən·tā′jəs) *adj.* Affording advantage; profitable; favorable; beneficial. See synonyms under EXPEDIENT, GOOD. — **ad′van·ta′geous·ly** *adv.* **—ad′van·ta′geous·ness** *n.*

ad·vec·tion (ad·vek′shən) *n. Meteorol.* Heat-transference by the horizontal motion of air currents. [< L *advectio, -onis* < *advehere* convey < *ad-* to + *vehere* carry]

ad·vent (ad′vent) *n.* A coming or arrival, as of any important event or person. [< L *adventus,* pp. of *advenire* < *ad-* to + *venire* come]

Ad·vent (ad′vent) *n.* **1** The birth of Christ. **2** The second coming of Christ. **3** The season including the four Sundays before Christmas.

Ad·vent·ist (ad′ven·tist, ad·ven′-) *n.* One who believes in the second coming of Christ, the Last Judgment, and the imminent end of the world: the term is now applied to a member of any of the following sects, all descended from the church founded by William Miller: **Advent Christian Church, Seventh-Day Adventists, Church of God (Adventist), Life and Advent Union.** See MILLERITE. **—Ad′vent·ism** *n.*

ad·ven·ti·ti·a (ad′ven·tish′ē·ə) *n.* The outermost covering of an organ or a blood vessel, composed of extrinsic connective tissue. **—ad′ven·ti′tial** *adj.*

ad·ven·ti·tious (ad′ven·tish′əs) *adj.* **1** Not inherent; extrinsic; accidental; casual. **2** Accidental; acquired, not inherited. **3** *Biol.* **a** Occurring in an unusual location: an *adventitious* root. **b** Adventitial. **c** Adventive. [< L *adventicius* coming from abroad, foreign. See ADVENT.] **—ad′ven·ti′tious·ly** *adv.* **—ad′ven·ti′tious·ness** *n.*

ad·ven·tive (ad·ven′tiv) *adj. Biol.* Exotic; not firmly established in a new environment. —*n.* An adventive organism.

Advent Sunday The Sunday nearest to St. Andrew's Day, the last day of November.

ad·ven·ture (ad·ven′chər) *v.* **·tured, ·tur·ing** *v.t.* **1** To venture upon; take the chance of. **2** To risk the loss of; imperil. —*v.i.* **3** To run risks. **4** To venture upon daring or dangerous undertakings. —*n.* **1** A hazardous or exciting experience; daring feat. **2** A commercial venture; speculation. **3** *Obs.* Danger; hazard; chance; fortune. See synonyms under ACCIDENT. [< OF *aventure* < L *adventura (res)* (a thing) about to happen < *advenire.* See ADVENT.]

ad·ven·tur·er (ad·ven′chər·ər) *n.* A seeker of adventures or fortune in new fields or by questionable means.

ad·ven·tur·ess (ad·ven′chər·is) *n.* **1** A woman adventurer. **2** A woman who attempts to gain wealth or social position by unscrupulous or equivocal means.

ad·ven·tur·ous (ad·ven′chər·əs) *adj.* **1** Disposed to seek adventures or take risks; venturesome. Also **ad·ven′ture·some** (-səm). **2** Attended with risk; hazardous. See synonyms under BRAVE. — **ad·ven′tur·ous·ly** *adv.* **—ad·ven′tur·ous·ness** *n.*

ad·verb (ad′vûrb) *n.* **1** Any of a class of words used to modify the meaning of a verb, adjective, or other adverb, in regard to time, place, manner, means, cause, degree, etc.: one of the eight traditional parts of speech. **2** Any word or phrase having this function. [< L *adverbium* < *ad-* to + *verbum* verb]

ad·ver·bi·al (ad·vûr′bē·əl) *adj.* Of, pertaining to, containing, used like an adverb, or tending to use adverbs. **—ad·ver·bi·al·i·ty** (ad·vûr′bē·al′ə·tē) *n.* **—ad·ver′bi·al·ly** *adv.*

ad·ver·sar·y (ad′vər·ser′ē) *n. pl.* **·sar·ies** One actively hostile; an opponent; enemy. See synonyms under ANTAGONIST, ENEMY. **—the Adversary** Satan. [< L *adversarius,* lit., one turned towards < *adversus.* See ADVERSE.]

ad·ver·sa·tive (ad·vûr′sə·tiv) *adj.* Expressing opposition or antithesis. —*n.* An antithetic word or proposition. **—ad·ver′sa·tive·ly** *adv.*

ad·verse (ad·vûrs′, ad′vûrs) *adj.* **1** Opposing or opposed; antagonistic; also, unpropitious; detrimental. **2** *Bot.* Turned toward the stem or main axis. **3** Opposite. See synonyms under INIMICAL. [< L *adversus* turned against, pp. of *advertere* < *ad-* to + *vertere* turn] **—ad·verse′ly** *adv.* — **ad·verse′ness** *n.*

ad·ver·si·ty (ad·vûr′sə·tē) *n. pl.* **·ties** A condition of hardship or affliction; misfortune; calamity. See synonyms under CATASTROPHE, MISFORTUNE. [< OF *aversite* < L *adversitas* < *adversus.* See ADVERSE.]

ad·vert (ad·vûrt′) *v.i.* To turn the attention; take notice; refer: with *to.* See synonyms under ALLUDE. [< L *advertere* < *ad-* to + *vertere* turn] — **ad·ver′tence, ad·ver′ten·cy** *n.*

ad·ver·tent (ad·vûr′tənt) *adj.* Giving attention; heedful. **—ad·ver′tent·ly** *adv.*

ad·ver·tise (ad′vər·tīz, ad′vər·tīz′) *v.* **·tised, ·tis·ing** *v.t.* **1** To make known by public notice; to proclaim the qualities of, as by publication or broadcasting, generally in order to sell. **2** *Obs.* To notify or warn. —*v.i.* **3** To inquire by public notice, as in a newspaper: with *for:* to *advertise* for a house. **4** To distribute or publish advertisements: The company *advertised* widely in national magazines. See synonyms under ANNOUNCE, INFORM, PUBLISH. Also **ad′ver·tize.** [< MF *advertiss-,* stem of *advertir* warn, give notice to < L *advertere.* See ADVERT.] — **ad′ver·tis′er** *n.*

ad·ver·tise·ment (ad′vər·tīz′mənt, ad·vûr′tis·mənt, -tiz-) *n.* **1** A public notice, as in a newspaper or on a radio or television program. **2** A giving notice; notification; information. Also **ad′ver·tize′ment.**

ad·ver·tis·ing (ad′vər·tī′zing) *n.* **1** Any system or method of attracting public notice to an event to be attended, or the desirability of commercial products for sale; promotion; also, advertisements collectively. **2** The business of writing and publicizing advertisements; promoting. Also **ad′ver·tiz′ing.**

add,āce,câre,pälm; end,ēven; it,īce; odd,ōpen,ôrder; tŏŏk,pōōl; up,bûrn; ə = a in *above,* e in *sicken,* i in *clarity,* o in *melon,* u in *focus* ; yōō = u in *fuse,* oi,oil; ou,pout; ch,check; g,go; ng,ring; th,thin; t͟h,this; zh,vision. Foreign sounds à,œ,ü,kh,ṅ; and ◆: see page xx. < from; + plus; ? possibly.

advertising man A man whose business is advertising.

ad·ver·tor·i·al (ad-vər-tôr′ē-əl; -tō′rē-) n. An editorial that includes elements of a commercial advertising message. [Blend of ADVERT(ISING) + (EDIT)ORIAL]

ad·vice (ad-vīs′) n. 1 Encouragement or dissuasion; counsel; suggestion. 2 Often pl. Information; notification. 3 Obs. Deliberation; forethought; hence, opinion. See synonyms under COUNSEL. [< OF avis view, opinion < L ad- to + visum, pp. of videre see]

ad·vis·a·ble (ad-vī′zə-bəl) adj. Proper to be advised or recommended; expedient. —**ad·vis′a·bil′i·ty**, **ad·vis′a·ble·ness** n. —**ad·vis′a·bly** adv.

ad·vise (ad-vīz′) v. **ad·vised**, **ad·vis·ing** v.t. 1 To give advice to; counsel. 2 To recommend: to advise a course of action. 3 To notify; inform, as of a transaction. 4 Obs. To consider; observe. — v.i. 5 To take counsel: with with: He advised with his lawyer. 6 To give advice. See synonyms under ADMONISH, INFORM¹. [< OF aviser < avis. See ADVICE.]

ad·vised (ad-vīzd′) adj. 1 Done with advice or counsel, or with deliberation and forethought; intended; deliberate; prudent. 2 Counseled. 3 Informed. See synonyms under CONSCIOUS.

ad·vis·ed·ly (ad-vī′zid-lē) adv. With forethought or advice; not hastily.

ad·vis·ee (ad-vī′zē, ad′vī-zē′) n. 1 One who is advised. 2 A student assigned to an advisor.

ad·vise·ment (ad-vīz′mənt) n. Consultation; deliberation.

ad·vis·er (ad-vī′zər) n. One who advises; specifically, a teacher in a school or college to whom certain students are assigned for periodic counsel. Also **ad·vi′sor**.

ad·vi·so·ry (ad-vī′zər-ē) adj. Having power to advise; containing or given as advice; not mandatory. —n. 1 A bulletin or report that advises about certain developments: a weather advisory. 2 A recommendation.

ad·vo·ca·cy (ad′və-kə-sē) n. The act of advocating or pleading a cause; a vindication; defense.

advocacy journalism Journalism that promotes a certain point of view, especially in news articles.

ad·vo·cate (ad′və-kāt) v.t. **·cat·ed**, **·cat·ing** To speak or write in favor of; defend; recommend. [< n.] —n. (ad′və-kit, -kāt) One who pleads the cause of another; an intercessor; defender; counselor. See synonyms under PLEAD. [< OF avocat < L advocatus one summoned to another < advocare < ad- to + vocare call] —**ad′vo·ca′tor** n. —**ad·voc·a·to·ry** (ad-vok′ə-tôr′ē, -tō′rē) adj.

ad·vo·ca·tion (ad′və-kā′shən) n. 1 A process in Scots law by which an action may be transferred from an inferior to a superior court without final judgment in the former. 2 Pleading; advocacy.

ad·vo·ca·tus di·ab·o·li (ad′və-kā′təs dī-ab′ə-lī) Latin The devil's advocate.

ad·vow·son (ad-vou′zən) n. In English law, the right of presentation to a vacant ecclesiastical benefice; patronage. [< OF avoeson < L advocatio. See ADVOCATE.]

ad·wom·an (ad′woom′ən) n. pl. **·wom·en** U.S. Colloq. A woman whose business is advertising; an advertising woman.

ad·y·na·mi·a (ad′ə-nā′mē-ə) n. Pathol. Lack of physical strength, resulting from disease. [< NL < Gk. a- without + dynamis strength]

ad·y·tum (ad′ə-təm) n. pl. **·ta** (-tə) 1 An inner or secret shrine in some ancient places of worship. 2 Hence, a sanctum. [< L < Gk. adyton, neut. of adytos not to be entered < a- no + dyein enter]

adze (adz) n. A hand cutting tool having its blade at right angles with its handle and usually curved: used for dressing timber, etc. —v.t. **adzed**, **adz·ing** To hew or dress with an adze. Also **adz**. [OE adesa]

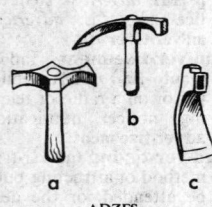

ADZES
a. Sculptor's.   b. Cooper's.   c. Carpenter's.

A·dzhar Autonomous Soviet Socialist Republic (ə-jär′, ä′jä-ristan) An administrative division of SW Georgian S.S.R.; 1,100 square miles; capital, Batum. Also **A·dzha·ri·stan** (ə-jä′ri-stan).

ad·zu·ki bean (ad-zōō′kē) See ADSUKI BEAN.

ae (ā) adj. Scot. One.

ae- For words not found here, see under E-.

æ 1 A digraph of Latin origin, equivalent to Greek ai: sometimes retained in the spelling of Greek and Latin proper names and used in certain scientific terms. 2 A digraph in Old English, symbolizing the sound of a in hat. Also printed as **ae**.

Æ Pen name of George William Russell, 1867–1935, Irish poet and artist. Also **A. E.**

Ae·a·cus (ē′ə-kəs) In Greek mythology, a son of Zeus and king of Aegina who ruled so justly that after his death he was made a judge in Hades. Also **Æ′a·cus**.

Ae·ae·a (ē-ē′ə) A legendary island between Italy and Sicily, mentioned in the Odyssey as the home of Circe. Also **Æ·æ′a**. — **Ae·ae′an** adj.

ae·ci·al stage (ē′shē-əl) The phase in the life stage of certain rust fungi in which aecia (spores) are formed.

ae·cid·i·um (ē-sid′ē-əm) n. pl. **·i·a** (-ē-ə) Bot. An aecium. [< NL < Gk. aikia injury] —**ae·cid′i·al** adj.

ae·ci·um (ē′sē-əm) n. Bot. The sorus developed from the haploid mycelium of certain rust fungi (Uridinales) and usually bearing spores in a chainlike formation. —**ae′ci·al** adj. [< NL < Gk. aikia injury]

a·e·des (ā-ē′dēz) n. Any of a genus (Aëdes) of mosquitoes which includes species that are vectors for yellow fever, dengue, and other diseases. [< NL < Gk. aēdēs unpleasant < a- not + hēdys sweet] —**a·e·dine** adj.

ae·dile (ē′dīl) n. A magistrate of ancient Rome who had charge of public lands, buildings, public spectacles, etc.: also spelled **edile**. Also **æ′dile**. [< L ædilis < ædes building] —**ae·dile·ship** n.

Ae·e·tes (ē-ē′tēz) In Greek mythology, king of Colchis; father of Medea and possessor of the Golden Fleece. Also **Æ·e′tes**.

Ae·ga·di·an Islands (ē-gā′dē-ən) The Egadi Islands. Also **Æ·ga′di·an; Ae·ga′de·an, Æ·.**

Ae·ga·tes (ē-gā′tēz) The Egadi Islands. Also **Æ·ga′tes.**

Ae·ge·an (i-jē′ən) adj. Of or pertaining to the Aegean Islands or the Aegean Sea; specifically, of or pertaining to the ancient civilization of this region: also Egean. Also **Æ·ge′an**.

Aegean Islands The islands of Asia Minor north of the Dodecanese Islands, comprising an administrative division of Greece; 1,506 square miles; capital, Mytilene, on Lesbos.

Aegean Sea An arm of the Mediterranean Sea between Greece and Asia Minor.

Ae·geus (ē′jōōs, ē′jē-əs) In Greek mythology, a king of Athens, father of Theseus. Also **Æ′geus**.

Ae·gid·i·us (ē-jid′ē-əs) Latin form of GILES. Also **Æ·gid′i·us**.

Ae·gi·na (ē-jī′nə) An island and its chief town in the Saronic Gulf (also **Gulf of Aegina**) of the Aegean Sea off eastern central Greece. Also **Æ·gi′na**. —**Ae·gi·ne·tan** (ē′jə-nē′tən) adj. & n.

Aegina marbles or **sculptures** A collection of sculptures the most important of which originally decorated the pediments of the temple of Aphaea, on the island of Aegina, built about 475 B.C. They were discovered in 1811.

Æ·gir (ē′jər, ā′jər) The Norse god of the sea. Also **Æ′ger**. [< ON]

ae·gis (ē′jis) n. 1 In Greek mythology, an attribute of Zeus used in various forms by several other gods, as Athena's goatskin cloak bearing Medusa's head. 2 Any shield or defensive armor. 3 A protecting influence or power; sponsorship: also spelled egis. Also **æ′gis**.

Ae·gis·thus (ē-jis′thəs) In Greek legend, the lover of Clytemnestra and her accomplice in the murder of Agamemnon. Also **Æ·gis′thus**.

Ae·gle (ē′glē) One of the Hesperides. Also **Æ′gle**.

Ae·gos·pot·a·mi (ē′gəs-pot′ə·mī) A river in ancient Thrace flowing into the Hellespont: at its mouth the Spartans destroyed the Athenian fleet (405 B.C.), resulting in the end of the Peloponnesian War. jl Also **Æ′gos·pot′a·mi; Ae′gos·pot′a·mos** (-məs), **Æ·.**

Ae·gyp·tus (ē-jip′təs) In Greek mythology, king of Egypt; brother of Danaus, whose daughters his sons married. See DANAIDES. Also **Æ·gyp′tus**.

Ae·gyp·tus (ē-jip′təs) An ancient name for Egypt. Also **Æ·gyp′tus**.

Æl·fric (al′frik), died 1020?, English monk and writer; abbot of Eynsham.

A·el·lo (ā-el′ō) One of the Harpies.

-aemia See -EMIA.

Ae·mil·i·us (ē-mil′ē-əs) Latin form of EMIL. Also **Æ·mil′i·us**.

Ae·ne·as (i-nē′əs) In Greek and Roman legend, a Trojan, son of Anchises and Venus, hero of the Aeneid: after the sack of Troy he wandered for seven years before reaching Latium where he founded the city of Lavinium. See ASCANIUS, DIDO. Also **Æ·ne′as**.

Ae·ne·as Sil·vi·us (i-nē′əs sil′vē-əs) See PIUS II. Also **Ae·ne′as Syl′vi·us**.

Ae·ne·id (i-nē′id) n. A Latin epic poem by Vergil narrating the adventures of Aeneas. Also **Æ·ne′id**.

a·e·ne·ous (ā-ē′nē-əs) adj. Having a golden-green or lustrous brassy color: said especially of insects. Also **a·e′ne·us**. [< L aeneus < aes copper, bronze]

ae·o·li·an (ē-ō′lē-ən) adj. Pertaining to or caused by the winds; wind-borne: also eolian.

Ae·o·li·an (ē-ō′lē-ən) adj. 1 Of or pertaining to ancient Aeolis in Asia Minor, its people, or their language; Aeolic. 2 Pertaining to Aeolus, Greek god of the winds. —n. 1 A member of one of the four major tribes of ancient Greece. The Aeolians settled in central Greece, Lesbos, and Aeolis. 2 Aeolic. Also spelled Eolian. Also **Æ·o′li·an**.

Aeolian harp A stringed instrument so constructed as to produce musical sounds when exposed to a current of air.

Aeolian Islands See LIPARI ISLANDS.

Ae·ol·ic (ē-ol′ik) n. A dialect of ancient Greek spoken in Aeolis (including Lesbos), Thessaly, and Boeotia, represented by the poetry of Sappho and Alcaeus. —adj. Aeolian. Also spelled Eolic. Also **Æ·ol′ic**.

ae·o·li·pile (ē-ol′ə-pīl) See EOLIPILE.

Ae·o·lis (ē′ə-lis) A country in ancient Greece and NW Asia Minor. Also **Æ′o·lis; Ae·o·li·a** (ē-ō′lē-ə).

ae·o·lo·trop·ic (ē′ə-lō-trop′ik) adj. Physics Anisotropic. [< Gk. aiolos varying + -TROPIC]

Ae·o·lus (ē′ə-ləs) 1 In Greek mythology, the god of the winds. 2 In Greek legend, a Thessalian king, son of Helen and ancestor of the Aeolians. Also **Æ′o·lus**.

ae·on (ē′ən, ē′on), **ae·o·ni·an** (ē-ō′nē-ən) See EON, etc.

Ae·qui·an (ē′kwē-ən) n. The Indo-European language of an early Italic people inhabiting Latium. [< L Aequi, pl.]

ae·quum (ē′kwəm) n. That quantity of food which is barely adequate to sustain an organism doing work. [< L < aequus even]

aer- Var. of AERO-.

ae·rar·i·an (ē-râr′ē-ən) adj. Fiscal; pertaining to the ancient Roman treasury. —n. A Roman citizen of the lowest rank, who had no right to vote, and paid only a poll tax. [< L aerarius < aerarium treasury < aes, aeris copper, money]

aer·as·the·ni·a (âr′əs-thē′nē-ə, ā′ər-əs-) n. Aeroneurosis. [< NL < AER- + Gk. astheneia weakness]

aer·ate (âr′āt, ā′ə-rāt) v.t. **·at·ed**, **·at·ing** 1 To supply or charge with air or gas. 2 To purify by exposure to air. 3 To oxygenate, as blood. [< AER- + -ATE²] —**aer·a′tion** n.

aer·a·tor (âr′ā-tər, ā′ə-rā′tər) n. 1 An apparatus for charging liquids with gas under pressure. 2 A device for supplying a stream of gas or air, as for fumigating, destroying fungi, etc.

aer·en·chy·ma (âr-eng′kə-mə, ā′ə-reng′kə-mə) n. Bot. A specialized tissue serving in some aquatic plants for buoyancy and aeration, and consisting of thin-walled cells with intercellular air spaces.

aeri- Var. of AERO-.

aer·i·al (âr′ē-əl, ā-ir′ē-əl) adj. 1 Of or in the air. 2 Like air; atmospheric. 3 Bot. Grow-

ing or living in the air and not in the soil or in water. 4 Airy; insubstantial; spiritual. 5 Existing or performed in the air. 6 Of, by, or for aircraft: *aerial* bombardment. See synonyms under AIRY. —*n.* (âr′ē·əl) An antenna, as in television and radio. [< L *aerius* airy < *aer* air] —**aer′i·al·ly** *adv.*

aerial bomb See under BOMB.

aer·i·al·ist (âr′ē·əl·ist, ā·ir′ē·əl-) *n.* One who performs feats of skill in the air, as a tightrope walker, trapeze artist, etc.

aer·i·al·i·ty (âr′ē·al′ə·tē, ā·ir′ē-) *n.* Tenuity, or want of substance; airiness.

aerial ladder An extension ladder commonly mounted on a truck, and operated by levers: used by firemen in saving life or property.

aerial train An airplane towing behind it one or more gliders.

aer·ie (âr′ē, ir′ē) *n.* 1 The nest of a predatory bird, as the eagle, on a crag. 2 The brood or young of such a bird. Also spelled *aery, eyry, eyrie.* [< Med.L *aeria* < OF *aire,* ? < L *area* open space] —**aer′ied** *adj.*

aer·if·er·ous (âr·if′ər·əs, ā′ə·rif′-) *adj.* Containing or conveying air. [< AERI- + -FEROUS]

aer·i·fi·ca·tion (âr′ə·fi·kā′shən, ā′ər·ə-) *n.* 1 The act or process of converting into air, gas, or vapor; the process of becoming air, gas, or vapor. 2 Purification by exposure to air; aeration. Also **aer′i·fac′tion.**

aer·i·form (âr′ə·fôrm, ā′ər·ə·fôrm′) *adj.* Like air; gaseous; unsubstantial; intangible.

aer·i·fy (âr′ə·fī, ā′ər·ə·fī) *v.t.* **·fied, ·fy·ing** 1 To aerate. 2 To change into a gaseous form.

aero- *combining form* 1 Air; of the air: *aerobiology.* 2 Of aircraft or flying: *aeromarine.* 3 Gas; of gases: *aerogen.* Also *aer-, aeri-.* [< Gk. *aēr* air]

aer·o·al·ler·gen (âr′ō·al′ər·jən, ā′ər·ō-) *n.* An airborne substance that is capable of producing an allergenic response in a sensitized subject. —**aer′o·al·ler·gen′ic** *adj.*

aer·o·bal·lis·tics (âr′ō·bə·lis′tiks, ā′ər·ō-) *n.* The ballistics of missiles dropped, launched, or fired from aircraft in flight. —**aer′o·bal·lis′tic** *adj.*

aer·o·bat·ics (âr′ə·bat′iks, ā′ər·ə-) *n.* Aerial maneuvers which are not necessary to normal flight voluntarily performed in aircraft; trick or stunt flying. [< AERO- + (ACRO)BATICS]

aer·o·ba·tion (âr′ə·bā′shən, ā′ər·ə-) *n. Aeron.* The performance of aerial feats; stunt flying; exhibition flying.

aer·obe (âr′ōb, ā′ər·ōb) *n.* A microorganism that can live only in the presence of free oxygen: opposed to *anaerobe.* [< AERO- + Gk. *bios* life]

aer·o·bic (âr·ō′bik, ā·ə·rō′-) *adj.* 1 Living in air. 2 Pertaining to aerobics. —**aer·o′bi·cal·ly** *adv.*

aer·o·bics (âr′ō′biks) *n. pl.* A system of calisthenics and other strenuous physical activities designed to improve the functioning of the lungs and heart by speeding up oxygen consumption and circulation.

aer·o·bi·ol·o·gy (âr′ō·bī·ol′ə·jē, ā′ər·ō-) *n.* The study of the dispersal of airborne bacteria, pollen grains, fungal spores, etc., and of airborne pollutants having biological effects. —**aer′o·bi′o·log′i·cal** *adj.*

aer·o·bi·o·scope (âr′ō·bī′ə·skōp, ā′ər·ō-) *n.* An instrument for the determination of the bacterial content of air.

aer·o·car·to·graph (âr′ō·kär′tə·graf, -gräf, ā′·ər·ō-) *n.* A mapmaking device that utilizes air photographs to show the contour and elevation of ground features.

aer·o·cy·cle (âr′ə·sī′kəl, ā′ər·ə-) *n.* A flying machine constructed on the helicopter principle but intended to carry only one man at low altitude and over a short flight range.

aer·o·do·net·ics (âr′ō·də·net′iks, ā′ər·ō-) *n.* The branch of dynamics that treats of gliding and soaring flight. [< AERO- + Gk. *donētos* shaken < *donein* shake]

aer·o·drome (âr′ə·drōm, ā′ər·ə-) *n.* Airdrome.

aer·o·dy·nam·ics (âr′ō·dī·nam′iks, ā′ər·ō-) *n.* The branch of physics that treats of the laws of motion of gases, especially atmospheric, under the influence of gravity and other mechanical forces, and of the mechanical effects produced by such motion. —**aer′o·dy·nam′ic** *adj.*

aer·o·dyne (âr′ə·dīn, ā′ər·ə-) *n.* Any aircraft which is heavier than air, as an airplane, glider, helicopter, etc. [< AERO- + Gk. *dynamis* power]

aer·o·e·las·tic·i·ty (âr′ō·i·las′tis′ə·tē, ā′ər·ō-) *n. Eng.* The effect of aerodynamic forces on elastic materials and structures exposed to the wind, especially steel and other metals, aircraft, bridges, and buildings. —**aer′o·e·las′tic** *adj.*

aer·o·e·las·tics (âr′ō·i·las′tiks, ā′ər·ō-) *n.* The study of the elastic deformations in the structural elements of aircraft and of the aerodynamic conditions leading to the maximum stability and control of these elements. —**aer′o·e·las′tic** *adj.*

aer·o·em·bo·lism (âr′ō·em′bə·liz′əm, ā′ər·ō-) *n.* 1 A bubble of air or other gas in the heart or in blood vessels. 2 Decompression sickness. Compare CAISSON DISEASE.

aer·o·foil (âr′ə·foil, ā′ər·ə-) *n.* Airfoil.

aer·o·gel (âr′ə·jel, ā′ər·ə-) *n.* A porous substance obtained from a gel by replacing the dispersed liquid phase with a gas.

aer·o·gen (âr′ə·jen, ā′ər·ə-) *n.* A microorganism that forms gas.

aer·o·gen·ic (âr′ə·jen′ik, ā′ər·ə-) *adj.* 1 Gas-producing: *aerogenic* bacteria. 2 Having the form of gas: *aerogenic* vaccine spray.

aer·o·gram (âr′ə·gram, ā′ər·ə-) *n.* 1 A wireless message; radiogram. 2 The record traced by a meteorograph.

aér·o·gramme (âr′ə·gram, ā′ər·ə-) *n.* An international airmail letter consisting of a single folded sheet: also, *Brit., air letter.* [< F]

aer·o·graph (âr′ə·graf, -gräf, ā′ər·ə-) *n.* A meteorograph.

aer·og·ra·pher (âr·og′rə·fər, ā′ə·rog′-) *n.* One skilled in aerography.

aer·og·ra·phy (âr·og′rə·fē, ā′ə·rog′-) *n.* A description of or treatise on the atmosphere and its phenomena. —**aer′o·graph′ic** or **·i·cal** *adj.* —**aer′o·graph′i·cal·ly** *adv.*

aer·o·hy·dro·plane (âr′ə·hī′drə·plān, ā′ər·ə-) See HYDROPLANE.

aer·o·lite (âr′ə·līt, ā′ər·ə-) *n.* A mass falling on the earth from celestial space and containing more stone than iron. See METEORITE. Also **aer′o·lith** (-lith). [< AERO- + Gk. *lithos* stone] —**aer′o·lit′ic** (-lit′ik) *adj.*

aer·ol·o·gy (âr·ol′ə·jē, ā′ə·rol′-) *n.* 1 *Physics* The science of the laws and phenomena of the atmosphere. 2 *Meteorol.* The study of the atmosphere in its vertical extent. —**aer·o·log·ic** (âr′ə·loj′ik, ā′ər·ə-) or **·i·cal** *adj.* —**aer·ol′o·gist** *n.*

aer·o·mag·net·ic (âr′ō·mag·net′ik, ā′ə·rō-) *adj.* Pertaining to magnetism in, or the action of magnetic force on, portions of the atmosphere, esp. the upper layers: an *aeromagnetic* survey.

aer·o·man·cy (âr′ə·man′sē, ā′ər·ə-) *n.* The art of divination or augury by atmospheric phenomena; hence, a forecasting of atmospheric changes. [< AERO- + Gk. *manteia* divination]

aer·o·ma·rine (âr′ō·mə·rēn′, ā′ər·ō-) *adj.* Pertaining to the navigation of aircraft over the ocean.

aer·o·me·chan·ics (âr′ō·mə·kan′iks, ā′ər·ō-) *n.* 1 The science that treats of equilibrium and motion of air and gases, including *aerostatics* and *aerodynamics.* 2 Pneumatics. —**aer′o·me·chan′ic** *adj. & n.*

aer·o·med·i·cine (âr′ō·med′ə·sən, ā′ər·ō-) *n.* 1 Aviation medicine. 2 Space medicine. —**aer′o·med′i·cal** *adj.*

aer·o·me·te·or·o·graph (âr′ō·mē′tē·ôr′ə·graf, -gräf, ā′ər·ō-) *n.* A device for recording atmospheric conditions, as temperature, pressure and moisture, wind velocities, etc.

aer·om·e·ter (âr·om′ə·tər, ā′ə·rom′ə·tər) *n.* An apparatus for weighing and estimating the density of air or other gases.

aer·om·e·try (âr·om′ə·trē, ā′ə·rom′-) *n.* The science of weighing and measuring air and other gases. —**aer·o·met·ric** (âr′ə·met′rik, ā′ər·ə-) *adj.*

aer·o·naut (âr′ə·nôt, ā′ər·ə-) *n.* 1 One who navigates the air; a balloonist or aviator. 2 A space traveler. [< F *aéronaute* < Gk. *aēr* air + *nautēs* sailor]

aer·o·nau·tic (âr′ə·nô′tik, ā′ər·ə-) *adj.* 1 Pertaining to, floating in, or navigating the air. 2 Pertaining to aeronautics. Also **aer′o·nau′ti·cal.**

aer·o·nau·tics (âr′ə·nô′tiks, ā′ər·ə-) *n.* 1 The science or art of navigating aircraft. 2 That branch of engineering which deals with the design, construction, operation, and performance characteristics of aircraft.

aer·o·neu·ro·sis (âr′ō·nōō·rō′sis, -nyōōq-, ā′·ər·ō-) *n. Pathol.* A condition of nervous exhaustion sometimes affecting airplane pilots, characterized by emotional tension, irritability, gastric distress, and insomnia. Also called **aerasthenia, flying fatigue.**

aer·on·o·my (âr on′ə·mē, ā′ər·on′-) *n.* The scientific study of the physics and chemistry of the earth or other orbiting body. —**aer′o·nom′ ·i·cal** *adj.*

aer·o·pause (âr′ə·pôz, ā′ər·ə-) *n. Meteorol.* The region of the atmosphere where the conditions of outer space are gradually approached: it is believed to extend from about 12 to 125 miles above the earth.

aer·o·pha·gi·a (âr′ə·fā′jē·ə, ā′ər·ə-) *n. Med.* The swallowing of air.

aer·o·phi·lat·e·ly (âr′ō·fi·lat′ə·lē, ā′ər·ō-) *n.* The collecting of air-mail stamps, covers, etc. —**aer′o·phi·lat′e·list** *n.*

aer·o·phobe (âr′ə·fōb, ā′ər·ə-) *n.* A person or organism evincing or affected by aerophobia.

aer·o·pho·bi·a (âr′ə·fō′bē·ə, ā′ər·ə-) *n.* 1 A morbid fear of fresh air and of airborne infection. 2 A morbid fear of flying. 3 *Biol.* Movement of an organism away from air or oxygen.

aer·o·phore (âr′ə·fôr, ā′ər·ə-) *n.* 1 An apparatus for inflating the lungs of a newborn infant to stimulate breathing. 2 A device for delivering air as needed to firemen, aviators, etc.

aer·o·pho·tog·ra·phy (âr′ō·fə·tog′rə·fē, ā′ər·ō-) *n.* Photography from aircraft.

aer·o·phys·ics (âr′ō·fiz′iks, ā′ər·ō-) *n.* Physical science considered with reference to the design, construction, and operation of aircraft, rockets, guided missiles, etc.: the physics of aeronautics and aviation.

aer·o·phyte (âr′ə·fīt, ā′ər·ə-) *n. Bot.* An epiphyte (def. 1).

aer·o·plane (âr′ə·plān, ā′ər·ə-) See AIRPLANE.

aer·o·scope (âr′ə·skōp, ā′ər·ə-) *n.* An instrument for collecting the minute particles in the atmosphere for microscopic examination. —**aer′o·scop′ic** (-skop′ik) *adj.*

aer·o·sid·er·ite (âr′ō·sid′ə·rīt, ā′ər·ō-) *n.* A meteorite of which iron is the chief constituent.

aer·o·sid·er·o·lite (âr′ō·sid′ər·ə·līt′, ā′ər·ō-) *n.* A meteorite that is both metallic and stony.

aer·o·sol (âr′ə·sōl, -sol, ā′ər·ə-) *n.* 1 A colloidal dispersion of solid or liquid particles in a gaseous medium. 2 A substance packaged under pressure along with a volatile propellant which, upon release through a nozzle, disperses fine particles of the substance in the air. —*adj.* Pertaining to, resembling, dispensing, or dispensed as an aerosol. Also **aer′o·sol′ic.** [< AERO- + SOL(UTION)]

aer·o·sol·ize (âr′ə·sol·īz, ā′ər·ə-) *v.t.* **·ized, ·iz·ing** To package with a propellant under pressure for dispersion as an aerosol. —**aer′o·sol′i·za′tion** *n.*

aer·o·space (âr′ō·spās, ā′ər·ō-) *n.* 1 The earth's atmosphere and outer space, considered as a single region in the operation of rockets, guided missiles, and spacecraft. 2 The study and investigation of this region, especially with reference to space travel.

aer·o·sphere (âr′ə·sfir, ā′ər·ə-) *n.* The entire atmosphere considered as a single gaseous shell surrounding the earth.

aer·o·stat (âr′ə·stat, ā′ər·ə-) *n.* Any aircraft which is lighter than air, as a balloon or dirigible. [< F *aérostat* < Gk *aēr* air + *statos* standing] —**aer′o·stat′ic** or **·i·cal** *adj.*

aer·o·stat·ics (âr′ə·stat′iks, ā′ər·ə-) *n.* 1 The branch of physics that treats of the mechanical properties of air and gases not in motion. 2 The art and science of operating lighter-than-air aircraft, as balloons and dirigibles: distinguished from *aviation.*

aer·o·sta·tion (âr′ə·stā′shən, ā′ər·ə-) *n.* **1** The art of raising and supporting bodies, as balloons, by means of fluids lighter than air: opposed to *aviation.* **2** *Obs.* Aerostatics. Compare AEROSTATICS.
aer·o·tax·is (âr′ə·tak′sis, ā′ər·ə-) *n. Biol.* Movement of an organism away from or toward a source of air or oxygen.
aer·o·ther·a·peu·tics (âr′ō·ther′ə·pyōō′tiks, ā′·ər·ō-) *n. Med.* A system of treating disease by varying the atmospheric pressure upon the patient or by changing the composition of the air. Also **aer′o·ther′a·py** (-ther′ə·pē).
aer·o·ther·mo·dy·nam·ics (âr′o·thûr′mō·dī·nam′iks, ā′ər·ō-) *n.* The branch of thermodynamics that deals with the relations between heat and mechanical energy in gases, especially in their applications to changes induced by the motions of bodies in the medium.
aer·o·tow (âr′ə·tō′, ā′ər·ə-) *v.t.* To tow (a glider or other aircraft) through the air. —*n.* The towing of an aircraft in this manner.
aer·ot·ro·pism (âr·ot′rə·piz′əm, ā′ə·rot′-) *n. Biol.* A change in orientation of a plant affected by differential growth of tissues in response to the presence of air or oxygen. —**aer·o·trop·ic** (âr′ə·trop′ik, ā′ər·ə-) *adj.*
ae·ru·gi·nous (i·rōō′jə·nəs) Resembling verdigris; bluish green. Also spelled *eruginous.* [<Latin *aerugo* <*aes* brass, copper]
aer·y[1] (âr′ē, ā′ər·ē) *adj.* Airy; aerial.
aer·y[2] (âr′ē, ir′ē) See AERIE.
aes (ēz) *n.* Money made of copper or bronze. [<L]
Aes·chi·nes (es′kə·nēz), 389–314 B.C., Athenian orator; rival of Demosthenes. Also **Æs′chi·nes.**
Aes·chy·le·an (es′kə·lē′ən) *adj.* Similar to, or in the style of, the tragedies of Aeschylus; hence, majestic; stately. Also **Æs′chy·le′an.**
Aes·chy·lus (es′kə·ləs), 525–456 B.C., Greek tragic dramatist. Also **Æs′chy·lus.**
Aes·cu·la·pi·an (es′kyə·lā′pē·ən) *adj.* Relating to Aesculapius; hence, pertaining to the art of healing; medical. —*n.* A disciple of Aesculapius; hence, a physician. Also spelled *Esculapian.*
Aes·cu·la·pi·us (es′kyə·lā′pē·əs) In Roman mythology, the god of medicine: identified with the Greek *Asclepius.* Also **Æs′cu·la′pi·us.**
Æ·sir (ā′sir, ē′-) *sing.* **As** The gods of the Teutonic pantheon collectively. See VAN[2].
Ae·sop (ē′səp, ē′sop) Greek author of fables, sixth century B.C. Also **Æ′sop.**
Ae·so·pi·an (ē·sō′pē·ən) *adj.* **1** Of or pertaining to Aesop; resembling the fables of Aesop. **2** Cryptic; phrased in figurative language or fable to carry a special meaning to the initiated: also spelled *Esopian.* Also **Æ·so′pi·an.**
aes·thete (es′thēt), **aes·thet·ic** (es·thet′ik) See ESTHETE, etc.
ae·ta·tis su·ae (ē·tā′tis sōō′ē) *Latin* Of his (or her) age; at a specified age. Also **æ·ta′tis su′æ.**
Æth·el·bert (ath′əl·bûrt) See ETHELBERT.
æth·el·ing (ath′əl·ing) See ATHELING.
Æth·el·red (ath′əl·red) See ETHELRED.
Ae·thi·o·pi·a (ē′thē·ō′pē·ə) See ETHIOPIA.
ae·thri·o·scope (ē′thrē·ə·skōp′) *n.* A thermometric instrument for measuring minute changes in the heat radiated from the sky. [<Gk. *aithria* clear sky + -SCOPE]
A·e·tian (ā·ē′shən) *n.* One of the party of extreme Arians that flourished in the latter half of the fourth century: so called from its leader, Aetius of Antioch.
Aet·na (et′nə) See ETNA. Also **Æt′na.**
Ae·to·li·a (ē·tō′lē·ə) A district of western Greece, part of modern Acarnania. Also **Æ·to′li·a.** *Greek* **Ai·to·li·a** (â′tô·lē′ä). —**Ae·to′li·an,** *adj. & n.*
af- Assimilated var. of AD-.
a·far (ə·fär′) *adv.* At, from, or to a distance; remotely. [<A-[1] on + FAR]
a·feard (ə·fird′) *adj. Dial.* Afraid; fearful. Also **a·feared′.**
a·fe·brile (ā·fē′brəl, ā·feb′rəl) *adj.* Free from fever.
aff (af) *adv. & prep. Scot.* Off; off from.
af·fa·ble (af′ə·bəl) *adj.* **1** Easy and courteous in manner; approachable. **2** Benign; mild. See synonyms under BLAND, FRIENDLY. [<F <L *affabilis,* lit., able to be spoken to <*affari* <*ad-* to + *fari* speak] —**af′fa·bil′i·ty, af′fa·ble·ness** *n.* —**af′fa·bly** *adv.*
af·fair (ə·fâr′) *n.* **1** Anything done or to be done; business; concern: often in plural. **2** An unimportant event, as a skirmish; matter; thing. **3** A vague or indefinite object or fact: The first ship was a rude *affair.* **4** See LOVE AFFAIR. See synonyms under BATTLE, BUSINESS, TRANSACTION. [<OF *afaire* <*a faire* to do <L *ad* to + *facere* do]
af·faire (à·fâr′) *n. French* Short for **affaire d'a·mour** (dà·mōōr′), a love affair, or **affaire de coeur** (də kœr′), affair of the heart.
af·faire d'hon·neur (à·fâr′ dô·nœr′) *French* A matter of honor; a duel.
af·fect[1] (ə·fekt′) *v.t.* **1** To act upon or have an effect upon; impress; influence. **2** To touch or move emotionally. **3** To attack or attaint: A disease *affects* the body. See synonyms under CONCERN, INFLUENCE. Compare EFFECT.
— *n.* **1** (af′ekt) *Psychol.* **a** That which tends to arouse emotion rather than to stimulate thought or perception. **b** The diffuse mental condition thus produced. **c** The fundamental controlling element in an emotional state. **2** *Obs.* Inward disposition; inclination. [<L *affectus,* pp. of *afficere* influence, attack <*ad-* to + *facere* do; def 1 of noun <G *affekt*]
af·fect[2] (ə·fekt′) *v.t.* **1** To have a liking for; show a preference for; fancy: to *affect* large hats. **2** To imitate or counterfeit for effect; make a show of one's liking or aptitude for: to *affect* a British accent; to *affect* omniscience. **3** To tend toward naturally; haunt; frequent: said of animals and plants. **4** *Obs.* To aim at; to aspire for or to. See synonyms under ASSUME, LIKE, PRETEND. [<F *affecter* <L *affectare* aim at, freq. of *afficere.* See AFFECT[1].]
af·fec·ta·tion (af′ek·tā′shən) *n.* **1** A studied pretense; shallow display: with *of:* an *affectation* of wealth. **2** Artificiality of manner or behavior; affectedness. See synonyms under HYPOCRISY, PRETENSE. [<L *affectatio, -onis* <*affectare.* See AFFECT[2].]
af·fect·ed[1] (ə·fek′tid) *adj.* **1** Acted upon, as by a drug. **2** Moved emotionally; influenced. **3** Attacked, as by disease; diseased. **4** *Math.* Adfected. [pp. of AFFECT[1]]
af·fect·ed[2] (ə·fek′tid) *adj.* **1** Assumed falsely or in outward semblance only; showing affectation. **2** Having a liking, inclination, or affection; inclined. **3** Fondly cherished; loved; frequented. See synonyms under FACTITIOUS, SQUEAMISH. [pp. of AFFECT[2]] —**af·fect′ed·ly** *adv.* —**af·fect′ed·ness** *n.*
af·fect·er (ə·fek′tər) *n.* One who affects or pretends.
af·fect·ing[1] (ə·fek′ting) *adj.* Having power to move the feelings; pathetic. —**af·fect′ing·ly** *adv.*
af·fect·ing[2] (ə·fek′ting) *adj. Obs.* **1** Showing love. **2** Pretending; falsely displaying.
af·fec·tion (ə·fek′shən) *n.* **1** *Often pl.* Good disposition, as towards another; fond attachment; kind feelings: usually distinguished from *love* as less powerful or intense. **2** *Often pl.* A mental state brought about by any influence; an emotion or feeling: to influence men by playing on their *affections.* **3** An abnormal state of the body; disease. **4** The act of affecting or influencing or the state of being influenced. **5** A property or attribute: Thought is said to be an *affection* of matter. **6** *Psychol.* Conscious perception of feeling or emotion: distinguished from *cognition.* **7** *Obs.* Constitutional inclination; tendency. See synonyms under ATTACHMENT, FRIENDSHIP, LOVE, INFLUENCE, DISEASE.
af·fec·tion·al (ə·fek′shən·əl) *adj.* Of or pertaining to affections. —**af·fec′tion·al·ly** *adv.*
af·fec·tion·ate (ə·fek′shən·it) *adj.* **1** Having or expressing love; loving; fond. **2** *Obs.* Favorably inclined. See synonyms under FRIENDLY. —**af·fec′tion·ate·ly** *adv.* —**af·fec′tion·ate·ness** *n.*
af·fec·tive (ə·fek′tiv) *adj.* **1** Pertaining to or exciting affection; emotional or stirring emotion. **2** *Psychol.* Pertaining to or arising from feeling or emotional reactions rather than from thought.
af·fec·tiv·i·ty (af′ek·tiv′ə·tē) *n. Psychol.* The relative intensity of response to a feeling or emotion.
af·fect·less (ə·fekt′lis) *adj.* Unfeeling; unemotional. —**af·fect′less·ly** *adv.* —**af·fect′less·ness** *n.*
af·fen·pin·scher (ä′fən·pin′shər) *n.* A toy terrier of monkeylike appearance, having a hard, wiry coat, usually black, a round head, a short, pointed muzzle, and a short tail. [<G, monkey terrier]
af·fer·ent (af′ər·ənt) *adj.* Conducting inward, or toward the center: said of those nerve processes which transmit sensory stimuli from receptor organs to the central nervous system: opposed to *efferent.* [<L *afferens, -entis,* ppr. of *afferre* <*ad-* to + *ferre* bear]
af·fet·tu·o·so (äf·fet′tōō·ō′sō) *adj. Music* Tender; soft; pathetic: designating a passage or piece to be rendered with feeling. [<Ital.]
af·fi·ance (ə·fī′əns) *v.t.* **·anced, ·anc·ing 1** To promise in marriage; betroth. **2** *Archaic* To pledge. —*n.* **1** A betrothal; pledge of faith. **2** *Obs.* Confidence. [<OF *afiancer* <*afiance* trust, confidence <*after* trust <Med.L *affidare* <L *ad-* to + *fidus* faithful]
af·fi·ant (ə·fī′ənt) *n. Law* One who makes an affidavit.
af·fi·da·vit (af′ə·dā′vit) *n.* **1** A voluntary sworn declaration, in writing, made before competent authority. **2** Any solemn or formal declaration. [<Med.L, he has stated on oath, perfect tense of *affidare.* See AFFIANCE.]
af·fil·i·ate (ə·fil′ē·āt) *v.* **·at·ed, ·at·ing** *v.t.* **1** To associate or unite, as a member or branch to a larger or principal body: with *to* or *with.* **2** To join or associate (oneself): with *with.* **3** To receive as a child; adopt. **4** To fix the legal paternity of. **5** To determine relations of, as the sources or branches of a field of study. —*v.i.* **6** To associate or ally oneself: with *with.* —*adj.* Affiliated. —*n.* Something affiliated. [<L *affiliatus,* pp. of *affiliare* adopt <*ad-* to + *filius* son]
af·fil·i·a·tion (ə·fil′ē·ā′shən) *n.* **1** The act of affiliating, or the state of being affiliated; association; friendly relationship; connection; adoption. **2** Combination; union.
af·fine (ə·fīn′) *n. Obs.* **1** A relative by marriage. **2** A kinsman. [<F *affin* <L *affinis. See* AFFINITY.]
af·fined (ə·fīnd′) *adj.* **1** Joined by artificial ties; allied; related by marriage. **2** *Obs.* Under obligation, due to some close relation. [<F *affiné* related <*affin.* See AFFINE.]
af·fin·i·ty (ə·fin′ə·tē) *n. pl.* **·ties 1** Any natural drawing or inclination; close relation or agreement. **2** *Biol.* A structural or physiologic likeness in different organisms indicative of a common origin. **3** Structural likenesses indicating a common origin, as in languages. **4** *Chem.* The force of attraction by which differing chemical elements unite to form compounds. **5** Connection through certain relations formed, as by church or state; especially, relationship through marriage (as opposed to blood relationship). **6** A Platonic or spiritual attraction held to exist between certain persons, especially between those of opposite sexes; also, the person exerting such attraction. [<L *affinitas, -tatis* <*affinis* adjacent, related <*ad-* to + *finis* end]
Synonyms: alliance, analogy, birth, blood, consanguinity, descent, family, kin, kind, kindred, race, relationship. *Kind* is broader than *kin,* denoting the most general *relationship,* as one of the whole human species in man*kind,* human*kind,* etc.; *kin* and *kindred* denote direct *relationship* that can be traced through either blood or marriage, especially the former; either of these words may signify collectively all persons of the same blood or members of the same family, relatives or relations. *Affinity* is *relationship* by marriage, *consanguinity* is *relationship* by blood. *Antonyms*: See ANTIPATHY.
af·firm (ə·fûrm′) *v.t.* **1** To declare or state positively; assert and maintain to be true; aver. **2** To confirm or ratify, as a judgment or law. —*v.i.* **3** *Law* To make a formal judicial declaration, but not under oath. [<OF *afermer* <L *affirmare* <*ad-* to + *firmare* make firm <*firmus* strong] —**af·firm′a·ble** *adj.* —**af·firm′a·bly** *adv.* —**af·firm′ance** *n.* —**af·firm′ant** *adj. & n.* —**af·firm′er** *n.*
Synonyms: assert, asseverate, aver, declare, depose, endorse, maintain, predicate, propound, protest, state, swear, tell, testify. *Affirm* has less of egotism than *assert,* more solemnity than *declare,* and more composure than *asseverate,* which is to *assert* emphatically. In legal usage, *affirm* differs from

swear in not invoking the name of God. See ALLEGE, ASSERT, STATE. *Antonyms:* contradict, deny, dispute, gainsay, negative, oppose, refute.

af·fir·ma·tion (af′ər·mā′shən) *n.* **1** The act of affirming, or that which is affirmed. **2** A declaration; statement; predication. **3** A solemn declaration made before a competent officer, in place of a judicial oath. **4** Confirmation; ratification. See synonyms under TESTIMONY.

af·firm·a·tive (ə·fûr′mə) ·tiv) *adj.* **1** Characterized by affirmation; asserting that the fact is so; ratifying; confirmative. **2** *Math.* Positive: an *affirmative* quantity. Also **af·firm·a·to·ry** (ə·fûr′mə·tôr′ē, -tō′re). —*n.* **1** A word or expression of affirmation or assent; that which affirms or asserts: to answer in the *affirmative*. **2** That side in a debate which affirms the proposition debated.

affirmative action *U.S.* A program that promotes the employment of women and of minority groups.

af·firm·a·tive·ly (ə·fûr′mə·tiv·lē) *adv.* In an affirmative manner; positively; on the affirmative side.

af·fix (ə·fiks′) *v.t.* **1** To fix or attach; fasten, as a seal; append, as a signature at the end of a document. **2** To connect with or lay upon, as blame, responsibility, etc. See synonyms under ADD. —*n.* (af′iks) **1** That which is attached, appended, or added. **2** *Ling.* A prefix, suffix, or infix. [<L *affixus,* pp. of *affigere* <*ad-* to + *figere* fasten]

af·fla·tus (ə·flā′təs) *n.* **1** The communication of supernatural knowledge, as in a state of exaltation: the divine *afflatus.* **2** Any creative inspiration or impulse. [<L, a breathing upon < *afflare* blow on < *ad-* to + *flare* blow] .

af·flict (ə·flikt′) *v.t.* **1** To distress with continued suffering; trouble. **2** *Obs.* To cast down; overthrow. See synonyms under CHASTEN, HURT. [<obs. *afflict,* adj., afflicted <L *afflictus,* pp. of *affligere* dash against, strike down < *ad-* to + *fligere* dash, strike]

af·flic·tion (ə·flik′shən) *n.* **1** The state of being afflicted; sore distress of body or mind. **2** That which causes great suffering or distress; misfortune; calamity. See synonyms under GRIEF, MISFORTUNE.

af·flic·tive (ə·flik′tiv) *adj.* Causing or involving pain or distress; grievous. See synonyms under TROUBLESOME. —**af·flic′tive·ly** *adv.*

af·flu·ence (af′lo͞o·əns) *n.* **1** A profuse or abundant supply, as of riches; wealth; abundance; opulence. **2** A flowing toward; concourse. [<F <L *affluentia* <*affluere.* See AFFLUENT.]

af·flu·ent (af′lo͞o·ənt) *adj.* **1** Abounding; abundant. **2** Wealthy; opulent. **3** Flowing freely; fluent. See synonyms under AMPLE. —*n.* A stream that flows into another; a tributary. [<L *affluens, -entis,* ppr. of *affluere* <*ad* - to + *fluere* flow] —**af′flu·ent·ly** *adv.*

af·flux (af′luks) *n.* A flowing toward a point, as blood to a tissue or organ; congestion. Also **af·flux′ion.** [<Med.L *affluxus* < *affluere.* See AFFLUENT.]

af·force (ə·fôrs′, ə·fō rs′) *v.t.* **af·forced, af·forc·ing** To reinforce, as a jury by the addition of new members. [<OF *aforcer* <L *ex* out + *fortis* strong] —**af·force′ment** *n.*

af·ford (ə·fôrd′, ə·fō rd′) *v.t.* **1** To have sufficient means for; be able to meet the expense of: Can you *afford* to go to Europe? **2** To incur without detriment: He can *afford* to suffer now. **3** To produce or furnish, as in behalf of; confer, as pleasure or profit: It *affords* me great delight to tell you this. [OE *geforthian* further, promote] —**af·ford′a·ble** *adj.*

af·for·est (ə·fôr′ist, ə·for′ist) *v.t.* To convert into a forest, as barren land. [<AD- + FOREST] —**af·for·es·ta·tion** (ə·fô r′is·tā′shən, ə·for′-) *n.*

af·fran·chise (ə·fran′chīz) *v.t.* **·chised, ·chis·ing** To enfranchise; liberate. [<F *affranchiss-,* stem of *affranchir* <*à* to + *franchir* free. See FRANCHISE.]

af·fray (ə·frā′) *n.* **1** A public brawl or fight; a disturbance of the peace. **2** *Law* The fighting in public of two or more persons in a manner that will naturally produce terror in others. See synonyms under ALTERCATION, QUARREL. —*v.t.* Archaic To cause to feel sudden fear; terrify; startle. [<OF *effrei, esfrei,* ult. <L *ex-* out + a Gmc. word for "peace" (cf. OHG *fridu*)]

af·fri·cate (af′ri·kit) *n.* Phonet. A complex sound consisting of a stop followed by the fricative release of breath at the point of contact, as *ch* (t + sh) in *church.* [<L *affricatus,* pp. of *affricare* <*ad-* against + *fricare* rub] —**af·fric·a·tive** (ə·frik′ə·tiv) *adj., n.*

af·fright (ə·frīt′) *Obs. v.t.* To strike with sudden fear; frighten. See synonyms under FRIGHTEN. —*n.* Sudden fear; also, a cause of terror. See synonyms under ALARM, FEAR, FRIGHT. [OE *āfyrhtan*] —**af·fright′ment** *n.*

af·front (ə·frunt′) *v.t.* **1** To insult openly; treat with insolence; offend by word or act. **2** To confront in defiance; accost. **3** *Archaic* To front in position; face toward. — *n.* **1** An open insult or indignity. **2** *Obs.* A meeting. See synonyms under OUTRAGE. [<OF *afronter* strike on the forehead <LL *affrontare* strike against <L *ad-* to + *frons* forehead] —**af·front′er** *n.* —**af·fron′tive** *adj.*

Synonyms (verb): aggravate, annoy, displease, exasperate, insult, irritate, offend, provoke, tease, vex, wound. *Aggravate* in the sense of *offend* is not in approved use. To *provoke,* literally to call out or challenge, is to begin a contest; one *provokes* another to violence. To *affront* is to offer some defiant offense or indignity, as it were to one's face. Compare PIQUE[1]. *Antonyms:* conciliate, content, gratify, honor, please.

af·fuse (ə·fyo͞oz′) *v.t.* **af·fused, af·fus·ing** *Archaic.* To pour on, as water. [<L *affusus,* pp. of *affundere* <*ad-* to + *fundere* pour]

af·fu·sion (ə·fyo͞o′zhən) *n.* A pouring on or into; a sprinkling, as in baptism.

af·ghan (af′gən, -gan) *n.* A soft wool coverlet, knitted or crocheted, often in many-colored geometrical patterns.

Af·ghan (af′gən, -gan) *n.* **1** A native of Afghanistan. **2** The dominant language of Afghanistan: also called *Pushtu.* **3** An Afghan hound. —*adj.* Of or pertaining to Afghanistan, its inhabitants, or their language.

Afghan hound An ancient breed of large hound originally from Egypt, having long, thick, silky hair and a pointed muzzle.

Af·ghan·i·stan (af·gan′ə·stan) An independent country of south central Asia; 250,000 square miles; capital, Kabul.

a·fi·cio·na·do (ə·fish′ə) ·nä′dō, ə·fis′ē-, ə·fē ′sē·ə-, *Sp.* ä·fē·thyō ·nä′thō, -fē·syō-) *n. pl.* **·dos** (-dōz, *Sp.* -thōs) An avid follower or fan, as of a sport or activity; devotee: an *aficionado* of horse racing. [<Sp.]

a·field (ə·fēld′) *adv.* **1** In or to the field; abroad. **2** Off the track; astray.

a·fire (ə·fīr′) *adv.* & adj . On fire.

a·flame (ə·flām′) *adv.* & adj. Flaming; glowing.

af·la·tox·in (af′lə·tok′sən) *n.* Any of several toxic carcinogens produced by certain strains of a fungus (*Aspergillus flavus*) growing on peanuts, corn, beans, etc.

AFL-CIO A United States labor organization with a membership of 16 million workers, created in 1955 as a result of a merger between the *American Federation of Labor* and the *Congress of Industrial Organizations.*

a·float (ə·flōt′) *adv.* & adj. **1** Floating on the surface of a liquid or a body of water. **2** Not aground or ashore. **2** In motion or circulation, as a rumor. **3** Adrift; unfixed. **4** Overflowed; flooded, as the deck of a ship.

à fond (á fôn′) *French* To the bottom; thoroughly.

a·foot (ə·fo͝ot′) *adv.* **1** On foot. **2** Able to walk. **3** In motion or progress; on the move; astir. [ME *on fot*]

a·fore (ə·fôr′, ə·fō r′) *adv., prep., & conj.* Before. [OE *onforan,* blended with *æt-foran* before. See ON, AT, and FORE.]

a·fore·hand (ə·fôr′hand′, ə·fōr′-) *adv.* & adj. Beforehand; prepared; supplied with what is needed for the future.

a·fore·said (ə·fôr′sed′, ə·fōr′-) *adj.* Said or mentioned before.

a·fore·thought (ə·fôr′thô t′, ə·fōr′-) *adj.* Intended, devised, contrived, or planned beforehand; premeditated. —*n.* Premeditation.

a·fore·time (ə·fôr′tīm′ , ə·fōr′-) *adv.* At a previous time; formerly.

a for·ti·o·ri (ā fôr′shē ·ôr′ī, ā fōr′shē·ō′rī, -rē) *Latin* By a stronger reason; all the more.

a·foul (ə·foul′) *adv. & adj.* In entanglement or collision; entangled. — **to run (or fall) afoul of** To become entangled with; get into difficulties with.

a·fraid (ə·frād′) *adj.* Filled with fear or apprehension; apprehensive; fearful. [Orig. pp. of AFFRAY]

A–frame (ā′frām′) *n.* A framework in the shape of the letter A, as that supporting a slanted roof.

a·fresh (ə·fresh′) *adv.* Once more; anew; again: We started *afresh.*

Af·ri·ca (af′ri·kə) *n.* The second largest continent, located in the eastern hemisphere south of Europe and joined to Asia by the Sinai peninsula; 11,500,000 square miles.

Af·ri·can (af′ri·kən) *n.* **1** A native or inhabitant of Africa. **2** A person of African ancestry, esp. a black person. **3** Of or pertaining to or characteristic of the continent of Africa or its people.

Africana (a-fri-′ka-nə) *n.pl.* Materials relating to African history and culture.

African American *n.* An American of black African descent.

Africanist *n.* A specialist in African languages or cultures.

Af·ri·can·ize (af′rə·kən·īz′) *v.t.* **·ized, ·iz·ing 1** To make African in character or nature. **2** To place under the control of Africans, especially of black Africans. —**Af′ri·can·i·za′tion** *n.*

African lily *n.* A greenhouse potted plant (*Agapanthus africanus*) from Africa, with deep blue or white flowers growing in umbellate clusters.

African sleeping sickness *n.* A disease confined to tropical Africa, caused by either of two species of trypanosomes (*Trypanosoma gambiense* or *T. rhodesiense*) usually transmitted by the bite of the tsetse fly and marked by recurrent fever and headaches, progressive lethargy, somnolence and death. Also called *sleeping sickness.* Also **African trypanosomiasis.**

African violet *n.* Any of a genus (*Saintpaulia*) of tropical African perennial herbs with purple, pink, or white flowers.

Af·ri·kaans (af′ri·käns′, -känz′) *n.* One of the official languages of the Republic of South Africa, which developed from the speech of 17th century Dutch settlers and contains many words of English, French, and Malay origin.

Af·ri·ka·ner (af′ri·kä′nər) *n.* A South African of European descent whose native language is Afrikaans.

Af·ro (af′rō) *n. pl.* **Af·ros** A hair style in which bushy hair is shaped into a full, rounded mass. —*adj.* Of, pertaining to, or influenced by African culture.

Afro- *combining form* Africa; African. [<L *Afer* an African]

Af·ro–A·mer·i·can (af′rō·ə·mer′ə·kən) *adj.* Of or pertaining to Americans of black African descent. —*n.* An Afro-American person.

aft (aft, äft) *adj.* Of or near the stern, or rear, of a vessel. — *adv.* Toward the rear; astern. [OE *æftan* behind]

af·ter (af′tər, äf′-) *adj.* **1** *Naut.* Farther aft; toward the stern. **2** Following in time or place; subsequent; later. —*adv.* **1** At a later time. **2** In the rear; behind. —*prep.* **1** In the rear of; farther back than; following: The prisoners followed *after* the soldiers. **2** Subsequently to; at a later period than: His will was read *after* his death. **3** In succession to; following repeatedly: the same routine day *after* day. **4** As a result of; subsequently to and because of: *After* their quarrel they decided to separate. **5** Notwithstanding; subsequently to and in spite of: *After* the best endeavors, one may fail. **6** Next below in order or importance: This man comes right *after* the king in power. **7** In search or pursuit of: to strive *after* wisdom. **8** According to the nature, wishes, or customs of; in conformity with: a man *after* my own heart. **9** In imitation of; in the manner of: a painting *after* Vermeer. **10** In honor, remembrance, or observance of: I was named *after* Lincoln. **11** In relation to; concerning: to inquire *after* someone's health. — *conj.* Following the time that: *After* I went home, I went to bed. [OE *æfter* behind]

After may appear as a combining form in

hyphemes or solidemes with the following meanings:

1 Following in place, order, or time:

after-acquired	**after-mentioned**
after-age	**after-named**
after-ages	**aftersails**
after-described	**after-specified**
after-designed	**after-supper**
after-knowledge	**after-written**
aftermast	**after-years**

2 Secondary; following the main occurrence:

aftercrop	**aftershock**
aftergrowth	**after-storm**
after-mass	**after-winter**

3 Following not at once; eventual; after delay:

aftereffect	**after-penitence**
after-fame	**after-reckoning**
after-glory	**after-remedy**

after all All things considered; on the whole.

af·ter·birth (af′tər·bûrth′, äf′-) *n.* The placenta and fetal membranes expelled from the uterus following delivery of mammalian offspring.

af·ter·bod·y (af′tər·bod′ē, äf′-) *n.* In rocketry, a section of a rocket or missile that continues to trail the nose cone or satellite from which it separates.

af·ter·brain (af′tər·brān′, äf′-) *n.* Hindbrain.

af·ter·burn·er (af′tər·bûr′nər, äf′-) *n. Aeron.* A device for injecting extra fuel into the exhaust system of a jet engine as a means of increasing the thrust.

af·ter·burn·ing (af′tər·bûr′ning, äf′-) *n. Aeron.* **1** An irregular burning of fuel occurring subsequently to the normal combustion of fuel in a rocket or jet engine. **2** The technique of using an afterburner.

af·ter·care (af′tər·kâr′, äf′-) *n.* Supplementary observation and treatment as needed of a person discharged from a program or a hospital or other institution.

af·ter·cool·er (af′tər·kōō′lər, äf′-) *n. Aeron.* A radiator designed to reduce the temperature of the fuel mixture in the supercharging system of a jet airplane flying at extreme altitudes.

af·ter·damp (af′tər·damp′, äf′-) *n.* A suffocating mixture of gases, chiefly nitrogen and carbon dioxide, found in mines after a fire or an explosion of firedamp.

af·ter·deck (af′tər·dek′, äf′-) *n. Naut.* That part of a deck aft of amidships.

af·ter-din·ner (af′tər·din′ər, äf′-) *adj.* **1** Occurring, made, or done after dinner: an *after-dinner* speech. **2** Served after dinner: *after-dinner* coffee.

af·ter·ef·fect (af′tər·ə·fekt′, äf′-) *n.* **1** An effect succeeding its cause after an interval. **2** A result following the initial effects of an agent, as a drug, X-rays, etc.

af·ter·glow (af′tər·glō′, äf′-) *n.* **1** A glow after a light has disappeared, as in metals cooling after being heated to incandescence or in the western sky after sunset. **2** The luminosity of a rarefied gas after the passage of an electric charge through it. **3** An agreeable feeling occurring after a pleasant or profitable experience.

af·ter·im·age (af′tər·im′ij, äf′-) *n.* **1** *Psychol.* The persistence of a visual sensation after the direct stimulus has been withdrawn from the retina. Also called *photogene.* **2** A similar effect of other senses.

af·ter·life (af′tər·līf′, äf′-) *n.* Life after death.

af·ter·math (af′tər·math, äf′-) *n.* **1** Results; consequences; especially, ill consequences. **2** *Agric.* The second grass crop of the season, after the first has been cut for hay; a second mowing. [< AFTER + MATH[1]]

af·ter·most (af′tər·mōst, äf′-) *adj.* **1** *Naut.* Nearest the stern: also **aft′most. 2** Last.

af·ter·noon (af′tər·nōōn′, äf′-) *n.* That part of the day between noon and sunset; hence, the closing part: the *afternoon* of life. —*adj.* Of, for, or occurring in the afternoon.

af·ter·pain (af′tər·pān′, äf′-) *n.* **1** A subsequent pain. **2** *pl.* The pains succeeding childbirth, due to contraction of the womb.

af·ter·piece (af′tər·pēs′, äf′-) *n.* **1** A farce or other short piece after a play. **2** *Naut.* The heel of a rudder.

af·ter·sen·sa·tion (af′tər·sen·sā′shən, äf′-) *n. Psychol.* Any sensory persistence after direct stimulation has ceased, as an afterimage, aftertaste, etc.

af·ter·shaft (af′tər·shaft′, äf′tər·shäft′) *n.* A secondary shaft of the feather in many birds, springing from near the junction of the quill with the rachis.

af·ter·taste (af′tər·tāst′, äf′-) *n.* A taste persisting in the mouth, as after a meal.

af·ter·thought (af′tər·thôt′, äf′-) *n.* **1** A later or more deliberate thought, as after decision or action. **2** A thought occurring too late to affect action in the matter to which it refers.

af·ter·time (af′tər·tīm′, äf′-) *n.* Time following the present; the future.

af·ter·ward (af′tər·wərd, äf′-) *adv.* In time following; subsequently. Also **af′ter·wards.** [OE *æfterweard*]

af·ter·world (af′tər·wûrld′, äf′-) *n.* The future world; also, the world after death.

af·to·sa (af·tō′sə) *n. SW U.S.* Foot-and-mouth disease. [< Sp., fem., aphthous]

ag- Assimilated var. of AD-.

Ag *chem.* Silver (symbol Ag). [L *argentum*]

a·ga (ä′gə) *n.* An officer of high military or civil rank in Mohammedan countries: also spelled *agha.* [< Turkish]

A·ga·des (ä′gə·des, ag′ə·dēz) A city in the Republic of the Niger. Also **A·ga·dez** (ä′gə·dēz, ag′ə-).

A·ga·dir (ä′gə·dir′, ag′ə-) A port in SW Morocco.

a·gain (ə·gen′, *esp. Brit.* ə·gān′) *adv.* **1** At a second or another time; once more; anew; afresh: to bring a subject to life *again.* **2** Once repeated: half as much *again.* **3** To the same place or over the same course; back, as in a previous condition: Here we are *again!* **4** In correspondence with something previous or preceding; in reply; in return: The valley echoed *again* to the sound of horns. **5** In the next place; further; moreover: *Again,* since the weather is uncertain, I may not be able to come. **6** On the other hand; from another point of view. [OE *ongegn*]

again and again Repeatedly.

a·gainst (ə·genst′, *esp. Brit.* ə·gānst′) *prep.* **1** In contact with and pressing upon: leaning *against* the wall. **2** In collision with: The ship was dashed *against* the rocks. **3** In front of; directly opposite: *against* the background of the sky. **4** In anticipation of; in preparation for: to be ready *against* the third day; to hoard wealth *against* old age. **5** In opposition to; contrary to: *against* my wishes. **6** In hostility to: fighting *against* the invader. **7** To the debit of: Charge it *against* my account. **8** In comparison with; contrasted with: my word *against* his. [OE *ongegn* + *-es,* adverbial genitive suffix + inorganic *-t*]

A·ga Khan (ä′gə kän′) A hereditary Mohammedan title passing to the heads of families descended from Ali.
—**Aga Khan III,** 1877–1957, leader of Ismaelian Mohammedans, succeeding his father, Aga Khan II, in 1885.

a·gal (ä·gäl′) *n. Arabic* A thick cord worn by Bedouins over the kaffiyeh to keep it in place.

ag·a·lac·ti·a (ag′ə·lak′shē·ə) *n. Pathol.* The failure or deficiency of milk secretion. [< NL < Gk. *agalaktia* < *a-* without + *gala, galaktos* milk]

a·gal·loch (ə·gal′ək, ag′ə·lok) *n.* The fragrant wood of a tree *(Aquilaria agallocha)* of Indochina and neighboring regions; the aloes or lignaloes of the Scriptures (*Num.* xxiv:5). Also called *aloes, lignaloes.* Also **a·gal·wood** ä′gəl·wŏŏd′, ag′əl-). [< NL *agallochum* < Gk. *agallochon* bitter aloe]

ag·al·mat·o·lite (ag′əl·mat′ə·līt) *n.* One of various soft waxy minerals, pagodite, pinite, or steatite, used for carvings by the Chinese. [< Gk. *agalma* statue, image + *lithos* stone]

ag·a·ma (ag′ə·mə) *n.* Any of various small terrestrial lizards of the family Agamidae, found in tropical regions of the Old World. [< Carib]

a·gam·ete (ā·gam′ēt) *n.* Any unicellular organism that reproduces asexually, as certain protozoans.

Ag·a·mem·non (ag′ə·mem′non, -nən) In Greek legend, king of Mycenae, brother of Menelaus and father of Orestes, Electra, and Iphigenia: chief of the Greek army in the Trojan war, he was killed on his return by his wife Clytemnestra and her lover Aegisthus.

a·gam·ic (ə·gam′ik) *adj.* Reproducing without the union of two sexes; parthenogenic; asexual. Also **ag·a·mous** (ag′ə·məs). [< Gk. *agamos* unmarried < *a-* without + *gamos* marriage] —**a·gam′i·cal·ly** *adv.*

a·gam·ma·glob·u·li·ne·mi·a (ā·gam′ə·glob′yə·lə·nē′mē·ə) *n.* Any congenital, acquired, or transient condition in which gamma globulins and antibodies are deficient or lacking in the blood.

ag·a·mo·gen·e·sis (ag′ə·mō·jen′ə·sis) *n.* Reproduction without the union of opposite sexual elements, as by budding, cell division, or parthenogenesis. [< NL < Gk. *agamos* unmarried + GENESIS] —**ag′a·mo·ge·net′ic** (-jə·net′ik) *adj.*

A·ga·ña (ä·gä′nyä) The capital of Guam.

Ag·a·nip·pe (ag′ə·nip′ē) A fountain on Mount Helicon, Greece, traditionally sacred to the Muses.

ag·a·pan·thus (ag′ə·pan′thəs) *n.* Any of a genus *(Agapanthus)* of South African plants of the lily family, bearing umbels of blue or white flowers; the African lily. [< NL < Gk. *agapē* love + *anthos* flower]

a·gape[1] (ə·gāp′, ə·gap′) *adv. & adj.* In a gaping state; gaping.

ag·a·pe[2] (ag′ə·pē) *n. pl.* **·pae** (-pē) The social meal or love feast of the primitive Christians which usually accompanied the Eucharist. [< Gk. *agapē* love]

a·gar (ä′gär, ā′gər, ä′gär) *n.* A gelatinous substance obtained from certain red algae and used as a gelling material in culture media and in the food industry. Also **a·gar-a·gar.** [< Malay *agar-agar*]

ag·a·ric (ag′ə·rik, ə·gar′ik) *n.* **1** Any of the various fungi (order Agaricales) bearing an umbrellalike fruiting body with gills on the underside, including the common edible mushroom *Agaricus campestris.* **2** The dried fruiting body of various fungi, used as touchwood, in medicine, etc. [< L *agaricum* < Gk. *agarikon,* named after *Agaria,* in Sarmatia] —**a·gar·i·ca·ceous** (ə·gar′i·kā′shəs) *adj.*

ag·a·ric·ic acid (ag′ə·ris′ik) The active principle of agaric, a white, odorless, tasteless crystalline powder, $C_{22}H_{40}O_7$, used in medicine for the relief of night sweats.

agaric mineral Rock milk.

A·gar·ta·la (ə·gûr′tə·lə) The capital of Tripura state, India.

Ag·as·siz (ag′ə·sē, *Fr.* à·gà·sē′), **Alexander,** 1835–1910, U.S. zoologist, born in Switzerland; son of **(Jean) Louis (Rodolphe),** 1807–73, U.S. naturalist and teacher, born in Switzerland.

ag·ate (ag′it) *n.* **1** A variegated waxy quartz or chalcedony, SiO_2, in which the colors are usually in bands. **2** A child's playing marble. **3** *Printing* 5 1/2 point type. See TYPOGRAPHY. **4** Any of several instruments, as the drawplate of goldwire drawers. **5** *Obs.* A very diminutive person; in allusion to the figures cut upon agates for rings. [< F < L *achates* < Gk. *achatēs* < *Achatēs,* a river in Sicily]

ag·ate·ware (ag′it·wâr′) *n.* **1** Pottery veined and mottled to resemble agate. **2** A kind of steel or iron kitchenware, enameled and grained to resemble agate pottery.

Ag·a·tha (ag′ə·thə; *Dan.* ä·gä′thə, *Du.* a·ga′ta) A feminine personal name. Also *Fr.* **A·gathe** (à·gàt′), *Ger.* **A·ga·the** (ä·gä′tə), *Ital., Sp.* **A·ga·ta** (ä′gä·tä), *Pg.* **A·ga·tha** (ä′gä·tä), *Sw.* **A·ga·ta** (ä·gä′tä), *Lat.* **Ag·a·the** (ag′ə·thē). [< Gk. *Agathē* good, kind]

A·gath·o·cles (ə·gath′ə·klēz), 361–289 B.C., tyrant of Syracuse.

ag·a·tho·de·mon (ag′ə·thō·dē′mən) *n.* A benevolent spirit; a good genius: opposed to *cacodemon.* [< Gk. *agathodaimōn* < *agathos* good + *daimōn* spirit]

ag·a·tize (ag′ə·tīz) *v.t.* **·tized, ·tiz·ing** To make into or cause to resemble agate or agateware.

à gauche (à gōsh′) *French* To, toward, or on the left (hand).

a·ga·ve (ə·gä′vē *or* ə·gā′vē) *n.* Any of a genus *(Agave)* of fleshy-leaved plants native to hot, desert areas of the Americas, as the century plant and the sisal. [< NL < Gk. *Agauē,* proper n., fem. of *agauos* noble]

a·gaze (ə·gāz′) *adv.* In the posture or attitude of gazing.

age (āj) *n.* **1** The entire period of life or existence, as of a person, thing, nation, etc. **2** The period or stage of life as measured by the time already or previously passed. **3** The closing period of life; decline of life; the state of being old. **4** Any period of life that fits or unfits for any function, office, duty, etc.; specifically, that time of life at which one legally becomes mature, independent, and responsible, usually 21 years; majority: used especially in the phrase **of age. 5** Any period of life naturally distinct; stage of life. **6** Any great and distinct period of

time in the history of man, of the earth, etc.; era; epoch; generation. **7** A century. **8** A long time; protracted period: He has been gone an *age.* **9** In poker, the eldest hand. **10** *Psychol.* The physical and mental development of a person, measured in years, in relation to the normal physical and mental development of an average child. —*v.* **aged, ag·ing** or **age·ing** *v.t.* **1** To make or cause to grow old. **2** In dyeing, to fix and distribute the mordant in, as fabric, by exposure to air or chemicals. —*v.i.* **3** To assume or show some characteristics of age; ripen: Tobacco *ages* in storing. [<OF *aage* <L *aetas* age, a span of life]

-age *suffix of nouns* **1** Collection or aggregate of: *baggage, leafage.* **2** Condition, office, service, or other relation or connection of: *drayage; pilgrimage.* [<OF <L *-aticum,* neut. adj. suffix]

a·ged (ā′jid *for defs.* 1, 2, 4; ājd *for def.* 3) *adj.* **1** Advanced in years; very old. **2** Of, like, or characteristic of old age. **3** Of or at the age of: a child, *aged* five. **4** *Geol.* Nearing base level reduction: said of configuration of ground. See synonyms under ANCIENT. **—a′ged·ly** *adv.* **—a′ged·ness** *n.*

a·gee (ə·jē′) *adv. & adj.* Awry; askew. [<A-[1] + GEE[2]]

age·ing (ā′jing) See AGING.

age-in-grade (āj′in·grād′) *n.* A military officer's age in relation to his rank: a consideration in qualifying him for field service.

age·ism (ā′jiz·əm) *n.* Discrimination or prejudice, esp. as directed against elderly people. **—age′ist** *n., adj.*

age·less (āj′lis) *adj.* **1** Not seeming to grow old. **2** Having no limits of duration.

age·long (āj′lông′, -long′) *adj.* Lasting a long time; everlasting: *agelong* myths.

a·gen·cy (ā′jən·sē) *n. pl.* **·cies 1** Active power or operation; activity. **2** Means; instrumentality. **3** The relation of an agent to his principal. **4** The business, office, or place of business, of an agent. **5** Any establishment where business is done for others. See synonyms under OPERATION. [<L *agentia* <*agere* do]

a·gen·da (ə·jen′də) *n. pl. of agendum* A record of things to be done, as items of business; a memorandum; specifically, a program of business to be done or papers to be read at a meeting: What's on the *agenda* for today?

a·gen·dum (ə·jen′dəm) *n. pl.* **·da** *Eccl.* A thing to be done, as a liturgical detail: opposed to *credendum,* a matter of belief. [<L, neut. gerundive of *agere* do]

a·gen·e·sis (ə·jen′ə·sis) *n.* **1** The absence of a tissue or organ due to a failure in development. **2** Sexual sterility or impotence. **3** Aplasia. Also **ag·e·ne·sia** (aj′ə·nē′zhə, -zhē·ə). [<A-[4] without + GENESIS]

age norm *Psychol.* The average score made on a standard set of tests by a random group of children of given age; the score typical for a child of stated age.

a·gent (ā′jənt) *n.* **1** One who or that which acts or has power to act; an efficient cause of anything; actor; doer. **2** One who or that which acts for another; a factor; steward; deputy. **3** Any force or substance having power to effect a material change in bodies, as a chemical, drug, or earth movement. **4** A means by which something is done. **5** One who transacts business for another: a literary *agent.* **6** A traveling salesman or canvasser. —*adj. Obs.* Acting: opposed to *passive.* [<L *agens, agentis,* ppr. of *agere* do]

Synonyms (noun): actor, cause, doer, factor, instrument, means, mover, operator, performer, promoter. In strict philosophical usage, the prime *mover* or *doer* of an act is the *agent.* Thus we speak of man as a free *agent.* But in common usage, especially in business, an *agent* is not the prime *actor,* but only an *instrument* or *factor,* acting under orders or instructions. Compare CAUSE. *Antonyms*: chief, inventor, originator, principal.

a·gen·tial (ā·jen′shəl) *adj.* Of or pertaining to an agent or agency.

Agent Orange A toxic herbicidal and defoliant mixture used extensively by the United States in military operations in Vietnam before its use was banned in early 1970.

a·gent pro·vo·ca·teur (à·zhäṅ′ prô·vô·kà·tœr′) *pl.* **a·gents pro·vo·ca·teurs** (à·zhäṅ′ prô·vô·kà·tœr′) *French* A secret agent implanted in an organization, as a trade union or political party, to incite its members to actions or declarations that will incur penalties or punishment.

age of consent The age of a girl before which sexual relations with her, regardless of her consent, constitute statutory rape.

age-old (āj′ōld′) *adj.* Extremely old; ancient: *age-old* traditions.

ag·e·o·tro·pism (aj′ē·ot′rə·piz′əm) *n. Bot.* Apogeotropism. **—ag·e·o·trop·ic** (aj′ē·ō·trop′ik) *adj.*

ag·er (ā′jər) *n.* **1** That which promotes age or produces an effect of age. **2** A boxlike vessel in which fabrics are treated with steam or ammonia fumes to fix the colors.

ag·e·ra·tum (aj′ə·rā′təm, ə·jer′ə·təm) *n.* **1** Any of a large genus (*Ageratum*) of tropical American herbs of the composite family with opposite petioled leaves and terminal cymes or panicles of blue or white flowers in small heads. **2** Any of several plants having similar heads of blue flowers. [<NL <Gk. *agēraton,* a kind of plant <*agēratos* ageless <*a-* not + *gēras* old age]

A·ges·i·la·us (ə·jes′ə·lā′əs), 444?–360 B.C., Spartan king.

a·geu·si·a (ə·gyo͞o′sē·ə) *n.* Loss or impairment of the sense of taste. Also **a·geus·ti·a** (ə·gyo͞os′tē·ə). [<NL <Gk. *a-* without + *geusis* taste] **—a·geu′sic** *adj.*

ag·ger (aj′ər) *n.* **1** A mound or heap; an earthwork; especially, in ancient Rome, the rampart of a fortified camp; a bank against a wall that overtops the defenses. **2** A military road. [<L]

Ag·gie (ag′ē) Diminutive of AGATHA.

ag·glom·er·ate (ə·glom′ə·rāt) *v.t. & v.i.* **·at·ed, ·at·ing** To gather, form, or grow into a ball or rounded mass. —*adj.* (ə·glom′ər·it, -ə·rāt) Gathered into a mass or heap; clustered densely. —*n.* (ə·glom′ər·it, -ə·rāt) **1** A heap or mass of things thrown together indiscriminately. **2** *Geol.* An unstratified mass of compacted volcanic debris with fragments of all sizes. [<L *agglomeratus,* pp. of *agglomerare* <*ad-* to + *glomerare* gather into a ball <*glomus* ball] **—ag·glom·er·at·ic** (ə·glom′ə·rat′ik), **ag·glom′er·a′tive** *adj.*

ag·glom·er·a·tion (ə·glom′ə·rā′shən) *n.* **1** The process of agglomerating. **2** The state or condition of being agglomerated. **3** A jumbled heap or mass.

ag·glu·ti·nant (ə·glo͞o′tə·nənt) *adj.* Tending to cause adhesion; sticky. —*n.* An adhesive substance.

ag·glu·ti·nate (ə·glo͞o′tə·nāt) *v.t. & v.i.* **·nat·ed, ·nat·ing 1** To unite, as with glue; join by adhesion. **2** *Ling.* To form (words) by agglutination. **3** To mass together, as living cells or bacteria, by agglutination. —*adj.* (ə·glo͞o′tə·nit, -nāt) Joined by adhesion. [<L *agglutinatus,* pp. of *agglutinare* glue to <*ag-* to + *glutinare* <*gluten* glue]

ag·glu·ti·na·tion (ə·glo͞o′tə·nā′shən) *n.* **1** Adhesion of distinct parts; a mass formed by adhesion. **2** *Ling.* In some languages, a combination of word elements without change of form or meaning to form new compound word elements. **3** The clumping together of particles, as red blood cells, bacteria, etc., suspended in blood serum or other medium.

ag·glu·ti·na·tive (ə·glo͞o′tə·nā′tiv) *adj.* **1** Tending toward, pertaining to, or characterized by agglutination. **2** *Ling.* Denoting a language, such as Turkish or Hungarian, in which words are formed by adding to a word root other word roots or simple words without change of form or loss of original meaning of the various elements.

ag·glu·ti·nin (ə·glo͞o′tə·nin) *n.* An antibody formed in blood serum which causes clumping of particles, as red corpuscles or bacteria, bearing the corresponding antigen.

ag·glu·tin·o·gen (ag′lo͞o·tin′ə·jən) *n.* An antigen that stimulates the formation of a specific corresponding antibody (agglutinin) when introduced into an animal body. **—ag′glu·tin′o·gen′ic** *adj.*

ag·grade (ə·grād′) *v.t.* **ag·grad·ed, ag·grad·ing** *Geol.* To add to or raise, as the bed of a river by the deposition of silt. [<AD- + GRADE] **—ag·gra·da·tion** (ag′rə·dā′shən) *n.*

ag·gran·dize (ə·gran′dīz, ag′rən·dīz) *v.t.* **·dized, ·diz·ing 1** To make great or greater; increase. **2** To increase the power or rank of (oneself): to *aggrandize* oneself at another's expense. **3** To make appear greater; exalt. [<F *agrandiss-,* stem of *agrandir* <L *ad-* to + *grandire* make great] **—ag·gran·dize·ment** (ə·gran′diz·mənt) *n.* **—ag·gran′diz·er** *n.*

ag·gra·vate (ag′rə·vāt) *v.t.* **·vat·ed, ·vat·ing 1** To make worse; increase, intensify, as an offense. **2** To make heavier or more burdensome, as a duty. **3** *Colloq.* To provoke or exasperate; arouse to anger. [<L *aggravatus,* pp. of *aggravare* make heavy or burdensome <*ad-* to + *gravare* make heavy <*gravis* heavy. Doublet of AGGRIEVE.] **—ag′gra·vat′ing** *adj.* **—ag′gra·vat′ing·ly** *adv.* **—ag′gra·va′tive** *adj.*

Synonyms: affront, enhance, heighten, increase, intensify, magnify. *Enhance* and *magnify* are most often used in the lofty and good sense; as, to *enhance* the glory of God; "I *magnify* mine office," *Rom.* xi 13. *Aggravate* is used always in the bad sense meaning to make worse what is already bad; as, to *aggravate* a fever or an enmity. See AFFRONT, INCREASE. *Antonyms*: alleviate, assuage, attenuate, diminish, lessen, palliate, reduce, soften.

aggravated assault *Law* Assault committed with the intention of committing an additional offense.

ag·gra·va·tion (ag′rə·vā′shən) *n.* **1** A making heavier or worse or the state of being aggravated. **2** Some extrinsic circumstance considered as increasing the atrocity of a crime. **3** *Colloq.* Exasperation; irritation.

ag·gre·gate (ag′rə·gāt) *v.t.* **·gat·ed, ·gat·ing 1** To bring or gather together, as into a mass, sum, or body; collect; mass. **2** To amount to; form a total of. See synonyms under AMASS. —*adj.* (ag′rə·git) **1** Collected into a sum, mass, or total; gathered into a whole; formed by collection; collective. **2** *Bot.* **a** Crowded close together in a dense cluster, as a flower head. **b** Formed of a coherent mass of drupelets, as a fruit. **3** *Geol.* Composed of distinct minerals separable by mechanical means, as granite. —*n.* (ag′rə·git) **1** The entire number, sum, mass, or quantity of something; amount; total, collection. **2** Material for making concrete. **—in the aggregate** Collectively; as a whole. [<L *aggregatus,* pp. of *aggregare,* lit., bring to the flock <*ad-* to + *gregare* collect <*grex* flock] **—ag′gre·ga′tive** *adj.* **—ag′gre·ga′tor** *n.*

Synonyms (noun): agglomeration, aggregation, amount, collection, entirety, heap, mass, sum, total, totality, whole. An *aggregate* of financial items is an *amount, sum,* or *total.* An *aggregate* or *aggregation* of material objects is a *collection, mass,* or *whole*; an *agglomeration* is a heterogeneous *mass. Collection* points rather to the differences, *mass* to the unity. We say a *collection* of minerals, a *mass* of rock. The result of multiplication is a product, the result of addition a *sum, total,* or *aggregate.*

ag·gre·ga·tion (ag′rə·gā′shən) *n.* **1** A collection into a whole; a mass; aggregate; whole. **2** The act of aggregating, or the state of being aggregated.

ag·gress (ə·gres′) *v.i.* To undertake an attack; begin a quarrel. [<L *aggressus,* pp. of *aggredi* approach, attack <*ad-* to + *gradi* step, go <*gradus* a step]

ag·gres·sion (ə·gresh′ən) *n.* **1** An unprovoked attack; encroachment. **2** Habitual aggressive action or practices. **3** *Psychoanal.* A primary instinct, generally associated with emotional states, to carry out action in a forceful way.

Synonyms: assault, attack, encroachment, incursion, intrusion, invasion, onslaught, trespass. An *attack* may be by word; an *aggression* is always by deed. An *assault* may be upon the person, an *aggression* is upon rights, possessions, etc. An *invasion* of a nation's territories is an act of *aggression*; an *intrusion* upon a neighboring estate is a *trespass. Onslaught* signifies intensely violent

assault, as by an army or a desperado, yet it is sometimes used of violent speech. *Antonyms*: defense, repulsion, resistance, retreat.

ag·gres·sive (ə·gres′iv) *adj.* **1** Disposed to begin an attack or encroachment. **2** Disposed to vigorous activity; assertive. **—ag·gres′sive·ly** *adv.* **—ag·gres′sive·ness** *n.*

ag·gres·sor (ə·gres′ər) *n.* One who commits an aggression or begins a quarrel.

ag·grieve (ə·grēv′) *v.t.* **ag·grieved, ag·griev·ing 1** To cause sorrow to; distress or afflict. **2** To give cause for just complaint, as by injustice. See synonyms under ABUSE. [<OF *agrever* <L *aggravare.* Doublet of AGGRAVATE.]

ag·grieved (ə·grēvd′) *adj.* **1** Subjected to ill-treatment; feeling an injury or injustice. **2** Injured, as by legal decision adversely infringing upon one's rights. **—ag·griev·ed·ness** (ə·grē′vid·nis) *n.*

a·gha (ä′gə) See AGA.

a·ghast (ə·gast′, ə·gäst′) *adj.* Struck dumb with horror. [pp. of obs. *agast* frighten, OE *ā-* A-[1] + *gæstan* terrify; spelling infl. by *ghost*]

ag·ile (aj′əl, aj′il) *adj.* **1** Able to move or act quickly and easily; active; nimble. **2** Characterized by quickness of perception or response; alert: an *agile* mind. See synonyms under ACTIVE, NIMBLE. [<F <L *agilis* <*agere* do, move] **—ag′ile·ly** *adv.* **—ag′ile·ness** *n.*

a·gil·i·ty (ə·jil′ə·tē) *n.* Quickness and readiness in movement or mind; nimbleness. [<F *agilité* <L *agilitas* <*agilis.* See AGILE.]

Ag·in·court (aj′in·kôrt, -kōrt; *Fr.* à·zhaṅ·kōōr′) A village in northern France: site of an English victory over the French, 1415.

ag·ing (ā′jing) *n.* **1** The process of acquiring characteristics of age. **2** *Biol.* The progressive breakdown of an organism or any of its parts through the cumulative effects of irreversible physicochemical changes acting over a period of time. **3** The effects of time on the properties of materials or substances. **4** Any means for obtaining such effects artificially, as the weathering of clay for bricks, or the acid treatment of bronze to obtain a patina. **5** *Metall.* A change in the properties of certain metals, as hardness and tensile strength, caused by heat treatment and cold working. **6** A method of steaming fabrics to develop and fix the colors. Also spelled *ageing.*

ag·i·o (aj′ē·ō) *n. pl.* **ag·i·os 1** The premium payable for the exchange of one kind or quality of money into another; exchange premium. **2** An allowance for depreciation of coin by wear. [<Ital. *aggio* exchange]

ag·i·o·tage (aj′ē·ə·tij) *n.* Brokerage; stockjobbing. [<F]

a·gist (ə·jist′) *v.t. Law* **1** To feed and care for, as horses or cattle, for hire. **2** To assess, as land or its owner, for a public purpose. [<OF *agister* <*a-* to (<L *ad-*) + *gister* lodge, ult. <L *jacere* lie] **—a·gist′ment** *n.*

ag·i·tate (aj′ə·tāt) *v.* **·tat·ed, ·tat·ing** *v.t.* **1** To shake or move irregularly. **2** To set or keep moving, as a fan. **3** To excite or endeavor to excite, as a crowd; perturb. **4** To discuss publicly and incessantly, as a controversial question. **5** *Archaic* To revolve in the mind; plan. *—v.i.* **6** To keep a subject or cause under continuous discussion, in order to excite public interest. [<L *agitatus*, pp. of *agitare* set in motion, freq. of *agere* move]

ag·i·ta·tion (aj′ə·tā′shən) *n.* **1** Violent motion. **2** Open, active discussion; urgent consideration. **3** Strong or tumultuous emotion. See synonyms under TUMULT.

a·gi·ta·to (ä′jē·tä′tō) *adj. & adv. Music* Stirring; restless; agitated: a direction in musical execution. [<Ital.]

ag·i·ta·tor (aj′ə·tā′tər) *n.* One who or that which agitates; specifically, one who promotes social change.

ag·it·prop (aj′it·prop′) *n.* **1** Communist political propaganda, as in a play, film, etc. **2** Any political propaganda. *—adj.* Pertaining to or of the nature of agitprop. [<Russ., Communist Party agency for agitation and propaganda]

A·gla·ia (ə·glā′ə) One of the three Graces.

a·glare (ə·glâr′) *adv.* In a glare.

a·gleam (ə·glēm′) *adv. & adj.* Bright; gleaming.

ag·let (ag′lit) *n.* A metal sheath or tag at the end of a lace or ribbon to facilitate threading; hence, any ornamental pendant: also spelled *aiglet.* [<F *aiguillette*, dim. of *aiguille* needle, ult. <L *acus*]

a·gley (ə·glē′, ə·glī′) *adv. Scot.* Aside; askew. Also **a·glee** (ə·glē′).

A·glos·sa (ə·glos′ə) *n. pl.* **1** A suborder of tailless amphibians without a tongue and with the Eustachian tubes confluent. **2** A group of headless and tongueless mollusks, including the clams, oysters, mussels, etc. [<NL <Gk. *aglōssos* without a tongue <*a-* without + *glōssa* tongue]

a·glow (ə·glō′) *adv. & adj.* In a glow; glowing.

ag·mi·nate (ag′mə·nit, -nāt) *adj.* Grouped in clusters. Also **ag′mi·nat′ed.** [<L *agmen, agminis* troop, crowd + -ATE[1]]

ag·nail (ag′nāl′) *n.* **1** A hangnail. **2** A painful swelling under or about a nail; whitlow. [OE *angnægl* <*ange* narrow, painful + *nægl* nail]

ag·nate (ag′nāt) *adj.* **1** Related on the male or the father's side. **2** Akin; similar. *—n.* A relative in the male line only. Compare COGNATE, ENATE. [<F *agnat* <L *agnatus* a relation (on the father's side), orig., added by birth, pp. of *agnasci* be born in addition to <*ad-* to + *nasci* be born] **—ag·nat·ic** (ag·nat′ik) *adj.* **—ag·nat′i·cal·ly** *adv.* **—ag·na·tion** (ag·nā′shən) *n.*

Ag·nes (ag′nis; *Dan., Du., Ger.* äg′nes) A feminine personal name. Also *Fr.* **A·gnès** (à·nyes′), *Ital.* **A·gne·se** (ä·nyā′zā). [<Gk., pure, sacred, or chaste]

Ag·ni (ug′nē, ag′nē) In Hindu mythology, the god of fire, representing also lightning and sun, according to the Vedas. Also **Ag′nis.** [<Skt.]

ag·no·men (ag·nō′mən) *n. pl.* **ag·nom·i·na** (ag·nom′ə·nə) An added name due to some special achievement; a nickname. [<L <*ad-* to + (*g*)*nomen* name] **—ag·nom′i·nal** *adj.*

ag·no·si·a (ag·nō′sē·ə) *n.* Impairment or loss of the ability to recognize or interpret sensory perceptions of familiar persons or things. [<NL <Gk. *a-* without + *gnōsis* knowing, knowledge] **—ag·no′sic** *adj.*

ag·nos·tic (ag·nos′tik) *adj.* Professing ignorance or the inability to know, especially in religion. *—n.* One who holds the theory of agnosticism. See synonyms under SKEPTIC. [<Gk. *agnōstos* unknowing, unknown <*a-* not + *gignōskein* know]

ag·nos·ti·cism (ag·nos′tə·siz′əm) *n.* **1** The doctrine of nescience, or the theory which maintains that man cannot have, and has not, any real or valid knowledge, but can know only impressions. **2** The theory that first truths, substance, cause, the human soul, and a First Cause, can neither be proved nor disproved, and must remain unknown or unknowable. **3** *Theol.* The theory that God is unknown or unknowable: distinguished from *atheism.*

ag·nus (ag′nəs) *n. pl.* **ag·ni** (ag′nī) The lamb as a Christian emblem; an Agnus Dei. [<L, lamb]

Ag·nus bell (ag′nəs) *Eccl.* The bell rung while the *Agnus Dei* is recited.

Ag·nus De·i (ag′nəs dē′ī, dā′ē) **1** *Eccl.* A figure of a lamb, as an emblem of Christ, often bearing a cross and banner. **2** In the Roman Catholic Church, a medallion or cake of wax stamped with this emblem and blessed by the Pope. **3** *Eccl.* **a** A prayer in the mass, beginning with the words *Agnus Dei.* **b** In Anglican and some other churches, a translation of this prayer, beginning "O Lamb of God." **4** A musical setting for this prayer. **5** In the Greek Church, a cloth bearing the figure of a lamb, used to cover the elements of the Eucharist. [<LL, Lamb of God. See *John* i 29.]

a·go (ə·gō′) *adv.* In the past; in time gone by; since. *—adj.* Gone by; past. [OE *āgān* past, gone away]

a·gog (ə·gog′) *adv. & adj.* In a state of eager curiosity; excited with interest or expectation. [<MF *en gogues* in a merry mood]

-agog *combining form* Leading, promoting, or inciting: *demagog, pedagog.* Also **-agogue.** [<Gk. *agōgos* leading]

ag·on (ag′ōn, -on) *n. pl.* **a·go·nes** (ə·gō′nēz) **1** One of the great national game festivals of ancient Greece, or the assembly at such a festival. **2** A division of the Greek drama in which the introduction or dramatized argument is carried on by the principal characters. [<Gk. *agōn* assembly, contest]

a·gone (ə·gôn′, ə·gon′) *adj. & adv. Obs.* Ago.

a·gon·ic (ə·gon′ik) *adj.* Having or forming no angle. [<Gk. *agōnos* <*a-* without + *gōnia* angle]

agonic line *Geog.* One of several lines on the earth's surface, on which the direction of the magnetic needle is truly north and south; a line of no magnetic declination.

ag·o·nist (ag′ə·nist) *n.* A contestant for a prize. [<AGON]

ag·o·nis·tic (ag′ə·nis′tik) *adj.* **1** Pertaining to athletic or polemic contest. **2** Striving for effect; strained. **3** Combative; polemic. Also **ag′o·nis′ti·cal.** **—ag′o·nis′ti·cal·ly** *adv.*

ag·o·nis·tics (ag′ə·nis′tiks) *n.* The art or science of athletic contests.

ag·o·nize (ag′ə·nīz) *v.* **·nized, ·niz·ing** *v.i.* **1** To be in or suffer extreme pain or anguish. **2** To make convulsive efforts, as in wrestling; strive. *—v.t.* **3** To subject to agony; torture. [<F *agoniser* <Med.L *agonizare* <Gk. *agōnizesthai* contend, strive <*agōn* contest]

ag·o·ny (ag′ə·nē) *n. pl.* **·nies 1** Intense suffering of body or mind; anguish; struggle. **2** Violent or very earnest contest or striving. **3** The suffering or struggle that precedes death. [<L *agonia* <Gk. *agōnia* <*agōn* contest]

Synonyms: ache, anguish, distress, pain, pang, paroxysm, suffering, throe, torment, torture. *Agony* and *anguish* express the uttermost *pain* or *suffering* of body or mind; *agony* that with which the sufferer struggles; *anguish*, that by which he is crushed. Compare AFFLICTION, GRIEF.

agony column A newspaper column devoted to messages or advertisements for missing friends and relatives.

ag·o·ra (ag′ər·ə) *n. pl.* **ag·o·rae** (-ər·ē) or **ag·o·ras 1** In ancient Greece, a popular assembly for political or other purposes. **2** A place of popular assembly; especially, the market place. [<Gk.]

ag·o·ra·pho·bi·a (ag′ər·ə·fō′bē·ə) *n.* Morbid fear of open spaces; fear of exposure to unidentified dangers.

A·gos·ti·no (ä′gōs·tē′nō) Italian form of AUGUSTINE.

a·gou·ti (ə·gōō′tē) *n. pl.* **·tis** or **·ties 1** A slender-limbed tropical American rodent (genus *Dasyprocta*), of grizzly color, little larger than a rabbit, with three hind toes. **2** A grizzled appearance of fur resulting from bands of light and dark coloration on each hair. Also **a·gou′ty.** [<F <Sp. *aguti* < Tupian]

AGOUTI (*def. 1*)

A·gra (ä′grä, ä′grə) **1** A district of western Uttar Pradesh state, India; 1,816 square miles; formerly a province of northern India. **2** A city, capital of Agra district, on the Jumna SE of Delhi: site of the Taj Mahal.

a·graffe (ə·graf′) *n.* **1** A hook or clasp; especially, an ornamental clasp used on armor or for fastening rich clothing. **2** A builders' cramp iron. Also **a·grafe′.** [<F]

A·gram (ä′gräm) The German name for ZAGREB.

a·gran·u·lo·cyte (ə·gran′yōō·lō·sīt) *n.* A type of leukocyte having the cytoplasm clear of granules.

a·gran·u·lo·cy·to·sis (ə·gran′yōō ·lō′sī·tō′sis) *n.* An acute febrile disease characterized by the absence or drastic reduction of granulocytes in the blood, often resulting from hypersensitivity to an administered drug.

ag·ra·pha (ag′rə·fə) *n. pl.* A collection of sayings ascribed to Jesus Christ, but not found in the Bible. See LOGIA. [<Gk. *agraphos* unwritten]

a·graph·i·a (ā·graf′ē·ə) *n.* A partial or total loss of the ability to write. [<NL <Gk. *a-* without + *graphein* write] **—a·graph′ic** *adj.*

a·grar·i·an (ə·grâr′ē·ən) *adj.* **1** Pertaining to land or its tenure or to a general distribution of lands. **2** Organizing or furthering agricultural interests and aid to farmers: an *agrarian* investment. *—n.* One who advocates agrarianism. [<L *agrarius* <*ager* field]

a·grar·i·an·ism (ə·grâr′ē·ən·iz′əm) *n.* **1** The theory or practice of equal distribution of lands. **2** Agitation or political dissension with the view of redistributing tenure of lands or of equalizing farm income, especially by the use of government controls.

a·gree (ə·grē′) *v.* **a·greed, a·gree·ing** *v.i.* **1** To give consent; accede: with *to.* **2** To come into or be in harmony. **3** To be of one mind; concur: with *with.* **4** To come to terms, as in the details of a transaction: with *about* or *on.* **5** To be acceptable or favorable; suit: with *with:* This food does not *agree* with him. **6** To conform or match, as scales of measurement. **7** *Gram.* To correspond in person, number, case, or gender. —*v.t.* **8** To grant as a concession: with a noun clause: I *agree* that the choice is difficult, but you must choose. [<OF *agreer* <*a gre* to one's liking <L *ad* to + *gratus* pleasing]

Synonyms: accede, accept, accord, acquiesce, admit, approve, assent, coincide, combine, comply, concur, consent, harmonize. *Agree* is the most general term of this group; to *concur* is to *agree* in general; to *coincide* is to *agree* in every particular. One *accepts* another's terms, *complies* with his wishes, *admits* his statement, *approves* his plan, *conforms* to his views of doctrine or duty, *accedes* or *consents* to his proposal. *Accede* expresses the more formal agreement, *consent* the more complete. One may silently *acquiesce* in that which does not meet his views, but which he does not care to contest. See ASSENT. *Antonyms:* contend, contradict, decline, demur, deny, differ, disagree, dispute, dissent, oppose, protest, refuse.

a·gree·a·ble (ə·grē′ə) ·bəl) *adj.* **1** Agreeing with or suited to the mind or senses; pleasurable; especially, of persons, giving pleasure by manner, bearing, or conversation. **2** Naturally or logically corresponding; suitable; correspondent; conformable: a truth *agreeable* to human reason. **3** Ready to agree; favorably inclined; giving assent; willing. **4** Being in accordance or conformity; conforming. —**a·gree′ a·bil′i·ty, a·gree′a·ble·ness** *n.* —**a·gree′a·bly** *adv.*

Synonyms: acceptable, amiable, comfortable, delightful, good, grateful, gratifying, pleasant, pleasing, welcome. See AMIABLE. *Antonyms:* disagreeable, hateful, obnoxious, offensive.

a·greed (ə·grēd′) *adj.* **1** Brought into or being in harmony; united. **2** Settled by consent, bargain, or contract. **3** Admitted or conceded; granted.

a·gree·ment (ə·grē′mənt) *n.* **1** The act of coming into accord, or the state of being in accord; conformity. **2** An arrangement or understanding between two or more parties as to a course of action; a covenant or treaty. **3** *Law* A contract. See synonyms under CONTRACT, HARMONY. **4** *Gram.* concord (def. 3).

a·gres·tial (ə·gres′chəl) *adj.* Growing wild on cultivated ground, as weeds. Also **a·gres·tal** (ə·gres′təl).

a·gres·tic (ə·gres′tik) *adj.* Rural; unpolished. Also **a·gres′ti·cal.** [<L *agrestis* <*ager* field]

ag·ri·bus·i·ness (ag′rə·biz′nis, -niz) *n.* All those commercial activities associated with agriculture, including the production, processing, and distribution of farm products and the manufacture of farm equipment. [<AGRI(CULTURE) + BUSINESS]

A·gric·o·la (ə·grik′ə·lə), **Gnaeus Julius,** 37–) 93, Roman governor of Britain.

ag·ri·cul·ture (ag′rə·kul′ chər) *n.* **1** The cultivation of the soil; the raising of food crops, breeding and raising of livestock, etc.; tillage; farming. **2** The science that treats of the cultivation of the soil. —**Department of Agriculture** An executive department of the U.S. government since 1899 (originally established 1862), headed by the Secretary of Agriculture, that acquires and diffuses information on agricultural subjects and administers laws to protect the farmer and consuming public. [<F<L *agricultura*<*ager* field + *cultura* cultivation] —**ag′ri·cul′tur·al** *adj.* — **ag′ri·cul′tur·al·ly** *adv.*

Synonyms: cultivation, culture, farming, floriculture, gardening, horticulture, husbandry, tillage. *Agriculture* is the generic term, including the science, the art, and the process of supplying human wants by raising the products of the soil, and by the associated industries; *farming* is the practice of *agriculture* as a business. We speak of the science of *agriculture,* the business of *farming:* scientific *agriculture* may be wholly in books; scientific *farming* is practiced upon the land.

ag·ri·cul·tur·ist (ag′rə·kul′chər·ist) *n.* One engaged in agriculture; a farmer; husbandman. Also **ag′ri·cul′tur·al·ist.**

A·gri·gen·to (ä′grē·jen′tō) A town in SW Sicily; site of Greek temples: formerly *Girgenti.* Ancient **Ag·ri·gen·tum** (ag′ri·jen′təm).

ag·ri·mo·ny (ag′rə·mō′ nē) *n.* **1** Any of several erect, perennial, rosaceous herbs (genus *Agrimonia)* having small yellow flowers on a long stalk and fruit covered with hooked hairs. **2** Any of several composite herbs of similar habit, as hemp agrimony, etc. [<L *agrimonia,* var. of *aragemonia* <Gk. *argemōnē*]

ag·ri·ol·o·gy (ag′rē·ol′ə·jē) *n.* That branch of ethnology concerned with illiterate peoples possessing a primitive technology. See ETHNOLOGY. [<Gk. *agrios* wild + -LOGY] —**ag·ri·o·log·i·cal** (ag′rē·ə·loj′i·kəl) *adj.* —**ag′ri·ol′o·gist** *n.*

A·grip·pa (ə·grip′ə), **Cornelius,** 1486–1535, German cabalistic philosopher and professor of magic. —**Agrippa, Herod** See HEROD AGRIPPA. —**Agrippa, Marcus Vipsanius,** 63–12 B.C., Roman statesman, geographer, and general.

Ag·rip·pi·na (ag′ri·pī′nə), 13? B.C.-A.D. 33, wife of Germanicus and mother of Caligula. —**Agrippina,** A.D. 15–59, daughter of preceding, mother of Nero.

Ag·rip·pin·i·an (ag′ri·pin′ē·ən) *n.* A follower of **Ag·rip·pi·nus** (ag′ri·pī′nəs), second century bishop of Carthage who taught rebaptism of heretics.

agro- *combining form* Of or pertaining to fields or agriculture: *agronomy.* [<Gk. < *agros* field]

ag·ro·bi·ol·o·gy (ag′rō·bī·ol′ə·jē) *n.* The quantitative study of plant life, especially in relation to the genetic and environmental factors which determine the vitality, growth, and yields of cultivated plants. —**ag·ro·bi·o·log·ic** (ag′rō·bī′ə·loj′ik) or **·i·cal** *adj.* —**ag′ro·bi′o·log′i·cal·ly** *adv.* —**ag′ro·bi·ol′o·gist** *n.*

ag·ro·chem·i·cal (ag′rō·kem′ə·kəl) *n.* Any chemical product, such as fertilizers or insecticides, used in agriculture. — *adj.* Pertaining to agrochemicals: the *agrochemical* industry.

ag·ro·cli·ma·tol·o·gy (ag′rō·klī′mə·tol′ ə·jē) *n.* The branch of climatology concerned with the effects of weather upon agricultural crops.

a·grol·o·gy (ə·grol′ə·jē) *n.* The science of soils, especially in its practical applications. —**ag·ro·log·ic** (ag′rə·loj′ik) or **·i·cal** *adj.* —**ag′ro·log′i·cal·ly** *adv.*

ag·ro·ma·ni·a (ag′rō·mā ′nē·ə) *n.* A morbid desire to live in open country, and especially in solitude.

ag·ro·nom·ic (ag′rə·nom′ik) *adj.* Of or pertaining to agronomy or agronomics. Also **ag′ro·Mnom′i·cal.**

ag·ro·nom·ics (ag′rə·nom′iks) *n.* **1** In political economy, the science that treats of the distribution and management of land, especially as a source of the wealth of a nation. **2** Agronomy.

a·gron·o·my (ə·gron′ə·mē) *n.* The application of scientific principles to the cultivation of land; scientific husbandry, especially in production of field crops. —**a·gron′o·mist** *n.* [<Gk. *agronomos* an overseer of lands <) *agros* field + *nemein* distribute, manage]

Synonyms: agriculture. *Agronomy* differs from *agriculture* in that it is concerned only with crop-production, while *agriculture* includes the improvement and care of animals and their products.

ag·ros·tol·o·gy (ag′rē·stol′ ə·jē) *n.* That branch of botany which treats of es. [<Gk. *agrōstis,* a kind of grass + -LOGY] —**a·gros·to·log·ic** (ə·gros′tə·loj′ik) **or ·i·cal** *adj.*

ag·ro·tech·ny (ag′rə·tek′ nē) *n.* The science of preserving farm products and processing them into manufactured edible foods.

a·ground (ə·ground′) *adv.* & adj. On the shore or bottom, as a vessel; stranded.

a·guar·di·en·te (ä·gwär′ dē·en′tā) *n.* **1** An inferior brandy made in Spain and Portugal. **2** Any common distilled liquor, as pulque or whisky. **3** A wood spirit drawn from cane refuse after the rum has been extracted: used as a drink by Cuban natives. [<Sp. <) *agua ardiente* burning water]

A·guas·ca·li·en·tes (ä′gwäs·kä·lē·en′tes) A state in central Mexico; 2,499 square miles; capital, Aguascalientes.

a·gue (ā′gyōō) *n.* **1** *Pathol.* A periodic malarial fever; intermittent fever; chills and fever. **2** A chill or paroxysm of violent shivering. [<OF <L *(febbris) acuta* an acute fever]

a·gue·weed (ā′gyōō·wēd′) *n.* A tall, slender gentian *(Gentiana quinquefolia)* with clusters of bluish purple or white tubular flowers.

A·gui·nal·do (ä′gē·nä l′dō), **Emilio,** 1869–1964, Filipino rebel leader.

a·gu·ish (ā′gyōō·ish) *adj.* Like, producing, or tending to produce ague; chilly; subject to ague. —**a′gu·ish·ly** *adv.* —**a′gu·ish·ness** *n.*

A·gul·has (ə·gul′əs, *Pg.* ə·gōōl′yəs), **Cape** The southernmost point of Africa, in the Republic of South Africa, on the dividing line between the Indian and Atlantic oceans.

a·gush (ə·gush′) *adj.* & adv. Gushing.

A·gus·tín (ä′gōōs·tē n′) Spanish form of AUGUSTINE.

ah (ä) *interj.* An exclamation expressive of various emotions, as surprise, triumph, satisfaction, contempt, compassion, or complaint.

a·ha [1] (ä′hä) *n.* A sunk fence; a ha–ha.

a·ha [2] (ä·hä′) *interj.* An exclamation expressing surprise, triumph, or mockery.

A·hab (ā′hab), died 897 B.C., seventh king of Israel.

A·has·u·e·rus (ə·haz′yōō ·ir′əs, ə·has′-) One of several Median and Persian kings mentioned) in the Old Testament; specifically, in the book of Esther, generally identified with Xerxes. See WANDERING JEW under JEW.

a·head (ə·hed′) *adv.* **1** At the head or front. **2** In advance. **3** Onward; forward: He pressed *ahead.* **4** Without restraint; headlong. —**ahead of** In advance of, as in time, rank, achievement, etc. —**to get ahead** To make one's way socially, financially, etc. [<A-[1] + HEAD]

a·heap (ə·hēp′) *adv.* In or into a heap.

a·hem (ə·hem′) *interj.* An exclamation to attract attention.

a·him·sa (ə·him′sä) *n.* The doctrine that all life is sacred, exemplified in the Jainist, Brahman, and Buddhist philosophies by strict nonviolence to all living things. [<Skt. *ahimsā* non-injury]

a·his·tor·i·cal (ā′his·tô r′ə·kəl, -tər′-) *adj.* Not historical; without regard for history.

Ah·mad·nag·ar (ä′məd·nug′ər) A district of east Bombay, India; 6,646 square miles; capital, Ahmadnagar. Also **Ah′med·nag′ar.**

Ah·med·a·bad (ä′məd·ä ·bäd′) A district of north Bombay, India; 3,800 square miles; capital, Ahmedabad. Also **Ah′mad·a·bad′.**

Ah·med Fu·ad (ä′med fōō·ä d′) See FUAD.

a·hold[1] (ə·hōld′) *adv.* Close to the wind: to lay a ship *ahold.*

a·hold [2] (ə·hōld) *U.S. Dialect* A hold (of): to get *ahold* of one's arm.

a·hoy (ə·hoi′) *interj.* Ho there! a call used in hailing: ship *ahoy!* [Var. of HOY]

Ah·ri·man (ä′ri·mən) In Zoroastrian religion, the principle of evil, source of death, disease, and disorder: opponent of Ormuzd.

a·hull (ə·hul′) *adv. Naut.* So as to lie under bare poles, helm lashed alee, and the bow nearly into the wind: said of a ship in heavy weather.

a·hun·gered (ə·hung′gərd) *adj. Archaic.* hungry.

A·hu·ra Maz·da (ä′hōō·rä mäz′dä) See ORMUZD.

Ah·waz (ä·wäz′) A city on the Karun in SW Iran.

a·i (ä′ē) *n.* A three-toed sloth of South America *(Bradypus tridactylus).* [<Tupian *ai, hai;* named from its cry]

ai·blins (ā′blinz) See ABLINS.

aid (ād) *v.t.* & v.i. To render assistance (to); help; succor. —*n.* **1** The act or result of helping or succoring, or the means employed; cooperation; assistance. **2** A person or thing that affords assistance; a helper; assistant; aide-de-camp. **3** *Law* A remedy; correction; also, a subsidy. **4** In medieval law, a pecuniary contribution by a feudal vassal to his lord, limited by Magna Carta to three special occasions. See synonyms under ADHERENT, AUXILIARY, HELP, SUBSIDY. [<OF *aider* <L

Synonyms (verb): abet, assist, befriend, cooperate, encourage, foster, help, second, serve, succor, support, sustain, uphold. *Help* expresses greater dependence and deeper need than *aid.* To *aid* is to *second* another's own exertions, but may fall short of the meaning of *help.* In law, to *aid* or *abet* makes one a principal. (Compare synonyms for ACCESSORY). To *cooperate* or *collaborate* implies complete or approximate equality, *collaborate* being used chiefly of literary or scientific work; to *assist* implies a subordinate and secondary relation. One *assists* a fallen friend to rise; he *cooperates* with him in helping others. We *encourage* the timid or despondent, *succor* those in danger, *support* the weak, *uphold* those who else might be shaken or cast down. Compare ABET, ACCESSORY, PROMOTE. *Antonyms*: counteract, discourage, hinder, obstruct, oppose, resist, thwart, withstand.

A·ï·da (ä·ē′də) The heroine and title of an opera (1871) by Giuseppe Verdi.

aid·ance (ād′ns) *n.* The act of aiding; assistance; help. **—aid′ant** *adj.*

aide (ād) *n.* **1** An officer of the personal staff of the head of a government. **2** An aide-de-camp. **3** A naval officer assisting a superior officer. [<F, assistant]

aide-de-camp (ād′də·kamp′) *n. pl.* **aides-de-camp** An officer of the personal staff of a general, who transmits his orders, bears confidential relationship to him, and attends to matters of etiquette and protocol. Also **aid-de-camp, aide.** [<F *aide de camp,* lit., field assistant]

Ai·din (ī·din′) See AYDIN.

AIDS (ādz) Acquired immunodeficiency syndrome.

ai·glet (ā′glit) See AGLET.

ai·gret (ā′gret, ā·gret′) *n.* **1** A heron, the egret. **2** A tuft of feathers or gems, worn on a helmet, headdress, etc. See EGRET. Also **ai′grette.** [<F *aigrette.* See EGRET.]

ai·guille (ā·gwēl′, ā′gwēl) *n.* **1** *Geol.* A sharp rocky mountain peak, as those of the Italian Alps near Mont Blanc. **2** A slender rock-perforating drill. [<F, needle]

ai·guil·lette (ā′gwi·let′) *n.* An ornamental shoulder tag; aglet; specifically, such a decoration on a uniform, consisting of bullion cord, loops, knots, and tassels. [<F, *aiguille* needle]

Ai·ken (ā′kin), **Conrad,** 1889–1973, U.S. poet.

ail (āl) *v.t.* To cause uneasiness or pain to; trouble; make ill. —*v.t.* To be somewhat ill; feel pain. ◆ Homophone: *ale.* [OE *eglan*] **—ail′ing** *adj.*

ai·lan·thus (ā·lan′thəs) *n.* **1** Any of a small genus *(Ailanthus)* of tall, deciduous trees, native to Asia and Australia, having pinnate leaves and staminate and pistillate flowers often on separate trees. **2** Tree of heaven. [<NL <Amboina *ailanto* tree of heaven]

Ai·leen (ī·lēn′, ā·lēn′) Irish form of HELEN

ai·le·ron (ā′lə·ron) *n.* **1** *Archit.* A wing wall shaped like a scroll to conceal the aisle of a church, or a half-gable formed by a penthouse roof. **2** *Aeron.* Any of several types of hinged and movable auxiliary surfaces of an airplane, usually located near the trailing edge of a wing and operated by the pilot to give a rolling motion about the longitudinal axis. [<F, dim. of *aile* wing]

ail·ment (āl′mənt) *n.* Indisposition of body or mind; slight illness.

Ail·sa Craig (āl′sə krāg) A basaltic columnar islet at the entrance of the Firth of Clyde, Scotland; 1,097 feet high.

ai·lu·ro·phile (ā·lo͝or′ə·fīl) *n.* A person who likes cats.

ai·lu·ro·pho·bi·a (ā·lo͝or′ə·fō′bē·ə) *n.* Morbid fear of cats. Also called *galeophobia, gatophobia.* [<Gk. *ailouros* cat + -PHOBIA]

aim (ām) *v.t.* **1** To direct, as a missile, blow, weapon, word, or act, toward or against some thing or person; point or level: to *aim* a gun at a man; to *aim* a speech at an offender. —*v.i.* **2** To have a purpose; endeavor earnestly: with the infinitive: to *aim* to please. **3** To direct a missile, weapon, etc.: We *aimed* and fired. —*n.* **1** The act of aiming, directing, or pointing a weapon, missile, remark, etc., at anything. **2** The line of direction of anything aimed. **3** The object or point aimed at or to be aimed at; a mark or target. **4** Design; purpose. **5** Conjecture; guess. [<OF *aesmer* <*a-* to (<L *ad-*) + *esmer* <L *aestimare* estimate]

Synonyms (noun): aspiration, design, determination, direction, end, endeavor, goal, inclination, intent, intention, mark, object, purpose, reason, tendency. The *aim* is the direction in which one shoots, or that which is aimed at. The *mark* is that at which one shoots; the *goal,* that toward which one moves or works. All indicate the direction of *endeavor.* The *end* is the point at which one expects or hopes to close his labors; the *object,* that which he would grasp as the reward of his labors. *Aspiration, design, endeavor, purpose,* referring to the mental acts by which the *aim* is attained, are often used as interchangeable with *aim.* Compare AMBITION, DESIGN, DIRECTION, PURPOSE. *Antonyms*: aimlessness, avoidance, carelessness, heedlessness, neglect, negligence, oversight, purposelessness, thoughtlessness.

Ai·mée (ā·mā′) French form of AMY.

aim·less (ām′lis) *adj.* Wanting in aim or purpose. **—aim′less·ly** *adv.* **—aim′less·ness** *n.*

a·in[1] (ä′yēn) See AYIN.

ain[2] (ān) *adj. Scot.* Own.

Ain (aṅ) A river in eastern France, flowing south 118 miles to the Rhône.

ain·sel′ (ān·sel′) *n. Scot.* Own self. Also **ain·sell′.**

Ains·worth (ānz′wûrth), **William Harrison,** 1805–82, English novelist.

ain't (ānt) *Illit. & Dial.* Am not; also used for *are not, is not, has not,* and *have not.*

◆ **ain't, aren't I** *Ain't* is used in dialog representing uneducated or homely speech. The emergence of the ungrammatical but idiomatic *aren't I* as a genteel substitute for *ain't I* shows the need for a colloquial contraction for *am not.* This need has not removed the stigma from *ain't,* though until a century ago it was good colloquial English and is still so considered by some in Scotland.

Ain·tab (īn·täb′) A former name for GAZIANTEP.

Ai·nu (ī′no͞o) *n.* **1** One of a primitive, aboriginal people of Japan, now found only in the northern parts. **2** The unclassified, unrelated language of the Ainu. Also **Ai·no** (ī′nō).

air (âr) *n.* **1** The atmosphere of the earth, consisting of a mixture of gases containing approximately 79 percent nitrogen, 19 percent oxygen, and small amounts of other gases including carbon dioxide, hydrogen, helium, argon, and methane. **2** The open space around and above the earth. **3** An atmospheric movement or current; breeze; wind. **4** Utterance abroad; publicity: to give *air* to one's views. **5** The medium through which radio waves are transmitted; airways. **6** The representation of atmosphere in painting; atmospheric perspective. **7** Something light and ethereal; wind. **8** Peculiar or characteristic appearance; mien; manner. **9** Assumed manner; affectation: to put on *airs.* **10** *Music* A melody as contrasted with a harmony; tune; especially, the leading or soprano part in a harmonized piece. **11** *Obs.* Breath. **12** *Obs.* Secret intelligence; private information. See synonyms under TUNE, WIND. **—in the air 1** Prevalent; abroad, as gossip; astir; in the making, as plans. **2** Without foundation in fact; unformed: The project is still *in the air.* **3** Excited; mentally upset. **—on the air** Broadcasting by radio; being broadcast. —*v.t.* **1** To expose to the air; admit air into so as to purify or dry; ventilate. **2** To make public; show off; display; exhibit. **3** *Colloq.* To broadcast by radio or television. ◆ Homophone: *heir.* [<OF <L *aer* <Gk. *aer* air, mist]

Air may appear as a combining form in hyphemes or solidemes, or as the first element in two-word phrases, with the following meanings:

1 By means of air or the air:

air-bred **air-dropped**
air-blasted **air-filled**
air-blown **air-formed**
air-cooling **air-insulated**
air-cured **air-slacked**
air-dried **air-spun**
air-driven

2 Of or pertaining to the atmospheric air:

air-breathing **airlike**
air-conveying **air-swallowing**
air-defiling **airward**
air-heating **airwise**

3 Conducting, confining, or regulating air:

air compressor **air filter**
airduct **air regulator**

4 Operating or operated by air, especially by the power of heated or compressed air:

air condenser **air hammer**
air drill **air motor**

5 Performed by or suitable for aircraft:

air action **air navigation**
air armament **air park**
air assault **air pickup**
air attack **air race**
air cover **air refueling**
air echelon **air rescue**
air express **air show**
air evacuation **air squadron**
air freight **air strike**
air group **air terminal**
air landing **air unit**
air meet **air war**

Synonyms (noun): appearance, bearing, behavior, carriage, demeanor, deportment, expression, fashion, look, manner, mien, port, pretense, sort, style, way. *Air* is that combination of qualities which makes the entire impression we receive in a person's presence; we say he has the *air* of a scholar, or the *air* of a villain. *Appearance* refers more to the dress and other externals. *Expression* and *look* especially refer to the face. *Expression* is oftenest applied to that which is habitual; as, a pleasant *expression; look* may be momentary; as, a *look* of dismay passed over his face. We may, however, speak of the *look* or *looks* as indicating all that we look at; as, he had the *look* of an adventurer. *Bearing* indicates often the expression of feeling or state of mind through bodily pose; as, a noble *bearing; port,* practically identical in meaning with *bearing,* is more exclusively a literary word. *Carriage,* the manner of holding the body, as in walking, is more completely physical than *bearing. Mien* is closely synonymous with *air,* but is a somewhat stilted or literary usage. Compare BEHAVIOR, PRETENSE.

A·ïr (ä·ir′) A mountainous region in the northern Niger: also *Asben, Azben.*

air alert A signal warning of the expected or imminent approach of enemy aircraft.

air·bag (âr′bag′) *n.* An automatically inflatable safety device installed beneath the dashboard of an automobile and designed to cushion passengers in case of a collision.

air base A base for operations by aircraft.

air bed *Brit.* A pneumatic rubber mattress for the sick.

air bladder 1 An air-filled sac situated under the spinal column of most fishes and serving as a hydrostatic device. Also called *swim bladder.* **2** Any sac filled with air or gas, as the flotation devices on bladderwrack and other seaweeds.

air·boat (âr′bōt′) *n.* A swamp boat.

air·borne (âr′bôrn′, -bōrn′) *adj.* **1** Transported in aircraft; specifically, designating specialized units of infantry or parachute troops so carried. **2** Aloft; no longer in contact with the ground. **3** Transported by air currents, as pollen, dust, etc.

air·bound (âr′bound′) *adj.* Impeded or stopped up by air, as an airplane motor.

air brake A brake operated by compressed air.

air·bra·sive (âr′brā′siv, -ziv) *adj.* Of or pertaining to a method of drilling teeth by means of a finely powdered abrasive pinpointed against the surface in a minute, controlled jet of air or other gas under high pressure.

air·brush (âr′brush′) *n.* An implement for spraying liquids by compressed air, especially one used by commercial artists and photographers for coating surfaces with a film of color.

air·burst (âr′bûrst′) *n.* An explosion in the air, as of a bomb or projectile.

air carrier An aircraft that carries freight.

air castle A visionary project; a daydream.

air chamber An enclosed space containing, or designed to contain, air for various mechanical or vital uses. Also **air cavity, air cell.**

air·cock (âr′kok′) *n. Mech.* A valve specially designed to control the flow of air.

air-con·di·tion (âr′kən·dish′ən) *v.t.* To equip with or ventilate by air-conditioning. **—air′-con·di′tioned** *adj.*

air-con·di·tion·ing (âr′kən·dish′ən·ing) *n.* A

system for treating air in buildings, dwellings, and other enclosed structures so as to maintain those conditions of temperature, humidity, and purity which are best adapted to technical operations, industrial processes, and personal comfort.

air-cool (âr'kōōl) v.t. To cool, as the cylinders of an engine, with a flow of air instead of water or other medium. —**air'-cooled'** adj.

air corridor An air lane, especially one established by international agreement.

air cover 1 A protection given by aircraft in military operations. **2** The aircraft giving this protection.

air-craft (âr'kraft', -kräft') n. Any form of craft designed for flight through or navigation in the air, as airplanes, dirigibles, balloons, helicopters, kites, and gliders.

aircraft carrier A large ship designed to carry aircraft, with a level upper flight deck usually extending beyond the bow and stern, serving as a mobile air base at sea: also called *flattop*.

air-craft-man (âr'kraft'mən, -kräft'-) n. pl. **·men** Brit. **1** Any of the four lower grades in the Royal Air Force. **2** One holding this rank.

air-crafts-man (âr'krafts'mən, -kräfts'-) n. pl. **·men** A skilled aircraft designer or builder.

air cushion 1 A bag inflated with air, especially one used as a pillow. **2** An air spring.

air cylinder 1 A nearly airtight cylinder having a piston playing in it: used to check the recoil of a gun. **2** A cylinder beneath a railway car, in which is compressed air which operates brakes. See BRAKE[1].

air defense All the measures taken to counteract aerial attack, including the use of fighter aircraft, barrage balloons, anti-aircraft artillery, blackouts, radar networks, etc.

air-dock (âr'dok') n. Aeron. A hangar equipped with ramps, bridges, conveyor belts, and hydraulic lifts for the rapid unloading of passengers and freight from large airliners.

air-drome (âr'drōm') n. Archaic An airport.

air-drop (âr'drop') n. Personnel, food, equipment, and other supplies dropped by parachute from an aircraft. —v.t. & v.i. **·dropped**, **·drop·ping** To drop (personnel, supplies, etc.) by parachute from an aircraft.

air-dry (âr'drī') v.t. **·dried**, **·dry·ing** To dry by exposing to the air.

Aire (âr) A river in western Yorkshire, England.

Aire·dale (âr'dāl) n. A large terrier with a wiry tan coat and black markings. See TERRIER. [from *Airedale*, the valley of the Aire River]

air embolism Aeroembolism (def. 1).

air engine An engine operated by the rapid thermal expansion of a controlled stream of compressed air.

air·er (âr'ər) n. Brit. A frame on which clothes are stretched to be aired or dried.

air-field (âr'fēld') n. An airport; specifically, the field or course of an airport.

air·flow (âr'flō') n. **1** A flow of air. **2** The air currents developed by the motion of an automobile, aircraft, etc.

air·foil (âr'foil') n. Aeron. A winglike surface designed to provide the maximum aerodynamic advantage for an airplane in flight.

air force The air arm of a country's defense forces. —**United States Air Force** The air force of the United States administered by the Department of the Air Force under the Department of Defense; established in 1947 and organized in 1951 to consist of the Regular Air Force, the Air Force Reserve, and the Air National Guard of the United States. Until 1947 it was part of the Army, under the title of the United States Army Air Force. See ROYAL AIR FORCE, ROYAL CANADIAN AIR FORCE, ROYAL AUSTRALIAN AIR FORCE.

air force academy A school where young men are trained for service in the air force; specifically, the United States Air Force Academy, Colorado Springs, Colo.

air-frame (âr'frām') n. An airplane complete except for the engine and its controls; a glider.

air gas Producer gas.

air gun A gun impelling a missile by compressed air.

air·head (âr'hed') n. **1** A position established in enemy territory that can be supplied and reinforced by air. **2** Slang A brainless person.

air·hole (âr'hōl') n. **1** A hole containing, or made by or for, gas or air. **2** A flaw in a casting. **3** An opening in the ice over a body of water. **4** Aeron. An air pocket. Also **air hole**.

air·i·ly (âr'ə·lē) adv. **1** In a light or airy manner; delicately. **2** In light spirits; jauntily; gaily.

air·i·ness (âr'ē·nis) n. The quality of being airy.

air·ing (âr'ing) n. **1** An exposure to the air, as for drying. **2** Public exposure or discussion. **3** Exercise in the air.

air jacket Mech. An air-filled compartment around some part of a machine, usually designed to control the transmission of heat.

air lane A lane for air traffic, especially one characterized by steady winds.

airles (ârlz), **air-penny** (âr'pen'ē) See ARLES.

air·less (âr'lis) adj. Destitute of air or of fresh air.

air letter 1 An airmail letter. **2** A sheet of lightweight writing paper for use in airmail letters. **3** Brit. An aerogramme.

air·lift (âr'lift') n. **1** The operation of transporting foodstuffs and other commodities into Berlin by airplane during the land blockade imposed by the U.S.S.R. in 1948. **2** Any similar operation for any purpose. **3** The load carried by such a transport method. —v.t. & v.i. To transport (food and supplies) by airplane, especially during a land blockade.

air·line (âr'līn) n. **1** The shortest distance between two points on the earth's surface. **2** A regular route traveled by aircraft carrying freight and passengers. **3** The business organization operating such a transport system. **4** A direct railroad route.

air·lin·er (âr'līn'ər) n. A large, passenger aircraft operated by an airline.

air layering A method of vegetative propagation by enclosing part of a branch or shoot in a moist wrapping until roots form and then detaching and planting it in earth.

air·lock (âr'lok') n. **1** An airtight antechamber, as of a submarine caisson, for graduating the air pressure.

air·log (âr'lôg', -log') n. An instrument for recording the linear travel of aircraft and guided missiles through the air.

air mail 1 Mail carried by airplane. **2** A system of carrying mail by airplane; particularly, a postal system in charge of forwarding of mail by aircraft. —**air'-mail'**, **air'mail'** adj.

air·man (âr'mən) n. pl. **air·men 1** Any person who is occupied with the navigation of an aircraft, whether as a pilot, mechanic, or other member of the operating crew. **2** Anyone charged with the inspection, repair, and overhauling of aircraft on the ground.

air mass Meteorol. Any extensive portion of the earth's atmosphere characterized by essentially uniform conditions of temperature, pressure, moisture, etc., along a horizontal plane.

Air Medal A decoration in the form of a bronze compass rose on which is an eagle carrying two lightning flashes in its talons: awarded for meritorious achievement while participating in an aerial flight: instituted September, 1939.

air meter A device for measuring the rate of flow of air or gas.

air mile A nautical mile by air.

air·mind·ed (âr'mīn'did) adj. Having an inclination for aeronautics or for the services of aircraft. —**air'-mind'ed·ness** n.

airn (ârn) n. Scot. Iron; also, an iron tool.

air·plane (âr'plān') n. A heavier-than-air flying craft, supported by aerodynamic forces acting upon fixed wings, and kept in flight by propellers or jet propulsion.

airplane cloth A cotton fabric plain-woven in varying weights, used for luggage, sportswear, etc.: originally made of unbleached linen for airplane wings.

air plant an epiphyte (def. 1).

air pocket Aeron. A sudden downward air current due to the sinking of a mass of heavy cooled air.

air pollution The contamination of the air, esp. by industrial waste gases, fuel exhaust, or smoke.

air·port (âr'pôrt', -pōrt') n. A field laid out as a base for aircraft, including all structures and appurtenances necessary for operation, housing, storage, repair, and maintenance: also called *airdrome*.

air·post (âr'pōst') n. Air mail.

air power The strength of a nation in terms of its command of the air in peace and war.

air·proof (âr'prōōf') adj. Impenetrable by air.

air pump A pump for exhausting, compressing, or transmitting air.

air raid An attack by military aircraft, especially bombers in mass formation.

air-raid shelter A place set aside and equipped for the protection of people during an air raid.

air-raid warden A person designated to exercise police authority during an air raid.

air rifle A rifle utilizing compressed air to propel a pellet or BB.

air sac 1 Ornithol. One of the membranous sacs filled with air in different parts of the body in birds, often extending through the bones and communicating with the lungs. **2** Entomol. Any of the large, thin-walled structures connected to the tracheal system in some insects. **3** An alveolus of the lungs.

air-scoop (âr'skōōp') n. A device for utilizing the air stream to maintain pressure and furnish ventilation within an airship.

air-screw (âr'skrōō) n. Brit. A power-driven propeller for use on aircraft, consisting of two or more helical blades.

air shaft An open shaft intended to secure proper ventilation of a building or other structure.

air·ship (âr'ship') n. **1** An aircraft, generally of large size, mechanically propelled and depending upon gases for flotation; a dirigible balloon. **2** Loosely, an airplane.

air-sick·ness (âr'sik'nis) Motion sickness experienced while flying. —**air'sick** adj.

air·space (âr'spās') n. **1** The atmosphere. **2** That portion of the atmosphere overlying a designated geographical area, considered as subject to territorial jurisdiction or international law in respect to its use by aircraft, guided missiles, rockets, etc.

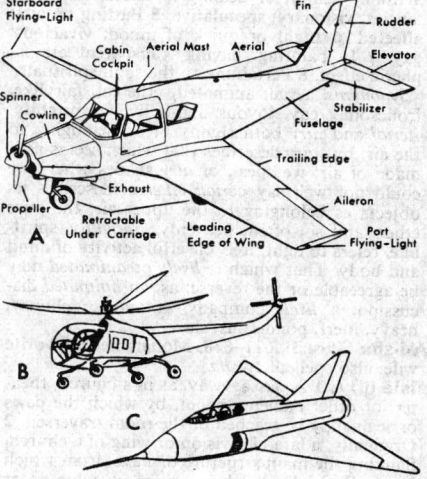

AIRPLANE SHOWING FUNCTIONAL PARTS
A. Four-passenger light plane.
B. Helicopter. *C.* Turbojet.

air speed The speed of an airplane with relation to the air: distinguished from *ground speed*.

air-speed meter An instrument for measuring the speed of aircraft in flight.

air-spray (âr'sprā) n. **1** A compressed-air device for spraying liquids on a prepared

surface. 2 The liquid used in such a device. **—air′-sprayed′** *adj.*

air·spring (âr′spring′) *n.* A device for resisting sudden pressure by the elasticity of compressed air.

air·stream (âr′strē′) *n.* A current or flow of air, especially one set up by the propeller or propellers of an aircraft.

air·strip (âr′strip′) *n.* A makeshift airfield, usually prepared from prefabricated materials for temporary use, as for landing fighter planes: also called *fighter strip.*

airt (ârt) *Scot. v.t.* To guide. *—n.* **1** A cardinal point of the compass. **2** The direction of the wind, or, poetically, the wind.

air thermometer A thermometer in which temperature differences are measured by the expansion and contraction of enclosed air or gas.

air·tight (âr′tīt′) *adj.* **1** Not allowing air to escape or enter. **2** Hence, having no weak places; flawless: an *airtight* argument.

air turbine A turbine operated by air currents fed to the vanes under pressure.

air-twist (âr′twist′) *n.* A spiral air-filled vein found in the stem of a glass vessel, formed by an elongation of an air bubble during the blowing process.

air umbrella A heavy concentration of military aircraft sent out to cover the movements and support the action of ground forces.

air valve *Mech.* **1** A valve, usually automatic, for the control of the flow of air. **2** An air cock.

air vesicle *Bot.* A large air chamber serving as a float in many water plants, especially in certain seaweeds.

air·way (âr′wā′) *n.* **1** Any passageway for air, as the windpipe, a ventilator shaft, etc. **2** *Aeron.* A specific route of travel selected for aircraft. **3** *pl. U.S. Colloq.* Channels for radio or television broadcasting.

air·wom·an (âr′wŏŏm′ən) *n. pl.* **air·wom·en** A woman aviator.

air·wor·thi·ness (âr′wûr′thē·nis) *n.* **1** Fitness for flight. **2** The status of one who has met certain requirements for flying an airplane.

air·wor·thy (âr′wûr′thē) *adj.* Being in fit condition for flight.

air·y (âr′ē) *adj.* **air·i·er, air·i·est 1** Of or pertaining to the air; in the air. **2** Open to or pervaded by the free air; breezy: an *airy* retreat. **3** Like or of the nature of air; as light as air; hence, immaterial; delicate; graceful; ethereal; buoyant: an *airy* evening dress, *airy* music, *airy* nothings. **4** Without reality, or dealing in unreal things or fancies; visionary; speculative. **5** Putting on airs; affected. **6** Light or quick of mood; vivacious; gay. **7** In painting, having transparent atmospheric effect. **8** Pertaining to the soul; spiritual.

Synonyms: aerial, animated, ethereal, fairylike, frolicsome, gay, joyous, light, lively, sprightly. *Aerial* and *airy* both signify of or belonging to the air, but *airy* describes that which seems as if made of air; we speak of *airy* shapes where we could not well say *aerial; ethereal* describes its objects as belonging to the upper air, the pure ether, and so, often, heavenly. *Sprightly,* spiritlike, refers to light, free, cheerful activity of mind and body. That which is *lively* or *animated* may be agreeable or the reverse; as, an *animated* discussion; a *lively* company. *Antonyms*: clumsy, heavy, inert, ponderous, slow.

A·i·sha (ä′i·shä), 611–678, Mohammed's favorite wife: also spelled *Ayesha.*

aisle (īl) *n.* **1** A passageway, as in a church, theater, or other audience-room, by which the pews or seats may be reached or the room traversed. **2** Originally, a lateral division or wing of a church, flanking the main structure or nave, from which it usually is divided by a range of columns or piers. **3** Any similar wing or passage, as in a forest. ◆ Homophone: *isle.* [< OF *aile, ele* wing (of a building) < L *ala* wing; spelling infl. by *isle*]

aisled (īld) *adj.* **1** Provided with aisles. **2** Placed in an aisle.

Aisne (ān, *Fr.* en) A river in northern France, flowing west 175 miles to the Oise.

ait (āt) *n. Brit. Dial.* A little island, especially one in a river. [OE *īggath, īgeoth*]

aitch (āch) *n.* The letter *H, h.*

aitch·bone (āch′bōn′) *n.* **1** The rump bone in cattle. **2** The cut of beef with this bone. [< OF *nache* buttock + BONE; ME *a nache bone* became *anache bone*]

aith (āth) *n. Scot.* An oath. Also **aithe.**

aits (āits) *n. pl. Scot.* Oats.

Ai·tu·ta·ki (ī′tōō·tä′kē) One of the Cook Islands in the South Pacific; 7 square miles.

ai·ver (ā′vər) *n. Scot.* A draft horse.

Aix-en-Pro·vence (eks′än·prô·väns′) A city in SE France.

Aix-la-Cha·pelle (āks′lä·shä·pel′, *Fr.* eks′lȧ·shȧ·pel′) French name for AACHEN.

ai·zle (ā′zəl) *n. Scot.* A hot cinder.

A·jac·cio (ä·yät′chō) A port in western Corsica; birthplace of Napoleon I.

a·jar[1] (ə·jär′) *adv. & adj.* Partly open, as a door. [ME *a-* on + *char,* OE *cerr* turn]

a·jar[2] (ə·jär′) *adv. & adj.* In a jarring or discordant condition; wanting in harmony. [< A-[1] + JAR[2]]

A·jax (ā′jaks) In the *Iliad,* the son of Telamon and the bravest of all the Greeks who besieged Troy, except Achilles.

Ajax the Lesser In the *Iliad,* son of the king of Locris, and one of Helen's suitors.

a·jee (ə·jē′) *adv. & adj. Scot.* Awry; askew; also, ajar: also spelled *agee.*

Aj mer (uj·mir′) or **Ajmer-Mer·wa·ra** (-mer·wä′rə) **1** Formerly, a chief commissioner's state in NW India, since 1956 part of Rajasthan. **2** A city in central Rajasthan, India, former capital of the state of Ajmer.

aj·o·wan (aj′ō·wən) *n.* The ripe fruit of a plant *(Trachyspermum ammi)* grown in Egypt, India, and Persia, cultivated as a source of thymol and cymene. [< native name]

a·kar·y·ote (ā·kar′ē·ōt) *n.* A cell having no nucleus, as a human erythrocyte. *—adj.* Lacking a nucleus.

Ak·bar (ak′bär), 1542–1605, Mogul emperor of Hindustan. Also **Ak·ber** (ak′bər).

Ak·bar Khan (ak′bär kän′), died 1849, Afghan leader.

a·kene (ā·kēn′) See ACHENE.

A·ken·side (ā′kən·sīd), **Mark,** 1721–70, English poet and physician.

Akh·na·ten (äk·nä′tən) See IKHNATON.

a·kim·bo (ə·kim′bō) *adv.* With the hands on hips and the elbows outward. [ME *in kene bowe* in a sharp bow]

a·kin (ə·kin′) *adj. & adv.* **1** Of the same kin; related by blood. **2** Of similar nature or qualities. See synonyms under ALIKE. [< A-[2] + KIN]

ak·i·ne·sis (ak′ə·nē′sis) *n.* **1** Impairment or loss of motor function. **2** Immobility due to any cause. Also **ak·i·ne·si·a** (ak′ə·nē′sē·ə). [< NL < Gk. *a-* without + *kinēsis* motion]**—ak′i·ne′sic** *adj.*

ak·i·nete (ak′ə·nēt) *n. Bot.* A non-motile, thick-walled resting spore in certain green algae. [< Gk. *akinētos* motionless] **—ak·i·net·ic** (ak′ə·net′ik) *adj.*

A·ki·ta (ä·kē·tä) A city on northern Honshu island, Japan.

Ak·kad (ak′ad, ä′käd) **1** A region of Mesopotamia occupying the northern part of Babylonia. **2** A city of Nimrod's kingdom. *Gen.* x 10. Also *Accad.*

Ak·ka·di·an (ə·kā′dē·ən, ə·kä′-) *n.* **1** One of the inhabitants of ancient Akkad. **2** The extinct group of East Semitic languages of Akkad, Assyria, and Babylonia, or any language of this group. *—adj.* **1** Of Akkad or its inhabitants. **2** Of the extinct Semitic languages of the Assyrians and Babylonians. Also spelled *Accadian.*

Ak·ker·man (ä·kir·män′) The former Russian and Turkish name for BELGOROD DNESTROVSKI.

Ak·kra (ak′rə) See ACCRA.

Ak·ron (ak′rən) A city in NE Ohio; world's largest rubber manufacturing center.

Ak·sum (äk·sōōm′) A town in northern Ethiopia, site of the ancient capital of Ethiopia: also *Axum.*

Ak·ti (ak′tē) The eastern prong of the Chalcidice peninsula of Greek Macedonia on the Aegean Sea; coextensive with Mount Athos: also *Acte.*

Ak·yab (ak·yab′, ak′yab) A port of Lower Burma at the mouth of the Kaladan River on the Bay of Bengal.

al-[1] *prefix* The: Arabic definite article, as in *Alkoran, algebra.*

al-[2] Assimilated var. of AD-.

-al[1] *suffix of adjectives and nouns* Of or pertaining to; characterized by; connected with: *personal, musical;* also in some nouns that were originally adjectives: *animal, rival.* [< L *-alis*]

-al[2] *suffix of nouns* The act of doing or the state of suffering that which is expressed by the verb stem: *betrayal, refusal.* [< OF *-aille* < L *-alia,* neut. pl. of *-alis*]

-al[3] *suffix Chem.* Denoting a compound having the properties of or derived from an aldehyde: *chloral.* [< AL(DEHYDE)]

Al *Chem.* Aluminum (symbol Al).

Al (al) Diminutive of ALBERT, ALFRED.

a·la (ā′lə) *n. pl.* **a·lae** (ā′lē) *Biol.* Any wing or winglike structure, as one of the lateral projections of the nose, one of the two side petals of a papilionaceous flower, a projection found on certain seeds, etc. [< L, wing]

à la (ä′lä, ä′lə; *Fr.* ȧ lȧ) **1** After the manner of: hair dressed *à la* Pompadour. **2** In Cooking, as done in; according to or prepared after the manner of: lobster *à la* Newburg. Also **a la.** [< F]

Al·a·bam·a (al′ə·bam′ə) A State in the SE United States, bordering on the Gulf of Mexico; 51,609 square miles; capital, Montgomery; entered the Union Dec. 14, 1819: nickname, *Cotton State:* abbr. AL **—Al·a·bam·i·an** (al′ə·bam′ē·ən), **Al′a·bam′an** *adj. & n.*

Alabama River A river in Alabama, flowing SW 320 miles to the Mobile river.

al·a·bas·ter (al′ə·bas′tər, -bäs′-) *n.* **1** A white or delicately tinted fine-grained gypsum. **2** A dense, translucent variety of calcite, sometimes banded like marble. *—adj.* Made of or like alabaster; smooth and white. [< L < Gk. *alabast(r)os* an alabaster box, ? from the name of a town in Egypt] **—al′a·bas′trine** (-trin) *adj.*

al·a·bas·ter-stone (al′ə·bas′tər·stōn′, -bäs′-) *n.* A hot-spring or cave deposit of aragonite.

à la bonne heure (ȧ lȧ bôn œr′) *French* Good; well done; literally, at a good hour.

à la carte (ä′ lə kärt′) By the card; in accordance with the bill of fare: said of meals at hotels, etc., each item having a separate price: contrasted with *table d'hôte.* [< F]

a·la·cha (ä·lä′chä) *n.* A lightweight Oriental fabric of silk or cotton. [< Turkish *ālājah*]

a·lack (ə·lak′) *interj. Archaic* An exclamation of regret or sorrow. Also **a·lack·a·day** (ə·lak′·ə·dā′). [< *ah* oh + *lack* failure, disgrace]

a·lac·ri·ty (ə·lak′rə·tē) *n.* Cheerful willingness and promptitude; facility. [< L *alacritas, -tatis* < *alacer* lively] **—a·lac′ri·tous** *adj.*

A·la Dagh (ä′lä däkh′) A mountain range north of Ankara, Turkey; highest point, 11,000 feet. Also **A·la Dag** (ä′lä däg′).

A·lad·din (ə·lad′n) A boy in the *Arabian Nights* who is able to cause one jinni to appear and do his bidding whenever he rubs a magic lamp, and another whenever he rubs a magic ring.

à la fin (ȧ lȧ faṅ′) *French* To or at the end; finally.

à la fran·çaise (ȧ lȧ fräṅ·sez′) *French* In the French style.

A·la·gez (ä′lə·gez′) An extinct volcano of Erivan, Armenian S.S.R.; 13,435 feet: also *Aragats.* Also **A·la·göz** (ä′lä·gœz′).

A·la·go·as (ä′lə·gō′əs) A state in eastern Brazil; 11,016 square miles; capital, Maceió.

Al Ah·sa See HASA, EL.

A·lai (ä·lī′) A mountain range of Kirghiz S.S.R., in the Tien Shan system.

a·la·li·a (ə·lā′lē·ə) *n.* Inability to speak, whether due to impairment or paralysis of the organs of speech or to brain damage. [< Gk. *a-* without + *lalia* talking] **—a·la·lic** *adj.*

A·la·mein (ä′lə·mān′, al′ə-), **El** A village of northern Egypt; site of a decisive British recovery and victory against Axis forces (1942) in World War II. Also **A′la·mein′.**

Al·a·man·ni (al′ə·man′ī) See ALEMANNI.

al·a·me·da (al′ə·mē′də, -mā′-) *n. SW U.S.* A shaded walk: so called because generally planted with *alamos* or poplar trees. [< Sp. < *álamo* poplar]

al·a·mo (al′ə·mō, ä′lə·mō) *n. pl.* **-mos** Any of various species of cottonwood. [< Sp.]

Al·a·mo (al′ə·mō) A Franciscan mission building, San Antonio, Texas; besieged and taken by Mexicans, 1836. **—Remember the Alamo!** A rallying cry for United States forces in the Mexican War (1848).

à la mode (ä′ lə mōd′, al′ə mōd′) **1** Literally, according to the mode; in the fashion. **2** Served with ice cream: pie *à la mode.* [< F].

Al·a·mo·gor·do (al′ə·mə·gôr′dō) A town in

southern New Mexico: site of the first atomic bomb trial explosion, July 16, 1945.

à la mort (á lá môr′) *French* Literally, to the death; hence, mortally ill in mind or body; mortally.

al·an (al′ən) *n.* **1** *Her.* A short-eared mastiff. **2** *Obs.* A wolfhound. Also **al·and** (al′ənd), **al·ant** (al′ənt). [< OF]

Å·land Islands (ō′län) See AALAND ISLANDS.

à la New·burg (á′ lə nōō′bûrg, nyōō′bûrg) Cooked with a sauce made of egg yolks, cream, sherry, and butter.

a·lang (ə·lang′) *adv. & prep. Scot.* Along.

à l'an·glaise (á län·glez′) *French* In the English style.

al·a·nine (al′ə·nēn, -nin) *n.* An amino acid, $C_3H_7NO_2$, occurring as a constituent of most proteins. [< AL(DEHYDE) + infix -an + -INE²]

a·lar (ā′lər) *adj.* Pertaining to an ala or wing; wing-shaped. [< L *alaris* < *ala* wing]

A·lar·cón (ä′lär·kōn′), **Pedro Antonio de,** 1833–91, Spanish poet.

Al·a·ric (al′ə·rik), 370?–410 A.D., king of the Visigoths who sacked Rome. —**Alaric II,** died 507, Visigoth king; issued legal code.

a·larm (ə·lärm′) *n.* **1** Sudden fear or apprehension arousing to defense or escape. **2** Any sound or signal to apprise of danger or arouse from sleep. **3** A mechanism, as of a clock, giving such signal. **4** A call to arms, to meet danger. **5** *Obs.* A sudden attack. —*v.t.* **1** To strike with sudden fear. **2** To arouse to a sense of danger; give warning to. See synonyms under FRIGHTEN. [< OF *alarme* < Ital. *all' arme* to arms] —**a·larm′a·ble** *adj.*

Synonyms (noun): affright, apprehension, consternation, dismay, disquiet, dread, fear, fright, panic, terror, timidity. *Alarm,* according to its derivation, is a sudden arousal to meet and repel danger and may be quite consistent with true courage. *Apprehension, disquiet,* and *dread* are in anticipation of danger; *consternation, dismay,* and *terror* are overwhelming *fear,* generally in the actual presence of that which is terrible. Compare FEAR. *Antonyms:* assurance, calmness, confidence, repose, security.

alarm clock A clock fitted with a bell which rings when a trip is sprung as the hands reach a predetermined hour.

a·larm·ing (ə·lär′ming) *adj.* Exciting alarm; causing fear and apprehension; disturbing: an *alarming* symptom. —**a·larm′ing·ly** *adv.*

a·larm·ist (ə·lär′mist) *n.* **1** One who needlessly excites or tries to excite alarm. **2** One who is easily or overeasily alarmed. —**a·larm′ism** *n.*

a·lar·um (ə·lar′əm, ə·lär′əm) *n. Obs.* An alarm.

a·la·ry (ā′lər·ē, al′ər·ē) *adj.* Pertaining to alae or wings; wing-shaped. [< L *alarius* < *ala* wing]

a·las (ə·las′, ə·läs′) *interj.* An exclamation of disappointment, regret, sorrow, etc. [< OF *a* ah! + *las* wretched < L *lassus* weary]

A·la·she·hir (ä′lä·she·hir′) A city in western Turkey, on the site of ancient *Philadelphia.* Also **A′la·se·hir′.**

a·las·ka (ə·las′kə) *n.* **1** A heavy rubber-topped overshoe. **2** A specially prepared yarn of wool and cotton, used as material for women's dresses and coats.

A·las·ka (ə·las′kə) A State of the United States in NW North America, including the Aleutian Islands and the Alexander Archipelago; 586, 400 square miles; capital, Juneau; entered the Union Jan. 3, 1959; —**A·las′kan** *adj. & n.*

Alaska, Gulf of A broad northern inlet of the Pacific on the south coast of Alaska between Alaska Peninsula and the Alexander Archipelago.

Alaska cod A species of cod found in the northern Pacific Ocean.

Alaska Highway A road from Dawson Creek, British Columbia, through the Yukon to Fairbanks, Alaska: built in 1942 as a United States military supply route; 1,527 miles: unofficially called *Alcan Highway.*

Alaskan malemute Any of a breed of working dog of arctic regions, having a strong, compact body, a coarse, heavy coat, and standing about two feet high at the shoulder.

Alaska Peninsula A long, narrow promontory of SW Alaska, extending about 400 miles between the Bering Sea and the Pacific.

Alaska Range A mountain range in south central Alaska; highest peak, 20,270 feet.

a·las·tor (ə·las′tər) *n.* Any avenging or relentless deity. [< Gk. *alastōr* < *a-* not + *lathein* forget]

A·la Tau (ä′lä tou′) The generic name for several series of mountain ranges in the Tien Shan system between Turkestan and Mongolia, U.S.S.R.

a·late (ā′lāt) *adj.* Having wings or structures resembling wings. Also **a′lat·ed.** [< L *alatus* < *ala* wing]

a·la·tion (ā·lā′shən) *n.* **1** The condition of being winged. **2** *Entomol.* The way in which an insect's wings are arranged.

Al·a·va (al′ə·və), **Cape** A promontory on the Pacific Ocean in NW Washington; western-most point on the United States mainland.

alb (alb) *n. Eccl.* A white linen vestment, reaching to the ankles, close-sleeved and girded at the waist, worn over the cassock and amice. [OE *albe* < L *alba (vestis)* white garment)]

al·ba¹ (al′bə) *n. Physiol.* The white substance of the central nervous system. [< NL < L, white]

al·ba² (äl′bə, al′bə) *n.* A short, formal lyric in Provençal troubadour literature, originally evoked by the necessity for lovers to separate when a watchman announced the dawn; aubade. [< Provençal, dawn]

ALB
As worn by a priest.

Al·ba (äl′bä), **Duke of,** 1508–82, Fernando Álvarez de Toledo, Spanish general: also spelled *Alva.*

Al·ba·ce·te (äl′vä·thā′tä) A province of SE central Spain; 5,738 square miles; capital, Albacete.

al·ba·core (al′bə·kôr, -kōr) *n. pl.* **·core** or **·cores** Any of various large scombroid fishes, especially a commercially important food and game fish (*Thunnus alalunga*) having very long pectoral fins. [< Pg. *albacor* < Arabic *al* the + *bukr* young camel]

Al·ba Lon·ga (al′bə lông′gə, long′gə) A city of ancient Latium, SE of Rome; traditional birthplace of Romulus and Remus.

Al·ba·ni·a (al·bā′nē·ə, -bān′yə) **1** A Balkan republic south of Yugoslavia; 10,629 square miles; capital, Tirana. *Albanian* **Shqip·ni** (shkyip·nē′). **2** *Obs.* Scotland. **3** An ancient country corresponding approximately to Azerbaijan S.S.R.

Al·ba·ni·an (al·bā′nē·ən, -bān′yən) *adj.* Of or pertaining to Albania, its people, or their language. —*n.* **1** A native or inhabitant of Albania. **2** The language of Albania, belonging to the Albanian subfamily of Indo-European languages.

Al·ba·ny (ôl′bə·nē) The capital of New York, a port on the Hudson River.

Albany River A river in north central Ontario, Canada, flowing about 600 miles eastward to James Bay.

al·ba·ta (al·bā′tə) *n.* A white German silver, consisting of nickel, copper, and zinc. [< NL, fem. pp. of *albare* make white < *albus* white]

al·ba·tross (al′bə·trôs, -tros) *n. pl.* **·tross·es** or **·tross** Any of a small family (Diomedeidae) of large web-footed sea birds with long, narrow wings and hooked beaks, confined mostly to the Southern Hemisphere. [Orig. *alcatras* frigate bird < Pg. *alcatraz* pelican < Arabic *al-ghattas* a sea eagle]

albatross cloth A smooth-faced woolen textile fabric of medium weight.

al·be·do (al·bē′dō) *n.* **1** *Astron.* The percentage of the total illumination of a planet or satellite which is reflected from its surface: the albedo of the moon is 7.2; of the

ALBATROSS
(Wing span up to 12 feet)

planet Mars, 14.8. **2** Reflectivity. **3** The white, spongy portion of the inner rind of citrus fruit that contains the substance pectin. [< L < *albus* white]

al·be·it (ôl·bē′it) *conj.* Even though; even if; notwithstanding; although. [ME *al be it* although it be]

Al·be·marle (al′bə·märl), **Duke of** See MONK.

Albemarle Sound An inlet of the Atlantic in NE North Carolina.

Al·bé·niz (äl·vā′nēth), **Isaac,** 1860–1909, Spanish composer and pianist.

al·ber·ca (äl·ber′kə) *n. SW U.S.* A pond; pool; also, a sink to carry off waste or dirty water. [< Sp.]

Al·ber·ich (äl′bər·ikh) **1** In Norse mythology, the king of the gnomes. **2** In the *Nibelungenlied,* the dwarf who guards the treasure of the Nibelungs.

Al·bert (al′bərt; *Fr.* ál·bâr′; *Ger., Sw.* äl′bert) A masculine personal name. Also *Ital., Sp.* **Al·ber·to** (äl·ber′tō); *Lat.* **Al·ber·tus** (al·bûr′təs). [< F < OHG *Adalbrecht* nobly bright] —**Albert I,** 1875–1934, king of the Belgians 1909–34. —**Albert, Prince,** 1819–61, Prince of Saxe-Coburg-Gotha, consort of Victoria of England. —**Albert of Brandenburg,** 1490–1545, archbishop of Magdeburg and elector of Mainz.

Albert, Lake Lake Edward (Africa). Also **Albert Edward Nyanza.**

Al·ber·ta (al·bûr′tə) Feminine of ALBERT.

Al·ber·ta (al·bûr′tə) A province in western Canada; 255,285 square miles; capital, Edmonton.

Al·ber·tan (al·bûr′tən) *n.* One from or living in Alberta.

Albert Edward, Mount A peak of the Owen Stanley Range, New Guinea; 13,000 feet.

al·bert·ite (al′bər·tīt) *n.* A jet-black, brittle hydrocarbon resembling coal and used as fuel. [from *Albert* County, New Brunswick + -ITE¹]

Albert Memorial A monument to Prince Albert in Kensington Gardens, London.

Al·ber·tus Mag·nus (al·bûr′təs mag′nəs), 1200?–80, Swabian medieval philosopher and theologian.

al·ber·type (al′bər·tīp) *n.* A picture printed in ink from a photographic plate of gelatin and albumin sensitized with potassium bichromate; also, the process by which the picture is produced. Also **albert type,** [after Joseph *Albert,* 1825–86, German inventor]

al·bes·cent (al·bes′ənt) *adj.* Growing white or moderately white; becoming whitish. [< L *albescens, -entis,* ppr. of *albescere* become white < *albus* white] —**al·bes′cence** *n.*

al·bi·ca·tion (al′bi·kā′shən) *n.* **1** The process of growing or becoming white. **2** *Bot.* The development of light patches or streaks on the foliage of plants. [< L *albicatus,* pp. of *albicare* whiten < *albus* white]

al·bi·fi·ca·tion (al′bə·fi·kā′shən) *n.* The process of making or changing to white. [< F < Med. L *albificatio, -onis,* < *albificare* make white < *albus* white]

Al·bi·gen·ses (al′bə·jen′sēz) *n. pl.* A sect of religious reformers during the 11th to 13th centuries in the south of France; suppressed for their heretical doctrines. Also *French* **Al·bi·geois** (äl·bē·zhwá′). [< Med. L, from *Albi,* a town in southern France]

Al·bi·gen·si·an (al′bə·jen′sē·ən, -shən) *adj.* Pertaining to the Albigenses. —*n.* One of the Albigenses.

al·bin·ism (al′bə·niz′əm) *n.* **1** An abnormal condition in human beings characterized by a genetically determined lack of pigment in certain cells of the skin, hair, and eyes, and giving a very white or pale appearance. **2** Deficient pigmentation in an animal or plant. **3** The state or condition of being an albino. —**al·bin·ic** (al·bin′ik) *adj.*

al·bi·no (al·bī′nō) *n. pl.* **·nos** A person, animal, or plant lacking normal pigmentation. [< Pg. < *albo* < L *albus* white]

Al·bi·on (al′bē·ən) England: an ancient name now generally only in literary use. [< L]

al·bite (al′bīt) *n.* A triclinic white feldspar, $NaAlSi_3O_8$, a common constituent of granite and other rocks. See FELDSPAR. [< L *albus*

white + -ITE¹] —**al·bit·i·cal** (al·bit′i·kəl) *adj.*

Al·boin (al′boin, -bō·in), died 573, founder and king of the Lombard dominion in Italy.

Al·bo·rak (al′bə·rak) The white mule on which Mohammed is said to have visited the seven heavens. [< Arabic *al-burāq*]

Al·borg (ôl′bôr) See AALBORG.

al·bor·noz (äl′bôr·nōth′) *n.* A burnoose. [< Sp.]

Al·brecht (äl′brekht) German form of ALBERT.

Al·bu·ca·sis (al′byōō·kā′sis). See ABUL KASIM.

al·bum (al′bəm) *n.* **1** A book for holding photographs or the like. **2** A blank book for registering names or preserving autographs, stamps, poetical selections, etc. **3** A printed compilation. **4** A single long-playing phonograph record. **5** A set of phonograph records or tape recordings. [< L, white tablet]

al·bu·men (al·byōō′mən) *n.* **1** The white of an egg. **2** *Bot.* The nutritive material that fills the space in a seed between the embryo and the seed coats; endosperm or perisperm. **3** Albumin. [< L, white of an egg < *albus* white]

al·bu·men·ize (al·byōō′mən·īz) *v.t.* **·ized, ·iz·ing** To treat with albumen.

al·bu·min (al·byōō′mən) *n.* Any of a group of simple proteins which are common in plant and animal tissues and which are soluble in water and coagulable by heat. [< F *albumine* < L *albumen, -inis*. See ALBUMEN.]

al·bu·min·ize (al·byōō′mən·īz) *v.t.* **·ized, ·iz·ing 1** To convert into albumin. **2** To coat or saturate with albumin. Also spelled *albumenize.* —**al·bu′min·i·za′tion** *n.* —**al·bu′min·iz′er** *n.*

al·bu·mi·noid (al·byōō′mə·noid) *adj.* Of or like albumen or albumin. —*n.* One of a diversified subclass of the simple proteins derived mainly from the supporting and connective animal tissues. Also **al·bu′me·noid.** —**al·bu′mi·noi′dal** *adj.*

al·bu·mi·nous (al·byōō′mə·nəs) *adj.* Of, pertaining to, like, or consisting of albumen or albumin. Also **al·bu′mi·nose** (-nōs).

al·bu·mi·nu·ri·a (al·byōō′mə·nŏōr′ē·ə, -nyŏōr′-) *n.* The presence of albumin in the urine. [< NL < ALBUMIN + Gk. *ouron* urine] —**al·bu′mi·nu′ric** *adj.*

al·bu·mose (al·byōō′mōs, al′byōō·mōs) *n.* Any of various albuminous products of the enzymatic hydrolysis of proteins during digestion.

Al·bu·quer·que (äl′bōō·ker′kə), **Affonso de,** 1453–1515, Portuguese navigator.

Al·bu·quer·que (al′bə·kûr′kē) A resort city on the Rio Grande in NW New Mexico.

al·bur·num (al·bûr′nəm) *n.* Sapwood. [< L < *albus* white]

Al·cae·us (al·sē′əs) A Greek poet of Mitylene; lived about 600 B.C. See ALCAIC. Also **Al·cæ′us.** —**Alcaeus** In Greek mythology, a king of Tiryns, son of Perseus and Andromeda; father of Amphitryon.

Al·ca·ic (al·kā′ik) *adj.* Of or pertaining to the poet Alcaeus or to his favorite meter, consisting of four strophes, each of four verses having four accents apiece. —*n.* Verse written in Alcaic strophes.

al·caide (al·kād′, *Sp.* äl·kä′ē·thä) *n.* **1** The governor of a Spanish, Portuguese, or Moorish castle or fortress. **2** The warden of a prison; a jailer. Also **al·cayde′.** [< Sp. < Arabic *al-qā′id* the leader]

al·cal·de (al·kal′dē, *Sp.* äl·käl′dä) *n.* A magistrate in a Spanish or Spanish-American pueblo or town; later, a chief magistrate or mayor. [< Sp. < Arabic *al-qādi* the judge]

Al·can Highway (al′kan) See ALASKA HIGHWAY.

Al·ca·traz (al′kə·traz) A small island in San Francisco Bay, California; former site of a Federal prison.

al·ca·zar (al·kaz′ər, al′kə·zär; *Sp.* äl·kä′thär) *n.* A Moorish castle in Spain; especially, **The Alcazar,** a Moorish palace in Seville, later used by the Spanish kings. [< Sp. < Arabic *al-qaṣr* the castle]

Al·ces·tis (al·ses′tis) In Greek mythology, the heroic wife of Admetus; she volunteered to die to save her husband's life but was rescued from Hades by Hercules.

al·che·mist (al′kə·mist) *n.* One skilled in or

practicing alchemy.

al·che·mis·tic (al′kə·mis′tik) *adj.* Of or pertaining to alchemy or alchemists; practicing alchemy. Also **al′che·mis′ti·cal.**

al·che·mize (al′kə·mīz) *v.t.* **·mized, ·miz·ing** To transmute by or as by alchemy.

al·che·my (al′kə·mē) *n.* **1** An ancient quasi-magical art through which practitioners sought a formula to cure any disease, confer eternal youth, and transmute base metals into gold. **2** Any cunning, mysterious, or preternatural process of changing the structure or appearance of things. [< OF *alkemie* < Med.L *alchimia* < Arabic *al-kīmiyā* < L Gk. *chēmeia* transmutation of metals, later prob. confused with *chymeia* pouring, infusion < *cheein* pour] —**al·chem·ic** (al·kem′ik) *adj.* —**al·chem′i·cal·ly** *adv.*

Al·ci·bi·a·des (al′sə·bī′ə·dēz), 450–404 B.C., Athenian general.

Al·ci·des (al·sī′dēz) Hercules: so named because he was the grandson of Alcaeus.

al·ci·dine (al′sə·dīn, -din) *n.* Any of a family (Alcidae) of web-footed sea birds of the Northern Hemisphere, including the auks, puffins, guillemots, etc. Also **al·cid.** —*adj.* Pertaining to or resembling an alcidine.

Alc·man (alk′mən) Spartan poet of the seventh century B.C.

Alc·me·ne (alk·mē′nē) In Greek mythology, the mother of Hercules by Zeus, who seduced her in the guise of her husband Amphitryon.

al·co·hol (al′kə·hôl, -hol) *n.* **1** A colorless, volatile, inflammable liquid, C_2H_5OH, produced commercially by the fermentation of cereal grains, molasses, and fruits, widely used as a solvent in industry and medicine, and as the intoxicating principle in beer, wine, and distilled liquor. Also called *ethanol, ethyl alcohol, grain alcohol.* **2** Any of a group of organic compounds containing one or more functional hydroxyl (OH) groups. **3** Any liquor containing ethyl alcohol. [< Med.L, orig., fine powder < Arabic *al-koh′l* the powdered antimony]

al·co·hol·ate (al′kə·hôl·āt, -hol-) *n.* **1** A type of alcohol in which the hydrogen of the hydroxyl is replaced by a metal. **2** An alcoholic compound or solution.

alcohol dehydrogenase An enzyme found in yeast and liver, necessary for the metabolism and production of alcohols.

al·co·hol·ic (al′kə·hôl′ik, -hol′-) *adj.* **1** Of, pertaining to, or containing alcohol. **2** Produced by alcohol: an *alcoholic* stupor. **3** Afflicted with alcoholism. —*n.* One who consumes alcohol compulsively. —**al·co·hol·i·cal·ly** *adv.*

al·co·hol·ic·i·ty (al′kə·hôl·is′ə·tē, -hol-) *n.* The quality of being alcoholic; alcoholic strength: the *alcoholicity* of a wine.

al·co·hol·ism (al′kə·hôl·iz·əm, -hol′-) *n.* Compulsive and habitual consumption of alcohol accompanied by varying degrees of deterioration, especially of the nervous and digestive systems.

al·co·hol·ize (al′kə·hôl·īz′, -hol-) *v.t.* **·ized, ·iz·ing 1** To change into alcohol. **2** To mix or saturate with alcohol. —**al′co·hol′i·za′tion** *n.*

al·co·hol·om·e·ter (al′kə·hôl·om′ə·tər, -hol-) *n.* An instrument, such as a modified hydrometer, for ascertaining the concentration of alcohol in a liquid. —**al′co·hol·om′e·try** *n.*

al·co·hol·y·sis (al′kə·hôl′ə·sis, -hol-) *n.* A decomposing by the action of alcohol.

Al·cor (al′kôr) See under MIZAR.

Al·co·ran (al′kō·rän′, -ran′) *n.* The Koran. —**Al′co·ran′ic** (-ran′ik) *adj.*

al·co·sol (al′kə·sōl, -sol) *n.* An alcoholic colloidal solution.

Al·cott (ôl′kət, -kot), **Amos Bronson,** 1799–1888, U.S. educator. —**Louisa May,** 1832–88, U.S. novelist; daughter of Amos B.

al·cove (al′kōv) *n.* **1** A recess connected with or at the side of a larger room, as to contain a bed. **2** Any embowered or secluded spot. **3** A niche in the face of a cliff or the wall of a building. [< F *alcove* < Sp. *alcoba* < Arabic *al-qobbah* the vaulted chamber]

Al·cuin (al′kwin), 735–804, English scholar and ecclesiastical reformer; friend and adviser of Charlemagne: in Old English spelled *Ealhwine.* Also **Al′cwin.**

Al·cy·o·ne (al·sī′ə·nē) **1** In Greek mythology: **a** The daughter of Aeolus who, mourning her husband Ceyx, cast herself into the sea and was changed into a kingfisher: also *Halcyone.* **b** One of the Pleiades. **2** *Astron.* The brightest star in the Pleiades.

Al·da (äl′də), **Frances,** 1885–1952, U.S. soprano born in New Zealand.

Al·dan (äl·dän′) A river in the Yakut Republic, U.S.S.R.; flowing north 1,767 miles to the Lena.

Al·deb·a·ran (al·deb′ə·rən) A red star, Alpha in the constellation Taurus; one of the 20 brightest stars, 1.06 magnitude. See STAR. [< Arabic *al-dabarān* the follower (i.e., of the Pleiades)]

al·de·hyde (al′də·hīd) *n.* **1** *Chem.* Any one of a group of aliphatic compounds derived from the alcohols, and intermediate between the alcohols and the acids; they have the general formula R-CHO. **2** Acetaldehyde. [< AL(COHOL) + DEHYD(ROGENIZED)]

Al·den (ôl′dən), **John,** 1599–1687, one of the original Pilgrim settlers of Plymouth Colony, 1620; the chief character in Longfellow's *Courtship of Miles Standish.*

al den·te (äl·den′tā) *Ital.* Cooked so as to be chewy; firm to the tooth.

al·der (ôl′dər) *n.* **1** Any of a genus (Alnus) of catkin-bearing shrubs and trees usually growing in moist areas in the Northern Hemisphere. **2** Any of various unrelated species resembling *Alnus* species. [OE *alor*]

al·der·man (ôl′dər·mən) *n. pl.* **·men 1** A member of a municipal legislative body, who usually also exercises certain judicial functions. **2** In England and Ireland, a member of the higher branch of a town council, as in a borough, whose office corresponds to that of the *bailie* in Scotland. [OE *ealdorman* head man] —**al′der·man·cy** (-mən·sē), **al′der·man·ship** *n.* —**al′der·man′ic** (-man′ik) *adj.*

al·der·man·ate (ôl′dər·mən·āt) *n.* **1** The position, dignity, or term of office of alderman. **2** Aldermen collectively.

Al·der·ney (ôl′dər·nē) The northernmost of the Channel Islands; 3 square miles: French *Aurigny.*

Alderney *n.* One of a breed of cattle originally peculiar to the island of Alderney.

Al·der·shot (ôl′dər·shot) A borough and permanent military camp, Hampshire, England.

Al·dine (ôl′dīn, al′-, -dēn) *adj.* Pertaining to or printed by the press of Aldus Manutius, Venetian editor and printer, or to his family (1494–1597): applied also to a modern series of books, and a style of display types. —*n.* A book printed by the Aldine press, noted for fine typography.

al·dol (al′dôl, -dol) *n. Chem.* A colorless liquid, $C_4H_8O_2$, a condensation product of acetaldehyde, or any of a group of similar aldehyde condensates. [< ALD(EHYDE) + (ALCOH)OL]

al·dol·ase (al′də·lās) *n.* An enzyme that appears in muscle tissue.

al·dose (al′dōs) *n. Chem.* Any of a class of monosaccharides containing in the molecule a group (CHO) that is characteristic of aldehydes.

al·dos·te·rone (al·dos′·tə·rōn) *n.* An adrenocortical steroid hormone, $C_{21}H_{28}O_5$, which regulates the metabolism of potassium and sodium.

al·dos·te·ron·ism (al·dos′tər·ə·niz′əm) *n.* Excessive secretion of aldosterone resulting in hypertension and loss of potassium through the kidneys.

Al·drich (ôl′drich), **Thomas Bailey,** 1836–1907, U.S. poet and novelist.

Al·drin (ôl′drin), **Edwin Eugene, Jr.,** born 1930, U.S. astronaut; one of the first two men to walk on the moon, July 20, 1969.

al·drin (al′drin) *n.* A powerful insecticide, $C_{12}H_8Cl_6$, derived from naphthalene, useful against insects that infest the soil, such as locusts and grasshoppers.

ale (āl) *n.* **1** A beverage made from a fermented infusion of malt, usually flavored with hops: ale resembles beer but generally has more body. **2** An English rural ale-drinking festival. ◆Homophone: *ail.* [OE *ealu*]

a·le·a·tor·ic (ā′lē·ə·tôr′ik, -tōr′-) *adj. Music* Made up of chance or random elements: *aleatoric* melodies.

a·le·a·to·ry (ā′lē·ə·tôr′ē, -tō′rē) *adj.* **1** Of or

pertaining to gambling or luck. **2** Dependent upon contingency. [< L *aleatorius* < *aleator* gambler < *alea* a die, chance]

a·lec·i·thal (ə-les′i-thəl) *adj.* Having no yolk, as the eggs of placental mammals. [< Gk. *a-* without + *lekithos* yolk]

Al·eck (al′ik) Diminutive of ALEXANDER.

A·lec·to (ə-lek′tō) One of the three Furies.

a·lee (ə-lē′) *adv. Naut.* At, on, or to the lee side of a vessel.

al·e·gar (al′ə-gər, ā′lə-) *n.* Sour ale; a vinegar produced by the fermentation of malt. [< ALE + (VINE)GAR]

ale·house (āl′hous′) *n.* A place where ale is sold to the public.

A·le·jan·dro (ä′lā-hän′drō) Spanish form of ALEXANDER. Also *fem.* **A′le·jan′dra** (-drä) or **A·le·jan·dri·na** (ä′lā-hän-drē′nä).

A·le·khine (ä-lyu′khin), **Alexander**, 1892–1946, French world chess champion born in Russia. Also **A·lje′chin**.

A·lek·san·dro·pol (ä-lyik-sän-drô′pəl) The former name of LENINAKAN.

A·lek·san·drovsk (ä-lyik-sän′drôfsk) **1** A port near Murmansk, NW U.S.S.R. **2** A Russian port in western Sakhalin Island. **3** Former name of ZAPOROZHE.

A·le·mán (ä′lā-män′), **Mateo**, 1547?–1610?, Spanish novelist. —**Miguel**, 1902–1983 Mexican lawyer; president of Mexico 1946–52.

Al·e·man·ni (al′ə-man′ī) *n.* A group of South Germanic tribes that fought against Rome in the third to fifth centuries; also spelled *Alamanni*, *Allemanni*.

Al·e·man·nic (al′ə-man′ik) *adj.* Of or pertaining to the Alemanni or their language. Also **Al′e·man′ni·an.** —*n.* The language of the ancient Alemanni: a dialect of Old High German. Also spelled *Alamannic*, *Allemannic*.

A·lem·bert (dá-län-bâr′), **Jean le Rond d′**, 1717–83, French mathematician and philosopher.

a·lem·bic (ə-lem′bik) *n.* **1** An apparatus of glass or metal formerly used in distilling. **2** Anything that tests, purifies, or transforms. [< OF *alambic* < L *alambicus* < Arabic *al-anbīq* the still < Gk. *ambix* a cup]

a·lem·bi·cate (ə-lem′bə-kāt) *v.t.* **·cat·ed**, **·cat·ing** To distill in an alembic.

A·len·çon (á-län-sôn′) A town in NW France.

A·len·çon lace (ə-len′sən, *Fr.* á-län-sôn′) A fine, needlepoint lace originally made in Alençon.

a·leph (ä′lif) *n.* The first letter in the Hebrew alphabet. Also **a′lef.** See ALPHABET.

A·lep·po (ə-lep′ō) A city of NW Syria, largest in the country. French **A·lep** (á-lep′).

a·lert (ə-lûrt′) *adj.* **1** Keenly watchful; on the look-out; ready for sudden action; vigilant. **2** Lively; nimble.
—*n.* **1** A warning against sudden attack; especially, a signal to prepare for an air raid or gas attack. **2** An alert attitude; guard; the period of preparedness for defense. **3** *Aeron.* The condition of an airplane which is manned and equipped to make a sortie. —**on the alert** On the look-out; ready. —*v.t.* To prepare for action; warn, as of a threatened attack or raid. [< F *alerte* < Ital. *all'erta* on the watch] —**a·lert′ly** *adv.* —**a·lert′ness** *n.*
  Synonyms (adj.): active, alive, brisk, bustling, nimble, prepared, prompt, ready, vigilant, watchful, wide-awake. *Alert, ready,* and *wide-awake* refer to a watchful promptness for action. *Ready* suggests preparation; the wandering Indian is *alert,* the trained soldier is *ready. Ready* expresses more life and vigor than *prepared.* The gun is *prepared;* the man is *ready. Prompt* expresses readiness for appointment or demand at the required moment. The good general is *ready* for emergencies, *alert* to perceive opportunity or peril, *prompt* to seize occasion. Compare ACTIVE, ALIVE, NIMBLE. *Antonyms:* drowsy, dull, heavy, inactive, slow, sluggish, stupid.

-ales *suffix Bot.* A feminine plural used to form the scientific names of plant orders. [< L, pl. of -ALIS]

A·les·san·dri·a (ä′les-sän′drē-ä) A city in northern Italy.

A·les·san·dro (ä′les-sän′drō) Italian form of ALEXANDER. Also *fem.* **A′les·san′dra** (-drä).

a·leu·ro·man·cy (ə-lōōr′ə-man′sē) *n.* Divination by means of flour or meal. [< F *aleuromancie* < Gk. *aleuron* flour + *manteia* divination]

a·leu·rone (ə-lōōr′ōn) *n. Bot.* An albuminoid substance found in minute solid granules in the seeds of some plants. In seeds of wheat and other cereals they form the outermost or **aleurone layer** of the endosperm. [< Gk. *aleuron* flour] —**al·eu·ron·ic** (al′yōō-ron′ik) *adj.*

Al·e·ut (al′ē-ōōt) *n. pl.* **Al·e·uts** or **Al·e·ut 1** A native of the Aleutian Islands belonging to either of two Eskimoan tribes called *Unungun.* **2** A subfamily of the Eskimo-Aleut family of languages; comprising the Aleutian Island dialects. —**A·leu·tian** (ə-lōō′shən), **A·leu′tic** *adj.*

A·leu·tian Islands (ə-lōō′shən) A chain of volcanic islands, extending some 1,100 miles from the tip of the Alaska Peninsula between the North Pacific and the Bering Sea. Also **A·leu′tians.**

Aleutian Range A mountain range of SW Alaska, extending along the Alaska Peninsula and continued by the Aleutian Islands.

al·e·vin (al′ə-vin) *n.* A young fish; particularly, a salmon hatchling. [< F < OF *alever* to rear < L *ad-* to + *levare* raise]

ale·wife (āl′wīf) *n. pl.* **·wives** A small North American anadromous fish of the herring family (*Pomolobus pseudoharengus*). [? < Am. Ind.]

Al·ex·an·der (al′ig-zan′dər, -zän′-; *Du., Ger.* ä′lek-sän′dər) **1** A masculine personal name. Also *Fr.* **A·lex·an·dre** (á-lek-sän′dr′), *Gk.* **A·lex·an·dros** (ä-leks′än-drōs), *Pg.* **A·lex·an·dre** (ä′leg-zän′drə)). **2** Name of many kings of Bulgaria, Greece, Russia, Scotland, Serbia, Yugoslavia, etc. **3** Appellation of eight popes. [< Gk., helper of men]
  —**Alexander I**, 1888–1934, king of Yugoslavia 1921–34.
  —**Alexander II**, 1818–81, czar of Russia 1855–81.
  —**Alexander III**, died 1181, real name Orlando Bandinelli, pope 1159–81.
  —**Alexander VI**, 1431?–1503, real name Rodrigo Borgia, pope 1492–1503.
  —**Alexander Nev·ski** (nev′skē, nef′-), 1220?–63, Russian hero.
  —**Alexander Se·ve·rus** (sə-vir′əs), 208?–235; Roman emperor 222–235.
  —**Alexander the Great**, 356–323 B.C., king of Macedon 336–323, conqueror of Asia.

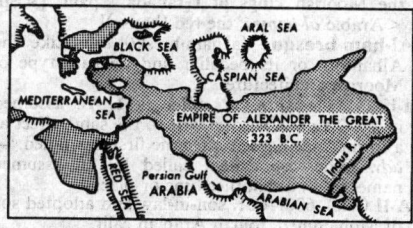

Al·ex·an·der (al′ig-zan′dər, -zän′-), **Sir Harold Rupert Leofric George**, 1891–1969, first Viscount Alexander of Tunis, British field marshal; governor general of Canada 1946–1952.

Alexander Archipelago A group of more than 1,000 islands, SE Alaska. Also **Alexander Islands.**

A·lex·an·dra (al′ig-zan′drə, -zän′-) A feminine personal name: feminine of ALEXANDER. Also **A·lex·an·dri·na** (al′ig-zan-drē′nə, -zän-), *Fr.* **A·lex·an·drine** (á-lek-sän-drēn′).
  —**Alexandra, Queen**, 1844–1925, wife of Edward VII of England.

Alexandra Nile See KAGERA.

Al·ex·an·dret·ta (al′ig-zan-dret′ə, -zän-) A former name for ISKENDERUN.

Al·ex·an·dri·a (al′ig-zan′drē-ə, -zän′-) The chief port and ancient capital of Egypt. *Arabic* **Al Is·kan·da·ri·ya** (al is-kan-da-rē′yə).

Al·ex·an·dri·an (al′ig-zan′drē-ən, -zän′-) *adj.* **1** Of or pertaining to Alexander the Great, his reign, or his conquests. **2** Of or pertaining to the Alexandrian school or its influence. **3** In prosody, Alexandrine. —*n.* **1** A native or inhabitant of Alexandria. **2** In prosody, an Alexandrine verse.

Alexandrian school 1 A late Hellenic school of literature, science, and philosophy, at Alexandria, Egypt, during the last three centuries B.C. **2** The school of Christian philosophers and theologians at Alexandria during the first five centuries A.D., which sought to combine Christianity and Greek philosophy, and so gave rise to Neoplatonism and Gnosticism.

Al·ex·an·drine (al′ig-zan′drin, -drēn, -zän′-) *n.* In prosody, a line of verse having six iambic feet with the caesura generally after the third. —*adj.* Of, composed of, or characterized by Alexandrines. Also *Alexandrian.*

al·ex·an·drite (al′ig-zan′drīt, -zän′-) *n.* A green variety of chrysoberyl, red by artificial light. [after *Alexander* II, czar of Russia]

A·lex·an·drou·po·lis (ä′lek-sän-drōō′pô-lēs) A port on the Aegean, NE Greece: formerly *Dedeagach.*

A·le·xan·drovsk (u-lyi-ksän′drôfsk) The former name for ZAPOROZHE.

a·lex·i·a (ə-lek′sē-ə) *n.* Loss of ability to grasp the significance of written or printed matter. Also called *word blindness.* [< NL < Gk. *a-* without + *lexis* speech < *legein* speak]

a·lex·ic (ə-lek′sik) *adj.* **1** Suffering from alexia. **2** Pertaining to alexin.

a·lex·in (ə-lek′sin) *n. Immunology* Complement. [< Gk. *alexein* ward off]

a·lex·i·phar·mic (ə-lek′si-fär′mik) *Med. adj.* Serving to ward off or resist poison; antidotal. —*n.* An antidote or poison preventive. [< Gk. *alexipharmakos* < *alexein* ward off + *pharmakon* poison]

A·lex·is Mi·khai·lo·vich (ə-lek′sis mē-khī′lə-vich), 1629–76, czar of Russia; father of Peter the Great.

Alexis Pe·tro·vich (pi-trô′vich), 1690–1718, Russian prince; son of Peter the Great.

A·lex·i·us I Com·ne·nus (ə-lek′sē-əs, kom-nē′nəs), 1048–1118, Byzantine emperor 1081–1118.

al·fal·fa (al-fal′fə) *n.* A perennial leguminous herb (*Medicago sativa*) having deep roots, compound pinnate leaves, and clusters of small purple flowers, widely grown for fodder. Also called *lucerne, purple medic.* [< Sp. < Arabic *alfaṣfaṣah* the best kind of fodder]

al·fa·qui (al′fə-kē′) *n.* A teacher of Mohammedan law or of the Koran; a priest of Islam. Also **al′fa·ki′** or **al′fa·quin′** (-kēn′). [< Sp. < Arabic *al-faqīh*]

Al·fie·ri (äl-fyä′rē), **Vittorio**, 1749–1803, Italian dramatic poet.

al·fil·e·ri·a (al-fil′ə-rē′ə) *n.* A biennial European weed (*Erodium cicutarium*) naturalized in North America, having leafy stems and rose or purple umbellate flowers. Also **alfilaria.** Also called *pin clover.* [< Am. Sp. < Sp. *alfiler* pin < Arabic *al-khilāl* the thorn]

Al·föld (ôl′fœld) The fertile central plain of Hungary.

Al·fon·so (äl-fôn′sō) **1** Italian and Spanish form of ALPHONSO. **2** One of many Spanish and Portuguese kings. Also *Dan., Ger.* **Alfons** (äl′fôns).
  —**Alfonso XIII**, 1886–1941, king of Spain 1886–1931; deposed.

al·for·ja (al-fôr′jə, *Sp.* äl-fôr′hä) *n.* **1** A leather pouch; saddle bag. **2** A cheek pouch, especially of the baboon. [< Sp. < Arabic *al-khorj*]

Al·fred (al′frid; *Dan.* äl′fred; *Du., Ger.* äl′fret; *Fr.* ál′fred′) A masculine personal name. Also *Ital., Pg., Sp.* **Al·fre·do** (äl-frä′dō), *Lat.* **Al·fre·dus** (äl-frē′dəs), *fem.* **Al·fre′da.** [OE *ælfred,* lit., elf counsel (i.e., good counselor)]
  —**Alfred the Great**, 849–901, king of the West Saxons; defeated the Danish invaders, built the first English navy, and is known as the father of English prose literature.

al·fres·co (al-fres′kō) *adv.* In the open air.

—*adj.* Occurring outdoors, as a meal. Also **al fresco.** [< Ital.]

al·gae (al′jē) *n. pl.* A large group of primitive, mostly aquatic, chlorophyll-bearing plants lacking specialized tissues and organs such as roots, stems, leaves, and flowers, and including forms ranging from giant seaweeds to single-celled diatoms and pond scums. [< L, seaweed] **—al·gal** (al′gəl) *adj.*

al·gar·ro·ba (al′gə·rō′bə) *n.* **1** The carob tree or its fruit, the carob bean. **2** A species of mesquite or its edible pods. Also **al′ga·ro′ba.** [< Sp. < Arabic *al-kharrūbah* the carob]

Al·gar·ve (äl·gär′və) The southernmost province of Portugal; 1,958 square miles; capital, Faro; formerly a Moorish kingdom.

al·ge·bra (al′jə·brə) *n.* **1** The branch of mathematics which treats of quantity and number in the abstract, and in which calculations are performed by means of letters and symbols: it includes the solution of equations of any degree. **2** A treatise on this subject. [< Ital. < Arabic *al-jebr* the reunion of broken parts, bone-setting]

al·ge·bra·ic (al′jə·brā′ik) *adj.* Pertaining to algebra. Also **al′ge·bra′i·cal. —al′ge·bra′i·cal·ly** *adv.*

al·ge·bra·ist (al′jə·brā′ist) *n.* One skilled in algebra.

Al·ge·cir·as (al′jə·sir′əs, *Sp.* äl′hā·thē′räs) A port in southern Spain, opposite Gibraltar.

al·ge·don·ic (al′jə·don′ik) *adj.* Characterized by or relating to the agreeable and the disagreeable. [< Gk. *algos* pain + *hēdonikos* pleasurable]

al·ge·don·ics (al′jə·don′iks) *n. Psychol.* The study of pain and pleasure in relation to human life.

Al·ger (al′jər), **Horatio,** 1834–99, U.S. writer of boys' stories.

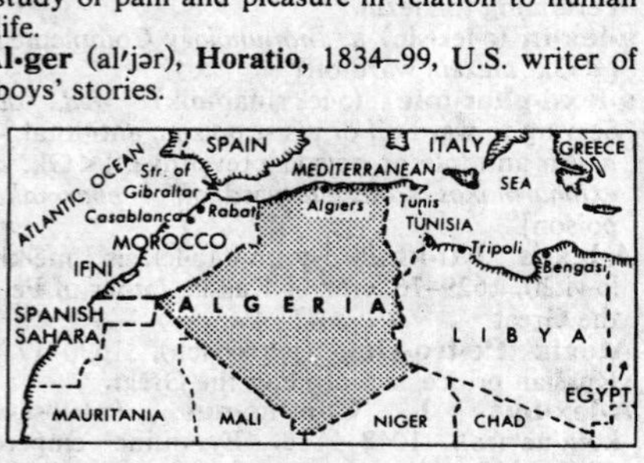

Al·ge·ri·a (al·jir′ē·ə) A republic in NW Africa, formerly a dependency of France; 919,352 square miles; capital, Algiers. *French* **Al·gé·rie** (ȧl·zhā·rē′). **—Al·ge′ri·an** *adj. & n.*

Al·ge·rine (al′jə·rēn′) *n.* **1** An inhabitant or native of Algeria, especially a native Berber, Arab, or Moor; an Algerian. **2** A pirate.

al·ge·rine (al′jə·rēn′) *n.* A soft woolen fabric or shawl with bright stripes.

Algerine War The war between the United States and the pirates of the Algerian coast, 1815.

Al·ger·non (al′jər·nən) A masculine personal name [? < OF *al grenon* with a mustache]

al·ge·si·a (al·jē′zē·ə) *n.* Sensitiveness to pain. [< Gk. *algos* pain]

al·get·ic (al·jet′ik) *adj.* Relating to or causing pain. [< Gk. *algein* feel pain]

-algia *suffix* Pain or disease of: *neuralgia.* [< Gk. *algos* pain]

al·gi·cide (al′jə·sīd) *n.* Any chemical agent used to kill algae. Also **al·gae·cide. —al·gi·cid·al** (al′jə·sī′dəl) *adj.*

al·gid (al′jid) *adj.* Cold; chilly: the *algid* stage of ague. [< F *algide* < L *algidus* cold < *algere* be cold] **—al·gid′i·ty** *n.*

Al·giers (al·jirz′) The capital of Algeria, a major port on the Mediterranean.

al·gin (al′jin) *n.* An insoluble, gelatinous acid obtained from various seaweeds, especially the giant kelp, used as an emulsifier and thickening agent. Also **alginic acid.** [< ALGA]

al·gi·nate (al′jə·nāt) *n.* Any of various salts of algin. —*adj.* Denoting any of various synthetic yarns or textile fibers made from algin or alginates.

al·goid (al′goid) *adj.* Of or like algae.

Al·gol (al′gol) The variable star Beta in Perseus: also called *Demon Star.* [< Arabic *al-ghūl* the ghoul, the demon]

al·go·lag·ni·a (al′gə·lag′nē·ə) *n. Psychiatry* Pleasure, specifically of a sexual nature, aroused by the infliction or the experiencing of pain. See MASOCHISM and SADISM. [< NL < Gk. *algos* pain + *lagneia* lust] **—al′go·lag′nic** *adj.* **—al′go·lag′nist** *n.*

al·gol·o·gy (al·gol′ə·jē) *n.* That branch of botany which treats of algae. [< L *alga* seaweed + -(O)LOGY] **—al·go·log·i·cal** (al′gə·loj′i·kəl) *adj.* **—al·gol′o·gist** *n.*

al·gom·e·ter (al·gom′ə·tər) *n.* An instrument to measure the intensity of pain. Also called *algesimeter.* [< Gk. *algos* pain + -METER] **—al·go·met·ric** (al′gə·met′·rik) or **·ri·cal** *adj.* **—al·gom′e·try** *n.*

Al·gon·ki·an (al·gong′kē·ən) *adj.* **1** *Geol.* Of, pertaining to, or characterized by a series of rock strata between the Archaean and the Cambrian; Proterozoic. **2** Former spelling of ALGONQUIAN.

Al·gon·qui·an (al·gong′kē·ən, -kwē·ən) *n.* **1** A large linguistic stock of North American Indians, formerly inhabiting the territory from Hudson Bay south to North Carolina and Tennessee, east of the Mississippi, including the Algonquin, Arapaho, Blackfoot, Cheyenne, Cree, Ojibwa, Micmac, Sauk, Delaware, Massachuset, and Shawnee tribes. **2** A member of one of the tribes belonging to this stock. —*adj.* Of or pertaining to the Algonquian family.

Al·gon·quin (al·gong′kin, -kwin) *n.* **1** A member of certain Algonquian tribes formerly inhabiting territory near the mouth of the Ottawa river, and of certain other tribes north of the St. Lawrence river. **2** The language spoken by these tribes, belonging to the East Central subfamily of Algonquian Indian languages. Also **Al·gon·kin** (al·gong′kin).

Algonquin Provincial Park A national park in SE Ontario, Canada; 2,740 square miles.

al·go·pho·bi·a (al′gə·fō′bē·ə) *n. Psychiatry* A morbid fear of pain. [< Gk. *algos* pain + -PHOBIA] **—al′go·pho′bic** *adj.*

al·gor (al′gôr) *n. Pathol.* Cold; chilliness; especially, an abnormal coldness, as in the early stages of a fever. [< L]

al·go·rism (al′gə·riz′əm) *n.* **1** The Arabic or decimal system of numeration. **2** Any method of computation using Arabic notation. **3** Arithmetic. Also **al·go·rithm** (al′gə·rith′əm). [< OF *algorisme* < Med.L *algorismus* < Arabic *al-Khowārazmi,* lit., the native of Khwārazm (Khiva), surname of a 9th cent. Arab mathematician]

al·gous (al′gəs) *adj.* Of, like, or filled with algae.

al·gua·zil (äl′gwä·zēl′) *n.* A Spanish officer of justice. [< Sp. < Arabic *al-wazīr* the vizier]

al·gum (al′gum) See ALMUG.

Al·ham·bra (al·ham′brə) The medieval palace of the Moorish kings at Granada, Spain. [< Sp. < Arabic *al-hamrā′* the red (house)]

Al·ham·bresque (al′ham·bresk′) *adj.* Like the Alhambra or its peculiar and delicate type of Moorish architecture.

a·li·as (ā′lē·əs) *n. pl.* **a·li·as·es 1** An assumed name. **2** *Law* A second writ to the same effect as a former one, issued after the first has failed. —*adv.* Otherwise called; called by an assumed name. [< L, at another time or place]

A·li (ä′lē), 600?–661, son-in-law and adopted son of Mohammed; fourth Arabian calif.

A·li Ba·ba (ä′lē bä′bä) In the *Arabian Nights,* the hero of the tale *Ali Baba and the Forty Thieves,* who gains entrance to a robbers' cave by crying out the magic words "Open sesame."

al·i·bi (al′ə·bī) *n.* **1** A form of defense by which the accused, in order to establish his innocence, undertakes to show that he was elsewhere when the crime was committed: He had a perfect *alibi.* **2** *Colloq.* Any excuse; especially, a poor and flimsy excuse. —*v.i. Colloq.* To make excuses for oneself. [< L, elsewhere]

al·i·bil·i·ty (al′ə·bil′ə·tē) *n.* Nutritive quality or value.

al·i·ble (al′ə·bəl) *adj.* Nourishing; nutritive. [< L *alibilis* < *alere* nourish]

A·li·can·te (ä′lē·kän′tā) A port in SE Spain; center of a wine-producing region.

Al·ice (al′is; *Fr.* ȧ·lēs′; *Ger.* ä·lē′sə) A feminine personal name. Also *Ital.* **A·li·cia** (ä·lē′chä), *Lat.* **A·li·ci·a** (ə·lē′shē·ə), *Sp.* **A·li·ci·a** (ä·lē′·thē·ä). [< Gmc. See ADELINE.]

Alice blue A light-blue color of slightly dusty hue. [after *Alice* Roosevelt Longworth, daughter of Theodore Roosevelt] **—Al′ice-blue′** *adj.*

al·i·cy·clic (al′i·sī′klik, -sik′lik) *adj.* Having both aliphatic and cyclic molecular structure or chemical properties. [< ALI(PHATIC) + CYCLIC]

al·i·dade (al′i·dād) *n.* **1** An auxiliary circle, frame, or movable arm, carrying microscopes or verniers, for reading the divisions of a graduated circle or arc. **2** A theodolite having such an arm. Also **al·i·dad** (al′i·dad). [< F < Med.L. *alhidada* < Arabic *al-'idādah* the revolving radius of a graduated circle]

al·ien (āl′yən, ā′lē·ən) *adj.* **1** Of another country; foreign. **2** Of foreign character; not similar; incongruous; inconsistent; also, unsympathetic. —*n.* **1** An unnaturalized foreign resident. **2** One of another race. **3** One estranged or excluded. **4** *Bot.* A plant native to one region maintaining itself under conditions prevailing in another. —*v.t.* **1** To transfer to another, as property. **2** To estrange. [< L *alienus* belonging to another]

Synonyms (adj.): conflicting, contradictory, contrary, contrasted, distant, foreign, hostile, opposed, remote, strange, unconnected, unlike. *Foreign* refers to difference of birth, *alien* to difference of allegiance. In their figurative use, that is *foreign* which is *remote, unlike,* or *unconnected*; that is *alien* which is *conflicting, hostile,* or *opposed. Antonyms*: akin, appropriate, apropos, essential, germane, pertinent, proper, relevant.

Synonyms (noun): foreigner, stranger. A naturalized citizen is not an *alien,* even if a *foreigner* by birth, and perhaps a *stranger* in the place where he resides. A person of foreign birth not naturalized is an *alien,* though he may have been long resident in the country, and ceased to be a stranger. He is an *alien* in one country if his allegiance is to another. *Antonyms*: citizen, countryman, native.

al·ien·a·ble (āl′yən·ə·bəl, ā′lē·ən-) *adj.* That can be made over or transferred, as property to the ownership of another. **—al′ien·a·bil′i·ty** *n.*

al·ien·age (āl′yən·ij, ā′lē·ən-) *n.* The state of being alien.

al·ien·ate (āl′yən·āt, ā′lē·ən-) *v.t.* **·at·ed, ·at·ing 1** To make indifferent or unfriendly; estrange: to *alienate* a friend. **2** To cause to feel estranged or withdrawn from society. **3** To make over; transfer, as property to the ownership of another. **4** To turn away, as affection or interest. **—al′ien·a′tor** *n.*

al·ien·a·tion (āl′yən·ā′shən, ā′lē·ən-) *n.* **1** The act of alienating, or the state of being alienated. **2** An anxious or resentful feeling of not belonging to or having a fit place in society. **3** An abnormal condition of indifference to or estrangement from others. **4** *Law* The transfer of property, or title, to another.

al·ien·ee (āl′yən·ē′, ā′lē·ən·ē′) *n.* One who takes over tranferred property.

al·ien·ism (āl′yən·iz′əm, ā′lē·ən-) *n.* Alienage.

al·ien·ist (āl′yən·ist, ā′lē·ən-) *n.* One skilled in the study or treatment of mental disorders: term used chiefly in medical jurisprudence. [< F *aliéniste,* ult. < L *alienus* foreign, strange]

al·ien·or (āl′yən·ər, ā′lē·ən·ôr′) *n. Law* One who alienates property to another; a vender. Also **al′ien·er.** [< AF]

a·lif (ä′lif) *n.* The first letter in the Arabic alphabet.

al·i·form (al′ə·fôrm, ā′lə·fôrm) *adj.* Wing-shaped; alar. [< L *ala* a wing + -FORM]

Al·i·garh (al′i·gûr′) A city in western Uttar Pradesh state, India.

a·light[1] (ə·līt′) *v.i.* **a·light·ed** or **a·lit, a·light·ing 1** To descend and come to rest; settle, as after flight. **2** To dismount, as from a horse or vehicle. **3** To come or fall upon by accident: with *on* or *upon.* [< OE *ālīhtan* < *ā-* out, off + *līhtan* alight, orig., make light]

a·light[2] (ə·līt′) *adj. & adv.* Lighted; lighted up; on fire; kindled. [ME *aliht,* pp. of *alihten* light up]

a·lign (ə·līn′), *v.t.* To arrange or place in a line; bring into line. —*v.i.* To fall into line. Also spelled *aline.* [< F *aligner* < *a-* to (< L *ad-*) + *ligne* line < L *linea*] **—a·lign·ment** *n.*

a·like (ə·līk′) *adj.* Having resemblance; like

one another; resembling, wholly or in part. *—adv.* In like manner. [OE *gelic, onlic*] **—a·like′ness** *n.*

Synonyms (adj.): akin, analogous, equal, equivalent, homogeneous, identical, kindred, like, resembling, similar, synonymous, uniform. Two or more objects are *alike* when each resembles the other or others; by modifiers *alike* may be made to express more or less resemblance; as, these houses are somewhat (that is, partially) *alike*; or, exactly (that is, in all respects) *alike*; or *alike* in color or structure. Substances are *homogeneous* which are made up of elements of the same kind, or which are the same in structure. To say "this is the *identical* man" is to say not merely that he is *similar* to the one in mind, but that he is the very *same* person. Things are *analogous* when they are *similar* in idea, plan, use, or character, but perhaps quite unlike in appearance; as, the gills of fishes are said to be *analogous* to the lungs in terrestrial animals. Compare IDENTICAL. *Antonyms*: different, dissimilar, distinct, heterogeneous, unlike.

al·i·ment (al′ə·mənt) *n.* Food; nutriment; sustenance. See synonyms under FOOD. *—v.t.* To furnish with food; nourish. [<L *alimentum* <*alere* nourish]**—al·i·men·tal** (al′ə·men′təl) *adj.* **—al′i·men′tal·ly** *adv.*

al·i·men·ta·ry (al′ə·men′tər·ē) *adj.* Supplying nourishment; connected with the function of nutrition.

alimentary canal The continuous digestive tube leading from the mouth through the esophagus, stomach, and intestines, having muscular walls which absorb nutrients and by peristalsis propel waste material to be discharged at the anus.

al·i·men·ta·tion (al′ə·men·tā′shən) *n.* **1** The act or process of supplying nutrition. **2** The act, process, or capacity of receiving nourishment or being nourished. **3** Maintenance; support.

al·i·men·ta·tive (al′ə·men′tə·tiv) *adj.* Of or pertaining to alimentation; nutritive.

al·i·mo·ny (al′ə·mō′nē) *n.* **1** *Law* The allowance made to a woman by order of court, from her husband's estate or income, for her maintenance after her divorce or legal separation from him, or during a suit therefor. The allowance made during suit is called **alimony pendente lite. 2** Maintenance; means of living or sustenance. [<L *alimonia* food, support <*alere* nourish]

a·line (ə·līn′) *v.* **a·lined, a·lin·ing** *v.t.* To arrange or place in a line; bring into line. *—v.i.* To fall into line. Also spelled *align.* [<F *aligner* <*a-* to (<L *ad-*) + *ligne* line <L *linea*]

a·line·ment (ə·līn′mənt) *n.* **1** Position or place in line; formation in line. **2** A straight line through two or more points. **3** *Eng.* The ground plan, as of a railroad. Also spelled *alignment.*

A·li Pa·sha (ä′lē pä·shä′), 1741–1822, Albanian warrior and leader: called the "Lion of Janina."

al·i·ped (al′ə·ped) *adj.* Having winglike membranes connecting the digits and the front and hind feet on each side, as a bat. *—n.* An aliped animal; a bat. [<L *alipes, -pedis* wing-footed <*ala* wing + *pes* foot]

al·i·phat·ic (al′ə·fat′ik) *adj.* Pertaining to or designating any organic compound of carbon and hydrogen having the carbon atoms connected in a straight or branched chain. [<Gk. *aleiphar, aleiphatos* fat, oil]

al·i·quant (al′ə·kwənt) *adj.* Contained in another number, but with remainder. [<L *aliquantus* some, somewhat <*alius* other + *quantus* how large, how much]

al·i·quot (al′ə·kwət) *adj.* Contained in another quantity an exact number of times. *—n.* A small aliquot portion of a measured volume or weight of a substance taken as a sample representing the whole. [<L *aliquot* <*alius* other + *quot* how many]

a·list (ə·list′) *adv. & adj.* In a canted or inclined position; listed over.

a·lit (ə·lit′) Past tense and past participle of ALIGHT[1].

a·lite (ā′līt) *n.* A component, consisting largely of calcium silicate, of the clinker produced in making portland cement. [<*A*, a rating + -LITE]

a·li·un·de (ā′lē·un′dē) *adv. Law Latin* From a source extrinsic to the principal matter; from elsewhere: Testimony to explain or contradict a written instrument from other sources than itself is evidence *aliunde.*

a·live (ə·līv′) *adj.* **1** In a living state, or a state in which the organs perform their functions; having life: said of organisms: opposed to *dead.* **2** In action, motion, or existence; in force, or operation; in full vigor. **3** In lively action; in an animated state; sprightly: *alive* with enthusiasm. **4** In a condition of attentiveness, sensitiveness, or susceptibility; open to impressions. **5** Abounding in life or living things, or in evidences of life: The hive was *alive* with bees. [OE *on līfe* in life]

Synonyms: active, alert, animate, animated, breathing, brisk, existent, existing, live, lively, living, quick, subsisting, vivacious. *Alive* applies to all degrees of life, from that which shows one to be barely *existing* or *existent* as a living thing, as when we say he is barely *alive,* to that which implies the utmost of vitality and power. So the word *quick,* which began by signifying "having life," is now mostly applied to energy of life as shown in swiftness of action. *Breathing* is capable of like contrast. We say of a dying man, "he is still *breathing*"; or we speak of a *breathing* statue, where we mean having, or seeming to have breath and life. Compare ACTIVE, ALERT, NIMBLE. *Antonyms*: dead, deceased, defunct, dispirited, dull, inanimate, lifeless, spiritless.

a·liz·a·rin (ə·liz′ə·rin) *n.* A basic orange-red crystalline coloring compound, $C_{14}H_8O_4$; used to dye cotton, wool, and silks various shades of red: formerly prepared from madder, now manufactured from anthraquinone. *—adj.* Designating any organic compound derived from anthraquinone: *alizarin* blue, *alizarin* crimson, *alizarin* green. Also **a·liz·a·rine** (ə·liz′ə·rin, -rēn). [<F *alizerine* <*alizari* madder]

al·ka·hest (al′kə·hest) *n.* The hypothetical universal solvent sought by the ancient alchemists. [A pseudo-Arabic word coined by Paracelsus]

al·ka·le·mi·a (al′kə·lē′mē·ə) *n. Pathol.* A reduction to below normal or safe limits of acidity in the blood; increased alkalinity. [<NL <ALKALI + -EMIA]

al·ka·les·cen·cy (al′kə·les′ən·sē) *n.* A tendency to become alkaline; slight alkalinity. Also **al′ka·les′cence.**

al·ka·les·cent (al′kə·les′ənt) *adj.* Becoming or tending to become alkaline. *—n.* An alkalescent compound.

al·ka·li (al′kə·lī) *n. pl.* **·lis** or **·lies 1** *Chem.* A compound of hydrogen and oxygen with any one of the elements lithium, sodium, potassium, rubidium, and cesium, or the ammonium radical, characterized by great solubility in water and capability of neutralizing acids and of turning red litmus paper blue. **2** Anything that will neutralize an acid, as lime, magnesia, etc. **3** Sodium carbonate. **4** Mineral matter, not including sodium chloride, found in natural waters and in soils. [<MF *alcali* <Arabic *al-qaliy* the ashes of saltwort]

al·kal·ic (al·kal′ik) *adj.* Containing or characterized by a considerable amount of the alkaline bases, especially soda and potash.

alkali flat *Geol.* An arid plain, permeated or incrusted with alkaline salts; the bed of an evaporated lake.

al·ka·li·fy (al′kə·lə·fī, al·kal′ə·fī) *v.t. & v.i.* **·fied, ·fy·ing** To change into or become alkaline or an alkali.

alkali metals Any of the metallic elements of group Ia of the periodic table, including lithium, sodium, potassium, rubidium, cesium, and francium.

al·ka·lim·e·ter (al′kə·lim′ə·tər) *n.* **1** An instrument for measuring the concentration or the amount of alkali in a solid or liquid. **2** An instrument for measuring the amount of carbon dioxide evolved in a reaction.

al·ka·lim·e·try (al′kə·lim′ə·trē) *n.* The determination of the percentage of alkali in a solution by a volumetric or other method.

al·ka·line (al′kə·līn, -lin) *adj.* **1** Of, pertaining to, or having the characteristics of an alkali; containing or produced by an alkali. **2** Having a pH greater than 7.

alkaline earth The oxide of any of the alkaline-earth metals.

al·ka·line-earth metals (al′kə·līn ûrth, -lin) A group of elements resembling the alkali metals but somewhat less reactive, usually including calcium, strontium, magnesium, and barium, and sometimes also other elements of group IIa of the periodic table.

al·ka·lin·i·ty (al′kə·lin′ə·tē) *n.* The state or quality of being alkaline.

al·ka·lize (al′kə·līz) *v.t. & v.i.* **·lized, ·liz·ing** To convert into or become alkali or alkaline. **—al′ka·li·za′tion** *n.*

al·ka·loid (al′kə·loid) *n.* Any of various nitrogenous bases of vegetable origin, usually having a toxic effect on animals, as strychnine, nicotine, or cocaine. **—al′ka·loi′dal** *adj.*

al·ka·lo·sis (al′kə·lō′sis) *n.* A higher concentration than normal of carbonate in body fluids.

al·kane (al′kān) *n.* Any of a homologous series of saturated aliphatic hydrocarbons having the general formula C_nH_{2n+2}, as methane, ethane, etc.

alkane series Methane series.

al·ka·net (al′kə·net) *n.* **1** A perennial plant *(Alkanna tinctoria)* or its roots, which yield a red dye. **2** The dye obtained from this plant, used as a chemical indicator. **3** Bugloss. **4** Puccoon. [<Sp. *alcaneta,* dim. of *alcana* henna <Arabic *al-hinnā′* the henna]

al·kene (al′kēn) *n.* Any of a series of unsaturated aliphatic hydrocarbons having the general formula C_nH_{2n} and containing a carbon-to-carbon double bond, as ethylene, propylene, etc. Also called *olefin.* [<ALK(YL) + -ENE]

Alk·maar (älk′mär) A city in NW Netherlands.

Al·ko·ran (al′kō·rän′, -ran′) *n.* The Koran. **—Al′ko·ran′ic** (-ran′ik) *adj.*

al·kyd (al′kid) Any of a group of adhesive resins made by combining an unsaturated organic acid and a polyhydric alcohol, used for paints and other surface coatings. Also **alkyd resin.**

al·kyl (al′kil) *n.* A univalent hydrocarbon radical having the general formula C_nH_{2n+1}, equivalent to an alkane molecule minus a hydrogen atom. Also **alkyl radical.** [<ALK(ALI) + -YL]

al·kyl·ate (al′kə·lāt) *v.t.* **·at·ed, ·at·ing** To introduce one or more alkyl groups into. *—n.* A product of alkylation, as a high-octane gasoline.

al·kyl·a·tion (al′kə·lā′shən) *n.* **1** The process of introducing one or more alkyl radicals into a compound by substitution or addition. **2** A refinery process for producing high-octane gasoline by forcing the combination of constituent alkanes and alkenes by the action of heat, pressure, and catalysts.

al·kyne (al′kīn) *n.* Any of a series of unsaturated aliphatic hydrocarbons having the general formula C_nH_{2n-2} and containing a carbon-to-carbon triple bond, as ethyne (acetylene) etc. Also **alkine.** [<ALKY(L) + -INE]

all (ôl) *adj.* **1** The entire substance or extent of: *all* Europe; *all* wisdom. **2** The entire number of; the individual components of, without exception: to be known to *all* men. **3** The greatest possible: in *all* haste. **4** Any whatever: beyond *all* doubt. **5** Every: used in phrases with *manner, sorts,* and *kinds: all* manner of men. **6** Nothing except: He was *all* skin and bones. See synonyms under EVERY. *—n.* **1** Everything that one has; entire interest or possession: to give one's *all.* **2** Whole being; totality. *—pron.* **1** Everyone: *All* are condemned. **2** Each one: When he questioned his students, *all* were ready with an answer. **3** Everything: *All* is in readiness. **4** Every part, as of a whole: *All* of it is gone. ◆Homophone; *awl.* [OE] **—above all** Primarily; of the first importance. **—after all 1** On the other hand. **2** In the long run; in spite of everything. **—all in all** All things considered; taken as a whole. **—at all. 1** In any way: I can't come *at all.* **2** To any degree or extent; no luck *at all.* **—for all** To the degree that: *For all* I care, you can go without me. **—for all of (me, you, him, her,** or **us)** As for: You can leave now, *for all of* me.**—in all** Including everything; all told. **—onceand for all** Once and no more; finally. *—adv.* **1** Wholly; entirely: fallen *all* to bits; running*all* the way; traveling *all* through the night. **2** Exclusively; only: That portion is *all*

three *all.* **—all along** All the time: I knew it *all along.* **—all but 1** Almost; on the verge of: I was *all but* exhausted by my trip. **2** Every one except: He took *all but* six. **—all in** *Colloq.* Wearied, as from exertion. **—all of** No less than; quite: It's *all of* ten miles. **—all out** Making every effort: They went *all out* for victory. **—all over 1** Finished; past and gone: The love affair is *all over* between us. **2** Everywhere; in all parts: He's been *all over.* **3** Typically; in every way: That's George *all over.* **—all the (better, more,** etc.) So much the (better, more, etc.) **—all up with** *Colloq.* Ended; without power to continue: It's *all up with* him.

al·la bre·ve (ä′lə brev′ā, *Ital.* äl′lä brā′vä) *Music* A measure of duple or quadruple time in which the beat is represented by the half note: performed twice as quickly as common time. Symbol C. [< Ital., lit., according to the breve]

all·ach·es·the·sia (al′ak·is·thē′zhə, -zhē·ə) *n.* A tactile sensation localized elsewhere than at the point of stimulation. Also *allesthesia.* [< Gk. *allachē* elsewhere + *aisthēsis* feeling]

Al·lah (al′ə, ä′lə) In the Moslem religion, the one supreme being; God. [< Arabic]

Al·la·ha·bad (al′ə·hə·bad′, ä′lə·hä·bäd′) A city on the Jumna River, capital of Uttar Pradesh state, India.

all-A·mer·i·can (ôl′ə·mer′ə·kən) *adj.* **1** Representative of America or of the United States. **2** Composed of the best in America: an *all-American* football team. **3** Of or composed of Americans exclusively. **4** Of all the Americas. **5** Within or confined to America or the United States. —*n.* **1** An imaginary or ideal team, as of football players, selected from the college players considered best in a season. **2** A player selected for such a team. **3** One of the best in America.

Al·lan-a-Dale (al′ən·ə·dāl′) In English legend, an outlaw of Robin Hood's band.

al·lan·toid (ə·lan′toid) *adj.* **1** Sausage-shaped. **2** Resembling or possessing an allantois. Also **al·lan·toi·dal** (al′ən·toi′dəl). [Gk. *allantoeidēs* < *allas* sausage + *eidos* form]

al·lan·to·in (ə·lan′tō·in) *n.* An oxidation product of uric acid, $C_4H_6N_4O_3$, occurring in allantoic fluid, fetal urine, and elsewhere, which promotes healing when applied to wounds.

al·lan·to·is (ə·lan′tō·is) *n.* A membranous, fluid-filled sac that develops from the hindgut in the embryos of reptiles, birds, and mammals. [< NL < *allantoides* < GK. See ALLANTOID.] —**al·lan·to·ic** (al′ən·tō′ik) *adj.*

all-a·round (ôl′ə·round′) *adj.* All-round.

al·la vos·tra sa·lu·te (äl′lä vôs′trä sä·lōō′tä) *Italian* To your health.

al·lay (ə·lā′) *v.t.* **al·layed, al·lay·ing 1** To lessen the violence or reduce the intensity of. **2** To lay to rest, as fears; pacify; calm. [OE *ālecgan* < *ā-* away + *lecgan* lay] **—al·lay′er** *n.*

Synonyms: abate, alleviate, appease, assuage, calm, compose, lessen, lighten, mitigate, moderate, mollify, pacify, palliate, quiet, reduce, relieve, soften, soothe, still, tranquilize. We *allay* suffering by using means to *soothe* and *tranquilize* the sufferer; we *alleviate* suffering by doing something toward removal of the cause. *Pacify* and *appease* signify to bring to peace; to *mollify* is to soften; to *mitigate* is to make mild; we *mollify* a temper, *mitigate* rage or pain. To *calm, quiet,* or *tranquilize* is to make still; *compose,* to adjust to a calm and settled condition; to *soothe* is to bring to pleased quietude. We *allay* excitement, *calm* agitation, *compose* our feelings, *pacify* the quarrelsome, *quiet* the clamorous, *soothe* grief or distress. Compare ALLEVIATE. *Antonyms*: agitate, arouse, excite, fan, kindle, provoke, rouse, stir.

all-clear (ôl′klir′) *n.* The signal indicating that an air raid is over.

al·le·cret (al′ə·kret) *n. Archaic* A breastplate with tassets, worn by light cavalry and infantry about the 16th century: also spelled *halecret.* [< MF *allecret, halcret*]

al·le·ga·tion (al′ə·gā′shən) *n.* The act of alleging. **2** That which is alleged; a formal assertion. **3** Something alleged without proof. **4** *Law* The assertion of a party to a suit, which he undertakes to prove. [< L *allegatio, -onis* < *allegare* send a message < *ad-* to + *legare* commission]

al·lege (ə·lej′) *v.t.* **al·leged, al·leg·ing 1** To assert to be true without proving; affirm. **2** To plead as an excuse, in support of or in opposition to a claim or accusation. **3** *Archaic* To cite or quote. [< AF *alegier,* OF *esligier* < L *ex-* out + *litigare* sue; infl. by L *allegare* (see ALLEGATION) and *lex* law] **—al·lege′a·ble** *adj.* **—al·leged′** *adj.* **—al·leg′er** *n.*

Synonyms: adduce, advance, affirm, assert, asseverate, assign, aver, cite, claim, declare, introduce, maintain, offer, plead, produce, say, state. To *allege* is formally to state as true, without proving. *Adduce* is a secondary word; nothing can be *adduced* in evidence until something has been *stated* or *alleged,* which the evidence is to sustain. An *alleged* fact stands open to question or doubt. When an *alleged* criminal is brought to trial, the counsel on either side are accustomed to *advance* a theory, and *adduce* the strongest possible evidence in its support; they will *produce* documents and witnesses, *cite* precedents, *assign* reasons, *introduce* suggestions, *offer* pleas. The accused will usually *assert* his innocence. Compare STATE. *Antonyms*: see AFFIRM.

al·leg·ed·ly (ə·lej′id·lē) *adv.* According to allegation.

Al·le·ghe·ny (al′ə·gā′nē) *adj.* Of or pertaining to the Allegheny Mountains or River. Also **Al′le·gha′ny.**

Allegheny Mountains A mountain range of the Appalachian system, extending from Pennsylvania to Virginia.

Allegheny River A river in western New York and Pennsylvania; flowing SW 325 miles to join with the Monongahela, forming the Ohio River.

Allegheny Series *Geol.* The middle Coal Measures of the eastern United States.

al·le·giance (ə·lē′jəns) *n.* **1** Fidelity, or an obligation of fidelity, to a government from a citizen, to a superior, or to a principle. **2** The obligation of fidelity in general. **3** *Archaic* The duty and obligation of a vassal holding lands by fealty to the superior lord. [ME *alegeaunce* < *a-* to (< L *ad-*) + OF *ligeance* < *liege.* See LIEGE.]

Synonyms: devotion, faithfulness, fealty, fidelity, homage, loyalty, obedience, subjection. The feudal uses of these words have mostly passed away with the state of society that gave them birth; but their origin still colors their present meaning. A patriotic American feels an enthusiastic *loyalty* to the Republic; he takes an oath of *allegiance* to the government, but his *loyalty* will lead him to do more than mere *allegiance* could demand; he pays *homage* to God or to those principles of right that are supreme; he acknowledges the duty of *obedience* to all rightful authority; he resents the idea of *subjection. Fealty,* except in poetic style, has given place to *faithfulness* or *fidelity. Antonyms*: disaffection, disloyalty, rebellion, sedition, treason.

al·le·giant (ə·lē′jənt) *adj. Obs.* Loyal; faithful.

al·le·gor·ic (al′ə·gôr′ik, -gor′-) *adj.* Pertaining to, appearing in, or containing allegory; figurative. Also **al′le·gor′i·cal. —al′le·gor′i·cal·ly** *adv.* **—al′le·gor′i·cal·ness** *n.*

al·le·go·rist (al′ə·gôr′ist, -gō′rist, al′ə·gər·ist) *n.* One who composes or uses allegories.**—al′·le·go·ris′tic** *adj.*

al·le·go·rize (al′ə·gə·rīz) *v.* **·rized, ·riz·ing** *v.t.* **1** To turn into an allegory; relate in the manner of an allegory. **2** To explain or interpret as an allegory. —*v.i.* **3** To make or use allegory. **—al·le·go·ri·za·tion** (al′ə·gôr′ə·zā′shən, -gor′-) *n.* **—al′le·go·riz′er** *n.*

al·le·go·ry (al′ə·gôr′ē, -gō′rē) *n. pl.* **·ries 1** The setting forth of a subject or the telling of a story in figurative or symbolic language requiring interpretation; especially, a narrative veiling a moral by symbolic devices, such as personification, metaphor, etc. **2** Any subject or story so presented. **3** Loosely, any symbolic representation in literature or art; an emblem. [< L *allegoria* < Gk. *allēgoria,* lit., a speaking otherwise < *allos* other + *agoreuein* speak in public assembly < *agora* forum]

Synonyms: fable, fiction, illustration, metaphor, parable, simile, story. The *allegory, parable,* or *fable* tells its story as if true, leaving the reader or hearer to discover its fictitious character and learn its lesson. The word *fiction* is applied almost exclusively to novels, short stories, or romances. An *allegory* or *parable* is a moral or religious tale, of which the moral lesson is the substance and all descriptions and incidents but accessories; the *parable* is generally briefer and less adorned than the *allegory.* A *fable* is generally brief, representing animals as the speakers and actors, and conveying some lesson of practical wisdom or shrewdness. Compare SIMILE, STORY. *Antonyms*: chronicle, fact, history, narrative, record.

al·le·gret·to (al′ə·gret′ō, *Ital.* äl′lā·gret′tō) *adj. & adv. Music* Rather fast: faster than *andante* but slower than *allegro.* —*n. pl.* **·tos** A movement in allegretto time. [< Ital.]

al·le·gro (ə·lā′grō, ə·leg′rō; *Ital.* äl·lā′grō) *adj. & adv. Music* Quick; lively: faster than *allegretto* but slower than *presto.* —*n. pl.* **·gros** A musical composition, movement, etc., in such tempo. [< Ital.]

allegro non tan·to (nōn tän′tō) *Music* Moderately lively. [< Ital.]

al·lele (ə·lēl′) *n. Genetics* An allelomorph.

al·le·lo·morph (ə·lē′lə·môrf, ə·lel′ə-) *n. Genetics* In Mendel's law, one of a pair of contrasted characters which become segregated in the formation of reproductive cells. [< Gk. *allēlōn* of one another + *morphē* form] **—al·le′lo·mor′·phic** *adj.* **—al·le′lo·mor′phism** *n.*

al·le·lu·ia (al′ə·lōō′yə) *n. & interj.* Hallelujah. Also **al′le·lu′iah.** [< L. See HALLELUJAH.] **—al·le·lu·iat·ic** (al′ə·lōō·yat′ik) *adj.*

Al·le·magne (ål·mån′y′) The French name for GERMANY.

al·le·mande (al′ə·mand′, *Fr.* ål·mäṅd′) *n.* **1** A stately processional dance in duple rhythm, originating in Germany. **2** The music for this. **3** *Music* A formal movement in various suites, resembling the dance chiefly in its duple rhythm. [< F, lit., German]

Al·le·man·ni (al′ə·man′ī) See ALEMANNI.

Al·len (al′ən), **Ethan,** 1737–89, American soldier, leader of the "Green Mountain Boys," a body of Vermont soldiers in the Revolution. **—Grant,** 1848–99, English author. **—Ira,** 1751–1814, American soldier and legislator; brother of Ethan.
—(William) Her·vey (hûr′vē), 1889–1949, U.S. novelist.

Al·len·by (al′ən·bē), **Edmund Henry,** 1861–1936, first viscount, British field marshal; commanded forces in Egypt and Palestine, 1917–18.

Al·len·stein (ä′len·shtīn) See OLSZTYN.

Al·len·town (al′ən·toun) A city in eastern Pennsylvania.

al·ler·gen (al′ər·jən) *n.* Any substance capable of producing allergy. **—al·ler·gen·ic** (al′ər·jen′·ik) *adj.*

al·ler·gic (ə·lûr′jik) *adj.* **1** Characteristic of or pertaining to allergy. **2** Highly susceptible to. **3** *Colloq.* Having an aversion to.

al·ler·gist (al′ər·jist) *n.* A specialist in the treatment of allergies.

al·ler·gy (al′ər·jē) *n. pl.* **·gies 1** A condition of exaggerated sensibility, as manifested by various physiologic reactions to an environmental substance or sensory stimulus that produces no reaction in nonsensitive individuals. **2** Anaphylaxis. [< NL *allergia* < Gk. *allos* other + *ergon* work]

al·les·the·sia (al′is·thē′zhə, -zhē·ə) See ALLACHESTHESIA.

al·leth·rin (ə·leth′rin) *n.* A synthetic liquid compound, used as an insecticide.

al·le·vi·ate (ə·lē′vē·āt) *v.t.* **·at·ed, ·at·ing** To make lighter or easier to bear; relieve, as pain; mitigate. [< L *alleviatus,* pp. of *alleviare* < *ad-* to + *levis* light]

Synonyms: abate, allay, assuage, lessen, lighten, mitigate, moderate, reduce, relieve, remove, soften. *Alleviate* is less than *relieve; relieve,* ordinarily, less than *remove. Assuage* is to sweeten; *mitigate,* to make milder; *moderate,* to bring within measure; *abate,* to beat down and so make less. We *abate* a fever; *lessen* anxiety; *moderate* passions or desires; *lighten* burdens; *mitigate* or *alleviate* pain; *reduce* inflammation; *soften, assuage,* or *moderate* grief; we *lighten* or *mitigate* punishments; we *relieve* suffering. Compare ALLAY. *Antonyms*: aggravate, augment, embitter, enhance, heighten, increase, intensify, magnify. **—al·le′vi·a′tion** *n.* **—al·le′·vi·a′tor** *n.*

al·le·vi·a·tive (ə·lē′vē·ā′tiv, ə·lē′vē·ə·tiv) *adj.*

Tending to alleviate. Also **al·le·vi·a·to·ry** (ə·lē′vē·ə·tôr′ē, -tō′rē). —*n.* Anything that alleviates.

al·ley[1] (al′ē) *n.* **1** A narrow passageway, street, path, or walk; especially, a narrow way behind city buildings, running parallel to a street. **2** A long narrow space for bowling, or the building containing it. See synonyms under WAY. [< OF *alee* a going, passage < *aler* go, ? < L *ambulare*]

al·ley[2] (al′ē) *n.* A large playing marble. [< ALABASTER]

alley cat A cat which forages for food in alleys, etc.

al·leyed (al′ēd) *adj.* Having an alley or alleys; having the form or nature of an alley.

Al·leyn (al′in), **Edward,** 1566–1626, English actor and producer.

al·ley·way (al′ē·wā′) *n.* A short or narrow passageway between buildings.

al·lez-vous-en (à·lā·vo͞o·zäṅ′) *French* Go away! Off with you!

all-fired (ôl′fīrd′) *U.S. Slang adj.* Excessive: an *all-fired* shame. —*adv.* Inordinately: He walked *all-fired* slow. [Alter. of *hell-fired*]

All Fools' Day The first of April: a day on which jokes and tricks are commonly practiced.

all fours 1 The four legs of a quadruped, or the arms and legs of a person. **2** Seven-up, a card game. **—to go** (or **be**) **on all fours 1** To move or crawl on all four limbs, as a baby. **2** To run smoothly, as a machine. **—to be on all fours with** To present an exact comparison or analogy with.

all hail All health! an exclamation in friendly salutation.

All-hal·low·mas (ôl′hal′ō·məs) *n.* The feast of All Saints.

All-hal·lows (ôl′hal′ōz) *n.* All Saints' Day, Nov. 1.

All-hal·low·tide (ôl′hal′ō·tīd) *n.* The season near Nov. 1.

all·heal (ôl′hēl′) *n.* Any of various plants reputed to have healing properties, as the selfheal and the garden heliotrope.

al·li·a·ceous (al′ē·ā′shəs) *adj.* **1** Pertaining to or belonging to a genus *(Allium)* of liliaceous herbs with a pungent odor, including the various species of onions, leeks, and garlic. **2** Having the taste or smell of onions or garlic. [< ALLIUM]

al·li·ance (ə·lī′əns) *n.* **1** A formal treaty or agreement between states or other parties. **2** The union so formed; any intimate relationship. [< OF *aliance* (MF *alliance*) < L *alligantia* < *alligare.* See ALLY.]

Synonyms: affinity, coalition, compact, confederacy, confederation, federation, fusion, kin, league, partnership, union. Commonly, *alliance* is a connection formed by treaty between sovereign states for mutual aid in war; *partnership* is a mercantile word. We speak of an alliance *with* a neighboring people; *against* the common enemy; *for* offense and defense; alliance *of, between,* or *among* nations. *Coalition* is oftenest used of political parties; *fusion* is now the more common word in this sense. In a *confederacy* or *confederation* there is an attempt to unite separate states in a general government without surrender of sovereignty. *Union* makes the separate states substantially one. *Federation* is a poetic and rhetorical word expressing something of the same thought. The United States is a federal *union.* See ASSOCIATION. *Antonyms*: antagonism, discord, disunion, divorce, enmity, hostility, schism, secession, separation, war.

Al·lie (al′ē) Diminutive of ALICE. Also **Al′ly.**

al·lied (ə·līd′) *adj.* **1** United, confederated, or leagued. **2** Morphologically, genetically, or otherwise related.

Al·lier (à·lyā′) **1** A river in central France, flowing NW 250 miles to the Loire. **2** A department of central France; 2,850 square miles; capital, Moulins.

Al·lies (al′īz, ə·līz′) See under ALLY.

al·li·ga·tion (al′ə·gā′shən) *n.* Formerly, the method of finding or rule for finding the relation between the prices of the ingredients in a mixture, their proportions, quality, and the price of the mixture. In **alligation alternate** the proportion is required, the other two quantities being given: in **alligation medial** the cost of the mixture is required. [< L *alligatio, -onis* < *alligare* < *ad-* to + *ligare* bind]

al·li·ga·tor (al′ə·gā′tər) *n.* **1** Either of two species of large, crocodilian reptiles (genus *Alligator),* found only in rivers and swamps of the southern United States and in the Yangtze River in China, having a shorter, blunter head than the crocodile and no lower teeth protruding when the jaw is closed. **2** Any crocodilian. **3** Leather made from the hide of an alligator. **4** A machine for squeezing ore, etc. [Earlier *alligarta* < Sp. *el lagarto* the lizard < L *lacertus*]

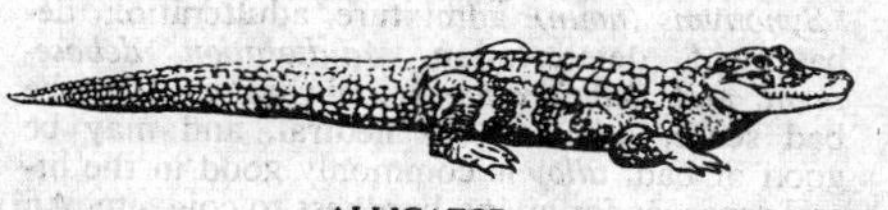

ALLIGATOR
(Length up to 18 feet)

alligator pear The avocado.

alligator snapping turtle A very large freshwater turtle *(Macrochelys temmincki)* having the head covered with plates and a fleshy extension on the tongue. Also **alligator snapper.**

all-im·por·tant (ôl′im·pôr′tənt) *adj.* Very important; crucial; necessary.

all-in·clu·sive (ôl′in·klo͞o′siv) *adj.* Including everything; general.

all-in-one (ôl′in·wun′) *n.* A woman's foundation garment, consisting of a brassière and girdle, with or without panties.

all in the wind 1 *Naut.* In line with the wind, so as not to draw, as the sails of a ship. **2** *Colloq.* Puzzled; nonplused; confused.

al·li·sion (ə·lizh′ən) *n. Naut.* The act of a vessel's striking or dashing against another: distinguished from *collision.* [< L *allisio, -onis* < *allidere* < *ad-* against + *lidere* strike violently]

Al·li·son (al′ə·sən), **Samuel King,** born 1900, U.S. physicist.

al·lit·er·ate (ə·lit′ə·rāt) *v.* **·at·ed, ·at·ing** *v.i.* **1** To speak alliteratively; use alliteration, as in the writing of verse. **2** To constitute alliteration: These two lines of verse *alliterate.* —*v.t.* **3** To make alliterative: to *alliterate* verses. [< AL-[2] to + L *littera* a letter (of the alphabet)]

al·lit·er·a·tion (ə·lit′ə·rā′shən) *n.* **1** The use or repetition of a succession of words with same initial letter or sound: Langland uses *alliteration* in his line "A fair field full of folk." **—al·lit·er·a·tive** (ə·lit′ə·rā′tiv, -ər·ə·tiv) *adj.* **—al·lit′er·a′tive·ly** *adv.* **—al·lit′er·a′tive·ness** *n.*

al·li·um (al′ē·əm) *n.* Any of a large genus *(Allium)* of liliaceous plants having a tunicate bulb, leafless scapes with flowers in a terminal umbel, and a pungent, onionlike smell, as onions, leeks, garlic, shallots, chives, etc. [< L]

allo- *combining form* **1** Other; alien: *allotheism,* worship of strange gods. **2** Variant; different: *allogeneic,* differing genetically. [< Gk. *allos* other]

al·lo·bar (al′ə·bär) *n. Meteorol.* An area above which the barometric pressure has changed during a specified interval. [ALLO- + Gk. *baros* weight, pressure] **—al·lo·bar·ic** (al′ə·bar′ik) *adj.*

al·lo·cate (al′ə·kāt) *v.t.* **·cat·ed, ·cat·ing 1** To set apart for a special purpose, as funds. **2** To apportion; assign, as a share or in shares. **3** To locate or localize, as a person or event. [< Med.L *allocatus,* pp. of *allocare* < L *ad-* to + *locare* place < *locus* a place] **—al·lo·ca·ble** (al′ə·kə·bəl) *adj.*

al·lo·ca·tion (al′ə·kā′shən) *n.* **1** An allocating or being allocated. **2** Something allocated.

al·lo·ca·tur (al′ō·kā′tər) *n. Law* The judicial indorsement of a writ or order. [< Med.L, lit., it is allowed]

al·loch·tho·nous (ə·lok′thə·nəs) *adj.* Originating, formed, or developed elsewhere: distinguished from *autochthonous.* [< ALLO- + Gk. *chthōn* earth, land]

al·lo·cu·tion (al′ə·kyo͞o′shən) *n.* A formal, official, or authoritative exhortation or address. [< L *allocutio, -onis* < *alloqui* < *ad-* to + *loqui* speak]

al·lo·di·al (ə·lō′dē·əl) *adj. Law* Pertaining to the absolute ownership of land, free from rent or service: opposed to *feudal.* Also spelled *alodial.*

al·lo·di·um (ə·lō′dē·əm) *n. pl.* **·di·a** (-dē·ə) *Law* **1** The interest or estate in lands held in absolute ownership; estates in fee simple. **2** Land so held. Also spelled *alodium.* [< Med.L *allodium, alodium* < OHG *alōd, allōd* entire property < *all* all + *ōt* property]

al·log·a·my (ə·log′ə·mē) *n. Bot.* Fecundation of a flower by pollen from another flower of the same species; cross-fertilization: opposed to *autogamy.* [< ALLO- + Gk. *gamos* marriage] **—al·log′a·mous** *adj.*

al·lo·ge·ne·ic (al′ə·jə·nē′ik) *adj.* Differing genetically to the extent of having the potential to initiate an immune reaction. Also **al·lo·gen·ic** (al′ə·jen′ik) *adj.*

al·lo·graft (al′ə·graft, -gräft) *n.* A graft of tissue from a donor who differs genetically but is of the same species as the recipient; homograft.

al·lom·er·ism (ə·lom′ər·iz′əm) *n.* Constancy of crystalline form with variation in chemical constitution. [< ALLO-[2] + Gk. *meros* a part] **—al·lom′er·ous** *adj.*

al·lom·e·try (ə·lom′ə·trē) *n.* The relative changes in dimension of organs and parts of the body during development and growth of the organism as a whole. **—al·lo·met·ric** (al′ə·met′rik) *adj.*

al·lo·morph (al′ə·môrf) *n.* **1** *Mineral.* **a** A pseudomorph formed without change of chemical composition, as calcite after aragonite. Compare PARAMORPHISM. **b** A variety of pseudomorph the constituents of which have been partially or totally changed, or one which has assumed a substitute constituent. **2** *Ling.* Any of the positional variants of a morpheme. [< ALLO- + Gk. *morphē* form] **—al′lo·mor′phic** *adj.* **—al′lo·mor′phism** *n.*

al·lons (à·lôṅ′) *French* Let's go! Come on!

al·lo·nym (al′ə·nim) *n.* **1** The name of one person taken by another, especially by an author; a false name. **2** A book under such a name. [< ALLO- + Gk. *onyma* name] **—al·lon·y·mous** (ə·lon′ə·məs) *adj.*

al·lo·path·ic (al′ə·path′ik) *adj.* Pertaining to, favoring, or practicing allopathy. **—al′lo·path′i·cal·ly** *adv.*

al·lop·a·thy (ə·lop′ə·thē) *n. Med.* The system of remedial treatment in which it is sought to cure a disease by producing a condition different from or incompatible with the effects of the disease: opposed to *homeopathy.* [< ALLO- + Gk. *pathos* suffering] **—al·lop′a·thist, al·lo·path** (al′ə·path) *n.*

al·lo·pat·ric (al′ə·pat′rik) *adj.* Occurring in isolated areas, as organisms of the same species; separated geographically.

al·lo·phane (al′ə·fān) *n.* An amorphous, translucent mineral of variable color, composed mainly of a hydrated aluminum silicate. [< Gk. *allophanēs* appearing otherwise < *allos* other + *phainesthai* appear; with ref. to its change of appearance under the blowpipe]

al·lo·phone (al′ə·fōn) *n. Phonet.* Any of the nondistinctive variants of a phoneme: The velar (k) of *coop* and the palatal (k) of *keep* are *allophones* of the phoneme /k/. [< ALLO- + Gk. *phōnē* a sound, voice]

al·lo·some (al′ə·sōm) *n.* **1** Sex chromosome. **2** Any aberrant chromosome. [< ALLO- + Gk. *sōma* body]

al·lot (ə·lot′) *v.t.* **al·lot·ted, al·lot·ting 1** To assign by lot; distribute so that the recipients have no choice: to *allot* duties. **2** To apportion or assign, as to a special function, person, or place: with *to*: to *allot* ten years to the acquisition of knowledge. [< OF *aloter* < *a-* to (< L *ad-*) + *lot.* See LOT.]

Synonyms: appoint, apportion, assign, award, destine, distribute, divide, give, grant, select. *Allot* applies to the giving of a definite thing; a portion or extent of time or space is *allotted. Appoint* may be used of time, space, or person; as the *appointed* day; the *appointed* place; an officer was *appointed* to this station. *Destine* fixes or assumes to fix what is considerably in the future; as, he *destines* his son to follow his own profession. *Assign* is rarely used of time, but rather of places, persons, or things. That which is *alloted, appointed,* or *assigned* is more or less arbitrary; that which is *awarded* is the due return for something the receiver has done, and he has right and claim to it, as, the medal was *awarded* for valor. *Antonyms*: appropriate, confiscate, deny, refuse, resume, retain, seize, withhold.

al·lot·ment (ə·lot′mənt) *n.* **1** The act of allotting or that which is allotted. **2** *U.S. Mil.* A portion of one's pay assigned to a member of the family. **3** A plot of land. **4** Destiny.

al·lo·trope (al′ə·trōp) *n.* One of the forms assumed by an allotropic substance: The diamond is an *allotrope* of carbon.

al·lo·trop·ic (al′ə·trop′ik) *adj.* Of, pertaining to, or having the property of allotropy: Ozone is an *allotropic* form of oxygen. Also **al′lo·trop′i·cal.** —**al′lo·trop′i·cal·ly** *adv.*

al·lot·ro·pism (ə·lot′rə·piz′əm) *n.* Allotropy.

al·lot·ro·py (ə·lot′rə·pē) *n.* The property shown by certain elements of having more than one physical form, usually due to different groupings of atoms stable under different conditions, especially different temperatures. [<Gk. *allotropia* variation <*allos* other + *tropos* turn, manner]

all′ ot·ta·va (äl ôt·tä′vä) *Music* A direction placed above or below the staff to indicate that the music is to be performed an octave higher or lower than written. Abbr. *8va.* [<Ital., lit., at the octave]

al·lot·tee (ə·lot′ē′) *n.* One to whom anything is allotted.

al·lot·ter·y (ə·lot′ər·ē) *n. Obs.* Allotment; share; portion.

all-out (ôl′out′) *adj.* Complete and entire; to the fullest extent.

all-o·ver (ôl′ō′vər) *adj.* Having, resembling, or pertaining to a pattern extending over the entire surface. —*n.* (ôl′ō′vər) A fabric or other substance having such a pattern.

all-o·ver·ish (ôl′ō′vər·ish) *adj. Colloq.* Ill; sick; vaguely apprehensive and unwell.

al·low (ə·lou′) *v.t.* **1** To put no obstacle in the way of; permit to occur or do: Children are *allowed* in the park; He *allowed* the flowers to wither. **2** To admit; grant, as something claimed; acknowledge as true or valid: I *allow* her ability, but not her right to exercise it. **3** To make an addition, deduction, or concession of, as for a consideration not formally appearing in the reckoning: to *allow* three pounds extra for waste; to *allow* customers a month to pay. **4** To grant; allot, as a share or portion: The emperor *allowed* him one hundred pounds a year. **5** *U.S. Dial.* To maintain; declare. **6** *Archaic* Approve; sanction. —*v.i.* **7** To permit the occurrence or realization of: with *of*: Your remark *allows* of several interpretations. **8** To bear in mind as a modifying or extenuating circumstance; make due allowance for: with *for*: to *allow* for traffic conditions in getting to the train on time. [<OF *alouer* place, use, assign <Med.L *allocare* (see ALLOCATE) and OF *alouer, aloer* approve <L *allaudare* extol <*ad-* to + *laudare* praise] —**al·lowed′** *adj.*

Synonyms: admit, concede, confess, endure, grant, let, permit, sanction, suffer, tolerate, yield. We *allow* that which we do not attempt to hinder; we *permit* that to which we give express authorization; we *concede* a right; *grant* a request; *permit* an inspection of accounts; *sanction* a marriage; *tolerate* the rudeness of a well-meaning clerk; *submit* to a surgical operation; *yield* to a demand or necessity against our wish or will. *Suffer,* in the sense of mild concession, is now becoming rare. Compare PERMISSION. *Antonyms*: deny, disallow, disapprove, forbid, protest, refuse, reject, resist, withstand. See synonyms for PROHIBIT.

al·low·a·ble (ə·lou′ə·bəl) *adj.* That can be allowed; permissible; admissible. —**al·low′a·ble·ness** *n.* —**al·low′a·bly** *adv.*

al·low·ance (ə·lou′əns) *n.* **1** An allowing or being allowed. **2** That which is allowed. **3** A limited amount or portion, as of an income or food, granted at regular intervals. **4** A sum or item put to one's credit in a transaction, as in consideration of the exchange of the used article or a purchase in volume; discount: The dealer will give you an *allowance* on your old car. **5** A difference permitted in excess or abatement, as of a specification: to make *allowances* for haste. **6** *Obs.* Acknowledgment. See synonyms under PERMISSION, SALARY, SUBSIDY. —*v.t.* **·anced, ·anc·ing 1** To put on an allowance; limit to a regular amount. **2** To supply in limited or meager quantities.

Al·lo·way (al′ə·wā) A village near Ayr, Scotland; birthplace of Robert Burns.

al·low·ed·ly (ə·lou′id·lē) *adv.* By general allowance or admission; admittedly.

al·loy (al′oi, ə·loi′) *n.* Any of numerous substances having metallic properties and consisting of two or more elements of which at least one is a metal. **2** Anything that reduces purity. —*v.t.* (ə·loi′) **1** To reduce the purity of, as a metal, by mixing with an alloy. **2** To combine (substances) to form an alloy. **3** To modify or debase, as by mixture with something inferior. —*v.i.* To become a constituent of an alloy: Carbon *alloys* with iron to form steel. [<F *aloi,* OF *alei* <*aleier* combine <L *alligare ad-* to + *ligare* bind]

Synonyms (noun): admixture, adulteration, debasement, deterioration. *Adulteration, debasement,* and *deterioration* are always used in the bad sense; *admixture* is neutral, and may be good or bad; *alloy* is commonly good in the literal sense, as for giving hardness to coin, etc. An excess of *alloy* virtually amounts to *adulteration*; but *adulteration* is commonly restricted to articles used for food, drink, medicine, and kindred uses.

Al·loy steel A steel having special properties due to a constituent in addition to carbon and iron.

all-purpose (ôl′pûr′pəs) *adj.* Generally useful; answering every purpose.

all-right (ôl′rīt′) *adj. Slang* **1** Dependable; honest; loyal. **2** Good; excellent.

all right 1 Satisfactory: His work is *all right.* **2** Correct, as a result in addition. **3** Uninjured; not hurt: Were you *all right* after your fall? **4** Certainly; without a doubt: I'll be there *all right!* **5** Yes: usually in answer to a question: May I leave now? *All right.* See ALRIGHT.

all-round (ôl′round′) *adj.* **1** Of comprehensive range or scope; complete in action or effect. **2** Excelling in all or many aspects or departments of the same business or ability; many-sided; versatile. Also *all-around.*

All Saints The festival of the Church commemorative of all saints and martyrs, occurring Nov. 1; All-hallows; All-hallowmas. In the Greek Church it is observed on the first Sunday after Pentecost. Also **All Saints' Day.**

all·seed (ôl′sēd′) *n.* Any of various small many-seeded plants, as knotgrass, goosefoot, flaxwort, etc.

All Souls In the Roman Catholic Church, a day of commemoration, occurring Nov. 2, on which special intercession is made for the souls of all the faithful departed. Also **All Souls' Day.**

all·spice (ôl′spīs′) *n.* **1** The aromatic dried berry of a West Indian tree; the pimento. **2** The sharply flavored, fragrant spice made from it. [So called because thought to combine the flavors of several spices]

all-star (ôl′stär′) *adj.* Consisting wholly of star performers, as the cast of a play.

All·ston (ôl′stən), **Washington,** 1779–1843, U.S. painter.

all the same Without difference, notwithstanding.

all-time (ôl′tīm′) *adj.* Perennially popular; likely to endure for all time: an *all-time* favorite.

all told When all are counted.

al·lude (ə·lo͞od′) *v.i.* **al·lud·ed, al·lud·ing** To refer without express mention; make indirect or casual reference: with *to.* [<L *alludere* play with, joke <*ad-* to + *ludere* play]

Synonyms: advert, hint, imply, indicate, insinuate, intimate, mention, point, refer, signify, suggest. *Allude* is erroneously used in the general sense of *mention* or *speak of.* We *allude* to a matter slightly, in passing; we *advert* to it when we turn from our path to treat it; we *refer* to it by any clear utterance or expression. One may *hint* at a thing in a friendly way, but what is *insinuated* is always unfavorable, generally both hostile and cowardly. One may *indicate* his wishes, *intimate* his plans, *imply* his opinion, *signify* his will, *suggest* a course of action. Compare SUGGESTION.

al·lure (ə·lo͝or′) *v.t.* & *v.i.* **al·lured, al·lur·ing** To draw with or as with a lure; attract or exercise attraction; entice. —*n.* That which allures; allurement. [<OF *alurer, aleurrer* <*a-* to (<L *ad-*)+ *leurre* lure. See LURE.] —**al·lur′er** *n.*

Synonyms (verb): attract, cajole, captivate, coax, decoy, draw, entice, inveigle, lure, seduce, tempt, win. One may *attract* without intent. One may *allure* to evil, but ordinarily to good. *Lure* is more akin to the physical nature and commonly used in an unfavorable sense. To *tempt* is to endeavor to lead one wrong; to *seduce* is to succeed in *winning* one from good to ill. *Win* may be used in a good sense, in which it surpasses the highest sense of *allure,* because it succeeds in that which *allure* attempts. *Coax* expresses the attraction of the person, not of the thing. A man may be *coaxed* to that which is by no means *alluring. Cajole* and *decoy* carry the idea of deceiving and ensnaring. To *inveigle* is to lead one blindly, as into folly or wrong. See DRAW, PERSUADE. *Antonyms*: chill, damp, deter, dissuade, repel, warn.

al·lure·ment (ə·lo͝or′mənt) *n.* **1** Enticement; fascination; attraction. **2** A charm or bait. **3** The act of alluring, as by some charm or bait.

al·lur·ing (ə·lo͝or′ing) *adj.* That draws as with a lure; attractive; fascinating. —**al·lur′ing·ly** *adv.* —**al·lur′ing·ness** *n.*

al·lu·sion (ə·lo͞o′zhən) *n.* **1** An alluding; indirect reference; suggestion. **2** A figure of speech consisting of a passing, but significant, reference to a well-known person, place, event etc. [<L *allusio, -onis* <*allusus,* pp. of *alludere.* See ALLUDE.]

al·lu·sive (ə·lo͞o′siv) *adj.* Having allusion to; suggestive; figurative. —**al·lu′sive·ly** *adv.* —**al·lu′sive·ness** *n.*

al·lu·vi·al (ə·lo͞o′vē·əl) *adj.* Pertaining to or composed of alluvium. —*n.* Alluvium.

alluvial cone *Geol.* The fan-shaped accumulation of detritus deposited where a river issues from a steep course upon flatland. Also called **alluvial fan.**

al·lu·vi·on (ə·lo͞o′vē·ən) *n.* **1** A flood deposit of earth; alluvium. **2** Inundation; flood. **3** The wash or flow of waves against the shore or banks. **4** *Law* The gradual increase of land by the action of flowing water. **5** *Geol.* A downpour of volcanic cinder mud. [<F <L *alluvio, -onis* a washing against, a flooding <*alluere* <*ad-* to + *luere* wash]

al·lu·vi·um (ə·lo͞o′vē·əm) *n. pl.* **·vi·a** (-vē·ə) or **·vi·ums** *Geol.* Deposits, as of sand or mud, transported and laid down by flowing water in river beds, flood-plains, lakes, and estuaries. [<L]

all wet *U.S. Slang* Completely wrong.

all wool *Colloq.* Absolutely genuine. —**all′-wool′** *adj.*

al·ly (ə·lī′) *v.* **al·lied, al·ly·ing** *v.t.* To unite or combine in an affinity, marriage, or association, by relationship, similarity of structure, treaty, or compact: generally in the passive with *to* or *with,* or used reflexively: The minister hoped to *ally* France with Spain against England; He *allied* himself with all liberal thinkers. —*v.i.* To enter into alliance; become allied. —*n.* (al′ī, ə·lī′) *pl.* **al·lies 1** A person or thing connected with another, usually in some relation of helpfulness or kinship; a state, sovereign, or chief leagued with another, as by treaty or common action. **2** Any friendly associate or helper. **3** An organism or substance associated with another by similarity of structure or properties. See synonyms under ACCESSORY, ADHERENT, ASSOCIATE, AUXILIARY. —**the Allies 1** The twenty-seven nations allied against the Central Powers in World War I; specifically, Russia, France, Great Britain, Italy, and Japan, adhering to the Declaration of London; the **Allied and Associated Powers** included twenty-two other nations, co-belligerent but not adhering to the Declaration. **2** The nations and governments-in-exile known as the United Nations in World War II. [<OF *alier* <L *alligare* <*ad-* to + *ligare* bind]

al·lyl (al′il) *n.* A univalent unsaturated radical, C_3H_5. [<L *allium* garlic + -YL] —**al·lyl·ic** (ə·lil′ik) *adj.*

allyl alcohol A pungent, flammable, poisonous liquid. CH_2:CH-CH_2OH.

allyl resin Any of a group of thermosetting synthetic resins derived from allyl compounds and used in laminated and molded plastic products.

allyl sulfide A colorless liquid, $(C_3H_5)_2S$, contained in garlic, onions, and other vegetables, giving them their characteristic taste and odor.

Al·ma (al′mə) A feminine personal name.

Al·ma A·ta (äl′mä ä′tä) The capital of Kazakh S.S.R.: formerly *Vyernyi.*

al·ma·cén (äl′mä·sān′) *n. pl.* **·ce·nes** (-sä′nās) *SW U.S.* **1** A warehouse. **2** A dockyard. [<Sp.]

Al·ma·dén (äl′mä·thän′) A city in south central Spain; site of several rich mercury mines.

Al·ma·gest (al′mə·jest) *n.* **1** Ptolemy's huge work on astronomy, explaining the celestial motions on the geocentric system: named from the title of the Arabian translation of this work made in 827. **2** In medieval science, any authoritative treatise, as upon astrology or alchemy. Also **al′ma·gest.** [< OF *almageste* < Arabic *al-majistī* < *al* the + Gk. *megistē (syntaxis)* the greatest (work)]

al·mah (al′mə) *n.* An Egyptian dancing and singing girl: also spelled *alme, almeh.* Also **al′ma.** [< Arabic *′ālimah* learned]

al·ma ma·ter (al′mə mä′tər, al′mə mā′tər, äl′mə mä′tər) The institution of learning which one has attended. [< L, fostering mother]

al·ma·nac (ôl′mə·nak) *n.* A yearly calendar giving the days of the week and month through the year, with weather forecasts, astronomical information, times of high and low tides, and other tabulated data. [< Med.L < Sp. < Arabic *al-manākh*]

al·man·dine (al′mən·dēn, -din) *n.* A deep red to brownish variety of garnet composed of iron aluminum silicate. Also **al′man·dite** (-dīt). [for *alabandine,* from *Alabanda,* city in Asia Minor]

Al·ma-Tad·e·ma (al′mə·tad′ə·mə), **Sir Lawrence,** 1836–1912, English painter; born in the Netherlands.

al·me, al·meh (al′me) See ALMAH.

al·me·mar (al·mē′mär) *n.* In a Jewish synagog, the platform from which the Pentateuch and the Prophets are read. [< Arabic *al-minbar* the pulpit]

Al·me·rí·a (äl′mā·rē′ə) A seaport in SE Spain on the **Gulf of Almería,** an arm of the Mediterranean.

Al·me·ri·cus (al′mə·rī′kəs) Latin form of EMERY.

al·might·y (ôl·mī′tē) *adj.* **1** Able to do all things; omnipotent. **2** Great; remarkable. —*adv. Slang* Exceedingly: *almighty* mad. —**the Almighty** God; the Supreme Being. [OE *ealmihtig* < *eal* all + *mihtig* mighty] —**al·might′i·ly** *adv.* —**al·might′i·ness** *n.*

almighty dollar *Colloq.* Money conceived of as having or imparting great power.

Al·mi·ra (al·mī′rə) A feminine personal name. [< Arabic, lofty, a princess]

Al·mo·hades (al′mə·hādz, -hadz) *n. pl.* **1** Followers of a strictly monotheistic reform among the Moslems of North Africa, founded by Mohammed ibn Tumart (died 1128). **2** The Moslem dynasty in North Africa and Spain founded by them, which lasted from 1145 to 1269. —**Al′mo·hade** *adj. & n.* [< Arabic *al-muwahhid* the one who professes monotheism]

Al·mon (al′mən) A masculine personal name. [< Hebrew, hidden]

al·mond (ä′mənd, am′ənd) *n.* **1** A small rosaceous tree (*Prunus amygdalus*) widely cultivated in warm temperate regions. **2** The nutlike edible seed of this tree. **3** Anything having a flattened oval shape resembling the almond seed. **4** A pale brown, the color of an almond shell. [< OF *almande, amande* < L *amygdala* < Gk. *amygdalē*]

al·mon·er (al′mən·ər, ä′mən-) *n.* An official dispenser of alms; formerly, a household chaplain, as of a prince. Also **alm·ner** (alm′·nər, äm′nər). [< OF *almosnier* < LL *eleemosynarius* pertaining to alms < L *eleemosyna* alms. See ALMS.]

al·mon·ry (al′mən·rē, ä′mən-) *n. pl.* **·ries** The residence of an almoner; a place where alms are dispensed.

Al·mo·ra·vides (al·môr′ə·vīdz, -mō′rə-) *n. pl.* A Moslem dynasty in Africa and Spain in the 11th and 12th centuries which began as a religious revival under Abdallah-ibn-Yasin and lasted from 1056 to 1145. [< Arabic *al-murābit*] **Al·mo′ra·vide** *adj & n.*

al·most (ôl′mōst′ ôl·mōst′) *adv.* Approximately; very nearly; all but. —*adj.* not quite: to have *almost* nothing. [OE *ealmæst.* See ALL, MOST.]

al·mous (al′məs, ä′məs, ô′məs) See AWMOUS.

alms (ämz) *n. sing. & pl.* A gift or gifts for the poor; charitable offerings; charity. Some self-explaining compounds have *alms* as their first element: *almsgiver, almsgiving, almsmoney,* etc. Collateral adjective: *eleemosynary.* [OE *ælmesse* < L *eleemosyna* alms < Gk. *eleēmosynē* < *eleos* pity]

alms·deed (ämz′dēd′) *n.* An act of charity.

alms·house (ämz′hous′) *n.* **1** A house where paupers are supported; a poorhouse. **2** In England, a house where deserving poor people are supported by charity, generally on a charitable foundation.

alms·man (ämz′mən) *n. pl.* **·men** (-mən) **1** One supported by charity. **2** *Obs.* A giver of alms. —**alms′wom′an** *n. fem.*

al·muce (al′myo͞os) *n.* A hood or hooded cape lined with fur, formerly worn by clergymen and monks: also spelled *amice.* [< OF *aumuce* < Med.L *almutia*]

ALMUCE
From tomb of
Philip the Bold
13th Cent.,
French.

al·mud (al·mo͞od′) *n.* A liquid and dry measure of Turkey, Spain, and some other countries, varying from about 2 to 32 quarts. Also **al·mude′.** [< Sp. < Arabic *al-mudd*]

al·mug (al′mug) *n.* A precious wood used for the making of harps, psalteries, etc.: also *algum.* [< Hebrew]

al·ni·co (al′nə·kō) *n.* Any of a group of ferrous alloys containing aluminum, nickel, and cobalt and having persistent magnetic properties.

a·lo·di·al (ə·lō′dē·əl), **a·lo·di·um** (-əm) See ALLODIAL, etc.

al·oe (al′ō) *n. pl.* **·oes 1** Any member of a genus (*Aloe*) of Old World plants of the lily family, some species of which furnish a drug, and others valuable fiber. **2** *pl.* (construed as singular) A bitter cathartic obtained from the juice of certain species of aloe. **3** *pl.* (construed as singular) Agalloch. [OE *aluwe* < L *aloe* < Gk. *aloē*]—**al·o·et·ic** (al′ō·et′ik) *adj.*

A·lo·fi (ä·lō′fē) See WALLIS AND FUTUNA ISLANDS.

a·loft (ə·lôft′, ə·loft′) *adv.* **1** In or to a high or higher place; on high; high up. **2** *Naut.* At or to the higher parts of a ship's rigging. [< ON *a lopt* (in the air)]

A·lo·gi·an (ə·lō′jē·ən) *n. pl.* **Al·o·gi** (al′ə·jī) or **A·lo·gi·ans** One of a sect of the second and third centuries that rejected the doctrine that Jesus is the Logos, and denied the authenticity of the Fourth Gospel and the Apocalypse. [< Med.L *alogiani* < Gk. *alogioi* < *a-* not + *logos* word]

a·lo·ha (ə·lō′ə, ä·lō′hä) *n. Hawaiian* Love: used also as a salutation and a farewell.

al·o·in (al′ō·in) *n.* A bitter crystalline substance of varying composition, obtained from aloes and forming its purgative principle.

A·lois (ə·lois′) See ALOYSIUS.

al·o·man·cy (al′ə·man′sē) See HALOMANCY.

a·lone (ə·lōn′) *adv.* **1** Without company; solitary. **2** Without equal; unique; unparalleled. **3** Excluding all others; solely; only. [ME *al one* all alone]

a·long (ə·lông′, ə·long′) *adv.* **1** Over, through, or following the length of in time or space; lengthwise. **2** Progressively onward in the course of motion. **3** In company or association: with *with:* I came *along* with my cousins. **4** Together; side by side: The donkey came *along* all the way. **5** Advanced in age or duration: well *along* in years. —**all along** The whole time; from the outset. — **along with** As well as; in addition to. —**right along** Continuously. —**to get along 1** To manage in spite of difficulties. **2** To go away: *Get along with you!* **3** To exist together in harmony: Her cat and dog *get along* very well. —*prep.* **1** In the line of; through or over the length of: The ship sailed *along* the coast. **2** At points throughout or over the length of: Trees are planted *along* the road. **3** During the course of; throughout: *along* the track of centuries. [OE *andlang*]

along of *Illit. & Dial.* Because of.

a·long·shore (ə·lông′shôr′, ə·long′-, -shōr′) *adv.* Along the shore, either on the water or on the land.

a·long·side (ə·lông′sīd′, ə·long′-) *adv.* Close to or along the side. —*prep.* Side by side with; at the side of.

A·lon·zo (ə·lon′zō) See ALPHONSO. Also *Sp.* **A·lon·so** (ä·lon′sō).

a·loof (ə·lo͞of′) *adj.* Distant, especially in manner

or interest; not in sympathy with or desiring to associate with others. —*adv.* At a distance; apart: to stand, keep, or hold aloof. [< A.[1] + *loof* < Du. *loef* LUFF] —**a·loof′ly** *adv.*

al·o·pe·ci·a (al′ə·pē′shē·ə, -sē·ə) *n.* Loss of hair; partial or total baldness. [< L, baldness, fox mange < Gk. *alōpekia* < *alōpēx* fox]

A·lost (ä·lôst′) A town in central Belgium NW of Brussels. *Flemish* **Aalst** (älst).

a·loud (ə·loud′) *adv.* Loudly or audibly.

a·low[1] (ə·lō′) *adv.* In or to a lower position; below: opposed to *aloft.*

a·low[2] (ə·lou′) *adv. Scot.* In a blaze; on fire. Also **a·lowe′.**

Al·o·ys·ius (al′ō·ish′əs, -is′ē·əs) A masculine personal name: also *Alois.* [See LOUIS.]

alp (alp) *n.* **1** Any peak of the Alps. **2** An alpine pasture. **3** A lofty mountain. [< L *Alpes* the Alps]

al·pac·a (al·pak′ə) *n.* **1** A domesticated ruminant (*Lama pacos*) of South America related to the guanaco and llama. **2** Its long, silky wool. **3** Cloth made from the wool of the alpaca. **4** A glossy, usually black fabric made of various fiber combinations other than alpaca wool. [< Sp. < Arabic *al* the + Peruvian *paco* name of the animal]

ALPACA
(About 3½ feet high
at the shoulder)

al·pen·glow (al′pən·glō) *n.* **1** The rosy light of the rising or setting sun, seen on the Alps or other mountains. **2** The reappearance of the sunset colors on a mountain summit after the original colors have faded. **3** A similar phenomenon preceding the regular sunrise coloration. [Trans. of G *Alpenglühen*]

al·pen·horn (al′pən·hôrn′) See ALPHORN.

al·pen·stock (al′pən·stok′) *n.* A long, iron-pointed staff, used by mountain-climbers. [< G, lit., alps stick]

al·pes·trine (al·pes′trin) *adj.* **1** Of, pertaining to, or growing on mountain heights below the limit of forest growth. **2** Subalpine. [< L *alpestris* < *Alpes* Alps]

al·pha (al′fə) *n.* **1** The first letter and vowel in the Greek alphabet (Α, α); corresponding to English a. As a numeral it denotes 1. **2** The beginning or first of anything. —**the alpha and omega** Both the first and the last; beginning and end; the sum total: used of Christ. *Rev.* i 8. —*adj.* **1** Designating the first in order of importance or discovery: *alpha* test. **2** *Chem.* Denoting a carbon atom next to a designated carbon in an organic molecule. **3** *Physics* Denoting the first of a series of radiations or emissions arranged in order of increasing frequency: *alpha* rays, *alpha* particle. [< Gk. < Hebrew *aleph* ox]

Al·pha (al′fə) *n. Astron.* The principal or brightest star in a constellation.

al·pha·bet (al′fə·bet) *n.* **1** The letters that form the elements of written language, in order as fixed by usage: in English, 26 in number. **2** Any system of characters or symbols representing the simple sounds of speech. See TABLE OF FOREIGN ALPHABETS on next page. **3** The simplest elements or rudiments of anything. —*v.t.* To alphabetize. [< L *alphabetum* < Gk. *alpha* a + *bēta* b]

al·pha·bet·ic (al′fə·bet′ik) *adj.* **1** Pertaining to, having, or expressed by an alphabet. **2** Arranged in the order of the alphabet. Also **al′pha·bet′i·cal.** —**al′pha·bet′i·cal·ly** *adv.*

al·pha·bet·ize (al·fə·bə·tīz′) *v.t.* **·ized, ·iz·ing 1** To put in alphabetical order. **2** To express by or furnish with an alphabet or alphabetic symbols. —**al′pha·bet·i·za′tion** (al′fə·bet′ə·zā′shən) *n.* —**al′pha·bet·iz′er** *n.*

Alpha Cen·tau·ri (sen·tôr′ē) *Astron.* The principal star in the constellation of Centaurus; the third brightest star in the heavens.

alpha helix A spiral arrangement of amino acids in certain protein molecules, forming a cylinder with side groups projecting outward.

TABLE OF FOREIGN ALPHABETS

(1) ARABIC			(2) HEBREW			(3) GREEK			(4) RUSSIAN			(5) GERMAN		
ا	alif	—[1]	א	aleph	—[6]	Α α	alpha	ä	А	а	ä	𝕬	α	ä
ب	ba	b	ב, בּ	beth	b, v	Β β	beta	b	Б	б	b	𝕭	b	e
ت	ta	t	ג, גּ	gimel	g, gh[3]	Γ γ	gamma	g	В	в	v	𝕮	c	k, ts, s
ث	sa	th	ד, דּ	daleth	d, ~~th~~	Δ δ	delta	d	Г	г	g	𝕯	d	d
ج	jim	j	ה	he	h	Ε ε	epsilon	e	Д	д	d	𝕰	e	e, ā
ح	ha	h	ו	vav	v	Ζ ζ	zeta	z	Е	е	e, ye	𝕱	f	f
خ	kha	kh	ז	zayin	z	Η η	eta	ā	Ж	ж	zh	𝕲	g	g
د	dal	d	ח	beth	kh	Θ θ	theta	th[9]	З	з	z	ℌ	h	h
ذ	zal	~~th~~	ט	teth	t	Ι ι	iota	ē	И	и	ē, yē	ℑ	i	i, ē
ر	ra	r	י	yod	y	Κ κ	kappa	k	Й	й	e[12]	𝕵	j	y
ز	za	z	ך, ך, כּ[8]	kaph	k[5], kh	Λ λ	lambda	l	К	к	k	𝕶	ł	k
س	sin	s	ל	lamed	l	Μ μ	mu	m	Л	л	l	𝕷	l	l
ش	shin	sh	ם, מ[8]	mem	m	Ν ν	nu	n	М	м	m	𝕸	m	m
ص	sad	s	ן, נ[8]	nun	n	Ξ ξ	xi	ks	Н	н	n	𝕹	n	n
ض	dad	d	ס	samek	s	Ο ο	omicron	o	О	о	ô, o	𝕺	o	ō, ŏ
ط	ta	t	ע	ayin	—[7]	Π π	pi	p	П	п	p	𝕻	ö	œ
ظ	za	z	ף, פ, פּ[8]	pe	p, f	Ρ ρ	rho	r	Р	р	r	𝕼(u)	q(u)	k(v)
ع	ain	—[2]	ץ, צ[8]	sade	s	Σ σ, ς[8]	sigma	s	С	с	s	𝕽	r	r
غ	ghain	gh[3]	ק	koph	k[4]	Τ τ	tau	t	Т	т	t	𝕾 ſ, ß[8]	s, z	
ف	fa	f	ר	resh	r	Υ υ	upsilon	ü, ōō	У	у	ōō	𝕿	t	t
ق	qaf	k[4]	שׂ, שׁ	sin, shin	s, sh	Φ φ	phi	f[10]	Ф	ф	f	𝖀	u	ōō, ŏŏ
ك	kaf	k[5]	ת, תּ	tav	t, th	Χ χ	chi	kh[11]	Х	х	kh	𝖁	ü	ü
ل	lam	l				Ψ ψ	psi	ps	Ц	ц	ts	𝖂	v	f
م	mim	m				Ω ω	omega	ō	Ч	ч	ch	𝖃	w	ks
ن	nun	n							Ш	ш	sh	𝖄	ŋ	ē, ü
ه	ha	h							Щ	щ	shch	𝖅	z	ts
و	waw	w							Ъ	ъ	—[13]			
ى	ya	y							Ы	ы	œ			
									Ь	ь	—[14]			
									Э	э	e			
									Ю	ю	yōō			
									Я	я	yä			

In each column the characters of the alphabet are given first, followed by the names of the characters in Arabic, Hebrew, and Greek. The last row in each column shows the approximate English sound represented by each character. Columns 3, 4, and 5 show the upper- and lower-case forms. The Arabic characters are given in their final, unconnected forms. The German style of letter, called *fraktur*, has, since the 1880's, been gradually replaced in German printing by the Latin letter.

[1] Functions as the bearer of hamza (the glottal stop), or as a lengthener of short *a*. [2] A voiced pharyngeal fricative. [3] A voiced velar fricative. [4] A uvular stop. [5] A voiceless velar stop. [6] A glottal stop, now usually silent, or pronounced according to the accompanying vowel points. [7] A pharyngeal fricative, now usually silent, or pronounced according to the accompanying vowel points. [8] The alternate form is restricted to the ends of words. [9], [10], [11] In classical Greek these were pronounced as aspirated stops similar to the sounds in foot*h*ill, ha*ph*azard, and bloc*kh*ouse.

[12] Appears only as the second vowel in a diphthong. [13] Formerly, a sign of non-palatalization of consonants at the ends of words; since 1918, used only between two syllables to indicate that they are separately pronounced. [14] A sign of palatalization of a preceding consonant.

---

alpha iron The common allotrope of iron, stable below 770° and having a cubic crystalline structure and magnetic properties.

al·pha·nu·mer·ic (al'fə·nŏō·mer'ik, -nyŏō-) *adj.* Able to use both letters and numbers: an *alphanumeric* computer.

alpha particle *Physics* The positively charged nucleus of the helium atom (H[4]), consisting of two protons and two neutrons; it is a product of disintegration of various isotopes of both natural and artificial radioactive elements.

alpha privative In Greek grammar, a prefix having negative or privative force, as in *atheos* godless. See A-[4], AN-[1]. ♦ The term is also applied to this prefix as naturalized in English, where it is sometimes used to express a shade of meaning different from that of the other negative prefixes, the Latin-derived *in-* and *non-*, and the native *un-*. *A-*, *an-*, as prefixed to terms or stems of Greek or Latin origin, often means "apart from" or "not concerned with,": An *amoral* approach to economics is one not concerned with moral is-

sues.

alpha ray *Physics* A stream of alpha particles, emitted with an initial velocity and over a mean range varying with the source and method of production.

alpha rhythm A frequency of 8 to 18 per second in brain waves, characteristic of a relaxed resting state in normal human adults.

alpha star *Physics* A starlike formation in a photographic emulsion, consisting of short heavy tracks identifying the paths of slow alpha particles emitted from a radioactive element.

al·pha·to·coph·er·ol (al'fə·tō·kof'ər·ōl, -ol) *n.* A light-yellow oily liquid obtained from wheat germ oil or produced synthetically and having potent vitamin E activity.

Al·phe·ratz (al'fə·rats') The brightest star in the constellation Andromeda: also called *Sirrah*.

Al·phe·us (al·fē'əs) In Greek mythology, a river god who fell in love with the nymph Arethusa, changing into a river to mingle with her when

she had become a fountain to escape him.

Al·phe·us (al·fē'əs) The chief river of the Peloponnesus, Greece, flowing NW 69 miles: formerly *Rouphia. Greek* **Al·fiós** (äl·fyôs').

Al·phon·so (al·fon'zō, -sō) A masculine personal name. Also *Fr.* **Al·phonse** (äl·fôns'), *Lat.* **Al·phon·sus** (al·fon'səs). See also ALFONSO.

alp·horn (alp'hôrn') *n.* A slightly curved, very sonorous horn, made of wood and from 7 to 12 feet long, used by cowherds in the Alps and formerly by Swiss soldiers: also *alpenhorn*. [< Gk. *alpenhorn* horn of the Alps]

Al·pine (al'pīn, -pin) *adj.* 1 Pertaining to or characteristic of the Alps. 2 Designating a European racial stock found in the Alps and adjacent districts, and marked by medium height, broad short skull and face, and brunette coloring. [< L *Alpinus*]

al·pine (al'pīn, -pin) *adj.* 1 Like an alp or mountain; lofty and towering: alpine *terrian*. 2 Occurring in regions above the timberline in mountains or tundra. —*n.* A plant native to treeless tundra or mountain tops.

habiting or growing in mountain regions above the limits of forest growth.

alpine garden A garden for alpine plants, especially a rock garden.

al·pi·nist (al′pə·nist) *n.* A climber of alps; a mountaineer. **—al′pi·nism** *n.*

Al·pi·no (äl·pē′nō) *n.* pl. **Al·pi·ni** (-pē′nē) A member of a body of Italian troops trained for Alpine or mountain warfare. [<Ital.]

Alps (alps) A mountain system of southern Europe, extending 680 miles from the Mediterranean coast of southern France to the Adriatic coast of Yugoslavia, separating the Po valley of northern Italy from the lowlands of France, Germany, and the Danubian plain; highest peak, 15,781 feet.

al·read·y (ôl·red′ē) *adv.* Before or by this time or the time mentioned; even now. [<ALL + READY]

al·right (ôl·rīt′) All right: a spelling not yet considered acceptable.

Al·sace (al·sās′, al′sas; *Fr.* äl·zäs′) A region and former province of France along the Rhine border of Germany: ancient **Al·sa·tia** (al·sā′shə): German *Elass.*

Al·sace-Lor·raine (al′sās·lə) ·rān′, al′ ·sas-; *Fr.* äl·zà s′· lô·ren′) A disputed (border region between NE France and SW Germany; ceded to Germany in 1871, regained by France in 1919, annexed by Germany in 1940, regained by France in 1945: German *Elsass-Lothringen.*

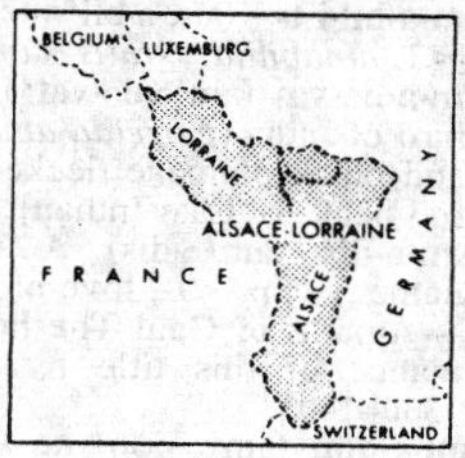

Al·sa·tia (al·sā′shə) A section of London, formerly a sanctuary for insolvent debtors and criminals: also called *Whitefriars.* [<Med.L <G *Elsass,* lit., foreign settlement]

Al·sa·tian (al·sā′shən) *adj.* **1** Of or pertaining to Alsace. **2** Of or pertaining to Alsatia. *—n.* **1** A native or inhabitant of Alsace. **2** A resident of Alsatia; hence, a debtor or criminal in sanctuary. **3** A German shepherd.

al·sike (al′sīk, -sik, ôl′-) *n.* A leguminous forage plant *(Trifolium hybridum)* with pink or white flowers. Also **Alsike clover.** [from *Alsike,* Swedish town]

Al·si·rat (al′sē·rät′) **1** In the Moslem religion, the bridge and only way to paradise over the abyss of hell: said to be finer than a hair and sharper than a razor. **2** In the Koran, the narrow path or correct way of religion. [<Arabic *al-ṣirāt* the road]

al·so (ôl′sō) *adv.* & cornj. **1** As something further tending in the same direction; besides; in addition: They *also* serve who only stand and wait. **2** In like manner; likewise: to provide for the pupils and *also* for the teachers. [OE *alswā, ealswā* all (wholly) so.]

al·so-ran (ôl′so-ran′) *n.* U.S. Colloq. **1** A horse that fails to win, place, or show in a race. **2** Hence, an unsuccessful candidate in an election or competition.

alt (alt) *Music adj.* Alto; high-pitched in the musical scale. *—n.* The octave next above the treble staff. **—in alt** In this octave. [<Ital. *alto* <L *al-tus* high]

Al·tai Mountains (al·tī′, äl-) A mountain system of central Asia at the juncture of China, Mongolia, and the U.S.S.R.; highest peak, 15,157 feet. Also **Al·tay′.**

Altai Territory A region of SW Siberia; 101,000 square miles; capital, Barnaul.

Al·ta·ian (al·tā′ən, -tī) ′-) *n.* One of the peoples of the Altai Mountains or of the Ural-Altaic linguistic group. *—adj.* Altaic.

Al·ta·ic (al·tā′ik) *n.* A family of agglutinative languages of Europe and Asia, generally considered to comprise the Turkic, Mongolian, and Manchu-Tungusic subfamilies: sometimes classified with Uralic in a Ural-Altaic family. *—adj.* **1** Of the Altai Mountains. **2** Pertaining to the peoples and languages of the Ural-Altaic stock; Turanian. Also *Altaian.*

Al·ta·ir (al·tä′ir, al·târ′) The brightest star in the constellation Aquila; one of the 20 brightest stars. See STAR. [<Arabic *al-ṭā′ir* the bird]

Al·ta·ma·ha River (ôl′tə·mə·hô′) A river in SE Georgia, flowing 137 miles SE to the Atlantic Ocean.

Al·ta·mi·ra (äl′tä·mē ′rä) A cave near Santander, in Spain, noted for the early Stone Age drawings on its walls.

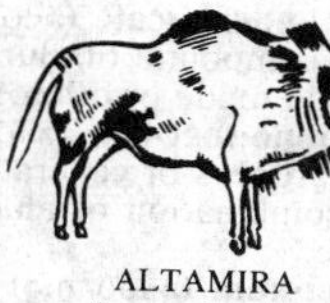

ALTAMIRA
A cave drawing.

al·tar (ôl′tər) *n.* **1** Any raised place or structure on which sacrifices may be offered or incense burned as an act of worship. **2** *Eccl.* The structure of wood or stone on which the elements are consecrated in the Eucharist; the communion table. **—to lead to the altar** To marry. ◆) Homophone: *alter.*([OE <L *altare* high altar <*altus* high]

Al·tar (ôl′tər) The constellation Ara.

al·tar·age (ôl′tər·ij) *n.* Eccl. **1** A revenue from altar offerings. **2** The endowment of an altar for general or special masses.

altar boy An attendant at the altar; acolyte.

altar bread *Eccl.* Bread used in the Eucharist, especially the unleavened wafer used in some churches.

al·tar·piece (ôl′tər·pē s′) *n.* A painting, mosaic, or bas-relief over and behind the altar; a reredos.

alt·az·i·muth (alt·az′ə·məth) *n.* Astron. An instrument with two graduated circles, one vertical and one horizontal, for measuring the altitude and azimuth of celestial bodies.

Alt·dorf (ält′dôrf) The capital of Uri canton in central Switzerland; scene of traditional exploits of William Tell.

Al·ten·burg (äl′tən·bo͝org) A city in eastern Thuringia, Germany.

al·ter (ôl′tər) *v.t.* **1** To cause to be different; change; modify; transform. **2** To castrate or spay. *—v.i.* **3** To become different; change, as in character or appearance. See synonyms under CHANGE. ◆Homophone: *altar.* [<MF *altérer* <Med.L *alterare* <L *alter* other]

al·ter·a·bil·i·ty (ôl′tə) r·ə·bil′ə·tē) *n.* Liability to or capacity for change.

al·ter·a·ble (ôl′tər·ə) ·bəl) *adj.* Capable of alteration. **—al·ter·a·bil·i·ty** (ôl′tər·ə·bil′ə·tē), **al′ ter·a·ble·ness** *n.* **—al′ter·a·bly** *adv.*

al·ter·a·tion (ôl′tə·rā ′shən) *n.* **1** The act or result of altering; or the state of being altered; modification; change. **2** *Geol.* Any change in the composition or texture of a rock occurring subsequent to its formation but not due to a cementing or induration of its original constituents. *—adj.* Of or pertaining to a geological alteration: Can *alteration* product. See synonyms under CHANGE.

al·ter·a·tive (ôl′tə·rā ′tiv) *adj.* **1** Tending to produce change. **2** *Med.* Tending to change gradually the bodily condition to a normal state. *—n.* An alterative medicine or treatment. Also **al·ter·ant** (ôl′tər·ənt).

al·ter·cate (ôl′tər·kāt, al′-) *v.i.* **·cat·ed, ·cat·ing** To dispute vehemently; wrangle. [<L *altercatus,* pp. of *altercari* <*alter* other]

al·ter·ca·tion (ôl′tər·kā′shən, al′-) *n.* Angry controversy; disputing; wrangling.

Synonyms: affray, brawl, broil, contention, controversy, debate, discussion, disputation, dispute, dissension, disturbance, fracas, quarrel, wrangle, wrangling. *Dispute* is preferably used of rights and claims; as, the title or the will is in *dispute; debate* and *discussion* refer rather to abstract matters, and may be entirely amicable. *Disputation* has a touch of bitterness. *Altercation, contention, controversy,* and *wrangle* are all words signifying more or less of ill-feeling; so is *dispute* in common speech; as, a sharp *dispute. Contention* and *controversy* are capable of a good sense in the learned or elevated style. See QUARREL. *Antonyms:* agreement, concord, consonance, harmony, unanimity, unity.

al·ter e·go (ôl′tər ē′gō, al′tər eg′ō) **1** Another self; a double. **2** An intimate friend. [<L, lit., other I]

al·ter i·dem (al′tər ī′dem) *Latin* Another self; a duplicate.

al·ter·nate (ôl′tər·nāt, al′-) *v.* **·nat·ed, ·nat·ing** *v.t.* **1** To arrange, use, or perform in alternation. **2** To cause to succeed and be succeeded by continuously: with *by* or *with:* to *alternate* a passive with an active style. *—v.i.* **3** To occur or appear alternately. **4** To take turns: to *alternate* on a job. **5** To pass from one thing or condition to another and back again repeatedly: Cycles of depression and inflation *alternate.* **6** *Electr.* To change from the positive to the negative direction and back rapidly; vibrate; pulsate. *—adj.* (ôl′tər·nit, al′-) **1** Existing, occurring, or following by turns; reciprocal. **2** Referring or pertaining to every other (of a series). **3** Alternative: an *alternate* method. **4** *Bot.* **a** Placed singly at regular intervals on opposite sides of the stem, as leaves. **b** Disposed by turn among other parts, as stamens opposite the intervals between petals. *—n.* (ô l′tər·nit, al′-) A substitute or second; especially, one substituting for another in the performance of a duty or in the filling of a position; a second choice. [<L *alternatus,* pp. of *alternare* <*alternus* every second one < *alter* other] **—al′ter·nate·ness** *n.*

alternate angle See under ANGLE.

al·ter·nate·ly (ôl′tər·nit·lē, al′-) *adv.* In alternate order or position; by turns.

alternating current See under CURRENT.

al·ter·na·tion (ôl′tər·nā′shən, al′-) *n.* Occurrence or action of two things or series of things in turn; passage from one place, state, or condition to another and back again: *alternation* between day and night.

alternation of generations Metagenesis.

al·ter·na·tive (ôl·tûr′nə·tiv, al-) *adj.* **1** Affording a choice between two things. **2** Of or pertaining to alternation; implying or involving an alternative: *alternative* conjunctions. **3** Occurring outside the boundaries of the established social, economic, or medical systems. *—n.* **1** Something that may or must be instead of something else; a choice between two things: used sometimes, loosely, of more than two. **2** One of the things to be chosen. **—al·ter′na·tive·ly** *adv.* **—al·ter′na·tive·ness** *n.*

Synonyms: choice, election, option, pick, preference, resource. A *choice* may be among many things; an *alternative* is in the strictest sense of *choice* between two things, but the usage is often extended to more than two. *Option* is the right or privilege of choosing; *choice* may be either the right to choose, the act of choosing, or the thing chosen. A *choice, pick, election,* or *preference* is that which suits one best; an *alternative* is that to which one is restricted; a *resource,* that to which one is glad to betake oneself. *Antonyms:* compulsion, necessity.

al·ter·na·tor (ôl′tər·nā ′tər, al′-) *n.* **1** One who or that which alternates. **2** *Electr.* A dynamo giving an alternating current. Also **al′ter·nat′ er.**

al·the·a (al·thē′ə) *n.* Any of a small but widely distributed genus *(Althaea)* of herbs with large flowers, including the hollyhock and the marshmallow. **2** The rose of Sharon (def. 2). Also **althaea.** [<L <Gk. *althaia* wild mallow]

Al·the·a (al·thē′ə) A feminine personal name. [<Gk., wholesome] **—Althaea** In Greek mythology, the wife of Oeneus and mother of Meleager.

alt·horn (alt′hôrn′) *n.* A wind instrument of the saxhorn class: used by military bands. [<ALT + HORN]

al·though (ôl·thō′) *conj.* Admitting or granting that; though: *Although* I believe the contrary, I accept your explanation. Also **al·tho′.** [<ALL + THOUGH]

alti- *combining from* High: *altiscope.* Also *alto-.* [<L < *altus* high]

al·ti·graph (al′tə·graf, -grä f) *n.* A recording altimeter.

al·tim·e·ter (al·tim′ə·tə) r, al′tə·mē′tər) *n.* **1** An aneroid barometer calibrated to permit accurate determination of altitudes above sea level, especially by aircraft pilots. **2** Any similar instrument operating by radio waves, etc. **—al·tim·ee·try** (al·tim′ə) ·trē) *n.*

al·ti·pla·no (äl′ti·plä′nō) *n.* High upland plateaus, especially in Andean countries. [<Sp. <Latin *altus* high + *planus* level]

al·ti·scope (al′tə·skōp) *n.* A periscope.

al·tis·o·nant (al·tis′ə·nənt) *adj.* High-sounding; pompous.

al·ti·tude (al′tə·to͞od; -tyo͞o d) *n.* **1** Vertical elevation above any given point, especially

add,āce,câre,pälm; end,ēven; it,īce; odd,ōpen,ôrder; to͝ok,po͞ol; up,bûrn; ə = a in *above*, e in *sicken*, i in *clarity*, o in *melon*, u in *focus*; yo͞o = u in *fuse*; oi,oil; ou,pout; ch,check; g,go; ng,ring; th,thin; th,this; zh,vision. Foreign sounds à,œ,ü,kh,ṅ; and ◆: see page xx. < from; + plus; ? possibly.

above mean sea level; height. **2** *Astron.* Angular elevation above the horizon. **3** *Geom.* The vertical distance from the base of a figure to its highest point. **4** A high or the highest point. See synonyms under HEIGHT. [<L *altitudo* <*altus* high]

altitude sickness A syndrome of varying severity due to inadequate atmospheric oxygen at the low barometric pressures obtaining at high altitudes and including hyperventilation, dizziness, nausea, etc.

al·ti·tu·di·nal (al'tə·to͞o'də·nəl, -tyo͞o'-) *adj.* Relating to altitude.

al·to (al'tō) *adj.* Sounding or ranging between tenor and treble. —*n. pl.* **·tos 1** The lowest female voice; contralto. **2** The highest male voice, or countertenor. **3** A singer who has an alto voice. **4** A tenor violin. **5** An althorn. [<Ital. <L *altus* high]

alto- See ALTI-.

al·to·cu·mu·lus (al'tō·kyo͞o'myə·ləs) *n.* Meteorol. A fleecy cloud, usually a rounded mass: also called *cumulocirrus.*

al·to·geth·er (ôl'tə·geth'ər, ôl'tə·geth'ər) *n.* A whole; also, the general effect; tout ensemble. **—in the altogether** *Colloq.* In the nude. —*adv.* **1** Completely; wholly; entirely. **2** With everything included; in all; all told. [<ALL + TOGETHER]

Al·to·na (äl'tō·nä) The major fishing port of Hamburg, Germany.

Al·too·na (al·to͞o'nə) A city in central Pennsylvania.

al·to-re·lie·vo (al'tō·ri·lē'vō) *n. pl.* **·vos** High relief; sculptured or carved work in which the carving, figures, etc., stand out very strongly from the background: contrasted with *bas-relief.* See RELIEF. [<Ital.]

al·to·ri·lie·vo (äl'tō·rē·lyä'vō) *n. pl.* **al·ti·ri·lie·vi** (äl'tē·rē·lyä'vē) *Italian* Alto-relievo.

al·to·stra·tus (al'tō·strā 'təs) *n.* Meteorol. A gray to bluish-gray cloud, usually forming a compact mass.

al·toun (ôl'to͞on) *n.* Scot. Old town.

al·tri·cial (al·trish'əl) *adj.* Having young that hatch in a naked and helpless state requiring care by one or both parent birds. Compare *precocial.* [<L *altrices,* pl. of *altrix* a nurse + -IAL]

al·tru·ism (al'tro͞o·iz'əm) *n.* **1** Devotion to the interests of others; disinterested benevolence: opposed to *egoism.* **2** *Biol.* Consistent behavior by individual organisms that tends to decrease the total reproductive output of the individual while enhancing that of other members of the group or species. [<F *altruisme,* ult. <L *alter* other]

al·tru·ist (al'tro͞o·ist) *n.* One devoted to or professing altruism.

al·tru·is·tic (al'tro͞o·is'tik) *adj.* Pertaining to altruism or altruists. **—al'tru·is'ti·cal·ly** *adv.*

al·u·del (al'yə·del) *n.* Chem. One of a series of pear-shaped vessels of glass or earthenware fitted one into another and used for condensation, as in subliming mercury. [<F <Sp. <Arabic *al-uthāl* the utensil]

A·luin (á·lwaṅ') French form of ALVIN. Also *Sp.* **A·lui·no** (ä·lwē'nō).

al·u·la (al'yə·lə) *n. pl.* **·lae** (lē) **1** *Ornithol.* A tuft of feathers on that part of a bird's wing homologous to the thumb. Also called *bastard wing.* **2** *Entomol.* A membranous lobe separated from the wing base in certain flies. [<NL, dim. of L *ala* wing] **—al'u·lar** *adj.*

al·um (al'əm) *n.* **1** An astringent white crystalline double salt of potassium and aluminum sulfates ($KAl(SO_4)_2 \cdot 12H_2O$) widely used in medicine, manufacturing and the arts. **2** Any of a class of double sulfates of a univalent metal such as potassium or sodium and a trivalent metal such as aluminum, chromium, iron, etc. [<OF <L *alumen*]

A·lum·bra·do (ä'lo͞om·brä 'dō) *n.* One of a Spanish sect of the 16th century. See ILLUMINATI. [<Sp., lit., illuminated]

a·lu·mi·na (ə·lo͞o'mə·nə) *n.* A native aluminum oxide (Al_2O_3), occurring as corundum and, in hydrated or impure form, as bauxite. [<NL <L *alumen, -minis* alum]

a·lu·min·ate (ə·lo͞o'mə) ·nāt) *n.* Any of several salts derived from aluminum hydroxide in which aluminum and oxygen together form a negative ion.

alumina trihydrate Aluminum hydroxide.

a·lu·mi·nif·er·ous (ə·lo͞o 'mə·nif'ər·əs) *adj.* Containing or yielding alum, alumina, or aluminum.

a·lu·mi·nize (ə·lo͞o'mə) ·nīz) *v.t.* **·nized, ·niz·ing** To cover with a film or coat of aluminum or an aluminum compound.

a·lu·mi·no·sil·i·cate (ə·lo͞o'mə·no·sil'ə·kit, -kāt) *n.* A compound of aluminum and silicon with a metal oxide or other radical.

a·lu·mi·no·ther·my (ə·lo͞o 'mə·nō·thûr'mē) *n.* The process of generating heat by the chemical combination of aluminum with a metallic oxide.

a·lu·mi·num (ə·lo͞o'mə) ·nəm) *n.* An abundant metallic element (symbol Al, atomic number 13) found only in combination, chiefly with oxygen, and having the useful properties of lightness and resistance to oxidation. Also *Brit.* **al·u·min·i·um** (al'yə·min'ē·əm). See PERIODIC TABLE. [<NL <L *alumen, -minis* alum] **—a·lu'mi·nous** *adj.*

aluminum bronze An alloy of aluminum and copper resembling pale gold: used in cheap jewelry, etc.

aluminum hydroxide The hydrated form of alumina, $Al_2O_3 \cdot 3H_2O$ or $Al(OH)_3$, formed as a gelatinous white precipitate when a soluble aluminum salt is treated with a soluble base. Also called *alumina trihydrate.*

aluminum oxide Alumina, Al_2O_3, specifically in the form of a white powder or colorless crystals.

aluminum sulfate A colorless, water-soluble salt, $Al_2(SO_4)_3$, used in water purification and in various manufacturing processes.

a·lum·na (ə·lum'nə) *n. pl.* **·nae** (-nē) A female graduate of a college or school. [<L, fem. of *alumnus*]

a·lum·nus (ə·lum'nəs) *n.* pl. **·ni** (-nī) **1** A male graduate of a college or school. **2** Originally, any pupil. [<L, foster son, pupil < *alere* nourish]

al·um·root (al'əm·ro͞ot', -ro͝ot') *n.* **1** Any of a genus *(Heuchera)* of North American perennial herbs having small clusters of greenish or purplish flowers, especially *H. americana,* or its astringent root. **2** The spotted cranesbill.

A·lun·dum (ə·lun'dəm) *n.* A fused crystalline alumina used as an abrasive: a trade name.

al·u·nite (al'yə·nīt) *n.* A mineral consisting chiefly of a basic potassium aluminum sulfate, used in the production of alum. Also **al'um·stone'.** [<F < *alun* <L *alumen* alum]

Al·u·re·dus (al'yo͞o·rē'dəs) Latin form of ALFRED.

al·u·ta·ceous (al'yə·tā'shəs) *adj.* Resembling tawed leather, as in its soft and pliable qualities or its pale-brown color; leathery. [<L *alutacius* <*aluta* soft leather]

Al·va (al'və, *Sp.* äl'vä), **Duke of** See ALBA.

Al·va·ra·do (äl'vä·rä 'thō), **Alonso de,** 1490?–) 1554, Spanish soldier, fought in Peru, and under Cortez in Mexico. **—Pedro de,** 1495–1541, Spanish officer, companion of Cortez in Mexico.

Al·va·rez (al'və·rez), **Luis Walter,** born 1911, U.S. physicist.

Ál·va·rez Quin·te·ro (äl'vä·räth kēn·tā'rō), **Joa·quín,** 1873–1944, and Serafí) n, 1871–1938, brothers, Spanish dramatists and journalists.

al·ve·o·lar (al·vē'ə·lər) *adj.* **1** Pertaining to or contining an alveolus or alveoli. **2** *Anat.* Denoting that part of the jaws in which the teeth are set. **3** *Phonet.* Formed with the tongue touching or near the alveolar ridge, as (t), (d), and (s) in English. —*n. Phonet.* A sound so produced.

alveolar arch *Anat.* The arch of the upper jawbone in vertebrates.

alveolar point In craniometry, the point situated between the two middle incisors of the upper jaw.

alveolar ridge *Anat.* The inwardly projecting bony ridge of the jaw just above the upper front teeth.

al·ve·o·late (al·vē'ə·lit, al'vē·ə-) *adj.* Having alveoli arranged like the cells of a honeycomb; deeply pitted. Also **al·ve·o·lat·ed** (al·vē'ə·lā'tid). **—al·ve'o·la'tion** *n.*

al·ve·o·lus (al·vē'ə·ləs) *n. pl.* **·li** (-lī) **1** A minute air sac at the end of each bronchiole in the lungs. **2** A tooth socket. **3** An acinus in a racemose gland. **4** One of the cells of a honeycomb. [<L, dim. of *alveus* a hollow]

al·ve·o·pal·a·tal (al·ve'ə) ·pal'ə·təl) *adj.* Intermediate between alveolar and palatal: *alveopalatal* sounds.

Al·vin (al'vin) A masculine personal name. Also *Ital.* **Al·vi·no** (äl·vē'nō).

al·vine (al'vin, -vīn) *adj.* Pertaining to the abdomen and the intestines. [<L *alvus* belly]

al·ways (ôl'wiz, -wāz) *adv.* **1** Perpetually; for all time; ceaselessly. **2** At every time; on all occasions: opposed to *sometimes.* Also *Archaic* or *Poetic* **al·way** (ôl'wā). [<ALL + WAY + adverbial genitive ending *-s*]

Al·win (al'win, *Ger.* äl'vin) See ALVIN.

a·lys·sum (ə·lis'əm) *n.* **1** Any of a large genus *(Alyssum)* of cruciferous plants bearing white or yellow flowers. **2** Sweet alyssum. [<NL <Gk. *alysson,* name of a plant, ? < *alyssos* curing madness < *a-* not + *lyssa* madness]

Alz·hei·mer's disease (älts'hī·mərz) *n.* A disease affecting mental stability by premature degeneration of the central nervous system.

am (am, *unstressed* əm) Present tense, first person singular, of BE. [OE *eom, am*]

Am *Chem.* Americium (symbol Am).

Am·a·bel (am'ə·bel) A feminine personal name. Also **A·mab·i·lis** (ə·mab'i·lis). [<L, fem., lovable]

am·a·bil·i·ty (am'ə·bil'ə·tē) *n.* Lovableness. [<L *amabilitas, -tatis* <*amabilis* lovely]

am·a·da·vat (am'ə·də·vat') *n.* A small singing bird of India *(Estrelda amandava),* having red and black plumage flecked with white, and a red beak. [<East Indian]

Am·a·dis (am'ə·dis) A masculine personal name. [<Sp. <L, love of God]

—Amadis of Gaul The hero in a Spanish romance of this title by Vasco de Lobeira, 1360–1403.

am·a·dou (am'ə·do͞o) *n.* A soft spongy combustible substance, prepared from several species of fungus (as *Boletus, Polyporus,* or *Hernandia*), found on old trees: used as tinder, especially after being steeped in a solution of saltpeter, and also as a styptic. [<F]

A·ma·ga·sa·ki (ä·mä·gä·sä·kē) A city on Osaka Bay in southern Honshu island, Japan.

a·mah (ä'mə, am'ə) *n.* In India and the Orient, a female attendant for children; especially, a wet-nurse. Also **a'ma.** [<Anglo-Indian]

A·mai·mon (ə·mā'mən, ə) ·mī'-) In medieval demonology, the devil of the East. Also **A·mamon** (ə·mā'mə) n), **A·may'mon.**

a·main (ə·mān') *adv.* Vehemently; forcibly; exceedingly; without delay; at full speed. [<A-[1] + MAIN[1]) strength]

à main ar·mée (à maṅ nà r·mā') *French* By force of arms.

a·maist (ə·māst') *adv.* Scot. Almost.

Am·a·lek (am'ə·lek) **1** Grandson of Esau. *Gen.* xxxvi 12. **2** The descendants of Amalek, a nation hostile to Israel. *Ex.* xvii 8–13. Also **Am'a·lech** (-lek).

Am·a·lek·ite (am'ə·lek·ī) t, ə·mal'ə·kīt) *n.* One of a nomad people dwelling in the desert south of Judah; a marauding tribe that warred against Israel. *Num.* xiii 29.

A·mal·fi (ä·mäl'fē) A town in southern Italy on the Gulf of Salerno.

a·mal·gam (ə·mal'gəm) *n.* **1** An alloy of mercury and one or more metals. **2** Any mixture or combination of two or more bodies, substances, or things. [<MF *amalgame* <) Med.L *amalgama* <Arabic *al-malgham* <) Gk. *malagma* an emollient < *malassein* soften]

a·mal·gam·a·ble (ə·mal'gə) ·mə·bəl) *adj.* Capable of forming an amalgam.

a·mal·ga·mate (ə·mal'gə·māt) *v.t.* & v.i. **·mated, ·mat·ing 1** To form an amalgam; unite in an alloy with mercury, as a metal. **2** To unite or combine: The four parts of the original are *amalgamated* into two. See synonyms under MIX, UNITE. **—a·mal·ga·ma·tive** (ə·mal'gə·mā'tiv) *adj.* **—a·mal·ga·ma·tor** (ə·mal'gə·mā'tər) *n.*

a·mal·ga·ma·tion (ə·mal' gə·mā'shən) *n.* **1** The forming of an amalgam. **2** A mingling of racial or ethnic stocks. **3** The removal of metals from their ores by treatment with mercury. **4** A substance formed by mixture.

A·ma·li·a (*Du., Ger.* ä·mä'lē·ä; *Ital.* ä·mä'lyä) Dutch, German, and Italian form of AMELIA.

Am·al·the·a (am'əl·thē'ə) In Greek mythology, the goat on whose milk Zeus was bred, one of whose horns, the **horn of Amalthea,** broken off by the god, became the *cornucopia,*

or horn of plenty. Also **Am′al·thae′a, Am′al·thæ′a.**

A·man·da (ə·man′də) A feminine personal name. Also *Fr.* **A·man·dine** (ä·män·dēn′). [< L, lovable]

a·man·i·ta (am′ə·nī′tə) *n.* Any of a genus (*Amanita*) of fleshy fungi that includes highly poisonous species sometimes mistaken for edible mushrooms. [< Gk. *amanitai*, a kind of fungus]

a·man·ta·dine (ə·man′tə·dēn) *n.* A compound, $C_{10}H_{17}N$, used to treat Parkinsonism and as an antiviral prophylactic against epidemic influenza.

a·man·u·en·sis (ə·man′yōō·en′sis) *n. pl.* **·ses** (-sēz) One who copies manuscript or takes dictation; a secretary. [< L < *a- (ab-)* from + *manus* hand]

A·ma·pá (ä·mə·pä′) A federal territory in northern Brazil; 53,057 square miles; capital, Macapá.

am·a·ranth (am′ə·ranth) *n.* **1** Any of a genus (*Amaranthus*) of weedy, mostly annual herbs, having spikes of small green or purplish flowers with a dry, persistent calyx. **2** A deep purplish hue. **3** An imaginary never-fading flower. [< L *amarantus* < Gk. *amarantos*, lit., unfading < *a-* not + *marainein* wither]

am·a·ran·thine (am′ə·ran′thin) *adj.* **1** Pertaining to, like, or containing amaranth. **2** Unfading; everlasting. **3** Of purplish hue.

Am·a·ryl·lis (am′ə·ril′is) In pastoral poetry, a country girl or shepherdess.

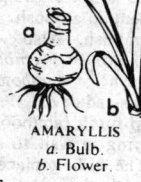

AMARYLLIS
a. Bulb.
b. Flower.

am·a·ryl·lis (am′ə·ril′is) *n.* **1** Any one of various bulbous South African plants of the genus *Amaryllis*, often cultivated for their large, lilylike flowers, as the belladonna lily. **2** Any of several similar liliaceous plants. [< L < Gk. *Amaryllis*, fem. personal name]

Am·a·sa (am′ə·sə, ə·mä′sə) A masculine personal name. [< Hebrew, a burden]
—**Amasa** Nephew of David; captain of the host of Absalom; slain by Joab. II *Sam.* xx 4.

a·mass (ə·mas′) *v.t.* To heap up; accumulate, especially as wealth or possessions for oneself. [< OF *amasser* < *a-* to (< L *ad-*) + *masser* pile up < L *massa* mass] —**a·mass′a·ble** *adj.* —**a·mass′er** *n.* —**a·mass′ment** *n.*
Synonyms: accumulate, aggregate, collect, gather. To *amass* is to bring together materials that make a mass, a great bulk or quantity, *accumulate* being commonly applied to the more gradual, *amass* to the more rapid gathering of money or materials. We say interest is *accumulated* rather than is *amassed;* a fortune may be rapidly *amassed* by shrewd speculations. *Aggregate* is now most commonly used of numbers and amounts; as, the expenses will *aggregate* a round million. Compare AGGREGATE. *n. Antonyms:* disperse, dissipate, divide, parcel, portion, scatter, spend, squander, waste.

A·ma·ta (ä·mä′tä) Italian form of AMY.

am·a·teur (am′ə·chŏŏr, -tŏŏr, -tyŏŏr, am′ə·tûr′) *adj.* **1** Pertaining to or done by an amateur. **2** Composed of amateurs: an *amateur* cast. **3** Not expert or professional. —*n.* **1** One who practices an art or science, not professionally, but for his own pleasure. **2** An athlete who has not engaged in contests for money, or used any athletic art as a means of livelihood. **3** One who does something without professional skill or ease. [< F < L *amator* lover < *amare* love]—**am′a·teur·ism** *n.*
Synonyms (noun): connoisseur, critic, dilettante, novice, tyro. Etymologically, the *amateur* is one who loves, the *connoisseur* one who knows. The *amateur* practices to some extent that in regard to which he may not be well informed; the *connoisseur* is well informed in regard to that which he may not practice at all. *Dilettante,* which had originally the sense of *amateur,* has come to denote one who is superficial, pretentious, and affected, whether in theory or practice.

am·a·teur·ish (am′ə·chŏŏr′ish, -tŏŏr′-, -tyŏŏr′-, -tûr′-) *adj.* Lacking the skill or perfection of an expert or professional. —**am′a·teur′ish·ly** *adv.* —**am′a·teur′ish·ness** *n.*

A·ma·ti (ä·mä′tē) *n.* A violin made by any of the Amati, a family of violinmakers at Cremona, Italy, in the 16th and 17th centuries, notably **Ni·cola** or **Nicolò**, 1596–1684.

am·a·tive (am′ə·tiv) *adj.* Pertaining to sexual love; amorous. [< L *amatus,* pp. of *amare* love] —**am′a·tive·ly** *adv.*

am·a·tive·ness (am′ə·tiv·nis) *n.* The propensity to love or to sexual passion.

am·a·tol (am′ə·tol, -tōl) *n.* An explosive mixture of variable proportions of ammonium nitrate and trinitrotoluene. [< AM(MONIUM) + TOL(UENE)]

Am·a·ton·ga·land (am′ə·tong′gə·land′) See TONGALAND.

am·a·to·ry (am′ə·tôr′ē, -tō′rē) *adj.* Characterized by or designed to excite love; expressing or given to sexual love; erotic, as a poem. Also **am′a·to′ri·al.** [< L *amatorius* < *amare* love]

am·au·ro·sis (am′ô·rō′sis) *n.* Total or partial loss of sight without apparent organic defect. [< Gk. *amaurōsis* < *amauros* dark] —**am·au·rot·ic** (am′ô-rot′ik) *adj.*

a·maze (ə·māz′) *v.t.* **a·mazed, a·maz·ing 1** To overwhelm, as by wonder or surprise; astonish greatly. **2** *Obs.* To puzzle; bewilder. [OE *āmasian*] —**a·mazed′** *adj.* —**a·maz·ed·ly** (ə·mā′zid·lē) *adv.* —**a·maz′ed·ness** *n.*

a·maze·ment (ə·māz′mənt) *n.* **1** Wonder; surprise; astonishment. **2** *Obs.* Stupefaction; frenzy; dementia. Also *Archaic* **a·maze′.**
Synonyms: admiration, astonishment, awe, bewilderment, confusion, consternation, perplexity, surprise, wonder. *Amazement* and *astonishment* both express the momentary overwhelming of the mind by that which is beyond expectation. *Awe* is the yielding of the mind to something supremely grand in character or formidable in power, and ranges from apprehension or dread to reverent worship. *Surprise* lies midway between *astonishment* and *amazement,* and usually concerns slighter matters. *Consternation* adds terror to *astonishment* or *amazement.* Compare PERPLEXITY. *Antonyms:* anticipation, calmness, composure, coolness, expectation, indifference, preparation, self-possession, steadiness.

a·maz·ing (ə·mā′zing) *adj.* Causing amazement; astonishing; wonderful. See synonyms under EXTRAORDINARY. —**a·maz′ing·ly** *adv.*

Am·a·zon (am′ə·zon, -zən) *n.* **1** In Greek mythology, one of a race of female warriors, said to have lived in Scythia, near the Black Sea. **2** A female warrior. **3** Any large, strong or athletic woman or girl. Also **am′a·zon** *n.* [< L < Gk. *Amazōn;* derived by the Greeks as < *a-* without + *mazos* breast, because of the fable that they cut off the right breast to facilitate the use of the bow]

Am·a·zon (am′ə·zon, -zən) A river in South America, carrying the largest volume of water

of any in the world and flowing about 3,300 miles from the Andes through northern Brazil to the Atlantic. *Spanish & Portugese* **A·ma·zo·nas** (Sp. ä′mä·sō′näs, Pg. ä·mə·zō′nəs).

Amazon ant Any of several species of ants of the genus *Polyergus* that capture the larvae or pupae of other species and raise them as workers.

A·ma·zo·nas (*Sp.* ä′mä·sō′näs, *Pg.* ä·mə·zō′nəs) **1** A state in NW Brazil; 614,913 square miles; capital, Manaus. **2** A commissary of SE Colombia; 48,008 square miles; capital, Letica. **3** A department of northern Peru; 13,948 square miles. **4** A territory of southern Venezuela; 67,857 square miles; capital, Puerto Ayacucho.

Am·a·zo·ni·an (am′ə·zō′nē·ən) *adj.* **1** Pertaining to the Amazons; warlike; masculine: said of women. **2** Pertaining to the Amazon River. —*n.* An Amazon.

am·a·zon·ite (am′ə·zən·it) *n.* A green variety of microcline often used as a gemstone. Also **Amazon stone.** [from the *Amazon* River]

am·bage (am′bij) *n. pl.* **am·bag·es** (am′bə·jiz, *Lat.* am·bā′jēz) **1** A winding or circuitous path. **2** *Usually pl.* An indirect method of proceeding. [< OF *ambages* < L *ambi-* around + *agere* go] —**am·ba·gious** (am·bā′jəs) *adj.* —**am·ba′gious·ly** *adv.* —**am·ba′gious·ness** *n.*

Am·ba·la (um·bä′lə) A city in eastern Punjab, India.

am·ba·ry (am·bä′rē) *n.* **1** A tropical malvaceous plant (*Hibiscus cannabinus*) cultivated in Asia for its tough fiber. **2** The hemplike fiber of this plant, used for sacking, cordage, etc. Also **am·ba′ri.** Also called *kenaf.* [< Hind. *ambārā*]

am·bas·sa·dor (am·bas′ə·dər, -dôr) *n.* **1** An accredited diplomatic agent of the highest rank, appointed as the representative of one government or state to another (**ambassador extraordinary and plenipotentiary**) or to represent a government or state at a particular function, as the wedding of a king (**ambassador extraordinary on special mission**). **2** Any personal representative or messenger. Also *embassador.* See synonyms under HERALD. —**ambassador-at-large** An ambassador accredited to no specific country or government. —**goodwill ambassador** Any person traveling in a foreign country to promote friendly relations and understanding. [< F *ambassadeur* < Ital. *ambasciatore*] —**am·bas·sa·do·ri·al** (am·bas′ə·dôr′ē·əl, -dō′rē-) *adj.* —**am·bas′sa·dor·ship** *n.*

am·bas·sa·dress (am·bas′ə·dris) *n.* **1** A woman ambassador. **2** The wife of an ambassador.

am·ber (am′bər) *n.* **1** A translucent yellow to reddish brown fossil resin of an extinct coniferous tree, used mainly as an ornament. **2** Anything the color of amber. **3** An amber-colored light used to produce the effect of sunlight, as on a stage. —*v.t.* **1** To encase or preserve in amber. **2** To give an amber color to. —*adj.* Pertaining to, like, or of the color of amber. [< F *ambre* < Arabic *'anbar* ambergris]

am·ber·gris (am′bər·grēs, -gris) *n.* An opaque, grayish, waxy morbid secretion from the intestines of the sperm whale, sometimes found floating on the ocean or lying on the shore: used in perfumery. [< F *ambre gris* gray amber]

am·ber·jack (am′bər·jak′) *n.* Any of several species of large carangoid food and game fishes (genus *Seriola*) found in warm areas of the western Atlantic.

am·ber·oid (am′bər·oid) See AMBROID.

ambi- *combining form* Both: *ambidextrous.* [< L *ambo* both]

am·bi·ance (am′bē·əns) *n.* Ambience. [< F]

am·bi·dex·ter (am′bə·dek′stər) *adj.* Ambidextrous. —*n.* **1** One who uses both hands equally well. **2** A double-dealer; hypocrite. [< Med. < L *ambo* both + *dexter* right (hand)] —**am′bi·dex′tral** (-dek′strəl) *adj.*

am·bi·dex·ter·i·ty (am′bə·dek·ster′ə·tē) *n.* **1** The state or quality of being ambidextrous. **2** Duplicity; trickery.

am·bi·dex·trous (am′bə·dek′strəs) *adj.* **1** Able to use both hands equally well. **2** Very dexterous or skilful. **3** Dissembling; double-dealing. —**am′bi·dex′trous·ly** *adv.* —**am′bi·dex′trous·ness** *n.*

am·bi·ence (am′bē·əns) *n.* The environment or pervading atmosphere of a place, situation, etc. Also *ench* **am·bi·ance** (än′·bē·äns′). [< L *ambiens* AMBIENT]

am·bi·ent (am′bē·ənt) *adj.* **1** Surrounding; encircling; encompassing. **2** Circulating. —*n.* Anything that encompasses. [< L *ambiens, -entis,* ppr. of *ambire* < *ambi-* around + *ire* go]

am·bi·gu·i·ty (am′bə·gyōō′ə·tē) *n. pl.* **·ties 1** The quality of being ambiguous; doubtfulness. **2** An expression or statement that can be variously interpreted.

am·big·u·ous (am·big′yōō·əs) *adj.* **1** Capable of being understood in more senses than one; having a double meaning; equivocal. **2** Doubtful or uncertain: a liquid of *ambiguous* nature. **3** Obscure, indistinct, as shadows. See synonyms under EQUIVOCAL, OBSCURE. [< L *ambiguus* < *ambigere* wander about < *ambi-* around + *agere* go] **—am·big′u·ous·ly** *adv.* **—am·big′u·ous·ness** *n.*

am·bit (am′bit) *n.* **1** That which bounds; a boundary. **2** Circumference; circuit. **3** Extent or sphere, as of actions or words; scope. [< L *ambitus* circuit < *ambire.* See AMBIENT.]

am·bi·ten·den·cy (am′bə·ten′dən·sē) *n. Psychol.* The state of having conflicting tendencies.

am·bi·tion (am·bish′ən) *n.* **1** Eager or inordinate desire, as for power, wealth, or distinction. **2** A strong desire to achieve something considered great or good: with *of* or the infinitive. **3** An object so desired or striven for. **4** *Obs.* A canvassing for an office or the like. *—v.t.* To desire and seek eagerly. [< L *ambitio, -onis* a going about (to solicit votes) < *ambire.* See AMBIENT.] **—am·bi′tion·less** *adj.*

Synonyms (noun): aspiration, competition, emulation, opposition, rivalry. *Aspiration* is the desire for excellence, pure and simple. *Ambition,* literally a going around to solicit votes, has primary reference to the award or approval of others, and is the eager desire for power, fame, or something deemed great and eminent. *Emulation* is not so much to win any excellence or success for itself as to equal or surpass other persons. Compare EMULATION. *Antonyms*: carelessness, contentment, humility, indifference, satisfaction.

am·bi·tious (am·bish′əs) *adj.* **1** Actuated or characterized by ambition. **2** Greatly desiring; eager for: with *of* or the infinitive. **3** Aspiring, as to a high or imposing position. **—am·bi′tious·ly** *adv.* **—am·bi′tious·ness** *n.*

am·biv·a·lence (am·biv′ə·ləns) *n. Psychol.* The state of being ambivalent.

am·biv·a·lent (am·biv′ə·lənt) *adj.* **1** Uncertain or subject to change, especially because affected by contradictory emotions or ideas: an *ambivalent* attitude. **2** *Psychol.* Experiencing contradictory and opposing emotions toward the same person at the same time, especially love and hate. [< AMBI- + L *valens, -entis,* ppr. of *valere* be strong, be worth]

am·bi·ver·sion (am′bə·vûr′zhən, -shən) *n. Psychol.* A condition intermediate between introversion and extroversion. [< AMBI- + *-version,* as in *introversion*]

am·bi·vert (am′bə·vûrt) *n. Psychol.* A personality type which is intermediate between the introvert and extrovert.

am·ble (am′bəl) *v.i.* **am·bled** (-bəld), **am·bling 1** To move, as a horse, by lifting the two feet on one side together, alternately with the two feet on the other. **2** To move with an easy, swaying motion resembling this gait; proceed leisurely. *—n.* **1** The single-foot. **2** An ambling movement, like that of a horse. [< OF *ambler* < L *ambulare* walk] **—am′bling** *adj.* **—am′bling·ly** *adv.*

am·bler (am′blər) *n.* One that ambles, especially an ambling horse.

am·blyg·o·nite (am·blig′ə·nīt) *n.* A white or greenish mineral found in cleavable masses consisting largely of basic lithium aluminum phosphate and constituting an important source of lithium. [< G *amblygonit* < Gk. *amblygōnios* having obtuse angles]

am·bly·o·pi·a (am′blē·ō′pē·ə) *n.* Dimness of vision, without discoverable disease or errors of refraction in the eye. [< NL < Gk. *amblys* dull + *ōps* eye] **—am·bly·op·ic** (am′blē·op′ik) *adj.*

am·bo (am′bō) *n. pl.* **am·bos** (am′bōz) or **am·bo·nes** (am·bō′nēz) In early Christian churches, a raised pulpitlike stand or desk, where parts of the service were read or chanted: usually two, one on each side of the nave. [< Gk. *ambōn* a rising ground]

am·bo·cep·tor (am′bə·sep′tər) *n. Bacteriol.* A thermostable agent supposed by Ehrlich to exist in blood serum and to assist in the destruction of pathogenic organisms by uniting them to another substance (the complement) also present in the blood. [< L *ambo* both + (RE)CEPTOR]

Am·boi·na (am·boi′nə) See AMBON. Also **Am·boy′na.**

Amboina wood A mottled wood obtained from any of several leguminous trees (genus *Pterocarpus*) of Asia and Africa, used in cabinetwork. Also **am·boy′na.** Also called *padauk.*

Am·boise (dän·bwäz′), **George d′,** 1460–1510, French cardinal and statesman.

Am·boise (äṅ·bwäz′) A town in west central France on the Loire; residence of the Valois kings from Charles VIII to Francis II.

Am·bon (äm′bôn) An Indonesian island SW of Ceram; 314 square miles; chief town, Amboina: also *Amboina, Amboyna.*

am·broid (am′broid) *n.* A reconstructed or imitation amber consisting of fragments of amber and sometimes other resins united by pressure and heat. Also *amberoid.*

Am·brose (am′brōz) A masculine personal name. Also *Dan., Du., Ger.* **Am·bro·si·us** (äm·brō′zē·ōōs), *Fr.* **Am·broise** (äṅ·brwäz′), *Ital.* **Am·bro·gio** (äm·brō′jō), *Sp., Pg.* **Am·bro·sio** (*Sp.* äm·brō′syō, *Pg.* äṅ·brō′zyōō), *Lat.* **Am·bro·si·us** (am·brō′zhē·əs, -zē·əs). [< Gk., divine, immortal] **—Ambrose, Saint,** 340?–397, bishop of Milan; one of the Latin fathers.

Ambrose Channel An entrance to New York Harbor: reckoning point for the time of a voyage in or out of New York.

am·bro·sia (am·brō′zhə, -zhē·ə) *n.* **1** The food of the gods, giving immortality. **2** Hence, any very delicious food or drink. **3** A richly perfumed salve or unguent. **4** *Bot.* Any of a genus *(Ambrosia)* of coarse herbs, weedy composite herbs comprising the ragweeds. [< L < Gk. *ambrosia* < *ambrotos* immortal < *a-* not + *brotos* mortal]

AMBROSIA (*def. 4*) (3 to 6 feet high)

am·bro·si·a·ceous (am·brō·zē·ā′shəs) *adj.* Belonging to the genus *Ambrosia,* comprising weedy herbs of the composite family, as the ragweeds.

am·bro·sial (am·brō′zhəl, -zhē·əl) *adj.* **1** Of or like ambrosia; fragrant; delicious. **2** Worthy of the gods; heavenly. Also **am·bro·sian** (am·brō′zhən, -zhē·ən). **—am·bro′sial·ly** *adv.*

Am·bro·sian (am·brō′zhən, -zhē·ən) *adj.* Of or attributed to St. Ambrose or resembling his style.

Ambrosian chant The mode of singing or chanting divine service introduced by St. Ambrose in the cathedral at Milan, but afterward superseded by the Gregorian system.

Ambrosian hymn Any metrical hymn written by St. Ambrose or characterized by his style.

Ambrosian liturgy *Eccl.* An ancient liturgy compiled by St. Ambrose, somewhat different from the Roman liturgy.

am·bro·type (am′brə·tīp′) *n.* A photograph made by an obsolete method in which a negative on a glass plate backed by a black surface appears positive because of light reflected from the silver in the negative. [< (James) *Ambro(se* Cutting), 1814–67, inventor + -TYPE]

am·bry (am′brē) *n. pl.* **·bries 1** A depository for goods, food, or money; pantry; cupboard; closet. **2** *Eccl.* A closet near the altar for the sacred vessels. **3** *Obs.* A library. Also **am·ber·y** (am′bər·ē). [ME *almarie, amerie, ambrie* < L *armarium* a chest, orig., a place for storing arms]

ambs·ace (āmz′ās′, amz′-) *n.* **1** Both aces, the lowest throw at dice. **2** Bad luck; misfortune. **3** Worthlessness; that which is next to nothing. [< OF *ambes as* < L *ambas as* double ace]

am·bu·cy·cle (am′byə·sī′kəl) *n.* A small ambulance attached like a side-car to a motorcycle. [< AMBU(LANCE) + (MOTOR)CYCLE]

am·bu·la·cral (am′byə·lā′krəl) *adj.* Of, pertaining to, or situated near an ambulacrum.

ambulacral feet The tube feet of echinoderms.

ambulacral groove A furrow on the oral surface of the radii of a starfish.

ambulacral ossicle An ossicle of which the sides of the ambulacral groove are formed.

ambulacral pore The aperture piercing the ambulacral plates of echinoids or between the contiguous ambulacral ossicles of asteroids, admitting the ducts of the pedicels or tube feet.

am·bu·la·crum (am′byə·lā′krəm) *n. pl.* **·cra** (-krə) Any of the radial series of perforated plates on the oral surface of echinoderms through which the tube feet are thrust. [< L, a covered walk < *ambulare* walk]

am·bu·lance (am′byə·ləns) *n.* **1** A covered vehicle for conveying the sick and wounded. **2** A moving or field hospital. **3** A boat or airplane for conveying sick and wounded personnel. [< F < *(hôpital) ambulant* walking (hospital) < L *ambulare* walk]

am·bu·lance-chas·er (am′byə·ləns·chā′sər) *n. U.S. Slang* A lawyer or his agent who seeks the victim of an accident to persuade him to institute a suit at law for damages.

am·bu·lant (am′byə·lənt) *adj.* Walking or moving about from place to place; shifting. [< L *ambulans, -antis,* ppr. of *ambulare* walk]

am·bu·late (am′byə·lāt) *v.i.* **·lat·ed, ·lat·ing** To walk about; move from place to place. [< L *ambulatus,* pp. of *ambulare* walk] **—am′bu·la′tion** *n.* **—am·bu·la·tive** (am′byə·lā′tiv, -lə·tiv) *adj.*

am·bu·la·to·ry (am′byə·lə·tôr′ē, -tō′rē) adj. **1** Pertaining to or for walking or walkers. **2** Able to walk, as an invalid. **3** Shifting; not fixed or stationary. **4** *Law* Alterable, as a writ or pleading until filed, or a will at any time during the testator's life. *—n. pl.* **·ries** A place, as a corridor, for walking.

am·bus·cade (am′bəs·kād′) *n.* **1** The act of hiding, or the state of being hidden, to surprise adversaries. **2** The place of hiding, or persons hidden; an ambush. *—v.t. & v.i.* **·cad·ed, ·cad·ing** To ambush. Also *Archaic* **am·bus·ca·do** (am′bəs·kā′dō). [< F *embuscade* < Ital. *imboscata* an ambush < *imboscare.* See AMBUSH.] **—am′bus·cad′er** *n.*

am·bush (am′bŏŏsh) *n.* **1** The act or condition of lying in wait to surprise or attack an enemy. **2** The hiding place or the persons hidden. Also **am′bush·ment.** *—v.t. & v.i.* **1** To hide in order to attack unexpectedly. **2** To attack from a hidden place; waylay. [< OF *embusche* < *embuschier* < Ital. *imboscare* place in a bush, set an ambush < L *in-* in + *boscus* a wood] **—am′bush·er** *n.*

Am·chit·ka (am·chit′kə) Easternmost of the Rat Islands in the Aleutian Islands group.

a·me·ba (ə·mē′bə) *n. pl.* **·bas** or **·bae** (-bē) Any of various naked protozoans of the genus *Amoeba* and other genera in the order Amoebidae, typically of indefinite shape, moving and feeding by the action of pseudopodia, and reproducing by fission. Also *amoeba.* [< NL < Gk. *amoibē* change] **—a·me′bic** *adj.*

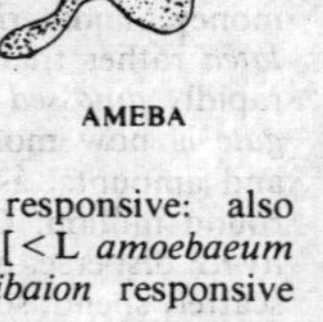

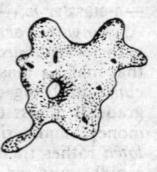

AMEBA

am·e·be·an (am′ə·bē′ən) *adj.* Alternately or reciprocally responsive: also spelled *amoebaean, amoebean.* [< L *amoebaeum (carmen)* < Gk. *(asma) amoibaion* responsive (song) < *amoibē* change]

am·e·bi·a·sis (am′ə·bī′ə·sis) *n.* Infection by a parasitic ameba, especially *Entamoeba histolytica,* usually manifested by severe intestinal symptoms. Also *amoebiasis.* [< NL < AMEBA + -IASIS]

amebic dysentery Severe amebiasis involving ulceration and bleeding of the colon and painful diarrhea.

a·me·bo·cyte (ə·mē′bō·sīt) *n.* Any wandering ameboid cell of a multicellular organism, as a leukocyte. Also *amoebocyte.*

a·me·boid (ə·mē′boid) *adj.* Resembling an ameba, as in its change of form: also spelled *amoeboid.*

a·meer (ə·mir′) *n.* **1** The sovereign of Afghanistan. **2** A Mohammedan prince or governor. Also **a·mir′.** [< Arabic *amīr* ruler]

am·el·corn (am′əl·kôrn′) *n.* An inferior kind of wheat *(Triticum sativum dicoccum)* cultivated in Europe mainly for the manufacture of starch; emmer. [< G *amelkorn* starch corn]

A·mel·ia (ə·mēl′yə, ə·mē′lē·ə; *Ital., Pg., Sp.* ä·mā′lyä) A feminine personal name. Also *Fr.* **A·mé·lie** (à·mā·lē′). [< Gmc., lit., industrious]

a·mel·io·rate (ə·mēl′yə·rāt) *v.t.* & *v.i.* **·rat·ed, ·rat·ing** To make or become better; meliorate; improve. See synonyms under AMEND. [< F *améliorer* < L *ad-* to + *meliorare* to better < *melior* better] —**a·mel·io·ra·ble** (ə·mēl′yə·rə·bəl) *adj.* —**a·mel′io·rant** (-rənt) *n.* —**a·mel·io·ra·tive** (ə·mēl′yə·rā′tiv, -rə·tiv) *adj.* —**a·mel′io·ra·tor** *n.*

a·mel·io·ra·tion (ə·mēl′yə·rā′shən) *n.* The act, process, or result of ameliorating, or the state of being ameliorated; improvement.

a·mel·o·blast (ə·mel′ə·blast) *n.* An epithelial cell, one of those producing the enamel of the teeth. [< OF *amail* enamel + -BLAST]

a·men (ā′men′, ä′-) *interj.* So it is; so be it. —*n.* **1** The word *amen* at the end of a prayer or hymn, meaning *so be it.* **2** Any expression of hearty assent or conviction. **3** A concluding act or word; termination. —*v.t.* **1** To say amen to; express hearty concurrence in or approval of. **2** To say or write that last word of; make an end of. —*adv. Obs.* Verily; truly. [< L < Gk. < Hebrew *āmēn* verily]

A·men (ā·men′) Christ, the true and faithful witness. *Rev.* iii 14.

A·men (ä′mən) In Egyptian mythology, the god of life and procreation, represented as having a ram's head; later identified with the sun-god, as the supreme deity, and called **Amen-Ra** (-rä′). Also spelled **Ammon, Amon.**

a·me·na·ble (ə·mē′nə·bəl, ə·men′ə-) *adj.* **1** Liable to be called to account; responsible to authority. **2** Submissive; tractable. **3** Capable of being tested or judged by rule or law. See synonyms under DOCILE. [< F *amener* bring to < *a-* to (< L *ad-*) + *mener* lead < L *minare* drive (with threats) < *minari* threaten] —**a·me′na·bil′i·ty, a·me′na·ble·ness** *n.* —**a·me′na·bly** *adv.*

amen corner *U.S.* The corner of a church laterally facing the pulpit, where, as in provincial regions of the United States, the deacons, who lead the responsive amens, usually sit.

a·mend (ə·mend′) *v.t.* **1** To change for the better; improve. **2** To free from faults; correct; reform. **3** To change or alter by authority: to *amend* a bill. **4** *Obs.* To mend or repair. —*v.i.* **5** To become better in conduct. [< OF *amender* < L *emendare* to free from faults < *ex-* from + *mendum* fault] —**a·mend′a·ble** *adj.*—**a·mend′a·ble·ness***n.* —**a·mend′er***n.*

Synonyms: advance, ameliorate, better, cleanse, correct, emend, improve, meliorate, mend, mitigate, purify, reclaim, rectify, reform, repair. To *amend* is to change for the better by removing faults, errors, or defects; it always refers to that which at some point falls short of a standard of excellence. *Advance, better,* and *improve* may refer either to what is quite imperfect or to what has reached a high degree of excellence. We *correct* evils, *reform* abuses, *rectify* incidental conditions of evil or error; we *ameliorate* poverty and misery, which we cannot wholly remove. We *mend* a tool, *repair* a building, *correct* proof; we *amend* character or conduct that is faulty, or a statement or law that is defective. Compare ALLAY, ALLEVIATE, EMEND. *Antonyms:* aggravate, blemish, corrupt, debase, depress, deteriorate, harm, impair, injure, mar, spoil, tarnish, vitiate.

a·mend·a·to·ry (ə·men′də·tôr′ē, -tō′rē) *adj.* Tending to amend; corrective.

a·mende (ə·mend′, *Fr.* ä·mänd′) *n.* A reparation or recantation. [< F]

a·mende ho·no·ra·ble (ä·mänd′ ô·nô·rá′bl′) *French* Public reparation or apology.

a·mend·ment (ə·mend′mənt) *n.* **1** Change for the better. **2** A removal of faults; correction. **3** The changing, as of a law, bill, or motion. **4** The statement of such a change, as in a clause or paragraph.

a·mends (ə·mendz′) *n. pl.* Reparation, as in satisfaction or compensation for loss, damage, or injury. See synonyms under RECOMPENSE. [< OF *amendes,* pl. of *amende* a fine < *amender.* See AMEND.]

A·men·ho·tep (ä′mən·hō′tep) Name of four Egyptian pharaohs.

—**Amenhotep III,** 1411–1375 B.C., conqueror, built temple at Karnak.

—**Amenhotep IV** See IKHNATON.

a·men·i·ty (ə·men′ə·tē) *n. pl.* **·ties 1** Agreeableness; pleasantness. **2** *pl.* Agreeable features or aspects, as of a place or scene. **3** *Often pl.* Any of the pleasant acts and courtesies of polite behavior. [< L *amoenitas, -tatis* < *amoenus* pleasant]

a·men·or·rhe·a (ā·men′ə·rē′ə) *n.* Abnormal suppression or absence of menstruation. [< NL < Gk. *a-* not + *mēn* month + *rheein* flow] —**a·men′or·rhe′ic, a·men′or·rhoe′ic** *adj.*

a men·sa et tho·ro (ā men′sə et thō′rō) *Latin* In law, a partial suspension by law of the marriage relations for some cause arising after marriage that renders it impossible for the parties to live together; a judicial separation; literally, from board and bed.

am·ent (am′ənt, ā′mənt) *n.* A catkin. [< L *amentum* a thong]

am·en·ta·ceous (am′ən·tā′shəs) *adj. Bot.* Like, pertaining to, or bearing catkins.

a·men·tia (ā·men′shə, -shē·ə) *n.* **1** Congenital lack of normal mental development; feeblemindedness. **2** Temporary insanity. [< L < *a- (ab-)* away + *mens* mind]

am·en·tif·er·ous (am′ən·tif′ər·əs) *adj. Bot.* Bearing aments, or catkins.

Am·er·a·sian (am′ər·ā′zhen) *adj.* Having both American and Asian parentage. —*n.* A person of American and Asian parentage.

a·merce (ə·mûrs′) *v.t.* **a·merced, a·merc·ing 1** To punish by an assessment or fine. **2** To punish, as by deprivation. [< AF *amercier* to fine < *a merci* at the mercy of] —**a·merce′a·ble** *adj.* —**a·merce′·ment** *n.* —**a·merc′er** *n.*

A·mer·i·ca (ə·mer′ə·kə) **1** The lands in the Western Hemisphere; specifically, either of the two continents, North America or South America. Also **the Americas. 2** The United States of America.

America A popular patriotic hymn written by S. F. Smith; also, the tune to which it is sung, that of the English "God Save the King."

A·mer·i·can (ə·mer′ə·kən) *adj.* **1** Pertaining to the continent or people of North or South America, or of the Western Hemisphere. **2** Pertaining to the United States of America, its history, government, people, etc. —*n.* **1** A citizen of the United States. **2** The English language as spoken and written in the United States; American English. **3** An inhabitant of America.

A·mer·i·ca·na (ə·mer′ə·kä′nə, -kan′ə, -kā′nə) *n. pl.* Things American, collectively; any collection of American literary papers, sayings, or other data, especially relating to American history and traditions.

American aloe The century plant.

American Beauty A hybrid perennial rose with large, deep red blossoms on long stems.

American cheese Any of several cheeses popular in the United States; especially, a mild yellow kind of Cheddar.

American crawl See under CRAWL[1]

American eagle The bald eagle, especially in reference to its symbolic function as the national emblem of The United States of America.

American Empire An American style of furniture popular in the first half of the 19th century, influenced by the neo-classical decorative art of the First French Empire.

American English The English language as used in the United States, with especial reference to pronunciation and vocabulary: also called *American.*

American Expeditionary Forces The United States Army troops in Europe during World War I. Abbr. *A.E.F.*

American Federation of Labor A federation of trade unions, founded in 1886, which merged in 1955 with the Congress of Industrial Organizations. Abbr. *AFL* or *A.F. of L.*

American Indian A member of one of the aboriginal races of America.

A·mer·i·can·ism (ə·mer′ə·kən·iz′əm) *n.* **1** A word, phrase, usage, or a trait, custom, or tradition peculiar to the people of the United States or to some of them. **2** Attachment to America or its institutions, traditions, and way of life.

A·mer·i·can·ist (ə·mer′ə·kən·ist) *n.* One who makes a special study of subjects pertaining to America, as its history, geography, or re-

sources.

American ivy The Virginia creeper.

A·mer·i·can·ize (ə·mer′ə·kən·īz′) *v.t.* & *v.i.* **·ized, ·iz·ing** To become or cause to become American in spirit or methods; imitate or become like the Americans, as in speech, customs, etc. —**A·mer·i·can·i·za′tion** *n.*

American Legion An organization of veterans of World War I and World War II, founded in 1919.

American Library Association An organization of librarians and libraries, founded in 1876. Abbr. *A.L.A.*

American plan At a hotel, the system of paying for room, meals, and other services at a fixed, inclusive rate. Compare EUROPEAN PLAN.

American Revolution See under REVOLUTION.

American Samoa See SAMOA.

American Veterans Committee An organization of veterans of World War II. Abbr. *AVC, A.V.C.*

American Veterans of World War II, Korea, and Vietnam An organization of veterans: also called *Amvets.*

America's Cup A trophy, won in England in 1851 by the schooner-yacht *America* in a race with British yachts, which has since become the chief trophy of international yacht racing, the races being held by custom when a challenge is issued by certain British or Canadian yacht clubs.

am·er·ic·i·um (am′ə·rish′ē·əm) *n.* A transuranium element (symbol Am, atomic number 95) produced in nuclear reactors by neutron bombardment of plutonium, the most stable isotope having mass number 243 and a half-life of 7370 years. See PERIODIC TABLE. [< NL, after *America*]

A·me·ri·go (ä′mā·rē′gō) Italian form of EMERY.

Amerigo Vespucci See VESPUCCI.

Am·er·in·di·an (am′ə·rin′dē·ən) *adj.* Of or pertaining to the American Indians or the Eskimos, individually or collectively. Also **Am′er·in′dic.** —*n.* An American Indian or Eskimo. Also **Am·er·ind** (am′ə·rind). [< AMER(ICAN) + INDIAN]

Ames (āmz), **Winthrop,** 1871–1937, U.S. theater producer.

ames·ace (āmz′ās′) See AMBSACE.

am·e·thyst (am′ə·thist) *n.* A violet to purple gemstone consisting of either quartz or corundum. **2** A violet to purple color. —*adj.* Violet or purple. [< OF *ametiste* < L *amethystus* < Gk. *amethystos* not drunken < *a-* not + *methystos* drunken < *methy* wine; from the ancient belief that a wearer of the stone would be unaffected by wine]

am·e·thys·tine (am′ə·this′tin, -tīn) *adj.* Of the color of an amethyst; violet; purple.

am·e·tro·pi·a (am′ə·trō′pē·ə) *n.* Any condition of the eye in which errors of refraction prevent focusing of images on the retina. [< NL < Gk. *ametros* irregular + *ōps* eye] —**am·e·trop·ic** (am′ə·trop′ik) *adj.*

Am·for·tas (äm·fôr′täs) In Wagner's *Parsifal,* chief knight of the Holy Grail. See PARSIFAL.

Am·ha·ra (äm·hä′rä) A former province of Ethiopia; divided in 1942 into two northern provinces.

Am·har·ic (am·har′ik, äm·hä′rik) *n.* A Southwest Semitic language spoken officially in Ethiopia. —*adj.* Of or pertaining to the inhabitants of Amhara, or to their language.

Am·herst (am′ûrst), **Baron Jeffrey,** 1717–1797, English general in French and Indian War; appointed governor general of British North America.

a·mi (á·mē′) *n. pl.* **a·mis** (á·mē′) *French* A friend.

am·i·a (am′ē·ə) *n.* A ganoid fish belonging to the genus *Amia,* of which it is the sole representative; the bowfin (*A. calva*). [< NL < Gk. *amia* kind of tunny]

a·mi·a·bil·i·ty (ā′mē·ə·bil′ə·tē) *n.* Sweetness of disposition; lovableness. Also **a′mi·a·ble·ness.**

a·mi·a·ble (ā′mē·ə·bəl) *adj.* **1** Pleasing in disposition, kind-hearted. **2** Free from irritation; friendly: an *amiable* rivalry. [< OF < L *amicabilis* friendly < *amicus* friend. Doublet of AMICABLE.] —**a′mi·a·bly** *adv.*

Synonyms: agreeable, attractive, benignant, charming, engaging, gentle, good-natured, kind, lovable, lovely, loving, pleasant, pleasing, sweet, winning, winsome. *Amiable* combines the senses of *lovable* or *lovely* and *loving*; *amiable* is a higher and stronger word than *good-natured* or *agreeable*. *Lovely* is often applied to externals; as, a *lovely* face. *Amiable* denotes a disposition desirous to cheer, please, and make happy. A selfish man of the world may have the art to be *agreeable*; a handsome, brilliant, and witty person may be *charming* or even *attractive*, while by no means *amiable*. *Antonyms*: acrimonious, churlish, crabbed, cruel, crusty, disagreeable, dogged, gruff, hateful, ill-conditioned, ill-humored, ill-natured, ill-tempered, morose, sour, sullen, surly, unamiable.

am·i·an·thus (am'ē·an'thəs) *n.* 1 A fine, silky asbestos. Also **am·i·an·tus.** [< L *amianthus* < Gk. *amiantos* (*lithos*), lit., unsoiled (stone), a stone like asbestos]

am·i·ca·ble (am'i·kə·bəl) *adj.* Showing or promoting good will; friendly; peaceable. [< L *amicabilis* < *amicus* friend. Doublet of AMIABLE.] —**am·i·ca·bil·i·ty** (am'i·kə·bil'ə·tē), **am'i·ca·ble·ness** *n.* —**am'i·ca·bly** *adv.*

Synonyms: cordial, favorable, friendly, hearty, kind, neighborly, sociable. The Anglo-Saxon *friendly* is stronger than the Latin *amicable*; that which is *amicable* may be merely formal; that which is *friendly* is from the heart. *Antonyms*: adverse, antagonistic, hostile, unfriendly.

amicable number See under NUMBER.

am·ice[1] (am'is) *n.* An ecclesiastical vestment consisting of a rectangular piece of fine white linen upon which a small cross is embroidered. It is the first garment put around the shoulders by the priest in vesting for mass. [< OF *amit* < L *amictus* cloak]

am·ice[2] See ALMUCE.

a·mid (ə·mid') *prep.* 1 In the midst of; among: He continued working *amid* the clamor of the crowd. 2 Mingled with or surrounded by: villages *amid* the woodlands. Also **amidst.** [OE *amiddan*, for *on middan* in the middle]

Synonyms: amidst, among, amongst, between, betwixt. *Amid* or *amidst* denotes surrounded by; *among* or *amongst*, mingled with. *Between* is said of two persons or objects, or of two groups of persons or objects. *Amid* denotes mere position; *among*, some active relation, as of companionship, hostility, etc. We say *among* (never *amid*) friends, or *among* (sometimes *amid*) enemies. *Antonyms*: beyond, outside, without.

am·ide (am'īd, -id) *n.* Any of a group of organic compounds containing the radical CONH₂. [< AM(MONIA) + -IDE] —**a·mid·ic** (ə·mid'ik) *adj.*

am·i·din (am'ə·din) *n.* A transparent gelatinous solution of starch in hot water. [< F *amidon* starch]

a·mid·most (ə·mid'mōst') *adv.* In the very middle. —*prep.* In the center of.

amido- *combining form Chem.* Used to indicate a compound containing both the NH₂ radical and an acid radical. [< AMIDE]

a·mi·do·gen (ə·mē'də·jən, ə·mid'ə-) *n.* The univalent radical, NH₂, known from its existence in various organic compounds.

am·i·dol (am'ə·dol, -dōl) *n.* A white crystalline powder, C₆H₃(NH₂)₂OH·HCl, used chiefly as a photographic developer.

a·mi·do·py·rine (ə·mē'dō·pī'rēn, am'ə·dō·pī'rēn, -rin) See AMINOPYRINE.

a·mid·ships (ə·mid'ships) *adv. Naut.* Halfway between stem and stern of a ship.

a·midst (ə·midst') *prep.* Amid. [ME *amidde* + adverbial genitive suffix -*s* + inorganic *t*]

Am·i·ens (am'ē·ənz, *Fr.* à·myan') A city of northern France on the Somme. —**Treaty of Amiens** An agreement among England, Holland, France, and Spain (1802), marking a period of peace in the Napoleonic Wars.

a·mi·go (ə·mē'gō) *n. pl.* **·gos** A friend; comrade. [< Sp.]

am·ine (am'in, ə·mēn') *n.* Any of a class of organic compounds theoretically derived from

ammonia by replacement of one or more hydrogen atoms by organic radicals. [< AM(MONIA) + -INE] —**am·in'ic** *adj.*

-amine *combining form Chem.* Used to denote an amine: methylamine.

a·mi·no (ə·mē'nō, am'ə·nō) *adj.* Containing the NH₂ group attached to a nonacid radical. [< AMINE]

amino- *combining form* Indicating a compound containing the group NH₂ attached to a nonacid radical.

amino acid Any of a group of some 80 organic compounds which contain one or more basic amino and acid carboxyl groups and which in some cases polymerize to form peptides and proteins.

am·i·no·ben·zo·ic acid Any of three isomeric derivatives of benzoic acid having the formula C₇H₇O₂N. See PARAAMINOBENZOIC ACID.

a·mi·no·plast (ə·mē'nə·plast) *n.* Any of a class of synthetic resins made from amido or amino compounds, as urea-formaldehyde.

a·mi·no·py·rine (ə·mē'nō·pī'rēn, am'ə·nō·pī'rēn, -rin) *n.* A colorless synthetic drug, C₁₃H₁₇ON₃, used as an anodyne and antipyretic in colds, rheumatism, neuritis, etc.: also called amidopyrine.

a·mir (ə·mir') See AMEER.

Am·ish (am'ish, ä'mish) *adj.* Relating to or designating the adherents of Jacob Ammann, a 17th century Mennonite. —*n. pl.* A sect of Mennonites, founded by Jacob Ammann: also spelled Omish.

a·miss (ə·mis') *adj.* Out of order or relation; wrong; improper: used predicatively: Something is *amiss*. —*adv.* 1 Improperly. 2 Erroneously. 3 Defectively. —**to take amiss** To take offense at; feel resentment toward. [ME *amis* < *a-* at + *mis* miss²]

am·i·to·sis (am'ə·tō'sis) *n.* Cell division by simple fission of the nucleus and cytoplasm without the formation and splitting of chromosomes. [< NL < A·⁴ without + MITOSIS] —**am·i·tot·ic** (am'ə·tot'ik) *adj.* —**am'i·tot'i·cal·ly** *adv.*

am·i·ty (am'ə·tē) *n. pl.* **·ties** Peaceful relations; mutual good will; friendship. See synonyms under FRIENDSHIP, HARMONY. [< MF *amitié*, ult. < L *amicus* friend]

Am·man (äm'män) The capital of Jordan.

am·me·ter (am'mē'tər) *n. Electr.* An amperemeter, an instrument for measuring the amperage of an electric current. [< AM(PERE) + -METER]

am·mine (am'ēn) *n. Chem.* 1 The ammonia molecule NH₃ in combination. 2 Any of various complex compounds containing the ammonia molecule. [< AMM(ONIA) + -INE]

am·mo·cete (am'ə·sēt) *n.* The prolonged larval stage of the lamprey, represented by an eyeless, transparent, wormlike filter feeder living in muddy river bottoms. Also **ammocoete.** [< Gk. *ammos* sand + *koitē* bed]

Am·mon (am'ən) The Greek and the Roman name for the Egyptian god AMEN: also *Zeus-Ammon, Jupiter-Ammon.*

Am·mon (am'ən) *n. pl.* A people descended from Ben Ammi, the son of Lot: chiefly in the phrase **children of Ammon.** *Deut.* ii 19. Also **Am·mon·ites** (am'ən·īts).

am·mo·nal (am'ə·nal) *n.* An explosive mixture containing TNT, ammonium nitrate, and aluminum powder. [< AMMON(IUM) + AL(UMI-NUM)]

am·mo·nia (ə·mōn'yə, ə·mō'nē·ə) *n.* 1 A colorless, pungent gas, NH₃, readily soluble in water to form an alkaline solution, produced in the decomposition of many organic nitrogenous compounds. 2 Ammonium hydroxide. [< SAL AMMONIAC]

am·mo·ni·ac[1] (ə·mō'nē·ak) *adj.* Of, containing, or resembling ammonia. Also **am·mo·ni·a·cal** (am'ə·nī'ə·kal).

am·mo·ni·ac[2] (ə·mō'nē·ak) *n.* A gum resin obtained from an umbelliferous plant (*Dorema acconiacum*) of Asia. Also called *gum ammoniac*. [< F < L *ammoniacum* < Gk. *ammōniakon*, a resinous gum said to come from a plant growing near the temple of *Ammon* in Libya]

am·mo·ni·ate (ə·mō'nē·āt) *v.t.* **·at·ed, ·at·ing** To treat or combine with ammonia. —*n.* (ə·mō'nē·it) A compound containing ammonia. —**am·mo'ni·a'tion** *n.*

am·mon·i·fi·ca·tion (ə·mon'ə·fi·kā'shən) *n.* 1 The addition of ammonia or ammonium salts, as in the form of fertilizer added to the soil. 2

The stage in the nitrogen cycle in which nitrogenous compounds are decomposed to form ammonia by the action of bacteria, fungi, etc.

am·mon·i·fy (ə·mon'ə·fī) *v.t. & v.i.* **·fied, ·fy·ing** To bring about or undergo ammonification.

am·mon·ite[1] (am'ən·īt) *n.* Any of various flat spiral shells of an extinct order (Ammonoidea) of cephalopods that flourished in the Mesozoic era. Also **am'mon·oid.** [< L *cornu Ammonis* horn of Ammon]

AMMONITE (European)

am·mon·ite[2] (am'ən·īt) *n.* 1 A fertilizer composed of animal wastes. 2 An explosive containing ammonium nitrate as the principal component. [< AMMON(IA) + -ITE¹]

Am·mon·ite (am'ən·īt) *n.* One of the people of Ammon.

am·mo·ni·um (ə·mō'nē·əm) *n. Chem.* The univalent radical NH₄, which in compounds formed from ammonia acts as an alkali metal. [< NL < AMMONIA]

ammonium chloride A white, crystalline salt, NH₄Cl, used as a flux in soldering and galvanizing and as an electrolyte in dry cells. Also called *sal ammoniac*.

ammonium hydroxide A compound, NH₄OH, formed in ordinary aqueous or caustic ammonia.

ammonium nitrate A colorless, crystalline, soluble salt, NH₄NO₃, used as an ingredient of explosives and in freezing mixtures.

ammonium sulfate A commercial salt, (NH₄)₂SO₄, manufactured from the ammoniac liquor produced in the manufacture of gas. It is used as a nitrogenous fertilizer.

am·mu·ni·tion (am'yə·nish'ən) *n.* 1 *Mil.* Any one of various articles used in the discharge of firearms and ordnance, as cartridges, shells, shot, rockets, primers, fuses, grenades, and chemicals. 2 Any resources for attack or defense. —*v.t.* To supply with ammunition. [< MF *amunition*, for *munition* (la munition taken as *l'amunition*) < L *munitio, -onis* < *munire* fortify]

am·ne·sia (am·nē'zhə, -zhē·ə) *n.* Loss or impairment of memory; morbid forgetfulness. [< NL < Gk. *amnēsia* forgetfulness < *a-* not + *mnasthai* remember] —**am·ne·sic** (am·nē'sik, -zik) *adj.*

am·ne·si·ac (am·nē'zhē·ak, -zē-) *n.* One suffering from amnesia. —*adj.* Pertaining to or causing loss of memory.

am·nes·tic (am·nes'tik) *n.* Any agent that produces amnesia. —*adj.* Amnesiac.

am·nes·ty (am'nəs·tē) *n. pl.* **·ties** 1 An official act of oblivion or pardon on the part of a government, absolving without trial all offenders or groups of offenders. 2 Intentional forgetfulness or overlooking, especially of wrongdoing. —*v.t.* **·tied, ·ty·ing** To pardon; grant amnesty to. [< F *amnestie* < L *amnestia* < Gk. *amnēstia* < *a-* not + *mnasthai* remember]

am·ni·o·cen·te·sis (am'nē·ō·sen·tē'sis) *n.* The sampling of amniotic fluid of a pregnant woman, as to detect chromosomal anomalies or to determine the sex of the fetus. [< AMNION + Gk. *kentein* to prick]

am·ni·on (am'nē·ən) *n. pl.* **·ni·ons** or **·ni·a** (-nē·ə) A tough, membranous, fluid-containing sac enclosing the embryo of birds, reptiles, and mammals. [< Gk. *amnion* the fetal envelope, dim. of *amnos* lamb] —**am·ni·on·ic** (am'nē·on'ik), **am·ni·ot·ic** (am'nē·ot'ik) *adj.*

am·ni·ote (am'nē·ōt) *n.* Any member of the three classes of animals (Reptilia, Aves, and Mammalia) in which the embryo is protected by an amnion. —*adj.* Of or pertaining to amniotes.

am·o·bar·bi·tal (am'ō·bär'bə·tôl) *n.* A bitter crystalline barbiturate, C₁₁H₁₈N₂O₃, used as a sedative and hypnotic.

am·o·di·a·quin (am'ō·dī'ə·kwin) *n.* A synthetic drug, C₂₀H₂₂ClN₃O, used chiefly to treat malaria.

a·mock, a·mok (ə·muk', ə·mok'), **a·moke** (ə·mōk'), etc. See AMUCK.

a·moe·ba (ə·mē'bə), **a·moe·bic** (ə·mē'bik), **a·moe·boid** (ə·mē'boid), etc. See AMEBA, etc.

am·oe·bae·an, am·oe·be·an (am'ə·bē'ən) See AMEBEAN.

a·mo·le (ə·mō'lā) *n.* 1 The roots or parts of certain plants, employed in Mexico and the

SW United States as a substitute for soap. **2** Any plant that produces such roots, as the century plant and the soap plant. [<Am. Sp. <Nahuatl]

A·mon (ä′mən) See AMEN.

among (ə·mung′) *prep.* **1** In the midst of: a house *among* the trees. **2** Mingled with; included within a mass or multitude: He was just one *among* hundreds. **3** In the class, group, number, or company of: one example *among* many. **4** In association with; connected with: Some truth may be found *among* many errors. **5** Shared by; affecting all of: money divided *among* the poor. **6** According to the customs of; in the country or time of: usage *among* educated people; a practice *among* the French. Also **amongst**. See synonyms under AMID, BETWEEN. [OE *on gemong* in the crowd]

a·mon·til·la·do (ə·mon′tə·lä′dō, *Sp.* ä·môn′tē·lyä′thō) *n.* A pale, dry kind of sherry. [<Sp., from *Montilla*, a town in southern Spain]

a·mor·al (ā·môr′əl, ā·mor′əl) *adj.* **1** Not subject to or concerned with moral or ethical judgment or distinctions. **2** Lacking a sense of right or wrong; lacking moral responsibility. [<A-[4] not + MORAL] **—a·mo·ral·i·ty** (ā′mə·ral′ə·tē) *n.*—**a·mor′al·ly** *adv.*

am·o·ret·to (am′ə·ret′ō) *n. pl.* **·ret·ti** (-ret′ē) A cupid. [<Ital., dim of *amore* love <L *amor*]

a·mo·ri·no (ä′mō·rē′nō) *n.* **·ni** (-nē) An amoretto.

am·o·rist (am′ə·rist) *n.* **1** A lover; one given to amours. **2** One who writes about romantic love. **—am′o·ris′tic** *adj.*

Am·o·rites (am′ə·rīts) One of the chief nations in the land of Canaan before its conquest by the Israelites. *Gen.* xv 16.

a·mo·ro·so (ä′mō·rō′sō) *adj. Music* Tender. —*adv. Music* Tenderly. —*n. pl.* **·si** (-sē) A gallant; lover. [<Ital., amorous]

am·o·rous (am′ə·rəs) *adj.* **1** Having a propensity for falling in love; influenced by sexual affection or appetite; loving; ardent in affection. **2** Of or pertaining to love; showing, springing from, or exciting to love or sexual desire. **3** In love; enamored: usually with *of.* [<OF <LL *amorosus* <L *amor* love] **—am′orous·ly** *adv.* **—am′o·rous·ness** *n.*

a·mor pa·tri·ae (ā′môr pā′tri·ē) *Latin* Love of native country; patriotism.

a·mor·phism (ə·môr′fiz·əm) *n.* The state or quality of being amorphous.

a·mor·phous (ə·môr′fəs) *adj.* **1** Without definite form or shape; structureless. **2** *Geol.* Found or occurring in masses lacking definite stratification. **3** Anomalous; unorganized. **4** Having no apparent fine structure; not crystalline. [<Gk. *amorphos* <*a-* without + *morphē* form] **—a·mor′phous·ly** *adv.* **—a·mor′phous·ness** *n.*

a·mort (ə·môrt′) *adj. & adv. Archaic* Without life or animation; dejected, as if dead.

am·or·ti·za·tion (am′ər·tə·zā′shən, ə·môr′tə·zā′shən) *n.* **1** An amortizing or being amortized. **2** The sum of money set aside or devoted to amortizing a debt.

am·or·tize (am′ər·tīz, ə·môr′tīz) *v.t.* **·tized, ·tiz·ing** **1** To extinguish, as a debt or liability, by payments to a sinking fund or creditor. **2** *Law* To sell and convey, as land, to a corporation having perpetual succession; alienate in mortmain. Also *Brit.* **am′or·tise**. [<OF *amortiss-*, stem of *amortir* extinguish, sell in mortmain <L *ad-* to + *mors, mortis* death] **—am·or·tiz·a·ble** (am′ər·tīz′ə·bəl, a·môr′tiz·ə·bəl) *adj.*

a·mor·tize·ment (ə·môr′tiz·mənt) *n.* **1** Amortization. **2** *Archaic* The finishing portion at the top of any part of a structure.

A·mos (ā′məs) A masculine personal name. [<Hebrew, ? borne by God]

—Amos A minor prophet, eighth century B.C., or the Old Testament book bearing his name.

a·mo·tion (ə·mō′shən) *n. Archaic.* A removal, as from office; deprivation of ownership. [<L *amotio, -onis* <*amotus*, pp. of *amovere.* See AMOVE.]

a·mount (ə·mount′) *n.* **1** A sum total; aggregate. **2** The value of the principal with the interest upon it, as in a loan. **3** The entire significance, value, or effect. **4** Quantity: a considerable *amount* of discussion. See synonyms under AGGREGATE. [<*v.*] —*v.i.* **1** To rise in number of quantity so as to reach: with *to*: This bill *amounts* to ten dollars. **2** To be equivalent in effect or importance: He doesn't *amount* to a row of beans. [<OF *amonter* <*amont* upward <*a mont* to the mountain <L *ad* to + *mons, montis* mountain]

a·mour (ə·mŏŏr′) *n.* A love affair; intrigue. [<F]

a·mour-pro·pre (á·mōōr′prô′pr′) *n. French* Self-love; self-esteem.

a·move (ə·mōōv′) *v.t.* **a·moved, a·mov·ing** *Law* To remove from a position or office. [<L *amovere* remove <*ab-* from + *movere* move]

A·moy (ə·moi′) **1** An island in Formosa Strait, Fukien Province, SE China. **2** A leading port and industrial center on Amoy island. Formerly *Szeming.*

amp (amp) *n. Colloq.* **1** Ampere. **2** An electrically amplified guitar.

AMP Symbol for adenosine monophosphate.

am·pe·lid·e·ous (am′pə·lid′ē·əs) *adj.* Of or relating to the vine family. [<NL *Ampelideae* the vine family <Gk. *ampelos* vine]

am·pe·lop·sis (am′pə·lop′sis) *n.* **1** Any member of a genus *(Ampelopsis)* of woody vines with small greenish flowers and alternate simple or compound leaves. [<NL <Gk. *ampelos* vine + *opsis* appearance]

am·per·age (am·pir′ij, am′pər·ij) *n.* The strength of an electric current in amperes.

am·pere (am′pir, am·pir′) *n. Electr.* The practical unit of electric-current strength; such a current as would be given with an electromotive force of one volt through a wire having a resistance of one ohm. **—international ampere** The current which on passing through a silver-nitrate solution will deposit silver at the rate of 0.001118 gram a second. [after A. M. *Ampère*]

Am·père (äṅ·pâr′), **André Marie,** 1775–1836, French physicist.

am·pere-hour (am′pir·our′) *n. Electr.* A quantity of electricity sufficient to furnish a current of an ampere for an hour.

am·pere-me·ter (am′pir·mē′tər) *n.* An ammeter. Also **am·pe·rom·e·ter** (am′pə·rom′ə·tər).

am·pere-turn (am′pir·tûrn′) *n. Electr.* An ampere flowing through one turn of a coil, considered with reference to electromagnetic effect. An electromagnet with 1,000 convolutions and a current of 5 amperes would have 5,000 ampere-turns.

am·per·sand (am′pər·sand, am′pər·sand′) *n.* The character (& or &) meaning *and.* [<*and per se and*, lit., & by itself = and]

am·phet·a·mine (am·fet′ə·mēn, -min) *n.*— **1** A colorless liquid, $C_9H_{13}N$, used as a stimulant of the central nervous system. **2** any of the various crystalline compounds of amphetamine used as drugs. [<*a(lpha)-m(ethyl)-ph(enyl)-et(hyl)-amine*]

amphi- *prefix* **1** On both or all sides; at both ends: *amphicoelous.* **2** Around: *amphigean.* **3** Of both kinds; in two ways: *amphibious.* [<Gk. <*amphi* around]

Am·phi·a·ra·us (am′fē·ə·rā′əs) See under SEVEN AGAINST THEBES.

am·phi·ar·thro·sis (am′fē·är·thrō′sis) *n. pl.* **·ses** (-sēz) *Anat.* An articulation in which bones are connected by intervening fibrocartilage permitting limited movement, as between adjacent vertebrae.

am·phi·as·ter (am′fē·as′tər) *n.* **1** *Biol.* That stage of cell division in which the chromatin filaments assume a radiate appearance at each end of the nuclear spindle; also, the figure so formed. **2** *Zool.* A spicule with two whorls of spines connected by a vertical axis, as in certain sponges. [<NL <AMPHI- + Gk. *astēr* star]

am·phib·i·an (am·fib′ē·n) *n. pl.* **·bi·ans** or **·bi·a** (def. 1) **1** Any of a class *(Amphibia)* of cold-blooded vertebrate organisms with smooth, moist skin, whose life cycle typically comprises tadpoles which hatch from eggs as aquatic, gilled, limbless forms and which metamorphose into terrestrial air-breathing adults with four limbs, as frogs, toads, newts, salamanders, etc. **2** Any amphibious organism. **3** An airplane constructed to rise from and alight on either land or water. **4** A craft capable of self-propulsion upon land and upon water. —*adj.* Amphibious.

am·phib·i·ol·o·gy (am·fib′ē·ol′ə·jē) *n. pl.* **·gies** **1** The scientific study of amphibians. **2** A treatise relating to this subject.

am·phib·i·ot·ic (am·fib′ē·ot′ik, am′fə·bī·ot′ik) *adj.* Having a life cycle with successive aquatic and terrestrial cycles.

am·phib·i·ous (am·fib′ē·əs) *adj.* **1** Living or adapted to life on land or in water. **2** Capable of operating on land or water: an *amphibious* tank. **3** Capable of operating on water and in the air: an *amphibious* airplane. **4** Of a mixed nature; connected with two ranks, classes, etc. [<Gk. *amphibios* having a double life <*amphi-* of two kinds + *bios* life] **—am·phib′i·ous·ly** *adv.* **—am·phib′i·ous·ness** *n.*

am·phi·blas·tu·la (am′fə·blas′chōō·lə) *n. Biol.* A blastula wherein the cells of one hemisphere differ from those of the other hemisphere, as in certain sponges.

am·phi·bole (am′fə·bōl) *n. Mineral.* Any of a class of variously colored hydrous silicates, consisting chiefly of calcium, magnesium, iron, aluminum, and sodium; tremolite, actinolite, asbestos, and hornblende are important varieties. [<F <L *amphibolus* ambiguous <Gk. *amphibolos* <*amphiballein* to throw around, to doubt <*amphi-* around + *ballein* throw]

am·phi·bol·ic (am′fə·bol′ik) *adj.* Pertaining to or like amphiboly; ambiguous. Also **am·phib·o·lous** (am·fib′ə·ləs).

am·phib·o·lite (am·fib′ə·līt) *n.* A rock consisting chiefly of amphibole and plagioclase, often with inclusions of garnet and quartz.

am·phi·bol·o·gy (am′fə·bol′ə·jē) *n. pl.* **·gies** An ambiguous phrase or sentence; ambiguity. [<F *amphibologie* <LL *amphibologia*, for L *amphibolia* <Gk. *amphibolia* ambiguity <*amphiballein.* See AMPHIBOLE.] **—am·phib·o·log·i·cal** (am·fib′ə·loj′i·kəl) *adj.*

am·phib·o·ly (am·fib′ə·lē) *n. pl.* **·lies** An ambiguous construction of language; a group of words admitting of two meanings. [<L *amphibolia.* See AMPHIBOLOGY.]

am·phi·brach (am′fə·brak) *n.* In prosody, a metrical foot, consisting of a long or accented syllable between two short or unaccented ones (˘ ¯ ˘). [<L *amphibrachys* <Gk. <*amphi-* at both ends + *brachys* short]

am·phi·car·pous (am′fə·kär′pəs) *adj. Bot.* Having fruit of two kinds, either in form or in period of ripening. Also **am′phi·car′pic**. [<AMPHI- + Gk. *karpos* fruit]

am·phi·chro·ic (am′fə·krō′ik) *adj.* Exhibiting either of two colors, as certain substances when subjected to tests with acids or alkalis. Also **am·phi·chro·mat·ic** (am′fə·krō·mat′ik). [<AMPHI- + Gk. *chroa* color]

am·phi·coe·lous (am′fə·sē′ləs) *adj. Zool.* Concave at both ends; biconcave, as the vertebrae of fishes and of certain extinct reptiles and birds. [<AMPHI- + Gk. *koilos* hollow]

am·phic·ty·on (am·fik′tē·ən) *n.* **1** A delegate to one of the ancient Greek amphictyonic councils. **2** The council as a body. [<L *amphictyones* <Gk. *amphiktyones* neighbors]

am·phic·ty·on·ic (am·fik′tē·on′ik) *adj.* Of or pertaining to an amphictyony.

am·phic·ty·o·ny (am·fik′tē·ə·nē) *n. pl.* **·nies** A league of ancient Greek states, allied in the worship of a common deity, as around a religious center or shrine, such as Delphi.

am·phi·cyr·tic (am′fə·sûr′tik) *adj.* Convex at both ends; biconvex. [<AMPHI- + Gk. *kyrtos* convex]

am·phi·dip·loid (am′fə·dip′loid) *n. Genetics* An interspecific hybrid having two diploid sets of chromosomes, one from each parent.—**am·phi·dip·loid·al** (am′f·dip′loi·dl) *adj.* **—am′phi·dip′loi·dy** *n.*

am·phi·ge·an (am′fə·jē′ən) *adj. Bot.* Extending around the globe in nearly the same latitude, as certain species of plants. [<AMPHI- + Gk. *gē* earth]

am·phi·gas·tri·um (am′fə·gas′trē·əm) *n. pl.* **·tri·a** (-tre·) A small, rudimentary leaf on the under surface of the stem of certain liverworts. [<AMPHI- + Gk. *gastēr* belly]

am·phi·gen·e·sis (am′fə·jen′ə·sis) *n.* **1** *Biol.* The merging of two gametes to form a fertilized cell or \zygote. **2** *Psychol.* Sexual response of a predominantly homosexual person

in regard to members of the opposite sex. **—am·phi·gen·ic** (am′fə·jen′ik) *adj.*

am·phig·e·nous (am·fij′ə·nəs) *adj. Bot.* Growing all around an object, as certain parasitic fungi; capable of developing in any direction permitted by the environment.

am·phi·go·ry (am′fə·gôr′ē, -gō′rē) *n. pl.* **·ries** A meaningless rigmarole with a semblance of sense; a burlesque, as one written in nonsensical verse. Also **am·phi·gou·ri** (am′fə·gōō′·rē) *pl.* **·ris** (-rēz). [< F *amphigouri;* ult. origin unknown] **—am·phi·gor·ic** (am′fə·gôr′ik, -gor′-) *adj.*

am·phil·o·gism (am·fil′ə·jiz′əm) *n. Obs.* A circumlocution. [< Gk. *amphilogos* < *amphi-* around + *logos* word]

am·phim·a·cer (am·fim′ə·sər) In prosody, a metrical foot consisting of one short or unaccented syllable between two long or accented ones (- ⏑ -): opposed to *amphibrach.* Also called *cretic.* [< L *amphimacrus* < Gk. *amphimakros* < *amphi-* on both sides + *makros* long]

am·phi·mix·is (am′fə·mik′sis) *n. Biol. The fusion of ovum and sperm in sexual reproduction. [< NL* AMPHI- + Gk. *mixis* a mingling] **—am·phi·mic·tic** (am′fə·mik′tik) *adj.* **—am′phi·mic′ti·cal·ly** *adv.*

am·phi·neur·an (am′fə·no-or′ən, -nyo-or′-) *n.* Any of a class of marine mollusks having bilateral symmetry and calcareous spicules that lie embedded in the cuticle, as the chitons.

Am·phi·on (am·fī′ən) In Greek mythology, a son of Jupiter and Antiope and husband of Niobe, who with his twin brother Zethus walled Thebes by the music of a magical lyre given him by Hermes.

am·phi·ox·us (am′fē·ok′səs) *n.* The lancelet. [< AMPHI- + Gk. *oxys* sharp]

am·phi·pod (am′fə·pod) *n.* Any of an order of small crustaceans *(Amphipoda)* having legs adapted to swimming and others adapted to walking and jumping, as the sand fleas. *—adj.* Of or pertaining to the amphipods. [< AMPHI- + Gk. *pous, podos* foot] **—am·phip·o·dan, am·phip′o·dous** *adj.*

am·phip·ro·style (am·fip′rə·stīl, am′fə·prō′stīl) *n.* A temple or other building of the classical period having at each end a columned portico but with no columns at the sides. *—adj.* Built like such a building: also **am·phip·ro·sty·lar** (am·fip′rə·stī′lər, am′fə·prō·stī′-). [< L *amphiprostylus* < Gk. *amphiprostylos* < *amphi-* on both sides + *prostylos* PROSTYLE]

am·phis·bae·na (am′fis·bē′nə) *n.* **1** A mythical serpent having a head at each end of the body and moving in either direction. **2** *Zool.* A tropical, legless lizard (family *Amphisbaenidae*) having head and tail much alike. [< L < Gk. *amphisbaina* < *amphis, amphi-* at both ends + *bainein* go] **—am′phis·bae′nic** *adj.*

am·phis·cians (am·fish′ənz) *n. pl. Archaic* The inhabitants of the torrid zone, whose shadows fall at one season to the north, at the other to the south. Also **am·phis·ci·i** (am·fish′ē·ī). [< Med.L *amphiscii* < Gk. *amphiskios* throwing a shadow both ways < *amphi-* on both sides + *skia* shadow]

am·phi·sty·lar (am′fə·stī′lər) *adj. Archit.* With columns at each end or on each side. [< AMPHI- + Gk. *stylos* pillar]

am·phi·the·a·ter (am′fə·thē′ə·tər) *n.* **1** An edifice of elliptical shape, constructed about a central open space or arena, with tiers of seats sloping upward. **2** Any structure of similar shape, as a natural area or theater having slopes or tiers of seats entirely surrounding a central space. **3** The place where a spectacle or battle takes place; scene of action. Also **am′phi·the′a·tre.** [< L *amphitheatrum* < Gk. *amphitheatron* < *amphi-* around + *theatron* theater]

am·phi·the·at·ri·cal (am′fə·thē·at′ri·kəl) *adj.* Of, pertaining to, resembling, or performed in an amphitheater. Also **am·phi·the·a·tral** (am′fə·thē′ə·trəl), **am·phi·the·at·ric** (am′fə·thē·at′rik). **—am′phi·the·at′ri·cal·ly** *adv.*

am·phi·the·ci·um (am′fə·thē′shē·əm, -sē·əm) *n. pl.* **·ci·a** (-shē·ə, -sē·ə) *Bot.* The outer layer of cells surrounding the endothecium in the spore case of mosses. [< NL < AMPHI- + Gk. *thēkion,* dim. of *thēkē* a case, container]

am·phit·ri·chous (am·fit′rə·kəs) *adj.* Having flagella at both ends, as certain bacteria. [< AMPHI- + Gk. *thrix, trichos* hair]

Am·phi·tri·te (am′fə·trī′tē) In Greek mythology, one of the Nereids, who became wife of Poseidon and goddess of the sea.

am·phit·ro·pous (am·fit′rə·pəs) *adj. Bot.* Half inverted with the hilum lateral: said of an ovule or seed. [< AMPHI- + -TROPOUS]

Am·phit·ry·on (am·fit′rē·ən) In Greek mythology, the husband of Alcmene.

am·phi·u·ma (am′fē·yōō′mə) *n. Zool.* Any of a genus *(Amphiuma)* of salamanders typical of the congo-snake family *(Amphiumidae).* [< NL < AMPHI- + Gk. *pneuma* breath]

am·pho·ra (am′fə·rə) *n. pl.* **·rae** (-rē) In ancient Greece, a tall, two-handled earthenware jar for wine or oil, narrow at the neck and the base. [< L < Gk. *amphoreus* < *amphi-* on both sides + *phoreus* bearer < *pherein* bear] **— am′pho·ral** *adj.*

AMPHORAE

am·phor·ic (am·fôr′ik, -for′-) *adj.* **1** Having a sound like that made by blowing into the mouth of an amphora. **2** Amphoral.

am·pho·ter·ic (am′fə·ter′ik) *adj.* Capable of reacting chemically as either an acid or a base. [< Gk. *amphoteros* both]

am·pho·ter·i·cin (am′fə·ter′ə·sin) *n.* An antibiotic produced by a soil actinomycete *(Streptomyces nodosus)* and having a component, amphotericin B, that is effective as a systemic fungicide.

am·pi·cil·lin (am′pə·sil′ən) *n.* A kind of penicillin that is especially effective against Gram-negative bacteria

am·ple (am′pəl) *adj.* **1** Of great dimensions or capacity; large; great in amount of degree. **2** More than enough; abundant; liberal. **3** Fully sufficient to meet all needs or requirements; adequate. [< F < L *amplus* large, abundant] **—am′ple·ness** *n.*

Synonyms: abundant, affluent, bountiful, complete, copious, enough, full, large, liberal, plenteous, plentiful, sufficient. That is *enough* which just meets a given demand; that is *ample* which gives a safe, but not a large, margin beyond; that is *abundant, affluent, bountiful, liberal, plentiful,* which is largely in excess of manifest need. Compare ENOUGH, LARGE, PLENTIFUL. *Antonyms*: deficient, inadequate, insufficient, niggardly, scant, small, stingy.

am·plex·i·caul (am·plek′si·kôl) *adj. Bot.* Clasping a stem, as the base of some leaves. [< NL *amplexicaulis* < L *amplexus* embracing + *caulis* stem]

am·pli·a·tive (am′plē·ā′tiv) *adj.* Supplementing, or adding to.

am·pli·fi·ca·tion (am′plə·fi·kā′shən) *n.* **1** An amplifying or being amplified; augmentation; addition. **2** An extended statement; the matter added to amplify a subject; details. **3** *Electr.* An increase in the voltage or power of an electric current. See synonyms under INCREASE.

am·pli·fi·er (am′plə·fī′ər) *n.* **1** One who or that which amplifies or increases. **2** A megaphonelike device for increasing the volume of sound. **3** *Electr.* A device for increasing the intensity of electric impulses by the control of power supplied by a local source, usually by means of vacuum tubes or dynamos. **4** A loudspeaker.

am·pli·fy (am′plə·fī) *v.* **·fied, ·fy·ing** *v.t.* **1** To enlarge or increase in scope, significance, or power. **2** To add to so as to make more complete, as by illustrations. **3** To exaggerate; magnify. **4** *Electr.* To increase the strength or amplitude of, as electromagnetic impulses. *—v.i.* **5** To make additional remarks; expatiate. [< F *amplifier* < L *amplificare* < *amplus* large + *facere* make] **—am·pli·fi·ca·tive** (am′plə·fi·kā′tiv, am·plif′i·kə·tiv), **am·plif·i·ca·to·ry** (am·plif′i·kə·tôr′ē, -tō′rē) *adj.*

Synonyms: augment, develop, dilate, enlarge, expand, expatiate, extend, increase, unfold, widen. *Amplify* is now chiefly applied to discourse or writing, signifying to make fuller in statement, as by stating fully what was before only implied, or by adding illustrations to make the meaning more readily apprehended, etc. We may *develop* a thought, *expand* an illustration, *extend* a discussion, *expatiate* on a hobby, *dilate* on some theme or incident, *enlarge* a volume, *unfold* a scheme, *widen* the range of treatment. Compare ADD. *Antonyms*: abbreviate, abridge, amputate, compress, condense, curtail, delete, epitomize, reduce, retrench, shorten, summarize, contract, tighten.

am·pli·tude (am′plə·tōōd, -tyōōd) *n.* **1** Greatness of extent; largeness; breadth; the state or quality of being ample: the *amplitude* of the oceans. **2** Fullness or completeness; abundance or richness: the *amplitude* of life. **3** Broad range or scope, as of mental capacity: an *amplitude* of talent. **4** *Astron.* The arc of the horizon between true east and west and the center of the sun, moon, or any star at its rising or setting. **5** *Physics* The extent of the swing of a vibrating body on each side of the mean position. **6** *Electr.* The peak value attained by an alternating current during one complete cycle. [< L *amplitudo* < *amplus* large]

amplitude modulation That form of radio transmission in which the carrier wave is modulated by varying the amplitude above and below a standard value in accordance with the signals to be transmitted. Compare FREQUENCY MODULATION.

am·ply (am′plē) *adv.* In an ample manner; largely; liberally; sufficiently.

am·poule (am·pōōl) *n. Med.* A small, hermetically sealed vial, usually made of glass, containing a medicament for injection or other use. Also **am·pule** (am′pyōōl), **am·pul** (am′pul). [< F < L *ampulla* ampulla (def. 3)]

am·pul·la (am·pul′ə) *n. pl.* **am·pul·lae** (-pul′ē) **1** *Eccl.* A flask for holding the consecrated oil used in confirmation, ordination, and extreme unction; specifically, that used in England at the consecration of kings. **2** The cruet used for the wine or water at mass. **3** An ancient Roman bottle or vase with a slender neck and flattened mouth, used to hold perfumes and oils and for carrying wine. **4** *Anat.* A small sac or dilated segment of a tube or gland. [< L, dim. of *amphora* jar] **—am·pul′lar** *adj.*

am·pul·la·ceous (am′pə·lā′shəs) *adj.* Of, pertaining to, or like an ampulla; bladder-shaped; inflated.

am·pu·tate (am′pyōō·tāt) *v.t.* **·tat·ed, ·tat·ing** **1** *Surg.* To remove by cutting, as a limb; cut off the whole or a part of. **2** To reduce; prune: to *amputate* funds for a project. [< L *amputatus,* pp. of *amputare* < *ambi-* around + *putare* trim, prune] **—am′·pu·ta′tion** *n.* **—am′pu·ta′tor** *n.*

am·pu·tee (am′pyōō·tē′) *n.* One who has had a limb or limbs removed by amputation.

am·ri·ta (um·rē′tə) *n.* In Hindu mythology: **1** The ambrosia of immortality, sometimes represented as the fruit of a tree or the cream of the ocean churned by the gods. **2** Immortality. Also **am·ree′ta.** [< Skt. *amṛta*]

Am·rit·sar (um·rit′sər) A city in western Punjab, India.

Am·ster·dam (am′stər·dam) A port on the Zuider Zee; constitutional capital and largest city of the Netherlands.

amt (ämt) *n.* An administrative territorial division of Denmark or Norway. [< G]

Am·trak (am′trak) *n.* A government-controlled public corporation, officially known as the National Railroad Passenger Corporation, created in 1970 to run the essential passenger service linking major U.S. cities which private enterprise is unable to provide.

a·muck (ə·muk′) *adj.* Possessed with murderous frenzy. *—adv.* In a violent or frenzied manner. **—to run amuck** To run about attacking everybody one meets. Also spelled *amock, amok, amoke.* [< Malay *amoq* engaging furiously in battle]

A·mu Dar·ya (ä·mōō′ där′yä) A principal river of central Asia, flowing 872 miles to the Aral Sea from the U.S.S.R.-Afghanistan border: ancient *Oxus:* Arabic *Jaihun.*

am·u·let (am′yə·lit) *n.* Anything worn about one's person to protect from witchcraft, accident, or ill luck; a charm. See synonyms under TALISMAN. [< L *amuletum* charm]

A·mund·sen (ä′mōōn·sən), **Ro·ald** (rō′äl), 1872–1928, Norwegian explorer; discovered South Pole, 1911.

A·mur (ä·mōōr′) A river in eastern Asia, flowing 1,767 miles to the Gulf of Sákhalin and forming the boundary between Manchuria and the U.S.S.R.

a·muse (ə·myōōz′) *v.t.* **a·mused, a·mus·ing** **1** To occupy pleasingly; entertain; divert: to *amuse* oneself by playing the guitar. **2** To cause to laugh or smile, as with pleasure. **3** *Archaic* To beguile; delude. [< F *amuser*

<*à* at (<L *ad-*) + OF *muser* stare] **—a·mus′a·ble** *adj.* **—a·mus′er** *n.*

a·muse·ment (ə·myōōz′mənt) *n.* **1** The state of being amused; the feeling of delight or joy, as in some diversion. **2** That which amuses, as an entertainment, game, or spectacle. See synonyms under COMFORT, ENTERTAINMENT, FROLIC, SPORT.

a·mus·ing (ə·myōō′zing) *adj.* **1** Entertaining or diverting. **2** Arousing laughter.

a·mu·sive (ə·myōō′ziv, -siv) *adj.* Having power to amuse; amusing.

Am·vets (am′vets′) American Veterans of World War II, Korea, and Vietnam.

A·my (ā′mē) A feminine personal name. [<L, beloved]

a·myg·da·la (ə·mig′də·lə) *n. pl.* **·lae** (-lē) **1** An almond. **2** An almond-shaped mass of gray matter in the anterior part of the temporal lobe of the brain. [<L <Gk. *amygdalē* almond]

a·myg·da·la·ceous (ə·mig′də·lā′shəs) *adj.* Allied to the almond.

a·myg·da·late (ə·mig′də·lit, -lāt) *adj.* Pertaining to or like almonds.

a·myg·dale (ə·mig′dāl) *n. Geol.* An almond-shaped cavity formed by expanding steam in volcanic and intrusive rocks, filled with mineral secretions which are often of commercial importance and of value in the determination of geologic time. [<Gk. *amygdalē* almond]

a·myg·dal·ic (am′ig·dal′ik) Of or pertaining to almonds.

a·myg·da·lin (ə·mig′də·lin) *n.* A white crystalline compound, $C_{20}H_{27}O_{11}N$, obtained from the kernel of bitter almonds and related plants and yielding on hydrolysis glucose, benzaldehyde, and hydrocyanic acid.

a·myg·da·line (ə·mig′də·lin, -līn) *adj.* Pertaining to or like almonds.

a·myg·da·loid (ə·mig′də·loid) *adj.* **1** Almond-shaped. **2** Pertaining to or of an amygdala. **3** *Geol.* Containing amygdales or resembling an amygdaloid rock. Also **a·myg′da·loi′dal.** *—n.* An igneous rock, usually basaltic, containing amygdales.

a·myg·dule (ə·mig′dyōōl) *n. Geol.* One of the mineral cavities in an amygdale.

am·yl (am′il) *n.* A univalent hydrocarbon radical, C_5H_{11}, having eight isomeric forms and entering into many organic compounds. Also called *pentyl.* [<Gk. *amylon* starch + -YL]

am·y·la·ceous (am′ə·lā′shəs) *adj.* Pertaining to or like starch; starchy.

amyl acetate A colorless, sweet-smelling, oily compound, $C_7H_{14}O_2$, used as a solvent and in flavors and perfumes. Also called *banana oil.*

amyl alcohol 1 A colorless liquid, $C_5H_{11}OH$, consisting of any one or a combination of any of eight isomeric alcohols.

am·y·lase (am′ə·lās) *n.* Any of several enzymes occurring in plants and animals which promote the conversion of starch and glycogen to sugar. [<AMYL + -ASE]

am·y·lene (am′ə·lēn) *n.* **1** A colorless volatile liquid, consisting of several olefins, obtained by distilling amyl alcohol with zinc chloride, and used as an anesthetic. **2** Any of the isomeric hydrocarbons, C_5H_{10}, belonging to the ethylene series. [<AMYL + -ENE]

a·myl·ic (ə·mil′ik) *adj.* Of, pertaining to, or derived from amyl.

amyl nitrite A volatile yellow liquid, $C_5H_{11}NO_2$, having a fruity odor, used by inhalation to relieve arterial spasms, as in angina pectoris.

amylo- *combining form* **1** Of starch: *amyloplast.* **2** Of amyl. Also, before vowels, **amyl-.** [def. 1 <AMYLUM; def. 2 <AMYL]

am·y·lo·dex·trin (am′ə·lō·dek′strən) *n.* A white, odorless powder formed by hydrolysis of starch, becoming reddish-brown in iodine solutions.

a·myl·o·gen (ə·mil′ə·jən) *n.* Starch granulose or granules that are soluble in water.

am·y·lo·gen·ic (am′ə·lō·jen′ik) *adj.* Pertaining to the biosynthesis of starch.

am·y·loid (am′ə·loid) *n.* **1** *Bot.* A gummy or starchlike substance formed in woody tissues in the process of lignification. **2** *Pathol.* Waxy matter formed in certain diseased tissues of the body, but not chemically related to starch. *—adj.* Like or containing starch. **—am′y·loi′dal** *adj.*

am·y·loi·do·sis (am′ə·loi·dō′sis) *n.* Deterioration of organic tissues with deposition of amyloids.

am·y·lol·y·sis (am′ə·lol′ə·sis) *n.* The hydrolysis of starch to sugar by the action of enzymes. **—am·y·lo·lyt·ic** (am′ə·lō·lit′ik) *adj.*

am·y·lo·pec·tin (am′ə·lō·pek′tin) *n.* An almost insoluble branched-chain carbohydrate polymer occurring on the surface of starch granules and staining violet with iodine.

am·y·lo·plast (am′ə·lō·plast′) *n. Bot.* **1** A starch-forming cell. **2** A leucoplastid or amylogenic body. Also **am′y·lo·plas′tid** (-plas′·tid),**am′y·lo·plas′tide** (-plas′tid, tīd).

am·y·lop·sin (am′ə·lop′sin) *n.* A constituent of pancreatic juice which promotes the conversion of starch to sugar. [<AMYLO- + (TRY)PSIN]

am·y·lose (am′ə·lōs) *n.* An unbranched carbohydrate polymer occurring as a water-soluble component of starch which turns blue in iodine.

am·y·lum (am′ə·ləm) *n.* Starch. [<L <Gk. *amylon* starch]

a·my·o·to·ni·a (ə·mī′ə·tō′nē·ə) *n.* Abnormal muscular flaccidity. [<NL <Gk. *a-* without + *mys, myos* muscle + *tonos* tone]

am·y·ot·ro·phy (am′e-ot′rə·fē) *n.* Atrophy of a muscle or muscles. [<Gk. *a-* without + *mys, myos* muscle + *trophē* nourishment]

Am·y·tal (am′ə·tal, -tôl) *n.* A proprietary name for amobarbital.

an[1] (an, *unstressed* ən) *indefinite article & adj.* **1** Each or any. **2** One; one kind of; one single. Used like the article *a,* but before words beginning with a vowel sound; as, *an* acorn, *an* honest man. **3** For each: The price is a dollar *an* apple. [OE *an* one]

an[2] (an, *unstressed* ən) *conj. Archaic* And, especially in the sense *and if,* or *if:* often written **an′.** See AND.

an-[1] *prefix* Without; not: *anacid, anarchy.* Also, before consonants except *h, a-* (called *alpha privative*). [<Gk.]

an-[2] Var. of ANA-.

an-[3] Assimilated var. of AD-.

-an *suffix* Used to form adjectives and nouns denoting connection with a country, person, group, doctrine, etc., as follows: **1** Pertaining to; belonging to: *human, sylvan.* **2** Originating in; living in: *Italian.* **3** Adhering to; following: *Lutheran.* [<L *-anus*]

a·na[1] (ā′nə, ä′nə) *n.* **1** A collection of notes, sketches, or scraps of literature bearing on some particular person, place, or subject. **2** The information in such a collection. See -ANA.

an·a[2] (an′ə) *adv. Med.* Of each a like amount: used in prescriptions. [<Gk. *ana* throughout]

A·na (ä′nä) Spanish form of ANN.

ana- *prefix* **1** Up; upward: *anadromous.* **2** Back; backward: *anapest.* **3** Anew: sometimes capable of being rendered *re-,* as *anabaptism,* rebaptism. **4** Throughout; thoroughly: *analysis.* Also, before vowels or *h, an-,* as in *anode.* [<Gk. <*ana* on]

-ana *suffix* Pertaining to: added to the names of notable persons, places, etc., to indicate a collection of materials, such as writings or anecdotes, about the subject: *Americana, Johnsoniana.* Also *-iana.* [<L, neut. pl. of *-anus.* See-AN]

an·a·bae·na (an′ə·bē′nə) *n. pl.* **·nas** Any of various blue-green algae of the genus *Anabaena,* sometimes imparting a disagreeable taste and odor to water supplies. [<NL <Gk. *anabainein.* See ANABASIS.]

An·a·bap·tist (an′ə·bap′tist) *n.* One of a sect that arose in Zurich in 1523 among the followers of Zwingli, who started the Reformation in Switzerland and advocated opposition to infant baptism, and believed that only such persons as had been baptized after a confession of faith in Christ constituted a real church. *—adj.* Of or pertaining to Anabaptists or Anabaptism. [<NL *anabaptista* <L *anabaptismus* <Gk. *anabaptismos* rebaptism <*anabaptizein* rebaptize <*ana-* anew + *baptizein* baptize] **—An′a·bap′tism***n.*

an·a·bas (an′ə·bas) *n.* Any of a genus *(Anabas)* of freshwater fishes of Africa and Asia adapted to using oxygen both in water and in the atmosphere, as the climbing perch, which *(Anabas scandens),* called the *climbing fish,* can travel on land and climb trees by means of its spinous gill covers. [<NL <Gk. *anabas* <*anabainein.* See ANABASIS.]

a·nab·a·sis (ə·nab′ə·sis) *n. pl.* **·ses** (-sēz) A military advance or incursion, as that of Cyrus the Younger, with 10,000 Greek auxiliaries, against Artaxerxes II in 401 B.C., described in Xenophon's *Anabasis.* [<Gk. <*anabainein* go up <*ana-* up + *bainein* go]

an·a·bat·ic (án′ə·bat′ik) *adj.* **1** Of or pertaining to an anabasis. **2** *Meteorol.* Rising upwards, as air currents.

an·a·bi·o·sis (an′ə·bī·ō′sis) *n.* A suspension of animation susceptible of resuscitation. [<NL <ANA- + Gk. *bios* life]

an·a·bi·ot·ic (an′ə·bī·ot′ik) *adj.* Lifeless, but capable of resuscitation.

an·a·bleps (an′ə·bleps) *n.* A fresh-water cyprinodont fish of tropical America having each eye divided into two segments, the upper portion adapted for vision in air, the lower for vision in water. Also called *four-eyed fish.* [<NL <Gk. *anablepein* look up]

ANABLEPS

an·a·bol·ic steroid (an′ə·bol′ik) Any of various synthetic drugs that stimulate the development of large and strong muscles.

a·nab·o·lism (ə·nab′ə·liz′əm) *n.* The phase of metabolism in which large and complex molecules are built up from smaller, simpler compounds. [<Gk. *anabolē* a heaping up <*ana-* up + *bolē* a stroke] **—an·a·bol·ic** (an′ə·bol′ik) *adj.*

an·a·branch (an′ə·branch, -bränch) *n. Geog.* An effluent of a stream which rejoins the main stream, forming an island between the two watercourses. [<*ana(stomosing) branch*]

an·a·car·di·a·ceous (an′ə·kär′dē·ā′shəs) *adj. Bot.* Designating a large family *(Anacardiaceae)* of trees or shrubs of the order *Sapindales,* the sumac family, with resinous, milky, acrid juice, alternate leaves, and small flowers. [<NL <ANA- similar to + Gk. *kardia* heart; with ref. to the shape of the fruit]

an·a·ca·thar·sis (an′ə·kə·thär′sis) *n. Med.* **1** Regurgitation; vomiting. **2** Expectoration. [<NL <Gk. *anakatharsis* <*ana-* up + *katharsis* purification]

a·nach·o·rism (ə·nak′ə·riz′əm) *n.* Something foreign to a country or unsuited to local conditions; a geographical error: compare with *anachronism.* [<ANA- + Gk. *chōros* country, place]

a·nach·ro·nism (ə·nak′rə·niz′əm) *n.* **1** A chronological error. **2** Something occurring or represented as occurring out of its proper time. [<F *anachronisme* <L *anachronismus* <Gk. *anachronismos* <*anachronizein* refer to a wrong time <*ana-* against + *chronos* time] **—an·a·chron·ic** (an′ə·kron′ik), **a·nach′·ro·nis′tic, a·nach′ro·nis′ti·cal, a·nach′ro·nous** *adj.*

an·ac·id (an·as′id) *adj. Med.* Lacking the normal degree of acidity: said especially of gastric secretions. **—an·a·cid·i·ty** (an′ə·sid′·ə·tē) *n.*

a·nac·la·sis (ə·nak′lə·sis) *n.* In prosody, the exchange of place of a short syllable with a preceding long one; thus, ⏑ ⏑ – ⏑ for – ⏑ ⏑ ⏑. [<NL <Gk. *anaklasis* <*anaklaein* bend back <*ana-* back + *klaein* break]

an·a·clas·tic (an′ə·klas′tik) *adj.* **1** *Optics* Pertaining to refraction or bending; caused by or causing refraction. **2** In prosody, characterized by anaclasis.

an·a·cli·nal (an′ə·klī′nəl) *adj. Geol.* Transverse to the course of underlying rocks and against the dip, as a valley. [<ANA- on + Gk. *klinein* lean]

an·a·cli·sis (an′ə·klī′sis, ə·nak′lə·sis) *n. Psychoanal.* A strong emotional dependence upon others, especially those who typify a child's first object of love or source of protection and support. [<NL <Gk. *anaklisis* <*anaklinein* lean upon <*ana-* upon + *klinein* lean]

an·a·clit·ic (an′ə·klit′ik) *adj.* **1** Needing support; dependent. **2** Exhibiting anaclisis.

an·a·co·lu·thon (an′ə·kə·lōō′thon) *n. pl.* **·thons** or **·tha** (-thə) **1** Violation of grammatical

sequence, as for the sake of energy or to express strong emotion. **2** An instance of this; a sentence in which anacoluthon occurs. [<Gk. *anakolouthos* lacking sequence <*an-* not + *akolouthos* following] **—an'a·co·lu'thic** *adj.*

an·a·con·da (an'ə·kon'də) *n.* **1** A very large nonvenomous, semiaquatic snake, *Eunectes murinus,* of tropical South America, which crushes its prey in its coils. **2** Any of very large constrictors. [Origin unknown]

An·a·con·da (an'ə·kon'də) A copper-mining city in SW Montana; site of the world's largest copper smelter.

A·nac·re·on (ə·nak'rē·ən, -on), 563?–478 B.C., Greek erotic poet.

A·nac·re·on·tic (ə·nak'rē·on'tik) *adj.* **1** Pertaining to or like the lyrics of Anacreon. **2** Praising love and wine; convivial; amatory. *—n.* A poem in the manner of Anacreon; amatory or convivial verse.

an·a·cru·sis (an'ə·krōō'sis) *n.* **1** In prosody, one or more unemphatic introductory syllables in a line of verse that would properly begin with a stressed syllable. **2** *Music* An upbeat. [<NL <Gk. *anakrousis* <*anakrouein* push back <*ana-* back + *krouein* strike] **—an·a·crus·tic** (an'ə·krus'tik) *adj.*

an·a·dem (an'ə·dem) *n.* A wreath for the head; garland; fillet. [<L *anadema* <Gk. *anadēma* <*anadein* wreathe <*ana-* up + *dein* bind]

an·a·di·plo·sis (an'ə·di·plō'sis) *n.* Rhetorical repetition, in which the ending of a sentence, line, or clause is repeated and emphasized at the beginning of the next. [<L <Gk. *anadiplōsis* <*ana-* again + *diploein* to double <*diploos* double]

a·nad·ro·mous (ə·nad'rə·məs) *adj.* Ascending upriver from the sea to spawn: said of fishes such as salmon. Compare *catadromous.* [<Gk. *anadromos* <*ana-* up + *dromos* a running <*dramein* run]

a·nae·mi·a (ə·nē'mē·ə), etc. See ANEMIA, etc.

an·aer·obe (an·âr'ōb, an·ā'ə·rōb) *n.* A microorganism that thrives in the absence of free oxygen. [<AN-[1] without + AERO- + Gk. *bios* life]

an·aer·o·bic (an'âr·ō'bik, -ob'ik, an'ā·ə·rō'bik, -rob'ik) *adj.* Living or functioning in the absence of free oxygen: *anaerobic* bacteria. **2** Containing no uncombined oxygen: an *anaerobic* environment. **—an'aer·o'bi·cal·ly** *adv.*

an·aer·o·phyte (an·âr'ə·fīt, an·ā'ər·ə-) *n. Bot.* A plant not requiring uncombined oxygen for respiration.

an·aes·the·sia (an'is·thē'zhə, -zhē·ə), **an·aes·thet·ic** (an'is·thet'ik), etc. See ANESTHESIA, etc.

an·a·glyph (an'ə·glif) *n.* **1** An ornament in low relief, as a cameo. **2** *Optics* A stereoscopic picture of an object produced in two colors, red and green, and from two angles, as from the right and the left eye: used to determine abnormal binocular vision. [<Gk. *anaglyphē* <*ana-* up + *glyphein* carve]

an·a·glyph·ic (an'ə·glif'ik) *adj.* Pertaining to, ornamented with, or executed in anaglyph. Also **an'a·glyph'i·cal, an·a·glyp·tic** (an'ə·glip'tik).

an·a·glyph·ics (an'ə·glif'iks) *n.* The art of carving anaglyphic decoration. Also **an·a·glyp·tics** (an'ə·glip'tiks).

an·a·glyph·o·scope (an'ə·glif'ə·skōp) *n. Optics* A device consisting of paired lenses or eyeglasses, one red and the other green, adapted to produce anaglyphs and to give ordinary pictures a stereoscopic effect.

an·a·go·ge (an'ə·gō'jē) *n.* Spiritual or mystical significance or interpretation of words, especially of the Scriptures. [<NL <Gk. *anagōgē* a leading up <*ana-* up + *agein* lead]

an·a·gog·ic (an'ə·goj'ik) *adj.* **1** Pertaining to or using anagoge; mystical: also **an'a·gog'i·cal. 2** *Psychoanal.* Pertaining to material from the psyche expressive of constructive ideals. **—an'a·gog'i·cal·ly** *adv.*

an·a·gram (an'ə·gram) *n.* **1** A word or phrase formed by transposing the letters of another word or phrase. **2** *pl.* A game in which the players make words by transposing or adding letters. [<NL *anagramma* <Gk. *ana-* anew + *gramma* a letter <*graphein* write] **—an·a·gram·mat·ic** (an'ə·grə·mat'ik) or **·i·cal** *adj.* **—an'a·gram·mat'i·cal·ly** *adv.*

an·a·gram·ma·tize (an'ə·gram'ə·tīz) *v.t.* **·tized, ·tiz·ing** To arrange as an anagram.

a·nal (ā'nəl) *adj.* **1 a** Of, pertaining to, or situated in the region of the anus. **b** Situated near the anus. **2** *Psychoanal.* **a** Of or relating to the second stage of psychosexual development of the child in which interest in excretion is dominant. **b** Of, pertaining to, or characterized by qualities in the adult, as orderliness or an inclination to hoard, regarded as typifying this stage of development. Compare GENITAL, ORAL.

a·nal·cime (a·nal'sim, -sīm) *n. Mineral.* An isometric white or pale zeolite. Also **a·nal'cite** (-sīt, -sit). [<AN-[1] not + Gk. *alkimos* strong]

an·a·lect (an'ə·lekt) *n. pl.* **an·a·lec·ta** (an'ə·lek'tə) or **·lects** A selection or fragment from a literary work or group of works: usually in the plural. [<L *analecta,* pl. <Gk. *analekta* <*analegein* collect <*ana-* up + *legein* gather] **—an'a·lec'tic** *adj.*

an·a·lep·tic (an'ə·lep'tik) *adj. Med.* Restorative or stimulating, especially to the central nervous system. *—n.* A medicine with analeptic properties. [<Gk. *analēptikos* restorative <*analambanein* recover <*ana-* up + *lambanein* take]

anal fin *Zool.* The unpaired median ventral fin just behind the anus in fishes: opposed to *dorsal fin.*

an·al·ge·si·a (an'əl·jē'zē·ə, -sē·ə) *n.* Insensibility to pain without loss of consciousness. [<NL <Gk. *analgēsia* <*an-* without + *algos* pain]

an·al·ge·sic (an'əl·jē'zik, -sik) *n.* A drug that prevents or relieves pain. *—adj.* Pertaining to or promoting analgesia.

an·a·log (an'ə·lôg, -log) *n.* **1** Anything analogous to something else. **2** *Biol.* An organ analogous to one in another species or group: distinguished from *homolog.* Also **an'a·logue.** [<F *analogue* <L *analogus.* See ANALOGY.]

analog computer A computing machine so designed and constructed as to provide information in terms of physical quantities analogous to those in which the problems are formulated. Compare DIGITAL COMPUTER.

an·a·log·i·cal (an'ə·loj'i·kəl) *adj.* Pertaining to, containing, or based on analogy. Also **an'a·log'ic. —an'a·log'i·cal·ly** *adv.*

a·nal·o·gist (ə·nal'ə·jist) *n.* One who uses or reasons from analogy.

a·nal·o·gize (ə·nal'ə·jīz) *v.* **·gized, ·giz·ing** *v.i.* To use or reason by analogy. *—v.t.* To show to be analogous.

a·nal·o·gous (ə·nal'ə·gəs) *adj.* **1** Resembling in certain respects. **2** *Biol.* Having a similar function but different in origin and structure, as the wings of birds and insects. See synonyms under ALIKE. **—a·nal'o·gous·ly** *adv.* **—a·nal'o·gous·ness** *n.*

a·nal·o·gy (ə·nal'ə·jē) *n. pl.* **·gies 1** Resemblance of properties or relations; similarity without identity. **2** Any similarity or agreement. **3** *Biol.* A similarity in function and superficial appearance, but not in origin: opposed to *homology.* **4** *Logic* Reasoning in which from certain observed and known relations or parallel resemblances others are inferred; reasoning that proceeds from the individual or particular to a coordinate individual or particular, thus involving both induction and deduction. **5** *Ling.* The formative process by which words take on inflections or constructions that are imitative of more familiar words and existing patterns without having undergone the same true linguistic development; as, the past tense of *climb* changed from the strong form *clomb* to the weak form *climbed* on analogy with the weak verbs. [<F *analogie* <L *analogia* <Gk. *analogia* <*analogos* proportionate, conformable <*ana-* according to + *logos* proportion]

Synonyms: coincidence, comparison, likeness, parity, proportion, relation, resemblance, semblance, similarity, simile, similitude. *Analogy* is specifically a *resemblance* of relations; a *resemblance* that may be reasoned from, so that from the *likeness* in certain respects we may infer that other and perhaps deeper relations exist. *Parity* of reasoning is said of an argument equally conclusive on subjects not strictly analogous. *Coincidence* is complete agreement in some one or more respects. *Similitude* is a rhetorical comparison of one thing to another with which it has some points in common. *Resemblance* and *similarity* are external or superficial, and may involve no deeper relation. Compare ALLEGORY. *Antonyms*: disagreement, disproportion, dissimilarity, incongruity, unlikeness.

an·al·pha·bet·ic (an·al'fə·bet'ik) *adj. & n.* Illiterate.

a·nal·y·sand (ə·nal'ə·sand) *n. Psychoanal.* The person who is being analyzed.

an·a·lyse (an'ə·līz) British spelling of ANALYZE.

a·nal·y·sis (ə·nal'ə·sis) *n. pl.* **·ses** (-sēz) **1** The resolution of a whole into its parts or elements: opposed to *synthesis.* **2** A statement of the results of this; logical synopsis. **3** A method of determining or describing the nature of a thing by resolving it into its parts: to study literature by the *analysis* of texts. **4** *Math.* **a** The process of resolving a problem into its first elements. **b** The investigation of the relations of variable or indeterminate quantities by means of symbols, including some branches of algebra and the differential and integral calculus. **5** *Chem.* **a** The identification of constituents of a compound, solution, mixture, or the like. See *qualitative analysis.* **b** The determination of the quantity or proportion of such constituents. See *quantitative analysis.* **c** A statement of the results of an analysis. **6** Psychoanalysis. See synonyms under ABRIDGMENT. Compare SYNTHESIS. [<Med.L <Gk. *analysis* <*ana-* throughout + *lysis* a loosing <*lyein* to loose]

analysis si·tus (sī'təs) Topology. [<NL, analysis of region]

an·a·lyst (an'ə·list) *n.* **1** One who analyzes or is skilled in analysis. **2** A psychoanalyst. ◆ Homophone: *annalist.*

an·a·lyt·ic (an'ə·lit'ik) *adj.* **1** Pertaining to, skilled in, or proceeding by analysis. **2** Resolving into constituent parts or first principles. **3** *Ling.* Describing a language, such as Modern English, that expresses grammatical relationships and the modification of word meanings by means of particles, auxiliaries, etc., rather than by inflection: opposed to *synthetic* or *inflectional.* Also **an'a·lyt'i·cal. —an'a·lyt'i·cal·ly** *adv.*

analytical balance An electronic or mechanical instrument for weighing substances to the nearest 0.1 milligram or less.

analytical psychology 1 The analysis of psychological phenomena by systematic introspection. **2** The systematic psychology and psychoanalytic methods originated by and associated with C. G. Jung.

analytic geometry Geometry in which position is represented analytically by a system of coordinates and the procedure by which solutions are obtained is largely algebraic.

an·a·lyt·ics (an'ə·lit'iks) *n.* **1** The science or use of analysis. **2** The part of logic concerned with analysis.

an·a·lyze (an'ə·līz) *v.t.* **·lyzed, ·lyz·ing 1** To resolve into constituent parts or elements. **2** To make an analysis of, as a chemical compound or a mathematical problem. **3** *Gram.* To separate (a sentence) into its grammatical elements. **4** To examine minutely or critically, as a text. Also *Brit.* **an'a·lyse.** [<F *analyser* <*analyse* <Med. L *analyses.* See ANALYSIS.] **—an'a·lyz'a·ble** *adj.* **—an'a·ly·za'tion** *n.* **—an'a·lyz'er** *n.*

A·nam (ə·nam', an'am) See ANNAM.

an·am·ne·sis (an'am·nē'sis) *n. pl.* **·ses** (·sēz) **1** *Psychol.* A reproducing in memory; recollection. **2** The complete medical history of a patient as obtained from all available sources. [<Gk. *anamnēsis* <*ana-* back + *mimnēskein* call to mind]

an·am·nes·tic (an'am·nes'tik) *adj.* **1** Stimulating the faculty of memory. **2** Pertaining to anamnesis.

anamnestic analysis Investigation of the mental history of a neurotic individual, particularly by the psychoanalytic methods developed by C. G. Jung.

anamnestic reaction A rapid increase in antibodies in an organism upon exposure to an antigen which had been encountered at some prior time. Also **anamnestic response.**

an·a·mor·phism (an'ə·môr'fiz·əm) *n.* **1** Distortion of shape. **2** *Biol.* Anamorphosis. [<ANA- up + Gk. *morphē* form]

an·a·mor·pho·scope (an'ə·môr'fə·skōp) *n.*

Optics A vertical cylindrical mirror for viewing an anamorphosis.

an·a·mor·pho·sis (an′ə·môr′fə·sis, -môr·fō′sis) *n.* 1 *Optics* A distorted representation of an object, unrecognizable except when viewed through a polyhedron or from a particular point, or when reflected from a specially constructed mirror, as an anamorphoscope. 2 *Biol.* An increase in complexity during the course of the evolution of an organism. Also call *anamorphism.* [<NL <Gk. *anamorphōsis* <Gk. *anamorphoein* <*ana-* again + *morphoein* form]

A·nan·da Ma·hi·dol (ä·nän′dä mä′hē·dôl′), 1925–46, king of Siam 1935–46.

an·an·drous (an·an′drəs) *adj. Bot.* Destitute of stamens, as a female flower.

An·a·ni·as (an′ə·nī′əs) 1 The husband of Sapphira; both fell dead after lying (*Acts* v 1–6); hence, any liar. 2 A disciple in Damascus who restored Paul's sight. *Acts* ix 10–18. 3 A high priest in Jerusalem who tried Paul. *Acts* xxiii 2–5.

an·an·thous (an·an′thəs) *adj. Bot.* Flowerless. [<AN-¹ without + Gk. *anthos* flower]

an·a·nym (an′ə·nim) *n.* A pseudonym consisting of a name written backwards, as *Niamert* for *Tremain.* [<Gk. *ana-* back + *onoma, onyma* name]

an·a·pest (an′ə·pest) *n.* 1 In prosody, a metrical foot consisting of two short or unaccented syllables followed by one long or accented syllable. 2 A line of verse made up of or characterized by such feet. Also **an′a·paest.** [<L *anapaestus* <Gk. *anapaistos* <*ana-* back + *paiein* strike] — **an′a·pes′tic** or **·ti·cal, an′a·paes′tic** or **·ti·cal** *adj.*

an·a·phase (an′ə·fāz) *n. Biol.* The stage of mitosis or meiosis in which the corresponding parts of the divided chromosomes move to opposite poles of the spindle. **an′a·pha′sic** *adj.* [ANA- up + PHASE]

a·naph·o·ra (ə·naf′ə·rə) *n.* The rhetorical device of repeating a word or phrase in the beginning of several successive verses, clauses, or sentences. [<L <Gk. *anaphora* <*ana-* back + *pherein* carry]

an·aph·ro·dis·i·a (an·af′rə·diz′ē·ə) *n.* Absence or impairment of sexual desire. [<NL <AN-¹ without + Gk. *aphrodisia* sexual pleasure <*Aphroditē*, the goddess of love]

an·aph·ro·dis·i·ac (an·af′rə·diz′ē·ak) *adj.* Of, pertaining to, or tending to produce anaphrodisia. —*n.* An anaphordisiac agent or treatment.

an·a·phy·lac·toid (an′ə·fə·lak′toid) *adj.* Similar to anaphylaxis.

an·a·phy·lax·is (an′ə·fə·lak′sis) *n.* Hypersensitivity to a foreign protein following injection of a small sensitizing dose. Also called *allergy.* [<NL <ANA- + (PRO)PHYLAXIS] —**an′a·phy·lac′tic** (-lak′tik) *adj.*

an·a·pla·sia (an′ə·plā′zhə, -zhē·ə) *n. Biol.* A reversion of cells to an undifferentiated or more primitive form, destroying their capacity for full development and functioning. [<NL <ANA- + -PLASIA]

an·a·plas·mo·sis (an′ə·plaz·mō′sis) *n.* A disease of domestic cattle and other ruminants due to a protozoan (genus *Anaplasma*) that inhabits red blood cells of the vertebrate host. [<NL <ANA- + PLASMA + -OSIS]

an·a·plas·tic (an′ə·plas′tik) *adj.* 1 *Surg.* Restoring lost or absent parts, as by transplanting tissue. 2 *Biol.* Of or pertaining to anaplasia.

an·a·plas·ty (an′ə·plas′tē) *n.* Plastic surgery. [<NL <Gk. *anaplastos* <*ana-* anew + *plassein* form]

an·ap·tot·ic (an′ap·tot′ik) *adj. Ling.* Losing or having lost inflections by phonetic decay: said of a language, as English. [<ANA- back + Gk. *ptōtikos* belonging to case < *ptōsis* a case]

an·ap·tyx·is (an′ap·tik′sis) *n.* The insertion of an extra vowel in a word so as to create another syllable, as in (fil′əm) for *film.* [<Gk. *anaptyxis* an unfolding <*ana-* back + *ptyssein* to fold]

A·na·pur·na (ä′nə·pŏŏr′nə) A mountain of the Himalaya range in north central Nepal; 26,502 feet: also *Annapurna.*

an·ar·chic (an·är′kik) *adj.* 1 Pertaining to or like anarchy. 2 Advocating anarchy. 3 Inducing anarchy; lawless. Also **an·ar′chi·cal.** —**an·ar′chi·cal·ly** *adv.*

an·ar·chism (an′ər·kiz′əm) *n.* 1 The theory that all forms of government are incompatible with individual and social liberty and should be abolished. 2 The methods, especially terroristic ones, of anarchists. —**philosophic anarchism** The advocacy of voluntary cooperation and mutual aid as a substitute for the coercive power of the state.

an·ar·chist (an′ər·kist) *n.* 1 One who believes in and advocates anarchism. 2 One who encourages or furthers anarchy. Also **an·arch** (an′ärk). — **an′ar·chis′tic** *adj.*

an·ar·chy (an′ər·kē) *n.* 1 Absence of government. 2 Lawless confusion and political disorder. 3 General disorder. See synonyms under DISORDER, REVOLUTION. [<Gk. *anarchia* <*anarchos* without a leader <*an-* without + *archos* leader, chief]

an·ar·thri·a (an·är′thrē·ə) *n.* Inability to utter articulate speech as a result of neural damage. — **an·ar′thric** *adj.*

an·ar·throus (an·är′thrəs) *adj.* 1 *Gram.* Used without the article: said of some Greek nouns in certain cases. 2 *Zool.* Lacking distinct joints. [<Gk. *anarthros* unjointed <*an-* without + *arthron* joint]

an·a·sar·ca (an′ə·sär′kə) *n.* A generalized swelling due to infiltration of serous fluid into body cavities and subcutaneous connective tissue. [<NL <Gk. *ana-* throughout + *sarx* flesh] —**an′a·sar′cous** *adj.*

An·as·ta·si·us I (an′ə·stā′shē·əs), 430?–518, Byzantine emperor 491–518.

—**Anastasius II**, died 721?, Byzantine emperor 713–716.

Anastasius IV, died 1154, real name Conrad, pope 1153–54.

an·as·tig·mat·ic (an·as′tig·mat′ik) *adj. Optics* 1 Not astigmatic; specifically, corrected for astigmatism, as a lens. 2 Pertaining to a compound photographic lens, each element of which is adapted to correct the astigmatism of the other. [<AN-¹ + ASTIGMATIC]

a·nas·to·mose (ə·nas′tə·mōz) *v.* **·mosed, ·mos·ing** *v.t.* To create an anastomosis. —*v.i.* To be connected by one or more anastomoses.

a·nas·to·mo·sis (ə·nas′tə·mō′sis) *n. pl.* **·ses** (-sēz) A natural or artificial connection, interlacing, or union of parts or branches of a system of blood vessels, leaf veins, rivers, or the like. Also called *inosculation.* [<NL <Gk. *anastomōsis* opening <*ana-* again + *stoma* mouth] — **a·nas′to·mot′ic** (-mot′ik) *adj.*

a·nas·tro·phe (ə·nas′trə·fē) *n.* In rhetoric, the inversion of the natural or usual order of words, as "homeward directly he went." Also **a·nas′·tro·phy.** [<Gk. *anastrophē* <*ana strephein* <*ana-* back + *strephein* turn]

an·a·tase (an′ə·tās, -tāz) *n.* A variously colored mineral consisting of tetragonal crystals of titanium oxide, TiO_2. Also called *octahedrite.* [<F <Gk. *anatasis* extension]

a·nath·e·ma (ə·nath′ə·mə) *n. pl.* **·mas** or **·ma·ta** (-mətə) 1 A formal ecclesiastical ban or curse, excommunicating a person or damning something, as a book or heresy. 2 Any curse or imprecation. 3 A person or thing excommunicated or damned. 4 A person or thing greatly disliked or detested. See synonyms under IMPRECATION. [<L <Gk. *anathema* a thing devoted (to evil) <*anatithenai* dedicate <*ana-* up + *tithenai* set, place]

anathema mar·a·nath·a (mar′ə·nath′ə) A formula formerly interpreted as an extreme curse: now considered an incorrect reading of I *Cor.* xvi 22. [<Gk. *anathema* a curse + Aramaic *Maranā′thā* Our Lord, come]

a·nath·e·ma·tize (ə·nath′ə·mə·tīz) *v.* **·tized, ·tiz·ing** *v.t.* To pronounce an anathema against. —*v.i.* To utter or express anathemas. —**a·nath′e·ma·ti·za′tion** *n.*

An·a·to·li·a (an′ə·tō′lē·ə) A mountainous peninsula comprising the westernmost part of Asia and almost all of Turkey; 287,117 square miles; formerly synonymous with Asia Minor. — **An′a·to′lic** *adj.*

An·a·to·li·an (an′ə·tō′lē·ən) *adj.* Pertaining to Anatolia or its people. —*n.* A family of languages of which Cuneiform Hittite is the best known: related to or descended from Indo-European. See INDO-HITTITE.

an·a·tom·i·cal (an′ə·tom′i·kəl) *adj.* 1 Pertaining to the structure of an organism. 2 Structural, especially as distinguished from functional. Also **an′a·tom′ic.** —**an′a·tom′i·cal·ly** *adv.*

a·nat·o·mist (ə·nat′ə·mist) *n.* One skilled in or a student of anatomy; a dissector.

a·nat·o·mize (ə·nat′ə·mīz) *v.t.* **·mized, ·miz·ing** 1 To dissect an animal or plant for the purpose of investigating the structure, position, and interrelationships of its parts. 2 To examine critically or minutely; analyze. —**a·nat′o·mi·za′·tion** *n.*

a·nat·o·my (ə·nat′ə·mē) *n. pl.* **·mies** 1 The science of the structure of organisms, as of the human body, and of the interrelations of their parts. 2 The art or practice of dissection in order to investigate the structure, position, and interrelationship of organs. 3 A textbook or treatise dealing with the art or practice of dissection. 4 A skeleton. 5 An anatomical model, showing the structure, position, and interrelationship of organs. 6 Any kind of analysis or close examination. [<F *anatomie* <L *anatomia* <Gk. *anatomia*, earlier *anatomē* dissection <*anatemnein* cut up <*ana-* up + *temnein* cut]

a·nat·ro·pous (ə·nat′rə·pəs) *adj. Bot.* Inverted, with the micropyle next to the hilum and the radicle inferior: said of an ovule. [<NL <ANA- + -TROPOUS]

a·nat·to (ä·nä′tō) *n.* Annatto. [<Cariban]

An·ax·ag·o·ras (an′ak·sag′ə·rəs), 500–428 B.C., Greek philosopher.

An·ax·i·man·der (an·ak′sə·man′dər), 610–546? B.C., Greek philosopher and astronomer.

An·ax·im·e·nes (an′ak·sim′ə·nēz), sixth century B.C. Greek philosopher.

An·cae·us (an·sē′əs) In Greek mythology, a son of Neptune who was told he would never drink the wine of his own vineyard. He scornfully started to drink, but was told there was a wild boar nearby, went out to kill it, and was killed himself; hence the proverb "There's many a slip between the cup and the lip."

-ance *suffix of nouns* Forming nouns of action, quality, state, or condition from adjectives in *-ant*, and also directly from verbs, as in abundance, resistance, forbearance. Compare -ANCY. [<F *-ance* <L *-antia, -entia*, a suffix used to form nouns from present participles; or directly from Latin]

◆ **-ance, -ence** The modern spelling of words in this group is unpredictable. The confusion arose originally in borrowings from Old French *(resistance, assistance)* where *-ance* had come to represent Latin *-entia*, as well as *-antia.* Since 1500, however, some of these have been altered back to *-ence* on the Latin model, as in the case of *dependence*, earlier *dependance.* Later Latin borrowings in French and in English (through French or directly from Latin) discriminate between *-ance* and *-ence* according to the vowel of the Latin original.

an·ces·tor (an′ses·tər) *n.* 1 One from whom descent is derived; especially, such person further back in the line than a grandparent; forefather; progenitor; forebear. 2 *Law* One who precedes another in the line of legal inheritance, whether or not a direct progenitor: correlative of *heir.* 3 *Biol.* An actual or hypothetical organism from which subsequent types have developed; a prototype. [<OF *ancestre* <L *antecessor* <*antecedere* <*ante-* before + *cedere* go]

an·ces·tral (an·ses′trəl) *adj.* Of, pertaining to, or inherited from an ancestor. —**an·ces′tral·ly** *adv.*

an·ces·tress (an′ses·tris) *n.* A female ancestor.

an·ces·try (an′ses·trē) *n. pl.* **·tries** 1 The line or body of ancestors; ancestors collectively. 2 Descent; ancestral lineage. 3 Noble or worthy lineage.

An·chi·ses (an·kī′sēz) In Roman legend, the father of Aeneas, rescued from burning Troy on his son's shoulders.

add,āce,câre,pälm; end,ēven; it,īce; odd,ōpen,ôrder; tŏŏk,pōōl; up,bûrn; ə = a in *above*, e in *sicken*, i in *clarity*, o in *melon*, u in *focus* ; yōō = u in *fuse*, oi,oil; ou,pout; ch,check; g,go; ng,ring; th,thin; th,this; zh,vision. Foreign sounds à,œ,ü,kh,ṅ; and ◆: see page xx. <from; + plus; ? possibly.

an·chor[1] (ang′kər) *n.* **1** A heavy implement, usually of iron or steel and having a long shank and two or more hooks or flukes that grip the sea bottom: used for holding fast a vessel by means of a connecting cable. **2** Any similar object used in such a manner for such a purpose. **3** Anything that makes stable or secure; anything depended on for support or security. **4** A military base from which an army operates. —**at anchor** Anchored, as a ship. —**to cast** (or **drop**) **anchor** To put down the anchor in order to hold fast a vessel. —**to ride at anchor** To be anchored, as a ship. —**to weigh anchor** To take up the anchor so as to sail away. —*v.t.* **1** To secure or make secure by an anchor. **2** To fix firmly. —*v.i.* **3** To come to anchor; lie at anchor, as a ship. **4** To become fixed; to hold oneself fast, as to a place. [OE *ancor* < L *ancora* < Gk. *ankyra*]

an·chor[2] (ang′kər) *n.* An anchorite.

an·chor·age (ang′kər·ij) *n.* **1** A place fit for or used for anchoring. **2** A coming to or lying at anchor. **3** That to which something is anchored; a means of support or security. **4** The fee charged for anchoring or the right to anchor, as in a harbor.

An·chor·age (ang′kər·ij) A southern Alaskan port, the largest city in Alaska.

an·cho·ress (ang′kə·ris) *n.* A woman anchorite.

anchor hold 1 The strength or grip with which an anchor holds. **2** The chief ground of trust; security; fixedness.

an·cho·rite (ang′kə·rīt) *n.* One who has withdrawn from the world; a religious recluse; hermit. Also **an′cho·ret** (-rit, -ret). [< L *anachoreta* < Gk. *anachōrētēs* < *anachōreein* retire, retreat < *ana-* back + *chōreein* withdraw] —**an′cho·rit′ic** (-rit′ik) *adj.*

an·chor·less (ang′kər·lis) *adj.* **1** Without an anchor. **2** Not settled or stable; drifting; insecure; without roots.

anchor man 1 An athlete, as in a relay race, who competes last for his team. **2** A television or radio broadcaster who coordinates the coverage of an event or program.

anchor watch *Naut.* The part of a crew set to watch while a vessel lies at anchor.

an·cho·vy (an′chō·vē, -chə·vē, an·chō′vē) *n. pl.* **·vies** Any of several very small, herring-like marine fishes (family Engraulidae) including some of commercial value as food or as a source of fishmeal. [< Sp., Pg. *anchova*, ? < Basque *anchua* < *antzua* dry]

an·cho·vy pear 1 A West Indian fruit tasting like the mango. **2** The tall unbranched tree (*Grias cauliflora*) of the myrtle family that bears this fruit.

an·chu·sa (ang·kyōō′sə, an·chōō′zə) *n.* Any plant of a genus (*Anchusa*) of hairy-stemmed plants, including various species of bugloss. [< NL < L < Gk. *anchousa*]

an·chu·sin (ang·kyōō′sin) *n.* A red resinous substance obtained from the root of various anchusas and other plants, used in dyeing.

an·chy·lose (ang′kə·los) *v.* **·losed**, **·los·ing** To ankylose.

an·chy·lo·sis (ang′kə·lō′sis) *n.* Ankylosis.

an·cienne no·blesse (äṅ·syen′ nô·bles′) *French* The old nobility; especially, that prior to the French Revolution.

an·cien ré·gime (äṅ·syaṅ′ rā·zhēm′) *French* A former political and social system; specifically, that system prevailing in France before the Revolution of 1789. Also **Ancient Regime.**

an·cient[1] (ān′shənt) *adj.* **1** Existing or occurring in times long gone by, especially before the fall of the Roman Empire of the West, in 476: opposed to *modern*: *ancient* history, *ancient* authors. **2** Belonging to or having existed from remote antiquity; of great age: *ancient* relics. **3** *Archaic* Venerable; sage. —*n.* **1** One who lived

in ancient times. **2** An ancient or venerable person. —**the ancients 1** The ancient Greeks, Romans, Hebrews, or other civilized nations of antiquity. **2** The ancient authors of Greece and Rome. [< OF *ancien*, ult. ·< L *ante* before] —**an′cient·ness** *n.*

Synonyms (adj.): aged, antiquated, antique, gray, hoary, immemorial, old, olden, time-honored, time-worn, venerable. *Ancient*, from the French, is the more stately; *old*, from the Anglo-Saxon, the more familiar word. *Venerable* expresses the involuntary reverence that we yield to the majestic and the long-enduring. See ANTIQUE, OLD. *Antonyms:* fresh, modern, new, novel, recent.

an·cient[2] (ān′shənt) *n.* An ensign, standard, or flag. **2** A flag standard-bearer. [Alter. of ENSIGN]

ancient light *Law* A window facing toward the property of another, which having been unobstructed for 20 years, gives the owner the right to its light and which, therefore, may not be obstructed by the erection of a building: a law in England and in some parts of the United States.

an·cient·ly (ān′shənt·lē) *adv.* In the distant past; of old.

Ancient of Days God. *Dan.* vii 9.

an·cil·lar·y (an′sə·ler′ē) *adj.* **1** Subordinate. **2** Auxiliary; serving to help. [< L *ancillaris* < *ancilla* maid]

an·cip·i·tal (an·sip′ə·təl) *adj. Bot.* Two-edged, as the stems of certain plants. Also **an·cip′i·tous.** [< L *anceps, ancipitis* two-headed < *an-* (*ambi-*) on both sides + *caput* head]

an·cis·troid (an·sis′troid) *adj.* Hook-shaped. [< Gk. *ankistron* a hook + -OID]

an·con (ang′kon) *n. pl.* **an·co·nes** (ang·kō′nēz) *Archit.* An elbow-shaped projection; a console, as for an ornament on a keystone. [< L < Gk. *ankōn* a bend, the elbow] —**an·co·nal** (ang′kə·nəl), **an·co·ne·al** (ang·kō′nē·əl) *adj.*

An·co·na (äng·kō′nä) A city in central Italy, on the Adriatic.

-ancy *suffix of nouns* A modern variant of -ANCE: *infancy, vacancy*: used to form new words expressing quality, state, or condition, or to fashion older nouns of quality in *-ance*, the latter being largely reserved for nouns of action: *constancy.* [< L *-antia*]

an·cy·los·to·mi·a·sis (an′sə·los′tə·mī′ə·sis) *n. pl.* **·ses** (·sēz) A condition in humans and some other mammals due to infestation by hookworms. Also called *hookworm disease.* [< NL < Gk. *ankylos* crooked + *stoma* mouth]

An·cy·ra (an·sī′rə) See ANKARA.

and (and, *unstressed* ənd, ən) *conj.* **1** Also; added to; as well as: a particle denoting addition, emphasis, or union, used as a connective between words, phrases, clauses, and sentences: shoes *and* ships *and* sealing wax; walking miles *and* miles; a horse both swift *and* strong. **2** As a result or consequence: Speak one word *and* you are a dead man! **3** To: in idiomatic use with *come, go, try*, etc.: Try *and* stop me; Come *and* see us; Go *and* find the answer. **4** *Archaic* Then: *And* she answered unto him. **5** *Obs.* If; in addition. See synonyms under BUT[1]. [OE]

an·dab·a·ta (an·dab′ə·tə) *n. pl.* **·tae** (-tē) One who fights blindly, or acts as if blindfolded; originally, in ancient Rome, a gladiator who fought wearing a helmet without eye openings. For illustration, see under GLADIATOR. Also **an·da·bate** (an′də·bāt). [< L]

an·dab·a·tar·i·an (an·dab′ə·târ′ē·ən) *adj.* Like the fights of a blindfolded gladiator or andabata; hence, misdirected, or blindly ineffectual.

An·da·lu·si·a (an′də·lōō′zhə, -shə) A region of southern Spain bordering on the Atlantic, the Strait of Gibraltar, and the Mediterranean. *Spanish* **An·da·lu·cí·a** (än′dä·lōō·thē′ä).

An·da·lu·sian (an′də·lōō′zhən, -shən) *adj.* Of or pertaining to Andalusia or its inhabitants. —*n.* **1** One of the inhabitants of Andalusia. **2** A dialect of southern Spain.

an·da·lu·site (an′də·lōō′sīt) *n.* A variously colored orthorhombic aluminum silicate, Al₂SiO₅, occurring in metamorphic rock. [from *Andalu-*

sia, region in Spain, where it was discovered]

An·da·man and Nic·o·bar Islands (an′də·mən; nik′ə·bär′) A chief commissioner's state of India in the east Bay of Bengal; 3,143 square miles; capital, Port Blair on South Andaman: comprising the northerly **Andaman Islands**; 2,508 square miles; and the southerly **Nicobar Islands**; 635 square miles.

An·da·ma·nese (an′də·mə·nēz′, -nēs′) *n. pl.* **·nese 1** Any of the Negrito people of the Andaman and Nicobar Islands. **2** The language of these people. —*adj.* Of or pertaining to this people or their language.

Andaman Sea An easterly part of the Bay of Bengal between the Malay Peninsula and the Andaman and Nicobar Islands.

an·dan·te (an·dan′tē, än·dän′tä) *adj. & adv. Music* Moderately slowly; slower than allegretto but faster than larghetto. —*n.* Music in andante tempo. [< Ital., lit., walking]

an·dan·ti·no (an′dan·tē′nō, än·dän-) *adj. & adv. Music* Slightly quicker than andante: originally, slower than andante, but now generally meaning not so slow as andante. —*n.* Music in andantino tempo. [< Ital., dim. of *andante*]

An·de·an (an·dē′ən, an′dē·ən) *adj.* Of or pertaining to the Andes Mountains.

An·der·lecht (än′dər·lekht) A city in central Belgium SW of Brussels.

An·ders (än′ders), **Wła·dy·sław** (vlä·di′släf), born 1892, Polish general.

An·der·sen (än′dər·sən), **Hans Christian**, 1805–75, Danish writer of fairy tales.

An·der·son (an′dər·sən), **Carl David**, born 1905, U.S. physicist. —**Marian**, born 1908, U.S. Negro contralto. —**Maxwell**, 1888–1959, U.S. playwright. —**Sherwood**, 1876–1941, U.S. author.

An·der·son·ville (an′dər·sən·vil) A village in SW Georgia; site of a Confederate prison for Union soldiers during the Civil War.

An·des (an′dēz) A mountain range in western South America, extending over 4,000 miles from Venezuela southward to Tierra del Fuego; highest peak, Aconcagua, 22,835 feet. *Spanish* **Los An·des** (lōs än′däs).

an·de·site (an′də·zīt) *n.* A volcanic rock, containing essentially plagioclase with biotite, hornblende, or augite. [from the *Andes* Mountains]

and·i·ron (and′ī′ərn) *n.* One of two iron, steel, etc., supports for wood to be burned in an open fireplace. Also called *firedog.* [< OF *andier*; infl. by IRON]

An·di·zhan (än·dē·zhän′) A city in eastern Uzbek S.S.R.

and/or Either *and* or *or*, according to the meaning intended: Place bills *and/or* coins in this container: a business and legal usage.

An·dor·ra (an·dôr′ə, -dor′ə) A republic between France and Spain, subject to the joint suzerainty of the president of France and the Bishop of Urgel, Spain; 191 square miles; capital, Andorra la Vella.

andr- *combining form* Variant of ANDRO-.

an·dra·dite (an′drə·dīt) *n.* A variety of garnet composed of calcium iron silicate, varying in color from green to brown or black. [after J. B. de *Andrada* e Silva, 1763?–1838, Brazilian geologist]

An·drás·sy (än′drä·shē), **Count Gyu·la** (dy·ōō′lä), father 1823–90, son, 1860–1929, Hungarian statesmen.

An·dré (än′drā, an′drē), **John**, 1751–80, British major, hanged as a spy during the American Revolution.

An·dre·a·nof Islands (än′drä·ä′nôf) An island group in the central Aleutians between Rat and Fox Islands.

An·dre·ev (än·drā′yef), **Leonid Nikolaievich**, 1871–1919, Russian writer.

An·drew (an′drōō) A masculine personal name. Also **An·dre·as** (an·drē′əs; *Dan.* än·dres′; *Du.*, *Ger.* än·drā′äs; *Lat.* an·drē·əs), *Fr.* **An·dré** (än·drā′), *Ital.* **An·dre·a** (än·drā′ä), *Pg.* **An·dre** (än·drā′), *Sp.* **An·drés** (än·drās′). [< Gk., man] —**Andrew, Saint**, One of the twelve Apostles; brother of Peter; martyred in Greece.

An·drewes (an′drōōz), **Lancelot**, 1555–1626, English bishop and scholar.

An·drews (an′drōōz), **Charles McLean**, 1863–1943, U.S. educator and historian. —**Roy Chapman**, 1884–1960, U.S. naturalist, explorer, and archeologist.

An·dri·a (än′drē·ä) A city in Apulia, southern Italy.

andro- *combining form* **1** Human: *androcephalous.* **2** Male; masculine: *andromorphous.* **3** *Bot.* Stamen; anther: *androecium.* [< Gk. *anēr, andros* man]

an·dro·cen·trism (an'drə·sen'triz·əm) *n.* Preoccupation with men and the activities of men to the exclusion of women in human affairs. — **an·dro·cen·tric** (an'drə·sen'trik) *adj.*

an·dro·ceph·a·lous (an'drə·sef'ə·ləs) *adj.* Having a human head, especially when joined to the body of an animal, as the Egyptian sphinx. [< ANDRO- + Gk. *kephalē* head]

An·dro·cles (an'drə·klēz) A Roman slave, first century A.D., whose life, according to legend, was spared in the arena by a lion that remembered him as the man who had once drawn a thorn from its paw. Also **An'dro·clus.**

an·dro·clin·i·um (an'drə·klin'ē·əm) *n. Bot.* Clinandrium. [< NL < ANDRO- + Gk. *klinē* a bed]

an·droc·ra·cy (an·drok'rə·sē) *n.* The rule of males; male supremacy. [< Greek *anēr, andros* man + *kratos* rule] — **an·dro·crat·ic** (an'drə·krat'ik) *adj.*

an·droe·ci·um (an·drē'shē·əm, -sē·əm) *n. pl.* **·ci·a** (-shē·ə, -sē·ə) *Bot.* The stamens of a flower collectively. [< NL < ANDRO- + Gk. *oikos* house] — **an·droe·cial** (an·drē'shəl) *adj.*

an·dro·gen (an'drə·jən) *n.* Any of various steroid hormones produced in the testes and the adrenal cortex which affect the development of masculine sexual characteristics. — **an·dro·gen·ic** (an'drə·jen'ik) *adj.*

an·drog·en·ize (an·droj'ə·nīz) *v.* **·ized, ·iz·ing.** To effect the development of masculine characteristics in, as by treatment with androgens. — **an'dro·gen·i·za'tion** *n.*

an·drog·e·nous (an·droj'ə·nəs) *adj.* Pertaining to or characterized by the production of male offspring.

An·dro·ge·us (an·drō'jē·əs) In Greek mythology, the son of Minos and Pasiphae, killed at Athens; to avenge him, Minos forced the Athenians to send a tribute of seven boys and seven girls every year, or every ninth year according to some traditions, to be thrown to the Minotaur. See MINOTAUR, THESEUS.

an·dro·gyne (an'drə·jin, -jīn) *n.* **1** A hermaphrodite. **2** *Bot.* An androgynous plant. [< MF < L *androgynus* < Gk. *androgynos* having the characteristics of both sexes < *anēr, andros* man + *gynē* woman]

an·drog·y·noid (an·droj'ə·noid) *adj.* Designating a male with hermaphroditic characteristics. [< ANDRO- + Gk. *gynē* woman]

an·drog·y·nous (an·droj'ə·nəs) *adj.* **1** Uniting the characteristics of both sexes; hermaphrodite. **2** *Bot.* Having the male and female flowers in the same cluster. **3** Undifferentiated as to sex, as in dress, bearing, etc.; unisex. Also **an·drog·y·nal** (an·droj'ə·nəl), **an·dro·gyn·ic** (an'·drə·jin'ik).

an·drog·y·ny (an·droj'ə·nē) *n.* Hermaphroditism.

an·droid (an'droid) *adj.* Having a human shape. —*n.* An automaton made to simulate a human being; a humanoid robot. [< NL *androides* < Gk. *androeidēs* manlike]

an·drol·o·gy (an·drol'ə·jē) *n.* The study of the male reproductive system and the disorders peculiar to it. — **an·drol'o·gist** *n.*

An·drom·a·che (an·drom'ə·kē) In Greek legend, the wife of Hector and mother of Astyanax, taken captive to Greece after the fall of Troy.

An·dro·med (an'drə·med) *n.* One of a system of meteors that seem to radiate from a point in the constellation Andromeda, called *Bielids*, because supposed to be the remains of Biela's comet. Also **An·dro·mede** (an'drə·mēd), **An·drom·e·did** (an·drom'ə·did).

An·drom·e·da (an·drom'ə·də) **1** In Greek mythology, the daughter of Cepheus and Cassiopeia, rescued from a sea monster and married by Perseus. **2** *Astron.* A northern constellation: see CONSTELLATION.

an·dro·mor·phous (an'drə·môr'fəs) *adj.* Having masculine shape or appearance. [< ANDRO- + Gk. *morphē* form]

An·dros (an'dros) The northernmost island of the Cyclades in the Aegean Sea; 145 square miles.

An·dros (an'drəs), **Sir Edmund,** 1637–1714, English colonial governor in America.

An·dros·cog·gin River (an'drə·skog'in) A river in New Hampshire and Maine; flowing SE 175 miles to the Kennebec River.

An·dros Island (an'dros) An island in the western Bahamas, largest of the group; 1,600 square miles.

an·dro·sphinx (an'drə·sfingks') *n.* A sphinx with a man's head and a lion's body. See SPHINX.

an·dro·spore (an'drə·spôr', -spōr') *n. Bot.* Microspore.

an·dros·ter·one (an·dros'tə·rōn) *n.* An androgenic sex hormone, $C_{19}H_{30}C_2$, typically present in the urine of men and women. [< ANDRO- + STER(OL) + -ONE]

-androus *suffix* **1** *Bot.* Having a stamen or stamens: *monandrous, diandrous.* **2** Pertaining to men: *polyandrous.* [< Gk. *anēr, andros* man]

and so forth Together with more of the same kind, or along the same line; et cetera.

And·va·re (än'dwä·rē) In Norse mythology, the dwarf from whom Loki stole the Nibelung treasure and the ring that carried the curse. Also **And'wa·ri.**

An·dy (an'dē) Diminutive of ANDREW.

ane (ān) *adj. & n. Scot.* One.

-ane[1] *suffix* Used primarily to differentiate words that have a corresponding form in -AN, as *human, humane.* [< L *-anus*]

-ane[2] *suffix Chem.* Denoting an open-chain saturated hydrocarbon compound of the methane series: *pentane.* [An arbitrary formation]

a·near (ə·nir') *v., adv. & prep. Poetic* or *Archaic* Near.

an·ec·do·ta (an'ik·dō'tə) *n. pl.* Unpublished historical details.

an·ec·dot·age (an'ik·dō'tij) *n.* **1** Anecdotes collectively. **2** *Colloq.* Old age: humorously considered the age for anecdotes.

an·ec·do·tal (an'ik·dō'tl) *adj.* Pertaining to, characterized by, or consisting of anecdotes. — **an'ec·do'tal·ly** *adv.*

an·ec·dote (an'ik·dōt) *n.* A brief account of some incident; a short narrative of an interesting or entertaining nature. See synonyms under STORY. [< Med.L *anecdota* < Gk. *anekdota,* neut. pl. of *anekdotos* unpublished < *an-* not + *ekdotos* published < *ekdidonai* give out, publish < *ek-* out + *didonai* give]

an·ec·dot·ic (an'ik·dot'ik) *adj.* **1** Anecdotal. **2** Habitually telling or given to anecdotes. Also **an'ec·dot'i·cal.** — **an'ec·dot'i·cal·ly** *adv.*

an·ec·dot·ist (an'ik·dō'tist) *n.* One who collects, publishes, or is given to telling anecdotes.

an·e·cho·ic (an'e·kō'ik) *adj.* **1** Without echoes. **2** Completely devoid of sound-wave reverberations: applied especially to researches in the problems of sound and acoustics.

a·nele (ə·nēl') *v.t.* **a·neled, a·nel·ing** *Archaic* To anoint, as in administering extreme unction or some other rite. [ME *anelien* < *an-* on + *ele* oil, OE *ele* oil < L *oleum*]

an·e·lec·tric (an'e·lek'trik) *adj.* Non-electric. —*n.* A non-electric substance.

a·ne·mi·a (ə·nē'mē·ə) *n.* A general or local deficiency in the amount or quality of red blood corpuscles or of hemoglobin in the blood or of both. Also spelled *anaemia.* [< NL < Gk. *anaimia* < *an-* without + *haima* blood]

a·ne·mic (ə·nē'mik) *adj.* **1** Of, having, or characterized by anemia. **2** Pale; without strength or vigor. Also spelled *anaemic.*

anemo- *combining form* Wind: *anemometer.* [< Gk. *anemos*]

a·nem·o·chore (ə·nem'ə·kôr, -kōr) *n. Bot.* A plant distributed by the wind.

a·nem·o·gram (ə·nem'ə·gram) *n.* A record made by an anemograph.

a·nem·o·graph (ə·nem'ə·graf, -gräf) *n. Meteorol.* An instrument that makes an automatic record of the velocity, force, or direction of the wind. — **a·nem'o·graph'ic** *adj.*

an·e·mog·ra·phy (an'ə·mog'rə·fē) *n. pl.* **·phies** *Meteorol.* **1** The art or act of recording automatically the velocity and direction of winds. **2** A description of or treatise on winds or their phenomena.

an·e·mol·o·gy (an'ə·mol'ə·jē) *n.* The branch of meteorological science that deals with the winds and related phenomena. — **an·e·mo·log·ic** (an'ə·mō·loj'ik) or **·i·cal** *adj.*

an·e·mom·e·ter (an'ə·mom'ə·tər) *n. Meteorol.* An instrument for measuring the force or velocity of wind. — **an·e·mo·met·ric** (an'ə·mō·met'rik) or **·ri·cal** *adj.*

ANEMOMETER

an·e·mom·e·ro·graph (an'ə·mō·met'rə·graf, -gräf) *n. Meteorol.* An anemograph, especially one that records both force and direction.

an·e·mom·e·try (an'ə·mom'ə·trē) *n. Meteorol.* The act or art of determining the velocity, force, and direction of the winds.

a·nem·o·ne (ə·nem'ə·nē) *n.* **1** Any of a genus (*Anemone*) of perennial herbs of cool and temperate regions having petal-like sepals instead of petals. **2** The sea anemone. [< Gk. *anemōnē* < *anemos* wind]

SEA ANEMONE *(def. 2)*
(3 to 5 inches in height)

an·e·moph·i·lous (an'ə·mof'ə·ləs) *adj.* Pollinated by wind-borne pollen. [< ANEMO- + Gk. *philos* loving]

an·e·moph·i·ly (an'ə·mof'ə·lē) *n.* Pollination by the wind.

a·nem·o·scope (ə·nem'ə·skōp) *n. Meteorol.* An instrument for determining the presence and direction of the wind.

an·e·mot·ro·pism (an'ə·mot'rə·piz'əm) *n.* The tropism of an organism with respect to the wind. — **an·e·mo·trop·ic** (an'ə·mō·trop'ik) *adj.*

an·en·ce·phal·ic (an·en'sə·fal'ik) *adj.* Lacking a brain. —*n.* A fetus with a rudimentary brain or none. [< Gk. *an-* without + *enkephalos* brain]

a·nent (ə·nent') *prep.* **1** *Archaic & Scot.* Concerning; in regard to. **2** *Obs.* On a line with. **3** *Obs.* Facing toward. [OE *onefen, onemn* near to + inorganic *-t*]

an·er·gy (an'ər·jē) *n.* **1** Lack of energy; inactivity. **2** Absent or reduced sensitivity to a specific allergen or antigen. [< NL *anergia* < Gk. *an-* without + *ergon* work] — **an·er·gic** (an·ûr'jik) *adj.*

an·er·oid (an'ə·roid) *adj.* Not containing or using a fluid. —*n.* An aneroid barometer. [< Gk. *a-* not + *nēros* wet + -OID]

aneroid altimeter An altimeter that uses air pressure to measure altitude.

aneroid barometer An instrument showing atmospheric pressure and approximate altitude above sea level by the movements of the elastic top of a chamber equipped with a calibrated dial and from which almost all the air has been removed.

an·es·the·sia (an'is·thē'zhə, -zhē·ə) *n.* **1** Partial or total loss of physical sensation, particularly of touch, due to disease or psychic disturbances. **2** Local or general insensibility to pain induced by the injection of an anesthetic drug, or the inhaling of an anesthetic gas. Also **an·es·the·sis** (an'is·thē'sis): also spelled *anaesthesia* [< NL < Gk. *anaisthēsia* insensibility < *an-* without + *aisthēsis* sensation]

an·es·the·si·ol·o·gy (an'is·thē'zē·ol'ə·jē) *n.* The branch of medicine that deals with the study and administration of anesthetics. Also spelled *anaesthesiology.* — **an'es·the'si·ol'o·gist** *n.*

an·es·thet·ic (an'is·thet'ik) *adj.* **1** Pertaining to or like anesthesia. **2** Producing anesthesia; making insensible to pain. —*n.* A drug or gas that causes unconsciousness or deadens sensation, as morphine, ether, chloroform, etc. Also spelled *anaesthetic.*

an·es·the·tist (ə·nes'thə·tist) *n.* A person trained to administer anesthetics: also spelled *anaesthetist.*

an·es·the·tize (ə·nes'thə·tīz) *v.t.* **·tized, ·tiz·ing** To induce anesthesia in; to render insensible, especially to pain: also spelled *anaesthetize.* — **an·es·the·ti·za·tion** (ə·nes'thə·tə·zā'shən, an'is·thet'ə-) *n.*

an·es·trus (an·es′trəs) *n.* The interval of sexual quiescence between successive periods of estrus. —**an·es·trous** *adj.*

an·e·thole (an′ə·thōl, -thol) *n.* A colorless crystalline compound, $C_{10}H_{12}O$, obtained from anise and fennel oils: used in perfumery and in medicine as an aromatic carminative. [< L *anethum* anise + -OLE]

an·eu·rysm (an′yə·riz′əm) *n.* A blood-filled, pulsating sac due to a localized abnormal dilatation of the wall of an artery. [< Gk. *aneurysma* < *ana-* up + *eurys* wide] —**an·eu·rys·mal** (an′yə·riz′məl) or **·ris′mal** *adj.*

a·new (ə·nōō′, ə·nyōō′) *adv.* 1 As a new act; in a new way. 2 Again; over again in a different way.

an·frac·tu·os·i·ty (an·frak′chōō·os′ə·tē) *n. pl.* **·ties** 1 The state or quality of being anfractuous. 2 A tortuous channel, depression, or process.

an·frac·tu·ous (an·frak′chōō·əs) *adj.* Tortuous; having many winding passages or grooves; sinuous. [< L *anfractuosus* < *anfractus* a winding < *an-* (ambi-) around + *frangere* break]

an·ga·ry (ang′gə·rē) *n.* In international law, the right of a warring nation, in case of need, to seize and use, or to destroy, neutral property, especially ships, the exercise of this right being subject to claim for compensation. Also **an·gar·i·a** (ang·gâr′ē·ə). [< F *angarie* < L *angaria* forced service to a lord < Gk. *angaros* courier]

an·gel (ān′jəl) *n.* 1 *Theol.* One of an order of spiritual beings endowed with immortality, attendant upon the Deity; a heavenly guardian, ministering spirit, or messenger. 2 A fallen spiritual being, also immortal. 3 In traditional and popular thought, the glorified spirit of a deceased person. 4 A pastor or bishop. *Rev.* ii 1. 5 A person of real or fancied angelic qualities. 6 In Christian Science, a message from Truth and Love; the inspiration of goodness, purity, and immortality, counteracting all evil, sensuality, and mortality. 7 A conventional representation of an angel, usually a youthful winged human figure in white robes with a halo. 8 A former English gold coin with the archangel Michael shown on it. 9 A guardian spirit or attendant. 10 *Colloq.* The financial backer of a play or of any enterprise. —*adj.* Angelic. [OE *engel* < L *angelus* < Gk. *angelos* messenger]

angel dust *Slang* Phencyclidine, especially when used illegally for psychedelic effect.

An·ge·le·no (an′jə·lē′nō) *n.* A native or inhabitant of Los Angeles.

An·gel Fall (ān′jəl) A waterfall in SE Venezuela, said to be the world's highest uninterrupted waterfall; 3,212 feet.

an·gel·fish (ān′jəl·fish′) *n. pl.* **·fish** or **·fish·es** 1 Any of various species of small, colorful, reef-dwelling fishes (family Chaetodontidae) with laterally compressed bodies. 2 The scalare.

ANGELFISH (def. 3)
(3 to 6 inches long)

angel food cake A delicate, spongy cake made without shortening or egg yolks. Also **angel cake**.

an·gel·hood (ān′jəl·hŏŏd) *n.* The state or nature of an angel.

an·gel·ic (an·jel′ik) *adj.* 1 Pertaining to, of, or consisting of angels; celestial. 2 Like an angel; pure; beautiful; saintly. Also **an·gel′i·cal**. [< L *angelicus* < Gk. *angelikos* < *angelos* messenger] —**an·gel′i·cal·ly** *adv.*

An·gel·i·ca (an·jel′i·kə; *Ger.* äng·gā′lē·kä, *Ital.* än·jel′ē·kä) See ANGELINA.

an·gel·i·ca (an·jel′i·kə) *n.* 1 Any of various plants of a genus (*Angelica*) widely distributed in the northern hemisphere, especially a species (*A. archangelica*) that yields an oil used as a flavoring agent. 2 A confection of candied angelica stalks. 3 A sweet white or pale-yellow fortified wine. [< Med.L (*herba*) *angelica* the angelic (herb); so called from its use against poisons]

an·gel·i·ca-tree (an·jel′i·kə·trē′) *n.* A shrub or small tree (*Aralia spinosa*) with prickly trunk and leaves, native to the eastern United States.

Also called *Hercules'-club.*

An·gel·i·co (än·jel′i·kō), **Fra**, 1387–1455, Giovanni da Fiesole, Italian painter and monk: original name *Guidi di Pietro.*

An·ge·li·na (an′jə·lī′nə, *Ger.* äng·gä·lē′nä) A feminine personal name. Also *Fr.* **An·gé·lique** (än·zhā·lēk′) or **An·gé·line** (än·zhā·lēn′). See also ANGELICA. [< Gk., angel]

an·gel·o·la·try (ān′jəl·ol′ə·trē) *n.* Angel-worship.

an·gel·ol·o·gy (ān′jəl·ol′ə·jē) *n.* The doctrine concerning angels; the branch of theology that treats of angels. —**an·gel·o·log·ic** (ān′·jəl·ə·loj′ik) or **·log′i·cal** *adj.*

angel shark A raylike shark of temperate seas (genus *Squatina*) having very large winglike pectoral fins.

an·ge·lus (an′jə·ləs) *n.* 1 In the Roman Catholic Church, a prayer said to commemorate the Annunciation: named from its first word. 2 A bell rung at morning, noon, and night as a call to recite this prayer: also called **angelus bell**. Also **An′ge·lus**. [< L]

an·ger (ang′gər) *n.* Violent vindictive passion; sudden and strong displeasure, as a result of injury, opposition, or mistreatment; wrath; ire. — *v.t.* 1 To make angry; enrage. 2 *Dial.* To inflame; make painful. See synonyms under INCENSE[1]. [< ON *angr* grief]

Synonyms (noun): animosity, choler, displeasure, exasperation, fury, hatred, impatience, indignation, ire, irritation, offense, passion, rage, resentment, temper, wrath. *Anger* is sharp, sudden, and, like all violent passions, necessarily brief. *Resentment* (a feeling back or feeling over again) is persistent brooding over injuries. *Rage* drives one beyond the bounds of prudence or discretion: *fury* is stronger yet, and sweeps one away into uncontrollable violence. *Anger* is personal and usually selfish. *Wrath* is deeper, more enduring than *anger*, and may be vengeful. *Indignation* is impersonal and unselfish *displeasure* at unworthy acts (L *indigna*), that is, at wrong as wrong. Pure *indignation* is not followed by regret, and is often a duty. See HATRED. *Antonyms*: forbearance, gentleness, long-suffering, patience, peace, peaceableness, peacefulness, self-control.

An·gers (an′jərz, ang′gərz; *Fr.* än·zhā′) A city of western France on the Maine.

An·ge·vin (an′jə·vin) *adj.* 1 Of or pertaining to Anjou. 2 Of or pertaining to the Plantagenet kings of England from 1154 to 1204. —*n.* 1 A native or inhabitant of Anjou. 2 A member of the royal house of Anjou. Also **An′ge·vine** (-vin, -vīn). [< F]

an·gi·na (an·jī′nə, an′jə·nə) *n.* 1 Any disease characterized by spasmodic suffocating pain, as quinsy, croup, etc. 2 Angina pectoris. [< L, quinsy < *angere* choke] —**an·gi′nal** *adj.* — **an·gi·nose** (an′jə·nōs) *adj.*

angina pec·to·ris (pek′tə·ris) Paroxysmal pain below the sternum and sometimes extending to the left shoulder and arm, due to inadequate blood and oxygen supplied to the heart. [< NL, angina of the chest]

angio- *combining form* 1 *Bot.* Seed vessel: *angiosperm.* 2 *Med.* Blood vessel; lymph vessel: *angiology.* Also, before vowels, **angi-**. [< Gk. *angeion* case, vessel, capsule]

an·gi·o·car·di·og·ra·phy (an′jē·ō·kär′dē·og′rə·fē) *n.* Radiography of the heart and connecting blood vessels of the chest following injection of a substance opaque to radiation. —**an′gi·o·car′di·o·graph′ic** *adj.*

an·gi·o·car·pous (an′jē·ə·kär′pəs) *adj. Bot.* 1 Having the fruit covered by a distinct envelope. 2 Having the fruit-bearing surface disposed inside the tissue of the sporocarp, as certain fungi, or lining the interior of cavities, as certain lichens. Also **an′gi·o·car′pic**. —**an·gi·o·car·py** (an′jē·ō·kär′pē) *n.*

an·gi·og·ra·phy (an′jē·og′rə·fē) *n.* Radiography of blood vessels following injection of a radiopaque substance. —**an·gi·o·gram** (an′jē·ō·gram) *n.* —**an′gi·o·graph′ic** (an′jē·ō·graf′ik) *adj.*

an·gi·ol·o·gy (an′jē·ol′ə·jē) *n.* That part of systematic anatomy which relates to blood and lymph vessels.

an·gi·o·ma (an′jē·ō′mə) *n. pl.* **·mas** or **·ma·ta** (-mə·tə) A tumor consisting of blood vessels and/or lymph vessels. [< NL < ANGI(O)- -OMA] —**an·gi·om·a·tous** (an′jē·om′ə·təs) *adj.*

an·gi·o·sperm (an′jē·ə·spûrm′) *n.* Any plant of a division (Magnoliophyta, formerly Angiospermae) of vascular seed plants in which the ovules are enclosed in an ovary. Also called *flowering plant.* **an′gi·o·sper′mous** *adj.*

an·gi·o·ten·sin (an′jē·ō·ten′sin) *n.* 1 Either of two peptide hormones that influence the constriction of blood vessels and the secretion of aldosterone. 2 A synthetic amide used in medicine as a pressor agent.

an·gi·ot·o·my (an′jē·ot′ə·mē) *n.* Incision into an artery or vein.

Ang·kor (ang′kôr) An assemblage of ruins in NW Cambodia; site of **Angkor Thom** (tôm), an ancient Khmer capital, and **Angkor Wat** or **Angkor Vat** (wät), the best preserved Khmer temple.

an·gle[1] (ang′gəl) *v.i.* **an·gled, an·gling** 1 To fish with a hook and line. 2 To try to get slyly or artfully: with *for.* [< *n.*] —*n. Obs.* A fish hook; fishing tackle. [OE *angel* fish hook]

an·gle[2] (ang′gəl) *n.* 1 *Geom.* **a** The figure formed by the meeting of two lines or of two or more surfaces; corner; point. **b** The figure, concept, or relation of two straight lines (sides) emanating from one point (the vertex).

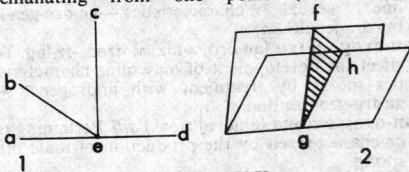

PLANE ANGLES

c The figure formed by the intersection of two straight lines or of two or more planes. See list of geometric angles below. 2 A secluded place resembling a corner; nook. 3 The point of view or aspect from which any object, question, or situation may be regarded. —**critical angle** 1 The least angle of incidence at which a ray is totally reflected. 2 *Aeron.* The angle of attack at which the airflow striking the under surface of an airplane changes abruptly, causing similar changes in lift and drag. —**gliding angle** *Aeron.* The angle the flight path of an airplane makes with the horizontal when flying in still air under the influence of gravity alone. —*v.* **an·gled, an·gling** *v.t.* 1 To move or turn at an angle or by angles: to *angle* a ball to avoid a hazard. 2 *Colloq.* To impart a particular bias or interpretation, as to a story or report. —*v.i.* 3 To proceed or turn itself at an angle or by angles: The road *angled* up the hill. [< F < L *angulus* a corner, angle]

PRINCIPAL GEOMETRIC ANGLES

—**acute angle** An angle less than a right angle.

—**adjacent angle** An angle having a common side with another angle and the same vertex.

—**alternate angle** Either of two non-adjacent interior or exterior angles formed on opposite sides of a line which crosses two other lines.

—**central angle** An angle whose vertex is the center of a circle and whose sides are radii.

—**complementary angle** One of two angles whose sum is a right angle.

—**conjugate angle** Either of two angles whose sum is a perigon.

—**dihedral angle** The relation of two intersecting planes, as measured by the difference in direction of perpendiculars to them.

—**exterior angle** 1 Any of four angles formed on the outside of two straight lines cut by a third line. 2 The angle formed between any side of a polygon and the extension of an adjacent side.

—**interior angle** 1 One of the four angles formed between two straight lines cut by a third line. 2 The angle formed in the interior of a polygon by two adjacent sides.

—**obtuse angle** An angle greater than a right angle.

—**plane angle** An angle made by lines lying in one plane.

—**reflex angle** An angle greater than a straight angle.

—right angle An angle whose sides are perpendicular to each other; an angle of 90°.

—solid angle The angle formed at the vertex of a cone or subtended at the point of intersection of three or more planes; equal to 4π steradians.

—spherical angle The angle formed at the intersection of two great circles on a sphere: its value is a measure of the difference in direction of the arcs of the intersecting circles.

—straight angle An angle of 180°, generated by two straight lines extending in opposite directions from the vertex.

—supplementary angle One of two angles whose sum is a straight angle.

An·gle (ang'gəl) n. 1 A member of a Germanic tribe which migrated from southern Denmark to Britain in the fifth and sixth centuries and founded the kingdoms of East anglia, Mercia, and Northumbria. 2 A national of any of the kingdoms in the parts of Britain settled by this tribe: from its descendants the country came to be called England (Angle-land). [<L *Anglus*, sing. of *Angli* <Gmc.]

an·gled (ang'gəld) adj. 1 Having angles. 2 Set or placed at an angle.

an·gle·doz·er (ang'gəl·dō 'zər) n. A tractorlike machine for leveling ground, scraping roads, etc., with its scraper adjusted to push the dirt off to one side.

angle iron A piece of iron in the form of an angle, especially a right angle, for joining or strengthening beams, girders, and corners, or as a component member of an iron structure. Also **an'gle·i'ron** n.

an·gle·me·ter (ang'gəl·mē 'tər) n. 1 A clinometer. 2 *Mech.* A device for determining the differences in angular velocity of the crank shaft of an engine during a revolution.

angle of attack *Aeron.* The acute angle between movement relative to air or wind and the chord of an airfoil, or the fore-and-aft axis of a body.

angle of incidence 1 *Optics* The angle at which a beam of light or sound strikes a surface relative to the perpendicular. 2 *Aeron.* The angle of attack.

angle of repose The inclination to the horizontal assumed by a heap of sand, gravel, or other loose particulate material when in equilibrium with gravity. Also called **angle of friction.**

angle of view *Optics* The angle formed by two lines drawn from the extremities of an object or scene to the center of a lens.

angle of yaw *Aeron.* The acute angle between the direction of the relative wind and the plane of symmetry of an aircraft.

angle plate *Mech.* One of two metal plates which may be securely bolted at right angles to each other as a support for tools or in machine-working.

an·gle·pod (ang'gəl·pod') n. A vine (genus *Vincetoxicum*) of the milkweed family, especially *V. gonocarpos* of the southern United States, bearing angular pods.

an·gler (ang'glər) n. 1 One of a family (*Lophiidae*) of fishes having a wide, froglike mouth and antennalike filaments attached to the head with which it angles for its prey: also called *frogfish.* 2 One who fishes with rod, hook, and line.

An·gle·sey (ang'gəl·sē) An island county of NW Wales; 275 square miles. Also **An'gle·sea.**

an·gle·site (ang'glə·sīt) n. A highly lustrous, white orthorhombic lead sulfate, PbSO₄. [from *Anglesey,* where first found]

an·gle·tube (ang'gəl·tōōb', -tyōōb') n. The tube which connects the facepiece of a gas mask to the hose.

an·gle·worm (ang'gəl·wûrm ') n. An earthworm commonly used as bait in angling.

An·gli·a (ang'glē·ə) The Latin name for ENGLAND.

An·gli·an (ang'glē·ən) adj. Pertaining to the Angles or their country. — n. The Northumbrian and Mercian dialects of Old English.

An·glic (ang'glik) n. A simplified form of English evolved for use as an auxiliary international language by R. E. Zachrisson, 1880–1937, Swedish linguist. — adj. Anglian.

An·gli·can (ang'glə·kən) adj. 1 Pertaining to the Church of England, the churches derived

from it, or the High-Church party in any of these. 2 Pertaining to England or that which is English. — n. A member of the Church of England or of any church derived from it; also, a High-Churchman. [<Med. L *Anglicanus* < *Anglicus* English <L *Angli* the Angles, the English]

An·gli·can·ism (ang'gli·kən·iz'əm) n. The doctrine, discipline, and practice of the Church of England.

Anglican orders Holy orders, as administered in the Church of England.

An·gli·ce (ang'glə·sē) adv. In English; according to the usage of the English language: Napoli, *Anglice* Naples. [<Med. L]

An·gli·cism (ang'glə·siz') m) n. 1 Any word, phrase, or idiom peculiarly English. 2 A word, phrase, or sense used in England, but not in accepted use in the United States; a Briticism. 3 Any trait or usage peculiarly English. 4 The state or quality of being English.

An·gli·cist (ang'glə·sist) n. An authority on or student of English language and literature.

An·gli·ci·za·tion (ang'glə·sə·zā'shən, -sī·zā'shən) n. 1 The act of making or becoming English in quality, character, or form. 2 The result or effect of Anglicizing.

An·gli·cize (ang'glə·sīz) v. ·cized, ·ciz·ing v.t. To give an English form, style, or idiom to. — v.i. To acquire some English trait or peculiarity; become like the English. Also *Brit.* **An'gli·cise.**

An·gli·form (ang'glə·fôrm) adj. Having English form.

An·gli·fy (ang'glə·fī) v.t. v.i. ·fied, ·fy·ing To Anglicize.

an·gling (ang'gling) n. The act or art of fishing with a hook, line, and rod.

An·glist (ang'glist) n. An authority of England.

Anglo- combining form English; English and: used in various adjectives and nouns indicating relations of language, interests, etc., between the countries concerned or natives of them: *Anglo-Asiatic, Anglo-Irish.* [<L *Anglus* an Angle, an Englishman]

An·glo (ang'glō) n. pl. ·glos *U.S.* An Anglo-American, especially as distinguished from a Mexican-American.

An·glo-Af·ri·can (ang'glō·af'rə·kən) adj. Designating a native of Africa of English descent.

An·glo-A·mer·i·can (ang'glō·ə·mer'ə·kən) adj. 1 Of or pertaining to England and America or the relations of the peoples of the two countries: *Anglo-American* trade. 2 Of or pertaining to the English people who have settled in America. — n. A native of England or a descendant of a native of England who has settled in the United States or in America.

An·glo-Boer War (ang'glō·bōr', -bor', -bōōr') See BOER WAR in table under WAR.

An·glo-Cath·o·lic (ang'glō·kath'ə·lik, -kath' lik) adj. 1 Of the Anglican Church, but emphasizing Catholic rather than Protestant tendencies. 2 Pertaining to the High-Church party in the Church of England or allied bodies. —**An·glo-Cath·ol·i·cism** (ang'glō·kə·thol'ə ·siz'əm) n.

An·glo-Chi·nese (ang'glō·chī) ·nēz', -chī nēs') adj. Of or pertaining to persons or things in China that are of English origin.

An·glo-French (ang'glō·french') adj. 1 Pertaining to the English and French jointly or to their countries. 2 Relating to Anglo-French. — n. The Norman dialect of Old French current in England from the Norman Conquest to the end of the 13th century: also called *Anglo-Norman, Norman French.* Abbr. *A.F., AF.*

An·glo-In·di·an (ang'glō·in'dē·ən) adj. 1 Pertaining to or between England and India. 2 Of the Anglo-Indians. 3 Having both English and East Indian characteristics: the *Anglo-Indian* style of living. — n. 1 An Englishman living in India. 2 A person of mixed English and Indian parentage. 3 The vocabulary, consisting of Anglicized native words, developed by British citizens in civil and military service in India: also called *Hobson-Jobson.*

An·glo-ma·ni·a (ang'glō·mā'nē·ə) n. Overfondness for or imitation of English manners, speech, institutions, or customs. —**An' glo·ma'ni·ac** (-ak) n.

An·glo-Nor·man (ang'glō·nô r'mən) adj. 1

English and Norman. 2 Pertaining to the Normans who settled in England after the Norman Conquest, their descendants, or their language. —n. 1 One of the Norman settlers in England after the Norman Conquest. 2 Anglo-French.

An·glo·phile (ang'glə·fil, -fil) n. A lover of England or its people, customs, institutions, or manners. — adj. Of or like Anglophiles. Also **An'glo·phil** (-fil).

An·glo·phobe (ang'glə·fōb) n. One who hates or distrusts England or English manners, people, institutions, or customs. — adj. Of or like Anglophobes. Also **An'glo·pho·bi·ac** (ang' glə·fō'bē·ak).

An·glo·pho·bi·a (ang'glə·fō'bē·ə) n. Hatred or dread of England or English customs, people, manners, or institutions. —**An'glo·pho'bic** (-fō'bik, -fob'ik) adj.

An·glo-Sax·on (ang'glō·sak'sən) n. 1 A member of one of the Germanic tribes (Angles, Saxons, and Jutes) that conquered Britain in the fifth and sixth centuries. 2 A member of the nation descended from these peoples which dominated England until the Norman Conquest. 3 Their West Germanic language; Old English. 4 Any one of English nationality or descent. 5 *Colloq.* Simple, pithy, unadorned English, free of scholarly borrowings or circumlocutions: the native element in the language being considered more forceful and direct. 6 *Colloq.* The short, vulgar words of the language, as used for their pungency. 7 Loosely, the modern English language. — adj. Of or pertaining to the Anglo-Saxons, their language, customs, or descendants. —**An'glo-Sax'on·ism** n.

Anglo-Saxon Chronicle A chronological prose history of England in Old English from early Christian times to 1154; especially those recensions to 892 usually accredited to Alfred.

An·go·la (ang·gō'lə) A country in western Africa; 481,351 square miles; capital, Loanda; formerly *Portuguese West Africa.*

An·go·ra (ang·gôr'ə, -gō 'rə, ang'gə·rə) See ANKARA.

An·go·ra (ang·gôr'ə, -gō 'rə) n. 1 An Angora goat. 2 The long, silky hair of this goat: when manufactured, often called *mohair.* 3 An imitation of Angora cloth made of rabbit hair. 4 A shawl, cloth, etc., made of Angora material or its imitations. 5 An Angora cat.

Angora cat A variety of cat, originally from Angora, with long, silky hair.

Angora goat A goat, originally from Angora, reared for its long, silky hair, known as **An·go·ra wool.**

an·gos·tu·ra bark (ang'gəs·tōōr'ə, -tyōor'ə) A bark from a South American tree (*Galipea officinalis*), used in the preparation of a tonic and flavoring. Also **An'gos·tu'ra.** [from *Angostura,* former name of Ciudad Bolívar]

Angostura bitters A bitter aromatic infusion, used as a flavoring, prepared from angostura bark and other roots, etc.: a trade name.

An·gou·l ême (än·gōō·lem') A city in western France.

An·gra do He·ro·ís·mo (äng'grə dōō ē·rōō·ēz' mōō) One of three districts in the Azores, comprising Terceira, S;atao Jorge, and Graciosa islands; 268 square miles; capital, Angra do Heroísmo, on Terceira.

An·gra Pe·que·na (ang'grə pē ·kwē'nə) The former name for LAU/U DERITZ.

an·gry (ang'grē) adj. ·gri·er, ·gri·est 1 Feeling, showing, or excited by anger; indignant. 2 Showing signs of anger; appearing to threaten: *angry* skies. 3 Badly inflamed: an *angry* sore. —**an·gri·ly** (ang'grə·lē) adv. —**an·gri·ness** n.

angst (ängst) n. Anxiety; dread. [<G]

ang·strom (ang'strəm) n. A unit for the measurement of wavelength, equal to a hundred millionth of a centimeter, or 0.003937 millionths of an inch. Also **angstrom unit.** [after A. J. *Ångström* m]

Ång·ström (ang'strəm, *Sw.* ōng'strœm), Anders Jonas, 1814–74, Swedish physicist.

an·gui·form (ang'gwə·fôrm) adj. Shaped like a snake. [<L *anguis* snake + -FORM]

An·guil·la (ang-gwil′ə) See St. Christopher, Nevis and Anguilla.

an·guil·li·form (ang-gwil′ə-fôrm) *adj.* Having the form of an eel. [< L *anguilla* eel + -FORM]

an·guine (ang′gwin) *adj.* Of, pertaining to, or like a snake. [< L *anguinus* < *anguis* snake]

an·guish (ang′gwish) *n.* Excruciating mental or bodily pain; agony; torture. See synonyms under AGONY, ANXIETY. —*v.t. & v.i.* To affect or suffer with anguish. [OF *anguisse* < L *angustia* tightness, difficulty < *angustus* narrow, tight]

an·gu·lar (ang′gyə-lər) *adj.* 1 Having, forming, or constituting an angle or angles; sharp-cornered; pointed. 2 Measured by an angle: *angular* motion. 3 Pertaining to angles. 4 Bony; gaunt and with little flesh, so as to be awkward or ungraceful. 5 Of a crabbed or unaccommodating disposition. [< L *angularis* < *angulus* corner, angle] —**an′gu·lar·ly** *adv.*

an·gu·lar·i·ty (ang′gyə-lar′ə-tē) *n. pl.* **·ties** 1 The state or condition of being angular. 2 *pl.* Angular outlines or corners. Also **an′gu·lar·ness.**

an·gu·late (ang′gyə-lit, -lāt) *adj.* Having angles; angular: used chiefly in botany: *angulate* leaves. Also **an′gu·lat′ed.** —*v.t. & v.i.* **·lat·ed, ·lat·ing** To make or become angular. [< L *angulatus,* pp. of *angulare* make angular < *angulus* corner, angle] —**an′gu·late·ly** *adv.*

an·gu·la·tion (ang′gyə-lā′shən) *n.* 1 The making of angles. 2 An angular formation or position.

An·gus (ang′gəs) A county in eastern Scotland; 874 square miles: formerly *Forfar.*

Angus Og (ōg) In Irish mythology, Angus the Young, god of love and beauty; son of Dagda.

an·gus·tate (ang-gus′tāt) *adj.* Compressed; narrowed. [< L *angustatus,* pp. of *angustare* narrow < *angustus* narrow]

ang·wan·ti·bo (äng′wän-tē′bō) *n.* A small, tailed primate *(Arctocebus calabarensis)* of African forests, having a small, pointed face.

An·halt (än′hält) A former state and duchy of central Germany; 898 square miles.

an·he·la·tion (an′hi-lā′shən) *n. Pathol.* Shortness of breath; difficult respiration; dyspnoea. [< F *anhélation* < L *anhelatio, -onis* < *anhelare* pant]

an·he·lous (an-hē′ləs) *adj.* Short-breathed; panting.

an·hi·dro·sis (an′hi-drō′sis) *n. Pathol.* Partial or complete lack of perspiration. Also **an·i·dro·sis** (an′i-drō′sis). [< NL < Gk. *an-* without + *hidrōs* perspiration] —**an·hi·drot·ic** (an′hi-drot′ik) *adj.*

an·hin·ga (an-hing′gə) *n.* The snakebird. [< Tupian]

An·hwei (än′hwā′) A province of eastern China; 54,000 square miles; divided after 1949 into **North Anhwei;** 40,000 square miles; capital, Hofei; and **South Anhwei;** 14,000 square miles; capital, Wuhu. Also **An·hui** (än′hwā′).

an·hy·drate (an-hī′drāt) *v.t.* **·drat·ed, ·drat·ing** To dehydrate.

an·hy·dride (an-hī′drīd, -drid) *n. Chem.* 1 Any organic or inorganic compound from which the water has been removed. 2 A non-metallic oxide to which water has been added, with formation of an *acid anhydride.* 3 A metallic oxide which forms a *basic anhydride* upon the addition of water. [See ANHYDROUS]

an·hy·drite (an-hī′drīt) *n.* An orthorhombic calcium sulfate, $CaSO_4$, found as a whitish or light-colored mineral.

an·hy·drous (an-hī′drəs) *adj. Chem.* Pertaining to or designating a compound which has no water in its composition, especially one having no water of crystallization. [< Gk. *anydros* waterless < *an-* without + *hydōr* water]

a·ni (ä′nē) *n.* Any of several species of birds of the cuckoo family (genus *Crotophaga*), generally black with metallic reflections, ranging from Florida southward. [< Tupian]

An·i·ak·chak (an′ē-ak′chak) A volcano in the Aleutian Range, SW Alaska; crater diameter, 6 miles.

a·nigh (ə-nī′) *adv. & prep.* Near; nigh; nigh to.

a·night (ə-nīt′) *adv.* At night; nightly. Also **a·nights′.**

an·il (an′il) *n.* 1 A West Indian indigo plant *(Indigofera suffruticosa).* 2 The indigo dye made from this plant. [< F < Pg. < Arabic *al-nil* the blue]

an·ile (an′īl, ā′nīl, an′il) *adj.* Like an old woman;

weak or feeble-minded. [< L *anilis* < *anus* old woman] —**a·nil·i·ty** (ə-nil′ə-tē) *n.*

an·i·line (an′ə-lin, -līn) *n.* A colorless oily compound, $C_6H_5NH_2$, the base from which many of the coal-tar dyes, resins, and varnishes are made. It may be regarded as derived from ammonia, NH_3, by replacing one molecule of hydrogen with the radical phenyl, C_6H_5, and is hence considered chemically as *phenylamine.* Aniline was originally obtained in the distillation of indigo, but is now chiefly made from nitrobenzene. —*adj.* Made of, derived from, or pertaining to aniline. Also **an·i·lin** (an′ə-lin). [< ANIL + -INE]

aniline red See MAGENTA.

an·i·mad·ver·sion (an′ə-mad·vûr′zhən, -shən) *n.* Criticism or censure; a censorious comment or reflection: with *on* or *upon.* [< L *animadversio, -onis* < *animadvertere.* See ANIMADVERT.] —**an′i·mad·ver′sive** (-siv) *adj.* —**an′i·mad·ver′sive·ness** *n.*

Synonyms: aspersion, blame, censure, chiding, comment, criticism, disapproval, rebuke, reflection, reprehension, reproof. *Comment* and *criticism* may be favorable as well as censorious; they imply no superiority or authority on the part of him who utters them; nor do *reflection* and *reprehension,* which are simply turning the mind back upon what is disapproved. *Reprehension* is calm and just, and with good intent; it is therefore a serious matter, however mild, and is capable of great force, as expressed in the phrase severe *reprehension. Reflection* is often from mere ill feeling, and is likely to be more personal and less impartial than *reprehension;* we often speak of unkind or unjust *reflections. Rebuke,* literally a stopping of the mouth, is administered to a forward or hasty person; *reproof* is administered to one intentionally or deliberately wrong; both words imply authority in the reprover. *Antonyms:* approbation, approval, commendation, encomium, eulogy, panegyric, praise.

an·i·mad·vert (an′ə-mad·vûrt′) *v.i.* 1 To comment critically, usually in an adverse sense: with *upon.* 2 *Obs.* To notice. [< L *animadvertere* take notice of < *animus* mind + *advertere* turn to. See ADVERT.]

an·i·mal (an′ə-məl) *n.* 1 A sentient living organism typically endowed with voluntary motion and sensation: distinguished from *plant.* 2 Any such creature as distinguished from man; a beast or brute. 3 A debased and bestial human being. 4 *pl.* Domestic quadrupeds. 5 Any creature but a bird, fish, or insect. —*adj.* 1 Of or pertaining to animals. 2 Bestial.

Synonyms (noun): beast, brute, fauna. An *animal* is a sentient being, distinct from inanimate matter and from vegetable life on the one side and from purely mental and spiritual existence on the other. Man is properly classified as an *animal,* but to call any individual man an *animal* is to imply that the animal nature has undue supremacy. The *brute* is the *animal* viewed as dull to all finer feeling; the *beast* is looked upon as a being of appetites. *Creature* is a word of wide signification, including inanimate objects, plants, animals, angels, or men as *divinely* created. The *animals* of a region are collectively called its *fauna. Antonyms:* angel, man, matter, mind, mineral, soul, spirit, vegetable.

animal act Any entertainment or demonstration featuring one or more performing animals.

animal charcoal Charcoal made from bones; bone-black.

animal crackers Small, sweetened cookies made in the shape of various animals.

an·i·mal·cu·la (an′ə-mal′kyə-lə) Plural of ANIMALCULUM.

an·i·mal·cu·lae (an′ə-mal′kyə-lē) Erroneous plural of *animalcula,* thought of as a feminine singular noun.

an·i·mal·cule (an′ə-mal′kyōōl) *n.* 1 A microscopic, usu. motile organism, as a paramecium, ameba, etc. 2 *Obs.* Any small animal, as a gnat. [< L *animalculum,* dim. of *animal* animal] **an′i·mal′cu·lar** (-kyə-lər) *adj.*

an·i·mal·cu·lism (an′ə-mal′kyə-liz′əm) *n.* An old biological theory that animalcules are the cause or source of vital phenomena and also of disease.

an·i·mal·cu·lum (an′ə-mal′kyə-ləm) *n. pl.* **·la** (-lə) An animalcule.

animal heat Heat generated by the chemical processes constantly going on in an animal organism: sustained at nearly uniform temperatures.

animal husbandry That branch of agriculture specializing in the breeding, raising, and care of farm animals.

an·i·mal·ism (an′ə-məl-iz′əm) *n.* 1 The state or condition of mere animals; the state of being actuated by sensual appetites only. 2 The belief or doctrine that man is entirely animal, having no soul or spirit.

an·i·mal·ist (an′ə-məl-ist) *n.* 1 An adherent to the doctrine of animalism. 2 A painter or sculptor of animals. —**an′i·mal·is′tic** *adj.*

an·i·mal·i·ty (an′ə-mal′ə-tē) *n.* 1 The animal qualities. 2 Animal life; the animal kingdom. 3 The merely animal nature, as distinguished from the moral and spiritual.

an·i·mal·i·za·tion (an′ə-məl·ə-zā′shən, -ī-zā′-) *n.* 1 The act of animalizing, or the state of being animalized. 2 *Ecol.* The number and kinds of animals, as horses, cattle, etc., in a country or district.

an·i·mal·ize (an′ə-məl·īz′) *v.t.* **·ized, ·iz·ing** 1 To render brutal; sensualize. 2 To change into animal matter, especially by digestive assimilation. 3 *Obs.* To give animal form to.

animal kingdom One of the three great divisions of nature, embracing all animal organisms: contrasted with the *mineral* and *vegetable* kingdoms; also, all animals, collectively.

an·i·mal·ly (an′ə-məl-ē) *adv.* 1 In an animal manner; with respect to the body; corporally, as distinguished from mentally. 2 With respect to the animal or animal spirits; physically, as distinguished from spiritually.

animal magnetism 1 Mesmerism. 2 Magnetic personal qualities. 3 Sensualism: usually with opprobrious implications.

animal spirits Vivaciousness; energy; the buoyancy of good health.

animal starch Glycogen.

an·i·mate (an′ə-māt) *v.t.* **·mat·ed, ·mat·ing** 1 To impart life to; make alive. 2 To move to action; incite; inspire: What motives *animated* him? 3 To produce activity or energy in: The wind *animated* the flags. See synonyms under ENCOURAGE, STIMULATE, STIR[1]. —*adj.* (an′ə-mit) 1 Possessing animal life; living. 2 Vivacious; lively. Also **an′i·mat′ed.** See synonyms under AIRY, ALIVE, EAGER, SANGUINE, VIVID. [< L *animatus,* pp. of *animare* to fill with breath, make alive < *anima* breath, soul] —**an′i·mat′ed·ly** *adv.*

animated cartoon See under CARTOON.

an·i·mat·er (an′ə-mā′tər) *n.* An animator.

an·i·mat·ing (an′ə-mā′ting) *adj.* Imparting life or animation; inspiring. —**an′i·mat′ing·ly** *adv.*

an·i·ma·tion (an′ə-mā′shən) *n.* 1 The act of imparting or the state of possessing life. 2 The state of being animated; liveliness; vivacity. 3 The process and technique of preparing the set of drawings to be filmed and exhibited as an animated cartoon. See synonyms under WARMTH.

an·i·ma·tive (an′ə-mā′tiv) *adj.* Enlivening; inspiring.

a·ni·ma·to (ä′nē-mä′tō) *adv. Music* With animation; in an animated manner: also *con anima.* [< Ital.]

an·i·ma·tor (an′ə-mā′tər) *n.* 1 One who or that which animates. 2 An artist who prepares a given set of drawings to be filmed as an animated cartoon.

an·i·mé (an′ə-mā, -mē) *n.* A hard fossilized resin obtained from the stem of an East African tree *(Hymenaea courbaril),* used in making flavorings, varnishes and lacquers. [< F < Sp., prob. < native name]

an·i·mism (an′ə-miz′əm) *n.* 1 The doctrine that the phenomena of animal life are produced by a soul or spiritual force distinct from matter. 2 The belief in the existence of spirit or soul, as distinct from matter. 3 The doctrine that inanimate objects and natural phenomena possess a personal life or soul. [< L *anima* soul] — **an′i·mist** *n.* —**an′i·mis′tic** *adj.*

an·i·mos·i·ty (an′ə-mos′ə-tē) *n. pl.* **·ties** Active and vehement enmity; hatred; ill will. See synonyms under ANGER, ENMITY, FEUD[1], HATRED, HOSTILITY. [< L *animositas, -tatis* high spirit, boldness < *animus* soul, mind, spirit]

an·i·mus (an′ə·məs) n. 1 Hostile feeling or intent; animosity. 2 The animating thought or purpose; disposition; temper. 3 Purpose; intention. [< L]

an·i·on (an′ī·ən) n. Chem. The electronegative constituent of an electrolyte, appearing at the anode of a voltaic cell; a negative ion: opposed to cation. [< Gk. anion (thing) going up, neut. of ppr. of anienai < ana- up + ienai go]

an·ise (an′is) n. 1 A small South European and North African plant (Pimpinella anisum) that furnishes aniseed. 2 Aniseed. Compare DILL. [< OF anis < L anisum < Gk. anison]

an·i·seed (an′i·sēd′) n. The fragrant seed of the anise plant, used in cookery and medicine.

an·i·sei·ko·ni·a (an′i·sī·kō′nē·ə, an·is′i-) n. Pathol. A disorder of vision in which the image perceived by one eye differs in form and size from that perceived by the other. [< Gk. anisos unequal + eikōn image]

an·i·sei·kon·ic (an·ī′si·kon′ik, an·is′i-) adj. 1 Pertaining to, characterized by, or serving to correct aniseikonia. 2 Optics Describing lenses designed to produce distorted images, especially in connection with the testing of vision.

an·i·sette (an′ə·zet′, -set′) n. A cordial made from or flavored with aniseed. [< F]

aniso- combining form Unequal; dissimilar: anisogamy. See ISO-. [< Gk. anisos unequal]

an·i·so·ga·mete (an·ī′sə·gə·mēt′) n. Heterogamete.

an·i·sog·a·my (an′ī·sog′ə·mē) n. Biol. A union of gametes similar in general type but unequal in size: opposed to isogamy. —**an′i·sog′a·mous** adj.

an·i·sole (an′ə·sōl) n. A colorless liquid compound, C₇H₈O, used as an insecticide and in the manufacture of perfumes. [< L anisum anise + -OLE¹]

an·i·so·mer·ic (an·ī′sə·mer′ik) adj. Chem. Composed of the same elements but in different proportions: opposed to isomeric.

an·i·som·er·ous (an′ī·som′ər·əs) adj. 1 Bot. Having an unequal number of parts in different floral whorls; unsymmetrical. 2 Zool. Having the ridges of contiguous molar teeth increasing by more than one, as in mastodons.

an·i·so·met·ric (an·ī′sə·met′rik) adj. Mineral. Not isometric; specifically, dissimilar in the direction of the different axes, as some crystals.

an·i·so·me·tro·pi·a (an·ī′sə·mə·trō′pē·ə) n. Pathol. Inequality in the refracting power of the eyes.

an·i·so·phyl·lous (an·ī′sə·fil′əs) adj. Bot. Having leaves of unequal size or unlike form.

an·i·so·phyl·ly (an·ī′sə·fil′ē) n. Bot. The property of having different leaves; particularly, the possession of leaves of different size and character on different sides of plagiotropic shoots.

an·i·so·spore (an·ī′sə·spôr′, -spōr′) n. Zool. A form of spore developed by colonial radiolarians, consisting of microspores and macrospores which probably copulate: opposed to isospore.

an·i·so·trop·ic (an·ī′sə·trop′ik) adj. 1 Physics Having different properties in different directions, as when a fibrous substance conducts heat more rapidly along its fibers than across them. 2 Bot. Responding unequally to external influences, as plant organs. 3 Optics Exhibiting double refraction, as a lens or mineral. Also eolitropic. Compare ISOTROPIC.

an·i·sot·ro·py (an·ī′sot′rə·pē) n. The property or state of being anisotropic. Also **an′i·sot′ro·pism** (-piz′əm).

A·ni·ta (ə·nē′tə) Diminutive of ANA.

An·jou (an′jōō, Fr. äṅ·zhōō′) A former province of western France; divided in 1790 into several departments.

Anjou A family of French nobles, originally ruling the duchy of Anjou, who succeeded to the English throne in 1154 upon the accession of Henry II, son of Geoffrey of Anjou. See PLANTAGENET.

An·ka·ra (äng′kə·rə, aṅg′-) The capital of Turkey since 1923, located in central Anatolia: ancient Ancyra: formerly Angora.

An·ka·ra·tra Highlands (äng′kä·rä′trä) A mountainous region of central Madagascar; highest point, 8,552 feet.

an·ker (ang′kər) n. A liquid measure of about 10 gallons. [< Du.]

an·ker·ite (ang′kər·īt) n. A mineral resembling dolomite, composed of a white, red, or grayish calcium-magnesium-iron carbonate crystallizing in the hexagonal system. [after Prof. Anker, Austrian mineralogist]

ankh (angk) n. In Egyptian art and mythology, a tau cross having a looped top: an emblem of generation; the ansate cross. For illustration see under CROSS. [< Egyptian ānkh life, soul]

An·king (än′king′) A city on the Yangtze River; former capital of Anhwei Province, China: formerly Hwaining.

an·kle (ang′kəl) n. Anat. 1 The joint connecting the foot and the leg. 2 The part of the leg between the foot and the calf near the ankle joint. [Prob. < ON, replacing OE anclēow]

an·kle·bone (ang′kəl·bōn′) n. Anat. The talus or astragalus. Also ankle bone.

an·klet (ang′klit) n. 1 An ornament or fetter for the ankle. 2 A short sock reaching just above the ankle.

an·kus (ang′kəs, -kəsh) n. An elephant goad consisting of a sharp spike and hook set on a short staff. Also **an·kush** (ang′kəsh). [< Hind.]

an·ky·lose (ang′kə·lōs) v.t. & v.i. ·losed, ·los·ing To unite or join by ankylosis: also spelled anchylose.

an·ky·lo·sis (ang′kə·lō′sis) n. 1 Anat. The knitting together or consolidation of two bones or parts of bones. 2 Pathol. The abnormal adhesion of bones, especially those forming a joint; stiffening of a joint. Also spelled anchylosis. [< NL < Gk. ankylōsis < ankylos crooked] — **an′ky·lot′ic** (-lot′ik) adj.

an·ky·los·to·mi·a·sis (ang′kə·los′tə·mī′ə·sis) See ANCYLOSTOMIASIS.

an·lace (an′lis) n. A broad two-edged dagger or short sword. Also **an′las**. [< OF alenas, alenaz dagger < alesne awl < Gmc.]

an·la·ge (än′lä·gə) n. 1 Biol. The first recognizable traces of an organ or part seen as an accumulation of cells in a developing embryo. 2 Basis; foundation; rudiment. Also **An′la·ge**. [< G, a laying on (foundation)]

Ann (an) A feminine personal name. Also Anne, An′na. See HANNAH. [< Hebrew, grace]

Ann, Cape A cape of NE Massachusetts.

an·na (an′ə) n. A copper coin of India, equal to one-sixteenth of a rupee. [< Hind. ānā]

An·na (an′ə; Dan., Du., Ger., Lat. ä′nä; Ital. än′nä) A feminine personal name. See ANN.

an·na·berg·ite (an′ə·bûr′gīt) n. An apple-green hydrous nickel arsenate crystallizing in the monoclinic system; nickelbloom. [from Annaberg, town in eastern Germany]

an·nal (an′əl) n. The record of a single year; an item or entry in a book of annals.

an·nal·ist (an′əl·ist) n. A writer of annals; a historian. ◆Homophone: analyst. —**an′nal·is′tic** adj.

an·nals (an′əlz) n. pl. 1 A record of events in their chronological order, year by year. 2 A narrative of events in which the order of time, rather than the causal relation, is followed or made prominent; chronicles. 3 A periodical publication of discoveries, transactions, etc. 4 History or records in general: the annals of crime. 5 In the Roman Catholic Church, masses said at stated intervals during the year. See synonyms under HISTORY. [< L annales (libri) yearly (record), chronicles < annus year]

An·nam (ə·nam′, an′am) A former empire and French protectorate. See CENTRAL VIETNAM.

An·na·mese (an′ə·mēz′, -mēs′) n. pl. **An·na·mese** 1 A native or inhabitant of Annam,

or the people of Annam collectively. 2 The language of Annam, including the Tonkinese and Cochin Chinese dialects: a member of the Mon-Khmer subfamily of the Austro-Asiatic family of languages. Also spelled Anamese. —adj. 1 Of Annam. 2 Of or pertaining to the inhabitants of Annam, their language, or their culture.

An·na·mite (an′ə·mīt) adj. & n. Annamese.

An·nap·o·lis (ə·nap′ə·lis) The capital of Maryland; seat of the United States Naval Academy.

Annapolis Royal A port on an arm of the Bay of Fundy, Nova Scotia.

An·na·pur·na (an′ə·pōōr′nə) See ANAPURNA.

Ann Ar·bor (an′ är′bər) A city in SE Michigan.

an·nates (an′āts, -its) n. pl. In the Roman Catholic Church, the first fruits, or the first year's revenue of bishops and certain other ecclesiastics, paid to the Pope on their appointment to a see or benefice. [< F annate < Med.L annata < L annus year]

an·nat·to (ä·nä′tō) 1 A small evergreen tree (Bixa orellana) of Central America, cultivated for its seeds. 2 A yellowish red dyestuff obtained from the pulp enclosing the seeds of the annatto tree, used to color foods, textiles, varnishes. Also anatto, arnatto.

Anne (an, Fr. än) A feminine personal name. See ANN.

—**Anne**, 1665–1714, English queen; last of the Stuarts.

—**Anne of Austria**, 1601–66, consort of Louis XIII of France; regent 1643–61 for her son, Louis XIV.

—**Anne of Bohemia**, 1366–94, wife of Richard II of England.

—**Anne Boleyn** See BOLEYN.

—**Anne of Cleves** (klēvz), 1515–57, fourth wife of Henry VIII.

—**Anne of Denmark**, 1574–1619, wife of James I of England.

an·neal (ə·nēl′) v.t. 1 To render tough, as something formerly brittle, by heating and then slowly cooling. 2 To toughen; render enduring, as the will. 3 Archaic To fix in place by heating and then cooling, as colors or enamel. [OE anǣlan burn]

an·nec·tent (ə·nek′tənt) adj. Connecting; joining on. [< L annectens, -entis, ppr. of annectere. See ANNEX.]

an·ne·lid (an′ə·lid) n. Zool. Any of a phylum (Annelida) of segmented invertebrates, including the earthworms, leeches, marine worms, etc. — adj. Of or pertaining to this phylum. [< NL < F annélide < anneler arrange in rings < OF annel a ring < L annellus for anellus, dim. of anulus a ring]

An·nel·i·dan (ə·nel′ə·dən) adj. & n. Annelid.

An·nette (ə·net′, Fr. ä·net′) Diminutive of ANN.

an·nex (ə·neks′) v.t. 1 To add or append, as an additional or minor part, to existing possessions; affix. 2 To attach, as an attribute, condition, or consequence: What punishment is annexed to vice? 3 Archaic To join; unite. —n. (an′eks) 1 An addition to a building; also, a nearby building used in addition to the main building. 2 A supplementary service or department. 3 An addition to a document; addendum. 4 Mil. An appendix to a combat order specifying the details prescribed in a given field or subject: an artillery annex. [< F annexer < L annexus, pp. of annectere tie together < ad- to + nectere tie] — **an·nex′a·ble** adj. —**an·nex′ive** adj.

an·nex·a·tion (an′ek·sā′shən) n. 1 An annexing or being annexed. 2 That which is annexed. 3 The permanent incorporation of newly acquired territory with the national domain. Also **an·nex′ment**.

An·nie (an′ē) Diminutive of ANN.

An·nie Oak·ley (an′ē ōk′lē) U.S. Slang A free pass to a theater, etc.: in allusion to the practice of punching a pass, which then resembled a small target after use by **Annie Oakley**, 1860–1926, U.S. markswoman.

an·ni·hi·late (ə·nī′ə·lāt) v.t. ·lat·ed, ·lat·ing 1 To destroy utterly. 2 To annul; abolish; make void. See synonyms under ABOLISH, EXTERMINATE. [< L annihilatus, pp. of annihilare < ad- to + nihil nothing] —**an·ni·hi·la·ble** (ə·nī′ə·lə·bəl) adj. —**an·ni′hi·la′tor** n.

an·ni·hi·la·tion (ə·nī′ə·lā′shən) *n.* An annihilating or being annihilated; extinction.

an·ni·hi·la·tion·ism (ə·nī′ə·lā′shən·iz′əm) *n.* *Theol.* The doctrine that the finally impenitent will be totally annihilated after death.

an·ni·hi·la·tion·ist (ə·nī′ə·lā′shən·ist) *n.* A believer in annihilation or annihilationism.

an·ni·hi·la·tive (ə·nī′ə·lā′tiv) *adj.* Tending to annihilate. Also **an·ni·hi·la·to·ry** (ə·nī′ə·lə·tôr′ē, -tō′rē).

an·ni·ver·sa·ry (an′ə·vûr′sər·ē) *n. pl.* **·ries 1** A day separated by a year or by an exact number of years from some past event. **2** A commemorative observance or celebration on such occasion. Wedding anniversaries are popularly named from the character of the presents regarded as appropriate to their celebration: **paper anniversary** (1st), **wooden anniversary** (5th), **tin anniversary** (10th), **crystal anniversary** (15th), **china anniversary** (20th), **silver anniversary** (25th), **golden anniversary** (50th), **diamond anniversary** (60th and 75th). *—adj.* **1** Recurring annually or at the same date every year. **2** Pertaining to or occurring on an anniversary. [<L *anniversarius* <*annus* year + *versus,* pp. of *vertere* turn]

Anniversary Day Australia Day.

an·no Chris·ti (an′ō kris′tī) *Latin* In the year of Christ.

an·no Dom·i·ni (an′ō dom′ə·nī) *Latin* In the year of our Lord or of the Christian era: abbr. *A.D.*

an·no mun·di (an′ō mun′dī) *Latin* In the year of the world: used in chronology, with the supposititious date of creation at 4004 B.C.

An·no·na (ə·nō′nə) In Roman mythology, the personification of fruitfulness and abundance, symbolized by a cornucopia and ears of grain.

an·no·tate (an′ō·tāt) *v.t.* **·tat·ed, ·tat·ing** To make explanatory or critical notes on or upon; to provide a commentary for, as a text. [<L *annotatus,* pp. of *annotare* <*ad-* to + *notare* note, mark <*nota* a mark] **—an′no·ta′tor** *n.*

an·no·ta·tion (an′ō·tā′shən) *n.* **1** An annotating or being annotated. **2** A critical or explanatory note; a comment.

an·no·ta·tive (an′ō·tā′tiv) *adj.* Of or marked by annotations. Also **an·no·ta·to·ry** (ə·nō′tə·tôr′ē, -tō′rē).

an·nounce (ə·nouns′) *v.t.* **an·nounced, an·nounc·ing 1** To make known publicly or officially; proclaim; publish. **2** To give notice of the approach or appearance of, as by a signal. **3** To make known to the senses: A roar *announced* the presence of the avalanche. **4** To serve as the announcer for, as a radio program. [<OF *anoncier* <L *annuntiare* <*ad-* to + *nuntiare* report <*nuntius* messenger]

Synonyms: advertise, communicate, declare, enunciate, herald, notify, proclaim, promulgate, propound, publish, report, reveal, speak. *Announce* is chiefly anticipatory; we *announce* a forthcoming book, a guest when he arrives. We *advertise* our business, *communicate* our intentions, *enunciate* our views; we *notify* an individual of a matter. We *propound* a question or an argument, *promulgate* the views of a sect or party. We *report* an interview, *reveal* a secret, *herald* the coming of some great event. *Declare* has often been an authoritative force; to *declare* war is to cause war to be. We *declare* war, *proclaim* peace. *Antonyms*: bury, conceal, hide, hush, secrete, suppress, withhold.

an·nounce·ment (ə·nouns′mənt) *n.* **1** An announcing or being announced. **2** That which is announced. **3** A printed declaration or publication.

an·nounc·er (ə·noun′sər) *n.* **1** One who announces. **2** A person who identifies the station from which a radio or television program is broadcast, introduces the performers and the program, etc.

an·noy (ə·noi′) *v.t.* **1** To be troublesome to; bother; irritate. **2** To do harm to or injure continuously or by repeated acts: Guerrilla fire *annoyed* the regiment. See synonyms under AFFRONT, HARASS. *—n. Obs.* Annoyance. [<OF *anuier, anoier* <L *in odio* in hatred] **—an·noy′er** *n.*

an·noy·ance (ə·noi′əns) *n.* **1** An annoying or being annoyed. **2** One who or that which annoys. See synonyms under ABOMINATION.

an·noy·ing (ə·noi′ing) *adj.* Vexatious, troublesome. See synonyms under TROUBLESOME. **—an·noy′ing·ly** *adv.* **—an·noy′ing·ness** *n.*

an·nu·al (an′yōō·əl) *adj.* **1** Returning, performed, or occurring every year. **2** Pertaining to the year; reckoned by the year. **3** *Bot.* Lasting or living only one year. *—n.* **1** A book or pamphlet issued once a year. **2** *Bot.* A plant living for a single year or season. **3** In the Roman Catholic Church, a yearly mass for a deceased person; also, the offering made for it. **4** *Archaic* A yearly payment. [<OF *annuel* <L *annualis* yearly <*annus* year]

an·nu·al·ly (an′yōō·əl·ē) *adv.* Year by year; yearly.

annual parallax See under PARALLAX.

annual ring Any of the concentric rings in a cross section of a tree trunk resulting from seasonal alternations of growth and quiescence. Also called *growth ring.*

an·nu·i·tant (ə·nōō′ə·tənt, ə·nyōō′-) *n.* One receiving, or entitled to receive, an annuity.

an·nu·it coep·tis (an′yōō·it sep′tis) *Latin* He (God) has favored our undertakings: motto on the reverse of the great seal of the United States.

an·nu·i·ty (ə·nōō′ə·tē, ə·nyōō′-) *n. pl.* **·ties 1** An annual allowance or income; also, the right to receive such an allowance or the duty of paying it. **2** The return from an investment of capital, with interest, in a series of yearly payments; especially, an agreed amount paid by an insurance company at stated intervals, usually monthly, in consideration of either a single premium or premiums paid over a period of years. [<F *annuité* <Med.L *annuitas, -tatis* <L *annus* year]

an·nul (ə·nul′) *v.t.* **an·nulled, an·nul·ling 1** To destroy the force of; declare void or invalid, as a law. **2** To reduce to nothing; extinguish: One loyalty may *annul* another in the mind. **3** To put an end or stop to, as a practice. [<OF *anuller* <LL *annullare* <L *ad-* to + *nullus* none] **—an·nul′la·ble** *adj.*

Synonyms: abolish, abrogate, cancel, destroy, extinguish, nullify, obliterate, quash, repeal, rescind, revoke. See ABOLISH, CANCEL. *Antonyms*: confirm, enact, establish, institute, maintain, preserve, sustain, uphold.

an·nu·lar (an′yə·lər) *adj.* **1** Pertaining to or formed like a ring; ring-shaped. **2** Marked with rings. [<L *annularis* <*annulus, anulus* ring] **—an′nu·lar·ly** *adv.*

annular eclipse *Astron.* A solar eclipse in which a narrow circular strip of the sun is visible beyond the dark mass of the moon.

annular ligament *Anat.* A ligament encircling the wrist or ankle.

an·nu·late (an′yə·lit, -lāt) *adj.* Furnished with rings; ringed. Also **an′nu·lat′ed.**

an·nu·la·tion (an′yə·lā′shən) *n.* **1** The act of forming rings. **2** A ringlike formation or segment, as in an annelid.

an·nu·let (an′yə·lit) *n.* **1** A small ring. **2** *Archit.* A small projecting circular molding, specifically, around the capital of a pillar. [<L *annulus* a ring + -ET]

an·nul·ment (ə·nul′mənt) *n.* **1** An annulling or being annulled. **2** An invalidation, as of a marriage.

an·nu·lose (an′yə·lōs) *adj.* Composed of or furnished with rings. [<L *annulus* a ring + -OSE]

an·nu·lus (an′yə·ləs) *n. pl.* **·li** (-lī) or **·lus·es 1** A ringlike body or figure. **2** *Geom.* The area between the circumferences of two concentric circles. **3** *Astron.* The thin, visible edge of the sun's disk as it appears around the body of the moon in an annular eclipse. [<L, a ring]

an·nun·ci·ate (ə·nun′shē·āt, -sē-) *v.t.* **·at·ed, ·at·ing** To announce. [<L *annuntiatus,* pp. of *annuntiare. See* ANNOUNCE.]

an·nun·ci·a·tion (ə·nun′sē·ā′shən, -shē-) *n.* **1** The act of announcing, or that which is announced; a proclamation.

An·nun·ci·a·tion (ə·nun′sē·ā′shən, -shē-) *n.* **1** The announcement of the Incarnation to the Virgin by an angel. *Luke* i 28–38. **2** The festival (March 25) commemorating this event.

annunciation lily The white or Madonna lily *(Lilium candidum),* often shown in pictures of the Annunciation.

an·nun·ci·a·tor (ə·nun′shē·ā′tər, -sē-) *n.* **1** A person or thing that announces. **2** An electrical indicator that shows a number or name when a bell is rung.

an·nus mi·rab·i·lis (an′əs mə·rab′ə·lis) *Latin* Wonderful year: used especially of the year 1666, notable in English history for the Dutch War and the Great Fire of London.

a·no·ci–as·so·ci·a·tion (ə·nō′sē·ə·sō′sē·ā′shən, -shē·ā′shən) *n. Surg.* A method in which the effects of surgical shock and exhaustion have been eliminated by the use of anesthetics, general and local. Also **a·no·ci·a·tion** (ə·nō′·sē·ā′shən, -shē-). See NOCI-ASSOCIATION. [<A-[4] not + L *nocere* harm + ASSOCIATION]

an·o·dal (an·ō′dəl) *adj.* Pertaining to an anode.

an·ode (an′ōd) *n. Electr.* The electrode through which current enters a non-metallic conductor and toward which electrons or anions flow from the cathode. It is positive for an electrolytic bath or vacuum tube, negative for a voltaic cell. [<Gk. *anodos* a way up <*ana-* up + *hodos* road, way]

an·od·ic (an·od′ik) *adj.* **1** Pertaining to an anode. **2** Proceeding upward.

an·o·dize (an′ə·dīz) *v.t.* **·dized, ·diz·ing** To oxidize or coat the surface of (a metal) by making it the anode of an electrolytic bath containing sodium phosphate or other suitable electrolyte.

an·o·dyne (an′ə·dīn) *adj.* Having power to allay pain; soothing. *—n.* Any drug that relieves pain or soothes. [<L *anodynus* <Gk. *anōdynos* <*an-* without + *odynē* pain]

a·noint (ə·noint′) *v.t.* **1** To smear with oil or any soft substance; pour or rub oil upon; apply ointment to. **2** To put oil on as a sign of consecration, as in a religious ceremony. [<OF *enoint,* pp. of *enoindre* <L *inungere* <*in-* on + *ungere* smear] **—a·noint′er** *n.* **—a·noint′ment** *n.*

an·o·lyte (an′ə·līt) *n.* In electrolysis, that portion of the electrolyte which is nearest the anode. [<ANO(DE) + (ELECTRO)LYTE]

a·nom·a·lism (ə·nom′ə·liz′əm) *n.* **1** That which is anomalous; an anomaly. **2** *Rare* The state or fact of being anomalous.

a·nom·a·lous (ə·nom′ə·ləs) *adj.* Deviating from the common rule; irregular; exceptional; abnormal. See synonyms under ABSURD, IRREGULAR, ODD. [<L *anomalus* <Gk. *anōmalos* <*an-* not + *homalos* even <*homos* same]**—a·nom′a·lous·ly** *adv.* **—a·nom′a·lous·ness** *n.*

a·nom·a·ly (ə·nom′ə·lē) *n. pl.* **·lies 1** Deviation from rule, type, or form; irregularity; anything abnormal. **2** *Astron.* **a** The angular distance of a planet from its perihelion, as seen from the sun. **b** The angle which measures apparent irregularities in the movement of a planet. [<L *anomalia* <Gk. *anōmalia* <*anōmalos.* See ANOMALOUS.] **—a·nom·a·lis·tic** (ə·nom′ə·lis′tik) or **·ti·cal** *adj.*

an·o·mie (an′ə·mē) *n.* An anxious awareness that the prevailing values of society have little or no personal relevance to one's condition; also, a condition of society characterized by the relative absence of norms or moral standards. [<F <Gk. *anomia* lawlessness <*a-* without (See A-[4]) + *nomos* law] **—a·nom·ic** (ə·nom′ik) *adj.*

a·non (ə·non′) *Archaic adv.* **1** In a little while; soon; presently. **2** Immediately. **3** At another time; again. **—ever and anon** Now and again. *—interj.* At once! [OE *on an* in one]

Anon. Abbreviation for ANONYMOUS.

an·o·nym (an′ə·nim) *n.* **1** An anonymous person or writer. **2** A pseudonym.

a·non·y·mous (ə·non′ə·məs) *adj.* Having no acknowledged name; bearing no name; of unknown authorship or agency. [<Gk. *anōnymos* <*an-* without + *onoma, onyma* name] **—an·o·nym·i·ty** (an′ə·nim′ə·tē), **a·non′y·mous·ness** *n.* **—a·non′y·mous·ly** *adv.*

a·noph·e·les (ə·nof′ə·lēz) *n.* Any of a genus *(Anopheles)* of mosquitoes of mostly tropical and subtropical distribution including numerous species that carry the malaria parasite and transmit the disease among humans. [<NL <Gk. *ānōphelēs* harmful] **—a·noph·e·line** (ə·nof′ə·līn, -lin) *adj.*

a·no·rak (ä′nə·räk) *n.* A warm, hooded jacket, worn in arctic climates. [<Eskimo *anoraq*]

an·o·rec·tic (an′ə·rek′tik) *n.* A person having anorexia. *—adj.* of or pertaining to anorexia.

an·o·rex·i·a (an′ə·rek′sē·ə) *n.* Absence of appetite, especially when accompanied by emotional stress and resulting in malnutrition and emaciation. Also **anorexia nervosa.** [<NL <Gk. *anorexia* <*an-* without + *orexis* appetite]

an·o·rex·ic (an′ə·rek′sik) *adj.* Avoiding food; suffering from anorexia. *—n.* An anorexic person.

an·or·thic (an·ôr′thik) *adj.* Triclinic. [<Gk. *an-* not + *orthos* straight]

an·or·thite (an-ôr'thīt) *n.* A triclinic feldspar, CaAl₂Si₂O₈, found in igneous rocks. [< AN-¹ + Gk. *orthos* straight + -ITE¹] —**an·or·thit·ic** (an'ôr-thit'ik) *adj.*

an·or·tho·scope (an-ôr'thə-skōp) *n.* An instrument by which distorted figures drawn on one of two revolving disks can be seen as normal images through slits in the other. [< AN-¹ + ORTHO- + -SCOPE]

an·or·tho·site (an-ôr'thə-sīt) *n. Geol.* A granular igneous rock composed essentially or wholly of plagioclase, which in the typical anorthosite is labradorite. [< AN-¹ + Gk. *orthos* straight + -ITE¹]

an·os·mi·a (an-oz'mē-ə, -os'-) *n. Pathol.* Loss of the sense of smell. [< NL < Gk. *an-* without + *osmē* smell] —**an·os'mic** *adj.*

an·oth·er (ə-nuth'ər) *adj. & pron.* 1 Not the same; distinct; different: often used as the correlative of *one*: One man's meat is *another* man's poison. 2 Different in character while of the same or similar substance: From that time I became *another* man. 3 Different in substance while of the same or similar character. 4 A further; an additional; one more. ◆ *Another* was originally written as two words, *an other*. As a pronoun its plural is *others*.

an·ox·e·mi·a (an'ok-sē'mē-ə) *n. Pathol.* Lack of oxygen in the blood. [< NL < AN-¹ + OX(YGEN) + -EMIA] —**an·ox·e'mic** *adj.*

an·ox·i·a (an-ok'sē-ə) *n. Pathol.* Oxygen deficiency; any condition characterized by defective or insufficient oxidation of the body tissues. [< AN-¹ + OX(YGEN) + -IA] —**an·ox'ic** *adj.*

an·sa (an'sə) *n. pl.* **·sae** (-sē) 1 *pl. Astron.* The apparent ends of Saturn's rings, which, seen obliquely, seem to project from the sides of the planet like handles. 2 A handle, as of a pitcher. [< L, a handle]

an·sate (an'sāt) *adj.* Having a handle. Also **an'sat·ed.** [< L *ansatus* < *ansa* a handle]

ansate cross See under CROSS.

An·schluss (än'shlŏŏs) *n. German* Political union.

An·selm (an'selm, *Ger.* än'selm) A masculine personal name. Also **An·sel** (an'səl), *Fr.* **An·selme** (än-selm'), *Ital., Sp.* **An·sel·mo** (än-sel'mō), *Pg.* **An·sel·mo** (än-sel'mŏŏ), *Lat.* **An·sel·mus** (an'selməs). [< Gmc., divine helmet] —**Anselm, Saint,** 1033–1109, archbishop of Canterbury.

An·ser (an'sər) *n.* 1 *Ornithol.* A genus of birds typical of *Anserinae*, a subfamily including the geese. 2 *Astron.* A small star in the constellation of the Fox and Goose (Vulpecula cum Ansere). See CONSTELLATION. [< L, goose]

an·ser·ine (an'sə-rīn, -sər-in) *adj.* 1 Pertaining to a goose; gooselike, as the human skin when chilled. 2 Silly; stupid. 3 Pertaining or belonging to the subfamily *Anserinae* of birds, the geese. Also **an'ser·ous.** —*n.* An organic substance, C₁₀H₁₆O₃N₄, obtained from the muscles of birds, fishes, and reptiles. [< L *anserinus* < *anser* a goose]

An·shan (än'shän') A city in southern Manchuria, China.

An·stey (an'stē), F. Pseudonym of Thomas Anstey Guthrie, 1856–1934, English writer.

an·swer (an'sər, än'-) *v.i.* 1 To reply or respond, as by words or actions. 2 To serve the purpose; prove successful: This solution *answers* best. 3 To be responsible or accountable: with *for.* I will *answer* for his honesty. 4 To correspond or match, as in appearance: with *to*: This man *answers* to your description. —*v.t.* 5 To speak, write, or act in response or reply to: to *answer* a letter. 6 To be sufficient for; fulfil: This rod *answers* the purpose. 7 To pay for; discharge, as a debt or liability: to *answer* damages. 8 To conform or correspond to; match: to *answer* a description. 9 *Law* To reply favorably to, as a petition or petitioner. —**to answer back** To reply emphatically or rudely; talk back, as in contradiction. —*n.* 1 A reply, especially one that is definite and final. 2 Any action in return or in kind; retaliation. 3 The result of a calculation or solution of a problem in mathematics. 4 *Law* The written defense of a defendant in an action to charges filed against him by the plaintiff in which he sets up matters of *fact* as defense in contradistinction to a *demurrer.* 5 *Music* The restatement of a musical theme or phrase by a different voice or instrument. [OE *andswerian*] —**an'swer·er** *n.*

Synonyms (noun): rejoinder, repartee, reply, response, retort. Anything said or done in return for some word, action, or suggestion of another may be called an *answer*, as the blow of an angry man, the movement of a bolt in a lock, an echo, etc. A *reply* is an unfolding, and ordinarily implies thought and intelligence. An *answer* to a charge or an argument effectually meets or disposes of it, as a *reply* may not do. See RESPONSE.

an·swer·a·ble (an'sər-ə-bəl, än'-) *adj.* 1 Liable to be called to account (*for* anything or *to* someone); responsible. 2 Requiring or admitting of answer; also, obligated to answer. 3 Corresponding; adequate; suitable. —**an'swer·a·ble·ness** *n.* —**an'swer·a·bly** *adv.*

ant (ant) *n.* A small social hymenopterous insect (family *Formicidae*); an emmet. The communities of ants are made up of winged males, females winged till after pairing, and wingless neuters or workers. For illustration see under INSECT (injurious). [OE *æmete*]

an't (ant, änt, änt) 1 Are not. 2 *Brit.* Am not. 3 *Illit. & Dial.* Is not; has not; have not.

ant- Var. of ANTI-.

-ant *suffix* 1 In the act or process of doing (what is denoted by the stem): used to form adjectives with nearly the meaning of the present participle: *militant, litigant,* etc. 2 One who or that which does (what is indicated by the stem): forming nouns of participial origin: *servant* one who serves. [< F *-ant* < L *-ans (-antis), -ens(-entis)*, present participial suffixes]

an·ta (an'tə) *n. pl.* **tae** (-tē) *Archit.* A pilaster, especially when forming the termination of a side wall continued beyond a transverse wall, or when placed on a wall to form a range of columns. [< L]

ant·ac·id (ant·as'id) *n. Med.* An alkaline remedy for stomach acidity. —*adj.* Correcting acidity. Also **an'ti·ac·id.**

An·tae·us (an-tē'əs) In Greek legend, a wrestler, invincible while in contact with the earth: crushed by Hercules, who lifted him into the air. Also **An·tæ'us.** —**An·tae'an** *adj.*

an·tag·o·nism (an·tag'ə-niz'əm) *n.* Mutual resistance; opposition; hostility. See synonyms under ANTIPATHY, ENMITY. [< Gk. *antagōnisma* < *antagōnizesthai.* See ANTAGONIZE.]

an·tag·o·nist (an·tag'ə-nist) *n.* 1 An adversary; opponent. See synonyms under ENEMY. 2 Any agent having an effect contrary to that of a similar agent, as a drug, muscle, hormone, etc.

an·tag·o·nis·tic (an·tag'ə-nis'tik) *adj.* Opposed; hostile. Also **an·tag·o·nis'ti·cal.** See synonyms under CONTRARY, INIMICAL. —**an·tag·o·nis'ti·cal·ly** *adv.*

an·tag·o·nize (an·tag'ə-nīz) *v.* **·nized, ·niz·ing** *v.t.* 1 To oppose, contend with, or struggle against. 2 To make unfriendly; to make an antagonist of. 3 To counteract; neutralize, as a force or action. —*v.i.* 4 To act antagonistically. See synonyms under CONTEND. [< Gk. *antagōnizesthai* struggle against < *anti-* against + *agōnizesthai* struggle, strive]

An·ta·ki·ya (än'tä-kē'yä) The Turkish and Arabic name for ANTIOCH. Also **An·ta·kya** (än'tä-kyä').

ant·al·gic (ant·al'jik) *adj.* Tending to alleviate pain. —*n.* An anodyne. [< ANT- + Gk. *algos* pain]

ant·al·ka·li (ant·al·kə·lī) *n. pl.* **·lis** or **·lies** Any substance able to neutralize alkalis, or counteract an alkaline tendency in the system. [< ANT- + ALKALI] —**ant·al'ka·line** (-līn, -lin) *adj. & n.*

An·tal·ya (än·täl'yä) A port in SW Anatolia, Turkey, on the **Gulf of Antalya**, an inlet of the Mediterranean: also *Adalia.*

An·ta·na·na·ri·vo (än'tə-nä'nə-rē'vō) The English name for TANANARIVE.

ant·arc·tic (ant·ärk'tik, -är'tik) *adj.* Pertaining to or designating the South Pole or the regions near it. [< L *antarcticus* < Gk. *antarktikos* southern < *anti-* opposite + *arktos* the Bear (a northern constellation), the north]

Ant·arc·ti·ca (ant·ärk'tə·kə, -är'-) A continent surrounding the South Pole of the earth, extending at certain points north of the antarctic circle and almost entirely covered by a vast ice sheet; over 5,000,000 square miles. Also **Antarctic Continent.**

Antarctic Archipelago See PALMER ARCHIPELAGO.

Antarctic Circle The boundary of the South Frigid Zone, 23°30' from the South Pole, including most of Antarctica.

Antarctic Ocean The ocean within the Antarctic Circle and bordering Antarctica.

Antarctic Zone The region, including most of Antarctica, enclosed by the Antarctic Circle.

An·tar·es (an-tār'ēz) A giant red star, Alpha in the constellation Scorpio; one of the 20 brightest stars, 1.22 magnitude. [< Gk. *Antarēs* < *anti-* similar to + *Arēs* Mars; with ref. to its color]

ant bear 1 The giant ant-eater (*Myrmecophaga jubata*), a large edentate mammal of tropical America that feeds wholly or chiefly on ants; it has a long snout, protrusible tongue, powerful digging claws, and a shaggy, black-banded coat. 2 The aardvark.

ant bird Any of numerous small birds of the family *Formicariidae*, of South America, which feed upon ants. Also called **ant'-catch'er.**

ant cow An aphid insect kept by ants as a source of food. The aphids yield a honeylike fluid on being stroked by the antennae of the ants.

an·te (an'tē) *v.t. & v.i.* **an·teed** or **an·ted, an·te·ing** 1 In poker, to put up, as a stake, before the cards are dealt. 2 *Slang* To pay (one's share). —**to ante up** *Slang* To ante. —*n.* 1 The stake put up in a game of poker. 2 A stake put up after the cards are dealt, but before drawing new ones. [< L, before]

ante- *prefix* 1 Before in time or order: *antenatal.* 2 Before in position; in front of: *antechamber.* [< L *ante* before]

The words in the following list are self-explanatory:

antebaptismal	anteporch
antebridal	anteresurrection
ante-Christian	anterevolutionary
antehuman	antespring
antemarital	ante-Victorian
ante-Norman	ante-war

an·te·a (an'tē-ə) *adv. Law Latin* Formerly; heretofore.

ant-eater (ant'ē'tər) *n.* 1 The ant bear. 2 One of several other mammals that feed partly on ants, as the tamandua, echidna, or aardvark. 3 An ant bird.

THE GIANT ANT-EATER (8 feet long over-all; 2 feet tall)

an·te·bel·lum (an'tē·bel'əm) *adj.* Of the time before the war, especially, before the Civil War in the United States. [< L *ante bellum* before the war]

an·te·bra·chi·um (an'tē·brā'kē·əm) *n. pl.* **·chi·a** (-kē·ə) *Anat.* The forearm. [< NL < ANTE- + L *brachium* arm]

an·te·cede (an'tə·sēd') *v.t. & v.i.* **·ced·ed, ·ced·ing** To go or come before, as in rank, place, or time; precede. [< L *antecedere* < *ante* before + *cedere* go]

an·te·ce·dence (an'tə·sēd'ns) *n.* 1 Precedence; going before; priority. 2 *Astron.* The apparent retrograde motion of a planet. Also **an'te·ce'den·cy.**

an·te·ce·dent (an'tə·sēd'nt) *adj.* 1 Going before; prior in time, place, or order; preceding; anterior: often with *to.* 2 *Geol.* Having a course across a fold or fault of the earth's surface: contrasted with *consequent.* —*n.* 1 One who or that which precedes or goes before. 2 *Gram.* The word, phrase, or clause to which a pronoun, especially a relative pronoun, refers. 3 *pl.* The facts, collectively, that have gone before in the history of a person or thing; also, ancestry. 4 *Math.* The first term of a ratio; in a proportion, the first and third terms. 5 *Logic* That upon which something else is based. See synonyms under CAUSE, PRECEDENT. [< L *antecedens, -entis,* ppr. of *antecedere.* See ANTECEDE.] —**an'te·ce'dent·ly** *adv.*

Synonyms (adj.): anterior, earlier, foregoing, former, introductory, precedent, preceding, preliminary, previous, prior. When used simply of time, *antecedent* and *previous* refer to that which happens at any prior time; *preceding* to that which is immediately or next before. See PREVIOUS. *Antonyms*: consequent, following, later, posterior, subsequent, succeeding.

an·te·ces·sor (an'tə·ses'ər) *n.* One who precedes or goes before; a leader; pioneer. [< L < *antecedere.* See ANTECEDE.]

an·te·cham·ber (an'ti·chām'bər) *n.* A room serving as an entranceway to another apartment.

an·te·chap·el (an'ti·chap'əl) *n.* The portion of a chapel outside of the rood screen; a vestibule or narthex.

an·te·choir (an'ti·kwīr') *n.* A portion of a chapel set apart just in front of the choir, enclosed, or partially enclosed, by a screen.

an·te·date (an'ti·dāt' *v.t.* **·dat·ed, ·dat·ing 1** To assign to a date earlier than the actual one, as a document; date back. **2** To be or occur earlier than; precede. **3** To cause to happen at or return to an earlier date; accelerate.

an·te·di·lu·vi·an (an'ti·di·lo͞o'vē·ən) *adj.* **1** Pertaining to the times, events, etc., before the Flood. **2** Antiquated; primitive. —*n.* **1** A person, animal, or plant that lived before the Flood. **2** An old or old-fashioned person. [< ANTE- + L *diluvium* deluge]

an·te·fix (an'ti·fiks) *n. pl.* **·fix·es** or **·fix·a** (-fik'sə) *Archit.* An upright ornament at the eaves of a tiled roof, to hide the joints between two adjacent rows of tiles, or at the edge of a frieze: sometimes also at the ridge, forming part of a cresting. [< L *antefixus.* See ANTE- and FIX.] —**an'te·fix'al** *adj.*

ANTEFIX

an·te·lope (an'tə·lōp) *n. pl.* **·lope** or **·lopes 1** Any one of various Old World hollow-horned ruminants of the family *Bovidae,* including the gazelle, chamois, gnu, etc. **2** The hide of such an animal. **3** *U.S.* The pronghorn. [< OF *antelop* < Med.L *antalopus* < LGk. *antholops*]

an·te·me·rid·i·an (an'ti·mə·rid'ē·ən) *adj.* Before noon; between midnight and the next noon.

an·te me·rid·i·em (an'tē mə·rid'ē·em) *Latin* Before the sun reaches the meridian, counted from the preceding midnight; before noon. Abbr. *a.m.* or *A.M.*

an·te mor·tem (an'tē môr'təm) *Latin* Before or immediately preceding death.

an·te·mun·dane (an'ti·mun'dān) *adj.* Pertaining to, existing, or occurring before the world's creation. [< ANTE- + L *mundus* world]

an·te·na·tal (an'ti·nāt'l) *adj.* Occurring or existing before birth; pertaining to conditions before birth.

an·ten·na (an·ten'ə) *n. pl.* **an·ten·nae** (an·ten'ē) *for def.* **1, an·ten·nas** *for def.* **2. 1** *Entomol.* One of the paired, lateral, movable, jointed appendages on the head of an insect or other arthropod. **2** *Telecom.* A system of wires upheld in a vertical or horizontal position by a mast or tower, for transmitting or receiving electromagnetic waves in wireless telegraphy, telephony, and radio. —**cage antenna** A radio antenna consisting of several wires arranged in parallel around a series of loops between two uprights and converging at each end. [< NL < L, a yard on which a sail is spread]

an·ten·nule (an·ten'yo͞ol) *n. Zool.* A small antenna or antennalike appendage. Also **an·ten·nu·la** (an·ten'yə·lə).

an·te·nup·tial (an'ti·nup'shəl, -chəl) *adj.* Previous to marriage; occurring or being before marriage.

an·te·pas·chal (an'ti·pas'kəl) *adj.* Occurring before the Passover or Easter.

an·te·past (an'ti·past, -päst) *n.* **1** Foretaste. **2** *Obs.* An appetizer. See synonyms under ANTICIPATION. [< ANTE- + L *pastus* food]

an·te·pen·di·um (an'ti·pen'dē·əm) *n. pl.* **·di·a** (-dē·ə) A covering, usually embroidered, for the front of the altar. [< Med.L < L *ante* before + *pendere* hang]

an·te·pe·nult (an'ti·pē'nult, -pi·nult') *n.* The last syllable but two of a word. Also **an·te·pe·nul·ti·ma** (an'ti·pi·nul'tə·mə).

an·te·pe·nul·ti·mate (an'ti·pi·nul'tə·mit) *adj.* Pertaining to the last but two of any series. —*n.* The antepenult.

an·te·pran·di·al (an'ti·pran'dē·əl) *adj.* Occurring or being before dinner.

an·te·ri·or (an·tir'ē·ər) *adj.* **1** Antecedent in time; prior; earlier: ages *anterior* to the Flood. **2** Farther front or forward, in space: an *anterior* cavity. **3** *Biol.* Situated in front: opposed to *posterior,* in the lower animals, relatively near the head; in man, toward the ventral side of the body. **4** *Bot.* Turned away from the main axis or stem, as the side of a leaf or flower; lower. [< L, compar. of *ante* before] —**an·te'ri·or·ly** *adv.*

Synonyms: former, forward, front, prior. *Anterior* is employed chiefly with reference to place. *Prior* bears exclusive reference to time. *Former* is used of time, or of position in written or printed matter, not of space in general. Compare ANTECEDENT, PREVIOUS. *Antonyms*: after, hind, hinder, hindmost, later, latter, posterior, subsequent, succeeding.

antero- *combining form* Anterior; placed in front. [< L *anterus* (assumed form)]

an·ter·o·in·fe·ri·or (an'tər·ō·in·fir'ē·ər) *adj.* Situated in front and below.

an·te·room (an'ti·ro͞om', -ro͝om') *n.* A waiting-room; antechamber.

an·ter·o·pos·te·ri·or (an'tər·ō·pos·tir'ē·ər) *adj.* **1** Of or pertaining to the front and rear; extending from front to rear. **2** Median.

an·te·type (an'ti·tīp') *n.* A preceding type; prototype.

an·te·ver·sion (an'ti·vûr'zhən, -shən) *n. Pathol.* A turning or tipping forward, as of the uterus.

an·te·vert (an'ti·vûrt') *v.t. Pathol.* To displace by turning or tipping forward, as an internal organ. [< L *antevertere* < *ante* before + *vertere* turn]

anth- Var. of ANTI-.

ant·he·li·on (ant·hē'lē·ən, an·thē'-) *n. pl.* **·li·a** (-lē·ə) *Astron.* A faint glory or series of diffraction rings about the shadow of an object cast by a low sun upon a cloud or fog bank; a mock sun. [< NL < Gk. *anthēlion* < *anti-* against + *hēlios* sun]

ant·he·lix (ant·hē'liks, an·thē'-) *n. pl.* **ant·hel·i·ces** (ant·hel'ə·sēz, an·thel'-) *Anat.* The inner curved ridge on the cartilage of the external ear: also *antihelix.* [< ANT- + HELIX]

an·thel·min·tic (an'thel·min'tik) *adj. Med.* Tending to expel intestinal worms. —*n.* A vermifuge. Also **an'thel·min'thic** (-thik). [< ANT- + Gk. *helmins, -inthos* worm]

an·them (an'thəm) *n.* **1** A musical composition, usually set to words from the Bible. **2** A joyous or triumphal song or hymn, or the music to which it is set. —*v.t.* To celebrate with, or sing as, an anthem. [OE *antefn* < LL *antiphona* < Gk. *antiphōna,* lit., things sounding in response < *anti-* against + *phōnē* voice. Doublet of ANTIPHON.]

an·the·mi·on (an·thē'mē·ən) *n. pl.* **·mi·a** (-mē·ə) The honeysuckle or palm-leaf pattern in decorative designs: common in Greek art. [< Gk., flower]

ANTHEMION

an·ther (an'thər) *n. Bot.* The pollen-bearing part of a stamen. [< F *anthère* < L *anthera,* a medicine obtained from flowers < Gk. *anthēra,* fem. of *antheros* flowery < *anthos* flower]

an'ther·id·i·o·phore (an'thə·rid'ē·ə·fôr', -fōr') *n. Bot.* An outgrowing part of a sexual plant bearing antheridia only, as in hepatic mosses.

an·ther·id·i·um (an'thə·rid'ē·əm) *n. pl.* **·ther·id·i·a** (-thə·rid'ē·ə) *Bot.* The male sexual organ in cryptogams, the analog of the anther in flowering plants. Also **an·ther·id** (an'thər·id). [< NL, dim. of Gk. *antheros* flowery] —**an'ther·id'i·al** *adj.*

an·ther·o·zo·id (an'thər·ə·zō'id, an'thər·ə·zoid') *n. Bot.* The male fecundating cell in cryptogams. It is a minute mass of protoplasm, provided with vibratory cilia, and produced in an antheridium. Also **an'ther·o·zo'oid** (-zō'oid). [< ANTHER + ZOOID] —**an'ther·o·zo'i·dal** (-zō'ə·dəl), **an'ther·o·zo·oi'dal** (-zō·oid'l) *adj.*

an·the·sis (an·thē'sis) *n. Bot.* The time or process of expansion in a flower; full bloom of a flower. [< NL < Gk. *anthēsis* full bloom < *antheein* bloom]

An·thes·te·ri·a (an'thes·tir'ē·ə) *n. pl.* A three days' festival in honor of Dionysus formerly held at Athens from the 11th to the 13th of **An'thes·te'ri·on** (-tir'ē·ən), a month nearly corresponding to February. [< Gk. *anthestēria* < *anthos* flower]

antho- *combining form* Flower: *anthophorous.* [< Gk. *anthos* a flower]

an·tho·ceph·a·lous (an'thō·sef'ə·ləs) *adj.* Having a head like a flower. [< ANTHO- + Gk. *kephalē* head]

An·thoc·er·os (an·thos'ər·əs) *n.* A genus of liverworts, especially the horned liverworts, the type of the order *Anthocerotales.* [< NL < ANTHO- + Gk. *keras* horn]

an·tho·cy·a·nin (an'thō·sī'ə·nin) *n.* The water-soluble coloring-matter of flowers, leaves, and other parts of plants which imparts red, violet, blue, blue-green, or green colors, dependent on the acidity or alkalinity of the cell sap: also called *cyanin, erythrophyll.* [< ANTHO- + Gk. *kyanos* blue]

an·tho·di·um (an·thō'dē·əm) *n. pl.* **·di·a** (-dē·ə) *Bot.* The flowering head of plants of the composite family: so called from the resemblance of the involucre to a calyx and of the ray florets, when present, to petals. [< NL < Gk. *anthōdēs* flowerlike < *anthos* a flower]

an·thoid (an'thoid) *adj.* Like a flower.

an·thol·o·gize (an·thol'ə·jīz) *v.* **·gized, ·giz·ing** *v.i.* To make an anthology or anthologies. —*v.t.* To put into an anthology or make an anthology of.

an·thol·o·gy (an·thol'ə·jē) *n. pl.* **·gies** A collection of choice or representative literary extracts. [< L *anthologia* < Gk. *anthologia* a garland, collection of poems < *anthos* flower + *legein* gather] —**an·tho·log·i·cal** (an'thə·loj'i·kəl) *adj.* —**an·thol'o·gist** *n.*

An·tho·ny (an'thə·nē, -tə-) A masculine personal name. See also ANTONY. [< L *Antonius,* the name of a Roman gens]

—**Anthony, Saint,** 251–356, one of the Christian fathers; founder of monastic life; born in Egypt.

—**Anthony of Padua, Saint,** 1195–1231, Franciscan monk.

An·tho·ny (an'thə·nē), **Susan Brownell,** 1820–1906, U.S. suffragist.

an·tho·phore (an'thə·fôr, -fōr) *n. Bot.* A stipe formed by the prolongation of an internode between the calyx and the corolla.

an·thoph·o·rous (an·thof'ər·əs) *adj.* Flower-bearing. [< Gk. *anthophoros* < *anthos* flower + *pherein* bear]

an·tho·tax·y (an'thə·tak'sē) *n. Bot.* The arrangement of flowers on the axis of inflorescence. [< ANTHO- + Gk. *taxis* arrangement]

an·tho·zo·an (an'thə·zō'ən) *n.* Any of a class (Anthozoa) of sessile, usually cylindrical, marine coelenterates, growing singly or in colonies, and including the sea anemones and corals. Also **anthozoon.** Also called *actinozoan.* —*adj.* Of or pertaining to the class *Anthozoa.* [< NL < ANTHO- + Gk. *zōein* live] —**an'tho·zo'ic** *adj.*

an·tho·zo·oid (an'thə·zō'oid) *n.* An individual polyp in a compound colony.

an·thra·cene (an'thrə·sēn) *n. Chem.* A blue fluorescent crystalline compound, $C_{14}H_{10}$, obtained in the last products of coal-tar distillation and used largely in the manufacture of alizarin and related dyes. [< Gk. *anthrax, -akos* coal + -ENE]

an·thra·cite (an'thrə·sīt) *n.* Mineral coal of nearly pure carbon which burns slowly and with little flame; hard coal. [< L *anthracites* < Gk. *anthrakitēs* coallike < *anthrax* coal] —**an·thra·cit·ic** (an'thrə·sit'ik) *adj.*

an·thrac·nose (an·thrak'nōs) *n.* A destructive disease of plants usually manifested by sharply defined discolored spots and caused by various fungi. [< Gk. *anthrax, -akos* coal, carbuncle + *nosos* disease]

an·thra·coid (an'thrə·koid) *adj.* **1** Resembling anthrax. **2** Like the precious carbuncle or like carbon.

an·thra·qui·none (an'thrə·kwi·nōn') *n.* A yellow crystalline compound, $C_{14}H_8O_2$, made from anthracene by oxidation with chromic and sulfuric acid: used in the manufacture of alizarin dyes and certain laxatives. [< Gk. *anthrax* coal + QUINONE]

an·thrax (an'thraks) *n. pl.* **·thra·ces** (-thrə·

sēz) **1** A carbuncle. **2** *Pathol.* An infectious and malignant febrile disease of man and some animals, caused by *Bacillus anthracis,* often with carbuncular swellings; splenic fever. **3** A bacillus found in the blood of those affected with splenic fever. **4** A gem stone of the ancients: probably the carbuncle. [< Gk., coal, carbuncle]

an·throp·ic (an·throp′ik) *adj.* Pertaining to the human species or the period of its existence. Also **an·throp′i·cal.**

anthropo- *combining form* Man; human: *anthropometry.* Also, before vowels, **anthrop-,** as in *anthropoid.* [< Gk. *anthrōpos* man]

an·thro·po·cen·tric (an′thrə·pō·sen′trik) *adj.* **1** Centering in man; regarding man as the central fact or final aim and end of the universe, or of any system: an *anthropocentric* philosophy. **2** Based on comparison with man: *anthropocentric* analysis of animal instincts.

an·thro·pog·e·ny (an′thrə·poj′ə·nē) *n.* The branch of anthropology that treats of the origin and development of man, either individually (ontogeny) or ethnically (phylogeny). See ANTHROPOLOGY. Also **an·thro·po·gen·e·sis** (an′thrə·pō·jen′ə·sis).

an·thro·pog·ra·phy (an′thrə·pog′rə·fē) *n.* The branch of anthropology that treats of the geographic distribution, variations, and peculiarities of the human race or its component parts; descriptive anthropology.

an·thro·poid (an′thrə·poid) *adj.* **1** Like a human being in form or other characteristics; manlike: said of the highest apes, as the gorilla, chimpanzee, and orang. **2** *Zool.* Of or pertaining to a suborder of primate mammals, including man, apes, and monkeys *(Anthropoidea).* Also **an′thro·poid′al.** —*n.* An anthropoid ape.

an·thro·pol·o·gy (an′thrə·pol′ə·jē) *n.* **1** The science of man in his physical, social, material, and cultural development, including the study of his origins, evolution, geographic distribution, ethnology, and communal forms. **2** The detailed study of the customs, beliefs, folkways, and superstitions of an ethnic group, especially on a comparative basis. —**an·thro·po·log·i·cal** (an′thrə·pə·loj′i·kəl) or **·log′ic** *adj.* —**an′thro·po·log′i·cal·ly** *adv.* —**an′thro·pol′o·gist** *n.*

an·thro·pom·e·try (an′thrə·pom′ə·trē) *n.* The science and technique of human measurements, specifically of anatomical and physiological features; also, the analysis and interpretation of the data so obtained. —**an·thro·po·met·ric** (an′thrə·pō·met′rik) or **·met′ri·cal** *adj.*

an·thro·po·mor·phic (an′thrə·pō·môr′fik) *adj.* Of or pertaining to anthropomorphism; having human form or human characteristics; manshaped.

an·thro·po·mor·phism (an′thrə·pō·môr′fiz·əm) *n.* The ascription of human attributes, feelings, conduct, or characteristics to God or any spiritual being, or to the powers of nature, etc. —**an′thro·po·mor′phist** *n.*

an·thro·po·mor·phize (an′thrə·pō·môr′fīz) *v.t.* & *v.i.* **·phized, ·phiz·ing** To endow (gods or natural objects) with human characteristics or qualities.

an·thro·po·mor·pho·sis (an′thrə·pō·môr′fə·sis) *n.* Transformation into human shape.

an·thro·po·mor·phous (an′thrə·pō·môr′fəs) *adj.* Having or resembling human form.

an·thro·pon·o·my (an′thrə·pon′ə·mē) *n.* The science of the laws that regulate the development of man in relation to environment and to other organisms. Also **an′thro·po·nom′ics**(-pō·nom′·iks). —**an′thro·po·nom′i·cal** *adj.*

an·thro·pop·a·thism (an′thrə·pop′ə·thiz′əm) *n.* **1** Anthropopathy. **2** An expression used in anthropopathy.

an·thro·pop·a·thy (an′thrə·pop′ə·thē) *n.* The attributing of human emotions, passions, suffering, etc., to God or to gods. [< Med. L *anthropopathia* < Gk. *anthrōpopatheia* humanity < *anthrōpos* man + *pathos* feeling]

an·thro·poph·a·gi (an′thrə·pof′ə·jī) *n. pl. sing.* **a·gus** (-ə·gəs) Eaters of human flesh; cannibals. [< L, pl. of *anthropophagus* < Gk. *anthrōpophagos* < *anthrōpos* man + *phagein* eat]

an·thro·po·phag·ic (an′thrə·pō·faj′ik) *adj.* Pertaining to the anthropophagi; man-eating. Also **an′thro·po·phag′i·cal.**

an·thro·poph·a·gite (an′thrə·pof′ə·jīt) *n.* A cannibal. Also **an′thro·poph′a·gist.**

an·thro·poph·a·gous (an′thrə·pof′ə·gəs) *adj.* Cannibalistic.

an·thro·poph·a·gy (an′thrə·pof′ə·jē) *n.* The eating of human flesh; cannibalism.

an·thro·po·zo·ic (an′thrə·pō·zō′ik) *adj. Geol.* Characterized by the existence of man: applied to the Quaternary period.

an·thu·ri·um (an·thoŏr′ē·əm) *n.* Any of a genus *(Anthurium)* of tropical American perennials of the arum family, with heart-shaped or lōbed leaves and densely flowered spathes. [< NL < Gk. *anthos* flower + *oura* tail]

an·ti (an′tī, an′tē) *n. pl.* **·tis** *Colloq.* One opposed to any proposed or enacted policy.

anti- *prefix*
1 Against; opposed to:

anti-abrasion	antileveling
anti-agglutinating	antilipase
anti-aggression	antiliturgical
anti-alien	antilottery
anti-Americanism	antimachine
anti-anarchic	anti-Malthusian
anti-aquatic	antimaterialist
anti-Aristotelian	antimerger
anti-ascetic	antimiasmatic
antibigotry	antimilitarism
anticaste	antimilitarist
anticensorship	antimiscegenation
anti-chafing	antimonarchist
antichurch	antimonopolist
anticivic	antimoral
anticlogging	antimusical
anticoagulating	antinational
anticombination	antinepotism
anticommercial	antinicotine
anticommunist	antinoise
anticonductor	anti-oxidase
anticonscription	anti-oxidizer
anticontagion	anti-oxygenating
anticontagious	antiparasitic
anticorrosive	anti-Platonic
anti-Darwinism	antiplethoric
antidemocratic	antipolitical
antidiastase	antipollution
antidogmatic	antipuritan
antidraft	antiradical
antidumping	antiradiation
antidynamic	antirationalism
antidynastic	antireformist
anti-empirical	antireligious
anti-episcopal	antirevolutionary
anti-erosion	antiromantic
anti-evangelical	antiroyalist
anti-evolutionist	antitrust
anti-expansionist	antischolastic
antifaction	antiscientific
antifanatic	antisensitizer
anti-Fascism	antisimoniacal
anti-Fascist	antiskid
antifat	antismoking
antifeminism	antistalling
antifeminist	antistatism
antiferment	antisubmarine
antifeudalism	antisuffragist
antiflash	antitarnish
antiforeign	antitartaric
antiforeignism	antitax
antigambling	antitobacco
antigrowth	antitorpedo
antihierarchist	anti-union
antihuman	antivaccinationist
antihypnotic	antivibratory
anti-imperialism	antivivisection
anti-imperialist	antivivisectionist
anti-imperialistic	anti-war
anti-intellectual	antiwaste
antilabor	antizealot
anti-Lamarckian	anti-Zionism

2 Opposite to; reverse:

anticyclic	antilogic
antihero	antipole

3 Rivaling; spurious:

anti-Caesar	anti-king
anticritic	anti-Messiah
anti-emperor	antiprophet

4 *Med.* Counteracting; curative; neutralizing:

anti-aphrodisiac	antibilious
anti-apoplectic	antibubonic
anti-arthritic	anticachectic
anti-asthmatic	anticarious

antibacterial	anticatalase
antibacteriolytic	anticatarrhal
anticolic	antipathogen
anticonvulsive	antipneumococcic
antidysenteric	antipruritic
anti-emetic	antirheumatic
anti-epileptic	antiscrofulous
anti-erysipelas	antiserum
antihemorrhoidal	antispirochetic
antihydrophobic	antistaphylococcic
antiluetic	antistreptococcal
antimalarial	antisudorific
antimephitic	antitetanic
antimicrobic	antithrombin
antimycotic	antityphoid
antinarcotic	antivirus

Anti- usually changes to *ant-* before words beginning with a vowel, as in *antacid,* and to *anth-* before the aspirate in words of Greek formation or analogy, as *anthelmintic.* [< Gk. < *anti* against]

an·ti·aer·i·al (an′tē·âr′ē·əl, -ā·ir′ē·əl) *adj.* Opposing attack from the air, as by parachute or glider troops.

an·ti·air·craft (an′tē·âr′kraft′, -âr′kräft′) *adj.* Opposed to or directed against aircraft: said especially of a type of gun or defense.

anti-àircraft artillery Fixed or mobile equipment used to spot, illuminate, and shoot at enemy aircraft, including sound locators, radar, searchlights, guns, etc.

an·ti·ar (an′tē·är) *n.* **1** The upas tree. **2** The acrid, virulent poison found in the gum of this tree, the glucoside antiarin, $C_{27}H_{42}O_{10}·4H_2O$, used as an arrow poison [< Javanese *antjar*]

an·ti·bi·o·sis (an′ti·bī·ō′sis) *n.* The condition of associated organisms in which one is detrimental to the other; antipathy.

an·ti·bi·ot·ic (an′ti·bī·ot′ik) *n.* **1** That which is antagonistic toward or destructive of life. **2** *Biochem.* **a** Any of a large class of substances produced by various micro-organisms and fungi that have the power of arresting the growth of other micro-organisms or of destroying them: some, as penicillin and streptomycin, are of value in the treatment of certain infectious diseases. **b** A chemical having similar properties produced by higher plants, some animals, and synthetically.

an·ti·bod·y (an′ti·bod′ē) *n. pl.* **·bod·ies** A globulin formed in the body in response to a foreign substance, as a protein or polysaccharide, and serving to neutralize the foreign substance.

an·tic (an′tik) *n.* **1** A prank; caper. **2** A clown; buffoon. **3** A grotesque figure or play. —*adj.* Odd; fantastic; ludicrous; incongruous. —*v.i.* **an·ticked, an·tick·ing** To play the clown; perform antics. Also *Obs.* **an′tick.** [< Ital. *antico* old (but used in the sense of grotesque) < L *antiquus.* Doublet of ANTIQUE.] —**an′tic·ly** *adv.*

an·ti·cat·a·lyst (an′ti·kat′ə·list) *n. Chem.* A catalyst which stops or retards a chemical reaction; a negative catalyst.

an·ti·cath·ode (an′ti·kath′ōd) *n.* The electrode in a vacuum or X-ray tube which receives and reflects the rays emitted from the cathode.

an·ti·chlor (an′ti·klôr, -klōr) *n.* Any substance, as sodium hyposulfite, used to neutralize the chlorine left in fabrics or the like after bleaching with hypochlorites. —**an′ti·chlo·ris′tic** *adj.*

An·ti·christ (an′ti·krīst′) *n.* Any opponent or enemy of Christ, whether a person or a power; specifically, a great enthroned antagonist, foretold in the Scriptures, who, as some have understood, is to precede the second coming of Christ: by some considered as evil personified. See I *John* ii 18.

an·ti·christ (an′ti·krīst′) *n.* **1** A false claimant of the attributes and characteristics of Christ. **2** A denier or opponent of Christ or Christianity. —**an·ti·chris·tian** (an′ti·kris′chən) *adj.*

an·tic·i·pant (an·tis′ə·pənt) *adj.* Coming or acting in advance; anticipating; expectant. —*n.* One who anticipates or expects.

an·tic·i·pate (an·tis′ə·pāt) *v.t.* **·pat·ed, ·pat·ing** **1** To experience or realize beforehand; expect; foresee: to *anticipate* a successful season. **2** To act or arrive sooner than. **3** To act or arrive sooner than so as to prevent; forestall: to *anticipate* an opponent's tactics. **4** To foresee and fulfil beforehand, as expectations.

5 To take or make use of beforehand, as income not yet available. 6 To discharge, as a debt or liability before it is due. 7 To cause to happen earlier; accelerate. [< L *anticipatus,* pp. of *anticipare* < *ante-* before + *capere* take] **—an·tic′i·pa′tor** *n.*

Synonyms: abide, apprehend, expect, forecast, foretaste, hope. We *expect* that which we have good reason to believe will happen. We *hope* for that which we much desire and somewhat *expect.* We *apprehend* what we both *expect* and fear. *Anticipate* is commonly used now, like *foretaste,* of that which we *expect* both with confidence and pleasure. In this use it is a stronger word than *hope;* I *hope* for a visit from my friend; I *expect* it when he writes that he is coming; and as the time draws near I *anticipate* it with pleasure. Compare ABIDE, PREVENT. *Antonyms*: distrust, doubt, dread, fear, recall, recollect, remember.

an·tic·i·pa·tion (an·tis′ə·pā′shən) *n.* **1** The act of anticipating; especially, a foreseeing or foretaste; expectation. **2** An instinctive prevision. **3** *Music* The introduction of a note

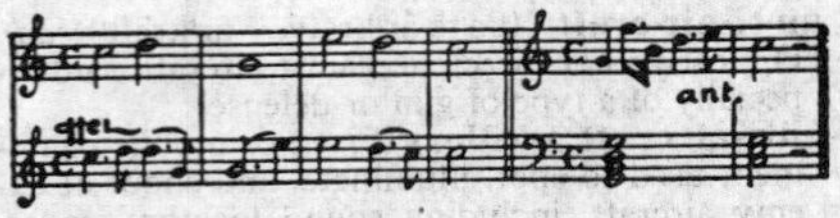

ANTICIPATION (*def. 3*)

before its expected place in the harmony.

Synonyms: antepast, apprehension, expectancy, expectation, foreboding, forecast, foresight, foretaste, forethought, hope, presentiment, prevision. *Expectation* may be either of good or evil; *presentiment* almost always, *apprehension* and *foreboding* always, of evil; *anticipation* and *antepast,* commonly of good. Thus, we speak of the pleasures of *anticipation.* A *foretaste* may be of good or evil, and is more than imaginary; it is a part actually received in advance. *Foresight* and *forethought* prevent future evil and secure future good by timely looking forward, and acting upon what is foreseen. Compare ANTICIPATE. *Antonyms*: astonishment, consummation, despair, doubt, dread, enjoyment, fear, realization, surprise, wonder.

an·tic·i·pa·tive (an·tis′ə·pā′tiv) *adj.* Anticipating; having the nature, quality, or habit of anticipation. **—an·tic′i·pa′tive·ly** *adv.*

an·tic·i·pa·to·ry (an·tis′ə·pə·tôr′ē, -tō′rē) *adj.* Pertaining to, showing, or embodying anticipation. **—an·tic′i·pa·to′ri·ly** *adv.*

an·ti·clas·tic (an′ti·klas′tik) *adj. Math.* Having opposite curvature in different directions; convex in one direction and concave in another. Compare SYNCLASTIC. [< ANTI- + Gk. *klastos* broken < *klaein* break]

an·ti·cler·i·cal (an′ti·kler′i·kəl) *adj.* Opposed to clerical influence; specifically, opposed to the Roman Catholic Church.

an·ti·cli·max (an′ti·klī′maks) *n.* **1** A real, apparent, or ludicrous decrease in the importance or impressiveness of what is said: opposed to *climax.* **2** Any sudden descent or fall contrasted with a previous rise. **—an′ti·cli·mac′tic** (-klī·mak′tik) *adj.*

an·ti·cli·nal (an′ti·klī′nəl) *adj. Geol.* Forming a bend with the convex side upward, as a rock stratum or group of strata: also **an′ti·clin′ic** (-klin′ik). *—n.* An anticlinal line, fold, or disposition of strata; a saddleback: also **an′ti·cline.** See SYNCLINAL. [< ANTI- + Gk. *klinein* slope]

an·ti·cli·no·ri·um (an′ti·klī·nôr′ē·əm, -nō′rē·əm) *n. pl.* **·no·ri·a** (-nôr′ē·ə, -nō′rē·ə) *Geol.* A system of roughly parallel folds in stratified rocks, having on the whole an anticlinal

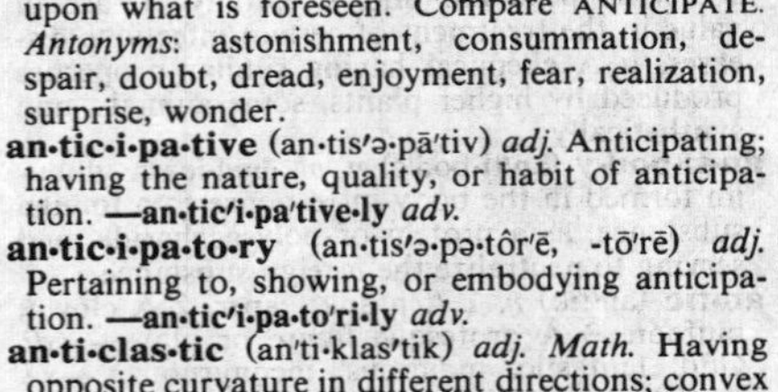

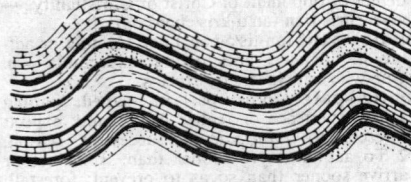

ANTICLINORIUM

structure and forming a great compound arch. [< NL < ANTI- + Gk. *klinein* slope + *oros* mountain]

antic mask See ANTIMASK.

an·ti·co·her·er (an′ti·kō·hir′ər) *n. Electr.* A wave-sensitive device which differs from the coherer in that its resistance increases, instead of decreases, under the action of electromagnetic waves. See DE-COHERER.

an·ti·cos·mon (an′ti·koz′mon) *n. Physics* The supposed fundamental particle from which the anticosmos developed, characterized by a nucleonic charge opposite to that of the cosmon.

an·ti·cos·mos (an′ti·koz′məs) *n. Physics* A cosmos composed entirely of antimatter and supposed to have been formed by the splitting of the universon into two distinct parts existing independently of each other in a condition of metastable equilibrium.

An·ti·cos·ti (an′ti·kôs′tē, -kos′-) An island in the Gulf of St. Lawrence, Quebec, Canada; about 3,043 square miles.

an·ti·cy·clone (an′ti·sī′klōn) *n. Meteorol.* An atmospheric condition of high central pressure relative to the surrounding area, with horizontal spiral currents flowing clockwise in the northern hemisphere, counterclockwise in the southern; also, the region subject to this condition.

an·ti·cy·clon·ic (an′ti·sī·klon′ik) *adj.* **1** Of or pertaining to an anticyclone. **2** Opposed to the cyclonic theory in meteorology.

an·ti·dote (an′ti·dōt) *n.* Anything that will counteract or remove the effects of poison, disease, or any evil. [< L *antidotum* < Gk. *antidoton* < *antidotos* given against < *anti-* against + *didonai* give] **—an′ti·do′tal** *adj.* **—an′ti·do′tal·ly** *adv.*

an·ti·drom·ic (an′ti·drom′ik) *adj. Physiol.* Denoting a movement or course opposed to the normal, as of a nerve impulse. [< ANTI- + Gk. *dromos* a running]

an·ti·en·er·gis·tic (an′tē·en′ər·jis′tik) *adj.* Resisting applied energy: contrasted with *synergistic.*

An·tie·tam (an·tē′təm) A village near Sharpsburg in western Maryland at the mouth of **Antietam Creek**; site of the fiercest day's battle of the Civil War, September 17, 1862.

an·ti·fe·brile (an′ti·fē′brəl, -feb′rəl) *adj.* Having the power to allay fever; antipyretic. *—n.* An antifebrile agent.

an·ti·fed·er·al (an′ti·fed′ər·əl, -fed′rəl) *adj.* Opposed to federalism: capitalized when used historically to mean opposed to the adoption of the U.S. Constitution in 1787–89.

an·ti·fed·er·al·ism (an′ti·fed′ər·əl·iz′əm, -fed′·rəl-) *n.* Opposition to federalism, especially to the Federal party. **—an′ti·fed′er·al·ist** *n.*

An·ti·fed·er·al·ist (an′ti·fed′ər·əl·ist, -fed′rəl-) *n.* A member of the political party that opposed the ratification of the U.S. Constitution. After it was ratified, the Antifederalists, led by Jefferson, opposed any extension of the powers of the Federal government.

an·ti·freeze (an′ti·frēz′) *n.* A liquid of low freezing point, added to or substituted for the cooling agent in combustion-engine radiators, to prevent freezing.

an·ti·fric·tion (an′ti·frik′shən) *adj.* Lessening or tending to lessen friction, as by lubricants or rollers. *—n.* **1** A lubricant. **2** A roller or other device for lessening friction. **—antifriction metal** Any alloy having a low coefficient of friction: used for bearing-surfaces.

an·ti·gen (an′tə·jən) *n.* Any of several substances, such as toxins, enzymes, proteins, which, injected into an organism, cause the development of antibodies. Also **an′ti·gene** (-jēn). **—an·ti·gen·ic** (an′tə·jen′ik) *adj.*

An·tig·o·ne (an·tig′ə·nē) In Greek legend, a daughter of Oedipus and Jocasta who accompanied her blinded father into exile and later was sentenced to death by her uncle Creon for illegally burying her brother Polynices.

An·tig·o·nus I (an·tig′ə·nəs), 382–301 B.C., general of Alexander the Great and king of Macedonia 306–301 B.C.: called "the Cyclops."

An·ti·gua (an·tē′gwə, -gə) A presidency of the Leeward Islands, comprising the island of Antigua (108 square miles) and its dependencies: Barbuda; 62 square miles; and Redonda; 1/2 square mile; capital, St. John's, on Antigua.

Antigua Guatemala A resort city in south central Guatemala; former capital of Guatemala. Also **Antigua.**

an·ti·he·lix (an′ti·hē′liks) See ANTHELIX.

an·ti·his·ta·mine (an′ti·his′tə·mēn, -min) *n. Med.* Any of certain drugs which neutralize the vasoconstrictor action of histamine in the body: used especially in the treatment of allergic conditions, as hay fever, asthma, etc., and of thecommon cold. **—an′ti·his′ta·min′ic** (-min′ik) *adj.*

an·ti·ic·er (an′tē·ī′sər) *n. Aeron.* A device for preventing the formation of ice on airplane wings and other exposed surfaces by the use of a spray delivering warm air or a special liquid preparation. Compare DE-ICER.

an·ti·ke·to·gen·e·sis (an′ti·kē′tə·jen′ə·sis) *n. Biochem.* The reduction or prevention of ketosis by the oxidation of sugar or allied substances in the body.

an·ti·knock (an′ti·nok′) *adj.* Tending to prevent detonation or pinging in an internal-combustion engine *—n.* Any agent, as tetraethyllead, having antiknock properties.

An·ti-Leb·a·non (an′ti·leb′ə·nən) A mountain range east of the Lebanon Mountains, on the Syria-Lebanon border.

an·ti·le·gal·ist (an′ti·lē′gəl·ist) *n.* One who repudiates law as the guide of human conduct.

an·ti·lip·oid (an′ti·lip′oid) *n.* An antibody which reacts with fatlike substances.

an·ti·lith·ic (an′ti·lith′ik) *Med. adj.* Efficacious against stones or calculi. *—n.* An agent which prevents or destroys urinary calculi. [< ANTI- + Gk. *lithos* stone]

An·til·les (an·til′ēz) The islands of the West Indies, except the Bahamas; divided into the **Greater Antilles**: Cuba, Hispaniola, Jamaica, and Puerto Rico; and the **Lesser Antilles**: Trinidad, the Leeward and Windward Islands, Barbados, and other islands: also *Caribbees.*

an·ti·log·a·rithm (an′ti·lôg′ə·rith′əm, -log′-) *n. Math.* The number corresponding to a given logarithm.

an·til·o·gous (an·til′ə·gəs) *adj. Physics* Designating that pole of a pyro-electric crystal which is negative while the crystal is being heated and positive as it cools. Compare ANALOGOUS. [< Gk. *antilogos* contradictory < *anti-* against + *legein* speak]

an·til·o·gy (an·til′ə·jē) *n. pl.* **·gies** Inconsistency in terms or ideas; contradiction.

an·ti·ma·cas·sar (an′ti·mə·kas′ər) *n.* A covering to prevent the soiling of the backs of chairs or sofas by contact with the hair; a tidy. [< ANTI- + MACASSAR (OIL)]

an·ti·mask (an′ti·mask′, -mäsk′) *n.* A grotesque interlude between the acts of a mask, often burlesquing it: also called *antic mask.* Also **an′ti·masque′.**

an·ti·mat·ter (an′ti·mat′ər) *n. Physics* Matter composed of antiparticles.

an·ti·mere (an′tə·mir) *n. Biol.* A part symmetrical with, or corresponding to, a part on the opposite side of the main axis; an opposite, symmetrical, or homotypic part, as an arm of a starfish, or the right or left half of a bilaterally symmetrical animal: also called *actinomere.* [< ANTI- + Gk. *meros* part] **—an·ti·mer·ic** (an′·tə·mer′ik) *adj.* **—an·tim·er·ism** (an·tim′ə·riz′·əm) *n.*

an·ti·mol·e·cule (an′ti·mol′ə·kyōōl) *n.* A molecule of antimatter.

an·ti·mo·nar·chic (an′ti·mə·när′kik) *adj.* Opposed to monarchism. Also **an′ti·mo·nar′chi·cal.**

an·ti·mo·ni·al (an′tē·mō′nē·əl) *adj.* Of or containing antimony. *—n.* A medicine, one of whose ingredients is antimony.

an·ti·mo·nic (an′tə·mō′nik, -mon′ik) *adj.* Of, pertaining to, or containing antimony, especially when combined in its higher or pentad valence: *antimonic* sulfide, Sb_2S_5.

an·ti·mo·nous (an′tə·mō′nəs) *adj.* Of, pertaining to, or containing antimony, especially in its lower valence: *antimonous* oxide, Sb_4O_6. Also **an′ti·mo′ni·ous.**

an·ti·mon·soon (an′ti·mon·sōōn′) *n. Meteorol.* The atmospheric current moving over a monsoon in an opposite direction to it.

an·ti·mo·ny (an′tə·mō′nē) *n.* A silver-white, brittle, flaky metallic element (symbol Sb, atomic number 51), sometimes found native, used chiefly in alloys. See PERIODIC TABLE. ◆ Collateral adjective: *stibial.* [< Med.L *antimonium,* ? < Arabic]

an·ti·mo·ny-glance (an′tə·mō′nē·glans′, -gläns′) *n.* Stibnite.

an·ti·mo·nyl (an′tə·mə·nil′) *n.* A univalent radical SbO, forming the base of several salts.

antimonyl potassium tartrate See TARTAR EMETIC.

an·ti·mu·ta·gen (an′ti·myōō′tə·jən) *n.* A chem-

ical regarded as having the property of inhibiting or decreasing the hereditary variability of micro–organisms and germ cells. [<ANTI- + L *mutare* alter + -GEN] — **an′ti·mu′ta·gen′ic** (-myōō′tə·jen′ik) *adj.*

an·ti·neu·tron (an′ti·nōō′tron, -nyōō′-) *n. Physics* An antiparticle having the same mass as a neutron, but having a reversed magnetic moment of equal magnitude.

an·tin·i·on (an·tin′ē·on) *n. Anat.* That point in the median line of the glabellum furthest removed from the inion: a craniometrical term. [<NL <ANTI- + INION]

an·ti·node (an′ti·nōd′) *n. Physics* The section that lies midway between the nodal points of a vibrating medium; a loop.

an·ti·no·mi·an (an′ti·nō′mē·ən) *n. Theol.* One holding that faith frees the Christian from the obligations of the moral law. —*adj.* Of or pertaining to this doctrine. — **an′ti·no′mi·an·ism** *n.*

an·tin·o·my (an·tin′ə·mē) *n. pl.* **·mies 1** Self–contradiction in a law; opposition of one law or rule to another. **2** Irreconcilability of seemingly necessary inferences or conclusions; paradox. [<L *antinomia* <Gk. *antinomia* <*anti-* against + *nomos* law]

An·tin·o·us (an·tin′ō·əs) In the *Odyssey,* the most insistent of Penelope's suitors and the first to be slain by Odysseus.

An·ti·och (an′tē·ok) An ancient city on the Orontes in southern Turkey; former capital of Syria: Arabic and Turkish *Antakiya* or *Antakya,* Roman *Caesarea.*

An·ti·o·chi·an (an′tē·ō′kē·ən) *adj.* **1** Of or pertaining to **Antiochus of Ascalon**, died 68 B.C., the founder of an eclectic school of philosophy uniting Platonic, Aristotelian, and Stoic doctrines. **2** Of or pertaining to Antioch.

An·ti·o·chus (an·tī′ə·kəs) Name of thirteen kings of the Seleucid dynasty in Syria, third to first century B.C.

— **Antiochus III,** 242–187 B.C., conquered Egypt and much of the Near East; defeated by the Romans at Magnesia, 190 B.C.: known as *Antiochus the Great.*

— **Antiochus IV,** died 163 B.C., attempted to suppress Judaism and brought on the Maccabean revolt: called "Epiphanes."

An·ti·o·pe (an·tī′ə·pē) **1** In Greek mythology, a maiden loved by Zeus in the form of a satyr, to whom she bore two sons, Amphion and Zethus. **2** Hippolyta, queen of the Amazons.

an·ti·par·tic·le (an′ti·pär′ti·kəl) *n. Physics* An elementary particle, as a positron, antiproton, antineutron, etc., equal in mass to another elementary particle, as an electron, proton, neutron, etc., but opposite to it in charge and in magnetic properties. Contact between a particle and its opposite results in mutual annihilation and the release of energy.

an·ti·pas·to (än′tē·päs′tō) *n.* A course of smoked or salted meat, fish, vegetables, etc., served as an appetizer. [<Ital. <*anti-* before (<L *ante*) + *pasto* food <L *pastus*]

An·tip·a·ter (an·tip′ə·tər), 398–319 B.C., regent of Macedonia.

— **Antipater,** died 43 B.C., procurator of Judea; father of Herod the Great.

an·tip·a·thet·ic (an·tip′ə·thet′ik, an′ti·pə-) *adj.* Having antipathy; naturally repugnant or opposed. Also **an·tip′a·thet′i·cal.** — **an·tip′a·thet′i·cal·ly** *adv.*

an·tip·a·thy (an·tip′ə·thē) *n. pl.* **·thies 1** An instinctive feeling of aversion or dislike. **2** One who or that which excites aversion. [<Gk. *antipatheia* <*anti-* against + *pathein* feel, suffer]

Synonyms: abhorrence, antagonism, aversion, detestation, disgust, dislike, distaste, hatred, hostility, loathing, opposition, repugnance, uncongeniality. *Antipathy, repugnance,* and *uncongeniality* are instinctive; other forms of *dislike* may be acquired or cherished for cause. Compare ACRIMONY, ANGER, HATRED. *Antonyms*: affinity, agreement, attraction, congeniality, harmony, kindliness, partiality, predilection, regard, sympathy.

an·ti–Pe·la·gi·an (an′ti·pi·lā′jē·ən) *Theol. adj.* Against Pelagius and his beliefs, as certain creeds or church decrees. —*n.* One who opposed Pelagius or his doctrines.

an·ti·pe·ri·od·ic (an′ti·pir′ē·od′ik) *Med. adj.* Remedial of periodic diseases, as quinine for malaria. —*n.* A remedy for such diseases.

an·ti·per·son·nel (an′ti·pûr′sə·nel′) *adj. Mil.* Designating weapons, such as bombs, mines, etc., which are employed against individuals rather than against defenses or mechanized equipment.

an·ti·per·spi·rant (an′ti·pûr′spə·rənt) *n.* A preparation which acts to diminish or prevent perspiration: an astringent applied to the skin.

an·ti·phlo·gis·tic (an′ti·flō·jis′tik) *Med. adj.* Capable of reducing inflammation. —*n.* A remedy for inflammation.

an·ti·phon (an′tə·fon) *n.* **1** A verse of a psalm or hymn said or chanted in response to another. **2** A composition consisting of passages for alternate singing or chanting. **3** A versicle chanted before, and often after, a psalm or canticle, and varying with the church season or feast. [<LL *antiphona* <Gk. *antiphona.* Doublet of ANTHEM.] — **an′ti·phon′ic** or **·i·cal** *adj.*

an·tiph·o·nal (an·tif′ə·nəl) *adj.* Of or pertaining to an antiphon. —*n.* An antiphonary. — **an·tiph′o·nal·ly** *adv.*

an·tiph·o·nar·y (an·tif′ə·ner′ē) *n. pl.* **·nar·ies** A book of antiphons. Also **an·tiph′o·nar** (-nər). —*adj.* Of or pertaining to a book of antiphons.

an·tiph·o·ny (an·tif′ə·nē) *n. pl.* **·nies 1** An anthem or other composition to be sung antiphonally. **2** Antiphonal singing. **3** In ancient Greek music, accompaniment in the octave.

an·tiph·ra·sis (an·tif′rə·sis) *n. pl.* **·ses** (-sēz) The use of a term in a sense opposite to its meaning; irony. [<L <Gk. *antiphrasis* <*antiphrazein* express by antithesis <*anti-* against + *phrazein* speak]

an·tip·o·dal (an·tip′ə·dəl) *adj.* **1** Pertaining to or situated on the opposite side of the earth. **2** Diametrically opposed. Also **an·tip·o·de·an** (an·tip′ə·dē′ən).

an·ti·pode (an′ti·pōd) *n.* An exact opposite.

an·tip·o·des (an·tip′ə·dēz) *n. pl.* **1** A place or region on the opposite side of the earth, or its inhabitants. **2** Any person or thing diametrically opposed to another, or at the opposite extreme from another. [<L <Gk. *antipodes,* pl. of *antipous* having the feet opposite <*anti-* opposite + *pous* foot]

An·tip·o·des (an·tip′ə·dēz) **1** A group of uninhabited islands SE of and belonging to New Zealand; 24 square miles: so called from their antipodal position to Greenwich, England. **2** Australasia.

an·ti·pope (an′ti·pōp′) *n.* A usurping pope or one not canonically elected.

an·ti·pro·ton (an′ti·prō′ton) *n. Physics* An antiparticle having the same mass as the proton, an equal but opposite charge, and a reversed magnetic moment of equal magnitude; its collision with a proton or neutron results in the liberation of energy equivalent to both particles.

an·ti·py·ic (an′ti·pī′ik) *Med. adj.* Preventive of suppuration. —*n.* A remedy against suppuration. [<ANTI- + Gk. *pyon* pus]

an·ti·py·ret·ic (an′ti·pī·ret′ik) *Med. adj.* Preventive or alleviative of fever. —*n.* A medicine to allay fever. [<ANTI- + Gk. *pyretos* fever]

an·ti·py·rine (an′ti·pī′rin, -rēn) *n.* A white crystalline compound, $C_{11}H_{12}N_2O$, used in medicine as an antipyretic. Also **an′ti·py′rin** (-rin).

an·ti·quar·i·an (an′ti·kwâr′ē·ən) *adj.* Pertaining to antiquity or to the knowledge of or collecting of antiquities. —*n.* An antiquary. — **an′ti·quar′i·an·ism** *n.*

an·ti·quar·y (an′ti·kwer′ē) *n. pl.* **·quar·ies** One who collects, examines, deals in, or studies ancient objects; one versed in ancient things, as relics, monuments, old manuscripts, etc. [<L *antiquarius* <*antiquus* ancient]

an·ti·quate (an′ti·kwāt) *v.t.* **·quat·ed, ·quat·ing 1** To make old, out of date, or obsolete. **2** To cause to look antique; give an old–fashioned air or style to. — **an′ti·qua′tion** *n.*

an·ti·quat·ed (an′ti·kwā′tid) *adj.* **1** Out of date; old–fashioned; obsolete. **2** Ancient; superannuated. See synonyms under ANCIENT, ANTIQUE.

an·tique (an·tēk′) *adj.* **1** Of, pertaining to, or having come down from ancient times. **2** In the style of ancient times. **3** Old; old–fashioned. **4** Pertaining or belonging to ancient Greece or Rome. —*n.* **1** The style of ancient art, or a specimen of it. **2** Any ancient object, as a piece of furniture, glass, etc. **3** A Roman–faced type with all the lines of nearly the same thickness. —*v.t.* **an·tiqued, an·ti·quing** To make seemingly old; give the appearance of antiquity to. [<F <L *antiquus* ancient <*ante* before. Doublet of ANTIC.] — **an·tique′ly** *adv.* — **an·tique′ness** *n.*

Synonyms (adj.): ancient, antiquated, old–fashioned, quaint, superannuated. *Antique* refers to an *ancient, antiquated* to a discarded style. The *antique* is that which is either *ancient* in fact or *ancient* in style. The *antiquated* is not so much out of date as out of vogue. *Old–fashioned* may be used approvingly or contemptuously. In the latter case it becomes a synonym for *antiquated;* in the good sense it approaches the meaning of *antique,* but indicates less duration. *Quaint* combines the idea of age with a pleasing oddity. The *antiquated* person is out of style and out of sympathy with the present generation by reason of age; the *superannuated* person is incapacitated for present activities by reason of age. Compare ANCIENT, OLD. *Antonyms*: fashionable, fresh, modern, modish, new, recent, stylish.

an·tiq·ui·ty (an·tik′wə·tē) *n. pl.* **·ties 1** The state or quality of being ancient. **2** Ancient times, people, or civilization. **3** Anything belonging to ancient times.

an·ti·re·mon·strant (an′ti·ri·mon′strənt) *n.* An opponent of remonstrance. —*adj.* Opposed to remonstrance.

An·ti·re·mon·strant (an′ti·ri·mon′strənt) *n.* A Dutch Calvinist who opposed the Arminian Remonstrance. —*adj.* Pertaining to such opposition.

an·ti–rent (an′ti·rent′) *adj.* **1** Opposed to payment of land rent. **2** Designating a concerted movement in Ireland in 1881, opposing the payment of rent to absentee landlords. — **an′ti–rent′er** *n.* — **an′ti–rent′ism** *n.*

An·ti–rent (an′ti·rent′) *adj.* Designating a political party in New York State (1839–47) opposed to paying farm rents to patroons.

an·tir·rhi·num (an′tə·rī′nəm) *n.* Any of a genus *(Antirrhinum)* of chiefly Old World herbs of the figwort family, including the common American snapdragon. [<NL <Gk. *antirrhinon* <*anti-* resembling + *rhis* nose]

an·ti·sab·ba·tar·i·an (an′ti·sab′ə·târ′ē·ən) *adj.* Of or pertaining to one who opposes the observance of the Sabbath. —*n.* One who denies the moral obligation to observe the Sabbath, or opposes its strict or puritanical observance.

An·ti–Sa·loon League (an′ti·sə·lōōn′) An organization, founded nationally in 1895, aiming to abolish the sale and use of liquor.

An·ti·sa·na (än′tē·sä′nä) A volcano in the Andes, north central Ecuador; 18,714 feet.

an·tis·cians (an·tish′ənz) *n. pl.* Dwellers on the same meridian on opposite sides of the equator, whose shadows at noon fall in opposite directions. Also **an·tis·ci·i** (an·tish′ē·ī). [<L *antiscii* <Gk. *antiskioi* <*anti-* opposite + *skia* shadow]

an·ti·scor·bu·tic (an′ti·skôr·byōō′tik) *Med. adj.* Relieving or preventing scurvy. —*n.* A remedy for scurvy.

an·ti–Sem·i·tism (an′ti·sem′ə·tiz′əm) *n.* Opposition to, prejudice or discrimination against, or intolerance of Jews, Jewish culture, etc. — **an′ti–Sem′ite** *n.* — **an′ti–Se·mit′ic** (-sə·mit′ik) *adj.* — **an′ti–Se·mit′i·cal·ly** *adv.*

an·ti·sep·sis (an′tə·sep′sis) *n.* **1** The condition in or method by which a substance, or organism, is kept sterile against the growth of pathogenic or putrefactive bacteria. **2** Listerism. [<NL <ANTI- + Gk. *sēpsis* putrefaction]

an·ti·sep·tic (an′tə·sep′tik) *adj.* **1** Of, pertaining to, or used in antisepsis. **2** Preventing or counteracting putrefaction, etc. Also **an′ti·sep′ti·cal.** —*n.* Any substance having antiseptic qualities, as solutions of carbolic acid and of corrosive sublimate. — **an′ti·sep′ti·cal·ly** *adv.* — **an′ti·sep′ti·cism** (-sep′tə·siz′əm) *n.*

an·ti·sep·ti·cize (an′tə·sep′tə·sīz) *v.t.* **·cized, ·ciz·ing** To render antiseptic; treat by the application of antiseptics.

an·ti·se·rum (an'ti·sir'əm) *n*. A serum which contains antibodies, the injection of which into the blood stream provides immunity from specific diseases.

an·ti·slav·er·y (an'ti·slā'vər·ē, -slāv'rē) *adj*. Opposed to human slavery. — *n*. Opposition to human slavery.

an·ti·so·cial (an'ti·sō'shəl) *adj*. 1 Averse to social intercourse or society. 2 Opposed to treating society as a unit; anarchistic. 3 Obstructive or disruptive of social good.

an·ti·so·cial·ist (an'ti·sō'shəl·ist) *n*. One hostile to socialistic teachings. — **an'ti·so'cial·is'·tic** *adj*.

an·ti·so·lar (an'ti·sō'lər) *adj*. 1 Situated or occurring at a point in the heavens 180 degrees from the sun in azimuth. 2 Diametrically opposite the sun, as the center of a rainbow.

an·ti·spas·mod·ic (an'ti·spaz·mod'ik) *adj*. Relieving or checking spasms. — *n*. An antispasmodic preparation, as ammonia, camphor, etc.

An·tis·the·nes (an·tis'thə·nēz) 444?–371? B.C., Greek philosopher; reputed founder of Cynic school.

an·tis·tro·phe (an·tis'trə·fē) *n*. 1 In ancient Greek poetry, the verses sung by the chorus in a play while returning from left to right, in answer to the previous strophe. 2 In classical prosody, the lines of an ode comprising a stanza and alternating with the strophe. 3 The second of two alternating metrical systems in a poem. [<Gk. *antistrophē* < *antistrephein* turn against < *anti-* against, opposite + *strephein* turn] — **an·ti·stroph·ic** (an'ti·strof'ik) *adj*.

an·ti·tank (an'ti·tangk') *adj*. *Mil*. Designed to combat tanks and other mechanized equipment: *anti-tank* guns.

an·ti·te·tan·ic (an'tī·te·tan'ik) *Med. adj*. Relieving or preventing tetanus. — *n*. A remedy for tetanus.

an·ti·the·ism (an'ti·thē'iz·əm) *n*. 1 Opposition to belief in God. 2 In philosophy and religion, opposition to theism.

an·tith·e·sis (an·tith'ə·sis) *n*. *pl*. **·ses** (-sēz) 1 The balancing of contrasted words or ideas against each other. 2 The direct contrary; a strong contrast. [<L <Gk. <*antitithenai* oppose < *anti-* against + *tithenai* place]

an·ti·thet·i·cal (an'tə·thet'i·kəl) *adj*. Directly opposed; strongly contrasted. Also **an'ti·thet'·ic**. — **an'ti·thet'i·cal·ly** *adv*.

an·ti·tox·in (an'ti·tok'sin) *n*. A substance, usually a protein, formed in the living tissues of a plant or animal, which neutralizes the bacterial poison that produced it. Also **an'ti·tox'ine** (-tok'sin, -sēn) — **an'ti·tox'ic** *adj*.

an·ti·trade (an'ti·trād') *Meteorol. n*. One of the upper air currents in the tropics, moving contrary to the trade winds. — *adj*. Pertaining to or designating such an air current.

an·tit·ra·gus (an·tit'rə·gəs) *n*. *pl*. **·gi** (-jī) *Anat*. The conical eminence behind the opening of the ear. [<ANTI- + TRAGUS]

an·ti·Trin·i·tar·i·an (an'ti·trin'ə·târ'ē·ən) *adj*. *Theol*. Opposing the doctrine of the Trinity. — *n*. One who opposes the doctrine of the Trinity.

an·ti·trust (an'ti·trust') *adj*. Pertaining to the regulation of or opposition to trusts, cartels, pools, monopolies, and other organizations and practices in restraint of trade.

an·ti·twi·light (an'ti·twī'līt) *n*. *Meteorol*. A pink or purplish light sometimes seen after sunset or before sunrise in the part of the sky opposite the sun.

an·ti·type (an'ti·tīp') *n*. 1 That which a type or symbol represents; the original of a type. 2 A person or event in the New Testament prefigured by one in the Old. [<Gk. *antitypos* < *anti-* corresponding to, against + *typos* stamp, type] — **an·ti·typ·al** (an'ti·tī'pəl), **an·ti·typ·ic** (an'ti·tip'ik) or **·i·cal** *adj*.

an·ti·ven·in (an'ti·ven'in) *n*. 1 The active principle of a serum which protects animals against snake poison or venom. 2 The serum. Also **an·ti·ven·ene**, **an·ti·ven·ine** (an'ti·ven'ēn, -və·nēn'). [<ANTI- + L *venenum* poison]

an·ti·vi·ral (an'ti·vī'rəl) *adj*. 1 Injurious to or destructive of viruses. 2 Counteracting a virus, as certain drugs.

an·ti·vi·rot·ic (an'ti·vī·rot'ik) *n*. A substance which destroys viruses or inhibits their development. — *adj*. Antiviral.

an·ti·world (an'ti·wûrld') *n*. *Physics* A hypothetical world or universe composed only of

antimatter: sometimes called *contra-terrene*.

ant·ler (ant'lər) *n*. 1 A deciduous bony outgrowth or horn on the head of various members of the deer family, usually branched. 2 Any one of its branches or tines. [<OF *antoillier*, ult. <L *ante-* before + *oculus* eye] — **ant'lered** *adj*.

Ant·li·a (ant'lē·ə) A southern constellation near Argo. See CONSTELLATION.

ant·li·on (ant'lī'ən) *n*. 1 An insect (family *Myrmeleontidae*) resembling a dragonfly; especially, its long-jawed, louselike larva, usually called *doodle-bug*, which buries itself in a funnel-shaped pit with only its jaws projecting and preys on ants and other insects. For illustration see under INSECT (beneficial). 2 A mythical animal, half lion, half ant.

ANTLERS
A. Rusine.
B., C., D. Rucervine: normal, intermediate, extreme.
E. Subelaphine.
F. Elaphine.
Tine: *a.* Brow *b.* Bez *c.* Royal

An·to·fa·gas·ta (än'tō·fä·gäs'tä) A port in northern Chile.

An·toine (än·twän') French form of ANTHONY.

An·toine, **Père** (pâr) See ANTONIO DE SEDILLA.

An·toi·nette (an'twə·net', -tə-; *Fr.* än·twä·net') French form of ANTONIA. Also *Ger.* **An·to·niet·te** (än·tō·nyet'ə), *Ital.* **An·to·niet·ta** (än'tō·nyet'tä).

An·ton (än'tōn) Danish, Dutch, German, and Swedish form of ANTHONY.

An·to·nes·cu (än'tō·nes'kōō), **Ion** (yon), 1882–1946, Rumanian general and political leader 1940–44; executed.

An·to·ni·a (an·tō'nē·ə) A feminine personal name; feminine of ANTHONY. Also *Fr.* **An·to·nie** (än·tô·nē'), *Ger.* **An·to·nie** (än·tō'nye), *Ital., Sp.* **An·to·ni·na** (än'tō·nē'nä).

An·to·ni·nus (an'tə·nī'nəs) See AURELIUS, MARCUS.

Antoninus Pi·us (pī'əs), A.D. 86–161, emperor of Rome A.D. 131–61.

An·to·nio (än·tō'nyō) Italian, Portuguese, and Spanish form of ANTHONY.
— **An·to·ni·o** (an·tō'nē·ō, -tōn'yō) One of several characters in Shakespeare's plays: in the *Merchant of Venice*, the merchant; in *Two Gentlemen of Verona*, father of Proteus; in *The Tempest*, Prospero's brother, who has usurped his dukedom; in *Twelfth Night*, a sea-captain; in *Much Ado About Nothing*, brother of Leonato, governor of Messina.

Antonio de Se·dil·la (thä sā·thē'lyä) 1748–1829, Spanish Capuchin priest in New Orleans, accused of trying to introduce the Inquisition: called *Père Antoine*.

An·to·ni·us (*Ger.* än·tō'nē·ōōs, *Lat.* an·tō'nē·əs) German and Latin form of ANTHONY.

an·to·no·ma·sia (an'tə·nō·mā'zhə, -zhē·ə) *n*. 1 The substitution of a title or epithet for a proper name, as *his Honor*, for a judge. 2 The use of the name of a representative individual for a class, as a *Cicero*, for an orator. [<L <Gk. <*antonomazein* name instead < *anti-* instead of + *onoma* name]

An·to·ny (an'tə·nē) See ANTHONY.
— **Antony, Mark**, 83–30 B.C., Roman general and triumvir: also *Marcus Antonius*.

an·to·nym (an'tə·nim) *n*. A word directly opposed to another in meaning: contrasted with *synonym*. [<Gk. *antōnymia* < *anti-* opposite + *onoma, onyma* name]

an·tre (an'tər) *n*. *Obs*. A cavern. [<F <L *antrum* <Gk. *antron* cave]

An·trim (an'trim) A county of Ulster province in NE Northern Ireland; 1,098 square miles; county seat, Belfast.

an·trorse (an·trôrs') *adj*. *Biol*. Directed forward or upward, as the short feathers hiding the nostrils in corvine birds. [<NL *antrorsus* <ANTERO- + L *versus*, pp. of *vertere* turn] — **an·trorse'ly** *adv*.

an·trum (an'trəm) *n*. *pl*. **·tra** (-trə) *Anat*. A cavity, usually in a bone. [<L <Gk. *antron* cave]

antrum of High·more (hī'môr, -mōr) *Anat*. A cavity in the upper jaw opening into the nose. [after Nathaniel *Highmore*, 1613–85, English anatomist]

an·trus·tion (an·trus'chən) *n*. A vassal follower and companion of the early Frankish princes. Compare THANE. [<F <Med. L *antrustio, -onis* <OHG *trōst* trust, protection] — **an·trus'tion·ship** *n*.

An·try·cide (an'tri·sīd) *n*. Proprietary name for a synthetic crystalline compound developed as a drug for use against trypanosomiasis in cattle, especially in tropical Africa.

An·tung (an'tŏŏng', *Chinese* än'dŏŏng') A port on the Yalu in southern Manchuria, capital of Liaotung province.

Ant·werp (ant'wûrp) A port on the Scheldt in northern Belgium: French *Anvers*. Flemish **Ant·wer·pen** (änt'ver·pən).

A·nu (ä'nōō) In Babylonian mythology, the sky god.

A·nu·bis (ə·nōō'bis, ə·nyōō'-) In Egyptian mythology, the jackal-headed conductor of the dead to judgment: identified with the Greek *Hermes*.

ANUBIS

A·nu·ra·dha·pu·ra (ə·nōō'rä·də·pŏŏr'ə) A Buddhist pilgrimage center in north central Ceylon; former capital of Ceylon.

a·nu·ran (ə·nŏŏr'ən, ə·nyŏŏr'-) *adj. & n. Zool.* Salientian. [<AN-[1] without + Gk. *oura* tail] — **a·nu'rous** *adj*.

an·u·re·sis (an'yŏŏ·rē'sis) *n*. Anury. — **an'u·ret'ic** (-ret'ik) *adj*.

an·u·ry (an'yŏŏ·rē) *n*. *Pathol*. Suppression or defective excretion of the urine. Also **a·nu·ri·a** (ə·nŏŏr'ē·ə, ə·nyŏŏr'-). [<NL *anuria* <Gk. *an-* without + *ouron* urine] — **a·nu·ric** (ə·nŏŏr'ik, ə·nyŏŏr'-) *adj*.

a·nus (ā'nəs) *n*. *Anat*. The opening at the lower extremity of the alimentary canal. [<L, orig. a ring]

An·vers (än·vâr') The French name for ANTWERP.

an·vil (an'vil) *n*. 1 A heavy block of iron or steel on which metal may be forged. 2 Anything similar to an anvil, as the lower contact of a telegraph key, etc. 3 *Anat*. The incus of the inner ear. 4 That part of the primer in a cartridge or shell which receives the impact of the firing pin and detonates the charge. 5 *Mech*. The fixed element of a measuring device, as in calipers. — *v.t. & v.i.* **an·viled** or **·villed**, **an·vil·ing** or **·vil·ling** To work at or shape on an anvil. [OE *anfilte*]

DOUBLE-BEAK ANVIL
a. Rounded beak. *b.* Flat beak. *c.* Cutter, or chisel hole.

an·vil·top (an'vil·top') *n*. *Meteorol*. A large, dense, anvil-shaped mass of cloud usually formed at the top of a cumulonimbus cloud preceding heavy showers or thunderstorms; incus (def. 2). For illustration see CLOUD.

anx·i·e·ty (ang·zī'ə·tē) *n*. *pl*. **·ties** 1 Disturbance of mind regarding some uncertain event; misgiving; worry. 2 Strained or solicitous desire, as for some object or purpose; eagerness. [<L *anxietas, -tatis* <*anxius*. See ANXIOUS.]

Synonyms: anguish, apprehension, care, concern, disquiet, disturbance, dread, fear, foreboding, fretfulness, fretting, misgiving, perplexity, solicitude, trouble, worry. *Anxiety* refers to some future event, always suggesting hopeful possibility, and thus differing from *apprehension, fear, dread, foreboding, terror,* all of which may be quite despairing. *Worry* is a more petty, restless, and manifest *anxiety; anxiety* may be quiet and silent; *worry* is communicated to all around. *Solicitude* is a milder *anxiety. Fretting* or *fretfulness* is a weak complaining without thought of accomplishing or changing anything, but merely as a relief to one's own *disquiet. Perplexity* often involves *anxiety*, but may be quite free from it. One feels anxiety *for* a friend's return; anxiety *about, for, in regard to,* or *concerning* the future. *Antonyms*: apathy, assurance, calmness, carelessness, confidence, ease, lightheartedness, nonchalance, satisfaction, tranquillity.

anx·ious (angk'shəs, ang'-) *adj*. 1 Troubled in mind respecting some uncertain matter; having anxiety: often with *about, at,* or *over:*

anxious about health; *anxious* at the delay; *anxious* over her safety. 2 Fraught with or causing anxiety; worrying; distressing: an *anxious* matter. 3 Intent; eagerly desirous; solicitous: with *for* or the infinitive with *to: anxious* for success; *anxious* to succeed. See synonyms under EAGER. [<L *anxius* < *angere* choke, distress] — **anx′·ious·ly** *adv.* — **anx′·ious·ness** *n.*

anxious seat *U.S.* The mourner's bench.

an·y (an′ē) *adj.* 1 One (person, thing, or part) indefinitely and indifferently; a; an; some; no matter what: at *any* price. 2 Some (individuals) of a number, class, or total. See synonyms under EVERY. —*pron.* One or more persons, things, or portions out of a number. —*adv.* Somewhat; in the least; at all: doing *any* better today. ◆ *Any,* in colloquial negative and interrogative sentences, is used absolutely to mean noticeably, at all: Did you hurt yourself *any?* [OE *ænig* < *ān* one]

an·y·bod·y (en′i·bod′ē, -bud′ē) *pron.* Any person whatever; anyone. —*n. pl.* **·bod·ies** 1 Any common or ordinary person. 2 A person of prestige or importance: He isn't *anybody.*

an·y·how (en′i·hou′) *adv.* 1 In any way whatever; by any means. 2 Notwithstanding; in any case: *Anyhow,* we did the best we could. 3 Carelessly.

any more 1 Anything added: Do not give me *any more.* 2 Now; from now on: He's not welcome *any more.*

any more than With more reason or likelihood than: I couldn't do that *any more than* I could fly.

an·y·one (en′i·wun′, -wən) *pron.* Any person. ◆ **any one, anyone** *Any one* is used to distinguish one person from others in the same group or class: *Any one* of these men may be guilty. *Anyone* (indefinite pronoun) means any person at all: Can *anyone* identify the culprit?

an·y·thing (en′i·thing′) *pron.* Any thing, event, or matter of any sort. —*n.* A thing of any kind. —*adv. Archaic* To any degree; in any way.

anything but By no means; far from: *anything but* safe.

an·y·way (en′i·wā′) *adv.* 1 No matter what happens; in any event. 2 Nevertheless; anyhow. 3 Carelessly; haphazardly.

an·y·ways (en′i·wāz′) *adv. Dial.* In any way; at all.

an·y·where (en′i·hwâr′) *adv.* In, at, or to any place whatever.

an·y·wise (en′i·wīz′) *adv.* In any manner.

An·zac (an′zak) *adj.* Pertaining to the *A* ustralian and *N* ew *Z* ealand *A* rmy *C* orps during World War I. —*n.* 1 A member of this army corps. 2 Any soldier from Australian or New Zealand.

An·zi·o (an′zē·ō, *Ital.* än′tsyō) A town on the west coast of Italy south of Rome; site of Allied beachhead in the invasion of Italy, World War II, January, 1944.

A-OK (ā′ō·kā′) *adj. Colloq.* Perfectly all right; just fine. Also **A′-o·kay′.**

A-one (ā′wun′) *n.* 1 First or highest class: said of a vessel to denote condition of its hull and equipment. Written **A-1.** 2 *Colloq.* Excellent; first-rate; superior.

A·o·ni·a (ā·ō′nē·ə) A district in ancient Greece including Mount Helicon, sacred to the Muses. — **A·o′ni·an** *adj.*

A·o·rang·i (ä′ō·räng′gē) See COOK, MOUNT.

a·o·rist (ā′ə·rist) *n.* A tense of Greek verbs simply expressing past action without further limitation as to completion, continuance, or repetition. Abbr. *aor.* [<Gk. *aoristos* indefinite < *a-* without + *horos* boundary]

a·o·ris·tic (ā′ə·ris′tik) *adj.* 1 Relating to the aorist tense. 2 Indefinite; undefined.

a·or·ta (ā·ôr′tə) *n. pl.* **·tas** or **·tae** (-tē) *Anat.* The great artery springing from the left ventricle of the heart and forming the main arterial trunk which distributes blood to all of the body except the lungs. [<NL <Gk. *aortē* < *aeirein* raise, heave] — **a·or′tal, a·or′tic** *adj.*

A·os·ta (ä·ôs′tä), **Duke of,** 1869–1931, Emanuele Filiberto, Italian general in World War I. — **Duke of,** 1898–1942, Amedeo Umberto, Italian general in World War II; son of preceding.

A·os·ta (ä·ôs′tä) A city in Piedmont, NW Italy, regional capital of Val d'Aosta.

a·ou·dad (ä′ōō·dad) *n.* The bearded argali (genus *Ammotragus*), a wild sheep of North Africa: also spelled *audad.* [<F <Berber *audad*]

ap-[1] Assimilated var. of AD-.

ap-[2] Var. of APO-.

a·pace (ə·pās′) *adv.* Rapidly; fast. [<A-[1] on + PACE]

A·pach·e (ə·pach′ē) *n. pl.* **A·pach·es** or **A·pach·e** One of a tribe of fierce North American Indians of Athapascan stock.

a·pache (ə·päsh′, ə·pash′; *Fr.* à·pash′) *n.* One of a band of lawless persons formerly frequenting the streets of Paris by night. [<F < *Apache*]

Apache State Nickname of ARIZONA.

ap·a·go·ge (ap′ə·gō′jē) *n.* 1 *Math.* The use of one proposition already demonstrated to prove another. 2 *Logic* Establishment of a thesis by showing its contrary to be absurd. [<Gk. *apagōgē* a leading away < *apagein* < *apo-* away + *agein* lead] — **ap′a·gog′ic** (-goj′ik) or **·i·cal** *adj.*

Ap·a·lach·ee Bay (ap′ə·lach′ē) A bay of the Gulf of Mexico in NW Florida.

Ap·a·lach·i·co·la River (ap′ə·lach′i·kō′lə) A river in NW Florida, flowing south 112 miles to the Gulf of Mexico.

ap·a·nage (ap′ə·nij) See APPANAGE.

a·pa·re·jo (ä′pä·rā′hō) *n. pl.* **·jos** (-hōz) *SW U.S.* A type of packsaddle with stuffed leather cushions. [<Sp.]

A·par·ri (ä·pä′rē) A port on Babuyan Channel in northern Luzon, Philippines.

a·part (ə·pärt′) *adv.* 1 So as to be separated in space or time, or from companionship, sympathy, or the like; aside. 2 So as to be isolated or separated for use of purpose. 3 So as to be independent logically or in thought. 4 Part from part; in pieces or to pieces; asunder. [<F *à part* <L *ad* to + *pars, partis* part]

a·part·heid (ə·pärt′hīt, -hāt) *n.* Racial segregation, especially as supported by law as an instrument of government policy. Specifically, enforced in the Republic of South Africa, was repealed after 1994 democratic elections. [<Afrikaans, apartness]

a·part·ment (ə·pärt′mənt) *n.* 1 A room or suite of rooms. 2 One of several similar suites of rooms in one building, equipped for housekeeping; a flat. [<F *appartement* <Ital. *appartamento,* ult. <L *ad* to + *pars, partis* part]

apartment house A multiple-dwelling building divided into a number of apartments.

a·pas·ti·a (ə·pas′tē·ə) *n. Psychiatry* Morbid abstention from food. [<Gk.] — **a·pas′tic** *adj.*

ap·as·tron (ap·as′tron) *n. Astron.* That point in the orbit of either member of a double star when the stars are at maximum distance from each other: opposed to *periastron.* [<AP- away from + Gk. *astron* star]

ap·a·tet·ic (ap′ə·tet′ik) *adj. Zool.* Having natural camouflage of imitative coloration or form. [<Gk. *apatētikos* deceiving < *apatē* deceit]

ap·a·thet·ic (ap′ə·thet′ik) *adj.* 1 Without emotion or feeling. 2 Indifferent; unconcerned; stolid. Also **ap′a·thet′i·cal.** — **ap′a·thet′i·cal·ly** *adv.*

ap·a·thy (ap′ə·thē) *n. pl.* **·thies** 1 Lack of feeling, emotion, or sensation; insensibility. 2 Indifference; lack of interest. [<L *apathia* <Gk. *apatheia* < *a-* without + *pathos* feeling < *pathein* feel]

Synonyms: calmness, composure, immobility, impassibility, indifference, insensibility, lethargy, phlegm, quietness, quietude, sluggishness, stillness, stoicism, tranquillity, unconcern, unfeelingness. *Composure* results ordinarily from force of will, or from perfect confidence in one's own resoures. *Indifference* is a want of interest; *insensibility* is a want of feeling; *unconcern* has reference to consequences. *Stoicism* is an intentional suppression of feeling and deadening of sensibilities, while *apathy* is involuntary, denoting a simple absence of emotion. Compare CALM, REST, STUPOR. *Antonyms:* agitation, alarm, anxiety, care, distress, disturbance, eagerness, emotion, excitement, feeling, frenzy, fury, passion, sensibility, sensitiveness, storm, susceptibility, sympathy, turbulence, vehemence, violence.

ap·a·tite (ap′ə·tīt) *n. Mineral.* A hexagonal, usually brown or green calcium phosphate of chlorine or fluorine. [<Gk. *apatē* deceit + -ITE[1]; because it was mistaken for other minerals]

ape (āp) *n.* 1 A large, tailless, Old World primate, as a gorilla or chimpanzee. 2 Loosely, any monkey. 3 A mimic. —*v.t.* **aped, ap·ing** To imitate; mimic. See synonyms under IMITATE. [OE *apa*]

a·peak (ə·pēk′) *adv. Naut.* In or nearly in a vertical position, as an anchor.

A·pel·doorn (ä′pəl·dōrn) A town in east central Netherlands.

A·pel·les (ə·pel′ēz) Greek painter of the fourth century B.C.

ape man Any of various primates resembling man, as Pithecanthropus.

Ap·en·nines (ap′ə·nīnz) A mountain range constituting most of the Italian peninsula south of the Po valley; highest peak, 9,560 feet.

a·pep·si·a (ā·pep′sē·ə, ə-) *n. Med.* Lack of capacity to digest. Also **a·pep′sy.** [<NL <Gk. *a-* not + *peptein* digest] — **a·pep′tic** (-tik) *adj.*

a·per·çu (à·per·sü′) *n. pl.* **a·per·çus** (-sü′) *French* 1 A glance. 2 An insight or perception. 3 An outline or conspectus.

a·pe·ri·ent (ə·pir′ē·ənt) *Med. adj.* Tending mildly to stimulate the action of the bowels; laxative. —*n.* A gently purgative remedy. Also **a·per·i·tive** (ə·per′ə·tiv). [<L *apeIiens, -entis,* ppr. of *aperire* open]

a·pe·ri·od·ic (ā′pir·ē·od′ik) *adj.* 1 *Pathol.* Not manifesting periodicity, as some diseases. 2 *Physics* **a** Without cyclic vibrations; not periodic. **b** Pertaining to any vibrating system whose oscillations are reduced or eliminated by sufficient damping, as the pointer of an indicating device which comes to a full stop without terminal vibration.

aperiodic antenna A radio antenna responding with a high degree of constancy to a wide range of frequencies.

aperiodic compass A magnetic compass whose needle assumes its final position in one movement and without any further fluctuation.

a·pe·ri·o·dic·i·ty (ā·pir′ē·ə·dis′ə·tē) *n.* Aperiodic condition.

a·pé·ri·tif (à·pā·rē·tēf′) *n. French* A drink of alcoholic liquor or wine taken as an appetizer.

a·pert (ə·pûrt′) *adj. Archaic* Open; undisguised. [<OF <L *apertus,* pp. of *aperire* open] — **a·pert′ly** *adv.* — **a·pert′ness** *n.*

ap·er·ture (ap′ər·chŏŏr, -chər) *n.* 1 An open passage; orifice; hole; cleft. 2 An opening, often adjustable in diameter, through which light enters the lens of a camera or other optical instrument. See synonyms under HOLE. [<L *apertura* < *apertus,* pp. of *aperire* open] — **ap′er·tur·al** *adj.* — **ap′er·tured** *adj.*

ap·er·y (ā′pər·ē) *n. pl.* **·er·ies** The act of aping; mimicry.

a·pet·al·ous (ā·pet′əl·əs) *adj. Bot.* 1 Without petals. 2 Pertaining to the *Apetalae,* a division of plants in which the flowers are without petals.

a·pex (ā′peks) *n. pl.* **a·pex·es** or **ap·i·ces** (ap′ə·sēz, ā′pə-) 1 The highest point; tip; top. 2 *Geom.* The vertex (of an angle). 3 Climax. 4 *Phonet.* The tip of the tongue. [<L]

aph- Var. of APO-.

a·pha·gi·a (ə·fā′jē·ə) *n. Pathol.* Loss of the power to swallow. [<NL <Gk. *a-* not + *phagein* eat]

a·pha·ki·a (ə·fā′kē·ə) *n. Pathol.* A condition of the eye marked by absence of the lens. Also **a·pha′ci·a.** [<NL <Gk. *a-* without + *phakē* lentil, lens of the eye]

a·phan·i·sis (ə·fan′ə·sis) *n. Psychoanal.* The fear of losing sexual potency. [<Gk., obliteration < *aphanizein* make unseen, destroy < *a-* not + *phainein* show]

aph·a·nite (af′ə·nīt) *n. Mineral.* A dense, fine-grained diabase with a compact texture. [<Gk. *aphanēs* unseen + -ITE[1]; so called because its grains are invisible to the naked eye] — **aph′·a·nit′ic** (-nit′ik) *adj.*

a·pha·sia (ə·fā′zhə, zhē·ə) *n.* Partial or total loss of the ability to articulate or understand language due to damage to the cerebral cortex. See

[<NL <Gk. *aphasia* <*aphatos* speechless <*a-* not + *phanai* speak] —**a·pha·sic** (ə·fā′zik, -sik), **a·pha·si·ac** (ə·fā′·zē·ak) *adj.* & *n.*

a·phe·li·on (ə·fē′lē·ən). *n. pl.* **·li·ons** or **·li·a** (-lē·ə). *Astron.* The point in an orbit of a planet or comet, farthest from the sun: opposed to *perihelion.* [<APH-(APO-) away from + Gk. *hēlios* sun] —**a·phe′li·an** (-ən) *adj.*

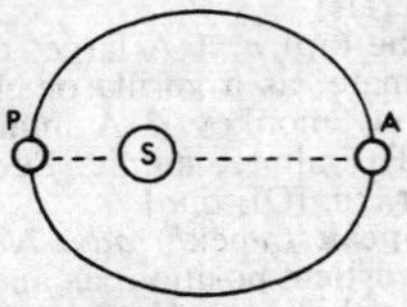

APHELION
P. Perihelion. *S.* Sun. *A.* Aphelion.

a·phe·li·o·trop·ic (ə·fē′lē·ə·trop′ik) *adj.* Turning away from the source of light; having negative heliotropism. [<APH- (APO-)+ HELIOTROPIC] —**a·phe′·li·o·trop′i·cal·ly** *adv.* —**a·phe·li·ot·ro·pism** (ə·fē′lē·ot′rə·piz′əm) *n.*

a·phe·mi·a (ə·fē′mē·ə) *n. Pathol.* A form of aphasia characterized by inability to name objects by speech, while retaining power to name them by writing. See SPEECH DISORDER. [<NL <Gk. *a-* without + *phēmē* voice] —**a·phem·ic** (ə·fem′ik) *adj.*

a·phen·go·scope (ə·feng′gə·skōp) *n.* A epidiascope. [<Gk. *aphengēs* without light (<*a-* without + *phengos* light) + -SCOPE]

a·pher·e·sis (ə·fer′ə·sis) *n.* The dropping of an unaccented syllable or sound from the beginning of a word, as in *squire* for *esquire*: opposite of *apocope.* Also **a·phaer′e·sis.** [<L *aphaeresis* <Gk. *aphairesis* <*aphairein* take away <*apo-* away + *hairein* take] —**aph·e·ret·ic** (af′ə·ret′ik) *adj.*

aph·e·sis (af′ə·sis) *n.* The gradual, developmental loss of a short or unaccented vowel at the beginning of a word, as in *mend* for *amend*: a form of apheresis. [< NL <Gk., a letting go <*aphienai* <*apo-* from + *hienai* send] —**a·phet·ic** (ə·fet′ik) *adj.*

a·phid (ā′fid, af′id) *n.* Any of a family *(Aphididae)* of numerous, small, juice-sucking insects, injurious to plants; a plant louse. [<APHIS]

a·phis (ā′fis, af′is) *n. pl.* **aph·i·des** (af′ə·dēz) A member of a genus *(Aphis)* especially injurious to fruits and vegetables. [<NL; origin uncertain]

aph·lo·gis·tic (af′lō·jis′tik, ā′flō-) *adj.* Flameless; giving light by incandescence, as a lamp. [<Gk. *aphlogistos* not flammable]

a·pho·ni·a (ə·fō′nē·ə, ā-) *n. Pathol.* Loss of voice, especially when due to organic or structural causes; hoarseness. [<NL <Gk. *aphōnia* <*a-* without + *phōnē* voice]

a·phon·ic (ə·fon′ik, ā-) *adj.* **1** *Pathol.* Affected with or characterized by aphonia. **2** *Phonet.* **a** Not representing a sound; lacking pronunciation. **b** Voiceless.

aph·o·rism (af′ə·riz′əm) *n.* **1** A brief, sententious statement of a truth or principle. **2** A proverb; maxim; precept. See synonyms under ADAGE. [<F *aphorisme* <Med. L *aphorismus* <Gk. *aphorismos* definition <*aphorizein* mark off, define <*apo-* from + *horizein* divide <*horos* boundary]

aph·o·ris·mic (af′ə·riz′mik) *adj.* Having the form of an aphorism; containing or abounding in aphorisms. Also —**aph·o·ris·mat·ic** (af′ə·riz·mat′ik).

aph·o·rist (af′ə·rist) *n.* A maker or user of aphorisms. —**aph′o·ris′tic** or **·ti·cal** *adj.* —**aph′o·ris′ti·cal·ly** *adv.*

aph·o·rize (af′ə·rīz) *v.i.* **·rized, ·riz·ing** To write or speak in aphorisms.

a·pho·tic (ā·fō′tik) *adj.* Without light; dark. [<Gk. *aphōs, aphōtos* <*a-* without + *phōs* light]

aphotic region That portion of any body of water lying at a depth beyond the reach of sunlight.

aph·ro·dis·i·a (af′rə·diz′ē·ə) *n. Pathol.* Excessive sexual desire.

aph·ro·dis·i·ac (af′rə·diz′ē·ak) *adj.* Arousing or increasing sexual desire or potency. —*n.* An aphrodisiac drug, food, etc. [<Gk. *aphrodisiakos* <*Aphroditē* goddess of love]

Aph·ro·di·te (af′rə·dī′tē) In Greek mythology, the daughter of Zeus and Dione, the goddess of love and beauty, said to have been born from the foam of the sea: identified with the Phoenician *Astarte* and the Roman *Venus.* [<Gk. *Aphroditē* the foam-born]

aph·ro·di·te (af′rə·dī′tē) *n.* A brilliantly colored butterfly *(Argynnis aphrodite)* of the United States.

aph·tha (af′thə) *n. pl.* **·thae** (-thē) *Pathol.* A small vesicle or speck, appearing in the mouth or stomach, caused by a fungous parasite. [<L <Gk.] —**aph′thous** *adj.*

aph·thoid (af′thoid) *adj.* Having the nature of or like an aphtha.

aph·tho·sis (af·thō′sis) *n. Pathol.* Any morbid condition marked by the presence of aphthae.

a·phyl·lous (ə·fil′əs, ā-) *adj. Bot.* Without leaves. Also **a·phyl·lose** (ə·fil′ōs, ā-). [<Gk. *aphyllos* <*a-* without + *phyllon* leaf]

a·phyl·ly (ə·fil′ē, ā-) *n. Bot.* Leaflessness.

A·pi·a (ä·pē′ä, ä′pē·ä) A port on Upolu Island, capital of Western Samoa.

a·pi·an (ā′pē·ən) *adj.* Of or pertaining to bees.

a·pi·ar·i·an (ā′pē·âr′ē·ən) *adj.* Of or relating to bees or the keeping of bees. —*n.* An apiarist.

a·pi·a·rist (ā′pē·ə·rist) *n.* A beekeeper.

a·pi·ar·y (ā′pē·er′ē) *n. pl.* **·ar·ies** **1** A place where bees are kept. **2** A set of hives, bees, and equipment. [<L *apiarium* <*apis* bee]

ap·i·cal (ap′i·kəl, ā′pi-) *adj.* **1** Situated at or belonging to the apex or top, as of a conical figure. **2** *Phonet.* Describing those consonants produced with the tip of the tongue, as (t), (d), and (s). Also **a·pi·cial** (ə·pish′əl). [<L *apex, apicis* tip]

apical cell *Bot.* In many cryptogamous plants, the cell which terminates the apex of roots and stems.

ap·i·ces (ap′ə·sēz, ā′pə-) A plural of APEX.

a·pi·cul·ture (ā′pi·kul′chər) *n.* Beekeeping. [<L *apis* bee + CULTURE] —**a′pi·cul′tur·ist** *n.*

a·pic·u·lus (ə·pik′yə·ləs) *n. pl.* **·li** (-lī) *Bot.* The point terminating a leaf. [<NL, dim. of L *apex* tip] —**a·pic′u·late** (-lit, -lāt) *adj.*

a·piece (ə·pēs′) *adv.* For each person or thing; to each one; each.

à pied (á pyeʹ) *French* On foot.

a·pi·ol·o·gy (ā′pē·ol′ə·jē) *n.* The study of bees. [<L *apis* bee + -(O)LOGY]

A·pis (ā′pis) A sacred bull worshiped by the ancient Egyptians. See SERAPIS.

ap·ish (ā′pish) *adj.* Like an ape; servilely imitative; foolish and tricky. —**ap′ish·ly** *adv.* —**ap′ish·ness** *n.*

A·pi·um (ā′pē·əm, ap′ē·əm) *n.* A genus of umbelliferous succulent herbs; celery. [<L, parsley]

a·piv·o·rous (ā·piv′ər·əs) *adj. Zool.* Bee-eating. [<L *apis* bee + -VOROUS]

a·pla·cen·tal (ā′plə·sen′təl, ap′lə-) *adj. Zool.* Without a placenta; implacental, as the monotremes and marsupials.

ap·la·nat·ic (ap′lə·nat′ik) *adj. Optics* Free from spherical or chromatic aberration. [<A-[4] not + *planatikos* wandering]

a·pla·sia (ə·plā′zhə, -zhē·ə) *n. Pathol.* **1** Partial or complete failure of tissue to grow. **2** Arrested development of parts of the body; congenital atrophy. [<NL <Gk. *a-* without + *plasis* a molding]

a·plas·tic (ā·plas′tik) *adj. Pathol.* Lacking the power of normal growth.

a·plomb (ə·plom′, *Fr.* à·plôn′) *n.* Assurance; self-confidence. [<F, perpendicularity, assurance <*à* according to + *plomb* plummet]

ap·noe·a (ap·nē′ə) *n. Pathol.* Suspension of respiration, partial or entire; suffocation. Also **ap·ne′a.** [<NL <Gk. *apnoia* <*a-* without + *pnoiē, pnoē* breath] —**ap·noe′al, ap·noe′ic** *adj.*

A·po (ä′pō), **Mount** A volcano in SE Mindanao; highest peak in the Philippines; 9,690 feet.

apo- *prefix* **1** Off; from; away: *apostasy.* **2** *Chem.* Used to indicate a derived compound: *apomorphine.* Also: *ap-* before vowels, as in *apagoge*; *aph-* before an aspirate, as in *aphelion.* [<Gk. <*apo* from, off]

a·poc·a·lypse (ə·pok′ə·lips) *n.* A prophecy or disclosure; any remarkable revelation. [<L *apocalypsis* <Gk. *apokalypsis* <*apokalyptein* disclose <*apo-* from + *kalyptein* cover] —**a·poc′·a·lyp′tic** (-lip′tik) or **·ti·cal** *adj.* —**a·poc′·a·lyp′ti·cal·ly** *adv.*

A·poc·a·lypse (ə·pok′ə·lips) The book of Revelation, the last book of the New Testament.

ap·o·carp (ap′ə·kärp) *n. Bot.* A gynoecium having separate carpels, as the distinct ovaries of the crowfoot family. [<APO- distinct + Gk. *karpos* fruit] —**ap′o·car′pous** *adj.*

ap·o·chro·mat·ic (ap′ə·krō·mat′ik) *adj. Optics* More exactly achromatic than an ordinary achromatic lens. —**ap′o·chro′ma·tism** (-krō′·mə·tiz′əm) *n.*

a·poc·o·pate (ə·pok′ə·pāt) *v.t.* **·pat·ed, ·pat·ing** To shorten by apocope. —*adj.* (ə·pok′ə·pit) Shortened by apocope. Also **a·poc′o·pat′ed** (-pā′·tid). —**a·poc′o·pa′tion** *n.*

a·poc·o·pe (ə·pok′ə·pē) *n.* A cutting off or elision of the last sound or syllable of a word. [<Gk. *apokopē* <*apokoptein* cut off <*apo-* off + *koptein* cut]

ap·o·crus·tic (ap′ə·krus′tik) *adj.* Having the power to repel; astringent. [<NL *apocrusticus* <Gk. *apokroustikos* <*apokrouein* beat off, repel]

A·poc·ry·pha (ə·pok′rə·fə) *n. pl.* **1** Fourteen books of the Septuagint in the Vulgate but not in the canonical Hebrew Scriptures nor in the Authorized Version. **2** One of the various collections of unauthenticated writings that abounded in the first and second centuries, proposed as additions to, but not admitted to the New Testament Gospels. [<LL, neut. pl. of *apocryphus* <Gk. *apokryphos* hidden <*apokryptein* <*apo-* away + *kryptein* hide] —**A·poc′ry·phal** *adj.*

a·poc·ry·phal (ə·pok′rə·fəl) *adj.* Of doubtful authenticity; spurious. —**a·poc′ry·phal·ly** *adv.* —**a·poc′ry·phal·ness** *n.*

a·poc·y·na·ceous (ə·pos′ə·nā′shəs) *adj. Bot.* Belonging to the dogbane family of herbaceous or woody plants *(Apocynaceae),* mainly tropical, with milky, mostly acrid juice and simple leaves, as Indian hemp, oleander, and periwinkle. [<NL *Apocynaceae* <Gk. *apokynon* dogbane <*apo-* from + *kyōn* dog]

a·poc·y·nin (ə·pos′ə·nin) *n. Chem.* An organic compound, $C_9H_{10}O_3$, forming one of the active principles of hemp dogbane. [<APOCYN(UM) + -IN]

A·poc·y·num (ə·pos′ə·nəm) *n.* Any of a genus of perennial herbs with a tough, fibrous bark and a milky juice, whose roots have medicinal qualities. [<NL, dogbane <Gk. *apo-* away + *kyōn, kynos* a dog]

ap·od (ap′əd) *n. Zool.* An animal without feet. Also **ap·o·dan** (ap′ə·dən). [<Gk. *apous, apodos* footless <*a-* without + *pous* foot]

ap·o·dac·tyl·ic (ap′ō·dak·til′ik) *adj. Pathol.* Without the use of the fingers. [<Gk. *apo-* away + *dactylos* a finger]

ap·o·dal (ap′ə·dəl) *adj. Zool.* **1** Without ventral fins. **2** Of or relating to an animal lacking distinct footlike appendages. **3** Of or relating to an order *(Apoda)* of holothurians without ambulacral feet.

ap·o·deic·tic (ap′ə·dīk′tik) *adj.* Apodictic. Also **ap′o·deic′ti·cal.** —**ap′o·deic′ti·cal·ly** *adv.*

ap·o·dic·tic (ap′ə·dik′tik) *adj.* Clearly demonstrable; indisputable. Also **ap′o·dic′ti·cal.** [<L *apodicticus* <Gk. *apodeiktikos* <*apodeiknynai* show by argument <*apo-* from + *deiknynai* show] —**ap′o·dic′ti·cal·ly** *adv.*

a·pod·o·sis (ə·pod′ə·sis) *n. pl.* **·ses** (-sēz) The conclusion in a conditional sentence; also, the clause expressing result in a sentence not conditional. [<Gk., a giving back <*apo-* back + *didonai* give]

a·pog·a·my (ə·pog′ə·mē) *n.* **1** *Bot.* **a** Absence of the sexual function in plants. **b** The development of the mature plant from the prothallium without intervention of sexual organs, as in certain of the higher cryptogams. **2** *Biol.* In evolution, the mating and interbreeding of segregated groups that do not differ significantly in character from other groups of their kind. [<APO- + Gk. *gamos* marriage] —**ap·o·gam·ic** (ap′ə·gam′ik) *adj.* —**a·pog′a·mous** *adj.*

ap·o·gee (ap′ə·jē) *n.* **1** *Astron.* The point in the orbit of the moon or of an artificial satellite where it is farthest from the earth; opposed to *perigee.* **2** The highest point; climax. [<F *apogée* <Gk. *apogaiou* <*apo-* away from + *gē, gaia* earth] —**ap·o·ge·al** (ap′ə·jē′əl), **ap′o·ge′an** *adj.*

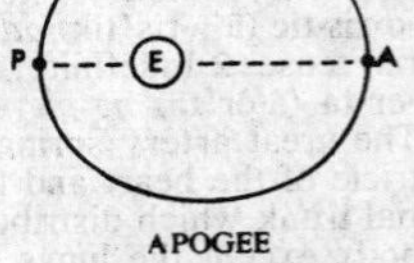

APOGEE
P. Perigee. *E.* Earth. *A.* Apogee.

ap·o·ge·ot·ro·pism (ap′ə·jē·ot′rə·piz′əm) *n. Bot.* The tendency to grow away from the earth, in opposition to gravitation, as plant stems and tree trunks; negative geotropism: also called *ageotropism.* [<APO- + GEOTRO-

PISM] — **ap·o·ge·o·trop·ic** (ap′ə·jē′ə·trop′ik) *adj.*

à point (à pwaṅ′) *French* To the point; exactly; just enough.

A·pol·lo (ə·pol′ō) **1** In Greek and Roman mythology, the god of music, poetry, prophecy, and medicine; the type of manly youth and beauty, later identified with *Helios.* **2** Any handsome young man. [<L <Gk. *Apollōn*]

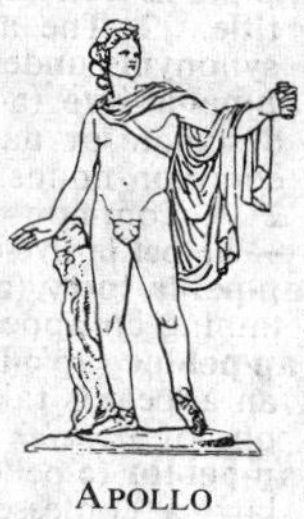

APOLLO
After the Apollo Belvedere in the Vatican.

Ap·ol·lo·ni·a (ap′ə·lō′nē·ə) An ancient port of western Cyrenaica on the Mediterranean.

Ap·ol·lo·ni·us Rho·di·us (ap′·ə·lō′nē·əs rō′dē·əs), late third to early second century B.C., Greek poet and grammarian.

A·pol·los (ə·pol′əs) First century Alexandrian Jew who continued the work of St. Paul at Corinth and Ephesus. *Acts* xviii 24.

A·pol·lyon (ə·pol′yən) The angel of the bottomless pit. *Rev.* ix 11. See also ABADDON. [<Gk. *apollyōn* destroying < *apollyein* destroy completely]

ap·o·log (ap′ə·lôg, -log) *n.* A fable or moral tale. Also **ap′o·logue.** See synonyms under FICTION. [<L *apologus* <Gk. *apologos* < *apo-* from + *logos* speech]

a·pol·o·get·ic (ə·pol′ə·jet′ik) *adj.* **1** Of the nature of an apology; excusing. **2** Defending or explaining. Also **a·pol′o·get′i·cal.** — *n.* An apology or defense. [<F *apologétique* <L *apologeticus* <Gk. *apologētikos* < *apologia* a speech in defense. See APOLOGY.] — **a·pol′o·get′i·cal·ly** *adv.*

a·pol·o·get·ics (ə·pol′ə·jet′iks) *n.* That branch of theology which deals with the defensive facts and proofs of Christianity.

ap·o·lo·gi·a (ap′ə·lō′jē·ə) *n.* A justification or defense. [<L <Gk.]

a·pol·o·gist (ə·pol′ə·jist) *n.* One who argues in defense of any person or cause.

a·pol·o·gize (ə·pol′ə·jīz) *v.i.* **·gized, ·giz·ing** **1** To offer or make excuse; acknowledge, with regret, any fault or offense. **2** To make a justification or formal defense in speech or writing. — **a·pol′o·giz′er** *n.*

a·pol·o·gy (ə·pol′ə·jē) *n. pl.* **·gies** **1** A formal acknowledgment, as of error, offense, or incivility. **2** Originally, a justification or defense. **3** A poor substitute. [<L *apologia* <Gk. *apologia* a speech in defense < *apo-* from + *logos* speech]

Synonyms: acknowledgment, confession, defense, exculpation, excuse, justification, plea, vindication. According to its present meaning, he who offers an *apology* admits himself, at least technically and seemingly, in the wrong. An *excuse* for a fault is an attempt at partial justification; as, one alleges haste as an *excuse* for carelessness. *Acknowledgment* is neutral, and may be either of fact, duty, obligation, etc., or of error or fault. *Confession* is a full *acknowledgment* of wrong, generally of a grave wrong, with or without *apology* or *excuse.* Compare CONFESS, DEFENSE. *Antonyms*: accusation, censure, charge, complaint, condemnation, imputation, injury, insult, offense, wrong.

ap·o·mix·is (ap′ə·mik′sis) *n.* **1** *Biol.* Parthenogenesis. **2** *Bot.* Reproduction from cells other than ovules. [<NL <APO- from + Gk. *mixis* a mingling] — **ap′o·mic′tic** (-mik′·tik) *adj.*

ap·o·mor·phine (ap′ə·môr′fēn, -fin) *n. Med.* A crystalline alkaloid, $C_{17}H_{17}O_2N$, obtained from morphine by removing one molecule of water: used as an emetic and expectorant.

ap·o·neu·ro·sis (ap′ə·nōō·rō′sis, -nyōō-) *n. pl.* **·ses** (-sēz) *Anat.* The white fibrous tissue investing or forming the end or attachment of certain muscles. [<Gk. *aponeurōsis* < *apo-* from + *neuron* a nerve] — **ap′o·neu·rot′ic** (-rot′ik) *adj.*

ap·o·pemp·tic (ap′ə·pemp′tik) *adj.* Bidding farewell; valedictory. — *n.* A farewell hymn or ode. [<Gk. *apopemptikos* < *apopempein* send away < *apo-* away + *pempein* send]

ap·o·pet·al·ous (ap′ə·pet′əl·əs) *adj. Bot.* Polypetalous; having separated petals.

a·poph·a·sis (ə·pof′ə·sis) *n.* A mentioning of something by denying that it will be mentioned. *Example*: I will not remind you of the following instance of his heroism. [<NL <Gk. *apophasis* denial < *apophanai* speak out, deny < *apo-* away + *phanai* speak]

ap·o·phthegm (ap′ə·them), etc. See APOTHEGM, etc.

a·poph·y·ge (ə·pof′ə·jē) *n. Archit.* **1** A concave curve in a column where the shaft rises from the base or joins the capital. **2** A hollow molding immediately below the echinus of some Doric capitals. [<Gk. *apophygē* escape < *apopheugein* flee away < *apo-* away + *pheugein* flee]

a·poph·yl·lite (ə·pof′ə·līt, ap′ə·fil′īt) *n. Chem.* A white, crystalline silicate of calcium and hydrogen, sometimes containing potassium and calcium. [<APO- + Gk. *phyllon* leaf + -ITE[1]]

ap·o·phyl·lous (ap′ə·fil′əs) *adj. Bot.* Composed of distinct floral leaves: said of a perianth. [<APO- + Gk. *phyllon* leaf]

a·poph·y·sis (ə·pof′ə·sis) *n. pl.* **·ses** (-sēz) **1** *Anat.* A bony protuberance, as of a vertebra. **2** *Zool.* In arthropods, any hardened process of the body wall. **3** *Geol.* A branching offshoot from an intrusion of igneous rock. [<NL <Gk. *apophysis* branch, offshoot < *apo-* from + *phyein* grow]

ap·o·plec·tic (ap′ə·plek′tik) *adj.* Pertaining to, affected with, or tending toward apoplexy. Also **ap′o·plec′ti·cal.** — *n.* A person subject to apoplexy.

ap·o·plex (ap′ə·pleks) *v.t. Obs.* To strike with apoplexy.

ap·o·plex·y (ap′ə·plek′sē) *n. Pathol.* **1** Sudden loss or diminution of sensation and of the power of voluntary motion, due to an acute vascular lesion of the brain, as from hemorrhage; a stroke of paralysis. **2** A sudden discharge of blood within an organ. [<OF *apoplexie* <L *apoplexia* <Gk. *apoplēxia* < *apoplēssein* disable by a stroke < *apo-* from, off + *plēssein* strike]

a·port (ə·pôrt′, ə·pōrt′) *adj. Naut.* On or toward the left or port side of a ship.

ap·o·sep·al·ous (ap′ə·sep′əl·əs) *adj. Bot.* Polysepalous.

ap·o·si·o·pe·sis (ap′ə·sī′ə·pē′sis) *n.* A sudden interruption of a thought in the middle of a sentence, as if the speaker or writer were unable or unwilling to continue. *Example*: When I perceived the delights of paradise — but who could describe them? [<L <Gk. *aposiōpēsis* < *aposiōpaein* < *apo-* from + *siōpaein* be silent] — **ap′o·si′o·pet′ic** (-pet′ik) *adj.*

a·pos·po·ry (ə·pos′pər·ē) *n. Bot.* **1** A loss of the sporogenous function. **2** The development of a new organism from or near the spore-producing organ without the intervention of spores, as in some ferns. [<APO- + SPORE] — **a·pos′po·rous** *adj.*

a·pos·ta·sy (ə·pos′tə·sē) *n. pl.* **·sies** Desertion of one's faith, religion, party, or principles. Also **a·pos′ta·cy.** [<L *apostasia* <Gk. *apostasia* a standing off, desertion < *apo-* away + *stasis* a standing]

a·pos·tate (ə·pos′tāt, -tit) *adj.* Guilty of apostasy; false. — *n.* One who apostatizes.

a·pos·ta·tize (ə·pos′tə·tīz) *v.i.* **·tized, ·tiz·ing** To forsake one's faith or principles.

ap·o·stem (ap′ə·stem) *n. Pathol.* An abscess. Also **ap′o·steme** (-stēm). [<Gk. *apostēma* separation (i.e., of pus) < *apostēnai* stand off < *apo-* from + *stēnai* stand]

a·pos·te·mate (ə·pos′tə·māt) *v.i.* **·mat·ed, ·mat·ing** *Obs.* To form an abscess.

a pos·te·ri·o·ri (ā′ pos·tir′ē·ôr′ī, -ō′rī) **1** Reasoning from facts to principles or from effect to cause: opposed to *a priori.* **2** Inductive; empirical. [<L, from what comes after]

a·pos·til (ə·pos′til) *n.* A marginal note; annotation. Also **a·pos′tille.** [<F *apostille*]

a·pos·tle (ə·pos′əl) *n.* **1** One of the twelve disciples originally commissioned by Christ to preach the gospel (*Matt.* x 2–4); later also denoting Matthias, who replaced Judas Iscariot (*Acts* i 26), and Paul (*Rom.* i 1). **2** One of a class of missionaries or preachers in the early church (1 *Cor.* xii 28). **3** A Christian missionary who first evangelizes a nation or place. **4** The earliest or foremost advocate of a cause. **5** In the Mormon Church, one of the twelve members of the church's administrative council. See PRESIDENCY (def. 4). [OE *apostol* <L *apostolus* <Gk. *apostolos* one sent forth, a messenger < *apostellein* < *apo-* from + *stellein* send] — **a·pos′tle·ship, a·pos·to·late** (ə·pos′tə·lit, -lāt) *n.*

Apostles' Creed A traditional and still widely accepted Christian confession of faith, beginning "I believe in God the Father Almighty": originally attributed to the twelve apostles, but now assigned to the fourth or fifth century.

ap·os·tol·ic (ap′ə·stol′ik) *adj.* **1** Of or pertaining to an apostle, the apostles, or their times. **2** According to the doctrine or practice of the apostles. **3** *Often cap.* Papal. Also **ap′os·tol′i·cal.** — **ap′os·tol′i·cism** (-ə·siz′·əm) *n.* — **a·pos·to·lic·i·ty** (ə·pos′tə·lis′ə·tē) *n.*

Apostolic Constitutions A fourth century collection of writings on ecclesiastical matters, claiming apostolic authorship, its final section comprising a collection of 85 regulations on church discipline and worship, the **Apostolic Canons.**

Apostolic Fathers **1** A group of early Christian writers, including Clement of Rome, Ignatius, Polycarp, and others who were younger contemporaries of the apostles. **2** An ancient collection of writings attributed to them.

Ap·os·tol·i·ci (ap′ə·stol′ə·sī) *n. pl.* **1** A third century Gnostic sect practicing a strict asceticism for which they claimed apostolic precedent. **2** A similar German sect of the 12th century. **3** An Italian sect of the 13th and 14th centuries which advocated absolute poverty and attacked the worldliness of the church. **4** An Anabaptist sect which practiced ceremonially the washing of feet. [<L, apostolic < *apostolus* APOSTLE]

apostolic see Any church or bishopric originally founded by an apostle.

Apostolic See **1** The Church of Rome, regarded as having been founded by St. Peter. **2** The papacy.

apostolic succession The regular and uninterrupted transmission of spiritual authority from the apostles, claimed for their bishops by the Anglican, Greek, Roman Catholic, and some other churches.

a·pos·tro·phe[1] (ə·pos′trə·fē) *n.* **1** A symbol (') above the line, to mark the omission of a letter or letters from a word, to indicate the possessive case, the end of a quotation, or the plural of figures or letters. **2** The omission so indicated. [<F <L *apostrophus* <Gk. *apostrophos*] — **ap·os·troph·ic** (ap′ə·strof′ik) *adj.*

a·pos·tro·phe[2] (ə·pos′trə·fē) *n.* **1** A digression from a discourse; specifically, a turning aside, as from an audience, to speak to an imaginary or absent person, an attribute, or the Deity. **2** *Bot.* The arrangement of chlorophyll granules (as on the lateral walls of leaf cells) when exposed to strong light: opposed to *epistrophe.* [<L <Gk. *apostrophē* a turning away < *apostrephein* < *apo-* from + *strephein* turn] — **ap·os·troph·ic** (ap′ə·strof′ik) *adj.*

a·pos·tro·phize[1] (ə·pos′trə·fīz) *v.i.* **·phized, ·phiz·ing** To use the apostrophe; shorten a word by omission.

a·pos·tro·phize[2] (ə·pos′trə·fīz) *v.t. & v.i.* **·phized, ·phiz·ing** To address by or in a rhetorical apostrophe; to speak or write an apostrophe. See synonyms under ADDRESS.

apothecaries' measure A system of liquid measure used in pharmacy. Units and values as used in the United States are as follows:

60 minims	=	1 fluid dram
8 fluid drams	=	1 fluid ounce
4 fluid ounces	=	1 gill
4 gills	=	1 pint
2 pints	=	1 quart
4 quarts	=	1 gallon

a·poth·e·car·y (ə·poth′ə·ker′ē) *n. pl.* **·car·ies** One who keeps drugs for sale and puts up prescriptions; a druggist; pharmacist. [<LL *apothecarius* storekeeper <L *apotheca* storehouse <Gk. *apothēkē* < *apotithenai* put away < *apo-* away + *tithenai* put]

ap·o·the·ci·um (ap′ə·thē′shē·əm, -sē·əm) *n. pl.* **·ci·a** (-shē·ə, -sē·ə) *Bot.* An open, more or less cup-shaped fruit body in which the asci–

bearing layer lies exposed during the maturing of the asci; an ascocarp. Also **ap·o·the·ce** (ap'ə·thē'sē, ap'ə·thēs). [<NL <Gk. *apothēkē* storehouse] **—ap'o·the'cial** (-shəl) *adj.*

ap·o·thegm (ap'ə·them) *n.* A terse, instructive, practical saying; a sententious maxim: also spelled *apophthegm.* See synonyms under ADAGE. [<Gk. *apophthegma* a thing uttered, a terse saying < *apophthengesthai* < *apo-* from + *phthengesthai* speak, utter] **—ap·o·theg·mat·ic** (ap'ə·theg·mat'ik) or **·i·cal** *adj.*

ap·o·them (ap'ə·them) *n. Geom.* The perpendicular from the center to any side of a regular polygon. [<APO- + Gk. *thema* that which is placed < *tithenai* place]

a·poth·e·o·sis (ə·poth'ē·ō'sis, ap'ə·thē'ə·sis) *n. pl.* **·ses** (-sēz) **1** Exaltation to divine honors; deification. **2** Supreme exaltation of any person, principle, etc., as if to divine honor. [<L <Gk. *apotheōsis* < *apo-* from + *theos* a god]

a·poth·e·o·size (ə·poth'ē·ə·sīz', ap'ə·thē'ə·sīz) *v.t.* **·sized, ·siz·ing** **1** To deify. **2** To glorify.

ap·o·tro·pa·ism (ap'ə·trō·pā'iz·əm) *n.* In folklore, the warding off of evil by incantations or ritual acts. [<Gk. *apotropaios* averting evil < *apo-* away + *trepein* turn]

ap·pal (ə·pôl') *v.t.* **ap·palled, ap·pal·ling** To fill with dismay or horror; terrify; shock. Also **ap·pall'.** See synonyms under FRIGHTEN. [<OF *apallir* become or make pale < *a-* to (<L *ad-*) + *pale* pale <L *pallidus.* See PALE, PALLID.]

Ap·pa·la·chi·an (ap'ə·lā'chē·ən, -chən, -lach'ən) *adj.* Of or pertaining to the Appalachian Mountains.

Appalachian Mountains A mountain system of eastern North America extending from Quebec to Alabama; highest peak, 6,684 feet.

Appalachian tea **1** The leaves of either of two shrubs, the inkberry and the withe rod, used for tea in some localities of the United States. **2** Either of these two plants.

Appalachian Trail A footpath for hikers, extending 2,050 miles along the crests of the Appalachian system from Maine to Georgia.

ap·pall·ing (ə·pô'ling) *adj.* Causing or apt to cause dismay or terror. **—ap·pall'ing·ly** *adv.*

ap·pa·loo·sa (ap'əlōō'sə) *n. Often cap.* One of a breed of Western saddle horses having a characteristically mottled appearance. [Prob. after *Palouse* Indians of the northwest]

ap·pa·nage (ap'ə·nij) *n.* **1** A dependent territory or property. **2** A natural accompaniment, attribute, or endowment. **3** A portion of land assigned by a king for support of his younger sons; the public allowance to the prince of a reigning house: also *apanage.* [<F *apanage* <OF *apaner* nourish <L *ad-* to + *panis* bread]

ap·pa·ra·tus (ap'ə·rā'təs, -rat'əs) *n. pl.* **·tus** or (rarely) **·tus·es** **1** A complex device or machine for a particular purpose: an X-ray *apparatus.* **2** An integrated assembly of tools, appliances, instruments, etc., operating to achieve a specified result. **3** *Physiol.* Those organs and parts of the body by means of which natural processes are carried on: digestive *apparatus.* [<L, preparation < *apparare* make ready < *ad-* to + *parare* prepare]

ap·pa·ra·tus bel·li (ap'ə·rā'təs bel'ī) *Latin* Materials of war.

apparatus crit·i·cus (krit'i·kəs) *Latin* Books, etc., used in literary work.

ap·par·el (ə·par'əl) *n.* **1** Raiment; clothing. **2** *Eccl.* Any oblong piece of embroidery ornamenting the alb and amice. **3** Things provided for special use; arrangements or furnishings, especially for a ship or a house. See synonyms under DRESS. **—***v.t.* **·eled** or **·elled, ·el·ing** or **·el·ling** **1** To clothe; dress. **2** *Archaic* To deck or equip. [<OF *apareil* preparation, provision < *apareiller* prepare, ult. <L *ad-* to + *par* equal]

ap·par·ent (ə·par'ənt, ə·pâr'-) *adj.* **1** Clearly perceived or perceivable; clear; evident; obvious; manifest; also, visible. **2** Seeming, in distinction from real or true. [<OF *aparant,* ppr. of *aparoir* appear <L *apparere.* See APPEAR.] **—ap·par'en·cy** *n.*

Synonyms: likely, presumable, probable, seeming. The *apparent* is that which appears, either that which is manifest, visible, certain, or that which is merely in seeming; as, the *apparent* motion of the sun around the earth. *Apparent* indicates less assurance than *probable* and more than *seeming.* See EVIDENT. *Antonyms*: doubtful, dubious, improbable, unimaginable, unlikely.

ap·par·ent·ly (ə·par'ənt·lē, ə·pâr'-) *adv.* Obviously or seemingly. Abbr. *appar.*

ap·pa·ri·tion (ap'ə·rish'ən) *n.* **1** A specter; phantom; ghost. **2** Any appearance, especially if remarkable; a phenomenon. **3** The act of appearing, or the state of being visible. **4** *Astron.* The period for most favorable observation of a planet, comet, or other heavenly body. [<MF <L *apparitio, -onis* < *apparere.* See APPEAR.] **—ap'pa·ri'tion·al** *adj.*

ap·par·i·tor (ə·par'ə·tər, ə·pâr'-) *n.* **1** Formerly, an official of a civil court. **2** In ecclesiastical law, an official who serves summonses and executes the processes of an ecclesiastical court. **3** *Brit.* The beadle of a university. [<L < *apparere* appear]

ap·par·te·ment (à·pàrt·män') *French* Living quarters; an apartment.

ap·peach (ə·pēch') *v.t. Obs.* To impeach; accuse. [ME *apechen,* var. of *empechen* <OF *empechier.* See IMPEACH.]

ap·peal (ə·pēl') *n.* **1** An earnest entreaty for aid, sympathy, or the like; prayer; supplication. **2** A quality or manner which elicits sympathy or attraction. **3** A resort to some higher power or final means, for sanction, proof, or aid. **4** *Law* **a** The carrying of a cause from a lower to a higher tribunal for a rehearing (see COURT OF APPEALS under COURT). **b** The right to do this. **c** A request to do this. **d** A case so carried. **4** In old English law, the accusation of a criminal by an accomplice. **5** In any parliamentary body, a reference to the house of a disputed decision made by the chairman. See synonyms under ADDRESS, PLEA, SUIT. **—***v.t.* **1** *Law* To refer or remove, as a case, to a higher court. **2** *Archaic* To challenge. **—***v.i.* **3** To make an earnest supplication or request, as for sympathy, corroboration, or aid. **4** To awaken a favorable response; be interesting: Does this idea *appeal* to you? **5** *Law* To remove a case, or request that a case be moved, to a higher court. **6** To resort or have recourse: with *to*: to *appeal* to reason to solve a difficulty. [<OF *apeler* <L *appellare* accost, call upon, var. of *appellere* < *ad-* to + *pellere* drive] **—ap·peal'a·ble** *adj.* **—ap·peal'er** *n.* **—ap·peal'ing·ly** *adv.*

ap·pear (ə·pir') *v.i.* **1** To come forth into view or public notice; become visible, plain, public, or certain. **2** To be visible. **3** To be published, as a book or other writing. **4** To seem, or seem likely. **5** *Law* To come into court in person or by attorney, and submit or object to its jurisdiction in a given cause. [<OF *aparoir* <L *apparere* < *ad-* to + *parere* come forth, appear]

ap·pear·ance (ə·pir'əns) *n.* **1** External show or aspect. **2** That which appears or seems; semblance. **3** *pl.* Circumstances or indications collectively. **4** A becoming manifest or public; advent; publication. **5** A coming formally into court. **6** A phenomenon. See synonyms under AIR[1], MANNER.

ap·pease (ə·pēz') *v.t.* **ap·peased, ap·peas·ing** **1** To reduce or bring to peace; placate; soothe, as by making concessions or yielding to demands. **2** To bribe, as an aggressor nation, with territorial or political concessions in order to avoid war or a break in diplomatic relations. **3** To satisfy or allay: *Appease* your hunger with this bread. See synonyms under ALLAY. [<OF *apaisier* < *a-* to (<L *ad-*) + *pais* peace <L *pax*] **—ap·peas'a·ble** *adj.* **—ap·peas'a·bly** *adv.* **—ap·peas'er** *n.* **—ap·peas'ing·ly** *adv.* **—ap·pea·sive** (ə·pē'siv) *adj.*

ap·pease·ment (ə·pēz'mənt) *n.* **1** The act of placating or pacifying. **2** The policy of making territorial or other concessions to potential aggressors in order to maintain peace.

ap·pel (à·pel') *n.* **1** In fencing, a feint, often accompanied by a stamp of the foot, to procure an opening. **2** In diplomatic correspondence, the salutation of the person addressed, as Sire, Excellency, etc. [<F, lit., a call]

ap·pel·la·ble (ə·pel'ə·bəl) *adj.* Appealable. **—ap·pel'la·bil'i·ty, ap·pel·lan·cy** (ə·pel'ən·sē) *n.*

ap·pel·lant (ə·pel'ənt) *adj. Law* Of or pertaining to an appeal; appellate. **—***n.* One who appeals, in any sense.

ap·pel·late (ə·pel'it) *adj. Law* Pertaining to or having jurisdiction of appeals: an *appellate* court. [<L *appellatus,* pp. of *appellare.* See APPEAL.]

ap·pel·la·tion (ap'ə·lā'shən) *n.* **1** A name or title. **2** The act of calling or naming. See synonyms under NAME.

ap·pel·la·tive (ə·pel'ə·tiv) *adj.* **1** Serving to designate or name. **2** Denoting a class, as common nouns. **—***n.* **1** A title; appellation. **2** A common noun. **—ap·pel'la·tive·ly** *adv.* **—ap·pel'la·tive·ness** *n.*

ap·pel·la·to·ry (ə·pel'ə·tôr'ē, -tō'rē) *adj.* Containing an appeal.

ap·pel·lee (ap'ə·lē') *n. Law* One against whom an appeal is taken; a defendant. [<F *appelé,* pp. of *appeler* appeal]

ap·pel·lor (ə·pel'ôr, ap'ə·lôr') *n.* In old English law, a confessed criminal who accused an accomplice. [<AF *apelour,* OF *apeleor* <L *appellator* one who appeals < *appellare.* See APPEAL.]

ap·pend (ə·pend') *v.t.* **1** To add, as something subordinate or supplemental. **2** To hang or attach: to *append* a seal. See synonyms under ADD. [<L *appendere* < *ad-* to + *pendere* hang]

ap·pend·age (ə·pen'dij) *n.* **1** Anything appended; a subordinate addition or adjunct: a mere *appendage.* **2** *Biol.* **a** Any part joined to or diverging from the axial trunk or from any adjunct of it. **b** A subordinate or subsidiary part, as a limb, tail, leaf, hair, etc.

Synonyms: accessory, accompaniment, addendum, addition, adjunct, appendix, appurtenance, attachment, auxiliary, concomitant, extension, increase, supplement. An *adjunct* constitutes no real part of the thing or system to which it is joined; an *appendage* is commonly a real, but not an essential or necessary, part of that with which it is connected; an *appurtenance* belongs subordinately to something by which it is employed, especially as an instrument to accomplish some purpose. An *attachment* in machinery is some mechanism that can be brought into optional connection with the principal movement; a hemmer is an *attachment* of a sewing machine. An *extension,* as of a railroad or of a franchise, adds to something already existing. See SUPPLEMENT.

ap·pen·dant (ə·pen'dənt) *adj.* **1** Hanging; attached; adjunct. **2** Associated with in a subordinate capacity. **3** Related by cause or purpose; consequent. **4** *Law* Belonging to a land grant or tenure as an added but lesser right. **—***n. Law* A subsidiary right attached to one more important. Also **ap·pen'dent.**

ap·pen·dec·to·my (ap'ən·dek'tə·mē) *n. pl.* **·mies** *Surg.* The excision of the vermiform appendix. Also **ap·pen·di·cec·to·my** (ə·pen'də·sek'tə·mē). [<APPENDIX + -ECTOMY]

ap·pen·di·ceal (ap'ən·dish'əl, ə·pen'də·se'əl) *adj. Anat.* Of or relating to the vermiform appendix.

ap·pen·di·ces (ə·pen'də·sēz) A plural of APPENDIX.

ap·pen·di·ci·tis (ə·pen'də·sī'tis) *n. Pathol.* Inflammation of the vermiform appendix.

ap·pen·di·cle (ə·pen'di·kəl) *n.* A small appendage. [<L *appendicula,* dim. of *appendix*]

ap·pen·dic·u·lar (ap'ən·dik'yə·lər) *adj.* **1** Of, pertaining to, or being an appendage or appendicle; appendiculate. **2** *Anat.* Of or pertaining to the limbs or appendages.

ap·pen·dic·u·late (ap'ən·dik'yə·lit, -lāt) *adj.* **1** Having appendages, as a leaf. **2** Of the nature of or forming an appendage.

ap·pen·dix (ə·pen'diks) *n. pl.* **·dix·es** or **·di·ces** (-də·sēz) **1** An addition or appendage, as of supplementary matter at the end of a book. **2** An appendage. **3** *Anat.* **a** The vermiform appendix. **b** A process or projection; an outgrowth or prolongation. **4** *Aeron.* A large tube hanging from a spherical balloon, through which the gas passes in or out. [<L, an appendage < *appendere.* See APPEND.]

Synonyms: addendum, addition, supplement. We add an *appendix* to a book, as a dictionary, to contain names, dates, lists, etc., which would encumber the text; we add a *supplement* to supply omissions, as, for instance, to bring it up to date. An *addition* might be matter interwoven in the body of the work, an index, plates, editorial notes, etc., which might be valuable *additions,* but are not within the meaning of *appendix* or *supplement.* See APPENDAGE.

appendix ver·mi·for·mis (vûr'mə·fôr'mis) See VERMIFORM APPENDIX.

ap·per·ceive (ap′ər·sēv′) *v.t.* **·ceived, ·ceiv·ing** *Psychol.* To perceive with conscious attention, integrating new experiences, concepts, ideas, etc., with the old. [<F *apercevoir* <L *ad-* to + *percipere.* See PERCEIVE.]

ap·per·cep·tion (ap′ər·sep′shən) *n.* **1** *Psychol.* **a** That kind of perception in which the mind is conscious of the act of perceiving. **b** The adding of other mental acts to perception proper, as interpretation, recognition, and classification. **c** An act of voluntary consciousness accompanied by self–consciousness; also, the coalescence of part of a new idea with an old one by modification. **2** The powers of intellect involved in the acquisition, conservation, and elaboration of knowledge; the understanding. [<F *aperception* < *apercevoir.* See APPERCEIVE.] — **ap′per·cep′tive** *adj.*

ap·per·son·a·tion (ə·pûr′sə·nā′shən) *n.* *Psychiatry* The compulsive identification with or impersonation of another person: noted in many mental disorders, especially dementia precox.

ap·per·tain (ap′ər·tān′) *v.i.* To pertain or belong as by custom, function, nature, right, or fitness; relate: with *to.* See synonyms under PERTAIN. [<OF *apertenir* <LL *appertinere* < *ad-* to + *pertinere.* See PERTAIN.]

ap·pe·tence (ap′ə·təns) **1** Strong craving or propensity. **2** Instinct or tendency: the *appetence* of ducks for water. **3** *Chem.* Affinity, as in atoms and molecules. Also **ap′pe·ten·cy.** See synonyms under APPETITE, DESIRE. [<L *appetentia* < *appetere.* See APPETITE.] — **ap′pe·tent** *adj.*

ap·pe·tite (ap′ə·tīt) *n.* **1** A desire for food or drink. **2** A craving or desire; strong liking. [<OF *appetit* <L *appetitus* < *appetere* strive for < *ad-* to + *petere* seek] — **ap′pe·ti′tive** *adj.*

Synonyms: appetence, craving, desire, disposition, impulse, inclination, liking, longing, lust, passion, proclivity, proneness, propensity, relish, thirst, zest. *Appetite* is used only of the demands of the physical system, unless otherwise expressly stated, as when we say an *appetite* for knowledge; *passion* includes all excitable impulses of our nature, as anger, fear, love, hatred, etc. *Appetite* is thus more animal than *passion*; we say an *appetite* for food, a *passion* for fame. Compare DESIRE. *Antonyms*: antipathy, aversion, detestation, disgust, dislike, disrelish, distaste, hatred, indifference, loathing, repugnance, repulsion. Compare ANTIPATHY.

ap·pe·tize (ap′ə·tīz) *v.t.* **·tized, ·tiz·ing** *Rare* To excite appetite or hunger in.

ap·pe·tiz·er (ap′ə·tī′zər) *n.* Anything that excites appetite or gives relish; specifically, food or drink served before a meal to stimulate the appetite. Also *Brit.* **ap′pe·tis′er.**

ap·pe·tiz·ing (ap′ə·tī′zing) *adj.* Giving relish; tempting to the appetite. Also *Brit.* **ap′pe·tis′ing.** — **ap′pe·tiz′ing·ly** *adv.*

Ap·pi·an (ap′ē·ən) *adj.* Pertaining to the Appii, a Roman family, or to any of its members.

Appian Way A paved road extending from Rome to Brundisium (modern *Brindisi*), begun in 312 B.C. by **Appius Claudius Caecus,** Roman consul, and still existing in part: Latin *Via Appia.*

Ap·pi·us Clau·di·us (ap′ē·əs klô′dē·əs) Roman consul and decemvir 451 B.C.

ap·plaud (ə·plôd′) *v.t.* & *v.i.* **1** To express approval, as of a performer, particularly by clapping the hands. **2** To commend; praise in an audible or visible manner. See synonyms under ADMIRE, PRAISE. [<L *applaudere* < *ad-* to + *plaudere* clap hands, strike] — **ap·plaud′er** *n.* — **ap·plaud′ing·ly** *adv.*

ap·plause (ə·plôz′) *n.* Acclamation; approval; praise; especially as shown by clapping the hands, shouting, etc. [<L *applausus,* pp. of *applaudere.* See APPLAUD.] — **ap·plau·sive** (ə·plô′siv) *adj.* — **ap·plau′sive·ly** *adv.*

Synonyms: acclaim, acclamation, cheering, cheers, eulogy, laudation, plaudit, praise. *Praise* is the expressed and hearty approval of an individual, or of a number or multitude, one by one; *applause,* the spontaneous outburst of many at once. *Applause* is expressed in any way, by clapping of hands, etc., as well as by the voice; *acclamation* is strictly by the voice alone. *Acclaim* is the more poetic term for *acclamation,* commonly understood in a loftier sense. *Plaudit* is a shout of *applause,* and is commonly used in the plural. See EULOGY, PRAISE. *Antonyms*: denunciation, derision, hissing, obloquy, scorn, vituperation.

ap·ple (ap′əl) *n.* **1** The fleshy edible fruit or pome of any variety of a widely distributed tree *(Malus malus)* of the rose family, usually of a roundish or conical shape with a depression at each end. **2** The similar fruit of several allied species of *Malus,* as *M. prunifolia* and *M. baccata,* the Siberian crab apple, and *M. coronaria,* the American crab apple. **3** A tree of any one of the species bearing apples as its natural fruit. **4** One of several fruits or plants with little or no resemblance to the apple: May *apple,* love *apple,* oak *apple,* etc. **5** In the Bible, the apple proper; also, a citron, apricot, pear, quince, or other fruit. [OE *æppel*]

apple blossom The flower of any species of the genus *Malus*: state flower of Arkansas and Michigan.

apple butter A thick, brown, spiced applesauce made from stewed apples.

apple cart A two–wheeled hand cart used for peddling apples, etc. — **to upset the apple cart** To ruin one's plans.

apple green A clear, light yellowish green.

ap·ple·jack (ap′əl·jak′) *n.* Brandy made from fermented cider.

ap·ple·john (ap′əl·jon′) *n.* *Obs.* A variety of apple considered to taste best when shriveled: said to ripen about St. John's Day: also called *John apple.*

apple of discord In Greek mythology, the golden apple inscribed "for the fairest," thrown among the gods by Eris; claimed by Hera, Aphrodite, and Athena, it was awarded by Paris to Aphrodite after she promised him Helen, fairest of women.

apple of Peru **1** An annual herb *(Nicandra physaloides)* of the nightshade family. **2** Jimsonweed.

apple of Sodom **1** The fruit of a plant said to have grown in the vicinity of the Dead Sea, of fair appearance, but disintegrating into ashes when plucked. **2** Hence, any bitter disappointment or disillusionment. Also called *Dead Sea fruit.*

apple of the eye **1** The pupil of the eye. **2** Something precious.

apple polisher *U.S. Slang* One who seeks favor by obsequious behavior, flattery, etc.

ap·ple·sauce (ap′əl·sôs′) *n.* **1** Apples stewed to a pulp. **2** *U.S. Slang* Nonsense; bunk.

Ap·ple·seed (ap′əl·sēd), **Johnny** Nickname of John Chapman, 1775?–1847, American pioneer, famous for distributing seeds to establish orchards in the Middle West.

Ap·ple·ton (ap′əl·tən), **Sir Edward Victor,** 1892–1965, English physicist.

Appleton layer A region of ionized air about 150 miles above sea level which acts as a reflector of certain wavelengths of sound: also called *F–layer.* [after E. V. *Appleton*]

ap·pli·ance (ə·plī′əns) *n.* **1** Something applied to effect a result; a machine or device; an instrument. **2** *Rare* An applying or being applied. **3** *Obs.* Compliance.

ap·pli·ca·ble (ap′li·kə·bəl) *adj.* Capable of or suitable for application; relevant; fitting. [<L *applicare* apply + -ABLE] — **ap′pli·ca·bil′i·ty, ap′pli·ca·ble·ness** *n.* — **ap′pli·ca·bly** *adv.*

ap·pli·cant (ap′li·kənt) *n.* One who applies, as for a position; a candidate.

ap·pli·ca·tion (ap′li·kā′shən) *n.* **1** The act of applying. **2** That which is applied, as a remedial agent. **3** That by which one applies; especially, a formal written request or demand; a requisition; request. **4** Appropriation to a particular use. **5** The testing or carrying into effect of a general law, truth, or precept by bringing it into relation with practical affairs; also, the capacity of being thus used. **6** The act, habit, or faculty of close and continuous attention. **7** The denoting or extending of a term, or the presenting of a proposition in a manner that combines logical strength with correctness of form. See synonyms under EXERCISE, INDUSTRY. [<L *applicatio, -onis* a joining to < *applicare.* See APPLY.]

ap·pli·ca·tive (ap′li·kā′tiv) *adj.* Applying or capable of being applied; pertaining to application; applicatory; practical.

ap·pli·ca·tor (ap′li·kā′tər) *n.* An instrument or utensil for applying medication, etc., in the form of liquids or pastes.

ap·pli·ca·to·ry (ap′li·kə·tôr′ē, -tō′rē) *adj.* **1** Fit for application. **2** Making application; practical.

ap·plied (ə·plīd′) *adj.* **1** Put in practice; utilized: opposed to *abstract* or *pure*: *applied* science. **2** Dealing with certain data or problems in a practical manner as opposed to a merely theoretical one: *applied* ethics.

ap·pli·er (ə·plī′ər) *n.* A person or thing that applies.

ap·pli·qué (ap′li·kā′) *adj.* Applied: said of ornaments, as in needlework, wood, metal, etc., cut out from one material and fastened to the surface of another. — *n.* Decoration or ornaments so applied. — *v.t.* **·quéd** (-kād′), **·qué·ing** (-kā′ing) To sew or decorate by sewing, as ornaments of one material to the surface of another. [<F]

ap·ply (ə·plī′) *v.* **ap·plied, ap·ply·ing** *v.t.* **1** To bring into contact with something; attach, as surfaces. **2** To devote or put to a particular use: to *apply* steam to navigation. **3** To connect, as an epithet, with a particular person or thing. **4** To give (oneself) wholly to; devote: to *apply* oneself to study. — *v.i.* **5** To make a request or petition; ask: with *for*: to *apply* for a position. **6** To have reference or appropriate relation; belong naturally: Your orders don't *apply* in an emergency. [<OF *aplier* <L *applicare* join to < *ad-* to + *plicare* fold]

ap·pog·gia·tu·ra (ə·poj′ə·tŏŏr′ə, -tyŏŏr′ə; *Ital.* äp·pôd′jä·tōō′rä) *n.* *Music* An ornament consisting of a single note preceding another note. [<Ital. < *appoggiare* lean upon, rest]

ap·point (ə·point′) *v.t.* **1** To name or select, as a person for a position, a time and place for an act or meeting, etc. **2** To ordain, as by decree; command; prescribe: These laws are *appointed* by God. **3** To fit out; equip; furnish: used chiefly in the past participle: a *well–appointed* yacht. **4** *Law* To establish as a trustee or guardian. See synonyms under ALLOT, APPORTION, INSTITUTE, SET. [<OF *apointer* arrange, settle <LL *appunctare* <L *ad-* to + *punctum* a point]

ap·point·ee (ə·poin′tē′) *n.* One appointed to an office or position.

ap·point·ment (ə·point′mənt) *n.* **1** An appointing or being appointed; position or service to which one is or may be appointed; station; office. **2** An agreement, as for meeting at a given time; an engagement. **3** Something agreed upon; direction; decree. **4** Anything for use or adornment; equipment. **5** *Law* A power or right to control or designate the disposition of property. **6** *Obs.* Preparation.

Ap·po·mat·tox (ap′ə·mat′əks) A village and county in central Virginia. At **Appomattox Court House,** established in 1940 as a national monument, Lee surrendered to Grant, April 9, 1865, virtually ending the Civil War.

Appomattox River A river of central Virginia, flowing east 137 miles to the James River.

ap·por·tion (ə·pôr′shən, ə·pōr′-) *v.t.* To divide and assign proportionally; allot. [<OF *apportionner* <LL *apportionare* <L *ad-* to + *portio, -onis* portion]

Synonyms: allot, appoint, appropriate, assign, deal, dispense, distribute, divide, grant, share. To *allot* or *assign* may be to make an arbitrary division; the same is true of *distribute* or *divide.* That which is *apportioned* is given by some fixed rule, which is meant to be uniform and fair. To *dispense* is to give out freely; as, the sun *dispenses* light and heat. One may *apportion* what he only holds in trust; he *shares* what is his own. Compare ALLOT. *Antonyms*: collect, consolidate, receive, retain.

ap·por·tion·ment (ə·pôr′shən·mənt, ə·pōr′-) *n.* **1** An apportioning or being apportioned; any proportional division or allotment. **2** *U.S.* The decision by law as to the number of representatives that a state may have in the Federal House of Representatives, or that a county or other political subdivision may have in a state legislature.

add, āce, câre, pälm; end, ēven; it, īce; odd, ōpen, ôrder; tŏŏk, pōōl; up, bûrn; ə = a in *above,* e in *sicken,* i in *clarity,* o in *melon,* u in *focus*; yōō = u in *fuse*; oi, oil; ou, pout; ch, check; g, go; ng, ring; th, thin; th, this; zh, vision. Foreign sounds à, œ, ü, kh, ṅ; and ◆: see page xx. < from; + plus; ? possibly.

ap·pose (ə·pōz′) *v.t.* **ap·posed, ap·pos·ing** **1** To apply or put, as one thing to another: with *to*: *appose* a seal to a document. **2** To arrange side by side. [<F *apposer* < *a-* to (<L *ad-*) + *poser* put. See POSE[1].] — **ap·pos′a·ble** *adj.*

ap·po·site (ap′ə·zit) *adj.* **1** Fit for or well adapted to the purpose; appropriate; pertinent; relevant: an *apposite* simile. **2** Placed or being in apposition; apposed. [<L *appositus,* pp. of *apponere* put near to < *ad-* to + *ponere* put] — **ap′po·site·ly** *adv.* — **ap′po·site·ness** *n.*

ap·po·si·tion (ap′ə·zish′ən) *n.* **1** *Gram.* The placing of one substantive beside another to add to or explain the first, as in *John, president* of the class. **2** A placing or being in immediate connection; application; addition. **3** *Biol.* Growth or increase by juxtaposition, as of tissue. — **ap′po·si′tion·al** *adj.* — **ap′po·si′tion·al·ly** *adv.*

ap·pos·i·tive (ə·poz′ə·tiv) *adj.* In or pertaining to a state of apposition. — *n.* A word or phrase in apposition. — **ap·pos′i·tive·ly** *adv.*

ap·prais·al (ə·prā′zəl) *n.* An appraising; official valuation. Also **ap·praise′ment.**

ap·praise (ə·prāz′) *v.t.* **ap·praised, ap·prais·ing** **1** To make an official valuation of; set a price or value on, especially by authority of law or agreement of interested parties. **2** To estimate the amount, quality, or worth of; judge. [<AP-[1] + PRAISE] — **ap·prais′a·ble** *adj.* — **ap·prais′er** *n.*

ap·pre·ci·a·ble (ə·prē′shē·ə·bəl, -shə·bəl) *adj.* Capable of being valued or estimated. — **ap·pre′ci·a·bly** *adv.*

ap·pre·ci·ate (ə·prē′shē·āt) *v.* **·at·ed, ·at·ing** *v.t.* **1** To form an estimate of, as to quality, etc. **2** To estimate correctly or adequately. **3** To consider highly; be keenly aware of or sensitive to. **4** To show gratitude for. **5** To raise or increase the price or value of. — *v.i.* **6** To rise in value. [<L *appretiatus,* pp. of *appretiare* appraise < *ad-* to + *pretium* price]

Synonyms: esteem, estimate, prize, value. A jeweler *estimates* an old ring as worth so much cash; the owner may *value* it beyond price, as a family heirloom, or he may *prize* it as the gift of an *esteemed* friend, without *appreciating* its commercial value. *Antonyms*: depreciate, despise, flout, misjudge, scorn, undervalue.

ap·pre·ci·a·tion (ə·prē′shē·ā′shən) *n.* **1** An appreciating; true or adequate estimation or recognition. **2** Increase in value.

ap·pre·ci·a·tive (ə·prē′shē·ā′tiv, -shə·tiv) *adj.* Capable of showing appreciation; manifesting appreciation. — **ap·pre′ci·a·tive·ly** *adv.* — **ap·pre′ci·a′tive·ness** *n.*

ap·pre·ci·a·tor (ə·prē′shē·ā′tər) *n.* **1** One who appreciates. **2** An apparatus by means of which the proportion of gluten in flour is determined.

ap·pre·ci·a·to·ry (ə·prē′shē·ə·tôr′ē, -tō′rē, -shə-) *adj.* Appreciative. — **ap·pre′ci·a·to′ri·ly** *adv.*

ap·pre·hend (ap′ri·hend′) *v.t.* **1** To lay hold of or grasp mentally; grasp a truth or statement; perceive. **2** To expect with anxious foreboding; look forward with fear or anxiety. **3** To arrest; seize in the name of the law. **4** *Obs.* To take hold of. [<L *apprehendere* < *ad-* to + *prehendere* seize] — **ap′pre·hend′er** *n.*

Synonyms: anticipate, arrest, catch, comprehend, conceive, grasp, imagine, know, perceive, understand. In strictness we *perceive* only what is presented through the senses. We *apprehend* what is presented to the mind by any means whatever. A child can *apprehend* the distinction between right and wrong, yet the philosopher cannot *comprehend* it in its fulness. Compare ALARM, IDEA. *Antonyms*: ignore, lose, misapprehend, miss, misunderstand, overlook.

ap·pre·hen·si·ble (ap′ri·hen′sə·bəl) *adj.* Capable of being apprehended. — **ap′pre·hen′si·bil′i·ty** *n.*

ap·pre·hen·sion (ap′ri·hen′shən) *n.* **1** Distrust or dread concerning the future; foreboding; misgiving; presentiment. **2** The power of apprehending; cognition; conception. **3** An estimate; idea; opinion. **4** Legal arrest. See synonyms under ALARM, ANTICIPATION, ANXIETY, FEAR, IDEA, KNOWLEDGE, UNDERSTANDING. [<L *apprehensio, -onis* < *apprehendere.* See APPREHEND.]

ap·pre·hen·sive (ap′ri·hen′siv) *adj.* **1** Anticipative of evil; anxious; fearful; suspicious. **2** Quick to apprehend. **3** Responsive to sense impressions. **4** Having cognizance; conscious. — **ap′pre·hen′sive·ly** *adv.* — **ap′pre·hen′sive·ness** *n.*

ap·pren·tice (ə·pren′tis) *n.* **1** One who is bound by a legal agreement to serve another for an agreed period of time in order to learn a trade or business. **2** Any learner or beginner. — *v.t.* **·ticed, ·tic·ing** To bind or take on as an apprentice. [<OF *aprentis* < *aprendre* teach <L *apprehendere* comprehend. See APPREHEND.] — **ap·pren′tice·ship** *n.*

ap·pressed (ə·prest′) *adj. Bot.* Pressed or applied closely against something, as leaves against a stem. [<L *appressus,* pp. of *apprimere* < *ad-* to + *premere* press]

ap·pres·sor (ə·pres′ər) *n. Bot.* The expansion at the tip of the hyphae of certain parasitic fungi, by means of which they fasten on to the host. Also **ap·pres·so·ri·um** (ap′rə·sôr′ē·əm, -sō′rē-).

ap·prise (ə·prīz′) *v.t.* **ap·prised, ap·pris·ing** To notify, as of an event; inform: also spelled *apprize.* See synonyms under INFORM. [<F *appris,* pp. of *apprendre* teach, inform <L *apprehendere.* See APPREHEND.] — **ap·prise′ment** *n.* — **ap·pris′er** *n.*

ap·prize[1] (ə·prīz′) *v.t.* **ap·prized, ap·priz·ing** Appraise. Also **ap·prise′.**

ap·prize[2] (ə·prīz′) *v.t.* **ap·prized, ap·priz·ing** Apprise. — **ap·prize′ment** *n.* — **ap·priz′er** *n.*

ap·proach (ə·prōch′) *v.i.* **1** To come near or nearer in time or space. — *v.t.* **2** To come or cause to come near or nearer to. **3** To make advances to; offer a solicitation, proposal, or bribe to. **4** To come close to; almost reach; approximate: to *approach* a solution; to *approach* Bluebeard in cruelty. — *n.* **1** The act of approaching; a coming nearer. **2** Nearness; approximation. **3** Opportunity, means, or way of approaching; access. **4** Advances, as to acquaintance, etc.; also, the manner in which any advance is made: a kindly *approach.* **5** In golf, the stroke made after the tee shot, which lands the player's ball on the putting green. **6** *pl. Mil.* Constructed works, trenches, etc., by which besiegers attack a fortified position. See synonyms under APPROXIMATION. [<OF *aprochier* <LL *appropiare* <L *ad-* to + *prope* near] — **ap·proach′a·bil′i·ty, ap·proach′a·ble·ness** *n.* — **ap·proach′a·ble** *adj.*

ap·pro·bate (ap′rə·bāt) *v.t.* **·bat·ed, ·bat·ing** **1** To approve. **2** To sanction formally or officially. See synonyms under PRAISE. [<L *approbatus,* pp. of *approbare.* See APPROVE.]

ap·pro·ba·tion (ap′rə·bā′shən) *n.* **1** The act of approving; approval; commendation. **2** *Eccl.* **a** Papal official approval of a religious order. **b** A bishop's official approval of a priest as confessor. **3** *Obs.* Proof; probation. See synonyms under PRAISE.

ap·pro·ba·tive (ap′rə·bā′tiv) *adj.* Expressing or implying approbation. Also **ap·pro·ba·to·ry** (ə·prō′bə·tôr′ē, -tō′rē). — **ap′pro·ba′tive·ness** *n.*

ap·pro·pri·a·ble (ə·prō′prē·ə·bəl) *adj.* That can be appropriated.

ap·pro·pri·ate (ə·prō′prē·it) *adj.* Suitable for or belonging to the person, circumstance, or place; fit; proper; relevant. — *v.t.* (ə·prō′prē·āt) **·at·ed, ·at·ing** **1** To set apart for a particular use. **2** To take for one's own use. See synonyms under ABSTRACT, APPORTION, ASSUME. [<L *appropriatus,* pp. of *appropriare* < *ad-* to + *proprius* one's own] — **ap·pro′pri·ate·ly** *adv.* — **ap·pro′pri·ate·ness** *n.* — **ap·pro′pri·a′tive** *adj.* — **ap·pro′pri·a′tor** *n.*

Synonyms (adj.): adapted, apt, becoming, befitting, congruous, fit, meet, pertinent, proper, suitable. *Antonyms*: inappropriate, incongruous, irrelevant, unfit, unsuitable.

ap·pro·pri·a·tion (ə·prō′prē·ā′shən) *n.* **1** Something, as money, appropriated, or set apart, as by a legislature, for a special use. **2** An appropriating or being appropriated.

ap·prov·al (ə·pro͞o′vəl) *n.* **1** An approving or being approved; approbation. **2** Official consent; sanction. **3** Favorable opinion; praise; commendation. See synonyms under PRAISE. — **on approval** For (a customer's) examination without obligation to purchase.

ap·prove[1] (ə·pro͞ov′) *v.* **ap·proved, ap·prov·ing** *v.t.* **1** To regard as worthy, proper, or right; be favorably disposed toward. **2** To confirm formally or authoritatively; sanction; ratify. **3** To show or prove (oneself) worthy of approval. **4** *Obs.* To prove by trial; test. — *v.i.* **5** To show or state approval: with *of*: He *approved* of my desire. See synonyms under ADMIRE, AGREE, ASSENT, JUSTIFY, LIKE, PRAISE, RATIFY. [<OF *aprover* <L *approbare* < *ad-* to + *probare* approve, prove < *probus* good] — **ap·prov′a·ble** *adj.* — **ap·prov′er** *n.* — **ap·prov′ing·ly** *adv.*

ap·prove[2] (ə·pro͞ov′) *v.t. Law* To turn to one's profit; appropriate, as waste or common land. [<OF *approuer* profit < *a* to + *pro* profit]

ap·prox·i·mal (ə·prok′sə·məl) *adj. Anat.* Close together: said of the surfaces of teeth.

ap·prox·i·mate (ə·prok′sə·mit) *adj.* **1** Nearly, but not exactly, accurate or complete. **2** Near. — *v.* (ə·prok′sə·māt) **·mat·ed, ·mat·ing** *v.t.* **1** To bring close to or cause to approach closely, as in time, space, or condition, without exact coincidence. **2** *Math.* To calculate a value progressively closer to exactitude: to *approximate* the square root of 6. — *v.i.* **3** To come near or close; be similar; That watch isn't the same as mine, but it *approximates.* [<L *approximatus,* pp. of *approximare* come near < *ad-* to + *proximus,* superl. of *prope* near] — **ap·prox′i·mate·ly** *adj.*

ap·prox·i·ma·tion (ə·prok′sə·mā′shən) *n.* **1** The act or process of approximating. **2** *Math.* A result sufficiently exact for a specified purpose.

Synonyms: approach, contiguity, likeness, nearness, neighborhood, propinquity, resemblance, similarity. *Approximation* expresses as near an approach to accuracy and certainty as the conditions in any given case make possible. *Resemblance* and *similarity* may be but superficial and apparent; *approximation* is real. *Approach* is a relative term, indicating that one has come nearer than before; *approximation* brings one really near. *Nearness, neighborhood,* and *propinquity* are commonly used of place; *approximation,* of mathematical calculations and abstract reasoning; we speak of *approach* to the shore, *nearness* to the town, *approximation* to the truth. *Antonyms*: difference, distance, error, remoteness, unlikeness, variation.

ap·prox·i·ma·tive (ə·prok′sə·mā′tiv, -mə·tiv) *adj.* Approaching almost to, but not quite; obtained by or involving approximation; approximate. — **ap·prox′i·ma′tive·ly** *adv.*

ap·pulse (ə·puls′) *n. Astron.* The approach of a heavenly body toward the meridian. [<L *appulsus* < *appellere* drive to < *ad-* to + *pellere* drive] — **ap·pul′sive** (-siv) *adj.*

ap·pul·sion (ə·pul′shən) *n.* The act of striking against.

ap·pur·te·nance (ə·pûr′tə·nəns) *n.* Something belonging or attached to something else as an accessory or adjunct. See synonyms under APPENDAGE. [<AF *apurtenance,* OF *apertenance* <L *appertinere.* See APPERTAIN.]

ap·pur·te·nant (ə·pûr′tə·nənt) *adj.* Appertaining or belonging, as by right; accessory. — *n.* An appurtenance.

A·pra Harbor (ä′prä) A harbor on the west coast of Guam: site of a United States naval base: also *Port Apra.*

a·prax·i·a (ə·prak′sē·ə, ā-) *n. Psychiatry* The inability to use or to understand the uses of things or to make purposeful movements, due to lesions in the cortical area of the brain. [<NL <Gk. *apraxia* inaction < *a-* not + *prassein* do]

a·près moi le dé·luge (à·pre mwà′ lə dā·lüzh′) *French* After me the deluge: attributed to Louis XV.

après–ski (äp′rā·skē′) *adj.* After skiing: usually applied to clothes or activities: *après–ski* boots; an *après–ski* fireside chat. [<F]

a·pri·cot (ā′pri·kot, ap′ri·kot) *n.* **1** A fruit (genus *Prunus*) of the rose family, intermediate between the peach and the plum. **2** The tree bearing this fruit. **3** A reddish–yellow color. [Earlier *apricock* (prob. directly <Pg.), *abricot* <F *abricot* <Pg. *albricoque* or Sp. *albaricoque* <Arabic *al-barqūq* <Med. Gk. *praikokion* <L *praecoquus* early ripe < *prae-* before + *coquere* cook]

A·pril (ā′prəl) The fourth month of the year, containing 30 days. [<L *Aprilis*]

April fool The subject of a practical joke on April 1, known as **April** (or **All**) **Fools' Day.**

a pri·o·ri (ā′ prī·ō′rī, ä′ prē·ôr′ē) **1** *Logic* Proceeding, as an argument, from cause to effect, or from an assumption to its logical conclusion: opposed to *a posteriori.* **2** Prior to, and thus independent of, experience; innate. **3** Previous to, or with insufficient, examination. See TRANSCENDENTAL. [<L, from what is before]

a·pri·or·i·ty (ā′prī·ôr′ə·tē, -or′-) *n.* The quality of being a priori, or not derived from experience.

a·pron (ā′prən, ā′pərn) *n.* **1** A covering to protect or adorn the front of a person's clothes, or any similar covering. **2** A part of the dress of a bishop or of the regalia of Masonic orders or other societies. **3** *Mech.* **a** Any of various overlapping pieces protecting parts of machines. **b** An endless band, as of cloth or leather, usually inclined, for conducting loose moving material, as grain in a separator. **4** *Eng.* **a** The platform or sill at the entrance to a dock. **b** The platform below a dam or in a sluiceway, or hinged to the river side of a fishing float. **5** *Geol.* A sheet of sand or gravel lying for some distance in front of the terminal moraines of a glacier. **6** *Aeron.* A hard-surfaced area in front of and around a hangar or aircraft shelter, to facilitate the handling of aircraft. **7** The part of a theater stage in front of the curtain. **8** *Mil.* **a** A movable screen of camouflage material, used to conceal artillery. **b** A network of barbed wire surrounding a post or stake in an entanglement. **9** A band of leather composing that part of an Oxford shoe which extends from the shank up and over the instep. —*v.t.* To cover or furnish with or as with an apron. [< OF *naperon,* dim. of *nape* cloth < L *mappa* cloth, napkin; in ME *a napron* became *an apron*] **—a′pron·like′** *adj.*

ap·ro·pos (ap′rə·pō′) *adj.* **1** Suited to the time, place, or occasion; pertinent; opportune: an *apropos* remark. —*adv.* **1** With reference or regard; in respect; as suggested by: with *of*: *apropos* of spring. **2** To the purpose; at the proper time; in the proper way; pertinently; appropriately: He spoke quite *apropos.* **3** By the way; incidentally: used to introduce a remark or observation. [< F *à propos* < *à* to + *propos* purpose]

ap·ro·sex·i·a (ap′rə·sek′sē·ə) *n.* *Psychiatry* Lack of power to concentrate the mind. [< NL < Gk. *aprosexia* lack of attention]

apse (aps) *n.* *Archit.* **1** An extending portion of an edifice, from the interior a recess and from the exterior a projection, usually semicircular with a half dome. **2** The eastern or altar end of a church. [< L *apsis* arch < Gk. *hapsis* a fastening, loop, wheel < *haptein* fasten]

Ap·she·ron (äp′shi·rôn′) A peninsula extending about 40 miles into the Caspian Sea from eastern Azerbaijan S.S.R.; site of the Baku oil fields.

ap·si·dal (ap′sə·dəl) *adj.* Of, pertaining to, like, or having an apse, apses, or apsides.

ap·sis (ap′sis) *n. pl.* **ap·si·des** (ap′sə·dēz) **1** *Astron.* A point of an eccentric orbit that is nearest to or farthest from the center of attraction, as the aphelion or perihelion of a planet. **2** *Geom.* The line joining these points to form the major axis of an ellipse. **3** An apse. **4** A reliquary. [< L. See APSE.]

apt (apt) *adj.* **1** Having a natural or habitual tendency; liable; likely. **2** Quick to learn; skilful. **3** Pertinent; apposite. [< L *aptus* fitted, suited] **—apt′ly** *adv.* **—apt′ness** *n.*

Synonyms: liable, likely. *Apt* inclines toward the meaning of *likely* and indicates an inherent inclination or ability. The distinction between *likely* and *liable* is that *likely* looks upon the probable event as favorable, *liable* as unfavorable; *likely* to succeed; *liable* to fail. See APPROPRIATE, CLEVER, LIKELY, SAGACIOUS.

Ap·ter·a (ap′tər·ə) *n. pl.* An order of small, primitive, wingless insects, formerly inclusive of many species now assigned to other orders. [< NL < Gk. *apteros* wingless < *a-* without + *pteron* wing]

ap·ter·al (ap′tər·əl) *adj.* **1** *Entomol.* Apterous. **2** *Archit.* Having no lateral ranges of columns, as a temple.

ap·ter·ous (ap′tər·əs) *adj.* **1** *Entomol.* Lacking wings, as the silverfish and other thysanurans. **2** *Bot.* Having no winglike expansions, as on a petiole or stem.

ap·ter·yx (ap′tər·iks) *n.* A New Zealand bird (genus *Apteryx*) with undeveloped wings, now nearly extinct. See KIWI. [< NL < Gk. *a-* without + *pteryx* wing] **—ap·ter·yg·i·al** (ap′tə·rij′ē·əl) *adj.*

ap·ti·tude (ap′tə·to͞od, -tyo͞od) *n.* **1** Natural or acquired adaptation, bent, or gift: an *aptitude* for being a gracious host. **2** General fitness. **3** Quickness of understanding; readiness: an *aptitude* for spelling. Also **apt′ness.** See synonyms under ABILITY, DEXTERITY. [< F < LL *aptitudo* < L *aptus* fitted, suited. Doublet of ATTITUDE.]

aptitude test *Psychol.* A test designed to indicate the ability or fitness of an individual to engage successfully in any of a number of specialized activities.

Ap·u·lei·us (ap′yə·lē′əs), **Lucius,** second century Roman satirist and philosopher.

A·pu·lia (ə·pyo͞o′lyə) A region of SE Italy; 7,469 square miles. *Italian* **Pu·glia** (po͞o′lyä).

A·pu·re (ä·po͞o′rā) A river in west central Venezuela, flowing east 350 miles to the Orinoco.

A·pu·rí·mac (ä′po͞o·rē′mäk) A river in southern Peru, flowing NW 550 miles to the Ucayali.

A·pus (ā′pəs) A southern constellation. See CONSTELLATION. [< NL < Gk. *apous* footless]

a·py·ret·ic (ā′pī·ret′ik, ap′ī-) *adj.* *Pathol.* Without fever. [< Gk. *apyretos* < *a-* without + *pyretos* fever]

A·qa·ba (ä′kä·bä) A town of south Jordan on the **Gulf of Aqaba,** the NE arm of the Red Sea. Ancient *Elath.*

aq·ua (ak′wə· ā′kwə) *n. pl. for def.* 1 **aq·uae** (ak′wē, ā′kwē) or **aq·uas,** *for def.* 2 **aq·uas** **1** Water. **2** A light bluish-green color; aquamarine. —*adj.* Light bluish-green. [< L]

aq·ua·cul·ture (ak′wə·kul′chər) *n.* The growing of plants or animals, especially fish or shellfish, in a body of water.

aqua for·tis (fôr′tis) Commercial nitric acid. Also **aq′ua·for′tis** *n.* [< L, strong water]

Aq·ua-lung (ak′wə·lung′) *n.* An underwater breathing apparatus or scuba: a trade name. Also **aq′ua·lung′.**

aq·ua·ma·rine (ak′wə·mə·rēn′) *n.* **1** A sea-green variety of precious beryl. **2** A bluish-green color. —*adj.* Bluish-green. [< L *aqua marina* sea water]

aq·ua·naut (ak′wə·nôt) *n.* One who explores or performs tasks underwater and is trained and equipped to live underwater over a period of time. [< L *aqua* water + *-naut* (< Gk. *nautēs* sailor), on analogy with *aeronaut, astronaut*]

aq·ua·plane (ak′wə·plān′) *n.* A board on which one stands while being towed over water by a motorboat. —*v.i.* **·planed, ·plan·ing** To ride an aquaplane.

aqua re·gi·a (rē′jē·ə) Nitrohydrochloric acid, a solvent for gold and platinum, and a powerful oxidizing agent. [< L, royal water]

aq·ua·relle (ak′wə·rel′) *n.* A kind of painting in transparent water colors. [< F < Ital. *acquerella* water color, dim. of *acqua* water < L *aqua*] —**aq′ua·rel′list** *n.*

a·quar·ium (ə·kwâr′ē·əm) *n. pl.* **a·quar·i·ums** or **a·quar·i·a** (ə·kwâr′ē·ə) **1** A tank, pond, or the like for the exhibition or study of aquatic animals or plants. **2** A public building containing such an exhibition. [< L, neut. sing. of *aquarius* pertaining to water < *aqua* water]

A·quar·i·us (ə·kwâr′ē·əs) **1** The eleventh sign of the zodiac; the Water-bearer. **2** A constellation of the zodiac. See CONSTELLATION. [< L]

a·quat·ic (ə·kwat′ik, ə·kwot′-) *adj.* Pertaining to, living in, growing in, or adapted to water. Also **a·quat′i·cal.** —*n.* **1** An aquatic animal or plant. **2** *pl.* Aquatic sports, as boating, etc. [< L *aquaticus* < *aqua* water]

aq·ua·tint (ak′wə·tint′) *n.* A form of engraving differing from an etching in that spaces instead of, or as well as, lines are bitten in by acid to give the effect of washes or tints in monochrome; also, an engraving printed from a plate so prepared. [< F *aquatinte* < Ital. *acqua tinta* dyed water < L *aqua tincta*]

a·qua·vit (ä′kwə·vēt) *n.* A Scandinavian liquor distilled from a grain or potato mash and flavored with caraway seed. Also **ak·va·vit** (äk′vä·vēt).

aqua vi·tae (vī′tē) **1** Alcohol. **2** Distilled spirits; whisky; brandy. [< L, water of life]

aq·ue·duct (ak′wə·dukt) *n.* **1** A water-conduit, particularly one for supplying a community from a distance. **2** A structure supporting a canal carried across a river or over low ground. **3** *Anat.* Any of several canals through which body liquids are conducted: the Fallopian *aqueduct.* [< L *aquaeductus* < *aqua* water + *ductus,* pp. of *ducere* lead]

aqueduct of Syl·vi·us (sil′vē·əs) *Anat.* The passage from the third to the fourth ventricle of the brain; the ventricle of the midbrain. Also called **a·quae·duc·tus cer·e·bri** (ak′wə·duk′təs ser′ə·brī).

a·que·ous (ā′kwē·əs, ak′wē-) *adj.* Pertaining to, made with, formed by, or containing water; watery.

aqueous humor *Physiol.* A clear, limpid, alkaline fluid that fills the anterior chamber of the eye from the cornea to the crystalline lens.

aqueous tension *Physics* The partial pressure due to the water vapor mixed with a gas measured over water. It is definite for each temperature.

aqui- *combining form* Water: *aquiferous.* [< L *aqua*]

aq·ui·cul·ture (ak′wi·kul′chər, ā′kwi-) *n.* Aquaculture.

aq·ui·fer (ak′wə·fər) *n.* *Geol.* Any water-bearing formation or group of formations, especially one that supplies ground water, wells, or springs.

a·quif·er·ous (ə·kwif′ər·əs) *adj.* Conveying or supplying water or watery fluid.

aq·ui·form (ak′wə·fôrm, ā′kwə-) *adj.* Like water; liquid.

aq·ui·fuge (ak′wə·fyo͞oj) *n.* *Geol.* A rock formation or structure which will neither absorb nor transmit water. [< AQUI- + L *fugere* flee]

Aq·ui·la (ak′wə·lə) A northern constellation, the Eagle. See CONSTELLATION. [< L, eagle]

aq·ui·le·gi·a (ak′wə·lē′jē·ə) *n.* Any of a genus (*Aquilegia*) of erect perennial plants of the crowfoot family; the columbine. [< NL < Med. L]

A·qui·le·ia (ä′kwē·lā′yä) A town in NE Italy; one of the chief cities of the Roman empire.

aq·ui·line (ak′wə·līn, -lin) *adj.* **1** Of or like an eagle. **2** Curving; hooked like an eagle's beak: an *aquiline* nose. [< L *aquilinus* < *aquila* eagle]

Aq·ui·lo (ak′wə·lō) In Roman mythology, the north or northeast wind. [< OF < L *Aquilo*]

A·qui·nas (ə·kwī′nəs), **Saint Thomas,** 1225?–1274, Italian Dominican monk and theologian.

Aq·ui·taine (ak′wə·tān′) A region of SW France; formerly a duchy, an independent kingdom, and the province of Guienne. Ancient **Aq·ui·ta·ni·a** (ak′wə·tā′nē·ə).

a·quose (ā′kwōs, ə·kwōs′) *adj.* Aqueous; watery.

a·quos·i·ty (ə·kwos′ə·tē) *n.* Moistness; wateriness.

ar (är) See ARE[2].

Ar *Chem.* Argon (symbol Ar).

ar- Assimilated var. of AD-.

-ar[1] *suffix* **1** Pertaining to; like: *regular, singular.* **2** The person or thing pertaining to: *scholar.* [ME *-er* < OF *-er,* F *-aire, -ier* < L *-aris* (in nouns *-are*), used for *-alis* when preceded by *l*]

-ar[2] *suffix* A form of -ARY, -ER[2]: refashioned in imitation of -AR[1]: *vicar,* ME *vicary, viker.*

-ar[3] *suffix* A form of -ER[1]: refashioned in imitation of -AR[2]: *pedlar.*

A·ra (ā′rə) A southern constellation, the Altar. See CONSTELLATION. [< L, altar]

Ar·ab (ar′əb) *n.* **1** A native or inhabitant of Arabia. **2** One of a Semitic people inhabiting Arabia from ancient times, commonly the nomadic Bedouins: now scattered and admixed with various other native peoples. **3** A horse of a graceful, intelligent breed originally native to Arabia. **4** A homeless street wanderer, especially a child; a street Arab. —*adj.* Arabian.

Ar·a·bel·la (ar′ə·bel′ə, *Ital.* ä′rä·bel′lä) A feminine personal name. Also **A·ra·belle** (*Fr.* à·rà·bel′, *Ger.* ä′rä·bel′ə), *Sp.* **A·ra·be·la** (ä′rä·bä′lä). [? < Gmc.]

ar·a·besque (ar′ə·besk′) *n.* **1** An ornament or design, as those used in Arabian or Moorish architecture, employing patterns of intertwined scrollwork, conventionalized leaves or flowers, etc., painted or sculptured in low relief. **2** In ballet, a position in which the

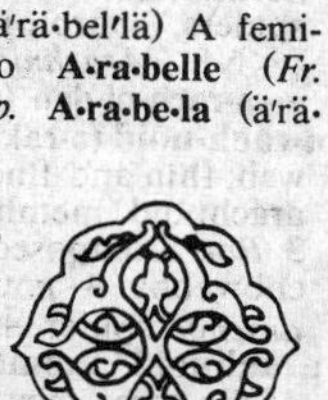

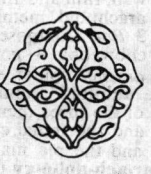

ARABESQUE

dancer extends one leg straight backward, one arm forward, and the other arm backward. **3** *Music* A short, lively composition in rondo form. — *adj.* Relating to, executed in, or resembling arabesque; fanciful; ornamental. Also **ar′a·besk′**. [<F <Ital. *arabesco* <*Arabo* Arab]

A·ra·bi·a (ə·rā′bē·ə) A peninsula of SW Asia, between the Red Sea and the Persian Gulf; 1,000,- 000 square miles; anciently divided into **Arabia De·ser·ta** (di·zûr′tə), northern Arabia, **Arabia Fe·lix** (fē′liks), generally restricted to Yemen, and **Arabia Pe·trae·a** (pe·trē′ə), NW Arabia.

A·ra·bi·an (ə·rā′bē·ən) *adj.* Of or pertaining to Arabia or the Arabs. — *n.* **1** A native or inhabitant of Arabia. **2** An Arab (def. 3).

Arabian Desert 1 The desert in eastern Egypt between the Nile and the Gulf of Suez. **2** Popularly, the desert in northern Arabia.

Arabian millet Johnson grass.

Arabian Nights A collection of stories from Arabia, India, Persia, etc., dating from the tenth century A.D.: also called *The Thousand and One Nights.*

Arabian Sea A broad arm of the Indian Ocean, between Arabia and India.

Ar·a·bic (ar′ə·bik) *adj.* Of or pertaining to Arabia, the Arabs, their language, culture, etc. — *n.* The Southwest Semitic language of the Arabians, now widely spread among Moslem nations.

ar·a·bic acid (ar′ə·bik) *Chem.* A white amorphous powder, $C_5H_{10}O·H_2O$, contained in gum arabic and other gums.

Arabic numerals The figures 1, 2, 3, 4, 5, 6, 7, 8, 9, and the zero (0). See NUMERAL.

a·rab·i·nose (ə·rab′ə·nōs, ar′ə·bə-) *n.* A colorless crystalline sugar of the pentose class, $C_5H_{10}O_5$, obtained from the gums of certain plants or by synthesis from glucose. [<ARAB-(IC) + -IN + -OSE]

Ar·a·bist (ar′ə·bist) *n.* A student of or one versed in Arabic, Arabic literature, science, medicine, etc.

A·ra·bi·stan (ä·rä′bē·stän′) A former name for KHUZISTAN.

ar·a·ble (ar′ə·bəl) *adj.* Capable of being plowed or cultivated. — *n.* Land fit for cultivation. [<L *arabilis* <*arare* plow] — **ar′a·bil′i·ty** *n.*

Arab League A confederation, established 1945, of the states of Iraq, Jordan (then *Trans-Jordan*), Lebanon, Saudi Arabia, the United Arab Republic (then *Egypt* and *Syria*), and Yemen; joined by 1959 by Libya, Morocco, Sudan, and Tunisia, and in 1961 by Kuwait.

Ar·a·by (ar′ə·bē) *Archaic* or *Poetic* Arabia.

A·ra·ca·jú (ä·rə·kə·zhōō′) A port of eastern Brazil, capital of Sergipe state.

a·ra·ceous (ə·rā′shəs) *adj.* Belonging to the arum family *(Araceae)* of plants, mainly tropical, and bearing flowers on a spadix which is usually surrounded by a spathe. [<AR(UM) + -ACEOUS]

A·rach·ne (ə·rak′nē) In Greek mythology, a Lydian girl who challenged Athena to a weaving contest and was changed by the goddess into a spider. [<L <Gk. *Arachnē* <*arachnē* spider]

a·rach·nid (ə·rak′nid) *n.* Any of a class *(Arachnida)* of arthropods, embracing the spiders, scorpions, harvestmen, mites, etc. [<NL *Arachnida* <Gk. *arachnē* spider] — **a·rach·ni·dan** (ə·rak′nə·dən) *adj.* & *n.*

a·rach·noid (ə·rak′noid) *adj.* **1** Like a spider's web; thin and fine. **2** Of or pertaining to the arachnoid membrane or to the *Arachnida.* **3** *Bot.* Composed of slender entangled hairs; cobwebby. — *n.* One of the *Arachnida.* [<Gk. *arachnē* spider + -OID]

arachnoid membrane *Anat.* The midmost of the three membranes enveloping the brain and the spinal cord: between the dura mater and the pia mater. Also **arachnoid tissue.**

ar·ach·nol·o·gy (ar′ak·nol′ə·jē) *n.* The branch of zoology which treats of the arachnids.

A·rad (ä·räd′) A city on the Mures in western Rumania.

A·ra·fu·ra Sea (ä′rä·fŏŏ′rä) A part of the Pacific Ocean between northern Australia and New Guinea.

A·ra·gats (ä·rä·gäts′) See ALAGEZ.

Ar·a·gon (ar′ə·gon) A region of NE Spain; 18,382 square miles; formerly an independent kingdom. *Spanish* **A·ra·gón** (ä′rä·gōn′).

Ar·a·go·nese (ar′ə·gə·nēz′, -nēs′) *adj.* Of or pertaining to Aragon, its people, or their language. — *n. pl.* **·nese 1** A native or inhabitant of Aragon. **2** The dialect of Spanish spoken in Aragon.

a·rag·o·nite (ə·rag′ə·nīt, ar′ə·gə-) *n.* A form of calcite crystallizing in the orthorhombic system. [from *Aragon,* Spain]

A·ra·guai·a (ä′rə·gwī′ə) A river in central Brazil, flowing north over 1,100 miles to the Atlantic. Also **A′ra·guay′a.**

A·ra·kan (ä′rä·kän′) An administrative division of SW Burma on the Bay of Bengal, containing the **Arakan Yo·ma** (yō′mə), a mountain range.

A·ral·do (ä·räl′dō) Italian form of HAROLD.

a·ra·li·a·ceous (ə·rā′lē·ā′shəs) *adj. Bot.* Relating to a family of polypetalous plants *(Araliaceae),* having more than two carpels and a drupaceous fruit, the English ivy and ginseng being the best-known species. [<NL]

Ar·al Sea A salt inland sea, bordered by Kazakhstan and Uzbekistan in Asia; one of the world's largest inland seas; 24,635 square miles. Also **Lake of Aral.**

Ar·am (âr′əm), **Eugene,** 1704–59, English philologist; executed for murder.

Ar·am (âr′əm) The Biblical name of an ancient country of SW Asia, generally identified with Syria. Also **Ar·a·me·a** (ar′ə·mē′ə).

Ar·a·ma·ic (ar′ə·mā′ik) *n.* **1** Any of a group of Northwest Semitic languages, embracing Biblical Aramaic (erroneously, Chaldee), Syriac, etc. **2** The language of the Jews in Palestine after the captivity and that spoken by Christ and his disciples. Also *Aramean.* — *adj.* Aramean.

Ar·a·me·an (ar′ə·mē′ən) *adj.* Of or pertaining to ancient Aram or Aramea, or its peoples, languages, etc. — *n.* **1** An inhabitant of Aram. **2** The Aramaic language, especially in the broad sense. See ARAMAIC. Also **Ar′a·mae′an.**

A·ra·ne·ae (ə·rā′ni·ē) *n. pl.* An order of arachnids; the spiders. [<L *aranea* spider]

a·ra·ne·ous (ə·rā′nē·əs) *adj.* Made up of or covered with slender tangled hairs; cobwebby. Also **a·ra′ne·ose** (-ōs).

A·ra·nha (ə·ru′nyə), **Oswaldo,** 1894–1960, Brazilian lawyer and diplomat; minister of foreign affairs 1938–44.

Ar·an Islands (ar′ən) A group of three islands off the SW coast of County Galway, Ireland, at the entrance to Galway Bay; 18 square miles: also *Arran Islands.*

A·ran·da (ə·ran′də) *n.* A native Australian language, spoken in an extensive area of central Australia.

A·ran·sas Pass (ə·ran′səs) A channel connecting **Aransas Bay,** an inlet of the Gulf of Mexico, with the Gulf Intracoastal Waterway in southern Texas.

Ar·an·y (ôr′ôn·y′), **Janos,** 1817–82, Hungarian poet.

A·rap·a·ho (ə·rap′ə·hō) *n. pl.* **·ho** or **·hoes** An Indian of a nomadic tribe of Algonquian stock. Also **A·rap′a·hoe.**

ar·a·pai·ma (ar′ə·pī′mə) *n.* A large South American fresh-water food fish *(Arapaima gigas)* sometimes over 400 pounds in weight and 15 feet long. [<Pg. <Tupian]

Ar·a·rat (ar′ə·rat), **Mount** The highest peak in eastern Turkey; 16,945 feet; traditional resting place of Noah's ark. *Gen* viii 4. *Turkish* **Ağ·ri Da·ği** (ä·rī′ dä·ī′).

ar·a·ro·ba (ar′ə·rō′bə) *n.* **1** Chrysarobin. **2** Zebrawood. [<Pg. <Tupian]

A·ras (ä·räs′) A river forming the border between the U.S.S.R. and Turkey and Iran, flowing east 666 miles to the Kara: ancient *Araxes. Russian* **A·raks** (ä·räks′).

A·rau·can (ə·rô′kən) *n.* **1** An Araucanian. **2** The language of the Araucanians.

A·rau·ca·ni·a (ar′ô·kā′nē·ə) A region of central Chile inhabited by the Araucanians.

Ar·au·ca·ni·an (ar′ô·kā′nē·ən) *n.* **1** One of the aboriginal Indian inhabitants of Araucania. **2** A family of South American Indian languages spoken in southern and central Chile and northern Argentina. — *adj.* Of or

pertaining to these people, their culture, or their language.

ar·au·ca·ri·a (ar′ô·kā′rē·ə) *n.* Any of a genus *(Araucaria)* of usually South American or Australian evergreen trees. [<NL <Sp. *Araucano* Araucanian]

A·ra·wak (ä′rä·wäk) *n.* Arawakan.

A·ra·wa·kan (ä′rä·wä′kən) *n.* **1** The most widely spread South American Indian linguistic stock, found from the headwaters of the Paraguay River, in southern Bolivia, to the northernmost part of the South American continent, and throughout the Antilles. **2** A member of any of the tribes speaking these languages. Also *Arawak.* — *adj.* Of or pertaining to this linguistic stock.

A·rax·es (ə·rak′sēz) The ancient name for the ARAS.

ar·ba·lest (är′bə·list) *n.* A medieval crossbow requiring a mechanical appliance to bend it.

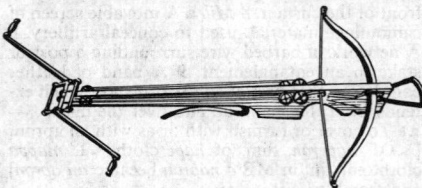

ARBALEST
With windlass for winding back bowstring.

Also **ar′ba·list.** [<OF *arbaleste* <L *arcuballista* <*arcus* a bow + *ballista.* See BALLISTA.] — **ar′ba·lest′er** *n.*

Ar·be·la (är·bē′lə) A city in ancient Assyria on the site of modern Erbil, near which, at Gaugamela, Alexander the Great defeated Darius in 331 B.C.

Ar·ber (är′bər), **Edward,** 1836–1912, English scholar and editor.

ar·bi·ter (är′bə·tər) *n.* **1** A chosen or appointed judge or umpire, as between parties in a dispute. **2** One who has matters under his sole control; an absolute and final judge. See synonyms under JUDGE. [<L, one who goes to see, a witness, judge <*ad-* to + *bitere, betere* go]

ar·bi·ter el·e·gan·ti·ae (är′bə·tər el′ə·gan′shi·ē) *Latin* A judge in matters of style. Also **arbiter el·e·gan·ti·a·rum** (el′ə·gan′shē·ā′rəm).

ar·bi·tra·ble (är′bə·trə·bəl) *adj.* Subject to, capable of, or suitable for arbitration.

ar·bi·trage (är′bə·trij, är′bə·träzh′) *n.* **1** The simultaneous buying and selling of the same thing, as stocks or bonds, in different markets, in order to profit by the difference between the prices ruling in such markets. **2** Arbitration. [<F <*arbitrer* arbitrate] — **ar·bi·trag·ist** (är′bə·trə·jist) *n.*

ar·bi·tral (är′bə·trəl) *adj.* Pertaining to an arbitrator or arbitration; subject to arbitration.

ar·bit·ra·ment (är·bit′rə·mənt) *n.* **1** The act of deciding by arbitration, or the decision of an arbitrator; an award. **2** Absolute and final decision by any power or authority to which a contest has been or may be appealed; also, the power or right to make such decision. Also **ar·bit′re·ment.** [<OF *arbitrement* <*arbitrer.* See ARBITRATE.]

ar·bi·trar·y (är′bə·trer′ē) *adj.* **1** Based on mere opinion or prejudice; capricious. **2** Absolute; despotic. **3** *Law* Not determined by statute; discretionary. [<L *arbitrarius* <*arbiter.* See ARBITER.] — **ar′bi·trar′i·ly** *adv.* — **ar′bi·trar′i·ness** *n.*

Synonyms: absolute, despotic, dictatorial, domineering, harsh, imperious, irresponsible, overbearing, peremptory, tyrannical, tyrannous. See ABSOLUTE, IMPERIOUS. *Antonyms:* constitutional, equitable, free, lenient, limited, mild, obliging, restrained, restricted.

ar·bi·trate (är′bə·trāt) *v.t.* & *v.i.* **·trat·ed,** **·trat·ing 1** To submit to or settle by arbitration. **2** To act as judge or arbitrator, as for a case. [<L *arbitratus,* pp. of *arbitrari* <*arbiter.* See ARBITER.] — **ar′bi·tra′tive** *adj.*

ar·bi·tra·tion (är′bə·trā′shən) *n.* The hearing and settlement of a dispute between two parties by the decision of a third party or court to which the matter is referred by the contestants as a means of avoiding war, a strike, a lawsuit, etc. See CONCILIATION, MEDIATION.

ar·bi·tra·tor (är′bə·trā′tər) *n.* **1** A person

chosen by agreement of parties to decide a dispute between them. **2** One empowered to decide a matter; an arbiter. See synonyms under JUDGE. [< L]

ar·bi·tress (är′bə·tris) *n.* A woman arbiter. Also **ar·bi·tra·trix** (är′bə·trā′triks).

Ar·blay (där′blā), **Madame d'** See BURNEY, FANNY.

ar·bo·lo·co (är′bō·lō′kō) *n.* A central American tree *(Montanoa lehmannii)* of the composite family, having a hard durable wood used for making billiard cues. [< Sp. *árbol* tree]

ar·bor¹ (är′bər) *n.* **1** A bower, as of latticework, supporting vines or trees; a place shaded by trees. **2** *Obs.* An orchard. Also *Brit.* **ar′bour.** [Earlier *erber, herber* < AF, var. of OF *erbier, herbier* < L *herbarium* a collection of herbs < *herba* grass, herb]

ar·bor² (är′bər) *n. pl.* **ar·bo·res** (är′bər-ēz) *for defs.* **1** and **3**, **ar·bors** *for def.* **2**. **1** A tree: used chiefly in botanical names. **2** *Mech.* **a** A shaft, mandrel, spindle, or axle, as of a circular saw, lathe, or watch wheel. **b** A principal support of a machine. **3** A pictured genealogical tree. [< L, tree]

Arbor Day A U.S. spring holiday observed in some States by planting trees.

ar·bo·re·al (är·bôr′ē·əl, -bō′rē-) *adj.* **1** Of or pertaining to a tree or trees; arborescent. **2** Living or situated among trees.

ar·bo·re·ous (är·bôr′ē·əs, -bō′rē-) *adj.* **1** Of the nature of or like a tree. **2** Forming a tree trunk, as distinguished from a shrub. **3** Having many trees; wooded.

ar·bo·res·cent (är′bə·res′ənt) *adj.* Treelike in character, appearance, or size; branching. — **ar′bo·res′cence** *n.*

ar·bo·re·tum (är′bə·rē′təm) *n. pl.* **·tums** or **·ta** (-tə) A botanical garden exhibiting trees for their scientific interest and educational value, and in association with appropriate wildlife features. [< L < *arbor* tree]

arbori- *combining form* Tree: *arboriform.* [< L *arbor* tree]

ar·bo·ri·cul·ture (är′bə·ri·kul′chər) *n.* The cultivation of trees or shrubs. — **ar′bo·ri·cul′tur·al** *adj.* — **ar′bo·ri·cul′tur·ist** *n.*

ar·bo·ri·form (är′bər·ə·fôrm, är·bôr′ə-, är·bor′ə-) *adj.* Formed like a tree.

ar·bor·i·za·tion (är′bər·ə·zā′shən, -ī·zā′-) *n.* The formation of a treelike arrangement or figure, as in some minerals and fossils.

ar·bor·ous (är′bər·əs) *adj.* Of, pertaining to, or formed by trees.

ar·bor·vi·tae (är′bər·vī′tē) *n.* **1** An evergreen shrub or tree of the genus *Thuya* or *Thuja*, of the pine family, especially *T. orientalis.* **2** *Anat.* The branching appearance of the white matter shown in a section of the cerebellum. [< L, tree of life]

ar·bus·cle (är′bus·əl) *n.* **1** A dwarf tree, or one between a shrub and a tree in size. **2** An arbuscule. [< L *arbuscula*, dim. of *arbor* tree]

ar·bus·cule (är·bus′kyōōl) *n. Zool.* A tuft, as of cilia, etc.

ar·bute (är′byōōt) *n.* **1** The European strawberry tree. **2** The arbutus. [< L *arbutus*]

Ar·buth·not (är′bəth·not, är·buth′nət), **John,** 1667–1735, Scottish satirist and physician.

ar·bu·tus (är·byōō′təs) *n.* **1** Any member of a small genus *(Arbutus)* of evergreen trees or shrubs of the heath family, whose bark, leaves, and fruit are used in drugs. **2** The trailing arbutus. [< L, strawberry tree]

arc (ärk) *n.* **1** Anything in the shape of an arch, of a curve, or of a part of a circle; a bow; arch. **2** *Geom.* A part of any algebraic curve, especially of a circle. **3** *Electr.* The bow of flame occurring in an arc light. **4** *Astron.* A part of the apparent path of a heavenly body. — *v.i.* **arced** or **arced** (ärkt), **arc·ing** or **arc·ing** (är′king) *Electr.* To form a voltaic arc. ◆ Homophone: *ark.* [< L *arcus* bow, arch. Doublet of ARCH¹.]

Arc, Jeanne d' (zhän därk) See JOAN OF ARC.

ar·cade (är·kād′) *n.* **1** *Archit.* **a** A vaulted roof. **b** An ornamental series or range of arches with their supporting columns or piers, standing against the face of a wall **(blind arcade)** or free, as a support of a ceiling, roof, etc. **2** A roofed passageway or street, especially one having

shops, etc., opening from it. **3** An avenue of trees, statues, etc. — *v.t.* **·cad·ed, ·cad·ing** To furnish with or form into an arcade or arcades. [< F < Med.L *arcata* < L *arcus* bow, arch]

Ar·ca·di·a (är·kā′dē·ə) **1** A nome of central Peloponnesus, Greece, traditionally associated with the pastoral pursuits of its ancient inhabitants. **2** Hence, any region of ideal rustic simplicity and contentment. *Modern Greek* **Ar·ka·dhi·a** (är′kä·thē′ä).

Ar·ca·di·an (är·kā′dē·ən) *adj.* **1** Of or pertaining to Arcadia. **2** Ideally rural or simple; pastoral. — *n.* **1** A native of or dweller in Arcadia. **2** One with simple, pastoral tastes.

Ar·ca·dy (är′kə·dē) *Archaic* or *Poetic* Arcadia.

ar·cane (är·kān′) *adj.* Secret; hidden. [< L *arcanus.* See ARCANUM.]

ar·ca·num (är·kā′nəm) *n. pl.* **·na** (-nə) **1** An inner secret or mystery. **2** One of the great secrets of nature which the alchemists sought to discover. **3** A secret remedy; an elixir. [< L, neut. of *arcanus* hidden < *arca* chest]

ar·ca·ture (är′kə·chŏŏr) *n.* **1** A small arcade formed by a series of little arches. **2** A blind arcade, used merely for ornament.

arc·bou·tant (är·bōō·täN′) *n. pl.* **arcs·bou·tants** (är·bōō·täN′) *French* An arched buttress.

arch¹ (ärch) *n.* **1** A curved structure spanning an opening, formed of wedge-shaped parts resting on supports at the two extremities. **2** Any similar structure or object; an archway.

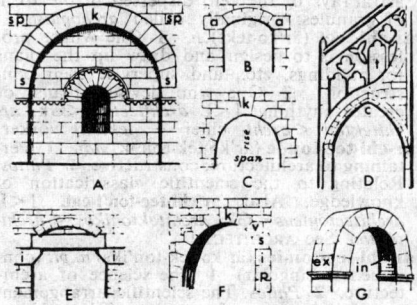

TYPES OF ARCHES

3 The form of an arch; a bowlike curve. **4** *Mech.* The height within the curve of an arched body, as through the central portion of a leaf spring. **5** *Aeron.* **a** The curve of a surface from front to rear. **b** A curved wing tip. **6** *Anat.* A curved or archlike part: the dental arch. **7** One of the major patterns into which all fingerprints are divided: subclassed as *plain, tented,* and *exceptional.* — *v.t.* **1** To cause to form an arch or arches. **2** To furnish with an arch or arches. **3** To span; extend over, as an arch. — *v.i.* **4** To form an arch or arches. [< OF *arche* < Med. L. *arca* < L *arcus* bow, arch. Doublet of ARC.]

arch² (ärch) *adj.* **1** Cunning; roguish; sly; coy. **2** Most eminent; chief. [< ARCH-] — **arch′ly** *adv.* — **arch′ness** *n.*

arch- *prefix* **1** Chief; principal: *archchancellor.* **2** Very great; extreme: *archknave.* Also **archi-,** as in *archidiaconal.* [OE *arce-, erce-* < L *arch-, arche-, archi-* < Gk. *archos* ruler]

Ar·chae·an (är·kē′ən) See ARCHEAN.

archaeo- See ARCHEO-.

ar·chae·ol·o·gy (är′kē·ol′ə·jē), etc. See ARCHEOLOGY, etc.

ar·chae·op·ter·yx (är′kē·op′tər·iks) *n.* A representative of a genus *(Archaeopteryx)* of fossil reptilian birds of the Upper Jurassic period, combining reptilian and avian characteristics. Also **ar′che·op′ter·yx.** [< NL < ARCHAEO- + Gk. *pteryx* wing]

Ar·chae·o·zo·ic (är′kē·ə·zō′ik) See ARCHEOZOIC.

ar·cha·ic (är·kā′ik) *adj.* **1** Belonging to a former period; no longer in use; antiquated. **2** Characterizing a word, an inflectional form, or a phrase found only in the older literature and in the Bible, but no longer in current use. Also **ar·cha′i·cal.** [< Gk. *archaikos* < *archaios* ancient]

ar·cha·ism (är′kē·iz′əm, -kā-) *n.* **1** An archaic word, idiom, or expression. **2** Archaic style or usage.

ar·cha·ist (är′kē·ist, -kā-) *n.* **1** One who uses or affects archaisms or the archaic. **2** One who studies antiquities; an archeologist.

ar·cha·is·tic (är′kē·is′tik, -kā-) *adj.* Of, pertaining to, or imitating the archaic; inclined to, characterized by, or affecting archaism.

ar·cha·ize (är′kē·īz, -kā-) *v.* **·ized, ·iz·ing** *v.t.* To make archaic or archaistic. — *v.i.* To use archaisms. Also *Brit.* **ar′cha·ise.** — **ar′cha·iz′er** *n.*

Ar·cham·bault (är·shäN·bō′) French form of ARCHIBALD.

arch·an·gel (ärk′ān′jəl) *n.* **1** An angel of highest rank; in Christian legend one of seven, in the Koran one of four, chief angels. **2** The garden angelica. **—the Archangel** In Christian legend, usually Michael. [< L *archangelus* < Gk. *archangelos* < *arch-* chief + *angelos* angel] — **arch·an·gel·ic** (ärk′an·jel′ik) or **·i·cal** *adj.*

Arch·an·gel (ärk′ān′jəl) See ARKHANGELSK.

Archangel Bay See DVINA BAY.

arch·bish·op (ärch′bish′əp) *n.* The chief bishop of an ecclesiastical province.

arch·bish·op·ric (ärch′bish′əp·rik) *n.* **1** The office, rank, term of office, or jurisdiction of an archbishop. **2** The ecclesiastical province over which an archbishop has jurisdiction.

arch·dea·con (ärch′dē′kən) *n. Eccl.* A church official who administers the property, temporal affairs, missionary work, etc., of a diocese under powers delegated from the bishop: chiefly an Anglican usage.

arch·dea·con·ate (ärch′dē′kən·it) *n.* The jurisdiction of an archdeacon.

arch·dea·con·ry (ärch′dē′kən·rē) *n. pl.* **·ries 1** The title, office, or dignity of an archdeacon. **2** An archdeacon's residence. Also **arch′dea′con·ship.**

arch·di·o·cese (ärch′dī′ə·sēs, -sis) *n.* The diocese or jurisdiction of an archbishop.

arch·du·cal (ärch′dōō′kəl, -dyōō′-) *adj.* Of or pertaining to an archduke or an archduchy.

arch·duch·ess (ärch′duch′is) *n.* **1** A princess of the former imperial family of Austria. **2** The wife or widow of an archduke.

arch·duch·y (ärch′duch′ē) *n. pl.* **·duch·ies** The territory ruled by an archduke. Also **arch′-duke′dom.**

arch·duke (ärch′dōōk′, -dyōōk′) *n.* A chief duke, especially a prince of the former imperial family of Austria.

Ar·che·an (är·kē′ən) *adj. Geol.* Pertaining to a rock group associated with the Archeozoic era of earth's history, consisting of the oldest stratified rocks, predominantly igneous and without fossil remains. Also **Ar·chae′an.** [< Gk. *archaios* ancient < *arche* beginning]

arched (ärcht) *adj.* **1** Having the form of an arch; characterized by arches. **2** Covered or furnished with arches.

ar·che·go·ni·o·phore (är′kə·gō′nē·ə·fôr′, -fōr′) *n. Bot.* A multicellular outgrowth of the thalloid shoot of liverworts bearing archegonia.

ar·che·go·ni·um (är′kə·gō′nē·əm) *n. pl.* **·ni·a** (-nē·ə) *Bot.* The female sexual organ of the higher cryptogams, the analog of the pistil of flowering plants, which has, when ready for fertilization, the form of a cellular sac or flask containing an egg-cell. Also **ar·che·gone** (är′kə·gōn). [< NL < Gk. *archegonos* primitive parent < *archos* chief, first + *gonos* offspring] — **ar′che·go′ni·al** *adj.* — **ar′che·go′ni·ate** (-it, -āt) *adj.*

Ar·che·la·us (är′kə·lā′əs) Ruler of Judea, son and successor of Herod. *Matt.* ii 22.

arch-en·e·my (ärch′en′ə·mē) *n. pl.* **·mies 1** Satan. **2** The principal enemy.

ar·chen·ter·on (är·ken′tər·on) *n. Biol.* The primitive enteron or alimentary cavity. [< ARCH(I)- + Gk. *enteron* intestine] — **ar·chen·ter·ic** (är′ken·ter′ik) *adj.*

archeo- *combining form* Ancient: *Archeozoic.* Also **archaeo-.** [< Gk. *archaios* ancient]

ar·che·o·as·tron·o·my (är′kē·ə·ə·stron′ə·mē) *n.* The astronomy of ancient cultures as deduced from archeological evidence.

ar·che·ol·o·gy (är′kē·ol′ə·jē) *n.* The science or study of history from the evidence of the relics and remains of early human cultures as

discovered chiefly by systematic excavations: also spelled *archaeology.* — **ar·che·o·log·i·cal** (är′kē·ə·loj′i·kəl) or **·log′ic** *adj.* — **ar′che·ol′o·gist** (-jist) *n.*

ar·che·op·ter·yx (är′kē·op′tər·iks) See ARCHAEOPTERYX.

Ar·che·o·zo·ic (är′kē·ə·zō′ik) *n. Geol.* The oldest of the eras making up the geological record. See chart under GEOLOGY. — *adj.* Belonging to or indicating this era. Also spelled *Archaeozoic* [<ARCHEO- + Gk. *zōon* animal]

arch·er (är′chər) *n.* One who shoots with a bow and arrow. [<OF *archier* <L *arcarius* bowman <*arcus* bow]

Arch·er (är′chər) The tenth sign of the zodiac. See SAGITTARIUS.

Ar·cher (är′chər), **William,** 1856–1924, Scottish critic and dramatist.

arch·er·fish (är′chər·fish′) *n. pl.* **·fish** or **·fish·es** A percomorph fish *(Toxotes jaculator)* of India and Polynesia, with the ability to shoot drops of water to bring down its insect prey.

arch·er·y (är′chər·ē) *n.* **1** The art or sport of shooting with the bow and arrows. **2** The weapons and outfit of the archer. **3** Archers collectively.

Arch·es National Monument (är′chiz) A group of wind-eroded rock formations in SE Utah, established as a national monument in 1929; 53 square miles.

ar·che·spore (är′kə·spôr, -spōr) *n. Bot.* The cell, or group of cells, from which the pollen mother cells are formed within a pollen sac, or the spore mother cells within a sporangium. Also **ar′che·spo′ri·um** (-spôr′ē·əm, spō′rē·əm). [<NL *archesporium* <ARCHI- + Gk. *sporos* seed] — **ar′che·spo′ri·al** *adj.*

ar·che·type (är′kə·tīp) *n.* An original or standard pattern or model; a prototype. See synonyms under EXAMPLE, IDEA, IDEAL, MODEL. [<L *archetypum* <Gk. *archetypon* pattern, model <*arche-* first + *typos* stamp, pattern] — **ar′che·typ′al** *adj.* — **ar′che·typ′ic** (-tip′ik) or **·i·cal** *adj.*

arch·fiend (ärch′fēnd′) *n.* A chief fiend; specifically, Satan.

archi– *prefix* **1** Var. of ARCH–. **2** *Biol.* Original; primitive: *archiblast.* [See ARCH-]

Ar·chi·bald (är′chə·bôld) A masculine personal name. Also *Lat.* **Ar·chi·bal·dus** (är′kə·bôl′dəs). [<Gmc., nobly bold]

ar·chi·blast (är′kə·blast) *n. Biol.* **1** The primitive portion of the blastoderm or germinal disk. **2** The epiblast. [<ARCHI- + Gk. *blastos* germ]

ar·chi·carp (är′kə·kärp) *n. Bot.* A female sex organ of certain fungi; an ascogonium. [<ARCHI- + Gk. *karpos* fruit]

ar·chi·di·ac·o·nal (är′ki·dī·ak′ə·nəl) *adj.* Pertaining to an archdeacon or an archdeaconry.

ar·chi·di·ac·o·nate (är′ki·dī·ak′ə·nāt) *n.* The office of an archdeacon.

Ar·chie (är′chē) Diminutive of ARCHIBALD. Also **Ar′chy.**

ar·chi·e·pis·co·pa·cy (är′kē·i·pis′kə·pə·sē) *n. pl.* **·cies** The rank and rule of an archbishop. Also **ar′chi·e·pis′co·pate** (-pāt).

ar·chi·e·pis·co·pal (är′kē·i·pis′kə·pəl) *adj.* Of or pertaining to an archbishop, his office, or residence.

ar·chil (är′kil) *n.* **1** A lichen of the Cape Verde and Canary Islands *(Rocella tinctoria),* yielding the dyestuff orchil. **2** The dyestuff obtained from this lichen; orchil. Also spelled *orchil.* [earlier *orchil* <OF *orchel, orcheil* <Ital. *orcello*]

Ar·chi·lo·chi·an (är′kə·lō′kē·ən) *adj.* Characteristic of or pertaining to the early Greek satiric poet Archilochus or the verse named after him. — *n.* The dactylic trimeter or tetrameter as used by Archilochus.

ar·chi·mage (är′kə·māj) *n.* **1** A chief magician; great wizard. **2** The chief priest of the Persian fire-worshipers. Also **ar·chi·ma·gus** (är′kə·mā′gəs). [<ARCHI- + Gk. *magos* magician]

ar·chi·man·drite (är′kə·man′drīt) *n.* In the Greek Orthodox Church: **1** The head of a monastery or of several monasteries. **2** A title of honor granted to distinguished celibate priests. [<L *archimandrita* <LGk. *archimandritēs* <*archi-* chief + *mandra* enclosure, monastery]

Ar·chim·bald (är′khim·bält) German form of ARCHIBALD.

Ar·chi·me·de·an (är′kə·mē′dē·ən, -mə·dē′ən) *adj.* Of, discovered by, or pertaining to Archimedes.

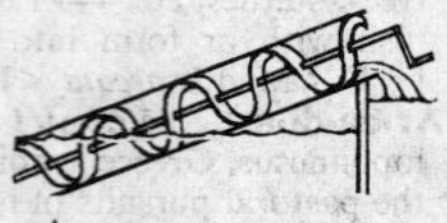

ARCHIMEDEAN SCREW

Archimedean screw *Mech.* A spiral conduit about an inclined axis, for raising liquid by rotation. Also **Archimedes′ screw.**

Ar·chi·me·des (är′kə·mē′dēz), 287?–212 B.C., Greek mathematician; born in Sicily.

ar·chi·mime (är′kə·mīm) *n.* In ancient Rome, the actor who impersonated the leading roles of satirical dramas.

ar·chine (är·shēn′) *n.* A Russian unit of linear measure, about 28 inches long.

arch·ing (är′ching) *n.* **1** An arch or series of arches. **2** The building of arches. **3** Any curve.

ar·chi·pel·a·go (är′kə·pel′ə·gō) *n. pl.* **·goes** or **·gos** A sea studded with many islands, or the islands collectively. [<Ital. *arcipelago,* ult. <Gk. *archi-* chief + *pelagos* sea; orig., with ref. to the Aegean Sea] — **ar·chi·pe·lag·ic** (är′kə·pə·laj′ik) *adj.*

Ar·chi·pel·a·go (är′kə·pel′ə·gō) The ancient name for the AEGEAN SEA.

Ar·chi·pen·ko (är′ki·peng′kō), **Alexander,** 1887–1964, Russian sculptor.

ar·chi·pho·neme (är′ki·fō′nēm) *n. Ling.* The total of relevant features common to two phonemes after neutralization.

ar·chi·plasm (är′kə·plaz′əm) *n. Biol.* The permanent substance of the spindle fibers and astral rays of the cell, dispersed in the form of granules: originally called *archoplasm.*

ar·chi·tect (är′kə·tekt) *n.* **1** One whose profession is to design and draw up the plans for buildings, etc., and supervise their construction. **2** One who devises, plans, or creates anything. [<L *architectus* <Gk. *architektōn* <*archi-* chief + *tektōn* worker]

ar·chi·tec·ton·ic (är′kə·tek·ton′ik) *adj.* **1** Pertaining to architecture; constructive. **2** *Philos.* Relating to the scientific classification of knowledge. Also **ar′chi·tec·ton′i·cal.** [<L *architectonicus* <Gk. *architektonikos* <*architektōn.* See ARCHITECT.]

ar·chi·tec·ton·ics (är′kə·tek·ton′iks) *n. pl.* (construed as singular) **1** The science of architecture. **2** *Philos.* The scientific arrangement and construction of systems of knowledge. **3** Structural design, as in works of music or art.

ar·chi·tec·ture (är′kə·tek′chər) *n.* **1** The science, art, or profession of designing and constructing buildings or other structures. **2** A style or system of building: Gothic *architecture.* **3** Construction or structure generally; any ordered arrangement of the parts of a system: the *architecture* of the universe. **4** A building, or buildings collectively. [<F <L *architectura* <*architectus.* See ARCHITECT.] — **ar′chi·tec′tur·al** *adj.* — **ar′chi·tec′tur·al·ly** *adv.*

ar·chi·trave (är′kə·trāv) *n. Archit.* **1** A chief beam; that part of an entablature which rests upon the column heads and supports the frieze. See illustration under ENTABLATURE. **2** A molded ornament, as of an arch; the archivolt, or the ornament skirting the head and sides of a door or window. [<F <Ital. <*archi-* chief (<Gk.) + *trave* beam <L *trabs*]

ar·chi·val (är·kī′vəl) *adj.* Of, pertaining to, or contained in archives.

ar·chives (är′kīvz) *n. pl.* **1** A place where public records and historical documents are kept. **2** Public records, documents, etc., as kept in such a depository. See synonyms under HISTORY. [<F *archives,* pl. of *archif* <L *archivum* <Gk. *archeion* a public office <*archē* government]

ar·chi·vist (är′kə·vist) *n.* A keeper of archives.

ar·chiv·ol·o·gy (är′kiv·ol′ə·jē) *n.* The science of maintaining and cataloging public documents. — **ar′chiv·ol′o·gist** *n.*

ar·chi·volt (är′kə·vōlt) *n. Archit.* **1** An ornamental molding following the outer curve of an arch. **2** An arch considered as supporting superincumbent weight. Also **ar′chi·vault** (-vôlt). [<Ital. *archivolto* an arched vault]

arch·let (ärch′lit) *n.* A little arch.

ar·chon (är′kon) *n.* **1** One of the nine chief magistrates of ancient Athens. **2** One of various magistrates or other officials in the Byzantine empire and modern Greece. **3** Any ruler or supreme commander. [<Gk. *archōn* <*archein* rule]

ar·chon·ship (är′kon·ship) *n.* The office or official term of an archon. Also **ar·chon·tate** (är′kən·tāt).

ar·cho·plasm (är′kə·plaz′əm) See ARCHIPLASM.

arch·priest (ärch′prēst′) *n.* **1** Formerly, the chief or senior priest of a cathedral chapter, serving as assistant to a bishop: later called a *dean.* **2** A rural dean. **3** A papal delegate appointed in 1598 as superior of Roman Catholic clergy in England: succeeded in 1623 by a vicar apostolic. — **arch′priest′hood, arch′priest′ship** *n.*

arch·way (ärch′wā′) *n.* An entrance or passage under an arch.

-archy *combining form* Rule; government: *heptarchy,* government by seven. [<Gk. *-archia* <*archos* ruler]

Ar·ci·bal·do (är′chē·bäl′dō) Italian form of ARCHIBALD.

ar·ci·form (är′sə·fôrm) *adj.* Shaped like an arc or bow. [<L *arcus* bow + -FORM]

arc light A lamp in which light of high intensity is produced between two adjacent electrodes connected with a powerful source of electricity. Also **arc lamp.**

ar·co·graph (är′kə·graf, -gräf) *n.* An instrument for drawing curves without striking them from a center point. [<L *arcus* arc + -GRAPH]

Ar·co·le (är′kō·lā) A village in northern Italy; scene of Napoleon's victory over the Austrians, 1796.

Ar·cot (är·kot′) A town in east central Madras state, India.

Arc·tal·pine (ärk·tal′pin) *adj.* **1** *Geog.* Of or pertaining to northern regions beyond the limits of tree growth; also, to mountain heights above the timber line. **2** *Ecol.* Designating those plant and animal forms which live beyond or above the limits of tree growth.

arc·tic (ärk′tik, är′tik) *adj.* **1** Pertaining to, suitable for, or characteristic of the North Pole or the regions, etc., near it. **2** Extremely cold; frigid. — *n.* **1** The region around the North Pole. **2** The Arctic Circle. **3** *pl. U.S.* Warm, waterproof overshoes. [Earlier *artik* <OF *artique* <L *articus, arcticus* <Gk. *arktikos* of the Bear (the northern constellation *Ursa Major*), northern <*arktos* bear]

Arctic Archipelago A north Canadian island group in the Arctic Ocean, comprising most of Franklin District, Northwest Territories. Also **Arctic Islands.**

Arctic char A salmonoid fish *(Salvelinus alpinus)* of Canada and Europe.

Arctic Circle The boundary of the North Frigid Zone, 23° 28′ from the North Pole.

Arctic Ocean An almost landlocked sea north of the Arctic Circle and surrounding the North Pole; 5,440,000 square miles.

Arc·tu·rus (ärk·tŏŏr′əs, -tyŏŏr′-) One of the 20 brightest stars, 0.24 magnitude and of an orange color; Alpha in the constellation Boötes. See STAR. [<L <Gk. *Arktouros* guardian of the bear <*arktos* a bear + *ouros* a guard]

ar·cu·ate (är′kyŏŏ·it, -āt) *adj.* Bent or curved like a bow; arched. Also **ar′cu·at′ed.** [<L *arcuatus,* pp. of *arcuare* curve like a bow <*arcus* a bow]

ar·cu·a·tion (är′kyŏŏ·ā′shən) *n.* **1** The act of curving or bending, or the state of being bent. **2** *Archit.* The use of arches; arched work.

ar·cus (är′kəs) *n. Meteorol.* A cloud resembling an arch: seen usually in cumulonimbus clouds. [<L, arch]

-ard *suffix of nouns* One who does something to excess or who is to be disparaged: *drunkard, coward*; sometimes changed to *-art: braggart.* [<OF *-ard, -art* <G *-hard, -hart* hardy]

ar·deb (är′deb) *n.* A unit of capacity for dry measure, used in Egypt and neighboring Moslem countries, varying from about 4 quarts to 8 bushels. [<Arabic]

Ar·de·bil (är′də·bēl′) A city in Azerbaijan, NW Iran. Also **Ar′da·bil′.**

Ar·den (är′dən), **Forest of** Formerly, a large wooded tract in Warwickshire, England.

ar·den·cy (är′dən·sē) *n.* The quality of being ardent; ardor; intensity; warmth.

Ar·dennes (är·den′) A wooded plateau, mostly in SW Belgium, extending into NE France. Also **Ardennes Forest.**

ar·dent (är′dənt) *adj.* **1** Vehement in emotion or action; passionate; zealous; intense. **2** Red;

glowing; flashing. **3** On fire; burning. [< L *ardens, -entis,* ppr. of *ardere* burn] —**ar′dent·ly** *adv.* —**ar′dent·ness.** *n.*

Synonyms: burning, eager, excitable, fervent, fervid, fierce, fiery, glowing, hot, impassioned, inflammable, intense, keen, longing, passionate, sanguine, vehement. See EAGER[1]. *Antonyms:* apathetic, calm, cold, cool, dispassionate, frigid, icy, indifferent, listless, phlegmatic, stolid, stony.

ardent spirits Alcoholic distilled liquors.

ar·dor (är′dər) *n.* **1** Warmth or intensity of passion or affection; eagerness; vehemence; zeal. **2** Great heat, as of fire, sun, or fever. Also *Brit.* **ar′dour.** See synonyms under ENTHUSIASM, WARMTH. [< L, a flame, fire < *ardere* burn]

ar·du·ous (är′joo·əs) *adj.* **1** Involving great labor, hardship, or difficulty; difficult. **2** Toiling strenuously; energetic. **3** Steep; hard to climb or surmount. [< L *arduus* steep] —**ar′·du·ous·ly** *adv.* —**ar′du·ous·ness** *n.*

Synonyms: difficult, exhausting, hard, laborious, onerous, severe, toilsome, trying. *Hard* may be active or passive; a thing may be *hard* to do or *hard* to bear. *Arduous* is always active. That which is *difficult* may require labor, or simply skill and address, as a *difficult* problem or puzzle. That which is *arduous* always requires persevering toil. *Antonyms:* easy, facile, light, pleasant, slight, trifling, trivial.

are[1] (är) *v.* First, second, and third person plural, present indicative, of the verb BE: also used as second person singular. [OE (Northumbrian) *aron*]

are[2] (âr, är) *n.* A measure of area in the metric system comprising a square dekameter or one hundred square meters. See METRIC SYSTEM. [< F < L *area.* Doublet of AREA.]

ar·e·a (âr′ē·ə) *n. pl.* **ar·e·as;** *for def.* 6, *often* **ar·e·ae** (âr′i·ē) **1** Any open space. **2** A tract or portion of the earth's surface; region. **3** Superficial extent; total outside surface. See SQUARE MEASURE. **4** A yard of a building; areaway. **5** Figuratively, the extent of anything; scope. **6** *Anat.* A section of the cerebral cortex with a specific motor or sensory function. [< L, an open space of level ground. Doublet of ARE[2].] —**ar′e·al** *adj.*

area bombing The bombing of a general region with no attempt to hit specific targets within that region. Compare PATTERN BOMBING, PRECISION BOMBING.

area code A three-digit number that identifies one of the telephone areas into which the United States is divided.

area fire Artillery fire or bombing designed to cover an entire area, either all at once or by part: distinguished from *precision fire.*

area rule *Aeron.* A design principle for improving the performance of supersonic air-craft by narrowing the fuselage in the area where the wings are attached.

area target A target for artillery fire or bombing that extends over a large area. Compare POINT TARGET.

ar·e·a·way (âr′ē·ə·wā′) *n.* **1** A small sunken court before basement windows or passageway to a basement door. **2** A passageway, as from one building or part of a building to another.

ar·e·ca (ar′i·kə, ə·rē′kə) *n.* **1** Any tree of a genus *(Areca)* of tropical palms, including the betel nut palm. **2** The fruit of such a tree. [< Pg. < Malayalam *ādekka*]

A·re·ci·bo (ä′rā·sē′bō) A port of NW Puerto Rico.

ar·e·ic (ar′ē·ik) *adj. Geog.* Pertaining to or designating a region of the earth contributing little or no surface drainage, as the Sahara. [< L *arere* be dry]

a·re·na (ə·rē′nə) *n.* **1** The central space for contestants in a Roman amphitheater. **2** Any place like this: The football players came into the *arena.* **3** A sphere of action or contest. [< L, sand, sandy place]

ar·e·na·ceous (ar′ə·nā′shəs) *adj.* **1** Pertaining to or like sand. **2** Full of or growing in sand; sandy. [< L *arenaceus* < *arena* sand]

arena theater A stage in the center of a room or auditorium, surrounded by seats and with out proscenium: also called *theater-in-the-round, central staging.*

ar·ene (ar′ēn) *n. Chem.* Any compound belonging to the class of aromatic hydrocarbon compounds. [< AR(OMATIC) + -ENE]

ar·e·nic·o·lous (ar′ə·nik′ə·ləs) *adj.* Living in sand. [< L *arena* sand + *colere* dwell]

aren't (ärnt) A contraction of *are not.* ◆ **Aren't I?** is condoned as a genteel colloquial substitute for the illiterate *Ain't I?,* though it is at variance with grammar.

areo- *combining form* Mars: *areography.* [< Gk. *Arēs*]

ar·e·o·cen·tric (âr′ē·ō·sen′trik) *adj.* Having reference to the planet Mars as a center or origin.

ar·e·og·ra·phy (âr′ē·og′rə·fē) *n.* A description of the physical features of the planet Mars.

a·re·o·la (ə·rē′ə·lə) *n. pl.* **·lae** (-lē) or **·las 1** *Bot.* A small space or interstice in a network of veins or vessels, as on leaves. **2** *Anat.* The colored circle about a nipple or about a vesicle; a depressed spot. Also **a·re·ole** (âr′ē·ōl). [< L, dim. of *area* open space] —**a·re′o·lar** *adj.*

areolar tissue *Anat.* Connective tissue composed of loose meshes of fibers enclosing irregular cavities; cellular tissue.

a·re·o·late (ə·rē′ə·lit, -lāt) *adj.* Marked off into areolae. Also **a·re′o·lat·ed.**

a·re·o·la·tion (ə·rē′ə·lā′shən) *n.* **1** The state of being areolate. **2** The arrangement of areolae. **3** A space containing areolae.

ar·e·ol·o·gy (âr′ē·ol′ə·jē) *n.* The scientific study of the planet Mars in all its aspects.

ar·e·om·e·ter (âr′ē·om′ə·tər) *n.* A hydrometer. [< Gk. *araios* thin + -METER]

Ar·e·op·a·gite (ar′ē·op′ə·jīt, -gīt) *n.* A member of the court of the Areopagus.

Ar·e·op·a·gus (ar′ē·op′ə·gəs) A hill NW of the Acropolis on which the highest court of ancient Athens held its sessions; hence, the court itself. [< L < Gk. *Areiopagos* < *Arēs* Mars + *pagos* hill]

A·re·qui·pa (ä′rä·kē′pä) A city in southern Peru.

Ar·es (âr′ēz) In Greek mythology, the god of war: identified with the Roman *Mars.*

a·rête (ə·rāt′) *n. Geog.* A sharp mountain spur or ridge. [< F < L *arista* awn of wheat, fishbone]

ar·e·thu·sa (ar′ə·thoo′zə, -sə) *n.* Any plant of a bulbous genus *(Arethusa)* of North American orchids, having a leafless or one-leaved scape and rose-colored flowers.

Ar·e·thu·sa (ar′ə·thoo′zə, -sə) In Greek mythology, a nymph who was changed into a fountain so that she might escape her pursuer Alpheus.

A·re·ti·no (ä′rā·tē′nō), **Pietro,** 1492–1556, Italian poet and courtier.

A·rez·zo (ä·ret′sō) A town in central Italy: ancient *Arretium.*

Ar·gae·us (är·jē′əs) The ancient name for ERCIYAS DAGI. Also **Ar·gæ′us.**

ar·gal[1] (är′gəl) See ARGOL.

ar·gal[2] (är′gəl) See ARGALI.

ar·gal[3] (är′gəl) *conj. Obs.* Therefore. [Alter. of L *ergo*]

ar·ga·la (är′gə·lə) *n.* **1** An adjutant bird. **2** A marabou. [< Hind. *hargīlā*]

ar·ga·li (är′gə·lē) *n. pl.* **·lis** or **·li 1** An Asiatic wild sheep *(Ovis ammon)* with large, thick, horns curved spirally **2** Any of several other wild sheep, as the **bearded argali** or aoudad; the **American argali** or big horn. [< Mongolian]

ARGALI
(4 feet tall at the shoulder; horn spread, about 3 feet)

Ar·gall (är′gôl, -gəl), **Sir Samuel,** died 1625, English mariner.

Ar·gand (ár·gän′), **Aimé,** 1755–1803, Swiss physician and chemist.

Argand burner (är′gənd) An oil or gas burner having a cylindrical wick supplied with air within as well as without to provide a maximum area of contact between the fuel and the flame. [after A. *Argand*]

Argand lamp A lamp using an Argand burner.

ar·gent (är′jənt) *n.* **1** *Her.* The white color of armorial bearings, symbolic of purity, innocence, etc. **2** Silver. **3** Silvery quality or color; whiteness. —*adj.* Like or made of silver; white; silvery: also **ar·gen·tal** (är·jen′təl). [< F < L *argentum* silver] —**ar·gen·te·ous** (är·jen′tē·əs).

ar·gen·tan (är′jən·tən) *n.* German silver. [< L *argentum* silver]

Ar·gen·tan (är·zhän·tän′) A town in Normandy, NW France; scene of a strategic battle of World War II, August, 1944.

ar·gen·tate (är′jən·tāt) *adj.* Silvery or shining white.

ar·gen·ta·tion (är′jən·tā′shən) *n.* A coating or plating with silver.

Ar·gen·teuil (är·zhän·tœ′y′) A city on the NW outskirts of Paris, France.

ar·gen·tic (är·jen′tik) *adj.* Containing or pertaining to silver, especially in its higher valence or ordinary proportion: *argentic* chloride, AgCl.

ar·gen·tif·er·ous (är′jən·tif′ər·əs) *adj.* Containing or producing silver: *argentiferous* ore.

Ar·gen·ti·na (är′jən·tē′nə) A republic of southern South America between the Andes and the Atlantic; 1,073,699 square miles; capital, Buenos Aires. Also **Argentine Republic** or **the Argentine.**

ar·gen·tine (är′jən·tin, -tīn) *n.* **1** Silver-white metal. **2** A precipitate of tin and zinc. **3** A pearly calcite. **4** The silvery substance obtained from fish scales and used in making artificial pearls. **5** Silver. —*adj.* Silvery. [< F *argentin* < < *argentum* silver]

Ar·gen·tine (är′jən·tēn, -tīn) *adj.* Of or pertaining to Argentina. —*n.* A native or citizen of Argentina. —**Ar·gen·tin·an** (är′jən·tin′·ē·ən) *n.*

ar·gen·tite (är′jən·tīt) *n.* An isometric, lead-gray, sectile silver sulfide, Ag₂S; silver glance; argyrite. [< L *argentum* silver + -ITE]

ar·gen·tol (är′jən·tōl, -tol) *n.* A silver salt, C₉N₅N(OH)SO₃Ag, used as an antiseptic and astringent. [< L *argentum* silver + -OL]

ar·gen·tous (är·jen′təs) *adj.* Of or pertaining to a compound containing univalent silver.

ar·gen·tum (är·jen′təm) *n. Chem.* Silver. [< L]

Ar·ges (är′jesh) A river of southern Rumania, flowing SE 180 miles to the Danube.

ar·gil (är′jil) *n.* **1** Potters' clay; white clay. **2** Aluminite. [< F *argile* < L *argilla* white clay < Gk. *argilla* < *argos* white] —**ar·gil·lif·er·ous** (är′jə·lif′ər·əs) *adj.*

ar·gil·la·ceous (är′jə·lā′shəs) *adj.* Containing, consisting of, or like clay; clayey.

ar·gil·lite (är′jə·līt) *n.* An argillaceous sedimentary rock, with or without slaty cleavage; mudrock: sometimes called *pelite* [< L *argilla* white clay + -ITE[1]]

ar·gil·lous (är·jil′əs) *adj.* Argillaceous; clayey.

ar·gi·nine (är′jə·nēn, -nin, -nīn) *n.* One of the amino acids essential to nutrition, C₆H₁₄O₂N₄, obtained from animal and vegetable proteins by hydrolysis or bacterial action. [< L *argentum* silver + -INE[2]]

Ar·gi·nu·sae (är′jə·noo′sē, -nyoo′-) The ancient name of three islands between Lesbos and Asia Minor; site of a naval battle in which the Athenians defeated the Spartans in 406 B.C. Also **Ar·gi·nu′sæ.**

Ar·give (är′jiv, -gīv) *adj.* **1** Of or pertaining to Argos or Argolis. **2** Greek. —*n.* **1** An inhabitant of Argos or Argolis. **2** A Greek, as in Homer.

ar·gle (är′gəl) *v.i. Scot.* To wrangle; argue. Also **ar′gle-bar′gle.**

Ar·go (är′gō) **1** In Greek legend, the ship in which Jason and the Argonauts sailed for the Golden Fleece. **2** *Astron.* A large southern constellation, the Ship, now generally divided into four parts.

ar·gol (är′gəl) *n.* Crude cream of tartar: the base of tartaric acid: also spelled *argal.* [ME *argoile*; origin unknown]

Ar·go·lis (är′gə·lis) A region of Greece in the NE Peloponnesus around the city of Argos, bordering on the **Gulf of Argolis,** an inlet of the Aegean.

ar·gon (är′gon) *n.* An inert gaseous element (symbol Ar, atomic number 18), constituting about 0.94% of the atmosphere. See PERIODIC TABLE. [< NL < Gk., neuter of *argos* idle, inert]

ar·go·naut (är′gə·nôt) *n. Zool.* The paper nautilus.

Ar·go·naut (är′gə·nôt) *n.* **1** In Greek legend, one who sailed with Jason in the ship Argo to find the Golden Fleece. **2** A gold-seeker who went to California in 1849. [< L *Argonauta* < Gk. *Argonautēs* < *Argo,* the ship + *nautēs* sailor] —**ar′go·nau′tic** *adj.*

Ar·gonne (är′gon, *Fr.* år·gôn′) A wooded ridge in northern France; site of several major battles of World War I. Also **Argonne Forest.**

Ar·gos (är′gos, -gəs) A city of NE Peloponnesus, traditionally the oldest city in Greece.

ar·go·sy (är′gə·sē) *n. pl.* **·sies 1** A large merchant ship. **2** A fleet of merchant vessels. [Earlier *ragusy* < *Ragusa,* Italian port which carried on extensive trade with England in the 16th C.]

ar·got (är′gō, -gət) *n.* **1** The secret language of the underworld. **2** The phraseology peculiar to any class or group. [< F] —**ar·got·ic** (är·got′ik) *adj.*

ar·gue (är′gyōō) *v.* **ar·gued, ar·gu·ing** *v.i.* **1** To urge reasons to support or contest a measure or opinion; reason. **2** To dispute or quarrel: Are you trying to *argue* with me? **3** To reason in opposition; raise objections: Don't stand there *arguing*—do as I say! —*v.t.* **4** To urge reasons for or against; discuss, as a proposal. **5** To contend or maintain, as by giving reasons: to *argue* that all men are equal. **6** To prove or indicate, as from evidence: His manner of speaking *argued* a good education. **7** To influence or convince, as by argument: to *argue* someone into buying a house. [< OF *arguer* < L *argutare,* freq. of *arguere* make clear, prove] —**ar′gu·a·ble** *adj.* —**ar·gu·er** *n.*

Synonyms: debate, demonstrate, discuss, dispute, prove, question, reason. To *argue* is to show the reasons for or against, so as to make a matter clear by reasoning; to *discuss* is to shake a matter apart for examination or analysis: One may *argue* or *discuss* a matter by himself; or with advocates, to make all clear; or with opponents, to *prove* his position and answer objections. We *argue* a case, *dispute* a bill. One side may do all the *arguing*; in *debating* both sides take part. See DISPUTE, PLEAD, REASON.

ar·gu·fy (är′gyə·fī) *v.* **·fied, ·fy·ing** *Colloq.* or *Dial.*—*v.t.* **1** To worry with arguing. —*v.i.* **2** To signify. **3** To argue, especially obstinately or merely for the sake of the argument. [< ARGUE + -FY]

ar·gu·ment (är′gyə·mənt) *n.* **1** A reason offered for or against something. **2** Something offered in proof; evidence. **3** A process of reasoning to establish or refute a position by the use of evidence; demonstration. **4** A contest in reasoning; debate; discussion. **5** *Logic* The middle term of a syllogism. **6** The plot or gist of a literary work. **7** *Stat.* A number given on the margin of a table to facilitate finding any of the included values. **8** *Math.* An independent variable from which another quantity can be deduced or on which its calculation depends. **9** *Obs.* The subject matter of a discourse or discussion; theme. See synonyms under REASON, REASONING. [< F < L *argumentum* < *arguere* make clear, prove]

ar·gu·men·ta·tion (är′gyə·men·tā′shən) *n.* **1** The methodical or logical setting forth of premises and the drawing of conclusions therefrom. **2** Interchange of argument; discussion; debate. **3** A sequence of arguments; process of reasoning.

ar·gu·men·ta·tive (är′gyə·men′tə·tiv) *adj.* Pertaining to, consisting of, or marked by argument; given to argumentation: an *argumentative* style. —**ar′gu·men′ta·tive·ly** *adv.* —**ar′gu·men′ta·tive·ness** *n.*

ar·gu·men·tum ad hom·i·nem (är′gyə·men′·təm ad hom′ə·nem) *Latin* Literally, an argument to the man; an argument addressed to feelings and prejudices rather than to reason.

Ar·gun (är′gōōn′) A river in NE Asia between the U.S.S.R. and Manchuria, flowing west 950 miles to the Shilka.

ar·gus (är′gəs) *n.* An East Indian pheasant (genus *Argus*).

Ar·gus (är′gəs) In Greek mythology, a giant with a hundred eyes: killed by Hermes, after which his eyes were put into the peacock's tail.

Ar·gus-eyed (är′gəs·īd′) *adj.* Sharp-sighted; vigilant.

ar·gute (är·gyōōt′) *adj.* **1** Quick or subtle; sharp; shrewd. **2** Shrill of sound. **3** *Bot.* Sharp-toothed, as a serrate leaf. [< L *argutus,* pp. of *arguere* make clear, prove]

Ar·gyle plaid (är′gīl) Plaid design of solid blocks or diamonds overlaid by a contrasting plaid. [from the tartan of the clan Campbell of *Argyll*]

Ar·gyll (är·gīl′) A country of western Scotland; 3,110 square miles. Also **Ar·gyll·shire** (är·gīl′·shir).

Ar·gyll (är·gīl′), **Duke of,** 1845–1914, John Douglas Sutherland Campbell, governor general of Canada 1878–83.

ar·gyr·o·dite (är·jir′ə·dīt) *n.* A steel-gray metallic silver mineral, Ag_6GeS_5, that crystallizes in the monoclinic system. [< Gk. *argyrōdēs* rich in silver < *argyros* silver]

Ar·gy·rol (är′jə·rōl, -rol) *n.* A compound of silver oxide and a protein, used as a local antiseptic in membranous infections: a trade name. [< Gk. *argyros* silver + -OL]

a·ri·a (ä′rē·ə, âr′ē·ə) *n.* **1** An air; melody. **2** An elaborate solo for single voice, as in an opera or oratorio, often with instrumental accompaniment. [< Ital. < L *aer* air]

-aria *suffix* Used in forming new Latin names, especially in zoological and botanical classifications. [< NL < L *-arius*]

Ar·i·ad·ne (ar′ē·ad′nē) In Greek mythology, the daughter of Minos and Pasiphae, who gave Theseus the thread by which he found his way out of the Labyrinth: when he fled Crete, Theseus took her with him, but later abandoned her on Naxos.

Ar·i·an (âr′ē·ən) *adj.* Of or pertaining to Arius or Arianism. —*n.* A believer in Arianism.

Ar·i·an (âr′ē·ən, ar′-, är′yən) See ARYAN.

-arian *suffix* Used in forming adjectives and adjectival nouns denoting occupation, age, sect, beliefs, etc.: *nonagenarian, predestinarian.* [< L *-arius* -ary + *-anus* -an]

Ar·i·an·ism (âr′ē·ən·iz′əm) *n.* The doctrines of Arius (fourth century) and his followers, denying that Christ is one substance with the Father.

A·ri·ca (ä·rē′kä) A port in northern Chile.

ar·id (ar′id) *adj.* **1** Parched with heat; dry. **2** Unfruitful; barren. **3** Without interest; dull. **4** Profitless. [< L *aridus* < *arere* be dry] —**a·rid·i·ty** (ə·rid′ə·tē), **ar′id·ness** *n.* —**ar′id·ly** *adv.*

ar·i·el (âr′ē·əl) *n.* An African gazelle *(Gazella dama).* Also **ariel gazelle.** [< Arabic *aryal*]

Ar·i·el (âr′ē·əl) A masculine personal name. [< Hebrew, lion of God]

—**Ariel** In medieval folklore, a spirit of the air.

—**Ariel** In Shakespeare's *Tempest,* an airy spirit employed by Prospero.

Ar·i·el (âr′ē·əl) The inner satellite of Uranus.

Ar·ies (âr′ēz, âr′ē·iz) **1** *Astron.* A constellation, the Ram. **2** In astrology, the first sign of the zodiac, which the sun enters on or about March 21st, the vernal equinox. See CONSTELLATION. [< L, the Ram]

ar·i·et·ta (ar′ē·et′ə) *n.* A short aria. Also **ar·i·ette** (ar′ē·et′). [< Ital.]

a·right (ə·rīt′) *adv.* In a right way; correctly; rightly; exactly.

A·ri·ka·ra (ə·rē′kər·ə) *n.* A member of a North American Indian tribe of Caddoan linguistic stock, formerly inhabiting the Dakotas.

ar·il (ar′il) *n. Bot.* An accessory covering of a seed, orginating at or around the funiculus, [< NL *arillus* < Med. L *arilli* dried grapes] —**ar·il·late** (ar′ə·lāt), **ar′il·lat′ed** *adj.*

ar·il·lode (ar′ə·lōd) *n. Bot.* A false aril; an outgrowth originating at or around the micropyle. [< NL *arillus* (see ARIL) + -ODE[2]]

Ar·i·ma·the·a (ar′ə·mə·thē′ə) A town of ancient Palestine, the home of Joseph, a disciple of Jesus, *Matt.* xxvii 57. Also **Ar′i·ma·thae′a.** —**Ar′·i·ma·the′an** *adj.*

A·rim·i·num (ə·rim′ə·nəm) The ancient name for RIMINI.

A·ri·on (ə·rī′on) Greek poet and musician of Lesbos, about 700 B.C.; reputed inventor of dithyrambic poetry.

ar·iose (ar′ē·ōs, ar′ē·ōs′) *adj. Music* Characteristic of a melody; songlike. [< Ital. *arioso* < *aria* air]

a·rio·so (ä·ryō′sō) *adj.* & *adv. Music* Of the nature or in the manner of both recitative and aria: said of a passage of dramatic or declamatory character emphasized by the libretto. [< Ital.]

A·ri·os·to (ä′rē·ôs′tō), **Lodovico,** 1474–1533, Italian poet.

-arious *suffix of adjectives* Connected with; pertaining to: *gregarious.* [< L *-arius* -ary + -OUS]

Ar·i·o·vis·tus (ar′ē·ō·vis′təs) Germanic chieftain of the first century B.C.; an opponent of Julius Caesar.

A·ri·pua·ña (ä′rē·pwa·nañ′) A river in western Brazil, flowing 400 miles north to the Madeira.

a·rise (ə·rīz′) *v.i.* **a·rose** (ə·rōz), **a·ris·en** (ə·riz′·ən), **a·ris·ing 1** To get up, as from a prone position. **2** To rise; ascend, as the sun above the horizon. **3** To spring forth; originate, as a river from its source. **4** To be born; come into being; appear. **5** *Poetic* To revive from death. [OE *ārisan* < *ā-* up + *rīsan* rise]

a·ris·ta (ə·ris′tə) *n. pl.* **·tae** (-tē) *Bot.* An awn or any similar bristly or beardlike appendage. [< L. Doublet of ARRIS.]

Ar·is·tae·us (ar′is·tē′əs) In Greek mythology, a son of Apollo, the tutelary deity of herdsmen and beekeepers. Also **Ar′is·tæ′us.**

Ar·is·tar·chus (ar′is·tär′kəs), 220–142 B.C., grammarian and critic of Alexandria.

—**Aristarchus of Samos** Greek astronomer of the third century B.C.

a·ris·tate (ə·ris′tāt) *adj. Bot.* Having a beard-like appendage; awned.

Ar·is·ti·des (ar′is·tī′dēz) Greek statesman and general in the fifth century B.C.: called "the Just."

Ar·is·tip·pus (ar′is·tip′əs), 435–366? B.C., Greek philosopher of Cyrene.

aristo- *combining form* Best, finest: *aristocracy.* [< Gk. *aristos*]

ar·is·toc·ra·cy (ar′is·tok′rə·sē) *n. pl.* **·cies 1** A hereditary nobility or privileged class, preeminent by birth or privilege and having prescriptive rank and rights. **2** The chief persons of a country; hence, any group preeminent in any way, as by virtue of wealth, talent, etc. **3** A state ruled by its best citizens. **4** The ruling class in such a state. [< L *aristocratia* < Gk. *aristokratia* < *aristos* best + *krateein* rule]

a·ris·to·crat (ə·ris′tə·krat, ar′is·tə·krat′) *n.* **1** A member of an aristocracy. **2** A proud and exclusive person. **3** One who prefers an aristocratic form of government. —**a·ris′to·crat′ic** or **·i·cal** *adj.* —**a·ris′to·crat′i·cal·ly** *adv.*

Ar·is·tol (ar′is·tōl, -tol) *n.* Proprietary name of a brand of thymol iodide. [< ARISTO- + -OL]

a·ris·to·lo·chi·a·ceous (ə·ris′tə·lō′kē·ā′shəs) *adj. Bot.* Belonging to a family *(Aristolochiaceae)* of tropical climbing plants with apetalous, irregular, pungent-smelling flowers. [< NL < L *aristolochia,* a plant deemed useful in childbirth < Gk. *aristolocheia* < *aristos* best + *locheia* childbirth]

Ar·is·toph·a·nes (ar′is·tof′ə·nēz), 450–380? B.C., Greek comic dramatist.

Ar·is·to·te·li·an (ar′is·tə·tē′lē·ən, -tə·tēl′yən, ə·ris′tə-) *adj.* Pertaining to or characteristic of Aristotle or his philosophy. —*n.* An adherent of Aristotle or of Aristotelianism.

Ar·is·to·te·li·an·ism (ar′is·tə·tē′lē·ən·iz′əm, -tēl′yən-, ə·ris′tə-) *n.* The philosophy or doctrines of Aristotle, especially as distinguished from Platonism by empirical or deductive reasoning.

Aristotelian logic 1 The deductive logic of Aristotle, characterized by the syllogism. **2** Logic considered from the standpoint of the form, rather than the content, of propositions.

Ar·is·tot·le (ar′is·tot′l), 384–322 B.C., Greek philosopher; pupil of Plato.

Aristotle's lantern *Zool.* The skeleton of the mouth parts of a sea urchin.

a·ris·to·type (ə·ris′tə·tīp) *n. Phot.* A print made on paper treated with mixed collodion and gelatin. [< ARISTO- + -TYPE]

a·ris·tu·late (ə·ris′chōō·lit, -lāt) *adj. Bot.* Having a small awn. [< L *arista* beard of grain]

ar·ith·man·cy (ar′ith·man′sē) *n.* Divination by numbers. [< Gk. *arithmos* number + *manteia* divination]

a·rith·me·tic (ə·rith′mə·tik) *n.* **1** The science of numbers and of computing with numbers under the four operations of addition, subtraction, multiplication, and division. **2** A treatise upon this science.

—**ar·ith·met·ic** (ar′ith·met′ik) *adj.* Of or pertaining to arithmetic: also **ar·ith·met′i·cal.**

[< L *arithmetica* < Gk. *(hē) arithmetikē (technē)* (the) counting (art) < *arithmeein* count, number < *arithmos* number] —**ar′ith·met′i·cal·ly** *adv.*

a·rith·me·ti·cian (ə·rith′mə·tish′ən, ar′ith-) *n.* One who uses or is skilled in arithmetic.

ar·ith·met·ic mean (ar′ith·met′ik) The sum of a group of measures, observations, magnitudes, scores, etc., divided by the total number of items in the group.

ar·ith·met·ic progression (ar′ith·met′ik) A sequence of terms such that each except the first differs from the preceding one by a constant quantity, either plus or minus, as 2, 4, 6, 8. See GEOMETRIC PROGRESSION. Also **arithmetical progression, arithmetic series, arithmetic sequence.**

a·rith·mo·ma·ni·a (ə·rith′mō·mā′nē·ə, -mān′yə) *n.* The impulse or desire to count everything. [< NL < Gk. *arithmos* number + -MANIA]

ar·ith·mom·e·ter (ar′ith·mom′ə·tər) *n.* A calculating machine.

-arium *suffix of nouns* **1** A place for: *herbarium.* **2** Connected with: *honorarium.* [< L < *-arius.* See -ARY.]

A·ri·us (ə·rī′əs, âr′ē·əs), 280?–336, Greek theologian; patriarch of Alexandria. See ARIANISM.

a ri·ve·der·ci (ä rē′vā·dâr′chē) *Italian* Until we meet again; so long.

Ar·i·zo·na (ar′ə·zō′nə) A State of the SW United States, bordering on Mexico; 113,909 square miles; capital, Phoenix; entered the Union Feb. 14, 1912; nickname *Apache State:* abbr. AZ — **Ar′i·zo′nan, Ar′i·zo′ni·an** (-nē-ən) *adj. & n.*

ark (ärk) *n.* **1** The ship of Noah (*Gen.* vi 14–22). **2** The chest containing the tables of the law (*Ex.* xxv 10): also called the **ark of the covenant. 3** The papyrus cradle of Moses (*Ex.* ii 3). **4** A flat-bottomed freight boat or scow; also, a large farm wagon. **5** *Dial.* A coffer, chest, or bin. ◆ *Homophone: arc.* [OE *arc* < L *arca* chest]

Ar·kan·san (är·kan′zən) *n.* A native or inhabitant of Arkansas.

Ar·kan·sas (är′kən·sô) **1** A State of the south central United States, just west of the Mississippi River; 53,102 square miles; capital, Little Rock; entered the Union June 15, 1836: nickname *Wonder State* or *Bear State:* abbr. AR **2** See QUAPAW.

Ar·kan·sas River (är′kən·sô, är·kan′zəs) A river rising in the Rocky Mountains of central Colorado and flowing SE 1,450 miles to the Mississippi in Arkansas.

Arkansas Traveler 1 Colonel Sandy Faulkner, 1803–74, an Arkansas cotton planter: alleged author of a famous dialog between a squatter and himself, the traveler. **2** Also, the dialog and the tune entitled *Arkansas Traveler.*

Ar·khan·gelsk (är·khän′gelsk) A city on the Dvina in NW Russian S.F.S.R.: also *Archangel.*

Ark·wright (ärk′rīt), **Sir Richard,** 1732–92, English cotton–manufacturer; invented the spinning jenny.

Arl·berg (ärl′berkh) An Alpine peak, 5,910 feet, in western Austria; winter sports center and site of the **Arlberg Tunnel,** 6⅜ miles.

Ar·len (är′lən), **Michael,** 1895–1956, English novelist born in Armenia: original name *Dikran Kouyoumdjian.*

arles (ärlz) *n. Brit. Dial.* **1** Money given in confirmation of a bargain: also **arles′–pen′ny. 2** An earnest or foretaste.

Arles (ärlz, *Fr.* árl) A city in SE France; site of Roman ruins. Ancient **Ar·e·las** (ar′ə·las).

Ar·ling·ton (är′ling·tən) An urban county of NE Virginia on the Potomac River opposite Washington, D.C.; site of a national cemetery containing the tomb of the Unknown Soldier.

Ar·liss (är′lis), **George,** 1868–1946, English actor.

Ar·lon (ár·lôn′) A city in SE Belgium, capital of Luxemburg province.

arm¹ (ärm) *n.* **1** *Anat.* **a** The upper limb of the human body, from the shoulder to the hand or wrist. **b** The part from the shoulder joint to the elbow joint. **2** The fore limb of vertebrates other than man. ◆ Collateral adjective: *brachial.* **3** An armlike part or appendage. **4** The part in contact with the

human arm: *arm* of a chair. **5** Anything branching out like an arm from the main body, or set apart or considered as a distinct part or branch; a subdivision: an *arm* of the sea. **6** *Naut.* **a** One of the projecting members of an anchor, ending in a fluke. **b** An end of a spar. **7** Strength to accomplish or aid; might: the *arm* of the law. — **arm in arm** With arms enlaced, as two persons walking together. — **at arm's length** At a distance, so as to keep from being friendly or intimate. — **with open arms** Cordially; warmly. [OE *arm, earm*]

arm² (ärm) *n.* **1** A weapon. **2** A distinct branch of the naval or military service: the air *arm.* — *v.t.* **1** To supply with instruments of warfare; equip, as with weapons or tools. **2** To make secure, as with a protective covering. — *v.i.* **3** To supply or equip oneself with weapons or other defensive means. **4** To supply oneself with the means necessary for an undertaking. [See ARMS]

ar·ma·da (är·mä′də, -mä′-) *n.* A fleet of warvessels. — **the Armada** The fleet sent against England by Spain in 1588. It was defeated by the English navy and almost entirely destroyed by storms: also called **Invincible Armada, Spanish Armada.** [< Sp. < L *armata* < *armare* arm. Doublet of ARMY.]

ar·ma·dil·lo (är′mə·dil′ō) *n. pl.* **·los** An American burrowing nocturnal mammal (family *Dasypodidae*) of the Edentate order, having an armorlike covering of jointed plates; especially, the nine–banded armadillo (*Dasypus novemcinctus*) of Mexico and Texas. [< Sp., dim. of *armado* armed < L *armatus,* pp. of *armare* arm]

ARMADILLO
(1 1/2 feet from head to tail;
tail about 1 foot)

Ar·ma·ged·don (är′mə·ged′n) **1** In Biblical prophecy, the scene of a great battle between the forces of good and evil, to occur at the end of the world. *Rev.* xvi 16. **2** Any great or decisive conflict. [< LL *Armagedon* < Gk. *Armageddon,* prob. < Hebrew *Megiddon* plain of Megiddo, a perennial battlefield]

Ar·magh (är·mä′) A county of Ulster province, southern Northern Ireland; 489 square miles; county seat, Armagh.

Ar·ma·gnac (ár·má·nyàk′) *n.* Brandy distilled from wine in the Armagnac region of SW France.

ar·ma·ment (är′mə·mənt) *n.* **1** A land or naval force. **2** The guns, munitions, and other military equipment of a fortification, military unit, airplane, vehicle, or vessel. **3** Equipment or the act of arming or equipping for war or battle. **4** The body of naval, air, and ground forces equipped for war, engaged in an expedition, or present in a given command area. **5** The aggregate of a nation's organized war power. See synonyms under ARMY. [< L *armamenta* implements, ship's tackle < *armare* arm]

Ar·mand (ár·män′) French form of HERMAN.

ar·ma·ture (är′mə·choor) *n.* **1** A piece of soft iron joining the poles of a magnet to prevent the loss of magnetic power. **2** *Electr.* **a** In a dynamo or motor, the cylindrical, laminated iron core carrying the coils of insulated wire to be revolved through the magnetic field. **b** The part of a relay, as a buzzer or bell, that vibrates when activated by a magnetic field. **3** *Biol.* **a** Protective covering for defense or offense, as the shells of animals, prickles on plants, etc. **b** A set of organs: the gastric *armature.* **4** *Archit.* Framing used to stiffen or brace. **5** In sculpture, a framework to support the clay or other substance used in modeling. **6** Arms; armor. — *v.t.* **·tured, ·tur·ing** To furnish or provide with an armature. [< F < L *armatura* armor < *armare* arm. Doublet of ARMOR.]

arm·band (ärm′band′) *n.* A brassard. Also **arm band.**

arm·chair (ärm′châr′) *n.* A chair with side supports for the arms or elbows.

armed (ärmd) *adj.* Equipped with arms; provided with or bearing weapons.

armed forces The combined military and naval forces of a nation; in the United States, the Army, Navy, Air Force, Marine Corps, and Coast Guard.

Ar·me·ni·a (är·mē′nē·ə, -mēn′yə) **1** A former kingdom of NE Asia Minor; generally understood to include eastern Turkey and the Armenian S.S.R. **2** A constituent republic (**Armenian S.S.R.**) of Transcaucasian U.S.S.R.; 11,500 square miles; capital, Erivan. *Armenian* **Ha·yas·dan** (hä′yäs·tän′, -dän′).

Ar·me·ni·an (är·mē′nē·ən, -mēn′yən) *adj.* Of or pertaining to the country, people, or language of Armenia. — *n.* **1** A native of Armenia. **2** The language of Armenia, belonging to the Armenian subfamily of Indo–European languages.

Ar·men·tières (ár·män·tyâr′) A town in northern France, near Lille; destroyed in heavy World War I fighting, 1918.

arm·er (är′mər) *n.* One who arms.

ar·met (är′met) *n.* A light steel helmet of the 15th and 16th centuries, with vizor and neckguard. [< F < OF *armette,* dim. of *arme* arm²]

arm·ful (ärm′fool′) *n. pl.* **·fuls** That which is held, or as much as can be held, in the arm or arms.

arm·hole (ärm′hōl′) *n.* An opening for the arm in a garment.

ar·mi·ger (är′mə·jər) *n.* **1** An armorbearer attending a knight; a squire. **2** A person entitled to bear heraldic arms. Also **ar·mig·e·ro** (är·mij′ə·rō). [< L < *arma* weapons + *gerere* bear]

ar·mil·lar·y (är′mə·ler′ē, är·mil′ə·rē) *adj.* Pertaining to or consisting of a ring or rings. [< L *armilla* arm ring, bracelet]

armillary sphere *Astron.* An arrangement of concentric rings in the form of a skeleton sphere, representing the relative positions of the ecliptic and other celestial circles.

arm·ing (är′ming) *n.* **1** The act of supplying with or taking arms. **2** That with which anything is armed. **3** *Naut.* Tallow on a sounding plummet to bring up matter from sea bottom. **4** *Her.* A coat of arms.

Ar·min·i·an·ism (är·min′ē·ən·iz′əm) *n. Theol.* The doctrines of Jacobus Arminius and his followers, opposed to Calvinism chiefly as holding a less rigorous view of predestination. — **Ar·min′i·an** *adj. & n.*

Ar·min·i·us (är·min′ē·əs) Latin form of HERMAN. — **Arminius,** 17 B.C.–A.D. 21, German national hero, defeated Roman governor Varus at battle of Teutoburger Wald, A.D. 9: sometimes called "Hermann."

Arminius, Jacobus, 1560–1609, Dutch Protestant theologian.

ar·mip·o·tent (är·mip′ə·tənt) *adj.* Mighty in arms. [< L *armipotens, -entis* < *arma* arms + *potens.* See POTENT.] — **ar·mip′o·tence** *n.*

ar·mi·stice (är′mə·stis) *n.* A temporary cessation, by mutual agreement, of hostilities; a truce. [< F < L *arma* arms + *stare* stand still]

Armistice Day See VETERANS DAY.

arm·let (ärm′lit) *n.* **1** A little arm, as of the sea. **2** An ornamental band worn around the upper arm. **3** A small, short sleeve. **4** *Archaic* A piece of armor for the arm.

ar·moire (är·mwär′) *n.* A large, movable, often ornate cabinet or cupboard; ambry. [< F < OF *aumoire* < L *armarium* a chest, orig., a place for storing arms]

ar·mor (är′mər) *n.* **1** A defensive covering, as of mail for a warrior, or of metallic plates for a war vessel, a tank, a deep–sea diver's suit, etc. **2** The aggregate of armored assault vehicles available to a military command. **3** *Biol.* The protective covering of various animals, as turtles, armadillos, and some fishes. See synonyms under ARMS. — *v.t. & v.i.* To furnish with or put on armor. Also *Brit.* **ar′mour.** [< OF *armeüre* < L *armatura.* Doublet of ARMATURE.]

ar·mor·bear·er (är′mər·bâr′ər) *n.* One bearing the arms of a warrior; a squire; armiger.

ar·mor–clad (är′mər·klad′) *adj.* Covered or plated with armor.

ar·mored (är′mərd) *adj.* **1** Protected by armor, as an automobile, a cruiser, or train. **2** Equipped with armored vehicles, as a military unit. Also *Brit.* **ar′moured.**

armored car 1 *Mil.* A motor vehicle protected by armor plate and used for reconnais-

sance, carrying ammunition or personnel, or as a self-propelled mount for machine-guns, anti-aircraft artillery, etc. **2** A small truck or other vehicle protected by light armor plate, used for transporting money, etc.

armored force A combination of tanks, armored cars, and other armored vehicles functioning as an offensive unit in modern warfare.

ar·mor·er (är′mər·ər) *n.* **1** A maker, repairer, or custodian of arms or armor. **2** A manufacturer of arms. **3** *Mil.* An enlisted man in charge of the repair, maintenance, and supply of small arms. Also *Brit.* **ar′mour·er.**

ar·mo·ri·al (är·môr′ē·əl, -mō′rē-) *adj.* Pertaining to heraldry or heraldic arms. —*n.* A treatise on heraldry.

Ar·mor·ic (är·môr′ik, -mor′-) *adj.* Of Armorica, its people, or their language. —*n.* Armorican.

Ar·mor·i·ca (är·môr′ə·kə, -mor′-) An ancient name for the NW part of France, later identified with Brittany.

Ar·mor·i·can (är·môr′ə·kən, -mor′-) *adj.* Armoric. —*n.* **1** A native or inhabitant of Armorica. **2** The language of Armorica, belonging to the Brythonic branch of Celtic languages; Breton. Also *Armoric.*

ar·mor-pierc·ing (är′mər·pir′sing) *adj.* Designating a type of projectile with a hard-shelled nose, designed to penetrate heavy armor and burst on the far side.

armor plate A protective covering of special high carbon steel alloy containing variable proportions of nickel, chrome, and manganese, forged under great pressure and given a hard surface. **—ar′mor-plat′ed** *adj.*

ar·mor·y[1] (är′mər·ē) *n. pl.* **·mor·ies 1** A place for the safekeeping of arms. **2** A building for the use of a body of militia, including general storage for arms and equipment, drill-rooms, etc. **3** *U.S.* A factory for making firearms. **4** *Archaic* Arms collectively; armor. **5** *Archaic* The craft or trade of the armorer. Also *Brit.* **ar′mour·y.** [Prob. < ARMOR]

ar·mor·y[2] (är′mər·ē) *n. Archaic* **1** Armorial bearings; heraldic arms. **2** Heraldry; the science of blazoning arms. [< OF *armoirie* < *armoier* blazoner < *armoier* blazon, publish a coat of arms]

ar·mour (är′mər), etc. See ARMOR, etc.

Ar·mour (är′mər), **Philip Danforth,** 1832–1901, U.S. meat packer.

ar·mo·zine (är′mə·zēn′) *n. Archaic* A plain silk, often used for clerical robes, etc. Also **ar′mo·zeen′** [< F *armoisin*]

arm·pit (ärm′pit′) *n.* The cavity under the arm at the shoulder; axilla.

arms (ärmz) *n. pl.* **1** Weapons collectively. **2** Warfare. **3** The official insignia or device of a state, person, or family. **4** Heraldic symbols. —**small arms** Firearms of small caliber, carried by hand, as pistols, rifles, machine-guns, etc. **—to arms!** Arm yourselves! Make ready for battle! **—to bear arms 1** To be provided with arms. **2** To serve as a member of the armed forces. **—under arms** Provided with weapons; ready for war. **—up in arms** Aroused and ready to fight. [< F *armes* < L *arma* weapons]

Synonyms: armor; weapons. *Arms* are implements of attack; *armor* is a defensive covering. Any vessel provided with cannon is an *armed* vessel; an *armored* ship is steel-clad. Anything that can be wielded in fight may be a *weapon; arms* are especially made and designed for conflict.

Arm·strong (ärm′strông, -strong), **Edwin Howard,** 1890–1954, U.S. electrical engineer. **—Neil Alden,** born 1930, U.S. astronaut; first man to walk on the moon, July 20, 1969. **—William George,** 1810–1900, Baron Armstrong of Cragside, English inventor and industrialist.

ar·mure (är′myŏŏr) *n.* A twilled fabric woven in ridges to resemble chain mail. [< F < OF *armeüre.* See ARMOR.]

ar·my (är′mē) *n. pl.* **ar·mies 1** A large organized body of men armed for military service on land. **2** The largest organized autonomous unit of the U.S. land forces, consisting of a headquarters, a variable number of corps, and auxiliary troops and trains: also called **field army. 3** Any large, united body: an *army* of ants. **4** A host. —**United States Army 1** The U.S. land military forces administered by the Department of the Army under the Department of Defense and including the Regular Army, the Army Reserve, and the National Guard of the United States. **2** Loosely, the Regular Army. [< OF *armee* < L *armata.* Doublet of ARMADA.]

Synonyms: armament, force, forces, host, legions, military, multitude, phalanx, soldiers, soldiery, troops. *Host* is used for any vast and orderly assemblage; as, the stars are called the heavenly *host. Multitude* expresses number without order or organization. Organization and unity rather than numbers are the essentials of an *army. Legion* and *phalanx* are applied by a kind of poetic license to modern *forces*; the plural *legions* is preferred to the singular. Any organized body of men by whom law is executed is a *force.*

Ar·my (är′mē) *n.* The total military land forces of a specified country, exclusive in some countries of the air forces: the British *Army,* the French *Army,* the American *Army,* etc.

Army Air Forces The air arm of the U.S. Army before establishment of the separate U.S. Air Force in 1947.

army ant A foraging ant.

army of occupation An army maintained in a defeated country to enforce the terms of surrender, keep the peace, etc.

Army of the United States 1 The body of personnel on active service in the United States Army, usually during wartime, composed of persons from the Regular Army appointed to a higher grade than their regular commissions, draftees, personnel or units of the Army Reserve and National Guard, and other components created for special purposes. **2** Loosely, United States Army.

army worm The larva of a moth (family *Phalaenidae*) which moves at times in vast destructive hosts, especially the larva of *Leucania unipuncta.*

ar·nat·to (är·nat·ō) *n.* Annatto.

Arne (ärn), **Thomas Augustine,** 1710–78, English composer.

Arn·hem (ärn′hem) The capital of Gilderland province on the lower Rhine, eastern Netherlands. *German* **Arn·heim** (ärn′him).

Arn·hem Land (är′nəm) A coastal region of Northern Territory, Australia; designated as an aboriginal reservation in 1931; about 31,200 square miles.

ar·ni·ca (är′ni·kə) *n.* **1** Any of a genus *(Arnica)* of widely distributed herbaceous perennials of the composite family, especially the common European arnica *(A. montana).* **2** A tincture prepared from the flower heads and roots of this herb, extensively used for sprains and bruises. [< NL]

Ar·no (är′nō) A river of central Italy, flowing 150 miles west to the Mediterranean.

Ar·nold (är′nəld, *Ger.* är′nôlt) A masculine personal name. Also *Fr.* **Ar·naud** (ȧr·nō′), *Ital.* **Ar·nol·do** (är·nôl′dō), *Sp.* **Ar·nal·do** (är·näl′dō). [< Gmc., eagle power]

—Ar·nold von Win·kel·ried (är′nôlt fôn ving′·kəl·rēt) Swiss hero said to have led the charge against the Austrians at the battle of Sempach, 1386.

Arnold, Benedict, 1741–1801, American Revolutionary general who became a traitor. **—Sir Edwin,** 1832–1904, English poet and Orientalist. **—Henry Harky,** 1886–1950, commanding general of United States Army Air Forces in World War II. **—Matthew,** 1822–88, English poet and critic. **—Thomas,** 1795–1842, English educator, father of preceding.

A·roe Islands (är′ōō) See ARU ISLANDS.

ar·oid (ăr′oid) *adj.* Araceous. Also **a·roi·de·ous** (ə·roi′dē·əs). —*n.* Any araceous plant. [< AR(UM) + -OID]

a·roint (ə·roint′) *v.i. Archaic* Avaunt! Begone!: used in the imperative, with reflexive *thee* or *ye.* Also **a·roynt′.** [Origin uncertain]

a·ro·ma (ə·rō′mə) *n.* **1** Fragrance, as from plants; agreeable odor. **2** Characteristic quality or style. [< L < Gk. *arōma* spice] **—a·ro·ma·tous** (ə·rō′mə·təs) *adj.*

ar·o·mat·ic (ar′ə·mat′ik) *adj.* **1** Having an aroma; fragrant; spicy. **2** *Chem.* Pertaining to a group of hydrocarbon compounds of the closed-ring formation and derived chiefly from benzene, as naphthalene: distinguished from *aliphatic.* Also **ar′o·mat′i·cal.** —*n.* **1** Any vegetable or drug of agreeable odor. **2** An aromatic chemical compound. **—ar′o·mat′i·cal·ly** *adv.*

a·ro·ma·tic·i·ty (ə·rō′mə·tis′ə·tē) *n. Chem.* The aromatic character of certain hydrocarbons as determined by their molecular structure rather than by their smell.

a·ro·ma·tize (ə·rō′mə·tīz) *v.t.* **·tized, ·tiz·ing 1** To make fragrant or aromatic. **2** *Chem.* To convert (an aliphatic hydrocarbon) into one of the aromatic group.

A·roos·took River (ə·rōōs′tŏŏk) A river in northern Maine, flowing east 140 miles to the St. John River.

Aroostook War A series of border skirmishes between citizens of Maine and of New Brunswick, leading to the settlement of the NE boundary of the United States in 1842.

a·rose (ə·rōz′) Past tense of ARISE.

A·rou·et (ȧ·rwe′), **François Marie** see VOLTAIRE.

a·round (ə·round′) *adv.* **1** So as to encompass or encircle all sides; in various directions. **2** So as to face the opposite way or different ways successively. **3** *U.S.* From place to place; here and there: to walk *around.* **4** *U.S. Colloq.* Nearby; in the vicinity: Wait *around* until I call. **5** In or to a particular place: Come *around* to see us again. **6** *U.S. Colloq.* Approximately; about: *around* fifty dollars. **—to come around 1** To revive; regain consciousness. **2** To become convinced, as of an opinion. **—to get around 1** To coax; wheedle; cajole. **2** To overcome; as an obstacle; hence, to evade or circumvent, as a law or rule. **—to get around to** To give attention to or accomplish: He'll *get around to* it in time. **—to have been around** *Colloq.* To be experienced in the ways of the world. —*prep.* **1** About the circuit of; encircling: to travel *around* the world. **2** In all or many directions about: a field of force *around* either magnetic pole. **3** On the other side of; to be reached or found by passing to the left or right of: the church *around* the corner. **4** Here and there in; in the region of; in various parts of: He wandered *around* the city. **5** Somewhere near or within: You'll find me *around* the house. **6** Approximately: The train leaves *around* midnight. [< A-[1] on + ROUND]

a·rous·al (ə·rou′zəl) *n.* An arousing; awakening.

a·rouse (ə·rouz′) *v.* **a·roused, a·rous·ing** *v.t.* **1** To stir up, as from sleep; awaken. **2** To excite, as to a state of high emotion; animate. —*v.i.* **3** To arouse oneself. See synonyms under ENCOURAGE, STIR. [< ROUSE, on analogy with *arise*]

a·row (ə·rō′) *adv.* In a row.

Arp (ärp), **Hans,** 1888–1966, German painter and sculptor: also **Jean Arp.**

Ar·pád (är′päd), died 907, Hungarian national hero.

ar·peg·gi·o (är·pej′·ē·ō, -pej′ō) *n. pl.* **·gi·os** *Music* **1** The sounding or playing of the notes of a chord in rapid succession instead of simultaneously, as in playing the harp. **2** A chord so played. [< Ital. < *arpeggiare* play on a harp < *arpa* a harp]

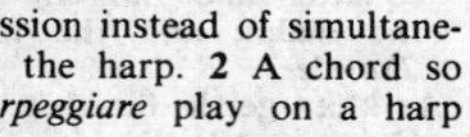

ARPEGGIO

ar·peg·gi·oed (är·pej′ē·ōd) *adj.* Sounded in the manner of an arpeggio.

ar·pent (är′pənt, *Fr.* ȧr·päṅ′) *n.* An old French measure of land, equivalent to about an acre: still used in Louisiana and in Quebec. Also **ar·pen** (är′pən). [< F]

ar·que·bus (är′kwə·bəs), etc. See HARQUEBUS, etc.

ar·rack (ar′ək) *n.* A strong Oriental liquor distilled from rice, molasses, etc. [< Arabic *'araq* sweat, juice]

ar·raign (ə·rān′) *v.t.* **1** *Law* To call into court and cause to answer to an indictment. **2** To call upon for an answer; accuse. —*n.* Accusation; indictment. [< AF *arainer,* OF *araisnier* < LL *arrationare* call to account < L *ad-* to + *ratio* reason] **—ar·raign′ment** *n.*

Synonyms (verb): accuse, censure, charge, cite, impeach, indict, summon. One may *charge* another with any fault, great or trifling, privately or publicly, formally or informally. *Accuse* suggests more of the formal and criminal. *Indict* and *arraign* apply strictly to judicial proceedings; an alleged criminal is *indicted* by the grand jury and *arraigned* before the court. *Censure* carries the idea of fault but not of crime; it may be private and individual, or public and official. A judge, a president, or other officer of high rank may be *impeached* before the appropriate

tribunal for high crimes; the veracity of a witness may be *impeached* by damaging evidence. One is arraigned *at* the bar, *before* the tribunal, *of* or *for* a crime, *on* or *upon* an indictment. *Antonyms*: acquit, condone, discharge, excuse, exonerate, forgive, overlook, pardon, release.

Ar·ran (ar'ən) An island in the Firth of Clyde, Buteshire, Scotland; 166 square miles.

ar·range (ə·rānj') *v.* **ar·ranged, ar·rang·ing** *v.t.* 1 To put in definite or proper order. 2 To adjust, as a conflict or dispute; settle. 3 To change or adapt, as a musical composition for other instruments or voices than those originally intended. —*v.i.* 4 To come to an agreement or understanding: often with *with.* 5 To see about the details; make plans: I was late, but he *arranged* accordingly. See synonyms under ADAPT, ADJUST, CLASSIFY, PREPARE, RANGE, REGULATE, SET, SETTLE. [< OF *arangier* < *a-* to (< L *ad-*) + *rangier* put in order < *rang* rank[1]. See RANK[1].]

ar·range·ment (ə·rānj'mənt) *n.* 1 An arranging or that which is arranged; disposition; order. 2 A preparation, measure, or plan. 3 Settlement, as of a dispute; adjustment. 4 The style in which something is arranged, as a stage scene or combination of colors; a system of parts arranged: the *arrangement* of a library or museum. 5 *Music* **a** The adaptation of a composition to other voices or instruments than those for which it was originally composed. **b** The composition so adapted.

Ar·ran Islands (ar'ən) See ARAN ISLANDS.

ar·rant (ar'ənt) *adj.* 1 Notoriously bad; unmitigated. 2 *Obs.* Wandering about. [Var. of ERRANT.] —**ar'rant·ly** *adv.*

ar·ras (ar'əs) *n.* 1 A tapestry. 2 A hanging for the walls of a room, especially one made of tapestry. [from *Arras*, France]

Ar·ras (ar'əs, *Fr.* à·räs') A city of northern France.

ar·ra·sene (ar'ə·sēn') *n.* An embroidery material of wool or silk. [< ARRAS]

ar·ras·tre (ä·räs'trā) *n.* 1 A crude apparatus for grinding and mixing ores. 2 In the Philippine Islands, lighterage, storage, and haulage, as of cargo. Also **ar·ras·tra** (ä·räs'trə). [< Sp.]

ar·ray (ə·rā') *n.* 1 Regular or proper order; arrangement, as for a battle, display, etc. 2 The persons or things arrayed, especially a military force. 3 Clothing; fine dress. 4 An orderly arrangement, as of brilliant objects, or a series of values in a statistical table. 5 In English history, the arming of militia: commission of *array.* —*v.t.* 1 To draw up in order of battle, as troops; set in order. 2 To adorn; dress, as for display. See synonyms under DRESS. [< AF *arai*, OF *arei* < *a-* to (< L *ad-*) + *rei* order < Gmc.]

ar·ray·al (ə·rā'əl) *n.* 1 The act or process of arraying; mustering of a force. 2 Anything arrayed; an array.

ar·rear·age (ə·rir'ij) *n.* 1 The state of being in arrears. 2 The amount in arrears. 3 *Rare* A thing kept in reserve.

ar·rear (ə·rir') *n.* 1 The state of being behind or behindhand, as with obligations, business, etc. 2 *Usually pl.* That which is behindhand; a part, as of a debt, overdue and unpaid. —**in arrears** (or **arrear**) Behind in meeting payment, fulfilling an obligation, etc. [< OF *arere* < L *ad-* to + *retro* backward]

ar·rest (ə·rest') *v.t.* 1 To stop suddenly; check, as the course, movement, or development of. 2 To take into custody by legal authority. 3 To attract and fix, as the attention; engage. —*n.* 1 An arresting or being arrested; especially, seizure by legal authority. 2 A device for arresting motion, as in a machine. [< OF *arester* < LL *arrestare* < L *ad-* to + *restare* stop, remain]
Synonyms (verb): apprehend, capture, catch, delay, hold, obstruct, restrain, secure, seize, stop. *Antonyms*: discharge, dismiss, free, liberate, release.

ar·rest·er (ə·res'tər) *n.* 1 One who or that which arrests. 2 In Scots law, one who makes an arrestment.

ar·rest·ing (ə·res'ting) *adj.* Notable; compelling attention.

arresting gear *Aeron.* A contrivance for bringing an airplane to an abrupt halt when landing in a small area, as on an aircraft carrier.

ar·rest·ment (ə·rest'mənt) *n.* 1 A stoppage, as of growth. 2 In Scots law, an attachment or garnishment of property or credits in the hands of a third party.

ar·rêt (ə·rā', ə·ret', *Fr.* à·re') *n. French* 1 An edict. 2 An arrest.

Ar·re·ti·um (ə·rē'shē·əm, -shəm) The ancient name for AREZZO.

Ar·rhe·ni·us (är·rā'nē·ōōs), **Svante A.,** 1859–1927, Swedish chemist.

ar·rhi·zal (ə·rī'zəl) *adj.* Rootless. Also **ar·rhi'zous** (-zəs). [< Gk. *arrhizos* < *a-* without + *rhiza* a root]

ar·rhyth·mi·a (ə·rith'mē·ə, ə·rith'-) *n. Pathol.* Irregularity of the heart or pulse. [< NL < Gk. *arrhythmia* lack of rhythm < *a-* without + *rhythmos* measure] —**ar·rhyth·mic** (ə·rith'mik, ə·rith'-) *adj.*

ar·ri·ère (ar'ē·âr, ə·rir') *n.* The rear: often used adjectively in the sense of dependent or subordinate: *arrière*-vassal. [< F. See ARREAR.]

ar·ri·ère-ban (ar'ē·âr·ban', *Fr.* à·ryâr·bän') *n.* 1 In the Middle Ages, the edict of a king summoning his vassals to military service. 2 The vassals thus summoned. [< F, ult. < OHG *hari, heri* army + *ban* edict]

ar·rière-guard (ə·rir'gärd') *n.* Rear guard. Also French **ar·rière-garde** (à·ryâr·gärd').

ar·rière-pen·sée (à·ryâr·pän·sā') *n. French* A mental reservation; concealed motive.

arrière tenant A tenant of a mesne lord.

ar·rie·ro (är·ryâ'rō) *n. Spanish* A muleteer.

Ar Ri·mal (är rē·mäl') See RUB AL KHALI.

ar·ris (ar'is) *n. Archit.* The sharp edge or ridge formed by the meeting of two surfaces, especially the sharp ridge between two channels of a Doric column. Also **ar'is.** [< OF *areste* < L *arista* awn, fishbone. Doublet of ARISTA.]

ar·ri·val (ə·rī'vəl) *n.* 1 The act of arriving. 2 One who or that which arrives or has arrived. See synonyms under ACCESSION.

ar·rive (ə·rīv') *v.i.* **ar·rived, ar·riv·ing** 1 To reach or come to a destination or place. 2 To come at length, by any stage or process: often with *at*: to *arrive* at an idea, fatherhood, etc. 3 To attain the circumstances of success or fame in the world. [< OF *ariver* < LL *arripare* come to shore < L *ad-* to + *ripa* shore]
Synonyms: attain, come, enter, land, reach. See ATTAIN. *Antonyms*: depart, embark, go, leave, start.

ar·ri·viste (à·rē·vēst') *n. French* A social climber or careerist.

ar·ro·ba (ä·rō'bä) *n.* 1 A liquid measure used in Spain, Mexico, etc., varying from 3.32 to 4.26 U.S. gallons. 2 A Spanish weight, equivalent to 25.37 pounds avoirdupois. 3 A Brazilian weight equivalent to 32.38 pounds avoirdupois. [< Sp. < Arabic *al-rub'* the quarter (part)]

Ar·roe Islands (är'rōō) See ARU ISLANDS.

ar·ro·gance (ar'ə·gəns) *n.* The quality or state of being arrogant; haughtiness; overbearing pride. Also **ar'ro·gan·cy.** [< OF < L *arrogantia.* See ARROGANT.]
Synonyms: assumption, assurance, disdain, haughtiness, insolence, presumption, pride, superciliousness, vanity. *Arrogance* claims much for itself and concedes little to others. *Pride* is an absorbing sense of one's own greatness. *Disdain* sees contemptuously the inferiority of others to oneself. *Presumption* claims place or privilege above one's right. *Assumption* quietly takes for granted superiority and privilege which others might or might not concede. *Vanity* intensely craves admiration and applause. *Superciliousness* silently manifests mingled *haughtiness* and *disdain. Insolence* is open and rude expression of contempt and hostility, generally from an inferior to a superior, as from a clerk to a customer. See ASSURANCE, IMPERTINENCE.

ar·ro·gant (ar'ə·gənt) *adj.* 1 Unduly or excessively proud; overbearing; haughty. 2 Characterized by or due to arrogance: *arrogant* proposals. See synonyms under DOGMATIC, IMPERIOUS. [< OF < L *arrogans, -antis,* ppr. of *arrogare.* See ARROGATE.] —**ar'ro·gant·ly** *adv.*

ar·ro·gate (ar'ə·gāt) *v.t.* **·gat·ed, ·gat·ing** 1 To claim, demand, or take unreasonably or presumptuously; assume; usurp. 2 To attribute or ascribe without reason: to *arrogate* a privilege. See synonyms under ASSUME. [< L *arrogatus,* pp. of *arrogare* claim for oneself < *ad-* to + *rogare* ask] —**ar'ro·ga'tion** *n.*

ar·ron·disse·ment (à·rôn·dēs·män') *n. pl.* **·ments** (-män') *French* 1 The chief subdivision of a French department. 2 A district: Paris is divided into 20 *arrondissements.*

ar·row (ar'ō) *n.* 1 A straight, slender shaft generally feathered at one end and with a pointed head at the other, to be shot from a bow. 2 Anything resembling an arrow in shape, function, speed, etc. 3 A sign or figure in the shape of an arrow, used to indicate directions, as on maps, charts, etc. ◆ Collateral adjective: *sagittal.* [OE *earh, arwe*]

Ar·row (ar'ō) The constellation Sagitta. See CONSTELLATION.

ar·row·head (ar'ō·hed') *n.* 1 The sharp-pointed head of an arrow. 2 Something resembling an arrowhead, as a mark used to point direction, etc. 3 *Archit.* The dart or tongue of an egg-and-dart molding. 4 *Bot.* Any aquatic plant of the genus *Sagittaria,* of the water-plantain family (*Alismaceae*), with arrow-shaped leaves. —**ar'row·head'ed** *adj.*

ar·row·root (ar'ō·rōōt', -root') *n.* 1 A nutritious starch obtained from the rhizomes of a tropical American plant (*Maranta arundinacea*). 2 The plant. 3 A similar starchy product from other tropical plants.

ar·row·wood (ar'ō·wood') *n.* One of various North American shrubs or small trees with many straight shoots or branches, used by the Indians for making arrows, as certain species of viburnum, flowering dogwood (*Cornus florida*), etc.

ar·row·worm (ar'ō·wûrm') *n. Zool.* A chaetognath, especially a pelagic species (*Sagitta bipunctata*) with a transparent body, capable of descent to great depths: also called *glassworm.*

ar·row·y (ar'ō·ē) *adj.* 1 Resembling an arrow or arrows in shape, appearance, or motion; swift; sharp; darting. 2 Full of or abounding in arrows.

ar·roy·o (ə·roi'ō) *n. pl.* **·os** (-ōz) *SW U.S.* 1 The steep-sided, flat channel of an intermittent stream. 2 The stream itself. 3 A deep, dry gulch. [< Sp.]

Ar·ru Islands (ä'rōō). See ARU ISLANDS.

Ar·sac·id (är·sas'id) *n. pl.* **·ids** or **·i·dae** (-ə·dē) Any ruler styled Arsaces of a dynasty in Parthia and Armenia, dating from about 250 B.C. to A.D. 224 in Parthia and to 428 in Armenia.

ar·se·nal (är'sə·nəl) *n.* A public repository or manufactory of arms and munitions of war. [< Ital. *arsenale* < Arabic *dār aṣ-ṣinā'ah* workshop]

ar·se·nate (är'sə·nāt, -nit) *n. Chem.* A salt of arsenic acid containing the trivalent radical AsO₄. Also **ar·se·ni·ate** (är·sē'nē·āt, -it).

ar·se·nic (är'sə·nik) *n.* 1 A poisonous element (symbol As, atomic number 33), existing in several allotropic forms, commonly as a gray, very brittle, crystalline, semimetallic substance. See PERIODIC TABLE. 2 A tasteless, poisonous compound, arsenic trioxide, As_2O_3, used in agricultural pesticides. 3 White arsenic or arsenic trioxide, As_2O_3, a tasteless, poisonous compound. —**ar·sen·ic** (är·sen'ik) *adj.* Arsenical. [< OF < L *arsenicum* < Gk. *arsenikon* yellow orpiment]

ar·sen·i·cal (är·sen'i·kəl) *adj.* Of, pertaining to, or containing arsenic. —*n.* Any preparation of arsenic used as an insecticide or drug.

ar·se·nide (är'sə·nīd, -nid) *n.* A compound of arsenic, in which arsenic is the electronegative constituent.

ar·se·nite (är'sə·nīt) *n.* A salt of arsenous acid.

ar·se·niu·ret·ed (är·sen'yə·ret'id, -yoo'-) *adj.* Chemically combined with arsenic to form an arsenide: *arseniureted* hydrogen. Also **ar·se'niu·ret'ted.**

ar·se·no·py·rite (är'sə·nō·pī'rīt, är·sen'ə-) *n.* A silver-white, orthorhombic, iron sulfarsenide, FeAsS: also called *mispickel.* [< ARSENIC + PYRITE]

ar·se·nous (är'sə-nəs) *adj.* Of, pertaining to, or containing arsenic, especially when combined in its triad valence: *arsenous* oxide, As₂O₃; *arsenous* sulfide, As₂S₃. Also **ar·se·ni·ous** (är·sē'nē·əs).

ars gra·ti·a ar·tis (ärz grä'shē·ə är'tis) *Latin* Art for art's sake.

ar·sine (är'sēn', är'sēn, är'sin) *n.* **1** A poisonous, inflammable, gaseous compound, AsH₃, with a nauseous odor, used as an agent of chemical warfare in shells, etc. **2** Any of various derivatives of this compound in which the hydrogen atom is replaced by a radical. [< ARS(ENIC) + -INE²]

Ar·sin·o·ë (är·sin'ō·ē) An ancient city of Upper Egypt west of the Nile.

ar·sis (är'sis) *n. pl.* **·ses** (-sēz) **1** In prosody: **a** The syllable that receives the ictus or stress of voice. **b** The stress itself. **c** In the original Greek usage, the raising of the foot in beating time, and hence the metrically unaccented part of the foot: the reverse of modern usage. **2** *Music* The unaccented part of a bar. [< L < Gk. *arsis* a lifting, raising < *airein* raise]

ars lon·ga, vi·ta brev·is (ärz lông'gə vī'tə brev'is) *Latin* Art long, life short.

ar·son (är'sən) *n. Law* The malicious burning of a dwelling or other structure belonging to another; also the similar burning of one's own property, including one's own, when insured, with the intent to defraud the insurers. [< OF < LL *arsio, -onis* a burning < L *arsus,* pp. of *ardere* burn]

Ar·son·val (dár·sôn·vál'), **Jacques Arsène d'** See D'ARSONVAL, JACQUES.

ars·phen·a·mine (ärs'fen·ə·mēn', ärs'fen·am'in) *n.* A yellow, crystalline arsenic compound, C₁₂H₁₄O₂N₂Cl₂As₂·2H₂O, first prepared by Paul Ehrlich as a treatment for syphilis and other spirillum infections, as relapsing fever, frambesia, etc.: also called *Salvarsan.* [< AR-S(ENIC) + PHEN(YL) + AMINE]

ars po·et·i·ca (ärz pō·et'i·kə) *Latin* The art of poetry.

art¹ (ärt) *n.* **1** The skilful, systematic arrangement or adaptation of means for the attainment of some end, especially by human endeavor as opposed to natural forces. **2** The practical application of knowledge or natural ability; skilled workmanship; mastery; dexterity. **3** A set or system of rules, principles, etc., devised for procuring some scientific, esthetic, or practical result, as by exercise; a branch of learning to be studied in order to be applied. **4 a** The application, or the principles of application, of skill, knowledge, etc., in a creative effort to produce works that have form or beauty, esthetic expression of feeling, etc., as in music, painting, sculpture, literature, architecture, and the dance. **b** Any particular branch of this, especially painting, drawing, etc. **c** The works thus created; statues; paintings, etc. **5** *Usually pl.* Any of certain branches of academic learning, as rhetoric, grammar, music, mathematics, etc.; the liberal arts, especially as distinguished from the sciences. **6** An illustration, as in a magazine or newspaper. **7** Craft; cunning; artfulness. **8** *Usually pl.* Stratagem; wiles; tricks. **9** An organized body of men trained in some trade or vocation; guild. **—fine arts** Those arts considered purely esthetic or expressive, as distinguished from the "useful arts": painting, drawing, sculpture, ceramics, architecture, literature, music, and the dance. **—household arts** The duties involved in managing a household. **—industrial arts** The technical skills used in industry, especially as subjects of study in schools. **—liberal arts** The course of study, including literature, philosophy, languages, history, etc., distinguished from professional or technical subjects, offered by an academic college: also called *arts*: a translation of Latin *artes liberales,* arts suitable for *liberi,* or free men. [< OF < L *ars, artis* skill] *Synonyms*: address, aptitude, artifice, business, cleverness, dexterity, esthetics, ingenuity, knack, science, skill, tact. In the highest sense, *art* has no synonym. The term *esthetics* denotes the theory of the beautiful which furnishes the basis of *art.* For subordinate senses, see ARTIFICE, BUSINESS. For the distinction between *science* and *art,* see synonyms for SCIENCE.

art² (ärt) Archaic or poetic second person

singular present tense of BE: used with *thou.*

Ar·ta·xerx·es (är'tə·zûrk'sēz) Name of three Persian kings. **—Artaxerxes II,** king of Persia 404–359 B.C., defeated his brother Cyrus at Cunaxa, 401.

art de·co (ärt de'kō) A style of decorative design characterized by ornateness, geometrical forms, asymmetry, and bold colors. Also **Art De'co.**

ar·tel (är·tel') *n.* **1** In pre–revolutionary Russia, an association of persons to carry out work in common. **2** In Soviet Russia, a cooperative organization of producers under government supervision: An agricultural *artel* is the same as a collective farm or kolkhoz. [< Russian]

Ar·te·mas (är'tə·məs) A masculine personal name.[< Gk.]

Ar·te·mis (är'tə·mis) In Greek mythology, the goddess of the chase and of the moon; twin sister of Apollo: identified with the Roman *Diana.*

ar·te·mis·i·a (är'tə·miz'ē·ə, -mish'ē·ə) *n.* **1** Any of a large genus (*Artemisia*) of bitter aromatic herbs of the composite family. **2** The sagebrush. [< L, mugwort < Gk.]

Ar·te·movsk (är·tyô'môfsk) A city in the eastern Ukrainian S.S.R.: formerly *Bakhmut.*

Ar·te·mus Ward (är'tə·məs wôrd) Pen name of Charles Farrar Browne, 1834–67, U.S. humorist.

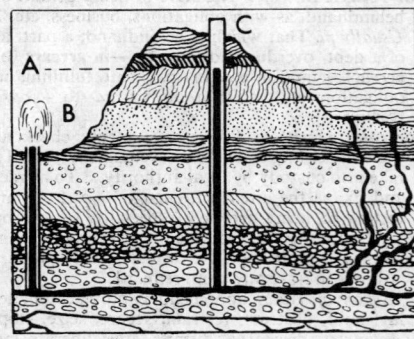

ARTEMIS
After a statue of Artemis and the Hind in the Louvre.

ar·ten·kreis (är'tən·krīs) *n. Ecol.* A group of species having a common origin and replacing each other within a given area; a polytypic species. [< G]

ar·te·ri·al (är·tir'ē·əl) *adj.* **1** Pertaining to, like, or contained or carried in the arteries or an artery. **2** *Physiol.* Pertaining to the blood which has undergone aeration in the lungs, distinguished by its bright red color. **3** Resembling an artery in having a main channel and a system of secondary branches: an *arterial* highway.

ar·te·ri·al·ize (är·tir'ē·əl·īz') *v.t.* **·ized, ·iz·ing** *Physiol.* To convert venous blood into arterial blood by oxygenation during its passage through the lungs in respiration. Also *Brit.* **ar·te'ri·al·ise'. —ar·te'ri·al·i·za'tion** *n.*

arterio– *combining form* Artery. [< Gk. *artēria*]

ar·te·ri·og·ra·phy (är·tir'ē·ogr'ə·fē) *n.* **1** The anatomy, description, etc., of the arteries or the arterial system. **2** The production of graphic representations of the action and state of the pulse.

ar·te·ri·ol·o·gy (är·tir'ē·ol'ə·jē) *n.* **1** The scientific study of the arteries in health and disease. **2** A treatise on the subject.

ar·te·ri·o·scle·ro·sis (är·tir'ē·ō·sklə·rō'sis) *n. Pathol.* The thickening and hardening of the walls of an artery, with impairment of blood circulation, as in old age. [< NL < ARTERIO- + SCLEROSIS] **—ar·te'ri·o·scle·rot'ic** (-rot'ik) *adj.*

ar·te·ri·ot·o·my (är·tir'ē·ot'ə·mē) *n.* **1** Dissection of arteries. **2** Any cutting or opening of an artery, as for letting blood.

ar·te·ri·tis (är'tə·rī'tis) *n. Pathol.* Inflammation of an artery or of its external coat.

ar·ter·y (är'tər·ē) *n. pl.* **·ter·ies 1** *Anat.* Any of a large number of muscular vessels conveying blood away from the heart to every part of the body. **2** Any principal channel in a communication or transportation network. **—** *v.t.* **·ter·ied, ·ter·y·ing** To supply with or as if with arteries; flow through, like an artery: Rivers *artery* the land. [< L *arteria* artery, windpipe < Gk. *artēria*]

ar·te·sian well (är·tē'zhən) A well bored down to a water–bearing stratum between impermeable strata, from a surface lower than the source of the water supply, so that the water pressure is great enough to force a flow of water out at the surface. [< F *artésien,* from *Artois,* town in France]

Ar·te·vel·de (är'tə·vel'də), **Jacob van,** 1290–1345, Flemish patriot; led insurgents at Ghent. **—Philip van,** 1340?–82, Flemish leader; son of Jacob. Also **Ar·te·veld** (är'tə·veld).

art·ful (ärt'fəl) *adj.* **1** Crafty; cunning; tricky.

2 Artificial; imitative. **3** Skilful; ingenious. See synonyms under INSIDIOUS. **—art'ful·ly** *adv.* **—art'ful·ness** *n.*

art history The study of the history of art, including painting, sculpture, and architecture. **—art historian**

ar·thral·gia (är·thral'jə) *n. Pathol.* Neuralgic pain in a joint. **—ar·thral'gic** (-jik) *adj.*

ar·thrit·ic (är·thrit'ik) *adj.* Pertaining to, having, or affected by arthritis.

ar·thri·tis (är·thrī'tis) *n. Pathol.* Inflammation of a joint. [< L < Gk. *arthritis* < *arthron* joint]

arthro– *combining form* Joint: *arthrography.* Also, before vowels, **arthr–,** as in *arthralgia.* [< Gk. *arthron*]

ar·thro·branch (är'thrə·brangk) *n. Zool.* A branchial plume grown to the membranous articulation between the coxa and body in crustaceans. Also **ar·thro·bran·chi·a** (är'thrə·brang'kē·ə). [< ARTHRO- + Gk. *branchia* gill]

ar·throc·a·ce (är·throk'ə·sē) *n.* **1** Disease of the joints, characterized by caries or dead bone. **2** An endemic disease that attacks very young animals, as calves, colts, etc. [< ARTHRO- + Gk. *kakē* illness]

ar·throd·e·sis (är·throd'ə·sis) *n. Surg.* The operation of fusing of the surfaces of joints; artificial ankylosis. [< NL < ARTHRO- + Gk. *desis* a joining]

ar·throg·ra·phy (är·throg'rə·fē) *n.* A scientific description of the joints.

ar·thro·mere (är'thrə·mir) *n. Zool.* Any typical segment in the body of an articulate invertebrate. [< ARTHRO- + -MERE]

ar·throp·a·thy (är·throp'ə·thē) *n.* Any disease of the joints.

ar·thro·plas·ty (är'thrə·plas'tē) *n. Surg.* A plastic operation on a joint or the formation of an artificial joint. **—ar'thro·plas'tic** *adj.*

ar·thro·pod (är'thrə·pod) *n. Zool.* Any of a large phylum (*Arthropoda*) of invertebrate animals characterized by jointed legs, chitinous exoskeletons, and segmented body parts, including insects, spiders, and crabs. **—** *adj.* Of or pertaining to the *Arthropoda.* [< ARTHRO- + Gk. *pous, podos* foot] **—ar·throp·o·dous** (är·throp'ə·dəs), **ar·throp'o·dal** *adj.*

ar·thro·sis (är·thrō'sis) *n. pl.* **·ses** (-sēz) **1** Articulation; connection of parts by joints. **2** *Pathol.* A degenerative condition of the joints.

ar·thro·spore (är'thrə·spôr, -spōr) *n.* **1** *Bot.* One of a series of spores in some algae and fungi, formed by fission and resembling a string of beads. **2** *Bacteriol.* An isolated vegetative cell in a resting state. **—ar'thro·spor'ic** (-spôr'ik, -spor'ik), **ar·thros·po·rous** (är·thros'pə·rəs) *adj.*

Ar·thur (är'thər, *Fr.* är·tür') A masculine personal name. Also *Lat.* **Ar·thu·rus** (är·tōōr'əs). **—Arthur** A legendary British king of the sixth century A.D., hero of the Round Table and subject of many romances. [? < Celtic, high admirable]

Ar·thur (är'thər), **Chester Alan,** 1830–86, president of the United States 1881–85, following the assassination of President Garfield.

ARTESIAN WELL
THROUGH GEOLOGICAL STRATA
A. Water level. *B.* Artesian well. *C.* Ordinary well.

Ar·thu·ri·an (är·thōōr'ē·ən) *adj.* Of or pertaining to King Arthur and his knights. See ROUND TABLE.

ar·ti·choke (är'tə·chōk) *n.* **1** A thistlelike garden plant (*Cynara scolymus*). **2** Its suc-

culent flower head, used as a vegetable. 3 The Jerusalem artichoke. [<Ital. *articiocco* <Arabic *al-kharshūf*]

ar·ti·cle (är′ti·kəl) *n.* 1 A particular object or substance; a material thing or class of things: an *article* of food; an *article* for sale. 2 A literary composition forming an independent part of a publication: an *article* in a newspaper. 3 A definite division; a distinct proposition, statement, or stipulation in a series of such, as in a constitution, an impeachment, or a treaty. 4 A complete item of religious belief; a point of doctrine, especially when forming a part of a statement of religious beliefs: the Thirty-nine *Articles.* 5 *Gram.* One of a class of auxiliary words inserted before a noun or a word used as a noun, or, in some languages, prefixed or suffixed to it, to limit or modify it in some way; as, English *a, an (indefinite article)* and *the (definite article).* 6 A definite part, as of a system; item; point. 7 *Archaic* A point of time; exact instant: the *article* of death. — *v.* **·cled, ·cling** *v.t.* 1 To bind by a written contract, as to an attorney for instruction in law; especially, to bind to service: to *article* a seaman for a voyage. 2 To set forth in articles; specify. 3 To charge specifically; accuse by formal articles. — *v.i.* 4 To make accusations: with *against.* [<F <L *articulus,* dim. of *artus* a joint]

Articles of Confederation The constitution of the 13 original American colonies, adopted by Congress in 1781 and replaced in 1788 by the Constitution.

Articles of War, Articles for the Government of the Navy See under UNIFORM CODE OF MILITARY JUSTICE.

ar·tic·u·lar (är·tik′yə·lər) *adj.* Pertaining to a joint or the joints.

ar·tic·u·late (är·tik′yə·lit) *adj.* 1 Jointed; segmented. 2 Particularized in articles; specific; distinct. 3 Divided into consecutive syllables so as to form speech. 4 Able to speak, especially to speak well or clearly. 5 Arranged with coherence; interrelated. Also **ar·tic′u·lat′ed** (-lā′tid). — *v.* (är·tik′yə·lāt) **·lat·ed, ·lat·ing.** *v.t.* 1 To utter distinctly, enunciate. 2 To give utterance to; express in words: to *articulate* your wrongs. 3 *Phonet.* To produce, as a speech sound, by the movement of the organs of speech. 4 To joint together; unite by joints. — *v.i.* 5 To speak distinctly. 6 *Phonet.* To produce a speech sound. 7 *Anat.* To form a joint: used with *with.* 8 *Obs.* To make terms. See synonyms under SPEAK. [<L *articulatus,* pp. of *articulare* divide into joints, utter distinctly < *articulus.* See ARTICLE.] — **ar·tic′u·late·ly** *adv.*

ar·tic·u·la·tion (är·tik′yə·lā′shən) *n.* 1 A jointing or being jointed together; also the manner or method of this. 2 A joint between two bones. 3 *Anat.* The union forming a joint, as of bones. 4 The utterance of articulate sounds; enunciation. 5 A speech sound, especially a consonant. 6 *Phonet.* The movements of the organs of speech in producing an articulate sound. 7 *Bot.* **a** A joint between two separable parts, as a leaf and a stem. **b** A node or the space between two nodes. — **ar·tic·u·la·to·ry** (är·tik′yə·lə·tôr′ē, -tō′rē) *adj.*

ar·tic·u·la·tor (är·tik′yə·lā′tər) *n.* 1 One who or that which articulates. 2 *Dent.* A device to secure proper articulation. 3 *Phonet.* A movable organ of speech, as the tongue.

articulatory phonetics See under PHONETICS.

ar·ti·fact (är′tə·fakt) *n.* 1 Anything made by human work or art. 2 *Biol.* A structure or appearance which is not normally present in a cell or tissue but is produced by artificial means. Also **ar′te·fact.** [<L *ars, artis* art, skill + *factus,* pp. of *facere* make]

ar·ti·fice (är′tə·fis) *n.* 1 Subtle or deceptive craft; trickery. 2 Skill; ingenuity. 3 An ingenious expedient; stratagem; maneuver. [<F <L *artificium* handicraft, skill < *ars* art + *facere* make]

Synonyms: art, blind, cheat, contrivance, craft, cunning, device, dodge, finesse, fraud, guile, imposture, invention, machination, maneuver, ruse, strategem, subterfuge, trick, wile. An *artifice, contrivance,* or *device* may be either good or bad. An *artifice* is a carefully and delicately prepared *contrivance* for doing indirectly what one could not well do directly. A *device* is something studied out for promoting an end, as in a mechanism. *Finesse* is especially subtle *contrivance,* delicate *artifice,* whether for good or evil. A *cheat* is a mean advantage in a bargain; a *fraud,* any form of covert robbery or injury. *Imposture* is a deceitful *contrivance* for securing charity, credit, or consideration. A *strategem* or *maneuver* may be good or bad. A *wile* is often but not necessarily evil. A *trick* is commonly low, injurious, and malicious, but the word is used playfully with less than its full meaning. A *ruse* or a *blind* may be quite innocent and harmless. *Antonyms*: artlessness, candor, fairness, frankness, guilelessness, honesty, ingenuousness, innocence, openness, simplicity, sincerity, truth.

ar·tif·i·cer (är·tif′ə·sər) *n.* 1 One who constructs with skill; a craftsman. 2 *Mil.* A worker in an artillery laboratory. 3 A skilful designer; an inventor.

ar·ti·fi·cial (är′tə·fish′əl) *adj.* 1 Produced by human art rather than by nature. 2 Made in imitation of or as a substitute for something natural: an *artificial* leg. 3 Not genuine or natural; affected. See synonyms under FACTITIOUS. [<L *artificialis* < *artificium.* See ARTIFICE.] — **ar′ti·fi′cial·ly** *adv.* — **ar′ti·fi′·cial·ness** *n.*

artificial horizon 1 *Aeron.* An instrument like a gyroscope, providing a surface always parallel to the true horizon and indicating the deviations of an aircraft from level flight. 2 *Astron.* A level reflector, as a surface of mercury, used to determine the altitude of celestial bodies.

artificial insemination Impregnation of the female with semen from the male without direct sexual contact: also called *eutelegenesis.*

ar·ti·fi·ci·al·i·ty (är′tə·fish′ē·al′ə·tē) *n. pl.* **·ties** 1 The character, fact, or state of being artificial. 2 Something artificial.

artificial language An arbitrary, auxiliary language devised for use in international communication.

ar·til·ler·y (är·til′ə·rē) *n.* 1 Guns of larger caliber than machine-guns: usually classified according to caliber as *light, medium,* and *heavy.* 2 Military units armed with such guns. 3 Branches of the United States Army composed of such units: Field *Artillery,* Coast *Artillery* Corps. 4 *U.S. Colloq.* Any small firearm. 5 The science of gunnery. 6 *Obs.* Implements of war. [<OF *artillerie* < *artiller* fortify]

ar·til·ler·y·man (är·til′ə·rē·mən) *n. pl.* **·men** (-mən) 1 One who studies artillery. 2 A soldier in the artillery. Also **ar·til′ler·ist.**

ar·ti·o·dac·tyl (är′tē·ō·dak′təl) *n.* A member of a mammalian order or suborder *(Artiodactyla)* of ungulate quadrupeds with two or four equal-hoofed digits to each foot, including the ruminants, hogs, etc. — *adj.* Of or pertaining to the *Artiodactyla*; having two or four digits to each foot. [<NL <Gk. *artios* even + *daktylos* finger, toe] — **ar′ti·o·dac′ty·lous** (-ləs) *adj.*

ar·ti·san (är′tə·zən) *n.* A trained or skilled workman; superior mechanic. [<F <Ital. *artigiano,* ult. <L *ars* art]

art·ist (är′tist) *n.* 1 One who is skilled in or who makes a profession of any of the fine arts. 2 Any professional public performer, as an actor, singer, etc. 3 One who does anything particularly well, as with a feeling for form, effect, etc. [<F *artiste* <Ital. *artista* <L *ars* art]

Synonyms: artificer, artisan, mechanic, operative, workman. The work of the *artist* is creative; that of the *artisan* mechanical. The *artificer* is between the two, putting more thought, intelligence, and taste into his work than the *artisan,* but less of the idealizing, creative power than the *artist.* The man who constructs anything by mere routine and rule is a *mechanic.* The man whose work involves thought, skill, and constructive power is an *artificer.* Those who operate machinery which is nearly automatic are *operators* or *operatives.*

ar·tiste (är·tēst′) *n.* A professional dancer, singer, or entertainer. [<F]

ar·tis·tic (är·tis′tik) *adj.* 1 Of or pertaining to art or artists. 2 Conforming or conformable to the principles of art; tastefully executed. 3 Fond of or sensitive to art. Also **ar·tis′ti·cal.** — **ar·tis′ti·cal·ly** *adv.*

art·ist·ry (är′tis·trē) *n.* 1 The pursuits or occupation of an artist. 2 Artistic characteristics or ability.

Ar·ti·um Bac·ca·lau·re·us (är′shē·əm bak′ə·lô′rē·əs) *Latin* Bachelor of Arts. Abbr. *A.B.* or *B.A.*

Ar·ti·um Ma·gis·ter (är′shē·əm mə·jis′tər) *Latin* Master of Arts. Abbr. *A.M.* or *M.A.*

art·less (ärt′lis) *adj.* 1 Without craft or deceit; unaffected. 2 Natural; simple. 3 Without art or skill; clumsy. 4 Without taste; ignorant. See synonyms under CANDID, INNOCENT, RUSTIC. — **art′less·ly** *adv.* — **art′less·ness** *n.*

Art Nou·veau (ärt nōō·vō′, *Fr.* àr nōō·vō′) A style of art and design of the late 19th and early 20th centuries characterized by curved and twisting shapes often representing natural objects. [<F, lit., new art]

Ar·tois (âr·twä′) A region and former province of northern France.

Ar·tu·ro (är·tōō′rō) Italian form of ARTHUR.

art·work (ärt′wûrk′) *n.* Illustrations, calligraphy, or other decorative elements accompanying printed text.

art·y (är′tē) *adj.* Pretending to be artistic; ostentatiously claiming artistic worth. — **art′i·ness** *n.*

Ar·tzy·ba·sheff (är′tsi·bä′shif), **Boris,** born 1899, U.S. illustrator born in Russia.

A·ru·ba (ä·rōō′bə) An island in the western group of the Netherlands West Indies; 69 square miles.

A·ru Islands (ä′rōō) An Indonesian island group in the Arafura Sea; 3,306 square miles: also *Aroe, Arro, Arru.*

ar·um (âr′əm) *n.* 1 Any of a genus *(Arum)* of araceous Old World herbs, especially the cuckoo pint. 2 One of various related plants, as the calla lily. [<L <Gk. *aron*]

Ar·un·del (ar′ən·dəl) A municipal borough in southern Sussex, England.

a·run·di·na·ceous (ə·run′də·nā′shəs) *adj. Bot.* Pertaining to a reed or reeds; reedlike. [<L *arundinaceus* < *arundo* reed]

ar·un·din·e·ous (ar′ən·din′ē·əs) *adj. Bot.* Abounding in or like reeds; reedy.

a·rus·pex (ə·rus′peks) See HARUSPEX.

A·ru·wi·mi (ä′rōō·wē′mē) A river in NE Belgian Congo, flowing 620 miles SW to the Congo.

ar·val[1] (är′vəl) *adj.* Of or pertaining to plowed land. [<L *arvalis* < *arare* plow]

ar·val[2] (är′vəl) *n. Brit. Archaic & Dial.* A funeral feast. Also **ar′vel.** [appar. <Scand.]

Arval Brethren In ancient Rome, a college of 12 priests who offered sacrifices to the goddess of the fields. [Trans. of L *Fratres Arvales*]

ar·y (âr′ē) *adj. Dial.* Any: opposite of *nary.*

-ary[1] *suffix of adjectives and nouns* 1 Connected with or pertaining to what is expressed in the root word: *elementary, honorary, secondary.* 2 A person employed as or engaged in: *apothecary, antiquary, secretary.* 3 A thing connected with or a place dedicated to: *dictionary, diary, sanctuary.* [<L *-arius, -arium*]

-ary[2] *suffix of adjectives* Of or pertaining to; belonging to: *military, salutary.* See -AR[1]. [<L *-aris*]

Ar·y·an (âr′ē·ən, ar′-, är′yən) *n.* 1 A member or descendant of a prehistoric people who spoke Indo-European. 2 In Nazi ideology, a Caucasian gentile, especially one of Nordic stock. 3 *Ling.* **a** The Indo-Iranian subfamily of Indo-European. **b** A former name for the parent language of the Indo-European family. — *adj.* 1 Of or pertaining to the Aryans or their languages. 2 In Nazi ideology, of or pertaining to Caucasian gentiles. Also spelled *Arian.* [<Skt. *ārya* noble]

Ar·y·an·ize (âr′ē·ən·īz′, ar′-, är′yən-) *v.t.* **·ized, ·iz·ing** 1 To make characteristically Aryan. 2 To free of all so-called non-Aryan elements or influences: a Nazi concept. Also **Ar′i·an·ize.**

ar·yl (ar′il) *adj. Chem.* Pertaining to any of a group of monovalent radicals derived from the aromatic hydrocarbon compounds, as phenyl, C_6H_5–. [<AR(OMATIC) + -YL]

ar·y·te·noid (ar′ə·tē′noid) *adj. Anat.* Of, connected with, or pertaining to two small

cartilages in the larynx mounted on the cricoid cartilage and attached posteriorly to the vocal bands, for the action of which they are largely responsible. Also **ar′y·te·noi′dal.** —*n.* An arytenoid cartilage. [< Gk. *arytainoeidēs* pitcher-shaped < *arytaina* pitcher + *eidos* form]

as[1] (az, *unstressed* əz) *adv.* **1** To the same extent or degree; equally: Do I look *as* pretty? **2** For instance; thus: to release, *as* prisoners, from confinement. —*conj.* **1** To the same extent, degree, or amount: Such a man *as* he cannot fail. **2** To the degree in which; in proportion to which: He became gentler *as* he grew older. **3** In the manner of; in the way that: Do *as* I tell you. **4** At the same time that; while: They sang *as* we left. **5** Because; considering that: *As* the weather was bad, the game was postponed. **6** However; though: Bad *as* it was, it might have been worse. See synonyms under BECAUSE. —*pron.* Who, which, or that, after *such, many,* and *same*: Such people *as* like sports will enjoy the game; He lost the same kind of pen *as* you have; As many *as* are here will receive tickets. [ME *as, als, alse,* OE *ealswā* entirely so, just as. See ALSO.] —**as . . . as** A correlative construction that indicates identity or equality of two things: *as* much *as, as* good *as.* —**as for** Concerning; in the case of. —**as if.** As it would if. Also **as though.** —**as is** *Colloq.* Just as it is; not guaranteed perfect: said of an article or commodity somewhat shopworn or damaged. —**as it were** So to speak; in a manner; in some sort. —**as to** Concerning. —**as well** Besides. —**as well as** Equally; just as much; in addition to. —**as yet** Up to the present time; hitherto; so far.

as[2] (as) *n. pl.* **as·ses** (as′iz) **1** An early Roman coin of copper or copper alloy: originally weighing about a pound. **2** An ancient Roman unit of weight of about one pound. [< L]

As (äs) In Norse mythology, any one of the gods *(Æsir)* who dwelt in Asgard.

As *Chem.* Arsenic (symbol As).

as- Assimilated var. of AD-.

A·sa (ā′sə) A masculine personal name. [< Hebrew, ·healer]

as·a·fet·i·da (as′ə·fet′ə·də) *n.* A fetid substance prepared from the juice of certain plants of the fennel family: used in medicine as an antispasmodic: also spelled *assafoetida.* Also **as′a·foet′·i·da.** [< Med.L *asa* mastic (< Persian *azā*) + L *foetida,* fem., ill-smelling]

As·a·hel (as′ə·hel, ā′sə-) A masculine personal name. [< Hebrew, made of God]

A·sa·hi·ga·wa (ä·sä·hē·gä·wä) A city on central Hokkaido island, Japan. Also **A·sa·hi·ka·wa** (-kä·wä).

A·sa·ma (ä·sä·mä) The highest and most violent of Japan's active volcanos, on central Honshu island; 8,200 feet.

A·saph (ā′saf, ā′səf) A Levite chief singer and musician of David's court. I *Chron.* xvi 7. [< Hebrew, collector] —**A·saph·ic** (ā·saf′ik) *adj.*

as·a·rum (as′ə·rəm) *n.* **1** The dried rootstock of a North American perennial herb *(Asarum canadense)* of the birthwort family; used as an aromatic and carminative. **2** The herb itself. [< L, hazelwort, wild spikenard < Gk. *asaron*]

As·ben (az·ben′) See AIR.

as·bes·tos (as·bes′təs, az-) *n.* **1** A white or light-gray mineral, obtained chiefly from actinolite and amphibole, occurring in long slender needles or fibrous masses which may be woven or shaped into acid-resisting, nonconducting, and fireproof articles: also called *earthflax, mountain cork.* **2** A fireproof curtain, as in a theater. —*adj.* Pertaining to, containing, or made of asbestos. Also **as·bes′·tus.** [< L < Gk., unquenchable < *a-* not + *sbennynai* quench; orig. applied to quicklime] —**as·bes·ti·form** (as·bes′tə·fôrm, az-) *adj.* —**as·bes·tine** (as·bes′tin, az-), **as·bes′tic** *adj.*

as·bes·to·sis (as′bes·tō′sis, az′-) *n. Pathol.* Pneumoconiosis caused by inhaling particles of asbestos.

as·bo·lin (as′bə·lin, az′-) *n.* A yellowish, acrid, oily organic compound obtained from wood soot. [< Gk. *asbolos* soot + -IN]

As·bur·y (az′ber′ē, -bər·ē), **Francis,** 1745–1816, English Methodist missionary and organizer in America.

As·ca·lon (as′kə·lon) See ASHKELON.

As·ca·ni·us (as·kā′nē·əs) In Roman legend, son of Aeneas and Creusa: reputed ancestor of the Caesars: also called *Iulus.*

as·ca·rid (as′kə·rid) *n. Zool.* A nematode worm of the genus *Ascaris,* as a roundworm or pinworm. [< Gk. *askaris, -idos* worm in the intestines]

as·cend (ə·send′) *v.i.* **1** To go or move upward; rise. **2** To rise by degrees, as from particulars to generals, from the present to the past, from the lower to the higher notes of a musical scale, etc. **3** To lie along an ascending slope: The path *ascends* sharply here. —*v.t.* **4** To move or slope upward on: to *ascend* a mountain. [< L *ascendere* < *ad-* to + *scandere* climb] —**as·cend′a·ble** or **·i·ble** *adj.*

as·cen·dence (ə·sen′dəns) *n.* Ascendency. Also **as·cen′dance.**

as·cen·den·cy (ə·sen′dən·sē) *n.* The quality, fact, or state of being in the ascendent; domination; sway. Also **as·cen′dan·cy.**

as·cen·dent (ə·sen′dənt) *adj.* **1** Ascending; rising. **2** Superior; dominant. **3** *Astron.* Coming to or above the horizon. **4** *Bot.* Ascending. See synonyms under PREDOMINANT. —*n.* **1** A position of supreme power; preeminence; domination. **2** In astrology: **a** The point of the ecliptic that is rising above the eastern horizon at any instant. **b** Horoscope. **3** *Rare* An ancestor: opposed to *descendant.* Also **as·cen′dant.** —**to be in the ascendent** To approach or occupy a predominating position; have controlling power, fame, influence, etc.

as·cend·er (ə·sen′dər) *n.* **1** One who or that which ascends. **2** *Printing* **a** The part of a letter that reaches into the top of the body of the type. **b** Any of such letters, as *b, d, h,* etc.

as·cend·ing (ə·sen′ding) *adj.* **1** Rising or directed upward. **2** *Bot.* Slanting or curving upward.

as·cen·sion (ə·sen′shən) *n.* **1** The act of ascending. **2** *Astron.* The elevating or rising of a star above the horizon in the celestial sphere. —**the Ascension** *Theol.* The bodily ascent of Christ into heaven after the Resurrection, commemorated on **Ascension Day** (also *Holy Thursday*), the fortieth day after Easter. [< L *ascensio, -onis* < *ascendere.* See ASCEND.] —**as·cen′sion·al** *adj.*

As·cen·sion (ə·sen′shən) **1** A British island in the South Atlantic, administered with St. Helena; 34 square miles. **2** A former name for PONAPE.

as·cen·sion·ist (ə·sen′shən·ist) *n.* One who makes ascensions, as a balloonist or a mountaineer.

as·cen·sive (ə·sen′siv) *adj.* **1** Tending upward. **2** Causing to rise. [< L *ascensus,* pp. of *ascendere.* See ASCEND.]

as·cent (ə·sent′) *n.* **1** The act of ascending or going up; a rising or soaring. **2** The act of climbing or traveling up, as a mountain. **3** The method or way of ascending; that by which one ascends, as the upward slope of a hill. **4** The amount or degree of upward slope: an *ascent* of 30°. **5** A rise in state, rank, or station; advancement, as in esteem or succession. **6** *Rare* A going back in time or genealogy. ◆ Homophone: *assent.* [< ASCEND, on analogy with *descent*]

as·cer·tain (as′ər·tān′) *v.t.* **1** To learn with certainty about; find out. **2** *Obs.* To make certain; determine; define. See synonyms under DISCOVER, KNOW. [< OF *acertener* < *a-* to (< L *ad-*) + *certain.* See CERTAIN.] —**as′cer·tain′·a·ble** *adj.* —**as′cer·tain′a·ble·ness** *n.* —**as′·cer·tain′a·bly** *adv.* —**as′cer·tain′ment** *n.*

as·cet·ic (ə·set′ik) *n.* **1** Originally, in the early church, one who renounced social life and comfort for solitude, self-mortification, and religious devotion; a hermit; recluse. **2** Hence, one who leads a very austere and self-denying life. —*adj.* Given to severe self-denial and austerity; practicing rigid abstinence and devotion. Also **as·cet′i·cal.** [< Gk. *askētikos* exercised, industrious, athletic < *askētēs* one who exercises (self-denial), a monk < *askeein* exercise] —**as·cet′i·cal·ly** *adv.*

as·cet·i·cism (ə·set′ə·siz′əm) *n.* **1** Ascetic belief and conduct. **2** The belief that one can attain to a high intellectual or spiritual level through solitude, mortification of the flesh, and devotional contemplation.

Asch (äsh), **Sholem,** 1880–1957, U.S. novelist and playwright in Yiddish, born in Poland.

As·cham (as′kəm), **Roger,** 1515–68, English classical scholar; tutor of Queen Elizabeth I.

as·ci (as′ī) Plural of ASCUS.

as·cians (ash′yənz) *n. pl.* Shadowless men: applied to inhabitants of the torrid zone, who twice in the year cast no shadow at noon. Also **as·ci·i** (ash′ē·ī). [< L *ascius* < Gk. *askios* without shadow < *a-* without + *skia* shadow]

as·cid·i·an (ə·sid′ē·ən) *n. Zool.* Any of a class (Ascidiacea) of solitary and colonial forms of tunicates in which the adults are sessile filter feeders that secrete a tunic of cellulose. Also called *sea squirt.*—*adj.* Of or pertaining to this class of animals. [< NL < ASCIDIUM]

as·cid·i·um (ə·sid′ē·əm) *n. pl.* **·cid·i·a** (-sid′ē·ə) *Bot.* A flask-shaped plant appendage. [< NL < Gk. *askidion,* dim. of *askos* bag, wine-skin]

as·cif·er·ous (ə·sif′ər·əs) *adj. Bot.* Bearing large cells or spore cases, as some ascomycetous fungi. Also **as·cig·er·ous** (ə·sij′ər·əs). [< ASCI + L *ferere* bear]

as·ci·tes (ə·sī′tēz) *n. Pathol.* Abdominal dropsy. [< L < Gk. *askitēs* < *askos* bag] —**as·cit·ic** (ə·sit′ik) or **·i·cal** *adj.*

as·cle·pi·a·da·ceous (as·klē′pē·ə·dā′shəs) *adj. Bot.* Belonging to a large family *(Asclepiadaceae)* of erect or twining plants, the milkweed family, having milky juice. [< NL *Asclepias,* a genus of plants < Gk. *asklēpias;* named after *Aesculapius*]

As·cle·pi·a·de·an (as·klē′pē·ə·dē′ən) *adj.* Of, pertaining to, or denoting a variety of classical verse, usually consisting of a spondee, two or three choriambi, and an iambus. —*n.* An Asclepiadean verse. [after *Asclepiades* of Samos, 3rd c. B.C. Greek lyric poet]

As·cle·pi·us (as·klē′pē·əs) In Greek mythology, the son of Apollo and god of medicine: identified with the Roman *Aesculapius.*

as·co·carp (as′kə·kärp) *n. Bot.* The sporocarp or fruit of ascomycetous fungi. [< Gk. *askos* bag + -CARP]

as·cog·e·nous (as·koj′ə·nəs) *adj. Bot.* Producing asci.

as·co·go·ni·um (as′kə·gō′nē·əm) *n. pl.* **·ni·a** (-nē·ə) *Bot.* The female reproductive organ before fertilization in certain of the lower cryptogams. [< NL < Gk. *askos* bag + *gonos* offspring]

as·co·my·ce·tous (as′kə·mi·sē′təs) *adj. Bot.* Belonging to a large class *(Ascomycetes)* of fungi having the spores formed in asci, including mildews and yeasts: many of the species cause destructive diseases of plants. [< NL *Ascomycetes* < ASCUS + -MYCETES]

a·scor·bic (ə·skôr′bik) See ANTISCORBUTIC.

ascorbic acid The scurvy-preventing vitamin C, a white, odorless, crystalline compound, $C_6H_8O_6$, present in citrus and other fresh fruits, tomatoes, potatoes, and green leafy vegetables, and also made synthetically from glucose.

as·co·spore (as′kə·spôr, -spōr) *n. Bot.* A spore developed within an ascus. —**as·cos·po·rous** (as·kos′pə·rəs), **as·co·spor·ic** (as′kə·spôr′ik, -spor′-) *adj.*

as·cot (as′kət, -kot) *n.* A kind of scarf or necktie, knotted so that the broad ends are laid one across the other. [from *Ascot*]

As·cot (as′kət, -kot) A village in Berkshire, England, near Windsor; site of annual races instituted in 1711.

as·cribe (ə·skrīb′) *v.t.* **as·cribed, as·crib·ing 1** To refer, as to a cause or source; attribute; impute. **2** To consider or declare as belonging or being due or appropriate; assign as a quality or attribute. See synonyms under ATTRIBUTE. [< L *ascribere* < *ad-* to + *scribere* write] —**as·crib·a·ble** (ə·skrī′bə·bəl) *adj.*

as·crip·tion (ə·skrip′shən) *n.* **1** An ascribing or being ascribed. **2** An expression ascribing, or that which is ascribed. **3** A text or sentence ascribing praise and glory to the Almighty. [< L *ascriptio, -onis* < *ascribere.* See ASCRIBE.]

As·cu·lum (as′kyə·ləm) An ancient town of southern Italy; scene of a Roman defeat by Pyrrhus of Epirus, 279 B.C.; modern **As·co·li Sa·tri·a·no** (äs′kô·lē sä′trē·ä′nō).

as·cus (as′kəs) *n. pl.* **as·ci** (as′ī) *Bot.* A large cell or spore case in ascomycetous fungi and lichens. [< NL < Gk. *askos* bag, wine-skin]

as·dic (az′dik) *n.* A hydrophone, operating through the reflection of sound waves under water. Also **AS′DIC.** [< A(LLIED) S(UBMARINE) D(ETECTION) I(NVESTIGATION) C(OMMITTEE)]

-ase *suffix Chem.* Used in naming enzymes, chiefly of vegetable origin: sometimes added to a part or the whole of the name of the compound which the enzyme decomposes: *amylase, casease,* etc. [< (DIAST)ASE]

a·sea (ə·sē′) *adv.* To or toward the sea; at sea.

a·se·mi·a (ə·sē′mē·ə) *n. Psychiatry* Loss of power to understand signs of communication. [< NL < A·⁴ without + Gk. *sēma* sign]

a·sep·sis (ə·sep′sis, ā-) *n. Med.* 1 Absence of or freedom from putrefactive infection. 2 The prevention of septic infection by the use of sterilized instruments, dressings, etc.

a·sep·tic (ə·sep′tik, ā-) *adj.* 1 Exempt from septic or blood poisoning conditions and from pathogenic micro-organisms. 2 Characterizing processes tending to remove such conditions. 3 Free from disease germs or tendency to putrefaction. —*n.* An aseptic preparation. —**a·sep′ti·cal·ly** *adv.*

a·sep·ti·cism (ə·sep′tə·siz′əm, ā-) *n.* The theory and practice of aseptic surgery.

a·sep·ti·cize (ə·sep′tə·sīz, ā-) *v.t.* ·cized, ·ciz·ing To make aseptic.

a·sex·u·al (ā·sek′shōō·əl) *adj. Biol.* 1 Having no distinct sexual organs; without sex. 2 Occurring or performed without commerce of the sexes; agamic: *asexual* methods of reproduction. —**a·sex·u·al·i·ty** (ā·sek′shōō·al′ə·tē) *n.* —**a·sex′u·al·ly** *adv.*

a·sex·u·al·i·za·tion (ā·sek′shōō·əl·ə·zā′shən, -ī·zā′-) *n.* The act of unsexing, as by castration.

As·gard (as′gärd, äs′-) In Norse mythology, the home of the Æsir; the residence of heroes slain in battle. See BIFROST. Also **As·garth** (äs′gärth), **As·gar·dhr** (äs′gär·thr′).

ash¹ (ash) *n.* 1 The powdery, whitish-gray residue of a substance that has been burnt. See ASHES. 2 *Geol.* Comminuted lava as ejected by a volcano. [OE *asce, æsce*]

ash² (ash) *n.* 1 Any of a widely distributed genus (*Fraxinus*) of trees of the olive family, as the American white ash (*F. alba*) and the European ash (*F. excelsior*). 2 Its light, tough, elastic wood. —*adj.* Made of ash wood. [OE *æsc*]

a·shamed (ə·shāmd′) *adj.* 1 Feeling shame; confused by consciousness of fault or impropriety; abashed. 2 Deterred by fear of shame; reluctant. [Orig. pp. of obs. v. *ashame* to shame or feel shame] —**a·sham·ed·ly** (ə·shā′·mid·lē) *adv.* —**a·sham′ed·ness** *n.*

A·shan·ti (ə·shan′tē, ə·shän′-) 1 A former native kingdom and British protectorate in western Africa, included since 1957 in Ghana. 2 A native of this region. 3 The Sudanic language spoken there: also called *Twi.* Also **A·shan′tee.**

Ash·bel (ash′bel) A masculine personal name. [< Hebrew, man of Baal]

Ash·bur·ton (ash′bûr′tən) A river in NW Australia, flowing 220 miles NW to Exmouth Gulf.

Ash·bur·ton (ash′bûr′tən), **Lord,** 1774–1848, Alexander Baring, English statesman and banker.

ash·cake (ash′kāk′) *n.* A cake, especially cornbread, baked in hot ashes.

ash·can (ash′kan′) *n.* 1 A large can or metal receptacle for cinders and ashes. 2 *U.S. Slang* A depth bomb.

ash·en¹ (ash′ən) *adj.* Of, pertaining to, or like ashes: pale in color; gray.

ash·en² (ash′ən) *adj.* Pertaining to or made of the wood of the ash tree.

Ash·er (ash′ər) The eighth son of Jacob. *Gen.* xxx 13.

ash·er·y (ash′ər·ē) *n. pl.* ·er·ies 1 A place of deposit for ashes. 2 A place where potash is made.

ash·es (ash′iz) *n. pl.* 1 The grayish-white, powdery particles, often intermixed with charred fragments, remaining after something has been burned. 2 The remains of the human body after cremation. 3 Any dead body; corpse. 4 Remains or ruins, as after destruction. 5 **The Ashes** A symbol of victory in international cricket matches between Australia and England. See ASH¹.

Ashe·ville (ash′vil) A resort city of western North Carolina.

a·shine (ə·shīn′) *adv.* Luminously. —*adj.* Shining.

Ash·ke·lon (ash′kə·lon) An ancient city on the Mediterranean coast of southern Palestine: also *Ascalon, Askalon.*

Ash·ke·naz·im (ash′kə·naz′im, äsh′kə·nä′zim) *n. pl.* The Jews settled in northern and central Europe: distinguished from the *Sephardim.* [< Hebrew] —**Ash′ke·naz′ic** *adj.*

Ash·kha·bad (äsh′khä·bäd′) The capital and largest city of Turkmen S.S.R., near the Iran border.

ash·lar (ash′lər) *n.* 1 In masonry, a rough-hewn block of stone. 2 A thin, dressed, squared stone, used for facing a wall. 3 Masonwork made of either kind of ashlar. Also **ash′ler.** [< OF *aiseler* < L *axilla,* dim. of *axis* board, plank]

ash·lar·ing (ash′lər·ing) *n.* 1 In carpentry, upright wooden plaster studs running from the floor of a garret to the rafters. 2 Ashlar masonry. Also **ash′ler·ing.**

ash·man (ash′man′) *n. pl.* ·men (-men′) A man who collects and removes ashes.

a·shore (ə·shôr′, ə·shōr′) *adv.* 1 To or on the shore. 2 On land; aground.

ash·ram (äsh′rəm) *n.* 1 In India, a Hindu hermitage or religious retreat. 2 A religious commune. 3 A commune of hippies. [< Skt. *āśrama* < *ā* toward + *śrama* exertion]

Ash·to·reth (ash′tə·reth) An ancient Phoenician and Syrian goddess of love and fertility: identified with *Astarte.*

ash·tray (ash′trā) *n.* A receptacle for the ashes and butts of cigars, cigarettes, and pipes. Also **ash tray.**

A·shur (ä′shoor, ash′ər) In Assyrian mythology, the chief deity, god of war and empire: also spelled *Asshur.*

A·shur (ä′shoor, ash′ər) See ASSYRIA.

A·shur·ba·ni·pal (ä′shoor·bä′ni·päl) Assyrian king 668–625 B.C.: known as *Sardanapalus.*

Ash Wednesday The first day of Lent: from the sprinkling of ashes on the heads of penitents.

ash·y (ash′ē) *adj.* **ash·i·er, ash·i·est** 1 Of, pertaining to, or like ashes; ash-covered. 2 Ash-colored; ashen.

A·sia (ā′zhə, ā′shə) The world's largest continent, bounded by Europe and the Pacific, Arctic, and Indian Oceans; 16,900,000 square miles.

Asia Minor The peninsula of extreme western Asia between the Black and the Mediterranean Seas, comprising most of Turkey in Asia: also *Anatolia.*

A·sian (ā′zhən, ā′shən) *adj.* Of, pertaining to, or characteristic of Asia or its peoples. —*n.* A native or inhabitant of Asia.

A·sian·ism (ā′zhən·iz′əm, ā′shən-) *n.* A florid literary and oratorical style of pre-Christian Hellenistic Asia. Compare ATTICISM.

A·si·arch (ā′shē·ärk) *n.* In the ancient Roman Empire, an official who presided over the religious rites and public games in the province of Asia. [< L *Asiarcha* < Gk. *Asiarchēs* < *Asia* Asia + *archos* ruler]

A·si·at·ic (ā′zhē·at′ik, ā′shē-) *adj. & n.* Asian. ♦ Especially in the ethnic sense *Asian* is now preferred to *Asiatic,* because of the supposed derogatory implications of the latter term.

Asiatic beetle A scarabaeid beetle (*Anomala orientalis*) destructive of sugarcane and grass roots, introduced from Japan into Hawaii and the NE United States.

Asiatic cholera See under CHOLERA.

a·side (ə·sīd′) *adv.* 1 On or to one side; apart; away. 2 Out of thought or use. 3 Away from the general company; in seclusion: He drew his friend *aside* to speak more intimately. 4 Away from one's person; down: He cast his weapon *aside.* 5 In reserve: Keep some *aside* for me. —**aside from 1** Excepting. 2 *U.S.* Apart from. —**to set aside** *Law* To declare of no authority, as a verdict, judgment, etc. —*n.* Something spoken privately, as a remark or speech by an actor supposed to be heard by the audience but not by the other actors. [< A·¹ on + SIDE]

as·i·nine (as′ə·nīn) *adj.* Pertaining to or like an ass, characterized as a stupid, silly animal. [< L *asininus* < *asinus* ass] —**as′i·nine′ly** *adv.* —**as·i·nin·i·ty** (as′ə·nin′ə·tē) *n.*

A·sir (ä·sir′) A mountainous region in western Arabia on the Red Sea between Hejaz and Yemen.

ask (ask, äsk) *v.t.* 1 To put a question to: Don't *ask* me. 2 To put a question about; inquire after: to *ask* someone the time. 3 To make a re-

quest for; solicit: to *ask* advice. 4 To need or require: This job *asks* more of me than I can give. 5 To state the price of; demand: They are *asking* three dollars a plate. 6 To invite: Were many guests *asked?* 7 *Archaic* To publish or proclaim, as the banns of marriage in a church. —*v.i.* 8 To make inquiries: with *for, after,* or *about.* 9 To make a request: How often must I *ask?* [OE *āscian*] —**ask′er** *n.* —**ask′ing** *n.*

Synonyms: beg, beseech, crave, demand, entreat, implore, petition, plead, pray, request, require, solicit, supplicate. One *asks* what he feels that he may fairly claim and reasonably expect; he *begs* for that to which he advances no claim but pity. *Entreat* implies a special earnestness of asking, and *beseech,* a still added and more humble intensity. To *supplicate* is to *ask,* as it were, on bended knees; to *implore,* with the added force of tears. *Crave* and *request* are somewhat formal terms; *crave* has almost disappeared from conversation. *Pray* is now used chiefly of address to the Supreme Being; *petition* is used of written request to persons in authority. *Beg* and *pray* are often used in polite forms of slight request; *beseech* was formerly so used. Compare DEMAND, INQUIRE. *Antonyms:* claim, command, deny, enforce, exact, extort, insist, refuse.

Ask (äsk) In Norse mythology, the first man, made from a tree by Odin, Hœner, and Loder.

As·ka·lon (as′kə·lon) See ASHKELON.

a·skance (ə·skans′) *adv.* 1 With a side glance; sidewise. 2 Disdainfully; distrustfully. Also **a·skant′.** [Origin unknown]

a·skew (ə·skyōō′) *adj.* Oblique. —*adv.* In an oblique position or manner; to one side. [< A·¹ on + SKEW]

Ask·ja (äsk′yä) An inactive volcano in east central Iceland; 4,754 feet.

a·slant (ə·slant′, ə·slänt′) *adj.* Slanting; oblique. —*adv.* In a slanting direction or position; obliquely. —*prep.* Across or over in a slanting direction or position; athwart.

a·sleep (ə·slēp′) *adj.* 1 In a state of sleep; sleeping. 2 Dormant; inactive. 3 Benumbed. 4 Dead. —*adv.* Into a sleeping condition: to fall *asleep.*

a·slope (ə·slōp′) *adj.* Sloping. —*adv.* In a sloping position.

As·ma·ra (äs·mä′rə) The capital of Eritrea.

As·mo·de·us (az′mə·dē′əs, as′-) In Jewish demonology, an evil, destructive spirit.

As·nières (ä·nyâr′) A northern suburb of Paris. Also **As·nières-sur-Seine** (-sür-sân′).

a·so·cial (ā·sō′shəl) *adj.* 1 Avoiding society; not gregarious. 2 Regardless of one's fellow beings; self-centered.

A·so·ka (ə·sō′kə), died 232 B.C., Buddhist king in India 273–232 B.C.

a·so·ma·tous (ā·sō′mə·təs, ə-) *adj.* Not having bodily form; disembodied; incorporeal. [< L *asomatus,* < Gk. *asōmatos* < *a-* without + *sōma* body]

A·so·san (ä·sō·sän) A group of five extinct volcanic cones on central Kyushu island, Japan; 5,223 feet; world's largest crater, 10 by 15 miles. Also **Mount A·so** (ä·sō).

asp¹ (asp) *n.* 1 The common European viper. 2 The haje. 3 The uraeus. [< OF *aspe* < L *aspis* < Gk.]

asp² (asp) *n.* The aspen.

as·par·a·gine (ə·spar′ə·jēn, -jin) *n.* An amino acid, $C_4H_8N_2O_3$, occurring as a constituent of many proteins.

as·par·a·gus (ə·spar′ə·gəs) *n.* 1 The succulent edible shoots of a cultivated variety of a perennial herb (*Asparagus officinalis*) of the lily family. 2 Any plant of this genus. [< L < Gk. *asparagos, aspharogos*]

asparagus beetle A beetle (*Crioceris asparagi*) harmful to asparagus shoots. See illustration under INSECT (*injurious*).

as·par·tame (as·pär′tām) *n.* A synthetic combination of the amino acids aspartic acid and phenylalanine, used as a sweetener in foods.

as·par·tic acid (as·pär′tik) A white crystalline amino acid, $C_4H_7O_4N$, found in plant and animal proteins. [< ASPARAGUS]

As·pa·sia (as·pā′zhə, -shə), 470?–410 B.C., Athenian courtesan, mistress of Pericles.

as·pect (as′pekt) *n.* **1** The look a person has; expression of countenance. **2** Appearance presented to the eye by something; look. **3** Appearance presented to the mind by circumstances, etc.; interpretation. **4** A looking or facing in a given direction. **5** The side or surface facing in a certain direction. **6** In astrology: **a** Any configuration of the planets. **b** The supposed resulting influence of this for good or evil. **7** *Gram.* A categorizing of the verb indicating, primarily, the nature of the action performed in regard to the passage of time, as in English *he ran* (perfective), *he was running* (imperfective or durative), and, in certain languages, the manner in which the action is performed, the intent of the subject, etc., as in Hebrew *'ākhal* he eats, *'ikkēl* he eats greedily. Aspect is shown in the various languages by means of auxiliaries, affixes, root changes, etc. **8** *Obs.* A look; glance. See synonyms under MANNER. [<L *aspectus,* pp. of *aspicere* look at <*ad-* at + *specere* look]

aspect ratio **1** *Telecom.* The numerical ratio of the width of a television frame to the height. **2** *Aeron.* The ratio of the square of the maximum span of an airfoil to the total wing area.

asp·en (as′pən) *n.* Any of several kinds of poplar of North America or Europe with leaves that tremble in the slightest breeze, especially the **quaking aspen** *(Populus tremuloides)* of North America: also *asp.* — *adj.* Of, like, or pertaining to the aspen; hence, shaking; tremulous. [OE *aspe*]

As·pen (as′pən) A resort and cultural center in west central Colorado.

as·per[1] (as′pər) *n.* A former Turkish silver coin, now only a money of account; equal to 1/120 of a piaster. [<F *aspre* <MGk. *aspron*]

as·per[2] (as′pər) *n.* In Greek grammar, a rough breathing (see under BREATHING). [<L *asper* rough]

as·per·ate (as′pə·rāt) *v.t.* **·at·ed, ·at·ing** To make harsh or uneven, as in sound or contour. [<L *asperatus,* pp. of *asperare* roughen <*asper* rough]

as·per·ges (ə·spûr′jēz) *n.* **1** A short service before the high mass on Sundays during which the celebrant sprinkles the altar and congregation with holy water. **2** An anthem, beginning "Asperges me", sung during this service. [<L, thou shalt sprinkle]

as·per·gill (as′pər·jil) *n.* In the Roman Catholic Church, a brush or other instrument used for sprinkling holy water: also *aspergillum.* See ASPERSORIUM. [<LL *aspergillum* <L *aspergere.* See ASPERSE.]

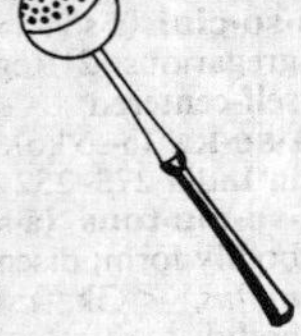

ASPERGILL

as·per·gil·lo·sis (as·pûr′jə·lō′sis) *n.* An infectious disease of animals and man, caused by any fungus of the genus *Aspergillus.*

as·per·gil·lum (as′pər·jil′əm) *n. pl.* **·gil·la** (-jil′ə) or **·gil·lums** Aspergill.

as·per·gil·lus (as′pər·jil′əs) *n. pl.* **·gil·li** (-jil′ī) *Bot.* Any of a genus *(Aspergillus)* of fungi belonging to the *Ascomycetes,* including the common mold fungus found on decaying vegetables, jellies, etc. [<NL; so named because of its resemblance to the ASPERGILL]

as·per·i·ty (as·per′ə·tē) *n. pl.* **·ties** **1** Roughness or harshness, as of surface, sound, style, etc. **2** Something uneven, harsh, or rough. **3** Bitterness or sharpness of temper; harsh feelings. See synonyms under ACRIMONY. [<OF *asprete* <L *asperitas, -tatis* roughness <*asper* rough]

a·sper·mous (ā·spûr′məs) *adj. Bot.* Without seeds. Also **a·sper·ma·tous** (ā·spûr′mə·təs). [<Gk. *aspermos* <*a-* without + *sperma* seed]

As·pern (äs′pûrn) A suburb of Vienna, Austria; site of Napoleon's defeat by the Austrians, 1809.

as·perse (ə·spûrs′) *v.t.* **as·persed** (ə·spûrst′), **as·pers·ing** **1** To spread false charges against; slander. **2** To besprinkle; bespatter. [<L *aspersus,* pp. of *aspergere* sprinkle on <*ad-* to + *spargere* sprinkle] — **as·pers′er, as·per′·sor** *n.* — **as·per′sive** (-siv) *adj.*

Synonyms: backbite, calumniate, decry, defame, depreciate, disparage, libel, malign, revile, slander, traduce, vilify. To *asperse* is to bespatter with injurious charges; to *defame* is to assail one's good name; to *malign* is to circulate studied and malicious attacks upon character; to *traduce* is to exhibit real or assumed traits in an odious light. *Antonyms*: defend, eulogize, extol, laud, praise.

as·per·sion (ə·spûr′zhən, -shən) *n.* **1** A slandering. **2** Slander; a slanderous report or charge. See synonyms under SCANDAL. **3** Sprinkling; specifically, baptism by sprinkling.

as·per·so·ri·um (as′pər·sôr′ē·əm, -sō′rē-) *n. pl.* **·so·ri·a** (-sôr′ē·ə, -sō′rē·ə) or **·so·ri·ums** **1** A font for holy water. **2** An aspergill. Also **as·per·so·ry** (as·pûr′sə·rē). [<LL <L *aspersus.* See ASPERSE.]

as·phalt (as′fôlt, -falt) *n.* **1** A bituminous, solid, brownish-black, odorous combustible mixture of different hydrocarbons occurring in superficial deposits in various parts of the world and also obtained as a residue in the refining of petroleum; mineral pitch. **2** A mixture of this with sand or gravel, used for paving, etc. Also **as·phal·tum** (as·fal′·təm), **as·phal′tus.** — *v.t.* To pave or cover with asphalt. [<LL *asphaltum* <Gk. *asphaltos,* ? <Semitic] — **as·phal·tic** (as·fôl′tik, -fal′-) *adj.*

as·pho·del (as′fə·del) *n.* **1** A plant (genus *Asphodelus*) of the lily family, bearing white or yellow flowers. **2** Any one of certain somewhat similar plants. [<L *asphodelus* <Gk. *asphodelos.* Doublet of DAFFODIL.]

as·phyx·i·a (as·fik′sē·ə) *n. Pathol.* A condition, characterized by loss of consciousness, caused by too little oxygen and too much carbon dioxide in the blood, generally as a result of suffocation. Also **as·phyx·y** (as·fik′sē). [<NL <Gk. *asphyxia* <*a-* not + *sphyzein* beat] — **as·phyx′i·al** *adj.*

as·phyx·i·ant (as·fik′sē·ənt) *adj.* Producing or tending to produce asphyxia. — *n.* An asphyxiant agent or condition.

as·phyx·i·ate (as·fik′sē·āt) *v.* **·at·ed, ·at·ing** *v.t.* **1** To cause asphyxia in. **2** To suffocate, as by drowning or causing to breathe noxious gases. — *v.i.* To undergo asphyxia. — **as·phyx′i·a′tion** *n.* — **as·phyx′i·a′tor** *n.*

as·pic[1] (as′pik) *n. Poetic* The asp. Also **as′pis.** [<F <L *aspis*]

as·pic[2] (as′pik) *n.* The spike lavender. See under LAVENDER. [<F <Provençal *espic* <L *spica* spike, ear of corn]

as·pic[3] (as′pik) *n.* A savory jelly of meat juice or vegetable juices, served as a relish or mold for meat, vegetables, etc. [<F; ult. origin uncertain]

as·pi·dis·tra (as′pə·dis′trə) *n.* Any of a small genus *(Aspidistra)* of smooth, stemless, Chinese and Japanese herbs of the lily family, with large, glossy, evergreen leaves: widely cultivated as a house plant. [<NL <Gk. *aspis, aspidos* shield + *astron* star]

As·pin·wall (as′pin·wôl) Former name of COLÓN, Panama.

as·pir·ant (ə·spīr′ənt, as′pər·ənt) *n.* One who aspires, as after honors or place; a candidate. — *adj.* Aspiring.

as·pi·rate (as′pə·rāt) *v.t.* **·rat·ed, ·rat·ing** **1** *Phonet.* **a** To utter with a breathing or as if preceded by the letter *h.* **b** In the articulation of a stop consonant, to follow with an explosive release of breath, as (p), (t), and (k) when in initial position. **2** *Med.* To draw out, as gas or fluid, from a vessel or cavity. — *n.* (as′pər·it) **1** *Phonet.* **a** The glottal fricative represented in English and many other languages by the letter *h.* **b** The sudden expulsion of breath in the release of a stop consonant before a vowel, as after the (p) in *pat.* **2** The rough breathing in Greek or the symbol (ʽ) indicating it. **3** Any consonant pronounced with a puff of breath. — *adj.* (as′pər·it) *Phonet.* Uttered with an aspirate or strong *h* sound: also **as′pi·rat′ed.** [<L *aspiratus,* pp. of *aspirare.* See ASPIRE.]

as·pi·ra·tion (as′pə·rā′shən) *n.* **1** The act of aspiring; exalted desire; high ambition. **2** The act or effect of aspirating; a breath. **3** *Med.* The use of an aspirator for remedial purposes. **4** *Phonet.* **a** The pronunciation of a consonant with an aspirate. **b** An aspirate. See synonyms under AIM, AMBITION, DESIRE.

as·pi·ra·tor (as′pə·rā′tər) *n.* **1** An appliance for producing a suction current of air or other gas. **2** *Med.* A device for drawing off fluid matter or gases from the body by suction.

as·pir·a·to·ry (ə·spīr′ə·tôr′ē, -tō′rē) *adj.* Of, pertaining to, or adapted for breathing or suction.

as·pire (ə·spīr′) *v.i.* **as·pired, as·pir·ing** **1** To have an earnest desire or ambition, as for something high and good: with *to.* **2** To long for; seek after: with *after.* **3** *Obs.* To reach or rise upward. [<L *aspirare* breathe on, attempt to reach <*ad-* to + *spirare* breathe] — **as·pir′ing** *adj.* — **as·pir′er** *n.*

as·pi·rin (as′pər·in) *n.* A white crystalline compound, the acetyl derivative of salicylic acid, $C_9H_8O_4$, having antipyretic and antirheumatic properties. [<A(CETYL) + SPIR(AEIC ACID), former name of salicylic acid, + -IN]

a·squint (ə·skwint′) *adj.* & *adv.* With sidelong glance. [<A-[1] on + SQUINT (of uncertain origin)]

As·quith (as′kwith), **Herbert Henry,** 1852–1928, English premier 1908–16; created Earl of Oxford and Asquith 1925.

ass[1] (as) *n.* **1** A long-eared equine quadruped *(Equus asinus)* smaller than the ordinary horse. **2** The Mongolian onager. **3** An obstinate or stupid person. [OE *assa,* ? <OIrish *assan* <L *asinus*]

ass[2] (äs) *n. Scot.* Ashes: also spelled *aise.*

ass[3] (as) *n. Slang* The buttocks: usually considered vulgar. [ME *ars* <OE *ærs, ears*]

as·sa·fet·i·da (as′ə·fet′ə·də) See ASAFETIDA.

as·sa·gai (as′ə·gī) *n.* **1** A light spear, used by Zulus, Kafirs, etc. **2** The assagai tree. — *v.t.* To pierce with an assagai. Also *assegai.* [<Sp. *azagaya* or Pg. *azagaia* <Arabic *az-zaghāyah* <*al* the + *zaghāyah* spear <native Berber word]

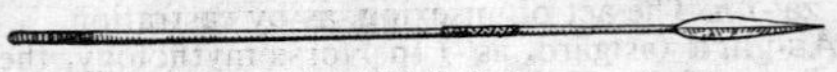

ASSAGAI

assagai tree A South African tree *(Curtisia faginea)* of the dogwood family, used for making spears.

as·sai[1] (ä·sä′ē) *n.* **1** A palm of the genus *Euterpe,* especially *E. edulis,* bearing a purple, fleshy fruit. **2** A drink made from this fruit. [<Pg. *assahy* <Tupian]

as·sai[2] (äs·sä′ē) *adv. Music* Very: Adagio *assai* means very slowly. [<Ital.]

as·sail (ə·sāl′) *v.t.* **1** To attack violently, as by force, argument, or censure; assault. **2** To approach, as a difficulty, with the intention of mastering. See synonyms under ATTACK. [<OF *asalir, asaillir* <LL *adsalire* leap upon <L *ad-* to + *salire* leap] — **as·sail′a·ble** *adj.* — **as·sail′a·ble·ness** *n.* — **as·sail′er** *n.*

as·sail·ant (ə·sā′lənt) *adj.* Attacking; hostile. — *n.* One who assails.

As·sam (a·sam′) A state in NE India; 54,951 square miles; capital, Shillong.

As·sa·mese (as′ə·mēz′, -mēs′) *adj.* Of or pertaining to Assam. — *n.* **1** A native or inhabitant of Assam. **2** The Indo-European, Indic language of the Assamese people.

Assam States A former political agency, comprising a number of small states, situated within Assam, India.

as·sas·sin (ə·sas′in) *n.* **1** One who kills, or tries to kill, secretly or treacherously. **2** One who undertakes to commit murder, particularly of a political figure, for a reward.

As·sas·sin (ə·sas′in) *n.* One of a secret order of hashish-eating Moslem fanatics who murdered Christian leaders in the time of the Crusades. [<F <Med. L *assassinus* <Arabic *hashshāshīn* hashish-eaters <*hashīsh* hashish]

as·sas·si·nate (ə·sas′ə·nāt) *v.t.* **·nat·ed, ·nat·ing** **1** To kill by secret or surprise assault. **2** To destroy or wound by treachery, as a reputation. See synonyms under KILL. — **as·sas′si·na′tion** *n.* — **as·sas′si·na′tor** *n.*

assassin bug Any of a predatory species of hemipterous insects (family *Reduviidae*) having a short curved beak: some species suck the blood of warm-blooded animals. See illustration under INSECT (beneficial).

assassin fly A hairy, predatory fly (family *Asilidae*), especially the common robber fly (genus *Erax*) of the United States. See illustration under INSECT (beneficial).

as·sault (ə·sôlt′) *n.* **1** Any violent attack, as an act, speech, or writing assailing a person or institution. **2** *Law* An unlawful attempt or offer to do bodily injury to another: distinguished from *battery.* **3** A rape. **4** *Mil.* A violent attack by troops, as upon a fortified place. See synonyms under AGGRESSION,

ATTACK. — *v.t.* & *v.i.* To attack with violence; make an assault (upon). [<OF *asaut* <L *ad-* to + *salire* leap] — **as·sault′er** *n.*

assault and battery *Law* The carrying out of an assault with force and violence; a beating.

assault boat *Mil.* A small craft used to transport attacking soldiers and their equipment across water.

as·say (ə·sā′, as′ā) *n.* **1** The chemical analysis or testing of an alloy or ore, to ascertain the ingredients and their proportions. **2** The substance to be so examined. **3** The result of such a test. **4** Any examination or testing. **5** *Obs.* Attempt; trial. — *v.t.* (ə·sā′) **1** To subject to chemical analysis; make an assay of. **2** To prove; test. **3** *Obs.* To attempt. — *v.i.* **4** To show by analysis a certain value or proportion, as of a precious metal: to *assay* low in platinum. [<OF *assai,* var. of *essai* trial <L *exagium* a weighing < *exigere* prove < *ex-* out + *agere* drive, do. Doublet of ESSAY.] — **as·say′er** *n.*

as·say·ing (ə·sā′ing) *n.* The process of making an assay.

as·se·gai (as′ə·gī) See ASSAGAI.

as·sem·blage (ə·sem′blij, *for def.* 4, *also Fr.* à·säṅ·blàzh′) *n.* **1** An assembling or being assembled. **2** Any gathering of persons or things; collection; assembly. **3** A fitting together, as parts of a machine. **4** A work of art created by assembling materials and objects; also, the technique of making such works. See synonyms under ASSEMBLY, COMPANY. [<F]

as·sem·ble (ə·sem′bəl) *v.t.* & *v.i.* **·bled, ·bling** **1** To collect or convene; come together; congregate, as a group or meeting. **2** To fit or join together, as the parts of a mechanism. See synonyms under CONVOKE. [<OF *as(s)embler* <L *assimulare* < *ad-* to + *simul* together] — **as·sem′bler** *n.*

as·sem·bly (ə·sem′blē) *n. pl.* **·blies** **1** An assembling or being assembled. **2** A number of persons met together for a common purpose. **3** The act or process of fitting together the parts of a machine, etc., especially where such parts are machine-made in great numbers so as to be interchangeable. **4** A unit made up of such parts. **5** The parts themselves, before or after being fitted together. **6** *Mil.* The signal calling troops to form ranks. [<OF *as(s)emblee* < *as(s)embler.* See ASSEMBLE.]

Synonyms: assemblage, collection, company, conclave, concourse, conference, congregation, convention, convocation, crowd, gathering, group, host, meeting, multitude. An *assemblage* may be of persons or of objects and is promiscuous and unorganized, an *assembly* is always of persons and is organized and united in some common purpose.

As·sem·bly (ə·sem′blē) *n.* In some states of the United States, the lower house of the legislature.

assembly line An arrangement of machines and workers in a factory, as along a moving track or belt, so that a number of specialized operations may be performed on a unit of work as it passes from one to another.

as·sem·bly·man (ə·sem′blē·mən) *n. pl.* **·men** (-men′, -mən) *U.S.* A member of a legislative assembly, especially of the lower house of a state legislature.

as·sent (ə·sent′) *v.i.* To express agreement, as with an abstract proposition; acquiesce; concur: usually with *to.* — *n.* **1** Mental concurrence or agreement. **2** Consent of will; acquiescence. ◆ Homophone: *ascent.* [<OF *as(s)enter* <L *assentare,* freq. of *assentire* < *ad-* to + *sentire* feel] — **as·sent′er** *n.*

Synonyms (verb): accede, accept, accord, acquiesce, admit, agree, approve, coincide, concur, consent, ratify, sustain, uphold. To *assent* is an act of the understanding; to *consent,* of the will. *Assent* is sometimes used for a mild or formal *consent.* See BELIEF. *Antonyms*: contradict, demur, deny, differ, disagree, disavow, disclaim, dissent, object, protest, question, refuse.

as·sen·ta·tion (as′en·tā′shən) *n.* Obsequious assent, as to the opinions of another.

as·sen·tor (ə·sen′tər) *n.* An assenter; specifically, in Great Britain, one who, as required by law, endorses the nomination of a candidate for Parliament.

as·sert (ə·sûrt′) *v.t.* **1** To state positively; affirm; declare. **2** To maintain as a right or claim, as by words or force. **3** To insist on the recognition of (oneself): He *asserted* himself at the conference. [<L *assertus,* pp. of *asserere* bind to, claim < *ad-* to + *serere* bind] — **as·sert′er, as·ser′tor** *n.*

Synonyms: affirm, allege, asseverate, aver, avouch, avow, claim, declare, maintain, pronounce, protest, say, state, tell. One may *assert* himself, his right, his belief, etc. *Assert* is controversial; *affirm, state,* and *tell* are simply declarative. See AFFIRM, ALLEGE. *Antonyms*: contradict, contravene, controvert, deny, disprove, dispute, gainsay, oppose, repudiate, retract, waive.

as·ser·tion (ə·sûr′shən) *n.* **1** The act of asserting. **2** A positive declaration without attempt at proof. **3** Insistence upon a right or claim. See synonyms under ASSURANCE.

as·ser·tive (ə·sûr′tiv) *adj.* **1** Of, pertaining to, or characterized by assertion. **2** Characterized by excessive assertion; overly insistent. — **as·ser′tive·ly** *adv.* — **as·ser′tive·ness** *n.*

as·ser·to·ry (ə·sûr′tər·ē) *adj.* Tending to assert.

asses′ bridge The fifth proposition of the first book of Euclid, stating that the angles opposite the equal sides of an isosceles triangle are equal: so called from the difficulty beginners are supposed to have in comprehending it: also called *pons asinorum.*

as·sess (ə·ses′) *v.t.* **1** To charge with a tax, fine, or other payment, as a person or property. **2** To determine the amount of, as a tax or other fine on a person or property. **3** To value, as property, for taxation. **4** To take stock of; evaluate: to *assess* the situation. See synonyms under TAX. [<OF *assesser* <LL *assessare* fix a tax <L *assidere* sit by (as a judge in court) < *ad-* to + *sedere* sit] — **as·sess′a·ble** *adj.*

as·sess·ment (ə·ses′mənt) *n.* **1** An assessing. **2** Apportionment or amount assessed. **3** The valuation of property for taxation.

as·ses·sor (ə·ses′ər) *n.* **1** One who makes assessments, as for taxation. **2** A specialist assisting a judge. **3** Any adviser or assistant. [<L, lit., one who sits beside, an assistant judge (in LL, an assessor of taxes) < *assidere.* See ASSESS.] — **as·ses·so·ri·al** (as′ə·sôr′ē·əl, -sō′rē-) *adj.*

as·set (as′et) *n.* **1** An item of property. **2** A person, thing, or quality regarded as useful or valuable: Her intelligence is an *asset.*

as·sets (as′ets) *n. pl.* **1** *Law* The property of a deceased person that is convertible into money and held for the payment of debts or legacies. **2** All the property, real and personal, of a person, of a corporation, or of a partnership, which is or may be chargeable with the debts or legacies of such parties or persons. **3** In accounting, the entries in a balance sheet showing all the property or resources of a person or business, as accounts receivable, inventory, deferred charges, and plant: opposed to *liabilities.* — **liquid assets** Such securities and assets as can be realized immediately. — **working assets** Non-permanent convertible invested funds. [<AF *asetz,* OF *asez* enough <L *ad-* to + *satis* enough]

as·sev·er·ate (ə·sev′ə·rāt) *v.t.* **·at·ed, ·at·ing** To affirm or aver emphatically or solemnly. See synonyms under AFFIRM, ALLEGE, ASSERT. [<L *asseveratus,* pp. of *asseverare* < *ad-* to + *severus* serious] — **as·sev′er·a′tion** *n.*

As·shur (ä′shŏŏr, ash′ər) **1** Ashur. **2** Assyria.

as·sib·i·late (ə·sib′ə·lāt) *v.t.* **·lat·ed, ·lat·ing** To utter with a sibilant or hissing sound; change into a sibilant. [<L *assibilatus,* pp. of *assibilare* < *ad-* to + *sibilare* hiss] — **as·sib′i·la′tion** *n.*

as·si·du·i·ty (as′ə·dōō′ə·tē, -dyōō′-) *n. pl.* **·ties** **1** Close and continuous application or effort. **2** *Usually pl.* Faithful personal attentions; carefulness; watchfulness. See synonyms under INDUSTRY.

as·sid·u·ous (ə·sij′ōō·əs) *adj.* **1** Devoted or constant, as a person. **2** Unremitting; persistent, as an action. See synonyms under BUSY, INDUSTRIOUS. [<L *assiduus* < *assidere* sit by < *ad-* to + *sedere* sit] — **as·sid′u·ous·ly** *adv.* — **as·sid′u·ous·ness** *n.*

as·sign (ə·sīn′) *v.t.* **1** To set apart, as for a particular function; designate. **2** To appoint or station: to *assign* a soldier to a post. **3** To allot: to *assign* a share to a participant. **4** To ascribe or attribute: to *assign* a date to an event. **5** *Law* To make over or transfer, as personal property, to another. **6** *Mil.* To allocate, as personnel, units or materiel, to a military unit as an integral unit thereof: distinguished from *attach.* See synonyms under ALLEGE, ALLOT, APPORTION, ATTRIBUTE, COMMIT, SET. — *n. Law Usually pl.* Assignee. [<OF *as(s)igner* <L *assignare* < *ad-* to + *signare* make a sign < *signum* sign]

as·sign·a·ble (ə·sī′nə·bəl) *adj.* **1** Capable of being assigned or allotted. **2** Legally transferable. **3** Attributable: Volcanoes are *assignable* to these geographical conditions. — **as·sign′a·bil′i·ty** *n.* — **as·sign′a·bly** *adv.*

as·sig·nat (as′ig·nat, *Fr.* à·sē·nyà′) *n.* A promissory note of the French revolutionary government circulated as currency (1789–96) against the security of confiscated lands. [<F <L *assignatus,* pp. of *assignare.* See ASSIGN.]

as·sig·na·tion (as′ig·nā′shən) *n.* **1** An assigning or being assigned. **2** Something assigned; assignment. **3** An appointment for meeting, especially a secret or illicit one as made by lovers. **4** *Law* An assignment. [<OF *assignacion* <L *assignatio, -onis* < *assignare.* See ASSIGN.]

as·sign·ee (ə·sī′nē′, as′ə·nē′) *n.* **1** *Law* A person to whom property, rights, or powers are transferred by another. **2** *Obs.* An agent or trustee.

as·sign·ment (ə·sīn′mənt) *n.* **1** An assigning or being assigned. **2** Anything assigned, as a lesson or task. **3** *Law* **a** The transfer of a claim, right, or property or the instrument or writing of transfer. **b** The claim, right, or property transferred.

assignment of error *Law* A specification of the errors contained in the complaint, made by the plaintiff on a writ of error.

as·sign·or (ə·sī′nôr′, as′ə·nôr′) *n. Law* One who assigns or makes an assignment of any property, right, or interest. Also **as·sign·er** (ə·sī′nər).

as·sim·i·la·ble (ə·sim′ə·lə·bəl) *adj.* Capable of being assimilated. — **as·sim′i·la·bil′i·ty** *n.*

as·sim·i·late (ə·sim′ə·lāt) *v.* **·lat·ed, ·lat·ing** *v.t.* **1** *Physiol.* To take up and incorporate, as food. **2** To make into a homogeneous part, as of a substance or system. **3** To make alike or similar; cause to resemble: to *assimilate* British law to the laws of Scotland. **4** *Phonet.* To cause (a sound) to undergo assimilation. — *v.i.* **5** To become alike or similar. **6** To become absorbed and assimilated. See synonyms under COMPARE. [<L *assimilatus,* pp. of *assimilare* < *ad-* to + *similare* make like < *similis* like]

as·sim·i·la·tion (ə·sim′ə·lā′shən) *n.* **1** The act or process of assimilating. **2** *Physiol.* The transformation of digested nutriment into an integral and homogeneous part of the solids or fluids of the organism. **3** *Bot.* The starch-making function of plants. Compare ANABOLISM. **4** *Phonet.* The process whereby a sound is changed or modified to cause it to approach, or become identical with, a neighboring sound, as in the pronunciation (hôrsh′shōō′) for *horseshoe.* **5** *Psychol.* The process by which all new experience, when received into consciousness, is modified so as to be incorporated with the results of previous conscious processes. **6** *Sociol.* The acceptance by one social group or community of cultural traits normally associated with another.

as·sim·i·la·tive (ə·sim′ə·lā′tiv) *adj.* Assimilating; characterized by or tending to assimilation. Also **as·sim·i·la·to·ry** (ə·sim′ə·lə·tôr′ē, -tō′rē).

As·sin·i·boin (ə·sin′ə·boin) *n. pl.* **·boins** or **·boin** **1** A member of a tribe of North American Indians of Siouan stock, formerly inhabiting parts of Montana, North Dakota, and Saskatchewan. **2** The language of this tribe.

As·sin·i·boine (ə·sin′ə·boin) **1** A river in eastern Saskatchewan, Canada, flowing SE 600 miles to Red River at Winnipeg. **2** A mountain of the Canadian Rockies, in Banff National Park; 11,870 feet.

As·si·si (ə·sē′zē, *Ital.* äs·sē′zē) A town in

Umbria, central Italy; birthplace of St. Francis.

as·sist (ə·sist') *v.t.* **1** To give succor or support to; render help or service to; relieve. **2** To act as subordinate or deputy to. — *v.i.* **3** To give help or support. **4** In baseball, to aid a teammate or partner in a play. — **to assist at** To be present at (a ceremony, entertainment, etc.). — *n.* In baseball, a play that helps to put out a runner. See synonyms under ABET, AID, HELP, SERVE. [<F *assister* <L *assistere* < *ad-* to + *sistere* cause to stand] — **as·sist'er, as·sis'tor** *n.*

as·sis·tance (ə·sis'təns) *n.* Help; aid; support; relief. See synonyms under HELP.

as·sis·tant (ə·sis'tənt) *adj.* **1** Holding a subordinate or auxiliary place, office, or rank. **2** Affording aid; assisting. — *n.* One who or that which assists; a deputy or subordinate; helper. See synonyms under ACCESSORY, AUXILIARY.

assistant professor A teacher in a college who ranks immediately below an associate professor.

As·siut (ä·syōōt') See ASYUT.

as·size (ə·siz') *n.* **1** Originally, a session of a court. **2** *pl.* **a** One of the regular sessions of the judges of a superior court for the trial of cases by jury in any county of England or Wales. **b** The time and place of such sessions. **3 a** A judicial inquest. **b** The writ by which it is instituted. **c** An action to be decided by such an inquest. **4** In Scots law, a trial by jury; also, the jury. **5** A statute or ordinance, or a rule prescribed by law or authority, as for the regulation of weights and measures or prices of commodities, etc. **6** A standard of weight, measure, price, etc. — **grand assize** In early English law, a trial by a jury of 12 knights instead of a trial by combat. — **great** (or **last**) **assize** The Last Judgment. [<OF *as(s)ise* < *aseeir* sit at, settle <L *assidere.* See ASSESS.]

assize of arms An English enactment of 1181 that every freeman should maintain arms suitable to his rank and station.

as·so·ci·a·ble (ə·sō'shē·ə·bəl, -shə·bəl) *adj.* Capable of being associated, connected, or joined. — **as·so'ci·a·bil'i·ty** *n.*

as·so·ci·ate (ə·sō'shē·it, -āt) *n.* **1** A companion; one who is habitually or frequently in the company or society of another. **2** A partner; one who is connected with another, as in some business, act, interest, office, or position. **3** Anything that habitually or frequently accompanies or is associated with something else; a concomitant. **4** One admitted to partial membership in an association, society, or institution. **5** In some educational institutions, one who has finished a course shorter than that set for a degree: an *associate* in arts. — *adj.* **1** Joined with another or others; united; allied; existing or occurring together; concomitant. **2** Having subordinate or secondary status or privileges: an *associate* professor; also, entitled to a limited or specified participation, as in rights, privileges, and functions: an *associate* member of a society. — *v.* (ə·sō'shē·āt) **·at·ed, ·at·ing** *v.t.* **1** To bring into company or relation; combine together. **2** To unite (oneself) with another or others, as in friendship or partnership. **3** To connect mentally: to *associate* poetry with madness. — *v.i.* **4** To join or be in company or relation: with *with:* She *associates* chiefly with musicians. **5** To unite, as nations in a league; combine. See synonyms under ATTRIBUTE, MIX, UNITE. [<L *associatus,* pp. of *associare* join to < *ad-* to + *sociare* join < *socius* ally]

Synonyms (noun): ally, chum, coadjutor, colleague, companion, comrade, consort, fellow, friend, helpmate, mate, partner, peer. An *associate,* as used officially, implies a chief, leader, or principal, to whom the *associate* is not fully equal in rank. *Associate* is popularly used for mere friendly relations, but oftener implies some work, enterprise, or pursuit in which the associated persons unite. We rarely speak of *associates* in crime or wrong, using *confederates* or *accomplices* instead. *Companion* gives itself with equal readiness to the good or the evil sense. *Peer* implies equality rather than companionship; as, a jury of his *peers.* *Comrade* expresses more fellowship and good feeling than *companion.* *Consort* is a word of equality and

dignity, as applied especially to the marriage relation. Compare ACCESSORY, ACQUAINTANCE, FRIENDSHIP. *Antonyms:* antagonist, enemy, foe, hinderer, opponent, opposer, rival, stranger.

Associated Press An organization for collecting news and distributing it to member newspapers. Abbr. *AP, A.P.*

associate professor A teacher in a college who ranks immediately above an assistant professor and immediately below a professor or adjunct professor.

as·so·ci·a·tion (ə·sō'sē·ā'shən, -shē-) *n.* **1** An associating or the act of associating. **2** The state of being associated; fellowship; companionship. **3** A body of persons associated for some common purpose; corporation; society; partnership. **4** *U.S.* An organized, unchartered body of persons analogous to but distinguished legally from a corporation. **5** *Chem.* An aggregate, as of molecules: $(H_2O)_2$ is an *association* of two molecules of water. **6** *Ecol.* A grouping of many plant species over a wide area, sharing a common habitat and similar geographic conditions: a forest *association.* **7** *Psychol.* **a** The connection or relation of ideas, feelings, etc., with each other, with objects suggesting them, or with subjects of thought, by means of which their succession in the mind is determined. **b** The process of establishing such a connection. **8** *Brit.* Association football. — **as·so'ci·a·tion·al** *adj.*

Synonyms: alliance, club, community, companionship, company, confederacy, confederation, conjunction, connection, corporation, familiarity, federation, fellowship, fraternity, friendship, lodge, partnership, society, union. We speak of an *alliance* of nations, a *club* of pleasure-seekers, a *community* of Shakers, a *company* of soldiers or of friends, a *confederacy, confederation, federation,* or *union* of states, a *partnership, corporation,* or *company* in business, a *conjunction* of planets, a religious, literary, or scientific *association* or *society.* See ACQUAINTANCE, ALLIANCE, ASSOCIATE, CLASS, FRIENDSHIP, INTERCOURSE. *Antonyms:* disconnection, disunion, independence, isolation, separateness, separation, severance, solitude.

association football Soccer.

as·so·ci·a·tive (ə·sō'shē·ā'tiv, -shē·ə-) *adj.* **1** Of, pertaining to, or characterized by association. **2** Causing association. — **as·so'ci·a'tive·ly** *adv.*

as·soil (ə·soil') *v.t. Archaic* **1** To absolve; acquit. **2** To atone for; remove. [<OF *assoil,* present indicative of *assoldre* <L *absolvere.* Doublet of ABSOLVE.]

as·so·nance (as'ə·nəns) *n.* **1** Resemblance in sound; specifically, in prosody, correspondence of the accented vowels, but not of the consonants, as in *main, came.* **2** Rough likeness; approximation. [<F <L *assonans,* ppr. of *assonare* sound to, respond to < *ad-* to + *sonare* sound] — **as'so·nant** *adj.* & *n.*

as·sort (ə·sôrt') *v.t.* **1** To distribute into groups or classes according to kinds; classify. **2** To furnish, as a warehouse, with a variety of goods, etc. — *v.i.* **3** To fall into groups or classes of the same kind. **4** To associate; consort: with *with.* [<OF *assorter* < *a-* to (<L *ad-*) + *sorte* sort <L *sors* lot] — **as·sort'a·tive** (ə·sôr'tə·tiv) *adj.*

as·sort·ed (ə·sôr'tid) *adj.* **1** Consisting of or arranged in various sorts or kinds; varied; miscellaneous. **2** Sorted out; classified. **3** Matched; suited.

as·sort·ment (ə·sôrt'mənt) *n.* **1** The act of assorting or a being assorted; classification. **2** A collection or group of various things; miscellany.

As·sou·an, As·su·an (äs·wän') See ASWAN.

as·suage (ə·swāj') *v.* **as·suaged, as·suag·ing** *v.t.* **1** To make less harsh or violent; soothe; calm, as an excited person. **2** To alleviate; allay, as feelings. — *v.i.* **3** *Obs.* To grow less; abate; subside. Also *Obs.* **as·swage'.** See synonyms under ALLAY, ALLEVIATE. [<OF *as(s)ouagier,* ult. <L *ad-* to + *suavis* sweet] — **as·suage'ment** *n.*

as·sua·sive (ə·swā'siv) *adj.* Soothing; alleviating. — *n.* An alleviative.

as·sume (ə·sōōm') *v.t.* **as·sumed, as·sum·ing** **1** To take up or adopt, as a style of dress, aspect, or character: to *assume* a haughty mien. **2** To undertake, as an office or duty.

3 To arrogate to oneself; usurp, as powers of state. **4** To take for granted; suppose to be a fact: to *assume* the sun will shine tomorrow. **5** To affect; pretend to have. [<L *assumere* take up, adopt < *ad-* to + *sumere* take] — **as·sum·a·ble** (ə·sōō'mə·bəl) *adj.*

Synonyms: accept, affect, appropriate, arrogate, claim, feign, postulate, presume, pretend, take, usurp. The distinctive idea of *assume* is to *take* by one's own independent volition, whether well or ill, rightfully or wrongfully. One may *accept* an obligation or *assume* an authority that properly belongs to him; if he *assumes* what does not belong to him, he is said to *arrogate* or *usurp* it. A man may *usurp* the substance of *power* in the most unpretending way; what he *arrogates* to himself he *assumes* with a haughty and overbearing manner. If he *takes* to himself the credit and appearance of qualities he does not possess, he is said to *affect* or *feign,* or to *pretend* to, the character he thus *assumes.* What a debater *postulates* he openly states and *takes* for granted without proof; what he *assumes* he may *take* for granted without mention. What a man *claims* he asserts his right to *take;* what he *assumes* he *takes.* See PRETEND. *Antonyms:* see synonyms for RENOUNCE.

as·sumed (ə·sōōmd') *adj.* **1** Taken for granted. **2** Pretended; fictitious.

as·sum·ing (ə·sōō'ming) *adj.* Presumptuous; arrogant.

as·sump·sit (ə·sump'sit) *n. Law* **1** A promise or contract not under seal. **2** An action to enforce this, or to recover damages for a breach of this. [<L, he undertook]

as·sump·tion (ə·sump'shən) *n.* **1** An assuming, or that which is assumed. **2** A taking for granted; supposition. **3** Presumption; arrogance. **4** *Logic* A minor premise. See synonyms under ARROGANCE, ASSURANCE, PRETENSE. — **the Assumption 1** *Theol.* The doctrine that the Virgin Mary was bodily taken up into heaven at her death. **2** A church feast, observed on August 15, commemorating this event. [<L *assumptio, -onis* < *assumere.* See ASSUME.]

as·sump·tive (ə·sump'tiv) *adj.* **1** Characterized by assumption. **2** That can be assumed. **3** Presumptuous. — **as·sump'tive·ly** *adv.*

as·sur·ance (ə·shŏŏr'əns) *n.* **1** The act of assuring; a being assured. **2** A positive or encouraging declaration. **3** Full confidence; undoubting conviction. **4** Self-confidence; firmness of mind. **5** Boldness; effrontery. **6** *Brit.* Insurance.

Synonyms: arrogance, assertion, assumption, boldness, confidence, effrontery, impudence, presumption, self-assertion, self-confidence, self-reliance, trust. *Confidence* is founded upon reasons; *assurance* is largely a matter of feeling. In the bad sense, *assurance* is a vicious courage, with belief of one's ability to outwit or defy others; it is less gross than *impudence,* which is (according to its etymology) a shameless *boldness. Assurance* appears in act or manner; *impudence,* in speech. *Effrontery* is *impudence* defiantly displayed. Compare BELIEF, CERTAINTY, EFFRONTERY, FAITH, IMPUDENCE, PRIDE. *Antonyms:* bashfulness, confusion, consternation, dismay, distrust, doubt, hesitancy, misgiving, shyness, timidity.

as·sure (ə·shŏŏr') *v.t.* **as·sured, as·sur·ing 1** To make sure or secure; establish against change: His poems *assured* his immortality. **2** To give confidence to; convince: His success *assured* him of the validity of his mission. **3** To offer assurances concerning; guarantee, as something risky. **4** To promise confidently: He *assured* his friends he would return. **5** To insure. See synonyms under CONFIRM. [<OF *aseurer* <LL *assecurare* <L *ad-* to + *securus* safe] — **as·sur'a·ble** *adj.*

as·sured (ə·shŏŏrd') *adj.* **1** Made certain; undoubted; sure. **2** Self-possessed; confident. **3** Insured. See synonyms under CONSCIOUS, SECURE, SURE. — *n.* An insured person or persons. — **as·sur·ed·ly** (ə·shŏŏr'id·lē) *adv.* — **as·sur'ed·ness** *n.*

as·sur·er (ə·shŏŏr'ər) *n.* **1** One who or that which assures. **2** *Brit.* An insurance underwriter. Also **as·sur'or.**

as·sur·gent (ə·sûr'jənt) *adj.* **1** Rising or tending to rise. **2** *Her.* Rising out of the sea. **3** *Bot.* Curving upward. [<L *assurgens,*

-entis. ppr. of *assurgere* < *ad-* to + *surgere* rise]
—**as·sur′gen·cy** n.

As·syr·i·a (ə-sir′ē-ə)
An ancient empire of
western Asia: capital,
Nineveh. Also *Ashur,
Asshur.*

As·syr·i·an (ə-sir′
ē-ən) *adj.* Of, pertain-
ing to, or characteris-
tic of Assyria or its
people. —*n.* 1 A na-
tive of Assyria or the
Assyrian empire. 2
The Semitic language spoken by the Assyrians.
As·syr·i·ol·o·gist (ə-sir′ē-ol′ə-jist) *n.* A student
of Assyriology. Also **As·syr·i·o·log** (ə-sir′ē-ə-lôg,
-log) or **-logue.**
As·syr·i·ol·o·gy (ə-sir′ē-ol′ə-jē) *n.* The study of
Assyrian civilization, history, and language; Assyrian archeology.
As·tar·te (as-tär′tē) In Phoenician mythology,
the goddess of love: identified with *Ashtoreth* and
the Greek *Aphrodite*. [< L < Gk. *Astartē* < Sem-
itic]
a·sta·si·a (ə-stā′zhē-ə, -zhə) *n. Pathol.* Inability to
stand erect. [< NL < A-⁴ without + Gk. *stasis* a
standing]
a·stat·ic (ā-stat′ik, ə-) *adj.* 1 *Physics* Being in neutral equilibrium; having no tendency toward any
change of position. 2 Unsteady. —**a·stat′i·cal·ly**
adv. —**a·stat·i·cism** (ā-stat′ə-siz′əm, ə-) *n.*
as·ta·tine (as′tə-tēn, -tin) *n.* An unstable element
(symbol At, atomic number 85) belonging to the
halogen group, produced by bombarding bismuth with alpha particles, the most stable isotope having mass number 210 and a half-life of
8.3 hours. See PERIODIC TABLE. [< Gk. *astatos*
unstable + -INE²]
as·ter (as′tər) *n.* 1 Any of a large genus (*Aster*) of
plants of the composite family, having alternate
leaves, and flowers with white, purple, or blue
rays and yellow disk. 2 One of various allied
plants, as the China aster. 3 *Biol.* The star-
shaped figure appearing in the cytoplasm of a
cell during mitosis and associated with the centrosome and spindle fibers. See OVUM. [< L
< Gk. *astēr* star]
aster- *combining form* Star: *asteroid*. Also
asteri-, astero-. [< Gk. *astēr*]
-aster *suffix* A contemptuous diminutive: *poetaster, criticaster.* [< L *-aster,* dim. *suffix*]
As·ter·a·ce·ae (as′tə-rā′sē-ē) Former name of the
COMPOSITAE.
as·ter·a·ceous (as′tə-rā′shəs) *adj.* Of, pertaining
to, or resembling an aster.
as·te·ri·a (as-tir′ē-ə) *n.* Any gemstone which
when properly cut exhibits asterism. [< L, a precious stone < Gk. *asterios* starry]
as·te·ri·al·ite (as-tir′ē-əl-īt′) *n.* A fossil starfish.
[< NL *Asterias* a starfish + Gk. *lithos* a rock,
stone]
as·te·ri·at·ed (as-tir′ē-ā′tid) *adj.* 1 Grouped like
stars. 2 Radiating, as the rays of a star. 3 *Mineral.* Exhibiting asterism, as certain sapphires.
as·te·ri·on (as-tir′ē-on) *n. Anat.* The point behind
the ear marking the junction of the temporal, occipital, and parietal bones. [< Gk., neut. of *asterios* starry]
as·ter·isk (as′tər-isk) *n.* 1 *Printing* A starlike figure (*) used to indicate omissions, footnotes, references, etc. 2 Anything shaped like a star. —*v.t.*
To mark with an asterisk. [< L *asteriscus* < Gk.
asteriskos, dim. of *astēr* star]
as·ter·ism (as′tər-iz′əm) *n.* 1 *Printing* **a** A group
of asterisks (***, ****). **b** A group of three asterisks set in front of a passage in the form of a triangle to call attention to it. 2 *Astron.* **a** A cluster
of stars. **b** A constellation. 3 *Mineral.* The property of some crystals of showing a starlike figure
by reflected or transmitted light.
a·stern (ə-stûrn′) *adv. Naut.* 1 In or at the stern.
2 In the rear; at any point behind a vessel. 3 To
the rear; backward.
a·ster·nal (ā-stûr′nəl) *adj. Anat.* 1 Not attached
to the sternum. 2 Not having a sternum.

as·ter·oid (as′tə-roid) *adj.* 1 Star-shaped. 2 *Bot.*
Pertaining to or like an aster. —*n.* 1 *Astron.* Any
of several hundred small planets between Mars
and Jupiter: also called *planetoid*. 2 *Zool.* A starfish. —**as′ter·oi′dal** *adj.*
As·ter·oi·de·a (as′tə-roi′dē-ə) *n. pl.* A class of
echinoderms, comprising the true starfishes.
[< NL < ASTEROID] —**as′ter·oi′de·an** *adj. & n.*
As·ter·o·pe (as-ter′ə-pē) See STEROPE.
as·the·ni·a (as-thē′nē-ə, as′thə-nī′ə) *n. Pathol.*
General debility; lack of bodily strength; weakness. Also **as·the·ny** (as′thə-nē). [< NL < Gk. *astheneia* < *a-* without + *sthenos* strength]
as·then·ic (as-then′ik) *n.* 1 One who is physically
weak or undeveloped. 2 *Anthropol.* One who is
characterized by a lean, generally tall figure, and
light muscular development. —*adj.* 1 Of or pertaining too an asthenic person or type. 2 Of, pertaining to, or characterized by asthenia. Also
as·then′i·cal *adj.*
as·the·no·pi·a (as′thə-nō′pē-ə) *n. Patho.* Weakness or fatigue of the visual organs. [< NL
< Gk. *asthenēs* weak + -OPIA]
as·the·no·sphere (as-then′ə-sfir) *n. Geol.* A layer
of dense, mobile, plastic rock underlying the lithosphere of the earth. —**as·then·o·spher·ic**
(as-then′ə-sfer′ik) *adj.*
asth·ma (az′mə, as′-) *n. Pathol.* A chronic respiratory disorder characterized by recurrent paroxysmal coughing, and a sense of constriction
due to spasmodic contractions of the bronchi.
[< Gk., a panting < *azein* breathe hard]
asth·mat·ic (az-mat′ik, as-) *adj.* Of, pertaining
to, or affected with asthma. Also **asth·mat′i·cal.**
—*n.* A person suffering from or subject to
asthma. —**asth·mat′i·cal·ly** *adv.*
As·ti (äs′tē) A town in Piedmont, NW Italy.
a·stig·ma·tism (ə-stig′mə-tiz′əm) *n.* A structural
defect of the eye or a lens such that the rays of
light from an object do not converge to a focus,
thus causing imperfect vision or images. [< A-⁴
without + Gk. *stigma* mark]
as·tig·mat·ic (as′tig-mat′ik) *adj.* 1 Of, having, or
characterized by astigmatism. 2 Correcting astigmatism.
a·stir (ə-stûr′) *adv. & adj.* Stirring; moving about.
As·ti spu·man·te (äs′tē spoō-män′tā) An Italian
sparkling wine, originally made in Asti.
As·to·lat (as′tə-lät, -lat) An English town in Arthurian legend.
a·stom·a·tous (ā-stom′ə-təs, ā-stō′mə-) *adj. Biol.*
Without a mouth or breathing pores. Also
as·to·mous (as′tə-məs). [< A-⁴ without + Gk.
stoma, stomatos mouth]
As·ton (as′tən), **Francis William,** 1877–1945,
English physicist.
a·ston·ish (ə-ston′ish) *v.t.* 1 To affect with wonder and surprise; amaze; confound. 2 *Obs.* To
stun or paralyze, as by a shock. [< OF *estoner*
< L *ex-* out + *tonare* thunder] —**a·ston′ish·er** *n.*
—**a·ston′ish·ing** *adj.* —**a·ston′ish·ing·ly** *adv.*
a·ston·ish·ment (ə-ston′ish-mənt) *n.* 1 An act of
astonishing or the state of being astonished; surprise; amazement. 2 An object or cause of such
emotion. See synonyms under AMAZEMENT. PER-
PLEXITY.
a·ston·y (ə-ston′ē) *v.t.* **a·ston·ied, a·ston·y·ing**
Obs. 1 To astound; astonish. 2 To stun. [See AS-
TONISH] —**a·ston′ied** *adj.*
As·tor (as′tər), **John Jacob,** 1763–1848, U.S. fur
merchant and capitalist. —**Lady,** 1879–1964, *née*
Nancy Langhorne, Viscountess Astor, first
woman member of the British House of Commons, born in the United States.
As·to·ri·a (as-tôr′ē-ə, -tō′rē-ə) A port at the
mouth of the Columbia River in NW Oregon.
a·stound (ə-stound′) *v.t.* To overwhelm or shock
with wonder or surprise; confound. —*adj. Obs.*
Amazed; astonished. [ME *astoned* stunned, pp.
of *astonien* < OF *estoner*. See ASTONISH.]
As·tra·chan (as′trə-kan, -kən) *n.* A variety of apple of Russian origin.
a·strad·dle (ə-strad′l) *adv. & adj.* In a straddling
position; astride.
As·trae·a (as-trē′ə) In Greek mythology, the
goddess of justice.
as·tra·gal (as′trə-gəl) *n.* 1 *Archit.* A small convex
molding in the form of a string of beads. 2 *Anat.*
The ankle bone or tarsus. 3 *pl.* Dice: orig-

inally made from such bones. [< L *astragalus*
< Gk. *astragalos*]
as·trag·a·lus (as-trag′ə-ləs) *n. pl.* **·li** (-lī) *Anat.*
The proximal bone of the foot, as in man or
other vertebrates; talus; anklebone. [< L < Gk.
astragalos] —**as·trag′a·lar** (-lər) *adj.*
as·tra·khan (as′trə-kan, -kən) *n.* 1 The pelts of
very young lambs, with tightly curled wool,
from the region near Astrakhan. 2 A fabric with
a curled pile imitative of these pelts. Also
as′tra·chan.
As·tra·khan (as′trə-kan, -kən) A city in SE Russian S.F.S.R., on the Volga Basin.
as·tral (as′trəl) *adj.* 1 Of, pertaining to, coming
from, or·like the stars; starry. 2 *Biol.* Of, pertaining to, or exhibiting an aster: an *astral* phase. 3
In alchemy, susceptible to influences from the
stars: *astral* gold. 4 In theosophy, pertaining to
or consisting of a supersensible substance supposed to pervade all space and to be refined beyond the tangible world. —*n.* 1 An astral body.
2 An astral lamp. [< LL *astralis* < L *astrum* star
< Gk. *astron*] —**as′tral·ly** *adv.*
astral body 1 Any fantasmal appearance of the
human body. 2 In theosophy, a counterpart of
the human body, composed of astral substance,
accompanying it in life, and surviving its death.
astral lamp An oil lamp with a ring-shaped reservoir so placed that its shadow is not cast directly below the flame.
a·strand (ə-strand′) *adv. & adj.* Aground;
stranded.
as·tra·pho·bi·a (as′trə-fō′bē-ə) *n.* Morbid fear of
thunder and lightning. Also **as·tra·po·pho·
bi·a** (as′trə-pə-fō′bē-ə). [< NL < Gk. *astrapē*
lightning + -PHOBIA]
a·stray (ə-strā′) *adv. & adj.* Away from the right
path; wandering in or into error or evil. [< OF
estraie, pp. of *estraier* < L *extra-* beyond + *vagare* wander]
as·trict (ə-strikt′) *v.t.* 1 To bind; restrict; limit. 2
To bind by moral or legal obligation, as an inheritance. [< L *astrictus,* pp. of *astringere.* See
ASTRINGE.] —**as·tric′tion** *n.*
as·tric·tive (ə-strik′tiv) *adj.* 1 Astringent; styptic. 2 *Obs.* Restrictive; obligatory. —*n.* An astringent. —**as·tric′tive·ly** *adv.* —**as·tric′
tive·ness** *n.*
a·stride (ə-strīd′) *adv. & adj.* 1 With one leg on
each side. 2 With the legs far apart. —*prep.* With
one leg on each side of: *astride* a horse.
as·tringe (ə-strinj′) *v.t.* **as·tringed, as·tring·ing** To
bind or draw together; compress; constrict. [< L
astringere < *ad-* to + *stringere* bind fast]
as·trin·gent (ə-strin′jənt) *adj.* 1 *Med.* Tending to
contract or draw together organic tissues; binding; styptic. 2 Harsh; stern; austere. —*n.* An astringent substance, as alum, tannin, etc. [< L *as-
tringens, -entis,* ppr. of *astringere.* See ASTRINGE.]
—**as·trin′gen·cy** *n.* —**as·trin′gent·ly** *adv.*
astro- *combining form* Star: *astrometry*. [< Gk.
astron star]
as·tro·bot·a·ny (as′trō-bot′ə-nē) *n.* The investigation of plant life on planets other than the
earth, especially on Mars. Also **as′tro·bo·tan′ics.**
—**as′tro·bot′an·ist** *n.*
as·tro·cyte (as′trə-sīt) *n. Biol.* 1 A star-shaped
cell, as of the neuroglia. 2 A bone corpuscle; osteoblast.
as·tro·dome (as′trə-dōm) *n.* A transparent
domelike structure incorporated in some aircraft
to facilitate observation of celestial bodies.
as·tro·ga·tion (as′trə-gā′shən) *n.* In space travel,
navigation by the stars. [< ASTRO- +
(NAVI)GATION] —**as′tro·ga′tor** *n.*
as·tro·labe (as′trə-lāb) *n.* An instrument formerly used for obtaining the altitudes of planets
and stars. [< OF *astrelabe* < Med.L *astrolabium*
< Gk. *astrolabon,* orig., star-taking < *astron* star
+ *lambanein* take]
as·trol·o·ger (ə-strol′ə-jər) *n.* 1 One who studies
astrology. 2 *Obs.* An astronomer.
as·trol·o·gy (ə-strol′ə-jē) *n.* 1 Originally, the
practical application of astronomy to human
uses. 2 The study professing to foretell the
future and interpret the influence of the
heavenly bodies upon the destinies of men.

[< L *astrologia* < Gk. *astrologia* < *astron* star + *logos* discourse < *legein* speak] **—as·tro·log·ic** (as'trə·loj'ik) or **·i·cal, as·trol'o·gous** (-gəs) *adj.* — **as'tro·log'i·cal·ly** *adv.*

as·tro·me·te·or·ol·o·gy (as'trō·mē'tē·ə·rol'ə·jē) *n.* The study of the supposed influence of the heavenly bodies on our atmosphere.

as·trom·e·try (ə·strom'ə·trē) *n.* That branch of astronomy which determines the apparent positions, motions, and magnitudes of the heavenly bodies.

as·tro·naut (as'trə·nôt) *n.* One who travels in space. [< ASTRO- + *(aero)naut*]

as·tro·nau·tics (as'trə·nô'tiks) *n.* The science of space travel.

as·tro·nav·i·ga·tion (as'trō·nav'ə·gā'shən) *n.* That part of navigation in which position is determined by observation of celestial bodies; nautical astonomy. **—as'tro·nav'i·ga'tor** *n.*

as·tron·o·mer (ə·stron'ə·mər) *n.* One learned or expert in astronomy; a skilled observer of the heavenly bodies.

as·tro·nom·ic (as'trə·nom'ik) *adj.* **1** Of or pertaining to astronomy. **2** Enormously or inconceivably large, like the quantities used in astronomy. Also **as'tro·nom'i·cal.** **—as'tro·nom'i·cal·ly** *adv.*

astronomical time (or **day**) See under TIME.

astronomical unit A space unit for expressing the distances of the stars, equal to the mean distance of the earth from the sun. Compare PARSEC.

astronomical year See under YEAR.

as·tron·o·my (ə·stron'ə·mē) *n.* **1** The science that treats of the heavenly bodies, their motions, magnitudes, distances, and physical constitution. **2** A treatise on this science. [< OF *astronomie* < L *astronomia* < Gk. *astronomia* < *astron* star + *nomos* law < *nemein* distribute, arrange]

as·tro·pho·tog·ra·phy (as'trō·fə·tog'rə·fē) *n.* The art or practice of photographing heavenly bodies. **—as·tro·pho·to·graph·ic** (as'trō·fō'tə·graf'ik) *adj.*

as·tro·pho·tom·e·ter (as'trō·fō·tom'ə·tər) *n.* An instrument for determining the brightness of stars by comparing them with a light source of standard brightness. **—as'tro·pho·tom'e·try** *n.* — **as·tro·pho·to·met·ri·cal** (as'trō·fō'tə·met'ri·kəl) *adj.*

as·tro·phys·ics (as'trō·fiz'iks) *n.* That branch of astronomy which treats of the physical constitution and properties of the heavenly bodies, especially as revealed by spectrum analysis. — **as'tro·phys'i·cal** *adj.* **—as·tro·phys·i·cist** (as'trō·fiz'ə·sist) *n.*

as·tro·sphere (as'trə·sfir) *n. Biol.* **1** That part of the aster which does not include the rays; the attraction sphere or centrosphere. **2** The whole aster excluding the centrosome.

As·tu·ri·as (as·tōōr'ē·əs, *Sp.* äs·tōō'ryäs) A region and former kingdom of NW Spain; 4,207 square miles.

as·tute (ə·stōōt', ə·styōōt') *adj.* Keen in discernment; acute; shrewd; sagacious, cunning. Also **as·tu·cious** (ə·stōō'shəs, ə·styōō'-), **as·tu'tious.** [< L *astutus* < *astus* cunning] **—as·tute'ly** *adv.* **—as·tute'ness** *n.*

Synonyms: acute, clear-sighted, crafty, cunning, discerning, discriminating, keen, knowing, penetrating, penetrative, perspicacious, sagacious, sharp, shrewd, subtile, subtle. *Acute* suggests the sharpness of the needle's point; *keen* the sharpness of the cutting edge. The *astute* mind adds to *acuteness* and *keenness* an element of cunning or finesse. *Knowing* has often a slightly invidious sense. See ACUTE, INTELLIGENT, KNOWING. *Antonyms*: blind, dull, idiotic, imbecile, shallow, short-sighted, stolid, stupid, undiscerning, unintelligent.

As·ty·a·nax (as·tī'ə·naks) In the *Iliad,* the son of Hector and Andromache, hurled from the battlements of Troy by the Greeks.

a·sty·lar (ā·stī'lər) *adj. Archit.* Having neither column nor pilaster. [< A-[4] without + Gk. *stylos* pillar]

A·sun·ción (ä·sōōn·syôn') The capital of Paraguay and principal port on the Paraguay River.

a·sun·der (ə·sun'dər) *adv.* **1** In or into a different place or direction. **2** Apart; into pieces. *—adj.* Separated; apart. [OE *on sundran.* See SUNDER.]

As·wan (äs·wän') A city on the Nile in southern Egypt; site of the **Aswan Dam** (1 1/4 miles long; 176 feet high): also *Assouan, Assuan*: ancient *Syene.*

a·swim (ə·swim') *adv.* & *adj.* Afloat; swimming.

a·swoon (ə·swōōn') *adv.* & *adj.* In a swooning state.

a·syl·lab·ic (ā'si·lab'ik) *adj.* Not syllabic.

a·sy·lum (ə·sī'ləm) *n. pl.* **·lums** or **·la** (-lə) **1** An institution for the care of some class of afflicted, unfortunate, aged, or destitute persons; a retreat. **2** A place of refuge; retreat; shelter. **3** An inviolable shelter from arrest or punishment, as a temple or church in ancient times. **4** The protection afforded by a sanctuary or refuge. See synonyms under REFUGE. **—right of asylum** In international law: **1** The right to protection from arrest, subject to the will of the official in charge, enjoyed by a person who takes refuge in a foreign embassy or ministry or on a foreign warship. **2** The right to sanctuary enjoyed by troops or naval vessels taking refuge in neutral territory or waters. **3** Formerly, the right to shelter from extradition granted a political refugee in a foreign country. [< L < Gk. *asylon* < *a-* without + *sylon* right of seizure]

a·sym·met·ric (ā'si·met'rik, as'i-) *adj.* **1** Not symmetrical. **2** *Chem.* Designating an atom with optical activity, each of whose valences is held by a different atom or radical. Also **a'·sym·met'ri·cal.** **—a'sym·met'ri·cal·ly** *adv.*

asymmetric carbon atom A carbon atom combined with four atoms or groups, no two of which are alike, as in the lactic acids.

a·sym·me·try (ā·sim'ə·trē) *n.* Lack of symmetry or proportion. [< Gk. *asymmetria* < *a-* without + *symmetria* symmetry]

a·symp·to·mat·ic (ā'simp·tə·mat'ik) *adj.* Without symptoms: an *asymptomatic* patient.

as·ymp·tote (as'im·tōt) *n. Math.* A straight line which an indefinitely extended curve continually approaches as a limit. [< Gk. *asymptōtos* not falling together < *a-* not + *syn-* together + *piptein* fall] **—as'ymp·tot'ic** (-tot'·ik) or **·i·cal** *adj.* — **as'ymp·tot'i·cal·ly** *adv.*

a·syn·chro·nism (ā·sing'krə·niz'əm) *n.* Lack of synchronism, or coincidence in time. — **a·syn'chro·nous** (-nəs) *adj.*

as·yn·det·ic (as'in·det'ik) *adj.* **1** Of or pertaining to asyndeton. **2** Without cross-references: said of a library catalog. **—as'yn·det'i·cal·ly** *adv.*

a·syn·de·ton (ə·sin'də·ton) *n.* In rhetoric, the omission of conjunctions between parts of a sentence, as "On your mark, get set, go!" Compare POLYSYNDETON. [< L < Gk. *asyndeton* < *a-* not + *syn-* together + *deein* bind]

a·syn·tac·tic (ā'sin·tak'tik) *adj.* Not according to syntax; ungrammatical.

as you were A drill command which directs soldiers to assume the position or resume the movement preceding the last command, or which cancels an earlier command that has not yet been executed.

As·yut (äs·yōōt') A city on the Nile, the largest of Upper Egypt: also *Assiut.*

at (at, *unstressed* ət) *prep.* **1** In the exact position of: the point *at* the center of the circle. **2** On or near the coming of: the train leaving *at* two; a man *at* sixty. **3** During the course or lapse of: *At* the moment the matter is uncertain. **4** In contact with; on; upon: *at* the bottom of the sea. **5** To or toward: Look *at* that sunset! **6** Through; by way of: smoke coming out *at* the windows. **7** Within the limits of; present in: to be *at* the ball grounds. **8** Engaged or occupied in: to be *at* work. **9** Attending: He was *at* the party. **10** In the state or condition of: a nation *at* war. **11** In the region or vicinity of; in proximity to: The car is *at* the door. **12** Viewed from; with an interval of: a target *at* sixty paces. **13** Having reference to: He winced *at* the thought. **14** In the manner of: *at* a trot. **15** In pursuit or quest of; in the direction of: to catch *at* straws. **16** Dependent upon: to be *at* an enemy's mercy. **17** According to: Proceed *at* your discretion. **18** To the extent of; amounting to: paying interest *at* two per cent; pencils *at* a dime apiece. [OE *æt*]

Synonyms: about, by, during, in, near, on, to, toward, with, within. As regards place, *at* is not used with names of countries; we say *in* England, *in* France, etc.; with names of cities and towns we use *at* when we think merely of the local or geographical point; when we think of inclusive space, we employ *in;* as, we arrived *at* Liverpool; there are few rich men *in* this village. As regards time, *at* is used of a point of time, as of the hour, minute, or second; as, the train leaves *at* 10:30 a.m.; *at* is also used of indefinite divisions of time involving some duration; as, *at* morning, noon, or night; to lie awake *at* night. We say *at* the hour, *on* the day, *in* the year. *On* with certain divisions of time has a special precision, signifying exactly *at,* neither before nor after; as, the train leaves *on* the hour.

At *Chem.* Astatine (symbol At).

at- Assimilated var. of AD-.

at·a·bal (at'ə·bal) *n.* A Moorish tabor or kettledrum. [< Sp. < Arabic *at-tabl* the drum]

At·a·brine (at'ə·brin, -brēn) *n.* Proprietary name for a brand of quinacrine.

A·ta·ca·ma Desert (ä'tä·kä'mä) An arid region of northern Chile, rich in natural nitrate deposits, extending 600 miles south from the border of Peru.

a·tac·a·mite (ə·tak'ə·mīt) *n.* A dark-green basic chloride of copper, crystallizing in the orthorhombic system. [from Atacama Desert]

at·a·ghan (at'ə·gan) See YATAGHAN.

A·ta·hual·pa (ä'tä·wäl'pä), died 1533, last Inca king of Peru.

a·ta·jo (ä·tä'hō) *n. SW U.S.* **1** A string of mules. **2** A cross-path shortening a road. [< Sp. *hatajo*]

At·a·lan·ta (at'ə·lan'tə) In Greek mythology, a maiden who agreed to marry any suitor who could outrun her, the losers being put to death. She was won by Hippomenes, who outwitted her by dropping three golden apples which she paused to pick up allowing him to outrun her.

at·a·man (at'ə·man) *n.* A Cossack chief; hetman. [< Russian *atamanu* < Polish *hetman* < G *hauptmann* captain < *haupt* head + *mann* man]

at·a·mas·co (at'ə·mas'kō) *n.* A low North American plant (genus *Zephyranthes*) of the amaryllis family, bearing a large white and pink flower. [< Algonquian]

atamasco lily The atamasco or an allied plant.

at·a·rac·tic (at'ə·rak'tik) *adj.* **1** Conducive to peace of mind. **2** *Med.* Having the power to tranquilize and to lessen nervous tension: said of certain drugs, as reserpine. Also **at'a·rax'ic** (-rak'sik). [< NL < Gk. *ataraktos* untroubled < *atarakteein* be calm. See ATARAXIA.]

at·a·rax·i·a (at'ə·rak'sē·ə) *n.* Freedom from anxiety; peace of mind. Also **at·a·rax·y** (at'ə·rak'sē). [< NL < Gk. *ataraxia* < *atarakteein* be calm < *a-* not + *tarattein* disturb, trouble]

A·ta·türk (ä·tä·türk') See KEMAL ATATÜRK.

a·taunt (ə·tônt') *adv. Naut.* **1** With all sails set; in full-rigged condition. **2** In order; shipshape. [< F *autant* as much (as possible)]

at·a·vism (at'ə·viz'əm) *n.* **1** Reversion to an earlier or primitive type. **2** *Biol.* Reversion. [< F *atavisme* < L *atavus* ancestor < *at-* beyond + *avus* grandfather] **—a·tav·ic** (ə·tav'ik) *adj.* — **at'a·vist** *n.* **—at'a·vis'tic** *adj.*

a·tax·i·a (ə·tak'sē·ə) *n. Pathol.* **1** Irregularity in muscular action through failure of muscular coordination. **2** Locomotor ataxia. Also **a·tax·y** (ə·tak'sē). [< NL < Gk. *ataxia* lack of order < *a-* not + *tattein* arrange]

a·tax·ic (ə·tak'sik) *adj.* Characteristic of or caused by ataxia. *—n.* One afflicted with ataxia.

a·tax·it·ic (ā'tak·sit'ik) *adj. Geol.* Of or pertaining to ore deposits occurring in unstratified form: opposed to *eutaxitic.*

a·tax·o·phe·mi·a (ə·tak'sə·fē'mē·ə) *n. Pathol.* Defective coordination of the muscles of speech.

At·ba·ra (ät'bä·rä) A river in Ethiopia and NE Sudan, flowing 500 miles NE to the Nile.

A·tchaf·a·lay·a River (ə·chaf'ə·lī'ə) A river of southern Louisiana constituting an outlet of the Red and Mississippi Rivers during high water and flowing SE 170 miles to **Atchafalaya Bay,** an arm of the Gulf of Mexico.

ate[1] (āt, *chiefly Brit.* et) Past tense of EAT.

a·te[2] (ā'tē) *n.* In ancient Greek culture, the fatal and reckless blindness inciting men to crime. [< GK. *atē*]

A·te (ā'tē) In Greek mythology, a goddess, variously regarded as a daughter of Zeus or of Eris, personifying men's reckless blindness, later associated with the punishment of crime.

-ate[1] *suffix* Forming: **1** Participial adjectives equivalent to those in *-ated*: *desolate, separate.* **2** Adjectives from nouns with the meaning "possessing or characterized by": *caudate, foliate.* **3** Verbs, originally from stems of Latin verbs of the first conjugation, and, by analogy, extended to other stems: *fascinate, assassinate.* **4** *Chem.* Verbs with the meaning "combine or treat with": *chlorinate.* [<L *-atus,* pp. ending of 1st conjugation verbs]

-ate[2] *suffix* Forming: **1** Nouns denoting office, function, or agent: *magistrate.* **2** Nouns denoting the object or result of an action: *mandate.* [<L *-atus,* suffix of nouns]

-ate[3] *suffix Chem.* Used to form the names of salts and esters derived from acids whose names end in *-ic: carbonate, nitrate.* [<L *-atum,* neut. of *-atus* -ATE[1]]

at ease A drill command authorizing soldiers to relax but not to talk or leave their places; also, the position assumed at this command.

a·tech·nic (ā·tek′nik) *adj.* Without technical knowledge. [<Gk. *atechnos* unskilled <*a-* without + *technē* skill]

at·el·ier (at′əl·yā, *Fr.* å·tə·lyā′) *n.* A workshop, especially of an artist; studio. [<F, orig., pile of chips <OF *astele* chip <LL *astella* <L *astula* chip, splinter]

a·te·li·o·sis (ə·tē′lē·ō′sis, ə·tel′ē-) *n. Pathol.* An incomplete development of body or mind; infantilism. [<Gk. *atelēs* imperfect + -OSIS] **—a·tel·ic** (ə·tel′ik) *adj.*

a tem·po (ä tem′pō) *Music* In the regular time; resuming the rate of speed originally indicated. [<Ital.]

a·tem·po·ral (ā·tem′pə·rəl) *adj.* Timeless; outside of or apart from time.

Ath·a·bas·can (ath′ə·bas′kən) See ATHAPASCAN.

Ath·a·bas·ka River (ath′ə·bas′kə) A river in Alberta, Canada, flowing 765 miles to **Lake Athabaska** in northern Alberta and Saskatchewan; 3,058 square miles.

Ath·a·li·ah (ath′ə·lī′ə) The wife of Jehoram who usurped the throne of Judah on the death of her husband and on that of his successor. II *Kings* xi 1–16.

Ath·a·mas (ath′ə·mas) In Greek legend, king of Thessaly, husband of Nephele, who, seized with madness, killed his own son.

ath·a·na·sia (ath′ə·nā′zhə, -zhē·ə) *n.* Deathlessness; immortality. Also **a·than·a·sy** (ə·than′ə·sē). [<Gk. <*a-* without + *thanatos* death]

Ath·a·na·sian creed (ath′ə·nā′zhən) A formulary of Christian belief called after Athanasius and formerly ascribed to his authorship, but now assigned to a later date.

Ath·a·na·sian·ist (ath′ə·nā′zhən·ist) *n.* An adherent of Athanasius or of the Athanasian creed.

Ath·a·na·sius (ath′ə·nā′shəs, -shē·əs), 298?–373, one of the fathers of the church; patriarch of Alexandria; opponent of Arianism.

Ath·a·pas·can (ath′ə·pas′kən) *n.* **1** A large North American Indian linguistic stock, including languages of Alaska and NW Canada, the Pacific coast (especially in Oregon and California), and the Apache and Navaho tribes of the southern SW United States. **2** A member of a tribe speaking these languages. Also *Athabascan.*

a·thart (ə·thôrt′) *adv. & prep.* Athwart. Also **a·thort′.**

a·the·ism (ā′thē·iz′əm) *n.* **1** The belief that there is no God. **2** The disbelief in the existence of God. **3** Godlessness in life or conduct. [<F *athéisme* <Gk. *atheos* <*a-* without + *theos* god]

a·the·ist (ā′thē·ist) *n.* One who denies or disbelieves in the existence of God. See synonyms under SKEPTIC.

a·the·is·tic (ā′thē·is′tik) *adj.* **1** Of or pertaining to atheism or atheists. **2** Given to atheism; godless. Also **a′the·is′ti·cal. —a′the·is′ti·cal·ly** *adv.*

athe·ling (ath′ə·ling) *n. Archaic* **1** A crown prince. **2** Any member of a noble family. Also spelled *ætheling.* [OE *ætheling* <*æthelu* noble ancestry]

Ath·el·stan (ath′əl·stan) A masculine personal name. Also **Ath′el·stane** (-stān). [OE *Æthelstan,* lit., noble stone]

—Athelstan, 895–940, Anglo-Saxon king; grandson of Alfred.

a·the·mat·ic (ā′thē·mat′ik) *adj. Ling.* Not attached to or not constituting a stem.

A·the·na (ə·thē′nə) In Greek mythology, the goddess of wisdom, war, and patroness of arts and crafts: identified with the Roman *Minerva.* Also **A·the·ne** (ə·thē′·nē). [<Gk. *Athēnē*]

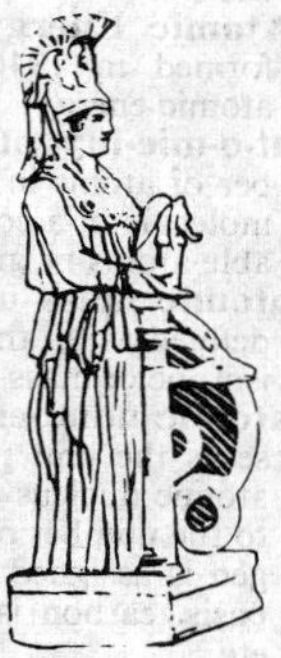

ATHENA
After a gold and ivory statuette; possibly by Phidias.

ath·e·ne·um (ath′ə·nē′əm) *n.* **1** A literary club, academy, or other institution for the promotion of learning. **2** A reading room, library, etc. Also **ath′e·nae′um.**

Ath·e·ne·um (ath′ə·nē′əm) *n.* **1** The temple of Athena at Athens. **2** An academy founded by Hadrian at Rome for the promotion of learning. Also **Ath′e·nae′um.** [<L <Gk. *Athenaion*]

A·the·ni·an (ə·thē′nē·ən) *adj.* Of or pertaining to Athens, or to its art or culture. *—n.* A native or citizen of Athens.

Ath·ens (ath′ənz) An ancient city in Attica and the present capital of Greece. *Greek* **A·the·nai, A·thi·nai** (ä·thē′nē).

a·ther·man·cy (ā·thûr′mən·sē) *n.* The state or quality of being athermanous.

a·ther·ma·nous (ā·thûr′mə·nəs) *adj.* Impervious to radiant heat. [<A-[4] without + Gk. *thermainein* heat <*thermos* hot]

ath·er·o·ma (ath′ə·rō′mə) *n. Pathol.* **1** A sebaceous cyst. **2** Arteriosclerosis accompanied by pronounced degenerative changes. [<L <Gk. *atherōma* <*atherē* gruel; with ref. to the encysted matter]

ath·er·o·scle·ro·sis (ath′ər·ō·sklə·rō′sis) *n. Pathol.* Hardening of the arteries, accompanied by degenerative tissue changes in the arterial walls. [<NL <Gk. *atherē* gruel + *sklēros* hard]

Ath·er·ton (ath′ər·tən), **Gertrude Franklin,** 1857–1948, *née* Horn, U.S. novelist.

ath·e·to·sis (ath′ə·tō′sis) *n. Pathol.* A derangement of the nervous system, in which the hands and feet, especially the fingers and toes, keep moving or twitching. [<Gk. *athetos* without position, unfixed <*a-* not + *tithenai* place]

a·thirst (ə·thûrst′) *adj.* **1** Wanting water; thirsty. **2** Keenly desirous; longing. [OE *ofthyrsted,* pp. of *ofthyrstan* <*of-,* intensive + *thyrstan* thirst]

ath·lete (ath′lēt) *n.* **1** One trained in acts or feats of physical strength and agility, as rowing, wrestling, etc. **2** In classical antiquity, a contestant in the public games. [<L *athleta* <Gk. *athlētēs* a contestant in the games <*athleein* contend for a prize <*athlos* a contest <*athlon* a prize]

athlete's foot Ringworm of the foot, caused by a parasitic fungus; dermophytosis.

ath·let·ic (ath·let′ik) *adj.* **1** Of, pertaining to, or like an athlete. **2** Strong; vigorous; muscular. **—ath·let′i·cal·ly** *adv.* **—ath·let·i·cism** (ath·let′ə·siz′əm) *n.*

ath·let·ics (ath·let′iks) *n. pl.* **1** Athletic games and exercises collectively. **2** A system of athletic training: usually construed as singular.

ath·o·dyd (ath′ō·did) *n.* Former name for a ramjet engine. [<A(ERO) TH(ERM)ODY(NAMIC) D(UCT)]

at-home (ət·hōm′) *n.* An informal party or reception given at one's home. *—adj.* For use at home; informal: *at-home clothing.*

Ath·os (ath′os, ā′thos), **Mount** The highest point on Chalcidice peninsula in Greek Macedonia, coextensive with the Akte prong; 6,670 feet; site of an autonomous monastic district; 131 square miles. *Greek* **Ha·gi·on O·ros** (ä′yē·ôn ô′rôs).

a·threp·si·a (ā·threp′sē·ə, -shə) *n.* **1** *Bacteriol.* Immunity from malignant tumors due to lack of food substance of tumor cells: also called *atrepsy.* **2** *Pathol.* Marasmus. [<NL <Gk. *a-* without + *threpsis* nourishment]

a·thrill (ə·thril′) *adj.* Thrilled.

a·thwart (ə·thwôrt′) *adv.* **1** From side to side; across. **2** So as to thwart; perversely. *—prep.* **1** Across the course of; from side to side of: The ship sailed *athwart* our course. **2** Contrary to; in opposition to: His action went *athwart* our plans. [<A-[1] on + THWART]

-atic *suffix* Of; of the kind of: used in adjectives of Latin or Greek origin: *erratic.* [<F *-atique* or <L *-aticus* <Gk. *-atikos*]

a·tilt (ə·tilt′) *adv. & adj.* **1** In a tilted manner; tilted up. **2** Like one tilting or making a lance thrust; hence, in spirited opposition.

at·i·my (at′ə·mē) *n.* Public dishonor or disgrace; deprivation of civic rights. [<Gk. *atimia* <*a-* without + *timē* honor]

-ation *suffix of nouns* **1** Action or process of: *creation.* **2** Condition or quality of: *affectation.* **3** Result of: *reformation.* Also *-ion, -tion.* ◆ **-ation** was originally found in English nouns borrowed from Latin, and is now used by analogy to form nouns on any stem, as in *starvation, thunderation.* [<F *-ation* or L *-atio, -ationis* <*-atus* -ATE[1] + *-io* -ION]

a·tip·toe (ə·tip′tō′) *adv.* On the tips of the toes.

A·ti·tlán (ä′tē·tlän′) **1** A town in SW Guatemala, on the south shore of **Lake Atitlán** (53 square miles). **2** An inactive volcano near Lake Atitlán; 11,565 feet.

-ative *suffix* Denoting relation, tendency, or characteristic: *tentative, remunerative, laxative.* [<F *-atif,* masc., *-ative,* fem. or <L *-ativus*]

At·ka (at′kə) The largest island of the Andreanof group in the Aleutian Islands.

At·kins (at′kinz), **Tommy** See TOMMY ATKINS.

At·lan·ta (at·lan′tə) A city in NW central Georgia; the state capital.

At·lan·te·an (at′lan·tē′ən) *adj.* **1** Pertaining to Atlas. **2** Pertaining to Atlantis. Also **At·lan·ti·an** (at·lan′tē·ən).

at·lan·tes (at·lan′tēz) *n. pl. Archit.* Male human figures, used in place of columns or pilasters. [<L <Gk. *Atlantes,* pl. of *Atlas*]

At·lan·tic (at·lan′tik) *adj.* **1** Of, near, in, or pertaining to the Atlantic Ocean. **2** Pertaining to or derived from Mount Atlas or the Atlas Mountains in NW Africa. *—n.* The Atlantic Ocean. [<L *Atlanticus* <Gk. *Atlantikos* pertaining to Atlas]

Atlantic Charter A statement resulting from a meeting at sea and issued in August 1941 by Churchill and Roosevelt, in which were set forth the basic aims of the Allied Nations for the peace after World War II.

Atlantic City A resort city on the Atlantic coast of SE New Jersey.

Atlantic Ocean The world's second largest ocean, extending from the Arctic to the Antarctic regions between the Americas and Europe and Africa; 31,500,000 square miles; divided by the equator into the **North Atlantic Ocean** and the **South Atlantic Ocean.**

At·lan·ti·des (at·lan′tə·dēz) *n. pl.* **1** The children of Atlas: the Pleiades, the Hesperides, etc. **2** The inhabitants of Atlantis.

At·lan·tis (at·lan′tis) A legenday island described by Plato as a center of civilization that was engulfed by the sea.

at·las (at′ləs) *n.* **1** A volume of maps usually bound together. **2** Hence, any bound collection of plates or engravings showing systematically the development of a subject, or any work producing such effect by tabular arrangement. **3** A large size of paper, 26 by 33 (34) inches. **4** *Anat.* The first cervical vertebra: so called after Atlas, who bore the world on his shoulders. **5** *Archit.* Any of the Atlantes. [def. 1 <ATLAS; because some early collections of maps contained a picture of Atlas supporting the heavens]

At·las (at′ləs) **1** In Greek mythology, a Titan supporting the pillars of heaven on his shoulders. **2** Anyone bearing a great burden. **3** An intercontinental ballistic missile of the U.S. Air Force. [<L <Gk. *Atlas* <*tlaein* bear]

Atlas beetle A large, olive-green Oriental beetle *(Chalcosoma atlas)* with two long, curved horns.

atlas grid A network of lines dividing an aerial photograph into squares to facilitate locating of points.

Atlas Mountains A range in NW Africa; highest peaks, over 15,000 feet.

at·latl (ät′lät·l) *n.* A throwing stick used to hurl a spear or harpoon at birds or aquatic animals. [<Nahuatl]

At·li (ät′lē) In the *Volsunga Saga,* a king who

married Gudrun and later murdered her brothers: identified with *Attila.*

at·man (ät′mən) *n.* In Hinduism, the soul, or selfhood; the spark in man emanating from divinity. **—Atman** The supreme soul from which all individual souls are derived and to which they return. [< Skt.]

atmo- *combining form* Vapor: *atmometer.* [< Gk. *atmos*]

at·mol·o·gy (at·mol′ə·jē) *n.* The science that treats of the laws of aqueous vapor. **— at·mo·log·ic** (at′mə·loj′ik) or **·i·cal** *adj.* **— at·mol′o·gist** *n.*

at·mol·y·sis (at·mol′ə·sis *n.* The act or process of partially separating mixtures of gases into their ingredients by virtue of their different diffusibility through porous substances. [< ATMO- + Gk. *lysis* a loosing]

at·mo·lyze (at′mə·līz) *v.t.* **·lyzed, ·lyz·ing** To separate by atmolysis. Also *Brit.* **at′mo·lyse. — at′mo·ly·za′tion** *n.* **—at′mo·lyz′er** *n.*

at·mom·e·ter (at·mom′ə·tər) *n.* An instrument for measuring rate of evaporation. **—at·mo·met·ric** (at′mə·met′rik) *adj.* **—at·mom′e·try** *n.*

at·mos·phere (at′məs·fir) *n.* **1** The mass or body of gases that surrounds the earth or any heavenly body. **2** The particular climatic condition of any place or region regarded as dependent on the air. **3** Any surrounding or pervasive element or influence: an *atmosphere* of gloom. **4** The prevailing tone of a poem, novel, painting, etc. **5** *Colloq.* An indefinable aura regarded as especially characteristic: This café has *atmosphere.* **6** *Physics* A conventional unit of pressure, the equivalent of the weight of a column of mercury 1 centimeter in diameter and 29.92 inches high at sea level, at a temperature of 0° C.: one atmosphere equals a pressure of 14.69 pounds per square inch. [< NL *atmosphaera* < Gk. *atmos* vapor + *sphaira* sphere]

at·mos·pher·ic (at′məs·fer′ik) *adj.* **1** Pertaining or belonging to or existing in atmosphere. **2** Dependent on, caused by, or resulting from the atmosphere. **3** Giving or creating atmosphere: *atmospheric* music. Also **at′mos·pher′i·cal.** See STATIC. **—at′mos·pher′i·cal·ly** *adv.*

at·mos·pher·ics (at′məs·fer′iks) *n.* Atmospheric conditions due to electromagnetic disturbances, especially as they affect radio transmission: also called *sferics, spherics.*

a·to·le (ä·tō′lā) *n. SW U.S.* Cornmeal mush. [< Sp. < Nahuatl]

at·oll (at′ôl, -ol, ə·tol′) *n.* A ring-shaped coral island and its associated reef, nearly or quite enclosing a lagoon. [< Malayalam *adal* closing, uniting]

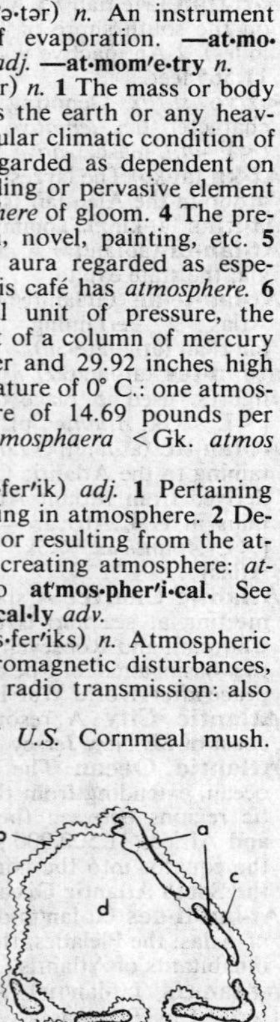

ATOLL
a. Islets. *b.* Barrier reef *c.* Fringing reef. *d.* Lagoon *e.* Passage.

at·om (at′əm) *n.* **1** *Chem.* The smallest part of an element capable of existing alone or in combination and which cannot be changed or destroyed in any chemical reaction: an *atom* of sulfur, carbon, etc.: distinguished from *molecule.* **2** *Physics* The electrically neutral combination of a nucleus and its complement of electrons to form a relatively stable, distinguishable unit, regarded as a unitary system. **3** A hypothetical entity admitting of no division into smaller parts. **4** An exceedingly small quantity or particle; iota. [< L *atomus* < Gk. *atomos* indivisible < *a-* not + *temnein* cut]

a·tom·ic (ə·tom′ik) *adj.* **1** Of or pertaining to an atom or atoms: also **a·tom′i·cal.** **2** Very minute; infinitesimal. **3** Of, characterized by or employing atomic energy: an *atomic* power plant. **— a·tom′i·cal·ly** *adv.*

atomic age The era characterized by the use and growing importance of atomic energy as a factor in human and social development. Also **Atomic Age.**

atomic bomb See under BOMB. Also **atom bomb.**

atomic clock A high-precision instrument for the measurement of time by a constant frequency associated with a selected line in the spectrum of ammonia gas or other suitable vibrator.

atomic energy The energy contained within the nucleus of the atom; especially, such energy when made available for human use by controlled nuclear fission or thermonuclear reactions.

Atomic Energy Commission A U.S. board formed in 1946 for the domestic control of atomic energy.

at·o·mic·i·ty (at′ə·mis′ə·tē) *n. Chem.* **1** The number of atoms in a molecule. **2** Valence. **3** In the molecule of a compound, the number of replaceable atoms or groups.

atomic mass unit *Physics* **1** A unit arbitrarily defined as 1/12 the mass of an atom of the carbon isotope of mass 12; a dalton. Abbr. *amu*

atomic number *Physics* A number which represents the unit positive charges (protons) in the atomic nucleus of each element and corresponds to the number of extra-nuclear electrons. Hydrogen is assigned an atomic number of 1; on this basis, carbon is 6, oxygen 8, iron 26, gold 79, etc.

atomic philosophy The philosophy, anciently expounded by Democritus, Epicurus, and Lucretius, which attempts to account for all material existence, or for the entire universe, as being composed of simple, indivisible atoms.

atomic pile Reactor.

atomic power Atomic energy as a source of power.

atomic structure *Physics* **1** The configuration of the atom. **2** The arrangement of atoms in a molecule or in bulk matter.

atomic submarine A nuclear submarine.

atomic theory **1** *Chem.* The doctrine that elements unite with one another, atom by atom, and in definite simple proportions by weight. **2** *Physics* The concept that all bulk matter is composed of atoms, and that the properties of matter are ultimately to be understood in terms of the properties and interactions of the component atoms.

atomic weight *Chem.* **a** Since 1961, the weight of an atom of an element relative to that of an atom of carbon, taken as 12.01115. **b** Formerly, the weight of an atom of an element relative to that of an atom of oxygen, taken as 16.

at·om·ism (at′əm·iz′əm) *n.* **1** The atomic philosophy. **2** The atomic theory. **—at′om·ist** *n.* **— at′om·is′tic** or **·ti·cal** *adj.*

at·om·ize (at′əm·īz) *v.t.* **·ized, ·iz·ing** **1** To reduce to or separate into atoms; pulverize. **2** To spray or reduce to a spray, as by an atomizer. Also *Brit.* **at′om·ise. —at′om·i·za′tion** *n.*

at·om·iz·er (at′əm·ī′zər) *n.* **1** An apparatus for reducing a liquid, especially medicine or perfume, to a spray.

at·om·me·ter (at′əm·mē′tər) *n.* The angstrom unit.

at·om·ol·o·gy (at′əm·ol′ə·jē) *n.* The study of atoms.

at·o·my[1] (at′ə·mē) *n. pl.* **·mies** *Archaic* **1** An atom. **2** A pigmy. [< L *atomi,* pl. of *atomus* atom]

at·o·my[2] (at′ə·mē) *n. pl.* **·mies** *Obs.* A skeleton or an emaciated person. [< ANATOMY (misunderstood as *an atomy*)]

a·to·nal (ā·tō′nəl) *adj. Music* Without tonality; lacking key. **—a·to′nal·ly** *adv.*

a·to·nal·ism (ā·tō′nəl·iz′əm) *n.* The theory of atonally composed music. **—a·to′nal·is′tic** *adj.*

a·to·nal·i·ty (ā′tō·nal′ə·tē) *n. Music* Lack of tonality; absence of key.

a·tone (ə·tōn′) *v.* **a·toned, a·ton·ing** *v.i.* **1** To make an expiation, as for sin or a sinner; make amends, reparation, or satisfaction. **2** *Obs.* To be at one, agree, *—v.t.* **3** *Rare* To expiate. **4** *Obs.* To propitiate; reconcile. [< earlier adverbial phrase *at one* in accord, short for *to set at one,* i.e., reconcile] **—a·ton′a·ble, a·tone′a·ble** *adj.* **—a·ton′er** *n.*

a·tone·ment (ə·tōn′mənt) *n.* **1** Satisfaction, reparation, or expiation made for wrong or injury; amends. **2** *Theol. Usually cap.* **a** The redemptive work of Christ. **b** The reconciliation between God and man effected by Christ's life, passion, and death. **3** In Christian Science, the exemplification of man's unity with God, whereby man reflects divine Truth, Life, and Love. **4** *Obs.* Reconciliation.

a·ton·ic (ə·ton′ik, ā-) *adj.* **1** Not accented, as a word or syllable. **2** Lacking tone or vigor. *—n.* An unaccented syllable or word. [< Gk. *atonos* slack < *a-* not + *teinein* stretch]

at·o·ny (at′ə·nē) *n.* **1** *Pathol.* Want of tone or power; abnormal relaxation, as of a muscle. **2** Lack of stress, as in a syllable. [< Gk. *atonia* slackness < *a-* not + *teinein* stretch]

a·top (ə·top′) *adv.* & *adj.* On or at the top. *— prep.* On the top of.

-atory *suffix of adjectives* Of or pertaining to; producing or produced by; of the nature of; expressing: *exclamatory.* [< L *-atorius* adj. suffix]

à toute force (à to͞ot fôrs′) *French* With all one's might.

à tout prix (à to͞o prē′) *French* At any price; whatever the cost.

ATP Symbol for adenosine triphosphate.

A·T·P·ase (ā′tē′pē′ās′) Adenosine triphosphatase.

at·ra·bil·ious (at′rə·bil′yəs) *adj.* Disposed to hypochondria; melancholy; splenetic. Also **at′ra·bil′i·ar** (-bil′ē·ər) [< L *atra bilis* black bile, a trans. of Gk. *melancholia.* See MELANCHOLY.] **— at′ra·bil′ious·ness** *n.*

at·ra·men·tal (at′rə·men′təl) *adj.* Of the nature of ink; inklike; inky. Also **at′ra·men′tous.** [< L *atramentum* ink < *ater* black]

A·trek (ä·trek′) A river in NE Iran, flowing west over 300 miles to its confluence with the Sumbar. Also **A·trak** (ä·trak′).

a·tre·ol (ā′trē·ōl, -ol) *n.* An aqueous solution of ammonium salts derived from organic acids, obtained as a black sirupy liquid, and used as a mild antiseptic. [< L *ater, atri* black + -OL]

at·rep·sy (at′rep·sē) See ATHREPSIA.

A·treus (ā′tro͞os, ā′trē·əs) In Greek legend, the son of Pelops and father of Agamemnon and Menelaus: to avenge the treachery of his brother Thyestes, who had seduced his wife and planned to murder him, Atreus killed his brother's sons and served them to their father at a banquet.

a·tri·al (ā′trē·əl) *adj.* Of or pertaining to an atrium.

at·ri·cho·sis (at′ri·kō′sis) *n. Pathol.* Loss of or failure to develop hair. [< NL < Gk. *atrichos* hairless (< *a-* without + *thrix* hair) + -OSIS]

at·ri·chous (at′ri·kəs) *adj. Biol.* Destitute of cilia.

a·tri·o·ven·tric·u·lar (ā′trē·ō·ven·trik′yə·lər) *adj.* Pertaining to the auricles and ventricles of the heart.

a·trip (ə·trip′) *adv.* & *adj. Naut.* **1** In a position for motion; just started from the bottom, as an anchor. **2** Properly hoisted and ready for trimming: said of a sail or a yard. **3** Freed from the fid and ready for lowering: said of a topmast. [< A-[1] on + TRIP]

a·tri·um (ā′trē·əm) *n. pl.* **a·tri·a** (ā′trē·ə) **1** The entrance hall or central open court of an ancient Roman house. **2** A court or hall. **3** *Anat.* One of the upper chambers of the heart through which venous blood is transmitted to the ventricles: also called *auricle.* **4** *Zool.* A cavity or sac. **— atrium of infection** *Med.* Any opening affording bacterial infection. [< L (def. 1)]

a·tro·cious (ə·trō′shəs) *adj.* **1** Outrageously wicked, criminal, vile, or cruel; heinous. **2** *Colloq.* Very bad or in bad taste: an *atrocious* remark. See synonyms under BARBAROUS, FLAGRANT, INFAMOUS. [< L *atrox, atrocis* harsh, cruel < *ater* black] **—a·tro′cious·ly** *adv.* **—a·tro′cious·ness** *n.*

a·troc·i·ty (ə·tros′ə·tē) *n. pl.* **·ties** **1** The state or quality of being atrocious. **2** An atrocious deed or act; cruelty or wickedness. **3** *Colloq.* A bad piece of work; something in very bad taste. [< L *atrocitas, -tatis* cruelty < *atrox.* See ATROCIOUS.]

at·ro·phied (at′rə·fēd) *adj.* Wasted away; withered.

at·ro·phy (at′rə·fē) *n. pl.* **·phies** *Pathol.* **1** A wasting or withering of the body or any of its parts. **2** A stoppage of growth or development, as of a part. *—v.* **·phied, ·phy·ing** *v.t.* To cause to waste away or wither; affect with atrophy. *—v.i.* To waste away; wither. [< F *atrophie* < L *atrophia* < Gk. *atrophia* < *a-* not + *trephein* nourish] **— a·troph·ic** (ə·trof′·ik), **at·ro·phous** (at′rə·fəs) *adj.*

at·ro·pine (at′rə·pēn, -pin) *n.* A crystalline, bitter, poisonous alkaloid, $C_{17}H_{23}O_3N$, found in the deadly nightshade and in the seeds of the thorn apple or jimsonweed: used in medicine as an antispasmodic and having the power of enlarging the pupil of the eye. Also **at′ro·pin** (-pin). [< NL *Atropa* the genus of belladonna < Gk. *Atropos.* See ATROPOS]

at·ro·pism (at′rə·piz′əm) *n.* A morbid state produced by overdoses of atropine.
At·ro·pos (at′rə·pos) One of the three Fates. [<Gk., inflexible <*a-* not + *trepein* turn]
at·ro·pous (at′rə·pəs) *adj. Bot.* Not inverted; erect, as an ovule. [<Gk. *atropos.* See ATROPOS.]
at·tac·ca (ät·täk′kä) *Music* Continue without pause. [<Ital.]
at·tach (ə·tach′) *v.t.* **1** To make fast to something; affix; fasten on. **2** To connect or join on as a part of something: He *attached* himself to the expedition. **3** To add or append, as a word or signature. **4** To attribute; add as appropriate to: to *attach* great importance to the outcome of an event. **5** *Law* To secure for legal jurisdiction; seize or arrest by legal process: to *attach* an employee's salary. **6** *Mil.* To allocate, as personnel, units, or materiel, to a military organization temporarily or as a non-integral part: The regiment *attached* a medical officer. **7** *Obs.* To seize. —*v.i.* **8** To be united in sympathy or affection: with *to*: to be *attached* to someone out of sympathy. **9** To belong, as a quality or circumstance; be incidental to: with *to*: Much interest *attaches* to this opinion. See synonyms under ADD, UNITE. [<OF *atachier* <*a-* to (<L *ad-*) + *tache* nail <Gmc. Related to ATTACK.] —**at·tach′a·ble** *adj.*
at·ta·ché (at′ə·shā′, *esp. Brit.* ə·tash′ā) *n.* A person regularly and officially attached to a diplomatic mission or staff: military *attaché*, naval *attaché*. [<F, pp. of *attacher* attach]
at·tach·ment (ə·tach′mənt) *n.* **1** An attaching or a being attached; adherence; affection. **2** That by which, or the point at which, anything is attached; a bond; band; tie. **3** Affection; devoted regard. **4** An appendage or adjunct. **5** *Law* **a** Seizure of a person or property. **b** The writ commanding this.
Synonyms: adherence, adhesion, affection, devotion, esteem, estimation, friendship, inclination, love, regard, tenderness, union. An *attachment* is an affection that binds a person to another person or thing; we speak of a man's *adherence* to his purpose, his *adhesion* to his party, or to anything to which he clings tenaciously, but with no special tenderness; of his *attachment* to his church, to the old homestead, or to any persons or objects that he may hold dear. *Inclination* expresses simply a tendency, which may be good or bad, yielded to or overcome; as, an *inclination* to study. *Regard* is more distant than *affection* or *attachment*, but closer and warmer than *esteem*; we speak of high esteem, kind *regard*. Compare ACQUAINTANCE, APPENDAGE, FRIENDSHIP, LOVE, UNION. *Antonyms*: alienation, animosity, antipathy, aversion, coolness, dislike, distance, divorce, enmity, estrangement, indifference, opposition, repugnance, separation, severance.
at·tack (ə·tak′) *v.t.* **1** To set upon suddenly; begin battle or conflict with. **2** To assail with hostile words; criticize, censure. **3** To begin work on; set about, as an undertaking, with the intention of completing. **4** To begin to affect seriously or injuriously; seize: Acid *attacks* metal; Disease *attacks* a person. —*v.i.* **5** To make an attack; begin battle: The enemy *attacked* at dawn. —*n.* **1** The act of assaulting: with *on* or *upon.* **2** The first movement toward any undertaking. **3** Any hostile, offensive part or action, as with troops. **4** A seizure, as by disease. **5** *Music* The manner of beginning a phrase or passage with decision and spirit. [<F *attaquer* <Ital. *attaccare*, ult. <same source as ATTACH]
Synonyms (verb): assail, assault, beleaguer, beset, besiege, charge, combat, encounter, invade. To *attack* is to begin hostilities of any kind. *Assail* and *assault,* while of the same original etymology, have diverged in meaning, so that *assault* alone retains the meaning of direct personal violence. One may *assail* another with reproaches; he *assaults* him with a blow, a brandished weapon, etc. To *encounter* is to meet face to face, and may be said either of the *attacking* or of the resisting force or person, or of both. *Antonyms*: aid, befriend, cover, defend, preserve, protect, resist, shelter, shield, support, sustain, uphold, withstand.
Synonyms (noun): aggression, assault, encroachment, incursion, infringement, intrusion, invasion, onset, onslaught, trespass. An *attack* may be by word; an *aggression* is always by deed, upon rights, possessions, etc. An *invasion* of a nation's territories is an act of *aggression*; an *intrusion* upon a neighboring estate is a *trespass*. *Onslaught* signifies intensely violent *assault*, as by an army or a desperado, but it is sometimes used of violent speech. See AGGRESSION. *Antonyms*: defense, repulsion, resistance, retreat, submission, surrender.
at·tain (ə·tān′) *v.t.* **1** To achieve, accomplish or gain, as a desired purpose or state. **2** To come to, as in time; arrive at: He *attained* a ripe old age. —**to attain to** To arrive at with effort; succeed in reaching: Few men have *attained to* power such as his. [<OF *ataindre* <L *attingere* reach <*ad-* to + *tangere* touch]
at·tain·a·ble (ə·tā′nə·bəl) *adj.* That can be attained; practicable; feasible. —**at·tain′a·bil′i·ty, at·tain′a·ble·ness** *n.*
at·tain·der (ə·tān′dər) *n.* **1** The loss of all civil rights of a person, as one dead in law, upon the pronouncing of sentence of death or of outlawry against him for a capital offense. **2** *Obs.* Dishonor. —**bill of attainder** A legal act making certain crimes punishable by attainder. [<OF *ataindre* attain, strike, accuse; infl. in meaning by F *taindre* stain]
at·tain·ment (ə·tān′mənt) *n.* **1** The act of attaining. **2** That which is attained; an acquisition, as of skill.
Synonyms: accomplishment, acquirement, acquisition. These words are oftenest used in the plural. *Accomplishments* are showy, graceful, pleasing; *acquirements* are substantial and useful; *attainments* are lofty and ennobling. *Acquisitions,* unless otherwise expressly stated, are understood to be of money or property. Compare WISDOM.
at·taint (ə·tānt′) *v.t.* **1** To inflict attainder upon; condemn. **2** To disgrace; taint; sully. **3** To touch or affect, as disease. **4** *Obs.* To accuse: with *of.* **5** *Obs.* To touch; hit, as in tilting. —*n.* **1** Imputation; stigma. **2** Attainder. [<OF *ataint*, pp. of *ataindre.* See ATTAIN.]
at·tain·ture (ə·tān′chər) *n. Obs.* **1** Imputation of dishonor. **2** Attainder.
at·tar (at′ər) *n.* The fragrant essential oil extracted from the petals of flowers, especially roses: also called *ottar.* [<Persian *'aṭar* <Arabic *'iṭr* perfume]
at·tem·per (ə·tem′pər) *v.t.* **1** To reduce or modify by or as by mixture. **2** To modify the temperature of. **3** To moderate or appease, as excited feelings. **4** To adapt (oneself) so as to harmonize. **5** *Obs.* To control; regulate. [<OF *atemprer* <L *attemperare* adjust <*ad-* to + *temperare* regulate]
at·tempt (ə·tempt′) *v.t.* **1** To make an effort or trial to perform or get; endeavor to effect; try. **2** *Archaic* To try to overcome, master, win, seduce, or take by force; attack; assault: to *attempt* the life of someone. **3** *Archaic* To attract by allurements; tempt. See synonyms under ENDEAVOR. —*n.* **1** A putting forth of effort; a trial; endeavor; essay. **2** An attack. See synonyms under ENDEAVOR [<OF *attenter, attempter* <L *attentare, attemptare* try <*ad-* toward + *tentare, temptare,* freq. of *tendere* stretch] —**at·tempt′a·ble** *adj.* —**at·tempt′a·bil′i·ty** *n.*
at·tend (ə·tend′) *v.t.* **1** To wait upon; minister to; visit or care for professionally. **2** To be present at or in, as a meeting. **3** To follow as a result. **4** To accompany. **5** *Archaic* To give heed; listen. **6** *Archaic* To await. See synonyms under FOLLOW, LISTEN, SERVE. [<OF *atendre* wait, expect <L *attendere* give heed to, consider <*ad-* toward + *tendere* stretch]
at·ten·dance (ə·ten′dəns) *n.* **1** An attending. **2** Those who attend; an audience or congregation; retinue. [<OF *atendance* <*atendre.* See ATTEND.]
at·ten·dant (ə·ten′dənt) *n.* **1** One who attends, especially as a servant; also, one who is present at a ceremony. **2** A concomitant; consequent. —*adj.* Following or accompanying; waiting upon.
at·tent (ə·tent′) *adj. Archaic* Eagerly attentive; intent. [<L *attentus*, pp. of *attendere.* See ATTEND.]
at·ten·tion (ə·ten′shən) *n.* **1** The act or faculty of attending. **2** Active consciousness; the power or faculty of mental concentration. **3** An act of courtesy or gallantry. **4** Practical consideration; care. **5** *Mil.* The prescribed position of readiness to obey orders; also, the order to assume this position. See synonyms under CARE, INDUSTRY. [<L *attentio, -onis* <*attendere.* See ATTEND.]
at·ten·tive (ə·ten′tiv) *adj.* **1** Of, pertaining to, giving, or showing attention; observant; thoughtful. **2** Courteous; gallant; polite. See synonyms under OBSEQUIOUS, THOUGHTFUL. —**at·ten′tive·ly** *adv.* —**at·ten′tive·ness** *n.*
at·ten·u·ant (ə·ten′yōō·ənt) *adj.* Making thin; diluting. —*n.* A medicine that dilutes the body fluids or thins the blood. [<L *attenuans, -antis*, ppr. of *attenuare.* See ATTENUATE.]
at·ten·u·ate (ə·ten′yōō·āt) *v.* **·at·ed, ·at·ing** *v.t.* **1** To make thin, small, or fine; draw out, as a wire. **2** To reduce in value, quantity, size, or strength; weaken; impair. **3** To reduce in density; rarefy, as a liquid or gas. **4** *Bacteriol.* To weaken the virulence of a micro-organism. —*v.i.* **5** To become thin, weak, rarefied, etc. —*adj.* (ə·ten′yōō·it) **1** Made thin; slender; rarefied; diluted. **2** *Bot.* Slender and tapering; narrow. [<L *attenuatus*, pp. of *attenuare* weaken <*ad-* + *tenuare* make thin <*tenuis* thin]
at·ten·u·a·tion (ə·ten′yōō·ā′shən) *n.* **1** The act or process of attenuating, or the state of being attenuated. **2** *Bacteriol.* Reduction of the virulence of micro-organisms by repeated cultivation in artificial media, exposure to light, etc.
at·test (ə·test′) *v.t.* **1** To confirm as accurate, true, or genuine; vouch for. **2** To certify, as by signature or oath. **3** To be proof of: His many works *attest* his industry. **4** To put upon oath. —*v.i.* **5** To bear witness; testify: with *to.* —*n.* One who or that which certifies or confirms; attestation. [<F *attester* <L *attestari* confirm <*ad-* to + *testari* bear witness]
at·tes·ta·tion (at′es·tā′shən) *n.* **1** A presenting (of something) as testimony. **2** Testimony; something presented as evidence.
at·tic (at′ik) *n.* **1** A half-story next the roof; a garret. **2** A low, decorative wall or structure, in classical style, above a cornice or entablature. [<F *attique,* orig. Athenian; from the false supposition that the attic was of Athenian origin]
At·tic (at′ik) *adj.* **1** Of or pertaining to Attica in ancient Greece. **2** Of, characteristic of, or pertaining to Athens; Athenian; characteristic of the Athenians; pertaining to the language, literature, art, or literary style of the Athenians. **3** Graceful; delicate; refined: *Attic* wit. —*n.* The dialect of Attica, closely related to Ionic, representing ancient Greek in its most refined form as used by Aeschylus, Sophocles, Euripides, and most of the great Greek writers. [<L *Atticus* <Gk. *Attikos* Athenian <*Attikē* Attica]
At·ti·ca (at′i·kə) A nome of east central Greece; 1,310 square miles; capital, Athens; formerly an ancient kingdom and republic of Greece.
Attic faith Inviolable faith.
At·ti·cism (at′ə·siz′əm) *n.* **1** An Attic idiom or characteristic. **2** A clear, concise, elegant expression. **3** A siding with the Athenians. **4** In Greek and Roman oratory, a style marked by simplicity of language and avoidance of rhetorical periods: contrasted with *Asianism.*
At·ti·cize (at′ə·sīz) *v.* **·cized, ·ciz·ing** *v.i.* **1** To conform to or copy Attic idiom, literary style, or customs. **2** To favor or to take the part of the Athenians. —*v.t.* **3** To cause to conform to or copy Athenian idiom, style, or customs. Also *Brit.* **At′ti·cise.**
Attic salt Delicate, refined, graceful wit. Also **Attic wit.**
At·ti·la (at′ə·lə), 406?–453, king of the Huns: called "the scourge of God."
at·tire (ə·tīr′) *v.t.* **at·tired, at·tir·ing** **1** To dress; array; adorn. **2** *Obs.* To equip. —*n.* **1** Dress or clothing; apparel; garments; costume; adornment. **2** *Her.* Antlers or horns.

as of a stag. See synonyms under DRESS. [< OF *atirer* arrange, adorn < *a-* in (< L *ad-*) + *tire* row, order (of uncertain origin)]

at·tire·ment (ə·tīr′mənt) *n.* Apparel; garb; attire.

At·tis (at′is) In classical mythology, a vegetation god worshipped with the Great Mother: an annual spring festival commemorated his death and resurrection. Also *Atys.*

at·ti·tude (at′ə·to͞od, -tyo͞od) *n.* **1** Position of the body, as suggesting some thought, feeling, or action. **2** State of mind, behavior, or conduct regarding some matter, as indicating opinion or purpose. **3** *Aeron.* The position of an airplane with reference to some plane, as the earth or the horizon; tilt or tip. **4** *Med.* The position of the fetus in the womb. [< F < Ital. *attitudine* < LL *aptitudo* fitness < L *aptus* fitted, suited. Doublet of APTITUDE.] **—at·ti·tu·di·nal** (at′ə·to͞o′də·nəl, -tyo͞o′-) *adj.*

Synonyms: pose, position, posture. A *posture* is assumed without any special reference to expression of feeling; *attitude* is the *position* appropriate to the expression of some feeling, whether consciously or unconsciously assumed. A *pose* is a *position* studied for artistic effect or considered with reference to such effect.

at·ti·tu·di·nize (at′ə·to͞o′də·nīz, -tyo͞o′-) *v.i.* **·nized, ·niz·ing** To pose for effect; strike an attitude. Also *Brit.* **at′ti·tu′di·nise.**

Att·lee (at′lē), **Clement Richard,** 1883–1967, Earl Attlee, British Labour Party leader; prime minister 1945–51.

at·torn (ə·tûrn′) *v.i.* **1** *Law* To agree to recognize a new owner of a property or estate and promise payment of rent to him. **2** In feudal law, to consent to the transfer of land by the lord of the fee and to the continuance of one's own holding under the new lord; also, to accord homage to a lord. [< OF *atorner* turn to, assign, appoint < *a-* to (< L *ad-*) + *torner* turn. See TURN.]

at·tor·ney (ə·tûr′nē) *n.* **1** A person empowered by another to act in his stead; especially, one legally qualified to prosecute and defend actions in a court of law; an attorney at law; a lawyer. **2** *Obs.* An agent. **—by attorney** By proxy. **—power of attorney** Legal written authority to transact business for another. **—prosecuting attorney** *U.S.* The law officer empowered to act in behalf of the government, whether state, county, or national, in prosecutions for penal offenses: also called **district attorney.** [< OF *atorné,* pp. of *atorner.* See ATTORN.] **—at·tor′ney·ship** *n.*

attorney at law An attorney who is qualified to prosecute and defend actions in a court of law: also called *public attorney.*

attorney general *pl.* **attorneys general, attorney generals** The chief law officer of a government.

Attorney General *U.S.* A cabinet officer who heads the Department of Justice and is chief legal adviser to the President.

attorney in fact An attorney who is limited to business out of court: also called *private attorney.*

at·torn·ment (ə·tûrn′mənt) *n.* In feudal law, the acknowledgment by the tenant of a new lord on the alienation of land; also, the acknowledgment by a bailee that he holds property for a new party. Compare ATTORN.

at·tract (ə·trakt′) *v.t.* **1** To draw to or cause to come near by some physical force, as magnetism, and without apparent mechanical connection. **2** To draw, as the admiration or attention of, by some winning influence; allure; entice. See synonyms under ALLURE, DRAW, INTEREST. [< L *attractus,* pp. of *attrahere* < *ad-* toward + *trahere* draw, drag] **—at·tract′a·ble** *adj.* **—at·tract′a·ble·ness, at·tract′a·bil′i·ty** *n.* **—at·tract′er, at·trac′tor** *n.*

at·trac·tile (ə·trak′təl) *adj.* Having power to attract.

at·trac·tion (ə·trak′shən) *n.* **1** The act or process of attracting, or that which attracts. **2** A physical force which, exerted between or among bodies, tends to make them approach each other or prevents their separating. Compare REPULSION. **3** Anything pleasing or alluring. See synonyms under INCLINATION, LOVE.

attraction sphere *Biol.* A minute spherical mass observed near the nucleus of many cells, that appears to control the phenomena of indirect division; centrosphere.

at·trac·tive (ə·trak′tiv) *adj.* Having the power or quality of attracting; drawing; pleasing; winning. See synonyms under AMIABLE, BEAUTIFUL, PLEASANT. **—at·trac′tive·ly** *adv.* **—at·trac′tive·ness** *n.*

at·tra·hent (at′rə·hənt) *adj.* **1** Drawing to or toward something. **2** *Anat.* Drawing a part forward. —*n.* **1** An external application that draws fluids to the place where it is applied. **2** A muscle that acts by drawing forward. [< L *attrahens, -entis,* ppr. of *attrahere.* See ATTRACT.]

at·trib·ute (ə·trib′yo͞ot) *v.t.* **·ut·ed, ·ut·ing** To consider or ascribe as belonging to, resulting from, owing to, or caused by; assign; refer: to *attribute* the invention of music to Orpheus; to *attribute* wisdom to gray hair.

—at·tri·bute (at′rə·byo͞ot) *n.* **1** That which is assigned or ascribed; a characteristic. **2** *Gram.* An adjective or its equivalent. **3** In art and mythology, a distinctive mark or symbol. [< L *attributus,* pp. of *attribuere* bestow, assign < *ad-* to + *tribuere* allot, give over] **—at·trib′u·ta·ble** *adj.*

Synonyms (verb): ascribe, assign, associate, charge, connect, impute, refer. We may *attribute* to a person either that which belongs to him or that which we merely suppose to be his. Where we are quite sure, we simply *refer* a matter to the cause or class to which it belongs or *ascribe* to one what is surely his, etc. We *associate* things which may have no necessary or causal relations; as, we may *associate* the striking of a clock with the serving of dinner. We *charge* a person with what we deem blameworthy. We may *impute* good or evil, but more commonly evil. *Antonyms*: deny, disconnect, dissociate, separate, sever, sunder.

Synonyms (noun): property, quality. A *quality* denotes what a thing really is in some one respect; an *attribute* is what we conceive a thing to be in some one respect; thus, while *attribute* may, *quality* must, express something of the real nature of that to which it is ascribed; we speak of the *attributes* of God, the *qualities* of matter. A *property* is what belongs especially to one thing as its own peculiar possession, in distinction from all other things; when we speak of the *qualities* or the *properties* of matter, *quality* is the more general, *property* the more limited term. Compare CHARACTERISTIC, EMBLEM, FIGURE. *Antonyms*: being, essence, nature, substance.

at·tri·bu·tion (at′rə·byo͞o′shən) *n.* **1** An attributing or being attributed. **2** An ascribed characteristic or quality; attribute.

at·trib·u·tive (ə·trib′yə·tiv) *adj.* **1** Pertaining to or of the nature of an attribute; expressing or assigning an attribute. **2** So ascribed, as a work of art: That canvas is an *attributive* Vermeer. **3** *Gram.* Expressing an attribute; in English, designating an adjective or its equivalent which stands before the noun it modifies, as opposed to a predicate adjective which follows a linking verb; as, in the expression "a silver watch," silver is an *attributive* adjective. —*n. Gram.* An attributive word. **—at·trib′u·tive·ly** *adj.* **—at·trib′u·tive·ness** *n.*

at·trite (ə·trīt′) *adj.* **1** Worn down by rubbing or friction. **2** *Theol.* Having attrition. Also **at·trit·ed** (ə·trī′tid). [< L *attritus,* pp. of *atterere.* See ATTRITION.]

at·tri·tion (ə·trish′ən) *n.* **1** A rubbing out or grinding down, as by friction. **2** A gradual wearing down or weakening: a war of *attrition.* **3** *Theol.* Repentance for sin, arising from inferior motives; imperfect contrition (see under CONTRITION). [< L *attritio, -onis* rubbing, friction < *atterere* rub away < *ad-* to, against + *terere* rub]

At·tu (at′to͞o) The westernmost island of the Aleutians, largest of the Near Islands.

at·tune (ə·to͞on′, ə·tyo͞on′) *v.t.* **at·tuned, at·tun·ing 1** To bring into accord with; harmonize. **2** To adjust to the right pitch, as a musical instrument; tune. See synonyms under ADAPT. [< AD- + TUNE]

A·tu·o·na (ä′to͞o·ō′nä) Capital of the Marquesas Islands, on Hiva Oa.

a·twain (ə·twān′) *adv.* In two; asunder. [< A-[1] on + TWAIN]

a·tween (ə·twēn′) *prep. Obs.* Between. [< A-[1] on + (BE)TWEEN]

a·twirl (ə·twûrl′) *adj.* & *adv.* In a twirl; twirling.

a·typ·ic (ā·tip′ik) *adj.* Not typical; without typical character; differing from the type; irregular. Also **a·typ′i·cal. —a·typ′i·cal·ly** *adv.*

Au *Chem.* Gold (symbol Au).

au·bade (ō·bäd′) *n. French* Morning music, as to announce the dawn. Compare SERENADE.

Aube (ōb) A river of north central France, flowing 140 miles NW to the Seine.

Au·ber (ō·bâr′), **Daniel François,** 1782–1871, French composer.

au·berge (ō·berzh′) *n. French* An inn.

Au·ber·vil·liers (ō·ber·vē·lyā′) An industrial suburb NE of Paris, France.

Au·bi·gné (dō·bē·nyā′), **Théodore Agrippa d'** 1552–1630, French poet and Huguenot soldier.

Au·brey (ô′brē) A masculine personal name. [< G *Alberich,* lit., elf-king]

Au·brey (ô′brē), **John,** 1626–97, English antiquary.

au·burn (ô′bûrn) *adj.* Reddish-brown: *auburn* hair. —*n.* An auburn color; a reddish-brown. [< OF *auborne, alborne* < LL *alburnus* whitish < L *albus* white; infl. in meaning by ME *brun* brown]

Au·bus·son (ō·bü·sôn′) A town in central France on the Creuse, noted for its tapestries and for a carpet of tapestry weave known as **Aubusson carpet.**

Au·chin·leck (ô′kin·lek), **Sir Claude John Eyre,** born 1884, British general in World War II.

Auck·land (ôk′lənd) A chief port and former capital of New Zealand, on North Island.

Auckland Islands A group of uninhabited islands south of and belonging to New Zealand; 234 square miles.

au con·traire (ō kôn·trâr′) *French* On the contrary.

au cou·rant (ō ko͞o·räN′) *French* Up to date; fashionable.

auc·tion (ôk′shən) *n.* **1** A public sale of property in which the price offered for individual items is increased by bids, until the highest bidder becomes the purchaser. **2** The bidding in bridge. **3** Auction bridge (see under BRIDGE[2]). —*v.t.* To sell by or at auction. **—to auction off** To sell by or at auction. [< L *auctio, -onis* an increase, a public sale (with increasing bids) < *augere* increase]

auction block *U.S.* A stand or block on which a slave was placed to be sold at auction. **—on the auction block** Up for forced or compulsory sale.

auc·tion·eer (ôk′shən·ir′) *n.* One who conducts an auction, usually as a business. —*v.t.* To sell by auction.

au·da·cious (ô·dā′shəs) *adj.* **1** Having or exhibiting an unabashed or fearless spirit; defiant of ordinary restraint, as of law or decorum. **2** Presumptuous; shameless; insolent. [< F *audacieux* < L *audacia.* See AUDACITY.] **—au·da′cious·ly** *adv.* **—au·da′cious·ness** *n.*

au·dac·i·ty (ô·das′ə·tē) *n. pl.* **·ties 1** The quality or state of being audacious. **2** An audacious act, remark, etc. See synonyms under EFFRONTERY, TEMERITY. [< L *audacia* boldness < *audax* bold, rash < *audere* dare]

Au·den (ô′dən), **W(ystan) H(ugh),** 1907–1973, U.S. poet born in England.

au·di·bil·i·ty (ô′də·bil′ə·tē) *n.* **1** Ability to be heard. **2** *Telecom.* The ratio of the strength of a transmitted signal to that of a barely audible signal.

au·di·ble (ô′də·bəl) *adj.* Perceptible by the ear; loud enough to be heard. [< Med. L *audibilis* < L *audire* hear] **—au′di·ble·ness** *n.* **—au′di·bly** *adv.*

au·di·ence (ô′dē·əns) *n.* **1** An assembly gathered to hear and see, as at a concert. **2** Those who are reached by a book, television program, etc. **3** The act of hearing; attention. **4** A formal hearing, interview, or conference. **5** Opportunity to be heard. [< OF < L *audientia* a hearing < *audire* hear]

au·di·ent (ô′dē·ənt) *adj.* Listening; hearing. [< L *audiens, -entis,* ppr. of *audire* hear]

au·dile (ô′dil, ô′dīl) *n. Psychol.* An individual having a tendency to form mental images derived from auditory sensations. —*adj.* Auditory. [< L *audire* hear + -ILE]

au·di·o (ô′dē·ō) *adj. Telecom.* **1** Of or pertaining to characteristics associated with sound waves. **2** Designating devices used in transmission or reception of sound waves: in television, distinguished from *video.* [< L *audire* hear]

audio- *combining form* Pertaining to hearing: *audiogram.* Also **audi-.** [<L *audire* hear]

au·di·o·cas·sette (ô′dē·ō·kə·set′; -ka·set′) *n.* Electronics. A cassette for the storage of audio material.

au·di·o·com·mu·ni·ca·tion (ô′dē·ō·kə·myoo′nə·kā′shən) *n.* **1** Vocal communication. **2** Any form of communication which utilizes electro-acoustic methods in the transmission, recording, and amplification of sound waves.

audio frequency A frequency of electrical, sound, or other wave vibrations coming within the range of normal human hearing, or from about 20 to 20,000 cycles a second.

au·di·o·gram (ô′dē·ō ·gram′) *n.* A graph to show the hearing level of a subject in relation to the minimum intensity of sounds perceptible to the normal ear.

au·di·om·e·ter (ô′dē·om′ə·tər) *n.* An instrument to gage and record the acuteness of hearing. **—au′di·o·met·ric** (ô′dē·ə·met′rik) *adj.* **— au′di·om′e·try** *n.*

au·di·o·phile (ô′dē·ə·fīl′) *n.* A specialist in or enthusiast of high-fidelity sound reproduction on radio, phonograph and tape recordings, etc.

au·di·o·vis·u·al (ô′dē·ō·vizh′oo·əl) *adj.* Pertaining to forms of instruction and entertainment other than books, as radio, television, motion pictures, photographs, recordings, etc.: *audio-visual* aids.

au·di·phone (ô′də·fōn) *n.* A device for directing sound through the bones of the head to the auditory nerve.

au·dit (ô′dit) *v.t.* **1** To examine, adjust, and certify, as accounts. **2** To attend as a listener: to *audit* a course in college. [< *n.*] —*n.* **1** An examination of an accounting document and of the evidence in support of its correctness. **2** A calling to account. **3** A settlement of accounts. **4** A balance sheet. **5** *Obs.* A hearing. [<L *auditus* a hearing < *audire* hear]

au·di·tion (ô·dish′ən) *n.* **1** The act or sense of hearing. **2** An audience or hearing; especially, a trial test or hearing, as of an actor or singer —*v.t.* To try out, as an actor or singer for a special role. —*v.i.* To demonstrate one's ability or talent when applying for an acting or singing job. [<L *auditio, -onis* a hearing < *audire* hear]

au·di·tor (ô′də·tər) *n.* **1** One who audits accounts. **2** One who listens; a hearer. **3** One who audits classes. —**au′di·tress** *n.* fem.

au·di·to·ri·um (ô′də·tôr′ē·əm), -tō′rē·əm *n. pl.* **·to·ri·ums** or **·to·ri·a** (-tôr′ē·ə, -tō′rē·ə) **1** The room or part of a building, as a church, theater, etc., occupied by the audience. **2** A building for concerts, public meetings, etc. [<L, lecture room, courtroom, orig. neut. of *auditorius.* See AUDITORY.]

au·di·to·ry (ô′də·tôr′ē, -tō′rē) *adj.* Of or pertaining to hearing or the organs or sense of hearing. —*n. pl.* **·ries** **1** An assembly of hearers; an audience. **2** An auditorium, particularly the nave of a church. [<L *auditorius* < *audire* hear] —au′di·to·ri·ly *adv.*

auditory canal *Anat.* The passage leading from the auricle to the tympanic membrane. See illustration under EAR.

Au·drey (ô′drē) A feminine personal name. —Saint Audrey See ETHELDREDA, SAINT. [<OF, ult. <Gmc., noble might]

Au·du·bon (ô′də·bon), **John James,** 1785–1851, U.S. ornithologist and painter.

Au·er (ou′ər), **Leopold,** 1845–) 1930, Hungarian violinist and teacher.

Au·er·bach (ou′ər·bäkh), **Berthold,** 1812–82, German novelist.

Au·er·städt (ou′ər·shtet) A village in east central Germany; scene of a French victory over the Prussians, 1806.

au fait (ō fe′) *French* Skilled, expert; well informed; literally, to the fact.

Auf·klä·rung (ouf′klâ′rŏŏ ng) *n.* German The Enlightenment.

au fond (ō fôn′) *French* Fundamentally; at bottom; essentially.

auf Wie·der·seh·en (ouf vē′dər·zā′ən) *German* Till we meet again; good-by for now.

Au·ge·an (ô·jē′ən) *adj.* **1** Of or pertaining to Augeas or his stables. **2** Exceedingly filthy; corrupt.

Augean stables In Greek mythology, the stables in which Augeas kept 3,000 oxen and which, uncleaned for 30 years, were cleaned in a day when Hercules turned the river Alpheus through them.

Au·ge·as (ô′jē·əs, ô·jē′əs) In Greek mythology, a king of Elis.

au·gen (ou′gən) *n. pl. Geol.* A rock formation which contains packed masses of eye-shaped particles. [<G, eyes]

au·gend (ô′jend) *n. Math.* A quantity or number to which another is to be added. See ADDEND. [<L *augendum,* neut. gerundive of *au-gere* increase]

au·ger (ô′gər) *n.* **1** A large tool with a spiral groove for boring holes in wood, etc. **2** An earth-boring tool. ◆Homophone: *augur.* [OE *nafugār,* lit., nave-borer < *nafu* nave of a wheel + *gār* borer, spear (*a nauger in ME becoming an auger*)]

AUGERS
a. Twisted. *b.* Posthole.
c. Ship. *d.* Chuck—shanked.
e. Gimlet. *f.* Expanding.

Au·ghra·bies Falls (ô·khrä′bēs, ō·grä′-) A waterfall in the Orange River, in Northern Cape Province, Republic of South Africa; 480 feet: also *King George's Falls.*

aught¹ (ôt) *n.* Anything; any part or item. —*adv.* By any chance; at all; in any respect. Also spelled *ought.* ◆Homophone: *ought.* [OE *āwiht* < *ā* ever + *wiht* thing]

aught² (ôt) *n.* The figure 0; cipher; a naught; nothing. ◆Homophone: *ought.* [*a naught* taken as an *aught*]

aught·lins (ôkht′linz) *adv. Scot.* In any measure; in the least.

Au·gier (ō·zhyä′), **Guillaume Victor Émile,** 1820–89, french dramatist.

au·gite (ô′jīt) *n. Mineral.* A dark-colored variety of aluminous rock-making pyroxene. [<L *augites,* a precious stone <Gk. *augitē s* < *augē* brightness, gleam (of a gem)] —au·git·tic (ô·jit′ik)

aug·ment (ôg·ment′) *v.t.* **1** To make greater, as in size, number, or amount; enlarge; intensify. **2** In Greek and Sanskrit grammar, to add the augment to. —*v.i.* To become greater, as in size, number, or amount. See synonyms under ADD, INCREASE. —*n.* (ôg′ment) **1** Increase; enlargement. **2** In Greek and Sanskrit grammar, a vowel prefixed to a verb, or a lengthening of the initial vowel, to indicate past time. [<F *augmenter* <L *augmentare* < *augmentum* an increase < *augere* increase] —**aug·ment′a·ble** *adj.* — **aug·ment′er** *n.*

aug·men·ta·tion (ôg′men·tā ′shən) *n.* **1** An augmenting or being augmented. **2** The result of augmenting; enlargement; increase; an addition. **2** *Music* The repetition of a theme in notes of twice the time value of those first used; opposite of *diminution.* See synonyms under ACCESSION, INCREASE.

aug·men·ta·tive (ôg·men′tə·tiv) *adj.* **1** Having the quality or power of augmenting. **2** *Gram.* Denoting greater size or intensity, as the suffix *-agne* in French *montagne* a mountain (from *mont* a hill). —*n. Gram.* An augmentative form. Also **aug·men′tive.** Abbr. *aug.*

aug·men·ted (ôg·men′tid) *adj. Music* Increased by a half step more than the corresponding major interval.

aug·men·tor (ôg·men′tər) *n. Aeron.* A duct for increasing the thrust of a jet engine by forcing the air-fuel mixture through a narrowed channel just behind the exit nozzle.

au gra·tin (ō grät′n, grat′n; *Fr.* ō grà·taṅ′) Sprinkled with breadcrumbs or grated cheese and baked until brown. [<F]

Augs·burg (ôgz′bûrg, *Ger.* ouks′bŏŏrkh) The capital of Swabia, SW Germany. Ancient **Au·gus·ta Vin·de·li·co·rum** (ô ·gus′tə vin·del′i·kô′rəm).

au·gur (ô′gər) *n.* **1** A religious official of ancient Rome whose duty it was to foretell future events by interpreting omens, such as the flights of birds, and to give advice on public affairs accordingly. **2** Hence, a prophet;

soothsayer. Also *Obs.* **au′gur·er.** —*v.t.* **1** To predict; divine; prognosticate from or as from signs and omens; also, to conjecture from indications. **2** To betoken; portend; to be an omen of. —*v.i.* **3** To conjecture from signs and omens. **4** To be an augury or omen. ◆Homophone: *auger.* [<L *augur* < *avis* bird + *-gar* (? akin to *garrire* talk, interpret)]

Synonyms (verb): betoken, bode, forbode, forecast, foretell, foretoken, portend, predict, pre- sage, prognosticate, prophesy. Persons only *divine, forecast, foretell, predict,* or *prophesy;* things only *betoken, foretoken,* or *portend;* either persons or things *augur, bode, forebode, presage,* or *prognosticate.* As regards the outcome, *bode, forebode,* and *portend* always refer to evil or misfortune; the other words are neutral, applying equally to good or ill. One may *augur* or *divine* from indications too slight to be explained; to *forecast* always denotes calculation. See PROPHESY. *Antonyms:* assure, demonstrate, determine, establish, insure, prove, warrant.

au·gu·ral (ô′gyə·rəl) *adj.* Of or pertaining to augurs or auguries.

au·gu·ry (ô′gyə·rē) *n. pl.* **·ries** **1** The art or practice of foretelling by signs or omens; divination. **2** A portent or omen; presage. **3** The rite or ceremony conducted by an augur.

au·gust (ô·gust′) *adj.* **1** Majestic; grand; imposing. **2** Of high birth or rank; venerable; eminent. See synonyms under AWFUL), GRAND, KINGLY. [<L *augustus* < *augere* increase, exalt] — **au·gust′ly** *adv.* — **au·gust′ness** *n.*

Au·gust (ô′gəst; *Dan., Ger., Sw.* ou′gŏŏst) A masculine personal name; variant of AUGUSTUS.

Au·gust (ô′gəst) The eighth month of the year, containing 31 days. [<L, after AUGUSTUS CAESAR]

Au·gus·ta (ô·gus′tə; *Ger.* ou·gŏŏs′tä, *Ital.* ou·gŏŏs′tä) A feminine personal name; feminine of AUGUSTUS). Also *Dan., Du., Ger.* **Au·gus·te** (ou·gŏŏs′tə). [<L, venerable] — **Augusta Victoria,** 1858–1921, German empress; wife of William II.

Au·gus·ta (ô·gus′tə) A city in south central Maine on the Kennebec River; the State capital.

Au·gus·tan (ô·gus′tən) *adj.* **1** Of or pertaining to the emperor Augustus or to his times. **2** Pertaining to any era which resembles that of Augustus in refinement and taste. **3** Classical; refined. **4** Pertaining to Augsburg. —*n.* A writer or artist of an Augustan age.

Augustan age 1 The period of the reign of Augustus, 27 B.C. to A.D. 14, the golden age of Roman literature. **2** A corresponding period in other literatures, as in England during the reign of Queen Anne.

Au·gus·tan·ism (ô·gus′tən·iz′əm) *n.* A characteristic or quality resembling those of the reign of Augustus, especially as shown by the literature of that period.

Au·gus·tine (ô′gəs·tēn, ô·gus′tin) A masculine personal name. Also **Au·gus·tin** (ô·gus′tən; *Fr.* ō·güs·taṅ′, *Ger.* ou′gŏŏ·stēn), *Lat.* **Au·gus·ti·nus** (ô′gəs·tī′nəs). [<L, venerable] — **Augustine, Saint,** 354–430, bishop of Hippo and a father of the church. — **Augustine, Saint,** died 604?, brought Christianity to England: also known as *Saint Austin.*

Au·gus·tin·i·an (ô′gəs·tin′ē·ən) *adj.* **1** Of or pertaining to St. Augustine or his doctrines. **2** Belonging to a monastic order named after St. Augustine or following his rule. —*n.* **1** A disciple of St. Augustine. **2** A member of any of the mendicant monastic orders named after St. Augustine: also **Au·gus·tin** (ô·gus′tin). —**Au′gus·tin′i·an·ism, Au·gus′tin·ism** *n.*

Augustinian canons An order of regular canons, originally of the Lateran Basilica in Rome, formerly numerous in England and Ireland.

Augustinian Hermits An order of mendicant friars, established in 1256 by Pope Alexander IV under an Augustinian rule: also called *Austin Friars.*

Au·gus·tus (ô·gus′təs) A masculine personal name. Also *Fr.* **Au·guste** (ō·güst′). [<L, venerable]

— Augustus Caesar, 63 B.C.–A.D. 14, Gaius Julius Caesar Octavianus, the first Roman emperor 27 B.C.–A.D. 14: before 27 B.C. called *Octavian.*

au jus (ō zhü′) *French* Served with its natural juice or gravy: said of meats.

auk (ôk) *n.* A short-winged, web-footed diving bird (family *Alcidae*) of northern seas. The **great auk** (*Plautus impennis*), now extinct, was black above and white below, had an oval white patch between the eyes and bill, and stood erect, two feet tall. The **razor-billed auk** (*Alca torda*) is smaller, with a white line extending between the eyes and bill. [<ON *ālka*]

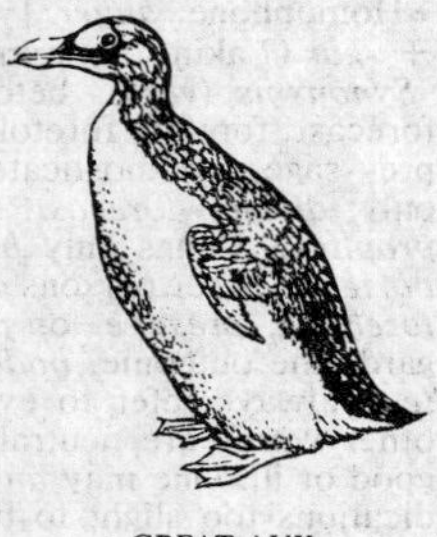
GREAT AUK

auk·let (ôk′lit) *n.* One of the smaller auks; especially, the crested auklet.

au lait (ō le′) *French* With milk.

auld (ôld) *adj. Scot.* Old.

Auld Cloot·ie (klo͞ot′ē, klo͞o′tē) *Scot.* The devil.

auld–far·rant (ôld′far′ənt) *adj. Scot.* Wise beyond one's years; sagacious. Also **auld–far·ran** (-far′ən).

Auld Horn·ie (hôr′nē) *Scot.* The devil.

auld lang syne (ôld′ lang sīn′, zīn′) *Scot.* Literally, old long since; hence, long ago.

au·lic (ô′lik) *adj.* Pertaining to a royal court. [<F *aulique* <L *aulicus* <Gk. *aulikos* < *aulē* a court]

Aulic Council In the Holy Roman Empire, the emperor's privy council: later the Austrian Council of State.

Au·lis (ô′lis) An ancient town in Boeotia, central Greece, on the Gulf of Euboea; traditional site for the sacrifice of Iphigenia and the embarkation of the Greeks for the Trojan War.

au na·tu·rel (ō nȧ·tü·rel′) *French* **1** Ungarnished; plainly cooked, as food. **2** In the nude.

aunt (ant, änt) *n.* **1** The sister of one's father or mother, or the wife of one's uncle. **2** An elderly woman: a familiar or affectionate use. [<OF *aunte, ante* <L *amita* paternal aunt]

aunt·y (an′tē, än′-) *n.* A familiar, diminutive form of AUNT. Also **aunt′ie.**

au pair (ō pâr) *Chiefly Brit.* **1** An arrangement whereby one receives room and board in a foreign household in exchange for doing certain chores, as housekeeping and the care of children: often used attributively: *au pair* girls. **2** *Colloq.* A girl participating in such an arrangement. [<F, lit., at par]

au·ra (ôr′ə) *n. pl.* **au·ras** or **au·rae** (ôr′ē) **1** An invisible emanation or exhalation. **2** A distinctive air or quality enveloping or characterizing a person or thing: an *aura* of wealth. **3** A gentle breeze. **4** *Electr.* **a** *Obs.* A subtile fluid supposed to surround an electrified body. **b** The current of air caused by a convective discharge from a sharp point. **5** *Pathol.* The sensory, motor, or psychic manifestations preceding an epileptic attack or other paroxysm. **6** In psychic research, the hypothetical emanations from living organisms. [<L, breeze <Gk. *aurē* breath]

au·ral[1] (ôr′əl) *adj.* Pertaining to the ear or the sense of hearing; auricular. [<L *auris* ear + -AL]

au·ral[2] (ôr′əl) *adj.* Pertaining to an aura.

au·rate[1] (ôr′āt) *adj.* Having ears or earlike expansions. Also **au′rat·ed.** [<L *auris* ear + -ATE[1]]

au·rate[2] (ôr′āt) *n.* A salt of auric acid, containing the trivalent radical AuO_3: ammonium *aurate* (fulminating gold). [<AUR(IC ACID) + -ATE[3]]

au·re·ate (ôr′ē·it) *adj.* Of the color of gold; golden. [<LL *aureatus* <L *aureus* < *aurum* gold]

Au·re·li·a (ô·rē′lē·ə, ô·rēl′yə; *Du., Ger.* ou·rā′lē·ä; *Ital., Sp.* ou·rā′lyä) A feminine personal name. Also *Fr.* **Au·ré·lie** (ō·rā·lē′). [<L, golden]

Au·re·li·an (ô·rē′lē·ən, ô·rēl′yən), 212?–275, Lucius Domitius Aurelianus, Roman emperor 270–275.

Au·re·li·us (ô·rē′lē·əs, ô·rēl′yəs) A masculine personal name. [<L, golden]

Aurelius, Marcus, 121–180, nephew, son-in-law and adopted son of Antoninus Pius; Roman emperor 161–180, and Stoic philosopher: full name: *Marcus Aurelius Antoninus.*

au·re·o·la (ô·rē′ə·lə) *n.* **1** In art, a radiance enveloping the whole figure or head of Christ or any sanctified being; a glory; halo; aureole. **2** A radiance, or something resembling or likened to it. **3** In the Roman Catholic Church, a reward added to the essential bliss of heaven for spiritual victories achieved on earth. [<L < *aureolus* golden, dim. of *aureus* < *aurum* gold]

au·re·ole (ôr′ē·ōl) *n.* **1** *Astron.* The corona of the sun; a halo surrounding the image of a brilliant body as seen in a telescope. **2** An aureola. [<L *aureolus.* See AUREOLA]

au·re·o·lin (ô·rē′ə·lin) *n.* A bright, permanent yellow pigment made from cobalt and potassium: used in water colors and oil paints. [<L *aureol(us)* golden + -IN]

Au·re·o·my·cin (ôr′ē·ō·mī′sin) *n.* Proprietary name for a brand of chlortetracycline: used as an antibiotic. [<L *aureus* golden (from its color) + Gk. *mykēs* fungus + -IN]

au·re·ous (ôr′ē·əs) *adj.* Of the color of gold; golden. [<L *aureus* golden < *aurum* gold]

au·re·us (ôr′ē·əs) *n. pl.* **au·re·i** (ôr′ē·ī) A gold coin of the Roman Empire, weighing, under Augustus, 1/42 of a libra.

au re·voir (ō rə·vwär′) *French* Good-by; till we meet again; literally, to the seeing again.

au·ric (ôr′ik) *adj.* Of, pertaining to, or containing gold, especially when combined in its highest or triad valency: *auric* chloride, $AuCl_3$. [<L *aurum* gold]

auric acid **1** Hydrated auric oxide, $Au(HO)_3$, which combines with bases to form aurates. **2** Auric oxide, a dark-brown powder, Au_2O_3, formed by heating auric hydroxide.

au·ri·cle (ôr′i·kəl) *n.* **1** *Anat.* **a** An atrium of the heart. **b** An auricular appendix. **c** The external ear; pinna. **2** An ear or ear-shaped appendage or part. **3** An ear trumpet. [<L *auricula,* dim. of *auris* ear] **— au′ri·cled** *adj.*

au·ric·u·la (ō·rik′yə·lə) *n. pl.* **·lae** (-lē) or **·las** **1** A primrose from the Alps (*Primula auricula*): also called *bear's-ear.* **2** A small ear-shaped appendage. [<L, dim. of *auris* ear]

au·ric·u·lar (ô·rik′yə·lər) *adj.* **1** Of or pertaining to the ear or the sense of hearing. **2** Intended for or perceived by the ear; audible; confidential. **3** Ear-shaped. **4** Of or pertaining to an auricle. **—** *n. Ornithol.* One of the feathers overlying the ear: usually in the plural.

au·ric·u·late (ô·rik′yə·lit, -lāt) *adj.* **1** Having ear-shaped appendages or projections. **2** *Bot.* Having rounded projections at the base, as a leaf. **3** Like an ear. Also **au·ric′u·lat′ed. — au·ric′u·late·ly** *adv.*

au·rif·er·ous (ô·rif′ər·əs) *adj.* Containing gold. [<L *aurifer* < *aurum* gold + *ferre* bear] **— au·rif′er·ous·ly** *adv.*

au·ri·flamme (ôr′ə·flam) See **ORIFLAMME.**

au·ri·form (ôr′ə·fôrm) *adj.* Shaped like or resembling an ear; ear-shaped. [<L *auris* ear + -FORM]

Au·ri·ga (ô·rī′gə) A northern constellation, the Charioteer or Wagoner. See CONSTELLATION. [<L, charioteer]

Au·rig·na·cian (ôr′ig·nā′shən) *adj. Anthropol.* Of or pertaining to an Upper Paleolithic culture appearing toward the end of the Pleistocene. It is associated with the rise of Cro-Magnon man in western Europe and is characterized by implements of flint, bone, and horn, delicately modeled ivory figurines, and early examples of cave painting. [from *Aurignac,* town in Haute-Garonne, France, where the relics were discovered]

Au·ri·gny (ō·rē·nyē′) The French name for ALDERNEY.

au·ri·lave (ôr′ə·lāv) *n.* An instrument with which to clean the ears. [<L *auris* ear + *lavare* wash]

Au·riol (ô·ryôl′), **Vincent,** 1884–1966, French lawyer; president of France 1947–54.

au·ris (ôr′is) *n. pl.* **au·res** (ôr′ēz) *Latin* The ear.

au·ri·scope (ôr′ə·skōp) *n.* An instrument for examining the ear. **— au·ris·co·py** (ô·ris′kə·pē) *n.*

au·rist (ôr′ist) *n.* A specialist in diseases of the ear.

au·rochs (ôr′oks) *n.* The extinct European bison; urus. [<G *auerochs* <OHG *ūrohso* < *ūr* the urus + *ohso* ox]

au·ro·ra (ô·rôr′ə, ō·rō′rə) *n.* **1** The dawn. **2** The early stage or development of anything. **3** *Meteorol.* A luminous, sometimes richly colored display of arcs, bands, streamers, etc., occasionally seen in the skies of high northern and southern latitudes: it is caused by electrical disturbances in the atmosphere: also **au·ro′ra po·la·ris** (pə·lâr′is). [<L, dawn]

Au·ro·ra (ô·rôr′ə, ō·rō′rə) In Roman mythology, the goddess of the dawn: identified with the Greek *Eos.*

aurora aus·tra·lis (ôs·trā′lis) *Meteorol.* The aurora as seen in far southern latitudes: also called *southern lights.* [<NL, southern aurora <L *auster* south wind]

aurora bo·re·al·is (bôr′ē·al′is, -ā′lis, bō′rē-) *Meteorol.* The aurora as seen in the high northern latitudes: also called *northern lights.* [<NL, northern aurora <Gk. *boreas* north wind]

au·ro·ral (ô·rôr′əl, ô·rō′rəl) *adj.* **1** Pertaining to or like the dawn; dawning; roseate. **2** Of, like, or caused by an aurora: an *auroral* display. Also **au·ro·re·an** (ô·rôr′ē·ən, ô·rō′rē-), **au·ro′ric. — au·ro′ral·ly** *adv.*

au·rous (ôr′əs) *adj.* Of, pertaining to, or containing gold, especially in its monad valency: *aurous* chloride, AuCl. See AURIC. [<L *aurum* gold]

au·rum (ôr′əm) *n.* Gold. [<L]

aurum po·tab·i·le (pō·tab′ə·lē) *Latin* Literally, potable gold: a medieval cordial containing minute grains of gold.

Au·sa·ble River (ô·sā′bəl) A river 20 miles long in NE New York, flowing through **Ausable Chasm,** a gorge 1 1/2 miles long, to Lake Champlain.

Au·schwitz (ou′shvits) The German name for Oświecim, a city in SW Poland; site of a German extermination camp in which about 4,000,000 victims, mostly Jews, were slaughtered during World War II.

aus·cul·tate (ôs′kəl·tāt) *v.t.* & *v.i.* **·tat·ed, ·tat·ing** *Med.* To examine by auscultation. [<L *auscultatus,* pp. of *auscultare* listen, give ear to] **— aus·cul·ta·tive** (ôs·kul′tə·tiv) *adj.*

aus·cul·ta·tion (ôs′kəl·tā′shən) *n.* **1** *Med.* The act, art, or process of listening, as with a stethoscope, for sounds produced in the chest, abdomen, etc., to determine any abnormal condition. **2** A listening.

aus·cul·ta·tor (ôs′kəl·tā′tər) *n.* **1** One skilled in or practicing auscultation. **2** A stethoscope. **3** One who listens. **— aus·cul·ta·to·ry** (ôs·kul′tə·tôr′ē, -tō′rē) *adj.*

Aus·gleich (ous′glīkh) *n. German* Adjustment; agreement; compromise; specifically, the treaty of 1867 between Austria and Hungary, which formulated the organization of the former dual monarchy into a political union.

aus·pex (ôs′peks) *n. pl.* **aus·pi·ces** (ôs′pə·sēz) An augur, soothsayer, or diviner of ancient Rome; especially, one who observed and interpreted the omens connected with the flight, singing, cries, or feeding, etc., of birds; a bird-viewer. [<L *auspex* < *avis* bird + *specere* look at, observe]

aus·pi·cate (ôs′pi·kāt) *v.t.* To initiate or begin, especially under favorable circumstances, as with a ceremony calculated to insure good luck. [<L *auspicatus,* pp. of *auspicari* take omens, begin < *auspex.* See AUSPEX.]

aus·pice (ôs′pis) *n. pl.* **aus·pi·ces** (ôs′pə·sēz) **1** *Usually pl.* Favoring influence or guidance; patronage. **2** An augury, omen, or sign, especially when taken from meteorological phenomena, the movements of birds, etc. **3** The observation of such omens, etc. [<F <L *auspicium* < *auspex.* See AUSPEX.]

aus·pi·cial (ôs·pish′əl) *adj.* **1** Pertaining to augury. **2** Auspicious.

aus·pi·cious (ôs·pish′əs) *adj.* **1** Of good omen; propitious. **2** Successful; prosperous; fortunate. **— aus·pi′cious·ly** *adv.* **— aus·pi′cious·ness** *n.*

Synonyms: encouraging, favorable, fortunate, happy, hopeful, lucky, opportune, promising, propitious, prosperous, successful. See PROPITIOUS. *Antonyms*: baleful, discouraging, hopeless, inauspicious, unfavorable, unpromising, unpropitious.

Aus·sig (ou′sikh) The German name for USTI NAD LABEM.

Aus·ten (ôs′tən), **Jane,** 1775–1817, English novelist.

aus·ten·ite (ôs′tən·īt) *n. Metall.* A solid solution of carbon in pure iron, used in the making of steel which is non-magnetic at ordi-

nary temperatures. [after Sir W. C. Roberts-*Austen*, 1843–1902, English metallurgist]— **aus'ten·it'ic** (-it'ik) *adj.*

Aus·ter (ôs'tər) *n. Poetic* **1** The south wind. **2** The south. [< L]

aus·tere (ô·stir') *adj.* **1** Severe, grave, or stern, as in aspect, disposition, judgment, or conduct. **2** Morally strict; abstemious; ascetic. **3** Sour and astringent. **4** Severely simple; unadorned. [< OF < L *austerus* < Gk. *austēros* harsh, bitter < *auein* dry] —**aus·tere'ly** *adv.*

Synonyms: hard, harsh, morose, relentless, rigid, rigorous, severe, stern, strict, unrelenting, unyielding. The *austere* person is severely simple or temperate, *strict* in self-restraint or discipline, and similarly *unrelenting* toward others. We speak of *austere* morality, *rigid* rules, *rigorous* discipline, *stern* commands, *severe* punishment, *harsh* speech or a *harsh* voice, *hard* requirements, *strict* injunctions, and *strict* obedience. *Strict* discipline holds one exactly and unflinchingly to the rule; *rigorous* discipline punishes severely any infraction of it.

aus·ter·i·ty (ô·ster'ə·tē) *n. pl.* **·ties** **1** Gravity or rigor in attitude or conduct toward others. **2** Severe self-restraint. **3** Rigid economy in expenditure. **4** *pl.* Austere acts or practices. Also **aus·tere'ness.**

Aus·ter·litz (ôs'tər·lits, *Ger.* ous'tər·lits) A town in Moravia, Czechoslovakia; site of Napoleon's greatest victory, in 1805, over the Russian and Austrian armies.

Aus·tin (ôs'tən) Var. of AUGUSTINE.

Aus·tin (ôs'tən) A city on the Colorado River; the capital of Texas.

Aus·tin (ôs'tən), **Alfred**, 1835–1913, English poet laureate 1896–1913. —**John**, 1790–1859, English jurist. —**Mary Hunter**, 1868–1934, U.S. writer. —**Stephen Fuller**, 1793–1836, U.S. colonizer in Texas. —**Warren Robinson**, 1877–1963, U.S. lawyer and politician.

Austin Friar An Augustinian Hermit.

aus·tral (ôs'trəl, os'-) *adj.* Southern; torrid. [< L *australis* southern < *auster* south wind]

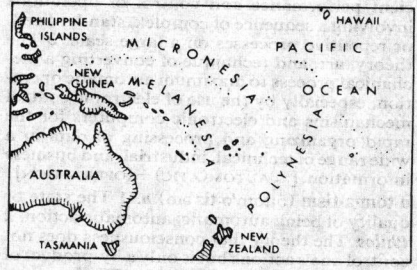

Aus·tral·a·sia (ôs'trəl·ā'zhə, -ā'shə, os'-) The islands of the South Pacific, including Australia, New Zealand, New Guinea, and adjacent islands; sometimes applied to all of Oceania. — **Aus'tral·a'sian** *adj. & n.*

Aus·tral English (ôs'trəl, os'-) Australian English.

Aus·tra·lia (ô·strāl'yə, o-) An island continent SE of Asia, comprising the **Commonwealth of Australia**, a self-governing member of the Commonwealth of Nations, consisting of a union of six states and two territories together with its dependencies; 2,948,366 square miles; capital, Canberra.

Australia Day An Australian holiday, January 26th, commemorating the landing of the British in 1788. Also *Anniversary Day*.

Aus·tra·lian (ô·strāl'yən, o-) *n.* **1** A native or naturalized inhabitant of Australia. **2** One of the Australian aborigines. **3** Any of the aboriginal languages of Australia. —*adj.* Designating a zoogeographical region including Australia, New Guinea and adjacent islands, New Zealand, and Polynesia.

Australian Alps A mountain range in SE New South Wales and eastern Victoria, Australia; highest peak, 7,316 feet.

Australian ballot See under BALLOT.

Australian Capital Territory A region within New South Wales containing Canberra, capital of Australia; 911 square miles; formerly *Federal Territory*.

Australian crawl See under CRAWL.

Australian English The English language as spoken and written in Australia: sometimes called *Austral English*.

Aus·tra·lian·ism (ô·strāl'yən·iz'əm, o-) *n.* **1** A trait, custom, or tradition of Australia or Australians. **2** A word, phrase, or usage characteristic of Australian English. **3** Devotion to Australia, its institutions, etc.

Australian pine Any of several species (genus *Casuarina*) of rapidly growing, dicotyledonous evergreen trees and shrubs having leaves reduced to whorls of pointed scales, native to Australia and established as a nuisance in southern Florida.

Aus·tral Islands (ôs'trəl) See TUBUAI ISLANDS.

Aus·tra·lite (ôs'trə·līt, os'-) *n.* A small, smooth lump of black glass, presumably a meteorite, found in the southern parts of Australia and elsewhere: also called *blackfellow's button*. Compare TEKTITE.

Aus·tra·loid (ôs'trə·loid) *adj.* Pertaining to, designating, or belonging to the ethnic group composed of the aborigines of Australia.

Aus·tra·lo·pi·the·cus (ôs·trā'lō·pi·thē'kəs) *n.* A genus of small-brained primates of the Pliocene and early Pleistocene, first identified from a fossil juvenile skull found in 1924 at Taungs, South Africa; subsequent remains confirm its position as a transitional form between ape and man. Also called *Taungs skull*. —**Aus·tra'lo·pi·the'cine** (-thē'sīn, -sin) *adj.* [< NL < L *australis* southern + Gk. *pithēkos* ape]

Aus·tri·a (ôs'trē·ə) A federal republic of central Europe; 32,375 square miles; capital Vienna; German *Österreich*. —**Aus'tri·an** *adj. & n.*

Aus·tri·a-Hun·ga·ry (ôs'trē·ə·hung'gə·rē) A former dual monarchy of central Europe, 1867–1918, comprising the Austrian empire, Hungary, and other crownlands.

Austro- *combining form* **1** Austrian: *Austro-Hungarian.* **2** Australian: *Austro-Malayan.*

Aus·tro-A·si·at·ic (ôs'trō·ā'zhē·at'ik, -ā'shē-) *n.* A family of languages of SE Asia, including the Mon-Khmer and Munda subfamilies. —*adj.* Of or pertaining to this linguistic family.

Aus·tro-Hun·gar·i·an (ôs'trō·hung·gâr'ē·ən) *adj.* Of or pertaining to Austria-Hungary.

Aus·tro-Ma·lay·an (ôs'trō·mə·lā'ən) *adj.* Of or pertaining to the Papuan subregion north of Australia, including islands from San Cristobal to Celebes.

Aus·tro·ne·sia (ôs'trō·nē'zhə, -shə) The islands of Indonesia, Melanesia, Micronesia, and Polynesia.

Aus·tro·ne·sian (ôs'trō·nē'zhən, -shən) *adj.* Of or pertaining to Austronesia, its inhabitants, or their languages. —*n.* A family of languages spoken throughout the Pacific in an area roughly bounded by Madagascar to the west, Easter Island to the east, Formosa to the north, and New Zealand to the south, but excluding Australia, Tasmania, and a large part of New Guinea. The Austronesian family is divided linguistically into three subfamilies: Indonesian or Malayan, Oceanic (including the Melanesian and Micronesian languages), and Polynesian. Also *Malayo-Polynesian*.

aut- Var. of AUTO-.[1]

au·ta·coid (ô'tə·koid) *n.* Hormone. [< AUT- + Gk. *akos* remedy + -OID]

au·tar·chy (ô'tär·kē) *n.* **1** Absolute rule or sovereignty or a country under such rule; unrestricted power; autocracy. **2** Self-government. **3** Autarky. [< Gk. *autarchos* absolute rule < *autos* self + *archein* rule] —**au·tar·chic** (ô·tär'kik) or **·chi·cal** *adj.*

au·tar·ky (ô'tär·kē) *n.* National economic self-sufficiency; a policy of establishing independence of imports from other countries: also *autarchy*. [< Gk. *autarkeia* self-sufficiency < *autos* self + *arkeein* suffice] —**au·tar·ki·cal** (ô·tär'ki·kəl) *adj.*

au·te·col·o·gy (ô'tē·kol'ə·jē) *n.* The ecology of individual organisms: distinguished from *synecology*.

au·teur (ō·tœr') *n.* A film director whose work is the product of personal vision and total production control. [< F, lit., author]

au·then·tic (ô·then'tik) *adj.* **1** According with the facts; authoritative; trustworthy; reliable. **2** Of undisputed origin; genuine. **3** *Law* Duly executed before the proper officer. Also **au·**

then'ti·cal. [< OF *autentique* < L *authenticus* < Gk. *authentikos* < *authentēs* the doer of a deed] —**au·then'ti·cal·ly** *adv.*

Synonyms: accepted, accredited, authoritative, authorized, certain, current, genuine, legitimate, original, real, received, sure, true, trustworthy, veritable. *Antonyms*: apocryphal, baseless, counterfeit, disputed, exploded, fabulous, false, fictitious, spurious, unauthorized.

au·then·ti·cate (ô·then'ti·kāt) *v.t.* **·cat·ed, ·cat·ing** **1** To make genuine, credible, or authoritative. **2** To give legal force or validity to. **3** To establish or certify, as a book or painting, to be the work of a certain person. —**au·then'ti·ca'tion** *n.*

au·then·ti·ca·tor (ô·then'ti·kā'tər) *n.* **1** One who or that which authenticates. **2** *Telecom.* A code signal transmitted with a radio message as a proof of genuineness.

au·then·tic·i·ty (ô'then·tis'ə·tē) *n.* The state or quality of being authentic, authoritative, or genuine. Also **au·then'tic·ness.**

au·thor (ô'thər) *n.* **1** An originator; first cause; creator. **2** The original writer, as of a book; also, one who makes literary compositions his profession. **3** An author's writings collectively. See synonyms under CAUSE. —*v.t. Informal* To be the author of; write. [< OF *autor* < L *auctor* originator, producer < *augere* increase] —**au'thor·ess** *n. fem.* —**au·tho·ri·al** (ô·thôr'ē·əl, ô·thō'rē-) *adj.*

au·thor·i·tar·i·an (ə·thôr'ə·târ'ē·ən, ə·thor'-) *adj.* Encouraging and upholding authority against individual freedom; specifically, relating to a type of government in which the individual and his rights are subordinated to interests of state. —*n.* A defender of the principle of authority or of a type of government organized on an authoritarian basis. —**au·thor'i·tar'i·an·ism** *n.*

au·thor·i·ta·tive (ə·thôr'ə·tā'tiv, ə·thor'-) *adj.* **1** Possessing or proceeding from proper authority; duly sanctioned. **2** Exercising authority; positive; commanding; dictatorial. See synonyms under ABSOLUTE, AUTHENTIC, DOGMATIC, IMPERIOUS. —**au·thor'i·ta'tive·ly** *adv.* —**au·thor'i·ta'tive·ness** *n.*

au·thor·i·ty (ə·thôr'ə·tē, ə·thor'-) *n. pl.* **·ties** **1** The right to command and to enforce obedience; the right to act officially. **2** Personal power that commands influence, respect, or confidence. **3** The person or persons in whom government or command is vested: often in the plural. **4** That which is or may be appealed to in support of action or belief, as an author, volume, etc. **5** An authoritative opinion, decision, or precedent. See synonyms under INFLUENCE, PERMISSION, PRECEDENT. [< F *autorité* < L *auctoritas, -tatis* power, authority < *augere* increase]

au·thor·i·za·tion (ô'thər·ə·zā'shən) *n.* **1** The act of conferring legality. **2** Formal legal power; sanction.

au·thor·ize (ô'thər·īz) *v.t.* **·ized, ·iz·ing** **1** To confer authority upon; empower; commission. **2** To warrant; justify. **3** To sanction; approve. **4** *Obs.* To vouch for. See JUSTIFY. —**au'thor·iz'er** *n.*

au·thor·ized (ô'thər·īzd) *adj.* **1** Endowed with authority; accepted as authoritative. **2** Formally or legally sanctioned.

Authorized Version The King James Bible. See under BIBLE.

au·thor·ship (ô'thər·ship) *n.* **1** The profession or occupation of an author. **2** Origin or source.

au·tism (ô'tiz·əm) *n. Psychol.* A tendency to morbid daydreaming and introspection uninfluenced by objective norms and realities. [< AUT- + -ISM] —**au·tis·tic** (ô·tis'tik) *adj.*

au·to (ô'tō) *U.S. Colloq.* An automobile. —*v.i.* To ride or travel by an automobile.

auto-[1] *combining form* **1** Arising from some process or action within the object; not induced by any stimulus from without; as in

autoagglutination	autofecundation
autocombustible	autohybridization
autoelectrolysis	autoinduction
autoelectrolytic	autoinhibitive
autoexcitation	autoluminescence

autoretardation **autosepticemia**
autorhythmic **autosymbolic**

2 Acting, acted, or directed upon the self; as in:

autoanalysis **autoimmunity**
autoanalytic **autolavage**

Also, before vowels, *aut-*, as in *autism.* [< Gk. *autos* self]

auto-² *combining form* Self-propelled: *auto-boat.* [< *automobile*]

au·to·bahn (ou′tō·bän) *n. pl.* **·bahns** or *German* **·bahn·en** In Germany, a superhighway.

au·to·bi·og·ra·phy (ô′tə·bī·og′rə·fē, -bē·og′-) *n. pl.* **·phies** The story of one's life written by oneself. See synonyms under HISTORY. —**au′to·bi·og′ra·pher** *n.* —**au·to·bi·o·graph·ic** (ô′tə·bī′ə·graf′ik) or **·i·cal** *adj.* —**au′to·bi′o·graph′i·cal·ly** *adv.*

au·to·boat (ô′tō·bōt) *n.* A boat propelled by motor power.

au·to·bus (ô′tō·bus) *n.* An omnibus propelled by motor power.

au·to·ceph·a·li (ô′tō·sef′ə·lī) *n. pl.* In the Greek Church, those churches or bishops rejecting patriarchal jurisdiction and claiming to be self-governing. [< Gk. *autokephalos* < *autos* self + *kephalē* head]

au·to·ceph·a·lous (ô′tō·sef′ə·ləs) *adj.* 1 *Eccl.* Independent of patriarchal or archiepiscopal jurisdiction. 2 Having jurisdiction as an independent head or chief. Also **au·to·ce·phal·ic** (ô′tō·sə·fal′ik).

au·to·chrome (ô′tə·krōm) *n.* A single plate for three-color photography.

au·toch·thon (ô·tok′thən) *n. pl.* **·thons** or **·tho·nes** (-thə·nēz) 1 Originally, one sprung from the earth itself. 2 *pl.* The aboriginal inhabitants. 3 *Ecol.* An indigenous animal or plant. [< Gk. *autochthōn* indigenous < *autos* self + *chthōn* earth, land]

au·toch·thon·ism (ô·tok′thən·iz′əm) *n.* Origin from the soil of a country; origination in or primitive occupation of a region. Also **au·toch·tho·ny** (ô·tok′thə·nē).

au·toch·tho·nous (ô·tok′thə·nəs) *adj.* 1 Sprung from the soil; native to a place; indigenous; aboriginal. 2 *Geol.* Of or pertaining to rocks which, with their constituents, have been formed *in situ,* as rock salt, stalactites, etc. Also **au·toch′tho·nal, au·toch·thon·ic** (ô′·tok·thon′ik). —**au·toch′tho·nous·ly** *adv.*

au·to·clave (ô′tə·klāv) *n.* 1 A strong gastight vessel in which chemical reactions can be effected under pressure. 2 An enclosed chamber for the sterilization of drugs, vaccines, instruments, etc., under specified pressure. 3 A steamtight cooking utensil; a pressure cooker. [< F < *auto-* AUTO-¹ + L *clavis* a key]

au·toc·ra·cy (ô·tok′rə·sē) *n.* 1 Absolute government by an individual; rule or authority of an autocrat. 2 A state ruled by an autocrat. 3 Complete power or dominance over others.

au·to·crat (ô′tə·krat) *n.* 1 A supreme ruler of unrestricted power. 2 One exercising unlimited power over others. 3 An arrogant, dictatorial person. [< F *autocrate* < Gk. *autokratēs* self-ruling, independent < *autos* self + *kratos* power] —**au′to·crat′ic** or **·i·cal** *adj.* —**au′to·crat′i·cal·ly** *adv.*

au·to-da-fé (ô′tō·də·fā′, ou′-) *n. pl.* **au·tos-da-fé** (ô′tōz-, ou′tōz-) The public announcement and execution of the sentence of the Inquisition, with the attendant ceremonies, as the burning of heretics at the stake, etc. Also *Spanish* **au·to de fe** (ou′tō dā fā′). [< Pg., lit., act of the faith]

au·to·de·tec·tor (ô′tō·di·tek′tər) *n. Electr.* An automatic coherer.

au·to·dyne (ô′tə·dīn) *adj. Telecom.* Designating the manner of producing oscillations in a detector tube so as to secure beats. See BEAT, HETERODYNE.

au·toe·cious (ô·tē′shəs) *adj. Bot.* 1 Having male and female reproductive organs on the same plant, as certain mosses. 2 Completing the whole development on a single host, as seen in certain rust fungi and other parasites: opposed to *heteroecious.* [< AUTO-¹ + Gk. *oikos* dwelling]

au·toe·cism (ô·tē′siz·əm) *n.* The condition of being autoecious.

au·to·er·o·tism (ô′tō·er′ə·tiz′əm) *n.* 1 *Psychoanal.* Sexual impulses taking one's own body as their object, without association with or stimulus from another person. 2 Masturbation. Also **au·to·e·rot·i·cism** (ô′tō·i·rot′ə·siz′·əm). [< AUTO-¹ + Gk. *erōs, erotos* love] —**au·to·e·rot·ic** (ô′tō·i·rot′ik) *adj.*

au·tog·a·mous (ô·tog′ə·məs) *adj. Bot.* Self-fertilized; capable of self-fertilization: said of certain flowers.

au·tog·a·my (ô·tog′ə·mē) *n.* 1 *Biol.* Self-fertilization; fecundation of a flower by its own pollen. 2 *Biol.* The union of closely related cells or of nuclei within a cell; karyogamy. [< AUTO-¹ + Gk. *gameein* marry]

au·to·gen·e·sis (ô′tō·jen′ə·sis) *n. Biol.* Spontaneous formation of a tissue or organism.

au·to·ge·net·ic (ô′tō·jə·net′ik) *adj.* 1 Of or pertaining to autogenesis. 2 *Geog.* Of, pertaining to, regulated by, or indicating a self-established system of drainage. —**au′to·ge·net′i·cal·ly** *adv.*

au·tog·e·nous (ô·toj′ə·nəs) *adj.* 1 Self-produced or independent. 2 *Physiol.* Developed within the body, as new tissue or skeletal parts. 3 *Mech.* Designating a process of soldering by means of a hydrogen flame. Also **au·to·gen·ic** (ô′tō·jen′ik). [< Gk. *autogenēs* self-produced]

autogenous vaccine Vaccine made from bacteria obtained from the person to be inoculated.

Au·to·gi·ro (ô′tə·jī′rō) *n. pl.* **·ros** An airplane having horizontal rotary airfoils which act only as a means of lift and support: a trade name. See GYROPLANE. [< AUTO-¹ + Gk. *gyros* a circle]

au·to·graft (ô′tō·graft′, -gräft) *n.* A mass of tissue transplanted from one site to another on the same organism. —*v.t.* To transplant (tissue) in making an autograft.

au·to·graph (ô′tə·graf, -gräf) *n.* 1 One's own handwriting or signature. 2 Something in one's own handwriting; a manuscript in an author's handwriting. —*v.t.* 1 To write one's name in or affix one's signature to. 2 To write in one's own handwriting. —*adj.* Written by one's own hand, as a will. [< L *autographum,* orig. neut. of *autographus* < Gk. *autographos* written with one's own hand < *autos* self + *graphein* write]

au·to·graph·ic (ô′tə·graf′ik) *adj.* 1 Of the nature of or like an autograph. 2 Written in one's own or the author's handwriting. 3 In telegraphy, recording or transmitting in facsimile. Also **au′to·graph′i·cal.** —**au′to·graph′·i·cal·ly** *adv.*

au·tog·ra·phy (ô·tog′rə·fē) *n.* 1 The writing of a document in one's own handwriting. 2 Autographs collectively. 3 One's own handwriting. 4 Facsimile reproduction.

au·to·harp (ô′tō·härp) *n.* A musical instrument resembling a zither, but having a piano scale and an arrangement of dampers enabling the player to produce the correct chords easily.

au·to·hyp·no·sis (ô′tō·hip·nō′sis) *n.* The state or condition of self-hypnotism.

au·to·im·mune (ô′′tō·i·myōōn′) *adj.* Caused by antibodies that operate against the body's own tissues: *autoimmune* diseases. —**au′to·im·mu′ni·ty** *n.*

au·to·in·fec·tion (ô′tō·in·fek′shən) *n. Pathol.* Infection due to agents or toxins generated in the body, as the infection causing peritonitis when perforation of the intestine occurs.

au·to·in·oc·u·la·tion (ô′tō·in·ok′yə·lā′shən) *n.* Inoculation with a virus or other morbid matter already present in one's own body. 2 The spreading of infection from a center to other portions of the same body.

au·to·in·tox·i·ca·tion (ô′tō·in·tok′sə·kā′shən) *n.* Autotoxemia.

au·to·ki·net·ic (ô′tō·ki·net′ik, -kī-) *adj.* Self-moving. [< Gk. *autokinētos* self-moved < *autos* self + *kineein* move]

au·to·load·ing (ô′tō·lō′ding) *adj.* Self-loading: said of firearms.

Au·tol·y·cus (ô·tol′i·kəs) A Greek astronomer and mathematician of the fourth century B.C. —**Autolycus** In Greek mythology, the son of Hermes, famous for his thievery, who could change the form of his plunder or render it invisible.

au·tol·y·sate (ô·tol′ə·sāt) *n.* A substance resulting from the autolysis of organic material.

au·to·ly·sin (ô′tə·lī′sin) *n. Biochem.* A substance which initiates or promotes autolysis.

au·tol·y·sis (ô·tol′ə·sis) *n.* 1 *Biochem.* The disintegration of cells and tissues after death by the action of enzymes already present: distinguished from *heterolysis.* 2 *Physiol.* Self-digestion of organic material. [< NL < AUTO-¹ + Gk. *lysis* dissolution < *lyein* loosen, dissolve] —**au·to·lyt·ic** (ô′tə·lit′ik) *adj.*

au·to·mat (ô′tə·mat) *n.* 1 An automatic device: applied to various articles, as a camera shutter, etc. 2 *U.S.* A restaurant in which food is automatically made available from a receptacle when money is deposited in a slot alongside.

au·to·mat·a·ble (ô′tə·mat′ə·bəl) *adj.* Suitable for or capable of automation: an *automatable* production process.

au·to·mate (ô′tə·māt) *v.* **·mat·ed, ·mat·ing** *v.t.* To adapt, as a machine, factory, or process, for automation. —*v.i.* To install or convert to automation equipment.

au·to·mat·ic (ô′tə·mat′ik) *adj.* 1 Self-moving, self-regulating, or self-acting. 2 Acting mechanically. 3 *Psychol.* Done from force of habit or without volition. 4 *Physiol.* Independent of the will, as a reflex action. 5 *Mech.* Having a self-acting mechanism by which certain operations are performed under predetermined conditions: an *automatic* pilot. Also **au′to·mat′i·cal, au·tom·a·tous** (ô·tom′ə·təs). —*n.* A self-acting machine, device, or weapon. See synonyms under SPONTANEOUS [< Gk. *automatos* acting of oneself. See AUTOMATON.] —**au′to·mat′i·cal·ly** *adv.*

au·tom·a·tic·i·ty (ô·tom′ə·tis′ə·tē) *n.* State or condition of being automatic.

automatic pilot *Aeron.* An automatic-control mechanism operating on the gyroscope principle: designed to keep an aircraft in level flight and on an even course: also called *gyro pilot, robot pilot.*

au·to·ma·tion (ô′tə·mā′shən) *n. Technol.* 1 The automatic transfer of one unit of a complex industrial assembly to a succession of self-acting machines each of which completes a specified stage in the total manufacturing process from crude material to finished product. 2 The application of fully automatic procedures in the efficient performance and control of operations involving a sequence of complex, standardized, or repetitive processes on a large scale. 3 The theory, art, and technique of converting a mechanical process to maximum automatic operation, especially by the use of electronic control mechanisms and electronic computers for the rapid organizing and processing of data in a wide range of technical, industrial, and business information. [< AUTOM(ATIC) + (OPER)ATION]

au·tom·a·tism (ô·tom′ə·tiz′əm) *n.* 1 The state or quality of being automatic; automatic action. 2 *Philos.* The theory that consciousness does not control one's actions but is only a by-product of physiological changes. 3 *Physiol.* The functioning or power of functioning of muscular or other processes in response to external stimuli but independent of conscious control, as winking. 4 *Biol.* Spontaneous activity of cells and tissues, as the beating of a heart freed from its nervous connections. 5 *Psychol.* **a** A condition in which actions are performed without the conscious knowledge or will of the subject. **b** Any such action. 6 Suspension of the conscious mind in order to release for expression the repressed ideas and images of the subconscious, as practiced by surrealist artists and writers. —**au·tom′a·tist** *n.*

au·tom·a·tize (ô·tom′ə·tīz) *v.t.* **·tized, ·tiz·ing** 1 To render automatic. 2 To reduce to an automaton.

au·tom·a·ton (ô·tom′ə·ton, -tən) *n. pl.* **·tons** or **·ta** (-tə) 1 A contrivance or apparatus that appears to function of itself by the action of a concealed mechanism. 2 Any living being whose actions are or appear to be involuntary or mechanical. 3 Anything capable of spontaneous movement or action. [< Gk. *automaton,* neut. of *automatos* acting of oneself, independent]

au·to·mo·bile (ô′tə·mə·bēl′, ô′tə·mə·bēl′, ô′tə·mō′bēl) *n.* A self-propelled vehicle; specifically, one driven by an internal-combustion engine or storage battery and independent of rails or tracks; a motorcar. —*v.i.* **·biled, bil·ing** To ride in or drive an automobile. —*adj.* (ô′tə·mō′bil) 1 Self-propelling. 2 Of or for automobiles. [< F]

au·to·mo·bil·ism (ô′tə·mə·bēl′iz·əm, -mō′bil·iz′əm) *n.* The practice of using motorcars; also, the acts and methods of those who use

them. —**au·to·mo·bil·ist** (ô'tə·mə·bēl'ist, -mō'·bil·ist) n.

au·to·mo·tive (ô'tə·mō'tiv) adj. 1 Self-propelling. 2 Of or for automobiles: *automotive* parts.

au·to·nom·ic (ô'tə·nom'ik) adj. 1 Autonomous. 2 *Biol.* Spontaneous: said of functions in plants and animals produced by inherent conditions. Also **au·to·nom'i·cal.** — **au·to·nom'i·cal·ly** adv.

autonomic nervous system A plexus of nerve ganglia and fibers originating in the spinal column and acting to innervate and control the efferent functions of all body tissues and organs not subject to voluntary control, as the heart, blood vessels, smooth muscle, glands, stomach, and intestines.

au·ton·o·mous (ô·ton'ə·məs) adj. 1 Independent; self-governing. 2 Of or pertaining to an autonomy. 3 *Biol.* Independent of any other organism. 4 *Bot.* Autonomic. [<Gk. *autonomos* independent < *autos* self + *nomos* law, rule] — **au·ton'o·mous·ly** adv.

au·ton·o·my (ô·ton'ə·mē) n. pl. **·mies** 1 The condition or quality of being autonomous; especially the power or right of self-government. 2 A self-governing community or local group in a particular sphere, as in religion, education, etc. 3 Self-determination, as of the will. [<Gk. *autonomia* independence <*autonomos.* See AUTONOMOUS.] — **au·ton'o·mist** n.

au·to·pho·bi·a (ô'tə·fō'bē·ə) n. Morbid fear of oneself or of being alone: also called *eremophobia, monophobia.* — **au·to·pho·bic** (ô'tə·fō'bik, -fob'ik) adj.

au·to·plas·ty (ô'tə·plas'tē) n. *Surg.* The operation of repairing wounds or diseased parts by means of living tissue from other parts of the same body. — **au'to·plas'tic** adj.

au·top·sy (ô'top·sē, ô'təp-) n. pl. **·sies** 1 Postmortem examination of a human body, especially to determine the cause of death for medical or legal purposes. Compare BIOPSY. 2 The act of seeing with one's own eyes. [<NL *autopsia* <Gk. *autopsia* a seeing for oneself < *autos* self + *opsis* a seeing]

au·top·tic (ô·top'tik) adj. 1 Seen with one's own eyes. 2 Of or as of an eyewitness. Also **au·top'ti·cal.**

au·to·ra·di·o·graph (ô'tō·rā'dē·ə·graf', -gräf') n. *Med.* A photograph taken by autoradiography: also called *radioautograph, radioautogram.*

au·to·ra·di·og·ra·phy (ô'tō·rā'dē·og'rə·fē) n. *Med.* Radiography which utilizes the emanations of radioactive elements or isotopes incorporated for the purpose of study and analysis in test material, as of a tissue: also called *radioautography.*

au·to·some (ô'tə·sōm) n. *Biol.* Any chromosome other than those which determine the sex of an organism. [<AUTO-¹ + (CHROMO)SOME] — **au'to·so'mal** adj.

au·to·sta·bil·i·ty (ô'tō·stə·bil'ə·tē) n. Stability owing to innate qualities, or to automatic machinery.

au·to·sug·gest·i·bil·i·ty (ô'tō·səg·jes'tə·bil'ə·tē) n. 1 The state or quality of being autosuggestive. 2 Ability to hypnotize oneself.

au·to·sug·ges·tion (ô'tō·səg·jes'chən) n. *Psychol.* Suggestion, particularly with a view to producing a condition of autohypnosis, emanating from self only. — **au'to·sug·ges'tive** adj.

au·tot·o·my (ô·tot'ə·mē) n. *Zool.* The spontaneous shedding of a part of an organism from the whole, as in starfish, salamanders, and crabs. [<AUTO-¹ + Gk. *tomē* a cutting < *temnein* cut]

au·to·tox·e·mi·a (ô'tō·tok·sē'mē·ə) n. The poisoning of self from noxious secretions of one's own body; autointoxication. Also **au'to·tox·ae'mi·a, au·to·tox·i·co·sis** (ô'tō·tok'si·kō'sis).

au·to·tox·in (ô'tō·tok'sin) n. Any toxin produced by changes of tissue within an organism. **au·to·tox·is** (ô'tō·tok'sis) n. Autotoxemia. Also **au·to·tox·i·ca·tion** (ô'tō·tok'si·kā'shən). — **au'·to·tox'ic** adj.

au·to·trans·form·er (ô'tō·trans·fôr'mər) n. *Electr.* An automatic compensator used with alternating-current motors, in which the motor is fed from different points in an impedance coil placed across the supply circuits; a compensator.

au·to·troph·ic (ô'tə·trof'ik) adj. *Bot.* Self-nourishing: said of green plants that make their own food by photosynthesis, and of bacteria which can grow without organic carbon and nitrogen. [<AUTO-¹ + Gk. *trophē* food < *trephein* nourish]

au·tot·ro·pism (ô·tot'rə·piz'əm) n. *Bot.* The tendency of the organs of a plant, uninfluenced from without, to grow in straight lines. [<AUTO-¹ + Gk. *tropē* a turning < *trepein* turn] — **au·to·trop·ic** (ô'tə·trop'ik) adj.

au·to·truck (ô'tō·truk) n. A motor-propelled truck.

au·to·type (ô'tə·tīp) n. 1 A photographic process by which pictures are produced in monochrome in a carbon pigment. 2 The print so produced. 3 A facsimile. — **au·to·typ·ic** (ô'tə·tip'ik) adj.

au·to·ty·pog·ra·phy (ô'tō·tī·pog'rə·fē) n. The art or process of drawing on gelatin, with a special ink, relief designs which are then transferred by pressure to soft metal plates from which copies may be printed.

au·to·ty·py (ô'tə·tī'pē) n. Reproduction by the autotype process.

au·tox·i·da·tion (ô·tok'sə·dā'shən) n. *Chem.* 1 Oxidation of a substance or compound on exposure to air. 2 Oxidation occurring only in the presence of a second substance which serves to complete the reaction.

au·tres temps, au·tres moeurs (ō'tr' tän'ō'tr' mœrs') *French* Other times, other customs.

au·tumn (ô'təm) n. 1 The third season of the year; in the northern hemisphere, September, October and November: often called *fall.* 2 A time of maturity and incipient decline. — adj. Autumnal. [Earlier *autumpne* <OF *autompne* <L *autumnus*; ult. origin uncertain]

au·tum·nal (ô·tum'nəl) adj. 1 Of, pertaining to, or like autumn; ripening or harvested in autumn. 2 Past maturity; denoting a later period of life; declining. — **au·tum'nal·ly** adv.

autumnal equinox See under EQUINOX.

au·tun·ite (ô'tən·īt) n. *Mineral.* A pearly, light-yellow, hydrous calcium-uranium phosphate, crystallizing in the orthorhombic system. [from *Autun*, a city in France]

Au·vergne (ō·vârn', ō·vûrn'; *Fr.* ō·vern'y') A region and former province of south central France.

Auvergne Mountains A range in south central France; highest peak, 6,188 feet.

aux (ō; *before vowel sounds* ōz) *French* To the; at the; according to: used before plurals.

aux·a·nom·e·ter (ôk'sə·nom'ə·tər) n. *Bot.* An instrument for measuring the growth of plants. [<Gk. *auxanein* increase, grow + -METER]

aux armes! (ō zȧrm') *French* To arms!

Aux Cayes (ō kā') See LES CAYES.

Aux·erre (ō·sâr') A city of north central France.

aux·il·ia·ry (ôg·zil'yər·ē, -zil'ər-) adj. 1 Giving or furnishing aid. 2 Subsidiary; accessory. — n. pl. **·ries** 1 One who or that which aids or helps; assistant; associate. 2 *Gram.* a A verb that helps to express the tense, mood, voice, or aspect of another verb, as *have* in "We *have* gone," *may* in "I *may* leave tomorrow": also called *helping verb.* Also **auxiliary verb.** b A word which functions as a subordinate element in a sentence and is fully meaningful only in association with the main words, as a preposition or conjunction. 3 pl. Foreign troops associated with those of a nation at war. 4 An auxiliary vessel. [<L *auxiliarius* < *auxilium* a help < *augere* increase]

Synonyms (noun): accessory, aid, ally, assistant, coadjutor, confederate, helper, mercenary, promoter, subordinate. *Allies* unite as equals; *auxiliaries*, in military usage, are troops of one nation uniting with the armies, and acting under the orders, of another. *Mercenaries* serve only for pay; *auxiliaries* often for reasons of state, policy, or patriotism as well. Compare ACCESSORY, APPENDAGE. *Antonyms:* antagonist, hinderer, opponent.

auxiliary vessel, ship, etc. 1 *Naut.* A vessel, yacht, etc., equipped with an engine and propeller as auxiliaries to its sails as motive power. 2 A naval vessel not designed for or

assigned to combat service, as a transport, hospital ship, tug, etc.

aux·i·mone (ôk'si·mōn) n. *Biochem.* One of several plant foods, analogous to vitamins, minute quantities of which are sufficient for plant nutrition. [<Gk. *auximos* assisting growth]

aux·in (ôk'sin) n. *Bot.* Any of a group of plant hormones which in minute quantities act to promote or modify the growth of plants, as in root and bud formation, stem curvature, and leaf drop. [<Gk. *auxein* increase + -IN]

aux·o·chrome (ôk'sə·krōm) n. *Chem.* Any of certain radicals which will convert a chromophore into an acidic or basic dye suitable for use in textile fabrics. [<Gk. *auxein* increase + -CHROME]

aux·o·spore (ôk'sə·spôr, -spōr) n. A comparatively large cell in diatoms. [<Gk. *auxein* increase + *sporos* seed]

a·va (ə·vä') adv. *Scot.* At all; of all.

a·vail (ə·vāl') n. 1 Utility for a purpose; benefit; good. 2 pl. Proceeds. See synonyms under PROFIT, UTILITY. — v.t. To assist or aid; profit. — v.i. To be of value or advantage; suffice. — **to avail oneself of** To take advantage of; utilize. [<OF a- to (<L *ad-*) + *valoir* <L *valere* be strong] — **a·vail'ing** adj. — **a·vail'ing·ly** adv.

a·vail·a·ble (ə·vā'lə·bəl) adj. 1 Capable of being used advantageously; usable; profitable; at one's disposal, as funds. 2 Of adequate power for a result; effectual; valid. — **a·vail'a·bil'i·ty, a·vail'a·ble·ness** n. — **a·vail'·a·bly** adv.

av·a·lanche (av'ə·lanch, -länch) n. 1 The fall of a mass of snow or ice down a mountain slope. 2 The mass so falling. 3 Something like an avalanche, as in power, destructiveness, etc. — v.i. To fall or slide like an avalanche. — v.t. To fall or come down upon like an avalanche. [<F <dial. F (Swiss) *lavenche* (of uncertain origin); infl. by OF *avaler* descend < *a val* to the valley <L *ad vallem*]

Av·a·lon (av'ə·lon) In Arthurian legend, the island tomb of King Arthur: generally identified with Glastonbury.

Av·a·lon Peninsula (av'ə·lon) The SE part of Newfoundland, connected with the mainland by an isthmus four miles wide; 4,000 square miles.

a·vant (ä·vänt', *Fr.* ȧ·vän') Before; forward: the first element in some compounds from the French. [<F *avant* before <LL *abante* <L *ab* from, + *ante* before]

a·vant–cou·ri·er (ə·vänt'kōōr'ē·ər) n. 1 One who is sent to give notice of the approach of another; a herald. Also *French* **a·vant-cou·reur** (ȧ·vän'kōō·rœr'). 2 pl. The scouts or advance guard of an army.

a·vant–garde (ȧ·vän·gȧrd') n. Vanguard: applied to the group of those who support or further the most recent trends or ideas in a movement. — adj. Of or pertaining to this group. [<F, lit., advance guard]

A·va·rau (ä'vä·rou') See PALMERSTON.

av·a·rice (av'ə·ris) n. Passion for riches; covetousness; greed. [<OF <L *avaritia* < *avarus* greedy < *avere* desire, crave]

av·a·ri·cious (av'ə·rish'əs) adj. Greedy of gain; grasping; miserly. — **av'a·ri'cious·ly** adv. — **av'a·ri'cious·ness** n.

Synonyms: close, covetous, greedy, miserly, niggardly, parsimonious, penurious, rapacious, sordid, stingy. The *avaricious* man desires both to get and to keep, the *covetous* man to get something away from its possessor; *miserly* and *niggardly* persons seek to gain by mean and petty savings; the *miserly* by stinting themselves, the *niggardly* by stinting others. *Parsimonious* and *penurious* may apply to one's outlay either for himself or for others; in the latter use, they are somewhat less harsh and reproachful terms than *niggardly*. *Greedy* and *stingy* are used not only of money, but often of other things, as food, etc. The *greedy* child tries to get everything for himself; the *stingy* child, to keep others from getting what he has. *Antonyms:* bountiful, free, generous, liberal, munificent, prodigal, wasteful.

a·vast (ə·vast', ə·väst') interj. *Naut.* Stop! hold! cease! [<Du. *hou' vast, houd vast* hold fast]

av·a·tar (av′ə·tär′) *n.* In Hindu mythology, the incarnation of a god. 2 Any concrete manifestation. [< Skt. *avatāra* descent]

a·vaunt (ə·vônt′, ə·vänt′) *interj. Archaic* Begone! away! [< OF *avant* forward < LL *abante* < *ab* from + *ante* before]

a·ve (ā′vē, ä′vā) *interj.* 1 Hail! 2 Farewell! —*n.* The salutation *ave.* [< L, hail or farewell]

A·ve (ā′vē, ä′vā) *n.* 1 A prayer of invocation to the Virgin Mary: also called *Ave Maria.* 2 The time when the Ave Maria is to be said, marked by the ringing of the Ave bell. Compare ANGELUS. 3 The small beads on a rosary, used to number the Aves repeated.

a·vec plai·sir (à·vek′ plā·zēr′) *French* With pleasure.

A·vel·la·ne·da (ä′vā·yä·nä′thä) A city in Argentina, a suburb of Buenos Aires.

A·ve Ma·ri·a (ä′vā mə·rē′ə, ä′vē) A Catholic prayer to the Virgin Mary, consisting of Biblical salutations (*Luke* i 28, 42) and a plea for her intercession. Also **A·ve Mar·y** (ā′vē mâr′ē). [< L, Hail Mary]

av·e·na·ceous (av′ə·nā′shəs) *adj.* Of, pertaining to, or resembling oats or kindred grasses. [< L *avenaceus* < *avena* oats]

a·venge (ə·venj′) *v.t.* **a·venged, a·veng·ing** 1 To take vengeance or exact exemplary punishment for, as in behalf of a person or persons. 2 To inflict revenge upon, as for an act or insult. —*v.i.* 3 To take vengeance. [< OF *avengier* < *a-* to (< L *ad-*) + *vengier* punish < L *vindicare* avenge] —**a·veng′er** *n.* —**a·veng′ing** *adj.* —**a·veng′ing·ly** *adv.*

Synonyms: punish, retaliate, revenge, vindicate, visit. To *avenge* is to *visit* some offense with fitting punishment; to *revenge* is to inflict harm or suffering upon another through personal anger and resentment. See REVENGE. *Antonyms*: see synonyms for PARDON.

av·ens (av′inz) 1 Any plant of the genus *Geum,* of the rose family, as *G. urbanum,* the yellow avens, or *G. rivale,* the purple avens. 2 A similar plant of some other genus, as the mountain avens. [< OF *avence;* of unknown origin]

Av·en·tine (av′ən·tīn, -tin) The Aventine Hill, one of the seven on which Rome was built. *Latin* **Mons Av·en·ti·nus** (monz av′ən·tī′nəs).

a·ven·tu·rine (ə·ven′chər·in) *n.* 1 An opaque, brown glass, flecked with fine metal particles. 2 A variety of quartz or feldspar containing shining particles, usually of mica or hematite: also called *sunstone.* Also **a·ven′tu·rin.** [< F < Ital. *avventurina* < *avventura* chance; def. 1 so called from its accidental discovery]

av·e·nue (av′ə·nyōō, -nōō) *n.* 1 A broad thoroughfare. 2 A way of approach, as to a building, bordered with trees or statues. 3 A mode of access. See synonyms under WAY. [< F *avenue,* orig. fem. pp. of *avenir* approach < L *advenire* < *ad-* toward + *venire* come]

a·ver (ə·vûr′) *v.t.* **a·verred, a·ver·ring** 1 To declare confidently as fact; affirm. 2 *Law* To assert formally; prove or justify (a plea). See synonyms under AFFIRM, ALLEGE, ASSERT, AVOW. [< OF *averer* confirm < L *ad-* to + *verus* true] —**a·ver′ment** *n.* —**a·ver′ra·ble** *adj.*

av·er·age (av′rij, av′ər·ij) *n.* 1 *Math.* **a** The quotient of any sum divided by the number of its terms; the arithmetic mean. **b** A number representing an array of values of which it is a function. 2 The ordinary rank, degree, or amount; general type. 3 In marine law: **a** The loss arising by damage to a ship or cargo. **b** The proportion of such loss falling to a single person in an equitable distribution among those interested. —*adj.* 1 Obtained by calculating the mean of several. 2 Medium; ordinary. —*v.* **·aged, ·ag·ing** *v.t.* 1 To fix or calculate as the mean. 2 To amount to or obtain an average of: He *averages* three dollars profit every hour. 3 To apportion on the average. —*v.i.* 4 To be or amount to an average. [< F *avarie* damage to a ship or its cargo (see *n.* def. 3) < Ital. *avaria;* ult. origin uncertain] —**av′er·age·ly** *adv.*

A·ver·no (ä·ver′nō) A crater lake 10 miles west of Naples, southern Italy; anciently regarded as the entrance to Hades. Ancient **A·ver·nus** (ə·vûr′nəs). [< L *Avernus* < Gk. *aornos* < *a-* without + *ornis* bird; so called because the volcanic vapors from the lake were said to kill birds that flew overhead] —**A·ver·ni·an** (ə·vûr′nē·ən), **A·ver·nal** (ə·vûr′·nəl) *adj.*

A·ver·rho·es (ə·ver′ō·ēz), 1126–98, Arab philosopher, born in Córdoba, Spain. Also **A·ver′ro·es.**

Av·er·rho·ism (av′ə·rō′iz·əm) *n.* The doctrines of Averrhoes and his disciples, chiefly consisting of a form of pantheism based on an interpretation of Aristotle. Also **Av′er·ro′ism.** —**Av′er·rho′ist** *n.* —**Av′er·rho·is′tic** *adj.*

a·verse (ə·vûrs′) *adj.* 1 Opposed; unfavorable; reluctant: with *to.* 2 *Bot.* Turned away from the main axis: opposed to *adverse.* See synonyms under INIMICAL. [< L *aversus,* pp. of *avertere* turn aside. See AVERT] —**a·verse′ly** *adv.* —**a·verse′ness** *n.*

a·ver·sion (ə·vûr′zhən, -shən) *n.* 1 Extreme dislike; opposition; antipathy. 2 That to which one is averse. See synonyms under ABOMINATION, ANTIPATHY, HATRED.

a·vert (ə·vûrt′) *v.t.* 1 To turn or direct away or aside from, as one's regard. 2 To prevent or ward off, as a danger. See synonyms under AVOID. [< OF *avertir* < L *avertere* turn aside < *ab-* away + *vertere* turn] —**a·vert′ed·ly** *adv.* —**a·vert′i·ble, a·vert′a·ble** *adj.*

A·ves (ā′vēz) *n. pl.* A class of the vertebrates which comprises the birds. See BIRD. [< L, pl. of *avis* bird]

A·ves·ta (ə·ves′tə) *n.* The sacred writings of Zoroastrianism. See ZEND-AVESTA.

A·ves·tan (ə·ves′tən) *n.* The ancient, Iranian language in which the Avesta was written. —*adj.* Of the Avesta or its language.

a·vi·an (ā′vē·ən) *adj.* Pertaining to birds. Also **a·vic·u·lar** (ə·vik′yə·lər). —*n.* A bird. [< L *avis* bird]

a·vi·ar·y (ā′vē·er′ē) *n. pl.* **·ar·ies** An enclosure or large cage for live birds. [< L *aviarium* < *avis* bird] —**a·vi·ar·ist** (ā′vē·er′ist, -ər·ist) *n.*

a·vi·ate (ā′vē·āt, av′ē-) *v.i.* **·at·ed, ·at·ing** To operate an aircraft. [Back formation < AVIATION]

a·vi·a·tion (ā′vē·ā′shən, av′ē-) *n.* 1 The act, science, or art of flying heavier-than-air aircraft. 2 The aircraft flown. [< F < L *avis* bird]

aviation medicine A branch of medicine that deals with the diagnosis, prevention, treatment, and cure of disorders caused by or associated with the conditions encountered in aviation; aeromedicine.

a·vi·a·tor (ā′vē·ā′tər, av′ē-) *n.* One who flies airplanes and other heavier-than-air aircraft; a pilot. —**a′vi·a′tress** (-tris) or **a·vi·a·trix** (ā′vē·ā′triks, av′ē-) *n. fem.*

Av·i·cen·na (av′ə·sen′ə), 980–1037, Arab physician and philosopher. Arabic **ibn-Sina** (ib′·ən·sē′nä).

a·vic·u·lar·i·um (ə·vik′yə·lâr′ē·əm) *n. pl.* **·lar·i·a** (-lâr′ē·ə) *Zool.* A prehensile, beaklike organ found in many polyzoans. [< NL < L *avicula,* dim. of *avis* bird]

a·vi·cul·ture (ā′vi·kul′chər, av′i-) *n.* The rearing of birds. [< L *avis* bird + CULTURE]

av·id (av′id) *adj.* Very desirous; eager; greedy. [< L *avidus* < *avere* crave] —**av′id·ly** *adv.*

av·i·din (av′ə·din) *n. Biochem.* A protein found in egg white which inhibits the action of biotin. [< AVID(ITY) + -IN; so called from its affinity for biotin]

a·vid·i·ty (ə·vid′ə·tē) *n.* 1 Extreme eagerness; greediness. 2 *Chem.* Affinity.

a·vi·fau·na (ā′və·fô′nə) *n. Ecol.* The birds of a given region: also called *ornis.* [< L *avis* bird + FAUNA] —**a′vi·fau′nal** *adj.*

av·i·ga·tion (av′ə·gā′shən) *n.* The handling and guidance of aircraft in the air. [< AVI(ATION) + (NAVI)GATION]

A·vi·gnon (à·vē·nyôn′) A city in SE France on the Rhone; papal seat, 1309–77.

a·vion (à·vyôn′) *n. French* An airplane.

a·vi·on·ics (ā′vē·on′iks, av′ē-) *n.* The study of the applications of electricity and electronics to aviation. [< AVI(ATION ELECTR)ONICS] —**a′vi·on′ic** *adj.*

a·vi·so (ə·vī′zo) *n. pl.* **·sos** 1 Advice; information. 2 A dispatch boat. [< Sp., information, advice]

a·vi·ta·min·o·sis (ā·vī′tə·min·ō′sis) *n. Pathol.* A condition caused by vitamin deficiency. [< A-[4] without + VITAMIN + -OSIS]

Av·lo·na (äv·lō′nä) A former name for VALONA.

av·o·ca·do (av′ə·kä′dō, ä′və-) *n. pl.* **·dos** 1 A tropical American evergreen tree (*Persea americana*) having leathery leaves and bearing large pear-shaped drupes with a dark leathery rind and bland, buttery flesh. 2 The edible fruit for which this tree is commercially cultivated. Also called *alligator pear.* [< Sp., alter. of AGUACATE < Nahuatl *ahuacatl*]

av·o·ca·tion (av′ə·kā′shən) *n.* 1 A casual or transient occupation; diversion; hobby. 2 One's business or vocation: now rarely used, to avoid confusion with def. 1. 3 *Obs.* A calling away; withdrawal. See synonyms under HOBBY. [< L *avocatio, -onis* a calling away, diversion < *ab-* away + *vocare* call]

a·voc·a·to·ry (ə·vok′ə·tôr′ē, -tō′rē) *adj.* Recalling; calling away or back: Letters *avocatory* are used by a sovereign to recall his citizens from a state with which he is at war.

av·o·cet (av′ə·set) *n.* A long-legged shore bird (genus *Recurvirostra*) having webbed feet and slender up-curved bill. Also **av′o·set.** [< F *avocette* < Ital. *avocetta*]

A·vo·ga·dro (ä′vō·gä′drō), **Amedeo,** 1776–1856, Conte di Quaregna, Italian physicist.

Avogadro number The actual number of molecules in one gram-molecule or the actual number of atoms in one gram-atom of an element or any pure substance. This number is 6.023×10^{23}. Also **Avogadro's constant.**

Avogadro's hypothesis or **rule** The rule that equal volumes of all gases, at the same temperature and pressure, contain the same number of molecules.

a·void (ə·void′) *v.t.* 1 To keep away or at a distance from; shun; evade, as an unpleasant duty. 2 *Law* To make void. 3 *Obs.* To void; empty. See synonyms under ESCAPE. [< AF *avoider,* OF *esvuidier* empty < *es-* out (< L *ex-*) + *vuidier* < L *viduare* empty, deprive] —**a·void′a·ble** *adj.* —**a·void′a·bly** *adv.* —**a·void′er** *n.*

a·void·ance (ə·void′ns) *n.* 1 The act of avoiding. 2 *Law* Annulment; a making void.

av·oir·du·pois (av′ər·də·poiz′) *n.* 1 The ordinary system of weights of the United States and Great Britain in which 16 ounces avoirdupois make a pound. See under WEIGHT. 2 *Colloq.* Weight; corpulence: a facetious use. [< OF *avoir de pois* goods of (i.e., sold by) weight < L *habere* have + *de* of + *pensum* weight]

A·von (ā′vən, av′ən) 1 A river in England, flowing SE 96 miles from Northampton past Stratford to the Severn at Tewksbury. 2 Any of several other rivers in England, Scotland, and Wales.

à vo·tre san·té (à vô′tr′ sän·tā′) *French* To your health.

a·vouch (ə·vouch′) *v.t.* 1 To vouch for; guarantee. 2 To affirm positively; proclaim. 3 To acknowledge; avow. See synonyms under ASSERT, AVOW. [< OF *avochier* affirm < L *advocare* call to one's aid, summon < *ad-* to + *vocare* call]

a·vow (ə·vou′) *v.t.* To declare openly, as facts; own or confess frankly; acknowledge: to *avow* oneself a conspirator. [< OF *avouer* < L *advocare* summon (< *ad-* to + *vocare* call) or LL *advotare* bind by oath < *ad-* to + *votare* freq. of *vovere* vow] —**a·vow′a·ble** *adj.* —**a·vow′·a·ble·ness** *n.* —**a·vow′a·bly** *adv.* —**a·vow′er** *n.*

Synonyms: acknowledge, admit, aver, avouch, confess, declare, own, proclaim, profess, protest, testify, witness. To *avow* is to declare boldly and openly, commonly as something one is ready to justify, maintain, or defend against challenge or opposition. A man *acknowledges* another's claim or his own promise; he *admits* an opponent's advantage or his own error; he *declares* either what he has seen or experienced or what he has received from another; he *avers* what he is sure of from his own knowledge or consciousness; he *avows* openly a belief or intention that he has silently held. Compare ACKNOWLEDGE, AFFIRM, ALLEGE, ASSERT, CONFESS, STATE. *Antonyms*: contradict, deny, disavow, disclaim, disown, ignore, repudiate.

a·vow·al (ə·vou′əl) *n.* Open declaration; frank admission or acknowledgment. See synonyms under BELIEF.

a·vowed (ə·voud′) *adj.* Openly acknowledged; plainly declared. See synonyms under OSTENSIBLE. —**a·vow·ed·ly** (ə·vou′id·lē) *adj.* —**a·vow′ed·ness** *n.*

a·vow·ry (ə·vou′rē) *n. pl.* **·ries** *Law* The acknowledgment and justification of the taking of the goods by the defendant in an action of replevin. [< OF *avouerie* < *avouer.* See AVOW.]

A·vranch·es (à·vränsh′) A town in Normandy, France, on the Gulf of Saint–Malo; site of a decisive Allied victory of World War II in 1944.

a·vulse (ə·vuls′) v.t. To remove forcibly; tear away. [<L avulsus, pp. of aveller < ab- away + vellere pull]

a·vul·sion (ə·vul′shən) n. 1 A pulling off or tearing away; forcible separation. 2 That which is torn away. 3 Law A sudden removal of the soil from the estate of one and its deposit upon or adjunction to the land of another by the violent action of water. The land thus torn away continues to be vested in the original owner. [<L avulsio, -onis < avellere. See AVULSE.]

a·vun·cu·lar (ə·vung′kyə·lər) adj. Of or pertaining to an uncle. [<L avunculus maternal uncle, dim. of avus grandfather]

a·vun·cu·late (ə·vung′kyə·lit, -lāt) n. Anthropol. A form of social relationship characteristic of certain clan societies, in which a close bond exists between male children and their maternal uncles. Compare AMITATE.

a·wa (à·wô′, ə·wä′) adv. Scot. Away.

a·wait (ə·wāt′) v.t. 1 To wait for; expect. 2 To be ready or in store for. See synonyms under ABIDE. [<OF awaitier watch for <a- to (<L ad-) + waitier watch <OHG wahtēn watch]

A·wa·ji (ä·wä·jē) A minor Japanese island between Harima Sea and Osaka Bay, and between Honshu and Shikoku islands; 228 square miles.

a·wake (ə·wāk′) adj. Not asleep; alert; vigilant. —v. a·woke or a·waked (ə·wākt′), a·waked or a·woke, a·wak·ing v.t. 1 To arouse from sleep. 2 To stir up; excite. —v.i. 3 To cease to sleep; become awake. 4 To become alert or aroused. See note under WAKE¹. [OE onwǣcnan rise from sleep <on- A-¹ + wæcnan rise and āwacian arise <ā- A-² + wacian watch]

a·wak·en (ə·wā′kən) v.t. & v.i. To awake. See note under WAKE¹. See synonyms under STIR. [OE onwǣcnan arise <on- A¹ + wæcnan rise] —a·wak′en·er n.

a·wak·en·ing (ə·wā′kən·ing) adj. Stirring; exciting. —n. 1 The act of waking. 2 An arousing of attention or interest; revival.

a·ward (ə·wôrd′) v.t. 1 To adjudge as due, as by legal decisions. 2 To bestow as the result of a contest or examination, as a prize. See synonyms under ALLOT. —n. 1 A decision, as by a judge, umpire, or arbitrator. 2 The document containing it. 3 That which is awarded. 4 A badge, medal, citation, or the like, given for meritorious service, as to a soldier. [<AF awarder, OF esguarder observe, examine <es- out (<L ex-) + guarder watch <Gmc.] —a·ward′a·ble adj. —a·ward′er n.

a·ware (ə·wâr′) adj. Possessing knowledge (of some fact or action); conscious; cognizant. See synonyms under CONSCIOUS, SURE. [OE gewær watchful] —a·ware′ness n.

a·wash (ə·wosh′, ə·wôsh′) adv. & adj. 1 Level with or just above the surface of the water. 2 Tossed or washed about by waves. 3 Covered or overflowed with water.

A·wash (ä′wäsh) A river in eastern Ethiopia, flowing 500 miles NE to Lake Abbé: formerly Hawash.

a·way (ə·wā′) adv. 1 From a given place; off. 2 Far; at or to a distance. 3 In another direction; aside. 4 Out of existence; at an end. 5 On and on continuously: to peg away at a task. 6 From one's keeping, attention, or possession. 7 At once, without hesitation: Fire away! —to do (or make) away with 1 To get rid of. 2 To kill. —adj. 1 Absent. 2 At a distance. —interj. Begone! [OE on weg on (one's) way]

awe¹ (ô) v.t. awed, aw·ing or awe·ing To impress with reverential fear. —n. 1 Reverential fear; dread mingled with veneration. 2 Obs. Overawing influence. 3 Obs. Dread; terror. See synonyms under AMAZEMENT, FEAR, REVERENCE, VENERATION. [<ON agi fear]

awe² (ô) v.t. Scot. To owe.

a·wea·ry (ə·wir′ē) adj. Wearied; weary.

a·weath·er (ə·weth′ər) adv. & adj. Naut. At, to, or toward the windward side.

a·wee (ə·wē′) adv. Scot. Awhile.

a·weel (ə·wēl′) interj. & adv. Scot. Well; well then!

a·weigh (ə·wā′) adv. Naut. Hanging with the flukes just clear of the bottom so that the vessel is free to move: said of an anchor.

awe·less (ô′lis) adj. Without fear; fearless. Also **aw′less**.

awe·some (ô′səm) adj. 1 Inspiring awe. 2 Characterized by or expressing awe; reverential. —awe′some·ly adv. —awe′some·ness n.

aw·ful (ô′fəl) adj. 1 Inspiring or suited to inspire awe; majestically or solemnly impressive. 2 Inspiring fear; terrible; dreadful. 3 Colloq. Exceedingly bad, monotonous, or unpleasant; ugly. 4 Colloq. Exceedingly great. 5 Filled with awe; reverential. Also Scot. **aw·fu'** (ô′fōō). —aw′ful·ness n.

Synonyms: alarming, appalling, august, dire, direful, dread, dreadful, fearful, frightful, grand, horrible, imposing, majestic, noble, portentous, shocking, solemn, stately, terrible, terrific. In careful speech *awful* should not be used of things which are merely disagreeable or annoying, nor of all that are *alarming* and *terrible*, but only of such as bring a solemn awe upon the soul, as in the presence of a superior power; as, the *awful* hush before a battle. We speak of an *exalted* station, a *grand* mountain, an *imposing* presence, a *majestic* cathedral, a *noble* mien, a *solemn* litany, a *stately* march, an *august* assembly. See FRIGHTFUL, GRAND. *Antonyms*: base, beggarly, commonplace, contemptible, despicable, humble, inferior, lowly, mean, paltry, undignified, vulgar.

aw·ful·ly (ô′fəl·ē) adv. 1 In an awful manner. 2 (ô′flē) Colloq. Excessively; very: *awfully* rich.

a·while (ə·hwīl′) adv. For a brief time. [OE āne hwīle a while]

a·whirl (ə·hwûrl′) adj. & adv. In a whirl; whirling.

awk·ward (ôk′wərd) adj. 1 Ungraceful in bearing. 2 Unskilful in action; bungling. 3 Embarrassing or perplexing. 4 Difficult or dangerous to deal with, as an opponent. 5 Inconvenient for use; uncomfortable. 6 Obs. Perverse; untoward. [<ON afug turned the wrong way + -WARD] —awk′ward·ly adv. —awk′ward·ness n.

Synonyms: boorish, bungling, clownish, clumsy, gawky, maladroit, uncouth, ungainly, unhandy, unskilful. *Awkward* is *offward*, turned the wrong way; it was anciently used of a back-handed blow in battle, of squinting eyes, etc. *Clumsy* originally signified benumbed, stiffened with cold; as, *clumsy* fingers, *clumsy* limbs. Thus, *awkward* primarily refers to action, *clumsy* to condition. See RUSTIC. *Antonyms*: adroit, clever, dexterous, handy, skilful.

awl (ôl) n. A pointed steel instrument for making small holes. ◆ Homophone: all. [OE ǣl, awel]

awl·wort (ôl′wûrt) n. A small stemless aquatic plant (*Subularia aquatica*) of the mustard family (*Brassicaceae*) having awl-shaped leaves.

aw·mous (ô′məs) n. Scot. Charity; alms.

awn (ôn) n. Bot. A bristlelike appendage of certain grasses; beard, as of wheat or rye. [<ON ǫgn chaff] —awned (ônd) adj. —awn′less adj. —awn′y, Scot. awn′ie adj.

awn·ing (ô′ning) n. 1 A rooflike cover, as of canvas, for protection from sun or rain. 2 A shelter resembling this. [Origin unknown]

a·woke (ə·wōk′) Past tense of AWAKE.

AWOL (as an acronym pronounced ā′wôl) Mil. Absent or absence without leave. Also awol, A.W.O.L., a.w.o.l.

a·wry (ə·rī′) adj. & adv. 1 Toward one side; crooked; distorted; obliquely. 2 Out of the right course; erroneously; perversely. [<A-¹ on + WRY]

ax¹ (aks) n. pl. ax·es 1 A tool with a bladed head mounted on a handle, used for chopping, hewing, etc. 2 An ax-hammer. See also ICE AX. —v.t. To cut, shape, trim, or fashion with an ax. —to have an ax to grind Colloq. To have a private purpose or interest to pursue. Also axe. [OE æx, eax] —ax′like′ adj.

ax² (aks) v.t. & v.i. Scot. To ask.

Ax·el Hei·berg (ak′səl hī′bûrg) The largest of the Sverdrup Islands in Franklin District of the Northwest Territories, Canada; 13,583 square miles.

ax·es¹ (ak′sēz) n. Plural of AXIS.

ax·es² (ak′siz) n. Plural of AX.

axes of an aircraft Aeron. Three fixed lines of reference, usually centroidal and mutually rectangular, called respectively the **longitudinal** (X) **axis**, the **vertical** (Z) **axis**, and the **lateral** (Y) **axis**.

ax–ham·mer (aks′ham′ər) n. A stonecutter's tool with cutting edges at either end of the head, or one cutting edge and one hammer face. —ax′–ham′mered adj.

ax·i·al (ak′sē·əl) adj. 1 Of, pertaining to, or constituting an axis. 2 On or along an axis.

axial angle 1 The angle between the optic axes of a biaxial crystal. 2 The angle between any two crystallographic axes.

axial cable Aeron. A wire running through the axis of a rigid airship from bow to stern.

ax·il (ak′sil) n. Bot. 1 The cavity or angle formed by the junction of the upper side of a leafstalk, branch, etc., with a stem or branch. 2 Anat. The axilla. [<L axilla armpit]

ax·ile (ak′sil, -sīl) adj. Of, pertaining to, or situated in, or in the line of, an axis.

ax·il·la (ak·sil′ə) n. pl. ax·il·lae (-sil′ē) 1 The armpit. 2 An axil. [<L]

ax·il·lar (ak′sə·lər) adj. Axillary. —n. Ornithol. One of the relatively long, stiff feathers on the undersurface of the wing of a bird.

ax·il·lar·y (ak′sə·ler′ē) adj. 1 Bot. Of, pertaining to, or situated in an axil or axilla: *axillary* buds. 2 Anat. Attached to a joint. —n. pl. ax·il·lar·ies An axillar.

ax·i·nite (ak′sə·nīt) n. An aluminum-calcium borosilicate, with varying amounts of iron and manganese. [Gk. axinē ax; from the resemblance of the crystals to an ax head]

ax·i·ol·o·gy (aks′ē·ol′ə·jē) n. Philos. The theory or study of values or of the nature of value. [<Gk. axios worthy + -LOGY]

ax·i·om (ak′sē·əm) n. 1 A self-evident or universally recognized truth. 2 An established principle or rule. 3 Logic & Math. A proposition assumed to be true without proof. [<F axiome <L axioma <Gk. axiōma a thing thought worthy, a self-evident thing < axioein think worthy < axios worthy]

Synonym: truism. Both the *axiom* and the *truism* are instantly seen to be true, and need no proof; but in an *axiom* there is progress of thought, while the *truism* simply says what is too manifest to need saying. Hence the *axiom* is valuable and useful, while the *truism* is weak and flat. Compare ADAGE, PROVERB. *Antonyms*: absurdity, contradiction, demonstration, nonsense, paradox, sophism.

ax·i·o·mat·ic (ak′sē·ə·mat′ik) adj. 1 Of, pertaining to, or resembling an axiom; self-evident. 2 Full of axioms; aphoristic, as a literary style. Also **ax′i·o·mat′i·cal**. —ax′i·o·mat′i·cal·ly adv.

Ax·i·os (äk′sē·ôs′) The Greek name for the VARDAR.

ax·is¹ (ak′sis) n. pl. ax·es (ak′sēz) 1 A line around which a turning body revolves or may be supposed to revolve. 2 Geom. a One of the principal lines through the center of a plane or solid figure, especially the longest or shortest, or a line as to which the plane figure or solid is symmetrical. b A fixed line along which distances are measured or to which positions are referred. 3 An imaginary line through the center of a drawing or sculpture for purposes of measurement or reference. 4 The central line about which parts of a body are symmetrically arranged. 5 Bot. The central body, part, line, or longitudinal support on, along, or above which organs or other parts are arranged. 6 Anat. a A short arterial trunk from which several nearly equal branches radiate. b The second cervical vertebra, or the large, blunt, toothlike odontoid process which surmounts it and forms a pivot on which the atlas and head turn. 7 One of the lines of reference meeting at the center of a crystal, and determining to which system it belongs. 8 Geol. The dominant central section of a mountain chain, or the line tracing the crest throughout its length. 9 Aeron. One of the three

axes of an aircraft. **10** An affiliation or coalition of two or more nations to promote and insure mutual interest, cooperation, and solidarity of front in their relations with foreign powers; also, the nations so affiliated. [<L, axis, axle]

ax·is[2] (ak′sis) *n.* A small deer (genus *Axis*) of southern Asia, having the body spotted with white. Also **axis deer.** [<L]

Ax·is (ak′sis) *n.* A coalition which developed from the Rome-Berlin Axis of 1936 and ultimately included Germany, Italy, Japan, Rumania, Bulgaria, Hungary, and others: opposed to the Allied and associated powers in World War II. Also **Axis Powers.**

axis cylinder *Anat.* The central conducting portion of a nerve fiber.

ax·le (ak′səl) *n.* **1** A crossbar supporting a vehicle, and on or with which its wheel or wheels turn: also called **ax′le·tree′. 2** A shaft or spindle on which a wheel is mounted and on or with which it turns. [ME *axel* in *axeltre* axletree <ON *öxultrē* <*öxull* axle + *trē* tree, bar] —**ax′led** *adj.*

ax·man (aks′mən) *n. pl.* **·men** (-mən) One who wields an ax; a woodman. Also **axe′man.**

Ax·min·ster (aks′min·stər) *n.* **1** A carpet with a long, soft pile; formerly made by hand in **Axminster,** a town of eastern Devonshire, England. **2** A carpet made in imitation of this.

ax·o·lotl (ak′sə·lot′l) *n.* A North American tailed amphibian (genus *Ambystoma*), as *A. mexicanum* of Mexican lakes and marshes, which retains its external gills, and breeds in a larval state. [<Sp. <Nahuatl, lit., servant of water]

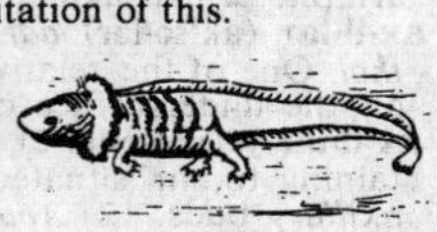

MEXICAN AXOLOTL
(From 6–9 inches long)

ax·on (ak′son) *n.* **1** *Zool.* The body axis of a vertebrate. **2** *Anat.* The axis-cylinder process of a nerve cell, usually carrying impulses away from the cells. See DENDRITE, NEURON. Also **ax·one** (ak′sōn). [<NL <Gk. *axōn* axis]

ax·seed (aks′sēd′) *n.* An Old World perennial crownvetch *(Coronilla varia)* with odd-pinnate leaves, and pink or white flowers, cultivated in the United States. [<AX + SEED: from the shape of the pods]

Ax·um (äk·sōōm′) See AKSUM.

ay[1] (ā) *adv. Poetic* Ever; always. Also *aye.* [<ON *ei* always]

ay[2] (ī) See AYE[1].

ay[3] (ā) *interj. Archaic* O! oh! ah!: an expression of sorrow, surprise, etc. [ME *ey, ei*]

A·ya·cu·cho (ä′yä·kōō′chō) A town in south central Peru; site of Sucre's victory over Spain, 1824, that secured Peruvian independence.

a·yah (ä′yə) *n. Anglo-Indian* A native nurse or lady's maid. [<Hind. *āya* <Pg. *aia* nurse]

ay·a·huas·ca (ī′ä·wäs′kä) *n.* A Brazilian plant *(Banisteria caapi)* whose alkaloid principle has powerful hallucinatory effects. See BANISTERINE. [<native Brazilian name]

a·ya·tol·lah (ä′yə·tō′lə) *n.* Title of the highest-ranking teacher of religion in Iran. [<Arabic *ayatollah* sign of God]

Ay·din (ī·din′) A town in western Turkey: also *Aidin.*

aye[1] (ī) *n.* An affirmative vote or voter. —*adv.* Yes; yea. Also *ay.* ◆ Homophone: *eye.*

aye[2] (ā) See AY[1].

aye-aye (ī′ī′) *n.* A nocturnal arboreal lemur (genus *Daubentonia*) of Madagascar, about the size of a cat and having rodentlike teeth. [<F <Malagasy *aiay;* so called from its cry]

A·ye·sha (ä′i·shä) See AISHA.

a·yin (ä′yēn) The sixteenth Hebrew letter. See ALPHABET.

Ayl·mer (āl′mər), **John,** 1521–94, English prelate.

Ay·ma·ra (ī′mä·rä′) *n.* One of a tribe of South American Indians, of highly developed pre-Incan culture, at the Aymaran linguistic stock: formerly occupying nearly all of Bolivia and Peru, and still comprising three-fourths of the population of Bolivia.

Ay·ma·ran (ī′mä·rän′) *adj.* Of or pertaining to a large and important linguistic stock of South American Indians inhabiting Bolivia and Peru.—*n.* The family of languages spoken by the Aymaran tribes: now largely superseded by Quechua.

Ay·mé (e·mā′), **Marcel,** born 1902, French novelist, dramatist, and short-story writer.

a·yont (ə·yont′) *prep. & adv. Scot & Brit. Dial.* Beyond; farther.

Ay·ot Saint Law·rence (ā′ət sānt lôr′əns, lor′əns) A town in Hertford, England; residence of George Bernard Shaw.

Ayr (âr) **1** A county in SW Scotland; 1,132 square miles: also **Ayr·shire** (âr′shir, -shər). **2** Its burgh, a port on the **Ayr River,** which flows 38 miles west to the Firth of Clyde.

Ayr·shire (âr′shir, -shər) *n.* One of a breed of dairy cattle especially adapted for milk production, originating in Ayrshire.

Ayr stone A very fine-grained stone widely employed in polishing sculptured marbles and also in fine metalwork: first found in Ayrshire. Also called *Scotch stone; water of Ayr.*

a·yun·ta·mien·to (ä·yōōn′tä·myen′tō) *n. pl.* **·tos** *SW U.S.* **1** A municipal council or legislative body of a town or city; town council. **2** City hall; municipal building. [<Sp.]

a·yur·ve·dism (ä′yōōr·vä′diz·əm) *n.* Medical treatment by plants and drugs indigenous to India: so called from the **Ayur Veda,** an ancient Hindu medical treatise sometimes regarded as a fifth Veda. [<Skt. *ayus* span of life + *vid* know] —**a′yur·ve′dist** *n.*

A·yut·tha·ya (ä·yōō′tä·yä) A former capital city in SE Thailand; site of early Thai ruins; destroyed, 1767. Also **A·yu′thi·a.**

az- Var. of AZO-.

a·zal·ea (ə·zāl′yə) *n.* A flowering shrub of the heath family (genus *Rhododendron,* formerly *Azalea*), especially the flame azalea *(R. calendulaceum)* with showy scarlet or orange flowers. [<NL <Gk. *azalea,* fem. of *azaleos* dry <*azein* parch, dry up; from its preference for dry soil]

a·zan (ä·zän′) *n. Arabic* In Moslem countries, the muezzin's call to prayer, usually given from the minaret of a mosque five times a day; also, the time spent in these prayers.

A·za·ña (ä·thä′nyä), **Manuel,** 1880–1940, president of the Spanish Republic 1936–39: full name *Azaña y Díez.*

Az·a·ri·ah (az′ə·rī′ə) A masculine personal name etymologically identical with *Eleazar:* 28 persons of this name are mentioned throughout the Old Testament. Also **Az·a·ri·as** (az′ə·rī′əs) [<Hebrew, helped by Jehovah]

az·a·role (az′ə·rōl) *n.* **1** The edible orange-red or yellow pomelike fruit of a Mediterranean shrub or tree *(Crataegus azarolus)* of the rose family. **2** The tree itself. [<F <Arabic *az-zu′rūr*]

A·za·zel (ə·zā′zəl, az′ə·zel) **1** In Mohammedan mythology, the chief among the Eblis who married the daughters of men. **2** In Milton's *Paradise Lost,* the standard-bearer of Satan. **3** The scapegoat sent into the wilderness as a sin atonement. *Lev.* xvi 21–28. [<Hebrew, scapegoat]

Az·ben (az·ben′) See AÏR.

a·zed·a·rach (ə·zed′ə·rak) *n.* **1** A large ornamental Eastern tree *(Melia azedarach)* of Asia and tropical America, with bipinnate leaves and panicles of lilac-colored flowers, succeeded by yellowish drupes: also called *Chinaberry tree, hagbush, pride of China.* **2** The bark from the roots of this tree, used as a cathartic, emetic, or vermifuge. [<F *azédarac,* ult. <Persian *āzād dirakht* noble tree]

a·ze·o·trope (ə·zē′ə·trōp) *n. Chem.* A mixture of substances, as water and hydrochloric acid, which has a constant boiling point at specified concentration. [<Gk. *a-* not + *zein* boil + *tropē* a turning] —**az·e·o·trop·ic** (az′ē·ō·trop′ik) *adj.*—**az·e·ot·ro·pism** (az′ē·ot′rə·piz′əm), **az′e·ot′ro·py** *n.*

A·zer·bai·jan (ä′zər·bī·jän′, az′ər-) **1** A constituent republic of the southern U.S.S.R., west of the Caspian Sea; 33,100 square miles; capital, Baku. Also **A′zer·bai·dzhan′.** Officially **Azerbaijan Soviet Socialist Republic. 2** A former province of NW Iran between Turkey and the Caspian Sea; 41,000 square miles; chief city, Tabriz.

A·zer·bai·ja·ni (ä′zər·bī·jä′nē, az′ər-) *n. pl.* **·ni** or **·nis** (-nēz) **1** A native or inhabitant of Azerbaijan. **2** The Turkic language of these people.

A·zil·ian (ə·zil′yən) *adj. Anthropol.* Designating a subdivision of Mesolithic culture associated with artifacts found in the **Mas d′A·zil** (mäs dä·zēl′), a village of southern France.

az·i·muth (az′ə·məth) *n.* **1** *Astron.* The arc of the horizon that a vertical plane passing through a heavenly body makes with the meridian of the place of observation. **2** *Mil.* **a** Direction to right or left of a horizontal plane. **b** That element in the movement of a bomb or guided missile to the right or left of its downward course: distinguished from *range.* [<F *azimut* <Arabic *assumūt* the ways, pl. of *samt* way] —**az·i·muth·al** (az′ə·muth′əl) *adj.* —**az′i·muth′al·ly** *adv.*

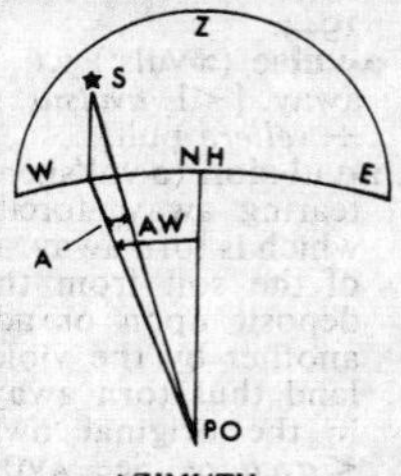

AZIMUTH
PO. Observation point. *A.* Altitude. *AW* Azimuth west. *W.* West. *E.* East. *NH.* North horizon. *Z.* Zenith. *S.* Star.

az·ine (az′ēn, -in) *n. Chem.* One of a class of nitrogenous heterocyclic compounds arranged in a six-membered ring, identified by the number of nitrogen atoms, as *diazine, triazine,* etc. [<AZ- + -INE[2]]

az·o (az′ō, ā′zō) *adj. Chem.* Containing nitrogen: an *azo* compound, *azo* dye. [<AZOTE]

azo- *combining form Chem.* Indicating the presence of nitrogen, especially in those organic compounds in which two atoms of nitrogen are connected with two similar radicals of the benzene series: *azobenzene,* C_6H_5N: NC_6H_5. Also, before vowels, *az-,* as in *azine.* [<AZOTE]

azo dye Any of an important class of coaltar dyes containing the azo radical N:N.

a·zo·ic (ə·zō′ik) *adj. Geol.* Of or pertaining to those periods on earth before life appeared; without organic remains. [<Gk. *azōos* lifeless <*a-* without + *zōē* life]

az·ole (az′ōl, ə·zōl′) *n. Chem.* Pyrrole. [<AZ(O)- + -OLE[1]]

az·on (az′on) *n.* A type of bomb equipped with control surfaces in the tail to permit radio guidance in azimuth only. [<*az(imuth) on(ly)*]

a·zon·ic (ā·zon′ik) *adj.* Not peculiar to any zone or region; not local.

A·zores (ə·zôrz′, ā′zôrz) Three island groups west of Portugal, divided into three Portuguese districts: *Angra do Heroísmo, Horta,* and *Ponta Delgada;* total area, 888 square miles. *Portuguese* **A·ço·res** (ə·sō′rēsh).

az·ote (az′ōt, ə·zōt′) *n.* Nitrogen: former name. [<F <Gk. *a-* not + *zōein* live; so called by Lavoisier from its inability to support life] —**az·ot·ed** (az′ō·tid, ə·zō′tid) *adj.*

az·oth (az′oth) *n.* **1** Mercury: the name given by the alchemists. **2** The universal remedy of Paracelsus. [<Arabic *az-zāūq* the quicksilver]

a·zot·ic (ə·zot′ik) *adj.* Of, pertaining to, or containing azote or nitrogen.

az·o·tize (az′ə·tīz) *v.t.* **·tized, ·tiz·ing** To nitrogenize.

A·zo·to·bac·ter (ə·zō′tō·bak′tər) *n.* A type of bacteria, chiefly *Clostridium pasteurianum,* which live in soil and have the power of fixing nitrogen, and thus contribute to soil fertility. Also **Az·o·bac·ter** (az′ō·bak′tər).

A·zov (ä·zôf′), **Sea of** A northern arm of the Black Sea in southern U.S.S.R.; 14,000 square miles. Also **A·zof′.**

Az·ra·el (az′rē·əl) In the Moslem and ancient Jewish mythology, the angel who separates the soul from the body at death. [<Hebrew, help of God]

Az·tec (az′tek) *n.* **1** One of tribe of Mexican Indians of Nahuatlan stock, founders of the Mexican Empire which was at its height when Cortés invaded the country in 1519. **2** Any of the Uto-Aztecan dialects spoken by the Aztecs; Nahuatl. —*adj.* Of or pertaining to the Aztec Indians, their language, culture, or empire: also **Az·tec·an** (az′tek·ən).

Aztec Ruins National Monument A group of pre-Columbian ruins in NW New Mexico, established as a national monument in 1923.

az·ure (azh′ər, ā′zhər) *adj.* **1** Like the blue of the sky; sky-blue. **2** Like the clear sky; cloudless; spotless. —*n.* **1** A clear sky-blue color or pigment. **2** *Poetic* The sky. **3** *Her.* Blue: represented in engraving by parallel

horizontal lines. [< OF *azur* < Arabic *al-lāzward* < Persian *lazhward* lapis lazuli]

az·u·rite (azh′ə-rīt) *n.* A vitreous, monoclinic, azure blue, basic copper carbonate: also called *blue bice.* 2 A gemstone.

a·zy·go·spore (ə-zī′gə-spôr, -spōr) *n. Bot.* A spore parthenogenetically formed in certain fungi, and resembling a zygospore. Also **a·zy′·go·sperm.**

az·y·gous (az′i-gəs) *adj. Biol.* Having no mate; occurring singly; not paired. [< Gk. *azygos* unpaired < *a-* without + *zygon* a yoke]

az·yme (az′īm, -im) *n.* Unleavened bread. Also **az·ym** (az′im). [< Gk. *azymos* unleavened < *a-* without + *zymē* leaven] —**a·zym·ic** (ə-zim′ik), **az·y·mous** (az′ə-məs) *adj.*

az·zi·mi·na (äd′zē-mē′nä) *n. Italian* Elaborate, metallic decoration in damask patterns.

B

b, B (bē) *n. pl.* **b's, B's** or **Bs, bs, bees** (bēz) 1 The second letter of the English alphabet: from Phoenician *beth,* through Greek *beta,* Roman *B.* 2 The sound of the letter *b,* the voiced bilabial stop. See ALPHABET. —*symbol* 1 *Music* **a** One of a series of tones, the seventh in the natural diatonic scale of C. **b** The pitch of this tone or the written note representing it. **c** A scale built upon B. 2 *Chem.* Boron (symbol B).

ba (bä) *n.* In Egyptian mythology, the soul, believed to depart from the body at death and expected to return to it: represented by a bird with a human head. [< Egyptian]

Ba *Chem.* Barium (symbol Ba).

ba' (bä, bô) *n. Scot.* A ball.

baa (bä, ba) *v.i.* **baaed, baa·ing** To bleat, as a sheep. —*n.* The bleat, as of a sheep. [Imit.]

Ba·al (bā′əl, bāl) *n. pl.* **Ba·al·im** (bā′əl-im) 1 Any of several ancient Semitic gods of fertility and flocks; a sun god. 2 An idol or false god. [< Hebrew *Ba'al* lord] —**Ba′al·ish** *adj.*

Baal·bek (bäl′bek) A tourist center in central Lebanon; site of ancient Phoenician temple to Baal: Greek *Heliopolis.*

Ba·al·ist (bā′əl-ist) *n.* 1 A worshiper of Baal. 2 A worshiper of idols. Also **Ba′al·ite** (-īt). —**Ba′al·ism** *n.*

Baan (bän) See PAAN.

Bab (bäb) *n.* The title of the founder of Babism.

Bab (bab) Diminutive of BARBARA.

ba·ba (bä′bä) *n.* A cake made with yeast and steeped in rum. Also *French* **ba·ba au rhum** (bȧ·bä′ ō rôm′). [< F, prob. < Polish *baba* grandmother]

Ba·bar (bä′bȧr) See BABER.

ba·bas·su (bä′bȧ-soo′) *n.* 1 A Brazilian palm tree (*Orbignya martiana*) bearing nuts yielding an oil used in making margarine, soap, etc. 2 The oil from this tree: also called **babassu oil.** [< native Brazilian name]

bab·bitt (bab′it) *v.t.* To line, bush, fill, or face with Babbitt metal. —**Babbitt metal.**

Bab·bitt (bab′it) *n.* A type of conventional American businessman, ambitious in his business, but otherwise provincial, mediocre, and smug: from George *Babbitt,* a character in Sinclair Lewis's novel *Babbitt* (1922).

Bab·bitt (bab′it), **Irving,** 1865–1933, U.S. scholar and critic.

Babbitt metal 1 A soft, white, anti-friction alloy of tin, copper, and antimony. 2 Any of a group of similar alloys. [after Isaac *Babbitt,* 1799–1862, U.S. metallurgist]

Bab·bitt·ry (bab′it-rē) *n.* The behavior or attitudes of Babbitts as a class or group.

bab·ble (bab′əl) *n.* 1 A murmuring or rippling sound, as of a stream. 2 Prattle, as of an infant. 3 A confusion of sounds, as of a crowd. 4 *Telecom.* The confused sound of cross-talk from a number of interfering radio channels. —*v.* **bab·bled, bab·bling** *v.t.* 1 To utter unintelligibly. 2 To blurt out; tell thoughtlessly or foolishly. —*v.i.* 3 To utter inarticulate sounds or meaningless noises, as a baby or idiot. 4 To murmur, as a brook. 5 To talk unwisely or foolishly. [ME *babelen*] —**bab′ble·ment** *n.* —**bab′bler** *n.*

Synonyms (verb): blab, blurt, cackle, chat, chatter, gabble, gossip, jabber, murmur, palaver, prate, prattle, tattle, twaddle. Most of these words are onomatopoetic. The *cackle* of a hen, the *gabble* of a goose, the *chatter* of a magpie, the *babble* of a running stream, as applied to human speech, indicate a rapid succession of what are to the listener meaningless sounds. *Blab* and *blurt* refer to the letting out of what the lips can no longer keep in. To *chat* is to talk in an easy, pleasant way, not without sense, but without special purpose; to *prattle* is to talk freely and artlessly, as children. To *prate* is to talk idly, presumptuously, or foolishly, but not necessarily incoherently. To *jabber* is to utter a rapid succession of unintelligible sounds, generally more noisy than *chattering.* To *gossip* is to talk of petty personal matters. To *twaddle* is to talk feeble nonsense. To *murmur* is to utter suppressed or even inarticulate sounds, suggesting the notes of a dove, or the sound of a running stream. Compare SPEAK.

babe (bāb) *n.* 1 An infant; baby. 2 *U.S. Colloq.* An artless person; one lacking experience, sophistication, or guile. 3 *U.S. Slang* A girl. [ME; of uncertain origin]

ba·bel (bā′bəl, bab′əl) *n.* A confusion of many voices or languages; tumult. Also **Ba′bel.**

Ba·bel (bā′bəl, bab′əl) An ancient city in Shinar. —**Tower of Babel** 1 A tower built by the descendants of Noah in Babel and intended to reach to heaven: God punished the builders for their presumption by confusing their language, preventing them from understanding each other and from completing the tower *Gen.* xi 9. 2 Any impractical scheme or structure; a visionary project.

Bab-el-Man-deb (bäb′el-män′deb) A strait between the Red Sea and the Gulf of Aden; 17 miles wide.

Ba·bel·thu·ap (bä′bəl-too′äp) Largest of the Palau Islands; 143 square miles.

Ba·ber (bä′bər), 1483–1530, founder of the Great Mogul dynasty in India: real name Zahir ed-Din Mohammed: also spelled *Babar, Babur.*

Ba·beuf (bȧ·bœf′), **François Emile,** 1760–97, French socialist.

Ba·bi (bä′bē) *n.* An adherent of Babism.

ba·bies'-breath (bā′bēz-breth) *n.* Baby's-breath.

Bab·ing·ton (bab′ing-tən), **Anthony,** 1561–86, English Roman Catholic conspirator against Queen Elizabeth.

ba·biche (bȧ-bēsh′) *n. Canadian* Rawhide thongs or lacings. [< Can. F]

bab·i·rus·a (bab′ə-roo′sə, bä′bə-) *n.* A wild hog (*Babirussa babirussa*) of SE Asia and the East Indies. The lower canines of the male pierce the upper lips and curve backwards. Also **bab′i·rous′sa, bab′i·rus′sa.** [< Malay *bābi* hog + *rūsa* deer]

Ba·bism (bä′biz·əm) *n.* The principles and practices of the Babis, a pantheistic Persian sect founded in 1844 by the Bab, Mirza Ali Mohammed ibn Radhik, 1824–50. Its philosophy recognizes the equality of the sexes and forbids polygamy, drinking, and mendicancy. [< Persian *bāb* gate] —**Ba·bite** (bä′bīt), **Ba′bist** *adj. & n.*

Ba·bol (bä-bôl′) A city in northern Iran near the Caspian Sea: formerly *Barfrush.* Also **Ba·bul** (bä-bool′).

ba·boon (ba-boon′) *n.* A large, terrestrial monkey (*Papio* and related genera) of Africa and Asia, having front and back legs of nearly equal length, doglike muzzle, large bare callosities on the buttocks, and usually a short tail. [< OF *babuin*] —**ba·boon′ish** *adj.*

BABOON
(About 30 inches high at the shoulder)

ba·boon·er·y (ba-boo′nər-ē) *n.* Baboonish antics or behavior.

Bab·son (bab′sən), **Roger Ward,** 1875–1967, U.S. statistician.

ba·bu (bä′boo) *n.* 1 A Hindu gentleman: a polite form of address, equivalent to *sir* or *Mr.* 2 In India, a native merchant or clerk who can write English. 3 A native of India with a smattering of English education: a derogatory term. Also **ba′boo.** [< Hind. *bābū,* a term of respect] —**ba′bu·ism** *n.*

ba·bul (bä-bool′) *n.* 1 An acacia (*Acacia arabica*) yielding a hard and heavy wood, and a gum used as a substitute for gum arabic. 2 The bark or gum of this acacia. Also **ba·bool′.** [< Hind., the acacia tree]

Ba·bur (bä′bər) See BABER.

ba·bush·ka (ba-boosh′kə) *n.* A woman's scarf, often made or folded in a triangular shape, worn as a hood with the ends tying under the chin. [< Russian, grandmother]

Ba·bu·yan Channel (bä′boo-yän′) The southernmost part of Luzon Strait, between Luzon and the Babuyan Islands.

Babuyan Islands A Philippine island group north of Luzon; 225 square miles.

ba·by (bā′bē) *n. pl.* **ba·bies** 1 A very young child of either sex; an infant. 2 The youngest or smallest member of a family or group. 3 One who has the appearance, behavior, or disposition of a young child, especially one with little courage or fortitude. 4 *Slang* A girl. 5 Any young animal. 6 *Obs.* A doll or puppet. —*adj.* 1 For a baby: *baby* shoes. 2 Childish; infantile: *baby* ways. 3 Small; diminutive; miniature. —*v.t.* **ba·bied, ba·by·ing** To treat as a baby; play tenderly with; pamper. —**ba′by·hood** *n.* —**ba′by·like′** *adj.* [ME *baby,* dim. of *babe* BABE]

ba·by-blue-eyes (bā′bē-bloo′īz′) *n.* Any of several annual plants (genus *Nemophila,* especially *N. menzies* of the Pacific Coast) with alternate leaves and showy sky-blue flowers: also called *blueball.* Also **baby blue-eyes.**

baby farm A place where babies may be boarded and cared for.

ba·by·ish (bā′bē-ish) *adj.* Childish; infantile. See synonyms under CHILDISH. —**ba′by·ish·ly** *adv.* —**ba′by·ish·ness** *n.*

Bab·y·lon (bab′ə-lən, -lon) 1 An ancient city of Mesopotamia on the Euphrates, capital of Babylonia from about 2100 B.C.; celebrated as a seat of wealth, luxury, and vice. 2 Any city or place of great wealth, luxury, or vice. 3 Any place of captivity: in allusion to the *Babylonian captivity.* —**Bab′y·lon′ic** (-lon′ik), **Bab′y·lo′nish** (-lō′nish) *adj.*

Bab·y·lo·ni·a (bab′ə-lō′nē-ə) An ancient empire of Mesopotamia; capital, Babylon; surrendered to Persia 538 B.C.

Bab·y·lo·ni·an (bab′ə-lō′nē-ən) *adj.* 1 Of, like, or pertaining to ancient Babylon or Babylonia. 2 Wicked; luxurious. —*n.* 1 A native or inhabitant of Babylonia. 2 The Semitic language of ancient Babylonia, belonging to the Akkadian group.

Babylonian captivity 1 The exile of the Jews deported by Nebuchadnezzar into Babylonia, 597 B.C. 2 The interval of forced residence of the Popes at Avignon, 1309–77. Also **Babylonian exile.**

ba·by's-breath (bā′bēz-breth′) *n.* 1 An Old World perennial (*Gypsophila paniculata*) with

numerous clusters of small, white or pink, fragrant flowers. 2 Any of certain other fragrant herbs, as the naturalized wild madder of the eastern United States: also spelled *babies'-breath.* Also **ba'by's-breath'.**

ba·by-sit (bā'bē·sit') *v.* **-sat, -sit·ting** To act as a baby sitter.

baby sitter (bā'bē sit'ər) *n.* A person employed to take care of young children during the hours when the parents are absent.

Ba·car·di (bə·kär'dē) *n.* A kind of Cuban rum. [after *Bacardi,* the original distillers]

bac·ca·lau·re·ate (bak'ə·lôr'ē·it) *n.* 1 The degree of bachelor of arts, bachelor of science, etc. 2 A sermon or address to a graduating class at commencement: also **baccalaureate sermon.** [< Med. L *baccalaureatus* < *baccalaureus,* var. of *baccalarius* a young farmer, ? < LL *bacca* cow; infl. in form by *bacca lauri* laurel berry. See BACHELOR]

bac·ca·rat (bak'ə·rä', bak'ə·rä) *n.* A card game of chance. The winnings are decided by comparison of hands with that of the banker. Also **bac'ca·ra'.** [< F *baccara,* a game of cards]

bac·cate (bak'āt) *adj. Bot.* 1 Like a berry. 2 Bearing berries. Also **bac'cat·ed.** [< L *baccatus* < *bacca* berry]

Bac·chae (bak'ē) 1 In Greek mythology, the female companions of Bacchus or Dionysus in his travels through the East. 2 Women taking part in the Dionysian celebrations. Also **Bac'chæ.**

bac·cha·nal (bak'ə·nəl) *n.* 1 A votary of Bacchus; hence, a drunken reveler. 2 *pl.* Bacchanalia. 3 A drunken revel; orgy. —*adj.* Bacchanalian. [< L *bacchanalis* of Bacchus < *Bacchus* god of wine]

bac·cha·na·li·a (bak'ə·nā'lē·ə, -nāl'yə) *n. pl.* Drunken revelries; orgies.

Bac·cha·na·li·a (bak'ə·nā'lē·ə, -nāl'yə) *n. pl.* An ancient Roman festival in honor of Bacchus.

bac·cha·na·li·an (bak'ə·nā'lē·ən, -nāl'yən) *adj.* Of, pertaining to, or indulging in orgies; carousing; uproariously drunk. —**bac'cha·na'li·an·ism** *n.*

bac·chant (bak'ənt) *n. pl.* **bac·chants** or **bac·chan·tes** (bə·kan'tēz) A votary of Bacchus; hence, a carouser; bacchanal. —*adj.* Given to drunkenness. [< L *bacchans, -antis* ppr. of *bacchari* celebrate the festival of Bacchus, carouse]

bac·chan·te (bə·kan'tē, bə·kant', bak'ənt) *n.* A female votary of Bacchus.

bac·chic (bak'ik) *adj.* Riotous; orgiastic; drunken. Also **bac'chi·cal.**

Bac·chic (bak'ik) *adj.* Of, pertaining to, or like Bacchus or his rites.

Bac·chus (bak'əs) In Roman mythology, the god of wine and revelry: identified with the Greek *Dionysus.*

bac·cif·er·ous (bak·sif'ər·əs) *adj. Bot.* Bearing or yielding berries. [< L *baccifer* bearing berries < *bacca* berry + *ferre* bear]

bac·ci·form (bak'sə·fôrm) *adj.* Berry-shaped. [< NL *bacciformis* berry-formed < *bacca* berry + -FORM]

Bac·cio del·la Por·ta (bät'chō del'lä pôr'tä) Fra Bartolommeo.

bac·civ·o·rous (bak·siv'ər·əs) *adj. Zool.* Feeding on berries. [< L *bacca* berry + *vorare* eat]

bach (bach) *v.i. Colloq.* To live as a bachelor; keep house alone or for oneself.

Bach (bäkh) A family of German musicians and composers, of whom the best known are **Johann Sebastian,** 1685–1750, and his sons, **Karl Philipp Emanuel,** 1714–88 and **Johann Christian,** 1735–82.

Ba·chan (bä·chän') See BATJAN.

bach·e·lor (bach'ə·lər, bach'lər) *n.* 1 An unmarried man. 2 One who has taken his first university or college degree. 3 A young knight serving under another's banner: also **bach'e·lor-at-arms'.** 4 A fresh-water fish, the crappie. 5 A young male fur seal kept from the breeding grounds by the older males: also called *holluschick.* [< OF *bacheler* < Med. L *baccalaris;* origin and meaning uncertain] —**bach'e·lor·hood'** *n.* —**bach'e·lor·ship'** *n.*

Bachelor of Arts 1 A degree given by a college or university to a person who has completed a four-year course or its equivalent in the humanities. 2 A person who has received this degree. Abbr. *B.A., A.B.*

Bachelor of Science 1 A degree given by a college or university to a person who has completed a four-year course or its equivalent, majoring in science rather than the humanities. 2 A person who has received this degree. Abbr. *B.S., B.Sc.*

bach·e·lor's-but·ton (bach'ə·lərz·but'n, bach'lərz-) *n.* Any of several plants with button-shaped flowers or flower heads, especially certain species of the genus *Centaurea,* as the cornflower *(C. cyanus).*

bac·il·lar·y (bas'ə·ler'ē) *adj.* 1 Rod-shaped: also **ba·cil·li·form** (bə·sil'ə·fôrm). 2 Pertaining to, characterized by, or due to bacilli: also **ba·cil·lar** (bə·sil'ər, bas'ə·lər).

ba·cil·lo·my·cin (bə·sil'ō·mī'sin) *n.* An antibiotic isolated from a soil organism *(Bacillus subtilis);* it has a strong action against fungi, especially those causing athlete's foot. [< BACILLUS + Gk. *mykēs* fungus + -IN]

ba·cil·lus (bə·sil'əs) *n. pl.* **ba·cil·li** (-sil'ī) 1 Any of a large and numerous class of straight, rod-shaped bacteria having both beneficial and pathogenic effects: distinguished from *coccus* and *spirillum* types. 2 Any of a family *(Bacillaceae)* of straight, rod-shaped, aerobic, spore-forming bacteria, occurring singly or in chains. 3 Loosely, a bacterium. For illustration see BACTERIA. [< NL < *bacillum,* dim. of *baculus* a stick]

bac·i·tra·cin (bas'ə·trā'sin) *n.* An antibiotic produced from a bacillus, used in the treatment of some bacterial skin infections.

back[1] (bak) *n.* 1 The part of the body nearest the spine; in man the hinder, in quadrupeds the upper part, extending from the neck to the base of the spine. ◆Collateral adjective: *dorsal, fergal.* 2 The backbone. 3 The rear or posterior part: Sit in the *back* of the car. 4 The farther or other side; the part away from the beholder: the *back* of the door. 5 The part which comes behind or is opposite to the part used in the ordinary movements of a thing: the *back* of a knife, the *back* of the hand. 6 The part of the leaves of a book sewed together into the binding; also, the part of the binding around this part. 7 The lining attached to the unexposed side of a thing, as for reinforcement. 8 In football, a member of the offensive or defensive backfield. 9 The ridge of a hill. 10 *Phonet.* The part of the tongue directly behind the front and below the velum. —**at one's back** Following closely. —**behind one's back** 1 Secretly. 2 Treacherously. —**in back of** *Colloq.* Behind; to the rear of. —**to be (flat) on one's back** To be helplessly ill. —**to get (or put) one's back up** To become (or make) angry or obstinate. —**to put one's back into** To exert all the physical strength of which one is capable. —**to turn one's back on** To show contempt or ill feeling toward by turning away from or ignoring. —**with one's back to the wall** Cornered; having no issue save by fighting one's way out. —*v.t.* 1 To cause to move or go backwards; force to the rear: often with *up.* 2 To form the back of; supply with a back. 3 To strengthen at the back. 4 To support, assist, or uphold; be in favor of: often with *up* . 5 To support financially. 6 To bet on the success or chances of. 7 To mount, sit, or ride on the back of, as a horse. 8 To write on the back of; address or endorse, as a check. —*v.i.* 9 To move or go backward: often with *up.* 10 To shift counterclockwise: said of the wind: opposed to *veer.* —**to back and fill** 1 *Naut.* To keep (a vessel) in mid-channel by alternately filling and spilling the sails, so as to be advanced by the current alone. 2 To be irresolute; vacillate. —**to back down** To withdraw from a position, abandon a claim, etc. —**to back off** To retreat, as from contact. —**to back out** To withdraw from or refuse to carry out an engagement or contest. —**to back water** 1 To retard the progress or reverse the motion of a vessel by reversing the action of the oars or of the propelling machinery. 2 To withdraw from a position; retract, as a claim. —*adj.* 1 In the rear; behind: a *back* room. 2 Distant; remote: the *back* country. 3 Of or for a date earlier than the present: *back* taxes. 4 In arrears; overdue, as a debt. 5 In a backward direction: a *back* thrust. 6 *Phonet.* Describing those vowels produced with the tongue pulled back in the mouth, as (o͞o) in *food.* [OE *bæc* back]

back[2] (bak) *adv.* 1 At, to, or toward the rear: to move *back.* 2 In, to, or toward a former place: to go *back* home. 3 In, to, or toward a former condition: My cold has come *back.* 4 In time past; ago: years *back.* 5 In return or retort: to talk *back.* 6 In reserve or concealment: to keep something *back.* —**back and forth** First in one direction and then in the opposite. —**back of** Behind. —**to go back on** *Colloq.* 1 To refuse to keep a promise or engagement. 2 To desert or betray (a cause). [< ABACK]

back[3] (bak) *n.* A brewer's tub or vat. [< Du. *bak* trough < F *bac* tub, basin]

back·ache (bak'āk') *n.* An ache or pain in one's back.

Back Bay A fashionable residential district of Boston.

back·bite (bak'bīt') *v.t.* & *v.i.* **·bit, ·bit·ten** or *Colloq.* **·bit, ·bit·ing** To revile or traduce behind one's back; slander. See synonyms under ASPERSE. —**back'bit'er** *n.* —**back'bit'ing** *n.*

back·blocks (bak'bloks') *n. pl. Australian* Inland farming areas.

back·board (bak'bôrd', -bōrd') *n.* 1 A board forming or supporting the back of something. 2 In basketball, the vertical board behind the basket to which it is attached.

back·bone (bak'bōn') *n.* 1 *Anat.* The spine or vertebral column. 2 Any main support or stiffening part; especially, the highest or most extensive mountain range of a region or a continent. 3 Firmness; resolution; courage. —**back'boned'** *adj.*

back-break·ing (bak'brā'king) *adj.* Physically exhausting; fatiguing.

back·chat (bak'chat') *Colloq.* Back talk.

back country Unpopulated or undeveloped areas adjoining settled areas.

back court 1 In tennis and other games, the rear part of the court. 2 In basketball, the defensive half of the court of each team.

back·cross (bak'krôs', -kros') *v.t.* & *v.i. Genetics* To cross (a hybrid offspring) with one of its parents. —*n.* The offspring of a hybrid and either of the parents.

back-door (bak'dôr', -dōr') *adj.* 1 Relating or belonging to the back door of a house. 2 Underhand; indirect; secret.

back·drop (bak'drop') *n.* The curtain hung at the rear of a stage, often painted to represent a scene. Also **back cloth.**

backed (bakt) *adj.* 1 Provided with or having a back, background, or backing: often used in composition: low-*backed.* 2 In weaving, having an extra weft, warp, or another ply of cloth woven or knitted on the back.

back·er (bak'ər) *n.* 1 One who or that which backs or furnishes a back to; especially, one who supports with money; a patron. 2 One who bets or gambles on a contestant. See synonyms under ADHERENT.

back·field (bak'fēld') *n.* 1 In American football, the players behind the forward linemen, consisting of the fullback, right and left halfbacks, and quarterback. 2 The area in which these players are regularly stationed.

back·fill (bak'fil') *n.* Soil and other material used to refill an excavation. —*v.t.* To refill (an excavation).

back·fire (bak'fīr') *n.* 1 A fire built to check an advancing forest or prairie fire by creating a barren area in its path. 2 Premature explosion in the cylinder of an internal-combustion engine. 3 An explosion in the back part of a gun. —*v.i.* **·fired, ·fir·ing** 1 To set or use a backfire. 2 To explode in a backfire. 3 To have consequences contrary to those desired: The plan to raise revenue by increasing the sales tax *backfired* when sales dropped off.

back-fo·cus (bak'fō'kəs) *n. Phot.* The distance from the main focus of a lens to its nearest face. —**back'-fo'cused** *adj.*

back formation *Ling.* 1 The creation, by analogy, of one word from another in cases where the original word would seem to be the derivative, as in the derivation of *emote* from *emotion.* 2 A word so formed.

back·gam·mon (bak'gam'ən, bak'gam'ən) *n.* 1 A game played by two persons, on a special board, the moves of the pieces being determined by dice throws: formerly called *tables.* 2 A victory in this game before the defeated player advances all his men beyond the first six points, resulting in a tripled score for the victor. —*v.t.* To win a backgammon from. [ME *back gamen* back game; because sometimes the pieces must go back to the start]

back·ground (bak'ground') *n.* 1 That part in

a picture which is behind the principal objects represented or which forms a setting. **2** Ground in the rear or distance. **3** A subordinate position; obscurity; retirement. **4** The aggregate of one's experiences, training, cultural environment, etc. **5** Music or sound effects employed in accompaniment to a dialog, recital, etc. **6** The events leading up to or causing a situation. **7** Information explaining a situation, person, etc.

back·hand (bak′hand′) *adj.* Backhanded. — *n.* **1** Handwriting that slopes toward the left. **2** The hand turned backward in making a stroke, as with a racket. **3** A stroke made with the hand turned backward, as in tennis. — *adv.* With a backhand stroke.

back·hand·ed (bak′han′did) *adj.* **1** Delivered or made with the back of the hand, or with back of the hand turned forward, as a stroke in tennis. **2** Equivocal; insincere; ironical: a *backhanded* compliment. **3** Sloping to the left, as handwriting. **4** Turned or twisted in a direction opposite to the normal, as a cable. — **back′hand′ed·ly** *adv.* — **back′hand′ed·ness** *n.*

back·house (bak′hous′) *n.* A building in the rear; a privy.

back·ing (bak′ing) *n.* **1** Support or assistance given to a person, cause, etc. **2** Supporters or promoters collectively. **3** Motion backward; the act of moving backward. **4** The back of anything, especially anything added at the back for extra support or strength. **5** The act of supporting or strengthening at or with the back. **6** *Law* Endorsement by a magistrate of a warrant.

back·lash (bak′lash′) *n.* **1** *Mech.* **a** The reaction or tendency to jar or recoil, as machinery subjected to sudden strain. **b** The amount of loose play in a part subject to such tendency or reaction. **2** In angling, a snarl or tangle of the line on a reel, as caused by a faulty cast. **3** A sudden, violent recoil or reaction, as of public opinion.

back·log (bak′lôg′, -log′) *n.* *U.S.* **1** A large log placed at the back of an open fireplace to maintain and concentrate the heat. **2** Any reserve, as of funds, business orders, etc.

back·most (bak′mōst) *adj.* Farthest to the rear; hindmost.

back number 1 An out-of-date issue of a magazine or newspaper. **2** *U.S. Colloq.* An old-fashioned, out-of-date person.

back·pack (bak′pak′) *n.* A pack or knapsack carried on the back, as by campers. — *v.t.* & *v.i.* To carry (equipment) in a backpack. — **back′pack′er** *n.*

back·rest (bak′rest′) *n.* A support for or at the back.

back·rope (bak′rōp′) *n.* *Naut.* A lateral stay from the martingale of a vessel to the bows.

back seat 1 A seat in the rear, as of a vehicle, theater, hall, etc. **2** Status of little or no importance: to take a *back seat.*

back-seat driver (bak′sēt′) A passenger in a vehicle who offers advice and directions for driving.

back·set (bak′set′) *n.* **1** A setback; relapse. **2** An eddy; backwater, as of a stream.

back·sheesh, back·shish (bak′shēsh) See BAKSHEESH.

back·side (bak′sīd′) *n.* The posterior part of a person or an animal; rump.

back·sight (bak′sīt′) *n.* **1** In surveying, a sight laid on a known point in order to determine the position or elevation of an instrument. **2** A sight laid on a previously taken instrument station from a newly located point.

back·slide (bak′slīd′) *v.i.* **·slid, ·slid** or **slid·den, ·slid·ing** To return to wrong or vicious ways or opinions after reformation or conversion; relapse; apostatize. — **back′slid′er** *n.*

back·spin (bak′spin′) *n.* Reverse rotation of a round object that is moving forward, causing it to rebound.

back·stage (bak′stāj′) *adv.* In or toward the portion of a theater behind the stage proper or acting area, including the wings, dressing rooms, etc. — *n.* The back portion of the stage. — *adj.* (bak′stāj′) Placed backstage, so as to be hidden.

back·stairs (bak′stârz′) *adj.* Indirect; underhanded. Also **back′stair′.**

back·stay (bak′stā′) *n.* **1** *Naut.* A stayrope supporting a mast of a vessel on the aft side.

2 A support for various mechanical purposes. **3** The leather band at the back and sides of a shoe above the heel and below the body of the counter.

back·stitch (bak′stich′) *n.* A stitch made by carrying the thread back half the length of the preceding stitch. — *v.t.* & *v.i.* To sew with backstitches.

back·stop (bak′stop′) *n.* A fence or screen to stop the ball from going too far in certain games, as baseball, tennis, etc.

back·strap (bak′strap′) *n.* The harness band extending from crupper to hames or saddle. See illustration under HARNESS.

back·stretch (bak′strech′) *n.* That part of a race course farthest from the spectators: opposite of *homestretch.*

back·stroke (bak′strōk′) *n.* **1** A blow or stroke in return; a backhanded stroke. **2** In swimming, a stroke executed while on one's back. — *v.* **·stroked, ·strok·ing** *v.t.* To strike, as a ball, with a backstroke. — *v.i.* To swim with a backstroke.

back·swept (bak′swept′) *adj. Aeron.* Sweptback.

back·sword (bak′sôrd′, -sōrd′) *n.* **1** A sword with one sharp edge; a broadsword. **2** A stick with a basket hilt, used in fencing practice or in single-stick play. **3** One who uses a backsword. — **back′sword′man, back′swords′man** *n.*

back talk Impudent retort; insolent answering back.

back·track (bak′trak′) *v.i. U.S.* **1** To retrace one's steps. **2** To withdraw from a position, undertaking, etc.

back·up (bak′up′) *n.* **1** A support or backing. **2** An accumulation, as of water or waste, caused by a stoppage. **3** A substitute held in readiness for contingent use: often used attributively: a *backup* plan; a *backup* quarterback. Also **back′-up′.**

back·ward (bak′wərd) *adj.* **1** Turned to the back or rear; reversed. **2** Retiring; bashful. **3** Slow in growth or development; retarded. **4** Late; slow; behindhand. **5** Done the reverse way. — *adv.* **1** In the direction of the back; to the rear. **2** Into time past; toward earlier times. **3** With the back foremost. **4** In reverse order. **5** From better to worse. Also **back′wards** *adv.* — **back′ward·ly** *adv.* — **back′ward·ness** *n.*

back·wash (bak′wosh′, -wôsh′) *n.* **1** The water moved backward, as by a boat, oars, etc. **2** The backward current of air set up by aircraft propellers. **3** Any condition resulting from some previous act, remark, etc.

back·wa·ter (bak′wô′tər, -wot′ər) *n.* **1** Water set, thrown, or held back, as by a dam, a current, etc.; also, the body of water held back. **2** Any place or condition regarded as stagnant, backward, etc.

back·woods (bak′wŏŏdz′) *n. pl. U.S.* Wild, heavily wooded, or sparsely settled districts. — *adj.* In, from, or like the backwoods: also **back′wood′.** — **back′woods′man** (-mən) *n.*

ba·con (bā′kən) *n.* **1** The salted and dried or smoked flesh of the hog, especially the back and sides. **2** *U.S. Colloq.* Money, profit, or gain from any undertaking: to bring home the *bacon.* [< OF < OHG *bacho, bakho* ham, side of bacon]

Ba·con (bā′kən), **Francis,** 1561–1626, first Baron Verulam, Viscount St. Albans, English

philosopher, essayist, and statesman. — **Nathaniel,** 1647–76, American colonial leader of a rebellion (1676) demanding governmental reforms. — **Roger,** 1214?-92?, English scientist and philosopher.

Ba·co·ni·an (bā·kō′nē·ən) *adj.* Of or pertaining to Francis Bacon, his philosophy, or his literary style. — *n.* One who believes in the philosophy of Francis Bacon or in the Baconian theory.

Baconian theory The theory that Francis Bacon wrote the plays attributed to Shakespeare.

ba·con·y (bā′kən·ē) *adj.* Like bacon; fatty.

bac·te·re·mi·a (bak′tə·rē′mē·ə) *n. Pathol.* The presence of bacteria in the blood.

bac·te·ri·a (bak·tir′ē·ə) Plural of BACTERIUM.

bac·te·ri·cide (bak·tir′ə·sīd) *n.* An agent destructive of bacteria. — **bac·te′ri·ci′dal** *adj.*

bac·te·rin (bak′tə·rin) *n.* A vaccine prepared from dead pathogenic bacteria. Also **bac′te·rine** (-rēn).

bacterio– *combining form* Of or pertaining to bacteria: *bacterioscopy.* [Gk. *baktērion,* dim. of *baktron* rod, staff]

bac·te·ri·ol·o·gy (bak·tir′ē·ol′ə·jē) *n.* The branch of biology and medicine that deals with bacteria. — **bac·te·ri·o·log·i·cal** (bak·tir′.ē·ə·loj′i·kəl) or **bac·te′ri·o·log′i·cal·ly** *adv.* — **bac·te′ri·ol′o·gist** *n.*

bac·te·ri·o·ly·sin (bak·tir′ē·ə·lī′sin) *n.* A specific antibody formed in the blood by the action of bacteria and having the power to disintegrate or dissolve them.

bac·te·ri·ol·y·sis (bak·tir′ē·ol′ə·sis) *n.* **1** Decomposition effected through bacteria without oxygen. **2** Destruction or breaking down of cells. — **bac·te·ri·o·lyt·ic** (bak·tir′ē·ə·lit′ik) *adj.*

bac·te·ri·o·phage (bak·tir′ē·ə·fāj′) *n.* An ultramicroscopic filter-passing agent which has the power of destroying bacteria and of inducing bacterial mutation.

bac·te·ri·os·co·py (bak·tir′ē·os′kə·pē) *n.* Microscopic study or investigation of bacteria. — **bac·te·ri·o·scop·ic** (bak·tir′ē·ə·skop′ik) or **·i·cal** *adj.* — **bac·te′ri·o·scop′i·cal·ly** *adv.* — **bac·te′ri·os′co·pist** *n.*

bac·te·ri·o·stat·ic (bak·tir′ē·ə·stat′ik) *adj.* Arresting the growth or development of bacteria.

bac·te·ri·um (bak·tir′ē·əm) *n. pl.* **·te·ri·a** (-tir′ē·ə) One of numerous widely distributed unicellular micro-organisms of the class *Schizomycetes;* autotrophic, heterotrophic, parasitic or saprophytic, they exhibit both plant and animal characteristics, and in their three varieties of *bacillus, coccus,* and *spirillum* range from the harmless and beneficial to the intensely virulent and lethal. [< NL < Gk. *baktērion,* dim. of *baktron* staff, stick] — **bac·te′ri·al** *adj.* — **bac·te′ri·al·ly** *adv.*

bac·ter·ize (bak′tər·īz) *v.t.* **·ized, iz·ing** To change by the action of bacteria. — **bac′ter·i·za′tion** *n.*

bac·ter·oid (bak′tə·roid) *adj.* Resembling the forms of bacteria. Also **bac′ter·oi′dal, bac·te·ri·oid** (bak·tir′ē·oid). — *n.* A bacterium found in tubercles on the roots of leguminous plants.

Bac·tra (bak′trə) *n.* The ancient name for BALKH.

Bac·tri·a (bak′trē·ə) A satrapy of the ancient Persian empire, lying partly in NE Afghanistan and partly in SW Asiatic U.S.S.R. — **Bac′·tri·an** *adj.* & *n.*

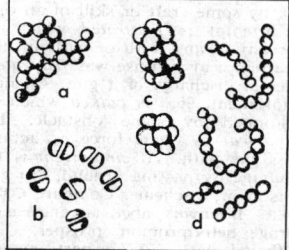

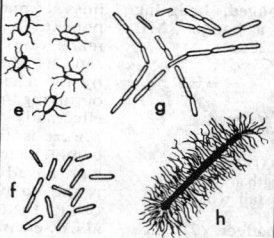

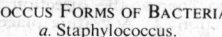

COCCUS FORMS OF BACTERIA
a. Staphylococcus.
b. Diplococcus.
c. Sarcina.
d. Streptococcus.

BACILLUS FORMS OF BACTERIA
e. Bacillus typhosus.
f. Bacillus sporagenes.
g. Bacillus subtilis.
h. Bacillus proteus.

SPIRILLUM FORMS OF BACTERIA
i. Spirillum undulam.
j. Species of spirochaete.
k. Thiospirillum.
l. Vibrio cholerae.

add,āce,câre,pälm; end,ēven; it,īce; odd,ōpen,ôrder; tŏŏk,pool; up,bûrn; ə = a in *above,* e in *sicken,* i in *clarity,* o in *melon,* u in *focus;* yōō = u in *fuse;* oi,oil; ou,pout; ch,check; g,go; ng,ring; th,thin; th,this; zh,vision. Foreign sounds å,œ,ü,kh,ṅ; and ◆: see page xx. < *from;* + *plus;* ? *possibly.*

ba·cu·li·form (bə·kyōō′lə·fôrm) *adj.* Shaped like a rod; straight. [<L *baculum* rod + -FORM]

bad[1] (bad) *adj.* **worse, worst 1** Not good in any manner or degree; not up to standard; unsatisfactory; inferior; poor: a *bad* meal; They played a *bad* game and lost. **2** Disagreeable; unpleasant: *bad* weather; *bad* manners. **3** Inadequate; deficient: *bad* wiring. **4** Lacking skill or proficiency: a *bad* musician. **5** Rotten; decaying: *bad* apples. **6** Immoral; corrupt; wicked. **7** Mischievous; naughty; ill-behaved: a *bad* child. **8** Incorrect; erroneous: *bad* grammar. **9** Injurious; harmful: a *bad* habit. **10** Severe: a *bad* sprain. **11** Sick; in poor health. **12** Injured or diseased; not sound: a *bad* knee; a *bad* heart. **13** Sorry; concerned: to feel *bad* about it. **14** Inexpedient; wrong; improper; inauspicious: He spoke at a *bad* time and regretted it later. **15** Invalid; illegal: a *bad* check. **16** In finance, outstanding and not collectable: a *bad* debt. —**in bad** *Colloq.* **1** In difficulty. **2** In disfavor. —**not bad** Rather good: also **not half bad, not so bad.** —*n.* **1** That which is bad. **2** Those who are bad, taken collectively. **3** A bad state or condition; bad luck; wickedness. —**to go to the bad** *Colloq.* To degenerate; become bad. —*adv. Colloq.* Badly. [ME *bad, baddle,* ? <OE *bæddel* effeminate man] —**bad′ness** *n.*

Synonyms (adj.): abominable, baleful, baneful, base, corrupt, corrupting, decayed, decaying, deceitful, deceptive, defective, deleterious, depraved, detrimental, dishonest, evil, false, foul, fraudulent, hurtful, ill, immoral, imperfect, incompetent, inferior, injurious, mean, mischievous, naughty, noxious, pernicious, poor, putrid, rascally, rotten, sad, saddening, scurvy, serious, severe, shabby, sinful, sorrowful, sorry, unfair, unfortunate, unhappy, unlucky, unprincipled, untrue, untrustworthy, unwelcome, unwholesome, unworthy, vile, villainous, wicked, worthless, wretched. See HARD, IMMORAL, PERNICIOUS. *Antonyms*: see synonyms for GOOD.

bad[2] (bad) Obsolete past tense of BID.

Ba·da·joz (bä·thä·hōth′) A province of western Spain, constituting Lower Estremadura; 8,360 square miles; capital, Badajoz.

Badb (biv) In Old Irish mythology, an evil spirit delighting in carnage, appearing as the crow that feeds on the slain after battle: also spelled *Bodb.*

bad blood Hostility; long-standing enmity; strife.

bad·der-locks (bad′ər·loks) *n.* An edible European seaweed *(Alaria esculenta).*

bade (bad) Past tense of BID.

Ba·den (bäd′n) A former state of SW Germany; after 1945 divided into (1) Baden, in the Federal Republic (1949); 3,842 square miles; capital, Freiburg; and (2) WÜRTTEMBERG-BADEN.

Ba·den-Ba·den (bäd′n·bäd′n) A resort city of southern Baden, Germany.

Ba·den-Pow·ell (bād′n·pō′əl), **Lord,** 1857–1941, Robert Stephenson Smyth, British general; founder of the Boy Scouts in 1908.

badge (baj) *n.* **1** A token, mark, decoration, or insignia of office, rank or membership. **2** Any distinguishing mark. **3** A ribbon worn on the field uniform to indicate award of a decoration, or a device to indicate branch, organization, rank, rating, or professional attainment. —*v.t.* **badged, badg·ing** To decorate or provide with a badge. [ME *bage, bagge*]

badg·er (baj′ər) *n.* **1** A small, burrowing, nocturnal, carnivorous mammal, with a broad body, short legs, and long-clawed toes. There are several species, including the **American badger** *(Taxidea americana),* the **European badger** *(Meles taxus),* and the balisaur and the ratel of Asia. **2** In Australia, the bandicoot, the rock wallaby, or the wombat. **3** The fur of a badger, or a brush made of its hair. —*v.t.* To worry or persecute persistently; bait; nag. [?<BADGE, with ref. to mark on head]

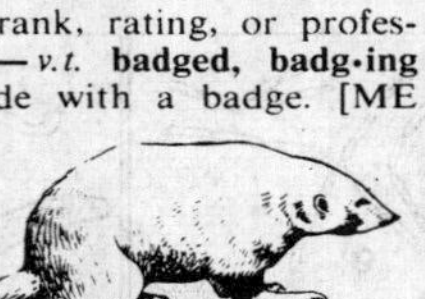

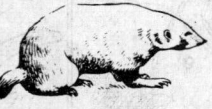

BADGER
(Body length about 2 feet, 4 inches: tail, 6 inches)

Badger State Nickname of WISCONSIN.

bad·i·nage (bad′ə·näzh′, bad′ə·nij) *n.* Playful raillery; banter. —*v.t.* **·naged, ·nag·ing** To subject to or tease with badinage. See synonyms under BANTER. [<F <*badiner* jest < *badin* silly, jesting <Provençal *bader* <LL *badare* gape]

bad·lands (bad′landz′) *n.* A barren area characterized by numerous ridges, peaks, and mesas cut by erosion.

Bad·lands (bad′landz′) An arid plateau in South Dakota, Nebraska, and North Dakota, eroded into peaks, pinnacles, and valleys. Also **Bad Lands.**

bad·ly (bad′lē) *adv.* **1** Improperly; imperfectly; incorrectly. **2** Unpleasantly. **3** Harmfully. **4** *Colloq.* Very much; greatly: I need to see you *badly.*

bad·man (bad′man′) *n.* A desperado.

bad·min·ton (bad′min·tən) *n.* **1** A game played by batting a shuttlecock back and forth over a high narrow net with a light racket. **2** A drink made with claret, sugar, and soda water. [from *Badminton* in England, the estate of the Duke of Beaufort]

bad-mouth (bad′mouth′) *v.t. U.S. Slang* To voice damaging criticism of; speak ill of.

Ba·do·glio (bä·dō′lyō), **Pietro,** 1871–1956, Italian marshal; premier 1943–44.

bad-tem·pered (bad′tem′pərd) *adj.* Having a bad temper; cross; irritable.

Bae·da (bē′də) See BEDE.

Bae·de·ker (bā′di·kər) *n.* **1** Any of a series of travelers' guidebooks issued by **Karl Baedeker,** 1801–59, German publisher, or his firm. **2** Loosely, any guidebook.

Baeke·land (bāk′lənd), **Leo Hendrik,** 1863–1944, U.S. chemist and inventor, born in Belgium. See BAKELITE.

Bae·yer (bā′yər), **Johann Friedrich Wilhelm Adolf von,** 1835–1917, German chemist.

baff (baf) *Scot. v.t. & v.i.* **1** To beat or strike. **2** In golf, to strike the ground under the ball with the sole of a wooden club so as to send the ball too high in the air. —*n.* **1** A stroke; blow. **2** In golf, a baffed stroke.

Baf·fin (baf′in), **William,** 1584–1622, English navigator.

Baffin Bay An arm of the North Atlantic between Greenland and the Northwest Territories, Canada.

Baffin Island The largest and most easterly island in the Arctic Archipelago, Northwest Territories, Canada; 197,754 square miles. Also **Baffin Land.**

baf·fle (baf′əl) *v.* **baf·fled, baf·fling** *v.t.* **1** To thwart or frustrate; defeat; perplex: Police detectives were completely *baffled* by the absence of a motive. **2** *Naut.* To beat back or hinder: The ship was *baffled* by the storm. —*v.i.* **3** To struggle to no avail: The gull *baffles* with the wind. —*n.* **1** A baffleplate. **2** A partition with a small central hole set in front of a radio loudspeaker to prevent excessive flow of air in either direction. **3** Any movable surface, as a board or blanket, used to control and direct sound effect in filming motion pictures. [Origin uncertain]—**baf′fle·ment** *n.* —**baf′fler** *n.* —**baf′fling** *adj.* —**baf′·fling·ly** *adv.*

Synonyms (verb): balk, circumvent, defeat, foil, frustrate, outgeneral, outmaneuver, outwit, thwart. All the words of this list imply *defeat* by something less than direct resistance. A plan, a scheme, or an opponent may be *baffled* by any artifice sufficient to prevent success. An attempt is *foiled* which is made to miss its mark by some craft or skill of an opponent. An attempt is *frustrated* which is made vain by any means, with or without design; as, the attempt at surprise was *frustrated* by the accidental discharge of a gun. An undertaking, movement, etc., is *balked* which is effectually stopped by some obstacle. To *thwart* is to *defeat* by some force or action coming across the path. To *circumvent* is to gain an advantage by passing around; "to get round" a person or a scheme. Compare CONQUER, HINDER. *Antonyms*: abet, advance, aid, assist, encourage, help, promote, prosper.

baf·fle·plate (baf′əl·plāt) *n.* **1** A partition, as in a furnace, to change the direction of the gases of combustion. **2** A grating placed in a pipe or channel to control eddies and secure a uniform flow of the liquid passing through it. **3** *Electronics* A metal plate serving to reduce the cross-section of electromagnetic waves passing through a guide.

baf·fy (baf′ē) *n. pl.* **·fies** A wooden golf club with a short shaft and deeply pitched face, for lofting the ball. [<BAFF]

Ba·fing (bä′fing) The unnavigable headstream of the Senegal in French West Africa, flowing NE about 350 miles.

bag (bag) *n.* **1** A sack or pouch. **2** A sac or similar structure in various animals, as the udder of a cow. **3** The amount a bag will hold. **4** The amount of game caught or killed. **5** The bulged part of any object, as of a sail. **6** *pl. Colloq.* Clothes, especially ill-fitting ones. **7** *pl. Brit. Colloq.* Men's slacks. **8** A purse. **9** A suitcase. **10** *Slang* One's personal interest or habit. **11** *Slang* A situation, matter, or problem. —**in the bag** *Slang* Virtually certain. —**to be left holding the bag** *U.S. Colloq.* To be left to assume full responsibility. —*v.* **bagged, bag·ging** *v.t.* **1** To put into a bag or bags. **2** To cause to fill out or bulge like a bag. **3** To capture or kill, as game. —*v.i.* **4** To bulge or swell like a bag. **5** To hang loosely. [?<ON *baggi* pack, bundle]

bag and baggage *Colloq.* **1** (With) all one's possessions. **2** Entirely; completely.

ba·gasse (bə·gas′) *n.* **1** The dry refuse of sugarcane after the juice has been expressed. **2** Similar refuse from other sources, as beets and olives: also called *megass, megasse.* Also **ba·gass′.** [<F <Sp. *bagazo* refuse of grapes, olives, etc., after pressing]

bag·a·telle (bag′ə·tel′) *n.* **1** A trifle; something of minor importance. **2** A game similar to billiards. **3** Pinball. **4** A short musical composition, especially for the piano. [<F < Ital. *bagatella,* dim. of *baga* sack]

Bage·hot (baj′ət), **Walter,** 1826–77, English economist and political writer.

ba·gel (bā′gəl) *n.* A doughnut-shaped roll of unsalted yeast simmered in water and baked. [<Yiddish <*beigen* bend, twist]

bag·gage (bag·ij) *n.* **1** The trunks, packages, etc., of a traveler. **2** An army's movable equipment. **3** A lively, pert, or impudent young woman. **4** *Archaic* A prostitute. [<OF *bagage* <*bague* bundle <Med. L *baga* sack]

bag·gage·mas·ter (bag′ij·mas′tər, -mäs′-) *n.* One in charge of receiving and sending baggage, as at a railway station.

bag·gie (bäg′ē, beg′ē) *n. Scot.* The stomach.

bag·ging (bag′ing) *n.* A coarse material for making bags.

bag·gy (bag′ē) *adj.* **bag·gi·er, bag·gi·est** Like a bag; loose; bulging or ill-fitting; puffy: a *baggy* dress. —**bag′gi·ly** *adv.* —**bag′gi·ness** *n.*

Bagh·dad (bag′dad, bäg·däd′) A city on the Tigris, capital of Iraq. Also **Bag′dad.**

Bagh·dad·i (bag·dad′ē, bäg·dä′dē) *n.* A native or inhabitant of Baghdad.

bag·man (bag′mən) *n. pl.* **·men** (-mən) *Brit.* A traveling salesman.

bagn·io (ban′yō, bän′-) *n.* **1** A brothel. **2** A bathhouse; a bath. **3** In the Orient, a prison. [<Ital. *bagno* <L *balneum* <Gk. *balaneion* bath]

bag·pipe (bag′pīp′) *n.* *Often pl.* A reed musical instrument in which the several drone pipes and the melody pipe with its finger stops are supplied with air from a windbag filled by a pipe to the player's mouth: now played chiefly in Scotland and Ireland. —**bag′·pip′er** *n.*

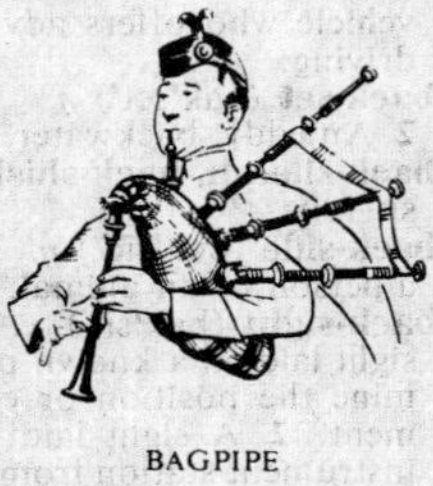

BAGPIPE

Ba·gra·ti·o·novsk (bä·grä·tyē·ô′nôfsk) A city on the Polish border of Russian S.F.S.R.: formerly *Eylau* in East Prussia, site of a battle between Napoleon and Russian and Prussian forces, 1807.

ba·guette (ba·get′) *n.* **1** *Archit.* A small, bead-shaped molding. **2** A gem or crystal cut in long, narrow, rectangular form. **3** This form. Also **ba·guet′.** [<F <Ital. *bacchetta* dim. of *bacchio* <L *baculum* staff, stick]

ba·guio (bä′gyō) *n. Spanish* A tropical cyclone in the Philippines.

Ba·gui·o (bag′ē·ō, bä′gē·ō) A city in northern Luzon, the summer capital of the Philippines.

bag·worm (bag′wûrm′) *n.* The larva of any of certain moths (family *Psychidae*), characterized by its baglike cocoon.

bah (bä, ba) *interj.* An exclamation expressing contempt, scorn, or dismissal.

ba·ha·dur (bə·hä′dŏŏr) *n.* A Hindu title of respect, generally given to European officers in state documents or ceremonies.

Ba·ha·i (bə·hä′ē) *n.* *pl.* **Ba·ha·is** A teacher or follower of Bahaism.

Ba·ha·ism (bə·hä′iz·əm) *n.* One of the two sectarian creeds of Babism, named after the elder brother of Mirza Yahva, Mirza Husayn Ali, who, as *Bahaullah,* proclaimed himself first successor to the Bab in 1863. — **Ba·ha′ist** *n.* & *adj.*

Ba·ha·ma Islands (bə·hä′mə, -hä′-) An island group in the western North Atlantic between Florida and Hispaniola, comprising a British colony; 4,375 square miles; capital, Nassau. Also **Ba·ha′mas.**

Ba·ha·sa Indonesia (bä·hä′sə) The official language of Indonesia, based on Malay.

Ba·ha·ul·lah (bä·hä′ŏŏl·lä′), 1817–92, Mirza Husayn Ali, Persian founder of Bahaism. Also **Ba·ha′ Ul·lah′.**

Ba·ha·wal·pur (bə·hä′wəl·pŏŏr) One of the Punjab states of western Pakistan; 15,918 square miles; capital, Bahawalpur.

Ba·hi·a (bə·ē′ə) **1** A coastal state of eastern Brazil; 217,688 square miles; capital, Salvador: also **Ba·ii′a, 2** Former name of SALVADOR, Brazil.

Ba·hi·a Blan·ca (bä·ē′ä vläng′kä) A port in southern Buenos Aires province, Argentina.

Bah·rein Islands (bä·rān′) An archipelago in the Persian Gulf near the coast of Saudi Arabia, comprising a sheikdom under British protection; 213 square miles; capital, Manameh. Also **Bah·rain′, Bah·rayn′.**

Bahr–el–Ab·iad (bär′el·ab′yäd), **–el–Az·raq** (-el·az′räk), **–el–Jeb·el** (-el·jeb′el) See under NILE.

Bahr–el–Yem·en (bär′el·yem′ən) The Arabic name for the RED SEA.

Bahr–en–Nil (bär′en·nēl′) See under NILE.

baht (bät) *n.* *pl.* **bahts** or **baht 1** The silver monetary unit of Thailand, equivalent to about 40 cents in U.S. currency: formerly called *tical.* **2** A tical, a Thai unit of weight. Also spelled *bat.*

Ba·ia (bä′yä) A village in Campania, southern Italy; site of ancient **Bai·ae** or **Bai·æ** (bä′ē), a favorite bathing resort of the Romans.

baik (bāk) *n. Scot.* **1** A biscuit. **2** Beck. —*v.t.* To bake.

Bai·kal The world's deepest freshwater lake, in southern Siberia, Russia; 12,150 square miles; greatest depth, 5,712 feet.

bail¹ (bāl) *n.* A scoop or bucket for dipping out fluids, as from a boat. —*v.t.* & *v.i.* **1** To dip (water) as from a boat, with or as with a bail. **2** To clear (a boat) of water by dipping out. — **to bail out** To jump from an airplane or other aircraft, usually with parachute, in order to land; to parachute. ◆ Homophone: *bale.* [<OF *baille* <LL *bacula,* dim. of *baca, bacca* shallow trough, tub]

bail² (bāl) *n.* **1** A partition between the stalls of a stable. **2** A frame to confine a cow's head while milking. **3** In cricket, one of the crosspieces of the wicket. **4** A crossbar. **5** A bailey. **6** *pl. Obs.* Palisades. ◆ Homophone: *bale.* — **to bail up** *Austral. Slang* **1** To hold up and rob. **2** To corner or accost someone. [<OF *baile* barrier, ? <*bailler* enclose, shut]

bail³ (bāl) *Law n.* **1** One who becomes surety for the debt or default of another, especially of a person under arrest. **2** The security or guaranty given or agreed upon. **3** Release, or the privilege of release, on bail. See synonyms under SECURITY. —*v.t.* **1** To release (an arrested person) on bail for appearance at a stipulated time: often with *out.* **2** To obtain the release of (an arrested person) on bail: usually with *out.* **3** To deliver, as goods, to another's disposition or care without transference of ownership. — **to go** (or **stand**) **bail for** To provide bail for. ◆ Homophone: *bale.* [<OF, power, custody <*baillier* guard, control <L *bajulare* carry, manage]

bail⁴ (bāl) *n.* **1** The semicircular handle of a pail, kettle, etc. **2** An arch–shaped support, as for holding up the cloth of a canopy. —*v.t.* To provide with a bail or handle. ◆ Homophone: *bale.* [<ON *beygla* hook, ring]

bail·a·ble (bā′lə·bəl) *adj. Law* Admitting of, or entitled to, bail.

Bai·lan Pass (bī·län′) See BELEN PASS.

Baile Atha Cli·ath (bal ä klē′ə) The Gaelic name for DUBLIN: literally, the town of the ford of the hurdles.

bail·ee (bā′lē′) *n. Law* One to whom property is bailed.

bail·er¹ (bā′lər) *n.* One who bails.

bail·er² (bā′lər) *n.* In cricket, a ball that strikes the bails.

bai·ley (bā′lē) *n.* *pl.* **bai·leys 1** The outer court of a castle, or any court of a fortress. **2** A court of justice or a prison. Also **bai′lie.**

Bai·ley (bā′lē), **Liberty Hyde,** 1858–1955, U.S. horticulturist and writer. — **Nathan** or **Nathaniel,** died 1742, English lexicographer.

Bailey bridge A portable bridge consisting of a series of interchangeable prefabricated steel panels in the form of lattices, over which a prepared roadway can be laid. [after Donald Colman *Bailey,* born 1901, English engineer]

bai·lie (bā′lē) *n.* **1** *Scot.* A municipal officer corresponding to an alderman in England. **2** *Obs.* A bailiff. [<OF *bailli* bailiff]

Bail·lie (bā′lē), **Joanna,** 1762–1851, Scottish dramatist and poet.

bai·liff (bā′lif) *n.* **1** An officer of court having custody of prisoners under arraignment. **2** A sheriff's deputy for serving processes and warrants of arrest. **3** A custodian of property and its management for the owner; steward; overseer. **4** *Brit.* A subordinate magistrate with jurisdiction limited to a certain district or to certain functions, as to keeping the peace in the hundreds. **5** The first civil officer in each of the Channel Islands. [<OF *baillif* <L *bajalus* porter, manager]

bai·li·wick (bā′lə·wik) *n.* **1** The office, jurisdiction, or district of a bailiff. **2** One's own special place or province. [<BAILI(E) + OE *wic* village]

bail·ment (bāl′mənt) *n. Law* The act of bailing an accused person, goods, etc.

bail·or (bā′lər, bā·lôr′) *n. Law* One who delivers goods, etc., in bailment.

bails·man (bālz′mən) *n.* *pl.* **·men** (-mən) One who provides bail for another.

bail–up (bāl′up′) *n. Austral. Slang* **1** A demand for money or attention. **2** A hold–up by bushrangers.

Bai·ly's beads (bā′lēz) *Astron.* A series of luminous points appearing along the advancing edge of the moon's disk just before totality in a solar eclipse. [after Francis *Baily,* 1774–1844, English astronomer]

Bain (bān), **Alexander,** 1818–1903, Scottish psychologist.

bain·ie (bā′nē) *adj. Scot.* Bony.

bain–ma·rie (baṅ·mà·rē′) *n.* *pl.* **bains–ma·rie** (baṅ-) *French* A water bath, especially as used in the preparation of drugs and in cookery.

Bai·ram (bī·räm′) *n.* Either of two Moslem festivals, one of which, the **Lesser Bairam,** is in the beginning of the tenth month, at the end of Ramadan, and lasts from one to three days, while the other, the **Greater Bairam,** of four days, is seventy days later. [<Turkish]

Baird (bârd), **John Logie,** 1888–1946, Scottish inventor.

Baird Mountains (bârd) A range in NW Alaska.

Bai·reuth (bī·roit′) See BAYREUTH.

bairn (bârn) *n. Scot.* A young child; a son or a daughter.

Bairns·fa·ther (bârnz′fä′thər), **Bruce,** 1888–1959, English soldier and cartoonist.

bairn·team (bârn′tēm′) *n. Scot.* Children; progeny; offspring.

bait¹ (bāt) *n.* **1** Food or other enticement placed as a lure in a trap, on a hook, etc. **2** Any allurement or enticement. **3** A halt on a journey for food or refreshment. —*v.t.* **1** To put food or some other lure on or in: to *bait* a trap. **2** To torment, as by setting dogs upon, for sport: to *bait* a bear. **3** To harass; heckle. **4** To lure; entice. **5** *Obs.* To feed (a horse, etc.) while resting. —*v.i.* **6** *Obs.* To stop for rest and refreshment. ◆ Homophone: *bate.* [<ON *beita* cause to bite] — **bait′er**

bait² (bāt) *n. Dial.* **1** A quantity; an amount. **2** Enough. ◆ Homophone: *bate.*

bait³ (bāt) See BATE.³

baith (bāth) *adj., pron., & conj. Scot.* Both.

baize (bāz) *n.* **1** A plain, loosely woven cotton

or woolen fabric, usually dyed green and napped to imitate felt: used for table covers, etc. **2** An article made of this fabric. [<OF *baies,* fem. pl. of *bai* chestnut–brown <L *badius*]

Ba·ja Ca·li·for·nia (bä′hä kä′lē·fôr′nyä) The Spanish name for LOWER CALIFORNIA.

Baj·er (bī′ər), **Fredrik,** 1837–1922, Danish statesman and writer.

ba·ju (bä′jŏŏ) A short jacket worn by men and women in Malay countries. [<Malay]

bake (bāk) *v.* **baked, bak·ing** *v.t.* **1** To cook by dry and continuous heat, as food in an oven. **2** To harden or vitrify by heat, as bricks or pottery. **3** *Obs.* To cake; harden. —*v.i.* **4** To bake bread, pastry, meat, or other food. **5** To become baked or hardened by heat, as soil. —*n.* **1** A baking or the amount baked. **2** *U.S.* A social gathering at which certain foods are baked and served. **3** *Scot.* A cracker. [OE *bacan*]

bake·house (bāk′hous′) *n.* A bakery.

Ba·ke·lite (bā′kə·līt) *n.* Trade name of a group of thermosetting plastics formed by the chemical reaction of phenol, formaldehyde, and their derivatives, having a wide range of properties and uses. [after L. H. *Baekeland*]

bak·er (bā′kər) *n.* **1** One who bakes and sells bread, cake, etc. **2** A portable oven.

Ba·ker (bā′kər), **Ernest Albert,** born 1869, English librarian and author. — **George Pierce,** 1866–1935, U.S. educator and editor. — **Newton Diehl,** 1871–1937, U.S. lawyer; secretary of war 1916–21. — **Ray Stannard,** 1870–1946, U.S. author: pseudonym *David Grayson.* — **Sir Samuel White,** 1821–93, English explorer in Africa.

Baker, Mount A peak in the Cascade Range, northern Washington; 10,750 feet.

Baker Island A United States possession (1936) in the Pacific Ocean near the equator, used as a refueling point; one square mile.

bakers' dozen Thirteen: from a former custom of giving an excess to make sure of avoiding the heavy penalties exacted for short weight or measure.

bak·er·y (bā′kər·ē, bāk′rē) *n.* *pl.* **·er·ies 1** A place for baking bread, cake, etc. **2** A shop where bread, cake, pastry, etc., are sold at retail: also **bake′shop.**

Bakh·mut (bäkh′mŏŏt) The former name of ARTEMOVSK.

bak·ing (bā′king) *n.* **1** The act of baking. **2** The quantity baked.

baking powder A finely powdered mixture of baking soda and an acid salt, giving off carbon dioxide when moist: it is used as a substitute for yeast in baking.

baking soda Sodium bicarbonate.

bak·sheesh (bak′shēsh) *n.* In India, Turkey, Egypt, and other countries, a gratuity or tip. —*v.t.* & *v.i.* To give a tip (to). Also spelled *backsheesh, backshish.* [<Persian *bakhshīsh* <*bakhshīdan* give]

Bakst (bäkst), **Leon Nikolaievich,** 1866?–1924, Russian painter and scenic designer.

Ba·ku The capital of Azerbaijan, pop. 1,700,000; an oil exporting port on the Caspian Sea.

Ba·ku·nin (bä·kŏŏ′nyin), **Mikhail,** 1814–76, Russian anarchist writer.

BAL (bal, *or pronounced as initials*) Proprietary name for a brand of dimercaprol, originally developed in England as an antidote to lewisite. [<B(RITISH) A(NTI-) L(EWISITE)]

Ba·laam (bā′ləm) A prophet, reproached by the ass he rode for cursing the Israelites. *Num.* xxii–xxiv.

Ba·la·ki·rev (bä·lä′ki·ryif), **Mili,** 1837–1910, Russian composer.

Bal·a·kla·va (bal′ə·klä′və) A Crimean port on the Black Sea, near which the Charge of the Light Brigade took place (1854).

bal·a·lai·ka (bal′ə·lī′kə) *n.* A Russian musical instrument having a triangular body, a guitar neck, and three strings. [<Russian]

BALALAIKA

bal·ance (bal′əns) *n.* **1** An instrument for weighing, often a bar pivoted on a central point according to the weight placed in or hung from a matched scale or pan at either end; scales: often used in the plural, either scale being called a *balance,* and the two a *pair of balances.* **2** The imaginary scales of destiny by which deeds and principles are weighed: a symbol of justice: Thou hast been weighed in the *balance* and found wanting. **3** The power to decide fate, value, etc., as by a balance. **4** A state of being in equilibrium; equipoise; equality. **5** Mental or emotional stability; sanity. **6** Harmonious proportion, as in the design or arrangement of parts in a work of art. **7** Something used to produce an equilibrium; counteracting influence; counterpoise. **8** The act of balancing or weighing. **9** Equality between the credit and debit totals of an account. **10** A difference between such totals; the excess on either side. **11** *U.S. Colloq.* Whatever is left over; remainder; surplus. **12** A balance wheel. **13** An instrument for measuring electricity or its effects by opposing some other force, as gravity. **14** A movement in dancing. See synonyms under REMAINDER. **—in the balance** Being judged; not yet settled. **—to strike a balance** To find or take an intermediate position; compromise. *—v.* **·anced, ·anc·ing** *v.t.* **1** To bring into or keep in equilibrium; poise. **2** To weigh in a balance. **3** To compare or weigh in the mind, as alternative courses of action; estimate the importance or consequence of. **4** To offset or counteract. **5** To keep or be in proportion to. **6** To be equal to. **7** To compute the difference between the debit and credit sides of (an account). **8** To reconcile, as by making certain entries, the debit and credit sides of (an account). **9** To adjust (an account) by paying what is owed. *—v.i.* **10** To be or come into equilibrium. **11** To be equal: The accounts *balance.* **12** To hesitate or waver; tilt: to *balance* on the edge of a chasm. **13** To move or lean back and forth as from one foot to another. [<F <L *bilanx, -ancis* having two plates <*bis* two + *lanx, lancis* dish, plate] **—bal′ance·a·ble** *adj.*

Bal·ance (bal′əns) The constellation Libra. See CONSTELLATION.

balanced load *Electr.* A distribution of power, current, and voltage over a polyphase circuit such that each phase of the circuit is balanced with respect to the others.

balanced surface *Aeron.* A control surface, as an aileron or rudder, part of which is forward of its pivot.

balance of payments The difference in payments made and received between a country and other countries, including costs of exports and imports of goods and services and the exchange of gold and capital.

balance of power A distribution of forces among nations such that no single nation or combination of nations will dominate or endanger any other.

balance of trade The difference in value between exports and imports of a country.

bal·anc·er (bal′ən·sər) *n.* **1** One who or that which balances. **2** A tightrope dancer; an acrobat. **3** *Entomol.* One of the paired halteres on each side of the thorax of certain dipterous insects. **4** An apparatus used to increase the precision of a radio direction finder.

balance-reef (bal′əns·rēf′) *Naut. v.t.* To reduce (a fore-and-aft sail) to the last reef. *—n.* A reef band diagonally across a fore-and-aft sail: the last reef on such a sail.

balance sheet A statement in tabular form to show assets and liabilities, profit and loss, etc., of a business at a specified date.

balance wheel The oscillating wheel of a watch or chronometer, which determines its rate of motion.

ba·lan·dran (bə·lan′drən) *n.* A wide wrap worn in the Middle Ages. Also **ba·lan·dra·na** (bə·lan′drə·nə). [<OF <Med. L *balandrana*]

Ba·lan·ga (bä·läng′gä) A town in southern Luzon, capital of Bataan province.

bal·as (bal′əs) *n.* A spinel having a rosy to yellowish color, used as a gemstone. [<OF *balais* <Arabic *balakhsh* <Persian *Badakhshan,* district where the gem is found]

bal·a·ta (bal′ə·tə) *n.* **1** The juice of the bullytree, used industrially as an elastic gum. **2** The tree. [<Sp. <Tupian]

Ba·la·ton (bä′lä·tōn), **Lake** A lake in western Hungary; 231 square miles: German *Plattensee.*

ba·laus·tine (bə·lôs′tin) *n.* The pomegranate, or its dried astringent flowers, bark, or rind. [<L *balaustium* pomegranate flower <Gk. *balaustion*]

Bal·bo (bäl′bō), **Italo,** 1896–1940, Italian general and aviator.

bal·bo·a (bal·bō′ə) *n.* A silver monetary unit of Panama, equivalent to about one U.S. dollar. [after Vasco de *Balboa*]

Bal·bo·a (bal·bō′ə) The port at the Pacific terminus of the Panama Canal, in Canal Zone.

Bal·bo·a (bal·bō′ə, *Sp.* bäl·vō′ä), **Vasco Nuñez de,** 1475?–1517, Spanish explorer; discovered the Pacific Ocean 1513.

Balboa Heights Administrative headquarters of Canal Zone.

bal·brig·gan (bal·brig′ən) *n.* **1** A fine, unbleached, knitted cotton hosiery fabric first made at Balbriggan, Eire. **2** A lightweight cotton fabric made in imitation of this. **3** *pl.* Clothes, especially underwear and hose, made of balbriggan. *—adj.* Made of balbriggan.

Bal·brig·gan (bal·brig′ən) A town on the Irish Sea 20 miles north of Dublin.

bal·bu·ti·es (bal·byōō′shi·ēz) *n.* A speech defect characterized by stuttering; stammering. [<NL <L *balbutire* stammer]

Balch (bôlch), **Emily Greene,** 1867–1961, U.S. economist and sociologist.

bal·co·ny (bal′kə·nē) *n. pl.* **·nies 1** A balustraded platform projecting from a wall of a building, usually before a window. **2** A projecting gallery inside a theater or other public building. [<Ital. *balcone* <*balco* a beam <OHG *balcho*] **—bal′co·nied** *adj.*

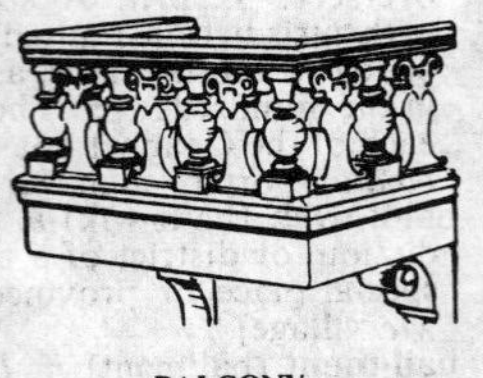

BALCONY WITH BALUSTRADE

bald (bôld) *adj.* **1** Without hair on the head. **2** Without natural covering or growth, as a mountain. **3** Unadorned; without embellishments. **4** Without disguise. **5** *Zool.* Having white feathers or fur on the head: the *bald* eagle. [? <Welsh *bāl* white] **—bald′ly** *adv.* **—bald′ness** *n.*

bal·da·chin (bal′də·kin, bôl′-) *n.* **1** A heavy, rich fabric, formerly made of silk and gold: also *baudekin.* **2** A canopy of such fabric, as one carried in religious processions. **3** *Archit.* A canopy of stone or metal, as over an altar or throne. Also **bal′da·quin.** [<F *baldaquin* <Ital. *baldacchino* <*Baldacco* Baghdad, where the cloth was first made]

bald cypress A timber tree (genus *Taxodium*) of the swampy regions of the southern United States, especially *T. distichum* and *T. ascendens.*

bald eagle A species of dark brown eagle (*Heliaeetus leucocephalus*), the adults having white head and tail feathers, formerly found throughout North America but in danger of extinction. Also called *American eagle.*

Bal·der (bôl′dər) In Norse mythology, god of sunlight, spring, and joy; son of Odin and Frigga. He was killed by the treachery of Loki. Also **Bal′dr.**

bal·der·dash (bôl′dər·dash) *n.* A meaningless flow of words; nonsense. [Origin uncertain]

bald-face (bôld′fās′) *n.* **1** The widgeon. **2** A horse having a white face.

bald-faced (bôld′fāst′) *adj.* **1** Having a white face or white markings on the face: said of animals. **2** Brash; undisguised: *bald-faced* lie.

bald·head (bôld′hed′) *n.* **1** One whose head is bald. **2** A breed of pigeons. **3** The widgeon. **4** The bald eagle.

bald-head·ed (bôld′hed′id) *adj.* Having a bald head. *—adv. U.S. Colloq.* Roughly, precipitately: to go at something *bald-headed.*

bald·ing (bôl′ding) *adj. U.S. Colloq.* Beginning to grow bald.

bald·pate (bôld′pāt′) *n.* A bald-headed person. **2** The widgeon. **—bald′-pat′ed** *adj.*

bal·dric (bôl′drik) *n.* A belt worn over one shoulder and across the breast, to support a sword, bugle, etc.: also spelled *bawdric.* Also **bal′drick.** [? <OF *baudrei*]

bald rush An American sedge (genus *Psilocarya*).

Bald·win (bôld′win) *n.* A red variety of winter apple.

Bald·win (bôld′win) A masculine personal name. Also *Dan., Ger.* **Bal·du·in** (bäl′dōō·ən); *Ital.* **Bal·do·vi·no** (bäl′dō·vē′nō); *Lat.* **Bal·du·i·nus** (bal′dōō·ī′nəs). [<Gmc., bold friend] **—Baldwin,** 1058–1118, king of Jerusalem 1100; fought in first crusade.

Bald·win (bôld′win), **James Mark,** 1861–1934, U.S. psychologist. **—Stanley,** 1867–1947, Earl Baldwin of Bewdly, prime minister of Great Britain, 1923–24, 1924–29, 1935–37.

Bald·y (bôl′dē) **1** Old Baldy. **2** A peak in northern New Mexico; 12,623 feet.

bale[1] (bāl) *n.* A large package of bulky goods corded or otherwise prepared for transportation. *—v.t.* **baled, bal·ing** To make into a bale or bales. ◆ Homophone: *bail.* [<OF *bale* round package, ? <OHG *balla* ball]

bale[2] (bāl) *n. Archaic* **1** That which causes ruin or sorrow; evil. **2** Pain; woe. ◆ Homophone: *bail.* [OE *bealu* evil, wickedness]

bale[3] (bāl) *n.* A balefire. ◆ Homophone: *bail.* [OE *bæl* fire, funeral pile]

Bâle (bäl) French name for BASEL.

Bal·e·ar·ic Islands (bal′ē·ar′ik, bə·lir′ik) A Spanish province in the western Mediterranean, comprising a group of four islands (Mallorca, Menorca, Iviza, and Formentera) and 11 islets; 1,936 square miles; capital, Palma, on Mallorca. *Spanish* **Is·las Ba·le·a·res** (ēz′läz vä·lā·ä′rās).

ba·leen (bə·lēn′) *n.* Whalebone. [<F *baleine* <L *balæna* <Gk. *phalaina* whale]

baleen knife A curved double-handled knife for splitting whalebone.

bale·fire (bāl′fīr′) *n.* **1** A signal fire; beacon. **2** A funeral pyre. **3** Any great outdoor fire. [OE *bælfyr* <*bæl* bale[3] + *fyr* fire]

bale·ful (bāl′fəl) *adj.* **1** Hurtful; malignant. **2** *Archaic* Sorrowful; miserable. See synonyms under BAD. **—bale′ful·ly** *adv.* **—bale′ful·ness** *n.*

bale hook A box hook.

bal·er (bā′lər) *n.* **1** One who or that which bales. **2** A baling machine.

Bal·four (bal′fŏŏr), **Arthur James,** 1848–1930, first Earl of Balfour, prime minister of Great Britain 1902–05.

Balfour Declaration A declaration issued by the British Government, November, 1917, favoring reestablishment of a Jewish "National Home" in Palestine.

Ba·li (bä′lē) One of the Lesser Sunda Islands, east of Java; 2,095 square miles; capital, Singaradja.

Ba·lik·pa·pan (bä′lik·pä′pän) A port and oil center on the eastern coast of the Indonesian part of Borneo.

Ba·li·nese (bä′lə·nēz′, -nēs′) *adj.* Of or pertaining to Bali, its people, or their language. *—n. pl.* **Ba·li·nese 1** A native or inhabitant of Bali. **2** The Indonesian language of Bali.

Ba·lin·tang Channel (bä′lēn·täng′) The central part of Luzon Strait, between the Batan and Babuyan Islands of north Luzon.

Bal·iol (bāl′yəl), **John de,** 1248–1315, king of Scotland. **—Edward,** died 1363, son of John; king of Scotland. Also spelled *Balliol.*

bal·i·saur (bal′ə·sôr) *n.* A long-tailed badger (*Arctonyx collaris*) of India and Siam. [<Hind. *bālusūr* <*bālu* sand + *sūr* hog]

Ba·lize (bə·lēz′) See BELIZE.

balk (bôk) *v.t.* **1** To render unsuccessful; thwart; frustrate. **2** *Obs.* To heap up in ridges or balks; also, to make a balk in (land). *—v.i.* **3** To stop short and refuse to proceed or take action. *—n.* **1** That which balks or hinders; an obstacle; hindrance. **2** An error; miss; blunder. **3** A feint or false motion, as a movement of the pitcher in baseball as if to pitch the ball, or the failure of a jumper to leap after taking his run. **4** A ridge left unplowed between furrows or between plowed strips of land. **5** A squared beam or timber. **6** The space between the balk line and the cushion of a billiard table. **7** One of the stringers or joist-shaped spars placed from boat to boat, upon which the chess or flooring of a pontoon bridge is placed. Also spelled *baulk.* See synonyms under ERROR. [OE *balca* bank, ridge]

Bal·kan (bôl′kən) *adj.* **1** Of or pertaining to the Balkan Peninsula, to the people of this region, their customs, etc. **2** Of or pertaining to the Balkan Mountains.

Balkan frame *Med.* A frame supported on four posts, with pulleys and slats for holding

up the legs in the treatment of fractures. [First used in the *Balkan* States]

bal·kan·ize (bôl′kən·īz) *v.t.* **·ized, ·iz·ing** To separate (a country) into small, dissenting political units or states, as the Balkans after World War I. Also **Bal′kan·ize.** — **bal′kan·i·za′tion** *n.*

Balkan Mountains A mountain range in Bulgaria, extending 350 miles westward from the Black Sea to the Yugoslav border; highest point, 7,793 feet.

Balkan Peninsula A peninsula of SE Europe lying south of the lower Danube and bounded by the Black, Aegean, Mediterranean, Ionian, and Adriatic Seas.

Balkan States The countries occupying the Balkan Peninsula: Albania, Bulgaria, Greece, Rumania, Yugoslavia, and the western part of Turkey. Also **the Balkans.**

Balkan Wars See table under WAR.

Balkh (bälkh) A town in northern Afghanistan, capital of ancient Bactria: ancient *Bactra.*

Bal·khash (bäl·käsh′) A salt lake in SE Kazakh S.S.R., 100 miles west of the Chinese border; 6,680 square miles.

Bal·kis (bal′kis) The Arabic name, used in the Koran, for the QUEEN OF SHEBA.

balk line (bôk) **1** In billiards, a line partitioning off a space in the corner, along the sides, or around the entire edge of the table. **2** In sports, especially track events, a line, progress beyond which counts as a trial.

balk·y (bô′kē) *adj.* **balk·i·er, balk·i·est** Disposed to stop suddenly or refuse to go: also spelled *baulky.* See synonyms under RESTIVE.

ball¹ (bôl) *n.* **1** A spherical or nearly spherical body. **2** Such a body, of any size and made of various substances, used in a number of games. **3** Any of several such games, especially baseball. **4** The mode of throwing or pitching a ball: a foul *ball,* a high or swift *ball.* **5** In baseball, a delivery by the pitcher in which the ball fails to pass over the home plate between the batsman's shoulder and knees and is not struck at by him: distinguished from *strike.* **6 Mil. a** Any spherical or conoid projectile, larger than a small shot. **b** Such projectiles collectively: to load with *ball.* **7** A roundish protuberance or part of something, especially of the human body or of some organ. **8** A planet or star, especially the earth. — **to be on the ball** *Slang* To be competent or efficient. — **to have something on the ball** *Slang* To have ability. — **to play ball 1** To begin or resume playing a ball game or some other activity. **2** *Colloq.* To cooperate. — *v.t. & v.i.* To form, gather, or wind into a ball: to *ball* worsted. — **to ball up** *Slang* To embarrass; confuse or become confused. ◆ Homophone: *bawl.* [<ON *böllr*]

ball² (bôl) *n.* A formal social assembly for dancing. ◆ Homophone: *bawl.* [<F *bal* a dance <*baler* < LL *ballare* dance]

Ball (bôl), **John,** died 1381, English priest; a leader of Wat Tyler's peasants' revolt.

bal·lad (bal′əd) *n.* **1** A narrative poem or song of popular origin in short stanzas, often with a refrain: originally handed down orally, often with changes and additions. **2** A sentimental song of several stanzas, in which the melody is usually repeated for each stanza. [<OF *balade* dancing song]

bal·lade (bə·läd′, ba-) *n.* A verse form consisting of three stanzas of eight or ten lines each and an envoy of four or five lines: the last line of each stanza and of the envoy is the same. **2** A musical composition, usually of romantic or dramatic nature, usually for piano or orchestra. [<OF *balade* dancing song]

bal·lad·eer (bal′ə·dir′) *n.* A ballad singer.

bal·lad·mon·ger (bal′əd·mung′gər, -mong′-) *n.* **1** A seller of popular ballads. **2** A poetaster.

bal·la·drom·ic (bal′ə·drom′ik) *adj.* Pursuing a course heading for the target: said of rockets and guided missiles. [<Gk. *ballein* hurl (a missile) + *dromos* course]

bal·lad·ry (bal′əd·rē) *n.* **1** Ballad poetry. **2** The art of making or singing ballads.

ballad stanza A four-line stanza used in ballads, generally riming the second and fourth lines.

ball and chain 1 A heavy metal ball fastened by a chain to a prisoner to keep him from escaping. **2** *Slang* One's wife or husband.

ball-and-sock·et joint (bôl′ən-sok′it) *Mech.* A joint composed of a sphere working in a bearing permitting a degree of free turning in any direction.

bal·lant (bal′ənt) *n. Scot.* A ballad.

Bal·lan·tyne (bal′ən·tīn), **James,** 1772–1833, Scottish printer.

Bal·la·rat (bal′ə·rat′) A city of central Victoria, Australia. Also **Bal·la·a·rat** (bal′ə·ə·rat′).

bal·last (bal′əst) *n.* **1** Any heavy substance, as sand, stone, etc., laid in the hold of a vessel or in the car of a balloon to steady it. **2** Gravel or broken stone laid down as a stabilizer for a railroad bed. **3** That which gives stability to character, morality, etc. — *v.t.* **1** To provide or fill with ballast. **2** To steady with or as if with ballast; stabilize. **3** *Obs.* To weigh down. [<ODan. *barlast* < *bar* bare, mere + *last* load]

ball bearing *Mech.* **1** A bearing in which the shaft at its points of support rests upon or is surrounded by small metal balls that turn freely as the shaft revolves: used to reduce friction. **2** Any of the metal balls in such a bearing.

ball cartridge *Mil.* Live ammunition as distinguished from blank ammunition.

ball cock *Mech.* A stopcock for regulating the supply of water, in which the valve is opened or shut by the rising or falling of a hollow floating ball.

BALL COCK

bal·le·ri·na (bal′ə·rē′nə) *n.* A female ballet dancer. [<Ital., fem. of *ballerino* dancer]

bal·let (bal′ā, ba·lā′) *n.* **1** An elaborate kind of dramatic group dance using conventionalized movements, often for narrative effects. **2** This style of dancing. **3** Dancers of ballet, especially a company of such dancers. **4** A danced interlude, as in an opera. **5** A musical composition written as an accompaniment to a ballet performance. [<F, dim. of *bal* a dance. See BALL².]

bal·let·o·mane (ba·let′ə·mān) *n.* A ballet enthusiast. [<F *ballet* + *-(o)mane* <Gk. *mania* enthusiasm.]

ball-flow·er (bôl′flou′ər) *n. Archit.* A ball-like ornament resembling a ball placed in a flower of which the petals form a globe around it.

ball-gov·er·nor (bôl′guv′ər·nər) *n.* Governor (def. 2).

bal·li·bun·tl (bal′i·bun′təl) *n.* **1** A lightweight, glossy straw, woven of buntal. **2** A hat made of this straw. [<*Baliuag* in the Philippine Islands + BUNTAL]

bal·lis·ta (bə·lis′tə) *n. pl.* **·tae** (-tē) An engine used in ancient and medieval warfare for

ROMAN BALLISTA

hurling missiles. [<L <Gk. *ballein* throw]

bal·lis·tic (bə·lis′tik) *adj.* Pertaining to projectiles or to ballistics.

ballistic coefficient A number which expresses the power of a projectile to maintain its velocity during flight.

ballistic curve The actual path of a projectile, as affected by wind, etc.

ballistic density A constant air density assumed to have the same effect upon a projectile in flight as the actual varying densities.

bal·lis·tics (bə·lis′tiks) *n.* The science that deals with the motion of projectiles, either while they are still in the bore (**interior ballistics**) or after they leave the muzzle (**ex-**

terior ballistics). — **bal·lis·ti·cian** (bal′ə·stish′ən) *n.*

ballistic table A table showing the character and values of the factors affecting the flight of a projectile, as range, angle of fire, muzzle velocity, time of flight, etc.

ballistic wave The compression of air immediately in front of a projectile in flight, regarded as a wave formation.

bal·lis·tite (bal′is·tīt) *n.* A nearly smokeless gunpowder invented by Alfred Nobel in 1888.

bal·lo·net (bal′ə·net′) *n.* **1** A small balloon. **2** An airtight bag set in the interior of a spherical or nonrigid dirigible balloon to maintain pressure on the outer envelope. [<F *ballonnet,* dim. of *ballon* balloon]

bal·loon (bə·lōōn′) *n.* **1** A large, airtight bag, inflated with gas lighter than air, designed to rise and float in the atmosphere: larger kinds have a car or basket attached, for carrying passengers, instruments, etc. Compare DIRIGIBLE, BLIMP. **2** A small inflatable rubber bag, used as a toy. **3** *Chem.* A spherical glass vessel. **4** A balloon-shaped outline connected with the mouth of a person, containing the words he is represented as speaking, as in comic strips. — **captive balloon** A balloon restrained from free flight by means of a cable that holds it to the ground. — **kite balloon** An elongated form of captive balloon, fitted with a tail appendage to keep it headed into the wind. — **observation balloon** A captive balloon used as an observation post. — **sounding balloon** A balloon sent up unmanned for obtaining meteorological data recorded on instruments which return to earth after the bursting of the balloon. Compare RADIOSONDE. — *v.i.* **1** To increase quickly in scope or magnitude; expand: The rumor *ballooned* into a scandal. **2** To swell out like a balloon, as a sail. **3** To travel or ascend in a balloon. — *v.t.* **4** To inflate or swell with air: A gust of wind *ballooned* the sail. [<Ital. *ballone* large ball < *balla* ball, sphere <Gmc.] — **bal·loon′ist** *n.*

balloon cloth A closely woven cotton fabric vulcanized with thin sheets of rubber so as to be airtight: used for balloons and dirigibles.

balloon foresail *Naut.* A light foresail set between the foretopmasthead and the jib-boom end, used mostly by yachts in light winds. Also **balloon jib.**

balloon sail A spinnaker or a balloon foresail.

balloon tire A pneumatic tire filled with air at low pressure for reducing the shock of bumps.

bal·loon-vine (bə·lōōn′vīn′) *n.* A tropical American climbing herb (*Cardiospermum halicacabum*), bearing inflated membranaceous three-celled pods; heartseed.

bal·lot (bal′ət) *n.* **1** A written or printed slip or ticket used in voting. **2** A little ball used in voting: the original sense. **3** The act or system of voting secretly by ballots or by voting machines. **4** The whole number of votes cast in an election. — **Australian ballot** A ballot bearing the names of all the candidates of all parties, so arranged as to insure absolute secrecy and liberty in polling votes. — *v.* **bal·lot·ed, bal·lot·ing** *v.i.* **1** To cast a ballot; vote or decide by ballot. **2** To draw lots or determine by lot: to *ballot* for position. — *v.t.* **3** To vote for or decide on by means of a ballot: to *ballot* a question. [<Ital. *ballotta,* dim. of *balla* ball. See BALLOON.]

bal·lotte·ment (bə·lot′mənt) *n. Med.* Impulse given to a body loosely suspended in a sac or cavity by which it rises on impact and returns again; sometimes applied in the diagnosis of pregnancy, floating kidney, etc. [<F *ballotter* toss < *ballotte* small ball]

ball-peen (bôl′pēn′) *n.* A hemispherical peen on a hammerhead, used especially for riveting. See illustration under HAMMER.

ball-play·er (bôl′plā′ər) *n. U.S.* A baseball player.

ball point pen A fountain pen having for a point a ball bearing that rolls against an ink cartridge and deposits a line on the writing surface.

ball·room (bôl′rōōm′, -rŏŏm′) *n.* A large room for dancing, especially one with a polished floor. [<BALL²]

ballroom dancing A kind of social dancing in which two people dance as partners.
ball turret *Aeron.* A ball-shaped projection on the bottom part of certain bombers, power-driven and containing machine-guns which can swing in any direction.
ball valve 1 A ball-shaped valve. 2 A valve controlled by a floating ball.
bal·ly (bal'ē) *adj. & adv. Brit. Slang* A euphemism for BLOODY.
bal·ly·hack (bal'ē-hak) *n. Slang* A smash; wreck. Also **bal'ly·wack** (-wak).
bal·ly·hoo (bal'ē·hōō) *n. Colloq.* 1 Noisy patter: the *ballyhoo* of a side-show announcer. 2 Any immoderate, unrestrained advertising. 3 Conspicuous noisiness of speech, manner, or habit. — *v.t. & v.i.* **·hooed, ·hoo·ing** To advocate or promote by means of ballyhoo. [Origin unknown]
balm (bäm) *n.* 1 An aromatic, resinous exudation from various trees or shrubs, used as medicine; balsam. 2 Any oily, fragrant, resinous substance. 3 Any tree or shrub yielding such a substance; especially, any tree of the genus *Commiphora.* 4 Any of various aromatic plants of the genus *Melissa,* especially *M. officinalis.* 5 Any pleasing fragrance. 6 Anything that soothes or heals. [<OF *basme* <L *balsamum* <Gk. *balsamon* ? <Semitic. Doublet of BALSAM.]
bal·ma·caan (bal'mə·kän') *n.* A loose overcoat with raglan sleeves, made of rough woolen cloth. [from *Balmacaan,* estate in Scotland]
balm of Gilead 1 Any of several Oriental trees of the myrrh family (genus *Commiphora).* 2 The fragrant balsam obtained from them. 3 The balsam fir, or the balm obtained from it. 4 A European shade tree (*Populus candicans).*
Bal·mor·al (bal·môr'əl, -mor'-) *n.* 1 A striped heavy woolen stuff. 2 A petticoat made of such material. 3 A brimless Scottish cap. 4 A laced walking shoe: also **bal·mor'al.** [from *Balmoral* Castle]
Balmoral Castle Royal residence in SW Aberdeenshire, Scotland: built by Queen Victoria in 1854.
Bal·mung (bäl'mŏŏng) In the *Nibelungenlied,* the sword which Siegfried took from the Nibelungs.
balm·y (bä'mē) *adj.* **balm·i·er, balm·i·est** 1 Having the qualities of balm; aromatic. 2 Healing; soothing; mild. 3 *Brit. Slang* Slightly crazy; overly foolish. — **balm'i·ly** *adv.* — **balm'i·ness** *n.*
bal·ne·al (bal'nē·əl) *adj.* Of or pertaining to baths and bathing. [<L *balneum* bath]
bal·ne·ol·o·gy (bal'nē·ol'ə·jē) *n.* The science of treating disease by baths and the waters of mineral springs. [<L *balneum* bath + -LOGY]
ba·lo·ney (bə·lō'nē) *n.* 1 *Slang* Stuff and nonsense; bunkum. 2 *Colloq.* Bologna sausage. Also spelled *boloney, bolony.* [def. 1 <BOLOGNA SAUSAGE]
Bal·or (bal'ôr) In Celtic mythology, a giant king of the Fomorians whose single eye killed whatever it looked at; blinded and slain by his grandson, Lug.
bal·sa (bôl'sə, bäl'-) *n.* 1 A tree (*Ochroma pyramidale*) of tropical America and the West Indies. 2 The very light wood from this tree: called *corkwood.* 3 A raft originally made of light logs fastened together by a platform. 4 A catamaran. [<Sp. *balza*]
bal·sam (bôl'səm) *n.* 1 Any of a group of fragrant oleoresins obtained chiefly from the exudations of various trees. 2 Any such tree. 3 Any fragrant ointment; balm. 4 An aromatic resin containing cinnamic and benzoic acid, or the tree that yields it. 5 A flowering plant of the genus *Impatiens,* especially the common garden annual *I. balsamina.* 6 Any soothing or healing agent or circumstance. 7 The balsam fir. — *v.t.* To anoint with balsam; salve. [<L *balsamum* <Gk. *balsamon* <Semitic. Doublet of BALM.] — **bal·sa·ma·ceous** (bôl'sə·mā'shəs) *adj.*
balsam fir A tree (*Abies balsamea*) of the pine family, growing in the northern United States and Canada and yielding the Canada balsam: also called *balm of Gilead.*
bal·sam·ic (bôl·sam'ik, bal-) *adj.* 1 Of, like, or containing balsam. 2 Soothing; balmy.
bal·sam·if·er·ous (bôl'sə·mif'ər·əs, bal'-) *adj.* Yielding balsam or balm.

bal·sa·mi·na·ceous (bôl'sə·mə·nā'shəs, bal'-) *adj.* Belonging to a family of plants (*Balsaminaceae*) composed of the genera *Impatiens* and *Hydrocera.*
balsam of Peru A balsam from a tropical American tree (*Myroxylon pereirae),* used as a perfume in medicine: also called *Peru balsam.*
balsam of To·lu (tə·lōō') An oleoresinous medicinal preparation obtained from a South American evergreen (*Myroxylon balsamum*), containing the volatile oil toluene: used as a basis for many cough mixtures.
balsam poplar The tacamahac (def. 2).
Bal·sas (bäl'säs), **Río de las** A large, unnavigable river in south central Mexico, flowing 450 miles SW to the Pacific.
Balt (bôlt) *n.* A native or inhabitant of the Baltic States.
Bal·tha·sar (bal·thä'zər, -thaz'ər) 1 One of the three Magi. Also **Bal·tha'zar.** 2 The alias of Portia in Shakespeare's *Merchant of Venice.*
Bal·tic (bôl'tik) *adj.* Of or pertaining to the Baltic Sea or the Baltic States. — *n.* A branch of the Balto-Slavic languages, including Lithuanian, Lettish (or Latvian), and Old Prussian (extinct).
Baltic Sea An inlet of the Atlantic enclosed by Sweden, Denmark, East Germany, West Germany, Poland, the U.S.S.R., and Finland; 163,000 square miles.

BALTIC SEA REGION

Baltic States A collective name for Lithuania, Latvia, and Estonia, formed in 1918 as independent republics from Russian provinces and governments; annexed in 1940 by the U.S.S.R.
Bal·ti·more (bôl'tə·môr, -mōr) A port in northern Maryland at the upper end of Chesapeake Bay.
Baltimore, Lord See CALVERT, GEORGE.
Baltimore oriole An American oriole (*Icterus galbula):* so named because the orange and black of the male were the colors of the coat of arms of Lord Baltimore.
Bal·to-Sla·vic (bôl'tō·slä'vik, -slav'ik) *n.* A subfamily of Indo-European languages, consisting of Baltic and Slavic branches.
Ba·lu·chi (bə·lōō'chē) *n.* The Indo-Iranian language of Baluchistan.
Ba·lu·chi·stan (bə·lōō'chə·stän', bə·lōō'chə·stan) A mountainous region of west Pakistan; 134,139 square miles: divided into Baluchistan proper, a province of Pakistan; 52,900 square miles; capital, Quetta; four princely states; and a small area on the SW coast belonging to Oman.
bal·us·ter (bal'əs·tər) *n.* 1 One of a set of small pillars that support a hand rail and form with the hand rail a balustrade. 2 One of the small columns forming a chair back. [<F *balustre* <Ital. *balaustro* baluster <*balaustra* pomegranate flower; so called from the resemblance in form]
bal·us·trade (bal'ə·strād') *n.* A hand rail supported by balusters. See illustration under BALCONY.
Bal·zac (bal'zak, bôl'-; *Fr.* bál·zák'), **Honoré de,** 1799–1850, French novelist and dramatist.
bam (bam) *Slang v.t.* To cheat; bamboozle. — *n.* A cheat, imposition, or deception.
Ba·ma·ko (bä·mä·kō') A city in west Africa; capital of Mali.
bam·bang (bäm'bäng) *n.* A Javanese musical instrument, similar to the xylophone. [<Malay]
Bam·berg (bäm'berkh) A city in northern Bavaria, Germany.
bam·bi·no (bam·bē'nō) *n. pl.* **·ni** (-nē) 1 A

little child; a baby. 2 A figure of the child Jesus. [<Ital., dim. of *bambo* simple, childish]
bam·boo (bam·bōō') *n.* 1 A tall, treelike or shrubby grass of tropical and semi-tropical regions (genus *Bambusa* or related genera). 2 The tough, hollow, jointed stem of this plant, widely used for building, furniture, utensils, etc. [<Malay *bambu*]
bam·boo·zle (bam·bōō'zəl) *v.* **·zled, ·zling** *v.t.* 1 To impose upon; mislead; cheat. 2 To perplex. — *v.i.* 3 To practice trickery or deception. [Origin unknown] — **bam·boo'zle·ment** *n.* — **bam·boo'zler** *n.*
bam·bou·la (bam·bōō'lə) *n.* 1 A primitive drum made of bamboo. 2 A dance performed by Negroes of Louisiana to the beating of this drum. [<Creole]
bam·bu·co (bam·bōō'kō) *n.* A South American dance originating with the Indians of Colombia, and introduced into the United States in the mid-twentieth century. [<Sp. <native name]
ban[1] (ban) *v.t.* 1 To forbid; to proscribe or prohibit. 2 To place under an ecclesiastical ban; excommunicate; anathematize; interdict. 3 *Archaic* To curse; execrate. — *n.* 1 An official proclamation or edict, especially one of prohibition. 2 *pl.* An announcement of intention to marry: often spelled *banns.* 3 Informal disapproval or prohibition, as by public opinion. 4 An ecclesiastical edict of excommunication or interdiction. 5 A sentence of outlawry or banishment. 6 The summoning of vassals to arms by a feudal lord; also, the forces so collected. 7 *Archaic* A curse or denunciation. [*v.* <OHG *bannan* curse, prohibit and Med. L *bannum* proclamation; *n.* <*v.* and OF *ban* <Med. L *bannum* <Gmc.]
ban[2] (ban) *v.t. Obs.* To summon; call forth; call for. [OE *bannan* proclaim]
ban[3] (ban) *n.* A fine muslin made in the East Indies, from the fiber of the banana leafstalk. [<BANANA]
ban[4] (ban) *n. Archaic* 1 The title of the ruler of the southern marches of Hungary. 2 The governor of Croatia and Slavonia. [<Serbo-Croatian *bān* lord, ruler]
ban[5] (bän) *n. pl.* **ba·ni** (bä'nē) A Rumanian copper coin, worth 1/100 of a leu.
ba·nal (bä'nəl, bə·nal', ban'əl) *adj.* Meaningless from overuse; commonplace; trivial. [<F <OF *ban* feudal summons (to service performed communally for a lord); hence ordinary, common] — **ba·nal·i·ty** (bə·nal'ə·tē) *n.* — **ba'nal·ly** *adv.*
ba·nan·a (bə·nan'ə) *n.* A large, herbaceous plant (*Musa paradisiaca sapientium*) growing 10 to 20 feet high, cultivated in tropical climates for its edible pulpy fruit which grows in long pendent clusters. 2 The fruit of this plant. [<Sp. <native African name]
banana oil 1 Iso-amyl acetate, $C_7H_{14}O_2$, a sweet-smelling, colorless, liquid ester widely used as a solvent and in artificial fruit flavors, cosmetics, etc.: also called *pear oil.* 2 *U.S. Slang* Fulsome flattery; cajolery.

BANANA PLANT
(From 10 to 20 feet high)

Ba·na·ras (bə·nä'rəs) A sacred city of the Hindus, on the Ganges River in SE Uttar Pradesh, India: formerly *Benares.*
Ba·nat (bä·nät') A region of SE Hungary formerly governed by a ban; divided (1920) into the **Rumanian Banat;** 6,975 square miles; the **Yugoslav Banat,** a small region of northern Serbia; and the **Hungarian Banat,** a small region near Szeged.
ba·nau·sic (bə·nô'sik) *adj. Rare* Suitable for a mechanic. [<Gk. *banausikos* mechanical <*banausos* artisan, mechanic]
Ban·bur·y (ban'ber·ē, bam'bər·ē) A municipal borough in northern Oxfordshire, England, famous for its cakes.
ban·ca (bäng'kä) *n.* In the Philippines, a form of dug-out canoe. [<Sp. <Tagalog *bangca*]
Ban·ca (bäng'kä) See BANGKA.

Ban·croft (ban′krôft, -kroft), **George,** 1800–1891, U.S. historian.

band[1] (band) *n.* **1** A flat flexible strip of any material used for binding. **2** Any strip of fabric used to finish, strengthen, or trim an article of dress. **3** *pl.* A pair of linen strips hanging from the front of the neck, worn with certain clerical or academical garments: also called **Geneva bands. 4** Any broad stripe of contrasting color, material, or surface. **5** *Physics* **a** Any of the broad stripes found in typical molecular spectra: seen as distinct lines upon high magnification. **b** A group of states whose energies are so closely spaced as to be unresolvable and which therefore provide a continuous range of energies throughout an interval. **6** *Electronics* A range of sound frequencies or wavelengths within two stated limits: the standard broadcast *band.* **7** *Mech.* A flexible driving belt, communicating motion between wheels by friction. **8** A circular strip or loop of metal; a ring: a golden *band* on one's finger. —*v.t.* **1** To unite or tie with a band; encircle. **2** To mark with a band, as birds; to mark with a stripe. [<F *bande* <OF *bende,* ult. <Gmc. Akin to BIND.]

band[2] (band) *n.* **1** A company of persons associated, organized, or bound together. **2** A company of persons organized to play musical instruments, especially wind and percussion instruments. **3** A group of certain instruments in an orchestra: the string *band.* **4** A drove of animals, nomadic peoples, etc., wandering together. —**to beat the band** *U.S. Colloq.* Inordinately; surpassingly: He shouted *to beat the band.* —*v.t.* To join or unite, as associates in a league or company: often with *together.* —*v.i.* To confederate. [<F *bande.* Akin to BIND.]

band[3] (band) *n.* That which binds, ties, or unites; a bond. [<ON. Akin to BIND.]

band·age (ban′dij) *n.* **1** A strip, usually of soft cloth, used in dressing wounds, etc. **2** Any band. —*v.t.* **·aged, ·ag·ing** To bind or cover with a bandage. [<F <*bande* band]

Band-Aid (band′ād′) *n.* A gauze patch attached to an adhesive strip, used to cover minor wounds: a trade name. Also **band′aid′.**

ban·da·lore (ban′də·lôr, -lōr) *n.* A toy worked by means of a spring which returns it to the hand on a cord when thrown. [Origin unknown]

ban·dan·na (ban·dan′ə) *n.* A large, bright-colored handkerchief with spots or figures. Also **ban·dan′a.** [<Hind. *bāndhnū* mode of dyeing <*bāndh* tie]

Ban·dar Shah·pur (bän·där′ shä·po͝or′) A port of SW Iran at the head of the Persian Gulf.

Ban·da Sea (bän′də, ban′-) A part of the Pacific Ocean bounded by the southern Moluccas, Celebes, and the Lesser Sunda Islands.

band·box (band′boks′) *n.* A light round or oval box, for carrying hats, etc.: originally used for collars (formerly called *bands*).

ban·deau (ban·dō′) *n. pl.* **·deaux** (-dōz′) **1** A narrow band, especially one worn about the hair; fillet. **2** A brassière. [<F <OF *bandel,* dim of *bande* band]

banded ant-eater A small Australian marsupial (*Myrmecobius fasciatus*), rust-red with white bands on the back: also called *numbat.*

band·er (ban′dər) *n.* One who belongs to a band or league.

ban·de·ril·la (bän′dā·rē′lyä) *n. Spanish* In bullfighting, a dart with streamers attached, stuck into the neck and shoulders of the bull.

ban·de·ril·le·ro (bän′dā·rē·lyā′rō) *n. Spanish* In bullfighting, one who places banderillas to infuriate the bull.

ban·de·role (ban′də·rōl) *n.* **1** A small flag, pennant, or streamer, as at the end of a lance, etc., often bearing an inscription. **2** In painting and sculpture, a ribbon or scroll bearing an inscription. **3** A banner over a tomb or carried at a funeral. Also **ban′de·rol**: also *banerole.* [<F <Ital. *banderuola,* dim. of *bandiera* banner]

ban·di·coot (ban′di·ko͞ot) *n.* **1** A large rat (*Mus* or *Nesokia bandicota*) of India and Ceylon, often over a foot in length. **2** A small insectivorous marsupial (genus *Parameles*) of Australia, Tasmania, etc. [<Telugu *pandikokku* pig-rat]

ban·dit (ban′dit) *n. pl.* **ban·dits** or **ban·dit·ti** (ban·dit′ē) A highwayman; brigand. See synonyms under ROBBER. [<Ital. *bandito,* pp. of *bandire* proscribe, outlaw] —**ban′dit·ry** *n.*

Ban·djer·ma·sin (bän′jər·mä′sin) See BANJERMASIN.

band·mas·ter (band′mas′tər, -mäs′tər) *n.* The conductor of a musical band.

ban·dog (ban′dôg′, -dog′) *n.* **1** A large, fierce dog, commonly kept chained as a watchdog. **2** A bloodhound or a mastiff. [<BAND[3] + DOG]

ban·do·leer (ban′də·lir′) *n.* **1** A broad band, usually of canvas webbing, with loops for holding cartridges, worn over the shoulder. **2** An ammunition box attached to this band. Also **ban′do·lier′.** [<F *bandoulière* <Ital. *bandoliera* shoulder belt, ult. <*banda* band]

ban·do·line (ban′də·lēn, -lin) *n.* A gummy liquid made from tragacanth and quince seeds: used for dressing the hair. [Origin uncertain]

ban·dore (ban·dôr′, -dōr′) *n.* An ancient lute-like musical instrument. [<Sp. *bandurria* <L *pandura* <Gk. *pandoura* lute]

band saw *Mech.* A saw consisting of a toothed endless belt on wheels.

band shell A concave, hemispherical bandstand for concerts.

bands·man (bandz′mən) *n. pl.* **·men** (-mən) A member of a musical band.

band·stand (band′stand′) *n.* An outdoor platform for a band of musicians, often roofed. Also **band stand.**

Ban·dung (bän′do͝ong) A city of western Java. *Dutch* **Ban′doeng.**

band·wag·on (band′wag′ən) *n.* A high, decorated wagon to carry a band in a parade. —**to climb on the bandwagon** To avow adherence publicly to a political principle or candidate evidently destined to win; adopt prevalent opinions and attitudes.

ban·dy (ban′dē) *v.t.* **ban·died, ban·dy·ing 1** To give and take; exchange, as blows, quips, or words: often with *about.* **2** To pass along; circulate: to *bandy* stories. **3** To pass, throw, or knock back and forth, as a ball. —*adj.* Crooked outward at the knees; curved; bowed. —*n. pl.* **ban·dies 1** A game resembling hockey; also, a crooked stick used in this game. **2** An ancient form of tennis. [Origin uncertain]

ban·dy-leg·ged (ban′dē·leg′id, -legd′) *adj.* Having crooked legs; bowlegged.

bane (bān) *n.* **1** Anything destructive or ruinous; ruin. **2** A deadly poison: now used only in composition: *henbane.* **3** *Obs.* Death. [OE *bana* murderer, destruction]

bane·ber·ry (bān′ber′ē, -bər·ē) *n. pl.* **·ries 1** The poisonous berry of any species of *Actaea.* **2** The plant bearing this berry.

bane·ful (bān′fəl) *adj.* Noxious; poisonous; injurious; deadly; ruinous. See synonyms under BAD, PERNICIOUS. —**bane′ful·ly** *adv.* —**bane′ful·ness** *n.*

Banff (bamf) **1** A mountainous county of NE Scotland; 630 square miles; county seat, Banff. Also **Banff·shire** (bamf′shir). **2** A resort town in **Banff National Park,** a scenic park in SW Alberta, Canada; 2,564 square miles.

bang[1] (bang) *n.* **1** A sudden or noisy blow, thump, whack, or explosion. **2** *Colloq.* A sudden spring; dash. **3** *U.S. Slang* Thrill; excitement: to get a *bang* out of flying. [<*v.*] —*adv.* **1** With a violent blow or loud and sudden noise. **2** All at once; abruptly. —*v.t.* **1** To beat or strike resoundingly. **2** To shut noisily, as a door. **3** To give a thrashing to; drub. —*v.i.* **4** To make a heavy, loud sound. **5** To strike noisily: The car *banged* into the wall. [<ON *banga* hammer, beat]

bang[2] (bang) *n.* Front hair cut straight across: usually in the plural. —*v.t.* To cut straight across, as the front hair. [<BANG[1], *adv.*; from the hair being cut off abruptly]

bang[3] (bang) See BHANG.

Ban·ga·lore (bang′gə·lôr′, -lōr′) The administrative capital of Mysore state, India.

ban·ga·lore torpedo (bang′gə·lôr, -lōr) *Mil.* A length of metal piping filled with high explosive and used chiefly to clear a safe path through a mine field or barbed-wire entanglements. [from *Bangalore*]

Bang·gai Archipelago (bäng·gī′) An Indonesian island group east of Celebes; 1,222 square miles.

Bang·ka (bäng′kä) An Indonesian island east of Sumatra; 4,600 square miles: also *Banca, Banka.*

bang·kok (bang′kok) *n.* **1** Smooth, lightweight, dull straw woven of buntal fibers. **2** An article made of this straw. [from *Bangkok*]

Bang·kok (bang′kok) A port on the Chao Phraya, capital of Thailand. *Siamese* **Krung Thep** (kro͝ong tep′).

Ban·gla Desh (bäng′glä desh′) A republic in southern Asia; 54,501 square miles; capital, Dacca.

ban·gle (bang′gəl) *n.* A decorative bracelet or anklet. [<Hind. *bangrī* glass bracelet]

Ban·gor (bang′gôr, -gər) **1** A city on the Penobscot River, central Maine. **2** A municipal borough of northern Caernarvonshire, Wales.

Bang's disease An infectious brucellosis in cattle, caused by a bacterium (*Brucella abortus*), often resulting in abortion. Compare UNDULANT FEVER. [after B. L. F. *Bang,* 1848–1932, Danish veterinarian]

bang·tail (bang′tāl′) *n.* **1** A horse's tail cut horizontally across. **2** *Slang* A horse, especially a race horse. [<BANG[2] + TAIL] —**bang′·tailed′** *adj.*

bang-up (bang′up′) *adj. Slang* Excellent.

Bang·we·u·lu (bang′wē·o͞o′lo͞o) A swampy lake in NE Northern Rhodesia; 3,800 square miles.

ba·ni (bä′nē) Plural of BAN[5].

ban·ian (ban′yən) *n.* **1** A Hindu merchant or trader belonging to a caste refusing to eat meat. **2** A loose shirt, jacket, or gown. **3** Banyan. [<Pg. <Arabic *banyān,* ult. <Skt. *vaṇij* merchant]

ban·ish (ban′ish) *v.t.* **1** To compel to leave a country by political decree; exile. **2** To expel, as from any customary or desired place; drive away; dismiss, as a thought from one's mind. [<OF *baniss-,* stem of *banir* <LL *banire* banish <*bannum* proclamation <Gmc.] —**ban′ish·er** *n.* —**ban′ish·ment** *n.*

Synonyms: ban, discharge, dislodge, dismiss, eject, evict, exile, expatriate, expel, ostracize, oust. From a country, a person may be *banished, exiled,* or *expatriated; banished* from any country where he may happen to be, but *expatriated* or *exiled* only from his own. One may *expatriate* or *exile* himself; he is *banished* by others. *Banish* is a word of wide import; one may *banish* disturbing thoughts; care may *banish* sleep. To *expel* is to drive out with violence, and often with disgrace. See EXTERMINATE.

ban·is·ter (ban′is·tər) *n.* **1** A baluster. **2** *pl.* A balustrade on a staircase. Also *bannister.* [Alter. of BALUSTER]

ban·is·ter·ine (ban·is′tər·ēn, -in) *n.* An alkaloid derivative, $C_{13}H_{12}ON_2$, of a South American plant (*Banisteriopsis caapi*): a hallucinating drug which has been used to treat encephalitis lethargica: also called *harmine.* [after John *Banister,* 17th c. American botanist]

Ba·ni·yas (bä′nē·yäs′) A village in SW Syria: ancient *Caesarea Philippi.*

Ban·jer·ma·sin (bän′jər·mä′sin) A town in SW Indonesian Borneo: also *Bandjermasin.*

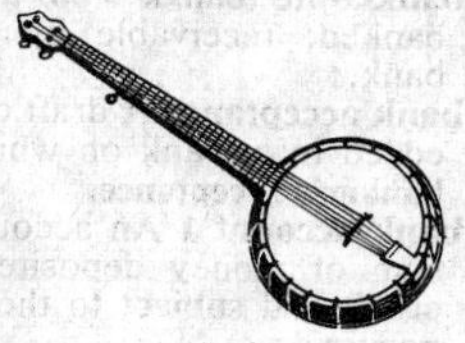
BANJO

ban·jo (ban′jō) *n. pl.* **·jos** A long-necked, stringed musical instrument having a hoop-shaped body covered on top with stretched skin and played by plucking the strings with the fingers or a plectrum. [Alter. of Sp. *bandurria.* See BANDORE.] —**ban′jo·ist** *n.*

banjo clock A 19th century American clock having a banjo-shaped case.

ban·jo·rine (ban′jə·rēn′) *n.* A musical instrument similar to the banjo, but tuned a fourth higher.

bank[1] (bangk) *n.* **1** Any moundlike formation or mass; ridge. **2** A steep acclivity; rising ground. **3** The slope of land at the edge of a watercourse or of any cut or channel: often in the plural. **4** A raised portion of the bed

of a river, lake, or ocean: the Newfoundland *banks;* also a shallow; sandbar; shoal. **5** The cushion of a billiard table. **6** *Aeron.* The sidewise inclination of an airplane in making a turn. **7** The ground at the top of the shaft of a mine. — *v.t.* **1** To enclose, cover, or protect by a bank, dike, or border; embank. **2** To heap up into a bank or mound. **3** To give an upward lateral slope to, as the curve of a road. **4** To incline (an airplane) laterally. **5** In billiards and pool, to cause (a ball) to rebound at an angle from a cushion; also, to pocket (a ball) in this manner. — *v.i.* **6** To form or lie in banks. **7** To incline an airplane laterally. **—to bank** (or **bank up**) **a fire** To cover a fire with ashes or earth so as to keep it alive but burning low. [ME *banke,* ult. <Gmc. Akin to BENCH.]

Synonyms (noun): beach, border, bound, brim, brink, coast, edge, marge, margin, rim, shore, strand. *Bank* is a general term for the land along the edge of a watercourse. A *beach* is a strip or expanse of incoherent wave-worn sand, which is often pebbly or full of boulders. *Strand* is a more poetic term for a wave-washed shore, especially as a place for landing or embarking; as, the keel grates on the *strand.* The whole line of a country or continent that borders the sea is a *coast. Shore* is any land, whether cliff, or sand, or marsh, bordering water. We do not speak of the *coast* of a river, nor of the *banks* of the ocean, though there may be *banks* by or under the sea. *Edge* is the line where land and water meet; as, the water's *edge. Brink* is the place from which one may fall; as, the *brink* of a precipice, the *brink* of ruin.

bank[2] (bangk) *n.* **1** An institution for lending, borrowing, exchanging, issuing , or caring for money. **2** An office or building used for banking purposes. **3** The funds of a gaming establishment or the fund held by the dealer or banker in some gambling games. **4** In some games, reserve piece from which the players are permitted to draw, as in dominoes. **5** A store or reserve supply of anything needed for future use or emergency: a blood *bank.* **6** Any place of storage. **7** *Obs.* A money-changer's table. — *v.t.* **1** To deposit in a bank. **2** To back financially or furnish funds for, as a business enterprise. — *v.i.* **3** To do business as or with a bank or banker. **4** In gambling, to keep the bank at a gambling table. **5** To have faith in; rely or count: with *on.* [<F *banque* <Ital. *banca* money-changer's table, ult. <Gmc.]

bank[3] (bangk) *n.* **1** A set of like articles grouped together in a line. **2** A rowers' bench in a galley; a thwart. **3** A horizontal rank of keys in a piano or organ. **4** In journalism, lines under a headline; deck. **5** *Printing* **a** The heavy sloping table on which type galleys or dead type are held. **b** A pressman's table for holding sheets. **c** The track along which the carriage of a printing press moves. — *v.t.* To bring together in a bank, as transformers. [<OF *banc* <LL *bancus* bench, ult. <Gmc. Akin to BENCH.]

Ban·ka (bäng′kä) See BANGKA.

bank·a·ble (bangk′ə·bə) *adj.* Capable of being banked; receivable by or acceptable to a bank.

bank acceptance A draft endorsed or acknowledged by a bank on which it is drawn. Also **banker's acceptance.**

bank account **1** An account with a bank. **2** A sum of money deposited in a bank to the credit and subject to the withdrawal of a depositor.

bank annuities The legal name for CONSOLS.

bank bill **1** A banknote. **2** A draft drawn on one bank by another: also **banker's bill.**

bank·book (bangk′bo͝ok′) *n.* A book in which a depositor's accounts are entered: held by the depositor and serving as a receipt for deposits: also called *passbook.*

bank discount A deduction beforehand of interest reckoned on the face of a bill or note.

bank·er[1] (bangk′ər) *n.* **1** A person or company that owns or manages a bank. **2** One who acts as dealer and keeps the bank, as in certain gambling games.

bank·er[2] (bangk′ər) *n.* A vessel or person engaged in cod-fishing on the Newfoundland banks.

bank·er[3] (bangk′ər) *n.* A stonemason's or sculptor's workbench.

bank holiday **1** *Brit.* Any of six holidays on which banks are legally closed, usually a general holiday. **2** Sunday or a legal holiday upon which banks are officially closed.

bank·ing (bangk′ing) *n.* The business of a bank or banker.

bank night *Colloq.* An evening when cash prizes are given by lottery to patrons of a motion-picture theater.

bank·note (bangk′nōt′) *n.* A promissory note, issued by a bank, payable on demand, and serving as currency.

Bank of the United States Either of two banking institutions (1791–1816 and 1817–36) that acted as fiscal agents of the U.S. government.

bank·pa·per (bangk′pā′pər) *n.* **1** Banknotes. **2** Negotiable, discountable commercial papers, as securities, bank drafts, bills of exchange, etc.

bank rate The rate of discount determined by banks.

bank·rupt (bangk′rupt) *n.* **1** A person unable to pay his debts or without credit or resources. **2** *Law* One who is unable to make payment of a just debt when due and demanded of him: a bankrupt is judicially declared insolvent and his property is administered for and divided among his creditors, under a bankruptcy law. — *adj.* **1** Unable to pay one's debts; insolvent. **2** Subject to the conditions of bankruptcy law. **3** Lacking in some quality. — *v.t.* To make bankrupt. [<F *banqueroute* <) Ital. *banca rotta* bankruptcy < *banca* bench + *rotta* broken <L *ruptus,* pp. of *rumpere* break]

bank·rupt·cy (bangk′rupt·sē, -rəp·sē) *n. pl.* **·cies** **1** The state of being insolvent; failure or inability to pay just debts. **2** Any complete ruin or failure.

bankrupt worm A threadworm (genus *Trichostrongylus*) which causes gastroenteritis in livestock: so called from the financial damage caused by this parasite.

Banks (bangks), **Sir Joseph,** 1743–1820, English explorer and naturalist.

bank·si·a (bangk′sē·ə) *n.* One of a genus *(Banksia)* of Australian evergreen trees or shrubs with leathery leaves and long, dense heads of yellow flowers. [after Sir Joseph *Banks*]

Bank·side (bangk′sīd) A district on the south bank of the Thames in London: site of Shakespeare's Globe Theater.

Banks Island Westernmost island in the Arctic Archipelago, Northwest Territories, Canada; approximately 26,000 square miles.

ban·ner (ban′ər) *n.* **1** A cloth bearing a device, suspended from a pole by a crossbar. **2** Any flag or standard. **3** *Bot.* The large upper petal of a papilionaceous blossom. **4** In journalism, a headline extending across the full width of a newspaper page. — *v.t.* To furnish with a banner. — *adj.* Leading; foremost; outstanding. [<OF *banere* <LL *bandum* banner, ult. <) Gmc.]

ban·ner·et[1] (ban′ə·ret′) *n.* A small banner. Also **ban′ner·ette′.**

ban·ner·et[2] (ban′ər·it, -et) *n.* **1** One of a grade of knights, next below a baron, entitled to lead vassals under his own banner. **2** The title of such a knight. Also **knight banneret.**

ban·ner·ole (ban′ə·rōl) See BANDEROLE.

ban·net (ban′it) *n. Scot.* A bonnet.

ban·nis·ter (ban′is·tər) See BANISTER.

ban·nock (ban′ək) *n. Scot. Brit. Dial.* A thin cake of meal baked on a griddle. [OE *bannuc* part, piece, bit]

Ban·nock·burn (ban′ək·bûrn) A village in NE Stirlingshire, Scotland; site of a battle, 1314, in which Robert Bruce defeated the English.

banns (banz) See BAN[1] (*n.* def. 2).

ban·quet (bang′kwit) *n.* **1** An elaborate or sumptuous feast. **2** A formal or ceremonial dinner, often followed by speeches. — *v.t. v.i.* To entertain at a banquet; feast sumptuously or formally. [<F, dim. of *banc* table] — **ban′quet·er** *n.*

ban·quette (bang·ket′) *n.* **1** *Mil.* A raised earthen platform or bank behind an earthwork, upon which soldiers stand to deliver their fire. See illustration under BASTION. **2** An upholstered bench, as along a wall in a restaurant. **3** Any bank, ledge, etc., as a shelf on a sideboard. **4** A sidewalk. [<F, dim. of *banc* bench]

Ban·quo (bang′kwō, -kō) In Shakespeare's *Macbeth,* a thane whose ghost appears only to Macbeth, his murderer.

bans (banz) See BAN[1] (*n.* def. 2).

ban·shee (ban′shē, ban·shē′) *n.* In Gaelic folklore, a supernatural being whose wailing outside a house was supposed to foretell a death in the family. [<Irish *bean sīdhe* < *bean* woman + *sīdhe* fairy]

ban·tam (ban′təm) *n.* **1** A breed of domestic fowl characterized by small size and pugnacity. Also **Ban′tam.** **2** Hence, a pugnacious person of small size. — *adj.* Like a bantam; small; combative. [from *Bantam,* Java]

Ban·tam (bän·täm′, ban′təm) A ruined town in NW Java, site of the first Dutch settlement in Indonesia.

ban·tam·weight (ban′təm·wā t′) *n.* A boxer or wrestler who weighs 118 pounds or less.

ban·ter (ban′tər) *n.* Good-humored ridicule; raillery; repartee. — *v.t.* To tease or ridicule good-naturedly. — *v.i.* To exchange good-natured repartee. [Origin unknown] **—ban′·ter·er** *n.* **—ban′ter·ing·ly** *adv.*

Synonyms (noun): badinage, chaff, derision, irony, jeering, mockery, raillery, ridicule, sarcasm, satire. *Banter* is the touching upon some unimportant fault or weakness of another in a way half to pique and half to please; *badinage* is delicate, refined *banter. Raillery* has more sharpness, but is usually good-humored and well-meant. *Irony,* the saying one thing that the reverse may be understood, may be either mild or bitter. *Ridicule* makes a person or thing the subject of contemptuous merriment; *derision* seeks to make the object derided seem utterly despicable—to laugh it to scorn. *Jeering* is loud, rude *ridicule,* as of a hostile crowd or mob. *Mockery* may include mimicry and personal violence, as well as scornful speech. A *satire* is a formal composition; a *sarcasm* may be an impromptu sentence. The *satire* shows up follies to keep people from them; the *sarcasm* hits them because they are foolish, without inquiring whether it will do good or harm. See MOCK, RIDICULE.

Ban·ting (ban′ting), **Sir Frederick Grant,** 1891–1941, Canadian physician; discovered insulin treatment for diabetes.

Ban·ting·ism (ban′ting·iz′əm) *n.* A method of reducing corpulence by dietetic treatment. [from William *Banting,* 1797–1878, English dietician.]

bant·ling (bant′ling) *n.* **1** A young child; infant. **2** A bastard. [<G *bänkling* bastard]

Ban·tu (ban′to͞o) *n. pl.* **Ban·tu** or **Ban·tus** (-to͞oz) **1** A family of Niger-Congo languages spoken in central and southern Africa. **2** A member of any of a group of African people who speak Bantu languages. **3** An offensive and vulgar term of contempt for black Africans of the Republic of South Africa.

Ban·ville (bā·vēl′), **Théodore de,** 1823–91, French poet and dramatist.

ban·yan (ban′yən) *n.* An East Indian fig-bearing tree *(Ficus benghalensis)* which sends down from its branches roots that develop into new trunks, thus producing a thick and shady grove: also spelled *banian.* [<BANIAN, from the use of the ground under the tree as a market place]

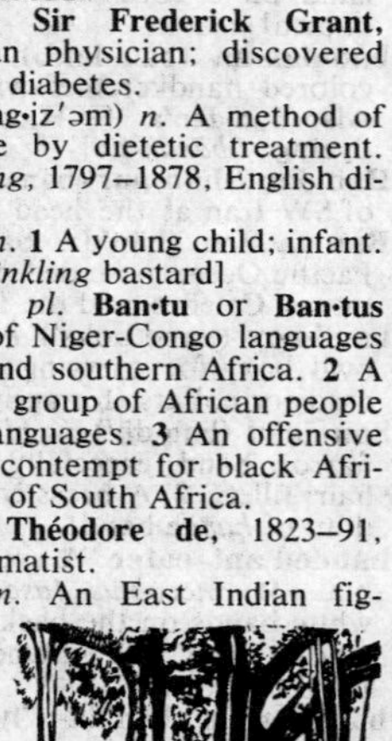

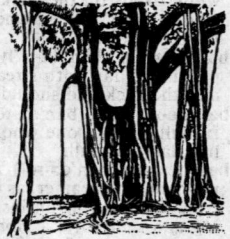

BANYAN TREE
(From 80 to 100 feet high)

ban·zai (bän′zī′) *interj.* A Japanese greeting, battle cry, or cheer, meaning: (May you live) ten thousand years!

banzai attack A desperate attempt to carry a position by infantry charge: used by the Japanese in World War II. Also **banzai charge.**

ba·o·bab (bā′ō·bab, bā′ō-) *n.* An African tree *(Adansonia digitata)* with a thick trunk, bearing edible, gourdlike fruit; the monkey-bread tree. [<native African name]

bap (bap) *n. Scot.* A loaf or roll of bread.

bap·tism (bap′tiz·əm) *n.* **1** The act of baptiz-

ing or of being baptized; specifically, a sacrament in which water is used to initiate the recipient into a Christian church, to symbolize purification, to acknowledge consecration to Christ, etc. **2** Any initiatory or purifying experience. **3** A religious ablution signifying a purification or consecration, as that by which proselytes were Judaized. **4** In Christian Science, purification by Spirit; submergence in Spirit. [<OF *baptesme* <LL *baptismus* <Gk. *baptismos* immersion] — **bap·tis·mal** (bap·tiz′məl) *adj.* — **bap·tis′mal·ly** *adv.*

baptismal name A name given to a person when he is baptized.

baptism of fire 1 In the Bible, baptism with the Holy Spirit; spiritual baptism. **2** Martyrdom. **3** A soldier's first experience under actual combat. **4** Any crucial ordeal or purifying experience or trial.

Bap·tist (bap′tist, *Ger.* bäp′-) A masculine personal name. Also *Fr.* **Bap·tiste** (bȧ·tēst′); *Lat.* **Bap·tis·ta** (bap·tis′tə). [<Gk., baptizer]

Bap·tist (bap′tist) *n.* **1** A member of various Protestant denominations holding that baptism should be given only to professed adult believers, and, generally, that baptism should be by immersion rather than by sprinkling. **2** One who baptizes. — **the Baptist** John the Baptist.

bap·tis·ter·y (bap′tis·tər·ē, -tis·trē) *n. pl.* **·ter·ies 1** A font or tank for baptism. **2** A part of a church or other building set apart for baptism. Also **bap′tis·try** (-trē).

bap·tize (bap·tīz′, bap′tīz) *v.t.* **·tized, ·tiz·ing 1** To immerse in water or pour water on in the Christian sacrament of baptism, symbolizing dedication to Christ, purification, and admission into a specific church. **2** To christen or name at the sacrament of baptism. **3** To cleanse; sanctify. **4** To consecrate or dedicate to special uses by some ceremony resembling baptism. Also *Brit.* **bap·tise′.** [<F *baptiser* <LL *baptizare* <Gk. *baptizein* immerse, wash] — **bap·tiz′er** *n.*

bar[1] (bär) *n.* **1** A piece of solid material, evenly shaped and long in proportion to its width and thickness: often used as a unit of quantity, a fastening, a barrier, etc. **2** Any barrier or obstruction. **3** A bank, as of sand, at the entrance to a river or harbor. **4** The enclosed place in court occupied by counsel; also, the place where a prisoner stands to plead; hence, the court or any place of justice, or anything considered as analogous; a judgment seat. **5** Lawyers collectively; the legal profession. **6** A room or a counter where liquors or refreshments are dispensed. **7** A stripe; a band, as of color or light. **8** *Music* **a** The vertical line that divides a staff into measures. **b** A double bar. **c** The unit of music between two bars; measure. **9** A horizontal timber or other

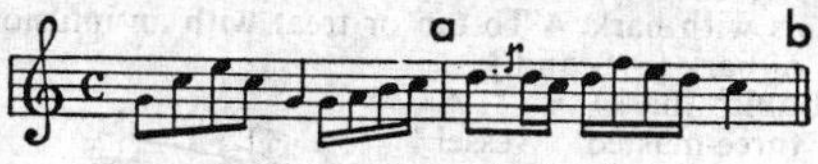

BARS IN MUSIC (*def. 8*)
a. Single. *b.* Double.

piece connecting two parts of a framework. **10** The solid metal mouthpiece of a horse's bridle; also, the space in front of a horse's upper molar teeth in which the bit is placed; also, that portion of a horse's foot that bends toward the frog. **11** In needlepoint, a transverse thread or group of threads passed from one side or corner of an opening to another: usually twisted or buttonholed and sometimes finished with knots. **12** *Law* The preventing or stopping of an action by showing that the plaintiff has no right of action. **13** *Her.* An ordinary formed by two parallel lines drawn horizontally across a shield, covering one fifth of the field. See synonyms under BARRIER, IMPEDIMENT, LOCK. — **the Bars** The Confederate flag. — *v.t.* **barred, bar·ring 1** To fasten, lock, or secure with or as with a bar. **2** To confine or shut out with or as with bars. **3** To obstruct or hinder: to *bar* the way. **4** To exclude or except. **5** To mark with bars. See synonyms under HINDER, OBSTRUCT. — *prep.* Barring; excepting: *bar* none. [<OF *barre* <LL *barra* bar]

bar[2] (bär) *n.* The cgs international unit of pressure, equal to 1,000,000 dynes a square centimeter or a pressure of 29.531 inches of mercury at 32° F. and in latitude 45°: sometimes incorrectly called *barye.* [<Gk. *baros* weight]

Ba·rab·bas (bə·rab′əs) A thief released in place of Jesus at the demand of the multitude. *Matt.* xxvii 16–21.

Ba·rac·a (bə·rak′ə) *n.* An interdenominational, world-wide organization of young men's Bible classes. [<Hebrew *berakah* blessing]

Bar·ak (bâr′ak) A warrior who, with Deborah, overcame Sisera and the Canaanites. *Judges* iv 6. [<Hebrew, lightning]

Bar·a·nof Island (bar′ə·nôf) An island in the Alexander Archipelago, SE Alaska; 1,607 square miles.

Ba·ra·nov (bä·rä′nôf), **Aleksandr Andreevich,** 1747–1819, Russian fur trader; first governor of Russian America (now Alaska).

Bá·rá·ny (bä′rä·ny′), **Robert,** 1876–1939, Austrian physician and otologist.

Bar·a·tar·i·a Bay (bar′ə·târ′ē·ə) A lagoon in extreme SE Louisiana, mouth of the Mississippi. Also **Barataria Bayou.**

bar·a·the·a (bar′ə·thē′ə) *n.* A soft fabric of silk combined with cotton or wool. [Origin uncertain]

barb[1] (bärb) *n.* **1** A backward-projecting point on a sharp weapon, as on an arrow, fish hook, or spear, intended to prevent easy extraction. **2** Any similar sharp point: the *barbs* on a barbed-wire fence. **3** *Bot.* A beard, as in certain grains and grasses; awn. **4** *Ornithol.* One of the lateral processes of a bird's feather. See illustration under FEATHER. **5** A band or scarf worn about the neck and covering the breast: the *barb* of a nun. **6** *pl.* Paps or folds of the mucous membrane under the tongue of cattle and horses. **7** *pl.* The disease characterized by their inflammation. **8** *Obs.* A beard. — *v.t.* To provide with a barb or barbs: to *barb* an arrow. [<F *barbe* <L *barba* beard]

barb[2] (bärb) *n.* **1** A horse of the breed introduced by the Moors from Barbary into Spain: noted for speed and endurance. **2** A blackish or dun pigeon with a short stout beak. [<F *barbe* <*Barbarie,* ult. <Arabic *Barbar* native of N. Africa]

Bar·ba·dos (bär·bā′dōz) An island in the West Indies east of the Windward Islands, comprising a British colony; 166 square miles; capital, Bridgetown. — **Bar·ba′di·an** *adj.* & *n.*

Barbados pride Flowerfence.

bar·bal (bär′bəl) *adj.* Of or pertaining to the beard. [<L *barba* beard]

Bar·ba·ra (bär′bə·rə, -brə; *Du., Ger., Ital.* bär′bä·rä) A feminine personal name. Also *Fr.* **Barbe** (bȧrb), *Sp.* **Bár·ba·ra** (bär′bä·rä). [<Gk., foreign, strange]

bar·bar·i·an (bär·bâr′ē·ən) *n.* **1** One whose state of culture is between savagery and civilization; a member of an uncivilized tribe or race. **2** Any rude, brutal, or uncultured person. **3** One destitute of, or not caring for, culture. **4** According to ancient Greek and Latin usage, a foreigner or outlander. — *adj.* **1** Uncivilized; cruel; barbarous. **2** Foreign; alien. See synonyms under BARBAROUS. — **bar·bar′i·an·ism** *n.*

bar·bar·ic (bär·bar′ik) *adj.* **1** Of or characteristic of barbarians. **2** Wild; uncivilized; crude. See synonyms under BARBAROUS. [<OF *barbarique* <L *barbaricus* <*barbarus* barbarian. See BARBAROUS.]

bar·ba·rism (bär′bə·riz′əm) *n.* **1** The stage between savagery and civilization. **2** Absence of culture; rudeness in manners, speech, living standards, etc. **3** The usage of words or forms not approved or standard in a language; also, an instance of this. See synonyms under LANGUAGE. **4** A barbarous act.

bar·bar·i·ty (bär·bar′ə·tē) *n. pl.* **·ties 1** Brutal or barbarous conduct. **2** A barbarous deed. **3** A barbarism of language.

bar·ba·rize (bär′bə·rīz) *v.* **·rized, ·riz·ing** *v.t.* To make barbarous; corrupt, as language, from classical standards. — *v.i.* To become barbarous.

Bar·ba·ros·sa (bär′bə·ros′ə) **1** The name of two brothers, Barbary pirates: **Horuk,** 1473?–1518, and **Khair-ed-Din,** 1466?–1546, rulers of Algiers. **2** The nickname (Latin, redbeard) of Frederick I of Germany.

bar·ba·rous (bär′bər·əs) *adj.* **1** Pertaining to or like a barbarian. **2** Uncultivated; lacking the refinements of advanced civilization; rude. **3** Cruel; brutal; savage. **4** Marked by barbarisms in speech; unpolished. **5** Rude or harsh in sound. **6** In Greek and Roman usage, of or pertaining to foreigners. [<L *barbarus* foreign, barbarian <Gk. *barbaros* non-Hellenic, foreign, rude] — **bar′ba·rous·ly** *adv.* — **bar′ba·rous·ness** *n.*

Synonyms: atrocious, barbarian, barbaric, brutal, cruel, inhuman, merciless, rude, savage, uncivilized, uncouth, untamed. *Barbarous* refers to the worst side of *barbarian* life, and to acts of cruelty. We may, however, say *barbarous* nations, *barbarous* tribes, without implying anything more than want of civilization and culture. *Antonyms*: civilized, courtly, cultured, delicate, elegant, graceful, humane, nice, polite, refined, tender, urbane.

Bar·ba·ry (bär′bər·ē) The Moslem countries of northern Africa west of Egypt, including the former Barbary States.

Barbary ape An easily trained, tailless ape (*Macaca sylvana*) of North Africa and southern Spain: also called *magot.*

Barbary Coast 1 The coastal region of Barbary. **2** A waterfront region of San Francisco before the earthquake of 1906, infamous for its saloons, gambling houses, and brothels.

Barbary States Formerly, Tripolitania, Algeria, Tunisia, and, generally, Morocco; centers of piracy until occupation by the European powers in the 19th century.

bar·bate (bär′bāt) *adj.* **1** Bearded. **2** *Bot.* Tufted with long hairs. [<L *barbatus* bearded <*barba* beard]

bar·be·cue (bär′bə·kyōō) *n.* **1** An outdoor feast at which the whole animal carcass is roasted over an open fire and served. **2** Any meat roasted on a spit over an open fire. — *v.t.* **·cued, ·cu·ing 1** To roast whole. **2** To roast (usually beef or pork) in large pieces or whole over an open fire or in a trench, often using a highly seasoned sauce. **3** To cook (meat) with a highly seasoned sauce. [<Sp. *barbacoa* <Taino *barbacoa* framework of sticks]

barbed (bärbd) *adj.* **1** Having a barb or barbs. **2** Pointed, piercing, or wounding: a *barbed* remark.

barbed wire Fence wire having barbs at intervals.

bar·bel (bär′bəl) *n.* **1** One of the soft filiform appendages to the jaws, chin, or nostrils of certain fishes: an organ of touch. **2** A carp-like Old World cyprinoid fish (genus *Barbes*). [<OF <LL *barbellus,* dim. of *barbus* barbel <*barba* beard]

bar·bel·late (bär′bə·lāt, bär·bel′it) *adj. Bot.* Having or studded with short, stiff hairs or bristles.

bar·ber (bär′bər) *n.* One who cuts the hair, shaves the beard, etc., as a business. — *v.t.* To cut or dress the hair of; shave or trim the beard of. ◆ Collateral adjective: *tonsorial.* [<OF *barbeor,* ult. <L *barba* beard]

Bar·ber (bär′bər), **Samuel,** born 1910, U.S. composer.

bar·ber·ry (bär′ber′ē, -bər·ē) *n.* **1** A shrub (genus *Berberis*) bearing yellow flowers and bright-red oblong berries. **2** Its fruit. [<Med. L *berberis, barbaris*]

bar·ber·shop (bär′bər·shop′) *n.* The place of business of a barber. — *adj. U.S.* Like, pertaining to, or characterized by close harmony, especially of male voices in sentimental songs.

bar·bet (bär′bit) *n.* **1** A tropical bird (family *Capitonidae*), having a broad bill surrounded by bristles at the base: related to the toucans: also called *scansorial barbet.* **2** A variety of small poodle. [<OF *barbet* <L *barbatus* bearded]

bar·bette (bär·bet′) *n.* **1** *Nav.* An armored cylinder protecting a revolving turret on a warship. **2** *Mil.* A platform from which cannon are fired over a parapet. [<F *barbette,* dim. of *barbe* beard]

bar·bi·can (bär′bi·kən) *n.* An outer fortification or outwork. See synonyms under RAMPART. [<F *barbacane*; ult. origin uncertain]

bar·bi·cel (bär′bə·sel) *n. Ornithol.* One of the very small simple processes fringing the lower edges of the barbule of a feather. [<NL *barbicella,* dim. of *barba* beard]

bar·bi·tal (bär′bə-tôl, -tal) *n.* A slow-acting and long-lasting barbiturate, $C_8H_{12}N_2O_3$, used as a sedative, hypnotic, and anticonvulsant. Also *Brit.* **bar′bi·tone** (-tōn).

bar·bit·u·rate (bär-bich′ər-it, bär′bə-tōōr′it, -tyōōr′it) *n.* Any of various derivatives of barbituric acid which act as depressants on the central nervous system and are often used as sedatives, hypnotics, and anticonvulsants.

bar·bi·tu·ric acid (bär′bə-tōōr′ik, -tyōōr′-) A synthetic compound, $C_4H_4O_3N_2$, from which barbiturates are derived. Also called *malonylurea*. [< NL (*Usnea*) *barbata* bearded (lichen) + -URIC]

Bar·bi·zon school (bär′bə-zon, *Fr.* bár-bē-zôn′) A group of French landscape painters of the 19th century, including Corot, Daubigny, Millet, and Théodore Rousseau. [from *Barbizon*, a village in NE France where they worked]

Bar·bour (bär′bər), **John**, 1320?–95, Scottish poet.

Bar·bu·da (bär-bōō′də) An island dependency of Antigua.

bar·bule (bär′byōōl) *n.* 1 A small barb or beard. 2 A process fringing the barb of a feather. [< L *barbula*, dim. of *barba* beard]

Bar·busse (bär-büs′), **Henri**, 1873–1935, French novelist.

Bar·ca (bär′kə) An influential Carthaginian family to which Hamilcar, Hannibal, and Hasdrubal belonged.

Bar·ca (bär′kə) 1 Cyrenaica. 2 The ancient name for BARCE.

bar car *U.S.* A railroad passenger car fitted out for serving drinks and short orders.

bar·ca·role (bär′kə-rōl) *n.* 1 A Venetian gondolier's song. 2 A melody in imitation of such a song. Also **bar′ca·rolle**. [< F *barcarolle* < Ital. *barcaruola* boatman's song < *barca* boat.]

Bar·ce (bär′chā) A town in western Cyrenaica, Libya: ancient *Barca*.

Bar·ce·lo·na (bär′sə-lō′nə, *Sp.* bär′thä-lō′nä) 1 A port of NE Spain. 2 A province in Catalonia, Spain; 2,975 square miles; capital, Barcelona. 3 A city of NE Venezuela.

Bar·clay (bär′klē), **Robert**, 1648–90, Scottish Quaker author.

Bar·clay de Tol·ly (bär-klī′ də tô′lyi), **Prince Mikhail**, 1761–1818, Russian field marshal.

bard[1] (bärd) *n.* 1 A Celtic poet and minstrel. 2 *Poetic* A poet. [< Celtic] —**bard′ic** *adj.*

bard[2] (bärd) *n.* Any piece of armor worn by horses. —*v.t.* To arm with bards. Also **barde**. [< F *barde*, ult. < Arabic *al-barda′ah* the packsaddle]

Bard of Avon William Shakespeare, born in Stratford-on-Avon.

bare[1] (bâr) *adj.* 1 Devoid of covering or dress; naked. 2 Destitute of or poorly provided with what is used or necessary; unfurnished. 3 Unarmed; unsheathed. 4 Not more than just suffices; mere. 5 Threadbare. 6 Exposed to view; made manifest or apparent; undisguised. 7 Lacking in embellishment or in interest or attraction; plain; meager: *bare* description. 8 Bareheaded; also, barefoot. See synonyms under BLANK. —*v.t.* **bared**, **bar·ing** To make or lay bare; reveal; expose. Homophone: *bear*. [OE *bær*]

bare[2] (bâr) Obsolete past tense of BEAR.

bare·back (bâr′bak′) *adj.* Riding a horse without a saddle. —*adv.* Without a saddle. —**bare′·backed** *adj.*

bare·faced (bâr′fāst′) *adj.* 1 Having the face bare. 2 Unconcealed; open. 3 Impudent; audacious. —**bare·fac·ed·ly** (bâr′fā′sid·lē, -fāst′lē) *adv.* —**bare′·fac′ed·ness** *n.*

bare·fit (bâr′fit) *adj. Scot.* Barefoot.

bare·foot (bâr′fōōt′) *adj. & adv.* With the feet bare. Also **bare′·foot′ed** *adj.*

ba·rege (bə-rezh′) *n.* A thin fabric of silk and worsted or cotton and worsted, used for veils, etc. [from *Barèges*, a French village]

bare·hand·ed (bâr′han′did) *adj.* With the hands uncovered. —*adv.* 1 In the act of committing a crime. 2 With the hands uncovered.

bare·head·ed (bâr′hed′id) *adj. & adv.* With head bare.

Ba·reil·ly (bə-rā′lē) A city in north central Uttar Pradesh, India, capital of Rohilkhand. Also **Ba·re′li.**

bare·leg·ged (bâr′leg′id, -legd′) *adj. & adv.* With the legs bare.

bare·ly (bâr′lē) *adv.* 1 Only just; scarcely. 2 Nakedly. 3 Openly; boldly; plainly. See synonyms under BUT.

Ba·rend (bä′rent) Dutch and German form of BERNARD.

Ba·rents (bä′rənts), **Willem**, died 1597, Dutch explorer.

Bar·ents Sea (bar′ənts, bä′rənts) An arm of the Artic Ocean north of Norway and European U.S.S.R.

bare·sark (bâr′särk) *n.* A berserk. —*adv.* Without armor. [Alter. of BERSERK]

Ba·ret·ti (bä-rāt′tē), **Giuseppi Marc Antonio**, 1719–89, Italian critic.

bar·fly (bär′flī′) *n. pl.* **·flies** *Slang* A habitual frequenter of barrooms.

Bar·frush (bär-frōōsh′) A former name for BABOL.

bar·gain (bär′gən) *n.* 1 A mutual agreement between persons, especially one to buy or sell goods. 2 That which is agreed upon or the terms of the agreement. 3 The agreement as it affects one of the parties to it: He made a bad *bargain*. 4 An article bought or offered at a price favorable to the buyer. See synonyms under CONTRACT. —**into the bargain** In addition to what was agreed; thrown in for good measure; besides. —**to strike a bargain** To come to an agreement. —*v.i.* 1 To discuss or haggle over terms for selling or buying. 2 To make a bargain; reach an agreement. —*v.t.* 3 To barter, as goods for others of equal value. —**to bargain for** To expect; count on: This is more than I *bargained for*. [< OF *bargaine;* ult. origin uncertain]

barge (bärj) *n.* 1 A flat-bottomed freight boat or lighter for harbors and inland waters, or other large boat, as for pleasure excursions. 2 A large and elegantly furnished boat, for pleasure or for state occasions. 3 *Nav.* A boat for the use of a flag officer. 4 *Obs.* In New England, a long, open vehicle, sometimes boat-shaped, for passengers. 5 A house-boat. —*v.* **barged**, **barg·ing** *v.t.* 1 To transport by barge. —*v.i.* 2 To move clumsily and slowly. 3 *Colloq.* To collide with: with *into*. 4 *Colloq.* To intrude; enter rudely: with *in* or *into*. [< OF < LL *barga*. Akin to BARK[3].]

barge·board (bärj′bôrd′, -bōrd′) *n.* A board, often ornate, attached along the barge couples and following the outline of a gable end.

barge couple One of a pair of outside rafters (**barge couples**) that support the projecting end of a gable roof.

barge course 1 The part of a gable roof projecting beyond the bargeboards or end wall. 2 A course of bricks laid edgewise to form the coping of a wall.

BARGEBOARD
a.a. Barge course.
b.b. Bargeboards.
c.c. Rafters.
d.d. Barge couples.

barge·man (bärj′mən) *n. pl.* **·men** (-mən) One who has charge of or is employed on a barge; a boatman or oarsman. Also *Brit.* **bar·gee** (bär-jē′).

bar·ghest (bär′gest) *n.* A goblin, often dog-shaped, whose appearance is supposed to forebode death or misfortune. [Cf. G *berggeist* gnome]

Bar·ham (bär′əm), **Richard Harris**, 1788–1845, English churchman and humorist: pen name *Thomas Ingoldsby.*

Bar Harbor A resort and port of entry on Mount Desert Island, Maine.

Ba·ri (bä′rē) A port on the Adriatic in southern Italy. Formerly **Bari del·le Pu·glie** (dăl′·lā pōō′lyä).

bar·i·a·trics (bar′ē-at′riks) *n.* The branch of medicine concerned with the treatment of the overweight. [< Gk. *baros* weight + -IATRICS]

bar·ic[1] (bar′ik) *adj.* Of or pertaining to weight, especially of air; barometric. [< Gk. *barys* heavy]

bar·ic[2] (bar′ik) *adj.* Of, pertaining to, derived from, or containing barium.

ba·ril·la (bə-ril′ə) *n.* 1 An impure sodium carbonate and sulfate obtained by burning certain land or marine plants; soda ash. 2 Any plant used in making soda ash, especially the saltwort. [< Sp. *barrilla* impure soda]

Bar·ing (bâr′ing), **Alexander** See ASHBURTON. —**Evelyn**, 1841–1917, first Earl of Cromer, English diplomat. —**Maurice**, 1874–1945, English novelist.

Bar·ing-Gould (bâr′ing-gōōld′), **Sabine**, 1834–1924, English clergyman and hymn-writer.

Ba·ri·sal (bu-ri-säl′) A city in SE Bengal, East Pakistan.

bar·ite (bâr′īt) *n.* A heavy, vitreous, usually white, orthorhombic barium sulfate, $BaSO_4$: also called *heavy spar.*

bar·i·tone (bar′ə-tōn) *n.* 1 A male voice of a register higher than bass and lower than tenor. 2 One having such a voice. 3 A brass wind instrument, used chiefly in military bands, having a similar range. —*adj.* 1 Of, like, or pertaining to a baritone. 2 Having the range of a baritone. Also spelled *barytone*. [< Ital. *baritono* < Gk. *barytonos* deep-sounding < *barys* deep + *tonos* tone]

bar·i·um (bâr′ē-əm) *n.* An element (symbol Ba, atomic number 56) of the alkaline-earth group, resembling calcium chemically and forming salts of which the water-soluble ones and the carbonate are poisonous. See PERIODIC TABLE. [< NL < Gk. *barys* heavy]

barium hydroxide A basic compound, Ba (OH)$_2$·$8H_2O$, that crystallizes in tetragonal prisms produced by rendering caustic barium carbonate or by dissolving the monoxide in water.

barium oxide *Chem.* A yellowish-white, poisonous alkaline compound, BaO, used in glassmaking and as a reagent: it forms barium hydroxide on the addition of water: also called *baryta.*

barium sulfate An insoluble compound, $BaSO_4$, produced synthetically as an insoluble white precipitate: used in roentgenology to facilitate X-ray pictures of the stomach and intestines.

barium yellow A pale, sulfur-yellow pigment with a greenish tone, made from barium chromate.

bark[1] (bärk) *n.* 1 The short, abrupt, explosive sound characteristically made by a dog. 2 Any sound like this. —*v.i.* 1 To utter a bark, as a dog, or to make a sound like a bark. 2 *Colloq.* To cough. 3 To speak loudly and sharply. 4 *U.S. Slang* To announce the attractions of a show at its entrance. —*v.t.* 5 To say roughly and curtly: He *barked* an order. —**to bark up the wrong tree** *Colloq.* To be mistaken as to one's object or the means of attaining it. [OE *beorcan*]

bark[2] (bärk) *n.* 1 The tissue covering the stems, branches, and roots of a tree or shrub, extending from the cambium layer to the outer surface. 2 This tissue removed from a particular species for its special medicinal or other properties. —*v.t.* 1 To remove the bark from; scrape; girdle. 2 To rub off or abrade the skin of. 3 To cover with or as with bark. 4 To tan or treat with an infusion of bark [< Scand.]

bark[3] (bärk) *n.* 1 A three-masted vessel square-rigged except for the mizzenmast, which is fore-and-aft rigged. 2 *Poetic* Any vessel or boat. Also spelled *barque*. [< F *barque* < LL *barca* bark]

BARK

bark beetle One of several small burrowing beetles (family *Scolytidae*) which breed between the bark and wood of trees, thus destroying the trees. See illustration under INSECT (injurious).

bar·keep·er (bär′kē′pər) *n.* 1 One who owns or manages a bar where alcoholic liquors are served. 2 A bartender. Also **bar′keep′**.

bar·ken·tine (bär′kən-tēn) *n.* A three-masted vessel square-rigged on the foremast and fore-and-aft rigged on the other two masts: also spelled *barquentine.*

bark·er[1] (bär′kər) *n.* 1 One who or that which barks or clamors. 2 A person stationed at the door of a shop or entrance to a show to attract patrons by loud, animated patter.

bark·er[2] (bär′kər) *n.* One who or that which removes bark from trees or works with bark.

Bar·kis (bär′kis) In Dickens's *David Copperfield*, a bashful carrier who is constantly declaring by deputy that "Barkis is willin'" to marry Clara Peggotty.

bark·it (bär′kit) *adj. Scot.* Barked; tanned.
Bark·la (bär′klə), **Charles Glover,** 1877–1944, English physicist.
bark·less (bärk′lis) *adj.* Unable to bark, as certain breeds of dogs.
Bark·ley (bärk′lē), **Alben William,** 1877–1956, U.S. lawyer, vice president of the United States 1949–53.
bark·y (bär′kē) *adj.* Covered with or resembling bark.
Bar-le-Duc (bär′lə-dük′) *n.* A preserve from seeded gooseberries or currants, originally made at **Bar-le-Duc,** a town of NE France.
Bar·let·ta (bär-let′tä) A port in Apulia, SE Italy, on the Adriatic.
bar·ley[1] (bär′lē) *n.* 1 A hardy, bearded cereal grass (*Hordeum vulgare*) of temperate regions, with long leaves, stout awns, and triple spikelets at the joints which distinguish it from wheat. 2 The grain borne by this grass. [OE *bærlīc*]
bar·ley[2] (bär′lē) *interj. Scot.* Truce!: a cry in children's games: also spelled *barly.*
bar·ley·corn (bär′lē-kô rn) *n.* 1 A grain of barley. 2 A unit of measure, originally the breadth of a barley grain, equal to one third of an inch. 3 A planed groove between moldings. —**John Barleycorn** A humorous personification of malt liquor, or of intoxicating liquors in general.
barley sugar A clear, brittle confection made by boiling sugar with a barley extract.
barley water A drink made by boiling barley in water, for invalids, etc.
Bar·low (bär′lō), **Jane,** 1860–1917, Irish novelist. —**Joel,** 1755–1812, U.S. poet and diplomat.
Barlow's disease Infantile scurvy. [after Sir Thomas *Barlow,* 19th c. English physician]
barm (bärm) *n.* The froth or foam rising on fermented malt liquors. [OE *beorma* yeast]
bar·maid (bär′mād′) *n.* A woman bartender.
Bar·me·cide (bär′mə·sīd) Any member of a former wealthy and princely family of Baghdad; specifically, in the *Arabian Nights,* the member of this family who served an imaginary feast to a beggar, setting only empty dishes before him.
Barmecide feast Any imaginary, illusory, or disappointing hospitality or generosity.
Bar·men (bär′mən) See **WUPPERTAL.**
bar miz·vah (bär mits′və) In Judaism, a boy commencing his thirteenth year, the age of religious duty and responsibility; also, the ceremony celebrating this: also spelled *bar mitzvah* or *mitzwah.*
barm·y (bär′mē) *adj.* **barm·i·er, barm·i·est** 1 Full of barm; frothy. 2 *Brit. Slang* Silly; flighty. Also *Scot.* **barm′ie.**
barn[1] (bärn) *n.* A building for storing hay, stabling livestock, etc. [OE *bern*]
barn[2] (bärn) *n. Physics* A unit of area used in measuring the cross-sections of atomic nuclei: equal to 10^{-24} square centimeter: so called in allusion to the phrase "He can't hit the side of a barn door."
Bar·na·bas (bär′nə·bəs; *Dan., Du., Ger., Lat.* bär′nä·bäs) A masculine personal name. Also **Bar·na·by** (bä r′nə·bē), *Fr.* **Bar·na·bé** (bär·nä·bā′), *Ital.* **Bar·na·ba** (bär′nä·bä) or **Bar·na** (bär′nä), *Pg.* **Bar·na·be** (bä r′nə·bā). [<Hebrew, son of consolation]
Barnabas, Saint (properly *Joses*) First century Christian apostle: reputed author of an apocryphal gospel and epistle.
bar·na·cle[1] (bär′nə·kəl) *n.* 1 A marine shellfish (order *Cirripedia*) that attaches itself to rocks, ship bottoms, etc.; especially, the **rock barnacle** (*Balanus balanoides*) and the **goose barnacle** (*Lepas fascicularis*), the latter so called because the barnacle goose was once supposed to hatch from it. 2 A European wild goose of northern seas (*Branta leucopsis*): also **barnacle goose.** 3 Something or someone that clings tenaciously; a persistent follower; a hanger-on. [ME *bernacle;* origin uncertain] —**bar′na·cled** *adj.*
bar·na·cle[2] (bär′nə·kəl) *n. Usually pl.* An instrument for pinching the nose of an unruly horse. [OF *bernacle,* dim. of *bernac* a bit]
Bar·nard (bär′nərd) See **BERNARD.**
Bar·nard (bär′nərd), **George Grey,** 1863–1938, U.S. sculptor. —**Henry,** 1811–1900, U.S.

educator.—**Christiaan Neethling,** 1922– , South African Surgeon.
Bar·na·ul (bär′nä·ōōl′) A city on the Ob, capital of Altai Territory in SW Siberia.
Barn·burn·er (bärn′bûr′nər) *n.* A member of one of the progressive factions of the Democratic party in New York state in 1842: opposed to the *Hunkers.*
barn dance 1 A dance held in a barn, especially with square dances, rural music, etc. 2 A country dance resembling the schottische.
Bar·ne·gat Bay (bär′nə·gat) An arm of the Atlantic extending about 30 miles along the coast of eastern New Jersey.
Barnes (bärnz), **Harry Elmer,** 1889–) 1968, U.S. sociologist and educator.
Bar·net (bär′nit) A town in southern Hertfordshire, England; site of a battle, 1471, between Yorkists and Lancastrians.
Bar·ne·veldt (bär′nə·velt), **Jan van Olden,** 1549–1619, Dutch patriot.
barn owl A North American owl (*Tyto alba pratincola*) with brownish upper parts and white underparts flecked with black: often found in barns, where it preys on mice.
Barns·ley (bärnz′lē) A county borough of southern Yorkshire, England.
barn·storm (bärn′stôrm′) *v.i.* 1 To tour rural districts, giving plays, making political speeches, etc. 2 To tour rural districts, giving exhibitions of stunt flying, short airplane excursions, etc. —**barn′storm′er** *n.*
barn′storm′ing *n.* [<BARN + STORM, *v.*]

BARN OWL
(15 to 17 inches tall.)

barn swallow The common swallow of North America and Europe: it frequently nests in the eaves of barns and other buildings.
Bar·num (bär′nəm), **P(hineas) T(aylor),** 1810–91, U.S. showman and circus proprietor.
barn·yard (bärn′yärd′) *n.* An enclosed space adjoining a barn.
baro- *combining form* Weight; atmospheric pressure: *barodynamics.* [<Gk. *baros* weight]
Ba·roc·chio (bä·rôk′kyō) See **BAROZZI, GIACOMO.**
bar·o·cy·clo·nom·e·ter (bar′ ō·sī′klə·nom′ə·tər) *n. Meterol.* An instrument for ascertaining the location, direction, distance, and movement of cyclones. [<BARO- + CYCLONE + -METER]
Ba·ro·da (bə·rō′də) A district of northern Bombay State; until 1948 a princely state in northern India; 8,236 square miles; capital, Baroda.
bar·o·dy·nam·ics (bar′ō·dī·nam′iks) *n.* The dynamics of heavy structures, as dams, bridges, etc., especially in relation to pressure and gravitation. —**bar′o·dy·nam′ic** *adj.*
bar·o·gram (bar′ə·gram) *n.* The record of a barograph.
bar·o·graph (bar′ə·graf, -gräf) *n.* An automatically recording barometer. —**bar′o·graph′ic** *adj.*
Ba·ro·ja (bä·rō′hä), **Pio,** 1872–1956, Spanish novelist.
ba·rom·e·ter (bə·rom′ə·tər) *n.* 1 An instrument for measuring atmospheric pressure: used for forecasting the weather, measuring elevations, etc. 2 Anything that indicates changes. —**bar·o·met·ric** (bar′ ə·met′rik) or **-ri·cal** *adj.* —**bar′o·met′ri·cal·ly** *adv.* —**ba·rom′e·try** *n.*
bar·on (bar′ən) *n.* 1 A member of the lowest order of hereditary nobility in several European countries; also, the dignity or rank itself. The title was used at first in England to designate one who held land by military or other honorable service. 2 *U.S.* One who has great power in a commercial field: a *coal* baron. 3 In the Middle Ages, a feudal tenant of the king; a noble.— ♦Homophone: **barren.** [<OF <LL *baro,-onis* man <Gmc.]
bar·on·age (bar′ən·ij) *n.* 1 Barons collectively. 2 The dignity or rank of a baron.
bar·on·ess (bar′ən·is) *n.* 1 The wife or widow of a baron. 2 A woman holding a barony in her own right.
bar·on·et (bar′ən·it, -ə·net) *n.* 1 An inheritable English title, below that of baron. 2 The bearer of the title, who is not a member of the nobility: A baronet is designated by "Sir" be-

fore the name and "Baronet" or the abbreviation "Bart." after.
bar·on·et·age (bar′ən·it·ij, -ə·net′-) *n.* 1 Baronets collectively. 2 The dignity or rank of a baronet.
bar·on·et·cy (bar′ən·it·sē, -ə·net′-) *n. pl.* **-cies** 1 The title or rank of a baronet. 2 The patent giving such rank.
ba·rong (bä·rông′, -rong′) *n.* In the Philippines, a cutlas cleaverlike weapon used by the Moros.
ba·ro·ni·al (bə·rō′nē ·əl) *adj.* Pertaining to or befitting a baron, a barony, or the order of barons.
bar·o·ny (bar′ə·nē) *n. pl.* **-nies** The rank, dignity, or domain of a baron.
ba·roque (bə·rōk′) *adj.* 1 Irregularly shaped: said of pearls. 2 Of, like, or characteristic of a style of art, architecture, and decoration characterized by extravagant and fantastic forms, curved rather than straight lines in ornament, and exaggerated and theatrical effects, as those developed in the 16th and 17th centuries in Europe. —*n.* 1 The baroque style. 2 An object, ornament, or design in this style. [<F <Pg. *barroco* rough or imperfect pearl]

BAROQUE (*def.* 2)
Venice: Church of Santa Maria della, Salute, 1631–56

bar·o·scope (bar′ə·skōp) *n.* 1 An instrument for approximately indicating atmospheric pressure; a weatherglass. 2 A device indicating the loss in weight of objects in air. — **bar′o·scop′ic** (-skop′ik) or **-i·cal** *adj.*
bar·o·switch (bar′ə·swich) *n. Meterol.* That component of a radiosonde apparatus which indicates pressure values during the ascent and, in a definite order, actuates the temperature, humidity, and other recording components.
Ba·rot·se·land (bə·rot′sē·land) A province of western Zambia; 63,000 square miles; capital, Mongu. Also **Western Province.**
ba·rouche (bə·rōōsh′) *n.* A four-wheeled, low-bodied pleasure-vehicle with folding top, two inside seats facing each other, and an upper outside seat for the driver. [<G *barutsche* <Ital. *baroccio* <L *bis* twice + *rota* wheel]
Ba·roz·zi (bä·rôt′tsē), **Giacomo,** 1507–73, Italian architect: also known as *Giacomo da Vignola.* Also *Barocchio.*
barque (bärk), **bar·quen·tine** (bär′kən·tēn) See **BARK**[3], **BARKENTINE.**
Bar·qui·si·me·to (bär′kē ·sē·mä′tō) A city in NW Venezuela.
bar·rack[1] (bar′ək) *n.* 1 *Usually pl.* A structure or group of structures for the lodgment of soldiers. 2 *Usually pl.* A temporary or rough shelter for a gang of laborers, etc. 3 A light adjustable roof for sheltering hay, etc. —*v.t. v.i.* To house in barracks. [ltF *baraque* <Ital. *baracca* soldiers' tent]
bar·rack[2] (bar′ək) *v.t. v.i. Austral.* To shout for or against (a group, team, etc.): often with *for* or *against.* [<dial. E]
barracks bag A soldier's cloth bag with a draw cord, for holding clothing and equipment. Also **barrack bag.**
bar·ra·coon (bar′ə·kōōn′) *n.* A barrack or enclosure for the confinement of slaves or convicts. [<Sp. *barracon,* aug. of *barraca* barrack]
bar·ra·cu·da (bar′ə·kōō′də) *n. pl.* **-da** or **-das** A voracious pike-like fish (genus *Sphyraena*) of tropical seas. The **great barracuda** (*S. barracuda*), found off the Florida coast, is often 8 feet long. [<Sp.]
bar·rage[1] (bär′ij) *n.* 1 The act of barring. 2 An artificial bar placed in a watercourse, to increase its depth for irrigating, etc. [<F < *barre* bar]
bar·rage[2] (bə·räzh′) *n.* 1 *Mil.* Concentrated fire on a part of any enemy's lines to prevent the advance of reinforcements. 2 *Mil.* A curtain of fire to close off part of the front

from enemy assault, isolate part of his position, or, by movable curtain, to protect advance of troops. **3** Any overwhelming attack, as of words or blows. **— balloon barrage** A curtain of captive balloons raised above a defense area to entangle enemy aircraft and prevent penetration of the area. **— box barrage** A curtain of artillery fire falling around an area and preventing the escape or reinforcement of troops. [<F *(tir de) barrage* barrage (fire)]

bar·ra·mun·da (bar′ə·mun′də) *n. pl.* **·da** or **·das** A large, edible, dipnoan mudfish *(Neoceratodus forsteri)* of Australia: also called *ceratodus.* Also **bar′ra·mun′di** (-dē). [<native Australian name]

bar·ran·ca (bə·rang′kə) *n. SW U.S.* A deep ravine or gorge. [<Sp.]

Bar·ran·quil·la (bär′räng·kē′yä) A port on the Magdalena, northern Colombia.

bar·ra·tor (bar′ə·tər) *n.* One guilty of barratry. Also **bar′ra·ter.**

bar·ra·try (bar′ə·trē) *n. pl.* **·tries** **1** Any wilful and unlawful act committed by the master or mariners of a ship, whereby the owners sustain injury. **2** In Scots law, the acceptance of a bribe by a judge. **3** The buying or selling of ecclesiastical positions. **4** *Law* The offense of exciting lawsuits; the stirring up of quarrels, spreading false rumors, etc. Also spelled *barretry.* [<OF *baraterie* misuse of office < *barat* fraud] **— bar′ra·trous** *adj.*

barred (bärd) *adj.* **1** Fastened with bars. **2** Obstructed by bars. **3** Made of bars. **4** Ornamented with bars; striped. **5** Prohibited; not allowed.

barred owl See under OWL.

bar·rel (bar′əl) *n.* **1** A large, round, wooden vessel, made with staves and hoops, having a flat base and top and slightly bulging sides. **2** As much as a barrel will hold: a varying measure of quantity. The standard U.S. barrel for fruits, vegetables, and other dry commodities contains 7,056 cubic inches. A barrel of petroleum contains 42 U.S. gallons. **3** Something resembling or having the form of a barrel. **4** *Ornithol.* The quill of a feather. **5** *Naut.* The rotating drum of a windlass, capstan, etc., around which the rope winds. **6** The cylindrical box containing the mainspring of a watch, around which the chain is wound. **7** In firearms, the tube through which the projectile is discharged. **8** The piston chamber of a pump. **— *v.* bar′reled** or **bar′relled, bar′rel·ing** or **bar′rel·ling** *v.t.* To put or pack in a barrel. **—*v.i. U.S. Slang*** To move at high speed. [<OF *baril;* ult. origin unknown]

barrel catch The mechanism which locks the barrel and cylinder of a revolver in firing position.

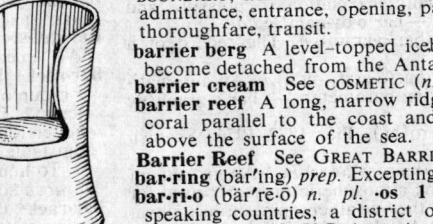

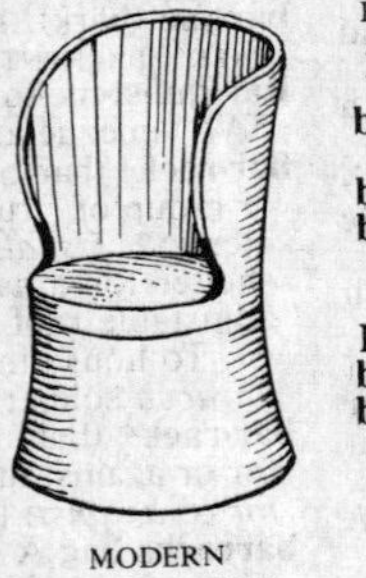
MODERN BARREL CHAIR

barrel chair An upholstered chair having a high, rounded back shaped like the vertical half of a barrel.

bar·rel·house (bar′əl·hous′) *n.* **1** A cheap drinking house. **2** An early style of jazz, originally played in barrelhouses.

barrel organ A hand organ.

barrel roll *Aeron.* A complete rotation of an airplane around its longitudinal axis.

bar·ren (bar′ən) *adj.* **1** Incapable of producing, or not producing, offspring; sterile. **2** Not producing fruit; unfruitful. **3** Unprofitable, as an enterprise. **4** Lacking in interest or attractiveness; dull. **5** Not producing; lacking: *barren* of creative effort. See synonyms under BLANK, MEAGER. **—*n.*** **1** A tract of barren land. **2** *Usually pl.* A tract of level land, having a sandy soil without trees and producing only scrubby growth. ◆Homophone *baron.* [<OF *baraigne*] **— bar′ren·ly** *adv.* **— bar′ren·ness** *n.*

Barren Grounds An arctic prairie region of northern Canada, extending west from Hudson Bay. Also **Barren Lands.**

Bar·rès (bà·res′), **Maurice,** 1862–1923, French novelist and essayist.

bar·ret (bar′it) *n.* **1** A biretta. **2** A flat cap formerly worn by soldiers. [<F *barrette* <LL *birettum* cap < *birrus* red cloak]

bar·re·try (bar′ə·trē) See BARRATRY.

bar·rette (bə·ret′) *n.* **1** A small bar or comb with a clasp used for keeping a woman's hair in place. **2** In fencing, the guard of a foil. [<F, dim. of *barre* bar]

bar·ret·ter (bar′it·ər, bə·ret′ər) *n. Electr.* A device for detecting electrical oscillations, consisting of an extremely fine, bulb-enclosed platinum wire loop, the resistance of which is increased by the heating effect of oscillations passing through it. Also **Barretter lamp.** [Origin uncertain]

bar·ri·cade (bar′ə·kād′, bar′ə·kād) *n.* **1** A barrier hastily built for obstruction or for defense. **2** Any obstruction or barrier closing a passage, as a street, a waterway, etc. See synonyms under BARRIER, RAMPART. **—*v.t.* ·cad·ed, ·cad·ing** To enclose, obstruct, or defend with a barricade or barricades. See synonyms under OBSTRUCT. [<F <Sp. *barricada* barrier < *barrica* barrel; the first barricades having been barrels filled with earth, stones, etc.] **— bar′ri·cad′er** *n.*

Bar·rie (bar′ē), **Sir James Matthew,** 1860–1937, Scottish novelist and playwright.

bar·ri·er (bar′ē·ər) *n.* **1** Any line of boundary and separation, natural or artificial, placed or serving as a limitation or obstruction. **2** Something that bars, keeps out, obstructs progress, or prevents encroachment: a *barrier* to ambition; a language *barrier.* **3** A palisade or stockade to defend the entrance to a fortified place. **4** A fortress on a frontier commanding a main passage into a country; a customs gate. **5** A fence or railing to shut out trespassers or strangers. **6** The narrow blank space which separates the frames of a motion-picture film or divides the sound track from the picture track. **7** *pl.* The palisades enclosing the ground for a tournament; the lists. **8** *Geog. Sometimes cap.* The part of the ice cap of Antarctica extending over the ocean beyond the land. [<OF *barriere* < *barre* bar]

Synonyms: bar, barricade, breastwork, bulwark, hindrance, obstacle, obstruction, parapet, prohibition, rampart, restraint, restriction. A *bar* is something that is or may be firmly fixed, ordinarily with intent to prevent entrance or egress; as, the *bars* of a prison cell. A *barrier* obstructs, but is not necessarily impassable. *Barricade* denotes some hastily piled obstruction, commonly an improvised street fortification. A *parapet* is a low or breast-high wall, as about the edge of a roof; in military use, such a wall for the protection of troops; a *rampart* is the embankment surrounding a fort, on which the *parapet* is raised; the word *rampart* is often used as including the *parapet. Bulwark* is a general word for any defensive wall, but in present technical use it signifies the raised side of a ship above the upper deck, topped by the rail. Compare BOUNDARY, IMPEDIMENT, RAMPART. *Antonyms*: admittance, entrance, opening, passage, road, thoroughfare, transit.

barrier berg A level-topped iceberg that has become detached from the Antarctic barrier.

barrier cream See COSMETIC (*n.* def. 3).

barrier reef A long, narrow ridge of rock or coral parallel to the coast and close to or above the surface of the sea.

Barrier Reef See GREAT BARRIER REEF.

bar·ring (bär′ing) *prep.* Excepting; apart from.

bar·ri·o (bär′rē·ō) *n. pl.* **·os** **1** In Spanish-speaking countries, a district or ward of a town or city. **2** *U.S.* A section of a city or town populated largely by Spanish-speaking people. [<Sp.]

bar·ris·ter (bar′is·tər) *n.* In English law, an advocate who argues cases in the courts, as distinguished from a *solicitor,* who prepares them. In the United States an attorney combines the two functions. [<BAR[1]]

bar·room (bär′ro͞om′, -ro͝om′) *n.* A room where alcoholic liquors are served across a counter.

Bar·ros (bär′ro͞osh), **João de,** 1496–1570, Portuguese historian.

bar·row[1] (bar′ō) *n.* **1** A frame, tray, or box, with or without a wheel or wheels, having handles or shafts by which it is pushed, pulled, or carried. **2** The load carried on or capacity of a barrow. **3** A wheelbarrow. **4** A push-cart. [OE *bearwe*]

bar·row[2] (bar′ō) *n.* **1** A burial mound; cairn. **2** A hill. [OE *beorg* hill, burial mound]

bar·row[3] (bar′ō) *n.* A castrated pig. [OE *bearg* pig]

Bar·row (bar′ō), **Isaac,** 1630–77, English mathematician and theologian.

Bar·row (bar′ō), **Point** A cape of the northernmost part of Alaska in the Arctic Ocean.

Bar·row-in-Fur·ness (bar′ō·in·fûr′nes) A county borough in NW Lancashire, England.

Bar·ry (bar′ē, *Fr.* bà·rē′), **du** See DU BARRY.

Bar·ry (bar′ē), **Philip,** 1896–1949, U.S. dramatist.

Bar·ry·more (bar′ə·môr, -mōr) A family of U.S. actors: **Maurice** (real name, Herbert Blythe), 1847–1905, father of **Lionel,** 1878–1954, **Ethel,** 1879–1959, **John,** 1882–1942.

bar sinister See BATON SINISTER under BATON.

Bart (bärt, *Fr.* bàr), **Jean,** 1651?–1702, French naval hero. Also **Barth.**

bar·tend·er (bär′ten′dər) *n.* One who serves liquors over a bar.

bar·ter (bär′tər) *v.i.* To trade by exchange of goods or services without use of money. **—*v.t.*** To trade (goods or services) for something of equal value. **—*n.*** The exchanging of commodities or a commodity given in exchange. See synonyms under BUSINESS. [<OF *barater* exchange] **— bar′ter·er** *n.*

Barth (bärt), **Heinrich,** 1821–65, German explorer. **— Karl,** 1886–1968, Swiss theologian.

Bar·thol·di (bär·thol′dē, *Fr.* bàr·tôl·dē′), **Frédéric Auguste,** 1834–1904, French sculptor of the Statue of Liberty.

Bar·thol·o·mew (bär·thol′ə·myo͞o) A masculine personal name. Also *Lat.* **Bar·thol·o·mae·us** (bär·tol′ə·mē′əs), *Fr.* **Bar·thé·le·my** (bàr·tāl·mē′) or **Bar·tho·lo·mé** (bàr·tô·lô·mā′), *Ital.* **Bar·to·lo·me·o** (bär·tō′lō·mâ′ō), *Pg.* **Bar·to·lo·meu** (bär·tō′lō·mā′o͞o), *Sp.* **Bar·to·lo·mé** (bär·tō′lō·mā′), *Du.* **Bar·thol·o·me·us** (bär·tôl′ō·mā′o͞os), *Ger.* **Bar·tho·lo·mä·us** (bär·tō′lō·mā′·o͞os) or **Bar·thel** (bär′təl). [<Hebrew, son of furrows]

— Bartholomew, Saint One of the twelve apostles, on whose feast day, August 24, in 1572 a slaughter of Huguenots (the **Massacre of St. Bartholomew**) occurred in France.

Bar·ti·mae·us (bär′tə·mē′əs) A beggar cured of blindness. *Mark* x 46–52. Also **Bar′ti·me′us.**

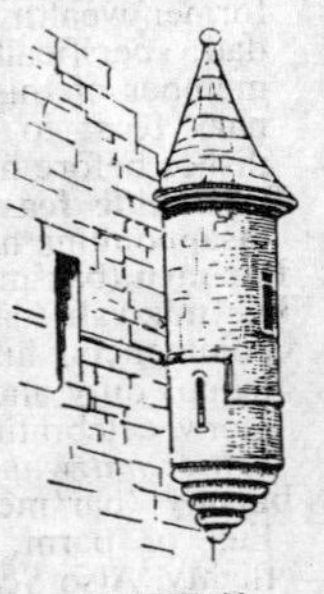
BARTIZAN ON A TOWER

bar·ti·zan (bär′tə·zən, bär′·tə·zan′) *n.* A turret, with loopholes, jutting out from a wall. [Alter. of *bratticing* <BRATTICE] **— bar·ti·zaned** (bär′tə·zənd, bär′tə·zand′) *adj.*

Bart·lett (bärt′lit) *n.* A variety of large, juicy pear developed in England about 1770 and introduced into America by Enoch Bartlett of Dorchester, Massachusetts. Also **Bartlett pear.**

Bart·lett (bärt′lit), **John,** 1820–1905, U. S. publisher; compiled *Familiar Quotations,* 1855. **— Josiah,** 1729–1795, American physician and Revolutionary leader. **— Robert Abram,** 1875–1946, Canadian Arctic explorer.

Bar·tok (bär′tôk), **Bé·la** (bā′lä), 1881–1945, Hungarian composer.

Bar·to·lom·me·o (bär′tō·lōm·mâ′ō), **Fra,** 1475–1517, Florentine painter: also known as *Baccio della Porta.*

Bar·ton (bär′tən), **Clara,** 1821–1912, founder of the American Red Cross.

Bar·tram (bär′trəm), **John,** 1699–1777, American botanist.

Bar·uch (bâr′ək) **1** The amanuensis of Jeremiah. *Jer.* xxxii–xxxvi. **2** A book in the Old Testament Apocrypha attributed to Baruch. [<Hebrew, blessed]

Ba·ruch (bə·ro͞ok′), **Bernard Mannes,** 1870–1965, U.S. financier and statesman.

Bar·won (bär′won) The upper Darling River, northern New South Wales, Australia.

bar·ye (bar′ē) *n.* In the cgs system, a unit expressing a pressure of one dyne a square centimeter. [<Gk. *barys* heavy]

Ba·rye (bà·rē′), **Antoine Louis,** 1795–1875, French sculptor.

bar·y·on (bar′ē·on) *n. Physics* Any strongly interacting particle whose spin is half an odd integer; a nucleon or hyperon. [<Gk. *barys* heavy + -ON]

bar·y·sphere (bar′i·sfir) *n. Geol.* The centrosphere. [<Gk. *barys* heavy + SPHERE]

ba·ry·ta (bə·rī′tə) *n.* Barium oxide. [<Gk. *barytēs* weight < *barys* heavy]

ba·ry·tes (bə·rī′tēz) *n.* Barite.

bar·y·tone[1] (bar′ə·tōn) *n.* In Greek grammar,

a word having the last syllable unaccented. [<Gk. *barytonos* unaccented]

bar·y·tone² (bar'ə·tōn) See BARITONE.

ba·sal (bā'səl) *adj.* **1** Pertaining to, of, or at the base. **2** Basic; fundamental. **3** *Physiol.* Designating a standard of reference or comparison: *basal* metabolism. **4** *Surg.* Serving to prepare for deeper levels of unconsciousness: *basal* anesthesia preliminary to surgical anesthesia. — **ba'sal·ly** *adv.*

basal metabolism *Physiol.* The minimum energy, measured in calories, required by the body at rest in maintaining essential vital activities.

basal age *Psychol.* The highest age level manifested in a completed series of mental tests graded to include items appropriate to each successive age level.

ba·salt (bə·sôlt', bas'ôlt) *n.* **1** A fine-grained, igneous, volcanic rock of high density and dark color, composed chiefly of plagioclase and pyroxene, usually exhibiting a columnar structure. **2** A black, unglazed pottery resembling basalt, developed by Josiah Wedgwood: also **ba·salt'ware'**. [<L *basaltes* dark marble] — **ba·sal'tic** *adj.*

bas-bleu (bä·blœ') *n. French* A bluestocking.

Bas·co (bäs'kō) Capital of Batanes province, Philippines.

bas·cule (bas'kyōol) *n.* A mechanical apparatus

BASCULE BRIDGE
Tower Bridge, London

of which each end counterbalances the other: used in a kind of drawbridge (**bascule bridge**) operated by a counterpoise. [<F, = see-saw]

base¹ (bās) *n.* **1** The lowest or supporting part of anything; bottom; foundation. **2** *Ling.* The form of a word used in making derivatives, as by adding prefixes or suffixes; root or stem. **3** A determining ingredient; a common element with which other more distinctive elements unite to form a product; essential or preponderant element or part of anything. **4** *Chem.* **a** A compound which is capable of so uniting with an acid to neutralize its acid properties and form a salt, as sodium hydroxide, NaOH. **b** A compound that yields hydroxyl ions in solution. **c** Any molecule or radical that takes up protons. **5** A basis of military or naval operations or of supplies. **6** In baseball, any one of the four points of the diamond; also, in certain other games, or in a race, the goal or starting point. **7** Any point, part, line, number, or quantity from which a reckoning, inference, or conclusion proceeds, or on which any other dimension depends; any principle or datum; a basis: the *base* of an argument, the *base* of a triangle. **8** A very accurately measured line on the earth's surface, from whose known length other lines in a survey are determined. **9** A number on which a mathematical system or calculation depends: In the Arabic notation, 10 is the *base* of the decimal system. **10** *Geom.* **a** That side of a rectilineal figure or that face of a solid on which the figure is conceived to be erected. **b** A side or face which has some special mark or character, or to which other parts are referred. **11** *Biol.* The end opposite to the apex; the point of attachment. **12** *Archit.* The lowest member of a structure, as the basement of a building, the plinth (when present) and base moldings of a column, or the lowest course of a wall; a pedestal. **13** The celluloid component of a motion-picture film. **14** *Her.* The lower part of the shield. — **off base 1** In baseball, not on the base one should be on. **2** *Colloq.* Utterly wrong about something. — *v.t.* **based, bas·ing 1** To place or ground

on a logical basis, as an argument, decision, or theory: with *on* or *upon*. **2** To make or form a base for. — *adj.* **1** Serving as a base: a *base* line. **2** Situated at or near the base: a *base* angle. ◆ Homophone: *bass²*. [<F <L *basis* <Gk. *basis* step, pedestal < *bainein* to go]

base² (bās) *adj.* **1** Low in sentiment, morals, or rank. **2** Low in value. **3** Alloyed, debased, or counterfeit, as money; not silver or gold: *base* metals. **4** *Music* Bass. **5** In English law, held by villeinage: opposed to *free*: said of a tenure of an estate. **6** *Obs.* Of humble or ignoble birth; also, illegitimate. **7** Menial; servile. **8** Not classical: said of languages. ◆ Homophone: *bass²*. [<OF *bas* <LL *bassus* low] — **base'ly** *adv.* — **base'ness** *n.*

Synonyms: abject, beggarly, cheap, contemptible, cringing, degraded, degrading, despicable, groveling, ignoble, infamous, low, low-minded, mean, mean-spirited, menial, miserable, obsequious, paltry, poor, poor-spirited, scurvy, servile, shabby, slavish, sneaking, sordid, squalid, subservient, vile, worthless, wretched. *Antonyms*: arrogant, conceited, dignified, eminent, esteemed, exalted, haughty, honorable, illustrious, independent, insolent, lofty, noble, pompous, princely, proud, self-assertive, self-conceited, self-reliant, self-respectful, supercilious, superior, supreme, vain, worthy.

base·ball (bās'bôl') *n.* **1** A game played with a wooden bat and a hard ball by two teams, properly of nine players each, one team being at bat and the other in the field, alternately,

N
M   B   O
L   J
K   I
C   *a*   A
d   H   *d*
    P
b   *c*   *b*
F   D   E
G
e
Q   Q

BASEBALL FIELD

a.   Diamond (90 feet x 90 feet).
b.   Players' line (75 feet x 75 feet).
c.   Three-foot line (48 x 3 feet).
d.   Coaches' lines.
e.   Catcher's lines.
A.   First base (15 inches x 15 inches).
B.   Second base (15 inches x 15 inches).
C.   Third base (15 inches x 15 inches).
D.   Home base (17 x 8 1/2 x 12 x 8 1/2 x 12 inches; five-sided).
E., F.   Batter's boxes.
G.   Catcher.
H.   Pitcher's plate (24 inches x 6 inches).
I.   First baseman.
J.   Second baseman.
K.   Third baseman.
L.   Shortstop.
M., N., O.   Outfielders.
P   Space to which base runner must confine himself.
Q.   Players' benches.

for a minimum of nine innings: the game is played on a field having four bases marking the course each player must take in scoring a run. **2** The ball used in this game.

base·board (bās'bôrd', -bōrd') *n.* **1** A board skirting the interior wall of a room, next to the floor. **2** A board forming the base of anything.

base·born (bās'bôrn') *adj.* **1** Born out of wedlock. **2** Of low birth; plebeian. **3** Mean.

base·burn·er (bās'bûr'nər) *n.* A coal stove or furnace in which the fuel is fed from above into a central fuel chamber.

base command *Mil.* An area organized for the unified administration of all military

operations carried on by the base or bases functioning within it.

Ba·se·dow's disease (bä'zə·dōz) Exophthalmic goiter. [after a 19th c. German physician]

base hit In baseball, a hit by which the batter reaches base without help of an opposing player's error or without forcing out a runner previously on base.

Ba·sel (bä'zəl) A city on the Rhine in northern Switzerland: ancient *Basilia*: also *Basle*: French *Bâle*.

base·less (bās'lis) *adj.* Without foundation in fact; unfounded; groundless. See synonyms under VAIN.

base level The lowest level of erosion possible to a watercourse in any geographical area.

base·man (bās'mən) *n. pl.* **·men** (-mən) A baseball player stationed at first, second, or third base.

base·ment (bās'mənt) *n.* **1** The lowest floor of a building, usually underground and just beneath the principal story. **2** The substructure or the basal portion of any building or other structure or member.

base metal 1 Any metal which oxidizes easily when exposed to or heated in air, as iron, lead, or tin: opposed to *noble metal*. **2** *Chem.* A metal whose hydroxide is soluble in water.

ba·sen·ji (bə·sen'jē) *n.* A small, barkless dog, similar in build to a fox terrier, with a smooth, reddish coat and white-tipped tail and feet. [<Afrikaans, bush thing]

BASENJI

base of operations *Mil.* A region or area from which a military force begins an offensive action and to which it falls back in case of withdrawal.

base runner In baseball, a member of the team at bat who has reached base.

bas·es¹ (bā'siz) Plural of BASE.

ba·ses² (bā'sēz) Plural of BASIS.

bash (bash) *v.t.* To strike heavily; smash in. — *n.* A smashing blow. [? Akin to Dan. *baske* thwack]

Ba·shan (bā'shən) A region east of the Jordan in ancient Palestine.

ba·shaw (bə·shô') *n.* **1** A Turkish official. **2** *Colloq.* An important or self-important personage. [<Turkish *bāshā*, var. of *pāshā*, ? < *bāsh* head]

bash·ful (bash'fəl) *adj.* **1** Shrinking from notice; shy; timid; diffident. **2** Characterized by or indicating sensitiveness and timid modesty. [<*bash*, var. of ABASH + -FUL] — **bash'ful·ly** *adv.* — **bash'ful·ness** *n.*

Ba·shi Channel (bä'shē) The northernmost part of Luzon Strait, between the Batan Islands and Taiwan.

bash·i·ba·zouk (bash'ē·bə·zōok') *n.* A member of a class of mounted Turkish irregular soldiers, noted for brutality. [<Turkish *bashi* headdress + *bozuq* disorderly]

Bash·kir Autonomous Soviet Socialist Republic (bäsh·kir') An administrative division of eastern European Russian S.F.S.R.; 55,400 square miles; capital, Ufa.

bash·lyk (bash'lik) *n.* A fitted cloth hood covering the head and ears. Also **bash'lik**. [<Russian]

ba·sic (bā'sik) *adj.* **1** Pertaining to, forming, or like a base or basis. **2** Essential; fundamental. **3** *Chem.* **a** Above normal in base-producing constituents: a *basic* salt. **b** Yielding hydroxyl ions when dissolved in an ionizing solvent. **c** Showing an alkaline reaction. **4** *Geol.* Containing comparatively little silica: said of igneous rocks, as basalt. **5** *Metall.* Designating the basic process of making steel. — *n.* In the U.S. Army, an enlisted man who has completed or is pursuing the minimum course of military training.

ba·si·cal·ly (bā'sik·lē) *adv.* Essentially; fundamentally.

Basic English A highly simplified form of English, devised by C. K. Ogden, intended for use as an international auxiliary language. It consists of 600 common nouns, 18 verbs, 150 adjectives, and 82 assorted pronouns, prepositions, conjunctions, and adverbs. The

850 words of the general vocabulary are supplemented by an additional 150 for scientific purposes. Also called **Basic.** [*Basic,* acronym for British, American, Scientific, International, Commercial]

ba·sic·i·ty (bā·sis′ə·tē) *n. Chem.* **1** The state or condition of being a base. **2** The ability of an acid to unite with one or more equivalents of a base, depending upon the number of replaceable hydrogen atoms contained in a molecule of the acid.

basic oxide A metallic oxide which is capable of interacting with an acid to form a salt, as calcium oxide or lime, CaO.

basic process A method of steelmaking which uses a furnace lined with a basic refractory material, as dolomite or magnesite: it yields a **basic slag** rich in lime and phosphorus.

ba·sid·i·o·my·ce·tous (bə·sid′ē·ō·mī·sē′təs) *adj. Bot.* Belonging to a class *(Basidiomycetes)* of fungi having the spores borne on basidia. It includes parasites and saprophytes: mushrooms, smuts, rusts, etc. [< BASIDIUM + Gk. *mykēs, -ētos* fungus]

ba·sid·i·um (bə·sid′ē·əm) *n. pl.* **·sid·i·a** (-sid′ē·ə) *Bot.* A mother cell in basidiomycetous fungi, on which spores (usually four) are borne at the extremity of slender stalks. [< NL < Gk. *baseidion,* dim. of *basis* base]

ba·si·fy (bā′sə·fī) *v.t.* **·fied, ·fy·ing** To change into a base by chemical means. — **ba′si·fi·ca′tion** *n.* — **ba′si·fi′er** *n.*

bas·il (baz′əl) *n.* **1** Any of certain aromatic plants of the mint family (genus *Ocimum*), especially the European *sweet basil (O. basilicum).* **2** The American mountain mint (genus *Pycnanthemum*) or **wild basil.** [< OF *basile* < L *basilicum* < Gk. *basilikon (phyton)* royal (plant), basil < *basileus* king]

Bas·il (baz′əl, bā′zəl) A masculine personal name. Also *Fr.* **Ba·sile** (bà·zēl′), *Lat.* **Ba·sil·i·us** (bə·sil′ē·əs; *Dan., Du., Ger., Sw.* bä·zē′lē·ōōs), *Ital., Pg., Sp.* **Ba·si·li·o** (bä·sē′lē·ō). [< Gk., kingly]

— **Basil the Great, Saint,** 329?–379, one of the four Greek doctors of the church; bishop of Caesarea.

Ba·si·lan (bä·sē′län) An island of the Philippines east of Mindanao; 494 square miles.

bas·i·lar (bas′ə·lər) *adj.* Pertaining to or situated at the base; basal. Also **bas·i·lar·y** (bas′ə·ler′ē).

basilar membrane *Anat.* The membrane separating the two vestibules of the cochlea of the ear and acting as a receptor of the sound vibrations transmitted by the auditory nerve.

Ba·sil·i·a (bə·zil′ē·ə) The ancient name for BASEL.

ba·sil·ic (bə·sil′ik) *adj.* **1** Pertaining to a basilica. **2** Royal. **3** *Anat.* Pertaining to the largest vein of the arm. Also **ba·sil′i·cal.** [< Gk. *basilikos* kingly]

ba·sil·i·ca (bə·sil′i·kə) *n.* **1** Originally, in ancient Athens, a portico used as a court of justice. **2** In ancient Rome, a rectangular building divided into nave and aisles: used as a hall of justice and adopted as the type of the earliest buildings for Christian worship. **3** A church shaped like a Roman basilica. **4** In the Roman Catholic Church, a church accorded certain liturgical privileges. [< L < Gk. *basilikē,* fem. of *basilikos* royal] — **ba·sil′i·can** *adj.*

Ba·sil·i·ca (bə·sil′i·kə) *n.* The Byzantine code of law of Basil I (9th century), chiefly adapted from that of Justinian: a plural used also as a singular. [< Gk. *basilika (nomima)* (laws) of Basil]

Ba·si·li·ca·ta (bä·sē′lē·kä′tä) A region of southern Italy at the instep of the Italian boot: ancient *Lucania.*

bas·i·lisk (bas′ə·lisk) *n.* **1** A fabled reptile of the African desert whose breath and look were fatal. **2** A tropical American lizard (genus *Basiliscus,* family *Iguanidae)* having an erectile crest and a dilatable pouch on the head. [< L *basiliscus* < Gk. *basiliskos,* dim. of *basileus* king]

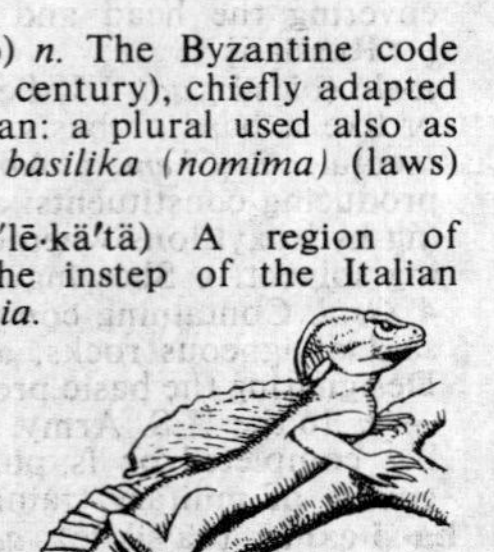

THE HOODED BASILISK

ba·sin (bā′sən) *n.* **1** A round, wide, shallow vessel, often with sloping sides, used especially for holding liquids. **2** The amount that a basin will hold. **3** A sink or wash bowl. **4** A depression in the earth's surface, as a valley, or the region drained by a river. **5** A depressed region in the floor of the ocean. **6** A comparatively circular and shallow area or arm of the sea: the Minas *Basin.* [< OF *bacin* < LL *bachinus* < *bacca* bowl] — **ba′sined** *adj.* — **ba′sin·like′** *adj.*

bas·i·net (bas′ə·nit, -net) *n.* A small, close-fitting helmet. [< OF *bacinet,* dim. of *bacin* basin]

ba·si·on (bā′sē·ən) *n. Anat.* The point where the anterior border of the foramen magnum of the skull cuts the median plane. [< Gk. *basis* base]

ba·sip·e·tal (bā·sip′ə·təl) *adj. Bot.* Growing in the direction of the base.

ba·sis (bā′sis) *n. pl.* **ba·ses** (bā′sēz) **1** That on which anything rests; support; foundation. **2** Fundamental principle. **3** The chief component or ingredient of a thing. [< L < Gk., base, pedestal]

bask (bask, bäsk) *v.i.* **1** To lie in and enjoy a pleasant warmth, as of the sun or a fire. **2** To enjoy or expose oneself to a benign influence, pleasant situation, etc.: to *bask* in the favor of a king. — *v.t.* **3** To expose to warmth. [< ON *badhask* bathe oneself]

Bas·ker·ville (bas′kər·vil), **John,** 1706–75, English printer and type founder; designer of the type face known by his name.

bas·ket (bas′kit, bäs′-) *n.* **1** A container made of interwoven twigs, splints, rushes, strips, etc. **2** Something resembling a basket, as the structure under a balloon for carrying passengers or ballast. **3** The amount a basket will hold; a basketful. **4** An openwork guard over the hilt of a sword: also **basket hilt.** **5** In basketball, either of the goals, consisting of a metal ring with a cord net suspended from it; also, the point or points made by throwing the ball through the basket. **6** *Mil.* The platform supporting the two operators of a tank turret, which rotates with the turret. [ME; origin unknown] — **bas′ket·like′** *adj.*

bas·ket·ball (bas′kit·bôl′, bäs′-) *n.* **1** An indoor game played by two teams of five men each, in which the object is to throw the ball through the elevated goal (basket) at the opponent's end of a zoned, oblong court.

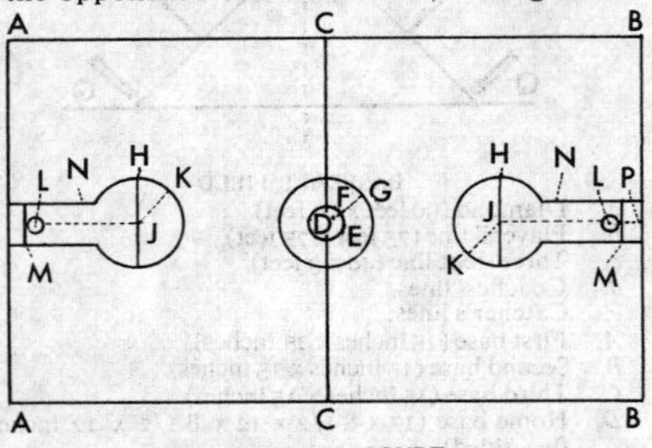

BASKETBALL COURT

C.	Center division line.	*N.*	Foul lines.
E.	Restraining circle.	*DF.*	Radius 2 feet.
H.	Free throw lines.	*DG.*	Radius 6 feet.
J.	Free throw circles.	*JK.*	Radius 6 feet.
L.	Baskets.	*JM.*	15 feet.
M.	Backboards.	*JP.*	19 feet.

AA, BB. End lines, vary from 35 to 50 feet.
AB, AB. Side lines, vary from 84 to 94 feet. The basket is raised 10 feet from playing floor.

On each team the players consist of a center, two forwards, and two guards. **2** The round, inflated leather ball used in this game.

basket dance *Anthropol.* A ceremonial dance centering the action on a basket held in the left hand of a woman dancer, who strews grain or meal from it as a symbol of vegetation fertility: danced in many culture areas of the Old and New World.

bas·ket·fish (bas′kit·fish′, bäs′-) *n.* A starfish (genus *Gorgonocephalus*) having many branched or interlacing arms: common off the New England coast.

Basket Maker One of a class of prehistoric cave-dwelling people of SW North America, of a culture more ancient than the cliff-dwellers or Pueblos, characterized by their basket-making and lack of pottery.

basket meeting *U.S.* A social gathering to which people bring their suppers in a basket.

bas·ket·ry (bas′kit·rē, bäs′-) *n.* **1** Baskets collectively; basketwork. **2** The art or craft of making baskets.

bas·ket·weave (bas′kit·wēv′, bäs′-) *n.* A weave with two or more warp and filling threads woven side by side to resemble a plaited basket.

bas·ket·work (bas′kit·wûrk′, bäs′-) *n.* A fabric or texture of woven or plaited osiers or twigs, or an imitation of it in some other substance; wickerwork.

basking shark A shark *(Cetorhinus maximus)* of the North Atlantic, attaining a length of over 30 feet and valued for its liver oil: named from its habit of basking on the surface of the water.

Basle (bäl) See BASEL.

ba·so·phile (bā′sə·fīl, -fil) *n. Biol.* A tissue or cell having a special affinity for basic staining dyes: also spelled *basiphile.* [< BASIC (dye) + -PHILE] — **ba·so·phil·ic** (bā′sə·fil′ik), **ba·soph·i·lous** (bā·sof′ə·ləs) *adj.*

ba·so·phil·i·a (bā′sə·fil′ē·ə) *n. Pathol.* A condition in which an excessive number of basophiles are present in the blood.

basque (bask) *n.* A woman's closely fitting bodice, separate from the dress skirt: originally from the Basque costume.

Basque (bask) *n.* **1** One of a people living in the western Pyrenees in Spain and France, of unknown racial origin but having such distinctive racial traits that they are believed to be unrelated to any other racial stock. **2** The agglutinative language of the Basque people, unrelated to any other language: possibly a survival of the lost ancient Iberian. — *adj.* Of or pertaining to the Basques or to their language, or to the Basque Provinces.

Basque Provinces Three provinces in northern Spain on the Bay of Biscay; combined area, 2,803 square miles. *Spanish* **Vas·con·ga·das** (väs′kōng·gä′thäs).

Bas·ra (bus′rə) A port of SE Iraq on the Shatt-el-Arab: also *Bassora, Bussora, Busra.* Also **Bas′rah.**

bas-re·lief (bä′ri·lēf′, bas′-) *n.* Sculpture or a piece of sculpture in which the figures project only slightly from the background: also called *basso-rilievo.* See RELIEF. [< F < Ital. *basso* low + *rilievo* relief]

Bas-Rhin (bä·raṅ′) A department of France in Alsace; 1,848 square miles; capital, Strasbourg.

bass[1] (bas) *n.* **1** One of various spiny-finned, marine and fresh-water food fishes, especially the European sea bass *(Dicentrarchus labrax),* the American striped bass *(Roccus lineatus),* and the black basses (genus *Micropterus).* **2** The European perch *(Perca fluviatilis).* **3** The cabrilla (def. 2). [OE *bærs*]

bass[2] (bās) *n. Music* **1** The lowest-pitched male singing voice. **2** A deep, low sound, as of this voice or of certain low-pitched instruments. **3** The notes in the lowest register of the piano, pipe organ, etc. **4** The lowest part in vocal or instrumental music. **5** One who sings or an instrument that plays such a part, especially a bass viol. **6** Such parts collectively. — *adj.* **1** Low in pitch; having a low musical range. **2** Pertaining to, for, or able to play bass. ◆ Homophone: *base.* [< OF *bas* low; infl. in spelling by Ital. *basso*]

bass[3] (bas) *n.* **1** The basswood. **2** Bast. [Alter. of BAST]

Bas·sa·ni·o (bə·sä′nē·ō) In Shakespeare's *Merchant of Venice,* Portia's successful suitor.

bass clef (bās) *Music* **1** The sign on a staff showing that the notes are below middle C. **2** The notes so shown.

bass drum (bās) The largest of the drums, beaten on both heads and having a deep sound: also called *double drum.*

Bas·sein (bä·sēn′, -sān′) A port on one of the mouths of the Irrawaddy, Lower Burma.

bas·set[1] (bas′it) *n.* A hound characterized by a long, low body, long head and nose, and short, heavy, crooked forelegs: used in hunting. Also **bas′set-hound′.** [< OF *basset,* fem. dim. of *bas* low]

bas·set[2] (bas′it) *Geol. n.* An outcropping. — *v.i.* **·set·ed, ·set·ing** To crop out; appear at the surface, as coal. [Origin uncertain]

Basse·terre (bäs·târ′) A town on St. Kitts, capital of the St. Christopher, Nevis and Anguilla presidency of the Leeward Islands.

Basse-Terre (bäs·târ′) **1** A port on the SW

coast of Basse-Terre island, capital of the French overseas department of Guadeloupe. **2** One of the twin islands comprising Guadeloupe department: also *Guadeloupe.*

bas·set-horn (bas′it·hôrn′) *n.* A tenor clarinet having a compass of three and a half octaves. It has four more low keys than the ordinary clarinet. [<Ital. *corno di bassetto* < *bassetto,* dim. of *basso* low + *corno* horn]

bass horn (bās) A tuba.

bas·si·net (bas′ə·net′) *n.* **1** A basket, usually with a hood over one end, used as a baby's cradle. **2** A small basket for holding the clothing of an infant. **3** A kind of perambulator. [<F, dim. of *bassin* basin]

bas·so (bas′ō, *Ital.* bäs′sō) *n. pl.* **bas·sos** (bas′ōz), *Ital.* **bas·si** (bäs′sē) **1** A bass singer. **2** The bass part. [<Ital., low]

bas·soon (ba·sōōn′, bə-) *n. Music* **1** A large, double-reed woodwind instrument with a long, curved mouthpiece. **2** An organ stop like a bassoon in its low tone. [<F *basson,* aug. of *bas* low]

basso pro·fun·do (prə·fun′dō, *Ital.* prō·fōōn′dō) **1** A singer who sings the deepest bass. **2** The lowest bass voice.

Bas·so·ra (bas′ə·rə) Basra. Also **Bas′so·rah.**

bas·so-re·lie·vo (bas′ō·ri·lē′vō) *n. pl.* **·vos** (-vōz) Bas-relief.

bas·so-ri·lie·vo (bäs′sō·ri·lyā′vō) *n. pl.* **·ri·lie·vi** (-ri·lyā′vē) *Italian* Bas-relief.

Bass Strait (bas) The passage between the coasts of the Australian mainland and Tasmania, from the Indian Ocean to the Tasman Sea.

bass viol (bās) *Music* **1** The double-bass. **2** The viola da gamba.

bass·wood (bas′wŏŏd′) *n.* The linden.

bast (bast) *n. Bot.* **1** The fibrous inner bark of trees or a cordage made from it: also called *bass.* **2** A vegetable tissue found especially in the inner bark of dicotyledons, composed of tough, spindle-shaped, thick-walled fibers or cells. **3** Phloem. [OE *bæst*]

bas·tard (bas′tərd) *n.* **1** An illegitimate child. **2** Any hybrid plant, tree, or animal. **3** Any spurious, irregular, inferior, or counterfeit thing. **4** A refuse sugar from previously boiled sirup. —*adj.* **1** Born out of wedlock. **2** False; spurious. **3** Resembling but not typical of the genuine thing: *bastard* mahogany. **4** Unusual in size, shape, or proportion; abnormal; irregular: *bastard* type. [<OF *bastard* < *fils de bast* packsaddle child; with ref. to the use of the saddle as a bed]

bas·tard·ize (bas′tər·dīz) *v.* **·ized, ·iz·ing** *v.t.* **1** To prove to be, or stigmatize as, a bastard. **2** To make degenerate; debase. —*v.i.* **3** To become debased. —**bas′tard·i·za′tion** *n.*

bas·tard·ly (bas′tərd·lē) *adj.* **1** Bastardlike; of illegitimate birth. **2** Debased; counterfeit.

bastard wing *Ornithol.* An alula.

bas·tard·y (bas′tər·dē) *n.* **1** The begetting of a bastard. **2** The state of being a bastard; illegitimacy.

baste[1] (bāst) *v.t.* **bast·ed, bast·ing** To sew loosely together, as with long, temporary stitches. [<OF *bastir* <OHG *bestan* sew with bast]

baste[2] (bāst) *v.t.* **bast·ed, bast·ing** To moisten (meat or fish) with drippings, butter, etc., while cooking. [<OF *basser* soak, moisten]

baste[3] (bāst) *v.t. Colloq.* **1** To cudgel; thrash. **2** To attack verbally; abuse. [prob. <Scand., cf. ON *beysta* beat]

Bas·tia (bäs′tyä) A port on the NE coast of Corsica; chief city and former capital of the island.

Bas·tien-Le·page (bȧs·tyaṅ′lə·pȧzh′), **Jules,** 1848–84, French painter.

bas·tille (bas·tēl′) *n.* **1** A prison; especially, one used as a government prison or operated tyrannically. **2** In ancient warfare, a small fortress. Also **bas·tile′.** [<OF, building]

Bas·tille (bas·tēl′, *Fr.* bȧs·tē′y′) A fortress in Paris, built in 1369 and stormed and destroyed in the French Revolution on July 14, 1789.

Bastille Day The national holiday of republican France, July 14, commemorating the fall and destruction of the Bastille.

bas·ti·na·do (bas′tə·nā′dō) *n. pl.* **·does** **1** A beating with a stick, usually on the soles of the feet: an Oriental punishment. **2** A stick or cudgel. —*v.t.* **·doed, ·do·ing** To beat with a stick, usually on the soles of the feet. See synonyms under BEAT. Also **bas′ti·nade′.** [<Sp. *bastonado* < *bastón* cudgel]

bast·ing (bās′ting) *n.* **1** The act of sewing loosely together. **2** *pl.* Long, loose, temporary stitches. **3** The thread used for this purpose. [<BASTE[1]]

bas·tion (bas′chən, -tē·ən) *n.* **1** In fortifications, a projecting work having two faces and two flanks so constructed that the adjacent curtain may be defended from it. **2** Any fortified or strongly defended place or position. [<F <Ital. *bastione* < *bastire* build] —**bas′tioned** *adj.*

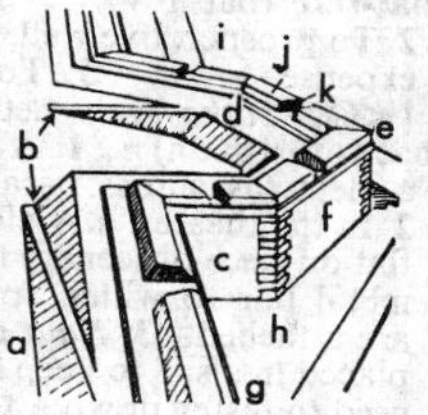

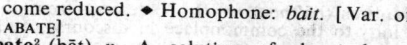

BASTION

a. Boulevard. *b.* Ramps. *c.* Flank. *d.* Banquette. *e.* Salient. *f.* Face of rampart. *g.* Berm. *h.* Moat. *i.* Glacis. *j.* Scarp. *k.* Embrasure in parapet.

The curtains extending from its flanks *(c)* are on both sides of the bastion.

Bas·togne (bas·tōn′, *Fr.* bȧs·tôn′y′) A town in SE Belgium; besieged and nearly destroyed during the German counter-offensive of World War II in December, 1944. *Flemish* **Bas·te·na·ken** (bäs′tə·nä′kən).

Ba·su·to·land (bə·sōō′tō·land′) A former British territory in southern Africa. See LESOTHO.

bat[1] (bat) *n.* **1** Any heavy cudgel or club. **2** Batting. **3** In baseball, cricket, and other games: **a** A stick or club for striking the ball, usually having one end wider or heavier than the other. **b** A turn at bat or the right to such a turn. **c** A racket, as in tennis. **d** The act of batting. **e** The batsman, as in cricket. **4** A fragment or lump of clay. **5** *Colloq.* A blow, as with a stick. **6** *Colloq.* Speed; rate of motion. **7** *Slang* A drunken carousal; a spree. —**at bat** In the act or position of batting. —**to go to bat for** *Colloq.* To defend or advocate the cause of. —*v.* **bat·ted, bat·ting** *v.i.* **1** In baseball, cricket, and other games: **a** To use a bat. **b** To take a turn at bat. **2** *Slang* To go hurriedly. —*v.t.* **3** To strike with or as with a bat. —**to bat around** *Slang* **1** To move or travel about. **2** To discuss, as a proposal or idea. **3** In baseball, to have the whole team bat in one inning. [OE *batt* cudgel]

bat[2] (bat) *n.* Any of numerous nocturnal flying mammals (order *Chiroptera*), having greatly elongated fore limbs and digits that support a thin wing membrane extending to the hind limbs and sometimes to the tail. —**blind as a bat** Altogether blind. —**to have bats in the belfry** *Slang* To be crazy. [ME *bakke,* ? <Scand.] —**bat′like′** *adj.*

bat[3] (bat) *v.t. Colloq.* To wink; flutter. —**not bat an eye** *Colloq.* Not show surprise or other reaction. [Var. of BATE[3]]

bat[4] (bät) See BAHT.

Ba·taan (bə·tan′, -tan′) A province in southern Luzon, Philippines; 517 square miles; capital, Balanga; occupying **Bataan Peninsula,** scene of World War II surrender of United States and Philippine forces to the Japanese, April, 1942.

Ba·tang (bä·täng′) Former name for PAAN.

Ba·tan·gas (bä·täng′gäs) A province in southern Luzon, Philippines; 1,192 square miles; capital, Batangas.

Ba·tan Islands (bä·tän′) An island group in the Philippines, constituting **Ba·ta·nes** (bä·tä′nās) province; total area, 76 square miles; capital, Basco.

Ba·ta·vi (bə·tā′vī) *n. pl.* An ancient Germanic people who inhabited the region about the mouths of the Rhine.

Ba·ta·vi·a (bə·tā′vē·ə, *Du.* bä·tä′vē·ä) A former name for JAKARTA. —**Ba·ta′vi·an** *adj.* & *n.*

batch[1] (bach) *n.* **1** The dough for one baking, or the quantity of bread, etc., baked. **2** The grain for one grinding; grist. **3** Any set of things made, done, dispatched, etc., at one time. **4** The amount of material, quantity of articles, etc., required for one operation. [ME *bacche.* Akin to BAKE.]

batch[2] (bach) *n. Slang* A bachelor.

bate[1] (bāt) *v.* **bat·ed, bat·ing** *v.t.* **1** To lessen the force or intensity of; moderate: to *bate* one's breath. **2** To deduct; take away. **3** *Obs.* To depress; decrease. —*v.i.* **4** To diminish; become reduced. ◆ Homophone: *bait.* [Var. of ABATE]

bate[2] (bāt) *n.* A solution of chemicals or manure containing natural or synthetic enzymes: used to soften skins or hides. —*v.t.* **1** To soak, as hides. **2** To separate and soften, as jute. ◆ Homophone: *bait.* [? <ON *beita* cause to bite. Akin to BAIT and BITE.]

bate[3] (bāt) *v.i.* **bat·ed, bat·ing** In falconry, to beat or flap the wings, as an impatient hawk: also spelled *bait.* ◆ Homophone: *bait.* [<F *battre* beat <L *battuere* strike, beat]

ba·teau (ba·tō′) *n. pl.* **·teaux** (-tōz′) **1** A light, flat-bottomed boat. **2** A pontoon for a floating bridge. [<F <OF *batel,* ult. <Gmc.]

bateau bridge A pontoon bridge.

Bates (bāts), **Katharine Lee,** 1859–1929, U.S. poet and educator.

Bate·son (bāt′sən), **William,** 1861–1926, English biologist.

bat·fish (bat′fish′) *n.* **1** A fish, as *Ogocephalus vespertilio* and other species of the Atlantic coast of the United States, resembling a bat. **2** The Pacific sting ray.

bat·fowl (bat′foul′) *v.i.* To catch birds at night by dazzling them with a light and netting or striking them down. —**bat′fowl′er** *n.* [<BAT[1] + FOWL]

bath[1] (bath, bäth) *n. pl.* **baths** (bathz, bäthz; baths, bäths) **1** The act of washing or immersing something, especially the body, in water or other liquid. ◆ Collateral adjective: *balneal.* **2** The liquid substance or element used for this. **3** The container for such a liquid; a bathtub. **4** A bathroom. **5** A set of rooms or a building for bathing: often in the plural. **6** An establishment or resort where bathing is part of a medical treatment: often in the plural. **7** *Chem.* An apparatus for applying steady heat or heat of a given degree. **8** *Phot.* Any solution, or the vessel containing it, in which photographic plates, etc., are immersed for treatment. **9** *Metall.* The molten material in a reverberatory furnace. **10** The condition of being soaked or covered with a liquid. —*v.t.* To place or wash in a bath; immerse. [OE *bæth*]

bath[2] (bath) *n.* An ancient Hebrew liquid measure, one tenth of a homer: equivalent to about 8 1/2 gallons. [<Hebrew]

Bath (bath, bäth) A city in NE Somersetshire, England, famous since Roman times for its hot springs.

Bath brick A fine calcareous and siliceous material, usually pressed into brick shape, used for polishing and cleansing metal objects: originally found near Bath, England.

Bath chair A hooded wheelchair for invalids. Also **bath chair.** [from *Bath,* England, where originally used]

bathe (bāth) *v.* **bathed, bath·ing** *v.t.* **1** To place in liquid; immerse. **2** To wash; wet. **3** To apply liquid to for comfort or healing; lave. **4** To cover or suffuse as with liquid: The hill was *bathed* in rosy light. —*v.i.* **5** To wash oneself; take a bath. **6** To go into or remain in water so as to swim or cool off. **7** To be covered or suffused as if with liquid. —*n. Brit.* The act of bathing, as in the sea. [OE *bathian*] —**bathe′a·ble** *adj.* —**bath′er** *n.*

ba·thet·ic (bə·thet′ik) *adj.* Pertaining to, exhibiting, or of the nature of bathos. [<BATHOS]

bath·house (bath′hous′, bäth′-) *n.* **1** A building with conveniences for taking baths. **2** A small structure at a bathing resort used as a dressing-room.

bath·ing suit (bāth′ing) A garment, sometimes consisting of two pieces, worn for swimming.

batho- *combining form* Depth: *bathometer.* [<Gk. *bathos* depth]

bath·o·lith (bath′ə·lith) *n. Geol.* A large irregular mass of intrusive igneous rock which has melted or forced its way into surrounding strata. Also **bath′o·lite** (-līt). —**bath′o·lith′ic, bath′o·lit′ic** (-lit′ik) *adj.*

ba·thom·e·ter (bə·thom′ə·tər) *n.* An apparatus for determining the depth of water, as by pressure. [<BATHO- + METER]

ba·thoph·i·lous (bə·thof′ə·ləs) *adj.* Of or pertaining to organisms adapted to life at great depths in the ocean. [<BATHO- + -PHILOUS]

bath·o·pho·bi·a (bath′ə·fō′bē·ə) *n. Psychiatry* Morbid fear of depths. Compare ACROPHOBIA. —**bath′o·pho′bic** (-fō′bik, -fob′ik) *adj.*

add, āce, câre, pälm; end, ēven; it, īce; odd, ōpen, ôrder; tŏŏk, pōōl; up, bûrn; ə = a in *above,* e in *sicken,* i in *clarity,* o in *melon,* u in *focus;* yōō = u in *fuse;* oi, oil; ou, pout; ch, check; g, go; ng, ring; th, thin; th, this; zh, vision. Foreign sounds à, œ, ü, kh, ṅ; and ◆: see page xx. < from; + plus; ? possibly.

ba·thos (bā′thos) *n.* **1** A descent from the lofty to the commonplace in discourse; anticlimax. **2** Insincere pathos; sentimentality. [<Gk. *bathos* depth < *bathys* deep]
bath·robe (bath′rōb′, bäth′-) *n.* A long, loose garment for wear before and after bathing.
bath·room (bath′rōōm′, -rōōm′, bäth′-) *n.* **1** A room in which to bathe. **2** A toilet (def. 4).
bath salts A perfumed mixture of crystal salts used to soften bath water.
Bath·she·ba (bath·shē′bə, bath′shi·bə) Wife of Uriah and later of David; mother of Solomon. II *Sam.* xi–xii.
bath·tub (bath′tub′, bäth′-) *n.* **1** A vessel in which to bathe. **2** Such a vessel installed as a permanent fixture in a bathroom.
Bath·urst (bath′ərst, bäth′-) **1** A municipality in east central New South Wales, Australia. **2** An Atlantic port, capital of Gambia, British West Africa.
bathy– *combining form* Deep: of the sea or ocean depths: *bathymeter; bathysphere.* [<Gk. *bathys* deep]
ba·thym·e·ter (bə·thim′ə·tər) See BATHOMETER.
ba·thym·e·try (bə·thim′ə·trē) *n.* The science or art of deep–sea sounding. **— bath·y·met·ric** (bath′ə·met′rik) *adj.*
bath·y·scaph (bath′ə·skaf) *n.* A bathysphere equipped with ballast for reaching ocean depths of over 12,000 feet and a gasoline–filled float for surfacing. [<BATHY- + Gk. *skaphē* bowl]
bath·y·seism (bath′ə·sī′zəm) *n.* An earthquake occurring at great depths. [<BATHY- + Gk. *seismos* earthquake]
bath·y·sphere (bath′ə·sfir) *n.* A spherical diving bell equipped with fused quartz windows for deep–sea observations.
ba·tik (bə·tēk′, bat′ik) *n.* **1** A process for coloring fabrics, originating in the East Indies, in which parts of a fabric are covered with melted wax so that only the uncovered portions will take the dye, the wax then being dissolved in boiling water. The process is often repeated to obtain multicolored designs. **2** The fabric so colored. Also *battik.* [<Malay]
bat·ing (bā′ting) *prep. Archaic* Making deduction for.
Ba·tis·ta y Zal·dí·var (bä·tēs′tä ē säl·dē′vär), **Fulgencio,** 1901–1973, Cuban soldier and politician; president 1940–44, 1950–58.
ba·tiste (bə·tēst′) *n.* **1** A sheer fabric made of cotton, silk, or spun rayon. The cotton batiste is sometimes mercerized. **2** A fine woolen fabric lighter than challis. **3** Originally, a fine linen cloth. [<F; after Jean *Baptiste,* 13th c. French linen weaver]
Ba·tjan (bä·chän′) An Indonesian island SW of Halmahera; 913 square miles: also *Bachan.*
bat·man (bat′mən, bä′mən) *n. pl.* **·men** (-mən) *Brit.* An officer's servant. [<F *bat* <OF *bast* packsaddle + MAN]
ba·ton (ba·ton′, bat′n; *Fr.* bȧ·tôn′) *n.* **1** A short official staff or truncheon borne as a weapon or as an emblem of authority or privilege: a marshal's *baton.* **2** *Music* A slender stick or rod used for beating time. **3** *Her.* A bend borne sinisterwise across the shield as a mark of bastardy: also **baton sinister,** erroneously *bar sinister.* [<F *bâton* <OF *baston* <LL *bastum* stick]
Bat·on Rouge (bat′n rōōzh′) A port on the Mississippi River, capital of Louisiana.
Ba·tra·chi·a (bə·trā′kē·ə) *n. pl.* Former name for AMPHIBIA. [<Gk. *batrachos* frog]
ba·tra·chi·an (bə·trā′kē·ən) *adj.* **1** Of or pertaining to the *Batrachia,* especially to the frogs and toads; amphibian. **2** Froglike. **—** *n.* One of the *Batrachia.*
bat·ra·chite (bat′rə·kīt) *n.* **1** A stone that is froglike in color. **2** A fossil batrachian.
bat·ra·choid (bat′rə·koid) *adj.* Froglike.
bats·man (bats′mən) *n. pl.* **·men** (-mən) In baseball or cricket, the batter.
batt (bat) See BATTING.
bat·tai·lous (bat′i·ləs) *adj. Obs.* Bellicose. [<OF *batailos* < *bataille* battle]
bat·ta·lia (bə·tāl′yə, -täl′-) *n. Obs.* **1** An army. **2** Order of battle.
bat·tal·ion (bə·tal′yən) *n.* **1** *Mil.* **a** A unit, normally part of a regiment, consisting of a headquarters and two or more companies, batteries, or comparable units. **b** A body of troops. **2** *Usually pl.* A large group or number. [<F *battaillon* <Ital. *battaglione* < *battaglia* battle]
Bat·tam·bang (bä′täm·bäng′) A town in western Cambodia.
bat·tels (bat′lz) *n. pl. Brit.* At Oxford University, a student's account with his college for provisions, etc. [Origin uncertain]
bat·ten[1] (bat′n) *v.i.* **1** To grow fat or thrive. **2** To prosper; live well, especially at another's expense. **—** *v.t.* **3** To make fat, as cattle. [<ON *batna* grow better, improve]
bat·ten[2] (bat′n) *n.* **1** A narrow strip of wood; a cleat, as across parallel boards in a door. **2** In the theater: **a** A cleat placed on a muslin flat or piece of scenery to stiffen it. **b** A round metal bar to which spotlights or floodlights are attached. **3** *Naut* **a** A thin strip of wood placed in a sail to keep it flat. **b** A similar strip used to fasten down a tarpaulin covering on a hatchway. **—** *v.t.* **1** To make, furnish, or strengthen with battens. **2** To fasten with battens. **— to batten down the hatches** *Naut.* To put tarpaulins over a hatchway and secure them by strips of wood. [Var. of BATON] **— bat′ten·er** *n.*
bat·ter[1] (bat′ər) *n.* **1** A heavy blow; also, repeated blows, or the condition resulting from them. **2** In ceramics, a mallet for beating a lump of plastic clay. **3** *Printing* **a** The breakage or marring of type or a plate. **b** The type thus broken. **c** The resulting defect in print. [< *v.*] **—** *v.t.* **1** To strike with repeated, violent blows. **2** To damage or injure with or as with such blows. **—** *v.i.* **3** To pound or beat with blow after blow; hammer. See synonyms under BEAT. [<F *battre* <L *battuere* beat]
bat·ter[2] (bat′ər) *n.* In baseball and cricket, the player whose turn it is to bat.
bat·ter[3] (bat′ər) *n.* A thick liquid mixture of eggs, flour, and milk, beaten up for use in cookery. [<OF *bature* beating < *battre* beat]
bat·ter[4] (bat′ər) *n.* An inward and upward slope of a wall, giving greater resistance to thrust or firmer base. **—** *v.t.* & *v.i.* To slope back from the base, as a wall. [Origin uncertain]
batter bread Spoonbread.
bat·ter·ing-ram (bat′ər·ing·ram′) *n.* A long, stout beam, with heavy head, used in ancient warfare for forcing gates and making breaches in walls, either carried by the assailants, or suspended in a frame.

BATTERING–RAM

Bat·ter·sea (bat′ər·sē) A metropolitan borough of London, on the south side of the Thames.
bat·ter·y (bat′ər·ē) *n. pl.* **·ter·ies** **1** *Mil.* **a** An earthwork or parapet for protecting one or more guns. **b** Two or more pieces of artillery constituting a tactical unit. **c** A unit of an artillery regiment equivalent to an infantry company, or their guns and other equipment. **2** *Nav.* The armament of a war vessel, or a special part of it. **3** *Electr.* **a** An arrangement of two or more primary cells, dynamos, etc., for the purpose of building up a strong electric current: a *battery* of Leyden jars. **b** Any of several types of such cells used to heat the filaments of a vacuum tube, provide current, or supply voltage: an A, B, or C *battery.* **4** *Law* The illegal beating or touching of another person. **5** In baseball, the pitcher and catcher together. **6** *Music* The percussion instruments of an orchestra, collectively. **7** *Optics* The group of prisms in a spectroscope. **8** Any unit, apparatus, or grouping in which a series or set of parts or components are assembled to serve a common end: a *battery* of tests. **9** The act of battering or beating. **10** The instrument for such an act. **— dry battery** *Electr.* A battery composed of cells whose contents are solid or nearly so; a dry pile. **— in battery** *Mil.* In firing position, after recovery from recoil: said of a heavy gun. [<F *batterie* < *battre* beat]
Battery, the A park at the southern extremity of Manhattan: so named from the guns mounted there in colonial and Revolutionary times. Also **Battery Park.**
battery cup A small metal cup which surrounds the cap (primer) of a shell or cartridge.
bat·tik (bə·tēk′, bat′ik) See BATIK.
bat·ting (bat′ing) *n.* **1** Wadded cotton or wool prepared in sheets or rolls: used for interlinings, stuffing mattresses, comforters, etc.: also *bat, batt.* **2** The act of one who bats.
Bat·tis·ta (bät·tēs′tä) Italian form of BAPTIST.
bat·tle (bat′l) *n.* **1** A combat between hostile armies or fleets; a military or naval engagement. **2** Armed combat. **3** Any fighting, conflict, or struggle: to do *battle* for a cause. **4** *Obs.* A battalion. **—** *v.* **bat·tled, bat·tling** *v.i.* To contend in or as in battle; struggle; strive. **—** *v.t.* To fight. See synonyms under CONTEND, DISPUTE. [<OF *bataille* <LL *battalia* gladiators' exercises < *battuere* beat] **— bat′tler** *n.*
Synonyms (noun): action, affair, bout, combat, conflict, contest, encounter, engagement, fight, skirmish, strife. *Conflict* is a general word which describes opponents, whether individuals or hosts, as dashed together. One continuous *conflict* between entire armies is a *battle.* Another *battle* may be fought upon the same field after a considerable interval; or a new *battle* may follow immediately, the armies meeting upon a new field. An *action* is brief and partial; a *battle* may last for days. *Engagement* is a somewhat formal expression for *battle.* A protracted war, including many *battles,* may be a stubborn *contest. Combat,* originally a hostile *encounter* between individuals, is now used also for extensive *engagements.* A *skirmish* is between small detachments or scattered troops. An *encounter* may be either purposed or accidental, between individuals or armed forces. *Fight* is a word of less dignity than *battle*; we should not ordinarily speak of Waterloo as a *fight,* unless where the word is used in the sense of fighting; as, I was in the thick of the *fight. Antonyms*: armistice, concord, peace, truce.
bat·tle-ax (bat′l·aks′) *n.* **1** A large ax formerly used in battle; a broad–ax. **2** *U.S. Slang* A formidable, disagreeable woman. Also **bat′tle–axe′.**
Battle Creek A city on the Kalamazoo River in SW Michigan.
battle cruiser A war vessel less heavily armored than a battleship, having cruiser speed and battleship armament.
battle cry **1** A shout used by troops in battle. **2** A slogan or identifying phrase used in any conflict or contest.
bat·tled (bat′ld) *adj. Obs.* Provided with battlements.
bat·tle·dore (bat′l·dôr, -dōr) *n.* **1** A flat paddle or bat, either of wood, webbed, or covered with parchment, used to drive a shuttlecock. **2** The game in which a shuttlecock is so batted: also **battledore and shuttlecock.** **—** *v.t.* & *v.i.* **·dored, ·doring** To drive or fly back and forth. [? <Provençal *batedor* an implement for beating]
battle fatigue *Psychiatry* A psychoneurotic condition, characterized by anxiety, depression, etc., occurring among soldiers engaged in active warfare: formerly called *shell shock*: also *combat fatigue.*
bat·tle·field (bat′l·fēld′) *n.* The ground on which a battle is fought. Also **bat′tle·ground′.**
bat·tle·ment (bat′l·mənt) *n.* A parapet indented along its upper line. **— bat·tle·ment′ed** (bat′l·men·tid) *adj.* [<OF *ba(s)tillier* fortify]

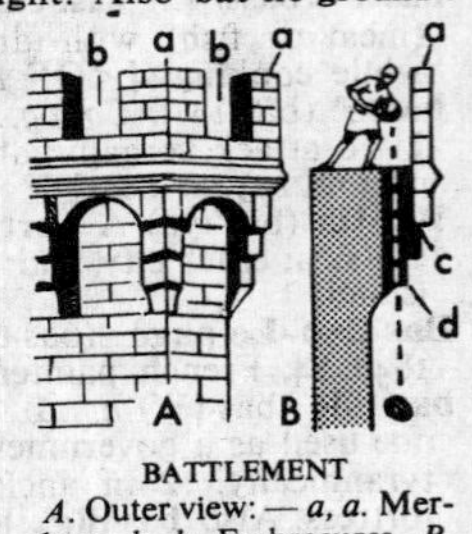

BATTLEMENT
A. Outer view: — *a, a.* Merlons; *b, b.* Embrasures. *B.* Cross–section: — showing use of corbel, *c,* for machicolation, *d.*

bat·tle·plane (bat′l·plān′) *n.* Formerly any airplane for combat use.
battle royal **1** A fight involving numerous combatants. **2** A protracted, rigorous battle.
bat·tle-scarred (bat′l·skärd′) *adj.* **1** Having scars, marks, etc., received in combat. **2** Having received the effects of a long and varied experience; experienced.
bat·tle·ship (bat′l·ship′) *n. Nav.* A vessel having a large displacement and radius of action, maximum armament and powerful batteries.
bat·tle·wag·on (bat′l·wag′ən) *n. Slang* A battleship.
bat·tol·o·gy (bə·tol′ə·jē) *n.* Unnecessary repetition in speaking or writing. [<Gk. *battologia*

stammering] **—bat·to·log·i·cal** (bat′ə·loj′i·kəl) *adj.* **—bat·tol′o·gist** *n.*

batts (bats, bäts) *n. pl. Scot.* Colic.

bat·tue (ba·tōō′, -tyōō′) *n.* **1** The driving of game from cover within reach of sportsmen previously posted. **2** A hunt so conducted. **3** Any wanton slaughter. [< F, fem. pp. of *battre* beat]

bat·ty (bat′ē) *adj.* **·ti·er, ·ti·est 1** Of, pertaining to, or like a bat. **2** *U.S. Slang* Crazy; foolish; odd.

Ba·tum (bə·tōōm′) A port on the Black Sea in Georgian S.S.R. near the Turkish frontier. *Georgian* **Ba·tu·mi** (bä·tōō′mē).

bau·bee (bô·bē′, bô′bē) See BAWBEE.

bau·ble (bô′bəl) *n.* **1** A worthless, showy trinket; gew-gaw; toy. **2** *Archaic* The wand of a jester. Also spelled *bawble.* See synonyms under GAUD. [< OF *baubel* toy, ? < L *bellus* pretty]

Bau·cis (bô′sis) In Greek mythology, a Phrygian peasant who, with Philemon, her husband, sheltered Zeus and Hermes.

baud (bôd) *n.* A unit of speed in telegraphy, based on the time interval required to transmit a given signal, usually the dot. [after J. M. E. *Baudot,* 1845–1903, French inventor]

bau·de·kin (bô′də·kin) See BALDACHIN (def. 1).

Baude·laire (bōd·lâr′), **Charles Pierre,** 1821–1867, French poet.

Bau·doin (bō·dwaṅ′) French form of BALDWIN. **—Baudoin,** born 1930, king of Belgium 1951–.

baud·rons (bôd′rənz) *n. Scot.* A cat.

Bau·er (bou′ər), **Harold,** 1873–1951, English pianist. **—Marion Eugenia,** 1887–1955, U.S. composer.

Bau·haus (bou′hous′) An institute of art study, design, and research, established by Walter Gropius in Weimar, Germany, in 1919: known for its experiments in associating technology and art.

bauk·ie (bô′kē) *n. Scot.* A bat.

bauld (bôld) *adj. Scot.* Bold; forward.

baulk (bôk) See BALK.

Baum (bôm), **Lyman Frank,** 1856–1919, U.S. children's story writer; author of *The Wizard of Oz.* **—(boum) Vicki,** 1889–1960, U.S. novelist born in Austria.

Bau·mé (bō·mā′) *n.* **1** A hydrometer for the measurement of the densities of liquids. **2** The scale used on this instrument. [after Antoine *Baumé,* 1728–1804, French pharmacist]

Bau·mes Law (bō′məs) A statute introduced in New York State in 1926 to curb crime: it provides for life imprisonment for fourth offenders. [after C. H. *Baumes,* 1863–1937, N.Y. legislator]

bau·son (bô′sən) *n. Archaic* A badger. [< OF *bausant* spotted]

bau·sond (bô′sənd) *adj. Scot.* Marked with white, especially on the face, as a horse. Also **bau′son-faced′.**

Bau·tis·ta (bou·tēs′tä) Spanish form of BAPTIST.

baux·ite (bôk′sīt, bō′zīt) *n.* A whitish to reddish brown material composed of hydrated aluminum oxides along with various siliceous, ferric, and other impurities and forming the principal commercial source of aluminum. [from Les *Baux,* town in southern France]

Ba·var·i·a (bə·vâr′ē·ə) A southeastern state of the Federal Republic of Germany; 27,119 square miles; capital, Munich; formerly a duchy, kingdom, and republic: German *Bayern.*

Ba·var·i·an (bə·vâr′ē·ən) *adj.* Of or pertaining to Bavaria, its people, or their dialect. **—n. 1** A native or inhabitant of Bavaria. **2** The High German dialect spoken in Bavaria.

baw·bee (bô·bē′, bô′bē) *n. Scot.* **1** A halfpenny. **2** *Archaic* A copper coin of 6d. Scots. Also spelled *baubee.*

baw·cock (bô′kok) *n. Archaic* A fine fellow. [< F *beau* beau + *coq* cock]

bawd (bôd) *n.* The keeper of a brothel; a procuress. [ME *bawde;* origin uncertain]

bawd·ry (bôd′rē) *n.* **1** Indecent language or behavior. **2** The occupation of a bawd.

bawd·y (bôd′ē) *adj.* **bawd·i·er, bawd·i·est** Of or like a bawd; obscene; indecent. **—bawd′i·ly** *adv.* **—bawd′i·ness** *n.*

bawd·y-house (bô′dē·hous′) *n.* A brothel.

---

bawl (bôl) *n.* A loud shout or outcry. **—v.t. 1** To proclaim or call out noisily; bellow. **2** *U.S. Slang* To berate: with *out.* **3** To cry for sale. **—v.i. 4** To weep or sob noisily. See synonyms under CALL. ◆ Homophone: *ball.* [< ON *baula* low, as a cow] **—bawl′er** *n.*

baw·tie (bô′tē) *n. Scot.* **1** A dog. **2** A hare. Also **baw′ty.**

Bax (baks), **Sir Arnold Edward Trevor,** 1883–1953, English composer.

Bax·ter (bak′stər), **Richard,** 1615–91, English Puritan minister and author.

bay¹ (bā) *n.* **1** A body of water partly enclosed by land; an arm of the sea. **2** A recess of low land between hills. **3** Land partly surrounded by woods. ◆ Homophone: *bey.* [< F *baie* < LL *baia*]

bay² (bā) *n.* **1** A space in a barn for storing hay or fodder. **2** *Engin.* A principal compartment or division, as the space between two piers or pontoons of a bridge. **3** *Archit.* **a** A division of a window between adjacent mullions. **b** Part of a vault between transverse ribs or of a ceiling between panel beams. **c** A vertical division of an arcade, as the space between two adjacent pillars. **4** The head of a canal lock. **5** *Naut.* The forward part of a ship between decks on each side: commonly used as a hospital. **6** *Aeron.* **a** A compartment in the body of an aircraft: a bomb *bay.* **b** A portion of the fuselage between adjoining struts, bulkheads, or frame positions. ◆ Homophone: *bey.* [< F *baie* gape, ult. < LL *badare*]

bay³ (bā) *adj.* Reddish-brown: said especially of horses. **—n. 1** A horse (or other animal) of this color. **2** This color. ◆ Homophone: *bey.* [< F *bai* < L *badius*]

bay⁴ (bā) *n.* **1** A deep bark or cry, as of dogs in hunting. **2** The situation of or as of a hunted creature compelled to turn on its pursuers. **3** The condition of being kept at a standstill or in check by an opponent, quarry, etc. **—at bay 1** Cornered; with no escape. **2** Held off: He kept his attackers *at bay.* **—to bring to bay** To force into a position from which there is no escape; corner and force to fight. **—v.i. 1** To utter a deep-throated, prolonged bark, as a hound. **—v.t. 2** To utter as with this bark: to *bay* defiance. **3** To pursue or beset with barking of this kind so as to bring to bay. ◆ Homophone: *bey.* [Var. of *abay* < OF *abai* a barking; ult. origin uncertain; in sense "at bay" appar. < OF *tenir a bay* hold in suspense < LL *badare* gape]

bay⁵ (bā) *n.* **1** Laurel (def. 1): also called *baytree.* **2** A laurel wreath, bestowed as a garland of honor, especially on a poet. **3** *pl.* Fame; poetic renown. **4** The bayberry. **5** Any of several plants resembling the laurels. **6** *U.S. Dial.* Low marshy ground abounding in bay and other shrubs: also **bay-gall** (bā′gôl′). ◆ Homophone: *bey.* [< F *baie* < L *baca* berry]

ba·ya·dere (bä′yə·dir′) *n.* **1** A dancing girl, especially one serving in a temple in India. **2** A fabric or pattern with stripes running crosswise. Also **ba′ya·deer′.** [< F *bayadère* < Pg. *bailadera* female dancer]

ba·ya·mo (bä·yä′mō) *n. Meteorol.* A violent wind blowing on the south coast of Cuba. [from *Bayamo,* town in eastern Cuba]

bay·ard (bā′ərd) *n.* **1** A bay horse. **2** Any horse: a humorous use. **—adj.** Bay in color. [< OF]

Bay·ard (bā′ərd) In medieval romance, a magical horse given to Rinaldo by Charlemagne.

Bay·ard (bā′ərd, *Fr.* bà·yàr′), **Chevalier de,** 1475–1524, Pierre du Terrail, heroic French soldier: called the knight "without fear and without reproach"; hence, a man of heroic courage and chivalry.

bay·ber·ry (bā′ber′ē, -bər·ē) *n. pl.* **·ber·ries 1** One of various trees, as the wax myrtle or laurel, or its fruit. **2** A tropical American tree (*Pimenta racemosa*) whose leaves are used in making bay rum. [< BAY⁵ + BERRY]

bay-cu·ru root (bī-kōō′rōō) The root of a tropical American plant (*Limonium brasiliense*) which yields a powerful astringent known as **bay-cu·rine** (bī-kōō′rēn, -rin). [< Tupian]

Bay·ern (bī′ərn) German name for BAVARIA.

Ba·yeux tapestry (bä·yœ′, *Fr.* bà·yœ′) A linen roll, 77 yards long and 20 inches wide,

---

embroidered in colored worsteds, depicting over 70 scenes in the life of William the Conqueror, traditionally ascribed to his queen, Matilda: now preserved at **Bayeux,** a town in Normandy, France.

Bayle (bel), **Pierre,** 1647–1706, French philosopher.

Bay·lor (bā′lər), **Robert Emmet,** 1793?–1873, U.S. jurist and Baptist preacher.

bay lynx The common wildcat of North America.

bay·o·net (bā′ə·nit, -net) *n.* A daggerlike weapon attachable to the muzzle of a musket

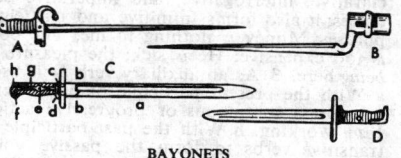

BAYONETS
A. One type of sword bayonet.
B. 18th–19th century bayonet.
C. Sword bayonet.
D. Type of United States Army bayonet.
a. Blade. *b.* Guard. *c.* Bayonet spring. *d.* Scabbard catch. *e.* Tang. *f.* Pommel. *g.* Bayonet catch. *h.* Undercut groove.

or rifle, for close fighting. **—v.t. ·net·ed, ·net·ing** To stab or pierce with a bayonet. [< F *bayonette,* from *Bayonne,* France, where first made]

Ba·yonne (bā·yōn′) **1** (*Fr.* bà·yôn′) A city in SW France near the Bay of Biscay. **2** A city in NE New Jersey.

bay·ou (bī′ōō) *n.* **1** A marshy inlet or outlet of a lake or bay. **2** A branch of a stream flowing through a delta. [< Choctaw *bayuk* small stream]

Bayou State Nickname of MISSISSIPPI.

Bay·reuth (bī·roit′) A city in NE Bavaria, capital of Upper Franconia: known for its annual Wagner music festivals.

bay rum An aromatic liquid used in medicines and cosmetics, originally obtained by distilling rum with the leaves of the bayberry, now consisting mainly of alcohol, water, and essential oils.

Bay State Nickname of MASSACHUSETTS.

bay-tree (bā′trē) *n.* **1** Bay⁵ (def. 1). **2** The magnolia of eastern North America.

bay window 1 A window structure projecting from the wall of a building and forming an extension within. **2** *Slang* A protruding abdomen.

bay·wood (bā′wŏŏd) *n.* A coarse mahogany from Honduras or the region around the Gulf of Campeche.

ba·zaar (bə·zär′) *n.* **1** An Oriental market place or range of shops. **2** A shop or store for the sale of miscellaneous wares. **3** A sale of miscellaneous articles, as for charity. Also **ba·zar′.** [< Persian *bāzār* market]

Ba·zaine (bà·zen′), **François Achille,** 1811–88, French marshal.

Ba·zin (bà·zaṅ′), **René,** 1853–1932, French novelist.

ba·zoo·ka (bə·zōō′kə) *n. Mil.* A long, tubular missile weapon which fires an explosive rocket, and is used for short-range action against tanks and fortifications. [from fancied resemblance to the *bazooka,* a comical musical instrument invented and named by Bob Burns, U.S. comedian]

BB A standard, commercial size of lead shot, 0.18 in. in diameter.

B battery *Electr.* The battery which supplies direct-current voltage to the plate and grid of a vacuum tube.

bdel·li·um (del′ē·əm) *n.* **1** A variety of gum resin resembling myrrh, yielded by various trees (genus *Commiphora*) of India and Africa; also, any of such trees. **2** A substance mentioned in the Old Testament, variously interpreted as crystal, carbuncle, pearl, or amber. [< L < Gk. *bdellion* a plant, and its fragrant gum]

Be *Chem.* Beryllium (symbol Be).

be (bē, *unstressed* bi) *v.i.* **been, be·ing** Present

---

indicative: *sing.* **am, are** (*Archaic* **art**), **is,** *pl.* **are;** past indicative: *sing.* **was, were** (*Archaic* **wast** or **wert**), **was,** *pl.* **were;** present subjunctive: **be;** past subjunctive: *sing.* **were, were** (*Archaic* **wert**), **were,** *pl.* **were** **1** As a substantive the verb **be** is used to mean: **a** To have existence, truth, or actuality: God *is;* There *are* bears in the zoo. **b** To take place; happen: The party *is* next week. **c** To stay or continue: She *was* here for one week. **d** To belong; befall: often with *to* or *unto*: Joy *be* unto you. **2** As a copulative verb *be* forms a link between the subject and predicate nominative or qualifying word or phrase in declarative, interrogative, and imperative sentences; it also forms infinitive and participial phrases: Money *is* nothing to me; The book *is* too expensive; He *is* sick; the pleasure of *being* here. **3** As an auxiliary verb *be* is used: **a** With the present participle of other verbs to express continuous or progressive action: I *am* working. **b** With the past participle of transitive verbs to form the passive voice: He *was* injured. **c** With the past participle of intransitive verbs to form the perfect tense: Christ *is* come; I *am* finished. **d** With the infinitive or present participle to express purpose, duty, possibility, futurity, etc.: We *are* to start on Monday; We *are* leaving Monday.
The verb is defective, and its conjugation is made up of fragments of three independent verbs, furnishing **be, am (are, is), was (were),** respectively. ◆ For usage as to the cases of personal pronouns following impersonal forms of the verb *to be,* see note under ME. [OE *bēon*]

be– *prefix* Used to form transitive verbs from nouns, adjectives, and verbs. [OE *be-, bi-*, var. of *bī* near, by]
Be– may appear as a prefix in hyphemes or solidemes, with the following meanings:
1 (from verbs) Around; all over; throughout; as in:

beclasp	**befreckle**	**beshackle**
beclog	**begirdle**	**beshadow**
beclothe	**bejumble**	**beshroud**
becompass	**bekiss**	**beslobber**
becrimson	**belick**	**besmother**
becrust	**bemingle**	**besmudge**
bedabble	**bemix**	**bespeckle**
bedarken	**berake**	**besprinkle**
bediaper	**bescour**	**betattered**
bedimple	**bescreen**	**bewrap**
befinger	**bescribble**	**bewreath**

2 (from verbs) Completely; thoroughly; as in:

beclamor	**beflatter**	**bescourge**
becrowd	**befluster**	**beshiver**
becudgel	**begall**	**besmear**
becurse	**beknotted**	**besoothe**
bedamn	**bemaddening**	**bethank**
bedeafened	**bemuddle**	**bethump**
bedrabble	**bemuzzle**	**betrample**
bedrench	**besanctify**	**beweary**
bedrug	**bescorch**	**bewidow**

3 (from verbs) Off; away from: *behead, bereave.*
4 (from intransitive verbs) About; at; on; over; against; for; as in:

bechatter	**behowl**	**beshout**
becrawl	**bejuggle**	**besmile**
bedrivel	**beleap**	**beswarm**
begaze	**bemurmur**	**bethunder**
begroan	**beshame**	**beweep**

5 (from adjectives and nouns) To make; cause to be; as in:

beclown	**bedumb**	**begrim**
becoward	**bedunce**	**beknight**
becripple	**bedwarf**	**bemonster**
bedirty	**befoul**	**besmooth**
bedoctor	**beglad**	**bespouse**

6 (from nouns) To provide with; affect by; cover with; as in:

beblister	**beflea**	**beslime**
beblood	**beflower**	**beslipper**
becap	**befringe**	**besmoke**
becarpet	**beglitter**	**besmut**
bechalk	**begloom**	**besnow**
becharm	**begulf**	**bethorn**
becloak	**bejewel**	**bewelcome**
becrime	**beliquor**	**bewhisker**
bedinner	**bemist**	**beworm**

7 (from nouns) To call; name; as in:

bebrother	**belady**	**berascal**
becoward	**bemadam**	**bescoundrel**
behypocrite	**bemonster**	**bevillain**

8 (from nouns) To furnish with, excessively or conspicuously (almost always in participial form); as in:

be–altared	**begarlanded**	**beruffled**
bebelted	**begartered**	**besainted**
bebuttoned	**behusbanded**	**beslaved**
becapped	**bejeweled**	**bespangled**
becarpeted	**belaced**	**bespectacled**
bechained	**bemedaled**	**bestarred**
becupided	**bemitered**	**besteepled**
becurtained	**bemottoed**	**bestrapped**
becushioned	**bepilgrimed**	**beswordeed**
bedaughtered	**berailroaded**	**betaxed**
bedotted	**beribboned**	**betinseled**
befathered	**beringed**	**be–uncled**
befeathered	**beringleted**	**be–uniformed**
beflowered	**berobed**	**bewinged**
befrilled	**berouged**	**bewrathed**

beach (bēch) *n.* **1** The sloping shore of a body of water; strand. **2** Loose pebbles on the shore; shingle. See synonyms under BANK, MARGIN. — *v.t.* & *v.i.* To drive or haul up (a boat or ship) on a beach; strand. ◆ Homophone: *beech.* [Origin unknown]

beach·comb·er (bēch′kō′mər) *n.* **1** A vagrant living on what he can find or beg around the wharves and beaches of ports, especially such a person in the South Sea islands. **2** A long wave rolling upon the beach.

beach flea A small amphipod crustacean (family *Talitridae*) that hops like a flea: found on sea beaches.

beach·grass (bēch′gras′, -gräs′) *n.* A tough, coarse grass (*Ammophila arenaria*) found on lake and ocean beaches: also called *marram.*

beach·head (bēch′hed′) *n. Mil.* **1** A position on a hostile shore established by an advance invasion force to make possible the landing of troops and supplies. **2** A fortified place on a beach.

beach–la–mar (bēch′lə·mär′) See BÊCHE–DE–MER.

beach·y (bē′chē) *adj.* Shingly; pebbly.

Beachy Head A chalk promontory in southern Sussex, England; 565 feet high.

bea·con (bē′kən) *n.* **1** Any prominent object, as a pole, tower, flag, or the like, set on a shore, shoal, buoy, reef, or in a similar position, as a guide or warning to mariners or others. **2** Something that serves as a conspicuous warning or a guide. **3** A lighthouse. **4** *Aeron.* Any of various marker, signal light, or radio devices used to establish and plot flight courses. See RADIO BEACON. — *v.t.* **1** To furnish with a beacon. **2** To light up (darkness, etc.). **3** To guide by a light or beacon. — *v.i.* **4** To shine or serve as a beacon. [OE *bēacen* sign, signal. Related to BECKON.]

Bea·cons·field (bē′kənz·fēld) See DISRAELI.

bead (bēd) *n.* **1** Any small, usually round piece of glass, wood, stone, etc., perforated and intended to be strung with others like it on a thread or attached to a fabric for decoration. **2** *pl.* A string of beads; especially, a rosary. **3** A bubble or bubbles on the surface of a liquid; froth. **4** A liquid drop, as of sweat. **5** A small spherical knob used as the front sight of a gun. **6** *Chem.* A small mass of borax or other flux, placed on a platinum wire to receive a substance for blowpipe testing **7** *Metall.* The spherical piece of refined metal resulting from cupellation. **8** *Archit.* **a** A molding composed of a row of half-oval ornaments resembling a string of beads. **b** A small convex molding. **9** That part of a pneumatic tire which grips the rim of a wheel. — **to draw a bead on** To take careful aim at. — **to tell (count,** or **say) one's beads** To recite prayers with a rosary. — *v.t.* To decorate with or as with beads or beading. — *v.i.* To collect in beads or drops. [OE *gebed* prayer]

bead·house (bēd′hous′) *n.* An almshouse or hospital in which the inmates were required to pray for the founders: also spelled *bedehouse.*

bead·ing (bē′ding) *n.* **1** *Archit.* **a** A bead. **b** Beads collectively. **2** A narrow openwork lace through which a ribbon may be run. **3** Beadwork.

bea·dle (bēd′l) *n.* **1** A minor parish officer in the Church of England whose duties include keeping order during services. **2** *Brit.* An official who leads university processions. **3** A court messenger. **4** The apparitor of a guild. [OF *bedel* messenger]

bea·dle·dom (bēd′l·dəm) *n.* **1** Beadles collectively, or their characteristics. **2** A show of petty and stupid officialism.

bead·roll (bēd′rōl′) *n.* **1** Originally, a list or catalog. **2** In the Roman Catholic Church, a list of persons to be prayed for.

bead–ru·by (bēd′rōō′bē) *n. pl.* **·bies** A small perennial herb (*Maianthemum canadense*) of northern North America with small crimson berries and four–lobed terminal flowers: akin to the Solomonseal.

beads·man (bēdz′mən) *n. pl.* **·men** (-mən) **1** *Brit.* The resident of an almshouse. **2** *Scot.* A privileged or licensed beggar receiving public alms. **3** One who prays for another, especially when hired to do so: also spelled *bedeman.* Also **bead′man.** — **beads′wom′an** *n. fem.*

bead·work (bēd′wûrk′) *n.* **1** Decorative work made with or of beads. **2** *Archit.* Beading.

bead·y (bē′dē) *adj.* **bead·i·er, bead·i·est** **1** Beadlike. **2** Full of or covered with beads. **3** Foamy.

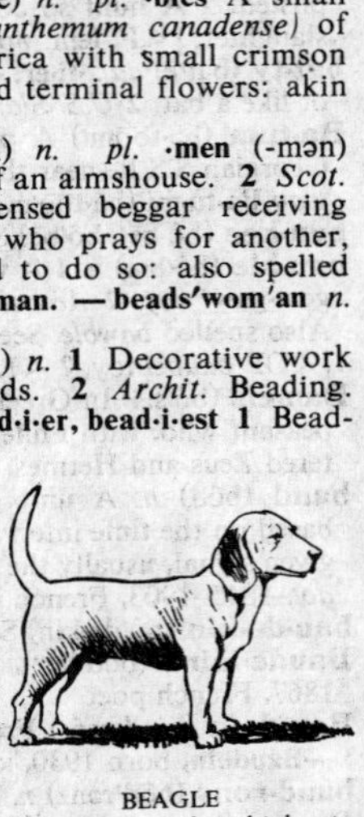
BEAGLE
(About 15 inches high at the shoulder)

bea·gle (bē′gəl) *n.* A small, short-coated hound with short legs and drooping ears. [ME *begle*; origin uncertain]

beak[1] (bēk) *n.* **1** The horny projecting mouth parts of birds; the bill or neb. **2** A beaklike part or organ, as the horny jaws of cephalopods and turtles, the elongated snout of various fishes, etc. **3** *Slang* The nose of a person. **4** *Naut.* That part of ancient warships fastened to the bow and used for piercing or ramming an enemy vessel. **5** *Archit.* A downward–projecting molding on the extreme edge of the lower member of a cornice to prevent the drip from working back under it. **6** Something projecting and pointed like a beak, as the spout of a pitcher. **7** That part of a retort or still which conducts the vapor to the worm or condenser. [<F *bec* <LL *beccus,* ult. <Celtic] — **beaked** (bēkt, bē′kid) *adj.* — **beak′less** *adj.* — **beak′like′** *adj.*

beak[2] (bēk) *n. Brit. Slang* **1** A policeman. **2** A magistrate. **3** At Eton, a master.

beak·er (bē′kər) *n.* **1** A large, wide–mouthed cup or goblet. **2** A cylindrical, flat–bottomed vessel of quartz, porcelain, aluminum, or thin annealed glass, having a flaring top: used in chemical analysis, etc. **3** The contents or capacity of a beaker. [<ON *bikarr*; spelling infl. by BEAK]

be–all (bē′ôl′) *n.* All that is to be; the whole of something.

beam (bēm) *n.* **1** A long, horizontal piece of wood, stone, or metal, forming part of the frame of a building or other structure. **2** The bar of a balance. **3** *Naut.* **a** One of the heavy pieces of timber or iron set transversely across a vessel to support the decks and stay the sides. **b** The greatest width of a vessel. **4** The widest part of anything. **5** A horizontal cylindrical bar, in a loom, upon which warp or woven goods are wound. **6** The pole of a carriage. **7** *Mech.* A horizontal bar that transmits power to the crankshaft through the connecting rod. **8** *Optics* A ray of light, or a group of nearly parallel rays. **9** *Aeron.* A continuous radio signal from a flying field to guide incoming pilots: also **radio beam.** **10** The main stem of a deer's antler. **11** The area of maximum sound clarity in front of a microphone. **12** The horizontal piece in a plow to which the share and the handles are attached. **13** A trough containing lights in the ceiling of a stage. — **off the beam** **1** *Aeron.* Not following the radio beam. **2** *Slang* On the wrong track; wrong. — **on the beam** **1** *Naut.* In a direction at right angles with the keel; abeam. **2** *Aeron.* Following the radio beam. **3** *Slang* In the right direction; just right; correct. — *v.t.* **1** To send out in or as in beams or rays. **2** In radio, to aim or transmit (a signal) in a specific direction: to *beam* a program to France. **3** *Aeron.* To guide (an airplane) to a destination by means of radio beams. — *v.i.* **4** To emit light. **5** To smile or grin radiantly. [OE, tree] — **beamed** *adj.* — **beam′less** *adj.* — **beam′like′** *adj.*

beam compass A drawing compass in which

the points are arranged to slide on a rod, instead of fixed on dividers.
beam-ends (bēm′endz′) *n. pl. Naut.* The ends of a ship's beams. **— on beam-ends 1** *Naut.* Canted over so far as to be in danger of overturning. **2** In an embarrassing or hopeless predicament.
beam·ing (bē′ming) *adj.* Radiant; bright; cheerful. See synonyms under BRIGHT. **— beam′·ing·ly** *adv.*
beam·ish (bē′mish) *adj.* Radiant; beaming with light. [<BEAM + -ISH; coined by Lewis Carroll in *Jabberwocky*]
beam-shy (bēm′shī′) *adj. Aeron.* Failing, through inexperience or nervousness, to locate the radio beam.
beam·y (bē′mē) *adj.* **beam·i·er, beam·i·est 1** Sending out beams of light; radiant. **2** Like a beam; massive. **3** *Naut.* Having much breadth of beam: said of vessels. **4** Antlered, as a stag.
bean (bēn) *n.* **1** The oval edible seed of any of various leguminous plants, especially of genus *Phaseolus*. **2** A plant that bears beans. **3** One of several beanlike seeds or plants. **4** *Slang* The head. — *v.t. U.S. Slang* To hit on the head, especially with a thrown object, as a baseball. [OE]
bean·bag (bēn′bag′) *n.* A small cloth bag filled with beans, used as a toy.
bean ball In baseball, a pitch aimed at the head of the batter.
bean beetle See MEXICAN BEAN BEETLE.
bean caper A small tree or shrub (*Zygophyllum fabago*) of the caltrop family, native to eastern Mediterranean regions, having flower buds which are used as capers.
bean·feast (bēn′fēst′) *n. Brit.* A free dinner given by an employer to his employees.
bean·o[1] (bē′nō) *n.* Bingo.
bean·o[2] (bē′nō) *n. Brit. Slang* A spree; a merry party. [<BEANFEAST]
bean·pole (bēn′pōl′) *n.* **1** A tall pole for a bean plant to climb on. **2** *Slang* A tall, thin person.
bean·stalk (bēn′stôk′) *n.* The principal stem of a bean plant.
bean tree 1 One of various trees or shrubs bearing beanlike pods, as the catalpa. **2** The Moreton Bay chestnut (*Castanospermum australe*) of Australia.
bear[1] (bâr) *v.* **bore** (*Archaic* **bare**), **borne** or **born, bear·ing** *v.t.* **1** To support; hold up. **2** To carry; convey. **3** To show visibly; carry: to *bear* a seal or a scar. **4** To conduct or guide. **5** To spread; disseminate: to *bear* tales. **6** To hold in the mind; maintain or entertain: to *bear* a grudge. **7** To suffer or endure; undergo. **8** To accept or acknowledge; assume, as responsibility or expense. **9** To produce; give birth to. **10** To conduct or comport (oneself). **11** To manage or carry (oneself or a part of oneself). **12** To press against or thrust back: The wind *bore* the ship backward. **13** To render; give: to *bear* witness. **14** To be able to withstand; allow: His story will not *bear* investigation. **15** To have or stand (in comparison or relation): with *to*: What relation does this *bear* to the other? **16** To possess as a right or power: to *bear* title. — *v.i.* **17** To carry burdens; convey. **18** To rest heavily; lean; press: His duties *bear* heavily upon him. **19** To endure patiently; suffer: often with *with*: *Bear* with me. **20** To produce fruit or young. **21** To move, point, or lie in a certain direction; take an aim or course: Later, we *bore* west. **22** To be relevant; have reference: with *on* or *upon*: The argument *bears* on the subject. See synonyms under ABIDE, CARRY, ENDURE, LEAN, PRODUCE, SUPPORT. **— to bear company** To accompany. **— to bear down** To force down; overpower or overcome. **— to bear down upon 1** *Naut.* To approach from the weather side: said of a vessel; hence, to approach. **2** To press hard; put pressure on. **— to bear in mind** To keep in recollection; remember. **— to bear out** To support; confirm; justify. **— to bear up** To keep up strength or spirits. **— to bear upon** To be trained upon, as cannon, so as to bring within the line of fire. [<OE *beran* carry, wear, bear, suffer]
bear[2] (bâr) *n.* **1** A large plantigrade carnivorous or omnivorous mammal (family *Ursidae*) with massive thick-furred body and short tail. ◆ Collateral adjective: *ursine*. **2** One of various other animals like or likened to a bear: the ant-*bear*. **3** The caterpillar of the tiger moth. **4** One of two constellations, the Great Bear or the Little Bear. **5** An ill-mannered or morose person. **6** A speculator who seeks to depress prices or who sells in the belief that there is likely to be a decline in prices. **7** *Mech.* A portable device for punching iron plates. **8** *Naut.* A weighted block of wood faced with sandstone and used for scouring the decks of a ship. **— Great Bear** A large northern constellation (*Ursa Major*). See CONSTELLATION. **— Little Bear** A northern constellation (*Ursa Minor*) including the polestar. See CONSTELLATION, POINTERS. **— the Bear** Russia. — *v.t.* To endeavor to depress the price of (stocks, etc.) by selling or offering to sell. ◆ Homophone: *bare*. [<OE *bera*]
bear[3] (bir) *n. Scot.* Four-rowed barley: also spelled *bere*.
bear·a·ble (bâr′ə·bəl) *adj.* Capable of being borne; endurable. **— bear′a·ble·ness** *n.* **— bear′·a·bly** *adv.*
bear-bait·ing (bâr′bā′ting) *n.* The sport of inciting dogs to attack a chained bear. **— bear′-bait′er** *n.*
bear·ber·ry (bâr′ber′ē, -bər·ē) *n.* **1** A trailing, thick-leaved evergreen plant (*Arctostaphylos uva-ursi*) of the heath family, having small red berries and astringent leaves. **2** The deciduous holly (*Ilex decidua*): also called *possumhaw*.
bear·cat (bâr′kat′) *n.* The panda (def. 1).
beard (bird) *n.* **1** The hair on a man's face, especially on the chin, usually excluding the mustache. **2** *Zool.* **a** The long hair on the chin of some animals, as the goat. **b** The feathers near the mouth of certain birds, as the turkey; the vibrissae. **3** Any similar growth or appendage. **4** *Bot.* A tuft of hairlike processes; an awn, as of grass. **5** The barb of an arrow, or of any hook. **6** *Ornithol.* The vane or barbs of a feather. **7** *U.S. Slang* In radio broadcasting, an error in performance, usually a misreading of a part. **8** *Printing* That part of a type which divides the face from the shoulder. — *v.t.* **1** To take by the beard; pull the beard of. **2** To defy courageously. **3** To furnish with a beard. [OE] **— beard′ed** *adj.* **— beard′less** *adj.* **— beard′·like′** *adj.*
Beard (bird), **Charles Austin,** 1874–1948, and his wife, **Mary Ritter,** 1876–1958, U.S. historians. **— Daniel Carter,** 1850–1941, founder of the Boy Scouts of America.
bearded eagle The lammergeier.
Beards·ley (birdz′lē), **Aubrey Vincent,** 1872–1898, English artist and illustrator.
beard tongue Penstemon.
bear·er (bâr′ər) *n.* **1** One who or that which bears, carries, or has in possession. **2** A person to whom a note, check, or draft is made payable without naming him; hence, as no endorsement is required, the person who presents such instrument for collection. **3** A tree or vine producing fruit. **4** A carrier or porter. **5** A pallbearer.
bear·gar·den (bâr′gär′dən) *n.* **1** A place where bears are exhibited or kept, especially for bear-baiting. **2** Any place or scene of tumult or strife.
bear·grass (bâr′gras′, -gräs) *n.* **1** Any of various species of *Yucca*. **2** The camas (*Camassia scilloides*) of Oregon. **3** A yucca-like plant (*Dasylirion texanum*) of the lily family of the SW United States.
bear·ing (bâr′ing) *n.* **1** Deportment; manner of conducting or carrying oneself. **2** The act, capacity, or period of producing. **3** That which is produced; crops; yield. **4** The act or capacity of enduring; endurance. **5** *Archit.* The part of an arch or beam that rests upon a support. **6** *Mech.* A part that rests on something, or on which something rests, or in which a pin, journal, etc., turns. **7** *Her.* A device or charge on a field. **8** The point of a compass in which an object is seen. **9** *Often pl.* The situation of an object relative to that of another, or of other points or places. **10** Reference or relation; connection: What *bearing* does his evidence have on the problem? See synonyms under AIR, BEHAVIOR, DIRECTION.
bearing rein A checkrein.
bear·ish (bâr′ish) *adj.* **1** Like a bear; rough; surly. **2** Tending to depress the price of stocks by offering to sell. **— bear′ish·ly** *adv.* **— bear′ish·ness** *n.*
bear-lead·er (bâr′lē′dər) *n.* **1** One who leads about a trained bear. **2** Hence, a young man's private tutor or traveling companion.
bear market In finance, a market in which prices decline.
Bé·arn (bā·ȧr′, -ärn′) A region and former province of SW France.
bé·ar·naise sauce (bā·ȧr·nâz′) A variation of hollandaise sauce made with chopped parsley and vinegar.
bear pit A place, usually a pit, where bears are kept, as in a zoological garden.
Bear River A river in Utah, Wyoming, and SE Idaho, flowing 350 miles from NE Utah to Great Salt Lake.
Bear State Nickname of ARKANSAS.
bear's-breech (bârz′brēch′) *n.* Any species of *Acanthus*; especially, the European *Acanthus spinosus*, having spiny leaves.
bear's-ear (bârz′ir′) *n.* The auricula.
bear's-foot (bârz′fo͝ot′) *n.* Helleboraster. Also **bears′foot′**.
bear·skin (bâr′skin′) *n.* **1** The skin of a bear or a coat or robe made of it. **2** A tall, black fur headdress worn as a part of some military uniforms. **3** A coarse, shaggy woolen cloth.
bear·wood (bâr′wo͝od′) *n.* Cascara buckthorn.
Be·as (bē′äs) A river in Punjab, NW India, flowing 285 miles SW to the Sutlej: also *Bias*.
beast (bēst) *n.* **1** Any animal except man. **2** Any large quadruped. **3** Animal characteristics or animal nature. **4** A cruel, rude, or filthy person. See synonyms under ANIMAL. [<OF *beste* <LL *besta* <L *bestia* beast] **— beast′like′** *adj.*
beast·ie (bēs′tē) *n. Scot.* A little beast: a term of endearment.
beast·ly (bēst′lē) *adj.* **1** Resembling a beast; brutish; vile; degraded. **2** *Colloq.* Disagreeable or unpleasant; nasty; abominable. See synonyms under BRUTISH. — *adv. Brit. Slang* Very. **— beast′li·ness** *n.*
beast marriage An incident in folklore in which a human being is married to a beast, in very primitive tales to an actual animal, in later elaborations to a human being doomed to exist in beast form.
beast of burden An animal used for carrying loads.
beat (bēt) *v.* **beat, beat·en** (*Colloq.* **beat**), **beat·ing** *v.t.* **1** To strike repeatedly; pound. **2** To punish by repeated blows; thrash; whip. **3** To dash or strike against, as wind or waves. **4** To make, as one's way, by repeated blows: to *beat* a path to the door. **5** To forge or shape by or as by hammering. **6** To make flat by tramping or treading, as a path. **7** To subdue or defeat; master. **8** To flap; flutter, as wings. **9.** *Music* To mark or measure with or as with a baton: to *beat* time. **10** To hunt over; search: to *beat* the countryside. **11** To sound (a signal) as on a drum. **12** To stir; turn (ingredients) over and over so as to make lighter or frothier. **13** *Colloq.* To baffle; perplex: It *beats* me. **14** *Slang* To defraud; swindle. — *v.i.* **15** To strike repeated blows. **16** To strike or smite as with blows: The sound *beats* on our ears. **17** To throb; pulsate. **18** To give forth sound, as when tapped or struck. **19** To sound a signal, as on a drum. **20** *Physics* To alternate in intensity so as to pulsate. **21** To be adaptable to beating: The yolk *beats* well. **22** To hunt through underbrush, etc., as for game. **23** To win a victory or contest. **24** *Naut.* To work against contrary winds or currents by tacking. **— to beat about** To search by one means and then another. **— to beat about the bush** To approach a subject in a round-about way. **— to beat a retreat** To give a signal for retreat, as by beat of drums; hence, to turn back; flee. **— to beat down** To force or persuade (a seller) to accept a lower price. **— to beat it** *Slang* To depart hastily. **— to beat the air** To make futile exertions. **— to beat up** *Colloq.* To thrash thoroughly. — *n.* **1** A stroke or blow, especially one producing sound or

serving as a signal. **2** A pulsation or throb, as of the pulse. **3** *Physics* **a** A regularly recurring pulsation or throb heard when two tones not quite in unison are sounded together: caused by the interference of sound waves. **b** A similar property belonging to light waves and other waves. **4** *Naut.* A tack. **5** *Music* **a** The unit of measure for indicating rhythm. **b** The gesture or symbol for this. **6** The stroke or tick of a watch or clock. **7** A round, line, or district regularly traversed, as by a sentry or a policeman. **8** A division of a county. **9** In newspaper slang, a scoop. **10** *U.S. Slang* A deadbeat (def. 1). **11** *Colloq.* A member of the Beat Generation. **—** *adj.* **1** *U.S. Colloq.* Fatigued; worn out. **2** Pertaining to the Beat Generation. [OE *bēatan*]

Synonyms (verb): bastinado, batter, belabor, bruise, castigate, chastise, conquer, cudgel, cuff, defeat, flog, overcome, pommel, pound, scourge, smite, strike, surpass, thrash, vanquish, whip, worst. *Strike* is the word for a single blow; to *beat* is to *strike* repeatedly. Others of the words above describe the manner of *beating*, as *bastinado*, to *beat* on the soles of the feet; *belabor*, to inflict an exhaustive *beating*; *cudgel*, to *beat* with a stick; *thrash* (originally identical with "thresh"), to *beat* with repeated blows, as wheat was *beaten* out with the old hand flail; to *pound* is to *beat* with a heavy, and *pommel* with a blunt, instrument. To *batter* and to *bruise* refer to the results of *beating*; that is *battered* which is broken or defaced by repeated blows; that is *bruised* which has suffered even one severe blow. To *beat* a combatant is to disable or dishearten him for further fighting. Hence *beat* becomes the synonym for every word which implies getting the advantage of another. Compare CONQUER, SUBDUE. *Antonyms*: fail, fall, surrender.

be·a·tae me·mo·ri·ae (bē·ā′tē me·mō′ri·ē) *Latin* Of blessed memory.

beat·en (bēt′n) *adj.* **1** Shaped by beating; having undergone blows. **2** Worn by use or travel: the *beaten* path. **3** Conquered or subdued; baffled.

beat·er (bē′tər) *n.* **1** One who or that which beats. **2** An implement or device for beating. **3** In hunting, one who arouses game and drives it from cover.

Beat Generation A group of post-World War II artists, writers, and musicians who seek spiritual fulfilment through sensual experience, disclaiming social responsibility to a hostile and thoroughly materialistic society.

be·a·tif·ic (bē′ə·tif′ik) *adj.* Making blessed or blissful. **—be′a·tif′i·cal·ly** *adv.*

be·at·i·fi·ca·tion (bē·at′ə·fi·kā′shən) *n.* **1** The act of blessing, or the state of being blessed or beatified. **2** In the Roman Catholic Church, an act of the Pope declaring a deceased person beatified *(beatus)* and worthy of a certain degree of public honor: usually the last step toward canonization.

be·at·i·fy (bē·at′ə·fī) *v.t.* **·fied, ·fy·ing** **1** To make supremely happy. **2** In the Roman Catholic Church, to declare as blessed and worthy of public honor by an act of the Pope. **3** To exalt above others. [<F *béatifier* <LL *beatificare* bless < *beatus* happy + *facere* make]

beat·ing (bē′ting) *n.* **1** The action of one who or that which beats, or the process involved. **2** Punishment by blows; flogging. **3** Pulsation; throbbing, as of the heart. **4** A defeat.

be·at·i·tude (bē·at′ə·tōōd, -tyōōd) *n.* **1** Supreme blessedness or felicity. **2** A blessing. **—the Beatitudes** Eight declarations of special blessedness pronounced by Jesus in the Sermon on the Mount. *Matt.* v 3–11. [<F *béatitude* <L *beatitudo* blessedness < *beatus* happy]

beat·nik (bēt′nik) *n.* A member of the Beat Generation.

beat-note (bēt′nōt′) *n.* An audible radio frequency caused by the interaction of two frequencies of different value.

Be·a·trice (bē′ə·tris, *Ital.* bā′ä·trē′chā) A feminine personal name. Also **Be·a·trix** (bē′ə·triks; *Dan., Du., Ger., Sw.* bā·ä′triks), *Fr.* **Bé·a·trice** or **Bé·a·trix** (bā·à·trēs′), *Pg., Sp.* **Be·a·triz** (*Pg.* bä′ä·trēsh′, *Sp.* -trēth′). [<L, she who makes happy]

—Beatrice The heroine of Shakespeare's *Much Ado About Nothing.*

—Beatrice The idealized and symbolic heroine of Dante's *Divine Comedy*: identified with **Beatrice Por·ti·na·ri** (pôr′tē·nä′rē), 1266–90, Florentine lady.

Beat·ty (bē′tē), **Lord David,** 1871–1936, first Earl of Brooksby and the North Sea; British admiral of the fleet in World War I. **—James,** 1735–1803, Scottish poet.

beau (bō) *n. pl.* **beaus** or **beaux** (bōz) **1** A dandy; fop. **2** An escort. **3** A lover; swain. ◆ Homophone: *bow*[3]. [<F <L *bellus* fine, pretty] **—beau′ish** *adj.*

Beau Brum·mell (brum′əl) A dandy or fop. [after George *("Beau") Brummell,* 1778–1840, English dandy]

Beau·clerc (bō′klâr) See HENRY I.

Beau·fort (bō′fərt), **Henry,** 1370?–1447, English cardinal.

Beau·fort scale (bō′fərt) *Meteorol.* A scale of wind velocities, ranging from 0 (calm) to 12 (hurricane). The wind velocity is measured by its pressure on a disk one square foot in area at a height of 33 feet in the open. See table below for scale as used by the U.S. Weather Bureau. [after Sir Francis *Beaufort,* 1774–1857, British admiral]

BEAUFORT SCALE

Code No.	*Description*	*Pressure lbs. per sq. ft.*	*Speed miles per hour.*
0	Calm	0.	Less than 1
1	Light air	.01	1–3
2	Light breeze	.08	4–7
3	Gentle breeze	.28	8–12
4	Moderate breeze	.67	13–18
5	Fresh breeze	1.31	19–24
6	Strong breeze	2.3	25–31
7	*Moderate gale	3.6	32–38
8	Fresh gale	5.4	39–46
9	Strong gale	7.7	47–54
10	Whole gale	10.5	55–63
11	Storm	14.	64–75
12	Hurricane	Above 17	Above 75

* Intermediate between breeze and gale.

Beaufort Sea That part of the Arctic Ocean between northern Alaska and the Arctic Archipelago.

beau geste (bō zhest′) *pl.* **beaux gestes** (bō zhest′) *French* **1** Literally, a fine gesture; hence, a kindly act. **2** A gesture of kindliness, often made for diplomatic or selfish reasons.

Beau·har·nais (bō·är·ne′), **Vicomte Alexandre de,** 1760–94, first husband of Empress Josephine. **—Eugène de,** 1781–1824, French general, son of preceding. **—Hortense Eugénie de,** 1783–1837, daughter of Josephine, wife of Louis Bonaparte; queen of Holland, mother of Napoleon III.

beau i·de·al (bō ī·dē′əl) **1** The highest conceivable standard of beauty or excellence. **2** A model of perfection or excellence. [<F *beau idéal* (the) ideal beautiful]

Beau·mar·chais (bō·mȧr·she′), **Pierre Augustin Caron de,** 1732–99, French dramatist.

beau monde (bō mônd′) *French* The fashionable world.

Beau·mont (bō′mont), **Francis,** 1584–1616, English dramatist who collaborated with John Fletcher. **—William,** 1785–1853, U.S. surgeon.

Beau·re·gard (bō′rə·gärd), **Pierre Gustave Toutant,** 1818–93, Confederate general in the Civil War.

beaut (byōōt) *n. U.S. Slang* Something beautiful: often used ironically: a *beaut* of a black eye.

beau·te·ous (byōō′tē·əs) *adj.* Beautiful. See synonyms under BEAUTIFUL. **—beau′te·ous·ly** *adv.* **—beau′te·ous·ness** *n.*

beau·ti·cian (byōō·tish′ən) *n.* One who works in a beauty parlor, or a person trained in hairdressing, manicuring, massaging, etc.

beau·ti·ful (byōō′tə·fəl) *adj.* Possessing beauty; conforming to esthetic standards, or arousing esthetic pleasure. **—** *n.* **1** Beauty in the abstract. **2** That which is beautiful. **—beau′ti·ful·ly** *adv.* **—beau′ti·ful·ness** *n.*

Synonyms (adj.): attractive, beauteous, bewitching, bonny, charming, comely, delightful, elegant, exquisite, fair, fine, graceful, handsome, lovely, picturesque, pretty. *Beautiful* implies softness of outline and delicacy of mold; it is opposed to all that is hard and rugged. *Pretty* expresses in a far less degree that which is pleasing to a refined taste. That is *handsome* which is superficially pleasing, and also well and harmoniously proportioned. *Handsome* is a term far inferior to *beautiful*; we may even say a *handsome* villain. *Fair* denotes what is bright, smooth, clear, and without blemish; as, a *fair* face. In a specific sense, *fair* has the sense of blond, as opposed to dark or brunette. One who possesses pleasing qualities may be *attractive* without beauty. *Comely* denotes an aspect that is smooth, genial, and wholesome, with fulness of contour and pleasing symmetry, while falling short of the *beautiful.* That is *picturesque* which would make a picture. See FINE, GRACEFUL, LOVELY. *Antonyms*: awkward, clumsy, deformed, disgusting, frightful, ghastly, grim, grisly, grotesque, hideous, horrid, odious, repulsive, shocking, ugly, unattractive, uncouth, ungainly, unlovely, unpleasant.

beau·ti·fy (byōō′tə·fī) *v.t.* & *v.i.* **·fied, ·fy·ing** To make or grow beautiful; embellish; adorn. See synonyms under ADORN, GARNISH. **—beau′·ti·fi·ca′tion** *n.* **—beau′ti·fied** *adj.* **—beau′ti·fi′er** *n.*

beau·ty (byōō′tē) *n. pl.* **·ties** **1** Any of those qualities of objects, sounds, emotional or intellectual concepts, behavior, etc., that gratify or arouse admiration to a high degree, especially by the perfection of form resulting from the harmonious combination of diverse elements in unity. **2** A person or thing that is beautiful, especially a woman. **3** A special grace or charm. [<OF *beaute,* ult. <L *bellus* handsome, fine, pretty]

beauty pack A face pack.

beauty parlor *U.S.* An establishment for the hairdressing, manicuring, cosmetic treatment, etc., of women. Also **beauty salon, beauty shop.**

beauty spot **1** A small black patch put on the face to enhance the brilliance of the complexion. **2** A mole or other natural mark resembling this. **3** Any place regarded as especially beautiful.

Beau·vais (bō·ve′) A cathedral city of northern France.

Beau·voir (bō·vwär′), **Simone de,** born 1908, French novelist.

beaux (bōz) Plural of BEAU.

Beaux (bō), **Cecilia,** 1863–1942, U.S. painter.

beaux-arts (bō·zàr′) *n. pl. French* The fine arts, as music, painting, sculpture, etc.

beaux-es·prits (bō·zes·prē′) Plural of BEL-ESPRIT.

beaux yeux (bō zyœ′) *French* Beautiful eyes; hence, a pretty face.

bea·ver[1] (bē′vər) *n.* **1** An amphibious rodent (family *Castoridae*), with a scaly, flat, oval tail and webbed hind feet, noted for skill in damming shallow streams: valued for its fur. **2** The fur of the beaver. **3** A high silk hat, originally made of this fur. **4** A heavy twill-woven woolen cloth with a napped finish, used for outer garments. [OE *beofor*]

BEAVER
(2 1/2 to 4 feet long, including tail)

bea·ver[2] (bē′vər) *n.* **1** A movable piece of medieval armor covering the lower part of the face, especially when worn with a vizor; later, both chinpiece and vizor. **2** *Slang* A beard. [<OF *bavière* child's bib < *bave* saliva]

bea·ver·board (bē′vər·bôrd′, -bōrd′) *n.* A light, stiff building material made of compressed or laminated wood pulp: used chiefly for walls and partitions.

Bea·ver·brook (bē′vər·brŏŏk), **Baron,** 1879–1964, William Maxwell Aitken, English publisher and statesman, born in Canada.

beaver cutting A place where the trees have been gnawed and leveled by beavers.

beaver dam A dam built by beavers.

beaver lodge A beaver den.

beaver pond A pond made by a beaver dam.

Beaver State Nickname of Oregon.

be·bee·rine (bi·bē′rēn, -rin) *n.* An amorphous alkaloid, $C_{18}H_{19}NO_3$, contained in the bark of the greenheart tree: used in medicine as a tonic and febrifuge. [<BEBEERU + -INE]

be·bee·ru (bi·bē′rōō) *n.* The greenheart tree. [<Sp. *bibiru* <Cariban]

Be·bel (bā′bəl), **Ferdinand August,** 1840–1913, German socialist.

be·bop (bē′bop′) *n.* A variety of jazz characterized by deliberate departures from key and extreme improvisation in rhythmic pattern, and sung with meaningless sounds. Also **be′bop′.**

be·calm (bi·käm′) *v.t.* **1** To make quiet or calm; still. **2** To cause to be motionless for lack of wind, as a ship: used in the passive: The ship was *becalmed* off Africa.

be·came (bi·kām) Past tense of BECOME.

be·cause (bi·kôz′) *conj.* For the reason that; on account of the fact that; since. [ME *bi cause* by cause]

Synonyms: as, for, since. *Because* is the most direct and complete word for giving the reason of a thing. *Since,* originally denoting succession in time, signifies a succession in a chain of reasoning, a natural inference or result. *As* indicates something like, coordinate, parallel. *Since* is weaker than *because; as* is weaker than *since:* either may introduce the reason before the main statement; thus, *since* or *as* you are going, I will accompany you. Often the weaker word is the more courteous, implying less constraint. *Antonyms:* although, however, nevertheless, notwithstanding, yet.

because of On account of; by reason of: He was unable to attend *because of* illness.

bec·ca·fi·co (bek′ə·fē′kō) *n. pl.* **·cos** Any of various small European birds, mostly warblers, supposed to eat figs; especially, the garden warbler *(Sylvia hortensis),* much esteemed as food. [<Ital. < *beccare* peck + *fico* <L *ficus* fig]

bé·cha·mel sauce (bā·shȧ·mel′) A white sauce made of cream, butter, flour, etc., and flavored with onion and seasonings. [after Louis de *Béchamel,* steward to Louis XIV, who invented it]

be·chance (bi·chans′, -chäns′) *v.t. & v.i.* **be·chanced, be·chanc·ing** To befall; happen by chance.

bêche-de-mer (bâsh·də·mâ r′) *n.* **1** The trepang. **2** A lingua franca of largely English vocabulary, used between Europeans and the natives of the SW Pacific: originally developed through commerce with trepang fishermen: also called *beach-la-mar.* [<F, sea spade]

Bech·u·a·na (bech′ŏŏ·ä′nə, bek′yŏŏ-) *n. pl.* **·a·na** or **·a·nas 1** One of an important Bantu tribe inhabiting the region between the Orange and Zambesi Rivers, SW Africa. **2** The Bantu language of this tribe.

Bech·u·a·na·land (bech′ŏŏ·ä′nə·land, bek′yŏŏ-) A former British protectorate in southern Africa. Now known as Botswana. See BOTSWANA.

Bechuanaland Protectorate Once a British protectorate in southern Africa, bounded by then Southern Rhodesia, the Union of South Africa, and South-West Africa; about 275,000 square miles; extraterritorial capital, Mafeking, in former Union of South Africa.

beck[1] (bek) *n.* A nod or other gesture of summons. **—at one's beck and call** Subject to one's slightest wish. — *v.t. & v.i.* **1** To beckon. **2** *Scot.* To recognize (a person) by a nod; bow or curtsy. [Var. of BECKON]

beck[2] (bek) *n.* A small brook, or the valley in which it runs. [<ON *bekkr* stream, brook]

beck·et (bek′it) *n.* **1** *Naut.* A device for holding a ship's spars, ropes, etc., in position, as a cleat, a strap, loop, or rope, or a small grommet. **2** *Slang* A trouser pocket. [Origin unknown]

Beck·et (bek′it,) **Thomas à, Saint,** 1117–70, English archbishop of Canterbury, murdered for his opposition to Henry II.

becket hitch *Naut.* A hitch or bend used when a rope is to be temporarily fastened to another rope or into an eye. Also **becket bend.**

Beck·ford (bek′fərd), **William,** 1759–1844, English writer.

beck·on (bek′ən) *v.t. & v.i.* **1** To signal, direct, or summon by sign or gesture. **2** To entice or lure. — *n.* A summoning gesture; beck. [OE *biecnan, beacnian* make signs <) *bēacen* a sign. Related to BEACON.]

be·cloud (bē·kloud′) *v.t.* **1** To obscure by a cloud or clouds; darken. **2** To confuse, as an issue.

be·come (bi·kum′) *v.* **be·came, be·come, be·com·ing** *v.i.* **1** To undergo development; grow to be: The chick *becomes* the chicken. **2** To come to be: The land *became* dry. — *v.t.* **3** To suit or befit: Your words do not *become* you. **4** To be suitable to; show to advantage: Your dress *becomes* you. **—to become of** To be the fate of: I don't know what *became of* him. [OE *becuman* happen, come about]

be·com·ing (bi·kum′ing) *adj.* **1** Appropriate; suitable. **2** Pleasing; adorning. **—be·com′·ing·ly** *adv.* **— be·com′ing·ness** *n.*

Synonyms: befitting, beseeming, comely, congruous, decent, decorous, fit, fitting, graceful, meet, neat, proper, seemly, suitable, worthy. That is *becoming* in dress which suits the complexion, figure, and other qualities of the wearer, so as to produce a pleasing effect. That is *decent* which does not offend modesty or propriety. That is *suitable* which is adapted to the age, station, situation, and other circumstances of the wearer. In conduct much the same rules apply. The dignity and gravity of a patriarch would not be *becoming* to a child; at a funeral lively, cheery sociability would not be *decorous,* while noisy hilarity would not be *decent. Meet* now expresses chiefly a moral fitness; as, *meet* for heaven. Compare APPROPRIATE. *Antonyms:* awkward, ill-becoming, ill-fitting, improper, indecent, indecorous, unbecoming, unfit, unseemly, unsuitable.

Becque·rel (bek·rel′) Family of French physicists, including **Antoine César,** 1788–1878, **Alexandre Edmond,** 1820–91, son of preceding, and **Antoine Henri,** 1852–1908, son of Alexandre Edmond.

Becquerel rays Rays emitted by radioactive substances. [after Antoine Henri *Becquerel,* who discovered them]

bed (bed) *n.* **1** An article of furniture to rest or sleep in or on: either the stuffed tick or mattress, on which the body rests, the mattress and bedclothes, the bedstead, or all combined; a couch. **2** Any place or thing used for a couch or for sleeping in or on. **3** Something likened to or serving as a bed, foundation, or support: the *bed* of a lake, a rocky *bed.* **4** The marriage bed; marriage. **5** Conjugal cohabitation, or the right to it. **6** A heavy horizontal mass of matter or a collection of closely massed objects, especially used as a foundation or support. **7** Anything resembling or used for a bed. **8** A part or surface that serves as a foundation. **9** The part of a printing press which supports the form, or a part from which work is fed to a machine. **10** A layer of mortar in which stones or bricks are to be laid. **11** A horizontal course of a stone wall. **12** The lower side of a slate, tile, or brick. **13** A plot of ground prepared for planting some particular thing, or the plants, etc., growing in such a plot. **14** A roadbed or a foundation for rails. **15** *Geol.* Any layer in a mass of stratified rock; a seam; a deposit, as of ore, parallel to the stratification. **16** A wagon body. — *v.* **bed·ded, bed·ding** *v.t.* **1** To furnish with a bed. **2** To put to bed. **3** To make a bed for; provide with litter: often with *down:* to *bed* cattle down. **4** To set out or plant in a bed or earth. **5** To have sexual intercourse with. **6** To lay flat or arrange in layers; to *bed* oysters. **7** To place firmly; embed. — *v.i.* **8** To go to bed. **9** To form a closely packed layer; stratify. [OE] **—bed′der** *n.* ◆ *Bed* may appear as a combining form, in hyphemes or solidemes, or as the first element in two-word phrases, which name things used for, in, or about a bed; as in:

bedchair	**bed light**	**bedquilt**
bedcover	**bedmaker**	**bed sock**
bedframe	**bedmaking**	**bedspring**
bedgown	**bedmate**	**bedstand**
bed jacket	**bed pad**	**bedtime**
bed lamp	**bedpost**	**bedwarmer**

be·daub (bi·dôb′) *v.t.* **1** To smear with something oily or sticky; soil. **2** To abuse; vilify. **3** To load with vulgar ornament or flattery.

be·daz·zle (bi·daz′əl) *v.t.* **·zled, ·zling 1** To blind by excess of light. **2** To bewilder; confuse.

bed·bug (bed′bug′) *n.* A bloodsucking hemipterous insect *(Cimex lectularius)* of reddish-brown color, infesting houses and especially beds. See illustration under INSECTS (injurious).

bed·cham·ber (bed′chām′bər) *n.* A sleeping apartment; a bedroom.

bed·clothes (bed′klōz′, -klō *th*z′) *n. pl.* Covering for a bed, as sheets, blankets, quilts, etc.

bed·ding (bed′ing) *n.* **1** The furnishings for a bedstead. **2** Straw or other litter for animals to sleep on. **3** A putting to bed. **4** That which forms a bed or foundation. **5** *Geol.* Stratification of rocks.

bedding plant Any plant used for placing in a bed, especially one conspicuous in its foliage or flowers and grown in masses with others.

Bed·does (bed′ōz), **Thomas Lovell,** 1803–49, English poet and dramatist.

Bede (bēd), **Saint,** 673–735, English theologian and historian: called "The Venerable Bede." Also *Be·da* (bē′də).

be·deck (bi·dek′) *v.t.* To deck; adorn; ornament. See synonyms under ADORN.

bede·man (bēd′mən) *n.* A beadsman.

be·dev·il (bi·dev′əl) *v.t.* **·iled** or **·illed, ·il·ing** or **·il·ling 1** To torment; worry. **2** To harass with diabolical treatment or abuse. **3** To spoil; corrupt, as by witchcraft. **4** To possess with or as with a devil; bewitch. **5** To make or transform into a devil. **—be·dev′il·ment** *n.*

be·dew (bi·dŏŏ′, -dyŏŏ′) *v.t.* To moisten with or as with dew.

bed·fel·low (bed′fel′ō) *n.* One who shares a bed with another.

Bed·ford (bed′fərd) A county in south central England; 473 square miles; county seat, Bedford. Also **Bed·ford·shire** (bed′fərd·shir, -shər), shortened form **Beds.**

Bed·ford (bed′fərd), **Duke of,** 1389–1435, John of Lancaster; English statesman; regent of France.

Bedford cord A strong rib-weave fabric having raised, lengthwise cords of wool, silk, cotton or rayon.

be·dight (bi·dīt′) *v.t.* **be·dight, be·dight·ing** *Archaic* To furnish with dress or ornament; adorn; apparel; bedeck.

be·dim (bi·dim′) *v.t.* **be·dimmed, be·dim·ming** To make dim; obscure.

Bed·i·vere (bed′ə·vir) In Arthurian legend, one of the knights of the Round Table.

be·diz·en (bi·diz′ən, -dī′zən) *v.t.* To dress or adorn with tawdry splendor. **—be·diz′en·ment** *n.*

bed·lam (bed′ləm) *n.* **1** An excited crowd. **2** An incoherent uproar. **3** A lunatic asylum; a madhouse. [<BEDLAM]

Bed·lam (bed′ləm) The hospital of St. Mary of Bethlehem in London, used for the insane. [Alter. of BETHLEHEM] **—Bed′lam·ite** (-īt) *n.*

bed·lam·ite (bed′ləm·īt) *n.* A lunatic.

bed linen Sheets, pillow cases, etc., for beds.

Bed·ling·ton terrier (bed′ling·tən) A muscular terrier used in hunting badgers, foxes, etc. See under TERRIER.

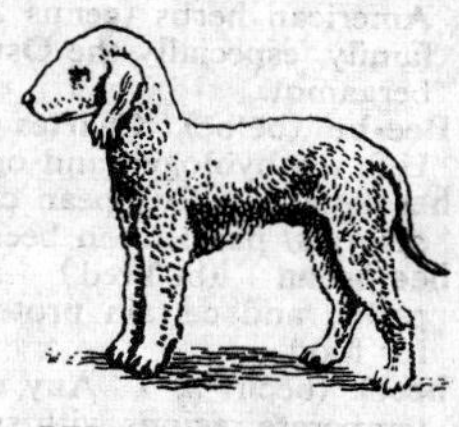

BEDLINGTON TERRIER
(About 16 inches high at the shoulder)

Bed·loe's Island (bed′lōz) A former name for LIBERTY ISLAND.

bed·mold·ing (bed′·mōl′ding) *n. Archit.* A molding, or one of a series of moldings, under the corona in a cornice.

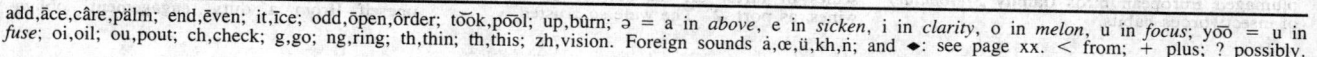

Bed·ou·in (bed′ŏŏ·in, -ēn) *n.* **1** One of the nomadic Arabs of Syria, Arabia, etc. **2** Such nomads collectively. **3** Any nomad or vagabond. — *adj.* **1** Of or pertaining to the Bedouins. **2** Roving; nomadic. Also spelled *Beduin.* [<F <Arabic *badāwīn* desert dweller < *badw* desert]

bed·pan (bed′pan′) *n.* **1** An earthenware or porcelain vessel to be used in bed by a sick person for urination or defecation. **2** A warming pan.

bed·plate (bed′plāt′) *n.* Mech. A plate or frame to which the lighter parts of a machine are bolted.

bed·post (bed′pōst′) *n.* One of the posts supporting a bedstead.

be·drag·gle (bi·drag′əl) *v.t. & v.i.* **·gled, ·gling** To make or become wet or soiled, as by dragging through mire.

bed·rid·den (bed′rid′ən) *adj.* Confined to bed, by sickness or weakness. Also **bed′rid′.** [OE *bedrida* <*bed* bed + *rida* rider]

bed·rock (bed′rok′) *n. Geol.* The solid rock underlying the looser materials of the earth's surface. —**down to bedrock 1** Down to the lowest limit: Prices dropped *down to bedrock.* **2** Down to fundamentals; down to the truth of the matter.

bed·roll (bed′rōl′) *n.* **1** Bedding compactly rolled to facilitate carrying. **2** The cover for a roll of bedding.

bed·room (bed′ro͞om′, -ro͝om′) *n.* A sleeping room.

bed·side (bed′sīd′) *n.* Place by a bed; the side of the bed. —*adj.* Pertaining to or suitable for the bedside: a *bedside* manner.

bed·sore (bed′sôr′, -sōr′) *n.* An ulcer on the body, caused by lying long in one position.

bed·spread (bed′spred′) *n.* A quilt or counterpane.

bed·spring (bed′spring′) *n.* The framework of springs supporting the mattress of a bed.

bed·staff (bed′staf′, -stäf′) *n. pl.* **·staves** (-stāvz′) **1** A stick or staff used in some way about a bed, as to smooth a featherbed or to spread the coverlets. **2** A bar at the side to keep the bedclothes in place.

bed·stead (bed′sted′) *n.* A framework for supporting a mattress, bedding, etc.

bed·straw (bed′strô′) *n.* Any of a genus *(Galium)* of woody herbs of the madder family with whorled sessile leaves and small flowers: so called because formerly used as stuffing in beds.

bed·time (bed′tīm′) *n.* The time for retiring to bed. —*adj.* Of or for this time: *bedtime* stories.

bed·ward (bed′wərd) *adv.* **1** Toward bed. **2** Toward bedtime. Also **bed′wards.**

bed–wet·ting (bed′wet′ing) *n.* Nocturnal enuresis.

Be·dzin (ben·jēn) A city in southern Poland. *German* **Bend·zin** (ben′tsēn), *Russian* **Ben·din** (byān′dyin).

bee[1] (bē) *n.* **1** Any of a large number of hymenopterous insects of the family *Apoidea,* solitary or social in habit, with smooth or hairy bodies, variously colored, and feeding largely upon nectar and pollen. **2** The common hive or honey bee *(Apis mellifera).* **3** A social gathering of neighbors for work or competitive activity: a quilting *bee.* —**to have a bee in one's bonnet** To be excessively concerned about or obsessed with one idea. [OE *beo*]

bee[2] (bē) *n. Naut.* A strip of timber or iron bolted to each side of the bowsprit of a vessel, through which to reeve the foretopmast stays. Also **bee block.** [OE *bēag* ring]

bee balm Any of various aromatic North American herbs (genus *Monarda*) of the mint family, especially the Oswego tea and the wild bergamot.

Bee·be (bē′bē), **Charles William,** 1877–1962, U.S. ichthyologist and ornithologist.

bee beetle A European clerid beetle *(Trichodes apiarius)* parasitic in beehives.

bee·bread (bē′bred′) *n.* A mixture of pollen and certain proteins as stored by bees for food.

beech (bēch) *n.* **1** Any of a family of trees of temperate regions with smooth, ash–gray bark, and bearing an edible nut; especially, the widely cultivated European beech *(Fagus sylvatica)* and the American beech *(F. grandifolia).* **2** One of various trees similar to the beech: the blue *beech (Carpinus caroliniana).* **3** The wood of this tree. ◆ Homophone: *beach.* [OE *bēce*] —**beech′en** *adj.*

Bee·cham (bē′chəm), **Sir Thomas,** 1879–1961, English orchestral conductor.

beech·drops (bēch′drops′) *n.* **1** A low–growing plant (genus *Epifagus*) of the broomrape family, parasitic on the roots of beech trees: also called *pinedrops.* **2** The squawroot.

Beech·er (bē′chər), **Henry Ward,** 1813–87, U.S. pulpit orator and writer. —**Lyman,** 1775–1863, U.S. theologian; father of preceding.

beech·mast (bēch′mast′, -mäst′) *n.* The nuts of the beech.

beech·nut (bēch′nut′) *n.* The edible nut of the beech.

bee–eat·er (bē′ē′tər) *n.* Any of certain bright–plumaged European birds (family *Meropidae*) of insectivorous habits.

beef (bēf) *n. pl.* **beeves** (bēvz) or **beefs** *for def.* **2; beefs** *for def.* **4 1** The flesh of a slaughtered adult bovine animal. **2** Any adult bovine animal, as an ox, cow, steer, bull, etc., fattened for the butcher. **3** *Colloq.* Muscular power; brawn. **4** *U.S. Slang* A complaint. —**bully beef** Canned or pickled beef. —**dried beef** Beef preserved by salting and drying, usually in smoke. —*v.i. U.S. Slang* To complain or grouse. [<OF *boef* <L *bos, bovis* ox]

beef·eat·er (bēf′ē′tər) *n.* **1** An eater of beef; hence, an Englishman (so called by the French), or a well–fed servant. **2** A bluebottle or fleshfly.

Beefeater One of the Yeomen of the Guard who attend the British sovereign on state occasions, or one of the similarly uniformed warders of the Tower of London.

beefed–up (bēft′up′) *adj. Colloq.* Strengthened or reinforced to increase load capacity: said of an aircraft.

beef·ing (bē′fing) *n.* **1** A kind of apple, so named because of its deep–red, beeflike color. **2** *U.S. Slang* Complaining.

bee·fly (bē′flī′) *n. pl.* **·flies** A hairy fly (family *Bombyliidae*) somewhat resembling a bee: the larvae destroy the young of wasps and other insects. For illustration see INSECTS (beneficial).

beef·steak (bēf′stāk′) *n.* A slice of beef suitable for broiling or frying.

beef tea A beverage made by boiling lean beef or from a beef extract.

beef·y (bē′fē) *adj.* **beef·i·er, beef·i·est 1** Like an ox; fat; dull. **2** *Colloq.* Brawny; muscular. —**beef′i·ness** *n.*

bee gum 1 A hollow gum tree in which bees nest. **2** A beehive, especially one made from a hollow gum tree.

bee·hive (bē′hīv′) *n.* **1** A hive for a colony of honey bees. **2** Any place filled with busy workers. **3** A woman's hair style in which the hair is coiled in a conical mound.

Beehive State Nickname of UTAH.

bee·keep·er (bē′kē′pər) *n.* One who keeps bees; an apiarist.

bee–kill·er (bē′kil′ər) *n.* One of several species of large flies (family *Asilidae*) that habitually prey on bees.

bee·line (bē′līn′) *n.* The shortest course from one place to another, as of a bee to its hive.

Be·el·ze·bub (bē·el′zə·bub) **1** The prince of the demons or of false gods; the devil. **2** In Milton's *Paradise Lost,* a chief of the lost angels ranking next to Satan. **3** A Semitic god, worshiped as the lord of flies: the original sense.

bee moth The honeycomb moth.

been (bin, *Brit.* bēn) Past participle of BE.

beep (bēp) *n.* A short, usually high–pitched mechanical or electronic sound used as a signal or warning. —*v.i.* **1** To make such a sound. —*v.t.* **2** To sound (a horn): taxi drivers *beeping* their horns. **3** To transmit (a message) by a beep or beeps. [Imit.]

bee plant Any plant valuable as a honey–producer; specifically, a spiderflower *(Cleome serrulata)* of the western United States, cultivated for bees, or a figwort, especially *Scrophularia fornica.*

beer (bir) *n.* **1** An alcoholic fermented liquor made from malt and hops. **2** A slightly fermented beverage made from the roots, etc., of various plants, as sassafras, ginger, spruce, etc. ◆ Homophone: *bier.* [OE *bēor*]

Beer·bohm (bir′bōm), **Max,** 1872–1956, English critic and caricaturist.

Beer·she·ba (bir·shē′bə, bir′shi·bə) A town in the Negev in southern Israel; in Biblical history it marked the southern limit of Palestine.

beer·y (bir′ē) *adj.* **1** Of, pertaining to, or like beer. **2** Stained or tainted with beer. **3** Addicted to or affected by beer: a *beery* voice. **4** Maudlin.

beest·ings (bēs′tingz) *n.* The first milk from a cow after calving; the colostrum: also spelled *biestings.* [OE *bȳsting*<*beost*]

bees·wax (bēz′waks′) *n.* A white or yellowish plastic substance, secreted by honey bees, from which they make the cells of their comb: widely used in medicine and the arts. —*v.t.* To smear with beeswax; wax.

bees·wing (bēz′wing′) *n.* **1** A filmy crust of scales of tartar on the surface of some old wines, as port. **2** The wine so crusted.

beet[1] (bēt) *n.* **1** The fleshy succulent root of a biennial herb of the goosefoot family (genus *Beta*); especially, the common or red beet *(B. vulgaris),* used as a vegetable, and the sugar beet *(B. saccharifera),* used in making sugar. **2** The plant. ◆ Homophone: *beat.* [OE *bēte* < L *beta*]

beet[2] (bēt) *v.t. Brit. Dial.* **1** To kindle or replenish, as a fire; hence, to rouse; stir. **2** *Obs.* To mend or amend; correct. Also **beete.** ◆ Homophone: *beat.* [OE *bētan* make better, amend]

Bee·tho·ven (bā′tō·vən), **Ludwig van,** 1770–1827, German composer.

bee·tle[1] (bēt′l) *n.* **1** Any coleopterous insect having biting mouth parts and hard, horny elytra that serve as a cover for the membranous posterior wings when at rest. For illustrations see under INSECT. **2** Loosely, any insect resembling a beetle. **3** A short–sighted or intellectually blind person; a blockhead. —*adj.* Shaggy; overhanging: a *beetle* brow: also **bee′tling.** —*v.i.* **·tled, ·tling** To jut out; overhang. [OE *bitula* <*bītan* bite]

bee·tle[2] (bēt′l) *n.* **1** A heavy wooden hammer or mallet; a maul. **2** A pestle or mallet for pounding clothes, or for various other purposes, as mashing potatoes. **3** A beetling machine. —*v.t.* **·tled, ·tling** To beat or stamp with or as with a beetle, mallet, beetling machine, etc. [OE *bīetel* mallet <*bēatan* beat]

bee·tle–browed (bēt′l·broud′) *adj.* Having prominent, overhanging eyebrows.

bee·tle–head·ed (bēt′l·hed′id) *adj.* Densely stupid or dull.

beetling machine A machine for stamping goods as they are wound over a roller.

bee tree 1 A hollow tree inhabited by bees; a bee gum. **2** The American linden *(Tilia americana),* or other tree with honey–bearing flowers.

beeves (bēvz) A plural of BEEF.

bee·wolf (bē′wo͝olf′) *n.* The larva of the bee beetle.

be·fall (bi·fôl′) *v.* **be·fell, be·fall·en, be·fall·ing** *v.i.* **1** To come about; happen; occur. **2** *Obs.* To fall as one's right or share; belong; be fitting. —*v.t.* **3** To happen to. [OE *bef(e)allan* fall]

be·fit (bi·fit′) *v.t.* **be·fit·ted, be·fit·ting** To be suited to; be appropriate for.

be·fit·ting (bi·fit′ing) *adj.* Becoming; adequate; suitable. See synonyms under APPROPRIATE, BECOMING. —**be·fit′ting·ly** *adv.*

be·fog (bi·fôg′, fog′) *v.t.* **be·fogged, be·fog·ging 1** To envelop in or as in fog. **2** To confuse; obscure.

be·fool (bi·fo͞ol′) *v.t.* **1** To make a dupe or fool of; hoodwink; delude. **2** To call or treat as a fool.

be·fore (bi·fôr′, -fōr′) *adv.* **1** In front; ahead. **2** Preceding in time; previously. **3** Earlier; sooner. —*prep.* **1** In front of; ahead of. **2** Face to face with; in the presence of: The prisoner stood *before* the court. **3** Prior to, in time; earlier or sooner than. **4** In advance of, as in rank, development, or attainment. **5** Demanding the attention of: The bill is *before* the senate. **6** In the cognizance or power of: *Before* God, I swear it. **7** Driven in front of; moved by: The ship sailed *before* the wind. —*conj.* **1** Previous to the time when; sooner than. **2** In preference to; rather than: They will die *before* yielding. [OE *beforan* in front of]

be·fore·hand (bi·fôr′hand′, -fōr′-) *adv. & adj.* In anticipation or advance; ahead of time.

before the mast Forward of the foremast: said of the common sailors, whose quarters are forward.

be·fore·time (bi·fôr′tīm′, -fōr′-) *adv.* In former time; formerly.

be·foul (bi·foul′) *v.t.* To make foul or dirty; sully.

be·friend (bi·frend′) *v.t.* **1** To be a friend to; stand by; help in time of need. **2** To become a friend to; make friends with. See synonyms under AID, HELP.

be·fud·dle (bi·fud′l) *v.t.* **·dled, ·dling** To confuse, as with liquor or glib arguments.

beg[1] (beg) *v.* **begged, beg·ging** *v.t.* **1** To ask for or solicit in charity. **2** To entreat of; beseech. —*v.i.* **3** To ask alms or charity. **4** To entreat humbly. —**to beg off** To free or attempt to free oneself (from a duty, engagement, obliga-

tion, etc.) by persuasion, excuse, or pleading. **— to beg the question** To take for granted the matter in dispute. **— to go begging 1** To fail of acceptance, adoption, or use: The office *went begging.* **2** To live the life of a beggar. [? <AF *begger* beg <OF *begard* mendicant friar. See BEGHARD.]

beg[2] (beg) *n.* A bey.

be·gan (bi·gan′) Past tense of BEGIN.

be·get (bi·get′) *v.t.* **be·got** (*Archaic* **be·gat**), **be·got·ten** or **be·got, be·get·ting 1** To procreate; be the father of. **2** To cause to be; occasion. [OE *begitan*] **— be·get′ter** *n.*

beg·gar (beg′ər) *n.* **1** One who asks alms, especially one who makes his living by begging. **2** A person in poor or impoverished circumstances; a pauper. **3** A fellow; rogue: used contemptuously or humorously: a sulky *beggar*; smart little *beggar.* — *v.t.* **1** To reduce to want; impoverish. **2** To outdo; exhaust the resources of: It *beggars* analysis. [<OF *begard* mendicant friar] **— beg′gar·dom, beg′gar·hood** *n.* **— beg′gar·er** *n.*

beg·gar·ly (beg′ər·lē) *adj.* **1** Miserably poor; like or characteristic of a beggar. **2** Mean; sordid; contemptible. **— beg′gar·li·ness** *n.*

beg·gar's–lice (beg′ərz·līs′) *n.* Any of various plants bearing prickly fruit which adheres readily to clothes, as bedstraws and stickseeds.

beg·gar·ticks (beg′ər·tiks′) *n.* **1** The bur marigold or its seed vessels. **2** Beggar's–lice. Also **beg′gar's–ticks′.**

beg·gar·weed (beg′ər·wēd′) *n.* **1** Any of several species of plants used for forage and a cover crop in the southern United States, especially the Florida beggarweed or clover *(Desmodium tortuosum).* **2** A low annual plant *(Spergula arvensis),* now cultivated in some regions for forage and fertilizing: also called *corn spurry.*

beg·gar·y (beg′ər·ē) *n.* **1** The state or condition of being a beggar; extreme indigence or deficiency, penury. **2** Beggars as a class. **3** The act or habit of begging. See synonyms under POVERTY.

Beg·hard (beg′ərd, bi·gärd′) *n.* A member of one of the several lay fraternities which arose in Flanders in the 13th century in imitation of the Beguines: in France called *Beguins.* [<Med. L *beghardus,* after Lambert *Begue,* 12th c., founder of the order of Beguines]

be·gin (bi·gin′) *v.* **be·gan, be·gun, be·gin·ning** *v.t.* **1** To commence or enter upon. **2** To give origin to; start. — *v.i.* **3** To start. **4** To come into being; arise. **5** To have the essentials or the ability: used with a negative: She doesn't *begin* to sing as well as her sister. [OE *beginnan*]

Synonyms: commence, inaugurate, initiate, undertake. See INSTITUTE.

be·gin·ner (bi·gin′ər) *n.* **1** A founder; originator. **2** One beginning to learn a trade or skill, study a new subject, etc.; a novice; tyro.

be·gin·ning (bi·gin′ing) *n.* **1** The starting point in space, time or action; origin. **2** The first stage or part. **3** The source or first cause of anything.

Synonyms: commencement, foundation, fountain, inauguration, inception, initiation, opening, origin, outset, rise, source, spring, start. The Latin *commencement* is more formal than the Anglo-Saxon *beginning*, as the verb *commence* is more formal than *begin. Commencement* is for the most part restricted to some form of action, while *beginning* has no restriction, but may be applied to whatever may be conceived of as having a first part, point, degree, etc. An *origin* is the point from which something starts or sets out, often involving causal connections; as the *origin* of a nation, government, or a family. A *source* is that which furnishes a first and continuous supply; as, the *source* of a river. A *rise* is thought of as in an action; we say that a lake is the *source* of a certain river, or that the river takes its *rise* from the lake. Compare CAUSE. *Antonyms*: see synonyms for END.

be·gird (bi·gûrd′) *v.t.* To gird; encircle; encompass. [OE *begyrdan*]

beg·ohm (beg′ōm′) *n.* One billion ohms, or one thousand megohms: a unit of electrical resistance. [< *beg-* billion (on analogy with *meg-* million) + OHM]

be·gone (bi·gôn′, -gon′) *interj.* Depart! Go away!

be·gon·ia (bi·gōn′yə) *n.* A plant of a large and widely distributed semitropical genus *(Begonia)* with brilliantly colored leaves and showy irregular flowers. [after Michel *Begon,* 1638–1710, French colonial administrator]

be·got (bi·got′) Past tense and past participle of BEGET.

be·got·ten (bi·got′n) A past participle of BEGET.

be·goud (bi·go͝od′) *Scot.* Past tense of BEGIN.

be·grime (bi·grīm′) *v.t.* **be·grimed, be·grim·ing** To soil; make dirty with grime.

be·grudge (bi·gruj′) *v.t.* **be·grudged, be·grudg·ing 1** To envy one the possession or enjoyment of (something). **2** To give or grant reluctantly. **— be·grudg′ing·ly** *adv.*

be·guile (bi·gīl′) *v.t.* **be·guiled, be·guil·ing 1** To deceive; mislead by guile. **2** To cheat; defraud: with *of* or *out of.* **3** To while away pleasantly, as time. **4** To charm; divert. See synonyms under DECEIVE, ENTERTAIN. **— be·guile′ment** *n.* **— be·guil′er** *n.*

Beg·uin (beg′in, *Fr.* bā·gaṅ′) *n.* A Beghard.

Beg·uine (beg′ēn, *Fr.* bā·gēn′) *n.* One of a lay Catholic sisterhood, originating in the Netherlands (12th century), devoted to a religious life, but not bound by irrevocable vows.

be·gum (bē′gəm) *n.* A Moslem princess, or woman of rank in India. [<Hind. *begam* <Turkish *bigim* princess]

be·gun (bi·gun′) Past participle of BEGIN.

be·half (bi·haf′, -häf′) *n.* The interest or defense (of anyone): preceded by *in, on,* or *upon.* [OE *be healfe* by the side (of)]

Be·har (bə·här′) See BIHAR.

be·have (bi·hāv′) *v.* **be·haved, be·hav·ing** *v.i.* **1** To comport oneself properly: Will you *behave?* **2** To act; conduct oneself or itself: The car *behaves* well. **3** To react to stimuli or environment. — *v.t.* **4** To conduct (oneself) properly or suitably. [ME *be-* thoroughly + *have* hold oneself, act]

be·hav·ior (bi·hāv′yər) *n.* **1** Manner of one's conduct; demeanor; deportment. **2** Manner or action of a machine, a chemical, substance, organ, organism, etc. **3** *Psychol.* The form of nervous, muscular, and emotional response of an individual to internal or external stimuli. Also *Brit.* **be·hav′iour.**

Synonyms: action, bearing, breeding, carriage, conduct, demeanor, deportment, manner, manners. *Behavior* is our *action* in the presence of others; *conduct* is a more general term, usually having ethical reference. *Demeanor* is the bodily expression, not only of feelings, but of moral states; as, a devout *demeanor. Breeding,* unless with some adverse limitation, denotes that *manner* and *conduct* which result from good birth and training. *Deportment* is *behavior* as related to a set of rules; as, the pupil's *deportment* was faultless. A person's *manner* may be that of a moment, or toward a single person: his *manners* are his habitual *behavior* toward or before others, especially in matters of etiquette and politeness; as, good *manners* are always pleasing. Compare AIR.

be·hav·ior·ism (bi·hāv′yər·iz′əm) *n. Psychol.* The theory that human behavior and activities are the result of individual reaction to definite objective stimuli or situations, and not of subjective factors. **— be·hav′ior·ist** *n.* **— be·hav′ior·is′tic** *adj.*

be·head (bi·hed′) *v.t.* To take the head from; decapitate. **— be·head′al** *n.*

be·held (bi·held′) Past tense and past participle of BEHOLD.

be·he·moth (bi·hē′məth, bē′ə-) *n.* In the Bible, a colossal beast, probably a hippopotamus. [<Hebrew *behēmōth,* pl. of *behēmāh* beast, ? <Egyptian *p-ehe-mah* water–ox]

be·hest (bi·hest′) *n.* An authoritative request; command. [OE *behæs* promise, vow]

be·hind (bi·hīnd′) *adv.* **1** In, toward, or at the rear; backward: looking *behind.* **2** In a previous place, condition, etc.: They left their regrets *behind.* **3** In time gone by: The days of youth are *behind.* **4** In reserve; to be made known: There is no evidence *behind.* **5** In arrears; not according to schedule: to fall *behind* in one's work. **6** Retarded in time, as a train or clock. — *prep.* **1** At the back or farther side of: The house is *behind* those trees. **2** To or toward the rear: Look *behind* you as you come. **3** Following after: The infantry came *behind* the cavalry. **4** Remaining after: He left a fortune *behind* him. **5** Later than: He stayed *behind* the others that day. **6** Sustaining; supporting: He has wealth *behind* him. **7** Inferior to, as in position, accomplishments, etc.; not so well advanced as: He is *behind* the others in his lessons. **8** Not yet revealed or made known about: something strange *behind* that remark. **— to put behind one** To refuse to accept or consider. — *n. Colloq.* The buttocks. [OE *behindan*]

be·hind·hand (bi·hīnd′hand′) *adv.* & *adj.* **1** Behind time; late. **2** In arrears. **3** In a backward state; not sufficiently advanced.

behind the times Old–fashioned; antiquated; out–of–date.

be·hint (bi·hint′) *adv.* & *prep. Scot.* Behind.

Be·his·tun (bā′hi·sto͞on′) A village in western Iran; near it is a bas–relief with inscriptions in Old Persian, Elamitic, and Assyrian: also *Bisutun.*

be·hold (bi·hōld′) *v.t.* **be·held, be·hold·ing** To look at or upon; observe. — *interj.* Look! See! See synonyms under LOOK. [OE *beh(e)aldan* hold] **— be·hold′er** *n.*

be·hold·en (bi·hōl′dən) *adj.* Indebted.

be·hoof (bi·ho͞of′) *n.* That which benefits; advantage; use. [OE *behōf* advantage]

be·hoove (bi·ho͞ov′) *v.* **be·hooved, be·hoov·ing** *v.t.* To be becoming to; be needful or right for: used impersonally: It *behooves* me to leave. — *v.i. Archaic* To be needful, essential or fit: used impersonally. Also **be·hove** (bi·hōv′). [OE *behōfian*] **— be·hoove′ful** *adj.*

Beh·ring (bā′ring), **Emil Adolf von,** 1854–1917, German physician, discoverer of diphtheria antitoxin.

Behring Sea See BERING SEA.

Behr·man (bâr′mən), **Samuel Nathaniel,** 1893–1973, U.S. playwright.

beige (bāzh) *n.* **1** The color of natural, undyed, unbleached wool. **2** A soft fabric of undyed, unbleached wool. — *adj.* Of the color of natural wool. [<F]

beik (bīk) *n.* See BIKE[2].

Bei·lan Pass (bī·län′) See BELEN PASS.

bein (bēn) *adj.* Bien.

be·ing (bē′ing) Present participle of BE. — *n.* **1** Any person or thing that exists or is conceived of as existing. **2** Existence, especially, conscious existence. **3** Essential nature of anything: His whole *being* is musical.

Be·ing (bē′ing) *n.* God: used often with qualifying words: the Supreme *Being.*

Bei·ra (bā′rə) **1** A former province of north central Portugal. **2** A port in central Mozambique.

Bei·rut (bā′ro͞ot, bā·ro͞ot′) A port on the Mediterranean and the capital of Lebanon: ancient *Berytus*: also *Beyrouth.*

Beith (bēth), **John Hay,** 1876–1952, English author: pen name *Ian Hay.*

Be·káa (bi·kä′) A rich agricultural region, constituting a province of central Lebanon: ancient *Coele–Syria*: also *El Bekáa.*

Bé·kés·csa·ba (bā′kāsh·chä′bä) A city in SE Hungary: also *Csaba.*

bel (bel) *n. Physics* A unit representing the ratio of the values of two amounts of power on a logarithmic scale to the base 10. [after A. G. *Bell*]

Bel (bāl) In Babylonian mythology, the god of heaven and earth.

Be·la (bā′lə) The capital of Las Bela, West Pakistan.

be·la·bor (bi·lā′bər) *v.t.* **1** To beat; thrash soundly. **2** To assail verbally. **3** *Obs.* To toil over; work at. See synonyms under BEAT. Also *Brit.* **be·la′bour.**

Be·las·co (bə·las′kō), **David,** 1854–1931, U.S. playwright and producer.

be·lat·ed (bi·lā′tid) *adj.* Delayed past the usual or proper time. **— be·lat′ed·ly** *adv.* **— be·lat′ed·ness** *n.*

be·lay (bi·lā′) *v.* **be·layed, be·lay·ing** *v.t.* **1** *Naut.* To make fast (a rope) by winding on a cleat or pin. **2** In mountain–climbing, to hitch (a rope) over a rock, piton, or other support. — *v.i.* **3** *Colloq.* To stop or hold; cease: *Belay* there. — *n.* A rock or other support, about which a rope may be hitched in

add,āce,câre,pälm; end,ēven; it,īce; odd,ōpen,ôrder; to͝ok,po͞ol; up,bûrn; ə = a in *above,* e in *sicken,* i in *clarity,* o in *melon,* u in *focus*; yo͞o = u in *fuse*; oi,oil; ou,pout; ch,check; g,go; ng,ring; th,thin; th,this; zh,vision. Foreign sounds á,œ,ü,kh,ṅ; and ◆: see page xx. < from; + plus; ? possibly.

order to provide security for a mountain climber; also, the state of being thus secured: He was in *belay.* [OE *belecgan*]

be·lay·ing-pin (bi·lā′ing·pin′) *n. Naut.* A movable pin of wood or metal to which running gear may be made fast.

bel can·to (bel kän′tō) The traditional Italian method of singing, characterized by ease of production and purity of tone. [<Ital., beautiful song]

belch (belch) *v.t.* & *v.i.* **1** To eject, throw out, or to come forth forcibly or violently; vomit. **2** To eject (gas) noisily from the stomach through the mouth; eructate. **—** *n.* An eructation. [OE *bealcian*] **—belch′er** *n.*

Belch (belch), **Sir Toby** The roistering uncle of Olivia in Shakespeare's *Twelfth Night.*

bel·cher (bel′chər) *n. Brit.* A garish neckcloth, especially a blue one with white spots. [after Jim *Belcher,* English boxer]

Bel·cher (bel′chər), **Jonathan,** 1681–1757, American governor of the colonies of Massachusetts, New Hampshire, and New Jersey.

beld (beld) *adj. Scot.* Bald.

bel·dam (bel′dəm) *n.* A forbidding or malicious old woman; a hag. Also **bel·dame** (bel′dəm, -dām′). [ME, grandmother < *bel* grand (<OF *bel* fine) + *dam* mother <OF *dame* lady]

be·lea·guer (bi·lē′gər) *v.t.* **1** To surround or shut in with an armed force. **2** To harass or annoy. See synonyms under ATTACK *verb.* [<Du. *belegeren* < *be-* about + *leger* camp] **—be·lea′guered** *adj.*

Be·lém (be·leṅ′) The capital of the state of Pará, northern Brazil: formerly *Pará.*

bel·em·nite (bel′əm·nīt) *n.* **1** *Paleontol.* The pointed cylindrical fossil shell of an extinct cephalopod related to the cuttlefish. **2** A thunderstone. [<NL *belemnites* <Gk. *belemnon* dart]

Be·len Pass (be·len′) A mountain defile in southern Turkey, identified with the Syrian Gates of antiquity: also *Bailan Pass, Beilan Pass.*

bel-es·prit (bel·es·prē′) *n. pl.* **beaux-es·prits** (bō·zes·prē′) *French* A person of culture or wit.

Bel·fast (bel′fast, -fäst) The capital of Northern Ireland; a county borough and port at the head of **Belfast Lough** (lôkh), an inlet between County Antrim and County Down.

Bel·fort (bel·fôr′) A town in eastern France commanding the Belfort Gap.

Bel·fort Gap (bel′fôr gap′) A strategic passageway from the Rhine valley to the Paris Basin: also *Burgundy Gate. French* **Trou·ée de Bel·fort** (trōō·ā′ də bel·fôr′).

bel·fry (bel′frē) *n. pl.* **·fries** **1** A tower in which a bell is hung. **2** The part containing the bell. [<OF *berfrei* tower, ult. <Gmc.] **—bel′fried** *adj.*

bel·ga (bel′gə) *n.* The unit of Belgian currency in foreign exchange, equal to five francs.

Bel·gae (bel′jē) *n. pl.* An ancient people, occupying, in Caesar's time, the region that is now Belgium and northern France.

Bel·gian (bel′jən, -jē·ən) *adj.* Of or pertaining to Belgium. **—** *n.* A native or citizen of Belgium.

Belgian Congo See ZAIRE REPUBLIC.

Belgian griffon A wire-haired toy dog, a type of Brussels griffon but with a black, or black mixed with brown or tan, coat.

Belgian hare A fancy strain of the common domestic rabbit, originally developed in England from Belgian stock.

Belgian marble Rance.

Bel·gic (bel′jik) *adj.* Of or pertaining to the ancient Belgae, to Belgium, or to the Netherlands.

Bel·gium (bel′jəm, -jē·əm) A constitutional monarchy of NW Europe; 11,779 square miles; capital, Brussels. *Flemish* **Bel·gi·ë** (bel′gē·ə); *French* **Bel·gique** (bel·zhēk′).

Bel·go·rod-Dnes·trov·ski A city in the Ukraine on the Dniester estuary; ancient Tyras; former Russian and Turkish Akkerman. *Rumanian* **Ce·ta·tea Al·bă** (che·tä′tyä äl′bə).

Bel·grade A port on the Danube, the capital of both Yugoslavia and Serbia; *Serbo-Croatian: Beograd.*

Bel·gra·vi·a (bel·grā′vē·ə) A formerly fashionable residential district of London surrounding Belgrade Square. **—Bel·gra′vi·an** *adj.* & *n.*

Be·li·al (bē′lē·əl, bēl′yəl) **1** The ancient Hebrew personification of lawlessness; the devil. **2** Any fiend: used by Milton in *Paradise Lost* as the name of one of the fallen angels.

be·lie (bi·lī′) *v.t.* **be·lied, be·ly·ing** **1** To misrepresent; disguise: His clothes *belie* his station. **2** To prove false; contradict: Her actions *belied* her words. **3** To disappoint; fail to fulfil: to *belie* hopes. **4** To traduce; slander. [OE *belēogan*] **—be·li′er** *n.*

be·lief (bi·lēf′) *n.* **1** Probable knowledge. **2** Mental conviction; acceptance of something as true or actual. **3** Confidence; trust in another's veracity. **4** That which is believed; creed. **5** Religious faith.

Synonyms: admission, assent, assurance, avowal, confidence, conviction, credence, credit, creed, opinion, reliance, trust. See DOCTRINE, FAITH, FANCY, IDEA. *Antonyms*: denial, disavowal, disbelief, dissent, distrust, doubt, misgiving, rejection, unbelief.

be·lieve (bi·lēv′) *v.* **be·lieved, be·liev·ing** *v.t.* **1** To accept as true or real. **2** To accept the word of (someone); credit with veracity. **3** To think; assume: with a clause as object: I *believe* that I will be there tomorrow. **—** *v.i.* **4** To accept the truth, existence, worth, etc., of something: with *in*: I *believe* in freedom. **5** To trust someone; have confidence: with *in*: The country *believes* in you. **6** To have religious faith. See synonyms under TRUST. [ME *beleven* < *be-* completely + *leven* <OE *gelēfen* believe] **—be·liev′a·ble** *adj.* **—be·liev′er** *n.* **—be·liev′ing** *adj.* **—be·liev′ing·ly** *adv.*

be·like (bi·līk′) *adv. Obs.* Perhaps; probably.

Be·lin·da (bi·lin′də) A feminine personal name. [<Gmc., serpent]

Bel·i·sar·i·us (bel′ə·sâr′ē·əs) 505?–565, Byzantine general.

be·lit·tle (bi·lit′l) *v.t.* **·tled, ·tling** To cause to seem small or less; disparage; minimize. See synonyms under DISPARAGE.

Be·li·tung (be·lē′tōōng) An Indonesian island between Borneo and Bangka; 1,866 square miles; chief town, Tanjungpandan: also *Billiton. Dutch* **Be·li·toeng** (be·lē′tōōng).

be·live (bi·līv′) *adv. Scot.* **1** Soon; anon. **2** Quickly; eagerly.

Be·lize (bə·lēz′) **1** The capital of British Honduras. *Spanish* **Be·li·ce** (bā·lē′sā). **2** Former name for BRITISH HONDURAS.

bell[1] (bel) *n.* **1** A hollow metallic instrument, usually cup-shaped, which gives forth a ringing sound when it is struck. **2** Anything in the shape of or suggesting a bell. **3** The lower termination of a tubular musical instrument. **4** A bell-shaped flower or corolla, the catkin of the hop, the body of a helmet, etc. **5** *Naut.* **a** A stroke on a bell to mark the time on shipboard. **b** *pl.* With a numeral prefixed, the time so marked, in half-hours, from one to eight, in each period of four hours beginning at midnight, 8 bells marking the commencement of each period. **—Liberty Bell** The first bell rung to announce the signing of the Declaration of Independence, July 4, 1776, in Philadelphia. **—** *v.t.* **1** To put a bell on. **2** To shape like a bell. **—** *v.i.* **3** To take the shape of a bell. **4** To blossom; be in bell, as hops. **—to bell the cat** To plan or perform a bold or rash act: from Aesop's fable about the mice who resolved in self-protection to hang a bell on the cat's neck. ◆ Homophone: *belle.* [OE *belle*]

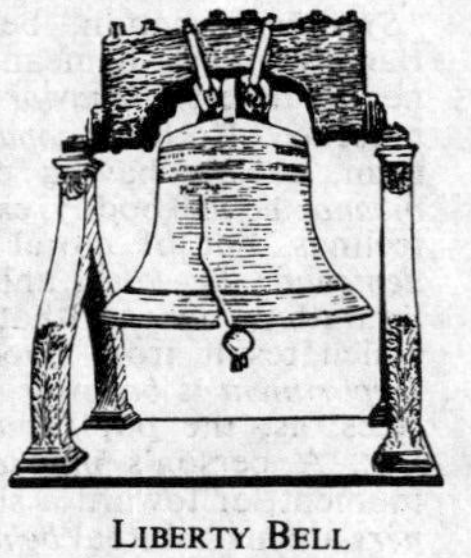

LIBERTY BELL

bell[2] (bel) *v.i.* To cry, as a buck or stag at rutting time. **—** *n.* The cry of a deer, bittern, etc.; also, a bellow. ◆ Homophone: *belle.* [OE *bellan* bellow]

Bell (bel), **Alexander Graham,** 1847–1922, U.S. physicist and inventor of the telephone, born in Scotland. **—Sir Charles,** 1774–1842, Scottish anatomist and surgeon.

bel·la·don·na (bel′ə·don′ə) *n.* **1** A perennial herb *(Atropa belladonna)* with purple-red flowers and shining black berries; deadly nightshade: the leaves and roots yield a number of poisonous alkaloids, as atropine, used in medicine. **2** The belladonna lily. [<Ital. *bella donna* beautiful lady]

belladonna lily An ornamental South African plant *(Amaryllis belladonna),* with large, showy, funnel-shaped flowers of pale rose color penciled with red.

Bel·la·my (bel′ə·mē), **Edward,** 1850–98, U.S. author.

Bel·lay (be·lā′), **Joachim du,** 1522–60, French poet.

bell·bird (bel′bûrd′) *n.* **1** One of various birds having a bell-like note; especially, the South American campanero *(Chasmorhynchus niveus),* with an erectile horn-shaped crest. **2** Any of various birds of Australia and New Zealand, as the honeyeater.

bell·boy (bel′boi′) *n.* A porter, man or boy, in a hotel. Also **bell·hop** (bel′hop′).

belle (bel) *n.* A beautiful and attractive woman; a reigning social beauty. ◆ Homophone: *bell.* [<F, fem. of *beau* beautiful]

Belle (bel) A feminine personal name.

Bel·leau Wood (bel′ō) A region in northern France, site of a notable American engagement (June, 1918) in World War I. *French* **Bois de Bel·leau** (bwä də be·lō′).

bel·leek (bə·lēk′) *n.* A thin, delicate pottery resembling porcelain, having an iridescent or pearly glaze: made originally at Belleek. Also **belleek ware.**

Bel·leek A town of NW County Fermanagh, Northern Ireland.

Belle Isle An island (20 square miles) at the entrance to the **Strait of Belle Isle,** the northern entrance to the Gulf of Saint Lawrence, lying between Labrador and Newfoundland.

Bel·ler·o·phon (bə·ler′ə·fon) In Greek mythology, a hero who slew the Chimera with the aid of the winged horse, Pegasus, and later perished in an attempt to scale heaven.

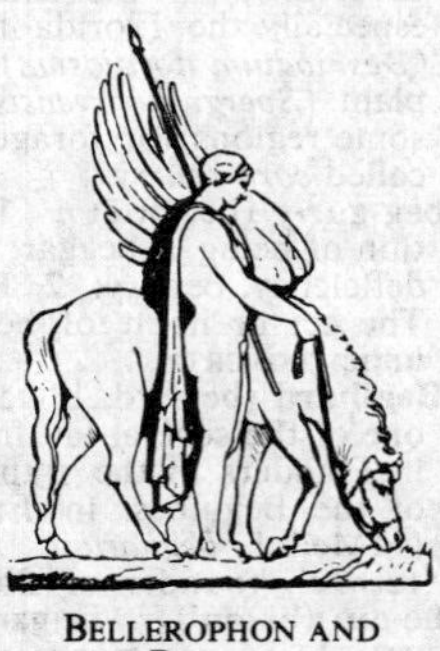

BELLEROPHON AND PEGASUS
After a sculpture in the Spada Palace, Rome.

belles-let·tres (bel′·let′rə) *n. pl.* Works of literary art, esthetic rather than informational or didactic; poetry, drama, fiction, etc.; the humanities. See synonyms under HUMANITY, LITERATURE. [<F, fine letters] **—bel·let′rist** (bel′let′rist) *n.* **—bel·le·tris′tic** (bel′le·tris′tik) *adj.*

bell·flow·er (bel′flou′ər) *n.* The campanula.

bel·li·cose (bel′ə·kōs) *adj.* Pugnacious; warlike. [<L *bellicosus* warlike < *bellum* war] **—bel′li·cose′ly** *adv.* **—bel′li·cos′i·ty** (-kos′ə·tē) *n.*

bel·lig·er·ent (bə·lij′ər·ənt) *adj.* **1** Warlike; bellicose. **2** Engaged in or pertaining to warfare. **—** *n.* A power or person engaged in legitimate warfare. [Earlier *belligerant* <F *belligérant* <L *belligerans, -antis,* ppr. of *belligare* wage war] **—bel·lig′er·en·cy, bel·lig′er·ence** *n.* **—bel·lig′er·ent·ly** *adv.*

bell·ing (bel′ing) *n. Dial.* A charivari.

Bel·ling·ham (bel′ing·ham) A city in NW Washington on **Bellingham Bay,** an inlet of the Pacific north of Seattle.

Bel·ling·ham (bel′ing·əm, -ham), **Richard,** 1592–1672, English lawyer and colonial governor of Massachusetts.

Bel·lings·hau·sen Sea (bel′ingz·hou′zən) That part of the South Pacific bordering Antarctica.

Bel·li·ni (bel·lē′nē) Name of three Venetian painters, **Jacopo,** 1400?–70?, and his two sons, **Gentile,** 1429?–1507, and **Giovanni,** 1430?–1516.

—Vincenzo, 1801–35, Italian composer.

bell jar A glass vessel having the shape of a bell, used to cover articles that may be injured by dust or air currents. Also **bell glass.**

bell·man (bel′mən) *n. pl.* **·men** (-mən) A town crier.

bell metal An alloy of copper and tin, used for the manufacture of bells.

bell-mouthed (bel′mouthd′, -moutht′) *adj.* Having a bell-shaped mouth, as a flask.

Bel·loc (bel′ok), **Hilaire,** 1870–1953, English writer born in France: full name *Joseph Hilaire Pierre Belloc.*

Bel·lo Ho·ri·zon·te (be′lô·rē·zôn′tē) Former name for BELO HORIZONTE.

Bel·lo·na (bə·lō′nə) In Roman mythology, the goddess of war, sister or wife of Mars.

bel·low (bel′ō) v.i. 1 To utter a loud, hollow sound; roar, as a bull. 2 To roar; shout: to *bellow* with anger. — v.t. 3 To utter with a loud, roaring voice. — n. A loud, hollow cry or roar. [ME *belwen*, ? <OE *bylgan*] — bel′low·er n.

bel·lows (bel′ōz, *earlier* bel′əs) n. 1 An instrument with an air chamber and flexible sides, for drawing in air and expelling it under strong pressure through a nozzle or tube.

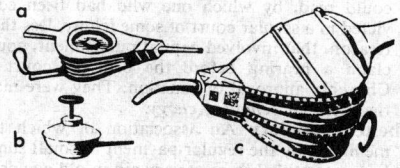

BELLOWS
a. Kitchen. *b.* For insect powders. *c.* Blacksmith's.

2 The expansible portion of a camera. 3 *Colloq.* The lungs. [OE *belg, belig* bag; a later plural from the same source as BELLY]

Bel·lows (bel′ōz), **George Wesley,** 1882–1925, U.S. painter and lithographer.

bell·weth·er (bel′weth′ər) n. 1 The wether that wears a bell and leads a flock of sheep. 2 One who leads a group, especially a thoughtless group, in any cause.

bell·wort (bel′wûrt′) n. 1 A plant of the lily family (genus *Uvularia*) having terminal, solitary, drooping flowers of a yellowish color with bell-shaped perianth. 2 Any plant of the bellflower family (*Campanulaceae*).

bel·ly (bel′ē) n. pl. **bel·lies** 1 *Anat.* a The anterior part of a vertebrate body, extending from the sternum to the pelvis and containing the organs below the diaphragm. b The under part of a quadruped or lower animal. c The abdomen. d The protuberance of a bulging muscle. 2 The stomach and its associated organs. 3 Appetite. 4 Anything resembling a belly; as, the *belly* of a flask, the *belly* of a wind-filled sail. 5 The sounding box of certain stringed instruments, as the violin, viola, etc. 6 *Obs.* The womb. — v.t. & v.i. **bel·lied, bel·ly·ing** To swell out or fill, as a sail. [OE *belg, belig* bag]

bel·ly·ache (bel′ē·āk′) n. Intestinal colic; pain in the bowels. — v.i. **·ached, ·ach·ing** *Slang* To complain sullenly.

bel·ly·band (bel′ē·band′) n. A transverse strap passing beneath a draft animal, to fasten the saddle, harness, etc., or hold the shafts; a girth. See illustration under HARNESS.

bel·ly·but·ton (bel′ē·but′n) n. *Colloq.* The navel.

bel·ly·ful (bel′ē·fŏŏl′) n. 1 Fullness resulting from much eating. 2 *Colloq.* An excessive fullness or surfeit of anything.

be·long (bi·lông′, -long′) v.i. 1 To be in the possession of someone: with *to*. 2 To be a part of or an appurtenance to something: with *to*: The screw *belongs* to this fan. 3 To have a proper place; be suitable: That lamp *belongs* in this room. 4 To have relation or be a member: with *to*: He *belongs* to the club. [ME *belongen* <*be-* completely + *longen*, OE *langian* go along with]

be·long·ing (bi·lông′ing, -long′-) n. 1 That which or one who belongs to a person or thing. 2 pl. Possessions; effects, as clothes, furniture, etc.

Be·lo·rus·sia The former name of the **Republic of Belorus.**

Be·lo·rus *Also* **Belarus** A republic in eastern Europe; 80,150 square miles; pop. 10,250,000; capital, Minsk; a member of the Commonwealth of Independent States. Formerly **White Russia,** the **Grand Duchy of Lithuania,** and the **Belorussian S.S.R.**

Be·lo·stok (bye·lə·stôk′) Russian name for BIAŁYSTOK.

be·love (bi·luv′) v.t. **be·loved, be·lov·ing** To

love: now only in the passive. [ME *biloven* <*be-* completely + *loven* love]

be·lov·ed (bi·luv′id, -luvd′) adj. Greatly loved; dear to the heart. — n. One greatly loved.

be·low (bi·lō′) adv. 1 In or to a lower place. 2 To a place under the floor or deck: Get *below!* 3 Farther down on a page or farther on in a list, book, etc. 4 On the earth, as distinguished from heaven. 5 In or to hell or Hades. 6 Lower in rank or authority: His case will be tried in the court *below.* — prep. 1 Farther down than: His apartment is *below* theirs. 2 Lower down in direction or course: the town *below* this one on the river. 3 Inferior to in degree, rank, value, etc.: The yield was *below* average. 4 Unworthy of. [<BE- + LOW[1]]

Bel·sen (bel′zən) A village in NW Germany, site of a large Nazi concentration camp and extermination center.

Bel·shaz·zar (bel·shaz′ər) The last Babylonian king, defeated and slain by Cyrus. He gave a banquet, **Belshazzar's Feast,** at which handwriting, foretelling the downfall of Babylonia, appeared on a wall. *Dan.* v.

belt (belt) n. 1 A band worn around the waist. 2 *Mech.* a A flexible band of leather or other material passing over two or more wheels and serving to transmit power in machinery and to communicate motion from one part to another. b A moving assembly line in a factory, intended to convey parts from one operation or worker to another. 3 Any broad, encircling band, region, etc. 4 *Ecol.* A characteristic zone or stretch of country favoring the development of a certain type of animal or plant life; a zone; strip; as, a forest *belt,* a corn *belt.* 5 A strait. 6 *Mil.* a A girdle of armor plates protecting a warship along the water line. b A strip of webbing designed to hold a weapon or to contain cartridges. 7 *Colloq.* A blow, as with the fist. — **below the belt** 1 In boxing, under the waistband. 2 Hence, unfairly; in violation of accepted codes. — **to tighten one's belt** To practice thrift; retrench; consume less food. — v.t. 1 To gird with or as with a belt. 2 To fasten with a belt: to *belt* on a sword. 3 To mark with belts or bands. 4 *Colloq.* To strike with force. [OE *belt* <L *balteus* girdle]

Bel·tane (bel′tān) n. 1 The Scottish name for May Day (old style). 2 The ancient Celtic festival celebrating the coming of summer, observed by the kindling of fires on the hills. [<Scotch Gaelic *bealtainn*]

belt·ed (bel′tid) adj. 1 Wearing a belt; distinguished by a belt. 2 Having a mark like a belt: the *belted* kingfisher.

Bel·ter (bel′tər) adj. Pertaining to or naming a type of furniture, usually of rosewood, carved in elaborate floral designs. [after John H. *Belter,* mid-19th c. New York cabinetmaker]

belt·ing (bel′ting) n. Belts collectively, or the material for belts.

belt line A transportation route encircling a city or district.

Bel·trán (bel·trän′) Spanish form of BERTRAM.

be·lu·ga (bə·lōō′gə) n. pl. **·ga** or **·gas** 1 A dolphin (*Delphinapterus leucas*) of arctic and sub-arctic seas; adults are of a white color and from 10 to 12 feet long: also called *white whale.* 2 The great white sturgeon (*Acipenser huso*), found in the Caspian Sea and the Black Sea; its roe is **Beluga caviar.** [<Russian *byelukha* <*byelo* white]

Be·lu·kha (bye·lōō′khə) The highest summit in the Altai Mountains, southern Siberia; 15,157 feet.

Be·lus (bē′ləs) 1 A legendary Assyrian king. 2 In Roman mythology, a king of Tyre, father of Dido and Pygmalion.

bel·ve·dere (bel′və·dir′) n. An elevated point of vantage affording an extensive view; especially, an upper story of an Italian building, open on one or more sides so as to command a view. — **the Belvedere** A part of the Vatican containing many famous works of art. [<Ital., beautiful view] — **bel′ve·dered′** adj.

be·ma (bē′mə) n. pl. **be·ma·ta** (bē′mə·tə) The enclosure about the altar; sanctuary; chancel, especially in the Eastern churches. [<Gk.

bema a step, a platform <*bainein* go, walk]

Bem·bo (bem′bō), **Pietro,** 1470–1547, Italian cardinal and scholar.

be·mean (bi·mēn′) v.t. To lower or abase (oneself).

be·mire (bi·mīr′) v.t. **be·mired, be·mir·ing** 1 To soil with or as with mud or mire. 2 To fix or stall in mud.

be·moan (bi·mōn′) v.t. 1 To express sympathy or pity for. 2 To lament, as a loss. — v.i. 3 To mourn or lament. See synonyms under MOURN. [OE *bemænan*] — **be·moan′a·ble** adj.

be·muse (bi·myōōz′) v.t. **·mused, ·mus·ing** To muddle or stupefy, as with drink.

be·mused (bi·myōōzd′) adj. 1 Stupefied; dazed. 2 Engrossed.

ben (ben) n. *Brit. Dial.* The inner room of a house. — prep. & adj. Within; in; inner. — **to be far ben with** To be intimate with. [OE *binnan* <*be-* by + *innan* within]

Ben (ben) Diminutive of BENJAMIN.

be·name (bi·nām′) v.t. **be·named, be·named** or **be·nempt** or **be·nempted, be·nam·ing** *Obs.* To name. [OE *benemnan*]

Be·na·res (bə·nä′riz) Former spelling of BANARAS.

Be·na·ven·te y Mar·ti·nez (bā′nä·vān′tä ē mär·tē′näth), **Jacinto,** 1866–1954, Spanish dramatist.

Ben·bow (ben′bō), **John,** 1653–1702, English admiral.

bench (bench) n. 1 A long, wooden seat, with or without a back. 2 A stout table for mechanical work. 3 The judges' seat in court; the judge or the judges collectively; the judiciary; also, the court. 4 A row of stalls on platforms or benches for the exhibition of animals, as dogs. 5 *Geog.* A terrace formed in rocks; also, elevated ground along the bank of a lake or river. — v.t. 1 To furnish with benches. 2 To seat on a bench. 3 To exhibit, as dogs at a dog show. 4 In sports, to remove (a player) from a game by sending him to a bench on the sidelines. [OE *benc.* Akin to BANK[1], BANK[3].]

bench·er (ben′chər) n. *Brit.* 1 A senior member of the English bar; a governor of one of the Inns of Court. 2 One of the populace; a loafer, as about taverns.

bench hook A clamp, usually of wood, for holding work upon a carpenter's bench.

bench·leg·ged (bench′leg′id, -legd′) adj. Having the legs wide apart: said of a dog or a horse.

Benchley (bench′lē), **Robert Charles,** 1889–1945, U.S. humorist.

bench·mark (bench′märk′) n. 1 A permanent reference mark fixed in the ground for use in surveys, tidal observations, etc. 2 A reference point serving as a standard for comparing or judging other things.

bench·root (bench′rōōt′, -rŏŏt′) n. *Bot.* A misshapen condition of roots caused by tenacious seed coats.

bench show An exhibition of animals, especially dogs, in stalls on benches, indoors.

bench warrant A warrant issued by the judge presiding at a session, directing that an offender be brought into court.

bend[1] (bend) v. **bent** (*Archaic* **bend·ed**), **bend·ing** v.t. 1 To cause to take the form of a curve; crook; bow. 2 To direct or turn, as one's course, in a certain direction; deflect. 3 To subdue; cause to yield, as to one's will. 4 To apply closely; concentrate, as the mind. 5 *Naut.* To tie; make fast, as a rope; place in position, as a sail. 6 *Archaic* To strain; make tense: with *up.* — v.i. 7 To assume the form of a bow. 8 To take a certain direction. 9 To bow in submission or respect; yield; conform. 10 To apply one's energies: with *to.* — n. 1 A curve or crook. 2 An act of bending or bowing. 3 A loop or knot by which a rope is fastened to any object. 4 A wale or rib. 5 *Scot.* A deep draft. [OE *bendan*]

Synonyms (verb): bias, crook, curve, deflect, deviate, diverge, incline, influence, mold, persuade, stoop, submit, turn, twine, twist, warp, yield. In some cases a thing is spoken of as *bent* where the parts make an angle; but oftener *to bend* is understood to be to draw to or through a curve; as, to *bend* a bow. To *submit* or *yield* is to *bend* or surrender to

another's wishes. To *incline* or *influence* is to *bend* another's wishes toward our own; to *persuade* is to draw them quite over. To *warp* is to *bend* slightly through the whole fiber, as a board in the sun. To *crook* is to *bend, turn,* or *twist* irregularly. *Deflect, deviate,* and *diverge* are said of any turning away from a direct line; *deviate* commonly of a slight and gradual movement, *diverge* of a more sharp and decided one. To *bias* is to influence feeling, opinion, or action in the direction of some prevailing (often unconscious) tendency; personal enmity against the accused will *bias* a witness or a juror so as to distort his view of the facts or motives involved in the case. *Mold* is a stronger word than *bend*; we may *bend* by a superior force that which resists the constraint; as, *bend* a bow; we *mold* something plastic entirely and permanently to some desired form. See TWIST.

bend[2] (bend) *n.* **1** *Her.* A band drawn diagonally across the shield from dexter chief to

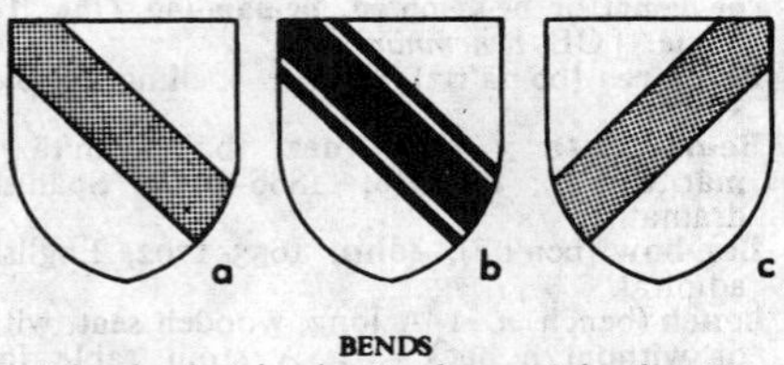

BENDS
***a.* A bend. *b.* A bend cottised. *c.* A bend sinister.**

sinister base. **2** In the leather trade, a butt cut in two. [OE *bend* strap; infl. in meaning by OF *bende* strip, band]

Ben·da (bän·dä′), **Julien,** 1867–1956, French philosopher.

Ben Da·vis (ben dā′vis) A variety of large, red, winter apple: used chiefly in cooking.

Ben Day (ben′ dā′) A process or method in photoengraving that produces a pattern of shaded areas of dots, lines, or other markings in an illustration; also, a background produced by this process. Also **ben′day′.** [after *Ben(jamin) Day,* 1838–1916, New York printer]

bend·er (ben′dər) *n.* **1** A person or thing that bends. **2** *Slang* A drinking spree. **3** *Brit. Slang* A sixpence.

Ben·di·go (ben′di·gō) A city in central Victoria, Australia.

Ben·dix (ben′diks), **Vincent,** 1882–1945, U.S. inventor and industrialist.

bends (bendz) *n. pl.* Decompression disease.

bend sinister *Her.* A bend drawn diagonally from sinister chief to dexter base: a mark of bastardy. Compare BATON SINISTER.

ben·dy (ben′dē) *n. Anglo-Indian* Okra.

bene[1] (bēn) *n. Obs.* A prayer. [OE *bēn*]

ben·e[2] (ben′ē) See BENNE.

be·neath (bi·nēth′) *adv.* **1** At a lower point; in a lower position. **2** On the underside of; underneath. —*prep.* **1** In a lower place or position than: a rock *beneath* the waves. **2** Pressed or crushed by: The ground gave *beneath* his foot. **3** Subdued or dominated by: *beneath* the yoke of the conqueror. **4** Influenced or controlled by: helpless *beneath* the ban. **5** Inferior to; unworthy of: His assignment was *beneath* his ability. **6** Unsuited to the dignity of; lower in rank than: She married *beneath* her station. [OE *beneathan*]

Synonyms (prep): below, under, underneath. *Under* strictly implies that another object is directly upon or over in a vertical line. *Below* signifies that one object is lower than another, so as to be looked down upon from it, or hidden from view by it; as, *below* (not *under* nor *beneath*) the horizon. *Under* has also the sense of being subject to or subjected to; as, *under* tutors and governors, *under* examination. *Antonyms*: see synonyms for ABOVE.

ben·e·cep·tor (ben′ə·sep′tər) *n. Physiol.* An element of the nervous system, as a receptor or sense organ, specialized in the transmission of pleasurable stimuli: opposed to *nociceptor.* [< NL < L *bene* well + *-ceptor,* as in RECEPTOR]

ben·e·dic·i·te (ben′ə·dis′ə·tē) *n.* A blessing; grace or thanksgiving, especially at table. —*interj.* Bless you! [< LL, bless ye, imperative of *benedicere* bless, commend]

Ben·e·dic·i·te (ben′ə·dis′ə·tē) *n.* The canticle beginning "O all ye works of the Lord, bless ye the Lord"; also, the music of this canticle.

Ben·e·dick (ben′ə·dik) In Shakespeare's *Much Ado About Nothing,* the hero, a bachelor, who eventually marries Beatrice.

ben·e·dict (ben′ə·dikt) *n.* A newly married man. Also **ben′e·dick.** [< BENEDICK]

Ben·e·dict (ben′ə·dikt) A masculine personal name. Also *Lat.* **Ben·e·dic·tus** (ben′ə·dik′təs), *Ital.* **Be·ne·det·to** (bā′nā·det′tō), *Pg., Sp.* **Be·ne·dic·to** (*Pg.* bā′nā·dē′tōō, *Sp.* bā′nā·dēk′tō), *Ger.* **Be·ne·dikt** (bā′nə·dikt). [< L, blessed]

—**Benedict** Name of 15 popes; notably: **Benedict XIV,** 1675–1758, real name Prospero Lambertini, pope 1740–58; and **Benedict XV,** 1854–1922, real name Giacomo della Chiesa, pope 1914–22.

—**Benedict, Saint,** 480–543, Italian monk; founder of the Benedictine Order.

Ben·e·dict (ben′ə·dikt), **Ruth Fulton,** 1887–1948, U.S. anthropologist.

Ben·e·dic·ta (ben′ə·dik′tə, *Pg.* bā′nā·dē′tə) A feminine personal name; feminine of BENEDICT. Also *Ger.* **Be·ne·dik·ta** (bā′nə·dik′tä), *Ital.* **Be·ne·det·ta** (bā′nā·det′tä). [< L, *fem.,* blessed]

ben·e·dic·tine (ben′ə·dik′tēn) *n.* A brandy liqueur formerly made at the Benedictine monastery at Fécamp, France.

Ben·e·dic·tine (ben′ə·dik′tin, -tēn) *adj.* Pertaining to St. Benedict or his order. —*n.* One of the order of monks established by St. Benedict at Subiaco, in Italy, about 530: sometimes called "Black Monks" from the color of their robes.

ben·e·dic·tion (ben′ə·dik′shən) *n.* **1** The act of blessing, as at the close of worship. **2** The invocation of divine favor upon a person. **3** Any of various formal ecclesiastical ceremonies of blessing; a dedication or consecration. **4** Divine grace or favor; the state of blessedness. **5** The giving of thanks before or after meals; grace. [< L *benedictio, -onis* < *benedicere* bless] —**ben′·e·dic′tive, ben·e·dic·to·ry** (ben′ə·dik′tər·ē) *adj.*

Ben·e·dic·tus (ben′ə·dik′təs) *n.* **1** Either of two canticles, *Luke* i 68–71, and *Matt.* xxi 9, each named from the first word, *benedictus,* "blessed," of its Latin version. **2** A musical setting of either canticle mentioned above.

ben·e·fac·tion (ben′ə·fak′shən) *n.* **1** A kindly or generous act; a gift or boon; beneficence. **2** The act of bestowing charity or conferring a benefit. See synonyms under GIFT. [< L *benefactio, -onis* < *benefacere* do well]

ben·e·fac·tor (ben′ə·fak′tər, ben′ə·fak′-) *n.* A friendly helper; a patron. —**ben′e·fac′tress** *n. fem.*

be·nef·ic (bə·nef′ik) *adj.* Beneficent; kindly. [< L *beneficus* generous]

ben·e·fice (ben′ə·fis) *n.* **1** An ecclesiastical living or preferment; a church office endowed with funds or property. **2** The revenue so devoted: generally limited to parsonages, rectories, vicarages, and donatives. **3** A feudal fee or life interest in a landed estate, subject to the will of the donor. —*v.t.* **·ficed, ·fic·ing** To invest with a benefice. [< OF < L *beneficium* favor]

be·nef·i·cence (bə·nef′ə·səns) *n.* **1** The quality of being beneficent; active goodness. **2** A beneficent act or gift. See synonyms under BENEVOLENCE. [< F *bénéficence* < L *beneficentia* < *beneficus* generous]

be·nef·i·cent (bə·nef′ə·sənt) *adj.* **1** Bringing about or doing good. **2** Characterized by charity and kindness. See synonyms under CHARITABLE. —**be·nef′i·cent·ly** *adv.*

ben·e·fi·cial (ben′ə·fish′əl) *adj.* **1** Benefiting or tending to benefit; conferring benefits; advantageous; helpful. **2** *Law* Entitled to receive the income of an estate without its title, custody, or control; as, a *beneficial* interest in land. [< F *bénéficial* < LL *beneficialis* < *beneficium* favor] —**ben′e·fi′cial·ly** *adv.* —**ben′e·fi′cial·ness** *n.*

ben·e·fi·ci·ar·y (ben′ə·fish′ē·er′ē, -fish′ər·ē) *adj.* **1** Pertaining to benefits or benevolence. **2** Of the nature of a charity or donation. **3** Held by feudal tenure or privilege. —*n. pl.* **·ar·ies 1** One who receives or uses a charitable provision or privilege. **2** The holder of a benefice or church living. **3** *Law* One who is lawfully entitled to the profits and proceeds of an estate or property, the title to which is vested in another, as in a trustee. **4** The person to whom the amount of an insurance policy or annuity is payable. [< L *beneficiarius* < *beneficium* favor]

ben·e·fit (ben′ə·fit) *n.* **1** Profit; advantage; promotion of welfare or prosperity; helpful result. **2** A benefaction or deed of kindness; favor bestowed; privilege. **3** A special theatrical or musical performance, at which the performers usually serve gratuitously, and the proceeds of which are bestowed on some particular person or on some charity. **4** Pecuniary aid extended by a benefit society. See synonyms under FAVOR, PROFIT, UTILITY. —*v.* **·fit·ed, ·fit·ing** *v.t.* To be helpful or useful to. —*v.i.* To profit; gain advantage. See synonyms under SERVE. [< AF *benfet,* OF *bienfait* < L *benefactum* good deed < *benefacere* do well]

benefit of clergy 1 *Law* A privilege accorded to the clergy and afterward extended to all who could read, by which one who had been convicted in a secular court of some felony, less than treason, that involved capital punishment, could claim a hearing before the bishop's court. **2** Churchly approval or sanction: They were married without *benefit of clergy.*

benefit society An association of which the members, by the regular payment of small sums, become entitled to pecuniary aid in old age or in time of sickness; in Great Britain called a *friendly society.* Also **benefit association.**

Ben·e·lux (ben′ə·luks) *n.* The customs union of Belgium, the Netherlands, and Luxembourg. [< BE(LGIUM) + NE(THERLANDS) + LUX(EMBOURG)]

be·nempt (bi·nempt′), **be·nempt·ed** (bi·nemp′·tid) Past participles of BENAME.

Be·neš (be′nesh), **Eduard,** 1884–1948, president of Czechoslovakia, 1935–38, 1946–48.

Be·nét (bi·nā′), **Stephen Vincent,** 1898–1943, U.S. poet. —**William Rose,** 1886–1950, brother of preceding, U. S. poet and critic.

Be·ne·ven·to (bā′nā·ven′tō) A town in Campania, southern Italy: ancient *Maleventum*; later **Be′ne·ven′tum** (-təm).

be·nev·o·lence (bə·nev′ə·ləns) *n.* **1** Desire for the well-being or comfort of others; love for mankind; charitableness. **2** Any act of kindness or well-doing; charity; humanity. **3** An enforced loan sometimes exacted by English sovereigns.

Synonyms: almsgiving, beneficence, benignity, bounty, charity, generosity, humanity, kindheartedness, kindliness, kindness, liberality, munificence, philanthropy, sympathy. Originally *beneficence* was the doing well, *benevolence* the wishing or willing well to others; but *benevolence* has come to include *beneficence* and to displace it. *Charity* is now almost universally applied to some form of *almsgiving* and is much more limited in meaning than *benevolence. Benignity* suggests some occult power of blessing, such as was formerly ascribed to the stars; we may say a good man has the air of *benignity. Kindness* and *tenderness* are personal; *benevolence* and *charity* are general. *Humanity* is *kindness* and *tenderness* toward man or beast. We speak of the *bounty* of a generous host, the *liberality* or *munificence* of the founder of a college, or of the *liberality* of a person toward holders of conflicting beliefs. *Philanthropy* applies to wide schemes for human welfare, often, but not always, involving large expenditures in *charity* or *benevolence.* Compare MERCY. *Antonyms*: barbarity, brutality, churlishness, greediness, harshness, illiberality, inhumanity, malevolence, malignity, niggardliness, selfishness, self-seeking, stinginess, unkindness.

be·nev·o·lent (bə·nev′ə·lənt) *adj.* **1** Characterized by benevolence. **2** Kindly, charitable; beneficent. See synonyms under CHARITABLE, GOOD, HUMANE. [< OF *benivolent* < L *benevolens, -entis* < *bene* well + *volens,* ppr. of *velle* wish] —**be·nev′o·lent·ly** *adv.*

Ben·gal (ben·gôl′, beng-) A former province of NE British India, divided (1947) into: (1) **East Bengal,** formerly a province of Pakistan; since 1972, the country of Bangla Desh; 54,501 square miles; capital, Dacca; (2) **West Bengal,** a constituent state of the republic of India; 29,476 square miles; capital, Calcutta. —**Ben·ga·lese** (ben′·gə·lēz′, -lēs′, beng′-) *adj. & n.*

Bengal, Bay of A broad arm of the Indian Ocean, between India and the Andaman Sea.

Ben·ga·li (ben·gô′lē, beng-) *adj.* Of or pertaining to Bengal. —*n.* **1** A native of Bengal.

2 The modern vernacular Indic language of Bengal.

ben·ga·line (beng'gə·lēn, beng'gə·lēn') *n.* A silk, wool, or rayon fabric of fine weave with widthwise cords. [<BENGAL]

Bengal light A colored fire much used in signaling. Also **Bengal fire.**

Ben·ga·si (ben·gä'zē, beng-) A port in NE Libya, co-capital of Libya, on the Gulf of Sidra: ancient *Berenice.* Also **Ben·gha'zi, Ben·ga'zi.**

Ben-Gur·i·on (ben·goor'ē·ən), **David,** 1886–1973, Russian-born Israeli statesman; prime minister of Israel 1948–53 and 1955–63.

Be·ni (bā'nē) A river of NW Bolivia, flowing north 600 miles to the Madeira river.

be·night·ed (bi·nī'tid) *adj.* **1** Involved in darkness or gloom, whether intellectual or moral; ignorant; unenlightened. **2** Overtaken by night. —**be·night'ed·ness** *n.*

be·nign (bi·nīn') *adj.* **1** Gracious; generous; kindly. **2** Soft; genial; propitious; mild. **3** *Pathol.* Of a mild type: opposed to *malignant:* a *benign* tumor or disease. See synonyms under BLAND, CHARITABLE, PROPITIOUS. [<OF *benigne* <L *benignus* kindly] —**be·nign'ly** *adv.*

be·nig·nant (bi·nig'nənt) *adj.* **1** Condescending; gentle; gracious. **2** Helpful; salutary. See synonyms under AMIABLE, CHARITABLE, HUMANE, MERCIFUL. [<BENIGN, on analogy with MALIGNANT] —**be·nig'nant·ly** *adv.*

be·nig·ni·ty (bi·nig'nə·tē) *n. pl.* **·ties** **1** Kindliness; beneficence: also **be·nig·nan·cy** (bi·nig'·nən·sē). **2** A gracious action or influence. See synonyms under BENEVOLENCE, MERCY.

Be·ni Has·san (bā'nē hä'sän) A village in Upper Egypt, on the east bank of the Nile; site of ancient rock tombs.

Be·nin (be·nēn') **1** An independent republic in western Africa; 44,290 square miles; capital, Porto-Novo: formerly *Dahomey.* **2** A river in southern Nigeria, flowing west 60 miles into the **Bight of Benin,** an Atlantic bay of the Gulf of Guinea on the coast of west central Africa. **3** A province in southern Nigeria; 8,627 square miles; capital, Benin City.

ben·i·son (ben'ə·zən, sən) *n.* A benediction; blessing. [<OF *beneison* <LL *benedictio, -onis* benediction]

Be·ni Suef (bā'nē swāf') A city in Upper Egypt on the west bank of the Nile. Also **Ba'ni Suwayf'.**

Be·ni·ta (bā·nē'tä) Spanish form of BENEDICTA.

ben·ja·min (ben'jə·mən) *n.* Benzoin (def. 1). [Alter. of BENZOIN]

Ben·ja·min (ben'jə·mən; *Dan., Ger.* ben'yä·mēn; *Fr.* ba·zhä·ma'; *Pg.* be·zhə·mē n') A masculine personal name. Also *Sp.* **Ben·ja·mín** (ben'hä·mēn'), *Ital.* **Ben·ia·mi·no** (ben'yä·mē'nō). [<Hebrew, son of the right hand]

Benjamin The youngest son of Jacob by Rachel: also, the tribe descended from him. *Gen.* xxxv 18.

Ben·ja·min (ben'jə·mən), **Judah Philip,** 1811–1884, American lawyer and Confederate cabinet member.

benjamin bush The spicebush; feverbush.

Ben·jy (ben'jē) Diminutive of BENJAMIN.

Ben·ku·len (ben·koo'lən) A port in SE Sumatra. *Indonesian* **Beng·ku·lu** (beng·koo'l;ov), *Dutch* **Ben·koe'len.**

Ben Lo·mond (ben lō'mənd) **1** A mountain in NW Stirlingshire, Scotland; 3,192 ft. **2** The highest mountain range in Tasmania; highest peak, Legge Tor, 5,160 ft.

ben·ne (ben'ē) *n.* An East Indian plant, the sesame, widely cultivated for its seeds which yield **benne oil:** also spelled **bene.** [<Malay *bijen* seed]

ben·net (ben'it) *n.* **1** The avens; especially, either of two American species (*Geum canadense* and *G. strictum*). **2** Herb-bennet. [<OF *(herbe) beneite* blessed (herb) <L *benedicta*]

Ben·net (ben'it) Variant of BENEDICT.

Ben·nett (ben'it), **(Enoch) Arnold,** 1867–1931, English novelist and playwright. —**James Gordon,** 1795–1872, U.S. journalist born in Scotland; founded New York *Herald* 1835. —**James Gordon,** 1841–1918, U.S. newspaper proprietor and editor; son of the preceding. —**Viscount Richard Bedford,** 1870–1947, Canadian prime minister 1930–35.

Ben Ne·vis (nē'vis, nev'is) A mountain in SW Invernessshire, Scotland; highest peak in Great Britain; 4,406 feet.

Ben·ning·ton (ben'ing·tən) A town in Vermont; near site of battle, 1777, in which American colonial forces defeated the British.

Ben·ny (ben'ē) Diminutive of BENJAMIN.

Be·noîte (bə·nwät') French form of BENEDICTA.

Ben·o·ni (ben·ō'nī) In the Bible, Benjamin: so called by Rachel. [<Hebrew, son of sorrow]

Be·no·ni (bə·nō'nī) A mining city in Gauteng, Republic of South Africa.

Ben·son (ben'sən), **Arthur Christopher,** 1862–1925, English educator and author. —**Edward Frederick,** 1867–1940, English novelist, brother of the preceding. —**Frank Weston,** 1862–1951, U.S. painter. —**William Shepherd,** 1855–1932, U.S. admiral.

bent¹ (bent) Past tense and past participle of BEND. — *adj.* **1** Deflected from a straight line; crooked. **2** Made fast to a spar or other object: said of a sail, etc. **3** Fixed in a course; set; as, on pleasure *bent.* — *n.* **1** The state of being inclined or the direction in which inclined; inclination; penchant; tendency; bias; disposition. **2** The degree of tension; limit of endurance or capacity. **3** *Engin.* A section of a framed building; a portion of a framework or scaffolding of a building, designed to carry both vertical and transverse loads. **4** A cast of the eye. **5** *Obs.* Concentrated force; impetus. See synonyms under INCLINATION.

bent² *n.* **1** One of various stiff wiry grasses (genus *Agrostis*): also **bent grass.** **2** The stiff flower stalk of various grasses. **3** *Brit.* The stalk or seeding spike of either of the two common species of plantain (*Plantago major* and *P. lanceolata*). **4** Land unenclosed and covered only with grass or sedge, as opposed to wood, a heath moor, or other waste land. [OE *beonet*]

Ben·tham (ben'thəm), **Jeremy,** 1748–1832, English jurist and philosopher.

Ben·tham·ism (ben'thəm·iz'əm) *n.* The political and ethical philosophy of Jeremy Bentham, who taught that nature has placed mankind under the governance of two sovereign masters, pain and pleasure, and that pleasure is the supreme end of life. —**Ben'tham·ite** (-īt) *n.*

ben·thos (ben'thos) *n. Ecol.* The whole assemblage of plants or animals living on the sea bottom: distinguished from *plankton.* [<Gk., the deep, depth of the sea] —**ben·thic** (ben'thik), **ben·thon·ic** (ben·thon'ik) *adj.*

ben·tho·scope (ben'thə·skōp) *n.* An undersea research apparatus resembling a bathysphere, but designed and built to withstand pressures at a depth of 10,000 feet: intended for the study of submarine life. [<Gk. *benthos* depth + -SCOPE]

Ben·tinck (ben'tingk), **Lord William Cavendish,** 1774–1839, son of William Henry, first governor general of India 1833. —**William Henry Cavendish,** 1738–1809, third duke of Portland; British prime minister 1783, 1807–1809.

Bent·ley (bent'lē), **Richard,** 1662–1742, English classical scholar.

Ben·ton (ben'tən), **Thomas Hart,** 1889–1975, U.S. painter.

Ben·ton·ville (ben'tən·vil) A town in central North Carolina; site of one of the final major engagements in the Civil War.

bent wood Designating a style of furniture constructed of wood sections curved and bent to desired shapes.

Be·nu·e (bā'noo·ā) A river in Nigeria; flowing about 800 miles to the Niger river: also *Binue.*

be·numb (bi·num') *v.t.* **1** To make numb; deaden. **2** To render insensible; stupefy. [OE *benumen*, pp. of *beniman* deprive. See NUMB.] —**be·numbed** (bi·numd') *adj.* —**be·numb'ment** *n.*

ben·zal·de·hyde (ben·zal'də·hīd) *n. Chem.* A colorless, highly refractive liquid, $C_7 H_6 O$, having the characteristic odor of essence of almonds. It is used largely in the dye and perfume industries. [<BENZ(OIN) + ALDEHYDE]

Ben·ze·drine (ben'zə·drēn, -drin) *n.* Proprietary name of a brand of amphetamine.

ben·zene (ben'zēn, ben·zēn') *n. Chem.* A colorless, volatile, inflammable, liquid hydrocarbon, $C_6 H_6$, obtained chiefly from coal tar by fractional distillation. It is useful as a solvent, as an illuminant in gas-manufacture, and is important as the starting point in the formation of the compounds of the benzene series. [<BENZOIN]

benzene ring *Chem.* The graphic formula of the aromatic hydrocarbon benzene. The hexagon formula shows six carbon atoms, each associated with a hydrogen atom one or more of which may be replaced to form any of a large class of benzene derivatives. Also **benzene nucleus.**

BENZENE RING

ben·zi·dine (ben'zə·dēn, -din) *n. Chem.* A crystalline hydrocarbon, $C_{12} H_{12} N_2$, synthesized from benzene derivatives: used in the preparation of dyes and as a test for blood. Also **ben'zi·din** (-din). [<BENZOIN]

ben·zine (ben'zēn, ben·zēn') *n.* A colorless inflammable liquid derived from crude petroleum by fractional distillation and consisting of various hydrocarbons. It is used as a solvent for fats, resins, etc., to cleanse clothing, and as a motor fuel: also called *petroleum spirit.* Sometimes confused with *benzene.* Also **ben'zin** (-zin), **ben·zo·line** (ben'zə·lēn).

ben·zo·ate (ben'zō·it, -āt) *n. Chem.* A salt of benzoic acid.

benzoate of soda Sodium benzoate.

ben·zo·ic (ben·zō'ik) *adj.* **1** Pertaining to or derived from benzoin. **2** Pertaining to benzoic acid.

benzoic acid *Chem.* An aromatic compound, $C_7 H_6 O_2$, contained in resins, as benzoin, and in coal-tar oil, etc., and obtained also by synthesis: used as a food preservative and in medicine.

ben·zo·in (ben'zō·in, -zoin) *n.* **1** A gum resin from various East Indian plants (genus *Styrax*), used in medicine and as a perfume: also called *benjamin.* **2** *Chem.* A crystalline chemical compound, $C_{14} H_{12} O_2$, obtained variously, as from benzaldehyde by the action of an alcoholic solution of potassium cyanide: also called *flowers of benzoin.* **3** Any plant of a small genus (*Lindera*) of North American and Asian shrubs or trees of the laurel family, including the spicebush. [<F *benjoin* <Pg. *beijoin* or Ital. *benzoi* <Arabic *lubān jāwī* incense of Java]

ben·zol (ben'zōl, -zol) *n.* A grade of crude benzene. Also **ben'zole** (-zōl).

ben·zo·phe·none (ben'zō·fē 'nōn) *n. Chem.* A crystalline compound, $C_{13} H_{10} O$, a ketone obtained variously, as from calcium benzoate by dry distillation. [<BENZENE + PHENOL + -ONE]

ben·zo·yl (ben'zō·il) *n. Chem.* The univalent organic radical, $C_6 H_5 CO$, derived from benzoic acid.

benzoyl peroxide *Chem.* A white, crystalline derivative of benzoic acid, $C_{12} H_{10} C_2 O_4$, used in bleaching oils, waxes, flour, etc.

ben·zyl (ben'zil) *n. Chem.* The univalent radical, $C_6 H_5 CH_2$, derived from toluene.

Be·o·grad (be·ô'gräd) The Serbo-Croatian name for BELGRADE.

Be·o·wulf (bā'ə·woolf) A warrior prince in an eighth century Anglo-Saxon epic poem, *Beowulf,* who kills the monsters Grendel and Grendel's mother and dies in old age of a wound received in battle with a dragon.

Bep·pu (bep'oo) A city on NE Kyushu, Japan.

be·queath (bi·kwēth', -kwēth') *v.t.* **1** *Law* To give, as personal property, by will; make a bequest of: compare DEVISE. **2** To hand down to posterity; transmit. **3** *Obs.* To devote. [OE *becwethan*]

be·quest (bi·kwest') *n.* The act of bequeathing or that which is bequeathed. See synonyms under GIFT. [ME *biqueste*]

Bé·ran·ger (bā·rä·zhā'), **Pierre Jean de,** 1780–1857, French lyric poet.

Be·rar (bā·rär') The SW division of Madhya Pradesh state, India, on the Deccan Plateau; 17,808 square miles; administrative center, Amraoti.

be·rate (bi·rāt′) *v.t.* **be·rat·ed, be·rat·ing** To chide severely; scold.

Ber·ber (bûr′bər) *n.* **1** A member of a group of Moslem tribes inhabiting northern Africa, especially the Kabyles of Algeria. **2** The Hamitic language of the Berbers, comprising the dialects spoken in Algeria, Tunisia, Morocco, and the Sahara, as Kabyle, Tuareg, etc. —*adj.* Of or pertaining to the Berbers or their language.

Ber·ber (bûr′bər) A town on the eastern bank of the Nile in northern Sudan.

Ber·ber·a (bûr′bər·ə) A port on the Gulf of Aden, former winter capital of British Somaliland.

Ber·ber·i (bûr′bər·ē) *n.* Nuba (def. 3).

ber·ber·i·da·ceous (bûr′bər·i·dā′shəs) *adj.* Pertaining or belonging to the barberry family of herbs and shrubs, as the May apple.

ber·ber·ine (bûr′bər·ēn, -in) *n.* A yellow crystalline bitter alkaloid, $C_{20}H_{19}O_5N$, contained in the bark of the barberry and some other plants: it is used in medicine as a tonic. Also **ber′ber·in** (-in). [<LL *berberis* barberry]

ber·ceuse (bâr·sœz′) *n. pl.* **·ceuses** (-sœz′) *Music* A cradle song. [<F]

Berch·tes·ga·den (berkh′tes·gä′dən) A resort village in Upper Bavaria; noted as the private retreat of Adolf Hitler.

Ber·di·chev (ber·dē′chef) A city in central Ukrainian S.S.R.

bere (bir) *n. Scot.* Barley.

be·reave (bi·rēv′) *v.t.* **be·reaved** or **be·reft** (bi·reft′), **be·reav·ing 1** To deprive, as of hope or happiness. **2** To leave desolate or saddened through loss: with *of*: He was *bereaved* of his father. Commonly in past participle: *bereaved* or *bereft* of a relative, but *bereft* of love or other immaterial object. **3** *Obs.* To despoil; rob. [OE *bereafian*]

be·reave·ment (bi·rēv′mənt) *n.* The act of bereaving, or the state of being bereaved; an afflictive loss, as by death. See synonyms under MISFORTUNE.

be·reft (bi·reft′) Alternative past tense and past participle of BEREAVE. —*adj.* Deprived: *bereft* of all hope.

Ber·e·ni·ce (ber′ə·nī′sē) A feminine personal name. Also spelled *Bernice.* [<Gk., victorious]
—**Berenice** Daughter of Herod Agrippa I. *Acts* xxv 13.

Ber·e·ni·ce (ber′ə·nī′sē) An ancient name for BENGASI.

Berenice's Locks or **Hair** Coma Berenices.

Ber·en·son (ber′ən·sən), **Bernard,** 1865–1959, U.S. art critic and writer born in Lithuania.

be·ret (bə·rā′, ber′ā) *n.* A soft, flat cap, usually of wool, originating in the Basque regions of France and Spain. [<F, ult. <LL *birettum* cap]

Ber·e·zi·na (ber′ə·zē′nə) A river in Belorussian S.S.R. flowing south 350 miles to the Dnieper; crossed by Napoleon (1812) at the battle of Borisov.

berg (bûrg) *n.* **1** An iceberg. **2** In South Africa, a mountain.

Berg (berkh), **Alban,** 1885–1935, Austrian composer.

Ber·ga·ma (ber′gə·mä) A town of western Turkey north of Smyrna, on the site of ancient Pergamum.

Ber·ga·mo (ber′gä·mō) A city in Lombardy, northern Italy.

ber·ga·mot[1] (bûr′gə·mot) *n.* **1** A tree *(Citrus bergamia)* of the rue family, the bergamot orange. **2** Its fruit, furnishing an oil used as a perfume. **3** Any of several plants of the mint family, as the horsemint in the United States, and *Mentha aquatica* and *Mentha citrata* (also called **bergamot-mint**) in England. **4** Snuff scented with bergamot. [? from *Bergamo,* Italy]

ber·ga·mot[2] (bûr′gə·mot) *n.* A minor variety of pear. [<F. *bergamote* <Ital. *bergamotta* <Turkish *beg-armūdi* prince's pear; spelling infl. by BERGAMOT[1]]

Ber·gen (bûr′gən, *Norw.* ber′gən) A port in SW Norway.

Ber·ge·rac (bâr·zhə·räk′) See CYRANO DE BERGERAC.

Bergh (bûrg), **Henry,** 1820–88, U.S. philanthropist; founded Society for Prevention of Cruelty to Animals, 1866.

Ber·gi·us (ber′gē·o͞os), **Friedrich,** 1884–1949, German chemist.

berg·schrund (bûrg′shrund, *Ger.* berkh′·shro͞ont) *n.* A crevasse or series of crevasses at the head of a glacier, near the base of the cliff against which the snow field lies. [<G]

Berg·son (berg′sən), **Henri Louis,** 1859–1941, French philosopher. —**Berg·so·ni·an** (berg·sō′nē·ən) *adj. & n.*

Berg·son·ism (berg′sən·iz′əm) *n.* The philosophy of Henri Bergson, who held that the world is a continuing process of creative evolution, hence, of inevitable novelty and change, rather than the result of fixed or unaltering laws of nature. Reality is the expression of the creative or vital force *(élan vital)* inherent in all organisms. Knowledge of reality comes through intuition rather than through analytical intellectual processes. Compare VITALISM.

Be·ri·a (be′rē·ə), **La·vren·ti** (lə·vren′tē) **Pavlovich,** 1899–1953, U.S.S.R. politician; executed. Also **Be′ri·ya.**

ber·i·ber·i (ber′ē·ber′ē) *n. Pathol.* An oriental disease of the peripheral nerves, characterized by partial paralysis, swelling of the legs, and general dropsy: due to the absence of vitamins of the B complex in a diet consisting principally of polished rice. [<Singhalese *beri* weakness] —**ber′i·ber′ic** *adj.*

be·rime (bi·rīm′) *v.t.* **·rimed, ·rim·ing 1** To mention or celebrate in rime. **2** To compose in rime. Also spelled *berhyme.*

Ber·ing Sea (bâr′ing, bir′-) An arm of the North Pacific Ocean between Alaska and Siberia, north of the Aleutian Islands: *Russian* **Be·ring·o·vo Mo·re** (be·ring′ə·və mô′re): connected by **Bering Strait** to the Arctic Ocean. Also *Behring Sea.*

Berke·le·ian·ism (bûrk·lē′ən·iz′əm, *Brit.* bärk-) *n.* The idealistic system of philosophy propounded by George Berkeley. —**Berke·le′ian** *adj. & n.*

Berke·ley (bûrk′lē, *Brit.* bärk′-), **George,** 1684–1753, English prelate and philosopher born in Ireland. —**Sir William,** 1606–77, English governor of Virginia.

berke·li·um (bûrk′lē·əm) *n.* A very rare, unstable element (symbol Bk, atomic number 97) of the actinide series, first obtained by bombarding americium with alpha particles, the most stable isotope having mass number 247 and a half-life of 1400 years. See PERIODIC TABLE. [from *Berkeley,* California, location of the University of California, where first produced]

Berk·shire (bûrk′shir, -shər) *n.* One of a breed of black-haired swine from Berkshire, England, of medium size, with short legs, broad, straight backs, square hams and shoulders, and short heads.

Berk·shire (bûrk′shir, -shər; *Brit.* bärk′-) A county in southern England; 725 square miles; county seat, Reading. Shortened form **Berks** (bûrks, *Brit.* bärks).

Berk·shire Hills (bûrk′shir, -shər) A wooded region of western Massachusetts; highest peak, 3,505 feet.

Ber·lich·ing·en (ber′likh·ing′ən), **Götz von** (gœts fôn), 1480–1562, German knight; the hero of Goethe's drama of the same name: called "Götz of the Iron Hand."

ber·lin (bər·lin′, bûr′lin) *n.* **1** An automobile of limousine type but with the driver's seat entirely enclosed: also **ber·line** (bər·lin′, *Fr.* ber·lēn′). **2** A four-wheeled covered carriage with a shelter seat behind. **3** Zephyr or worsted for knitting: also **Berlin wool.** [from *Berlin,* Germany]

Ber·lin (bər·lin′, *Ger.* ber·lēn′) A city of central Prussia and the largest city in Germany, of which it was the capital until 1945; the eastern sector is the capital of the German Democratic Republic.

Ber·lin (bər·lin′), **Irving,** born 1888, U.S. song writer.

Ber·li·oz (ber′lē·ōz, *Fr.* bâr·lyôz′), **Hector,** 1803–69, French composer.

berm (bûrm) *n.* **1** The bank of a canal opposite the towpath. **2** A horizontal ledge part way up a slope; bench. **3** A ledge dug near the top of a trench to support beams and prevent caving in of the sides. **4** A narrow, level ledge at the outside foot of a parapet, to retain material which might otherwise fall from the slope into the moat. **5** The outside or downhill side of a ditch or trench. For illustration see BASTION. Also **berme.** [<F *berme*]

Ber·me·jo (ber·me′hō) A river in northern Argentina, flowing about 650 miles to the Paraguay.

Ber·mu·da (bər·myo͞o′də) An island group in the western North Atlantic, comprising a British colony; 22 square miles; capital, Hamilton. Also **Ber·mu′das.** —**Ber·mu·di·an** (bər·myo͞o′dē·ən) *adj. & n.*

Bermuda shorts Shorts which extend to just above the knees.

Bern (bûrn, bern) The capital of Switzerland. Also **Berne.**

Ber·na·be (ber′nä·bā′) Spanish form of BARNABAS.

Ber·na·dette (bûr′nə·det′, *Fr.* ber·nȧ·det′), **Saint,** 1844–79, Bernadette Soubirous, a French maiden who saw a vision of the Virgin Mary at Lourdes; canonized 1933.

Ber·na·dotte (bûr′nə·dot, *Fr.* ber·nȧ·dôt′) Family name of royal house of Sweden, founded by **Jean Baptiste Jules Bernadotte,** 1764–1844, French marshal, who became king of Sweden as Charles XIV John, in 1818.

Ber·nard (bûr′nərd, bər·närd′) A masculine personal name. Also *Fr.* **Ber·nard** (ber·nȧr′) or **Ber·nar·din** (ber·nȧr·daṅ′), *Ital., Sp.* **Ber·nar·do** (*Ital.* ber·när′dō, *Sp.* -thō), *Lat.* **Ber·nar·dus** (bər·när′dəs). [<OHG, hardy bear]
—**Bernard of Clairvaux, Saint,** 1091–1153, French Cistercian monk, founder of the monastery of Clairvaux.
—**Bernard of Cluny,** 1122–56, French Benedictine monk and hymn writer.

Ber·nard (ber·nȧr′), **Claude,** 1812–78, French physiologist.

Ber·nar·din de Saint-Pierre (ber·nȧr·daṅ′ də saṅ·pyâr′), **Jacques Henri,** 1737–1814, French novelist and author.

Ber·nar·dine (bûr′nər·din, -dēn) *adj.* Pertaining to St. Bernard of Clairvaux, 1091–1153, or to the Cistercian order founded by him. —*n.* A Cistercian monk.

Bern·burg (bern′bo͝orkh) A city in Saxony-Anhalt, East Germany.

Ber·ners (bûr′nərz), **Lord,** 1883–1950, Gerald Hugh Tyrwhitt-Wilson, English composer and painter.

Ber·nese (bûr·nēz′, -nēs′) *adj.* Of or pertaining to Bern, Switzerland. —*n.* **1** A resident of Bern, Switzerland. **2** A Swiss mountain dog, characterized by a short, compact body, straight forelegs, long, soft coat, and usually with white feet and with white blaze on face and chest.

Bernese Alps The northern division of the Swiss Alps; highest peak, 14,026 feet: also *Bernese Oberland.* (See OBERLAND).

Bern·hard (bern′härt) Danish and German form of BERNARD. Also *Du.* **Bern·har·dus** (bern′·här·doos).

Bern·hardt (bûrn′härt, *Fr.* ber·nȧr′), **Sarah,** 1844–1923, French actress: original name Rosine Bernard.

Ber·nice (bər·nēs′, bûr′nis) See BERENICE.

Ber·ni·ci·a (bər·nish′ē·ə) An Anglian kingdom founded in 547; later included in Northumbria.

ber·ni·cle (bûr′ni·kəl, bär′-) *n.* The barnacle goose.

Ber·ni·na (ber·nē′nä), **Piz** (pēts) Highest peak (13,304 feet) of the **Bernina Alps,** a part of the Rhaetian Alps, Switzerland; traversed by **Bernina Pass,** elevation, 7,645 feet.

Ber·ni·ni (ber·nē′nē), **Giovanni Lorenzo,** 1598–1680, Italian sculptor and architect.

Ber·noul·li (*Fr.* ber·no͞o·yē′, *Ger.* ber·no͞o′lē), **Jacob** (or **Jacques**), 1654–1705, Swiss mathematician. —**Daniel,** 1700–82, nephew of the preceding, Swiss mathematician.

Bern·stein (bern′stīn), **Henry Léon,** 1876–1953, French dramatist.

Bern·storff (bern′shtôrf), **Count Johann Heinrich von,** 1862–1939, German diplomat.

ber·ret·ta (bə·ret′ə) *n.* A biretta.

ber·ry (ber′ē) *n. pl.* **ber·ries 1** Any small, succulent fruit: the black*berry,* straw*berry,* goose*berry.* **2** *Bot.* A simple fruit with the seeds in a juicy pulp, as the tomato, grape, and currant. ◆ Collateral adjective: *baccate.* **3** A coffee bean; also, the dry kernel of various grains. **4** Something likened to a berry, as an egg of a crustacean. **5** *Slang* A dollar. —*v.i.* **ber·ried, ber·ry·ing 1** To form or bear berries. **2** To gather berries. ◆ Homophone: *bury.* [OE *berie*] —**ber′ried** *adj.*

Ber·ry (be·rē′) A region and former province of central France. Also **Ber·ri′.**

Ber·sa·glie·re (ber′sä·lye′rā) *n. pl.* **·ri** (-rē) *Italian* A marksman; rifleman; specifically,

one of a special corps of sharpshooters in the Italian army.

ber·seem (bər-sēm′) *n.* A clover (*Trifolium alexandrinum*) grown as forage in Egypt and the United States. [< Arabic *birshīm* clover]

ber·serk (bûr′sûrk, bər-sûrk′) *n.* 1 In Norse mythology, a furious fighter, who could assume the form of wild beasts, and whom fire and iron could not harm; hence figuratively, one who fights with frenzied fury. 2 A freebooter. Also **ber′serk·er.** —*adj.* Violently or frenziedly destructive. —**to go berserk** To run wild; have a fit of destructive rage. [< ON *berserkr* bear-shirt]

Bert (bûrt) Diminutive of ALBERT, BERTRAM, HERBERT.

berth (bûrth) *n.* 1 A bunk or bed in a vessel or sleeping-car, etc. 2 Any place in which a vessel may lie at anchor or at a dock; sea room. 3 A place or engagement on a vessel. 4 Office or employment in general. —**to give a wide berth to** To avoid; keep out of the way of. —*v.t. & v.i.* 1 To provide with or occupy a bed. 2 *Naut.* To provide with or come to an anchorage. ◆ Homophone: *birth.* [Origin unknown]

ber·tha (bûr′thə) *n.* A deep collar falling from the bodice neckline over the shoulders; in imitation of a short shoulder cape formerly so called. [after Charlemagne's mother]

Ber·tha (bûr′thə; *Du., Ger., Sw.* ber′tä) A feminine personal name. Also *Fr.* **Berthe** (bert), *Ital., Sp.* **Ber·ta** (ber′tä). [< Gmc., bright or famous]

Ber·tie (bûr′tē) Diminutive of ALBERT, BERTRAM, HERBERT.

Ber·the·lot (ber-tə-lō′), **Pierre Eugène Marcelin**, 1827–1907, French chemist.

Ber·til·lon system (bûr′tə-lon, *Fr.* ber-tē-yôn′) A system of coded physical measurements, later extended to include personal characteristics, such as the color of the eyes, scars, deformities, and the like (sometimes, also, photographs), used as a means for identification, especially as applied to criminals. [after Alphonse *Bertillon,* 1853–1914, French anthropologist]

Ber·tin (ber-tan′), **Exupère Joseph,** 1712–81, French anatomist.

Ber·tram (bûr′trəm) A masculine personal name. Also *Fr.* **Bertrand** (ber-trän′), *Ital.* **Ber·tran·do** (ber-trän′dō), *Pg.* **Ber·trão** (ber-troun′), *Ger.* **Ber·tram** (ber′träm) or **Ber·trand** (ber′tränt). [< Gmc., fair, illustrious]

Ber·wick (ber′ik) A county in SE Scotland; 457 square miles; county seat, Duns. Also **Ber′wick·shire** (-shir, -shər).

Berwick-on-Tweed A municipal borough in northern Northumberland, England. Also **Berwick-upon-Tweed.**

ber·yl (ber′əl) *n.* A vitreous, green or emerald-green, light-blue, yellow, pink, or white silicate of aluminum and beryllium crystallizing in the hexagonal system. The aquamarine and emerald varieties are used as gems. [< OF < L *beryllus* < Gk. *bēryllos* beryl] —**ber′yl·line** (ber′ə-lin, -līn) *adj.*

be·ryl·li·um (bə-ril′ē-əm) *n.* A hard, very light metallic element (symbol Be, atomic number 4), transparent to X rays and highly toxic, whether in compounds or metallic form. See PERIODIC TABLE. [< NL < L *beryllus* beryl]

Be·ry·tus (bə-rī′təs) The ancient name for BEIRUT.

Ber·ze·li·us (bər-zē′lē-əs, *Sw.* ber-sä′lē-ŏŏs), **Baron Jöns Jacob,** 1779–1848, Swedish chemist.

Bes (bes) In Egyptian mythology, a god presiding over art, the dance, and music, and having power to avert witchcraft.

Be·san·çon (bə-zän-sôn′) A city in eastern France; ancient *Vesontio.*

Bes·ant (bez′ənt), **Annie,** 1847–1933, *née* Wood, English theosophist.

—Besant (bi-zant′), **Sir Walter,** 1836–1901, English novelist and historian.

be·seech (bi-sēch′) *v.t.* **be·sought, be·seech·ing** 1 To entreat earnestly; implore. 2 To beg for earnestly; plead. See synonyms under ASK, PLEAD. [OE *bēsēcan*] —**be·seech′ing** *adj.* —**be·seech′ing·ly** *adv.* —**be·seech′ing·ness** *n.*

be·seem (bi-sēm′) *v.i.* To be fitting or appropriate: used impersonally: It ill *beseems* you to speak thus. —**be·seem′ing** *adj.*

be·seen (bi-sēn′) *adj. Obs.* 1 Clad; adorned. 2 Accomplished; versed.

be·set (bi-set′) *v.t.* **be·set, be·set·ting** 1 To attack on all sides; harass. 2 To hem in; encircle. 3 To set or stud with, as gems. See synonyms under ATTACK. [OE *besettan*] —**be·set′ment** *n.*

be·set·ting (bi-set′ing) *adj.* Constantly attacking or troubling.

be·show (bi-shō′) *n.* The black candlefish (*Anoplopoma fimbria*), of the Pacific coast of the U.S. [< N. Am. Ind. *bishowk*]

be·shrew (bi-shrōō′) *v.t. Obs.* To wish ill to; execrate: a mild imprecation.

be·side (bi-sīd′) *prep.* 1 At the side of; in proximity to: a path *beside* the river. 2 In comparison with: My merit is little *beside* yours. 3 Away or apart from: This discussion is *beside* the point. 4 Other than; over and above: I have no treasure *beside* this. —**beside oneself** Out of one's senses, as from anger, fear, etc. —*adv.* In addition to; besides. See synonyms under ADJACENT. [OE *be sidan* by the side (of)]

be·sides (bi-sīdz′) *adv.* 1 In addition; as well: There are, *besides,* some remarkable books here. 2 Moreover; furthermore: He is rich; *besides,* he is virtuous. 3 Not included in that mentioned; otherwise; else: Loving me, her heart is stone to all the world *besides.* —*prep.* 1 In addition to; other than: *Besides* this we have much more. 2 Beyond; apart from: I care for nothing *besides* this.

be·siege (bi-sēj′) *v.t.* **be·sieged, be·sieg·ing** 1 To beset or surround; lay siege to, as a castle. 2 To crowd around; block. 3 To harass or overwhelm, as with invitations or prayers. See synonyms under ATTACK. —**be·sieg′er** *n.* —**be·siege′ment** *n.*

Bes·kid Mountains (bes′kid, bes-kēd′) A mountain group of the Carpathians along the Czechoslovak-Polish border; highest point, 5,658 feet. Also **Bes′kids.**

be·smear (bi-smir′) *v.t.* To smear over; sully.

be·smirch (bi-smûrch′) *v.t.* 1 To soil; stain. 2 To sully; dishonor, as a reputation. —**be·smirch′er** *n.* —**be·smirch′ment** *n.*

be·som[1] (bē′zəm) *n.* 1 A bundle of twigs used as a broom; any agency that cleanses or abolishes. 2 The broom (*Cytisus scoparius*). [OE *besma* broom]

be·som[2] (bē′zəm, biz′əm) *n. Scot.* A drab; slattern; street woman.

be·sot (bi-sot′) *v.t.* **be·sot·ted, be·sot·ting** 1 To stupefy, as with drink. 2 To make foolish or stupid. 3 To infatuate. —**be·sot′ted** *adj.*

be·sought (bi-sôt′) Past tense and past participle of BESEECH.

be·span·gle (bi-spang′gəl) *v.t.* **·gled, ·gling** To decorate with or as with spangles.

be·spat·ter (bi-spat′ər) *v.t.* 1 To cover or soil by spattering. 2 To spatter about. 3 To besmirch; sully.

be·speak (bi-spēk′) *v.t.* **be·spoke** (*Archaic* **be·spake**), **be·spoke** or **be·spo·ken, be·speak·ing** 1 To ask or arrange for in advance; reserve. 2 To give evidence of; indicate: His face *bespeaks* his happy lot. 3 To foretell; foreshadow: The present *bespeaks* a sad future. 4 *Obs.* To speak to. [OE *bisprecan*]

be·spec·ta·cled (bi-spek′tə-kəld) *adj.* Wearing glasses.

be·spoke (bi-spōk′) Past tense and alternative past participle of BESPEAK. —*adj. Brit.* Ordered ahead of time; made to order, as a suit of clothing.

be·spread (bi-spred′) *v.t.* **be·spread, be·spreading** To cover or spread thickly.

be·sprent (bi-sprent′) *adj. Obs.* Besprinkled; strewed. [OE, pp. of *besprengan* sprinkle]

be·sprin·kle (bi-spring′kəl) *v.t.* **·kled, ·kling** To scatter or spread over by sprinkling.

Bess (bes) Diminutive of ELIZABETH. Also **Bes·sie** (bes′ē), **Bes′sy.**

Bes·sa·ra·bi·a (bes′ə-rā′bē-ə) A region of SW European U.S.S.R.; about 18,000 square miles; formerly a Rumanian province. *Rumanian* **Ba·sa·ra·bia** (bä′sä-rä′byä). —**Bes′sa·ra′bi·an** *adj. & n.*

Bes·sel method (bes′əl) A method of determining one's position by sighting through

points on a map correctly oriented to the corresponding features of the terrain. [after Friedrich *Bessel,* 1784–1846, German astronomer]

Bes·se·mer (bes′ə-mər) *n.* Steel prepared by the Bessemer process. [after Sir Henry *Bessemer,* 1813–98, British engineer]

Bessemer converter *Metall.* A large pear-shaped vessel for containing the molten iron to be converted into steel by the Bessemer process.

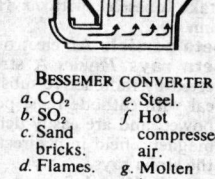

BESSEMER CONVERTER

a. CO_2	*e.* Steel.
b. SO_2	*f* Hot
c. Sand	compressed
bricks.	air.
d. Flames.	*g.* Molten
	iron.

Bessemer process *Metall.* 1 A process for eliminating the carbon and silicon from pig iron by forcing a blast of air through the molten metal preparatory to its conversion into steel or ingot iron. 2 A similar process for eliminating sulfur from copper matte.

best (best) *adj.* [*Superlative of* GOOD] 1 Excelling all others in a given quality. 2 Most advantageous, desirable, or serviceable. 3 Most; largest; as, the *best* part of an hour. —*n.* The most excellent thing, part, etc.; the highest degree or state; the utmost. —*adv.* [*Superlative of* WELL] 1 In the most excellent or suitable manner. 2 With the most favorable result. 3 To the utmost degree. —*v.t.* To defeat; overcome. [OE *betst*]

be·stain (bi-stān′) *v.t.* Mark with stains.

be·stead (bi-sted′) *v.t.* **be·stead·ed** or **be·sted, be·stead·ing** To be of service to; help.

bes·tial (bes′chəl, best′yəl) *adj.* 1 Pertaining to or like beasts or a beast; animal. 2 Having the qualities of an animal; brutish; sensual; depraved. 3 Irrational; rude; savage. See synonyms under BRUTISH. [< OF < L *bestialis* < *bestia* beast] —**bes′tial·ly** *adv.*

bes·ti·al·i·ty (bes′chē-al′ə-tē, -tē-al′-) *n.* 1 The quality or state of being bestial. 2 Character or conduct befitting beasts. 3 Human sexual relations with an animal; sodomy.

bes·tial·ize (bes′chəl-īz, best′yəl-) *v.t.* **·ized, ·iz·ing** To brutalize.

bes·ti·ar·y (bes′tē-er′ē) *n. pl.* **·ar·ies** A medieval allegory or moralizing treatise on animals.

be·stir (bi-stûr′) *v.t.* **be·stirred, be·stir·ring** To incite or rouse to activity.

best man The chief groomsman at a wedding.

be·stow (bi-stō′) *v.t.* 1 To present as a gift: with *on* or *upon.* 2 To expend; apply: He *bestowed* his life on science. 3 *Obs.* To give in marriage. 4 *Obs.* To deposit; store; also, to house; lodge. See synonyms under GIVE. [ME *bistowen* < *bi-* to, upon + *stowen* place] —**be·stow′a·ble** *adj.* —**be·stow′al** or **be·stow′ment** *n.*

be·strad·dle (bi-strad′l) *v.t.* **·dled, ·dling** To bestride; straddle.

be·strew (bi-strōō′) *v.t.* **be·strewed, be·strewed** or **be·strewn, be·strew·ing** 1 To cover or strew (a surface). 2 To scatter about. 3 To lie scattered over. Also **be·strow** (bi-strō′). [OE *bestreowian*]

be·stride (bi-strīd′) *v.t.* **be·strode, be·strid·den, be·strid·ing** 1 To mount; sit astride of; ride astride; straddle. 2 To stride over or across.

best-sell·er (best′sel′ər) *n.* A book or phonograph record currently selling in large numbers.

bet (bet) *v.* **bet** or (less commonly) **bet·ted, bet·ting** *v.t.* 1 To stake or pledge (money, etc.) in support of an opinion or on an uncertain outcome, as of a race. 2 To declare as in a bet: I'll *bet* he doesn't come. —*v.i.* 3 To place a wager. —**you bet** *U.S. Slang* Certainly. —*n.* 1 The act of betting; a wager. 2 The stake in any wager. 3 That on which the bet is placed: The black horse is the best *bet.* [Origin uncertain]

be·ta (bā′tə, bē′-) *n.* 1 The second letter of the Greek alphabet (B, β): corresponding to English *b.* As a numeral it denotes 2. 2 The second object in any order of arrangement

or classification, as, in astronomy the second brightest star in a constellation, in chemistry the second of a group of isomeric compounds, in botany the second subspecies, etc. [< Gk.]

be·ta-block·er (bā′tə·blok′ər) *n.* A drug that relieves heart stress by inhibiting absorption of adrenalin by the heart and blood vessels.

Beta Cen·tau·ri (sen·tôr′ē) The star Beta in the constellation of Centaurus; one of the 20 brightest stars, 0.86 magnitude.

be·ta·ine (bē′tə·ēn, -in) *n. Chem.* A crystalline alkaloid compound, $C_5H_{11}O_2N \cdot H_2O$ related to glycine, found in the beet and various other plants. [< L *beta* beet]

be·take (bi·tāk′) *v.t.* **be·took, be·tak·en, be·tak·ing** 1 To resort or have recourse: used reflexively: with *to*: She *betook* herself to prayer. 2 To go; take (oneself): with *to*: He *betook* himself to an inn.

beta particle An electron.

beta rays *Physics* A stream of electrons projected by radioactive substances. They are identical with cathode rays, possess great penetrative power, and are easily deflected by an electric or magnetic field in a direction opposite to that of the alpha rays.

beta rhythm A frequency of 13 to 30 per second in brain waves, characteristic of an alert or aroused state in the normal human adult.

be·ta·tron (bā′tə·tron) *n.* An electromagnetic apparatus for liberating electrons and accelerating them in a quarter-cycle alternating field to the required velocity for discharge against a chosen target. [< BETA (RAY) + (ELEC)TRON]

be·ta·tro·pic (bā′tə·trō′pik, -trop′ik) *adj. Physics* 1 Of or pertaining to a difference of one beta particle in the nucleus of an atom. 2 Designating either of two atoms, one of which has been formed by the ejection of a beta particle from the nucleus, with an increase of 1 in the nuclear charge. [< BETA (PARTICLE) + -TROPIC]

be·tel (bēt′l) *n.* A climbing plant *(Piper betle)* of Asia, the leaves of which are chewed by the natives of Malaya and other Asian countries. See BETELNUT. [< Pg. *betel* < Malay *vettila*]

Be·tel·geuse (bē′təl·jōōz, bet′əl·jœz) A giant red star, Alpha in the constellation of Orion. It is an irregular variable with a magnitude of 1.2. Also **Be′tel·guese, Be′tel·geux.** [< F *Bételgeuse* < Arabic *bat al-jauza*, ? shoulder of the giant]

be·tel·nut (bēt′l·nut′) *n.* The astringent seed of an East Indian palm, the **betel palm** *(Areca catechu)*, used for chewing with betel leaves.

bête noire (bāt′ nwär′, *Fr.* bet nwär′) Anything real or imaginary that is an object of hate or dread; a bugaboo. [< F, black beast]

beth (beth) The second Hebrew letter. See ALPHABET.

Beth (beth) Diminutive of ELIZABETH.

be·thank·it (bi·thang′kit) *n. Scot.* Grace said at table: elliptical for *God be thanked.*

Beth·a·ny (beth′ə·nē) In the New Testament, a village in Palestine near Jerusalem, mentioned as the home of Lazarus, Martha, and Mary.

beth·el (beth′əl) *n.* 1 A seamen's church or chapel, floating or on shore. 2 *Brit.* A dissenters' chapel. 3 A hallowed place. [< Hebrew *bēth-ēl* house of God]

Beth·el (beth′əl) An ancient town of Palestine, near Jerusalem. *Gen.* xxviii 19.

Be·thes·da (bə·thez′də) *n.* 1 A pool in Jerusalem reputed to have healing properties. *John* v 2. 2 A meeting house; chapel.

be·think (bi·thingk′) *v.* **be·thought, be·think·ing** *v.t.* To remind (oneself); bear in mind; consider: generally used reflexively: *Bethink* yourself of what you are. *—v.i. Archaic* To meditate.

Beth·le·hem (beth′lē·əm, -lə·hem) 1 An ancient town in Judea, SW of Jerusalem; birthplace of Jesus. *Matt.* ii 1. 2 A town in Palestine on the same site. 3 A manufacturing city on the Lehigh River in eastern Pennsylvania **—Beth′le·hem·ite′** *n.*

Beth·mann-Holl·weg (bāt′män·hōl′väkh), **Theobald von,** 1856–1921, German chancellor 1909–17.

Beth·nal Green (beth′nəl) A metropolitan borough of London north of the Thames.

be·thought (bi·thôt′) Past tense and past participle of BETHINK.

Beth·sa·i·da (beth·sā′ə·də) A ruined town on the northern shore of the Sea of Galilee, Palestine. *John* i 44. Also **Bethsaida of Galilee.**

Bé·thune (bā·tün′) A town of northern France.

be·tide (bi·tīd′) *v.t.* & *v.i.* **be·tid·ed, be·tid·ing** To happen (to) or befall. See synonyms under HAPPEN. [ME *betiden*]

be·times (bi·tīmz′) *adv.* In good season or time; also, soon. Also *Obs.* **be·time′.** [ME *betymes* in time, seasonably]

Be·ti·o (bā′tsē·ō, bāt′shē·ō) An islet SW of Tarawa; World War II capital of the Gilbert and Ellice Islands Colony.

bê·tise (be·tēz′) *n. French* 1 A stupid thing; an absurdity. 2 Stupidity; nonsense.

be·to·ken (bi·tō′kən) *v.t.* 1 To be a sign of; portend. 2 To give evidence of; indicate. See synonyms under AUGUR, IMPORT. [ME *bitacnien*] **— be·to′ken·er** *n.*

bé·ton (bā·tôn′) *n. French* A concrete of lime, sand, and cement.

bet·o·ny (bet′ə·nē) *n. pl.* **·nies** 1 A European herb (genus *Stachys,* formerly *Betonica)* of the mint family, once used as an emetic. 2 One of various other plants, as a British species of figwort (the water *betony*), etc. [< F *bétoine* < L *betonica*, var. of *vettonica* < *Vettones,* a people of Portugal]

be·took (bi·tŏŏk′) Past tense of BETAKE.

be·tray (bi·trā′) *v.t.* 1 To deliver up to an enemy; be a traitor to. 2 To prove faithless to; disappoint: to *betray* a trust. 3 To disclose, as secret information. 4 To reveal unwittingly: to *betray* ignorance. 5 To deceive; seduce and desert. 6 To indicate; show: The smoke *betrays* a fire. See synonyms under DECEIVE. [ME *bitraien* < *bi* over, to + OF *trair* < L *tradere* deliver, give up] **— be·tray′al, be·tray′ment** *n.* **—be·tray′er** *n.*

be·troth (bi·trōth′, -trôth′) *v.t.* 1 To engage to marry; affiance. 2 To contract to give in marriage. [ME *bitreuthien* < *bi-* + *treuthe* truth]

be·troth·al (bi·trō′thəl, -trôth′əl) *n.* 1 The act of betrothing, or the state of being betrothed. 2 Engagement or contract to marry. Also **be·troth′·ment.**

be·trothed (bi·trōthd′, -trôtht′) *adj.* Engaged to be married; affianced. *—n.* A person engaged to be married.

Bet·sy (bet′sē) Diminutive of ELIZABETH.

bet·ter[1] (bet′ər) *adj.* [Comparative of GOOD] 1 Superior in excellence, amount, or value; excelling or surpassing. 2 Larger; greater: the *better* half of the cake. 3 Improved in health; convalescent. *—n.* 1 That which is in any way better; also, advantage; superiority. 2 A superior, as in ability, rank, age, etc. *—v.t.* 1 To make better; improve. 2 To surpass; excel. *—v.i.* 3 To grow better. See synonyms under AMEND. *—adv.* [Comparative of WELL] 1 In a superior manner; more thoroughly or correctly; in a higher degree. 2 *Colloq.* More: We've been here *better* than a week. [OE *betera*]

bet·ter[2] (bet′ər) *n.* One who lays wagers. Also **bet′tor.**

bet·ter·ment (bet′ər·mənt) *n.* 1 Improvement. 2 An addition to the value of real property.

Bet·ter·ton (bet′ər·tən), **Thomas,** 1635?–1710, English actor and producer; said to have inaugurated scene-shifting.

Bet·ty (bet′ē) Diminutive of ELIZABETH.

bet·u·la·ceous (bech′ŏŏ·lā′shəs) *adj.* Belonging to a family *(Betulaceae)* of trees and shrubs including the birch, the alder, and the hazel. [< L *betula* birch]

be·tween (bi·twēn′) *adv.* In intervening time, space, position, or relation; at or during intervals: Rest periods were few and far *between.* **—in between** In an intermediate position or state; undecided. *—prep.* 1 In or at some point within the space separating two places or objects: He stepped *between* the combatants. 2 Intermediate in relation to qualities, conditions, periods of time, etc.: a flavor *between* sweet and sour; Come *between* one and two. 3 Involving in or as in joint or reciprocal action or relation: They had only five dollars *between* them. 4 Connecting, as in continuous extent or motion: the plane *between* New York and Paris. 5 One or the other of: How can you choose *between* them? 6 As a result of: *Between* her job and her housework, she had little time for her children. [OE *betweonan* < *be-* by + *tweonan* < *twā* two]

Synonym (prep.): among. In strict usage *between* is used only of two objects; *among* of more than two; divide the money *between* the two, *among* the three. *Between* is, however, used at times of more than two objects, particularly when some reciprocal relation is denoted; as, a treaty *between* the three powers. See AMID.

between the devil and the deep (blue) sea Intermediate between unpleasant alternatives.

between you and me Confidentially.

be·twixt (bi·twikst′) *adv.* & *prep. Archaic* or *Poetic* Between. See synonyms under AMID. [OE *betweohs* twofold < *be* by + *-tweohs* < *twā* two]

betwixt and between In an intermediate state or position; neither the one nor the other.

beuk (byŏŏk) *n. Scot.* Book.

Beu·lah (byōō′lə) A feminine personal name. [< Hebrew *be'ūlāh* married]

Beu·lah (byōō′lə) The land of Israel. *Isa.* lxii 4. **—Land of Beulah** In Bunyan's *Pilgrim's Progress,* the land of rest where pilgrims abide till death.

Bev or **bev** (bev) *n. Physics.* Billion (10^9) electron volts.

bev·a·tron (bev′ə·tron) *n. Physics* An atom-smashing machine resembling the synchrotron in operating principle but capable of accelerating protons to an energy level in excess of one billion electron volts; a proton synchrotron: also called *cosmotron.* [< B(ILLION) E(LECTRON) V(OLTS) + (ELEC)TRON]

bev·el (bev′əl) *n.* 1 An inclination of two surfaces other than 90°, as at the edge of a timber, etc. 2 An adjustable instrument for measuring angles: also **bevel square.** *—adj.* Oblique; slanting; beveled. *—v.* **bev·eled** or **bev·elled, bev·el·ing** or **bev·el·ling** *v.t.* To cut or bring to a bevel. *—v.i.* To slant. [? < OF. Cf. F *beveau.*]

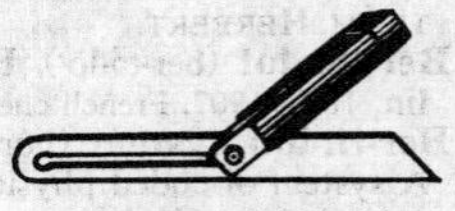
BEVEL SQUARE

bevel gear *Mech.* A gear having beveled teeth, as for transmitting rotary motion at an angle. See illustration under COGWHEEL.

bev·er·age (bev′rij, bev′ər·ij) *n.* Drink; that which is drunk. [< OF *bevrage* < *beivre* drinking < L *bibere* drink]

Bev·er·idge (bev′ər·ij), **Albert Jeremiah,** 1862–1927, U.S. politician and historian. **—Sir William** 1879–1963 English economist.

Beveridge plan A proposal (1942) for the unification of the various types of social insurance in Great Britain: formulated by Sir William Beveridge.

Bev·er·ly Hills (bev′ər·lē) A residential city in California, on the western boundary of Los Angeles.

Bevin (bev′in), **Ernest,** 1884–1951, English labor leader and politician.

bev·y (bev′ē) *n. pl.* **·ies** 1 A small group of persons, usually of girls or women. 2 A flock of birds, especially of quail, grouse, or larks. 3 A small herd, especially of roes. See synonyms under FLOCK. [ME *bevey;* origin uncertain]

be·wail (bi·wāl′) *v.t.* & *v.i.* To mourn; lament. See synonyms under MOURN.

be·ware (bi·wâr′) *v.t.* & *v.i.* **be·wared, be·war·ing** To look out (for); be cautious or wary (of): often with *of, lest, that, not, how.* [OE *wær* cautious; orig. *be ware* be on guard, be cautious]

be·wil·der (bi·wil′dər) *v.t.* 1 To confuse utterly; perplex. 2 *Archaic* To cause to lose the way or course. See synonyms under ABASH. **— be·wil′dered** *adj.* **—be·wil′dered·ly** *adv.* **— be·wil′der·ing** *adj.* **—be·wil′der·ing·ly** *adv.*

be·wil·der·ment (bi·wil′dər·mənt) *n.* 1 A state or condition of being bewildered. 2 A confusion; entanglement. See synonyms under PERPLEXITY.

be·witch (bi·wich′) *v.t.* 1 To gain power over by charms or incantations. 2 To attract irresistibly; charm; fascinate. See synonyms under CHARM. **—be·witch′er** *n.* **—be·witch′·ment, be·witch′er·y** *n.*

be·witch·ing (bi·wich′ing) *adj.* Charming; captivating. See synonyms under BEAUTIFUL. **— be·witch′ing·ly** *adv.*

be·wray (bi·rā′) *v.t. Obs.* To disclose; betray.

[ME *bewreien* <*be-* + *wreien*, OE *wrēgan* accuse]
bey (bā) *n.* **1** The governor of a minor Turkish province or district. **2** A native ruler of Tunis. **3** A Turkish title of respect. Also spelled *beg.* ◆ Homophone: *bay.* [<Turkish *beg* lord] —**bey′i·cal** *adj.*
Beyle (bāl), **Marie Henri.** See STENDHAL.
bey·lik (bā′lik) *n.* **1** The authority of a bey. **2** The district ruled by a bey. Also **bey′lic.**
be·yond (bi·yond′) *prep.* **1** Farther or more distant than; on or to the far side of: the house *beyond* the turn of the road. **2** Extending further than: staying *beyond* his usual hour. **3** Out of the reach or scope of: Algebra is *beyond* me. **4** Surpassing; superior to; exceeding: a woman lovely *beyond* description. —*adv.* Farther on or away; at a distance. —**the (great) beyond** Whatever comes after death. [OE *begeondan* <*be-* near + *geondan* yonder]
Bey·routh (bā′rōōt, bā·rōōt′) See BEIRUT.
bez·ant (bez′ənt, bə·zant′) *n.* **1** The solidus (def. 1). **2** *Archit.* A flat disk used in ornamentation. Also spelled *byzant.* [<OF *besant* <L *Byzantius* Byzantine]
bez antler (bez, bāz) The second branch of a deer's antler, the one above the brow antler. Also **bez tine.** For illustration see ANTLER. [<OF *bes-* <L *bis* twice]
bez·el (bez′əl) *n.* **1** A bevel on the edge of a cutting tool. **2** That part of a cut gem which is above the girdle, including the table and surrounding facets. **3** A groove and flange made to receive a beveled edge, as of a watch crystal. **4** A flat, engraved gold seal. [? <OF. Cf. F *biseau.*]
Bé·ziers (bā·zyā′) A city in southern France.
be·zique (bə·zēk′) *n.* A game of cards based on the declaring of certain combinations upon taking a trick: also, such a combination in this game. [<F *bésigue*]
be·zoar (bē′zôr, -zōr) *n.* **1** A concretion found in the stomach and intestines of ruminants and some other animals, formerly supposed to have medicinal value. **2** *Obs.* An antidote or panacea. [<NL <Persian *pādzahr* <*pād* expelling + *zahr* poison]
Bha·ga·vad-Gi·ta (bug′ə·vəd·gē′tä) *n.* A sacred Hindu text consisting of philosophical dialog in the *Mahabharata,* expounding the duties of caste and the yoga doctrines of devotion to the Supreme Spirit. [<Skt., Song of the Blessed One (i.e., Krishna)]
Bha·mo (bä′mō) A district of Upper Burma; 4,148 square miles; capital, Bhamo.
bhang (bang) *n.* **1** Indian hemp. **2** The dried leaves and capsules of the Indian hemp: used for their intoxicant and narcotic properties. Also spelled *bang.* [<Hind. <Skt. *bhangā* hemp]
Bha·rat (bu′rut) The ancient name for INDIA.
Bhat·pa·ra (bät·pä′rə) A city in West Bengal, India; an ancient seat of Sanskrit learning.
Bhau·nag·ar (bou·nug′ər) **1** A former princely state on the west coast of India. **2** A port on the Gulf of Cambay; former capital of the state. Also **Bhav·nag′ar** (bou-).
bhees·tee (bēs′tē) *n.* In India, a native water carrier. Also **bhees′tie, bhis′tie.** [<Hind. *bhistī* <Persian *bihishti,* lit., one from heaven]
Bho·pal (bō·päl′) A chief commissioner's state in central India; 6,921 square miles; capital, Bhopal.
Bhu·ba·nes·war (bōō′və·nesh′vər) A town and pilgrimage site in eastern India; capital of Orissa. Also **Bhu′va·nesh′war.**
Bhu·tan (bōō·tän′) A semi-independent kingdom between NE India and Tibet; 18,000 square miles; capital Punaka.
Bhu·tan·ese (bōō′tən·ēz′, -ēs′) *n. pl.* **·ese 1** A native of Bhutan. **2** The Sino-Tibetan language of Bhutan. —*adj.* Of or pertaining to Bhutan, its people, or their language.
Bi *Chem.* Bismuth (symbol Bi).
bi- *prefix* **1** Twice; doubly; two; especially, occurring twice or having two; as in:

biangulate	**bicephalic**	**biradiate**
bicapitate	**biciliate**	**bispiral**
bicellular	**bicolumnar**	**bistipular**
bicentral	**biflorate**	**bistipulate**

2 *Chem.* **a** Having two equivalents of the substance named: *bichloride.* **b** Indicating the presence of the named component in double the ordinary proportion, or the doubling of a radical, etc., in an organic compound. Also: *bin-* before a vowel, as in *binaural; bis-* before *c, s,* as in *bissextile.* [<L *bi-* <*bis* twice]
bi·a·cu·mi·nate (bī′ə·kyōō′mə·nāt) *adj. Bot.* Two-pointed.
Bi·a·fra (bē·ä′frə), **Bight of** A bay of the western Gulf of Guinea, Africa.
Bi·ak (bē·yäk′) The largest of the Schouten Islands; 948 square miles.
Bia·lys·tok (byä·lis′tôk) A city in NE Poland. *Russian* **Be·lo·stok** (byi·lə·stôk′).
Bian·ca (byäng′kä) The Italian form of BLANCH.
Bian·co (byäng′kō), **Mon·te** (môn′tā) Italian name for MONT BLANC.
bi·an·gu·lar (bī·ang′gyə·lər) *adj.* Having two angles.
bi·an·nu·al (bī·an′yōō·əl) *adj.* Occurring twice a year; semiannual. —**bi·an′nu·al·ly** *adv.*
bi·an·nu·late (bī·an′yə·lāt, -lit) *adj. Zool.* Having two rings or bands, as of color.
Bi·ar·ritz (bē′ə·rits, *Fr.* byȧ·rēts′) A resort town in SW France on the Bay of Biscay.
bi·as (bī′əs) *n. pl.* **bi·as·es** or **bi·as·ses 1** A line, cut, or seam running obliquely across the threads of a fabric: a dress sewn on the *bias.* **2** A mental predilection or prejudice. See synonyms under INCLINATION, PREJUDICE. **3** *Electronics* A grid bias. **4** In bowling, a lopsided shape of a ball, causing it to swerve; also, the swerving course of such a ball. —*adj.* Cut, running, set, or folded diagonally; slanting. —*adv.* Slantingly; diagonally. —*v.t.* **bi·ased** or **bi·assed, bi·as·ing** or **bi·as·sing 1** To influence or affect unduly or unfairly. **2** *Electronics* To impose a steady negative potential upon (a grid). [<F *biais* oblique]
Bi·as (bē′äs) See BEAS.
bi·au·ric·u·lar (bī′ô·rik′yə·lər) *adj.* **1** Of or pertaining to two auricles. **2** Biauriculate. **3** Having two ears.
bi·au·ric·u·late (bī′ô·rik′yə·lit) *adj. Anat.* Having two auricles, as the heart.
bi·ax·i·al (bī·ak′sē·əl) *adj.* Having two axes, as a crystal. Also **bi·ax·al** (bī·ak′səl). —**bi·ax′i·al·ly** *adv.*
bib (bib) *v.t.* & *v.i.* **bibbed, bib·bing** *Obs.* To drink; tipple. —*n.* **1** A cloth worn under the chin by children at meals to catch drink or food that is dribbled. **2** A waistpiece attached to a woman's apron. **3** A bibcock. [<L *bibere* drink]
bib and tucker *Colloq.* Clothes.
bi·ba·sic (bī·bā′sik) *adj.* Dibasic.
bibb (bib) *n. Naut.* A cleat or bracket bolted to the hounds of a mast of a vessel to support the trestletrees. **2** A bibcock. [<BIB (*n.* def. 1)]
bib·ber (bib′ər) *n.* A tippler.
bib·cock (bib′kok′) *n.* A cock or faucet having the nozzle bent downward.
bibe·lot (bib′lō, *Fr.* bēb·lō′) *n.* A small, decorative, or curious article of virtu or object of art. [<F]
bi·bi·va·lent (bī′bī·vā′lənt, bī·biv′ə-) *adj. Chem.* Pertaining to or designating an electrolyte that breaks down into two bivalent ions.
Bi·ble (bī′bəl) *n.* **1** The writings of the Old and New Testaments, as accepted by the Christian Church as a divine revelation: in certain churches embracing also parts of the Apocrypha. **2** A copy of this. **3** The Old Testament Scriptures in the form accepted by the Jews. **4** Any book, record, or history considered authoritative: in this sense usually not capitalized. —**Douai Bible** An English translation of the Latin Vulgate by members of the English College at Douai, 1582–1610; revised and altered for modern use in the Roman Catholic Church: also **Douay Bible.** —**King James Bible** A revision of the English Bible proposed by King James I in 1604, the work of 50 revisors, published in 1611; the most widely used Protestant version of the Bible in English-speaking countries: also called *Authorized Version.* Compare REVISED VERSION. [<OF <L *biblia* <Gk., pl. of *biblion* book]
Bible paper See INDIA PAPER.
Bib·li·cal (bib′li·kəl) *adj.* **1** Pertaining to, like, quoted, or derived from the Bible. **2** In harmony with the Bible. Also **bib′li·cal.** —**Bib′li·cal·ly** *adv.*
Bib·li·cist (bib′lə·sist) *n.* **1** A person thoroughly versed in the Bible. **2** One who adheres to the letter of the Bible.
biblio- *combining form* Of or pertaining to a book or books, or to the Bible: *bibliophile, bibliomancy.* [<Gk. *biblion* book]
bib·li·o·film (bib′lē·ə·film′) *n.* A kind of microfilm used especially to reproduce rare or much-used books, etc.
bib·li·og·ra·phy (bib′lē·og′rə·fē) *n. pl.* **·phies 1** The description and history of books including details of authorship, editions, dates, typography, etc.; also a book containing such descriptions. **2** A list of the works of an author, or of the literature bearing on a particular subject. —**bib′li·og′ra·pher, bib′li·o·graph′** *n.* —**bib·li·o·graph·ic** (bib′lē·ə·graf′ik) or **·i·cal** *adj.* [<BIBLIO- + -GRAPHY]
bib·li·ol·a·try (bib′lē·ol′ə·trē) *n.* **1** Extravagant homage paid to the letter of the Bible. **2** Excessive worship of books. [<BIBLIO- + Gk. *latreia* worship] —**bib′li·ol′a·ter** *n.* —**bib′li·ol′a·trous** *adj.*
bib·li·o·man·cy (bib′lē·ō·man′sē) *n.* Divination by means of reference to some passage taken at random from a book, usually the Bible.
bib·li·o·ma·ni·a (bib′lē·ō·mā′nē·ə) *n.* An intense passion for collecting and owning books. —**bib′li·o·ma′ni·ac** (-ak) *n.* & *adj.*
bib·li·op·e·gy (bib′lē·op′ə·jē) *n.* The art or practice of bookbinding. [<*biblio-* + Gk. *pēgnynai* fasten, join]
bib·li·o·phile (bib′lē·ə·fīl′, -fil′) *n.* One who loves books. Also **bib′li·o·phil′** (fil′), **bib·li·oph·i·list** (bib′lē·of′ə·list). —**bib′li·oph′i·lism** *n.* —**bib′li·oph′i·lis′tic** *adj.*
bib·li·o·pole (bib′lē·ə·pōl′) *n.* A dealer in rare books. Also **bib·li·op·o·list** (bib′lē·op′ə·list). [<L *bibliopola* <Gk. *bibliopōlēs* bookseller <*biblion* book + *pōleein* sell] —**bib′li·o·pol′ic** (-pol′ik) or **·i·cal** *adj.* —**bib′li·op′o·lism** *n.*
bib·li·o·ther·a·py (bib′lē·ō·ther′ə·pē) *n. Pathol.* The treatment of certain nervous and mental disorders by the reading of selected books. —**bib′li·o·ther′a·pist** *n.*
Bib·list (bib′list, bī′blist) *n.* A Biblicist.
bib·u·lous (bib′yə·ləs) *adj.* **1** Given to drink; fond of drinking. **2** Taking up moisture readily; absorbent. [<L *bibulus* drinking readily <*bibere* drink] —**bib′u·los′i·ty** (-los′ə·tē) *n.* —**bib′u·lous·ly** *adv.* —**bib′u·lous·ness** *n.*
bi·cam·er·al (bī·kam′ər·əl) *adj.* Consisting of two chambers, houses, or branches, as a legislature.
bi·cap·su·lar (bī·kap′sə·lər, -syə-) *adj. Bot.* **1** Having two capsules. **2** Having a two-celled capsule.
bi·car·bo·nate (bī·kär′bə·nit, -nāt) *n. Chem.* A salt of carbonic acid in which one of the hydrogen atoms is replaced by a metal: sodium *bicarbonate.*
bice (bīs) *n.* **1** A blue or green pigment made from varieties of basic copper carbonate ore. **bice green** is now usually called malachite green and **blue bice,** azurite. **2** The color of any of these pigments. [<OF *bis* dark-colored]
bi·cen·te·nar·y (bī·sen′tə·ner′ē, bī′sen·ten′ər·ē) *adj.* **1** Occurring once in 200 years. **2** Lasting or consisting of 200 years. —*n. pl.* **·nar·ies 1** A period of 200 years. **2** A 200th anniversary. Also **bi·cen·ten·ni·al** (bī′sen·ten′ē·əl).
bi·ceph·a·lous (bī·sef′ə·ləs) *adj. Biol.* Having two heads.
bi·ceps (bī′seps) *n. pl.* **bi·ceps** *Anat.* **1** The large front muscle, or flexor, of the upper arm, the **biceps bra·chi·i** (brā′kē·ī). **2** The large flexor muscle at the back of the thigh, the **biceps cru·ris** (krōōr′is). **3** Loosely, muscular strength. [<L, two-headed <*bis* twofold + *caput* head]
Bi·chat (bē·shȧ′), **Marie François Xavier,** 1771–1802, French anatomist; founder of histology.
biche (bēch) *n.* A Mexican hairless dog. [<Nahuatl, naked]
bi·chlo·ride (bī·klôr′īd, -id, -klō′rīd, -rid) *n. Chem.* **1** A salt in which there are two atoms of chlorine. **2** Bichloride of mercury, or corrosive sublimate, a dangerous poison used as a disinfectant.
bi·chro·mate (bī·krō′māt, -mit) *n. Chem.* **1** Dichromate. **2** Potassium dichromate.
bi·cip·i·tal (bī·sip′ə·təl) *adj. Anat.* **1** Having

two heads. 2 Pertaining to the biceps. Also **bi·cip′i·tous** (-təs).

bick·er[1] (bik′ər) *v.i.* 1 To dispute petulantly; wrangle. 2 To flow noisily, as a brook; gurgle. 3 To flicker, as a flame; twinkle. —*n.* 1 A petulant or angry dispute; a petty altercation: also **bick·er·ing.** 2 A clattering, babbling noise. 3 A flicker, or a tremulous or unsteady motion. See synonyms under QUARREL. [ME *bikeren;* origin uncertain] —**bick′er·er** *n.*

bick·er[2] (bik′ər) *n. Scot.* A wooden vessel for food or drink. [Var. of BEAKER]

Bi·col (bi·kōl′) *n.* 1 One of a Malayan people, inhabiting SE Luzon and professing Christianity before the Spanish conquest. 2 The Indonesian language of these people. Also spelled *Bikol.*

bi·col·or (bī′kul′ər) *adj.* Having two colors.

bi·con·cave (bī·kon′kāv, -kong′-, bī′kon·kāv′) *adj.* Concave on both sides.

bi·con·vex (bī·kon′veks, bī′kon·veks′) *adj.* Convex on both sides.

bi·corn (bī′kôrn) *n.* 1 A two-cornered, crescent-shaped hat with upturned brim; specifically, the two-cornered hat worn by French gendarmes: also **bi·corne.** 2 A two-horned animal: compare UNICORN. —*adj.* Two-horned; two-pronged; having two hornlike projections: also **bi·cor·nous** (bī·kôr′nəs), **bi·cor·nu·ate** (bī·kôr′nyōō·āt). [< L *bicornis* < *bis* twofold + *cornus* horn]

bi·cor·po·ral (bī·kôr′pər·əl) *adj.* Double-bodied, as certain signs of the zodiac. Also **bi·cor·po·re·al** (bī′kôr·pôr′ē·əl, -pō′rē-).

bi·cron (bī′kron) *n.* The one-billionth part of a meter; micromillimeter.

bi·cul·tur·al·ism (bī·kul′chə·rə·liz′əm) *n.* The policy of union between two separate cultures within one nation.

bi·cus·pid (bī·kus′pid) *adj.* 1 Having two cusps or points. 2 Double-pointed, as a premolar tooth, the valve at the left auricular opening of the heart, or a curve or crescent: also **bi·cus′pi·dal** (-dəl), **bi·cus′pi·date** (-dāt). —*n.* A premolar tooth, of which there are eight in the normal human jaws, two between each cuspid and the first molar tooth. Also **bi·cus′pis.** [< L *bis* twofold + *cuspis, -idis* point]

bi·cy·cle (bī′sik·əl) *n.* A two-wheeled vehicle with the wheels in tandem, a saddle or saddles, a steering handle, and propelled by foot pedals or a motor. —*v.i.* **·cled, ·cling** To ride a bicycle. Also *cycle.* [< L *bis* twofold + Gk. *kyklos* wheel] —**bi′cy·cler, bi′cy·clist** *n.*

bi·cy·clic (bī·sī′klik, -sik′lik) *adj.* 1 Pertaining to bicycles or bicycling. 2 *Bot.* Disposed in two cycles or whorls: also **bi·cy′cli·cal.**

bid (bid) *n.* 1 An offer to pay or accept a price. 2 The amount offered. 3 In card games, the number of tricks or points that a player engages to make; also, a player's turn to bid. 4 An effort to acquire, win, or attain: He made a *bid* for the governorship. 5 *Colloq.* An invitation. —*v.* **bade** (*Archaic* **bad**) *for defs.* 3, 4, 6 or **bid** *for defs.* 1, 2, 5, 7, **bid·den** or **bid, bid·ding** *v.t.* 1 To make an offer of (a price), as at an auction or for a contract. 2 In card games, to declare (the number of tricks one will engage to take) and specify (the trump suit or no-trump under which the hand will be played): I *bid* six spades. 3 To command; order. 4 To invite. 5 *U.S. Colloq.* To invite to join: The fraternity will *bid* you. 6 To utter, as a greeting or farewell: I *bid* you good day. —*v.i.* 7 To offer a price. —**to bid fair** To seem probable. —**to bid in** At an auction, to attempt to raise the price (of an object) by competing with spurious bids. —**to bid up** To increase the price by offering higher bids. [Fusion of OE *biddan* ask, demand and *bēodan* proclaim, command]

bi·dar·ka (bī·där′kə) *n.* A skin-covered canoe used by natives of Alaska. [< Russian *baidarka,* dim. of *baidara* canoe]

Bi·dault (bē·dō′), **Georges**, born 1899, French statesman.

bid·da·ble (bid′ə·bəl) *adj.* 1 Of sufficient value to offer a bid on, as a bridge hand. 2 Inclined to do as bidden; obedient; docile.

bid·der (bid′ər) *n.* 1 One who makes a bid. 2 In contract bridge, the player who first names the trump suit, or no-trump, in which a hand is played; the declarer.

bid·ding (bid′ing) *n.* 1 A notification or command. 2 A solicitation or invitation. 3 The making of a bid or bids, as at a sale, in the game of contract bridge, etc.; bids collectively.

Bid·dle (bid′l) A prominent Philadelphia family, including **Nicholas**, 1786–1844, financier; **Francis**, 1886–1968 U.S. attorney general 1941–45; **George**, 1885–1973 brother of Francis, painter. —**John**, 1615–62, founder of Unitarianism in England.

bid·dy[1] (bid′ē) *n. pl.* **·dies** A chicken; especially, a hen. [Origin uncertain]

bid·dy[2] (bid′ē) *n. pl.* **·dies** *U.S. Colloq.* A female domestic; strictly, an Irish servant girl. [< BIDDY]

Bid·dy (bid′ē) Diminutive of BRIDGET.

bide (bīd) *v.* **bid·ed** (*Archaic* **bode**), **bid·ing** *v.t.* 1 To endure; withstand: to *bide* a storm. 2 *Archaic* To tolerate; submit to. —*v.i.* 3 To dwell; abide; stay. —**to bide one's time** To await the most favorable opportunity. See synonyms under ABIDE. [OE *bīdan* wait, stay]

bi·den·tate (bī·den′tāt) *adj.* Having two teeth or toothlike processes. Also **bi·den′tal.**

bi·det (bi·dā′) *n.* A small porcelain commode with running water, used for cleansing the genital and anal areas. [< F]

bi·di·a·lect·al·ism (bī′dī·ə·lek′tə·liz′əm) *n.* The use of two distinct dialects of a single language.

bid·ing (bī′ding) *n.* 1 An awaiting; expectation. 2 Residence; habitation.

bid·ri (bid′rē) *n.* An alloy of copper, lead, and tin used for making **bidri ware**, an Indian ware damascened with silver or gold. Also **bid′ree, bid′der·y.** [from *Bidar,* town in India]

Bie·der·mei·er (bē′dər·mī′ər) *adj.* Of or pertaining to a style of German furniture of the first half of the 19th century, based on French Empire forms. [after Gottlieb *Biedermeier,* character invented by L. Eichrodt, 1827–92, German poet]

Bie·la (bē′lä), **Baron Wilhelm von**, 1782–1856, German astronomer.

bield (bēld) *Scot. v.t.* To protect. —*n.* A shelter. —**bield′y** *adj.*

Bie·le·feld (bē′lə·felt) A city in NW Germany.

Bie·lid (bē′lid) See ANDROMED.

bien (bēn) *adj. Scot.* 1 Well-to-do; comfortably off, as a farmer. 2 Comfortably furnished; cosy, as a house. Also spelled *bein.* [< F *bien* well]

bien en·ten·du (byaṅ näṅ·täṅ·dü′) *French* Of course; lit., well understood.

bi·en·ni·al (bī·en′ē·əl) *adj.* 1 Occurring every second year. 2 Lasting or living for two years. —*n.* 1 *Bot.* A plant that produces leaves and roots the first year and flowers and fruit the second, then dies. 2 An event occurring once in two years. [< L *biennis* < *bis* twofold + *annus* year] —**bi·en′ni·al·ly** *adv.*

bien·ve·nue (byaṅ·və·nü′) *n. French* A welcome.

Bien·ville (byaṅ·vēl′), **Sieur de**, Jean Baptiste Le Moyne, 1680–1768, French governor of Louisiana and founder of New Orleans.

bier[1] (bir) *n.* A framework for carrrying a corpse to the grave; a coffin. ◆ Homophone: *beer.* [OE *bǽr*]

bier[2] (bēr) *n. German* Beer.

Bierce (birs), **Ambrose Gwinnett**, 1842–1914?, U.S. journalist and author.

Bie·rut (bye′rōōt), **Bo·le·slaw** (bô·le′släf), born 1892, president of Poland 1947–52; premier 1952–54.

biest·ings (bēs′tingz) *n.* Beestings.

bi·fa·cial (bī·fā′shəl) *adj.* 1 Having two fronts, as an effigy on a medal. 2 *Bot.* Having the opposite faces unlike, as a leaf. 3 Being alike on the opposite surfaces.

bi·far·i·ous (bī·fâr′ē·əs) *adj.* 1 Two-ranked. 2 *Bot.* Disposed in two vertical rows, as leaves on a branch. [< LL *bifarius* double < *bis* twofold + *fari* speak] —**bi·far′i·ous·ly** *adv.*

biff (bif) *Slang v.t.* To give a blow. —*n.* A whack; blow. [Imit.]

bif·fin (bif′in) *n. Brit.* 1 A cooking apple: a Norfolk *biffin.* 2 A baked apple flattened into a cake. [Var. of BEEFING]

bi·fid (bī′fid) *adj.* Doubly cleft: forked. Also **bif·i·date** (bif′i·dāt), **bif′i·dat′ed.** [< L *bifidus* < *bis* twofold + *findere* split] —**bi·fid·i·ty** (bī·fid′ə·tē) *n.* —**bi′fid·ly** *adv.*

bi·fi·lar (bī·fī′lər) *adj.* Formed of, having, or supported by two threads. —*n.* A bifilar micrometer. [< BI- + L *filum* thread] —**bi·fi′lar·ly** *adv.*

bi·flag·el·late (bī·flaj′ə·lāt) *adj. Zool.* Having two flagella or whiplike processes.

bi·flex (bī′fleks) *adj.* Bent in two places; alternately convex and concave. [< BI- + L *flexus,* pp. of *flectere* bend]

bi·fo·cal (bī·fō′kəl) *adj. Optics* Having two foci: said of a lens ground of both near and far vision. [< BI- + L *focus* hearth, focus of a lens]

bi·fo·cals (bī·fō′kəlz, bī′fō·kəlz) *n. pl.* Eyeglasses with bifocal lenses ground for distant vision in the upper portion of the lenses and for near vision in the lower.

bi·fold (bī′fōld′) *adj.* Twofold.

bi·fo·li·ate (bī·fō′lē·it) *adj. Bot.* Having two leaves.

bi·fo·li·o·late (bī·fō′lē·ə·lāt′) *adj. Bot.* Having two leaflets.

bi·fo·rate (bī·fôr′āt, -fō′rāt) *adj.* Having two perforations. [< BI- + L *foratus,* pp. of *forare* bore]

bi·forked (bī′fôrkt′) *adj.* Bifurcate.

bi·form (bī′fôrm′) *adj.* Having or combining the characteristics of two distinct forms, as the Minotaur. Also **bi′formed′.**

Bif·rost (bēf′rost) In Norse mythology, the bridge of the rainbow between Asgard and Midgard.

bi·fur·cate (bī′fər·kāt, bī·fûr′kāt) *v.t. & v.i.* **·cat·ed, ·cat·ing** To fork; divide into two branches or stems. —*adj.* (bī′fər·kāt, bī·fûr′·kit) Forked: also **bi′fur·cat′ed, bi·fur·cous** (bī·fûr′kəs). [< BI- + L *furca* fork] —**bi′fur·cate·ly** (-kit·lē) *adv.* —**bi′fur·ca′tion** *n.*

big[1] (big) *adj.* **big·ger, big·gest** 1 Of great size, amount, or intensity; large; bulky. 2 Fruitful; pregnant. 3 Full to overflowing; teeming. 4 Puffed up; pompous. 5 Important: a *big* day in his life. 6 Generous; magnanimous. See synonyms under LARGE. —*adj. Colloq.* Pompously; extravagantly: to talk *big.* [ME; origin uncertain] —**big′gish** *adj.* —**big′ly** *adv.* —**big′ness** *n.*

big[2] (big) *v.t. & v.i. Scot.* To build. Also **bigg.**

big·a·mist (big′ə·mist) *n.* One guilty of bigamy.

big·a·mous (big′ə·məs) *adj.* 1 Guilty of or living in bigamy. 2 Involving bigamy. —**big′a·mous·ly** *adv.*

big·a·my (big′ə·mē) *n.* The criminal offense of marrying any other person while having a legal spouse living. [< OF *bigamie* < LL *bigamus* < *bis* twice + Gk. *gamos* wedding]—**bi·gam·ic** (bī·gam′ik) *adj.*

big·ar·reau (big′ə·rō, big′ə·rō′) *n.* A type of sweet, firm-fleshed, heart-shaped cherry. Also **big·a·roon** (big′ə·rōōn′). [< F < *bigarré,* pp. of *bigarrer* variegate]

big bang theory Astronomical theory that the universe began in a single, gigantic explosion of flammable gases.

Big Ben 1 A bell which strikes the hour in the Westminster clock in the tower of the Houses of Parliament, London. 2 The clock itself.

Big Bend National Park A government reservation (1,082 square miles) in westernmost Texas, established in 1944 in **Big Bend**, the wide angle of the Rio Grande forming the Mexican border.

Big Dipper A group of seven stars resembling a dipper in outline in the constellation Ursa Major.

Big-end·i·an (big·en′dē·ən) *n.* A partisan in small matters of dispute: from Swift's *Gulliver's Travels,* in which one religious party (the *Big-endians*) of Lilliput opposed the other (the Little-endians) by maintaining that boiled eggs should be broken at the big end.

bigg (big) *n. Scot.* 1 The four-rowed barley (*Hordeum vulgare*), a hardy species grown in high latitudes. 2 Loosely, barley. Also **big.** [< ON *bygg*]

big game 1 Large wild animals hunted for sport. 2 *Colloq.* The objective of any important or difficult undertaking.

big·gin (big′in) *n.* 1 A head covering; especially, a child's cap. 2 *Brit.* The coif of a sergeant at law. 3 *Brit. Dial.* A nightcap. [< F *beguin* cap, orig. worn by the Beguines]

big·ging (big′in) *n. Scot.* 1 A house; residence. 2 The act of building. Also **big′gin.** [< BIG[2]]

big·gi·ty (big′ə·tē) *adj. U.S. Dial.* Conceited; pompous; uppity.

big·head (big′hed′) *n.* 1 *Colloq.* Inflated conceit; pomposity. 2 A bulging of the skull of an animal, due to osteomalacia. 3 A contagious inflammation of the lungs and intestines of young turkeys.

big·head·ed fly (big′hed′id) A fly (family *Pipunculidae*) with a large hemispherical head

almost completely covered by two large compound eyes. The larvae destroy leafhoppers. See illustration under INSECT (beneficial).

big-heart·ed (big′här′tid) *adj.* Generous; charitable.

big·horn (big′hôrn′) *n.* *pl.* **·horns** or **·horn** The Rocky Mountain sheep (*Ovis canadensis*), remarkable for its large horns: also called *American argali.*

Bighorn Mountains A range of the Rockies in southern Montana and northern Wyoming; highest peak, 13,165 feet.

Bighorn River A river in northern Wyoming and southern Montana, flowing north 461 miles to the Yellowstone River.

bight (bīt) *n.* **1** A slightly receding bay; a small recess in a bay. **2** A bend in a river, or the like. **3** A loop or turn in a rope, as around a post, the two ends being fast. **4** A bending or angle. —*v.t.* To secure (a load, sail, etc.) as with a bight. ◆ Homophone: *bite.* [OE *byht* corner, bay < *būgan* bend]

Big Inch A 24-inch oil pipeline, 1,400 miles from Longview, Texas, to the Atlantic seaboard.

big money *U.S. Colloq.* A large amount of money; huge profits.

big·no·ni·a (big·nō′nē·ə) *n.* Any of a genus (*Bignonia*) of woody climbing plants, mostly of tropical America, with clusters of large, trumpet-shaped flowers. [after A. J. *Bignon,* 1711–72, librarian to Louis XV]

big·no·ni·a·ceous (big·nō′nē·ā′shəs) *adj.* Of or belonging to the *Bignoniaceae,* or bignonia family, a large group of trees, shrubs, and woody vines characterized by trumpet-shaped flowers.

big·ot (big′ət) *n.* An illiberal or intolerant adherent of a religious creed or of any party or opinion. [<F]

big·ot·ed (big′ət·id) *adj.* Stubbornly attached to a creed, party, system, or opinion. —**big′·ot·ed·ly** *adv.*

big·ot·ry (big′ət·rē) *n.* *pl.* **·ries** Obstinate and intolerant attachment to a cause or creed. See synonyms under FANATICISM.

big shot *Slang* A person of importance.

Big Stone Lake A narrow lake between NE South Dakota and western Minnesota; 25 miles long.

Big Thomp·son River (tomp′sən) A river in northern Colorado, flowing 78 miles east to the South Platte River.

big top *U.S. Colloq.* The main tent of a circus.

big tree The redwood of California.

big wheel *U.S. Slang* A person of importance.

big·wig (big′wig′) *n.* *Colloq.* A person of importance: in allusion to the big wigs formerly worn by people of consequence in England.

Bi·har (bi·här′) **1** A constituent state of NE India; 70,368 square miles; capital, Patna; formerly **Bihar and Orissa,** a province of British India. **2** A city in north central Bihar.

Bi·ha·ri (bi·hä′rē) *n.* **1** A native of Bihar. **2** The Sanskritic language spoken in NE India, belonging to the Indic branch of the Indo-Iranian languages.

bi-hour·ly (bī·our′lē) *adj.* Occuring once in two hours.

Biisk (bēsk) See BISK.

bi·jou (bē′zhōō, bē·zhōō′) *n.* *pl.* **bi·joux** (bē′·zhōōz, bē·zhōōz′) A jewel; a trinket. [<F]

bi·jou·te·rie (bē·zhōō′tər·ē) *n.* Jewelry; especially, an article of fine workmanship.

bi·ju·gate (bī′jōō·gāt, bī·jōō′git) *adj. Bot.* Two-paired, as a pinnate leaf with two pairs of leaflets. Also **bi·ju·gous** (bī′jōō·gəs).

Bi·ka·ner (bē′kə·nēr′) A city in northern Rajasthan; former capital of a princely state of the same name now included in Rajasthan.

bike[1] (bīk) *n.* *Colloq.* A bicycle. [Alter. of BICYCLE]

bike[2] (bīk) *n.* *Scot.* A nest or swarm of wild bees, wasps, ants, etc.; hence, a swarm; a crowd: also spelled *byke, beik.*

bi·ki·ni (bi·kē′nē) *n.* An extremely abbreviated or scanty bathing suit.

Bi·ki·ni (bi·kē′nē) An atoll in the Marshall islands; 2 square miles; site of U.S. atomic bomb tests, July 1946.

Bi·kol (bi·kōl′) *n.* Bicol.

bi·la·bi·al (bī·lā′bē·əl) *adj.* **1** *Phonet.* Articulated with both lips, as certain consonants. **2** Having two lips. —*n.* *Phonet.* A speech sound formed with both lips, as (b), (p), (m), and (w).

bi·la·bi·ate (bī·lā′bē·āt, -it) *adj. Bot.* Two-lipped: said of a corolla.

bil·an·der (bil′ən·dər, bī′lən-) *n.* A small two-masted vessel having a lateen mainsail: used principally on the canals in the Low Countries. [<Du. *bylander*]

bi·lat·er·al (bī·lat′ər·əl) *adj.* Pertaining to two sides; two-sided: a *bilateral* agreement. —**bi·lat′er·al·ly** *adv.* —**bi·lat′er·al·ness** *n.*

Bil·ba·o (bil·bä′ō) A port in northern Spain on **Bilbao Bay,** an inlet of the Bay of Biscay.

bil·ber·ry (bil′ber′ē, -bər·ē) *n.* **1** The European whortleberry. **2** Its blue-black fruit. [<Scand. Cf. Dan. *böllebær*]

bil·bo (bil′bō) *n.* *pl.* **·boes** **1** A finely tempered Spanish sword made at Bilbao. **2** A fetter consisting of two sliding shackles attached to an iron bar. [from BILBAO]

bile (bīl) *n.* **1** *Physiol.* A bitter viscid fluid, yellowish in man and green in herbivores, secreted by the liver. **2** Anger; peevishness. [<L *bilis* bile, anger]

bi·lec·tion (bī·lek′shən) *n.* Bolection.

bile ducts *Physiol.* The excretory ducts of the gall bladder.

bile·stone (bīl′stōn′) *n.* *Pathol.* A biliary calculus; gallstone.

bilge (bilj) *n.* **1** *Naut.* The rounded part of a ship's bottom; specifically, that part extending from the keel to the point from which the sides rise vertically. **2** The bulge of a barrel. **3** Bilge water. **4** *Slang* Stupid or trivial chatter or writing. —*v.t.* & *v.i.* **bilged, bilg·ing** **1** To break open the bottom of (a vessel). **2** To bulge or cause to bulge. [Var. of BULGE]

bilge·keel (bilj′kēl′) *n.* *Naut.* An outside keel set lengthwise on each side of the bilge of a vessel to lessen rolling. Also **bilge′piece′.**

bilge water Foul water that collects in the bilge of a ship.

bilg·y (bil′jē) *adj.* Resembling bilge water, as in smell.

bil·har·zi·a·sis (bil′här·zī′ə·sis) *n.* Schistosomiasis. [after Theodore M. *Bilharz,* 1825–1862, German parasitologist]

bil·i·ar·y (bil′ē·er′ē) *adj.* Pertaining to or conveying bile.

bi·lin·e·ar (bī·lin′ē·ər) *adj.* Formed of or related to two lines.

bi·lin·gual (bī·ling′gwəl) *adj.* **1** Recorded or expressed in two languages. **2** Speaking two languages. —**bi·lin′gual·ly** *adv.* —**bi·lin′gual·ism** *n.*

bil·ious (bil′yəs) *adj.* **1** *Pathol.* Suffering from real or supposed disorder of the liver. **2** Of, pertaining to, containing, or consisting of bile. **3** Ill-natured; cross. [<F *bilieux* <L *biliosus*] —**bil′ious·ly** *adv.* —**bil′ious·ness** *n.*

bi·lit·er·al (bī·lit′ər·əl) *adj.* Composed of two letters. —**bi·lit′er·al·ism** *n.*

-bility *suffix* Forming nouns of quality from adjectives in *-ble*: *probability* from *probable.* [<F *-bilité* <L *-bilitas, -tatis*]

bilk (bilk) *v.t.* **1** To cheat; swindle; evade payment to. **2** To escape; dodge. **3** To balk. —*n.* **1** A swindler; deadbeat. **2** A trick; a hoax. [Origin unknown] —**bilk′er** *n.*

bill[1] (bil) *n.* **1** A statement of an account or of money due. **2** A banknote or treasury note: a ten-dollar *bill.* **3** A list of items: a *bill* of fare. **4** The draft of a proposed law. **5** *Law* A paper filed in a court calling for some specific action. **6** Some public notice or advertisement; the program of a theatrical performance. **7** *Brit.* A bill of exchange. **8** Loosely, a promissory note. **9** In Scots law, a petition to the court of sessions. **10** *Obs.* Any writing; a billet; petition. See synonyms under MONEY. —*v.t.* **1** To enter in a bill; charge. **2** To present a bill to. **3** To advertise by bills or placards. [<LL *billa,* var. of *bulla.* See BULL[2].]

bill[2] (bil) *n.* A beak, as of a bird. —*v.i.* To join bills, as doves; caress. —**to bill and coo** To caress lovingly; make love in soft murmuring tones. [OE *bile*]

bill[3] (bil) *n.* **1** A hook-shaped instrument used by gardeners in pruning: also **bill′hook′.** **2** An ancient weapon with a hook-shaped blade; a halberd. **3** The point or peak of the fluke of an anchor. [OE *bill* sword, ax]

bill[4] (bil) *n.* **1** A bellow or roar. **2** A boom, as of the bittern. [Var. of BELL[2]]

Bill (bil) Diminutive of WILLIAM.

bill·a·ble (bil′ə·bəl) *adj.* Indictable.

bil·la·bong (bil′ə·bong) *n.* *Austral.* **1** A blind branch or channel leading from a river; an incomplete anabranch. **2** A pool of stagnant water or the backwaters of a stream. [<native Australian *billa* water + *bong* dead]

bill·board (bil′bôrd′, -bōrd′) *n.* A board, panel, or tablet intended for the display of posters or placards; a bulletin board.

bil·let[1] (bil′it) *n.* **1** A written missive; a note. **2** A requisition on a household to maintain a soldier. **3** The place where soldiers are so lodged. **4** *Brit.* A position; appointment. —*v.t.* & *v.i.* **1** To lodge (soldiers), or to be quartered or lodged, in a private house. **2** To serve with a missive. [<OF *billete,* dim. of *bille* <L *bulla* seal, document] —**bil′let·er** *n.*

bil·let[2] (bil′it) *n.* **1** A stick, as of firewood. **2** Any short, thick stick. **3** *Archit.* One of a series of short, cylindrical ornaments, forming part of a molding. **4** A harness strap that passes through a buckle; also, the loop or pocket for receiving such a strap after it passes through the buckle. **5** *Metall.* A bloom of iron or steel drawn into a small bar. [<OF *billete,* dim. of *bille* log]

bil·let d'a·mour (bē·ye dà·mōōr′) *French* Love letter; billet-doux.

bil·let-doux (bil′ē·dōō′, *Fr.* bē·ye·dōō′) *n.* *pl.* **bil·lets-doux** (bil′ē·dōōz′, *Fr.* bē·ye·dōō′) A love letter; lover's note. [<F, lit., sweet note]

bill·fish (bil′fish′) *n.* *pl.* **·fish** or **·fish·es** One of various fishes having elongated jaws; especially, the saury or skipper, or the spearfish.

bill·fold (bil′fōld′) *n.* A folding case for paper money.

bill·head (bil′hed′) *n.* A heading on paper used for making out bills or itemized statements.

bil·liard (bil′yərd) *n.* *U.S. Colloq.* A carom. —*adj.* Of or pertaining to billiards: *billiard* cue, *billiard* player.

bil·liards (bil′yərdz) *n.* A game played with hard elastic or ivory balls (**billiard balls**) propelled by cues on an oblong, cloth-covered, cushion-edged table. [<F *billard* <OF *billart* cue < *bille* log] —**bil′liard·ist** *n.*

bill·ing (bil′ing) *n.* **1** The listing of performers or acts on a theater billboard, playbill, etc. **2** The relative eminence given to an actor or an act on such a listing.

Bil·lings (bil′ingz), **Josh** Pen name of Henry Wheeler Shaw, 1818–85, U.S. humorist.

bil·lings·gate (bil′ingz·gāt) *n.* Vulgar and abusive language. [from *Billingsgate* fish market, London]

bil·lion (bil′yən) *n.* **1** A thousand millions (1,000,000,000). **2** *Brit.* A million millions (1,000,000,000,000). [<F] —**bil·lionth** (bil′·yənth) *adj.* & *n.*

bil·lion·aire (bil′yən·âr′) *n.* One who owns property worth a billion of money.

Bil·li·ton (bi·lē′ton) See BELITUNG.

Bill·jim (bil′jim) *n.* The typical Australian: a nickname.

bill of exchange. See under EXCHANGE.

bill of fare A list of the dishes provided at a meal; a menu.

bill of health An official certificate of the crew's health issued to a ship's master on departure from a port.

bill of lading A written acknowledgment of goods received for transportation.

bill of rights **1** A formal summary and declaration of the fundamental principles of government and of the rights of individuals. **2** *Often cap.* The first ten amendments to the U.S. Constitution. **3** *Often cap.* The declaration of rights setting forth those fundamental principles of the British constitution, the observance of which was to be imposed upon William and Mary upon their acceptance of the crown in 1689.

bill of sale An instrument by which the transfer of title to personal property is declared and established.

bil·lon (bil′ən) *n.* **1** An alloy of gold or silver with some baser metal, generally copper or tin. **2** A low alloy of silver with a large proportion of copper, used in making tokens and medals. [<F <OF *bille* log]

bil·low (bil′ō) *n.* **1** A great wave of the sea; a

storm wave. 2 Any wave, as of sound, etc. 3 *pl.* The sea. — *v.i.* To rise or roll in billows; surge; swell. [<ON *bylgja*] — **bil′low·y** *adj.* — **bil′low·i·ness** *n.*

bill·post·er (bil′pōs′tər) *n.* A person whose occupation it is to post bills on walls, fences, etc. Also **bill′stick′er.** — **bill′post′ing, bill′·stick′ing** *n.*

bil·ly[1] (bil′ē) *n. pl.* **bil·lies** 1 A short bludgeon; a policeman's club. 2 A slubbing machine, used in the manufacture of textiles. [<*Billy,* a nickname for William]

bil·ly[2] (bil′ē) *n. Scot.* A comrade; crony; chum; also, a young fellow. Also **bil′lie.**

bil·ly[3] (bil′ē) *n. Austral.* A can used for heating water. [<native Australian *billa* water]

bil·ly·cock (bil′ē·kok′) *n. Brit.* A low-crowned felt hat; derby. Also **billycock hat.**

billy goat A male goat.

Billy the Kid Sobriquet of William H. Bonney, 1859–81, notorious Western cattle thief and murderer.

bi·lo·bate (bī·lō′bāt) *adj.* Divided into or having two lobes. Also **bi·lo′bat·ed.**

bi·lo·ca·tion (bī′lō·kā′shən) *n.* The power of being in two places at the same time.

bi·loc·u·lar (bī·lok′yə·lər) *adj. Biol.* Two-celled; divided into two cells.

Bi·lox·i (bi·lok′sē) *n.* One of a tribe of North American Indians of Siouan stock.

Bi·lox·i (bi·lok′sē) A city in SE Mississippi, on a peninsula in **Biloxi Bay,** an arm of Mississippi Sound.

bil·sted (bil′sted) *n. U.S.* The sweetgum.

bil·tong (bil′tong) *n.* Dried and cured meat of the ox, antelope, or buffalo, cut into strips and eaten raw. [<Afrikaans *bil* buttock + *tong* tongue; because it is cut mostly from the rump and resembles smoked tongue]

bim·a·nous (bim′ə·nəs, bī·mā′-) *adj.* Two-handed. [<NL *bimanus* <L *bis* twofold + *manus* hand]

bi·man·u·al (bī·man′yōō·əl) *adj.* Employing both hands. — **bi·man′u·al·ly** *adv.*

bi·men·sal (bī·men′səl) *adj.* Bimonthly.

bi·mes·tri·al (bī·mes′trē·əl) *adj.* Lasting two months. [<L *bimestris*]

bi·met·al·ism (bī·met′əl·iz′əm) *n.* The concurrent use of both gold and silver as the standard of currency and value. Also **bi·met′·al·lism.** — **bi·met′al·ist, bi·met′al·list** *n.*

bi·me·tal·lic (bī′mə·tal′ik) *adj.* 1 Consisting of or relating to two metals. 2 Having a double metallic coin standard. 3 Of or pertaining to bimetalism. [<F *bimétallique*]

Bim·i·ni Islands (bim′ə·nē) An island group in the NW Bahamas; 9 square miles; the legendary fountain of youth sought by Ponce de Leon was said to be here. Also **Bim′i·nis.**

bi·mo·lec·u·lar (bī′mə·lek′yə·lər) *adj. Chem.* Relating to two molecules: a *bimolecular* reaction.

bi·month·ly (bī·munth′lē) *adj.* & *adv.* Occurring once in two months. — *n.* A publication issued once in two months.

bi·mo·tored (bī·mō′tərd) *adj.* Having two motors, as an airplane.

bin (bin) *n.* 1 An enclosed place or large receptacle for holding meal, coal, etc. 2 A compartment in a wine cellar. 3 A basket used by hop pickers. — *v.t.* **binned, bin·ning** To store or deposit in a bin. [OE *binn* basket, crib <Celtic]

bin- Var. of BI-.

bi·nal (bī′nəl) *adj.* Double; twofold. [<L *bini* two]

bi·na·ry (bī′nə·rē) *adj.* 1 Pertaining to, characterized by, or made up of two; double; paired. 2 *Astron.* Denoting a pair of stars revolving about a common center. — *n. pl.* **·ries** 1 A combination of two things; a couple; duality. 2 A binary star. [<L *binarius* <*bini* two, double]

binary star See under STAR.

binary system 1 A method of counting which has 2 for its base: still in use among certain primitive tribes of Australia and Africa. 2 *Math.* A system of numeration which can express any number by means of two digits, 0 and 1, in various combinations: applied especially in the operation of digital computers.

bi·nate (bī′nāt) *adj. Bot.* Being or growing in couples or pairs. [<NL *binatus* paired <L *bini* double, two by two] — **bi′nate·ly** *adv.*

bi·na·tion (bi·nā′shən) *n.* In the Roman Catholic Church, celebration of two masses within the same day by the same priest. [<Med. L *binatio, -onis* duplication <*bini* double]

bin·au·ral (bin·ôr′əl) *adj.* 1 Hearing with both ears. 2 Designating an apparatus for communicating faint or distant sounds simultaneously to both ears: a *binaural* stethoscope. 3 Two-eared. 4 Stereophonic.

bind (bīnd) *v.* **bound, bound** (*Archaic* **bound·en**), **bind·ing** *v.t.* 1 To tie together; make fast by tying. 2 To encircle, as with a belt. 3 To bandage; swathe: often with *up.* 4 To cause to cohere; cement. 5 To strengthen or ornament at the edge, as a garment. 6 To fasten together and secure within a cover, as a book. 7 To make irrevocable; seal, as a bargain. 8 To constrain or oblige to do or not to do, as by moral or legal authority: often with *over.* 9 To make constipated or costive. 10 To apprentice: often with *out.* — *v.i.* 11 To tie up anything: to reap and *bind.* 12 To cohere; stick together. 13 To have binding force; be obligatory. 14 To become stiff or hard, as cement; jam, as gears. — **to bind over** *Law* To hold under bond for appearance at a future time. — *n.* 1 That which fastens, ties, or binds. 2 *Music* A curved line, tie, or brace. [OE *bindan*]

Synonyms (verb): compel, engage, fasten, fetter, fix, oblige, restrain, restrict, secure, shackle, tie. *Binding* is primarily by something flexible, as a cord or bandage drawn closely around an object or a group of objects, as when we *bind* up a wounded limb. We *bind* a sheaf of wheat with a cord; we *tie* the cord in a knot; we *fasten* by any means that will make things hold together, as a board by nails or a door by a lock. *Bind* has an extensive figurative use. One is *bound* by conscience or honor; he is *obliged* by some imperious necessity; *engaged* by his own promise; *compelled* by physical force or its moral equivalent. *Antonyms*: free, loose, unbind, unfasten, unloose, untie.

bind·er (bīn′dər) *n.* 1 One who or that which binds. 2 One who binds books. 3 *Agric.* A device on a reaping machine for binding grain. 4 An attachment on a sewing machine to secure an edging. 5 A surety or written pledge for payment or performance of a contract. 6 A folder in which sheets of paper may be fastened, as for a notebook. 7 In painting, a material used to cause the pigment to adhere to a surface, as solutions of gum, glue, or casein, oils and resins, and (in fresco painting) lime. 8 In construction, a beam of steel or wood serving to support the bridging joists in a floor. 9 *Metall.* A substance used to promote the cohesion of crushed ore particles or finely powdered metallic dust before or in the process of sintering. 10 The cord or braiding which binds the edges of a fabric.

bind·er·y (bīn′dər·ē) *n. pl.* **·er·ies** A place where books are bound.

bind·ing (bīn′ding) *adj.* Causing to be bound; obligatory. — *n.* 1 The act of fastening or joining. 2 Anything that binds objects to each other, as the cover of a book. 3 Any thickening substance added to a mixture to cause the various ingredients to adhere; a binder. 4 A strip sewed over an edge for protection. 5 A course of masonry by which adjoining parts are secured. — **bind′ing·ly** *adv.* — **bind′ing·ness** *n.*

binding energy *Physics* The energy associated with the loss of mass occurring when the constituent particles of an atomic nucleus are closely bound together.

bind·weed (bīnd′wēd′) *n.* Any plant of the genus *Convolvulus,* or similar plant of strong twining habit.

bine (bīn) *n.* A flexible shoot or climbing stem of a plant; specifically, a hop vine: used of other climbers, in composition: wood*bine.* [Var. of BIND]

Bi·net-Si·mon (bi·nā′sī′mən, *Fr.* bē·ne′sē·môn′) **scale** *Psychol.* A system of rating the intelligence and mental development of children according to their performance in carefully selected and graded tests: used in the determination of mental age. See also STANFORD REVISION. [after Alfred *Binet,* 1857–1911, and Théodore *Simon,* born 1873, French psychologists]

bing[1] (bing) *interj.* A word imitating any sharp metallic sound, as of a rifle shot. — *n.* The sound thus produced. — *v.i.* To make this sound: The guns *binged* away. [Imit.]

bing[2] (bing) *n. Scot.* & *Brit. Dial.* A pile or heap of anything. [<ON *bingr* heap]

binge (binj) *n. Slang* A drunken carousal; spree. [? <dial. E *binge* soak]

Bing·en (bing′ən) A town on the Rhine in Rhineland-Palatinate, Germany.

Bing·ham·ton (bing′əm·tən) A city on the Susquehanna River in south central New York.

bin·go (bing′gō) *n.* A variety of keno: also called *beano.* [Origin unknown]

Binh·dinh (bin′din′) A town in southern Vietnam. Also **Binh Dinh.**

bin·it (bin′it) *n.* Bit[4].

bin·na·cle (bin′ə·kəl) *n. Naut.* A stand or case for a ship's compass: placed usually before the steering wheel. [Var. of *bittacle* <Pg. *bitacola* <LL *habitaculum* little house]

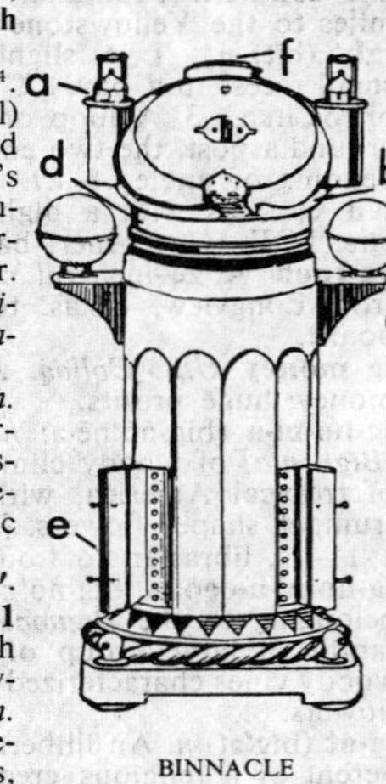

BINNACLE
a. Lamp.
b. Hood.
c. Quadrilateral sphere.
d. Compass chamber.
e. Magnet chamber.
f. Window to admit light to compass chamber.

bin·nogue (bin′ōg) *n.* A headdress formerly worn by peasant women in Ireland. [<Irish Gaelic *beannōg*]

bin·oc·u·lar (bə·nok′yə·lər, bī-) *adj.* 1 Pertaining to both eyes at once. 2 Having two eyes. — *n. Often pl.* A telescope, opera glass, etc., adapted for use by both eyes at once. Also **bin·o·cle** (bin′ə·kəl). — **bin·oc′u·lar′i·ty** (-lar′ə·tē) *n.* — **bin·oc′u·lar·ly** *adv.*

bi·no·mi·al (bī·nō′mē·əl) *adj.* Consisting of two names or terms. — *n.* 1 *Math.* An algebraic expression having two terms. 2 In taxonomy, a name consisting of two words, one indicating the genus, the other the species of a plant or animal. [<Med. L *binomius* having two names] — **bi·no′mi·al·ly** *adv.*

binomial system The system which assigns to every plant and animal a Latinized scientific name consisting of two terms, the first indicating the genus and the second the species: *Latrodectus mactans,* the black-widow spider. Also **binomial nomenclature.**

binomial theorem *Math.* The theorem stating the general form of any power of an algebraic binomial.

bi·nom·i·nal (bī·nom′ə·nəl) *adj.* Of, having, or characterized by two names.

bi·nu·cle·ate (bī·nōō′klē·āt, -nyōō′-) *adj.* Having two nuclei, as a cell. Also **bi·nu′cle·ar, bi·nu′cle·at′ed.**

Bin·ue (bin′wā) See BENUE.

Bin·yon (bin′yən), **Laurence,** 1869–1943, English poet and art critic.

bio- *combining form* Life: *biology, biography.* [<Gk. *bios* life]

bi·o·aer·a·tion (bī′ō·âr·ā′shən, -ā′ə·rā′-) *n.* A method of purifying sewage by aerating it in specially designed centrifugal pumps.

bi·o·as·say (bī′ō·as′ā) *n.* The determination of the properties and effects of a drug by testing it under controlled conditions in the bodies of standard laboratory animals.

Bí·o-Bí·o (bē′ō·bē′ō) A river in south central Chile, flowing 240 miles to the Pacific.

bi·o·blast (bī′ə·blast) *n.* Bioplast.

bi·o·cat·a·lyst (bī′ō·kat′ə·list) *n.* An enzyme.

bi·oc·el·late (bī·os′ə·lāt, bī′ō·sel′it) *adj. Biol.* Having two eyelike marks or ocelli. [<BI- + OCELLATE]

bi·o·chem·is·try (bī′ō·kem′is·trē) *n.* That branch of chemistry relating to vital processes, their mode of action, and their products. — **bi′o·chem′ic, bi′o·chem′i·cal** *adj.* — **bi′o·chem′i·cal·ly** *adv.* — **bi′o·chem′ist** *n.*

bi·o·chore (bī′ə·kôr, -kōr) *n. Ecol.* 1 That region of the earth having a climate favorable to life. 2 A climatic boundary for a given plant group. [<Gk. *bios* life + *chōrē* land, country] — **bi′o·chor′ic** *adj.*

bi·o·ci·dal (bī′ə·sīd′l) *adj.* Destructive of life, as certain poisons and antibiotics.

bi·o·coe·no·sis (bī′ō·sē·nō′sis) *n. Ecol.* An association of plants and animals in a given habitat and under similar environmental conditions. Also **bi·o·ce·nose** (bī′ō·sē′nōs). [< BIO- + Gk. *koinōsis* sharing] —**bi′o·coe·not′ic** (-not′·ik) *adj.*

bi·o·de·grad·a·ble (bī′ō·di′grā′də·bəl) *adj. Chem.* Capable of being broken down, as a compound, by bacterial action. [< BIO- + DEGRADABLE]

bi·o·dy·nam·ics (bī′ō·dī·nam′iks) *n.* The branch of biology that treats of the activities of living organisms. —**bi′o·dy·nam′ic** or **·i·cal** *adj.*

bi·o·e·lec·tric·i·ty (bī′ō·i·lek′tris′ə·tē) *n.* Those phenomena of electricity which are associated with and characteristic of living matter. — **bi′o·e·lec′tri·cal** *adj.*

bi·o·eth·ics (bī′ō·eth′iks) *n. pl. (construed as sing.)* The study of the ethical implications of medical practice, especially in regard to the preservation of human life. —**bi′o·eth′i·cal** *adj.* — **bi′o·eth′i·cist** (-eth′ə·sist) *n.*

bi·o·feed·back (bī′ō·fēd′bak) *n.* Voluntary control by feedback of involuntary functions, as heart rate.

bi·o·gen (bī′ə·jən) *n. Biochem.* The hypothetical large protein molecular unit assumed to be active in the functioning of body tissues.

bi·o·gen·e·sis (bī′ō·jen′ə·sis) *n.* **1** The doctrine that life is generated from living organisms only. **2** Such generation itself: opposed to *abiogenesis*. Also **bi·og·e·ny** (bī·oj′ə·nē). —**bi′o·ge·net′ic** (bī′ō·jə·net′ik) or **·i·cal** *adj.* —**bi′o·ge·net′i·cal·ly** *adv.*

bi·o·ge·og·ra·phy (bī′ō·jē·og′rə·fē) *n.* The science of the geographical distribution of living organisms. —**bi′o·ge′o·graph′ic** (bī′ə·graf′ik) or **·i·cal** *adj.* —**bi′o·ge′o·graph′i·cal·ly** *adv.*

bi·og·ra·pher (bī·og′rə·fər, bē-) *n.* One who writes an account of a person's life.

bi·og·ra·phy (bī·og′rə·fē, bē-) *n. pl.* **·phies** **1** A written account of a person's life. **2** That form of literature dealing with the facts and events of individual experience. **3** Biographies collectively. See synonyms under HISTORY. [< LGk. *biographia* < *bios* life + *graphein* write] —**bi′o·graph′ic** (bī′ə·graf′ik) or **·i·cal** *adj.* —**bi′o·graph′i·cal·ly** *adv.*

bi·o·log·i·cal (bī′ə·loj′i·kəl) *adj.* **1** Of or pertaining to biology, or to the science of vital functions, structures, and processes. **2** Used for or produced by biological research or practice. Also **bi′o·log′ic.** —**bi′o·log′i·cal·ly** *adv.*

biological engineering The artificial selection of different strains of a plant or animal species to improve the structure, function, or yield of an organism, esp. a plant or animal of economic importance.

bi·o·log·i·cals (bī′ə·loj′i·kəlz) *n. pl.* Drugs and medicinal preparations obtained from animal tissues and other organic sources.

bi·ol·o·gism (bī·ol′ə·jiz′əm) *n. Philos.* The doctrine that biological methods are applicable to the entire field of human experience.

bi·ol·o·gist (bī·ol′ə·jist) *n.* One having special knowledge of biology.

bi·ol·o·gy (bī·ol′ə·jē) *n.* The science of life and of the origin, structure, reproduction, growth, and development of living organisms collectively: its two main divisions are botany and zoology. [< BIO- + -LOGY]

bi·o·lu·mi·nes·cence (bī′ō·lōō′mə·nes′əns) *n.* The emission of light by living organisms, as fireflies, certain fungi, and deep-sea fishes. —**bi′o·lu′mi·nes′cent** *adj.*

bi·ol·y·sis (bī·ol′ə·sis) *n.* The dissolution of life. [< BIO- + Gk. *lysis* loosing] —**bi′o·lyt·ic** (bī′ə·lit′ik) *adj.*

bi·o·mass (bī′ō·mas′) *n.* The total amount of plant material in a given area, esp. when considered as an energy source.

bi·o·me·chan·ics (bī′ō·mə·kan′iks) *n.* The study of the mechanics of living organisms, especially under conditions of sudden, violent, or prolonged strain. —**bi′o·me·chan′i·cal** or **·i·cal** *adj.* —**bi′o·me·chan′i·cal·ly** *adv.*

bi·om·e·try (bī·om′ə·trē) *n.* **1** A measuring or calculating of the probable duration of human life. **2** Biology from a statistical point of view, especially with reference to problems of variation: also **bi·o·met·rics** (bī′ə·met′riks). [< BIO +

·METRY] —**bi′o·met′ric** or **·ri·cal** *adj.* —**bi′o·met′ri·cal·ly** *adv.*

bi·on·ics (bī·on′iks) *n.* The science of relating the functioning of biological systems to the development of electronic devices. [< BIO- + (ELECTR)ONICS]

bi·o·nom·ics (bī′ə·nom′iks) *n.* The branch of biology treating of habits and adaptation; ecology. —**bi′o·nom′ic** or **·i·cal** *adj.* —**bi′o·nom′·i·cal·ly** *adv.* —**bi·on·o·mist** (bī·on′ə·mist) *n.*

bi·o·phys·ics (bī′ō·fiz′iks) *n.* The study of biological function, structure, and organization in relation to and by the methods of physics. — **bi′o·phys′i·cal** *adj.*

bi·o·plasm (bī′ō·plaz′əm) *n.* Formative living matter; protoplasm.

bi·op·sy (bī′op·sē) *n. Med.* The clinical and diagnostic examination of tissue and other material excised from the living subject: opposed to *autopsy, necropsy.* [< BIO- + Gk. *opsis* sight] —**bi·op′sic** (bī·op′sik) *adj.*

bi·o·psy·chol·o·gy (bī′ō·sī·kol′ə·jē) *n.* Psychobiology.

bi·o·rhythm (bī′ō·rith′əm) *n.* Any cyclic pattern of activity in an organism. —**bi′o·rhyth′mic** *adj.* —**bi′o·rhyth·mic·i·ty** (bī′ō·rith′mis′ə·tē) *n.*

bi·o·scope (bī′ō·skōp) *n.* **1** A motion-picture projector. **2** An instrument used in bioscopy.

bi·os·co·py (bī·os′kə·pē) *n. Med.* An examination to ascertain whether life exists or has ceased. [< BIO- + -SCOPY] —**bi·o·scop·ic** (bī′ə·skop′ik) *adj.*

-biosis *combining form* Method of living: *aerobiosis, symbiosis.* [< Gk. *biōsis* < *bios* life]

bi·os·o·phy (bī·os′ə·fē) *n.* A system of character development and national and international peace education. [< Gk. *bios* life + *sophia* knowledge]

bi·o·sphere (bī′ə·sfir) *n.* That portion of the earth and its environment within which life in any of its forms is manifested.

bi·o·stat·ics (bī′ō·stat′iks) *n.* The branch of biology that treats of the potentialities of organisms or of structure as related to function: distinguished from *biodynamics.* —**bi′o·stat′ic** or **·i·cal** *adj.*

bi·o·syn·the·sis (bī′ō·sin′thə·sis) *n.* The chemical synthesis of organic materials, especially of a fibrous nature, from elementary living units or cells. —**bi·o·syn·thet·ic** (bī′ō·sin·thet′·ik) *adj.*

bi·o·ta (bī·ō′tə) *n. Ecol.* The combined fauna and flora of any geographical area or geological period. [< Gk. *biotē* life, living < *bios* life]

bi·o·tech·nol·o·gy (bī′ō·tek·nol′jē) *n.* The application of industrial techniques to the exploitation of biological processes.

bi·ot·ic (bī·ot′ik) *adj.* Pertaining to life. Also **bi·ot′i·cal.**

biotic potential **1** *Biol.* The inherent capacity of an organism to survive and reproduce under given or optimum conditions. **2** A measure of the innate vitality of a species confronted by an unfavorable or hostile environment.

bi·ot·ics (bī·ot′iks) *n.* The science of the functions of living organisms.

bi·o·tin (bī′ə·tin) *n. Biochem.* A crystalline acid, $C_{10}H_{16}O_3N_2S$, forming part of the vitamin B complex: it is essential in preventing the death of animals from an excess of egg white in the diet: also called *vitamin H.*

bi·o·tite (bī′ə·tīt) *n.* A common, brown or dark-green magnesium iron mica. [after J. B. *Biot,* 1774–1862, French physicist] —**bi′o·tit′ic** (-tit′ik) *adj.*

bi·o·tope (bī′ə·tōp) *n. Ecol.* An area, usually small and of uniform environmental conditions, characterized by relatively stable biotypes. [< BIO- + Gk. *topos* region]

bi·o·tox·ic (bī′ō·tok′sik) *adj.* Of or pertaining to natural poisons produced by plants and animals.

bi·o·type (bī′ə·tīp) *n. Biol.* **1** A race or strain that breeds true or almost true. **2** A group of individuals all of which have the same genotype. —**bi′o·typ′ic** (-tip′ik) *adj.* —**bi′o·ty·pol′o·gy** (-tī·pol′ə·jē) *n.*

bi·pa·ri·e·tal (bī′pə·rī′ə·təl) *adj. Anat.* Of or pertaining to the two parietal bones.

bip·a·rous (bip′ə·rəs) *adj.* **1** *Bot.* Having two

lateral axes, as certain cymes. **2** *Zool.* Bringing forth two at a birth. [< BI- + -PAROUS]

bi·par·ti·san (bī·pär′tə·zən) *adj.* Composed of, pertaining to, or advocated by representatives of two political parties. —**bi·par′ti·san·ship** *n.*

bi·par·tite (bī·pär′tīt) *adj.* **1** Consisting of two corresponding parts. **2** *Bot.* Two-parted almost to the base, as certain leaves. Also **bi·part′ed.** — **bi·par′tite·ly** *adv.* —**bi·par·ti·tion** (bī′pär·tish′ən) *n.*

bi·ped (bī′ped) *n.* An animal having two feet. —*adj.* Two-footed: also **bi·pe·dal** (bī′pə·dəl, bip′ə-). [< L *bipes, bipedis* two-footed]

bi·pet·al·ous (bī·pet′əl·əs) *adj. Bot.* Dipetalous.

bi·phen·yl (bī·fen′əl, -fē′nəl) *n. Chem.* A colorless crystalline hydrocarbon, $C_6H_5 \cdot C_6H_5$, found in coal tar: used in lacquers and as a preservative of citrus fruit. Also called *diphenyl.*

bi·pin·nate (bī·pin′āt) *adj. Bot.* Twice or doubly pinnate, as a leaf. Also **bi·pin′nat·ed.** — **bi·pin′nate·ly** *adv.*

bi·plane (bī′plān) *n. Aeron.* A type of airplane having two parallel connected wings arranged one above the other: distinguished from *monoplane* and *triplane.*

bi·pod (bī′pod) *n.* A two-legged rest or stand, as for a rifle or machine-gun. [< BI- + -POD]

bi·po·lar (bī·pō′lər) *adj.* **1** Relating to or possessing two poles. **2** *Biol.* **a** Describing marine organisms found in both polar regions but nowhere else. **b** Having two prolongations of cell matter: said of nerve cells. —**bi·po·lar·i·ty** (bī′pō·lar′ə·tē) *n.*

bi·pro·pel·lant (bī′prə·pel′ənt) *n.* A propellant for rockets consisting of two chemicals, each of which is fed separately into the combustion chamber.

bi·quad·rate (bī·kwod′rāt) *n. Math.* A fourth power or the square of a square.

bi·quad·rat·ic (bī′kwod·rat′ik) *Math. adj.* Containing or referring to a fourth power. —*n.* **1** A fourth power. **2** A biquadratic equation.

bi·ra·di·al (bī·rā′dē·əl) *adj. Biol.* Having the radii set bilaterally and radially, as certain sea anemones.

birch (bûrch) *n.* **1** Any of an important genus (*Betula*) of deciduous trees and shrubs of the northern hemisphere, often having outer bark easily separable in sheets. **2** A rod or twig from a birch tree, used as a whip. **3** The tough, close-grained hardwood of the birch tree. —*v.t.* To whip with a birch rod; flog. —*adj.* Composed or fashioned of birch: also **birch·en.** [OE *birce*]

bird (bûrd) *n.* **1** A warm-blooded, feathered, egg-laying vertebrate (class *Aves*), having the

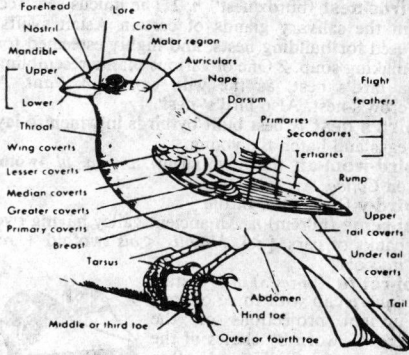

BIRD
Nomenclature for anatomical parts

forelimbs modified as wings. ♦ Collateral adjective: *avian.* **2** A game bird; in England, a partridge. **3** *Obs.* The young of a fowl; a nestling. **4** *Slang* A peculiar or remarkable person. **5** *U.S. Slang* A hiss, or other call of disapproval, by an audience; usually in the phrases *to give* (one) *the bird, to get the bird.* **6** A clay pigeon; also, the shuttlecock in badminton. —**for the birds** *Slang* Worthless. —*v.t.* To trap or shoot birds. [OE *bridd*]

bird-call (bûrd′kôl) *n.* **1** An instrument for decoying birds by imitating their notes. **2** A bird's note in calling.

bird dog A dog that is trained to locate birds and retrieve them for hunters; specifically, a setter or pointer.

bird·grass (bûrd′gras′, -gräs′) *n.* **1** A North American grass *(Poa trivialis),* much cultivated for lawns. **2** Knotgrass.

bird·house (bûrd′hous′) *n.* **1** A small house or enclosure for birds; an aviary. **2** A small house, placed in trees, etc., in which birds may nest. Also **bird house.**

bird·ie (bûr′dē) *n.* **1** A small bird. **2** A whistling birdlike chirp, as on a radio transmission line, or in the body of an automobile, etc. **3** In golf, one stroke less than par in playing a hole.

bird·lime (bûrd′līm′) *n.* A sticky substance made from the inner bark of the holly or mistletoe: smeared on twigs to catch small birds. —*v.t.* **·limed, ·lim·ing** To smear or snare with birdlime; trap.

bird·man (bûrd′man′, -mən) *n. pl.* **·men** (-men′, -mən) **1** *Colloq.* An aviator. **2** A fowler. **3** An ornithologist.

bird of Minerva The owl.

bird of paradise A bird of New Guinea *(Paradisea apoda),* noted for the curious form and beauty of the plumage in the male.

bird of passage A bird that migrates with the changing seasons.

bird of prey Any of various raptorial birds, as an eagle, hawk, vulture, falcon, etc.

bird·pep·per (bûrd′pep′ər) *n.* Capsicum (def. 2).

birds·eye (bûrdz′ī′) *adj.* **1** Marked with spots resembling birds' eyes: *birdseye* cotton, *birdseye* maple. **2** Seen at a glance, and from above: a *birdseye* view; also, cursory. —*n.* **1** A plant with small, bright-colored flowers, the birdseye primrose *(Primula farinosa).* **2** The germander speedwell. **3** A textile fabric woven in a pattern of small eyelike indentations. **4** Any of various fabrics having such a pattern. Also **bird's′-eye′.**

bird's-foot (bûrdz′fo͝ot′) *n.* **1** Any plant of the genus *Ornithopus,* of the bean family, bearing curving pods. **2** Any one of various other plants, as a South African spurge *(Euphorbia ornithopus).*

bird's-foot fern A fern *(Pellaea mucronata)* from California, with tufted, deltoid, bipinnatifid fronds, 4 to 6 inches long, on rigid, dark chestnut-brown stipes.

bird's-foot trefoil Any plant of the genus *Lotus;* especially, the common species *(L. corniculatus)* of the Old World, a hardy perennial trailer.

bird's-foot violet A large-flowered pedate violet *(Viola pedata)* with large, pale-blue or purple, beardless flowers. See under VIOLET.

birds·nest (bûrdz′nest′) *n.* **1** The mucus secreted in the salivary glands of certain Asian swifts, used for building nests, and highly esteemed for making soup. **2** One of various plants resembling a bird's nest, as the wild carrot. **3** *Naut.* A crow's-nest. Also **bird's′-nest′.**

bird's nest A nest built by birds in which to lay eggs and hatch the young.

bird·wom·an (bûrd′wo͝om′ən) *n. fem. pl.* **·wom·en** *Colloq.* An aviatrix.

bird·y (bûr′dē) *n.* Birdie.

bi·reme (bī′rēm) *n.* An ancient galley having two banks of oars. [< L *biremis* < *bis* twofold + *remus* oar]

bi·ret·ta (bi·ret′ə) *n.* A stiff, square cap with three or four upright projections on the crown, worn by clerics of the Roman Catholic and other churches: also spelled *berretta.* [< Ital. *berretta* or Sp. *birreta* < LL *birretum* cap, dim. of *birrus* cape, cloak]

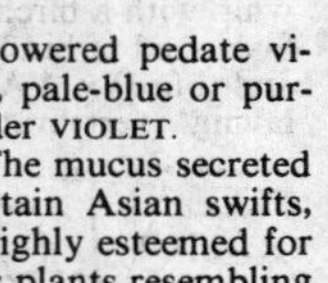

BIRETTA FOR PRIESTS

Bir·git·ta (bir·git′ə) Swedish form of BRIDGET.

bi·rit·u·al·ism (bī·rich′o͞o·əl·iz′əm) *n.* In the Roman Catholic Church, the use of a non-Latin rite, permitted a priest in cases of necessity.

birk (bûrk, birk) *n. Scot.* The birch. **—birk′en, birk′in** *adj.*

Birk·beck (bûrk′bek), **George,** 1776–1841, English physician; founder of mechanics' institutions.

Bir·ken·head (bûr′kən·hed) A county borough in NW Cheshire, England, on the Mersey River opposite Liverpool.

Bir·ken·head (bûr′kən·hed), **Earl of,** 1872–1930, Frederick Edwin Smith, English jurist and statesman.

birl (bûrl) *v.t & v.i.* **1** To rotate rapidly. **2** To spin with a humming sound. —*n.* A droning noise. ◆ Homophone: *burl.* [Blend of BIRR and WHIRL]

birle (bûrl, birl) *v.t. & v.i. Brit. Dial.* To ply with drink; carouse: also spelled *byrl.* Also **birl.** [OE *byrelian* pour out drink < *byrele* cupbearer]

birl·ing (bûr′ling) *n.* A game between two lumberjacks in which each stands on an end of a floating log and rotates it with his feet so as to dislodge his opponent. [Origin uncertain]

Bir·ming·ham 1 (bûr′ming·əm) A county borough and city of NW Warwickshire, England. **2** (bûr′ming·ham) A manufacturing city in north central Alabama.

Bir·ney (bûr′nē), **James G.,** 1792–1857, U.S. abolitionist.

Bi·ro·bi·dzhan (bir′ō·bi·jän′) An administrative division of the U.S.S.R. on the NE border of Manchuria; 13,800 square miles; capital, Birobidzhan: also *Jewish Autonomous Oblast.* Also **Bi′ro·bi·jan′.**

Bi·ron (byē′rən), **Ernst Johann,** 1690–1772, Russian statesman.

birr (bûr) *n. Scot.* **1** Onward rush; momentum; emphatic and rapid utterance. **2** A whirring or buzzing sound. **3** *Obs.* A rushing wind. —*v.i.* To move with or make a whirring noise. ◆ Homophones: *bur, burr.* [< ON *byrr* favorable wind]

Bir·rell (bir′əl), **Augustine,** 1850–1933, English author.

birse (bûrs, *Scot.* birs) *Scot.* **1** A bristle; collectively, bristles. **2** Short hair, as of the head or beard. **—to set up one's birse** To make one angry.

birth (bûrth) *n.* **1** The fact or act of being born; nativity. **2** A beginning; an origin. **3** The bringing forth of offspring; parturition. **4** Ancestry or descent; lineage; also, the class into which one is born. **5** Offspring; issue. See synonyms under AFFINITY, KIN. ◆ Homophone: *berth.* [< ON *byrth*] **—to give birth** To produce offspring.

birth canal *Anat.* The passage through which a child is delivered at birth, extending from the cervix uteri to the vulva.

birth control The regulation of conception by employing preventive methods or devices.

birth·day (bûrth′dā′) *n.* The day of one's birth or its anniversary: used also adjectively.

birth·mark (bûrth′märk′) *n.* A mark or stain existing on the body from birth; a nevus.

birth·place (bûrth′plās′) *n.* The place of one's birth or of origin in general.

birth rate The number of births per 1,000 inhabitants of a given district in any given period.

birth·right (bûrth′rīt′) *n.* Native right or privilege.

birth·root (bûrth′ro͞ot′, -ro͝ot′) *n.* Any of a genus *(Trillium)* of typically North American perennial herbs of the lily family; especially, *T. erectum,* which has astringent tuberlike rootstocks: sometimes used to hasten parturition.

birth·stone (bûrth′stōn′) *n.* A jewel identified with a particular month of the year: thought to bring good luck when worn by a person whose birthday falls in that month.

birth trauma *Psychoanal.* The deep psychic anxiety assumed to be implanted in a child at the moment of and by the act of birth: sometimes considered the basis for subsequent psychoneurotic disorders.

birth tree In folklore, a tree planted at the birth of a child in the belief that its welfare has some mysterious connection with the welfare of the child all his life.

birth·wort (bûrth′wûrt′) *n.* **1** Any plant of the genus *Aristolochia;* especially, *A. clematitis* of Europe, with stimulant tonic roots used as aromatic bitters. **2** Birthroot.

bis (bis) *adv.* **1** Twice: noting duplication or repetition. **2** Encore: a call for the repetition of a performance. [< L]

bis- Var. of BI-.

Bi·sa·yan (bē·sä′yən) See VISAYAN.

Bisayan Islands The Visayan Islands. Also **Bi·sa·yas** (bē·sä′yəz).

Bis·cay (bis′kā, -kē) One of the Basque provinces of northern Spain; 858 square miles; on the **Bay of Biscay,** a wide inlet of the Atlantic indenting the coast of western Europe from Brittany, France, to NW Spain: Spanish *Vizcaya.*

Bis·cayne Bay (bis′kān, bis·kān′) A shallow arm of the Atlantic south of Miami, Florida.

bis·cuit (bis′kit) *n.* **1** A kind of shortened bread baked in small cakes, raised with baking powder or soda. **2** *Brit.* A sweetened cracker or cookie. **3** Unglazed pottery which has been fired in the oven; bisque. [< OF *bescoit* < *bes* twice (< L *bis*) + *coit,* pp. of *cuire* cook < L *coquere*]

bis·cuit·root (bis′kit·ro͞ot′, -ro͝ot′) *n.* Wild parsley.

bise (bēz) *n.* **1** A cold northerly wind in Switzerland and parts of France, destructive to vegetation. **2** Misfortune; disaster.

bi·sect (bī·sekt′) *v.t.* **1** To cut into two parts; halve. **2** *Geom.* To divide into two parts of equal size. —*v.i.* **3** To fork, as a road. [< BI- + L *sectus,* pp. of *secare* cut] **—bi·sec′tion** *n.* **—bi·sec′tion·al** *adj.* **—bi·sec′tion·al·ly** *adv.*

bi·sec·tor (bī·sek′tər) *n.* **1** That which bisects. **2** *Geom.* A line or plane that bisects an angle or another line.

bi·sec·trix (bī·sek′triks) *n. pl.* **bi·sec·tri·ces** (bī′sek·trī′sēz) **1** The line bisecting the angle formed by the optic axes of a crystal. **2** A bisector.

bi·ser·rate (bī·ser′āt, -it) *adj.* **1** *Bot.* Doubly serrate, as a leaf. **2** *Entomol.* Serrate on both sides, as the antenna of an insect.

bi·sex·u·al (bī·sek′sho͞o·əl) *adj.* **1** *Biol.* Having the organs of both sexes. **2** *Bot.* Hermaphroditic, as a flower with both stamens and pistils. **3** Showing characters derived from both parents, as a hybrid. **4** *Psychol.* Equally attracted by both sexes. **—bi·sex′u·al·ism** *n.* **—bi·sex′u·al·ly** *adv.*

bish·op (bish′əp) *n.* **1** A spiritual overseer in the Christian church; in various churches, a clergyman of the highest order, and head of a diocese. **2** A hot drink made with mulled wine, sugar, oranges, etc. **3** A chessman, often carved to represent a miter, which may be moved diagonally any number of unoccupied squares of the same color. [OE *biscop* < LL *episcopus* bishop < Gk. *episkopos* overseer]

BISHOP (*def.* 3)

bish·op·ric (bish′əp·rik) *n.* The office or the diocese of a bishop.

bish·ops·cap (bish′əps·kap′) *n.* Any species of miterwort; especially, *Mitella diphylla.* Also **bish′op's-cap′.**

Bi·si·tun (bē′sə·to͞on′) See BEHISTUN.

Bisk (bēsk) A city in central Altai Territory, Russian S.F.S.R.: also *Biisk.*

Bis·marck (biz′märk) The capital of North Dakota, a city on the Missouri River.

Bis·marck (biz′märk, *Ger.* bis′-), **Prince Karl Otto Eduard Leopold von,** 1815–98, German statesman; founder of the German Empire.

Bismarck Archipelago An island group in the United Nations Trust Territory of New Guinea, comprising New Britain, New Ireland, Lavongai, and the Admiralty Islands; total, 19,200 square miles.

Bismarck Mountains A range in NE New Guinea; highest peak, 14,107 feet.

Bismarck Sea The SW arm of the Pacific enclosed by the Bismarck Archipelago.

bis·muth (biz′məth) *n.* A heavy, grayish, brittle, metallic element (symbol Bi, atomic number 83) used in alloys and in medicines and cosmetics. See PERIODIC TABLE. [< G] **—bis·muth·al** (biz′məth·əl) *adj.*

bis·mu·thic (biz·myo͞o′thik, -muth′ik) *adj. Chem.* Containing bismuth in its highest valence.

bis·muth·ous (biz′məth·əs) *adj. Chem.* Containing bismuth in its lowest valence.

bi·son (bī′sən, -zən) *n.* A bovine ruminant, nearly related to the true ox; especially, the North American buffalo *(Bos* or *Bison bison). B. bonasus* is the European bison. [< L *bison* wild ox, ult. < Gmc.]

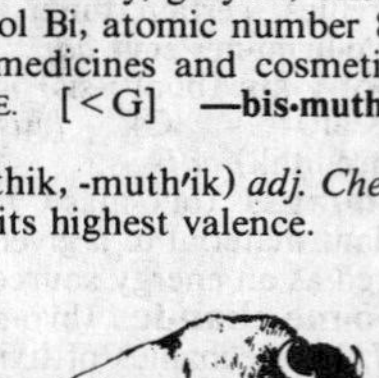

NORTH AMERICAN BISON (Up to 5 3/4 feet high at the shoulders)

bisque[1] (bisk) *n.* **1** A thick, rich soup made from meat or fish, especially shellfish. **2** A kind of ice-cream containing crushed macaroons. Also **bisk.** [<F]

bisque[2] (bisk) *n.* **1** In ceramics, biscuit. **2** Any of several shades of pinkish-beige. [< BISCUIT]

bisque[3] (bisk) *n.* An advantage given to an opponent in various games, as lawn tennis, consisting of a point or stroke to be taken at any time. [<F]

Bis·sau (bi·sou′) A port; the capital of Guinea-Bissau, formerly Portuguese Guinea, transferred here in 1941 from Bolama.

bis·sex·tile (bi·seks′təl, -tīl) *adj.* **1** Pertaining to the extra day occurring in leap year. **2** Pertaining to a leap year. —*n.* A leap year. [<L *bisextilis* intercalary <*bis* twice + *sextilis* sixth; so called because the sixth day before March 1 was doubled in leap year in the Julian calendar]

bis·ter (bis′tər) *n.* **1** A non-permanent, yellowish-brown pigment made from beechwood soot: used chiefly as a water-color wash. **2** A dark-brown color. Also **bis′tre.** [<F *bistre* dark brown] —**bis′tered** *adj.*

bis·tort (bis′tôrt) *n.* **1** A perennial herb *(Polygonum bistorta)* of Europe and Asia, with creeping rootstocks having astringent properties: also called *snakeweed.* **2** An allied herb, the Virginia bistort *(Tovara virginiana).* [<F <L *bis* twice + *tortus,* pp. of *torquere* twist]

bis·tou·ry (bis′to͝o·rē) *n. pl.* **·ries** *Surg.* A narrow-bladed knife for making minor incisions. [<OF *bistorie* dagger]

bis·tro (bis′trō, *Fr.* bē·strō′) *n. Colloq.* **1** A small night club or bar. **2** A restaurant or tavern where wine is served. [<F]

bi·sul·cate (bī·sul′kāt) *adj.* **1** Cleft in two; cloven-hoofed. **2** Two-grooved. Also **bi·sul′cat·ed.** [<L *bisulcus* <*bis* twofold + *sulcus* furrow]

bi·sul·fate (bī·sul′fāt) *n. Chem.* An acid sulfate containing the group HSO_4.

bi·sul·fide (bī·sul′fīd) *n.* Disulfide. Also **bi·sul′phide.**

bi·sul·fite (bī·sul′fīt) *n. Chem.* A salt of sulfurous acid in which the metal has replaced half the hydrogen in the acid: sodium *bisulfite,* $NaHSO_3$. Also **bi·sul′phite.**

Bi·su·tun (bē′sə·to͞on′) See BEHISTUN.

bi·sym·met·ri·cal (bī′si·met′ri·kəl) *adj.* Bilaterally symmetrical. Also **bi′sym·met′ric.** —**bi′sym·met′ri·cal·ly** *adv.* —**bi·sym·met·ry** (bī·sim′ə·trē) *n.*

bit[1] (bit) *n.* **1** A small piece, portion, or fragment; a little. **2** The smallest quantity; a whit; jot. **3** A small quantity of food; a morsel; taste; bite. **4** In Great Britain, a small coin, usually of a named value: a threepenny *bit.* **5** In the United States, the Spanish real or its equivalent, 12½ cents. **6** A short time. **7** *Slang* A typical or standard practice, procedure, or way of acting. —**a long bit** *U.S. Dial.* 15 cents. —**a short bit** *U.S. Dial.* 10 cents. —**two bits** *U.S. Colloq.* 25 cents. [OE *bita* <*bītan* bite]

Synonyms: dole, driblet, drop, installment, item, mite, morsel, particle, scrap.

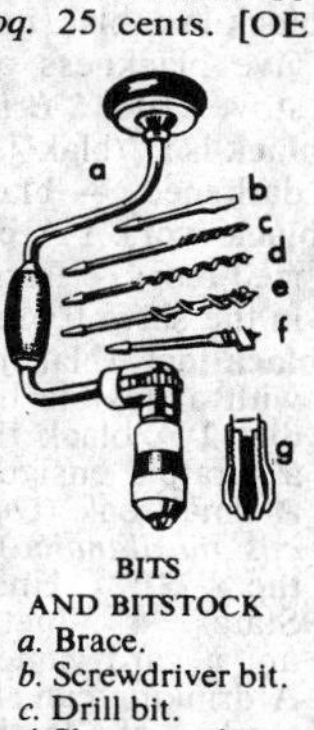

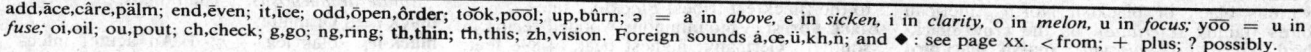

BITS AND BITSTOCK
a. Brace.
b. Screwdriver bit.
c. Drill bit.
d. Ship auger bit.
e. Auger bit.
f. Expanding bit.
g. Cross-section of chuck for holding bits.

bit[2] (bit) *n.* **1** A wood-boring tool adapted to be used with a stock or brace. **2** The metallic mouthpiece of a bridle. **3** Anything that controls or holds in subjection. **4** One of various objects somewhat like a boring bit or a bridle bit. **5** The part of a key that engages the bolt or tumblers of a lock. **6** The cutting blade of a plane. —*v.t.* **bit·ted, bit·ting 1** To put a bit in the mouth of; train, as a horse, to the use of a bit. **2** To curb; restrain. **3** To make a bit on (a key). [OE *bite* a biting <*bītan* bite]

bit[3] (bit) Past tense of BITE.

bit[4] (bit) *n. Telecom.* A single unit of information; specifically, one of the coded digital signals forming part of a complete message in the operation of an electronic computing machine: also called *binit.* [<B(INARY) (DIG)IT]

bi·tar·trate (bī·tär′trāt) *n. Chem.* A salt containing the univalent tartaric acid radical $C_4H_5O_6$; acid tartrate: potassium *bitartrate.*

bitch (bich) *n.* **1** The female of the dog or other canine animal. **2** *Slang* Wench; hussy: an abusive epithet, often implying lewdness. —*v.i. Slang* To complain. —**to bitch up** *Slang* To botch. [OE *bicce*]

bite (bīt) *v.* **bit, bit·ten** or *Colloq.* **bit, bit·ing** *v.t.* **1** To seize, tear, or wound with the teeth. **2** To cut or tear off with or as with the teeth: usually with *off:* He *bit* off his words. **3** To cut or pierce, as with a sword. **4** To sting, as mosquitoes. **5** To cause to smart, as a cold wind. **6** To eat into; corrode, as acid. **7** To grip; take hold of. **8** To cheat; trick. —*v.i.* **9** To seize or cut into something with the teeth. **10** To sting; have the effect of biting, as mustard. **11** To take firm hold; grip. **12** To take a bait, as fish. **13** To be tricked; accept a deceptive offer. —**to bite off more than one can chew** To attempt something beyond one's capabilities. —**to bite the dust** (or **ground**) To be vanquished or slain. —*n.* **1** The act of biting, or the hurt inflicted by biting; also, a painful sensation; smart. **2** A morsel of food; mouthful. **3** The grip or hold taken by a tool or piece of mechanism. ◆ Homophone: *bight.* [OE *bītan*] —**bit′a·ble, bite′a·ble** *adj.* —**bit′er** *n.*

Bi·thyn·i·a (bi·thin′ē·ə) An ancient country in NW Asia Minor.

bit·ing (bī′ting) *adj.* Keen; pungent; stinging. See synonyms under BITTER. —**bit′ing·ly** *adv.* —**bit′ing·ness** *n.*

Bi·tolj (bē′tôl·y′) A town in southern Yugoslavia. Also **Bi·tol** (bē′tôl). Turkish **Mon·as·tir** (mun·əs·tēr′).

bit part A small role in a play.

bit·stock (bit′stok′) *n.* A brace for a bit. For illustration see BIT.

bitt (bit) *n. Naut.* A post or vertical timber on a ship's deck, to which cables, etc., are made fast: usually in pairs. —*v.t.* To take a turn of (a cable) around a bitt or pair of bitts. [? <ON *biti* beam]

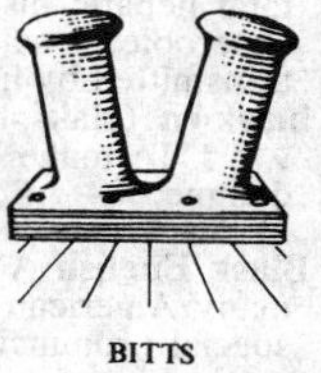

BITTS

bit·ten (bit′n) Past participle of BITE.

bit·ter[1] (bit′ər) *adj.* **1** Having a peculiar acrid taste, as quinine. **2** Producing pain of body or mind; keen; poignant; severe. **3** Feeling or showing hate or resentment. **4** Stinging; sharp; severe: said of words. —*n.* **1** That which is bitter; bitterness. **2** *pl.* A bitter vegetable tonic, usually spirituous. **3** *Brit.* Bitter beer. —*v.t. & v.i.* To make or become bitter. [OE *biter* <*bītan* bite] —**bit′ter·ish** *adj.* —**bit′ter·ly** *adv.* —**bit′ter·ness** *n.*

Synonyms (adj.): acerb, acetous, acid, acidulated, acidulous, acrid, acrimonious, biting, caustic, cutting, harsh, irate, pungent, savage, sharp, sour, stinging, tart, vinegarish, virulent. *Acid, sour,* and *bitter* agree in being contrasted with *sweet,* but *acid* or *sour* applies to the taste of vinegar or lemon juice; *bitter* to that of quassia, quinine, or strychnine. *Acrid* is nearly allied to *bitter. Pungent* suggests the effect of pepper or snuff on the organs of taste or smell; as, a *pungent* odor. *Caustic* indicates the corroding effect of some strong chemical, as nitrate of silver. In a figurative sense we say a *sour* face, *sharp* words, *bitter* complaints, *caustic* wit, *cutting* irony, *biting* sarcasm, a *stinging* taunt, *harsh* judgment, a *tart* reply. *Harsh* carries the idea of intentional and severe unkindness, *bitter* of a severity that arises from real or supposed ill-treatment. *Tart* and *sharp* utterances may proceed merely from a wit recklessly keen; *cutting, stinging,* or *biting* speech indicates more or less of hostile intent. The *caustic* utterance is meant to burn. Compare MALICIOUS, MOROSE. *Antonyms*: dulcet, honeyed, luscious, nectared, saccharine, sweet.

bit·ter[2] (bit′ər) *n. Naut.* A turn of the cable round a mooring bitt. [<BITT]

bitter apple The colocynth.

bitter end 1 *Naut.* The extreme end of a cable or rope, attached to the bitt. **2** The last extremity, as defeat or death.

bit·ter-ènd·er (bit′ər·en′dər) *n.* One who determines to continue a political, social, or any struggle to the end.

Bitter Lakes Two lakes in NE Egypt, joined and traversed by the Suez Canal.

bit·tern[1] (bit′ərn) *n.* A small, speckled, pale-buff heron *(Botaurus lentiginosus)* of North America, which utters a booming note in the breeding season. —**least bittern** The American dwarf bittern *(Ixobrychus exilis).* [<OF *butor,* ? <L *butio, -onis* a hawk]

bit·tern[2] (bit′ərn) *n.* **1** In salt manufacture, the waste liquor remaining after crystallization from brine. **2** A bitter mixture of quassia.

bitter principle Any of numerous bitter substances found in plants and not yet chemically classified.

bit·ter-root (bit′ər·ro͞ot′, -ro͝ot′) *n.* **1** An herb *(Lewisia rediviva)* with nutritious roots: State flower of Montana. **2** Any one of certain other North American plants, as the dogbane.

Bit·ter·root Range (bit′ər·ro͞ot′, -ro͝ot′) A range of the Rockies along the Idaho-Montana border; highest peak, 10,175 feet.

bit·ter·sweet (bit′ər·swēt′) *n.* **1** A coarse trailing plant, the woody nightshade, having oval bright-red berries. Its twigs and root have a taste at first bitter and afterward sweetish. **2** A shrubby or climbing plant *(Celastrus scandens),* with green flowers succeeded by orange pods that display a red aril. —*adj.* Combining bitter and sweet.

bit·ter·weed (bit′ər·wēd′) *n.* **1** A ragweed; especially, *Ambrosia artemisifolia.* **2** Any of various other plants yielding a bitter principle, as the horseweed and sneezeweed.

Bit·u·mas·tic (bich′o͝o·mas′tik) *n.* A quick-drying, bituminous paint resistant to heat and chemical fumes: a trade name.

bi·tu·men (bi·to͞o′mən, -tyo͞o′-, bich′o͝o·mən) *n.* **1** Any native mixture of solid and semi-solid hydrocarbons, as naphtha or asphalt. **2** A brown paint made by mixing asphalt with a drying oil: used by artists. [<L] —**bi·tu·mi·noid** (bi·to͞o′mə·noid, -tyo͞o′-) *adj.*

bi·tu·mi·nize (bi·to͞o′mə·nīz, -tyo͞o′-) *v.t.* **·ized, ·iz·ing** To render bituminous; treat with bitumen. —**bi·tu′mi·ni·za′tion** *n.*

bi·tu·mi·nous (bi·to͞o′mə·nəs, -tyo͞o′-) *adj.* **1** Of, pertaining to, or containing bitumen. **2** Containing, as coal, many volatile hydrocarbons.

bi·va·lence (bī·vā′ləns, biv′ə-) *n. Chem.* The property of having a valence of two. Also **bi·va′len·cy.**

bi·va·lent (bī·vā′lənt, biv′ə-) *adj.* **1** *Chem.* **a** Having a valence of two, or twice that of a univalent. **b** Having two valences: also *divalent.* **2** *Biol.* Composed of or characterizing chromatin rods representing two chromosomes joined end to end. [<BI- + L *valens, -entis,* ppr. of *valere* have power]

bi·valve (bī′valv′) *n.* **1** *Zool.* An acephalous mollusk having a shell of two lateral valves. **2** *Bot.* A seed vessel that splits into two parts, as a pea pod. —*adj.* Having two valves, as a mollusk or seed vessel: also **bi′valved′, bi·val·vous** (bī·val′vəs), **bi·val·vu·lar** (bī·val′vyə·lər).

biv·ou·ac (biv′o͞o·ak, biv′wak) *n.* A temporary encampment with or without shelter. —*v.i.* **biv·ou·acked, biv·ou·ack·ing** To encamp for the night with or without tents. [<F <G *beiwacht* guard]

Bi·wa (bē·wä), **Lake** The largest lake in Japan, located in southern Honshu; 261 square miles. *Japanese* **Bi·wa-ko** (bē·wä·kō).

bi·week·ly (bī·wēk′lē) *adj.* **1** Occurring or appearing once in two weeks. **2** Semiweekly. —*n.* A publication issued every other week.

bi·year·ly (bī·yir′lē) *adj. & adv.* **1** Occurring twice within one year. **2** Biennial.

bi·zarre (bi·zär′) *adj.* Grotesque; odd; fantastic. See synonyms under ODD. [<F, ? ult.< Basque] —**bi·zarre′ly** *adv.* —**bi·zarre′ness** *n.*

Bi·zen (bē·zen) A former province of SW Honshu, Japan; famous for pottery known as **Bi·zen·ware** (biz′ən·wâr′).

Bi·zer·te (bi·zûr′tə, *Fr.* bē·zert′) The northernmost city in Africa, a port in northern Tunisia; ancient *Hippo Zarytus.* Also **Bi·zer′ta.**

Bi·zet (bē·zā′), **Georges,** 1838–75, French composer: original name *Alexandre César Léopold Bizet.*

bizz (biz) *v.i. Scot.* To buzz.

Björn·son (byœrn′sən), **Björn·stjer·ne** (byœrn′·styâr·nə), 1832–1910, Norwegian poet, novelist, and dramatist.

Björns·son (byœrs′sôn), **Sveinn**, 1881–1952, Icelandic statesman; president of Iceland 1945–52.

Bk *Chem.* Berkelium (symbol Bk).

blab (blab) *v.t. & v.i.* **blabbed, blab·bing 1** To tell or repeat indiscreetly. **2** To prattle. See synonyms under BABBLE. [< *n*] — *n.* **1** One who betrays confidence. **2** Idle chatter. [ME *blabbe* idle talker] — **blab′ber** *n.*

blab·ber·mouth (blab′ər·mouth′) *n.* One who talks too much and can't be trusted to keep secrets.

black (blak) *adj.* **1** Having little or no power to reflect light: of the color of jet: the opposite of *white.* **2** Belonging to a group having dark skin. **3** Of or relating to the African American people or their culture: *black power, black studies, black pride.* **4** Swarthy; somber; dark. **5** Destitute of light; gloomy; dismal; forbidding. **6** Soiled; stained. **7** Evil; malignant; wicked; deadly; slanderous; malicious; threatening: a *black*-hearted wretch. **8** Wearing black garments: *black* monks. See synonyms under DARK. — *n.* **1** The absence of or complete absorption of light; the darkest of all colors. **2** Something that is black; also, mourning apparel or drapery. **3** A stain. **4** A member of the so-called black race. — **in the black** In the credit column of an account: converse of *in the red.* — *v.t. & v.i.* **1** To make or become black. **2** To blacken and polish. — **to black out 1** To extinguish or screen all light. **2** To lose vision or consciousness temporarily. **3** To censor; delete by scoring through. See BLACKOUT. [OE *blæc* dark] — **black′ly** *adv.* — **black′ness** *n.*

Black (blak), **Hugo La Fayette**, 1886–1971, associate justice of the United States Supreme Court 1937–1971.

black-and-blue (blak′ən-bloo′) *adj.* Discolored: said of skin that has been bruised.

Black and Tan Formerly, the auxiliary division of the Royal Irish Constabulary: so called from its uniform and accouterments.

black and white Writing or printing.

black art Necromancy; magic.

black·ball (blak′bôl′) *v.t.* **1** To use one's vote to ban from membership. **2** To exclude or ostracize: *blackballed* from the television industry. — *n.* **1** A single negative vote resulting in the rejection of an application for membership. **2** Any willful exclusion or act of ostracism. [<BLACK + BALL¹ from the use of a black ball to signify a negative vote during balloting] — **black′·ball′er** *n.*

black bass 1 A voracious fresh-water percoid fish (genus *Micropterus*) of the eastern United States and Canada. **2** The black sea bass (family *Serranidae*) of the North Atlantic; the blackwill.

black bear The common American bear (*Euarctos americanus*).

black belt *U.S.* **1** The highest degree of proficiency in judo or karate. **2** A person holding this degree. **3** A section of certain states in the U.S., especially of Alabama and Mississippi, characterized by rich black soil. **4** An area densely populated by blacks.

black·ber·ry (blak′ber′ē, -bər·ē) *n. pl.* **·ber·ries 1** The black, edible fruit of certain shrubs (genus *Rubus*) of the rose family. **2** Any of the plants producing it.

blackberry lily A perennial herb (*Belamcanda chinensis*) of the iris family: so called from its ripened seed vessel, which resembles a blackberry.

black bindweed 1 A twining, perennial vine (*Tamus communis*) of the yam family, with long angular stems and a small red fruit; the European black bryony. **2** An herbaceous twining plant (*Polygonum convolvulus*) growing as a weed in the United States.

black birch A species (*Betula lenta*) of birch of eastern North America with aromatic twigs and dark brown bark that becomes furrowed with age. Also called *sweet birch.*

black·bird (blak′bûrd′) *n.* **1** A common European thrush (*Turdus merula*), the male of which is black, with a yellow bill. **2** One of various black or blackish North American birds (family *Icteridae*), as the **crow blackbird** (*Quiscalus quiscula*), **marsh blackbird** (*Agelaius phoeniceus*), etc.

black·board (blak′bôrd′, -bōrd′) *n.* A blackened surface, for marking upon with chalk.

black body *Physics* **1** An ideal body that completely absorbs all radiant energy incident upon it. **2** The blackened interior of an opaque box or chamber with a very narrow slit.

black book A book or record of misdemeanors kept at some universities. — **to be in one's black book** To be in disfavor.

black·boy (blak′boi′) *n.* The grasstree.

black buck 1 The common Indian antelope (*Antilope cervicapra*) of a prevailing blackish-brown color. **2** The sable antelope (*Hippotragus niger*) of South Africa.

Black·burn (blak′bərn) A county borough in central Lancashire, England.

Blackburn, Mount A peak in southern Alaska; 16,140 feet.

Black Canyon 1 A gorge of the Colorado River, between Arizona and Nevada; site of Hoover Dam. See MEAD, LAKE. **2** A gorge of the Gunnison River in SW Colorado, a 10-mile section of which is included in **Black Canyon of the Gunnison National Monument**, established 1933.

black·cap (blak′kap′) *n.* **1** Any of several birds having a black crown, as the European warbler, chickadee, etc. **2** The black raspberry, or its fruit.

black·cock (blak′kok′) *n.* The male of the heath grouse.

black country A highly industrialized region of England in Staffordshire, Warwickshire, and Worcestershire.

black·damp (blak′damp′) *n.* Chokedamp.

black death A bubonic plague of exceptional virulence and duration prevalent in Asia and Europe in the 14th century.

black diamond 1 Mineral coal: only in plural. **2** Carbonado or bort.

black disease An acute, infectious, generally fatal hepatic disease of sheep, caused by an anaerobic bacterium (*Clostridium novyi*) transmitted by liver flukes.

black·en (blak′ən) *v.* **black·ened, black·en·ing** *v.t.* **1** To make black or dark. **2** To slander; defame. — *v.i.* **3** To become black; darken. — **black′en·er** *n.*

Black English A dialect of English spoken by many American blacks, and distinguished by special pronunciation, vocabulary, and grammatical or syntactic structure.

black eye 1 An eye with a black iris. **2** An eye having the adjacent surface discolored by a blow or bruise. **3** *Colloq.* A bad reputation. — **black′-eyed′** *adj.*

black-eyed Susan 1 One of the coneflowers (*Rudbeckia hirta*): the State flower of Maryland: also known as *yellow daisy.* **2** The bladder ketmia.

black·face (blak′fās′) *n.* **1** Makeup worn by a performer playing a black character, esp. in a minstrel show. **2** A performer wearing such makeup.

Black·feet (blak′fēt′) *n. pl. sing.* **·foot** A confederacy of Algonquian North American Indian tribes, consisting of the Siksika or Blackfeet, the Kainah, and the Piegan, formerly inhabiting the territory between the Saskatchewan and Missouri Rivers, now on reservations in Alberta and Montana.

black·fel·low (blak′fel′ō) *n.* An Australian aborigine.

black·fel·low's button (blak′fel·ōz) *Austral.* An Australite.

black·fish (blak′fish′) *n.* **1** One of various dark-colored cetaceans, as the pilot whale (genus *Globicephala*). **2** One of various fishes, as the tautog, the black sea bass, etc. **3** A food fish (*Dallia pectoralis*) of northern Alaskan and Siberian waters.

black flag See under FLAG.

black·fly (blak′flī′) *n.* **1** Any of certain small, stocky, dark-colored, biting flies (genus *Simulium*) having aquatic larvae, especially common in forested mountainous regions; especially, *S. hirtipes* of North America. **2** The buffalo gnat.

Black·foot (blak′foot′) *n.* A member of any of the tribes of North American Indians known as Blackfeet. — *adj.* Pertaining or belonging to the Blackfeet tribes: *Blackfoot* tales.

Black Forest A mountainous wooded region in southern Germany; highest peak, 4,898 feet: German *Schwarzwald.*

Black Friar A Dominican: so named from his black cloak.

Black·fri·ars (blak′frī′ərz) An area in the SW angle of old London city, England: named for the large number of Dominican monasteries in the district.

black frost A frost severe enough to turn vegetation black.

black·guard (blag′ərd, -ärd) *n.* A low, vicious fellow; a scoundrel. — *v.t.* To revile; vilify. — *v.i.* To act like a blackguard. — *adj.* Of or like a blackguard; base; vile: also **black′guard·ly.** [< *black guard*, orig., the scullions and low menials of a great house or army; later applied to any base person] — **black′guard·ism** *n.*

black·gum (blak′gum′) *n.* A large tree (*Nyssa sylvatica*) of the dogwood family, with an ovoid, blue-black drupe and close-grained wood hard to split; pepperidge; sour gum.

Black Hand 1 A society of anarchists in Spain, repressed in 1883. **2** A secret organization in the United States, especially of Italians, for the purpose of vengeance or blackmail. See MAFIA.

black·haw (blak′hô′) *n.* **1** The black oval drupe of certain species of *Viburnum.* **2** The sweet viburnum or sheepberry.

Black Hawk, 1767–1838, American Indian chief who fought against the United States in 1831–32.

black·head (blak′hed′) *n.* **1** An American scaup duck. **2** An infectious, often fatal protozoan disease of turkeys and certain wildfowl: it attacks chiefly the liver and intestines. **3** A facial blemish; comedo.

black·heart (blak′härt′) *n.* **1** A variety of early black cherry. **2** A blackening of the internal tissues of various trees and of the potato.

black·heart·ed (blak′här′tid) *adj.* Malign; wicked.

Black Hills A mountainous region in SW South Dakota and NE Wyoming; highest point, 7,242 feet; about 6,000 square miles.

black hole 1 A dark cell or dungeon. **2** A military lock-up: in allusion to the Black Hole in Fort William, at Calcutta, a room 18 feet square, into which 146 British subjects were forced on the night of June 20, 1756, of whom 123 died of asphyxia before morning. **3** A hypothetical hole in space into which stars and other celestial objects that have condensed to a certain radius collapse under the influence of gravity.

black horehound A fetid herb (*Ballota nigra*) of the mint family.

black·ing (blak′ing) *n.* **1** A preparation used to give blackness or luster, or both, to shoes, stoves, etc. **2** *Brit.* Shoe polish.

black·ish (blak′ish) *adj.* Somewhat black; darkened. — **black′ish·ly** *adv.*

black ivory 1 A pigment composed of carbonized ivory. **2** Formerly, blacks as merchandise in the slave trade.

black·jack (blak′jak′) *n.* **1** A small bludgeon with a flexible handle. **2** A black flag; a pirate's ensign. **3** A small oak (*Quercus marilandica*) of the SE United States. **4** Vingt-et-un: a card game. **5** A drinking can, formerly of leather, now of japanned metal. **6** Sphalerite or zincblende. **7** Caramel: used to color soups, wines, etc. — *v.t.* **1** To strike with a blackjack. **2** To coerce by threat.

BLACKJACK (def. 2)

black·ja·pan (blak′jə·pan′) *n.* Japan black.

black knot 1 A disease of plum and cherry trees, producing black knotlike excrescences on the branches, caused by a fungus (*Sphaeria morbosa*). **2** The fungus.

black lead Graphite.

black·leg (blak′leg′) *n.* **1** An acute, infectious, often fatal disease of young cattle,

caused by an anaerobic bacterium (*Clostridium chauvoei*) and characterized by fever and loss of appetite accompanied by swellings or tumors under the skin. **2** An injurious disease of cabbage and other cruciferous plants; also, a bacterial rot of potatoes. **3** A professional swindler or gambler; a cheat; sharper. **4** *Brit. Colloq.* A strikebreaker.

black letter *Printing* The Gothic or Old English letter.

𝕿𝖍𝖎𝖘 𝖑𝖎𝖓𝖊 𝖎𝖘 𝖎𝖓 𝖇𝖑𝖆𝖈𝖐 𝖑𝖊𝖙𝖙𝖊𝖗.

black·let·ter (blak′let′ər) *adj.* **1** Of or pertaining to manuscript printed or written in black letter. **2** Unfortunate or unlucky: a *black-letter* day. Also **black′·let′tered.**

black·light (blak′līt′) *n. Physics.* Ultraviolet radiation capable of exciting fluorescence in properly treated materials or objects.

black·list (blak′list′) *n.* A list of persons or organizations under suspicion or censure, or refused approval for any cause. — *v.t.* To place the name of (a person) on or as on a blacklist.

black lung A form of pneumoconiosis that afflicts coal miners.

black·ly (blak′lē) *adv.* In a manner showing blackness or darkness; gloomily; threateningly.

black Magellanic cloud *Astron.* One of several dark spaces in the Milky Way, especially one near the Southern Cross.

black magic See under MAGIC.

black·mail (blak′māl′) *n.* **1** Extortion by threats of public accusation or of exposure. **2** *Scot.* A tax formerly paid to bandits to insure immunity from pillage. — *v.t.* **1** To levy blackmail upon. **2** To force (a person to do something) as by threats: with *into*. [<BLACK + MAIL³] — **black′mail′er** *n.*

Black Ma·ri·a (mə·rī′ə) *Colloq.* A prison van or police patrol wagon.

black mark A mark or symbol used to record failure or bad conduct.

black market A place or firm where merchandise is offered for sale contrary to legal restrictions, or in quantities or at terms contrary to such restrictions. Also **black bourse.**

black match Strands of twine impregnated with gunpowder, used to ignite fireworks, etc.

black measles *Pathol.* A severe form of measles, marked by very dark eruptions.

black medic An annual herb of the bean family (*Medicago lupulina*) with yellow flowers and curved pods: also called *hop clover.*

Black Mountains The highest range of the Appalachians and a spur of the Blue Ridge Mountains in western North Carolina; highest point, 6,684 feet.

Black Muslim *n.* A member of a chiefly black group that follows Islamic religious beliefs.

black nationalist *n.* A member of a group of militant blacks who advocate separatism from whites and the creation of self-governing black communities.

black nightshade The common nightshade.

black·out (blak′out′) *n.* **1** A defensive or precautionary measure against aerial attack, consisting of the extinguishment or screening of all lights visible from the air. **2** *Physiol.* The partial or complete loss of vision and sometimes of consciousness, experienced by airplane pilots during rapid changes in velocity. **3** In theatrics, a fade-out or cut-out, as of part of a scene, eliminating it from view. **4** An official ban on the publication of news in war time, imposed for security reasons.

Black Panther *n.* A member of a militant black American organization of the same name.

black·poll (blak′pōl′) *n.* A North American wood warbler (*Dendroica striata*), the male of which has glossy black plumage on the top of the head.

Black·pool (blak′pool′) A county borough in west Lancashire, England; a seaside resort.

black·pot (blak′pot′) *n.* In ceramics, a type of coarse, unglazed pottery, manufactured chiefly in England.

black power The power of black Americans to establish their rights by collective action.

Black Prince See under EDWARD.

black racer The blacksnake.

Black River A river in Northern Vietnam, flowing 500 miles SE to the Red River: Annamese *Song Bo.*

Black Rod 1 *Brit.* An officer of the royal household, who acts as messenger from the House of Lords to the House of Commons. **2** An usher in the legislatures of British colonies and dominions.

black rot Leaf spot.

Black Sea A large inland sea between Europe and Asia, connected with the Mediterranean by the Bosporus, the Sea of Marmara, and the Dardanelles; 159,000 square miles: also *Euxine Sea.* Ancient **Pon·tus Eux·i·nus** (pon′təs yōōk·sī′nəs).

black sheep 1 One, among a herd of white sheep, that is black. **2** An evil-disposed or disreputable member of an otherwise decent family or society.

Black Shirt 1 A member of the Italian Fascist party, in allusion to the black shirts worn by members. **2** A member of the Nazi Schutzstaffel.

black·smith (blak′smith′) *n.* A workman who works in or welds wrought iron. Compare WHITESMITH.

black·snake (blak′snāk′) *n.* **1** A large, agile, non-venomous snake of the eastern United States (*Coluber constrictor*) with smooth, satiny, black scales; the black racer. **2** A dangerous Australian snake (*Pseudechis porphyriacus*) with blue-black scales and a venom similar to that of the cobra. **3** A heavy pliant whip of braided leather or rawhide.

black spruce A North American evergreen tree (*Picea mariana*) with deep blue-green foliage and firmly attached cones.

Black·stone (blak′stōn′, -stən), **Sir William,** 1723–80, English jurist.

black·thorn (blak′thôrn′) *n.* **1** A thorny European shrub (*Prunus spinosa*) of the rose family: the sloe. **2** A cane made from its wood. **3** An American hawthorn (*Crataegus calpodendron*).

black tie 1 A black bow tie. **2** A tuxedo and its correct accessories. **3** A phrase used on invitations to indicate semiformal dress.

black·top (blak′top′) *n.* Asphalt used for paving. — *v.t.* **-topped, -top·ping** To surface with blacktop.

black tracker *Austral.* An Australian aborigine used by police to track down a lost or wanted person in rough country.

black vomit 1 Yellow fever. **2** The dark bloody matter vomited in its later stages.

black walnut See under WALNUT.

Black Watch A regiment of the British Army, officially known as the Royal Highlanders: so called because of their somber tartan.

black·wa·ter fever (blak′wô′tər, -wot′ər) *Pathol.* A dangerous form of malaria characterized by the excretion of black or dark red urine; malarial hematuria.

black·weed (blak′wēd′) *n.* The ragweed.

Black·well's Island (blak′welz, -wəlz) Former name for WELFARE ISLAND.

black whale The blackfish (*Globicephala melaena*): also called *pilot whale.*

black widow A medium-sized, venomous female spider (*Latrodectus mactans*) common in dark, sheltered places in the United States, having a black body with an hourglass-shaped red mark on the abdomen: so called from its color and its habit of eating its mate.

black·will (blak′wil′) *n.* The black bass.

black·wood (blak′wood′) *n.* The black mangrove of Florida and tropical America (*Rhizophora mangle*).

blad (blad, bläd) *n. Scot.* A fragment or portion.

blad·der (blad′ər) *n.* **1** *Anat.* **a** A distensible membranous sac in the anterior part of the pelvic cavity, for the temporary retention of urine. **b** Some part or organ of analogous structure. ◆Collateral adjective: *vesical.* **2** *Biol.* An air vessel or an air cell in some seaweeds. **3** Anything puffed out, empty, or unsubstantial. **4** A blister or pustule. [OE *blædre*]

bladder campion A perennial herb (*Silene latifolia*) belonging to the pink family, and having the calyx much inflated.

blad·der·fish (blad′ər·fish′) *n.* The globefish.

bladder ket·mi·a (ket′mē·ə) **1** The flower-of-

an-hour, a European annual (*Hibiscus trionum*) of the mallow family, naturalized in America, with ephemeral pale yellow flowers and a purple-veined, bladderlike calyx. **2** The black-eyed Susan. Also **bladder ket·mie** (ket′mē).

blad·der·nose (blad′ər·nōz′) *n.* The hooded seal.

blad·der·nut (blad′ər·nut′) *n.* **1** Any plant of the genus *Staphylea* of the soapberry family, with large, inflated, three-lobed pods. **2** A seed pod of one of these plants.

blad·der·worm (blad′ər·wûrm′) *n. Zool.* An encysted larval tapeworm; a scolex; hydatid.

blad·der·wort (blad′ər·wûrt′) *n.* Any aquatic herb of the genus *Utricularia*, usually having little bladders on the leaves, in which minute organisms are trapped for nutriment.

blad·der·wrack (blad′ər·rak′) *n.* Any rockweed of the genus *Fucus*. See FUCUS.

blad·der·y (blad′ər·ē) *adj.* **1** Like a bladder. **2** Covered with or having bladders or vesicles.

blade (blād) *n.* **1** The flat, cutting part of any edged tool or weapon. **2** The thin, flat part of any instrument or utensil, as of an oar, screw propeller, plow, etc. **3** *Bot.* The leaf of grasses or certain other plants, especially, a leaf of Indian corn. **4** A rakish young man; wild, reckless fellow. **5** A swordsman; also, a sword. **6** *Phonet.* The upper flat part of the tongue immediately behind the tip and directly below the alveolar ridge. **7** The expanded or broad flat part of a leaf, petal, etc.; the lamina. **8** *Anat.* The shoulder blade or scapula. [OE *blæd* blade of a oar or sword] — **blad′ed** *adj.*

blae (blā, blē) *adj. Scot.* Blackish-blue or bluish-gray; livid; also, cloudy; bleak.

Bla·go·vesh·chensk (blä′gō·vyesh′chensk) A city on the Amur, Russian S.F.S.R.

blah (blä) *n. Slang* Excessive hyperbole; fustian; buncombe. — *adj.* Uninteresting; dull: a *blah* story.

blain (blān) *n. Pathol.* A pustular tumor; a blister. [OE *blegen*]

Blaine (blān), **James Gillespie,** 1830–93, U.S. statesman.

Blake (blāk), **Robert,** 1599–1657, English admiral. — **William,** 1757–1827, English painter, poet, and mystic.

blam·a·ble (blā′mə·bəl) *adj.* Deserving blame; culpable; faulty. — **blam′a·ble·ness** *n.* — **blam′a·bly** *adv.*

blame (blām) *v.t.* **blamed, blam·ing 1** To accuse of fault or error: often with *for.* **2** To find fault with; reproach. **3** To place the responsibility for (an action or error): with *on.* — **to be to blame** To be at fault. — *n.* Faultfinding; censure; also, the fault; culpability. See synonyms under ANIMADVERSION. [<OF *blasmer* <LL *blasphemare* revile, reproach <Gk. *blasphēmeein.* Doublet of BLASPHEME.]

Synonyms (verb): censure, chide, condemn, rebuke, reprehend, reproach, reprobate, reprove. We blame a person *for* a fault, or lay the blame *upon* him. See CONDEMN, REPROVE. Compare ARRAIGN. *Antonyms:* acquit, approve, eulogize, exculpate, exonerate, extol, laud, praise.

blamed (blāmd) *adj. U.S. Dial.* Damned: a *blamed* fool: a euphemism. — *adv.* Very: exceedingly: *blamed* hot.

blame·ful (blām′fəl) *adj.* **1** Deserving of blame. **2** Imputing blame. — **blame′ful·ly** *adv.* — **blame′ful·ness** *n.*

blame·less (blām′lis) *adj.* Innocent; guiltless. See synonyms under PERFECT. — **blame′less·ly** *adv.* — **blame′less·ness** *n.*

blame·wor·thy (blām′wûr′thē) *adj.* Deserving of blame. — **blame′wor′thi·ness** *n.*

Bla·mey (blā′mē), **Sir Thomas Albert,** 1884–1951, Australian general.

Blanc (blängk, blangk; *Fr.* blän), **Cape** A cape of Tunisia on the northernmost tip of Africa. *French* **Cap Blanc** (kàp blän′).

Blanc (blän), **Jean Joseph Charles Louis,** 1811–82, French socialist and historian.

Blanc, Mont See MONT BLANC.

Blan·ca Peak (blang′kə) Highest peak in the Sangre de Cristo Mountains, southern Colorado; 14,363 feet.

blanc fixe (bläṅ fēks′) Fine-grained barium sulfate, used as a base in making certain pigments, and in water colors, where it retains its white color.

blanch[1] (blanch, blänch) *v.t.* **1** To remove the color from; bleach. **2** To cause to turn pale, as from fear or anger. **3** To remove the skin of, as almonds, by scalding. **4** To whiten, as meat, by scalding. **5** *Bot.* To bleach by removing from light, as celery or endives. **6** *Metall.* To whiten or brighten (metals), as with acids or by coating with tin. —*v.i.* **7** To turn or become white or pale. See synonyms under BLEACH. —*adj.* **1** In heraldry, white; argent. **2** In English law, based on a slight payment, often in silver: said of tenures. **3** In Scottish law, designating a merely nominal quit-rent, as a pair of gloves, or the tenure thus held. [<F *blanchir* <*blanc* white] —**blanch′er** *n.*

blanch[2] (blanch, blänch) *v.t.* To turn, as a deer, aside or back. [Var. of BLENCH[1]]

Blanch (blanch, blänch) A feminine personal name. Also **Blanche,** *Fr.* **Blanche** (bläṅsh), *Ital.* **Bian·ca** (byäng′kä), *Sp.* **Blan·ca** (bläng′·kä). [<Gmc., white, shining]

blanc·mange (blə·mänzh′, -mäṅzh′) *n.* A whitish, jellylike preparation of milk, eggs, sugar, cornstarch, flavoring, etc.: used for desserts, etc. [<F *blanc-manger* white food]

Blan·co (blang′kō), **Cape** The westernmost point of Oregon.

bland (bland) *adj.* **1** Affable in manner; gentle; suave. **2** Mild; balmy; genial. **3** Not stimulating or irritating. **4** Smooth and mild in flavor; as, a *bland* sauce. [<L *blandus* mild]—**bland′ly** *adv.* —**bland′ness** *n.*

Synonyms: affable, balmy, benign, complaisant, courteous, genial, gentle, gracious, mild, smooth, soft, tender. *Antonyms*: acrid, biting, brusk, curt, harsh, rough, rude.

Blan·ding's turtle (blan′dingz) The emyd. [after William *Blanding,* 19th c. U.S. herpetologist]

blan·dish (blan′dish) *v.t.* To wheedle; flatter; cajole. [<OF *blandiss-*, stem of *blandir* flatter < L *blandiri* <*blandus* mild, gentle] —**blan′·dish·er** *n.*

blan·dish·ment (blan′dish·mənt) *n.* Soothing, caressing, or flattering speech or action; cajolery.

blank (blangk) *adj.* **1** Wholly or partly free from writing or print. **2** Lacking in ornament, variety, interest, or results. **3** Empty; void. **4** Without expression or animation: a *blank* stare. **5** Without rime: *blank* verse. **6** Disconcerted; confused. **7** Utter; downright. **8** Pale or white; colorless. **9** Having no finishing cuts, slots, grooves, teeth, or the like; unfinished: common in such phrases as *blank arcade, arch, file, key, saw, window,* etc. —*n.* **1** A paper containing no written or printed matter. **2** A written or printed paper with blank spaces. **3** A vacant space; void interval. **4** A lottery ticket which has drawn no prize; a disappointing result. **5** A partially prepared piece, as of wood or metal, ready for forming into a finished object, as a coin, key, button, etc. **6** The central white spot of a target; bull's-eye. **7** A blank verse. **8** A blank cartridge. —*v.t.* **1** To delete; invalidate: often with *out.* **2** In games, to prevent (an opponent) from scoring. **3** *Archaic* To disconcert; put out of countenance. [<F *blanc* white, ult. <Gmc.] —**blank′ly** *adv.* —**blank′ness** *n.*

Synonyms (adj.): bare, barren, clear, empty, plain, unfilled, unlimited, unmarked, unsigned. See BLEAK, VACANT.

Blan·ka (bläng′kä) Swedish form of BLANCH.

blank·book (blangk′bŏŏk′) *n.* A book with blank leaves, for accounts, memoranda, etc.

blank cartridge A cartridge loaded only with powder.

blank check *Colloq.* Carte blanche.

blank endorsement The writing of one's name as an indorser across the back of a negotiable instrument, without any words of restriction or contingency, making it payable to bearer.

blan·ket (blang′kit) *n.* **1** A heavy woolen covering, as of a bed. **2** A robe of like material used, by Indians, as a garment, or for horses, etc., as a protection. **3** A sheet of other material, as cotton, of like appearance. **4** Anything that covers, conceals, or protects: a *blanket* of snow; a *blanket* of smoke; a *blanket* of rubber. —*adj.* **1** Designating anything which covers a wide range or large number of interrelated names, conditions, objects, items, or the like; covering every phase of a subject; all-embracing: a *blanket* ballot; *blanket* injunction. **2** Using blankets for garments: a *blanket* Indian. —*v.t.* **1** To cover with or as with a blanket. **2** To cover or apply uniformly: The new law *blankets* the nation. **3** To obscure or suppress; interfere: A strong broadcast *blankets* a weak one. **4** *Naut.* To deprive (a sailboat) of wind by passing close on the windward side. **5** To toss in a blanket as sport or punishment. [<OF *blankete,* dim. of *blanc* white; orig. a white or undyed cloth]

blank verse Verse without rime; specifically, iambic pentameter verse, the principal verse form in English epic and dramatic poetry.

blan·quette (bläṅ·ket′) *n.* A stew of veal, lamb, chicken, or any white meat served in an egg sauce, garnished with mushrooms and onions. [<F <*blanc* white]

blare (blâr) *v.t. & v.i.* **blared, blar·ing 1** To sound loudly, as a trumpet. **2** To announce loudly. —*n.* **1** A loud brazen sound. See synonyms under NOISE. **2** Brightness or glare, as of color. [Prob. imit.]

blar·ney (blär′nē) *n.* Wheedling flattery. —*v.t. & v.i.* To flatter, cajole, or wheedle. [<BLARNEY STONE]

Blar·ney (blär′nē) A village in central County Cork, Ireland.

Blarney Stone A stone in a 15th century castle in Blarney, Ireland, which, when kissed, reputedly endows one with invincible eloquence.

Blas·co-I·bá·ñez (bläs′kō-ē·vä′nyāth), **Vicente,** 1867–1928, Spanish novelist.

bla·sé (blä·zā′, blä′zā) *adj.* Sated with pleasure; wearied or worn out, as by dissipation; indifferent. [<F, pp. of *blaser* satiate]

blas·pheme (blas·fēm′) *v.* **·phemed, ·phem·ing** —*v.t.* **1** To speak in an impious or irreverent manner of (God or sacred things). **2** To speak ill of; malign. —*v.i.* **3** To utter blasphemy. [<OF *blasfemer* <LL *blasphemare* <Gk. *blasphēmein* revile <*blasphēmos* evil-speaking. Doublet of BLAME.]

blas·phe·mous (blas′fə·məs) *adj.* Impious; irreverent; profane. See synonyms under PROFANE. —**blas′phe·mous·ly** *adv.* —**blas′phe·mous·ness** *n.*

blas·phe·my (blas′fə·mē) *n. pl.* **·mies 1** Evil or profane speaking of God or sacred things; claiming the attributes of God. **2** In the Old Testament, any attempt to lessen reverence for the name of Jehovah. **3** Any irreverent act or utterance. See synonyms under OATH.

blast (blast, bläst) *v.t.* **1** To rend in pieces by or as by explosion. **2** To cause to wither or shrivel; destroy. —*n.* **1** A strong or sudden wind. **2** *Metall.* The strong artificial current of air in a blast furnace. **3** The discharge of an explosive, or its effect. **4** The charge of dynamite or other explosive used in shattering rocks, as for a building foundation, tunnel, etc. **5** A loud, sudden sound, as of a trumpet. **6** A blight or blighting influence. **7** The draft of air near the muzzle of a cannon at its discharge. **8** *Slang* A party. **9** *Slang* An important or surprising event or occasion. **10** *Slang* A drink of hard liquor. See synonyms under RUPTURE. —**in blast** In operation: said of a smelting furnace. —**at full blast** At capacity operation or maximum speed. [OE *blæst* blowing. Akin to BLOW[1].] —**blast′er** *n.*

-blast *combining form Biol.* Growth; sprout: *ameloblast.* [<Gk. *blastos* bud]

blast·ed (blas′tid, bläs′-) *adj.* **1** Blighted; withered or destroyed. **2** *Colloq.* Confounded: a euphemistic oath.

blas·te·ma (blas·tē′mə) *n. pl.* **·ma·ta** (-mə·tə) Embryonic protoplasm; the formative material of an ovum. [<Gk. *blastēma* offspring]

blast furnace *Metall.* A smelting furnace in which the fire is intensified by an air blast.

blast·ing (blas′ting, bläs′-) *n.* **1** The act of rending by charges of explosives. **2** A blighting or withering. **3** *Telecom.* The distortion resulting from the imposing on a microphone or loudspeaker of a greater volume of sound than can be properly transmitted.

blasting gelatin A high explosive, made by dissolving collodion cotton in nine times its weight of nitroglycerin.

blast·ment (blast′mənt, bläst′-) *n. Obs.* A blast; a blight.

blasto- *combining form Biol.* Growth, sprout: *blastoderm.* Also, before vowels, **blast-.** [<Gk. *blastos* a sprout]

blas·to·cele (blas′tə·sēl) *n. Biol.* The cavity of the blastodermic vesicle. Also **blas′to·coele.**

blas·to·cyst (blas′tə·sist) *n.* The blastula.

blas·to·derm (blas′tə·dûrm) *n. Biol.* The germinal disk. [<BLASTO- + Gk. *derma* skin] —**blas′to·der′mic** *adj.*

blas·to·disk (blas′tə·disk) *n. Biol.* A nucleated disk of protoplasm which forms on the surface of the yolk mass in certain eggs. Also **blas′·to·disc.**

blast-off (blast′ôf′) *n.* The launching of a rocket or missile.

blas·to·gen·e·sis (blas′tə·jen′ə·sis) *n. Biol.* **1** Origin from the germ plasm: opposed to *pangenesis.* **2**. Reproduction by budding. —**blas′·to·gen′ic** *adj.*

blas·to·mere (blas′tə·mir) *n. Biol.* One of the large number of small cells formed during the cleavage of the fertilized ovum. —**blas′to·mer′·ic** (-mer′ik) *adj.*

blas·to·pore (blas′tə·pôr, -pōr) *n. Biol.* The exterior opening of the primitive intestine. —**blas′to·por′ic** (-pôr′ik, -por′ik) *adj.*

blas·to·sphere (blas′tə·sfir) *n. Biol.* **1** The blastodermic vesicle of the mammalian egg. **2** A blastula.

blas·tu·la (blas′chŏŏ·lə) *n. pl.* **·lae** (-lē) *Biol.* The stage of the embryo just preceding the formation of the gastrula; a hollow sphere of one layer of blastomeres enclosing a blastocele or segmentation cavity. [<NL <Gk. *blastos* sprout] —**blas′tu·lar** *adj.*

blat (blat) *v.* **blat·ted, blat·ting** *v.t. Colloq.* To utter heedlessly; blurt out. —*v.i.* To bleat, as a sheep. [Var. of BLEAT]

bla·tant (blā′tənt) *adj.* **1** Loud or noisy; offensively loud or clamorous. **2** Making a bellowing or bleating noise: said of animals. **3** Tumid; pretentious; obtrusive. [Coined by Edmund Spenser. Cf. L *blatire* babble; ME *blait* bleat.] —**bla′tan·cy** *n.* —**bla′tant·ly** *adv.*

blath·er (blath′ər) *v.t. & v.i.* To talk garrulously or foolishly. —*n.* Foolish talk; nonsense. Also spelled *blether.* Also **blat·ter** (blat′ər). [<ON *blathra* talk stupidly <*blathr* nonsense]

blath·er·skite (blath′ər·skīt) *n.* **1** A blustering, noisy fellow; a hoodlum. **2** Blustering talk; balderdash. **3** The ruddy duck. [<BLETHER + SKATE[3]]

blau·bok (blou′bok) *n. pl.* **·bok** or **·boks 1** An extinct South African antelope *(Hippotragus leucophaeus)* with bluish hair. **2** A South African antelope (genus *Cephalopus*) about the size of a rabbit. [<Afrikaans]

Bla·vat·sky (blə·vät′skē), **Helena Petrovna,** 1831–91, Russian theosophist.

blaw (blô) *v.t. & v.i. Scot.* To blow.

blawn (blôn) *Scot.* Blown.

blaze[1] (blāz) *v.* **blazed, blaz·ing** *v.i.* **1** To burn brightly. **2** To burn as with emotion: to *blaze* with anger. **3** To shine; be resplendent. —*v.t.* **4** *Rare* To cause to flame or shine brightly. See synonyms under BURN. —**to blaze away** To keep on firing; hence, to go on or proceed with anything. —*n.* **1** A vivid glowing flame; fire. **2** Brightness or brilliance and heat; effulgence; also, glare. **3** Excitement or ardor. See synonyms under FIRE, LIGHT. [OE *blæse* firebrand]

blaze[2] (blāz) *v.t.* **blazed, blaz·ing 1** To mark (a tree) by chipping off a piece of bark. **2** To mark out (a path) in this way. —*n.* **1** A white spot on the face of an animal, as a horse. **2** A mark chipped on a tree, to indicate a path; a path so indicated. [Akin to ON *blesi* white spot on a horse's face]

blaze[3] (blāz) *v.t.* **blazed, blaz·ing 1** To publish abroad or noise about. **2** *Obs.* To blare forth. [ON *blāsa* blow]

blaz·er (blā′zər) *n.* **1** A lightweight jacket of flannel or silk in vivid colors, usually worn in outdoor sports. **2** A dish with a small brazier under it for hot coals. **3** *Colloq.* That which blazes.

blazing star 1 A smooth herb *(Chamaelirium luteum)* of the lily family, with wandlike racemes of white flowers: also called *fairy wand.* **2** One of various perennial herbs of the genus *Liatris,* of the composite family, especially *L. squarrosa.* **3** *Her.* A six-pointed star with the tail of a comet, used as a bearing. **4** *Obs.* A comet. **5** In the western United States, a stampede of animals. **6** A center of interest; cynosure.

bla·zon (blā′zən) n. 1 Her. A coat of arms or armorial bearing, or a banner bearing such representation; a technical description or a graphic representation of armorial bearings. 2 A proclaiming or publishing abroad. 3 Ostentatious display. — v.t. 1 To inscribe or adorn, as with names or symbols. 2 Her. To describe technically or paint (coats of arms). 3 To proclaim; publish. See synonyms under PUBLISH. [<F blason coat of arms, shield] — bla′zon·er n. — bla′zon·ment n.

bla·zon·ry (blā′zən·rē) n. 1 The art of describing or depicting heraldic devices. 2 A coat of arms. 3 Decoration; show.

-ble See -ABLE.

bleach (blēch) v.t. 1 To deprive of color, as by exposure to the sun or chemicals; whiten. 2 To make pale: Fear bleached his face. — v.i. 3 To become colorless, pale or white. — n. 1 An act or the act of bleaching; also, the result of the act or degree of bleaching obtained. 2 A fluid or powder used as a bleaching agent. [OE blǣcean]
Synonyms (verb): blanch, whiten, whitewash. To whiten is to make white in general, but commonly it means to overspread with white coloring matter. Bleach and blanch both signify to whiten by depriving of color, the former permanently (as linen), the latter either permanently (as, to blanch celery) or temporarily (as, to blanch the cheek with fear). To whitewash is to whiten the surface of, literally with whitewash, or figuratively with false praise or by minimizing a fault. Antonyms: blacken, color, darken, dye, soil, stain.

bleach·er (blē′chər) n. 1 One who or that which bleaches. 2 Usually pl. An outdoor uncovered seat or stand for spectators.

bleach·er·y (blē′chər·ē) n. pl. ·er·ies A place where bleaching is done.

bleach·ing (blē′ching) n. The process of whitening, as textile fibers and fabrics, by treatment with chemicals or exposure to the sun and weather.

bleaching powder A white or grayish-white powder with a slight odor of hypochlorous acid, formed by treating slaked lime with chlorine, and used for bleaching and as a disinfectant: also called chloride of lime.

bleak¹ (blēk) adj. 1 Exposed to wind and weather; bare; barren; dreary. 2 Cold, cutting, or penetrating. [<ON bleikja pale] —bleak′ish adj. —bleak′ly adv. —bleak′ness n.
Synonyms: blank, cheerless, chill, cold, cutting, desolate, dreary, exposed, piercing, stormy, unsheltered, waste, wild, windy. Antonyms: balmy, bright, cheerful, genial, homelike, mild, sheltered, sunny, warm.

bleak² (blēk) n. pl. bleak or bleaks A small European cyprinoid fish (genus Alburnus), whose scales are lined with a silvery pigment used in making artificial pearls. [<ON bleikja]

blear (blir) adj. 1 Dimmed, as by tears or rheum; dull. 2 Causing dimness of sight; also, dim; obscure; indistinct; hazy. — v.t. 1 To dim or inflame (the eyes). 2 To obscure, as the face with tears; blur. 3 To mislead; hoodwink. — n. That which renders vision indistinct; also, a blurry condition or look. [ME blere. Akin to LG bleer-oged blear-eyed.] — blear′y adj. — blear′i·ness n.

blear-eyed (blir′īd′) adj. 1 Having inflamed or rheumy eyes. 2 Weak-sighted. Also blear′y-eyed′.

bleat (blēt) n. The cry of the sheep, goat, or calf; also, any sound resembling it. — v.i. 1 To cry, as a sheep or goat. 2 To speak with such a sound, as with fear or in complaint. — v.t. 3 To utter with the sound of a bleat. 4 To babble foolishly; prate. [OE blǣtan] —bleat′er n. —bleat′ing adj. —bleat′. ing·ly adv.

bleb (bleb) n. A blister, or bladderlike body; a bulla. [ME bleb; imit.] — bleb′by adj.

bled (bled) Past tense and past participle of BLEED.

Bled (bled) A village and resort in NW Slovenia, Yugoslavia, on the shores of Bled Lake.

bleed (blēd) v. bled, bleed·ing v.t. 1 To draw blood from; leech. 2 To exude, as sap, blood, or other fluid. 3 To draw sap or other fluid from. 4 To empty of liquid or gaseous matter. 5 To extort money from; overcharge.

6 In bookbinding, to trim (a page) too closely, so as to cut into or mar the printed or engraved matter. — v.i. 7 To lose or shed blood. 8 To exude sap or other fluid. 9 To suffer wounds or die, as in battle: He bled for his country. 10 To feel grief, sympathy, or anguish. 11 To suffer by extortion; be overcharged. 12 To be cut into, as a printed page. 13 To run, as dyes in wet cloth. — to bleed (someone) white To extort money from in very large amounts. — n. 1 A page or plate so trimmed as to cut the printing or engraving. 2 The part of a page or plate on which printing or an illustration extends beyond the usual printing edge. [OE blēdan]

bleed·er (blē′dər) n. 1 One who or that which bleeds. 2 A person who bleeds profusely from slight wounds; a hemophiliac.

bleeding heart 1 Any of various plants having racemes of pink, drooping, heart-shaped flowers; especially, the ornamental garden herb (Dicentra spectabilis). 2 Colloq. One whose political views are unduly influenced by sympathy for alleged suffering.

BLEEDING HEART (From 1 to 3 feet tall.)

bleek·bok (blēk′bok) n. An antelope, the oribi. [<Afrikaans]

blel·lum (blel′əm) n. Scot. A noisy talker.

blem·ish (blem′ish) v.t. To mar the perfection of; sully. — n. A disfiguring defect; also, moral reproach or stain. [<OF blemiss-, stem of blemir make livid <blême pale, wan] —blem′. ish·er n.
Synonyms (noun): blot, blur, brand, crack, daub, defacement, defect, deformity, dent, disfigurement, disgrace, dishonor, fault, flaw, imperfection, injury, reproach, smirch, soil, speck, spot, stain, stigma, taint, tarnish. A blemish is superficial; a flaw or taint is in structure or substance. In the moral sense, a blemish comes from one's own ill-doing; a brand or stigma is inflicted by others; as, the brand of infamy; we speak of a blot or stain upon reputation; a flaw or taint in character. A defect is the want or lack of something; fault, primarily a failing, is something that fails of an apparent intent or disappoints a natural expectation. See INJURY.

Blem·my·es (blem′mē·ēz) n. pl. A fabled people of ancient Libya who had no heads, but eyes and mouth placed in the breast.

blench¹ (blench) v.i. 1 To shrink back; flinch. 2 Obs. To turn aside. [OE blencan deceive] — blench′er n.

blench² (blench) See BLANCH.

blend (blend) v. blend·ed or blent, blend·ing v.t. 1 To mix, as paints or whiskies, so as to obtain a combined product of a desired quality, taste, color, or consistency. 2 To prepare by such process. — v.i. 3 To mix; intermingle. 4 To pass or shade imperceptibly into each other, as colors. 5 To harmonize; suit one another. See synonyms under MIX, UNITE. — n. 1 The act or result of mixing; a mixture. 2 Ling. A word resulting from the combining of parts of two distinct words of generally similar meaning, as brunch from breakfast and lunch: also called portmanteau word, telescope word. [Fusion of OE blendan, var. of blandan mix and ON blanda mingle]

blende (blend) n. 1 Sphalerite; zinc sulfide. 2 One of a number of rather bright minerals, generally a compound of sulfur with a metallic element. [<G blendendes erz deceptive ore] — blend′ous, blend′y adj.

blend·er (blen′dər) An automatic electrical device that mixes and blends foods, paints, cement, etc.

Blen·heim (blen′əm) See under SPANIEL.

Blen·heim (blen′əm) A village in western Bavaria, Germany; scene of Marlborough's and Eugene of Savoy's victory in an important battle, 1704, in the War of the Spanish Succession: German Blindheim.

Blenheim Park An estate and parish in central Oxfordshire, England; site of Blenheim Palace, voted by Parliament as a grant to the Duke of Marlborough for his victory at Blenheim and built by Vanbrugh, 1705–16.

Blen·ner·has·set (blen′ər·has′it), Harman, 1764–1831, Anglo-American lawyer involved with Aaron Burr in a plot to conquer Texas and Mexico.

blen·ny (blen′ē) n. pl. blen·nies A small percoid marine fish (family Blennidae) having the pelvic fins placed close together below the throat. [<L blennius <Gk. blennos slime]

bleph·a·ri·tis (blef′ə·rī′tis) n. Pathol. Inflammation of the eyelids.

blepharo- combining form Anat., Pathol. Eyelid. Also, before vowels, blephar-, as in blepharitis. [<Gk. blepharon eyelid]

Blé·riot (blā·ryō′), Louis, 1872–1936, French aviator and designer.

bles·bok (bles′bok) n. pl. ·bok or ·boks A large South African antelope (Damaliscus albifrons), of a prevailing violet color and having a white blaze extending over its face. Also bles·buck (-buk). [<Afrikaans]

bless (bles) v.t. blessed or blest, bless·ing 1 To consecrate; make holy by religious rite. 2 To honor and exalt; glorify. 3 To sanctify or protect by making the sign of the cross over. 4 To invoke God's favor upon (a person or thing). 5 To bestow happiness or prosperity upon; make happy. 6 To endow, as with a gift: She was blessed with a beautiful face. 7 To guard; protect: used as an exclamation: God bless me; Bless me! See synonyms under PRAISE. [OE blēdsian consecrate (with blood) <blōd blood] — bless′er n.

bless·ed (bles′id, blest) adj. 1 Being in enjoyment of felicity in heaven; beatified. 2 Worthy of veneration or of blessing. 3 Joyful; healing. 4 Happy; favored. 5 Confounded, cursed, or the like: a euphemistic, ironical, or merely intensive use: not a blessed cent. Also blest (blest). See synonyms under HAPPY, HOLY. — bless′ed·ly adv.

blessed event Colloq. The birth of a baby.

bless·ed·ness (bles′id·nis) n. The state of one who is blessed; felicity. — single blessedness The unmarried state.

Bless·ed Sacrament (bles′id) In the Roman Catholic Church, the consecrated elements in the mass, especially the Host.

bless·ing (bles′ing) n. 1 That which makes happy or prosperous; a gift of divine favor. 2 A benediction. 3 Grateful adoration; worship. 4 Cursing or scolding: a euphemism. See synonyms under FAVOR, MERCY.

blest (blest) adj. Blessed.

blet (blet) v.i. blet·ted, blet·ting To decay internally, as a fleshy fruit after ripening. — n. Incipient decay in overripe fruit. [<F blet overripe]

bleth·er (bleth′ər) n. Scot. Blather.

blew (bloo) Past tense of BLOW.

Bli·da (blē′də) A city in north central Algeria.

Bligh (blī), William, 1754–1817, British naval officer.

blight (blīt) n. 1 Any of a number of destructive plant diseases, as mildew, rust, smut, etc. 2 Anything that withers hopes or prospects; also, the act of ruining or destroying. 3 A minute insect, usually an aphis, injurious to trees. 4 A deteriorating influence or condition affecting use, development, and value, as of real estate. — v.t. 1 To cause to decay; blast. 2 To ruin; frustrate. — v.i. 3 To suffer blight. [Origin unknown]

Bligh·ty (blī′tē) n. Brit. Slang 1 England; hence, home. 2 A wound severe enough to necessitate one's being sent to England for treatment. [Alter. of Hindustani Bilāyati foreign country]

blimp (blimp) n. Colloq. 1 A non-rigid, lighter-than-air, dirigible balloon. 2 The soundproof cover enclosing a motion-picture camera: also called bungalow. [<Type B-Limp, a kind of British dirigible]

blind (blīnd) adj. 1 Without the power of seeing. 2 Lacking in perception or judgment. 3 Acting or proceeding at random. 4 Difficult to understand or trace; illegible; unintelligible. 5 Having no opening or outlet: a blind ditch. 6 Having but one opening; open at one end only: a blind alley. 7 Difficult to find or follow: a blind path. 8 Of or relating to blind persons as a class. 9 Dark; obscure. — to go it blind 1 To bet in a poker game before looking at one's hand. 2 Hence,

to undertake anything without reasonable inquiry. — *n.* **1** Something that obstructs vision or shuts off light; particularly, a window shade; a screen or shutter. **2** A subterfuge; ruse. **3** One who is, or those who are, blind. **4** A place of ambush; hiding place. **5** A baggage car with no end door: also **blind baggage.** See synonyms under ARTIFICE. — *v.t.* **1** To make blind. **2** To dazzle. **3** To deprive of judgment or discernment. **4** To darken; obscure. **5** To outshine; eclipse. [OE]

blind alley 1 An alley, road, etc., open at one end only. **2** Any search, occupation, or the like, in which progress is blocked.

blind date A date with a person whom one has not previously seen or met, usually arranged by a third person.

blind·er (blīn′dər) *n.* **1** One who or that which blinds. **2** A flap on the side of a horse's bridle, to obstruct his side view: also called *blinker.* For illustration see HARNESS.

blind·fish (blīnd′fish′) *n.* A fish of subterranean streams without functional eyes; especially, the cavefish *(Amblyopsis spelaeus),* found in the Mammoth Cave of Kentucky.

blind·fold (blīnd′fōld′) *v.t.* **1** To cover or bandage the eyes of. **2** To hoodwink; mislead. — *n.* A bandage, etc., over the eyes. — *adj.* **1** Having the eyes bandaged. **2** Having the mental vision darkened; rash. Also **blind′·fold′ed** *adj.* [ME *blindfellen* < *blind* blind + *fellen* strike; infl. in spelling by FOLD]

blind gut The cecum.

Blind·heim (blint′hīm) German name for BLENHEIM.

blind hinge A shutter hinge constructed so that the shutter or other piece hinged thereby closes itself by its own weight when not held open. For illustration see under HINGE.

blind·ing (blīn′ding) *adj.* Making blind or as if blind, physically or mentally: *blinding* tears; *blinding* passions. — **blind′ing·ly** *adv.*

blind·ly (blīnd′lē) *adv.* Without sight or without foresight; recklessly.

blind·man's–buff (blīnd′manz′buf′) *n.* A game in which one who is blindfolded must catch and identify someone.

blind poker A game of poker in which bets are made before the hands are seen.

blind side The weakest or most vulnerable side.

blind spot 1 *Anat.* A small area on the retina of the eye that is insensible to light because of the entrance of the fibers of the optic nerve. **2** A subject or a phase of thought in which one is unable to be objective or critical.

blind staggers Staggers (def. 1).

blind·sto·ry (blīnd′stôr′ē, -stō′rē) *n. pl.* **·sto·ries** A story without windows; the triforium.

blind tiger *Slang* A place where intoxicants are illegally served and sold. Also **blind pig.**

blind·worm (blīnd′wûrm′) *n.* A small, limbless, snakelike lizard with very small but perfect eyes; especially the slowworm *(Anguis fragilis)* of Europe and Africa.

blink (blingk) *v.i.* **1** To wink rapidly. **2** To look with half–closed eyes, as in sunlight; squint. **3** To twinkle; glimmer; also, to flash on and off. **4** To ignore something: He *blinked* at the law. — *v.t.* **5** To cause to wink. **6** To shut the eyes to; evade: to *blink* matters. **7** To send (a message) by blinker light. — *n.* **1** A glance or glimpse. **2** A shimmer or glimmer. **3** Light reflected from floating ice; iceblink. [<Du. *blinken*]

blink·er (blingk′ər) *n.* **1** One who or that which blinks. **2** A blinker light. **3** *pl.* Goggles. **4** A horse's blinder.

blinker light 1 A light set to blink at regular intervals, usually as a warning. **2** A light used to signal messages.

blin·tze (blin′tsə) *n.* A thin pancake folded about a filling, as of cheese. Also **blintz** (blints). [<Yiddish]

blip (blip) *n.* **1** *Telecom.* A visual display of a radar echo. **2** A short, sharp sound. — *v.i.* **blipped, blip·ping 1** To make blips. — *v.t.* **2** To delete (speech) from a videotape, as in censoring, thus creating a discontinuity: to *blip* swearwords. [Imit.]

bliss (blis) *n.* **1** Superlative happiness; heavenly joy. **2** Gladness; joy. **3** A cause of delight. See synonyms under HAPPINESS, RAPTURE. [OE *bliths* < *blithe* joyous] — **bliss′ful** *adj.* — **bliss′ful·ly** *adv.* — **bliss′ful·ness** *n.*

blis·ter (blis′tər) *n.* **1** A thin vesicle, especially one on the skin, containing watery matter, as from a scald, bruise, etc. **2** A similar vesicle on a plant, on steel, or on a painted surface. **3** Any substance used for blistering. **4** *Nav.* A bulge on the hull of a warship below the waterline to protect it from torpedoes. **5** *Aeron.* A bulge or projection from the fuselage of certain aircraft, containing guns and used for observation. — *v.t.* **1** To produce a blister or blisters upon. **2** To rebuke; lash with words. — *v.i.* **3** To become blistered. [OF *blestre* <ON *blāstr* swelling]

blister beetle 1 A beetle (family *Meloidae*), yielding a vesicating substance; especially, the Spanish fly. **2** A long, slender beetle (genus *Epicauta*), widely distributed in the United States, especially *E. pennsylvanicus,* very destructive of the potato. See illustrations under INSECTS (injurious).

blis·tered (blis′tərd) *adj.* **1** Having blisters. **2** Covered with raised spots resembling blisters. **3** Having slits which reveal material of a different color or a different type of material, especially in 16th century costumes.

blister gas *Mil.* A gaseous vesicant used in warfare.

blister rust A serious disease of pine trees, especially the white–pine blister rust, caused by a fungus (genus *Cronartium*) that raises blisters on the bark.

blis·ter·y (blis′tər·ē) *adj.* Marked by or full of blisters.

blithe (blīth) *adj.* Characterized by gladness or mirth; joyous; gay; merry; sprightly. See synonyms under CHEERFUL, HAPPY, MERRY. [OE] — **blithe′ly** *adv.*

blithe·some (blīth′səm) *adj.* Showing or imparting gladness; cheerful; merry. See synonyms under HAPPY. — **blithe′some·ly** *adv.* — **blithe′some·ness** *n.*

blitz (blits) *v.t. Colloq.* To attack with sudden and overwhelming force. — *n.* Sudden force; lightninglike destruction. — *adj.* Lightning-like. [<G, lightning]

blitz·krieg (blits′krēg) *n.* **1** Lightning war. **2** Sudden overwhelming attack with powerful force. [<G]

bliz·zard (bliz′ərd) *n. Meteorol.* **1** A high, cold wind accompanied by blinding snow. **2** A severe and heavy snowstorm of long duration. [< dial.E *blizzer* sudden blow, flash of lightning]

bloat[1] (blōt) *v.t.* **1** To cause to swell, as with fluid or gas. **2** To puff up; make proud or vain. — *v.i.* **3** To swell; become puffed up. — *n.* **1** One who is bloated; a drunkard. **2** An accumulation of gas in the rumen or intestinal tract of an animal brought on by the fermentation of green forage. — *adj.* Bloated; puffed; swollen. [ME *blout,* ? <ON *blautr* soft, soaked]

bloat[2] (blōt) *v.t.* To cure, as herring, by half-drying in smoke. — *adj.* Smoke–cured: a *bloat* herring. [ME *blote,* ? <ON *blautr* soft, soaked]

bloat·ed (blō′tid) *adj.* **1** Swollen with fluid or gas. **2** Turgid; edematous. **3** Puffed up; conceited.

bloat·er (blō′tər) *n.* **1** A selected smoked herring. **2** A whitefish *(Argyrosomus prognathus)* of the Great Lakes of North America.

blob (blob) *n.* **1** A soft, globular mass; a drop, as of viscous liquid; a blotch or daub. **2** A noise like that made by a fish flopping in water. — *v.* **blobbed, blob·bing** *v.t.* **1** To smear with ink or color; blur. — *v.i.* **2** To rise in bubbles or produce bubbles. **3** To flop, as a fish in water. [Imit.]

bloc (blok) *n.* A group, as of politicians, combined to foster special interests or to obstruct legislative action: originally, a combination of members of different political parties in the French Chamber of Deputies. Compare BLOCK[2]. [<F]

Bloch (blok, *Ger.* blôkh), **Ernest,** 1880–1959, U.S. composer born in Switzerland.

block[1] (blok) *n.* **1** A solid piece of wood, metal, or other material. **2** A wooden log or the like upon which chopping is done. **3** A temporary support; shore. **4** The stand on which slaves were sold at auction. **5** A wooden billet on which condemned persons are beheaded. **6** The form or piece on which the final shape is given to a hat body, or one on which a hat is placed to be ironed. **7** A wooden support for a wig: a barbers' *block.* **8** A continuous portion of land: a 10–acre *block.* **9** A sheave or pulley, or set of pulleys, in a frame or shell. **10** The land and buildings enclosed in a single square, or the like, bounded by streets; the distance along a street from

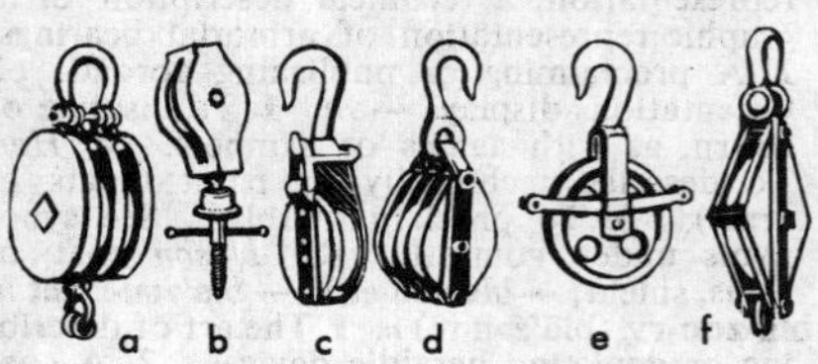

TYPES OF BLOCKS

a. Tackle. *b.* Dock. *c.* Link snatch. *d.* Triple–sheave steel. *e.* Gin. *f.* Square–cheeked.

one cross–street to another. **11** A group acting or considered as a unit: a *block* of theater seats; the Asian *block* of nations. **12** *Austral.* The public promenade of a city; also, one of the sections into which the public lands available for settlement are divided. **13** A section of a railroad controlled by signals. **14** A set, as of tickets, shares of stock, etc., handled as a unit. — *v.t.* **1** To shape into blocks. **2** To shape, mold, or stamp with a block, as a hat. **3** To secure or strengthen with blocks. — **to block out** To plan broadly without details. — **to block up** To raise on blocks. [<F *bloc,* ult. <Gmc.]

block[2] (blok) *n.* **1** That which hinders or obstructs, or the condition of being obstructed; an obstruction. **2** In sports, interference. **3** The blocking of a ball with a bat, as in cricket. **4** *Pathol.* An obstruction, as of a nerve or blood vessel. — *v.t.* **1** To obstruct; stop or impede the progress of. **2** To stop with or as with a block; blockade: often with *up.* **3** In sports, to hinder the movements of (an opposing player), usually by bodily contact; also, to stop (a ball), as with the body. **4** *Physiol.* To stop (a nerve) from functioning, as with an anesthetic. — *v.i.* **5** To act so as to hinder. See synonyms under HINDER. — **to block out** To obscure from view. — **to block up** To fill (an area or space) so as to prevent movement into or through. [<F *bloquer* obstruct < *bloc* block, ult. <Gmc.]

block·ade (blo·kād′) *v.t.* **·ad·ed, ·ad·ing** To close to traffic or communication by military or naval force; obstruct. — *n.* **1** The investing of a coast by a hostile naval force with intent to close it to maritime commerce. **2** A blockading force. **3** Any hindrance or obstruction to action. — **to run the blockade** To elude blockading forces. [<BLOCK[2]]

block·ad·er (blo·kā′dər) *n.* One who or that which blockades, as a warship.

blockade runner 1 A vessel engaged in passing through a blockade. **2** The captain of such a vessel, or a member of the crew.

block·bust·er (blok′bus′tər) *n.* **1** An aerial bomb capable of devastating a large area. **2** *U.S.* One who engages in blockbusting.

block·bust·ing (blok′bust′ing) *n. U.S.* The practice of inducing home owners to sell hastily and often at a loss by arousing the fear that the sale of nearby homes to members of a minority group will lower the values of their houses.

block·er (blok′ər) *n.* **1** One who or that which blocks. **2** In football, a player who obstructs an opposing tackler.

block front In American furniture, a form of front, as in a desk or chest of drawers, characterized by three vertical panels, the center concave, the end panels convex or blocked. — **block′–front′** *adj.*

block·head (blok′hed′) *n.* A stupid person.

block·house (blok′hous′) *n.* **1** A fortification, formerly of logs and heavy timbers, now of concrete or other very resistant material, having loopholes from which to fire guns. **2** *U.S.* A house made of hewn logs set square.

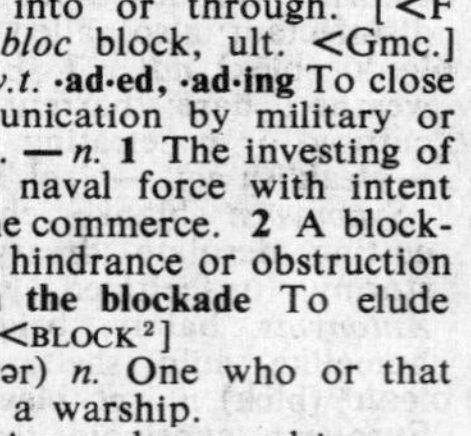

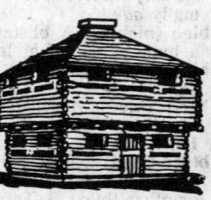

BLOCKHOUSE

block·ish (blok′ish) *adj.* Like a block; stupid; dull. Also **block′like′.**

Block Island An island resort off the south coast of and belonging to Rhode Island.

block lava Lava in the form of angular blocks with sharp, rough surfaces.

block letter 1 Printing type cut from wood. 2 A style of printing without serifs, resembling letters cut from wood. — **block-let-ter** (blok′·let′·ər) *adj.*

block-line (blok′lin′) *n.* A line passing over one or more blocks and pulleys.

block plane A small carpenter's plane for trimming wood across the grain.

block printing A method of printing from wooden blocks on which designs have been engraved.

block signal A signal functioning as part of a block system.

block system A system of regulating the running of trains on a railway, by automatic signals or otherwise, in which the track is divided into sections called blocks, on any one of which, ordinarily, only one train at a time is allowed.

block tin 1 Tin cast in ingots. 2 Pure tin as distinguished from tin plate.

block-y (blok′ē) *adj.* ·i·er, ·i·est 1 Unequally shaded, as if printed in blocks. 2 Short and stout; stocky.

Bloem-fon-tein (bloom′fon·tān) A city, capital of Orange Free State province and judicial capital of the Republic of South Africa.

Blois (blwä) A city on the Loire, north central France.

bloke (blōk) *n. Brit. Slang* A fellow; guy.

Blom-i-don (blom′i·dən), **Cape** A headland on the north coast of Nova Scotia.

blond (blond) *adj.* 1 Having a fair skin with light eyes and hair. 2 Flaxen or golden, as hair. — *n.* A blond person: feminine **blonde** (blond). 2 A variety of silk lace. [<F, yellow-haired <Med.L *blondus*, prob. <Gmc.]

blood (blud) *n.* 1 The chemically complex and usually red fluid that circulates through the vascular system of most vertebrates. Consisting essentially of semi-solid corpuscles suspended in plasma, it delivers oxygen and nutrients to all the cells and tissues, distributes internal secretions, removes waste products, guards against infection, and helps to maintain homeostasis of the organism. ◆Collateral adjective: *hemal.* 2 Kinship by descent; race; especially, noble lineage. Compare FULL BLOOD, HALF BLOOD. 3 Vitality; temperament; mood. 4 Bloodshed; war; murder. 5 A dashing fellow; gallant. 6 One of various red liquids, as the sap of some trees. 7 A blood horse. 8 The life blood of a sacrificial victim, especially as in the atonement of Christ. See synonyms under AFFINITY, KIN. — *v.t.* 1 To draw blood from; bleed. 2 To give (a hunting dog) its first sight or smell of blood; also, to give (troops) their first experience of battle. — *adj.* Blooded; of superior breed: a fine *blood mare.* [OE *blōd*]

blood-and-thun-der (blud′ən·thun′dər) *adj.* Characterized by violence and bloodshed; sensational; melodramatic: said of certain fiction or drama.

blood bank *Med.* A reserve of blood, either in liquid form classified according to blood groups, or in the form of dried plasma, for use in transfusion.

blood bath A massacre; slaughter.

blood-bol-tered (blud′bōl′tərd) *adj.* Daubed or clotted with blood.

blood count *Med.* A measure giving the number and proportion of red and white cells in a given sample of blood: used for clinical and diagnostic purposes.

blood-cur-dling (blud′kurd′ling) *adj.* Terrifying or horrifying enough to curdle or congeal the blood.

blood-ed (blud′id) *adj.* 1 Having blood or temper of a specified character: cold-*blooded.* 2 Having pure blood or lineage; thoroughbred.

blood group *Physiol.* One of four great classes into which all human beings may be divided on the basis of specific genetic differences in the composition and properties of blood: in the classification of Landsteiner, they are designated as AB, A, B, and O. Also **blood type.**

blood-guilt (blud′gilt′) *n.* The crime of unrighteous bloodshed. — **blood′guilt′i·ness** *n.* — **blood′guilt′y** *adj.*

blood heat *Physiol.* The normal temperature of human blood, about 98.6°F. or 37°C.

blood-hound (blud′hound′) *n.* A large hound with an unusual ability to follow a scent: characterized by a powerful body, straight and large-boned forelegs, and loose skin: often used to track fugitives: also called *sleuthhound.*

blood-less (blud′lis) *adj.* 1 Having no blood; without color; pale. 2 Lifeless. 3 Cold-hearted. 4 Without bloodshed. — **blood′less-ly** *adv.* — **blood′less-ness** *n.*

blood-let-ting (blud′let′ing) *n.* Bleeding for a therapeutic purpose. — **blood′let′ter** *n.*

blood-line (blud′līn′) *n.* Strain or pedigree, as of livestock.

blood-mo-bile (blud′mə·bēl) *n.* An automobile or other vehicle equipped to obtain and carry supplies of blood for emergency transfusion.

blood money Money paid to a hired murderer, or, as compensation, to the kin of a murdered man.

blood plasma *Physiol.* The liquid part of the blood, containing all the components of whole blood except hemoglobin.

blood platelet *Physiol.* A thrombocyte; one of the minute circular or oval bodies found in the blood of higher vertebrates, essential to the coagulating process.

blood poisoning Introduction of virulent bacteria into the blood stream, usually from a local infection, such as a boil or wound; septicemia.

blood pressure *Physiol.* The pressure of the blood on the walls of the arteries, varying with the force of the heart action, resilience of the arteries and blood vessels, amount and viscosity of blood, etc.

blood pudding An article of food composed of swine's blood, coagulated by cooking, intermingled with particles of fat and usually stuffed into skins. Also **blood sausage.**

blood-red (blud′red′) *adj.* Colored with or like blood. See synonyms under BLOODY.

blood relation A person of the same stock or parentage; a kinsman by birth.

blood-root (blud′root′, -root′) *n.* 1 A low perennial North American herb (*Sanguinaria canadensis*), having pale green leaves, a single white or pink flower, and a thick rhizome with abundant red, acrid juice. Also called *red puccoon.*

blood-shed (blud′shed′) *n.* The shedding of blood; slaughter; carnage. Also **blood′shed′-ding.** — **blood′shed′der** *n.*

blood-shot (blud′shot′) *adj.* Suffused or shot with blood; red and inflamed or irritated: said of the eye.

blood-stain (blud′stān′) *n.* A spot produced by blood. — *v.t.* To stain with blood. — **blood′-stained′** *adj.*

blood-stone (blud′stōn′) *n.* A stone of green chalcedony flecked with particles of red jasper: often cut as a gem.

blood-stream (blud′strēm′) *n.* The stream of blood coursing through a living body.

blood-suck-er (blud′suk′ər) *n.* 1 An animal that sucks blood, as a leech. 2 A cruel extortioner. — **blood′suck′ing** *adj.*

blood test *Med.* Any of various procedures for indicating the presence of blood under set conditions, or for determining its specific type or its condition in health or disease.

blood-thirst-y (blud′thûrs′tē) *adj.* Thirsting for blood; murderous; cruel. — **blood′thirst′i·ly** *adv.* — **blood′thirst′i·ness** *n.*

blood transfusion *Med.* The transfer of a quantity of the blood from one person into the vascular system of another.

blood type Blood group.

blood vessel Any tubular canal in which the blood circulates: an artery, vein, or capillary.

blood-wood (blud′wood′) *n.* 1 Haematoxylon. 2 Any of various other woods characterized by a red or reddish heartwood, especially the Jamaica ironwood (*Laplacea haematoxylon*) valued as timber, and the bloodwood cacique (*Brosimum caloxylon*), used by the Panama Indians as a tribal medicine.

blood-worm (blud′wûrm′) *n.* Any of various annelid worms (genera *Polycirrus* and *Enoplobranchus*), having long, slender bodies and bright-red blood: found in mud and shallow water.

blood-wort (blud′wûrt′) *n.* 1 Any plant of the family *Haemodoraceae.* 2 The salad burnet

(*Sanguisorba minor*). 3 The red-veined dock (genus *Rumex*). 4 Bloodroot.

blood-y (blud′ē) *adj.* **blood·i·er, blood·i·est** 1 Covered or stained with blood: also **blood′ied.** 2 Consisting of, containing, or mixed with blood. 3 Characterized by or delighting in bloodshed; saguinary; bloodthirsty. 4 Red like blood; suggesting blood. 5 *Brit. Slang* Damned; accursed; confounded: also used adverbially, meaning very, exceedingly, damnably; as, not *bloody* likely: a low vulgarism. — *v.t.* **blood·ied, blood·y·ing** To smear or stain with blood. — **blood′i·ly** *adv.* — **blood′i·ness** *n.*

Synonyms (adj.): blood-dyed, blood-red, blood-stained, crimson, gory, reeking, sanguinary. *Bloody* is commonly used in the literal, *sanguinary* in the figurative sense. We say a *sanguinary* or *bloody* battle, a *sanguinary* temper, a *bloody* weapon, a *bloody* field. *Crimson* refers to the color of blood; *gory* signifies covered or daubed with gore, or clotted blood, and always keeps the physical signification. *Reeking,* which is capable of other meanings, is often used alone to signify wet with steaming blood; as a *reeking* blade. *Antonyms:* bloodless, calm, conciliatory, gentle, harmless, peaceable, peaceful, tranquil, unwarlike.

bloody shirt The bloodstained shirt of one who has been killed, exhibited to incite or perpetuate vengeance: used especially as the symbol of enmity between the North and South after the Civil War. — **to wave the bloody shirt** To keep alive or incite hostility by displaying the bloodstained shirts of those slain by an enemy: often used figuratively.

bloom¹ (bloom) *n.* 1 The act of florescence or the state of being in flower. 2 A growing or flourishing condition; freshness; also, flush; glow. 3 A flower; blossom; also, flowers collectively. 4 *Bot.* The powdery, waxy substance on certain fruits, as the plum or grape, and on certain leaves, as those of the cabbage. 5 A clouded appearance on a varnished surface. 6 A yellow appearance on tanned leather. 7 A fluorescence seen in lubricating oils. 8 *Phot.* A moist film on the surface of a lens, film, or glass plate. 9 A fine variety of sundried raisin: also **bloom raisin.** 10 An earthy mineral, usually bright-colored, and ordinarily a decomposition product. — *v.i.* 1 To bear flowers; blossom. 2 To glow with health and beauty; be at one's prime. 3 To glow with a warm color; be rosy. — *v.t.* 4 To bring into bloom; cause to flourish. 5 To invest with a warm color. 6 To cloud, as a varnished surface. [<ON *blōm* flower, blossom. Akin to BLOSSOM.]

bloom² (bloom) *n. Metall.* A mass of malleable iron from which the slag has been forced by hammer or roller. 2 A lump of melted glass. [OE *bloma* lump of metal]

bloom-er¹ (bloo′mər) *n.* 1 A costume of loose trousers under a short skirt; also, a woman so dressed. 2 *pl.* Loose, wide knickerbockers gathered at the knees: worn by women. 3 *pl.* Canvas guards attached to turrets of battleships and enclosing the barrels of turret guns to keep out dampness. [after Mrs. Amelia Bloomer, U.S. feminist reformer, 1818–94, who first proposed it]

bloom-er² (bloo′mər) *n. Slang* A bad mistake; an error. [? <Australian slang *a bloom(ing) er(ror)*]

bloom-er-y (bloo′mər·ē) *n. pl.* **·er·ies** *Metall.* 1 An apparatus or establishment for making malleable iron directly from the ore. 2 A puddling furnace.

Bloom-field (bloom′fēld), **Leonard,** 1887–1949, U.S. linguist.

bloom-ing (bloo′ming) *adj.* Coming into flower; hence, fresh and beautiful; prosperous. See synonyms under FRESH. — **bloom′ing-ly** *adv.* — **bloom′ing-ness** *n.*

bloom-y (bloo′mē) *adj.* 1 Abounding in blooms; flowery. 2 Covered with bloom, as a fruit.

bloop (bloop) *n.* In sound reproduction of motion pictures, the dull thud caused by a poorly made patch of material placed over a splice in the sound track. [Imit.]

bloop-er (bloo′pər) *n.* 1 *U.S. Slang* An error

or blunder. **2** In baseball: **a** A weakly hit fly ball reaching just beyond the infield. **b** A high, weakly thrown pitch. [Imit.]

blos·som (blos′əm) *n.* **1** A flower, especially one of a plant yielding edible fruit. **2** The state or period of flowering; bloom. **3** *Geol.* A weathered or decomposed outcrop of a coal bed or mineral bed. — *v.i.* **1** To come into blossom; bloom. **2** To prosper; thrive. See synonyms under FLOURISH. [OE *blostma.* Akin to BLOOM.] — **blos′som·less** *adj.* — **blos′·som·y** *adj.*

blot[1] (blot) *n.* **1** A spot or stain, as of ink. **2** Reproach; blemish; a stain on a reputation. **3** An erasure. See synonyms under BLEMISH, STAIN. — *v.* **blot·ted, blot·ting** *v.t.* **1** To spot, as with ink; stain. **2** To disgrace; sully. **3** To mark over or obliterate, as writing: often with *out.* **4** To dry with blotting paper. **5** To obscure; darken: usually with *out.* **6** To paint roughly; daub. — *v.i.* **7** To spread in a blot or blots, as ink. **8** To become blotted; acquire spots. **9** To absorb: This paper *blots* well. [ME *blotte*; origin uncertain]

blot[2] (blot) *n.* **1** In backgammon, an exposed man liable to be forfeited. **2** Any exposed point; a weak spot. [Origin uncertain]

blotch (bloch) *n.* **1** A spot or blot. **2** An inflamed eruption on the skin. — *v.t.* To mark or cover with blotches. [Blend of BLOT[1] and BOTCH[2]] — **blotch′y** *adj.*

blot·ter (blot′ər) *n.* **1** A sheet, pad, or book of blotting paper. **2** The daily record of arrests and charges in a police station. **3** Anything that blots or defiles.

blotting paper Unsized paper for absorbing excess ink.

Blount (blunt), **Charles,** 1563–1605?, Earl of Devonshire; English statesman; suppressed Irish rebellion, 1603.

blouse (blous, blouz) *n.* **1** A woman's loose waist or bodice of various types, extending from the neck to the waist or below, and worn tucked into the skirt or outside. **2** A loose, knee-length shirt or frock, usually belted at the waist, worn chiefly by French workmen. **3** A U.S. Army service coat. [<F; ult. origin uncertain]

bloused (bloust, blouzd) *adj.* **1** Wearing a blouse. **2** Made loose like a blouse, as a waist.

blow[1] (blō) *v.* **blew, blown, blow·ing** *v.t.* **1** To move by a current of air. **2** To overthrow or extinguish by a current of air. **3** To emit, as air or smoke, from the mouth. **4** To force air upon, as from the mouth: often with *up*: to *blow up* a fire. **5** To empty or clear by forcing air through, as pipes. **6** To cause to sound, as a bugle or horn. **7** To sound (a signal): The bugle *blew* taps. **8** To form or shape, as by inflating: to *blow* glass. **9** To put out of breath, as a horse. **10** To shatter or destroy by or as by explosion: usually with *up, down, out, through,* etc.: to *blow out* a tire; to *blow down* a pole; to *blow* a hole *through* a wall; to *blow up* a house. **11** To melt (a fuse). **12** To lay eggs in, as flies in meat. **13** *Slang* To spend (money) lavishly; also, to treat or entertain: I'll *blow* you to a meal. **14** *Slang* To leave; go out of. **15** *Slang* To damn: a euphemism: Well, I'll be *blowed.* — *v.i.* **16** To be in motion: said of wind or air. **17** To move in a current of air; be carried by the wind. **18** To emit a current or jet of air, water, steam, etc. **19** To sound by being blown: The bugle *blew* at dawn. **20** To fail or become useless, as by melting: The fuse *blew.* **21** To explode: usually with *up, down, to,* etc.: The engine *blew up.* **22** To pant; gasp for breath. **23** *Colloq.* To talk boastfully. **24** *Slang* To leave; go. — **to blow a fuse** *Colloq.* To lose self-control; become enraged. — **to blow hot and cold** *Colloq.* To vacillate; be uncertain. — **to blow off** **1** To let off steam, as from a boiler. **2** *Slang* To speak in anger, as to relieve pent-up emotion. — **to blow out** To subside; become less intense: The storm will *blow* itself *out.* — **to blow over** To pass, as a storm; subside. — **to blow up** **1** To inflate. **2** To enlarge, as a photographic print. **3** *Colloq.* To lose self-control; become enraged. **4** To arise; become increasingly intense, as a storm. — *n.* **1** The act of blowing; a blast; gale. **2** The oviposition of a fly; a flyblow. **3** *Metall.* A single blast of the Bessemer converter, or the quantity of metal acted on at one time. **4** *Mining* The violent inrush of gas from or into a coal seam; also, the collapse of a mine roof. **5** *Slang* Boastfulness: oratorical *blow.* **6** Time to get the breath; the act of getting the breath when winded. [OE *blāwan.* Akin to BLAST.]

blow[2] (blō) *n.* **1** A sudden or violent stroke; thump; thwack. **2** A sudden misfortune. **3** A hostile or combative act: usually in the plural: coming to *blows.* — **at a** (or **one**) **blow** By a single stroke or action; all at one time. — **to come to blows** To start fighting one another. [ME *blaw*]

Synonyms: box, buffet, calamity, concussion, cuff, cut, disaster, hit, knock, lash, misfortune, rap, shock, stripe, stroke, thump. A *blow* is a sudden impact, as of a fist or a club; a *stroke* is a sweeping movement: the *stroke* of a sword, of an oar, of the arm in swimming. A *slap* is given with the open hand, a *lash* with a whip, thong, or the like; we speak also of the *cut* of a whip. A *cuff* is a somewhat sidelong *blow,* generally with the open hand: a *cuff* or *box* on the ear. In the metaphorical sense, *blow* is used for sudden, stunning, staggering *calamity* or sorrow; *stroke* for sweeping *disaster,* and also for sweeping achievement and success. We say a *stroke* of paralysis, or a *stroke* of genius. We speak of the *buffets* of adverse fortune. *Shock* is used of that which is at once sudden, violent, and prostrating; we speak of a *shock* of electricity, the *shock* of an amputation, a *shock* of surprise. Compare BEAT, MISFORTUNE.

blow[3] (blō) *v.* **blew, blown, blow·ing** *v.t.* **1** To cause to bloom, as a plant. **2** To produce, as flowers. — *v.i.* **3** To bloom; blossom. — *n.* **1** The state of flowering. **2** A mass of blossoms; blossoms in general. [OE *blowan* blossom]

blow–back (blō′bak′) *n.* **1** The escape from the rear of a gun of gases formed by discharge of the projectile. **2** A defective cartridge or primer causing this escape.

blow·by (blō′bī′) *n.* **1** The exhaust fumes of a car, truck, etc. **2** A device on the car, etc., to reduce such fumes.

blow·er (blō′ər) *n.* **1** One who or that which blows. **2** A device for forcing a draft of air through a building, furnace, machinery, etc. **3** *Slang* A boaster.

blow·fish (blō′fish′) *n. pl.* **·fish** or **·fish·es** **1** The walleyed perch. **2** A swellfish or any like fish which can puff up its body.

blow·fly (blō′flī′) *n. pl.* **·flies** Any of several metallic-blue or -green flies (family *Calliphoridae*), whose larvae live in carrion or in the wounds of living animals.

blow·gun (blō′gun′) *n.* A long tube through which a missile, as an arrow, may be blown by the breath.

blow–hard (blō′härd′) *Slang n.* A braggart. — *adj.* Boastful.

blow·hole (blō′hōl′) *n.* **1** *Zool.* The nasal openings in the heads of certain cetaceans. **2** *Geol.* A small crater formed on the surface of a lava flow for the escape of gas, etc. **3** A vent for the release of gas and bad air, as from mines. **4** *Metall.* A defect in a metal casting due to an air bubble caught during solidification. **5** A hole in the ice to which seals, whales, etc., come to breathe.

blow·ing (blō′ing) *n.* **1** The action of emitting or applying a current of air. **2** The act or sound of breathing, especially hard breathing, as of an animal. **3** *Metall.* An inrush of steam or gas through molten metal.

blown[1] (blōn) Past participle of BLOW[1]. — *adj.* **1** Winded from overexertion. **2** Spoiled, as food, by exposure, keeping, or oviposition; tainted. **3** Inflated or swollen with gas. **4** Made with a blowpipe: *blown* glass.

blown[2] (blōn) Past participle of BLOW[3]. — *adj.* In full flower or bloom.

blow·off (blō′ôf′, -of′) *n.* **1** The expelling of water, vapor, etc. **2** An apparatus for blowing off steam, water, etc., as from boilers.

blow·out (blō′out′) *n.* **1** *Electr.* The explosive destruction of a fuse by an overcharge. **2** *Slang* A formal entertainment that becomes disorderly; also, an elaborate social function or, especially, an elaborate meal. **3** A puncture in or bursting of an automobile tire. **4** A flameout.

blow·pipe (blō′pīp′) *n.* **1** A tube by which air or gas is blown through a flame for the purpose of fusing, heating, or melting something. **2** A blowtube (def. 3). **3** A blowgun.

blowse (blouz) *n. Obs.* A fat, red-faced woman. [Origin uncertain]

blow·torch (blō′tôrch′) *n.* An apparatus for vaporizing a combustible fluid under pressure and expelling it from a nozzle as a long, intensely hot flame: used for soldering, etc.

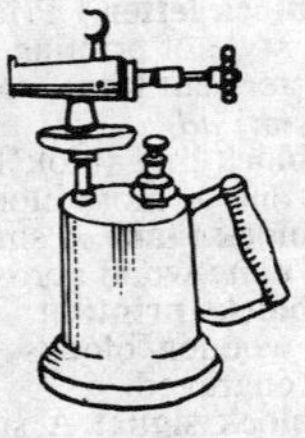

BLOWTORCH

blow·tube (blō′to͞ob′, -tyo͞ob′) *n.* **1** A pea-shooter. **2** A blowgun. **3** A tube used for blowing molten glass into the desired shape.

blow–up (blō′up′) *n.* **1** An explosion. **2** *Colloq.* Bankruptcy. **3** *Colloq.* Loss of self-control. **4** An enlargement, as of a photograph, page of print, etc. **5** A rapid increase in the intensity or spread of a fire.

blow·y (blō′ē) *adj.* **blow·i·er, blow·i·est** Windy.

blowz·y (blou′zē) *adj.* **·i·er, ·i·est** **1** Slatternly or unkempt; slovenly. **2** Having a red or flushed face. Also **blows·y** (blou′zē), **blowzed** (blouzd). [<BLOWSE]

blub·ber[1] (blub′ər) *v.t.* **1** To disfigure, wet, or swell with weeping. **2** To utter sobbingly. — *v.i.* **3** Weep and sob noisily. [ME *blubren*] — **blub′ber·er** *n.* — **blub′ber·ing·ly** *adv.*

blub·ber[2] (blub′ər) *n.* **1** *Zool.* The layer of fat beneath the skin of a cetacean, used as a source of oil. **2** The act of blubbering. [ME *bluber*]

blub·ber·y (blub′ər·ē) *adj.* **1** Like blubber; very fat. **2** Swollen, as cheeks; protruding.

blu·cher (blo͞o′chər, -kər) *n.* **1** A half boot, or high shoe. **2** A shoe in which there is no front seam, the upper meeting above in two projecting flaps. [after BLÜCHER]

Blü·cher (blo͞o′chər, -kər, *Ger.* blü′khər), **Gebhard Leberecht von,** 1742–1819, German field marshal commanding Prussian army at Waterloo.

blude (blüd) *n. Scot.* Blood.

bludg·eon (bluj′ən) *n.* A short club, commonly loaded at one end, used as a weapon. — *v.t.* **1** To strike with or as with a bludgeon. **2** To coerce; bully. [Origin unknown]

blue (blo͞o) *adj.* **blu·er, blu·est** **1** Having the color of the clear sky. **2** Dismal; dreary; melancholy; despondent; also, depressing; discouraging: Things look *blue.* **3** Severe or Puritanic; strict: *blue* laws. **4** Faithful; genuine; sterling: He is true *blue.* **5** Livid, as from contusion, cold, or fear. **6** Devoted to literature; pedantic: said of women. **7** Denoting venous blood that shows through the skin. **8** Designating a flame, as of a candle, where the red glare is absent: said to be an omen of the presence of evil spirits. — *n.* **1** One of the chief colors of the spectrum, between green and violet; the color of the clear sky; azure. **2** The coloring matter or pigment used for imparting a blue color. **3** A blueprint. **4** One who wears blue clothing or insignia. **5** *pl.* See BLUES. **6** The bluish-gray winter coat of a deer. **7** A small butterfly of the family *Lycaenidae.* **8** A bluestocking. — **out of the blue** At an unexpected time and from an unsuspected source; completely unforeseen. — *v.t.* **blued, blu·ing** **1** To make blue. **2** To treat with bluing. [<OF *bleu,* ult. <Gmc.] — **blue′ly** *adv.* — **blue′ness** *n.*

Blue (blo͞o) *n.* **1** A soldier of the Federal Army in the American Civil War. Compare GRAY. **2** *Brit.* An athlete wearing the colors of his university in contests between Oxford (dark blue) and Cambridge (light blue). **3** *Brit.* A member of the Royal Horse Guard.

blue–and–white (blo͞o′ən·hwīt′) *n.* Nanking porcelain.

blue baby An infant born with cyanosis resulting from a congenital heart lesion or from defective expansion of the lung.

blue·ball (blo͞o′bôl′) *n.* Baby-blue-eyes.

Blue·beard (blo͞o′bird′) In folklore, a man who married and then murdered his wives one after another.

blue·bell (blo͞o′bel′) *n.* **1** Any one of various plants that bear blue bell-shaped flowers. **2** The grape hyacinth. **3** The Virginia cowslip. **4** The wood hyacinth. **5** The harebell.

blue·ber·ry (blo͞o′ber′ē, -bər·ē) *n. pl.* **·ries** **1** A many-seeded, edible, blue or black American berry of the genus *Vaccinium.* **2** The plant that bears it. Compare HUCKLEBERRY.

blue·bill (blo͞o′bil′) *n.* The scaup duck.

blue·bird (blo͞o′bûrd′) *n.* A small American passerine bird (genus *Sialia*), with a prevailing blue plumage, especially the eastern bluebird *(S. sialis)* common in North America, and the Mexican bluebird *(S. mexicana)*.
blue blindness Tritanopia.
blue blood 1 Blood of a supposed finer or purer kind. 2 Aristocratic lineage, character, or bearing. 3 A person of noble or aristocratic family. **—blue′-blood′ed** *adj.*
blue·bon·net (blo͞o′bon′it) *n.* 1 The cornflower. 2 An annual leguminous herb *(Lupinus subcarnosus)* with blue flowers: the State flower of Texas. 3 A woolen cap worn by the Scots; hence, a Scot.
blue·book (blo͞o′bo͝ok′) *n.* 1 A register of names of persons employed by the U.S. government. 2 A classified register, as of persons in high society. 3 *Brit.* A governmental publication, issued in blue covers.
blue·bot·tle (blo͞o′bot′l) *n.* 1 A blowfly (family *Callephoridae*) with a brilliant metallic–blue or –green abdomen. 2 Any of various flowers, wild or cultivated, with tubular florets, blue, violet, etc., each borne on a tall, slender stalk. 3 The cornflower.
blue·cap (blo͞o′kap′) *n.* 1 The bluebonnet. 2 A bluish titmouse. 3 A Scot.
blue chip 1 In poker, a blue–colored chip of high value. 2 A high–priced common–stock issue of a leading company that pays regular dividends. **—blue′–chip′** *adj.*
blue·coat (blo͞o′kōt′) *n.* A person wearing a blue uniform, as a policeman; during the Civil War, a Union soldier. **—blue′-coat′ed** *adj.*
blue cohosh See under COHOSH.
blue–col·lar (blo͞o′kol′ər) *adj.* Of, pertaining to, or designating employees engaged in physical or manual work that requires them to wear rough–textured, dark, or special clothing for protection or as a uniform. Compare WHITE–COLLAR.
Blue Cross 1 *U.S.* A non–profit organization providing hospital insurance. 2 *Brit.* An organization devoted to the humane treatment of animals, especially of horses and dogs.
blue·curls (blo͞o′kûrlz′) *n.* 1 Any herb of the genus *Trichostema*, of the mint family: from its resemblance to pennyroyal, called *bastard pennyroyal.* 2 The selfheal (def. 1).
blue devils 1 Great depression of spirits; despondency; morbid melancholy. 2 Delirium tremens.
blue–eyed (blo͞o′īd′) *adj.* Having blue eyes.
blue–eyed grass Delicate grasslike plants *(Sisyrinchium angustifolium)* of the iris family, with blue flowers on slender, winged scapes.
Blue·fields (blo͞o′fēldz′) A port in SE Nicaragua.
blue·fish (blo͞o′fish′) *n. pl.* **·fish** or **·fish·es** 1 A voracious food fish *(Pomatomus saltatrix)* common along the Atlantic Coast of the United States. 2 One of various other fishes of a bluish color, as the cunner.
blue flag See under FLAG[2].
blue fox A small fox of Arctic regions *(Alopex lagopus)* whose pelt acquires a bluish color in summer.
blue·gill (blo͞o′gil′) *n.* An edible American fresh–water sunfish *(Lepomis pallidus)* ranging from the Great Lakes to Florida and Mexico.
blue grass (blo͞o′gras′, -gräs′) *n.* 1 One of various grasses (genus *Poa*); esp., the Kentucky bluegrass *(P. pratensis)* with many running rootstocks. 2 Traditional country music, esp. of the southern United States.
Bluegrass Country A region of central Kentucky. Also **the Bluegrass.**
Bluegrass State Nickname of KENTUCKY.
blue–green algae (blo͞o′grēn′) Primitive unicellular and unspecialized algae (class *Cyanophyceae*) in which the chlorophyll is mixed with a blue pigment: they give a scum to the surface of stagnant water.
Blue Grotto A wave–cut cave on the north shore of Capri, famous for the blue reflections of the sea within it.
blue grouse Any of several grouse of western North America (genus *Dendrogapus*), with dusky gray or blackish plumage: also called *dusky grouse, sooty grouse.*
blue·gum (blo͞o′gum′) *n.* Any of several eucalyptus trees with aromatic bitter astringent leaves.
blue hen's chickens Natives of the State of Delaware.
blue·ing (blo͞o′ing) See BLUING.
blue·jack (blo͞o′jak′) *n.* 1 Blue vitriol. 2 A small oak *(Quercus cinerea)* of the southern United States.
blue·jack·et (blo͞o′jak′it) *n.* An enlisted man in the U.S. Navy.
blue jay A small, crested corvine bird *(Cyanocitta cristata)* of eastern North America.
blue jeans Trousers made of blue denim or a similar fabric.
blue law A law proscribing or dictating private personal behavior in the interests of a narrow moral code; specifically, any such law common in the early American colonies; also, any law regulating the observance of Sunday as a day of rest.
blue·line (blo͞o′līn′) *n.* Either of two blue lines across a hockey rink between the center of the rink and each goal.
blue mold A destructive rotting disease of apples and citrus fruits, caused respectively by the fungi *Penicillium expansum* and *P. digitatum. P. crustaceum* or *glaucum* is the typical blue–green mold of bread, cheese, etc.: also called *green mold.*
blue Monday Monday conceived as gloomy because of the resumption of work.
blue moon A period of time considered as occurring when the moon is blue; hence, never. **—once in a blue moon** Seldom or hardly ever.
Blue Mountains 1 A wooded range in NE Oregon, highest point, 6,500 feet. 2 An extensive plateau west of Sydney, Australia; highest point, Bird's Rock, 3,871 feet.
blue movie, a pornographic motion picture.
Blue Nile See NILE.
blue·nose (blo͞o′nōz′) *n.* 1 *Usually cap. Canadian* A Nova Scotian person or vessel. 2 A puritanical person.
blue–pen·cil (blo͞o′pen′səl) *v.t.* 1 To edit or revise (a manuscript) with or as with a blue pencil. 2 *Colloq.* To veto; disapprove; censor.
blue peter A square, blue flag with a white rectangle in the center. In the International Maritime Code it signifies the letter P. It is also raised to indicate that a ship is sailing within 24 hours. [<*blue (re)peater*]
blue plate 1 A dinner plate divided by ridges into sections for holding apart several kinds of food. 2 A main course, as of meat and vegetables, listed as a single item on a menu.
Blue Point An oyster from off the shore of Blue Point, Great South Bay, Long Island, New York.
blue·print (blo͞o′print′) *n.* 1 A ferricyanide positive photographic print from a transparent negative original. 2 A plan or drawing made by printing on sensitized paper, the drawing showing in white lines on a blue ground. 3 Any detailed plan. **—***v.t.* To make a blueprint of.
blue racer A greenish–gray variety of the American blacksnake.
blue ribbon 1 The badge of the Order of the Garter. 2 A badge indicating the first competitive prize; a prize; an honor. **—blue′–rib′-bon·er, blue′–rib′bon·ist** *n.*
blue–rib·bon (blo͞o′rib′ən) *adj.* 1 Having high skill or intelligence. 2 Having special qualifications: a *blue–ribbon* jury.
Blue Ridge The SE portion of the Appalachian Mountains extending from Virginia into northern Georgia. Also **Blue Ridge Mountains.**
blues (blo͞oz) *n. pl.* 1 Downcast or depressed feeling; melancholy. 2 A type of popular song written in minor keys, and characterized by slow jazz rhythms and melancholy words. [Short for BLUE DEVILS]
blue–sky laws (blo͞o′skī′) Laws enacted to prevent the sale of worthless stocks and bonds by corporations, etc., to the public.
blue·stock·ing (blo͞o′stok′ing) *adj.* Pertaining to or characteristic of a learned woman, or one affecting literary tastes. **—***n.* A learned or literary woman.
blue·stone (blo͞o′stōn′) *n.* 1 Blue vitriol. 2 A bluish sandstone, used for paving and building. 3 Any stone of a blue–gray color.
blue streak *Colloq.* 1 Speed as swift as lightning. 2 Light caused by swift motion. 3 Rapid and incessant language: to talk a *blue streak.*
blu·et (blo͞o′it) *n.* 1 One of various plants having blue flowers. 2 A delicate meadow flower of the madder family *(Houstonia caerulea).* 3 In England, a garden flower of the composite family. [<F *bleuet,* dim. of *bleu* blue]
blue vitriol A deep blue, crystalline copper sulfate, $CuSO_4 \cdot 5H_2O$, used in electric batteries, calico–printing, etc.: also called *bluestone.*
blue·weed (blo͞o′wēd′) *n.* A rough, bristly herb, viper's–bugloss *(Echium vulgare)* of the borage family, with showy blue flowers, naturalized in the United States from Europe.
blue·wood (blo͞o′wo͝od′) *n.* A shrub or small tree *(Condalia obovata)* of the buckthorn family, of the SW United States.
bluff[1] (bluf) *v.t.* 1 To fool or deceive by putting on a bold front. 2 To frighten with empty threats. 3 In poker, to attempt to deceive (an opponent) by betting heavily on a poor hand. **—***v.i.* 4 To pretend to knowledge, ability, strength, etc., which one does not have. **—to bluff one's way** To obtain (an object) by bluffing. **—***n.* 1 Bold speech or manner intended to overawe, impress, or deceive. 2 Pretense; deceit. 3 A pretender. [? <Du. *bluffen* deceive, mislead] **—bluff′er** *n.*
bluff[2] (bluf) *n.* A bold, steep headland; a steep bank. **—***adj.* 1 Blunt, frank, and hearty; rude or abrupt, but kindly. 2 Presenting an upright, broad, flattened front: said of a ship's bows or a water frontage. [? <Du. *blaf* flat, as in *blaf aensicht* broad flatface] **—bluff′ly** *adv.* **—bluff′ness** *n.*
Synonyms (adj.): abrupt, blunt, blustering, bold, brusk, coarse, discourteous, frank, impolite, inconsiderate, open, plain–spoken, rough, rude, uncivil, unmannerly. *Bluff* is a word of good meaning, as are *frank* and *open.* The *bluff* man talks and laughs loudly and freely, with no thought of annoying or giving pain to others. The *blunt* man often says things which he is perfectly aware are disagreeable, either from a defiant indifference to others' feelings, or from the pleasure of tormenting; *blunt,* in this use, is allied in meaning with *impolite, inconsiderate, rough, rude, uncivil,* and *unmannerly.* Compare BLUNT, CANDID. *Antonyms*: bland, courteous, genial, polished, polite, refined, reserved, urbane.
bluid (blüd) *n. Scot.* Blood.
blu·ing (blo͞o′ing) *n.* 1 The giving of a blue tint to; also, the tint so given. 2 The blue coloring matter used in laundry work to counteract the yellow tinge of linen. Also **blue′ing.**
blu·ish (blo͞o′ish) *adj.* Somewhat blue. Also **blue′ish. —blu′ish·ness** *n.*
Blum (blo͞om), **Léon,** 1872–1950, French Socialist leader; premier 1936–37; provisional president 1946.
blume (blüm) *v.i. Scot.* To blossom.
Blu·men·bach (blo͞o′mən·bäkh), **Johann Friedrich,** 1752–1840, German anthropologist.
blun·der (blun′dər) *n.* A stupid mistake. See synonyms under ERROR. **—***v.i.* 1 To proceed carelessly or awkwardly; stumble; bungle. 2 To make a stupid and awkward mistake; err egregiously. **—***v.t.* 3 To confuse (two things); jumble. [ME *blondren* mix up, confuse. Akin to BLIND and BLEND.] **—blun′der·er** *n.* **—blun′der·ing·ly** *adv.*
blun·der·buss (blun′dər·bus) *n.* 1 An old–fashioned, short gun with large bore and flaring mouth. 2 A noisy blusterer. [Blend of BLUNDER and Du. *donderbus* thunder box]

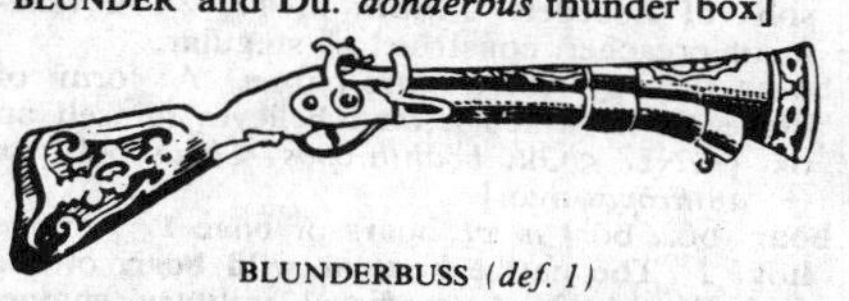

BLUNDERBUSS *(def. 1)*

blung·er (blun′jər) *n.* 1 A wooden implement shaped like a spatula, but much larger, used in mixing clay with water in the manufacture of ceramics. 2 A pug mill. See under PUG[1].
blunt (blunt) *adj.* 1 Having a thick end or edge; not sharp or piercing. 2 Abrupt in manner; plain–spoken; unceremonious; brusk. 3 Slow of wit; dull. **—***v.t.* & *v.i.* 1 To make or become blunt or dull. 2 To make or be-

come less keen or poignant. [ME *blunt*; origin unknown]—**blunt'ly** *adv.* —**blunt'ness** *n.*
Synonyms (adj.): dull, edgeless, obtuse, pointless, round, smooth, thick. See BLUFF. *Antonyms*: acute, keen, pointed, sharp.
blunt·ie (blun'tē) *n. Scot.* A blockhead; stupid fellow. Also **blunt'y**.
Bluntsch·li (blŏŏnch'lē), **Johann Kaspar,** 1808–81, Swiss legal scholar.
blur (blûr) *n.* **1** A smeared or indistinct marking or figure. **2** A blemish; also, a moral stain. See synonyms under BLEMISH. —*v.* **blurred, blur·ring** *v.t.* **1** To stain; blemish. **2** To make obscure or indistinct in outline. **3** To impair the perceptiveness of; render insensitive. —*v.i.* **4** To become obscure. **5** To smear; make blurs. —**blur'ry** *adj.*
blurb (blûrb) *n.* A publisher's statement concerning an author or a book, containing a description of its chief characteristics, frequently excessively commendatory. [Coined by Gelett Burgess]
blurt (blûrt) *v.t.* To utter abruptly; burst out with as if on impulse. See synonyms under BABBLE. —*n.* An ejaculatory utterance; abrupt exclamation. [? Blend of BLOW and SPURT]
blush (blush) *v.i.* **1** To redden, especially in the face; flush. **2** To become red or rosy, as flowers. **3** To feel shame or regret: usually with *at* or *for.* —*v.t.* **4** To make red. **5** To exhibit or make known by blushing: She *blushed* her pride. —*n.* **1** A reddening of the face from modesty, shame, or confusion. **2** A red or rosy tint; flush. **3** A glance; glimpse; view: obsolete except in the phrase *at* or *on first blush.* —*adj.* Colored like one blushing: a *blush* rose. [OE *blyscan* redden]—**blush'ful** *adj.* —**blush'ing** *adj.*
blush·er (blush'ər) *n.* **1** One who blushes. **2** A cosmetic to give the skin a rosy color.
blus·ter (blus'tər) *n.* **1** Boisterous talk or swagger. **2** A fitful and noisy blowing of the wind; blast. See synonyms under TUMULT. —*v.i.* **1** To blow gustily and with violence and noise, as the wind. **2** To utter loud, empty threats; swagger noisily. —*v.t.* **3** To utter noisily and boisterously. **4** To force or bully by blustering. [Cf. ON *blāstr* blast, blowing] —**blus'ter·er** *n.*
blus·ter·ing (blus'tər·ing) *adj.* **1** Windy; disagreeable. **2** Noisy; swaggering. See synonyms under BLUFF, NOISY. —**blus'ter·ing·ly** *adv.*
blus·ter·y (blus'tər·ē) *adj.* Stormy; rough; violent; given to bluster. Also **blus'ter·ous, blus'·trous.**
B'nai B'rith (bə·nā' brith') A Jewish fraternal organization. [<Hebrew, sons of the covenant]
bo·a (bō'ə) *n. pl.* **bo·as 1** Any of several nonvenomous serpents (family *Boidae*) having vestigial hind legs in the form of stout spurs, including the anaconda and the python. **2** A tropical American snake *(Constrictor constrictor),* distinguished from a python and notable for the crushing power of its coils: also **boa constrictor. 3** A long feather or fur neckpiece for women. [<L]
Bo·ab·dil (bō'əb·dēl'), died 1533?, last of the Moorish rulers of Granada 1482–92.
Bo·a·di·ce·a (bō'ə·də·sē'ə), died A.D. 62, British queen, suffered defeat by Romans and poisoned herself.
Bo·a·ner·ges (bō'ə·nûr'jēz) **1** Literally, sons of thunder: name given by Jesus to the two sons of Zebedee. *Mark* iii 17. **2** A vehement preacher: construed as singular.
bo·an·thro·py (bō·an'thrə·pē) *n.* A form of dementia in which a man believes himself an ox. [<NL <Gk. *boanthrōpos* <*bous* bull, ox + *anthrōpos* man]
boar (bôr, bōr) *n. pl.* **boars** or **boar 1** A male hog. **2** The native hog, or **wild boar,** of the Old World. **3** A medieval military engine. ◆ Homophone: *bore.* [OE *bār*] —**boar'ish** *n.*
board (bôrd, bōrd) *n.* **1**A flat piece of wood whose length is much greater than its width. **2** A table, spread for serving food; the food served. **3** Meals regularly furnished for pay. **4** An organized official body: a *board* of directors; also, a table at which the sessions of a council are held. **5** *pl.* The stage of a theater. **6** Pasteboard; a pasteboard bookcover. **7** A thin slab of wood, cardboard, or the like for a specific purpose: a *chessboard.* **8** *Naut.* **a** The deck or side of a vessel: *on board.* **b** The course followed by a vessel while tacking. **9** A wooden rack in the box office of a theater containing tickets: sometimes arranged according to the seating plan. **10** A bulletin board for notices of rehearsals. **11** *Telecom.* The control panel connected with all the microphones on a radio broadcast, and operated by the engineer in the control room. **12** The wooden enclosure of a hockey rink. —**binder's board** Board used by bookbinders; a single-ply pasteboard made from a base stock of kiln- or plate-dried mixed papers and ranging in thickness from .03 to .30 of an inch. —**on board** On or in a vessel; also, on or in a conveyance: He jumped *on board* the train. —**to go by the board 1** To go over the ship's side: said of a mast broken off short. **2** To go to utter wreck or ruin. —**to tread the boards** To appear as an actor. —*v.t.* **1** To cover or enclose with boards. **2** To furnish with meals or meals and lodging for pay. **3** To place (someone) where meals are provided, as in a boarding school. **4** *Naut.* To come alongside or go on board of (a ship), usually for hostile purposes. **5** To enter, as a ship or train. **6** *Obs.* To approach; accost. —*v.i.* **7** To take meals or meals and lodging. **8** *Naut.* To tack. [OE *bord*]
board·er (bôr'dər, bōr'-) *n.* **1** A person who receives regular meals, or meals and lodging at a fixed place, for pay. **2** One detailed to board an enemy's ship.
board foot *pl.* **board feet** The contents of a board 1 foot square and 1 inch thick; 144 cubic inches, or 2359.8 cubic centimeters: the common unit of measure for logs and lumber in the United States.
board·ing (bôr'ding, bōr'-) *n.* **1** Boards collectively; a structure of boards. **2** The obtaining of food, or food and lodging, regularly for pay. **3** The act of going on board a ship, a train, etc. **4** The operation of softening leather and developing the grain by rubbing the surfaces together. **5** The shaping of hosiery on heated metal boards.
boarding house A house for keeping boarders.
boarding school A school in which pupils are boarded: opposed to *day school.*
board measure A system of cubic measure applied to boards, the unit of which is the board foot.
board of trade 1 An association of merchants, bankers, etc., to promote business interests. **2** In England, a special committee of the privy council on commerce.
board rule A graduated stick for determining the number of board feet in boards of given widths and lengths.
board school In England, an undenominational elementary school having a parliamentary grant andaged by a school board.
board·walk (bôrd'wôk', bōrd'-) *n.* A promenade along a beach.
boar·fish (bôr'fish', bōr'-) *n.* Any one of several marine fishes (order *Zeomorphi*) related to the John Dory, having a hoglike snout.
boar·hound (bôr'hound', bōr'-) *n.* A dog used for hunting boars, usually the Great Dane.
boar·ish (bôr'ish, bōr'ish) *adj.* **1** Pertaining to or characteristic of a boar. **2** Swinish; rough; brutal. —**boar'ish·ly** *adv.* —**boar'ish·ness** *n.*
Bo·as (bō'äz), **Franz,** 1858–1942, U.S. anthropologist born in Germany.
boast[1] (bōst) *v.i.* **1** To vaunt or extol the deeds or abilities of oneself or of another; brag. —*v.t.* **2** To vaunt or extol (deeds or abilities); brag about. **3** To be proud to possess; take pride in: The school *boasts* a new laboratory. See synonyms under FLAUNT. —*n.* **1** A boastful speech. **2** A source of pride. [ME *bosten*; origin unknown]
boast[2] (bōst) *v.t.* **1** In masonry, to pare, as stone, with a broad chisel. **2** In sculpture, to block out, as a statue, before finishing in detail. [Origin uncertain]
boast·er (bōs'tər) *n.* **1** One who exults. **2** A boasting chisel.
boast·ful (bōst'fəl) *adj.* Characterized by or addicted to boasting. —**boast'ful·ly** *adv.* —**boast'ful·ness** *n.*
boast·ing[1] (bōs'ting) *adj.* Exulting; bragging; ostentatious. —**boast'ing·ly** *adv.*
boast·ing[2] (bōs'ting) *n.* The dressing of stone with a boaster.
boat (bōt) *n.* **1** A small, open watercraft propelled by oars, sails, or an engine. **2** *Colloq.* Any watercraft of any size, ranging from a rowboat to an ocean liner. **3** Any article, as a dish, resembling a boat. —**to be in the same boat** To be equally involved; to run the same risks; in the same situation. —*v.i.* **1** To travel by boat. **2** To go boating for pleasure. —*v.t.* **3** To transport or place in a boat: to *boat* oars. [OE *bāt*]
boat·a·ble (bō'tə·bəl) *adj.* **1** Navigable by boats. **2** Transportable by boat.
boat·age (bō'tij) *n.* **1** Carriage by boat, or the charge for such carriage. **2** The carrying capacity of a ship's boats.
boat·bill (bōt'bil') *n.* A tropical American wading bird *(Cochlearius cochlearius)* related to the night herons, with a greatly depressed bill excessively widened laterally.
boat hook A pole having a sharp point and a hook: used in holding a boat to or pushing it off from some object, etc. For illustration see HOOK.
boat·house (bōt'hous') *n.* A building along the water used for storing boats.
boat·ing (bō'ting) *n.* **1** Boats collectively. **2** use of or transportation by boats, etc.; rowing; cruising; sailing.
boat·load (bōt'lōd') *n.* **1** The full amount that a boat can hold. **2** The load carried by a boat.
boat·man (bōt'mən) *n. pl.* **·men 1** One who manages, rows, or works on a boat. **2** An aquatic insect (family *Corixidae*) of which one pair of legs is long and oarlike: also **boat bug. 3** An aquatic insect (family *Notonectidae*) that swims on its back. —**boat'man·ship** *n.*
boat·swain (bō'sən, *rarely* bōt'swān') *n.* **1** A subordinate officer of a vessel, who has general charge of the rigging, anchors, etc., and whose business it is to pipe the crew to duty with his whistle, which is his badge. **2** On a fighting ship, a warrant officer, trained in seamanship. Also spelled *bosun.*
boatswain's chair A short board slung by rope, used as a seat by a seaman working aloft, and also by painters on the outside of houses.

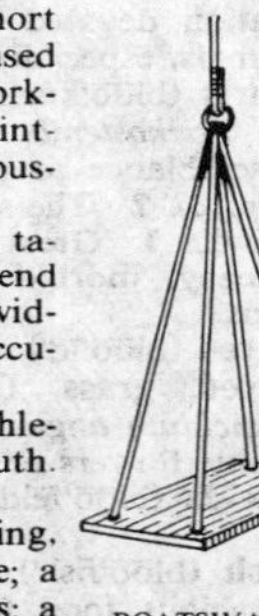
BOATSWAIN'S CHAIR

boat·tail (bōt'tāl') *n.* A tapering, streamlined rear end of a shell or bomb, providing greater range and accuracy.
Bo·az (bō'az) A Bethlehemite who married Ruth. *Ruth* iii 10.
bob[1] (bob) *n.* **1** In fishing, a cork or float on a line; a set or gang of fish hooks; a grapple. **2** A large, ball-shaped bait for eels, catfish, etc., made by stringing angleworms, rags, etc. **3** A grub or worm used for bait. **4** A small, pendent object, as on a pendulum. **5** A jerky bow or curtsy; any short, jerky movement. **6** A style of haircut for women or children cut short to fall about the ears. **7** The docked tail of a horse. **8** *sing. & pl. Brit. Colloq.* A shilling. **9** *Scot.* A bunch; cluster; nosegay, **10** A short, stout sleigh-runner; also, a bobsled. **11** The refrain of a song. —*v.* **bobbed, bob·bing** *v.t.* **1** To move up and down: to *bob* the head. **2** To effect by moving up and down: to *bob* a curtsy. **3** To cut short, as hair. —*v.i.* **4** To move up and down with an irregular motion. **5** To curtsy. **6** To fish (for eels) with a bob. —**to bob up** To appear or emerge suddenly. [ME *bobbe* a hanging cluster; origin uncertain] —**bob'ber** *n.*
bob[2] (bob) *v.t.* **bobbed, bob·bing** To strike lightly and quickly; tap. —*n. Obs.* A rap or blow; a shake or jog. [ME *bobben*; origin unknown]
bob[3] (bob) *v.t. Obs.* **1** To mock. **2** To delude; cheat. —*n.* A trick; also, a jeer or taunt; jibe. [OF *bober*]
Bob (bob), **Bob·by** (bob'ē) Diminutives of ROBERT.
Bo·ba·dil·la (bō'vä·thē'lyä), **Francisco de,** died 1502, Spanish viceroy of the Indies; arrested Columbus.
bobbed (bobd) *adj.* **1** Cut short, as the hair of a child or of a woman. **2** Docked, as a horse's tail.

bob·ber·y (bob′ər·ē) *n. Anglo–Indian* A disturbance; tumult.

bob·bin (bob′in) *n.* **1** A slender spool to hold weft or thread in spinning, weaving, or in machine sewing. **2** A small piece of wood attached to the end of a latchstring. **3** A small pin or spool used in making bobbin lace to steady the threads. **4** A cord or braid used in haberdashery. [<F *bobine*]

Bob·bin–and–Joan (bob′in·ən·jōn′) *n.* The cuckoo pint.

bob·bi·net (bob′ə·net′) *n.* An open reticulated fabric; a machine–made lace.

bobbin lace A hand–made lace in which several bobbins are used to form a pattern, as on a pillow. Also *pillow lace.*

bob·ble (bob′əl) *n.* **1** *Brit. Colloq.* A slight swell or sea. **2** *U.S. Slang* A fumble or miss. —*v.t.* **·bled, ·bling** *U.S. Slang* To mishandle; drop: He *bobbled* the ball. [Freq. of BOB[1]]

bob·by (bob′ē) *n. pl.* **·bies** *Brit. Colloq.* A policeman. [after Sir Robert *(Bobby)* Peel]

bobby pin A metal hairpin so shaped as to clasp and hold the hair tightly: used with bobbed hair. Also **bobbie pin.**

bobby socks *Colloq.* Ankle–length socks worn by girls.

bobby sox·er (sok′sər) *U.S. Colloq.* A young girl who is a devotee of the changing fads and fashions current among adolescents.

bob·cat (bob′kat′) *n.* The American lynx.

bob·o·link (bob′ə·lingk) *n.* An American thrushlike singing bird *(Dolichonyx oryzivorus),* the male having in spring black plumage with white or buff markings: also called *ricebird.* [Imit.; from its call]

Bo·bruisk (bə·brōō′isk) A city in central Belorussia. Also **Bo·bruysk′.**

bob·sled (bob′sled′) *n.* **1** Either of two short sleds or pairs of runners connected tandem by a top plank. **2** The entire vehicle so formed. Also *bob.* —*v.i.* To go coasting on a bobsled. Also **bob′sleigh′** (-slā′).

bob·stay (bob′stā′) *n. Naut.* A chain or rope from the end of the bowsprit to the stem, to counteract the strain of the forestays.

bob·tail (bob′tāl′) *n.* **1** A short tail or a tail cut short. **2** An animal with such a tail. **3** The rabble; common herd. **4** Dishonorable discharge from military service. —*adj.* Having the tail docked; inadequate; incomplete. —*v.t.* To cut the tail of; dock. —**bob′tailed′** *adj.*

bob·white (bob′hwīt′) *n.* The North American quail *(Colinus virginianus);* also, its cry. [Imit.; from its call]

bo·cac·cio (bə·kä′chō) *n.* A rockfish *(Sebastodes paucispinis)* of the California coast. [< Ital. *boccaccio* <*boccaccia* large mouth]

Boc·cac·ci·o (bō·kä′che·ō, *Ital.* bok·kät′chō), **Giovanni,** 1313–75, Italian writer and poet, author of the *Decameron.*

Boc·che·ri·ni (bok′kä·rē′nē), **Luigi,** 1743–1805, Italian composer.

boc·cie (boch′ē) *n.* An Italian variety of lawn bowling, played on a small court. Also **boc·ci** (boch′ē, *Ital.* bôt′chē), **boc·cia** (boch′ə, *Ital.* bôt′chä) [<Ital. *bocce* bowls, pl. of *boccia* ball]

Boche (bosh, *Fr.* bôsh) *n. French Slang* **1** A German: a derogatory term. **2** A bloodthirsty rioter or revolutionist. **3** A blockhead. Also **boche.** [? Alter. of F *caboche* thickhead, hardhead]

Bo·chum (bō′khoom) A city in North Rhine–Westphalia, West Germany.

bock (bok) *v.i. Scot. & Brit. Dial.* To retch; vomit; belch; gush.

bock beer (bok) An extra strong beer brewed in the winter and served in early spring. Also **bock.** [<G *bockbier* <*Eimbockbier,* from *Einbeck,* town in Hanover]

Böck·lin (bœk·lēn′), **Arnold,** 1827–1901, Swiss painter.

Bodb (bov) See BADB.

bod·dle (bod′l) *n.* Bodle.

bode[1] (bod) Archaic past tense and past participle of BIDE.

bode[2] (bod) *v.* **bod·ed, bod·ing** *v.t.* **1** To be a token of; presage, as good, evil, etc. **2** *Obs.* To predict; foretell. —*v.i.* **3** To presage good or ill. See synonyms under AUGUR. [OE *bodian* announce] —**bode′ment** *n.*

bo·de·ga (bō·dē′gə, *Sp.* bo·thā′gä) *n.* A wine shop or warehouse. [<Sp.]

Bo·den·see (bō′dən·zā) German name for CONSTANCE, LAKE.

bo·dhi·satt·va (bō′di·sat′wə) *n.* In Buddhism, a candidate for Buddhaship; one who, by his virtues and meditations, is held to be a future Buddha or savior of the world. [<Skt. < *bodhi* knowledge + *sattva* essence]

bod·ice (bod′is) *n.* **1** The waist of a woman's dress. **2** A woman's ornamental laced waist. **3** *Obs.* A corset laced in front. [Var. of *bodies,* pl. of BODY]

bod·ied (bod′ēd) *adj.* Having a body: usually with an adjective forming a compound word: full–*bodied.*

bod·i·less (bod′i·lis) *adj.* Having no body; without material form; incorporeal.

bod·i·ly (bod′ə·lē) *adj.* **1** Pertaining to the body. **2** Corporeal; material. See synonyms under PHYSICAL. —*adv.* **1** In the body; in person. **2** All together; in one mass; wholly; completely.

bod·ing (bō′ding) *adj.* Portending evil; ominous. —*n.* An omen; presage, especially of evil. —**bod′ing·ly** *adv.*

bod·kin (bod′kin) *n.* **1** An instrument for drawing tape through a hem. **2** A pointed instrument for piercing holes in cloth, etc. **3** A pin for fastening the hair. **4** A pointed instrument for picking type from a form. **5** *Obs.* A stiletto. [ME *boydekin* dagger; origin unknown]

bod·le (bod′l) *n. Scot.* **1** An old Scotch copper coin worth about one third of a cent; the smallest coin. **2** A trifle. Also spelled *boddle.* [? after *Bothwell,* a Scotch mintmaster]

Bod·lei·an (bod·lē′ən, bod′lē·ən) *adj.* Of or pertaining to the library of the University of Oxford, England, restored in the seventeenth century by Sir Thomas Bodley, 1544–1613. Also **Bod·ley′an.**

Bo·do·ni (bō·dō′nē), **Giambattista,** 1740–1813, Italian printer.

Bo·drum (bō·drōōm′) A Turkish town on the site of ancient Halicarnassus.

bod·y (bod′ē) *n. pl.* **bod·ies** **1** The entire physical part of a man or other animal, living or dead. **2** A corpse, cadaver, or carcass. **3** The trunk, or main part, of an animal or person, distinguished from the limbs and head. **4** A person; an individual: *somebody.* **5** The principal part or mass of anything. **6** The main part of a legal document as distinguished from the recitals and other introductory parts. **7** The box of a vehicle. **8** A mass of matter: the celestial *bodies.* **9** *Geom.* A solid. **10** A collection of persons, things, facts, or the like, as one whole. **11** Opacity, density, or consistency; substance: a wine with *body.* **12** That part of a garment that covers the body; waist. **13** Matter, as opposed to spirit. **14** *Printing* The size or depth of type, as distinguished from its face or style. **15** *Naut.* The hull of a ship; also, a section of it when seen from different points: the fore *body.* **16** *Aeron.* The supporting frame of an airplane, where the planes are fixed, and on which are the mechanical apparatus, seats, etc.; fuselage. —*v.t.* **bod·ied, bod·y·ing** **1** To furnish with or as with a body. **2** To exhibit in bodily form; represent. [OE *bodig*]

Synonyms (noun): ashes, carcass, clay, corpse, dust, form, frame, remains, system, trunk. *Body* denotes the entire physical structure, considered as a whole, of man or animal; *form* looks upon it as a thing of shape and outline, perhaps of beauty; *frame* regards it as supported by its bony framework; *system* views it as an assemblage of many related and harmonious organs. *Body, form, frame,* and *system* may be either dead or living; *clay* and *dust* are ordinarily used only of the dead. *Corpse* is the plain technical word for a dead body still retaining its unity; *remains* may be used after any lapse of time. *Carcass* applies only to the *body* of an animal, or of a human being regarded with contempt and loathing. Compare COMPANY, MASS. *Antonyms:* intellect, intelligence, mind, soul, spirit.

body corporate An association of persons duly incorporated for a specific purpose or enterprise; a corporation.

bod·y·guard (bod′ē·gärd′) *n.* A guard of the person, as of a king; also, a retinue.

body language The unconscious gestures and postures of the body as a form of communication.

body linen Shirts, underwear, etc., made of linen or cotton.

body politic The state or nation as an organized political body; the people, taken collectively.

bod·y–snatch·er (bod′ē·snach′ər) *n.* One who illegally and surreptitiously removes bodies from the grave; a grave–robber; resurrectionist. —**bod′y–snatch′ing** *n.*

Boece (bois), **Hector,** 1465?–1536, Scottish historian.

Boe·ing (bō′ing), **William Edward,** 1881–1956, U.S. airplane designer and manufacturer.

Boe·o·tia (bē·ō′shə, -shē·ə) A nome of east central Greece; 1,300 square miles; capital, Levadia; comprised an ancient republic. Also **Bœ·o′tia.** *Greek* **Voio·ti·a** (vyô·tē′ä).

Boe·o·tian (bē·ō′shən) *adj.* **1** Of or pertaining to Boeotia, noted for the rusticity of its people. **2** Dull; clownish. —*n.* **1** A native of Boeotia. **2** A dull–witted person.

Boer (bôr, bôr, boor) *n.* A Dutch colonist, or person of Dutch descent in South Africa. [< Du., farmer]

Boer·haa·ve (bōōr′hä·və), **Hermann,** 1668–1738, Dutch physician; professor of botany, medicine, and chemistry.

Boer War See table under WAR.

Bo·e·thi·us (bō·ē′thē·əs), **Anicius,** 475?–525, Roman philosopher. Also **Bo·e·ti·us** (bō·ē′shē·əs) and, formerly, **Bo·ece** (bō·ēs′).

bog (bog, bôg) *n.* Wet and spongy ground; marsh; morass. —*v.t. & v.i.* **bogged, bog·ging** To sink or stick in a bog: often with *down.* [<Irish, soft] —**bog′gish** *adj.* —**bog′gish·ness** *n.*

bo·gan (bō′gən) *n. Canadian* A backwater or tributary.

bog asphodel Any species of *Narthecium* of the lily family; especially, the American *N. americanum* and *N. californicum,* and the Old World Lancashire asphodel *(N. ossifragum).*

bog·bean (bog′bēn′, bôg′-) *n.* The buckbean.

bo·gey[1] (bō′gē) *n. pl.* **bo·geys** In golf: **1** An estimated standard score. **2** One stroke over par on a hole. Also **bo′gie.** [after Col. *Bogey,* an imaginary partner who plays a faultless game]

bo·gey[2] (bō′gē) *n.* Bogy[1].

bog·gle (bog′əl) *v.* **bog·gled, bog·gling** *v.i.* **1** To hesitate, as from doubt or scruples; shrink back. **2** To start with fright, as a horse. **3** To equivocate; dissemble. **4** To work in a clumsy manner; fumble. —*v.t.* **5** To make a botch of; bungle. —*n.* **1** The act of shying, as of a horse. **2** A scruple; objection; difficulty. **3** *Colloq.* A bungle. [<BOGLE] —**bog′gler** *n.*

bog·gy (bog′ē, bôg′ē) *adj.* **bog·gi·er, bog·gi·est** Swampy; miry. —**bog′gi·ness** *n.*

bo·gie[1] (bō′gē) *n.* **1** A railway truck mounted on one axle and two wheels or two axles and four wheels. **2** One of the small rollers or wheels that distribute the weight of a tractor or tank along the track. Also **bo′gy.** [<dial. E. (Northern), a kind of truck or cart]

bo·gie[2] (bō′gē) See BOGY[1].

bog iron An impure ferruginous deposit formed in swampy or marshy ground by the oxidizing action of bacteria and algae.

bo·gle (bō′gəl) *n.* A hobgoblin or bogy; bugbear. Also **bog·gle** (bog′əl). [? Akin to BUG[2]]

bog oak Wood of the trunks of oaks, sunk and preserved in the peat bogs.

bog orchid **1** The addermouth. **2** A European orchid *(Malaxis paludosa)* having small green flowers. Also **bog orchis.**

bog ore An iron hydroxide ore, as limonite, from marshy places.

Bo·go·tá (bō′gə·tä′) **1** The capital of Colombia. **2** A river in central Colombia, flowing 120 miles SW to the Magdalena: also *Funza.*

bog·trot·ter (bog′trot′ər, bôg′-) *n.* **1** One who trots over or lives among bogs. **2** Humorously, an Irish peasant.

bo·gus (bō′gəs) *n. U.S.* **1** An apparatus used in making counterfeit coins. **2** Counterfeit money. **3** Any counterfeit article. —*adj.* Counterfeit; spurious; fake. [Origin unknown]

bog·wood (bog′wood′, bôg′-) *n.* Wood of trees buried and preserved in peat bogs; bog oak.

bo·gy[1] (bō′gē) *n. pl.* **bo·gies** A goblin; bug-

bear. Also **bo′gie, bo′gey.** [? Akin to BUG[2]] **— bo′gey·ism** *n.*

bo·gy[2] (bō′gē) See BOGIE[1].

bo·hea (bō·hē′) *n.* A black tea: once applied to the choicest picking, then to black tea, now to the poorest grade. [from the *Wu-i* Hills (pronounced bo͞o′ē) of China]

Bo·he·mi·a (bō·hē′mē·ə) A historic province of western Czechoslovakia; with Moravia and Silesia comprising one of the two constituent states (Slovakia is the other) of Czechoslovakia; 20,102 square miles; capital Prague; formerly a kingdom: German *Böhmen,* Czech *Cechy.*

Bo·he·mi·an (bō·hē′mē·ən) *adj.* **1** Relating to Bohemia. **2** Leading the life of a Bohemian; unconventional. *—n.* **1** An inhabitant of Bohemia. **2** A gipsy. **3** A person, usually of artistic or literary tastes, who lives in a more or less unconventional manner: also **bo·he′mi·an. 4** A former name for the Czech dialect of Czechoslovakian. **— Bo·he′mi·an·ism** *n.*

Bohemian Brethren A religious association or sect that arose in the 15th century, the original of the Moravian Church.

Bohemian Forest A wooded mountain range along the Czechoslovak–German border.

Böh·me (bœ′mə), **Jacob,** 1575–1624, German mystic. Also **Böhm** (bœm).

Bo·hol (bō·hôl′) One of the Visayan Islands of the south central Philippines; 1,492 square miles.

Bohr (bōr), **Niels,** 1885–1962, Danish physicist.

Bohr theory *Physics* The theory that the spectrum lines of an atom are indicators of the energy changes produced in it by the jumps of electrons from one orbit to another.

bo·hunk (bō′hungk) *n. U.S. Slang* A foreign-born laborer, especially one of central European extraction: also called *hunky*: a prejudicial term. [<BO(HEMIAN) + HUNG(ARIAN)]

Bo·iar·do (bō·yär′dō), **Matteo Maria,** 1434?–1494, Count of Scandiano, Italian poet. Also spelled *Bojardo.*

Bo·i·dae (bō′ə·dē) *n. pl.* A family of nonvenomous snakes extensive in warm regions, including the largest living species, as the python, anaconda, etc. [<NL <L *boa* serpent]

Boiel·dieu (bwȧl·dyœ′), **François Adrien,** 1775–1834, French composer.

boil[1] (boil) *v.i.* **1** To be agitated, as a liquid, by gaseous bubbles rising to the surface; also said of the container in reference to the contents: The kettle *boils.* **2** To reach the boiling point. **3** To undergo the action of a boiling liquid, as meat. **4** To be agitated; to seethe: The water *boiled* with sharks. **5** To be stirred or agitated, as by violent emotion. *— v.t.* **6** To bring to the boiling point. **7** To cook or cleanse by boiling: to *boil* rice; to *boil* shirts. **8** To separate by means of evaporation caused by boiling: to *boil* sugar. **— to boil away** To evaporate in boiling. **— to boil down 1** To reduce in bulk by boiling. **2** To condense; edit. **— to boil over 1** To overflow (the container) while boiling. **2** To become enraged. *— n.* **1** The act or state of boiling. **2** An immersion in boiling water. [<OF *boillir* <L *bullire* boil]

boil[2] (boil) *n. Pathol.* A purulent and painful nodule of bacterial origin lodged beneath the skin; a furuncle. [OE *byl, byle*]

Boi·leau–Des·pré·aux (bwȧ·lō′dā·prā·ō′), **Nicolas,** 1636–1711, French poet and critic: called *Boileau.*

boiled shirt *U.S. Colloq.* **1** A man's white or, especially, dress shirt. **2** A pretentious person: also often called *stuffed shirt.*

boil·er (boi′lər) *n.* **1** A utensil in which food or liquid is boiled. **2** A closed vessel, usually cylindrical, used in generating steam, as for motive power. **3** A receptacle for hot–water storage; a hot–water tank. **4** One who boils.

boil·er·plate (boi′lər·plāt′) *n.* **1** Iron plate for making boilers. **2** *U.S.* Material in stereotype or mat form sent out to newspapers; filler.

boiler scale Layers of calcium sulfate and other mineral wastes deposited by the action of water on the inner surfaces of boilers.

boil·ing (boi′ling) *n.* **1** The state or process of ebullition. **2** A thing boiled or to be boiled.

boiling point The temperature at which the vapor pressure in a liquid equals the external pressure; at normal atmospheric pressure the boiling point of water is 212° F.

Bois de Bou·logne (bwä′ də bo͞o·lōn′, *Fr.* bwäd·bo͞o·lôn′y′) A park and fashionable pleasure ground in Paris, France. Also **the Bois.**

Boi·se (boi′zē, -sē) The capital of Idaho, in the SW part of the State.

boise·rie (bwäz′rē) *n.* Woodwork; specifically, carved wall paneling characteristic of 17th and 18th century French interiors. [<F]

Bois–le–Duc (bwä·lə·dük′) The French name for s' HERTOGENBOSCH.

bois·ter·ous (bois′tər·əs) *adj.* **1** Vociferous and rude; tempestuous; unrestrained. **2** *Obs.* Rough; coarse; big; rank. See synonyms under NOISY, TURBULENT. [ME *boistous*; origin unknown] **— bois′ter·ous·ly** *adv.* **— bois′ter·ous·ness** *n.*

Bo·i·to (bō′ē·tō), **Arrigo,** 1842–1918, Italian composer and librettist.

Boj·a·dor (boj′ə·dōr′), **Cape** A headland of Spanish West Africa in the Atlantic.

Bo·jar·do (bō·yär′dō) See BOIARDO.

Boj·er (boi′ər), **Johan,** born 1872, Norwegian author.

Bok (bok), **Edward William,** 1863–1930, U.S. editor born in Holland.

Bo·kha·ra (bō·kä′rə) See BUKHARA.

Bokhara clover See under MELILOT.

bo·la (bō′lə) *n.* A missile weapon, consisting of balls fastened to cords and used in South America in hunting cattle and large game. Also **bo·las** (bō′ləs). [<Sp., a ball]

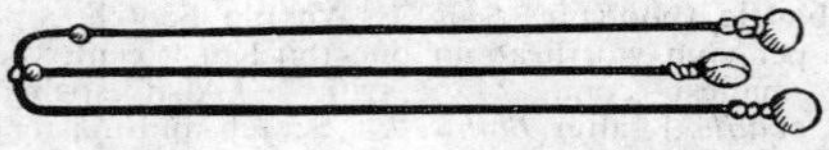

BOLA

Bo·la·ma (bo͞o·lä′mə) A city in Portuguese Guinea; capital until 1941.

Bo·lan Pass (bō·län′) A narrow gorge in central Baluchistan, West Pakistan; historical gateway to India for invaders and traders.

bo·lar (bō′lər) *adj.* Pertaining to or consisting of bole; clayey. Also **bo·lar·y** (bō′lər·ē).

bold (bōld) *adj.* **1** Possessing, showing, or requiring courage; audacious; fearless; spirited. **2** Presuming; forward; brazen. **3** Regardless of conventions; striking; vigorous; as language. **4** Clear; prominent; in high relief: *bold* sculpture, *bold* outlines. **5** Abrupt; steep, as a cliff. **6** Having a swift, strong current: a *bold* stream. See synonyms under BLUFF, BRAVE, IMMODEST, IMPUDENT. **— to make bold** To take the liberty; venture. [OE *bald*] **— bold′ly** *adv.* **— bold′ness** *n.*

bold·face (bōld′fās′) *n.* **1** An impudent person. **2** *Printing* A type in which the lines have been thickened to give a very black impression, often used for emphasis: also called *blackface.* **— bold′–faced′** *adj.*

bole[1] (bōl) *n.* The trunk of a tree. ◆ Homophone: *bowl.* [<ON *bolr*]

bole[2] (bōl) *n.* A fine, compact, soft clay. ◆ Homophone: *bowl.* [<LL *bolus* <Gk. *bōlos* clod of earth]

bole[3] (bōl) *n. Scot.* & *Irish* A small rectangular recess in the wall of a room, or an unglazed aperture in a wall; a locker. ◆ Homophone: *bowl.*

bo·lec·tion (bō·lek′shən) *n. Archit.* A molding following the outside edge of a panel and projecting beyond the face of the frame in which the panel is held: also called *bilection.* [Origin unknown]

bo·le·ro (bō·lâr′ō) *n. pl.* **·ros 1** A short jacket open at the front, worn over a blouse or the like. **2** A Spanish dance, usually accompanied by castanets; also, the music for it. [<Sp.]

bo·le·tus (bō·lē′təs) *n.* One of a genus *(Boletus)* of fleshy, quick–rotting fungi of the family *Polyporaceae,* widely distributed in the United States. [<L *boletus* <Gk. *bōlitēs* mushroom]

Bol·eyn (bo͝ol′in), **Anne,** 1507–36, second wife of Henry VIII of England; beheaded. Also spelled *Bullen.*

bo·lide (bō′līd, -lid) *n.* A brilliant shooting star; a meteor, especially one that explodes. [<F <L *bolis, -idis* meteor <Gk. *bōlis* missile < *ballein* hurl]

Bol·ing·broke (bol′ing·brook, bo͝ol′-), 1367–1413, Henry of Lancaster, later Henry IV of England: Shakespeare's *Bolingbroke.*

Bolingbroke, Viscount, 1678–1751, Henry Saint John, English prime minister.

bol·i·var (bol′ə·vər, *Sp.* bō·lē′vär) *n. pl.* **bol·i·vars,** *Sp.* **bo·li·va·res** (bō′lē·vä′rās) The monetary unit of Venezuela. [after Simón *Bolívar*]

Bo·li·var (bō·lē′vär), **Ciudad** See CIUDAD BOLÍVAR.

Bol·í·var (bol′ə·vər, *Sp.* bō·lē′vär), **Simón,** 1783–1830, Venezuelan patriot: called "the liberator of South America."

bo·liv·i·a (bə·liv′ē·ə) *n.* A soft woolen or worsted pile fabric, with finish resembling velvet or plush. [from *Bolivia*]

Bo·liv·i·a (bə·liv′ē·ə) A republic of South America; 412,777 square miles; constitutional and judiciary capital, Sucre; de facto capital and chief city, La Paz. **— Bo·liv′i·an** *adj.* & *n.*

bo·li·via·no (bō·lē′vyä′nō) *n. pl.* **·nos** (-nōs) The monetary unit of Bolivia.

boll (bōl) *n.* **1** *Bot.* A round pod or seed capsule, as of flax or cotton. **2** A knob. *— v.i.* To form pods. [Var. of BOWL[1]]

Bol·land (bol′ənd), **John,** 1596–1665, Flemish Jesuit writer. Also **Bol·lan·dus** (bə·lan′dəs).

bol·lard (bol′ərd) *n.* **1** *Naut.* A vertical post, as on a wharf, to which to attach a hawser. **2** *Aeron.* A similar post located on the hull or float of a seaplane for mooring purposes. [? <BOLE[1] + -ARD]

bol·lix (bol′iks) *v.t.* **·lixed, ·lix·ing** *Slang* To bungle; botch; make a mess of: usually with *up.* [Alter. of earlier *ballocks* testicles, dim. pl. of BALL]

boll weevil A grayish curculio *(Anthonomus grandis)* that infests and destroys cotton bolls. For illustration see under INSECTS (injurious).

boll·worm (bōl′wûrm′) *n.* **1** The very destructive larva of a pale–brown moth *(Platyedra gossypiella)* that feeds on cotton bolls. **2** The corn–ear worm.

bo·lo (bō′lō) *n. pl.* **·los** (-lōz) A heavy, single-edged, cutlaslike weapon used by natives of the Philippine Islands. [<Sp. <Visayan]

Bo·lo·gna (bō·lō′nyä) A city of north central Italy. **— Bo·lo·gnese** (bō′lə·nēz′, -nēs′) *adj.* & *n.*

Bo·lo·gna sausage (bə·lō′nə, -lōn′yə, -lō′nē) A highly seasoned sausage of mixed meats. Also *Colloq. baloney.*

Bo·lo·gna stone (bə·lōn′yə) Barium sulfate occurring in round masses and exhibiting phosphorescence after calcination.

bo·lo·graph (bō′lə·graf, -gräf) *Physics* A continuous automatic record of the temperature indications of the bolometer. Compare BOLOMETER. [<Gk. *bolē* ray of light + -GRAPH] **— bo′lo·graph′ic** *adj.* **— bo′lo·graph′i·cal·ly** *adv.* **— bo·log·ra·phy** (bō·log′rə·fē) *n.*

bo·lom·e·ter (bō·lom′ə·tər) *n. Physics* An instrument for the measurement of minute differences of radiant energy by changes in the electric resistance of a blackened conductor exposed to it. [<Gk. *bolē* ray of light + -METER] **— bo·lo·met·ric** (bō′lə·met′rik) *adj.*

bo·lo·ney (bə·lō′nē) See BALONEY. Also **bo·lo′ny.**

Bol·sha·ya (bol·shä′yə) The Russian name for MCKINLEY, MOUNT.

Bol·she·vik (bōl′shə·vik, bol′-) *n. pl.* **Bol·she·viks** or **Bol·she·vi·ki** (bōl′shə·vē′kē, bol′-) **1** A member of the radical and dominant branch of the Russian Social Democratic Party: since 1918, called the *Communist Party.* Compare MENSHEVIK. **2** Loosely, any radical or any communist. Also **bol′she·vik.** [<Russian *bolshe* greater; referring to the majority group in the party]

Bol·she·vism (bōl′shə·viz′əm, bol′-) *n.* **1** The Marxian doctrines and policies of the Bolsheviki. **2** A government based on these policies. Also **bol′she·vism. — Bol′she·vist** *n.* **— Bol′she·vis′tic** *adj.*

bol·son (bōl′sən) *n. SW U.S.* A low, enclosed basin of ground surrounded by hills. [<Sp. *bolsón,* aug. of *bolso* purse]

bol·ster (bōl′stər) *n.* **1** A long, narrow pillow as wide as a bed. **2** A pad used as a support or for protection. **3** Anything shaped like or used as a bolster. **4** *Archit.* **a** The lateral part of the volute of an Ionic capital. **b** A crosspiece of an arch centering, running from rib to rib and bearing the voussoirs. **5** *Mech.* A steel block which supports the die in a punching machine. *— v.t.* **1** To support with a pillow. **2** To prop up, as something ready to fall: with *up.* **3** To furnish with padding. [OE] **— bol′ster·er** *n.*

bolt[1] (bōlt) *n.* **1** A sliding bar or piece for fastening a door, etc. **2** A pin or rod used for holding anything in its place. **3** An arrow. **4** A long cylindrical shot for a cannon, or the like. **5** Anything coming suddenly; as, a

thunderbolt. **6** A refusal to support a party, candidate, or policy. **7** A sudden start, departure, or spring. **8** A roll of cloth containing a certain number of yards, usually 30 or 40; also, a roll of wallpaper. **9** *Obs.* **—a bolt from the blue** A sudden and wholly unexpected event. **—to shoot one's bolt** To do one's utmost; perform at the top of one's ability. **—v.i. 1** To move, go, or spring suddenly: usually with *out* or *from*: He *bolted* from the room. **2** To start suddenly; break from control and run away. **3** *U.S.* To break away, as from a political party; refuse to support party policy. **—v.t. 4** To fasten with or as with bolts. **5** *U.S.* To break away from, as a political party. **6** To chew and swallow hurriedly; gulp, as food. **7** To arrange or roll into bolts, as cloth. **8** To blurt out; say impulsively or hastily. **—adv.** Like an arrow; swiftly; straight. [OE *bolt* an arrow for a crossbow, the bolt of a door]

bolt² (bōlt) *n.* A rotating cylindrical or prismoidal frame, covered with silk or the like with very regular meshes, for sifting flour. **—v.t. 1** To sift; pass through a sieve. **2** To examine as by sifting. [< OF *bulter, buleter* sift < *burete,* dim. of *bure* coarse cloth]

bol·tel (bōl′təl) *n. Archit.* **1** A shaft of a clustered pillar; a shaft engaged in a jamb. **2** A convex molding, semicircular or quadrantal in cross–section. [Origin uncertain. Cf. BOLT¹.]

bolt·er¹ (bōl′tər) *n.* **1** One who or that which bolts. **2** A horse given to shying or running away. **3** A person who refuses to support a political nomination.

bolt·er² (bōl′tər) *n.* A sifter for meal or flour.

bolt·head (bōlt′hed′) *n.* **1** *Chem.* A spherical glass vessel with a long, narrow neck: also called *matrass, receiver.* **2** The head of a bolt.

Bol·ton (bōl′tən) A county borough in south central Lancashire, England. Also **Bolton-le-Moors** (-lə-mŏŏrz′).

bol·to·ni·a (bōl·tō′nē·ə) *n.* Any member of a genus (*Boltonia*) of tall, erect perennials of the composite family native in the eastern United States, Europe, and Asia, with alternate leaves and white to purplish asterlike flowers. [< NL, after James *Bolton,* 18th c. English botanist]

bolt·rope (bōlt′rōp′) *n. Naut.* A rope forming the border of a sail.

bolt upright In an erect position.

Boltz·mann (bōlts′män), **Ludwig,** 1844–1906, Austrian physicist.

bo·lus (bō′ləs) *n. pl.* **bo·lus·es 1** A large pill. **2** Any dose hard to swallow. **3** Any rounded mass. [< L < Gk. *bōlos* clod of earth, lump]

Bol·za·no (bōl·tsä′nō) A province of northern Italy; 3,090 square miles; capital, Bolzano.

Bo·ma (bō′mə) A port at the mouth of the Congo.

bomb (bom) *n.* **1** *Mil.* A hollow projectile containing explosive, incendiary, or chemical material to be discharged by concussion or by a time fuze. **2** Any similar receptacle, of any shape, containing an explosive: a dynamite *bomb.* **3** *Geol.* A roughly shaped spherical or ellipsoidal mass of lava hurled from a volcano during an explosive eruption. **4** An unexpected occurrence. **5** *U.S. Slang* A complete failure; flop; dud; disaster. **6** *Football* A long forward pass. See also GRENADE, MINE, SHELL. **—aerial bomb** Any bomb dropped from an airplane. **—atomic bomb** A bomb of formidable destructive power, utilizing the energy released by the continuing fission of atomic nuclei, especially those of radioactive elements, as uranium: also called **A–bomb, atom bomb. —chemical bomb** A bomb which discharges noxious chemicals, fumes, and the like. **—de-**

AERIAL BOMB.
a. Metal vanes.
b. Steel walls.
c. Bursting charge.
d. Booster charge.
e. Fuze.
f. Steel base.

molition bomb A high–explosive bomb used to destroy buildings and installations. **—depth bomb** A drum–shaped bomb which explodes under water at a desired depth: used against underwater mines and submarines: also called *ashcan; depth charge.* **—fragmentation bomb** A shrapnel–like bomb for use against ground troops and personnel. **—hung bomb** A bomb that fails to be released from an aircraft. **—incendiary bomb** A bomb filled with any of various inflammable materials as gasoline, oil, powdered magnesium, etc. **—robot bomb** A high–explosive bomb equipped with a jet–propulsion engine or rocket mechanism permitting it to travel under its own power after being launched on the target: also called *guided missile, pilotless plane.* Also **buzz bomb, flying bomb, rocket bomb. —v.t. 1** To attack or destroy with or as with bombs. **—v.i. 2** *U.S. Slang* To fail utterly. [< F *bombe* < Ital. *bomba* < L *bombus* loud sound < Gk. *bombos* hollow noise]

bom·ba·ca·ceous (bom′bə·kā′shəs) *adj. Bot.* Of or pertaining to a family (*Bombacaceae*) of trees native in the American tropics, with dry or fleshy fruit, some yielding a cottony fiber; the silk–cotton family. [< LL *bombax* cotton. See BOMBAST.]

bom·bard (bombärd′) *v.t.* **1** To attack with bombs or shells. **2** To attack or press as with bombs: to *bombard* with questions. **3** To expose (substances) to the effect of radiation or to the impact of high–energy atomic particles. **—n.** (bom′bärd) **1** The earliest form of cannon. **2** A leather liquor jug; blackjack. [< MF *bombarder* < **bom·bard′er** *n.* **—bom·bard′ment** *n.*

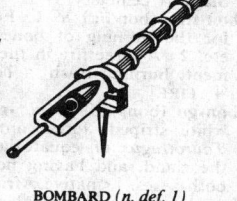

BOMBARD (*n.* def. 1)

bom·bar·dier (bom′bər·dir′) *n.* **1** *Mil.* **a** The member of the crew of a bomber who operates the bombsight and releases bombs. **b** An artilleryman in charge of mortars, etc. **2** A ground beetle (*Brachinus tscherniki*) which, on irritation, ejects an acrid liquid. [< F]

bom·bar·don (bom′bər·dən, bom·bär′dən) *n.* **1** A wind instrument of the bassoon type, used as a bass for an oboe or hautboy; a bass saxhorn. **2** A pedal reed stop on the organ with 16–foot tone. [< Ital. *bombardone*]

bom·bast (bom′bast) *n.* **1** Grandiloquent language; rant. **2** *Obs.* Stuffing; filling. [< OF *bombace* cotton padding < LL *bombax, –acis,* earlier *bambax* cotton < LGk. *bambax* (infl. by Gk. *bambyx* silk) < Gk. *pambax* < Persian *pambak* cotton]

bom·bas·tic (bom·bas′tik) *adj.* Inflated; grandiloquent. Also **bom·bas′ti·cal. —bom·bas′·ti·cal·ly** *adv.*

Bom·bay (bom·bā′) **1** A constituent state of western India; 115,570 square miles; formerly a presidency of British India. **2** Its capital, a port on the Arabian Sea.

Bombay hemp Sunn.

bom·ba·zine (bom′bə·zēn′, bom′bə·zēn) *n.* A fine twilled fabric usually with silk or artificial silk warp and worsted filling. Also **bom′ba·sine′.** [< F *bombasin* < LL *bombasinum* < *bombax* cotton. See BOMBAST.]

bomb bay A compartment in military aircraft in which bombs are carried and from which they are dropped.

bomb–bay door (bom′bā′) A door at the bottom of a bomber, opened when bombs are to be released. Also **bomb door.**

bombe (bônb) *n.* A confection in the form of a ball; especially, a mold containing different kinds of ice–cream. [< F, bomb; so called from its shape]

bombed (bombd) *adj. U.S. Slang* Drunk.

bomb·er (bom′ər) *n.* **1** A soldier who throws bombs. **2** An airplane employed in bombing. **—dive bomber** A fast, bomb–carrying airplane which, with motors running, dives toward its target and drops its bombs at close range. **—medium bomber** An airplane equipped to carry a moderately heavy bomb

load over a moderate distance.

bom·bo (bom′bō) *n. Austral. Slang* Cheap wine.

bom·bo·ra (bom·bôr′ə) *n. Austral.* A dangerous area of broken water, as near the base of a cliff with submerged rocks. Also **bom·boor′a** (-bŏŏr′ə). [< native Australian]

bomb·proof (bom′prŏŏf′) *adj.* So constructed as to resist injury from bombs. **—n.** A structure or chamber for refuge from bombs.

bomb rack See under RACK¹.

bomb·shell (bom′shel) *n.* A bomb (def. 1).

bomb·sight (bom′sīt) *n. Mil.* An instrument for aiming aerial bombs.

bomb–throw·er (bom′thrō′ər) *n. Mil.* **1** A gun of the howitzer type used in firing heavy shells. **2** A catapult–like military engine for throwing bombs.

bom·by·cid (bom′bə·sid) *n.* A moth or the larva of any moth belonging to the family *Bombycidae.* [See BOMBYX]

bom·byx (bom′biks) *n.* A silkworm (genus *Bombyx*). [< L < Gk. *bombyx* silkworm] **—bom·bic** (bom′bik) *adj.*

Bo·mu (bō′mŏŏ) A river forming the border between Zaïre and Central African Republic, flowing 450 miles west to the Ubangi: also *M'bomu.*

Bon (bōn) A Japanese festival celebrated in July, honoring the ancestral household spirits: sometimes called *Feast of Lanterns.*

Bon (bon, *Fr.* bôn), **Cape** A promontory of Tunisia; 50 miles long. *Arabic* **Ras Ad·dar** (räs ä·där′).

Bo·na (bō′nə) A former name for BÔNE.

bo·na·ci (bō′nä·sē′) *n.* One of various important food fishes of the grouper type found in Floridian and West Indian waters, especially the **bonaci cardinal** (*Mycteroperca venenosa apua*). [< Am.Sp. *bonasi* < native name]

Bo·na De·a (bō′nə dē′ə) In Roman mythology, the goddess of fertility and chastity: often identified with *Maia:* also called *Fauna.* [< L, the good goddess]

bo·na–fide (bō′nə·fīd′, -fī′dē) *adj.* **1** Acting or carried out in good faith: *bona–fide* transactions. **2** Legitimate: *bona–fide* owners. [< L *bona fide* in good faith]

Bon–aire (bô·nâr′) An island in the western group of the Netherlands West Indies; 95 square miles; chief town, Kralendijk. *Spanish* **Buen Ai·re** (bwän i′rā).

bon a·mi (bôn′ nà·mē′) *French* Good friend; sweetheart. **—bonne a·mie** (bôn′ à·mē′) *fem.*

bo·nan·za (bə·nan′zə) *n.* **1** A rich mine, vein, or find of ore. **2** Any profitable operation. [< Sp., success < L *bonus* good]

Bo·na·parte (bō′nə·pärt) Name of a prominent Corsican French family: **Napoleon,** 1769–1821, French military leader and conqueror 1795–1815, emperor of the French 1804–15, as *Napoleon I;* his brothers, **Joseph,** 1768–1844, king of Naples 1806, of Spain 1808; **Louis,** 1778–1846, king of Holland 1806; **Lucien,** 1775–1840, Prince de Canino; his son **François Charles Joseph,** 1811–32, *Napoleon II,* although he never ascended the throne: often called "l'Aiglon" (the Eaglet); his nephew **Louis Napoleon,** 1808–73, emperor of France 1852–71, as *Napoleon III,* deposed 1871. Also spelled **Buo·na·par·te** (bwô′nä·pär′tə).

Bo·na·part·ist (bō′nə·pär′tist) *adj.* Of or pertaining to the Imperial cause in France. **—n.** An adherent of Napoleon Bonaparte or the Imperial cause. **—Bo·na·part′ism** *n.*

Bon·ar Law (bon′ər lô) See LAW, BONAR.

bo·na·sus (bə·nā′səs) *n.* The European bison; aurochs. [< L < Gk. *bonasos* bison]

Bon·a·ven·tu·ra (bon′ə·ven·tŏŏr′ə,-tyŏŏr′ə), **Saint,** 1221–74, Giovanni di Fidanza, Italian Franciscan monk and theologian. Also **Bon·a·ven·ture** (bon′ə·ven′chər).

bon–bon (bon′bon′, *Fr.* bôn·bôn′) *n.* A sugared candy. [< F < *bon* good]

bon·bon·nière (bôn′bô·nyâr′) *n. French* A decorated box, dish, or small metal box for confections.

bond (bond) *n.* **1** That which binds; a band; tie. **2** *pl.* Fetters; captivity. **3** An obligation or constraint. **4** *Law* An obligation in writing under seal. **5** An interest–bearing debt certificate. **6** In insurance, a policy covering losses suffered through the acts of an employee. **7** The condition of being bonded. See BONDED (def. 2). **8** Bail; a surety. **9** In building,

timbers or stones which help to bind together. **10** *Chem.* A unit of combining power between the atoms of a molecule, associated with the energy of electrons. **11** The attachment of an adhesive material at the interface of two surfaces. **12** Bond paper. —**bottled in bond** *U.S.* A straight, 100-proof whiskey at least 4 years old, bottled under government supervision before payment of taxes. —**debenture bond** **1** A bond acknowledging loan indebtedness and securing repayment out of some designated fund or income. **2** A certificate issued by customs officials stating that an importer is entitled to a drawback on goods imported and afterward exported. **3** A bond for the payment of money stipulating that government securities or the stock of a corporate company shall be held as security. —**indemnity bond** A release signed by a shipper, relieving a railroad of responsibility. —*v.t.* **1** To put a certified debt upon; mortgage. **2** To furnish bond for; be surety for (someone). **3** To place, as goods or an employee, under bond (*n.* def. 6); guarantee. **4** In masonry, to place, as bricks, in interlocking patterns, so as to strengthen a wall, etc. —*v.i.* **5** To interlock or cohere, as bricks. —*adj.* Subject to servitude; enslaved. [Var. of BAND[1]]

bond·age (bon′dij) *n.* **1** Compulsory servitude; slavery; imprisonment. **2** Captivity; subjection. **3** In old English law, villenage.

Synonyms: captivity, enthralment, serfdom, servitude, slavery, subjection, subjugation, thraldom. See FETTER.

bond·ed (bon′did) *adj.* **1** Hypothecated for payment of bonds; mortgaged. **2** Held in bond for payment of duties. **3** Secured by bonds, as a debt. **4** Held close together, as by a strong adhesive or by chemical action.

bonded warehouse A warehouse for bonded goods.

bond·er (bon′dər) *n.* **1** One who bonds, puts goods into bond, or owns goods in bond. **2** A stone or a brick extending through a wall and binding it together: also **bond′stone′**.

bond·hold·er (bond′hōl′dər) *n.* One owning or holding bonds. —**bond′hold′ing** *adj. & n.*

bond·maid (bond′mād′) *n.* A female slave.

bond·man (bond′mən) *n. pl.* **·men** (-mən) **1** A male slave or serf. **2** A villein. Also **bonds′·man.**—**bond′wom′an, bonds′wom′an** *n. fem.*

bond paper A stiff, strong, uncalendered paper of superior fiber: used in printing bonds and banknotes, for business letters, etc.

bond·ser·vant (bond′sûr′vənt) *n.* One in servitude without wages; slave. Also **bond′slave′**.

bonds·man (bondz′mən) *n. pl.* **·men** (-mən) **1** One bound as security for another. **2** A bondman.

bon·duc·nut (bon′duk·nut′) *n.* The prickly seed of the nickernut tree. [<F *bonduc* <Arabic *bunduq* hazelnut]

bone (bōn) *n.* **1** *Anat.* **a** A hard, dense, porous structure composed of calcium salts (mainly of phosphate) and organic materials, forming the skeleton of vertebrate animals. **b** A separate piece of the skeleton of a vertebrate animal. ◆Collateral adjective: *osteal.* **2** *pl.* The skeleton as a whole; mortal remains. **3** One of various objects made of bone or similar material; specifically, one of a pair of dice; also, one of a pair of clappers, as used by minstrels; also, whalebone in a waist or corset. **4** *pl. U.S.* The end man on the right in a minstrel show (who plays the bones). **5** A ground of contention. **6** *pl. Slang* Dice. —**to feel in (one's) bones** To be sure of; have an intuition of. —**to have a bone to pick** To have grounds for complaint or dispute. —**to make no bones about** To have no scruples about; find no difficulty with. —**to point** (or **sing**) **a bone at** *Austral.*To invoke death or disaster upon (someone) by an aboriginal ritual. —*v.* **boned, bon·ing.** *v.t.* **1** To remove the bones from. **2** To stiffen with whalebone. **3** To fertilize with bonedust. —*v.i.* **4** *Slang* To study intensely: often with *up*: to *bone up* for an exam. **5** *Austral.* To bring misfortune to; jinx. [OE *bān*]

Bône (bōn) A port of NE Algeria: ancient *Hippo Regius*: formerly *Bona.*

Bone (bōn), **Sir Muirhead,** 1876–1953, Scottish etcher and painter.

bone ash A white, friable substance, the ash of bones, composed mainly of calcium phosphate: used in cupellation, china-making, and other arts. Also **bone earth.**

bone-black (bōn′blak′) *n.* A black pigment made by calcining finely ground bones in airtight containers; animal charcoal.

bone china Porcelain in which bone ash is used.

bone conduction The transmission of sounds to the inner ear by means of the bones of the skull rather than through the auditory canal.

bone·head (bōn′hed′) *n. Colloq.* A slow-witted, stupid person.

bone house An elevated, covered platform on which certain American Indians stored the bones of their dead to await burial.

bone meal Pulverized bone, used as fertilizer.

bone of contention A cause or subject of disagreement; a reason for argument.

bone oil A viscid oily substance obtained from bones by dry distillation: used in disinfectants and insecticides.

bon·er (bō′nər) *n. Slang* An error; faux pas.

bone·set (bōn′set′) *n.* A bitter tonic and diaphoretic herb of the genus *Eupatorium*: also called *thoroughwort.*

bone·set·ter (bōn′set′ər) *n.* **1** One who sets broken bones, especially one who does so without regular surgical training. **2** *Colloq.* A doctor. —**bone′set′ting** *n.*

bone·yard (bōn′yärd′) *n.* **1** A place where the bones of horses and cattle are collected. **2** The reserve pieces in a game of dominoes. **3** *Slang* A cemetery.

bon·fire (bon′fīr′) *n.* **1** Formerly, a large fire for the burning of bones, as a funeral pile, etc. **2** A large fire in the open air for amusement, burning trash, a beacon, etc. [<BONE + FIRE]

bon·go (bong′gō) *n. pl.* **·gos** A large, reddish, white-striped, forest antelope of the genus *Taurotragus* of equatorial Africa, related to the eland, and having heavy, lyrate horns in both sexes. [<native African name]

bon·go drums (bong′gō) A pair of drums, attached together and played with the hands, originally from Africa. Also **bon′gos.**

Bon·heur (bô·nœr′), **Rosa,** 1822–99, French painter: full name *Marie Rosalie Bonheur.*

bon·ho·mie (bon′ə·mē′, *Fr.* bô·nô·mē′) *n.* Genial nature or manner; good fellowship. Also **bon′hom·mie′.** [<F]

bon·i·face (bon′ə·fās) *n.* An innkeeper; hotel landlord. [after *Boniface,* innkeeper in Farquhar's *Beaux' Stratagem*]

Bon·i·face (bon′ə·fās) Name of nine popes; especially **Boniface VIII,** 1228–1303, real name Benedict Cajetan, pope 1294–1303; emphasized the temporal supremacy of the papacy. —**Boniface, Saint,** 680–755, English monk, apostle to Germany.

Bo·nin Islands (bō′nin) As island group in the North Pacific, SE of Japan; 40 square miles; administered by the United States after World War II; restored to Japan in 1968. Japanese name *Ogasawara Jima.*

bo·ni·to (bə·nē′tō) *n. pl.* **·tos** or **·toes** **1** One of various large, mackerel-like marine fishes of the Atlantic and Pacific (genus *Sarda*), as the California bonito (*S. lineolata).* **2** The skipjack. [<Sp.]

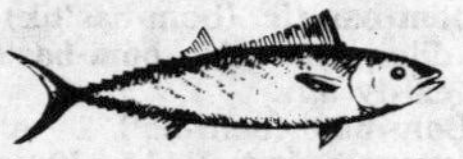

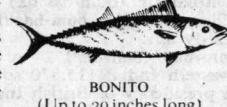

BONITO
(Up to 30 inches long)

bon jour (bôn zhōōr′) *French* Good day; good morning.

bon mot (bôn mō′) *pl.* **bons mots** (bôn mōz′, *Fr.* mō′) A clever saying; terse witticism. [<F]

Bonn (bon) A city on the Rhine in North Rhine-Westphalia; capital of the German Federal Republic.

Bon·nard (bô·när′), **Pierre,** 1867–1947, French painter.

bonne (bôn) *n. French* A housemaid or nursemaid.

bonne foi (bôn fwá′) *French* Good faith.

bon·net (bon′it) *n.* **1** A covering, or an article of apparel, for the head. **2** An outdoor headdress for women. **3** A brimless cap for men and boys, worn especially in Scotland. **4** An American Indian headdress of feathers. **5** The velvet cap lining a crown or coronet. **6** A gambler's or auctioneer's decoy. **7** The yellow waterlily. **8** One of various constructions or devices having a form or use analogous to that of a bonnet. **9** A cover or plate which can be removed to inspect a valve or other part of machinery in a chamber. **10** Any metal hood, canopy, projection, or cowl. **11** *Naut.* A supplementary sail laced to the foot of a jib of a vessel in light winds. **12** *Brit.* The hood of an automobile. —*v.t.* To cover with or as with a bonnet. [<OF *(chapel de), bonet* (cap of) bonet (a fabric) < Med. L *bonetus*]

Bon·net (bô·ne′), **Georges,** 1889–1973, French diplomat.—**Henri,** 1888–1978, French historian and diplomat.

bonnet pepper A shrub *(Capsicum frutescens),* native to tropical America, grown as a source of paprika: also called *cluster red pepper.*

bon·net·piece (bon′it·pēs′) *n.* A coin of James V of Scotland, bearing a figure of the king's head wearing a bonnet.

bon·net rouge (bô·ne rōōzh′) *pl.* **bon·nets rouges** (bô·ne rōōzh′) *French* **1** The red cap of the French revolutionists of 1793. **2** A radical republican, anarchist, or communist.

Bon·ne·ville (bon′ə·vil), **Lake** A large body of water that covered Utah, extending into Nevada and Idaho, in prehistoric times.

Bonneville Dam A dam in the Columbia River between Washington and Oregon; 170 feet high; completed 1937.

bon·ny (bon′ē) *adj.* **bon·ni·er, bon·ni·est** **1** Having homelike beauty; sweet and fair. **2** Blithe; merry; cheery. **3** *Scot.* Fine; spacious. **4** *Brit. Dial.* Healthy; robust; plump. Also **bon′nie.** See synonyms under BEAUTIFUL. [< F *bon* good] —**bon′ni·ly** *adv.* —**bon′ni·ness** *n.*

bon·ny·clab·ber (bon′ē·klab′ər) *n.* Milk curdled by natural souring. [<Irish *bainne clabair* <*bainne* milk + *clabair* clabber < *claba* thick]

Bo·no·mi (bō·nō′mē), **Ivanoe,** 1873–1951, Italian Socialist; premier 1921–22, 1944–45.

bon·sai (bon′sī, bōn′-) *n. pl.* **·sai** **1** A dwarfed tree or shrub trained, as by pruning, into a pleasing design. **2** The art of creating such trees or shrubs. [<Japanese]

bon soir (bôn swär′) *French* Good evening; good night.

bon·spiel (bon′spēl, -spəl) *n. Scot.* A match game; especially,a curling or golf match. Also **bon′spell** (-spəl).

bon·te·bok (bon′tə·bok) *n. pl.* **·bok** or **·boks** A nearly extinct South African antelope of the genus *Damaliscus*; the pied antelope. [< Afrikaans <*bont* pied + *bok* buck, deer]

bon-ton (bôn·tôn′) *n.* **1** The fashionable world. **2** Good style or breeding. [<F, good tone]

bo·nus (bō′nəs) *n. pl.* **bo·nus·es** **1** An allowance in addition to what is usual, current, or stipulated: a *bonus* on stocks. **2** Compensation, as for the obtaining of a loan. **3** A grant, as of money, insurance, etc., made by a government to citizens who have rendered military service. **4** A payment out of surplus, made by a life-insurance company to its policy holders. See synonyms under SUBSIDY. [<L, good]

bon vi·vant (bôn vē·vän′) *pl.* **bons vi·vants** (bôn vē·vän′) **1** A high liver; an epicure. **2** A boon companion. [<F]

bon vo·yage (bôn vwá·yázh′) *French* A pleasant voyage or trip.

bon·y (bō′nē) *adj.* **bon·i·er, bon·i·est** **1** Of, like, pertaining to, or consisting of bone or bones. **2** Having prominent bones; thin; gaunt. —**bon′i·ness** *n.*

bonze (bonz) *n.* A Buddhist monk. [<F <Pg. *bonzo*<Japanese <Chinese *fan seng* religious person]

bon·zer (bon′zər) *n. Austral. Slang* Something unusually good;a stroke of good luck.

boo (bōō) *n. & interj.* A vocal sound made to indicate contempt or to frighten. —*v.* **booed, boo·ing** *v.i.* To utter *boos.* —*v.t.* To shout *boo* at, either to startle or to express contempt for.

boob (bōōb) *n. U.S. Slang* A gullible person; simpleton; booby.

boobs (bōōbz) *n. pl. Slang* The female breasts.

boob tube *Slang* **1** Television. **2** A television set.

boo·by (bōō′bē) *n. pl.* **boo·bies** **1** A dull fellow; dunce. **2** In some games, the person who makes the poorest score. **3** A gannet or swimming bird of warm seas related to the pelican, especially *Sula piscator* of the coasts of the tropical and subtropical Americas: named from its apparent stupidity. [<Sp. *bobo* fool <L *balbus* stupid, dull]

booby hatch 1 *Naut.* A small hatch giving access inside a vessel without removing the main hatches. 2 *Slang* An insane asylum.

booby prize A mock award, given in good-natured derision, for the worst score or performance in a contest, game, etc.

booby trap A concealed mechanism designed to operate and cause damage when inadvertently disturbed; specifically, a mine actuated by movements of the enemy.

boo·dle (bo͞od'l) *n.* 1 *U.S. Slang* Money. 2 A bribery fund; corruption money. 3 Public plunder. 4 Caboodle. 5 Counterfeit money. —*v.i.* **·dled, ·dling** To receive money corruptly. [Cf. Du. *boedel* property] —**boo'dler** *n.*

boo·dling (bo͞od'ling) *n.* The use of bribery in politics.

boog·er (bo͝og'ər) *n.* 1 A hobgoblin. 2 *U.S. Slang* A person who is subject to contemptuous derision; also, one held in pitying affection: also *bugger.* [Origin unknown]

boog·ie–woog·ie (bo͝og'ē·wo͝og'ē) *n.* 1 A style of jazz piano–playing characterized by a rhythmic, ostinato bass with melodic inventions rhapsodizing in the treble. 2 A piece of music in this style. —*adj.* Of, in, or pertaining to this style. [Origin unknown]

boo·hoo (bo͞o·ho͞o') *v.i.* **·hooed, ·hoo·ing** To weep loudly. —*n. pl.* **·hoos** Noisy sobbing. [Imit.]

book (bo͝ok) *n.* 1 A number of sheets of paper bound or stitched together; especially, a printed and bound volume. 2 A literary composition or treatise of some length. 3 Any one of the writings of which the Bible is made up. 4 A subdivision of a literary composition or treatise. 5 A list of horses entered in a race, with the odds laid for and against them. 6 A booklike pack of gold leaf. 7 The words of a play or opera; a libretto: The music of the new opera is good, but the *book* is poor. 8 In whist and similar games, six tricks taken by one side; in other games, all the cards of one set. 9 A business record or register, as a ledger, etc.: often in the plural: The *books* show a steady loss. 10 A volume prepared for written entries. 11 Anything considered as a record or a setting forth of truth: the *book* of nature. 12 A bundle of tobacco leaves cut in half longitudinally and without the stems. —**by the book** According to rule; unoriginal; also, literal. —**like a book** Thoroughly: He knows the town *like a book.* —**the book** The telephone directory. —**the Book** The Bible. —**by the book** According to the correct form; in the usual manner. —**to throw the book at** *Slang* 1 To sentence a lawbreaker to the maximum penalties for all charges against him. 2 To punish or reprimand severely. —*v.t.* 1 To enter or list in a book. 2 To arrange for beforehand, as accommodations or seats. 3 To engage, as actors or a play, for performance. 4 To make a record of charges against (someone) on a police blotter. [<OE *bōc*]

book·bind·er (bo͝ok'bīn'dər) *n.* One whose trade is the binding of books.

book·bind·er·y (bo͝ok'bīn'dər·ē) *n. pl.* **·er·ies** A place where books are bound.

book·bind·ing (bo͝ok'bīn'ding) *n.* The art or trade of binding books.

book·case (bo͝ok'kās') *n.* A case containing shelves for holding books.

book–end (bo͝ok'end') *n.* A support or prop used to hold upright a row of books.

book·ie (bo͝ok'ē) *n. Slang* In gambling, a bookmaker.

book·ing (bo͝ok'ing) *n.* 1 The act or process of registering in a book, rarely of forming into a book. 2 The buying of a passage ticket. 3 The engaging of actors for dramatic productions; also, any part thus contracted for. 4 A contracting to present a play at a theater; the contract or play itself.

book·ish (bo͝ok'ish) *adj.* 1 Fond of books; book–learned. 2 Pedantic; unpractical. —**book'ish·ly** *adv.* —**book'ish·ness** *n.*

book jacket A removable cover to protect the binding of a book, usually designed to aid in displaying and advertising it.

book·keep·er (bo͝ok'kē'pər) *n.* One who keeps accounts; an accountant.

book·keep·ing (bo͝ok'kē'ping) *n.* The art, method, or practice of recording business transactions systematically.

book·land (bo͝ok'land') *n.* A freehold as held by deed charter.

book–learn·ing (bo͝ok'lûr'ning) *n.* 1 The knowledge of, or obtained from, books. 2 Mere literary culture or attainment as opposed to practical experience.

book·let (bo͝ok'lit) *n.* A small book, often paperbound.

book·lore (bo͝ok'lôr', -lōr') *n.* Book–learning.

book louse Any of various small, fragile, winged or wingless insects (order *Corrodentia*) which damage books by eating away the paste and glue of the bindings.

book·mak·er (bo͝ok'mā'kər) *n.* 1 One who compiles, prints, or binds books. 2 A professional betting man, especially as connected with the turf.

book·man (bo͝ok'mən) *n. pl.* **·men** (-mən) 1 One versed in books; a scholar. 2 One who publishes or sells books.

book·mark (bo͝ok'märk') *n.* Any object, as a ribbon, to be placed between or in the leaves of a book to mark a place for ready reference.

book·mo·bile (bo͝ok'mə·bēl) *n.* A motor truck equipped with shelves for the transport, display, and loan of books forming part of a traveling library. [<BOOK + (AUTO)MOBILE]

book·plate (bo͝ok'plāt') *n.* 1 An engraved label, often artistic in design, placed on or in a book to indicate ownership or proper place in a library. 2 An electrotype or stereotype of a page of a book.

book·rack (bo͝ok'rak') *n.* 1 A frame to hold an open book: also **book'rest'.** 2 A framework to hold books, as on a table.

book review An article or essay discussing or critically examining a book.

book scorpion A small, flattened arachnid (order *Chelonethida*), especially the common house scorpion *(Chelifer cancroides),* found in old books, etc.

book·sell·er (bo͝ok'sel'ər) *n.* One who sells books.

book·shop (bo͝ok'shop') *n.* A shop where books are sold; bookstore.

book·stack (bo͝ok'stak') *n.* A tall rack containing shelves for books in a library.

book·stall (bo͝ok'stôl') *n.* A stall or stand where books are sold.

book·stand (bo͝ok'stand') *n.* 1 A rack for books. 2 A bookstall.

book·store (bo͝ok'stôr', -stōr') *n.* A store for the sale of books.

book·work (bo͝ok'wûrk') *n.* Work involving reading or writing in books.

book·worm (bo͝ok'wûrm') *n.* 1 A person exclusively devoted to books and study. 2 Any of various insects destructive to books, especially one of the order *Corrodentia.*

boom[1] (bo͞om) *n.* 1 *Naut.* A spar holding the foot of a fore–and–aft sail, or that attached to a yard or to another boom to extend it. 2 A chain of logs to intercept or retard the advance of a vessel, to confine timbers, sawlogs, etc. 3 A pole set up to mark a navigable channel. 4 A long mobile beam projecting from the foot of a derrick to carry a load raised from its outer end. —**to lower the boom** *Slang* To act decisively to correct abuses; crack down. —*v.t.* 1 To extend (a sail) by means of a boom: with *out.* 2 To shove off or away, as a vessel from a wharf: with *off.* 3 To equip (a river, lake, etc.) with a barrier to stop floating logs. [<Du. *boom* tree, beam. Akin to BEAM.]

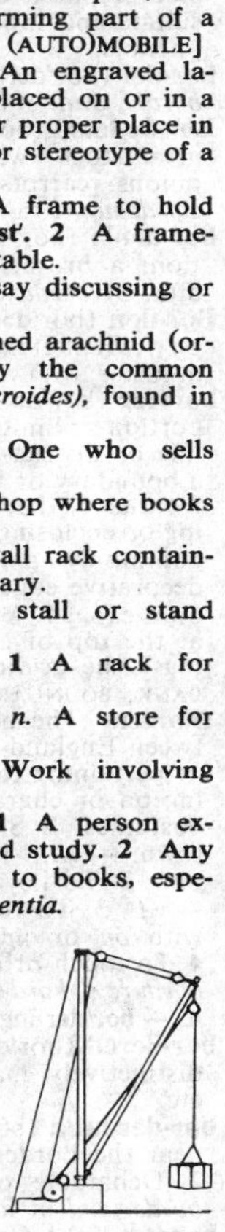

BOOM *(def. 4)*

boom[2] (bo͞om) *v.i.* 1 To emit a deep, resonant sound, as cannon or drums. 2 To hum loudly, as bees. 3 To rush swiftly or in tumult. 4 To grow rapidly; flourish. —*v.t.* 5 To utter or sound in a deep resonant tone: to *boom* the hour. 6 To extol; praise or advertise vigorously. 7 To cause to flourish: Prosperous times *boomed* my business. 8 To rush, as logs, down a river. —*n.* 1 A deep, reverberating sound, as of a supersonic aircraft, waves, etc. 2 Any sudden or rapid growth or popularity. [Imit. Cf. G *bummen* hum, Gk. *bombos* hollow noise.]

boom·e·rang (bo͞o'mə·rang) *n.* 1 A curved, wooden missile weapon originated in Australia, one form of which will return to the thrower. 2 Any proceeding that recoils upon the originator. —*v.i.* To react harmfully on the doer or user. [<native Australian name]

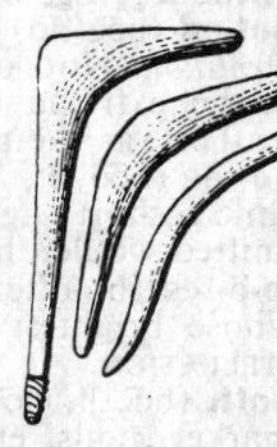

BOOMERANGS

boom town A town that has sprung up quickly, or one that has suddenly increased in population, as from a discovery of gold or oil.

boon[1] (bo͞on) *n.* 1 A good thing bestowed; favor; blessing. 2 *Obs.* A petition. See synonyms under FAVOR. [<ON *bon* petition]

boon[2] (bo͞on) *adj.* 1 Possessing convivial qualities; genial; jovial. 2 Benign; bounteous. [<F *bon* <L *bonus* good]

boon·docks (bo͞on'doks') *n. pl. U.S. Slang* An uncivilized, out–of–the–way, or backwards area: used with *the.* [<Tagalog *bundok* mountain]

boon·dog·gle (bo͞on'dôg'əl, -dog'əl) *v.i.* **·dog·gled, ·dog·gling** *U.S. Colloq.* To work, especially for the government, on wasteful or unnecessary projects. —*n.* A wasteful or worthless project. [Origin uncertain] —**boon'·dog'gler** *n.* —**boon'dog'gling** *n.*

Boone (bo͞on), **Daniel,** 1735?–1820, American frontiersman in Kentucky and Missouri.

boor (bo͝or) *n.* 1 A coarse rustic. 2 An ill-bred fellow. 3 A peasant, especially a Dutch peasant. [<Du. *boer* farmer, rustic]

boor·ish (bo͝or'ish) *adj.* Rude; clownish. See synonyms under AWKWARD, RUSTIC. —**boor'·ish·ly** *adv.* —**boor'ish** *n.*

boost (bo͞ost) *v.t. U.S.* 1 To raise by or as by pushing from beneath or behind. 2 *Slang* To speak in praise of; help by speaking well of. 3 *Colloq.* To increase: to *boost* prices. —*n.* 1 A lift; help. 2 *Colloq.* An increase. [Origin uncertain]

boost·er (bo͞os'tər) *n.* 1 Any device for increasing the power or thrust of an engine, mechanism, etc. 2 *U.S. Colloq.* One who gives enthusiastic support to a person, organization, community, or cause. 3 The first stage of a multistage rocket, the source of thrust during takeoff. 4 A booster shot. 5 *Slang* A professional shoplifter.

booster shot Another injection, as of a vaccine, to reinforce immunity, administered at an interval after the initial dose.

boot[1] (bo͞ot) *n.* 1 A leather covering for the foot and leg. 2 A high shoe. 3 *Brit.* A compartment in an automobile, coach, etc., for carrying baggage. 4 A medieval instrument of torture, compressing the foot and leg. 5 A ring–shaped appliance put on the leg of a horse to prevent interference. 6 A leather flap fastened to the dashboard of an open carriage, to be drawn up as a shield from rain or mud. 7 A carbine bucket fitted to a military saddle. 8 A box encasing the lower pulley in a grain elevator. 9 The part of a reed pipe containing the reed, as of an organ. 10 *Ornithol.* A tarsal envelope of a bird, as in thrushes. 11 *Bot.* The lowest leaf–bearing segment of a stalk of wheat. 12 *Colloq.* In the U.S. Navy, a new recruit, or one but recently arrived from a training station. —**big in one's boots** Proud. —**the boot is on the other foot** The case is reversed. —**to get the boot on the wrong foot** —To make a mistake in attribution, interpretation, etc. —**to die with one's boots on** 1 To die by violence; die fighting. 2 To die working, *i.e.,* without ever resting. —**to get the boot** *Slang* To be discharged. —*v.t.* 1 To put boots on. 2 To torture with the boot. 3 To kick; also, in football, to punt. 4 *Slang* To dismiss; fire; eject: often with *out.* [<OF *bote*]

boot[2] (bo͞ot) *v.i. Obs.* To be of avail. —*v.t. Obs.* To benefit. —*n.* 1 Something over and above given in barter. 2 Advantage; resource; help. —**to boot** In addition; over and above. [OE *bōt* profit]

boot·black (bo͞ot'blak') *n.* One who cleans and blacks boots.

boot camp The primary training station for enlisted naval personnel; so called because

of the leggings or *boots* worn by the recruits.
boot·ed (bo͞o′tid) *adj.* 1 Wearing boots. 2 *Ornithol.* Not divided into scutella except at the extreme lower portion; covered with feathers, as the tarsi of some birds.
boo·tee (bo͞o·tē′, bo͞o′tē) *n.* 1 A woman's or child's short, light boot; a half-boot. 2 A knitted woolen boot for a baby.
Bo·ö·tes (bō·ō′tēz) A northern constellation, whose brightest star is Arcturus. See CONSTELLATION.
booth (bo͞oth, bo͞oth) *n.* 1 A stall at a fair, market, polls, etc. 2 A temporary shelter. [ME *bothe,* ult. <Scand.]
Booth (bo͞oth) Family of English reformers and religious leaders, including **William,** 1829–1912, founder of the Salvation Army: known as *General Booth*; **Ballington,** 1859–1940, son of William, founder of the Volunteers of America; **Evangeline Cory,** 1865–1950, daughter of William; **William Bramwell,** 1856–1929, son of William.
— **Edwin Thomas,** 1833–93, U.S. actor.
— **John Wilkes,** 1838–65, U.S. actor, brother of preceding, assassinated Abraham Lincoln.
Boo·thi·a (bo͞o′thē·ə), **Gulf of** An inlet of the Arctic Ocean between Boothia Peninsula and Baffin Island.
Boothia Peninsula The most northerly part of the North American continent, extending north 190 miles into the Arctic Ocean from Northwest Territories, Canada. Formerly **Boothia Fe·lix** (fē′liks).
boot·jack (bo͞ot′jak′) *n.* A forked implement by which a boot may be held by the heel while the wearer withdraws his foot.
Boo·tle (bo͞ot′l) A county borough adjoining Liverpool, England.
boot·leg (bo͞ot′leg′) *v.t. & v.i.* **·legged, ·leg·ging** To make, sell, or carry for sale (liquor, etc.) illegally; smuggle. — *adj.* Unlawful: *bootleg* whisky. — *n.* 1 The part of a boot above the instep. 2 Liquor, or other merchandise, that is unlawfully carried, produced, sold, or offered for sale. Compare BLACK MARKET. [With ref. to the smuggling of liquor in bootlegs] — **boot′leg′ger** *n.*
boot·leg·ging (bo͞ot′leg′ing) *n.* The act of producing, carrying, selling, or offering for sale liquor or other merchandise in violation of the law.
boot·less (bo͞ot′lis) *adj.* Profitless; useless; unavailing. — **boot′less·ly** *adv.* — **boot′less·ness** *n.*
boot·lick (bo͞ot′lik′) *v.t. & v.i.* To flatter servilely; to toady. — **boot′lick′er** *n.* — **boot′lick′ing** *n. & adj.*
boots (bo͞ots) *n. Brit.* A hotel bootblack.
boot–tree (bo͞ot′trē′) *n.* An apparatus for stretching or shaping boots, or for keeping them in shape.
boo·ty (bo͞o′tē) *n. pl.* **boo·ties** 1 The spoil of war; plunder. 2 Gain. See synonyms under PLUNDER. [<F *butin* <MLG]
booze (bo͞oz) *n.* 1 Strong drink; liquor. 2 A drunken spree; carouse. [< *v.*] — *v.i.* **boozed, booz·ing** To drink to excess; tipple. Also **boose, bouse.** [<MDu. *busen* drink, tipple] — **boozed** *adj.* — **booz′er** *n.*
booz·y (bo͞o′zē) *adj.* Somewhat intoxicated; tipsy. Also **boos′y.** — **booz′i·ly** *adv.* — **booz′i·ness** *n.*
bop[1] (bop) *v.t.* **bopped, bop·ping** *Slang* To hit or strike. [Imit.]
bop[2] (bop) See BE-BOP.
bo–peep (bō·pēp′) *n.* The game of peek–a–boo.
Bo·peep (bō·pēp′), **Little** The little nursery–rime shepherdess who lost her sheep.
bo·ra (bō′rə) *n. Meteorol.* A blustering dry wind from the Julian Alps, blowing over the Adriatic in winter. See BOREAS. [<Ital.]
bo·rac·ic (bə·ras′ik) *adj.* Boric.
bo·ra·cite (bôr′ə·sīt, bō′rə-) A vitreous, white, translucent chloride and borate of magnesium, $Mg_7Cl_2B_{16}O_{30}$, that crystallizes in the isometric system.
bor·age (bûr′ij, bôr′-, bor′-) *n.* An erect, rough European herb *(borago officinalis)* with blue flowers, used medicinally. [<Med. L *borrago* < *borra, burra* rough hair]
bo·rag·i·na·ceous (bə·raj′ə·nā′shəs) *adj. Bot.* Of or pertaining to the borage family *(Boraginaceae)* of herbs, shrubs, or trees, including the forget–me–not, alkanet, and heliotrope.
Bor·ah (bôr′ə, bō′rə), **William Edgar,** 1865–1940, U.S. lawyer; senator from Idaho.
bo·rane (bôr′ān, bō′rān) *n. Chem.* Boron hydride, BH_3, forming part of many boron compounds and their organic derivatives.
Bo·rås (bo͞o·rōs′) A city in SW Sweden.
bo·rate (bôr′āt, bō′rāt) *n. Chem.* A salt of boric acid. — **bo′rat·ed** *adj.*
bo·rax (bôr′aks, bō′raks) *n.* A white crystalline compound, $Na_2B_4O_7 \cdot 10H_2O$, with a sweetish, alkaline taste, found native as tincal, and used as an antiseptic, in preserving food, in medicine, and as a flux, also of value in glass–manufacture and certain smelting operations. [<OF *boras* <Med. L *borax* <Arabic *bōraq* <Persian *būrah*]
bo·ra·zon (bôr′ə·zon, bō′rə-) *n. Chem.* A crystalline compound of boron and nitrogen, BN, produced under extremely high temperature and pressure: it equals the diamond in hardness but has a much higher melting point. [<BOR(ON) + AZO- + *-n*]
Bor·deaux (bôr·dō′) A port of SW France on the Garonne.
Bor·deaux (bôr·dō′) *n.* A white or red wine produced in the vicinity of Bordeaux, France. Red Bordeaux is often called *claret.*
Bordeaux mixture A fungicide and insecticide prepared by mixing solutions of copper sulfate and lime, or of copper arsenate and phenols.
bor·del (bôr′dəl) *n. Archaic* A brothel. [<OF *bordel,* dim. of *borde* cottage, hut, ult. <Gmc.]
Bor·de·laise (bôr·də·lâz′) *n.* A sauce made of meat stock, white wine, and flavored with onions, carrots, thyme, and garlic. [from *Bordeaux,* France]
bor·del·lo (bôr·del′ō) *n.* A house of prostitution; a brothel. [<Ital. <Med. L *bordellus,* dim. of *borda* cottage]
Bor·den (bôr′dən), **Sir Robert Laird,** 1854–1937, Canadian lawyer and statesman; prime minister 1911–20.
bor·der (bôr′dər) *n.* 1 A margin or edge; outer portion or limit; brink; verge. 2 The frontier line or district of a country or state; hence, a boundary or frontier, especially the western frontier of the United States. 3 A surrounding or enclosing strip of ground in a garden, commonly planted with flowers; also, a decorative edge or margin: a *border* of lace on a cap. 4 A shallow drop curtain hanging at the top of a stage set, to conceal lights, mask the gridiron, etc. See synonyms under BANK, BOUNDARY, MARGIN. — **the Border** or **Borders** The boundary and nearby land between England and Scotland. — *adj.* 1 Of or pertaining to a territorial border. 2 Living on or characteristic of a frontier: *border* costumes. 3 Situated on a frontier: a *border* town. — *v.t.* 1 To put a border or edging on. 2 To lie next to; form a boundary to. — *v.i.* 3 To resemble; have the appearance: with *on* or *upon*: That *borders* on piracy. 4 To touch or abut: with *on* or *upon.* [<OF *bordure* < *bord* edge, ult. <Gmc.] — **bor′der·er** *n.* — **bor′der·ing** *adj.*
bor·dered (bôr′dərd) *adj.* Having a border distinctively marked in structure, coloring, etc.
bor·der·land (bôr′dər·land′) *n.* 1 Land on or near the border of two adjoining countries. 2 Debatable or indeterminate ground: the *borderland* of history.
border light One of a series of overhead stage lights masked by a border.
bor·der·line (bôr′dər·līn′) *n.* A line of demarcation. Also **border line.** — *adj.* Difficult to classify, such as might conceivably fall into one or another category.
border rider A freebooter on the borders of England and Scotland.
border ruffian A pro–slave partisan in Missouri (1854–58) who crossed into Kansas to vote illegally, and by acts of violence kept anti–slavers from voting.
Bor·det (bôr·de′), **Jules,** 1870–1961, Belgian bacteriologist and physiologist.
bor·dure (bôr′jər) *n. Her.* A border around a shield. See SUBORDINARY. [<F]
bore[1] (bôr, bōr) *v.* **bored, bor·ing** *v.t.* 1 To make a hole in or through, as with a drill. 2 To make (a tunnel, hole, well, etc.) by or as by drilling. 3 To advance or force (one's way). 4 To weary by monotony, iteration, etc.; tire. — *v.i.* 5 To make a hole, etc., by or as by drilling. 6 To admit of being drilled: This wood *bores* easily. 7 To force one's way; advance by persistent motion. — *n.* 1 A hole made by or as if by boring. 2 The interior diameter of a firearm or cylinder. 3 Caliber. 4 A tiresome person or thing; an annoyance. See synonyms under HOLE. ◆ Homophone: *boar.* [*v.*, OE *borian* < *bor* auger; *n.* < *v.* + ON *bora* hole]
bore[2] (bôr, bōr) *n.* A high crested wave caused by the rush of flood tide up a river, as in the Amazon or the Bay of Fundy. Compare EAGER[2]. ◆ Homophone: *boar.* [<ON *bāra* billow]
bore[3] (bôr, bōr) Past tense of BEAR.
bo·re·al (bôr′ē·əl, bō′rē-) *adj.* Pertaining to the north or the north wind. [<LL *borealis* <BOREAS]
Bo·re·al (bôr′ē·əl, bō′rē-) *adj.* 1 Pertaining to or designating a climatic period of the Mesolithic Baltic culture, centering around 6,000 B.C. 2 Describing a subdivision of the Holarctic region, including the great belt of coniferous forests extending from New England to Alaska.
Bo·re·as (bôr′ē·əs, bō′rē-) *n.* In Greek mythology, the north wind. [<Gk.]
bore·dom (bôr′dəm, bōr′-) *n.* 1 The condition of being bored; ennui. 2 *Rare* The habit of being a bore. 3 *Rare* Bores as a class.
bor·er (bôr′ər, bō′rər) *n.* 1 One who or that which bores. 2 A beetle, moth, or worm that burrows in plants, wood, etc.; especially, the **metallic wood borer** (family *Buprestidae*), the **palm borer** (family *Bostrichidae*), the **maple borer** (family *Cerambycidae*). For illustration see INSECTS (injurious). 3 The shipworm.
Bor·ge·se (bôr·jā′zā), **Giuseppe Antonio,** 1882–1952, U.S. author, born in Sicily.
Bor·ghe·se (bôr·gā′zā) A noble family in the Republic of Siena and later at Rome, flourishing in the 16th and 17th centuries.
Bor·gia (bôr′jä) Aristocratic Spanish family, a branch of which emigrated to Italy.
— **Alfonso,** 1378–1458; became Pope Calixtus III, 1455–58.
— **Cesare,** 1478–1507, Duc de Valentinois, Italian cardinal, soldier, and adventurer.
— **Francisco de,** 1510–72, Spanish Jesuit, third general of the order; canonized 1671.
— **Lucrezia,** 1480–1519, sister of Cesare, and wife of Alfonso, Duke of Esté; heroine of opera by Donizetti.
— **Rodrigo Lanzol y,** 1431–1503; became Pope Alexander VI, 1492–1503.
Bor·glum (bôr′gləm), **Gut·zon** (gut′sən), 1867–1941, U.S. sculptor; full name *John Gutzon de la Mothe Borglum.*
Bo·ri· (bō′rē), **Lucrezia,** 1888–1960, Spanish operatic soprano.
bo·ric (bôr′ik, bō′rik) *adj. Chem.* Of, pertaining to, or derived from boron: also called *boracic.*
boric acid *Chem.* A white crystalline compound, H_3BO_3, obtained in volcanic lagoons of Tuscany, Italy, and by treating borax with sulfuric acid: used as a preservative, and mild antiseptic. Also **bo·rac′ic acid.**
bo·ride (bôr′īd, bō′rīd) *n.* A combination of boron with another element or radical.
bor·ing (bôr′ing, bō′ring) *n.* 1 The act or process of making a hole with or as with a boring tool. 2 A hole so made; a bore hole. 3 *pl.* Material removed by boring.
Bo·ris (bôr′is, bō′ris) A masculine personal name. [<Russian]
— **Boris III,** 1894–1943, king of Bulgaria 1918–43.
Bo·ri·sov (bo·ryē′sôf) A city on the Berezina in Byelorussia NE of Minsk.
born (bôrn) *adj.* 1 Brought forth or into being, as offspring. 2 Natural; ingrained: a *born* musician. [OE *boren,* pp. of *beran* bear]
borne (bôrn, bōrn) Past participle of BEAR.
Bor·ne·o (bôr′nē·ō, bōr′-) The third largest island in the world, between Sumatra and Celebes; 286,969 square miles: divided into (1) *Sabah*; (2) *Sarawak*; (3) *Brunei*; and (4) Borneo, a part of the Republic of Indonesia; 208,285 square miles; chief town, Banjermasin: formerly *Dutch Borneo. Indonesian* **Ka·li·man·tan** (kä′lē·män′tän).
bor·ne·ol (bôr′nē·ōl, -ol, bōr′-) *n. Chem.* A translucent crystalline solid, $C_{10}H_{18}O$, found in cavities in the trunk of a large tree *(Dryobalanops aromatica)* of Borneo and Sumatra: also called *camphol.* [<BORNE(O) + -OL]
Born·holm (bôrn′hōlm) A Danish island in the Baltic Sea; 228 square miles; chief port, Rönne.
born·ite (bôr′nīt) *n.* A metallic, reddish–brown, copper–iron sulfide showing purple

tarnish: also called *horseflesh ore, peacock copper*. [after Ignaz von *Born*, 1742-91, Austrian metallurgist]

Bor·nu (bôr·nōō′) A province of NE Nigeria, 900 square miles; capital, Maiduguri; formerly a Moslem native kingdom.

Bo·ro·bu·dur (bō′rō·bōō·dōōr′) Site of a huge, ruined Buddhist temple in central Java. Also **Bo′ro·boe·doer′**.

Bor·o·din (bôr′ə·dēn, *Russian* bə·rô·dyēn′), **Alexander Porphyrievich**, 1834-87, Russian composer.

Bor·o·di·no (bôr′ə·dē′nō, *Russian* bə·rə·dyi·nô′) A village near Moscow; site of one of Napoleon's important victories over the Russians, 1812.

bo·ron (bôr′on, bō′ron) *n.* A non-metallic element (symbol B) obtained as an odorless and very infusible powder, **amorphous boron**, from its oxide and in octahedral or prismatic diamondlike crystals, **crystalline** or **adamantine boron**, from amorphous boron heated with aluminum. See ELEMENT. [<BOR(AX) + (CARB)ON]

boron carbide *Chem.* A compound of carbon and boron, B₄C, an extremely hard material, often used in cutting tools.

bo·ro·sil·i·cate (bôr′ə·sil′ə·kit, -kāt, bō′rə-) *n. Chem.* A salt in which both boric and silicic acids are united with a base.

bor·ough (bûr′ō) *n.* **1** An incorporated village or town; a subdivision of a city, having a limited self-government; specifically, one of the five administrative divisions of New York, N.Y. **2** *Brit.* A municipal corporation, not a city, endowed by royal charter with certain privileges, a **municipal borough**; a town, whether corporate or not, entitled to representation in Parliament, a **parliamentary borough**. **3** *Obs.* Any town. ♦ Homophone: **burrow**. [OE *burg, burh* fort, town, ult. <Gmc. Related to BOURG, BURG.]

bor·ough–Eng·lish (bûr′ō·ing′glish) *n.* An old custom in certain parts of England by which the youngest son, or, in default of issue, the youngest brother, inherits the estate.

bor·ough·mon·ger (bûr′ō·mung′gər, -mong′-) *n.* One who trades in borough representation in Parliament.

bor·row (bôr′ō, bor′ō) *v.t.* **1** To take or obtain (something) on a promise to return it or its equivalent. **2** To adopt for one's own use, as words or ideas. **3** *Math.* In subtraction, to add ten to any figure of the minuend, at the same time withdrawing one from the next figure of the process. — *v.i.* **4** To borrow something. — *n.* **1** A place, as a bank of earth, where material is removed to be used as filling elsewhere. **2** *Obs.* A pledge; surety; the act of borrowing. [OE *borgian* give a pledge, borrow <*borg* pledge] — **bor′row·er** *n.*

Bor·row (bôr′ō, bor′ō), **George Henry**, 1803-1881, English writer and authority on Romany language and customs.

borscht (bôrsht) *n.* A Russian beet soup, often served with sour cream and eaten hot or cold. Also **borsch** (bôrsh). [<Russian]

borscht circuit A series of summer resorts, chiefly in the Catskill Mountains, where professional entertainment is provided for the guests: so called from a characteristic item of the cuisine of these resorts.

bort (bôrt) *n.* An impure diamond, used only for cutting and polishing: often called *carbonado*. Also **bortz** (bôrts). [? <OF *bort* bastard] — **bort′y** *adj.*

Bo·rus·sian (bō·rush′ən) *n.* The Old Prussian language. See also PRUSSIAN.

bo·ryl (bôr′əl, bō′rəl) *n. Chem.* The boron radical H₂B. [<BOR(ON) + -YL]

bor·zoi (bôr′zoi) *n.* A breed of Russian hounds, generally resembling the greyhound, but with a long, silky coat, usually white: also called *Russian wolfhound*. [<Russian, swift]

Bo·san·quet (bō′zən·ket), **Bernard**, 1848-1923, English philosopher.

bos·cage (bos′kij) *n.* A mass of shrubbery; a thicket; clump. Also **bos′kage**. [<OF, ult. <Gmc. Akin to BUSH.]

Bosch (bos), **Hieronymus**, 1450?-1516, Dutch painter. Also **Jerom Bos**.

— **Bosch** (bôsh), **Karl**, 1874-1940, German chemist.

bosch·bok (bosh′bok) *n.* A bushbuck. Also

bosh′bok. [<Du. *bosch* wood + *bok* buck]

bosch·vark (bosh′värk) *n.* A wild hog of South Africa (*Potamochoerus choeropotamus*); the bush pig. [<Du. *bosch* wood + *vark* pig]

Bose (bōs), **Sir Jagadis Chandra**, 1858-1937, Indian physicist and plant physiologist.

bosh¹ (bosh) *n. Colloq.* Empty words; nonsense. [<Turkish, empty, worthless]

bosh² (bosh) *n. Metall.* **1** That part of one of the sloping sides of a blast furnace extending from the belly to the hearth. **2** A trough for cooling ingots, etc. [Cf. G *böschung* slope]

bosk (bosk) *n.* A thicket of bushes; a small wood. [ME, var. of *busk* bush] — **bosk′i·ness** *n.*

bos·ket (bos′kit) *n.* A cluster of trees in a garden; a thicket. Also **bos′quet**. [<F *bosquet* <Ital. *boschetto*, dim. of *bosco* wood, ult. <Gmc.]

Bos·ni·a and Her·ze·go·vi·na (boz′nē·ə; her′tsə·gō·vē′nə) A republic founded from Yugoslavia; 19,999 square miles; capital, Sarajevo; formerly under Turkish rule, later annexed to Austria-Hungary: divided into two regions, **Bosnia** in the north and Herzegovina in the south.

Bos·ni·an (boz′nē·ən) *adj.* Of or belonging to Bosnia: — *n.* **1** A native of Bosnia; especially, one of the Slavic people inhabiting the region around the northern Adriatic. **2** The language spoken by the Bosnians.

bos·om (bŏŏz′əm, bōō′zəm) *n.* **1** The breast of a human being, especially that of a woman. **2** The breast with the arms, considered as an enclosure in embracing. **3** That portion of a garment covering the breast, as a shirt front, or the receptacle which it forms. **4** The breast as the seat of affection. **5** Any deep or enclosed place or supporting surface, suggesting, in purpose or function, the human breast: *the bosom of the earth.* — *adj.* **1** Close, as if held to the bosom; confidential; intimate; cherished: a *bosom* friend. **2** Cherished in secret: a *bosom* sin. — *v.t.* **1** To have or cherish in the bosom; embrace. **2** To hide in the bosom; conceal. [OE *bōsm*]

Bos·po·rus (bos′pə·rəs) A strait between the Black Sea and the Sea of Marmara, separating European from Asian Turkey; 17 miles long. Also **Bos·pho·rus** (bos′fə·rəs). *Turkish* **Ka·ra·de·niz Bo·ğa·zi** (kä′rä·deng·ēz′ bō′ä·zi′).

boss¹ (bôs, bos) *n.* **1** *U.S. Colloq.* A superintendent or employer of workmen; manager; foreman. **2** Any employer or any director of the work of others. **3** *U.S.* An organizer or dictator of a political party. See synonyms under MASTER. — *adj.* Being at the head of a working force; superintending; also, expert; master: *boss* shoemaker. — *v.t. & v.i.* **1** To have control (of) or supervision (over). **2** To domineer. [<Du. *baas* master]

boss² (bôs, bos) *n.* **1** A circular prominence; a knob; stud. **2** *Archit.* An ornament, sometimes a pendant, at the intersection of the ribs of a groined arch, or in any similar position. **3** *Mech.* An enlargement of a shaft to couple with a wheel or another shaft. **4** *Geol.* A domelike mass of igneous rock. — *v.t.* **1** To work with bosses. **2** To ornament with bosses. [<OF *boce* bump, knob]

BOSS (def. 2)

boss³ (bos, bôs) *n.* **1** A calf or a cow. **2** A word used to call a calf or a cow. Also **boss′y**. [Cf. L *bos* cow]

bos·set (bôs′it, bos′-) *n.* A small protuberance, boss, or knob. [<F *bossette*, dim. of *bosse* knob]

boss·ism (bôs′iz·əm, bos′-) *n.* Political party management by bosses; acts, arts, or practices of bosses.

boss rule Domination of voters by political leaders.

Bos·suet (bô·swe′), **Jacques Bénigne**, 1627-1704, French bishop and writer.

boss·y¹ (bôs′ē, bos′ē) *adj. Colloq.* **boss·i·er**, **boss·i·est** Like a boss; domineering.

boss·y² (bôs′ē, bos′ē) *adj.* Decorated with or as with bosses.

bos·ton (bôs′tən, bos′-) *n.* **1** A game of cards,

somewhat resembling whist; also, a bid to make five tricks, the lowest in the game. **2** A form of the waltz. [from *Boston*, Mass.]

Bos·ton (bôs′tən, bos′-) **1** A New England port on Boston Bay; capital of Massachusetts. **2** A municipal borough and port in eastern Lincolnshire, England. — **Bos·to·ni·an** (bôs·tō′nē·ən, bos-) *n. & adj.*

Boston bag A small handbag opening at the top and having a handle at each side of the opening.

Boston Bay The inner portion of Massachusetts Bay.

Bos·ton·ese (bôs′tən·ēz′, -ēs′) *n.* Speech characteristic of Boston, Massachusetts.

Boston Harbor The northern arm of Boston Bay.

Boston Massacre A riot in Boston, Mass., March 5, 1770, during which several colonials were killed and others wounded by British troops.

Boston Mountains The ruggedest section of the Ozarks, in Oklahoma and Arkansas.

Boston rocker An American 19th century rocking chair having an up-curved wooden seat and a high back with spindles held at the top by a wide rail.

Boston Tea Party An uprising in Boston, Mass., in 1773, against the British customs officials, during which colonists, disguised as Indians, boarded British ships in the harbor and dumped chests of tea overboard.

bo·sun (bō′sən) *n.* Boatswain.

Bos·well (boz′wel, -wəl), **James**, 1740-95, Scottish lawyer and writer; biographer of Samuel Johnson.

Bos·worth Field (boz′wûrth) A region in western Leicestershire, England; scene of the final battle, in 1485, in the Wars of the Roses.

bot (bot) *n.* The larva of a botfly. Also spelled *bott*. [Origin unknown]

bo·ta (bō′tə) *n.* A Portuguese wine cask or butt, holding about 128 gallons. [<Pg.]

bo·tan·i·cal (bə·tan′i·kəl) *adj.* **1** Of or pertaining to botany. **2** Connected with the study or cultivation of plants. Also **bo·tan′ic**. [<F *botanique* <Gk. *botanikos* <*botanē* plant, pasture <*boskein* feed, graze] — **bo·tan′i·cal·ly** *adv.*

bot·a·nist (bot′ə·nist) *n.* A student of or one versed in botany.

bot·a·nize (bot′ə·nīz) *v.* **·nized**, **·niz·ing** *v.i.* **1** To study botanical specimens. **2** To gather plants for study. — *v.t.* **3** To explore in search of botanical specimens. — **bot′a·niz′er** *n.*

bot·a·ny (bot′ə·nē) *n. pl.* **·nies 1** That division of biology which treats of plants with reference to their structure, functions, classification, etc. **2** The total plant life of a country, region, zone, etc.: the *botany* of Oceania. **3** The characteristics of a group of plants treated collectively: the *botany* of orchids.

Botany Bay An inlet of the Pacific south of Sydney, Australia; formerly site of a British penal colony.

Botany wool Wool from the Merino sheep: so called from Botany Bay, Australia, the original source of this quality of wool. Also **Botany** or **botany**.

botch¹ (boch) *v.t.* **1** To patch or mend clumsily. **2** To bungle; do or say ineptly. — *n.* A bungled piece of work; a bad job; an ill-finished patch. [ME *bocchen*; origin unknown] — **botch′er** *n.* — **botch′er·y** *n.*

botch² (boch) *n. Brit. Dial.* A superficial swelling or ulcer; a boil. [<OF *boche*, var. of *boce* knob, lump]

botch·y (boch′ē) *adj.* Imperfect; botched; poorly done. — **botch′i·ly** *adv.*

bote (bōt) *n. Obs.* **1** In English law, a fine or compensation: *manbote*, a fine paid for killing a man. **2** In English law, a privilege to use things needful for repair or subsistence, etc.: *hedgebote, housebote*, etc. **3** Boot; remedy; relief. ♦ Homophone: **boat**. [OE *bot* benefit]

bot·fly (bot′flī′) *n.* A fly of the family Gasterophilidae or Oestridae, the larvae of which are parasitic in vertebrates, especially the **horse botfly** (*Gasterophilus intestinalis*). For illustration see under INSECTS (injurious).

both (bōth) *adj.* The two inclusively or together: *Both* girls laughed. — *pron.* The two; the one and the other; the pair: *Both* of the girls were there. — *adv. & conj.* Equally; alike;

as well: with *and:* The bill passed *both* the House and the Senate. [<ON *badhir*]

Synonyms: twain, two. As an adjective or pronoun *both* emphasizes the idea of *two* and should not be connected with or refer to more than two objects. But as a conjunction *both* has a more extended meaning than it has as an adjective or a pronoun; thus, it is permissible to say, "He lost all his livestock–*both* horses, cows and sheep." When so used it emphasizes the extent or comprehensiveness of the assertion. *Twain* is a nearly obsolete form of *two. The two,* or *the twain,* is practically equivalent to *both; both,* however, expresses a closer unity. Compare EVERY.

Bo·tha (bō′tə), **Louis,** 1862–1919, South African statesman; premier 1910–19.

both·er (both′ər) *v.t.* **1** To pester; give trouble to. **2** To confuse; fluster. —*v.i.* **3** To trouble or concern oneself. —*n.* A source of annoyance; petty perplexity; vexation. [? dial. E (Irish) var. of POTHER]

both·er·a·tion (both′ə·rā′shən) *n. Colloq.* Annoyance; vexation.

both·er·some (both′ər·səm) *adj.* Causing bother or perplexity.

Both·ni·a (both′nē·ə), **Gulf of** A northern arm of the Baltic Sea between Sweden and Finland.

bot·o·né (bot′ə·nā) *adj. Her.* Having an ornament of three leaf–shaped or button–shaped projections. Also **bot·o·née, bot·o·ny** (bot′ə·nē). [<OF *botonné,* pp. of *botonner* bud, button]

bo tree (bō) *Anglo–Indian* The sacred Buddhist fig tree or pipal *(Ficus religiosa).* [<Skt. *bodhi(-taru)* perfect knowledge (tree)]

bot·ry·oi·dal (bot′rē·oid′l) *adj.* Like a cluster of grapes. Also **bot′ry·oid.** [<Gk. *botryoeidēs* <*botrys* cluster of grapes + *eidos* form, shape] —**bot′ry·oi′dal·ly** *adv.*

bot·ry·ose (bot′rē·ōs) *adj.* **1** *Bot.* Designating an indeterminate form of inflorescence, as the raceme, corymb, umbel, capitulum, etc. **2** Botryoidal.

bots (bots) *n.* A disease of horses, sheep, etc., caused by the botfly.

Bot·swa·na (bot·swä′nä) An independent member of the Commonwealth of Nations in southern Africa; 222,000 sq. mi.; capital, Gaberones; formerly *Bechuanaland Protectorate.*

bott (bot) *n.* A bot.

Bot·ti·cel·li (bot′ə·chel′ē, *Ital.* bōt′tē·chel′lē), **Alessandro,** 1447?–1515, Florentine painter: real name *Filipepi.*

bot·tle (bot′l) *n.* **1** A vessel for holding, carrying, and pouring liquids, having a neck and a narrow mouth that can be stopped. **2** As much as a bottle will hold: also **bot′tle·ful. 3** In the U.S., a unit of capacity for wines or spirits, equal to approximately 26 fluid ounces. **4** The act or habit of drinking intoxicants. —**to hit the bottle** To drink to excess. —*v.t.* **·tled, ·tling 1** To put into a bottle or bottles. **2** To restrain; shut in, as if in a bottle: often with *up* or *in.* [<OF *bouteille, botel* <LL *buticula* flask, dim. of *butis* vat, vessel] —**bot′tler** *n.*

bottle cap A small, round, usually metal lid covering the opening of a bottle.

bottled in bond See under BOND.

bottle glass Green glass.

bottle green A dark, dull green, like the color of bottle glass.

bottle imp 1 A Cartesian devil. **2** An imp or spirit shut up in a bottle. See ALADDIN.

bot·tle·neck (bot′l·nek′) *n.* **1** A narrow or congested way. **2** Any condition that retards progress.

bot·tle·nose (bot′l·nōz′) *n.* One of various dolphins, especially *Tursiops truncatus* of the North Atlantic, about 10 feet long.

bot·tle·stone (bot′l·stōn′) *n.* A mineral, sometimes used as a gemstone, having the characteristics of ordinary bottle glass; chrysolite; moldavite.

bot·tle·tree (bot′l·trē′) *n.* A Queensland tree *(Brachychiton rupestre)* the trunk of which is swollen out like a bottle, or the similar *B. populneum* of Victoria.

bot·tom (bot′əm) *n.* **1** The lowest part of anything; undersurface; base; support. **2** The ground beneath a body of water. **3** The real meaning; base; root; the foundation or basis of any state of affairs; idea; plan: to knock the *bottom* out of an argument. **4** Lowland along a river: often in plural. **5** *Naut.* The part of a vessel below the water line; hence, a vessel. **6** The part of the body on which one sits; the posterior; buttocks. **7** Residuum or dregs. **8** Endurance; stamina; grit. **9** All of a shoe below the upper. —*adj.* Lowest; fundamental; basal. —*v.t.* **1** To provide with a bottom. **2** To base or found: with *on* or *upon.* **3** To fathom; comprehend. —*v.i.* **4** To be founded; rest. **5** To touch or rest upon the bottom. [OE *botm*]

bottom dollar *U.S.* One's last and only dollar.

bottom land Lowland along a river.

bot·tom·less (bot′əm·lis) *adj.* **1** Having no bottom. **2** Unfathomable. **3** Baseless; visionary.

bottom line 1 *Colloq.* The line of a business accounting statement showing net profit or loss: with *the.* **2** *U.S. Slang* The condition or status of any enterprise after assets and liabilities have been calculated: with *the.*

bot·tom·ry (bot′əm·rē) *n.* A maritime contract whereby the owner or master of a vessel borrows money, pledging the vessel as security.

bot·u·lin (boch′o͝o·lin) *n.* A highly active nerve poison formed by an anerobic bacterium *(Clostridium botulines)* and sometimes present in spoiled or improperly prepared food; it has the property of resisting the action of gastrointestinal secretions.

bot·u·lism (boch′o͝o·liz′əm) *n.* Poisoning caused by eating spoiled food or food improperly prepared or canned, caused by botulin and characterized by acute gastrointestinal and nervous disorders. [<L *botulus* sausage; so called because the bacteria were first isolated from spoiled sausage]

bou·chée (bo͞o·shā′) *n. French* A small cake, tart shell, or puff, filled with cream, marmalade or forcemeat, and sometimes glazed.

Bou·cher (bo͞o·shā′), **François,** 1703–70, French painter.

Bou·ci·cault (bo͞o′si·kō), **Dion,** 1822–90, U.S. dramatist and actor born in Ireland.

bou·clé (bo͞o·klā′) *n.* A wool, rayon, cotton, silk, linen, or combination fabric woven or knitted with a looped or knotted surface. [<F, pp. of *boucler* buckle, curl]

bou·doir (bo͞o′dwär, bo͞o·dwär′) *n.* A lady's private sitting–room. [<F, lit., pouting room <*bouder* pout, sulk] —**bou·doir·esque** (bo͞o′·dwär·esk′) *adj.*

bouf·fant (bo͞o·fänt′) *adj.* Puffed–out; flaring: a *bouffant* skirt. —*n.* A woman's hairstyle in which the hair hangs straight from the top of the head and puffs out over the ears and neck to frame the face. [<F, ppr. of *bouffer* swell]

bouffe (bo͞of) *n.* Opera bouffe. [<F *(opéra) bouffe* comic (opera) <Ital. *buffa* joke, jest]

Bou·gain·ville (bo͞o′gən·vil) The largest of the Solomon Islands, comprising with Buka a part of the United Nations Trust Territory of New Guinea; 3,880 square miles.

Bou·gain·ville (bo͞o·gaṅ·vēl′), **Louis Antoine de,** 1729–1811, French navigator, 1766–69.

bou·gain·vil·le·a (bo͞o′gən·vil′ē·ə) *n.* Any of a genus *(Bougainvillea)* of small climbing shrubs: widely cultivated as hothouse plants. [after L. A. de *Bougainville*]

bough (bou) *n.* **1** A limb of a tree. **2** *Obs.* The gallows. ◆ Homophones: *bow*[1] and *bow*[2]. [OE *bog* shoulder, bough. Akin to BOW[1].]

bought (bôt) Past tense and past participle of BUY.

bought·en (bôt′n) *adj. Dial.* Bought at a store or shop: opposed to *home–made.*

bou·gie (bo͞o′jē, -zhē) *n.* **1** *Med.* **a** A smooth, slender, flexible instrument to be introduced into a canal of the body, for removing obstructions, etc. **b** A suppository. **2** A wax candle. [from *Bougie,* a town in Algeria, where the candles were made]

Bou·gue·reau (bo͞o·grō′), **Adolphe William,** 1825–1905, French painter.

bouil·la·baisse (bo͞ol′yə·bās′, *Fr.* bo͞o·yà·bes′) *n.* A chowder made of several varieties of fish and crustaceans, flavored with wine and saffron. [<F <Provençal *bouiabaisso* <*boui* boil + *abaisso* settle, go down]

bouil·lon (bo͞ol′yon, -yən; *Fr.* bo͞o·yôṅ′) *n.* **1** Clear soup from beef, chicken, or other meats. **2** A special preparation used as a culture medium for bacteria. [<F<*bouillir* boil]

Bou·lan·ger (bo͞o·läṅ·zhā′), **Georges Ernest,** 1837–91, French general.

—**Nadia,** 1887–1979, French musician; professor of harmony and counterpoint.

boul·der (bōl′dər) *n.* A large stone moved by natural agencies from its original bed. Also **bowl′der.** [ME *bulderston* <Scand. Cf. Sw. *bullersten* rumbling stone (in a stream).]

Boul·der (bōl′dər) A university city in northern Colorado.

Boulder Canyon A gorge of the Colorado River above Hoover Dam, now covered by Lake Mead.

Boulder Dam The former name of HOOVER DAM.

bou·le[1] (bo͞o′lē) *n. Greek* **1** An ancient Greek legislative council. **2** The modern Greek legislative assembly, especially the lower house. Also spelled *bule.*

boule[2] (bo͞ol) *n.* A small mass of fused alumina, usually pear–shaped, and tinted to resemble the natural ruby, sapphire, etc. [<F, ball]

boul·e·vard (bool′ə·värd, bo͞o′lə-) *n.* **1** A broad city avenue, often planted with trees. **2** The decorative plot of trees, turf, or shrubbery along such an avenue. **3** Originally, a rampart; hence, a street laid out on the site of former ramparts. [<F <G *bollwerk* fortification. Akin to BULWARK.]

bou·le·ver·se·ment (bo͞ol·vers·mäṅ′) *n. French* An overthrow; confusion; convulsion.

Bou·logne (bo͞o·lōn′, *Fr.* bo͞o·lôn′y′) A port of northern France on the English Channel. Also **Boulogne–sur–Mer** (-sür·mâr′).

Bou·logne–Bil·lan·court (bo͞o·lôn′y′·bē·yäṅ·ko͞or′) A city on the Seine River, SW of Paris, France.

bounce (bouns) *v.* **bounced, bounc·ing** *v.t.* **1** To cause to bound or rebound. **2** To cause to move noisily; bang; thump. **3** *U.S. Slang* To eject forcibly. **4** *U.S. Slang* To discharge from employment. —*v.i.* **5** To bound or rebound. **6** To move suddenly and violently; jump or spring. **7** To move hurriedly: with *out of* or *into.* **8** *Informal* To be returned because of insufficient funds: said of a check. —*n.* **1** A sudden, or violent spring or leap; a bounding or elastic motion; rebound. **2** *Colloq.* Enthusiasm; vivacity; spirit; verve. **3** *Slang* Dismissal; discharge; expulsion. **4** A heavy blow; a bang. **5** *Brit. Colloq.* An audacious lie; a bouncer; boastful exaggeration; bluster; swagger. [ME *bunsen* <MLG. Cf. Du. *bonzen.*]

bounc·er (boun′sər) *n.* **1** A large or strong person or thing. **2** One who or that which bounces. **3** *U.S. Colloq.* A strong man employed in a theater, saloon, etc., to throw out objectionable customers. **4** An audacious lie; also, a braggart.

bounc·ing (boun′sing) *adj.* **1** Strong and active. **2** Large; strapping; buxom. **3** Exaggerated; boastful.

bouncing Bet The soapwort.

bound[1] (bound) *v.i.* **1** To strike and spring back from a surface, as a ball. **2** To leap; move by a series of leaps. —*v.t.* **3** To cause to rebound. —*n.* **1** A light elastic leap or spring; also, a rebound. **2** The distance passed over in a leap or bound. See synonyms under LEAP. [<F *bondir* leap]

bound[2] (bound) *v.t.* **1** To set limits to; restrict. **2** To form the boundary of. **3** To describe or name the boundaries of. —*v.i.* **4** To adjoin. See synonyms under CIRCUMSCRIBE, LIMIT. [<*n.*] —*n.* **1** That which circumscribes or limits; boundary. **2** *pl.* The district included within a boundary or limits. See synonyms under BANK, BOUNDARY. [<OF *bonne, bonde* <LL *bodina* limit. Related to BOURN[1].]

bound[3] (bound) Past tense and past participle of BIND.—*adj.* **1** Made fast; tied; confined in bonds. **2** Constrained or compelled. **3** Having a cover or binding. **4** Apprenticed. **5** *Colloq.* Determined; resolved. **6** Constipated.

bound[4] (bound) *adj.* Having one's course directed; on the way; destined: with *for* or *to.* [<ON *buinn* <*bua* prepare]

bound·a·ry (boun′də·rē, -drē) *n. pl.* **·ries 1** A limiting or dividing line or mark. **2** Any object serving to indicate a limit or confine.

Synonyms: barrier, border, bound, bourn, bourne, confines, edge, enclosure, frontier, landmark, limit, line, marches, marge, margin, term, termination, verge. The *boundary* was originally the *landmark,* that which marked off one piece of territory from another. The *bound* is the *limit,* marked or unmarked. Now, however, the difference between the two words has come to be simply one of usage. As regards territory, we speak of the *boundaries* of a nation or of an estate; the *bounds* of a college,

a ball ground, etc. A *barrier* is something that bars ingress or egress. A *barrier* may be a *boundary*, as was the Great Wall of China for many centuries. *Bourn*, or *bourne*, is a poetical expression for *bound* or *boundary*. A *border* is a strip, as of land, along the *boundary*. A *border* is a sharp terminal line, as where river or ocean meets the land. *Limit* is now used almost wholly in the figurative sense; the *limit* of discussion, of time, of jurisdiction. *Line* is a military term: within the *lines*, or through the *lines*, of an army. Compare BARRIER, END, MARGIN.

boundary layer 1 *Aeron.* A tenuous stratum or film of air in contact with the surface of an airfoil. **2** *Physics* Any layer of fluid close to the surface of a body in a moving stream that reduces the pressure of impact.

boundary rider *Austral.* An employe of a sheep or cattle station who patrols boundaries to prevent the straying of stock or to inspect fences.

bound·en (boun′dən) *adj.* **1** Obligatory; necessary, as a duty. **2** *Obs.* Under obligations; obliged. [Var. of BOUND³]

bound·er (boun′dər) *n.* **1** One who fixes or marks bounds. **2** *Colloq.* One whose manners, etc., are offensive; a cad.

bound form *Ling.* A morpheme which occurs only as part of a larger form, as the *-s* in *cats* and the *-ing* in *looking*: opposed to *free form.*

bound·less (bound′lis) *adj.* Having no limit; vast; measureless; infinite. See synonyms under INFINITE. —**bound′less·ly** *adv.* —**bound′less·ness** *n.*

bound-out (bound′out′) *adj.* Indentured; apprenticed.

boun·te·ous (boun′tē·əs) *adj.* **1** Giving freely and largely; generous; beneficent. **2** Marked by liberality or bounty; plentiful. —**boun′te·ous·ly** *adv.* —**boun′te·ous·ness** *n.*

boun·ti·ful (boun′tə·fəl) *adj.* **1** Bounteous; generous. **2** Abundant; displaying abundance. See synonyms under AMPLE, GENEROUS. —**boun′ti·ful·ly** *adv.* —**boun′ti·ful·ness** *n.*

boun·ty (boun′tē) *n. pl.* **·ties 1** Liberality in giving or bestowing; munificence. **2** Gifts or favors generously bestowed. **3** A grant or allowance from a government, as for fisheries, manufactures, exports, enlistment, etc. **4** A reward paid by a government to encourage the killing of predatory animals (formerly also of Indians). See synonyms under BENEVOLENCE, GIFT, SUBSIDY. [< OF *bonté* < L *bonitas, -tatis* goodness]

boun·ty-fed (boun′tē-fed′) *adj.* Aided and encouraged by government grants or premiums; subsidized: *bounty-fed* industries.

boun·ty-jump·er (boun′tē-jum′pər) *n.* One who, having enlisted for the bounty, deserts as soon as possible, as in the Civil War.

bounty land Land given as a bounty for military service.

bounty money Money given as a bounty, especially for military service.

bou·quet (bō·kā′, bōō·kā′ for def. 1; bōō·kā′ for def. 2) *n.* **1** A bunch of flowers; a nosegay. **2** Delicate odor; particularly, the distinctive aroma of a wine. [< F < OF *boschet,* dim. of *bosc* wood, ult. < Gmc.]

bou·quet gar·ni (bōō·ke′ gár·nē′) *French* A bundle of herbs and vegetables used for seasoning.

Bour·bon (bōōr′bən) **1** A dynasty that reigned over France, 1589–1792, 1815–48. **2** A member of the deposed royal house of France, or of the Spanish or Neapolitan branches of the same family. **3** One who is stubbornly conservative in politics; one opposed to progressive movement. —**Bour′bon·ism** *n.* —**Bour′bon·ist** *n.*

Bour·bon (bōōr′bən, *Fr.* bōōr·bôn′), **Charles,** 1490–1527, French general under Charles V: called "Connétable de Bourbon."

Bour·bon Island (bōōr′bən) A former name for RÉUNION ISLAND.

Bour·bon whisky (bûr′bən) Whisky distilled from corn and barley, originally in Bourbon County, Ky. Also **bour′bon.**

bourd (bōōrd) *n. Scot.* A jest; anecdote; also, merriment.

bour·don¹ (bōōr′dən) *n.* **1** An organ stop, commonly of 16-foot tone. **2** The drone of a bag-

pipe. **3** A humming, monotonous, or continuous sound. —*v.i.* To drone a melody. [< Med. L *burdo* drone]

bour·don² (bōōr′dən) *n. Obs.* A pilgrim's staff. [< F]

bourg (boorg) *n.* A fortified medieval town; a Continental market town. [< F < LL *burgus,* ult. < Gmc. Related to BOROUGH.]

bour·geois¹ (bōōr′zhwä, bōōr·zhwä′) *adj.* Of or pertaining to the commercial or middle class, as distinguished from the nobility or from the working class: used by some writers as signifying uncultivated; ill-bred; common. —*n. pl.* **·geois 1** A citizen; a member of the commercial or middle class; a townsman; tradesman. **2** A 14th century coin. **3** In radical circles, anyone who owns property. [< F < OF *burgeis.* Doublet of BURGESS.]

bour·geois² (bər·jois′) *n.* A size of type: about 9-point. [? after a French printer]

Bour·geois (bōōr·zhwä′), **Léon Victor,** 1851–1925, French statesman.

bour·geoi·sie (bōōr·zhwä·zē′) *n.* **1** The middle class of society, especially in France: used collectively. **2** That class of society having private property. used especially by radical socialists. [< F < *bourgeois* middle class]

bour·geon (bûr′jən) *v. & n.* Burgeon.

Bourges (boorzh) A city in central France.

Bour·get (bōōr·zhe′), **Paul,** 1852–1935, French novelist, poet, and critic.

Bour·gogne (bōōr·gôn′y′) The French name for BURGUNDY.

Bour·gui·gnonne (bōōr·gē·nyôn′) *adj.* Prepared in a red wine sauce garnished with mushrooms and small onions. [< F, Burgundian]

bourn¹ (bôrn, bōrn, bōōrn) *n.* **1** That which limits; bound; goal; end: the *bourn* of man's life. **2** *Obs.* Realm; region; domain. Also **bourne.** See synonyms under BOUNDARY. [< F *borne* < OF *bodne* < LL *bodina* limit. Related to BOUND².]

bourn² (bôrn, bōrn, bōōrn) *n.* A brook or rivulet: used also in combination: *Eastbourne.* Compare BURN². Also **bourne.** [Var. of BURN²]

Bourne·mouth (bôrn′məth, bōrn′-) A county borough and seaside resort in SW Hampshire, England.

bourre·let (bōōr·lā′) *n.* A ridgelike band between the ogive and body of a shell, fitting closely to the bore of the gun and centering the projectile. [< F]

bourse (boors) *n.* An exchange or money market: applied to Continental stock exchanges, and especially to the Paris stock exchange. [< F, purse < LL *bursa* bag]

bour·tree (bōōr′trē) *n. Scot.* The European elder tree (*Sambucus nigra*).

bouse¹ (bōōz, bouz) *n. & v.i.* Booze.

bouse² (bous, bouz) *v. Naut.* To lift or haul with blocks and tackle: also spelled *bowse.* [Origin unknown]

bou·stro·phe·don (bōō′strə·fēd′n, bou′-) *n.* The early Greek method of writing, alternately from right to left and from left to right, as in inscriptions. [< Gk. *boustrophēdon* turning like oxen (in plowing) < *bous* ox + *strephein* turn] —**bou·stroph·e·don·ic** (bōō·strofə·don′ik, bou-), **bou·stroph·ic** (bōō·strof′ik, bou-) *adj.*

bous·y (bōō′zē, bou′-) *adj.* Boozy.

bout (bout) *n.* **1** A single turn, as in mowing a field. **2** A set-to or contest, as at boxing, etc. **3** A fit of drunkenness, reveling, or illness. **4** A bend or turn, as of a rope; bight. See synonyms under BATTLE. [Var. of ME *bought* bending, turn. Cf. LG *bucht* bend, turn.]

bou·tique (bōō·tēk′) *n. French* A small retail store in which dress accessories are sold.

bou·ton·nière (bōō′tə·nyâr′) *n.* A buttonhole bouquet, or a single flower worn in the buttonhole. [< F]

Bou·vier (bōō·vir′), **John,** 1787–1851, U.S. jurist born in Italy.

bou·vier des Flan·dres (bōō·vyā′ dā flän′dr′) A breed of powerfully built, medium-sized working dog, native to Belgium. [< F, cowherd of Flanders]

bou·zou·ki (bə·zōō′kē) *n.* A mandolinlike stringed instrument having a very long neck. [< New Gk. *mpouzouki*]

Bo·ve·ri (bō·vā′rē), **Theodor,** 1862–1915, German zoologist.

bo·vid (bō′vid) *n. Zool.* One of the *Bovidae.*

Bo·vi·dae (bō′vi·dē) *n. pl.* A family of ruminants, generally embracing those having paired hollow horns ensheathing horn cores, as antelopes, cattle, sheep, goats, etc.: distinguished from the deer family especially by non-deciduous, unbranched horns. [< L *bos, bovis* ox]

bo·vine (bō′vīn, -vin) *adj.* **1** Of or pertaining to the *Bovidae* or the genus *Bos.* **2** Oxlike; slow; patient; dull. —*n.* A bovine animal, as an ox, cow, etc. [< LL *bovinus* < L *bos* ox]

bow¹ (bou) *n.* **1** The forward part of a vessel; also, the front part of an airship. **2** The forward oarsman of a boat. —Homophone: *bough.* [< Dan. *bov* bow of a ship. Akin to BOUGH.]

bow² (bou) *v.* **bowed, bow·ing** *v.t.* **1** To bend (the head, knee, etc.), as in reverence, courtesy, or assent. **2** To express with bows: to *bow* agreement. **3** To escort with bows: He *bowed* us into the room. **4** To cause to yield; coerce: He *bowed* her to his will. **5** To weigh down; cause to stoop: Fatigue *bowed* his head. —*v.i.* **6** To bend the head, knee, etc., as in reverence, courtesy, or assent. **7** To express thanks, greeting, agreement, etc., by bowing. **8** To bend or incline downward: The waves *bowed* over and broke. **9** To submit; yield. —**to bow out** To withdraw; resign. —*n.* An inclination of the body or head forward and downward, as in salutation or worship. ◆Homophone: *bough.* [OE *bugan* bow, bend, flee] —**bow′er** *n.*

bow³ (bō) *n.* **1** A bend or curve, or something bent or curved. **2** A rainbow. **3** A weapon made from a strip of elastic wood or other pliable material, bent by a cord and projecting an arrow by its recoil when suddenly released; also, an archer. **4** *Music* A rod having parallel hairs strained between raised ends, used with a violin or other stringed instrument by drawing across the strings; also, the movement or mode of moving this. **5** A knot with a loop or loops, as of ribbon, etc. **6** Any one of various bow-shaped objects. **7** A U-shaped wooden piece passing upward through a yoke and retained by pins; oxbow. **8** *Geom.* A polygonal or curved projection from a straight line or wall on the ground plane. **9** Either of the rims of a pair of spectacles or one of the curved supports passing over the ears. —*adj.* Bent; curved; bowed. —*v.t. & v.i.* **bow·ed, bow·ing 1** To bend into the shape of a bow. **2** *Music* To play (a stringed instrument) with a bow. ◆Homophone: *beau.* [OE *boga*] —**bow′er** *n.*

bow arm (bō) In playing a violin, the right arm; in archery, the left.

Bow bells (bō) The bells of St. Mary-le-Bow, in Cheapside, London, within sound of which cockneys were said to be born; hence, the region within London called *cockneydom.*

Bow china (bō) A delicate ware made at Stratford-le-Bow, near London, in the 18th century.

bow compass (bō) *Geom.* A pair of very small compasses, properly having, instead of a joint, a curved metal strip between the legs, for drawing small circles or arcs of small radius.

Bow·ditch (bou′dich), **Nathaniel,** 1773–1838, U.S. mathematician and navigator.

bowd·ler·ize (boud′lər·īz) *v.t.* **·ized, ·iz·ing** To expurgate or edit prudishly. [after Dr. Thomas *Bowdler's* "family" edition of Shakespeare (1818)] —**bowd′ler·i·za′tion** *n.* —**bowd′ler·ism** *n.*

Bow·doin (bōd′n), **James,** 1726–90, American patriot.

bow·el (bou′əl, boul) *n.* **1** An intestine. **2** *pl.* The intestines or entrails collectively. **3** *pl.* The inner part of anything: the *bowels* of the earth. **4** *pl.* The intestinal regions, formerly considered as the seat of the tender emotions; hence, pity; compassion; heart. —*v.t.* **·eled** or **·elled, ·el·ing** or **·el·ling** To remove the bowels from; disembowel. [< OF *boel* < L *botellus,* dim. of *botulus* sausage]

bow·er¹ (bou′ər) *n.* **1** A shady recess; a retired dwelling; a rustic cottage. **2** A private apartment; boudoir. **3** An arbor. —*v.t.* To enclose in or as in a bower; embower. [OE *bur* chamber] —**bow′er·y** *adj.*

bow·er² (bou′ər) *n.* Either of the two highest cards (the knave of trumps or **right bower** and

the knave of the same color or **left bower**) in the game of euchre, unless the joker is used, which is then usually called the **best bower.** [<G *bauer* peasant, knave in a deck of cards]

bower[3] (bou′ər) *n. Naut.* A large anchor carried on the bow of a vessel. Also **bower anchor.**

bow·er·bird (bou′ər·bûrd′) *n.* An Australian bird that builds a bower or playhouse to attract the female, ornamenting it with shells, feathers, etc.; especially, the **great bowerbird** *(Chlamydera nuchalis).*

bow·er·y (bou′ər·ē) *n. pl.* **·er·ies** A farm or plantation: so called by the Dutch settlers of New York. [<Du. *bouwerij* farm <*bouwer, boer* farmer]

Bow·er·y (bou′ər·ē), **the** A street and section in New York City occupying the site of Governor Stuyvesant's farm or bowery: noted for its saloons, shabby hotels, and cheap shops.

bow·fin (bō′fin′) *n.* A small, predaceous, ganoid fish *(Amia calva),* having a long dorsal fin, being the sole member of the family Amiidae, which inhabits lakes and sluggish fresh water in North America. Also called *amia, mudfish, dogfish.*

bow·head (bō′hed′) *n.* The right whale.

bow·ie knife (bō′ē, bo͞o′ē) A strong hunting knife with two-edged point, hilt, crosspiece, and sheath: its invention is usually attributed to James Bowie, 1799–1836, Texan fighter who died at the Alamo; his brother, Rezin P. Bowie, also claimed to be the inventor.

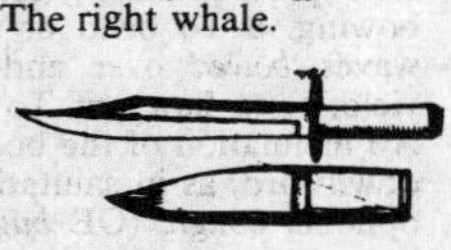

BOWIE KNIFE AND SHEATH

bow-key (bō′kē′) *n.* The wooden pin which fastens the oxbow to the yoke: also called *bowpin.*

bow·knot (bō′not′) *n.* An ornamental slipknot made by doubling ribbon, cord, fabric, etc., into one or more loops, usually tied so as to leave ends free to draw the loops easily through the knot. See illustration under KNOT.

bowl[1] (bōl) *n.* **1** A concave domestic vessel, nearly hemispherical and larger than a cup. **2** The amount it will hold. **3** A drinking-vessel for wine, etc. **4** A large goblet. **5** Anything shaped like a bowl, as a stadium. ◆ Homophone: *bole.* [OE *bolla*]

bowl[2] (bōl) *v.t.* **1** To strike or hit with or as with a bowl; knock down. **2** To roll (a ball). **3** To carry or transport on or as on wheels. **4** In cricket, to put out (the batsman): with *out.* —*v.i.* **5** To play at bowls. **6** To throw or roll a bowl or round object. **7** In cricket, to deliver the ball to the batsman. **8** To move smoothly and swiftly: usually with *along:* The ship *bowled* along. **—to bowl over** To cause to be confused or helpless; knock down or out. —*n.* **1** A large wooden ball for playing bowls or tenpins. **2** A turn or inning at a game of bowls. **3** A roller in a knitting machine. ◆ Homophone: *bole.* [<F *boule* ball <L *bulla* bubble]

bowl·der (bōl′dər) *n.* Boulder.

bow·leg (bō′leg′) *n.* A leg bent in an outward curve. **—bow′leg′ged** *adj.*

bowl·er (bō′lər) *n.* **1** One who plays bowls. **2** The player who delivers the ball. **3** *Brit.* A low-crowned, stiff felt hat; a derby hat.

Bowles (bōlz), **Samuel,** father 1797–1851, and son 1826–78, U.S. newspaper editors and publishers. **—Chester,** born 1901, U.S. public administrator and diplomat.

bow·line (bō′lin, -lin′) *n.* **1** *Naut.* A rope to keep the weather edge of a vessel's square sail forward when sailing close-hauled. **2** A knot. **—on a bowline** Close-hauled to the wind; said of a vessel.

bowl·ing (bō′ling) *n.* **1** A game played on a narrow lane along which a ball is rolled in an attempt to knock down ten pins at the far end of the lane. **2** Any of various similar games. **3** The playing of any of these games.

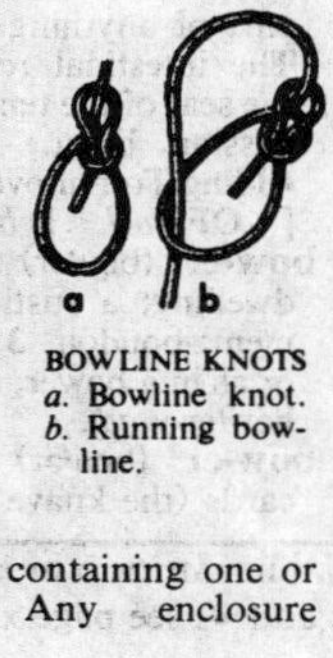

BOWLINE KNOTS
a. Bowline knot.
b. Running bowline.

bowling alley 1 A long, narrow, planked space for playing at tenpins. **2** A building containing one or more such alleys. **3** Any enclosure for playing bowls.

bowling ball A hard, heavy ball used in the game of bowling, usually having three finger holes for gripping.

bowling green A smooth lawn for playing at bowls.

Bowling Green 1 A small park at the foot of Broadway, New York City. **2** A city in southern Kentucky.

bowls (bōlz) *n. pl. (construed as sing.)* Any of various bowling games, especially one (also called **lawn bowling**) played outdoors with weighted balls rolled at a stationary ball.

bow·man[1] (bō′mən) *n. pl.* **·men** (-mən) An archer.

bow·man[2] (bou′mən) *n. pl.* **·men** (-mən) The oarsman nearest the bow.

bow pen (bō) *Geom.* A pair of jointless compasses carrying a pen or pencil: used for drawing very small circles.

bow·pin (bō′pin′) *n.* A bow-key.

bowse (bo͞oz, bouz) See BOUSE[2].

bow·shot (bō′shot′) *n.* The distance which an arrow may be sent from the bow.

bow·sprit (bou′sprit′, bō′-) *n. Naut.* A spar projecting forward from the bow of a vessel.

bow·string (bō′string′) *n.* **1** The string of a bow. **2** A string for strangling criminals. **3** Execution by strangling. —*v.t.* To execute by strangling; garrotte.

bowstring hemp A perennial, erect herb of the lily family (genus *Sansevieria*) with narrow white or yellowish-white flowers and hemplike fiber.

bow't (bōt) *adj. Scot.* Bowed; crooked; bent.

bow·tie (bō′tī′) *n.* A necktie worn in a bowknot.

bow window (bō) A projecting window built up from the ground level, properly one of curved ground plan. Compare BAY WINDOW.

bow-wow (bou′wou′) *n.* **1** The bark of a dog, or an imitation of it. **2** A dog: a child's word. **3** *pl. Colloq.* Ruin; damnation: going to the *bow-wows.* —*v.i.* To bark.

bow·yer (bō′yər) *n.* A maker or seller of bows.

box[1] (boks) *n.* **1** A receptacle or case of wood or other material, usually having a lid. **2** Any of various objects or receptacles resembling a box. **3** *Mech.* An axle bearing, casing, or other enclosed cavity. **4** The raised seat of a coach, the body of a wagon, etc. **5** A building, structure, or compartment with some resemblance or analogy to a box, as a compartment in a theater, restaurant, etc. **6** The quantity contained in a box or that a box will hold. **7** Either of the rectangular spaces on a baseball field in which the batsman or pitcher stands. **8** A gift or present packed in a box. **9** A box stall for a horse or bovine animal. **10** A flag house, sentry house, or similar small building for a watchman or the like. **11** A small house in the country; a shooting-box. **12** The place in a courtroom where the jury, a prisoner, or witnesses are railed in. **13** A cavity made in the trunk of a tree to collect its sap, as in extracting turpentine, etc. **14** A difficulty or predicament. —*v.t.* **1** To put into or enclose in a box: often with *up.* **2** To furnish with a bushing or box. **3** To boxhaul. **4** To fit into a mortise, as a tenon. **—to box the compass 1** To recite in order the 32 points of the compass. **2** To make a complete revolution; adopt successively all possible opinions on a question. [OE <Med. L *buxis,* blend of L *buxus* boxwood and *pyxis* box (both <Gk. *pyxos* boxwood). Doublet of PYX.] **—box′er** *n.*

box[2] (boks) *v.t.* **1** To cuff or buffet, especially about the ears and side of the head. **2** To fight (another) in a boxing match. —*v.i.* **3** To fight in a boxing match. **4** To be a prize fighter. —*n.* A slap or cuff with the hand on the ear or the cheek. See synonyms under BLOW [ME; origin uncertain]

box[3] (boks) *n.* A small evergreen tree or shrub (genus *Buxus*) of the Old World, cultivated as a border or hedge; especially, any variety of *B. sempervirens.* [OE <L *buxus* <Gk. *pyxos* boxwood]

box·ber·ry (boks′ber′ē, -bər·ē) *n. pl.* **·ber·ries 1** The checkerberry or wintergreen. **2** The partridgeberry.

box calf Tanned calfskin with square markings on the grain produced by lengthwise and crosswise rolling.

box·car (boks′kär′) *n.* A railway car shaped like a rectangular box, for carrying freight.

box coat 1 A coachman's heavy overcoat. **2** A greatcoat, especially one worn by travelers on the tops of coaches. **3** A loosely fitting overcoat, snug only at the shoulders.

box elder A North American tree of the maple family *(Acer negundo)* having leaves with 3 or 5 compound leaflets.

box·er[1] (bok′sər) *n.* A pugilist.

box·er[2] (bok′sər) *n.* A breed of medium-sized dog, related to the bulldog, characterized by a short, sturdy body, smooth coat, fawn or brindle in color, and a black mask. [Alter. of G *-beisser* in *Bullenbeisser* bulldog]

Box·er (bok′sər) *n.* A member of a Chinese secret society, active in 1900, which aimed to rid China of foreigners by force.

box·haul (boks′hôl′) *v.t. Naut.* To veer (a square-rigged vessel) round instead of tacking: done when tacking is impracticable.

box hook A sickle-shaped hook with a wooden handle, usually T-shaped, used for gripping and moving heavy boxes or bales of merchandise, waste, etc.: also called *bale hook.*

box·ing[1] (bok′sing) *n.* The act or practice of sparring, as with gloves; pugilism.

box·ing[2] (bok′sing) *n.* **1** The act of enclosing in a box. **2** Material from which to make boxes. **3** A casing or niche, as for window shutters.

Boxing Day The first weekday after Christmas, a British legal holiday on which presents (Christmas boxes) are given to employees, letter-carriers, etc.

boxing glove A glove with padded back, for boxing.

boxing match A prize fight or sparring contest.

box iron A smoothing and pressing iron containing a receptacle for a heater: distinguished from *sad-iron.*

box kite A kite having two rectangular, box-shaped, covered frames fitted together.

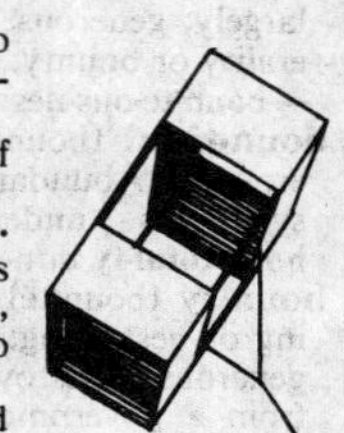

BOX KITE

box office The ticket office of a theater, etc.

box-of·fice (boks′ôf′is, -of′-is) *adj.* Of such a character as to attract large audiences, and, therefore, destined to make large profits.

box pleat Material folded twice and in opposite directions, the edges turned under and meeting. Also **box plait.**

box set A series of wooden frames covered with canvas, assembled to form the three walls of an interior stage setting.

box spring A mattress foundation consisting of an upholstered wood or metal frame set with an arrangement of coil springs to provide resiliency.

box stall A large, boxed-in stall for horses or cattle, in which they do not have to be tied.

box·thorn (boks′thôrn′) *n.* Any of various evergreen or deciduous ornamental plants (genus *Lycium)* of the nightshade family, with long, drooping, flowering branches and usually scarlet berries, especially *L. halimifolium*: also called *matrimony vine.*

box·wood (boks′wo͝od′) *n.* **1** The hard, close-grained, durable wood of the box evergreen shrub (genus *Buxus*). **2** The shrub.

boy (boi) *n.* **1** A male child; lad; youth; son. **2** *pl.* Comrades; fellows. **3** A male servant, especially a personal servant: often used of Orientals or Africans. [ME *boi;* origin unknown]

bo·yar (bō·yär′, boi′ər) *n.* **1** A member of a class of the old Russian aristocracy, abolished in the time of Peter the Great. **2** In Rumania, one of a privileged class. Also **bo·yard** (bō·yärd′, boi′ərd). [<Russian *boyarin* noble]

boy·cott (boi′kot) *v.t.* **1** To combine together in refusing to deal or associate with, so as to punish or coerce. **2** To refuse to use or buy. —*n.* The act, pressure, or an instance of boycotting. [after Capt. C. *Boycott,* 1832–1897, landlord's agent in Ireland, who was first victim, 1880]

boy friend *Colloq.* **1** A girl's or woman's sweetheart, favorite male companion, etc. **2** A male friend. Also **boy·friend** (boi′frend′).

boy·hood (boi′ho͝od) *n.* **1** The state or period of being a boy. **2** Boys collectively.

boy·ish (boi′ish) *adj.* Of, pertaining to, or like boys or boyhood. See synonyms under YOUTHFUL. **—boy′ish·ly** *adv.* **—boy′ish·ness** *n.*

Boyle (boil), **Robert,** 1627–91, English chemist and physicist, born in Ireland.

Boyle's law *Physics* The statement that the volume of a gas kept at constant temperature varies inversely as the pressure. [after Robert *Boyle*]

Boyne (boin) A river in NE Ireland, flowing NE 70 miles to the Irish Sea.

boy scout 1 A member of the **Boy Scouts,** an organization for training boys between the ages of 12 and 19 in self-reliance and good citizenship through a program of constructive, recreational training: initiated in England in 1908 by Lieut. Gen. Sir Robert Baden-Powell. 2 A member of the Boy Scouts of America, incorporated in 1910.

boy·sen·ber·ry (boi′zən·ber′ē) *n. pl.* **·ries 1** A hybrid plant obtained by crossing the blackberry, raspberry, and loganberry. 2 Its edible fruit, resembling the raspberry in taste. [after Rudolph *Boysen,* 20th c. U.S. horticulturist, the originator]

Boz (boz) An early pen name of Charles Dickens.

Boz·ca·a·da (bôz·jä′ä·dä′) The Turkish name for TENEDOS. Also **Boz·ca Island** (bôz′jä).

bo·zo (bō′zō) *n. U.S. Slang* A fellow; guy.

Boz·za·ris (bot′sä·rēs, bō·zar′is), **Marcos,** 1788–1823, Greek patriot.

Br *Chem.* Bromine (symbol Br).

bra (brä) *n.* A brassière.

Bra·ban·çon griffon (brȧ·bän·sôṅ′) A toy dog similar to the Brussels griffon except that its coat is short and smooth, reddish-brown or black mixed with reddish-brown.

Bra·ban·çonne (brȧ·bän·sôn′) The national anthem of the Belgians since 1830. [< F < *Brabant,* province in Belgium]

Bra·bant (brə·bant′, brä′bənt) A former duchy, now divided into North Brabant, Netherlands, and Brabant province in Belgium; 1,268 square miles; capital, Brussels.

brab·ble (brab′əl) *v.i.* **·bled, ·bling** To quarrel noisily about trifles. [? < Du. *brabbelen* jabber] — **brab′ble·ment** *n.*

brac·cate (brak′āt) *adj. Ornithol.* Having the feet feathered down to the claws, as certain birds. [< L *bracatus* wearing breeches < *bracae* breeches]

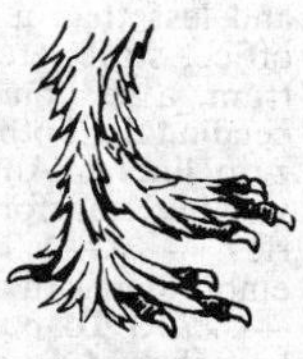
BRACCATE CLAWS

brace (brās) *v.* **braced, brac·ing** *v.t.* 1 To make firm or steady; strengthen by or as by equipping with braces. 2 To make ready to withstand pressure, impact, assault, etc. 3 To tie or fasten firmly, as with straps. 4 To stimulate; enliven. 5 *Naut.* To turn (the yards) by means of the braces. 6 *Slang* To ask a loan or favor from. —*v.i.* 7 To strain against pressure. **—to brace up** *Colloq.* To rouse one's courage or resolution. —*n.* 1 A support, as of wood or metal, to hold something firmly in place. 2 A cranklike handle, as for a bit. 3 A clasp or clamp used for connecting, fastening, etc. 4 A doubly curved line (⏞), used in writing and printing to connect words, lines, or staves of music. 5 A pair; couple; two: a *brace* of ducks, etc. 6 The state of being braced; tension. 7 *Naut.* A rope fastened to a yardarm and reaching the deck, to swing the yard for the wind and to hold it in place. 8 *pl. Brit.* Suspenders. [< OF *bracier* embrace < *brace, brache* two arms < L *brachia,* pl. of *brachium* arm]

brace·let (brās′lit) *n.* 1 An ornamental band encircling the wrist or arm. 2 *Colloq.* A handcuff. [< OF, dim. of *bracel* < L *brachiale* bracelet < *brachium* arm]

brac·er (brā′sər) *n.* 1 That which braces or steadies; a band; support. 2 A protective covering for the forearm in archery. 3 A tonic; stimulant. 4 A stimulating drink.

bra·ce·ro (brə·sâr′ō) *n. pl.* **·ros** A Mexican laborer brought into the United States under contract for seasonal farm work. [< Sp., day laborer]

brach (brach, brak) *n. Archaic* A hound bitch. Also **brach·et** (brach′it). [< OF *brachet* hunting dog < OHG]

bra·chi·al (brā′kē·əl, brak′ē-) *adj.* 1 Of or pertaining to the arm, especially the upper arm. 2 *Zool.* Of, pertaining to, or designating the armlike appendages or brachia of various invertebrates. 3 Armlike. [< L *brachialis* < *brachium* arm]

bra·chi·ate (brā′kē·it, -āt, brak′ē-) *adj. Bot.* Having branches in pairs, each pair forming a right line with each other, and standing at right angles to the stem, or widely diverging. —*v.i.* (-āt) **·at·ed, ·at·ing** *Zool.* To move by a swinging motion of the arms, as from branch to branch of trees: said especially of certain arboreal apes not fully adapted to the erect posture and bipedal locomotion. [< L *brachiatus* having arms < *brachium* arm] **—bra′chi·a′tion** *n.*

brachio- *combining form* Arm; of the arm: *brachiotomy.* Also, before vowels, **brachi-.** [< Gk. *brachiōn* arm]

bra·chi·ot·o·my (brā′kē·ot′ə·mē, brak′ē-) *n. Surg.* The cutting off or removal of an arm.

bra·chi·o·pod (brā′kē·ə·pod′, brak′ē-) *n. Zool.* One of a phylum or class *(Brachiopoda)* of nearly extinct molluscoid marine animals having a bivalve shell and a pair of brachial appendages rising from the sides of the mouth; a lamp shell. — **bra·chi·op·o·dous** (brā′kē·op′ə·dəs, brak′ē-) *adj.*

bra·chis·to·chrone (brə·kis′tə·krōn) *n. Physics* The line of motion along which a particle acted upon by a constraining force will move from one given point to another in the shortest time: also spelled *brachystochrone.* [< Gk. *brachistos* shortest + *chronos* time]

bra·chi·um (brā′kē·əm, brak′ē-) *n. pl.* **bra·chi·a** (brā′kē·ə, brak′ē-) 1 The upper arm, or its homolog in any animal. 2 Any armlike process or appendage. [< L]

brachy- *combining form* Short: *brachycranic.* [< Gk. *brachys* short]

brach·y·ce·phal·ic (brak′i·sə·fal′ik) *adj.* 1 *Anat.* Having a short skull of excessive breadth; round-headed. 2 In anthropometry, characterized by a skull whose cephalic index is at least 80. Also **brach·y·ceph·a·lous** (brak′·ē·sef′ə·ləs). [< NL *brachycephalicus* < Gk. *brachykephalos* < *brachys* short + *kephalē* head] **—brach′y·ceph′a·ly** *n.*

brach·y·cra·nic (brak′i·krā′nik) *adj.* Brachycephalic. [< BRACHY- + Gk. *kranion* head]

brach·y·dac·tyl·ic (brak′i·dak·til′ik) *adj.* Having abnormally short fingers or toes. [< Gk. *brachydaktylos* < *brachys* short + *daktylos* finger] — **brach′y·dac′tyl·ism** (-dak′təl·iz′əm) *n.*

brach·y·dome (brak′i·dōm) See under DOME (def. 4).

brach·y·dro·mic (brak′i·drō′mik) *adj.* Taking a deflected or slanting path with reference to the target; heading short: said of guided missiles. [< Gk. *brachydromos* < *brachys* short + *dromos* course]

bra·chyl·o·gy (brə·kil′ə·jē) *n.* Brevity and conciseness of speech; an abridged form of expression; especially, omission of a word necessary for correct grammatical expression. [< Gk. *brachylogia* < *brachys* short + *-logia* speech]

bra·chyp·ter·ous (brə·kip′tər·əs) *adj. Ornithol.* Having short wings. [< Gk. *brachypteros* < *brachys* short + *pteron* wing]

brach·y·u·ran (brak′i·yŏŏr′ən) *adj. Zool.* Of or relating to a suborder *(Brachyura)* of decapods, comprising the crabs. Also **brach′y·u′rous** (-yŏŏr′əs). —*n.* A short-tailed crustacean. [< NL *brachyura* < Gk. *brachys* short + *oura* tail]

brac·ing[1] (brā′sing) *adj.* Imparting tone or vigor; invigorating; tonic.

brac·ing[2] (brā′sing) *n.* 1 The act of bracing, or the state of being braced. 2 A system of braces, as in bridge-building.

brack·en (brak′ən) *n.* 1 A brake or other large fern. 2 Brakes collectively. [ME *braken* < Scand. Cf. Sw. *bräken* fern.]

brack·et (brak′it) *n.* 1 A piece projecting from a wall to support a shelf or other weight. 2 A projecting gas fixture or lamp holder, etc. 3 A brace used to strengthen an angle. 4 *Printing* One of two marks [ ], used to enclose any part of the text. 5 A vinculum. 6 A number of persons considered as a group because of some common characteristics: the high-income *bracket.* —*v.t.* 1 To provide or support with a bracket or brackets. 2 To enclose within brackets. 3 To group or categorize together. 4 *Mil.* To fire both over and short of (a target). [< Sp. *bragueta,* dim. of *braga* < L *bracae,* pl., breeches]

brack·et·ing (brak′it·ing) *n.* 1 Wooden skeleton pieces to which the lath and plaster forming the surface of a cornice are fastened, and which give shape to the latter. 2 The act of furnishing with brackets. 3 A series of brackets.

brack·ish (brak′ish) *adj.* 1 Somewhat saline, as a mixture of salt water and fresh; briny. 2 Distasteful. [< Du. *brak* salty] **—brack′ish·ness** *n.*

bract (brakt) *n. Bot.* A modified leaf in a flower cluster or subtending a flower. [< L *bractea* thin metal plate] — **brac·te·al** (brak′tē·əl) *adj.*

BRACT Surrounding a composite flower.

brac·te·ate (brak′tē·it, -āt) *adj. Bot.* Having bracts.

brac·te·o·late (brak′tē·ə·lāt′) *adj. Bot.* Having bracteoles.

brac·te·ole (brak′tē·ōl) *n. Bot.* A diminutive bract. Also **bract·let** (brakt′lit).

brad (brad) *n.* A small and slender nail, often having, in place of head, a projection on one side. [< ON *broddr* spike]

brad-awl (brad′ôl′) *n.* A short, non-tapering awl, with a cutting edge on the end.

Brad·dock (brad′ək), **Edward,** 1695?–1755, English general in French and Indian War.

Brad·ford (brad′fərd) A county borough in SW Yorkshire, England.

Brad·ford (brad′fərd), **Ga·ma·li·el** (gə·mā′lē·əl), 1863–1932, U.S. biographer. **—Roark** (rôrk, rōrk), 1896–1948, U.S. novelist and short-story writer. **—William,** 1590–1657, Pilgrim governor of Plymouth Colony. **—William,** 1722–91, American printer: called "Patriot Printer of 1776."

Brad·ley (brad′lē), **Francis Herbert,** 1846–1924, English philosopher. **—Henry,** 1845–1923, English lexicographer. **—Omar Nelson,** born 1893, U.S. general.

Brad·street (brad′strēt), **Anne,** 1612–72, *née* Dudley, first woman poet in America. **—Simon,** 1603–97, colonial governor of Massachusetts; husband of Anne.

brady- *combining form* Slow: *bradycardia.* [< Gk. *bradys* slow]

brad·y·car·di·a (brad′i·kär′dē·ə) *n. Pathol.* Slowness of the heartbeat, indicated by a pulse rate of 60 or less. [< NL < BRADY- + Gk. *kardia* heart] **—brad′y·car′dic** *adj.*

brae (brā) *n. Scot.* A bank; hillside; slope. ◆ Homophone: *bray.*

brag (brag) *v.* **bragged, brag·ging** *v.i.* To vaunt oneself or one's deeds or abilities. —*v.t.* To declare or assert boastfully; boast of. —*n.* 1 The act of bragging; boastfulness; boastful language. 2 The thing bragged of; boast. 3 A person who brags. 4 A game of cards resembling poker. — *adj.* 1 To be bragged about: a *brag* crop. 2 *Obs.* Boastful; also, spirited; valiant. [Origin uncertain] **—brag′ger** *n.*

Bra·ga (brä′gə), **Teófilo,** 1843–1924, Portuguese reformer and author.

Bra·gan·ça (brə·gaṅ′sə) A city in northern Portugal, site of the castle of the Bragançás, former royal family of Portugal. Also **Bra·gan·za** (brə·gan′zə).

Bragg (brag), **Braxton,** 1817–76, Confederate general. **—Sir William Henry,** 1862–1942, English physicist and chemist. **—William Lawrence,** 1890-1971, English physicist: son of the preceding.

brag·ga·do·ci·o (brag′ə·dō′shē·ō) *n. pl.* **·ci·os 1** Pretentious boasting. 2 One who talks boastfully; a swaggerer. [after *Braggadochio,* a boastful character in Spenser's *Faerie Queene*]

brag·gart (brag′ərt) *n.* A vain boaster. —*adj.* Overboastful. **—brag′gart·ism** *n.*

brag·get (brag′it) *n.* An ancient drink of ale and honey fermented with yeast; later, mulled ale sweetened and spiced. [< Welsh *bragawd*]

Bragg method *Physics* A method for studying and analyzing crystal structure by means of X-rays: originated by Sir W. H. Bragg.

Bra·gi (brä′gē) In Norse mythology, the god of poetry, son of Odin, husband of Ithunn, and one of the original Æsir. Also **Bra·ge** (brä′gə).

Bra·he (brä′ə), **Ty·cho** (tü′kō), 1546–1601, Danish astronomer.

Brah·ma[1] (brä'mə) n. 1 In Hindu religion, the absolute primordial essence; the supreme soul of the universe, self-existent, absolute, and eternal, from which all things emanate and to which all return. 2 God, conceived of as comprising the Hindu trinity Brahma, Vishnu, and Siva; also, specifically, the personification of the first of the trinity, as supreme creator. [<Skt. *Brahmā*]

Brah·ma[2] (brä'mə, brā'-) n. A large variety of the domestic hen of an Asian breed. [from *Brahmaputra*]

Brah·man (brä'mən) n. pl. **·mans** 1 A member of the first of the four Hindu castes of India; the sacerdotal class: also spelled *Brahmin*. 2 A species of cattle originally imported from India and bred in the southern United States. [<Skt. *brāhmana* < *brahman* praise, worship] — **Brah·man·i** (brä·man'ik) or **·i·cal** adj.

Brah·man·ism (brä'mən·iz'əm) n. The religious and social system of the Brahmans: also spelled *Brahminism*. — **Brah'man·ist** n.

Brah·man·y (brä'mən·ē) adj. Held sacred according to Brahmanic rites, or consecrated to the use of Brahmans: said especially of certain animals and trees: *Brahmany* bull, fig tree, etc. Also **Brah'min·y.**

Brahmany bull The white male zebu.

Brah·ma·pu·tra (brä'mə·pōō'trə) A river of southern Asia, flowing 1,800 miles across Tibet, SW China, Assam, and East Pakistan to the Bay of Bengal.

Brah·min (brä'min) n. 1 Brahman (def. 1). 2 An aristocrat; a highly cultured person; specifically, an ultra-intellectual New Englander.

Bra·min·ism (brä'min·iz'əm) n. 1 Brahmanism. 2 The attitude, mannerisms, etc., of Brahmins.

Brahms (brämz, *Ger.* bräms), **Johannes,** 1833–97, German composer.

Bra·hu·i (brä·hōō'ē) n. A Dravidian language spoken in eastern Baluchistan.

braid[1] (brād) v.t. 1 To weave together or intertwine several strands of; plait. 2 To bind or ornament (the hair) with ribbons, etc. 3 To form by braiding: to *braid* a mat. 4 To ornament (garments) with braid. — n. 1 A narrow, flat tape or strip for binding or ornamenting fabrics. 2 Anything braided or plaited: a *braid* of hair. 3 A string or band used in arranging the hair. [OE *bregdan* brandish, weave, braid] — **braid'er** n.

braid[2] (brād) adj. *Scot.* Broad.

braid·ing (brā'ding) n. 1 Braids collectively. 2 Embroidery done with braid.

brail (brāl) n. 1 *Naut.* One of the ropes for gathering up the foot and leeches of a foreand-aft sail for furling. 2 A leather fastening for a hawk's wing. — v.t. 1 *Naut.* To haul in (a sail) by means of brails: usually with *up*. 2 To fasten with a brail, as a hawk's wing. [<OF *braiel* <L *bracale* a belt for breeches < *bracae* breeches]

Brǎ·i·la (bro·ē'lä) A city on the Danube in eastern Rumania.

Braille (brāl) n. A system of printing or writing

BRAILLE ALPHABET

for the blind in which the characters consist of raised dots to be read by the fingers; also, the characters themselves. See POINT SYSTEM (def. 2). [after Louis *Braille*, 1809–52, French educator, who invented it]

brain (brān) n. 1 *Anat.* The enlarged and greatly modified portion of the central nervous system contained within the cranium of vertebrates: its functions are shared between the two cerebral hemispheres, the cerebellum, and the medulla oblongata, which are of great development in higher mammals and in man. 2 Mind; intellect: often in the plural. 3 *Zool.* The principal regulating ganglion of invertebrates. See synonyms under MIND. — **to have on the brain** To be obsessed by. — v.t. To dash out the brains of. [OE *brægen*]

brain·child (brān'chīld') n. An idea, project, or other product of the mind considered as belonging to its creator.

brain·fag (brān'fag') n. Extreme mental fatigue.

brain fever Inflammation of the meninges.

brain·less (brān'lis) adj. 1 Without a brain. 2 Destitute of intelligence; senseless. — **brain'less·ly** adv. — **brain'less·ness** n.

brain·pan (brān'pan') n. The bony case enclosing the brain; cranium; skull.

brain·sick (brān'sik') adj. Mentally disordered; whimsical. — **brain'sick'ly** adv. — **brain'sick'ness** n.

brain·stem (brān'stem') n. All the brain except the cerebellum and the cerebral cortex; that is, the segmental apparatus.

brain storm 1 Cerebral disturbance of a sudden and violent character. 2 *Colloq.* Any momentary confusion of mind. 3 *Colloq.* A burst of inspiration.

brain trust Any group of experts or, derisively, of pretended experts: used in 1933 to designate the group of educators in political science and economy who advised President Franklin D. Roosevelt.

brain·wash (brān'wosh', -wôsh') v.t. To alter the convictions, beliefs, etc., of by means of brainwashing.

brain·wash·ing (brān'wosh'ing, -wôsh'ing) n. 1 Indoctrination. 2 The systematic alteration of personal convictions, beliefs, habits, and attitudes to follow politically acceptable lines.

brain wave 1 *Physiol.* A rhythmical fluctuation of electrical potential between different parts of the brain. 2 *Colloq.* A sudden inspiration.

brain·work (brān'wûrk') n. Work involving primarily the use of the mind, rather than manual or mechanical skills. — **brain'work'er** n.

brain·y (brā'nē) adj. **brain·i·er, brain·i·est** Possessed of brains; mentally able; smart. — **brain'i·ly** adv. — **brain'i·ness** n.

braise (brāz) v.t. **braised, brais·ing** To cook (meat) by searing till brown and then simmering in a covered pan. [<F *braiser* < *braise* charcoal]

brais·er (brā'zər) n. A covered kettle or pan used in braising.

braize (brāz) n. A European sparoid fish (genus *Pagrus*). [Origin uncertain]

brake[1] (brāk) n. 1 A device for retarding or arresting the motion of a vehicle, a wheel, etc. 2 A harrow. 3 An instrument for separating the fiber of flax, hemp, etc., by bruising. 4 A lever for working a pump or other machine. 5 A baker's kneading machine. 6 A framework to hold a horse's foot while it is being shod. 7 A machine for extracting juice from fruits and vegetables. 8 An old instrument of torture. — v. **braked, brak·ing** v.t. 1 To apply a brake to; reduce the speed of. 2 To bruise and crush, as flax. 3 To pulverize (clods) with a harrow. 4 To knead (dough). — v.i. 5 To operate a brake or brakes. ◆Homophone: *break*. [MDu. *braeke* brake for flax; infl. in meaning by F *brac*, var. of *bras* arm, and by BREAK]

brake[2] (brāk) n. Break (def. 7).

brake[3] (brāk) n. 1 A variety of fern; bracken. 2 A canebrake. ◆Homophone: *break*. [ME < *braken* BRACKEN]

brake[4] (brāk) n. A thicket. ◆Homophone: *break*. [Cf. MLG *brake* stumps, broken branches]

brake[5] (brāk) Archaic past tense of BREAK.

brake·age (brā'kij) n. The action or controlling power of a brake.

brake band A flexible band or strap which encircles a brake drum and grips it when tightened.

brake drum A metal drum attached to the axle or transmission shaft of a vehicle and connecting with the brake mechanism.

brake horsepower The effective horsepower of an engine, as measured by a brake or dynamometer attached to the driving shaft.

brake lining The friction-producing material with which the working parts of a brake are lined.

brake·man (brāk'mən) n. pl. **·men** (-mən) One who tends a brake or brakes on a railroad car or in a mine. Also **brakes'man.**

brake shoe A brake lining.

brake wheel A hand wheel on the roof of a railroad car for controlling the brakes.

brake·y (brā'kē) n. *Slang* A brakeman on a train.

Brak·pan (brak'pan) A town in Gauteng, Republic of South Africa.

bra·ky (brā'kē) adj. Overgrown with bracken or brushwood.

Bra·man·te (brä·män'tā), **Donato d'Agnolo,** 1444–1514, Italian architect and painter.

bram·ble (bram'bəl) n. 1 The European blackberry, or any other species of the genus *Rubus*. 2 Any prickly plant or shrub. [OE *bræmble*. Akin to BROOM.] — **bram'bly** adj.

bram·bling (bram'bling) n. The European mountain finch (*Fringilla montifringilla*).

bran (bran) n. 1 The coarse, outer coat of cereals, as separated from the flour by sifting or bolting. 2 Grain by-products as used for cattle feed. [<OF *bran, bren*]

Bran (bran) 1 A mythical king of Britain. 2 In Celtic mythology, a god of the underworld. 3 In Icelandic saga, the faithful hound of Frithiof.

branch (branch, bränch) n. 1 A secondary stem of a tree, shrub, or the like; a limb: distinguished from *twig*; an offshoot. 2 A separate part; side issue; division; department. 3 *Geog.* A tributary stream; in the southern United States, any stream of water smaller than a river. 4 Anything having an analogy to a branch, as one of the subdivisions of a deer's antler, a part of a family, a subhead of a general subject, etc. 5 A local division of a highway, railroad, etc., connecting with a main line. 6 *Archit.* One of the ribs in the Gothic style of vaulting. 7 A division used in classifying the subdivisions of linguistic families and stocks, including more than a group and less than a stock. 8 A subordinate local office, store, etc. 9 *Physics* **a** In a band spectrum, a section of the component lines proceeding in both directions from a common zero line. **b** Any of the subdivisions due to varying transformations of a radioactive series. — v.t. 1 To divide into branches. 2 To embroider with a pattern of flowers or foliage. — v.i. 3 To put forth branches; divide into branches. 4 To spring off from the main part; come out from the trunk, etc. — **to branch off** 1 To separate into branches; fork, as a road. 2 To diverge; go off on a tangent. — **to branch out** To extend or expand, as one's business or interests. — adj. Diverging from or tributary to a trunk, stock, or main part. [<F *branche* <LL *branca* paw]

bran·chi·a (brang'kē·ə) n. pl. **·chi·ae** (-ki·ē) 1 *Zool.* A gill. 2 pl. Gills or gill-like appendages; respiratory organs of fish, used in breathing the air contained in water. [<L <Gk. *branchia*, pl., gills] — **bran'chi·al** adj.

branchial cleft Gill slit.

bran·chi·ate (brang'kē·it, -āt) adj. Having gills.

branchio- *combining form* Gills: branchiopod. Also, before vowels, **branchi-.** [<Gk. *branchia*, pl., gills of fishes]

bran·chi·o·pod (brang'kē·ə·pod') n. One of a group (*Branchiopoda*) of aquatic crustaceans having a typically elongated body and many pairs of leaflike thoracic appendages having a respiratory function. [<BRANCHIO- + Gk. *pous, podos* foot]

Bran·cusi (bron'kōōsh), **Constantin,** 1876–1957, Rumanian sculptor.

brand (brand) v.t. 1 To mark with or as with a hot iron. 2 To stigmatize; mark as infamous. [< n.] — n. 1 A burning stick; firebrand. 2 A mark burned with a hot iron. 3 A name or trademark used to identify a product or group of products of a particular manufacturer. 4 A herd of cattle marked with a certain brand. 5 Quality; kind. 6 A branding iron. 7 *Archaic* A sword. 8 *Bot.* A pustular appearance of plants, caused by a parasitic fungus. See synonyms under BLEMISH, BURN. [OE. torch, sword. Akin to BURN[1].] — **brand'er** n.

Bran·deis (bran'dīs), **Louis Dembitz,** 1856–1941, U.S. jurist.

bran·den·burg (bran'dən·bûrg) n. 1 One of a series of ornamental loops worn on an outer

garment in the place of buttons; a frog. **2** A facing of embroidery on a military coat: usually in parallel bars. [from *Brandenburg*]

Bran·den·burg (bran'dən·bûrg, *Ger.* brän'dən·bŏŏrkh) A state in the German Democratic Republic; 10,416 square miles; capital, Potsdam; formerly a province of Prussia.

brand·er[1] (bran'dər) *n.* **1** One who or that which brands. **2** *Dial.* A support of a grain stack. [<BRAND]

brand·er[2] (bran'dər) *n.* **1** *Scot.* A gridiron. **2** *Dial.* A stand for a kettle; trivet. [ME *brandire* < *branden* burn + *ire* iron]

Bran·des (brän'des), **Georg Morris Cohen,** 1842–1927, Danish literary critic.

brand goose The brant.

bran·died (bran'dēd) *adj.* Mixed, flavored with, or preserved in brandy: *brandied* cherries.

branding iron An iron for burning in a brand. Also **brand iron.**

RRR Ⴑ Oᖶ ᗰ ᴀᴀˣ Ᾱ

BRANDING IRON AND CATTLE BRANDS

bran·dish (bran'dish) *v.t.* To wave, shake, or flourish triumphantly, menacingly, or defiantly. See synonyms under SHAKE. — *n.* A flourish, as with a weapon. [<OF *brandiss-*, stem of *brandir* < *brand* sword] — **brand'ish·er** *n.*

brand·ling (brand'ling) *n. Brit.* A small red earthworm (*Eisenia foetida*), used as bait. [<BRAND, *n.* + -LING]

brand-new (brand'nōo', -nyōo') *adj.* Quite new; fresh and bright: also *bran-new.*

bran·dy (bran'dē) *n. pl.* **bran·dies** An alcoholic liquor distilled from wine and also from the fermented juice of fruits other than the grape. — *v.t.* **bran·died, bran·dy·ing** **1** To mix, flavor, strengthen, or preserve with brandy. **2** To serve or refresh with brandy. [<Du. *brandewijn* brandy, lit., distilled wine]

brandy sling A drink made of brandy, water, sugar, and lemon juice.

brandy smash A drink made of brandy, crushed ice, and mint sprigs.

Bran·dy·wine (bran'di·wīn') A creek in SE Pennsylvania and northern Delaware; site of Washington's defeat by the British, 1777.

Brang·wyn (brang'win), **Sir Frank,** 1867–1956, English painter, etcher, and illustrator.

branle (bränl) *n.* A form of dance in vogue in France in the 16th and 17th centuries, still performed by French Canadians. [<F < *branler* shake]

bran-new (bran'nōo', -nyōo') *adj.* Brand-new.

bran·ny (bran'ē) *adj.* Made of, containing, or like bran.

brant (brant) *n. pl.* **brants** or **brant** A small, dark-colored wild goose (*Branta bernicla*) of the coasts of Europe and eastern North America, breeding only within the Arctic Circle, coming south in great flocks in autumn. Also **brant goose.** [? <ON *brandgās* sheldrake]

Brant (brant), **Joseph,** 1742–1807, Mohawk chief who fought for the British against the American colonists.

bran·tail (bran'tāl') *n.* The European redstart.

Bran·ting (brän'ting), **Karl Hjalmar,** 1860–1925, Swedish statesman.

Bran·tôme (brän·tôm'), **Seigneur de,** 1540?–1614, Pierre de Bourdeilles, French historian.

Braque (bråk), **Georges,** 1882–1963, French painter.

brash[1] (brash) *adj.* Brittle: said of wood or timber. [Cf. dial. E (Northern) *brassish* brittle]

brash[2] (brash) *adj.* **1** Quick-tempered; irascible; hasty; rash. **2** Saucy; pert. **3** Active; quick. [Cf. G *barsch* harsh and Sw. *barsk* impetuous] — **brash'ly** *adv.* — **brash'ness** *n.*

brash[3] (brash) *n.* **1** A transient attack of sickness, especially one arising from a disordered stomach. **2** A rash or eruption. **3** An attack; bout; brush. **4** *Brit. Dial.* A shower of rain. [? Blend of BREAK and CRASH, DASH, SPLASH, etc.] — **brash'i·ness** *n.* — **brash'y** *adj.*

brash[4] (brash) *n.* **1** A heap of rubbish. **2** Any brittle wood. [Prob. <F *brèche* rubble]

bra·sier (brā'zhər) *n.* Brazier.

Bra·sí·li·a (brə·zē'lē·ə) The capital of Brazil, in a Federal District in the central part.

bras·i·lin (braz'ə·lin) *n. Chem.* Brazilin.

Bra·şov (brä·shôv') The Rumanian name for STALIN. Also **Bra·shov'.**

brass (bras, bräs) *n.* **1** An alloy essentially of copper and zinc, harder than copper, ductile, and capable of being hammered into thin leaves. **2** Formerly, any alloy of copper, especially one with tin. **3** An ornament or utensil of brass, as a candlestick, doorknob, etc.: chiefly in the plural. **4** The brass wind instruments of an orchestra collectively. **5** *Colloq.* Impudence; effrontery. **6** *Slang* Money. **7** A bearing box or bush, properly of a copper alloy. **8** A monumental tablet of brass. **9** *Colloq.* High-ranking military officers collectively. [OE *bræs*]

brass·age (bras'ij, bräs'-) *n.* The mintage fee for coining. Compare SEIGNIORAGE. [<F < *brasser* stir (fused metal)]

brass·ard (bras'ärd, brə·särd') *n.* **1** A cloth band worn on the left arm by military police, umpires at maneuvers, and others, bearing insignia which denote the special duties of the wearer. **2** A piece of armor for the arm. Also **bras·sart** (bras'ərt). [<F < *bras* arm]

brass band A band of musicians using mostly brass instruments.

brass hat *Colloq.* **1** A high-ranking officer in the armed services. **2** Hence, a person in high position in business, government, etc.

bras·si·ca·ceous (bras'i·kā'shəs) *adj. Bot.* Of, pertaining, or belonging to a genus (*Brassica*) of erect, tall, branched herbs of the mustard family, yielding many edible plants, as cabbages, turnips, and radishes. [<L *brassica* cabbage]

bras·sière (brə·zir') *n.* A woman's undergarment shaped to support the breasts. [<F, shoulder strap < *bras* arm]

brass tacks *Colloq.* Concrete facts; details.

brass winds *Music* The wind instruments of a band or orchestra that are made of metal: distinguished from *woodwinds;* specifically, the trumpet, horn, trombone, and tuba.

brass·y (bras'ē, bräs'ē) *adj.* **brass·i·er, brass·i·est** **1** Covered with, made of, or like brass. **2** Impudent; shameless. **3** Debased; degenerate. — *n. pl.* **brass·ies** A wooden golf club with a brass plate on the sole: also **brass'ie.** — **brass'i·ly** *adv.* — **brass'i·ness** *n.*

brat[1] (brat) *n.* A child: now only contemptuously. [? <BRAT[2] (def. 1)]

brat[2] (brat) *n. Scot.* **1** An apron; bib; rag or clout. **2** The scum on boiled milk, porridge, etc. [OE *bratt*, ult. <Celtic]

Bra·ti·sla·va (brä'ti·slä'və) A city on the Danube in SW Czechoslovakia; capital of Slovakia: Hungarian *Pozsony,* German *Pressburg.*

brat·tice (brat'is) *n.* **1** A plank partition; especially, inside planking in a mine. **2** In old fortifications, a temporary parapet or breastwork. — *v.t.* **brat·ticed, brat·tic·ing** To furnish with a brattice. [<OF *bretesche,* ult. <Gmc.]

brat·tle (brat'l) *v.i.* **·tled, ·tling** **1** To make a rattling or clattering noise. **2** To run with clatter; scamper noisily. — *n.* A rattling or clattering noise. [Imit.]

brat·wurst (brät'wûrst, -vûrst, brat'-) *n.* A small German sausage made mainly of pork or of pork and veal and various seasonings. [<G < *brat* fried + *wurst* sausage]

Braun (broun), **Karl Ferdinand,** 1850–1918, German physicist and inventor in wireless telegraphy.

Braun·schweig (broun'shvīkh) The German name for BRUNSWICK.

bra·va·do (brə·vä'dō) *n. pl.* **·dos** or **·does** Arrogant defiance or menace; affectation of reckless bravery. [<Sp. *bravada* < *bravo* brave]

brave (brāv) *adj.* **brav·er, brav·est** **1** Having or showing courage; intrepid; courageous. **2** Having elegance; showy; splendid. **3** *Obs.* Excellent. — *v.* **braved, brav·ing** *v.t.* **1** To meet or face with courage and fortitude. **2** To defy; challenge. **3** *Obs.* To make splendid. — *v.i.* **4** *Obs.* To boast. — *n.* **1** A man of courage; a soldier. **2** A North American Indian warrior. **3** A bully; bravo. **4** *Obs.*

A boast or defiance. [<F <Ital. *bravo,* ? <L *barbarus* wild, fierce] — **brave'ly** *adv.* — **brave'ness** *n.*

Synonyms (*adj.*): adventurous, bold, chivalric, chivalrous, courageous, daring, dauntless, doughty, fearless, gallant, heroic, intrepid, undaunted, undismayed, valiant, venturesome. The *adventurous* man goes in quest of danger; the *bold* man stands out and faces danger or censure audaciously; the *brave* man combines confidence with firm resolution in presence of danger; the *chivalrous* man puts himself in peril for others' protection. The *daring* step out to defy danger; the *dauntless* will not flinch before anything that may come to them; the *doughty* will give and take limitless hard knocks; the *venturesome* may be simply heedless, reckless, or ignorant. The *fearless* and *intrepid* possess unshaken nerves in any place of danger. *Courageous* is more than *brave,* adding a moral element; the *courageous* man steadily encounters perils to which he may be keenly sensitive, at the call of duty; the *gallant* are *brave* in a dashing, showy, and splendid way; the *valiant* not only dare great dangers, but achieve great results; the *heroic* are nobly *daring* and *dauntless,* truly *chivalrous,* sublimely *courageous.* Compare CALM. *Antonyms:* afraid, cowardly, craven, cringing, faint-hearted, fearful, frightened, pusillanimous, shrinking, timid, timorous.

brav·er·y (brā'vər·ē) *n. pl.* **·er·ies** **1** The quality or state of being brave; valor; gallantry; heroism. **2** Elegance of attire; show; splendor; beauty. **3** *Obs.* Ostentation; bravado. See synonyms under COURAGE.

bra·vis·si·mo (brä·vis'sē·mō) *interj. Italian* Excellent! splendid!

bra·vo[1] (brä'vō) *interj.* Good! well done! — *n. pl.* **·vos** A shout of "bravo!" [<Ital. See BRAVE.]

bra·vo[2] (brä'vō, brä'-) *n. pl.* **·voes** or **·vos** A daring villain; hired assassin; bandit. [<Ital. See BRAVE.]

bra·vu·ra (brə·vyŏŏr'ə, *Ital.* brä·vōō'rä) *n.* **1** *Music* A passage in a composition that requires dashing and brilliant execution; also, a brilliant style of execution. **2** Any pretentious attempt or display; dashing or daring style. [<Ital., dash, daring < *bravo* BRAVE]

braw (brô, brä) *adj. Scot.* Brave or bravely dressed; splendid; handsome; fine. — **braw'ly,** *Obs.* **braw'lie** *adv.*

brawl[1] (brôl) *n.* **1** A noisy quarrel or wrangle; a row. **2** A roaring stream. See synonyms under ALTERCATION, QUARREL. — *v.i.* **1** To quarrel noisily; fight. **2** To move noisily, as water. [ME *braulen,* ? <LG; cf. Du. *brallen*] — **brawl'er** *n.* — **brawl'ing·ly** *adv.*

brawl[2] (brôl) *n.* A dance in which one or two dancers lead the others; also, the music for it. [<F *branle* < *branler* shake, sway]

brawn (brôn) *n.* **1** Flesh; firm muscle; strength. **2** The flesh of the boar, especially when boiled, pickled, and pressed. **3** The arm, calf of the leg, or buttock. [OF *braon* slice of flesh, ult. <Gmc.]

brawn·y (brô'nē) *adj.* **brawn·i·er, brawn·i·est** Having or characterized by firm muscle; strong. — **brawn'i·ness** *n.*

braws (brôz, bräz) *n. pl. Scot.* Finery; best clothes.

brax·y (brak'sē) *n.* **1** A carbuncular fever of sheep, caused by a bacterium (*Clostridium septicum*). **2** A sheep affected with this disease. — *adj.* Affected with braxy. [Cf. OE *bræc* sickness, rheum]

bray[1] (brā) *v.t.* **1** To utter in a loud, harsh manner. — *v.i.* **2** To give forth a loud, harsh cry, as an ass. **3** To sound harshly, as a trumpet. — *n.* Any loud, harsh sound, as the cry of an ass. ◆ Homophone: *brae.* [<OF *braire* cry out] — **bray'er** *n.*

bray[2] (brā) *v.t.* To bruise, pound, or mix, as in a mortar. ◆ Homophone: *brae.* [<OF *breier,* ult. <Gmc.]

bray·er (brā'ər) *n.* A roller mounted for use by hand, to spread ink evenly over a printing surface. [See BRAY[2]]

bra·ye·ra (brə·yâr'ə) *n.* Cusso. [after A. *Brayer,* 1775?–1848, French physician]

bra·za (brä'thä, -sä) *n.* A Spanish measure of

length equivalent to 5.48 feet; in Argentina, 5.68 feet. [<Sp.]

braze[1] (brāz) *v.t.* **brazed, braz·ing 1** To make of brass. **2** To make hard like brass. **3** To ornament with or as with brass. **4** *Poetic* To color as with brass. [OE *brasian* <*bræs* brass]

braze[2] (brāz) *v.t.* **brazed, braz·ing** *Metall.* To join the surfaces of similar or dissimilar metals by partial fusion with a layer of a soldering alloy applied under very high temperature. [<F *braser* solder <OF, burn, ult. <Gmc; infl. in meaning by BRAZE[1]] — **braz′er** *n.*

bra·zen (brā′zən) *adj.* **1** Made of, colored like, or resembling brass. **2** Sounding like brass. **3** Impudent; shameless. See synonyms under IMMODEST, IMPUDENT. —*v.t.* **1** To face or treat with effrontery or impudence: with *out.* **2** To make bold or reckless. —**bra′zen·ly** *adv.* —**bra′zen·ness** *n.*

brazen age In classical mythology, a period of war and violence when Neptune reigned: distinguished from *bronze age.*

bra·zen·face (brā′zən·fās′) *n.* A person marked by boldness or impudence.

brazen sea The great bronze laver in Solomon's temple at Jerusalem: also called *molten sea.*

bra·zier[1] (brā′zhər) *n.* A worker in brass: also spelled *brasier.* [ME *brasiere*]

bra·zier[2] (brā′zhər) *n.* An open pan for holding live coals: also spelled *brasier.* [<F *braiser* <*braise* hot coals]

bra·zil (brə·zil′) *n.* **1** The red wood of a Brazilian tree *(Caesalpinia echinata),* or of several related species: used as a dyestuff. **2** A dyewood from several nearly allied genera. **3** The dye obtained from the wood. **4** The Oriental sapanwood *(C. sappan).* Also **bra·zil′wood′.** [<Sp. *brasil,* or Ital. *brasile,* an Oriental dyewood]

Bra·zil (brə·zil′) A republic in South America; 3,287,842 square miles; capital, Brasília: officially **The United States of Brazil.** *Portuguese* **Es·ta·dos U·ni·dos do Bra·sil** (ēsh·tä′thōōz ōō·nē′·thōōz thōō brə·zil′). —**Bra·zil′ian** *adj. & n.*

braz·i·let·to (braz′i·let′ō) *n.* An inferior variety of brazilwood from certain West Indian and South American trees, as *Caesalpinia brasiliensis* and *C. crista,* and several other tropical species. [<Sp. *brasilete,* dim. of *brasil* BRAZIL]

braz·i·lin (braz′ə·lin) *n. Chem.* A crystalline compound, $C_{16}H_{14}O_5$, contained in brazilwood, sapanwood, and other woods of the genus *Caesalpinia,* of which it is the red coloring principle. Also spelled *brasilin.*

Brazil nut One of the triangular edible seeds of a South American tree *(Bertholletia excelsa).*

brazing solder A brass alloy of high tensile strength used to make brazing joints.

brazing tongs Clamping irons used in brazing.

Bra·zos River (brä′zəs, brā′-) A river in central Texas, flowing SE about 800 miles to the Gulf of Mexico.

Braz·za·ville (braz′ə·vil, *Fr.* brà·zà·vēl′) A city on the Congo, capital of the Congo Republic.

breach (brēch) *n.* **1** The act of breaking; infraction; infringement. **2** Violation of duty, right, or legal obligation. **3** A gap or break, as in a wall, dike, etc. **4** A rupture of amicable relations; dissension; quarrel. **5** The breaking of waves or surf; a surge. **6** The leaping of a whale from the water. **7** *Obs.* An injury; wound. —*v.t.* To make a breach in; break through. ◆Homophone: *breech.* [<OE *bryce* breaking; infl. in form by F *brèche* fragment, piece. Akin to BREAK.]

Synonyms (noun): chasm, chink, cleft, crack, cranny, crevice, fissure, flaw, hole, opening, rent, rupture. Compare BREAK, GAP, HOLE, QUARREL, RUPTURE. *Antonyms*: adhesion, connection, contact, contiguity, union, unity.

breach of promise Failure to fulfil a promise, especially a promise to marry.

breach·y (brē′chē) *adj.* **1** Apt to break out of an enclosure: said of livestock. **2** Full of breaches.

bread (bred) *n.* **1** An article of food made with flour or meal: commonly raised with yeast, kneaded, and baked. **2** Food in general; also, the necessaries of life. **3** Beebread. **4** *Slang* Money. —**light bread** Bread made with wheat flour and leavened with yeast. —*v.t.* To dress with bread crumbs before cooking. [OE. bit, crumb]—**bread′ed** *adj.*

bread and butter 1 Bread spread with butter. **2** *Colloq.* Subsistence; maintenance; livelihood.

bread–and–but·ter (bred′ən·but′ər) *adj.* **1** Actuated by personal need; mercenary; *bread–and–butter* candidates. **2** Youthful; immature or unformed: a *bread–and–butter* miss. **3** Prosaic. **4** Expressing gratitude for hospitality: a *bread–and–butter* letter.

bread basket 1 A basket or tray for carrying bread or rolls. **2** *Colloq.* The stomach.

bread·fruit (bred′frōōt′) *n.* **1** The fruit of a moraceous tree of the South Sea Islands *(Artocarpus altilis),* which, when roasted, resembles bread. **2** The tree.

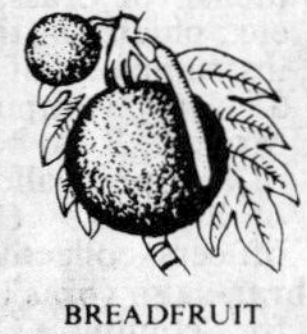

BREADFRUIT
(Fruit: 4–8 inches in diameter)

bread·line (bred′lin′) *n.* A line of persons waiting for charitable donations of bread or other food.

bread mold A mold developed on bread by a black fungus *(Rhizopus nigricans).*

bread·nut (bred′nut′) *n.* The edible fruit of a West Indian tree *(Brosimum alicastrum)* of the mulberry family.

bread riot A people's riot caused by extreme hunger.

bread·root (bred′rōōt′, -root′) *n.* **1** A leguminous plant *(Psoralea esculenta)* of the plains of the United States. **2** Its starchy, edible root.

bread·stuff (bred′stuf′) *n.* **1** Material for bread; grain, meal, or flour. **2** *pl.* Such materials collectively. **3** Bread.

breadth (bredth, bretth) *n.* **1** Measure or distance from side to side; as distinguished from length and thickness; width. **2** Catholicity; liberality. **3** That which has breadth; especially, a piece of a fabric of the full width. **4** The impression, in art, of largeness and comprehensiveness. [OE *braedu* <*brad* broad; *-th* added on analogy with *length*]

breadth·wise (bredth′wīz′, bretth′-) *adv.* In the direction of the breadth. Also **breadth′ways′** (-wāz′).

bread·win·ner (bred′win′ər) *n.* One who supports himself and others by his earnings; a producer.

break (brāk) *v.* **broke** (*Archaic* **brake**), **bro·ken** (*Archaic* **broke**), **break·ing** *v.t.* **1** To separate into pieces or make a fracture in; divide into fragments; shatter. **2** To part; sever, as a rope or bonds. **3** To disable or render useless by shattering or crushing. **4** To puncture or pierce the surface of (the skin). **5** To part the surface of, as ground or water. **6** To violate: to *break* a contract or a law. **7** To diminish the force of; moderate by interrupting: to *break* a fall. **8** To dispel or interrupt, as darkness or silence. **9** To destroy the order, continuity, or completeness of: to *break* step. **10** To interrupt the course of, as a journey; disconnect, as an electrical circuit. **11** To terminate forcibly; overwhelm: to *break* a strike. **12** To open forcibly (an entrance or way), as into or through a barrier. **13** To escape from: to *break* jail. **14** To surpass; excel, as a record. **15** To subdue or destroy the spirit or health of, as with toil or discipline. **16** To demote; reduce in rank or status. **17** To make bankrupt or short of money. **18** To discontinue (a habit): usually with *off.* **19** To cause (someone) to discontinue a habit: to *break* a child of biting his nails. **20** To tell; announce, as news. **21** *Law* **a** To enter (a shop or house) illegally. **b** To invalidate (a will) by court action. —*v.i.* **22** To become divided into fragments or pieces. **23** To dissolve and disperse; come apart: The clouds *broke.* **24** To become unusable or inoperative: The pencil *broke.* **25** To be grief–stricken, as the heart. **26** To burst away; free oneself: He *broke* free from the crowd. **27** To appear above the surface, as a periscope or arm. **28** To come into being or evidence, as the day. **29** To become bankrupt or short of funds. **30** To change or alter in direction, course, etc.: The horse *broke* from the track. **31** In baseball, to curve near the plate: said of the ball. **32** To crack, as a boy's voice. **33** *Music* To change from one quality of tone to another. —**to break bread** To take or share a meal. —**to break down 1** To become inoperative. **2** To have a physical or nervous collapse. **3** To give way to grief or strong feelings. **4** To overcome, as opposition. **5** To analyze. —**to break in** To cause to obey. —**to break into** (or **in**) **1** To interrupt or intervene. **2** To enter by force. —**to break in on** (or **upon**) To interrupt.—**to break off 1** To stop or cease, as from doing something. **2** To sever (relations); discontinue. **3** To become separate or detached. —**to break out 1** To start; have inception, as a fire or plague. **2** To have an eruption or rash, as the skin. **3** To make an escape, as from prison. —**to break out into** (or **forth in, into,** etc.) To begin to do or perform: The birds *broke* into song. —**to break up 1** To disperse; scatter: The meeting *broke up.* **2** To dismantle; take apart. **3** To put an end to; stop. **4** To distress: The loss *broke up* the old man. **5** To sever or discontinue relations: They decided to *break up.* —**to break with** To sever relations. —*n.* **1** An opening or breach; tear; fracture. **2** A starting or opening out: The *break* of day. **3** That which causes an opening, breach, or interruption. **4** *Electr.* **a** An apparatus for interrupting the flow or reversing the direction of an electric current. **b** The interruption of the current. **5** *Printing* A place where one paragraph ends and another begins. **6** In prosody, a caesura. **7** A high, four–wheeled carriage or wagonette: also brake. **8** A breach of continuity; interruption; especially, an interruption of physical continuity. **9** In writing, address, verse, etc., an interruption in the text or thought, as by an omission, or a space left to be filled out, or by a digression or aposiopesis. **10** A rupture of friendship; a falling out. **11** A sudden decline in prices. **12** *Music* The point where the chest tone changes to the head tone in singing; hence, sometimes, the point where one register or quality of voice changes to another, as alto to soprano; a similar point in the tones of a musical instrument. **13** In pool, the first play; the shot that scatters the balls. **14** In bowling, the act of playing a frame without making a strike or a spare. **15** In baseball or cricket, a deflection of the ball from a straight course when thrown. **16** In billiards, pool, and croquet, an uninterrupted series of successful shots. **17** *Colloq.* An unfortunate remark or ill–considered reaction: He made a bad *break.* **18** *Colloq.* An opportunity; a piece of luck, good or bad. **19** An agitation on the surface of water caused by the rising of a fish. **20** A dash or run; especially, an attempt to escape. **21** A sudden change in the gait of a horse. ◆ Homophone: *brake.* [OE *brecan.* Akin to BREACH.]

Synonyms (verb): bankrupt, burst, cashier, crack, crush, demolish, destroy, fracture, rend, rive, rupture, sever, shatter, shiver, smash, split, sunder, transgress. To *break* is to divide sharply, with severance of particles, as by a blow or strain. To *burst* is ordinarily to *break* by pressure from within, as a bombshell.To *crush* is to *break* by pressure from without, as an egg shell. To *crack* is to *break* without complete severance of parts. *Fracture* has a somewhat similar sense. A *shattered* object is *broken* suddenly and in numerous directions, as a vase is *shattered* by a blow. A *shivered* glass is *broken* into numerous minute, needle-like fragments. To *smash* is to *break* thoroughly to pieces with a crashing sound by some sudden act of violence. To *split* is to part, as wood in the way of the grain, or of other natural cleavage. To *rupture* is to cause to part less violently and completely than by explosion. To *demolish* is to beat down, as a mound, building, fortress, etc.; to *destroy* is to put by any process beyond restoration physically, mentally, or morally. Compare REND, RUPTURE. *Antonyms*: attach, bind, fasten, join, mend, repair, secure, unite, weld.

break·a·ble (brā′kə·bəl) *adj.* Capable of being broken. See synonyms under FRAGILE. —**break′a·ble·ness** *n.*

break·age (brā′kij) *n.* **1** A breaking, or the state of being broken. **2** Articles broken. **3** Compensation for damage or loss due to articles broken in shipment or use.

break–a·way (brāk′ə·wā′) *n.* **1** A motion–

picture set or prop so designed as to break apart quickly. **2** In pugilism, a separation of the antagonists. **3** The start of the contestants in a race.

break·bone (brāk′bōn′) n. Pathol. Dengue. Also **breakbone fever.**

break·down (brāk′doun′) n. **1** The act of breaking down; a collapse, as of a machine, one's health, etc. **2** A shuffling, stamping dance. **3** Chem. Decomposition or analysis of compounds. **4** The arrangement of large groups, as of facts, figures, operations, and processes, into categories permitting more efficient interpretation or management. Also **break′–down′.**

break·er (brā′kər) n. **1** One who or that which breaks. **2** A wave of the sea that breaks on a beach, etc. **3** A structure in which large masses of anthracite coal are broken up, sorted in various sizes, and cleaned for the market. **4** A strip of rubberized fabric attached to a pneumatic tire before the tread is put on, serving to distribute the pressure of the tire in contact with the ground. **5** Naut. A small barrel or cask containing drinking water for those in a lifeboat.

break·fast (brek′fəst) n. **1** The first meal of the day. **2** That with which a fast is broken; a meal. — v.t. To give a breakfast to; furnish with a breakfast. — v.i. To eat breakfast. —**break′fast·er** n.

breakfast food Any of various kinds of cereal eaten at breakfast; especially, a cereal prepared to be eaten without cooking.

break·front (brāk′frunt′) n. A cabinet, bookcase, or the like, having a central section which extends forward from those at either side.

break–in (brāk′in′) n. The act of breaking into a place, as to commit burglary.

breaking and entering Law Burglary; housebreaking.

break·neck (brāk′nek′) adj. Likely to break the neck; dangerous to life and limb: at breakneck speed.

break·o·ver (brāk′ō′vər) n. The front of a forest fire that jumps across a natural barrier or control line set to confine its range of devastation: also called slopover.

break·through (brāk′thrōō′) n. **1** A decisive or dramatic advance, especially in research, knowledge, understanding, etc. **2** Mil. An attack that penetrates an enemy's defensive system into the rear area.

break·up (brāk′up′) n. **1** The act of breaking up. **2** Canadian The time when the ice breaks up in the northern streams; spring.

break·wa·ter (brāk′wô′tər, -wot′ər) n. A mole or wall for protecting a harbor or beach from the force of waves.

bream¹ (brēm) n. pl. **breams** or **bream 1** A European fresh-water fish (Abramis brama), with deep, compressed body. **2** Any of various fresh-water sunfishes, especially the blue bream (Leponis pallidus). **3** A porgy or sailor's-choice (Lagodon rhomboides). [< F brême < OF bresme, ult. < Gmc.]

bream² (brēm) v.t. Naut. To clean (a ship's bottom) of barnacles, seaweed, etc., by heating the pitch and then scraping. [Akin to BRAMBLE and BROOM]

breast (brest) n. **1** Anat. The front of the chest from the neck to the abdomen. **2** One of the mammary glands; a teat. **3** That part of a garment that covers the breast. **4** The seat of the affections, etc.; the mind or heart. **5** Anything likened to the human or animal breast. **6** The front of a plow moldboard. **7** The working face of a mine, from which material is being, or may be, removed. —**to make a clean breast of** To make a complete confession of. — v.t. **1** To encounter or oppose with the breast. **2** To meet or oppose boldly; advance against: to breast one's problems. [OE brēost]

breast·bone (brest′bōn′) n. Anat. A bone in the front part of the chest, with which some of the ribs are joined; the sternum.

Breast·ed (bres′tid), **James Henry,** 1865–1935, U.S. Egyptologist.

breast–feed (brest′fēd′) v.t. & v.i. —**fed,** —**feed·ing** To suckle.

breast·it (brēs′tit) adj. Scot. Breasted.

breast·pin (brest′pin′) n. A pin worn at the breast to close a garment; brooch; scarfpin.

breast·plate (brest′plāt′) n. **1** A piece of defensive plate armor for the breast; also, a metalworker's protective plate. **2** A strap crossing a horse's breast. **3** A square piece of linen cloth, embroidered with gold, adorned with twelve precious stones symbolizing the twelve tribes of Israel, worn by the Jewish high priest. **4** The plastron of a turtle.

breast pocket A pocket in a garment situated over the breast, as the inside pocket of a jacket.

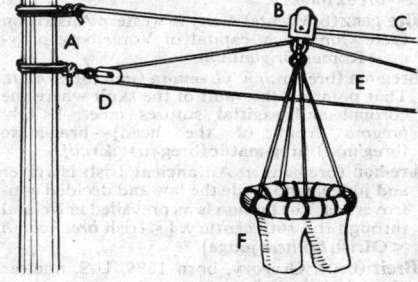

BREASTPLATE

breast pump A suction instrument for drawing milk from the breast.

breast·stroke (brest′strōk′) n. In swimming, a stroke made while lying face down, the arms being simultaneously thrust forward from the breast under or on the surface, then brought laterally back to the sides, the legs at the same time being moved in a frog kick. —**breast′–strok·er** n.

breast·work (brest′wûrk′) n. A low, temporary, defensive work, usually breast–high; a parapet. See synonyms under BARRIER, RAMPART.

breath (breth) n. **1** Air inhaled or exhaled in respiration. **2** A single act of respiration: He drew a long breath. **3** Power to breathe, or to breathe freely; life. **4** The time of a single respiration; an instant. **5** Something resembling breath; a gentle movement of air; an exhalation. **6** Some slight thing, as a word or a rumor. **7** Phonet. An exhalation of air without vibration of the vocal cords, as in the production of (p) and (f). **8** The moisture condensed on cold objects or in cold air caused by the act of breathing. **9** Anything caused by breathing, as an utterance. **10** Time to breathe; delay; intermission; respite. —**in the same breath** At the same moment; without a pause or break. —**to take one's breath away** To overawe; produce sudden emotion. —**under one's breath** In a whisper. [OE brǣth vapor, odor]

breath·a·lys·er (breth′ə·lī′zər) n. A balloonlike device that measures the alcoholic content of blood by analyzing expelled breath, used especially to test motorists for intoxication. [< BREATH + (AN)ALYSER, Brit. spelling of analyzer; the device was originated in Britain]

breathe (brēth) v. **breathed** (brēthd), **breath·ing** v.t. **1** To inhale and exhale, as air; respire. **2** To emit by breathing. **3** To utter; whisper. **4** To express; manifest. **5** Phonet. To utter with the breath only, without vibration of the vocal cords. **6** To exhaust; put out of breath. **7** To inject or infuse by or as by breathing: to breathe new life into a project. — v.i. **8** To inhale and exhale air; respire. **9** To be alive; exist. **10** To exhale, as fragrance. **11** To pause for breath. **12** To move gently, as breezes. **13** To allow air to penetrate: said of a fabric or garment. [ME brethen < breth breath]—**breath′a·ble** adj.

breath·er (brē′thər) n. **1** One who or that which breathes. **2** Colloq. That which exercises or exhausts the breath, as a run. **3** Colloq. A brief rest period: to take a breather during a workout.

breath·ing (brē′thing) adj. Respiring; living. See synonyms under ALIVE. — n. **1** The act of respiration; a breath. **2** Time to take breath. **3** Exercise that quickens the breath. **4** Gram. An aspiration; aspirate. In Greek the **rough breathing** (ʽ) over an initial vowel indicates the sound equivalent to our letter h; the **smooth breathing** (ʼ), its absence.

breath·less (breth′lis) adj. **1** Out of breath. **2** Intense or eager, as if holding the breath. **3** Without breath; dead. —**breath′less·ly** adv. —**breath′less·ness** n.

breath·tak·ing (breth′tā′king) adj. Astounding; overawing.

breath·y (breth′ē) adj. Characterized by audible breathing; aspirate.

brec·ci·a (brech′ē·ə, bresh′-) n. Geol. A rock made up of angular fragments embedded in a matrix which may or may not be of the same nature or origin. [< Ital., gravel] —**brec·ci·at·ed** (brech′ē·ā′tid, bresh′-) adj.

brech·am (brekh′əm) n. Scot. A draft–horse collar.

brech·an (brek′ən) n. Scot. Bracken. Also **breck′an.**

Brecht (brekht), **Bertolt,** 1898–1956, German playwright and poet.

Breck·in·ridge (brek′in·rij), **John Cabell,** 1821–75, U.S. statesman.

Breck·nock (brek′nok) The county seat of Brecknockshire. Also **Brec·on** (brek′ən).

Breck·nock·shire (brek′nok·shir) A county in SE central Wales; 733 square miles. Also **Breck′nock.**

bred (bred) Past tense and past participle of BREED.

Bre·da (brā·dä′) A town in SW Netherlands.

brede (brēd) n. **1** Obs. A braid or twist. **2** A piece of braiding or embroidery. [Var. of BRAID¹, n.]

bree (brē) n. Scot. Broth; brew; moisture: also called broo: also spelled brie.

breech (brēch) n. **1** The posterior and lower part of the body; the buttocks. **2** The rear end of a gun, cannon, etc. — v.t. (brēch, brich) **1** To clothe with breeches. **2** To provide with a breech, as a gun. **3** To fasten by a breeching, as a ship's cannon. **4** Obs. To flog on the breech. ◆ Homophone: breach. [OE brec, pl., breeches]

breech·block (brēch′blok′) n. The movable piece which closes the breech of a breech-loading firearm, but is withdrawn to insert the cartridge, and replaced before firing.

breech·cloth (brēch′klôth′, -kloth′) n. A loincloth. Also **breech′clout** (-klout′).

breech·es (brich′iz) n. pl. **1** A garment for men, covering the waist, hips, and thighs. **2** Trousers. [OE brec breeches]

breeches buoy Naut. A life-saving apparatus, consisting of canvas breeches, attachable at the waist to a ring–shaped lifebuoy, to be slung and run upon a rope stretched from the shore to a wrecked vessel.

BREECHES BUOY
A. Mast of vessel.
B. Traveling block.
C. Hawser running from mast to shore.
D. Tailblock.
E. Whip, or endless line, by which buoy is hauled to and from shore.
F. Breeches buoy.

breech·ing (brich′ing, brē′ching) n. **1** A holdback strap passing behind a horse's haunches. For illustration see HARNESS. **2** The parts composing the breech of a gun. **3** A heavy rope used for securing a ship's cannon. **4** A flogging.

breech·load·er (brēch′lō′dər) n. A firearm the load of which is inserted at the breech. —**breech′load′ing** adj.

breed (brēd) v. **bred, breed·ing** v.t. **1** To produce (offspring); give birth to; hatch. **2** To cause; favor the development of: Familiarity breeds contempt. **3** To cause to give birth; develop new strains in: He breeds horses. **4** To bring up; train, as to a profession. — v.i. **5** To produce young; procreate. **6** To originate or be caused: Militarism breeds in armies. See synonyms under PRODUCE. — n. **1** The progeny of one stock; a race or strain of animals deliberately cultivated by man. **2** A sort or kind. **3** The character or degree of perfection possessed by a wine. [OE brēdan < brod brood. Related to BROOD.]

breed·er (brē′dər) n. **1** One who or that which breeds or produces; author; source. **2** One who manages the breeding of animals. **3** An

animal suitable, or intended primarily for, reproductive purposes.

breeder reactor *Physics* An apparatus for the generation of atomic energy in which the fuel is converted into more fissionable material than is consumed. Compare REACTOR (def. 4).

breed·ing (brē'ding) *n*. **1** The generating, bearing, or training of young. **2** Nurture or its effect on character and behavior. **3** Manners, especially good manners. See synonyms under BEHAVIOR, EDUCATION, NUTURE.

Breed's Hill (brēdz) A hill near Bunker Hill. See BUNKER HILL.

breeks (brēks) *n. pl. Scot*. Breeches. —**breek'less** *adj*.

breeze[1] (brēz) *n*. **1** A moderate current of air; a gentle wind. See BEAUFORT SCALE. **2** *Brit. Colloq*. A flutter of excitement; agitation; disturbance. **3** A vague rumor; whisper. See synonyms under WIND. **4** *Slang* Ease; facility: The horse won in a *breeze*. —*v.i.* **breezed, breez·ing 1** To blow moderately; begin to blow: It's *breezing* up. **2** *Slang* To go or proceed quickly and blithely. —**to breeze in** *Slang* To enter in an airy, vivacious manner. —**to breeze up** To spring up, as a wind; also, to grow stronger. [< Sp. and Pg. *brisa, briza* northeast wind]

breeze[2] (brēz) *n*. A gadfly or a botfly. [OE *breosa* gadfly]

breeze[3] (brēz) *n. Brit*. Refuse cinders, small coke, or fine coal used in burning bricks in a kiln. [? < F *braise* hot embers]

breeze·way (brēz'wā') *n*. A roofed, open passageway from house to garage or between two buildings.

breez·ing (brē'zing) *n*. The blurring of a motion picture on the screen caused by distorted focus, uneven shrinkage of film, or unevenly placed track perforations.

breez·y (brē'zē) *adj*. **breez·i·er, breez·i·est 1** Like a breeze; airy; windy. **2** Brisk or animated. **3** Somewhat pert; brash. —**breez'i·ly** *adv*. —**breez'i·ness** *n*.

Bre·genz (brā'gents) A city in western Austria on Lake Constance, capital of Vorarlberg province: Roman *Brigantium*.

breg·ma (breg'mə) *n. pl*. **·ma·ta** (-mə·tə) *n. Anat*. That point on the vault of the skull where the coronal and sagittal sutures meet. [< Gk. *bregma* front of the head]—**breg·mate** (breg'māt), **breg·mat·ic** (breg·mat'ik) *adj*.

bre·hon (brē'hən) *n*. An ancient Irish lawgiver and judge, who made the law and decided controversies. The **brehon laws** prevailed in Ireland through the 16th century. [< Irish *breitheamh* < OIrish *brithem* judge]

Breit (brīt), **Gregory**, born 1899, U.S. nuclear physicist born in Russia.

Brei·ten·feld (brī'tən·felt) A district near Leipzig, in east central Germany; scene of Swedish victory in the Thirty Years' War.

Breiz (brez) The Breton name for BRITTANY.

bre·loque (brə·lôk') *n. French* A charm, seal, or other ornament for wearing on a watch chain.

Brem·en (brem'ən, brā'mən) A state of northern Germany; 156 square miles; including the cities of Bremerhaven and Bremen, a port on the Weser.

Brem·er·ha·ven (brem'ər·hā'vən, *Ger*. brā'mər·hä'fən) The ocean port of Bremen.

Bren gun (bren) *Mil*. A fast, accurate machine-gun, introduced into the British Army in World War II. [< *Br(no)*, Czechoslovakia, where first made, + *En(field)*, England, where perfected]

Bren·nan (bren'ən), **William J(oseph)**, born 1906, U.S. jurist; associate justice of the Supreme Court 1956.

Bren·ner Pass (bren'ər) Lowest of the main Alpine passes, on the Austrian-Italian border, 4,495 feet. *Italian* **Pas·so Bren·ne·ro** (päs'sō bren·nā'rō).

brent (brent) *adj. Scot*. Smooth; unwrinkled; also, high; prominent: said of the forehead.

Brere·ton (brâr'tən), **Lewis Hyde**, 1890–1967, U.S. general.

Br'er Rabbit (brûr, brer) Brother Rabbit: the principal figure in the animal folktales told by Uncle Remus. See UNCLE REMUS.

Bres (bres) In Old Irish mythology, a handsome Fomorian king who married Brigid, and later instigated the war between the Fomorians and the gods.

Bre·scia (brā'shä) A city in Lombardy, Italy.

Bresh·kov·sky (bresh·kôf'skē), **Catherine**, 1844–1934, Russian revolutionist.

Bres·lau (bres'lou, brez'-) The German name for WROCLAW.

Brest (brest) **1** A port and naval station in NW France. **2** A city on the Bug in Belorussia: Polish *Brześ̄Rnad Bugiem*; until 1921 **Brest-Li·tovsk** (-li·tôfsk'); Russo-German peace treaty signed here, 1918.

Bre·tagne (brə·tàn'y') French name for BRITTANY.

breth·ren (breth'rən) *n. pl*. **1** Brothers. **2** Members of a brotherhood. [ME, pl.]

Bret·on (bret'n) *adj*. Of or pertaining to Brittany, its inhabitants, or their language. —*n*. **1** A native of Brittany. **2** The language of the Bretons, belonging to the Brythonic branch of the Celtic languages: also called *Armorican*.

Bre·ton (brə·tôn'), **André**, 1896–1966, French surrealist poet and critic. —**Jules Adolphe**, 1827–1906, French painter and author.

Bret·ton Woods (bret'n) A village in north central New Hampshire; site of an international monetary conference, September, 1944.

Breu·ghel (broe'gəl) See BRUEGHEL.

breve (brēv) *n*. **1** A mark (˘) placed over a vowel to indicate that it has a short sound, as the *a* in *hat* compare MACRON); or, in prosody, placed over a syllable to show that it is not stressed. **2** A royal or papal commission or mandate; brief. **3** A judicial writ or brief. **4** *Music* A note equivalent to two whole notes, or the sign for it. [< Ital. < L *brevis* short]

bre·vet (brə·vet', *esp. Brit*. brev'it) *n. Mil*. **1** A commission advancing an officer in honorary rank without advance in pay or in command. **2** A commission or promotion awarded for achievement, usually on the field of battle. —*v.t.* **bre·vet·ted** or **bre·vet·ed, bre·vet·ting** or **bre·vet·ing** To raise in rank by brevet. —*adj*. Held or conferred by brevet; holding rank by brevet; brevetted. [< OF *brevet*, dim. of *bref* letter, document]

bre·vet·cy (brə·vet'sē) *n. pl*. **·cies** Brevet rank.

brevi- *combining form* Short: *brevipennate*. [< L *brevis* short]

bre·vi·ar·y (brē'vē·er'ē, brev'ē-) *n. pl*. **·ar·ies** *Eccl*. A book of daily offices and prayers for the canonical hours. [< L *breviarium* abridgment < *brevis* short]

bre·vier (brə·vir') *n. Printing* A size of type, about 8-point. [? < G, breviary; with ref. to its use in breviaries]

brev·i·lin·e·al (brev'i·lin'ē·əl) *adj*. Denoting a type of body built along broad, short lines: opposed to *longilineal*. [< BREVI- + L *linea* line]

brev·i·pen·nate (brev'i·pen'āt) *adj. Ornithol*. Short-winged, as the ostrich, cassowary, etc. —*n*. A brevipennate bird, as the auk, guillemot, etc. [< BREVI- + L *penna* wing]

brev·i·ros·trate (brev'i·ros'trāt) *adj. Ornithol*. Having a short bill or beak. Also **brev'i·ros'tral**. [< BREVI- + L *n. rostrum* beak]

brev·i·ty (brev'ə·tə) *n. pl*. **·ties 1** Shortness of duration; brief time. **2** Condensation of language; conciseness. [< L *brevitas,* —*tatis* < *brevis* short]

brew (brōō) *v.t.* **1** To make, as beer or ale, by steeping, boiling, and fermentation of malt, hops, etc. **2** To make (any beverage) as by boiling or mixing. **3** To concoct; devise, as mischief. —*v.i.* **4** To make ale, beer, or the like. —**to be brewing** To be imminent; gather, as a storm, trouble, etc. —*n*. That which is brewed; the product of brewing. [OE *breōwan*. Related to BROTH.]—**brew'er** *n*.

brew·age (brōō'ij) *n*. **1** The process of brewing. **2** A drink prepared by brewing or mixing. **3** A concocted plot.

brew·er·y (brōō'ər·ē) *n. pl*. **·er·ies** An establishment for brewing.

brew·ing (brōō'ing) *n*. **1** Brewage. **2** The amount of liquor brewed at one time. **3** A mixture; concoction. **4** A gathering of storm clouds.

brew·is (brōō'is) *n*. **1** Bread or oatmeal soaked in pot liquor, hot milk, or the like. **2** Thickened broth. **3** In New England, porridge made of brown bread, milk, and butter. [ME *browes* < OF *brouet*, dim. of *breu, bro* broth; infl. by BREW]

Brew·ster (brōō'stər), **William**, 1567–1644, one of the Pilgrim Fathers.

Brewster chair An early New England type of chair with heavy turned posts and spindles ar-

ranged in tiers in the back and below the seat in front: named for William Brewster.

Brezh·nev (bryezh·nyôf'), **Leonid Ilyich**, 1906–82, Soviet statesman; first secretary of the Communist party 1964–82.

Bri·an (brī'ən) A masculine personal name. Also *Ital*. **Bri·a·no** (brē·ä'nō). [< Celtic, strong]

Bri·an Bo·ru (brī'ən bô·rōō', bô·rōō') 926–1014, a king of Ireland, killed at battle of Clontarf. Also **Brian Bo·roimhe'**.

Bri·and (brē·äṅ'), **Aristide**, 1862–1932, French statesman.

Bri·ansk (brē·ansk') See BRYANSK.

bri·ar (brī'ər), **bri·ar·root** (-rōōt', -rŏŏt'), **bri·ar·wood** (-wŏŏd') See BRIER, etc.

bri·ard (brē·ärd') *n*. A breed of French work dog with a large head, pointed muzzle, heavily boned legs, and long, stiff coat. [< F, a native of Brie, France]

Bri·ar·e·us (brī·âr'ē·əs) One of the Hecatoncheires. —**Bri·ar'e·an** *adj*.

bribe (brīb) *n*. **1** Any gift or emolument used corruptly to influence public or official action. **2** Anything that seduces or allures; an allurement. See synonyms under GIFT. —*v*. **bribed, brib·ing** *v.t.* **1** To offer or give a bribe to. **2** To gain or influence by means of bribery. —*v.i.* **3** To give bribes. [< OF, piece of bread given a beggar]—**brib'a·ble** *adj*. —**brib'er** *n*.

brib·er·y (brī'bər·ē) *n. pl*. **·er·ies** The giving, offering, or accepting of a bribe.

bric-à-brac (brik'ə·brak) *n*. Objects of curiosity or decoration; rarities; antiques; knickknacks. [< F]

brick (brik) *n*. **1** A molded block of clay, sun-baked or kiln-burned in various shapes and sizes, but usually about 8 1/2 x 4 x 2 1/2 inches: used for building, paving, etc. **2** Bricks collectively; also, any object shaped like a brick. **3** *Colloq*. An admirable or first-rate fellow. —*v.t.* **1** To build or line with bricks. **2** To cover or wall in with bricks: with *up* or *in*. [< OF *brique* fragment, bit, ult. < Gmc. Cf. OE *bryce* fragment.]

brick·bat (brik'bat') *n*. A piece of a brick, especially when used as a missile.

brick·kiln (brik'kil', -kiln') *n*. A structure in which bricks are burnt.

brick·lay·er (brik'lā'ər) *n*. One who builds with bricks. —**brick'lay ing** *n*.

brick·le (brik'əl) *adj*. **1** *Dial*. Changeable; fickle: *brickle* weather. **2** *Brit. Dial*. Brittle.

brick red Any of several shades of dull, yellowish- or brownish-red, like the color of the common red clay brick. —**brick-red** (brik'red') *adj*.

brick·work (brik'wûrk') *n*. Any construction of bricks laid in courses.

brick·yard (brik'yärd') *n*. A place where bricks are made.

bri·cole (bri·kōl', brik'əl) *n*. **1** A harness worn by men for dragging field guns over ground where horses cannot be used. **2** A side stroke against the wall of a tennis court. **3** A cushion shot in billiards. **4** A medieval military engine for throwing stones or darts. [< F]

bri·dal (brīd'l) *adj*. Pertaining to a bride or a wedding; nuptial. —*n*. A marriage festival; wedding. See synonyms under MATRIMONIAL. ◆ Homophone: *bridle*. [OE *brȳldeala* wedding feast]

Bri·dal·veil (brīd'l·vāl') A cataract in Yosemite National Park, California; 620 feet.

bri·dal·wreath (brīd'l·rēth') *n*. A spring-flowering shrub (*Spiraea prunifolia*) of the rose family, with umbels of white flowers and ovate-oblong leaves.

bride[1] (brīd) *n*. A newly married woman, or a woman about to be married. [OE *brȳd*]

bride[2] (brīd) *n*. **1** A loop, tie, etc., made in lace or needlework; also, a bonnet string. **2** *Obs*. A bridle. [< F, bridle, string]

Bride (brīd), **Saint** See BRIGID, SAINT.

bride·groom (brīd'grōōm', -grŏŏm') *n*. A man newly married or about to be married. [OE *brȳdguma* < *brȳ* bride + *guma* man; infl. in ME by *grome* lad, groom]

brides·maid (brīdz'mād') *n*. A young, usually unmarried woman who attends a bride at her wedding.

brides·man (brīdz'mən) *n. pl*. **·men** (-mən) A groomsman.

bride·well (brīd'wel, -wəl) *n*. A house of correction; a lock-up. [from St. *Bride's well*, in London, near which a prison was located]

bridge[1] (brij) *n.* **1** A structure erected to afford passage for pedestrians, vehicles, railroad trains, etc., across a waterway, a railroad, a ravine, etc.; a raised support. **2** *Naut.* An observation platform or partial deck built across and above a ship's deck for the use of the officers, the pilot, etc. **3** Something likened to a bridge. **4** The arched or central portion of the nose. **5** The part of a pair of spectacles or eyeglasses crossing over or resting upon this portion of the nose. **6** A block for raising the strings of a musical instrument, as a violin or guitar. **7** *Anat.* The pons Varolii. **8** A low, vertical, crosswise division wall, as in a boiler setting or a metallurgic furnace. **9** A mounting for holding false teeth, attached to adjoining teeth on each side. **10** *Electr.* A device used in measuring electrical resistance. **11** In billiards or pool, the hand or a notched support for a billiard cue, used when a player is about to strike a ball. **12** In the theater, a platform immediately inside the teaser, for suspending lights and providing space for electricians, etc. — **to burn one's bridges** To cut off all possibility of retreat. — **suspension bridge** Any bridge in which the roadway is hung from cables strong-

SUSPENSION BRIDGE
Brooklyn Bridge spanning East River, New York

ly anchored over towers and without support from below. See also under BASCULE, CANTILEVER, DRAWBRIDGE, PONTOON. — *v.t.* **bridged**, **bridg·ing 1** To construct a bridge or bridges over. **2** To make a passage over or across by a bridge; get over. [OE *brycg*]
bridge[2] (brij) *n.* A card game similar to whist, except that the dealer, or his partner (the dummy), has the right to name the trump. Odd tricks vary in value according to the suit declared. Partners first scoring 30 win the game. Also BRIDGE WHIST. — **auction bridge** A variety of the game of bridge, in which, instead of the dealer or his partner having the declaration, it goes to the player who undertakes to score the highest number of points. — **contract bridge** A variation of bridge in which the declarer, if successful, scores toward game only the tricks named in the bid; the awards are high, and failure is heavily penalized. — **duplicate bridge** The game of bridge, auction bridge, or contract bridge in which a series of hands is played over again, each side holding the cards previously held by its opponent. [Origin uncertain]
bridge·board (brij′bôrd′, -bōrd′) *n.* A notched board to which stair treads and risers are fastened.
bridge·head (brij′hed′) *n.* **1** *Mil.* A position on or near the bank of a river or defile that is established by advance troops of an attacking force to protect and cover the crossing of the main body of troops over the river or defile. **2** Loosely, a beachhead.
Bridge of Sighs 1 A covered bridge in Venice, over which condemned prisoners formerly passed to the place of execution. **2** *U.S.* The covered passageway, now destroyed, between the Tombs prison and the Criminal Courts building, New York City.
Bridge·port (brij′pôrt, -pōrt) A city on Long Island Sound, SW Connecticut.
Bridg·es (brij′iz), **Robert,** 1844–1930, English physician and poet laureate. — **Calvin Blackman,** 1889–1938, U.S. geneticist.
Bridg·et (brij′it) A feminine personal name. — **Bridget, Saint** (of Ireland) See BRIGID. — **Bridget, Saint** (of Sweden), 1303?–73, Roman Catholic nun; founder of the order of St. Saviour, or the Brigittines: also spelled *Birgitta* or *Brigitta.*

Bridge·town (brij′toun) The capital of Barbados, British West Indies.
bridge·work (brij′wûrk) *n.* **1** *Dent.* A partial denture, variously attached to the natural teeth. **2** The construction of bridges.
bridg·ing (brij′ing) *n.* Wooden struts or braces between joists or other beams to keep them apart and to stiffen the structure.
Bridg·man (brij′mən), **Percy Williams,** 1882–1961, U.S. physicist.
bri·dle (brīd′l) *n.* **1** The head harness of a horse, including bit and reins. **2** Anything that restrains, limits, or guides movement, action, or development; a check; also, a curb. **3** The clevis of a plow. **4** *Anat.* A ligament or frenum attaching two parts or surfaces of an organism to each other. **5** A former instrument of torture, used for scolds. **6** *Aeron.* In the handling of airships and dirigibles, a sling of cordage or wire with ends fixed at two different points, to the bight of which a single line may be attached, movable or fixed, thus distributing the pull of the single line to two points or more in the case of a multiple bridle. **7** A span of mooring cables. — *v.* **bri·dled, bri·dling** *v.t.* **1** To put a bridle on. **2** To check or control with or as with a bridle. — *v.i.* **3** To raise the head and draw in the chin through resentment, pride, etc. See synonyms under REPRESS, RESTRAIN, SUBDUE. ◆ Homophone: *bridal.* [OE *brīdel*] — **bri′dler** *n.*
bridle hand The left hand, in which the reins are usually held.
bri·dle·path (brīd′l·path′, -päth′) *n.* A path intended only for saddle horses or pack-animals.
bri·dle·wise (brīd′l·wīz′) *adj.* Answering the pressure of the bridle rein on the neck, instead of on the bit: said of a horse.
bri·doon (bri·dōōn′) *n.* A snaffle and rein of a military bridle used in connection with, or acting independently of, the curb bit and its rein. [<F *bridon* snaffle, bit < *bride* bridle, check]
brie (brē) *n. Scot.* Bree.
Brie (brē) *n.* A soft, white, creamy cheese, mold- or bacteria-ripened. [from *Brie*-Comte–Robert, town in central France, where first made]
brief (brēf) *adj.* **1** Short in time or space; quickly passing. **2** Of few words; concise; also, curt or abrupt in speech. **3** Curtailed in extent; limited. See synonyms under TERSE, TRANSIENT. — *n.* **1** Any short or abridged statement; a summary. **2** *Law* A concise statement in writing of the law and authorities relied upon in trying a cause; also, a memorandum of all the material facts of a client's case prepared for the instruction of counsel. **3** In the Roman Catholic Church, a letter from the Pope; less formal than a bull. **4** Briefing; in short. — **in brief** Briefly; in short. — **to hold a brief for** To be on the side of; champion; aid. — *v.t.* **1** To epitomize; make a summary of. **2** To instruct or advise in advance: He *briefed* his salesmen on the coming campaign. **3** *Brit.* To inform by a legal brief. **4** *Brit.* To retain as counsel. — *adv. Obs.* Shortly; briefly. [<OF *bref* <L *brevis* short] — **brief′ly** *adv.* — **brief′ness** *n.*
brief·case (brēf′kās′) *n.* A leather portfolio for carrying briefs, commercial papers, manuscripts, etc.
brief·ing (brē′fing) *n.* Final instructions given to aircraft pilots and crew members before a flight or raid.
brief·less (brēf′lis) *adj.* Having no briefs or clients.
Bri·enz (brē·ents′) A village in central Switzerland, on the **Lake of Brienz** (11 square miles).
bri·er (brī′ər) *n.* **1** A prickly bush or shrub, especially of the rose family, as the sweetbrier. **2** A pipe of brier-root. **3** A thorn or prickle; also, the white or tree heath. Also spelled *briar.* [OE *brēr*] — **bri′er·y** *adj.*
bri·er-root (brī′ər·rōōt′, -rŏŏt′) *n.* The root of the white or tree heath of southern Europe (*Erica arborea*), used in making tobacco pipes. Also spelled *briar-root.*
bri·er-wood (brī′ər·wŏŏd′) *n.* **1** The wood of the brier-root. **2** A pipe made from it. Also spelled *briarwood.*

Bri·eux (brē·œ′), **Eugène,** 1858–1932, French dramatist.
brig[1] (brig) *n. Naut.* A two-masted ship, square-rigged on both masts. [Short for BRIGANTINE]
brig[2] (brig) *n. Scot.* A bridge.
brig[3] (brig) *n.* A place of confinement on shipboard. [Origin unknown]
bri·gade (bri·gād′) *n.* **1** *Mil.* A tactical unit intermediate between a regiment and a division, commanded by a brigadier general. **2** Any considerable body of persons more or less organized: a fire *brigade*. — *v.t.* **bri·gad·ed, bri·gad·ing 1** To form into a brigade. **2** To classify or combine. [<Ital. *brigata* company, crew < *brigare* brawl, fight]
brig·a·dier (brig′ə·dir′) *n.* **1** See under GENERAL. **2** In some European armies, a cavalry subaltern whose rank corresponds with that of an infantry corporal.
brig·and (brig′ənd) *n.* A robber; a bandit; especially, one of a band of outlaws and plunderers. See synonyms under ROBBER. [<F <Ital. *brigante* fighter < *brigare* brawl, fight] — **brig′and·age** (-ij) *n.* ← **brig′and·ish** *adj.* — **brig′and·ism** *n.*
brig·an·dine (brig′ən·dēn, -dīn) *n.* A medieval coat of mail made of metal plates, scales, or rings, sewn upon linen, leather, or the like. [<MF, armor for fighter < *brigand.* See BRIGAND.]
brig·an·tine (brig′ən·tēn, -tīn) *n. Naut.* A two-masted vessel, square-rigged on the foremast, and fore-and-aft rigged on the mainmast: also called *hermaphrodite brig, jackass brig.* [<MF *brigandin* a fighting vessel <Ital. *brigantino* < *brigare* fight]
Bri·gan·ti·um (bri·gan′shē·əm) The Roman name for BREGENZ.
Briggs (brigz), **Lyman James,** 1874–1963, U.S. physicist.

BRIG

bright (brīt) *adj.* **1** Emitting or reflecting much light; shining; sparkling. **2** Possessing or showing quick intelligence or sparkling wit; quick-witted. **3** Full of or marked by gladness, prosperity, or hope; cheery; auspicious. **4** Illustrious; glorious. **5** Of brilliant color; clear and transparent. **6** Resplendent with excellence or beauty. **7** Watchful; alert. — *adv.* Brightly: The moon shines *bright*. — *n. Poetic* Brilliancy; splendor; brightness. [OE *beorht, briht*] — **bright′ly** *adv.*
Synonyms (*adj.*): beaming, brilliant, burnished, cheerful, cheering, cheery, effulgent, flashing, gleaming, glorious, glowing, luminous, lustrous, radiant, refulgent, resplendent, shining, sparkling, splendid, sunny, sunshiny. See CHEERFUL, CLEVER, FRESH, HAPPY, INTELLIGENT, VIVID. Compare LIGHT. Antonyms: See synonyms under DARK.
Bright (brīt), **John,** 1811–89, English Quaker, statesman, and free-trade advocate.
bright·en (brīt′n) *v.t. & v.i.* To make or become bright or brighter. **2** To make or become cheerful: The outlook is *brightening*. — **bright′en·er** *n.*
bright·ness (brīt′nis) *n.* **1** The state, quality, or condition of being bright, in any sense. **2** The luminous intensity of any surface in a given direction, per unit of projected area of the surface as viewed in that direction. **3** That attribute of a color which identifies it as equivalent to some member of the achromatic color series, ranging from black or very dim, to white or very bright. Compare LIGHTNESS, HUE, SATURATION. See COLOR.
Brigh·ton (brīt′n) **1** A county borough and seaside resort in southern Sussex, England. **2** A resort city in southern Victoria, Australia.
Bright's disease *Pathol.* A disease characterized by degeneration of the kidneys and imperfect elimination of uric acid from the system. [after Richard *Bright,* 1789–1858, English physician]
bright·work (brīt′wûrk′) *n.* Those parts of a

machine, building, etc., in which the metal is made bright, as by planing, turning, or polishing.

Brig·id (brij′id, brē′id), **Saint,** 453?–523, patroness of Ireland; identified with **Brigid,** ancient Irish goddess of fire, fertility, and the manual arts: also *Bride, Bridget.*

Bri·git·te (brē·git′ə) German form of BRIDGET. Also *Fr.* **Bri·gitte** (brē·zhēt′).

brill (bril) *n. pl.* **brill** or **brills** A flatfish of Europe *(Bothus* or *Scophthalmus rhombus)* related to the turbot. [Prob. <Cornish *brilli* mackerel]

Bril·lat–Sa·va·rin (brē·yȧ′sȧ·vȧ·raṅ′), **Anthelme,** 1755–1826, French writer and epicure.

bril·liance (bril′yəns) *n.* **1** The quality of being brilliant; brightness; radiance; luster. **2** The presence of many rich overtones and high frequencies in a sound record made under suitable conditions. **3** A high degree of insight or understanding; skill and finish of execution in artistic performance, creative work, etc. **4** In colorimetry, lightness. Also **bril′lian·cy.**

bril·liant (bril′yənt) *adj.* **1** Sparkling or glowing with luster or light; very bright. **2** Showy; accomplished; illustrious; splendid: a *brilliant* mind, *brilliant* record. — *n.* **1** A diamond of the finest cut, or one possessing a single large face surrounded by a bezel of 33 facets and, below the girdle, a pavilion of 25 facets. For illustration see DIAMOND. **2** *Printing* A small type, about 3 1/2–point. [<MF *brillant,* ppr. of *briller* sparkle, ? <L *beryllus* beryl] — **bril′liant·ly** *adv.* — **bril′liant·ness** *n.*

bril·lian·tine (bril′yən·tēn) *n.* **1** A smooth, fine, wiry fabric in plain or twill weave, having a cotton warp and worsted or mohair filling. **2** A mixture of oil and perfume, used to impart a gloss to the hair.

brim (brim) *n.* **1** The rim of a cup. **2** The margin of a river. **3** A projecting rim, as of a hat. See synonyms under BANK, MARGIN. — *v.t.* & *v.i.* **brimmed, brim·ming** To fill or be filled to the brim. — **to brim over** To fill to the brim and overflow. [OE *brim* seashore]

brim·ful (brim′fo͝ol′, brim′fo͝ol′) *adj.* Full to the brim; brimming.

brim·mer (brim′ər) *n.* A vessel full to the brim; a brimming cup.

brim·stone (brim′stōn′) *n.* **1** Sulfur in its solid state or in some form derived from the solid state. **2** A spitfire; scold. [OE *brynstān* < *bryn-* burning (< *brinnen* burn) + *stān* stone] — **brim′ston′y** *adj.*

brin (brin) *n.* One of the radiating sticks of a fan.

brind·ed (brin′did) *adj.* Irregularly streaked; brindled. [Akin to BRAND]

Brin·di·si (brēn′dē·zē) A port of Apulia, SE Italy: ancient *Brundisium.*

brin·dle (brin′dəl) *adj.* Brindled. — *n.* A brindled color, or a brindled animal.

brin·dled (brin′dəld) *adj.* Tawny or grayish with irregular streaks or spots; also, barred; streaked. [Var. of BRINDED]

brine (brīn) *n.* **1** Water saturated or strongly impregnated with salt, as the water of the sea, that of salt wells and springs. **2** Saline water in which meats are preserved. **3** The water of the sea; ocean. **4** Tears. **5** A solution of sodium or calcium chloride used as a refrigerant in the making of ice. — *v.t.* **brined, brin·ing** To treat with brine; steep in brine. [OE *brȳne*] — **brin′ish** *adj.*

Bri·nell hardness (bri·nel′) *Metall.* The hardness of a metal, alloy, or similar material as measured by the area of indentation produced on its surface by a rigid steel ball of given diameter acted upon by a given force. [after J. A. *Brinell,* 1849–1925, Swedish engineer]

brine pit A salt spring, or a well the water of which yields salt on evaporation.

bring (bring) *v.t.* **brought, bring·ing** **1** To convey or cause (a person or thing) to come with oneself to or toward a place: *Bring* your friend to the party. **2** To cause to come about; involve as a consequence: War *brings* destruction. **3** To introduce into the mind; cause to appear: He *brought* her face into his thoughts. **4** To cause (a person) to adopt or admit, as a persuasion, course of action, etc.: He *brought* her to his point of view. **5** To sell for: The house *brought* a good price. **6** *Law* **a** To prefer, as a charge. **b** To institute: to *bring* suit. **c** To set forth, as evidence or an argument. — **to bring about** **1** To accomplish; cause to happen. **2** *Naut.* To reverse; turn, as a ship. — **to bring around** (or **round**) **1** To cause to adopt or admit, as an opinion or persuasion. **2** To revive; restore to consciousness. — **to bring down** **1** To cause to fall. **2** To fell by wounding or killing. — **to bring down the house** To evoke wild applause or acclaim. — **to bring forth** **1** To give birth. **2** To produce (foliage). — **to bring forward** **1** To adduce, as an argument. **2** In bookkeeping, to carry, as a sum, from one page or column to another. — **to bring home** To prove conclusively, so as to be understood. — **to bring home the bacon** *Colloq.* **1** To provide support or livelihood. **2** To gain a desired end or object. — **to bring in** **1** To import. **2** To render or submit (a verdict). **3** To yield or produce, as profits. — **to bring off** To do successfully. — **to bring on** **1** To cause; lead to. **2** To produce; cause to appear: *Bring on* the dancing girls! — **to bring out** **1** To reveal; cause to be evident, as the truth. **2** To publish or produce, as a book or play. **3** To introduce, as a young girl to society. — **to bring to** **1** To revive; restore to consciousness. **2** *Naut.* To cause (a ship) to come up into the wind and lie to. — **to bring to bear** To cause to have reference, application, or influence. — **to bring up** **1** To rear; educate. **2** To suggest or call attention to, as a subject. **3** To cough or vomit up. [OE *bringan*] — **bring′er** *n.*

bring·ing–up (bring′ing·up′) *n.* Care, training, and education of a person in childhood. See also UPBRINGING.

brink (bringk) *n.* **1** The verge of a steep place, or of a dangerous condition, action, event, or time. **2** The margin of any water; bank; shore. See synonyms under BANK, MARGIN. [ME *brenk* <Scand.]

brink·man·ship (bringk′mən·ship) *n.* A willingness to expose oneself to major risk to achieve some end; especially, a national policy embodying such a position. [<BRINK + *-manship,* on analogy with *showmanship,* etc.]

brin·y (brī′nē) *adj.* **brin·i·er, brin·i·est** Of the nature of brine; salty. — *n. Colloq.* The ocean: a dip in the *briny.* — **brin′i·ness** *n.*

bri·o (brē′ō) *n. Music* Spirit; vivacity: usually in the phrase *con brio.* [<Ital.]

bri·oche (brē′ōsh, -osh, *Fr.* brē·ôsh′) *n.* A soft, sweet roll made of butter, eggs, flour, and yeast. [<F]

bri·o·lette (brē′ə·let′) *n.* A gemstone cut with triangular or long facets, generally pear– or drop–shaped. For illustration see DIAMOND. [<F < *brillant* diamond]

bri·quet (bri·ket′) *n.* A block of compressed coal dust, used as fuel. Also **bri·quette′.** [<F *briquette,* dim. of *brique* brick]

bri·sance (brē·zäṅs′) *n.* The shattering effect of a high–explosive shell or of any blasting substance, usually measured in terms of detonating velocity. [<F *brisant,* ppr. of *briser* crush]

Bris·bane (briz′bān, -bən) The capital and principal port of Queensland, Australia.

Bri·se·is (brī·sē′is) In the *Iliad,* Achilles' concubine, whose seizure by Agamemnon led to a quarrel between the two men.

brisk (brisk) *adj.* **1** Moving, acting, or taking place rapidly; quick. **2** Energetic; vivacious; spirited; lively. **3** Sharp or stimulating, as cold air. **4** Sparkling; effervescent: said of liquors. See synonyms under ACTIVE, ALERT, ALIVE, NIMBLE. — *v.t.* & *v.i.* To make or become lively; animate: with *up.* [Cf. F *brusque* abrupt, sudden] — **brisk′ly** *adv.* — **brisk′ness** *n.*

bris·ket (bris′kit) *n.* The breast of a quadruped, especially of one whose flesh is used as food. [OF *bruschet,* ult. <Gmc.]

bris·ling (bris′ling) *n.* The sprat. [<Scand.]

bris·tle (bris′əl) *n.* **1** A coarse, stiff hair, as of swine. **2** *Bot.* A slender, stiff hair; morphologically, a trichome. — *v.* **bris·tled, bris·tling** *v.i.* **1** To erect the bristles, as an animal when aroused: often with *up.* **2** To show anger, irritation, etc., as by stiffening the body: often with *up.* **3** To be thickly set as with bristles: The plain *bristled* with bayonets. — *v.t.* **4** To erect as or like bristles: often with *up*: A cock *bristles* up his crest. **5** To cover or line as with bristles. **6** To agitate; ruffle violently: The storm *bristled* the lake. [ME *bristel,* OE *byrst*] — **bris′tly** *adj.*

bris·tle·tail (bris′əl·tāl′) *n.* The silverfish.

Bris·tol (bris′təl) A county borough and port in SW Gloucestershire, England.

Bristol board A fine quality of calendered cardboard. [from *Bristol*]

Bristol Channel An inlet of the Atlantic between Wales and SW England.

brit (brit) *n. pl.* **brit** A young herring, once thought to be a species. [Origin unknown]

Brit·ain (brit′n) Great Britain. Abbr. *Brit.*; *Br.*

bri·tan·ni·a (bri·tan′ē·ə, -tan′yə) *n. Metall.* A silver–white alloy of tin, copper, and antimony: used for cheap tableware. Also **Britannia metal.** [from *Britannia*]

Bri·tan·ni·a (bri·tan′ē·ə, -tan′yə) **1** The Roman name for Britain. **2** Great Britain, Ireland, and the Dominions. **3** A female figure representing Great Britain or the British Empire.

Bri·tan·nic (bri·tan′ik) *adj.* Of or pertaining to Great Britain; British. [<L *Britannicus*]

Brit·i·cism (brit′ə·siz′əm) *n.* A word, expression, or usage characteristic of Great Britain or the British. Also *Britishism, Britticism.*

Brit·ish (brit′ish) *adj.* **1** Pertaining to Great Britain, the United Kingdom, or the British Empire. **2** Of or pertaining to the ancient Britons, the original Celtic people of Britain. — *n.* **1** *pl.* The people of Great Britain or of the British Empire. **2** The language of the ancient Britons; Brythonic. [OE *Brettisc* <*Bret* a Briton].

British America **1** Canada: also **British North America.** **2** All British possessions in or adjacent to North or South America.

British Bechuanaland See BECHUANALAND.

British Columbia The westernmost province of Canada; 366,255 square miles; capital, Victoria. Abbr. *B.C.*

British Commonwealth of Nations A political association comprising the United Kingdom, Australia, Canada, Ceylon, Cyprus, Gambia, Ghana, India, Jamaica, Malawi, Malaysia, New Zealand, Nigeria, Pakistan, Sierra Leone, Tanzania, Trinidad and Tobago, Uganda, Western Samoa, and Zambia, and including the dependencies of member nations: officially *The Commonwealth.* Also *Commonwealth of Nations.*

British East Africa A former association of territories including Kenya, Tanganyika, Uganda, and Zanzibar. Abbr. *B.E.A.*

British Empire The sovereign states under the British Crown, comprising those in the BRITISH COMMONWEALTH OF NATIONS with their dependencies, colonies, territories, etc.

Brit·ish·er (brit′ish·ər) *n.* A native or subject of Great Britain.

British Guiana A British crown colony on the NE coast of South America; 83,000 square miles; capital, Georgetown.

British Honduras A British crown colony in Central America south of Yucatán peninsula; 8,866 square miles; capital, Belize. Formerly *Belize.*

British India Formerly, the territories in India subject to British law.

British Isles Great Britain, Ireland, Isle of Man, and the Channel Islands.

Brit·ish·ism (brit′ish·iz′əm) See BRITICISM.

British Malaya Formerly, the British possessions and dependencies in Malaya; now substantially the same as the FEDERATION OF MALAYA.

British New Guinea The former name of PAPUA.

British North America Act The act of Parliament that in 1867 created the Government of Canada for the federation of Ontario, Quebec, Nova Scotia, and New Brunswick. Manitoba joined in 1870, British Columbia in 1871, Prince Edward Island in 1873, Alberta and Saskatchewan in 1905, and Newfoundland in 1949.

British North Borneo See NORTH BORNEO.

British Solomon Islands See SOLOMON ISLANDS.

British Somaliland See SOMALILAND.

British thermal unit *Physics* The quantity of heat required to raise the temperature of one pound of water one degree Fahrenheit: at a starting temperature of 60° F. it is equal to 1054.6 joules. Abbr. *B.T.U.*

British Togoland See GHANA.

British Virgin Islands A presidency of the British colony of the Leeward Islands, comprising about 30 islands; 67 square miles; capital, Road Town.

British West Africa An association of territories including Cameroons, Gambia, Gold

Coast, Nigeria, Sierra Leone, and Togoland. Abbr. *B.W.A.*

British West Indies The possessions of Great Britain in the West Indies, including Bahamas, Bermuda, Jamaica, Trinidad, Tobago, and islands in the Lesser Antilles. Abbr. *B.W.I.*

Brit·on (brit′n) *n.* **1** One of any of the tribes inhabiting ancient Britain before the Anglo-Saxon invasion, probably belonging to the Brythonic branch of the Celts. **2** A native or citizen of Great Britain; an Englishman. [< OF *Breton* < L *Britto, -onis* < Celtic]

Brit·ta·ny (brit′ə·nē) A region and former province of western France, occupying the peninsula between the English Channel and the Bay of Biscay: French *Bretagne*, Breton *Breiz.*

Brit·ten (brit′n), **(Edward) Benjamin,** 1913–1976, English composer.

Brit·ti·cism (brit′ə·siz′əm) See BRITICISM.

brit·tle (brit′l) *adj.* Liable to break or snap; frangible; fragile. [ME *britel.* Akin to OE *bryttian* divide.] **—brit′tle·ness** *n.*

Brit·ton (brit′n), **Nathaniel Lord,** 1859–1934, U.S. botanist.

britz·ska (brits′kə) *n.* A light, four-wheeled carriage with calash top. Also **brits′ka, britz′·ka.** [< Polish *bryczka,* dim. of *bryka* freight wagon]

Brno (bûr′nô) The second largest city in Czechoslovakia; former capital of Moravia.

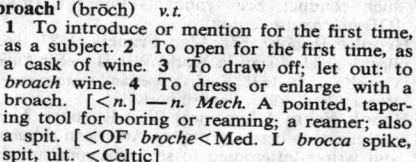
BRITZSKA

broach[1] (brōch) *v.t.* **1** To introduce or mention for the first time, as a subject. **2** To open for the first time, as a cask of wine. **3** To draw off; let out: to *broach* wine. **4** To dress or enlarge with a broach. [< *n.*] **—*n. Mech.* A pointed, tapering tool for boring or reaming; a reamer; also a spit. [< OF *broche* < Med. L *brocca* spike, spit, ult. < Celtic]

broach[2] (brōch) *v.t. & v.i.* To veer. **—to broach to** *Naut.* To fall off with the wind and waves, especially broadside to the wind and waves, and thus risk capsizing. [? < BROACH[1], *v.*]

broach·er (brō′chər) *n.* One who or that which broaches.

broad (brôd) *adj.* **1** Extended in lateral measurement; of unusual width; wide; expanded; vast. **2** Of wide range, sympathy, etc. **3** Widely diffused; comprehensive: a *broad* education. **4** Catholic; liberal; tolerant: *broad* views. **5** Strongly dialectal; also, rude and vigorous, as speech. **6** Strongly defined; plain; clear: a *broad* hint. **7** Loose; indelicate; bold. **8** Denoting the chief features of a thing; not detailed: a *broad* outline. **9** *Phonet.* Formed with the oral passage wide open and the tongue low and flat, as the *a* in *calm*; open. See synonyms under LARGE. **—*n.* 1** The broad part of anything. **2** A former English gold coin; a broadpiece. **3** A type of incandescent flood lamp used on motion-picture sets; a broadside. **4** The broadening out of a river over flat land; a fenny lake. **5** *Slang* A woman or girl. **—*adv.* Completely; fully. [OE *brād*] **—broad′ly** *adv.*

broad arrow 1 A broad-headed arrow. **2** A mark shaped like a barbed arrow placed on British government property, as convicts' uniforms, ordnance stores, etc.

broad–ax (brôd′aks′) *n.* An ax with broad edge and short handle. Also **broad′–axe′.**

broad·bean (brôd′bēn′) *n.* The large, usually flat, orbicular or angular, seed of a strong, erect annual vine (*Vicia faba*) of the Old World.

broad·bill (brôd′bil′) *n.* **1** The scaup duck. **2** The shoveler duck. **3** The European spoonbill. **4** The swordfish.

BROADBILL *(def 3)*

broad·brim (brôd′brim′) *n.* A hat with a broad brim.

Broad·brim (brôd′brim′) *n. Colloq.* A Friend or Quaker.

broad·cast (brôd′kast′, -käst′) *v.* **·cast** or **·casted, ·cast·ing** *v.t.* **1** To send or transmit (music, newscasts, etc.) by radio or television. **2** To scatter or cast, as seed, over a wide area; sow. **3** To disseminate; make public, as gossip. **—*v.i.* 4** To speak, sing, etc., for broadcasting purposes. **—*adj.* 1** Transmitted by radio. **2** Cast or scattered abroad, as seeds. **—*n.* 1** *Telecom.* **a** The process of transmitting a program by radio. **b** A radio program. **c** The time period of a broadcast. **2** A casting or scattering of seed, etc., over the ground. **—*adv.* By scattering abroad, or so as to scatter abroad or disseminate.

broad·cast·er (brôd′kas′tər, -käs′-) *n.* **1** One who owns or operates a broadcasting station. **2** One who makes broadcasts.

Broad Church The liberal wing of the Church of England, or, by extension, of any church. **—Broad′–Church′** *adj.* **—Broad′–Church′ism** *n.* **—Broad′–Church′man** *n.*

broad·cloth (brôd′klôth′, -kloth′) *n.* **1** A fine quality of woven wool, napped and calendered, in plain or twill weave: used for suits, skirts, etc. **2** A closely woven fabric of silk, cotton, etc., in plain weave with a light crosswise rib: used for shirts, dresses, etc.

broad·en (brôd′n) *v.t. & v.i.* To make or become broad or broader.

broad–gage (brôd′gāj′) *adj.* **1** Having a gage wider than the standard gage of 56½ inches, as a railway. **2** Broad-minde Also **broad′–gauge′, broad′–gaged′, broad′–gauged′.**

broad hatchet A hatchet with a broad blade. For illustration see HATCHET.

broad·horn (brôd′hôrn′) *n.* **1** A large flatboat, used formerly on the Mississippi and Ohio Rivers. **2** A Rocky Mountain sheep. **3** One of a herd of Texas longhorn cattle.

broad·ish (brôd′dish) *adj.* Somewhat broad.

broad jump A jump for distance; a long jump.

broad·leaf (brôd′lēf′) *n.* **1** A tree (*Terminalia catappa*) of the myrobalan family, of Jamaica, with almondlike fruit. **2** Any variety of tobacco plant suitable for cigarmaking, having especially broad leaves.

broad–minded (brôd′mīn′did) *adj.* Liberal in beliefs and opinions; tolerant; free from bigotry and prejudice. **—broad′–mind′ed·ly** *adv.* **—broad′–mind′ed·ness** *n.*

broad–piece (brôd′pēs′) *n.* An English gold coin of James II.

Broads (brôdz), **The** A region of marshy lakes in Norfolk (**the Norfolk Broads**) and Suffolk (**the Suffolk Broads**), England.

broad seal The official seal of a government.

broad·side (brôd′sīd′) *n.* **1** All the guns on one side of a man-of-war, or their simultaneous discharge. **2** Any sweeping attack; hence, a volley of abuse or denunciation. **3** *Naut.* A vessel's side above the water line. **4** A large sheet of paper, printed on one side: also **broad′sheet′.** **5** The broad, unbroken surface of anything. **6** The side of an animal between the ham and the shoulder, used as meat; specifically, a side of bacon. **7** A flood lamp: see BROAD (*n.* def. 3). **—*adv.* With the broadside turned, presented, or exposed.

Broad·stairs (brôd′stârz) A resort town in NE Kent, England.

broad·sword (brôd′sôrd′, -sōrd′) *n.* A sword with a broad cutting blade and obtuse point.

broad·tail (brôd′tāl′) *n.* **1** A family of fat-tailed sheep. **2** The pelt of very young fat-tailed lambs, whose soft, lustrous fur lacks the tight curl characteristic of older lambs and sheep.

Broad·way (brôd′wā) **1** A street running north and south through New York City, famous for its brightly lighted entertainment district. **2** The New York entertainment industry. **—*adj.* Situated on, characteristic of, or like Broadway in New York.

Brob·ding·nag (brob′ding·nag) The giants' country in Swift's *Gulliver's Travels.* **—Brob′·ding·nag′i·an** (-nag′ē·ən) *adj. & n.*

Bro·ca (brô·kä′), **Paul,** 1824–80, French surgeon.

Broca's area *Anat.* A convolution located on the left frontal lobe of the brain: its function

is the coordination of the sensory and motor processes involved in speech. [after Paul *Broca*]

bro·cade (brō·kād′) *n.* A rich fabric of satin or twill background interwoven with raised flower or figure design in silken or gold or silver threads. **—*v.t.* cad·ed, ·cad·ing** To weave (a cloth) with a raised design or figure. [< Sp. *brocado* < Med. L *broccata,* fem. pp. of *broccare* embroider] **—bro·cad′ed** *adj.*

broc·a·tel (brok′ə·tel′) *n.* A brocaded fabric of silk, wool, cotton, or the like, with a more highly raised pattern than in brocade. Also **broc′a·telle′.** [< F *brocatelle* < Ital. *broccatello,* dim. of *broccato* brocade]

broc·co·li (brok′ə·lē) *n.* A hardy variety of cauliflower which does not head, of which the green sprouts and tender stalks are eaten. [< Ital., pl. of *broccolo* cabbage sprout]

broch (brokh) *n.* A type of corbelled stone tower of the Bronze Age found in Scotland. [< ON *borg* castle]

bro·ché (brō·shā′) *adj.* Woven with a raised design; embossed; brocaded; stitched, as a book. [< F *broché,* pp. of *brocher* stitch, brocade]

bro·chette (brō·shet′) *n.* A small spit used in roasting; a skewer. [< OF, dim. of *broche* skewer, spit]

bro·chure (brō·shoor′) *n.* A pamphlet; anything written or published in pamphlet form. [< F < *brocher* stitch]

brock (brok) *n.* **1** A badger. **2** *Brit. Dial.* A foul, dirty fellow. [OE *broc*]

Brock·en (brok′ən) The highest peak of the Harz Mountains in central Germany; 3,747 feet; famous for its "specter," caused by its shadow cast on clouds. Also **Blocks·berg** (blôks′·berk).

brock·et (brok′it) *n.* **1** A stag in its second year with its first horns as simple spikes. **2** A small deer of tropical America (genus *Mazama*). [< F *brocart* < *broche* tine of antlers]

Brock·ton (brok′tən) A city in eastern Massachusetts.

brod (brod) *n. Scot.* A prod; goad.

Brod·ribb (brod′rib), **John Henry** See IRVING, SIR HENRY.

bro·gan (brō′gən) *n.* A coarse, heavy shoe kept on the foot by side flaps laced or buckled over a short tongue. [< Irish *brōgan,* dim. of *brōg* shoe]

brög·ger·ite (brœg′ər·īt) *n.* A variety of uraninite from which helium has been obtained. [after W. C. *Brögger,* 1851–1940, Norwegian mineralogist]

Bro·glie (brôl′y′), **de** See DE BROGLIE.

brogue[1] (brōg) *n.* A dialectal pronunciation of English, especially that of the Irish people. [< Irish *barróg* defect of speech]

brogue[2] (brōg) *n.* **1** A heavy oxford with low heels, decorated with stitchings, pinkings, and perforations. **2** A rude shoe of untanned hide with the hair outside, tied with thongs: worn formerly in Ireland and the Scottish Highlands. [< Irish *brōg* brogue (def. 2)]

brogue[3] (brōg) *n. Scot.* A fraud; cheating trick.

broi·der (broi′dər) *v.t. Obs.* To embroider. [< MF *broder* stitch; infl. by ME *broid,* var. of *braid*] **—broi′der·y** *n.*

broil[1] (broil) *v.t.* **1** To cook, as meat, by subjecting to direct heat. **2** To expose to great heat; scorch. **—*v.i.* 3** To be exposed to great heat; cook. **4** To become impatient; burn with anger. **—*n.* 1** Something broiled. **2** A broiling heat. [< OF *bruiller*]

broil[2] (broil) *n.* A turmoil; noisy quarrel; brawl. See synonyms under ALTERCATION, QUARREL. **—*v.i.* To engage in a broil; brawl; quarrel. [< F *brouiller* confuse]

broil·er (broil′ər) *n.* **1** A device for broiling, as a gridiron. **2** A chicken suitable for broiling. **3** *Colloq.* A very hot day.

broil·ing (broi′ling) *adj.* Extremely hot; torrid. **—broil′ing·ly** *adv.*

bro·kage (brō′kij) *n.* Brokerage. [< AF *brocage*]

broke[1] (brōk) *v.i.* **broked, brok·ing** To act as a broker.

broke[2] (brōk) Past tense and archaic past participle of BREAK. **—*adj.* 1** Ruined; bankrupt. **2** *Colloq.* Without any money. **—go for broke** *Slang* To risk everything on an uncertain course of action.

bro·ken (brō′kən) Past participle of BREAK. — *adj.* **1** Separated forcibly into parts; fractured; shattered; ruptured. **2** Crushed in feeling or spirit; humbled; contrite. **3** Reduced to subjection; trained. **4** Made infirm; weakened. **5** Violated, transgressed, or disobeyed. **6** Reduced or shattered in estate or fortune; ruined; bankrupt. **7** Incomplete or interrupted, as sleep, utterance, etc. **8** Disordered or disarranged, as troops. **9** Rough, rugged, or irregular: *broken* ground; also, plowed or dug up, as land. **10** Faultily spoken: *broken* English. **—bro′ken·ly** *adv.* — **bro′ken·ness** *n.*

bro·ken-down (brō′kən·doun′) *adj.* **1** Broken in health or strength; ruined; wrecked. **2** Having the parts or a part broken; powerless: a *broken-down* engine.

bro·ken·heart·ed (brō′kən·här′tid) *adj.* Overwhelmed or crushed in spirit, as by sorrow or grief.

Broken Hill A city in western New South Wales, Australia.

broken wind Wind-broken respiration; the heaves.

bro·ken-wind·ed (brō′kən·win′did) *adj.* **1** Habitually short of breath. **2** Affected with the heaves, as a horse.

bro·ker (brō′kər) *n.* One who buys and sells for another on commission or who arranges for the negotiation of contracts of various types; especially, a stockbroker. [<AF *brocour* <OF *brochier* tap, broach (a wine cask)]

bro·ker·age (brō′kər·ij) *n.* The business or commission of a broker.

brom- Var. of BROMO-.

bro·ma (brō′mə) *n.* **1** The dry powder of cacao seeds after the oil has been expressed. **2** A beverage prepared therefrom. **3** *Med.* Solid food. [<Gk. *brōma* food]

brom·ac·e·tone (brom·as′ə·tōn) *n. Chem.* A colorless volatile liquid, C_3H_5OBr, of toxic properties: used as a tear gas in World War I.

bro·mal (brō′məl) *n. Chem.* A colorless liquid compound resembling chloral, C_2HBr_3O, with a pungent taste and penetrating odor: obtained by the action of bromine on alcohol and used in medicine as a hypnotic and anodyne. [<BROM- + AL(COHOL)]

bro·mate (brō′māt) *Chem. n.* A salt of bromic acid containing the univalent BrO_3 radical. —*v.t.* **·mat·ed, ·mat·ing** To combine, saturate, or impregnate with bromine.

bro·ma·tol·o·gy (brō′mə·tol′ə·jē) *n.* The study of food and diet. [<Gk. *brōma, -atos* + -LOGY]

bro·mat·o·ther·a·py (brō·mat′ə·ther′ə·pē) *n. Med.* The treatment of disease by means of food. Also **bro′ma·ther′a·py** (brō′mə-). [<Gk. *brōma, -atos* + THERAPY]

Brom·berg (brôm′berkh) The German name for BYDGOSZCZ.

brome·grass (brōm′gras′, -gräs′) *n.* Any grass of the genus *Bromus,* widely cultivated for hay and pasturage. Also **brome.** [<Gk. *bromos* oats]

bro·me·li·a·ceous (brō·mē′lē·ā′shəs) *adj. Bot.* Belonging to a family *(Bromeliaceae)* of tropical or subtropical American monocotyledonous plants, including the Spanish moss and the pineapple. [<NL *Bromeliaceae,* after Olaf *Bromel,* 1639–1705, Swedish botanist]

Brom·field (brom′fēld), **Louis,** 1896–1956, U.S. novelist.

bromic (brō′mik) *adj. Chem.* Of, pertaining to, or containing bromine, especially in its higher valence.

bro·mide[1] (brō′mīd, -mid) *n.* **1** *Chem.* A compound of bromine with an element or an organic radical; a salt of hydrobromic acid: potassium *bromide,* KBr. **2** A photograph printed on paper, etc., that has been subjected to the effects of bromide of silver. Also **bro′mid** (-mid). [<BROM(INE) + -IDE]

bro·mide[2] (brō′mīd, -mid) *n. Colloq.* **1** One who utters platitudes; a commonplace bore. **2** A platitude; a dull remark. [<BROMIDE[1]; with ref. to the sedative effect of some bromides] — **bro·mid·ic** (brō·mid′ik) *adj.*

bro·mi·nate (brō′mə·nāt) *v.t.* **·nat·ed, ·nat·ing** To bromate.

bro·mine (brō′mēn, -min) *n.* A heavy, reddish-brown non-metallic liquid element (symbol Br, atomic number 35) belonging to the halogen group and having a toxic, suffocating vapor. See PERIODIC TABLE. Also **bro′min** (-min). [<F *brome* (<Gk. *brōmos* stench) + -INE]

bro·mism (brō′miz·əm) *n. Pathol.* Chronic poisoning by bromides.

bro·mize (brō′mīz) *v.t.* **·mized, ·miz·ing** *Chem.* To combine, impregnate, or treat with bromine or a bromide.

bromo- *combining form* Used to indicate the presence of bromine as a principal element in chemical compounds. Also, before vowels, *brom-*. [<BROMINE]

bron·chi (brong′kī) *Anat.* Plural of BRONCHUS.

bron·chi·a (brong′kē·ə) *n. pl. Anat.* The bronchial tubes. [<LL <Gk. *bronchia* bronchial tubes]

bron·chi·al (brong′kē·əl) *adj. Anat.* Of or pertaining to the chief air passages of the lungs.

bronchial tubes *Anat.* The subdivisions of the trachea conveying air into the lungs.

bron·chi·tis (brong·kī′tis) *n. Pathol.* Inflammation of the bronchial tubes, or, loosely, of the bronchi or trachea. [<BRONCH(O)- + -ITIS] — **bron·chit·ic** (brong·kit′ik) *adj.*

broncho- *combining form* Windpipe: *bronchoscope.* Also, before vowels, **bronch-.** [<Gk. *bronchos*]

bron·cho·cele (brong′kə·sēl) *n.* Goiter. [<Gk. *bronchokēlē* tumor in the throat <*bronchos* windpipe + *kēlē* tumor]

bron·cho·pneu·mon·ia (brong′kō·nōō·mōn′yə, -nyōō-) *n. Pathol.* Bronchitis complicated with inflammation of the surrounding substance of the lungs; catarrhal pneumonia.

bron·cho·scope (brong′kə·skōp) *n. Med.* An instrument for inspecting or treating the interior of the bronchi. **—bron·chos·co·py** (brong·kos′kə·pē) *n.*

bron·chot·o·my (brong·kot′ə·mē) *n. Surg.* The operation of making an incision into the windpipe; tracheotomy. [<BRONCHO- + -TOMY]

bron·chus (brong′kəs) *n. pl.* **·chi** (-kī) *Anat.* One of the two forked branches of the trachea. [<Gk. *bronchos* windpipe]

bron·co (brong′kō) *n. pl.* **·cos** A small, wild, or partly broken horse of the western United States. —*adj.* **1** Consisting of, or like broncos. **2** Wild; unruly. Also **bron′cho.** [<Sp. *bronco* rough]

bron·co·bust·er (brong′kō·bus′tər) *n. U.S. Colloq.* One who breaks a bronco to the saddle. Also **bron′cho·bust′er.**

Bronk (brongk), **Detlev W.,** 1897–1975, U.S. neurophysiologist.

Bron·të (bron′tē) Name of three English novelists, sisters: **Anne,** 1820–49; **Charlotte,** 1816–1855; **Emily Jane,** 1818–48. Pseudonyms, respectively, *Acton, Currer,* and *Ellis Bell.*

bron·tides (bron′tīdz) *n. pl. Meteorol.* Brief, thunderlike noises accompanying the activity of faint earthquakes in seismic regions. [<Gk. *brontē* thunder + *-eidēs* like, similar to]

bron·to·sau·rus (bron′tə·sôr′əs) *n. Paleontol.* A huge, herbivorous dinosaur (order *Sauropoda*) of the Jurassic period, found fossil in western North America. [Gk. *brontē* thunder + *sauros* lizard]

BRONTOSAURUS
(Up to 70 feet in length, 20 tons in weight)

Bronx (brongks), **the** A mainland borough of New York City.

Bronx cheer *U.S. Slang* A voiced and forced expulsion of the breath through nearly-closed lips to express contempt or derision.

bronze (bronz) *n.* **1** *Metall.* **a** A reddish-brown alloy essentially of copper and tin, used in making bells and statues. **b** A similar alloy of copper and some other metal, as aluminum or manganese. **2** A pigment of the color of bronze. **3** A statue or bust cast in bronze. —*v.* **bronzed, bronz·ing** *v.t.* To harden or color like bronze; make brown. —*v.i.* To become brown or tan. [<MF <Ital. *bronzo, bronzino,* ? <L *(aes) Brundisinum* (alloy) of Brundisium] **—bronz′y** *adj.*

bronze age A mythological period of time characterized by violence and war, following the silver age of Zeus; often called *brazen age.*

Bronze Age *Archeol.* A period of time following the Stone Age and preceding the Iron Age during which weapons and other implements were made of bronze.

Bronze Star A U.S. military decoration in the form of a bronze star having a much smaller raised star in the center: awarded for heroic or meritorious achievement not involving participation in an aerial flight.

broo (brōō) *n. Scot.* Juice; broth: also *bree.*

brooch (brōch, brōōch) *n.* An ornamental pin for wearing on the breast. [Var. of BROACH[1], *n.*]

brood (brōōd) *n.* **1** All the young birds of a single hatching; also, offspring; progeny. **2** Species; kind; race. See synonyms under FLOCK. —*v.t.* **1** To sit upon or incubate (eggs). **2** To protect (young) by covering with the wings. —*v.i.* **3** To sit on eggs; incubate. **4** To meditate or ponder moodily and deeply: usually with *on* or *upon.* — *adj.* Kept for breeding purposes: a *brood* mare [OE *brod.* Related to BREED.]

brood·er (brōō′dər) *n.* **1** A covered and warmed receptacle, usually with an outside run, for protecting chicks reared without a hen. **2** One who broods over things in thought.

brood mare A mare used for breeding.

brood·y (brōō′dē) *adj.* **brood·i·er, brood·i·est** **1** Inclined to brood, or sit on eggs, as a hen. **2** Prolific; capable of breeding. **3** Meditative; moody.

brook[1] (brŏŏk) *n.* A small, natural stream, smaller than a river or creek; a rivulet. See synonyms under STREAM. [OE brōc]

brook[2] (brŏŏk) *v.t.* To put up with; endure; tolerate: usually with the negative: I cannot *brook* such conduct. See synonyms under ENDURE. [OE *brūcan* use, enjoy]

Brooke (brŏŏk), **Sir Alan Francis,** 1883–1963, British chief of staff in World War II. **—Sir Fulke Greville,** 1554–1628, English poet and statesman. — **Rupert,** 1887–1915, English poet.

Brook Farm A farm near West Roxbury, Massachusetts, where a group of American scholars and writers attempted to set up a communistic community, 1841–47.

brook·let (brŏŏk′lit) *n.* A little brook.

(brŏŏk′lin) A borough of New York City on the western end of Long Island.

Brooks (brŏŏks), **Phillips,** 1835–93, U.S. divine and writer. **—Van Wyck,** 1886–1963, U.S. biographer and critic. **—William Robert,** 1844–1921, U.S. astronomer; discovered 23 comets.

Brooks Range The northernmost part of the Rocky Mountains, in northern Alaska, forming a watershed between the Yukon River and the Arctic Ocean; highest point, 9,239 feet.

brook trout **1** The speckled trout *(Salvelinus fontinalis)* of eastern North America. **2** The European brown trout *(Salmo trutta).*

brook·weed (brŏŏk′wēd′) *n.* Either of two water pimpernels, the European *(Samolus valerandi),* or the American *(S. floribundus).*

broom (brōōm, brŏŏm) *n.* **1** A brush attached to a long handle for sweeping: made chiefly of broomcorn. **2** Any of various shrubs (genus *Cytisus*) of the pea family, especially the **Scotch broom** *(C. scoparius),* with yellow flowers and stiff green branches. —*v.t.* To remove with a broom; sweep. [OE *brōm* broom. Akin to BRAMBLE.] **—broom′y** *adj.*

broom·corn (brōōm′kôrn′, brŏŏm′-) *n.* A canelike grass (genus *Sorghum*) of which brooms are made.

broom·rape (brōōm′rāp′, brŏŏm′-) *n.* Any of various Old World fleshy herbs (genus *Orobanche,* family *Orobanchaceae*), destitute of green foliage and parasitic on the roots of other plants.

broom·stick (brōōm′stik′, brŏŏm′-) *n.* The handle of a broom.

broose (brōōz) *n. Scot.* A race for a prize at a wedding, as practiced in the Highlands.

brose (brōz) *n. Scot.* Porridge hastily made by pouring boiling water, or sometimes milk, beef broth, or the like, on meal, and stirring them together. **—bro′sy** *adj.*

broth (brôth, broth) *n.* **1** A fluid food made by boiling flesh, vegetables, etc., in water; a thin or strained soup. **2** *Irish Colloq.* A manly boy or young man of good character. **—a broth of a boy** A fine fellow. [OE. Related to BREW.]

broth·el (broth′əl, broth′-, brôth′əl, brôth′-) *n.* A house of prostitution. [ME, a worthless

person, OE *brothen*, pp. of *breothan* ruin, decay; infl. by BORDEL]

broth·er (bruth′ər) *n. pl.* **broth·ers** or *Archaic* **breth·ren 1** A male person having the same parent as another or others. Sons of the same two parents are **full** or **whole brothers**; those having only one parent in common are *half-brothers.* **2** A person of the same descent, profession, trade, company, etc., with another or others; one having the same racial heritage; a kinsman. **3** A fellow human being. **4** One closely united with another or others by religious, political, or family bond. **5** One of a male religious order; a monk. **6** *U.S. Colloq.* A black man; a fellow black. —*v.t.* To treat or address as a brother. [OE *brōthor*]

broth·er·hood (bruth′ər·hŏŏd) *n.* **1** Fraternal relationship; the state of being brothers. **2** A society, fraternity, guild, etc. **3** A body of persons of the same occupation, profession, etc.

broth·er-in-law (bruth′ər·in·lô′) *n. pl.* **broth·ers-in-law** A brother of a husband or wife, a sister's husband, or, loosely, a wife's sister's husband.

Brother Jonathan The people of the United States collectively: said to be from Washington's frequent allusion to Jonathan Trumbull by this name.

broth·er·ly (bruth′ər·lē) *adj.* Pertaining to or like a brother; fraternal; affectionate. See synonyms under FRIENDLY. —*adv.* Like a brother; kindly. —**broth′er·li·ness** *n.*

brougham (brŏŏm, brŏŏ′əm, brō′əm) *n.* **1** A closed, four-wheeled carriage with front wheels turning short on a pivot, seating two or more persons, and having a high, uncovered driver's seat: drawn by one or two horses. **2** An electric automobile built on these lines, but seating four or five persons. **3** An automobile with a limousine body and the driver's seat outside. [after Lord Henry *Brougham*, 1778–1868, British statesman]

BROUGHAM

brought (brôt) Past tense and past participle of BRING.

brou·ha·ha (brŏŏ′hä·hä) *n.* Hubbub; uproar; hurly-burly. [< F]

brow (brou) *n.* **1** The front upper part of the head; the forehead. **2** The eyebrow. **3** The countenance in general. **4** The upper edge of a cliff or the like. [OE *brū*]

brow antler The branch of an antler nearest the brow. For illustration see ANTLER.

brow·band (brou′band′) *n.* **1** A band about the brow. **2** A band, as of a bridle, passing across a horse's forehead. For illustration see HARNESS.

brow·beat (brou′bēt′) *v.t.* **·beat**, **·beat·en**, **·beat·ing** To intimidate by a stern, overbearing manner; bully. See synonyms under FRIGHTEN.

brown (broun) *n.* **1** A dark color, shading toward red, yellow, or black, as the color of faded leaves. **2** A pigment or dye used to produce it; a thing or part that is brown. —*adj.* Of the dusky or tanned color known as brown. —**to do up brown** *Slang* To do thoroughly and perfectly. —*v.t. & v.i.* To make or become brown; tan, as by sunbathing. [OE *brun*] —**brown′ish** *adj.* —**brown′ness** *n.*

Brown (broun), **Charles Brockden,** 1771–1810, American novelist. —**John,** 1800–59, American abolitionist, led raid on arsenal at Harpers Ferry to establish stronghold for escaped slaves; hanged for treason.

brown algae any members of a division of plants (Phaeophyta) consisting of multicellular, mostly marine algae containing a brown pigment that masks the green color of chlorophyll, such as kelp, gulfweed, and rockweed.

brown bagging 1 The practice of carrying in a small paper bag one's own liquor into a restaurant, where its sale is prohibited. **2** The practice of taking one's lunch to work in a brown paper bag.

brown Bess The bronzed flint musket formerly used in the British Army.

brown Betty Baked pudding made of bread crumbs, apple, and milk and sweetened.

brown bread 1 Bread made of unbolted wheat flour; Graham bread. **2** Bread made of rye flour and corn meal.

brown coal Lignite.

Browne (broun), **Charles Far·rar** (far′ər). See ARTEMUS WARD. —**Sir Thomas,** 1605–82, English physician and writer.

Brown·i·an movement (brou′nē·ən) *Physics* The rapid oscillatory movement of small particles when suspended in liquids. Also **Brownian motion.** [after Robert *Brown*, 1773–1858, English botanist, who discovered it]

brown·ie (brou′nē) *n.* **1** A homely, good-natured sprite, supposed to haunt farmhouses and do useful work at night. **2** A small, flat chocolate cake with nuts, usually square.

Brown·ie (brou′nē) *n.* A junior girl scout of the age group seven through nine.

Brown·ing (brou′ning), **Elizabeth Barrett,** 1806–61, English poet; wife of Robert. —**Robert,** 1812–89, English poet.

Browning automatic rifle An air-cooled, gas-operated, self-loading rifle, firing from a magazine: it is both automatic and semi-automatic. [after John Moses *Browning*, 1855–1926, U.S. inventor]

Browning machine-gun A machine-gun used by the U.S. Army, firing .30 or .50 caliber ammunition.

Brown·ist (brou′nist) *n.* A follower of Robert Browne, a Puritan, who separated from the Church of England about 1580. —**Brown′ism** *n.* —**Brown·is′tic** or **·ti·cal** *adj.*

brown lung Byssinosis.

brown-out (broun′out′) *n.* **1** A partial diminishing of lights as a defensive measure against aerial attacks. **2** Any diminution of electric power.

brown recluse A small, brown, venomous spider (*Loxosceles reclusa*) with a violin-shaped mark on its back.

brown rice Unpolished rice grains, with the bran layers and most of the grains intact.

brown rot A serious disease of stone fruits caused by a fungus of the *Sclerotinia* genus.

Brown Shirt 1 A member of the Sturmabteilung. **2** A Nazi.

brown·stone (broun′stōn′) *n.* A brownish-red sandstone used for building. —*adj.* **1** Made of brownstone. **2** Pertaining to the well-to-do class: the *brownstone* vote.

brownstone front A house having a front of brownstone.

brown study Deep meditation; absent-mindedness.

brown sugar Sugar that is unrefined or partly refined.

Browns·ville (brounz′vil) A port on the Rio Grande in southern Texas.

Brown Swiss A type of hardy dairy cattle originating in Switzerland.

brown·tail (broun′tāl′) *n.* A white European moth (*Euproctis chrysorrhoea*), reddish-brown at the posterior end: its larvae defoliate shade trees. Also **brown′-tailed′ moth.**

brown thrasher See under THRASHER.

browse (brouz) *v.* **browsed**, **brows·ing** *v.t.* **1** To crop; nibble at (leaves, grasses, etc.). **2** To graze on. —*v.i.* **3** To feed on grasses, leaves, etc. **4** To dip into books, etc., for casual reading. [< *n.*, or < MF *brouster* browse] —*n.* **1** Growing shoots or twigs used as fodder. **2** The act or process of browsing. [< MF *broust* bud, sprout] —**brows·er** *n.*

Broz (brōz) See TITO.

Bruce (brŏŏs), **Sir David,** 1855–1931, English physician and bacteriologist. —**Robert the,** 1274–1329, king of Scotland; defeated Edward II at Bannockburn: also known as *Robert I, Robert Bruce.* —**Viscount Stanley Melbourne,** born 1883, Australian statesman; prime minister 1923–29.

bru·cel·lo·sis (brŏŏ′sə·lō′sis) *n.* Undulant fever. [after Sir David *Bruce*]

bru·cine (brŏŏ′sēn, -sin) *n. Chem.* A bitter poisonous crystalline alkaloid, $C_{23}H_{26}O_4N_2H_2O$, found with strychnine, in the seed and bark of the nux vomica, and in other species of the same genus (*Strychnos*). Also **bru′cin** (-sin). [after J. *Bruce*, 1730–94, Scottish explorer in Africa]

bru·cite (brŏŏ′sīt) *n.* A magnesium hydrate, $Mg(OH)_2$. [after Archibald *Bruce*, 1777–1818, U.S. mineralogist]

Bruck·ner (brook′nər), **Anton,** 1824–96, Austrian composer.

Brue·ghel (broi′gəl) Family of Flemish painters, especially, **Peter,** 1520?–69, known as *the Elder,* and his sons, **Peter,** 1564?–1638?, known as *the Younger,* and **Jan,** 1568–1625. Also spelled *Breughel, Bruegel.*

Bruges (brŏŏzh, brŏŏ′jiz) A city of NW Belgium, capital of West Flanders province. *Flemish* **Brug·ge** (braekh′ə).

bru·in (brŏŏ′in) *n.* A bear; especially, a brown bear. [< Du., brown]

bruise (brŏŏz) *v.* **bruised**, **bruis·ing** *v.t.* **1** To injure, as by a blow, without breaking the surface of the skin; contuse. **2** To dent or mar the surface of. **3** To hurt or offend slightly, as feelings. **4** To crush; pound small, as with a mortar and pestle. —*v.i.* **5** To become discolored as the result of a blow. —*n.* A surface injury caused by violent contact, usually with discoloration of the skin but without laceration or fracture; contusion. [Fusion of OE *brȳsan* crush and OF *bruisier* break, shatter]

bruis·er (brŏŏ′zər) *n.* **1** One who bruises. **2** A professional pugilist. **3** A pugnacious ruffian; a bully.

bruit (brŏŏt) *v.t.* To noise abroad; talk about: used mainly in the passive. See synonyms under PUBLISH. [< *n.*]—*n.* **1** *Obs.* A rumor noised abroad. **2** A din; clamor. **3** *Med.* A sound, generally abnormal, heard in auscultation. ◆ Homophone: *brute.* [< F *bruit* noise < *bruire* roar, make a noise, ? < L *rugire* roar, bellow] —**bruit′er** *n.*

Bru·maire (brü·mâr′) The second month in the calendar of the first French republic. See CALENDAR (Republican). [< F < *brume* fog, mist]

bru·mal (brŏŏ′məl) *adj.* Wintry. [< L *brumalis* wintry]

brum·by (brum′bē) *Austral.* A wild horse.

brume (brŏŏm) *n.* Fog; mist. [< F < L *bruma* winter] —**bru·mous** (brŏŏ′məs) *adj.*

brum·ma·gem (brum′ə·jəm) *adj.* Cheap and showy; spurious, bogus. —*n.* An imitation; a sham; especially, cheap, imitation jewelry. [Alter. of *Birmingham*, England, where cheap jewelry was made]

Brum·mell (brum′əl), **George Bryan.** See BEAU BRUMMELL.

brunch (brunch) *n.* A late morning meal combining breakfast and lunch. [Blend of BREAKFAST and LUNCH]

Brun·dis·i·um (brun·diz′ē·əm) An ancient name for BRINDISI.

Bru·nei (broo·nī′) A sultanate under British protection in NW Borneo; 2,226 square miles; capital, Brunei.

Bru·nel·les·chi (brŏŏ′nel·les′kē), **Filippo,** 1377–1446, Italian architect and sculptor. Also **Bru′nel·les′co** (-les′kō).

bru·net (brŏŏ·net′) *n.* A man or boy of dark complexion, eyes, and hair. —*adj.* Brunette.

bru·nette (brŏŏ·net′) *adj.* Dark-hued; having dark complexion, hair, and eyes. —*n.* A woman or girl of dark complexion, eyes, and hair. [< F, fem. dim. of *brun* brown]

Brun·hild (brŏŏn′hild, *Ger.* brŏŏn′hilt) In the *Nibelungenlied,* a queen of Iceland, married to Gunther, for whom she is won by Siegfried: discovering the deceit of her conquest, she persuades Hagen to avenge her by murdering Siegfried. Compare BRÜNNEHILDE, BRYNHILD.

Brü·ning (brü′ning), **Heinrich,** 1885–1970, German statesman, chancellor of Germany 1930–32. Also **Brue′ning.**

Brünn (brün) The German name for BRNO.

Brünne·hil·de (brün·hil′də) In Wagner's *Ring of the Nibelung,* a Valkyrie who incurs the anger of Wotan for assisting Siegmund and is put in a trance in a flame-encircled fastness, but is eventually released by Siegfried. Compare BRUNHILD, BRYNHILD.

Bru·no (brŏŏ′nō) A masculine personal name. [< OHG, brown]

—**Bruno, Saint,** 1030?–1101, German monk, founder of the Carthusian order, 1086.

Bru·no (brŏŏ′nō), **Giordano,** 1548?–1600, Italian philosopher; burned as a heretic. —**Bru·nis′tic** (brŏŏ·nis′tik) *adj.*

Bru·no·ni·an (broo͞·nō′nē·ən) *n.* An adherent of the **Brunonian theory,** now obsolete, that disease is a result of defective stimuli. [after John *Brown,* 1735–88, Scottish physician]

brun·stane (brun′stān) *n. Scot.* Brimstone.

Bruns·wick (brunz′wik) **1** A port in SE Georgia. **2** A former duchy and state of north central Germany; also, its former capital, a city in Lower Saxony: German *Braunschweig.*

Bruns·wick–black (brunz′wik·blak′) *n.* Japan (def. 2).

brunt (brunt) *n.* **1** The main force, shock, strain, or stress of a blow, an attack, etc.; the hardest part. **2** *Obs.* A blow; assault; collision. [? <ON *bruna* advance quickly, as a fire]

Bru·sa (broo͞′sä) A city in NW Turkey in Asia: ancient *Prusa*: also *Bursa.*

brush[1] (brush) *n.* **1** An implement having bristles, hair, feathers, wire, or other flexible fibrous material, fixed in a handle or a back, and used for sweeping, scrubbing, painting, cleansing, smoothing, etc. **2** The act of brushing. **3** A light, grazing touch. **4** A skirmish; a short, brisk fight. **5** Brushwork. **6** Any object resembling a brush, as the bushy tail or bushy part of the tail of various animals, especially the fox. **7** *Elect.* **a** A strip of metal, bundle of wire, or bunch of slit metal plates, bearing on the commutator cylinder of a dynamo, for carrying off the current or for an external current through a motor. **b** A brush discharge. **8** A brushlike appearance in certain phenomena of polarized light. —*v.t.* **1** To use a brush on; sweep, polish, smooth, paint, etc., with or as with a brush. **2** To remove with or as with a brush. **3** To touch lightly in passing; touch upon briefly. —*v.i.* **4** To move lightly and quickly, often with a touch: to *brush* past someone. **— to brush aside** To deny consideration to. **— to brush up 1** To refresh one's knowledge of. **2** To renovate; refurbish. **— to brush up against** To come into slight contact with. [<OF *brosse* butcher-broom, brush, ? <Gmc.]

brush[2] (brush) *n.* **1** A growth of small trees and shrubs; hence, wooded country sparsely settled; backwoods. **2** Lopped-off bushes or branches of trees; brushwood. [<OF *broche,* ? <Gmc.]

brush discharge *Electr.* A discharge of low luminosity which issues in brushlike form from the terminals of an electric circuit. Compare CORONA (def. 6).

brushed wool A knit or woven woolen fabric on which a nap has been raised by a process using circular brushes.

brush fire 1 A fire in the brush. **2** A fire built of brushwood.

brush hook A hook for cutting brush.

brush–off (brush′ôf′, -of′) *n. U.S. Colloq.* An abrupt refusal or dismissal.

brush–tail possum (brush′tāl′) A marsupial (*Trichosurus vulpecula fuliginosis*) of Tasmania, about two feet high and largest of the Australian possums.

brush turkey A jungle fowl of Australia or New Guinea; especially, the Australian *Alectura lathami,* about the size of a turkey but having a bright-yellow wattle.

brush wheel A wheel with bristles, buff leather, etc., on its periphery: used to rotate a similar wheel, or for cleaning, polishing, etc.

brush·wood (brush′wo͝od′) *n.* **1** A low thicket; underwood. **2** Cut bushes, or branches.

brush·work (brush′wûrk′) *n.* A painter's characteristic style or way of applying paint with a brush.

brush·y (brush′ē) *adj.* **brush·i·er, brush·i·est 1** Covered with brushwood. **2** Resembling a brush; shaggy; rough; bushy.

Bru·si·lov (broo͞·sē′lôf), **Alexei Alexeivich,** 1853–1926, Russian general in World War I.

brusk (brusk, *esp. Brit.* bro͝osk) *adj.* Rude or curt; abrupt; blunt; rough. See synonyms under BLUFF. Also **brusque.** [<MF *brusque* <Ital. *brusco* rough, rude] **— brusk′ly** *adv.* **— brusk′ness** *n.*

brus·que·rie (brus′kə·rē, *Fr.* brüs·kə·rē′) *n.* Bluntness; bruskness; a brusk act or speech.

Brus·sels (brus′əlz) The capital of Belgium and of the province of Brabant. *French* **Brux·elles** (brü·sel′, brük·sel′); *Flemish* **Brus·sel** (brœs′əl).

Brussels carpet A machine-made worsted carpet of linen or cotton and linen web.

Brussels griffon A toy dog of European origin, having a flat face and shaggy, reddish-brown hair. See BELGIAN GRIFFON, BRABANÇON GRIFFON.

Brussels lace Net lace, made by machine, with designs separately made and appliquéd upon it.

BRUSSELS LACE

Brussels sprouts 1 A cultivated variety of wild cabbage (*Brassica oleracea gemmifera*), with blistered leaves and stems covered with heads like little cabbages. **2** The small edible heads or sprouts of this plant.

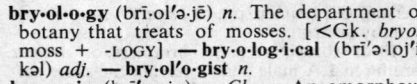

brut (brüt) *adj.* Dry: said of wines. [<F, lit., rough, raw <L *brutus* rough, rude]

Brut (broo͞t) Legendary king of Britain; great-grandson of Aeneas and founder of the British race. See LAYAMON. Also **Brute, Bru′tus.**

bru·tal (broo͞t′l) *adj.* **1** Characteristic of or like a brute; cruel; savage. **2** Unfeeling; rude; coarse. See synonyms under BARBAROUS, BRUTISH. [<L *brutus* stupid] **— bru′tal·ly** *adv.*

bru·tal·i·ty (broo͞·tal′ə·tē) *n. pl.* **·ties 1** The state or quality of being brutal; cruelty. **2** A brutal or cruel act.

bru·tal·ize (broo͞′təl·īz) *v.t.* & *v.i.* **·ized, ·iz·ing** To make or become brutal. **— bru′tal·i·za′tion** *n.*

brute (broo͞t) *n.* **1** Any animal other than man, as a horse, dog, etc. **2** A brutal person. See synonyms under ANIMAL. —*adj.* **1** Wanting the rational faculty; merely animal. **2** Unintelligent; also, sensual; brutal. **3** Merely material; inanimate. ◆ Homophone: *bruit.* [<F *brut* <L *brutus* stupid]

bru·ti·fy (broo͞′tə·fī) *v.t.* & *v.i.* **·fied, ·fy·ing** To brutalize.

brut·ish (broo͞′tish) *adj.* **1** Pertaining to, characteristic of, or resembling brutes. **2** Stupid; irrational; sensual; gross. **— brut′ish·ly** *adv.* **— brut′ish·ness, brut′ism** *n.*

Synonyms: animal, base, beastly, bestial, brutal, brute, carnal, coarse, ignorant, imbruted, insensible, lascivious, sensual, sottish, stolid, stupid, swinish, unintellectual, unspiritual, vile. A *brutish* man simply follows his *animal* instincts, without special inclination to do harm; the *brutal* have always a spirit of malice and cruelty. *Brute* or *animal* simply indicates what a brute or an animal might possess; *animal* leans more to the side of sensuality, *brute* to that of force, as appears in the familiar phrase "*brute* force." Hunger is an *animal* appetite; a *brute* impulse may prompt one to strike a blow in anger. *Bestial* implies an intensified and degrading animalism. *Beastly* refers largely to the outward and visible consequences of excess; as, *beastly* drunkenness. Compare ANIMAL. *Antonyms*: elevated, enlightened, exalted, grand, great, humane, intellectual, intelligent, noble, refined, spiritual.

Brut·ti·um (brut′ē·əm) The ancient Roman name for CALABRIA.

Bru·tus (broo͞′təs), **Marcus Junius,** 85–42 B.C., Roman republican leader, one of Caesar's assassins.

brux·ism (bruk′siz·əm) *n.* A grinding or gnashing of the teeth in sleep or for other than chewing purposes: injurious to dental health. [<Gk. *bruchē* gnashing (of teeth) < *bruchein* gnash]

Bry·an (brī′ən) Variant of BRIAN.

Bry·an (brī′ən), **William Jennings,** 1860–1925, U.S. statesman and orator.

Bry·ansk (brē·ansk′) A city in western Russian S.F.S.R.: also *Briansk.*

Bry·ant (brī′ənt), **William Cullen,** 1794–1878, U.S. poet.

Bryce (brīs), **James,** 1838–1922, Viscount Bryce of Dechmont, British diplomat and writer.

Bryce Canyon National Park (brīs) A region of wide canyons and eroded pinnacles in SW Utah; 56 square miles; established 1928.

Bryn·hild (brün′hilt) In the *Volsunga Saga* and in William Morris's *Sigurd the Volsung,* a Valkyrie who is thrown into an enchanted sleep by Odin, from which she is awakened by Sigurd. Compare BRUNHILD, BRÜNNEHILDE.

bry·o·chore (brī′ə·kôr, -kōr) *n. Ecol.* The tundra region characteristic of Siberia and arctic North America. [<Gk. *bryon* moss + *chorē* country, region]

bry·ol·o·gy (brī·ol′ə·jē) *n.* The department of botany that treats of mosses. [<Gk. *bryon* moss + -LOGY] **— bry·o·log·i·cal** (brī′ə·loj′i·kəl) *adj.* **— bry·ol′o·gist** *n.*

bry·o·nin (brī′ə·nin) *n. Chem.* An amorphous bitter glucoside, $C_{48}H_{66}O_{18}$, contained in the root of bryony: used in medicine.

bry·o·ny (brī′ə·nē) *n.* A common English herb (genus *Bryonia*) of the gourd family, with white or yellowish flowers and black or red berries. [<Gk. *bryōnē*]

bry·o·phyte (brī′ə·fīt) *n. Bot.* Any moss or liverwort of the phylum *Bryophyta.* [Gk. *bryon* moss + -PHYTE] **— bry′o·phyt′ic** (-fit′ik) *adj.*

bry·o·zo·an (brī′ə·zō′ən) *n. Zool.* One of a phylum or class (*Bryozoa*) of small aquatic animals which generate by budding, usually found in permanent colonies: of delicately branched or mosslike formation, or else of flat, crustlike growth. [<Gk. *bryon* moss + *zōon* organism]

Bryth·on (brith′ən) *n.* A Briton; specifically, a Welshman or a Celt of the Brythonic group. [<Welsh]

Bry·thon·ic (bri·thon′ik) *adj.* Of or pertaining to the Brythons or to their languages. —*n.* That branch of the Celtic languages which includes Welsh, Breton, and the extinct Cornish; Cymric: distinguished from *Goidelic.*

Brześć nad Bu·giem (bzheshch näd boo͞′gyem) The Polish name for BREST (def. 2).

bub (bub) *n. Colloq.* A small boy; youngster; young man: used in direct address. [Alter. of BROTHER]

bu·bal (byoo͞′bəl) *n.* A large antelope (genus *Alcelaphus*), especially the North African **bubal hartebeest** (*A. boselaphus*). Also **bu·bale** (byoo͞′bəl), **bu·ba·lis** (byoo͞′bə·lis). [<L *bubalus* <Gk. *boubalos* African antelope. Related to BUFFALO.]

bu·ba·line (byoo͞′bə·līn, -lin) *adj.* **1** Resembling the bubal. **2** Of, pertaining to, or like a buffalo.

bub·ble (bub′əl) *n.* **1** A vesicle of cohesive liquid, filled with air or other gas. **2** A globule of air or other gas in any confined space, as in a liquid or solid substance. **3** Anything unsubstantial; a delusion; cheat; fraud. **4** The process or sound of bubbling. [< *v.*] —*v.* **·bled, ·bling** *v.t.* **1** To form bubbles in, as a liquid. **2** To emit or utter by or as by bubbling: He *bubbled* the good news. **3** *Archaic* To cheat; swindle. —*v.i.* **4** To form bubbles; rise in bubbles. **5** To move or flow with a gurgling sound. **6** To express emotion, joy, etc., with a gurgling sound: He *bubbled* with glee. [ME *buble*; prob. imit.] **— bub′bly** *adj.*

bubble and squeak *Brit.* Cabbage and meat fried together. Also **bub′ble-and-squeak′** *n.*

bub·bler (bub′lər) *n.* A drinking fountain fitted with a vertical nozzle from which water flows in a small stream.

bubble sextant *Aeron.* A sextant in which an artificial horizon is represented by the position of a bubble in an instrument similar to a carpenter's level.

bu·bo (byoo͞′bō) *n. pl.* **bu·boes** *Pathol.* An inflammatory swelling of a lymph gland in the groin, especially one due to venereal infection. [<LL <Gk. *boubōn* groin] **— bu·bon·ic** (byoo͞·bon′ik) *adj.*

bubonic plague *Pathol.* A malignant, contagious, epidemic disease, characterized by fever, vomiting, diarrhea, and buboes: it is caused by a bacterium of the genus *Pasteurella* transmitted to man by fleas which have been infected by rats.

bu·bon·o·cele (byoo͞·bon′ə·sēl) *n. Pathol.* Inguinal hernia. [<Gk. *boubōnokēlē* < *boubōn* groin + *kēlē* abscess]

Bu·ca·ra·man·ga (boo͞′kä·rä·mäng′gä) A city in north central Colombia.

buc·cal (buk′əl) *adj. Anat.* **1** Of or pertaining to the cheek: the *buccal* artery. **2** Pertaining to the mouth; oral. [<L *bucca* cheek]

buc·ca·neer (buk′ə·nir′) *n.* **1** A pirate or freebooter. **2** One of the piratical rovers of the 17th and 18th centuries who preyed upon the Spaniards, along the Spanish coasts of America. See synonyms under ROBBER. [<F *boucanier,* orig. one of the hunters of wild oxen in Haiti, who later turned to piracy <Tupian *boucan* a frame for the smoking and curing of meat]

buc·ci·na·tor (buk′sə·nā′tər) *n. Anat.* A muscle

of the middle cheek, used in blowing. [<L, trumpeter <*buccina* trumpet]

Bu·cen·taur (byōo·sen′tôr) *n.* **1** The state barge of Venice, used by the Doge on Ascension Day. **2** A mythical monster, half bull and half man. [<Ital. *bucentoro,* ? <Med. Gk. *boukentauros* bucentaur < Gk. *bous* bull + *kentauros* centaur; with ref. to the vessel's figurehead]

BUCENTAUR

Bu·ceph·a·lus (byōo·sef′ə·ləs) The war horse of Alexander the Great. [<L <Gk. *boukephalos* bull-headed < *bous* bull, ox + *kephalē* head]

Bu·cer (bōo′tsər), **Martin,** 1491–1551, German Lutheran reformer: also *Butzer.*

Buch·an (buk′ən), **John,** 1875–1940, first Baron Tweedsmuir, Scottish writer and statesman.

Bu·chan·an (byōo·kan′ən), **James,** 1791–1868, president of the United States 1857–61.

Bu·cha·rest (bōo′kə·rest, byōo′-) The capital of Rumania. *Rumanian* **Bu·cu·res·ti** (bōo·kōo·resht′)

Buch·en·wald (bookh′ən·wôld, *Ger.* bookh′ən·vält) Site of a notorious Nazi concentration and extermination camp near Weimar, Germany.

Buch·man·ism (book′mən·iz′əm) *n.* A religious movement founded by **Frank Buchman,** 1878–1961, U.S. evangelist: also called *Oxford Group* movement. — **Buch′man·ite** (-īt) *n.*

Buch·ner (bookh′nər), **Eduard,** 1860–1917, German chemist.

buck¹ (buk) *n.* **1** The male of certain animals, as of antelopes, deer, goats, rabbits, and rats. **2** A dashing fellow; a young blood. **3** An adult male Negro or Indian. — *v.i.* **1** To leap upward suddenly and come down with the legs stiff, as a horse or pack-animal, in an attempt to dislodge rider or burden. **2** *U.S. Colloq.* To resist stubbornly; object. **3** *U.S. Colloq.* To move with jerks and jolts: said of vehicles. **4** To provide resistance against which a rivet may be driven or some other pounding or pushing work done. — *v.t.* **5** To throw (a rider) by bucking. **6** *U.S. Colloq.* To butt with the head. **7** *U.S. Colloq.* To resist stubbornly; oppose. **8** To provide resistance for pounding or pushing (a rivet, etc.). **9** In football, to charge into (the opponent's line) with the ball. — **to buck up** *Colloq.* To encourage or become encouraged. [Fusion of OE *buc* he-goat and *bucca* male deer]

buck² (buk) *n.* **1** A sawhorse. **2** A padded frame in the shape of a sawhorse, used by gymnasts. [<Du. *zaagbok* sawbuck]

buck³ (buk) *n.* **1** A buckskin, formerly taken as a standard of value by North American Indians. **2** *U.S. Slang* A dollar.

buck⁴ (buk) *n. Brit.* Suds or lye, for washing clothes; also, the clothes washed. [< *v.*] — *v.t. Dial.* To wash or bleach in lye. [ME *bouken.* Akin to LG *büken* steep in lye]

buck⁵ (buk) *n.* **1** In card games, an object placed before a player as a reminder of his turn to deal. **2** In poker, a marker occasionally put into a jackpot, indicating that he who receives the buck must order another jackpot when it is his deal. — **to pass the buck** *U.S. Colloq.* To shift responsibility, blame, etc., from oneself to someone else. [Origin uncertain]

Buck (buk), **Dudley,** 1839–1909, U.S. composer. — **Pearl S.,** 1892–1973, U.S. novelist.

buck-and-wing (buk′ən·wing′) *n.* An intricate, fast tap dance.

buck·a·roo (buk′ə·rōo, buk′ə·rōo′) *n.* A cowboy. Also **buck·ay·ro** (buk·ā′rō). [Alter. of Sp. *vaquero* cowboy]

buck·bean (buk′bēn′) *n.* A perennial herb (*Menyanthes trifoliata*) of the gentian family, having racemed white or reddish flowers: also called *bogbean.*

buck·ber·ry (buk′ber·ē, -bər·ē) *n.* **1** A small, wild, black huckleberry (*Gaylussacia ursina*) native in SE United States. **2** The deerberry

(*Vaccineum stamineum*) common in eastern North America.

buck·board (buk′bôrd′, -bōrd′) *n.* A light, four-wheeled, horse-drawn vehicle having a long flexible board in place of body and springs. Also **buck′wag·on.**

BUCKBOARD

[<BUCK, *v.* (def. 3) + BOARD]

buck·een (buk·ēn′) *n.* In Ireland, formerly, a young man of the impoverished gentry, or a younger son of the poorer aristocracy who aped the wealthy.

buck·er (buk′ər) *n.* **1** One who or that which bucks. **2** *U.S. Slang* One who bolts from a political party.

buck·et (buk′it) *n.* **1** A deep cylindrical vessel, with a bail, for dipping or carrying liquids; a pail. **2** As much as a bucket will hold: also **buck′et·ful.** **3** A compartment on a water wheel, or the like. **4** A piston, as in a lifting pump, with a valve opening upward. — *v.t. & v.i.* **1** To draw or carry in a bucket. **2** *Colloq.* To ride (a horse) hard. **3** To move along rapidly. — **to kick the bucket** *Slang* To die. [? <OF *buket* kind of tub; infl. by OE *bucc* pitcher]

bucket seat A single, low, often adjustable seat with a rounded back: used in racing and sports cars, airplanes, etc.

buck·et-shop (buk′it·shop′) *n.* An office for gambling in fractional lots of stocks, grain, etc., with no delivery of securities or commodities sold or purchased.

buck·eye (buk′ī′) *n.* **1** The horse chestnut of the United States. **2** The glossy brown seed or nut of this tree. [<BUCK¹ + EYE]

Buck·eye (buk′ī′) *n.* A native or inhabitant of Ohio.

Buckeye State Nickname of OHIO.

buck fever *U.S. Colloq.* The state of excitement felt by an inexperienced hunter when first sighting game.

buck·horn (buk′hôrn′) *n.* The horn of a buck deer: often used to make knife handles, buttons, etc.

buck·hound (buk′hound′) *n.* **1** A large hound formerly used for hunting bucks. **2** The Scottish deerhound: also called *staghound.*

buck·ie (buk′ē) *n. Scot.* **1** A seashell, as that of the whelk. **2** A mischievous fellow.

Buck·ing·ham (buk′ing·əm) A county in southern England; 749 square miles; county seat, Aylesbury. Also **Buck′ing·ham·shire′** (-shir′); shortened form **Bucks.**

Buck·ing·ham (buk′ing·əm), **Duke of,** 1592–1628, George Villiers, English courtier. — **Duke of,** 1628–87, George Villiers, English statesman, son of the preceding.

buck·ish (buk′ish) *adj.* Dapper; foppish.

buck·le¹ (buk′əl) *n.* **1** A metal frame with movable tongue for fastening together two loose ends, as of straps, etc. **2** An ornament for shoes, etc., devised like a buckle. — *v.t.* **1** To fasten or attach with or as with a buckle. **2** To apply (oneself) assiduously. — *v.i.* **3** To apply oneself vigorously: often with *down* to or *to.* **4** To fight; grapple. [<F *boucle* cheekstrap, boss of a shield <L *buccula,* dim. of *bucca* cheek]

buck·le² (buk′əl) *v.t. & v.i.* **·led, ·ling** To bend under pressure; warp, curl, or crumple. — *n.* A bend; in mechanics, a permanent distortion or bend. [<F *boucler* bulge]

Buck·le (buk′əl), **Henry Thomas,** 1821–62, English historian.

buck·ler (buk′lər) *n.* **1** A shield; especially, a small round shield. **2** One who defends or protects; one who shields. **3** A protective covering on various animals. — *v.t.* To shield, as with a buckler; defend; protect. [OF *boucler* having a boss]

Buck·ley's chance (buk′lēz) *Austral. Slang* No chance at all, or very little chance, of success.

Buck·ner (buk′nər), **Simon Bolivar,** 1823–1914, American Confederate general and politician. — **Simon Bolivar,** 1886–1945, U.S. general, son of the preceding.

buck·o (buk′ō) *n. pl.* **·oes 1** A bully; blusterer. **buck private** *U.S. Colloq.* An enlisted man of the lowest rank in the U.S. Army.

buck·ra (buk′rə) *adj.* White, or belonging to a white man; like or characteristic of white people: a term used among the Negroes of Africa, the West Indies, and the southern United States: a *buckra* house, *buckra* manners. — *n.* A white man. [<Efik *mbākara*]

buck·ram (buk′rəm) *n.* **1** A coarse, glue-sized cotton fabric, for stiffening garments, and for bookbinding. **2** Stiffness of manner. **3** Originally, a fine linen or cotton fabric. — *adj.* Of or like buckram; stiff; precise. — *v.t.* To stiffen with or as with buckram. [Cf. OF *boquerant*]

buck·saw (buk′sô′) *n.* A saw set in an adjustable H-shaped frame, used for sawing firewood on a buck.

buck·shee (buk′shē) *adj. Brit. Slang* Gratis. [See BAKSHEESH]

buck·shot (buk′shot′) *n.* Shot of a large size, used in hunting deer and other large game.

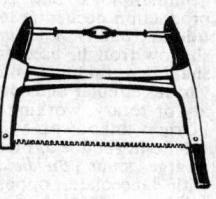

BUCKSAW

buck·skin (buk′skin′) *n.* **1** The skin of a buck: also **buck skin.** **2** A soft, strong, grayish-yellow leather, formerly made from deerskins, now chiefly from sheepskins. **3** *pl.* Breeches or a suit made of such skin. **4** A person clad in such skin; especially, one of the American soldiers in the Revolution. **5** A horse of a buckskin color. **6** A cream-colored woolen cloth of close weave: also **buckskin cloth.**

buck·thorn (buk′thôrn′) *n.* A shrub or small tree of the genus *Rhamnus,* having alternate pinnately veined leaves and axillary flowers. — **southern buckthorn** A tree (*Bumelia lycioides*) of the southern United States. [<BUCK¹ + THORN]

buck·tooth (buk′tōoth′) *n. pl.* **·teeth** A projecting tooth. [<BUCK¹ + TOOTH]

buck·toothed (buk′tōotht′, -tōothd′) *adj.* Having projecting teeth.

buck·wheat (buk′hwēt′) *n.* A plant of the genus *Fagopyrum,* yielding triangular seeds used as fodder and for flour. **2** Its seeds. **3** The flour. [OE *bōc* beech + WHEAT, from resemblance of seeds to beech seeds]

buck·y diaphragm (buk′ē) In roentgenography, an apparatus for preventing secondary X-rays from affecting the plate, thus ensuring a clearer picture. [after Gustav *Bucky,* 1880–1963, German-American roentgenologist]

bu·col·ic (byōo·kol′ik) *adj.* Pertaining to or like shepherds or herdsmen; pastoral; rustic: also **bu·col′i·cal.** — *n.* **1** A pastoral poem. **2** A rustic; farmer: humorous usage. See synonyms under RUSTIC. [<L *bucolicus* <Gk. *boukolikos* < *boukolos* herdsman < *bous* ox] — **bu·col′i·cal·ly** *adv.*

Bu·co·vi·na (bōo′kə·vē′nə) The Rumanian spelling of BUKOVINA.

bud¹ (bud) *n.* **1** *Bot.* **a** An undeveloped stem, branch, or shoot of a plant, with rudimentary leaves or unexpanded flowers. **b** The act or stage of budding. **2** *Zool.* A budlike projection, as in polyps, etc., developing into a new individual; also, a budlike part. **3** Any immature person or thing. — **to nip in the bud** To stop in the initial stage. — *v.* **bud·ded, bud·ding** *v.t.* **1** To put forth as buds. **2** To graft by inserting a bud of (a tree or plant) into the stock of another type of tree or plant. **3** To cause to bud. — *v.i.* **4** To put forth buds. **5** To begin to grow or develop. [ME *budde;* origin uncertain] — **bud′der** *n.*

bud² (bud) *n. U.S. Colloq.* A term of direct address to a man or boy. Also **buddy.** [Alter. of BROTHER]

Bu·da·pest (bōo′də·pest) The capital of Hungary, on the Danube.

Bud·dha (bood′ə, bōo′də) *n.* Literally, the Enlightened; an incarnation of selflessness, virtue, and wisdom; specifically, Gautama Siddhartha, 563?–483? B.C., the founder of Buddhism, regarded by his followers as the last of a series of deified religious teachers of central and eastern Asia. [<Skt.]

Bud·dhism (bood′iz·əm, bōo′diz-) *n.* A mystical and ascetic religious faith of eastern Asia, founded in northern India by Buddha in the sixth century B.C., teaching that Nirvana,

which is the conquest of self and subsequent freedom from sorrow and mortality, is reached by the Eightfold Path of right belief, right resolution, right speech, right action, right living, right effort, right thinking, and peace of mind through meditation. — **Bud′·dhist** *adj.* & *n.* — **Bud·dhis′tic** or **·ti·cal** *adj.*

bud·ding (bud′ing) *n.* **1** *Zool.* A mode of asexual reproduction, as in various polyps, ascidians, etc., in which a small part of the substance of the parent is protruded as a bud or gemma and develops into a new organism; gemmation. **2** *Bot.* A similar mode of reproduction occurring in some cryptogams.

bud·dle (bud′l) *n. Mining* **1** An inclined shallow trough, used for separating ores by shaking or raking in running water. **2** One of various circular and conical machines, stationary or rotary, working on the same principle. [Origin unknown]

bud·dle·ia (bud·lē′ə, bud′lē·ə) *n.* Any plant of a large genus *(Buddleia)* of shrubs or herbs, with lanceolate, opposite leaves and small yellow or purplish flowers: native in warm regions of America, Asia, and southern Africa: also called *butterfly bush.* [after Adam *Buddle,* died 1715, English botanist]

bud·dy (bud′ē) *n. pl.* **·dies** *Colloq.* **1** Brother. **2** Pal; chum; companion. **3** Little boy: used in direct address. [See BUD[2]]

Bu·dën·ny (bo͞o·den′ē, *Russian* bo͞o·dyôn′i), **Semyon Mikhailovich,** born 1883?, Russian general in Revolution of 1917 and marshal in World War II.

budge[1] (buj) *v.t.* & *v.i.* **budged, budg·ing** To move or stir slightly: usually with the negative. — *n.* A slight movement. [<F *bouger* stir, move]

budge[2] (buj) *n.* **1** Lambskin with the wool side out: formerly used for edgings on the gowns of scholastics, etc. **2** A leather bag made with the wool side out. — *adj.* **1** Trimmed with budge, or wearing budge. **2** Hence, pompous; imposing; formal. [Origin uncertain]

budg·et (buj′it) *n.* **1** A statement of probable revenue and expenditure and of financial proposals for the ensuing year as presented to or passed upon by a legislative body. **2** A summary of probable income for a given period, as of a family or an individual, with approximate allowances for certain expenditures over that period. **3** A collection or store, as of news, anecdotes, etc. **4** A small sack or its contents; hence, a loose bundle. — *v.t.* **1** To determine in advance the expenditure of (time, money, etc.) over a period of time. **2** To put on or into a budget: He *budgeted* his trip. [<F *bougette,* dim. of *bouge* <L *bulga* leather bag] — **budg·et·ar·y** (buj′ə·ter′ē) *adj.* — **budg′et·er** *n.*

Bud·weis (bo͞ot′vīs) The German name for ČESKÉ BUDEJOVICE.

Bu·ell (byo͞o′əl), **Don Carlos,** 1818–98, U.S. general.

Bue·na Vis·ta (bwā′nə vis′tə) A village in SE Coahuila, Mexico; scene of United States victory, 1847, in the Mexican War.

Bue·nos Ai·res (bwā′nəs ī′riz, bō′nəs âr′ēz) **1** A province in eastern Argentina; 116,322 square miles; capital, La Plata. **2** The largest city of Latin America, a federal district and port on the La Plata, capital of Argentina; 77 square miles: a native of the city is known as a *Porteño.*

buff[1] (buf) *n.* **1** A thick, soft, flexible leather, undyed and unglazed, made from the skins of buffalo, elk, oxen, etc: also **buff leather.** **2** Its color, a light yellow. **3** A coat made of buff leather. **4** *Colloq.* The bare skin; the nude: in the *buff.* **5** A stick or wheel covered with leather, velvet, etc., and used with emery and other powders in polishing: also **buff′er.** — *adj.* Made of, or of the color of, buff leather; brownish-yellow. — *v.t.* **1** To clean or polish with or as with a buff. **2** In leather-making, to shave, as cowskin, on the grain side until very thin, producing an imitation of calf leather. **3** To make buff in color. [<F *buffle* buffalo]

buff[2] (buf) *n.* A blow; buffet: only in *blind-man's-buff.* — *v.t.* **1** To deaden the shock of. **2** To strike; buffet. — *v.i.* **3** To act as a buffer. [<OF *buffe* blow]

buff[3] (buf) *n.* **1** Originally, a voluntary, unofficial auxiliary of a fire department. **2** One who rushes to attend fires. **3** An enthusiast in any special field, who attends all possible events: a theater *buff.* [? Special use of BUFF[1]]

buf·fa·lo (buf′ə·lō) *n. pl.* **·loes** or **·los** **1** A large Old World ox, now extensively domesticated, one of which, the African **Cape buffalo** *(Syncerus caffer),* has horns that broaden at the base. ◆ Collateral adjective: *bubaline.* **2** The Indian water buffalo. **3** The North American bison. **4** A buffalo robe. **5** A buffalo fish. **6** *Naut.* One of the bulwarks on each side of the stem of the forecastle deck in the extreme bow. — *v.t. U.S. Slang* To overawe; hoodwink. [<Ital. <L *bufalus,* var. of *bubalus* <Gk. *boubalos* buffalo. Related to BUBAL.]

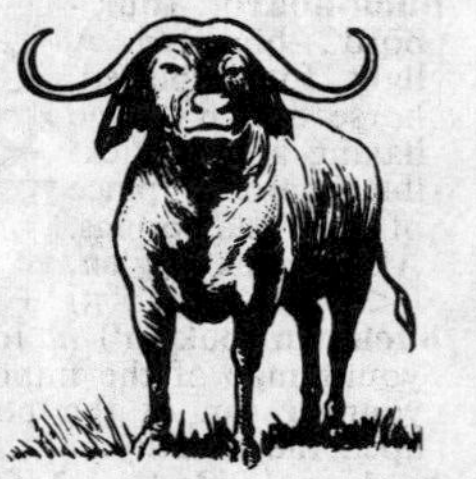

AFRICAN OR CAPE BUFFALO

Buf·fa·lo (buf′ə·lō) A city in western New York at the eastern end of Lake Erie.

buf·fa·lo·ber·ry (buf′ə·lō·ber′ē) *n.* The edible crimson berry of either of two American shrubs, the thorny silverleaf *(Shepherdia argentea)* or the russet buffaloberry *(S. canadensis).*

Buffalo Bill See CODY, WILLIAM F.

buffalo bug The carpet beetle. Also **buffalo moth.**

buffalo fish A large, carplike, fresh-water fish (genus *Ictiobus*) of the sucker family, native in North America: named from its humped back, resembling that of a buffalo.

buffalo gnat A small, black, winged insect (*Simulium* and related genera) which attacks all warm-blooded animals, usually in swarms: also called *black fly.*

buf·fa·lo·grass (buf′ə·lō·gras′, -gräs′) *n.* **1** A low, creeping grass *(Buchloë dactyloides)* covering large prairies east of the Rocky Mountains, highly esteemed for winter forage. **2** The curly mesquite *(Hilaria belangeri)* of the SW United States and Central America.

Buffalo Indian A Plains Indian.

buffalo robe The skin of the North American bison, dressed with the hair on for use as a lap robe.

buff·er[1] (buf′ər) *n.* One who or that which buffs. [<BUFF[1], *v.*]

buff·er[2] (buf′ər) *n.* A device for lessening the shock of concussion. [<BUFF[2], *v.*]

buffer state A small country situated between two larger rival powers regarded as less likely to open hostilities with each other because they have no common boundary.

buf·fet[1] (bo͞o·fā′, *Brit.* buf′it) *n.* **1** A sideboard; also, a cupboard for china, glassware, etc. **2** A counter or bar for serving lunch or refreshments; also, a public lunchroom. [<F]

buf·fet[2] (buf′it) *v.t.* **1** To strike or cuff, as with the hand. **2** To strike repeatedly; knock about. **3** To force (a way) by pushing or striking, as through a crowd. — *v.i.* **4** To fight; struggle. **5** To force a way. — *n.* A blow; cuff; assault. [<OF *buffet,* dim. of *buffe* blow, slap] — **buf′fet·er** *n.*

buf·fet car (bo͞o·fā′) A parlor car or sleeping car on a train equipped with a small kitchen.

buf·fet supper (bo͞o·fā′) A light meal at which the guests serve themselves. Also **buffet lunch.**

buff·ing wheel (buf′ing) Buff[1] (def. 5).

buf·fle·head (buf′əl·hed′) *n.* A North American duck *(Charitonetta albeola)* having the feathers of the head elongated, and with plumage black above and white below: also called *butterball.* [<F *buffle* buffalo + HEAD]

buf·fo (bo͞o′fō, *Ital.* bo͞of′fō) *n. pl.* **·fi** (-fē) A comic actor in opera; comic singer: usually a bass. [<Ital., foolish, comic]

Buf·fon (bü·fôṅ′), **Comte de,** 1707–88, Georges Louis Leclerc, French naturalist.

buf·foon (bu·fo͞on′) *n.* A clown; one given to jokes, coarse pranks, etc. [<F *buffon* <Ital. *buffone* clown <*buffa* jest] — **buf·foon′er·y** *n.* — **buf·foon′ish** *adj.*

buff·skin (buf′skin′) *n.* Buff[1] (def. 1).

buff·y (buf′ē) *adj.* **1** Of a buff color. **2** Characterized by or resembling buff. **3** Designating or pertaining to a buffy coat.

buffy coat *Physiol.* A yellowish or grayish coat formed on coagulating blood.

Bu·fo (byo͞o′fō) *n.* A genus of toads. [<L *bufo* toad]

bug[1] (bug) *n.* **1** Any of an order *(Hemiptera)* or suborder *(Heteroptera)* of terrestrial or aquatic insects with piercing, sucking mouth parts, wingless or with two pairs of wings, the anterior pair typically horny with an apical membranous part, as the stinkbug, squashbug, bedbug. For illustrations see under INSECT. **2** Loosely, any insect or small arthropod. **3** *Often pl. U.S. Colloq.* Any small but troublesome defect in the design, structure, or operation of an instrument, motor, machine, or the like. **4** *Slang* An enthusiast; a monomaniac. **5** *Colloq.* A pathogenic microorganism. **6** *Colloq.* A miniature electronic microphone, used in wiretapping, etc. — *v.* **bugged, bug·ging** *v.i.* **1** To stare; stick out: said of eyes. — *v.t.* **2** *Colloq.* To fix an electronic eavesdropping device in (a room, etc.) or to a (wire, etc.). **3** *U.S. Slang* To annoy or anger; also, to bewilder or puzzle. — **to bug off** *U.S. Slang* Go away! Get lost! — **to bug out** *U.S. Slang* To quit, especially hastily or ignominiously. [Origin unknown]

bug[2] (bug) *n. Obs.* A specter; bugbear. [ME *bugge* scarecrow. Cf. Welsh *bwg* ghost.]

Bug (bo͝og) **1** A river in southern Ukrainian S.S.R., flowing 532 miles SE to the Black Sea; also **Southern Bug.** *Russian* **Yuzh·nyy Bug** (yo͝ozh′nē bo͝ok′). **2** A river rising in western Ukrainian S.S.R., flowing about 500 miles NW to form the Poland–U.S.S.R. border: also **Western Bug.** *Russian* **Za·pad·nyy Bug** (zä′pəd·nē bo͝ok′).

bug·a·boo (bug′ə·bo͞o) *n. pl.* **·boos** A bugbear. [<BUG[2] + BOO]

Bu·gan·da (byo͞o·gan′də) A kingdom under British protection, comprising a province of southern Uganda; 25,631 square miles; capital, Kampala.

bug·bane (bug′bān′) *n.* A perennial herb (genus *Cimicifuga*) of the crowfoot family, as the **European bugbane,** *C. foetida,* used to drive away vermin, or the **American bugbane,** *C. americana.*

bug·bear (bug′bâr′) *n.* An imaginary object of terror; a specter: also called *bugaboo.* [<BUG[2] + BEAR[2]]

bug·eye (bug′ī′) *n. Naut.* A centerboard sailing vessel of shallow draft, fore-and-aft rigged on two raked masts: used in dredging oysters in Chesapeake Bay.

bug-eyed (bug′īd′) *adj. Slang* With the eyes bulging out, as from astonishment.

bug·ger (bug′ər) *n.* **1** One guilty of sodomy. **2** A contemptible person. **3** *U.S. Slang* A chap; person; child: used in mild or humorous disparagement. [<OF *boulgre* <Med. L *Bulgarus* a Bulgarian; with ref. to a Bulgarian sect of heretics (11th c.) to whom sodomy was imputed]

bug·ger·y (bug′ər·ē) *n.* Sodomy.

bug·gy[1] (bug′ē) *n. pl.* **·gies** **1** A light, four-wheeled, horse-drawn vehicle with a hood. **2** The caboose of a freight train. [Origin uncertain]

bug·gy[2] (bug′ē) *adj.* **·gi·er, ·gi·est** **1** Infested with bugs. **2** *Slang* Crazy. — **bug′gi·ness** *n.*

bug·house (bug′hous′) *U.S. Slang* *n.* An asylum for the insane. — *adj.* Crazy; insane.

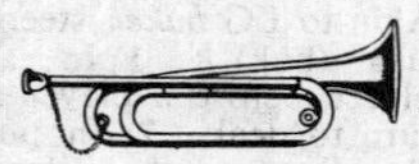

BUGLE

Bu·gin·vil·lae·a (bo͞o′gən·vil′ē·ə) *n.* Bougainvillea.

bu·gle[1] (byo͞o′gəl) *n.* **1** A brass wind instrument resembling a horn or trumpet, with or without keys or valves. **2** A huntsman's horn. — *v.t.* & *v.i.* **bu·gled, bu·gling** **1** To summon with or as with a bugle. **2** To sound a bugle. [<OF <L *buculus,* dim. of *bos* ox; because first made from the horns of oxen] — **bu′gler** *n.*

bu·gle[2] (byo͞o′gəl) *n.* A tube-shaped glass bead, commonly black, used for ornamenting garments. — *adj.* Of, resembling, or adorned with bugles. [Origin uncertain] — **bu′gled** *adj.*

bu·gle[3] (byo͞o′gəl) *n.* A British plant of the mint family (genus *Ajuga*), especially the **carpet bugle** *(A. reptans).* [<F <LL *bugula*]

bu·gle·weed (byo͞o′gəl·wēd′) *n.* Any of several herbs (genus *Lycopus*); especially, **sweet Virginia bugleweed** *(L. virginicus)* used medicinally, and **bitter American bugleweed** *(L. americanus).*

bug·light (bug′līt′) *n.* **1** A small lighthouse. **2** A small flashlight.

bu·gloss (byo͞o′glos, -glôs) *n.* Any of various genera (as *Anchusa, Lycopsis,* and *Echium*) of coarse, hairy, boraginaceous plants having funnel-shaped, blue flowers. Also called *alkanet, oxtongue.* [<F *buglosse* <L *buglossa* <Gk. *bouglossos* <*bous* bull, ox + *glossa* tongue]

bug·seed (bug′sēd′) *n.* A low, branching annual herb *(Corispermum hyssopifolium)* of the goosefoot family, the flat seeds of which resemble bugs.

bu·hach (byo͞o′hach) *n.* The powdered flower heads of pyrethrum, used as an insect powder. [Origin uncertain]

buhl (bo͞ol) *n.* Metal or tortoise shell inlaid in furniture; also, cabinetwork so decorated. Also **buhl′work′.** [after A. C. *Boulle,* 1642–1732, French cabinetmaker]

buhr·stone (bûr′stōn′) *n.* Burrstone.

build (bild) *v.* **built** (*Archaic* **build·ed**), **build·ing** *v.t.* **1** To construct, erect, or make by assembling separate parts or materials. **2** To establish and increase: to *build* a business. **3** To found; make a basis for: We *build* our hopes on peace. **4** In cards, to form sequences or combinations of cards, as by suit or number. —*v.i.* **5** To be in the business of building. **6** To base or form an idea, theory, etc.: with *on* or *upon.* **—to build up 1** To renew; strengthen, as health or physique. **2** To fill, as an area, with houses. See synonyms under CONSTRUCT. —*n.* **1** The manner or style in which anything is built; form; figure. **2** A cumulative increase in power and effectiveness, as of a dramatic performance as the climax is approached. [OE *byldan* <*bold* house]

build·er (bil′dər) *n.* **1** One who or that which builds. **2** One who follows the occupation of building, or who controls or directs the actual work of building. **3** An abrasive or other substance added to soap to increase its cleansing effect.

build·ing (bil′ding) *n.* **1** An edifice for any use; that which is built, as a dwelling house, barn, etc. **2** The occupation, business, or art of constructing. **3** The act or process of erecting or establishing. See synonyms under HOUSE.

building and loan association A society, usually an incorporated joint-stock company, organized to aid some of its members in building homes or other edifices with money lent or subscribed by all the members.

build-up (bild′up′) *n.* **1** A gradual accumulation or increase, as of buildings. **2** *Mil.* The accumulation of troops or materiel in a given area. **3** In forestry, the steady acceleration of a fire under conditions favoring its spread and in spite of attempts at effective control. **4** *Colloq.* An enhancement of reputation, as by praise or favorable publicity.

built-in (bilt′in′) *adj.* Made part of or permanently attached to the structure, as of a house or room.

buird·ly (bürd′lē) *adj. Scot.* Large and well made; stately; burly; stalwart; sturdy; stout.

Buis·son (bwē·sôṅ′), **Ferdinand,** 1841–1932, French educator.

Bui·ten·zorg (bœi′tən·zôrkh) The Dutch name for BOGOR.

Bu·ka (bo͞o′kə) One of the Solomon Islands, comprising, with Bougainville, a part of the United Nations Trust Territory of New Guinea; 220 square miles.

Bu·kha·ra (bo͞o·kä′rə) A division of central Uzbek S.S.R.; 49,600 square miles; capital, Bukhara; also *Bokhara.*

Bu·kha·rin (bo͞o·khä′rin), **Nicolai Ivanovich,** 1888–1938, U.S.S.R. revolutionist and editor; executed for treason.

Bu·ko·vi·na (bo͞o′kə·vē′nə) A region of eastern Europe in NE Rumania and western Ukrainian S.S.R.; formerly an Austrian duchy: Rumanian *Bucovina. German* **Bu·ko·wi·na** (bo͞o′kō·vē′nä).

Bul (bo͞ol) See HESHWAN.

Bu·la·wa·yo (bo͞o′lə·wä′yō) A city in SW Zimbabwe also *Buluwayo.*

bulb (bulb) *n.* **1** *Bot.* **a** A leaf bud comprised of a cluster of thickened, scalelike leaves, growing usually underground and sending forth roots from the lower face, as the onion or lily. **b** Any of several underground stems resembling bulbs, as the corm of a crocus or a dahlia tuber. **2** Any protuberance resembling a plant bulb, as the bulb at the root of a hair (see illustration under HAIR), the enlarged end of a thermometer tube, etc. **3** *Electr.* An evacuated glass container holding the filament of an incandescent electric light. **4** A vacuum tube. **5** *Anat.* The medulla oblongata. [<L *bulbus* <Gk. *bolbos* bulbous root] **—bul·ba·ceous** (bul·bā′·shəs) *adj.* **—bul′bous** *adj.*

bul·bar (bul′bər) *adj.* Of or pertaining to a bulb, especially the bulb of the medulla oblongata: *bulbar* paralysis.

bul·bif·er·ous (bul·bif′ər·əs) *adj.* Producing bulbs. [<NL *bulbifer* <L *bulbus* bulb + *ferre* bear]

bulb·i·form (bul′bə·fôrm) *adj.* Having the form of a bulb.

bul·bil (bul′bil) *n.* **1** A small bulb. **2** *Bot.* An aerial, deciduous, fleshy leaf bud, capable of developing into a new individual, as in the tiger lily: also **bul′bel** (-bel). [<NL *bulbillus,* dim. of *bulbus* bulb]

bul·bul (bo͞ol′bo͞ol) *n.* **1** Any of various thrushlike birds (family *Pycnonotidae*) of the tropics of the Old World, with short legs, rounded wings, and typically dull coloration. **2** The Persian nightingale (genus *Luscinia*). [<Persian <Arabic]

Bul·finch (bo͞ol′finch), **Charles,** 1763–1844, American architect. **—Thomas,** 1796–1867, compiler of myths; son of the preceding.

Bul·ga·nin (bo͞ol·gä′nyin), **Nikolai Aleksandrovich,** 1895–1975, U.S.S.R. marshal; premier 1955–58.

Bul·gar (bul′gär, bo͞ol′-) *n.* **1** A Bulgarian. **2** The Bulgarian language.

Bul·gar·i·a (bul·gâr′ē·ə, bo͞ol-) A state in SE Europe; 142,471 square miles; capital, Sofia: officially **People's Republic of Bulgaria.** *Bulgarian* **Bl·ga·ri·ya** (bul·gä′rē·yä).

Bul·gar·i·an (bul·gâr′ē·ən, bo͞ol-) *adj.* Of or pertaining to Bulgaria, the Bulgarians, or to their language. —*n.* **1** A native or citizen of Bulgaria. **2** One of an ancient people considered to be of Mongolian stock, who, in the 7th century, migrated from the region west of the Ural Mountains and north of the Caspian Sea, and settled Bulgaria. **3** The language of the Bulgarians, belonging to the South Slavic group of the Balto-Slavic languages.

bulge (bulj) *v.t.* & *v.i.* **bulged, bulg·ing** To make or be protuberant; swell out. [<*n.*] —*n.* **1** The most convex part, as of a cask. **2** A protuberant part; swelling. **3** *U.S. Colloq.* Advantage; especially, a slight but telling advantage. **—to get the bulge on** *U.S. Colloq.* To gain the advantage over. [<OF *boulge*] **—bulg′y** *adj.* **—bulg′i·ness** *n.*

Bulge (bulj), **Battle of the** The last major German counter-offensive of World War II, repulsed in January, 1945, during which the line of combat formed a deep bulge on the Belgian front.

bulg·er (bul′jər) *n.* **1** In golf, a driver or a brassy having a convex face: also **bulger driver. 2** A stick used in hockey, having a flat-faced, heavy head with a convex back.

bu·lim·i·a (byo͞o·lim′ē·ə) *n. Pathol.* Insatiable appetite, or the disease of which this is a characteristic. [<Gk. *boulimia* great hunger <*bou-* ox-like, great + *limos* hunger] **—bu·lim′ic** *adj.*

bulk[1] (bulk) *n.* **1** The substance or body of anything material considered with reference to its magnitude, as of a ship, a man, an elephant, etc. **2** A large body; mass; volume; size. **3** Greater or principal part; main body; majority. **4** *Naut.* The whole space in a ship's hold for stowing goods; also, the whole cargo. See synonyms under MAGNITUDE, MASS. **—in bulk** Loose; in mass; not in boxes, bales, sacks, or packages. —*v.i.* **1** To have an appearance of largeness or weight; be of importance: The weather *bulks* large in our plans. **2** *Obs.* To swell; expand: with *up.* —*v.t.* **3** To cause to expand or grow large: with *out.* [Cf. ON *būlki* heap, cargo, and Dan. *bulk* lump]

bulk[2] (bulk) *n.* A projecting part of a building; a framework in front of a shop; stall. [?<ON *bōlkr* beam]

bulk·age (bul′kij) *n. Physiol.* The non-assimilable accessory of food elements, such as vegetable fiber, that stimulates intestinal activity.

bulk·head (bulk′hed′) *n.* **1** *Naut.* One of various partitions in a vessel, to separate it into rooms or to divide the hold into watertight compartments. **2** A partition of stone or wood to keep back earth, gas, etc., as in a mine. **3** A horizontal or sloping door outside a house, giving entrance to the cellar. **4** A framework or casing to cover a staircase or elevator shaft. **—bulk′head′ed** *adj.*

bulk·y (bul′kē) *adj.* **bulk·i·er, bulk·i·est** Huge; large; massive; unwieldy. **—bulk′i·ly** *adv.* **—bulk′i·ness** *n.*

bull[1] (bo͞ol) *n.* **1** The male of domestic cattle or of some other animals, as of the elephant, moose, giraffe, whale, seal, etc. ◆ Collateral adjective: *taurine.* **2** A dealer who seeks or expects higher prices, and buys stocks or bonds accordingly. **3** One possessing characteristics suggestive of a bull. **4** *U.S. Slang* A policeman or detective, usually in plain clothes. —*v.t.* **1** To attempt to raise the price of or in. **2** To push or force (a way). —*v.i.* **3** To go up in price: said of stocks, etc. **4** *Slang* To go or push ahead: to *bull* through a crowd. —*adj.* **1** Large; bull-like; male. **2** Going up or advancing: a *bull* market. [ME *bule;* cf. OE *bulluc* bullock]

bull[2] (bo͞ol) *n.* **1** An official and authoritative document issued by the Pope, usually an edict, decree, or other proclamation, sealed with a bulla. **2** Bulla (def. 1). [<L *bulla* edict, seal]

bull[3] (bo͞ol) *n.* A ridiculous blunder in speech. [?<F *boule* lie, deceit <L *bulla* bubble]

bull[4] (bo͞ol) *n. Slang* Nonsense; bluff.

Bull (bo͞ol) The constellation and astrological sign Taurus. See CONSTELLATION.

Bull (bo͞ol), **Ole Bornemann,** 1810–80, Norwegian violinist.

bul·la (bo͞ol′ə, bul′ə) *n. pl.* **bul·lae** (bool′·ē, bul′ē) **1** A seal of lead, used by the Pope, or of gold or other metal used by the Greek and early German emperors and sovereigns. **2** *Pathol.* A small blister or large vesicle filled with watery serum; a bleb. [<L, seal]

bul·lar·i·um (bo͞ol·âr′ē·əm) *n.* A collection of papal bulls. [<Med. L]

bul·late (bo͞ol′āt, -it, bul′-) *adj.* **1** *Biol.* Having blisterlike prominences, as a leaf or surface. **2** *Anat.* Swollen; inflated. [<L *bullatus* <*bulla* bubble]

bull-bait·ing (bo͞ol′bā′ting) *n.* The setting of dogs upon bulls: a former English sport.

bull·bat (bo͞ol′bat′) *n.* The nighthawk (genus *Chordeiles*): named from the noise it makes while flying.

bull·dog (bo͞ol′dôg′, -dog′) *n.* **1** A medium-sized, short-haired, powerful dog, originally bred in England for use in bull-baiting: also called *English bulldog.* **2** A pistol; especially, a short-barreled revolver of large caliber: also, formerly, a cannon. —*adj.* Resembling a bulldog; courageous; tenacious. —*v.t. U.S. Colloq.* To throw (a steer) by gripping its horns and twisting its neck.

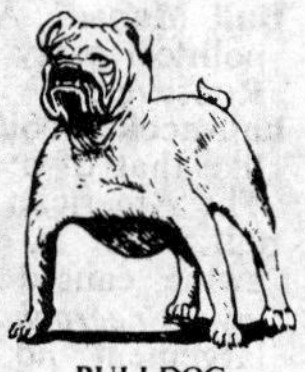

BULLDOG (About 16 inches high at the shoulders)

bulldog edition The early edition of a morning newspaper, often appearing the evening before, for distribution out of town.

bull·doze (bo͞ol′dōz′) *v.* **·dozed, ·doz·ing** *v.t.* **1** *U.S. Slang* To intimidate; bully. **2** To clear, dig, scrape, etc., with a bulldozer. —*v.i.* **3** To operate a bulldozer. [?<BULL, *adj.* + DOSE, with ref. to the violent or excessive treatment given to the victim.]

bull·doz·er (bo͞ol′dō′zər) *n.* **1** A powerful, tractor-driven machine equipped with a heavy steel blade: used for clearing wooded areas and moving soil in road construction. **2** A power-driven machine for stamping heads on wires and small rods. **3** *U.S. Slang* One who bulldozes.

bull dust *Austral.* **1** Dry silt. **2** *Slang* Nonsense; foolish chatter; bluff.

Bul·len (bo͞ol′ən), **Anne** See BOLEYN.

Bull·ers of Buch·an (bo͝ol′ərz əv bukh′ən) A large, hollow rock formation on the east coast of Scotland into which the sea rushes at high tide; 200 feet deep and 50 feet in diameter.
bul·let (bo͝ol′it) *n.* **1** A small projectile for a firearm. **2** Any small ball. [<F *boulette,* dim. of *boule* ball]
bul·le·tin (bo͝ol′ə·tən) *n.* **1** A brief official summary. **2** A brief news statement, issued in printed form, as in a newspaper, or by word of mouth, as transmitted by radio. **3** A periodical publication, as of the proceedings of a society. —*v.t.* To make public by bulletin. [<F <Ital. *bulletino,* double dim. of *bulla* <L, edict] —**bul′le·tin·ist** *n.*
bul·let·proof (bo͝ol′it·pro͞of′) *adj.* Not penetrable by bullets.
bull·fight (bo͝ol′fīt′) *n.* A combat in an arena between men and a bull or bulls, popular among the Spanish, Portuguese, and Spanish Americans. —**bull′fight′ing** *n.* —**bull′fight′er** *n.*
bull·finch[1] (bo͝ol′finch′) *n.* **1** A European singing bird (genus *Pyrrhula*) having a short, stout bill and red breast. **2** Any of certain American grosbeaks. [<BULL, *adj.* + FINCH]
bull·finch[2] (bo͝ol′finch′) *n. Brit.* A strong high hedge. [Prob. alter. of BULL FENCE]
bull·frog (bo͝ol′frog′, -frôg′) *n.* A large North American frog *(Rana catesbiana)* with a deep bass croak.
bull·head (bo͝ol′hed′) *n.* **1** One of various fishes (genus *Ameiurus*) with a broad head, as the horned pout *(A. nebulosus).* **2** The sculpin. **3** A plover (family *Charadriidae*). **4** The goldeneye duck *(Glaucionetta clangula).* **5** An obstinate, stupid person.
bull–head·ed (bo͝ol′hed′id) *adj.* Stupid and obstinate.
bull·horn (bo͝ol′hôrn′) *n.* An electrical, hand-held voice amplifier resembling a megaphone.
bul·lion[1] (bo͝ol′yən) *n.* Gold or silver uncoined or in mass, as in bars, plates, or the like. See synonyms under MONEY. [<AF *bullion,* OF *bouillon* boiling, melting < *bouillir* boil; ? infl. by OF *billon* base metal]
bul·lion[2] (bo͝ol′yən) *n.* A heavy, twisted, cord fringe, especially that of which the cords are covered with fine gold or silver wire. [<OF *bouillon* <L *bulla* bubble]
bull·ish[1] (bo͝ol′ish) *adj.* **1** Of or characteristic of a bull. **2** Characterized by or suggesting a trend toward higher prices, as in the stock market; also, hopeful of such a trend. **3** Confidently optimistic. —**bull′ish·ly** *adv.* —**bull′ish·ness** *n.*
bull·ish[2] (bo͝ol′ish) *adj.* Having the character of a bull or blunder.
Bul·litt (bo͝ol′it), **William Christian,** 1891–1967, U.S. diplomat.
bull moose The male moose.
Bull Moose A member of the Progressive political party formed in 1912 by Theodore Roosevelt.
bull·neck (bo͝ol′nek′) *n.* **1** A short, thick neck like that of a bull. **2** The canvasback. **3** The American scaup duck.
bull nose A form of rhinitis occurring in swine, caused by a micro-organism *(Actinomyces necrophorus)* and characterized by enlargement and necrosis of the nose.
bul·lock (bo͝ol′ək) *n.* **1** A gelded bull; a steer or an ox. **2** Formerly, a bull calf. [OE *bulluc*]
bull·pen (bo͝ol′pen′) *n. U.S.* **1** An enclosure for one or more bulls; also, an enclosure for a bullfight. **2** *Colloq.* A corral for temporary detention of prisoners; hence, a jail. **3** *Colloq.* The living quarters in a lumber camp. **4** A place of practice for baseball pitchers who may be needed in an emergency.
bull·pout (bo͝ol′pout′) *n.* A catfish; bullhead.
bull·ring (bo͝ol′ring′) *n.* A circular enclosure for bullfights.
bull·roar·er (bo͝ol′rôr′ər, -rōr′-) *n.* **1** A toy consisting of a small slat of wood fastened to a thong or string, to be whirled in the air to produce a roaring sound. **2** A larger device of this kind used by Australian aborigines in their religious rites.
Bull Run A creek in NE Virginia; scene of Civil War battles, 1861 and 1862, in which Union forces were defeated. See MANASSAS.
bull's–eye (bo͝olz′ī′) *n.* **1** The center of a target, or a shot that hits it. **2** A circular window or mirror. **3** A thick disk or lens of glass, or a lantern fitted with one. **4** *Naut.* A small wooden block perforated for ropes. **5** A thick, rounded lump of candy, usually flavored with peppermint. **6** An old-fashioned, thick, open-faced watch. **7** A depression or wave in mirror glass which causes a distortion of the image. **8** *Meteorol.* **a** A small area of clear sky marking the center of a cyclone storm; the eye of the storm. **b** A small detached cloud indicating the top of a developing bull's-eye squall.
bull's–eye squall *Meteorol.* A fair-weather squall off the coasts of South Africa: usually identified by the detached cloud marking the peak of its invisible vortex.
bull snake A gopher snake.
bull–strong (bo͝ol′strông′, -strong′) *adj.* Strong enough to hold a bull: said of fences.
bull terrier See under TERRIER.
bull–tongue (bo͝ol′tung′) *n.* In cotton farming, a heavy plow with a nearly vertical moldboard.
bull·weed (bo͝ol′wēd′) *n.* Knapweed.
bull·whip (bo͝ol′hwip′) *n.* A long, tough whip used by teamsters. —*v.t.* **·whipped, ·whip·ping** To strike or beat with a bullwhip.
bul·ly[1] (bo͝ol′ē) *adj.* **bul·li·er, bul·li·est** **1** *Colloq.* Excellent, admirable. **2** Quarrelsome; blustering. **3** Jolly; dashing; gallant. —*n. pl.* **bul·lies** **1** A quarrelsome, swaggering, cowardly fellow; one who terrorizes or threatens those weaker than himself. **2** *Archaic* A hired ruffian. **3** *Obs.* A pimp. **4** *Obs.* Sweetheart; darling: a term formerly applied to both sexes. —*interj.* Well done! —*v.* **bul·lied, bul·ly·ing** *v.t.* To coerce by threats; intimidate. —*v.i.* To be quarrelsome and blustering. [Cf. Du. *boel* friend, lover]
bul·ly[2] (bo͝ol′ē) *n.* Canned or pickled beef. Also **bul′ly·beef′.** [Prob. <F *bouilli,* pp. of *bouillir* boil]
bul·ly·boy (bo͝ol′ē·boi′) *n.* A jovial fellow.
bul·ly·rag (bo͝ol′ē·rag′) *v.t.* **·ragged, ·rag·ging** To bully; intimidate. [? <BULLY, *v.* + RAG[1]]
bul·ly·tree (bo͝ol′ē·trē′) *n.* One of several tropical American trees yielding balata gum, especially *Manilkara bidentata.* Also **bul′let·wood′.**
Bü·low (bü′lō), **Prince Bernhard von,** 1849–1929, German chancellor 1900–09. —**Friedrich Wilhelm von,** 1755–1816, Prussian general at the battle of Waterloo. —**Hans Guido,** 1830–94, German orchestral conductor and composer.
bul·rush (bo͝ol′rush′) *n.* **1** A tall, rushlike plant growing in damp ground or water, as the tall sedge *(Scirpus lacustris),* the common American rush *(Juncus effusus),* and the common English cat-tail *(Typha latifolia).* **2** Papyrus. *Exodus* ii 3. [<BULL[1], *adj.* + RUSH[2]]
bul·wark (bo͝ol′wərk) *n.* **1** A defensive wall or rampart; fortification. **2** Any safeguard or defense. **3** *Naut.* The raised side of a ship, above the upper deck: usually in the plural. See synonyms under BARRIER, DEFENSE, RAMPART. —*v.t.* To surround and fortify with, or as with, a bulwark. [<MHG *bolwerc.* Akin to BOULEVARD.]
Bul·wer (bo͝ol′wər), **William Henry Lytton Earle,** 1801–72, Baron Dalling and Bulwer, English diplomat.
Bul·wer–Lyt·ton (bo͝ol′wər·lit′n) See LYTTON.
bum[1] (bum) *n.* **1** *U.S. Colloq.* A worthless or dissolute loafer; tramp. **2** A spree; debauch. —**on the bum** **1** Out of order; broken. **2** Living as a vagrant. —*adj.* Bad; inferior. —*v.* **bummed, bum·ming** *v.i.* **1** To live by sponging from others. **2** To live idly and in dissipation. —*v.t.* **3** To get by begging: to *bum* a ride. [Short for *bummer,* alter. of G *bummler* loafer, dawdler] —**bum′mer** *n.*
bum[2] (bum) *v.i.* **bummed, bum·ming** *Brit. Dial.* To hum, as a top. [Var. of BOOM[2]]
bum[3] (bum) *n. Brit. Slang* The buttocks. [ME *bom;* origin uncertain]
bum·bai·liff (bum′bā′lif) *n. Brit.* A sheriff's deputy or county-court bailiff whose duties are to levy and attach. Also **bum′bail′ey** (-bā′·lē). [<BUM[3] + BAILIFF; because he follows closely behind a person]
bum·ble (bum′bəl) *v.t.* & *v.i.* **·bled, ·bling** To bungle; confuse, especially in an officious manner. [Imit.] —**bum′bling** *adj.* & *n.*
bum·ble·bee (bum′bəl·bē′) *n.* Any of certain large, hairy, social bees (family *Bombidae*). [< dial. E *bumble,* freq. of BUM[2] + BEE[1]]
bum·ble·foot (bum′bəl·fo͝ot′) *n.* A suppurative swelling of the foot in domestic fowls, arising from a bacterial infection of a cut or bruise.
bum·boat (bum′bōt′) *n.* A boat employed in peddling provisions and small wares among vessels in port or offshore. [<LG *bumboot* broad-beamed boat]
bum·kin (bum′kin) *n. Naut.* A projecting boom on a vessel, placed at each side of the bow to haul the foretack to, or on the quarter, for the standing part of the mainbrace, or over the stern to extend the mizzen sail: also *bumpkin.* [<Du. *boomkin,* dim. of *boom* tree, beam]
bum·ming[1] (bum′ing) *n.* **1** Carousing. **2** Living like a bum.
bum·ming[2] (bum′ing) *adj. Scot.* Humming.
bump (bump) *v.t.* **1** To come into contact with; knock into. **2** To cause to knock into or against. **3** *U.S. Colloq.* To displace, as from a position or seat. —*v.i.* **4** To come into contact; knock together. **5** To move or proceed with jerks and jolts. —**to bump off** *Slang* To kill, especially with a gun. —*n.* **1** A violent impact or collision; a heavy blow. **2** A protuberance like that caused by a blow. **3** The act of bumping. **4** One of the protuberances of the human head said to denote a certain faculty. **5** *Aeron.* A gust of wind striking the surface of an aircraft with the effect of a sharp blow. [Imit.]
bump·er[1] (bum′pər) *n.* **1** Something that either bumps or causes a bump. **2** A buffer, as on a railroad car. **3** A guard on the front or rear of an automobile to attenuate the shock of collision.
bump·er[2] (bum′pər) *n.* A cup or glass filled to the brim. —*adj.* Unusually full or large: a *bumper* crop. —*v.t.* **1** To fill to the brim. **2** To drink toasts to. —*v.i.* **3** To drink from bumpers. [? Alter. of F *bombarde* large cup, infl. in form by BUMP]
bump·i·ness (bum′pē·nis) *n.* **1** The state or condition of being bumpy. **2** *Aeron.* A condition of irregular atmospheric density, as from rising or falling air currents, which results in sudden jolts to aircraft.
bump·kin (bump′kin) *n.* **1** An awkward rustic; a clown; a lout. **2** A bumkin. [? <Du. *boomkin* little tree, block. Cf. BLOCKHEAD.]
bumps (bumps) *n. pl.* In motion pictures, a series of low-frequency sounds caused by irregularities in the sound track.
bump·tious (bump′shəs) *adj.* Aggressively and offensively self-conceited. —**bump′tious·ly** *adv.* —**bump′tious·ness** *n.*
bump·y (bum′pē) *adj.* **bump·i·er, bump·i·est** Having bumps or bumpiness; jolty. —**bump′i·ly** *adv.* —**bump′i·ness** *n.*
bum's rush *Slang* Forced expulsion or ejection, as of an undesirable person.
bun[1] (bun) *n.* **1** A small bread roll, sometimes sweetened or glazed with sugar, containing currants, citron, etc. **2** *Brit.* A small sweet cake. **3** A roll of hair shaped like a bun and worn at the nape of the neck. [ME *bunne;* origin uncertain]
bun[2] (bun) *n. Brit. Dial.* A rabbit's tail; hence, a rabbit or squirrel. [Cf. Irish *bun* stump]
bu·na (bo͞o′nə, byo͞o′-) *n. Chem.* A synthetic rubber made by the polymerization of butadiene with certain other substances, as styrene. Also **Bu′na.** [<BU(TADIENE) + NA(TRIUM)]
bunch (bunch) *n.* **1** A compact collection, usually of objects of the same kind; also, a group; cluster. **2** A hunch; hump; protuberance. —*v.t.* & *v.i.* **1** To make into or form bunches or groups. **2** To gather, as in pleats or folds. [ME *bonche, bunche;* origin unknown]
bunch·ber·ry (bunch′ber′ē, -bər·ē) *n. pl.* **·ries** The dwarf cornel *(Cornus canadensis)* with bright red, closely clustered berries.
Bunche (bunch), **Ralph Johnson,** 1904–1971, U.S. educator and United Nations statesman.
bunch·flow·er (bunch′flou′ər) *n.* A plant *(Melanthium virginicum)* of the lily family of the United States, having linear leaves and a pyramidal panicle of greenish flowers.
bunch grass Any of various grasses growing in clumps or tufts.
bun·co (bung′kō) *n. U.S. Colloq.* A swindling game in which confederates join to rob a stranger. —*v.t.* To swindle or bilk. Also spelled *bunko.* [Prob. <Sp. *banco,* a card game]
bun·combe (bung′kəm) *n.* **1** Bombastic speechmaking or any specious utterance for political effect. **2** Humbug. Also spelled *bunkum.* [from *Buncombe* County, N.C., whose Congressman (1819–21) often insisted

on making empty, unimportant speeches "for Buncombe"]

bun·co–steer·er (bung′kō-stir′ər) *n. U.S. Slang* A swindler.

bund[1] (bund) *n.* **1** An embankment or dike. **2** A thoroughfare along a waterfront. **— the Bund,** an esplanade in Shanghai, China. [<Hind. *band*]

bund[2] (bŏond, bund; *Ger.* bŏont) *n.* A confederation; league; a society. [<G]

Bund (bŏont) *n. pl.* **Bün·de** (bün′də) **1** A confederation of German states established in 1867. **2** The German–American Bund, a former pro–Nazi organization in the United States.

Bun·del·khand (bŏon′dəl·khund) A region in Vindhya Pradesh and Uttar Pradesh states, central India; formerly a subdivision, **Bundel- khand Agency,** of the Central India Agency, including about 30 native states.

bun·der (bun′dər) *n. Anglo–Indian* In the Orient, a landing place: the Apollo *bunder* at Bombay. [<Hind. *bandar*]

Bun·des·rat (bŏon′dəs·rät′) *n.* A federal council, as formerly in Germany or Austria. Also **Bun′des·rath′.** [<G, lit., council of the league]

bun·dle (bun′dəl) *n.* **1** A number of things or a quantity of anything bound together. **2** Anything folded or wrapped and tied up; a package. **3** A group; collection. **4** *Bot.* A cluster of one or more elementary tissues lying across other tissues: also called *vascular bundle*. ◆ Collateral adjective: *fascicular.* — *v.* ·**dled,** ·**dling** *v.t.* **1** To tie, roll or otherwise secure in a bundle. **2** To send away or place in summarily or in haste: with *away, off, out,* or *into.* — *v.i.* **3** To leave or proceed hastily or in a bustling manner: They *bundled* down the stairs. **4** To practice bundling. [<MDu. *bondel*, dim. of *bond* group. Akin to BIND.] **— bun′dler** *n.*

bun·dling (bun′dling) *n.* An old courting custom, prevalent in New England, in which sweethearts lay or slept together in bed without undressing.

bung (bung) *n.* **1** A stopper for the large hole through which a cask is filled. **2** Bunghole. **3** A large sac between the small intestine and the colon of beef viscera. — *v.t.* **1** To close with or as with a bung: often with *up* or *down.* **2** *Slang* To damage; maul: usually with *up.* [<MDu. *bonghe*]

bun·ga·low (bung′gə·lō) *n.* **1** In India, a one-storied house with wide verandas. **2** A small house or cottage, usually with one or one and a half stories. **3** The blimp of a motion-picture camera. [<Hind. *banglā* Bengalese <*Banga* Bengal]

bun·gee (bung·gē′) *n. Aeron.* An apparatus, operated by the pilot of an aircraft, which restricts or controls the action of certain movable parts, as a bomb-bay door. [Origin uncertain]

bung·hole (bung′hōl) *n.* A hole in a keg or barrel from which liquid is tapped. [<MDu. *bonghe* a stopper, plug + HOLE]

bun·gle (bung′gəl) *v.t. & v.i.* ·**gled,** ·**gling** To work, make, or do (something) clumsily; botch. — *n.* An awkward, clumsy, and imperfect job or performance; botch. **— bun′gler** *n.* **— bun′gle·some** (-səm) *adj.* **— bun′gling** *adj.* **— bun′gling·ly** *adv.* [Cf. Sw. *bangla* work ineffectually]

Bun·gu·ran Islands (bŏong′ŏo·rän′) An Indonesian island group in the South China Sea; total, 816 square miles: also *Natuna Islands. Dutch* **Boen′goe·ran′ Islands.**

Bu·nin (bŏo′nyin), **Ivan Alexeyevich,** 1870–1953, Russian novelist and poet.

bun·ion (bun′yən) *n. Pathol.* A painful swelling of the foot, usually at the outer side of the base of the great toe: at first an enlarged bursa, eventually producing a distortion of the bony structure. [Akin to OF *bugne* swelling]

bunk[1] (bungk) *n.* **1** A small compartment, shelf, box, or recess, etc., used as a sleeping place, as in a vessel, lodging house, sleeping car, etc. **2** A piece of timber across a lumberman's sled; also, the sled so arranged. — *v.i.* **1** To sleep in a bunk. **2** To share a bed. [Cf. MDu. *banc* bench, shelf and BANK[3] (def. 2)]

bunk[2] (bungk) *n. Slang* Inflated or empty speech; balderdash. [Short for BUNCOMBE]

bun·ker (bung′kər) *n.* **1** A large bin, as for coal on a ship. **2** A box or chest that serves also for a seat. **3** In golf, a sandy hollow or a mound of earth serving as an obstacle on a course. **4** *Mil.* A steel and concrete fortification, usually underground. **b** A bulwark of earth erected to protect a gun emplacement. — *v.i.* To fill the coal bunkers of a ship. — *v.t.* In golf, to drive (a ball) into a bunker. [Cf. OSw. *bunke* hold of a ship and BANK[3] (def. 2)]

Bun·ker Hill (bung′kər) A hill in Charlestown, Massachusetts, near which (on *Breed's Hill*) occurred the first organized engagement of the Revolutionary War, June 17, 1775.

bunk·house (bungk′hous′) *n.* A structure used as sleeping quarters.

bunk·mate (bungk′māt′) *n.* One who shares a bunk. Also **bunk·ie** (bung′kē), **bunk′y.**

bun·ko (bung′kō), **bun·kum** (bung′kəm) See BUNCO, BUNCOMBE.

bunn (bun) *n.* Bun[1].

Bun·ner (bun′ər), **Henry Cuyler,** 1855–96, U.S. humorist.

bun·ny (bun′ē) *n. pl.* ·**nies** A rabbit or squirrel: a pet name. [<BUN[2]]

bun·ny–hug (bun′ē·hug′) *n. U.S.* A dance in ragtime rhythm, popular in about 1910.

Bun·sen (bun′sən, *Ger.* bŏon′zən), **Robert William Eberhard,** 1811–99, German chemist and inventor.

Bun·sen burner (bun′sən) A type of gas burner in which a mixture of gas and air is burned at the top of a short metal tube, producing a very hot flame. [after R. W. E. Bunsen]

bunt[1] (bunt) *v.t. & v.i.* **1** To strike or push as with horns; butt. **2** In baseball, to bat (the ball) lightly to the infield, without swinging the bat. — *n.* **1** A push or shove; a butt. **2** In baseball, a short hit to the infield, made by allowing a pitched ball to bounce off a loosely held bat. [Nasalized var. of BUTT[1]]

bunt[2] (bunt) *n.* **1** *Naut.* The middle or belly-ing portion of a square sail. **2** The middle, sagging part of a fishnet. **3** *Naut.* The middle part of a yard. — *v.t. Naut.* To haul up the middle part of (a square sail) in furling. **1** To swell out; belly. [Origin unknown]

bunt[3] (bunt) *n.* **1** A parasitic fungus (*Tilletia foetens*), a species of smut, which destroys the grains of wheat by converting the interior into a fetid black powder. **2** The disease caused by it: also called *stinking smut.* [Origin unknown]

bun·tal (bŏon·täl′) *n.* A white Philippine fiber obtained from unopened palm-leaf stems, from which a fine straw is woven. [<Tagalog]

bunt·ing[1] (bun′ting) *n.* **1** A light woolen stuff used for flags. **2** A light cotton fabric resembling cheesecloth. **3** Flags, banners, etc., collectively. [? ME *bonten* sift]

bunt·ing[2] (bun′ting) *n.* One of various birds related to the finches and sparrows: the indigo and snow *buntings.* [ME *bountyng*; origin unknown]

bunt·line (bunt′lin, -līn) *n. Naut.* A rope used in hauling a square sail of a vessel up to the yard for furling.

bun·ya–bun·ya (bun′yə·bun′yə) *n.* An evergreen tree of Australia (*Araucaria bidwillii*), of the pine family: its cones contain edible seeds. Also **bun′ya.** [<native name]

Bun·yan (bun′yən), **John,** 1628–88, English preacher and author of *Pilgrim's Progress.* **— Paul** See PAUL BUNYAN.

Bun·yip (bun′yip) *n.* In Australian folklore, a bellowing water monster who lives at the bottom of lakes and water holes, into which he draws his human victims.

Buo·na·par·te (bwô′nä·pär′tā) See BONAPARTE.

Buo·nar·ro·ti (bwô′när·rô′tē) See MICHELANGELO.

buoy (boi, bŏo′ē) *n.* **1** *Naut.* A float moored on a dangerous rock or shoal or at the edge of a channel, as a guide to navigators. Many are named according to shape or function: **can buoy** (cylindrical); **nun buoy** (conical);

spar buoy (a spar anchored at one end); **bell buoy, whistling buoy** (buoys devised to sound with the motion of the waves: used to mark dangerous shoals or harbor entrances, respectively). **2** Any device or object for keeping a person in the water afloat: also called *lifebuoy.* Compare BREECHES BUOY. — *v.t.*

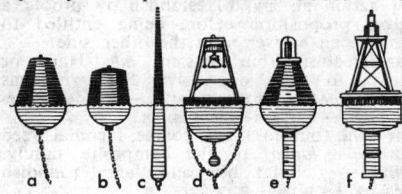

TYPES OF BUOYS

a. Nun buoy. *b.* Can buoy. *c.* Spar buoy. *d.* Bell buoy. *e.* Whistling buoy. *f.* Gas–lighted buoy.

1 To keep from sinking in a liquid; keep afloat. **2** To sustain the courage or heart of; encourage: usually with *up.* **3** *Naut.* To mark, as a channel, with buoys. [<MDu. *boeie*]

buoy·age (boi′ij, bŏo′ē·ij) *n.* **1** Buoys collectively. **2** A system of buoys.

buoy·an·cy (boi′ən·sē, bŏo′yən·sē) *n.* **1** The property of keeping afloat. **2** Power or tendency of a liquid or gas to keep an object afloat. **3** Resultant upward pressure of fluid on an immersed or floating body. **4** Elasticity of spirits; cheerfulness. Also **buoy′-ance.**

buoy·ant (boi′ənt, bŏo′yənt) *adj.* **1** Having buoyancy. **2** Vivacious; cheerful; hopeful. See synonyms under CHEERFUL, HAPPY, SANGUINE. [Prob. <Sp. *boyante* <*boyar* float] **— buoy′ant·ly** *adv.*

bu·pres·tid (byŏo-pres′tid) *n.* Any of a family (*Buprestidae*) of brilliantly colored beetles with the first and second vertical segments confluent and membranous-lobed tarsi, and whose larvae are destructive woodborers. [<L *buprestis* <Gk. *bouprēstis* <*bous* ox + *prēthein* swell]

bur[1] (bûr) **1** *Bot.* A rough or prickly flower head, or the like, as of the chestnut and burdock. **2** The burdock or other plant that bears burs. **3** A protuberance; lump; specifically, a knot or excrescence on a tree. **4** An impediment or unwelcome adherent. — *v.t.* **burred, bur·ring** To remove burs from, as wool. Also spelled *burr.* ◆ Homophones: *birr, burr.* [<Scand. Cf. Dan. *borre* bur.]

bur[2] (bûr) See BURR[1].

bu·ran (bŏo-rän′) *n. Meteorol.* A violent windstorm of Siberia and the Russian steppes: a hot duststorm in summer and a blizzard in winter. Also **bu·ra** (bŏo-rä′). [<Russian]

Bur·bage (bûr′bij), **Richard,** 1567?–1619, English actor; associate of Shakespeare.

Bur·bank (bûr′bangk), **Luther,** 1849–1926, U.S. horticulturist.

bur·ble (bûr′bəl) *v.i.* ·**bled,** ·**bling** **1** To bubble; gurgle. **2** To talk excitedly and confusedly. [ME; imit.]

bur·bling (bûr′bling) *n. Aeron.* A turbulence in the airflow around an airplane, especially such as to increase the drag.

bur·bot (bûr′bət) *n. pl.* ·**bots** or ·**bot** A freshwater fish (*Lota lota*) of the northern hemisphere, with barbels on the nose and chin: also called *ling.* [<F *bourbotte*, ult. <L *barbata* bearded; infl. in form by TURBOT]

Burch·field (bûrch′fēld), **Charles Ephraim,** 1893–1967, U.S. painter.

Burck·hardt (bŏork′härt), **Jakob,** 1818–97, Swiss cultural historian. **— Johann Ludwig,** 1784–1817, Swiss traveler.

burd (bûrd) *n. Brit. Dial.* A maiden. Also **burd·ie** (bûr′dē). [ME *burde*; origin uncertain]

bur·den[1] (bûr′dən) *n.* **1** Something heavy that is borne or carried; responsibility; a load. **2** *Naut.* **a** The carrying capacity of a vessel. **b** The weight of the cargo. **3** The employment of carrying loads: beasts of *burden.* — *v.t.* To load or overload; oppress, as with care: *burdened* with responsibilities. See synonyms under LOAD. Also spelled *burthen.* [OE *byrthen* load]

bur·den[2] (bûr′dən) *n.* **1** Something often repeated or dwelt upon; the prevailing idea or

tone: The *burden* of the speech was a desire for war. **2** A refrain repeated at the end of every stanza of a song. **3** The drone of a bagpipe. Also spelled *burthen.* [<F *bourdon* bass <LL *burdo* drone]

burden of proof The obligation resting upon one or other of the parties to a controversy, or action at law, to establish by proofs a given proposition before being entitled to receive an answer from the other side.

bur·den·some (bûr′dən·səm) *adj.* Hard or heavy to bear; oppressive. See synonyms under HEAVY, TROUBLESOME. **— bur′den·some·ly** *adv.* **— bur′den·some·ness** *n.*

bur·dock (bûr′dok) *n.* A coarse, biennial weed *(Arctium lappa)* of the composite family, with a globular bur and large roundish leaves. [<BUR + DOCK[4]]

bu·reau (byŏŏr′ō) *n. pl.* **bu·reaus** or **bu·reaux** (byŏŏr′ōz) **1** A chest of drawers for clothing, etc., commonly provided with a mirror. **2** A public department. **3** An organized staff of literary workers, etc.; also, the place where the work is done. **4** A writing desk; escritoire. [<F, cloth-covered desk <OF *burel* coarse woolen cloth]

bu·reauc·ra·cy (byŏŏ·rok′rə·sē) *n. pl.* **·cies** **1** Government by bureaus, especially by rigid and arbitrary routine. **2** Government officials collectively.

bu·reau·crat (byŏŏr′ə·krat) *n.* **1** A member of a bureaucracy. **2** An official who governs by rigid routine. **— bu′reau·crat′ic** ·or **·i·cal** *adj.* **— bu′reau·crat′i·cal·ly** *adv.*

bu·rette (byŏŏ·ret′) *n.* **1** *Chem.* A finely graduated glass tube from which a small quantity of a solution can be drawn off at a time. **2** A decorated cruet; an altar cruet. Also **bu·ret′.** [<F, dim. of *buire* vase <OF *buise* drink]

burg (bûrg) *n.* **1** *Colloq.* A town; city. **2** *Archaic* A fortified place. [OE *burg.* Related to BOROUGH.]

bur·gage (bûr′gij) *n.* **1** In feudal law, a tenure by which houses and lands in an ancient borough were held of the lord at a certain yearly rent; land so held. **2** A form of tenure by which property in royal burgs is held of the king for the nominal service of watching and warding. [<OF <Med. L *burgagium* < *burgus* town <Gmc.]

Bur·gas (bŏŏr·gäs′) A port on the **Gulf of Burgas,** the westernmost inlet of the Black Sea in eastern Bulgaria.

bur·gee (bûr′jē) *n. Naut.* A triangular or swallow-tailed pennant flown on vessels for identification. [Origin unknown]

Bur·gen·land (bŏŏr′gən·länt) An autonomous province of eastern Austria; 1,526 square miles; capital, Eisenstadt.

bur·geon (bûr′jən) *v.t.* & *v.i.* To put forth (buds or shoots); sprout. [< *n.*] **—** *n.* **1** A bud; sprout. **2** A boss for protecting the binding of a book. Also spelled *bourgeon.* [<OF *burjon*]

Burg·er (bûr′gər), **Warren Earl,** born 1907, U.S. jurist; chief justice of the Supreme Court 1969–.

bur·gess (bûr′jis) *n.* **1** A freeman, citizen, or officer of a borough or burg. **2** In colonial times, a member of the lower house of the legislature, the **House of Burgesses,** of Maryland or Virginia: now called *delegate.* **3** *Brit.* Formerly, a member of Parliament for a borough or university. [<OF *burgeis* < *bourg* town <Gmc. Doublet of BOURGEOIS[1].] **— bur′gess-ship** *n.*

Bur·gess (bûr′jis), **(Frank) Gelett,** 1866–1951, U.S. humorist and illustrator.

burgh (bûrg, *Scot.* bûr′ō, -ə) *n.* **1** In Scots law, a corporate body erected by charter of the sovereign, consisting of the inhabitants of the district designated in the charter; a borough. **2** *Archaic* A castle or fortification. [Var. of BOROUGH] **— burgh·al** (bûr′gəl) *adj.*

Burgh (bûrg), **Hubert de,** died 1243, English statesman.

burgh·er (bûr′gər) *n.* **1** A citizen of a burgh. **2** An early Dutch inhabitant or citizen of New York. [<Du. *burger* < *burg* town. Akin to BURGESS.]

Burgh·ley (bûr′lē), **Lord** See CECIL. Also **Bur′leigh.**

bur·glar (bûr′glər) *n.* One who commits a burglary. See synonyms under ROBBER. [<Med. L *burglator* ? <OF *bourg* dwelling (<Gmc.) + *laire* robbery (<L *latro* robber)]

burglar alarm A device, usually electric, by which an alarm is given, by bell, gong, flashing light, etc., upon forcible intrusion of a building, safe, etc.

bur·glar·i·ous (bər·glâr′ē·əs) *adj.* Relating to or of the nature of a burglary. **— bur·glar′i·ous·ly** *adv.*

bur·glar·ize (bûr′glə·rīz) *v.t.* **·ized, ·iz·ing** **1** To commit burglary upon. **2** To enter or steal by burglary.

bur·gla·ry (bûr′glər·ē) *n. pl.* **·ries** The breaking and entering of a building (primarily of a dwelling, by night), with felonious intent.

bur·gle (bûr′gəl) *v.t.* & *v.i.* **·gled ·gling** *Colloq.* To commit burglary; burglarize. [Back formation <BURGLAR]

bur·go·mas·ter (bûr′gə·mas′tər, -mäs′-) *n.* **1** A Dutch, Flemish, German, or Austrian municipal magistrate; a mayor. **2** A large arctic gull *(Larus hyperboreus).* [<Du. *burgemeester*]

bur·go·net (bûr′gə·net) *n. Archaic* A light, open helmet. [<OF *bourguignotte* Burgundian <*Bourgogne* Burgundy, where first used]

bur·goo (bûr′gōō, bər·gōō′) *n. pl.* **·goos** **1** A kind of oatmeal porridge or mush formerly served at sea. **2** *U.S. Dial.* A thick, highly seasoned soup or stew of meat; also, the meals at which this is served, especially picnics and barbecues. Also **bur′gout** (-gōō). [Cf. Turkish *burghul* porridge]

Bur·gos (bŏŏr′gōs) A city in northern Spain; capital of the former kingdom of Castile.

Bur·goyne (bər·goin′), **John,** 1723–92, English general, surrendered to Gates at Saratoga, 1777.

bur·grave (bûr′grāv) *n.* The governor or lord of a fortified town or a military fortress. [<G *burg* walled town + *graf* count]

Bur·gun·dy (bûr′gən·dē) A region of east central France; formerly a kingdom, duchy, and province: French *Bourgogne.* **— Bur·gun·di·an** (bər·gun′dē·ən) *adj.* & *n.*

Bur·gun·dy (bûr′gən·dē) *n. pl.* **·dies** A kind of red or white wine originally made in Burgundy.

Burgundy Gate The Belfort Gap. *French* **Porte de Bourgogne** (pôrt də bŏŏr·gôn′y′).

bur·i·al (ber′ē·əl) *n.* The burying of a dead body; sepulture. [OE *byrgels* tomb]

bur·i·er (ber′ē·ər) *n.* One who or that which buries.

bu·rin (byŏŏr′in) *n.* **1** An engraver's tool; graver. **2** The style or manner of execution of an engraver.

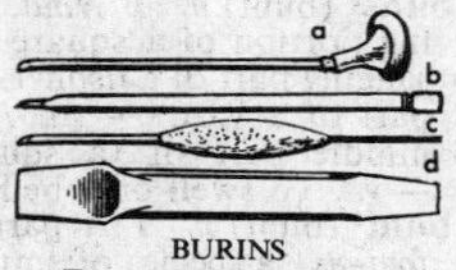

BURINS
a. For engraving on wood.
b. For carving copper or stone.
c. For carving steel.
d. For use by mechanics.

burke (bûrk) *v.t.* **burked, burk·ing** **1** To murder by suffocating, so as to leave no marks. **2** To get rid of by quietly suppressing; dispose of. [after William *Burke,* 1792–1829, Irish murderer who sold his victims' bodies for dissection]

Burke (bûrk), **Edmund,** 1729–97, British orator, writer, and statesman born in Ireland.

burl (bûrl) *n.* **1** A knot or lump in wool or cloth. **2** A large, wartlike excrescence, usually a flattened hemisphere, formed on the trunks of trees. **3** A veneer made from it. **—** *v.t.* To dress (cloth) by removing burls, loose thread, etc. ◆ Homophone: *birl.* [<OF *bourle* tuft of wool <L *burra* shaggy hair] **— burled** *adj.* **— burl′er** *n.*

bur·lap (bûr′lap) *n.* A coarse fabric resembling canvas, made of jute, flax, hemp, or cotton: used for wrapping, bagging, etc. [Origin uncertain]

bur·lesque (bər·lesk′) *n.* **1** Ludicrous imitation or representation; broad caricature; travesty. **2** A product of such imitation, as a literary or dramatic work intended to produce laughter by its caricature or satire. **3** *U.S.* A theatrical entertainment marked by low comedy, strip-tease, etc. See synonyms under CARICATURE. **—** *v.* **·lesqued, ·les·quing** *v.t.* To represent by grotesque parody or ridicule. **—** *v.i.* To use burlesque. **—** *adj.* Marked by ludicrous incongruity or broad caricature. [<F <Ital. *burlesco* < *burla* joke] **— bur·les′quer** *n.*

bur·ley (bûr′lē) *n.* A fine, light tobacco used chiefly in plug form for chewing, and grown principally in Kentucky. Also **Bur′ley.** [? after *Burley,* name of a grower]

Bur·lin·game (bûr′lin·gām, -ling·gām), **Anson,** 1820–70, U.S. diplomat.

Bur·ling·ton (bûr′ling·tən) The largest city in Vermont, on Lake Champlain.

bur·ly[1] (bûr′lē) *adj.* **bur·li·er, bur·li·est** Large of body; bulky; stout; lusty. See synonyms under CORPULENT. [ME *borlich;* origin unknown] **— bur′li·ly** *adv.* **— bur′li·ness** *n.*

bur·ly[2] (bûr′lē) *adj.* Having burls or knots, as a tree.

Bur·ma The former name of Myanmar, a country in SE Asia bordered by India and Bangladesh on the western side and China, Laos, and Thailand on the east; 261,228 square miles; capital, Rangoon (Yangon); pop. 43,000,000; the coastal border is on the Bay of Bengal. Formerly **the Union of Burma,** (1948–1989). Although the borders remained the same after 1989, the name was changed to reflect the non-Burmese population of the country. *adj.* & *n.* **— Burman.**

Bur·mese *n.* **1** *usu. pl.* The ethnic Burmans from Myanmar (Burma), or their language. The other ethnic groups of Myanmar are the Karens, Shans, Kachins, Chins, and Chinese. **2** A native or inhabitant of Burma. **3** The Sino-Tibetan language of Burma, written in the Pali alphabet. **—** *adj.* **-mese** Of or pertaining to the ethnic Burmans, or their language.

burn[1] (bûrn) *v.* **burned** or **burnt, burn·ing** *v.t.* **1** To destroy or consume by fire. **2** To set afire; ignite. **3** To injure or kill by fire; execute by fire. **4** To injure or damage by friction, heat, steam, etc.; scald; wither. **5** To produce by fire, as a hole in a suit. **6** To brand; also, to cauterize. **7** To finish or harden by intense heat; fire. **8** To use; employ, so as to give off light, heat, etc. **9** To cause a feeling of heat in: The pepper *burned* his tongue. **10** To sunburn. **11** *Chem.* To cause to undergo combustion. **12** *Slang* To electrocute. **13** *Slang* To cheat. **—** *v.i.* **14** To be on fire; blaze. **15** To be destroyed or scorched by fire; undergo change by fire. **16** To give off light, heat, etc.; shine. **17** To die by fire. **18** To appear or feel hot: He *burns* with fever. **19** To be eager, excited, or inflamed. **20** *Chem.* To oxidize; undergo combustion. **21** *Slang* To be electrocuted. **— to burn down** To be razed by fire. **— to burn one's fingers** To suffer from taking part in. **— to burn out** **1** To become extinguished through lack of fuel. **2** To destroy or wear out by heat, friction, etc. **3** To burn up the house, store, or property of. **4** To drive out by heat. **— to burn the candle at both ends** To exhaust one's strength by overwork or dissipation. **— to burn up** **1** To consume by fire. **2** *Slang* To make or become irritated or enraged. **—** *n.* **1** An effect or injury from burning; a burnt place. **2** A brand. **3** The process of burning. **4** *Usually pl.* A defective area in window glass caused by overheating in the annealing furnace. **5** A place where vegetation has been burned away, in a forest, on the prairie, etc. [Fusion of OE *beornan* be on fire and OE *bærnan* set afire]

Synonyms (verb): blaze, brand, cauterize, char, consume, cremate, flame, flash, ignite, incinerate, kindle, scorch, singe. To *burn* is to effect either partial change or complete combustion: to *burn* wood in the fire; to *burn* one's hand on a hot stove; the sun *burns* the face. One *brands* with a hot iron, but *cauterizes* with some corrosive substance, as silver nitrate. *Cremate* is now used specifically for *consuming* a dead body by intense heat. To *kindle* is to *ignite,* the scientific word for the same thing. To *scorch* and to *singe* are superficial, and to *char* usually so. Both *kindle* and *burn* have extensive figurative use. Compare LIGHT. *Antonyms*: cool, extinguish, smother, stifle, subdue.

burn[2] (bûrn) *n. Scot.* A brook or rivulet: also spelled *bourn, bourne.*

Burne-Jones (bûrn′jōnz′), **Sir Edward,** 1833–98, English painter.

burn·er (bûr′nər) *n.* **1** One who or that which burns. **2** The light-giving or flame-giving part of a lamp, etc.

bur·net (bûr′nit) *n.* Any of several perennial herbs (genus *Sanguisorba*) of the rose family, with alternate, pinnate leaves and small flowers in a dense head or spike. [Var. of BRUNETTE]

Bur·nett (bər·net′), **Frances Hodgson,** 1849–1924, U.S. novelist.

Bur·ney (bûr'nē), **Fanny,** 1752–1840, Madame d'Arblay, English novelist: original name Frances Burney.

bur·nie (bûr'nē) n. Scot. A little burn; brooklet.

burn·ing (bûr'ning) adj. Consuming or being consumed by fire; intense; vehement; exciting. See synonyms under ARDENT, EAGER, HOT. — n. 1 A state or sensation of inflammation. 2 A destruction or putting to death by fire. 3 The baking, as of brick or pottery. See synonyms under FIRE.

burn·ing·bush (bûr'ning·boŏsh') n. 1 The wahoo. 2 The strawberry bush.

burning glass A convex lens for concentrating the sun's rays upon an object so as to heat or ignite it.

bur·nish (bûr'nish) v.t. & v.i. To polish by friction; make or become brilliant or shining. — n. Polish; luster; brightness. [OF burniss-, stem of burnir polish] — **bur'nish·ment** n.

bur·nish·er (bûr'nish-ər) n. 1 One who burnishes. 2 A tool with a smooth, rounded head used for giving a lustrous surface to metal, porcelain, etc. 3 A tool used to soften the hard lines of an engraving.

Burn·ley (bûrn'lē) A county borough in eastern Lancashire, England.

bur·noose (bər·noōs', bûr'noōs) n. A cloak with hood, worn by Arabs and Moors. Also **bur·nous', bur·nus'.** [<F burnous <Arabic burnus]

burn·out (bûrn'out') n. 1 Agric. A severe parching of the soil in areas subjected to prolonged or excessive solar heat. 2 The point at which one of the parts of a rocket or guided missile drops off the main assembly after having completed its work.

BURNOOSE

Burns (bûrnz), **Robert,** 1759–1796, Scottish poet.

burn·sides (bûrn'sīdz) n. pl. Side whiskers and mustache worn with closely shaven chin. [after Ambrose E. Burnside, 1824–81, U.S. major general]

burnt (bûrnt) A past tense and past participle of BURN. — adj. 1 Affected or consumed by fire; charred. 2 Diseased, as grain.

burnt cork A paste of powdered charred cork mixed with water: formerly used by actors to simulate Negro coloring.

burnt ocher A permanent, brick-red pigment made by heating ocher in a furnace.

burnt offering An animal, food, etc., burnt upon an altar as a sacrifice or offering to a god.

burnt orange A shade of light orange, with a brownish cast.

burnt sienna Raw sienna, calcined or roasted, noted for its dark brown color: used as an artist's pigment.

burnt umber A reddish-brown pigment made by calcining raw umber.

burp (bûrp) n. Colloq. A belch. — v.t. & v.i. To belch or cause to belch. [Imit.]

burr¹ (bûr) 1 A roughness or rough edge, especially one left on metal in casting or cutting. 2 A tool or device that raises a burr. 3 A dentist's drill with rough knothead: also **burr drill.** 4 A millstone made of burrstone: also spelled **buhr.** 5 The lobe of the ear. 6 A metal ring on the staff of a lance or handle of a battle-ax to keep the hand from slipping. 7 A halo around the moon or a star. 8 A blank punched out of a sheet of metal. 9 A washer to be slipped upon the end of a rivet before swaging, as in riveting leather. 10 A partly vitrified brick. 11 A hard lump of ore imbedded in a vein of softer material. 12 Bur¹. — v.t. 1 To form a rough edge on. 2 To remove a rough edge from. — v.i. 3 To operate a dentist's drill. Also spelled bur. ◆ Homophone: birr [Var. of BUR¹]

burr² (bûr) n. 1 A rough guttural sound of r caused by the vibration of the uvula against the back part of the tongue: common in the north of England, but not to be confused with the Scottish trill. 2 Any rough, dialectal pronunciation: the Scottish burr. 3 A whirring sound; a buzz. — v.t. To pronounce with a rough or guttural articulation. — v.i. 2 To speak with a burr. 3 To whir. Also spelled bur. ◆ Homophone: birr. [Imit.]

Burr (bûr), **Aaron,** 1756–1836, American lawyer and statesman; vice president of the United States 1801–05.

bur reed An herb (genus Sparganium), with ribbon-shaped leaves and spherical burlike fruit.

bur·ro (bûr'ō, boŏr'ō) n. pl. ·ros A small donkey, used as a pack animal. [<Sp.]

Bur·roughs (bûr'ōz), **John,** 1837–1921, U.S. naturalist and writer.

bur·row (bûr'ō) n. 1 A hole made in and under the ground, as by a rabbit, etc., for habitation. 2 A mound or barrow. — v.t. 1 To make by burrowing. 2 To perforate with or as with burrows. — v.i. 3 To live or hide in or as in a burrow. 4 To make a burrow or hole. 5 To dig into, under, or through something; bore. ◆ Homophone: borough. [ME borow. Related to BOROUGH.] — **bur'row·er** n.

burrowing owl Ground owl.

burr·stone (bûr'stōn) n. A cellular, compact siliceous rock used for making millstones: also spelled **buhrstone, burstone.**

bur·ry (bûr'ē) adj. Having or resembling burs; rough; prickly.

bur·sa (bûr'sə) n. pl. ·sae (-sē) 1 Anat. A pouch or saclike cavity; especially, one containing a viscid fluid and located at points of friction in the bodies of vertebrates. 2 Pathol. A cyst or abnormal sac. [<Med. L, sack, pouch]

Bur·sa (boŏr'sä) See BRUSA.

bur·sal (bûr'səl) adj. 1 Of or pertaining to a bursa. 2 Of or pertaining to the public revenue.

bur·sar (bûr'sər, -sär) n. A treasurer, as of a college. [<Med. L bursarius treasurer] — **bur·sar·i·al** (bər·sâr'ē·əl) adj.

bur·sa·ry (bûr'sər·ē) n. pl. ·ries 1 The treasury of a public institution or a religious order. 2 Scot. A grant for the maintenance of beneficiary students.

Bur·schen·schaft (boŏr'shən·shäft') n. pl. ·schaf·ten (-shäf'tən) German A students' association, especially one operated as a social organization; a fraternity.

burse (bûrs) n. 1 A purse. 2 Eccl. A lined case used to carry the folded corporal to and from the altar. 3 A scholarship. [<F bourse <LL bursa wallet <Gk. byrsa hide]

bur·seed (bûr'sēd') n. An Old World stickseed (Lappula echinata), naturalized in Canada and the northern United States.

bur·ser·a·ceous (bûr'sə·rā'shəs) adj. Bot. Designating or belonging to a small family (Burseraceae) of tropical balsamiferous or resinous polypetalous trees or shrubs with alternate compound leaves: the resin, leaves, and roots are used medicinally. [<NL Burseraceae, after J. Burser, 1603–89, German botanist]

bur·si·form (bûr'sə·fôrm) adj. Pouch-shaped; saclike.

bur·si·tis (bər·sī'tis) n. Pathol. Inflammation of a bursa.

burst (bûrst) v. **burst, burst·ing** v.i. 1 To break open or come apart suddenly and violently; explode, as from internal force. 2 To be full to the point of breaking open; bulge. 3 To issue forth or enter suddenly or violently. 4 To appear, begin; become audible or evident, etc.: A sound burst upon their ears. 5 To give sudden expression to passion, grief, etc.: to burst into tears; also, to be filled with violent emotion: He was bursting with rage. — v.t. 6 To cause to break open suddenly or violently; force open; puncture. 7 To fill or cause to swell to the point of breaking open. — n. 1 A sudden or violent explosion, rending, or disruption. 2 Mil. a The explosion of a bomb or shell on impact or in the air. b The number of bullets fired by one pressure on the trigger of an automatic weapon: a short burst. 3 A sudden effort; spurt; rush. 4 A sudden opening to view; prospect. [OE berstan]

burst·er (bûr'stər) n. 1 One who bursts. 2 Mil. An explosive which breaks open and scatters the contents of chemical shells, bombs, or mines.

bur·stone (bûr'stōn') See BURRSTONE.

bur·then (bûr'thən) See BURDEN.

bur·ton (bûr'tən) n. Naut. A light hoisting tackle, usually one kept hooked to the pendant at the topmasthead of a vessel. [Origin uncertain]

Bur·ton (bûr'tən), **Harold Hitz,** born 1888, U.S. jurist; associate justice of the Supreme Court 1945–59. — **Sir Richard Francis,** 1821–1890, English traveler and writer. — **Robert,** 1577–1640, English scholar, author, and clergyman.

Bur·ton-up·on-Trent (bûr'tən·ə·pon'trent') A county borough in eastern Staffordshire, England. Also **Bur'ton-on'-Trent'.**

Bu·ru (boŏ'roō) An Indonesian island in the Banda Sea west of Ceram; 3,668 square miles. Dutch **Boe·roe** (boŏ'roō).

Bu·run·di (boŏ·roŏn'dē) A kingdom in central Africa, part of the former UN Trust Territory of Ruanda-Urundi; 10,747 square miles; pop. about 2,000,000; capital, Usumbura.

Bu·ru·shas·ki (boŏ'roō·shas'kē) n. An unrelated language spoken in NW India.

bur·weed (bûr'wēd') n. Any of various weeds bearing burlike fruits, as the burdock.

bur·y¹ (ber'ē) v.t. **bur·ied, bur·y·ing** 1 To put (a dead body) in a grave, tomb, or the sea; perform burial rites for; inter. 2 To cover, as for concealment. 3 To end; put out of mind: to bury a friendship or a difference. 4 To occupy deeply; engross: He buried himself in study. ◆ Homophone: berry. [OE byrgan]

Synonyms: conceal, cover, entomb, hide, inter, overwhelm. Anything which is effectually covered and hidden under any mass or accumulation is buried. Money is buried in the ground; a body is buried in the sea; a paper is buried under other documents. Whatever is buried is hidden or concealed; but there are many ways of hiding or concealing a thing without burying it. So a person may be covered with wraps, and not buried under them. Bury may be used of any object, entomb and inter only of a dead body. Compare HIDE, IMMERSE. Antonyms: disclose, disinter, exhume, expose, raise, restore, reveal, show, uncover.

bur·y² (ber'ē) n. Obs. A borough; castle; manor: often in composition: Salisbury. ◆ Homophone: berry. [Var. of BOROUGH]

Bur·y (ber'ē) A county borough in SE Lancashire, England.

Bur·yat–Mon·gol Autonomous S.S.R. (boŏr·yät'mong'gəl) An autonomous republic in southern Siberia, Russian S.F.S.R.; 135,700 square miles; capital, Ulan-Ude.

burying beetle Sexton (def. 2).

bur·y·ing-ground (ber'ē·ing·ground') n. A cemetery.

Bur·y St. Ed·munds (ber'ē sänt ed'məndz) A municipal borough in Suffolk, England.

bus (bus) n. pl. **bus·es** or **bus·ses** 1 A large motor vehicle that carries passengers; an omnibus. 2 Colloq. An automobile. — v. **bused** or **bussed, bus·ing** or **bus·sing** v.t. 1 To transport by bus. — v.i. 2 To go by bus. 3 Colloq. To do the work of a bus boy. [Short form of OMNIBUS]

bus bar Electr. A short bar of copper or aluminum, usually uninsulated, forming a connection between two or more electrical circuits: also called omnibus bar.

bus boy An employee in a restaurant whose duty it is to clear tables of soiled dishes, assist the waiters, etc.

bus·by (buz'bē) n. pl. ·bies A tall fur cap worn as part of the full-dress uniform of British hussars, artillerymen, and engineers. [Origin uncertain]

bush¹ (boŏsh) n. 1 A low, treelike or thickly branching shrub. 2 A scrubby growth, or land covered by scrub; a forest with undergrowth. 3 A bough: used as a sign for a tavern; hence, a tavern. 4 A fox's brush. 5 A bushy growth, as of hair. — **the bush** 1 Country covered with thick woods and dense undergrowth. 2 A rural, arid, scrub-

BUSBY

covered region, especially of Australia. —*v.i.* **1** To grow or branch as or like a bush. **2** To be or become bushy. —*v.t.* **3** To protect (plants) with bushes or bushwood set round about; support with bushes. —*adj. U.S. Slang* Bush-league; small-time. [<ON *buskr*]

bush[2] (bōōsh) *v.t.* To line with a bushing, as an axle bearing, a pivot hole, etc. —*n.* A bushing. [<MDu. *busse* box]

bush baby Any of several species (genera *Galago* and *Euoticus*) of small, agile, gregarious nocturnal primates of African forests, having fluffy fir, long tails, and large eyes. Also **bush-baby.** Also called *galago.*

bush·boy (bōōsh′boi′) *n.* A bushman.

bush·buck (bōōsh′buk′) *n.* A small South African forest antelope *(Tragelaphus sylvaticus)*: also *boschbok.* Also **bush′goat′.**

bush clover A North American plant *(Lespedeza capitata)* with an erect, woolly stem.

bush cranberry The cranberry tree.

bushed (bōōsht) *adj. Colloq.* **1** Exhausted; worn out. **2** *Austral.* Lost; confused.

bush·el[1] (bōōsh′əl) *n.* **1** A measure of capacity; four pecks, 35.238 liters, or 2150.42 cubic inches. **2** A vessel holding that amount. [<OF *boissel,* dim. of *boiste* box]

bush·el[2] (bōōsh′əl) *v.t. & v.i.* To mend or alter, as men's clothes. [Cf. G *bosseln* do small jobs] —**bush′el·er, bush′el·ler** *n.* —**bush′el·man** (-mən) *n.*

bush·el·ing (bōōsh′əl·ing) *n.* The repairing of garments.

bush·ham·mer (bōōsh′ham′ər) *n.* A mason's hammer, used in dressing stone.

bush honeysuckle Any of various small shrubs (genus *Diervilla*) having opposite leaves and sweet-scented, reddish-yellow flowers.

bush hook A long pole with a sharp, hooked blade at the end, for cutting brush or limbs.

bu·shi·do (bōō′shē·dō) *n.* The code of the medieval Japanese Samurai, prescribing rigorous military training and practice, severe self-discipline, concern for personal honor, and loyalty to superiors and country. Also **Bu′shi·do.** [<Japanese, way of the warrior]

bush·ing (bōōsh′ing) *n.* **1** A metallic lining for a hole, as in the hub of a wheel, designed to insulate or to prevent abrasion between parts. **2** A tube for insertion in a pump barrel or a pulley bore to reduce the diameter. **3** *Electr.* A lining inserted in a socket to protect an electric current.

bush jacket A hip-length jacket of strong material with a belt and four pockets.

bush·land (bōōsh′land′) *n. Canadian* Unsettled northern forest land.

bush league *U.S. Slang* **1** In baseball, a minor league. **2** Anything minor or second-rate. —**bush′-league′** *adj.*

bush-lea·guer (bōōsh′lē′gər) *n. U.S. Slang* **1** A player in a bush league. **2** Any person working or acting in a petty way.

bush·man (bōōsh′mən) *n. pl.* **·men** (-mən) *Austral.* A dweller or farmer in the bush.

Bush·man (bōōsh′mən) *n. pl.* **·men** (-mən) **1** One of a nomadic people of South Africa, considered to be related to the Pygmies. **2** The language of the Bushmen comprising many dialects, characterized by clicks, and forming a subfamily of the Khoisan family of African languages. [<Du. *boschjesman*]

bush·mas·ter (bōōsh′mas′tər, -mäs′-) *n.* A large and venomous pit viper *(Lachesis mutus)* of Central America and tropical South America, sometimes 12 feet long.

bush pig Boschvark.

bush·rang·er (bōōsh′rān′jər) *n.* **1** One who lives as a wanderer in the bush. **2** *Austral.* A robber or brigand; originally, an outlaw living in the bush.

bush·whack (bōōsh′hwak′) *v.i.* **1** To cut bushes or underbrush with a bushwhacker. **2** To ride or range in the bush; fight in the bush, as a guerrilla. [<Du. *boschwachter* forest-keeper; infl. by WHACK]

bush·whack·er (bōōsh′hwak′ər) *n.* **1** One who ranges or fights in the bush. **2** A Confederate guerrilla. **3** A stout scythe for cutting bushes; also, one who uses it. **4** A backwoodsman. **5** *Austral.* A dweller or worker in the bush.

bush·whack·ing (bōōsh′hwak′ing) *n.* **1** Pulling a boat against the current by grabbing bushes. **2** Using underhand methods in politics. **3** Marauding; guerrilla fighting.

bush·y (bōōsh′ē) *adj.* **bush·i·er, bush·i·est 1** Covered with or full of bushes. **2** Like a bush; shaggy. —**bush′i·ly** *adv.* —**bush′i·ness** *n.*

bus·ied (biz′ēd) Past tense and past participle of BUSY.

bus·i·ly (biz′ə·lē) *adv.* In a busy manner; industriously.

busi·ness (biz′nis) *n.* **1** A pursuit or occupation; trade; profession; calling. **2** Commercial affairs. **3** A matter or affair. **4** Interest; concern; duty. **5** A commercial enterprise or establishment. **6** Those details other than and exclusive of dialog, by which actors portray their parts and interpret a play. **7** (biz′ē·nis) *Obs.* The state of being busy: now *busyness.* —**to mean business** To be serious. [OE *bysignis*] —**busi·ness·like** *adj.*

Synonyms: art, avocation, barter, calling, commerce, concern, craft, duty, employment, handicraft, industry, job, labor, occupation, profession, trade, trading, traffic, vocation, work. A *business* is what one follows regularly and for profit; an *occupation* is what he is engaged in, either continuously or temporarily, for any purpose, whether of profit, or of amusement, learning, philanthropy, etc. *Pursuit* is an *occupation* which one follows with ardor. A *profession* implies scholarship; as, the learned *professions.* A *vocation* or a *calling* is that to which one feels himself called, as by special fitness or sense of duty, often now also used to characterize an occupation or profession; an *avocation* is a secondary interest, including hobbies and other activities whether for pleasure or profit, that interrupt one's *vocation* or *business* or that may parallel and eventually become a vocation. A job is a piece of *business* viewed and paid for as a single undertaking; colloquially, any regular *employment* is often termed a *job. Trade* and *commerce* may be used as equivalents, but *trade* may have a more limited application; as, the *trade* of a village, the *commerce* of a nation; in the special sense, a *trade* is an *occupation* involving manual training and skilled labor. *Barter* is the direct exchange of commodities without use of money. *Work* is any application of energy to secure a result, or the result thus secured; we may speak of the *work* of an artist, or of a janitor. A single branch of productive *work* is called an *industry*; as, the steel *industry. Labor* is ordinarily used, in this connection, for unskilled *work; employment* for *work* done in the service of another. *Art* in the industrial sense is a system of rules and methods for accomplishing some practical result; as, the *art* of printing; collectively, the *arts.* A *craft* is some occupation requiring technical skill or manual dexterity, or the persons, collectively, engaged in its exercise; as, the weaver's *craft.* Compare ACTION, DUTY, TRAFFIC, TRANSACTION, WORK. *Antonyms*: idleness, inaction, inactivity, indolence, leisure, unemployment, vacation.

business card A card printed with one's name, business, and business address.

business English 1 English as used in business procedure. **2** A course in such English, including spelling, composition, etc.

business letter A letter about a business transaction, often following a certain form.

busi·ness·man (biz′nis·man′) *n. pl.* **·men** (-men′) One engaged in commercial or industrial activity. —**busi′ness·wom′an** *n. fem.*

bus·ing (bus′ing) *n.* **1** Transporting by bus. **2** The transportation of pupils by bus to schools other than in their own neighborhoods, in order to have racial balance in those schools.

busk[1] (busk) *n.* **1** A thin, elastic strip of wood, whalebone, or steel, placed in a corset or the like. **2** A corset. [<F *busc* ? <LL *boscum* bush, wood]

busk[2] (busk) *v.t. Scot.* or *Obs.* **1** To dress. **2** To prepare. [<ON *buask* get ready] —**busk′er** *n.*

busk·er (buskər) *n. Brit.* An itinerant musician or entertainer.

bus·kin (bus′kin) *n.* **1** A high shoe or half-boot reaching half-way to the knee, and strapped or laced to the ankle. **2** A laced half-boot, worn by Athenian tragic actors. **3** Tragedy. Compare SOCK[1]. [Origin uncertain]

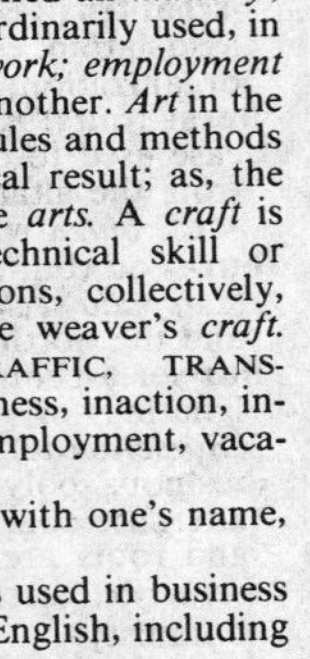

BUSKIN

bus·kined (bus′kind) *adj.* **1** Having the feet laced in buskins, as on the stage. **2** Of or pertaining to the tragic drama. **3** Tragic, lofty, dignified.

bus·kit (bus′kit) *adj. Scot.* **1** Clothed. **2** Prepared; made ready.

bus·man (bus′mən) *n. pl.* **·men** (-mən) One who operates a bus.

busman's holiday A holiday spent by choice in activity similar to one's regular work.

Bus·ra (bus′rə) Basra. Also **Bus′rah.**

buss[1] (bus) *Colloq. n.* A kiss; smack. —*v.t. & v.i.* To kiss heartily. [Imit. Cf. dial. G *bussen,* Sw. *puss,* Sp. *buz* (? <L *basiare*)]

buss[2] (bōōs, bōōs) *n. Scot.* A bush.

buss·es (bus′iz) A plural of BUS.

Bus·so·ra (bus′ə·rə) Basra. Also **Bus′so·rah.**

bust[1] (bust) *n.* **1** The human chest or breast. **2** A piece of statuary representing the human head, shoulders, and breast. [<F *buste* <Ital. *busto* trunk of the body]

bust[2] (bust) *Slang v.t.* **1** To burst. **2** To tame; train, as a horse. **3** To make bankrupt or short of funds. **4** To reduce in rank; demote. **5** To hit; strike. —*v.i.* **6** To burst. **7** To become bankrupt or short of funds. —*n.* **1** A bankruptcy. **2** Any failure; flop; dud. **3** A spree of any kind. **4** An arrest. [Alter. of BURST]

bus·tard (bus′tərd) *n.* Any member of a family *(Otididae)* of large Old World game birds related to the plovers and cranes, especially the **great bustard** *(Otis tarda),* the largest European land bird. [<OF *bistarde, oustarde* <L *avis tarda,* lit., slow bird]

bust·er (bus′tər) *n.* **1** *Slang* Something great, large, or remarkable; a person of exceptional ability. **2** *Slang* A spree; a bust. **3** *U.S. Colloq.* Little boy: used in direct address. —**southerly buster** *Austral.* **1** A powerful southerly wind. **2** A mixed alcoholic drink.

bus·tic (bus′tik) *n.* A tree *(Dipholis salicifolia)* of southern Florida, with a very hard, strong, close-grained wood. [Origin unknown]

bus·tle[1] (bus′əl) *n.* Excited activity; noisy stir; fuss. See synonyms under TUMULT. —*v.t. & v.i.* **·tled, ·tling** To hurry noisily; make a stir or fuss [? Related to BUSK[2]]

bus·tle[2] (bus′əl) *n.* **1** A frame or pad, formerly worn by women on the back below the waist to distend the skirts. **2** Fullness, as of gathered material, a bow, etc., worn over the back of a skirt below the waist. [? <BUSTLE[1]]

bus·tling (bus′ling) *adj.* Active; agitated. See synonyms under ACTIVE, ALERT, BUSY. —**bus′·tling·ly** *adv.*

bus·y (biz′ē) *adj.* **bus·i·er, bus·i·est 1** Intensely active; constantly or habitually occupied. **2** Temporarily engaged; not at leisure. **3** Officiously active; prying; meddling. **4** Pertaining to or filled with business. **5** Engaged: said of a telephone line or number. —*v.t.* **bus·ied, bus·y·ing** To make or be busy; occupy (oneself). See synonyms under OCCUPY. [OE *bysig* active]

Synonyms(adj.): active, assiduous, bustling, diligent, employed, engaged, industrious, occupied. *Busy* applies to an activity which may be temporary, *industrious* to a habit of life. *Diligent* indicates also a disposition, which is ordinarily habitual, and suggests more of heartiness and volition than *industrious.* We say one is a *diligent,* rather than an *industrious* reader. The *assiduous* worker gives patient and unremitting devotion to a task until it is done, or until nothing more can be done. Compare ACTIVE, INDUSTRIOUS, INDUSTRY. *Antonyms*: dilatory, dull, idle, inactive, indolent, lazy, listless, negligent, remiss, slack, slothful.

bus·y·bod·y (biz′ē·bod′ē) *n. pl.* **·bodies** One who officiously meddles with the affairs of others.

bus·y·ness (biz′ē·nis) *n.* The state of being busy: distinguished from *business.*

busy signal In a dial telephone, the sharp, recurrent buzzing tone indicating that the number called is already connected on another line. Compare DIAL TONE.

bus·y·work (biz′ē·wûrk′) *n.* Unnecessary work that is done only to keep one busy.

but[1] (but, *unstressed* bət) *conj.* **1** On the other hand; yet: I thought him honest, *but* he was lying. **2** Unless; if not: It never rains *but* it pours. **3** Excepting: Nothing would satisfy him *but* I come along. **4** Other than; otherwise than: I cannot choose *but* hear. **5** That:We don't doubt *but* matters will improve. **6** That . . . not: He is not so strong *but* a little

exercise will do him good. 7 Who . . . not; which . . . not: Few sought his advice *but* were enlightened by it. —*prep.* With the exception of; save: owning nothing *but* his clothes. —*adv.* 1 Only; just: If I had *but* thought. 2 Merely; not otherwise than: She is *but* a child. **—all but** Almost: He is *all but* well. **—but for** Were it not for; without: *But for* me, how would you have succeeded? **—but what** 1 But that; but those which: There are no events *but what* have meaning. 2 *Colloq.* But that: I don't know *but what* I will. —*n.* A verbal objection; exception; condition: without any ifs or *buts.* [OE *buten* < *be* by + *ūtan* outside]

Synonyms (conj.): and, barely, besides, except, further, however, just, merely, moreover, nevertheless, notwithstanding, only, provided, save, still, that, though, unless, yet. *But* ranges from the faintest contrast to absolute negation; as, I am willing to go, *but* (on the other hand) content to stay; he is not an honest man, *but* (on the contrary) a villain. *Except* and *excepting* are slightly more emphatic than *but.* Such expressions as "words are *but* breath" (nothing *but*) may be referred to the restrictive use by ellipsis. *But* never becomes a full synonym for *and; and* adds something, *but* adds something different; "brave *and* tender" implies that tenderness is natural to the brave; "brave *but* tender" implies that bravery and tenderness are rarely combined. The omission or insertion of *but* often reverses the meaning. "I have no fear *that* he will do it" and "I have no fear *but that* he will do it" have contrary senses, the former indicating the feeling of certainty *that he will not do it,* and the latter the feeling of certainty *that he will do it.* Where ambiguity or haziness results from the use of *but that,* it can ordinarily be avoided by recasting the sentence. Compare NOTWITHSTANDING.

but[2] (but) *n. Brit.* Any of various kinds of flatfish, especially the halibut and flounder: also spelled *butt.* [? < Gmc. Cf. Du. *bot* flounder, Sw. *butta* turbot.]

but[3] (but) *v.t.* & *v.i.* **but·ted, but·ting** To abut.

but[4] (but) *n. Scot.* The kitchen or outer room of a two-roomed house. **—to be but and ben with** To live in close intimacy with.

but[5] (but) See BUTT[4].

bu·ta·di·ene (byōō'tə·dī'ēn, -dī·ēn') *n. Chem.* A hydrocarbon, C_4H_6, closely related to isoprene, variously prepared from acetylene, petroleum, or alcohol: an important component in the manufacture of synthetic rubber. [< BUTANE + DI-[3] + -ENE]

bu·tane (byōō'tān, byōō·tān') *n. Chem.* A colorless, inflammable, gaseous compound, C_4H_{10}, of the aliphatic hydrocarbon series, contained in petroleum and formed synthetically by the action of zinc on ethyl iodide. [< L *butyrum* butter]

bu·tane·thi·ol (byōō'tān·thī'ōl, -ol) *n.* Butyl mercaptan. [< BUTANE + THIOL]

bu·ta·no·ic acid (byōō'tə·nō'ik) Butyric acid.

bu·ta·nol (byōō'tə·nôl, -nol) *n.* Butyl alcohol. [< BUTAN(E) + (ALCOH)OL]

bu·ta·none (byōō'tə·nōn) *n. Chem.* An inflammable colorless ketone, C_4H_8O, used in making plastics and as a solvent. [< BUTAN(E) + -ONE]

Bu·ta·ri·ta·ri (bōō·tä'rē·tä'rē) An atoll of the northern Gilbert Islands; 4 square miles: also *Makin.*

butch (bŏŏch) *adj. Slang* Masculine, as in appearance or manner: said of one who adopts a masculine role, especially a female homosexual. —*n.* 1 A closely cropped haircut for boys or men. 2 *Slang* A butch woman, especially a lesbian. [Prob. < *Butch,* a boy's nickname, often applied to young toughs]

butch·er (bŏŏch'ər) *n.* 1 One who slaughters animals or deals in meats for food. 2 A bloody or cruel murderer. 3 A vendor of candy, cigarettes, newspapers, etc., on trains. 4 In journalism, a copyreader. —*v.t.* 1 To slaughter or dress (animals) for market. 2 To kill (people or game) barbarously or brutally. 3 *Slang* To ruin by bungling treatment; botch. See synonyms under KILL. [< OF *bouchier* man who slaughters bucks < *boc* buck, he-goat] **—butch'er·er** *n.*

butch·er·bird (bŏŏch'ər·bûrd') *n.* A shrike: named from its habit of impaling its prey upon thorns.

butch·er·broom (bŏŏch'ər·brŏŏm', -brōōm') *n.* Any plant of the genus *Ruscus* of the lily family; especially, *R. aculeatus,* a low, evergreen shrub with leathery, leaflike branches bearing scarlet berries: also **butch'er's-broom'.**

butch·er·y (bŏŏch'ər·ē) *n. pl.* **·er·ies** 1 Wanton or wholesale slaughter. 2 A slaughterhouse. 3 Butcher's trade. 4 The result of butchering. See synonyms under MASSACRE.

bute (byōōt) See BUTTE.

Bute (byōōt) 1 A county in SW Scotland; 218 square miles; capital, Rothesay: also **Bute'shire** (-shir). 2 An island in the Firth of Clyde, Scotland; 47 square miles.

bu·te·o (byōō'tē·ō) *n.* Any of the numerous large, thickset hawks of the genus *Buteo,* having broad wings and rounded tails. Also called *buzzard.*

but·ler (but'lər) *n.* 1 A man servant in charge of the dining-room, wine, plate, etc. 2 Formerly, an official in charge of a royal wine cellar. [< OF *bouteillier* cupbearer < Med. L *buticularius* < *buticula* bottle] **—but'ler·ship** *n.*

Butler (but'lər), **Benjamin Franklin,** 1818–1893, U.S. general. **—Joseph,** 1692–1752, English theologian. **—Nicholas Murray,** 1862–1947, U.S. educator, president of Columbia University, New York, 1902–45. **—Pierce,** 1866–1939, U.S. jurist, associate justice of the Supreme Court 1923–39. **—Samuel,** 1612–1680, English satirical poet. **—Samuel,** 1835–1902, English novelist. **—Smedley Darlington,** 1881–1940, U.S. general.

butler's pantry A room between the kitchen and the dining-room, arranged for storage, serving, etc.

but·ler·y (but'lər·ē) *n. pl.* **·ler·ies** The butler's pantry.

butt[1] (but) *v.t.* 1 To strike with or as with the head or horns; ram. 2 To touch or bump against. 3 To cause to abut. 4 To abut on. 5 To join two things at the end; attach (one thing) to another, as a beam to a wall. —*v.i.* 6 To make a butting motion; move by butting. 7 To project; jut out. 8 To make a butt joint. 9 To be or lie adjacent; abut. —*n.* 1 A stroke, thrust, or push with or as with the head. 2 A thrust in fencing. **—to butt in** *Colloq.* To interrupt; interfere. [< OF *abouter* strike, ult. < Gmc.]

butt[2] (but) *n.* 1 A target, as for a rifle range. 2 *Often pl.* The range itself. 3 The shelter for the score-keeper on a rifle range. 4 The retaining wall placed behind a target to stop the bullets: also *target butt.* 5 A target for ridicule or criticism. 6 A limit; bound. [< OF *but* end, goal, ult. < Gmc.]

butt[3] (but) *n.* 1 The larger or thicker end of anything, as of a log. 2 That end or edge of a piece of timber where it comes squarely against another piece, or the joint thus formed. 3 A hinge. 4 The thick part of a tanned hide of leather. 5 The large end of the loin in beef. 6 *U.S. Colloq.* The buttocks. 7 The unused end of a cigar or cigarette. [Akin to Dan. *but* blunt, Du. *bot* short, stumpy]

butt[4] (but) *n.* 1 A large cask. 2 A measure of wine, 126 U.S. gallons. Also *but.* [< OF *boute*]

butt[5] (but) See BUT[2].

butte (byōōt) *n. Geog.* A conspicuous hill or natural turret, especially one with steep sides and a flattened top: also *bute.* [< F]

Butte (byōōt) A copper mining city in SW Montana.

but·ter[1] (but'ər) *n.* 1 The fatty constituent of milk, separated by churning into a soft, whitish-yellow solid; also, this substance prepared and processed for cooking and table use. 2 A substance having the consistency or other qualities of butter, as the chlorides of some metals, a fruit preserve of a semisolid consistency: apple *butter,* and certain easily fused vegetable oils: peanut *butter.* **—to look as if butter would not melt in one's mouth** To look innocent. —*v.t.* 1 To put butter on. 2 *Colloq.* To flatter: usually with *up.* **—to know which side one's bread is buttered on** To be aware of the true sources of one's fortune or security and to behave accordingly. [OE *butere,* ult. < Gk. *boutyron* < *bous* cow + *tyros* cheese]

butt·er[2] (but'ər) *n.* A person or animal that butts.

but·ter-and-eggs (but'ər·ən·egz') *n.* Any of various plants having two shades of yellow in the flower, as the toadflax in the United States, and a species of narcissus in England.

but·ter·ball (but'ər·bôl') *n.* 1 The bufflehead. 2 *Colloq.* A very fat person.

butter bean 1 Wax bean 2 *Southern U.S.* Lima bean.

but·ter·bough (but'ər·bou') *n.* The inkwood.

but·ter·burr (but'ər·bûr') *n.* An Old World herb (genus *Petasites*), with round or roundish leaves often a foot wide. Also **but'ter·bur'.**

but·ter·cup (but'ər·kup') *n.* 1 One of various species of crowfoot (genus *Ranunculus*), as *R. acris* and *R. bulbosus,* with yellow, cup-shaped flowers. 2 The flower. Also **but'ter·flow'er.**

but·ter·fat (but'ər·fat') *n.* The fatty substance obtained from the milk of mammals, consisting of the glycerides of various fatty acids.

but·ter·fin·gers (but'ər·fing'gərz) *n.* An inept or clumsy person; one who drops things easily. **—but'ter·fin'gered** *adj.*

but·ter·fish (but'ər·fish') *n. pl.* **·fish** or **·fish·es** One of various marine food fishes of the North Atlantic with an oily skin, as the dollarfish: also called *pumpkinseed.*

but·ter·fly (but'ər·flī') *n. pl.* **·flies** 1 A diurnal lepidopterous insect (division *Rhopalocera*) with large, often brightly colored wings, club-shaped antennae, and slender body. Compare MOTH. 2 A gay idler or trifler. [OE *buttorflēoge*]

butterfly bush Buddleia.

butterfly fish *n.* 1 One of various tropical marine fishes (family *Chaetodontidae*) having brightly colored bodies. 2 A brilliantly colored Chinese fish *(Macropodus viridiauratus).*

butterfly stroke In swimming, a stroke made while lying face down, the arms being brought forward laterally above the water: performed in conjunction with a fishtail kick.

butterfly table A small drop-leaf table, the leaves supported by brackets that resemble a butterfly's wings.

butterfly tie A bow tie.

butterfly valve *Mech.* 1 A valve resembling a double clack valve, composed of two semicircular pieces attached to a cross-rib in the pump bucket. 2 A disk turning on a diametral axis, used as a damper in a pipe.

butterfly weed 1 A bushy species of milkweed *(Asclepias tuberosa),* common in the United States and Canada, and conspicuous in midsummer by its large masses of orange-red flowers: also called *orange* or *vermilion milkweed.* 2 A native North American plant *(Gaura coccinea)* of the primrose family, with small pink, red, or white flowers. 3 Pleurisy root.

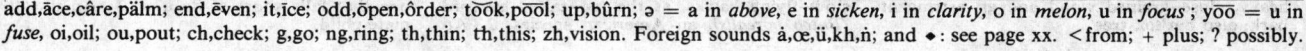

BUTTERFLY WEED (*def. 1*)

but·ter·ine (but'ər·ēn, -in) *n.* Artificial butter; oleomargarine.

butter knife A small, blunt-edged knife for cutting or spreading butter.

but·ter·milk (but'ər·milk') *n.* The sour liquid left after the butterfat has been separated from milk or cream.

but·ter·nut (but'ər·nut') *n.* 1 The oily, edible nut of the North American white walnut *(Juglans cinerea).* 2 The tree, or its cathartic inner bark. 3 An oily, nutlike seed of a tall tree *(Caryocar nuciferum),* native in British Guiana, having a hard, brown, tubercled shell: also called *souari nut.* 4 The dye obtained from the bark and roots of the butternut tree. 5 A Confederate soldier; also, a Southern sympathizer in the Civil War. 6 Cloth or a garment dyed with butternut.

but·ter·scotch (but'ər·skoch') *n.* 1 Hard, sticky candy made with brown sugar, butter, and flavoring. 2 A flavoring extract consisting of similar ingredients. —*adj.* Made of or flavored with butterscotch.

but·ter·weed (but′ər·wēd′) *n.* **1** The horseweed. **2** A groundsel *(Senecio lobatus)* of the southern United States. **3** The Indian mallow.

but·ter·wort (but′ər·wûrt′) *n.* Any of several small stemless herbs (genus *Pinguicula*), with broad fleshy leaves that secrete a greasy substance in which insects are captured.

but·ter·y[1] (but′ər·ē) *adj.* **1** Containing, like, or smeared with butter. **2** Grossly flattering; adulating.

but·ter·y[2] (but′ər·ē, but′rē) *n. pl.* **·ter·ies 1** A pantry; a wine cellar. **2** In English universities, a place in each college from which the students are supplied with provisions. [<OF *boterie* <LL *botaria* <*butta* bottle]

butt hinge A hinge composed of two plates or leaves which are screwed to the abutting surfaces of the door and the jamb. For illustration see under HINGE.

but·ting (but′ing) *n.* An abuttal.

butt joint A joint made by placing the component parts end to end and holding them in place either by welding or by side plates riveted thereto.

but·tock (but′ək) *n.* **1** *Naut.* The hinder part of a ship's hull. **2** *Anat.* **a** Either of the two fleshy prominences which form the rump. **b** *pl.* The rump. ◆ Collateral adjective: *gluteal.* [Dim. of BUTT[3]]

but·ton (but′n) *n.* **1** A knob or disk, as of bone or metal, which, when forced through a narrow opening, or buttonhole, fastens one part of a garment to another. **2** Anything resembling a button, as an emblem of membership, usually worn in the lapel, a political emblem on a celluloid disk, etc. **3** A pivoted fastener for a door, window, etc. **4** A knob or protuberance, as for operating an electric bell, at the end of a foil, etc. **5** *pl. Brit. Colloq.* A boy in attendance; a page: so called from the buttons on his uniform. **6** *Metall.* A small globular or disklike mass of metal found in a crucible after fusion. **7** *Bot.* **a** A bud or other like protuberance on a plant. **b** The small round flower head of some composite plants. **c** A small seed vessel. **d** The head of an immature mushroom. **8** *Zool.* **a** The bud that forms at the initial stage of a stag's horns. **b** The small round knob at the end of the rattles of a rattlesnake. **9** *U.S.* A guessing game. **10** *Slang* The point of the jaw. **11** *pl. Slang* Wits: Some of his *buttons* are missing. —*v.t.* **1** To fasten with or as with a button or buttons. **2** To provide with buttons. —*v.i.* **3** To admit of being buttoned. **4** To bud or form heads, as a cauliflower. [<OF *boton* button, bud] —**but′ton·er** *n.* —**but′ton·like′** *adj.*

but·ton·bush (but′n·boosh′) *n.* A North American shrub *(Cephalanthus occidentalis)*: so called from its spherical white flower heads.

but·ton·hole (but′n·hōl′) *n.* A slit to receive and hold a button. —*v.t.* **·holed, ·hol·ing 1** To work buttonholes in. **2** To sew with a buttonhole stitch. **3** To detain by conversation; importune. —**but′ton·hol′·er** *n.*

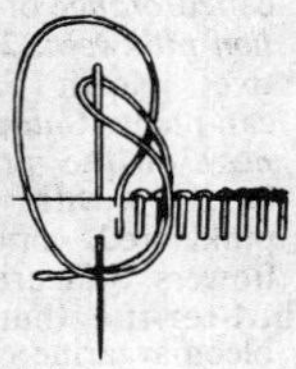

BUTTONHOLE STITCH

buttonhole stitch A perpendicular stitch fastened with a loop at the top, worked in a row or series for making a firm edge as in buttonholes: also called *close stitch.*

but·ton·hook (but′n·hook′) *n.* A hook for buttoning gloves or shoes.

but·ton·mold (but′n·mōld′) *n.* A disk of wood or other material which is made into a button by covering with fabric, leather, etc.

button snakeroot 1 Any of several plants (genus *Liatris*): so called from the small round flower heads. **2** A stout-stemmed plant *(Eryngium aquaticum)*, with linear leaves and globose heads of flowers.

button spider The black widow.

but·ton·weed (but′n·wēd′) *n.* **1** The knapweed. **2** The Indian mallow.

but·ton·wood (but′n·wood′) *n.* **1** The sycamore or plane tree of the United States: also **but′ton·ball′. 2** A tree or shrub of tropical America and Africa *(Conocarpus erecta)* with heavy, close-grained wood and an astringent bark: also **but′ton·tree′.**

but·ton·y (but′ən·ē) *adj.* Of the nature of, like, or covered with buttons.

butt plate A plate, usually corrugated to prevent slipping on the shoulder, attached to the end of a gunstock.

but·tress (but′ris) *n.* **1** *Archit.* A structure built against a wall to strengthen it. **2** Any support or prop: *buttresses* to faith. **3** Any formation suggesting a buttress. **4** A projecting rock or hillside. **5** A horny growth on a horse's hoof. See synonyms under PROP. —**flying buttress** *Archit.* A rampant arch extending from a wall or pier to a supporting abutment, usually receiving the thrust of another arch on the other side of the wall, which it supports by its upper end. —*v.t.* **1** *Archit.* To support with a buttress. **2** To prop up; sustain; fortify: *buttressed* by her religious convictions. [<OF *bouterez,* nominative sing. of *bouteret* <*bouter* push, thrust]

butt shaft An arrow with a blunt head.

butt·weld (but′weld′) *n.* A weld made between two abutting ends or edges without overlapping.

Bu·tung (bōō′toong) An Indonesian island just SE of Celebes; 1,759 square miles: also *Buton.*

bu·tyl (byōō′til) *n. Chem.* A univalent hydrocarbon radical, C_4H_9, from butane. [<BUT(YRIC) + -YL]

butyl alcohol *Chem.* Any of three isomeric alcohols derived from butane, and having the formula C_4H_9OH: also *butanol.*

bu·ty·lene (byōō′tə·lēn) *n. Chem.* A gaseous hydrocarbon, C_4H_8, of the olefin series, existing in three isomeric modifications: an ingredient of synthetic rubber.

butyl mercaptan *Chem.* A noxious sulfur compound, C_4H_9SH: used in dilutions to protect stored foods against rats, and as a warning agent in natural-gas service: also *butanethiol.*

bu·ty·ra·ceous (byōō′tə·rā′shəs) *adj.* Having the nature, qualities, or appearance of butter; buttery. Also **bu·ty·rous** (byōō′tər·əs). [<L *butyrum.* See BUTTER[1].]

bu·ty·rate (byōō′tə·rāt) *n. Chem.* A salt or ester of butyric acid.

bu·tyr·ic (byōō·tir′ik) *adj.* Of, pertaining to, or derived from butter. [<L *butyrum.* See BUTTER[1].]

butyric acid *Chem.* Either of two isomeric acids, C_3H_7COOH, especially one found as an ester in butter and certain oils, and free in rancid butter, perspiration, etc.: also *butanoic acid.*

bu·ty·rin (byōō′tər·in) *n. Chem.* Any one of three analogous compounds formed by treating glycerol with butyric acid at a high temperature.

bux·om (buk′səm) *adj.* **1** Characterized by health and vigor; plump; comely: said of women. **2** Having a large bosom. [OE *buhsum* pliant. Akin to OE *bugan* bend, bow.] —**bux′om·ly** *adv.* —**bux′om·ness** *n.*

buy (bī) *v.* **bought, buy·ing** *v.t.* **1** To obtain for a price; purchase. **2** To be a price for. **3** To obtain by an exchange or sacrifice: to *buy* wisdom with experience. **4** To bribe; corrupt. **5** *Slang* To believe or accept, as an excuse. —*v.i.* **6** To make purchases; be a purchaser. —**to buy in 1** To buy from the owner, as at an auction when bids are too low. **2** To buy stock or an interest, as in a company. **3** *Slang* To pay money as a price for joining. —**to buy off** To obtain a promise of nonintervention by bribing. —**to buy out** To purchase the stock, interests, etc., of, as in a business. —*n. Colloq.* **1** Anything bought or about to be bought. **2** A bargain. [OE *bycgan*] —**buy′a·ble** *adj.* —**buy′er** *n.*

buzz[1] (buz) *v.i.* **1** To make a humming, vibrating sound, as a bee or hummingbird. **2** To talk, discuss, or gossip excitedly: The town *buzzed* with the news. **3** To move from place to place; bustle about. —*v.t.* **4** To utter or express in a buzzing manner; gossip. **5** To cause to buzz, as wings. **6** *Colloq.* To fly an airplane low over: He *buzzed* the ship. **7** *Colloq.* To call on the telephone. —*n.* **1** A low murmur, as of bees, talk, or distant sounds. **2** Rumor; gossip. **3** *Colloq.* A telephone call. [Imit.]

buzz[2] (buz) *v.t. Brit.* To drain to the last drop. [Origin unknown]

buzzard (buz′ərd) *n.* **1** One of several large, slow-flying hawks, as the **red-tailed buzzard** *(Buteo borealis),* an American species. **2** An American vulture; the turkey buzzard. [<OF *busart,* prob. <L *buteo* hawk]

buz·zard[2] (buz′ərd) *n. Brit. Dial.* A noisy insect, as a cockchafer, dor beetle, etc. [<BUZZ[1] + -ARD]

buzzard dollar The silver dollar of 412½ grains coined under the Bland bill, 1878: in allusion to the design of the eagle on the reverse.

Buzzards Bay An inlet of the Atlantic in southern Massachusetts.

buzz bomb See under BOMB.

buzz·er (buz′ər) *n.* **1** One who or that which buzzes. **2** An electric signal making a buzzing sound, as on a telephone switchboard.

buzz saw A circular saw: so called from the sound it emits.

buzz·wig (buz′wig′) *n.* **1** A large, thick wig. **2** A person who wears such a wig. **3** A person of importance.

Bwa·na (bwä′nä) *n.* Master; sir. [<Swahili <Arabic *Abuna* our father]

by (bī) *prep.* **1** Next to; near: the house *by* the road. **2** Along the course of: the railroad tracks *by* the river. **3** Past or beyond: The train flashed *by* us. **4** In the course of; during: birds flying *by* night. **5** Not later than: Be here *by* four tomorrow. **6** For the period of; according to: They work *by* the day. **7** As a result of the effort, means, or action of: a play written *by* Shakespeare; a house struck *by* lightning. **8** With the perception of: a loss felt *by* all. **9** By means of: leading a child *by* the hand. **10** In consequence of: a case won *by* default. **11** As a means of conveyance; via: Mail your letters *by* air. **12** To the extent or amount of: insects *by* the thousands. **13** On the basis of: a road four miles long *by* actual measurement. **14** Considered according to: advancing step *by* step; reading word *by* word. **15** With reference to: to do well *by* one's friends. **16** Multiplied by: a room ten *by* twelve. **17** In the name of: swearing *by* all that is sacred. —*adv.* **1** In the presence or vicinity; at hand; near; as, to keep one's sword *by.* **2** Up to and beyond something; past: the train roared *by.* **3** Apart; aside, as discarded or saved for future use: to lay something *by.* **4** At or into a person's house, store, etc.: to stop *by.* —*adj. & n.* Bye. [OE *bī* near, about]

Synonyms (prep.): through, with. *By* refers to the agent; *through,* to the means, cause, or condition; *with,* to the instrument. *By* commonly refers to persons; *with,* to things; *through* may refer to either. The road having become impassable *through* long disuse, a way was opened *by* pioneers *with* axes. *By,* however, may be applied to any object which is viewed as partaking of action and agency; as, the metal was corroded *by* the acid; skill is gained *by* practice. "His friends were displeased *by* the selection of another chairman" means that the action displeased them; "His friends were displeased *with* the selection," etc., means that the man selected was not their choice. *Through* implies a more distant connection than *by* or *with,* and more intervening elements. Material objects are perceived *by* the mind *through* the senses. *By* is in frequent use after call, judge, know, measure, perceive, see, seem, take, understand, etc., to indicate the determining object; as, to call *by* name; I judge *by* his dress that he is poor; I saw *by* his glance that he was a rogue. *Accompanied* and *attended* take *by* of persons, *with* (commonly) of things; we say, *surrounded by.*

by– *combining form* **1** Secondary; inferior; incidental: *by-product.* **2** Near; close: *bystander.* **3** Aside; out of the way: *byway.*

By (bī), **John,** 1781–1836, Canadian military engineer; founder of Ottawa.

by all means Certainly; on every account.

by and by 1 At some time in the future; soon; before long. **2** *Obs.* At once; immediately.

by–and–by (bī′ən·bī′) *n.* Future time; hereafter.

by and large 1 Generally speaking; on the whole. **2** *Naut.* Alternatively well up to and off from the wind: This boat sails well *by and large.*

by–bid·der (bī′bid′ər) *n.* A person who runs up prices at an auction for the seller or owner. —**by′–bid′ding** *n.*

by–blow (bī′blō′) *n.* **1** A side or chance blow; one that falls short of its aim. **2** An illegitimate child.

Byd·goszcz (bid'gôshch) A city in north central Poland: German *Bromberg.*

bye (bī) *n.* **1** Something of minor or secondary importance; a side issue. **2** In cricket, a run made on a ball missed by the batsman and which has passed the wicket-keeper. **3** The position of a person who is assigned no opponent and automatically advances to the next round, as in the preliminary pairings of a tennis tournament. **4** In golf, any hole or holes remaining unplayed when the match ends. —*adj.* Not principal or main; secondary. Also **by.** [Var. of BY]

bye-bye (bī'bī') *interj.* A child's word for good-bye. Also **bye.**

Bye·la·ya A river in Bashkortostan, flowing 882 miles to the Kama river; also **Belaya.**

by-e·lec·tion (bī'i·lek'shən) *n. Brit.* A parliamentary election between general elections, held to fill a vacancy.

Bye·lo·rus·sia See **Belorus.**

bye-low (bī'lō) *adv. & interj.* Hush!: a child's word, used in lullabies.

by·gone (bī'gôn', -gon') *adj.* Gone by; former; past; out-of-date. —*n.* Something past; that which has gone by: usually in the plural.

byke (bīk) See BIKE².

by-lane (bī'lān') *n.* **1** A byway. **2** A side passage in a mine.

by-law (bī'lô') *n.* **1** A rule or law adopted by an association, a corporation, or the like, which is subordinate to a constitution or charter. **2** *Obs.* An accessory law. [ME *bilawe* < *by, bi* village (< ON *bȳr*) + *lawe* law; infl. by BY]

by-line (bī'līn') *n.* The line at the head of an article in a newspaper, etc., giving the name of the writer.

by-name (bī'nām') *n.* **1** A secondary name; surname; sobriquet. **2** A nickname; epithet.

Byng (bing), **George,** 1663–1733, British admiral. —**Julian Hedworth George,** 1862–1935, Viscount Byng of Vimy, British field marshal.

by-pass (bī'pas', -päs') *n.* **1** Any road, path, or route connecting two points in a course other than that normally used; a detour. **2** A device to lead a flow of gas or liquid around a pipe, fixed connection, or obstacle. **3** An electric switch. —*v.t.* **1** To go around (an obstacle). **2** To provide with a by-pass.

by·past (bī'past', -päst') *adj.* Bygone.

by-path (bī'path', -päth') *n.* A side, secluded, or secondary path.

by-play (bī'plā') *n.* **1** Action on the stage conducted through asides or dumb show as an accompaniment to the main action. **2** Any diversion from the main action.

by-prod·uct (bī'prod'əkt) *n.* Any material or product contingent upon or incidental to a manufacturing process: Bagasse is a *by-product* in the making of cane sugar.

Byrd (bûrd), **Harry Flood,** 1887–1966, U.S. politician. —**Richard Evelyn,** 1888–1957, U.S. rear admiral, aviator, polar explorer, and writer: brother of the preceding. —**William,** 1674–1744, Virginia planter and author. —**William,** 1543?–1623, English composer.

byre (bīr) *n.* A cow stable. [OE, stall, shed]

byrl (bûrl, birl) See BIRLE.

Byrnes (bûrnz), **James Francis,** 1879–1972, U.S. statesman; secretary of state 1945–47.

byr·nie (bûr'nē) *n. Archaic* A coat of mail. [Var. of ME *brynie*]

by-road (bī'rōd') *n.* **1** A back road or crossroad; a private way. **2** Secret means.

By·ron (bī'rən), **Lord,** 1788–1824, George Gordon Noel Byron, sixth baron, English poet.

By·ron·ic (bī·ron'ik) *adj.* Of or pertaining to Lord Byron or his writings. **2** Like or characteristic of Byron or his style: proud, romantic, passionate, etc. Also **By·ro·ni·an** (bī·rō'nē·ən), **By·ron'i·cal.**

bys·si·no·sis (bis'ə·nō'sis) *n.* A pulmonary disease caused by the inhalation of cotton dust in mills. [< Latin *byssinum* linen + -OSIS]

bys·sus (bis'əs) *n. pl.* **bys·sus·es** or **bys·si** (bis'ī) **1** Formerly, any costly white stuff of cotton, silk, or linen. **2** *Zool.* A bunch of silky thread secreted by the foot of certain stationary bivalve mollusks, as mussels, and serving as a means of attachment to an anchorage. **3** *Bot.* A filamentous fungus of the obsolete group *Byssi.* [< L < Gk. *byssos* fine linen]

by·stand·er (bī'stan'dər) *n.* One who stands by; a looker-on. See synonyms under SPECTATOR.

by-street (bī'strēt') *n.* A side street; a byway.

by-talk (bī'tôk') *n.* Incidental talk; small talk.

byte (bīt) *n.* A group of eight bits in a computer memory that form a character, a symbol, or a keyboard function. [< B(INAR)Y (DIGIT)E(IGHT)]

by the bye Incidentally; by the way. Also **by the by.**

by the way Incidentally; by the bye.

By·tom (bi'tôm) Polish name for BEUTHEN.

by·wa·ter (bī'wô'tər, -wot'ər) *n.* A diamond that is slightly yellowish or off color. [< BY, *adv.* (def. 3) + WATER (def. 5)]

By·wa·ter (bī'wô·tər), **Ingram,** 1840–1914, English classical scholar.

by·way (bī'wā') *n.* A branch or side road.

by·word (bī'wûrd') *n.* **1** A phrase, person, institution, etc., that has become an object of derision or mockery. **2** A nickname. **3** A trite saying; proverbial phrase. See synonyms under ADAGE. [OE *biword* proverb]

by·work (bī'wûrk') *n.* Work for odd hours during leisure time.

byz·ant (biz'ənt) See BEZANT.

Byz·an·tine (biz'ən·tēn, -tīn, bi·zan'tin) *adj.* **1** Of or pertaining to Byzantium. **2** Pertaining to a style of architecture developed in the Byzantine Empire during the fourth century, characterized by the round arch springing from four columns or piers, and in which the dome rests on

BYZANTINE ARCHITECTURE
Santa Sophia, Constantinople, A.D. 538.

pendentives, with centralized plans, colorful mosaics, and rich decoration. For illustration see under CAPITAL. —*n.* A native or inhabitant of Byzantium. Also **By·zan·ti·an** (bi·zan'·shē·ən, -shən). [< L *Byzantinus* < *Byzantium*]

Byzantine Empire The eastern part of the later Roman Empire (395–1453): Arabic *Rum:* also *Byzantium, Eastern Empire, Eastern Roman Empire.*

Byzantine rite Religious ceremonies as performed by the Greek Orthodox Church.

By·zan·ti·um (bi·zan'shē·əm, -tē·əm) **1** A former name for ISTANBUL. **2** The Byzantine Empire.

Bzu·ra (bzōō'rä) A river in central Poland, flowing 85 miles NE to the Vistula.

C

c, C (sē) *n. pl.* **c's** or **cs, C's Cs, cees** (sēz) **1** The third letter of the English alphabet: from Phoenician *gimel,* through Hebrew *gimel,* Greek *gamma,* Roman C or G. **2** The sound of the letter c. See ALPHABET. —*symbol* **1** In Roman notation, the numeral 100. See under NUMERAL. **2** *Chem.* Carbon (symbol C). **3** *Music* **a** The tonic note of the natural musical scale, do. **b** The pitch of this tone or the written note representing it. **c** The scale built upon C. **d** Common or 4–4 time.

Ca *Chem.* Calcium (symbol Ca).

ca' (kô) *v.t. Scot.* **1** To call. **2** To drive, as cattle. Also spelled **caw.**

Caa·ba (kä'bə, kä'ə·bə) See KAABA.

cab¹ (kab) *n.* **1** A one-horse public carriage. **2** A taxicab. **3** The covered part of a locomotive or motortruck. [Short form of CABRIOLET]

cab² (kab) *n.* A Hebrew measure equivalent to about two quarts: also spelled **kab.**

ca·bal (kə·bal') *n.* **1** A number of persons secretly united for some private purpose. **2** Intrigue; conspiracy. —*v.i.* **ca·balled, ca·bal·ling** To form a cabal; plot. [< MF *cabale* < Med. L *cabbala* < Hebrew *qabbālāh* tradition]

Synonyms (*noun*): combination, conclave, confederacy, conspiracy, crew, faction, gang, junto. See CONSPIRACY.

cab·a·la (kab'ə·lə, kə·bä'lə) *n.* **1** The mystic theosophy of the Hebrews. **2** Any secret, occult, or mystic system. Often spelled *cabbala, kabala, kabbala.* [< Hebrew *qabbālāh* tradition < *qābal* receive] —**ca·bal'ic** *adj.* —**cab·a·lism** (kab'ə·liz'əm) *n.*

cab·a·list (kab'ə·list) *n.* **1** A student of the cabala. **2** A mystic; occultist.

cab·a·lis·tic (kab'ə·lis'tik) *adj.* **1** Pertaining to the cabala. **2** Having a mystic sense; mysterious. Also **cab·a·lis'ti·cal.** See synonyms under MYSTERIOUS. —**cab·a·lis'ti·cal·ly** *adv.*

ca·bal·la·da (kä'bəl·yä'də) *SW U.S.* A herd of horses or mules.

cab·al·le·ro (kab'əl·yâr'ō) *n. pl.* **·ros 1** A Spanish gentleman; cavalier: used with as broad a signification as the English word *gentleman.* **2** *SW U.S.* **a** A lady's escort. **b** A horseman.

cab·al·line (kab'ə·līn, -lin) *adj.* Of, pertaining to, or suited to horses: *caballine* aloes. [< L *caballinus* < *caballus* horse]

caballine fountain The fountain Hippocrene; hence, a fountain of inspiration. Also **caballine spring.**

ca·ba·na (kə·bä'nə, -ban'ə; *Sp.* kä·bä'nyä) *n.* **1** A small cabin. **2** A bathhouse on a beach. Also **ca·ba'ña.** [< Sp.]

Ca·ba·na·tuan (kə·bä'nə·twän') A town in central Luzon; site of a Japanese prisoner of war camp in World War II.

ca·bane (kə·ban') *n. Aeron.* **1** A framework to support the wings of an airplane at the fuselage. **2** The system of trusses supporting the overhang of a wing. [< F, cabin]

cab·a·ret (kab'ə·rā') *n.* **1** A restaurant or café which provides singing, dancing, etc., as entertainment for its patrons. **2** Entertainment of this type. **3** A tavern or wine shop. **4** A tea or coffee set, including tray and dishes. [< F]

cab·as (kab'ə, kə·bä') *n.* **1** A rush basket. **2** A woman's workbag or basket. [< F]

cab·as·set (kab'ə·set) *n.* An open helmet with a rounded top and narrow brim. [< F, dim. of *cabas* basket]

cab·bage¹ (kab'ij) *n.* **1** The close-leaved head formed by certain brassicaceous plants. **2** The plant (*Brassica oleracea*) producing it. **3** The large terminal leaf bud of the cabbage palm used as a vegetable. —*v.i.* **·baged, ·bag·ing** To form a head, as cabbage; to grow into a head. [< OF *caboche* < L *caput* head]

---

cab·bage[2] (kab′ij) *v.t.* & *v.i.* **·baged, ·bag·ing** To pilfer; take dishonestly; purloin: said originally of a tailor who appropriated a part of his customers' cloth. —*n.* Cloth appropriated by a tailor in cutting out garments; hence, anything purloined. [Origin uncertain]
cabbage bug The harlequin bug.
cabbage butterfly Any of several butterflies (genus *Pieris*) whose larvae feed on plants of the mustard family; especially *P. rapae,* the green larvae of which destroy cabbage. For illustration see under INSECT (injurious).
cabbage green The soft, grayish blue-green color of cabbage leaves.
cabbage palm 1 A palm with a terminal leaf bud used as a vegetable, as the cabbage palm *(Sabal palmetto)* of Florida. **2** The feather palm *(Ptychosperma elegans)* of Australia. **3** The fan palm.
cab·ba·la (kab′ə·lə, kə·bä′lə), etc. See CABALA.
cab·by (kab′ē) *n. pl.* **·bies** *Colloq.* A cabman.
Cab·ell (kab′əl), **James Branch,** 1879–1958, U.S. novelist.
ca·ber (kā′bər) *n. Scot.* A mastlike pole, generally the stem of a tree, used in the Highland athletic game **tossing the caber:** also spelled *kabar, kebar.*
Ca·be·za de Va·ca (kä·vā′thä thā vä′kä), **Alvar Núñez,** 1490?–1559?, Spanish explorer of North and South America.
cab·in (kab′in) *n.* **1** A small, rude house; hut. **2** A compartment in a vessel for officers or passengers. **3** *Aeron.* The enclosed space in an airplane for passengers, pilot, etc.; the cockpit. see synonyms under, HOUSE, HUT. —*v.t. & v.i.* To shut up or dwell in or as in a cabin; crib; hamper. [<F *cabane* <LL *capanna* cabin]
cabin boy A boy who waits on the officers and passengers of a vessel.
cabin class A class of accommodations for steamship passengers, higher than tourist class, lower than first class.
Ca·bin·da (kə·bin′də) An exclave of Angola north of the Congo on the Gulf of Guinea; about 3,000 square miles.
cab·i·net (kab′ə·nit) *n.* **1** The body of official advisers of a king, president, or chief of state. **2** A council, or the chamber in which it meets. **3** A room for works of art, etc.; also, the articles collected. **4** A piece of furniture fitted with shelves and drawers. **5** *Obs.* A little cabin. **6** A small private room; a study or closet. —*adj.* **1** Pertaining to or suitable for a cabinet in any sense. **2** Secret; confidential. [<F <Ital. *gabinetto* closet, chest of drawers; in def. 4, dim. of CABIN]
cab·i·net·mak·er (kab′ə·nit·mā′kər) *n.* One who does fine woodworking, as for cabinets, furniture, etc.
cab·i·net·work (kab′ə·nit·wûrk′) *n.* The work of a cabinetmaker; expert woodwork.
ca·ble (kā′bəl) *n.* **1** *Naut.* **a** A heavy rope or chain, as for mooring vessels, etc. **b** A cable's length. **2** *Electr.* An insulated electrical conductor or group of conductors, protected by a waterproof coat, as for a submarine telegraph. **3** A cablegram. —*v.t.* **ca·bled, ca·bling 1** To fasten, as by a cable; tie fast. **2** To equip with cable or cables. **3** To send, as a message, by submarine telegraph. —*v.i.* **4** To communicate by submarine telegraph. [Akin to F *câble,* Sp. *cable* <LL *capulum,* *caplum* rope <*capere* take, grasp]
Ca·ble (kā′bəl), **George Washington,** 1844–1925, U.S. writer.
cable car A car or cage, pulled by an overhead or underground cable.
ca·ble·gram (kā′bəl·gram) *n.* A telegraphic dispatch sent by cable.
ca·ble-laid (kā′bəl·lād′) *adj.* Made up of three three-stranded ropes twisted together left-handed: a ropemaking term.
cable railroad A railroad in which the cars are attached to an endless moving cable by means of an adjustable grip usually passing through a slot in the roadway.
cable's length A unit of nautical measure: in the United States 720 feet, in England 608 feet.
ca·blet (kā′blit) *n.* A cable rope less than 10 inches in circumference: a hawser. [Dim. of CABLE]
cable TV or **cable television** A system for transmitting television programs by coaxial cable to individual subscribers. Abbr. CATV
cab·man (kab′mən) *n. pl.* **·men** (-mən) The driver of a cab.
ca·bob (kə·bob′) See KABAB.
ca·boched (kə·bosht′) *adj. Her.* Full-faced: said of the head of a stag, bull, or other beast. Also **ca·boshed′.** [<OF *caboché,* pp. of *cabocher* cut off the head <L *caput* head]
cab·o·chon (kab′ə·shon, *Fr.* kȧ·bô·shôn′) *adj.* Cut convex and highly polished but not faceted. —*n.* Any gem so cut. **—en cabochon** Cut and polished but not faceted: said of gems. [<F, aug. of *caboche* head]
Ca·bo Ju·bi (kä′vō ho͞o′vē) A headland of Spanish West Africa opposite the Canary Islands; site of Villa Bens. *English* **Cape Ju·by** (jo͞o′bē).
ca·boo·dle (kə·bo͞od′l) *n. Colloq.* Aggregate or collection; lot; usually with an intensive, as **the whole caboodle, the whole kit and caboodle.** [Prob. intens. form of BOODLE]
ca·boose (kə·bo͞os′) *n.* **1** *U.S.* A car on a freight train or work train equipped with stove and bunks for the use of the train crew or work crew. **2** *Brit.* The cook's galley on a ship. Also spelled *camboose.* [<MDu. *cabuse* cook's galley]
Cab·ot (kab′ət), **John,** 1451?–98, Venetian navigator in English service; discovered American continent (Labrador) 1497. **—Sebastian,** 1474–1557, English navigator: son of preceding.
cab·o·tage (kab′ə·tij) *n.* **1** Coastwise navigation; coast pilotage; coasting trade. **2** Air transport passengers and goods within the same national territory. [<F]
Ca·bral (kə·vräl′), **Pedro Álvarez,** 1460?–1526?, Portuguese navigator; claimed Brazil for Portugal.
ca·bres·ta (kä·bres′tä), **ca·bres·to** (-tō) See CABESTRO.
ca·bril·la (kə·bril′ə, *Sp.* kä·brē′yä) *n.* **1** One of various serranoid food fishes; specifically, one of the groupers (genus *Epinephelus*) common on the West Indian and Florida coasts. **2** A fish of the genus *Paralabrax,* as the California rock bass *(P. clathratus).* ob<Sp.]
Ca·bri·ni (kä·brē′nē), **Saint Frances Xavier,** 1850–1917, first U.S. citizen canonized, 1946: known as *Mother Cabrini.*
cab·ri·ole (kab′rē·ōl) *n.* A curved, tapering leg, often with a decorative foot: characteristic of Chippendale and Queen Anne furniture. [<MF. See CABRIOLET.]
cab·ri·o·let (kab′rē·ə·lā′, -let′) *n.* **1** A one-horse covered carriage with two seats; a cab. **2** An automobile of the coupé type, having a collapsible top. [<F, dim. of MF *cabriole* leap <Ital. *capriola* <L *capreolus* wild goat]
cab·stand (kab′stand′) *n.* A specified place where cabs are stationed for hire.
ca' can·ny (kä kan′ē, kô) **1** *Brit.* A deliberate slowing down of production on the part of workers. **2** *Scot.* Go warily.
ca·ca·o (kə·kā′ō, -kä′ō) *n. pl.* **·ca·os 1** The large, nutritive seeds of a small evergreen tropical American tree *(Theobroma cacao):* also called *chocolate nuts.* **2** the sweet-scented, yellowish oil of this tree, widely used in medicine and cosmetics, and in making cocoa and chocolate. **3** The tree producing these nuts or seeds: also called *chocolate tree.* [<Sp. <Nahuatl *cacauatl* cacao]
cacao butter A hard, yellowish, fatty substance obtained from cacao beans, consisting chiefly of glycerides of stearic, palmitic, and lauric acid: used for soap, cosmetics, etc.: also called *cocoa butter.*
cac·cia·to·re (käch′ə·tôr′ē, -tō′rē) *adj.* Stewed in tomatoes and wine: chicken *cacciatore.* [<Italian]
Cá·ce·res (kä′thä·rās) A province of western Spain, constituting Upper Estremadura; 7,699 square miles; capital, Cáceres.
cach·a·lot (kash′ə·lot, -lō) *n.* The sperm whale. [<F, prob. <dial. F *cachalut* toothed]
cache (kash) *v.t.* **cached, cach·ing** To conceal or store, as in the earth; hide in a secret place. —*n.* A place for hiding or storing provisions, equipment, etc.; also, the things stored or hidden. [<F <*cacher* hide]
ca·chec·tic (kə·kek′tik) *adj.* Of, pertaining to, or affected with cachexia. Also **ca·chec′ti·cal.** [<MF *cachectique* <L *cachecticus* <Gk. *kachektikos*]
cache·pot (kash′pot, *Fr.* kȧsh·pō′) *n.* A jardinière or an ornamental pot or a casing concealing an ordinary flowerpot. [<F]
ca·chet (ka·shā′, kash′ā) *n.* **1** A seal. **2** A distinctive mark; stamp of individuality. **3** A hollow wafer used for enclosing nauseous medicine. **4** A stamped or printed mark, picture, etc., put on mail as a slogan, commemoration mark, etc. See LETTRE DE CACHET. [<F <*cacher* hide]
ca·chex·i·a (kə·kek′sē·ə) *n. Pathol.* Malnutrition and general bad health, characterized by a waxy or sallow complexion, as in cancer, tuberculosis, etc. Also **ca·chex·y** (kə·kek′sē). [<LL *cachexia* <Gk. *kachexia* poor condition or state <*kakos* bad + *-hexia* <*echein* hold oneself, be]
cach·in·nate (kak′ə·nāt) *v.i.* **·nat·ed, ·nat·ing** To laugh immoderately or noisily. [<L *cachinnatus,* pp. of *cachinnare* laugh loudly] **—cach′in·na′tion** *n.*
cach·o·long (kash′ə·long) *n.* An opaque white, yellowish, or reddish variety of opal. [<Kalmuck *kaschschilon* beautiful stone]
ca·chou (kə·sho͞o′, ka-) *n.* **1** An aromatic pill or pastille, used to perfume the breath. **2** Catechu. [<F <Malay *kāchū* catechu]
ca·chu·cha (kä·cho͞o′chä) *n. Spanish* An Andalusian dance or dance tune in 3–4 time, resembling the bolero.
ca·cique (kə·sēk′) *n.* **1** A prince or chief among the Indians of the West Indies, Mexico, Peru, etc. **2** An oriole of the warmer parts of America. Also spelled *cazique.* [<Sp. <native Haitian word for "chief"]
cack·le (kak′əl) *v.* **·led, ·ling** *v.i.* **1** To make a shrill cry, as a hen that has laid an egg. **2** To laugh or talk with a sound resembling this cry. —*v.t.* **3** To utter in a cackling manner. —*n.* **1** The shrill, broken cry made by a hen after laying an egg; the gabbling of a goose. **2** Idle talk; chattering or chuckling. See synonyms under BABBLE. [Imit.] **—cack′ler** *n.*
caco- *combining form* Bad; diseased; vile: *cacography.* [<Gk. *kakos* bad, evil]
cac·o·de·mon (kak′ə·dē′mən) *n.* **1** A devil, or evil spirit. **2** One supposedly possessed by an evil spirit. Also **cac′o·dae′mon.** [<Gk. *kakodaimōn* evil genius]
cac·o·dyl (kak′ə·dil, -dēl,) *n.* **1** *Chem.* The univalent arsenic radical, C_2H_6As, which unites with oxygen, sulfur, chlorine, etc., to form stinking, poisonous compounds. **2** A colorless, poisonous, stinking liquid, some of whose derivatives are used as accelerators in making rubber. [<Gk. *kakōdia* (<*kakos* bad + *ozein* smell) + -YL] **—cac′o·dyl′ic** (-dil′ik) *adj.*
cac·o·e·thes (kak′ō·ē′thēz) *n.* **1** A bad propensity or habit; a mania. **2** *Pathol.* A malignant ulcer. [<L <Gk. *kakoēthēs* <*kakos* bad + *ēthos* habit, disposition]
cacoethes lo·quen·di (lō·kwen′dī) *Latin* A passion for talking.
cac·o·gen·ics (kak′ə·jen′iks) *n.* The scientific study of race degeneration; also, race degeneration, as from inbreeding or inferior mating. [<CACO- + (EU)GENICS] **—cac′o·gen′ic** *adj.*
ca·cog·ra·phy (kə·kog′rə·fē) *n.* Bad handwriting or spelling. **—ca·cog′ra·pher** *n.* **—cac·o·graph·ic** (kak′ə·graf′ik) or **·i·cal** *adj.*
ca·col·o·gy (kə·kol′ə·jē) *n.* Mischoice or misuse of words; bad pronunciation or speech. [<Gk. *kakologia* bad style, abuse]
cac·o·mis·tle (kak′ə·mis′əl) *n.* A long-tailed, raccoonlike carnivore (genus *Bassariscus*); especially, *B. astutus* of Mexico and adjacent parts of the United States. Also **cac′o·mis′cle, cac′o·mix′l** (-mis′əl, -mik′səl), **cac′o·mix′le.** [<Sp. <Nahuatl *tlacomiztli*]
ca·coph·o·nous (kə·kof′ə·nəs) *adj.* **1** Having a harsh, discordant, disagreeable sound: opposed to *euphonious.* **2** *Music* Discordant; dissonant: opposed to *harmonious. Also* **cac·o·phon·ic** (kak′ə·fon′ik) or **·i·cal —ca·coph′o·nous·ly, cac′o·phon′i·cal·ly** *adv.*
ca·coph·o·ny (kə·kof′ə·nē) *n.* **1** Discord; a disagreeable sound. **2** The use of harsh combinations of sounds, words, etc., in speech. **3** *Music* Dissonance; also, the frequent use of dissonance. [<F *cacaphonie* <Gk. *kakophlōnia* <*kakos* bad + *phōneein* sound]
cac·ta·ceous (kak·tā′shəs) *adj. Bot.* Of or belonging to the cactus family *(Cactaceae).*
cac·tus (kak′təs) *n. pl.* **·tus·es** or **·ti** (-tī) Any one of various polypetalous, green, fleshy, mostly leafless and spiny plants of the family *Cactaceae,* native in arid regions of America, often having showy flowers. [<L <Gk. *kaktos* a prickly plant]

ca·cu·men (kə·kyōō'mən) *n.* The apex or top. [<L]

ca·cu·mi·nal (kə·kyōō'mə·nəl) *adj.* 1 Pertaining to the top, as of a plant. 2 *Phonet.* Describing those consonants pronounced with the tip of the tongue turned up and back toward the hard palate, as *t* and *d* in the Indic and Dravidian languages; cerebral; retroflex. —*n. Phonet.* A consonant so formed.

Ca·cus (kā'kəs) In Roman mythology, a giant, son of Vulcan, who stole the cattle of Hercules and was killed by him.

cad (kad) *n.* 1 A vulgar, ill-bred, obtrusive person; one not behaving as a gentleman. 2 *Obs.* In England, one who caters to the sports of public-school boys or university students; at Oxford, a townsman. 3 *Obs.* The conductor of an omnibus. [Short form of CADET] —**cad'dish** *adj.* —**cad'dish·ly** *adv.* —**cad'dish·ness** *n.*

ca·das·ter (kə·das'tər) *n.* A register, survey, or map of the extent, ownership, value, etc., of the lands of a country, as a basis of taxation. Also **ca·das'tre.** [<F *cadastre* <LL *capitastrum* tax register <*caput* head] —**ca·das'tral** *adj.* —**cad·as·tra'tion** (kad'əs·trā'shən) *n.*

ca·dav·er (kə·dav'ər, -dā'vər) *n.* A dead body; especially, that of a human being intended for dissection; a corpse. [<L]

ca·dav·er·ine (kə·dav'ər·in, -ēn) *n. Biochem.* A thick, colorless, liquid ptomaine, $C_5H_{14}N_2$, of noxious odor, formed by putrefying animal tissue.

ca·dav·er·ous (kə·dav'ər·əs) *adj.* Like a corpse; pale; ghastly; gaunt. Also **ca·dav'er·ic.** —**ca·dav'er·ous·ly** *adv.* —**ca·dav'er·ous·ness** *n.*

cad·die (kad'ē) *n.* A messenger or errand boy, especially one paid to carry clubs for golf players. —*v.i.* **·died, ·dy·ing** To act as a caddie. Also spelled *caddy.* [<CADET]

cad·dis (kad'is) *n.* 1 A coarse, sergelike fabric. 2 A narrow, tapelike worsted fabric for bindings, etc. 3 Worsted yarn; crewel. Also **cad'dice.** [<MF *cadis,* a woolen fabric]

cad·dis fly (kad'is) Any of certain four-winged insects (order *Trichoptera*): their aquatic larvae, known as **caddis worms,** construct, inhabit, and carry cylindrical, silklined cases covered with sand, gravel, etc. [Origin uncertain]

Cad·do (kad'ō) *n. pl.* **·do** or **·does** A member of a North American Indian confederacy belonging to the southern group of the Caddoan linguistic stock, formerly living along the Red River in Louisiana, Arkansas, and eastern Texas: now in Oklahoma.

Cad·do·an (kad'ō·ən) *n.* A North American Indian linguistic stock formerly numerous west of the Mississippi, and including the Arikaras of the Dakotas, the tribes of the Pawnee confederacy of Nebraska and Kansas, the Caddo of Oklahoma, Arkansas, Louisiana, and Texas, and the Wichita of Oklahoma and Texas.

cad·dy¹ (kad'ē) *n. pl.* **·dies** 1 A receptacle for tea. 2 A small box or case. [<Malay *kati,* a measure of weight, equal to 1 1/4 lbs.]

cad·dy² (kad'ē) See CADDIE.

cade¹ (kād) *adj.* 1 Brought up by hand: a *cade* colt. 2 Coddled. [Origin unknown]

cade² (kād) *n.* A large, bushy shrub (*Juniperus oxycedrus*) of Mediterranean regions: its wood yields a brown, thick liquid having a tarry odor, known as **cade oil,** used in soaps and medicinally. [<F]

cade³ (kād) *n. Obs.* A barrel or keg, especially for herring. [<F L *cadus* <Gk. *kados* jar]

Cade (kād), **John,** died 1450, English rebel: known as *Jack Cade.*

ca·delle (kə·del') *n.* A small, black beetle (*Tenebrioides mauritanicus*) which in both larval and adult stages feeds upon stored grain. [<F]

ca·dence (kād'ns) *n.* 1 Rhythmic or measured flow or movement, as in poetry, music, oratory. 2 *Mil.* Uniform pace and time in marching expressed in so many steps to the minute; measure; beat. 3 Modulation, as of the voice or of elemental sounds; also, a fall of the voice, as at a period. 4 Intonation or inflection of the speaking voice as distinctive of a language or locality. 5 *Music* a A succession of chords naturally closing a musical phrase or period: the **perfect, com-**plete,** or **whole cadence,** proper at the end of a movement; the **imperfect** or **half cadence,** often a reversal of the dominant perfect. **b** A cadenza. See synonyms under TUNE. [<F <Ital. *cadenza* <LL *cadentia* a falling <*cadere* fall. Doublet of CHANCE, CADENZA.] —**ca'denced** *adj.*

ca·den·cy (kād'n·sē) *n. pl.* **·cies** 1 Cadence; rhythm. 2 *Her.* The relative position of the younger members of the same family or branches of the same house.

ca·dent (kād'nt) *adj.* 1 Having cadence or rhythm. 2 *Obs.* Falling.

ca·den·za (kə·den'zə, *Ital.* kä·dent'sä) *n. Music* An embellishment or flourish, prepared or improvised, for a solo voice or an instrument, before the close of a movement or between divisions of a movement, especially in the first movement of a concerto. [<Ital. Doublet of CADENCE, CHANCE.]

ca·det (kə·det') *n.* 1 A student at a military or naval school. 2 A student in training at the United States Military or Coast Guard Academy for commissioning as an officer: at the United States Air Force Academy the official designation is **Air Force cadet.** 3 A younger son or brother in a noble family. 4 *Archaic.* A gentleman who entered the army without a commission so as to gain military experience and thus earn a commission. 5 *Colloq.* A pander or pimp; whoremonger. [<F, ult. <dim. of L *caput* head, chief]

Ca·det (kə·det') *n.* A member of the Constitutional Democratic party of Russia, formed about 1905. [< Russian *Kadet* <*K(onsti tutsionalnyie)* + *D(emokrati)*]

ca·det·ship (kə·det'ship) *n.* 1 The state or condition of being a cadet. 2 Appointment as cadet. Also **ca·det'cy.**

ca·dette (kä·det') *n. fem.* 1 *French* A younger daughter or sister in a noble family. 2 In New Zealand, a young woman who has passed a competitive test and been appointed to the civil service.

cadet teacher A college student who does practice teaching in public schools.

cadge (kaj) *v.* **cadged, cadg·ing** *v.i. Brit. Dial.* To go about as a peddler or beggar. —*v.t. Colloq.* To beg; sponge. [? Var. of CATCH]

cadg·y (kaj'ē) *adj.* 1 Cheerful; frolicsome. 2 Wanton; amorous. [Origin uncertain]

ca·di (kä'dē,kä'-) *n. pl.* **·dis** In Moslem communities, a chief judge or magistrate whose decisions are based on Moslem law: also spelled *kadi.* [<Arabic *qādī*]

Cad·il·lac (kad'ə·lak, *Fr.* kà·dē·yàk'), **Antoine de la Mothe,** 1657?–1730, French explorer; founded Detroit.

Cá·diz (kə·diz', kā'diz, *Sp.* kä'thēth) 1 A province of SW Spain; 2,827 square miles. 2 Its capital, a port on the Atlantic coast of Andalusia.

Cádiz, Gulf of A wide Atlantic inlet of the SW Iberian Peninsula.

Cad·man (kad'mən), **Charles Wakefield,** 1884–1946, U.S. composer.

Cad·me·an (kad·mē'ən) *adj.* Of or pertaining to Cadmus.

Cadmean victory A victory that is ruinous to the victor.

cad·mi·um (kad'mē·əm) *n.* A soft, bluish-white, toxic metallic element (symbol Cd, atomic number 48) occurring in zinc ores and used in the manufacture of fusible alloys, in electroplating, and in controlling fission in nuclear reactors. See PERIODIC TABLE. [<NL <L *cadmia* zinc ore <Gk. *kadmeia(gē)*]

cadmium sulfide A pigment, CdS, varying in hue from lemon to orange: also **cadmium yellow** or **cadmium orange.**

Cad·mus (kad'məs) In Greek mythology, a Phoenician prince who killed a dragon sacred to Ares and sowed its teeth on the site of Thebes: from these teeth sprang up armed men who fought and destroyed each other except for five who helped him found the city. Cadmus introduced the Phoenician alphabet into Greece.

Ca·dor·na (kä·dôr'nä), **Count Luigi,** 1850–1928, Italian general: commander in chief in World War I.

cad·re (kad'rē, *Fr.* kä'dr') *n.* 1 The officers and men necessary to establish and train a military unit. 2 Trained personnel essential in the conduct and management of an organization, enterprise, etc. 3 A nucleus; skeleton; framework. [F, frame of a picture <Ital. *quadro* <L *quadrum* square]

ca·du·ce·us (kə·dōō'sē·əs, -dyōō'-) *n. pl.* **·ce·i** (-sē·ī) 1 The wand or staff of Mercury, the messenger of the gods. 2 A similar wand used in the armed services as the emblem of the medical corps or department; also often used as the symbol of the medical profession. [<L <Gk. (Doric) *karykion* herald's staff] —**ca·du'ce·an** *adj.*

CADUCEUS

ca·du·ci·ty (kə·dōō'sə·tē, -dyōō'-) *n.* 1 The state or quality of being caducous. 2 Old age; senility.

ca·du·cous (kə·dōō'kəs, -dyōō'-) *adj.* 1 *Biol.* Dropping or falling off, especially at an early stage of development, as the sepals of a poppy or the gills of salamanders, etc. 2 Having a tendency to fall or perish; perishable. [<L *caducus* falling <*cadere* fall]

Cad·wal·la·der (kad·wol'ə·dər) A masculine personal name. Also **Cad·wal'a·der.** [Welsh, battle arranger]

cae- For words not found here, see under CE-.

cae·cil·i·an (si·sil'ē·ən) *n.* One of a family (*Caecilidae*) of tropical, burrowing, legless amphibians, resembling worms or small snakes. [<L *caecilia,* a kind of lizard]

Cae·cil·i·us (si·sil'ē·əs) Latin form of CECIL.

cae·cum (sē'kəm), etc. See CECUM, etc.

Cæd·mon (kad'mən) Seventh century English poet, the first to write in the vernacular.

Cae·li·an (sē'lē·ən) One of the seven hills of Rome. Also **Cæ'li·an.**

Caen (kän) A port in Normandy, NW France.

cae·o·ma (sē·ō'mə) *n. Bot.* An aecium of a fungus (genus *Caeoma*) of the *Uredinales.* [<NL <Gk. *kaiein* burn; with ref. to its color]

caer·i·mo·ni·a·ri·us (serī·mō'nē·â·rē·əs) *n. pl.* **·ri·i** (-rē·ī) A director of ceremonies in solemn offices, as in Roman Catholic cathedral services. [<L *caerimonia* ceremony]

Caer·le·on (kär·lē'ən) An urban district in Monmouth, England, on the Usk; identified with Camelot.

Caer·nar·von (kär·när'vən) A county of NW Wales; 569 square miles; county town, Caernarvon: also *Carnarvon.* Also **Caer·nar'von·shire** (-shir).

caes·al·pin·i·a·ceous (sez'al·pin'ē·ā'shəs, ses'-) *adj. Bot.* Belonging to a genus (*Caesalpinia*) of tropical trees, shrubs, or herbs of the bean family. [<after A. *Caesalpinus,* 1519–1603, Italian botanist]

Cae·sar (sē'zər) 1 A masculine personal name: also spelled *Cesar.* 2 The title of any one of the Roman emperors from Augustus to Hadrian. 3 Any powerful emperor or despot.
—**Caesar, Gaius Julius,** 100–44 B.C., Roman general, statesman, and historian.

Caes·a·re·a (ses'ə·rē'ə, sez'-) An ancient port in Palestine, site of the Sdot Yam settlement. Also **Caesarea Palestine; Caesarea Maritime.** Also **Cæs'a·re'a.**

Caesarea Maz·a·ca (maz'ə·kə) The ancient name for KAYSERI.

Cae·sar·e·an (si·zâr'ē·ən) *adj.* Pertaining to Caesar. —*n.* A Caesarean operation. Also spelled *Cesarean, Cesarian.* Also **Cae·sar'i·an.**

Caesarean operation *Surg.* The delivery of a child by section of the abdominal walls and the womb of the mother when ordinary delivery is apparently impossible: reported to have been performed at the birth of Julius Caesar: also spelled *Cesarean.* Also **Caesarean section.**

Caesarea Phi·lip·pi (fi·lip'ī, fil'i·pī) The ancient name for BANIYAS.

Cae·sar·ism (sē'zər·iz'əm) *n.* Government like that of the Caesars; imperialism; military despotism. —**Cae'sar·ist** *n.*

cae·si·um (sē'zē·əm) See CESIUM.

caes·tus (ses′təs) See CESTUS.
cae·su·ra (si·zhōōr′ə, -zyōōr′ə) *n. pl.* **·su·ras** or **·su·rae** (-zhōōr′ē, -zyōōr′ē) **1** In prosody, a break or pause in the middle of a foot, usually near the middle of a verse. **2** A break or interruption. **3** *Music* A rest or pause indicating a rhythmic division point in an air or melody; also, the stressed note preceding. Also spelled *cesura.* [< L, cutting, caesura < *caedere* cut] — **cae·su′ral** *adj.*
Cae·ti·té (kī·tē·tā′) A city in central Bahia, eastern Brazil.
ca·fé (kə·fā′, ka-) *n.* **1** A coffee house; restaurant. **2** A barroom. **3** Coffee. [< F]
ca·fé au lait (kà·fā′ ō lā′) *French* **1** Coffee made with scalded milk. **2** A light brown.
ca·fé noir (kà·fā′ nwàr′) *French* Black coffee.
café society The set customarily frequenting cafés or night clubs, especially in New York City.
caf·e·te·ri·a (kaf′ə·tir′ē·ə) *n.* A restaurant where the patrons wait upon themselves. [< Am. Sp., coffee store]
caf·fe·ic (ka·fē′ik) *adj.* Of, pertaining to, or derived from coffee. [< F *caféique* < *café* coffee]
caf·feine (kaf′ēn, *in technical usage* kaf′ē·in) *n. Chem.* A crystallizable, slightly bitter alkaloid, $C_8H_{10}N_4O_2 \cdot H_2O$, found in the leaves and berries of coffee, and chemically identical with theine: used as a stimulant and diuretic. [< F *caféine* < *café* coffee]
Caf·fer (kaf′ər) See KAFFIR. Also **Caf′fre.**
Caf·fer·y (kaf′rē, kaf′ər·ē), **Jefferson**, 1886—1974, U.S. diplomat.
caf·fe·tan·nic (kaf′ē·tan′ik) *adj. Chem.* Of, pertaining to, or derived from caffeine and tannin together. Also **caf′fe·o·tan′nic** (kaf′ē·ō·tan′ik). [< CAFFE(INE) + TANNIC]
caf·tan (kaf′tən, käf·tän′) *n.* An undercoat having long sleeves and a sash, worn in Mediterranean countries: also spelled *kaftan.* [< F *cafetan* < Turkish *qaftān*]
Ca·ga·yan (kä′gä·yän′) **1** A province of northern Luzon, Philippines; 3,470 square miles. **2** An island in the Sulu Sea, belonging to Palawan province, Philippines. **3** The largest river of the Philippines, flowing about 220 miles north across Luzon to Babuyan Channel. *Spanish* **Ri·o Gran·de de Ca·ga·yan** (rē′ō grän′dā thā kä′gä·yän′).
Cagayan Sulu Island An island in the Sulu Sea NE of Borneo, belonging to Sulu province, Philippines; 26 square miles.
cage (kāj) *n.* **1** A structure, with openwork of wire or bars, as for confining birds or beasts. **2** A room or place enclosed by a grating, for confining prisoners. **3** Any lockup, prison, or place of confinement, or anything that confines or imprisons. **4** Any cagelike structure, framework, or grating, as a timber framework lining a shaft. **5** A platform, elevator car, or the like, protected by gratings. **6** A wire mask worn by the catcher in baseball. **7** The iron or steel skeleton frame of a high building. **8** A table from which quick-firing guns are discharged. **9** An enclosure in a gymnasium for interior baseball practice. —*v.t.* **caged, cag·ing** To shut up in or as in a cage; confine; imprison. [< OF < L *cavea* < *cavus* empty, hollow]
cage·ling (kāj′ling) *n.* A caged bird.
ca·gey (kā′jē) *adj. Colloq.* **ca·gi·er, ca·gi·est** Shrewd; wary of being duped. Also **ca′gy.** — **ca′gi·ly** *adv.* —**ca′gi·ness** *n.*
Ca·glia·ri (kä′lyä·rē) The capital of Sardinia, a port on the **Gulf of Cagliari**, an inlet of the Mediterranean in southern Sardinia.
Ca·glia·ri (kä′lyä·rē), **Paolo** See VERONESE.
Ca·glio·stro (kä·lyô′strō), **Count Alessandro di**, 1743–95: Sicilian adventurer and supposed magician: real name *Giuseppe Balsamo.*
Ca·gou·lard (kà·gōō·làr′) *n.* A member of a secret French organization whose conspiracy to overthrow the government and eventually restore the monarchy in France was exposed in 1937. [< F *cagoule* monk's hood < L *cuculla* hood]
ca·hier (kä·yā′) *n.* **1** A memorial, report of proceedings, or the like. **2** A quarter of a quire of writing paper. **3** A few leaves, as of printed matter, loosely stitched together; a number of a book issued in parts. [< F < OF *quaier* < L *quaterni* by fours < *quattuor* four]
ca·hoots (kə·hōōts′) *n. pl. U.S. Slang* Partnership; close cooperation; collusion: to be in *cahoots.* [? < F *cahute* cabin]
Cai·a·phas (kā′ə·fəs, kī′-) A Jewish high priest: presided at the council which condemned Jesus. *Matt.* xxvi 57–68.
Cai·cos (kī′kōs) See TURKS AND CAICOS ISLANDS.
Caill·laux (kà·yō′), **Joseph Marie**, 1863–1944, French politician.
cai·man (kā′mən) *n. pl.* **·mans** A tropical American crocodilian (genus *Caiman*) closely related to the alligator, as the **spectacled caiman** *(C. sclerops),* having prominent ridges above the upper eyelid. Also spelled *cayman.* [< Sp., probably < a Carib word]
cain (kān) See KAIN.
Cain (kān) **1** The eldest son of Adam, who slew his brother Abel. *Gen.* iv 1–10. **2** Hence, a fratricide or murderer. **—to raise Cain** *Slang* To raise a rumpus; make a noisy disturbance.
ca·in·ca root (kə·ing′kə) The root of the tropical American snowberry: the bark of this root yields a glycoside used as a purgative. Also **ca·hin·ca root** (kə·hing′kə).
Caine (kān), **(Sir Thomas Henry) Hall**, 1853–1931, English novelist.
Cain·ite (kā′nīt) *n.* A member of a heretical sect of the second century which professed reverence for Cain, Esau, and other wicked Old Testament characters. **—Cain′ism** *n.* **—Cain·it·ic** (kā·nit′ik) *adj.*
Cai·no·zo·ic (kī′nə·zō′ik) See CENOZOIC.
ca·ique (kä·ēk′) *n.* **1** A long, narrow, pointed skiff with from two to ten oars, used on the Bosporus. **2** A small Levantine sailing vessel. [< F < Ital. *caicco* < Turkish *qāyiq*]
ça i·ra (sà′ ē·rà′) *French* Literally, it will go, meaning it will succeed: the refrain of a popular song of the French Revolution.
caird (kârd) *n. Scot.* A tinker; gipsy.
Caird (kârd), **Edward**, 1835–1908, Scottish philosopher.
Caird Coast (kârd) The part of Antarctica on the SE coast of the Weddell Sea.
Cai·rene (kī′ren, kī·rēn′) *n.* One born or living in Cairo. —*adj.* Pertaining to Cairo.
cairn (kârn) *n.* A mound or heap of stones for a memorial or a marker. [< Scottish Gaelic *carn* heap of stones] **—cairned** *adj.*
cairn·gorm (kârn′gôrm) *n.* A smoky, yellow to brown variety of quartz; smoky quartz. [from *Cairngorm* Mountains]
Cairn·gorm Mountains (kârn′gôrm) A range in Inverness and Banffshire, Scotland; highest peak, 4,296 feet.
Cairn terrier (kârn) See under TERRIER.
Cai·ro (kī′rō) **1** The capital of Egypt and the largest city of Africa, on the east bank of the Nile at the head of its delta: an inhabitant of the city known as a **Cai·rene** (kī·rēn′). **2** (kâr′ō) A city in Illinois at the confluence of the Mississippi and Ohio Rivers.
cais·son (kā′sən, -son) *n.* **1** An ammunition chest or wagon. **2** A two-wheeled vehicle carrying such a chest to serve a gun in firing position with its immediate needs in ammunition. **3** A large watertight chamber within which work is done under water, as on a bridge pier. **4** A watertight box, or other apparatus, to be placed beneath a sunken vessel and inflated in order to raise it. **5** A gate for closing the entrance to a drydock. [< F, aug. of *caisse* box, chest]

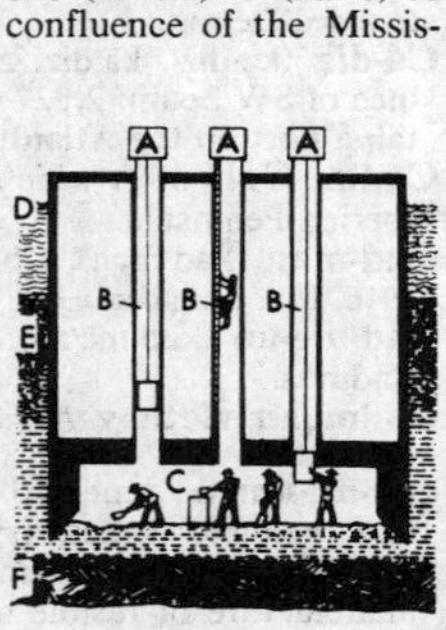

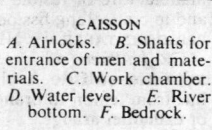

CAISSON
A. Airlocks. *B.* Shafts for entrance of men and materials. *C.* Work chamber. *D.* Water level. *E.* River bottom. *F.* Bedrock.

caisson disease Decompression sickness.
Caith·ness (kāth′nes, kāth·nes′) A county of NE Scotland; 686 square miles; capital, Wick. Also **Caith′ness·shire** (-shir).
cai·tiff (kā′tif) *n.* A base wretch. —*adj.* Vile; basely wicked. [< AF *caitif* weak, wretched < L *captivus.* Doublet of CAPTIVE.]
Cai·us (kā′əs, kī′-) See GAIUS.
Caius (kēz), **John**, 1510–72, English physician and educator.
Ca·jal (kä·häl′) See RAMÓN Y CAJAL.
Ca·ja·mar·ca (kä′hä·mär′kä) A city in NW Peru.
caj·e·put (kaj′ə·pət) *n.* **1** The California laurel *(Umbellularia californica).* **2** The cajuput. [< Malay *kāyupūtih* < *kāyu* tree + *pūtih* white]
ca·jole (kə·jōl′) *v.* **ca·joled, ca·jol·ing** *v.t.* To persuade or coax with flattery or delusive promises. —*v.i.* To wheedle; to practice cajolery. See synonyms under ALLURE. [< F *cajoler*] — **ca·jole′ment** *n.* **—ca·jol′er** *n.* **—ca·jol′ing·ly** *adv.*
ca·jol·er·y (kə·jō′lər·ē) *n. pl.* **·er·ies** The act of cajoling; the art or practice of wheedling by flattery.
ca·jon (kä·hōn′) *n. pl.* **ca·jo·nes** (kä·hō′nās) *SW U.S.* A canyon or narrow gorge with steep sides. [< Sp.]
Ca·jun (kā′jən) *n.* A reputed descendant of the Acadian French in Louisiana. [Alter. of ACADIAN]
caj·u·put (kaj′ə·pət) *n.* **1** A small tree *(Melaleuca leucadendron)* of the myrtle family, native in the Moluccas. **2** A greenish-yellow, odorous oil distilled from the fresh leaves and twigs of this tree: used chiefly in the treatment of skin diseases. Also **caj′a·put.** Sometimes spelled *cajeput, kajeput.* [See CAJEPUT]
cake (kāk) *n.* **1** A baked mixture of flour, eggs, milk, etc.: distinguished from bread or pudding. **2** A small or thin mass of dough, etc., baked or fried: *pancake.* **3** A hardened mass of any material: a *cake* of soap, etc. **4** *Pathol.* A morbid hardening or coagulation in the body. **—to take the cake** *Colloq.* To take the prize; be the best of or at something. —*v.t.* & *v.i.* **caked, cak·ing** To form into a hardened mass. [< ON *kaka*]
cakes and ale A carefree way of life; soft, easy living.
cake urchin A sea urchin (family *Clypeastridae*) having a disklike body with a raised central surface and a mass of velvety spines.
cake·walk (kāk′wôk′) *n.* **1** Originally, a promenade or march of American Negro origin in which a cake is awarded as prize for the most original steps. **2** A dance based on this or the music for such a dance. —*v.i.* To do a cakewalk; strut. **—cake′walk′er** *n.*
cal·a·bar (kal′ə·bär) *n.* **1** The pelt of the gray Siberian squirrel. **2** The squirrel. Also **cal′a·ber** (-bər). [< F *Calabre* Calabria]
Cal·a·bar (kal′ə·bär′, kal′ə·bär) A port in SE Nigeria, formerly **Old Calabar,** on the **Calabar River,** flowing 70 miles SW to the Gulf of Guinea.
Calabar bean The highly poisonous seed of an African twining climber *(Physostigma venenosum)* of the bean family, the source of physostigmine: also called, from its use as a native test for crime or witchcraft, *ordeal bean.*
cal·a·bash (kal′ə·bash) *n.* **1** The calabash tree. **2** Any vessel, pipe, or utensil made from the calabash gourd. [< F *calebasse* < Sp. *calabaza* pumpkin < Persian *kharbuz* melon]

CALABASH
A. Gourd.
B. Portion used in making pipe.
C. Finished pipe with meerschaum bowl.

calabash gourd The common gourd from the calabash tree, used for making pipes, etc.
calabash tree **1** A tropical American tree *(Lagenaria siceraria)* of the trumpet-flower family, bearing a gourdlike fruit or calabash. **2** A tropical American tree *(Crescentia cujete)* of the bignonia family, with a hard-shelled, gourdlike fruit. **3** The African baobab.
cal·a·ba·zil·la (kal′ə·bə·sēl′yə) *n.* A squash *(Cucurbita foetidissima),* the macerated root of which is used as a remedy for hemorrhoids and the pulp of its green fruit as soap. [< Sp., dim. of *calabaza* gourd]
cal·a·boose (kal′ə·bōōs) *n. U.S. Colloq.* A jail; lockup. [< Sp. *calaboza*]
Ca·la·bri·a (kə·lā′brē·ə, *Ital.* kä·lä′bryä) A region of southern Italy; 5,828 square miles, occupying the toe of the Italian boot: ancient *Bruttium.* — **Ca·la′bri·an** *adj* & *n.*
ca·la·di·um (kə·lā′dē·əm) *n.* One of a genus *(Caladium)* of tuberous tropical American herbs of the arum family with large, varie-

gated sagittate leaves. [< NL < Malay *kelādy*]

Ca·lah (kā′lə) The biblical name for KALAKH.

Cal·ais (kal′ā, ka·lā′, kal′is; *Fr.* kà·le′) A French port on the English Channel, facing Dover.

cal·a·man·co (kal′ə·mang′kō) *n.* **1** A glossy, woolen, Flemish fabric, or a garment made from it. **2** A glazed linen stuff. Also spelled *calimanco.* [< Sp.]

cal·a·man·der (kal′ə·man′dər) *n.* The wood of various trees of the ebony family, especially the rare *Diospyros quaesita* of Ceylon, finely veined, hard, and valued for cabinetwork. [Alter. of *Coromandel* (Coast)]

cal·a·mar·y (kal′ə·mâr′ē, -mər·ē) *n. pl.* **·mar·ies** A squid. [< L *calamarius* < *calamus* pen < Gk. *kalamos* reed]

Ca·la·mian Islands (kä′lä·myän′) A Philippine island group between Mindoro and Palawan; 600 square miles. *Spanish* **Is·las Ca·la·mi·a·nes** (ēs′läs kä′lä·myä′nās).

cal·am·bak (cal·am·bak′) *n.* A wood used in fine inlay work; also called *aloes wood.*

cal·a·mif·er·ous (kal′ə·mif′ər·əs) *adj.* Bearing reeds [< CALAMUS + L *ferre* bear]

ca·lam·i·form (kə·lam′ə·fôrm) *adj.* Shaped like a reed.

cal·a·mine (kal′ə·mīn, -min) *n.* **1** Hemimorphite. **2** Smithsonite. **3** A native zinc carbonate, a pink powder much used in the form of a zinc and ferric oxide as a lotion or ointment for the treatment of skin ailments.—*v.t.* **·mined, ·min·ing** To apply calamine to. [< F < LL *calamina* < L *cadmia.* See CADMIUM.]

cal·a·mint (kal′ə·mint) *n.* A menthaceous plant (genus *Satureia*) of the north temperate zone, especially *S. calamintha.* Also **calamint balm.** [< MF *calament* < Med. L *calamentum* < L *calaminthe* < Gk. *kalaminthē*]

cal·a·mite (kal′ə·mīt) *n.* A fossil plant (genus *Calamites,* division *Pteridophyta*) of the later Paleozoic era, resembling the modern horsetails in general appearance but growing to a height of 100 feet and more. [< NL *calamites* < L *calamus* reed]

ca·lam·i·tous (kə·lam′ə·təs) *adj.* Disastrous; causing or resulting in a calamity. **—ca·lam′i·tous·ly** *adv.*

ca·lam·i·ty (kə·lam′ə·tē) *n. pl.* **·ties 1** A misfortune or disaster. **2** A state or time of affliction, adversity, or disaster. See synonyms under ACCIDENT, ADVERSITY, BLOW, CATASTROPHE, MISFORTUNE. [< F *calamité* < L *calamitas*]

Ca·lam·i·ty Jane (kə·lam′ə·tē jān′), 1852?–1903, U.S. frontier marksman: real name *Martha Jane Burke, née* Canary.

cal·a·mus (kal′ə·məs) *n. pl.* **·mi** (-mī) **1** The sweetflag. **2** The quill of a feather. [< L < Gk. *kalamos* reed]

Cal·a·mus (kal′ə·məs) *n.* A genus of oriental climbing palms; the climbing rattans. [See CALAMUS]

ca·lan·do (kä·län′dō) *adj.* & *adv. Music* Diminishing in strength of tone and in rapidity. [< Ital.]

ca·lash (kəl·ash′) *n.* **1** A low-wheeled light carriage with folding top. **2** A folding carriage top or hood. **3** A woman's hood supported by hoops, to be pulled over the head or folded back, fashionable in the 18th century. Also spelled *calèche.* [< F *calèche,* ult. < Slavic]

CALASH (*def. 3*)

cal·a·thus (kal′ə·thəs) *n. pl.* (-thī) In ancient Greece, a vase-shaped basket for fruit: regarded as a symbol of fruitfulness, as on statues of Demeter, etc. [< L < Gk. *kalathos* basket]

cal·a·ver·ite (kal′ə·vâr′īt) *n.* A telluride of gold and silver, usually granular in structure, with a silvery-white metallic luster: an important ore of gold. [from *Calaveras* County, Calif.]

Ca·la·yan (kä′lä·yän′) The largest of the Babuyan Islands, Philippines; 73 square miles.

cal·ca·ne·um (kal·kā′nē·əm) *n. pl.* **·ne·a** (-nē·ə) *Anat.* The heel bone. See illustration under FOOT. Also **cal·ca′ne·us.** [< L < *calx* heel]

cal·car[1] (kal′kär) *n.* **1** A calcining oven. **2** An annealing oven. [< L *calcaria* limekiln]

cal·car[2] (kal′kär) *n. pl.* **cal·car·i·a** (kal·kâr′ē·ə) *Biol.* A spur, or spurlike projection, as at the base of a petal or on the leg or wing of a bird. [< L, spur < *calx* heel]

cal·ca·rate (kal′kə·rāt, -rit) *adj. Biol.* Having a calcar, or spur; spurred. Also **cal′ca·rat′ed.**

cal·car·e·ous (kal·kâr′ē·əs) *adj.* **1** Composed of, containing, or of the nature of limestone or calcium carbonate. **2** Containing calcium. [< L *calcarius* of lime < *calx* lime]

cal·ca·rif·er·ous (kal′kə·rif′ər·əs) *adj. Biol.* Bearing spurs.

cal·ce·ate (kal′sē·āt, -it) *adj.* Wearing shoes; shod: said of certain religious orders. [< L *calceatus,* pp. of *calceare* shoe]

cal·ced·o·ny (kal·sed′ə·nē) See CHALCEDONY.

cal·ce·i·form (kal′sē·ə·fôrm′) *adj. Bot.* Calceolate.

cal·ce·o·lar·i·a (kal′sē·ə·lâr′ē·ə) *n.* A member of a large genus *(Calceolaria)* of herbs and shrubs of the figwort family, with opposite leaves and small axillary or racemose flowers having the lowest petal the longest: also called *slipperwort.* [< L *calceolus,* dim. of *calceus* shoe]

cal·ce·o·late (kal′sē·ə·lāt) *adj. Bot.* Slipper-shaped. **—cal′ce·o·late′ly** *adv.*

cal·ces (kal′sēz) A plural of CALX.

Cal·chas (kal′kəs) In the *Iliad,* a priest of Apollo who accompanied the Greeks to Troy.

calci- *combining form* Lime: *calciferous.* [< L *calx, calcis* lime]

cal·cic (kal′sik) *adj.* Of, pertaining to, or containing calcium or lime. [< L *calx* lime]

cal·cic·o·lous (kal·sik′ə·ləs) *adj. Ecol.* Growing upon limestone: said of certain plants. [< CALCI- + L *colere* cultivate, dwell]

cal·ci·co·sis (kal′si·kō′sis) *n. Pathol.* A disease of the lungs occurring among workers in limestone dust. [< L *calx* lime + -OSIS]

cal·cif·er·ol (kal·sif′ər·ōl, -ol) *n. Biochem.* The anti-rachitic vitamin D_2, a white, crystalline, fat-soluble, accessory food factor, $C_{28}H_{44}O$, formed by the ultraviolet irradiation of ergosterol: found in fish oils, milk, eggs, etc. [< CALCIFER(OUS) + (ERGOSTER)OL]

cal·cif·er·ous (kal·sif′ər·əs) *adj.* Yielding or containing calcium carbonate, as rocks. Also **cal·cif·ic** (kal·sif′ik).

cal·ci·fi·ca·tion (kal′sə·fi·kā′shən) *n.* **1** Conversion into chalk, or into stony or bony substance, by the deposition of lime salts, as in petrifaction and ossification. **2** Such a lime formation. **3** *Pathol.* A petrifactive retrogression observed in tissue which has degenerated. **4** The accumulation by a surface soil of sufficient calcium to bring soil colloids close to saturation, as in Chernozem soils.

cal·ci·form[1] (kal′sə·fôrm) *adj.* **1** *Obs.* Having the form of lime or chalk. **2** Pebble-shaped.

cal·ci·form[2] (kal′sə·fôrm) *adj.* Having a projection like a heel. [< L *calx* heel + -FORM]

cal·cif·u·gous (kal·sif′yə·gəs) *adj. Ecol.* Not growing on limestone: said of certain saxicolous lichens. Also **cal·cif′u·gal.** [< CALCI- + L *fugere* flee]

cal·ci·fy (kal′sə·fī) *v.t.* & *v.i.* **·fied, ·fy·ing** To make or become stony by the deposit of lime salts.

cal·ci·mine (kal′sə·mīn, -min) *n.* A white or tinted wash consisting of whiting, or zinc white, with glue and water, for ceilings, walls, etc. —*v.t.* **·mined, ·min·ing** To apply calcimine to. Also spelled *kalsomine.* [< L *calx* lime]

cal·cin·a·to·ry (kal·sin′ə·tôr′ē, -tō′rē) *adj.* For calcining. —*n. pl.* **·ries** An apparatus for calcining, as a calcining furnace. [< LL *calcinatorium* < *calcinare* calcine]

cal·cine (kal′sīn, -sin) *v.* **·cined, ·cin·ing** *v.t.* **1** To expel volatile matter (as carbon dioxide or water) from (a substance) by heat, for the purpose of rendering it friable: to *calcine* limestone. **2** To reduce to a calx, as copper ore, by subjecting to heat; roast. —*v.i.* **3** To become changed by the action of dry heat into a friable powder. Also **cal′cin·ize.** [< F *calciner* < Med. L *calcinare* < L *calx* lime] **—cal′cined** *adj.* **—cal·ci·na·tion** (kal′sə·nā′shən) *n.*

cal·ciph·i·lous (kal·sif′ə·ləs) *adj. Ecol.* Thriving on chalk; lime-loving: said of plants that grow best in soils containing lime. [< CALCI- + Gk. *philos* loving < *phileein* love]

cal·ciph·o·bous (kal·sif′ə·bəs) *adj. Ecol.* Not thriving on soils rich in lime. [< CALCI- + Gk. *-phobos* fearing < *phobeein* fear]

cal·cite (kal′sīt) *n.* A widely diffused calcium carbonate, $CaCO_3$, usually colorless or whitish in hexagonal crystals: massive varieties include chalk, limestone, and marble. See ICELAND SPAR. **—cal·cit·ic** (kal·sit′ik) *adj.*

cal·ci·tra·tion (kal′sə·trā′shən) *n.* Kicking. See RECALCITRATE. [< L *calcitrare* kick]

cal·ci·um (kal′sē·əm) *n.* An abundant, silvery-white metallic element (symbol Ca, atomic number 20) belonging to the alkaline-earth group and forming an essential constituent of living organisms. See PERIODIC TABLE. [< L *calx* lime]

calcium carbide *Chem.* A compound, CaC_2, made from quicklime and carbon in an electric furnace: treated with water it yields acetylene. Also **calcium acetylide.**

calcium carbonate *Chem.* A fine white amorphous powder, $CaCO_3$: used in toothpowders and dental cements.

calcium chloride *Chem.* A white, very deliquescent, hygroscopic salt, $CaCl_2$: used as a drying agent, preservative, refrigerant, and to prevent dust.

calcium cyanamide *Chem.* A compound, $CaCN_2$, produced in the electric furnace from the nitrogen of the air; an artificial fertilizer.

calcium fluoride *Chem.* A white powder, CaF_2, which becomes luminous on the application of heat: used for etching glass and in the manufacture of enamels.

calcium hydroxide *Chem.* Slaked lime, $Ca(OH)_2$: also used in solution; limewater.

calcium light A powerful light produced by the incandescence of lime in an oxyhydrogen flame; the Drummond light: limelight.

calcium phosphate *Chem.* Any of a class of earthy phosphates formed in various animal tissues and otherwise; especially, tribasic calcium phosphate or bone ash, $Ca_3(PO_4)_2$, used as an antacid, polishing agent, etc.

calcium sulfate *Chem.* A white compound, $CaSO_4$, occurring in nature as anhydrite and as gypsum.

cal·cog·ra·phy (kal·kog′rə·fē) *n.* The art of drawing with colored chalks or pastels. [< L *calx, calcis* chalk, lime + -GRAPHY] **—cal·co·graph·ic** (kal′kə·graf′ik) *adj.*

calc·sin·ter (kalk′sin′tər) *n.* A loose deposit of massive calcite in caverns or river beds; travertine. [< G *kalksinter* < *kalk* chalk (< L *calx* lime) + *sinter* slag]

calc·spar (kalk′spär′) *n.* Crystallized carbonate of lime. [< CALC(AREOUS) + SPAR[3]]

calc·tuff (kalk′tuf′) *n. Geol.* A porous deposit of carbonate of lime found in calcareous springs. Also **calc·tu·fa** (kalk′to͞o′fə, -tyo͞o′-). [< CALC(AREOUS) + TUFA]

cal·cu·la·ble (kal′kyə·lə·bəl) *adj.* Capable of being calculated, estimated, or forecast; reliable. **—cal′cu·la·bly** *adv.*

cal·cu·late (kal′kyə·lāt) *v.* **·lat·ed, ·lat·ing** *v.t.* **1** To determine by computation; arrive at by arithmetical means. **2** To predict or ascertain beforehand, as by computation: to *calculate* an eclipse. **3** To adapt or fit, as to a purpose or function: used chiefly in the passive: a truck *calculated* to carry a two-ton load. **4** To estimate or determine after deliberation; reckon: He *calculated* his chances. —*v.i.* **5** To perform a mathematical process; compute. **6** *U.S. Dial.* & *Colloq.* To suppose or believe; think. **—to calculate on** *Colloq.* To depend or rely on. [< LL *calculatus,* pp. of *calculare* reckon < *calculus* pebble < *calx* lime; with ref. to the use of pebbles in counting]

Synonyms: account, compute, consider, count, deem, enumerate, estimate, number, rate, reckon. *Number* is the generic term. To *count* is to *number* one by one. To *calculate* is to use more complicated processes, as multiplication, division, etc. *Compute* allows more of the element of probability, which is still more strongly expressed by *estimate*; as, to *estimate* the cost of a proposed building. To *enumerate* is to mention item by item; as to *enumerate* one's grievances. To *rate* is to

estimate by comparison, as if the object were one of a series. We *count* upon a desired future; we do not *count* upon the undesired. As applied to the present we *reckon* or *count* a thing precious or worthless. Compare ESTEEM.

cal·cu·lat·ing (kal′kyə·lā′ting) *adj.* **1** Inclined to reckon or estimate, especially for one's own chances or interests; planning; scheming: a *calculating* politician. **2** Designed for computation: a *calculating* machine.

calculating machine A keyboard machine that automatically adds, subtracts, multiplies, and divides a series of numbers recorded by the operator.

cal·cu·la·tion (kal′kyə·lā′shən) *n.* **1** The act or art of computing. **2** A computation; reckoning. **3** An estimate of probability; a forecast or deduction; the result of calculating. **4** Shrewd caution; prudence.

cal·cu·la·tive (kal′kyə·lā′tiv) *adj.* Of or pertaining to calculation; given to calculation.

cal·cu·la·tor (kal′kyə·lā′tər) *n.* **1** One who calculates. **2** A calculating machine or set of tables.

cal·cu·lous (kal′kyə·ləs) *adj.* **1** Stony; gritty. **2** Pertaining to, like, or affected with calculus. [<L *calculosus* gritty, pebbly]

cal·cu·lus (kal′kyə·ləs) *n. pl.* **·li** (-lī) or **·lus·es** **1** *Pathol.* A stonelike concretion, as in the bladder. **2** *Math.* A method of calculating by the use of a highly specialized system of algebraic symbols. **— differential calculus** That branch of analysis which investigates the infinitesimal changes of constantly varying quantities when the relations between the quantities are given. **— integral calculus** That branch of analysis which, from the relations among the infinitesimal changes or variations of quantities, deduces relations among the quantities themselves, as in finding the area enclosed by a given curve. [<L, a pebble (used in counting)]

Cal·cut·ta (kal·kut′ə) A port on the Hooghly; the largest city in India, and the capital of West Bengal.

cal·dar·i·um (kal·dâr′ē·əm) *n. pl.* **·dar·i·a** (-dâr′ē·ə) In ancient Rome, a room for the hot bath. [<L < *calidus* hot]

Cal·de·cott (kôl′də·kət), **Randolph,** 1846–86, English artist and illustrator.

cal·de·ra (kal·dē′rə, *Sp.* käl·dā′rä) *n.* **1** *Geol.* A large, roughly circular depression, in many cases with a partially broken-down rim, formed by the explosive disruption of a volcanic cone, or by the collapse of a crater floor. **2** A large caldron. [<Sp.]

Cal·de·rón de la Bar·ca (käl′dā·rōn′ thā lä vär′kä), **Pedro,** 1600–81, Spanish dramatist.

cal·dron (kôl′drən) *n.* A large kettle or boiler: also spelled *cauldron.* [<AF *caudron* <L *caldaria* kettle < *calidus* hot]

Cald·well (kôld′wel, -wəl), **Erskine,** born 1903, U.S. writer.

Ca·leb (kā′ləb) A masculine personal name. [<Hebrew, dog]
— Caleb The associate of Joshua in spying on the land of Canaan. *Num.* xiii 30.

ca·lèche (kà·lesh′) See CALASH.

Cal·e·do·ni·a (kal′ə·dō′nē·ə, -dōn′yə) The Roman name for the part of England north of the Firths of Clyde and Forth; now used poetically to mean all of Scotland. **— Cal′e·do′ni·an** *adj.* & *n.*

Caledonian Canal A waterway from Moray Firth to Loch Linnhe, Argyllshire, Scotland; 60 1/2 miles.

cal·e·fa·cient (kal′ə·fā′shənt) *adj.* Causing heat or warmth. **—** *n. Med.* Something that produces heat or warmth, as a mustard plaster. [<L *calefaciens, -entis,* ppr. of *calefacere* < *calere* be warm + *facere* make, cause] **— cal′e·fac′tion** (-fak′shən) *n.* **— cal′e·fac′tive** *adj.*

cal·e·fac·to·ry (kal′ə·fak′tər·ē) *adj.* Adapted or used for heating or warming; communicating warmth. **—** *n.* An artificially warmed room in a monastery.

ca·len·dal (kə·len′dəl) *adj.* Of or pertaining to the Roman calends or the first day of any month. [<L *calendae* first day of the month]

cal·en·dar (kal′ən·dər) *n.* **1** A systematic arrangement of subdivisions of time, as years, months, days, weeks, etc. **2** An almanac. **3** A schedule or list of things or events classified or chronologically arranged: a *calendar* of causes for trial in court. **4** *Obs.* A guide; example; model. **—** *v.t.* To register in a calendar or list; place in the calendar of saints; digest and index, as documents. ◆ Homophone: *calender.* [<L *calendarium* account book < *calendae* calends]
— Chinese calendar An ancient calendar, no longer in official use, with days and years reckoned in cycles of sixty. Each year consists of twelve lunar months, with adjustment to the solar year by periodic intercalation.
— ecclesiastical calendar A lunisolar calendar reckoning the year from the first Sunday in Advent: used for regulating the dates of church feasts.
— Gregorian calendar The calendar now in general use in most parts of the world; first prescribed in 1582 by Pope Gregory XIII to correct the Julian year to the solar year; adopted in England Sept. 3/14, 1752, the first being the *Old Style (O.S.)* date and the last being the *New Style (N.S.).* (Thus, although George Washington's birthday is commemorated on February 22, he was born on February 11, 1732, by the Old Style calendar.)
— Hebrew calendar The present-day calendar of the Jews, based on a lunar month, and adjusted to the solar year by intercalating the month Veadar between Adar and Nisan 7 times in a 19-year cycle. The months, having alternately 30 and 29 days, are Tishri, Heshwan, Kislew, Tebet, Shebat, Adar, Nisan, Iyyar, Siwan, Tammuz, Ab, and Elul; Heshwan and Kislew, however, may add or lose a day respectively as needed. The year now begins on Tishri 1, though anciently it began in Nisan. The Hebrew calendar reckons the creation at 3760 years 3 months B.C., as compared with Archbishop Ussher's 4004 B.C.
— Hindu calendar A solar calendar, reckoned in 12 months, each beginning when the sun enters a new sign of the zodiac.
— Julian calendar The calendar prescribed by Julius Caesar, which, though using the bissextile year, was in error one day in 128 years. The months, after some changes by Augustus, had the length now in use in Europe and America.
— Mohammedan calendar A lunar calendar of 12 months dating from A.D. 622 (July 15), the year of the Hegira. There is no seasonal intercalation, the seasons retrogressing in a period of 32 1/2 years. The names of the months, alternately 29 and 30 days, are Muharram (30 days), Saphar, Rabia 1, Rabia 2, Jomada 1, Jomada 2, Rajab, Shaaban, Ramadan, Shawwal, Dulkaada, and Dulheggia.
— perpetual calendar A calendar by which the day of the week for any given date may be ascertained during a widely extended period of time.
— Republican or **Revolutionary calendar** The calendar instituted on Oct. 5, 1793, by the first French Republic, and abolished Dec. 31, 1805. Its scheme divided the year into 12 months of 30 days each, with five (in leap years, six) supplementary days (*sansculottides*) at the end of the last month. The first year (Year I) began Sept. 22, 1792. The months were: Vendémiaire, Brumaire, Frimaire, Nivose, Pluviose, Ventose, Germinal, Floréal, Prairial, Messidor, Thermidor (or Fervidor), and Fructidor.
— Roman calendar A lunar calendar, attributed to Numa. The day of the new moon was the *calends,* and the day of the full moon the *ides* (the 13th or 15th of the month). Days were reckoned backward from these dates and from the *nones,* ninth day before the ides by inclusive reckoning.
— world calendar A proposed reformed calendar designed to equalize the lengths of the quarters of the year, each to have one month of 31 and two of 30 days. It provides for extra days to conform to solar time.

cal·en·der[1] (kal′ən·dər) *n.* A machine for giving a gloss to cloth, paper, etc., by pressing between rollers. **—** *v.t.* To press in a calender. ◆ Homophone: *calendar.* [<F *calendre* <L *cylindrus* <Gk. *kylindros* roller] **— cal′en·dered** *adj.* **— cal′en·der·er** *n.*

cal·en·der[2] (kal′ən·dər) *n.* A mendicant dervish of Persia or Turkey. ◆ Homophone: *calendar.* [<Persian *qalandar*]

cal·ends (kal′əndz) *n. pl.* The first day of the Roman month: also spelled *kalends.* **— at** (or **on) the Greek calends** At a date that will never come, the Greeks having had no calends. [<L *calendae* calends]

ca·len·du·la (kə·len′jŏŏ·lə) *n.* **1** Any of a small genus (*Calendula*) of annual or perennial herbs of the composite family, the pot marigolds, having alternate entire leaves, and heads of yellow or orange flowers. **2** The dried florets of this plant, containing a bitter principle used to promote the healing of wounds. [<NL, dim. of *calendae* calends; because it blooms almost every month]

cal·en·ture (kal′ən·chŏŏr) *n. Pathol.* **1** A tropical remittent fever caused by extreme heat and accompanied by delirium and hallucinations. **2** Sunstroke. [<F <Sp. *calentura* fever <L *calere* be warm]

ca·le·sa (kä·lā′sä) *n. Spanish* A small, two-wheeled carriage; Spanish chaise; cab.

ca·les·cence (kə·les′əns) *n.* The condition of growing warm; increasing warmth. [<L *calescens, -entis,* ppr. of *calescere,* inceptive of *calere* be warm] **— ca·les′cent** *adj.*

calf[1] (kaf, käf) *n. pl.* **calves** (kavz, kävz) **1** The young of the cow or various other bovine animals. ◆ Collateral adjective: *vituline.* **2** The young of various large mammals, as the elephant, whale, hippopotamus, etc. **3** The skin of the calf, or leather made from it: also *calfskin.* **4** *Colloq.* A raw, gawky, witless young person; a blockhead; dolt. **5** A floating fragment of ice near an iceberg. **— the golden calf** **1** The molten image made by Aaron and worshiped by the Israelites. *Ex.* xxxii. **2** Riches, as unduly prized; mammon. [OE *cealf*]

calf[2] (kaf, käf) *n. pl.* **calves** (kavz, kävz) The muscular hinder part of the human leg below the knee. ◆ Collateral adjective: *sural.* [<ON *kálfi*]

calf love *Colloq.* Adolescent or immature love felt by a boy for a girl or a girl for a boy.

calf's-foot jelly (kafs′fŏŏt′, käfs′-) A gelatinous deposit sometimes found between the bones of calves' feet and processed by boiling: also spelled *calvesfoot jelly.*

calf's-head (kafs·hed) *n.* The pitcherplant.

calf·skin (kaf′skin′, käf′-) *n.* **1** The skin or hide of a calf. **2** A kind of fine leather made from the skin of a calf. Also *calf.*

Cal·ga·ry (kal′gər·ē) A city in southern Alberta, Canada.

Cal·houn (kal·hōōn′), **John Caldwell,** 1782–1850, U.S. statesman.

Ca·li (kä′lē) A city in western Colombia.

Cal·i·ban (kal′ə·ban) In Shakespeare's *The Tempest,* a deformed savage slave of Prospero.

cal·i·ber (kal′ə·bər) *n.* **1** The internal diameter of a tube. **2** *Mil.* **a** The internal diameter of the barrel of a gun, cannon, etc., expressed in decimals of an inch for small arms, millimeters for rifles, centimeters for cannon. **b** The diameter of a bullet, shell, etc. **c** The ratio of the length of a gun's bore to its diameter: a unit of length. **3** Degree of individual capacity or intellectual power; personal ability, quality, or worth. Also **cal′i·bre.** [<F *calibre,* ? <Arabic *qālib* mold, form]

cal·i·brate (kal′ə·brāt) *v.t.* **·brat·ed, ·brat·ing** **1** To graduate the tube of (a measuring instrument) into appropriate units. **2** To determine the reading of (such an instrument). **3** To ascertain the caliber of. [Cf. F *calibrer*] **— cal′i·bra′tion** *n.* **— cal′i·bra′tor** *n.*

Cal·i·burn (kal′ə·bûrn), **Cal·i·bur·no** (kal′ə·bûr′nō) See EXCALIBUR.

cal·i·ces (kal′ə·sēz) Plural of CALIX.

ca·li·che (kä·lē′chā) *n.* **1** The native, impure sodium nitrate of Chile, $NaNO_3$; Chile saltpeter. **2** A calcareous sediment typical of soils in warm, semiarid, or desert regions. [<Am. Sp.]

cal·i·cle (kal′i·kəl) *n. Zool.* A small, cup-shaped part or organ, as a polyp cell in corals or a hydrotheca in hydrozoans; a calycle. [<L *caliculus,* dim. of *calix* cup]

cal·i·co (kal′i·kō) *n. pl.* **·coes** or **·cos** **1** Any cheap cotton cloth printed in bright colors. **2** *Brit.* White cotton cloth. **—** *adj.* **1** Made of calico: a *calico* dress. **2** Resembling printed calico; dappled or streaked; variegated: a *calico* cat. [from *Calicut*]

cal·i·co·back (kal′i·kō·bak′) *n.* **1** The turnstone. **2** The harlequin bug. **3** The calico bass.

calico bass A varicolored food fish (*Pomoxys sparoides*) of the Mississippi Valley, etc.: also called *strawberry bass.*

cal·i·co·bush (kal′i·kō·boŏsh′) *n*. The mountain laurel. Also **cal′i·co·tree′**.

ca·lic·u·la (kə·lik′yə·lə) See CALYCLE.

Cal·i·cut (kal′ə·kut) A port in SW Madras, India.

ca·lif (kā′lif, kal′if), **cal·i·fate** (kal′ə·fāt, -fit), etc. See CALIPH, etc.

Cal·i·for·nia (kal′ə·fôrn′yə, -fôr′nē·ə) A Pacific State of the United States; 156,803 square miles; capital, Sacramento; entered the Union Sept. 9, 1850: nickname *Golden State.* Abbr. CA

California, Gulf of An arm of the Pacific, between Mexico and Lower California.

California, Lower See LOWER CALIFORNIA.

California condor A large, rare vulturine bird (*Gymnogyps californianus*), native within a restricted range of the mountains of southern California.

California fuchsia A perennial herbaceous shrub (*Zauschneria californica*), with large scarlet flowers.

Cal·i·for·nian (kal′ə·fôrn′yən, -fôr′nē·ən) *adj*. Of or pertaining to California. —*n*. 1 A native or inhabitant of California. 2 An aboriginal of California. 3 One of the original Spanish settlers of California.

California poppy Any of several plants of the poppy family; specifically, the yellow-flowered *Eschscholtzia californica*, State flower of California; the creamcups and the mission poppy.

cal·i·for·nite (kal′ə·fôr′nīt) *n*. A compact variety of vesuvianite, resembling jade, found in California.

cal·i·for·ni·um (kal′ə·fôr′nē·əm) *n*. A synthetic radioactive element (symbol Cf, atomic number 98), having isotopic mass numbers from 242 to 253 and half-lives ranging from 3.7 minutes to approximately 800 years. See PERIODIC TABLE. [< from the University of *California*, where first produced]

ca·lig·i·nous (kə·lij′ə·nəs) *adj*. Obscure; dark; dim. [< L *caliginosus* misty, dark < *caligo* fog, darkness] —**ca·lig′i·nous·ly** *adv*. —**ca·lig′i·nous·ness, ca·lig·i·nos′i·ty** (-nos′ə·tē) *n*.

ca·lig·ra·phy (kə·lig′rə·fē) See CALLIGRAPHY

Ca·lig·u·la (kə·lig′yə·lə), 12–41, Roman emperor 37–41; assassinated: real name *Gaius Caesar*.

cal·i·man·co (kal′ə·mang′kō) See CALAMANCO.

cal·i·pash (kal′ə·pash, kal′ə·pash′) *n*. The part of a turtle next to the upper shell, a greenish gelatinous substance esteemed as a table delicacy: also spelled *callipash*. [? Alter. of Sp. *carapacho* carapace]

cal·i·pee (kal′ə·pē, kal′ə·pē′) *n*. The part of a turtle next the lower shell, a yellowish gelatinous edible substance: also spelled *callipee*. [Cf. CALIPASH.]

cal·i·per (kal′ə·pər) *n*. 1 An instrument like a pair of compasses, usually with curved legs, for measuring diameters: usually in the plural: also **caliper compass.** 2 A caliper rule. —*v.t. & v.i.* To measure by using calipers. Also spelled *calliper*. [Var. of CALIBER]

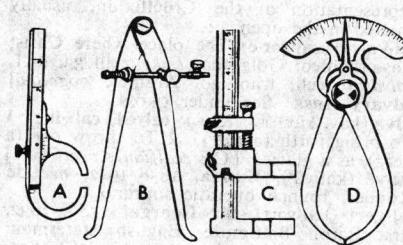

TYPES OF CALIPERS
A. Graduating.   *B.* Inside.
C. Square or beam.   *D.* Outside-adjusting.

caliper rule 1 A caliper for determining the weight of a ball from its diameter, and vice versa. 2 A scaled rule with sliding jaw.

ca·liph (kā′lif, kal′if) *n*. The spiritual and civil head of a Moslem state: title taken by the sultans of Turkey, abolished in 1924: also spelled *calif, kalif, khalif*. [< F *caliphe.* < Arabic *khalifah* successor (to Mohammed)] —**cal·i·phate** (kal′ə·fāt, -fit) *n*.

cal·i·sa·ya (kal′ə·sā′ə) *n*. Cinchona; specifically, the species rich in quinine, *Cinchona calisaya*: also called *yellowbark*. [< Sp. < Quechua]

cal·is·then·ics (kal′is·then′iks) *n. pl.* 1 Light gymnastics to promote grace and health: construed as plural. 2 The science of such exercises: construed as singular. Also spelled *callisthenics*. [< Gk. *kalli-* < *kalos* beautiful + *sthenos* strength] —**cal′is·then′ic** *adj*.

ca·lix (kā′liks kal′iks) *n. pl.* **cal·i·ces** (kāl′ə·sēz) 1 A cup; hence, any cup-shaped organ or part. 2 *Eccl.* A chalice. Compare CALYX. [< L, cup]

Ca·lix·tine (kə·lik′stin) *n*. One of a Hussite sect in Bohemia in the 15th century, who demanded the cup in the Eucharist for the laity and also a limitation of the exclusive rights of the clergy. [< L *calix* cup]

Ca·lix·tus (kə·lik′stəs), **Georg**, 1586–1656, German Lutheran theologian, advocate of a united Protestant church: original name *Georg Callisen*.

calk[1] (kôk) *v.t.* 1 *Naut.* To make tight, as a boat's seams, by plugging with soft material, as oakum or hemp fiber. 2 To hammer or fasten together, as the edges of the plates of a boiler. 3 To plug up the crevices of, as a window frame. Also spelled *caulk*. [< OF *cauquer* < L *calcare* tread] —**calk′ing** *n*.

calk[2] (kôk) *n*. 1 A spur on a horse's shoe to prevent slipping. 2 A plate with sharp points worn on the sole of a person's boot or shoe to prevent slipping. Also **calk′er, calk′in.** —*v.t.* 1 To furnish with calks. 2 To wound with a calk. [Prob. < L *calx* heel]

calk·er (kô′kər) *n*. 1 One who calks the seams of a vessel or a boiler. 2 A tool used for calking.

call (kôl) *v.t.* 1 To appeal to by word of mouth. 2 To utter or read aloud. 3 To summon in any way; convoke, as Congress; convene; invoke solemnly: to *call* God to witness. 4 To designate or characterize in any way; name; style; suppose; assume to be so much. 5 To read aloud from a list of names: *Call* the roll. 6 To arouse, as from sleep. 7 To designate for a special work: to *call* to the ministry. 8 To lure (birds or animals) by imitating their cry with a whistle, call, or other imitative means. 9 To insist upon payment of, as by written notice. 10 To communicate by telephone. 11 To fix the time for; bring to action: to *call* a case to court. 12 *Colloq.* In the game of pool, to designate (a shot), before making the play. 13 In baseball, to stop or suspend (a game) because of rain, darkness, etc. —*v.i.* 14 To lift up the voice in address, command, or entreaty; send out a cry of summons; appeal; sound a signal. 15 To communicate by telephone: I will *call* tomorrow. 16 To make a brief visit, stop or stay: followed by *at, on*, or *upon*: The steamer *calls* at Southampton. 17 In poker, to demand a show of hands, upon staking an amount equal to the bet of each previous player. 18 In whist and other card games, to make a demand or give a signal, as for trumps or for a particular card. 19 To ask for a showdown on anything. —**to call back** 1 To summon back; recall; revoke; retract. 2 To call in return, as by telephone. —**to call one's bluff** To take a challenge; ask for a showdown. —**to call down** 1 To pray heaven to send or cause to descend: to *call down* the wrath of the gods. 2 To rebuke; reprimand. —**to call off** 1 To count; announce. 2 To cancel. —**to call out** 1 To shout. 2 To bring an actor or actress out before the curtains by applause. 3 To summon workers to go out on strike. —**to call up** 1 To bring before the memory or mind's eye. 2 To bring up for action or discussion, as a legislative measure. 3 To demand payment of, as amounts due on shares. 4 To notify to appear before some tribunal, as a court; cite. 5 To notify to appear for induction into the armed forces; also, to summon (troops) for active service. 6 To summon to stand up and speak. 7 To communicate with by telephone. —*n*. 1 A shout or cry to attract attention or response. 2 A lifting up of the voice in speech or other utterance; specifically, a thing called or indicated. 3 A summons or invitation; also, a roll call, a bugle call, or telephone call. 4 A requirement; claim; right; obligation: the *call* of duty. 5 A brief visit. 6 An assessment or demand; specifically, a contract requiring, in consideration of money paid, the delivery of some article named, as stocks, at a certain price. Compare PUT *n*. (def. 2). 7 A request by a govern-

ment or corporation that holders of its redeemable bonds present them for payment. 8 An assessment on the members of a corporation or joint-stock company for the payment of subscription instalments, or for cash to meet losses. 9 A blast on a hunting horn to encourage the hounds. 10 The characteristic cry of an animal or a bird. 11 *Law* A visible natural object or an established point mentioned in the descriptive part of a deed for tracing a line of vision or boundary: a *call* of the deed. 12 An inward urge to a certain line of work; a vocation. 13 *Colloq.* Right or occasion for: You've no *call* to do that. 14 In poker, a demand for a show of hands: made only after equaling preceding bets. 15 A notice of rehearsals, instructions to actors, etc., posted on the callboard. —**at (or on) call** Payable on demand, or without previous notice, as a loan or deposit. —**to have the call** To have the advantage; also, to be the leader in popular favor. —**within call** Readily accessible or within hearing; also, subject to call. ♦ Homophone: *caul*. [< ON *kalla*]

Synonyms (*verb*): bawl, bellow, clamor, cry, ejaculate, exclaim, roar, scream, shout, shriek, vociferate, yell. To *call* is to send out the voice in order to attract another's attention, either by word or by inarticulate utterance. Animals *call* their mates, or their young; a man *calls* his dog, his horse, etc. The sense is extended to include summons by bell or other audible signal. To *shout* is to *call* or *exclaim* with the fullest volume of sustained voice; to *scream* or *shriek* is to utter a shriller cry. We *shout* words; in *screaming, shrieking*, or *yelling* there is often no attempt at articulation. To *bawl* is to utter senseless, noisy cries, like a child in pain or anger. *Bellow* and *roar* are applied to the utterances of animals, and only figuratively to those of persons. To *clamor* is to utter with noisy iteration; it applies also to the confused cries of a multitude. To *vociferate* is commonly applied to loud, excited speech. One may *exclaim, or ejaculate* with no thought of others' presence; when he *calls*, it is to attract another's attention. See CONVOKE, EXCLAIM. *Antonyms*, harken, hush, list, listen.

cal·la (kal′ə) *n*. 1 A South African plant (*Zantedeschia aethiopica*) of the arum family, with a large, milk-white spathe that resembles a flower: also called *lily-of-the-Nile*. 2 A marsh plant of North America and Europe (*Calla palustris*) bearing red berries in dense clusters. Also **calla lily.** [< L *calla*, a plant name]

cal·lant (kä′lənt) *n. Scot.* A lad; youth. Also **cal·lan** (kä′lən).

Cal·la·o (kä·yä′ō) A port on **Callao Bay**, an inlet of the Pacific in western Peru.

call-back (kôl′bak′) *n*. The recall of a product by its manufacturer in order to correct previously undetected defects.

call·board (kôl′bôrd′, -bōrd′) *n*. A theater bulletin board for posting notices of rehearsals, instructions, etc.

call·boy (kôl′boi′) *n*. 1 A boy who answers calls, in a hotel or on board ship; a bellboy. 2 A boy who calls actors to go on stage.

call-down (kôl′doun′) *n*. A rebuke or scolding.

call·er[1] (kô′lər) *n*. 1 One who or that which calls. 2 One making a brief, formal visit. 3 A head waiter. 4 In square dancing, one who calls the successive steps of a set.

cal·ler[2] (kal′ər, kä′lər) *Scot. v.t.* To freshen; cool. —*adj*. 1 Cool or refreshing. 2 Fresh.

Cal·les (kä′yās), **Plutarco Elias**, 1877–1945, Mexican general; president 1924–28.

call girl *Colloq.* A prostitute who goes to assignations in response to telephone calls.

calli- For words not found here, see under CALI-.

cal·li·graph (kal′ə·graf, -gräf) *n*. A specimen of beautiful or ornamental penmanship.

cal·lig·ra·phy (kə·lig′rə·fē) *n*. 1 Beautiful pen-

manship. 2 Handwriting in general. [<Gk. *kalligraphia* <*kalos* beautiful + *graphein* write] —**cal·lig′ra·pher, cal·lig′ra·phist** *n.* —**cal·li·graph·ic** (kal′ə·graf′ik) *adj.* —**cal′li·graph′·i·cal·ly** *adv.*

Cal·lim·a·chus (kə·lim′ə·kəs) Fifth century B.C. Greek sculptor.

call·ing (kô′ling) *n.* 1 A speaking, crying, or shouting to command attention. 2 A convocation or summoning. 3 A solemn appointment or summons. 4 Habitual occupation; profession; vocation; business. 5 Social condition or status; rank.

calling card A small card, printed or engraved with one's name: used to announce a visit or call.

cal·li·o·pe (kə·lī′ə·pē, kal′ē·ōp) *n.* A musical instrument consisting of a series of steam whistles played by means of a keyboard; a steam organ. [after *Calliope*]

Cal·li·o·pe (kə·lī′ə·pē) The Muse of eloquence and epic poetry. [<L <Gk. *Kalliopē* the beautiful-voiced <*kalos* beautiful + *ops* voice]

cal·li·op·sis (kal′ē·op′sis) See COREOPSIS.

cal·li·per (kal′ə·pər) See CALIPER.

cal·li·pyg·i·an (kal′ə·pij′ē·ən) *adj.* Having beautiful buttocks. Also **cal′li·py′gous** (-pī′·gəs). [<Gk. *kallipygos* <*kalos* beautiful + *pygē* buttocks]

Cal·lis·the·nes (kə·lis′thə·nēz), 360?–328? B.C., Greek philosopher and historian.

cal·lis·then·ics (kal′is·then′iks) See CALISTHENICS.

Cal·lis·to (kə·lis′tō) 1 In Greek and Roman mythology, a nymph loved by Zeus and transformed into a bear by Artemis or Hera: set as Ursa Major among the stars by Zeus. 2 *Astron.* The fifth satellite of Jupiter: the largest satellite in the solar system.

Cal·lis·tra·tus (kə·lis′trə·təs), died 355 B.C., Athenian orator and general.

cal·li·type (kal′ə·tīp′) *v.t.* **·typed, ·typ·ing** To make a copy of (reading matter) on printing plates by photoengraving typewritten sheets. [<*calli-* beautiful (<Gk. *kalos*) + -TYPE] —**cal′li·typ′y** *n.*

call letters The code letters identifying a radio or television transmitting station.

call loan A loan of money to be repaid on demand, or call, at any time.

call money See under MONEY.

call number A classifying number employed by libraries to indicate the subject and author of a book and its place on the shelves.

cal·lose (kal′ōs) *n. Biochem.* A hard, thick, insoluble carbohydrate assumed to develop in the cell walls of certain plants. [<L *callosus* hard-skinned]

cal·los·i·ty (kə·los′ə·tē) *n. pl.* **·ties** 1 *Physiol.* A thickened, hardened portion of the skin, produced by or as by pressure or friction. 2 *Biol.* A hard or thickened part, as on the legs of horses, on or in a plant, etc.; a callus. 3 Hardness; insensibility.

cal·lous (kal′əs) *adj.* 1 Thickened and hardened, as the skin by friction or pressure. 2 Hardened in feeling; insensible; unfeeling. See synonyms under HARD. ◆ Homophone: *callus.* [<L *callosus* <*callus* hard skin] —**cal·loused** (kal′əst) *adj.* —**cal′lous·ly** *adv.* —**cal′·lous·ness** *n.*

cal·low (kal′ō) *adj.* 1 Unfledged; not yet feathered, as a bird. 2 Inexperienced; youthful. 3 Of or pertaining to an unfledged bird or a youth. [OE *calu* bare, bald]

call rate The interest rate on call loans.

call slip A printed form on which a library patron writes his request for a desired book.

cal·lus (kal′əs) *n. pl.* **·lus·es** 1 A callosity or thickening. 2 *Physiol.* The new bony tissue between and around the fractured ends of a broken bone in the process of reuniting. 3 *Bot.* The parenchymatous tissue which forms over a cut on a stem and protects the exposed wood. —*v.i.* To form a callosity or callus. ◆ Homophone: *callous.* [<L, hard skin]

calm (käm) *adj.* Free from disturbance or agitation; without motion; in repose; also, unmoved by passion or emotion; serene. —*n.* 1 Stillness; serenity. 2 Lack of wind or motion. See synonyms under REST. —*v.t.* To bring into repose; still; soothe. —*v.i.* To become quiet or placid. See synonyms under ALLAY, SETTLE. [<MF *calme* <Ital. *calma* <LL *cauma* heat of the day <Gk. *kauma* heat; with ref. to the rest or siesta at midday] —**calm′ly** *adv.* —**calm′ness** *n.*

Synonyms (adj.): collected, composed, cool, dispassionate, imperturbable, peaceful, placid, quiet, sedate, self-controlled, self-possessed, serene, smooth, still, tranquil, undisturbed, unruffled. That is *calm* which is free from disturbance or agitation; in the physical sense, free from violent motion or action; in the mental or spiritual sense, free from excited or disturbing emotion or passion. We speak of a *calm* sea, a *placid* lake, a *serene* sky, a *still* night, a *quiet* day, a *quiet* home. We speak, also, of *still* waters, *smooth* sailing, which are different modes of expressing freedom from manifest agitation. *Cool,* in this connection, always suggests the recognition of some form of danger or risk. One may be *calm* by assured superiority to danger, by ignorance of its existence or of its magnitude, or by indifference to the result, or by the apathy of hopelessness, as we speak of the *calmness* of despair; one is *cool* who, while intensely alive to danger or need, has all his faculties concentrated on the means of meeting or overcoming it; a *calm* boxer would probably be an easy victim, while a *cool* boxer would be a dangerous antagonist. *Cool* is stronger than *composed* or *collected.* One is *composed* who has subdued excited feeling; he is *collected* when he has every thought, feeling, or perception awake and at command. *Tranquil* refers to a present state, *placid* to a prevailing tendency. We speak of a *tranquil* mind, a *placid* disposition. The *serene* spirit dwells as if in the clear upper air, above all storm or agitation. See PACIFIC, SOBER. *Antonyms*: agitated, boisterous, disturbed, excited, fierce, frantic, frenzied, furious, heated, passionate, raging, roused, ruffled, stormy, turbulent, violent, wild, wrathful.

cal·ma·tive (kal′mə·tiv, kä′mə-) *adj.* Having a soothing effect; sedative. —*n.* A sedative; tranquilizer.

calm·y (kä′mē) *adj. Obs.* Calm.

cal·o·mel (kal′ə·mel, -məl) *n. Med.* Mercurous chloride, HgCl, a heavy, white, tasteless compound: used as a purgative. [<F <Gk. *kalos* beautiful + *melas* black]

cal·o·mon·din (kal′ə·mon′din) *n.* A hardy orange (*Citrus mitis*) with a small, acid, orange-red fruit.

Ca·lo·o·can (kä′lô·ô′kän) A municipality of southern Luzon, Philippines.

Ca·loo·sa·hatch·ee River (kə·lo͞o′sə·hach′ē) A river in southern Florida, flowing 75 miles SW to the Gulf of Mexico.

cal·o·res·cence (kal′ə·res′əns) *n. Physics* The generation of visible light from invisible heat radiation, as by directing a stream of infrared rays upon a thin platinum plate. [<L *calor* heat + -ESCENCE]

ca·lor·ic (kə·lôr′ik, -lor′-) *adj.* Of or pertaining to heat. —*n.* 1 Heat. 2 Formerly, a supposed principle of heat. [<F *calorique* <L *calor* heat]

cal·o·ric·i·ty (kal′ə·ris′ə·tē) *n.* The power of developing heat, possessed by animals.

cal·o·rie (kal′ə·rē) *n.* 1 One of two recognized units of heat used especially to express the heat- or energy-producing content of foods. The **great, greater, large,** or **kilogram calorie** is the amount of heat required to raise the temperature of one kilogram of water 1° C. The **lesser, small,** or **gram calorie** is the amount of heat required to raise one gram of water 1° C. 2 *Physiol.* The large calorie, used as a measure of the energy value of foods or the heat output of organisms. Also **cal′o·ry.** [<F *calorie* <L *calor* heat]

cal·o·rif·ic (kal′ə·rif′ik) *adj.* 1 Able to produce heat; heating. 2 Carrying or conducting heat; thermal. Also **cal′o·rif′i·cal.** [<F *calorifique* <L *calorificus*]

ca·lor·i·fi·ca·tion (kə·lôr′ə·fi·kā′shən, -lor′-) *n.* The production of heat.

calorific power The heat resulting from complete combustion of a gram of fuel. Also **calorific value.**

cal·o·rif·ics (kal′ə·rif′iks) *n.* 1 The science of heating. 2 The branch of physics that treats of heat.

cal·o·rim·e·ter (kal′ə·rim′ə·tər) *n.* Any apparatus for measuring the quantity of heat generated by friction, combustion, or chemical change. —**bomb calorimeter** A calorimeter in the form of a steel-walled container in which measured quantities of fuel or other substances may be burned to determine their calorific value. [<L *calor* heat + -METER] —**ca·lor·i·met·ric** (kə·lôr′ə·met′rik, -lor′-) or **·met′ri·cal** *adj.* —**cal′o·rim′e·try** *n.*

ca·lotte (kə·lot′) *n.* 1 A skullcap worn by the Roman Catholic clergy. 2 Any small, close-fitting cap. [<F <Ital. *calotta,* prob. <Gk. *kalyptra* veil, hood <*kalyptein* cover]

cal·o·yer (kal′ə·yər, kə·loi′ər) *n.* A monk of the Eastern Church, especially one of the order of St. Basil. [<F <Ital. *caloiero* venerable <LGk. *kalogēros* <*kalos* fair + *gerōn* old]

cal·pac (kal′pak) *n.* A black sheepskin or felt cap worn by Armenians, Turks, etc.: also spelled *kalpac.* Also **cal′pack.** [<Turkish *qālpāq*]

Cal·ta·nis·set·ta (käl′tä·nēs·sāt′tä) A city in central Sicily.

cal·trop (kal′trəp) *n.* 1 *Mil.* A small iron instrument shaped like a ball from which four sharp-pointed curved spikes project and are so mounted that one is always upright: formerly used to impede cavalry or infantry. 2 One of various plants with spiny heads or fruit that entangle the feet, as the **hairy caltrop** (*Kalestroemia hirsutissima*), the puncturevine, the star thistle, and the water chestnut. Also **cal′trap** (-trəp). [OE *coltetraeppe* <L *calx* heel + LL *trappa* trap]

cal·u·met (kal′yə·met, kal′yə·met′) *n.* A tobacco pipe with a long, ornamented reed stem, and, usually, a red clay bowl: used by American Indians in religious and magic ceremonies, to ratify war and peace treaties, etc.: often called *peace pipe.* [<F, pipe stem <L *calamellus,* dim. of *calamus* reed]

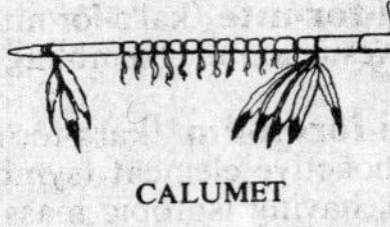
CALUMET

ca·lum·ni·ate (kə·lum′nē·āt) *v.t. & v.i.* **·at·ed, ·at·ing** To accuse falsely; defame; slander. See synonyms under ASPERSE, REVILE. [<L *calumniatus,* pp. of *calumniari* slander <*calumnia* slander] —**ca·lum′ni·a′tion** *n.* —**ca·lum′ni·a′tor** *n.* —**ca·lum·ni·a·to·ry** (kə·lum′·nē·ə·tôr′ē, -tō′rē).

ca·lum·ni·ous (kə·lum′nē·əs) *adj.* Slanderous; defamatory. —**ca·lum′ni·ous·ly** *adv.*

cal·um·ny (kal′əm·nē) *n. pl.* **·nies** A false, malicious, and injurious accusation or report; defamation; slander. See synonyms under SCANDAL. [<MF *calomnie* <L *calumnia* slander. Doublet of CHALLENGE.]

cal·u·tron (kal′yə·tron) *n.* An electromagnetic device for the separation of isotopes, especially in the study and production of atomic energy. [<CAL(IFORNIA) U(NIVERSITY) (CYCLO)TRON]

Cal·va·dos (kål·vå·dōs′) *n.* A French brandy made from cider. [from *Calvados,* a department in NW France]

cal·var·i·a (kal·vâr′ē·ə) *n. Anat.* The vaulted upper portion of the cranium. Also **cal·var′·i·um** (-ē·əm). [<L, skull]

cal·va·ry (kal′vər·ē) *n. pl.* **·ries** A sculptured representation of the Crucifixion, usually erected in the open air.

Cal·va·ry (kal′vər·ē) The place where Christ was crucified; Golgotha. *Luke* xxiii 33. [<L *calvaria* skull, trans. of Aramaic *gogolthā*]

Calvary cross See under CROSS.

calve (kav, käv) *v.t. & v.i.* **calved, calv·ing** 1 To bring forth (a calf). 2 To throw off (a berg), as a glacier. [OE *cealfian* <*cealf* calf]

Cal·vé (kål·vā′), **Emma,** 1858–1942, *née* de Roquer, French operatic soprano.

Cal·vert (kal′vərt), **Sir George,** 1580?–1632, first Baron Baltimore, English statesman; founder of Maryland. —**Leonard,** 1606?–1647, English statesman; first governor of Maryland, son of the preceding.

calves (kavz, kävz) Plural of CALF.

Cal·vin (kal′vin, *Fr.* kål·vaṅ′) A masculine personal name. Also *Lat.* **Cal·vi·nus** (kal·vī′nəs), *Sp.* **Cal·vo** (käl′vō).

Cal·vin (kal′vin), **John,** 1509–64, French Protestant reformer.

Cal·vin·ism (kal′vin·iz′əm) *n.* 1 *Theol.* a The system or doctrines of John Calvin, emphasizing the depravity and helplessness of man, the sovereignty of God, and predestination, and characterized by an austere moral code. b Any later system based upon the teachings of Calvin. 2 Belief in or support for such a system. —**Cal′vin·ist** *n.*

Cal·vin·is·tic (cal′vin·is′tik) *adj.* 1 Pertaining

to Calvinism or Calvinists. 2 Austere: strict; severe. —**Cal'vin·is'ti·cal** adj. —**Cal'vin·is'ti·cal·ly** adv.

cal·vi·ti·es (kal·vish'i·ēz) n. Baldness, especially on the top or back of the head. [< L < calvus bald]

calx (kalks) n. pl. **calx·es** or **cal·ces** (kal'sēz) 1 The residue from the calcination of minerals. 2 Lime or chalk. [< L]

cal·y·ces (kal'ə·sēz, kā'lə-) A plural of CALYX.

cal·y·cine (kal'ə·sin, -sīn) adj. 1 Of or pertaining to a calyx. 2 Of the nature of, situated on, or like a calyx. Also **ca·lyc·i·nal** (kə·lis'ə·nəl). [< L calyx. See CALYX.]

cal·y·cle (kal'i·kəl) n. Bot. An accessory calyx outside of the true calyx: also called calicula. [< L caliculus, dim. of calyx]

ca·lyc·u·lar (kə·lik'yə·lər) adj. Having calycles. Also **ca·lyc'u·late** (-lāt, -lit).

ca·lyc·u·lus (kə·lik'yə·ləs) See CALYCLE.

Cal·y·don (kal'ə·don) An ancient city in Aetolia, west central Greece, on the **Gulf of Calydon**, modern Gulf of Patras. —**Cal·y·do·ni·an** (kal'ə·dō'nē·ən, -dōn'yən) adj. & n.

Calydonian boar In Greek mythology, a great boar sent by Artemis to ravage Calydon. See MELEAGER, OENEUS.

ca·lyp·so[1] (kə·lip'sō) n. Any orchid of the genus Cytherea, having only one species (C. bulbosa), growing in boggy regions of northern Europe and North America. [after Calypso]

ca·lyp·so[2] (kə·lip'sō) n. A type of song, originally improvised and sung by natives of Trinidad, dealing with topical, sexual, or humorous themes and achieving its effect by only approximate rime, flexible syllabic emphasis, and colloquial language. [Origin uncertain]

Ca·lyp·so (kə·lip'sō) In the Odyssey, a nymph who kept Odysseus for seven years on the island of Ogygia when he had been shipwrecked.

ca·lyp·tra (kə·lip'trə) n. 1 A hood or lid. 2 Bot. a In mosses, the hood or covering of the capsule. b In flowering plants, any similar hood-shaped organ. Also **ca·lyp'ter** (-tər). [< NL < Gk. kalyptra veil < kalyptein cover]

ca·lyp·trate (kə·lip'trāt) adj. Covered with, having, or like a calyptra.

ca·lyx (kā'liks, kal'iks) n. pl. **ca·lyx·es** or **cal·y·ces** (kal'ə·sēz, kā'lə-) 1 The outermost series of leaflike parts of a flower, individually called sepals: usually green and more or less leaf-shaped, but frequently colored and shaped. Compare COROLLA. 2 Zool. A cup-shaped part or organ. Compare CALIX. [< L < Gk. kalyx husk, pod]

cam[1] (kam) n. Mech. A rotating piece of irregular shape, as on a wheel in a machine: used to change the direction of the motion of another part moving against it, as rotary into reciprocating or variable motion. [< Du. cam tooth, cog of a wheel]

cam[2] (käm) Scot. Past tense of COME.

Cam (kam) A river in Cambridgeshire, England, flowing north 40 miles to the Ouse: also Granta.

Ca·ma·cho (kä·mä'chō), (**Manuel**) 'Avila, 1897–1955, president of Mexico 1940–46.

Ca·ma·güey (kä'mä·gwā') A city in eastern Cuba.

ca·ma·ieu (kà·mà·yœ') n. French 1 A cameo. 2 Painting in one color or in different shades of one color. —**en camaieu** In monochrome.

ca·mail (kə·māl') n. A piece of chain mail depending from a basinet and protecting the neck and shoulders; also, a hood of mail. [< F] —**ca·mailed'** adj.

ca·ma·ra·de·rie (kä'mə·rä'dər·ē) n. Comradeship; loyalty; fellowship. Also **com'rade·ry**. [< F]

cam·a·ril·la (kam'ə·ril'ə, Sp. kä'mä·rēl'yä) n. 1 A group of unofficial advisers, as of a king; a clique of persons exercising political powers secretly and unofficially; a cabal. 2 A little chamber; especially, the audience chamber of a king. [< Sp., dim. of camara chamber]

cam·as (kam'əs) n. 1 Any of several North American bulbous herbs of the lily family (genus Camassia); especially, C. quamash, having an edible bulb. 2 The death camas. Sometimes spelled cammas, quamash. Also **cam'ass**. [< Chinook jargon]

Cam·bay (kam·bā') A town of northern Bombay state, India; capital of the former princely state of Cambay, on the **Gulf of Cambay**, an inlet of the Arabian Sea between Bombay and Kathiawar peninsula.

cam·ber (kam'bər) v.t. To cut or bend to a slight upward convex form. —v.i. To have or assume a slight upward convex curve, as a ship's deck. —n. A slight upward bend or convexity, as of a timber or an airfoil; a slight central rise. [< MF cambrer arch < L camerare < camera curved roof, vault]

Cam·ber·well (kam'bər·wel) A metropolitan borough in SE London.

Camberwell beauty A mourning cloak butterfly.

cam·bist (kam'bist) n. 1 A manual giving the moneys, weights, and measures of different countries, and their equivalents. 2 One versed in exchange values. [< F cambiste < Ital. cambista b < LL cambiare exchange]

cam·bi·um (kam'bē·əm) n. Bot. A zone of cells which generate new phloem and xylem in the stems and roots of many vascular plants. For illustration see EXOGEN. [< LL, exchange] **cam·bi·al** (kam'bē·əl) adj.

Cam·bo·di·a (kam·bō'dē·ə) See KHMER REPUBLIC.

Cam·bo·di·an (kam·bō'dē·ən) adj. Pertaining to Khmer Republic (Cambodia), its people, or their language. —n. A native or inhabitant of Khmer Republic.

cam·boose (kam·bōōs') See CABOOSE.

Cam·brai (kän·bre') A city of northern France.

Cam·bri·a (kam'brē·ə) The ancient Roman name for WALES.

Cam·bri·an (kam'brē·ən) adj. 1 Of or pertaining to Cambria or Wales; Welsh. 2 Geol. Of or pertaining to the earliest of the periods of the Paleozoic era. See chart under GEOLOGY. —n. 1 The Cambrian strata or period. 2 A Welshman.

Cambrian Mountains A mountain range throughout Wales.

cam·bric (kām'brik) n. 1 A fine white linen fabric or a similar fabric of cotton. 2 A coarse cotton fabric used for linings. [< Flemish Kameryk Cambrai]

cambric tea n. A drink made of sweetened hot water and milk, sometimes flavored with a little tea.

Cam·bridge (kām'brij) 1 A county of SE England; with Ely 867 square miles; county seat, Cambridge, site of Cambridge University. Also **Cam'bridge·shire** (-shir). 2 A city in eastern Massachusetts, site of Harvard University. A native of either the county or the city, or a student at or graduate of either university, is known as a Cantabrigian.

Cam·by·ses (kam·bī'sēz), died 521? B.C., king of Persia 529?–522 B.C., son of Cyrus the Great.

cam·cord·er (kam'kôr'dər) n. A portable TV camera and videotape recorder combination.

Cam·den (kam'dən) 1 A port of entry on the Delaware River in SW New Jersey. 2 A town in central South Carolina; scene of Revolutionary War battles, 1780–81.

Cam·den (kam'dən), **William**, 1551–1623, English antiquary and historian.

came[1] (kām) Past tense of COME.

came[2] (kām) n. Brit. A leaden sash bar or grooved strip for fastening together panes in latticed or stained glass windows. [Prob. var. of CAM[1]]

cam·el (kam'əl) n. 1 A large Asian or African ruminant (genus Camelus) with a humped back, capable of subsisting for extended periods of time without water: used as a beast of burden. There are two species, the **Arabian camel** or **dromedary**, having one hump, and the **Bactrian camel** (C. bactrianus), having two. 2 A buoyant, watertight contrivance for lifting wrecks, etc. [OE < L camelus < Gk. kamēlos < Semitic] —**cam'el·ish** adj.

cam·el·eer (kam'əl·ir') n. A camel driver or a soldier mounted on a camel.

CAMELS
A. Arabian.   B. Bactrian.
(7–9 feet tall)

ca·mel·lia (kə·mēl'yə, mel'ē·ə) n. A tropical Asian tree or shrub (Camellia or Thea japonica) with glossy leaves and white, pink, red, or variegated flowers: also called Japan rose. [after George Joseph Kamel, 1661–1706, Jesuit traveler]

ca·mel·o·pard (kə·mel'ə·pärd) n. Archaic The giraffe. [< L camelopardus < Gk. kamēlopardalis < kamēlos camel + pardalis leopard]

Ca·mel·o·par·da·lis (kə·mel'ə·pär'də·lis) A northern constellation, the Giraffe, between Ursa Major and Cassiopeia. See CONSTELLATION. Also **Ca·mel'o·pard, Ca·mel'o·par'dus** (-dəs)

Cam·e·lot (kam'ə·lot) In Arthurian legend, the seat of King Arthur's court: identified with Caerleon and Winchester.

cam·el's-hair (kam'əlz·hâr') n. A heavy, warm, tan cloth made of camel's hair, sometimes mixed with wool or other fibers. —adj. Made of, like, or the color of camel's-hair. Also **cam'el·hair'**.

Cam·em·bert (kam'əm·bâr, Fr. kà·män·bâr') n. A rich, creamy, soft cheese. [from Camembert, town in NW France]

Ca·me·nae (kə·mē'nē) n. pl. In Roman mythology, prophetic nymphs of springs or fountains: later identified with the Greek Muses.

cam·e·o (kam'ē·ō) n. 1 A striated stone (as onyx or agate) or shell, carved in relief so as to show the design on differently colored layers. 2 The art of so carving. Compare INTAGLIO. 3 A brief appearance by an actor or actress in a film or play. —adj. Miniature; on a small scale. [< Ital. cammeo; ult. origin unknown]

cameo glass n. Glass fused in layers of different colors and cut in relief like a cameo: also called **onyx glass**.

cam·er·a (kam'ər·ə, kam'rə) n. pl. **·er·as** for defs. 1 and 2, **·er·ae** for defs. 3, 4, 5, 6. 1 A lightproof chamber or box in which the image of an exterior object is projected upon a sensitized plate or film through a shuttered opening usually equipped with a lens or lenses. 2 An enclosed unit containing the special light-sensitive vacuum tube which converts optical images into electrical impulses for television transmission. 3 A chamber, as of the heart. 4 In Italy, a legislative chamber; also, the financial department of the papal curia. 5 Law A judge's chamber or private room. 6 A camera obscura. —**in camera** Law Not in public court; privately; secretly. [< L, vaulted room < Gk. kamara. Doublet of CHAMBER.]

camera gun A camera mounted on a machine-gun frame in an airplane, and used in gunnery practice to record each shot.

cam·er·al (kam'ər·əl) adj. Pertaining to a camera, chamber, public office, or treasury.

cam·er·al·is·tics (kam'ər·əl·is'tiks) n. The science of state finances. —**cam'er·al·ist** n. —**cam·er·al·is'tic** adj.

camera lu·ci·da (lōō'si·də) A device by which the image of a body seems to be projected on a sheet of paper or other surface, so that it may be traced.

cam·er·a·man (kam'ər·ə·man', kam'rə-) n. pl. **·men** (-men') The operator of a camera, especially a motion-picture camera.

camera ob·scu·ra (ob·skyōōr'ə) A darkened box in which the real image of an object, received through a small aperture, is projected upon a plane surface, for viewing, tracing, or photographing.

CAMERA LUCIDA
a. Eyepiece.
b. Mirror.
c. Glass slide.
d. Image here.

cam·er·lin·go (kam'ər·ling'gō) n. In the Roman Catholic Church, the cardinal who administers the finances and secular interests of the Pope. Also **cam'er·len'go** (-leng'gō). [< Ital. camerlingo chamberlain < L camera chamber]

Cam·e·ro·ni·an (kam'ə·rō'nē·ən) n. A follower of **Richard Cameron**, died 1680, Scottish Presbyterian preacher and Covenanter.

Cam·er·on of Loch·iel (kam'ər·ən əv lokh·ēl'), **Sir Ewen**, 1629–1719, Scottish chieftain.

— Donald, 1695?–1748, Scottish chieftain and soldier; grandson of the preceding.

Cam·e·roon (kam′ə·ro͞on′) **1** A volcanic mountain group in south Cameroons; the highest in western Africa; highest point 13,350 feet. **2** An estuarial inlet of the Gulf of Guinea in the Cameroons coast.

Cameroons, British A former United Nations Trust Territory. See CAMEROUN, NIGERIA.

Cameroons, French See CAMEROUN.

Cam·e·roun (kam′ə·ro͞on, kam′ro͞on) An independent republic in western Africa, including the southern part of the former British Cameroons; 184,252 square miles; capital, Yaoundé; formerly French Cameroons, a United Nations Trust Territory.

Ca·mi·guin (kä′mē·gēn′) **1** One of the Babuyan Islands, northern Philippines; 63 square miles; site of **Mount Camiguin,** an active volcano; 2,372 feet. **2** An island in the southern Philippines; 96 square miles; site of Hibokhibok.

Ca·mil·la (kə·mil′ə, *Ital.* kä·mēl′lä) A feminine personal name. Also *Fr.* **Ca·mille** (kȧ·mēl′), *Sp.* **Ca·mi·la** (kä·mē′lä). [<L, fem., attendant at a sacrifice]
— Camilla In Roman legend, the virgin queen of the Volscians who aided Turnus against Aeneas.

cam·i·on (kam′ē·ən, *Fr.* kȧ·myôṅ′) *n.* A military motor truck. [<F]

ca·mi·sa (kä·mē′sä) *n. SW U.S.* A chemise; shirt; specifically, a thin waist worn by women. [<Sp.]

cam·i·sa·do (kam′i·sä′dō) *n. Obs.* A night attack by soldiers wearing shirts over their armor for mutual recognition; also, a shirt so worn. Also **cam′i·sade′** (-sād′). [<Sp. *camisada* < *camisa* shirt]

Cam·i·sard (kam′i·zärd) *n.* One of the French Calvinists who fought for civil and religious liberties after the revocation of the Edict of Nantes in 1685. [<F, lit., a smockwearer]

ca·mise (kə·mēs′) *n.* A loose shirt; a light, loose gown. Compare CHEMISE. Also **ca·mis·i·a** (kə·mis′ē·ə). [<Arabic *qamīṣ* <LL *camisa* shirt]

cam·i·sole (kam′ə·sōl) *n.* **1** Formerly, a woman's wrapper. **2** A woman's fancy underwaist or corset cover. **3** A straitjacket having long sleeves that can be tied behind the patient's back. **4** Formerly, a man's jacket or jersey with sleeves. [<F <Sp. *camisola,* dim. of *camisa* shirt]

Cam·lan (kam′lən) In Arthurian legend, the battlefield where King Arthur was killed.

cam·let (kam′lit) *n.* **1** A stiff, closely woven fabric of camel's–hair, or an imitation of it. **2** A garment made from this fabric. [<MF *camelot* <OF *chamelot,* ? <Arabic *khamlat* nap, pile on cloth]

Cam·maerts (käm′ärts), **Émile,** 1878–1953, Belgian poet.

cam·mas (kam′as) See CAMAS.

Cam·o·ëns (kam′ō·ens), **Luis de,** 1524–80, Portuguese poet. Also *Pg.* **Ca·mões** (kə·moiṅsh′).

cam·o·mile (kam′ə·mīl) *n.* **1** A strongly scented bitter herb of the genus *Anthemis*; especially, the European perennial *(A. nobilis)* whose bitter, aromatic flowers and leaves are used in medicine. **2** Any plant of a genus *(Matricaria)* of widely distributed herbs of the composite family. Also spelled *chamomile.* **— wild** (or **stinking) camomile** Mayweed. [<F *camomille* <L *chamomilla* <Gk. *chamaimēlon* < *chamai* on the ground + *mēlon* apple]

Ca·mor·ra (kə·môr′ə, -mor′ə; *Ital.* kä·môr′·rä) *n.* A secret society of Naples, Italy, practicing violence and extortion. See MAFIA. **— Ca·mor′rism** *n.* **— Ca·mor′rist** *n.*

cam·ou·flage (kam′ə·fläzh) *n.* **1** *Mil.* Disguise by masking, as artillery, with an arbor of leaves built around a gun; also, artificial scenery, etc., painted on canvas to conceal military installations and movements. **2** *Nav.* Disguise by painting, as ships, as protection from attack by submarines, etc. **3** Any disguise or pretense. **—** *v.t.* & *v.i.* **·flaged, ·flag·ing** To hide or obscure, as with disguises. [<F < *camoufler* disguise] **— cam′ou·flag′er** *n.*

ca·mou·flet (kȧ·mo͞o·fle′) *n. Mil.* A small underground cavity caused by the explosion of a deeply buried mine or bomb which shows little or no surface effect; also, an explosive that will make such a cavity. [<F]

cam·ou·fleur (kam′ə·flər, *Fr.* kȧ·mo͞o·flœr′) *n. Mil.* One who constructs or paints camouflage. [<F]

camp[1] (kamp) *n.* **1** A group of tents or other shelters, as for soldiers or hunters, or the place so occupied; also, a single tent, cabin, etc. **2** An army encamped; hence, military life or the field of battle. **3** A chapter or lodge of various fraternal organizations. **4** A new community or town hastily gathered around the mines: so called because the people originally lived in tents. **5** A group of buildings for temporary (usually summer) habitation, built on a lake, or seashore, or in the mountains. **6** A stage of a journey. **7** A place where open–air religious or political meetings are held. **8** A body of persons who support or defend a policy, theory, or doctrine: Avarice dominates the *camp* of the profiteers. **9** A mass of facts or arguments arrayed in support or defense of a policy, theory, or doctrine. **—** *v.t.* **1** To shelter or station, as troops, in a camp. **—** *v.i.* **2** To form an encampment. **3** To live temporarily in a camp. **4** To hold stubbornly to a position: Strikers *camped* in front of the factory. **— to camp down** To settle down. **— to camp on the trail of** To follow closely; dog. **— to camp out** To sleep in a tent; live in the open. [<MF <Ital. *campo* field <L *campus* level plain]

camp[2] (kamp) *n.* **1** A comical style or quality typically perceived in banal, flamboyant, or patently artificial gestures, appearances, literary works, etc., that intentionally or unwittingly seem to parody themselves. **2** A person, thing, aspect, etc., marked by this style or quality. **—** *adj.* Of or characterized by camp, or by a ready appreciation of camp: the *camp* sensibility; in the *camp* tradition of Hollywood's gangster films. **—** *v.i. Slang* **1** To behave, dress, etc., in a theatrical or bizarre way to get attention. **—** *v.t.* **2** To invest with a camp quality: to *camp* the play up with weird effects. [? < dial. E *camp* or *kemp* bold, impetuous fellow]

Cam·pa·gna (käm·pä′nyə) A lowland surrounding Rome; about 800 square miles. Also **Campagna di Ro·ma** (dē rō′mä).

cam·paign (kam·pān′) *n.* **1** A series of connected military actions or maneuvers conducted for a particular objective, in a particular area, etc. **2** A series of connected political, commercial, or other activities designed to bring about a result: a welfare *campaign.* **—** *v.i.* To serve, operate in, or conduct a campaign. [<F *campagne* open country, field <Med. L *compania* <L *campus*]

cam·paign·er (kam·pā′nər) *n.* **1** One who campaigns. **2** A person of long experience in campaigns; a veteran.

cam·pa·ne·ro (käm′pä·nā′rō) *n.* The bellbird of South America. [<Sp., bellman <LL *campana* bell]

Cam·pa·nia (kam·pā′nē·ə, *Ital.* käm·pä′nyä) A region of southern Italy; 5,249 square miles; capital, Naples. **— Cam·pa′ni·an** *adj.* & *n.*

cam·pan·i·form (kam·pan′ə·fôrm) *adj.* Bell-shaped; campanulate. [<LL *campana* bell + -FORM]

cam·pa·ni·le (kam′pə·nē′lē, *Ital.* -nē′lā) *n. pl.* **·ni·les** or **·ni·li** (-nē′lē) A bell tower, especially a detached one. [<Ital. <LL *campana* bell]

cam·pa·nol·o·gy (kam′pə·nol′ə·jē) *n.* The science and art of casting and ringing bells. [<LL *campana* bell + -LOGY] **— cam′pa·nol′o·gist** *n.*

cam·pan·u·la (kam·pan′yə·lə) *n.* **1** A member of a very large genus of plants *(Campanula),* the bellflowers, as the bluebell of Scotland, Canterbury bell, etc. **2** *Zool.* A bell-shaped structure. [<NL, dim. of LL *campana* bell]

campanula blue The bluish–mauve color of various campanulas or bellflowers.

cam·pan·u·la·ceous (kam·pan′yə·lā′shəs) *adj. Bot.* Belonging to the bellflower family *(Campanulaceae)* of herbs, shrubs, and trees.

cam·pan·u·late (kam·pan′yə·lit, -lāt) *adj.* Bell-shaped, as a corolla.

Camp·bell (kam′bəl, kam′əl), **Alexander,** 1788–1866, U.S. theologian born in Ireland; founder of the Disciples of Christ. **Thomas,** 1777–1844, Scottish poet. **— Thomas,** 1763–1854, U.S. theologian born in Ireland; co-founder, with his son Alexander, of the Disciples of Christ.

Camp·bell–Ban·ner·man (kam′bəl·ban′ər·mən, kam′əl-), **Sir Henry,** 1836–1908, British statesman; prime minister 1905–08.

Camp·bel·lite (kam′əl·īt, kam′bəl-) *n.* A member of the Disciples of Christ, founded by Thomas and Alexander Campbell. The name *Campbellite* is rejected by the denomination.

camp chair A light, folding chair.

Cam·pe·a·dor (käm·pā′ä·thōr′), **El** See CID.

Cam·pe·che (kam·pē′chē, *Sp.* käm·pā′chā) A state in SE Mexico; 19,672 square miles; capital, Campeche.

Campeche, Gulf of The SW part of the Gulf of Mexico.

camp·er (kamp′ər) *n.* **1** One who camps out or lives in a camp. **2** A member of a camp, as a summer camp for children. **3** A vehicle affording shelter and usually sleeping accommodations for travelers and campers: also **camper wagon.**

cam·pes·tral (kam·pes′trəl) *adj.* Growing in or pertaining to the fields or open country. [<L *campestris* < *campus* field]

camp·fire (kamp′fīr′) *n.* **1** A fire in an outdoor camp, for cooking, warmth, etc. **2** A fire in a camp used as the center of social evening gatherings. **3** A meeting or social gathering; especially, a reunion. Also **camp fire.**

campfire girl A girl between 12 and 20 years of age, belonging to the **Camp Fire Girls of America,** an organization incorporated in 1914 for promoting the health and welfare of young women by encouraging outdoor life, etc.

camp follower **1** A civilian who follows an army about, usually a merchant or prostitute. **2** One who supports a movement, etc., without formally belonging to it; hanger–on.

camp·ground (kamp′ground′) *n.* An area used for a camp or a camp meeting.

cam·phene (kam′fēn, kam·fēn′) *n. Chem.* One of a series, $C_{10}H_{16}$, of solid hydrocarbons similar to camphor, isomeric with oil of turpentine: used as a camphor substitute. [<CAMPHOR]

cam·pho·gen (kam′fə·jen) *n. Chem.* Cymene.

cam·phol (kam′fōl, -fol) *n. Chem.* Borneol.

cam·phor (kam′fər) *n.* A white, volatile, translucent crystalline compound, $C_{10}H_{16}O$, with a penetrating, fragrant odor and pungent taste, distilled from the wood and bark of the camphor tree and also obtained by organic synthesis: used in medicine as a sedative, as an antispasmodic, in liniments, etc., and in the chemical and plastics industries. [<F *camphre* <Arabic *kāfūr* <Malay *kāpūr*] **— cam·phor·ic** (kam·fôr′ik, -for′-) *adj.*

cam·phor·ate (kam′fə·rāt) *v.t.* **·at·ed, ·at·ing** To treat or saturate with camphor.

camphor ball A moth ball.

camphor ice A mixture of camphor, white wax, spermaceti, and castor oil: used for chapped skin, etc.

camphor tree **1** A large evergreen tree of eastern Asia *(Cinnamomum camphora)* yielding the camphor of commerce. **2** A tree of Borneo, Sumatra, and Malaya *(Dryobalanops aromatica)* yielding borneol.

Cam·pi·na Gran·de (kaṅm·pē′nə graṅn′di) A city in NE Brazil.

Cam·pi·nas (kaṅm·pē′nəs) A city in SE Brazil.

camp·ing (kamp′ing) *n.* The act or practice of living outdoors, as in tents or without any shelter, especially for recreation.

cam·pi·on (kam′pē·ən) *n.* One of various herbs of the pink family, as the **rose campion.** [Origin uncertain]

Cam·pi·on (kam′pē·ən), **Thomas,** 1567–1619, English poet.

camp meeting A prolonged series of religious meetings held in a grove or field, usually in a tent.

cam·po[1] (kam′pō, käm′-) *n.* *pl.* **·pi** (-pē) In Italy, an open space in a town. [<Ital.]

cam·po[2] (kam′pō, käm′-) *n. pl.* **·pos** In South American countries, an open, level plain, with scattered shrubbery and trees. [<Sp.]

Cam·po·bel·lo (kam′pō·bel′ō) An island in SW New Brunswick, eastern Canada, in the Bay of Fundy.

Cam·po·for·mi·do (käm′pō·fôr′mē·dō) A town in NE Italy. Also **Cam′po·for′mio** (-fôr′myō).

Cam·pos (kaṅm′po͞os) A city in SE Brazil.

cam·po san·to (käm′pō sän′tō) *Italian* A cemetery; literally, holy field.

Campo Santo The cathedral cemetery at Pisa, Italy, to which earth from Mount Calvary was brought.

camp stool A light, folding stool or seat.

cam·pus (kam′pəs) *n.* **1** *U.S.* The grounds of a school or college or the court enclosed by

the buildings. 2 In ancient Rome, an open field where military drills, games, etc., were held. [<L, field]

cam·py·lot·ro·pal (kam'pi·lot'rə·pəl) *adj. Bot.* Bent on itself so as to bring the true apex or micropyle down to the base or hilum: said of an ovule. Also **cam'py·lot'ro·pous** (-pəs). [< NL <Gk. *kampylos* bent + *tropos* direction <*trepein* turn]

cam shaft The shaft to which a cam is attached.

Ca·mus (kȧ·mü'), **Albert,** 1913–1960, French writer.

cam·wood (kam'wo͝od') *n.* The red wood of a tree *(Baphia nitida)* of western Africa, used in dyeing. [? <native African name]

can[1] (kan, *unstressed* kən) *v.* Present: *sing.* **can, can** (*Archaic* **canst**), **can,** *pl.* **can**; past: **could** A defective verb now used only in the present and past tenses as an auxiliary followed by the infinitive without *to,* or elliptically with the infinitive unexpressed, in the following senses: **1** To be able to. **2** To know how to. **3** To have the right to. **4** *Colloq.* To be permitted to; may. [OE *cunnan* know, be able]

◆ **can, may** In informal speech and writing, *can* is now acceptable in the sense of *may,* to express permission, especially in questions or negative statements: *Can* I leave now? You *cannot.* At the formal level, the distinction between *can* and *may* is still observed: *can,* to express ability to perform, either mentally or physically; *may,* to denote permission.

can[2] (kan) *n.* **1** A vessel for holding or carrying liquids. **2** A vessel of tin-plated iron or other metal, in which fruit, meat, tobacco, or the like is sealed, often hermetically: called *tin* in Great Britain. **3** A drinking mug or cup; a tankard. **4** A radio headphone. **5** *Slang* Jail; prison. **6** *Slang* Toilet; bathroom. **7** *Slang* Buttocks; backside. **—in the can** Ready for distribution or exhibition: said of a motion picture.—*v.t.* **canned, can·ning 1** To put up or preserve in cans, glass jars, or the like. **2** *Slang* To dismiss; discharge; also, to expel from school. **3** To preserve for reproduction, as on a phonograph record: *canned* music. **4** *Slang* To suppress; jail; imprison. [OE *canne* cup] **—can'ner** *n.*

Ca·na (kā'nə) A Biblical locality in northern Palestine; scene of Christ's first miracle. *John* ii 1. Also **Cana of Galilee.**

Ca·naan (kā'nən) The fourth son of Ham.

Ca·naan (kā'nən) The Israelite name of the part of Palestine between the Jordan and the Mediterranean; the Promised Land.

Ca·naan·ite (kā'nən·īt) *n.* **1** A dweller in the land of Canaan prior to the Israelite conquest. **2** A descendant of Canaan, son of Ham. **Ca'naan·it'ish** (-ī'tish), **Ca'naan·it'ic** (-it'ik) *adj.*

ca·ña·da (kä·nyä'də) *n. SW U.S.* A narrow canyon. [<Sp.]

Can·a·da (kan'ə·də) A self-governing member of the Commonwealth of Nations, comprising ten provinces and two territories in North America; 3,851,809 square miles; capital, Ottawa: also *British North America.*

Canada balsam A yellowish turpentine derived from the balsam fir.

Canada bluegrass Wiregrass.

Canada goose See under GOOSE.

Canada jay A non-migratory, sooty-gray bird of the crow family *(Perisoreus canadensis),* native in Canada and the NE United States: also called *venison bird.*

Canada lily An American lily *(Lilium canadense)* with drooping orange or yellow flowers, sometimes spotted with brown: also called *meadow lily.*

Canada thistle See under THISTLE.

Ca·na·di·an (kə·nā'dē·ən) *adj.* Of or pertaining to Canada or its inhabitants, their industries, products, etc.—*n.* A native of Canada or a legally constituted citizen of Canada.

Canadian English The English language as spoken and written in Canada.

Canadian French The French language as spoken and written by French Canadians.

Ca·na·di·a·nism (kə·nā'dē·ən·iz'əm) *n.* **1** A trait, custom, or tradition characteristic of the people of Canada or some of them. **2** A word, phrase, or usage especially characteristic of Canadian English or French. **3** Devotion to Canada, its institutions, etc.

Canadian River A river in the SW United States, flowing 906 miles east to the Arkansas River.

Canadian Shield The shield-shaped region of Archean rock in central Canada and Greenland on which the later strata rest; approximately 2,000,000 square miles: also *Laurentian Plateau.*

ca·naille (kə·nāl', *Fr.* kȧ·nä'y') *n.* The rabble; mob. [<F <Ital. *canaglia* pack of dogs <L *canis* dog]

ca·nal (kə·nal') *n.* **1** An artificial inland waterway connecting two navigable bodies of water. **2** An artificial channel for irrigating tracts of land. **3** Any channel, groove, passage, or duct: the auditory *canal.* **4** *Zool.* A groove, as for the siphon in the shells of gastropods, or a pore, as in sponges, etc. **5** *Astron.* One of the peculiar markings visible on the face of the planet Mars. **—central canal** The ventricle of the spinal cord. —*v.t.* **ca·nalled** or **ca·naled, ca·nal·ling** or **ca·nal·ing** To build a canal or canals across or through; canalize. [<MF <L *canalis* groove. Doublet of CHANNEL.]

ca·nal·age (kə·nal'ij) *n.* **1** The construction of canals. **2** Canals collectively. **3** A charge for transportation through a canal.

canal boat A long barge, principally used on canals and drawn either by electric power or by horses or mules on a towpath.

Ca·nal du Nord (kȧ·nȧl' dü nôr') See SAINT-QUENTIN CANAL.

ca·nal·er (kə·nal'ər) *n.* **1** One who works on a canal boat. **2** A canal boat. Also **ca·nal'·ler.**

Ca·na·let·to (kä'nä·let'tō), **Antonio,** 1697–1768, Venetian painter. Also **Ca·na·le** (kä·nä'lā).

can·a·lic·u·late (kan'ə·lik'yə·lit, -lāt) *adj.* Channeled or grooved. Also **can'a·lic'u·lar** (-lər), **can'a·lic'u·lat'ed.**

can·a·lic·u·lus (kan'ə·lik'yə·ləs) *n. pl.* **·li** (-lī) *Anat.* A small tube or canal, as in a bone. [< L *canaliculus,* dim. of *canalis* pipe, groove]

ca·nal·ize (kə·nal'īz, kan'əl·īz) *v.t.* **·ized, ·iz·ing 1** To convert into a canal, as a stream or chain of lakes. **2** To furnish with a canal, or a system of canals, or waterways. **3** To furnish with an outlet. **—ca·nal·i·za·tion** (kə·nal'ə·zā'shən, kan'ə·lə-) *n.*

canal rays *Physics* A stream of positively charged ions emitted from the anode of a vacuum tube and emerging through openings in the cathode: also called *positive rays.*

Canal Zone A strip of territory leased in perpetuity to the United States by the Republic of Panama, extending five miles on each side of the Panama Canal, across the Isthmus of Panama; 648 square miles; administrative headquarters, Balboa Heights.

Can·an·dai·gua Lake (kan'ən·dā'gwə) One of the Finger Lakes in western New York.

Ca·nan·ga oil (kə·nang'gə) A volatile oil used in perfume, obtained from the ylang-ylang.

can·a·pé (kan'ə·pē, -pā; *Fr.* kȧ·nȧ·pā') *n.* Bread, fried or toasted, on which relishes are served. [<F, sofa, couch]

Ca·na·ra (kä'nə·rə, kə·nä'rə) A former spelling of KANARA.

ca·nard (kə·närd', *Fr.* kȧ·när') *n.* **1** A fabricated, sensational story; newspaper hoax. **2** *Aeron.* An airplane which has the controlling surfaces, etc., in front of the wings. [<F]

Ca·na·rese (kä'nə·rēz', -rēs') See KANARESE.

ca·nar·y (kə·nâr'ē) *n. pl.* **·nar·ies 1** A small finch *(Serinus canarius)* originally native in the Canary Islands, having generally yellow plumage: popular as a cage bird for its song. **2** A bright yellow color: also **canary yellow. 3** A sweet, white wine from the Canary Islands. **4** An old French dance in rapid time. —*v.i.* To dance the canary.[<F *canarie* <Sp. *canario* < L *Canaria (Insula)* Dog (Island) <*canis* dog; so called from a breed of dogs found there]

ca·nar·y·grass (kə·nâr'ē·gras', -gräs') *n.* A grass *(Phalaris canariensis)* native in the Canary Islands and cultivated for its seeds, which are used as food for cage birds.

Canary Islands An island group off the NW coast of Africa, comprising two Spanish provinces; 2,894 square miles. Also **Canaries.** *Spanish* **Is·las Ca·na·rias** (ēz'läs kä·nä'ryäs).

canary seed Seed used as food for canaries and other cage birds.

ca·nas·ta (kə·nas'tə) *n.* A card game based on the principles of rummy, for two to six players, using a double deck of cards.[<Sp., basket]

ca·nas·ter (kə·nas'tər) *n.* A coarse-grained tobacco formerly packed in rush baskets. [< Sp. *canastro* <Gk.*kanastron* rush basket]

Ca·nav·er·al (kə·nav'ər·əl), **Cape** See KENNEDY, CAPE.

Can·ber·ra (kan'bər·ə) The capital of the Commonwealth of Australia, in Australian Capital Territory: formerly *Yass-Canberra.*

can but Have no other course than to. See CANNOT BUT.

Can·by (kan'bē), **Henry Seidel,** 1878–1961, U.S. editor and writer.

can·can (kan'kan', *Fr.* käṅ·käṅ')*n.* A Parisian dance, introduced about 1830, in which the figures of the quadrille are diversified by high kicking and other wild or suggestive movements. [<F, gossip] **—can'can'ing** *adj.*

can·cel (kan'səl) *v.t.* **can·celed** or **·celled, can·cel·ing** or **·cel·ling 1** To mark out or off, as by drawing or stamping lines across written matter to signify that it is to be omitted; blot or strike out; obliterate. **2** To remove, as by cutting out; suppress, as pages of a book. **3** To render null and void; annul, revoke, or set aside. **4** To make up for; compensate; neutralize; countervail. **5** To mark or ink (a postage stamp) to show that it has been used. **6** *Math.* To eliminate (a common factor, as a figure or quantity) from the numerator and denominator of a fraction, or from both sides of an equation. —*n.* In printing and bookbinding, the striking or cutting out, omission, or suppression of a leaf, leaves, or any part of any printed matter or work; also, any printed matter thus suppressed, or the matter substituted for that stricken out. [<MF *canceller* <L *cancellare* cross out<*cancelli,* dim. pl. of *cancer* lattice]

Synonyms (verb): abolish, abrogate, annul, discharge, efface, erase, expunge, nullify, obliterate, quash, remove, repeal, rescind, revoke, vacate. *Cancel, efface, erase, expunge,* and *obliterate* have as their first meaning the removal of written characters or other forms of record. To *cancel* is, literally, to make a lattice by cross lines, exactly our English *cross out*; to *efface* is to rub off, smooth away the face of, as of an inscription; to *expunge* is to punch out with some sharp instrument, so as to show that the words are no longer part of the writing; to *obliterate* is to cover over or remove, as a letter, as was done by reversing the Roman stylus, and rubbing out with the rounded end what had been written with the point on the waxen tablet. What has been *canceled, erased, expunged,* may perhaps still be traced; what is *obliterated* is gone forever, as if it had never been. The figurative use of the words keeps close to the primary sense. Compare ABOLISH, ANNUL. *Antonyms*: approve, confirm, enact, enforce, establish, maintain, perpetuate, record, reenact, sustain, uphold.

can·cel·a·ble (kan'səl·ə·bəl) *adj.* That can be canceled. Also **can'cel·la·ble.**

can·cel·er (kan'səl·ər) *n.* **1** A person or thing that cancels. **2** A device for canceling. Also **can'cel·ler.**

can·cel·late (kan'sə·lāt) *adj.* **1** *Anat.* Latticelike in structure; also, having reticulations, as certain bones, or parts of bones. **2** Chambered; cell-like. Also **can'cel·lat'ed, can'cel·lous** (-ləs).

can·cel·la·tion (kan'sə·lā'shən) *n.* **1** That which is canceled. **2** The mark which cancels. **3** A network formed by small interlacing bars; a reticulation.

can·cel·li (kan·sel'ī) *n. pl.* **1** Bars of latticework, as in a latticed window or in the screen separating the choir from the nave of a church. **2** Bars in the railing of a court. **3** Reticulations; especially, the latticework of bony spicules that forms the spongy or interior portion of a bone.

can·cer (kan'sər) *n.* **1** *Pathol.* A malignant neoplasm or tumor, characterized by a morbid proliferation of epithelial cells in various parts of the body, spreading into adjacent tissue, with consequent progressive degeneration which often ends fatally: also called *carci-*

noma, sarcoma. 2 Any inveterate and spreading evil. **—colloid cancer** A variety of cancer which chiefly attacks the alimentary canal, uterus, or peritoneum. *—v.t.* To eat or penetrate like a cancer. [<L, crab]
Can·cer (kan′sər) The Crab, the fourth sign of the zodiac, which the sun enters at the summer solstice. See CONSTELLATION. **—Tropic of Cancer** See under TROPIC.
can·cer·ate (kan′sə·rāt) *v.i.* **·at·ed, ·at·ing** *Pathol.* To become cancerous; develop into a cancer. **—can′cer·a′tion** *n.*
can·cer·ous (kan′sər·əs) *adj.* 1 *Pathol.* Pertaining to, of the nature of, or affected with a cancer. 2 Virulent; incurable.
can·cer·root (kan′sər·rōōt′, -rŏŏt′) *n.* Beechdrops: so called from its supposed value in the external treatment of cancerous ulcer.
can·croid (kang′kroid) *adj.* 1 Like a crab. 2 Resembling a cancer. *—n. Pathol.* An epithelioma of the skin.
can·del·a (kan·del′ə) *n. Physics* A unit of luminous intensity equal to that of 1/60 square centimeter of a black body operating at the temperature of solidification of platinum: also called *candle, standard candle.* Abbr. *cd*
can·de·la·brum (kan′də·lä′brəm, -lā′-) *n. pl.* **·bra** or **·brums** A large, branched candlestick. Also **can′de·la′bra** *pl.* **·bras.** [<L <*candela* candle]
can·dent (kan′dənt) *adj.* Glowing with heat; incandescent. [<L *candens, -entis,* ppr. of *candere* glow]
can·des·cence (kan·des′əns) *n.* Incandescence. **—can·des′cent** *adj.*
Can·di·a (kan′dē·ə) 1 The largest city in Crete, a port on the **Gulf of Candia,** a bay of the Aegean in northern Crete: Greek *Hērakleion.* 2 A former name for CRETE.
can·did (kan′did) *adj.* 1 Sincere; ingenuous; frank. 2 Impartial; fair. 3 *Obs.* White; also, pure. [<MF *candide* pure, honest <L *candidus* <*candere* gleam, shine] **—can′did·ly** *adv.* **—can′did·ness** *n.*
Synonyms: aboveboard, artless, fair, frank, guileless, honest, impartial, ingenuous, innocent, naive, open, simple, sincere, straightforward, transparent, truthful, unbiased, unprejudiced, unreserved, unsophisticated. A *candid* statement is meant to be true to the real facts and just to all parties; a *fair* statement is really so. *Fair* is applied to the conduct but *candid* is not; as, *fair* treatment, a *fair* field and no favor. One who is *frank* has a fearless and unconstrained truthfulness. *Honest* and *ingenuous* unite in expressing total lack of deceit. On the other hand, *artless, guileless, naive, simple,* and *unsophisticated* express the goodness which comes from want of the knowledge or thought of evil. *Sincere* applies to the feelings as being all that one's words would imply. See HONEST. *Antonyms*: adroit, artful, crafty, cunning, deceitful, designing, diplomatic, foxy, insincere, intriguing, knowing, maneuvering, sharp, shrewd, sly, subtle, tricky, wily.
can·di·date (kan′də·dāt, -dit) *n.* A nominee or aspirant for any position or honor. [<L *candidatus* wearing white <*candidus* white; because office-seekers in Rome wore white togas] **—can·di·da·cy** (kan′də·də·sē), **can′di·date′ship, can·di·da·ture** (kan′də·də·chər, -dā′·chər) *n.*
candid camera A small camera with a fast lens, used for taking informal pictures of unposed subjects.
Can·dide (kän·dēd′) Hero of Voltaire's romance *Candide* (1759), which satirizes the optimistic theory that this is "the best of all possible worlds."
can·died (kan′dēd) *adj.* 1 Converted into candy; preserved in sugar. 2 Coated with something resembling sugar; frosted. 3 Flattering; honeyed; sugared.
Can·di·ot (kan′dē·ot) *adj.* Cretan; of or pertaining to Candia. *—n.* A Cretan. Also **Can′·di·ote** (-ōt).
can·dle (kan′dəl) *n.* 1 A cylinder of tallow, wax, or other solid fat, containing a wick, to give light when burning. 2 Anything like a candle in shape or purpose. 3 *Mil.* A cylindrical container which, when ignited, emits a cloud of smoke or gas. 4 *Physics* A candela. **—to hold a candle to** To compare with favorably: used in the negative. *—v.t.* **·dled, ·dling** 1 To test (eggs) by holding between the eye and a light, translucency indicating soundness. 2 To test (bottled wines) for clarity. [OE *candel* <L *candela* <*candere* shine, gleam] **—can′dler** *n.*
can·dle·ber·ry (kan′dəl·ber′ē) *n. pl.* **·ries** 1 The wax myrtle or bayberry. 2 Its fruit. 3 An East Indian and Polynesian tree *(Aleurites moluccana);* the candlenut.
candleberry cactus The ocotillo.
can·dle·fish (kan′dəl·fish′) *n.* An edible, oily smeltlike marine fish *(Thaleichthys pacificus)* of the northern Pacific, which, when dried, may be burned as a candle.
can·dle–foot (kan′dəl·fŏŏt′) *n.* Foot–candle.
can·dle·light (kan′dəl·līt′) *n.* 1 Light given by a candle. 2 The time of day when candles are first needed; early evening. Also **candle light, can′dle·light′ing.**
Can·dle·mas (kan′dəl·məs) *n.* The feast of the Purification, or of the Presentation of Christ in the temple, held on Feb. 2; also, the day itself. Also **Candlemas Day.** [OE *candelmæsse* <*candel* candle + *mæsse* mass]
can·dle·mold (kan′dəl·mōld′) *n.* A tin mold with multiple tubular compartments in which to insert wicks and pour melted tallow or wax for making candles.

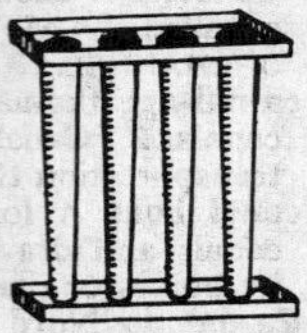

CANDLEMOLD

can·dle·nut (kan′dəl·nut′) *n.* 1 The candleberry (def. 3). 2 The fruit of this tree, burned as candles by the natives of Polynesia.
can·dle·pin (kan′dəl·pin′) *n.* A slender, nearly cylindrical pin used in a bowling game called **candlepins.**
can·dle·pow·er (kan′dəl·pou′ər) *n.* The illuminating power of a standard candle: used as a measure of other illuminants.
can·dle·stand (kan′dəl·stand′) *n.* A small table fitted with candle holders, or on which to set a candlestick.
can·dle·stick (kan′dəl·stik′) *n.* A support for a candle or candles. [OE *candelsticca* <*candel* candle + *sticca* stick]
can·dle·wick (kan′dəl·wik′) *n.* The wick of a candle, or the soft, twisted fibers from which wicks are made; candlewicking. [OE *candelweoca* <*candel* candle + *weoca* wick]
can·dle·wick·ing (kan′dəl·wik′ing) *n.* 1 Thick, soft, cotton thread used to make wicks for candles. 2 Tuftings of such threads worked into a fabric, usually in the form of a design, to give a napped surface.
can·dle·wood (kan′dəl·wŏŏd′) *n.* 1 Any of several trees or shrubs, as the ocotillo *(Fouquiera splendens).* 2 Any resinous wood finely split so as to give light when burned on the hearth.
Can·dolle (kän·dôl′), **Augustin Pyrame de,** 1778–1841, Swiss botanist.
can·dor (kan′dər) *n.* 1 Freedom from mental reservation or prejudice. 2 Openness; frankness; impartiality; fairness. 3 *Obs.* Brightness; fairness. Also *Brit.* **can′dour.** See synonyms under VERACITY. [<L, sincerity, purity < *candere* gleam, shine]
c–and–w or **C–and–W** Country–and western music.
can·dy (kan′dē) *n. pl.* **·dies** 1 Sugar or molasses crystallized by evaporation; also, a confection of sugar or molasses crystals. 2 Any of numerous confections in various colors, flavors, and forms, and consisting chiefly of cane or beet or other sugar to which has been added chocolate, milk products, fruits, fruit extracts, nuts, or the like; also, such confections collectively: usually called *sweets* in Great Britain. *—v.* **·died, ·dy·ing** *v.t.* 1 To cause to form into crystals of sugar. 2 To preserve by boiling or coating with sugar, as orange peels. 3 To render pleasant; sweeten. 4 To overlay with any crystalline substance, as ice or sugar. *—v.i.* 5 To become crystallized into or covered with sugar. [Short for *sugar candy* <F *(sucre) candi* <Arabic *qandī* made of sugar <*qand* sugar, ult. <Skt.]
Can·dy (kan′dē) A former spelling of KANDY.
can·dy–pull (kan′dē·pŏŏl′) *n.* A party at which pulling taffy candy is the chief entertainment.
can·dy·tuft (kan′dē·tuft′) *n.* A plant of the mustard family (genus *Iberis*) with white, pink, or purple flowers.
cane (kān) *n.* 1 A walking stick. 2 A stem of cane grass. 3 The stem of a raspberry or allied plant. 4 Any rod, especially one used for flogging. *—v.t.* **caned, can·ing** 1 To strike or beat with a cane. 2 To bottom or back with cane, as a chair. [<OF <L *canna* <Gk. *kanna* reed <Semitic] **—can′er** *n.*
Ca·ne·a (kä·nē′ä) The capital of Crete, a port on the **Gulf of Canea,** a bay of the Aegean in western Crete: ancient *Cydonia*: Greek *Khania.*
cane blade A blade or stalk of cane grass.
cane·brake (kān′brāk′) *n.* Land overgrown with canes.
cane grass Any of various plants with slender, flexible stems, usually jointed, as the rattan or sugarcane.
ca·nel·la (kə·nel′ə) *n.* The pale, orange–yellow, aromatic inner bark of a tropical American tree *(Canella winterana)*: used as a tonic and condiment. Also **canella bark.** [<Med. L, dim. of *canna* reed]
cane patch A small field of cane grass.
ca·neph·o·rus (kə·nef′ə·rəs) *n. pl.* **·ri** (-rī) The basket–bearer: an Athenian maiden selected to carry the baskets of sacred utensils in the processions of Demeter, Bacchus, and Athena: a frequent subject in Greek art. Also **ca·neph′·o·ros** (-ros), **ca·neph′o·ra** (-rə). [<L *canephora* <Gk. *kanēphoros* <*kaneon* basket + *pherein* carry]
ca·nes·cence (kə·nes′əns) *n.* A whitish color; hoariness.
ca·nes·cent (kə·nes′ənt) *adj.* Becoming, or tending to become, white or hoary. [<L *canescens, -entis,* ppr. of *canescere,* inceptive of *canere* be white]
cane sugar Sucrose obtained from the sugarcane.
Ca·nes Ve·nat·i·ci (kā′nēz vi·nat′ə·sī) A northern constellation, the Hunting Dogs, near Boötes. See CONSTELLATION.
Ca·ney (kä·nā′), **El** See EL CANEY.
Can·field (kan′fēld), **Dorothy,** 1879–1958, U.S. author: married name *Fisher.*
cangue (kang) *n.* A heavy wooden collar or yoke, formerly worn around the neck by convicts in China as a punishment. [<F <Pg. *cango*]
Ca·nic·u·la (kə·nik′yə·lə) The star Sirius; the Dog Star.
ca·nic·u·lar (kə·nik′yə·lər) *adj.* 1 Relating to the Dog Star or to dog days. 2 Relating to a dog: used humorously. [<L *canicularis* < *caniculus,* dim. of *canis* dog]
can·i·kin (kan′ə·kin) See CANNIKIN.
ca·nine (kā′nīn) *adj.* 1 Of, pertaining to, or like a dog. 2 *Zool.* Of or pertaining to the dog family (*Canidae*). 3 Of or pertaining to a canine tooth. *—n.* 1 A dog or other canine animal. 2 A canine tooth. [<L *caninus* <*canis* dog]
canine tooth *Anat.* A tooth growing directly behind the intermaxillary suture in the upper jaw, or the opposite one of the lower jaw; an eyetooth of the upper jaw, or stomach tooth of the lower jaw.
can·ions (kan′yənz) *n. pl.* Sausagelike rolls worn in the 16th and 17th centuries as ornaments around the bottoms of breeches' legs. [<Sp. *cañon,* aug. of *caña* tube,]
Ca·nis (kā′nis) *n. Zool.* The genus including the dog (wild and domestic), the wolf, the fox, and the jackal. [<L, dog]
Ca·nis Ma·jor (kā′nis mā′jər) A northern constellation, the Greater Dog: contains the bright star, Sirius. See CONSTELLATION.
Canis Mi·nor (mī′nər) A northern constellation, the Lesser Dog, including the star Procyon, used by navigators. See CONSTELLATION.
can·is·ter (kan′is·tər) *n.* 1 A metal case, as for tea, coffee, or spices. 2 Shot or bullets packed in a metallic cylinder, to be fired from a cannon; case shot; shrapnel. [<L *canistrum* basket <Gk. *kanastron* <*kanna* reed]
ca·ni·ti·es (kə·nish′i·ēz) *n.* The turning gray of the hair. [<L <*canus* white]
can·ji·ar (kan′jē·är) *n.* A poniard: also spelled *khanjar.* Also **can·jar** (kan′jär). [<Arabic *khanjar*]
can·ker (kang′kər) *n.* 1 *Pathol.* Any ulcer with a tendency to gangrene; a group of small ulcers in the mouth. 2 A disease of fruit trees. 3 Any secret or spreading evil. 4 A disease affecting the feet of horses, characterized by the discharge of an evil–smelling exudate. 5 An inflammation of the external ear in cats and dogs. 6 The cankerworm. 7 *Obs.* The dog rose; also **canker blossom.** *—v.t.* 1 To infect with canker. 2 To eat away or into like a canker; corrode; corrupt. *—v.t.* 3 To

fester with or be attacked by a canker. [<AF *cancre* <L *cancer* crab, ulcer]

can·kered (kang′kərd) *adj.* **1** Affected by or as by canker. **2** Corrupted; malignant; venomous.

can·ker·ous (kang′kər·əs) *adj.* **1** Of the nature of a canker; gangrenous. **2** Causing canker. **3** Corroding; corrupting.

canker rash Scarlet fever.

can·ker·root (kang′kər·ro͞ot′, -ro͝ot′) *n.* One of several plants with astringent roots, as the marsh rosemary.

can·ker·worm (kang′kər·wûrm′) *n.* Any of several insect larvae which destroy fruit and shade trees; especially, the measuring worms of the family *Geometridae.*

can·ker·y (kang′kər·ē) *adj.* **1** Affected with canker. **2** *Scot.* Crabbed; cross; vexatious.

can·na[1] (kan′ə) *n.* Any of a genus (*Canna*) of erect, mostly tropical American plants with red or yellow irregular flowers. [<L <Gk. *kanna* reed] **— can·na·ceous** (kə·nā′shəs) *adj.*

can·na[2] (kän′nə) *Scot.* Cannot.

can·na·bin (kan′ə·bin) *n.* A white, poisonous crystalline resin in Indian hemp, of which it is believed to be the active narcotic principle.

can·nab·in·ol (kə·nab′ə·nōl, -nol) *n. Chem.* The principal resinous ingredient of *Cannabis sativa,* $C_{21}H_{30}O_2$, a thick, reddish-yellow oil, subject to deterioration on exposure to air.

Can·na·bis (kan′ə·bis) *n.* **1** A genus of plants of the mulberry family having only one known species, Indian hemp, from the flowering tops of which are derived the resinous alkaloids noted for their narcotic properties. **2** Hashish. [<L <Gk. *kannabis* hemp]

Can·nae (kan′ē) An ancient town of southern Italy; scene of Hannibal's victory over the Romans, 216 B.C. Also **Can′næ.**

canned (kand) *adj.* **1** Preserved in a can or jar. **2** *Slang* Recorded: *canned* music.

can·nel (kan′əl) *n.* A bituminous coal, rich in gas, with low heating power: also called *kennel.* Also **cannel coal.** [Alter. of *candle coal*]

can·ne·lon (kȧn·lôṅ′) *n. French* **1** A hollow roll of puff paste. **2** A roll of richly seasoned chopped meat, either fried or baked.

can·ne·lure (kan′ə·lo͝or) *n.* A groove or a fluting, especially around the rim of a bullet or the head of a rimless cartridge case. [<F] **— can′ne·lured** *adj.*

can·ner·y (kan′ər·ē) *n. pl.* **·ner·ies** A factory or other establishment where foods are canned.

Cannes (kan, kanz; *Fr.* kȧn) A port and resort city on the Riviera, SE France.

can·ni·bal (kan′ə·bəl) *n.* **1** A human being who eats human flesh. **2** An animal that devours members of its own species. **—** *adj.* Of or like cannibals or their feasts. [<Sp. *Canibales,* var. of *Caribes* Caribs] **— can′ni·bal·ism** *n.* **— can·ni·bal·ic** (kan′ə·bal′ik), **can′ni·bal·is′tic** *adj.* **— can′ni·bal·is′ti·cal·ly** *adv.*

can·ni·bal·ize (kan′ə·bəl·īz′) *v.t.* **·ized, ·iz·ing** *Mil.* To take parts from (tanks, airplanes, etc.) in order to repair other damaged equipment and vehicles. **— can′ni·bal·i·za′tion** *n.*

can·nie (kan′ē) *Scot.* See CANNY.

can·ni·kin (kan′ə·kin) *n.* **1** A small can or drinking cup. **2** A small wooden pail. Also spelled *canikin.* [Dim. of CAN[2]]

can·ning (kan′ing) *n.* The act, process, or business of preserving fruits, vegetables, meats, etc., in hermetically sealed tin cans, glass jars, etc.

Can·ning (kan′ing), **George,** 1770–1827, English statesman. **— Charles John,** 1812–62, first viceroy of India; son of the preceding. **— Stratford,** 1786–1880, Viscount Stratford de Redcliffe, British diplomat.

can·non (kan′ən) *n. pl.* **·nons** or **·non** **1** *Mil.* **a** A large tubular weapon for discharging a heavy projectile; especially, one mounted on a carriage, movable or fixed. **b** A big artillery gun. **c** Artillery collectively. **2** The great bone between the fetlock and knee or hock of the horse and allied animals: also **cannon bone.** **3** A carom. **4** *Mech.* A loose metallic sleeve on a shaft. **5** A smooth round bit for a horse: also **cannon bit.** **6** The ear of a bell; one of the parts by which it is hung. **—** *v.t.* **1** To attack with cannon shot. **2** In billiards, to cause to carom. **3** To cause to rebound from one object to another. **—** *v.i.* **4** To fire cannon repeatedly. **5** In billiards, to make a carom. **6** To rebound from one object to another. ◆ Homophone: *canon.* [<OF *canon* <Ital. *cannone,* aug. of *canna* tube, pipe]

Can·non (kan′ən), **Annie Jump,** 1863–1941, U.S. astronomer. **— Joseph Gurney,** 1836–1926, U.S. politician, member of the House of Representatives 1873–91, 1893–1913, 1915–1923.

can·non·ade (kan′ən·ād′) *v.* **·ad·ed, ·ad·ing** *v.t.* To attack with cannon shot. **—** *v.i.* To fire cannon repeatedly. **—** *n.* A continued attack with or discharge of cannon.

cannon ball Any missile to be shot from a cannon; originally, a spherical solid shot.

can·non·eer (kan′ən·ir′) *n.* **1** An artilleryman belonging to a gun squad. **2** A soldier who serves as gunner. Also **can′non·ier′.**

cannon fodder Soldiers, as considered expendable in wartime.

can·non·ry (kan′ən·rē) *n.* Artillery; also, its discharge.

cannon shot **1** A shot or projectile for a cannon; a cannon ball. **2** The distance which the shot of a cannon may achieve.

can·not (ka′not) *v.i.* Am, is, or are not able to.

cannot but Have no alternative except to: objected to by some as a double negative, but long established in formal literary usage.

can·nu·la (kan′yə·lə) *n. Med.* A tube to be inserted by means of a trocar into a cavity, through which pus, etc., may escape or medicine be introduced: also spelled *canula.* [<L, dim. of *canna* reed, tube] **— can′nu·lar** *adj.*

can·nu·late (kan′yə·lāt) *v.t.* **·lat·ed, ·lat·ing** To make hollow or tubular. **—** *adj.* (kan′yə·lit, -lāt) Tubular. Also spelled *canulate.*

cannulated needle *Surg.* A ligating needle having a bore through which the wire or thread may pass.

can·ny (kan′ē) *adj.* **can·ni·er, can·ni·est** **1** Careful in determining or acting; prudent; knowing; thrifty; shrewd. **2** Skilful; clever. **3** Lucky; safe. **4** Quiet; sly; dry: said of humor as characteristically Scottish. **5** Comfortable; cozy; snug. Also spelled *cannie.* [<CAN (def. 3)] **— can′ni·ly** *adv.* **— can′ni·ness** *n.*

Ca·no (kä′nō), **Alonso,** 1601–67, Spanish painter, sculptor, and architect.

ca·noe (kə·no͞o′) *n.* **1** A small, long, narrow boat, pointed at both ends, made from a hollowed log, bark, light wood, or animal skins, and propelled by paddles: used by primitive peoples. **2** A modern adaptation of this, made of canvas, light wood, or aluminum. Compare illustration under CATAMARAN. **—** *v.t.* **1** To convey by canoe. **—** *v.i.* **2** To paddle, sail, or travel in a canoe. **3** To operate a canoe. [<Sp. <Taino *canoa* boat] **— ca·noe′ing** *n.* **— ca·noe′ist** *n.*

A B C
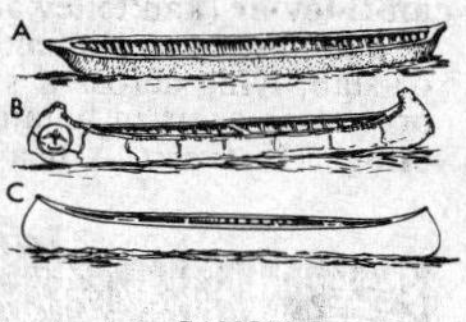

CANOES
A. Dugout. *B.* Birch bark. *C.* Modern.

ca·noe·wood (kə·no͞o′wo͝od′) *n.* Tulipwood.

can·on[1] (kan′ən) *n.* **1** A rule or law; standard; criterion. **2** The books of the Bible that are recognized by the Church as inspired. **3** The list of an author's works which are accepted as genuine: the Shakespearian *canon.* **4** *Eccl.* An official list or catalog, as of the saints recognized by a church, or of the members of a cathedral chapter. **5** *Eccl.* A rule of faith or discipline, especially one enacted by a church council and (in the Roman Catholic Church) ratified by the Pope. **6** *Often cap.* The portion of the mass between the Sanctus and the Lord's Prayer. **7** *Printing* A size of type nearly four times as large as pica; 48-point type. See PICA. **8** *Music* A composition having voices or parts wherein each voice or part in turn takes up the same melody (called the subject), and all combine to make harmony: the strictest form of musical imitation. **9** One of the metal loops at the top of a bell, by which it is hung. See synonyms under LAW, RULE. ◆ Homophone: *cannon.* [OE <L <Gk. *kanōn* rule, straight rod]

can·on[2] (kan′ən) *n.* A member of the chapter of a cathedral or collegiate church. ◆ Homophone: *cannon.* [OE *canonic* <LL *canonicus* cleric < *canon* rule. See CANON[1].]

cañ·on (kan′yən, *Sp.* kä·nyōn′) See CANYON.

ca·non·i·cal (kə·non′i·kəl) *adj.* **1** Belonging to or characteristic of the canon of Scripture. **2** Regular; lawful; accepted or approved. Also **ca·non′ic.** [<Med. L *canonicalis* <LL *canonicus* <L *canon.* See CANON[1].] **— ca·non′·i·cal·ly** *adv.*

canonical age The age required by canon law for ordination or for the performance of any particular act.

canonical hours **1** *Eccl.* The seven stated daily periods, fixed by canon, for prayer and devotion. They are named respectively matins (including nocturns and lauds), prime, tierce, sext, nones, vespers, and compline. **2** *Brit.* The hours (from 8 a.m. to 3 p.m.) during which marriage may be legally performed in parish churches.

ca·non·i·cals (kə·non′i·kəlz) *n. pl.* The habits or robes prescribed by canon to be worn by the clergy when they officiate.

ca·non·i·cate (kə·non′i·kāt, -kit) *n.* The office of a canon.

can·on·ic·i·ty (kan′ən·is′ə·tē) *n.* **1** The quality of being canonical. **2** Conformity to the canon; orthodoxy.

can·on·ist (kan′ən·ist) *n.* One skilled in canon law. **— can′on·is′tic** or **·ti·cal** *adj.*

can·on·i·za·tion (kan′ən·ə·zā′shən, -ī·zā′-) *n.* **1** The formal enrolling of a deceased and beatified person in the Roman Catholic canon, or calendar of saints. **2** The act of canonizing or regarding as a saint; the state of being canonized.

can·on·ize (kan′ən·īz) *v.t.* **·ized, ·iz·ing** **1** To place (a deceased person) in the canon, or catalog of saints; declare to be or regard as a saint. **2** To recognize as part of the canon of Scripture. **3** To sanction as being conformable to the canons of the Church. **4** To give or ascribe glory to; glorify.

canon law The body of ecclesiastical law by which a church is governed.

can·on·ry (kan′ən·rē) *n. pl.* **·ries** **1** The office or dignity of a canon; the benefice of a canon. **2** Canons collectively. Also **can′on·ship.**

can–o·pen·er (kan′ō′pən·ər) *n.* A device for opening cans, especially those containing food.

Ca·no·pic (kə·nō′pik) *adj.* Of or pertaining to Canopus.

Canopic vase or **jar** A vase with a top in the form of a human head: used in ancient Egypt to hold the viscera of embalmed bodies: also called **Canopic urn.**

Ca·no·pus (kə·nō′pəs) One of the 20 brightest stars, −0.86 magnitude; Alpha in the constellation Carina. See STAR. [<L]

Ca·no·pus (kə·nō′pəs) A port in ancient Egypt NE of Alexandria.

can·o·py (kan′ə·pē) *n. pl.* **·pies** **1** A covering suspended over a throne, bed, shrine, or the like, or held over a person in a procession. **2** Any covering overhead, as the arch of the sky. **3** An ornamental feature covering a niche, or an altar or tomb, or placed over a statue. **4** *Aeron.* **a** The main lifting surface of a parachute, whose unfolding reduces the velocity of descent. **b** The semicircular sliding panel enclosing the cockpit cowling of an airplane. **—** *v.t.* **·pied, ·py·ing** To cover with or as with a canopy. [<F *canapé* sofa <L *canopeum* mosquito net <Gk. *kōnōpeion* bed with mosquito net < *kōnōps* mosquito]

ca·no·rous (kə·nôr′əs, -nō′rəs) *adj.* Having a singing quality; tuneful; melodious; musical. [<L *canorus* < *canor* song < *canere* sing] **— ca·no′rous·ly** *adv.*

Ca·nos·sa (kə·nos′ə, *Ital.* kä·nôs′sä) A ruined castle in north central Italy; scene of Henry IV's penance before Gregory VII in 1077. **— to go to Canossa** To do penance; be reconciled.

Ca·no·va (kä·nō′vä), **Antonio,** 1757–1822, Italian sculptor.

Cá·no·vas del Cas·til·lo (kä′nō·väs t͟hel käs·tē′lyō), **Antonio,** 1828–97, Spanish statesman and writer.

can·so (kan·sō′) *n. pl.* **·sos** A lyric poem in Provençal troubadour literature, characterized by great formal elaboration and generally concerning themes of mundane gallantry (*canso d'amor*): also spelled *canzo.* [<Provençal <L *cantio* < *canere* sing]

Can·so (kan′sō), **Cape** The easternmost point

of the Nova Scotia peninsula. — **Strait of Canso** The strait between Cape Breton Island and the mainland of Nova Scotia. Also **Canso Strait.**

canst (kanst) Can: obsolescent or poetic second person singular, present tense of CAN: used with *thou.*

cant[1] (kant) *n.* 1 An inclination or tipping; a slope or set to one side. 2 A motion that produces a slant or an overturn. 3 A salient angle, as of a bolthead. 4 A slant surface, as one produced by cutting off a corner or edge. — *v.t.* 1 To set slantingly; tip up; tilt. 2 To give a bevel to. 3 To throw out or off; also, to jerk; toss. — *v.i.* 4 To tilt; slant. — *adj.* 1 Oblique; slanting. 2 Having canted sides or corners. [Prob. <OF <Med. L *cantus* corner, side]

cant[2] (kant) *n.* 1 Hypocritical or ostentatious religious talk. 2 Any technical or professional jargon: legal *cant.* 3 The secret language of thieves, gipsies, beggars, etc.; argot. 4 Any jargon employed for secrecy. 5 Hackneyed phraseology assumed as a fashion or for effect. 6 Whining speech, especially of beggars. See synonyms under HYPOCRISY, SLANG.— *v.t.* 1 To say with affected religiousness or in a hypocritical way. — *v.i.* 2 To chant; whine, as a beggar. 3 To talk with hypocritical or exaggerated unction, especially about religion. — *adj.* Like cant; insincere; hypocritical. [< AF, singing <L *cantus* song <*canere* sing] — **cant'er** *n.*

cant[3] (kant) *adj. Scot. & Brit. Dial.* Bold; brisk; lively.

can't (kant, känt) Cannot: a contraction.

can·ta·bi·le (kän·tä′bē·lā) *Music adj.* Melodious; flowing. — *n.* Music characterized by flowing melody. [<Ital.]

Can·ta·bri·an Mountains (kan·tā′brē·ən) A range in northern Spain; highest peak, 8,687 feet. *Spanish* **Cor·dil·le·ra Can·tá·bri·ca** (kôr′thē·lyä′rä kän·tä′vrē·kä).

Can·ta·brig·i·an (kan·tə·brij′ē·ən) *adj.* 1 Of or pertaining to Cambridge, England, or its university. 2 Of or pertaining to Cambridge, Massachusetts, or to Harvard University. — *n.* 1 A resident of Cambridge, England; also, a student or graduate of Cambridge University. 2 A student or graduate of Harvard University, or a resident of Cambridge, Massachusetts. [<LL *Cantabrigia* Cambridge]

can·ta·lev·er (kan′tə·lev·ər, -lē′vər) See CANTILEVER.

can·ta·loupe (kan′tə·lōp) *n.* A variety of muskmelon (*Cucumis melo cantalupensis*). Also **can′ta·loup.** [<F from *Cantalupo,* Italian castle where first grown in Europe]

can·tank·er·ous (kan·tang′kər·əs) *adj.* Quarrelsome; ill-natured; perverse. [ME *contak* strife] — **can·tank′er·ous·ly** *adv.* — **can·tank′er·ous·ness** *n.*

can·tar (kan′tär) *n.* A unit of weight in Moslem countries, commonly between 100 and 130 pounds: also spelled *kantar.* [<Sp. *cantaro* <Arabic *qintar* hundredweight, ult. <L *centenarius* hundredfold]

can·ta·ta (kən·tä′tə) *n. Music* A choral composition in the style of an oratorio or drama, sung but not acted. [<Ital.]

Can·ta·te (kan·tä′tē) The 98th Psalm (97th in the Douai version), used as an alternative canticle in the Book of Common Prayer at Evening Prayer: so called from the first words in Latin, *Cantate Domino* (Sing unto the Lord).

Cantate Sunday The fourth Sunday after Easter, the introit for which is the first verse of the Cantate.

can·ta·tri·ce (kän′tä·trē′chä) *n. pl.* **·tri·ci** (-trē′chē) *Ital.* A female professional singer.

cant·dog (kant′dôg′, -dog′) *n.* A cant-hook.

can·teen (kan·tēn′) *n.* 1 A small, metal flask for water, coffee, etc. 2 A refreshment and liquor shop; formerly, a shop at a military camp where soldiers might buy provisions. See POST EXCHANGE. 3 An entertainment center or club operated by civilians for enlisted personnel of Army, Navy, Air Force, Marine, and other military units. [<F *cantine* <Ital. *cantina* cellar]

can·ter (kan′tər) *n.* A moderate, easy gallop. — *v.t. & v.i.* To ride or go at an easy gallop. [Short for *Canterbury gallop;* with ref. to the pace of pilgrims riding to Canterbury.] — **can′ter·er** *n.*

Can·ter·bur·y (kan′tər·ber′ē) 1 A county

borough and archbishopric in Kent, England; seat of the primate of the English Church. 2 A provincial district of eastern South Island, New Zealand; 13,940 square miles.

Canterbury bell One of various cultivated bellflowers, especially *Campanula medium.*

Canterbury gallop A canter: the original term. Also **Canterbury pace, rack,** or **trot.**

Canterbury Tales An uncompleted work (1387–1400) by Chaucer, consisting of a series of tales, largely in verse, told by a group of pilgrims to each other on their way to Canterbury.

can·thar·i·des (kan·thar′ə·dēz) *n.* The dried powder obtained by crushing the Spanish fly or blister beetle: used externally as a rubefacient and vesicant and internally as a diuretic and aphrodisiac. [See CANTHARIS]

can·thar·i·din (kan·thar′ə·din) *n. Chem.* The bitter crystalline anhydride principle, $C_{10}H_{12}O_4$, contained in cantharides: a powerful blistering agent. Also **can·thar′i·dine** (-din, -dēn).

can·thar·is (kan′thə·ris) *n. pl.* **can·thar·i·des** (kan·thar′ə·dēz) The Spanish fly. [<L <Gk. *kantharis*]

cant–hook (kant′·hook′) *n.* A lever equipped with a hook for handling logs.

can·thus (kan′thəs) *n. pl.* **·thi** (-thī) *Anat.* The angle at the outer or inner junction of the eyelids. [<L <Gk. *kanthos*]

CANT–HOOK

can·ti·cle (kan′ti·kəl) *n.* A non-metrical hymn, as one with words taken directly from the Bible text, to be chanted, as in certain church services. [<L *canticulum,* dim. of *canticum* song]

Can·ti·cles (kan′ti·kəlz) The Song of Solomon.

Can·ti·gny (kän·tē·nyē′) A village in northern France; scene of the first engagement of U.S. troops in World War I, May 27–28, 1918.

can·ti·lev·er (kan′tə·lev′ər) *n.* 1 *Engin.* One of two long structural members, as a truss, beam, or slab, lying across a support, with the two projecting arms in balance, as in a **cantilever bridge.** 2 *Archit.* A heavy bracket supporting

CANTILEVER BRIDGE

a balcony, or the like. 3 *Aeron.* A form of airfoil without external bracing. — *v.t. & v.i.* To project (a building member) outward and in balance beyond the base. Sometimes spelled *cantalever.* Also **can′ti·liv′er** (-liv′ər). [Origin uncertain]

can·til·late (kan′tə·lāt) *v.t. & v.i.* **·lat·ed, ·lat·ing** To recite by intoning or chanting: said especially of the manner of rendering the service in Jewish or other rituals. [<L *cantillatus,* pp. of *cantillare* sing low, hum < *cantare* sing] — **can′til·la′tion** *n.*

can·ti·na (kan·tē′nə) *n. SW U.S.* A place where liquor is sold; a bar or saloon. [<Sp.]

can·tle (kan′təl) *n.* 1 A piece cut or broken off; a segment; corner. 2 The hind bow of a saddle. [<AF *cantel* <LL *cantellus,* dim. of *cantus* corner]

can·to (kan′tō) *n. pl.* **·tos** 1 A division of an extended poem. 2 *Archaic* The part of a musical score to which the melody is assigned; the air. [<Ital. <L *cantus* song]

can·ton (kan′tən, -ton, kan·ton′) *n.* 1 A district of the Swiss confederation. 2 A subdivision of an arrondissement in France. 3 The rectangular part of a flag next the staff. 4 *Her.* The diminutive of the quarter, occupying one third of the chief, usually on the dexter side of the shield. 5 An assemblage of village communities. — *v.t.* 1 To divide into

cantons. 2 To sever; separate. 3 To assign to quarters, as military troops. [<OF <Ital. *cantone,* aug. of *canto* corner <L *cantus*] — **can·ton·al** (kan′tən·əl) *adj.*

Can·ton[1] (kan·ton′) A port on the Canton River, the capital of Kwangtung province, southern China: Chinese *Kwangchow.* 2 (kan′tən) A city in NE Ohio.

Canton crêpe (kan′tən) A soft silk crêpe, having more body than crêpe de Chine. [from *Canton,* China]

can·toned (kan′tənd) *adj.* 1 *Her.* Placed in the midst of four bearings or groups of bearings on a shield, as a cross, or having a single canton, as a shield. 2 *Mil.* Assigned to quarters, as soldiers.

Can·ton·ese (kan′tən·ēz′, -ēs′) *n. pl.* **·ese** 1 A native of Canton, China. 2 The Chinese language spoken in Kwangtung province and other parts of southern China.

canton flannel (kan′tən) A heavy cotton fabric having a long nap, usually on one side only: used for undergarments, infants' nightwear, etc. [from *Canton,* China]

Can·ton Island (kan′tən) The largest and northernmost of the Phoenix Islands, comprising a condominium (1939) of the United States and Great Britain; 3 1/2 square miles.

can·ton·ment (kan·ton′mənt, -tōn′-, kan′tən·mənt; *Brit.* kan·tōon′mənt) *n.* 1 A group of wooden buildings for housing troops; a military station 2 The act of cantoning troops. [<F *cantonnement* < *cantonner* quarter]

Can·ton River (kan·ton′) A river in southern Kwangtung province, China, flowing 110 miles to the South China Sea: also *Pearl River:* Chinese *Chu Kiang.*

can·tor (kan′tər, -tôr) *n.* 1 A precentor; a chief singer. 2 A liturgical singer in a synagog. [<L]

can·trip (kan′trip) *n. Scot.* 1 An incantation; charm; piece of witchcraft. 2 A mischievous trick or mad prank.

cant timber *Naut.* One of the heavy timbers forming part of a ship's hull at either end and supported by the deadwood.

can·tus (kan′təs) *n. pl.* **can·tus** 1 A style of church song. 2 The principal voice of a polyphonic work. [<L, song, singing]

cantus fir·mus (fûr′məs) 1 The plain song or chant. 2 *Music* The fixed, simple melody to which other parts are added to make a polyphonic work.

can·ty (kan′tē) *adj. Scot.* Brisk; glad; lively. Also **can′tie.**

Ca·nuck (kə·nuk′) *Slang adj.* Canadian. — *n.* 1 A Canadian. 2 A French Canadian. Also **Ca·nuck′er.**

can·u·la (kan′yə·lə) See CANNULA.

can·u·late (kan′yə·lāt) See CANNULATE.

Ca·nute (kə·nōōt′, -nyōōt′), 994?–1035, king of England 1016?–35 and of Denmark 1018–1035: also spelled *Cnut, Knut.*

can·vas (kan′vəs) *n.* 1 A heavy, strong cloth of various grades, used for sails, tents, etc. 2 A piece of such cloth; a sail. 3 A strong, closely woven cloth stretched on a frame and prepared for the reception of colors, as in paintings. 4 A painting. 5 A square-meshed fabric of linen, silk, or the like, on which embroidery or tapestry is worked with a needle. 6 A tent; especially, a circus tent. — **under canvas** 1 With sails set. 2 In tents. ◆ Homophone: **canvass.** [<AF *canevas* <L *cannabis* hemp]

can·vas·back (kan′vəs·bak′) *n.* A North American sea duck (*Nyroca valisineria*) with a grayish white back, highly esteemed for its flesh.

can·vass (kan′vəs) *n.* 1 The going about to solicit orders, interest, or votes. 2 A political campaign. 3 A survey taken to ascertain sentiment. 4 A detailed examination; especially, a sifting of votes in an election; a recount. — *v.t.* 1 To go about an area to solicit, as votes. 2 To scrutinize; examine; sift. — *v.i.* 3 To go about seeking votes, orders or the like: to *canvass* for votes. See synonyms under EXAMINE. ◆ Homophone: **canvas.** [<CANVAS; with ref. to the earlier use of canvas for sifting] — **can′vass·er** *n.*

can·y (kā′nē) *adj.* Full of canes; made of cane.

can·yon (kan′yən) *n.* A deep gorge or ravine, with steep or precipitous sides: also spelled *cañon.* See synonyms under VALLEY. [<Sp. *cañón*]

Canyon de Chelly National Monument

(də shā′) A region of cliff-dweller ruins in NE Arizona; established as a national park in 1931.

can·zo (kan·sō′) See CANSO.

can·zo·ne (kän·tsō′nä) *n. pl.* **·ni** (-nē) 1 A Provençal or Italian ballad or song. 2 The music for such a song. [<Ital. <L *cantio* song]

can·zo·net (kanzə·net′) *n.* A short song; light air. [<Ital. *canzonetta*, dim of *canzone* song]

caout·chouc (koo′chook, koo·chook′) *n.* Rubber; especially, crude rubber. [<F <Tupian *caú-uchú*]

cap¹ (kap) *n.* 1 A covering to be worn on the head; specifically, a brimless head covering, often with a shade or vizor in front. 2 A head covering for a woman or an infant made of lace or some soft fabric. 3 Any headgear of unique design to distinguish some order, office, dignity, or characteristic of the wearer. 4 Anything resembling or used as a cap: a bottle *cap*. 5 The primer of a cartridge or shell case. 6 *Bot.* The pileus of a mushroom. 7 The top of an oil well. 8 Any of various large sizes of writing paper. See FOOLSCAP, LEGAL CAP. 9 *Archit.* The upper member of a column or pilaster; a capital. —**test cap** A protective covering for the exposed end of a cable, excluding dirt, moisture, etc. —**to set one's cap for** To try to win as a suitor or husband. —*v.t.* **capped, cap·ping** 1 To put a cap on, as the head. 2 To fit the top or summit of with a cover: Bees *cap* their cells. 3 To serve as a cap to; lie on top of; crown: The cloud *capped* the mountain. 4 To add the final touch to; complete. 5 To excel; top. —**to cap the climax** To surpass the climax; exceed the limit. [OE *cæppe* <LL *cappa* hooded cloak, cap, prob. < *caput* head]

cap² (kap) *n. Colloq.* A capital letter.

ca·pa·bil·i·ty (kāpə·bil′ə·tē) *n. pl.* **·ties** 1 The state or quality of being capable; capacity; ability. 2 Susceptibility to some particular form of use, treatment, or development. 3 *Usually pl.* A feature or condition that may be improved or developed. See synonyms under ABILITY.

Ca·pa·blan·ca (käpä·vläng′kä), José Raoul, 1882–1942, Cuban world chess champion: full name *Capablanca y Granperra*.

ca·pa·ble (kā′pə·bəl) *adj.* 1 Having adequate ability or capacity to do or to receive; efficient; able; qualified; competent. 2 *Obs.* Comprehensive. 3 Adaptable; susceptible: with *of*. See synonyms under CLEVER, COMPETENT. [<F <LL *capabilis* <L *capere* take, receive] —**ca′pa·ble·ness** *n.* —**ca′pa·bly** *adv.*

ca·pa·cious (kə·pā′shəs) *adj.* Able to contain or receive much; spacious; roomy. See synonyms under LARGE. [<L *capax, -acis* able to hold, roomy < *capere* take] —**ca·pa′cious·ly** *adv.* —**ca·pa′cious·ness** *n.*

ca·pac·i·tance (kə·pas′ə·təns) *n. Electr.* 1 In a conductor or system of conductors, the ratio of electrical charge to a resulting potential. 2 That property of a body expressed by the amount of electricity required to give it a potential greater than its surroundings. [<CAPACI(TY) + (REAC)TANCE]

ca·pac·i·tate (kə·pas′ə·tāt) *v.t.* **·tat·ed, ·tat·ing** 1 To render capable. 2 To qualify according to law.

ca·pac·i·tive (kə·pas′ə·tiv) *adj. Electr.* Of or relating to capacitance.

ca·pac·i·tor (kə·pas′ə·tər) *n.* A device for accumulating and holding a charge of electricity, consisting of two conductors separated by a dielectric and having equal, opposite charges.

ca·pac·i·ty (kə·pas′ə·tē) *n. pl.* **·ties** 1 Ability to receive or contain; cubic extent; carrying power or space. 2 Adequate mental power to receive, understand, etc.; also, ability; talent; capability. 3 Specific position, character, or office. 4 Legal qualification. 5 *Electr.* **a** Capacitance. **b** The output of an electric generator. See synonyms under ABILITY, POWER. [<F *capacité* <L *capacitas, -tatis* < *capax*. See CAPACIOUS .]

cap and bells A cap ornamented with little bells, worn by a fool or court jester.

cap and gown The apparel worn at some academic ceremonies, consisting of a flat cap (*mortarboard*) and a long, dark gown: often used figuratively for the academic life.

Cap·a·neus (kap′ə·noos, -nyoos, kə·pā′nē·əs) See SEVEN AGAINST THEBES.

cap-a-pie (kapə·pē′) *adv.* From head to foot. Also **cap-à-pie′**. [<OF]

ca·par·i·son (kə·par′ə·sən) *n.* 1 Decorative trappings for a horse. 2 Showy or sumptuous apparel. —*v.t.* To put ornamental trappings on; clothe richly. [<OF *caparasson* <Sp. *caparazón* <LL *cappa* cape]

Synonyms (noun): accouterments, harness, housings, trappings. *Harness* was formerly used of the armor of a knight as well as of a horse; it is now used almost exclusively of the equipment of a horse when attached to a vehicle. We speak of the *accouterments* of a soldier. *Caparison* and *trappings* denote the ornamental outfit of a horse, or, in a humorous sense, showy human apparel. Compare ARMS, DRESS.

cape¹ (kāp) *n.* A point of land extending into the sea or a lake. —**the Cape** 1 The Cape of Good Hope. 2 *U.S.* Cape Cod. [<F *cap* <L *caput* head]

cape² (kāp) *n.* A circular, sleeveless upper garment; a short cloak. [<F <LL *cappa*] —**caped** (kāpt) *adj.*

Cape Bret·on Island (brit′n, bret′n) An island off the NE end of Nova Scotia; 3,975 square miles.

Cape Coast A port on the Gulf of Guinea, former capital of Gold Coast Colony. Formerly **Cape Coast Castle**.

Cape Cod 1 See COD, CAPE. 2 A style of cottage developed chiefly on Cape Cod in the 18th and early 19th centuries, typically a one-story wooden cottage with a gable roof.

Cape Cod Canal A canal, 13 miles long, across Cape Cod from Buzzards Bay Cape Cod Bay.

Cape Colony A former administrative division of the Republic of South Africa. See CAPE OF GOOD HOPE PROVINCE.

Cape Dutch Afrikaans.

Cape Fear River See FEAR, CAPE.

Cape-Horn·er (kāphôr′nər) *n.* A vessel whose run is around Cape Horn. See HORN, CAPE.

Ča·pek (chä′pek), Karel, 1890–1938, Czech playwright and novelist.

cap·e·lin (kap′ə·lin) *n. pl.* **·lin** or **·lins** A small, edible fish (*Mallotus villosus*) of the smelt family, with many-rayed pectoral fins, found in northern seas: much used as cod bait: also spelled **caplin**. [<F *caplan, capelan*]

Ca·pel·la (kə·pel′ə) One of the 20 brightest stars, 0.21 magnitude and of a yellow color; Alpha in the constellation Auriga. See STAR. [<L, she-goat]

Cape of Good Hope See GOODHOPE, CAPE OF.

Cape of Good Hope Province A former province of the Republic of South Africa roughly corresponding to the Eastern, Western, and Northern Cape provinces; formerly *Cape Colony*.

ca·per¹ (kā′pər) *n.* 1 A leaping or frisking; a skip or jump; prank; antic. 2 Any wild or fantastic action activity. —**to cut a caper** (or **capers**) To caper; frolic. — *v.i.* To leap playfully; frisk. See synonyms under FROLIC. [Short for CAPRIOLE] —**cap′per·er**

ca·per² (kā′pər) *n.* 1 The flower bud of a low shrub of Mediterranean countries, used as a condiment. 2 The shrub (*Capparis spinosa*) producing it. [<L *capparis* <Gk. *kapparis*]

cap·er·cail·lie (kapər·kāl′yē) *n.* A large, black European grouse (*Tetrao urogallus*). Also **cap·er·cail′zie** (-yē, -zē). [<Scottish Gaelic *capull-coille* horse of the wood]

Ca·per·na·um (kə·pûr′nē·əm) A Biblical locality in NE Palestine by the Sea of Galilee. *Matt.* iv 13.

Cape Sable 1 See SABLE, CAPE. 2 See under SABLE ISLAND.

cape·skin (kāp′skin) *n.* A kind of leather made from lamb or sheep skins, originally from the Cape of Good Hope: used especially for gloves.

Ca·pet (kā′pit, kap′it) See HUGH CAPET.

Ca·pe·tian (kə·pē′shən) *adj.* 1 Pertaining to or descended from Hugh Capet, or pertaining to the dynasty founded by him which ruled France until 1328, or to the collateral branches of that dynasty which ruled until 1792. See HUGHCAPET. —*n.* A descendant, direct or indirect, of Hugh Capet.

Cape Town A port on Table Bay, capital of

West Cape Province, Republic of South Africa. Also **Cape′town**.

Cape Verde See VERDE, CAPE.

Cape Verde Islands A Portuguese overseas province west of Cape Verde, comprising two groups of islands; 1,557 square miles; capital, Praia, on São Tiago. *Portuguese* **I·lhas do Ca·bo Ver·de** (ē′lyəz hthoo kä′voo vâr′di).

Cape York Peninsula The NE part of Queensland, Australia.

Cap Hai·tien (käp hä′shən) A port in northern Haiti. Also **Le Cap** (lə kä′). *French* **Cap Ha·ï·tien** (kä·pä·ē·sya′).

ca·pi·as (kā′pē·əs, kap′ē·əs) *n. pl.* **·as·es** *Law* A judicial writ issued to an officer, commanding him to take and hold in custody the person named therein subject to the order of the court; a writ of arrest. [<L, you may take]

cap·il·la·ceous (kapə·lā′shəs) *adj.* Hairlike; capillary. [<L *capillaceus* < *capillus* hair]

cap·il·lar·i·ty (kapə·lar′ə·tē) *n.* 1 The state or quality of being capillary. 2 *Physics* The interaction between the molecules of a liquid and those of a solid: a form of surface tension. When the adhesive force is stronger the liquid will tend to rise above mean level at the points of contact, as water in clean glass; when cohesion dominates, the liquid will tend to fall below this level, as mercury. [<F *capillarité*]

cap·il·lar·y (kap′ə·lerē) *adj.* 1 Of, pertaining to, or like hair; fine; slender. 2 Having a hairlike bore, as a tube or vessel; also, pertaining to such a tube. —*n. pl.* **·lar·ies** 1 *Anat.* A minute vessel, as those connecting the arteries and veins. 2 Any tube with a fine bore. [<L *capillaris* < *capillus* hair]

capillary attraction and repulsion Capillarity.

cap·il·li·ti·um (kapə·lish′ē·əm) *n. pl.* **·ti·a** (-lish′ē·ə) *Bot.* The sterile, branching or anastomosing, threadlike tubes or filaments mixed with the spores in a sporangium, or fruit body, as in myxomycetes. [<L < *capillus* hair]

Ca·pis·tra·no (käpi·strä′nō) *n.* A native or inhabitant of Capri.

cap·i·ta (kap′ə·tə) Plural of CAPUT.

cap·i·tal¹ (kap′ə·təl) *adj.* 1 Standing at the head or beginning; chief; principal. 2 Excellent; admirable. 3 Of or pertaining to the death penalty; punishable with death. 4 Of or pertaining to funds or capital. See synonyms under EXCELLENT, GOOD. —*n.* 1 The chief city or town of a country, state, province, etc., usually the seat of government. 2 A capital letter. 3 Wealth employed in or available for producing more wealth. 4 Property used in the business of a firm or corporation at a valuation on which profits and dividends are calculated. 5 The aggregate of the products of industry directly available for the support of human existence or for promoting additional production. 6 Possessors of wealth, as a class. 7 Any resource or circumstance that can be utilized for an ambitious objective. —Homophone: *capitol.* [<F <L *capitalis* < *caput* head]

CAPITALS

A. Doric.
  a. Abacus. *b.* Echinus.
  c. Channeled shaft.
B. Egyptian.
C. Ionic.
D. Corinthian.
E. Byzantine.
F. Romanesque.

cap·i·tal² (kap′ə·təl) *n. Archit.* The upper member of a column or pillar. —Homophone: *capitol.* [<L *capitellum*, double dim of *caput* head]

capital account A statement of the amount and value of a business at a given time, consisting of two columns representing assets and liabilities balanced by profit and loss, indicating a surplus or a deficit.

capital expenditure Expenditure for permanent additions or improvements to property, as opposed to money spent for repairs.

capital gain Profit from the sale of capital investments, such as stocks, real estate, etc.
capital goods Materials used in industry in the production of consumers' goods.
cap·i·tal·ism (kap'ə·təl·iz'əm) *n.* **1** An economic system in which the means of production and distribution are for the most part privately owned and operated for private profit. **2** The possession and concentration of private capital and its resulting power and influence.
cap·i·tal·ist (kap'ə·təl·ist) *n.* **1** One who shares in or adheres to capitalism. **2** An owner of capital; especially, one who has large means employed in productive enterprise. **3** Loosely, any person of apparent wealth. —**cap'i·tal·is'tic** *adj.* —**cap'i·tal·is'ti·cal·ly** *adv.*
cap·i·tal·i·za·tion (kap'ə·təl·ə·zā'shən, -ī·zā'-) *n.* **1** The act or process of capitalizing. **2** The value of the entire property of a business, usually represented by the stock or shares issued as permanent liabilities of the business.
cap·i·tal·ize (kap'ə·təl·īz) *v.t.* **·ized, ·iz·ing** **1** To begin with capital letters, or write or print in capital letters. **2** To convert into capital or cash. **3** To convert (a periodical payment) into a sum in hand; compute the value of in a single payment or capital sum. **4** To invest for profit; provide capital. **5** To organize on a basis of capital. **6** To profit by: with *on:* He *capitalized* on his enemy's errors.
capital letter In writing and printing, the form of the alphabetic letter used at the beginning of a sentence, with proper names, etc.: in printing called *cap* or *upper case letter* as distinguished from *lower case letter.* Compare CASE[2] (def. 3). —**small capital** A letter used in printing having the same form as but of smaller size than the CAPITAL of the same font: also called *small cap.* In this dictionary cross–references are in SMALL CAPITALS.
capital levy A tax on capital; a property tax: distinguished from *income tax.*
cap·i·tal·ly (kap'ə·təl·ē) *adv.* **1** Firstly; chiefly. **2** Excellently. **3** So as to deserve death.
capital punishment The death penalty for a crime.
capital ship A warship of large size (including aircraft carriers) carrying guns of over 8–inch caliber; battleship or battle cruiser.
capital stock The amount of property owned by an individual or a corporation: distinguished from *income.*
cap·i·tate (kap'ə·tāt) *adj.* **1** *Bot.* Head–shaped; headed: a *capitate* flower. **2** *Zool.* Enlarged terminally, or knobbed at the end, as tentacles. [<L *capitatus* having a head < *caput* head]
cap·i·ta·tion (kap'ə·tā'shən) *n.* **1** An individual assessment or tax; a poll tax. **2** Any count or fee per capita. [<LL *capitatio, -onis* poll tax <L *caput* head]
cap·i·tol (kap'ə·təl) *n.* The building in which a State legislature convenes; a statehouse. ◆ Homophone: *capital.*
Cap·i·tol (kap'ə·təl) **1** The official building of the U.S. Congress in Washington. **2** The temple of Jupiter Maximus in ancient Rome, or the Capitoline Hill on which it stood. [< L *Capitolium* the Capitoline <*caput* head]
Capitol Hill **1** The site of the Capitol in Washington, D.C. **2** The U.S. Congress.
Cap·i·to·line (kap'ə·tə·līn') *adj.* Pertaining to the Roman Capitol, to its presiding god, Jupiter Capitolinus, or to the Capitoline Hill. —*n.* One of the seven hills of Rome: site of the Temple of Jupiter and of the Tarpeian rock.
ca·pit·u·lar (kə·pich'o͞o·lər) *adj.* **1** Of or belonging to a cathedral chapter; capitulary. **2** *Bot.* Of, pertaining to, or growing in a capitulum. —*n.* **1** Any of the collections of laws issued by Charlemagne and his successors. **2** A member of a cathedral chapter. [<L *capitularis* <*capitulum* chapter, dim. f *caput* head]
ca·pit·u·lar·y (kə·pich'o͞o·ler'ē) *adj.* Relating to an ecclesiastical hapter. —*n. pl.* **·lar·ies** A capitular.
ca·pit·u·late (kə·pich'o͞o·lāt) *v.* **·lat·ed, ·lat·ing** *v.t.* To surrender, as a fort or army, to an enemy on stipulated conditions. —*v.i.* To surrender on stipulated terms; make terms. —*adj.* (kə·pich'o͞o·lit, -lāt) *Bot.* Headed; having a capitulum. [<L *capitulatus,* pp. of *capitulare* draw up in chapters, arrange terms] —**ca·pit'·u·la'tor** *n.* —**ca·pit·u·la·to·ry** (kə·pich'o͞o·lə·tôr'ē, tō'rē) *adj.*
ca·pit·u·la·tion (kə·pich'o͞o·lā'shən) *n.* **1** A conditional surrender, or the instrument embodying it; a charter or treaty. **2** A statement, summary, or enumeration.
ca·pit·u·lum (kə·pich'o͞o·ləm) *n. pl.* **·la** (-lə) **1** *Bot.* In phanerogams, a close, head–shaped cluster of sessile flowers, as in the button daisy. See illustration under INFLORESCENCE. **2** *Anat.* A small rounded body, as at the head of a rib. **3** *Zool.* The headlike part of ticks and mites. **4** *Entomol.* The enlarged tip of the antenna or mouth of certain insects. [< L, dim. of *caput* head]
ca·po (kä'po) *n. Slang* The head of one of the units or branches of the Mafia.
ca·po das·tro (kä'pō däs'trō) A clamp or nut attached to the finger board of a guitar to raise uniformly the pitch of the strings. Also **capo tas·to** (täs'tō). [<Ital. *capo di tastro* cap for the keys]
ca·pon (kā'pon, -pən) *n.* A rooster gelded to improve the flesh for eating. [OE *capun* <L *capo, -onis*]
cap·o·ral[1] (kap'ə·ral') *n.* A form of cut tobacco. [<F *(tabac du) caporal* corporal's tobacco]
ca·po·ral[2] (kä'pō·räl') *n. SW U.S.* One who supervises laborers; a boss. [<Sp.]
Cap·o·ret·to (kap'ə·ret'ō, *Ital.* kä'pō·ret'tō) A town in NW Slovenia, Yugoslavia; in Italy until 1947; scene of Italian defeat (1917) of World War I. *Serbo–Croatian* **Ko·ba·rid** (kō'·bä·rēd).
ca·pot (kə·pot') *n.* The winning of all the tricks in the game of piquet. —*v.t.* **ca·pot·ted, ca·pot·ting** To win all the tricks from. [<F]
ca·pote (kə·pōt') *n.* **1** A hooded coat or cloak. **2** The adjustable top of a vehicle, as a buggy; hood. **3** A bonnet. [<F, dim. of *cape* cape, hood]
Ca·po·te (kə·pō'tē), **Truman,** born 1924, U.S. author.
ca·pouch (kə·po͞osh', -po͞och') See CAPUCHE.
Cap·pa·do·ci·a (kap'ə·dō'shē·ə, -shə) An ancient region of Asia Minor. —**Cap'pa·do'·ci·an** *adj. & n.*
cap·pa·ri·da·ceous (kap'ə·ri·dā'shəs) *adj. Bot.* Belonging to a family *(Capparidaceae)* of herbs and shrubs, the caper family. [<L *capparis* caper]
cap·per (kap'ər) *n.* **1** One who or that which caps. **2** A maker or seller of caps. **3** *U.S. Slang* A person employed by gamblers as a decoy; also, a professional or hired "bidder–up" at an auction.
cap pistol A toy pistol with a hammer for firing caps.
Cap·ra (kap'rə), **Frank,** born 1897, U.S. motion–picture director born in Sicily.
cap·re·o·late (kap'rē·ə·lāt, kə·prē'-) *adj. Bot.* Like or bearing a tendril. [<L *capreolus* tendril]
Ca·pri (kä'prē, kə·prē') A resort island at the SE entrance of the Bay of Naples; 4 square miles: a native of the island is known as a *Capistrano.*
Ca·pri blue A vivid turquoise blue: so called from the tones of the Blue Grotto of Capri.
cap·ric (kap'rik) *adj.* Of, pertaining to, derived from, or like a goat. [<L *caper, capri* goat]
capric acid *Chem.* A colorless crystalline compound, $C_{10}H_{20}O_2$ of goatlike odor, found in butter, coconut oil, etc.: used in perfumery.
ca·pric·ci·o (kə·prē'chē·ō, *Ital.* kä·prēt'chō) *n. pl.* **·ci·os** or *Ital.* **ca·pric·ci** (kä·prēt'chē) **1** *Music* A composition of lively and spirited mood and fancifully irregular in form. **2** A prank. [<Ital. <*capro* goat <L *caper*]
ca·pric·ci·o·so (kə·prē'chē·ō'sō, *Ital.* kä'prēt·chō'sō) *adj. Music* Fanciful; lively; irregular; fantastic. [<Ital.]
ca·price (kə·prēs') *n.* **1** A sudden unreasonable change of mood or opinion; a whim. **2** Any sudden, arbitrary act or fanciful idea. **3** The mood or state of mind that causes sudden changes or fancies. **4** A capriccio. See synonyms under FANCY, WHIM. [<F <Ital. *capriccio.* See CAPRICCIO.]
ca·pri·cious (kə·prish'əs, kə·prē'shəs) *adj.* Characterized by or resulting from caprice; fickle; whimsical; inconstant; unpredictable; also, fanciful. See synonyms under IRRESOLUTE. [<F *capricieux*] —**ca·pri'cious·ly** *adv.* —**ca·pri'cious·ness** *n.*
Cap·ri·corn (kap'rə·kôrn) **1** The tenth sign of the zodiac, entered by the sun at the winter solstice. **2** A zodiacal constellation; the Goat. See CONSTELLATION. Also **Cap'ri·cor'nus** (-kôr' nəs). [<L *capricornus* <*caper* goat + *cornu* horn]
cap·ri·fi·ca·tion (kap'rə·fi·kā'shən) *n.* **1** The process and effect of exposing the cultivated fig, at the time when the flowers are within the growing fruit, to the attack of a chalcid insect that infests the wild fig, so as to hasten the ripening and improve the quality of the fruit. **2** Artificial fertilization of the fig or date by this method. [<L *caprificatio, -onis* <*caprificare* ripen figs <*caprificus* wild fig]
cap·ri·fo·li·a·ceous (kap'ri·fō'lē·ā'shəs) *adj. Bot.* Belonging to the honeysuckle family *(Caprifoliaceae)* of herbs, woody shrubs, and vines. [<Med. L *caprifolium* honeysuckle <L *caper* goat + *folium* leaf]
cap·ri·form (kap'rə·fôrm) *adj.* Having the form or appearance of a goat. [<L *caper, capri* goat +-FORM]
cap·ri·ole (kap'rē·ōl) *n.* An upward leap made by a trained horse while standing. —*v.i.* **·oled, ·ol·ing** To perform a capriole; leap upward. [<F <Ital. *capriola,* dim. of *capra* she–goat <L *capra*]
Capri pants Tight–fitting women's trousers, worn informally. Also **Capris.**
ca·pro·ic (kə·prō'ik) *adj.* Of or pertaining to a goat.
caproic acid *Chem.* A colorless, inflammable fatty acid, $C_6H_{12}O_2$, derived from butter and other sources: used in organic synthesis.
cap·sa·i·cin (kap·sā'ə·sin) *n. Chem.* A white crystalline compound, $C_{18}H_{27}O_3N$, extracted from cayenne pepper: used in medicine as a rubefacient. [<NL *capsicum*]
cap screw A screw bolt with a long thread and, generally, a square head: used to secure cylinder covers, etc.
Cap·si·an (kap'sē·ən) *adj. Anthropol.* Denoting an Upper Paleolithic culture roughly contemporaneous with the Magdalenian.
cap·si·cum (kap'si·kəm) *n.* **1** An herb or shrub of the nightshade family (genus *Capsicum*), including the common red and other peppers producing many–seeded pods prepared as condiments or gastric stimulants. **2** The fruit of these plants. [<L *capsa* box (from the shape of the fruit)]
cap·size (kap·sīz', kap'sīz) *v.t. & v.i.* **·sized, ·siz·ing** To upset or overturn. [? <Sp. *capuzar* sink a ship by the head <*cabo* head]
cap·stan (kap'stən) *n. Naut.* A drum–like apparatus for hoisting anchors or other weights by exerting traction upon a cable. [<F *cabestan* <L *capistrum* halter < *capere* hold]

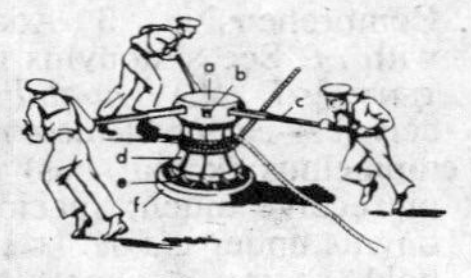

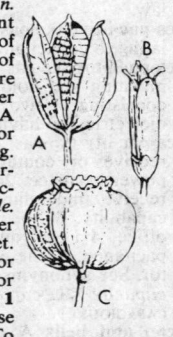

CAPSTAN
a. Drumhead. *b.* Bar-hole. *c.* Capstan bar. *d.* Barrel. *e.* Pawls. *f.* Pawl-rim.

capstan bar A lever used in turning a capstan.
cap·stone (kap'stōn') *n.* Copestone.
cap·su·late (kap'sə·lāt, -syo͞o-) *adj.* **1** Enclosed in a capsule. **2** Having or formed into a capsule or capsules. Also **cap'su·lat'ed.** [<NL *capsulatus* <L *capsula,* dim. of *capsa* box] —**cap'su·la'·tion** *n.*
cap·sule (kap'səl, -syo͞ol) *n.* **1** *Bot.* **a** A dry dehiscent seed vessel made up of more than one carpel, as of a pink or a lily. **b** The spore case of a moss or other cryptogam. **2** *Med.* A small gelatinous case for containing a dose of a drug. **3** *Biol.* A capsulelike organ, membrane, or structure: the suprarenal *capsule.* **4** The cargo or passenger container of a space rocket. **5** A metallic shell, cap, or seal, as of a cartridge or percussion cap. —*v.t.* **1** To furnish with or enclose in or as in a capsule. **2** To summarize. —*adj.* Small and compact; condensed; brief. [<F<L *capsula,* dim. of *capsa* box] —**cap·su·lar** (kap'sə·lər, -syo͞o-) *adj.*

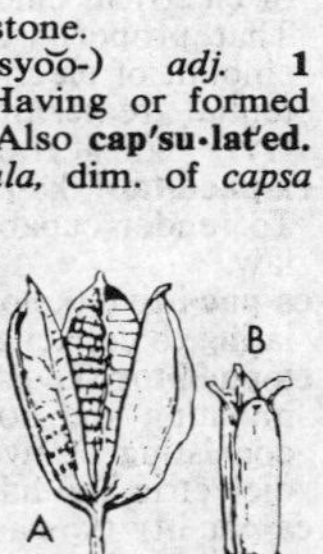

CAPSULES
A. Iris.
B. Carnation.
C. Poppy.

cap·tain (kap'tən, -tin) *n.* **1** One at the head of or in command of others; a chief; leader; comman-

der. **2** The master or commander of a vessel, regardless of rank. **3** In the U.S. Army, Air Force, or Marine Corps, a commissioned officer ranking next above a first lieutenant and next below a major. **4** In the U.S. Navy and Coast Guard, a commissioned officer ranking next above a commander and next below a rear admiral: equal in rank to a colonel in the Army, Air Force, or Marine Corps. See table under GRADE. See synonyms under CHIEF, MASTER. — *v.t.* To be captain over; act as captain to; command; manage; lead. [<OF *capitaine* <LL *capitaneus* <L *caput* head. Doublet of CHIEFTAIN.] — **cap′·tain·cy, cap′tain·ship** *n.*

Captain Lynch Lynch law.

cap·tion (kap′shən) *n.* **1** The title or introductory part of a legal document, showing time, place, circumstances, authority, etc., or a notary's affidavit, endorsed or affixed. **2** A heading of a chapter, section, document, etc. **3** The title of an illustration. **4** The subtitle in a motion picture. **5** *Obs.* Any seizure or capture. — *v.t.* To provide a caption for. [<L *captio*, *-onis* seizure, deception, sophism < *capere* take; in senses 1–4 infl. in meaning by L *caput* head]

cap·tious (kap′shəs) *adj.* **1** Apt to find fault; hypercritical. **2** Perplexing; sophistical. [<L *captiosus* fallacious < *captio* sophism < *capere* take] — **cap′tious·ly** *adv.* — **cap′tious·ness** *n.*
Synonyms: carping, caviling, censorious, critical, cross, cynical, faultfinding, hypercritical. *Antonyms:* appreciative, approving, commendatory, eulogistic, flattering, laudatory.

cap·ti·vate (kap′tə·vāt) *v.t.* **·vat·ed, ·vat·ing** **1** To charm; win; fascinate. **2** *Obs.* To capture; subdue. See synonyms under ALLURE, CHARM. [<L *captivatus*, pp. of *captivare* capture < *captivus* CAPTIVE] — **cap′ti·va′tion** *n.* — **cap′ti·va′tor** *n.*

cap·tive (kap′tiv) *n.* **1** One captured and held in confinement or restraint; a prisoner. **2** One who is held captive in will and feeling. — *adj.* **1** Taken prisoner, as in war; held in confinement or bondage. **2** Charmed or subdued in will or feeling. [<F *captif* <L *captivus* < *capere* take. Doublet of CAITIFF.]

captive audience Any audience which has little or no choice but to watch or listen to something, as a radio broadcast on a public vehicle.

captive balloon See under BALLOON.

cap·tiv·i·ty (kap·tiv′ə·tē) *n.* The state of being held captive; thraldom. See synonyms under BONDAGE.

cap·tor (kap′tər) *n.* One who takes or holds captive.

cap·ture (kap′chər) *v.t.* **·tured, ·tur·ing** **1** To take captive; seize and hold or carry off, as in war. **2** To take possession of; catch; gain; win. See synonyms under ARREST, CATCH. — *n.* **1** A capturing, or being captured. **2** The person or thing captured. [<MF <L *captura* < *capere* take]

Cap·u·a (kap′yo͞o·ə, *Ital.* kä′pwä) A town in southern Italy. — **Cap′u·an** *adj. & n.*

ca·puche (kə·po͞osh′, -po͞och′) *n.* A hood or cowl; especially, that worn by a Capuchin friar: also spelled capouch. [<F <Ital. *cappuccio*, aug. of *cappa* hood]

cap·u·chin (kap′yo͞o·chin, -shin) *n.* **1** A woman's hooded cloak, or hood. **2** A long-tailed South American ceboid monkey (genus *Cebus*) whose head is covered with a cowllike growth of hair. [<Ital. *cappuccino* < *cappuccio*]

Cap·u·chin (kap′yo͞o·chin, -shin) *n.* A member of a branch of the Franciscan order, wearing a habit with a distinctive capuche. [<F <*capuche* CAPUCHE]

Cap·u·let (kap′yə·let, -lit) The family of Juliet, in Shakespeare's *Romeo and Juliet.*

ca·put (kā′pət, kap′ət) *n. pl.* **cap·i·ta** (kap′ə·tə) **1** The head; also, any rounded extremity of an organ; top. **2** *Law* The person; a citizen; one holding civil rights; the status of a citizen before the law. **3** The former governing council of Cambridge University in England. [<L, head]

caput mor·tu·um (môr′cho͞o·əm) *Archaic* Colcothar. [<L, dead head]

cap·y·ba·ra (kap′i·bä′rə) *n.* A South American

rodent (*Hydrochoerus capybara*) about 4 feet long, with coarse, dark brown fur, webbed feet, and a stumpy tail: it frequents the borders of lakes and rivers. [<Sp. *capibara* <Tupian *kapigwara*]

Ca·que·ta (kä′kä·tä′) See JAPURÁ.

car (kär) *n.* **1** A vehicle for use on tracks. **2** Any wheeled vehicle, as an automobile. **3** *Poetic* A chariot. **4** The contents of a car; carload. **5** The cage of an elevator. **6** The basket of a balloon or the like. **7** A floating box for live fish. [<AF *carre* <LL *carra*, var. of *carrus* wagon, ult. <Celtic]

Car (kär) A group of stars in Ursa Major: also called *The Northern Car.*

ca·ra·ba·o (kä′rə·bä′ō) *n. pl.* **·ba·os** or **·ba·o** In the Philippines, a water buffalo. [<Sp. <Malay *karbau*]

car·a·bid (kar′ə·bid) *n.* Any of an extensive family (*Carabidae*) of predatory ground beetles, variously colored and usually nocturnal, including the caterpillar hunters. [< NL <L *carabus* small crab <Gk. *karabos* crayfish]

CARABAO
(5 to 5 1/2 feet high at the shoulder)

car·a·bin (kar′ə·bin), **car·a·bine** (-bīn) See CARBINE.

car·a·bin·eer, car·a·bin·ier (kar′ə·bin·ir′) See CARABINEER.

ca·ra·bi·nie·re (kä′rä·bē·nyä′rā) *n. pl.* **·nie·ri** (-nyä′rē) A member of the Italian military police, recruited from the regular army for a term of five years. [<Ital.]

car·a·cal (kar′ə·kal) *n.* **1** The Persian lynx (*Felis* or *Lynx caracal*) of SW Asia and the greater part of Africa, somewhat larger than a fox, reddish-brown with black-tipped ears. **2** Its pelt or fur. [<F <Turkish *qarah qulaq* < *qarah* black + *qulaq* ear]

Car·a·cal·la (kar′ə·kal′ə), 188–217, Marcus Aurelius Antoninus, Roman emperor 212–217.

ca·ra·ca·ra (kä′rə·kä′rə) *n.* A large, vulturelike hawk of South America: **Audubon's caracara** (*Polyborus cheriway*) sometimes reaches as far north as the southern borders of the United States. [<Sp. <Tupian]

Ca·ra·cas (kə·rä′kəs, -rak′əs; *Sp.* kä·rä′käs) The largest city and capital of Venezuela.

car·ack (kar′ək) *n.* A large Portuguese or Spanish merchant vessel, frequently armed, in use from the 15th to the 17th century: also spelled carrack. [<OF *carraque* <Med. L *carraca*, ? <Arabic *qaraqīr*, pl. of *qorqūr* merchant ship]

car·a·cole (kar′ə·kōl) *n.* A sudden half turn to the right or left made by a horseman in riding; curvet. — *v.* **·coled, ·col·ing** *v.t. Rare* To cause to curvet or half-wheel: He was fond of *caracoling* his horse. — *v.i.* To make or cause one's horse to make caracoles; prance; wheel in line of files, as cavalry. Also **car′a·col** (-kol). [<F <Ital. *caracollo*]

Ca·rac·ta·cus (kə·rak′tə·kəs) British chieftain of about A.D. 50. Also *Welsh* **Ca·rad·oc** (kə·rad′ək).

car·a·cul (kar′ə·kəl) See KARAKUL.

ca·rafe (kə·raf′, -räf′) *n.* A glass water bottle; decanter. [<F, ? <Arabic *gharafa* draw water]

car·a·geen, car·a·gheen (kar′ə·gēn), etc. See CARRAGEEN, etc.

car·a·mel (kar′ə·məl, -mel, kär′məl) *n.* **1** A confection, variously colored and flavored, composed of sugar, butter, and other ingredients. **2** Burnt sugar; the brown or black, soluble material obtained by heating sugar or molasses, or from starch by converting it into glucose: used to color soups, liquids, gravies, and the like. **3** A reddish tan, the color of burnt sugar. [<F, alter. of OF *calemele* <Med. L *calamellus*, alter. of *canna mellis* sugarcane, under the infl. of L *calamus* reed]

car·a·mel·ize (kar′ə·məl·īz′, kär′məl-) *v.t.* **·ized, ·iz·ing** To heat (sugar) slowly until melted and brown. — **car′a·mel·i·za′tion** *n.*

ca·ran·goid (kə·rang′goid) *adj.* Belonging to a family (*Carangidae*) of fishes having a rudimentary dorsal fin, and usually two anal spines

forming a detached portion, as in cavallies, pompanos, etc. — *n.* Any member of this family. [<NL *caranx*, *-angis* <Sp. *carangue* flatfish]

car·a·pace (kar′ə·pās) *n.* **1** *Zool.* The hard bony or chitinous outer case on the back of various animals, as of a turtle or a lobster. **2** Any protective, umbrellalike covering. Also **car′a·pax** (-paks). [<F <Sp. *carapacho*] — **car′a·pa′cic** (-pā′sik) *adj.*

ca·ras·sow (kə·ras′ō) See CURASSOW.

car·at (kar′ət) *n.* **1** A unit of weight for gems: one metric carat is 200 milligrams, or 3.086 grains. **2** Loosely, a karat. ◆ Homophone: carrot. [<F <Ital. *carato* <Arabic *qīrāt* weight of 4 grains <Gk. *keration* seed, small weight]

ca·ra·te (kä·rä′tā) *n.* Pinta.

Ca·ra·vag·gio (kä′rä·väd′jō), **Michelangelo Amerighi da,** 1569–1609, Italian painter.

car·a·van (kar′ə·van) *n.* **1** An Oriental armed company of traders, pilgrims, etc. **2** A traveling company or menagerie. **3** A van; a house on wheels. **4** A company of people traveling together with wagons, pack horses, etc. **5** A train of wagons or pack horses, or of motor vehicles. [<F *caravane* <Persian *kārwān* caravan]

car·a·van·sa·ry (kar′ə·van′sə·rē) *n. pl.* **·ries** **1** A large square building enclosing a court for the shelter of caravans in Oriental countries. **2** A hostelry or inn. Also **car′a·van′se·rai** (-rī, -rā), **car′a·van′se·ry.** [<F *caravansérai* <Persian *kārwānsarāī* <*kārwān* caravan + *sarāī* inn]

car·a·vel (kar′ə·vel) *n.* A fleet vessel of Spain and Portugal in the 15th century: sometimes

CARAVELS
A. The *Santa Maria* of Columbus.
B. A caravel, showing the set of the sails.

spelled carvel. Also **car′a·velle.** [<MF *caravelle* <Sp. *carabela*, dim. of *caraba* boat <L *carabus* <Gk. *korabus*]

car·a·way (kar′ə·wā) *n.* A European biennial herb (*Carum carvi*) of the parsley family: its fruits, called **caraway seeds,** are small, spicy, aromatic seeds used for flavoring food. [<Sp. *alcarahueya* <Arabic *al* the + *karwīyā* caraway <Gk. *karon*]

carb– Var. of CARBO–.

car·ba·mate (kär′bə·māt, kär·bam′āt) *n. Chem.* A salt or ester of carbamic acid containing the univalent NH_2COO radical.

car·bam·ic (kär·bam′ik) *adj. Chem.* Of, pertaining to, or derived from the amide of carbonic acid and the amide radical NH_2.

carbamic acid *Chem.* A theoretical compound, NH_2COOH, known only by its salts and esters.

car·bam·ide (kär·bam′īd, -id, kär′bə·mīd) *n. Chem.* Urea or one of its isomers. Also **car·bam′id** (-id). [<CARB– + AMIDE]

car barn A building or shed for street or railroad cars.

car·ba·zole (kär′bə·zōl) *n. Chem.* A white crystalline compound, $C_{12}H_9N$, derived from coal tar: used in dyes and as a stabilizer in making explosives. [<CARB– + AZOLE]

car·bide (kär′bīd, -bid) *n. Chem.* A compound of carbon with a more positive element: calcium carbide, CaC_2.

car·bine (kär′bīn, -bēn) *n. Mil.* A light, short-barreled rifle originally devised for mounted troops. A magazine-fed, gas-operated carbine weighing about five pounds was adopted in the United States in World War II for certain ranks previously armed with pistols. Also spelled carabin, carabine. [<F *carabine*]

car·bi·neer (kär′bə·nir′) *n.* A soldier armed with a carbine: also spelled carabineer, carabinier.

car·bi·nol (kär′bə·nōl, -nol) *n. Chem.* Methanol. [< G; name given to wood alcohol by Adolf Kolbe, German chemist, 1818–84]
carbo- *combining form* Carbon: *carbohydrate.* Also, before vowels, *carb-.* [< L *carbo* coal]
car·bo·hy·drate (kär′bō·hī′drāt) *n. Biochem.* Any one of a group of compounds containing carbon combined with hydrogen and oxygen in the form of an aldose or a ketose, essential in the metabolism of plants and animals. The carbohydrates include sugars, starches, and cellulose.
car·bo·late (kär′bə·lāt) *n. Chem.* An ester of carbolic acid.
car·bo·lat·ed (kär′bə·lā′tid) *adj.* Carbolized.
car·bol·ic (kär·bol′ik) *adj. Chem.* **1** Of, pertaining to, or derived from carbon and oil. **2** Of or pertaining to coal-tar oil. [< CARB- + L *oleum* oil]
carbolic acid Phenol (def. 2).
car·bo·lize (kär′bə·līz) *v.t.* **·lized, ·liz·ing** *Chem.* To treat or impregnate with carbolic acid.
Car·bo·loy (kär′bə·loi) *n.* A cemented tungsten carbide, just under the diamond in hardness: used for high-speed machine tools: a trade name.
car·bon (kär′bən) *n.* **1** A nonmetallic element (symbol C, atomic number 6) found free as diamond, graphite, and amorphous carbon, and having the property of forming stable rings and long chains which are the basis of millions of organic compounds. See PERIODIC TABLE. **2** *Electr.* A rod of carbon, used as an electrode in an arc light. **3** A piece of carbon paper. **4** A carbon copy. —*adj.* **1** Of, pertaining to, or like carbon. **2** Treated with carbon: *carbon* paper. [< F *carbone* < L *carbo, -onis* coal]
carbon 13 *Physics* A heavy carbon isotope of mass 13, used as a tracer element in the study of physiological processes.
carbon 14 *Physics* Radiocarbon.
car·bo·na·ceous (kär′bə·nā′shəs) *adj.* Of, pertaining to, or yielding carbon.
car·bo·na·do[1] (kär′bə·nā′dō) *n. pl.* **·does** or **·dos** A bird, fish, or piece of meat scored and broiled. —*v.t.* **·doed, ·do·ing** *Obs.* **1** To hack or slash. **2** To score and broil. [< Sp. *carbonada* < *carbón* coal < L *carbo*]
car·bo·na·do[2] (kär′bə·nā′dō) *n. pl.* **·does** Bort. [< Pg., carbonated]
Car·bo·na·ri (kär′bō·nä′rē) *n. pl. of* **Car·bo·na·ro** (-rō) Members of a Neapolitan anti-French secret society of the 19th century. [< Ital. < L *carbonarius* charcoal burner < *carbo* coal] —**Car′bo·na′rism** (-nä′riz·əm) *n.*
car·bon·ate (kär′bə·nāt) *Chem. v.t.* **·at·ed, ·at·ing** **1** To charge with carbonic acid. **2** To carbonize. —*n.* (kär′bə·nāt, -nit) A salt or ester of carbonic acid.
carbon bisulfide Carbon disulfide.
carbon black A deep, smooth, permanent black pigment made of pure carbon: also called *lampblack, ivory black.*
carbon copy **1** A copy of a typewritten letter, etc., made by means of carbon paper. **2** An exact replica; duplicate.
carbon cycle **1** *Physics* A 6-stage thermonuclear process taking place in the interior of stars, by which hydrogen is transformed into helium through the catalytic action of carbon and nitrogen. Compare PROTON-PROTON REACTION. **2** *Biol.* The biological elaboration and destruction in the biosphere of carbon compounds derived from atmospheric carbon dioxide by photosynthesis.
Car·bon·dale (kär′bən·dāl) A city in NE Pennsylvania.
carbon dioxide A heavy, colorless, non-flammable gas, CO_2, formed by the oxidation of carbon, by the interaction of carbonates and acids, and in the respiration of plants and animals. It is irrespirable, extinguishes fire, and is moderately soluble in water.
carbon disulfide *Chem.* A colorless, limpid, volatile, and highly inflammable liquid, CS_2, with a disagreeable odor: used as a solvent for oils, resins, etc., and for the extermination of vermin.
car·bon·ic (kär·bon′ik) *adj.* Of, pertaining to, or obtained from carbon.
carbonic acid *Chem.* A weak, unstable dibasic acid, H_2CO_3, existing only in solution and readily dissociating into water and carbon dioxide.
car·bon·ic-ac·id gas (kär·bon′ik·as′id) Carbon dioxide.
car·bon·if·er·ous (kär′bə·nif′ər·əs) *adj.* Of, pertaining to, containing, or yielding carbon or coal.
Car·bon·if·er·ous (kär′bə·nif′ər·əs) *adj. Geol.* Of or pertaining to a period of the Upper Paleozoic era succeeding the Devonian, characterized by the formation of extensive coal beds. In North America the Carboniferous system of strata is divided into the Mississippian, Pennsylvanian, and Permian series. See chart under GEOLOGY.
car·bon·i·za·tion (kär′bən·ə·zā′shən, -ī·zā′-) *n.* The conversion of organic matter, as wood, into coal or charcoal.
car·bon·ize (kär′bən·īz) *v.t.* **·ized, ·iz·ing** **1** To reduce to carbon; char. **2** To coat with carbon, as paper. **3** To charge with carbon.
carbonized cloth Cloth charred in a vacuum: used for high electrical resistance.
car·bon·iz·er (kär′bən·ī′zər) *n.* Carburetor (def. 1).
carbon monoxide *Chem.* A colorless, odorless gas, CO, formed by the incomplete oxidation of carbon. It burns with a blue flame to form carbon dioxide, and is highly poisonous when inhaled, since it combines with the hemoglobin of the blood to the exclusion of oxygen.
carbon paper Tissue paper so prepared with carbon or other material that it will reproduce on paper underneath a copy of anything impressed upon it, as by pencil or typewriter. Also **carbon tissue.**
carbon process A photographic printing process employing a tissue or film of gelatin colored with a permanent and insoluble pigment. Also **carbon printing.**
carbon tetrachloride *Chem.* A colorless, nonflammable liquid, CCl_4, produced by the action of chlorine on carbon disulfide: used as a solvent, local anesthetic, fire extinguisher, cleaning fluid.
car·bon·yl (kär′bən·il) *n. Chem.* **1** A bivalent organic radical, CO, known only in combination. **2** A compound of a metal and carbon monoxide: nickel *carbonyl.* —**car′bon·yl′ic** *adj.*
carbonyl chloride *Chem.* Phosgene.
car·bo·ra (kär·bôr′ə, -bō′rə) *n.* An Australian worm that bores into timber, as of piers, exposed at low tide. [< native Australian]
Car·bo·run·dum (kär′bə·run′dəm) *n.* An abrasive of silicon carbide: a trade name.
car·box·yl (kär·bok′sil) *n. Chem.* A univalent acid radical, COOH, characteristic of nearly all organic acids. [< CARB(ON) + OX(YGEN) + -YL] —**car·box·yl·ic** (kär′bok·sil′ik) *adj.*
car·box·y·lase (kär·bok′sə·lās) *n. Biochem.* An enzyme found in yeast which splits carbon dioxide from the carboxyl group of amino acids. [< CARBOXYL + -ASE]
car·boy (kär′boi) *n.* A large glass bottle enclosed in a box or in wickerwork: used as a container for corrosive acids, etc. [< Persian *qarāba* demijohn]
car·bun·cle (kär′bung·kəl) *n.* **1** *Pathol.* An inflammation of the subcutaneous tissue, resembling a boil but larger and more painful. **2** A red garnet cut without facets and concave below, to show the color. **3** Any deep red gem. [< AF < L *carbunculus,* dim. of *carbo* coal] —**car·bun·cu·lar** (kär·bung′kyə·lar) *adj.*
car·bu·ret (kär′bə·rāt, -byə·ret) *v.t.* **·ret·ed** or **·ret·ted, ·ret·ing** or **·ret·ting** To carburize; combine chemically with carbon. [< NL *carburetum* carbide] —**car·bu·re·tion** (kär′bə·rā′shən, -byə·resh′ən) *n.*
car·bu·re·tor (kär′bə·rā′tər, -byə·ret′ər) *n.* **1** An apparatus used to charge air or gas with volatilized hydrocarbons to give it illuminating power: also called *carbonizer.* **2** A device for carrying a current of air through or over a liquid fuel, so that the air may take up the vapor to form the explosive mixture, as in internal-combustion engines. **3** A hydrocarbon so used. Also **car·bu·ret·tor** (kär′byə·ret′·ər), **car′bu·ret′ter.**
car·bu·rize (kär′bə·rīz, -byə-) *v.t.* **·rized, ·riz·ing** **1** To combine or impregnate with carbon, as gas to increase its illuminating power. **2** *Metall.* To impregnate the surface layer of (low-carbon steel) with carbon: a stage in casehardening. Also *Brit.* **car′bu·rise.** [< F *carbure* carbide + -IZE] —**car′bu·ri·za′tion** *n.* —**car′bu·riz′er** *n.*
car·byl·a·mine (kär′bil·ə·mēn′, -am′in) *n. Chem.* An organic compound containing the radical -NC.
car·ca·jou (kär′kə·jōō, -zhōō) *n.* The wolverine. [< dial. F (Canadian) < native Algonquian name]
car·ca·net (kär′kə·net) *n.* **1** An ornamental collar or necklace of gold set with jewels. **2** A jeweled circlet formerly worn in the hair. [< F, dim. of *carcan* iron collar worn by prisoners < Med. L *carcanum* < Gmc.] —**car′ca·net′ed** or **car′ca·net′ted** *adj.*
car·cass (kär′kəs) *n.* **1** The dead body of an animal. **2** The human body: a contemptuous or humorous use. **3** Something from which the vital principle, importance, or value has departed; lifeless or worthless remains. **4** A framework or skeleton, as of a construction. Also **car′case.** See synonyms under BODY. [< AF *carcas* < Med. L *carcasium* infl. in form by MF *carcasse* a corpse < Ital. *carcassa*]
Car·cas·sonne (kȧr·kȧ·sôn′) A city in southern France.
car·cel (kär′səl) *n.* The light of a Carcel lamp burning 42 grams of colza oil an hour with a flame 40 millimeters high: a photometric standard, equal to 9.6 international candles. [after B. G. *Carcel,* 1750–1812, French inventor]
Carcel lamp A lamp in which colza oil is constantly pumped up to the wick: used in lighthouses and as a photometric standard.
Car·cha·ri·as (kär·kā′rē·əs) *n.* The typical genus of a family of sharks *(Carcharinidae).* [< NL < Gk. *karcharias* a saw-toothed shark]
Car·che·mish (kär′kə·mish, kär·kē′-) An ancient city of the Hittites in southern Turkey.
car·cin·o·gen (kär′sin′ə·jen) *n.* A cancer-producing substance. —**car·cin·o·gen·ic** (kär′sən·ə·jen′ik) *adj.*
car·ci·no·ma (kär′sə·nō′mə) *n. pl.* **·mas** or **·ma·ta** (-mə·tə) A cancer; a malignant tumor that arises from epithelial cells and spreads by metastasis. [< L < Gk. *karkinoma* < *karkinos* cancer] —**car′ci·nom′a·tous** (-nom′ə·təs, -nō′mə-) *adj.*
card[1] (kärd) *n.* **1** A piece of cardboard bearing, or intended to bear, written or printed words, symbols, etc.: used for social and business purposes. **2** A piece of cardboard imprinted with symbols, for use in certain games of chance and skill: in such use specifically called a **playing card.** **3** *pl.* Any or all games played with playing cards. **4** A small advertisement or published statement printed on a card. **5** A chart giving a table of information, etc. **6** A program or a menu; hence, an authorized announcement of a coming event. **7** *Naut.* The dial of a compass. **8** *Colloq.* A person manifesting some peculiarity: He is a queer *card.* **9** Cardboard. —**on the cards** **1** Listed on the program; scheduled to occur. **2** Possible; likely to happen. —**to put one's cards on the table** To reveal one's intentions or resources with complete frankness. —*v.t.* **1** To fasten or write upon a card or cards. **2** To provide with a card. [< F *carte* < Ital. *carta* card, sheet of paper < L *charta* paper < Gk. *chartēs.* Doublet of CHART.]
card[2] (kärd) *n.* **1** A wire-toothed brush for combining and cleansing wool and other fiber. **2** A similar instrument for currying cattle and horses. —*v.t.* To comb, dress, or cleanse with a card. [< MF *carde* < Ital. *carda* < Med. L < *cardus* < L *carduus* thistle] —**card′er** *n.*
car·da·mom (kär′də·məm) *n.* **1** The fruit of an East Indian or Chinese plant of the ginger family *(Elettaria cardamomum)* having aromatic seeds, used as a condiment. **2** One of the plants yielding this fruit. Also **car′da·mon** (-mən), **car′da·mum.** [< L *cardamomum* < Gk. *kardamōmon* < *kardamon* cress + *amōmon* spice]
card·board (kärd′bôrd′, -bōrd′) *n.* A thin, stiff pasteboard used for making cards, boxes, etc. —*adj.* **1** Made of cardboard. **2** Flimsy; insubstantial.
card·case (kärd′kās′) *n.* **1** A case to hold playing or other cards; specifically, a pocket case for calling cards. **2** In library use, a case of drawers for card catalogs, etc.
card catalog A catalog made out on cards, especially for library books.
Cár·de·nas (kär′thā·näs) A port in western Cuba.
Cár·de·nas (kär′thā·näs), **Lá·za·ro** (lä′sä·rō), 1895–1970, president of Mexico 1934–40.
card file A systematic arrangement of cards containing records or other data.
cardi- -Var. of CARDIO-.

car·di·a (kär′dē·ə) *n. Anat.* The upper orifice of the stomach, where the esophagus discharges. [<Gk. *kardia* heart]

car·di·ac (kär′dē·ak) *Med. adj.* **1** Pertaining to, situated near, or affecting the heart or the cardia. **2** Of, pertaining to, or designating the upper esophageal orifice of the stomach. Also **car·di·a·cal** (kär·dī′ə·kəl). —*n.* **1** One suffering from a heart disease. **2** A cardiac remedy or stimulant; a cordial.

cardiac neurosis *Psychiatry* Abnormal heart action due primarily to nervous disorder or emotional disturbance, without pathological change.

car·di·al·gi·a (kär′dē·al′jē·ə) *n. Pathol.* A burning sensation of the stomach, caused by indigestion; gastric neuralgia; heartburn: once thought to be an affliction of the heart. Also **car′di·al′gy.** [<NL <Gk. *kardialgia* <*kardia* heart + *algos* pain] **—car′di·al′gic** *adj.*

Car·diff (kär′dif) A county borough and port in SE Wales, capital of Glamorganshire.

Cardiff giant A rude statue of gypsum dug up in 1869 near Cardiff, in central New York, exhibited as a prehistoric human fossil, and later proved a hoax.

car·di·gan (kär′də·gən) *n.* A jacket of knitted wool; a sweater opening down the front. Also **cardigan jacket** or **sweater.** [after the seventh Earl of *Cardigan* (1797–1868)]

Car·di·gan (kär′də·gən) A county in western Wales; 693 square miles; capital, Cardigan. Also **Car′di·gan·shire′** (-shir′).

car·di·nal (kär′də·nəl) *adj.* **1** Of prime importance; chief; fundamental; principal. **2** Of a deep scarlet color. **3** Of or relating to a cardinal or cardinals. —*n.* **1** One of the ecclesiastical body of the Roman Catholic Church known as the sacred college, an electoral college by which the Pope is elected and which constitutes his chief advisory council; a prince and senator of the Church. **2** A cardinal bird. **3** A short, hooded cloak worn by women in the 18th century. **4** A deep scarlet, the color of a cardinal's cassock. **5** A dyestuff, derived from magenta, for dyeing cardinal-red. **6** A cardinal number. [<F <L *cardinalis* important <*cardo* hinge] **—car′di·nal·ly** *adv.*

car·di·nal·ate (kär′də·nəl·āt′) *n.* The rank, dignity, or term of office of a cardinal. Also **car′di·nal·ship′.**

cardinal bird A North American bright-red, crested finch (genus *Richmondena*); especially, the common redbird of the eastern United States. Also **cardinal grosbeak.**

cardinal flower A perennial North American herb *(Lobelia cardinalis)* having large red flowers: also called *red lobelia.*

car·di·nal·i·ty (kär′də·nal′ə·tē) *n. Math.* The property of being expressible by a cardinal number, as any finite or restricted series of numbers.

cardinal number See under NUMBER.

cardinal point Any one of the four principal points of the compass.

cardinal sins See SEVEN DEADLY SINS.

cardinal virtues Virtues of the first importance or rank, as the "natural virtues" of ancient philosophy: justice, prudence, temperance, and fortitude; with the "theological virtues," faith, hope, and charity, these form the seven cardinal virtues of medieval and modern writers.

card index An index made out on cards filed in alphabetical order.

card·ing (kär′ding) *n.* **1** The preparing of wool, flax, or cotton fibers before drawing or spinning. **2** Material as it comes from the carding machine.

carding machine A machine for carding cotton, wool, flax, etc., by the action of wire-toothed cylinders. Also **carding engine.**

cardio- *combining form* Heart: *cardiogram.* Also, before vowels, *cardi-.* [<Gk. *kardia* heart]

car·di·o·gram (kär′dē·ə·gram′) *n.* The graphic record of heart movements produced by the cardiograph.

car·di·o·graph (kär′dē·ə·graf′, -gräf′) *n.* An instrument for tracing and recording the force of the movements of the heart. **—car′di·o·graph′ic** *adj.* **—car·di·og·ra·phy** (kär′dē·og′rə·fē) *n.*

car·di·oid (kär′dē·oid) *Math.* A heart-shaped curve generated by a point in the circumference of a circle which rolls on another fixed circle of the same size.

car·di·ol·o·gy (kär′dē·ol′ə·jē) *n.* The science of the heart and its physiology and pathology.

car·di·o·pul·mo·nar·y (kär′dē·ō·po͝ol′mə·ner′ē) *adj.* Pertaining to or affecting the heart and lungs: *cardiopulmonary* resuscitation. Also *cardiorespiratory.*

cardiopulmonary resuscitation (kär′dē·ō·po͝ol′mə·ner·ē, -pul′-) A first-aid method of restoring the heartbeat and breathing by alternately compressing the chest and applying mouth-to-mouth insufflation. Also *CPR.*

car·di·o·res·pi·ra·to·ry (kär′dē·ō·res′pər·ə·tôr·ē, -ri·spīr·ə-) *adj.* Cardiopulmonary.

car·di·ot·o·my (kär′dē·ot′ə·mē) *n. Surg.* Incision of the heart or of the cardiac end of the esophagus.

car·di·o·vas·cu·lar (kär′dē·ō·vas′kyə·lər) *adj.* Pertaining to or affecting the heart and the blood vessels: *cardiovascular* disease.

car·di·tis (kär·dī′tis) *n. Pathol.* Inflammation of the muscular substance of the heart.

car·doon (kär·do͞on′) *n.* A perennial plant of the Mediterranean region *(Cynara carduncullus),* allied to the artichoke and eaten as a vegetable. [<MF *cardon* <Ital. *cardone,* aug. of *cardo* thistle <L *carduus*]

Car·do·zo (kär·dō′zō), **Benjamin Nathan,** 1870–1938, U.S. jurist and author; associate justice, U.S. Supreme Court 1932–38.

cards (kärdz) *n. pl.* **1** Any game played with playing cards. **2** The playing of such a game.

card·sharp (kärd′shärp′) *n.* One who cheats at cards, especially as a profession. Also **card′·sharp′er. —card′sharp′ing** *n.*

car·du·a·ceous (kär′jo͞o·ā′shəs) *adj. Bot.* Of or belonging to the thistle group (formerly the *Carduaceae*) of the composite family, having heavy-headed radiate flowers. [<NL <L *carduus* thistle]

care (kâr) *v.i.* **cared, car·ing 1** To have or show regard, interest or concern as respecting some person, thing, or event. **2** To be wishful or inclined: Do you *care* to read this book? **3** To mind or be concerned; harbor an objection: used chiefly in negative or conditional expressions: I don't *care* if it rains. **—to care for 1** To protect or provide for; guard; watch over. **2** To be interested in or concerned for some person or thing; also, to feel affection for; hold in high regard or esteem. —*n.* **1** A state of oppressive anxiety or concern; solicitude. **2** Responsible charge or oversight. **3** Watchful regard or attention; heed. **4** Any object of solicitude or guardianship. **5** Affliction; distress. [OE *carian*] **—car′er** *n.*

Synonyms (noun): anxiety, attention, caution, charge, circumspection, concern, direction, forethought, heed, management, oversight, perplexity, precaution, prudence, solicitude, trouble, vigilance, wariness, watchfulness, worry. *Care* inclines to the positive, *caution* to the negative; *care* is shown in doing, *caution* largely in not doing. *Precaution* is allied with *care, prudence* with *caution*; a man rides a dangerous horse with *care*; caution may keep him from mounting the horse; *precaution* looks to the saddle girths, bit, and bridle, and all that may make the rider secure. *Circumspection* is watchful observation and calculation, but without the timidity implied in *caution. Concern* denotes a serious interest, milder than *anxiety*; as, *concern* for the safety of a ship at sea. *Heed* implies *attention* without disquiet; it is now largely displaced by *attention* and *care. Solicitude* involves especially the element of personal concern for another not expressed in *anxiety,* and of hopefulness not implied in *care. Watchfulness* recognizes the possibility of danger, *wariness* the probability. A man who is not influenced by *caution* to keep out of danger may display great *wariness* in the midst of it. *Care* has also the sense of responsibility, with possible control, as expressed in *charge, management, oversight*; as, these children are under my *care*; send the money to me in *care* of the firm. Compare ALARM, ANXIETY, OVERSIGHT, PRUDENCE. *Antonyms*: carelessness, disregard, heedlessness, inattention, indifference, neglect, negligence, omission, oversight, recklessness, remissness, slight.

CARE (kâr) A non-profit organization begun after World War II to send food and clothing parcels overseas to the needy. [<C(OOPERATIVE FOR) A(MERICAN) R(EMITTANCES) E(VERYWHERE)]

ca·reen (kə·rēn′) *v.t.* **1** To cause to turn over to one side; heel over, as for repairing or cleaning the bottom of: to *careen* a ship. **2** To clean, repair, or calk (a careened ship.) —*v.i.* **3** To heel over, as a vessel in the wind. **4** To clean, repair, or calk a ship when turned on one side. **5** To lurch or twist from side to side: The car *careened* down the slope. —*n.* **1** The act of inclining a ship to one side. **2** The cleaning or repairing of a ship that is turned over. **3** A careening. [<F *cariner, caréner* <*carène* keel of a ship <L *carina*] **—ca·reen′er** *n.*

ca·reen·age (kə·rē′nij) *n.* **1** The charge for careening. **2** A place where a ship is careened for repairs.

ca·reer (kə·rir′) *n.* **1** A free and swift course; a swift run or charge. **2** A complete course or progress extending through the life or a portion of it, especially when abounding in remarkable actions or incidents: His was a remarkable *career.* **3** A course of business, activity, or enterprise; especially, a course of professional life or employment. **4** A short, rapid gallop or encounter, as in a tournament; a charge; an assault. **5** *Obs.* Originally, a racecourse. —*v.i.* To move with a swift, free, and headlong motion. [<F *carrière* racecourse <LL *carraria (via)* road for carriages <*carrus* wagon] **—ca·reer′er** *n.*

Synonyms (noun): achievement, charge, course, flight, passage, race, rush. Compare BUSINESS.

ca·reer·ist (kə·rir′ist) *n.* A person chiefly or exclusively concerned with advancing himself professionally. **—ca·reer′ism** *n.*

career woman A woman devoted to a business or professional career.

care·free (kâr′frē′) *adj.* Free of troubles; without responsibilities; light-hearted.

care·ful (kâr′fəl) *adj.* **1** Exercising, marked by, or done with care. **2** Attentive and prudent; circumspect. See synonyms under PRECISE, THOUGHTFUL. **—care′ful·ly** *adv.* **—care′ful·ness** *n.*

care·less (kâr′lis) *adj.* **1** Neglectful; indifferent; heedless. **2** Free from solicitude or anxiety; light-hearted. **3** Negligent; unconcerned. **4** Not studied or constrained; easy: a *careless* attitude. See synonyms under CURSORY, IMPROVIDENT, IMPRUDENT, INATTENTIVE, SECURE. **—care′less·ly** *adv.* **—care′less·ness** *n.*

ca·ress (kə·res′) *n.* A gentle, affectionate movement; an expression of affection or attachment by touching, as by patting, embracing, or stroking. —*v.t.* To touch or handle lovingly; fondle; embrace; pet. [<F *caresse* <Ital. *carezza* <L *carus* dear] **—ca·ress′er** *n.* **—ca·ress′ing** *adj.* **—ca·ress′ive** *adj.*

Synonyms (verb): coddle, embrace, flatter, fondle, kiss, pamper, pet. To *caress* is less than to *embrace. Fondling* is always by touch; *caressing* may be also by words, or other tender and pleasing attentions. See PAMPER.

car·et (kar′ət) *n.* A sign (^) placed below a line to denote an omission. [<L, it is missing]

care·tak·er (kâr′tā′kər) *n.* **1** One who takes care of a place, thing, or person. **2** One employed to watch over property or keep it in order, as a house in the absence of its owner, or the property of an insolvent, to see that nothing is removed.

care-worn (kâr′wôrn′) *adj.* Harassed with troubles or worries.

car·fare (kär′fâr′) *n.* The charge for a ride on a bus, streetcar, etc.

car·ga·dor (kär′gə·dôr) *n.* **1** *SW U.S.* A loader and driver of pack animals. **2** In the U.S. Army, the member of a pack train who supervises packers in their duties. [<Sp.]

car·go (kär′gō) *n. pl.* **·goes** or **·gos 1** Goods and merchandise taken on board a vessel; lading. **2** Load. [<Sp. <LL *carricum* load <*carricare* load <*carrus* wagon]

cargo vessel 1 A vessel of the merchant marine, carrying goods or merchandise exclusive of passengers or animals. **2** A naval vessel for transporting goods.

car·hop (kär′hop′) *n. Colloq.* A waiter or waitress at a drive-in restaurant.

Car·i·a (kâr′ē·ə) An ancient region of SW Asia Minor.

Car·ib (kar′ib) *n.* One of a Cariban tribe of Indians formerly found in Brazil, Guiana, Venezuela, and the Lesser Antilles; now surviving in small numbers on the coasts of Guiana, Venezuela, Dominica, Honduras, Guatemala, and Nicaragua. [<Sp. *Caribe* Carib, cannibal <Cariban *caribe* brave]

Car·ib·an (kar′ə·bən) *adj.* Of or pertaining to a linguistic family of South American and Caribbean coastal Indians. — *n.* This family of languages.

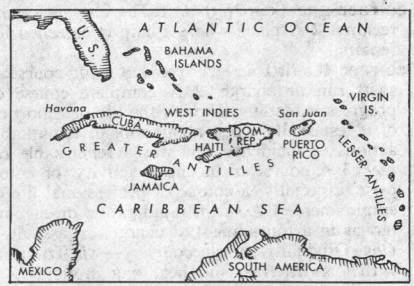

Car·ib·be·an (kar′ə·bē′ən, kə·rib′ē·ən) *n.* A Carib Indian. — *adj.* 1 Of or pertaining to the Caribbean Sea. 2 Of the Carib Indians, their language, culture, etc.

Caribbean Sea An arm of the Atlantic between the West Indies and Central and South America.

car·i·be (kar′ə·bē, *Sp.* kä·rē′bä) *n.* A carnivorous, fresh-water characin fish of tropical South America (genus *Serrasalmo*), with massive jaws and sharp trenchant teeth. They are attracted by blood, and, in schools, will attack man or the larger animals: also called *piranha, piraya.* [<Sp., cannibal]

Car·i·bees (kar′ə·bēz) The Lesser Antilles.

Car·i·boo Mountains (kar′ə·boo) A range of the Rockies in British Columbia, Canada; highest peak, 11,750 feet.

car·i·bou (kar′ə·boo) *n.* The North American reindeer. The **woodland caribou** (*Rangifer caribou*) is found from Maine to Lake Superior and northward, and the smaller and lighter colored (sometimes white) **Barren Grounds caribou** (*R. arcticus*) in the treeless arctic regions. [<Canadian F <Algonquian *khalibu* pawer, scratcher]

CARIBOU
(About 4 feet high at the shoulder)

car·i·ca·ture (kar′i·kə·choor, -chər) *n.* 1 A picture or description deliberately making use of ridiculous exaggeration or distortion; burlesque. 2 The act or art of caricaturing. 3 A poor, inept, or badly distorted likeness or imitation. — *v.t.* **·tured, ·tur·ing** To represent so as to make ridiculous; travesty; burlesque. [<F <Ital. *caricatura,* lit., an overloading <*caricare* load, exaggerate] — **car′-i·ca·tur′al** *adj.* — **car′i·ca·tur′ist** *n.*

Synonyms (noun): burlesque, exaggeration, extravaganza, imitation, mimicry, parody, take-off, travesty.

car·i·es (kâr′ēz, -i·ēz) *n. Pathol.* Ulceration and decay of a bone or of a tooth. [<L]

car·il·lon (kar′ə·lon, kə·ril′yən) *n.* 1 A set of bells so hung and arranged as to be capable of being played upon, either by hand or by machinery, as a musical instrument. 2 A small instrument provided with bells, played upon by means of a pianoforte keyboard. 3 An air arranged for a chime of bells, or any rapid ringing of changes on a chime. — *v.i.* **·lonned, ·lon·ning** To play a carillon. [<F <Med. L *quadrilio, -onis* set of four bells]

car·il·lon·neur (kar′ə·lə·nûr′) *n.* One who plays a carillon. [<F]

ca·ri·na (kə·rī′nə) *n.* *pl.* **·nae** (-nē) *Biol.* In certain plants and animals, a keel or keel-shaped formation. [<L, keel] — **ca·ri′nal** *adj.*

Ca·ri·na (kə·rī′nə) A southern constellation, formerly part of the larger one, Argo Navis:

Canopus is its principal star. See CONSTELLATION.

car·i·nate (kar′ə·nāt) *adj. Biol.* Having a carina; keeled; keel-shaped: said especially of birds having a breastbone. Compare RATITE. Also **car′i·nat′ed.** [<L *carinatus,* pp. of *carinare* supply with a keel]

Ca·rin·thi·a (kə·rin′thē·ə) A province of southern Austria; formerly a duchy; 3,681 square miles; capital, Klagenfurt: German *Kärnten.* — **Ca·rin′thi·an** *adj.* & *n.*

car·i·o·ca (kar′ē·ō′kə) *n.* A South American dance. [See CARIOCAN]

Car·i·o·can (kar′ē·ō′kən) *n.* A resident of Rio de Janeiro, Brazil. Also **Car′i·o′ca.** [from Serra de *Carioca,* a mountain range near the city]

car·i·ole (kar′ē·ōl) *n.* A small carriage: also spelled *carriole.* [<F <Ital. *carriuola,* dim. of *carra* cart, wagon]

car·i·op·sis (kar′ē·op′sis) See CARYOPSIS.

car·i·ous (kâr′ē·əs) *adj.* Affected with caries; decayed. Also **car·ied** (kâr′ēd). See synonyms under ROTTEN. — **car′i·os′i·ty** (-os′ə·tē), **car′·i·ous·ness** *n.*

cark (kärk) *Archaic v.t. & v.i.* To fill or be filled with anxiety: *carked* with care. — *n.* A burden of care. [<AF *carkier,* ult. <L *carricare.* See CHARGE.] — **cark′ing** *adj.*

carl (kärl) *n. Archaic* 1 A rustic. 2 *Scot.* A boor; churl. 3 A feudal serf. Also **carle.** [<ON *karl* man, freeman. Akin to CHURL.]

Carl (kärl) A masculine personal name. [<OHG *karl* freeman]

Carle·ton (kärl′tən), **Guy,** 1724–1808, Baron Dorchester, British general and administrator in America.

carl hemp *Bot.* The seed-bearing or female hemp plant: so named because formerly supposed to be the male. Also **carl.**

car·lie (kär′lē) *n. Scot.* A little man; a precocious boy.

car·lin (kär′lin) *n. Scot.* An old woman.

car·line[1] (kär′lin) *adj.* Of or pertaining to a genus (*Carlina*) of thistles. — *n.* A plant of the genus *Carlina.* [? after *Charlemagne,* whose soldiers were supposedly cured of a plague with it]

car·line[2] (kär′lin) *n.* 1 *Naut.* A short fore-and-aft timber connecting the beams on which the deck of a vessel is laid. 2 One of the cross-pieces supporting the roof boards of a railway car; rafter. Also **car′ling** (-ling). [Cf. F *carlingue*]

Car·lisle (kär·līl′) A city in NW England, county town of Cumberland.

Carl·ist (kär′list) *n.* 1 In France, a supporter of Charles X and his line. 2 In Spain, a supporter of the pretender, Don Carlos de Borbón, 1788–1855, and of his representatives. — **Carl′ism** *n.*

Car·lo (kär′lō) Italian form of CHARLES.

car·load (kär′lōd′) *n.* A minimum load carried by a railroad freight car at a lesser rate (a **carload rate**) than for a smaller shipment: a unit of measure of varying tonnage.

carload lot A freight shipment meeting the official minimum weight for a carload amount.

Car·los (kär′lōs), **Don,** 1788–1855, pretender to the Spanish throne: full name *Carlos María Isidro de Borbón.*

Car·los (kär′lōs) Spanish form of CHARLES.

car·lot (kär′lət) *n. Obs.* A carl or churl; peasant. [<CARL]

Car·lo·ta (kär·lō′tä), 1840–1927, Marie Charlotte Amélie, wife of Maximilian, Archduke of Austria; empress of Mexico 1864–67.

Car·lot·ta (kär·lot′tä) Italian form of CHARLOTTE. Also *Sp.* **Car·lo·ta** (kär·lō′tä).

Car·lo·vin·gi·an (kär′lə·vin′jē·ən) *adj.* Of or pertaining to the dynasty or family of Charlemagne. — *n.* A member of the royal house of Charlemagne or a sovereign in that line. Also called *Caroline, Carolingian.*

Car·low (kär′lō) A county of Leinster province, SE Ireland; 346 square miles; county seat, Carlow.

Carls·bad (kärlz′bad, *Ger.* kärls′bät) See KARLSBAD.

Carls·bad Caverns National Park (kärlz′bad) A series of immense, subterranean limestone caves in SE New Mexico; 77 square miles; established 1930.

Carl·son (kärl′sən), **Anton Julius,** 1875–1956, U.S. physiologist born in Sweden. — **Evans Fordyce,** 1896–1947, U.S. general.

Carls·ruh·e (kärls′rōō′ə) See KARLSRUHE.

Car·lyle (kär·līl′), **Thomas,** 1795–1881, Scottish essayist and historian.

Car·ma·gnole (kär′mən·yōl′, *Fr.* kär·má·nyôl′) *n.* 1 A wild dance and song of the French revolutionists of 1789. 2 The coat and general costume worn by them. 3 A soldier of the French Revolution. [<F, from *Carmagnola,* a town in Piedmont occupied by the revolutionists]

car·man (kär′mən) *n. pl.* **·men** (-mən) 1 One who drives a car. 2 One who drives a cart.

Car·man (kär′mən), **(William) Bliss,** 1861–1929, Canadian poet.

Car·ma·ni·a (kär·mā′nē·ə) The ancient name for KERMAN.

Car·mar·then (kär·mär′thən) A county in southern Wales; 920 square miles; county seat, Carmarthen: also **Car·mar′then·shire** (-shir), **Caer·mar′then.**

Car·mel (kär′məl), **Mount** A mountain in NW Israel; 1,791 feet.

car·mel·ite (kär′məl·īt) *n.* 1 A fine, usually beige or gray, woolen stuff. 2 A variety of pear. [<CARMELITE]

Car·mel·ite (kär′məl·īt) *n.* 1 An inhabitant of Carmel. I *Sam.* xxx 5. 2 A member of the mendicant order of Our Lady of Mt. Carmel (*White Friars*) founded in Syria in 1156. 3 A nun of this order. — *adj.* Of or relating to the Carmelites. — **Car·mel·it·ess** (kär′məl·it′is) *n. fem.*

car·min·a·tive (kär·min′ə·tiv, kär′mə·nā′tiv) *Med. adj.* Tending to relieve flatulence; warming. — *n.* A remedy for flatulence. [<L *carminatus,* pp. of *carminare* cleanse]

car·mine (kär′min, -mīn) *n.* 1 A rich purplish-red color. 2 An impermanent lake pigment prepared from cochineal; rouge. [<F *carmin* <Med. L *carminus,* contraction of *carmesinus* <OSp. *carmesin.* Doublet of CRIMSON.] — **car·min·ic** (kär·min′ik) *adj.*

Car·mo·na (kär·mō′nə), **Antonio Oscar,** 1869–1951, Portuguese general; president of Portugal 1926–51.

car·nage (kär′nij) *n.* 1 Extensive and bloody slaughter; massacre. 2 *Obs.* The bodies of the slain. See synonyms under MASSACRE. [<MF <Ital. *carnaggio* <LL *carnaticum* <L *caro, carnis* flesh, meat]

car·nal (kär′nəl) *adj.* 1 Pertaining to the fleshly nature or to bodily appetites. 2 Sensual; sexual. 3 Pertaining to the flesh or to the body; not spiritual; hence, worldly. See synonyms under BRUTISH. [<LL *carnalis* fleshly <*caro, carnis* flesh] — **car′nal·ist** *n.* — **car·nal·i·ty** (kär·nal′ə·tē) *n.* — **car′nal·ly** *adv.*

car·nal·lite (kär′nəl·īt) *n.* A massive, milk-white, hydrous chloride of magnesium and potassium: an important source of potassium. [after R. von *Carnall,* 1804–74, German mineralogist]

Car·nar·von (kär·när′vən) See CAERNARVON.

car·nas·si·al (kär·nas′ē·əl) *adj.* Adapted for tearing flesh; sectorial: specifically said of the last upper premolar and the first lower molar in carnivores. — *n.* A carnassial tooth. [<F *carnassier* carnivorous <Provençal *carnacier* <*carnaza* flesh <L *caro, carnis* flesh]

Car·nat·ic (kär·nat′ik) A region of SE Madras, India. Also **Kar·nat′ic.**

car·na·tion (kär·nā′shən) *n.* 1 The perennial, herbaceous, fragrant flower of any of the many cultivated varieties of the pink family (genus *Dianthus*), especially the clove pink or scarlet carnation (*D. caryophyllus*): State flower of Ohio. 2 A light pink, bright rose, or scarlet color. 3 *Obs.* In painting, the flesh tints in the human face and figure. [<F, flesh pink <L *carnatio, -onis* fleshiness <*caro, carnis* flesh]

car·nau·ba (kär·nou′bə) *n.* 1 The Brazilian wax palm (*Copernicia cerifera*). 2 The greenish or yellow wax from its leaves, used as a polish and for making phonograph records. [<Pg. <Tupian]

Car·ne·gie (kär·nā′gē, -neg′ē, kär′nə·gē), **Andrew,** 1837–1919, U.S. industrialist and philanthropist born in Scotland.

Carnegie Institution An institution for investigation, research, and discovery, founded at Washington, D.C., 1902, by Andrew Carnegie.

car·nel·ian (kär·nēl′yən) *n.* A clear red chalcedony, often cut as a gem: also spelled *cornelian.* [Earlier *cornelian* <MF *corneline* <Med. L *corneolus, cornelius* chalcedony]

Car·nic Alps (kär′nik) A range of the eastern

Alps along the Austro–Italian border; highest peak, 9,219 feet.

car·ni·fy (kär′nə·fī) v.t. & v.i. **·fied, ·fy·ing** 1 To change to a fleshlike consistency. 2 To form into flesh; grow fleshy. [<L *carnificare* <*caro, carnis* flesh + *facere* make] — **car′·ni·fi·ca′tion** n.

Car·ni·o·la (kär′nē·ō′lə) A former duchy of Austria; 3,845 square miles; since 1947 included in Yugoslavia.

car·ni·val (kär′nə·vəl) n. 1 A period of festival and gaiety immediately preceding Lent, observed in Roman Catholic countries and in some cities in the United States, especially by the Latin peoples. It commonly lasts from three days to a week, Shrove Tuesday being the conclusion, and is marked by street revelry, masking, pageants, and the like. 2 Any gay festival, wild revel, or masquerade. 3 Riotous sport and confusion. 4 A traveling amusement show, with merry–go–round, ferris wheel, side shows, etc. [<Ital. *carnivale* < Med. L *carnelevarium* <L *caro, carnis* flesh + *levare* remove]

Car·niv·o·ra (kär·niv′ə·rə) n. pl. An order of flesh–eating mammals.

car·ni·vore (kär′nə·vôr, -vōr) n. 1 One of the *Carnivora.* 2 An insectivorous plant.

car·niv·o·rous (kär·niv′ə·rəs) adj. 1 Eating or living on flesh. 2 Of or pertaining to the *Carnivora.* [<L *carnivorus* <*caro, carnis* flesh + *vorare* eat, devour] — **car·niv′o·rous·ly** adv. — **car·niv′o·rous·ness** n.

car·nos·i·ty (kär·nos′ə·tē) n. pl. **·ties** Pathol. An abnormal fleshy growth or excrescence upon any bodily organ. [<OF *carnosité* < Med. L *carnositas, -tatis* <*carnosus* fleshy]

Car·not cycle (kär·nō′) Physics. A thermodynamic cycle consisting of four reversible changes in the operation of an ideal heat engine working at maximum efficiency. [after N. L. S. *Carnot,* 1796–1832, French physicist]

car·no·tite (kär′nə·tīt) n. A yellow, earthy vanadate containing potassium, uranium, and slight traces of radium, found in western Colorado: one of the sources of uranium [after M. A. *Carnot,* Inspector General of Mines in France]

car·ob (kar′əb) n. 1 An evergreen tree of the Mediterranean region (*Ceratonia siliqua*). 2 Its long, sickle–shaped, fleshy pods, used for fodder: sometimes called *St. John's bread:* also **carob bean.** [<F *caroube* <Arabic *kharrūbah* bean pods]

ca·roche (kə·rōch′, -rōsh′) n. 1 A carriage of the 16th and 17th centuries. Also **ca·roach′, ca·roch′:** sometimes spelled *carroch.* 2 A carroccio. [<MF *carroche* <Ital. *carroccio,* aug. of *carro* chariot <L *carrus* wagon]

car·ol (kar′əl) v. **·oled** or **·olled, ·ol·ing** or **·ol·ing** v.t. 1 To utter in song, as a bird; sing. 2 To celebrate or praise in song. — v.i. 3 To sing in a cheerful or joyous strain; warble. 4 To sing. — n. 1 A song of joy or praise; especially, a Christmas song. 2 The warbling of birds. 3 Obs. A dance performed in a circle; also, the song accompanying it. See synonyms under SING. [<OF *carole,* prob. <L *choraules* a flutist <Gk. *choraulēs* <*choros* a dance + *aulein* play the flute <*aulos* a flute] — **car′ol·er, car′ol·ler** n.

Car·ol (kar′əl) A masculine or feminine personal name. [<Med. L *Carolus*]

— **Carol II,** 1893–1953, king of Rumania 1930–40; abdicated.

Car·o·le·an (kar′ə·lē′ən) adj. Of, or pertaining to the furniture and decoration of the period of Charles II of England. [<Med. L *Carolus* Charles]

Car·o·let·ta (kar′ə·let′ə) Latin form of CHARLOTTE.

Car·o·li·na (kar′ə·lī′nə) An English colonial settlement, divided in 1729 into what is now North and South Carolina. — adj. Of, pertaining to, or from North or South Carolina.

Carolina dove The mourning dove.

Carolina parrot An extinct American parakeet (*Conuropsis carolinensis*), native to the Carolinas.

Carolina pink The pinkroot.

Carolina potato The common sweet potato.

Car·o·li·nas (kar′ə·lī′nəs), **the** 1 North and South Carolina. 2 The Caroline Islands.

Car·o·line (kar′ə·lin, -lin; *Fr.* kȧ·rō·lēn′; *Dan.*.

Ger. kä′rō·lē′nə) A feminine personal name. Also **Car′o·lyn,** *Ital., Sp.* **Ca·ro·li·na** (kä′rō·lē′nä). [<F]

— **Caroline Amelia Elizabeth,** 1768–1821, British queen; wife of George IV.

— **Caroline Wilhelmina,** 1683–1737, British queen; wife of George II.

Car·o·line (kar′ə·lin, -lin) adj. 1 Pertaining to Charles I and II of England and their times, or to Charles I of Spain. 2 Carlovingian. [<Med. L *Carolinus* < *Carolus* Charles]

Caroline Island A British possession in the Line Islands. Formerly **Thorn·ton Island** (thôrn′tən).

Caroline Islands An island group east of the Philippines, comprising part of the United Nations Trust Territory of the Pacific Islands; 510 square miles; Japanese mandate, 1919–1944; formerly **New Philippines:** administered as the **Western Carolinas,** capitals, Palau and Yap; and the **Eastern Carolinas,** capitals, Ponape and Truk: also *the Carolinas.* Also **the Car′o·lines.**

Car·o·lin·gi·an (kar′ə·lin′jē·ən) See CAR-LOVINGIAN.

Car·o·lin·i·an (kar′ə·lin′ē·ən) adj. 1 Of or pertaining to North Carolina or South Carolina. 2 Carlovingian. — n. A native or naturalized citizen of North or South Carolina.

car·o·lus (kar′ə·ləs) n. pl. **·lus·es** or **·li** (-lī) An ancient English gold coin of the value of about twenty shillings. [<Med. L, *Charles*]

Car·o·lus (kar′ə·ləs) Latin form of CHARLES.

car·om (kar′əm) v.t. To cause to make a glancing movement: He *caromed* one ball off the other. — v.i. To make a glancing movement: The car *caromed* off the wall. — n. 1 In billiards, the impact of one ball against two others in succession, or the stroke producing it. 2 In other games, the glancing of one object from another: in England, this word has been altered to *cannon.* Also spelled *carrom.* [<F *carambole*]

Ca·ro·ní (kä′rō·nē′) A river of SE Venezuela, flowing 430 miles NW to the Orinoco.

car·o·tene (kar′ə·tēn) n. Biochem. A deep-yellow or red crystalline hydrocarbon, $C_{40}H_{56}$, which acts as a plant pigment: it occurs also in various animal tissues, and is changed in the body to vitamin A. Also **car′o·tin** (-tin): sometimes spelled *carrotin.* [<L *carota* carrot]

ca·rot·e·noid (kə·rot′ə·noid) n. Biochem. One of a large variety of nitrogen–free, light-yellow to deep–red lipochrome pigments found in plant and animal tissues. Also **ca·rot′i·noid.**

ca·rot·id (kə·rot′id) adj. Anat. Of, pertaining to, or near one of the two major arteries on each side of the neck. Also **ca·rot′i·dal.** [<Gk. *karōtides,* pl. <*karoein* stupefy; so called from the belief that pressure on them would cause unconsciousness]

ca·rotte (ka·rot′) n. A roll of tobacco; especially, the perique tobacco of Louisiana. [<F, carrot]

ca·rou·sal (kə·rou′zəl) n. A jovial feast or banquet; boisterous or drunken revelry. See synonyms under FROLIC.

ca·rouse (kə·rouz′) v.i. **ca·roused, ca·rous·ing** To drink deeply, freely, and jovially; engage in a carousal. — n. 1 A carousal. 2 Obs. The draining of a full bumper of liquor. See synonyms under FROLIC. [<G *gar aus (trinken)* (drink) all out] — **ca·rous′er** n.

car·ou·sel (kar′ə·sel′, -zel′) n. 1 A merry–go-round. 2 A tournament, tilting match, or military pageant. Also spelled *carrousel.* [<F *carrousel* <Ital. *carosello* tournament]

carp¹ (kärp) v.i. To find fault unreasonably; complain; cavil. [<ON *karpa* boast] — **carp′·er** n.

carp² (kärp) n. pl. **carp** or **carps** 1 A fresh-water food fish (*Cyprinus carpio*), originally of China but now widely distributed in Europe and America. 2 Any of various other cyprinoid fishes, as dace, minnows, and goldfish. [<OF *carpe* <LL *carpa*]

–carp combining form Fruit; fruit (or seed) vessel: *pericarp.* [Gk. *karpos* fruit]

car·pal (kär′pəl) adj. Anat. Of, pertaining to, or near the wrist. — n. A carpal bone. [<NL *carpalis* <L *carpus* wrist <Gk. *karpos*]

car·pa·le (kär·pā′lē) n. pl. **·li·a** (-lē·ə) Anat. A bone of the carpus or wrist; especially, one articulating with the metacarpal bones. [<NL, neut. of *carpalis* CARPAL]

Car·pa·thi·an Mountains (kär·pā′thē·ən) A range of central and eastern Europe, enclosing the Great Hungarian Plain; highest peak, 8,737 feet. Also the **Car·pa′thi·ans.**

Car·pa·tho·U·kraine (kär·pā′thō·yoō·krān′) See RUTHENIA.

car·pe di·em (kär′pē dī′em) Latin Enjoy the present; seize today's opportunities; literally, seize the day.

car·pel (kär′pəl) n. Bot. A simple pistil or seed vessel. See illustration under FRUIT. Also **car·pel·lum** (kär·pel′əm). [<NL *carpellum* <Gk. *karpos* fruit] — **car·pel·lar·y** (kär′pə·ler′ē) adj.

car·pel·late (kär′pə·lāt) adj. Bot. Possessing, or like, carpels.

Car·pen·tar·i·a (kär′pən·târ′ē·ə), **Gulf of** An arm of the Arafura Sea indenting the NE coast of Australia.

car·pen·ter (kär′pən·tər) n. An artificer who builds with timber or wood, as in the construction of houses, ships, and other wooden structures. — v.t. To make by carpentry. — v.i. To work with wood. [<AF *carpentier* <LL *carpentarius* carpenter, wagon–maker <L *carpentum* two–wheeled carriage] — **car′pen·ter·ing** n. — **car′pen·try** n.

Car·pen·ter (kär′pən·tər), **John Alden,** 1876–1951, U.S. composer.

carpenter bee A large, hairy, solitary bee (genus *Xylocopa*) that bores tunnels in wood for its nest, as *X. violacea* of Europe or *X. virginica* of the United States.

carpenter moth A large, light–brown moth (*Prionoxystus robiniae*), with two blue horizontal bars on its wings, whose larvae, called **carpenter worms,** bore beneath the bark of certain trees.

car·pet (kär′pit) n. 1 A heavy ornamental floor covering; also, the fabric used for it. 2 Any smooth surface upon which one may walk. — **on the carpet** Colloq. Subjected to reproof or reprimand. — v.t. To cover with or as with a carpet. [<OF *carpite* <LL *carpita* thick woolen covering < *carpere* pluck]

car·pet·bag (kär′pit·bag′) n. A handbag for travelers; especially, one made of carpeting.

car·pet·bag·ger (kär′pit·bag′ər) n. A person traveling with all his possessions in a carpet-bag: said originally of unscrupulous itinerant bankers of the West; later, of political or profit–seeking adventurers who infested the South after the Civil War. Compare SCAL-AWAG. — **car′pet·bag′ger·y, car′pet·bag′gism** n.

carpet beetle A beetle (*Attagenus piceus*) whose reddish–brown larvae are destructive of carpets, woolen fabrics, and animal products. Also called *buffalo bug.* See illustration under INSECTS (injurious). Also **carpet bug.**

car·pet·ing (kär′pit·ing) n. 1 Material or fabric used for carpets; carpets collectively. 2 The act of covering with, or as with, a carpet.

carpet knight One knighted for other than military achievements; a stay–at–home soldier: used contemptuously.

car·pet–sweep·er (kär′pit·swē′pər) n. A hand-operated apparatus for sweeping carpets: when pushed over the floor a revolving brush sweeps the dirt into a dustpan.

carpet weed A procumbent North American herbaceous annual (*Mollugo verticillata*), the leaves of which, clustered in whorls, form mats on the ground.

car·phol·o·gy (kär·fol′ə·jē) n. Pathol. A delirious, automatic picking at the bedclothes in forms of low fever. [<Gk. *karphologia* < *karphos* straw + *legein* pick, collect]

–carpic combining form See –CARPOUS.

carp·ing (kär′ping) adj. Censorious; fault-finding. — **carp′ing·ly** adv.

carpo– combining form Fruit: *carpology.* [<Gk. *karpos* fruit]

car·pog·e·nous (kär·poj′ə·nəs) adj. Bot. Fruit-producing: said of the cell or groups of cells from which the spores are formed in certain algae. [<CARPO- + -GENOUS]

car·po·go·ni·um (kär′pə·gō′nē·əm) n. pl. **·ni·a** (-nē·ə) Bot. The female organ of certain algae; especially, in the red algae, the carpogenous

cell or cells of the procarp which, after fertilization, develop a sporocarp. [<CARPO- + -GONIUM] — **car′po·go′ni·al** *adj.*

car·pol·o·gy (kär·pol′ə·jē) *n.* That department of botany which treats of fruits in general. [<CARPO- + -LOGY] — **car·po·log·i·cal** (kär′·pə·loj′i·kəl) *adj.* — **car·pol′o·gist** *n.*

car·poph·a·gous (kär·pof′ə·gəs) *adj.* Frugivorous; fruit-eating. [<CARPO- + -PHAGOUS]

car·po·phore (kär′pə·fôr, -fōr) *n. Bot.* **1** In flowering plants, a portion of the receptacle prolonged between the carpels, as in the geraniums and many umbelliferous plants. **2** In fungi, any fruit-bearing structure or organ.

car·port (kär′pôrt′, -pōrt′) *n.* A roof projecting from the side of a building, used as a shelter for motor vehicles.

-carpous *combining form* Having a certain kind or number of fruits: *acrocarpous.* Also *-carpic.* [<Gk. *karpos* fruit]

car·pus (kär′pəs) *n. pl.* **·pi** (-pī) **1** *Anat.* The wrist. **2** *Zool.* A part analogous to or like a wrist. [<NL <Gk. *karpos* wrist]

Car·rac·ci (kär·rät′chē) A family of Italian painters: **Agostino,** 1557–1602; **Annibale,** 1560–1609; **Ludovico,** 1555–1619.

car·rack (kar′ək) See CARACK.

car·ra·geen (kar′ə·gēn) *n.* A small, purplish, edible marine alga *(Chondrus crispus)*, the Irish moss of commerce: used in medicine as a demulcent. Often spelled *carageen, carageen, carrigeen.* Also **car′ra·gheen.** [from *Carragheen,* near Waterford, Ireland]

Car·ran·za (kär·rän′sä), **Ve·nus·tia·no** (vā′·nōō·styä′nō), 1859–1920, president of Mexico 1915–20; assassinated.

Car·ra·ra (kə·rä′rə, *Ital.* kär·rä′rä) A city in central Italy; famous for the white marble quarried nearby.

Car·rel (kə·rel′, kar′əl), **Alexis,** 1873–1944, French surgeon and physiologist, active in the United States.

car·rell (kar′əl) *n.* A small space, as among the stacks in a library, for solitary study. Also **car′rel.** [Var. of CAROL]

Car·rère (kə·râr′), **John Merven,** 1858–1911, U.S. architect.

car·re·ta (kä·rā′tə) *n. SW U.S.* A long, narrow cart. [<Sp.]

car·riage (kar′ij) *n.* **1** A wheeled vehicle for carrying persons. **2** That which carries something, as in a machine. **3** Transportation; the charge for, or cost of, carrying. **4** Deportment; bearing. **5** The carrying of a besieged place. **6** The act of carrying. **7** Execution; management; control. **8** *Obs.* That which is carried. **9** *Obs.* Import; meaning. Compare BEHAVIOR. See synonyms under AIR, MANNER. [<AF *cariage* < *carier* CARRY]

carriage dog A Dalmatian.

carriage trade The wealthy patrons of a restaurant, theater, etc.: so called because of the former association of wealth with private carriages.

car·rick bend (kar′ik) *Naut.* A knot used for joining two hawsers, etc.

carrick bitt *Naut.* One of the two vertical posts on a ship's deck that support the ends of a windlass.

Car·rick·fer·gus (kar′ik·fûr′gəs) A port and municipal borough of County Antrim in eastern Northern Ireland.

Car·rick-on-Shan·non (kar′ik·on·shan′ən) The county town of County Leitrim, Ireland.

Car·rie (kar′ē) Diminutive of CAROLINE, CATHERINE.

car·ried (kar′ēd) Past tense and past participle of CARRY.

car·ri·er (kar′ē·ər) *n.* **1** One who or that which carries; hence, a person or company that undertakes to carry persons or goods for hire, as a railroad company, etc.; also, one who carries or delivers messages, letters, etc. **2** A carrier pigeon. **3** A conduit. **4** *Chem.* A material used as an intermediary or vehicle, as a catalytic agent acting to transfer an element between compounds. **5** *Mech.* A device or attachment that conveys, drives, moves, or supports something. **6** A ship for carrying aircraft. **7** *Bacteriol.* One who is immune to a disease but transmits it to others by carrying the bacteria in his body. **8** A carrier wave. — **common carrier** A person or company that undertakes to carry persons or goods for pay when called to do so, whether by land, air, or water, and that is liable for all loss or damage during transportation except such losses as arise from natural causes.

carrier pigeon A homing pigeon.

carrier wave *Telecom.* The current, wave frequency, or voltage transmitted in various forms of electrical communication; especially, in radio, the wave which is subjected to amplitude or frequency modulation.

car·ri·ole (kar′ē·ōl) See CARIOLE.

car·ri·on (kar′ē·ən) *n.* Dead and putrefying flesh; a carcass. — *adj.* **1** Feeding on carrion. **2** Like or pertaining to carrion; putrefying. [<AF *caroigne,* ult. <L *caro, carnis* flesh]

carrion crow **1** The common crow *(Corvus corone)* of Europe. **2** The black vulture *(Coragyps atratus)* of the southern United States, Mexico, and Central America.

car·ritch (kar′ich) *n. Scot.* A catechism; catechizing. [Alter. of CATECHISM]

car·roc·cio (kär·rôt′chō) *n. pl.* **·ci** (-chē) *n. Italian* The great car or chariot on which the standard of any of the medieval Italian republics was borne in battle: also *caroche.*

car·roch (kə·rōch′, -rōsh′) See CAROCHE.

Car·roll (kar′əl), **Charles,** 1737–1832, American patriot; signed the Declaration of Independence. — **Lewis** See DODGSON. — **Paul Vincent,** 1900–1968, Irish playwright.

car·rom (kar′əm) See CAROM.

car·ro·ma·ta (kär′rō·mä′tä) *n.* In the Philippines, a light, narrow, two-wheeled, covered vehicle, usually pulled by a single horse. [<Sp. *carromato* < *carro* cart]

car·ro·nade (kar′ə·nād′) *n.* Formerly, a short, chambered ordnance piece of large caliber and short range. [from the *Carron* ironworks, Scotland]

car·ron oil (kar′ən) A mixture of limewater and linseed oil: used for treating burns. [from the *Carron* ironworks, Scotland]

car·rot[1] (kar′ət) *n.* **1** The long, reddish-yellow, edible root of an umbelliferous plant *(Daucus carota).* **2** The plant itself. ◆ Homophone: *carat.* [<F *carotte* <L *carota* <Gk. *karōton*]

car·rot[2] (kar′ət) *v.t.* To brush (furs) with a mercury and nitric acid solution, in order to prepare the fibers for the operations of matting and felting: so called from the yellowish color of the furs when dried. ◆ Homophone: *carat.* [<CARROT[1]] — **car′rot·ing** *n.*

car·ro·tin (kar′ə·tin) See CAROTENE.

car·rot·y (kar′ət·ē) *adj.* **1** Like a carrot. **2** Having red hair.

car·rou·sel (kar′ə·sel′, -zel′) See CAROUSEL.

car·ry (kar′ē) *v.* **·ried, ·ry·ing** *v.t.* **1** To bear from one place to another; transport; convey. **2** To have or bear upon or about one's person or in one's mind. **3** To serve as a means of conveyance or transportation: The wind *carries* sounds. **4** To lead; urge; move; influence: Love for art *carried* him abroad. **5** To win; capture. **6** To bear up; sustain; hold in position: The ship *carries* sail well. **7** To conduct (oneself) or demean (oneself); behave. **8** To transfer, as a number or figure, to another column, or, as in bookkeeping, from one account book to another. **9** To have or keep on hand: We *carry* a full stock. **10** To win, as an election; win the support of. **11** To be pregnant with. **12** To bear, as crops, or sustain, as cattle. **13** To give support to, as evidence; corroborate; confirm. **14** To extend; continue: He *carries* this farce too far. **15** In golf, to cover or pass, as a distance or object, in one stroke. **16** In hunting, to follow or trail by scent. **17** *U.S. Dial.* To conduct; escort. — *v.i.* **18** To act as bearer or carrier: fetch and *carry.* **19** To have or exert impelling or propelling power: The rifle *carries* nearly a mile. **20** To hold the head and neck habitually in a given manner: The horse *carries* well. **21** In falconry, to fly off with the game. — **to carry all before one** To meet with unimpeded and uniform success. — **to carry arms** **1** To belong to the army. **2** To bear weapons. **3** To hold a weapon in a prescribed position against the shoulder. — **to carry away** **1** To move the feelings greatly; enchant, as with passion or rapture. **2** To break off, as from a ship; lose by breaking off in a collision or gale. — **to carry forward** **1** To progress or proceed with. **2** In bookkeeping, to transfer, as an item, to the next column or page. — **to carry off** **1** To cause to die. **2** To win, as a prize or honor. **3** To face consequences boldly; brazen out. **4** To abduct. — **to carry on** **1** To keep up; keep going; continue. **2** To behave in a free, frolicsome manner. **3** To perpetuate; continue, as a tradition. — **to carry out** To accomplish; bring to completion. — **to carry over** **1** In bookkeeping, to repeat, as an item, on another page or in another column. **2** To influence to join the opposed party. — **to carry through** **1** To carry to completion or success. **2** To sustain or support to the end. — *n. pl.* **·ries** **1** A portage, as between navigable streams; also, the act of carrying, as a canoe, luggage, etc. **2** The range of a gun or a projectile; also, the distance covered by a projectile, as a golf ball. **3** *Mil.* The position of carry arms, or carry swords, etc. [<AF *carier* <LL *carricare* <L *carrus* cart. Doublet of CHARGE.]

Synonyms (verb): bear, bring, convey, lift, move, remove, sustain, take, transmit, transport. A person may *bear* a load when either in motion or at rest; he *carries* it only when in motion. The stooping Atlas *bears* the world on his shoulders; swiftly moving Time *carries* the hourglass and scythe; a person may be said either to *bear* or to *carry* a scar, since it is upon him whether in motion or at rest. If an object is to be *moved* from the place we occupy, we say *carry*; if to the place we occupy, we say *bring.* A messenger *carries* a letter to a correspondent, and *brings* an answer. *Take* is often used in this sense in place of *carry*; as, *take* that letter to the office. *Carry* often signifies to *transport* by personal strength, without reference to the direction; as, that is more than he can *carry*; yet even so, it would not be admissible to say *carry* it to me, or *carry* it here; in such case we must say *bring.* To *lift* is simply to raise an object from its support, if only for an instant, with no reference to holding or moving; one may be able to *lift* what he cannot *carry.* The figurative uses of *carry* are very numerous; as, to *carry* an election, *carry* the country, *carry* (in the sense of *capture*) a fort, *carry* an audience, *carry* a stock of goods, etc. Compare CONVEY, KEEP, SUPPORT. *Antonym*: drop.

car·ry-all (kar′ē·ôl′) *n.* **1** A one-horse, four-wheeled covered vehicle. **2** A closed automobile having two seats arranged lengthwise and facing each other. [Alter. of CARIOLE]

carrying charge In instalment buying, the interest charged on the unpaid balance.

car·ry-o·ver (kar′ē·ō′vər) *n.* **1** The item or entry in bookkeeping repeated from the bottom of one page to the top of the next. **2** The remainder of a crop, supply of stock, etc., to be disposed of along with the next crop or lot.

carse (kärs, kers) *n. Scot.* A stretch of intervale along a river; alluvial land.

car-sick (kär′sik′) *adj.* Nauseated from riding in a car or train.

Car·so (kär′sō) A limestone plateau in NW Yugoslavia and Trieste: German *Karst. Serbo-Croatian* **Kras** (kräs).

Car·son (kär′sən), **Christopher,** 1809–68, U.S. frontiersman: known as *Kit Carson.* — **Edward Henry,** 1854–1935, Baron Carson of Duncairn, English jurist and statesman.

Car·son City (kär′sən) The capital of Nevada.

Car·stensz (kär′stənz), **Mount** The highest peak in New Guinea and the highest island peak in the world, in west central New Guinea; about 16,400 feet.

cart (kärt) *n.* **1** A heavy two-wheeled vehicle, for carrying loads. **2** A light two-wheeled pleasure vehicle with springs. **3** Loosely, any two- or four-wheeled vehicle. — *v.t.* To convey or carry in or as in a cart. — *v.i.* To drive or use a cart. [OE *cræt*] — **cart′er** *n.*

cart·age (kär′tij) *n.* The act of or price charged for carting.

Car·ta·ge·na (kär′tə·jē′nə, *Sp.* kär′tä·hā′nä) **1** A port in SE Spain. **2** A port in northern Colombia on the **Bay of Cartagena,** an arm of the Caribbean.

carte[1] (kärt) *n.* **1** A card or paper. **2** *Scot.* A playing card. **3** A bill of fare. [<F, card]

carte[2] (kärt) See QUARTE.

Carte (kärt), **Richard D'Oy·ly** (doi′lē), 1844–1901, English theatrical impresario.

carte blanche (kärt′ blänsh′, *Fr.* kȧrt bläṅsh′) *n. pl.* **cartes blanches** (kärts′ blänsh′, *Fr.* kȧrt bläṅsh′) **1** An authorization signed in blank to be filled in at discretion. **2** Unrestricted authority. [<F, white card]

carte de vi·site (kärt′ də vē·zēt′) *pl.* **cartes**

de visite (kärt) **1** A visiting card. **2** A small photograph on a card formerly used as a visiting card. [< F]

car·tel (kär·tel′, kär′təl) *n.* **1** A written official agreement between governments, especially when at war, as for the exchange of prisoners. **2** A written challenge to single combat. **3** An international combination of independent enterprises in the same branch of production, aiming at a monopolistic control of the market by means of weakening or eliminating competition. Compare MONOPOLY, SYNDICATE, TRUST. **4** An agreement among states to maintain mutually beneficial customs rates or otherwise act as a unit for a common purpose. See ANSCHLUSS. [< F < Ital. *cartello,* dim. of *carta* paper]

Car·ter (kär′tər), **Howard,** 1873–1939, English archeologist. **—Jimmy (James Earl),** born 1924, 39th president of the United States, 1977–81.

Car·ter·et (kär′tər·it), **John,** 1690–1763, first Earl Granville, English statesman.

Car·te·sian (kär·tē′zhən) *adj.* Of or pertaining to René Descartes, a French philosopher and geometer of the 17th century, or to his doctrines and methods. *—n.* A follower of Descartes, or believer in his doctrines. [< NL *Cartesianus* < *Cartesius,* Latinized form of *Descartes*] **—Car·te′sian·ism** *n.*

Cartesian coordinate system *Geom.* **1** A plane system for indicating the curve of an equation graphically by means of two axes, graduated in both directions from the origin: when intersecting at right angles, the coordinates are called *rectangular,* when intersecting at any angle other than 90°, the coordinates are called *oblique.* **2** A three-dimensional system for indicating the shape of a solid by means of three planes intersecting at right angles to each other at a point called the origin: from the three points of reference required, any point in space with coordinates *x, y,* and *z* can be located. See illustration under OCTANT. Also called *rectangular coordinate system.*

Cartesian devil A hollow figure partly filled with air, and immersed in water in a glass jar, the jar being provided with an elastic cover, by pressure upon which the immersed figure is made to sink, rising again when the pressure is removed: sometimes called *bottle imp.* Also **Cartesian diver, Cartesian imp.**

Car·thage (kär′thij) An ancient city-state in North Africa near modern Tunis; destroyed by the Romans in 146 B.C. Ancient **Car·tha·go** (kär·thā′gō, -tä′-).

Car·tha·gin·i·an (kär′thə·jin′ē·ən) *adj.* Of or pertaining to Carthage. *—n.* A native or inhabitant of Carthage.

Carthaginian peace A peace on drastically severe terms: so called in allusion to the Roman destruction of Carthage (146 B.C.).

Carthaginian Wars See PUNIC WARS in table under WAR.

Car·thu·sian (kär·thōō′zhən) *n.* A monk or nun of the order founded in 1086 in Chartreuse in the French Alps. *—adj.* Of or pertaining to the order of Carthusians. [< Med. L *Cartusianus* < *Carturissium* Chartreuse]

Car·tier (kär·tyā′), **Sir George Etienne,** 1814–1873, Canadian statesman. **—Jacques,** 1491–1557, French navigator; discoverer of the St. Lawrence River 1535.

car·ti·lage (kär′tə·lij) *n Biol.* **1** A tough, elastic supporting tissue in animals, composed of cells embedded in an opalescent matrix, either homogeneous or fibrous; gristle. **2** A structure or part consisting of cartilage. [< MF < L *cartilago* gristle]

car·ti·lag·i·nous (kär′tə·laj′ə·nəs) *adj.* **1** Of or like cartilage; gristly. **2** Having a gristly skeleton, as sharks.

Car·tist (kär′tist) *n.* A supporter of the Constitution in Spain or Portugal. [< Sp. *carta* charter]

cart·load (kärt′lōd′) *n.* **1** As much as a cart will hold. **2** The contents of a cart.

car·to·gram (kär′tə·gram) *n.* A map giving statistical information by means of comparative diagrams. [< F *cartogramme*]

car·tog·ra·phy (kär·tog′rə·fē) *n.* The science, technology, or art of drawing or compiling, maps or charts. [< *carto-* map (< L *charta*) + -GRAPHY] **—car·to·graph** (kär′tə·graf, -gräf) *n.* **—car·tog′ra·pher** *n.* **—car′to·graph′ic** or **·i·cal** *adj.*

car·ton (kär′tən) *n.* **1** A pasteboard box. **2** Pasteboard. **3** A white disk within the bull's-eye of a target or a shot striking it. [< F. See CARTOON.]

car·toon (kär·tōōn′) *n.* **1** A drawing or caricature as in a newspaper or periodical; especially, one intended to affect public opinion as to some matter or person. **2** A sketch for a fresco or mosaic. **3** A comic strip. **4** A motion-picture film, called an **animated cartoon,** made by photographing a series of carefully prepared black-and-white or colored drawings, each representing a further stage in the action of the film, which is usually synchronized for sound effects and music. See synonyms under PICTURE. *—v.t.* To make a caricature or cartoon of; satirize pictorially. *—v.i.* To make cartoons. [< F *carton* < Ital. *cartone* pasteboard, aug. of *carta* card < L *charta* paper] **—car·toon′ist** *n.*

car·toph·i·ly (kär·tof′ə·lē) *n. U.S.* The collecting of illustrative cards, as those enclosed in packages of retail goods: a humorous term. [< *carto-* card (< F *carte*) + Gk. *philia* < *phileein* love] **—car·toph′i·list** *n.*

car·touche (kär·tōōsh′) *n.* **1** An oblong or oval figure containing the name of a king, queen, or deity, as on ancient Egyptian monuments and papyri. **2** *Archit.* An ornamental tablet or scroll with inscription or emblem; a scroll-shaped bracket, etc. **3** A cartridge; a cartridge box; an ammunition bag. **4** The case containing the inflammable materials in some fireworks. **5** *Astron.* A curve exhibiting the varying visibility of an object, as of a canal on Mars. Also **car·touch′.** [< F < Ital. *cartoccio,* aug. of *carta* card < L *charta* paper]

car·tridge (kär′trij) *n.* **1** An explosive charge for a pistol, rifle, machine gun, or other small arm, consisting of primer, gunpowder, cardboard or metal case, and projectile or projectiles. **2** *Phot.* A roll of protected sensitized films. **—blank cartridge** A cartridge containing powder but no projectile. [Alter. of CARTOUCHE]

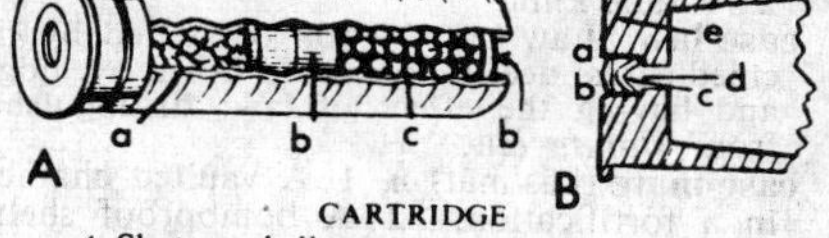

CARTRIDGE

A. Shotgun shell.
a. Powder. *b., b.* Wads. *c.* Shot.
B. Section of center-fire metallic rifle or pistol cartridge case.
a. Primer–cup. *b.* Percussion composition.
c. Anvil. *d.* Vent. *e.* Base of case.

cartridge belt A belt having loops or pockets for cartridges or cartridge clips.

cartridge clip Clip[1] (def. 6).

car·tu·lar·y (kär′chōō·ler′ē) *n. pl.* **·lar·ies** **1** A collection or a register of charters, etc., as of a monastery. **2** An officer in charge of such records. Also spelled *chartulary.* [< LL *cartularium*]

cart·wheel (kärt′hwēl′) *n.* **1** *U.S. Colloq.* A silver dollar. **2** *Aeron.* A flight maneuver which causes an airplane to rotate about its long axis while describing an inverted U in the air: a variation of the half-roll. **3** A lateral handspring.

Cart·wright (kärt′rīt), **Edmond,** 1743–1823, English clergyman and inventor of the power loom, etc. **—Thomas,** 1535–1603, English Puritan clergyman.

ca·ru·ca (ka·rōō′kə) *n.* **1** A plow. **2** A plow team of four oxen or horses yoked abreast. [< Med. L *carruca* a plow]

car·u·cage (kar′ə·kij) *n.* In old English law, a tax imposed on every plow or on every carucate.

car·u·cate (kar′ə·kāt) *n.* A Norman measure of land: the amount of land that could be plowed in a year and a day by one caruca, usually about 120 acres.

car·un·cle (kar′ung·kəl, kə·rung′-) *n.* **1** *Zool.* A fleshy excrescence, as a cock's comb. **2** *Bot.* A protuberant growth of the seed coat at or near the hilum. Also **ca·run·cu·la** (kə·rung′kyə·lə). [< MF < L *caruncula,* dim. of *caro, carnis* flesh] **—ca·run·cu·lar** (kə·rung′kyə·lər) or **·late** (-lit, -lāt) or **·lous** (-ləs) *adj.*

Ca·ru·so (kə·rōō′sō, *Ital.* kä·rōō′zō), **Enrico,** 1873–1921, Italian operatic tenor.

car·va·crol (kär′və·krōl, -krol) *n. Chem.* A colorless, oily, aromatic liquid, $C_{10}H_{14}O$, obtained from origan, camphor, thyme, and other plants of the mint family: used in perfumery and in medicine as an antiseptic. [< F *carvi* caraway + L *acer, acris* biting + -OL]

carve (kärv) *v.* **carved, carv·ing** *v.t.* **1** To cut figures or designs upon. **2** To make by cutting or chiseling. **3** To cut up, as cooked meat; divide. *—v.i.* **4** To make carved work or figures. **5** To cut up cooked meat served at table. See synonyms under CUT. *—n.* A cut or stroke in carving. [OE *ceorfan*] **—carv′er** *n.*

car·vel (kär′vəl) *n.* A caravel. [See CARAVEL]

car·vel-built (kär′vəl·bilt′) *adj. Naut.* Built with carvel joints: distinguished from *clinker-built.* See illustration under CLINKER-BUILT.

carvel joint *Naut.* A flush joint, as of two planks or plates in a vessel's side.

carv·en (kär′vən) *adj. Poetic* or *Archaic* Wrought by carving or graving; carved.

Car·ver (kär′vər), **George Washington,** 1864?–1943, U.S. Negro scientist. **—John,** 1575–1621, English Pilgrim father; first governor of Plymouth Colony.

Carver chair A type of early American chair with turned posts and spindles, and usually having a rush seat: named for one owned by John Carver.

carv·ing (kär′ving) *n.* **1** The act of one who carves. **2** That which is carved; sculpture.

Car·y (kâr′ē), **Alice,** 1820–71, U.S. poet and novelist. **—Henry Francis,** 1772–1844, English clergyman and poet. **—Phoebe,** 1824–71, U.S. poet, sister of Alice. **—Joyce,** 1889–1957, English novelist.

car·y·at·id (kar′ē·at′·id) *n. pl.* **·ids** or **·i·des** (-ə·dēz) *Archit.* A supporting column in the form of a sculptured female figure. [< L *Caryatis,* -*ides* < Gk. *Karyiatis* a priestess of Artemis at Karyai, town of Laconia, Greece] **—car·y·at·i·dal** (kar′ē·at′ə·dəl), **car·y·at·i·de·an** (kar′ē·at′ə·dē′·ən), **car·y·a·tid·ic** (kar′ē·ə·tid′ik) *adj.*

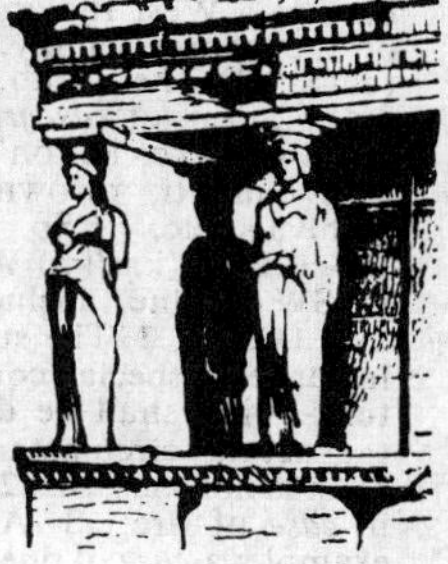

CARYATIDS

caryo- See KARYO-.

car·y·o·ki·ne·sis (kar′·ē·ō·ki·nē′sis) See KARYOKINESIS

car·y·o·phyl·la·ceous (kar′ē·ō·fi·lā′shəs) *adj. Bot.* **1** Pertaining or belonging to a family *(Caryophyllaceae)* of herbs, the pink family, characterized by stems enlarged at the nodes, opposite entire leaves, and perfect or rarely dioecious flowers: also called *silenaceous.* **2** Having a tubular calyx with five long-clawed petals. [< NL < Gk. *karyophyllon* < *karyon* nut + *phyllon* leaf]

car·y·op·sis (kar′ē·op′sis) *n. pl.* **·op·ses** (-op′sēz) or **·op·si·des** (-op′sə·dēz) *Bot.* A seedlike fruit, as the grains of wheat and rye: also spelled *cariopsis.* [< Gk. *karyon* nut + Gk. *opsis* appearance]

car·y·o·tin (kar′ē·ō′tin) See KARYOTIN.

Ca·sa·ba (kə·sä′bə) *n.* A winter variety of muskmelon with sweet white flesh and yellow rind: also spelled *Cassaba.* Also **Casaba melon.** [from *Kasaba,* a town in western Turkey]

Cas·a·blan·ca (kas′ə·blang′kə, kä′sə·bläng′kə) A port and the largest city of Morocco: Arabic *Dar-el-beida.*

Cas·a Gran·de National Monument (kas′ə·gran′dē) A region of prehistoric ruins in southern Arizona, including **Casa Grande,** an adobe watchtower built in 1350; established as a national park in 1918.

Ca·sals (kä·säls′), **Pablo,** 1876–1973, Spanish violoncellist, conductor, and composer.

Cas·a·no·va (kas′ə·nō′və, kaz′-; *Ital.* kä′sä·nō′vä), **Giovanni Giacomo,** 1725–98, Italian adventurer, known for his *Memoirs*: full surname *Casanova de Seingalt.*

Ca·sau·bon (kə·sô′bən, *Fr.* kȧ·zō·bôn′), **Isaac,**

1559–1614, French scholar and theologian.
ca·sa·va (kə·sä′və) See CASSAVA.
Cas·bah (käz′bä) The native quarter of Algiers or of other cities with a large Arab population. Also spelled *Kasbah.*
cas·ca·bel (kas′kə·bel) *n.* **1** A knob or breeching loop behind the breech of a cannon, to facilitate handling. **2** A rattlesnake or its rattle. Also **cas′ca·ble** (-bəl). [<Sp.]
cas·cade (kas·kād′) *n.* **1** A fall of water over steeply slanting rocks, or one of a series of such falls. **2** Anything resembling a waterfall, as the lace trimming of a dress. **3** *Chem.* A connection in series of two or more electrolytic cells or tanks so arranged as to produce a flow of the electrolyte from higher to lower levels. **4** *Physics* A successive operation, as cooling a gas by utilizing the effect of a previously expanded gas. —*v.i.* **·cad·ed, ·cad·ing** To fall in the form of a waterfall; form cascades. [<F <Ital. *cascata* <*cascare* fall <L *cadere*]
cascade amplification *Electronics* An amplifying system in which two or more vacuum tube units are connected to form a number of stages, each stage deriving its input from the output of the one preceding.
cascade control *Electr.* A method of turning street lights on and off in sections, each section being controlled by the energizing and de-energizing of preceding sections.
Cascade Range A range of mountains in Oregon, Washington, and British Columbia; highest peak, 14,408 feet.
cas·car·a buckthorn (kas·kâr′ə) A buckthorn (*Rhamnus purshiana*) of the NW United States: its bark yields **cascara sa·gra·da** (sə·grā′də), used as a laxative: also called *bearwood.* Also **cas·car′a.** [<Sp. *cáscara* bark]
cas·ca·ril·la (kas′kə·ril′ə) *n.* **1** The aromatic bark of a West Indian shrub (*Croton eluteria*) of the spurge family, sometimes used as a tonic. **2** The shrub. Also **cascarilla bark.** [<Sp., dim. of *cáscara* bark]
cas·ca·ron (kas′kə·rōn′) *n.* An eggshell filled with confetti, thrown by revelers at balls, carnivals, etc. [<Sp. *cascarón* eggshell]
Cas·co Bay (kas′kō) An inlet of the Atlantic in SW Maine, including Portland Harbor.
case[1] (kās) *n.* **1** The state of things in a given instance; a special condition of affairs; juncture: What shall be done in this *case*?; also, the actual circumstance; the fact or facts: Such is not the *case.* **2** An event; contingency: in *case* of fire. **3** A particular instance or example: a *case* of pneumonia; a *case* of fraud. **4** *Law* A cause of action; a suit; an action. **5** State; physical condition or situation; plight. **6** *Gram.* **a** The syntactical relationship of a noun, pronoun, or adjective to other words in a sentence, as indicated, generally, in inflected languages, by declensional endings or, in non-inflected languages, by prepositions and word order. **b** The form of a word indicating this relationship. **c** These relationships or forms as a group. Evidence would indicate that primitive Indo-European had eight cases—nominative, genitive, dative, accusative, ablative, instrumental, locative, and vocative. See SUBJECTIVE, POSSESSIVE, and OBJECTIVE for the cases surviving in Modern English. **7** *Colloq.* A peculiar or exceptional person. See synonyms under EVENT, PRECEDENT, SAMPLE. —**in any case** No matter what; regardless. —**in case** In the event that; if. [<F *cas* <L *casus* event <*cadere* fall; the grammatical cases (def. 6) were thought of as "falling" from the nominative]
case[2] (kās) *n.* **1** A box, sheath, bag, or other covering in which something is or may be kept. **2** A box and the quantity or number contained in it; a set. **3** *Printing* A tray, with compartments for holding type. Cases are commonly made in pairs, called **upper** or **cap case,** for capital letters, and **lower case,** for small letters, respectively. **4** The frame or casing for a door, window, etc., or a hollow box beside a casing, as for sash weights. **5** *Archit.* An outer facing of a building, as of stone over brick. **6** The cavity in the upper anterior part of the head of a sperm whale containing the spermaceti. **7** In bookbinding, a binding or cover made separately. **8** *Her.* The skin of an animal. **9** *Obs.* The clothes of a person; also, the exterior, in any sense. **10** *Obs.* A brace or pair, as of pistols. —*v.t.* **cased, cas·ing 1** To cover with a case; incase. **2** *Slang* To look over; inspect. **3** *Obs.* To flay. [<AF *casse* <L *capsa* box <*capere* take, hold]
ca·se·ase (kā′sē·ās) *n. Biochem.* A tryptic enzyme of bacterial origin which dissolves casein and hastens ripening in cheese. [<CASE(IN) + -ASE]
ca·se·ate (kā′sē·āt) *v.i.* **·at·ed, ·at·ing** To become cheesy; undergo caseation. [<L *caseatus* mixed with cheese <*caseus* cheese]
ca·se·a·tion (kā′sē·ā′shən) *n.* **1** Conversion into cheese or curd; coagulation. **2** *Pathol.* Caseous degeneration, as of the tissues.
ca·se·fy (kā′sə·fī) *v.t.* & *v.i.* **·fied, ·fy·ing** To make or become like cheese. [<L *caseus* cheese]
case·hard·en (kās′här′dən) *v.t.* **1** *Metall.* To harden by carburizing the surface of (iron), followed by quenching. **2** To make callous or insensible to influences, especially good influences.
case history The record of an individual, as made and filed by hospitals, social agencies, insurance companies, etc., giving the salient facts on health, family, financial condition, economic and social status.
ca·se·in (kā′sē·in, -sēn) *n. Biochem.* A phosphoprotein found especially in milk, constituting the principal ingredient in cheese: a white friable substance of acid character, used in preparing cotton cloth for calico printing, as an adhesive in certain varieties of cement, and as an important ingredient in plastics and synthetic resins. [<L *caseus* cheese] —**ca·se·ic** (kā′sē·ik) *adj.*
ca·se·in·o·gen (kā′sē·in′ə·jen, kā·sē′nə-) *n.* The casein-bearing protein of milk. [<CASEIN + -GEN]
case knife 1 A knife provided with a sheath. **2** A table knife.
case law Law based upon or settled by decided cases; decisions handed down by judges and having the effect of law: distinguished from *statute law.*
case·mate (kās′māt) *n.* **1** A vaulted chamber in a fortification. **2** A bombproof shelter from which guns fire through openings, or an armored bulkhead on shipboard, with openings for guns. [<F <Ital. *casamatta,* ? <Gk. *chasmata,* pl. of *chasma* opening] —**case′·mat′ed** *adj.*
case·ment (kās′mənt) *n.* **1** The sash of a window when arranged to open on hinges at the side, or a window arranged with such sashes. **2** A case; covering; incasement. [<OF *encassement*] —**case′ment·ed** *adj.*
Case·ment (kās′mənt), **Sir Roger,** 1864–1916, Irish patriot, hanged by the British for treason.
ca·se·ose (kā′sē·ōs) *n. Biochem.* An intermediary product in the hydration of caseins, either artificial or in the digestive process: one of the proteoses. [<L *caseus* cheese]
ca·se·ous (kā′sē·əs) *adj.* Of, pertaining to, or like cheese; cheesy.
ca·sern (kə·zûrn′) *n.* A barrack of soldiers in a garrison town. Also **ca·serne′.** [<F *caserne* <Sp. *caserna* small hut <L *quaterna* four each]
Ca·ser·ta (kä·zer′tä) A town in Campania, southern Italy.
case shot An assortment of small shot, as shrapnel or canister, enclosed in a metal case.
case system A system of teaching law in which selected cases form the basis for study, supplemented by textbooks.
case·work (kās′wûrk′) *n.* The investigation and guidance by a social worker of the cases of maladjusted individuals and families. —**case′·work′er** *n.*
case·worm (kās′wûrm′) *n.* A caddis worm.
Ca·sey Jones (kā′sē jōnz′), 1864–1900, John Luther Jones, U.S. railroad hero who died in a train wreck.
cash[1] (kash) *n.* **1** Current money in hand or readily available. **2** Money paid down; immediate payment: five percent discount for *cash.* See synonyms under MONEY. —*v.t.* To convert into ready money, as a check; give or receive money for. —**to cash in 1** In gambling, to turn in one's chips and receive cash. **2** *U.S. Slang* To die. —**to cash in on** To turn to advantage; make a profit from. [<F *caisse* cash box, cash <Ital. *cassa* <L *capsa* box] —**cash′a·ble** *adj.*
cash[2] (kash) *n. pl.* **cash** Any of various little coins used as small change in parts of the East Indies and China; especially, a Chinese coin made of copper and lead, with a square hole in the middle. [<Pg. *caixa* <Tamil *kāsu* small coin]
cash·a (kash′ə) *n.* A soft woolen fabric similar to flannel, with an admixture of Cashmere goat's hair. [Prob. <CASHMERE]
cash-and-car·ry (kash′ən·kar′ē) *adj.* Operated on a system of cash purchase and no delivery.
ca·shaw (kə·shô′) *n.* **1** The honey mesquite. **2** The cushaw. [Var. of CUSHAW]
cash basis A system of bookkeeping that includes only cash receipts as income and only cash payments as expense: opposed to *accrual basis.*
cash·book (kash′bo͝ok′) *n.* A book devoted to a cash account.
cash discount A discount from the purchase price allowed the purchaser provided he pays within a stipulated period.
cash·ew (kash′o͞o, kə·sho͞o′) *n.* **1** A tropical American tree (genus *Anacardium*) now naturalized in Africa and Asia. **2** Its small, kidney-shaped, edible fruit, the **cashew nut.** [<F *acajou* <Tupian *acajoba*]
cash·ier[1] (ka·shir′) *n.* **1** A custodian of money; especially, one who has charge of the receipts, disbursements, cash on hand, etc., of a banking or mercantile house. **2** A paymaster. [<F *caissier* <*caisse.* See CASH[1].]
cash·ier[2] (ka·shir′) *v.t.* **1** To dismiss in disgrace, as a military officer. **2** To discard. See synonyms under BREAK. [<Du. *casseren* <F *casser* <LL *cassare* annul and L *quassare* destroy]
cashier's check A check drawn by a bank's cashier upon its own funds.
cash·mere (kash′mir) *n.* **1** A fine wool obtained from Cashmere goats. **2** A soft fabric made from this or similar wool. **3** A dress, shawl, etc., made of cashmere. [from *Kashmir,* India]
Cash·mere (kash·mir′, kash′mir) See KASHMIR.
Cashmere goat A variety of goat originally native in Kashmir.
cash on delivery Immediate cash payment to the bearer on delivery of goods: abbr. *C.O.D.*
ca·shoo (kə·sho͞o′) See CATECHU.
cash register An automatic mechanical device with keyboard, for recording, adding, and displaying the amount of cash placed in its money drawer.
cas·i·mere, cas·i·mire (kas′ə·mir) See CASSIMERE.
cas·ing (kā′sing) *n.* **1** That with which a thing or place is incased or lined, as a wall of firebrick on the door of a kiln. **2** The framework around a door or window. **3** The outer covering or shoe of an automobile tire. **4** *pl.* The intestines of cattle, hogs, etc., cleaned and salted for use as sausage containers. [<CASE[2]]
ca·si·no (kə·sē′nō) *n.* **1** A room or building for public amusement, dancing, gambling, etc. **2** In Italy, a summerhouse, or the like; also, a house built in imitation of the Italian casino. **3** A game of cards for from two to four players: also spelled *cassino.* [<Ital., dim. of *casa* house]
Ca·si·quia·re (kä′sē·kyä′rā) A river in southern Venezuela, flowing 140 miles SW, linking the Orinoco and Amazon basins.
cask (kask, käsk) *n.* **1** A barrel-shaped wooden vessel or receptacle, made of staves, hoops, and flat heads. A cask for liquor or liquids may be larger or smaller than a barrel, and is usually of heavier material. **2** The quantity a cask will hold. **3** *Obs.* A casket. ◆ Homophone: *casque.* [<Sp. *casco* skull, potsherd, cask, ? ult. <L *quassare* break. Related to *casque.*]
cas·ket (kas′kit, käs′-) *n.* **1** A small box or chest, as for jewels or other valuables. **2** A coffin. —*v.t.* To enclose in or as in a casket. [<F *cassette* <*casse* chest; form infl. by CASK]
Cas·lon (kaz′lən) *n.* A style of type created by the English type founder **William Caslon,** 1692–1766.
Cas·par Milque·toast (kas′pər milk′tōst′) A creation by H. T. Webster, U.S. cartoonist, of a painfully timid man; hence, any apologetic or non-assertive person; a milksop.
Cas·per (kas′pər) A masculine personal name. Also **Cas′par.** [? <Persian, master of the treasure]
Cas·per (kas′pər) A city in central Wyoming.

Cas·pi·an Sea (kas′pē·ən) The largest salt-water lake and inland sea in the world, between SE Europe and SW Asia in the U.S.S.R. and Iran; 163,800 square miles.

casque (kask) *n.* **1** Any piece of armor to cover the head. **2** A helmet. **3** A helmet-like protuberance, as the bony crest of a cassowary or the horny process of a hornbill. ◆ Homophone: *cask.* [<F, ult. <L *quassare.* Related to CASK.] **— casqued** (kaskt) *adj.*

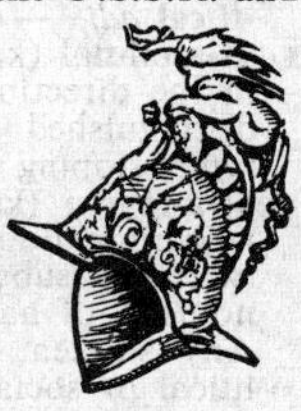

CASQUE
Surmounted by a crest.

cas·quette (kas·ket′) *n.* A woman's brimless hat. [<F, dim. of *casque* helmet]

Cass (kas), **Lewis,** 1782–1866, U.S. statesman.

Cas·sa·ba (kə·sä′bə) See CASABA.

Cas·san·dra (kə·san′drə) In Greek mythology, a daughter of Priam whose prophecies were fated by Apollo always to be true but never to be believed; hence, anyone who utters unheeded prophecies of disaster.

cas·sa·reep (kas′ə·rēp) *n.* A condiment made from the juice of the cassava plant. [<F *cassiry* <Tupian *cachiri*]

cas·sa·tion (ka·sā′shən) *n.* **1** The act of making null or abrogating, as a judgment or decree. **2** *Music* A composition in several movements, similar to a suite. [<F <LL *cassatio, -onis* < *cassare* annul <L *cassus* empty]

Cas·satt (kə·sat′), **Mary,** 1855–1926, U.S. painter.

cas·sa·va (kə·sä′və) *n.* **1** One of several tropical American shrubs or herbs (genus *Manihot*), cultivated for their edible roots; especially, the sweet cassava *(M. dulcis)* and the bitter cassava *(M. exculens)*; manioc. **2** A starch made from the roots of these plants, valued as the source of tapioca. Also spelled *casava.* [<F *cassave* <Taino *casavi*]

casse (kas) *n.* A darkening in the color of wines due to the chemical action of excess iron or copper. [<F, a breaking]

Cas·se·grain·i·an (kas′ə·grā′nē·ən) *adj. Astron.* Describing a type of reflecting telescope which employs a hyperbolic mirror inside the prime focus to form an image which passes through an aperture in the primary mirror at the bottom of the tube. [after N. *Cassegrain,* 17th c. French physician, who invented it in 1672]

Cas·sel (kas′əl, *Ger.* käs′əl) See KASSEL.

cas·se·role (kas′ə·rōl) *n.* **1** A saucepan. **2** A baking dish of earthenware, glass, etc., in which food may be baked and served: food so served is said to be **en casserole.** **3** A dish with a handle used by chemists. [<F]

cas·sette (kə·set′, ka-) *n.* **1** *Photog.* A light-proof magazine for holding a sensitized plate or film in a camera or X-ray device. **2** *Electronics* A cartridge containing magnetic tape for the storage of audio or video material, as for use in a tape recorder or television receiver. [<F, lit., small box]

cas·sia (kash′ə) *n.* **1** A coarse variety of cinnamon, especially that obtained from the bark of *Cinnamomum cassia*: also **cassia bark.** **2** The tree yielding it. **3** Any of a large genus *(Cassia)* of shrubs or herbs of the senna family. **4** A medicinal product of a plant of the genus *Cassia*; especially, the laxative pulp obtained from the pods of *C. fistula* of the East Indies. Compare SENNA. [<L <Gk. *kasia* <Hebrew *qetsi'ah* < *qātsa'* strip off bark]

cas·si·mere (kas′ə·mir) *n.* A woolen cloth for men's wear: also called *kerseymere*: also spelled *casimere, casimire.* [<F *casimir* cashmere]

cas·si·no (kə·sē′no) See CASINO (def. 3).

Cas·si·no (kə·sē′nō, *Ital.* käs·sē′nō) A town in central Italy; site of Benedictine **Monte Cassino Abbey** and scene of German resistance to the Allied advance on Rome in World War II, 1943–44.

cas·si·o·ber·ry (kas′ē·ō·ber′ē) *n. pl.* **·ries** **1** The shining black edible drupe of a North American shrub *(Viburnum obovatum).* **2** The yaupon or its fruit. [<N. Am. Ind.]

Cas·si·o·do·rus (kas′ē·ō·dō′rəs), **Flavius Magnus Aurelius,** died 575? A.D., Roman statesman and historian.

Cas·si·o·pe·ia (kas′ē·ə·pē′ə) **1** In Greek mythology, the wife of Cepheus and mother of Andromeda. **2** A constellation near the north pole: from the arrangement of its five brightest stars in the form of an irregular W, also called **Cassiopeia's Chair.** See CONSTELLATION.

cas·sis (kä·sēs′) *n.* **1** The black currant of Europe. **2** A cordial made from black currants. [<F]

cas·sit·e·rite (kə·sit′ə·rīt) *n.* A tetragonal, brown to black tin dioxide, SnO_2: the most important ore of tin. [<Gk. *kassiteros* tin]

Cas·sius Lon·gi·nus (kash′əs lon·jī′nəs), **Gaius,** died 42 B.C. Roman general, conspirator against Caesar.

cas·sock (kas′ək) *n.* **1** A close-fitting garment, reaching to the feet, worn by the Roman Catholic and many of the Protestant clergy. **2** A short garment or loose jacket worn under the Geneva gown by Presbyterian ministers. **3** A clergyman or the clerical office. **4** *Obs.* Any long coat or gown; especially, a military cloak. [<MF *casaque* <Ital. *casacca* greatcoat] **— cas·socked** (kas′əkt) *adj.*

cas·so·ne (käs·sô′nā) *n. Italian* A large chest, usually with painted, carved, or inlaid decoration.

cas·so·war·y (kas′ə·wer′ē) *n. pl.* **·war·ies** A large, three-toed, ratite bird of Australia and New Guinea (genus *Casuarius*), related to the emu. [<Malay *kasuāri*]

cast (kast, käst) *v.* **cast, cast·ing** *v.t.* **1** To throw with force; drive by force, as from the hand or from an engine; fling; hurl. **2** To place as if by throwing; put with violence or force, as by the sea or wind: The waves *cast* us on the beach. **3** To throw up, as with a shovel: to *cast* a mound of earth. **4** To throw down; defeat; especially with the feet upward: He *cast* his enemy to the ground. **5** To deposit; give: He *cast* his vote. **6** To draw by chance; throw, as dice. **7** To cause to fall upon or over; throw in a particular direction; emit: *cast* a shadow. **8** To throw out or forth; get rid of. **9** To let down; put out; let drop: to *cast* anchor. **10** To abandon or shed, as in the process of growth; molt. **11** To give birth to, especially prematurely; drop: The mare *cast* her foal. **12** *Metall.* To shape in a mold; make a cast of; found. **13** To stereotype or electroplate. **14** To assign roles, as in a play; to assign to a part. **15** To add; total, as a column of figures. **16** To calculate mathematically: He *cast* his horoscope. **17** *Law* To defeat in a suit. **18** To winnow, as grain, by throwing in the air. **19** To reject; discard; disqualify: to *cast* horses for bad temper. **20** In falconry, to place upon the perch. **21** *Naut.* To turn, as a ship, to another course. **— *v.i.*** **22** To revolve something in the mind; scheme; consider: to *cast* about for a solution. **23** To anticipate; forecast; conjecture. **24** *Metall.* To take shape in a mold, as metal. **25** To add up a column of figures; make a computation: with *up.* **26** To throw a fish line. **27** *Naut.* To turn from the wind; fall off, as in getting under way; to tack; put about. **28** To warp, as timber. **29** In hunting, to make a detour or run, as a dog, in search of a lost scent or trail. **30** To swarm, as bees. **— to cast about** **1** To consider ways and means; scheme. **2** To warp; tack. **— to cast away** To discard; reject. **— to cast down** **1** To overthrow; destroy. **2** To cause to feel dejection; discourage; depress. **— to cast off** **1** To reject or discard. **2** To let go, as a ship from a dock. **— *n.*** **1** The act of throwing or casting: a *cast* of a fly in angling. **2** A throw of dice; also, the number or total thrown. **3** The distance to which a thing may be thrown: a stone's *cast.* **4** Anything that is thrown out or off, as an insect's skin, the dung of an earthworm, the undigested matter ejected from the stomach of an owl or hawk. **5** In angling, a leader, sometimes including the flies. **6** An object founded or run in or as in a mold, as of metal, plaster, wax, etc. **7** *Pathol.* A morbid substance molded as in one of the urinary tubules: a renal *cast.* **8** A stereotype or electrotype plate. **9** A reverse copy, in plaster of Paris or similar material, of a mold: usually distinguished from a *casting,* which is of iron or other metal or alloy. **10** The material run into molds at one operation. **11** An impression as of a harder in a softer body: a *cast* of a man's face. **12** An impressed form of the inner surface of an animal or plant, either of the bony outline or particularly of the organs of an animal: distinguished from *mold.* **13** A characteristic formation or inclination; also, stamp; type; kind; sort. **14** Shade; dash; tinge: white, with a bluish *cast.* **15** A twist or perversion; warp; squint. **16** The distribution of parts to performers in a play; also, the performers collectively. **17** In hunting, a detour in search of the scent. **18** A stroke or turn: a *cast* of one's skill. **19** A pair of hawks or other birds. **20** A course or change in a course. **21** A forecast or conjecture. **22** A contrivance; scheme. **23** A look; turning of a glance in a certain direction. ◆ Homophone: *caste.* [<ON *kasta* throw]

Cas·ta·li·a (kas·tā′lē·ə) A fountain on Mount Parnassus, near Delphi, sacred to Apollo and the Muses, and supposed to give inspiration to those who drank of it. Also **Cas·ta·ly** (kas′tə·lē). **— Cas·ta′li·an** *adj.*

cas·ta·net (kas′tə·net′) *n.* One of a pair of small concave disks of wood or ivory, clapped together with the fingers, as an accompaniment to song or dance. [<Sp. *castañeta,* dim. of *castaña* <L *castanea* chestnut]

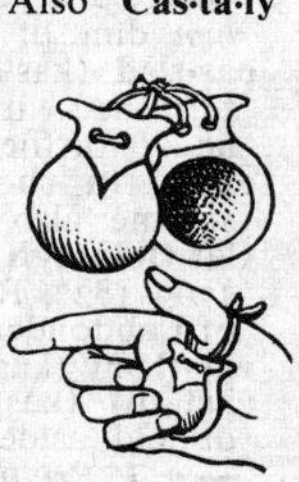

CASTANETS

cast·a·way (kast′ə·wā′, käst′-) *adj.* **1** Adrift; shipwrecked. **2** Thrown away; discarded. **— *n.*** One who is wrecked, adrift, or abandoned; an outcast.

caste (kast, käst) *n.* **1** One of the hereditary classes into which Hindu society is divided in India. **2** The principle or practice of such division or the position it confers. **3** The division of society on artificial grounds; a social class. **4** Reputation; standing. See synonyms under CLASS. **— to lose caste** To lose one's former or rightful position in a community; lose standing. ◆ Homophone: *cast.* [<Pg. *casta* unmixed breed <L *castus* pure]

cas·tel·lan (kas′tə·lən) *n.* The keeper or commander of a castle; a chatelain. [<AF *castelain* <L *castellanus* < *castellum* castle]

cas·tel·lat·ed (kas′tə·lā′tid) *adj.* **1** Having battlements; built like a castle; fortified. **2** Having a castle or castles. [<Med. L *castellatus,* pp. of *castellare* build a castle <L *castellum* castle] **— cas′tel·la′tion** *n.*

Cas·tel·lón de la Pla·na (käs′tā·lyōn′ dā lä plä′nä) A port in eastern Spain.

Cas·tel·ros·so (käs·tel·rōs′sō) See KASTELLORIZO.

cas·tel·ry (kas′əl·rē, käs′-) *n. pl.* **·ries** **1** The government, tenure, or jurisdiction of a castle. **2** The territory subject to the lord of the castle. Also spelled *castlery.*

Cas·tel·ve·tro (käs·tel′vā′trō), **Lodovico,** 1505–71, Italian critic.

cast·er (kas′tər, käs′-) *n.* **1** One who or that which casts. **2** A cruet for condiments. **3** A swiveling roller fastened under an article of furniture, or a similar mounting for wheels, etc. **4** An axle offset on a motor vehicle. Also *castor* for defs. 2 and 3.

cas·ti·gate (kas′tə·gāt) *v.t.* **·gat·ed, ·gat·ing** To punish with or as with the rod; chastise. See synonyms under BEAT, CHASTEN. [<L *castigatus,* pp. of *castigare* chasten, ult. < *castus* pure] **— cas′ti·ga′tion** *n.* **— cas′ti·ga′tor** *n.* **— cas·ti·ga·to·ry** (kas′ti·gə·tôr′ē, -tō′rē) *adj.*

Cas·ti·glio·ne (käs′tē·lyō′nā), **Count Bal·das·sa·re** (bäl′däs·sä′rā), 1478–1529, Italian diplomat; author of *The Courtier.*

Cas·tile (kas·tēl′) A region and former kingdom in northern and central Spain. *Spanish* **Cas·til·la** (käs·tē′lyä).

Cas·tile soap (kas′tēl, kas·tēl′) A hard, white, odorless soap made with olive oil.

Cas·til·ian (kas·til′yən) *n.* **1** A citizen of Castile. **2** The official and literary form of Spanish as used in Spain; originally, the dialect of Castile. **—*adj.*** Pertaining to Castile: in Spanish, **cas·tel·la·no** (käs′tā·lyä′nō).

cast·ing (kas′ting, käs′-) *n.* **1** The act of cast-

ing. 2 That which is cast. 3 Any substance, as metal or plastics, cast in a mold.

casting vote See under VOTE.

cast iron *Metall.* Commercial iron produced in a blast furnace and containing a large proportion of carbon. It may be hard and brittle or soft and strong.

cast–i·ron (kast′ī′ərn, käst′-) *adj.* 1 Made of cast iron. 2 Like cast iron; rigid; unyielding.

cas·tle (kas′əl, käs′-) *n.* 1 A strong fortress. 2 Any massive or imposing building; hence, any place of defense and security. 3 A castle-shaped chessman; a rook. 4 A close helmet; casque. 5 A wooden tower on the back of an elephant. See synonyms under FORTIFICATION. — *v.* **·tled, ·tling** *v.t.* 1 To place in or as in a castle; fortify. 2 In chess, to move the king two squares to the right or left, at the same time bringing the castle (rook) from that side of the board toward which the king is moved to the square over which the king has passed. — *v.i.* 3 In chess, to move the castle and king in this manner. [Fusion of OE *castel* village and AF *castel* castle, both <L *castellum*, dim. of *castrum* camp, fort]

cas·tled (kas′əld, käs′-) *adj.* 1 Having or furnished with a castle or castles. 2 Castellated; fortified.

castle in the air A fanciful, impractical scheme: also called **castle in Spain.**

Cas·tle·reagh (kas′əl·rā, käs′-), **Viscount,** 1769–1822, Robert Stewart, second Marquis of Londonderry, English statesman.

cas·tle·ry (kas′əl·rē, käs′-) See CASTELRY.

cast–off (kast′ôf′, -of′, käst′-) *adj.* Thrown or laid aside; discarded: *cast–off* garments. — *n.* 1 *Printing* A computation of the space required by any matter to be printed. 2 A person or thing no longer wanted or used.

cas·tor[1] (kas′tər, käs′-) *n.* 1 A beaver, or its fur. 2 A hat of beaver or other fur; also, a silk hat. 3 An oily odorous secretion of beavers: used in medicine and perfumery: also **cas·to·re·um** (kas·tôr′ē·əm, -tō′rē·əm). [<L <Gk. *kastōr* beaver]

cas·tor[2] (kas′tər, käs′-) See CASTER (defs. 2 and 3).

Cas·tor and Pol·lux (kas′tər, käs′-; pol′əks) 1 In Greek mythology, the Dioscuri, twin sons of Leda and brothers of Helen and Clytemnestra, set by Zeus among the stars. 2 *Astron.* The two brightest stars in the constellation Gemini.

castor bean 1 The seed of the castor-oil plant. 2 The plant.

castor oil A viscous fixed oil, colorless or pale yellow, extracted from the seeds of the castor-oil plant: used as a cathartic and lubricant.

cas·tor-oil plant (kas′tər·oil′, käs′-) A herbaceous plant *(Ricinus communis)* of the spurge family, native in India but widely naturalized in warm climates, yielding the castor bean: also called *palma–Christi.*

cas·tra·me·ta·tion (kas′trə·mə·tā′shən) *n.* The art or act of, or plan for, laying out a camp, especially an army camp. [<F *castramétation* <L *castrum* camp + *metari* measure, lay out]

cas·trate (kas′trāt) *v.t.* **·trat·ed, ·trat·ing** 1 To remove the testicles from; emasculate; geld. 2 To remove the ovaries from; spay. 3 To expurgate, as a book; mutilate. [<L *castratus,* pp. of *castrare* castrate] — **cas·tra′tion** *n.*

Cas·tries (kàs·trē′, käs′trēs) The capital of St. Lucia, Windward Islands: also *Port Castries.*

Cas·tri·o·ta (kas′trē·ō′tə), **George.** See SCANDERBEG.

Cas·tro (käs′trō, kas′-), **Fidel,** born 1926, Cuban revolutionary leader; premier 1959–.

Cas·tro·ism (kas′trō·iz·əm) *n.* The revolutionary doctrines and practices associated with Fidel Castro.

Ca·strop–Rau·xel (käs′trəp·rouk′səl) A city in the Ruhr valley, North Rhine–Westphalia, Germany.

cast steel *Metall.* Steel cast in molds to provide special machine parts or other articles.

cas·u·al (kazh′o͞o·əl) *adj.* 1 Occurring by chance; accidental; unusual. 2 Occurring at irregular intervals; occasional. 3 *Brit.* Of or pertaining to laborers, vagrants, or paupers who receive temporary aid or shelter. 4 Nonchalant; careless. 5 Unmethodical; haphazard. 6 Of, pertaining to, or caused by accident; a *casual* patient. 7 Informal: *casual* clothes. 8 *Obs.* Precarious. See synonyms under INCIDENTAL. — *n.* 1 A casual laborer, patient, or pauper. 2 A chance visitor. 3 *Mil.* A soldier subject to individual regulation because of his physical separation from an organization or lack of assignment or attachment to one. [<F *casuel* <L *casualis* < *casus* accident < *cadere* fall] — **cas′u·al·ly** *adv.* — **cas′u·al·ness** *n.*

cas·u·al·ism (kazh′o͞o·əl·iz′əm) *n.* The doctrine that chance prevails in all things. — **cas′u·al·ist** *n.*

cas·u·al·ty (kazh′o͞o·əl·tē) *n. pl.* **·ties** 1 A fatal or serious accident. 2 A chance occurrence. 3 *Mil.* **a** A soldier missing in action or removed from active duty by death, wounds, or capture. **b** *pl.* Losses arising from death, wounds, illness, capture, or desertion. See synonyms under ACCIDENT, HAZARD.

casual water Water which has temporarily accumulated on a golf course, but is not treated as a hazard except where it lodges in a bunker.

cas·u·ist (kazh′o͞o·ist) *n.* A theologian, philosopher, etc., who studies or resolves ethical problems or cases of conscience involving a seeming conflict of right and wrong: often used derogatorily. [<F *casuiste* <L *casus* event, case]

cas·u·is·tic (kazh′o͞o·is′tik) *adj.* 1 Pertaining to a casuist or casuistry. 2 Sophistical; equivocal. Also **cas′u·is′ti·cal.** — **cas′u·is′ti·cal·ly** *adv.*

cas·u·ist·ry (kazh′o͞o·is·trē) *n. pl.* **·ries** 1 The science or doctrine of resolving doubtful cases of conscience or questions of right and wrong according to the injunctions of sacred books or of individual authority or social conventions: often used derogatorily. 2 Sophistical or equivocal reasoning.

ca·sus (kā′səs) *n. Law.* 1 That which happens; an occurrence. 2 An accident or calamity. 3 An occasion; case. [<L]

ca·sus bel·li (kā′səs bel′ī) *Latin* An occurrence held to warrant hostilities; a cause for war.

cat (kat) *n.* 1 A domesticated carnivorous mammal *(Felis domestica)* with retractile claws: it kills mice and rats and is of worldwide distribution in various breeds. ◆ Collateral adjective: *feline.* 2 Any animal of the cat family *(Felidae),* as a lion, tiger, lynx, ocelot, etc. 3 *Naut.* A purchase for hoisting an anchor. 4 A whip with nine lashes; a cat-o′–nine–tails. 5 A catboat. 6 A double-pointed piece of wood used in the game of tipcat; also, the game. 7 A game of ball, called from the number of batters *one old* (or *o′*) *cat, two old cat,* etc. 8 *Colloq.* A spiteful woman given to gossip and scandal. 9 *Colloq.* A prostitute. 10 *U.S. Colloq.* A Caterpillar tractor. 11 *U.S. Slang* A musician in a jazz band. — **to let the cat out of the bag** To divulge a secret. — **see which way the cat jumps** See how things turn out. — *v.t.* **cat·ted, cat·ting** To hoist or raise to and fasten at the cathead, as an anchor. 2 To flog with a cat-o′–nine–tails. [OE *cat, catte*]

cata– *prefix* 1 Down; against; upon: *cataclysm.* 2 Back; over: *cataphonic.* 3 With a pejorative or intensive sense: *cataphyllon.* Also, before vowels, **cat–;** before *h, cath–.* [<Gk. *kata-* < *kata* down, against, back]

ca·tab·a·sis (kə·tab′ə·sis) *n. pl.* **·ses** (-sēz) 1 A going downward; descent: opposed to *anabasis.* 2 *Pathol.* The decreasing of a disease. [<Gk. *katabasis* < *kata-* down + *bainein* go] — **cat·a·bat·ic** (kat′ə·bat′ik) *adj.*

ca·tab·o·lism (kə·tab′ə·liz′əm) *n. Biol.* The series of changes by which living matter or protoplasm breaks down into less complex and more stable substances within a cell or organism; destructive metabolism: opposed to *anabolism.* Also spelled *katabolism.* [<Gk. *katabolē* destruction < *kata-* down + *ballein* throw] — **cat·a·bol·ic** (kat′ə·bol′ik) *adj.* — **cat′a·bol′i·cal·ly** *adv.*

ca·tab·o·lite (kə·tab′ə·līt) *n.* Any product resulting from catabolism.

cat·a·caus·tic (kat′ə·kôs′tik) *adj. Optics* Denoting a caustic curve formed by reflected rays of light: opposed to *diacaustic.* — *n.* A catacaustic curve. [<CATA- + CAUSTIC (def. 3)]

cat·a·chre·sis (kat′ə·krē′sis) *n.* 1 The misuse of a word; application of a meaning to a word not its own, as *asset* used in the sense of *advantage*; also, a mixed or strained metaphor. 2 The use of a wrong form of a word, through a misunderstanding of its etymology. [<L <Gk. *katachrēsis* < *kata-* against + *chraesthai* use] — **cat·a·chres·tic** (kat′ə·kres′tik) or **·ti·cal** *adj.* — **cat′a·chres′ti·cal·ly** *adv.*

cat·a·cli·nal (kat′ə·klī′nəl) *adj. Geol.* Running in the direction of the dip: said of a valley: distinguished from *anaclinal.* [<Gk. *kataklinēs* sloping < *kata-* down + *klinein* bend]

cat·a·clysm (kat′ə·kliz′əm) *n.* 1 An overwhelming flood. 2 *Geol.* Any violent and extensive subversion of the ordinary phenomena of nature on the earth's surface. 3 Any sudden overwhelming change or political or social upheaval. See synonyms under CATASTROPHE. [<Gk. *kataklysmos* flood < *kata-* down + *klyzein* wash] — **cat·a·clys·mal** (kat′ə·kliz′məl), **cat′a·clys′mic, cat′a·clys·mat′ic** (-kliz·mat′ik) *adj.*

cat·a·comb (kat′ə·kōm) *n. Usually pl.* A long underground gallery with excavations in its sides for tombs or in which human bones are stacked or piled. [<F *catacombe* <LL *catacumbas*]

ca·tad·ro·mous (kə·tad′rə·məs) *adj. Zool.* Running down: said of fishes that go down rivers to the sea to spawn: opposed to *anadromous.* [<CATA- + -DROMOUS]

cat·a·falque (kat′ə·falk) *n.* 1 A temporary raised structure or staging that supports the coffin, usually draped, of a deceased personage lying in state. 2 The drapery on or the hangings over it. 3 A stately funeral car. [<F <Ital. *catafalco*]

Cat·a·lan (kat′ə·lan, -lən) *adj.* Of or pertaining to Catalonia, a former province of Spain, its people, or their language. — *n.* 1 One of Catalonian descent or blood. 2 The Romance language of Catalonia and Valencia, closely related to Provençal.

cat·a·lase (kat′ə·lās) *n. Biochem.* An animal and vegetable enzyme which decomposes hydrogen peroxide into water and oxygen. [<CATAL(YSIS) + -ASE]

Ça·tal·ca (chä′täl·jä′) A town near Istanbul, Turkey: also *Chatalja.*

cat·a·lec·tic (kat′ə·lek′tik) *adj.* In prosody, describing a line of verse which terminates in an incomplete foot. [<Gk. *katalēktikos* < *kata-* wholly + *lēgein* stop]

cat·a·lep·sy (kat′ə·lep′sē) *n. Psychiatry* Inordinate maintenance of physical postures; muscular rigidity: common in certain nervous diseases, especially hysteria and schizophrenia. [<Med. L *catalepsia* <Gk. *katalēpsis* < *kata-* upon + *lēpsis* seizure < *lambanein* grasp] — **cat′a·lep′tic** (-lep′tik) *adj.* & *n.*

Cat·a·li·na Island (kat′ə·lē′nə) See SANTA CATALINA.

cat·a·lo (kat′ə·lō) *n. pl.* **·loes** or **·los** A fertile hybrid between the bison and the domestic cow: also spelled *cattalo.* [<CAT(TLE) + (BUFF)ALO]

cat·a·log (kat′ə·lôg, -log) *n.* 1 A list or enumeration of names, persons or things, usually in alphabetical order, sometimes with accompanying description. 2 A publication listing wares for sale by a commercial establishment: a mail–order *catalog.* See synonyms under RECORD. — *v.* **·loged, ·log·ing** *v.t.* To make an alphabetical list of; insert in a catalog. — *v.i.* To work upon or make such a list. [<F <LL *catalogus* <Gk. *katalogos* list < *kata-* down + *legein* select, choose] — **cat′a·log′er, cat′a·log′ist** *n.*

cat·a·logue (kat′ə·lôg, -log) *n., v.t.* & *v.i.* **·logued, ·logu·ing** Catalog. — **cat′a·logu′er, cat′a·logu′ist** *n.*

ca·ta·logue rai·son·né (kà·tà·lôg′ re·zô·nā′) *French* A catalog or list classified by subjects, often with explanatory notes.

Cat·a·lo·ni·a (kat′ə·lō′nē·ə) A region of NE Spain; 12,332 square miles. *Spanish* **Ca·ta·lu·ña** (kä′tä·lo͞o′nyä). — **Cat′a·lo′ni·an** *adj.* & *n.*

ca·tal·pa (kə·tal′pə) *n.* A tree (genus *Catalpa*) of the bignonia family of China, Japan, and North America, having large, ovate leaves, large, fragrant bell–shaped flowers, and long slender pods. [<N. Am. Ind.]

ca·tal·y·sis (kə·tal′ə·sis) *n. pl.* **·ses** (-sēz) *Chem.* An alteration in the speed of a chemical reaction effected by the presence of an agent or substance that itself remains stable. [<Gk. *katalysis* dissolution < *kata-* wholly, completely + *lyein* loosen] — **cat·a·lyt·ic** (kat′ə·lit′ik) *adj.* & *n.*

cat·a·lyst (kat′ə·list) *n. Chem.* Any substance or agent that causes catalysis. A **positive cata-**

lyst accelerates the speed of the reaction; a **negative catalyst** retards it.

cat·a·lyze (kat′ə·līz) v.t. **·lyzed**, **·lyz·ing** To submit to or decompose by catalysis. — **cat′a·lyz′er** n.

cat·a·ma·ran (kat′ə·mə·ran′) n. Naut. **1** A long, narrow raft of logs, often with an outrigger. **2** A life raft of two pointed metal cylinders connected by a platform. **3** A boat having twin hulls. [<Tamil *kaṭṭa–maram* tied wood]

CATAMARAN
Twin-hulled
Tahitian
war canoe.

Ca·ta·mar·ca (kä′tä·mär′kä) A province of NW Argentina; 45,829 square miles; capital, Catamarca.

cat·a·me·ni·a (kat′ə·mē′nē·ə) n. pl. Physiol. The menses. [<Gk. *katamēnia*, neut. pl. of *katamēnios* monthly < *kata*- by + *mēn* month] — **cat′a·me′ni·al** adj.

cat·a·mite (kat′ə·mīt) n. A boy used in pederasty. [<L *Catamitus*, alter. of Gk. *Ganymēdēs*, the cupbearer of Zeus]

cat·am·ne·sis (kat′əm·nē′sis) n. Med. The history of a patient subsequent to his illness and recovery: distinguished from *anamnesis*. [<NL <Gk. *kata*- down + *-mnēsis* recollection < *mimnēskein* remember] — **cat′am·nes′tic** (-nes′tik) adj.

cat·a·mount (kat′ə·mount) n. **1** A wildcat. **2** A cougar or lynx. **3** A catamountain. [Short form of CATAMOUNTAIN]

cat·a·moun·tain (kat′ə·moun′tən) n. **1** A catamount. **2** One of various wildcats, as a leopard or panther. [Short form of *cat of the mountain*]

Ca·ta·nia (kä·tä′nyä) The second largest city in Sicily, a port on the **Gulf of Catania**, an inlet of the Ionian Sea in eastern Sicily.

Ca·tan·za·ro (kä′tän·dzä′rō) A port in SE Calabria, Italy.

cat·a·phon·ic (kat′ə·fon′ik) adj. Physics Relating to or produced by the reflection of sound. [CATA- + Gk. *phōnē* sound]

cat·a·phon·ics (kat′ə·fon′iks) n. Physics The study of the reflection of sound.

cat·a·pho·re·sis (kat′ə·fə·rē′sis) n. **1** The movement of medicinal substances in or through living tissue under the influence of an electric field. **2** Electrophoresis. [<NL <Gk. *kata*- down + *phorēsis* carrying < *pherein* bear, carry] — **cat′a·pho·ret′ic** (-ret′ik) adj.

cat·a·phyll (kat′ə·fil) n. Bot. A rudimentary or scalelike leaf which forms the covering of a bud. [<CATA- + Gk. *phyllon* leaf]

cat·a·pla·si·a (kat′ə·plā′zhē·ə, -zē·ə) n. Pathol. A reversion of cells or tissues to a more primitive or embryonic form. Also **ca·tap·la·sis** (kə·tap′lə·sis). [<NL <Gk. *kata*- back + *-plasia* a molding < *plassein* form, mold]

cat·a·plasm (kat′ə·plaz′əm) n. A soothing poultice, often medicated. [<Gk. *kataplasma*]

cat·a·plex·y (kat′ə·plek′sē) n. Psychiatry A temporary paroxysmic rigidity of the muscles often caused by sudden emotional shock. [<Gk. *kataplēxis* amazement < *kataplēssein* astound < *kata*- down + *plēssein* strike] — **cat′a·plec′tic** (-plek′tik) adj.

cat·a·pult (kat′ə·pult) n. **1** An engine of

CATAPULT
For ship-borne airplanes.

ancient warfare for throwing bombs, grenades, stones, spears, or arrows. **2** A toy con-

sisting of an elastic band attached to the prongs of a forked stick: used by boys for throwing missiles. **3** Aeron. A device for launching an airplane at flight speed, as from the deck of a ship not having a flight deck. — v.t. To hurl from or as from a catapult. — v.i. To hurtle through the air as if from a catapult. [<L *catapulta* <Gk. *katapeltēs* < *kata*- down + *pallein* brandish, hurl]

cat·a·ract (kat′ə·rakt) n. **1** A waterfall of great size. **2** Pathol. Opacity of the crystalline lens of the eye. **3** A heavy downpour or flood of water; a deluge. [<F *cataracte* <L *cataracta* <Gk. *kataraktēs* < *kata*- down + *arassein* fall headlong]

ca·tarrh (kə·tär′) n. Pathol. Excessive secretion from an inflamed mucous membrane, especially of the air passages of the throat and head. [<F *catarrhe* <L *catarrhus* <Gk. *katarrhoos* < *kata*- down + *rheein* flow] — **ca·tarrh′al** adj. — **ca·tarrh′ous** adj.

ca·tas·ta·sis (kə·tas′tə·sis) n. pl. **·ses** (-sēz) **1** In the ancient drama, the heightened part of the action that prepares for the catastrophe. **2** In oratory, the exordium of a speech, especially the part designed to conciliate the audience. [<Gk. *katastasis* settled condition < *kata*- down + *stasis* a settling < *histanai* stand]

ca·tas·tro·phe (kə·tas′trə·fē) n. **1** Any final event; a fatal conclusion; great and sudden misfortune. **2** In a drama, the conclusion or unraveling of the plot; the dénouement. **3** A sudden, violent change, especially of the earth's surface; cataclysm. [<Gk. *katastrophē* < *kata*- over, down + *strephein* turn] — **cat·a·stroph·ic** (kat′ə·strof′ik) adj.

Synonyms: calamity, cataclysm, dénouement, disaster, mischance, misfortune, mishap, sequel. A *cataclysm* or *catastrophe* is some great convulsion or momentous event that may or may not be a cause of misery to man. In *calamity*, or *disaster*, the thought of human suffering is always present. It has been held by many geologists that numerous *catastrophes* or *cataclysms* antedated the existence of man. In literature the final event of a drama is the *catastrophe*, or *dénouement*. *Misfortune* ordinarily suggests less of suddenness and violence than *calamity* or *disaster*, and is especially applied to that which is lingering or enduring in its effects. Pestilence is a *calamity*; a defeat in battle, a shipwreck, a failure in business are *disasters*; sickness, loss of property are *misfortunes*; failure to meet a friend is a *mischance*; the breaking of a teacup is a *mishap*. Compare ACCIDENT, MISFORTUNE. *Antonyms:* benefit, blessing, boon, comfort, favor, help, pleasure, privilege, prosperity, success.

ca·tas·tro·phism (kə·tas′trə·fiz′əm) n. Geol. The theory or doctrine which attributes the principal stratigraphic and paleontological changes of the earth to sudden and violent physical upheavals. — **ca·tas′tro·phist** n.

cat·a·to·ni·a (kat′ə·tō′nē·ə) n. Psychiatry A complex of symptoms typical of schizophrenia, characterized by stupor, muscular rigidity, and occasional mental agitation. [<NL < *kata*- down + *tonos* tension, tone < *teinein* stretch] — **cat·a·ton·ic** (-ton′ik) adj.

cat·a·wam·pus (kat′ə·wom′pəs) U.S. Colloq. adj. **1** Malicious; resentful. **2** Askew; cater-cornered. — n. **1** A malicious person. **2** A hobgoblin or bogy. Also spelled *cattywampus*. [Origin unknown]

Ca·taw·ba (kə·tô′bə) n. **1** One of a tribe of North American Indians, the most important eastern tribe of Siouan linguistic stock, formerly occupying the region along the Catawba River, South Carolina. **2** An American red grape. **3** A dry white wine made from it.

Catawba River A river rising in North Carolina and flowing 295 miles south to South Carolina, where it is called the Wateree.

cat·bird (kat′bûrd′) n. A small slate-colored North American songbird (*Dumetella carolinensis*), related to the mockingbird: named from its catlike cry.

catbird seat U.S. Colloq. The most advantageous and powerful position.

cat·block (kat′blok′) n. Naut. A heavy hoisting block used in catting an anchor.

cat·boat (kat′bōt′) n. Naut. A small one-masted sailboat, usually equipped with a centerboard and having its mast stepped well forward and carrying a single fore-and-aft sail with boom and gaff.

cat·bri·er (kat′brī′ər) n. Any of certain woody vines of the genus *Smilax*, especially the greenbrier.

cat·call (kat′kôl′) n. A shrill, discordant call or whistle, in token of impatience or derision. — v.t. To deride or express disapproval of with catcalls. — v.i. To utter catcalls.

catch (kach) v. **caught**, **catch·ing** v.t. **1** To take, seize, or come upon, as something departing or fleeing; take captive; capture. **2** To entrap; ensnare. **3** To captivate, gain, or hold. **4** To apprehend or perceive clearly. **5** To surprise; detect, as in a misdeed. **6** To contract; incur, as a disease. **7** To arrive at or take, as a train or boat, just before its departure. **8** To arrest the motion of; entangle. **9** To grasp and retain. **10** To perceive, as something fleeting, with momentary distinction: to *catch* sight of. **11** To reach, as a person, with a blow: She *caught* him a box on the ear. — v.i. **12** To make a movement of grasping or seizing: He *caught* at the idea. **13** In baseball, to act as catcher. **14** To become entangled or fastened. **15** To be communicated or communicable, as a disease or enthusiasm. **16** To take fire; kindle; ignite. **17** Naut. To catch the wind: an elliptical expression. — **to catch it** Colloq. To receive a reprimand, scolding, drubbing, or the like. — **to catch (one) napping** To take off guard; outwit. — **to catch on** Colloq. **1** To understand. **2** To become popular or fashionable. — **to catch out 1** In baseball, to put a batter out by catching the ball. **2** To discover (someone) in error. — **to catch up 1** To overtake. **2** To regain by or as if by overtaking: to *catch up* on one's lessons. — **to catch up with** (or **up to**) To overtake. — n. **1** The act of catching; the act of grasping or seizing; specifically, the act of catching a batted or thrown ball before it reaches the ground, as in baseball, cricket, etc.; also a catcher. **2** A hold or grip, as in wrestling. **3** That which catches or fastens; a fastening. **4** That which is or may be caught or gained, such as a person or thing worth obtaining, as in marriage. **5** The amount of fish or the like caught at one time or in a given period. **6** The state in which or the extent to which a crop germinates. **7** An artful trick or question. **8** An impediment; a break, as in the voice or breathing. **9** Music A round; also, a scrap of song. — adj. Attracting or meant to attract notice; catchy; a *catch* phrase. [<AF *cachier* <LL *captiare*, freq. of *capere* take, hold. Doublet of CHASE.]

Synonyms (verb): apprehend, capture, clasp, clutch, comprehend, discover, ensnare, entrap, grasp, grip, gripe, overtake, secure, seize, snatch, take. To *catch* is to come up with or take possession of something departing, fugitive, or illusive. We *catch* a runaway horse, a flying ball, a mouse in a trap. To "catch at" is to attempt to *catch*, often unsuccessfully. We *clutch* with a swift, tenacious movement of the fingers; we *grasp* with a firm closure of the whole hand; we *grip* or *gripe* with the strongest muscular closure of the whole hand possible to exert. We *clasp* in the arms. We *snatch* with a quick, sudden, and usually a surprising motion. In the figurative sense, *catch* is used of any act that brings a person or thing into our power or possession; as, to *catch* a criminal in the act; to *catch* an idea, in the sense of *apprehend* or *comprehend*. Compare ARREST, GRASP. *Antonyms:* lose, miss, release, restore.

catch–all (kach′ôl′) n. A bag or the like to hold odds and ends.

catch basin A filter at the entrance to a drain or sewer to stop matter which might clog the pipes.

catch crop Agric. A quick-growing crop raised between two main crops, when the ground would otherwise be idle.

catch·er (kach′ər) n. **1** One who or that which catches. **2** In baseball, the player stationed behind home plate to catch balls that pass the batter.

catch·fly (kach′flī′) *n.* Any one of several weeds (genus *Silene*) of the pink family, the stem and calyx of which exude a viscid fluid which holds small insects alighting on it.

catch·ing (kach′ing) *adj.* **1** Infectious. **2** Captivating

catch·ment (kach′mənt) *n.* **1** Drainage. **2** The collection of water over a natural drainage area. **3** The water so collected.

catchment basin *Geog.* The area drained by a river or river system. Also **catchment area.**

catch·pen·ny (kach′pen′ē) *adj.* Cheap, poor, and showy. —*n. pl.* **·nies** An inferior article, made to attract buyers.

catch·pole (kach′pōl′) *n.* **1** A medieval weapon for catching a person out of arm's reach. **2** One who arrests for debt; a bailiff; taxgatherer: also **catch′poll.** [<Med. L *cacepollus* chaser of fowl]

catch·up (kach′əp, kech′-) See KETCHUP.

catch·weed (kach′wēd′) *n.* Cleavers.

catch·weight (kach′wāt′) *n.* In certain sports, the weight of a contestant as determined by his own discretion, rather than by rule or agreement.

catch·word (kach′wûrd′) *n.* **1** A word or phrase to catch the popular fancy or attention, especially, a word or phrase used as a slogan in a political campaign. **2** In the theater, a cue. **3** A word so placed as to catch the attention. **4** An isolated word at the bottom of a page in old books, inserted to connect the text with the beginning of the next page. **5** A word at the head of a page or column, as of a dictionary, encyclopedia, etc.

catch·y (kach′ē) *adj.* **·i·er, ·i·est 1** Attractive; taking. **2** Entangling; deceptive, puzzling. **3** Broken; fitful.

cate (kāt) *n. Archaic* Delicate or luxurious food: usually in plural. [Earlier *acate* <AF *acat* provision, purchase <*acater* buy]

cat·e·che·sis (kat′ə·kē′sis) *n. pl.* **·ses** (-sēz) **1** Oral instruction in the elements of Christianity, as given to a catechumen; catechizing. **2** A catechetic discourse or writing. [<Gk. *katēchēsis* instruction]

cat·e·chet·ic (kat′ə·ket′ik) *adj.* **1** Of or pertaining to oral instruction: consisting of question and answer. **2** Of or pertaining to instruction in the elementary doctrines of Christianity. Also **cat′e·chet′i·cal.**

cat·e·chin (kat′ə·chin, -kin) *n. Chem.* An amorphous yellow powder, $C_{15}H_{14}O_6 \cdot 4H_2O$, contained in catechu: used in dyeing.

cat·e·chism (kat′ə·kiz′əm) *n.* **1** A short treatise giving in catechetic form an outline of the fundamental principles of a religious creed. **2** Any brief manual of instruction by questions and answers; an examination of candidates by interrogatories. **3** Catechetic instruction, especially in religious doctrine. [<Med. L *catechismus* <Gk. *katēchizein* instruct]

cat·e·chist (kat′ə·kist) *n.* One who teaches by question and answer; especially, an instructor of catechumens or new converts. Also **cat′e·chiz′er, cat′e·chis′er.** —**cat′e·chis′tic** or **·ti·cal** *adj.*

cat·e·chize (kat′ə·kīz) *v.t.* **·chized, ·chiz·ing 1** To interrogate seriously as to conduct or belief. **2** To question in a searching manner, especially with a view to judgment or reproof. **3** To give systematic oral instruction to; instruct in elementary truths of religion; teach by means of a catechism. **4** To teach the catechism to, as in preparation for confirmation. Also **cat′e·chise.** [<L *catechizare* instruct <Gk. *katēchizein*] —**cat′e·chi·za′tion** *n.*

cat·e·chol (kat′ə·chōl, -kōl) *n. Chem.* Pyrocatechol. [<CATECHU]

cat·e·chol·a·mine (kat′ə·chōl′ə·mēn, -kōl′-) *n.* Any of various amines chemically related to pyrocatechol and having a hormonal effect on the sympathetic nervous system, including epinephrine, norepinephrine, and dopamine.

cat·e·chu (kat′ə·choo͞) *n.* A resinous astringent and tanning extract prepared from the wood of various Asian and East Indian plants, especially *Acacia catechu.* Also called *cashoo, cutch.* [<NL <Malay *kachu*] —**cat′e·chu′ic** *adj.*

cat·e·chu·men (kat′ə·kyoo͞′mən) *n.* **1** One who is under instruction in the elements of Christianity; especially, a new or a young convert in the ancient church; a beginner. **2** One undergoing initiation in any science, art, set of opinions, etc. [<L *catechumenus* <Gk. *katēchoumenos,* ppr. passive of *katēchēein* instruct] —**cat′e·chu′me·nal, cat·e·chu·men·i·cal** (kat′ə·kyoo͞·men′i·kəl) *adj.*

cat·e·gor·e·mat·ic (kat′ə·gôr′ə·mat′ik, -gor′-) *adj. Logic* Capable of being used alone as the complete subject or predicate of a proposition: opposed to *syncategorematic.* [<Gk. *katēgorēma* logical predicate]

cat·e·gor·i·cal (kat′ə·gôr′i·kəl, -gor′-) *adj.* **1** Without qualification; absolute; unequivocal. **2** or pertaining to a category; in the form of a category. —**cat′e·gor′i·cal·ly** *adv.* —**cat′e·gor′i·cal·ness** *n.*

categorical imperative *Philos.* The principle established by Immanuel Kant, which states, "Act in such a way that the maxim of your will can simultaneously apply as the basis for a universal law."

cat·e·go·rize (kat′ə·gə·rīz′) *v.t.* **·rized, ·riz·ing 1** To put into categories. **2** To treat categorically.

cat·e·go·ry (kat′ə·gôr′ē, -gō′rē) *n. pl.* **·ries 1** Any comprehensive class or description of things. **2** A class, condition, or predicament. **3** One of the several forms of conception or knowledge that together embrace everything predicable or existent. [<L *categoria* <Gk. *katēgoria* <*katēgoreein* allege, predicate <*kata-* against + *agora* public assembly]

cat·e·lec·trot·o·nus (kat′ə·lek·trot′ō·nəs) *Physiol.* A state of increased tension produced in a nerve fiber or muscle at the negative pole of an electric current passing through it. [<CAT(HODE) + ELECTROTONUS]

ca·te·na (kə·tē′nə) *n. pl.* **·nae** (-nē) A chain or closely connected series, usually with reference to succession in time; specifically, a series of excerpts from the works of the fathers of the Church to clear up some point, as of Scriptural exegesis. [<L, chain]

cat·e·nar·y (kat′ə·ner′ē, kə·tē′nə·rē) *n. pl.* **·ies** *Math.* The curve formed by a perfectly flexible, inextensible, infinitely slender cord suspended from two points not in the same vertical line; especially, the common catenary, represented by a chain freely suspended from two fixed points. —*adj.* Relating to or like a catenary or a chain: also **cat·e·nar·i·an** (kat′·ə·nâr′ē·ən). [<L *catenarius* <*catena* chain]

cat·e·nate (kat′ə·nāt) *v.t.* **·nat·ed, ·nat·ing** To connect like the links of a chain; form into a chain; link together. —**cat′e·na′tion** *n.*

cat·e·noid (kat′ə·noid) *n. Math.* The surface formed by the rotation of a catenary about its axis.

ca·ten·u·late (kə·ten′yə·lāt, -lit) *adj.* Consisting of little links; made up of parts united end to end in a chainlike series. [<L *catenula,* dim. of *catena* chain]

ca·ter (kā′tər) *v.t.* **1** To furnish food or entertainment. **2** To provide for the gratification of any need or taste. See synonyms under PROVIDE. [<AF *acater* buy <LL *acceptare* <*ad-* toward + *captare* grasp, seize] —**ca′ter·er** *n.*

cat·er·cor·nered (kat′ər·kôr′nərd) *adj.* Placed cornerwise or diagonally; diagonal: also *cattycornered, kitty-cornered.* Also **cat′er·cor′ner.** [<*cater* diagonally <F *quatre* four <L *quattuor* + CORNERED]

ca·ter-cous·in (kā′tər·kuz′ən) *n. Obs.* **1** A fourth cousin; remote relative. **2** An intimate friend. [Origin uncertain]

cat·er·pil·lar (kat′ər·pil′ər) *n.* **1** The larva of a butterfly or moth (order *Lepidoptera*), or of certain other insects, as the sawfly. **2** Something resembling a caterpillar or its system of locomotion, as a car fitted with supplementary wheels or a device on the principle of the endless chain. [<AF *catepelose* hairy cat <L *catta* cat + *pilosus* <*pilum* hair]

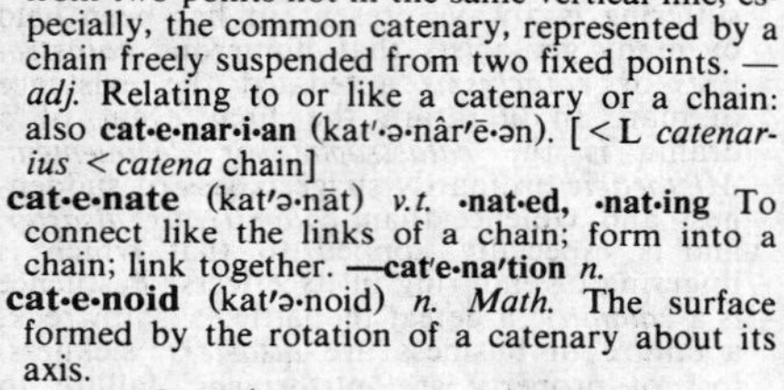

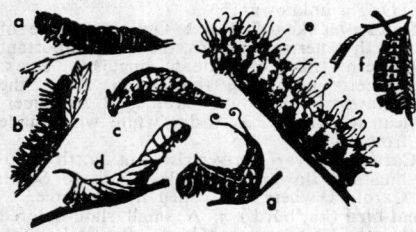

CATERPILLAR
a. Swallowtail butterfly. *b.* Mourning cloak butterfly. *c.* Emperor moth. *d.* Puss moth. *e.* Eyed hawk moth. *f.* Great peacock moth. *g.* Pale tussock moth.

Cat·er·pil·lar (kat′ər·pil′ər) *n.* A tractor whose driving wheels gear with self-laid, wide metal belts whereby its weight is distributed over a large area, permitting the tractor to move over soft or rough terrain: a trade name.

caterpillar hunter Any of a genus *(Calosoma)* of carabid beetles which prey on caterpillars, especially *C. scrutator,* having dark green elytra. For illustration see INSECTS (beneficial).

cat·er·waul (kat′ər·wôl) *v.i.* **1** To utter the discordant cry peculiar to cats at rutting time. **2** To make any discordant screeching. **3** To argue or dispute noisily. —*n.* The cry of cats at rutting time; also, any similar cry. [ME *caterwawen* <*cater* cat (cf. G *kater* tomcat) + *wawen* wail, howl] —**cat′er·waul′ing** *n.*

Cates (kāts), **Clifton Bledsoe,** born 1893, U.S. Marine Corps general.

Cates·by (kāts′bē), **Mark,** 1679?–1749, English naturalist.

cat-eye (kat′ī′) *n.* A small knot in wood, usually one less than one fourth of an inch in diameter: also called *pin knot.*

cat·face (kat′fās′) *n.* A lesion on the surface of a tree caused by an injury or wound that has not completely healed.

cat·fall (kat′fôl′) *n. Naut.* The tackle for raising an anchor to the cathead.

cat·fish (kat′fish′) *n. pl.* **·fish** or **·fish·es 1** One of numerous silurid fishes, usually carnivorous and of fresh-water habitat, having sensitive barbels around the mouth to enable them to find their prey in muddy waters. **2** Any of many other teleost fishes, as the bullhead.

cat-foot·ed (kat′foot′id) *adj.* **1** Having digitigrade feet with retractile claws like a cat's. **2** Soft; stealthy.

cat·gut (kat′gut′) *n.* **1** A very tough cord, made from the intestines of certain animals, as sheep, and used for stringing musical instruments, making surgical ligatures, etc. **2** A violin or fiddle; hence, stringed instruments generally: a humorous use. **3** A leguminous perennial *(Tephrosia virginiana),* native in the eastern half of the United States.

cath- Var. of CATA-.

Cath·a·ri (kath′ə·rī) *n. pl.* Various Christian sects aiming at or claiming peculiar purity of life or doctrine, as the *Novatians* (3rd century), the *Albigenses* (12th century), and various others. [<Med.L <Gk. *katharos* pure] —**Cath′a·rist** (-rist) *n.* —**Cath′a·rism** *n.*

Cath·a·ri·na (kath′ə·rī′nə, *Pg.* kä′tə·rē′nə) See CATHERINE. Also **Cath·a·rine** (kath′ə·rin, kath′rin).

ca·thar·sis (kə·thär′sis) *n.* **1** *Med.* Purgation or cleansing of any passage of the body, especially of the alimentary canal. **2** A word used by Aristotle to express the effect of tragic drama in purifying and relieving the emotions. **3** *Psychoanal.* Abreaction. Also spelled *katharsis.* [<Gk. *katharsis* cleansing <*katharos* pure]

ca·thar·tic (kə·thär′tik) *adj.* Purgative; purifying: also **ca·thar′ti·cal.** —*n.* A purgative medicine. [<Gk. *kathartikos* <*katharos* pure] —**ca·thar′ti·cal·ly** *adv.*

Ca·thay (ka·thā′) *Poetic* or *Archaic* China.

cat·head (kat′hed′) *n. Naut.* A beam of wood or iron, projecting over the bow, by which the anchor is supported clear of the ship.

ca·the·dra (kə·thē′drə, kath′ə-) *n.* **1** A bishop's seat or throne in the cathedral or chief church of his diocese; hence, the see or dignity of a bishop. **2** A professor's chair. —**ex cathedra** *Latin* **1** Literally, from the seat: applied to a pronouncement on faith or morals by the Pope as head of the Roman Catholic Church. **2** With authority: also used attributively, meaning "officially spoken": an *ex cathedra* pronouncement. [<L <Gk. *kathedra* <*kata* down + *hedra* seat. Doublet of CHAIR.]

ca·the·dral (kə·thē′drəl) *n.* **1** The church containing the cathedra or official chair of the bishop; the mother church of a diocese. **2** Any large or important church. —*adj.* **1** Pertaining to or containing a bishop's chair or see. **2** Of or pertaining to any chair of authority; authoritative; dogmatic. **3** Of, pertaining to, belonging to, or resembling a cathedral: a *cathedral* choir.

cathedral schools Elementary schools founded by the bishops of the Middle Ages and erected close to their cathedrals.

Cath·er (kath′ər), **Willa Sibert**, 1876–1947, U.S. author.

Cath·e·rine (kath′ə·rin, kath′rin, *Fr.* kȧ·trēn′) A feminine personal name. [<Gk.; meaning uncertain]
  —**Catherine, Saint** A virgin of Alexandria who, in the fourth century, professed Christianity and died by torture on the wheel.
  —**Catherine I,** 1680?–1727, empress of Russia; wife of Peter the Great.
  —**Catherine II,** 1729–96; empress of Russia 1762–96: known as **Catherine the Great.**
  —**Catherine de Medici** See MEDICI.
  —**Catherine of Aragon,** 1485–1536, first wife of Henry VIII of England; divorced 1533.
  —**Catherine of Braganza,** 1638–1705, queen of Charles II of England.

Catherine, Mount See KATHERINA, GEBEL.

catherine wheel 1 A rotating firework; a pin-wheel, especially a large, showy one. **2** *Her.* The figure of a wheel with the tire armed with hooks, to represent the legendary instrument of St. Catherine's martyrdom.

cath·e·ter (kath′ə·tər) *n. Med.* A slender, tubular, surgical instrument for introduction into canals or passages. [<L <Gk. *kathetēr* < *kata-* down + *hienai* send, let go]

cath·e·ter·ize (kath′ə·tər·īz′) *v.t.* **·ized, ·iz·ing** To introduce a catheter into.

ca·thex·is (kə·thek′sis) *n. Psychoanal.* **1** Concentration of psychic energy upon the self, another person, a phantasy, idea, or object. **2** The investment or charging of an idea or emotion with significance. [<Gk. *kathexis* holding < *kata-* thoroughly + *echein* hold, have; trans. of G *besetzung*]

cath·ode (kath′ōd) *n. Electr.* The electrode through which negative ions leave a non—metallic conductor and toward which positive ions flow from the anode. It is negative for a battery, electrolytic bath, or a vacuum tube, but positive for a voltaic cell: also spelled *kathode.* [< Gk. *kathodos* a way down < *kata-* down + *hodos* road, way] —**ca·thod·ic** (kə·thod′ik) or·i ·**cal** *adj.*

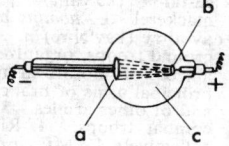

CATHODE–RAY TUBE
a. Cathode.
b. Anode.
c. Vacuum.

cathode rays *Physics* A stream of electrons that pass from a cathode to the opposite wall of a vacuum discharge tube when it is excited by a current of electricity, or by a series of spark discharges.

cathode–ray tube *Electronics* A special type of electron tube in which a beam of electrons is focused by an electric or magnetic field and deflected so as to impinge upon a sensitized screen, forming an image, as on a television receiver.

cath·o·lic (kath′ə·lik, kath′lik) *adj.* **1** Broadminded, as in belief, tastes, or views; liberal; comprehensive; large. **2** Universal in reach; general. [<L *catholicus* <Gk. *katholikos* universal < *kata-* thoroughly + *holos* whole] —**ca·thol·i·cal·ly** (kə·thol′ik·lē) *adv.* —**cath·o·lic·i·ty** (kath′ə·lis′ə·tē) *n.*

Cath·o·lic (kath′ə·lik, kath′lik) *adj.* **1** Universal; of, pertaining to, belonging or addressed to all Christians: a *Catholic* epistle; the *Catholic* faith. **2** Describing the ancient, undivided Christian Church; in accordance with the decrees of the seven ecumenical councils; not heretical or schismatic: the *Catholic* fathers; a *Catholic* creed. **3** Designating the western or Latin Church as opposed to the eastern or Greek Church after their final separation in 1472; not Orthodox. **4** Describing those churches which, after the Reformation and in modern times, claim to have the apostolic doctrine, discipline, orders, and sacraments of the ancient undivided church, and including the Anglican, Eastern Orthodox, Old Catholic, and Roman Churches. —*n.* **1** A member of the Catholic Church, in any of the above senses. **2** Specifically, a Roman Catholic. —**Cath·o·lic ·i·ty** (kath′ə·lis′ə·tē) *n.*

Catholic Church The Roman Catholic Church.

Catholic Emancipation Act An act of the English Parliament, passed in 1829, removing certain civil disabilities from Roman Catholics in Great Britain and Ireland.

Ca·thol·i·cism (kə·thol′ə·siz′əm) *n.* **1** The doctrine, system, and practice of the Church universal. **2** The system, doctrine, and practice of the Roman Catholic Church.

ca·thol·i·cize (kə·thol′ə·sīz) *v.t. & v.i.* **·cized, ·ciz·ing** To make or become catholic or Catholic.

ca·thol·i·con (kə·thol′ə·kən) *n.* A supposed universal remedy; a panacea. [<LL <Gk. *katholikos* universal]

cath·o·lyte (kath′ə·līt) *n. Chem.* The liquid formed near the cathode during electrolysis. [<CATHO(DE)+ (ELECTRO)LYTE]

cat·house (kat′hous′) *n. Slang* A house of prostitution; brothel.

Cat·i·line (kat′ə·līn), 108?–62 B.C., Roman conspirator, denounced by Cicero: full name *Lucius Sergius Catilina.*

cat·i·on (kat′ī′ən) *n. Chem.* **1** A positively charged particle which in electrolysis moves toward the cathode or is deposited there. **2** A positive ion, molecule, or radical. Also spelled *kation.* [<Gk. *kation*, ppr. neut. of *katienai* < *kata-* down + *ienai* go]

cat·kin (kat′kin) *n. Bot.* A deciduous scaly spike of flowers, as in the willow; an ament. [<MDu. *katteken*, dim. of *katte* cat]

cat·like (kat′līk′) *adj.* **1** Like a cat; feline. **2** Noiseless; stealthy.

cat·ling (kat′ling) *n.* **1** Catgut. **2** *pl.* Stringed instruments. **3** A kitten.

cat·nap (kat′nap′) *n.* A short doze, usually taken sitting up.

cat·nip (kat′nip) *n.* An aromatic herb (*Nepeta cataria*) of the mint family, of which cats are fond. Also **cat′mint′.**

Ca·to (kā′tō), **Marcus Porcius** Name of two Roman statesmen: **Cato the Elder,** 234–149 B.C., advocate of the destruction of Carthage, known as **Cato the Censor;** and his great–grandson **Cato the Younger,** 95–46 B.C., Stoic philosopher, supporter of Pompey against Caesar.

cat·o′·moun·tain (kat′ə·moun′tən) See CATA-MOUNT.

cat·o′·nine–tails (kat′ə·nīn′tālz′) *n.* A whip with nine lashes.

ca·top·trics (kə·top′triks) *n.* That branch of optics which treats of the reflection of light and the formation of images by mirrors. [< Gk. *katoptrikos* < *katoptron* mirror]—**ca·top′·tric** or **·tri·cal** *adj.*

cat owl The great horned owl.

cat rig The rig of a catboat, consisting of one mast far forward and one sail with a long boom and a gaff. —**cat′–rigged′** *adj.*

cat's cradle A game played with a loop of string stretched over the fingers and transferred from one player's hands to another's, so as to produce intricate geometrical arrangements.

cat's–eye (kats′ī′) *n.* A gemstone, usually chrysoberyl or quartz, which shows a line of light across the dome when cut en cabochon.

Cats·kill Mountains (kats′kil) A range of the Appalachians in SE New York; highest peak, 4,205 feet. Also the **Catskills.**

cat's–paw (kats′pô′) *n.* **1** A person used as a tool or dupe. **2** A light wind which barely ruffles the water. **3** *Naut.* A twisting hitch in the bight of a rope. Also **cats′paw′.**

cat·sup (kat′səp, kech′əp) See KETCHUP.

Catt (kat), **Carrie Chapman,** 1859–1947, *née* Lane, U.S. suffragist.

cat–tail (kat′tāl′) *n.* **1** A perennial aquatic plant (genus *Typha*), with long leaves, flowers in cylindrical terminal spikes, and downy fruit: used in making mats; chair seats, etc. **2** *Brit.* Timothy grass. **3** A catkin or ament. **4** A cirrus cloud.

cat·ta·lo (kat′ə·lō) See CATALO.

Cat·ta·ro (kät′tä·rō) The Italian name for KOTOR.

catted chimney A chimney built of sticks and clay.

Cat·te·gat (kat′ə·gat) See KATTEGAT.

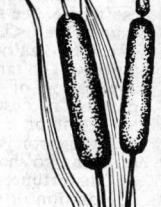

CAT–TAIL
(From 3 to 6 feet tall)

Cat·tell (kə·tel′), **James McKeen** 1860–1944, U.S. psychologist and editor.

cat·tle (kat′l) *n.* **1** Domesticated bovine animals. **2** Formerly, all livestock, as horses, sheep, goats, etc. **3** Human beings: a contemptuous term. **4** *Obs.* Vermin, birds, etc. [<AF *catel* <LL *captale* <L *capitale* capital, wealth. Doublet of CHATTEL.]

cat·tle·man (kat′l·mən) *n. pl.* **·men** (-mən) One who raises cattle.

cat·tle·ya (kat′lē·ə) *n.* Any of a genus (*Cattleya*) of tropical American orchids, widely cultivated in many horticultural varieties and esteemed for their showy, variously colored flowers. [<NL, after William *Cattley,* English botanist]

cat·ty[1] (kat′ē) *n. pl.* **·ties** An Oriental and Asiatic weight varying in different countries but equivalent to about 1 1/3 pounds avoirdupois: also called *chang.* Also **cat′tie.** [<Malay *kāti*]

cat·ty[2] (kat′ē) *adj.* **·ti·er, ·ti·est 1** Pertaining to cats. **2** *Colloq.* Malicious; spiteful; backbiting. —**cat′ti·ly** *adv.* —**cat′ti·ness** *n.*

cat·ty–cor·nered (kat′ē–kôr′nərd) See CATER–CORNERED.

Ca·tul·lus (kə·tul′əs), **Gaius Valerius,** 84–54? B.C., Roman poet.

cat·walk (kat′wôk′) *n.* **1** Any narrow walking space, as at the side of a bridge, in an aircraft, near the ceiling of the stage in a theater, etc.

cat–whisk·er (kat′hwis′kər) *n. Electronics* A fine, sharp–pointed wire used to make contact with a sensitive point on the surface of a crystal detector.

Cau·ca (kou′kä) A river in Colombia, flowing 600 miles north to the Magdalena.

Cau·ca·sian (kô·kā′zhən, -shən, -kash′ən) *n.* **1** A member of the white–skinned division of the human race: so called from a skull found in the Caucasus, which was taken as establishing the type. **2** A member of the native peoples of the Caucasus region. **3** A family of languages spoken in the Caucasus region, including Georgian and Circassian: unrelated to the Indo–European, Semitic, Hamitic, Uralic, or Altaic families. —*adj.* **1** Belonging to the region of the Caucasus mountains, its inhabitants, or their languages. **2** Caucasoid. Also **Cau·cas·ic** (kô·kas′ik).

Cau·ca·soid (kô′kə·soid) *adj. Anthropol.* Of or pertaining to the so–called white race, characterized by a skin color ranging from very white to dark brown; variable in stature, body build, eye color, head hair, and cephalic index, with moderate to profuse body hair and generally narrow to medium–broad, high–bridged nose. —*n.* A member of this ethnic group; a Caucasian.

Cau·ca·sus 1 A mountain range between the Black and Caspian Seas; highest peak, 16,512 feet. **2** A region in southern Russia between the Black and Caspian Seas; divided by the Caucasus mountains into Northern Caucasus and Transcaucasia. Also **Cau·ca·sia.** (kô·kā′zhə, -shə, -kash′ə).

Caucasus In·di·cus (in′di·kəs) The ancient name for the HINDU KUSH.

cau·cus (kô′kəs) *n.* **1** A private or preliminary meeting of members of a political party to select candidates or plan a campaign; a primary. **2** *Brit.* A political committee or other body in charge of shaping political policies, or of a local canvass or election. —*v.i.* **cau·cused** or **·cussed, ·cus·ing** or **·cus·sing** To meet in or hold a caucus. [from the *Caucus* Club, Boston, Mass., prob. <Algonquian *caucawasu* advisor]

cau·da (kô′də) *n. pl.* **·dae** (-dē) A tail, or tail–like appendage. [<L, tail]

cau·dad (kô′dad) *adv. Zool.* Toward the tail: opposed to *cephalad.*

cau·dal (kôd′l) *adj. Zool.* **1** Of, pertaining to, or near the tail or posterior part of the body. **2** Having the nature or form of a tail. —**cau′dal·ly** *adv.*

Cau·da·ta (kô·dā′tə) *n. pl.* An order of amphibians with naked skin, limbs, and a tail, including salamanders and newts: formerly called *Urodela.*

cau·date (kô′dāt) *adj. Zool.* Having a tail or tail–like appendage or extremity. Also **cau′·dat·ed.** [<L *caudatus* <*cauda* tail]

cau·dex (kô′deks) *n.* *pl.* **·di·ces** (-də·sēz) or **·dex·es** *Bot.* 1 The woody axis or trunk of a tree. 2 The woody base of a perennial plant. [<L, var. of *codex* trunk of a tree]
cau·dil·lo (kou·thē′lyō, -thē′yō) *n.* *Spanish* A chief; leader. — **el Caudillo** The head of the Spanish state: title applied to Francisco Franco (1939–).
Cau·dine Forks (kô′dīn) Two narrow passes in the Apennines, southern Italy.
cau·dle (kôd′l) *n.* A warm drink of gruel with wine, eggs, etc., for invalids. [<AF *caudel* <Med. L *caldellum,* dim. of *caldum, calidum* warm, hot]
cau·dron (kô′drən) *n.* *Scot.* A caldron.
cauf (kôf) *n.* *Scot.* A calf: also spelled *cawf.*
caught (kôt) Past tense and past participle of CATCH.
cauk (kôk) *n.* *Scot.* Chalk; limestone: also spelled *cawk.*
cauk an' keel (kôk′ ən kēl′) *Scot.* Chalk and red clay used to mark sheep.
caul (kôl) *n.* *Anat.* 1 That part of the amniotic sac which sometimes envelops the head of a newly born child. 2 The great omentum. ◆ Homophone: *call.* [<OF *cale* cap]
Cau·lain·court (kō·laṅ·kōōr′), **Marquis Armand Augustine Louis de,** 1772–1827, French general and diplomat.
cauld (kôld, käld, kôd) *adj.* & *n.* *Scot.* Cold.
caul·dron (kôl′drən) See CALDRON.
cau·les·cent (kô·les′ənt) *adj.* *Bot.* Having a clearly defined stem. [<L *caulis* stem + -ESCENT]
cau·li·cle (kô′li·kəl) *n.* *Bot.* A little stem; specifically, the rudimentary stem in the embryo of a seed. [<L *cauliculus,* dim. of *caulis* CAULIS]
cau·li·flo·rous (kô′lə·flôr′əs, -flō′rəs) *adj.* *Bot.* Characterized by a growth of flowers; borne on the main stem, as flowers and fruits. [<L *caulis* stem + *florus* flowering]
cau·li·flow·er (kô′lə·flou′ər, kol′i-) *n.* 1 The fleshy, edible head formed by the young flowers of a variety of cabbage (*Brassica oleracea botrytis*). 2 The plant bearing this. [<NL *cauliflora* flowering cabbage; infl. in form by FLOWER]
cau·li·form (kô′lə·fôrm) *adj.* *Bot.* Shaped like a stem.
cau·line (kô′lin, -līn) *adj.* *Bot.* Of, pertaining to, or growing on a stem. [<NL *caulinus* <L *caulis* CAULIS]
cau·lis (kô′lis) *n.* *pl.* **·les** (-lēz) *Bot.* The stem of a plant. [<L <Gk. *kaulos* stem of a plant]
caulk (kôk) See CALK[1].
cau·lome (kô′lōm) *n.* *Bot.* The axial portion or stem of a plant as distinguished from phyllome, trichome, and root. [<Gk. *kaulos* stalk + -OME] — **cau·lom·ic** (kô·lom′ik) *adj.*
caup (kôp) *n.* *Scot.* A bowl; cup.
caus·al (kô′zəl) *adj.* Pertaining to, constituting, involving, or expressing a cause. — *n.* A word expressive of cause or reason. [<L *causalis* of a cause < *causa* cause] — **caus′al·ly** *adv.*
cau·sal·gi·a (kô·zal′jē·ə) *n.* *Pathol.* A burning pain, such as often follows injuries of the nerves; neuralgia with severe local pain. [<NL <Gk. *kausos* heat < *kaiein* burn + *-algia* pain < *algeein* hurt]
cau·sal·i·ty (kô·zal′ə·tē) *n.* *pl.* **·ties** 1 The relation of cause and effect. 2 Causal action or agency. See synonyms under CAUSE.
cau·sa si·ne qua non (kô′zə sī′nē kwā non′) *Latin* A condition which is indispensable; a prerequisite; literally, cause without which not.
cau·sa·tion (kô·zā′shən) *n.* 1 The act, process, or agency of causing. 2 The relation of cause and effect. 3 The active force of the principle of causality. 4 Causative power or agency. See synonyms under CAUSE. [<L *causatio, -onis* < *causari* bring about < *causa* cause]
caus·a·tive (kô′zə·tiv) *adj.* 1 Effective as a cause. 2 *Gram.* Expressing cause or agency; indicating that the subject causes the action: *en-* in *enfeeble* is a *causative* prefix; *lay* (cause to lie) is a *causative* verb. — *n.* *Gram.* A form that expresses or suggests causation. [<F *causatif* <L *causativus* < *causa* cause] — **caus′a·tive·ly** *adv.* — **caus′a·tive·ness** *n.*
cause (kôz) *n.* 1 The power or efficient agent producing any thing or event. 2 Any occasion or condition upon the occurrence of which an event takes place. 3 Any rational ground for choice or action; reason. 4 A great enterprise, movement, principle, or aim. 5 *Law* An action or suit; also, a ground of action. 6 *Obs.* Behalf; interest. 7 *Philos.* The object or end for which anything is done or made; purpose; aim. — *v.t.* **caused, caus·ing** To be the cause of; produce; effect; induce; compel. [<F <L *causa* cause, legal case] — **caus′a·ble** *adj.* — **cause′less** *adj.* — **caus′er** *n.*

Synonyms (noun): actor, agent, antecedent, author, causality, causation, condition, creator, designer, former, fountain, motive, occasion, origin, originator, power, precedent, reason, source, spring. The efficient *cause,* that which makes anything to be or be done, is the common meaning of the word, as in the saying "There is no effect without a *cause.*" Every man instinctively recognizes himself acting through will as the *cause* of his own actions. The *Creator* is the Great First *Cause* of all things. A *condition* is something that necessarily precedes a result, but does not produce it. An *antecedent* simply precedes a result, with or without any agency in producing it; as, Monday is the invariable *antecedent* of Tuesday, but not the *cause* of it. The direct antonym of *cause* is *effect,* while that of *antecedent* is *consequent.* An *occasion* is some event which brings a *cause* into action at a particular moment; gravitation and heat are the *causes* of an avalanche; the steep incline of the mountain side is a necessary *condition. Causality* is the doctrine or principle of causes, *causation* the action or working of causes. *Motive* is an impulse of an intelligent being which incites to action, and, if unchecked, is a *cause* of action. Compare DESIGN, REASON. *Antonyms*: consequence, creation, development, effect, end, event, fruit, issue, outcome, outgrowth, product, result.

cause cé·lè·bre (kōz sā·leb′r′) *French* 1 A famous legal case. 2 Any well-known controversial issue.
cau·se·rie (kō′zə·rē′, *Fr.* kōz·rē′) *n.* 1 Light conversation; informal discussion. 2 A free, unconventional treatment or criticism of a subject; conversational criticism. [<F]
cause·way (kôz′wā′) *n.* 1 A raised road or way, as over marshy ground. 2 A sidewalk above the street level. 3 A highway. — *v.t.* 1 To make a causeway for or through, as a marshy tract. 2 To pave, as a road. [<AF *caucie* <LL *calciata,* pp. of *calciare* tread, stamp down <L *calx, calcis* heel + WAY]
cau·sey (kô′zē) *n.* *pl.* **·seys** *Scot.* & *Brit. Dial.* A paved way, street, or highway.
caus·tic (kôs′tik) *adj.* 1 Capable of corroding or eating away tissues; burning; corrosive. 2 Causing to smart; stinging; biting; sarcastic and severe. 3 *Optics* **a** Designating a surface to which all rays emitted from one point and reflected or refracted from a curved surface are tangents: so called because along such a surface the heating effect is at the maximum. **b** Designating a curve formed by such a surface. — *n.* 1 A caustic substance. 2 *Optics* A caustic curve or surface. Also **caus′ti·cal.** See synonyms under BITTER. [<L *causticus* <Gk. *kaustikos* < *kausos* burning < *kaiein* burn] — **caus′ti·cal·ly** *adv.*
caus·tic·i·ty (kôs·tis′ə·tē) *n.* 1 The quality or state of being caustic. 2 Severity of language. See synonyms under ACRIMONY.
caustic potash Potassium hydroxide.
caustic soda Sodium hydroxide.
cau·ter·ant (kô′tər·ənt) *adj.* Of or pertaining to cautery or a caustic. — *n.* A cauterizing substance.
cau·ter·ize (kô′tər·īz) *v.t.* **·ized, ·iz·ing** 1 To sear with a caustic drug or a heated iron. 2 To make callous or insensible. Also *Brit.* **cau′ter·ise.** See synonyms under BURN. [<LL *cauterizare* <L *cauterium.* See CAUTERY.] — **cau′ter·i·za′tion, cau′ter·ism** *n.*
cau·ter·y (kô′tər·ē) *n.* *pl.* **·ter·ies** 1 *Med.* The application of a caustic, especially for the purpose of destroying tissue. 2 A cauterizing agent or a searing iron. [<L *cauterium* branding iron <Gk. *kautērion* < *kaiein* burn]
cau·tion (kô′shən) *n.* 1 Care to avoid injury or misfortune; prudence; wariness. 2 An admonition or warning. 3 *Colloq.* A person or thing that alarms, astonishes, or provokes great admiration. — *v.t.* To advise to be prudent; warn. See synonyms under ADMONISH. [<OF <L *cautio, -onis* < *cavere* beware, take heed]
cau·tion·ar·y (kô′shən·er′ē) *adj.* Constituting or conveying a warning; admonitory.
cau·tious (kô′shəs) *adj.* Exercising or manifesting caution; wary; prudent. — **cau′tious·ly** *adv.* — **cau′tious·ness** *n.*
Cau·ver·y (kô′vər·ē) See KAVERI.
Cau·vin (kō·vaṅ′) French form of CALVIN
ca·val (kā′vəl) *adj.* 1 Of or pertaining to a cavity. 2 Large and hollow. [<L *cavus* hollow]
cav·al·cade (kav′əl·kād′, kav′əl·kād) *n.* A company of riders; a parade. See synonyms under PROCESSION. [<MF <Ital. *cavalcata* < *cavalcare* ride on horseback <LL *caballicare* <L *caballus* horse, nag]
cav·a·lier (kav′ə·lir′) *n.* 1 A horseman; knight. 2 A lover; escort; gallant. — *adj.* 1 Free and easy; offhand. 2 Haughty; supercilious. — *v.t.* To escort or play the gallant to, as a lady. — *v.i.* To behave in a cavalier fashion; show arrogance. Also *Obs.* **cav·a·le·ro** (kav′ə·lā′rō), **cav′a·lie′ro** (-lyā′rō). [<MF <Ital. *cavaliere* <LL *caballarius* < *caballus* horse, nag. Doublet of CHEVALIER.]
Cav·a·lier (kav′ə·lir′) *n.* A supporter or member of the court party during the reign of Charles I of England; a royalist: opposed to *Roundhead.* — *adj.* Pertaining to the Cavaliers. — **cav′a·lier′ism** *n.*
cav·a·lier·ly (kav′ə·lir′lē) *adj.* Like or characteristic of a cavalier; gallant; also, haughty. — *adv.* After the manner of a cavalier; disdainfully; haughtily.
Cavalier poets A group of English lyric poets, mainly at the court of Charles I, including Herrick, Carew, Lovelace, and Suckling.
ca·val·ly (kə·val′ē) *n.* *pl.* **·lies** 1 A carangoid fish (genus *Caranx*); especially, a food fish (*C. hippos*) of the Atlantic. 2 The cero. Also **ca·val·la** (kə·val′ə). [<Sp. *caballa* horse mackerel <L *caballus* horse]
cav·al·ry (kav′əl·rē) *n.* *pl.* **·ries** 1 Mobile ground troops, organized in mounted, mechanized, or motorized units. 2 One of the principal arms or branches of the U.S. Army and of other armies. 3 Organized, mounted combat troops. 4 Riders, horsemen, etc., collectively. [<MF *cavallerie* <Ital. *cavalleria* <LL *caballarius* horseman < *caballus* horse. Doublet of CHIVALRY.] — **cav′al·ry·man** (-mən) *n.*
ca·van (kä·vän′) *n.* A measure used in the Philippines: approximately equal to 75 liters or 2 1/2 bushels. [<Sp. *cabán*]
Cav·an (kav′ən) A county of southern Ulster province, Ireland; 730 square miles; county seat, Cavan.
cav·a·ti·na (kav′ə·tē′nə, *Ital.* kä′vä·tē′nä) *n.* *Music* A short and simple kind of aria; especially, a song without a second part. [<Ital.]
cave (kāv) *n.* 1 A natural cavity beneath the earth's surface or in a mountain; a cavern; den. ◆ Collateral adjective: *spelean.* 2 In English politics, a member of a party which seceded from the Liberals in 1866: so called from the application by John Bright of the expression **Cave of Adullam** (I *Sam.* xxii 1, 2) in referring to this party; hence, a seceder or a seceding group. See synonyms under HOLE. — *v.* **caved, cav·ing** *v.t.* 1 To hollow out. 2 To cause to fall down or in, or to become hollow by a partial falling away. 3 To place in or as in a cave. — *v.i.* 4 To fall in or down; give way, as ground when undermined. — **to cave in** 1 To fall in or down, as when undermined; cause to fall in, as by undermining. 2 *Colloq.* To yield utterly; give in, as to argument, hardship, or strain. [<OF <L *cava* < *cavus* hollow]
ca·ve·at (kā′vē·at) *n.* 1 *Law* A formal notification to a court or officer not to take a certain step till the notifier is heard. 2 A description of an invention that is not fully perfected, formerly filed in the U.S. Patent Office, which entitled the person filing it to three months' notice before the issuing of a patent for a like invention to another. 3 A caution. [<L, let him beware]
ca·ve·at emp·tor (kā′vē·at emp′tôr) *Latin* Let the purchaser beware: implying that the purchase is made at his own risk.
ca·ve·a·tor (kā′vē·ā′tər) *n.* One who enters a caveat.
ca·ve ca·nem (kā′vē kā′nəm) *Latin* Beware of the dog.
cave·fish (kāv′fish′) *n.* *pl.* **·fish** or **·fish·es** Blindfish.
cave–in (kāv′in′) *n.* A collapse or falling in, as

of a mine or tunnel; also, the site of such a collapse.

Cav·ell (kav'əl), **Edith**, 1865–1915, English nurse executed by the Germans in World War I for helping Allied soldiers to escape from occupied Belgium.

cave man 1 A Paleolithic man; a cave dweller. **2** *Colloq.* A man who is rough and brutal, especially in his approach to women.

cav·en·dish (kav'ən-dish) *n.* A brand of American plug tobacco. [after *Cavendish,* proper name]

Cav·en·dish (kav'ən-dish), **Henry,** 1731?–1810, English chemist and physicist. —**William,** 1640–1707, first Duke of Devonshire, English statesman.

cav·ern (kav'ərn) *n.* A large cave; a den; cavity. —*v.t.* **1** To make like a cavern; hollow out. **2** To enclose, shut up, or place in or as in a cavern. [< F *caverne* < L *caverna* < *cavus* hollow]

cav·er·nic·o·lous (kav'ər-nik'ə-ləs) *adj.* Living in caves: *cavernicolous* fish. [< L *caverna* cavern + *colere* dwell + -OUS]

cav·ern·ous (kav'ər-nəs) *adj.* **1** Consisting of or containing caverns; like a cavern; hollow. **2** Hollow-sounding. **3** Pertaining to rocks having cavities or various sizes and shapes. —**cav'ern·ous·ly** *adv.*

cav·es·son (kav'ə-sən) *n.* A headstall furnished with a noseband having rings attached for a rein or cord by which a trainer on foot directs a horse in circles about him. [< F *caveçon* < Ital. *cavezzone,* aug. of *cavezza* halter]

ca·vet·to (kə-vet'ō, *Ital.* kä-vet'tō) *n. pl.* **·ti** (-tē) or **·tos** *Archit.* A molding having a concave profile of not more than 90° curvature, terminating in a vertical fillet, with a projection usually about equal to its altitude. [< Ital., dim. of *cavo* hollow < L *cavus*]

cav·i·ar (kav'ē-är, kä'vē-) *n.* A relish consisting of the roe of sturgeon or other fish, either in the natural state and salted, or pressed and salted, especially as prepared in Russia: considered a delicacy. —**caviar to the general** Something too esoteric to appeal to the popular taste. Also **cav'i·are.** [< F < Turkish *khavyar*]

cav·i·corn (kav'ə-kôrn) *adj. Zool.* Having hollow horns. —*n.* Any one of the hollow-horned ruminants. [< L *cavus* hollow + *cornu* horn]

ca·vie (kā'vē) *n. Scot.* A hencoop; chicken house.

cav·il (kav'əl) *v.* **cav·iled** or **·illed, cav·il·ing** or **·il·ling** *v.t.* To find fault with. —*v.i.* To pick flaws or raise trivial objections; argue or object captiously: with *at* or *about.* —*n.* A captious objection; caviling. [< MF *caviller* < L *cavillari* < *cavilla* a jeering, a scoffing] —**cav'il·er, cav'il·ler** *n.* —**cav'il·ing, cav'il·ling** *adj.* —**cav'il·ing·ly, cav'il·ling·ly** *adv.*

cav·i·ta·tion (kav'ə-tā'shən) *n. Physics* The formation of vapor cavities in the water flowing around the blades of a propeller, due to excessive speed of rotation, and resulting in structural damage or a loss of efficiency. [< CAVITY]

Ca·vi·te (kä-vē'tā) A province in southern Luzon, Philippines; 498 square miles; capital, Cavite.

cav·i·ty (kav'ə-tē) *n. pl.* **·ties 1** A hollow or sunken space; hole. **2** A natural hollow in the body. **3** A hollow place in a tooth, especially one caused by decay. [< MF *cavité* < LL *cavitas, -tatis* a hollow < *cavus* hollow, empty]

ca·vort (kə-vôrt') *v.i.* **1** To act up; cut up. **2** To prance and show off, as a horse; curvet. **3** To run and prance without control. [Origin unknown]

Ca·vour (kä-vōōr'), **Count Camillo Benso di,** 1810–61, Italian statesman.

ca·vy (kā'vē) *n. pl.* **·vies** A small South American burrowing rodent with the tail absent or rudimentary, as the guinea pig (*Cavia cobaya*), the **restless cavy** (*C. porcellus*), the **southern cavy** (*C. australis*), common on the Patagonian coast, and the harelike **Patagonian cavy** (*Dolichotis patagonica*). —**giant cavy** The capybara. [< NL *Cavia* < Cariban]

caw¹ (kô) *v.i.* To cry or call: said of crows, rooks, etc.; cry like a crow. —*n.* The cry of a crow, raven, rook, etc. [Imit.]

caw² (kô) See CA'.

cawk (kôk) *n. Scot.* Chalk.

Cawn·pore (kôn-pôr', -pōr') A former name for KANPUR. Also **Cawn·pur** (kôn-pōōr').

Ca·xi·as (kə-shē'əs) See DUQUE DE CAXIAS.

Cax·ton (kak'stən) *n.* **1** Any book printed by William Caxton, 1422–91, scholar and translator, who introduced printing into England. **2** *Printing* A style of type imitating that of Caxton.

cay (kā, kē) *n.* A coastal rock or sandy islet, as in the Gulf of Mexico. See KEY². [< Sp. *cayo* shoal]

Cay·enne (kī-en', kā-) The capital of French Guiana.

cayenne pepper A pungent red powder made from the fruit of various capsicums; red pepper. Also **cay·enne'.**

Cayes (kā) See LES CAYES.

cay·man (kā'mən) *n. pl.* **·mans** See CAIMAN.

Cay·mans (kā'mənz, kī-mänz') A West Indies island group, comprising a dependency of Jamaica; 92 square miles. Also **Cayman Islands.**

cay·ote (kī'ōt) See COYOTE.

Ca·yu·ga (kə-yōō'gə, kī-) *n. pl.* **·ga** or **·gas** A member of a tribe of North American Indians of Iroquoian linguistic stock formerly dwelling around Lake Cayuga, N.Y., the smallest tribe of the confederation known as the Five Nations: now chiefly on reservations in Ontario.

Ca·yu·ga Lake (kə-yōō'gə, kī-) One of the Finger Lakes in west central New York.

cay·use (kī-yōōs') *n.* **1** An Indian pony. **2** A horse of little value: a humorous or derogatory term. [after the *Cayuse* Indians]

Cay·use (kī-yōōs') *n.* A member of a tribe of North American Indians formerly inhabiting Oregon: now almost extinct.

ca·zique (kə-zēk') See CACIQUE.

C-bi·as (sē'bī'əs) See GRID BIAS.

Cd *Chem.* Cadmium (symbol Cd).

Ce *Chem.* Cerium (symbol Ce).

Ce·a (sē'ə) See CEOS.

Ce·a·rá (sā'ä-rä') A state in NE Brazil; 59,168 square miles; capital, Fortaleza.

Ceará rubber The coagulated latex of a tropical American tree (*Manihot glaziovi*).

cease (sēs) *v.* **ceased, ceas·ing** *v.t.* To leave off or discontinue, as one's own actions. —*v.i.* To come to an end; stop; desist. —*n.* End; stopping: obsolete except after *without.* [< F *cesser* < L *cessare* stop < *cedere* withdraw, yield] —**cease'less** *adj.* —**cease'less·ly** *adv.* —**cease'less·ness** *n.*

Synonyms (verb): abstain, conclude, desist, discontinue, end, finish, intermit, pause, quit, refrain, stop, terminate. Strains of music may gradually or suddenly *cease.* A man *quits* work on the instant; he may *discontinue* a practice gradually; he *quits* suddenly and completely; he *stops* short in what he may or may not resume; he *pauses* in what he will probably resume. What *intermits* or is *intermitted* returns again, as a fever that *intermits.* Compare ABANDON, DIE, END, REST. *Antonyms:* begin, commence, inaugurate, initiate, institute, originate, start.

ceb·a·dil·la (seb'ə-dil'ə) See SABADILLA.

ce·boid (sē'boid) *adj. Zool.* Pertaining to or describing any member of a superfamily or group (*Ceboidea*) of monkeys believed to have evolved from the prosimians isolated in South America, and including the marmosets, capuchins, tamarins, sapajous, and spider monkeys. —*n.* A member of this superfamily or group: also **ce·bid** (sē'bid, seb'id). [< NL < Gk. *kēbos,* a long-tailed monkey]

Ce·bu (sā-bōō') One of the Visayan Islands, Philippines; 1,703 square miles; chief port and principal city, Cebu.

Cech·y (chekh'ē) The Czech name for BOHEMIA.

Ce·cil (sē'səl, ses'əl) A masculine personal name. [< L, poor-sighted]

Ce·cil (ses'əl, sis'-), **(Edgar Algernon) Robert,** born 1864, Viscount Cecil of Chelwood, English statesman. —**Lord David,** born 1902, English biographer. —**Robert,** 1563?–1612, Earl of Salisbury and Viscount Cranborne, English statesman. —**Robert Arthur Gas-**

coyne See SALISBURY. —**William,** 1520–98, Baron Burghley, English statesman.

Ce·cil·i·a (si-sil'ē-ə, -sil'yə; *Ital.* chä-chēl'yä; *Pg.* sä-sēl'yə; *Sp.* thä-thēl'yä) A feminine personal name. Also **Cec·i·ly** (ses'ə-lē), *Fr.* **Cé·cile** (sā-sēl'). [< L. See CECIL.]

—**Cecilia, Saint,** died 230?, a Roman virgin who professed Christianity and suffered martyrdom in Sicily; patroness of music; her day is Nov. 22.

ce·cro·pi·a moth (si-krō'pē-ə) A large, strikingly marked moth (*Samia cecropia*) common in the eastern United States. [< NL *Cecropia,* genus of an American mulberry tree, named after *Cecrops*]

Ce·crops (sē'krops) In Greek legend, the first king of Attica and founder of Athens, represented as half man, half dragon.

ce·cum sē'kəm) *n. pl.* **ce·ca** (sē'kə) *Anat.* A blind pouch, or cavity, open at one end, especially that situated between the large and small intestines; the blind gut. Also spelled *caecum.* [< L < *caecus* blind] —**ce'cal** *adj.*

ce·dar (sē'dər) *n.* **1** A large tree of the pine family (genus *Cedrus*) having evergreen leaves and fragrant wood. There are several varieties, as the **cedar of Lebanon** (*C. libani*), **deodar cedar** (*C. deodara*), etc. **2** The American red cedar. **3** The arbor vitae. **4** Spanish cedar (*Cedrela odorata*), a deciduous tree of the mahogany family, whose wood is used for cigar boxes. **5** The wood of these and related trees. —*adj.* Pertaining to or made of cedar. [< OF *cedre* < L *cedrus* < Gk. *kedros*]

ce·dar·bird (sē'dər-bûrd') *n.* The common American waxwing. Also **cedar waxwing.**

Cedar Breaks National Monument (brāks) A region of SW Utah; 10 square miles; established 1933.

cedar brown A warm, light brown, the color of cedar wood.

cedar chest A storage chest for woolens, made of cedar wood, for protection from moths.

ce·darn (sē'dərn) *adj.* **1** Of, pertaining to, or made of cedar. **2** Lined or bordered with cedars. Also **ce'dared.**

Cedar Rapids A city in eastern Iowa.

ce·dar·wood (sē'dər-wood') *n.* The wood from any species of cedar.

cedarwood oil A colorless to pale- or greenish-yellow essential oil obtained by the distillation of cedarwood: used in medicine and in perfumes and insecticides.

cede (sēd) *v.t.* **ced·ed, ced·ing 1** To yield or give up. **2** To surrender title to; transfer: said especially of territory. See synonyms under ABANDON, GIVE. ◆Homophone: *seed.* [< MF *céder* < L *cedere* withdraw, yield]

ce·dil·la (si-dil'ə) *n.* A mark put under the letter *c* (ç) in some French words to indicate that it is to be sounded as (s). [< Sp., dim. of *zeda,* the letter *z* < Gk. *zēta;* orig., a small *z* placed next to a *c* to indicate its sound]

Ced·ric (sed'rik, sē'drik) A masculine personal name. [< Celtic, war chief]

ced·u·la (sej'oo-lə, *Sp.* thā'thoo'lä) *n.* **1** An obligation of the government in certain Spanish-American countries. **2** In the Philippines, a personal registration tax certificate; also, the tax itself. [< Sp. *cédula* note, bill]

cee (sē) *n.* The letter *c.*

ce·i·ba (sā'i-bä, sī'bə) *n.* A West Indian and Mexican tree (*Ceiba pentandra*), yielding kapok. [< Sp. < Arawakan]

ceil (sēl) *v.t.* **1** To furnish with a ceiling; line the roof of. **2** To sheathe internally; line, as an apartment. ◆Homophone: *seal.* [< F *ciel* roof, canopy < L *caelum* heaven, sky]

ceil·ing (sē'ling) *n.* **1** The overhead covering of a room. **2** Internal sheathing, as of a vessel. **3** The act of one who ceils. **4** *Aeron.* **a** The maximum height to which a given aircraft can be driven. **b** The upward limit of visibility for flying; the distance, expressed in hundreds of feet, between the ground and the base of an overcast or broken cloud formation. **5** The top limit of anything; specifically, the highest price that can be charged for a given thing. —**absolute ceiling** *Aeron.* The greatest altitude above sea level

at which an airplane can sustain horizontal flight under standard air conditions. **—service ceiling** *Aeron.* The maximum height beyond which an airplane under normal conditions may not climb faster than 100 feet a minute.

ceil·om·e·ter (sē·lom′ə·tər) *n. Meteorol.* A photoelectric device used with a mercury-vapor lamp to determine the ceiling height of clouds under all weather conditions.

ce·ja (sā′hä) *n. SW U.S.* The cliff edge or margin of a mesa. [<Sp.]

cel·a·don (sel′ə·don) *n.* **1** A Chinese porcelain famous for its gray-green glaze. **2** A delicate grayish-green color. [<F *céladon*]

Ce·lae·no (se·lē′nō) **1** In Greek mythology, one of the Harpies. **2** One of the Pleiades.

cel·an·dine (sel′ən·dīn) *n.* **1** A European perennial *(Chelidonium majus)* of the poppy family, with yellow flowers. **2** The pilewort. [<OF *celidoine* <L *chelidonia* <Gk. *chelidonion* <*chelidōn* a swallow]

ce·la·tion (sə·lā′shən) *n. Med.* The concealing of pregnancy, or of the birth of a child. [<L *celatio, -onis* <*celare* conceal]

-cele[1] *combining form* Tumor or hernia: *gastrocele.* [<Gk. *kēlē* tumor]

-cele[2] *combining form* Cavity; hollow space: *blastocele.* Also spelled *-coele.* [<Gk. *koilos* hollow]

Cel·e·bes (sel′ə·bēz, sə·lē′bēz) An Indonesian island east of Borneo; 69,277 square miles; chief city, Makassar. *Indonesian* **Su·la·we·si** (so͞o′lä·wä′sē).

Celebes Sea A part of the Pacific bounded by Celebes, Borneo, and Mindanao.

cel·e·brant (sel′ə·brənt) *n.* **1** One who celebrates. **2** The officiating priest at a mass.

cel·e·brate (sel′ə·brāt) *v.* **·brat·ed, ·brat·ing** *v.t.* **1** To observe, as a festival or occasion, with demonstrations of respect or rejoicing. **2** To make known or famous; extol, as in song or poem: to *celebrate* a hero. **3** To perform a ceremony publicly and as ordained, as with solemn rites. *—v.i.* **4** To observe or commemorate a day or event. **5** To observe the Eucharist. [<L *celebratus,* pp. of *celebrare* celebrate, honor <*celeber* famous] **—cel′e·brat′er** or **·bra′tor** *n.*

Synonyms (verb): commemorate, keep, observe, solemnize. To *celebrate* any event or occasion is to make some demonstration of respect or rejoicing because of or in memory of it, or to perform such public rites or ceremonies as it properly demands. We *celebrate* the birth, *commemorate* the death of one beloved or honored. We *celebrate* a national anniversary with music, song, firing of guns and ringing of bells; we *commemorate* by any solemn and thoughtful service, or by a monument or other enduring memorial. We *keep* the Sabbath, *solemnize* a marriage, *observe* an anniversary; we *celebrate* or *observe* the Lord's Supper in which believers *commemorate* the sufferings and death of Christ. See KEEP, PRAISE. *Antonyms*: contemn, despise, dishonor, disregard, forget, ignore, neglect, overlook, profane, violate.

cel·e·brat·ed (sel′ə·brā′tid) *adj.* **1** Famous; renowned. **2** Performed or observed with customary rites.

Synonyms: distinguished, eminent, exalted, famed, famous, glorious, illustrious, noted, renowned. See ILLUSTRIOUS. *Antonyms*: degraded, disgraced mean, obscure, unknown.

cel·e·bra·tion (sel′ə·brā′shən) *n.* **1** The act of celebrating. **2** Things done in commemoration of any event.

ce·leb·ri·ty (sə·leb′rə·tē) *n. pl.* **·ties 1** The state or quality of being celebrated; fame. **2** A famous or much publicized person. See synonyms under FAME.

ce·ler·i·ty (sə·ler′ə·tē) *n.* Quickness of motion; speed; rapidity. [<F *célérité* <L *celeritas, -tatis* <*celer* swift]

cel·er·y (sel′ər·ē, sel′rē) *n.* A biennial herb *(Apium graveolens),* whose blanched stems are used as a vegetable or salad. [<F *céleri* <Ital. *sellari,* pl. of *sellaro* <L *selinon* parsley <Gk.]

ce·les·ta (sə·les′tə) *n.* A musical instrument, with keyboard of five octaves and hammers that strike steel plates. [<F *célesta*]

Ce·leste (sə·lest′) A feminine personal name. Also **Ce·les·tine** (se·les′tēn, -tin, sel′is·tīn), *Fr.* **Cé·les·tine** (sā·les·tēn′). [<F <L, heavenly]

ce·les·tial (sə·les′chəl) *adj.* **1** Of or pertaining to the sky or heavens. **2** Heavenly; divine. *—n.* A heavenly being. [<OF <L *caelestis* heavenly <*caelum* sky, heaven] **—ce·les′tial·ly** *adv.*

Ce·les·tial (sə·les′chəl) *adj.* Chinese. *—n.* A Chinese.

celestial body A star, planet, comet, etc.

Celestial Empire The former Chinese Empire: translation of *Tien Chao,* Heavenly Dynasty.

celestial equator *Astron.* The great circle in which the plane of the earth's equator cuts the celestial sphere: also called *equinoctial circle* or *line.*

celestial globe A globe whose surface depicts the geography of the heavens, fixed stars, constellations, etc.; a spherical representation of the heavens.

celestial navigation. Celonavigation.

celestial pole Either of the two points where the earth's axis of rotation pierces the celestial sphere.

celestial sphere The spherical surface on which the heavenly bodies seem to lie: conceived by astronomers as of infinite diameter and enclosing the universe.

Cel·es·tine (sel′is·tīn, sə·les′tīn, -tin) Name of five popes; notably, **Celestine V, 1214?–96,** real name Pietro di Murrhone, elected pope 1294; abdicated after five months.

Cel·es·tine (sel′is·tīn, sə·les′tīn, -tin) *n.* A member of a Benedictine order of hermits founded in 1264 by Celestine V, before his papacy. Also **Cel·es·tin·i·an** (sel′is·tin′ē·ən).

cel·es·tite (sel′is·tīt) *n.* A vitreous, white, often bluish orthorhombic strontium sulfate, $SrSo_4$. Also **cel′es·tine** (-tin, -tīn). [<L *caelestis* heavenly; from its blue color]

Cel·ia (sēl′yə, sē′lē·ə; *Ital.* chā′lyä) A feminine personal name. Also *Fr.* **Cé·lie** (sā·lē′). [<CECILIA]

ce·li·ac (sē′lē·ak) *adj.* Of or pertaining to the abdomen: also spelled *coeliac.* [<L *coeliacus* <Gk. *koiliakos* <*koilia* belly, abdomen <*koilos* hollow]

cel·i·ba·cy (sel′ə·bə·sē) *n.* The state of being unmarried; specifically, abstinence from marriage in accordance with religious vows. [<L *caelebs* unmarried]

cel·i·bate (sel′ə·bit, -bāt) *adj.* **1** Unmarried. **2** Vowed to remain single. *—n.* An unmarried person.

cell (sel) *n.* **1** A small, close room, especially one for a prisoner. **2** *Entomol.* **a** A small space or cavity bounded by the veins or nerves on the surface of an insect's wing. **b** A single compartment of a honeycomb. **3** *Biol.* **a** One of the cases or cuplike cavities containing an individual zoospore. **b** A small, often microscopic mass of protoplasm, variously differentiated in composition, structure, and function, usually containing a central nucleus and enclosed within a semipermeable wall (plant) or membrane (animal). It is the

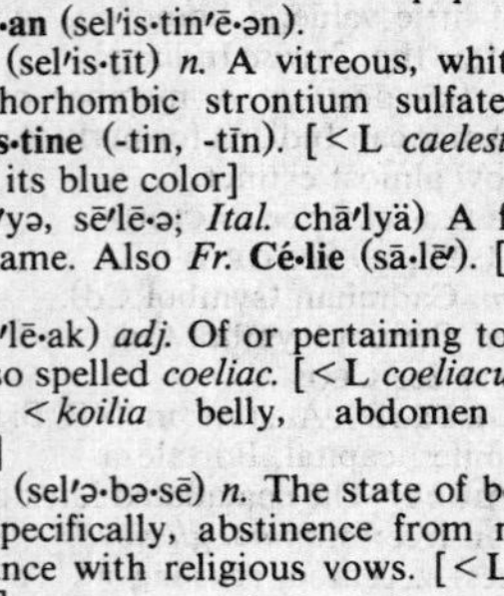

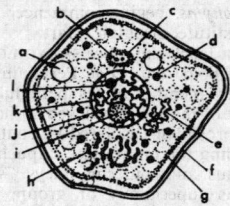

TYPICAL CELL

a.	Vacuole.	*g.*	Plasma membrane.
b.	Centriole.	*h.*	Chondriosome.
c.	Centrosphere.	*i.*	Nucleolus.
d.	Metaplasm.	*j.*	Nuclear sap.
e.	Golgi body.	*k.*	Chromatin.
f.	Cell wall.	*l.*	Karyosome.

fundamental unit of all organisms and the physicochemical basis both of individual development and of organic evolution from the simplest protozoa to the most complex forms of plant and animal life. **4** *Bot.* **a** The cavity of an anther, containing pollen. **b** The seed-bearing cavity of an ovary or pericarp. **5** *Electr.* The unit of a battery, consisting of electrodes in contact with an electrolyte and in which an electric potential is developed by means of chemical action: a voltaic *cell.* **6** *Crystall.* The fundamental structural element of a crystalline lattice: also called *unit cell.* **7** *Aeron.* **a** The full assembly of parts on either side of the fuselage of a biplane. **b** The gas compartment of a balloon or dirigible. **8** A body of persons forming a single unit in an organization of similar groups. **9** A small monastery or nunnery dependent on a larger one. **10** The room occupied by a monk or a nun. ◆Homophone: *sell.* [<OF *celle* <L cella]

cel·la (sel′ə) *n. pl.* **cel·lae** (sel′ē) The enclosed interior of a temple. [<L, small room]

cel·lar (sel′ər) *n.* **1** An underground room usually under a building: used for storage. **2** A room for storing wines; hence, the wines. *—v.t.* To put or keep in or as in a cellar. [<OF *celier* <L *cellarium* pantry <*cella* cell, small room]

cel·lar·age (sel′ər·ij) *n.* **1** A cellar or cellars. **2** Storage in a cellar or the charge for it.

cel·lar·er (sel′ər·ər) *n.* **1** The keeper of a cellar, as in a monastery. **2** A butler. **3** A wine merchant.

cel·lar·et (sel′ə·ret′) *n.* A case or small cabinet for bottles or decanters, glasses, etc. Also **cel′lar·ette′.**

cell-block (sel′blok′) *n.* In prisons, a group of cells considered as and divided off into a unit.

Cel·le (tsel′ə) A city in Lower Saxony, NW Germany.

cell fusion *Biol.* The artificial creation of a cell containing replicating genetic elements from disparate sources.

Cel·li·ni (chə·lē′nē, *Ital.* chel·lē′nē), **Benvenuto,** 1500–71, Italian sculptor and goldsmith, known for his autobiography.

cel·lo (chel′ō) *n. pl.* **·los** A violoncello. Also **′cel′lo.** [Short for VIOLONCELLO] **—cel′list** *n.*

cel·loi·din (sə·loi′din) *n.* A substance composed of pyroxylin, used for embedding microscopic specimens so that they may be cut in thin sections. [<CELL(ULOSE) + -OID + -IN]

cel·lo·phane (sel′ə·fān) *n.* A specially treated regenerated cellulose which has been processed in thin, transparent, and impermeable strips or sheets, variously colored. [<CELL(ULOSE) + -PHANE]

cel·lu·lar (sel′yə·lər) *adj.* **1** Of, pertaining to, or like a cell or cells. **2** Consisting of or containing cells. [<NL *cellularis* <L *cellula.* See CELLULE.]

cel·lule (sel′yo͞ol) *n.* **1** *Biol.* A small cell, as on a leaf or the wings of an insect. **2** *Aeron.* A boxlike rectangular area in a biplane or triplane formed by the planes or the struts between. [<L *cellula,* dim, of *cella* cell, small room]

cel·lu·li·tis (sel′yə·lī′tis) *n. Pathol.* Inflammation of the cellular tissue.

Cel·lu·loid (sel′yə·loid) *n.* A hard, elastic, inflammable plastic compound, made by subjecting gun cotton (pyroxylin) mixed with camphor and other substances to hydraulic pressure: a trade name.

cel·lu·lose (sel′yə·lōs) *n. Biochem.* An amorphous white carbohydrate, $(C_6H_{10}O_5)x$, isomeric with starch, insoluble in all ordinary solvents, and forming the fundamental material of the structure of plants. *—adj.* Containing cells. [<L *cellula.* See CELLULE.]

cellulose acetate *Chem.* **1** An acetic acid ester of cellulose: when coagulated or solidified it is used in making artificial leather and synthetic textile yarns and fabrics. **2** Acetate rayon.

cellulose nitrate *Chem.* A nitric acid ester of cellulose, its properties depending upon the nitrogen content: used in the manufacture of explosives and lacquers: also called *nitrocellulose.*

cel·lu·lous (sel′yə·ləs) *adj.* Consisting or full of cells.

ce·lom (sē′ləm) See COELOM.

cel·o·nav·i·ga·tion (sel′ō·nav′ə·gā′shən) *n.* That part of navigation in which position is determined by observation of celestial bodies; nautical astronomy: also called *astronavigation.* [<L *caelum* sky + NAVIGATION]

Cel·o·tex (sel′ə·teks) *n.* A sound-absorbing and heat-insulating board made by compressing bagasse into sheets: a trade name.

Cel·si·us scale (sel′sē·əs) A temperature scale in which the freezing point of water is 0° and the boiling point 100°: term now preferred to *centigrade scale.* [after Anders *Celsius,* 1701–44, Swedish astronomer]

Cel·sus (sel′səs) Epicurean philosopher of the

second century. — **Aurelius Cornelius,** Roman medical writer of the first century.

celt (selt) *n. Archeol.* A prehistoric or primitive implement or weapon of stone or bronze. [<LL *celtis* stone chisel]

CELT
Side. Front.

Celt (selt, kelt) *n.* **1** A person of Celtic linguistic stock, now represented by the Irish, Welsh, Highland Scots, Manx, Cornish, and Bretons, formerly by the ancient Gauls and Britons. **2** One of an ancient people of central and western Europe, known to the Greeks as *Keltoi* and to the Romans as *Celtae,* described as being fair and of great stature. Also spelled *Kelt.*

Celt·ic (sel′tik, kel′-) *n.* A subfamily of the Indo-European family of languages, including ancient Gaulish, the Brythonic or Cymric branch (Cornish, Welsh, Breton), and the Goidelic or Gaelic branch (Irish, Scottish Highland Gaelic, Manx). — *adj.* Of or pertaining to the Celtic peoples, their languages, or culture. Also spelled *Keltic.*

Celtic cross See under CROSS.

Celt·i·cism (sel′tə·siz′əm, kel′-) *n.* **1** A custom, idiom, or peculiarity of the Celts. **2** Devotion to Celtic customs.

Celt·i·cist (sel′tə·sist, kel′-) *n.* An authority on or scholar in the Celtic languages and literature.

Celtic renaissance 1 The resurgence of Irish national spirit, interest in Old Irish literature, and the creation of new, which began in the 1890's, led by Lady Augusta Gregory, Æ, Douglas Hyde, W. B. Yeats, John M. Synge, etc. **2** The revival of Irish Gaelic as the national language in the schools and business of the Irish Free State.

Celt·ism (sel′tiz·əm, kel′-) *n.* The Celtic temperament or spirit.

Celt·ist (sel′tist, kel′-) *n.* An authority on the Celts.

ce·ment (si·ment′) *n.* **1** Any substance, as a preparation of glue, red lead, or lime, the hardening of which causes objects between which it is applied to adhere firmly. **2** Any compound or substance applied in the form of a mortar and used for producing a hard and stony mass, smooth, waterproof surface, coating, filling, or lining, as for a floor or cistern. Ordinary cement is made by heating limestone and clay, or a natural rock containing both materials in right proportions. When it will harden under water, it is called **hydraulic cement. 3** That which serves to bind together persons or interests; bond of union. **4** *Metall.* **a** A finely divided metal obtained by precipitation: *cement silver.* **b** The substance in which iron is packed in the process of cementation. **5** Auriferous gravel held together by a clayey or silicic bond; also, the binding substance. **6** The glassy base of an igneous rock. **7** Cementum. — **Portland cement** A hydraulic cement made by calcining limestone with clayey matter, such as chalk and river mud. — *v.t.* **1** To unite or join with or as with cement. **2** To cover or coat with cement, as a cistern. — *v.i.* **3** To become united by means of cement; cohere. [<OF *ciment* <L *caementum* rough stone, stone chip < *caedere* cut] — **ce·ment′er** *n.*

ce·men·ta·tion (sē′mən·tā′shən, sem′ən-) *n.* **1** The act of cementing; result of cementing. **2** *Metall.* **a** A process of making steel by heating wrought iron in charcoal until it is carburized, or in making so-called malleable iron by heating cast iron in a bed of red hematite until it is partly decarburized. **b** The method of precipitating a metal from its solution, as the precipitation of metallic copper from a copper sulfate solution by means of metallic iron.

ce·ment·ite (si·men′tīt) *n. Metall.* Iron combined with carbon as it exists in steel before hardening; carbide of iron, Fe_3C.

ce·ment·um (si·men′təm) *n. Anat.* The layer of bony tissue developed over the roots of the

teeth about the fifth month after birth: also called *cement.* [<L]

cem·e·ter·y (sem′ə·ter′ē) *n. pl.* **·ter·ies** A place for the burial of the dead; formerly, a churchyard or a catacomb; now, usually, a large parklike enclosure, laid out and kept for purposes of interment. [<L *cemeterium* <Gk. *koimētērion* < *koimaein* put to sleep]

cen·a·cle (sen′ə·kəl) *n.* **1** A small supper room, usually on an upper story. **2** The room in which the Last Supper of Jesus and His disciples was held. [<F *cénacle* <L *cenaculum* < *cena* dinner]

Cen·ci (chen′chē), **Beatrice,** 1577–99, Roman lady, executed as an accessory to her father's murder.

ce·nes·the·sia (sē′nis·thē′zhə, -zhē·ə, sen′is-) *n. Psychol.* The diffuse internal awareness of bodily existence, caused by the interaction of numerous unlocalized sensations whose aggregate expression may be of any degree of pain or pleasure. Also **ce′nes·the′sis.** Sometimes spelled *coenesthesia, coenesthesis.* [<CEN(O)- + Gk. *aisthēsis* feeling] — **ce′nes·thet′ic** (-thet′ik) *adj.*

Ce·nis (sə·nē′), **Mont** (môn) An Alpine pass in SE France on the Italian frontier; site of the **Mont Cenis tunnel** between France and Italy; 8 1/2 miles. *Italian* **Mon·te Ce·ni·sio** (môn′tā chā·nē′zyō).

ceno- *combining form* Common: *cenobite.* Also spelled *coeno-.* Also, before vowels, **cen-.** [<Gk. *koinos* common]

cen·o·bite (sen′ə·bīt, sē′nə-) *n.* A monk; a member of a religious community (convent or monastery), as distinguished from a religious recluse, or *anchorite:* also spelled *coenobite.* [<LL *coenobita* < *coenobium* CENOBIUM] — **cen·o·bit′ic** (-bit′ik) or **·i·cal** *adj.* — **cen·o·bit·ism** (sen′ə·bit·iz′əm, sē′nə-) *n.*

ce·no·bi·um (si·nō′bē·əm) *n. pl.* **·bi·a** (-bē·ə) The abode of a society that has all things in common; especially, a monastery or other such religious community. Also **cen·o·by** (sen′ə·bē, sē′nə-). [<LL *coenobium* <Gk. *koinobion* < *koinos* common + *bios* life]

cen·o·gen·e·sis (sen′ə·jen′ə·sis, sē′nə-) *n. Biol.* A form of development in which the characters of an individual organism are not typical of the group to which it belongs: opposed to *palingenesis.* Also spelled *coenogenesis, kenogenesis.* [<CENO- + Gk. *genesis* origin] — **cen·o·ge·net·ic** (sen′ə·jə·net′ik, sē′nə-) *adj.*

ce·nog·o·nal (si·nog′ə·nəl) *adj.* **1** Having one or more angles in common. **2** *Mineral.* Pertaining to or describing different crystals some of whose angles have identical values. [<Gk. *koinos* common + *gōnia* angle]

cen·o·taph (sen′ə·taf, -täf) *n.* **1** An empty tomb. **2** A monument erected to the dead but not containing the remains. [<MF *cénotaphe* <L *cenotaphium* <Gk. *kenotaphion* < *kenos* empty + *taphos* tomb] — **cen·o·taph′ic** *adj.*

Ce·no·zo·ic (sē′nə·zō′ik, sen′ə-) *adj. Geol.* Of or pertaining to the fourth and latest of the eras of geologic time, following the Mesozoic, and extending to and including the present. The Cenozoic rocks are customarily divided into the Tertiary and Quaternary (or Pleistocene) systems. See chart under GEOLOGY. — *n.* The Cenozoic period: called also the *age of mammals.* Also spelled *Caenozoic, Cainozoic.* [<Gk. *kainos* new + *zōē* life]

cense (sens) *v.t.* **censed, cens·ing 1** To perfume with incense. **2** To offer burning incense to. [<INCENSE²]

cen·ser (sen′sər) *n.* A vessel for burning incense, especially in religious ceremonies; thurible. ◆ Homophone: *censor.* [<OF *censier,* short for *encensier* <Med. L *incensarium* < *incensum* incense]

cen·sor (sen′sər) *n.* **1** An official examiner of manuscripts and plays empowered to prohibit their publication or performance if offensive to the government or subversive of good morals. **2** An official who examines despatches, letters, etc., and, if necessary, prohibits forwarding or publication, especially in time of war. **3** Anyone who censures or arraigns; a critic. **4** In ancient Rome, one of two magistrates who kept the public register of citizens and of their property, and were entrusted with the supervision of public man-

ners and morals. **5** *Psychoanal.* The subconscious mental force that disguises painful or unwanted memories and complexes or prevents them from rising to conscious recognition. — *v.t* To act as censor of; delete. ◆ Homophone: *censer.* [<L < *censere* judge] — **cen·so·ri·al** (sen·sôr′ē·əl, -sō′rē-) *adj.*

cen·so·ri·ous (sen·sôr′ē·əs, -sō′rē-) *adj.* **1** Given to censure; judging severely; faultfinding. **2** Containing or involving censure, as remarks. See synonyms under CAPTIOUS. — **cen·so′ri·ous·ly** *adv.* — **cen·so′ri·ous·ness** *n.*

cen·sor·ship (sen′sər·ship) *n.* **1** The office, term, power, system, or act of a censor or critic. **2** *Psychoanal.* The aggregate of selective agencies, both unconscious and deliberate, which are responsible for the suppression of unpleasant memories and thoughts, for the inhibition of impulses and behavior deemed improper, and for the exercise of discipline over the tendencies of the primitive ego or id.

cen·sur·a·ble (sen′shər·ə·bəl) *adj.* Deserving censure; culpable; blameworthy. — **cen′sur·a·ble·ness** *n.* — **cen′sur·a·bly** *adv.*

cen·sure (sen′shər) *n.* **1** Disapproval; condemnation or blame; adverse criticism. **2** Reprimand or discipline by ecclesiastical or political authority. **3** Critical recension of a literary work; revision. **4** *Obs.* A formal judgment or judicial sentence; opinion. — *v.t.* **·sured, ·sur·ing 1** To express disapproval of; condemn; blame. **2** To punish by a public reprimand, with or without some other penalty. **3** *Obs.* To pass judgment upon. [<F <L *censura* < *censere* judge] — **cen′sur·er** *n.*

cen·sus (sen′səs) *n. pl.* **cen·sus·es 1** An official numbering of the people of a country or district, embracing statistics of nativity, age, sex, employment, possessions, etc.; also, the printed record of it. **2** In ancient Rome, a similar enumeration of the people, but with special reference to their property, in order to determine taxation. [<L < *censere* assess] — **cen·su·al** (sen′shoo·əl) *adj.*

cent (sent) *n.* **1** The hundredth part of a dollar. In the United States it is legal tender for all sums not exceeding twenty-five cents. **2** Centum or cento, hundred: used only in *per cent,* etc. **3** The hundredth part of a standard unit in other money systems, as of the florin of the Netherlands. Equivalent forms are the centavo, centesimo, and centime. **4** *Music* A unit of pitch equal to one one-hundredth of the interval between any two successive semi-tones of the equally tempered scale: An octave contains 1200 *cents.* ◆ Homophone: *scent.* [<F <L *centum* hundred]

cen·tal (sen′təl) *adj.* **1** Of or pertaining to a hundred. **2** Counting by the hundred. — *n. Rare* A hundredweight. [<L *centum* hundred]

cen·tare (sen′târ, *Fr.* säɴ·târ′) *n.* A measure of land area, equal to one square meter: also spelled *centiare.* See METRIC SYSTEM. [<F *centi-* hundredth (<L *centum* hundred) + *are* ARE²]

cen·taur (sen′tôr) **1** In Greek mythology, one of a race of monsters, having the head, arms, and torso of a man united to the body and legs of a horse. **2** An expert horseman. [<L *Centaurus* <Gk. *Kentauros*]

Cen·tau·rus (sen·tôr′əs) A constellation of the southern sky which contains **Alpha Centauri,** the third brightest star known. See CONSTELLATION. Also **Cen′taur.**

cen·tau·ry (sen′tô·rē) *n. pl.* **·ries 1** One of certain small, mostly annual herbs (genera *Centaurium* and *Sabatia*) of the gentian family, with opposite leaves and clusters of rose, purple, or pink flowers, especially the Old World *C. umbellatum,* reputed to have

CENTAUR

medicinal properties. 2 A milkwort (*Polygala polygama*). [< L *centaureum* < Gk. *kentaureion*]

cen·ta·vo (sen·tä′vō) *n. pl.* **·vos** (-vōz, *Sp.* -vōs) 1 A small nickel or copper coin of the Philippines, Mexico, and other countries of Latin America, usually equal to the hundredth part of a peso. 2 A similar coin of Portugal and Brazil, equal to the hundredth part of an escudo. [< Sp.]

cen·te·nar·i·an (sen′tə·nâr′ē·ən) *n.* One who has reached the age of one hundred years. —*adj.* Of or pertaining to a hundred years, or to a hundredth anniversary.

cen·te·nar·y (sen′tə·ner′ē, sen·ten′ə·rē) *adj.* 1 Of or pertaining to a hundred or a century. 2 Completing a century. —*n. pl.* **·nar·ies** 1 A hundredth anniversary. 2 A period of a hundred years. [< L *centenarius* hundredfold < *centum* hundred]

cen·ten·ni·al (sen·ten′ē·əl) *adj.* 1 Of or pertaining to a hundredth anniversary. 2 A hundred years old or more. —*n.* 1 A hundredth anniversary; also, its celebration. 2 A period of a hundred years; centennium. [< L *centum* hundred + *annus* a year] —**cen·ten′ni·al·ly** *adv.*

Centennial State Nickname of COLORADO.

cen·ten·ni·um (sen·ten′ē·əm) *n.* A century.

cen·ter (sen′tər) *n.* 1 *Geom.* a The point within a circle or sphere equally distant from any point on the circumference or surface. b The point within a regular polygon equidistant from the vertices. 2 The middle: the *center* of the town. 3 The point, object, or place about which things cluster or to which they converge. 4 A fixed point or line about which a thing or things revolve; point of attraction or convergence; focal point: the *center* of interest. 5 The point of divergence, emanation, or radiation; nucleus; origin. 6 The earth considered as the center of the universe; the center of the earth. 7 The part of a target nearest the bull's-eye, or a shot striking this part. 8 The middle part of an army in order of battle, occupying the front between the wings. 9 *Mech.* a One of two conical points, as in a lathe, between which an object is held and rotated on an axial line. The one at the end from which the object is rotated is the **live center,** the other the **dead center.** b The depression in a piece of revolving work, as a shaft, into which the conical point enters to support it. 10 The person who takes the middle position of the forward line in many athletic games, as football, basketball, etc. 11 Any place considered the hub of a specific activity: a manufacturing *center.* —*v.t.* 1 To place in the center. 2 To supply with a center. 3 To draw or converge in one place; concentrate. 4 In football, to pass the ball from the line to a backfield player. 5 To determine the center of; shape a lens so as to have it thickest in the center. —*v.i.* 6 To be in or at the center; have a focal point: The riots *centered* in the industrial section of the city. 7 To gather or converge, as toward a center: The crowds *centered* in the square. —*adj.* Central; middle. Also spelled *centre.* [< L *centrum* < Gk. *kentron* point (i.e., around which a circle is described)]

Synonyms (noun): middle, midst. We speak of the *center* of a circle, the *middle* of a room or the street. The *center* is equally distant from every point of the circumference of a circle, or from the opposite boundaries on each axis of a parallelogram, etc.; *middle* is more general and less definite. The *center* is a point; the *middle* may be a line or a space. We say *at the center; in the middle. Midst* commonly implies a group or multitude of surrounding objects. Compare synonyms for AMID. *Antonyms:* bound, boundary, circumference, perimeter, rim.

Cen·ter (sen′tər) *n.* In some European legislatures, the members sitting on the middle benches, a position generally assigned to those of moderate views: also spelled *Centre.*

cen·ter·bit (sen′tər·bit′) *n.* A bit with a cutting edge that revolves about a central point.

cen·ter·board (sen′tər·bôrd′, -bōrd′) *n. Naut.* 1 In certain fore-and-aft vessels, a movable device which can be lowered through a watertight slot so as to prevent leeway. 2 A boat furnished with this device.

cen·ter·ing (sen′tər·ing) *n.* 1 The act or operation of bringing an object within the

focus of a microscope, telescope, etc. 2 A temporary support of an arch or other part of a building. Also **cen′tring.**

center of mass *Physics* 1 That point in a body at which all its mass can be concentrated without altering the effect of gravitation upon it. 2 The point in which a body near the earth's surface, acted upon by gravity or other parallel forces, is balanced in all positions: commonly known as **center of gravity.**

cen·ter·piece (sen′tər·pēs′) *n.* An ornament in the center of a table, ceiling, etc., or between other ornaments: also spelled *centrepiece.*

center table A medium-sized table of almost any shape, finished on all sides to stand in the center of a room.

cen·tes·i·mal (sen·tes′ə·məl) *adj.* 1 Hundredth; of or divided into hundredths. 2 Pertaining to progression by hundreds. [< L *centesimus* hundredth] —**cen·tes′i·mal·ly** *adv.*

cen·tes·i·mo (sen·tes′ə·mō; *Ital.* chen·tes′ē·mō, & *Sp.* sen·tes′ē·mō) 1 *pl.* **·mi** (-mē) An Italian coin, equal to the hundredth part of a lira. 2 *pl.* **·mos** (-mōz, *Sp.* -mōs) A small Uruguayan coin, equal to the hundredth part of a peso.

centi- *combining form* 1 Hundred: *centipede.* 2 In the metric system, hundredth: *centiliter.* [< L *centum* hundred]

cen·ti·are (sen′tē·âr) See CENTARE.

cen·ti·grade (sen′tə·grād) *adj.* Graduated to a scale of a hundred. On the **centigrade scale** (now called the *Celsius scale*) the freezing point of water at normal atmospheric pressure is 0° and its boiling point 100°. The distance between those two points in the Fahrenheit and Réaumur is 180° and 80° respectively. See TEMPERATURE. [< F < L *centum* hundred + *gradus* step, degree]

cen·ti·gram (sen′tə·gram) *n.* The hundredth part of a gram. See METRIC SYSTEM. Also **cen′ti·gramme.** [< F *centigramme*]

cen·tile (sen′til, -til) See PERCENTILE.

cen·ti·li·ter (sen′tə·lē′tər) *n.* The hundredth part of a liter. See METRIC SYSTEM. Also **cen′ti·li′tre** [< F *centilitre*]

Cen·ti·man·us (sen′tə·man′əs) In Roman mythology, a hundred-handed giant: identified with the Greek *Hecatoncheires.*

cen·time (sän′tēm, *Fr.* sän·tēm′) *n.* In France, Belgium, and Switzerland, a hundredth of a franc; also, a coin of this value. [< F < OF *centisme* < L *centesimus* hundredth]

cen·ti·me·ter (sen′tə·mē′tər) *n.* The hundredth part of a meter. See METRIC SYSTEM. Also **cen′ti·me′tre.** [< F *centimètre*]

cen·ti·me·ter-gram-sec·ond (sen′tə·mē′tər·gram′sek′ənd) See CGS.

cen·ti·mo (sen′tə·mō) *n. pl.* **·mos** The hundredth part of a Spanish peseta.

cen·ti·pede (sen′tə·pēd) *n.* Any of a class (Chilopoda) of carnivorous, predatory arthropods having elongate, segmented bodies bearing a pair of legs on each segment, the front pair being modified into poison claws. Also called *chilopod.* [< F < L *centipeda* < *centum* hundred + *pes, pedis* foot]

cen·ti·poise (sen′tə·poiz) *n.* The hundredth part of a poise. [< CENTI- + POISE²]

cen·ti·stere (sen′tə·stir) *n.* A hundredth of a stere. See METRIC SYSTEM. [< F *centistère*]

cent·ner (sent′nər) *n.* 1 The hundredweight of various European countries, or 110.23 pounds, equal to 50 kilograms. 2 *Metall.* A hundred pounds. 3 In assaying, one dram. —**metric centner** Quintal. [< G *centner, zentner* hundredweight < L *centenarius* of a hundred]

cen·to (sen′tō) *n. pl.* **·tos** 1 A writing composed of selections from various authors or from different works of the same author. 2 *Obs.* Patchwork. [< L, patchwork cloak]

cen·tral (sen′trəl) *adj.* 1 Of or pertaining to, equidistant or acting from, the center. 2 Being a dominant or controlling factor, element, etc.; chief. 3 Constituting the principal point; a *central* event in history. 4 *Phonet.* Formed with a tongue position intermediate between front and back: said of vowels. —*n.* 1 *Colloq.* A telephone exchange; also, the operator in charge of it. 2 In Latin America, a sugar mill grinding for a number of plantations. [< L *centralis* < *centrum* center] —**cen′tral·ly** *adv.* —**cen′tral·ness** *n.*

Central African Republic An independent republic of the French Community; 238,244 square miles; capital, Bangui; formerly

Ubangi-Shari, a French overseas territory.

Central America A narrow, winding strip of land between North America proper and

the South American continent, generally understood to include Guatemala, British Honduras, Honduras, El Salvador, Nicaragua, Costa Rica, and Panama.

central angle See under ANGLE.

Central Asia See SOVIET CENTRAL ASIA.

central heating A system of heating a building by piping hot steam, water, or air from a central source to heat distributors located in separate rooms, apartments, etc.

Central India A former political agency in India, including a large number of princely states; 51,946 square miles.

cen·tral·ism (sen′trəl·iz′əm) *n.* Concentration of control in a central authority, especially of government control. —**cen′tral·ist** *n. & adj.* —**cen′tral·is′tic** *adj.*

cen·tral·i·ty (sen·tral′ə·tē) *n.* 1 The state of being central. 2 Tendency toward or situation at a center.

cen·tral·ize (sen′trəl·īz) *v.* **·ized, ·iz·ing** *v.t.* 1 To make central; bring to a center; concentrate. 2 To concentrate (power or control) in one authority. —*v.i.* 3 To come to a center; concentrate. —**cen′tral·i·za′tion** *n.* —**cen′tral·iz′er** *n.*

Central Kar·roo (kə·rōō′) See GREAT KARROO.

Central Powers The countries opposed to the Allied Nations in World War I: Germany, Austria-Hungary, Bulgaria, and Turkey.

Central Provinces and Berar The former name for MADHYA PRADESH.

central spindle *Biol.* The fibrous portions of protoplasm lying between the asters in a karyokinetic division of a cell, and about which the chromosomes are grouped.

central staging See ARENA THEATER.

Central Standard Time See STANDARD TIME. Abbr. *C.S.T.*

Central Valley The great longitudinal trough in California between the Coast Ranges and the Sierra Nevada: also *Great Valley.*

Central Vietnam Former Annam, now a constituent part of Vietnam.

cen·tre (sen′tər) *n., v.t. & v.i.* **·tred, ·tring** Center.

Cen·tre (sen′tər) See CENTER.

Centre, the *Austral.* The central region of Australia, from 1926–31 a separate administrative area.

centri- *combining form* Center: equivalent of CENTRO-: used in words of Latin origin, as in *centrifugal.* [< L *centrum* center]

cen·tric (sen′trik) *adj.* 1 Central; centrally situated. 2 Belonging to or described around a center. 3 *Physiol.* Related to or connected with a nerve center. Also **cen′tri·cal.** —**cen·tri·cal·i·ty** (sen′tri·kal′ə·tē) *n.,* **cen·tric·i·ty** (sen·tris′ə·tē) *n.* —**cen′tri·cal·ly** *adv.*

cen·trif·u·gal (sen·trif′yə·gəl, -ə·gəl) *adj.* 1 Directed or tending away from a center; radiating; opposed to *centripetal.* 2 Employing centrifugal force: a *centrifugal* pump. 3 *Bot.* a Developing from the center or apex outward, or toward the base; determinate. b Turned from the center toward the side of a fruit, as a radicle. 4 *Physiol.* Leading away from the central nervous system; efferent. —*n.* 1 The drum-

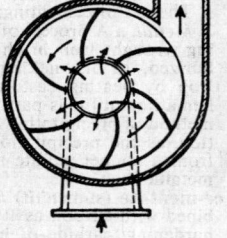

CENTRIFUGAL (*n. def. 1*)

like rotary part of a centrifuge or other centrifugal machine. 2 *pl.* Sugars from which the molasses has been removed by a centrifugal machine: also **centrifugal sugar.** [<NL *centrifugus* <L *centrum* center + *fugere* flee] **—cen·trif′u·gal·ly** *adv.*

centrifugal force *Physics* The inertial reaction of a body against a force constraining it to move in a curved path.

cen·tri·fuge (sen′trə·fyo͞oj) *n.* A rotary machine, with accessory containers, tubes, etc., for the separation by controlled centrifugal force of substances having different densities. *—v.t.* **·fuged, ·fug·ing** To subject to the action of a centrifuge. **—cen·trif·u·ga·tion** (sen·trif′yə·gā′shən, -ə·gā′-) *n.*

cen·tri·ole (sen′trē·ōl) *n. Biol.* A minute structure, frequently double, enclosed within the centrosome which forms the center of the aster in cell division, and with which it makes up the central body. For illustration see under CELL. [<CENTRI- + -OLE[2]]

cen·trip·e·tal (sen·trip′ə·təl) *adj.* **1** Directed, tending, or drawing toward a center: *centripetal* force. **2** Acting by drawing toward a center: a *centripetal* pump. **3** *Bot.* **a** Developing from without toward the center or in the direction of the apex. **b** Turned toward the axis of the fruit, as a radicle. **4** *Physiol.* Conducting toward the central nervous system; afferent. [<NL *centripetus* <*centrum* center + *petere* seek]

centripetal force *Physics* A force attracting a body toward a center around which it revolves.

cen·trist (sen′trist) *n.* One who takes the middle position in politics, especially in France.

centro- *combining form* Center: used in words of Greek origin, as in *centrosphere.* Also, before vowels, **centr-.** [<Gk. *kentron* center]

cen·tro·bar·ic (sen′trə·bar′ik) *adj. Physics* Relating to the center of gravity of a body. [<CENTRO- + Gk. *baros* weight]

cen·troid (sen′troid) *n.* **1** *Physics* Center of mass. **2** *Mech.* The point at which the area of a body may be concentrated without altering the moment of any line in its plane, as the center of a square or the intersections of the median lines of a triangle.

cen·tro·some (sen′trə·sōm) *n. Biol.* The small area of protoplasm at the center of each aster in cell division: it contains the centrioles. [<CENTRO- + Gk. *sōma* body] **—cen′tro·som′ic** (-som′ik) *adj.*

cen·tro·sphere (sen′trə·sfir′) *n.* **1** *Geol.* The central portion of the terrestrial globe. Compare HYDROSPHERE, LITHOSPHERE. **2** *Biol.* In living cells, the sphere from which the astral rays diverge, and which surrounds the centrosome, if any. For illustration see under CELL.

cen·trum (sen′trəm) *n. pl.* **·trums** or **·tra** (-trə) **1** A center or central mass. **2** *Zool.* The body of a vertebra. [<L]

cen·tum (ken′təm) *n.* One of the two main divisions of the Indo-European languages; namely, the western division, including the Hellenic, Italic, Celtic, and Germanic languages and dialects, in which the proto-Indo-European palatalized velar stop (k) is retained as a velar, as in the Latin word *centum* "hundred." Compare SATEM. See INDO-EUROPEAN.

cen·tum·vir (sen·tum′vər) *n. pl.* **·virs** or **·vi·ri** (-və·rī) In ancient Rome, one of the judges (105 to 180 in number) appointed yearly to try common causes. [<L <*centum* hundred + *vir* man] **—cen·tum′vi·ral** *adj.*

cen·tum·vi·rate (sen·tum′və·rāt) *n.* **1** The office or term of a centumvir. **2** The centumviri as a body. **3** Any body of 100 men.

cen·tu·ple (sen′tə·pəl, sen·to͞o′pəl, -tyo͞o′-) *v.t.* **·pled, ·pling** To increase a hundredfold. *—adj.* Increased a hundredfold. [<F <L *centuplus* hundredfold]

cen·tu·pli·cate (sen·to͞o′plə·kāt, -tyo͞o′-) *v.t.* **·cat·ed, ·cat·ing** To multiply by a hundred; centuple. *—adj. & n.* (-kit) Hundredfold. [<LL *centuplicatus,* pp. of *centuplicare* increase a hundredfold <*centuplex* hundredfold]

cen·tu·ri·al (sen·to͝or′ē·əl, -tyo͝or′-) *adj.* **1** Of or pertaining to a century of the Roman army or people. **2** Of or pertaining to a hundred years.

cen·tu·ried (sen′chə·rēd) *adj.* **1** Continued or maintained for one or more than one century. **2** Having endured for hundreds of years.

cen·tu·ri·on (sen·to͝or′ē·ən, -tyo͝or′-) *n.* A captain of a century in the ancient Roman army. [<L *centurio, -onis*]

cen·tu·ry (sen′chə·rē) *n. pl.* **·ries 1** One hundred consecutive years, reckoning from a specific date. **2** A period of 100 years in any system of chronology, especially in reckoning from the first year of the Christian era: the twentieth *century,* A.D. 1901–2000. **3** A body of Roman foot soldiers (at one time 100 men); one sixtieth of a legion; also, one of the 193 divisions into which the Roman people were divided according to their incomes. **4** A hundred; hundred things of the same kind collectively. [<L *centuria* <*centum* hundred]

century plant An agave *(Agave americana)* which flowers once in twenty or thirty years and then dies. Also called *American aloe.*

ceorl (cheôrl, kyûrl) *n.* In ancient England, a freeman of the lowest rank; a churl. [OE] **—ceorl′ish** *adj.*

Ce·os (sē′os) The ancient name for KEOS: also *Cea.*

ce·pha·e·line (si·fā′ə·lēn, -lin) *n. Chem.* A white, crystalline alkaloid, $C_{28}H_{38}O_4N_2$, from ipecac: regarded as more powerful than emetine. [<NL *cephaelis,* genus name of ipecac]

ceph·a·lad (sef′ə·lad) *adv. Zool.* Toward the head of an animal body: opposed to *caudad.* [<Gk. *kephalē* head]

ceph·a·lal·gia (sef′ə·lal′jē·ə) *n.* A headache. [<Gk. *kephalē* head + *algos* pain]

ce·phal·ic (sə·fal′ik) *adj.* **1** Of, pertaining to, on, in, or near the head. **2** Performing the functions of a head. **3** Relatively nearer the head or the end of the body where the head is situated: the *cephalic* end of the sternum. [<Gk. *kephalē* head]

-cephalic *combining form* Head; skull: *brachycephalic.* [<Gk. *kephalē* head]

cephalic index *Anat.* The figure that expresses the ratio of the greatest breadth of the human skull to the greatest length, the former being multiplied by 100. Skulls are usually designated as *brachycephalic, mesocephalic,* and *dolichocephalic:* also called *cranial index.*

ceph·a·lin (sef′ə·lin) *n. Biochem.* A yellowish amorphous phospholipid obtained from the brain substance or spinal cord of mammals, which acts as a blood coagulant: also spelled *kephalin.*

ceph·a·li·za·tion (sef′ə·lə·zā′shən, -lī·zā′-) *n. Zool.* Concentration or localization of functions, powers, or parts in or toward the head: the *cephalization* of the vertebrate nervous system.

cephalo- *combining form* Head: *cephalometer.* Also, before vowels, **cephal-.** [<Gk. *kephalē* head]

ceph·a·lo·cau·dal (sef′ə·lō·kô′dəl) *adj. Anat.* Of or pertaining to the head or tail, or to the long axis of the body. Also **ceph′a·lo·cer′cal** (-sûr′kəl). [<CEPHALO- + L *cauda* tail]

ceph·a·lo·chor·date (sef′ə·lō·kôr′dāt) *adj. Zool.* Having the notochord continued into the head: said especially of the lancelets. Also **ceph′a·lo·chor′dal.** *—n.* An animal having such a notochord.

ceph·a·lom·e·ter (sef′ə·lom′ə·tər) *n.* An instrument for measuring the head or skull, as for ascertaining the size of a fetal head (in parturition); craniometer. [<CEPHALO- + Gk. *metron* measure] **—ceph′a·lom′e·try** *n.*

Ceph·a·lo·ni·a (sef′ə·lō′nē·ə, -lōn′yə) One of the Ionian Islands, western Greece; 289 square miles; capital, Argostoli: Greek *Kephallenia.*

ceph·a·lo·pod (sef′ə·lə·pod′) *n.* Any of a class (Cephalopoda) of predaceous marine mollusks, including squids, octopuses, cuttlefish, and nautiluses, having a clearly defined head and eyes and tentacles surrounding the mouth. *—adj.* Of or pertaining to the class Cephalopoda. **—ceph·a·lop·o·dan** (sef′ə·lop′ə·dən) *adj. & n.* **—ceph·a·lop·o·dous** (sef′ə·lop′ə·dəs) *adj.*

ceph·a·lo·tho·rax (sef′ə·lō·thôr′aks, -thō′raks) *n. Zool.* The anterior portion of certain arthropods, as crustaceans and arachnids, consisting of the united head and thorax. **—ceph′a·lo·tho·rac′ic** (-thə·ras′ik) *adj.*

ceph·a·lous (sef′ə·ləs) *adj.* Having a head.

-cephalous *combining form* Headed: *hydrocephalous.* [<Gk. *kephalē* head]

Ce·phas (sē′fəs) A masculine personal name. *John* i 42. [<Aramaic, a stone]

Ceph·e·id variable (sef′ē·id) *Astron.* Any of a class of variable stars characterized by a uniform, relatively short-term cycle of brightness associated with corresponding internal changes: so called from the star Delta in the constellation of Cepheus.

Ce·pheus (sē′fyo͞os, -fē·əs) **1** In Greek legend, a king of Ethiopia, husband of Cassiopeia and father of Andromeda. **2** A northern constellation near Draco and Cassiopeia. See CONSTELLATION.

ce·ra·ceous (si·rā′shəs) *adj.* Of the nature of or like wax; waxy. [<L *cera* wax]

Ce·ram (si·ram′; *Du.* sā′ram, *Pg.* sə·rañ′) An Indonesian island in the Banda Sea west of New Guinea; 6,622 square miles.

ce·ram·al (sə·ram′əl) *n. Metall.* A combination of metals, as iron and cobalt, with ceramic materials such as boron or titanium carbide, developed to provide alloys resistant to very high temperatures, as on the blades of turbine airplane engines. [<CERAM(IC) AL(LOY)]

ce·ram·ic (sə·ram′ik) *adj.* Pertaining to pottery and to articles made of clay that have been fired and baked. Also spelled *keramic.* [<Gk. *keramikos* <*keramos* potters' clay]

ce·ram·ics (sə·ram′iks) *n.* **1** The art of molding, modeling, and baking in clay: construed as singular. **2** Objects made of fired and baked clay: construed as plural. **—cer·a·mist** (ser′ə·mist) *n.*

Ceram Sea An arm of the Pacific north of Ceram, extending from Obi to New Guinea.

ce·rar·gy·rite (sə·rär′jə·rīt) *n.* An isometric, brown, easily sectile silver chloride, AgCl; horn silver. [<Gk. *keras* horn + *argyros* silver]

ce·ras·tes (sə·ras′tēz) *n.* A horned viper of North Africa and the Near East *(Cerastes cornutus).* [<L <Gk. *kerastēs* <*keras* horn]

ce·rate (sir′āt) *n.* A medicated ointment of oil or lard mixed with resin, wax, etc. Cerates are intermediate in consistency between ointments and plasters. [<L *ceratus,* pp. of *cerare* smear with wax <*cera* wax]

ce·rat·ed (sir′ā·tid) *adj.* Covered with wax.

cerato- *combining form* Horn; of or like horn: *ceratodus.* Also, before vowels, **cerat-.** [<Gk. *keras, -atos* horn]

ce·rat·o·dus (sə·rat′ə·dəs, ser′ə·tō′dəs) *n.* The barramunda. [<NL <Gk. *keras* horn + *odous* tooth]

cer·a·toid (ser′ə·toid) *adj.* **1** Horny; horn-shaped. **2** Of or pertaining to a superfamily *(Ceratoidea)* of mostly small deep-sea fishes having luminescent organs.

Cer·ber·us (sûr′bər·əs) In Greek and Roman mythology, the three-headed dog guarding the portals of Hades. **—Cer·be·re·an** (sər·bir′ē·ən) *adj.*

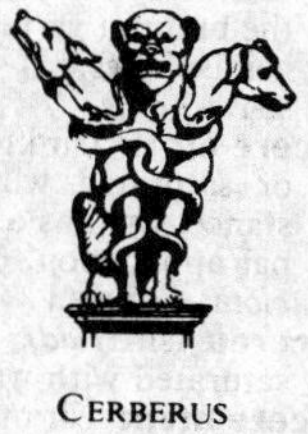

CERBERUS

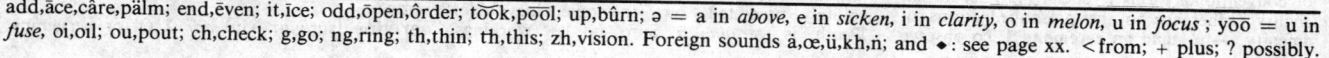

cer·car·i·a (sər·kâr′ē·ə) *n. pl.* **·car·i·ae** (-kâr′i·ē) *Zool.* A larval, parasitic form of a trematode worm, originating as a bud from a birth stage and having a tail that is lost in the adult. [<NL <Gk. *kerkos* tail] **—cer·car′i·al** *adj.* **—cer·car′i·an** *adj. & n.*

cer·co·pi·the·coid (sûr′kō·pi·thē′koid) *adj. Zool.* Relating to or describing any of a superfamily or group *(Cercopithecoidea)* of Old World monkeys evolved from prosimian stock by adaptive radiation and including macaques, mandrills, baboons, langurs, and Barbary apes. *—n.* A member of this group. [<NL <L *cercopithecus* <Gk. *kerkopithēkos* <*kerkos* tail + *pithēkos* ape]

cer·cus (sûr′kəs) *n. pl.* **·ci** (-sī) *Entomol.* One of a pair of anal appendages found in many insects, as in the cockroach. [<NL <Gk. *kerkos* tail]

cere[1] (sir) *v.t.* **cered, cer·ing 1** *Obs.* To cover with or as with wax; to wax. **2** To wrap in cerecloth; wrap (a dead body). ◆ Homophones: *sear, sere.* [<F *cirer* <L *cerare* smear with wax <*cera* wax]

cere[2] (sir) *n. Ornithol.* A waxlike, fleshy area about the bill, in parrots and birds of prey, containing the nostrils. ◆Homophones: *sear, sere.* [<F *cire* <L *cera* wax]

ce·re·al (sir′ē·əl) *n.* **1** An edible starchy grain yielded by certain plants of the grass family, as rice, wheat, rye, oats, etc. **2** Any of the plants yielding such grains. **3** A breakfast food made from a cereal grain. —*adj.* Pertaining to edible grain. ◆Homophone: *serial.* [<L *cerealis* of grain <*Ceres,* goddess of grain]

cer·e·bel·lum (ser′ə·bel′əm) *n. pl.* **·bel·lums** or **·bel·la** (-bel′ə) The massive, dorsally located organ of the central nervous system forming that part of the brain below and behind the cerebrum. It consists of a central lobe and two lateral lobes and acts as the coordination center of voluntary movements, posture, and equilibrium. [<L, dim. of *cerebrum* brain] —**cer′e·bel′lar** *adj.*

cer·e·bral (ser′ə·brəl, sə·rē′-) *adj.* **1** Of or pertaining to the cerebrum or the brain. **2** Appealing to the intellect; requiring mental activity; intellectual. **3** *Phonet.* Cacuminal. —*n. Phonet.* A cerebral consonant, as *ṭ* and *ḍ* in the Indic languages. [<F *cérébral* <L *cerebrum* brain]

cerebral hemisphere *Anat.* One of the two halves into which the brain is divided.

cerebral palsy *Pathol.* Any paralysis affecting the ability to control movement and caused by brain lesions resulting from prenatal defect or birth injury.

cer·e·brate (ser′ə·brāt) *v.* **·brat·ed, ·brat·ing** *v.t.* **1** To perform by brain action. —*v.i.* **2** To have or manifest brain action. **3** To think. [<L *cerebrum* brain]

cer·e·bra·tion (ser′ə·brā′shən) *n.* **1** The functional activity of the cerebrum. **2** The act of thinking; thought.

cer·e·brin (ser′ə·brin) *n.* A cerebroside found in brain substance and isolated as a yellowish-white powder, $C_{17}H_{33}NO_3$.

cer·e·bri·tis (ser′ə·brī′tis) *n. Pathol.* Inflammation of the cerebrum.

cerebro- *combining form* Brain; pertaining to the brain: *cerebrospinal.* Also, before vowels, **cerebr-** [<L *cerebrum* brain]

cer·e·bro·side (ser′ə·brō·sīd′) *n. Biochem.* A nitrogenous fatty substance found in brain and nerve tissue, containing galactose and forming a series of complex fatty acids, as phrenosin: also called *galactolipin.* [<CEREBR(O)- + -OSE + -IDE]

cer·e·bro·spi·nal (ser′ə·brō·spī′nəl) *adj.* Of or pertaining to the brain and spinal cord.

cerebrospinal fever Meningitis.

cer·e·brum (ser′ə·brəm) *n. pl.* **·bra** (-brə) or **·brums** The enlarged upper and anterior part of the brain in vertebrates, consisting of two lateral hemispheres. [<L] —**cer·e·bric** (ser′ə·brik, sə·rē′-) *adj.*

cere·cloth (sir′klôth′, -kloth′) *n.* A cloth coated or saturated with wax or some gummy substance, used as a waterproof covering, a medicinal application, or a winding sheet. [orig. *cered cloth* <CERE[1]]

cered (sird) *adj.* **1** Having a cere. **2** Smeared or saturated with wax.

cere·ment (sir′mənt) *n.* A cerecloth; a garment or wrapping for the dead; usually in the plural. [<F *cirement* a waxing <*cirer* CERE[1]]

cer·e·mo·ni·al (ser′ə·mō′nē·əl) *adj.* Of or pertaining to ceremony; ritual; formal. —*n.* **1** A system of rules of ceremony; ritual; also, social etiquette. **2** A ceremony. See synonyms under FORM. —**cer′e·mo′ni·al·ism** *n.* —**cer′e·mo′ni·al·ist** *n.* —**cer′e·mo′ni·al·ly** *adv.*

cer·e·mo·ni·ous (ser′ə·mō′nē·əs) *adj.* **1** Observant of or conducted with ceremony; formal. **2** Conventional; studiously polite. **3** Ceremonial. —**cer′e·mo′ni·ous·ly** *adv.* —**cer′e·mo′ni·ous·ness** *n.*

cer·e·mo·ny (ser′ə·mō′nē) *n. pl.* **·nies** **1** A formal or symbolical act or observance, or a series of them, as on religious and state occasions. **2** The doing of some formal act in the manner prescribed by authority or usage: the *ceremonies* at an ordination, inauguration, or coronation. **3** Mere outward form. **4** Observance of etiquette or conventional forms in social matters; formal civility; adherence to the prescribed forms of amenity. —**to stand on ceremony 1** To observe conventions. **2** To be formal, stiff, or uncordial. See synonyms under FORM, SACRAMENT. [<OF *cerymonie* <L *caerimonia* awe, veneration]

Ce·ren·kov effect (se·ren′kôf) *Physics* The emission of light by a charged particle passing through a medium with a velocity greater than the velocity of light in that medium. Also **Cerenkov radiation.** [after P. A. *Cerenkov,* U.S.S.R. physicist]

Ce·res (sir′ēz) **1** In Roman mythology, the goddess of grain and harvests: identified with the Greek *Demeter.* **2** *Astron.* The first of the asteroids to be discovered.

cer·e·sin (ser′ə·sin) *n.* Ozocerite. [<L *cera* wax]

ce·re·us (sir′ē·əs) *n.* Any of a genus of cactuses *(Cereus)* having large lateral tubular flowers, often nocturnal, whence several have the name of *night-blooming cereus.* [<L *cereus* waxy <*cera* wax]

ce·ri·a (sir′ē·ə) *n. Chem.* An infusible compound, CeO_2, used in the manufacture of incandescent mantles; cerium dioxide.

ce·rif·er·ous (sə·rif′ər·əs) *adj.* Yielding or producing wax. [<L *cera* wax + *ferre* bear]

Ce·ri·go (chā′rē·gō) The Italian name for KYTHERA.

cer·iph (ser′if) See SERIF.

ce·rise (sə·rēz′, -rēs′) *adj.* Of a vivid red. —*n.* A vivid red color. [<F, cherry]

ce·rite (sir′īt) *n.* A resinous, brown, orthorhombic hydrous cerium silicate. [<CERIUM]

ce·ri·um (sir′ē·əm) *n.* A silvery-white, ductile, highly reactive and electropositive metallic element (symbol Ce, atomic number 58), being the most abundant of the lanthanide series. See PERIODIC TABLE. [after the asteroid *Ceres*]

cerium metals A subgroup of the lanthanide series of elements, including lanthanum, cerium, praseodymium, neodymium, illinium, samarium, europium, and gadolinium.

cer·met (sûr′met) *n.* An alloy of a heat-resistant compound and a metal, used for strength and to withstand high temperatures. [<CER(AMIC) + MET(AL)]

Cer·nă·u·ţi (cher′nə·o͞ots′) The Rumanian name for CHERNOVTSY.

cer·nu·ous (sûr′nyo͞o·əs) *adj. Bot.* Drooping or nodding, as a flower. [<L *cernuus* stooping]

ce·ro (sir′ō) *n. pl.* **·ros** A scombroid fish *(Scomberomorus regalis,* or *S. cavalla)* closely related to, but larger than, the Spanish mackerel. The **common cero** *(S. regalis)* weighs as much as 20 pounds, and the **spotted** or **king cero** *(S. cavalla)* up to 100 pounds. See PINTADO. [<Sp. *sierra* <L *serra* saw]

cero- *combining form* Wax: *cerotype.* Also, before vowels, **cer-.** [<L *cera* or Gk. *kēros* wax]

ce·rog·ra·phy (si·rog′rə·fē) *n.* **1** The art of engraving or writing on wax. **2** Painting by the encaustic method. **3** The wax process of printing. [<Gk. *kērographia* <*kēros* wax + *graphein* write] —**ce·ro·graph** (sir′ə·graf, -gräf) *n.* —**ce′ro·graph′ic** *adj.* —**ce·rog′ra·phist** *n.*

ce·roon (sə·ro͞on′) See SEROON.

ce·ro·plas·tic (sir′ə·plas′tik) *adj.* **1** Pertaining to or of the nature of wax modeling. **2** Modeled in wax. [<Gk. *kēroplastikos* <*kēros* wax + *plassein* mold]

ce·rot·ic (si·rot′ik) *adj.* Of, pertaining to, or derived from beeswax, as **cerotic acid,** $C_{26}H_{53}COOH$. [<Gk. *kērōtos* waxed <*kēros* wax]

cer·o·type (sir′ə·tīp′, ser′-) *n.* **1** A process of engraving in which a metal plate is coated with wax, which is cut away according to some design, and a cast made therefrom in plaster. **2** A printing plate so produced.

ce·rous[1] (sir′əs) *adj. Chem.* Of, pertaining to, or containing cerium in its lower valence.

ce·rous[2] (sir′əs) *adj.* Of the nature of a cere.

Cer·ro de Pas·co (ser′rō thā päs′kō) **1** A town in central Peru. **2** A peak of the Peruvian Andes in this vicinity; 15,100 feet.

Cer·ro Gor·do (ser′ō gôr′dō) A mountain pass NE of Mexico City.

cer·tain (sûr′tən) *adj.* **1** Established as fact or truth so as to be absolutely known, accepted as true, and depended upon; beyond doubt or question; demonstrable; true. **2** Absolutely confident as to truth or reality; sure; convinced. **3** Definitely settled so as not to be variable or fluctuating; fixed; determined; stated. **4** That may be absolutely predicted; sure to come; inevitable: Death is *certain.* **5** Sure in its workings or results; reliable; effectual. **6** Determinate, but not particularized or named; indefinite, but assumed to be determinable: a *certain* man. See synonyms under AUTHENTIC, CONSCIOUS, INCONTESTABLE, SECURE, SURE. [<OF <L *certus* <*cernere* determine]

cer·tain·ly (sûr′tən·lē) *adv.* With certainty; surely.

cer·tain·ty (sûr′tən·tē) *n. pl.* **·ties** **1** The quality or fact of being certain. **2** A known truth. **3** Precision; accuracy.

Synonyms: assurance, certitude, confidence, conviction, demonstration, evidence, infallibility, positiveness, proof, surety. See DEMONSTRATION. Compare ASSURANCE. *Antonyms:* conjecture, doubt, dubiousness, hesitation, indecision, misgiving, precariousness, uncertainty.

cer·tes (sûr′tēz) *adv. Archaic* Truly; certainly; verily. [<OF <*a certes* <L *certus.* See CERTAIN.]

cer·tif·i·cate (sər·tif′ə·kit) *n.* **1** A written declaration or testimonial. **2** A writing signed and legally authenticated. **3** A writing or statement certifying that the one named therein has satisfactorily completed a certain educational course. —**gold** (or **silver**) **certificates** Certificates issued by the U.S. government, and used as currency, on the basis of gold (or silver) bullion of equal amounts deposited with the government for their redemption. —*v.t.* (-kāt) **·cat·ed, ·cat·ing** To furnish with or attest by a certificate. [<Med. L *certificatus,* pp. of *certificare.* See CERTIFY.] —**cer·tif·i·ca·to·ry** (sər·tif′ə·kə·tôr′ē, -tō′rē) *adj.*

certificate of deposit A statement issued by a bank certifying that a person has a specified sum on deposit.

cer·ti·fi·ca·tion (sûr′tə·fi·kā′shən) *n.* **1** The act of certifying; the guaranteeing of the truth or validity of; attestation. **2** A certified statement; a certificate.

certified check A check marked or stamped, as by a bank official, to certify that it is genuine and that it represents an account having sufficient funds for the bank to guarantee its payment.

certified milk Milk produced and bottled under sanitary conditions, in compliance with all State and municipal regulations.

certified public accountant See under ACCOUNTANT.

cer·ti·fy (sûr′tə·fī) *v.* **·fied, ·fy·ing** *v.t.* **1** To give certain knowledge of; attest. **2** To assert as a matter of fact; assure. **3** To give a certificate of, as insanity. —*v.i.* **4** To make attestation as to truth or excellence. [<F *certifier* <Med.L *certificare* attest <L *certus* certain + *facere* make] —**cer′ti·fi′a·ble** *adj.* —**cer′ti·fi′er** *n.*

cer·ti·o·ra·ri (sûr′shē·ə·râr′ē, -râr′ī) *n. Law* A writ from a superior to an inferior court, directing a certified record of its proceedings in a designated case to be sent up for review. [<LL, to be certified]

cer·ti·tude (sûr′tə·to͞od, -tyo͞od) *n.* **1** Perfect assurance; confidence. **2** Assured fact or reality; sureness and precision. See synonyms under CERTAINTY. [<Med.L *certitudo* <L *certus.* See CERTAIN.]

ce·ru·le·an (sə·ro͞o′lē·ən) *adj. & n.* Sky blue. [<L *caeruleus* dark blue]

cerulean blue A light-blue pigment made from the combined oxides of cobalt and tin.

ce·ru·men (sə·ro͞o′mən) *n.* Earwax. [<NL <L *cera* wax] —**ce·ru′mi·nous** *adj.*

ce·ruse (sir′o͞os, sə·ro͞os′) *n.* **1** White lead. **2** A cosmetic made from it. [<F *céruse* <L *cerussa*]

ce·rus·site (sir′ə·sīt) *n.* An orthorhombic, white to grayish-black lead carbonate, $PbCO_3$. Also **ce′ru·site.**

Cer·van·tes (sər·van′tēz, *Sp.* ther·vän′tās), **Miguel de,** 1547–1616, Spanish novelist and dramatist; author of *Don Quixote*: full surname *Cervantes Saavedra.*

cer·vi·cal (sûr′vi·kəl) *adj. Anat.* Of, pertaining to, or situated in or near the neck or cervix: *cervical* vertebrae. [<L *cervix, -icis* neck]

cervico- *combining form* Neck: *cervicofacial.* Also, before vowels, **cervic-.** [<L *cervix, -icis* neck]

cer·vi·co·fa·cial (sûr′vi·kō·fā′shəl) *adj. Anat.* Pertaining to the neck and the face.

Cer·vin (ser·vaṅ′), **Mont** (môṅ) See MATTERHORN.

cer·vine (sûr′vin, -vin) *adj.* **1** Of or pertaining

to deer. **2** Designating the subfamily (*Cervinae*) of deer representing the typical deer. [< L *cervinus* < *cervus* deer]

cer·vix (sûr′viks) *n. pl.* **cer·vix·es** or **cer·vi·ces** (sər·vī′sēz, sûr′və·sēz) **1** The neck. **2** The cervix uteri. **3** A necklike part. [< L]

cer·vix u·ter·i (sûr′viks yōō′tər·ī) *Anat.* The constricted neck of the uterus which distends during parturition.

cer·void (sûr′void) *adj.* Resembling a deer. [< L *cervus* deer + —OID]

Cer·y·ne·ia (ser′ə·nē′ə) A city in ancient Achaea.

Ce·sar (sē′zər) See CAESAR. Also *Fr.* **Cé·sar** (sā·zär′), *Ital.* **Ce·sa·re** (chā′zä·rā), *Pg.* **Ce·sar** (sā′zär), *Sp.* **Cé·sar** (thā′sär).

Ce·sar·e·an (si·zâr′ē·ən) See CAESAREAN. Also **Ce·sar′i·an.**

Ce·sar·e·vitch (si·zär′ə·vich) See CZAREVITCH.

Ce·se·na (chā·zā′nä) A town in north central Italy.

ce·si·ous (sē′zē·əs) *adj.* Pale greenish-blue: also spelled *caesious.* [< L *caesius* bluish-gray]

ce·si·um (sē′zē·əm) *n.* A steel-gray, ductile metallic element (symbol Cs, atomic number 55) that is the most electropositive of the alkali metals. See PERIODIC TABLE. [< L *caesius* bluish-gray]

Ces·ké Bu·dě·jo·vi·ce (ches′ke bōō′dye-yŏ′vi·tse) A city in southern Bohemia, Czechoslovakia: German *Budweis.*

ces·pi·tose (ses′pə·tōs) *adj. Bot.* Growing in tufts or clumps, as a plant; matted; turfy: also spelled *caespitose.* [< L *caespes, caespitis* turf] — **ces′pi·tose·ly** *adv.*

ces·pi·tous (ses′pə·təs) *adj.* Cespitose.

cess[1] (ses) *n. Brit. Dial.* A public rate; tax; assessment. —*v.t.* To tax; assess; rate. [Short for ASSESS]

cess[2] (ses) *n. Irish* Luck; success: used in the phrase **bad cess to** Bad luck to. [? Short for SUCCESS]

ces·sa·tion (se·sā′shən) *n.* A ceasing; stop; pause. See synonyms under END, REST. [< L *cessatio, -onis* < *cessare* stop]

ces·sion (sesh′ən) *n.* **1** The act of ceding; surrender. **2** An assignment of property or rights to another or others. **3** The ceding of territory by a nation or state; also, the territory ceded. ♦ Homophone: *session.* [< L *cessio, -onis* surrender < *cessus* pp. of *cedere* yield]

ces·sion·ar·y (sesh′ən·er′ē) *adj.* Giving up; surrendering. —*n.* An assignee or grantee.

cess·pool (ses′pōōl) *n.* **1** A covered well or pit for the drainage from sinks, etc. **2** Any repository of filth. Also spelled *sesspool.* Also **cess′pit.** [Origin uncertain]

ces·ta (ses′tə, *Sp.* thäs′tä) *n.* In jai alai, a curved wicker racket attached to the hand. [< Sp.]

c'est-à-dire (se·tà·dēr′) *French* That is to say.

c'est la guerre (se lä gâr′) *French* It is war; hence, it cannot be helped.

c'est la vie (se lä vē′) *French* That is life.

ces·tode (ses′tōd) *n.* A tapeworm. [< Gk. *kestos* girdle] —**ces·toid** (ses′toid) *adj.*

c'est se·lon (se sə·lôn′) *French* That depends (on the circumstances).

c'est une au·tre chose (se tün ō′tr′ shōz) *French* That is another thing, or a different matter.

ces·tus[1] (ses′təs) *n. pl.* **ces·tus** An ancient Roman device of thongs, often weighted, wound about the hands by boxers: also spelled *caestus.* [< L *caestus* < *caedere* kill]

ces·tus[2] (ses′təs) *n. pl.* **·ti** (-tī) **1** A belt or girdle. **2** In classical mythology, the girdle of Aphrodite, which could awaken love in whoever beheld it. [< L < Gk. *kestos*]

CESTUS

ce·su·ra (si·zhŏŏr′ə, -zyŏŏr′ə) See CAESURA.

Ce·ta·cea (si·tā′shə) *n. pl.* An order of aquatic mammals, especially those of a fishlike form with teeth conic or absent: the whales, dolphins, and porpoises. [< L *cetus* < Gk. *kētos* whale] — **ce·ta′cean** *adj. & n.* —**ce·ta′ceous** *adj.*

ce·tane (sē′tān) *n. Chem.* A saturated hydrocarbon of the methane series, $C_{16}H_{34}$: used as fuel for diesel engines. [< L *cetus* whale]

cetane number *Chem.* A measure of the performance characteristics of diesel engine fuels. It is the percentage of cetane (value = 100) in a mixture of cetane and *alpha*-methylnaphthalene (value = 0) which gives the same ignition performance as the fuel being tested. Compare OCTANE NUMBER.

Ce·ta·tea Al·ba (che·tä′tyä äl′bə) See BELGOROD DNESTROVSKI.

ce·te·ris pa·ri·bus (set′ər·is pär′i·bəs) *Latin* Other things being equal.

Ce·tin·je (tse′tin·ye) The former capital of Montenegro, now in Yugoslavia.

ce·tol·o·gy (si·tol′ə·jē) *n.* The branch of zoology dealing with whales. [< Gk. *kētos* + -LOGY] — **ce·to·log·i·cal** (sē′tə·loj′i·kəl) *adj.* —**ce·tol′o·gist** *n.*

Cette (set) See SÈTE.

Ce·tus (sē′təs) A southern constellation, the Sea Monster. See CONSTELLATION. [< L, the whale]

Ceu·ta (syōō′tə, sōō′-; *Sp.* thä′ōō·tä) A port and an enclave in Morocco opposite Gibraltar; 7 1/2 square miles.

cev·a·dil·la (sev′ə·dil′ə) See SABADILLA.

Cé·vennes (sā·ven′) A mountain range west of the Rhone in southern France; highest peak, 5,755 feet.

Cey·lon (si·lon′) See SRI LANKA. —**Cey·lon·ese** (sē′lən·ēz′, -ēs′) *adj. & n.*

Ceylon moss A red seaweed of the East Indies (*Gracilaria lichenoides*), a principal source of agar-agar.

Ce·yx (sē′iks) In Greek mythology, the husband of Alcyone.

Cé·zanne (sā·zàn′), **Paul**, 1839–1906, French painter.

Cf *Chem.* Californium (symbol Cf).

cgs The centimeter-gram-second system of measurement in which the unit of length is the centimeter, the unit of mass the gram, and the unit of time one second. Thus, the cgs unit of force is the dyne, of work the erg, etc. Also **c.g.s., C.G.S.**

chab·a·zite (kab′ə·zīt) *n.* A rhombohedral, white or flesh-colored hydrous silicate of calcium and aluminum. Also **chab′a·site** (-sīt). [< F *chabazie,* alter. of Gk. *chalazios,* a precious stone < *chalaza* hail]

cha·blis (shà·blē′) *n.* A dry, white, Burgundy wine made in the region of **Chablis,** a town in north central France.

cha·bouk (chä′bōōk) *n.* A horsewhip; specifically, a long whip used in the Orient for corporal punishment. Also **cha′buk.** [< Persian *chābuk* horsewhip]

chace (chäs) See CHASE[1] *n.*

chac·ma (chak′mə) *n.* A large, black and gray South African baboon (*Papio porcarius*). [< Hottentot]

Cha·co (chä′kō) An interior province of northern Argentina; 38,041 square miles; capital, Resistencia.

Cha·co Canyon National Monument (chä′kō) A region of NW New Mexico containing cliff-dweller ruins; 33 square miles; established as a national park in 1907.

cha·conne (shà·kôn′) *n.* A slow dance of the 18th century; also, the music for it. [< F < Sp. *chacona*]

cha·cun à son goût (shà·kœn nä sôn gōō′) *French* Each to his own taste.

Chad (chad) An independent republic of the French Community in north central Africa; 501,000 square miles; capital, Fort-Lamy; formerly a French overseas territory.

Chad (chad), **Lake** A lake in NW central Africa; 4,000 square miles in dry, 8,000 in rainy season.

Chad·i·an (chad′ē·ən) *adj.* Pertaining to Chad. —*n.* A native or citizen of Chad.

Chad·wick (chad′wik), **George Whitefield**, 1854–1931, U.S. composer and conductor. —**Sir James**, 1891–1974, English physicist.

Chaer·o·ne·a (ker′ə·nē′ə) An ancient Boeotian city of central Greece; scene of victories of Philip of Macedon over Athens and Thebes, 338 B.C., and of Sulla over Mithridates, 86 B.C. Also **Chær′o·ne′a.**

chae·ta (kē′tə) *n. pl.* **·tae** (-tē) *Zool.* A bristle or seta. [< NL < Gk. *chaitē* hair]

chaeto- *combining form* Hair: *chaetopod.* Also, before vowels, **chaet-.** [< Gk. *chaitē* hair, bristle]

chae·to·don (kē′tə·don) *n.* One of a family (*Chaetodontidae*) of fishes having the dorsal fins stiff and spiny, including certain angelfishes of West Indies and Florida waters. [< NL < Gk. *chaitē* bristle + *odous, odontos* tooth]

chae·tog·nath (kē′tog·nath) *n. Zool.* Any of a phylum (*Chaetognatha*) of small, active, widely distributed marine animals having characteristic bristles around the mouth and elongate, arrow-shaped, almost transparent bodies adapted for swift motion through the water. [< NL < Gk. *chaitē* hair + *gnathos* jaw].

chae·to·pod (kē′tə·pod) *n. Zool.* Any of a class (*Chaetopoda*) of annelid worms having conspicuous segments provided with locomotor organs and setae, including clamworms and earthworms. [< NL < Gk. *chaitē* + *pous, podos* foot]

chafe (chāf) *v.* **chafed, chaf·ing** *v.t.* **1** To abrade or make sore by rubbing; gall. **2** To make warm by rubbing. **3** To fret; irritate; annoy. —*v.i.* **4** To be irritated; fret; fume. —*n.* **1** Soreness or wear from friction; friction. **2** Irritation or vexation; restlessness. [< OF *chaufer* warm < L *calefacere* < *calere* be warm + *facere* make] —**chaf·er** *n.*

chaf·er (chā′fər) *n.* The cockchafer or other scarabaeid beetle. Also **chaf·fer** (chaf′ər). [OE *ceafor*]

chaff[1] (chaf, chäf) *n.* **1** The external envelopes or husks of grain. **2** Straw or hay cut fine. **3** Refuse; trifles collectively. See synonyms under WASTE. [OE *ceaf*]

chaff[2] (chaf, chäf) *v.t.* To poke fun at; ridicule. —*n.* Good-natured raillery; banter. See synonyms under BANTER, RIDICULE, MOCK. [Origin uncertain] —**chaff′er** *n.*

Chaf·fee (chaf′ē), **Adna Romanza**, 1884–1941, U.S. major general; organized the first mechanized brigade.

chaf·fer (chaf′ər) *v.t.* **1** *Obs.* To buy or sell; barter. **2** To say idly; bandy. —*v.i.* **3** To haggle about price; bargain. **4** To talk idly. [< *n.*] —*n.* **1** A disputatious bargaining. **2** *Obs.* Trade; traffic. [ME *chapfare,* OE *cēap* bargain + *faru* going] —**chaf′fer·er** *n.*

chaf·finch (chaf′inch) *n.* A European song finch (*Fringilla caelebs*), popular as a cage bird. [< CHAFF[1] + FINCH]

chaff·y (chaf′ē, chäf′ē) *adj.* **1** Of, pertaining to, or like chaff. **2** *Bot.* Paleaceous. **3** Light as chaff; unsubstantial; empty.

chaf·ing dish (chā′fing) A vessel with a heating apparatus beneath it, to cook or keep hot its contents at the table.

chaft (chaft, chäft) *n. Scot. & Brit. Dial.* **1** A jaw. **2** *pl.* The jaw bones; chops.

Cha·gall (shə·gäl′), **Marc**, born 1887, Russian painter, active in France.

Cha·gas disease (chä′gäs) *Pathol.* A form of trypanosomiasis prevalent in South and Central America, communicated by the bite of the assassin bug. [after C. *Chagas,* 1879–1934, Brazilian physician]

Cha·gres (chä′gres) A river in the Panama Canal Zone, largely utilized by the Panama Canal.

Chagres fever *Pathol.* A malignant malaria endemic along the Chagres.

cha·grin (shə·grin′) *n.* Distress or vexation caused by disappointment, failure, or wounded pride; mortification. —*v.t.* To humiliate; mortify: used in the passive. [< F. See SHAGREEN.]

Synonyms (noun): confusion, disappointment, discomposure, dismay, humiliation, mortification, shame, vexation. *Chagrin* unites *disappointment* with some degree of *humiliation.* A rainy day may bring *disappointment;* needless failure in some enterprise brings *chagrin. Shame* involves the consciousness of fault, guilt, or impropriety; *chagrin* of failure of judgment, or harm to reputation. A consciousness that one has displayed his own ignorance will cause him *mortification;* if there was a design to deceive, the exposure will cover him with *shame.* Compare ABASH.

Antonyms: delight, exultation, glory, rejoicing, triumph.

Cha·har (chä′här) A province of northern China, 45,000 square miles; capital, Kalgan.

chain (chān) *n.* **1** A series of connected rings or links, serving to bind, drag, hold, or ornament. **2** Shackles; bonds; enthralment: usually in the plural. **3** Any connected series; a succession. **4** A range of mountains. **5** A measuring line or tape of 100 links; the **engineer's** (or **Ramden's**) **chain** is 100 feet long; the **surveyor's** (or **Gunter's**) **chain** is 66 feet long. **6** The warp threads of a fabric; also, the pattern chain of a loom. **7** *pl. Naut.* The flat iron bars on the side of a ship that receive the strain of the shrouds; a chain plate or channel plate. **8** *Chem.* A series of atoms of the same or different kinds, linked together and acting as a unit. See CLOSED CHAIN, OPEN CHAIN, SIDE CHAIN. **9** A series of associated stores, banks, etc. — *v.t.* **1** To fasten, as with a chain; also, to bring into or hold in subjection; enthrall. **2** In surveying, to measure with a chain. [<OF *chaeine* <L *catena*] — **chain′less** *adj.*

Chain (chān), **Ernest Boris,** born 1906, German pathologist, active in England.

chain gang A gang of convicts chained together while doing hard labor.

chain letter **1** A letter written to a group of people and sent from one to another in rotation, each recipient adding to it before forwarding it to the next. **2** A letter, duplicates of which are sent by one person to two or more others, each of whom forwards it to two or more others.

chain lightning **1** Forked or zigzag lightning. **2** *U.S. Slang* Cheap whisky.

chain mail See under MAIL[2].

chain·man (chān′mən) *n. pl.* **·men** (-mən) In surveying, a man who carries one end of the measuring chain. Also **chain′bear′er.**

chain pump A pump that raises water by means of buckets or disks on an endless chain passing under water and up over a wheel.

chain reaction *Physics* **1** A series of reactions each of which develops from the energy released by the previous reaction within the system. **2** The spontaneous explosive fission of atomic nuclei through the repeated capture of free neutrons, as in an atomic bomb or in the controlled generation of atomic energy.

chain shot Cannon balls or half-balls chained together: formerly used in warfare.

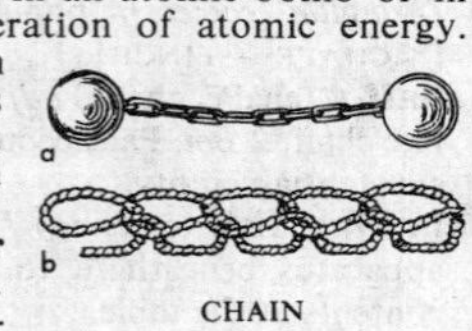

CHAIN
a. Chain shot.
b. Chain stitch.

chain-smok·er (chān′smō′kər) *n.* One who smokes cigars or cigarettes in unending succession.

chain stitch **1** In sewing, a loop stitch. **2** A chainlike stitch used in crocheting, embroidery, etc. Also **chain′work′.**

chain store A retail store selling the same type of goods, food, etc., as a number of other like stores, all of which are under the same management or ownership.

chain·wale (chān′wāl, chā′nəl) See CHANNEL[2].

chair (châr) *n.* **1** A movable or stationary seat, usually with four legs and a back and for one person. **2** A seat of office, as of a professor or moderator. **3** An office or officer; a chairman. **4** An iron block for holding railroad tracks in place. **5** The seat with long projecting arms on which the glassblower rolls his blowpipe; also, the set of men working with him. **6** *Obs.* A sedan. — *v.t.* **1** To put into a chair; install in office. **2** To preside over (a meeting). **3** In England, to carry in a chair in public; bear in triumph in a chair. [<F *chaiere* <L *cathedra.* Doublet of CATHEDRA.]

chair car A railroad passenger car equipped with comfortable single armchairs instead of the usual double seats; a parlor car.

chair·man (châr′mən) *n. pl.* **·men** (-mən) **1** One who presides over an assembly, committee, etc. **2** *Obs.* One of the carriers of a sedan chair. — *v.t.* To take the chair at (a meeting); preside over.

chair rail A wooden molding running around the walls of a room to protect them against damage from the backs of chairs.

chair-ta·ble (châr′tā′bəl) See TABLE-CHAIR.

chair·wom·an (châr′wŏŏm′ən) *n. pl.* **·wom·en** (-wim′ən) A woman who presides over an assembly, committee, etc.

chaise (shāz) *n.* **1** A two-wheeled, one-horse vehicle for two persons, having a calash top, and the body usually hung on long leather straps. **2** A light, four-wheeled carriage, usually open. *Chay,* or *shay,* was formerly a common colloquial variant, from the notion that *chaise* was a plural form. [<F, var. of *chair* chair]

chaise-longue (shāz′lông′, *Fr.* shez lôṅg′) *n.* A couchlike chair having a backrest at one end and the seat prolonged to support the sitter's outstretched legs. [<F, lit., long chair]

cha·la·za (kə·lā′zə) *n. pl.* **·zas** or **·zae** (-zē) **1** *Biol.* One of the two spirally twisted albuminous threads that are attached to each end of the lining membrane of an egg and keep the yolk in position with the germinating spot uppermost. See illustration under EGG. **2** *Bot.* The part of an ovule where the coats are united to each other and to the nucellus. [<NL <Gk., hailstone, small lump]

Chal·ce·don (kal′sə·don, kal·sē′dən) An ancient Greek port in Asia Minor on the Bosporus; site of modern Turkish *Kadikoy.*

chal·ced·o·ny (kal·sed′ə·nē, kal′sə·dō′nē) *n. pl.* **·nies** A waxy, translucent, crypto-crystalline variety of quartz: also spelled *calcedony.* [from *Chalcedon*]

chal·ced·o·nyx (kal·sed′ə·niks, kal′sə·don′iks) *n.* A variety of agate in which white and gray layers alternate. [<CHALCED(ONY) + ONYX]

chal·cid (kal′sid) *n.* A tiny hymenopterous fly (family *Chalcididae*) whose larvae are parasitic on the larvae of other insects. Also **chalcid fly.** [<NL <Gk. *chalkos* copper; with ref. to its color]

Chal·cid·i·ce (kal·sid′ə·sē) A peninsula of NE Greece extending into the Aegean. *Modern Greek* **Khal·ki·di·ki** (khäl′kē·thē·kē′).

Chal·cis (kal′sis, Gk. khäl·kēs′) A city on Euboea, eastern Greece: Greek *Khalkis.* Also **Chal·kis** (kal′kis).

chalco- *combining form* Copper; brass: *chalcography.* [<Gk. *chalkos* copper]

chal·co·cite (kal′kə·sīt) *n.* An orthorhombic, metallic, blackish-gray copper sulfide, Cu_2S: also called *copper glance.*

chal·cog·ra·phy (kal·kog′rə·fē) *n.* The art of engraving on plates of copper or steel; line engraving. [<CHALCO- + -GRAPHY] — **chal·co·graph** (kal′kə·graf, -gräf) *n.* — **chal·cog′ra·pher** *n.* — **chal′co·graph′ic** *adj.* — **chal·cog′ra·phist** *n.*

chal·co·py·rite (kal′kə·pī′rīt, -pir′īt) *n.* A tetragonal, metallic, brass-yellow copper-iron sulfide, $CuFeS_2$; copper pyrites.

Chal·de·a (kal·dē′ə) In Biblical geography, the southernmost part of the valley of the Tigris and the Euphrates: sometimes extended to include Babylonia. Also **Chal·dae′a.**

Chal·de·an (kal·dē′ən) *n.* **1 a** A native of Chaldea. **b** One of an ancient Semitic people of the Tigris and Euphrates Valley, who conquered and ruled Babylon. **c** A Babylonian. **2** One versed in the occult learning of the Chaldeans; an astrologer; hence, a magician. **3** The ancient Semitic language of the Chaldeans. — *adj.* Of or pertaining to Chaldea, the Chaldeans, or their language or culture: also **Chal·da·ic** (kal·dā′ik). Also **Chal·dae′an.**

Chal·dee (kal·dē′, kal′dē) *n.* **1** A Chaldean. **2** Biblical Aramaic: erroneous use. — *adj.* Chaldean: also **Chal·da·ic** (kal·dā′ik).

chal·der (chôl′dər) *n. Scot.* A former measure of 32 to 96 bushels. [<OF *chaldere* <L *caldaria* pot for boiling <*calidus* warm, hot]

chal·dron (chôl′drən) *n.* A weight or measure for coal and coke: in England 32 to 36 bushels; in the United States 36 bushels or 1.268 cubic meters. [Var. of CALDRON]

cha·let (sha·lā′, shal′ā) *n.* **1** A small building made of planks or of squared timbers, having a gently sloping and projecting roof, built by herdsmen in the Alpine regions of central Europe, especially in Switzerland. **2** A Swiss cottage with a projecting roof. **3** Any house built in this style. [<F]

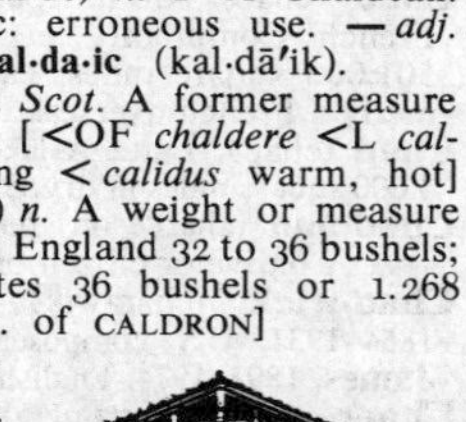

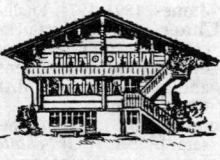

CHALET

Cha·leur Bay (shə lŏŏr′, -lûr′) An inlet of the Gulf of Saint Lawrence between the Gaspé Peninsula and New Brunswick.

Cha·lia·pin (shä·lyä′pin), **Feodor Ivanovich,** 1873–1938, Russian basso.

chal·ice (chal′is) *n.* **1** A consecrated cup used in the celebration or administration of the Lord's Supper. **2** Any drinking cup, goblet, or bowl. **3** *Bot.* A cup-shaped flower. [<OF <L *calix, calicis* cup]

chal·iced (chal′ist) *adj. Bot.* Having a cup-shaped flower.

chal·i·co·there (kal′i·kō·thir′) *n. Paleontol.* One of a family (*Chalicotheridae*) of extinct ungulates resembling both the horse and rhinoceros and having legs ending in three-clawed hoofs. [<NL <Gk. *chalix* gravel + *thēr* wild beast]

chalk (chôk) *n.* **1** A soft, grayish-white or yellowish compact limestone, largely composed of the shells of foraminifers. **2** A piece of chalk or chalklike material, either natural or artificial and frequently colored, used for marking or drawing. **3** A score in a game, because often recorded with chalk. **4** A debit, formerly often marked with chalk upon the wall or door, as of an ale house. — *v.t.* **1** To put chalk on or in; also, to mark with chalk; to bleach. **2** To record, as charges or debits; score. **3** To put an official mark on. — **to chalk up** **1** To raise the price of. **2** To score. **3** To give credit. — *adj.* Made with chalk. [OE *cealc* <L *calx* limestone] — **chalk′i·ness** *n.* — **chalk′y** *adj.*

chalk·board (chôk′bôrd′, -bōrd′) *n.* A flat surface of hard material for marking upon with chalk, used for classroom instruction.

chal·ki·tis (kal·kī′tis) *n. Pathol.* An inflammation of the eyes caused by rubbing the eyes with hands that have been working on or with brass. [<NL <Gk. *chalkos* brass]

chalk·stone (chôk′stōn′) *n.* **1** *Pathol.* A gouty concretion in the joints. **2** A piece of chalk.

chal·lenge (chal′ənj) *v.* **·lenged, ·leng·ing** *v.t.* **1** To dare to a contest or trial of superiority. **2** To invite to personal combat: to *challenge* to a duel. **3** To invite or defy, as scrutiny or proof: to *challenge* criticism. **4** To claim as due, as attention or respect. **5** To call in question; dispute; object to, as a choice of jurors. **6** *Mil.* To stop and demand a countersign of, as a sentry does. — *v.i.* **7** To utter or make a challenge. **8** In hunting, to open and cry, as hounds on picking up the scent. — *n.* **1** A call or defiance to personal contest; a dare or summons to fight, especially to a duel. **2** A formal objection or exception to a person or thing. **3** *Mil.* A sentry's call, requiring one to halt and give the countersign. **4** *Telecom.* An electromagnetic signal requesting identification, as in radar communication. [<OF *chalenger* <LL *calumniare* accuse falsely <*calumnia* slander. Doublet of CALUMNY.] — **chal′lenge·a·ble** *adj.* — **chal′leng·er** *n.*

chal·lis (shal′ē) *n.* A light dress fabric, usually printed. Also **chal′lie.** [Origin uncertain]

Chal·mers (chä′mərz), **Alexander,** 1759–1834, Scottish biographer and editor. — **Thomas,** 1780–1847, Scottish divine and writer.

Chal·na Anchorage (chäl′nə) See PORT JINNAH.

chal·one (kal′ōn) See COLYONE.

Châ·lons-sur-Marne (shä·lôṅ′sür·märn′) A city in NE France; scene of the defeat of Attila, 451 A.D.

Cha·lon-sur-Saône (shä·lôṅ′sür·sōn′) A town in eastern France.

chal·u·meau (shal′yə·mō′, *Fr.* shà·lü·mō′) *n.* **1** The lowest register of the clarinet. **2** An old, single-reed wind instrument from which the clarinet developed. [<F <OF *chalemel* <L *calamellus,* dim. of *calamus* reed]

cha·lutz (khä·lōōts′) See HALUTZ.

Chal·y·be·an (kal′ə·bē′ən, kə·lib′ē·ən) *adj.* Of or pertaining to the ancient **Chal·y·bes** (kal′ə·bēz), a people of Asia Minor, famous for their work in iron and steel. [<L *chalybeius* <Gk. *chalybēis* <*chalyps, chalybos* steel]

cha·lyb·e·ate (kə·lib′ē·āt, -it) *adj.* **1** Impregnated with compounds of iron: said of mineral waters. **2** Resembling iron in taste or action. — *n.* A medicine or water containing iron in solution. [<NL *chalybeatus* <L *chalybeius.* See CHALYBEAN.]

chal·y·bite (kal′ə·bīt) *n.* Siderite.

cham (kam) *n. Archaic* A Tatar or Mogul ruler; a khan. [<F <Turkish *khān* ruler]

cha·made (shə·mād′) *n. Mil.* A signal, made with drum or trumpet, for a parley. [<F <Pg. *chamada* < *chamar* <L *clamare* cry out, shout]

Cham·bal (chum′bəl) A river in west central India, flowing 550 miles NE to the Jumna.

cham·ber (chām′bər) *n.* **1** A room in a dwelling house; especially, a bedroom. **2** *pl.* A suite of rooms or offices for the use of one person; specifically, a lawyer's or judge's office or apartment. **3** Lodgings. **4** A hall where an assembly or council meets; also, the assembly itself: the *chamber* of commerce. **5** The popular branch of a legislature. **6** An enclosed space at the breech of a gun containing the explosive charge; also, one of the cavities in the cartridge cylinder of a revolver. **7** A room in which a monarch or other great personage gives audience. **8** *Anat.* A space enclosing the aqueous humor of the eye, separated by the iris into an anterior and a posterior chamber. **9** A chamber pot. **10** A lock on a canal. — **cloud chamber** *Physics* An enclosed receptacle containing air or gas saturated with water vapor whose sudden cooling indicates the presence of ions as condensation nuclei of water droplets. The movements of these nuclei are revealed by the cloud tracks marked out by the droplets. Also **expansion chamber, fog chamber.** — **lower chamber** The lower house of a bicameral legislature. — **upper chamber** The upper house of a bicameral legislature. — *v.t.* **1** To make chambers in, as a gun. **2** To fit into a chamber; also, to fit compactly, as shot in a cartridge. [<F *chambre* <L *camera* vaulted room <Gk. *kamara.* Doublet of CAMERA.] — **cham′bered** *adj.*

chamber concert A concert of chamber music.

cham·ber·lain (chām′bər·lin) *n.* **1** A high European court official. **2** A steward or treasurer of a corporation or municipality. **3** *Obs.* The chamber attendant of a monarch or lord. [<OF *chamberlenc* <OHG *chamarlinc* < *chamara* room <L *camera.* See CHAMBER.] — **cham′ber·lain·ship′** *n.*

Cham·ber·lain (chām′bər·lin), **Joseph,** 1836–1914, English statesman. — **Sir (Joseph) Austen,** 1863–1937, son of the preceding, English statesman. — **(Arthur) Neville,** 1869–1940, brother of Austen, English statesman; prime minister 1937–40.

Cham·ber·lin (chām′bər·lin), **Thomas Chrowder,** 1843–1928, U.S. geologist.

cham·ber·maid (chām′bər·mād′) *n.* A woman whose work is taking care of the bedrooms in a hotel.

chamber music Music written for a small number of instruments (less than ten), suitable for performance in a small room or hall.

chamber of commerce An association of merchants and businessmen for the protection and regulation of commerce.

chamber pot A portable receptacle used in a bedchamber as a toilet.

Cham·bers (chām′bərz), **Robert,** 1802–71, Scottish publisher and editor.

Cham·bord (shän·bôr′) A village in north central France; site of a celebrated chateau built by Francis I.

cham·bray (sham′brā) *n.* A strong cotton fabric woven with colored warp and white filling that gives a changeable colored surface. [from *Cambrai,* France]

cha·me·le·on (kə·mē′lē·ən, -mēl′yən) *n.* **1** A tropical tree lizard (genus *Chamaeleon*) with a long protrusible tongue, prehensile limbs and tail, and the power of changing its color. **2** A person of changeable character or habits like a chameleon. [<L *chamaeleon* <Gk. *chamaileōn* < *chamai* on the ground + *leōn* lion] — **cha·me·le·on·ic** (kə·mē′lē·on′ik) *adj.*

Cha·me·le·on (kə·mē′lē·ən, -mēl′yən) A southern constellation. Also **Cha·mae′le·on.** See CONSTELLATION.

cham·fer (chām′fər) *v.t.* **1** To cut a channel in. **2** To bevel. [< *n.*] — *n.* A groove or channel; a bevel. [<F *chanfrein* <OF *chanfraindre* cut off an edge]

cham·frin (chām′frin) *n.* Armor for the front of a war horse's head. Also **cham·fron** (cham′fron). [<OF *chanfrain*]

Cha·mi·nade (shà·mē·nàd′), **Cécile Louise**

Stéphanie, 1861–1944, French composer.

Cha·mis·so (shà·mē′sō), **Adalbert von,** 1781–1838, German poet, born in France.

cham·ois (sham′ē, *Fr.* shà·mwä′) *n. pl.* **·ois** **1** A mountain antelope of Europe, the Caucasus, and western Asia (*Rupicapra rupicapra*). **2** A soft leather originally prepared from the skin of the chamois, now from sheep, goats, deer, etc.: also spelled *shammy, shamois.* Also **cham′my. 3** The color of this leather, a yellowish-beige. — *v.t.* **1** To dress (leather or skin) like chamois. **2** To clean or dry with a chamois skin, as an automobile. [<F]

CHAMOIS
(About 2 1/2 feet at the shoulder)

cham·o·mile (kam′ə·mīl) See CAMOMILE.

Cha·mo·nix (sham′ə·nē, *Fr.* shà·mô·nē′) The valley of the Arve north of Mont Blanc, France; site of **Chamonix–Mont-Blanc,** a resort town. Also **Cha·mou·ni** (sham′ōō·nē, *Fr.* shà·mōō·nē′).

Cha·mor·ro Var·gas (chä·môr′rō vär′gäs), **Emiliano,** 1871–1966, Nicaraguan general; president of Nicaragua 1917–20, 1926.

champ[1] (champ) *v.t.* **1** To crush and chew noisily; munch. **2** To bite upon restlessly. **3** *Scot.* To mash, as potatoes; trample underfoot. — *v.i.* **4** To make a biting or chewing movement with the jaws. — *n.* The action of chewing or biting. [Prob. imit.]

champ[2] (champ) *n. Slang* Champion.

cham·pa·col (cham′pə·kōl, -kol) *n. Chem.* A white, crystalline, camphorlike substance, $C_{15}H_{26}O$, extracted from the wood of the champak tree. [<CHAMPAK + -OL[1]]

cham·pagne (sham·pān′) *n.* **1** A sparkling white wine made from grapes grown in the area of the former province of Champagne. **2** A still, white wine from this region. **3** Any light, effervescent wine made in imitation of French champagne. **4** The color of champagne, a pale, tawny or greenish yellow.

Cham·pagne (sham·pān′, *Fr.* shäN·pän′y′) A region and former province of NE France.

cham·paign (sham·pān′) *n.* **1** Flat and open ground; clear, level country; a plain. **2** Figuratively, field of observation; expanse. **3** *Obs.* An area of unenclosed or common land. **4** *Archaic* The field of military operation. — *adj.* Of or pertaining to level ground or open country. [<OF *champaigne* <Med. L *campania.* See CAMPAIGN.]

cham·pak (cham′pak, chum′puk) *n.* An Indian tree (*Michelia champaca*) of the magnolia family, bearing golden-yellow fragrant flowers, and whose wood yields champacol. Also **cham′pac.** [<Skt. *campaka*]

cham·per·ty (cham′pər·tē) *n. pl.* **·ties** *Law* A bargain made by one not a party to the suit to bear expenses of litigation in consideration of a share of the matter sued for. [<F *champart* <OF <L *campi pars* share of the field] — **cham′per·tous** *adj.*

cham·pi·gnon (sham·pin′yən, *Fr.* shäN·pē·nyôN′) *n.* **1** The fairy-ring mushroom (*Marasmius oreades*). **2** In France, a mushroom or fungus. [<F, ult. <L *campania* < *campus* field]

cham·pi·on (cham′pē·ən) *n.* **1** Originally, one who fights in behalf of another; one who defends a person, principle, etc. **2** The victor in an open contest. **3** Something of highest excellence; anything which has been given first prize. — *adj.* Acknowledged superior to all competitors; holding the first prize, or having first excellence. — *v.t.* To defend; advocate; stand up for the rights of. [<OF <LL *campio, -onis* fighter <L *campus* field] — **cham′pi·on·ess** *n. fem.*

cham·pi·on·ship (cham′pē·ən·ship′) *n.* **1** The state of being a champion; supremacy. **2** The position or honor of a champion. **3** The act of championing; advocacy; defense.

Cham·plain (sham·plān′), **Lake** A lake between New York and Vermont; 435 square miles; 107 miles long.

Cham·plain (sham·plān′, *Fr.* shäN·plaN′), **Samuel de,** 1570–1635, French explorer; founder of Quebec.

champ·le·vé (shämp′lə·vā′) *n.* **1** An enamelware produced by cutting depressions in a metal plate, leaving a ridge between them which forms the outline of a design, the hollows then being filled with enamel powder or paste and fired. **2** The process of making this ware, or an article so made. [<F, pp. of *champlever* engrave < *champ* surface + *lever* raise]

Cham·pol·lion (shäN·pô·lyôN′), **Jean François,** 1790–1832, French Egyptologist; deciphered hieroglyphic system.
— **Champollion-Fi·geac** (-fē·zhàk′), **Jean Jacques,** 1778–1867, French archeologist, brother of the preceding.

Champs É·ly·sées (shäN zā·lē·zā′) *French* A fashionable avenue in Paris, France; literally, the Elysian Fields.

chance (chans, chäns) *n.* **1** The unknown or the undefined cause of events not subject to calculation; luck; fortune. **2** An unknown agency, assumed to account for unusual or unexplained events. **3** The operation of this agency: often personified or, in antiquity, deified. **4** A fortuitous event; an accident. **5** A favorable conjuncture of circumstances; opportunity. **6** Undetermined probability in general; contingency. See synonyms under ACCIDENT, HAZARD, PROBABILITY. — *v.* **chanced, chanc·ing** *v.i.* **1** To occur accidentally; happen. — *v.t.* **2** To take the chance of; hazard: I'll *chance* it. **3** *Archaic* To befall; happen to. — **to chance upon** To find unexpectedly or undesignedly; come upon; stumble over. — *adj.* Occurring by chance; casual; accidental. [<OF *cheance* <LL *cadentia.* Doublet of CADENCE, CADENZA.]

chance·ful (chans′fəl, chäns′-) *adj.* **1** Full of chance or chances; eventful. **2** *Obs.* Dependent on chance.

chan·cel (chan′səl, chän′-) *n.* The space in a church reserved for the officiating clergy and the choir, often separated from the rest of the building by a screen or railing. [<OF <LL *cancellus* < *cancelli,* pl., lattice, railing; because it is so enclosed]

chan·cel·ler·y (chan′sə·lər·ē, chän′-, chans′lər·ē, chäns′-) *n. pl.* **·ries 1** The office or dignity of a chancellor. **2** The building or room in which a chancellor has his office. **3** A court and its officials. **4** The office of an embassy or legation. Also **chan·cel·ry** (chan′səl·rē, chän′-).

chan·cel·lor (chan′sə·lər, chän′-, chans′lər, chäns′-) *n.* **1** A high officer of state or of a university. **2** A judicial officer sitting in a court of chancery or equity. **3** In Germany, formerly, the president of the Federal Council. **4** In France, formerly, the keeper of the great seal and president of the Councils. **5** A chief secretary, as of an embassy. **6** A keeper of the great seal under the Eastern Empire, the Holy Roman Empire, etc. Also **chan′cel·or.** — **lord high chancellor** In Great Britain, the highest judicial officer of the crown. Also **lord chancellor.** [<OF *chancelier* <LL *cancellarius* one who stands at the bar in a court < *cancelli.* See CHANCEL.] — **chan′cel·lor·ship′** *n.*

chancellor of the Exchequer The minister of finance in the British cabinet.

Chan·cel·lors·ville (chan′sə·lôrz·vil′, chän′-) A village in NE Virginia; scene of a Union defeat in a Civil War battle of 1863.

chance-med·ley (chans′med′lē, chäns′-) *n.* **1** *Law* Unpremeditated wounding or killing in self-defense in a casual affray; homicide upon sudden encounter. **2** A haphazard combination or mixture; any inadvertent act. [<OF *chance medlée* mixed case or event < *chance* CHANCE + *medlée,* pp. of *medler* mix]

chan·cer·y (chan′sər·ē, chän′-) *n. pl.* **·cer·ies 1** In the United States, a court of equity, as distinguished from a common-law court. **2** *Brit.* Previously to 1873, the court presided over by the Lord High Chancellor of England, the highest court next to the House of Lords; since the Judicature Act of 1873, one of the five divisions of the High Court of Justice.

3 A court of records; archives. 4 A chancellery. 5 The business and legal offices of a Roman Catholic diocese or archdiocese. 6 A wrestling hold. **— in chancery 1** Pending in a court of chancery; also, under the supervision of the Lord Chancellor. 2 In a hopeless predicament. 3 In boxing, said of the head caught and held under the arm of an opponent. [<OF *chancellerie* < *chancelier.* See CHANCELLOR.]

chan·ci·fy (chan′sə·fī, chän′-) *v.* **·fied, ·fy·ing** *v.t.* 1 To make fully random, as by the thorough mixing of an array of lottery tickets. — *v.i.* 2 To become fully random. 3 In the theory of games, to provide for the equiprobability of any in a series of results or events by deliberately altering the number, range, or effect of chance factors. [<CHANCE + -FY]

chan·cre (shang′kər) *n. Pathol.* A primary syphilitic lesion resembling a sore with a hard base. [<F <L *cancer* crab, ulcer] **— chan·crous** (shang′krəs) *adj.*

chan·croid (shang′kroid) *n. Pathol.* A venereal sore resembling chancre, but not infecting the system; soft chancre.

chanc·y (chan′sē, chän′-) *adj.* **·i·er, ·i·est 1** *Colloq.* Subject to chance; risky. 2 *Scot.* Favored by chance; auspicious; favorable.

chan·de·lier (shan′də·lir′) *n.* A branched support for lights, as a gas or electric fixture, suspended from a ceiling. [<F <Med. L *candelarius* <L *candela* candle]

chan·delle (shan·del′) *n. Aeron.* An abrupt climbing turn of an airplane, utilizing momentum to gain altitude while the direction of flight is changed. [<F]

Chan·der·na·gore (chun′dər·nə·gôr′) A free city and former French settlement on the Hooghly in West Bengal, India. *French* **Chan·der·na·gor** (shäṅ·der·nȧ·gôr′).

chan·dler (chan′dlər, chän′-) *n.* 1 A trader; dealer: ship *chandler.* 2 In England, a retailer of common groceries, provisions, and the like; a petty shopkeeper. 3 One who makes or sells candles: tallow *chandler.* [<F *chandelier* chandler, candlestick. See CHANDELIER.]

chan·dler·y (chan′dlər·ē, chän′-) *n. pl.* **·dler·ies** 1 The goods sold by a chandler: often in the plural. 2 A chandler's shop. 3 A place for keeping candles.

Chan·dra·gup·ta (chun′drə·gŏŏp′tə) **I,** fourth century B.C., Indian ruler of the Maurya kingdom: also *Sandrocottus.* **— II,** 383?–413, Indian ruler of the Gupta dynasty.

chang (chang) See CATTY[1].

Chang·chow (chäng′jō′) 1 A former name for LUNGKI. 2 A city in southern Kiangsu province, China.

Chang·chun (chäng′chŏŏn′) A city in western Kirin province of Manchuria: formerly *Hsinking.*

change (chānj) *v.* **changed, chang·ing** *v.t.* 1 To make different; alter; transmute. 2 To exchange; interchange: to *change* places. 3 To give or cause another to give the equivalent of, as money, in smaller units or foreign currency. 4 To put other garments, coverings, etc., on: to *change* the bed. — *v.i.* 5 To become different; vary. 6 To enter upon a new phase: the moon has *changed.* 7 To make a change or exchange. 8 To transfer from one train to another. 9 To put on other garments. **— to change color** To blush or turn pale. **— to change front 1** In a military sense, to face a different way; alter the direction of a line of attack. 2 To adopt a new line of argument. 3 To alter one's attitude or principles. **— to change hands** To pass from one possessor to another. — *n.* 1 The act or fact of changing; alteration; substitution or something used in substitution. 2 A place for general transaction of business; an exchange. 3 The money returned to a purchaser who has given a bill or coin of greater value than his purchase. 4 Money of smaller denomination given in exchange for larger; small coins collectively. 5 A passage from one phase to another: the *change* of the moon. 6 *Music* **a** A modulation or variation of key. **b** Any order, other than that of the diatonic scale, in which a peal of bells is struck: usually in the plural. 7 *Obs.* Want of constancy; caprice. 8 Religious conversion. **— to ring the changes 1** To operate a chime of bells so as to produce a variety of tuneful combinations. 2 To repeat something with every possible variation of language and illustration. [<OF *changer* <LL *cambiare* exchange] **— chang′er** *n.*

Synonyms (verb): alter, commute, convert, exchange, metamorphose, modify, qualify, shift, substitute, transfigure, transform, transmute, turn, vary, veer. To *change* is to make a thing other than it has been; to *exchange,* to put or take something else in its place; to *alter* is ordinarily to *change* partially. To *exchange* is often to transfer ownership; as, to *exchange* city for country property. *Change* is often used in the sense of *exchange*; as, to *change* horses. To *transmute* is to *change* the qualities while the substance remains the same; as, to *transmute* baser metals into gold. To *transform* is to *change* form or appearance, with or without deeper and more essential change. *Transfigure* is, as in its Scriptural use, to *change* in an exalted and glorious spiritual way. To *metamorphose* is to make some remarkable change, as of a caterpillar into a butterfly, or of the crystalline structure of rocks, hence called "metamorphic rocks." To *vary* is to *change* from time to time, often capriciously. To *commute* is to put something easier, lighter, milder, etc., in place of that which is *commuted*; as, to *commute* daily fares on a railway to a monthy payment. To *convert* is primarily to *turn* about, and signifies to *change* in form, character, use, etc.; iron is *converted* into steel, joy into grief, etc. *Turn* is a popular word for *change* in any sense short of the meaning of *exchange,* being often equivalent to *alter, convert, transform, transmute,* etc. We *modify* a statement by some limitation, *qualify* it by some addition. See CONVEY. *Antonyms*: abide, bide, continue, endure, hold, keep, persist, remain, retain, stay.

Synonyms (noun): alteration, conversion, diversity, innovation, mutation, novelty, regeneration, renewal, renewing, revolution, transformation, transition, transmutation, variation, variety, vicissitude. *Mutation* is a more formal word for *change,* often suggesting repeated or continual *change*; as, the *mutations* of fortune. *Revolution* is specifically and most commonly a *change* of government. *Variation* is a partial *change* in form, qualities, position, or action; as, the *variation* of the magnetic needle or of the pulse. *Vicissitude* is sharp, sudden, or violent *change*; as, the *vicissitudes* of politics. *Transition* is change by passing from one place or state to another, especially in a natural, regular, or orderly way; as, the *transition* from spring to summer. An *innovation* is a *change* that breaks in upon an established order or custom. See MOTION. *Antonyms*: constancy, continuance, firmness, fixedness, fixity, identity, invariability, permanence, persistence, steadiness, unchangeableness, uniformity.

change·a·ble (chān′jə·bəl) *adj.* 1 Capable of being changed; alterable. 2 Likely to change or vary; inconstant. 3 Reflecting light so as to appear of different color from different points of view. See synonyms under FICKLE, MOBILE. **— change·a·bil·i·ty** (chān′jə·bil′ə·tē), **change′a·ble·ness** *n.* **— change′a·bly** *adv.*

change·ful (chānj′fəl) *adj.* Full of or given to change; variable. See synonyms under FICKLE. **— change′ful·ly** *adv.* **— change′ful·ness** *n.*

change·less (chānj′lis) *adj.* 1 Without change; monotonous. 2 Constant; enduring; unchanging. **— change′less·ly** *adv.* **— change′less·ness** *n.*

change·ling (chānj′ling) *n.* 1 An ill-favored or stupid child believed to have been substituted, especially by supernatural or demonic agency, for a normal or beautiful child. 2 A fickle person: used also adjectivally. 3 *Obs.* A silly or weak-minded person; simpleton; imbecile.

change of life The menopause.

change–ring·ing (chānj′ring′ing) *n.* The art or science of producing every possible variation in the ringing of a set of bells, starting from the time the bells leave the position of rounds to the time they return to it.

Chang·hua (chäng′hwä′) A city in west central Taiwan.

Chang·jin (chäng·jin) A river in northern Korea, flowing 160 miles NE; **Changjin reservoir** in its upper course was the site of fierce fighting in the Korean war, 1950. *Japanese* **Cho·sin** (chō·shin).

Chang·sha (chäng′shä′) A port of eastern China, capital of Hunan province.

Chang·teh (chäng′du′) A city in NW Hunan province, central China.

Chang Tso·lin (jäng′ tsō′lin′), 1873–1928, Chinese general.

Chan·kiang (chän′jyäng′) A municipality of SW Kwangtung province, China; leased to France, 1898–1945: French *Kwangchowan.*

chan·nel[1] (chan′əl) *n.* 1 The bed of a stream. 2 A wide strait: the English *Channel.* 3 Any groove or passage. 4 *Naut.* The deep part of a river, harbor, strait, or estuary, where the current or tide is strongest; especially, a navigable passage between the shoal parts. 5 That through which anything flows or passes: a news *channel.* 6 *Telecom.* **a** A path for the transmission of telegraph, telephone, and radio communications. **b** A wave band of specified frequency over which radio and television messages or programs are transmitted. 7 A flanged iron beam having a bracket-shaped section: also **channel bar.** 8 In motion pictures, a complete assemblage of all the necessary recording equipment. — *v.t.* **chan·neled** or **·nelled, chan·nel·ing** or **·nel·ling** 1 To cut or wear channels in. 2 To convey through or as through a channel. [<OF *chanel* <L *canalis* groove. Doublet of CANAL.]

chan·nel[2] (chan′əl) *n. Naut.* A flat piece of wood or iron attached to the side of a vessel, to spread the shrouds and keep them clear of the bulwarks: originally called *chainwale.* [Alter. of *chainwale* <CHAIN (def. 7) + WALE (def. 2)]

Channel Islands A group of British islands in the English Channel off the coast of Normandy, including Jersey, Guernsey, Alderney, and Sark; 75 square miles. *French* **Iles Normandes** (ēl nôr·mäṅd′).

Chan·ning (chan′ing), **William Ellery,** 1780–1842, U.S. Unitarian divine and writer.

chan·son (shan′sən, *Fr.* shäṅ·sôṅ′) *n.* A song. [<F <L *cantio, -onis* song < *canere* sing]

chan·son de geste (shäṅ·sôṅ′ də zhest′) An Old French epic tale in verse, generally written in assonant verse of ten syllables a line, arranged in irregular stanzas, and dealing with ancient French history and legend. The most celebrated one is the *Chanson de Roland.* [<F, song of noble deeds]

chant (chant, chänt) *n.* 1 A melody adapted to words without strict rhythm, or containing both recitative and rhythm: the most ancient and simple form of choral music. 2 A psalm or canticle so recited. 3 A song; melody. 4 Any measured monotonous singing or reciting of words. 5 A singing intonation in speech; twang. [< *v.*] — *v.t.* 1 To sing to a chant; intone, as in public worship. 2 To celebrate in song: to *chant* the praises of. 3 To say repetitiously and monotonously; harp upon. — *v.i.* 4 To sing chants. 5 To make melody; sing. 6 To talk monotonously and continuously. Also spelled *chaunt.* [<OF *chanter* <L *cantare,* freq. of *canere* sing]

chant·age (chan′tij, chän′-; *Fr.* shäṅ·tȧzh′) *n.* The extortion of money by threats of exposure; blackmailing. [<F]

chant·er (chan′tər, chän′-) *n.* 1 A singer; especially, a singer in a chantry; a chorister; precentor. 2 The fingerpipe of a bagpipe: distinguished from *drone.* 3 The hedge sparrow. Also **chan′tor.**

chan·te·relle[1] (shäṅ·trel′) *n. Music* The highest string of certain stringed instruments, as a violin. [<F]

chan·te·relle[2] (shan′tə·rel′, chan′-) *n.* An edible yellow mushroom (*Cantharellus cibrius*), with a short stem. [<F <NL *cantharellus,* dim. of *cantharus* drinking cup <Gk. *kantharos*]

chan·teuse (shäṅ·tœz′) *n. French* A woman singer.

chant·ey (shan′tē, chan′-) *n. pl.* **·eys** A rhythmical working song of sailors: also spelled *shanty.* [Alter. of F *chantez,* imperative of *chanter* sing]

chan·ti·cleer (chan′tə·klir) *n.* A cock: used as a proper name. [<OF *chantecler* (name of the cock in the medieval "Reynard the Fox") < *chanter* sing, crow + *cler* aloud]

Chan·til·ly (shan·til′ē, *Fr.* shäṅ·tē·yē′) A town in northern France.

Chantilly lace A fine variety of lace formerly produced in Chantilly, France.

chant ro·yal (shäṅ rwä·yȧl′) A lyric poem, related to the ballade, consisting of five 11-

line stanzas with an 8-line envoy, the stanzas and the envoy having the last line identical. [<F]

chan·try (chan′trē, chän′-) *n. pl.* **·tries 1** A chapel in or attached to a church or monastery, endowed for maintaining daily masses for the soul of the founder or of others nominated by him (the chapel usually containing the tomb of the founder). **2** Formerly, the endowment itself. **3** A chapel for subsidiary church services. [<OF *chanterie* <*chanter.* See CHANT.]

Cha·nu·ca (khä′noo·kä) See HANUKKAH.

Chao·an (chou′än′) A city in SE China on the Han. Formerly **Chao·chow** (chou′jō′).

Chao K'uang-yin (jou′kwäng′yin′), died 976, Chinese emperor; founder of Sung dynasty.

Chao Phra·ya (chou′ prä·yä′) The chief river of Thailand, flowing 140 miles south to the Gulf of Siam: also *Mae Nam, Menam.*

cha·os (kā′os) *n.* **1** A condition of utter disorder and confusion, as the unformed primal state of the universe. **2** Any thing or condition of which the elements or parts are in utter disorder and confusion. **3** *Obs.* Any vast gulf or chasm; an unfathomable abyss. [<L <Gk., abyss <*chainein* gape, yawn]

cha·ot·ic (kā·ot′ik) *adj.* **1** Of, pertaining to, or like chaos. **2** Unformed; completely disordered. Also **cha·ot′i·cal.** —**cha·ot′i·cal·ly** *adv.*

chap[1] (chap) *n.* **1** *Colloq.* A fellow; lad. **2** *Obs.* A chapman; a dealer; buyer. [Short for CHAPMAN]

chap[2] (chap) *v.* **chapped** or **chapt, chap·ping** *v.t.* **1** To cause to split, crack, or become rough. **2** *Scot.* To strike with a hammer; pound on. —*v.i.* **3** To split, crack, or redden. **4** *Scot.* To beat or knock, as on a door; to strike, as a clock. —**to chap out** *Scot.* To summon by a tap, as on the window. —*n.* **1** A crack or roughened place in the skin. **2** *Scot.* A rap on the door; a knock of any sort. [ME *chappen.* Related to CHIP, CHOP.]

chap[3] (chap, chop) *n.* **1** A jaw. **2** *pl.* The mouth and cheeks. **3** The jaw of a vise. Also spelled *chop.* [Cf. ME *chaftjaw*]

cha·pa·re·jos (chä′pä·rā′hōs) *n. pl. SW U.S.* Chaps. Also **cha·pa·ra·jos** (chä′pä·rä′·hōs), **cha·par·re·ras** (chä′·pär·rā′räs). [<Sp.]

chap·ar·ral (chap′ə·ral′) *n.* A thicket of dwarf oak, low thorny shrubs, etc. [<Sp. <*chaparra* evergreen oak]

chaparral cock The roadrunner.

chaparral pea A thorny shrub of California *(Pickeringia montana)* of the pea family, growing densely over chaparrals.

chap·book (chap′book′) *n.* One of a former class of cheap popular books sold by chapmen.

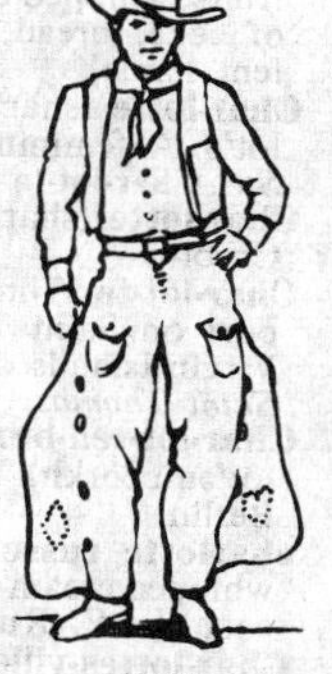
CHAPS

chape (chāp) *n.* **1** A metal tip, as of a scabbard, or an outer case, as of a mold. **2** The backpiece by which a buckle is fastened to a strap or the like; any attaching loop of metal or leather. [<F <LL *capa, cappa* cap]

cha·peau (sha·pō′, *Fr.* shä·pō′) *n. pl.* **·peaux** (-pōz′, *Fr.* -pō′) or **peaus** (-pōz′) A hat.

chapeau bras (brä) A soft, three-cornered dress hat that can be folded and carried under the arm: worn commonly in the 18th century and still with court and diplomatic dress. [<F <*chapeau* hat + *bras* arm]

chap·el (chap′əl) *n.* **1** A place of worship other than a large and regular church. **2** A compartment or recess of a church, where independent services may be held. **3** Any place of worship not connected with the state or established church. **4** In England, any dissenting church. **5** A building or large room in a university, college, or school, for religious services; also, the services. **6** An official choir or orchestra, as of a court or nobleman's establishment. **7** The body of journeymen printers in a given office usually organized under a chairman, known in Great Britain as the *father of the chapel.* **8** *Archaic* A printing house. [<OF *chapele* <Med. L *capella,* dim. of *cappa* cloak; orig., a sanctuary where the cloak of St. Martin was kept as a relic]

chap·el·mas·ter (chap′əl·mas′tər, -mäs′-) See KAPELLMEISTER.

chap·er·on (shap′ə·rōn) *n.* **1** A woman who acts as attendant or protector of a young unmarried woman in public. **2** An older person who attends a social function to maintain its decorum and propriety. —*v.t.* To attend (a young unmarried woman) in mixed company; act as chaperon to. Also **chap′er·one.** [<F, hood <*chape* cape; because she protects her charges from harm] —**chap·er·on·age** (shap′ə·rō′nij) *n.*

chap·fall·en (chap′fô′lən, chop′-) *adj.* **1** Having the chap or jaw drooping. **2** Dejected; crestfallen. Also spelled *chop-fallen.*

chap·i·ter (chap′i·tər) *n. Archit.* The capital of a pillar. See CAPITAL[2]. [<F *chapitre.* See CHAPTER.]

chap·lain (chap′lin) *n.* **1** A clergyman with special functions, such as conducting religious services in a legislative assembly, in a regiment, or on board a ship. **2** A clergyman attached to a chapel for permanent or occasional duty. [<OF *chapelain* <Med. L *cappellanus* <*cappella* CHAPEL] —**chap′lain·cy, chap′lain·ship** *n.*

chap·let (chap′lit) *n.* **1** A wreath or garland for the head. **2** A necklace. **3** A rosary, or, more strictly, the third part of a rosary, or fifty-five beads. **4** A string of beads, or anything resembling it, as an astragal molding, or a rope of frog or toad spawn. [<OF *chapelet,* double dim. of *chape* hood <LL *cappa* hooded cape]

Chap·lin (chap′lən), **Charles Spencer,** 1889–1977, English motion-picture actor and producer, active in the United States.

chap·man (chap′mən) *n. pl.* **·men** (-mən) **1** peddler. **2** *Obs.* A buyer; dealer; merchant. [OE *ceapman* <*ceap* business + *man* man]

Chap·man (chap′mən), **Frank Michler,** 1864–1945, U.S. ornithologist. —**George,** 1557–1634, English poet, dramatist, and translator of Homer. —**John** See APPLESEED, JOHNNY.

chaps (shaps, chaps) *n. pl. U.S.* Leather overalls without a seat, worn over trousers by cowboys to protect the legs: also called *chaparejos.* [Short for CHAPAREJOS]

chap·ter (chap′tər) *n.* **1** A division of a book or treatise, usually marked by a number and heading. **2** The body of clergy connected with a cathedral or other collegiate church; also, a council of such body, or their place of assembly. **3** *Eccl.* The meeting of any order. **4** In certain church services, a short Scriptural passage read immediately after the psalms. **5** A branch of a club, brotherhood, or other association, especially of a college fraternity or sorority. —**cathedral chapter** The personnel of canons attached to a cathedral. —**conventual chapter** The assembly of the clergy of one house or of an entire order for the purpose of regulating domestic affairs. —*v.t.* To divide into chapters, as a book. [<F *chapitre* <OF *chapitle* <L *capitulum,* dim. of *caput* head, capital, chapter]

chapter house A house of assembly for a chapter or a fraternity; especially, such a structure connected with a cathedral.

Cha·pul·te·pec (chə·pool′tə·pek) A fortified hill SW of Mexico City; captured (1847) by U.S. forces in the Mexican War.

cha·que·ta (chä·kā′tä) *n. SW U.S.* A jacket, usually of leather, worn by cowboys, especially when riding in a bushy region. [<Sp.]

char[1] (chär) *n. Brit.* A chore; an odd job; also, work done by the day. —*v.i.* **charred, char·ring** To perform arduous work, as cleaning and scrubbing; serve as a charwoman. Also spelled *chare.* [OE *cerr* turn of work]

char[2] (chär) *v.* **charred, char·ring** *v.t.* **1** To burn or scorch the surface of, as timber. **2** To convert into charcoal by incomplete combustion. —*v.i.* **3** To become charred. See synonyms under BURN. —*n.* Charcoal. [? <CHARCOAL]

char[3] (chär) *n. pl.* **chars** or **char** Any fish (genus *Salvelinus*) characterized by small scales and having red spots, as the brook trout: also spelled *charr.* [<Scottish Gaelic *ceara* blood-red]

char·a·banc (shar′ə·bangk, -bang) *n. pl.* **char·a·bancs** A long open vehicle with transverse seats. [<F *char à bancs* car with benches]

char·a·cin (kar′ə·sin) *n. Zool.* Any of a large and diversified family of fishes *(Characinidae)* native to South America and Africa, including the voracious caribe and many popular aquarium species. [<NL *Characinidae* <Gk. *charax* a sea fish <*charassein* sharpen, whet]

char·ac·ter (kar′ik·tər) *n.* **1** The combination of qualities distinguishing any person or class of persons; any distinctive mark or trait, or such marks or traits collectively, belonging to any person, class, or race; the individuality which is the product of nature, habits, and environment. **2** High qualities; moral force. **3** Reputation. **4** A representation; assumed part; role. **5** One assuming a certain role. **6** Position; status. **7** The person holding or represented as holding a certain position or rank. **8** A figure engraved, written, or printed; mark; sign; letter. **9** A style of handwriting or printing. **10** A form of secret writing; a cipher. **11** Fidelity and vigor in artistic representation of characteristic features. **12** An individual considered as possessing a combination of distinctive features; a personage; also, popularly, a humorous or eccentric person. **13** A representation or characterization, as of one's qualities or abilities; especially, a written testimonial given by an employer to an employee to aid in obtaining employment. **14** That by which a thing is especially known or distinguished; a quality; property: Ductility is a *character* of gold. **15** *Genetics* Any structural or functional trait in an organism regarded as the expression of a gene or genes. [<F *caractère* <L *character* <Gk. *charaktēr* stamp, mark <*charassein* carve, sharpen, engrave]

character actor An actor who plays the part of a character markedly different from himself in age, temperament, manner, etc.

char·ac·ter·is·tic (kar′ik·tə·ris′tik) *adj.* **1** Distinguishing or contributing to distinguish; marking; characterizing; showing the character, traits, and disposition of; typical. **2** Constituting or pertaining to the character. See synonyms under PARTICULAR. —*n.* **1** A distinctive feature; peculiarity. **2** The integral part of a logarithm; index. —**char′ac·ter·is′ti·cal** *adj.* —**char′ac·ter·is′ti·cal·ly** *adv.*

Synonyms (noun): attribute, character, distinction, feature, indication, mark, peculiarity, property, quality, sign, singularity, trace, trait. Compare ATTRIBUTE, CHARACTER, MARK.

char·ac·ter·ize (kar′ik·tə·rīz′) *v.t.* **·ized, iz·ing 1** To describe by qualities or peculiarities; designate. **2** To be a mark or peculiarity of; distinguish. **3** To supply character to. —**char′ac·ter·i·za′tion** *n.* —**char′ac·ter·iz′er** *n.*

char·ac·ter·o·log·i·cal (kar′ik·tər·ə·loj′ə·kəl) *adj.* Pertaining to the study of character or personality: *characterological* features. —**char′ac·ter·ol′o·gy** *n.*

character sketch 1 A literary profile of a person or a type of personality. **2** In the theater, a short impersonation.

char·ac·ter·y (kar′ik·tər·ē, -trē) *n. pl.* **·ter·ies** A system of characters or signs; mode; representation.

char·ac·to·nym (ka·rak′tə·nim) *n.* A word or name indicating the principal charateristic, occupation, or other distinguishing mark of a person; an epithet. [<CHARACTER + Gk. *onoma* name]

cha·rade (shə·rād′) *n.* A guessing game in which each syllable of a word, and finally the whole word, is acted in pantomime or represented in tableau. [<F <Provençal *charrado* chatter <*charra* chatter, prattle]

char·bon (shär′bən) *n. Pathol.* Anthrax. [<F <L *carbo, -onis* coal]

char·coal (chär′kōl′) *n.* **1** A black, porous, odorless carbonaceous substance, burning with little or no flame, obtained by the imperfect combustion of organic matter, as of wood: it is used as a fuel, an adsorbent, a filter, etc. **2** A drawing pencil or crayon made of charcoal dust. **3** A drawing made in charcoal. —*v.t.* **1** To write, draw, mark, or blacken with or as with charcoal. **2** To subject to or suffocate with charcoal fumes. [ME *charcole;* origin unknown]

add,āce,câre,pälm; end,ēven; it,īce; odd,ōpen,ôrder; to͝ok,po͞ol; up,bûrn; ə = a in *above,* e in *sicken,* i in *clarity,* o in *melon,* u in *focus;* yo͞o = u in *fuse,* oi,oil; ou,pout; ch,check; g,go; ng,ring; th,thin; th,this; zh,vision. Foreign sounds à,œ,ü,kh,ṅ; and ◆: see page xx. <from; + plus; ? possibly.

Char·cot (shàr·kō′), **Jean Martin**, 1825–93, French physician and specialist in nervous diseases.

chard (chärd) *n.* **1** The blanched leaves, leafstalks, or midribs of certain plants, as of the artichoke: used as a vegetable. **2** A variety of white beet (*Beta vulgaris cicla*) cultivated for its large leaves and leafstalks, which are used for salad and as a vegetable: also called *Swiss chard, leaf beet.* [<F *carde* <L *carduus* thistle]

Char·din (shàr·dan′), **Jean Baptiste Simeon**, 1699–1779, French painter.

chare (châr) See CHAR¹.

Cha·rente (shà·ränt′) A river in western France, flowing 220 miles west to the Bay of Biscay.

charge (chärj) *v.* **charged, charg·ing** *v.t.* **1** To lay or impose a load upon; to burden. **2** To put something into or upon; fill. **3** To exhort or instruct solemnly or authoritatively: to *charge* a jury. **4** *Electr.* To replenish, as a storage battery. **5** To accuse: with *with:* They *charged* him with reckless driving. **6** To make an onset against or attack upon, as a fort. **7** To emblazon, as with heraldic emblems. **8** To set or state, as a price. **9** To set down or record, as a debt to be paid or accounted for. **10** To load, as a weapon. — *v.i.* **11** To demand or fix a price: Do you *charge* for your services? **12** To debit. **13** To make an onset: *Charge!* **14** To crouch or lie down, as hunting dogs. —**to charge off** To regard or write off as a loss. —**to be in charge of 1** To have the responsibility or control of. **2** To be under the supervision or control of. See synonyms under ARRAIGN, ATTACK, ATTRIBUTE, LOAD. — *n.* **1** The quantity of gunpowder, fuel, etc., put or to be put into a firearm, a furnace, etc. **2** The quantity of static electricity present in a saturated storage battery. **3** *Physics* The energy, measured in electrostatic units, present in an atomic particle, as the proton, electron, meson, etc. **4** Care and custody of that which is under one's care. **5** A price. **6** An entry of indebtedness. **7** A tax; expense; cost. **8** An address of instruction or admonition: the *charge* to a jury. **9** An accusation. **10** An impetuous attack or onslaught; also, the signal for it. **11** *Her.* A figure or device; a bearing. **12** *Obs.* A burden; load. See synonyms under CARE, CAREER, LOAD, OVERSIGHT, PRICE. [<OF *chargier* <LL *carricare* carry <*carrus* cart. Doublet of CARRY.]

char·gé (shàr·zhā′) *n.* A chargé d'affaires. [<F]

charge·a·ble (chär′jə·bəl) *adj.* **1** Capable of being or rightfully to be charged, as an obligation, expense, accusation, etc. **2** Liable to be charged or rendered subject to some duty, expense, etc.; responsible or indictable. **3** *Obs.* Burdensome; also, important.

charge account An account against which the purchase of merchandise in a store is charged.

char·gé d'af·faires (shàr·zhā′ də·fâr′, *Fr.* shàr·zhā′ dà·fâr′) *pl.* **char·gés d'af·faires** (shàr·zhāz′ də·fâr′, *Fr.* shàr·zhā′ dà·fâr′) **1** A person who temporarily assumes the command of a diplomatic mission in the absence of the regularly appointed chief: in full *chargé d'affaires ad interim.* **2** A diplomatic representative of the fourth rank accredited by one foreign minister to another, and not to the chief of state. Compare MINISTER RESIDENT, DIPLOMATIC AGENT.

char·gé des af·faires (shàr·zhā′ dā·zà·fâr′) A person who has custody of the archives or other property of a mission in a country with which formal diplomatic relations are not maintained. He has no diplomatic status or immunity, and his relations with the foreign government are purely informal.

Charge of the Light Brigade Tennyson's poem commemorating the heroic British charge at Balaklava during the Crimean War.

charg·er (chär′jər) *n.* **1** One who or that which charges; especially, a war horse. **2** An apparatus for charging electric storage batteries. **3** A large shallow dish for meat.

Cha·ri (shà·rē′) The French name for the SHARI.

char·i·ly (châr′ə·lē) *adv.* In a chary manner; warily.

char·i·ness (châr′ē·nis) *n.* **1** The quality of being chary. **2** Integrity; scrupulousness.

Char·ing Cross (châr′ing) A district at the west end of the Strand in London, England.

char·i·ot (char′ē·ət) *n.* **1** An ancient two–wheeled vehicle used in war and in racing. **2** An ornate four–wheeled carriage. — *v.t.* & *v.i.* To convey, ride, or drive in or as in a chariot. [<OF, aug. of *char* car <L *carrus* cart, wagon]

ETRUSCAN WAR CHARIOT OF BRONZE

char·i·o·teer (char′ē·ə·tir′) *n.* One who drives a chariot. — *v.t.* To act as driver of (a vehicle) or for (a person).

Char·i·o·teer (char′ē·ə·tir′) The constellation Auriga.

cha·ris·ma (kə·riz′mə) *n.* **1** *Theol.* A gift or power bestowed by the Holy Spirit for use in the propagation of the truth or the edification of the church and its adherents. **2** The aggregate of those special gifts of mind and character which are the source of the personal power of exceptional individuals and upon which they depend for their capacity to sustain the allegiance of, and exercise decisive authority over, large masses of people. Also **char·ism** (kar′iz·əm). [<Gk., grace, favor] — **char·is·mat·ic** (kar′iz·mat′ik) *adj.*

char·i·ta·ble (char′ə·tə·bəl) *adj.* **1** Of, pertaining to, or characterized by charity. **2** Generous in gifts to the poor; liberal. **3** Characterized by love and good will; tolerant; benevolent; kindly; lenient. — **char′i·ta·ble·ness** *n.* — **char′i·ta·bly** *adv.*

Synonyms: beneficent, benevolent, benign, benignant, compassionate, considerate, forgiving, indulgent, kind, lenient, liberal, loving, merciful, mild, patient, placable. *Antonyms:* implacable, relentless, revengeful, unforgiving.

char·i·ty (char′ə·tē) *n. pl.* **·ties 1** Liberality to the poor. **2** Almsgiving; alms. **3** An institution for the help of the needy. **4** Readiness to overlook faults; tolerance; leniency. **5** Spiritual benevolence; Christian love. **6** *Law* A gift of real or personal property for the public benefit. See synonyms under BENEVOLENCE, LOVE. [<OF *charité* <L *caritas, -tatis* love <*carus* dear]

cha·riv·a·ri (shə·riv′ə·rē′, shiv′ə·rē′, shä′rē·vä′rē) *n.* A noisy and discordant burlesque serenade, as to a newly married couple or an unpopular personage, performed with tin pans, horns, kettles, etc.: also spelled *shivaree.* [<F]

chark (chärk) See CHAR². [Back formation from CHARCOAL]

char·kha (chûr′kə, chär′-) *n.* The spinning wheel of India. Also **char′ka.** [<Hind. *carkhā*]

char·la·tan (shär′lə·tən) *n.* A pretender to knowledge or skill, especially to medical knowledge; quack. — **char′la·tan′ic** (-tan′ik) *adj.* — **char′la·tan·ry, char′la·tan·ism** *n.* [<F <Ital. *ciarlatano* babbler <*ciarlare* babble <*ciarla* chat, idle talk]

Char·le·magne (shär′lə·mān), 742–814, king of the Franks 768–814; emperor of the West, 800–814: known as *Charles the Great.*

Char·le·roi (shär′lə·rwä′) A town in SW Belgium; site of the first battle of World War I (1914). Also **Char·le·roy** (shär′lə·rwä′).

Charles (chärlz, *Fr.* shàrl) A masculine personal name. See CARLO, CARLOS, KARL. [<F <L *Carolus* <Gmc., a freeman]
— **Charles I**, 1600–49, Charles Stuart, king of England 1625–49; beheaded.
— **Charles I of Anjou**, 1226–85, king of Sicily 1265–82; of Naples 1266–85.
— **Charles II**, 1630–85, king of England 1660–85.
— **Charles V**, 1337–80, king of France 1364–80: known as *Charles the Wise.*
— **Charles V**, 1500–58, emperor of Germany 1519–56, and, as Charles I, king of Spain 1516–56; abdicated.
— **Charles VII**, 1403–61, king of France 1422–61.
— **Charles IX**, 1550–74, king of France 1560–74.
— **Charles X**, 1757–1836, king of France 1824–30.

— **Charles XII**, 1682–1718, king of Sweden 1697–1718.
— **Charles Edward Stuart** See STUART, CHARLES EDWARD.
— **Charles Mar·tel** (mär·tel′), 688–741, Frankish ruler; grandfather of Charlemagne: called "The Hammer."
— **Charles the Great** See CHARLEMAGNE.

Charles, Cape The northern point at the entrance of Chesapeake Bay, Virginia.

Charles (chärl), **Jacques Alexandre César**, 1746–1823, French aeronaut and physicist.

Charles River A river in eastern Massachusetts, flowing 60 miles to Boston Harbor.

Charles's law (chärl′ziz) *Physics* The statement that the volume of a gas kept at constant pressure varies directly with the absolute temperature: exact only for perfect gases: also called *Gay–Lussac law.* [after J. A. C. *Charles*]

Charles's Wain See under WAIN.

Charles·ton (chärlz′tən) **1** A port in SE South Carolina. **2** The capital of West Virginia.

Charles·ton (chärlz′tən) *n.* A fast dance in four-four time; also, the music for it. [from *Charleston*, S.C.]

Charles·town (chärlz′toun) Formerly a city, now part of Boston, Massachusetts; site of Bunker Hill.

Char·le·voix (shär′lə·voi) A resort city in NW Michigan.

Char·le·voix (shàr·lə·vwä′), **Pierre F. X. de**, 1682–1761, French Jesuit missionary in Canada.

Char·ley (chär′lē) Diminutive of CHARLES. Also **Char′lie.**

char·ley–horse (chär′lē·hôrs′) *n. U.S. Colloq.* A rupture or severe strain in the muscles of the leg or arm, caused by excessive exertion. [Origin unknown]

char·lock (chär′lək) *n.* Wild mustard (*Brassica arvensis*): often a troublesome weed. [OE *cerlic*]

char·lotte (shär′lət) *n.* A dessert made of fruits, whipped cream, custard, etc., in a mold of cake, bread, or crumbs. [<F, from the fem. name]

Char·lotte (shär′lət; *Fr.* shär·lôt′; *Ger.* shär·lot′ə) A feminine personal name. Also *Dan., Sw.* **Char·lot·ta** (shär·lot′ä). [<F]

Char·lotte (shär′lət) A city in southern North Carolina.

Char·lot·te A·ma·li·e (shär·lot′ə ə·mä′lē·ə) A port on Saint Thomas Island, capital of the Virgin Islands of the United States: formerly *Saint Thomas.*

Char·lot·ten·burg (shär·lot′ən·bûrg, *Ger.* shär·lôt′ən·boŏrkh) The chief residential district of Berlin.

charlotte russe (rōōs) A dessert made of whipped cream or custard in a mold of sponge cake. [<F, Russian charlotte]

Char·lottes·ville (shär′ləts·vil) A city in central Virginia.

Char·lotte·town (shär′lət·toun) A port, capital of Prince Edward Island province, Canada.

charm¹ (chärm) *v.t.* **1** To attract irresistibly; bewitch; enchant. **2** To influence as by magic power; soothe; assuage. **3** To influence the senses or mind of by some quality or attraction, as beauty; delight. **4** To protect as by a spell: a *charmed* life. — *v.i.* **5** To be pleasing or fascinating. **6** To act as a charm; work as a spell. **7** To use spells or incantations. [<n.] — *n.* **1** The power of alluring or delighting; fascination. **2** That which charms; beauty; appeal. **3** A magical spell. **4** A small ornament worn on a watchguard, bracelet, etc., for decoration, to avert evil, or to insure good fortune. **5** Originally, the chanting of a verse supposed to possess magical power; an incantation. See synonyms under TALISMAN. [<F *charme* <L *carmen* song, incantation] — **charm′er** *n.*

Synonyms (verb): bewitch, captivate, delight, enchant, enrapture, entice, entrance, fascinate. See RAVISH. *Antonyms:* annoy, disenchant, disgust, distress, disturb, irritate, repel.

charm² (chärm) *n. Obs.* Singing, especially of birds; hence, song or melody. [ME *cherme*, var. of *chirm* CHIRM]

char·meuse (shär·mœz′) *n.* A soft, light fabric with satin weave, having a dull back and semilustrous surface. [<F]

charm·ing (chär′ming) *adj.* **1** Having power to charm. **2** Enchanting; fascinating; bewitching. — **charm′ing·ly** *adv.* — **charm′ing·ness** *n.*

Synonyms: bewitching, captivating, delightful, enchanting, enrapturing, entrancing, fascinating, winning. That is *charming* or *bewitching* which is adapted to win others as if by a magic spell. *Enchanting, enrapturing, entrancing* represent the influence as not only supernatural, but irresistible and *delightful.* That which is *fascinating* may win without delighting, as a serpent its prey; we can speak of horrible *fascination. Charming* applies only to what is external to oneself; *delightful* may apply to personal experiences or emotions as well; we speak of a *charming* manner, a *charming* dress, but of *delightful* anticipations. Compare AMIABLE, BEAUTIFUL, LOVELY.

char·nel (chär′nəl) *n.* A burying place; cemetery; mortuary; also, a sepulcher. —*adj.* Fitted or used for the reception of dead bodies. [<OF <LL *carnalis* fleshly < *caro, carnis* flesh]

charnel house A room or vault, sometimes in a church, for or filled with dead bodies or with bones.

Charn·wood (chärn′wo͝od), **Baron,** 1864–1945, Godfrey Rathbone Benson, English biographer.

Char·on (kâr′ən) **1** In Greek mythology, the ferryman who carried the dead over the river Styx to Hades. **2** A ferryman: a humorous use.

Char·pen·tier (shȧr·päṅ·tyā′), **Gustave,** 1860–1956, French composer.

char·poy (chär′poi′) *n.* The typical bedstead or cot of India, usually having a bamboo frame interlaced with twine. Also **char·pai** (chär′pī′). [<Hind. *chārpāī* < *chār* four + *pāī* foot]

char·qued (chär′kid) *adj.* Dried or jerked: said of meat. See JERK[2]. [<Sp. *charqué,* var. of *charquí* dried beef]

char·qui (chär′kē) *n.* Thin strips of sun-dried meat; jerked beef: also called *jerky.* Also **char′qué.** [<Sp. *charquí* <Quechua *echarqui* dried beef]

charr (chär) See CHAR[3].

char·ry (chär′ē) *adj.* **·ri·er, ·ri·est** Pertaining to or like charcoal.

chart (chärt) *n.* **1** A map on which selected features or characteristics are clearly indicated; especially, one for the use of navigators, aviators, and meteorologists. **2** A sheet showing facts graphically or in tabular form. **3** An outline or diagram having some geographical or physical application. **4** A graph showing changes and variation of temperature, population, circulation of publications, death rate, etc. —*v.t.* To map out; lay out on a chart. [<OF *charte* <L *charta* <Gk. *chartē* leaf of paper. Doublet of CARD.]

char·ta (kär′tə) *n.* *pl.* **·tae** (-tē) A sheet of paper impregnated with medicines, applied externally. [<L *charta* paper]

char·ter (chär′tər) *n.* **1** An act of incorporation of a municipality, company, institution, or the like. **2** A writing permitting the establishment of a branch or chapter of a society. **3** A document granting special rights or privileges. **4** A lease, as of a vessel, or the contract by which it is leased: also **char′ter·par′ty. 5** Written evidence of agreement or contract, as a deed. —*v.t.* **1** To hire by charter. **2** To hire by contract, as a train or car. **3** To establish by charter; give a charter to, as a bank, railroad, colony, etc. [<OF *chartre* <L *chartula,* dim. of *charta* paper] —**char′ter·er** *n.*

char·ter·age (chär′tər·ij) *n.* The act or business of chartering vessels; shipbrokerage; also, a shipbroker's fee.

charter colony In American history, a colony established under a royal charter, which freed it from direct parliamentary control, as Massachusetts.

chartered accountant See under ACCOUNTANT.

Char·ter·house (chär′tər·hous′) A school and asylum established in London in 1611 in a suppressed Carthusian monastery.

charter member An original member of a corporation, or of an order or society.

Charter of the United Nations The charter adopted by the United Nations Conference on International Organization at San Francisco, April–June, 1945, making the United Nations a permanent organization, and establishing the General Assembly, the Security Council, the Economic and Social Council, the Trusteeship Council, the International Court of Justice, and the Secretariat as its component parts. See UNITED NATIONS, INTERNATIONAL COURT OF JUSTICE under COURT.

Char·ters Towers (chär′tərz) A town in Queensland, Australia.

Chart·ism (chär′tiz·əm) *n.* **1** A movement for democratic social and political reform in England, based on principles embodied in the *People's Charter* (1838). **2** The principles of this movement. —**Chart′ist** *n.*

chart·less (chärt′lis) *adj.* **1** Not laid down in a chart. **2** Without a chart. **3** Unguided.

char·tog·ra·pher (kär·tog′rə·fər) See CARTOGRAPHER.

Chartres (shȧr′tr′) A city in NW France; noted for its 11th–13th century Gothic cathedral.

char·treuse (shȧr·trœz′) *n.* **1** A yellow, pale green, or white liqueur made by the Carthusian monks. **2** (*also* shär·tro͞oz′) A pale yellowish-green color. —*adj.* Of this color. [from CHARTREUSE]

Char·treuse (shȧr·trœz′) A Carthusian monastery, especially **La Grande Chartreuse,** the original house of the Carthusian order, near Grenoble, France.

Char·treux (shȧr·trœ′) *n. Obs.* A Carthusian monk. [<F]

char·tu·lar·y (kär′cho͞o·ler′ē) See CARTULARY.

char·wom·an (chär′wo͝om′ən) *n.* *pl.* **·wom·en** A woman employed to do cleaning, scrubbing, etc., as in office buildings. [<CHAR[1] + WOMAN]

char·y (chȃr′ē) *adj.* **char·i·er, char·i·est 1** Cautious; wary. **2** Careful; prudent; sparing; hence, stingy. [OE *cearig* sorrowful, sad < *cearu* care]

Cha·ryb·dis (kə·rib′dis) In Greek mythology, a monster dwelling in a whirlpool on the Sicilian coast opposite the rock Scylla. See SCYLLA.

chase[1] (chās) *v.* **chased, chas·ing** *v.t.* **1** To pursue with intent to catch, capture, or molest. **2** To drive away; dispel: often with *away, out* or *off.* **3** To hunt, as deer. **4** To drive by pursuing: He *chased* the hens into the coop. —*v.i.* **5** To follow in pursuit. **6** *Colloq.* To rush; go hurriedly. —*n.* **1** Earnest pursuit; also, that which is pursued; the prey or quarry. **2** The practice of hunting. **3** *Archaic* The right to hunt on a certain tract. **4** Hunters collectively; the hunt. **5** *Brit.* A private game preserve. **6** In court tennis, a scoring stroke, as when the ball bounces a second time in certain parts of the court. Also spelled *chace.* [<OF *chacier* <LL *captiare,* freq. of *capere* take, hold. Doublet of CATCH.] —**chas′ing** *n.*

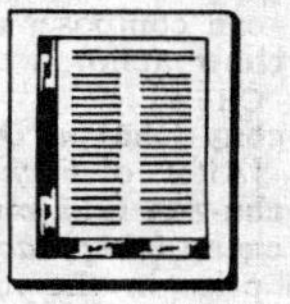
CHASE[2] (*n. def. 1*)

chase[2] (chās) *n.* **1** *Printing* A strong rectangular metal frame into which pages of type are fastened for printing. **2** The part of a cannon between the trunnions and the swell of the muzzle. **3** A groove or slot: the *chase* of a water wheel. **4** A longitudinal groove for a tenon or tongue; a form of rabbet. **5** The circular trough of a cider mill, where the apples are crushed by the runner. —*v.t.* **chased, chas·ing** To ornament by indenting; also, to form by embossing, indenting, etc.: to *chase* silverware. [<F *châsse, chas* <OF *chasse* <L *capsa* box] —**chas′er** *n.*

Chase (chās), **Mary Ellen,** born 1887, U.S. educator and author. —**Salmon Portland,** 1808–73, U.S. lawyer; chief justice of the United States 1864–73.

chas·er (chā′sər) *n.* **1** One who chases or pursues; a hunter. **2** A steeplechaser. **3** A pursuing or following airplane or vessel. **4** A gun at the bow or stern of such a vessel for use in pursuit of or by another vessel: a bow *chaser* and a stern *chaser.* **5** *U.S. Colloq.* A drink of water or of some mild beverage taken after or with whisky, rum, etc. **6** A small quantity of alcoholic liquor taken at the end of a meal; a chasse.

chasm (kaz′əm) *n.* **1** A yawning hollow; deep gorge. **2** An abrupt interruption of continuity; a gap or void. See synonyms under BREACH, HOLE. [<Gk. *chasma* < *chainein* gape, open wide] —**chas·mal** (kaz′məl) *adj.*

chasse[1] (shȧs) *n.* A small glass of alcoholic liquor served at the end of a meal. Also *French* **chasse-ca·fé** (-kȧ·fā′). [Short for *chasse-café* < *chasser* chase + *café* (the taste of) coffee]

chasse[2] (shäs) *n.* A casket for the relics of a saint. [<F *châsse* <L *capsa* box]

chas·sé (sha·sā′) *n.* In dancing, a movement across or to right and left. —*v.i.* **chas·séd, chas·sé·ing** To perform a chassé. Also popularly called *sashay.* [<F, pp. of *chasser* chase]

chasse·pot (shȧs·pō′) *n.* A French breechloading rifled needle gun. [after A. A. *Chassepot,* 1833–1905, French inventor]

chas·seur (sha·sûr′) *n.* **1** A light-armed soldier of cavalry or infantry. **2** A semimilitary household servitor among the European nobility. **3** A huntsman. **4** A hotel servant. [<F, hunter < *chasser* <OF *chacier* CHASE[1]]

Chas·si·dim (khä·sē′dim) *n.* *pl.* of **Chas·sid** (khä′sid) Also Jewish mystics: also spelled *Hasidim.* [<Hebrew, pious] —**Chas·si·dic** (khä·sē′dik) *adj.*

chas·sis (shas′ē, chas′ē) *n.* *pl.* **chas·sis** (shas′ēz, chas′-) **1** The frame and springs of a motor vehicle; also, all other mechanical parts of the car, including the wheels and motor. **2** *Aeron.* The landing gear of an aircraft; the wheels, floats, or other structures which support the main weight of an airplane. **3** In radio: **a** The metal framework to which the tubes and other components of a receiver, amplifier, etc., are attached. **b** The assembled framework and components. **4** In coast artillery, a movable railway for running the top carriage of a gun into and out of firing position. [<F *châssis* < *chas.* See CHASE[2].]

chaste (chāst) *adj.* **1** Free from sexual impurity; virtuous. **2** Pure in thought. **3** Pure in style; free from literary or artistic extravagances. **4** *Obs.* Unmarried; single. See synonyms under MODEST, PURE. [<OF *chaste* <L *castus* pure] —**chaste′ly** *adv.* —**chaste′ness** *n.*

chast·en (chā′sən) *v.t.* **1** To discipline by punishment or affliction; chastise. **2** To moderate; soften; temper. **3** To refine; purify. —**chast′en·er** *n.* —**chast′en·ing** *n.*

Synonyms: afflict, castigate, chastise, correct, discipline, humble, punish, purify, refine, soften, subdue, try. *Castigate* and *chastise* refer strictly to corporal punishment, although both are somewhat archaic. *Punish* is distinctly retributive in sense; *chasten,* wholly corrective and merciful in intent and result. See REPRESS, REPROVE. [<OF *chastier* <L *castigare* correct. See CASTIGATE.]

chas·tise (chas·tīz′) *v.t.* **·tised, ·tis·ing 1** To punish, especially with the rod; whip. **2** To refine or subdue; chasten. See synonyms under BEAT, CHASTEN. [ME *chastisen*] —**chas·tis′a·ble** *adj.* —**chas·tise·ment** (chas′tiz·mənt, chas·tīz′-) *n.* —**chas·tis′er** *n.*

chas·ti·ty (chas′tə·tē) *n.* **1** The state or quality of being chaste; purity. **2** Virginity or celibacy. See synonyms under VIRTUE. [<OF *chasteté* <L *castitas, -tatis* purity < *castus* pure]

chastity belt A fettered girdle worn by women in the Middle Ages to prohibit sexual intercourse during the absence of their husbands.

chas·u·ble (chaz′yə·bəl, chas′-) *n.* The outer vestment worn by a priest in celebrating the mass or Eucharist: a sleeveless mantle falling low in front and behind, and having a cross on the back. [<F <Med. L *casubula,* var. of *casula* cloak <L, dim. of *casa* house]

chat[1] (chat) *v.i.* **chat·ted, chat·ting** To converse in an easy or gossipy manner; talk familiarly. —*n.* **1** Easy and familiar speech; informal conversation. **2** Any of several singing birds: so called from their notes. See synonyms under CONVERSATION. [Short for CHATTER]

chat[2] (chat) *n. Bot.* The inflorescence, catkin, or seed of various plants, as the ament of the pine, the samara of the maple, etc. [<F, cat; so called from its appearance]

Cha·tal·ja (chä′täl·jä′) See ÇATALCA.

cha·teau (sha·tō′, *Fr.* shä·tō′) *n.* *pl.* **·teaux** (-tōz′, *Fr.* -tō′) **1** A French castle or manor house. **2** A house on a country estate, particularly a large house resembling a French manor. Also *French* **châ·teau′.** [<F <OF *chastel* <L *castellum* CASTLE]

Châ·teau·bri·and (shȧ·tō·brē·äṅ′), **François**

René, 1768–1848, Vicomte de Chateaubriand, French writer and diplomat.

Châ·teau·roux (shä·tō·ro͞o′) A town in central France.

Châ·teau–Thier·ry (shä·tō′tye·rē′) A town in northern France; scene of heavy fighting (1918) in World War I.

château wine Any wine made, named for, and usually bottled on, the estate of a château in France where the grapes are grown, particularly those near Bordeaux.

chat·e·lain (shat′ə·lān) See CASTELLAN.

chat·e·laine (shat′ə·lān) *n.* **1** A chain, hanging from a woman's belt to hold small articles; also, a clasp to hold a watch or purse. **2** The mistress of a chateau or castle. [<F *châtelaine,* fem. of *châtelain* CASTELLAN]

Cha·tel·per·ro·ni·an (sha·tel′pə·rō′nē·ən) *adj. Anthropol.* Describing a culture stage of the Upper Paleolithic closely related to and merging with the Aurignacian: also called *Lower Perigordian.* [from *Chatelperron* town in southern France where artifacts were found]

Chat·ham (chat′əm) A municipal borough and port in Kent, England.

Chat·ham (chat′əm), **Earl of.** See PITT.

Chat·ham Island (chat′əm) See SAN CRISTÓBAL ISLAND.

Chatham Islands Two New Zealand Islands, **Chatham** and **Pitt,** east of South Island; total, 372 square miles.

Chatham Strait A navigable channel of SE Alaska through the Alexander Archipelago.

Châ·til·lon (shä·tē·yôn′) A town of north central France. Also **Châtillon–sous–Bag·neux** (-so͞o·bȧ·nyœ′)

cha·toy·ant (shə·toi′ənt, *Fr.* shȧ·twȧ·yäñ) *adj.* **1** Possessing a changeable luster, like that of a cat's eye in the dark. **2** Exhibiting a narrow band of light, as certain gemstones when cut and polished. —*n.* A stone having such a luster; cat's–eye. [<F, ppr. of *chatoyer* change, as a cat's eye] —**cha·toy′an·cy** *n.*

Cha·tri·an (shȧ·trē·äñ′), **Alexandre** See ERCKMANN–CHATRIAN.

Chat·ta·hoo·chee River (chat′ə·ho͞o′chē) A river forming the boundary between southern Georgia and Alabama, flowing 235 miles SW to the Apalachicola.

Chat·ta·noo·ga (chat′ə·no͞o′gə) A city in SE Tennessee; scene of decisive Union victories (1863) in the Civil War.

chat·tel (chat′l) *n. Law* **1** An article of personal property; a movable. **2** Any interest or right in land less than a freehold; a leasehold estate in lands for a determinate period: called a **chattel real.** As distinguished from freeholds, chattels real are regarded as personal property; but, as being interests in real property, they are so designated to distinguish them from other chattels, which are called **chattels personal.** **3** *Archaic* A bondman; serf. See synonyms under PROPERTY. [<OF *chatel* <L *capitale* property <*caput* head. Doublet of CATTLE.]

chattel mortgage A conditional transfer of rights in movable property as security for a debt or obligation, insuring the debtor reversion of ownership upon payment of the obligation.

chat·ter (chat′ər) *v.i.* **1** To click together rapidly, as the teeth in shivering. **2** To talk rapidly and trivially; blather. **3** To make rapid and indistinct sounds, as a monkey or squirrel. **4** To clatter or vibrate while operating improperly, as a power tool. —*v.t.* **5** To utter in a trivial or chattering manner. See synonyms under BABBLE. —*n.* **1** Idle prattle. **2** Jabbering, as of a monkey. **3** A rattling of the teeth. **4** The jar or vibration of a chattering tool. [Imit.]

chat·ter·box (chat′ər·boks′) *n.* A voluble talker.

chat·ter·er (chat′ər·ər) *n.* **1** One who or that which chatters. **2** A passerine bird, as a waxwing, especially the Bohemian waxwing.

Chat·ter·ji (chä′tər·jē), **Bankim Chandra,** 1838–94, Indian novelist.

chatter marks **1** *Mech.* Irregular, very fine tool markings caused by vibration of a tool. **2** *Geol.* Transverse crescent–shaped marks in a continuous series, sometimes occurring in deeply gouged glacial striae as the result of vibration.

Chat·ter·ton (chat′ər·tən), **Thomas,** 1752–1770, English poet.

chat·ty[1] (chat′ē) *adj.* **·ti·er, ·ti·est** Given to chat; loquacious. —**chat′ti·ly** *adv.* —**chat′ti·ness** *n.*

chat·ty[2] (chat′ē) *n. pl.* **·ties** An East Indian porous water jar. [<Hind. *chāṭī*]

Chau·cer (chô′sər), **Geoffrey,** 1340?–1400, English poet.

Chau·ce·ri·an (chô·sir′ē·ən) *adj.* Of, related to, or characteristic of Chaucer or his writings. —*n.* A student or admirer of Chaucer.

chauf·fer (chô′fər, shô′-) *n.* A small chemical furnace. Also **chau′fer.** [Var. of CHAFER]

chauf·feur (shō′fər, shō·fûr′) *n.* One who drives or operates an automobile; especially, one whose work is to drive an automobile for someone else. [<F, stoker <*chauffer* warm]

chaul·moo·gra (chôl·mo͞o′grə) *n.* An East Indian and Malayan tree *(Taraktogenos kurzii,* family *Flacourtiaceae),* from whose seeds is extracted the yellowish **chaulmoogra oil,** used in the treatment of leprosy and other skin diseases. Also **chaul·mu′gra.** [<Bengali *cāulmugrā*]

Chau·mont (shō·môn′) A city in NE France, capital of Haute–Mar department.

Chaun·cey (chôn′sē, chän′-) A masculine personal name. [<OF, chancellor]

chaunt (chônt, chänt) See CHANT.

Chau·pa·ya (chou·pä′yä) See MENAM.

chausses (shōs) *n. Archaic.* **1** Medieval leg harness or hose of mail. **2** Tight pantaloons covering the hips, legs, and feet. [<OF *chauces*<L *calceus* boot <*calx, calcis* heel]

Chaus·son (shō·sôn′), **Ernest,** 1855–99, French composer.

chaus·sure (shō·sür′) *n.* Foot covering. [<F < L *calceare* shoe <*calceus.* See CHAUSSES.]

chau·tau·qua (shə·tô′kwə) *n. U.S.* Any educational association, especially one of a number holding sessions in a circuit of communities. [from *Chautauqua*]

Chau·tau·qua (shə·tô′kwə) A summer resort, seat of an educational association, **Chautauqua Institution,** on **Lake Chautauqua,** 18 miles long, in western New York.

chau·vin·ist (shō′vən·ist) *n.* **1** Anyone absurdly jealous of his country's honor or puffed up with an exaggerated sense of national glory; an extravagant glorifier of his country. **2** One who is belligerently attached to his own race, group, etc.: white *chauvinist.* [after Nicolas *Chauvin,* an extremely devoted soldier and overzealous supporter of Napoleon Bonaparte] —**chau′vin·ism** *n.* —**chau′vin·is′tic** *adj.* —**chau′vin·is′ti·cal·ly** *adv.*

Cha·vannes (shȧ·vȧn′) See PUVIS DE CHAVANNES.

Chá·vez (chä′vās), **Carlos,** 1899–1978, Mexican composer and conductor.

chaw (chô) *v.t. & n. Dial.* Chew. [Var. of CHEW]

chay (shā) *n. Dial.* A chaise: also spelled *shay.* [Alter. of F *chaise* chair]

cha·zan (khä′zən) See HAZZAN.

cheap (chēp) *adj.* **1** Bearing or bringing a low price in the market; that may be bought at low price; inexpensive. **2** Obtainable at a low rate. **3** Depreciated: said of money. **4** Being of little value; hence, poor; of inferior quality. **5** Not esteemed. **6** Low: a *cheap* person. **7** Embarrassed; sheepish. See synonyms under BASE, COMMON. —*n. Obs.* **1** A market; still used in combination in some place names: *Cheap*side and East*cheap* in London. **2** A bargain. —*adv.* In a cheap manner [Earlier *good cheap* a bargain <OE *ceap* business, trade] —**cheap′ly** *adv.* —**cheap′·ness** *n.*

cheap·en (chē′pən) *v.t.* **1** To make cheap or cheaper. **2** *Obs.* To chaffer or bargain for. **3** To bring into contempt, belittle, or disparage. —*v.i.* **4** To become cheap. —**cheap′en·er** *n.*

Cheap·side (chēp′sīd) A district of London, a market center in the Middle Ages and the site of the Mermaid Tavern.

cheap·skate (chēp′skāt′) *n. U.S. Slang* An unpleasant, miserly person.

cheat (chēt) *v.t.* **1** To deceive or defraud. **2** To impose upon; delude; trick. **3** To elude or escape; foil: to *cheat* the hangman. —*v.i.* **4** To practice fraud or act dishonestly. —**to cheat on** *Slang* To be sexually unfaithful to. —*n.* **1** An act of cheating; fraud; imposture. **2** *Law* The obtaining of property by imposture: indictable at common law when the act injures the public welfare. **3** A systematic cheater; swindler. **4** Any of several types of bromegrass: so called because they resemble the grain among which they grow. See CHESS[2]. **5** An article or object of fictitious value; a sham. See synonyms under ARTIFICE, FRAUD, HYPOCRITE. [ME *chete,* short for *achete* escheat] —**cheat′ing** *adj.* —**cheat′ing·ly** *adv.*

cheat·er (chē′tər) *n.* **1** One who cheats; swindler; defrauder. **2** *pl. U.S. Slang* Spectacles; eyeglasses.

che·bec (chi·bek′) *n.* The least flycatcher. [Imit.]

Che·bok·sa·ry (chi·bok·sä′rē) A port on the Volga, capital of Chuvash Autonomous S.S.R.

che·cha·ko (chē·chä′kō) See CHEECHAKO.

check (chek) *n.* **1** A sudden stopping or arrest; rebuff; reverse; delay. **2** Any person or thing that controls or restrains. **3** A checkrein. **4** A written order for money, drawn upon a bank or banker: also *Brit. cheque.* **5** A numbered tag, etc., used in duplicate to identify the owner of article. **6** Any examination, test, or comparison for verification; also, a mark for verification or identification. **7** A square in a checkered surface; also, any checkered pattern or fabric having a checkered pattern. **8** In chess, an attack upon or menace to the king. **9** In mining, a slight fault. **10** A chip used in games. **11** A crack, as in timber, caused by uneven seasoning, or, in steel, caused by uneven tempering. **12** A notch or rabbet in a piece of wood or stone into which another piece fits. **13** A curb on administrative power, as a constitutional right: the *checks* and balances of republican government. **14** A bill in a restaurant. **15** *Obs.* Rebuke; reproof. See synonyms under ANIMADVERSION, REPROOF. —*v.t.* **1** To stop or restrain forcibly or suddenly. **2** To curb; hold in restraint, as with a checkrein. **3** To ascertain correctness of, as by comparison; investigate. **4** To mark with a check or checks. **5** To mark with a pattern of criss–crosses, as cloth. **6** To cause to crack; to make checks or chinks in. **7** To rebuke; rebuff; repulse: They *checked* the attack. **8** In chess, to put an opponent's king in check. **9** To deposit temporarily for safekeeping: to *check* one's luggage. **10** *Agric.* To plant so as to form checkrows. —*v.i.* **11** pause or make a stop. **12** To crack, as paint. **13** To agree item for item: My figures *check* with yours. **14** In chess, to give check to a king. **15** *U.S.* To draw on a checking account. **16** In hunting, to pause, as hounds, to locate a lost scent. **17** In falconry, to forsake proper quarry for baser game: with *at.* —**to check in** *U.S.* To register as a guest at a hotel. —**to check out** *U.S.* **1** To pay one's bill and leave, as from a hotel; also, to depart; die. **2** To investigate or confirm. **3** To be true or as expected, upon investigation. **4** To count and charge for (merchandise). **5** test the performance of. —**to check up** **1** To test; examine: often with *on.* **2** To put a checkrein on. —*interj.* **1** An exclamation proclaiming that the opponent's king is in check. **2** Correct; that is right. —*adj.* **1** Checkered. **2** Serving to verify or confirm: a *check* test. [<OF *eschek* defeat, check <Arabic *shāh* king <Persian; orig. from chess, indicating the king was in danger]

check·book (chek′bo͝ok′) *n.* A book of bank checks in blank, usually with marginal stubs for date, amount, and name of payee.

checked (chekt) *adj.* **1** Marked with squares: *checked* gingham. **2** Made of a fabric marked or woven in squares: a *checked* suit. **3** Restrained; stopped; kept in check.

check·er (chek′ər) *n.* **1** A piece in the game of checkers, usually a small disk. **2** One of the squares in a checkered surface. **3** *pl.* A game for two persons played with 24 pieces upon a checkerboard; draughts. **4** One who checks; especially, one who inspects, counts, or supervises the disposal of merchandise, as in a market. **5** The cultivated service tree. **6** The wild European service tree *(S. torminalis)*: also called **checkertree.** **7** The fruit of either tree. —*v.t.* **1** To mark with squares or crossed lines. **2** To mark with vicissitudes; diversify. Also *Brit. chequer.* [<OF *eschequier* chessboard <Med. L *scaccarium* < *scacci* chess <Arabic *shāq.* See CHECK.]

check·er·ber·ry (chek′ər·ber′ē) *n. pl.* **·ries** **1** The wintergreen. **2** Its red berry. **3** Loosely, the partridgeberry.

check·er·board (chek′ər·bôrd′, -bōrd′) *n.* A

board divided into 64 squares, used in playing checkers or chess.

check·ered (chek′ərd) *adj.* **1** Divided into squares of different colors; checked, as with black and white. **2** Showing any alternating spaces of color or of light and darkness. **3** Marked by vicissitudes; alternating, as between good and evil fortune.

checking account A bank account against which a depositor may draw checks.

check list 1 A list by which something may be confirmed or verified; specifically, a roll or list of voters used at the polls on election days for checking off the names of those who vote. **2** A list of plants, animals, minerals, fossils, etc., usually limited to one natural division, for students and collectors, to check when recognized or acquired.

check·mate (chek′māt′) *v.t.* **·mat·ed, ·mat·ing 1** In chess, to put (an opponent's king) in check from which no escape is possible, thus winning the game: commonly shortened to *mate.* **2** Hence, to defeat by a skilful maneuver. See synonyms under CONQUER. — *n.* **1** The act or position of checkmating. **2** Complete defeat. [<OF *eschec mat* <Arabic *al-shāh māt* the king is dead <Persian]

check-off (chek′ôf′, -of′) *n.* The collection of trade–union dues by deduction at source from the pay of each employee, the employer's accounting office serving as collecting agent. Also **check′-off′.**

check·out (chek′out′) *n.* **1** The series of actions by which the condition or performance of someone or something is tested. **2** The operation or act of examining and charging for purchases, as in a market.

check·rein (chek′rān′) *n.* **1** A rein from the bit of the bridle to the saddle of a harness to keep a horse's head up. **2** The branch rein connecting a driving rein of one horse to the bit of his mate in a double team. Also **check′line′.**

check·room (chek′rōōm′, -rŏŏm′) *n.* A room in a railway station, restaurant, theater, etc., where small packages, coats, hats, luggage, etc., may be left temporarily.

check·row (chek′rō′) *n.* One of the standing rows, as of trees, in a farm or orchard that partition it into squares. — *v.t.* To plant in this fashion.

checks and balances Complementary or balanced powers among the branches of a government, as among the legislative, executive, and judiciary branches.

check–up (chek′up′) *n.* A thorough examination or testing of a living organism, the operation of a mechanism or machine, the progress of work or the finished work of a person or group, etc., to ascertain health, accuracy, value, etc.

check valve *Mech.* A one–way valve, as in a boiler, which closes automatically to prevent return of fluid passing through it. See illustration under HYDRAULIC RAM.

Ched·dar (ched′ər) *n.* Any of several types of white to yellow, hard, smooth cheese. Also **Cheddar cheese.** [from *Cheddar,* Somersetshire, England]

ched·dite (ched′īt, shed′-) *n.* An explosive used in blasting, consisting essentially of nitrated naphthalene containing a chlorate or perchlorate mixed with an oily substance, as castor oil. [from *Chedde,* France]

chee·cha·ko (chē-chä′kō) *n. U.S. Dial.* In Alaska and the NW United States, a newly arrived miner; a newcomer; tenderfoot: also spelled *chechako.* Also **chee·cha′co.** [<Chinook *t′shi* new + *chakho* come]

cheek (chēk) *n.* **1** Either side of the face below the eye and above the mouth. ◆ Collateral adjective: *buccal.* **2** A side or part analogous to the side of a face: the *cheek* of a vise. **3** *Naut.* One of two corresponding projections on either side of a mast, supporting the trestletrees. **4** *Colloq.* Assurance; impudence. — *v.t. Brit. Colloq.* To confront or address impudently. [OE *cēce, cēace*]

cheek by jowl 1 With cheek close to cheek. **2** Closely juxtaposed. **3** Confidential; intimate. Also *Scot.* **cheek for chow.**

cheek·y (chē′kē) *adj.* **cheek·i·er, cheek·i·est** Impudent; brazen. — **cheek′i·ly** *adv.* — **cheek′·i·ness** *n.*

chee·la (chē′lä) See CHELA[1].

cheep (chēp) *v.t. & v.i.* To utter in a faint, shrill tone; chirp; peep. — *n.* A weak chirp or squeak, as of a young bird. [Imit.] — **cheep·er** *n.*

cheer (chir) *n.* **1** A shout of applause or encouragement. **2** State of mind: Be of good *cheer.* **3** Cheerfulness. **4** Something that promotes cheerfulness. **5** Provisions for a feast. **6** *Obs.* Expression of countenance; look. See synonyms under APPLAUSE, ENTERTAINMENT, HAPPINESS. — *v.t.* **1** To make cheerful; fill with joy; comfort: often with *up.* **2** To applaud or salute with cheers. **3** To urge with words or cries; encourage; incite: often with *on.* **4** To act on like cheer; invigorate: The cup that *cheers.* — *v.i.* **5** To be or become cheerful, happy or glad: with *up.* **6** To utter cheers. **7** *Obs.* To be affected; feel; fare. See synonyms under ENCOURAGE, ENTERTAIN, REJOICE. [<OF *chiere, chere* face, countenance <LL *cara*] — **cheer′er** *n.* — **cheer′ing** *adj.*

cheer·ful (chir′fəl) *adj.* **1** In good spirits; joyous; lively. **2** Willing. — **cheer′ful·ly** *adv.* — **cheer′ful·ness** *n.*

Synonyms: blithe, bright, buoyant, cheering, cheery, gay, genial, happy, jocund, joyous, lively, merry, mirthful, smiling, sprightly, sunny. See BRIGHT, COMFORTABLE, GOOD, HAPPY.

cheer·i·o (chir′ē-ō) *interj. & n. Brit.* **1** Hello! **2** Goodbye! Also **cheer′o.**

cheer·less (chir′lis) *adj.* Destitute of cheer; gloomy. See synonyms under BLEAK. — **cheer′less·ly** *adv.* — **cheer′less·ness** *n.*

cheer·ly (chir′lē) *adv. Archaic* Cheerfully; heartily; cheerily.

cheer·y (chir′ē) *adj.* **cheer·i·er, cheer·i·est 1** Abounding in cheerfulness. **2** Fitted to cheer; cheering. See synonyms under BRIGHT, CHEERFUL, COMFORTABLE, HAPPY. — **cheer′i·ly** *adv.* — **cheer′i·ness** *n.*

cheese[1] (chēz) *n.* **1** The pressed curd of milk, variously prepared and flavored; also, a cake or mass of this substance. **2** Any of various substances ground and compacted like cheese, as headcheese. [OE *cēse* <L *caseus* cheese]

cheese[2] (chēz) *v.t. Slang* To stop; quit: leave off: especially in the imperative: *Cheese* it! Run away! [Alter. of CEASE]

cheese[3] (chēz) *n. Slang* The correct or most important thing or person. [Prob. <Persian *chiz* thing]

cheese·cake (chēz′kāk′) *n.* **1** A cake containing sweetened curds, eggs, milk, etc.: also **cheese cake.** **2** *Slang* The display of a girl's legs, as in photographs.

cheese·cloth (chēz′klôth′, -kloth′) *n.* A thin cotton fabric, originally used for wrapping a cheese after pressing.

cheese mite A minute acarid infesting cheese, flour, and milk.

cheese·par·ing (chēz′pâr′ing) *adj.* Miserly; parsimonious. — *n.* **1** A paring of cheese. **2** Something of no value. **3** Any mean or stingy practice or disposition.

chees·y (chē′zē) *adj.* **·i·er, ·i·est 1** Made of or similar to cheese. **2** *Slang* Of inferior grade; second–rate.

chee·tah (chē′tə) *n.* An animal (*Acinonyx jubatus*) of the cat family, resembling the leopard, native to SW Asia and northern Africa: often tamed and trained to hunt antelope. Also spelled *chetah.* [<Hind. *chītā* leopard]

chef (shef) *n.* **1** A head cook. **2** Any cook. **3** A chief or director. [<F]

chef de cui·sine (də kwē-zēn′) *French* Chief cook; head chef.

chef–d′oeu·vre (she-dœ′vr′) *n. pl.* **chefs–d′oeu·vre** (she-) *French* A masterpiece; the most important work of an artist, writer, etc.

Che·foo (chē′fōō′) Yentai. Also **Chih′fu′.**

cheg·oe (cheg′ō) See CHIGOE.

cheilo–, etc. See CHILO–, etc.

cheiro–, etc. See CHIRO–, etc.

Chei·ron (kī′ron) See CHIRON.

Che·ju (chā′jōō′) A Korean island in the East China Sea; 713 square miles: formerly *Quelpart.*

Che·ka (chā′kä) *n.* A Soviet extraordinary commission working as secret police against counter–revolution: superseded by the OGPU in 1922. [<Russian *Che* C + *Ka* K, initials of *Chrezvychainaya Komissya* extraordinary commission]

Che·khov (chek′ôf), **Anton Pavlovich,** 1860–1904, Russian dramatist and short–story writer. Also **Che′kov, Che′koff.**

Che·kiang (che′kyang′, *Chinese* ju′jyäng′) A province in eastern China; 40,000 square miles; capital, Hangchow. Also **Che′chiang′.**

che·la[1] (chā′lä) *n. Anglo–Indian* A disciple or novice; especially, the disciple of a holy man. Also spelled *cheela.* [<Hind. *chelā* disciple <Skt. *chetaka* servant, slave]

che·la[2] (kē′lə) *n. pl.* **·lae** (-lē) *Zool* A terminal pincerlike claw in crustaceans and arachnids, as in lobsters and scorpions. [<NL <Gk. *chēlē* claw]

che·late (kē′lāt) *adj. Zool.* Having a chela or pincerlike claw; cheliform. — *n. Chem.* A compound which has been subjected to chelation.

che·la·tion (kē-lā′shən) *n. Chem.* The inactivation of metallic ions in a solution by an organic reagent with whose molecules they are strongly bound in a ring structure giving maximum stability for specified uses. [<Gk. *chēlē* claw]

che·li·form (kē′lə-fôrm, kel′ə-) *adj. Zool.* Having the form of a chela of a lobster; pincerlike.

Chel·le·an (shel′ē-ən) *adj. Anthropol.* Describing a culture stage of the Paleolithic Age, now more frequently assigned to the Abbevillian, Clactonian, and the earlier portion of the Acheulean. [from *Chelles,* France, where artifacts were first found]

Chelm (khelm) A city in eastern Poland: Russian *Kholm.*

Chelms·ford (chelms′fərd, chelmz′-, chemz′-) A municipal borough, county seat of Essex, England.

che·loid (kē′loid) See KELOID.

Che·lo·ni·a (ki-lō′nē-ə) *n.* An order of reptiles with external skeletons and toothless jaws, including tortoises and turtles. [<NL <Gk. *chelonē* tortoise] — **che·lo′ni·an** *adj. & n.*

Chel·sea (chel′sē) A metropolitan borough of SW London.

Chelsea china A fine, decorated china produced at Chelsea, England, from about 1745 to 1770.

Chel·ten·ham (chelt′nəm) A municipal borough in north central Gloucestershire, England.

Che·lya·binsk (chi-lyä′byinsk) A city in west central Russian S.F.S.R., in Asia.

Che·lyus·kin (chi-lyōōs′kin), **Cape** The northernmost point of Asia, on the Taimur Peninsula.

chem·i·cal (kem′i·kəl) *adj.* **1** Of or pertaining to chemistry or its phenomena, laws, operations, or results: *chemical* analysis. **2** Obtained by or used in chemistry. Also *Obs.* **chem′ic.** — *n.* A substance obtained by or used in a chemical process. — **chem′i·cal·ly** *adv.*

chemical agent 1 Any of numerous chemical compounds used to effect a given purpose. **2** *Mil.* A poison gas, incendiary substance, or screening smoke.

chemical bomb See under BOMB.

chemical bond The force, usually exerted by shared electrons, which holds atoms together in a molecule.

chemical engineering That branch of engineering which studies, develops, and supervises the applications of chemistry to industrial processes.

chemical warfare The technique of using chemical agents, such as burning or poisonous gases, incendiary materials, etc., in defensive or offensive warfare.

chem·i·cide (kem′ə·sīd) *n.* Any of various preparations intended to kill pests or vermin by chemical action.

chem·i·cul·ti·va·tion (kem′i·kul′tə·vā′shən) *n.* The treatment of crops with special chemicals in order to destroy injurious weeds and insect pests.

chem·i·lu·mi·nes·cence (kem′i·lōō′mə·nes′əns) *n.* The emission of light from a substance undergoing a chemical reaction. — **chem′i·lu′mi·nes′cent** *adj.*

che·min de fer (shə·man′ də fâr′) *French* **1** Literally, road of iron; a railroad. **2** A form of baccarat.

che·mise (shə·mēz′) *n.* **1** A woman's undergarment. **2** A muslin surgical dressing used mainly in rectal or bladder operations. **3** A dress style. [<F <LL *camisia* shirt]

chem·i·sette (shem'i·zet') *n.* An ornamental neckpiece or dickey usually made of muslin or lace, worn by women to fill in the open neck of a dress. [<F, dim. of *chemise* CHEMISE]

chem·ism (kem'iz·əm) *n.* Chemical affinity or attraction; chemical properties or activities collectively.

chem·i·sorb (kem'i·sôrb, -zôrb) *v.t.* To adsorb or take up by chemical means. —*v.i.* To be adsorbed in this manner, especially in the presence of a catalyst. —**chem'i·sorp'tion** *n.*

chem·ist (kem'ist) *n.* 1 One versed in chemistry. 2 *Brit.* A druggist. 3 *Obs.* An alchemist. [<ALCHEMIST]

chem·is·try (kem'is·trē) *n.* 1 That science which treats of the structure, composition, and properties of substances and of the transformations which they undergo. 2 Chemical composition or processes.

Chem·nitz (kem'nits) A city in east central Germany.

chemo- *combining form* Chemical; of or with chemicals or chemical reactions: *chemotherapy.* Also, before vowels, **chem-; chemi-,** as in *chemicide.* [<CHEMICAL]

chem·o·cep·tor (kem'ō·sep'tər) *n.* 1 *Physiol.* An organ or nerve element of the body specialized to receive and transmit chemical stimuli, as those of smell and taste. 2 *Biol.* Those receptors within a cell which are supposed to have the power of fixing chemicals. Also **chem'o·re·cep'tor.** [<CHEMO- + (RE)CEPTOR]

chem·o·sphere (kem'ə·sfir') *n.* A region of the atmosphere ranging from 26 to 70 miles above the earth and marked by predominant photochemical activity.

chem·o·sur·ger·y (kem'ō·sûr'jər·ē) *n.* A medical technique which utilizes chemistry, surgery, and microscopic analysis, especially in the treatment of skin cancers.

chem·o·syn·the·sis (kem'ō·sin'thə·sis) *n.* The formation of organic compounds from inorganic constituents by the energy derived from chemical changes. —**chem·o·syn·thet·ic** (kem'-ō·sin·thet'ik) *adj.*

chem·o·tax·is (kem'ō·tak'sis) *n. Biol.* The property which certain motile living cells possess of approaching (**positive chemotaxis**) or moving away from (**negative chemotaxis**) chemical substances; also called *chemotropism.* [<CHEMO-+ Gk. *taxis* order < *tattein* arrange] —**chem·o·tac·tic** (-tak'tik) *adj.*—**chem'·o·tac'ti·cal·ly** *adv.*

chem·o·ther·a·peu·tant (kem'ō·ther'ə·pyoo'tant) *n.* Any substance used in the prevention, treatment, and cure of diseases by chemotherapy.

chem·o·ther·a·py (kem'ō·ther'ə·pē) *n. Med.* The treatment of diseases by the chemical disinfection of affected organs and tissues, especially through the use of synthetic drugs whose action is specific against certain pathogenic micro-organisms but non-toxic to the patient. Also **chem'o·ther'a·peu'tics.** —**chem'o·ther'a·peu'tic** *adj.*—**chem'o·ther'a·peu'tist** *n.*

che·mot·ro·pism (ki·mot'rə·piz'əm) *n.* 1 *Biol.* The response of a plant or animal organism to a chemical reaction, as by unequal growth or directed movements. 2 Chemotaxis. [< CHEMO- + TROPISM] —**chem·o·trop·ic** (kem'ō·trop'ik) *adj.*

Che·mul·po (che·mool'pō) See INCHON. Also **Che·mul·pho** (-pō).

chem·ur·gy (kem'ər·jē) *n.* The chemical exploitation of organic raw materials, especially agricultural products, in the industrial development of new products. [<CHEM(O)- + -URGY] —**chem·ur·gic** (kem·ûr'jik) *adj.* — **chem·ur'gi·cal** *adj.*

Che·nab (chi·nab') A river of NW India, flowing 675 miles west to the Sutlej.

Cheng·teh (chung'du') A city in Manchuria, capital of Jehol province.

Cheng·tu (chung'doo') The capital of Szechwan province, southern China.

Ché·nier (shā·nyā'), **André Marie de,** 1762–1794, French poet, born at Constantinople.

che·nille (shə·nēl') *n.* 1 A soft, fluffy cord or yarn of silk, rayon, cotton, wool, etc., having a fuzzy pile on all sides: used for embroidery, fringes, tassels, etc. 2 Any fabric made with such yarns, used for rugs, etc. [<F, caterpillar <L *canicula,* dim. of *canis* dog; from its fuzzy appearance]

Chen·nault (shə·nôlt'), **Claire Lee,** 1890–1958, U.S. aviator; major general in World War II.

che·no·pod (kē'nə·pod, ken'ə-) *n.* Any plant of the goosefoot family, including American wormseed (*Chenopodium anthelminticum*), used as a remedy for intestinal worms. [<NL *chenopodium* <Gk. *chēn, chēnos* goose + *pous, podos*foot] —**che·no·po·di·a·ceous** (kē'nə·pō'dē·ā'shəs, ken'ə-) *adj.*

Che·ops (kē'ops) Egyptian king of the fourth dynasty; builder of the Great Pyramid at Gizeh: also *Khufu.*

cheque (chek) See CHECK (*n.* def. 4).

chequ·er, etc. (chek'ər) See CHECKER, etc.

Cher (shâr) A river in central France, flowing 200 miles NW to the Loire.

cher a·mi (shâr á·mē') *French* Dear friend. — **chère a·mie** (shâr á·mē') *fem.*

Cher·bourg (sher'boorg, *Fr.* sher·boor') A port on the English Channel in northern France.

Cherbourg Peninsula See COTENTIN PENINSULA.

cher·chez la femme (sher·shā' lá fám') *French* Seek the woman: implying that a woman is the motive for a specified action.

Cher·i·bon (cher'i·bon') See TJIREBON.

cher·ish (cher'ish) *v.t.* 1 To care for kindly; hold dear; treat with tenderness; foster. 2 To entertain fondly, as a hope or an idea; hold closely to. [<F *chériss-,* stem of *chérir* hold dear <*cher* dear <L *carus*] —**cher'ish·er** *n.*

Synonyms: cheer, comfort, encourage, entertain, foster, harbor, nourish, nurse, nurture, protect, shelter, treasure, value. To *cherish* is both to hold dear and to treat as dear. To *nurse* is to tend the helpless or feeble. To *nourish* is strictly to sustain and build up by food; to *nurture* includes mental and spiritual training with love and tenderness; to *foster* is simply to maintain and care for.

Cher·kas·sy (chir·kä'sē) A city on the Dnieper in central Ukrainian S.S.R.

Cher·kess Autonomous Region (cher·kes') A district of SE European S.F.S.R.; 1,500 square miles; capital, Cherkessk.

Cher·kessk (cher·kesk') The capital of Cherkess Autonomous Region, on the Kuban.

Cher·ni·gov (chir·nyē'gôf) A city on the Desna in northern Ukrainian S.S.R. Also **Cher·ni'·gof.**

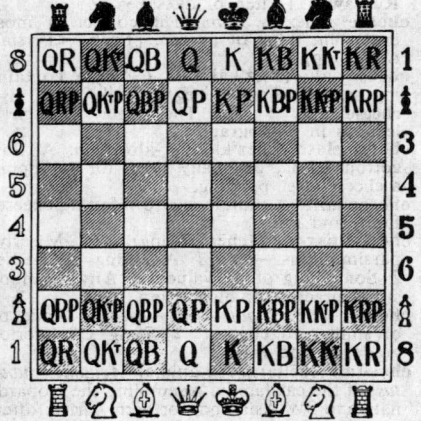

CHESSBOARD
As at the beginning of a game.

B—Bishop   Kt (or N)—Knight   Q—Queen
K—King   P—Pawn   R—Rook

In chess notation the ranks (horizontal rows of squares) are numbered 1–8 reading away from each player, and each file (vertical row) is named for the piece standing at its head. The symbol for each piece is opposite the square it occupies at the beginning of the game, excepting the pawns, which are indicated at each end of the pawn rows. Bishops, knights, and rooks are named for the king or queen, according to their positions at the start. Pawns are named for the pieces they stand in front of.

Cher·nov·sy (cher·nôf'tsē) A city on the Prut in western Ukrainian S.S.R.: Rumanian *Cernauți,* German *Czernowitz.*

cher·no·zem (cher'nə·zem) *n.* A soil typical of temperate subhumid grasslands, consisting of a very dark to black surface layer rich in organic materials overlying a layer of accumulated lime. [< Russian *chernozemu* black soil]

Cher·o·kee (cher'ə·kē, cher'ə·kē') *n. pl.* **·kee** or **·kees** 1 One of a great tribe of Iroquoian Indians formerly occupying northern Georgia and North Carolina, now dwelling in Oklahoma: the most advanced in culture of the North American Indians. 2 The Iroquoian language of this tribe.

Cherokee rose A Chinese rose (*Rosa laevigata*) of trailing habit and having large, solitary white flowers, naturalized in the southern United States and the West Indies: the State flower of Georgia.

che·root (shə·root') *n.* A cigar cut square at both ends, generally of Manila or East Indian make: also spelled *sheroot.* [<F *cheroute* < Tamil *shuruttu* roll, cigar]

cher·ry (cher'ē) *n. pl.* **·ries** 1 Any of various trees (genus *Prunus*) of the rose family, related to the plum and the peach and bearing small, round, or heart-shaped drupes enclosing a smooth pit; especially, the sweet cherry (*P. avium*), the sour cherry (*P. cerasus*), and the wild black cherry (*P. serotina*). 2 The wood or fruit of a cherry tree. 3 A bright-red color resembling that of certain cherries: also **cherry red.** —*adj.* 1 Like a cherry; red. 2 Made of cherry wood. [ME *chery,* back formation from AF *cherise* (mistaken for a plural) <L *cerasus* cherry tree < Gk. *kerasos*]

cher·ry·bird (cher'ē·bûrd') *n.* The waxwing.

cherry bomb A red, round, highly explosive firecracker.

cherry bounce Brandy and sugar, in which cherries have been steeped.

cherry picker Any of several types of crane with a large bucket at the end of an articulated arm and mounted on a truck.

cherry stone 1 The pit of a cherry. 2 A small quahaug.

cher·so·nese (kûr'sə·nēz, -nēs) *n.* A peninsula. [<L *chersonesus* <Gk. *chersonēsos* <*chersos* dry + *nēsos* island]

chert (chûrt) *n.* A dull-colored, impure cryptocrystalline quartz or chalcedony: also called *hornstone.* [Origin uncertain]

cher·ub (cher'əb) *n. pl.* **cher·ubs** *for defs.* 1 *and* 2, **cher·u·bim** (cher'ə·bim, -yə·bim) *for defs.* 3 *and* 4. 1 In art, the representation of a beautiful winged child, or the winged head of a child, the accepted type of the angelic cherub. 2 Hence, a beautiful child or infant. 3 One of an order of angelic beings ranking second to the seraphim in the celestial hierarchy. 4 In Scripture, an angelic being, especially as represented on the ark of the covenant, typifying the presence and power of the Deity. See *Ps.* xviii 10; *Ezek.* x; *Heb.* ix 5. [<LL <Hebrew *kerūbh,* an angelic being] —**che·ru·bic** (chə·roo'bik) *or* **·bi·cal** *adj.* —**che·ru'bi·cal·ly** *adv.*

Che·ru·bi·ni (kā'roo·bē'nē), **Maria Luigi,** 1760 –1842, Italian composer.

cher·vil (chûr'vəl) *n.* 1 Either of two European garden herbs (*Anthriscus cerefolium* or *Chaerophyllum bulbosum*) of the parsley family, the young leaves of which are used for soups, salads, etc. 2 Any one of several other plants of the same family: the great or sweet chervil (*Myrrhis odorata*). [OE *cerfille* <L *caerefolium* <Gk. *chairephyllon*]

cher·vo·nets (cher·vô'nets) *n. pl.* **·vont·si** (-vônt'sē) A gold monetary unit of the U.S.S.R., equivalent to ten rubles: no longer used. [<Russian]

Ches·a·peake Bay (ches'ə·pēk) A large arm of the Atlantic, running northward into Maryland.

Chesh·ire (chesh'ər, -ir) A county in western England, 1,019 square miles; county seat, Chester.

Cheshire *n.* A kind of crumbly Cheddar: also **Cheshire cheese.** [from *Cheshire,* England]

Cheshire cat In Lewis Carroll's *Alice's Adventures in Wonderland,* a grinning cat that disappeared by gradually fading away until only its grin remained.

chess (ches) *n.* A game of skill played by two persons on a checkered board (a **chess'board**) divided into 64 squares, with 16 pieces on each side. The aim of each player, proceeding by alternate moves, is to checkmate his op-

ponent's king. [<OF *eschès*, pl. of *eschec*. See CHECK]

chess² (ches) *n.* 1 Any of several kinds of brome grass, especially *Bromus secalinus*, a pernicious weed in grain fields in America and Europe: also called *cheat*. 2 The darnel. [Origin uncertain]

chess³ (ches) *n.* The deck planks of a pontoon bridge. [Origin uncertain]

chest (chest) *n.* 1 A box of wood, metal, or other material, usually large, and having a hinged lid: used for valuables, tools, personal possessions, etc. 2 A receptacle for gases, liquids, etc.: a steam *chest*. 3 The part of the body enclosed by the ribs; the thorax. ◆ Collateral adjective: *pectoral*. 4 A case for packing certain commodities: a *chest* for indigo. 5 The quantity ordinarily carried in certain chests: a *chest* of tea. 6 A public treasury or fund; coffer; also, the funds contained there: the community *chest*. —**to get off one's chest** *Colloq.* To experience the relief of expressing openly (an emotion, opinion, etc.) that one has previously been at pains to withhold. [OE *cest* <L *cista* <Gk. *kistē* basket, box]

Ches·ter (ches'tər) A masculine personal name. [<L, dweller in camp, i.e., soldier]

Ches·ter (ches'tər) 1 The county seat of Cheshire, England. Ancient **De·va·na Cas·tra** (di·vā'nə kas'trə). 2 A city on the Delaware River in eastern Pennsylvania.

ches·ter·field (ches'tər·fēld) *n.* 1 A single-breasted topcoat of knee length, generally with concealed buttons and a velvet collar. 2 A type of overstuffed sofa. [after an Earl of *Chesterfield* of the 19th c.]

Ches·ter·field (ches'tər·fēld), **Lord**, 1694–1773, Philip Dormer Stanhope, fourth Earl of Chesterfield, English statesman and author.

Ches·ter·field·i·an (ches'tər·fēl'dē·ən) *adj.* 1 Of or pertaining to Lord Chesterfield. 2 Suave; polished; elegant.

Ches·ter·ton (ches'tər·tən), **Gilbert Keith**, 1874–1936, English author.

Chester white One of a breed of pigs first developed in Chester County, Pa.

chest·nut (ches'nut', -nət) *n.* 1 An edible nut, growing in a prickly bur. 2 Any of various trees (genus *Castanea*) of the beech family that bear this nut. 3 One of certain other trees: the horse *chestnut*. 4 A reddish-brown color; also, a horse of such a color. 5 *Colloq.* A worn-out joke; hence, anything trite. 6 A small, horny, wartlike callosity on the inner surface of the leg, as of a horse. —*adj.* 1 Reddish-brown. 2 Made of the wood of the chestnut tree. Also **ches'nut'**. [ME *chesten*, var. of *chesteine* <OF *chastaine* <L *castanea* <Gk. *kastanea* + NUT]

chest of drawers A piece of furniture consisting of a frame containing a set of drawers for storing linens, wearing apparel, etc.

chest on chest A chest of drawers in two sections, one placed upon the other which is usually wider and has feet.

chest register The lower or chest tones of the human voice.

chest·y (ches'tē) *adj.* *Colloq.* **chest·i·er, chest·i·est** 1 Having a large chest, lung capacity, etc. 2 Proud; self-important.

che·tah (chē'tə) See CHEETAH.

cheth (kheth) See HETH.

Chet·nik (chet'nik) *n.* *pl.* **Chet·ni·ci** (chet'nē·tsē) or **Chet·niks** A Serbian nationalist guerrilla in World War II. [<Serbo-Croatian]

che·val-de-frise (shə·val'də·frēz') *n.* *pl.* **che·vaux-de-frise** (shə·vō'-) 1 A portable obstacle of barbed wire supported on a sawhorse construction. 2 Formerly, an obstacle or obstruction of projecting spikes, used to hinder the progress of cavalry. [<F, lit., horse of Friesland; because first used by the Frisians]

che·va·let (shə·və·lā') *n.* The bridge of a stringed instrument. [<F, dim. of *cheval* horse]

che·val glass (shə·val') A full-length mirror mounted on horizontal pivots in a frame.

chev·a·lier (shev'ə·lir') *n.* 1 A knight or cavalier; especially, a French knight or nobleman. 2 *Obs.* A gallant gentleman; chivalrous man. 3 A member of the French Legion of Honor or other order of knighthood. 4 A

cadet of the old French nobility who went into the army. 5 *Her.* An armed knight mounted. [<F <LL *caballarius*. Doublet of CAVALIER.]

che·vals (shə·valz') *n. pl.* Riding breeches.

che·ve·lure (shəv·lür') *n.* *French* A head of hair.

chev·i·ot (shev'ē·ət) *n.* A type of rough woolen cloth of twill weave, used for suits, overcoats, etc., originally made from the wool of the Cheviot sheep.

Chev·i·ot (chev'ē·ət, chē'vē-) *n.* One of a breed of large mountain sheep, originating in the Cheviot Hills, much esteemed for their wool.

Chev·i·ot Hills (chev'ē·ət, chē'vē-) A range on the boundary between Scotland and England; highest peak, 2,676 feet.

chev·on (shev'ən) *n.* Goat flesh used as food. [<F *chèv(re)* goat, she-goat + (*mout*)*on* sheep]

chev·ron (shev'rən) *n.* 1 A V-shaped insigne, made of cloth and worn on the sleeve to indicate rank, rating, wounds, or length of service: used in the U.S. Army, the police force, etc. In the U.S. service, the rank of corporal is indicated by two chevrons, sergeant by three. 2 Any V-shaped mark or zigzag pattern, especially as used in Romanesque architecture: also **chevron molding**. 3 *Her.* An honorable ordinary. [<OF <Med. L *capro, -onis* rafter <L *caper* goat]

CHEVRONS
Sergeant—Army
a. United States.
b. Great Britain.
c. France.

chev·ro·tain (shev'rə·tān, -tin) *n.* A small, deerlike, hornless ruminant (family *Tragulidae*) of Africa and Asia; the mouse deer. [<F < OF *chevrot*, dim. of *chèvre* she-goat <L *capra*, fem. of *caper* goat]

chev·y¹ (chev'ē) *n.* *pl.* **chev·ies** *Brit.* 1 A hunt; chase. 2 The game of prisoner's base. 3 A cry or shout in hunting. —*v.* **chev·ied, chev·y·ing.** —*v.i.* To chase about; race; scamper. —*v.t.* To worry; harass; torment. Also **chev'ey**: sometimes spelled *chivy, chivvy*. [Prob. <*Chevy* Chase]

chev·y² (chev'ē) See SHIV.

Chev·y Chase (chev'ē) An old English ballad dealing with the battle of Otterburn.

chew (chōō) *v.t.* 1 To cut or grind with the teeth. 2 To meditate upon; consider carefully. —*v.i.* 3 To perform the act of cutting or grinding with the teeth: with *on* or *upon*. 4 To meditate: with *on* or *upon*. 5 *Colloq.* To use chewing tobacco continually. —**chew out** *Slang* To scold or reprimand severely. —**chew the fat** or **rag** *Slang* To chat; gossip. —*n.* The act of chewing, or that which is chewed; as a quid; cud: a *chew* of tobacco. [OE *cēowan*] —**chew'er** *n.*

chewing gum See under GUM.

che·wink (chi·wingk') *n.* One of several finches or buntings; especially, the towhee of the eastern United States. [Imit.]

chew·y (chōō'ē) *adj.* **chew·i·er, chew·i·est** Relatively soft and requiring chewing: Caramels are *chewy*. [<CHEW + -Y]

Chey·enne (shī·en') *n.* *pl.* **·enne** or **·ennes** One of an Algonquian tribe of North American Indians formerly inhabiting territory which is now Wyoming, Nebraska, and the western Dakotas: now on reservations in Montana and Oklahoma.

Chey·enne (shī·en') The capital of Wyoming.

Cheyenne River A river in Wyoming and South Dakota, flowing 527 miles NE to the Missouri.

Chey·ne (chā'nē), **Thomas Kelly**, 1841–1915, English Bible scholar and editor.

chez (shā) *prep.* *French* At; at the home of; by.

Chhat·tis·garh (chut'is·gär) A former native states agency in NE India.

chi (kī) The twenty-second letter in the Greek alphabet (see ALPHABET), transliterated into Latin, English, and German by *ch*.

chi·a (chē'ə) *n.* *SW U.S.* A Californian and Mexican herb (*Salvia columbariae*) of the mint family, whose seeds yield a beverage and an oil, **chia oil**. [<Sp. Nahuatl]

Chia·mus·su (jyä'mōō'sōō') See KIAMUSZE.

Chi·an (kī'ə) *adj.* Of, pertaining to, or produced in Chios: *Chian* wine. —*n.* A native of Chios.

Chiang Kai-shek (chäng' kī'shek', chang'; *Chinese* jyäng'), 1887–1975, Chinese generalissimo and statesman; head of the Nationalist government of the Republic of China: real name *Chiang Chung-cheng*. —**Madame Chiang Kai-shek** See under SOONG.

Chiang·mai (chyäng'mī') A city in northern Thailand: also *Chiengmai*.

chian·ti (kyän'tē) *n.* A red or white table wine from the Monti Chianti region; also, any similar wine.

Chian·ti (kyän'tē), **Mon·ti** (môn'tē) A small range of the Apennines in Tuscany, Italy; highest peak, 2,930 feet.

Chi·a·pas (chē·ä'päs) A state in southern Mexico; 28,732 square miles; capital, Tuxtla.

chi·a·ro·scu·ro (kē·är'ə·skyōōr'ō) *n.* *pl.* **·ros** 1 The distribution and treatment of lights and shades in a picture. 2 A kind of painting or drawing using only light and shade to achieve its effects of depth, design, etc. 3 The characteristic use or mastery of light and shade by an artist. Also called *clair-obscure*. Also **chi·a·ro·scu·ro** (kē·är'ə·ō·skyōōr'ō). [<Ital. < *chiaro* clear (<L *clarus*) + *oscuro* dim, obscure (<L *obscurus*)—**chi·a·ro·scu'rist** *n.*

chi·asm (kī'az·əm) *n.* 1 *Anat.* An intersecting or X-like commissure which unites the optic nerves at the base of the brain. 2 *Genetics* The point of intersection of two chromosomes. Also **chi·as·ma** (kī·az'mə). [<NL *chiasma* <Gk. <*chiazein* mark with a chi] —**chi·as'mal, chi·as'mic** *adj.*

chi·as·ma·ty·py (kī·az'mə·tī'pē) *n.* *Genetics* The intertwining of two homologous chromosomes during side-by-side conjugation of the chromosome threads in meiosis, resulting in blending and possible crossing over at points of contact. [<Gk. *chiasma* crossing + *typos* impression]—**chi·as'ma·type'** *adj. & n.*

chi·as·mus (kī·az'məs) *n.* In rhetoric, a contrast by parallelism in reverse order, as in Pope's "they fall successive, and successive rise." [<Gk. *chiasmos* <*chiazein* mark crosswise]

chi·as·to·lite (kī·as'tə·līt) *n.* *Mineral.* An andalusite in which the crystals in transverse section appear crossed or checkered: also called *macle*. [<Gk. *chiastos* crossed]

chiaus (chous, choush) *n.* A Turkish official messenger or sergeantat arms: also *choush*. [< Turkish *chāush*]

Chia·yi (jyä'yē') A city in west central Taiwan: also *Kiayi*. *Japanese* **Ka·gi** (kä·gē).

Chi·ba (chē·bä) A city on central Honshu island, Japan.

Chib·cha (chib'chə) *n.* An Indian belonging to an important linguistic stock, the **Chibchan**, of South and Central American Indians, formerly occupying territory from Honduras southward and eastward through Nicaragua, Costa Rica, Panama, and Colombia; specifically, an Indian of the Chibchan tribes of Colombia: next highest in culture to the Incas at the time of the Spanish conquest. —**Chib'chan** *adj. & n.*

chi·bouk (chi·bōōk', -bŏŏk') *n.* A Turkish pipe having a long straight stem, and a bowl of red clay. Also **chi·bouque', chi·buk'**. [<F *chiboque* <Turkish *chibūk*]

chic (shēk, shik) *adj.* Smart; stylish; elegant. —*n.* Originality, elegance, and taste, as in dress; smartness. [<F]

Chi·ca·go (shi·kä'gō, -kô'-) A city in NE Illinois on Lake Michigan.

chi·ca·lo·te (chē·kä·lō'tä) *n.* A prickly poppy (*Argemone platyceras*) of the SW United States. [<Sp. <Nahuatl *chicalotl*]

chi·cane (shi·kān') *v.* **·caned, ·can·ing** *v.t.* 1 To overreach by trickery. 2 To quibble about. —*v.i.* 3 To resort to quibbles, shifts, or tricks. —*n.* 1 Mean, petty trickery, with pretense of fairness. 2 A bridge or whist hand containing no trumps. [<F *chicaner*]

chi·can·er·y (shi·kā'nər·ē) *n.* *pl.* **·er·ies** 1 The use of mean or paltry artifices, subterfuges, or shifts; especially, legal trickery or underhandedness. 2 A trick or dodge.

Chi·ca·no (chi·kä'nō) *n.* *pl.* **·nos** *U.S.* A Mexican-American.

Chich·a·gof Island (chich'ə·gôf) An island in

the Alexander Archipelago, SE Alaska; 2,104 square miles.

Chi·chén–It·zá (chē·chen′ēt·sä′) A ruined Maya city of Yucatán, Mexico.

Chich·es·ter (chich′is·tər) The county town of West Sussex, England.

chick (chik) *n.* **1** A young chicken. **2** A child. **3** *Slang* A young woman. [Short for CHICKEN]

chick·a·dee (chik′ə·dē) *n.* An American titmouse (genus *Penthestes*) without a crest and with the top of the head and the throat black or dark–colored; especially, the **black–capped chickadee** (*P. atricapillus*) of eastern North America. [Imit. of its cry]

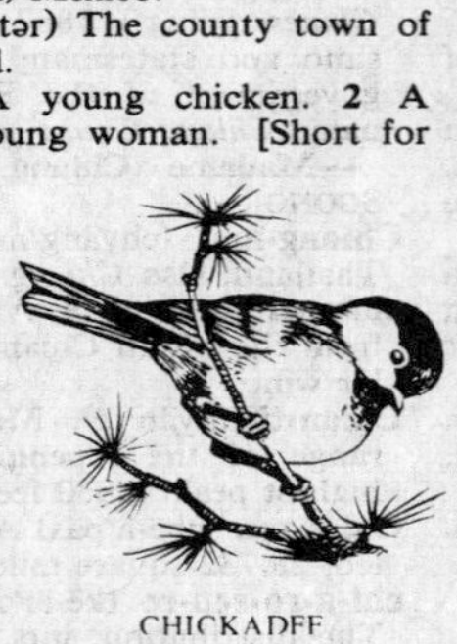
CHICKADEE

Chick·a·hom·i·ny River (chik′ə·hom′ə·nē) A river in eastern Virginia, flowing SE 90 miles to the James River.

Chick·a·mau·ga (chik′ə·mô′gə) A city in NW Georgia on **Chickamauga Creek**; scene of Civil War battle, 1863.

chick·a·ree (chik′ə·rē) *n.* The American red squirrel (*Sciurus hudsonicus*), smallest of the tree–climbing diurnal squirrels. [Imit. of its cry]

Chick·a·saw (chik′ə·sô) *n. pl.* **·saw** or **·saws** One of a tribe of Muskhogean North American Indians formerly occupying the country along the Mississippi River and eastward: now dwelling in Oklahoma.

chick·en (chik′ən) *n.* **1** The young of the common domestic fowl. **2** Loosely, a fowl of any age; also, its flesh used as food. **3** *Colloq.* A child; an inexperienced person. —*adj.* **1** Containing, made from, or flavored with chicken. **2** *Slang* Cowardly. —**to chicken out** *Slang* To refrain from doing something because of fear or cowardice. [< OE *cȳcen*]

chick·en–breast (chik′ən·brest′) *n. Pathol.* A malformed, prominent sternum or breastbone, with lateral flattening of the chest; pigeon breast. —**chick′en–breast′ed** *adj.*

chicken feed *Slang* A petty sum of money.

chicken hawk One of various hawks that prey on poultry; especially, the eastern goshawk (*Astur atricapillus*), Cooper's hawk, and the red–tailed hawk of the eastern United States.

chick·en–heart·ed (chik′ən·här′tid) *adj.* Faint–hearted or cowardly.

chick·en–liv·ered (chik′ən·liv′ərd) *adj.* Cowardly or timorous.

chicken louse One of a species of wingless insects (order *Mallophaga*, the bird lice) that live on chickens, where they feed on feathers and the epidermis. For illustration see INSECTS (injurious).

chicken pox *Pathol.* A contagious disease, principally of children, caused by a virus and characterized by eruptions, a slight fever, and a typically brief course; varicella.

chick·pea (chik′pē′) *n.* **1** A plant (*Cicer arietenum*) of Mediterranean regions and central Asia. **2** Its edible seed, enclosed in short, hairy pods: widely used as a food in Asia and Latin America; Egyptian pea. [Alter. of ME *chich–pease* < F *pois chiche* < *pois* pease + *chiche* < L *cicer*, a small pea]

chick·weed (chik′wēd′) *n.* A spreading, white–flowered, Old World starwort (*Stellaria media*), used for feeding caged birds.

chic·le (chik′əl) *n.* **1** The milky juice of the sapodilla: used as the basic principle of chewing gum. **2** A gum prepared from it. Also **chicle gum.** [< Sp. < Nahuatl *chictli*]

chi·co (chē′kō) *n. pl.* **·cos** The western American greasewood (*Sarcobatus vermiculatus*). [< Sp. *chicalote*]

chic·o·ry (chik′ə·rē) *n. pl.* **·ries 1** A perennial herb of the composite family (*Cichorium intybus*) with pink, white, or azure flowers: naturalized in the United States. **2** Its dried, roasted, and ground roots, used for mixing with coffee or as a coffee substitute. Also spelled *chiccory*. [< F *cichorée* < L *cicorium* < Gk. *kichora*]

chi·co·te (chē·kō′tā) *n. SW U.S.* A whip with a short wooden handle, used by cowboys. Also **chi·co·ta** (chē·kō′tä). [< Sp.]

chide (chīd) *v.t. & v.i.* **chid·ed** or **chid** (chid), **chid·ed** or **chid** or **chid·den** (chid′n), **chid·ing** To scold; utter words of reproof or reprimand. See synonyms under BLAME, REPROVE. [OE *cīdan*] —**chid′er** *n.*

chief (chēf) *n.* **1** A ruler, leader, head, principal actor or agent, or principal part of anything, as of a tribe, party, army, fleet, police force, government bureau, or establishment of any kind. **2** An official superior to another or others in office or authority; one having authority. **3** One who or that which is specially eminent, esteemed, efficient, or active. **4** *Her.* The upper part of a shield. See illustration under ESCUTCHEON. —*adj.* **1** Highest in rank or authority. **2** Principal, most important, or most eminent, in any respect. **3** Most distinguished, influential, valuable, or active. **4** Main; foremost; leading; greatest. See synonyms under FIRST, PARAMOUNT, PREDOMINANT. —**in chief 1** At the head; in or having the highest place or authority: used in titles: commander *in chief*. **2** Chiefly. [< OF *chef, chief* < L *caput* head]

Synonyms (noun): captain, chieftain, commander, head, leader, master, principal, ruler, sachem. A *chief* is either the *ruler* of a tribe or the *head* of some department of established government; as, the *chief* of police. The word is colloquially applied to one holding some analogous position in literary or mercantile life, etc. *Chieftain* is now mainly employed in poetic and literary use; it has special historic application to the *head* of a Scottish clan. A *leader* is one who is voluntarily followed because of ability to overcome and control, or as the choice of a party. A *master* is one who can enforce obedience. The highest officer of any considerable military force is called the *commander*; of all the forces of a nation, the *commander in chief*. See MASTER. *Antonyms*: adherent, attendant, follower, minion, retainer, satellite, subaltern, subordinate, vassal.

chief justice The presiding judge of a court composed of several justices.

Chief Justice The official head of the U.S. Supreme urt.

chief·ly (chēf′lē) *adv.* **1** Most of all or above all; preeminently; especially; particularly. **2** Generally; usually.

chief magistrate The highest administrative official of civil affairs in a community; also, loosely, the president of the United States.

Chief of Staff 1 The senior officer or head of a staff. **2** *U.S.* The principal staff officer in assistance to a command officer in higher military echelons. Compare EXECUTIVE OFFICER. **3** The ranking officer in the U.S. Army or in the U.S. Air Force, immediately under the secretary of his department.

chief·tain (chēf′tən) *n.* **1** The head of a Highland clan. **2** Any chief; leader. See synonyms under CHIEF. [< OF *chevetain* < LL *capitaneus* < L *caput* head. Doublet of CAPTAIN.] —**chief′tain·cy, chief′tain·ship** *n.*

chiel (chēl) *n. Scot.* A lad; a fellow; a child. Also **chield** (chēld).

Chieng·mai (chyeng′mī′) See CHIANGMAI.

Ch'ien–lung (chyen′loong′) Imperial title of Hung–li, 1711–99, fourth Ch'ing emperor, 1736–96: also *Kien Lung*.

chiff·chaff (chif′chaf′, -chäf′) *n.* A small, brownish–white, Old World warbler (*Phylloscopus rufus*), known for its peculiar cry. [Imit.]

chif·fon (shi·fon′) *n.* **1** A sheer silk or rayon fabric. **2** *Obs.* Any decorative object worn by women, as a ribbon or sash. [< F, dim. of *chiffe* rag]

chif·fo·nier (shif′ə·nir′) *n.* **1** An ornamental cabinet. **2** A high chest of drawers. Also **chif′fon·nier′.** [< F < *chiffon* CHIFFON]

chif·fo·robe (shif′ə·rōb) *n.* An article of furniture having a wardrobe compartment alongside a chest of drawers. [< CHIFFO(NIER) + (WARD)ROBE]

Chif·ley (chif′lē), **Joseph Benedict,** 1885–1951, Australian politician; prime minister of Australia 1945–49.

chig·e·tai (chig′ə·tī) See DZIGGETAI.

chig·ger (chig′ər) *n.* **1** Any of certain mites of the southern United States whose larvae burrow under the skin: also spelled *jigger*. **2** The chigoe. [Alter. of CHIGOE]

chi·gnon (shēn′yon, *Fr.* shē·nyôṅ′) *n.* A knot or roll of hair worn at the back of the head by women. [< F]

chig·oe (chig′ō) *n.* **1** A flea (*Tunga penetrans*) of the West Indies and South America. The female burrows under the skin, especially of the feet, causing sores: also called *chigger* or *jigger*. **2** The chigger. Also spelled *chegoe*. [< F *chique* < Cariban]

Chih·li (chē′lē′, *Chinese* ju′lē′) A former name for HOPEH, China.

Chihli, Gulf of An arm of the Yellow Sea in NE China; connected with the Yellow Sea by the **Strait of Chihli.**

Chi·hua·hua (chi·wä′wä) A state in northern Mexico; 94,831 square miles; capital, Chihuahua.

Chi·hua·hua (chi·wä′wä) *n.* One of an ancient breed of very small, smooth–coated dog with large, pointed ears, originally native to Mexico. [from *Chihuahua*, Mexico]

chil·blain (chil′blān) *n. Pathol.* An inflammation of the hands or feet, caused by exposure to cold; erythema. [< CHILL + BLAIN] —**chil′blained** *adj.*

child (chīld) *n. pl.* **chil·dren 1** An offspring of either sex of human parents; a son or daughter. **2** A young person of either sex at any age less than maturity, but most commonly one between infancy and youth. **3** A descendant in any degree: the *Children* of Israel. **4** A childish person; one immature in judgment or discretion. **5** A person or thing considered as an offspring or product: Poems are the *children* of fancy. **6** A follower or disciple. **7** *Law* A legitimate son or daughter. In some States, as in Louisiana, the term includes all descendants in the direct line. —**with child** Pregnant; enceinte. [OE *cild*] —**child′less** *adj.*

Child (chīld), **Francis James,** 1825–96, American scholar; authority on the English and Scottish ballad.

child·bear·ing (chīld′bâr′ing) *n.* Producing or giving birth to children.

child·bed (chīld′bed′) *n.* The state of a woman who is in labor or confined to bed as the result of it.

child·birth (chīld′bûrth′) *n.* Parturition. Also **child′bear′ing.**

childe (chīld) *n. Archaic* A youth of noble or gentle birth, especially one training to be a knight. [Var. of CHILD]

Chil·der·mas (chil′dər·məs) Holy Innocents' Day (December 28th), commemorating Herod's slaughter of the children of Bethlehem. *Matt.* ii 16. Also **Childermas Day.** [OE *cildra*, genitive pl. of *cild* child + *mæsse* mass]

child·hood (chīld′hood) *n.* The state or time of being a child. —**second childhood** A time or state in which the physical and mental powers are enfeebled or impaired by old age; dotage.

child·ing (chīl′ding) *adj.* **1** Child–bearing; pregnant; hence, fruitful; productive. **2** *Bot.* Having young blossoms clustered around an older blossom.

child·ish (chīl′dish) *adj.* **1** Of, pertaining to, or characteristic of a child. **2** Puerile; petty; mentally or physically weak. —**child′ish·ly** *adv.* —**child′ish·ness** *n.*

Synonyms: babyish, childlike, foolish, imbecile, infantile, paltry, petty, puerile, silly, trifling, trivial. *Childlike* refers to the lovable qualities, *childish* to the less desirable traits of childhood. See YOUTHFUL. *Antonyms*: bold, manly, masculine, mature, resolute, strong, vigorous, virile.

child labor 1 Work done by children. **2** The employment of minors under 14 or 16 in industry.

child·like (chīld′līk′) *adj.* **1** Like a child. **2** Artless; confiding. **3** Docile; submissive. Also **child′ly.** See synonyms under CHILDISH, YOUTHFUL. —**child′like′ness** *n.*

child·ness (chīld′nis) *n.* Childish nature, humor, character, or manners.

chil·dren (chil′drən) Plural of CHILD.

Children of Israel The descendants of Jacob; Israelites; the Jews.

Children's Crusade An ill–fated expedition (1212) of some 70,000 German and French children to recover Jerusalem from the Saracens.

child's play Any easy or simple activity.

chil·e (chil′ē) *n.* The acrid red pod or fruit of certain peppers, especially *Capsicum frutescens*, the source of red or cayenne pepper: also spelled *chilli, chilly*. Also **chil′i.** [< Sp. < Nahuatl *chilli*]

Chil·e (chil′ē, *Sp.* chē′lā) A republic on the SW

coast of South America; 286,396 square miles; capital, Santiago. —**Chil′e·an** *adj. & n.*

chil·e con car·ne (chil′ē kon kär′nē) A Mexican dish of red peppers minced and mixed with meat, beans, spices, etc. [< Sp., chile with meat]

Chile saltpeter See under SALTPETER.

chile sauce A spiced condiment sauce made with tomatoes, red peppers, etc.

chil·i·ad (kil′ē·ad) *n.* **1** A thousand. **2** A period of a thousand years; a millennium. [< L chilias < Gk. chilias, -ados < chilioi thousand]

chil·i·arch (kil′ē·ärk) *n.* In Greek antiquity, a commander of a thousand men. [< Gk. chiliarchos < chilioi thousand + archos leader]

chil·i·asm (kil′ē·az′əm) *n.* The doctrine that Christ will reign upon earth a thousand years; the millennium. [< Gk. chiliasmos < chilias. See CHILIAD.] —**chil′i·ast** *n.* —**chil′i·as′tic** *adj.*

Chil·koot Pass (chil′kōōt) A mountain pass from SE Alaska to the Yukon valley; elevation, 3,502 feet.

chill (chil) *n.* **1** A sensation of cold, as that which precedes a fever, often with shivering or shaking. **2** A disagreeable feeling of coldness. **3** A check to ardor, joy, or the like. **4** *Metall.* A metal mold so constructed as to cool suddenly the surface of iron cast therein: also called *coquille.* —*v.t.* **1** To reduce to a low temperature. **2** To make chilly; seize with a chill. **3** To discourage; dispirit; check, as ardor. **4** To harden (metal) by sudden cooling. —*v.i.* **5** To become cold. **6** To be stricken with a chill. **7** To harden by sudden cooling, as metal. —*adj.* **1** Moderately, unpleasantly, or injuriously cold; chilly. **2** Somewhat affected by cold; feeling cold. **3** Cold in manner or disposition; distant; formal. **4** Dispiriting; discouraging. See synonyms under BLEAK. [OE ciele, cyle] —**chill′ing·ly** *adv.* —**chill′ness** *n.*

Chil·lán (chē·yän′) A city in south central Chile.

chill·er (chil′ər) *n.* **1** One who or that which chills. **2** *Metall.* One who sprays hot molds with water in steelworking. **3** *Slang* A horror story or moving picture.

chil·li (chil′ē) See CHILE.

Chil·ling·worth (chil′ing·wûrth), **William,** 1602–44, English theologian.

Chil·lon (shi·lon′, *Fr.* shē·yôn′) A castle on the eastern shore of Lake Geneva; prison of François de Bonnivard, 1496–1570, hero of Byron's poem *The Prisoner of Chillon.*

chill·y[1] (chil′ē) *adj.* **chill·i·er, chill·i·est 1** Producing or feeling cold. **2** Disheartening; depressing. **3** Not genial or cordial; unfriendly. —**chil′li·ly** *adv.* —**chil′li·ness** *n.*

chill·y[2] (chil′ē) See CHILE.

chilo- *combining form* Lip: *Chilopoda.* Also, before vowels, **chil-.** [< Gk. cheilos lip]

chi·lo·pod (kī′lə·pod) *n.* Centipede. —**chi·lop·o·dan** (kī·lop′ə·dən) *adj. & n.*

chi·lo·pod·ol·o·gy (kī′lə·pə·dol′ə·gē) *n.* The branch of zoology concerned with centipedes. —**chi′lo·po·dol′o·gist** *n.*

Chil·tern Hundreds (chil′tərn) *Brit.* **1** An ancient, now purely nominal sinecure under the British crown, for which, by a legal fiction, a member of Parliament applies when he wishes to retire. **2** The hundreds of Burnham, Desborough, and Stoke in Buckinghamshire, England. See HUNDRED (*n.* def. 2).

Chi·lung (jē′lōōng′) See KEELUNG.

Chil·wa (chil′wä) A shallow lake between Mozambique and SE Nyasaland, length 30 miles: also *Shirwa.*

Chi·mae·ra (kə·mir′ə, kī-) *n.* **1** A genus of fishes related to the sharks and rays, having a smooth skin, jaws equipped with solid dental plates, and a short anterior dorsal fin with a spine in front. **2** Chimera. [Var. of CHIMERA] —**chi·mae′rid** *n.*

Chim·bo·ra·zo (chim′bō·rä′zō) An inactive volcano in central Ecuador; 20,577 feet.

chime[1] (chīm) *v.* **chimed, chim·ing** *v.t.* **1** To cause to ring musically; play tunefully with or upon, as by striking. **2** To announce, as the hour, by the sound of bells. **3** To summon, welcome, or send by chiming. **4** To recite in unison or cadence. —*v.i.* **5** To ring out in harmony or unison, as bells. **6** To extract melodious sound, as by striking a bell or set of bells. **7** To harmonize; agree: with *with:* Her remarks *chimed* with his intentions. **8** To recite or intone in cadence. —**to chime in 1** To be in accord with; agree. **2** To take part in or interrupt, as a conversation. —*n.* **1** A set of bells

tuned to a scale. **2** The mechanism for ringing the changes on bells; also, the music from such bells. **3** Accord; harmony. [ME chimbe, chime, alter. of OE cimbal < L cymbalum cymbal] —**chim′er** *n.*

chime[2] (chīm) *n.* **1** The edge or brim of a cask, barrel, or tub: also *chine.* **2** A channel in a vessel's deck. —*v.t.* To make a chime in (a stave, etc.). Also **chimb** (chīm). [OE cimb- edge, as in cimbing a joint]

chi·me·ra (kə·mir′ə, kī-) *n.* **1** An absurd creation of the imagination; a groundless or impracticable conception or fancy; any horrible fancy. **2** *Bot.* A novel or unusual plant growth caused by the grafting of tissue from two or more plants; a graft hybrid of mixed characteristics. **3** *Biol.* An organism incorporating cells of more than one genotype. Also **chi·mae′ra.** [See CHIMERA]

Chi·me·ra (kə·mir′ə, kī-) In Greek mythology, a fire-breathing monster, part lion, part goat, and part serpent, which was killed by Bellerophon: also spelled *Chimaera.* [< L chimaera < Gk. chimaira she-goat]

chi·mere (chi·mir′, shi-) *n.* **1** The sleeveless upper robe of a bishop. **2** *Obs.* A loose upper robe. Also **chim·ar** (chim′ər, shim′-), **chim′er.** [< OF chamarre]

chi·mer·i·cal (kə·mer′i·kəl, kī-) *adj.* **1** Like a chimera; imaginary; fanciful. **2** Impracticable; visionary. See synonyms under FANCIFUL, IMAGINARY, ROMANTIC. Also **chi·mer′ic.** —**chi·mer′i·cal·ly** *adv.*

Chim·kent (chim·kent′) A city in southern Kazakh S.S.R.

chim·la (chim′lə) *n. Scot.* A chimney. Also **chim·ley** (chim′lē).

chim·ney (chim′nē) *n.* **1** A flue for the smoke or gases from a fire. **2** A structure containing it, or something resembling such a structure. **3** A tube for enclosing a flame, as of a lamp. **4** *Obs.* A fireplace, hearth, or forge. **5** *Geol.* **a** A formation of rock shaped like a chimney; specifically, a cleft in a steep mountain cliff or rock wall, wide enough to admit a climber's body and which can be ascended by pressure against the opposite sides. **b** A long spur of ore extending downward through the main vein; a pipe. [< OF cheminée < LL caminata < L caminus furnace, oven < Gk. kaminos]

chimney corner 1 The space between the jamb or side of a large, old-fashioned fireplace and the fire, where one might sit. **2** The fireside.

chimney money See HEARTH MONEY.

chim·ney·piece (chim′nē·pēs′) *n.* **1** A mantelpiece. **2** *Obs.* An ornament, as a picture, placed over a fireplace.

chimney pot A pipe on the top of a chimney, to improve the draft.

chimney swallow 1 The chimney swift. **2** The European swallow.

chim·ney·sweep (chim′nē·swēp′) *n.* One who cleans chimneys, especially by the old method of ascending the flue. Also **chim′ney·sweep′er.**

chimney swift An American swift that nests in chimneys. See under SWIFT.

chim·pan·zee (chim′pan·zē′, chim·pan′zē) *n.* A West African arboreal anthropoid ape (*Pan troglodytes*), about 5 feet in height, with very large ears, dark-brown hair, smaller, less erect, and more intelligent than the gorilla. [< native West African name]

chin (chin) *n.* **1** *Anat.* The central and anterior part of the lower jaw. ◆ Collateral adjectives: *genial*[1], *mental.* **2** *Entomol.* The second sclerite of the labium of an insect. **3** *Zool.* A small ciliated muscular process below the mouth, as in certain rotifers (genus *Pedalion*). —*v.* **chinned, chin·ning** *v.t.* To lift (oneself) by the hands until the chin is level with the hands. —*v.i. U.S. Colloq.* To talk idly. [OE cin]

CHIMPANZEE
(About 4 1/2 feet standing erect)

chi·na (chī′nə) *n.* Porcelain or porcelain ware, originally from China. Also **chi′na·ware′.** —*adj.* Relating to or made of porcelain.

Chi·na (chī′nə) A country of eastern Asia, the most populous and second largest in the world; 3,800,000 square miles; divided (1949) into the **People's Republic of China;** capital, Peking; and the **Republic of China;** temporary capital, Taipei, on Taiwan. Abbr. *Chin., Ch.*

China aster An erect hairy plant (*Callistephus chinensis*) of the composite family, with terminal heads and rayed flowers: cultivated in many varieties.

china bark 1 Cinchona bark. **2** Quillai.

chi·na·ber·ry (chī′nə·ber′ē) *n. pl.* **·ries** The baccate fruit of the chinaberry tree (def. 2).

chinaberry tree 1 The azedarach. **2** Either of two trees (*Sapindus saponaria* and *S. marginatus*) of the soapberry family: found in Mexico and the SW United States, where each is known as the **China tree.**

china closet A closet, cupboard, or cabinet, often with glass front and sides, for household china.

Chi·na·man (chī′nə·mən) *n. pl.* **·men** (-mən) One of the Chinese: an offensive term.

Chinaman's chance *Colloq.* The merest chance.

Chi·nan (jē′nän′) See TSINAN.

China Sea The part of the Pacific bordering on China, divided by Taiwan into the *East China Sea* and the *South China Sea.*

China squash See CUSHAW.

Chi·na·town (chī′nə·toun′) The Chinese quarter of any city outside China, especially of San Francisco and of New York City.

chin·ca·pin (ching′kə·pin) See CHINKAPIN.

chinch (chinch) *n.* **1** A small, brown and black hemipterous insect (*Blissus leucopterus*) destructive to grain: also **chinch bug. 2** The bedbug. [< Sp. chinche < L cimex bug]

chin·chil·la (chin·chil′ə) *n.* **1** A small rodent (*Chinchilla laniger*) native in the Andes, about the size of a squirrel, having a soft pearl-gray fur. **2** The valuable fur of this rodent. **3** A heavy, woolen, twilled fabric used for coating, having a napped surface that is rolled into little tufts or nubs: originally woven to resemble chinchilla fur. [< Sp., ? alter. of Quechua sinchi strong]

Chin·chow (jin′jō′) A city in SW Manchuria, capital of Liaosi province: also *Kinchow.*

chin·cough (chin′kôf′, -kof′) *n.* Whooping cough.

Chin·dwin (chin′dwin′) A river in upper Burma, flowing over 500 miles south to the Irrawaddy.

chine[1] (chīn) *n.* **1** The spine, backbone, or back. **2** A piece of meat from the back. **3** A ridge. —*v.t.* **chined, chin·ing 1** To cut through the backbone of; cut into chines. **2** To cut up. [< OF eschine backbone < Gmc.]

chine[2] (chīn) See CHIME[2].

chine[3] (chīn) *n. Geog.* A deep or narrow ravine or fissure. [OE cinu]

Chi·nee (chī·nē′) *n. Slang* A Chinese: an illiterate or humorous usage.

Chi·nese (chī·nēz′, -nēs′) *adj.* Of or pertaining to the Chinese Republic or China, its people, or their languages. —*n. pl.* **·nese 1** A native or naturalized inhabitant of China. **2** The standard language of China, based on the language spoken in Peking; Mandarin. **3** A subfamily of the Sino-Tibetan family of languages, including the many languages and dialects spoken in China, as those of Peking, Canton, Amoy, Foochow, etc. **4** Any of these languages or dialects, some of which are mutually unintelligible.

Chinese blue Prussian blue.

Chinese carved lacquer Lacquer built up in layers, frequently colored vermilion with ground cinnabar, and carved: also called *cinnabar lacquer, Peking lacquer.*

Chinese Chippendale See under CHIPPENDALE.

Chinese Empire China as ruled by various

imperial dynasties until the founding of the Chinese Republic, 1912.

Chinese ink India ink.

Chinese lantern A collapsible lantern made of thin, brightly colored paper.

Chinese puzzle 1 An intricate puzzle originally made by the Chinese. **2** Any problem difficult to solve.

Chinese red 1 Chrome red. **2** Vermilion. Also **Chinese vermilion.**

Chinese Republic See CHINA.

Chinese Revolution See under REVOLUTION.

Chinese Turkestan See under TURKESTAN.

Chinese Wall See GREAT WALL OF CHINA.

Chinese wax The yellowish-white, tasteless, waxy secretion of an insect *(Ceroplastes ceriferus)* deposited on the branches and twigs of a certain Chinese ash tree: used in candles, as a furniture polish, and as a sizing material: also called *insect wax.*

Chinese white 1 A pigment composed of barium sulfate. **2** Very thick zinc oxide used as a pigment.

Chinese windlass See under WINDLASS.

Chinese wood oil Oil from the tung tree.

Ching·hai (ching′hī′) See TSINGHAI.

Chin Hills (chin) A mountain range of Upper Burma; highest point, 10,018 feet.

chink[1] (chingk) A small, narrow cleft; crevice. —*v.t.* **1** To make cracks or fissures in. **2** To fill the cracks of, as a wall; plug up. —*v.i.* **3** To open in clefts or cracks; crack. [ME *chynke*] **—chink′y** *adj.*

chink[2] (chingk) *n.* **1** A short, sharp, metallic sound. **2** *Slang* Coin; ready money; cash. —*v.t. & v.i.* To make or cause to make a short, sharp, clinking sound by striking together, as coins. [Imit.]

Chink (chingk) *n. Slang* A Chinese: a contemptuous usage.

chin·ka·pin (ching′kə·pin) *n.* **1** Any of several trees (genus *Castanea*) of the United States; especially, the dwarf chestnut *(C. pumila)* and the giant chinkapin *(Castanopsis chrysophylla)* of the Pacific coast. **2** The edible nut of any of these trees. Also **chin′qua·pin**: sometimes spelled *chincapin.* [<N. Am. Ind.]

Chin·kiang (chin′kyang′) A port of eastern China, on the Yangtze.

Chin·ne·reth (kin′ə·reth), **Sea of** The Old Testament name for the SEA OF GALILEE.

chi·no (chē′nō) *n.* **1** A strong, mercerized cotton fabric with a twilled weave. **2** *pl.* Trousers or slacks made of this material. [<Sp., toasted; with ref. to the original tan color]

Chino- *combining form* Belonging to or connected with China (the country): *Chino-Japanese.* See SINO-.

chi·noi·se·rie (shē·nwȧz·rē′) *n. French* **1** A Chinese mannerism or characteristic. **2** An object of Chinese origin or Chinese art or decoration, especially as imitated in the occidental decorative arts.

chi·nook (chi·nŏŏk′, -nŏŏk′) *n. Meteorol.* **1** A warm wind of the Oregon and Washington coasts; first named because it came from the direction of Chinook territory. **2** A warm, dry wind that descends the eastern slopes of the Rocky Mountains in the NW United States and western Canada. **3** Any warm wind occurring during the cold season in the western United States: often called *snow-eater.*

Chi·nook (chi·nŏŏk′, -nŏŏk′) *n. pl.* **·nook** or **·nooks 1** One of a tribe of North American Indians of the Chinook linguistic stock, formerly occupying the region of the Columbia River, Oregon. **2** A family of American Indian languages spoken by the Chinook. **3** Chinook jargon. **—Chi·nook′an** *adj.*

Chinook jargon A lingua franca comprised of words from Chinook and other Indian languages, mixed with English and French: formerly used as a commercial language by traders and Indians from Oregon to Alaska.

Chinook salmon The quinnat.

chintz (chints) *n.* A cotton fabric printed in various colors and usually glazed. Also **chints.** [<Hind. *chīnt* <Skt. *chitra* variegated]

chintz·y (chints′ē) *adj.* **chintz·i·er, chintz·i·est 1** Decorated with chintz. **2** *Colloq.* Cheap; sleazy. **3** *Slang* Stingy.

Chi·os (kī′os) A Greek island in the Aegean off the western coast of Asia Minor; 320 square miles: Greek *Khios. Italian* **Sci·o** (shē′ō), *Turkish* **Sa·kis-A·da·si** (sä·kiz′ä·dä·si′)

chip[1] (chip) *n.* **1** A small piece cut or broken off. **2** A small disk or counter used in games, as in poker. **3** One of the dried droppings of animals available as fuel: usually in the plural: buffalo *chips.* **4** Anything insipid, vain, or worthless. **5** An overdone piece of meat, etc. **6** A small, crisp morsel: potato *chips.* **7** A crack produced by chipping. **8** A very small piece of silicon on which integrated circuits can be printed. **—a chip off the old block** *Colloq.* A child that resembles either of its parents. —*v.* **chipped, chip·ping** *v.t.* **1** To break or scale off a part of, as a piece of china. **2** To chop or cut, as with an ax or chisel. **3** To hew or shape by cutting off pieces. **4** *Obs.* To pare, as a crust of bread. —*v.i.* **5** To scale off in small pieces. **6** In golf, to hit a chip shot. **—to chip in 1** *Colloq.* To contribute, as help or money. **2** In poker, to put chips in as one's ante or bet. [ME *chippe.* Related to CHAP, CHOP.] **—chip′per** *n.*

chip[2] (chip) *v.i.* To cheep. —*n.* A squeak or weak chirp, as of a bird or mouse. [Imit.]

chip[3] (chip) *n.* In wrestling, a leg movement to trip one's opponent. [Cf. ON *kippa* a pull, sudden motion]

chip·munk (chip′mungk) *n.* Any of various striped North American rodents of the squirrel family of terrestrial or burrowing habits; especially, the common *Tamias striatus* of the eastern United States and Canada, and the genus *Eutamias* of the West, having many subspecies: also called *ground squirrel, striped squirrel.* Also **chip·muck** (chip′muk), **chipping squirrel.** [<N. Am. Ind.]

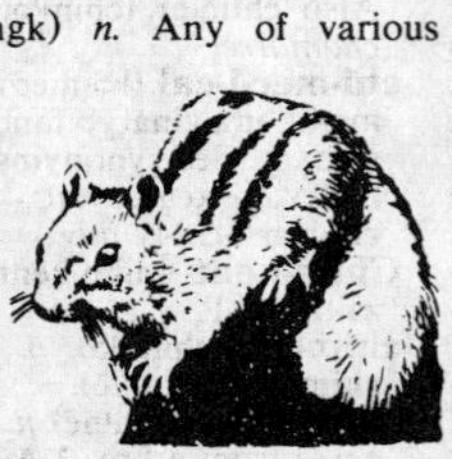

CHIPMUNK
(About 6 1/2 inches long; tail, 4 1/2 inches)

chipped (chipt) *adj.* Smoked and sliced thin, as beef.

Chip·pen·dale (chip′ən·dāl) *adj.* Pertaining to or naming a graceful, rococo style of furniture. —**Chinese Chippendale** Chippendale furniture characterized by the adaptations of Chinese forms and motifs. [after Thomas *Chippendale,* 1718–79, English cabinetmaker]

chip·per (chip′ər) *v.i.* **1** To chirp, as a bird; twitter; babble, as a brook. **2** To talk quickly, in a heated way; be rude. —*adj.* **1** Brisk; hearty; cheerful. **2** Neat; spruce; smart. [<CHIP[2]]

Chip·pe·wa (chip′ə·wä, -wā, -wə) *n. pl.* **·wa** or **·was** Ojibwa. Also **Chip·pe·way** (chip′ə·wā).

Chippewa River A river in west central Wisconsin, flowing 200 miles SW to the Mississippi.

chipping sparrow A small common sparrow *(Spizella passerina)* of eastern North America, with a reddish-brown cap.

chip·py (chip′ē) *n. pl.* **·pies 1** The chipping sparrow. **2** A squirrel or chipmunk. **3** *Slang* **a** A promiscuous girl or woman. **b** A prostitute.

chip shot In golf, a short, lofted shot made in approaching the green.

chi·ral·i·ty (kī·ral′ə·tē) *n. Chem., Physics.* The property by which a form is distinguishable from its mirror image; handedness. [<Gk. *cheir* hand] **—chi·ral** (kī′rəl) *adj.*

Chi·ri·co (kē′rē·kō), **Giorgio di,** 1888–1978, Italian painter.

chir·i·men (chir′i·men) *n.* A Japanese silk crêpe fabric. [<Japanese]

chirk (chûrk) *v.i.* **1** *Scot.* To make a screeching or gritting noise; creak; shriek. **2** *Colloq.* To be or become cheerful: with *up.* [OE *cearcian* creak]

chirm (chûrm) *n.* Twittering; warbling, as of many birds or insects. —*v.i.* To make a twittering sound. [OE *cirm* <*cirman* cry out]

chiro- *combining form* Hand; of or with the hand: *chirograph.* Also, before vowels, **chir-**: also spelled *cheiro-.* [<Gk. *cheir, cheiros* hand]

chi·rog·no·my (kī·rog′nə·mē) *n.* The study of the hand as a means of interpreting character and personality. [<CHIRO- + -GNOMY]

chi·rog·nos·tic (kī′rog·nos′tik) *adj.* Having the ability to distinguish between the right and left sides of the body. [<CHIRO- + Gk. *gignōskein* know]

chi·ro·graph (kī′rə·graf, -gräf) *n. Law* A legal paper, as an acknowledgment of a debt written in the handwriting of the borrower.

chi·rog·ra·phy (kī·rog′rə·fē) *n.* The art, style, or character of handwriting. **—chi·rog′ra·pher** *n.* **—chi·ro·graph·ic** (kī′rə·graf′ik) or **·i·cal** *adj.*

chi·ro·man·cy (kī′rə·man′sē) *n.* Palmistry. **—chi′ro·man′cer, chi′ro·mant** *n.*

Chi·ron (kī′ron) In Greek mythology, the wisest of the centaurs, tutor of Achilles and Asclepius: also *Cheiron.*

chi·ron·ja (chē·rōn′hä) *n.* A citrus fruit produced by crossing the grapefruit with the orange. [<Am. Sp. *china* orange + *toronja* grapefruit]

chi·ro·plas·ty (kī′rə·plas′tē) *n.* Plastic surgery of the hand.

chi·rop·o·dy (kə·rop′ə·dē, kī-) *n.* The treatment of ailments of the foot, as bunions, corns, etc. See PODIATRY. [<CHIRO- + Gk. *pous, podos* foot] **—chi·rop′o·dist** *n.*

chi·ro·prac·tic (kī′rə·prak′tik) *n.* A method of therapy based on the theory that disease is mainly due to a malfunction of the nerves which may be corrected by manipulation of bodily structures, especially the spinal column. [<CHIRO- + Gk. *praktikos* effective <*prattein* do, act] **—chi·ro·prac·tor** (kī′rə·prak′tər) *n.*

chi·rop·ter (kī·rop′tər) *n.* A bat; any member of the order Chiroptera. [<CHIRO- + Gk. *pteron* wing] **—chi·rop′ter·an** *adj. & n.*

chirp (chûrp) *v.i.* **1** To give a short, acute cry, as a sparrow, locust, or cricket; to cheep, as a young bird. **2** To make a similar sound, as in urging a horse. **3** To talk in a quick and cheerful manner. —*v.t.* **4** To utter with a quick, sharp sound. —*n.* A short, sharp sound, as made by some birds and insects. [ME *chirpen,* var. of *chirken* CHIRK] **—chirp′er,** *n.* **—chirp′ing·ly** *adv.*

chirr (chûr) *v.i.* To make a sharp trilling sound, as that of the grasshopper, cicada, and some birds: chirp. —*n.* The trilling sound made by crickets, locusts, cicadas, etc. Also **chirre.** [Imit.]

chir·rup (chir′əp) *v.i.* **1** To chirp continuously or repeatedly, as a bird. **2** To chirp with the lips, as in urging or calling a horse. —*v.t.* **3** To utter with chirps. —*n.* A chirp; a cheery sound. [<CHIRP] **—chir′rup·y** *adj.*

chi·rur·geon (kī·rûr′jən) *n. Archaic* A surgeon. [<OF *cirurgien* <LL *chirurgicus* <L *chirurgus* <Gk. *cheirourgos* <*cheir* hand + *ergon* work] **—chi·rur′ger·y** *n.* **—chi·rur′gic** or **·gi·cal** *adj.*

chis·el (chiz′əl) *n.* A cutting tool with a beveled edge, used for cutting, engraving, or mortising metal, stone, or wood. —*v.* **chis·eled** or **·elled, chis·el·ing** or **·el·ling** *v.t.* **1** To cut, engrave, or carve, as with a chisel. **2** *Colloq.* To cheat; swindle. **3** *Colloq.* To obtain by dishonest or unfair methods. —*v.i.* **4** To use a chisel. **5** *Colloq.* To use dishonest or unfair methods. [<AF, ult. <L *caedere* cut] **—chis′el·er** or **chis′el·ler** *n.*

chis·eled (chiz′əld) *adj.* Distinctly outlined; finely molded with, or as with, a chisel; clearcut. Also **chis′elled.**

Chi·shi·ma Ret·to (chē·shē·mä ret·tō) The Japanese name for the KURILE ISLANDS.

Chis·holm Trail (chiz′əm) An old cattle trail from San Antonio, Texas, to Abilene, Kansas.

Chi·şi·nău (kē′shē·nu′ŏŏ) The Rumanian name for KISHINEV.

Chis·le·hurst and Sid·cup (chiz′əl·hûrst; sid′kup) A residential district of NW Kent, England.

Chis·leu (kis′lef) See KISLEW.

chit[1] (chit) *n.* **1** *Brit.* A note; letter; memorandum. **2** A voucher of a small sum owed, as for food or drink; restaurant check. Also **chit′ty.** [<Hind. *chiṭṭhī* note]

chit[2] (chit) *n. Brit. Dial.* A budding shoot. —*v.i.* **chit·ted, chit·ting** To sprout, as a seed or plant. [OE *cith* sprig]

chit[3] (chit) *n.* A pert child, girl, or young woman. [ME *chitt.* ? Related to CAT.]

Chi·ta (chē·tä′) A city near the Mongolian border of Russian S.F.S.R.

chit-chat (chit′chat′) *n.* **1** Informal or familiar talk. **2** Gossip.

chi·tin (kī′tin) *n. Biochem.* A colorless, horny, amorphous polysaccharide, intermediate between proteins and carbohydrates, forming the principal constituent of the hard covering of insects and crustaceans. [<F *chitine* <Gk. *chitōn* tunic] **—chi′ti·nous** *adj.*

chi·ton (kīʹtən) *n.* **1** A gown or tunic worn by men and women in ancient Greece. **2** Any of a family (*Chitonidae*) of gastropods, found mostly on rocks. [< Gk.]

Chi·tral (chi·trälʹ) A princely state in West Pakistan; 4,000 square miles; capital, Chitral.

Chit·ta·gong (chitʹə·gong) The main port of Bangladesh.

chit·ter (chitʹər) *v.i.* **1** *Obs.* To twitter. **2** *Scot.* To shiver, as with cold. [Var. of CHATTER]

chit·ter·ling (chitʹər·ling) *n.* **1** *pl.* The small intestine of pigs or calves, especially as prepared as food: also **chitʹling.** **2** *pl.* Shreds: torn to *chitterlings.* **3** *Archaic* A short frill having wrinkled folds. [Cf. G *kutteln* entrails]

Chiu·si (kyo͞oʹsē) A town in Tuscany, central Italy: ancient *Clusium.*

chiv (chiv) See SHIV.

chiv·al·rous (shivʹəl·rəs) *adj.* **1** Having the qualities of the ideal knight: gallant, courteous, generous, brave, etc. **2** Pertaining to the feudal system of chivalry. See synonyms under BRAVE. — **chivʹal·rous·ly** *adv.* — **chivʹal·rous·ness** *n.*

chiv·al·ry (shivʹəl·rē) *n.* **1** The feudal system of knighthood; knight-errantry; also, the spirit and customs of medieval knight-errantry. **2** Disinterested courtesy; bravery; magnanimity. **3** A body of knights, warriors, or gallant gentlemen. **4** *Obs.* Mounted and armed fighting men. [< OF *chevalerie* < LL *caballarius* cavalier. Doublet of CAVALRY.] — **chivʹal·ric** (shivʹəl·rik, shi·valʹrik) *adj.*

chiv·a·ree (shivʹə·rēʹ) See CHARIVARI.

chive (chiv) *n.* A perennial herb (*Allium schoenoprasum*) allied to the leek and onion: used as a flavoring in cooking. Also **chive garlic.** [< AF < L *cepa* onion]

chiv·y (chivʹē) *v.t. & v.i.* To chevy. Also **chivʹvy.**

chlam·y·date (klamʹə·dāt) *adj. Zool.* Having a mantle, as certain mollusks. [< L *chlamydatus* cloaked < Gk. *chlamys, -ydos* cloak]

chla·myd·e·ous (klə·midʹē·əs) *adj. Bot.* Pertaining to the floral envelope of a plant. [< Gk. *chlamys, -ydos* cloak]

chlam·y·do·spore (klamʹi·dō·spôr´, -spōr´) *n.* **1** *Bot.* A non-sexual accessory spore in certain fungi, possessing a very thick membrane. **2** *Zool.* A spore with protective envelope, as formed by fission from an encysted protozoan. [< Gk. *chlamys, -ydos* cloak + -SPORE]

chla·mys (klāʹmis, klamʹis) *n. pl.* **chla·mys·es** or **chlam·y·des** (klamʹy·dēz) A short cloak caught up on the shoulder, worn by hunters, soldiers, and horsemen in ancient Greece.

chlo·an·thite (klō·anʹthīt) *n.* A tin-white arsenide of nickel, NiAs₂. [< Gk. *chloanthēs* budding < *chloē* bud, sprout]

Chlod·wig (klōtʹvikh) See CLOVIS.

Chlo·e (klōʹē) A feminine personal name. See DAPHNIS AND CHLOE. [< Gk., bud, sprout]

chlor- Var. of CHLORO-.

chlor·a·cet·o·phe·none (klôrʹə·setʹō·fi·nōn´, klōrʹ-) *n. Chem.* A colorless, crystalline compound, C₈H₇ClO, with an odor of apple blossoms: it is used as a lacrimator and harassing agent in chemical warfare. Symbol, CN. [< CHLORO- + ACETO- + PHEN(YL) + -ONE]

chlor·ac·ne (klôr·akʹnē, klōr-) *n.* A severe skin disorder resembling acne and caused by exposure to chlorinated organic compounds, especially dioxin.

chlo·ral (klôrʹəl, klōrʹəl) *n. Chem.* **1** A colorless, oily, liquid compound, CCl₃·CHO, with a penetrating odor, obtained variously, as by the action of chlorine on alcohol. **2** A white crystalline pungent compound, CCl₃CHO·H₂O, used medicinally as a hypnotic, etc., which in large doses acts as a poison, paralyzing the heart: also **chloral hydrate.** [< CHLOR(INE) + AL(COHOL)]

chlo·ra·mine-T (klôrʹə·mēn·tē´, klōrʹə-) *n. Chem.* A white crystalline compound, C₇H₇SO₂NClNa, used as a surgical antiseptic and decontaminating agent for mustard gas. [< CHLOR- + -AMINE]

chlo·ram·phen·i·col (klôrʹam·fenʹi·kōl, -kol, klōrʹam-) *n. Chem.* A crystalline nitrogenous compound, C₁₁H₁₂Cl₂O₅N₂, obtained from a soil bacillus (*Streptomyces venezuelae*) and also made synthetically: used as an antibiotic in the treatment of certain viral, bacterial, and rickettsial diseases. [< CHLOR- + AM(IDE) + PHE(NOL) + NI(TROGEN) + (GLY)COL]

chlo·ran·thy (klə·ranʹthē) *n. Bot.* The transformation into leaflike organs of the parts of a flower. [< CHLOR- + Gk. *anthos* flower]

chlo·rate (klôrʹāt, klōrʹāt) *n. Chem.* A salt of chloric acid containing the univalent ClO₃ radical.

chlor·dane (klôrʹdān, klōrʹ-) *n.* An oily, chlorinated hydrocarbon, C₁₀H₆Cl₈, used as an insecticide and very toxic to humans, being absorbable through the skin. Also **chlorʹdan.**

chlo·ren·chy·ma (klə·rengʹkə·mə) *n. Bot.* Stem tissue of a plant containing chlorophyll. [< CHLOR(OPHYLL) + (PAR)ENCHYMA]

chlo·ric (klôrʹik, klōrʹik) *adj. Chem.* Of, pertaining to, or combined with chlorine: said specifically of chlorine compounds containing relatively more oxygen than the chlorous compounds.

chloric acid *Chem.* A monobasic, pungent acid, HClO₃, like nitric acid in oxidizing properties, but much less stable.

chlo·ride (klôrʹīd, -id, klōrʹīd, -rid) *n. Chem.* A compound of chlorine with a more positive element or radical, as hydrogen *chloride* (muriatic acid) or sodium *chloride* (common salt). — **chlo·rid·ic** (klə·ridʹik) *adj.*

chloride of lime *Chem.* A disinfecting and bleaching agent made by the action of chlorine gas on slaked lime; bleaching powder.

chlo·rin·ate (klôrʹə·nāt, klōrʹə-) *v.t.* **·at·ed, ·at·ing** *Chem.* To treat, impregnate, or cause to combine with chlorine, as in whitening fabrics or separating gold from ore. — *n.* A soluble bleaching compound made by subjecting potassium or sodium hydroxide to the action of chlorine. — **chlo·rin·aʹtion** *n.* — **chlo·rin·aʹtor** *n.*

chlo·rine (klôrʹēn, -in, klōrʹēn, -rin) *n.* A greenish-yellow, poisonous, readily liquefiable gaseous element (symbol Cl, atomic number 17), a very chemically active member of the halogens and an essential constituent of living organisms. See PERIODIC TABLE. [< Gk. *chlōros* green]

chlo·rin·i·ty (klə·rinʹə·tē) *n.* A measure of the total amount of chlorine per kilogram of sea water: it bears a constant relation to salinity according to the formula S = 0.03 × 1.805 × C.

chlo·rite (klôrʹīt, klōrʹīt) *n.* **1** Any one of several green hydrous silicates, closely related to the micas. **2** One of the salts of chlorous acid. [< Gk. *chlōritis* greenstone]

chloro- *combining form* **1** Light-green: *chlorophyll.* **2** Chlorine: *chlorohydrin.* Also, before vowels, *chlor-.* [< Gk. *chlōros* green]

chlo·ro·a·ce·tic acid (klôrʹō·ə·sēʹtik, -ə·setʹik, klōrʹō-) *Chem.* A colorless, corrosive compound, CH₂ClCOOH, derived from acetic acid in the form of deliquescent crystals: used chiefly in the synthesis of dyestuffs and in medicine as a caustic.

chlo·ro·form (klôrʹə·fôrm, klōrʹə-) *n. Chem.* A colorless, volatile, sweetish liquid compound, CHCl₃, used as an anesthetic and anodyne and as a solvent of wax, resin, plastics, etc. — *v.t.* **1** To administer chloroform to. **2** To anesthetize or kill with chloroform. [< CHLORO- + FORM(YL)]

chlo·ro·hy·drin (klôrʹə·hīʹdrin, klōrʹə-) *n. Chem.* Any of a group of organic compounds containing the hydroxyl radical and chlorine.

chlor·o·meth·ane (klôrʹə·methʹān, klōrʹ-) *n.* Methyl chloride.

Chlo·ro·my·ce·tin (klôrʹə·mī·sēʹtən, klōrʹə-) Proprietary name for a brand of chloramphenicol, used as an antibiotic.

chlo·ro·phane (klôrʹə·fān, klōrʹə-) *n.* A variety of fluorite emitting a green phosphorescence when heated. [< CHLORO- + Gk. *phainein* appear]

chlo·ro·phyll (klôrʹə·fil, klōrʹə-) *n. Biochem.* The green nitrogenous coloring matter contained in the chloroplasts of plants and essential to their growth by photosynthesis of carbohydrates. It occurs in two forms: the bluish-green **chlorophyll-A,** C₅₅H₇₂O₅N₄Mg, the most abundant form; and the yellowish-green **chlorophyll-B,** C₅₅H₇₀O₆N₄Mg: some derivatives are used as dyes, in cosmetics, and in medicine as vulneraries. Also **chloʹro·phyl.** [< CHLORO- + Gk. *phyllon* leaf] — **chlo·ro·phyl·la·ceous** (klôrʹə·fi·lāʹshəs, klōrʹə-), **chloʹro·phylʹlose** (-filʹōs), **chloʹro·phylʹlous** (-filʹəs) *adj.*

chlo·ro·plast (klôrʹə·plast, klōrʹə-) *n. Bot.* One of the flattened bodies or plastids containing chlorophyll found in the cell cytoplasm of plants. Also **chloʹro·plasʹtid.** [< CHLORO- + PLAST(ID)]

chlo·ro·prene (klôrʹə·prēn, klōrʹə-) *n. Chem.* A colorless liquid, C₄H₅Cl, synthesized from acetylene and chlorine: in its polymerized forms it yields a number of compounds essential in the making of synthetic rubber. [< CHLORO- + (ISO)PRENE]

chlo·ro·sis (klə·rōʹsis) *n.* **1** *Pathol.* An anemic disease affecting young women, characterized by a greenish pallor, hysteria, etc.; greensickness. **2** *Bot.* The blanching or etiolation of plants, usually caused by lack of iron and other mineral salts. [< NL < Gk. *chlōros* green] — **chlo·rotʹic** (klə·rotʹik) *adj.*

chlo·rous (klôrʹəs, klōrʹəs) *adj. Chem.* Of, pertaining to, or combined with chlorine: *chlorous* acid.

chlor·pic·rin (klôrʹpikʹrin, klôr-) *n. Chem.* A colorless, oily liquid, CCl₃NO₂, obtained by distilling chloride of lime with picric acid; nitrochloroform: its nauseous vapor is called *vomiting gas.* Symbol, PS. Also **chloʹro·picʹrin.**

chlor·pro·ma·zine (klôrʹprōʹmə·zēn, -zin, klōr-) *n. Med.* A synthetic ataractic drug used in the control of severe excitement in psychiatric cases, particularly of the manic-depressive type. [A composite word from dimethyl amino*propyl* *chloro*phenothi*azine* hydrochloride]

chlor·sul·fon·ic acid (klôrʹsul·fonʹik, klōrʹ-) *Chem.* A colorless, fuming liquid, HClSO₃, used as a smoke-producer in chemical warfare. Symbol, FS.

chlor·tet·ra·cy·cline (klôrʹtetʹrə·sīʹklin, klōrʹ-) *n. Chem.* An organic compound chemically related to tetracycline, obtained from the soil bacillus *Streptomyces aureofaciens:* used as an antibiotic, chiefly in the form known as Aureomycin.

cho·an·o·cyte (kō·anʹə·sīt) *n.* Collar cell. [< Gk. *choanē* funnel + -CYTE]

chock (chok) *n.* **1** A block or wedge, so placed as to prevent or limit motion. **2** *Naut.* A heavy piece of metal or wood fastened to a deck, or the like, and having jaws through which a rope or cable may pass. — *v.t.* To fit or wedge in tightly, as a boat, barrel, or wheel. — *adv.* **1** Completely: He stood *chock* still. **2** All the way: *chock* to the edge. [< AF *choque* log]

CHOCK

chock·a·block (chokʹə·blokʹ) *adj.* **1** Drawn to the limit, with blocks touching: said of a tackle. **2** Close together; crowded. — *adv.* Close; very near.

chock-full (chokʹfo͝olʹ) *adj.* **1** Completely full; full to crowding or choking. **2** Deeply moved with emotion. Also *choke-full.* [ME *chokke-fulle*]

chock·stone (chokʹstōn) *n. Geol.* A block or mass of loose rock wedged in a mountain chimney.

choc·o·late (chôkʹlit, chôkʹə·lit, chokʹ-) *n.* **1** Cacao nuts roasted and ground without removing the fat, usually sweetened and flavored. **2** A beverage or confection made from this preparation. **3** Dark-brown color. — *adj.* Flavored, made with, or colored like chocolate. [< Sp. < Nahuatl *chocólatl*]

Choc·taw (chokʹtô) *n. pl.* **·taw** or **·taws 1** One of a tribe of North American Indians of Muskhogean linguistic stock, formerly living between the Mobile and Mississippi Rivers: now in Oklahoma. **2** The language of this tribe.

choice (chois) *n.* **1** The act, fact, power, or privilege of choosing; selection. **2** One who

or that which is chosen or to be chosen; preference. 3 A number or a variety from which to choose; also, an alternative. 4 The power to prefer or select. 5 The right or privilege to choose; option. 6 The best part. See synonyms, under ALTERNATIVE. —*adj.* **choic·er, choic·est 1** Meriting, preference; select; elegant; excellent; also, precious. 2 Dainty; fastidious. 3 *Dial.* Careful of; fond of. [< OF *choisir* choose] **—choice′ly** *adv.* **—choice′ness** *n.*

Synonyms (adj.): cherished, chosen, costly, dainty, elegant, excellent, exquisite, nice, picked, precious, rare, select. See EXCELLENT. *Antonyms*: cheap, common, inferior, mean, ordinary, poor, valueless, worthless.

choir (kwīr) *n.* 1 A body of trained singers or that part of a church occupied by them; chancel. 2 Originally, any band or organized company, especially of dancers or singers. 3 One of the nine orders in the angelic hierarchy. —*v.i.* To sing, as in a choir. —*v.t.* To sing or utter in chorus. Also spelled *quire.* ◆ Homophone: *quire.* [< OF *cuer* < L *chorus*; infl. in form by F *choeur.* Doublet of CHORUS.]

choir boy A young boy who sings in a choir.

choir loft A gallery in a church set aside for the choir.

choir·mas·ter (kwīr′mas′tər, -mäs′-) *n.* One who directs or trains a choir.

Choi·seul (shwȧ·zœl′) Northeasternmost of the British Solomon Islands; about 1,500 square miles.

Choi·seul (shwȧ·zœl′), **Duc Étienne de,** 1719–1785, French statesman.

choke (chōk) *v.* **choked, chok·ing** *v.t.* 1 To stop the breathing of by obstructing or constricting the windpipe; strangle. 2 To keep back; suppress. 3 To fill completely. 4 To obstruct or close up by filling. 5 To retard the progress, growth, or action of. 6 To make a chokebore. 7 To lessen the air intake of the carburetor in order to enrich the fuel mixture of (a gasoline engine). —*v.i.* 8 To become suffocated or stifled. 9 To become clogged, fouled, or obstructed. —*n.* 1 The act of choking. 2 The narrowest part of a chokebored gun. 3 A device to control the supply of oxygen to a gasoline engine. 4 A choke coil. [OE *aceōcian*]

choke·ber·ry (chōk′ber′ē, -bər·ē) *n. pl.* **·ries** 1 A North American shrub (genus *Aronia*) of the rose family. 2 The small, red or purple astringent fruit of this shrub.

choke·bore (chōk′bôr′, -bōr) *n.* 1 The bore of a shotgun narrowed at the muzzle. 2 A gun so bored.

choke·cher·ry (chōk′cher′ē) *n. pl.* **·ries** A North American wild cherry *(Prunus virginiana).*

choke coil *Electr.* A low-resistance coil of sufficient inductance to limit or suppress any fluctuating current without impeding the flow of a steady current.

choke·damp (chōk′damp′) *n.* A nonexplosive, asphyxiating atmosphere deficient in oxygen, found in mines, wells, etc. Also called *black-damp.*

choke-full (chōk′fool′) See CHOCK-FULL.

chok·er (chō′kər) 1 One who or that which chokes. 2 *Colloq.* A wide white tie or neck cloth worn high around the throat. 3 A person who wears such a tie; especially, a minister. 4 A small fur neckpiece, closely fitting the neck. 5 A closely fitting necklace.

chok·ing (chō′king) *adj.* 1 Causing strangling; stifling. 2 Strained with emotion: said of the voice. **—chok′ing·ly** *adv.*

chok·y (chō′kē) *adj.* **chok·i·er, chok·i·est 1** Suffocating; causing suffocation; stifling. 2 Somewhat choked: a *choky* voice. Also **chok′ey.**

chol·a·gog (kol′ə·gôg, -gog) *n. Med.* A purgative causing evacuations of bile. [< Gk. *cholagogos* < *cholē* bile + *agein* lead] **—chol·a·gog·ic** (kol′ə·goj′ik) *adj.* & *n.*

cho·lan·gi·ot·o·my (kə·lan′jē·ot′ə·mē) *n. Surg.* The opening of a bile duct through the substance of the liver, to remove gallstones. [< CHOLE- + ANGIO- + -TOMY]

chol·an·gi·tis (kol′an·jī′tis) *n. Pathol.* Inflammation of the biliary ducts. Also **chol′an·gei′tis.** [< CHOL- + ANGI(O)- + -ITIS]

chole- *combining form* Bile; gall: *cholesterol.* Also, before vowels, **chol-:** also **cholo-.** [< Gk. *cholē bile*]

chol·e·cyst (kol′ə·sist) *n. Anat.* The gall bladder. [< NL *cholecystis* < Gk. *cholē* gall + *kystis* bladder]

cho·led·o·cho·plas·ty (kə·led′ə·kō·plas′tē) *n.* Plastic surgery on the bile duct. [< NL *choledochus* bile duct (< Gk. *cholē* bile + *dechesthai* contain) + -PLASTY] **—cho·led′o·cho·plas′tic** *adj.*

cho·le·mi·a (kə·lē′mē·ə) *n. Pathol.* The presence of bile in the blood; jaundice. Also **cho·lae′·mi·a.** [< CHOLE- + -EMIA]

chol·er (kol′ər) *n.* 1 Anger or hastiness of temper: formerly believed to be caused by disturbance of the liver or gall bladder. 2 *Obs.* Bile; also, biliousness. See synonyms under ANGER. [< OF *colère* < L *cholera* CHOLERA]

chol·er·a (kol′ər·ə) *n. Pathol.* An acute, infectious, chiefly epidemic disease, occurring in many forms and characterized principally by serious intestinal disorders: it is caused by a bacterium *(Vibrio comma)* and in its more malignant forms, as Asiatic cholera, is usually fatal. [< L < Gk., cholera morbus (in Hippocrates)]

cholera in·fan·tum (in·fan′təm) *Pathol.* A warm-weather, non-contagious, often fatal diarrhea of children, possibly caused by the bacterium *Vibrio proteus.* [< L, cholera of infants]

cholera mor·bus (môr′bəs) *Pathol.* Acute gastroenteritis, a warm-weather complaint. Also **cholera nos·tras** (nos′tras). [< L, cholera disease]

chol·er·ic (kol′ər·ik, kə·ler′ik) *adj.* 1 Of a bilious temperament; in a bilious condition. 2 Easily provoked; irascible. 3 Of the nature of anger. See synonyms under HOT.

cho·les·ter·ol (kə·les′tə·rōl) *n. Biochem.* A fatty monatomic crystalline alcohol. $C_{27}H_{45}OH$, derived principally from bile and present in most gallstones: it is found also in the blood, brain and nerve tissue, kidneys, liver, etc. Also **cho·les′ter·in.** [< CHOLE- + Gk. *stereos* solid + -OL[2]]

cho·lic acid (kō′lik, kol′ik) *Biochem.* A white, bitter crystalline acid; $C_{24}H_{40}O_5$, found in bile acids and in animal excrements.

cho·line (kō′lēn, kol′ēn, -in) *n.* An alkaline compound, $C_5H_{15}NO_2$, forming a part of the vitamin B complex and used in the biosynthesis of acetylcholine.

chol·la (chōl′yä) *n.* A variety of the prickly-pear cactus *(Cylindropuntia)* having spiny cylindrical stems: it is a frequent pest on stock ranges in the SW United States. [< Sp.]

chon·dri·fy (kon′drə·fī) *v.t.* & *v.i.* **·fied, ·fy·ing** To convert into or become cartilage. **—chon′·dri·fi·ca′tion** *n.*

chon·dri·o·some (kon′drē·ə·sōm) *n. Biol.* A small granular body found, alone or in clusters, in the cytoplasm of a cell and subject to rapid changes both in shape and position: also called *mitochondria.* See illustration under CELL. [< Gk. *chondrion,* dim. of *chondros* cartilage + *sōma* body]

chon·drite (kon′drīt) *n.* A stony meteorite containing chondrules. **—chon·drit·ic** (kon·drit′ik) *adj.*

chondro- *combining form* 1 Cartilage: chondrotomy. 2 Grain: *chondr*ule. Also, before vowels, **chondr-.** [< Gk. *chondros* cartilage]

chon·droid (kon′droid) *adj.* Resembling cartilage.

chon·dro·ma (kon·drō′mə) *n. pl.* **·mas** or **·ma·ta** (-mə·tə) *Pathol.* A cartilaginous tumor.

Chon·dros·te·i (kon·dros′tē·ī) *n. pl.* An order of fishes with cartilaginous skeletons, as the paddle fishes and sturgeons. [< NL < Gk. *chondros* cartilage + *osteon* bone] **—chon·dros′te·an** *adj.* & *n.*

chon·drot·o·my (kon·drot′ə·mē) *n. Surg.* The cutting of cartilages. [< CHONDRO- + -TOMY]

chon·drule (kon′drōōl) *n.* Any of the small, rounded beads of various mineral composition found embedded in chondrites.

Chong·jin (chông·jin) A port of North Korea. *Japanese* **Sei·shin** (sā·shēn).

Chong·ju (chông·jōō) A city of South Korea. *Japanese* **Sei·shu** (sā·shōō).

choose (chōōz) *v.* **chose, cho·sen, choos·ing** *v.t.* 1 To select as most desirable; take by preference; elect. 2 To desire or have a preference for. 3 To please or think proper (to do something): with infinitive as object. —*v.i.* 4 To make selection or decision. 5 To have an alternate. **—cannot choose but** Has no alternative choice. **—to pick and choose** To select with great deliberation. [OE *cēosan*] **—choos′er** *n.*

Synonyms: cull, elect, pick, prefer, select. *Prefer* indicates a state of desire and approval; *choose,* an act of will. Prudence or generosity may lead one to *choose* what he does not *prefer. Select* implies a careful consideration of the reasons for preference and choice. Among objects so nearly alike that we have no reason to *prefer* any one to another, we may simply *choose* the nearest, but we could not be said to *select* it. Aside from theology, *elect* is popularly confined to the political sense; as, a free people *elect* their own rulers. *Cull* means to collect, as well as to *select.* In a garden we *cull* the choicest flowers. To *pick* is to *choose* for special fitness; as, a guard of *picked* men; *chosen,* in this sense, is somewhat archaic. *Antonyms*: decline, disclaim, dismiss, leave, refuse, reject.

choos·y (chōō′ze) *adj.* **choos·i·er, choos·i·est** *Colloq.* Disposed to be particular or fussy in one's choices.

chop[1] (chop) *v.* **chopped, chop·ping** *v.t.* 1 To cut or make by strokes of a sharp tool; hew. 2 To cut up in small pieces; mince. 3 To utter jerkily; cut short. 4 To make a cutting, downward stroke at (the ball), as in tennis. —*v.i.* 5 To make cutting strokes, as with an ax. 6 To interrupt abruptly, as in conversation: with *in*: to *chop in* with a remark. 7 To go, come, or move with sudden or violent motion. —*n.* 1 A cut of meat, chopped off, usually containing a rib. 2 A cleft or fissure; a crack, especially in the lip. 3 The act of chopping. 4 A tool for chopping. 5 A sudden bite or snap. 6 A sudden motion of waves; also, a choppy sea. 7 In boxing, a short, sharp, downward punch. 8 In tennis or cricket, a sharp, cutting, downward stroke. [ME *choppen.* Related to CHAP, CHIP.]

chop[2] (chop) *v.t.* 1 *Obs.* To barter; exchange. —*v.i.* 2 To veer suddenly; shift, as the wind; vacillate. 3 *Obs.* To bargain; barter. [ME *choppen.* Related to CHEAP.]

chop[3] (chop) *n.* 1 A jaw. 2 *pl.* The jaws and the parts about the mouth. 3 *pl.* The entrance or mouth of a harbor, channel, valley, etc.; especially, the entrance of the English Channel from the Atlantic. —*v.t.* 1 To seize with the jaws; snap. 2 To utter quickly and sharply. Also spelled *chap.* [Var. of CHAP[3]]

chop[4] (chop) *n.* 1 An official stamp or seal in India, China, etc.; hence, a clearance, passport, or permit. 2 *Anglo-Indian* Brand or quality. **—first chop** *Slang* Superior brand or quality. [< Hind. *chhāp* stamp]

chop chop! (chop′ chop′) In Pidgin English, quickly! in a hurry!

chop-fal·len (chop′fô′lən) See CHAP-FALLEN

chop house An eating house specializing in serving chops and steaks.

chop·house (chop′hous′) *n.* A Chinese custom house.

Cho·pin (shō′pan, *Fr.* shō·paṅ′), **Frédéric François,** 1810–49, Polish composer and pianist, active in France.

cho·pine (chō·pēn′, chop′in) *n.* A high clog worn under a shoe. Also **chop·in** (chop′·in). [< Sp. *chapin* < *chapa* metal plate]

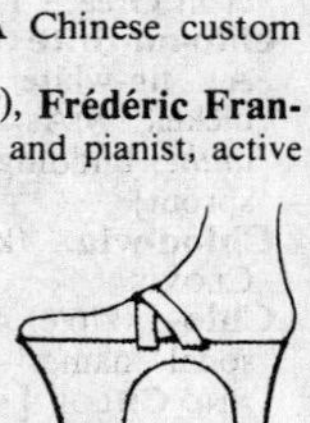
CHOPINE
Sixteenth century

chop·log·ic (chop′loj′ik) *n.* 1 Hair-splitting argument. 2 *Obs.* A contentious, argumentative person.

chop·per (chop′ər) *n.* 1 One who or that which chops. 2 *Telecom.* A device, usually one that rotates, used to interrupt a continuous-wave radio signal in a transmitter or receiver. 3 *pl. Slang* Teeth. 4 *Slang* A helicopter.

chop·ping (chop′ing) *adj.* 1 Shifting suddenly, as a wind. 2 Full of short, broken waves.

chop·py[1] (chop′ē) *adj.* **·pi·er, ·pi·est** Full of cracks, chops, or fissures.

chop·py[2] (chop′ē) *adj.* 1 Full of short, rough waves. 2 Variable; shifting, as wind.

chop shop A place where stolen cars are disassembled so that their parts can be sold.

chop·sticks (chop′stiks′) *n. pl.* Slender rods of ivory or wood, used in pairs, in China, Japan, etc., to convey food to the mouth. [< Pidgin English *chop* quick + STICK; trans. of Chinese name]

chop-su·ey (chop′sōō′ē) *n.* A Chinese-American dish consisting of fried or stewed meat or

chicken, bean sprouts, onions, celery, mushrooms, etc., cooked in their own juices and served with rice. [<Chinese *tsa-sui*, lit., mixed pieces]

cho·ra·gus (kō·rā′gəs) *n. pl.* **·gi** (-jī) **1** In ancient Greece, the leader of a chorus, as at the performance of a play. **2** Any leader of a chorus or band. Also **cho·re·gus** (kō·rē′gəs). [<L <Gk. *chorēgos* <*choros* chorus + *agein* lead] —**cho·rag·ic** (kō·raj′ik) *adj.*

cho·ral[1] (kə·ral′) *n.* A hymn characterized by a simple melody and firm rhythm, and often sung in unison. Also **cho·rale**′. [<G *choral*]

cho·ral[2] (kôr′əl, kō′rəl) *adj.* **1** Pertaining to a chorus or choir. **2** Written for or sung by a chorus. [<Med. L *choralis* <L *chorus* CHORUS] —**cho′ral·ly** *adv.*

Cho·ras·mi·a (kə·raz′mē·ə) A province of ancient Persia, extending from the Oxus to the Caspian Sea.

chord[1] (kôrd) *n. Music* A combination of three or more tones sounded together according to the laws of harmony. The most important chords are the **common chord**, consisting of a fundamental tone with its major or minor third and its perfect fifth, and the **chord of the seventh**, called the dominant seventh. —*v.i.* To be in harmony or accord. ◆ Homophone: *cord*. [Earlier *cord*, short for ACCORD; form infl. by CHORD[2]]

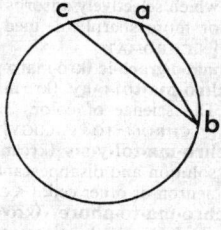

CHORD
cb and *ab* are chords.

chord[2] (kôrd) *n.* **1** A string or cord of a musical instrument; hence, emotional response or reaction. **2** *Geom.* A straight line connecting the extremities of an arc; a secant; the portion of a straight line contained by its intersections with a curve. **3** *Eng.* One of the principal members of a bridge truss, horizontal or inclined. **4** *Anat.* A tendon, a connective ligament. **5** *Aeron.* The length of an airplane. ◆ Homophone: *cord*. [<L *chorda* <Gk. *chordē* string of a musical instrument. Doublet of CORD.] —**chord′al** *adj.*

Chor·da·ta (kôr·dā′tə) *n. pl.* A phylum of the animal kingdom which includes the vertebrates and whose members are characterized by an internal skeleton (which in primitive forms is a slender, axial rod, the *notochord*), a dorsally located central nervous system, and gill slits, present in the embryos of terrestrial forms. [<NL <*chorda* CHORD[2]] —**chor·date** (kôr′dāt) *adj. & n.*

chore (chôr, chōr) *n.* **1** A small job. **2** *pl.* The routine duties of a household or farm. **3** An unpleasant or hard task. [Var. of CHAR[1]]

-chore *combining form Bot.* Denoting a plant that is distributed in a specified manner: *anemochore*. [<Gk. *chōrein* spread]

cho·re·a (kô·rē′ə, kō-) *n. Pathol.* A nervous disease characterized by involuntary muscular twitching; St. Vitus's dance. [<NL <Gk. *choreia* dance] —**cho·re′al** *adj.*

cho·re·o·graph (kôr′ē·ə·graf, kō′rē-) *v.t.* To provide the choreography for.

cho·re·og·ra·phy (kôr′ē·og′rə·fē, kō′rē-) *n.* **1** The art of devising ballets and incidental dances. **2** The written representation of figures and steps of dancing. **3** The art of dancing; ballet. Also **cho·reg·ra·phy** (kə·reg′rə·fē). [<Gk. *choreia* dance + -GRAPHY] —**cho′re·og′ra·pher** *n.* —**cho·re·o·graph′ic** *adj.*

cho·re·ol·o·gy (kôr′ē·ol′ə·jē, kō′rē-) *n.* The systematic study and analysis of choreographic notation or dance-scores.

cho·re·o·ma·ni·a (kôr′ē·ə·mā′nē·ə, -mān′yə, kō′rē-) *n.* A morbid craving to dance, often communal and epidemic and characterized by hysterical religious exaltation; dancing mania. [<Gk. *choreia* dance + -MANIA] —**cho′re·o·man′ic** *adj.*

cho·ri·amb (kôr′ē·amb, kō′rē-) *n.* In prosody, a metrical foot of four syllables, the second and third short and the others long (–‿‿–). Also **cho·ri·am·bus** (kôr′ē·am′bəs, kō′rē-) [<L *choriambus* <Gk. *choriambos* <*choreios*

trochee + *iambos* iambus] —**cho′ri·am′bic** *adj. & n.*

cho·ric (kôr′ik, kō′rik) *adj.* Relating to or like a chorus.

cho·rine (kôr′ēn, kō′rēn) *n. Colloq.* A chorus girl.

cho·ri·on (kôr′ē·on, kō′rē-) *n.* **1** *Anat.* The external protective and nutritive membrane that invests the fetus of the higher vertebrates and attaches it to the uterus. **2** *Entomol.* The outer case of an insect egg. [<Gk. *chorion*]

cho·ri·pet·al·ous (kôr′ē·pet′əl·əs, kō′rē-) *adj. Bot.* Having free, unconnected petals; polypetalous. [<Gk. *chōris* apart + *petalon* leaf]

cho·rist (kôr′ist, kō′rist) *n.* A member of a chorus. —**cho·ris·tic** (kə·ris′tik) *adj.*

chor·is·ter (kôr′is·tər, kor′-) *n.* **1** A member of a choir; specifically, a male singer in a church choir. **2** A leader of a choir or of congregational singing; a precentor. **3** Any singer, as a bird.

cho·rog·ra·phy (kô·rog′rə·fē, kō-) *n. pl.* **·phies** **1** The delineation or mapping of regions. **2** A map or chart of any particular region. [<Gk. *chōros* region + -GRAPHY] —**cho·rog′ra·pher** *n.* —**cho·ro·graph·ic** (kôr′ə·graf′ik, kō′rə) or **·i·cal** *adj.* —**cho′ro·graph′i·cal·ly** *adv.*

cho·roid (kôr′oid, kō′roid) *adj. Anat.* Resembling the chorion: said of highly vascular membranes. —*n.* The choroid coat, the middle or vascular tunic of the eyeball. See illustration under EYE. Also **cho·ri·oid** (kôr′ē·oid, kō′rē-).

cho·rol·o·gy (kô·rol′ə·jē, kō-) *n. Ecol.* The study of the migrations of plants and animals, especially in relation to areas of distribution. [<Gk. *chōros* region + -LOGY]

cho·ro·script (kôr′ə·skript, kō′rə-) *n.* A system of choreographic notation devised for the correct teaching and permanent recording of the steps and figures of a dance: also called *dance script*. [<Gk. *choros* dance + SCRIPT]

chor·tle (chôr′təl) *v.i.* **·tled** **·tling** To chuckle or make a loud noise expressive of joy. —*n.* A chuckle; joyful vocal sound. [Blend of CHUCKLE and SNORT; coined by Lewis Carroll in *Through the Looking-Glass*]

cho·rus (kôr′əs, kō′rəs) *n.* **1** A musical composition, usually in parts, for performance by a large group of singers. **2** A body of singers, or singers and dancers, who perform together in concerts, opera, ballet, musical comedy, etc. **3** Any group of individuals singing or speaking something together simultaneously; also, that which is thus uttered. **4** The part of a work written for or performed by a chorus; the burden or refrain of a song, which others join a soloist in singing. **5** In ancient Greece, a ceremonial dance, accompanied by the singing of odes, and performed in honor of Dionysus. **6** In Greek drama, a body of actors who through song, dance, and dialog commented upon and sometimes took part in the main action of a play; also, the parts of a play so performed. **7** In later drama, especially the Elizabethan, a single actor who recites the prolog and epilog and comments upon the plot. —*v.t. & v.i.* **cho·rused** or **·russed**, **cho·rus·ing** or **·rus·sing** To sing or speak in concert. [<L <Gk. *choros* dance. Doublet of CHOIR.]

chorus girl A woman performing in the chorus of a musical comedy, cabaret, etc.

Cho·rzów (khô′zhoof) A city in southern Poland: formerly *Królewska Huta*.

chose[1] (chōz) Past tense of CHOOSE.

chose[2] (shōz) *n. Law* Anything that is personal property. [<F, thing <L *causa* matter, cause]

chose ju·gée (shōz zhü·zhā′) *French* An adjudicated case; hence, any matter which has been decided.

cho·sen (chō′zən) Past participle of CHOOSE.—*adj.* **1** Made an object of choice; selected. **2** Worthy of special preference; select; choice. **3** *Theol.* Elect.

Cho·sen (chō′sen) The Japanese name for KOREA.

chosen people The Israelites. *Deut.* xiv 2.

Cho·ta Nag·pur (chō′tə näg′pŏŏr) A plateau region mainly in Madhya Pradesh and Bihar states, India.

chou (shōō) *n. pl.* **choux** (shōō) *French* A cabbage.

Chou (jō) An early Chinese imperial dynasty (1122?–249 B.C.)

Chou En-lai (jō′ en′lī′), 1898–1976, Chinese premier and foreign minister of the People's Republic of China 1949–76.

chough (chuf) *n.* A bird of the crow family, especially the red-legged or Cornish chough (*Pyrrhocorax pyrrhocorax*) with black plumage and red beak and feet. ◆ Homophone: *chuff*. [ME *choghe*.]

chouse (chous) *v.t.* **choused, chous·ing** *Colloq.* To cheat; swindle. [<*n.*] —*n.* **1** *Obs.* A sharper; swindler. **2** *Obs.* A dupe. [<Turkish *chaush* messenger; ? with ref. to a dishonest 17th c. Turkish agent in London]

choush (choush) See CHIAUS.

chow[1] (chou) *n.* **1** A medium-sized, heavy-coated, muscular dog native to China, having a thick coat of brown or black, a massive head, and characteristically blue-black tongue: also *chow-chow*. **2** *Slang* Food. [Short for CHOW-CHOW]

CHOW
(20 inches high at its shoulder)

chow[2] (chou) *n.* A Chinese subordinate district or its chief city: used frequently in combination in place names: *Foochow*.

chow[3] (chou) *n. Scot.* The jowl.

chow-chow (chou′chou′) *n.* **1** A relish consisting of a mixture of chopped-up vegetables pickled in mustard. **2** A chow dog. —*adj.* Miscellaneous; mingled. [<Pidgin English]

chow·der (chou′dər) *n.* **1** A dish, usually of clams or fish stewed with vegetables, often in milk. **2** A picnic, usually on the seashore, where chowder is served. [<F *chaudière* kettle <L *caldaria*. See CALDRON.]

chow-mein (chou′mān′) *n.* A Chinese–American dish consisting of a stew of shredded chicken or meat, onions, mushrooms, celery, bean sprouts, etc., served with fried noodles. [<Chinese *ch'ao* fry + *mien* flour]

chow·ry (chou′rē) *n. pl.* **·ries** *Anglo–Indian* A fly flapper originally made from the bushy tail of a yak: formerly a symbol of royalty in eastern Asia. [<Hind. *chaunrī*]

chre·ma·tis·tic (krē′mə·tis′tik) *adj.* Of or pertaining to the accumulation of wealth; money -making. [<Gk. *chrēmatistikos* <*chrēmatizein* deal with, transact <*chrēma* money]

chre·ma·tis·tics (krē′mə·tis′tiks) *n.* The branch of economics that treats of the accumulation of wealth; also, political economy as a whole.

chres·ard (kres′ərd) *n. Ecol.* The available water of the soil: opposed to *echard*. [<Gk. *chrēsthai* use + *ardeia* irrigation]

Chres·tien de Troyes (krā·tyan′ də trwä′), 1140?–91, French poet; the first author to relate original versions of the Arthurian legends. Also **Chré·tien′ de Troyes′**.

chres·tom·a·thy (kres·tom′ə·thē) *n. pl.* **·thies** A collection of choice extracts; especially, one compiled for instruction in a language. [<Gk. *chrēstos* useful + *manthanein* learn]

Chré·tien (krā·tyan′) French form of CHRISTIAN, personal name. Also **Chres·tien** (krā·tyan′).

Chris (kris) Diminutive of CHRISTIAN or of CHRISTOPHER.

chrism (kriz′əm) *n.* **1** An unguent of oil and balm used for anointing at baptism, confirmation, unction, etc., in the Greek Orthodox and Roman Catholic Churches. **2** Loosely, any unguent. Also spelled *chrisom*. [OE *crisma* < LL *chrisma* <Gk. <*chriein* anoint. Doublet of CREAM.] —**chris·mal** (kriz′məl) *adj.*

chris·ma·to·ry (kriz′mə·tôr′ē, -tō′rē) *n. pl.* **·ries** A vessel or container for chrism. [<Med. L *chrismatorium* <*chrisma* chrism]

chris·om (kriz′əm) *n.* **1** A baptismal or christening robe. **2** Chrism. [Var. of CHRISM]

chrisom child 1 An innocent baby; a newborn child. **2** A child who dies within a month after baptism: formerly buried in its baptismal robe.

Chris·sie (kris′ē) Diminutive of CHRISTIANA.

Christ (krīst) *n.* **1** The Anointed; the Messiah: the deliverer of Israel whose coming was foretold by the Hebrew prophets. **2** Specifically, a title of Jesus of Nazareth, regarded as fulfilling this prophecy: at first used as a title *(Jesus the Christ)* but later a proper name *(Jesus Christ).* **3** In Christian Science, the divine manifestation of God, which comes to the flesh to destroy incarnate error. [OE *Crist* < L *Christus* < Gk. *Christos* (< *chriein* anoint); trans. of Hebrew *māshīach* anointed] **—Christ′li·ness** *n.* **—Christ′ly** *adj.*

Chris·ta·bel (kris′tə·bel) A feminine personal name. [< *Christ* + L *bella* beautiful]

Christ·church (krīst′chûrch) A city on the eastern coast of South Island, New ealand.

christ-cross (kris′krôs′, -kros′) *n.* **1** The mark of the cross (+), formerly placed before the alphabet in hornbooks, before and after treatises, inscriptions, etc. **2** *Brit. Dial.* A mark or cross made by a person who cannot sign his name. **3** *Obs.* The alphabet; christ-cross-row. See CRISS-CROSS. [< *Christ's cross*]

christ-cross-row (kris′krôs′rō′, -kros′-) *n. Obs.* The alphabet: so called because once printed with a cross at the beginning. Also **criss′-cross′-row′.**

chris·ten (kris′ən) *v.t.* **1** To name in baptism: He was *christened* John. **2** To administer the rite of Christian baptism to. **3** To give a name to in baptism, or in some ceremony considered as analogous; dedicate; hence, in general, to name: The ship was *christened.* **4** To use for the first time. [OE *cristnian* < *cristen* CHRISTIAN]

Chris·ten·dom (kris′ən·dəm) *n.* **1** Christian lands, or Christians collectively; the Christian world. **2** *Obs.* Christianity.

chris·ten·ing (kris′ən·ing) *n.* **1** Any Christian baptismal ceremony. **2** Specifically, the baptizing and naming of an infant.

Christ·hood (krīst′ho͝od) *n.* The condition of being the Christ; the Messiahship.

Chris·tian (kris′chən) *adj.* **1** Professing or following the religion of Christ. **2** Relating to or derived from Christ or his doctrine. **3** Manifesting the spirit of Christ or of his teachings. **4** Characteristic of Christianity or Christendom. **5** *Colloq.* Human; civilized; decent. —*n.* **1** One who believes in or professes belief in Jesus as the Christ; a member of the Christian church. **2** A disciple of Jesus of Nazareth; one whose profession and life conform to the example and teaching of Jesus. **3** *Colloq.* Any human being as distinguished from a brute: That dog knows as much as a *Christian.* **4** *Colloq.* A civilized, decent, or respectable person. **5** *U.S.* A Campbellite; a member of the Disciples of Christ. [OE *cristen* < LL *christianus* < *Christus* CHRIST] **—Chris′tian·ly** *adv.*

Chris·tian (kris′chən; *Dan., Ger.* kris′tē·än) A masculine personal name. [< L]
—Christian The central character in Bunyan's *Pilgrim's Progress.*
—Christian X, 1870–1947, king of Denmark 1912–47.

Chris·ti·an·a (kris′tē·an′ə) A feminine personal name. Also *Ger.* **Chris·ti·a·ne** (kris′tē·ä′nə). [< L]

Christian Brothers A Roman Catholic lay order devoted to education; also called *Brothers of the Christian Schools.*

Christian era The period beginning January 1, 754 A.U.C., or nine months and seven days after March 25, 753 A.U.C., calculated by Dionysius Exiguus in A.D. 527 as the date of Christ's incarnation, now placed four to six years earlier.

Chris·ti·a·ni·a (kris′tē·ä′nē·ə) *n.* In skiing, a turn effected by shifting the weight to one advanced ski and turning its tip outward: also called *Christy.*

Chris·tia·ni·a (kris·tyä′nē·ä) A former name for OSLO.

Chris·tian·ism (kris′chən·iz′əm) *n.* Christianity.

Chris·ti·an·i·ty (kris′chē·an′ə·tē) *n.* **1** The Christian religion. **2** Christians collectively. **3** The state of being a Christian.

Chris·tian·ize (kris′chən·īz) *v.* **·ized, ·iz·ing** *v.t.* **1** To convert to Christianity. **2** To imbue with Christian ideas, principles, and faith. —*v.i.* **3** *Rare* To adopt Christianity; become Christian. **—Chris′tian·i·za′tion** *n.* **—Chris′tian·iz′er** *n.*

Christian name A baptismal name; first or given name: distinguished from *family name* or *surname.*

Christians See DISCIPLES OF CHRIST.

Christian Science A religious system embodying metaphysical healing, founded in 1866 by Mary Baker Eddy and based on her exposition of the Scriptures: officially called the **Church of Christ, Scientist.**

Chris·tians·haab (krēs′tyäns·hôp) A settlement on the west coast of Greenland; founded 1743.

Chris·tian·sted (kris′chən·sted) The capital of St. Croix in the Virgin Islands; former capital of the Danish West Indies.

Chris·ti·na (kris·tē′nə, *Pg.* krēs·tē′nə) A feminine personal name. Also **Chris·tine** (kris·tēn′; *Fr.* krēs·tēn′; *Ger.* kris·tē′nə). [Var. of CHRISTIANA]
—Christina, 1626–89, queen of Sweden, 1632–54.

Christ·less (krīst′lis) *adj.* **1** Without Christ or his spirit. **2** Without faith in Christ; unchristian. **—Christ′less·ness** *n.*

Christ·like (krīst′līk′) *adj.* **1** Resembling Christ or like that of Christ. **2** Having the spirit of Christ. **—Christ′like′ness** *n.*

Christ·mas (kris′məs) *n.* **1** The 25th of December, held as the anniversary of the birth of Jesus Christ: widely observed as a holy day or a holiday. Also **Christmas Day. 2** A church festival observed annually at this date in memory of the birth of Jesus Christ; the Feast of the Nativity; especially, the anniversary day, the 25th of December. The season of Christmas extends from Christmas Eve (Dec. 24) to Epiphany (Jan. 6), and is known as **Christmastide.** [< CHRIST + MASS[2]]

Christmas box 1 A box of Christmas gifts sent to an absent person. **2** *Brit.* A gratuity given at Christmas.

Christmas Eve The evening of December 24, before Christmas Day.

Christmas Island 1 An island SW of Java, comprising part of the British crown colony of Singapore; 60 square miles. **2** The largest atoll in the Line Islands district of the Gilbert and Ellice Islands Colony; 220 square miles.

Christmas rose The white-flowering hellebore: so called because its single roselike flowers bloom from December to February.

Christmas tree An evergreen tree decorated with ornaments and lights at Christmas.

Chris·tol·o·gy (kris·tol′ə·jē) *n.* The branch of theology that treats of the person and attributes of Christ. **2** Loosely, any theory or doctrine concerning Christ. [< CHRIST + -LOGY] **—Chris·to·log·i·cal** (kris′tə·loj′i·kəl) *adj.*

Chris·tophe (krēs·tôf′), **Henri,** 1767–1820, Negro king of Haiti 1811–20.

Chris·to·pher (kris′tə·fər) A masculine personal name. Also *Lat.* **Chris·toph·o·rus** (kris·tof′ə·rəs), *Fr.* **Chris·tophe** (krēs·tôf′), *Pg.* **Chris·to·vão** (krēs′tō·vouṅ′), *Ger.* **Chris·to·pho·rus** (kris′tō·fôr′əs) or **Chris·toph** (kris′tôf). [< Gk., bearer of Christ]
—Christopher, Saint A Christian martyr of the third century.

Christ's-thorn (krīsts′thôrn′) *n.* **1** A Palestinian shrub of the buckthorn family *(Paliurus spina-cristi),* with long sharp thorns: so called from a belief that Christ's crown of thorns was made of it: also called *Jew's-thorn.* **2** The jujube.

Chris·ty (kris′tē) Dim. of CHRISTIAN, personal name.

Chris·ty (kris′tē) See CHRISTIANIA (ski turn).

Chris·ty (kris′tē), **Howard Chandler,** 1873–1952, U.S. illustrator and painter.

chrom- Var. of CHROMO-.

chro·ma (krō′mə) *n.* Color intensity; the degree of hue and saturation in a color other than white, black, or gray. [< Gk. *chrōma* color]

chro·maf·fin (krō·maf′in) *adj. Biol.* Having the property of staining when treated with dichromate.

chro·mate (krō′māt) *n. Chem.* A salt of chromic acid.

chro·mat·ic (krō·mat′ik) *adj.* **1** Pertaining to color or colors. **2** *Music* Using or proceeding by semitones. Also **chro·mat′i·cal.**

chromatic aberration See under ABERRATION.

chro·ma·tic·i·ty (krō′mə·tis′ə·tē) *n. Physics* That quality of a color which is defined by its dominant or complementary wavelength taken together with its purity.

chro·mat·ics (krō·mat′iks) *n.* The science of colors.

chromatic scale *Music* The diatonic scale proceeding by semitones.

chro·ma·tid (krō′mə·tid) *n. Biol.* One of the four members of a tetrad formed by the longitudinal splitting of a chromosome during meiosis.

chro·ma·tin (krō′mə·tin) *n. Biol.* The deeply staining filamentous material in the protoplasm of the cell nucleus: during mitosis chromatin develops into chromosomes: also called *chromoplasm.* See illustration under CELL. [< Gk. *chrōma, -atos* color]

chro·ma·tism (krō′mə·tiz′əm) *n.* **1** *Optics* Chromatic aberration. **2** *Bot.* The assumption by normally green plant organs, as leaves, of a color approximating that of the petals. Also **chro·mism** (krō′miz·əm).

chromato- *combining form* Color; coloring or pigmentation: *chromatoscope.* Also, before vowels, **chromat-.** [< Gk. *chrōma, -atos* color]

chro·mat·o·gram (krō·mat′ə·gram) *n. Chem.* The complete array of distinctively colored bands produced by chromatography.

chro·ma·tog·ra·phy (krō′mə·tog′rə·fē) *n. Chem.* A method for the separation and analysis of small quantities of substances by passing a solution through a column of finely divided powder which selectively adsorbs the constituents in one or more sharply defined, often colored bands. [< CHROMATO- + -GRAPHY] **—chro·mat·o·graph·ic** (krō·mat′ə·graf′ik) *adj.*

chro·ma·tol·o·gy (krō′mə·tol′ə·jē) *n. pl.* **·gies 1** The science of color. **2** A treatise on colors. [< CHROMATO- + -LOGY]

chro·ma·tol·y·sis (krō′mə·tol′ə·sis) *n. Biol.* The solution and disappearance of chromatin from a neuron or other cell. [< CHROMATO- + -LYSIS]

chro·ma·to·phore (krō′mə·tə·fôr′, -fōr′) *n.* **1** *Zool.* One of the pigment-bearing sacs with contractile walls by which changes of color are effected in various animals, as in chameleons; a pigment cell. **2** *Bot.* A pigment-bearing plastid found in diatoms and other plants. **—chro·ma·to·phor·ic** (krō′mə·tə·fôr′ik, -for′-), **chro·ma·toph·o·rous** (krō′mə·tof′ə·rəs) *adj.*

chrome (krōm) *n.* **1** Chrome yellow. **2** Chromium. —*v.t.* **chromed, chrom·ing** To subject to the action of a solution of potassium dichromate. [< F < Gk. *chrōma* color]

-chrome *combining form* **1** Color; colored: *polychrome.* **2** *Chem.* Chromium: *ferrochrome.* [Gk. *chrōma* color]

chrome alum *Chem.* Any double sulfate of chromium with potassium, sodium, or ammonium: *chrome alum ammonium,* $Cr(NH_4)(SO_4)_2 \cdot 12H_2O$, a dark, violet-red compound used as a mordant in dyeing.

chrome green 1 A green pigment derived from chromic oxide, Cr_2O_3. **2** The color of this, a dull, dark green.

chrome red A pigment made from basic lead chromate.

chrome steel *Metall.* A very hard steel alloyed with chromium: when the chrome is 12 percent or more, the resulting alloy is known as *stainless steel.* Also **chromium steel.**

chrome yellow 1 *Chem.* A yellow pigment consisting of natural lead chromate, $PbCrO_4$. **2** Any of several shades of yellow ranging from lemon to deep orange.

chro·mic (krō′mik) *adj.* **1** *Chem.* Of, from, or pertaining to chromium. **2** Pertaining to compounds in which chromium is present in its higher valency.

chromic acid *Chem.* A hypothetical acid, H_2CrO_4, known only in solution and forming chromates.

chromic oxide *Chem.* A green compound, Cr_2O_3; chromium sesquioxide: used as a pigment.

chro·mi·nance (krō′mə·nəns) *n. Physics* The colorimetric difference between a given color and a reference color of equal brightness and specified chromaticity.

chro·mite (krō′mīt) *n.* Chromic iron ore, $FeCr_2O_4$, a valuable source of chromium.

chro·mi·um (krō′mē·əm) *n.* A grayish-white, very hard metallic element (symbol Cr): used in making alloys, pigments, as a mordant, etc. See ELEMENT. [< Gk. *chrōma* color; so called from its many brightly colored, poisonous compounds]

chromium trioxide *Chem.* A red crystalline

substance, CrO_3; chromic anhydride: a powerful oxidizing agent.

chro·mo (krō′mō) *n. pl.* **·mos** A picture printed in colors; a chromolithograph. [Short for CHROMOLITHOGRAPH]

chromo– *combining form* **1** Color; in or with color: *chromophotography.* **2** *Chem.* Chromium: *chromotype.* Also, before vowels, **chrom–**. [< Gk. *chrōma* color]

chro·mo·gen (krō′mə·jen) *n.* **1** *Chem.* **a** Any organic coloring matter or substance capable of yielding a dye. **b** Any dye derived from naphthalene which develops a brown color on wool by oxidation. **2** *Biol.* Any substance in an animal or plant which under certain conditions becomes colored or deepens its hue. — **chro′mo·gen′ic** *adj.*

chro·mo·gen·e·sis (krō′mō·jen′ə·sis) *n.* The origin or development of color.

chro·mo·lith·o·graph (krō′mō·lith′ə·graf, -gräf) *n.* A print in colors obtained by chromolithography. — **chro·mo·li·thog·ra·pher** (krō′mō·li·thog′rə·fər) *n.* — **chro′mo·lith′o·graph′ic** *adj.*

chro·mo·li·thog·ra·phy (krō′mō·li·thog′rə·fē) *n.* The process of reproducing a colored original from a set of stones by lithography.

chro·mo·mere (krō′mə·mir) *n. Biol.* One of the granules of chromatin forming the chromosome.

chro·mo·phore (krō′mə·fôr, -fōr) *n. Chem.* A group of atoms so arranged as to produce the colors of dyestuffs when combined under proper conditions with hydrocarbon radicals. — **chro·mo·phor·ic** (krō′mə·fôr′ik, -for′-), **chro·moph·o·rous** (krō·mof′ə·rəs) *adj.*

chro·mo·pho·to·graph (krō′mō·fō′tə·graf, -gräf) *n.* A photograph in colors.

chro·mo·pho·tog·ra·phy (krō′mō·fə·tog′rə·fē) *n.* Photography in colors.

chro·mo·plasm (krō′mə·plaz′əm) *n.* Chromatin.

chro·mo·plast (krō′mə·plast) *n. Bot.* A colored protoplasmic granule of a color other than green.

chro·mo·some (krō′mə·sōm) *n. Biol.* One of the deeply staining, rod– or loop–shaped bodies into which the chromatin of the cell nucleus divides during mitosis, generally of a fixed number for any given species: regarded as a carrier of the genes or units of heredity. See HAPLOID, POLYPLOID. — **accessory chromosome** A chromosome of which the shape, size, and purpose differ from those of other chromosomes of the same cell. [< CHROMO– + –SOME²]

chro·mo·sphere (krō′mə·sfir′) *n. Astron.* An envelope of incandescent red gas surrounding the sun beyond the photosphere: it is composed chiefly of hydrogen and helium. — **chro·mo·spher·ic** (krō′mə·sfer′ik) *adj.*

chro·mo·type (krō′mə·tīp′) *n.* **1** A photographic process in which some salt of chromium is the sensitive agent. **2** A chromolithograph. **3** A photograph in colors. Also **chro′ma·type′.**

chro·mous (krō′məs) *adj. Chem.* Of or pertaining to chromium in its lower valence.

chro·nax·y (krō′nak·sē) *n. Physiol.* The time that a current of twice the rheobase requires to excite a muscle, nerve fiber, etc. Also **chro′nax·ie, chro·nax·i·a** (krō·nak′sē·ə). [< CHRON(O)– + Gk. *axia* value]

chron·ic (kron′ik) *adj.* **1** Continuing for a long period. **2** Inveterate; habitual: a *chronic* complainer. **3** Prolonged; lingering: said of a disease: opposed to *acute.* Also **chron′i·cal.** [< F *chronique* < L *chronicus* < Gk. *chronikos* of time < *chronos* time] — **chron′i·cal·ly** *adv.*

chron·i·cle (kron′i·kəl) *n.* A register of events in the order of time; a historical record chronologically arranged. See synonyms under HISTORY, RECORDS. — *v.t.* **·cled, ·cling** To record. [< AF *cronicle* < L *chronica,* neut. pl. of *chronicus.* See CHRONIC.] — **chron′i·cler** *n.*

Chron·i·cles (kron′i·kəlz) The two books of the Old Testament following *Kings.*

chrono– *combining form* Time: *chronograph.* Also, before vowels, **chron–**. [< Gk. *chronos* time]

chron·o·gram (kron′ə·gram) *n.* **1** A record of a chronograph. **2** A writing or an inscription recording a date in numeral letters.

chron·o·graph (kron′ə·graf, -gräf) *n.* An instrument for recording graphically the moment or duration of an event, measuring intervals of time, etc.

chron·o·log·i·cal (kron′ə·loj′i·kəl) *adj.* **1** Occurring or recorded in temporal sequence, as a series of events. **2** Pertaining to or occupied with the science of time. Also **chron′o·log′ic.** — **chron′o·log′i·cal·ly** *adv.*

chro·nol·o·gy (krə·nol′ə·jē) *n. pl.* **·gies 1** The science that treats of the measurement of time, or the order of events. **2** Any particular chronological system. **3** Any tabulated arrangement of events of historical or scientific import, in the order of the time of their occurrence. [< CHRONO– + –LOGY] — **chro·nol′o·ger, chro·nol′o·gist** *n.*

chro·nom·e·ter (krə·nom′ə·tər) *n.* A portable timekeeping instrument of high precision and accuracy for use in navigation and scientific work. [< CHRONO– + –METER] — **chron·o·met·ric** (kron′ə·met′rik) or **·ri·cal** *adj.* — **chron′o·met′ri·cal·ly** *adv.*

chro·nom·e·try (krə·nom′ə·trē) *n.* **1** The measurement of time. **2** The science or method of measuring time.

chron·o·scope (kron′ə·skōp) *n.* A chronograph or the like for measuring a minute interval of time. — **chron·o·scop·ic** (kron′ə·skop′ik) *adj.*

–chrous *combining form* Having (a certain) color: *isochrous.* [< Gk. *chrōs, chroos* color]

chrys– Var. of CHRYSO–.

chrys·a·lid (kris′ə·lid) *n.* A chrysalis; especially, the intermediate or pupal stage in butterflies. — *adj.* Of, pertaining to, or like a chrysalis: also **chrys·al·i·dal** (kri·sal′ə·dal).

chrys·a·lis (kris′ə·lis) *n. pl.* **chrys·a·lis·es** or **chry·sal·i·des** (kri·sal′ə·dēz) *Entomol.* **1** The pupa of an insect, especially of a butterfly; the capsule–enclosed stage between caterpillar and butterfly during which the individual develops and from which the winged adult emerges. See illustration under PUPA. **2** Anything in an undeveloped or transitory stage. [< L < Gk. *chrysallis* golden sheath of a butterfly < *chrysos* gold]

chrys·an·i·line (kris·an′ə·lin, -līn) *n. Chem.* A coal–tar dyestuff, $C_{19}H_{15}N_3$, obtained from rosaniline, that gives a golden–yellow color.

chrys·an·the·mum (kri·san′thə·məm) *n.* **1** Any of a genus of perennials (*Chrysanthemum*) of the composite family, some cultivated varieties of which have large heads of showy flowers of various colors. **2** The flower. [< L < Gk. *chrysanthemon* marigold, lit., golden flower]

chrys·a·ro·bin (kris′ə·rō′bin) *n. Chem.* An orange–yellow compound, $C_{15}H_{12}O_3$, which forms the essential principle of Goa powder. Also **chrys·a·ro·bi·num** (kris′ə·rō′bi·nəm). [< CHRYS– + Tupian *araroba* bark]

Chry·se·is (krī·sē′is) In the *Iliad,* the daughter of a priest of Apollo, given as a slave to Agamemnon: she was returned after Apollo sent a plague upon the Greeks.

chrys·e·le·phan·tine (kris′el·ə·fan′tin) *adj.* Made or covered with gold and ivory, as certain ancient Greek statues. [< Gk. *chryselephantinos* of gold and ivory < *chrysos* gold + *elephas* ivory]

chrys·ene (kris′ēn′) *n. Chem.* A reddish–violet, fluorescent crystalline compound, $C_{18}H_{12}$, contained in coal tar and other substances.

chryso– *combining form* Gold; of a golden color: *chrysolite.* Also, before vowels, **chrys–**. [< Gk. *chrysos* gold]

chrys·o·ber·yl (kris′ə·ber′əl) *n.* A vitreous, yellowish or greenish, transparent to translucent beryllium aluminate: used as a gem. [< L *chrysoberyllus* < Gk. *chrysoberyllos* < *chrysos* gold + *beryllos* beryl]

chrys·o·lite (kris′ə·līt) *n.* A vitreous, orthorhombic, olive–green, transparent to translucent magnesium iron silicate, $(Mg,Fe)_2SiO_4$: used as a gem: also called *olivine.* [< OF *crisolite* < Med. L *crisolitus* < L *chrysolithus* < Gk. *chrysolithos* < *chrysos* gold] — **chrys·o·lit·ic** (kris′ə·lit′ik) *adj.*

chrys·o·prase (kris′ə·prāz) *n.* A semiprecious, apple–green variety of chalcedony, colored by nickel oxide: used as a gem. [< OF *crisopace* < L *chrysoprasus* < Gk. *chrysoprasos* < *chrysos* gold + *prason* leek]

Chrys·os·tom (kris′əs·təm, kris·os′təm), **Saint**

John, 345?–407, Greek Church father; patriarch of Constantinople 398–404.

Chrys·o·tham·nus (kris′ə·tham′nəs) *n.* A genus of low, flowering shrubs related to the aster group of the *Compositae* and native in western North America. Certain species, especially *C. nauseosus,* yield a rubber latex. [< CHRYSO– + Gk. *thamnos* bush]

chrys·o·tile (kris′ə·til) *n.* A fibrous, silky variety of serpentine. [< CHRYSO– + Gk. *tilos* hair, fiber]

chtho·ni·an (thō′nē·ən) *adj.* **1** Of, pertaining to, or being in the nether world; underground; subterranean. **2** Specifically, pertaining to the Greek underworld gods as distinguished from those of Olympus. Also **chthon·ic** (thon′ik). [< Gk. *chthōn* the earth]

Chu (choō) A river in Kirghiz and Kazakh S.S.R., flowing 700 miles NW.

chub (chub) *n. pl.* **chubs** or **chub 1** A European carplike fish of the cyprinoid order (genus *Leuciscus*). **2** One of various other fishes, as the fallfish, tautog, etc. [ME *chubbe;* origin unknown]

chu·bas·co (choō·bäs′kō) *n. Meteorol.* A violent thunder squall along the west coast of Central America. [< Sp.]

chub·by (chub′ē) *adj.* **·bi·er, ·bi·est** Plump; rounded. [< CHUB] — **chub′bi·ness** *n.*

Chu·but (choō·voōt′) A national territory of southern Argentina; 65,669 square miles; capital, Rawson; drained by the **Chubut River,** flowing 500 miles SE to the Atlantic.

chuck¹ (chuk) *n.* **1** A chick; hen. **2** A short clucking sound; a cluck. **3** *Archaic* An endearing sound or word. — *v.i.* To cluck, as a fowl does, or as in calling fowls. [Imit.]

chuck² (chuk) *v.t.* **1** To pat or tap affectionately or playfully, as under the chin. **2** To throw or pitch: to *chuck* a baseball. **3** *Colloq.* To throw away; discard. **4** *Colloq.* To throw out forcibly; eject: with *out.* **5** *Brit. Slang* To quit: He *chucked* his job. — *n.* **1** A playful pat, throw, or toss. **2** *Brit.* A game of pitch–and–toss, played with coins or pebbles: also called **chuck′–far′thing.** [Cf. F *choquer* shake, jolt]

chuck³ (chuk) *n.* **1** *Mech.* A clamp, chock,

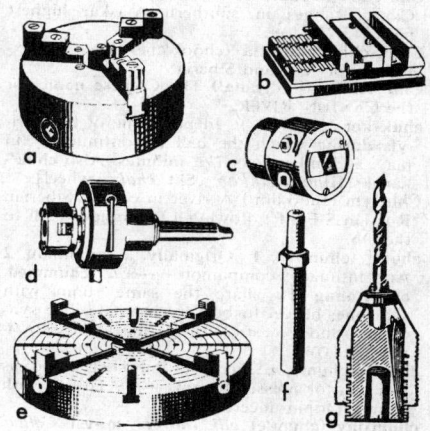

CHUCKS
a. Geared scroll chuck.
b. Planer chuck.
c. Drill chuck.
d. Tapping chuck.
e. Independent reversible–jaw lathe chuck.
f. Beach drill chuck.
g. Sectional view of drill chuck.

or wedge to hold a tool, as a drill. See illustration under BIT. **2** The part of a beef extending from the neck to the shoulder blade. **3** *Colloq.* **a** Food. **b** A meal. **c** Mealtime. — *v.t.* To place or fix in or by means of a chuck; do with a chuck. [Var. of CHOCK]

chuck–a–luck (chuk′ə·luk′) *n.* A gambling game employing three dice. Also **chuck′–luck′.**

chuck–full (chuk′foōl′) *adj.* Chock–full.

chuck·hole (chuk′hōl′) *n. U.S. Dial.* A mudhole in a road.

chuck·ie (chuk'ē) *n. Scot.* **1** A chuckiestone; jackstone. **2** The game of chuck. Also **chuck'y.**

chuck·ie·stone (chuk'ē·stōn') *n. Scot.* **1** A pebble suitable for use in the game of chuck. **2** *pl.* A game played with such stones. Also **chuck'stone'.**

chuck·le[1] (chuk'əl) *v.i.* **·led, ·ling 1** To laugh quietly, especially to oneself. **2** To cluck, as a hen. —*n.* A low, suppressed, or broken laugh. [Freq. of CHUCK[1]] —**chuck'ler** *n.*

chuck·le[2] (chuk'əl) *adj.* Thick or clumsy. [? < CHUCK[3] (def. 1)]

chuck·le·head (chuk'əl·hed') *n. Colloq.* A stupid fellow; blockhead. —**chuck'le·head'ed** *adj.*

chuck wagon *U.S.* A food wagon that carries provisions and cooking equipment around to cowboys, harvest hands, etc.

chuck·wal·la (chuk'wol'ə) *n.* A large, herbivorous lizard *(Sauromalus ater)* of the deserts of the SW United States. Also **chuck·a·wal·la** (chuk'ə·wol'ə). [<N. Am. Ind.]

chuck–will's–wid·ow (chuk'wilz'wid'ō) *n.* A large goatsucker *(Caprimulgus carolinensis)* of the southern United States: so called from its note.

chuck·y (chuk'ē) *n. Scot.* **1** A chicken; fowl. **2** A little chick.

chud·der (chud'ər) *n. Anglo–Indian* A large, square shawl of fine wool, made in India. Also **chud'dar.** [<Hind. *chadar* square piece of cloth]

Chud·sko·e (cho͞ot'skə·yə) The Russian name for PEIPUS.

chu·fa (cho͞o'fə) *n.* **1** A sedge *(Cyperus esculentus)* whose tuberous roots are eaten in southern Europe. **2** One of the tubers. [< Sp.]

chuff (chuf) *n. Brit. Dial.* **1** A rustic. **2** A boor. **3** A coarse, churlish fellow. **4** A miser. —*adj.* Gruff; crusty: also **chuf'fy.** ◆ Homophone: *chough.* [Origin unknown]

chuf·fy (chuf'ē) *adj.* Chubby; plump. Also **chuf'fie.** —**chuf'fi·ly** *adv.* —**chuf'fi·ness** *n.*

chug (chug) *n.* An explosive sound, as of the exhaust of an engine.—*v.i.* **chugged, chug·ging** To work or go with a series of small explosions: The old car *chugged* along. [Imit.]

Chu·gach Mountains (cho͞o'gak) A part of the Coast Ranges in southern Alaska; highest peak, 13,250 feet.

Chuk·chi Peninsula (cho͝ok'chē) The NE extremity of Asia and Siberia.

Chu–Kiang (jo͞o'jyäng') The Chinese name for the CANTON RIVER.

chuk·ker (chuk'ər) *n.* In polo, one of the periods during which the ball is continuously in play: a chukker lasts 7½ minutes. Also **chuk'·kar.** [<Hind. *chakkar* <Skt. *chakra* wheel]

Chu·lym (cho͞o·lim') A river in central Siberian Russian S.F.S.R., flowing 1,000 miles north to the Ob.

chum[1] (chum) *n.* **1** Originally, a roommate. **2** An intimate companion. —*v.i.* **chummed, chum·ming** To share the same room with someone; hence, to be very intimate. See synonyms under ASSOCIATE [? Short for CHAMBER FELLOW]

chum[2] (chum) *n.* Pieces of oily fish, used as fish bait, or pressed for oil. —*v.i.* To fish with chum. [Origin uncertain]

chum·my (chum'ē) *adj.* **·mi·er, ·mi·est** *Colloq.* Friendly; intimate. —**chum'mi·ly** *adv.*

chump[1] (chump) *n.* **1** A chunk of wood. **2** The thick end, as of a loin of mutton. **3** The head: a humorous use. **4** *Colloq.* A stupid or unskilful person. —**off his chump** *Brit. Slang* Out of his senses; silly. [? Var. of CHUNK]

chump[2] (chump) *v.t.* To chew; munch. [< CHAMP[1]

Chun·chon (cho͞on·chôn) A city in northern South Korea. *Japanese* **Shun·sen** (shoon·sen).

Chung·king (cho͝ong'king') A port on the Yangtze, capital of China in World War II.

chunk (chungk) *n.* **1** A short, stout thing, person, or animal; especially, a short, thick piece of wood. **2** A lump or large piece of anything. —*v.t.* **1** To throw clods of earth, stones, etc., at. **2** To throw, as clods of earth, stones, etc. **3** To put (chunks of wood) on a fire. [Var. of CHUCK]

chunk·er (chung'kər) *n.* A coal boat on a canal.

chunk·y (chung'kē) *adj.* **chunk·i·er, chunk·i·est 1** Short and thick–set; stocky. **2** In a chunk or chunks.

Chur (ko͞or) A town in eastern Switzerland, capital of Grisons canton. *French* **Coire** (kwär).

church (chûrch) *n.* **1** A building for Christian worship. **2** Regular religious services; public worship. **3** A local congregation of Christians. **4** *Usually cap.* A distinct body of Christians having a common faith and discipline; a denomination: the Episcopal *Church.* **5** All Christian believers collectively. **6** Ecclesiastical organization and authority, as distinguished from secular authority: the separation of *church* and state. **7** The clerical profession; holy orders. **8** Any religious body or society. —*v.t.* **1** To call to account before the congregation; to reprimand or punish publicly according to church discipline. **2** To conduct a religious service for (a person, especially a woman after childbirth). [OE *circe,* ult. <Gk. *kyriakon (doma)* the Lord's (house) < *kyrios* Lord]

church–go·er (chûrch'gō'ər) *n.* One who goes regularly to church. —**church'–go'ing** *adj.* & *n.*

Church·ill (chûrch'il, -əl) A port at the mouth of **Churchill River,** flowing 1,000 miles NE to Hudson Bay in northern Manitoba, Canada.

Church·ill (chûrch'il, -əl), **John** See MARLBOROUGH. —**Lord Randolph (Henry Spencer),** 1849–95, British statesman. —**Winston,** 1871–1947, U.S. novelist. —**Sir Winston (Leonard Spencer),** 1874–1965, British statesman; prime minister, 1940–45; 1951–55.

church·ing (chûr'ching) *n.* **1** A woman's appearance in church, to return thanks after confinement; also, the service for this occasion. **2** The process of subjecting to church discipline.

church·ly (chûrch'lē) *adj.* **1** Of, pertaining to, or suitable to a church. **2** Devoted to church polity and ritual. **3** Not secular. —**church'·li·ness** *n.*

church·man (chûrch'mən) *n. pl.* **·men** (-mən) **1** A devoted supporter or member of a church, especially of an established church. **2** *Obs.* A clergyman; ecclesiastic. —**church'·man·ly** *adj.* —**church'man·ship** *n.* —**church'·wom'an** *n. fem.*

Church of Christ, Scientist See CHRISTIAN SCIENCE.

Church of England The church established and endowed by law as the national church of England: also called *Anglican Church.*

Church of God Any of various small religious groups in the United States, for the most part unrelated.

Church of God, Adventist See under ADVENTIST.

Church Slavonic See under SLAVONIC.

church text *Printing* Old English type.

church·war·den (chûrch'wôr'dən) *n.* **1** In the Church of England, an elected lay officer who assists in the administration of a parish, and acts as its legal representative. **2** In the Protestant Episcopal Church, one of two elected lay officers of a vestry who, with the other vestrymen, administer the property and temporal affairs of the parish, and represent the congregation on certain occasions. **3** A long–stemmed clay pipe. Also **church warden.**

church·yard (chûrch'yärd') *n.* The yard or graveyard of a church; a cemetery.

churl (chûrl) *n.* **1** A low–bred, surly fellow. **2** A miserly or niggardly person. **3** A peasant. **4** In England of Saxon times, a freeman of low degree. [OE *ceorl.* Akin to CARL.]

churl·ish (chûr'lish) *adj.* **1** Of or like a churl; rude; boorish. **2** Hard to work or manage; intractable. See synonyms under HAUGHTY, MOROSE. —**churl'ish·ly** *adv.* —**churl'ish·ness** *n.*

churn (chûrn) *n.* **1** A vessel in which milk or cream is agitated to separate the oily globules and gather them as butter. **2** Any vessel or receptacle similar in shape to a milk churn. —*v.t.* **1** To stir or agitate (cream or milk), as in a churn, to make butter. **2** To make by agitation, as butter. **3** To agitate violently: The oars *churned* the water. —*v.i.* **4** To stir or agitate cream or milk in making butter. **5** To produce or be in violent agitation; seethe. [OE *cyrin*] —**churn'er** *n.*

churn·ing (chûr'ning) *n.* **1** The process of churning. **2** The butter churned at one time. **3** *Med.* A splashing sound from the chest sometimes heard in pleural effusion and resembling the sound made by a churn.

churr (chûr) *n.* The whirring sound made by certain birds, as the partridge or nightjar, or insects, as the cockchafer. —*v.t.* To utter with a churr. —*v.i.* To utter a low trill or similar vibrant sound, as a partridge. [Imit.]

Chur·ri·guer·esque (cho͞o·re'gər·esk') *adj.* **1** Pertaining to or in the style of **José Chur·ri·gue·ra** (cho͞or're·gä'rä), 1650–1723, Spanish architect. **2** Highly ornate; rococo.

Chu·ru·bus·co (cho͞o'ro͞o·boos'kō) A suburb SE of Mexico City; site of a battle of the Mexican War, 1847.

chute (sho͞ot) *n.* **1** A narrow, rocky rapid in a river. **2** A sluice through a dam for logs. **3** A passageway for fish through a dam. **4** An inclined trough or slide for grain, ore, coal, mail, baggage, etc. **5** A narrow pen for branding or shipping cattle. **6** A precipitous slide in an amusement park. **7** A toboggan slide. **8** *Colloq.* A parachute. —*v.t.* & *v.i.* **chut·ed, chut·ing** To descend or cause to descend (on) a chute. ◆ Homophone: *shoot.* [< F. fall]

Chu Teh (jo͞o' du'), 1886–1976, Chinese Communist military leader.

chut·ney (chut'nē) *n.* A piquant relish of fruit, spices, etc. Also **chut'nee.** [<Hind. *chatni*]

chutz·pah (ho͞ots'pə, kho͞ots'-) *n. U.S. Slang* Brazen effrontery; gall. [<Yiddish <Hebrew]

Chu·vash (cho͞o'väsh) *n. pl.* **Chu·vash·es** or **Chu·vash 1** One of a Bulgarian people living chiefly in the Chuvash Autonomous S.S.R. **2** The Turkic language of these people.

Chuvash Autonomous S.S.R. An administrative division of central European Russian S.F.S.R.; 7,100 square miles; capital, Cheboksary.

Chu Yüan–chang (jo͞o' yo͞o·än'jäng') Imperial title of Hung Wu, 1328–98, Chinese emperor 1368–98; founder of the Ming dynasty.

Chu·zen·ji (cho͞o·zen·jē) A lake in central Honshu island, Japan; altitude, 4,000 feet: also *Tyuzenzi.*

chyle (kīl) *n. Physiol.* The milky emulsion of lymph and fat taken up from the intestines during digestion and passed from the thoracic duct into the veins, where it mixes with the blood. [<F <L *chylus* <Gk. *chylos* juice < *cheein* pour]—**chy·la·ceous** (kī·lā'shəs), **chy·lous** (kī'ləs) *adj.*

chyme (kīm) *n. Physiol.* The partly digested food in liquid form as it passes from the stomach into the small intestines. [<L *chymus*<Gk. *chymos* juice <*cheein* pour] —**chy·mous** (kī'məs) *adj.*

chym·ic (kim'ik), **chym·ist** (kim'ist), etc. Archaic spellings for CHEMIC, CHEMIST.

chy·mif·er·ous (kī·mif'ər·əs) *adj.* Conveying or containing chyme. [<CHYME + -(I)FEROUS]

chy·mo·sin (kī'mə·sin) *n.* Rennin. [<CHYME + (PEP)SIN]

Cia·no (chä'nō), **Count Ga·le·az·zo** (gä'lā·ät'·tsō), 1903–44, son–in–law of Mussolini; Fascist foreign minister of Italy 1936–43; executed.

Cib·ber (sib'ər), **Colley,** 1671–1757, English dramatist and poet laureate.

cib·ol (sib'əl) *n.* **1** The Welsh onion *(Allium fistulosum)* having hollow stems and a very small bulb: also spelled *sybo.* **2** The shallot. Also **cib'oule.** [<L *ciboule* <LL *cepulla* bed of onions <L *cepa* onion]

Ci·bo·la (sē'bō·lä), **Seven Cities of** See SEVEN CITIES OF CIBOLA.

ci·bo·ri·um (si·bôr'ē·əm, -bō'rē-) *n. pl.* **·bo·ri·a** (-bôr'ē·ə, -bō'rē·ə) **1** An arched canopy over an altar; especially, a baldachin supported on four pillars. **2** A receptacle for the wafers of the Eucharist. [<Med. L <Gk. *kibōrion* cup]

ci·ca·da (si·kā'də, -kä'-) *n. pl.* **·das** or **·dae** (-dē) A large homopterous insect (family *Cicadidae*), the male being equipped at the base of the abdomen with vibrating membranes and sound chambers that produce a loud, shrill sound. The larvae develop underground. Often called *locust.* [<L]

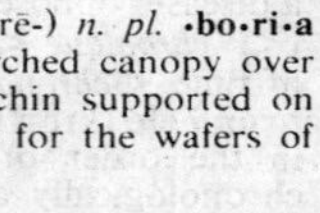

CICADA

cicada killer A digger wasp *(Sphecius speciosus)* that preys upon the cicada. For illustration see under INSECTS (beneficial).

ci·ca·la (si·kä'lə) *n.* A cicada.[<Ital.]

cic·a·tric·le (sik'ə·trik'əl), *n.* **1** *Biol.* The

germinating point in the yolk of an egg or in the embryo of a seed; the tread of an egg: also **cic·a·tri·cule** (sik′ə·tri·kyōōl′). 2 *Bot.* A small scar, as that left by the stem of a detached leaf. [< L *cicatricula,* dim. of *cicatrix* scar]

cic·a·trix (sik′ə·triks) *n. pl.* **cic·a·tri·ces** (sik′·ə·trī′sēz) 1 *Med.* A scar or seam consisting of new tissue formed in the healing of wounded or ulcerous parts and remaining after their cure: also **cic·a·trice** (sik′ə·tris). 2 *Biol.* A scar or scar-like marking, as that left on the interior of a bivalve shell by the attachment of the adductors, or that left by the fall of a leaf or other organ. [< L] **—cic·a·tri·cial** (sik′ə·trish′əl), **ci·cat·ri·cose** (si·kat′ri·kōs) *adj.*

cic·a·trize (sik′ə·trīz) *v.t. & v.i.* **·trized, ·triz·ing** To heal or become healed by the formation of a scar. **—cic′a·tri·za′tion** *n.*

cic·e·ly (sis′ə′lē) *n. pl.* **·lies** A fragrant perennial herb *(Myrrhis odorata)* of the parsley family. — **fool's-cicely** Fool's-parsley. [< L *seselis* < Gk.; infl. in form by *Cecily,* a feminine name]

cic·e·ro (sis′ə·rō) *n. Printing* A unit of typographical measurement in Europe, similar to the pica but slightly larger: from the type size used in an edition of Cicero printed in 1458.

Cic·e·ro (sis′ə·rō), **Marcus Tullius,** 106–43 B.C., Roman orator, author, and politician: sometimes called *Tully.*

cic·e·ro·ne (sis′ə·rō′nē, *Ital.* chē′chā·rō′nā) *n. pl.* **·nes,** *Ital.* **·ni** (-nē) A guide who explains to tourists and sightseers the curiosities and antiquities of a place; a local guide. [< Ital., Cicero; with ref. to the usual talkativeness of a guide]

Cic·e·ro·ni·an (sis′ə·rō′nē·ən) *adj.* Of or pertaining to Cicero or to his rhetorical style; polished; eloquent.

cich·lid (sik′lid) *n.* One of a family *(Cichlidae)* of spiny-finned, fresh-water fishes with a compressed oblong body, interrupted lateral line, and single nostril. [< NL *Cichlidae* < Gk. *kichlē,* a sea fish]

ci·cho·ri·a·ceous (si·kō′rē·ā′shəs) *adj. Bot.* Of or pertaining to the chicory family *(Cichoriaceae)* of herbs and shrubs, yielding a milky juice, which, in some species, has narcotic properties. [< NL *Cichoriaceae* < L *cichorium* chicory < Gk. *kichōrion*]

ci·cis·be·o (si·sis′bē·ō, *Ital.* chē′chēz·bā′ō) *n. pl.* **·be·i** (-bi·ē, *Ital.* -bā′ē) The acknowledged gallant of a married woman. [< Ital.]

Cid (sid, *Sp.* thēth), **the,** 1044?–99, Rodrigo Díaz, Count of Bivar, a Christian champion in the wars with the Moors in Spain; hero of a 12th century epic: also called *El Cid Campeador.*

-cidal *combining form* Killing; able to kill: *homicidal.* [< L *caedere* kill]

-cide *combining form* 1 Killer or destroyer of: *regicide.* 2 Murder or killing of: *parricide.* [def. 1 < L *-cida* killer < *caedere* kill; def. 2 < L *-cidium* slaughter < *caedere*]

ci·der (sī′dər) *n.* The expressed juice of apples used to make vinegar, and as a beverage before fermentation **(sweet cider)** or after fermentation **(hard cider)**. [< OF *sidre* < LL *sicera* strong drink < Hebrew *shēkār*]

ci-de·vant (sē·də·vän′) *adj. French* Former.

Cien·fue·gos (syen·fwā′gōs) A port in south central Cuba.

ci·gar (si·gär′) *n.* A small roll of tobacco leaves prepared and shaped for smoking. [< Sp. *cigarro*]

cig·a·rette (sig′ə·ret′, sig′ə·ret) *n.* 1 A small roll of finely cut tobacco in thin paper or, rarely, in tobacco leaf. 2 A similar roll with medicinal filling. Also **cig′a·ret′.** [< F, dim. of *cigare* cigar]

cigar fish A carangoid food fish *(Decapterus punctatus)* found in the West Indies and along the Atlantic Coast of the United States: also called *round robin.*

cil·i·a (sil′ē·ə) Plural of CILIUM.

cil·i·ar·y (sil′ē·er′ē) *adj.* 1 Of, pertaining to, or like cilia. 2 *Anat.* **a** Pertaining to or situated near the eyelashes. **b** Pertaining to the set of muscle fibers which are attached to ligaments supporting the lens of the eye. [< L *cilium* eyelid]

cil·i·ate (sil′ē·it, -āt) *adj. Biol.* Having cilia or motile hairlike processes: *ciliate* leaves. Also **cil′i·at′ed.** *—n. Zool.* One of a class *(Ciliata)* of infusorians possessing cilia in both young and adult stages.

cil·ice (sil′is) *n.* 1 A coarse cloth, originally made of goats' hair. 2 A shirt made of this; a hair shirt, formerly worn by monks and others in doing penance. [< F < L *cilicium* < Gk. *Kilikia* Cilicia, where the cloth was woven] **—ci·li·cious** (si·lish′əs) *adj.*

Ci·li·cia (si·lish′ə) An ancient country in SE Asia Minor: also *Little Armenia.*

Ci·li·cian (si·lish′ən) *adj.* Belonging to Cilicia. — *n.* An inhabitant or a native of Cilicia.

Cilician Gates The ancient name for GÜLEK BOGHAZ. *Latin* **Ci·li·ci·ae Py·lae** (si·lish′i·ē pī′lē).

cil·i·o·late (sil′ē·ə·lit, -lāt) *adj.* Fringed with small cilia.

cil·i·um (sil′ē·əm) *n. pl.* **cil·i·a** (sil′ē·ə) 1 *Biol.* A vibratile, microscopic, hairlike process on the surface of a cell, organ, plant, etc. 2 An eyelash. [< L, eyelid]

Ci·ma·bu·e (chē′mä·bōō′ā), **Giovanni,** 1240–1302, Florentine painter.

Cim·ar·ron River (sim′ə·rōn′, sim′ə·rōn, -ron) A river rising in NE New Mexico and flowing 692 miles east to the Arkansas River.

Cim·bri·an Cher·so·nese (sim′brē·ən kûr′sə·nēz′) Jutland. Also **Cim·bric Chersonese** (sim′brik).

ci·mex (sī′meks) *n. pl.* **cim·i·ces** (sim′ə·sēz) An insect of the genus *Cimex;* a bedbug. [< L, bug]

cim·i·tar or **cim·i·ter** (sim′ə·tər) See SCIMITAR.

Cim·mer·i·an (si·mir′ē·ən) *adj.* Densely dark; shrouded in gloom: with reference to the **Cim·me·ri·i** (si·mir′ē·ī), a mythical people mentioned by Homer as living in perpetual darkness. *—n.* 1 One of the mythical Cimmerii. 2 A member of a nomadic tribe of the Crimea which overran Asia Minor in the seventh century B.C.

Ci·mon (sī′mən), 507?–449 B.C., Athenian general and statesman.

cinch[1] (sinch) *n. U.S.* 1 A saddle girth, as of horsehair. 2 *Colloq.* A tight grip. 3 *Slang* A sure thing; a certainty. 4 *Slang* An easy thing to do. *—v.t.* 1 To fasten a saddle girth around. 2 *Slang* To get a tight hold upon; make sure of. *—v.i.* 3 To tighten a saddle girth: often with *up.* [< Sp. *cincha* girth < L *cingula* girdle < *cingere* bind]

cinch[2] (sinch) *n.* A game of cards in which the five of trumps is the most important card. [Prob. < Sp. *cinco* five]

cin·cho·na (sin·kō′nə) *n.* 1 Any of various Peruvian trees and shrubs (genus *Cinchona)* of the madder family, now widely cultivated in India and Java as a source of quinine and related alkaloids. 2 The bark of any of these trees. [after the Countess of *Cinchón,* 1576–1639, wife of the viceroy of Peru] **—cin·chon·ic** (sin·kon′ik) *adj.*

cin·chon·i·dine (sin·kon′ə·dēn, -din) *n. Chem.* A crystalline, bitter alkaloid, $C_{19}H_{22}N_2O$, derived from cinchona, isomeric with cinchonine, but less powerful: used medicinally.

cin·cho·nine (sin′kə·nēn, -nin) *n. Chem.* A crystalline alkaloid, $C_{19}H_{22}N_2O$, derived from cinchona, similar to cinchonidine, of which it is an isomer.

cin·cho·nism (sin′kə·niz′əm) *n. Pathol.* An abnormal condition caused by overdoses of cinchona, characterized by buzzing in the head, giddiness, deafness, and temporary loss of sight.

cin·cho·nize (sin′kə·nīz) *v.t.* **·nized, ·niz·ing** To bring under the influence of cinchona or quinine. **—cin′cho·ni·za′tion** *n.*

Cin·cin·nat·i (sin′sə·nat′ē, -nat′ə) A city on the Ohio River in SW Ohio.

Cin·cin·na·tus (sin′sə·nā′təs), **Lucius Quinctius,** 519?–439 B.C., Roman patriot.

cinc·ture (singk′chər) *n.* 1 Something bound about the waist; a belt or girdle. 2 Any covering about the loins: The savages wore a *cincture* of leaves. 3 Anything that encircles or encloses; also, the act of cincturing. *—v.t.* **·tured, ·tur·ing** To surround with or as with a cincture; gird. [< L *cinctura* < *cingere* gird]

cin·der (sin′dər) *n.* 1 Any partly burned combustible substance, before it has been reduced to ashes, especially when combustion has entirely ceased. 2 A thoroughly charred bit of wood, coal, or the like; an ember. 3 *pl.* Ashes. 4 A scale of iron oxide thrown off in forging; also, light slag. 5 *pl. Geol.* Fragments of scoriaceous lava explosively ejected from a volcano during an eruption; scoria. *—v.t.* To burn or reduce to a cinder. [OE *sinder;* infl. in form by L *cinis, cineris* ash] **—cin′der·ry** *adj.*

Cin·der·el·la (sin′dər·el′ə) 1 Heroine of a fairy tale, who, though treated as a servant by her stepmother and stepsisters, is aided by her fairy godmother to attend a court ball and finally marries a prince. 2 Any girl whose beauty or merit becomes known only after a period of neglect.

cin·e·ma (sin′ə·mə) *n.* 1 A motion-picture theater. 2 A motion picture or motion pictures collectively. 3 The art or business of making or exhibiting motion pictures. [Short for CINEMATOGRAPH]

Cin·e·ma·Scope (sin′ə·mə·skōp′) *n.* A motion-picture process employing a special type of lens to project a panoramic, three-dimensional image upon a wide, curved screen: a trade name.

cin·e·mat·ic (sin′ə·mat′ik) *adj.* Of, pertaining to, or suitable for motion-picture presentation. — **cin′e·mat′i·cal·ly** *adv.*

cin·e·mat·o·graph (sin′ə·mat′ə·graf, -gräf) *n.* A camera for producing motion pictures, so constructed that a large number of separate exposures or frames are made in very rapid succession: also called *kinetograph.* — *v.t. & v.i.* To take photographs of (something) with a motion-picture camera: also **cin·e·ma·tize** (sin′ə·mə·tīz′). [< Gk. *kinēma, -atos* movement + -GRAPH]

cin·e·ma·tog·ra·phy (sin′ə·mə·tog′rə·fē) *n.* The art and process of making motion pictures. **—cin′e·ma·tog′ra·pher** *n.* **—cin·e·mat·o·graph·ic** (sin′ə·mat′ə·graf′ik) *adj.* **—cin′e·mat′o·graph′·i·cal·ly** *adv.*

cin·e·ma·tome (sin′ə·mə·tōm′) *n.* An apparatus by means of which very thin sections of rock or other solid material may be sliced and then photographed on motion-picture film.

ci·ne·ma ve·ri·té (sin′ə·mə ver·ə·tā′) A kind of motion-picture technique that emphasizes realism and spontaneity. [< French *cinéma-vérité* truth cinema]

cin·e·o·graph (sin′ē·ə·graf, -gräf) *n.* A motion picture; kineograph. [< Gk. *kineein* move + -GRAPH]

cin·e·ol (sin′ē·ōl, -ol) *n.* Eucalyptol. Also **cin′e·ole** (-ōl) [Transposition of NL *ole(um) cin(ae)* oil of wormwood]

Cin·e·ram·a (sin′ə·ram′ə, -rä′mə) *n.* A motion picture having a very wide angle of projection to give the effect of panoramic vision: a trade name. [< CINE(MA PANO)RAMA]

cin·e·rar·i·a (sin′ə·râr′ē·ə) *n.* A cultivated, ornamental plant *(Senecio cruentus)* of the composite family, originally from the Canary Islands, having heart-shaped leaves and showy white, red, or purple flowers. [< NL < L, fem. of *cinerarius* ashy < *cinis, cineris* ash]

cin·e·rar·i·um (sin′ə·râr′ē·əm) *n. pl.* **·rar·i·a** (-râr′ē·ə) A niche in a tomb or other place for an urn containing the ashes of a cremated body. [< L] **—cin·er·ar·y** (sin′ə·rer′ē) *adj.*

cin·er·a·tor (sin′ə·rā′tər) *n.* Incinerator.

cin·e·ri·tious (sin′ə·rish′əs) *adj.* Of the nature of ashes; ashen: said of ash-colored brain- or nerve-substance. Also **ci·ne·re·ous** (si·nir′ē·əs). [< L *cineritius* ashen]

cin·gu·lum (sing′gyə·ləm) *n. pl.* **·la** (-lə) *Zool.* A band, zone, or girdle, as of the carapace of an armadillo, of a tooth near the gum, the clitellum of an earthworm, or a raised spiral line on certain univalves. [< L < *cingere* gird] **—cin·gu·late** (sing′gyə·lit, -lāt) or **cin′·gu·lat′ed** *adj.*

cin·na·bar (sin′ə·bär) *n.* 1 A crystallized red mercuric sulfide, HgS, the chief ore of mercury. 2 A mixture formed by subliming mercury and sulfur, known as **artificial cinnabar:** used as a pigment, called *vermilion.* [< L *cinnabaris* < Gk. *kinnabari,* ult. < Persian *zinifrah*]

cinnabar lacquer Chinese carved lacquer.

cin·nam·ic (si·nam′ik, sin′ə·mik) *adj.* Of, per-

taining to, or derived from cinnamon. Also **cin·na·mon·ic** (sin′ə·mon′ik).

cinnamic acid *Chem.* A colorless, crystalline, volatile compound, $C_9H_8O_2$, contained in cinnamon and various balsams, and made synthetically.

cin·na·mon (sin′ə·mən) *n.* **1** The aromatic inner bark of any of several tropical trees of the laurel family, used as a spice. **2** Any tree that yields cinnamon; especially, *Cinnamomum zeylanicum,* cultivated in Ceylon, Java, etc. **3** Cassia. **4** A shade of light reddish-brown. [<L *cinnamomum* <Gk. *kinnamōmon* <Hebrew *qinnāmōn*]

cinnamon bear A cinnamon-colored variety of the American black bear.

cinnamon stone A cinnamon-colored garnet; essonite.

cin·na·myl (sin′ə·mil) *n. Chem.* The univalent radical, C_9H_9, an important constituent of many compounds used in making soap, perfumes, drugs, etc. [<CINNAM(ON) + -YL]

cin·quain (sing·kān′) *n.* A stanza of five lines. [<F]

cinque (singk) *n.* The number five, in cards or dice; also, the throw in dice that turns up five. [<F *cinq* <L *quinque* five]

cin·que·cen·tist (ching′kwə·chen′tist) *n.* **1** An Italian artist or writer of the 16th century. **2** An imitator or student of 16th century art or style. [<Ital. *cinquecentista* < *cinquecento* five hundred, short for *mil cinque cento* fifteen hundred, i.e., the 16th century]

cin·que·cen·to (ching′kwə·chen′tō) *n.* The 16th century, especially with reference to Italy, or its art and literature; the Renaissance. [<Ital. <*(mil)cinquecento* (one thousand) five hundred]

cinque·foil (singk′foil) *n.* **1** *Archit.* A five-cusped ornament or window; a five-leaved rosette. **2** *Bot.* Any one of several species of a genus *(Potentilla)* of plants of the rose family, with five-lobed leaves. [<F <L *quinque* five + *folium* leaf]

CINQUEFOIL

cinque·pace (singk′pās) *n.* An old French dance with a five-step movement.

Cinque Ports (singk) An association of maritime towns in southern England, including Dover, Hastings, Hythe, Romney, and Sandwich, which formerly furnished men and ships for the king's service in return for special privileges. [<OF *cinq porz* five ports]

Cin·tra (sēnn′trə) A town and royal residence of central Portugal: also *Sintra.*

ci·on (sī′ən) *n. Bot.* A piece cut from a plant or tree; a twig or shoot used for grafting. See SCION. [Var. of SCION]

-cion Var. of -TION.

Ci·pan·go (si·pang′gō) *Poetic* Japan: a name used by Marco Polo.

ci·pher (sī′fər) *n.* **1** The character 0, the symbol of the absence of quantity, in numerical notation; zero. **2** A person or thing of no value or importance. **3** A cryptogram made by rearranging the individual characters of a plain text or by substituting others in their place. **4** The method of making such a cryptogram; also, the key for deciphering it. **5** A monogram; a character consisting of two or more interwoven or interlaced letters. **6** Any numerical character; a number. Also spelled *cypher.* — *v.t.* **1** To calculate arithmetically. **2** To write in characters of hidden meaning; encipher. **3** To add a cipher to. — *v.i.* **4** To work out arithmetical examples. [<OF *cyfre* <Arabic *ṣifr.* Doublet of ZERO.]

cip·o·lin (sip′ə·lin) *n.* An Italian marble having layers of alternating white and green. [<F <Ital. *cipollino,* dim. of *cipolla* onion; with ref. to its layered structure]

cir·ca (sûr′kə) *prep. Latin* About; around: used to indicate approximate dates.

cir·ca·di·an (sər·kā′dē·ən) *adj. Biol.* Pertaining to or designating those vital processes in plants and animals that tend to recur in cycles of approximately 24 hours. [<L *circa* around + *dies* day]

Cir·cas·sia (sər·kash′ə, -kash′ē·ə) A region of the NW Caucasus, Russian S.F.S.R.

Cir·cas·sian (sər·kash′ən, -kash′ē·ən) *n.* **1** A person belonging to one of a group of tribes of the Caucasus region. **2** The agglutinative language of these tribes, belonging to the Northwest Caucasian group of the Caucasian languages. — *adj.* Of or pertaining to Circassia, the Circassians, or their language: also **Cir·cas·sic** (sər·kas′ik).

Circassian walnut See under WALNUT.

Cir·ce (sûr′sē) In the *Odyssey,* an enchantress who transformed the companions of Odysseus into swine by a magic drink.

Cir·ce·an (sər·sē′ən) *adj.* **1** Of, pertaining to, or characteristic of Circe. **2** Bewitching and degrading.

cir·ci·nate (sûr′sə·nāt) *adj.* **1** Ringed; ring-shaped. **2** *Bot.* Rolled inward from the apex into a coil. [<L *circinatus,* pp. of *circinare* make round < *circinus* circle] — **cir′ci·nate′ly** *adv.*

cir·cle (sûr′kəl) *n.* **1** A plane figure bounded by a curved line everywhere equally distant from the center; also, the circumference of such a figure. **2** A circular object or arrangement of objects, or whatever is included within it; an enclosure; ring; halo: a *circle* around the moon. **3** Loosely, a round or spherical body. **4** An association of persons having the same interests or pursuits; a set; class; coterie. **5** A series ending at the starting point; a repeated succession; hence, a completed series or system: the *circle* of the months. **6** A circular path or course; circuit. **7** An indirect statement; circumlocution. **8** *Logic* A form of argument in which the conclusion is virtually assumed to prove the premise and vice versa: also called *argument in a circle.* **9** In some European countries, an administrative governmental district. **10** An astronomical or other instrument whose important parts are graduated circles. **11** A circus ring. **12** A tier of seats or gallery in a theater: the dress *circle.* **13** A crown; diadem. **14** *Astron.* The orbit of a heavenly body; formerly, the supposed sphere of a planet or other body. **15** The domain of a special influence. — *v.* **·cled, ·cling** *v.t.* **1** To enclose with or as with a circle; encompass; surround. **2** To move around, as in a circle: The dog *circles* the field. — *v.i.* **3** To move in a circle; revolve. [<L *circulus,* dim. of *circus* ring] — **cir′cler** *n.*

cir·clet (sûr′klit) *n.* A small ring or ring-shaped object, especially as used as a personal ornament. [<F *cerclet,* dim. of *cercle* ring; infl. in form by CIRCLE]

cir·cuit (sûr′kit) *n.* **1** A passing or traveling round; a revolution. **2** A journey from place to place, as by a judge or clergyman, in the discharge of duties. **3** A district or route within certain limits or boundaries; especially, a division assigned to a peripatetic judge for the holding of courts at stated intervals. **4** The persons undertaking these peripatetic journeys, as the judges. **5** In the Methodist Church, and in the Evangelical Association, a district in charge of an itinerant minister. **6** Distance around; compass; circumference. **7** *Electr.* **a** The entire course traversed by an electric current. When it is complete, so that the current will flow, it is a **made** or **closed circuit;** when interrupted, so that the current stops, it is a **broken** or **open circuit. b** The complete assembly of generators, conductors, vacuum tubes, switches, etc., by which an electric current is transmitted. **8** A circuit court. See under COURT. **9** A radio transmission and reception system. — **to ride the circuit** To travel an assigned route in the capacity of minister, lawyer, judge, etc. — *v.t.* & *v.i.* To go or move in a circuit. [<F <L *circuitus* < *circumire* < *circum-* around + *ire* go]

circuit binding A style of bookbinding in which the sides of a book are made to overlap the edge of the pages to protect them from injury.

circuit breaker *Electr.* A switch or relay for breaking a circuit under specified or abnormal conditions of current flow.

circuit judge A judge of a circuit court.

cir·cu·i·tous (sər·kyōō′ə·təs) *adj.* Of the nature of a circuit; indirect; round-about. — **cir·cu′·i·tous·ly** *adv.* — **cir·cu′i·tous·ness** *n.*

circuit rider A minister who preaches at churches on a circuit or district route.

cir·cuit·ry (sûr′kit·rē) *n.* The design and arrangement of circuits in any device, instrument, or system carrying an electric current: radio *circuitry.*

cir·cu·i·ty (sər·kyōō′ə·tē) *n. pl.* **·ties** **1** Movement in a circuit; circular form or movement. **2** Indirectness; round-about procedure or speech.

cir·cu·lar (sûr′kyə·lər) *adj.* **1** Forming, or bounded by, a circle; round. **2** Moving or occurring in a circle or round. **3** Ending at the point of beginning. **4** Constantly repeated in the same or similar order: *circular* motion. **5** Intended for public circulation. **6** Circuitous; devious; indirect. — *n.* A communication for general circulation; a circular letter or announcement, such as a printed advertisement. See synonyms under ROUND. [<L *circularis* < *circulus* CIRCLE] — **cir·cu·lar·i·ty** (sûr′kyə·lar′ə·tē), **cir′cu·lar·ness** *n.* — **cir′cu·lar·ly** *adv.*

cir·cu·lar·ize (sûr′kyə·lə·rīz′) *v.t.* **·ized, ·iz·ing** **1** To make circular. **2** To ply with circulars. — **cir′cu·lar·i·za′tion** *n.* — **cir′cu·lar·iz′er** *n.*

circular measure A system of measurement for circles:

60 seconds of an arc (60″)	=	1 minute of an arc (1′)
60 minutes of an arc	=	1 degree (1°)
90 degrees	=	1 quadrant
4 quadrants (360°)	=	1 circle

circular mil A unit of measurement for the cross-sectional area of wires, equal to the area of a circle having a diameter of 1 mil.

circular sailing *Naut.* Sailing by the arc of a great circle: also called *great-circle sailing.*

circular saw A disk-shaped saw having a toothed edge, rotated at high speed by a motor.

circular triangle *Geom.* A triangle whose sides are formed by the arcs of a circle.

cir·cu·late (sûr′kyə·lāt) *v.* **·lat·ed, ·lat·ing** *v.t.* **1** To spread about; disseminate, as news. — *v.i.* **2** To move by a circuitous course back to the starting point, as the blood through the body. **3** To spread abroad, or become diffused. **4** *Colloq.* To travel about. **5** To repeat indefinitely a number or set of numbers in a decimal quantity. See synonyms under SPREAD. [<L *circulatus,* pp. of *circulari* form a circle < *circulus* CIRCLE] — **cir′cu·la′tor** *n.*

circulating decimal A decimal number in which one or more digits are repeated indefinitely, as 0.444 . . . , 0.16353535 . . . , 0.824-37437 . . . : also called *recurring decimal, repeating decimal.*

circulating medium Currency used in exchange.

cir·cu·la·tion (sûr′kyə·lā′shən) *n.* **1** The act of circulating or state of being circulated. **2** Motion around or through something back to the starting point: the *circulation* of the blood. **3** Transmission; diffusion; dissemination. **4** The extent or amount of distribution; number of copies issued, as of a paper or periodical, etc. **5** A current medium of exchange, as coin, etc. [<L *circulatio, -onis* < *circulari.* See CIRCULATE.] — **cir′cu·la′tive** *adj.* — **cir·cu·la·to·ry** (sûr′kyə·lə·tôr′ē, -tō′rē) *adj.*

circum- *prefix*

1 About; around; on all sides; surrounding:

circumagitate
circumanal
circumbasal
circumcircle
circumesophagal
circumfulgent
circumgenital
circumhorizontal
circummedullary
circummigration
circumnatant
circumnuclear
circumocular
circumoral
circumscrive
circumspheral
circumtropical
circumundulate

2 Revolving around:

circumlunar
circumsolar

[<L *circum-* around, about < *circus* circle]

cir·cum·am·bi·ent (sûr′kəm·am′bē·ənt) *adj.* Extending or going around; encompassing. — **cir′cum·am′bi·ence, cir′cum·am′bi·en·cy** *n.*

cir·cum·am·bu·late (sûr′kəm·am′byə·lāt) *v.t.* & *v.i.* **·lat·ed, ·lat·ing** To walk around. [<L *circumambulatus,* pp. of *circumambulare* < *circum-* around + *ambulare* walk] — **cir′cum·am′bu·la′tion** *n.* — **cir′cum·am′bu·la′tor** *n.*

cir·cum·ben·di·bus (sûr′kəm·ben′di·bəs) *n.* A round-about course or method; circumlocution: a humorous usage. [Coined from L *circum* + BEND + L *-ibus*]

cir·cum·cise (sûr′kəm·sīz) *v.t.* **·cised, ·cis·ing** **1** To cut off the prepuce or, in females, the inner labia of, especially as a religious rite. **2** In the Bible, to purify from sin; to cleanse spiritually. [<OF *circonciser* <L *circumcisus,*

pp. of *circumcidere* < *circum-* around + *caedere* cut] — **cir′cum·cis′er** *n.*

cir·cum·ci·sion (sûr′kəm·sizh′ən) *n.* **1** The act of circumcising; the initiatory rite of Judaism, also practiced by Moslems. **2** Figuratively, spiritual purification. **3** Those purified under this rite; the Jewish people. — **Feast of the Circumcision** The festival of the circumcision of Jesus, observed on Jan. 1.

cir·cum·fer·ence (sər·kum′fər·əns) *n.* **1** The boundary line of a circle. **2** Distance around; circuit; compass. [<L *circumferentia* < *circum-* around + *ferre* bear] — **cir·cum·fer·en·tial** (sər·kum′fər·en′shəl) *adj.* — **cir·cum′·fer·en′tial·ly** *adv.*

cir·cum·flex (sûr′kəm·fleks) *n.* A mark (ˆ ˜ ˆ) used over a letter to indicate the combination of a rising with a falling tone or to mark a long vowel, contraction, etc., or used as a diacritical mark in phonetics. In the pronunciations in this dictionary, the circumflex is used over *a* to indicate the vowel sound in *care* (kâr), over *o* for the vowel in *fall* (fôl), and over *u* for the vowel in *earn* (ûrn). — *adj.* **1** Pronounced or marked with the circumflex accent. **2** Bent in a curvilinear manner, as certain vessels and nerves. — *v.t.* **1** To utter with a circumflex intonation or accent; mark with a circumflex. **2** To wind around; bend about. [<L *circumflexus,* pp. of *circumflectere* < *circum-* around + *flectere* bend] — **cir·cum·flex·ion** (sûr′kəm·flek′shən) *n.*

cir·cum·flu·ent (sər·kum′floo·ənt) *adj.* **1** Flowing around; surrounding. **2** Surrounded by, or as by, water. Also **cir·cum′flu·ous.** [<L *circumfluens, -entis,* ppr. of *circumfluere* < *circum-* around + *fluere* flow]

cir·cum·fuse (sûr′kəm·fyooz′) *v.t.* **·fused, ·fus·ing** **1** To pour, scatter, or spread about. **2** To surround, as with a liquid. [<L *circumfusus,* pp. of *circumfundere* < *circum-* around + *fundere* pour] — **cir·cum·fu·sion** (sûr′kəm·fyoo′zhən) *n.*

cir·cum·gy·rate (sûr′kəm·jī′rāt) *v.t.* & *v.i.* **·rat·ed, ·rat·ing** To turn or roll about. [< CIRCUM- + L *gyratus,* pp. of *gyrare* spin]

cir·cum·gy·ra·tion (sûr′kəm·jī·rā′shən) *n.* The act of turning around; rotation; motion in a circular course. — **cir·cum·gy·ra·to·ry** (sûr′·kəm·jī′rə·tôr′ē, -tō′rē) *adj.*

cir·cum·ja·cent (sûr′kəm·jā′sənt) *adj.* Bordering on all sides; surrounding. [<L *circumjacens, -entis,* ppr. of *circumjacere* < *circum-* around + *jacere* lie] — **cir′cum·ja′cence, cir′·cum·ja′cen·cy** *n.*

cir·cum·lo·cu·tion (sûr′kəm·lō·kyoo′shən) *n.* Indirect or round-about expression; the use of superfluous words. [<L *circumlocutio, -onis* < *circum-* around + *locutio* speaking < *loqui* speak] — **cir·cum·loc·u·tory** (sûr′kəm·lok′yə·tôr′ē, -tō′rē) *adj.*

Synonyms (noun): diffuseness, periphrasis, pleonasm, prolixity, redundance, redundancy, surplusage, tautology, tediousness, verbiage, verbosity, wordiness. *Circumlocution* is the more common, *periphrasis* the more technical word. *Diffuseness* is a scattering both of words and thought; *redundance* or *redundancy* is an overflow. *Prolixity* goes into endless petty details, without selection or perspective. *Pleonasm* may be an emphatic, *tautology* is a useless repetition of a word or words. "I saw it with my eyes" is a *pleonasm*; "all the members agreed unanimously" is *tautology.* *Verbiage* is the use of mere words without thought. *Verbosity* and *wordiness* denote an excess of words in proportion to the thought. *Antonyms*: brevity, compactness, conciseness, condensation, directness, succinctness, terseness.

cir·cum·mure (sûr′kəm·myoor′) *v.t.* **·mured, mur·ing** To wall around. [<CIRCUM- + LL *murare* build a wall <L *murus* wall]

cir·cum·nav·i·gate (sûr′kəm·nav′ə·gāt) *v.t.* **·gat·ed, ·gat·ing** To sail around. [<L *circumnavigatus,* pp. of *circumnavigare* < *circum-* around + *navigare* sail] — **cir·cum·nav·i·ga·ble** (sûr′kəm·nav′ə·gə·bəl) *adj.* — **cir′cum·nav′i·ga′tion** *n.* — **cir′cum·nav′i·ga′tor** *n.*

cir·cum·nu·ta·tion (sûr′kəm·nyoo·tā′shən) *n.* *Bot.* A nodding or turning successively in all directions, as observed in the tips of young and growing plant organs, such as tendrils, stems, or roots. [<CIRCUM- + L *nutatio, -onis* a nodding < *nutare* nod]

cir·cum·po·lar (sûr′kəm·pō′lər) *adj.* Near or surrounding one of the terrestrial or celestial poles: applied specifically to stars revolving about the pole without setting.

cir·cum·pose (sûr′kəm·pōz′) *v.t.* **·posed, ·pos·ing** To place around. — **cir·cum·po·si·tion** (sûr′kəm·pə·zish′ən) *n.*

cir·cum·ro·tate (sûr′kəm·rō′tāt) *v.i.* **·tat·ed, ·tat·ing** To turn in the manner of a wheel; revolve. — **cir·cum·ro·ta·to·ry** (sûr′kəm·rō′·tə·tôr′ē, -tō′rē), **cir′cum·ro′ta·ry** (-rō′tə·rē) *adj.* — **cir′cum·ro·ta′tion** *n.*

cir·cum·scis·sile (sûr′kəm·sis′il) *adj.* *Bot.* Dehiscent, as a capsule, in a transverse circular line, so that the top separates like a lid, as in the common purslane. [<L *circumscissus,* pp. of *circumscindere* < *circum-* around + *scindere* cut]

cir·cum·scribe (sûr′kəm·skrīb′) *v.t.* **·scribed, scrib·ing** **1** To draw a line or figure around; encircle. **2** To mark out the limits of; define. **3** To confine within bounds; restrict. **4** *Geom.* **a** To surround with or as with a figure that touches at every possible point: to *circumscribe* a triangle with a circle. **b** To cause to surround a figure thus: to *circumscribe* a circle about a triangle. [<L *circumscribere* < *circum-* around + *scribere* write] — **cir′·cum·scrib′a·ble** *adj.* — **cir′cum·scrib′er** *n.*

Synonyms: bound, confine, define, delineate, describe, designate, enclose, fence, limit, restrict. See RESTRAIN. *Antonyms*: dilate, distend, enlarge, expand, open.

cir·cum·scrip·tion (sûr′kəm·skrip′shən) *n.* **1** The act of circumscribing. **2** The state of being limited or bounded; limitation; restriction. **3** The line marking the external boundary of an object; surrounding margin or edge; periphery. **4** The space or district circumscribed. **5** *Obs.* Definition; description. **6** *Obs.* Something written around, as an inscription surrounding a coin. [<L *circumscriptio, -onis* < *circumscribere.* See CIRCUMSCRIBE.] — **cir′cum·scrip′tive** *adj.*

cir·cum·so·lar (sûr′kəm·sō′lər) *adj.* Near, revolving about, or surrounding, the sun.

cir·cum·spect (sûr′kəm·spekt) *adj.* Attentive to everything; watchful in all directions, as against danger or error; cautious; wary. See synonyms under THOUGHTFUL. [<L *circumspectus,* pp. of *circumspicere* < *circum-* around + *specere* look] — **cir′cum·spect′ly** *adv.* — **cir′cum·spect′ness** *n.*

cir·cum·spec·tion (sûr′kəm·spek′shən) *n.* Cautious and careful observation with a view to wise conduct. See synonyms under CARE, PRUDENCE.

cir·cum·spec·tive (sûr′kəm·spek′tiv) *adj.* Cautious; watchful.

cir·cum·stance (sûr′kəm·stans) *n.* **1** Something existing or occurring incidentally to some other fact or event; a related or concomitant act or thing; an accessory detail. **2** An event, happening, or fact, especially if incidental or subordinate: a *circumstance* in English history. **3** *pl.* The surrounding facts, means, influences, etc., especially as related to one's support and way of living. **4** Environment: He is the victim of *circumstance*; also, environment with reference to state or condition resulting from adventitious surroundings. **5** That which is unessential or of no account; detail; circumstantiality. **6** *Archaic* Formal show or display; ceremony; pomp. — **under no circumstances** Never; under no conditions. — **under the circumstances** Since such is the case; things being as they are or were. — *v.t.* **·stanced, ·stanc·ing** **1** To place in or under limiting circumstances or conditions: chiefly in past participle. **2** *Obs.* To set forth circumstantially; relate with details. [<OF <L *circumstantia* < *circumstare* < *circum-* around + *stare* stand]

Synonyms (noun): accompaniment, concomitant, detail, event, fact, feature, incident, item, occurrence, particular, point, position, situation. A *circumstance* is something existing or occurring in connection with or relation to some other fact or event, modifying or throwing light upon the principal matter without affecting its essential character; an *accompaniment* is something that unites with the principal matter, but is not necessary to it; as, the piano *accompaniment* to a song; a *concomitant* goes with a thing in natural connection, but in a subordinate capacity, or perhaps in contrast. A *circumstance* is not strictly, nor usually, an occasion, condition, effect, or result. Nor is the *circumstance* properly an *incident.* All the *circumstances* make up the *situation.* Compare ACCIDENT, CAUSE, EVENT.

cir·cum·stanced (sûr′kəm·stanst) *adj.* **1** Being in or under certain conditions. **2** Supported by conditions, facts, details, etc., as an argument.

cir·cum·stan·tial (sûr′kəm·stan′shəl) *adj.* **1** Consisting of details; minute; particular. **2** Pertaining to or dependent on circumstances; indirect; presumptive. **3** Having to do with one's circumstances: *circumstantial* prosperity. **4** Incidental or casual; not essential. **5** *Archaic* Full of circumstance or display; ceremonial. See synonyms under MINUTE, PARTICULAR.

circumstantial evidence See under EVIDENCE.

cir·cum·stan·ti·al·i·ty (sûr′kəm·stan′shē·al′·ə·tē) *n. pl.* **·ties** **1** The quality or characteristic of being particular, detailed, or minute. **2** A particular matter; a detail.

cir·cum·stan·tial·ly (sûr′kəm·stan′shəl·ē) *adv.* At length; minutely.

cir·cum·stan·ti·ate (sûr′kəm·stan′shē·āt) *v.t.* **·at·ed, ·at·ing** To set forth or establish by circumstances or in detail.

cir·cum·val·late (sûr′kəm·val′āt) *v.t.* **·lat·ed, ·lat·ing** To surround with a rampart or a trench. —*adj.* Enclosed by or as by a wall or rampart: *circumvallate* papillae. [<L *circumvallatus,* pp. of *circumvallare* < *circum-* around + *vallare* fortify < *vallum* rampart] — **cir′cum·val·la′tion** *n.*

cir·cum·vent (sûr′kəm·vent′) *v.t.* **1** To get around; get the better of, as by craft, artifice, or fraud; outwit. **2** To surround or entrap, as an enemy, by craft or strategem. **3** To pass around: to *circumvent* a town. **4** To forestall (an occurrence or happening). See synonyms under BAFFLE, DECEIVE. [<L *circumventus,* pp. of *circumvenire* < *circum-* around + *venire* come] — **cir′cum·ven′tive** *adj.* — **cir′·cum·ven′tion** *n.*

cir·cum·ven·tor (sûr′kəm·ven′tər) *n.* **1** One who circumvents. **2** A surveying instrument having at the top a compass box, used for laying out horizontal angles. Also **cir′cum·vent′er.**

cir·cum·vo·lu·tion (sûr′kəm·və·loo′shən) *n.* **1** The act of winding. **2** A single fold or turn of something wound. **3** A turning round an axis or center; rotation; revolution. **4** Convolution; sinuosity. [<L *circumvolutus,* pp. of *circumvolvere* < *circum-* around + *volvere* turn, spin]

cir·cum·volve (sûr′kəm·volv′) *v.t.* & *v.i.* **·volved, ·volv·ing** To revolve.

cir·cus (sûr′kəs) *n.* **1** A traveling show in which feats of horsemanship, tumbling, and strength, as well as clowns, wild animals, etc., are exhibited; also, a performance of such a show. **2** The circular, tented enclosure in which such a show is commonly held. **3** The troupe of performers in such a show. **4** In ancient Rome, a large oval or oblong enclosure with tiers of seats around it, used for races, games, etc. **5** *Brit.* A circle formed by bow-shaped rows of houses. **6** *Colloq.* Any person or thing regarded as uproariously entertaining. [<L, a ring, racecourse <Gk. *kirkos.* Doublet of CIRQUE.]

Cir·cus Max·i·mus (sûr′kəs mak′si·məs) A large arena built around 330 B.C. in ancient Rome, used for chariot races, gladiatorial contests, etc.

Ci·re·na·i·ca (chē′rā·nä′ē·kä) The Italian name for CYRENAICA.

Ci·ren·ces·ter (sis′i·tər, sī′rən·ses′tər) An urban district of SE Gloucestershire, England; site of Roman ruins.

Ci·re·ne (chē·rā′nā) Italian name for CYRENE.

Ci·ri·lo (thē·rē′lō) Spanish form of CYRIL. Also *Ital.* **Ci·ril·lo** (chē·rēl′lō).

cirque (sûrk) *n.* **1** A circular enclosure; circus. **2** *Geol.* A circular valley with precipitous walls, usually formed by the action of glaciers. **3** A circlet; ring: a poetical usage. [<F <L *circus.* Doublet of CIRCUS.]

cir·rate (sir′āt) *adj.* Having curls or cirri. [<L *cirratus* < *cirrus* curl]
cir·rho·sis (si·rō′sis) *n. Pathol.* An abnormal formation of connective tissue, with wasting of the proper tissue of the liver or other organ. [<NL <Gk. *kirrhos* tawny; with ref. to the color of the cirrhotic liver] — **cir·rhot·ic** (si·rot′ik) *adj.*
cir·ri (sir′ī) Plural of CIRRUS.
cir·ri·ped (sir′ə·ped) *n.* One of an order *(Cirripedia)* of crustaceans which become attached or parasitic in the adult stage, as the barnacles. — *adj.* Of or pertaining to this order.
cirro– *combining form* Cirrus: *cirrostratus.* Also **cirri–.** [<L *cirrus* curl]
cir·ro·cu·mu·lus (sir′ō·kyōō′myə·ləs) *n. Meteorol.* A mass of fleecy, globular cloudlets in contact with one another, with an average height of 5 miles; mackerel sky. — **cir′ro·cu′mu·lar** or **cir′ro·cu′mu·lous** or **cir·ro·cu·mu·la·tive** (sir′ō·kyōō′myə·lā′tiv, -lə·tiv) *adj.*
cir·ro·stra·tus (sir′ō·strā′təs) *n. Meteorol.* A fine, whitish veil of cloud with an average height of 6 miles. — **cir′ro·stra′tive** *adj.*
cir·rous (sir′əs) *adj.* **1** Having or like cirri. **2** Of or pertaining to a cirrus cloud. Also **cir·rose** (sir′ōs).
cir·rus (sir′əs) *n. pl.* **cir·ri** (sir′ī) **1** *Meteorol.* A type of white, wispy cloud, usually consisting of ice crystals and having an average height of 7 miles, seen in tufts or feathery–shaped bands across the sky. **2** *Bot.* A tendril. **3** *Zool.* A threadlike appendage serving as an organ of touch. [<L, ringlet]
cir·soid (sûr′soid) *adj.* Resembling a varix; varicose. [<Gk. *kirsos* a dilated vein]
cir·sot·o·my (sər·sot′ə·mē) *n. Surg.* The incision of varicose veins. [<Gk. *kirsos* dilated vein + -TOMY]
Cis (sis) Diminutive of CECILIA. Also **Cis′sie.**
cis– *prefix* **1** On this side of: opposed to TRANS– or ULTRA–: *cisatlantic.* **2** Since; following: opposed to PRE–: *cis–Elizabethan.* [<L *cis* on this side]
cis·al·pine (sis·al′pīn, -pin) *adj.* On the Roman side of the Alps. [<L *cisalpinus* < *cis* on this side + *Alpes* the Alps]
Cisalpine Gaul An ancient name for northern Italy.
cis·at·lan·tic (sis′ət·lan′tik) *adj.* On this side of the Atlantic: opposed to *transatlantic.*
Cis·cau·ca·sia (sis′kô·kā′zhə, -shə) See NORTHERN CAUCASUS.
cis·co (sis′kō) *n. pl.* **·coes** or **·cos** A whitefish (genus *Leucichthys*) of North America; especially, the lake herring (*L. artedi*) of Lakes Michigan and Ontario. [? <N. Am. Ind.]
cis·lu·nar (sis·lōō′nər) *adj.* On this side of the moon.
cis·mon·tane (sis·mon′tān) *adj.* **1** On this side of the mountains. **2** Cisalpine. Opposed to *ultramontane.* [<L *cismontanus* < *cis* on this side + *mons, montis* a mountain]
cis·soid (sis′oid) *Math. n.* A curve *GAP* intersecting a circle at the two extremities of a diameter and having a cusp the apex of which is at the point on the circumference where the perpendicular bisector of the diameter falls: the curve traces the locus of a point moving so that a straight line *BC* drawn through the apex of the cusp at *A* through the curve at any point *P* intersects the tangent *DEF* (with *E* on the circumference diametrically opposite to *A*) at point *M*, so that *AP* = *NM*. — *adj.* Contained within two curves that intersect each other, as an angle: opposed to *sistroid*: The angle interior to both curves is a *cissoid* angle; the exterior and opposite a *sistroid.* [<Gk. *kissoeidēs* like ivy < *kissos* ivy + *eidos* form]

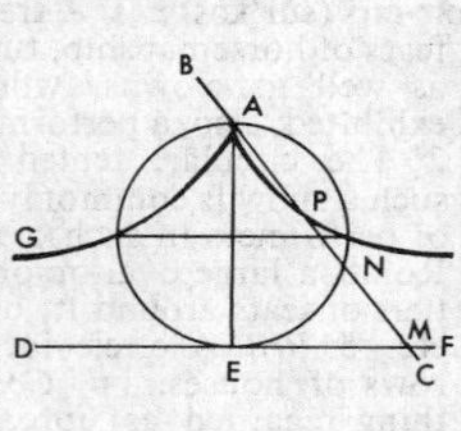

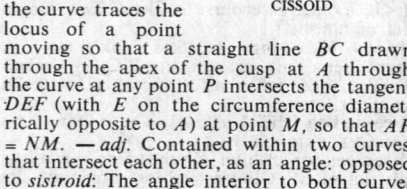

CISSOID

cist[1] (sist) *n.* A casket; box. [<L *cista* CHEST]
cist[2] (sist, kist) *n.* A small sepulchral chamber, or chest, made of flat stones; a kistvaen. [< Welsh, chest <L *cista* chest]
cis·ta·ceous (sis·tā′shəs) *adj. Bot.* Designating the rockrose family *(Cistaceae)* of shrubby or herbaceous plants, with regular, perfect, often showy flowers. [<NL *Cistaceae* <Gk. *kistos* rockrose]
Cis·ter·cian (sis·tûr′shən) *n.* A monk of an order founded in 1098 at Cistercium (modern *Citeaux*), France, as an offshoot of the Benedictines. — *adj.* Of or pertaining to this order.
cis·tern (sis′tərn) *n.* **1** A reservoir, usually of masonry, wood, or metal, for storing water or other liquids; also, any natural reservoir. **2** Any analogous receptacle in which fluid is stored. **3** *Anat.* A large lymph space; a sac. [<OF *cisterne* <L *cisterna* < *cista* chest]
cis·tus (sis′təs) *n.* A plant of a genus *(Cistus)* of European evergreen shrubs of the rockrose family: gum ladanum is produced by several species. [<Gk. *kistos* rockrose]
cist·vaen (kist′vīn) See KISTVAEN.
cit (sit) *n. Archaic* A resident of a city; citizen.
cit·a·del (sit′ə·dəl, -del) *n.* **1** A fortress commanding a city. **2** Any strong fortress. **3** The heavily plated central casemate containing the guns in a war vessel. See synonyms under FORTIFICATION. [<F *citadelle* <Ital. *cittadella,* dim. of *città* city]
ci·ta·tion (sī·tā′shən) *n.* **1** The act of citing, or a passage quoted. **2** A public commendation for exceptional military conduct or achievement. **3** *Law* A judicial summons. **4** Recounting; enumeration. [<F <L *citatio, -onis* < *citare* CITE] — **ci·ta·to·ry** (sī′tə·tôr′ē, -tō′rē) *adj.*
cite (sīt) *v.t.* **cit·ed, cit·ing** **1** To quote or refer to as an authority, illustration, or exemplification for proof or support. **2** To refer to specifically, as in a military report. **3** *Law* To summon to appear, as before a tribunal. See synonyms under ALLEGE, ARRAIGN, QUOTE. ◆ Homophones: *sight, site.* [<F *citer* <L *citare,* freq. of *cire* call] — **cit′a·ble, cite′a·ble** *adj.*
Ci·thae·ron (si·thē′ron) A mountain of east central Greece, regarded as sacred to Dionysus; 4,623 feet: Greek *Kithairon.* Formerly **El·a·ti·as** (el′ə·tī′əs).
cith·a·ra (sith′ə·rə) *n.* **1** An ancient Greek stringed instrument with a wooden case, the strings extending to the base from a crosspiece connecting the straight hollow arms: the instrument of professional musicians. **2** Loosely, any of the stringed instruments of ancient Greece. Also spelled *kithara.* [<L <Gk. *kithara.* Doublet of GUITAR and ZITHER.]

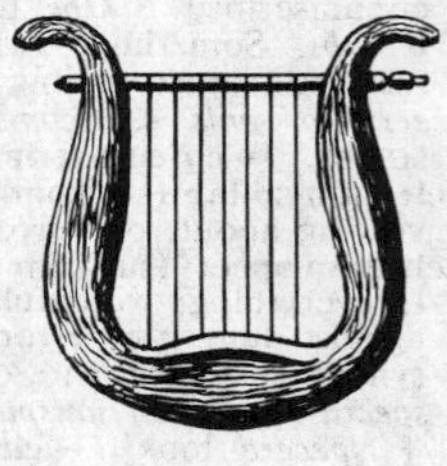
CITHARA

cith·er (sith′ər) *n.* **1** A zither. **2** A cithern. **3** A cithara.
cith·ern (sith′ərn) *n.* A medieval lute or guitar having wire strings plucked with a plectrum: the original of the zither: also spelled *cittern, zittern.* [Blend of CITHER and GITTERN]
cit·i·fied (sit′i·fīd) *adj.* Having the ways and means of city life; following city fashions: also spelled *cityfied.*
cit·i·zen (sit′ə·zən) *n.* **1** A native or naturalized person owing allegiance to, and entitled to protection from, a government: opposed to *alien.* **2** A resident of a city or town. **3** A private person; one who is not a public officer nor a soldier; a civilian. [<AF *citezein,* var. of OF *citeain* < *cité* CITY] — **cit′i·zen·ess** *n. fem.*
cit·i·zen·ry (sit′ə·zən·rē) *n.* Citizens collectively.
cit·i·zen·ship (sit′ə·zən·ship′) *n.* The status of a citizen, with its rights and duties; state of being a citizen.
Cit·lal·té·petl (sēt′läl·tā′pet·l) See ORIZABA, PICO DE.
citra– *prefix* On this side; cis–. [<L]
cit·ral (sit′rəl) *n. Chem.* An oily liquid aldehyde, $C_{10}H_{16}O$, contained in geranium, lemon, and other oils: used as a flavoring extract and in perfumery; geranial. [<CITR(US) + AL(DEHYDE)]
cit·rate (sit′rāt, -rit, sī′trāt) *n. Chem.* A salt of citric acid.
cit·re·ous (sit′rē·əs) *adj.* Having the yellow color of a citron or lemon; citrine. [<L *citreus* < *citrus* citron tree]
cit·ric (sit′rik) *adj.* Derived from lemons, oranges, or similar fruits.
citric acid *Chem.* A white, crystalline, sharply sour compound, $C_6H_8O_7$, contained in various fruits, and obtained from lemons, limes, and sour oranges, etc., and also made synthetically.
cit·ri·cul·ture (sit′ri·kul′chər) *n.* The cultivation of oranges, lemons, grapefruit, and other citrus fruits. — **cit′ri·cul′tur·ist** *n.*
cit·rin (sit′rin) *n. Biochem.* A constituent of vitamin P, consisting of a mixture of glycosides and occurring in citrus fruits.
cit·rine (sit′rin) *adj.* **1** Having the yellow color of a citron or lemon. **2** Pertaining to the citron, lemon, and allied trees. — *n.* **1** Citron color. **2** A light–yellow, vitreous variety of quartz so fused as to resemble topaz. [<F *citrin*]
cit·ron (sit′rən) *n.* **1** A fruit like a lemon, but larger and less acid. **2** The tree *(Citrus medica)* producing this fruit. **3** A watermelon *(Citrullus vulgaris citroides),* with a small, hard–fleshed fruit. **4** The rind of either of these fruits, preserved and used in confections. [<F <Ital. *citrone* <L *citrus* citrus tree]
cit·ron·el·la (sit′rə·nel′ə) *n.* A grass *(Cymbopogon nardus)* cultivated in Ceylon, yielding **citronella oil,** which is used in perfumery, in cooking for flavoring, and as protection against mosquitos. Also **citronella grass.** [< NL <CITRON; so called from its odor]
cit·ron·el·lal (sit′rə·nel′al) *n. Chem.* An unsaturated aldehyde, $C_9H_{17}CHO$, found in citronella oil and other essential oils: used in making soaps and perfumes.
citron wood **1** The wood of the sandarac tree, used in cabinetwork. **2** The wood of the citron tree.
cit·rus (sit′rəs) *adj.* Of or pertaining to a genus *(Citrus)* of trees or shrubs of the rue family, cultivated for their fruits. Also **cit′rous.** [<L, citron tree]
citrus fruits Fruits of the genus *Citrus*: the orange, lemon, lime, citron, grapefruit, etc.
Cit·tà del Va·ti·ca·no (chēt·tä′ del vä′tē·kä′nō) The Italian name for VATICAN CITY.
Cit·tà Vec·chia (chēt·tä′ vek′kyä) The Maltese name of MDINA. Also **Città No·ta·bi·le** (nō·tä′bē·lā).
cit·tern (sit′ərn) See CITHERN.
cit·y (sit′ē) *n. pl.* **cit·ies** **1** A place inhabited by a large, permanent, organized community. **2** In the United States and Canada, a municipality of the first class, governed by a mayor and aldermen and created by charter. **3** Any one of the ancient Greek city–states. **4** The people of a city, collectively. **5** In ancient times, a citadel or central walled section used by the dwellers in a district as a market, a place of worship or festivity, and a refuge in time of invasion. — **The City** That part of London which is governed by the Lord Mayor and corporation; also, the financial center of this district. [<F *cité* <L *civitas* < *civis* citizen]
city block **1** A division of a city bounded by four streets. **2** A unit of measure as long as this. **3** The distance along one side of it.
cit·y–bred (sit′ē·bred′) *adj.* Brought up in a city.
city editor On a newspaper, the editor having charge of the city news and the reportorial staff.
city father One who directs the public affairs of a city; a mayor, councilman, etc.
cit·y·fied (sit′i·fīd) See CITIFIED.
city hall **1** An administrative building of a city in which the chief government offices are situated. **2** The city government presently in office. **3** Bureaucratic procedures or officials characterized as obstinately unresponsive: Go fight *city hall.*
city manager An administrator not publicly elected but appointed by a city council to act as manager of the city.
City of God Heaven.
City of Seven Hills Rome.
city planning Public control of the physical development of a city, as by regulation of the size and use of buildings and streets, location of parks and public facilities, etc.
cit·y·scape (sit′ē·skāp′) *n.* A view of a city, as in a painting.
cit·y–state (sit′ē·stāt′) *n.* A state consisting of an independent city, having sovereignty over contiguous territories, as in ancient Greece.
cit·y·ward (sit′ē·wərd) *adj.* Directed toward the city. — *adv.* In the direction of the city.
Ciu·dad Bo·lí·var (syōō·thäth′ bō·lē′vär) A port on the Orinoco, SE Venezuela.
Ciudad Juá·rez (hwä′rās) A city in northern Mexico, on the Rio Grande; formerly *El Paso del Norte.* Also **Juárez.**
Ciudad Tru·jil·lo (trōō·hē′yō) The name of

the capital of the Dominican Republic from 1936–61, when its original name of Santo Domingo was restored.
Ciudad Vic·to·ria (vēk·tō′ryä) The capital of Tamaulipas state, Mexico.
civ·et (siv′it) *n.* **1** A substance of musklike odor, secreted by certain glands of the civet cat: used as a perfume. **2** A foxlike carnivore of Africa (genus *Viverra*), dark grey in color and banded and spotted with black, that secretes this substance: also **civet cat. 3** The fur of this animal. See ZIBET. [< MF *civette* < Arabic *zabād*]
civ·ic (siv′ik)*adj.* Of or pertaining to a city, a citizen, or citizenship; civil. [< L *civicus* < *civis* citizen]
civ·ics (siv′iks) *n.* The science of government.
civ·il (siv′əl) *adj.* **1** Observing the social proprieties; decently polite; not rude. **2** Of or pertaining to civil or everyday life: distinguished from *ecclesiastical, naval, military.* **3** Pertaining to citizens or to the state, or to relations between the citizen and the state or between citizens, as regulated by law; belonging to private legal rights; established by law: distinguished from *criminal, political,* or *natural*: civil rights. **4** Occurring within the state or between citizens; intestine: *civil* war. **5** In accordance with the requirements of civilization; civilized. **6** Of or pertaining to civil law. See CIVIL LAW. See synonyms under POLITE. [< F < L *civilis* < *civis* citizen] **—civ′il·ly** *adv.*
civil day See CIVIL TIME under TIME
civil death The total deprivation of civil rights and standing, as by life imprisonment, etc.
civil defense A program of action by civilians for the protection of the population and the maintenance of essential services in the event of overt enemy action, as nuclear bombardment.
civil disobedience Passive resistance.
civil engineer A professional engineer trained to design and build roads, bridges, tunnels, harbors, canals, docks, irrigation systems, and other public works.
ci·vil·ian (sə·vil′yən) *n.* **1** One who follows the pursuits of civil life, as distinguished from military, naval, or clerical. **2** *Obs.* One learned in the Roman or civil law. *—adj.* Of or pertaining to a civilian or civil life. [< OF *civilien* < L *civilis.* See CIVIL.]
ci·vil·i·ty (sə·vil′ə·tē) *n. pl.* **·ties 1** The quality of being civil; courtesy; cold or formal politeness. **2** A civil act or speech. **3** *pl.* The amenities of social life. See synonyms under FAVOR.
civ·i·li·za·tion (siv′ə·lə·zā′shən, -lī·zā′-) *n.* **1** The state of human society regarded as having reached a high level of intellectual, social, and cultural development. **2** The countries and peoples considered to have reached this stage. **3** A stage in the cultural development of any specific people, country, or geographical region: Greek *civilization;* a primitive *civilization.* See CULTURE.
civ·i·lize (siv′ə·līz) *v.t.* **·lized, ·liz·ing** To bring into a state of civilization; educate from savagery; refine. Also *Brit.* **civ′i·lise. —civ′i·lized** *adj.* **—civ′i·liz′er** *n.*
civil law See under LAW[1].
civil liberty Freedom of the individual citizen from government control or restraint of, or interference with, his property, opinions, or affairs, except as the public good may require.
civil list 1 That part of the revenue annually appropriated in the United States for the salaries and expenses of civil officers and the government. **2** The body of such officers. **3** In Great Britain and elsewhere, the amount voted by the legislature for the personal and household expenses of the sovereign.
civil marriage A marriage solemnized as a civil contract, as distinguished from an ecclesiastical marriage considered as a sacrament.
civil rights Private, non-political privileges; specifically, exemption from involuntary servitude, as established by the 13th and 14th amendments to the U.S. Constitution and by certain acts of Congress.
civil servant One employed in the civil service.
civil service 1 The branches of governmental service that are neither military, naval, legislative, or judicial. **2** The body of persons employed in these branches.
civil time See under TIME.
civil war War between parties of the same government, between states within a nation, between fellow citizens, etc.
Civil War See table under WAR.
civ·ism (siv′iz·əm) *n.* Devotion to the public weal; good citizenship.
Ci·vi·ta·vec·chia (chē·vē·tä·vek′kyä) A city on the Tyrrhenian Sea, the chief port for Rome.
Cl *Chem.* Chlorine (symbol Cl).
clab·ber[1] (klab′ər) *n.* Milk curdled by souring. *—v.t. & v.i.* To curdle, as milk. [Short for BONNYCLABBER]
clab·ber[2] (klab′ər) *n.* Mire; mud. [< Irish *clabar*]
clach·an (klakh′ən) *n. Scot.* A Highland hamlet; also, a village inn or a village church. Also **clach** (klakh).
clack (klak) *v.t.* **1** To strike together so as to make a cracking sound; clap; rattle. **2** To utter heedlessly; babble. *—v.i.* **3** To make a rattling, clapping, or cracking sound. **4** To talk hastily or continually; chatter. **5** To cluck or cackle, as a hen. *—n.* **1** A sharp, short, clapping sound, or something producing it. **2** Continual and confused talk; chatter. **3** *Slang* The tongue: Hold your *clack*; hence, a gossip. [Imit.] **—clack′er** *n.*
Clack·man·nan (klak·man′ən) A country in east central Scotland; 54.6 square miles; county seat, Clackmannan. Also **Clack·man′nan·shire** (-shir).
clack valve *Mech.* A valve hinged at one edge, permitting flow of fluid in one direction only. See illustration under HYDRAULIC.
Clac·to·ni·an (klak·tō′nē·ən) *adj. Anthropol.* Pertaining to a culture stage of the Lower Paleolithic, roughly contemporaneous with the Abbevillian but characterized by stone tools of a more advanced flake type. [from *Clacton,* England, where artifacts were found]
clad (klad) Past tense of CLOTHE. *—adj.* Clothed.
cla·dis·tics (klə·dis′tiks) *n.* A branch of biology dealing with the evolutionary interrelationships of organisms. [< Gk. *klados* sprout + (STAT)ISTICS]
clad·o·phyll (klad′ə·fil) *n. Bot.* A leaflike branch stemming from the axil of a leaf. Also **clad·ode** (klad′ōd). [< Gk. *klados* branch + *phyllos* leaf]
claim (klām) *v.t.* **1** To demand on the ground or right; affirm to be one's due; assert ownership or title to. **2** To hold to be true against implied denial or doubt. **3** To require or deserve: The problem *claims* our attention. *—v.i.* **4** To derive a right; make a claim, especially by descent: He *claims* from royal lineage. See synonyms under ALLEGE, ASSERT, ASSUME, DEMAND. *—n.* **1** The demand for something as due or on the ground of right; the assertion of a right; a right or title. **2** An assertion, as of a fact. **3** A tract of government land, petitioned for, marked out, and claimed by a settler. **4** A piece of public land staked out by a miner to be worked by him. See synonyms under RIGHT. **—Court of Claims** See under COURT. [< OF *clamer* call, claim < L *clamare* declare] **—claim′a·ble** *adj.* **—claim′er** *n.*
claim·ant (klā′mənt) *n.* One who makes a legal claim or asserts a right, title, etc.
claiming race A horse race in which any horse entered is subject to the claim of right to buy for a given price by any registrant starting a horse in that meeting
claim-jum·per (klām′jum′pər) *n.* One who seizes another's claim.
clair de lune (klâr′ də lün′) **1** In ceramics, a faint, grayish-blue glaze applied to certain varieties of Chinese porcelain. **2** The color of this glaze. [< F, moonlight] **—clair′-de-lune′** *adj.*
Claire (klâr) French form of CLARA.
clair-ob·scure (klâr′əb·skyŏŏr′) See CHIAROSCURO.
clair·schach (klär′shäkh) *n.* An ancient Irish harp; especially, a festival harp having from 29 to 58 strings. [< Irish *clairseach* harp]
clair·voy·ance (klâr·voi′əns) *n.* **1** The ability to see things not visible to the normal human eye; second sight. **2** Intuitive sagacity or perception; mind-reading. [< F] **—clair·voy′ant** *adj. & n.*
claise (klāz) *n. Scot.* Clothes. Also **claithes** (klāz).
claith (klāth) *n. Scot.* Cloth.
clam[1] (klam) *n.* **1** Any of various bivalve mollusks; especially, the edible quahog of North Atlantic American coasts, and the **long** or **soft clam** *(Mya arenaria)* of the southern Atlantic coasts. **2** *U.S. Colloq.* An uncommunicative person. **—giant clam** A huge bivalve mollusk *(Tridacna gigas)* of the Indian and Pacific Oceans: the shell may exceed 3 feet in length and weigh more than 500 pounds. *—v.i.* **clammed, clam·ming** to hunt for or dig clams. **—to clam up** *U.S. Slang* To maintain silence, as a criminal under interrogation. [Short for *clamshell* < *clam* a clamp, OE *clamm* + SHELL]

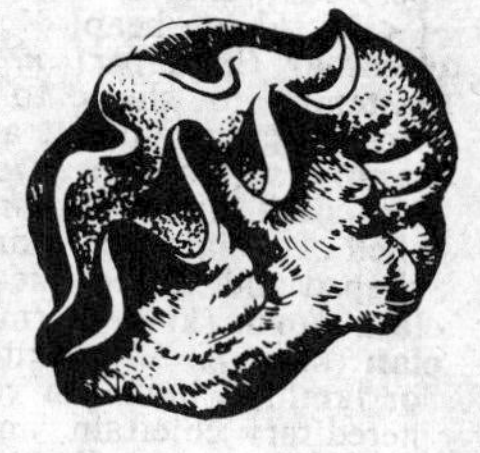

GIANT CLAM

clam[2] (klam) *Brit. Dial. v.t.* To smear with a sticky substance; glue or stick: to *clam* paper to the wall. *—v.i.* To be sticky or clammy; be damp or cold. *—adj.* Sticky. *—n.* **1** Clamminess; cold dampness. **2** A sticky substance. [Cf. OE *clæman* smear, Du. *klam* sticky]
clam[3] (klam) *n.* A clamp, as of bricks. [OE *clamm* grip, grasp]
clam[4] (klam) *Brit. n.* The simultaneous ringing of all the bells in a chime; hence, clangor; clamor. *—v.i.* **1** To ring all the bells of a chime together. **2** To muffle or jangle a bell. [Imit.]
cla·mant (klā′mənt) *adj.* **1** Calling for help or remedy; crying; insistent. **2** Clamorous; resounding: a poetic usage. [< L *clamans, -antis,* ppr. of *clamare* cry out]
clam·a·to·ri·al (klam′ə·tôr′ē·əl, -tō′rē) *adj. Ornithol.* Relating to a suborder *(Clamatores)* of raucous-voiced passerine birds, as the kingbirds. [< NL *Clamatores* < L *clamare* cry out]
clam·bake (klam′bāk′) *n.* **1** A picnic where roasted clams are the principal dish: especially common at the seashore in New England, where the clams, often with other articles of food, are usually cooked on hot stones, sometimes in a hole covered with seaweed. **2** The meal served at such a picnic. **3** *U.S. Slang* A radio broadcast that breaks down because of bad handling and mistakes; any poor broadcast. **4** *U.S. Slang* An informal gathering of jazz musicians to improvise music for their own enjoyment.
clam·ber (klam′bər) *v.t. & v.i.* To climb up, down, or along by using hands and feet; also, to climb by attaching tendrils, as certain vines. [Akin to CLIMB] **—clam′ber·er** *n.*
clam·jam·fer·y (klam·jam′fər·ē) *n. Scot.* **1** Rubbish; trumpery. **2** Worthless people. Also **clam·jam·phrie** (klam·jam′frē).
clam·my (klam′ē) *adj.* **·mi·er, ·mi·est 1** Damp and cold. **2** Soft and sticky. [< CLAM[2] *adj.*] **—clam′mi·ly** *adv.* **—clam′mi·ness** *n.*
clam·or[1] (klam′ər) *n.* **1** Any loud, repeated outcry, din, or noise; vociferation; noisy confusion of voices. **2** A continuous, vehement objecting or demanding; public outcry. See synonyms under NOISE. *—v.t.* **1** To utter with loud outcry. **2** To move or drive by clamor. *—v.i.* **3** To make loud outcries, demands, or complaints; vociferate. Also *Brit.* **clam′our.** [< OF < L < *clamare* cry out] **—clam′or·er** *n.*
clam·or[2] (klam′ər) *v.t. & v.i. Obs.* To stop the noise of; silence: often with *down.* Also *Brit.* **clam′our.** [< CLAM[4]]
clam·or·ous (klam′ər·əs) *adj.* Making or made with clamor; noisy. See synonyms under NOISY. **—clam′or·ous·ly** *adv.* **—clam′or·ous·ness** *n.*
clamp[1] (klamp) *n.* A device for compressing, holding in position, or binding together two or more parts. *—v.t.* To join or bind with or as with a clamp. [< M Du. *klampe*]

clamp[2] (klamp) *v.i.* To walk heavily; tramp. —*n.* A heavy tread; tramp. [Imit.]

clamp[3] (klamp) *n.* **1** *Brit.* A kiln with impervious walls. **2** A pile or heap, as of ore. [<Du. *klamp* heap]

clamp·er (klam′pər) *n.* An attachment for fastening to shoes to prevent the wearer from slipping on ice; a creeper.

clamp·ers (klam′pərz) *n. pl. Scot.* Pliers.

clam·shell (klam′shel′) *n.* **1** The shell or half-shell of a clam. **2** A dredging box or bucket shaped and hinged like the shell of a clam.

clam·worm (klam′wûrm′) *n.* Nereis.

clan (klan) *n.* **1** A united group of relatives, or families, having a common ancestor, one hereditary chieftain, and the same surname, especially in the Scottish Highlands. **2** In certain primitive societies, a body of kindred related in only one line, the members of which do not intermarry, having its own council, property, religion, etc.; an exogamous subdivision of a tribe: also called *sib.* **3** A clique, or set of persons; a fraternity; club. See synonyms under CLASS. [<Scottish Gaelic *clann*]

clan·des·tine (klan·des′tin) *adj.* Kept secret for a purpose; concealed; surreptitious; furtive; underhand. See synonyms under SECRET. [<L *clandestinus* < *clam* in secret] —**clan·des′tine·ly** *adv.* —**clan·des′tine·ness** *n.*

clang (klang) *v.t.* **1** To cause to send forth a loud, ringing metallic sound. —*v.i.* **2** To send forth such a sound: The bells *clanged.* **3** To strike together with such a sound: The shields *clanged* together. —*n.* **1** A ringing sound, as of metal struck. **2** In acoustics, a tone with its overtones; acoustic color; timbre. **3** The ringing call of cranes or geese. [Prob. imit. Cf. L *clangere.*]

clan·gor (klang′gər, klang′ər) *n.* Repeated clanging; a clanging or noisy ringing; clamor. —*v.i.* To ring noisily; clang. Also *Brit.* **clan′gour.** [<L < *clangere* clang] —**clan′gor·ous** *adj.* —**clan′gor·ous·ly** *adv.*

clank (klangk) *n.* An abrupt, short, harsh, metallic sound. —*v.t.* & *v.i.* To emit, or cause to emit, a clank. [Blend of CLANG and CLINK]

clan·nish (klan′ish) *adj.* **1** Like a clan; disposed to cling together. **2** Bound by family tradition, class, or clan prejudice, etc.; narrow. —**clan′nish·ly** *adv.* —**clan′nish·ness** *n.*

clan·ship (klan′ship) *n.* Union under a chief.

clans·man (klanz′mən) *n. pl.* **·men** (-mən) A member of a clan or of the same clan.

clap[1] (klap) *v.* **clapped** or **clapt, clap·ping** *v.t.* **1** To strike together with a sharp, explosive sound. **2** To applaud by clapping the hands. **3** To strike suddenly, as in greeting. **4** To place quickly or suddenly. **5** To make or build hastily: often with *together* or *up.* **6** To flap, as wings. **7** *Obs.* To shut, as a door or window. —*v.i.* **8** To come together with a sharp, explosive sound, as flat surfaces. **9** To applaud by striking the hands together. **10** *Archaic* To close with a clapping sound. —**to clap eyes on** To see. —*n.* **1** A sharp sudden noise, as of two hard flat objects coming together. **2** The act of striking sharply together flatwise: a *clap* of the hands. **3** A sudden, but slight blow with the flat of the hand; a slap. **4** *Obs.* A sudden stroke or event. [OE *clæppan*]

clap[2] (klap) *n.* Gonorrhea: usually with *the*: a vulgarism. [<OF *clapoir* a venereal sore]

clap·board (klab′ərd, klap′bôrd′, -bōrd′) *n.* **1** A lapping weatherboard, usually with one edge thicker than the other. **2** A rived roofing board larger than a shingle. —*v.t.* To cover with clapboards. [Partial trans. of MDu. *klapholt* barrel stave]

clap·per (klap′ər) *n.* **1** One who or that which claps, as the tongue of a bell, or either of a pair of sticks, bones, or the like, held between the fingers and struck together, as an accompaniment to music. **2** *Slang* The tongue; also, the mouth.

clap·per·claw (klap′ər·klô′) *v.t.* & *v.i.* **1** *Obs.* To slap, scratch, and claw; attack with tooth and nail. **2** To scold vehemently.

clap·trap (klap′trap) *n.* **1** Any device, language, or conduct designed to evoke applause. **2** Cheap, sensational, or unworthy artifice.

claque (klak) *n.* Hired applauders in a theater. **2** Any set of persons concerting to praise or applaud from interested motives. [<F < *claquer* clap]

Clar·a (klar′ə, klâr′ə; *Du., Ger., Pg., Sp.* klä′rä) A feminine personal name. [<L, famous]

clar·a·bel·la (klar′ə·bel′ə) *n.* An organ stop with open wooden pipes, giving a soft, sweet tone. [<L *clarus* clear + *bellus* pretty]

clar·ain (klâr·ān′) *n. Geol.* A type of bituminous coal having a finely banded structure of translucent materials which impart a bright, silky luster. [<L *clarus* clear + (FUS)AIN]

Clare (klâr) Diminutive of CLARA or CLARISSA. —**Clare of Assisi, Saint** Italian founder of the Order of Poor Clares in 1212, under the rule given to her by Saint Francis.

Clare (klâr) A county in Munster province, western Ireland; 1,231 square miles; county seat, Ennis.

Clar·ence (klar′əns) A masculine personal name. [after the Duke of *Clarence*] —**Clarence, Duke of,** 1449–78, George Plantagenet, brother of Edward IV and Richard III of England; murdered.

clar·ence (klar′əns) *n.* A four-wheeled, closed carriage, having seats for four persons inside and, usually, a glass front. [after the Duke of *Clarence*, later William IV of England]

clar·en·don (klar′ən·dən) *n. Printing* A style of type having a somewhat heavy and condensed face. [from the *Clarendon* Press, Oxford, England]

Clar·en·don (klar′ən·dən), **Earl of,** 1609–74, Edward Hyde, English royalist statesman, historian, premier, and lord chancellor.

clar·et (klar′ət) *n.* **1** Any red table wine; especially, one from the region around Bordeaux. **2** A loose color term for various shades ranging from ruby to a deep purplish-red. [<OF *(vin)claret* clear (wine) < *cler* <L *clarus* bright]

Clar·i·bel (klar′ə·bel) A feminine personal name. [<L, brightly fair]

Clar·ice (klar′is, klə·rēs′) See CLARISSA.

clar·i·fy (klar′ə·fī) *v.* **·fied, ·fy·ing** *v.t.* **1** To make clear or understandable. **2** To free from impurities, as wines or fats. —*v.i.* **3** To become clear or transparent. **4** To become understandable or clear: The situation *clarified.* See synonyms under PURIFY. [<OF *clarifier* <LL *clarificare* < *clarus* clear + *facere* make] —**clar′i·fi·ca′tion** *n.* —**clar′i·fi′er** *n.*

clar·i·net (klar′ə·net′) *n.* **1** A cylindrical wood-

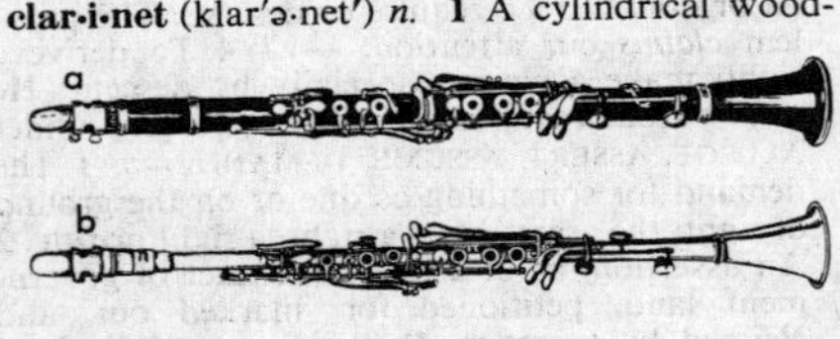

CLARINETS
a. Wood.
b. Metal.

wind instrument with bell mouth, having a single reed mouthpiece, finger holes, and keys. Clarinets are made in various keys and sizes: those in B♭ and A are used in both orchestras and jazz bands; those in C and E♭ are used in jazz bands only. **2** An organ stop having a sound similar to that of a clarinet. Also **clar·i·o·net** (klar′ē·ə·net′). —**bass clarinet** A large clarinet pitched an octave lower than the common B♭ clarinet. [<F *clarinette,* dim. of *clarine* bell] —**clar′i·net′ist** or **clar′i·net′·tist** *n.*

clar·i·on (klar′ē·ən) *n.* **1** A small trumpet. **2** The sound of a trumpet, or any sound resembling it. —*v.t.* & *v.i.* To proclaim with or as with a clarion; blow a clarion. —*adj.* Shrill; clear. [<OF *claron, clairon* <L *clarus* clear]

Cla·ris·sa (klə·ris′ə; *Ger.* klä·ris′ä, *Ital.* klä·rēs′sä) A feminine personal name. Also *Clarice.* [<L, famous]

clar·i·ty (klar′ə·tē) *n.* Clearness as of sight, language, understanding, etc.

Clark (klärk), **Champ,** 1850–1921, James Beauchamp Clark, U.S. politician. —**George Rogers,** 1752–1818, American soldier and pioneer. —**Mark Wayne,** born 1896, U.S. general. —**Thomas Campbell,** born 1899, U.S. jurist; associate justice of the Supreme Court. —**William,** 1770–1838, brother of George Rogers; with Meriwether Lewis, led expedition to Columbia River, 1804–06.

Clark Fork River A river in Montana and Idaho, flowing 360 miles NW in the Columbia River system.

cla·ro (klä′rō) *adj.* Light in color and mild: said of cigars. [<Sp.]

clart·y (klär′tē) *adj.* **clart·i·er, clart·i·est** *Brit. Dial.* Dirty; sticky. [Origin unknown]

clar·y (klâr′ē) *n. pl.* **clar·ies** Any of several species of sage; especially, the common clary (*Salvia sclarea*), native in Italy, Syria, etc.; and the wild English or vervain clary (*S. verbenaca*). [<F *sclarée* <Med. L *sclarea*]

clash (klash) *v.t.* **1** To strike or dash together or against with a confused, harsh, metallic sound. —*v.i.* **2** To collide with loud and confused noise; to collide. **3** To conflict; be in opposition. —*n.* A confused, resounding, metallic noise, as of striking or colliding; collision; conflict, opposition. See synonyms under COLLISION [Imit. Cf. CLAP, DASH.]

clasp (klasp, kläsp) *n.* **1** A fastening by which things are bound together. **2** A firm grasp or embrace. **3** A small bar affixed to the ribbon of a military decoration: a **battle clasp** designates the campaign in which the wearer has taken part, a **service clasp** the country in which he has served. See synonyms under LOCK. —*v.t.* **1** To take hold of with an encircling grasp; embrace. **2** To fasten with or as with a clasp. **3** To grasp firmly in or with the hand. See synonyms under CATCH, EMBRACE, GRASP. [ME *claspe;* origin unknown]

clasp·er (klas′pər, kläs′-) *n.* **1** One who or that which clasps. **2** *Zool.* **a** One of the paired organs accessory to copulation in various animals, as the external genital organs in male insects, etc. **b** One of the grooved cartilaginous appendages to the ventral fins of sharks, rays, etc.

clasp knife A knife with a blade that folds into the handle; a pocket knife.

class (klas, kläs) *n.* **1** A number or body of persons with common characteristics: the educated *class.* **2** Social rank; caste. **3** A group of students under one teacher, or pursuing a study together; a group of students in a school or college having the same standing and graduating together. **4** *Biol.* A group of plants or animals standing below a phylum and above an order. **5** A number of objects, facts, or events having common accidental or essential properties; a set; kind. **6** A grading according to quality, value, or rank: first-*class* mail; to travel second-*class.* **7** *Slang* Superiority; elegance. —**the classes** The wealthier, more educated, or higher social classes. —*v.t.* To arrange or group according to characteristics or properties; assign to a class; classify. —*v.i. Rare* To be placed or ranked, as in a class. [<F *classe* <L *classis* group, class]

Synonyms (noun): association, caste, circle, clan, clique, club, company, coterie, grade, order, rank, set. A *caste* is hereditary; a *class* may be independent of lineage or descent; membership in a *caste* is normally for life, and hereditary; membership in a *class* may be very transient; a religious and ceremonial sacredness attaches to the *caste,* but not to the *class. Grade* implies some regular scale of valuation; as, the coarser and finer *grades* of wool. A *coterie* is a small company of persons of similar tastes. A *clique* is always fractional, implying some greater gathering of which it it is a part; the *association* breaks up into *cliques.* A *set,* while exclusive, is more intensive than a *clique,* and chiefly of persons who are united by common social station, etc. *Circle* is similar in meaning to *set,* but of wider application; we speak of scientific as well as of social *circles.*

class-con·scious·ness (klas′kon′shəs·nis, kläs′-) *n.* Awareness among a social group of its own nature, interests, and unity. —**class′-con′·scious** *adj.*

class day A day set apart, during school or college commencements, for exercises and ceremonies relating to and conducted by the graduating class.

clas·sic (klas′ik) *adj.* **1** Belonging to the first class or rank in literature or art. **2** Pertaining to standard and authoritative principles and forms in art, literature, music, etc. **3** Connected with or made famous by the ancient Greek or Latin authors. Compare ROMANTIC. **4** Balanced; formal; finished; regular; simple; austere: a term variously interpreted, and often opposed to *romantic.* **5** Having literary or historical traditions: *classic* lands. See synonyms under PURE. —*n.* **1** A work of literature or art, generally recognized

as excellent; especially, one of Greek or Roman workmanship or authorship. 2 *Rare* One who is familiar with classical literature. 3 Any author whose work is generally accepted as being a standard of excellence. — **the classics** Greek and Roman literature and authors. [<L *classicus* of the first rank < *classis* order, class]

clas·si·cal (klas′i·kəl) *adj.* 1 Of, pertaining to, or characteristic of ancient Greek and Roman art and literature. 2 Learned in, or based on Greek and Latin: a *classical* education. 3 Formal; finished; polished; modeled after Greek and Roman forms: often opposed to *romantic.* 4 Being of or modeled after the best in art, music, or literature. 5 *Music* **a** Following strict and established form, as a fugue or sonata. **b** Composed by the great masters. 6 *Physics* Pertaining to or describing those physical theories based upon or derived from Newtonian mechanics, especially as distinguished from relativity theory and quantum mechanics. — **clas′si·cal·ly** *adv.*

clas·si·cal·ism (klas′i·kəl·iz′əm) *n.* 1 Adherence to, imitation or knowledge of Greek or Roman art, literature, or antiquities. 2 Classicism.

clas·si·cal·i·ty (klas′ə·kal′ə·tē) *n.* 1 The quality of being classical. 2 An instance, exemplification, or piece of classicality; a classical characteristic. 3 Classicism. Also **clas′si·cal·ness.**

clas·si·cism (klas′ə·siz′əm) *n.* 1 Classic principles and style. 2 Any idiom found in the classics. 3 Adherence to or imitation of the classic style in literature or art. 4 Classical scholarship.

clas·si·cist (klas′ə·sist) *n.* 1 One versed in the classics. 2 An adherent or imitator of classic style.

clas·si·cize (klas′ə·sīz) *v.* **·cized, ·ciz·ing** *v.t.* To make classic. — *v.i.* To affect the classic style.

clas·si·fi·ca·tion (klas′ə·fə·kā′shən) *n.* 1 The act, process, or result of classifying. 2 Taxonomy. 3 Systematics. 4 The systematic arrangement of books, documents, archives, and other printed material in accordance with categories, as of subject, author, time, etc.

clas·si·fi·ca·to·ry (klas′ə·fə·kā′tər·ē, klə·sif′ə·kə·tôr′ē, -tō′rē) *adj.* Of or pertaining to classification; taxonomical.

clas·si·fy (klas′ə·fī) *v.t.* **·fied, ·fy·ing** 1 To arrange or put in a class or classes on the basis of resemblance or differences. 2 To declare or designate as of aid to an enemy and restrict as to circulation or use, as a document, weapon, or item of information. [<L *classis* class + -FY] — **clas′si·fi′a·ble** *adj.* — **clas′si·fi′er** *n.*

clas·sis (klas′is) *n. pl.* **clas·ses** (klas′ēz) 1 A court in the Dutch and German Reformed churches, composed of ministers and ruling elders. 2 The district it represents. [<L]

class·mate (klas′māt′, kläs′-) *n.* A member of the same class in school or college.

class·room (klas′ro͞om′, -ro͝om′, kläs′-) *n.* 1 A room allotted to a certain class in a school. 2 A room in a school or college in which recitations and lectures are held.

class struggle The conflict between classes in society; particularly, the economic struggle for power between employers, as a general class or group, and employees.

class·y (klas′ē) *adj. Slang* **class·i·er, class·i·est** Grand; elegant.

clas·tic (klas′tik) *adj.* 1 *Biol.* Breaking, separating, or dividing into parts: a *clastic* cell. 2 Something that may be taken apart and reassembled: a *clastic* anatomical model. 3 *Geol.* Composed of fragments, especially of preexisting rocks: distinguished from *crystalline.* [<Gk. *klastos* broken]

clath·rate (klath′rāt) *n. Chem.* Any of a class of organic compounds whose molecules are so interlocked through hydrogen bonds as to form 3-dimensional lattices exhibiting trigonal symmetry. — *adj.* 1 Designating such a compound. 2 Having a latticelike appearance. [<L *clathri* lattice]

clat·ter (klat′ər) *v.i.* 1 To make a rattling noise or racket; give out short, sharp noises rapidly or repeatedly. 2 To advance, go, or proceed with a rattling noise. 3 To chatter; tattle. — *v.t.* 4 To cause to make a rattling noise. — *n.* 1 A rattling noise. 2 Noisy talk; chatter. See synonyms under NOISE. [OE *clatrung* a clattering noise] — **clat′ter·er** *n.*

Claude (klôd, *Fr.* klōd) A masculine personal name. See CLAUDIUS.

Claude Lor·rain (klōd lô·raṅ′) See LORRAIN, CLAUDE.

Clau·del (klō·del′), **Paul,** 1868–1955, French diplomat, poet, and dramatist.

Clau·di·a (klô′dē·ə; *Du., Ger., Ital., Sw.* klou′dē·ä; *Sp.* klou′thē·ä) A feminine personal name: feminine of CLAUDIUS.

Clau·di·an (klô′dē·ən) *adj.* Of or pertaining to the Roman emperors of the Claudius family (Tiberius, Caligula, Claudius, and Nero, A.D. 14–68).

Clau·di·an (klô′dē·ən), 365–408, Latin epic poet. Also *Latin* **Clau·di·us Clau·di·a·nus** (klô′dē·əs klô′dē·ā′nəs).

clau·di·cant (klô′di·kənt) *adj. Obs.* Limping; lame. [<L *claudicans, -antis,* ppr. of *claudicare* limp < *claudus* lame]

clau·di·ca·tion (klô′di·kā′shən) *n.* A limp or the act of limping.

Clau·dine (klō·dēn′) French form of CLAUDIA.

Clau·di·us (klô′dē·əs; *Dan., Du., Ger., Sw.* klou′dē·o͞os) A masculine personal name. Also *Ital., Sp.* **Clau·di·o** (*Ital.* klou′dē·ō, *Sp.* -thē·ō). [<L, lame]

— **Claudius** In Shakespeare's *Hamlet,* king of Denmark, Hamlet's stepfather and uncle.

— **Claudius, Appius,** Roman decemvir. See APPIUS.

— **Claudius I,** 10 B.C.–A.D. 54, Tiberius Claudius Drusus, Roman emperor 41–54; successor to Caligula.

— **Claudius II,** 214–270, Marcus Aurelius Claudius, Roman emperor 268–270.

Clau·di·us (klou′dē·o͞os), **Matthias,** 1740–1815, German poet.

claught (klôkht) *Scot. v.t.* To seize; clutch. — *n.* 1 A grasp; clutch. 2 A handful.

clause (klôz) *n.* 1 *Gram.* A group of words containing a subject and predicate, but forming a subordinate part of a compound or complex sentence: distinguished from *phrase.* 2 A distinct part of a composition, as a paragraph or article. 3 A separate statement or proviso in a legal or state document. — **principal clause** *Gram.* The clause which contains the main predication of a sentence. — **relative clause** *Gram.* A subordinate clause introduced by a relative pronoun. — **subordinate** (or **dependent**) **clause** *Gram.* A clause which has the effect of a noun, adjective, or adverb in the structure of a sentence. [<OF <Med. L *clausa* <L *clausus,* pp. of *claudere* close] — **claus′al** *adj.*

Clau·se·witz (klou′zə·vits), **Karl von,** 1780–1831, Prussian general and writer.

Clau·si·us (klou′zē·əs), **Rudolf Julius Emanuel,** 1822–88, German physicist.

claus·tral (klôs′trəl) *adj.* Cloistral.

claus·tro·pho·bi·a (klôs′trə·fō′bē·ə) *n. Psychiatry* Morbid fear of enclosed or confined places. [<L *claustrum* a closed place + -PHOBIA] — **claus′tro·pho′bic** *adj.*

clau·su·ra (klô·zho͞o′rə) *n.* In the Roman Catholic Church, the rule which separates part of a monastery or convent from outsiders. [<L, a barrier < *claudere* close]

claut (klôt) *Scot. n.* 1 A rake, hoe, etc. 2 A grasping clutch. 3 A handful. 4 A lump or piece. — *v.t.* To scratch; scrape; rake.

cla·vate (klā′vāt) *adj. Biol.* Denoting an organ or part having a thickened or bulbous end; club-shaped. Also **cla′vat·ed.** [<L *clavatus,* pp. of *clavare* stud with nails; infl. in meaning by L *clava* club] — **cla′vate·ly** *adv.*

clave (klāv) Archaic past tense of CLEAVE[1] and CLEAVE[2].

clav·e·cin (klav′ə·sin) *n.* A harpsichord. [<F] — **clav′e·cin·ist** *n.*

cla·ver (klā′vər, klav′ər) *v.t. Scot.* To talk idly; gossip. — *n.* Foolish or empty talk; gossip.

clav·i·chord (klav′ə·kôrd) *n.* A keyboard musical instrument whose tones are produced by the blow of brass pins on horizontal strings: a forerunner of the piano. [<Med. L *clavichordium* <L *clavis* key + *chorda* string]

clav·i·cle (klav′ə·kəl) *n. Anat.* The bone connecting the shoulder blade and breastbone; collar bone. [<L *clavicula,* dim. of *clavis* key] — **cla·vic·u·lar** (klə·vik′yə·lər) *adj.*

clav·i·corn (klav′ə·kôrn) *adj. Entomol.* Of, pertaining to, or belonging to a superfamily of beetles (*Staphylinoidea,* formerly *Clavicornia*) having club-shaped antennae. [<NL *Clavicornia* <L *clava* club + *cornu* horn] — **clav·i·cor·nate** (klav′ə·kôr′nāt) *adj.*

clav·i·er (klav′ē·ər, klə·vir′ *for defs. 1 and 3;* klə·vir′ *for def. 2*) *n.* 1 A keyboard. 2 Any keyboard stringed instrument, as a clavichord, etc.; especially, a piano. 3 A dummy keyboard: used for the perfection of technique. [<F, keyboard <L *clavis* key]

clav·i·form (klav′ə·fôrm) *adj.* Club-shaped; clavate. [<L *clava* club + -FORM]

claw (klô) *n.* 1 *Zool.* **a** A sharp, usually curved, horny nail on the toe of a bird, mammal, or reptile. **b** A limb terminating in a claw or pincers, as in certain insects and crustaceans. 2 Anything sharp and hooked. 3 A stroke, clutch, or scratch from or as with claws. — *v.t. & v.i.* To tear, scratch, dig, pull, etc., as with claws. [OE *clawu*]

claw hammer 1 A hammer with one end of its head forked and curved like a claw for drawing nails. See illustration under HAMMER. 2 *Colloq.* A swallowtail coat or dress coat: from its shape.

claw hatchet A hatchet having the head forked at one end. See illustration under HATCHET.

clax·on (klak′sən) See KLAXON.

clay (klā) *n.* 1 A common earth of various colors and fine texture, compact and brittle when dry, but plastic and tenacious when wet. It is a hydrous aluminum silicate, generally mixed with powdered feldspar, quartz, sand, iron oxides, and various other minerals. 2 Earth in general. 3 Earth as a symbol of the human body; also, the body itself. See synonyms under BODY. — *v.t.* To cover, mix, or treat with clay. [OE *clæg*] — **clay′ish** *adj.*

Clay (klā), **Henry,** 1777–1852, U.S. statesman and orator.

clay·bank (klā′bangk′) *n.* 1 A bank of clay: also **clay′bluff′.** 2 A yellowish-brown color. 3 A horse of this color.

clay-eat·er (klā′ē′tər) *n.* 1 A person who eats clay. Compare GEOPHAGY. 2 *U.S. Slang* A poor white of North or South Carolina: a contemptuous use.

clay·ey (klā′ē) *adj.* **clay·i·er, clay·i·est** Of, like, abounding in, mixed or covered with clay.

clay·more (klā′môr, -mōr) *n.* A double-edged broadsword of the Scottish Highlanders. [<Scottish Gaelic *claidheamh* sword + *mor* great]

clay pigeon In trapshooting, a saucer-shaped disk of some brittle material, as baked clay, projected from a trap as a flying target.

clay stone 1 One of the concretionary nodules found in alluvial clay. 2 A dull-colored igneous rock containing feldspar and clay in a compact mass.

Clay·ton (klā′tən), **John Middleton,** 1796–1856, U.S. lawyer and statesman.

clay·to·ni·a (klā·tō′nē·ə) *n.* One of a genus (*Claytonia*) of low herbs of the purslane family: also called *springbeauty.* [after John *Clayton,* 1693–1773, botanist, of Virginia]

-cle *suffix of nouns* Small; minute: *particle; corpuscle.* [<F <L *-culus,* dim. suffix]

clean (klēn) *adj.* 1 Free from dirt, soil, impurity, or defilement; unblemished; pure. 2 Ginned: *clean* cotton. 3 Free from bungling; dexterous; complete: He's a *clean* shot. 4 Well-proportioned; symmetrical. 5 Ceremonially pure; conforming to the ceremonial law. 6 Completely cleared or rid of something. 7 Having no imperfection; perfect; whole. 8 Clear: a *clean* title to land. 9 In baseball, without error. — *v.t.* 1 To purify or cleanse; to free from dirt or impurities. 2 To draw and prepare (fowl, game, etc.) for cooking. — *v.i.* 3 To undergo or perform the act of cleaning. — **to clean out** 1 To clear of trash or rubbish. 2 To force out; overcome: to *clean* the gangsters *out* of town. 3 To empty (a place) of contents or occupants: The crowd *cleaned out* the store. 4 *Colloq.* To leave without money: The depression *cleaned* him *out.* — **to clean up** 1 To remove dirt; put in order: Today we *clean up.* 2 *Colloq.* To win a large amount or make large profits. 3 *Colloq.* To defeat: to *clean up* the enemy.

4 To remove undesirable persons or scandalous activities from: to *clean up* politics. — *adv.* In a clean manner; unqualifiedly, wholly. [OE *clæne* clear, pure] — **clean′a·ble** *adj.* — **clean′ness** *n.*

clean–cut (klēn′kut′) *adj.* 1 Cut with smooth edge or surface; made with skill and neatness. 2 Sharply defined. 3 Clear. 4 Neat in appearance; trim: a *clean–cut* young man.

clean·er (klē′nər) *n.* 1 One who or that which cleans. 2 Any substance or mechanical device which removes dirt.

clean·ly (klen′lē) *adj.* 1 Habitually and carefully clean; neat; tidy; clean. 2 Cleansing. — *adv.* (klēn′lē) In a clean manner. — **clean·li·ness** (klen′lē·nis) *n.*

cleanse (klenz) *v.t.* **cleansed, cleans·ing** To free from dirt or defilement; clean; purge. [OE *clænsian* < *clæne* clean] — **cleans′er** *n.*

Synonyms: brush, clean, disinfect, dust, mop, purify, rinse, scour, scrub, sponge, sweep, wash, wipe. *Cleanse* implies a worse condition to start from, and more to do, than *clean*; as, Hercules *cleansed* the Augean stables. *Cleanse* and *purify* are used extensively in a moral sense; *wash* in that sense is archaic. See AMEND, PURIFY. *Antonyms*: befoul, besmear, besmirch, bespatter, contaminate, corrupt, debase, defile, deprave, pollute, soil, spoil, stain, sully, taint, vitiate.

Cle·an·thes (klē·an′thēz) Greek Stoic philosopher of the third century B.C.

clean–up (klēn′up′) *n.* 1 *U.S. Colloq.* A big financial success. 2 In mining, the periodic collecting of gold or other mineral from the gravel in the sluices.

clear (klir) *adj.* 1 Free from anything that dims or darkens; light. 2 Unclouded; distinct; intelligible. 3 Able to see, discern, or discriminate: a *clear* mind. 4 Free from obstruction or hindrance. 5 Free from encumbrance, responsibility, or guilt. 6 Free from adulteration, defect, or blemish. 7 Without deduction; net. 8 Undisturbed; serene. 9 Plain; evident. 10 Free from uncertainty. 11 Without trees or underbrush, as land. 12 Without knots or imperfections, as lumber or shingles. — *v.t.* 1 To make clear; brighten. 2 To free from foreign matter, impurities, blemishes, or muddiness. 3 To remove, as obstructions, in making clear: to *clear* dishes from the table. 4 To disentangle: to *clear* a rope. 5 To free from imputations or accusations of guilt; acquit. 6 To free from doubt or ambiguity; make plain. 7 To free from debt by payment. 8 To pass or get by or over without touching: to *clear* a fence. 9 To obtain or give clearance, as for a ship or cargo. 10 To net or gain over and above expenses. 11 To pass through a clearing–house, as a check. — *v.i.* 12 To become free from fog, cloud, or obscurity; grow bright; become fair. 13 To pass away, as mist or fog. 14 To settle accounts by exchange of bills and checks, as in a clearing–house. — **to clear for action** To prepare for battle by clearing the decks. — **to clear in** (or **inward**) *Naut.* To discharge cargo. — **to clear out** 1 To leave port, as a ship. 2 To empty. 3 *Colloq.* To leave; depart. — **to clear the air** To dispel emotional tensions or disagreements. — **to clear the land** *Naut.* To get beyond danger of land and shoals into sea room. — **to clear up** 1 To grow fair, as the weather. 2 To free from confusion or mystery. 3 To free from obligation. — *adv.* Wholly; completely; quite; clearly; plainly. — *n.* 1 Unbroken or unobstructed distance or space; clearance. 2 Inside measurements, from boundary to boundary. — **in the clear** 1 In plain language; not written in code or cipher: said of military messages. 2 Innocent; not liable. 3 Free from limitations or obstructions. [<OF *cler* <L *clarus* clear, bright] — **clear′a·ble** *adj.* — **clear′ly** *adv.*

Synonyms (adj.): apparent, diaphanous, distinct, evident, explicit, intelligible, limpid, lucid, manifest, obvious, pellucid, perspicuous, plain, straightforward, translucent, transparent, unadorned, unambiguous, unequivocal, unmistakable. A substance is said to be *clear* that offers no impediment to vision, is not dim, dark, or obscure; *transparent*, when objects are readily seen through it; we speak of a stream as *clear* when we think of the water itself, as *transparent* with reference to the ease with which we see the pebbles at the bottom. *Clear* is said of that which comes to the senses without dimness, dulness, obstruction, or obscurity; hence, the word is used for that which is free from any kind of obstruction; as, a *clear* field. *Lucid* and *pellucid* refer to a shining clearness, as of crystal. *Translucent* is less than *transparent*; a *translucent* body allows light to pass through, but may not permit forms and colors to be distinguished. *Limpid* refers to a liquid clearness, or that which suggests it; as, *limpid* streams. That which is *distinct* is well–defined, as in outline. That is *plain* which is level to the thought, so that one goes straight on without difficulty or hindrance; as, *plain* language; a *plain* statement. *Perspicuous* is often equivalent to *plain*, but *plain* never wholly loses the meaning of *unadorned*, so that we can say the style is *perspicuous* even if highly ornate, when we could not call it at once ornate and *plain*. Compare APPARENT, BLANK, EVIDENT, FINE, FREE, INNOCENT, MANIFEST, PLAIN, PURE, SURE, VIVID. *Antonyms*: ambiguous, cloudy, dim, dubious, foggy, indistinct, mysterious, obscure, opaque, turbid, unintelligible, vague.

Clear, Cape The southernmost point of Ireland, in County Cork.

clear·ance (klir′əns) *n.* 1 The act or process of clearing. 2 A certificate permitting a vessel to sail; also, the obtaining or granting of such permission. 3 The space by which a moving vehicle, machine, or part clears something. 4 The passage of checks, bank drafts, etc., through the clearing–house.

Cle·ar·chus (klē·är′kəs) Spartan general of the fifth century B.C., treacherously killed by Persians in 401 B.C.

clear–cut (klir′kut′) *adj.* 1 Distinctly and sharply outlined. 2 Concise; plainly put.

clear–eyed (klir′īd′) *adj.* 1 Having bright, clear eyes; keen–sighted. 2 Acute; wise.

clear–head·ed (klir′hed′id) *adj.* Not mentally confused or befogged; clear in understanding; sensible. — **clear′–head′ed·ness** *n.*

clear·ing (klir′ing) *n.* 1 A making or becoming clear. 2 That which is clear or cleared; a tract of land cleared of trees, underbrush, etc. 3 The settlement of balances between banks arising from the interchange of checks, drafts, etc., carried on at a clearing–house. 4 *pl.* The total of checks, drafts, etc., presented daily at a clearing–house.

clear·ing–house (klir′ing·hous′) *n.* An office where bankers exchange drafts and checks and adjust balances.

clear·ness (klir′nis) *n.* 1 The state or quality of being clear; distinctness to sight or understanding. 2 Transparence. 3 In rhetoric, that property of style by means of which thought is so presented as to be immediately understood, depending on precision and simplicity of diction and sentence structure.

clear–sight·ed (klir′sī′tid) *adj.* Of keen vision; having accurate perception and good judgment; discerning. — **clear′–sight′ed·ly** *adv.* — **clear′–sight′ed·ness** *n.*

clear·starch (klir′stärch′) *v.t.* To stiffen with clear or pure starch. — **clear′starch′er** *n.*

clear·sto·ry (klir′stôr′ē, -stō′rē) See CLERESTORY.

clear text Plain text.

clear·way (klir′wā′) *n. Aeron.* An unobstructed area beyond the stopway of an airport to permit safe landing of an aircraft that fails to attain a proper altitude.

clear·weed (klir′wēd′) *n.* Richweed.

clear·wing (klir′wing′) *n.* A moth of the families *Aegeriidae* or *Sphingidae*, having nearly transparent wings.

cleat (klēt) *n.* 1 A strip of wood or iron fastened across a surface, or nailed against a wall, to strengthen, support, or prevent slipping. 2 *Naut.* **a** A piece of metal or wood with arms, usually fastened in place by a bolt, on which to belay a rope. **b** A wedgelike piece of wood fastened to a spar to keep rigging from slipping up or down. 3 A piece of metal or leather fastened to the underside of a shoe to prevent slipping: used by athletes. 4 A spurlike attachment used to grip a pole or tree in climbing. — *v.t.* 1 To furnish or strengthen with a cleat or cleats. 2 *Naut.* To fasten (rope, etc.) to or with a cleat. [ME *clete*. Akin to CLOT.]

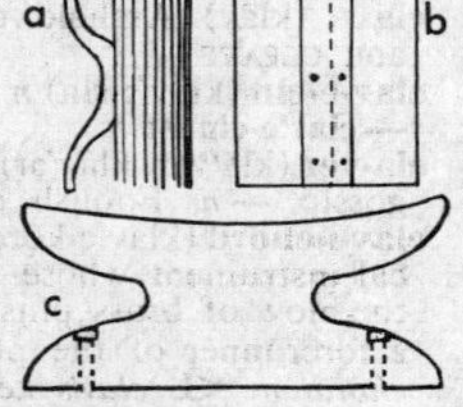

TYPES OF CLEATS
a. Pole. *b.* Surface.
c. Deck.

cleav·age (klē′vij) *n.* 1 A cleaving or being cleft; a split; cleft; division or the manner in which a thing divides. 2 *Mineral.* A tendency in certain rocks or crystals to divide or split in certain directions. 3 *Biol.* The process of division of a fertilized ovum by which the original single cell becomes a mass of smaller cells.

cleave[1] (klēv) *v.* **cleft** or **cleaved** or **clove** (*Archaic* **clave**), **cleft** or **cleaved** or **clo·ven** (*Archaic* **clove**), **cleav·ing** *v.t.* 1 To sunder, as with an ax or wedge; split, especially along structural lines or with the grain. 2 To make or achieve by cutting. 3 To pass through; penetrate. — *v.i.* 4 To split or divide by natural lines of cleavage. 5 To pass; make one's way: with *through*. [OE *clēofan*] — **cleav′a·ble** *adj.*

cleave[2] (klēv) *v.i.* **cleaved** (*Archaic* **clave**), **cleaved, cleav·ing** 1 To stick fast; adhere. 2 To be faithful: with *to*. [OE *cleofian, clifian*]

cleav·er (klē′vər) *n.* 1 One who or that which cleaves. 2 A butcher's chopper.

cleav·ers (klē′vərz) *n. pl.* A species of bedstraw (*Galium aparine*), so called because of the hooked prickles on stem and fruit: also called *catchweed*.

cleck (klek) *v.t.* & *v.i. Scot.* To hatch; litter.

cleck·in (klek′in) *n. Scot.* A brood; litter.

cle·don·ism (klē′də·niz′əm) *n.* Avoidance of the use of words considered ominous or unlucky; the practice of using euphemisms. [<Gk. *klēdōn* omen]

cleed (klēd) *Scot. v.t.* To shelter; clothe. — *n.* A garment; dress.

cleek (klēk) *v.t.* & *v.i. Scot.* 1 To clutch; hook. 2 To marry. — *n.* 1 A large hook; a crooked staff. 2 A golf club with an iron head.

clef (klef) *n.* In musical notation, a symbol placed upon the staff to determine the pitch: namely, **treble** or **G clef**, **bass** or **F clef**, and the **tenor** or **C clef** of ancient music. [<F <L *clavis* key]

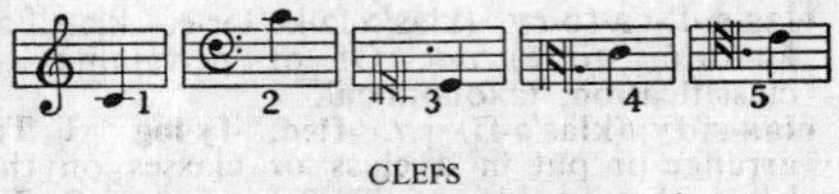

CLEFS
Showing position of Middle C on each:
1. Treble or G clef. *2.* Bass or F clef.
3., 4., 5., C clefs (Soprano, Alto, Tenor).

cleft (kleft) *v.* A past tense and past participle of CLEAVE[1]. — *adj.* 1 Divided partially or completely. 2 *Bot.* Divided about half–way down: said of leaves. — *n.* 1 An opening made by cleaving; a fissure in a rock; crevice; rift. 2 A chap or crack in the human skin. 3 The space between the two parts of a horse's foot. See synonyms under BREACH. [ME *clift*. Related to CLEAVE[1].]

cleft palate A congenital longitudinal fissure in the roof of the mouth.

Cleis·the·nes (klīs′thə·nēz) Athenian statesman of the sixth century B.C.: also spelled *Clisthenes*.

cleisto– *combining form* Closed: *cleistogamous*. Also, before vowels, **cleist–**. [<Gk. *kleistos* closed < *kleiein* close]

cleis·tog·a·mous (klīs·tog′ə·məs) *adj. Bot.* Closed or non–expanding and self–fertilizing: said of certain closed flowers, as some violets: also spelled *clistogamous*. Also **cleis·to·gam·ic** (klīs′tə·gam′ik). [<CLEISTO– + –GAMOUS]

cleis·tog·a·my (klīs·tog′ə·mē) *n. Bot.* Self–fertilization; self–pollination.

clem·a·tis (klem′ə·tis) *n.* 1 A plant of a large genus (*Clematis*) of perennial shrubs or vines of the crowfoot family. 2 Any vine of a related genus (*Atragene*). [<Gk. *klēmatis*, dim. of *klēma* vine]

Cle·men·ceau (klem′ən·sō′, *Fr.* kle·män·sō′) **Georges Eugène**, 1841–1929, French statesman; premier 1906–09; 1917–20.

clem·en·cy (klem′ən·sē) *n. pl.* **·cies** 1 Mildness of temper, especially toward offenders; leniency; mercy. 2 Mildness of climate,

weather, etc. See synonyms under MERCY. [<L *clementia* <*clemens* mild]

Clem·ens (klem′ənz), **Samuel Langhorne** See MARK TWAIN.

clem·ent (klem′ənt) *adj.* **1** Lenient; merciful. **2** Mild or pleasant: said of weather. See synonyms under HUMANE. [<L *clemens, -entis* mild, merciful] —**clem′ent·ly** *adv.*

Clem·ent (klem′ənt) A masculine personal name. Also *Fr.* **Clé·ment** (klā·mäṅ′); *Ital., Sp.* **Cle·men·te** (klā·men′tā); *Ger.* **Cle·mens** (klā′·mens). [<L, merciful]

—**Clement** The name of 17 popes.

—**Clement I** Third bishop of Rome; pope 90?–99?: called "Clement of Rome."

—**Clement V,** 1264–1314, real name Bertrand d'Agoust, pope 1305–14; removed the papal seat to Avignon, 1309.

—**Clement VII,** 1478?–1534, real name Giulio de' Medici, pope 1523–34; by a bull against Henry VIII caused the severance of the English church from Rome.

—**Clement XIV,** 1705–74, real name Giovanni Ganganelli, pope 1769–74; decreed the suppression of the Jesuits, 1773.

—**Clement of Alexandria,** 150?–220?, Greek Christian theologian.

Clem·en·ti·na (klem′ən·tē′nə, *Ital.* klā′men·tē′nä) A feminine personal name. Also **Clem·en·tine** (klem′ən·tēn, -tīn; *Ger.* klem′ən·te′nə), *Fr.* **Clé·men·tine** (klā·mäṅ·tēn′). [<L, merciful]

Clem·en·tine (klem′ən·tin, -tīn) *adj.* Of or pertaining to any of several popes and theologians named Clement.

clench (klench) *v.t.* **1** To grasp or grip firmly; clamp: to *clench* something in a vise. **2** To close tightly or lock, as the fist or teeth. **3** To clinch, as a nail. **4** *Naut.* To fasten by making a clinch. —*n.* A clenching; clinch. [OE *-clenc(e)an* in *beclencan* hold fast]

Cle·o·bu·lus (klē′ō·byōō′ləs) Greek lyric poet of the sixth century B.C.

cle·o·me (klē·ō′mē) *n.* Any of a large genus (*Cleome*) of woody or herbaceous plants of the caper family, with solitary or racemose, often showy, white, yellow, or purple flowers: also called *spiderflower.* [<LL, a plant]

Cle·om·e·nes (klē·om′ə·nēz) Name of three kings of Sparta; especially **Cleomenes III,** reigned 235–219? B.C.

Cle·on (klē′on) Athenian demagog of the fifth century B.C.

Cle·o·pat·ra (klē′ə·pat′rə, -pā′trə, -pä′trə), 69–30 B.C., queen of Egypt; loved by Julius Caesar and Mark Antony.

Cleopatra's Needle The popular name for either of two Egyptian obelisks, one in Central Park in New York City, the other in London, England.

Cle·os·tra·tus (klē·os′trə·təs), died 432 B.C., Greek astronomer.

clepe (klēp) *v.t.* **cleped** or **clept, clep·ing** *Archaic* To name; call: in the past participle also spelled *ycleped, yclept.* [OE *cleopian*]

clep·sy·dra (klep′sə·drə) *n. pl.* **·dras** or **·drae** (-drē) An ancient instrument for measuring time by the regulated flow of water; a water clock. [<L <Gk. *klepsydra* <*kleptein* steal + *hydōr* water]

clep·to·ma·ni·a (klep′tə·mā′nē·ə) See KLEPTOMANIA.

clere·sto·ry (klir′stôr′ē, -stō′rē) *n. Archit.* **1** The highest story of the nave and choir of a church, with windows opening above the aisle roofs, etc. **2** A similar story or elevated part in the roofs of other structures. Also **clere′sto′rey:** sometimes spelled *clearstory.* [<earlier *clere* clear + STORY]

cler·gy (klûr′jē) *n. pl.* **·gies** **1** The group of people ordained for service in a Christian church: distinguished from *laity.* **2** *Brit.* The ministers of the Established Church. —**regular clergy** The body of ecclesiastics of the Roman Catholic Church bound by monastic rules: distinguished from **secular clergy,** those not bound by such rules. [<OF *clergie* <*clerc* clerk, cleric <LL *clericus*]

cler·gy·man (klûr′jē·mən) *n. pl.* **·men** (-mən) One of the clergy; an ordained minister.

cler·ic (kler′ik) *adj.* Clerical. —*n.* **1** A member of the clergy. **2** A member of a clerical party. [<LL *clericus*]

cler·i·cal (kler′i·kəl) *adj.* **1** Of, belonging to, or characterizing the clergy. **2** Of or pertaining to a clerk or penmanship; composed of clerks: a *clerical* staff. —*n.* **1** A cleric. **2** One of a party seeking to preserve or extend the authority of the church in social or political matters. —**cler′i·cal·ly** *adv.*

cler·i·cal·ism (kler′i·kəl·iz′əm) *n.* The principle or policy of clerical control over education, marriage laws, etc. —**cler′i·cal·ist** *adj.* & *n.*

cler·id (kler′id) *n.* Any of a family (*Cleridae*) of small, slender, soft-bodied, variously colored coleopterous insects. [<NL *Cleridae* <Gk. *klēros,* a type of beetle]

cler·i·hew (kler′ə·hyōō) *n.* A satiric or comic poem in two couplets concerning some well-known personage whose name furnishes one of the rimes. [after Edmund *Clerihew* Bentley, 1875–1956, English writer, the originator]

cler·i·sy (kler′ə·sē) *n.* The literate, or well-educated class. [<Med. L *clericia*]

clerk (klûrk, *Brit.* klärk) *n.* **1** An officer or employee of a court, legislative body, corporation, society, commercial establishment, or the like, charged with the care of its records, correspondence, and accounts; a secretary. **2** A salesman or saleswoman in a store. **3** A hotel employee who assigns guests to their rooms. **4** In the Anglican Church, one who leads in the responses. **5** *Obs.* A clergyman or cleric; anciently, any person who could read or write. —*v.i.* To work or act as clerk. [OE *clerc* <LL *clericus* <Gk. *klērikos* <*klēros* lot, portion] —**clerk′li·ness** *n.* —**clerk′ly** *adj.* & *adv.* —**clerk′ship** *n.*

Cler·mont-Fer·rand (kler·môṅ′fe·räṅ′) A city of central France.

cleve·ite (klēv′īt) *n.* A radioactive variety of uraninite that is rich in uranium oxide and contains yttrium earths and helium. [after Per *Cleve,* 1840–1905, Swedish chemist]

Cleve·land (klēv′lənd), **(Stephen) Grover,** 1837–1908, U.S. statesman, president of the United States 1885–89, 1893–97.

Cleve·land (klēv′lənd) A city in NE Ohio on Lake Erie.

clev·er (klev′ər) *adj.* **1** Ready and adroit with hand or brain; dexterous; capable; quick-witted; talented. **2** *U.S. Dial.* Good-natured; obliging. **3** *U.S. Dial.* Finely built; well-trained, as a horse. **4** *Dial.* Honest. **5** *Obs.* Handy; convenient; agreeable. [Cf. ME *cliver* adroit] —**clev′er·ly** *adv.* —**clev′er·ness** *n.*

Synonyms: able, adroit, apt, bright, capable, dexterous, expert, gifted, happy, ingenious, intellectual, intelligent, keen, knowing, quick, quick-witted, sharp, skilful, smart, talented. *Clever,* as used in England, implies an aptitude for study or learning, and for excellent while not preeminent mental achievement. The early New England usage as implying simple and weak good nature has largely affected the use of the word throughout the United States. *Smart,* indicating dashing ability, is now coming to have a suggestion of unscrupulousness, similar to that of the word *sharp.* The discriminating use of such words as *able, gifted, talented,* etc., is preferable to an excessive use of the word *clever.* Compare ABILITY, ACUMEN, BRIGHT, INTELLIGENT, KNOWING. *Antonyms*: awkward, bungling, clumsy, dull, foolish, idiotic, ignorant, senseless, slow, stupid, thick-headed, witless.

Cleves (klēvz) A city in North Rhine-Westphalia, Germany; seat of a former duchy: German *Kleve.*

clev·is (klev′is) *n.* A U-shaped or stirrup-shaped piece of iron for attaching the draft chain to the end of a plow beam, wagon tongue, whiffletree, etc. [Akin to CLEAVE[1]]

clew (klōō) *n.* **1** A thread that guides through a maze. **2** Something that leads to the solution of a mystery: in this sense now spelled *clue.* **3** *Naut.* A lower corner of a square sail or the lower aft corner of a fore-and-aft sail; also, a loop at the corner. **4** *pl.* The small cords by which the two ends of a hammock are slung. **5** A ball of yarn, thread, or the like. —*v.t.* **1** To move or fasten by or as by a clew or clew line. **2** To coil into a ball; roll up into a bunch. [OE *cleowan*]

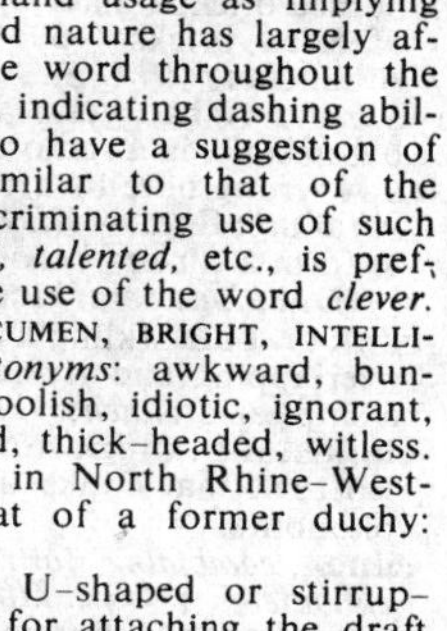

HAMMOCK CLEWS

clew line *Naut.* A rope by which the clew of a sail is run up to the yards.

cli·ché (klē·shā′) *n.* **1** A fixed or stereotyped expression which has lost its significance through frequent repetition. **2** *Printing* **a** An electrotype or stereotype plate. **b** A printing block made by the half-tone or similar process. —*adj.* Being a cliché; hackneyed. [<F, pp. of *clicher* stereotype]

Cli·chy (klē·shē′) A suburb of Paris, France. Also **Cli·chy-la-Ga·renne** (-là·gà·ren′).

click (klik) *n.* **1** A short, sharp, or dull metallic sound, as that made by the latch of a door. **2** A detent or stop; a pawl. **3** *Phonet.* An articulation occurring in the Hottentot and Bushman languages, produced by the sudden withdrawal of the tip or side of the tongue from the teeth or palate. **4** The trip, in wrestling, in which an opponent's foot is knocked from under him. —*v.t.* **1** To cause to make a click or clicks. —*v.i.* **2** To produce a click or succession of clicks. **3** *Slang* To succeed: The show *clicked.* **4** *Slang* To suit exactly; agree. [Imit.] —**click′er** *n.*

click beetle An elaterid; a snapping beetle. For illustration see INSECT (injurious).

cli·ent (klī′ənt) *n.* **1** One in whose interest a lawyer acts. **2** Hence, one who engages the services of any professional adviser. **3** Loosely, a customer or patron. **4** A dependent or follower, as of an ancient Roman patrician. [<L *cliens, -entis,* var. of *cluens,* ppr. of *cluere* hear, listen] —**cli′en·cy** *n.* —**cli·en·tal** (klī·en′təl, klī′ən·təl) *adj.*

cli·en·tele (klī′ən·tel′) *n.* A body of clients, dependents, customers, or adherents; a following. Also **cli·ent·age** (klī′ən·tij). [<F]

cliff (klif) *n.* A high steep face of rock, as on the seashore; a precipice. [OE *clif*]

cliff-dwell·er (klif′dwel′ər) *n.* **1** One of certain aboriginal North American Indian tribes of the SW United States and NW Mexico who built their dwellings in natural or excavated recesses in the sides of cliffs and canyons: antecedents of the tribes now known as Pueblo Indians. **2** *U.S. Colloq.* A person who lives in a city apartment house. —**cliff′-dwell′ing** *n.*

cliff·hang·er (klif′hang′ər) *n.* **1** A situation marked by suspense or uncertainty of outcome. **2** A serialized drama marked by suspense at the end of each episode. Also **cliff′-hang′er.** —**cliff′hang′ing** *adj.* & *n.*

Clif·ford (klif′ərd) A masculine personal name. [from a surname]

cliff swallow A North American swallow (*Petrochelidon albifrons*) which builds mud nests under the eaves of buildings or against cliffs.

cliff·y (klif′ē) *adj.* Abounding in or resembling cliffs; craggy.

Clif·ton (klif′tən) A masculine personal name. [from a surname]

cli·mac·ter·ic (klī·mak′tər·ik, klī′mak·ter′ik) *n.* **1** A critical year or period, or one of marked change, as in human life. **2** The menopause. —**grand climacteric** One's sixty-third year. —*adj.* **1** Of or pertaining to a climax; climactic. **2** Pertaining to or designating a critical year or period; marking, or marked by, a crisis. Also **cli·mac·ter·i·cal** (klī′mak·ter′i·kəl). [<L *climactericus* <Gk. *klimakterikos* <*klimaktēr* rung of a ladder]

cli·ma·gram (klī′mə·gram) *n. Meteorol.* Any graphic diagram representing one or more climatic elements of a region.

cli·mate (klī′mit) *n.* **1** The temperature, humidity, precipitation, winds, radiation, and other meteorological conditions characteristic of a locality or region over an extended period of time. **2** A region characterized by a certain average temperature, rainfall, dryness, etc. **3** Any region. **4** A prevailing or dominant trend in social affairs: *climate* of opinion. [<OF *climat* <LL *clima* <Gk. *klima, -atos* region, zone <*klinein* slope] —**cli·mat·ic** (klī·mat′ik) or **·i·cal** *adj.*

climato- *combining form* Climate; pertaining to climate or climatic conditions: *climatology.*

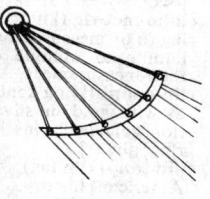

Also, before vowels, **climat-**. [<Gk. *klima, -atos* region]

cli·ma·tol·o·gy (klī'mə·tol'ə·jē) *n.* The science of climate. — **cli·ma·to·log·ic** (klī'mə·tə·loj'ik) or **·i·cal** *adj.* — **cli'ma·tol'o·gist** *n.*

cli·ma·to·ther·a·py (klī'mə·tō·ther'ə·pē) *n.* The treatment of diseases by subjecting patients to appropriate climate.

cli·max (klī'maks) *n.* 1 A progressive increase in force throughout a rhetorical or musical passage, culminating at the close. 2 *Ecol.* A relatively stable community of plants and animals dominant in a given locality. 3 Loosely, the culmination; acme. — *v.t. & v.i.* To reach or bring to a climax; culminate. [<L <Gk. *klimax* ladder] — **cli·mac·tic** (klī·mak'tik) or **·ti·cal** *adj.*

climb (klīm) *v.* **climbed** (*Archaic* **clomb**), **climb·ing** *v.t.* 1 To ascend or descend, especially by means of the hands and feet; go up or down by holding or getting a foothold; mount. — *v.i.* 2 To mount, rise, or go up, especially by using the hands and feet. 3 To rise by effort, as in position or dignity. 4 To incline or slope upward. 5 To rise during growth, as certain vines, by entwining a support or clinging by means of tendrils. — *n.* 1 The act or process of climbing. ◆ Collateral adjective: *scansorial.* 2 A place that can be ascended only by climbing. — Homophone: *clime.* [OE *climban*] — **climb'a·ble** *adj.*

climb·er (klī'mər) *n.* 1 One who or that which climbs. 2 *Bot.* A plant that supports its growth by its tendrils, rootlets, or the like. 3 *Colloq.* A social climber.

climbing fish See ANABAS.

climbing irons Iron bars bearing spur points, for strapping to the boots or legs, to aid in climbing telegraph poles, trees, glaciers, etc. See CLEAT *n.* Also **climb·ers** (klī'mərz).

clime (klīm) *n. Poetic* A country; region; climate. ◆ Homophone: *climb.* [<L *clima* CLIMATE]

cli·nan·dri·um (kli·nan'drē·əm) *n. pl.* **·dri·a** (-drē·ə) *Bot.* A depression in the summit of the column in certain orchids, in which the anther is lodged. [<NL <Gk. *klinē* bed + *anēr, andros* man]

cli·nan·thi·um (kli·nan'thē·əm) *n. pl.* **·thi·a** (-thē·ə) *Bot.* The receptacle in the heads of composite plants. [<NL <Gk. *klinē* bed + *anthos* flower]

clinch (klinch) *v.t.* 1 To secure firmly, as a nail or staple, by bending down the protruding point. 2 To fasten together by this means. 3 To grapple with. 4 To confirm, as a bargain or agreement. 5 *Naut.* To fasten by making a clinch. — *v.i.* 6 To take a strong, close hold; grapple, as combatants, with one another. 7 *Slang* To embrace or hug. — *n.* 1 A clinching, or that which clinches; especially, a clinched nail or bolt; a clamp. 2 A decisive or conclusive argument. 3 *Naut.* A rope knot made by a half-hitch and seizings: called an **inside** or an **outside clinch**. 4 A grip or struggle at close quarters, as in boxing. 5 *Slang* A close embrace. Also called *clench.* [Var. of CLENCH]

Clinch River (klinch) A river in Virginia and Tennessee, flowing 300 miles SW through the Great Appalachian Valley into Norris Reservoir.

clinch·er (klin'chər) *n.* 1 One who or that which clinches. 2 A person or device that clinches nails; a clencher. 3 A nail made for clinching. 4 *Colloq.* The final unanswerable proof in or as in an argument.

clinch·er-built (klin'chər-bilt') *adj.* Clincherbuilt.

clincher rim A rim of an automobile wheel with turned-in edges, to grip and hold a clincher tire.

clincher tire A tire with flanges on each side of the inner circumference fitting into turned-over edges of the wheel rim.

cline (klīn) *n. Ecol.* A graded series of changes in a biotype, induced by corresponding gradual alterations in the environmental factors operating within a large area. [<Gk. *klinein* slope, bend]

cling (kling) *v.i.* **clung, cling·ing** 1 To hold on to something firmly, as by grasping, embracing, or winding round. 2 To remain in contact; resist separation: with *together.* 3 To stick to or continue tenaciously, as in the memory; be loyal. 4 To adhere closely; stick. [OE *clingan*] — **cling'er** *n.* — **cling'y** *adj.*

cling·fish (kling'fish') *n. pl.* **·fish** or **·fish·es** Any of a group of small marine fishes (family *Gobiesocidae*) having a large central suction disk by which they cling to rocks, shells, etc.

cling·ing (kling'ing) *adj.* Adhering closely, as a garment. — **cling'ing·ly** *adv.*

clinging vine A woman who displays extreme dependence on a man in an attempt to gain his sympathy, attentions, protection, etc.

Cling·mans Dome (kling'mənz) One of the Great Smoky Mountains between Tennessee and North Carolina; 6,642 feet.

cling·stone (kling'stōn') *n.* A variety of peach in which the pulp adheres to the stone.

clin·ic (klin'ik) *n.* 1 The teaching of medicine and surgery by treatment of or operation upon the patients in the presence of a class in a hospital or dispensary. 2 A class receiving such instruction. 3 An infirmary or dispensary connected with a hospital or medical college, for the treatment of non-resident patients. [<F *clinique* <L *clinicus* <Gk. *klinikos* <*klinē* bed <*klinein* recline]

clin·i·cal (klin'i·kəl) *adj.* 1 Of or pertaining to a sickbed or a clinic. 2 Pertaining to the practical, experimental method of medical education by the observation and treatment of patients in clinics. 3 Administered to one on a deathbed or sickbed: *clinical* baptism. — **clin'i·cal·ly** *adv.*

clinical thermometer See under THERMOMETER.

cli·ni·cian (kli·nish'ən) *n.* An active practitioner of medicine: distinguished from a teacher or from one who is consulted only at his office.

clink¹ (klingk) *v.t.* 1 To cause to make a short, slight, ringing sound. 2 *Scot. & Brit. Dial.* To clinch; rivet. — *v.i.* 3 To make a short, slight, ringing sound. 4 To rime or jingle. — *n.* 1 A tinkle, as of glass or small metallic bodies in collision. 2 *Scot.* Money; chink. 3 The shrill note of certain birds, as the whinchat. 4 A rime or jingle. [Imit. Cf. MDu. *klinken.*]

clink² (klingk) *n. Slang* A prison. [? after *Clink* prison in London]

clink·er (kling'kər) *n.* 1 A thing that clinks, especially the earthy residue left by coal in burning. 2 A large, irregular porous fragment of lava. 3 A brick impregnated with niter and burned very hard. 4 A vitrified or over-burned brick; a mass of fused bricks. 5 A clincher. 6 *U.S. Slang* a A bad verbal mistake in a radio or television broadcast. b A wrong note in a musical performance. c A failure; flop. — *v.t. & v.i.* To form or cause to form a clinker; become clogged with clinker. [<Du. *klinckaerd,* kind of brick]

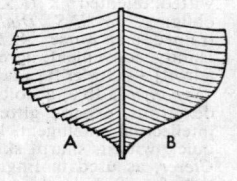

CLINKER-BUILT
In shipbuilding.
A. Clinker-built.
B. Carvel-built.

clink·er-built (kling'kər·bilt') *adj.* Built with overlapping and riveted planks or plates, as a ship: also *clincher-built.*

clink·stone (klingk'stōn') *n.* A compact, grayish rock that clinks like metal when struck; phonolite.

clino- *combining form* Bend; slope; incline: *clinometer.* [<Gk. *klinein* bend]

cli·nom·e·ter (kli·nom'ə·tər, kli-) *n.* An instrument for determining angular inclination, as of guns, slopes, etc.: also *anglemeter.* [<CLINO- + -METER]

cli·no·met·ric (klī'nə·met'rik) *adj.* 1 Pertaining to or measured by the clinometer. 2 Pertaining to oblique crystalline forms or to their measurement. Also **cli'no·met'ri·cal.**

clin·quant (kling'kənt) *adj.* Glittering with or as with gold or silver; tinseled. — *n.* Imitation gold leaf; tinsel. [<F, ppr. of *clinquer* ring, glitter]

Clin·ton (klin'tən) A family prominent in American history, including **James,** 1736-1812, general in American Revolution; **George,** 1739-1812, brother of James, governor of New York, and vice president of the United States; **De Witt,** 1769-1828, son of James, lawer and statesman.

— **Sir Henry,** 1738-95, British commander

in chief in the American Revolution, 1778-1782.

clin·to·ni·a (klin·tō'nē·ə) *n.* A plant of a small genus (*Clintonia*) of perennial herbs of the lily family, having broadly lanceolate, radical leaves, and a naked scape, bearing usually an umbel of flowers succeeded by berries. [after De Witt *Clinton*]

Cli·o (klī'ō) The Muse of history. [<Gk. *kleein* celebrate, make famous]

cli·o·met·rics (klī'ō·met'riks) *n.pl.* (*construed as sing.*) The systematic application of statistical methods to the study of history, as in the collection and analysis of quantitative data. [< CLIO + METRICS] — **cli'o·met'ric** *adj.* — **cli·o·me·tri·cian** (klī'ō·mə·trish'ən) *n.*

clip¹ (klip) *n.* 1 Any appliance that clasps, grips, or holds fast. 2 *Med.* An appliance for stopping the bleeding of arteries, etc. 3 A flange on a horseshoe, projecting upward above the calk. 4 A spring clasp for holding letters, papers, etc.: also **paper clip.** 5 A pinching device for stopping the flow of a fluid in a flexible tube. 6 A metal container holding cartridges for a rapid-fire gun, as an automatic rifle: also **cartridge clip.** — *v.t.* **clipped, clip·ping** 1 *Archaic* To clasp; embrace. 2 To encircle; hold tightly. [OE *clyppan* clasp]

clip² (klip) *v.t.* **clipped, clip·ping** 1 To cut or trim with shears or scissors, as hair or fleece. 2 To snip a part from, as a coin. 3 To cut short; curtail: to *clip* the ends of words. 4 *Colloq.* To strike with a sharp blow. 5 In football, to hurl oneself illegally across the backs of the legs of (an opponent who is not carrying the ball.) 6 *Slang* To cheat or defraud. — *v.i.* 7 To cut or trim. 8 *Colloq.* To run or move swiftly. — **to clip the wings of** To check the aspirations or ambitions of. — *n.* 1 The act of clipping, or that which is clipped off. 2 The wool yielded at one shearing or season. 3 *Colloq.* A blow with the hand or fist; a swinging or glancing hit. 4 *Colloq.* A quick pace: going at a good *clip.* 5 *pl.* Shears; snuffers. 6 *Colloq.* An effort or attempt. [<ON *klippa*]

clip·board (klip'bôrd', bōrd') *n.* A small board for writing and having a spring clip for holding paper in place.

clipped form A shortened form of a polysyllabic word, as *bus* for *omnibus,* *gym* for *gymnasium,* or *exam* for *examination.* Also **clipped word.**

clip·per (klip'ər) *n.* 1 One who or that which clips. 2 One who clips coins. 3 An instrument for clipping hair. 4 *pl.* Shears; especially, pruning shears or sheep shears. 5 *Naut.* A certain type of sailing vessel built for speed, with tall, aft-raked masts: also **clipper ship.** 6 *Colloq.* One who or that which moves swiftly, as a swift horse, a sled, or smart person.

Clip·per·ton Island (klip'ər·tən) A Pacific Island SW of Mexico, awarded to France in 1931; .6 square mile.

clip·ping (klip'ing) *adj.* 1 That cuts or clips. 2 That moves rapidly. — *n.* 1 The act of one who or that which clips. 2 That which is cut off or cut by clipping: a newspaper *clipping.*

clique (klēk, klik) *n.* An exclusive or clannish set; coterie. — *v.i.* **cliqued, cli·quing** To unite in a clique; act clannishly. See synonyms under CLASS. [<F <*cliquer* click, clap]

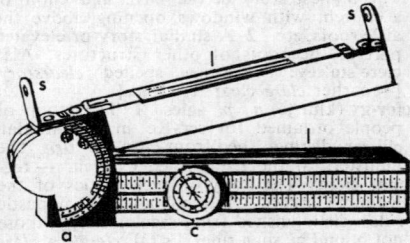

CLINOMETER
s., s. Sights. *l., l.* Levels. *a.* Sliding scale.
c. Compass for taking bearings of objects.

cli·quish (klē'kish, klik'ish) *adj.* Inclined to form cliques; exclusive. Also **cli'quey, cli'quy.** — **cli'quish·ly** *adv.* — **cli'quish·ness** *n.*

cli·sere (klī'sir) *n. Ecol.* A series of climax formations or zones which follow each other

in a particular region as a consequence of a distinct change of climate. [< CLI(MATE) + SERE[2]]
clish·ma·clav·er (klish′mə·klav′ər) *n. Scot.* Foolish talk; gossip.
clis·tase (klis′tās) *n. Ecol.* The state or condition of vegetation in a given layer of fossil plant deposits, indicating a climatic change. [< CLI(MAX), def. 2 + STASE
Clis·the·nes (klis′thə·nēz) See CLEISTHENES.
clis·tog·a·mous (klis·tog′ə·məs) See CLEISTOGAMOUS.
cli·tel·lum (kli·tel′əm) *n.* The swollen, glandular portion of the skin in some earthworms. [< NL < L *clitellae* packsaddle]
clith·ro·pho·bi·a (klith′rə·fō′bē·ə) *n.* Claustrophobia. [< Gk. *kleithron* bar + -PHOBIA]
cli·to·ris (klī′tə·ris, klit′ə-) *n. Anat.* An erectile organ of the female of most vertebrates, at the anterior part of the vulva: the homolog of the penis. [NL < Gk. *kleitoris* < *kleiein* close, confine]
Clive (klīv), **Robert,** 1725–74, Baron Clive of Plassey, English general and statesman, founded the empire of British India.
cli·vers (klī′vərz) See CLEAVERS.
clo·a·ca (klō·ā′kə) *n. pl.* **·cae** (-sē) **1** *Zool.* The common cavity into which the various ducts of the body open in certain fishes, reptiles, insects, etc. **2** A sewer; sink; privy; a general receptacle for or repository of filth. [< L, a drain] —**clo·a′cal** *adj.*
cloak (klōk) *n.* **1** A loose outer garment. **2** Something that covers or hides; a pretext; disguise; mask. See synonyms under PRETENSE. —*v.t.* To cover with a cloak; disguise; conceal. See synonyms under HIDE, MASK, PALLIATE. [< OF *cloque, cloke* < Med. L *cloca* bell, cape; so called from its bell-like shape. Doublet of CLOCK.]
cloak·room (klōk′rōōm′, -rŏŏm′) *n.* A room where hats, coats, luggage, etc., are cared for temporarily.
clob·ber (klob′ər) *v.t. Slang* To beat or trounce; strike (someone) severely. [? Freq. of CLUB[1], *v.*]
cloche (klōsh, *Fr.* klôsh) *n.* **1** A woman's close-fitting, bell-shaped hat. **2** A portable translucent cover for the protection and forcing of young plants. [< F, bell]
clock[1] (klok) *n.* **1** An instrument for measuring and indicating time by mechanical movements; a timepiece. **2** Any clocklike, mechanical, registering device for recording distance, output, etc. —**what o'clock, six o'clock,** etc. See O'CLOCK. —*v.t.* To determine the rate of speed of an automobile or of any racing event by means of a stopwatch. [< MDu. *clocke* < OF *cloque, cloche* bell < Med. L *cloca.* Doublet of CLOAK.]
clock[2] (klok) *n.* An embroidered ornament on the side of a stocking or sock at the ankle. —*v.t.* To ornament with clocks. [Origin uncertain]
clock·mak·er (klok′mā′kər) *n.* One who makes or repairs clocks.
clock·wise (klok′wīz′) *adj. & adv.* Moving in the direction traveled by the hands of a clock.
clock·work (klok′wûrk′) *n.* The machinery of a clock, or any similar mechanism. —**like clockwork** With regularity and precision.
clod (klod) *n.* **1** A lump of earth, clay, etc.; hence, the soil. **2** Anything earthy, as the body of man compared with his soul. **3** The cut of beef on the back part of the foreshoulder above the shank. **4** A dull, stupid fellow, —*v.t.* **clod·ded, clod·ding 1** To throw clods or stones at. —*v.i.* **2** To turn into clods; clot; coagulate. [Var. of CLOT] —**clod′dish** *adj.* —**clod′dish·ness** *n.* —**clod′dy** *adj.*
clod·hop·per (klod′hop′ər) *n.* **1** A plowman; rustic; lout. **2** *pl.* Large, heavy shoes, such as those worn by plowmen, farm workers, etc.
Clo·do·ve·o (klō′thō·vā′ō) Spanish form of CLOVIS.
clod·pate (klod′pāt′) *n.* A blockhead; a stupid person. Also **clod·poll** (klod′pōl′), **clod′pole′.**
clog (klog) *n.* **1** Anything that impedes motion, as a block attached to an animal or a vehicle. **2** An encumbrance; a hindrance. **3** A wooden-soled shoe. **4** A clog dance. See synonyms under IMPEDIMENT, LOAD. —*v.* **clogged, clog·ging** —*v.t.* **1** To choke up or obstruct. **2** To place impediments in the way of; hinder. **3** To fasten a clog to; hamper the movements of by a clog; hobble. —*v.i.* **4** To become choked up. **5** To be retarded or hindered. **6** To adhere in a mass; coagulate. **7** To perform a clog dance. See synonyms under HINDER, OBSTRUCT. [ME *clogge* block of wood] —**clog′gy** *adj.* —**clog′gi·ness** *n.*
clog almanac An early form of calendar made by cutting notches on the edges of a square block of wood, brass, or horn, and engraving devices upon it: also called *runic staff.*
clog dance A dance performed with clogs or other shoes, the clatter of which emphasizes the rhythm of the music.
cloi·son·né (kloi′zə·nā′) *n.* **1** A method of producing designs in enamel by laying out the pattern with strips of flat wire and filling the interstices with enamel paste, which is then fused in place. **2** The ware so produced. —*adj.* Of, pertaining to, or made by this method. [< F < *cloison* a partition]
clois·ter (klois′tər) *n.* **1** A covered walk, generally following the walls of buildings enclosing a quadrangle, as in a monastery or college. **2** A building devoted to the secluded life; a monastery; convent. **3** Monastic life. —*v.t.* **1** To seclude; confine, as in a cloister. **2** To provide with cloisters. [OF *cloistre* < L *claustrum* enclosed place] —**clois′ter·er** *n.* —**clois′tral** *adj.*

Synonyms (noun): abbey, convent, friary, hermitage, monastery, nunnery, priory. *Cloister, abbey, convent,* and *priory* are for either sex; a *friary* is always for men, a *nunnery* for women, a *monastery* commonly for men. A *priory* (governed by a prior or prioress) is inferior to an *abbey* (governed by an abbot or abbess). The word *monastery* lays stress upon the loneliness; *convent* emphasizes the association of its inmates. A *hermitage* was originally for a single recluse, but the word came to be applied to collections of hermits' cells.

clois·tered (klois′tərd) *adj.* **1** Built with cloisters. **2** Living in cloisters: *cloistered* nuns. **3** Concealed or withdrawn from the world.
clois·tress (klois′tris) *n.* A nun.
clomb (klōm) Archaic past tense and past participle of CLIMB.
clone (klōn) *n.* **1** A group of organisms derived from a single individual by asexual means. **2** An exact genetic replica of an organism. **3** A duplicate. Also **clon** (klōn, klon). —*v.t.* **cloned, clon·ing 1** To produce in the form of a clone. **2** To produce a clone. [< Gk. *klōn* sprout, twig] —**clon′al** *adj.*
clon·ing (klōn′ing) *n.* The production of progeny that is genetically identical with a single progenitor.
clo·nus (klō′nəs) *n. Pathol.* A form of muscular convulsion, characterized by violent contraction and relaxation. [< Gk. *klonos* motion] —**clon·ic** (klon′ik) *adj.* —**clo·nic·i·ty** (klə·nis′ə·tē) *n.*
cloot (klōōt) *n. Scot.* A cloven hoof, or one of its parts.
Cloot (klōōt) *Scot.* The devil. Also **Cloo·tie** (klōō′tē).
Clootz (klōts), **Baron Jean Baptiste,** 1755–94, French revolutionary leader, born in Prussia: called *Anacharsis Clootz.*
close (klōs) *adj.* **clos·er, clos·est 1** Enclosed or partly enclosed; shut in or about; confined; encompassed by limits, walls, or bounds; hence, kept in confinement: a *close* prisoner. **2** Closed so as to confine, restrict, or keep out something; fast shut: a *close* box. **3** Near or near together, in space, time, etc.: The two houses were *close* to each other. **4** Divided by small intervals: a *close* sequence of events. **5** Marked by nearness in space, order, or arrangement: marching in *close* order. **6** Dense; compact: a *close* fabric. **7** Affectionately associated; trusty; intimate: a *close* friend. **8** Exactly or literally executed; near in thought or performance to some aim, purpose, or standard: a *close* copy. That shot was *close.* **9** Narrowly confined or attentive to some object; watchful; strict; searching: a *close* search. **10** Nearly even or equal, without much difference in favor of either side: a *close* election. **11** Concealing one's thoughts and feelings; secretive; reticent. **12** Not liberal; stingy. **13** Ill-ventilated; heavy; stifling; dense: *close* weather. **14** *Colloq.* Difficult to obtain; tight: said of money or the money market. **15** Shut or restricted by law; not open or free: a *close* season for fishing; a *close* corporation. **16** Fitting tightly or snugly: a *close* cap. **17** Near to the surface: a *close* shave. **18** *Phonet.* Describing those vowels pronounced with a part of the tongue relatively close to the palate, as the (ē) in *seat*; high: opposed to *open.* See synonyms under ADJACENT, AVARICIOUS, FIRM, IMMEDIATE, IMPENETRABLE, TACITURN. —*v.* (klōz) **closed, clos·ing** *v.t.* **1** To shut, as a door. **2** To fill or obstruct, as an opening or passage. **3** To bring the parts of together, as a knife or book. **4** To bring into contact; join, as parts of an electric circuit. **5** To bring to an end; terminate. **6** To shut in; enclose. —*v.i.* **7** To become shut or closed. **8** To come to an end. **9** To grapple; come to close quarters. **10** To join; coalesce; unite. **11** To come to an agreement. **12** To be worth at the end of a business day: Stocks *closed* at an average three points higher. —**to close down 1** To come upon; enfold: Night *closed down.* **2** To suppress: The law *closed down* on gambling. **3** To discontinue a business or venture. —**to close in** To advance and surround. —**to close out** *U.S.* To sell all of, as goods, usually at a reduced price. —**to close up** To make all final arrangements: to *close up* one's affairs. —*n.* (klōz) **1** The end; conclusion. **2** A grapple. **3** A junction; meeting. **4** (klōs) Any place shut in or enclosed, as by a fence; specifically, the precinct of a cathedral or abbey. **5** (klōs) *Law* Land adjoining a house. **6** (klōs) An interest in the soil entitling the holders to damages in event of trespass. —**to break close** To trespass. —*adv.* (klōs) Closely. [< OF *clos,* pp. of *clore* close < L *claudere* close] —**close·ly** (klōs′lē) *adv.* —**close·ness** (klōs′nis) *n.* —**clos·er** (klō′zər) *n.*
close-bod·ied (klōs′bod′ēd) *adj.* **1** Fitting closely, as the body of a coat. **2** Close-grained.
close call (klōs) *U.S.* A narrow escape.
closed chain (klōzd) *Chem.* Atoms of a molecule arranged in a cyclical form and represented by the symbol of a ring, as in benzene and aromatic compounds.
closed corporation A business enterprise in which the stock ownership is vested in a few persons. Also **close corporation** (klōs).
closed season That part of the year during which it is unlawful to catch or kill certain varieties of fish or game.
closed shop An establishment in which all the employees are union members.
closed syllable See under SYLLABLE.
close·fist·ed (klōs′fis′tid) *adj.* Stingy; miserly. —**close′fist′ed·ness** *n.*
close-fit·ting (klōs′fit′ing) *adj.* Fitting so tightly as to show the contours of the body.
close-grained (klōs′grānd′) *adj.* Compact in growth or structure; solid: said of wood, crystals, etc.
close-hauled (klōs′hôld′) *adj. & adv. Naut.* With the sails set for sailing as close to the wind as possible.
close-mouthed (klōs′mouthd′, -moutht′) *adj.* Not given to imparting formation; taciturn; uncommunicative.
close-or·der drill (klōs′ôr′dər) *Mil.* A systematic exercise in information marching and in the formal handling of arms.
close quarters 1 In fighting, an encounter at close range or hand-to-hand. **2** A small, confined space or lodgment.
close shave *Colloq.* A narrow escape; close call.
close stitch The buttonhole stitch.
close-stool (klōs′stōōl′) *n.* A covered box containing a commode.
clos·et (kloz′it) *n.* **1** A small chamber, side room, or recess for storage of clothes, linen, etc., or for privacy. **2** The private chamber of a ruler, used as a council chamber, or as a chapel for devotion. **3** A watercloset; privy. —*v.t.* **clos·et·ed, clos·et·ing** To shut up or conceal in or as in a closet, especially for privacy: usually used with a reflexive pronoun. —*adj.* **1** Private; confidential. **2** Based on theory rather than practice: *closet* strategy. [< OF, dim. of *clos.* See CLOSE.]
closet drama A play or dramatic poem writ-

ten solely, or chiefly, for reading rather than performance.

close-up (klōs′up′) *n.* **1** In motion pictures and television, a picture of a character or a scene taken with the camera at close range. **2** A close look or view.

clos·trid·i·um (klos·trid′ē·əm) *n. pl.* **·trid·i·a** (-trid′ē·ə) *n. Bacteriol.* Any of a genus *(Clostridium)* of rod-shaped, spore-bearing, anaerobic bacteria, including pathogenic forms causing botulism, gas gangrene, and tetanus. [<NL <Gk. *klōstēr* spindle]

clo·sure (klō′zhər) *n.* **1** A proceeding to stop debate in a deliberative body in order to secure a prompt vote: also *cloture.* Compare PREVIOUS QUESTION. **2** A closing or shutting up: the *closure* of a shop. **3** *Obs.* That which closes or encloses; enclosure. — *v.t.* **clo·sured, clo·sur·ing** To apply closure to (a debate, etc.). [<OF <L *clausura* a closing < *claudere* close]

clot (klot) *n.* **1** A coagulated mass. **2** A thick, viscid, or coagulated mass of blood. — *v.t.* & *v.i.* **clot·ted, clot·ting** To form into clots; coagulate; mat, fill, or cover with clots. [OE *clott* lump, mass] — **clot′ty, clot′ted** *adj.*

cloth (klôth, kloth) *n. pl.* **cloths** (klôthz, klothz, klôths, kloths) **1** A woven fabric of wool, cotton, rayon, etc.; a piece of such fabric. **2** A piece of cloth for a special use, as a tablecloth. **3** *Naut.* A sail, or a breadth of the canvas that goes to make up a sail. **4** *Obs.* Raiment; clothes. — **the cloth** Clerical attire; hence, the clerical office; the clergy. [OE *clath*]

clothe (klōth) *v.t.* **clothed** or **clad, cloth·ing** **1** To cover or provide with clothes; dress. **2** To cover as if with clothing; invest. [OE *clathian*]

clothes (klōz, klōthz) *n. pl* **1** The articles of raiment worn by human beings; garments collectively; raiment; clothing. **2** Covering for a bed; bedclothes. See synonyms under DRESS. [OE *clathas,* pl. of *clath* cloth]

clothes hanger A metal, plastic, or wooden device on which a garment may be hung.

clothes·horse (klōz′hôrs′, klōthz′-) *n.* **1** A frame on which to hang or dry clothes. **2** *Slang* A person regarded as excessively concerned with dress or as having little ability except for dressing well.

clothes·line (klōz′līn′, klōthz′-) *n.* A cord, rope, or wire on which to hang clothes to dry.

clothes moth Any of various moths, especially of the family *Tineidae,* whose larvae are destructive of wool, fur, and other animal products. For illustration see under INSECT (injurious).

clothes·pin (klōz′pin′, klōthz′-) *n.* A peg or clamp with which to fasten clothes on a line.

clothes·press (klōz′pres′, klōthz′-) *n.* A closet or chest for clothes; wardrobe.

clothes·tree (klōz′trē′, klōthz′-) *n.* A stand having arms or hooks on which to hang hats, coats, etc.

cloth·ier (klōth′yər) *n.* One who makes or sells cloths or clothing.

cloth·ing (klō′thing) *n.* **1** Dress collectively; apparel. **2** A covering.

Clo·tho (klō′thō) One of the three Fates. [<Gk. *klōthein* spin]

cloth-yard (klôth′yärd′, kloth′-) *n.* A rod used for measuring cloth, formerly 27 inches, now equal in length to the standard yard of 36 inches.

cloth-yard shaft An early English arrow for the longbow, a cloth-yard in length.

clo·ture (klō′chər) See CLOSURE (def. 1).

cloud (kloud) *n.* **1** *Meteorol.* A mass of visible vapor or an aggregation of watery or icy particles, floating in the atmosphere at various heights and exhibiting a large variety of shapes, which partly aid in the determination of weather conditions. In the International Code, clouds have been classified, according to height and typical formation, into four families and ten genera. See table below. **2** Something that darkens, obscures, dims, confuses, or threatens. **3** A dimmed appearance; a spot. **4** *Law* A defect; blemish: a *cloud* on a title. **5** A great multitude; a cloudlike mass: a *cloud* of arrows. — **in the clouds 1** Imaginary; fanciful. **2** Impractical. — *v.t.* **1** To cover with or as with clouds; dim; obscure. **2** To render gloomy or troubled. **3** To cover with obloquy or disgrace. **4** To variegate, as marble. — *v.i.* **5** To be overcast with or as with clouds. [OE *clūd* rocky mass, hill] — **cloud′less** *adj.* — **cloud′less·ly** *adv.*

CLOUD TABLE—INTERNATIONAL CODE

Families: A: high clouds, from 20,000 feet up; B: middle clouds, 6,500–20,000 feet; C: low clouds, near surface to 6,500 feet; D: vertical displacement clouds, 1,600–20,000 feet.

Type	*Symbol*	*Family*	*Av. ht. miles*
Altocumulus	Ac	B	2 1/2
Altostratus	As	B	3 1/2
Cirrocumulus	Cc	A	5
Cirrostratus	Cs	A	6
Cirrus	Ci	A	7
Cumulonimbus	Cb	D	4
Cumulus	Cu	D	2
Nimbostratus	Ns	C	1/4
Stratocumulus	Sc	C	1
Stratus	St	C	1/4

The following variations of the International Code are also accepted in the U.S. Weather Bureau procedure: *altocumulus castellatus* (Acc), *cumulonimbus mammatus* (Cm), *fractocumulus* (Fc), and *fractostratus* (Fs).

cloud attack In chemical warfare, a gas attack made with aircraft or by igniting chemical candles.

cloud band In Chinese art, a wavy ribbonlike conventionalization of a cloud.

cloud·ber·ry (kloud′ber′ē) *n. pl.* **·ries** An arctic or alpine species of raspberry *(Rubus chamaemorus)* producing an amber-colored fruit.

cloud·burst (kloud′bûrst′) *n.* A sudden flood of rain, as if a whole cloud had been discharged at once.

cloud-capped (kloud′kapt′) *adj.* Having clouds encircling the top.

cloud chamber See under CHAMBER.

cloud-drift (kloud′drift′) *n.* A mass of broken and flying clouds. Also **cloud′rack′.**

cloud·land (kloud′land′) *n.* The realm of fancy and dreams or of theory and speculation.

cloud·let (kloud′lit) *n.* A little cloud.

cloud·y (klou′dē) *adj.* **cloud·i·er, cloud·i·est** **1** Overspread with clouds. **2** Of or like a cloud or clouds. **3** Obscure; vague; confused. **4** Gloomy; sullen. **5** Not limpid or clear. **6** Marked with cloudlike spots. — **cloud′i·ly** *adv.* — **cloud′i·ness** *n.*

Clou·et (kloo·e′), **François,** 1516?–72, son of Jean, court painter to King Francis I. — **Jean,** 1485–1541, French painter.

clough (kluf, klou) *n.* A gorge or ravine. [ME *clough, cloghe,* OE (assumed) *cloh*]

Clough (kluf), **Arthur Hugh,** 1819–61, English poet.

clour (kloor) *v.t. Scot.* To knock; thump; dent. — *n.* A blow, bump, or bash on the head.

clout[1] (klout) *n.* **1** A piece of cloth or leather; patch; rag. **2** *Often pl.* A swaddling cloth. **3** The center of a target. **4** An iron plate. **5** A short, stout nail for boot or shoe soles; a flat-headed nail for fastening iron plates: also called **clout nail. 6** *Colloq.* A heavy blow or cuff with the hand. **7** In baseball, a long hit to the outfield. **8** *U.S. Slang* Influence or power; especially, political weight; pull. — *v.t.* **1** *Colloq.* To hit or strike, as with the hand; cuff. **2** To patch or bandage crudely. **3** To protect with an iron plate. **4** To stud with iron nails. [OE *clut*]

clout[2] (klout) *n. Brit. Dial.* A stupid, loutish person; clod. [<Du. *kluit* clod]

clout·ed (klou′tid) *adj.* Clotted: said of cream.

clout·er·ly (klou′tər·lē) *adj. Brit. Dial.* Unhandy; clumsy.

clove[1] (klōv) *n.* A dried flower bud of a tropical evergreen tree *(Syzygium aromaticum),* the **clovetree** of the myrtle family: used as a spice. [<OF *clou (de girofle)* nail (of clove) <L *clavus* nail; so called from its shape]

clove[2] (klōv) A past tense and archaic past participle of CLEAVE[1].

clove[3] (klōv) *n. Bot.* One of the small bulbs formed in the axis of the scale of a mother bulb, as in garlic. [OE *clufu*]

clove-hitch (klōv′hich′) *n. Naut.* A knot consisting of two half-hitches, with the ends of the rope going in opposite directions: used for fastening a rope around a spar. See illustration under HITCH.

clo·ven (klō′vən) *adj.* Parted; split. See CLEAVE[1].

clo·ven-hoofed (klō′vən·hooft′, -hooft′) *adj.* **1** Having the foot cleft or divided, as cattle: also **clo′ven-foot′ed. 2** Satanic; bearing the mark of the evil one.

clove pink Any of several varieties of *Dianthus caryophyllus* having a sweet clovelike odor. Also **clove gilliflower.**

clo·ver (klō′vər) *n.* **1** Any of several species of plants (genus *Trifolium*) of the legume family, having dense flower heads and the leaves divided into three leaflets; especially, the common **red clover** *(T. pratense)* used for forage and adopted as the State flower of Vermont. **2** Any of certain other plants of the legume family, as melilot. — **in clover** **1** Originally, in good pasture, as cattle in a clover field. **2** Prosperous; having an abundance. [OE *clāfre* trefoil]

clo·ver·leaf (klō′vər·lēf′) *n.* **1** An open automobile of early style, seating three or four persons, with entrance only through doors in front of forward seats. **2** A highway intersection designed so as to route traffic without interference, by means of a system of curving ramps from one level to another, in the form of a four-leaf clover. **3** *Aeron.* A testing maneuver in which an airplane flies in a course or pattern like a double figure-8 or a highway cloverleaf.

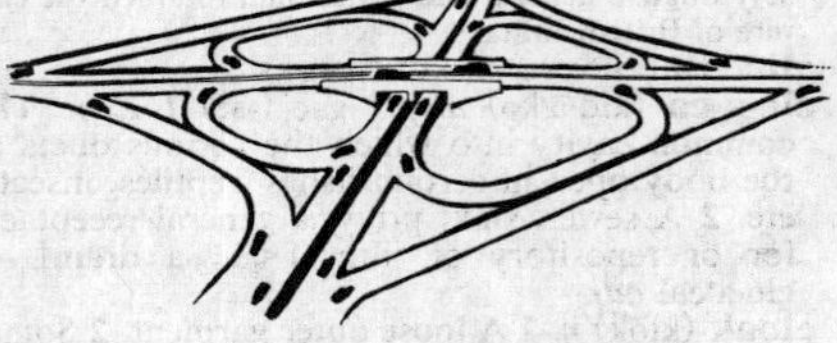

CLOVERLEAF

Clo·vis (klō′vis), 466–511, king of the Franks 481–511; traditional founder of the French kingdom: also called *Chlodwig.*

clown (kloun) *n.* **1** A professional buffoon in a play or circus, who entertains by antics, jokes, tricks, etc.; a zany; a jester. **2** A coarse or vulgar fellow; boor. **3** A countryman. — *v.i.* To behave like a clown. [Earlier *cloune* <MLG. Cf. Du. *kloen,* dial. Frisian *klönne*] — **clown′er·y** *n.*

clown·ish (klou′nish) *adj.* Of or like a clown; rude; ill-bred. See synonyms under AWKWARD. — **clown′ish·ly** *adv.* — **clown′ish·ness** *n.*

clown·ism (klou′niz·əm) *n.* Clownish gait and behavior, especially in certain psychiatric disorders.

cloy (kloi) *v.t.* To satiate, as with sweetness; surfeit. See synonyms under SATISFY. [Var. of earlier *accloy* <OF *encloyer* nail up, block, overload <LL *inclavare* nail < *clavus* a nail] — **cloy′ing·ly** *adv.* — **cloy′ing·ness** *n.*

club[1] (klub) *n.* **1** A stout stick or staff; cudgel; truncheon. **2** A staff with curved head of metal or wood used in golf, hockey, etc. **3 a** A three-lobed spot on a playing card. **b** A card so marked. **c** *pl.* The suit so marked. **4** *Naut.* A small spar by means of which a good set is given to a gaff topsail or a staysail; also, a similar spar on a staysail or jib to which the sheet is made fast. **5** *Entomol.* A clavate organ or part. — **Indian clubs** Bottle-shaped wooden clubs used in gymnastics. — *v.* **clubbed, club·bing** *v.t.* **1** To beat, as with a stick or club. **2** *Archaic* To gather into a clublike mass, as hair. — *v.i.* **3** *Archaic* To gather in a mass. — **to club a rifle** or **musket** or **gun** To turn a firearm so that the stock is uppermost and may be used as a club. [<ON *klubba.* Akin to CLUMP.]

club[2] (klub) *n.* **1** An organization of persons for social intercourse or other common object. **2** A house or room reserved for the meetings of such an organization. — *v.* **clubbed, club·bing** *v.t.* To contribute for a common purpose; make common stock of: to *club* resources. — *v.i.* To combine with a common object; form a club: often with *together.* — *adj.* Of, pertaining to, or belonging to a club; *club* grounds. [Special meaning of CLUB[1]]

club·ba·ble (klub′ə·bəl) *adj. Colloq.* Having tastes or qualities suited to club life; sociable. Also **club′a·ble.**

club car A railroad passenger car furnished with easy chairs, card tables, a buffet or bar, etc.

club·foot (klub′foot′) *n. pl.* **·feet** **1** Congenital

distortion of the foot; talipes. 2 A foot so affected. **—club′foot′ed** *adj.*

club·grass (klub′gras′, -gräs′) *n.* The cat-tail.

club·hand (klub′hand′) *n.* 1 A deformity of the hand, analogous to clubfoot; talipomanus. 2 A hand so deformed.

club·haul (klub′hôl′) *v.t. Naut.* To put (a vessel) about when in danger of drifting on a lee shore, by letting go the lee anchor, hauling to windward by the hawser, when the vessel's head has come into the wind, and cutting the hawser when the sails are trimmed on the new tack.

club·house (klub′hous′) *n.* The building occupied by a club.

club·man (klub′mən, -man′) *n. pl.* **·men** (-mən, -men′) A man who is a member of a club or clubs, especially one who frequents fashionable places of entertainment.

club·moss (klub′môs′, -mos′) *n.* A widely distributed evergreen herb (genus *Lycopodium*).

club sandwich A sandwich containing three or more layers of bread filled with meat, lettuce, tomatoes, mayonnaise, etc.

club steak A small beefsteak cut from the loin.

club topsail *Naut.* A sail, as a gaff topsail, extended on the foot by a club.

club·wom·an (klub′wo͝om′ən) *n. pl.* **·wom·en** (-wim′ən) A woman who is a member of a club or clubs, especially one who devotes much time to club social affairs.

cluck (kluk) *v.t.* 1 To call by clucking, as chickens. 2 To utter with a like sound: to *cluck* disapproval. *—v.i.* 3 To make the noise of a hen calling her chicks or brooding. 4 To make a sound of suction in the side of the mouth, as in urging a horse; make any sound similar to a cluck. *—n.* 1 A sound like that made by a brooding hen to call her chicks. 2 A hen. 3 *Slang* A person resembling a hen in stupidity. [Imit.]

clue (klo͞o) *n.* A guiding fact or idea which leads to the solution of a problem or mystery. See CLEW. [Var. of CLEW]

Cluj (klo͞ozh) A city in west central Rumania; former capital of Transylvania: German *Klausenburg,* Hungarian *Kolozsvár.*

Clum·ber spaniel (klum′bər) See under SPANIEL.

clump (klump) *n.* 1 A thick cluster; tuft; lump. 2 A dull sound, as of heavy tramping. 3 An irregular, clumsy, thick piece or mass. 4 *Bacteriol.* A mass of bacteria in a state of rest, as by the agency of agglutinins. *—v.t.* 1 To place or plant in a cluster or group. 2 To put an extra sole on (a shoe). 3 *Bacteriol.* To cluster together, as bacteria. *—v.i.* 4 To walk clumsily and noisily. 5 To form clumps. [<LG. Cf. Du. *klomp.* Akin to CLUB.] **—clump′y, clump′ish** *adj.*

clum·sy (klum′zē) *adj.* **·si·er, ·si·est** 1 Lacking dexterity, ease, or grace; awkward. 2 Rudely constructed; ill-contrived, so as to be unwieldy; ungainly. See synonyms under AWKWARD. [ME *clumsed,* pp. of *clumsen* be numb (with cold) <Scand. Cf. dial. Sw. *klumsen* benumbed.] **—clum′si·ly** *adv.* **—clum′si·ness** *n.*

clung (klung) Past tense and past participle of CLING.

Clu·ny (klü·nē′) A town in east central France; site of remains of a medieval Benedictine abbey.

clu·pe·id (klo͞o′pē·id) *n.* 1 Any one of a family of teleost fishes *(Clupeidae)* having compressed bodies, including the herrings, shads, etc. *—adj.* Pertaining to the *Clupeidae.* [<NL *Clupeidae* <L *clupea,* a kind of small fish]

clu·pe·oid (klo͞o′pē·oid) *adj.* Herringlike. *—n.* A fish of the herring family.

Clu·si·um (klo͞o′zhē·əm, -zē·əm) The ancient name for CHIUSI.

clus·ter (klus′tər) *n.* 1 A group or bunch, as of grapes. 2 A group of bombs dropped simultaneously. 3 An assembly; congregation. 4 In pyrotechnic illumination, a group of stars burning at the same time. *—v.t.* 1 To bring forth in or collect into clusters. 2 To provide with clusters. *—v.i.* 3 To grow in clusters, as grapes. 4 To gather in a cluster or clusters. [OE *clyster*] **—clus′tered** *adj.* **—clus′ter·y** *adj.*

cluster redpepper Bonnet pepper.

clutch[1] (kluch) *v.t.* 1 To seize eagerly; snatch, as with hands or talons. 2 To grasp and hold firmly. *—v.i.* 3 To attempt to seize, snatch, or reach: with *at:* to *clutch at* shadows. *—n.* 1 A tight, powerful grasp. 2 *pl.* Cruel, powerful claws or hands; hence, rapacious or cruel power: to fall into the *clutches* of an enemy. 3 A talon, paw, claw, or hand. 4 *Mech.* Any of variously constructed and operated devices for coupling two working parts; also, any appliance suitable for seizing and holding. See synonyms under CATCH. [ME *clucchen,* var. of *clicche,* OE *clyccan* grasp]

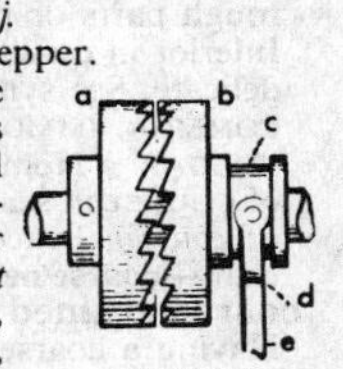

CLUTCH
a. Fixed member.
b. Slidable and splined member.
c. Collar.
d. Fork.
e. Lever.
The fork is controlled by the lever which slides *b* into connection with *a.*

clutch[2] (kluch) *n.* A sitting of eggs; a brood of chickens. *—v.t.* To hatch [<ON *klekja* hatch]

Clu·tha (klo͞o′thə) The largest river of South Island, New Zealand, flowing 210 miles SE to the Pacific.

clut·ter (klut′ər) *n.* 1 A disordered state or collection; litter. 2 A clattering, confused noise; chattering. *—v.t.* 1 To litter, heap, or pile in a confused manner: often with *up.* *—v.i.* 2 To be littered or strewn with objects in a disorderly manner. 3 To run or move with bustle or confusion; clatter. 4 To speak hurriedly and inexactly. [Var. of earlier *clotter,* freq. of CLOT]

Clyde (klīd), **Baron** See CAMPBELL, SIR COLIN.

Clyde (klīd) A river in SW Scotland, flowing 106 miles NW to the **Firth of Clyde,** its delta on the North Channel.

Clydes·dale (klīdz′dāl) *n.* A breed of draft horses originating in the valley of the Clyde, Scotland.

Cly·mer (klī′mər), **George,** 1739–1813, American patriot; legislator; signer, from Pennsylvania, of the Declaration of Independence.

clyp·e·ate (klip′ē·āt) *adj.* 1 Shield-shaped: also **clyp·e·i·form** (klip′ē·ə·fôrm′). 2 Having a clypeus. Also **clyp′e·at′ed.**

clyp·e·us (klip′ē·əs) *n. pl.* **clyp·e·i** (klip′ē·ī) 1 *Entomol.* A shieldlike plate on the front part of the head of an insect. 2 *Bot.* A band encircling the perithecium of certain fungi. [<L, shield]

clys·ter (klis′tər) *n. Med.* An intestinal injection; enema. [<F *clystère* <Gk. *klystēr* <*klyzein* wash out, rinse]

Cly·tem·nes·tra (klī′təm·nes′trə) In Greek legend the wife of Agamemnon who, with her lover Aegisthus, killed her husband on his return from the Trojan War and was herself killed by her son Orestes. Also **Cly′taem·nes′tra.**

Cm *Chem.* Curium (symbol Cm).

Cni·dus (nī′dəs) An ancient Greek city in SW Asia Minor. Also **Cni′dos.**

Cnos·sus (nos′əs) An ancient city of Crete, its capital during the Minoan period: also *Knossos.* Also **Cnos′sos.**

Cnut (kno͞ot) See CANUTE.

Co *Chem.* Cobalt (symbol Co).

co-[1] *prefix* With; together; joint or jointly: used with verbs, nouns, adjectives, and adverbs. See the foot of the page for a list of self-explanatory words containing the prefix *co-.* [<L *co-,* var. of *com-* before *gn, h,* and vowels <*cum* with]

co-[2] *prefix* 1 *Math.* Of the complement: *cosine.* 2 *Astron.* Complement of: *codeclination.* [<L *complementum* complement]

co·a·cer·vate (kō′ə·sûr′vāt, kō·as′ər-) *n. Chem.* The material precipitated in coacervation. [<L *coacervatus,* pp. of *coacervare* pile up <*co-* together + *acervus* heap]

co·ac·er·va·tion (kō·as′ər·vā′shən) *n. Chem.* The precipitation of minute liquid droplets from a mixture of two hydrophilic colloids having opposite electric charges.

coach (kōch) *n.* 1 A large four-wheeled closed carriage. 2 A two-door, two-seated, closed automobile. 3 A stagecoach. 4 A passenger bus. 5 A railway passenger car, usually providing the lowest-priced accommodations on a train. 6 A private tutor. 7 A trainer and director in athletics. 7 In baseball, a member of the team at bat stationed near first or third base to advise the base runners. *—v.t.* 1 To tutor or train; prepare by training or drilling. 2 To place or carry in a coach. 3 In baseball, to direct base runners in their movements, as from first or third base. *—v.i.* 4 To study with or be trained by a coach or trainer. 5 To act as coach or trainer. 6 To ride or drive in a coach. [<MF *coche* <Magyar *kocsi* of Kocs, a Hungarian village where first used]

coach-and-four (kōch′ən·fôr′, -fōr′) *n.* A coach drawn by four horses.

coach dog A Dalmatian.

coach·er (kō′chər) *n.* 1 One who coaches. 2 In baseball, a coach. 3 A coach horse. 4 *Obs.* A coachman.

coach horse A horse suitable for drawing a coach.

coach·man (kōch′mən) *n. pl.* **·men** (-mən) 1 One who drives a coach or a carriage. 2 In angling, a variety of artificial fly.

co·act (kō·akt′) *v.i.* To act or work together. **—co·ac′tion** *n.* **—co·ac′tive** *adj.*

co·act (kō·akt′) *v.t.* To force; compel; coerce. [<L *coactus,* pp. of *cogere* compel <*co-* together + *agere* do, drive]

co·ac·tion (kō·ak′shən) *n.* The exertion of force in compulsion or restraint.

co·ac·tive (kō·ak′tiv) *adj.* Having power to compel or constrain; compulsory.

co·ad·ju·tant (kō·aj′ə·tənt) *adj.* Cooperating. *—n.* An assistant; colleague. [<CO- + L *adjutans, -antis,* ppr. of *adjutare* help]

co·ad·ju·tor (kō·aj′ə·tər, kō′ə·jo͞o′tər) *n.* An associate in action; a co-worker or colleague, especially one appointed to assist in official duties, as the assistant of a bishop. See synonyms under ACCESSORY, ASSOCIATE, AUXILIARY. **—co·ad′ju·tress, co·ad′ju·trix** *n. fem.*

co·ad·u·nate (kō·aj′ə·nāt) *v.t.* To join together. *adj.* (kō·aj′ə·nit, -nāt) *Biol.* Closely joined, especially during the growth of an organ or part. [<L *coadunatus,* pp. of *coadunare* unite <*co-* together + *ad* to + *unus* one] **—co·ad′u·na′tion** *n.* **—co·ad′u·na′tive** *adj.*

co·ae·val (kō·ē′vəl) See COEVAL.

co·ag·u·lant (kō·ag′yə·lənt) *n.* A coagulation agent, as rennet. [<L *coagulans, -antis,* ppr. of *coagulare* curdle]

co·ag·u·late (kō·ag′yə·lāt) *v.t.* & *v.i.* **·lat·ed, ·lat·ing** To change from a liquid state into a clot or jelly, as blood. [<L *coagulatus,* pp. of *coagulare* curdle] **—co·ag′u·la·bil′i·ty** *n.* **—co·ag·u·la·ble** (kō·ag′yə·lə·bəl) *adj.* **—co·ag′u·la′tion** *n.* **—co·ag′u·la′tive** *adj.* **—co·ag′u·la′tor** *n.*

co·ag·u·lum (kō·ag′yə·ləm) *n. pl.* **·la** (-lə) Any coagulated mass, as a gel, curd, or clot. [<L, that which binds together]

Co·a·hui·la (kō′ä·wē′lä) A state in northern Mexico; 58,067 square miles; capital, Saltillo.

coak (kōk) See COKE[1].

coal (kōl) *n.* 1 A black, brittle, compact, amorphous substance of variable physical and chemical composition, produced by the carbonization of prehistoric vegetation: found in beds or veins in the earth and used as fuel; the principal varieties are bituminous coal, anthracite, and lignite. 2 A piece of coal as broken for use; such pieces collectively: in Great Britain commonly used in the plural. 3 A fragment of burned wood; charcoal. 4 An ember. **—to haul, rake,** etc., **over the coals** To criticize; reprimand. *—v.t.* 1 To supply with coal. 2 To reduce to coal, as wood, by burning. *—v.i.* 3 To take in coal. ◆ Homophone: *cole.* [OE *col*]

Coal may appear as a combining form in

coadequate	**coadmire**	**coagitate**	**coambassador**	**coapparition**	**coapprover**	**coassessor**
coadminister	**coadmit**	**coagitation**	**coanimate**	**coappear**	**coarbiter**	**coassignee**
coadministration	**coadventure**	**coagitator**	**coannex**	**coappearance**	**coarrange**	**coassist**
coadministrator	**coagency**	**coagriculturist**	**coannihilate**	**coappriser**	**coarrangement**	**coassistance**
coadmiration	**coagent**	**co-allied**	**coapostate**	**coapprove**	**coassession**	**coassistant**

add,āce,câre,pälm; end,ēven; it,īce; odd,ōpen,ôrder; to͝ok,po͞ol; up,bûrn; ə = a in *above,* e in *sicken,* i in *clarity,* o in *melon,* u in *focus* ; yo͞o = u in *fuse,* oi,oil; ou,pout; ch,check; g,go; ng,ring; th,thin; th,this; zh,vision. Foreign sounds á,œ,ü,kh,ń; and ◆: see page xx. <from; + plus; ? possibly.

hyphemes or in solidemes, or in two-word phrases, as in:

coal ashes	coal-dark	coal-heaver
coal barge	coal-dealer	coal-laden
coalbin	coal-dealing	coal mine
coal-black	coal deposit	coal-miner
coal-blue	coal-digger	coal-mining
coalbox	coal-digging	coalmonger
coal bunker	coal district	coal-producing
coal-burner	coal dust	coal-rationing
coal-burning	coal-eyed	coal-rich
coal chute	coalfield	coalshed
coal-consumer	coal-fired	coal strata
coal-consuming	coal furnace	coalyard

coal bank A vein of coal at the surface.

coal bed A receptacle or place for coals, as in a forge. See illustration under FORGE.

coal car A railroad car designed to carry coal, as from a mine.

coal·er (kōl′ər) n. One who or that which supplies or transports coal; a collier.

co·a·lesce (kō′ə·les′) v.i. **·lesced**, **·lesc·ing** To grow or come together into one; fuse; blend. See synonyms under UNITE. [< L *coalescere* unite < *co-* together + *alescere*, inceptive of *alere* grow up] —**co′a·les′cence** n. —**co′a·les′cent** adj.

coal·fish (kōl′fish′) n. pl. **·fish** or **·fish·es** 1 A dark-colored food fish (*Pollachius virens*) of the cod family; the common pollack of the Atlantic. 2 The sablefish.

coal gas 1 The poisonous gas produced by the combustion of coal. **2** A gas used for illuminating and heating: produced by the distillation of bituminous coal and consisting chiefly of methane, carbon monoxide, and hydrogen.

coal·hole (kōl′hōl′) n. **1** A place for storing coal. **2** A covered hole in a sidewalk, through which coal is chuted to a bin or cellar.

coal·ing (kō′ling) n. **1** The burning of wood into charcoal; also, the place where this is done. **2** Loading with coal.

coaling station A place where boats or trains stop to take on coal.

co·a·li·tion (kō′ə·lish′ən) n. **1** An alliance of persons, parties, or states. **2** Coalescence. See synonyms under ALLIANCE, UNION. [< L *coalitio*, *-onis* < *coalescere*. See COALESCE.] —**co′a·li′tion·ist** n.

Coal Measures A division of the Carboniferous series containing workable beds of coal.

coal oil Kerosene.

coal·pit (kōl′pit′) n. **1** A pit from which coal is obtained. **2** A pit for making charcoal.

coal·sack (kōl′sak′) n. **1** A sack for coal. **2** *Astron.* One of several dark spaces in the Milky Way, especially **the Coalsack,** a large space near the Large and Small Magellanic clouds in the constellation of the Southern Cross.

coal scuttle A bucketlike container with a lip and a handle, used for containing and carrying coal.

coal tar The black viscid pitch distilled from bituminous coal, and yielding a large variety of organic compounds used in the making of dyestuffs, explosives, flavoring extracts, drugs, plastics, etc. —**coal′-tar′** adj.

coam·ing (kō′ming) n. *Naut.* **1** A raised curb about a hatchway, well, or skylight, to keep water from entering: also spelled *combing.* **2** One of the pieces in such a curb. [Origin unknown]

co·arc·tate (kō·ärk′tāt) adj. **1** *Bot.* Crowded together, as a panicle of flowers; compressed. **2** *Entomol.* Constricted at the base, as the abdomen of an insect. [< L *coarctatus*, pp. of *coarctare*, var. of *coartare* confine, constrain < *co-* together + *artus* crowded]

co·arc·ta·tion (kō′ärk·tā′shən) n. Stricture or contraction, as of a cavity or orifice.

coarse (kôrs, kōrs) adj. **1** Composed of large or rough parts or particles; not fine or delicate. **2** Inferior in quality; common. **3** Low; vulgar; indelicate. See synonyms under BLUFF, BRUTISH, COMMON, IMMODEST, LARGE, ROUGH, RUSTIC, VULGAR. ◆ Homophone: *course.* [Adjectival use of COURSE in sense "customary sequence" (as in *of course*); hence, usual, ordinary] —**coarse′ly** adv. —**coarse′ness** n.

coarse-grained (kôrs′grānd′, kōrs′-) adj. **1** Having a coarse grain or texture. **2** Crude; indelicate; low.

coars·en (kôr′sən, kōr′-) v.t. & v.i. To make or become coarse.

coast (kōst) n. **1** The land next to the sea; the seashore. **2** *Obs.* A region; boundary: used chiefly in the plural. **3** A slope suitable for sliding, as on a sled; also, a slide down it. —**the Coast** *U.S.* That part of the United States bordering on the Pacific Ocean. —**the coast is clear** There is no danger or difficulty now. —v.t. **1** To sail or travel along, as a coast or border. —v.i. **2** To sail or travel along a coast or littoral, keeping in sight of land; to travel from port to port along a coast. **3** To slide or ride down a slope by force of gravity alone, as on a sled or bicycle. **4** To continue moving on momentum after the source of power has been stopped. **5** To move or behave aimlessly. [< OF *coste* < L *costa* rib, flank]

coast·al (kōs′təl) adj. **1** Of or pertaining to the coast. **2** Bordering or skirting a coastline.

coast artillery Units of heavy artillery, fixed or movable, for defense against hostile ships.

coast·er (kōs′tər) n. **1** One who or that which coasts, as a person or vessel engaged in the coasting trade. **2** A sled or toboggan. **3** Formerly, a tray used in passing a decanter around a dining table. **4** A small disk of glass or other material on which to set a drinking glass to protect the surface underneath from moisture or heat.

coaster brake A free-wheel clutch brake on a bicycle, operated by reversing the pressure on the pedals.

coast guard 1 Naval or military coast police. **2** A member of this police. —**United States Coast Guard** A police or military force stationed along the coasts to enforce customs, immigration, and navigation laws and maintain an ice patrol. It operates in wartime within the U.S. Navy and at other times under the Department of the Treasury.

coast·ing (kōs′ting) n. **1** The act of sliding down a snow-covered hill or track on a sled. **2** The act of going down grade by force of gravity, as on a bicycle or in a car. **3** Trade up and down the same coast from port to port: also **coasting trade.**

Coast Mountains A range in western British Columbia and southern Alaska; highest point, 13,260 feet.

Coast Province A region of SE Kenya on the Indian Ocean; 26,651 square miles; capital, Mombasa.

Coast Ranges A mountain belt of western North America, extending along the Pacific coast from Alaska into Lower California; highest peak, 19,850 feet.

coast·ward (kōst′wərd) adj. Directed or facing toward the coast. —adv. Toward the coast: also **coast′wards.**

coast·wise (kōst′wīz′) adj. Following or along the coast. —adv. By way of or along the coast: also **coast′ways.**

coat (kōt) n. **1** A sleeved outer garment opening down the front, of varying length: worn as part of an outfit or as an out-of-door covering over one's usual clothing. **2** Any outer covering, as the fur of an animal, a layer of ice or paint, etc. **3** A coat of arms. **4** *Dial.* A skirt; petticoat. **5** *Obs.* The distinctive vesture of an order of men; cloth. —v.t. To cover with or as with a coat, as of paint. [< OF *cote* < Med. L *cota* garment] —**coat′less** adj.

coat·ed (kō′tid) adj. **1** Having a covering, layer, or coat. **2** In papermaking, having a calendered surface of mineral matter, as sizing or china clay.

coat·ee (kō·tē′) n. A short coat.

Coates (kōts), **Albert,** 1882–1954, English conductor born in Russia. —**Joseph Gordon,** 1878–1943, New Zealand statesman.

co·a·ti (kō·ä′tē) n. pl. **·tis** A carnivorous, raccoonlike mammal (genus *Nasua*) of tropical America, with mobile snout, plantigrade feet, elongated body, and a long, ringed tail. Also **co·a·ti·mon·di, co·a·ti·mun·di** (-mun′dē). [< Tupian]

coat·ing (kō′ting) n. **1** A covering layer; coat. **2** Cloth for coats.

coat of arms The armorial bearings of a person or family.

coat of mail See under MAIL².

coat·tail (kōt′tāl′) n. **1** The loose hinder part of a coat below the waist. **2** *Usually pl.* The pendent, tapering, rear part of a man's dress coat.

Co·at·za·co·al·cos (kō·ät′sä·kō·äl′kōs) A city on the Gulf of Campeche in Veracruz state, SE Mexico: formerly *Puerto Mexico.*

coax (kōks) v.t. **1** To persuade or seek to persuade by gentleness and tact; wheedle. **2** To obtain by coaxing or cajolery. —v.i. **3** To use persuasion or cajolery. See synonyms under ALLURE, PERSUADE. —n. One who coaxes. —**coax′er** n. —**coax′ing·ly** adv. [< Earlier *cokes* a fool, dupe; origin unknown]

co·ax·i·al (kō·ak′sē·əl) adj. Having a common axis or coincident axes: also **co·ax·al** (kō·ak′səl).

coaxial cable A conducting wire for the transmission of radio or television signals or of multiple telegraph or telephone messages; held in the center of a metal tube by a series of closely-spaced disks, every element of the assembly being well insulated.

cob¹ (kob) n. **1** A roundish mass, heap, or lump, as a piece of coal or stone. **2** The woody spike of an ear of corn around which the kernels grow; a corncob. **3** A strong, thick-set, short-legged horse. **4** The male of the swan. **5** *Brit. Dial.* A leading man; a leader. [ME *cobbe*; origin uncertain]

cob² (kob) n. *Brit.* A gull, especially the great black-backed gull (*Larus marinus*). Also **cobb.** [Cf. Du. *kobbe* gull]

co·balt (kō′bôlt) n. A hard, brittle, magnetic metallic element (symbol Co, atomic number 27) usually found in iron and nickel ores, used in alloys, and biologically essential for the activity of several enzymes. See PERIODIC TABLE. [< G *kobalt*, var. of *kobold* goblin; so called by early miners who thought it a worthless, injurious ore]

cobalt bloom Erythrite.

cobalt blue 1 A permanent deep-blue pigment resembling ultramarine, made from the oxides of cobalt and aluminum. **2** An intense, pure blue.

co·bal·tic (kō·bôl′tik) adj. *Chem.* Designating a compound containing cobalt in its higher valence.

co·bal·tite (kō·bôl′tīt, kō′bôl·tīt) n. A metallic, silver-white, brittle cobalt sulfarsenide, CoAsS. Also **co·bal·tine** (kō′bôl·tēn, -tin).

co·bal·tous (kō·bôl′təs) adj. *Chem.* Designating a compound containing cobalt in its lower valence.

Cobb (kob), **Irvin Shrewsbury,** 1876–1944, U.S. humorist.

cob·ber (kob′ər) *Austral. Slang* A friend; companion; workfellow.

Cob·bett (kob′it), **William,** 1762–1835, English political economist.

cob·ble¹ (kob′əl) n. **1** A cobblestone. **2** A lump of coal as big as a cobblestone. —v.t. To pave with cobblestones. [Akin to COB¹]

cob·ble² (kob′əl) v. **·bled, ·bling** v.t. **1** To make, patch, or repair, as boots or shoes. **2** To put together roughly. —v.i. **3** To work as a shoemaker. [Origin uncertain]

cob·ble³ (kob′əl) See COBLE.

cob·bler¹ (kob′lər) n. **1** A shoemaker. **2** A clumsy workman. [< COBBLE²]

cob·bler² (kob′lər) n. **1** An iced drink made of wine, sugar, fruit juices, etc. **2** A deep-dish fruit pie with no bottom crust. [Origin unknown]

cob·ble·stone (kob′əl·stōn′) n. A rounded stone formerly much used for paving. [See COBBLE¹]

cob coal A large round piece of coal; also, coal in such pieces or lumps.

Cob·den·ism (kob′dən·iz′əm) n. The policies of free trade, international peace, and aloof-

coassume	co-attribution	co-believer	co-constituent	cocreditor	co-derive	coeffect
co-attend	co-auditor	coclause	co-contractor	cocurator	co-descendant	co-embody
co-attest	co-author	co-connection	co-covenanter	co-debtor	co-dominion	coembrace
co-attestation	co-authority	co-conscious	cocreate	co-defendant	co-edify	coeminency
co-attribute	co-authorship	co-conspirator	cocreator	co-delinquent	co-editor	coemperor

ness from the European struggle for supremacy, advanced by **Richard Cobden,** 1804–1865, English statesman and political economist.

co·bel·lig·er·ent (kō'bə·lij'ər·ənt) *n.* A country fighting on the same side with another, or others, against a common enemy: distinguished from an *ally* in international usage in that it is not bound by an alliance.

Cóbh (kōv) A port in SW Ireland: formerly *Queenstown.*

Cob·ham (kob'əm), **Lord,** 1360?–1417, John Oldcastle, English Lollard leader.

cob·le (kob'əl) *n.* **1** *Brit.* A flat-bottomed fishing boat. **2** *Scot.* A flat-bottomed rowboat. Also spelled **cobble.** [OE (Northumbrian) *cuopl*]

Co·blenz (kō'blents) A city at the junction of the Rhine and Moselle in western Germany: also *Koblenz.*

cob·nut (kob'nut') *n.* **1** A large nut from a cultivated variety of hazel tree *(Corylus avellana grandis).* **2** The tree producing it. **3** A children's game played with such nuts. [? <COB[1] (def. 1) + NUT]

co·bra[1] (kō'brə) *n.* Any of a genus *(Naja)* of very venomous snakes of Asia and Africa that when excited can dilate their necks into a broad hood; especially, the **spectacled cobra** *(N. naja)* of India, and the **king cobra** *(Ophiophagus hannah),* the largest known of all venomous snakes. [<Pg. <L *colubra* snake]

co·bra[2] (kob'rə) See COPRA.

COBRA
a. Indian or spectacled cobra.
b. Back of head, showing markings or "spectacles."
(Up to 6 feet in length)

co·bra·de·ca·pel·lo (kō'brə·dē·kə·pel'ō) *n. pl.* **co·bras·de·ca·pel·lo** The spectacled snake. [<Pg., snake with a hood]

Co·burg (kō'bûrg, *Ger.* kō'bŏŏrkh) A city in Upper Franconia, central Germany: also *Koburg.*

cob·web (kob'web') *n.* **1** The network of fine thread spun by a spider; also, a single thread of this. **2** A snare, or anything fine-spun or flimsy. —*v.t.* **cob·webbed, cob·web·bing** To cover with or as with cobwebs. [ME *coppeweb* <*coppe* spider + WEB] —**cob'web'ber·y** *n.*

cob·work (kob'wûrk') *n.* A structure of logs laid crosswise, with ends secured by dovetailing.

co·ca (kō'kə) *n.* **1** The dried leaves of a South American shrub (genus *Erythroxylon*), yielding cocaine and other alkaloids and sometimes chewed for their stimulant properties. **2** Either of the two species of this shrub which yield these alkaloids. [<Sp. <Quechua]

co·caine (kō·kān', kō'kān; *in technical usage* kō'kə·ēn) *n.* A white, bitter, crystalline alkaloid, $C_{17}H_{21}NO_4$, contained in coca leaves: used in medicine as a local anesthetic and as a narcotic. Also **co·cain'.** [<COCA]

co·cain·ism (kō·kā'niz·əm, kō'kə·niz'əm) *n. Pathol.* A morbid condition produced by the excessive use of cocaine; cocaine poisoning.

co·cain·ize (kō·kā'nīz, kō'kə·nīz) *v.t.* **·ized, ·iz·ing** To bring under the specific effect of cocaine. —**co·cain'i·za'tion** *n.*

co·car·box·yl·ase (kō'kär·bok'səl·ās) *n.* A coenzyme necessary in the production and activity of carboxylase.

co·car·cin·o·gen (kō'kär'sin'ə·jən) *n.* Any noncarcinogenic agent that enhances the action of a carcinogen.

coc·cid (kok'sid) *n. Entomol.* Any member of a superfamily *(Coccoidae)* of hemipterous insects,

including mealybugs and scale insects. [<NL *Coccoidae* <Gk. *kokkos* berry]

coc·cid·i·oi·dal granuloma (kok·sid'ē·oid'l) A disease caused by a fungus (genus *Coccidioides*) superficially resembling tuberculosis, which affects the lymph nodes of some animals and of man. [<NL *Coccidioides* <Gk. *kokkos* a berry + *eidos* form]

coc·cid·i·o·sis (kok·sid'ē·ō'sis) *n.* One of a group of specific infectious diseases caused by protozoan parasites (order *Coccidia*) which attack the epithelial tissue of animals, birds, and, rarely, man. [<NL *Coccidia* (<Gk. *kokkos* a berry) + -OSIS]

coc·cif·er·ous (kok·sif'ər·əs) *adj. Bot.* Bearing or producing berries. [<Gk. *kokkos* berry + -(I)FEROUS]

coc·coid (kok'oid) *adj. Bacteriol.* Like a coccus: applied to certain forms of bacteria which tend to be round in form.

coc·co·lith (kok'ə·lith) *n. Geol.* A minute oval or rounded body often abundant in deep-sea mud. [<Gk. *kokkos* berry + -LITH]

coc·cu·lus in·di·cus (kok'yə·ləs in'də·kəs) The fishberry.

coc·cus (kok'əs) *n. pl.* **coc·ci** (kok'sī) **1** *Bot.* **a** One of the dry, one-seeded portions into which a schizocarp splits. **b** A spore mother cell in which the spores are contained for a time after their maturity. **2** *Bacteriol.* One of the principal forms of bacteria, characterized by an ovoid or spherical shape: often used in combination: *streptococcus.* See illustration under BACTERIUM. **3** *Entomol.* One of a genus *(Coccus)* of scale insects. [<NL <Gk. *kokkos* berry]

coc·cyx (kok'siks) *n. pl.* **coc·cy·ges** (kok·sī'jēz) *Anat.* The caudal end of the spine. [<L <Gk. *kokkyx* cuckoo; from a fancied resemblance to a cuckoo's bill] —**coc·cyg·e·al** (kok·sij'ē·əl) *adj.*

Co·cha·bam·ba (kō'chä·bäm'bä) A city in central Bolivia.

Co·chin (kō'chin') An administrative division of northern Travancore-Cochin, southern India; 1,493 square miles; capital, Ernakulam.

Co·chin (kō'chin, koch'in) *n.* A variety of large domestic fowl, of Asiatic origin, having heavily feathered legs. Also **Co'chin·chi'na.**

Cochin China A former name of SOUTH VIETNAM.

coch·i·neal (koch'ə·nēl', koch'ə·nēl) *n.* A coloring matter yielding a brilliant scarlet dye, consisting of the dried bodies of the female *Dactylopius coccus,* a scale insect of tropical America and of Java. [<F *cochenille* <Sp. *cochinilla* <L *coccineus* scarlet <*coccus* a berry, grain of kermes <Gk. *kokkos*]

coch·le·a (kok'lē·ə) *n. pl.* **·le·ae** (-li·ē) *Anat.* A winding cavity in the internal ear, containing the essential organs of hearing. See illustration under EAR. [<L *cochlea* snail] —**coch'le·ar** *adj.*

coch·le·ate (kok'lē·āt) *adj.* Spirally twisted like a snail shell. Also **coch'le·at'ed.**

co·ci·na (kō·sē'nä) *n. SW U.S.* A kitchen. [<Sp.]

co·ci·ne·ra (kō'sē·nä'rä) *n. SW U.S.* A cook. [<Sp.]

cock[1] (kok) *n.* **1** A full-grown male of the domestic fowl. **2** Any male bird. **3** A leader; champion. **4** A weathercock. **5** A faucet, often with the nozzle bent downward. **6** In a firearm, the hammer; also, the position at which the hammer rests when raised. **7** A significant jaunty tip or upward turn; a bending or pricking up, as of a hat brim, the ears, eyes, etc. —*v.t.* **1** To raise the cock or hammer of (a firearm) preparatory to firing. **2** To turn up or to one side alertly, jauntily, or inquiringly, as the head, eye, ears, etc. —*v.i.* **3** To raise the hammer of a firearm. **4** To stick up; be prominent. —*adj.* Male: a *cock* lobster. [OE *cocc*]

cock[2] (kok) *n.* A small conical pile of straw or hay. —*v.t.* To arrange in piles or cocks, as hay. [<ON *kökkr* lump, heap]

cock[3] (kok) *n.* A ship's small boat; cockboat. [<F *coque*]

cock·ade (kok·ād') *n.* A rosette, knot of ribbon, or the like, worn on the hat. [<MF *coquarde* <*coq* cock] —**cock·ad'ed** *adj.*

Cockade State Nickname of MARYLAND.

cock·a·doo·dle·doo (kok'ə·dōōd'l·dōō') *n.* The characteristic crow of a cock; hence, a rooster.

cock·a·hoop (kok'ə·hōōp', -hōōp') *adj.* **1** Elated; exultant. **2** Boastful. —*adv.* Triumphantly. [Origin uncertain]

Cock·aigne (kok·ān') *n.* **1** An imaginary region of luxury and ease. **2** Cockneydom. Also **Cock·agne'.** [<OF *cocaigne;* ult. origin uncertain]

cock·a·lo·rum (kok'ə·lôr'əm, -lō'rəm) *n.* A self-important little man. [Cf. Du. *kockeloeren* crow]

cock·and·bull (kok'ən·bool') *adj.* Highly improbable; incredible: a *cock-and-bull* story.

cock·a·tiel (kok'ə·tēl') *n.* An Australian cockatoo of the genus *Leptolophus,* especially *L. hollandicus.* Also **cock'a·teel'.** [<Du. *kaketielje*]

cock·a·too (kok'ə·tōō', kok'ə·tōō) *n. pl.* **·toos** Any of various, bright-colored, crested parrots of the East Indies or Australia, especially one of the genus *Kakatoë.* [<Du. *kaketoe* <Malay *kākatūa;* infl. in form by COCK]

cock·a·trice (kok'ə·tris) *n.* **1** A fabulous serpent, said to be hatched from a cock's egg, deadly to those who felt its breath or met its glance. Compare **basilisk. 2** In the Bible, an unidentified species of deadly serpent. [<OF *cocatris,* infl. by *coq* cock, <Med. L *calcatrix* (<L *calcare* tread, walk), used to translate Gk. *ichneumōn* ICHNEUMON]

cock·boat (kok'bōt') *n.* A small rowboat: also called *cock.* [<COCK[3] + BOAT]

cock·chaf·er (kok'chā'fər) *n.* Any of a widely distributed family *(Melolonthidae)* of scarabaeoid beetles, especially *Melolontha melolontha,* a large, European variety destructive to vegetation. [<COCK[1] (def. 3) + CHAFER]

cock·crow (kok'krō') *n.* The early morning. Also **cock'crow'ing.**

cocked hat (kokt) **1** A hat with the brim turned up, especially one turned up in three places; a three-cornered hat. **2** A game of bowls played with three pins. —**to knock into a cocked hat** To demolish; ruin.

cock·er[1] (kok'ər) *n.* **1** A cocker spaniel. See under SPANIEL. **2** A cockfighter.

cock·er[2] (kok'ər) *v.t.* To spoil by indulgence; coddle. [Prob. <Scand. Cf. Norw. *kokla* crow, fuss over, pamper.]

cock·er·el (kok'ər·əl) *n.* A young cock. [Dim. of COCK[1]]

Cock·er·mouth (kok'ər·muth) A town in Cumberland County, England; birthplace of Wordsworth.

cock·eye (kok'ī') *n.* A squinting eye.

cock·eye bob (kok'ī') *Austral. Slang* A willy willy (def. 1).

cock·eyed (kok'īd') *adj.* **1** Cross-eyed. **2** *Slang* Off center; askew. **3** Absurd; crazy. **4** Drunk; intoxicated.

cock·fight (kok'fīt') *n.* A battle between cocks, especially between gamecocks. Also **cock'match'.** —**cock'fight'er** *n.* —**cock'fight'ing** *adj. & n.*

cock·horse (kok'hôrs') *n.* A child's rocking-horse, hobbyhorse, or the like.

cock·i·ness (kok'ē·nis) *n.* Jauntiness; also, conceit.

cock·ing (kok'ing) *n.* **1** Cockfighting. **2** The shooting of woodcocks.

cock·ish (kok'ish) *adj.* **1** Cocklike; cocky. **2** Strutting; self-assertive. —**cock'ish·ly** *adv.* —**cock'ish·ness** *n.*

cock·le[1] (kok'əl) *n.* **1** An edible European bivalve mollusk *(Cardium edule).* **2** The cockleshell. **3** A confection made with sugar

COCKATOO
(About 12 inches tall)

coemploy	coendure	coerect	coestate	coexecutant	cofeoffer	coheritor
coenact	coepiscopacy	coerectant	coeternal	coexecutor	coheir	co-incline
coenactor	coequate	coessential	coeternally	coexert	coheiress	co-include
coenamor	coequated	coestablish	coexchange	coexertion	coheirship	co-incorporate
coenamorment	coequation	coestablishment	coexchangeable	coextend	coheritage	co-idemnify

and flour. **4** The fire chamber or dome of a hot-air furnace. **5** A shallow boat. **— cockles of one's heart** The depths or bottom of one's heart, or feelings. — *v.t.* & *v.i.* **cock·led, cock·ling** To wrinkle; pucker. [<F *coquille* <L *conchylium* shell <Gk. *conchylion*, dim. of *conchylē* shell, mussel]

cock·le[2] (kok′əl) *n.* A grass that grows among grain; the darnel. [OE *coccel*]

cock·le·boat (kok′əl·bōt′) *n.* A cockboat or cockle.

cock·le·bur (kok′əl·bûr′) *n.* **1** A low-branching, rank weed (genus *Xanthium*) of the composite family, with hard ovoid or oblong two-celled burs about an inch long. **2** *Brit.* The burdock.

cock·le·shell (kok′əl·shel′) *n.* **1** The shell of a cockle; especially, one valve of a scallop's shell worn in a pilgrim's hat. **2** A scallop shell. **3** A frail, light boat.

cock·loft (kok′lôft′, -loft′) *n.* A loft or attic under a roof. [Origin uncertain]

cock·ney (kok′nē) *n.* **1** One born in the East End of London, traditionally within the sound of the bells of St. Mary-le-Bow Church, in Cheapside, and speaking a characteristic dialect. **2** One having the traits or dialect of such a person; especially, an uneducated yet pretentious city person. **4** The characteristic dialect or accent of East End Londoners. **5** *Obs.* A petted child; an effeminate youth. — *adj.* Of or like cockneys or their speech. [ME *cokeney*, lit., cock's egg < *coken* cock's + OE *æg* egg; later, a pampered child, a soft or effeminate person, a city man] **— cock′ney·ish** *adj.* **— cock′ney·ism** *n.*

cock·ney·dom (kok′nē·dəm) *n.* The sphere or realm of cockneys; London and its suburbs.

cock·ney·ese (kok′nē·ēz′, -ēs′) *n.* Cockney dialect.

cock·ney·fy (kok′ni·fī) *v.t.* **·fied, ·fy·ing** Cause to resemble a cockney in speech or manners.

cock of the plains A large grouse (*Centrocercus urophasianus*): also called *sage cock, prairie cock.*

cock of the walk One who has overcome all opposition; leader or chief in any group. Also **cock of the loft.**

cock·pit (kok′pit′) *n.* **1** A pit or ring for cockfighting; hence, any place where many battles have taken place. **2** An apartment for the wounded in a warship. **3** *Naut.* In small yachts, a space lower than the rest of the deck. **4** *Aeron.* In some airplanes, an enclosed space for the pilot and co-pilot or a passenger. **5** *Obs.* The pit of a theater.

cock·roach (kok′rōch′) *n.* Any of a large group of swift-running, chiefly nocturnal insects (families *Blattidae* and *Phyllodromidae*) of world-wide distribution, having flat, oval, variously colored bodies, biting mouth parts, and a typically offensive odor, including such household pests as the Croton bug, the dark-brown Oriental cockroach (*Blatta orientalis*) and the large, winged American cockroach (*Periplaneta americana*). For illustration see INSECTS (injurious). [<Sp. *cucaracha*]

cocks·comb (koks′kōm′) *n.* **1** A plant (genus *Celosia*) with red flowers, suggesting the comb of a cock. **2** A coxcomb (def. 1). **3** A scarlet ridge on a jester's cap; also, the cap. Also spelled *coxcomb.*

cocks·head (koks′hed′) *n.* An annual shrubby herb (*Onobrychis caputgalli*) of the Mediterranean region, with purple flowers and small, crested, spine-bearing pods.

cock·shut (kok′shut′) *n.* *Obs.* Twilight.

cock·shy (kok′shī′) *n.* *pl.* **·shies** *Brit. Colloq.* **1** A mark to be shied or thrown at, as at fairs. **2** A throw, as at a mark.

cock·spur (kok′spûr′) *n.* **1** A spur on the leg of a cock. **2** A kind of hawthorn (*Crataegus crusgalli*) with long thorns: also **cockspur thorn.**

cock·sure (kok′shŏŏr′) *adj.* **1** Absolutely sure. **2** Self-confident; presumptuously sure. **3** *Obs.* Perfectly safe. **— cock′sure′ness** *n.*

cock·swain (kok′sən, -swān′) See COXSWAIN.

cock·tail[1] (kok′tāl′) *n.* **1** A short, mixed, alcoholic drink, variously flavored and prepared. **2** An appetizer, as chilled, diced fruits, fruit juices, or sea food seasoned with a highly spiced sauce. [? Alter. of F *coquetel*, a mixed drink popular in the 18th c.]

cock·tail[2] (kok′tāl′) *n.* **1** A horse with a docked tail. **2** An underbred horse. **3** A person of low breeding. [<COCK[1] (def. 1) + TAIL; with ref. to the appearance of a horse's docked tail]

cock-up (kok′up′) *n.* **1** A turned-up or cocked part or point of anything. **2** A cocked hat.

cock·y[1] (kok′ē) *adj.* **cock·i·er, cock·i·est** *Colloq.* Pert or forward; confident or overconfident; conceited; snobbish. **— cock′i·ly** *adv.*

cock·y[2] (kok′ē) *n.* *Austral.* A small farmer: cow *cocky*; cane *cocky*; bee *cocky.*

co·co (kō′kō) *n.* *pl.* **·cos** A widely distributed tropical palm tree (*Cocos nucifera*) that produces coconuts. Also **coco palm, coconut palm.** — *adj.* Made of coco fiber. [<Pg., grinning face; with ref. to the eyes of a coconut]

co·coa (kō′kō) *n.* **1** A powder made from the roasted, husked seed kernels of the cacao; chocolate. **2** A beverage made from it. **3** The light reddish-brown color of cocoa powder. [Alter. of CACAO]

cocoa butter Cacao butter.

co·co·bo·lo (kō′kō·bō′lō) *n.* Granadillo. [<Sp.]

co·co·grass (kō′kō·gras′, -gräs′) *n.* The nut-grass.

co·con·scious·ness (kō·kon′shəs·nis) *n.* *Psychol.* A latent or accompanying consciousness, on the fringe of awareness. **— co·con′scious** *adj.* **— co·con′scious·ly** *adv.*

co·co·nut (kō′kə·nut′, -nət) *n.* **1** The fruit of the coco palm, a white-meated seed enclosed in a hard shell, and containing a milky liquid. **2** *Slang* The head or skull. Also **co′coa·nut′.**

coconut palm The coco or coco palm.

co·coon (kə·kōōn′) *n.* **1** The envelope spun by the larvae of certain insects, as silkworms, in which they are enclosed in the pupal or chrysalis state. **2** Any analogous structure, as the egg-bearing case of spiders, earthworms, etc. **3** *Mil.* The weatherproof covering of cellophane or quick-drying synthetic resin in which military or other heavy equipment may be sealed during transport or when not in use. — *v.t.* To envelop or place in a cocoon. [<F *cocon* < *coque* shell]

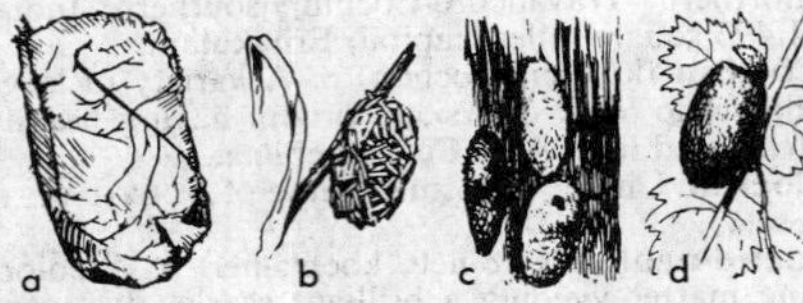

COCOONS
a. American silkworm. *b.* Caddis fly. *c.* Weevil under bark. *d.* Sawfly.

Co·cos Islands (kō′kōs) An island group SW of Java, comprising a dependency of Australia; 1.5 square miles: also *Keeling Islands.* Also **Co′cos-Kee′ling.**

co·cotte (kō·kot′, kə-) *n.* A young woman of dubious character or loose morals. [<F]

Coc·teau (kok·tō′), **Jean,** 1891–1963, French dramatist, novelist, critic, and poet.

coc·tion (kok′shən) *n.* The act or process of boiling. [<L *coctio, -onis* <*coquere* cook]

co·cur·ric·u·lum (kō′kə·rik′yə·ləm) *n.* The extra-curricular activities of students in the modern secondary school, such as athletics, student councils, clubs, fraternities, etc. **— co′cur·ric′u·lar** *adj.*

Co·cy·tus (kō·sī′təs) In Greek mythology, the river of wailing, one of the five rivers surrounding Hades.

cod[1] (kod) *n.* **1** An important gadoid food fish (*Gadus callarias*) of the North Atlantic, found especially from Newfoundland to Norway. **2** Any other gadoid fish. [Origin unknown]

cod[2] (kod) *n.* **1** A pod or husk. **2** A bag or envelope. **3** *Scot.* A pillow or cushion. [OE *codd* bag]

Cod (kod), **Cape** A peninsula of SE Massachusetts projecting 65 miles into the Atlantic and enclosing **Cape Cod Bay.**

co·da (kō′də) *n.* An independent musical passage, introduced at the conclusion of a movement, forming a more decided and usually somewhat elaborate termination; the finale of a sonata movement or of a fugue. [<Ital. <L *cauda* tail]

cod·der (kod′ər) *n.* A person or vessel occupied in codfishing.

cod·dle (kod′l) *v.t.* **·dled, ·dling** **1** To seethe or simmer in water; cook gently. **2** To treat as a baby or an invalid; pamper. See synonyms under CARESS, PAMPER. [? Akin to CAUDLE] **— cod′dler** *n.*

code (kōd) *n.* **1** A systematized body of law. **2** A system of signals, characters, or symbols with arbitrary, conventionalized meanings, used in communication: Language is a form of *code.* **3** A set of prearranged symbols, usually letters, used for purposes of secrecy or brevity in transmitting messages: the meanings of the symbols are given in a code book. Compare CIPHER. **4** A system of rules and regulations for the purpose of ensuring adequate standards of practice and uniformity in workmanship. See synonyms under LAW, LEGISLATION. **— civil code** A code regulating the civil relations of citizens. **— criminal** or **penal code** A code defining crimes and prescribing the method and degree of punishment. **— telegraphic code** A code convenient for use in telegraphing; specifically, the Morse or the International code, consisting of dots and dashes. — *v.t.* **cod·ed, cod·ing** **1** To systematize as laws; make a digest of. **2** To put into the symbols of a code. [<F <L *codex* writing tablet]

code beacon *Aeron.* A beacon which assists aviators in maintaining their flight course by flashing signals in code.

co·dec·li·na·tion (kō′dek·lə·nā′shən) *n.* *Astron.* The complement of the angle of declination: also called *polar distance.* [<CO-[2] + DECLINATION]

co·deine (kō′dēn, kō′di·ēn) *n.* *Chem.* A white crystalline alkaloid, $C_{18}H_{21}NO_3$, derived from morphine and widely used in medicine as a mild narcotic. Also **co·de·in** (kō′dē·in, kō′·dēn), **co·de·ia** (kō·dē′ə). [<Gk. *kōdeia* head of a poppy]

Code Na·po·lé·on (kôd nȧ·pô·lā·ôṅ′) The body of French civil law, put in force by Napoleon I between 1804–07.

co·dex (kō′deks) *n.* *pl.* **co·di·ces** (kō′də·sēz, kod′ə-) **1** A medieval manuscript in leaf form: distinguished from *scroll.* **2** A collection of canons or of formulas. **3** A code of laws. [<L, writing tablet]

Co·dex Ju·ris Ca·non·i·ci (kō′deks jŏŏr′is kə·non′ə·sī) A compilation of legislation of the Roman Catholic Church: in effect since 1918.

codg·er (koj′ər) *n.* *Colloq.* **1** A chap; a fellow. **2** A testy or eccentric old man. [Prob. var. of *cadger.* See CADGE.]

co·di·ces (kō′də·sēz, kod′ə-) Plural of CODEX.

cod·i·cil (kod′ə·səl) *n.* A supplement to a will. [<L *codicillus*, dim. of *codex* writing tablet] **— cod·i·cil·la·ry** (kod′ə·sil′ə·rē) *adj.*

cod·i·fy (kod′ə·fī, kō′də-) *v.t.* **·fied, ·fy·ing** To systematize, as laws. **— cod′i·fi·ca′tion** *n.* **— cod′i·fi′er** *n.*

cod·ling[1] (kod′ling) *n.* **1** A young cod. **2** A gadoid fish (genus *Phycis*) with filamentous ventral fins of two or three rays; a hake. [Dim. of COD[1]]

cod·ling[2] (kod′ling) *n.* **1** One of a group of varieties of cooking apple, elongated and tapering. **2** Formerly, any hard apple for stewing. Also **cod·lin** (kod′lin). [ME *querdling*; origin uncertain]

codling moth A moth (*Carpocapsa pomonella*) whose larvae, the apple worms, feed on the interior of apples, pears, quinces, and several other fruits. For illustration see under INSECT (injurious). Also **codlin moth.**

cod-liv·er oil (kod′liv′ər) Oil from the livers of cod, especially rich in vitamins A and D: used in cases of malnutrition.

---

co-indicate
co-infer
co-inhabit
co-inhabitant
co-inhabitor
co-inhere
co-inheritance
co-inheritor
co-inmate
co-inspire
co-inter
co-interest
co-intersect
co-inventor
co-involve
co-laborer
co-latitudinal
co-legatee
co-legislator
colunar
co-meddle
comortgagee
comourner
co-oblige
co-occupy
co-organize
co-original
co-originality
co-owner
co-ownership
co-parent
co-partner
co-passionate
co-pastor
co-patentee

cod·piece (kod'pēs') *n.* An ornamented bag or flap attached to the front of the tight breeches worn by men of the 15th and 16th centuries. [ME *cod* scrotum + PIECE]
co·dress (kō'dres) *n.* A radiotelegraph message in which the address is given in the same code system as the body of the message. Compare PLAINDRESS. [<CO(DE) + (AD)DRESS]
Co·dy (kō'dē), **William Frederick,** 1846–1917, U.S. plainsman, army scout, and showman: called "Buffalo Bill."
co·ed (kō'ed') *n. Colloq.* A young woman being educated at the same institution with young men. —*adj. Colloq.* Co-educational. Also **co'ed'.**
co·ed·u·ca·tion (kō'ej·ōō·kā'shən) *n.* The education of both sexes together in the same classes or institution. —**co'–ed·u·ca'tion·al** *adj.*
co·ee-bird (kō'ē·bûrd') *n.* The koel.
co·ef·fi·cient (kō'ə·fish'ənt) *n.* **1** A cooperating agent. **2** *Math.* A number or letter put before an algebraic expression and multiplying it. **3** *Physics* A number indicating the degree of magnitude, or the kind and amount of change under given conditions. —*adj.* Jointly efficient; acting together to a common end. —**co'ef·fi'cien·cy** *n.*
coefficient of friction *Physics* A number expressing the ratio between the force required to move one surface along another and the force, normal to the surfaces, pressing them together.
coe·la·canth (sē'lə·kanth) *n. Zool.* A large-bodied, hollow-spined crossopterygian fish, one species of which (*Latimeria chalumnae*) still survives. [<COEL(O)- + Gk. *akantha* spine]

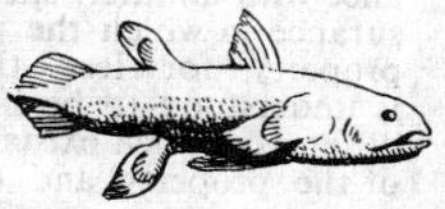
COELACANTH
(From 4 to 5 1/2 feet in length)

-coele See -CELE[2].
coe·len·ter·ate (si·len'tə·rāt) *n.* Any of a phylum of invertebrate animals (*Coelenterata*) having an enteric cavity occupying the entire interior of the body and functioning as a vascular as well as a digestive system: the phylum includes sea anemones, corals, jellyfish, and hydras. —*adj.* Belonging or pertaining to the *Coelenterata.* [<COEL(O)- + Gk. *enteron* intestine] —**coe·len·ter·ic** (sē'len·ter'ik) *adj.*
coe·len·ter·on (si·len'tə·ron) *n. pl.* **·ter·a** (-tər·ə) *Zool.* The primitive intestinal cavity of coelenterates; the archenteron.
Coe·le-Syr·i·a (sē'lē·sir'ē·ə) An ancient name for BEKÁA.
coe·li·ac (sē'lē·ak) See CELIAC.
coelo- *combining form* Cavity; cavity of the body, or of an organ. Also, before vowels, **coel-.** [<Gk. *koilos* hollow]
coe·lom (sē'ləm) *n. Zool.* The body cavity of a metazoan; the space between the viscera and the body wall. Also **coe·lome** (sē'lōm). [<Gk. *koilōma* cavity <*koilos* hollow]
coe·lo·stat (sē'lə·stat) *n. Astron.* An instrument consisting of a mirror driven by clockwork and mounted in such a way as to keep the same celestial image reflected continuously to the eyepiece or camera attachment of a fixed telescope. [<L *caelum* heavens + *status* a standing <*stare* stand]
coe·nes·the·sia (sē'nis·thē'zhə, -zhē·ə, sen'is-) See CENESTHESIA.
coeno- See CENO-.
coe·no·cyte (sē'nə·sīt, sen'ə-) *n. Bot.* An aggregation of protoplasmic units enclosed within a common wall: exemplified in the lower algae and fungi.
coe·nure (sē'nyŏŏr) *n.* The many-headed bladderworm or larval stage of a dog tapeworm (*Taenia coenurus*), attacking the brain of sheep and producing gid or staggers. Also **coe·nu·rus** (si·nyŏŏr'əs). [<COEN(O)- + Gk. *oura* tail]
co·en·zyme (kō·en'zīm, -zim) *n. Biochem.* Any substance present in a fermenting mixture that increases the activity of the enzyme.
co·e·qual (kō·ē'kwəl) *adj.* Of the same value, age, size, or importance; equal and conjoined. —*n.* The equal of another or others. —**co·e·qual·i·ty** (kō'i·kwol'ə·tē) *n.* —**co·e'qual·ly** *adv.*
co·erce (kō·ûrs') *v.* **co·erced, co·erc·ing** *v.t.* **1** To constrain by force, law, authority, or fear; compel. **2** To bring into subjection or under control by superior force; repress. **3** To bring about by coercion: to *coerce* obedience. —*v.i.* **4** To use coercive measures, as in government. See synonyms under COMPEL. [<L *coercere* <*co-* together + *arcere* shut up, restrain] —**co·er'ci·ble** *adj.*
co·er·cion (kō·ûr'shən) *n.* **1** Forcible constraint or restraint, moral or physical; compulsion. **2** Government by force. —**co·er·cion·ar·y** (kō·ûr'shən·er'ē) *adj.* —**co·er'cion·ist** *n.*
co·er·cive (kō·ûr'siv) *adj.* Serving or tending to coerce. —**co·er'cive·ly** *adv.* —**co·er'cive·ness** *n.*
coercive force See under FORCE.
co·e·ta·ne·ous (kō'i·tā'nē·əs) *adj.* Originating at the same time; of equal age; contemporary. [<LL *coetaneus* <*co-* together + *aetas* age] —**co'e·ta'ne·ous·ly** *adv.* —**co'e·ta'ne·ous·ness** *n.*
Coeur de Li·on (kûr' də lē'ən) "Lion-heart": epithet applied to Richard I of England. [<F]
co·e·val (kō·ē'vəl) *adj.* Of or belonging to the same age: usually implying remote time or long duration. —*n.* One of the same age; a contemporary. Also spelled *coaeval.* [<LL *coaevus* <*co-* together + *aevus* age] —**co·e'·val·ly** *adv.*
co·ex·ist (kō'ig·zist') *v.i.* To exist together, in the same place or at the same time. —**co'ex·ist'ent** *adj.*
co·ex·ist·ence (kō'ig·zis'təns) *n.* **1** The state of coexisting. **2** The simultaneous existence of two (or more) societies, nations, etc., which differ in ideology but which agree, often tacitly, to non-interference in each other's political affairs.
coff (kof) *v.t.* **coft, coff·ing** *Scot.* To buy.
cof·fee (kôf'ē, kof'ē) *n.* **1** The seeds or beans enclosed in the dark berrylike fruit of a tropical evergreen shrub (genus *Coffea*), native in Asia and Africa and widely grown in Brazil. **2** A beverage made from the roasted and ground beans of this plant. **3** The shrub or tree itself. **4** The brown color of coffee, especially of coffee when containing milk or cream. —**black coffee** Coffee taken without milk or cream. [<Ital. *caffè* <Turkish *qahveh* <Arabic *qahwah*]
coffee break A recess from work for the purpose of taking coffee or other refreshments.
cof·fee-cake (kôf'ē·kāk', kof'ē-) *n.* Any of several kinds of cake often containing raisins or nuts, topped with melted sugar, cinnamon, or butter crumbs, and eaten with coffee.
coffee house A house where coffee and other refreshments are served; a café.
coffee mill A hand mill for grinding roasted coffee beans; a coffee grinder.
coffee nut The Kentucky coffee tree or its fruit.
coffee pot A covered vessel in which coffee is prepared or served.
coffee shop A public restaurant or room in a hotel or a restaurant where coffee and food are served. Also **coffee room.**
coffee table Any low table, generally placed in front of a sofa, for serving refreshments.
coffee tree **1** The cascara buckthorn. **2** The Kentucky coffee tree.
coffee weed Chicory.
cof·fer (kôf'ər, kof'-) *n.* **1** A chest or box; strongbox; safe. **2** *pl.* A treasury; financial resources. **3** A decorative, sunk panel in a dome or vault. **4** A canal-lock chamber; a caisson. —*v.t.* **1** To place in a coffer. **2** To adorn with coffers, or form in coffers, as a ceiling. [<F *coffre* <L *cophinus.* See COFFIN.]
cof·fer·dam (kôf'ər·dam', kof'-) *n.* **1** A temporary enclosing dam built in the water and pumped dry, to protect workmen. **2** A watertight structure attached to a ship's side when repairs are made below the water line.
cof·fin (kôf'in, kof'-) *n.* **1** The case in which a corpse is buried. **2** The part of a horse's hoof below the coronet. —*v.t.* To put into or as into a coffin. [<OF *cofin* <L *cophinus* <Gk. *kophinos* basket]
Cof·fin (kôf'in, kof'-), **Robert Peter Tristram,** 1892–1955, U.S. poet and author.
coffin bone The bone of a horse's foot that is enclosed within the hoof.
cof·fle (kof'əl) *n.* A gang of animals or slaves, chained together for marching or sale. —*v.t.* **·fled, ·fling** To form into a coffle. [<Arabic *qāfilah* caravan]
coft (koft) Past tense of COFF.
cog[1] (kog) *n.* **1** *Mech.* A tooth or one of a series of teeth projecting from the surface of a wheel or gear to impart or receive motion. **2** A tenon on a joist or beam to fit a mortise on another. **3** A person regarded as making a minor or insignificant contribution to the working of a large organization or process. [<Scand. Cf. Sw. *kugge* cog.]
cog[2] (kog) *v.* **cogged, cog·ging** *v.t.* **1** To load or mishandle, as dice, in order to cheat. **2** *Obs.* To mislead or deceive. —*v.i.* **3** To cheat, as with loaded dice. —*n.* A trick; imposition; a lie. [Origin unknown]
cog[3] (kog, kōg) *n.* **1** A small rowboat or fishing vessel; cockboat. **2** Formerly, a broadly built transport or other vessel: also spelled *cogue.* [<OF *cogue*]
co·gent (kō'jənt) *adj.* Compelling belief, assent, or action; forcible; convincing. See synonyms under POWERFUL. [<L *cogens, -entis,* ppr. of *cogere* compel. See COACT.]
cog·ger (kog'ər) *n. Brit.* **1** A sharper. **2** A flatterer. [< COG[2]]
cog·gie (kog'ē) *n. Brit. Dial.* A small wooden bowl.
cog·ging (kog'ing) *n. Metall.* The operation of reducing a metal ingot to a billet by application of a forging press or hammer.
cog·i·tate (koj'ə·tāt) *v.* **·tat·ed, ·tat·ing** *v.t.* To think over; ponder; meditate. —*v.t.* To think about or upon; devise. See synonyms under MUSE. [<L *cogitatus,* pp. of *cogitare* think <*co-* together + *agitare* consider] —**cog·i·ta·ble** (koj'ə·tə·bəl) *adj.* —**cog'i·ta'tor** *n.*
cog·i·ta·tion (koj'ə·tā'shən) *n.* Consideration; reflection; thought. [<OF *cogitacion* <L *cogitatio, -onis* <*cogitare.* See COGITATE.]
cog·i·ta·tive (koj'ə·tā'tiv) *adj.* Capable of cogitation; reflective; contemplative. —**cog'i·ta'tive·ly** *adv.* —**cog'i·ta'tive·ness** *n.*
co·gi·to er·go sum (koj'i·tō ûr'gō sum') *Latin* I think, therefore I exist: the basic proposition of Descartes' philosophy.
co·gnac (kōn'yak, kon'-) *n.* **1** Brandy distilled from wine produced in the Cognac region of western France. **2** Any brandy.
cog·nate (kog'nāt) *adj.* **1** Allied by blood; kindred; especially, related through females only. **2** Allied by derivation from the same source; belonging to the same stock or root: English *cold* and Latin *gelidus* are *cognate* words. **3** Allied in radical characteristics; having the same nature or quality. —*n.* One who or that which is closely related to other persons or things. [<L *cognatus* <*co-* together + *(g)natus,* pp. of *(g)nasci* be born]
cog·na·tion (kog·nā'shən) *n.* Relationship by blood or derivation.
cog·ni·tion (kog·nish'ən) *n.* **1** The act, power, or faculty of apprehending, knowing, or perceiving. **2** Knowledge; a conception, perception, or notion. [<L *cognitio, -onis* knowledge <*cognoscere* know <*co-* together + *(g)noscere* know] —**cog·ni'tion·al** *adj.* —**cog·ni·tive** (kog'nə·tiv) *adj.*
cog·ni·za·ble (kog'nə·zə·bəl, kon'ə-) *adj.* Capable of being known or of being judicially tried or examined. —**cog'ni·za·bly** *adv.*
cog·ni·zance (kog'nə·zəns, kon'ə-) *n.* **1** Apprehension or perception; knowledge; recog-

co-patron
co-patroness
co-petitioner
co-plaintiff
co-plant
co-please
co-plot
co-project
co-promote
co-proprietor
coraise
co-rector
co-redeem
co-regency
co-regnant
co-reign
co-rejoice
co-religionist
co-renounce
co-residence
co-resonant
co-revel
co-revolve
coriparian
cosettle
cosheathe
cosigner
cosound
cosovereign
cospecies
co-tenant
co-traitor
co-translate
co-trustee
co-worker

add,āce,câre,pälm; end,ēven; it,īce; odd,ōpen,ôrder; tŏŏk,pōōl; up,bûrn; ə = a in *above,* e in *sicken,* i in *clarity,* o in *melon,* u in *focus;* yōō = u in *fuse;* oi,oil; ou,pout; ch,check; g,go; ng,ring; th,thin; th,this; zh,vision. Foreign sounds à,œ,ü,kh,ṅ; and ◆: see page xx. < from; + plus; ? possibly.

nition; also, the range or sphere of what can be known by observation. 2 *Law* Knowledge on which a judge acts without requiring proof; judicial notice, as of statutes or public events. 3 Jurisdiction. 4 *Law* Acknowledgment of a fine of land and tenements; a confession. [<OF *conoisance* <*conistre* know <L *cognoscere*. See COGNITION.]

cog·ni·zant (kog′nə·zənt, kon′ə-) *adj.* Having knowledge; aware: with *of.* See synonyms under CONSCIOUS.

cog·nize (kog′nīz) *v.t.* **·nized, ·niz·ing** To know, perceive, or recognize. See synonyms under KNOW. Also *Brit.* **cog′nise.** [<L *cognoscere* know. See COGNITION.]

cog·no·men (kog·nō′mən) *n. pl.* **·no·mens** or **·nom·i·na** (-nom′ə·nə) 1 In ancient Rome, the last of three names; a surname used to denote some physical or mental characteristic: Publius Ovidius *Naso.* 2 A surname. 3 Loosely, any name, nickname, or appellation. See synonyms under NAME. [<L <*co-* together + *(g)nomen* name] — **cog·nom·i·nal** (kog·nom′ə·nəl) *adj.*

co·gno·scen·te (kō′nyō·shen′tā) *n. pl.* **·ti** (-tē) A connoisseur: also spelled *conoscente.* [<Ital.]

cog·nos·ci·ble (kog·nos′ə·bəl) *adj.* Capable of being known, recognized, or ascertained; knowable. [<L *cognoscere.* See COGNITION.] — **cog·nos′ci·bil′i·ty** *n.*

cog·no·vit (kog·nō′vit) *n. Law* A written acknowledgment, by a defendant, that the plaintiff's demand is just. [<L *cognovit (actionem)* he has acknowledged (the action)]

co·gon (kə·gōn′) *n.* A tall, rank grass (*Imperata cylindrica*) of the Philippines: used for fodder and in thatching. [<Sp. *cogón* < Tagalog]

cog rail *n.* A cogged center rail with a cogwheel that permits a locomotive to make steep ascents. Also **cog′-rail′way.**

cogue (kog, kōg) See COG[3].

cog·way (kog′wā′) *n.* A rack railway.

cog·wheel (kog′hwēl′) *n.* A wheel with cogs; a gearwheel.

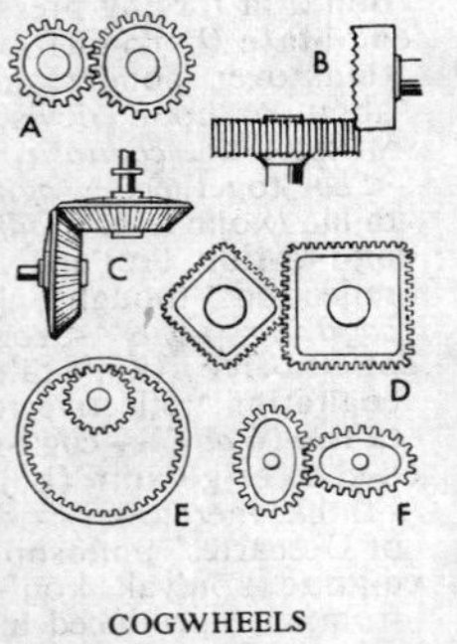

COGWHEELS
A. Spur-gears.
B. Spur and crown gears.
C. Bevel-gears.
D. Square gears.
E. Annular gears.
F. Elliptical gears.

co·hab·it (kō·hab′it) *v.i.* 1 To live together, usually illegally, as husband and wife. 2 *Obs.* To inhabit together the same place or country. [<LL *cohabitare* <*co-* together + *habitare* live] — **co·hab′i·tant, co·hab′it·er** *n.* — **co·hab′i·ta′tion** *n.*

Co·han (kō·han′), **George M(ichael),** 1878–1942, U.S. playwright and actor.

Co·hee (kō′hē) *n. U.S.* Formerly, a settler in western Virginia and western Pennsylvania. [? <dial. E (Scottish) *quo′ he* quoth he; with ref. to a characteristic phrase in their speech]

Co·hen (kō′ən), **Morris,** 1880–1947, U.S. philosopher and logician of science, born in Russia.

co·here (kō·hir′) *v.i.* **co·hered, co·her·ing** 1 To stick or hold firmly together. 2 To be logically consistent or connected. 3 To be coherent, as the parts of an address. 4 *Obs.* To agree. See synonyms under UNITE. [<L *cohaerere* <*co-* together + *haerere* stick]

co·her·ence (kō·hir′əns) *n.* 1 A sticking to or a sticking together; union; conjunction. See COHESION (def. 2). 2 Logical consistency; agreement: also **co·her′en·cy.** 3 *Physics* That relation of coincidence between two sets of waves, as light or sound waves, which will produce interference phenomena. [<MF *cohérence* <L *cohaerentia* <*cohaerere* COHERE]

co·her·ent (kō·hir′ənt) *adj.* 1 Cleaving or sticking together. 2 Logically consistent. — **co·her′ent·ly** *adv.*

co·her·er (kō·hir′ər) *n.* A device formerly employed to detect radio waves, in which loosely touching metallic particles in a glass tube are made to cohere closely under the action of the wave, thus momentarily completing a local electric signaling circuit.

co·he·sion (kō·hē′zhən) *n.* 1 The act or state of cohering; union; consistency. 2 *Physics* That force by which molecules of the same kind or of the same body are held together so that the substance or body resists separation: distinguished from *adhesion.* 3 *Bot.* The joining of one part with another. [<F *cohésion* <L *cohaerere* COHERE]

co·he·sive (kō·hē′siv) *adj.* Belonging to, having, or exerting the property of cohesion; causing to cleave. — **co·he′sive·ly** *adv.* — **co·he′sive·ness** *n.*

Cohn (kōn), **Ferdinand Julius,** 1828–98, German botanist: called "the founder of bacteriology."

co·ho·bate (kō′hō·bāt) *v.t.* **·bat·ed, ·bat·ing** To redistil by restoring the distillate to the retort, to mingle again with the matter there. [<Med. L *cohobatus,* pp. of *cohobare,* ? <Arabic *ka′aba* repeat]

co·hoes (kō·äs′) *n. U.S. Dial.* Land originally overgrown with pine. Also **co·hos′.** [<Du. <Algonquian *koowa,* a small pine tree]

co·hog (kō′hôg, -hog) See QUAHAUG.

co·honk (kə·hôngk′, -hongk′) *n.* 1 The Canada goose. 2 *Obs.* The season, beginning in October, when this wild goose makes its appearance. [Imit. of its call]

co·hort (kō′hôrt) *n.* 1 The tenth of an ancient Roman military legion, 400 to 600 men. 2 A band of soldiers. 3 Any group of associates. 4 A companion or follower. [<L *cohors, cohortis.* Doublet of COURT.]

co·hosh (kō′hosh, kō·hosh′) *n.* 1 Either of two North American herbs, sometimes used medicinally; especially, the **blue cohosh** (*Caulophyllum thalictroides*), often called *squawroot,* and the black snakeroot or **black cohosh** (*Cimicifuga racemosa*). 2 The baneberry. [<N. Am. Ind.]

co·hune (kō·hōōn′) *n.* A feather-leaved palm (*Orbignya cohune*) of Central and South America, from which a fatty oil is obtained. Also **cohune palm.** [< native Honduran name]

Coi (koi), **Song** (sông) The Annamese name for the RED RIVER, Vietnam.

coif (koif) *n.* 1 Any close-fitting cap, hood, or headdress; especially, a close-fitting hood or skull cap for either sex, tied under the chin. 2 In England, an inner skull cap of lawn, formerly worn by sergeants at law; hence, the office or rank of a sergeant at law. 3 A soldier's thick skull cap of steel or leather, worn under the helmet. — *v.t.* To put a coif on; invest with or as with a coif. [<OF *coife* <LL *cofia* <Gmc.]

coif·feur (kwä·fœr′) *n. French* A male hairdresser. — **coif·feuse** (kwä·fœz′) *n. fem.*

coif·fure (kwä·fyōōr′, *Fr.* kwä·für′) *n.* 1 An arrangement or dressing of the hair. 2 A headdress. [<F <OF *coife* COIF.]

coign (koin) *n.* A projecting angle or stone; a corner. Also **coigne.** [Var. of QUOIN]

coign of vantage An advantageous position.

coil[1] (koil) *n.* 1 A ring or spiral formed by winding. 2 An involvement; a perplexity. 3 A spiral pipe, or a series of pipes, forming a continuous conduit which reverses two or more times. 4 An induction coil. — **Ruhmkorff coil** An induction coil with circuit breaker for use with direct and constant current. [<*v.*] — *v.t.* 1 To wind spirally or in rings; wind round and round. 2 To enwrap with coils, as a lasso or the folds of a boa constrictor. — *v.i.* 3 To form rings or coils. 4 To move in spirals, as a hawk. [<OF *coillir* <L *colligere.* See COLLECT.] — **coil′er** *n.*

coil[2] (koil) *n. Archaic* Confusion or tumult; turmoil. [Origin unknown]

Coim·ba·tore (koim′bə·tôr′) A city in SW Madras state, India.

Co·im·bra (kō·im′brə) A city in north central Portugal; former capital of Portugal and site of the **University of Coimbra** (founded at Lisbon in 1290, established here in 1537).

coin (koin) *n.* 1 A piece of metal stamped by government authority, for use as money. 2 Metal currency, collectively. 3 Kind or means of recompense. 4 A corner; quoin. See synonyms under MONEY. — *v.t.* 1 To stamp or mint (coins) from metal. 2 To make into coins, as metal. 3 To originate or invent, as a word or phrase. 4 *Colloq.* To make or gain rapidly: to *coin* money. — *v.i.* 5 *Brit. Colloq.* To counterfeit money. [<F, wedge, die <L *cuneus* wedge] — **coin′a·ble** *adj.* — **coin′er** *n.*

coin·age (koi′nij) *n.* 1 The making of coins, or the coins made; the system of coins of a country. 2 The cost or charge for coining money. 3 The act of fabricating, or the thing fabricated. 4 *Ling.* An artificially created word, as *blurb.*

co·in·cide (kō′in·sīd′) *v.i.* **·cid·ed, ·cid·ing** 1 To correspond because of identity in parts, elements, space occupied, or position. 2 To agree exactly; be of one opinion, idea, or interest. 3 To occur at the same time; endure an equal span of time. See synonyms under AGREE, ASSENT. [<MF *coincider* <Med. L *coincidere* <L *co-* together + *incidere* < *in-* upon + *cadere* fall]

co·in·ci·dence (kō·in′sə·dəns) *n.* 1 The fact or condition of coinciding; correspondence. 2 A remarkable occurrence of events, ideas, etc., at the same time or in the same way, apparently by mere accident. 3 *Geom.* Exact correspondence in space or in time. See synonyms under ANALOGY.

co·in·ci·dent (kō·in′sə·dənt) *adj.* 1 Agreeing or coinciding as in position, extent, time, etc.; concurring. 2 Exactly corresponding; identical. — **co·in′ci·dent·ly** *adv.*

co·in·ci·den·tal (kō·in′sə·den′təl) *adj.* Characterized by or involving coincidence. — **co·in′ci·den′tal·ly** *adv.*

co·in·sur·ance (kō′in·shōōr′əns) *n.* Joint insurance with another; specifically, a form of insurance in which the person who insures his property for less than its entire value is understood to be his own insurer for the difference which exists between the true value of the property and the amount of the insurance.

co·in·sure (kō′in·shōōr′) *v.t.* & *v.i.* **·sured, ·sur·ing** 1 To insure with another or others. 2 To insure according to the specific terms of coinsurance.

Coin·treau (kwaṅ·trō′) An orange-flavored liqueur with a curaçao base: a trade name.

coir (koir) *n.* Coconut-husk fiber, used in making cables, ropes, matting, etc.: also called *kyar.* [<Malay *kāyar* rope]

coi·stril (koi′strəl) *n. Archaic* 1 A groom; lackey. 2 A low fellow. Also **coi′strel.** [? <OF *coustillier* soldier]

co·i·tion (kō·ish′ən) *n.* Sexual intercourse; copulation. Also **co·i·tus** (kō′i·təs). [<L *coitio, -onis*: *co-* together + *ire* go]

coke[1] (kōk) *n.* A solid, carbonaceous fuel obtained by distilling the volatile constituents from coal by heating in ovens or retorts. — *v.t.* & *v.i.* **coked, cok·ing** To change or be changed into coke. Also spelled *coak.* [? ME *colke*; origin uncertain]

coke[2] (kōk) *n. Slang* Cocaine.

coke[3] (kōk) *n. Colloq.* A carbonated soft drink. [<*Coke,* short for *Coca-Cola,* a trade name]

Coke (kŏŏk, kōk), **Sir Edward,** 1552–1634, lord chief justice of England. — **Thomas,** 1747–1814, English preacher; first bishop of Methodist Episcopal Church in America.

col (kol) *n.* 1 *Geog.* A depression between two mountains; a gap in a ridge, serving as a pass from one valley to another: also called *saddle.* 2 *Meteorol.* A necklike area of low pressure between two anticyclones. [<F <L *collum* neck]

col-[1] Assimilated var. of COM-.

col-[2] Var. of COLO-.

co·la (kō′lə) *n.* 1 A small African tree (*Cola acuminata*), naturalized in the West Indies: also **co′la·nut′ tree.** 2 The seed of this tree or the extract of it, yielding caffeine and other substances, said to have tonic and antiseptic qualities: used in the manufacture of beverages: also **co′la·nut′.** Also spelled *kola.* [NL < native African name]

col·an·der (kul′ən·dər, kol′-) *n.* A perforated vessel for straining liquids, etc.: also spelled *cullender.* [Cf. Sp. *colador* <L *colare* strain]

co·lat·i·tude (kō·lat′ə·tōōd, -tyōōd) *n.* In navigation, the complement of the latitude; distance in degrees from the nearest pole. [<CO-[2] + LATITUDE]

Col·bert (kôl·bâr′), **Jean Baptiste,** 1619–83, French statesman and financier.

Col·by (kōl′bē), **Bainbridge,** 1869–1950, U.S. lawyer and statesman.

col·can·non (kəl·kan′ən, kôl′kan·ən) *n.* An Irish dish of potatoes and greens cooked

together. [< Irish *cāl ceannain* white-headed cabbage]

Col·ches·ter (kōl′ches′tər, -chis·tər) A municipal borough of NE Essex, England.

col·chi·cine (kol′chə·sēn, kol′kə-) *n.* A pale-yellow, bitter, poisonous alkaloid, $C_{22}H_{25}O_6N$, obtained from the roots of the colchicum: used in medicine.

col·chi·cum (kol′chə·kəm, kol′kə-) *n.* **1** A plant of a genus *(Colchicum)* of Old World bulbous plants of the lily family. **2** The corm or the seed of *C. autumnale,* the autumn crocus or meadow saffron, which yields colchicine. **3** A medical preparation made from this. [< L < Gk. *kolchikon* < *Kolchis* Colchis, home of the legendary sorceress Medea]

Col·chis (kol′kis) A lowland region of western Georgian S.S.R.; identified with a legendary kingdom east of the Black Sea, the land of the Golden Fleece.

col·co·thar (kol′kə·thər) *n.* A dark-red ferric oxide formed by heating ferrous sulfate: used as a polish and as the pigment Indian red. [< Med. L < Arabic *qolqotār*]

cold (kōld) *adj.* **1** Of a relatively low temperature as compared with a normal or standard temperature, or with the normal temperature of the human body. **2** Having no perceptible heat; gelid; frigid. **3** Dead. **4** Having the sensation due to too rapid loss of heat from the body. **5** Feeling no warmth or not sufficient warmth; chilled; chilly. **6** Having little or no liveliness, ardor, or enthusiasm; displaying no feeling or passion; unmoved; stolid; indifferent. **7** Lacking signs of life; unconscious: to be knocked *cold.* **8** Chilling or depressing to the spirits; awakening no enthusiasm; not cordial; disappointing; frigid; discouraging. **9** Weak to the taste; wanting sharpness or pungency. **10** Lacking odor or freshness: a *cold* trail. **11** Distant from the object sought; wide of the mark: said of a seeker in a game, or a guesser. **12** Bluish in tone or effect; not suggestive of warmth. —*n.* **1** A low temperature. **2** Lack of heat, or the sensation caused by it. **3** A catarrhal affection of the respiratory tract, often following exposure to cold, dampness, or draft. **4** Temperature below the freezing point. **5** The sensation characterized by lack of enthusiasm, or by fear or dejection. [OE *cald*] —**cold′ly** *adv.* —**cold′ness** *n.*

cold blood **1** Blood not warmed by exercise or emotion. **2** Heartlessness or deliberate cruelty. —**in cold blood** Without feeling; pitilessly; not prompted by impulse or excitement.

cold-blood·ed (kōld′blud′id) *adj.* **1** Lacking body heat; frigid; sensitive to cold. **2** *Zool.* Having a variable temperature dependent on the temperature of the surrounding medium, as a fish or reptile; ectothermic. **3** Unfeeling; heartless; deliberately cruel. —**cold′-blood′ed·ly** *adv.* —**cold′-blood′ed·ness** *n.*

cold chisel A chisel of tempered steel for cutting cold metal.

cold cream A cleansing and soothing ointment for the skin.

cold deck A deck of cards prearranged to the advantage of a certain player.

cold-drawn (kōld′drôn′) *adj.* Stretched or drawn while cold: *cold-drawn* steel wire.

cold feet *Colloq.* Loss of courage; timidity. —**to get cold feet** *Colloq.* To lose courage.

cold·frame (kōld′frām′) *n.* A wooden frame set into the ground and having a glass top: used to protect plants against cold.

cold front *Meteorol.* The irregular, forward edge of a cold air mass advancing beneath and against a warmer mass.

cold-ham·mer (kōld′ham′ər) *v.t.* To hammer when cold, as metals.

Cold Harbor A village in eastern Virginia; scene of Civil War battles, 1862, 1864.

cold light Light which is not produced by incandescence or combustion, as phosphorescent light.

cold pack **1** *Med.* A wrapping of cold, wet blankets or sheets about a patient as a means of therapy. **2** A canning process in which raw food is packed in cans or jars, which are then heated for sealing and cooking.

cold rubber A synthetic rubber, chemically related to buna, which has been polymerized at low temperatures of 41° F. or less to impart better wearing qualities and greater resistance to abrasion.

cold shoulder *Colloq.* A deliberate slight or show of indifference.

cold snap A sudden, short interval of very cold weather.

cold sore An eruption about the mouth or nostrils, often accompanying a cold or fever: a form of herpes.

cold storage The storage of perishable food, furs, etc. in a refrigerated chamber.

cold turkey *U.S. Slang* **1** The abrupt and total deprivation of a substance, as a narcotic drug or cigarettes, from one addicted to its use. **2** Blunt, candid talk, often unwelcome to the listener.

cold war Intense rivalry between nations in diplomacy, economic strategy, and military preparedness, falling just short of armed conflict.

cold wave *Meteorol.* An unusual drop in temperature; a spell of very cold weather, usually traveling along a specified course.

cole (kōl) *n.* A plant of the same genus as the cabbage, especially rape *(Brassica napus).* Also **cole·wort** (kōl′wûrt′). ◆Homophone: *coal.* [OE *cawl* < L *caulis* cabbage]

Cole (kōl), **G(eorge) D(ouglas) H(oward),** 1889–1959, English historian, sociologist, and economist.
—**Thomas,** 1801–48, U.S. painter born in England.

co·lec·to·my (kə·lek′tə·mē) *n. Surg.* The excision of all or part of the colon.

cole·man·ite (kōl′mən·īt) *n.* A colorless, transparent, hydrous calcium borate, $Ca_2B_6O_{11} \cdot 5H_2O$, occurring massive or in monoclinic crystals: used in the manufacture of borax. [after W.T. *Coleman,* 1824–93, of California]

Co·le·op·ter·a (kō′lē·op′tər·ə, kol′ē-) *n. pl.* A large, cosmopolitan order of insects, including the beetles and weevils, having horny front wings that fit as cases over the hind wings. [< NL < Gk. *koleos* sheath + *pteron* wing] —**co′le·op′ter, co′le·op′ter·an** *n.* —**co′le·op′ter·ous, co′le·op′ter·al** *adj.*

co·le·op·tile (kō′lē·op′til, kol′ē-) *n. Bot.* The first leaf appearing above the ground in grass seedlings. [< NL < Gk. *koleos* sheath + *ptilon* feather]

co·le·o·rhi·za (kō′lē·ə·rī′zə, kol′ē-) *n. pl.* **·zae** (-zē) *Bot.* The root sheath in certain plants, through which the radicle bursts in germination. [< NL < Gk. *koleos* sheath + *rhiza* root]

Cole·ridge (kōl′rij), **Samuel Taylor,** 1772–1834, English poet, critic, and philosopher.

Coles (kōlz), **Elisha,** 1640?–80, English teacher and encyclopedist.

cole·seed (kōl′sēd′) *n.* Colza.

cole·slaw (kōl′slô′) *n.* A salad made of finely shredded, raw cabbage. [< Du. *kool sla* cabbage salad]

co·les·see (kō′les·ē′) *n.* A joint lessee; cotenant.

co·les·sor (kō′les′ôr, kō′les·ôr′) *n.* One of the makers of a lease.

Cö·les·ti·ne (tsœ′les·tē′nə) German form of CELESTINE.

Col·et (kol′it), **John,** 1467?–1519, English humanist.

Co·lette (kō·let′) Pseudonym of Sidonie Gabrielle Claudine, 1873–1954, French writer and novelist.

co·le·us (kō′lē·əs) *n.* A plant of a large genus *(Coleus)* of tropical African and East Indian herbs or shrubs of the mint family, cultivated for their showy foliage. [< NL < Gk. *koleos* sheath]

cole·wort (kōl′wûrt′) *n.* A plant of the cabbage genus; rape or kale.

Col·fax (kōl′faks), **Schuyler,** 1823–85, vice president of the United States 1869–73.

col·ic (kol′ik) *n.* Acute spasmodic pain in the bowels. —*adj.* **1** Pertaining to, near, or affecting the bowels. **2** Pertaining to or like colic. [< F *colique* < L *colicus* sick with colic < Gk. *kōlikos* < *kolon* colon] —**col′ick·y** *adj.*

colic root **1** The intensely bitter tonic and stomachic root of a North American herb *(Aletris farinosa)* of the lily family. **2** The root of the wild yam or of the blazing star.

colic weed One of several plants, as dutchman's-breeches, the squirrel corn, or the pale corydalis *(Corydalis sempervirens).*

Co·li·gny (kô·lē·nyē′), **Gaspard de,** 1519–72, French admiral and Huguenot leader. Also **Co·li·gni′.**

Co·li·ma (kō·lē′mä) A state in western Mexico; 2,010 square miles; capital, Colima; site of the **Vol·cán de Colima** (vōl·kän′), a smoking volcano; 12,631 feet.

col·in (kol′in) *n.* An American quail (genus *Colinus*), especially the bobwhite. [< Am. Sp. *colín* < Nahuatl]

—coline See -COLOUS.

Col·i·se·um (kol′ə·sē′əm) See COLOSSEUM.

col·i·se·um (kol′ə·sē′əm) *n.* A large stadium or amphitheater.

co·li·tis (kə·lī′tis) *n. Pathol.* Inflammation of the colon: also called *colonitis.* [< COL(O)- + -ITIS]

col·lab·o·rate (kə·lab′ə·rāt) *v.i.* **·rat·ed, ·rat·ing** **1** To labor or cooperate with another, especially in literary or scientific pursuits. **2** To cooperate willingly and traitorously with the enemy; be a collaborationist. [< LL *collaboratus,* pp. of *collaborare* < L *com-* with + *laborare* work] —**col·lab′o·ra′tion** *n.* —**col·lab′o·ra′tive** *adj.* —**col·lab′o·ra′tor** *n.*

col·lab·o·ra·tion·ist (kə·lab′ə·rā′shən·ist) *n.* A citizen of a country invaded or occupied by foreign troops who cooperates with the enemy.

col·lage (kə·läzh′) *n.* **1** A composition of flat objects, as newspaper, cloth, cardboard, etc., pasted together on a surface and often combined with related lines and color for artistic effect. **2** The clarifying or fining of a wine by means of an albuminous substance. [< F, pasting < *colle* glue < L *colla* < Gk. *kolla*]

col·la·gen (kol′ə·jen) *n. Biochem.* A protein forming the chief constituent of the connective tissues of the body, as cartilage, skin, bone, hair, etc. [< Gk. *kolla* glue + -GEN]

col·lapse (kə·laps′) *v.* **·lapsed, ·laps·ing** *v.i.* **1** To give way; cave in. **2** To fail utterly; come to ruin. **3** To assume a more compact form by the folding in of parts, as of camp chairs. **4** To lose health or strength completely, as from exhaustion or disease; become suddenly and completely prostrated. **5** To lose courage or boldness; sink suddenly from notice. —*v.t.* **6** To cause to collapse. —*n.* **1** A falling or sinking together. **2** Extreme prostration. **3** Utter failure; ruin. [< L *collapsus,* pp. of *collabi* < *com-* together + *labi* fall] —**col·laps′i·ble** or **·a·ble** *adj.* —**col·laps′i·bil′i·ty** *n.*

col·lar (kol′ər) *n.* **1** An article worn about the neck, as a band or circlet of some fabric, worn as an article of dress; the neckpiece of a garment. **2** A band of leather or metal for the neck of an animal. **3** *Biol.* **a** A ring or band on or about anything, as in certain plants and insects. **b** A growth of fur or ring of color about the neck of an animal. **4** *Mech.* Any of various cylindrical or ring-shaped devices used to limit or control the action of machine parts, secure stability, etc. —*v.t.* **1** To grasp by or provide with a collar. **2** To take possession of; capture. [< AF *coler* < L *collare* < *collum* neck]

collar bone The clavicle.

collar cell *Zool.* A flagellate cell having the base of the flagellum surrounded by a collar-like expansion, as in certain infusorians and sponges: also called *choanocyte.*

col·lard (kol′ərd) *n.* A variety of cabbage that does not gather its edible leaves into a head. [Alter. of *colewort.* See COLE.]

col·lar·et (kol′ər·et′) *n.* A small collar; also, a narrow fichu of lace or the like. Also **col′lar·ette′.** [< F *collerette,* dim. of *collier* collar]

col·la·sir·i (kol′ə·sir′ē, *Sp.* kô′lyä·sē′rē) *n. pl.* Among the modern Aymara Indians, specialized magicians and medicine men who are bonesetters, who diagnose disease by divination from the viscera of animals brought into contact with the patient, and claim to effect cures by magical transference of the disease to the animal or object. [< Aymaran]

col·late (kə·lāt′, kol′āt) *v.t.* **·lat·ed, ·lat·ing** **1** To compare critically, as writings or facts. **2** In bookbinding, to examine (the gathered sheets to be bound) in order to verify and correct their arrangement. **3** In bibliography,

add,āce,câre,pälm; end,ēven; it,īce; odd,ōpen,ôrder; tŏŏk,pōōl; up,bûrn; ə = a in *above,* e in *sicken,* i in *clarity,* o in *melon,* u in *focus* ; yōō = u in *fuse,* oi,oil; ou,pout; ch,check; g,go; ng,ring; th,thin; th,this; zh,vision. Foreign sounds á,œ,ü,kh,ṅ; and ◆: see page xx. < from; + plus; ? possibly.

to examine (the pages of a book) to see that none are missing or out of order. **4** To appoint or admit (a cleric) to a benefice. See synonyms under COMPARE. [<L *collatus,* pp. to *conferre* < *com-* together + *ferre* bear, carry]

col·lat·er·al (kə·lat′ər·əl) *adj.* **1** Subordinately connected; attendant or secondary; incidental. **2** Corroborative; confirmatory. **3** Being or lying alongside; parallel; bordering. **4** Descended from the same ancestor in a different line: distinguished from *lineal.* **5** Pertaining to property, as stocks or bonds, deposited as security additional to one's personal obligation: a *collateral* note. See synonyms under INCIDENTAL. —*n.* **1** Collateral security, which in case of default, is subject to immediate forfeiture, without recourse to legal proceedings. See COLLATERAL SECURITY. **2** A kinsman or kinswoman descended from the same ancestor in a different line. **3** An accompanying or subordinate fact, condition, or part. **4** *Anat.* A part connected with or derived from a main branch: the *collaterals* of a nerve fiber. See synonyms under SECURITY. [<Med. L *collateralis* < *com-* together + *lateralis* lateral < *latus, -eris* side] —**col·lat′er·al·ly** *adv.*

collateral security Property, money, etc., hypothecated as security additional to one's personal obligation.

col·la·tion (kə·lā′shən) *n.* **1** A collating; comparison. **2** The collection and critical comparison of writings or the published result of such a comparison. **3** In bookbinding, the examination of the collected sheets of a book before binding, to detect errors in arrangement. **4** A lunch or light repast: originally confined to the light evening refection of monks; also, the light supper permitted in seasons of fast, such as Lent. **5** The presentation of a clergyman to a church living. **6** In civil law, the return to an estate of property advanced to an heir, with a view to a common distribution of the whole. [<OF *collacion* <L *collatio, -onis* < *conferre.* See COLLATE.]

col·la·tive (kə·lā′tiv) *adj.* **1** Collating. **2** Bestowed, bestowable, or held by collation: said especially of a church living of which the bishop is patron.

col·la·tor (kə·lā′tər) *n.* An extensible, compartmentalized device used in offices to facilitate gathering the pages of duplicated material in proper order.

col·league (kol′ēg) *n.* A fellow member of an official body; an associate in office. See synonyms under ACCESSORY, ASSOCIATE. [<F *collègue* <L *collega* < *com-* together + *legere* choose] —**col′league·ship** *n.*

col·lect[1] (kə·lekt′) *v.t.* **1** To gather or come together; assemble. **2** To bring together as for a hobby, as stamps or books. **3** To gather or obtain payments of money. **4** To regain control of; bring or call back: to *collect* one's wits. —*v.i.* **5** To assemble or congregate, as people; accumulate, as sand. **6** To gather payments or donations. See synonyms under AMASS, CONVOKE. —*adj.* To be paid for on delivery: a telegram sent *collect.* [<F *collecter* <L *colligere* < *com-* together + *legere* choose] —**col·lect′a·ble** or **·i·ble** *adj.*

col·lect[2] (kol′ekt) *n.* A formal, condensed prayer used in several western liturgies, usually containing a single petition and varying with the season or occasion. [<F *collecte* <L *collecta* a gathering together < *colligere.* See COLLECT[1].]

col·lec·ta·ne·a (kol′ek·tā′nē·ə) *n. pl.* Passages selected from different authors; a miscellany. [<L, (things) gathered together]

col·lect·ed (kə·lek′tid) *adj.* **1** Assembled; gathered. **2** Composed; self-possessed. See synonyms under CALM, SOBER. —**col·lect′ed·ly** *adv.* —**col·lect′ed·ness** *n.*

col·lec·tion (kə·lek′shən) *n.* **1** A collecting; a group of collected objects or individuals. **2** An aggregation; accumulation. **3** A sum of money solicited and contributed, as for church expenses, missions, charity, or the like. **4** The act of receiving or enforcing payment, or the amount of such payment. **5** The act of collecting one's thoughts, feelings, etc., or the resultant state; composure. See synonyms under AGGREGATE, ASSEMBLY, COMPANY. [<L *collectio, -onis* < *colligere* COLLECT]

col·lec·tive (kə·lek′tiv) *adj.* **1** Relating to, consisting of, or denoting an aggregate or group: opposed to *individual.* **2** Having the power or quality of bringing together. **3** *Gram.* Denoting in the singular number a collection or aggregate of individuals: The word "army" is a *collective* noun. —*n.* **1** *Gram.* A singular noun naming a collection or group. It takes either a singular or a plural verb, according as it refers to the objects composing it as one aggregate (**collective singular**) or as separate individuals (**collective plural**): The audience *was* large; The audience *were* divided in opinion. **2** A collection or gathering. **3** Any collective enterprise. —**col·lec′tive·ly** *adv.* —**col·lec′tive·ness** *n.*

collective bargaining Negotiation between organized workers and their employer or employers for reaching an agreement on working conditions, wages, hours, etc.

collective farm A farm worked and managed by cooperative labor, and in which the machinery and buildings are communally or state-owned.

collective fruit *Bot.* A fruit which is the product of a number of distinct flowers growing in a compact mass, as a mulberry or a pineapple: also called *multiple fruit.*

collective security Maintenance of world peace by the concerted action of all countries toward an aggressor or potential aggressor, as by the imposition of sanctions or the formation of alliances.

col·lec·tiv·ism (kə·lek′tiv·iz′əm) *n.* The doctrine that the people as a whole should own or control the material and means of production, or the spirit which determines production by the masses rather than by individuals. Compare SOCIALISM. —**col·lec′·tiv·ist** *adj.* & *n.* —**col·lec′tiv·is′tic** *adj.*

col·lec·tiv·i·ty (kol′ek·tiv′ə·tē) *n.* **1** The whole taken together; the quality or state of being collective. **2** The people as a body. **3** Collectivism.

col·lec·tiv·ize (kə·lek′tiv·īz) *v.t.* **·ized, ·iz·ing** To organize (an agricultural settlement, industry, economy, etc.) on a collectivist basis, so that management and labor function cooperatively, the material and means of production being owned communally. —**col·lec′tiv·i·za′tion** *n.*

col·lec·tor (kə·lek′tər) *n.* **1** One who or that which collects. **2** One who receives taxes, duties, etc., or collects debts. —**col·lec′tor·ship** *n.*

col·leen (kol′ēn, kə·lēn′) *n.* A girl. [<Irish *cailín,* dim. of *caile* countrywoman]

col·lege (kol′ij) *n.* **1** An incorporated school for instruction in the liberal arts or professional studies; a school of higher learning that grants degrees at the completion of courses of study; one of the educational institutions of a university; especially one that offers a general, four-year course toward the bachelor's degree: distinguished from graduate and professional schools. **2** A building, or collection of buildings, owned and used by a college. **3** A body of associates or colleagues. **4** A course of lectures or studies. **5** *Brit. Slang* A prison. **6** Any assemblage or gathering: a *college* of bees. [<OF *collège* <L *collegium* body of associates < *collega* COLLEAGUE[1]]

College of Cardinals The body of cardinal-bishops, cardinal-priests, and cardinal-deacons, varying in number up to 70, who constitute the papal council and electorate: also called *Sacred College.*

col·leg·er (kol′ij·ər) *n.* **1** A member of a college. **2** A pupil at Eton College, England, supported by endowment of the college.

college widow A woman who has been popular with several college generations of male students.

col·le·gi·al (kə·lē′jē·əl) *adj.* Collegiate.

col·le·gian (kə·lē′jən, -jē·ən) *n.* **1** A member or attendant of a college; a college student. **2** *Brit. Slang* A prisoner or jailbird.

col·le·giate (kə·lē′jit, -jē·it) *adj.* Pertaining to, like or conducted like, or connected with a college or colleges. —*n.* A collegian. —**col·le′giate·ly** *adv.*

collegiate church **1** An association of churches having pastors in common: the *Collegiate* Dutch Church. **2** A Roman Catholic or an Anglican church, not a cathedral, which has a chapter of canons. **3** A Scottish church served by two or more joint incumbents.

Col·lem·bo·la (kə·lem′bə·lə) *n. pl.* An order of small, primitive, wingless insects with chewing mouth parts, adhesive ventral tubes, and a tail-like organ used in jumping; the springtails. [<NL <Gk. *kolla* glue + *embolon* wedge, peg]

col·len·chy·ma (kə·leng′kə·mə) *n. Bot.* A form of thick-walled, elastic plant tissue, composed of elongated cells strongly thickened at the angles with colloidal material. [<NL <Gk. *kolla* glue + *enchyma* infusion]

Col·le·o·ni (kôl′lā·ō′nē), **Bartolommeo,** 1400–1474, Venetian commander born in Bergamo, Italy; subject of notable equestrian statue by Verrocchio.

col·let (kol′it) *n.* **1** *Mech.* A collar, clutch, or clamping-piece, as for a rod. **2** The ring or rim in which a gem is set. **3** The circular flange which supports the inner terminal of the balance spring in a watch. **4** Culet. —*v.t.* **·let·ed, ·let·ing** To place in or furnish with a collet. [<F, dim. of *col* neck <L *collum*]

col·lide (kə·līd′) *v.i.* **·lid·ed, ·lid·ing** **1** To come together with violent impact; crash. **2** To come into conflict; clash. [<L *collidere* < *com-* together + *laedere* strike]

col·lie (kol′ē) *n.* A breed of large shepherd dogs which originated in Scotland, characterized by a long, narrow head and tapering nose and an abundant long-haired coat. [Prob. <Scottish Gaelic *cuilean* puppy]

col·lied (kol′ēd) *adj. Obs.* Blackened, as with soot; coal-black.

col·lier (kol′yər) *n.* **1** A coal-miner. **2** A vessel employed in carrying coal; also, one of the crew. **3** Formerly, a dealer in coal. [ME *colier* <OE *col* coal + -IER]

Col·lier (kol′yər), **Jeremy,** 1650–1726, English clergyman. —**Peter Fenelon,** 1849–1909, U.S. publisher; founded *Collier's Weekly,* 1896.

col·lier·y (kol′yər·ē) *n. pl.* **·lier·ies** **1** A coal mine. **2** The coal trade.

col·lie·shang·ie (kol′ē·shang′ē) *n. Scot.* A wrangle; brawl; hubbub.

col·li·gate (kol′ə·gāt) *v.t.* **·gat·ed, ·gat·ing** **1** To tie, group, or fasten together. **2** *Logic* To bind together (facts) by means of some suitable conception or explanation: Certain material phenomena are *colligated* by the law of gravity. [<L *colligatus,* pp. of *colligare* < *com-* together + *ligare* bind] —**col′li·ga′tion** *n.* —**col′li·ga′tive** *adj.*

col·li·mate (kol′ə·māt) *v.t.* **·mat·ed, ·mat·ing** **1** To bring into line. **2** To adjust the line of sight of, as of a telescope or other optical instrument. **3** To make parallel, as refracted rays of light or a gunsight with the axis of the gun's barrel. [<L *collimatus,* alter. of *collineatus,* pp. of *collineare* < *com-* together + *lineare* align] —**col′li·ma′tion** *n.*

col·li·ma·tor (kol′ə·mā′tər) *n. Optics* A device used to obtain parallel rays of light, as a fixed telescope or the convex lens and slit used in a spectroscope.

col·lin·e·ar (kə·lin′ē·ər) *adj.* Being in the same straight line: said of three or more points. —**col·lin′e·ar·ly** *adv.*

Col·ling·wood (kol′ing·wŏŏd) A city in SE Australia near Melbourne.

Col·lins (kol′inz), **Michael,** 1890–1922, Irish patriot. —**Michael,** born 1930, U.S. astronaut; member of first space flight to land men on the moon, July 16–24, 1969. —**William,** 1721–59, English poet. —**Wilkie,** 1824–89, English novelist: full name *William Wilkie Collins.*

col·lin·si·a (kə·lin′sē·ə, -zē·ə) *n.* **1** An annual or biennial plant (genus *Collinsia*) of the figwort family with whorled leaves. **2** Any of the variously colored flowers of this plant. [after Z. *Collins,* 1764–1831, U.S. botanist]

col·li·sion (kə·lizh′ən) *n.* **1** The act of colliding. **2** Violent contact; clashing; antagonism. [<LL *collisio, -onis* < *collidere* COLLIDE]

Synonyms: clash, clashing, concussion, conflict, contact, encounter, impact, meeting, opposition, shock. *Collision* is the result of motion or action and is sudden and momentary; *contact* may be a condition of rest and be continuous and permanent. *Impact* is the blow given by the striking body. *Concussion* is often by transmitted force rather than by direct *impact*; an explosion of dynamite shatters neighboring windows by *concussion.* *Shock* is the result of *collision.* *Opposition* is used chiefly of persons, less frequently of opinions or interests; *conflict* is used indifferently of all. See ENCOUNTER. *Antonyms*:

agreement, amity, coincidence, concert, concord, concurrence, conformity, harmony, unison, unity.

col·lo·cate (kol′ō·kāt) *v.t.* **·cat·ed, ·cat·ing** To put in certain order; arrange together. [< L *collocatus,* pp. of *collocare* < *com-* together + *locare* place] **—col′lo·ca′tion** *n.*

col·lo·di·on (kə·lō′dē·ən) *n.* A solution of guncotton or pyroxylin in ether and alcohol, deposited as a film on the evaporation of the ether, and used as a coating for wounds and for photographic plates. Also **col·lo·di·um** (kə·lō′·dē·əm). [< Gk. *kollōdēs* gluelike]

col·logue (kə·lōg′) *v.i.* **·logued, ·lo·guing** *Brit. Dial.* **1** To confer secretly; plot. **2** *Obs.* To use flattery and deceit; cajole; wheedle. [Prob. < F *colloque* conference < L *colloquium*]

col·loid (kol′oid) *n.* **1** Any gluelike or jellylike substance, as gelatin, starch, raw egg white, etc., which diffuses not at all or very slowly through vegetable and animal membranes, and whose components do not separate as in a true solution or simple mixture: distinguished from *crystalloid.* **2** *Chem.* A state of matter in which very finely divided particles of one substance (the *disperse phase*) are suspended in another (the *dispersion medium*) in such manner and degree that the electrical and surface properties acquire special importance. **3** *Med.* A translucent, gelatinous substance resulting from certain forms of tissue degeneration. *—adj.* Of or pertaining to a colloid or the colloid state: also **col·loi·dal** (kə·loid′l). [< Gk. *kollōdēs* gluelike] **—col·loi·dal·i·ty** (kol′oi·dal′ə·tē) *n.*

colloid system *Chem.* Any aggregate of substances exhibiting the properties of a colloid, as sols, gels, emulsions, etc. Eight of these systems are known, occurring in solid, liquid, and gaseous forms, each identified in terms of the relationship existing between the disperse phase and the dispersion medium. See table below.

COLLOID SYSTEMS

Components	*Term*	*Example*
Solid in solid	solid sol	alloys, paper
Solid in liquid	suspension	paints
Solid in gas	smoke	iodine vapor
Liquid in solid	gel	celluloid, glue, gelatin
Liquid in liquid	emulsion	milk, blood
Liquid in gas	fog	clouds, steam
Gas in solid	solid foam	pumice, rubber
Gas in liquid	foam	lather, froth
Gas in gas		(No example known)

col·lop (kol′əp) *n.* **1** A slice or morsel of meat for stewing. **2** A small portion or piece of anything. [Cf. Sw. *kalops* slices of stewed beef]

col·lo·qui·al (kə·lō′kwē·əl) *adj.* **1** Characteristic of or suitable to the informal language of ordinary conversation or familiar writing, but inappropriate for use on the formal level. Colloquial language is widely used by the educated in informal discourse and is not to be confused with substandard speech. **2** Conversational. Abbr. *colloq.* **—col·lo′qui·al·ly** *adv.* **—col·lo′qui·al·ness** *n.*

col·lo·qui·al·ism (kə·lō′kwē·əl·iz′əm) *n.* **1** An expression or form of speech of the type used in informal conversation. **2** Informal, conversational style.

col·lo·quy (kol′ə·kwē) *n. pl.* **·quies 1** An informal conference; conversation. **2** A literary work written in conversational or dialog form. [< L *colloquium* conversation < *com-* together + *loqui* speak] **—col′lo·quist** *n.*

col·lo·type (kol′ə·tīp) *n.* **1** A photomechanical printing process in which the negative is printed on a plate covered with a light-sensitive gelatin coat which is then rendered selectively ink-repellent by treatment with glycerin and salt water. **2** A print or plate made by this process. *—v.t.* **·typed, ·typ·ing** To make a collotype of. [< Gk. *kolla* glue + -TYPE] **—col·lo·typ·ic** (kol′ə·tip′ik) *adj.* **—col·lo·typ·y** (kol′ə·tī′pē) *n.*

col·lude (kə·lōōd′) *v.i.* **·lud·ed, ·lud·ing** To cooperate secretly; conspire; connive. [< L *colludere* < *com-* together + *ludere* play, trick] **—col·lud′er** *n.*

col·lu·sion (kə·lōō′zhən) *n.* Cooperation in fraud. [< L *collusio, -onis* < *colludere* COLLUDE]

col·lu·sive (kə·lōō′siv) *adj.* Fraudulently concerted or devised. **—col·lu′sive·ly** *adv.* **—col·lu′sive·ness** *n.*

col·ly (kol′ē) *Brit. Dial. n.* Coal dust; soot. *—v.t.* **·lied, ·ly·ing** To blacken as with coal smut or soot; begrime. [ME *colie,* OE *col* coal]

col·lyr·i·um (kə·lir′ē·əm) *n.* A medicated eyewash or eye salve. [< L < Gk. *kollyrion* poultice, dim. of *kollyra* bread]

Col·mar (kōl′mär, *Fr.* kôl·màr′) A city of eastern France, capital of Haut-Rhin department. *German* **Kol·mar** (kōl′mär).

colo- *combining form* Colon: *colotomy.* Also, before vowels, *col-.* [< Gk. *kolon* colon]

Co·lô·a·ne (kōō·lō′ə·nə) See under MACAO.

col·o·cynth (kol′ə·sinth) *n.* **1** A Mediterranean vine *(Citrullus colocynthis)* of the gourd family. **2** Its small gourdlike fruit from which is obtained a cathartic drug: also called *bitter apple, coloquintida.* [< L *colocynthis* < Gk. *kolokynthē* gourd]

co·logne (kə·lōn′) *n.* A toilet water consisting of alcohol scented with aromatic oils: often called *eau de Cologne.* Also **Cologne water.** [from *Cologne*]

Co·logne (kə·lōn′) A city in North Rhine-Westphalia, Germany, on the Rhine: German *Köln.*

Co·lombes (kô·lônb′) A NW suburb of Paris, France.

Co·lom·bi·a (kə·lum′bē·ə, *Sp.* kō·lōm′byä) A republic in NW South America; 439,828 square miles; capital, Bogotá. **—Co·lom′bi·an** *adj.* & *n.*

Co·lom·bo (kə·lum′bō) The capital of Sri Lanka; a port on the west coast.

co·lon[1] (kō′lən) *n. pl.* **co·lons** *for def.* **1,** cola (kō′lə) *for def.* **2 1** A punctuation mark (:) indicating a pause greater than a semicolon, but less than a period: used as a sign of apposition or equality to connect one clause with another that explains it, as in introducing an enumeration or catalog; also used after a word introducing a speech, quotation, etc., in expressing clock time, in citations, and in mathematical proportions. **2** In ancient prosody, a member or section of a rhythmical period. [< Gk. *kōlon* member, limb, clause]

co·lon[2] (kō′lən) *n. pl.* **co·lons** or **co·la** (kō′lə) *Anat.* The portion of the large intestine between the cecum and the rectum. [< Gk. *kolon*] **—co·lon·ic** (kə·lon′ik) *adj.*

co·lon[3] (kō·lōn′) *n. pl.* **co·lons** (kō·lōnz′), *Sp.* **co·lo·nes** (kō·lō′nās) The monetary unit of Costa Rica and El Salvador.

Co·lón (kō·lōn′) A port of Panama at the Atlantic entrance to the Panama Canal: formerly *Aspinwall.*

Co·lón (kō·lōn′), **Cristóbal** See COLUMBUS, CHRISTOPHER.

Co·lón Archipelago (kō·lōn′) The official name for the GALAPAGOS ISLANDS.

colo·nel (kûr′nəl) *n.* A commissioned officer of the sixth rank in the U.S. Army, U.S. Air Force, or U.S. Marine Corps, ranking next above a lieutenant colonel and next below a brigadier general. **—lieutenant colonel** A commissioned officer of the fifth rank in the U.S. Army, U.S. Air Force, or U.S. Marine Corps, ranking next above a major and next below a colonel. ◆ Homophone: *kernel.* [Earlier *coronel* < F *coronnel* < Ital. *colonnello* < *colonna* column of soldiers] **—colo′nel·cy, colo′nel·ship** *n.*

co·lo·ni·al (kə·lō′nē·əl) *adj.* **1** Of, pertaining to, produced in or living in, like, or forming a colony or colonies, especially one of the thirteen British Colonies that became the United States. **2** Characteristic of colonial times; antique. *—n.* A citizen or inhabitant of a colony. **—co·lo′ni·al·ly** *adv.*

co·lo·ni·al·ism (kə·lō′nē·əl·iz′əm) *n.* The policy of a nation seeking to acquire, extend, or retain overseas dependencies; imperialism.

col·o·nist (kol′ə·nist) *n.* **1** A member or inhabitant of a colony. **2** A settler or founder of a colony.

col·o·ni·tis (kol′ə·nī′tis) See COLITIS.

col·o·ni·za·tion·ist (kol′ə·nə·zā′shən·ist, -nī·zā′-) *n.* An advocate of colonization; specifically, one of the American anti-slavery reformers who favored colonizing emancipated Negroes in Liberia.

col·o·nize (kol′ə·nīz) *v.* **·nized, ·niz·ing** *v.t.* **1** To settle a colony or colonies in. **2** To establish or place as colonists. *—v.i.* **3** To establish or unite in a colony or colonies. **4** To settle in colonies. Also *Brit.* **col′o·nise. —col′o·ni·za′tion** *n.* **—col′o·niz′er** *n.*

col·on·nade (kol′ə·nād′) *n. Archit.* A range of columns connected by an entablature. [< F < *colonne* column] **—col′on·nad′ed** *adj.*

col·on·nette (kol′ə·net′) *n.* **1** *Archaic* A small column. **2** *Anat.* A small column of bone. [< F, dim. of *colonne* column]

col·o·ny (kol′ə·nē) *n. pl.* **·nies 1** A body of emigrants or their descendants in a remote region under the control of a parent country. In Great Britain the term *colony* designates a region that has a responsible government, whether or not it has an elective legislature. **2** Any aggregation of individuals in a common group, as of alien residents in a country, or of bees, beavers, etc. **3** The territory occupied by early settlers or their descendants. **4** *Biol.* A group of organisms of the same species, usually from the same parent cell, functioning in close association and with varying degrees of independence, as certain bacteria, protozoans, and algae. **5** *Ecol.* **a** Two or more species of plants developing in a locality as a result of invasion. **b** A group of plants isolated from others of the same species, but growing in the same locality. [< L *colonia* < *colonus* farmer]

col·o·phon (kol′ə·fon, -fən) *n.* An inscription or device, often ornamental, as the publisher's distinctive emblem, at the beginning or end of books. [< LL < Gk. *kolophon* summit]

Col·o·phon (kol′ə·fon) An ancient city NW of Ephesus, Asia Minor.

col·o·pho·ny (kol′ə·fō′nē, kə·lof′ə·nē) *n.* Rosin. [< L *colophonia (resina)* (rosin) from Colophon] **—col·o·phon·ic** (kol′ə·fon′ik) *adj.*

col·o·quin·ti·da (kol′ə·kwin′ti·də) See COLOCYNTH.

col·or (kul′ər) *n.* **1** A visual attribute of bodies or substances distinct from their spatial characteristics and depending upon the spectral composition of the wavelengths of radiant energy capable of stimulating the retina and its associated neural mechanisms. **Achromatic colors** include black and white and the entire series of intermediate grays, varying only in *lightness* and *brightness.* **Chromatic colors** may also vary in *hue,* as red, green, blue, and purple; and in *saturation.* **2** A paint, dyestuff, or pigment, as used in industry and the arts. **3** An appearance; semblance; pretense; disguise. **4** *pl.* An ensign or flag of a nation, also of a military or naval unit, as a regiment, warship, etc. **5** *pl.* In the U.S. Navy, the salute made to the national flag when it is hoisted in the morning and lowered in the evening. **6** The hue of the human skin; complexion: equal rights regardless of race, creed, or *color.* **7** In art, coloring. **8** *Music* Timbre; clang; also, the tone, or characteristic effect, of a composition, as produced by specific harmonic, rhythmic, or melodic means. **9** *Law* An apparent or prima-facie right, authority, etc. **10** A small particle or trace of gold in auriferous sand or gravel. **11** Liveliness or animation, vividness, especially in literary work. **—complementary color 1** Either of a pair of spectrum colors which when combined give a white or nearly white light. **2** One of two pigments whose mixture produces a third color, as blue and yellow blended to produce green. **—primary colors 1** The principal colors in which white light is separated by a prism; the colors of the rainbow. **2** The colors red, yellow, green, and blue, by mixing which any desired color or hue may be obtained; to these white and black may be added. *—v.t.* **1** To apply or give color, as by painting, staining, or dyeing. **2** To misrepresent by distortion or exaggeration. **3** To modify in nature or character. *—v.i.* **4** To take on or change color, as ripening fruit. **5** To blush or flush. Also *Brit.* **col′our** [< OF *colour* < L *color*] **—col′or·a·ble** *adj.* **—col′or·a·bly** *adv.* **—col′or·er** *n.*

Col·o·ra·dan (kol′ə·rä′dən, -rad′ən) *n.* A na-

tive or citizen of Colorado. —*adj.* Of or pertaining to Colorado.

col·o·ra·do (kol′ə·rä′dō) *adj.* **1** Denoting medium strength and color: said of cigars. **2** Red; reddish: used in geographic names. [<Sp., colored, red]

Col·o·ra·do (kol′ə·rä′dō, -rad′ō) A western State of the United States; 103,967 square miles; capital, Denver; entered the Union Aug. 1, 1876: nicknamed *Centennial State* : abbr. CO

Colorado beetle The potato beetle.

Colorado Desert An arid region in SE California and northern Lower California.

Colorado River 1 A river of the SW United States, flowing 1,400 miles SW to the northern tip of the Gulf of California. **2** A river in Texas, flowing 900 miles SE to the Gulf of Mexico: also **Eastern Colorado River.**

col·o·ra·tion (kul′ə·rä′shən) *n.* Particular marking or arrangement of colors, as in an animal or plant; coloring.

col·o·ra·tu·ra (kul′ər·ə·tŏŏr′ə,-tyŏŏr′ə) *n.* The effect of giving color to vocal music, by means of grace notes, runs, trills, or other florid decoration. **2** The runs, etc., themselves. —*adj.* Characterized by or suitable for coloratura. Also **col·o·ra·ture** (kul′ər·ə·choor). [<Ital. *coloratura* ration]

coloratura soprano 1 A clear, high voice of flexible range. **2** A singer with such a voice.

col·or·blind (kul′ər·blīnd′) *adj.* Totally or partially unable to discriminate between hues as distinguished from light or shade.

col·or·blind·ness (kul′ər·blīnd′nis) *n.* Achromatopsia.

col·or·cast (kul′ər·kast′, -käst′) *n.* A television broadcast in color.

color corrector An electronic device used in the preparation of precision color negatives in photoengraving.

color diagram A graphic chart or table which illustrates the interrelations of colors in respect of hue, lightness, saturation, etc. When in three dimensions, such a diagram is called a **color solid** or **color pyramid.**

col·ored (kul′ərd) *adj.* **1** Having color. **2** Embellished or exaggerated; prejudiced; specious. **3** Of a race other than the white, especially black; taken to be offensive. **4** Of mixed race; taken to be offensive.

col·or·fast (kul′ər·fast′, -fäst′) *adj.* Retaining color of dye or paint substantially unfaded when fabric or surface is subjected to the action of water, cleaning fluid, or a reasonable amount of light; resistant to fading: *colorfast* fabrics; a *colorfast* paint job.

color filter A layer of substance, in solid, liquid, or gaseous form, which will absorb a certain wavelength of light: used in photography to change the relative intensities of impinging light waves. Also called **color screen.**

col·or·ful (kul′ər·fəl) *adj.* **1** Full of colors, especially contrasting colors; bright: a *colorful* scene. **2** In literature, vivid; animated: a *colorful* plot. — **col′or·ful·ly** *adv.* — **col′or·ful·ness** *n.*

color guard In the U.S. Army, Navy, and Air Force, the flagbearers and guards who conduct the colors in a ceremony.

col·or·if·ic (kul′ə·rif′ik) *adj.* Pertaining to the production or imparting of color. [<F *colorifique*]

col·or·im·e·ter (kul′ə·rim′ ə·tər) *n.* An apparatus for determining the hue, purity, and brightness of a color, especially as compared with a specified standard: used in chemical analysis and in medicine. [<COLOR + -(I) METER] — **col·or·i· met′ric** (kul′ər·ə·met′rik) or **·ri·cal** *adj.* — **col′or·i·met′ri·cal·ly** *adv.*

col·or·im·e·try (kul′ə·rim′ə·trē) *n.* The measurement and analysis of color by comparison with a standard or in terms of physical and spectral characteristics.

color index 1 *Astron.* The difference between the photographic and visual magnitude of a star. **2** *Med.* A number expressing the amount of hemoglobin in the red blood cells. **3** *Mineral.* A number indicating the percentage of light to dark and heavy minerals in igneous rock: also called **color ratio.**

col·or·ing (kul′ər·ing) *n.* **1** The imparting of color, or that which imparts color. **2** The general color of anything; coloration; style of ap-

plying colors. **3** Peculiar style or air. **4** Appearance; especially, false appearance.

col·or·ist (kul′ər·ist) *n.* **1** One who uses color. **2** An artist skilled in the use of color.

col·or·ize (kul′ər·īz) *v.t.* **-ized, -iz·ing** To add color to originally black-and-white movies by means of computer-enhanced techniques. — **col′or·i· za′tion** *n.*

col·or·less (kul′ər·lis) *adj.* **1** Without color. **2** Dull; uninteresting. See synonyms under PALE.

color scheme An arrangement of colors according to a planned design, as in a room.

color sergeant See under SERGEANT.

color temperature *Physics* The temperature of a blackbody when its color exactly matches that of a given source of radiation.

color wheel A wheel designed to exhibit the proportion of primary colors in any shade of color.

Co·los·sae (kə·los′ē) An ancient city of SW Phrygia, Asia Minor.

co·los·sal (kə·los′əl) *adj.* Enormous; huge; tremendous. See synonyms under IMMENSE. — **co·los′sal·ly** *adv.*

Col·os·se·um (kol′ə·sē′əm) The Flavian amphitheater in Rome, built by Vespasian and Titus in A.D. 75–80: also spelled *Coliseum.*

Co·los·sian (kə·losh′ən) *adj.* Pertaining to Colossae, in ancient Phrygia. —*n.* **1** A native or inhabitant of Colossae. **2** *pl.* Saint Paul's epistle to the Colossians, a book of the New Testament.

co·los·sus (kə·los′əs) *n. pl.* **co·los·si** (kə·los′ī) or **co·los·sus·es 1** A gigantic statue. **2** Any strikingly huge or great person or object. [<L <Gk. *kolossos* gigantic statue]

Colossus of Rhodes A 100-foot bronze statue of Helios set at the entrance to the harbor of ancient Rhodes in 285 B.C. See SEVEN WONDERS OF THE WORLD.

co·los·to·my (kə·los′tə·mē) *n. pl.* **·mies** *Surg.* The formation of an artificial opening into the colon. [<COLO- + -STOMY]

co·los·trum (kə·los′trəm) *n.* The first milk of a mammal after parturition; beestings. [<L]

col·our (kul′ər) See COLOR.

-colous *combining form* Dwelling in or inhabiting: *arenicolous.* [<L *colere* dwell, inhabit]

col·pi·tis (kol·pī′tis) *n.* Inflammation of the vagina; vaginitis. [<Gk. *kolpos* womb + -ITIS]

col·por·tage (kol′pôr·tij) *n.* A colporteur's work.

col·por·teur (kol′pôr·tər) *n.* **1** A peddler, especially one who hawks books, almanacs, etc., in country districts. **2** A traveling agent of a religious society, who sells or gives away Bibles, tracts, etc. [<F < *colporter* peddle < *col* neck + *porter* carry]

colt (kōlt) *n.* **1** A young horse, ass, etc.; specifically, a young male horse. **2** A frisky person. [OE] — **colt′ish** *adj.*

Colt (kōlt) *n.* A kind of pistol or revolver: a trade name. [after Samuel *Colt,* 1814–) 62, U.S. inventor]

col·ter (kōl′tər) *n.* A blade or disk on the beam of a plow, to cut the sod: also spelled *coulter.* [OE *culter* <L *culter* knife]

colts·foot (kōlts′foot′) *n. pl.* **·foots** A low, perennial, Old World herb of the composite family (*Tussilago farfara*), bearing yellow flowers: formerly used in medicine.

col·u·brine (kol′yə·brīn, -brin) *adj.* **1** Of, pertaining to, or like a snake. **2** Of or pertaining to a widely distributed family of snakes (*Colubridae*); especially to the subfamily *Colubrinae,* which includes the typically nonvenomous snakes, as the garter snake, blacksnake, etc. [<L *colubrinus* < *coluber* snake]

co·lu·go (kə·lōō′gō) *n. pl.* **·gos** The flying lemur.

Col·um (kol′əm), **Padraic,** 1881–1972, Irish poet and playwright.

Co·lum·ba (kə·lum′bə) A southern constellation, the Dove. See CONSTELLATION.

Co·lum·ba (kə·lum′bə), **Saint,** 521–597, Irish monk and missionary in Caledonia.

Co·lum·bae (kə·lum′bē) *n. pl.* An extensive suborder of birds of the order *Columbiformes,* including pigeons and doves. [<L *columba* dove]

Co·lum·ban (kə·lum′bən), **Saint,** 543?–615, Irish monk and missionary in France, Switzerland, and Italy.

col·um·bar·i·um (kol′əm·bâr′ē·əm) *n. pl.* **·bar·i·a** (-bâr′ē·ə) **1** A dovecot; also, a pigeonhole in a dovecot: also **col·um·bar·y** (kol′ əm·ber′ē). **2** In ancient Rome, a sepulcher with niches for cinerary urns. [<L < *columba* dove]

COLUMBARIUM

Co·lum·bi·a (kə·lum′bē·ə) *n. Poetic* The personification of the United States of America. [after Christopher *Columbus*]

Co·lum·bi·a (kə·lum′bē·ə) The capital of South Carolina.

Columbia, Cape A promontory of Ellesmere Island in the Arctic Ocean, the northernmost point of Canada.

Columbia, District of See DISTRICT OF COLUMBIA.

co·lum·bi·ad (kə·lum′bē·ad) *n.* A heavy smooth-bore cannon first used in the War of 1812: now obsolete. [from *Columbia,* the United States]

Co·lum·bi·ad (kə·lum′bē·ad) *n.* An epic of America; especially, *The Columbiad* in 12 books, by Joel Barlow, 1807.

Co·lum·bi·an (kə·lum′bē·ən) *adj.* **1** Of or pertaining to Columbia (the United States). **2** Pertaining to Christopher Columbus.

Co·lum·bi·an (kə·lum′bē·ən) *n. Printing* A style and size of type, 16-point.

Columbia River A river in SW Canada and NW United States, flowing 1,200 miles to the Pacific Ocean.

col·um·bine (kol′əm·bīn) *n.* A herbaceous plant (genus *Aquilegia*) of the crowfoot family with variously colored flowers of five petals; especially the **Colorado columbine** (*A. coerulea*), State flower of Colorado. — *adj.* Dovelike. [<F <Med. L *columbinus* dovelike < *columba* dove; from the resemblance of its flowers to a flock of doves]

Col·um·bine (kol′əm·bīn) A stock character in pantomimes: the daughter of Pantaloon and the sweetheart of Harlequin.

COLUMBINE

co·lum·bite (kə·lum′bīt) *n.* A black, brittle mineral, containing variable proportions of niobium and tantalum, associated with iron and manganese.

co·lum·bi·um (kə·lum′bē·əm) *n.* Former name for the element niobium. [<NL < *Columbia,* the United States]

Co·lum·bus (kə·lum′bəs) The capital of Ohio.

Co·lum·bus (kə·lum′bəs), **Christopher,** 1446–1506, Italian navigator; discovered America for Spain, Oct. 12, 1492. Spanish *Cristóbal Colón.*

Columbus Day October 12, a holiday observed in most States of the United States in commemoration of the discovery of America by Christopher Columbus in 1492: also called *Discovery Day.*

col·u·mel·la (kol′yə·mel′ə) *n. pl.* **·mel·lae** (-mel′ē) *Biol.* A little rod, pillar, or central axis, as the central rod of the cochlea, the axial pillar of a spiral shell, etc. Also **col·u·mel**

(kol′yə·mel). [<L, dim. of *columna* column] — **col′u·mel′lar** *adj.* — **col·u·mel·li·form** (kol′-yə·mel′ə·fôrm) *adj.*

col·umn (kol′əm) *n.* **1** *Archit.* A vertical shaft or pillar, usually having a base and a capital, and primarily for the support of superincumbent weight. **2** Any object or structure resembling a column in form position, or use: th spinal *column*; a *column* of vapor. **3** *Printing* A vertical series of lines, separated from adjoining columns by a rule or a blank space. **4** *Mil.* A unit of troops in single file, or formed several lines abreast. **5** *Naut.* A fleet of ships in single file. **6** A department of a newspaper in which a special writer presents a daily article of contemporary comment. See synonyms under PROCESSION. [<L *columna*] — **col·umned** (kol′əmd) *adj.*

co·lum·nar (kə·lum′nər) *adj.* **1** Of, pertaining to, or having the form of a column or columns; like the shaft of a column. **2** *Geol.* Describing the six-sided structural formation characteristic of basaltic rock.

co·lum·ni·a·tion (kə·lum′nē·ā′shən) *n.* Grouping of columns; columns collectively.

col·um·nist (kol′əm·nist, -əm·ist) *n.* A journalist who writes or conducts a special column on a daily newspaper.

co·lure (kə·lyŏŏr′, kō′lyŏŏr) *n.* *Astron.* One of the two great circles of the celestial sphere at right angles to each other, intersecting at the poles and passing through the equinoxes and the solstices respectively. [<L *colurus* <Gk. *kolouros* <*kolos* docked + *oura* tail; because their lower parts are cut off by the horizon]

Col·ville River (kol′vil) A river of northern Alaska, flowing 375 miles NE to the Beaufort Sea.

Col·vin (kol′vin), **Sir Sidney**, 1845–1927, English author.

co·ly (kō′lē) *n.* *pl.* **co·lies** The long-tailed African mousebird, one of a genus (*Colius*) having four toes and a strong, slightly curved beak. [<NL *colius* <Gk. *kolios*, a green woodpecker]

co·ly·one (kō′lē·ōn) *n.* *Biochem.* A secretion which has the property of inhibiting the action of some organ, tissue, or part of the body: distinguished from *hormone*: also called *chalone*. [<Gk. *kōlyōn*, ppr. of *kōlyein* hinder]

col·za (kol′zə) *n.* The summer rape or coleseed whose seeds produce rape oil. [<F <Du. *koolzaad* <*kool* cabbage + *zaad* a seed]

colza oil Rape oil.

com- *prefix* With; together: *combine*, *compare*. Also: *co-* before *gn*, *h*, and vowels; *col-* before *l*, as in *collide*; *con-* before *c*, *d*, *f*, *g*, *j*, *n*, *q*, *s*, *t*, *v*, as in *concur*, *confluence*, *connect*, *conspire*; *cor-* before *r*, as in *correspond*. [<L *com-* <*cum* with]

co·ma[1] (kō′mə) *n.* *pl.* **co·mas** A state of unconsciousness with slow, heavy breathing: sometimes called by the names of the conditions or diseases that cause them: **diabetic coma** (occurring in diabetes), **uremic coma** (from excess of urea), etc. **2** Stupor; lethargy. [<NL <Gk. *kōma* deep sleep]

co·ma[2] (kō′mə) *n.* *pl.* **co·mae** (kō′mē) **1** *Astron.*

Column illustration labels:

ROMAN
COLUMN WITH
ENTABLATURE (*a.–c.*)
a. Cornice.
b. Frieze.
c. Architrave.
d. Capital (in Corinthian style)
e. Astragal.
f. Shaft.
g. Base.
From the Pantheon, Rome

The nebulosity around the nucleus of a comet. **2** *Bot.* A tuft of silky hairs, as at the end of certain seeds. **3** *Optics* The hazy border surrounding an object viewed through an imperfect lens. [<L, hair <Gk. *komē*] — **co′mal** *adj.*

Co·ma Ber·e·ni·ces (kō′mə ber′ə·nī′sēz) A northern constellation, Berenice's Hair, near Boötes. See CONSTELLATION.

Co·man·che (kō·man′chē) *n.* *pl.* **·ches 1** One of a tribe of North American Indians of Shoshonean stock; plains Indians: formerly roaming territory between Kansas and northern Mexico, now in Oklahoma. **2** The Uto-Aztecan language of this tribe.

Co·man·che·an (kō·man′chē·ən) *adj.* *Geol.* Of or pertaining to the Comanche series and to the epoch during which the series was deposited; Shastan. — *n.* **1** *Geol.* **a** An epoch of the Mesozoic between the Jurassic and the Cretaceous. **b** The Comanche series of rocks. Also called *Shastan*.

Comanche series *Geol.* The Lower Cretaceous series of rocks in the region of the Gulf of Mexico. [from *Comanche*, a town and county in central Texas]

co·mate[1] (kō′māt) *adj.* **1** *Bot.* Having a coma. **2** *Entomol.* Hairy, as the heads of certain insects.

co·mate[2] (kō·māt′, kō′māt) *n.* A mate; companion.

co·ma·tose (kō′mə·tōs, kom′ə-) *adj.* **1** Relating to or affected with coma. **2** Lethargic; torpid; abnormally sleepy. Also **co·ma·tous** (kō′mə·təs, kom′ə-). — **co′ma·tose′ly** *adv.* — **co′ma·tose′ness** *n.*

co·mat·u·la (kō·mat′yə·lə) *n.* *Zool.* One of a genus (*Comatula*) of free-swimming crinoids, with plumelike arms: also called *feather star*. Also **co·mat′u·lid**. [<NL <L *comatulus*, dim. of *comatus* having hair <*coma* hair]

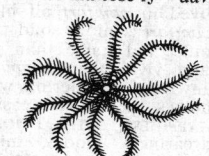

COMATULA
(Mostly microscopic: some up to 2/3 of an inch)

comb[1] (kōm) *n.* **1** A thin piece of horn, metal, ivory, or the like, with teeth, for cleansing, dressing, or fastening the hair. **2** Something resembling such a comb in appearance or use, as a currycomb or a card for dressing wool or flax. **3** The fleshy crest on the head of a fowl. **4** The crest of a hill or wave. **5** Honeycomb. **6** That part of a gunstock in which the cheek rests. **7** The ridge of a roof. — *v.t.* **1** To dress, disentangle, or smoothe out with or as with a comb, as hair; clear or cleanse with a comb. **2** To card, as wool or flax. **3** In painting, to grain with a comb. **4** To search carefully and exhaustively. — *v.i.* **5** To crest and break: said of waves. [OE *camb*]

comb[2] (kōm) See COOMB.

com·bat (kom′bat, kum′-) *n.* A battle or fight; struggle; contest; duel. — **close combat** Hand-to-hand fighting. — **single combat** A fight between two persons; a duel. — *v.* (kəm·bat′) **·bat·ed** or **·bat·ted**, **·bat·ing** or **·bat·ting** *v.t.* **1** To fight or contend with; oppose in battle. **2** To resist. — *v.i.* **3** To do battle; struggle: with *with* or *against*. See synonyms under ATTACK, BATTLE, CONTEND, DISPUTE, OPPOSE. [<F <*combattre* <L *com-* with + *batuere* fight, beat] — **com·bat·a·ble** (kəm·bat′ə·bəl, kom′bat·ə-bəl) *adj.* — **com·bat·er** (kom′bat·ər, kum′-, kəm·bat′ər) *n.*

com·bat·ant (kəm·bat′ənt, kom′bə·tənt, kum′-) *n.* One engaged in or prepared for combat or hostilities. — *adj.* Fighting; battling; ready or disposed to combat. [<OF *combatant*, ppr. of *combattre* COMBAT]

combat fatigue Battle fatigue.

com·bat·ive (kəm·bat′iv, kom′bə·tiv, kum′-) *adj.* Inclined or eager to fight; pugnacious. — **com·bat′ive·ly** *adv.* — **com·bat′ive·ness** *n.*

comb·er (kō′mər) *n.* **1** One who or that which combs wool, flax, etc. **2** A long crested wave; a breaker.

com·bi·na·tion (kom′bə·nā′shən) *n.* **1** A joining together; union; alliance. **2** A compound or group. **3** *pl.* Underwear made in one piece. **4** The series of numbers or letters forming the key symbol to a keyless lock or

---

combination lock; also, the mechanism operated by such a sequence. **5** *Math.* A group of several things or symbols in which the order of arrangement is immaterial. **6** *Chem.* The union of elements in certain fixed proportions, or the compound thus resulting. **7** An alliance of politicians, or merchants, etc., to protect or further a common interest, activity, or advantage. **8** An alliance of corporations; a combine or monopoly. **9** A railroad car divided into a baggage and a passenger section. See synonyms under CABAL, UNION. [<MF <LL *combinatio, -onis* a joining by twos <*combinare*. See COMBINE.] — **com′bi·na′tion·al** *adj.*

com·bi·na·tive (kom′bə·nā′tiv, kəm·bī′nə-) *adj.* **1** Relating to or effecting combination; tending to combine. **2** Designating those branches of algebra which depend on the theory of combinations. Also **com·bi·na·to·ri·al** (kəm·bī′nə·tôr′ē·əl, -tō′rē-).

com·bine (kəm·bīn′) *v.t.* & *v.i.* **·bined, ·bin·ing 1** To bring or come into a close union; blend; compound; unite. **2** To unite by affinity. **3** To enter into chemical combination: Oxygen and hydrogen *combine* to form water. See synonyms under MIX, UNITE. — *n.* (kom′bīn) **1** *Colloq.* An association of persons to raise prices or obstruct the course of trade, or to gain or keep political control, often by unfair or dishonest means; a trust; ring; cabal. **2** A farm machine which combines the processes of heading, threshing, and cleaning grain while harvesting it in the field. [<LL *combinare* <*com-* together + *bini* two by two] — **com·bin′a·ble** *adj.* — **com·bin′er** *n.*

comb·ing (kō′ming) *n.* **1** The act of combing, or what is removed by or from a comb. **2** A coaming.

combining form The stem of a word, usually of Greek or Latin origin (*tele-* and *-phone* in *telephone*), or in an English word unchanged (*over* in *overeat*), used in combination with other forms to create compounds.

comb jelly A ctenophore.

com·bust (kəm·bust′) *adj.* In astrology, obscured by proximity to the sun, as a planet or star. [<OF <L *combustus*, pp. of *comburere* burn up]

com·bus·ti·ble (kəm·bus′tə·bəl) *adj.* **1** Susceptible of combustion; inflammable. **2** Excitable; fiery. — *n.* Any substance that will readily burn, as pitch or coal. — **com·bus′ti·ble·ness, com·bus′ti·bil′i·ty** *n.*

com·bus·tion (kəm·bus′chən) *n.* **1** The action or operation of burning; the state of being on fire. **2** *Chem.* The combination of a substance with oxygen, accompanied by the generation of heat and sometimes light. **3** *Physiol.* Oxidation, as of fuel, or of food in the body. **4** Disturbance; tumult. See synonyms under FIRE. [<LL *combustio, -onis* <*comburere* burn up] — **com·bus′tive** *adj.*

com·bus·tor (kəm·bus′tər) *n.* The chamber of a jet-propulsion engine in which combustion occurs.

comb·y (kō′mē) *adj.* Resembling a comb or honeycomb.

come (kum) *v.* **came, come, com·ing** *v.i.* **1** To move to or toward a position or place from a point further away: opposed to *go*. **2** To move to or toward the speaker: *Come* here. **3** In the imperative, to move mentally where the speaker wills: almost an interjectional sense: *Come*, let us make a visit. **4** To arrive as the result of motion or progress: They *came* to land. **5** To attain to an end or completion: Thy kingdom *come*. **6** To arrive at some state or condition; develop. **7** To advance or move into view; become perceptible: Her color *comes* and goes. **8** To draw near in time; be present; arrive: When Christmas *comes*. **9** To arrive in due course or in orderly progression. **10** To proceed or emanate as from a source. **11** To exist as an effect or result: This *comes* of trifling. **12** To happen or befall: *Come* what may, I'll do it. **13** To get or prove to be; become: The sign *came* true. **14** To reach or extend: with *to*. **15** To be offered, obtainable, or produced: The car *comes* in many colors. **16** To be favorably inclined; yield. — *v.t.* **17** *Slang* To play the part of; act; also, to perpetrate: He *comes* a joke on us. **18** *Naut.* To loosen: with *up*:

---

to *come up* the standing rigging. **19** *Brit. Dial.* To fit or suit; become. **— to come about** **1** To take place; happen. **2** *Naut.* To turn in order to proceed on the opposite tack. **— to come by** **1** To pass near. **2** To get, acquire, or obtain. **— to come in** **1** To give birth to a calf. **2** To join a group in some special activity. **— to come it over** *Colloq.* To outwit or humble (someone). **— to come out** **1** To speak frankly; declare one's views. **2** To pass through a contest or competition: to *come out* first. **3** To make one's début in society. **— to come through** **1** To produce (the expected thing); achieve; win. **2** To experience. **— to come to** **1** To recover consciousness; revive; be resuscitated; also, return to, as one's senses. **2** *Naut.* **a** To anchor. **b** To bring a ship close to the wind. **3** To turn sharply to the left: said of a team of oxen or horses. **4** To amount to: The bill *came to* five dollars. [OE *cuman*]

come-at-a·ble (kum·at′ə·bəl) *adj. Colloq.* Easily accessible, as a person; readily acquired or procured, as an object; attainable.

come-back (kum′bak′) *n.* **1** *Colloq.* Recovery of health or supremacy, after illness, failure, or deposition. **2** *Slang* A smart retort. **3** *Slang* Grounds for complaint; recourse: The customer has no *come-back.*

co·me·di·an (kə·mē′dē·ən) *n.* **1** A comic actor; one who plays comic parts or in comedies. **2** An entertainer who tells jokes, sings comic songs, etc. **3** One who writes comedies. **4** One who is or tries to be amusing. **— co·me·di·enne** (kə·mē′dē·en′) *n. fem.*

com·e·do (kom′ə·dō) *n. pl.* **com·e·dos** or **com·e·do·nes** (kom′ə·dō′nēz) A condition of the sebaceous glands, in which the secretion is retained in the follicle; a blackhead. [<L, glutton < *comedere* eat up < *com-* + *edere* eat]

come-down (kum′doun′) *n.* A descent to a lower condition or position; downfall.

com·e·dy (kom′ə·dē) *n. pl.* **·dies** **1** A drama or other literary work with a happy ending. **2** A play or other work of literature, motion pictures, television, radio, etc., characterized by a humorous treatment of characters, situation, etc., and having a happy ending; an entertaining drama: distinguished from the problematic, tragic, or serious. **2** The art of writing, producing, or acting in such plays, motion pictures, etc. **3** Comedies collectively, especially as a branch of the drama. **4** Any comic or ludicrous incident or series of incidents. [<MF *comédie* <L *comoedia* <Gk. *kōmōdia* < *kōmos* revel + *aeidein* sing]

come-hith·er (kum′hith′ər) *U.S. Slang adj.* Alluring; able to attract: a *come-hither* look. — *n.* Lure; attraction.

come·ly (kum′lē) *adj.* **·li·er, ·li·est** **1** Pleasing in person; handsome; graceful. **2** *Obs.* Suitable; becoming; decorous. See synonyms under BEAUTIFUL, BECOMING. [OE *cȳmlic*] **— come′li·ly** *adv.* **— come′li·ness** *n.*

Co·me·ni·us (kō·mē′nē·əs), **John Amos,** 1592–1670, Moravian educational reformer and bishop: also called *Komensky.*

come-on (kum′on′, -ôn′) *n. Slang* **1** Someone or something that lures or inveigles. **2** A beckoning look or gesture.

com·er (kum′ər) *n.* **1** One who comes or arrives. **2** *Colloq.* A person, animal, or thing capable of further growth or development; someone or something showing great promise. **— all comers** All applicants, contestants, etc.: to maintain a position against *all comers.*

co·mes·ti·ble (kə·mes′tə·bəl) *adj.* Edible; pertaining to food. — *n.* An eatable: usually in the plural. [<F <LL *comestibilis* < *comedere.* See COMEDO.]

com·et (kom′it) *n. Astron.* A celestial body drawn within the sun's gravitational field and occasionally close enough to the earth or bright enough to be observed by the naked eye. It consists of a nucleus of more or less condensed material, accompanied by a tenuous coma which always points in a direction away from the sun. A number of periodic comets are now known: among them are **Biela's comet,** with a period of 7 years; **Encke's comet,** period 3 years; **Halley's comet,** period 76 years. [OE *cometa* <L <Gk. *komētēs* long-haired < *komē* hair] **— com·et·ar·y** (kom′ə·ter′ē), **co·met·ic** (kə·met′ik) *adj.*

co·meth·er (kə·meth′ər) *n. Colloq.* **1** An affair; a subject for discussion or feeling. **2** Friendly relations; fellowship. **— to put the** (or **one's**) **comether on** To persuade by flattery; cajole. [Alter. of *come hither*]

com·et-seek·er (kom′it·sē′kər) *n. Astron.* A small telescope usually with an aperture of 3 to 5 inches, of short focal length, mounted to search for comets. Also **com′et-find′er.**

come-up·pance (kum′up′əns) *n. Colloq.* Deserved punishment; retribution.

com·fit (kum′fit, kom′-) *n.* A sweetmeat; confection. Also **com·fi·ture** (kum′fi·chŏŏr, kom′-). [<F *confit* <L *confectus.* Related to CONFECT.]

com·fort (kum′fərt) *n.* **1** Freedom or relief from pain, annoyance, or want; also, anything that contributes to such relief. **2** Relief from sorrow or distress; consolation; also, one who or that which comforts or consoles. **3** A thick, quilted bedcover; a comforter. [< *v.*] — *v.t.* **1** To give cheer or encouragement to; encourage; console; solace. **2** *Law* To countenance; abet. See synonyms under CHERISH, CONSOLE. [<OF *conforter* <LL *confortare* strengthen < *com-* with + *fortis* strong] **— com′fort·ing** *adj.* **— com′fort·ing·ly** *adv.* **— com′fort·less** *adj.*

Synonyms (noun): abundance, amusement, cheer, contentment, ease, enjoyment, happiness, opulence, pleasure, plenty, satisfaction, sufficiency. *Comfort* may be used of simple freedom from pain, annoyance, or privation, with no implication of any previous trouble, sorrow, or want. Thus, we may say one has lived in *comfort* all his life. In this sense, *comfort* is more solid than *amusement,* more quiet and stable than *pleasure,* less positive and vivid than *happiness. Comfort* is also any relief of suffering, want, or sorrow, which makes the distress easier to be borne. See HAPPINESS, SATISFACTION. *Antonyms*: dearth, dreariness, gloom, misery, need, poverty, suffering, want, wretchedness.

com·fort·a·ble (kum′fər·tə·bəl, kumf′tə·bəl) *adj.* **1** Having or imparting comfort. **2** Out of pain; free from suffering. **3** *Colloq.* Moderate; enough: a *comfortable* income. **4** *Obs.* Comforting. — *n.* A wadded bedquilt or comforter. **— com′fort·a·ble·ness** *n.* **— com′fort·a·bly** *adv.*

Synonyms (adj.): agreeable, cheerful, cheery, commodious, contented, convenient, genial, pleasant, satisfactory, satisfied, snug. A person is *comfortable* in mind when *contented* and measurably *satisfied.* A little additional brightness makes him *cheerful.* He is *comfortable* in body when free from pain; quiet, at ease, at rest. He is *comfortable* in circumstances, or in *comfortable* circumstances, when things about him are generally *agreeable* and *satisfactory,* usually with the suggestion of sufficient means to secure that result. *Antonyms*: cheerless, disagreeable, discontented, dissatisfied, distressed, dreary, forlorn, miserable, suffering, uncomfortable, wretched.

com·fort·er (kum′fər·tər) *n.* **1** One who comforts; a consoler. **2** A thick, quilted bedcover. **3** A long woolen scarf. See JOB'S COMFORTER.

Com·fort·er (kum′fər·tər) The Holy Spirit.

comfort station A public rest-room.

com·frey (kum′frē) *n. pl.* **·freys** **1** A rough, hairy herb (genus *Symphytum*) of the borage family. **2** Its root, containing tannin: used in medicine. [<OF *confirie*]

com·ic (kom′ik) *adj.* **1** Pertaining to, like, or connected with comedy. **2** Provoking or meant to provoke mirth; funny; ludicrous. **3** Acting in or composing comedy. See synonyms under HUMOROUS. — *n.* **1** A comical person or thing; especially, a comic actor. **2** A book or motion picture made up of comic strips. **3** *pl. Colloq.* The comic strips of a newspaper. **4** The comic side of art, life, etc. [<L *comicus* <Gk. *kōmikos* < *kōmos* revelry]

com·i·cal (kom′i·kəl) *adj.* **1** Causing amusement; ludicrous; diverting. **2** *Obs.* Of or pertaining to comedy. See synonyms under HUMOROUS, ODD, RIDICULOUS. **— com′i·cal·ly** *adv.* **— com·i·cal·i·ty** (kom′ə·kal′ə·tē), **com′i·cal·ness** *n.*

comic book A magazine of comic strips, usually containing one or more complete stories.

comic strip A strip of cartoons printed in newspapers, magazines, etc., and picturing a serial sequence of comic, dramatic, or historical incidents.

Co·mines (kô·mēn′), **Philippe de,** 1445?–1509, French historian. Also **Com·mines′.**

Com·in·form (kom′in·fôrm) *n.* The Communist Information Bureau, established in September, 1947, for the purpose of coordinating the policies and activities of the various national Communist parties. The original nine members were the Communist parties of Yugoslavia, Bulgaria, Hungary, Czechoslovakia, Poland, Italy, France, Rumania, and the U.S.S.R.: dissolved in April, 1956. [<COM(MUNIST) INFORM(ATION)]

com·ing (kum′ing) *adj.* **1** Approaching, especially in time: the *coming* year. **2** On the way to fame or note: He is the *coming* man. **3** Growing; increasing: a *coming* appetite. — *n.* The act of approaching; arrival; advent.

com·ing-out (kum′ing·out′) *n. Colloq.* Entrance into society; debut.

Com·in·tern (kom′in·tûrn) *n.* The Third International, formed at Moscow in 1919, and dissolved in 1943: also spelled *Komintern.* [<COM(MUNIST) INTERN(ATIONAL)]

com·i·ta·tus (kom′ə·tā′təs) *n.* **1** In Roman and medieval history, the retinue of a prince or chieftain, acting as companions and protectors in exchange for maintenance. **2** In old English law, a county or shire; also, an earldom. [<L, a company]

co·mi·ti·a (kə·mish′ē·ə) *n.* In ancient Rome, one of three assemblies for election or legislation. [<L, pl. of *comitium* a place of assembly < *com-* together + *ire* go] **— co·mi·tial** (kə·mish′əl) *adj.*

co·mi·ti·um (kə·mish′ē·əm) *n. pl.* **co·mi·ti·a** (kə·mish′ē·ə) The place of meeting for the comitia of ancient Rome in the Forum adjoining the Sacred Way at the foot of the Capitol. [<L]

com·i·ty (kom′ə·tē) *n.* **1** Kindly consideration for others; friendliness; good will; courtesy. **2** The recognition which one jurisdiction accords within its territory to the laws of another. See synonyms under FRIENDSHIP. [<L *comitas, -tatis* courtesy < *comis* kind]

com·ma (kom′ə) *n.* **1** A punctuation mark (,) indicating separation in ideas or construction within a sentence. **2** A clause, or short group of words, cut off by itself. **3** Any pause or separation. [<L <Gk. *komma* short phrase < *koptein* cut]

comma bacillus *Bacteriol.* A comma-shaped bacillus (*Vibrio comma* or *cholerae*), the causative agent of Asiatic cholera. See illustration under BACTERIUM.

com·mand (kə·mand′, -mänd′) *v.t.* **1** To order, require or enjoin with authority. **2** To control or direct authoritatively; rule; have at one's disposal or use. **3** To overlook, as from a height; guard. **4** To exact as being due or proper. — *v.i.* **5** To be in authority; rule. **6** To overlook something from a superior position. See synonyms under DICTATE, GOVERN, INFLUENCE. — *n.* **1** The right to command; the authority exercised by an individual over others through his rank or ability; also, the act of commanding. **2** An order; commandment. **3** The troops or district under the command of one person. **4** Dominating power; hence, range of view; control; mastery. **5** In the U.S. Air Force, a unit, usually a wing or more, directed by an officer; also, its base of operations. **6** The distance between the bore of a gun and the adjacent ground. [<OF *comander* <LL *commandare* < *com-* thoroughly + *mandare* order, charge. Related to COMMEND.]

com·man·dant (kom′ən·dant′, -dänt′) *n.* A commanding officer, as of a service school, military district, etc.

command car A fast, maneuverable automobile of the convertible type, used in the field by a commander and his staff.

com·man·deer (kom′ən·dir′) *v.t.* **1** To force into military service. **2** To take possession of or requisition by force for public use, especially under military necessity; sequester; confiscate. **3** To take over by force or by threat of force. [<Afrikaans *kommandeeren* command]

com·mand·er (kə·man′dər, -män′-) *n.* **1** One in command; a military leader. **2** In the U.S. Army, the commanding officer of a post or unit. **3** In the U.S. Navy, an officer ranking next above a lieutenant commander and next

below a captain: equivalent in rank to a lieu-tenant colonel in the U.S. Army. — **lieutenant commander** In the U.S. Navy, an officer rank-ing next above a lieutenant and next below a commander: equivalent in rank to a major in the U.S. Army.

Com·mand·er (kə·man′dər, -män′-) *n.* 1 The chief officer of various orders, as Knights Templar, Grand Army posts, etc. 2 A mem-ber of a higher class in certain orders, as of knighthood.

commander in chief 1 An officer command-ing all the armed forces in a certain theater of war. 2 Formerly, the officer commanding the armed forces of an American Colony: often the governor.

Commander in Chief 1 The President of the United States. 2 The highest officer of the American Revolutionary armies: George Washington.

Commander Islands See KOMANDORSKI IS-LANDS.

com·mand·er·y (kə·man′dər·ē, -män′-) *n. pl.* **·der·ies** 1 *U.S.* A lodge of various orders, as of the Knights Templar, etc.; also, a divi-sion of a military officers' veterans' organi-zation. 2 The rank of commander in an order of knighthood. 3 A district or estate under the authority of a commander; especially, a district or estate in charge of a member of a medieval order of knights; also, the house or priory of such an order: a *commandery* of the Knights of Malta.

com·mand·ing (kə·man′ding, -män′-) *adj.* 1 Fitted to command; impressive; authoritative; dignified. 2 Having a wide, overlooking view or advantageous position. See synonyms un-der IMPERIOUS, POWERFUL, PREDOMINANT. — **com·mand′ing·ly** *adv.*

com·mand·ment (kə·mand′mənt, -mänd′-) *n.* An authoritative mandate; edict; order; law; especially, a command of God, and specifi-cally one of the divisions of the decalog or moral law. See synonyms under LAW. — **the Ten Commandments** The ten precepts given by God to Moses on Mount Sinai as recorded in *Exodus* xx 1–17; the decalog.

command module *Aerospace* A part of a space vehicle that houses the crew and navigational systems and is equipped for reentry.

com·man·do (kə·man′dō, -män′-) *n. pl.* **·dos** or **·does** 1 A special fighting force trained for quick, destructive raids into enemy ter-ritory. 2 A member of such a unit. 3 In South Africa, a militia force; also, a raid. [<Afrikaans <Pg., a group commanded <*commandar* command <LL *commandare.* See COMMAND.]

command performance A theatrical or musi-cal performance presented at royal request.

com·meas·ure (kə·mezh′ər) *v.t.* To be coex-tensive with or equal to. — **com·meas′ur·a·ble** *adj.*

com·me·dia dell' ar·te (kôm·me′dyä del är′te) A dramatic genre originating in 16th century Italy, characterized by improvisation of dia-log, conventional plots, and standard charac-ters such as Pantaloon, Harlequin, Pulcinella, Columbine, etc.

comme il faut (kô mēl fō′) *French* As it should be; correct; in good form.

com·mem·o·rate (kə·mem′ə·rāt) *v.t.* **·rat·ed, ·rat·ing** To celebrate or signalize the memory of; keep in remembrance. Also **com·mem′o·rize.** See synonyms under CELEBRATE. [<L *commemoratus,* pp. of *commemorare* recall <*com-* together + *memorare* remember] — **com·mem·o·ra·ble** (kə·mem′ə·rə·bəl) *adj.* — **com·mem·o·ra·to·ry** (kə·mem′ə·rə·tôr′ē, -tō′rē) *adj.* — **com·mem′o·ra′tor** *n.*

com·mem·o·ra·tion (kə·mem′ə·rā′shən) *n.* The act of commemorating, or that which com-memorates; a commemorative observance, celebration, recital, or action of any kind; a memorial. — **com·mem′o·ra′tion·al** *adj.*

com·mence (kə·mens′) *v.t. & v.i.* **·menced, ·menc·ing** To give origin to; begin; initiate; have or make a beginning; originate; start. See synonyms under INSTITUTE. [<OF *co-mencer* <L *com-* together + *initiare* begin <*in-* in + *ire* go] — **com·menc′er** *n.*

com·mence·ment (kə·mens′mənt) *n.* 1 A beginning; origin. 2 A celebration of the

completion of a school or college course, when degrees are conferred; also, the day so observed. See synonyms under BEGINNING.

com·mend (kə·mend′) *v.t.* 1 To express a favorable opinion of; approve; praise. 2 To recommend; accredit. 3 To present the re-gards of. 4 To commit with confidence; en-trust. 5 To place under the protection of a feudal lord. 6 To bestow *in commendam.* See synonyms under PRAISE. [<L *commendare* <*com-* thoroughly + *mandare* order, charge. Related to COMMAND.] — **com·mend′a·ble** *adj.* — **com·mend′a·ble·ness** *n.* — **com·mend′a·bly** *adv.*

com·men·dam (kə·men′dam) *n.* 1 The right to enjoy the revenues of a religious house or institution in the absence of a superior or during a vacancy (**in commendam**): abolished in England by act of Parliament in 1836. See COMMENDATOR. 2 The benefice so held. [<Med. L *(dare in) commendam* (give in) trust <*commendare.* See COMMEND.]

com·men·da·tion (kom′en·dā′shən) *n.* 1 The act of commending; approbation. 2 Some-thing that commends. 3 *Obs.* A message of good will; a greeting. See synonyms under EULOGY. [<L *commendatio, -onis* <*commen-dare.* See COMMEND.]

com·men·da·tor (kom′ən·dā′tər) *n.* One who held a benefice *in commendam.*

com·mend·a·to·ry (kə·men′də·tôr′ē, -tō′rē) *adj.* 1 Expressing commendation; serving to com-mend. 2 Holding a benefice as a commen-dator.

com·men·sal (kə·men′səl) *adj.* 1 Eating at the same table. 2 *Biol.* Associated or living with another in close but non-parasitic rela-tionship, as a sea anemone attached to the shell of a hermit crab. — *n.* 1 A table com-panion. 2 A commensal organism. [<Med. L *commensalis* <*com-* together + *mensa* table] — **com·men′sal·ism** *n.* — **com·men·sal·i·ty** (kom′-en·sal′ə·tē) *n.* — **com·men′sal·ly** *adv.*

com·men·su·ra·ble (kə·men′shər·ə·bəl, -sər·ə-) *adj.* 1 Measurable by a common unit. 2 Proportionate. [<LL *commensurabilis* <*com-* together + *mensurabilis* measurable] — **com·men′su·ra·bil′i·ty, com·men′su·ra·ble·ness** *n.* — **com·men′su·ra·bly** *adv.*

com·men·su·rate (kə·men′shə·rit, -sə·rit) *adj.* 1 Commensurable. 2 In proper proportion; proportionate. 3 Sufficient for the purpose or occasion. 4 Adequate; of equal extent. See synonyms under ADEQUATE. [<LL *com-mensuratus,* pp. of *commensurare* <*com-* together + *mensurare* measure] — **com·men′-su·rate·ly** *adv.* — **com·men′su·rate·ness** *n.*

com·men·su·ra·tion (kə·men′shə·rā′shən, -sə-rā′-) *n.* 1 The act of proportioning, or the state of being proportioned. 2 Measurement by comparison.

com·ment (kom′ent) *v.i.* To make expository or critical notes or remarks; make reflections or observations. — *v.t.* To make comments or remarks upon; explain or annotate. [<*n.*] — *n.* 1 A note in explanation or criticism. 2 A remark made in observation or criticism. 3 Talk; conversation; gossip. See synonyms under ANIMADVERSION, REMARK. [<OF <L *commentum* invention <*comminisci* contrive) — **com′ment·er** *n.*

com·men·tar·y (kom′ən·ter′ē) *n. pl.* **·tar·ies** 1 A treatise in annotation or explanation, as of the Scriptures; a series or body of com-ments; exposition. 2 Anything explanatory or illustrative; systematic exposition. 3 A historical narrative or chronological record of events; journal of official acts: the Royal *Commentaries* of Peru. See synonyms under DEFINITION. [<L *commentarius* notebook <*commentari,* freq. of *comminisci* contrive; devise] — **com·men·tar·i·al** (kom′ən·târ′ē·əl) *adj.*

com·men·ta·tor (kom′ən·tā′tər) *n.* 1 A writer of commentaries; an annotator; expounder. 2 One who discusses current events, espe-cially over the radio at regular periods. 3 An actor who serves as a link between audi-ence and players by appropriate commentaries on the action of the play. See synonyms under COMMENTARY.]

com·merce (kom′ərs) *n.* 1 Exchange of goods, products, or property, as between states or nations; extended trade. 2 Familiar or social

intercourse. 3 A card game in which the hands are varied by exchanging cards. 4 Sex-ual intercourse. See synonyms under BUSINESS, INTERCOURSE. — **Department of Commerce** An executive department of the U.S. govern-ment established in 1913 (from 1903 to 1913 part of the Department of Commerce and Labor), headed by the Secretary of Com-merce, which fosters, promotes, and develops foreign and domestic commerce, the mining, manufacturing, shipping, and fishing indus-tries, and transportation facilities. — *v.i.* (kə·mûrs′) **·merced, ·merc·ing** To have inter-course; associate; commune. [<F <L *com-mercium* <*com-* together + *merx, mercis* wares] — **com·merc′er** *n.*

com·mer·cial (kə·mûr′shəl) *adj.* 1 Of or be-longing to trade or commerce; mercantile. 2 Made or put up for the market: *commercial* sulfur. 3 Having financial gain as an object: a *commercial* novel. — *n.* In radio and tele-vision, an advertisement. — **com·mer′cial·ly** *adv.*

commercial college A business college.

commercial high school A high school spe-cializing in business subjects.

com·mer·cial·ism (kə·mûr′shəl·iz′əm) *n.* The spirit, methods, or principles of trade; the domination of life by such practices or aims. — **com·mer′cial·ist** *n.* — **com·mer′cial·is′tic** *adj.*

com·mer·cial·ize (kə·mûr′shəl·īz) *v.t.* **·ized, ·iz·ing** To make a matter of trade; put on a commercial basis. — **com·mer′cial·i·za′-tion** *n.*

commercial paper Mercantile paper.

commercial traveler A traveling salesman.

com·merge (kə·mûrj′) *v.t. & v.i.* **·merged, ·merg·ing** To merge together; commingle. — **com·mer′gence** *n.*

com·mi·na·tion (kom′ə·nā′shən) *n.* A denun-ciation or threatening. [<L *comminatio, -onis* <*comminari* <*com-* thoroughly + *minari* threaten]

com·min·a·to·ry (kə·min′ə·tôr′ē, -tō′rē, kom′-in·ə-) *adj.* Threatening punishment or ven-geance.

com·min·gle (kə·ming′gəl) *v.t. & v.i.* **·gled, ·gling** To mix together; mingle. See synonyms under MIX.

com·mi·nute (kom′ə·nōōt, -nyōōt) *v.t.* **·nut·ed, ·nut·ing** To reduce to minute particles; pul-verize; triturate. [<L *comminutus,* pp. of *comminuere* <*com-* thoroughly + *minuere* lessen]

com·mi·nu·tion (kom′ə·nōō′shən, -nyōō′-) *n.* 1 Trituration; pulverization; diminution by a gradual wearing or reduction, as by slicing, rasping, etc. 2 *Surg.* A fracture in which the bones are badly crushed or splintered.

com·mis·er·a·ble (kə·miz′ər·ə·bəl) *adj.* Worthy of commiseration; pitiable.

com·mis·er·ate (kə·miz′ə·rāt) *v.* **·at·ed, ·at·ing** *v.t.* To feel or manifest pity for; sympathize. — *v.i.* To condole with *with.* [<L *com-miseratus,* pp. of *commiserari* <*com-* with + *miserari* feel pity] — **com·mis′er·a′tive** *adj.* — **com·mis′er·a′tive·ly** *adv.* — **com·mis′er·a′-tor** *n.*

com·mis·er·a·tion (kə·miz′ə·rā′shən) *n.* 1 The act of commiserating. 2 A feeling or ex-pression of sympathy, pity, sorrow, or regret; compassion. See synonyms under PITY.

com·mis·sar (kom′ə·sär, kom′ə·sär′) *n.* For-merly, a cabinet minister or an official in charge of a commissariat of the Soviet gov-ernment. [<F *commissaire* <Med. L *commis-sarius* <L *committere.* See COMMIT.]

com·mis·sar·i·at (kom′ə·sar′ē·ət) *n.* 1 *Mil.* An army department supplying food and other necessaries. 2 The supply department of a club, household, or the like. 3 The of-ficers and employees of the commissary de-partment collectively. 4 The supplies fur-nished, as food, equipage, etc.; food supply. 5 Formerly, a major department of the gov-ernment of the U.S.S.R.: now called *Ministry.* [<F <Med. L *commissarius.* See COMMISSAR.]

com·mis·sar·y (kom′ə·ser′ē) *n. pl.* **·sar·ies** 1 A commissioner. 2 An army officer in charge of subsistence, etc. 3 A church officer ap-pointed by a bishop to exercise spiritual juris-diction or hold an ecclesiastical court in dis-tant parts of a diocese. 4 A store selling food and general provisions, as at a lumber camp.

5 An administrative division or territory, especially one in Colombia. 6 A wagon carrying food and provisions. — *adj.* Pertaining to, of, housing, or from a commissary. [<Med. L *commissarius.* See COMMISSAR.] **— com·mis·sar·i·al** (kom′ə·sâr′ē·əl) *adj.* **— com′·mis·sar′y·ship** *n.*

com·mis·sion (kə·mish′ən) *n.* 1 The act of committing, doing, or perpetrating; positive doing: contrasted with *omission.* 2 The act of entrusting; the matter entrusted; a trust; charge. 3 A certificate which confers a particular authority; specifically, a document issued by the president of the United States conferring rank and authority as an officer in the armed forces. 4 The rank or authority so conferred. 5 A body of persons acting under public authority. 6 The transaction of business for another under his authority; agency; also, an item of business so transacted. 7 The compensation of an agent. **— to put in** (or **into**) **commission** 1 To put in direct command of a designated officer, as a ship of war, for active service. 2 *Brit.* To entrust temporarily to a commission, as the great seal or the functions of a high office. **— to put out of commission** 1 To render unfit for use; to best or defeat thoroughly. 2 To retire the officers and crew of a naval vessel from active service, either permanently or temporarily. — *v.t.* 1 To give rank or authority to, as an officer. 2 To put into active service, as a ship of war. 3 To appoint; empower; delegate. [<OF <L *commissio, -onis* <*committere* COMMIT] **— com·mis′sion·al, com·mis·sion·ar·y** (kə·mish′ən·er′ē) *adj.*

commissioned officer See under OFFICER.

com·mis·sion·er (kə·mish′ən·ər) *n.* 1 A person who holds a commission to perform certain acts. 2 A member of a commission. 3 A public official appointed as head of an executive department, usually on a state or municipal level. **— com·mis′sion·er·ship′** *n.*

commission house A business house that buys and sells goods as an agent for others for a fee.

commission merchant One who buys and sells goods, either as an agent for a commission, or as a trader or merchant for his own account.

com·mis·sion·naire (kə·mish′ən·âr′) *n. Brit.* 1 The head doorman of a hotel. 2 Formerly, one of a body of disabled and pensioned soldiers, organized in London in 1859, employed as trusty porters, doorkeepers, etc.

commission plan A form of municipal government in which legislative, executive, and administrative powers are in a small elected commission or council, each municipal department being in charge of one commissioner: often called *Galveston plan.*

com·mis·sure (kom′ə·shŏŏr) *n.* 1 The point of union of two bodies, parts, or organs, as at the angle of the lips, etc. 2 A junction; seam; closure. 3 *Anat.* A tract or band of nerve fibers uniting corresponding right and left parts of the brain and spinal column. 4 *Bot.* The face or edge by which two carpels adhere. [<F <L *commissura* a joining < *committere* COMMIT] **— com·mis·su·ral** (kə·mish′yə·rəl, kom′·ə·sŏŏr′əl) *adj.*

com·mit (kə·mit′) *v.t.* **·mit·ted, ·mit·ting** 1 To do; perpetrate. 2 To place in trust or custody; consign; entrust; especially, to consign to an institution or prison. 3 To consign to any person, place, or use. 4 To devote; pledge; hence, to involve, compromise, or bind (oneself). 5 To consign for future reference, preservation, or disposal: to *commit* a speech to memory or to writing; *Commit* these bones to the earth. 6 To refer, as to a committee for consideration or report: a parliamentary term. [<L *committere* join, entrust < *com-* together + *mittere* send] **— com·mit′ta·ble** *adj.*

Synonyms: assign, confide, consign, entrust, relegate, trust. *Commit* is to give in charge, put into care or keeping; to *confide* or *entrust* is to *commit* especially to one's fidelity, *confide* being used chiefly of mental or spiritual, *entrust* also of material things; we *assign* a duty, *confide* a secret, *entrust* a treasure; we *commit* thoughts to writing; *commit* a paper to the flames. *Consign* is a formal word in mercantile use; as, to *consign* goods to an agent. See LEARN, TRUST. *Antonyms*: get, obtain, receive, secure, take.

com·mit·ment (kə·mit′mənt) *n.* 1 The act or process of entrusting or consigning for safekeeping. 2 An act of engagement or pledging. 3 The act of doing; perpetration. 4 *Law* A warrant (*mittimus*) for imprisonment; also, the state of being committed or act of committing to prison. 5 The act of referring a bill to a legislative body. 6 Liability incurred through buying or selling stocks, bonds, etc., or by agreeing to buy or sell. Also **com·mit′tal.**

com·mit·tee (kə·mit′ē) *n.* 1 A person or persons appointed by a larger number to act upon some matter. 2 One or more members of a legislative body appointed to investigate and report on a matter under discussion. 3 *Law* A person or persons appointed by a court to care for the person or property of another.

com·mit·tee·man (kə·mit′ē·mən) *n. pl.* **·men** (-mən) A member of a committee. **— com·mit′tee·wom′an** *n. fem.*

committee of the whole A committee consisting of all the members, as of a legislative body, sitting in deliberation on a given matter, but without legislative action, presided over by some member not the regular presiding officer.

com·mix (kə·miks′) *v.t.* & *v.i.* **·mixed** or **·mixt, ·mix·ing** To mingle or mix; intermix; blend. [Back formation < *commixt* <L *commixtus,* pp. of *commiscere* < *com-* together + *miscere* mix]

com·mix·ture (kə·miks′chər) *n.* 1 A mixture. 2 The act or process of mixing. 3 The state of being mingled.

com·mode (kə·mōd′) *n.* 1 A low chest of drawers; a cabinet. 2 A covered washstand. 3 A low chair or cabinet enclosing a chamber pot; a night-chair. 4 A woman's high headdress, worn about 1700. [<F]

COMMODE (*def. 4*)

com·mo·di·ous (kə·mō′dē·əs) *adj* Well adapted to serve the purpose for supplying needs; especially, affording ample accommodation; convenient; spacious. See synonyms under COMFORTABLE, CONVENIENT, LARGE. [<Med. L *commodiosus* <L *commodus* convenient] **— com·mo′di·ous·ly** *adv.* **— com·mo′di·ous·ness** *n.*

com·mod·i·ty (kə·mod′ə·tē) *n. pl.* **·ties** 1 A movable article of trade or convenience; an element of economic wealth. 2 Something bought and sold. 3 *Obs.* Convenience; suitability; conveniency; profit. [<MF *commodité* <L *commoditas, -tatis* convenience]

commodity money The currency of a suggested financial system, the unit of which, the **commodity dollar,** has a gold value determined at regular intervals by an index number based on the market prices of certain commodities.

com·mo·dore (kom′ə·dôr, -dōr) *n.* 1 In the U.S. Navy, an officer next above a captain and next below a rear admiral: a rank no longer in use since World War II. 2 In the British Navy, the commander of a squadron or division of a fleet, often having the temporary rank and pay of a rear admiral. 3 A title given to the senior captain of a naval squadron or of a fleet of merchantmen; also to the presiding officer of a yacht club. [Earlier *commandore*? <Du. *kommandeur*]

Com·mo·dus (kom′ə·dəs), **Lucius Aelius Aurelius,** 161–192, Roman emperor 180–192.

com·mon (kom′ən) *adj.* 1 Often occurring, met, or seen; frequent or usual; not distinguished or separated from the ordinary; customary; regular: a *common* occurrence. 2 Pertaining to, connected with, or participated in by two or more persons or things; joint. 3 Belonging to the public: the *common* schools. 4 The most prevalent or familiar: the *common* crow. 5 Commonplace; not excellent or distinguished in tone or quality; banal; coarse; vulgar; low. 6 *Gram.* **a** Of either gender. **b** Applicable to any individual of a class. See COMMON NOUN under NOUN. 7 Secular; profane; polluted. 8 In prosody, either long or short; doubtful in quantity. 9 Public or general; widespread: *common* knowledge. 10 *Anat.* Formed by or having similar relations with two or more organs: the *common* carotid artery. 11 *Math.* Referring to a number or quantity belonging equally to two or more quantities: a *common* denominator. — *n.* 1 Land generally, or a tract of land, considered as the property of the public, in which all persons enjoy equal rights; also, land owned by a town; land open to the use of all. 2 *Law* A profit or right of one person in the land of another: used in some specific phrases: **common of estovers** (wood necessary for the house or farm), **common of pasture, common of piscary** (fishing), **common of turbary** (cutting turf). 3 *Eccl. Sometimes cap.* The office composed of psalms, antiphons, lessons, etc., which can be used for any of certain classes of feasts: the *common* of virgins. [<OF *comun* <L *communis* common] **— com′mon·ly** *adv.* **— com′mon·ness** *n.*

Synonyms (adj.): cheap, coarse, commonplace, customary, familiar, frequent, general, habitual, low, mean, normal, ordinary, popular, public, threadbare, trite, universal, usual, vile, vulgar. See FREQUENT, GENERAL, HABITUAL, MUTUAL, NORMAL, TRITE, USUAL. *Antonyms*: exceptional, infrequent, odd, peculiar, rare, singular, unusual.

For the following terms, see under the second element:

common council	common multiple
common denominator	common noun
common divisor	common school

com·mon·a·ble (kom′ən·ə·bəl) *adj.* 1 *Law* Entitled to common as of right: applied to beasts essential to the plowing or manuring of land, as horses, oxen, cows, and sheep. 2 Held in common: said of land.

com·mon·age (kom′ən·ij) *n.* 1 A common right to the use of lands; a tenancy of several persons in common to the same property. 2 Land held in common. 3 The common people; the untitled.

com·mon·al·ty (kom′ən·əl·tē) *n. pl.* **·ties** 1 The common people; the lower classes as opposed to persons of title or rank; the commons. 2 A body corporate; corporation: the mayor, *commonalty,* and citizens of London.

common carrier An individual or company which, for a fee, provides public transport.

com·mon·er (kom′ən·ər) *n.* 1 One of the commonalty; any subject not a peer. 2 In certain English universities, a student not dependent on the university foundation. 3 One who has a joint right in common ground. 4 Formerly, a member of the House of Commons.

common fraction See under FRACTION.

com·mon–law marriage (kom′ən·lô′) A marriage, or an agreement of marriage, substantiated by writings or conduct, instead of by church or civil ceremony.

Common Market Any of several customs unions, especially the European Economic Community.

common measure 1 In prosody, a four-line stanza in which iambic lines of four stresses and three stresses alternate, usually rhyming the first with the third and the second with the fourth lines: also called *hymnal stanza.* 2 *Music* Common time.

common meter In prosody, common measure.

com·mon·place (kom′ən·plās′) *adj.* Not remarkable or interesting; ordinary; trite. See synonyms under COMMON, GENERAL, TRITE. — *n.* 1 A trite remark; familiar truth; platitude; truism. 2 A note jotted down for reference; a memorandum. 3 Formerly, a book containing a methodical collection of notes, passages, etc.: also called **commonplace book** 4 Commonplace quality; ordinariness. [Trans. of L *locus communis* <Gk. *koinos topos* a general theme or argument].

Common Prayer, Book of The book of ritual used in public worship in the Anglican Churches. See under PRAYER.

com·mons (kom′ənz) *n. pl.* 1 The common people; commonalty. 2 A company eating at a common table, as in a college; the provisions so furnished; hence, allowance of food; rations; fare. 3 The dining hall in a college.

Com·mons (kom′ənz) *n. pl.* The legislators of the lower house, the House of Commons, of the British Parliament.

common sense 1 Practical understanding; capacity to see and take things in their right light; sound judgment. 2 Ordinary mental capacity. —**com'mon–sense'** *adj.*
common time See under TIME. Also **common measure.**
com·mon·weal (kom'ən·wel') *n.* 1 The general welfare. 2 *Obs.* A commonwealth.
com·mon·wealth (kom'ən·welth') *n.* 1 The people of a state; the state. 2 A state in which the people rule; a republic; the official title of four States of the United States: the *Commonwealth* of Kentucky, of Massachusetts, of Pennsylvania, and of Virginia; also, the official title of Puerto Rico. 3 A body of persons united by some common interest and viewed as equals in authority. See synonyms under PEOPLE.
Commonwealth Day May 24, the anniversary of Queen Victoria's birthday: observed throughout the British Commonwealth of Nations: formerly called *Empire Day.*
Commonwealth of Australia See AUSTRALIA.
Commonwealth of England The republic established in England after the execution of Charles I in 1649 and continued till 1653, when Cromwell assumed the protectorate.
Commonwealth of Nations See BRITISH COMMONWEALTH OF NATIONS.
com·mo·tion (kə·mō'shən) *n.* 1 A violent agitation; excitement. 2 Popular tumult; social disorder; riot. See synonyms under TUMULT. [<L *commotio, -onis* <*commovere* <*com-* thoroughly + *movere* move]
com·move (kə·mo͞ov') *v.t.* **·moved, ·mov·ing** To put in motion or commotion.
com·mu·nal (kom'yə·nəl, kə·myo͞o'nəl) *adj.* 1 Of or pertaining to a commune. 2 Common; public; belonging to a community. —**com·mu'nal·ly** *adv.*
com·mu·nal·ism (kom'yə·nəl·iz'əm, kə·myo͞o'·nəl-) *n.* 1 In France, the theory that each commune should be self–governing and the state a mere federation of communes; hence, local self–government. 2 Communal ownership of goods and property. —**com'mu·nal·ist** *n.* —**com'mu·nal·is'tic** *adj.*
com·mu·nal·i·ty (kom'yə·nal'ə·tē) *n.* The state of being a member of a community.
com·mu·nal·ize (kom'yə·nəl·īz, kə·myo͞o'·nəl·īz) *v.t.* **·ized, ·iz·ing** To render communal; make municipal property of. —**com'mu·nal·i·za'tion** *n.* —**com'mu·nal·iz'er** *n.*
Com·mu·nard (kom'yə·närd) *n.* An adherent of the Paris Commune of 1871. [<F]
com·mune[1] (kə·myo͞on') *v.i.* **·muned, ·mun·ing** 1 To converse or confer intimately. 2 To partake of the Eucharist. —*n.* (kom'yo͞on) Intimate intercourse; communion. [<OF *comuner* share <*comun* COMMON]
com·mune[2] (kom'yo͞on) *n.* 1 A political division of France, governed by a mayor and a council; the people and the government of such a district; also, a similar division elsewhere, as in Italy and Spain. 2 A self–governing community; also, the people of such a community. 3 The commonalty. [<F <L *communis* common]
Com·mune (kom'yo͞on) *n.* 1 The revolutionary committee, elected by the communes, which ruled Paris in 1789–93. 2 The Communards who ruled Paris after the departure of the Germans, 1871. Also **Commune of Paris.**
com·mu·ni·ca·ble (kə·myo͞o'nə·kə·bəl) *adj.* 1 Capable of being communicated or imparted. 2 *Obs.* Ready to communicate; communicative. —**com·mu'ni·ca·bil'i·ty, com·mu'ni·ca·ble·ness** *n.* —**com·mu'ni·ca·bly** *adv.*
com·mu·ni·cant (kə·myo͞o'nə·kənt) *n.* 1 One who communicates or imparts, as information. 2 One who partakes or has a right to partake of the Lord's Supper. —*adj.* Communicating. [<L *communicans, -antis,* ppr. of *communicare.* See COMMUNICATE.]
com·mu·ni·cate (kə·myo͞o'nə·kāt) *v.* **·cat·ed, ·cat·ing** *v.t.* 1 To make another or others partakers of; impart; transmit, as news, a disease, or an idea. 2 To administer the communion to. —*v.i.* 3 To make or hold communication. 4 To be connected, as rooms. 5 To partake of communion. See synonyms under ANNOUNCE, GIVE, INFORM, PUBLISH. [<L *communicatus,* pp. of *communicare* share < *communis* common] —**com·mu'ni·ca'tor** *n.* —**com·mu·ni·ca·to·ry** (kə·myo͞o'·nə·kə·tô'rē) *adj.*
com·mu·ni·ca·tion (kə·myo͞o'nə·kā'shən) *n.* 1 The act of communicating; intercourse; exchange of ideas, conveyance of information, etc.; correspondence. 2 That which is communicated; a letter or message. 3 Means of communicating, as a highway or passage; also, a telephone, telegraph, or radio system, etc. 4 Eucharistic communion. See synonyms under CONVERSATION, INTERCOURSE.
communication satellite An artificial satellite, as the Telstar or Relay, put into orbit to serve as a relay station for radio or television transmissions.
communications gap A failure of understanding, usually because of a lack of information, esp. between different age groups, economic classes, political factions, or the like.
communication theory Information theory.
com·mu·ni·ca·tive (kə·myo͞o'nə·kā'tiv, -kə·tiv) *adj.* 1 Ready to communicate; frank; talkative. 2 Of or pertaining to communication. —**com·mu'ni·ca'tive·ly** *adv.*—**com·mu'ni·ca'tive·ness** *n.*
com·mun·ion (kə·myo͞on'yən) *n.* 1 The act of communing or sharing. 2 Sympathetic intercourse; fellowship. 3 The religious fellowship existing between man and God, between Christians, between a Christian and the church, or between autonomous churches. 4 A body or denomination of Christians having a common faith and discipline. 5 *Usually cap.* The Eucharist, or the act of celebrating or partaking of it: often called *Holy Communion.* 6 An antiphon said or chanted after the distribution of the Sacrament. See synonyms under CONVERSATION, INTERCOURSE, SACRAMENT, SECT. [<OF<L *communio, -onis* <*communis* common]
com·mun·ion·ist (kə·myo͞on'yən·ist) *n.* 1 One who has a theory as to the conditions on which a person should be admitted to church communion. 2 A member of a communion. 3 A communicant.
com·mu·ni·qué (kə·myo͞o'nə·kā') *n.* An official message, announcement, etc. [<F]
com·mu·nism (kom'yə·niz'əm) *n.* 1 A social system in which there is community of goods. 2 A theory of social change conceived by Karl Marx, directed to the ideal of a classless society. As developed by Lenin and others, it advocates seizure of power by a conspiratorial political party, maintenance of power during an interim period by stern suppression of internal opposition, centralized public ownership of almost all productive property and the sharing of the products of labor, and mmitment to the ultimate goal of a world–wide communist state. 3 Any social theory that calls for the abolition of private property and control by the community over economic affairs. 4 *Often cap.* **a** The system in force in any state based on this theory. **b** The doctrines and practices of the Communist party of any state; specifically, of the Communist party of the U.S.S.R. —**com'mu·nist** *n.*
Com·mu·nist (kom'yə·nist) *n.* 1 A member of the Communist party, especially in the U.S.S.R. 2 In other countries, a person who endorses, supports, or advocates communism or who belongs to any party or group that advocates the establishment of some type of communism: also **communist.** 3 A Communard.
com·mu·nis·tic (kom'yə·nis'tik) *adj.* 1 Pertaining to or like communism. 2 Tending to, favoring, or in accordance with communism. 3 Shared in common. 4 Occupying the same nest in common, as in certain birds. Also **com'mu·nis'ti·cal.** —**com'mu·nis'ti·cal·ly** *adv.*
Communist Manifesto A pamphlet written in 1848 by Karl Marx and Friedrich Engels, regarded as the first statement of the principles of modern communism.
Communist party 1 The dominant party in Russia since 1917, originally the majority left wing of the Social Democratic party and previously called the Bolshevik party. 2 Any political party advocating communism. See THIRD INTERNATIONAL under INTERNATIONAL.
com·mu·ni·ty (kə·myo͞o'nə·tē) *n. pl.* **·ties** 1 The people who reside in one locality and are subject to the same laws, have the same interests, etc. 2 A body politic. 3 The public; society at large. 4 A group of plants or animals living in a common dwelling under common conditions; also, the region in which they live. 5 A sharing or participation. 6 Identity or likeness: *community* of interest. 7 Common ownership, possession, or enjoyment of property. See synonyms under ASSOCIATION, PEOPLE. [<L *communitas, -tatis* fellowship <*communis* common]
community antenna television A television reception service in which a signal received at a master antenna is distributed to subscribers by cable. Abbr. *CATV*
community center The building or grounds used by a community for its social and recreational activities.
community chest A general fund for charity and public welfare to which individual contributions are made, and which is drawn upon by different organizations.
community church *U.S.* A non-denominational or interdenominational church for the use of a whole community.
com·mu·nize (kom'yə·nīz) *v.t.* **·nized, ·niz·ing** 1 To make common; make public property. 2 To make or cause to become communistic. —**com'mu·ni·za'tion** *n.*
com·mu·tate (kom'yə·tāt) *v.t.* **·tat·ed, ·tat·ing** *Electr.* To alter or reverse the direction of (a current).
com·mu·ta·tion (kom'yə·tā'shən) *n.* 1 A substitution of one kind of payment or service for another; also, the payment or service substituted. 2 *Law* A reduction or change of penalty. 3 *Electr.* The action of a commutator. 4 Daily or periodic travel on a commutation ticket. [<L *commutatio, -onis* < *commutare* change, alter <*com-* thoroughly + *mutare* change]
commutation ticket A railway or other ticket issued at a reduced rate for a specified number of trips within a certain period of time.
com·mu·ta·tive (kə·myo͞o'tə·tiv, kom'yə·tā'tiv) *adj.* Of or characterized by commutation.
com·mu·ta·tor (kom'yə·tā'tər) *n. Electr.* 1 Any contrivance for reversing the direction of the current in an electric circuit. 2 An assembly of individually insulated segments connected with the armature of a dynamo or generator and serving to collect and transmit the induced current.
com·mute (kə·myo͞ot') *v.* **·mut·ed, ·mut·ing** *v.t.* 1 To exchange reciprocally for something else. 2 To exchange for something less severe: to *commute* a sentence, debt, or payment. 3 To pay in gross at a reduced rate, as an annuity or railroad fare, instead of in successive payments. 4 *Electr.* To commutate. —*v.i.* 5 *Archaic* To serve as or be a substitute. 6 To pay a railroad fare, etc., in gross at a reduced rate. 7 To use a commutation ticket; specifically, to make daily or regular trips to and from work. See synonyms under CHANGE. —*n. U.S. Colloq.* A commuter's trip, or its duration or distance: a two–hour *commute.* [<L *commutare.* See COMMUTATION.] —**com·mut'a·ble** *adj.* —**com·mut'a·ble·ness, com·mut'a·bil'i·ty** *n.*
com·mut·er (kə·myo͞o'tər) *n.* One whose home and place of work are in different communities and who regularly travels between them, as a suburbanite who works in the city.
com·mu·tu·al (kə·myo͞o'cho͞o·əl) *adj.* Reciprocal; mutual.
Co·mo (kō'mō) A province in Lombardy, Italy; 798 square miles; capital, Como.
Como, Lake A lake in Como province, Lombardy; 30 miles long: famous for its beauty. *Italian* **La·go di Co·mo** (lä'gō dē kō'mō).
Com·o·rin (kom'ə·rin), **Cape** The southernmost point of India.
Com·o·ro Islands (kom'ə·rō) A volcanic archipelago NW of Madagascar, formerly a French overseas territory but since 1975 an independent republic; 838 sq. mi.; capital, Moroni.
co·mose (kō'mōs) *adj. Bot.* Having hairs; hairy; tufted; comate. Also **co·mous** (kō'məs). [<L *comosus* <*coma* hair]
com·pact[1] (kəm·pakt', kom'pakt) *adj.* 1 Closely and firmly united; pressed together; solid; dense; also, fine–grained. 2 Condensed; brief; terse. 3 Packed into a small space.

4 Compound; made up: with *of.* See synonyms under FIRM, HARD, STRONG, TERSE. —*v.t.* (kəm-pakt′) To pack or press closely; compress; unite closely; condense. —*n.* (kom′pakt) A small, hinged box for face powder and sometimes rouge, carried in a woman's purse. [< L *compactus,* pp. of *compangere* < *com-* together + *pangere* fasten]—**com·pact′ly** *adv.* —**com·pact′ness** *n.*

com·pact² (kom′pakt) *n.* A covenant, agreement, or contract. See synonyms under ALLIANCE, CONTRACT. [< L *compactum* < *compacisci* < *com-* together + *pacisci* agree]

compact disc A small digital disc on which sound has been recorded, to be replayed on an electronic device utilizing a beam of laser light that reads and reproduces the original sound with a very high level of quality.

com·pa·dre (kom-pä′drā) *n. SW U.S.* A close male companion: used also as a term of address. [< Sp.]

com·pan·ion¹ (kəm-pan′yən) *n.* **1** One who or that which accompanies; a comrade; associate. **2** A person, usually a woman, employed for company and assistance not of a menial nature. **3** A mate; one of a pair. See synonyms under ACCESSORY, ASSOCIATE. —*v.t.* To be a companion to; accompany; associate with. [< OF *compagnon* < LL *companio, -onis* < L *com-* together + *panis* bread]

com·pan·ion² (kəm-pan′yən) *n. Naut.* A companionway; also, the wooden hood over a companionway. [< Du. *kampanje* quarter-deck]

com·pan·ion·a·ble (kəm-pan′yən-ə-bəl) *adj.* Fitted for companionship; inclined to be friendly; sociable. —**com·pan·ion·a·bil′i·ty** *n.* —**com·pan′ion·a·bly** *adv.*

com·pan·ion·ate (kəm-pan′yən-it) *adj.* Of or pertaining to companionship or association; hence, agreed upon; shared.

companionate marriage A proposed form of marriage in which a couple agree not to have children until they are sure they wish to stay married, and which permits divorce by mutual consent.

com·pan·ion·ship (kəm-pan′yən-ship) *n.* The state of being a companion; fellowship; association. See synonyms under ACQUAINTANCE, ASSOCIATION.

com·pan·ion·way (kəm-pan′yən-wā′) *n. Naut.* A staircase leading from the deck of a ship to a cabin.

com·pa·ny (kum′pə-nē) *n. pl.* **·nies** **1** The society or presence of another or others; fellowship; association. **2** One or more guests or visitors; persons met for social purposes; society. **3** An assemblage or corporation. **4** A partner or partners not named. **5** A number of persons forming a corporation, guild, or partnership, or associated for some common purpose. **6** The person or persons with whom one has companionship: keeping bad *company.* **7** *Mil.* A body of men commanded by a captain, larger than a platoon and smaller than a battalion: the basic military unit, equivalent to a battery or troop. **8** *Naut.* The whole crew of a ship: a ship's *company.* **9** The entire body of actors and actresses in a play or a theater; cast; a troupe. **10** *Obs.* Friendship **—to keep company (with)** To be sweethearts (with); court. **—to part company (with)** To end friendship or association (with). —*v.t.* & *v.i.* **·nied, ·ny·ing** *Archaic* To keep or be in company (with); accompany; associate (with). [OF *compagnie* < *compagnon* COMPANION]

Synonyms (noun): assemblage, assembly, body, collection, conclave, concourse, conference, congregation, convention, convocation, crowd, gathering, group, host, meeting, multitude, throng. *Company* is used to include any association of those united permanently or temporarily, for business, pleasure, festivity, travel, etc., or by sorrow, misfortune, or wrong; *company* implies more unity of feeling and purpose than *crowd,* and is a less formal and more familiar word than *assemblage* or *assembly.* An *assemblage* may be of persons or of objects; an *assembly* is usually of persons. *Collection, crowd, gathering, group,* and *multitude* have the unorganized and promiscuous character of the *assemblage;* the other terms come under the general idea of *assembly. Body* is used of a number of persons so organized and unified that they can be thought of as one whole. *Congregation* is now

almost exclusively religious. *Gathering* refers to a coming together, commonly of numbers from far and near; as, the *gathering* of the Scottish clans. See ASSEMBLY, ASSOCIATION, CLASS, FLOCK. *Antonyms:* dispersion, loneliness, privacy, retirement, seclusion, solitude.

company union A union of workers formed within an industrial establishment, having no affiliation with any other recognized trade union, and usually considered to be dominated by the employer of its members.

com·pa·ra·ble (kom′pər-ə-bəl) *adj.* **1** Capable of comparison. **2** Worthy of comparison. —**com′pa·ra·ble·ness, com·pa·ra·bil′i·ty** *n.* —**com′pa·ra·bly** *adv.*

com·par·a·tive (kəm-par′ə-tiv) *adj.* **1** Pertaining to, resulting from or using comparison. **2** Estimated by comparison; relative. **3** Almost but not quite. **4** *Gram.* Expressing a degree of an adjective or adverb higher than the positive and lower than the superlative. —*n. Gram.* The comparative degree, or a word or form by which it is expressed: "Better" is the *comparative* of "good." *Abbr. comp.* [< L *comparativus* < *comparare* COMPARE]—**com·par′a·tive·ly** *adv.*

comparative linguistics See under LINGUISTICS.

com·pa·ra·tor (kom′pə-rā′tər) *n.* An instrument for automatically comparing data of length, distance, colors, etc.

com·pare (kəm-pâr′) *v.* **·pared, ·par·ing** *v.t.* **1** To represent or speak of as similar, analogous, or equal: with *to.* **2** To examine so as to perceive similarity or dissimilarity; state the resemblance or difference of: with *with.* **3** *Gram.* To state the degrees of comparison of (an adjective or adverb). —*v.i.* **4** To be worthy of comparison: with *with.* **5** To vie or compete. —*n. Archaic* or *Poetic* Comparison: usually in the phrase *beyond compare.* [< F *comparer* < L *comparare* < *com-* together + *par* equal]

Synonyms (verb): assimilate, collate, liken, parallel. See CONTRAST. To compare one thing *to* another is to liken or suggest as being similar; to compare one thing *with* another is to make a detailed analysis of points of similarity or difference.

com·par·i·son (kəm-par′ə-sən) *n.* **1** A comparing; an estimate or statement of relative likeness or unlikeness. **2** *Gram.* That inflection of adjectives or adverbs which indicates differences of degree. There are three **degrees of comparison,** the positive, comparative, and superlative, the last two being regularly expressed by adding *-er* or *-est* to the positive (except in words of three syllables or more), or by using *more* or *most, less* or *least,* before it. **3** That which in its relation to something else serves as an illustration or example; a parallel: an act without *comparison.* **4** Any rhetorical figure that sets forth the points of similarity or contrast between one person or thing and another, such as a simile or metaphor. See synonyms under ANALOGY, SIMILE. [< OF *comparaison* < L *comparatio, -onis* < *comparare* COMPARE]

com·part (kəm-pärt′) *v.t.* To divide into compartments; partition. [< OF *compartir* < L *compartiri* < *com-* together + *pars, partis* part]

com·part·ment (kəm-pärt′mənt) *n.* **1** One of the parts into which an enclosed space is subdivided by lines or partitions. **2** Any separate section or chamber: watertight *compartments.* **3** In railway passenger cars, a small, private division with sleeping accommodations. [< F *compartiment* < Ital. *compartimento* < *compartiri.* See COMPART.]

com·part·men·tal·ize (kom′pärt-men′təl-īz) *v.t.* **·ized, ·iz·ing** To divide into compartments.

com·pass (kum′pəs, kom′-) *n.* **1** Extent within limits; area; reach; scope. **2** A boundary, circumference, or circuit. **3** The range of a voice or instrument. **4** An instrument for determining directions by the pointing to magnetic north of a magnetic needle free to turn in a horizontal plane, and carrying a marked card, as in the **mariner's compass. 5** A radio compass. Compare illustrations under BINNACLE, CLINOMETER. **6** *Obs.* A circular course or journey; round; circuit. **7** Compasses. —*v.t.* **1** To go around; make a circuit of. **2** To surround; encompass. **3** To grasp mentally; comprehend. **4** To plot or scheme. **5** To attain or accomplish; achieve. **6** *Obs.* To cause to curve; bend into circular form.

[< OF *compas,* ult. < L *com-* together + *passus* step]—**com′pass·a·ble** *adj.*

compass card The circular card or dial resting on the pivot of a mariner's compass, on which the 32 points and 360 degrees of the circle are marked. Also **compass dial.**

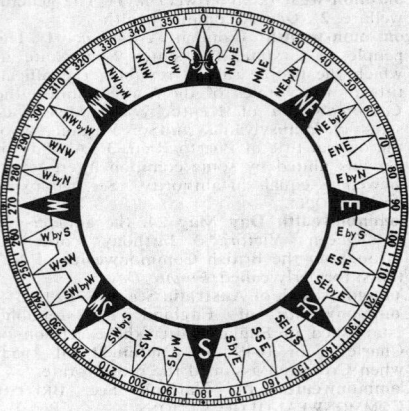

COMPASS CARD
The letters are abbreviations of the compass points; to the right of north (at top of card and not lettered) they are read: (N) *north,* (N by E) *north by east,* (NNE) *north-northeast,* (NE by N) *northeast by north,* etc.

com·pass·es (kum′pəs-iz, kom′-) *n. pl.* An instrument having two branches or legs, usually pointed, and hinged at the top by a pivoted joint, used for taking or marking measurements, describing circles, etc. Also **pair of compasses.**

compass heading *Aeron.* A specified flight course which the pilot follows by compass indications.

com·pas·sion (kəm-pash′ən) *n.* Pity for suffering, with desire to help or to spare; commiseration; sympathy. See synonyms under MERCY, PITY. [< MF < LL *compassio, -onis* < L *com-* together + *pati* feel, suffer]

com·pas·sion·ate (kəm-pash′ən-it) *adj.* **1** Feeling compassion or pity; merciful; sympathetic. **2** *Obs.* Pitiable; piteous. See synonyms under CHARITABLE, HUMANE, MERCIFUL. —*v.t.* (kəm-pash′ən-āt) **·at·ed, ·at·ing** To have compassion for; to pity. —**com·pas′sion·ate·ly** *adv.* —**com·pas′sion·ate·ness** *n.*

compass plant 1 A tall, rough, bristly herb (*Silphium laciniatum*) of North American prairies, belonging to the composite family and having large leaves lying in a vertical position with their edges turned north and south. **2** The prickly lettuce (*Lactuca serriola*).

com·pat·i·ble (kəm-pat′ə-bəl) *adj.* **1** Capable of existing together; congruous; congenial. **2** Describing a television set adapted to produce images in color or in black and white. [< F < Med. L *compatibilis* < L *com-* together + *pati* suffer] —**com·pat′i·bil′i·ty, com·pat′i·ble·ness** *n.* —**com·pat′i·bly** *adv.*

com·pa·tri·ot (kəm-pā′trē-ət, -pat′rē-ət) *n.* **1** A fellow countryman. **2** *Colloq.* A colleague. —*adj.* Having the same country. [< F *compatriote* < LL *compatriota* < L *com-* together + *patria* native land]—**com·pa′tri·ot·ism** *n.*

com·peer (kəm-pir′, kom′pir) *n.* **1** One of equal rank; a peer. **2** A comrade; associate. —*v.t. Obs.* To be the compeer of; equal; rival; match. [< OF *comper* < L *compar* equal < *com-* with + *par* equal]

com·pel (kəm-pel′) *v.t.* **·pelled, ·pel·ling 1** To drive or urge irresistibly; constrain. **2** To force to yield; subdue. **3** To obtain by force; exact. **4** *Obs.* To seize; overpower; extort. **5** To drive together; gather in a company; herd; drive. [< L *compellere* < *com-* together + *pellere* drive]—**com·pel′la·ble** *adj.* —**com·pel′la·bly** *adv.* —**com·pel′ler** *n.*

Synonyms: coerce, constrain, drive, force, make, necessitate, oblige. See ACTUATE, BIND, MAKE. Compare DRIVE, INFLUENCE. *Antonyms:* see synonyms under HINDER.

com·pel·la·tion (kom′pə-lā′shən) *n.* **1** Form of address; appellation. **2** The act of address-

ing or accosting; an address. [< L *compellatio, -onis* < *compellare* accost]

com·pend (kom′pend) *n.* A compendium. See synonyms under ABRIDGMENT.

com·pen·di·ous (kəm·pen′dē·əs) *adj.* Briefly stated; succinct; concise; containing the substance in narrow compass. See synonyms under TERSE. [< L *compendiosus* brief < *compendium* COMPENDIUM] **—com·pen′di·ous·ly** *adv.* **—com·pen′di·ous·ness** *n.*

com·pen·di·um (kəm·pen′dē·əm) *n. pl.* **·di·ums** or **·di·a** (-dē·ə) An abridgment; abstract; a brief, comprehensive summary. See synonyms under ABBREVIATION, ABRIDGMENT. [< L < *compendere* < *com-* together + *pendere* weigh]

com·pen·sa·ble (kəm·pen′sə·bəl) *adj.* Entitled to be or capable of being compensated.

com·pen·sate (kom′pən·sāt) *v.* **·sat·ed, ·sat·ing** *v.t.* **1** To make suitable amends to or for; requite; remunerate. **2** To counterbalance or make up for; offset. **3** To stabilize the purchasing power of (a monetary unit) by varying gold content to counteract price fluctuations. **4** *Mech.* To provide with a counterbalancing or neutralizing device, as for a variation. *—v.i.* **5** To make returns or amends; serve as an equivalent or substitute. See synonyms under PAY, REQUITE. [< L *compensatus,* pp. of *compensare* < *com-* together + *pensare,* freq. of *pendere* weigh] **—com·pen·sa·tive** (kəm·pen′sə·tiv), **com·pen·sa·to·ry** (kəm·pen′sə·tôr′ē, -tō′rē) *adj.*

com·pen·sa·tion (kom′pən·sā′shən) *n.* **1** The act of compensating, or that which compensates; payment; amends. **2** *Mech.* A means of counteracting variations, as of temperature; neutralizing opposing forces, as of magnetic attraction; or maintaining equilibrium. **3** *Psychol.* A form of behavior whereby an individual disguises or conceals an unpleasant sensation, feeling, or trait by giving prominence to one having desirable results. **4** *Biol.* The correction, by biological processes or medical means, of serious defects in the structure and functions of an organism or a human body. **—workmen's compensation 1** Damages recoverable from an employer by an employee in case of accident. **2** Government insurance against illness, accident, or unemployment. **—com′pen·sa′tion·al** *adj.*

com·pen·sa·tor (kom′pən·sā′tər) *n.* **1** One who or that which compensates. **2** A device for neutralizing the influence of local attraction upon a compass needle. **3** An automatic apparatus for equalizing the pressure of gas in retorts or mains. **4** *Electronics* A device which automatically compensates for errors in a direction finder. **5** *Physics* A device for measuring the components of polarized light.

com·pete (kəm·pēt′) *v.i.* **·pet·ed, ·pet·ing** To contend with another or others for a prize; engage in a contest or competition; vie. See synonyms under CONTEND. [< L *competere* strive < *com-* together + *petere* seek]

com·pe·tence (kom′pə·təns) *n.* **1** The state of being competent; ability. **2** Sufficient means for comfortable living; a moderate income. **3** *Law* Qualification or admissibility; legal capacity, authority, or jurisdiction: the *competence* of a tribunal. Also **com′pe·ten·cy.** See synonyms under ABILITY.

com·pe·tent (kom′pə·tənt) *adj.* **1** Having sufficient ability or authority. **2** Possessing the requisite natural or legal qualifications; qualified. **3** Sufficient; adequate. [< MF *competent* < L *competens, -entis,* ppr. of *competere* be fit, be proper < *com-* together + *petere* go, seek] **—com′pe·tent·ly** *adv.* **—com′pe·tent·ness** *n.*

Synonyms: able, adapted, adequate, capable, fit, qualified. One is *competent* who has all the natural powers, physical or mental, to meet the demands of a situation or work; the word is widely used of ability to meet all requirements, natural, legal, or other; as, a *competent* knowledge of a subject; a court of *competent* jurisdiction. *Qualified* refers to acquired abilities; a *qualified* teacher may be no longer *competent,* by reason of ill health. *Able* and *capable* suggest general ability and reserved power, *able* being the higher word of the two. An *able* man will do something well in any position. A *capable* man will come up to any ordinary demand. Compare ADEQUATE, GOOD. *Antonyms*: disqualified, inadequate, incompetent, unequal, unfit, unqualified.

com·pe·ti·tion (kom′pə·tish′ən) *n.* **1** Contention of two or more for the same object or for superiority; rivalry. **2** The independent endeavor of two or more persons to obtain the business patronage of a third by offering more advantageous terms; also, the conditions which this endeavor produces.

Synonyms: contest, emulation, opposition, rivalry. *Competition* is the striving for something that is sought by another at the same time. *Emulation* regards the abstract, *competition* the concrete; *rivalry* is the same in essential meaning with *competition,* but differs in the nature of the objects contested for. We speak of *competition* in business, *emulation* in scholarship, *rivalry* in love, politics, etc. *Competition* may be friendly, *rivalry* is commonly hostile. Compare AMBITION, EMULATION. *Antonyms*: agreement, association, alliance, combination, confederacy, harmony, monopoly, union. In business and commercial use, the chief antonym of *competition* is *monopoly,* which by bringing all engaged in an industry under a single control forbids them to compete. [< L *competitio, -onis* < *competere* COMPETE]

com·pet·i·tive (kəm·pet′ə·tiv) *adj.* Pertaining to or characterized by competition. **—com·pet′i·tive·ly** *adv.* **—com·pet′i·tive·ness** *n.*

com·pet·i·tor (kəm·pet′ə·tər) *n.* **1** One who or that which competes; especially, one striving for the same thing as another, in business, athletics, etc. **2** *Obs.* An associate; confederate. See synonyms under ENEMY. **—com·pet′i·tor·ship′** *n.* **—com·pet·i·to·ry** (kəm·pet′ə·tôr′ē, -tō′rē) *adj.*

Com·piègne (kôn·pyen′y′) A town in northern France, near the **Forest of Compiègne,** scene of the signing of armistices between the Allies and Germany, 1918, and Germany and France, 1940.

com·pi·la·tion (kom′pə·lā′shən) *n.* **1** The act or process of collecting materials for making a book, statistical table, etc. **2** That which is compiled, as a book made up of material gathered from other books: *compilations* of verse. [< F < L *compilatio, -onis* < *compilare.* See COMPILE.]

com·pile (kəm·pīl′) *v.t.* **·piled, ·pil·ing 1** To compose (a literary work, etc.) from other works. **2** To gather (materials borrowed or transcribed) into a volume or into orderly form. [< L *compilare* < *com-* thoroughly + *pilare* strip, plunder; prob. infl. in meaning by PILE] **—com·pi·la·to·ry** (kəm·pī′lə·tôr′ē, -tō′rē) *adj.* **—com·pil′er** *n.*

com·pla·cen·cy (kəm·plā′sən·sē) *n. pl.* **·cies 1** Satisfaction; self-approval. **2** Equanimity. Also **com·pla′cence.** See synonyms under SATISFACTION.

com·pla·cent (kəm·plā′sənt) *adj.* **1** Feeling or showing complacency or satisfaction; especially, pleased or satisfied with oneself; smug. **2** *Obs.* Disposed to please; complaisant. [< L *complacens, -entis,* ppr. of *complacere* < *com-* thoroughly + *placere* please. Doublet of COMPLAISANT.] **—com·pla′cent·ly** *adv.*

com·plain (kəm·plān′) *v.i.* **1** To express a sense of ill-treatment or of pain, grief, etc.; murmur; find fault; present a grievance. **2** To make a formal accusation; present a charge or complaint. [< F *complaindre* < LL *complangere* < *com-* thoroughly + *plangere* beat (the beast in grief)] **—com·plain′er** *n.*

Synonyms: croak, deplore, growl, grumble, grunt, murmur, remonstrate, repine. To *complain* is to give utterance to dissatisfaction or objection, express a sense of wrong or ill-treatment. One *complains* of a real or assumed grievance; he may *murmur* through mere peevishness or ill temper; he *repines,* with vain distress, at the inevitable. *Complaining* is by speech or writing; *murmuring* is commonly said of half-repressed utterance; *repining* of the mental act alone. One may *complain* of an offense to the offender or to others; he *remonstrates* with the offender only. *Complain* has a legal meaning, which the other words have not, signifying to make a formal accusation, present a specific charge; the same is true of the noun *complaint. Antonyms*: applaud, approve, commend, eulogize, laud, praise.

com·plain·ant (kəm·plā′nənt) *n.* One who complains; especially, one who enters a formal complaint before a magistrate or other authority; a plaintiff or petitioner. [< F *complaignant* a plaintiff, orig. ppr. of *complaindre* COMPLAIN]

com·plaint (kəm·plānt′) *n.* **1** A statement of wrong, grievance, or injury. **2** *Law* The first paper setting forth the plaintiff's cause of action. **3** The act of complaining. **4** A grievance. **5** A physical ailment; disease. See synonyms under DISEASE, ILLNESS. [< F *complainte* < *complaindre* COMPLAIN]

com·plai·sant (kəm·plā′zənt, kom′plə·zant) *adj.* Showing a desire or endeavor to please; yielding; compliant. See synonyms under BLAND, FRIENDLY, POLITE. [< F, ppr. of *complaire* please < L *complacere.* Doublet of COMPLACENT.] **—com·plai′sance** *n.* **—com·plai′sant·ly** *adv.* **—com·plai′sant·ness** *n.*

com·pla·nate (kom′plə·nāt) *adj.* **1** Leveled; flattened. **2** *Bot.* Lying in the same plane, as certain leaves. [< L *complanatus,* pp. of *complanare* < *com-* together + *planare* make level] **—com′pla·na′tion** *n.*

com·plect (kəm·plekt′) *v.t.* To join by weaving; interweave. [< L *complecti* < *com-* together + *plecti* twine, weave]

com·plect·ed (kəm·plek′tid) *adj. U.S. Dial.* Complexioned: used only in compounds: light-*complected.*

com·ple·ment (kom′plə·mənt) *n.* **1** That which fills up or completes; that which must be added to complete a symmetrical whole. **2** Full number: The vessel has her *complement* of men. **3** An addition or appendage; an accessory. **4** *Geom.* The amount by which an angle falls short of 90 degrees. **5** *Gram.* A word or phrase used after a verb of incomplete predication to complete the meaning of the sentence. A **subjective complement** describes or identifies the subject, as the noun *president* in *He is president* or in *He was elected president* or as the adjective *happy* in *She is happy* or in *She was made happy.* An **objective complement** describes or identifies the direct object, as the noun *president* in *They elected him president* or the adjective *happy* in *It made her happy.* **6** *Music* A musical interval which, with the interval already given, will complete an octave. **7** *Immunology* A complex system of unstable, heat-sensitive proteins normally present in human and other serums where it reacts with specific antibodies to destroy related antigens. Also called *alexin.* *—v.t.* To add or form a complement to; supplement; make complete; supply a lack in. ◆ Homophone: *compliment.* [< L *complementum* < *complere* COMPLETE] **—com·ple·men·tal** (kom′plə·men′təl) *adj.* **—com′ple·ment′er** *n.*

com·ple·men·ta·ry (kom′plə·men′tər·ē, -trē) *adj.* **1** Serving as a complement; helping to constitute a whole or to supply a lack; completing complemental. **2** Mutually providing each other's needs. **3** *Geom.* Furnishing the complement of another: see COMPLEMENTARY ANGLE under ANGLE.

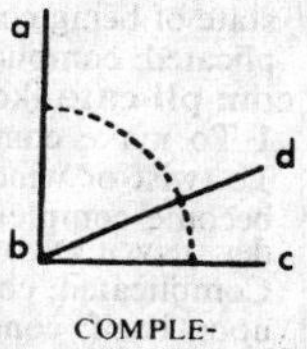

COMPLEMENTARY ANGLES
abd and *dbc* are complementary

complementary cell *Bot.* One of the cellular components of the lenticel in plants.

complementary color See under COLOR.

com·plete (kəm·plēt′) *adj.* **1** Having all needed or normal parts, elements, or details; lacking nothing; entire; perfect; full. **2** Thoroughly wrought; finished. See synonyms under AMPLE, IMPLICIT, RADICAL, RIPE. *—v.t.* **·plet·ed, ·plet·ing** To make complete; accomplish; finish; fulfil. See synonyms under ACCOMPLISH, EFFECT, END. [< L *completus,* pp. of *complere* < *com-* thoroughly + *plere* fill] **—com·plete′ly** *adv.* **—com·plete′ness** *n.* **—com·ple′tive** *adj.*

com·ple·tion (kəm·plē′shən) *n.* **1** The act of completing, or the state of being completed.

2 Accomplishment; fulfilment. See synonyms under END.

com·plex (kəm·pleks′, kom′pleks) *adj.* **1** Consisting of various parts or elements; composite. **2** Complicated; involved; intricate. —*n.* (kom′·pleks) **1** Something composite or complicated; a complication; collection. **2** *Psychoanal.* A group or cluster of interrelated and usually repressed ideas with strong emotional content which compels the individual to adopt abnormal patterns of thought and behavior. [< L *complexus,* pp. of *complectere* < *com-* together + *plectere* twist] —**com·plex′ly** *adv.* —**com·plex′ness** *n.*

Synonyms (adj.): abstruse, complicated, composite, compound, confused, conglomerate, entangled, heterogeneous, intricate, involved, manifold, mingled, mixed, multiform, tangled. That is *complex* which is made up of a number of connected parts. That is *compound* in which the parts are not merely connected, but combined into a single substance. In a *composite* object the different parts have less of unity than in that which is *complex* or *compound,* and maintain their distinct individuality. In a *heterogeneous* body, mass, or collection, unlike parts or particles are intermingled, often without apparent order or plan. *Conglomerate* (literally, globed together) is said of a *confused* mingling of masses or lumps of various substances. Things are *involved* which are rolled together so as not to be easily separated, either in thought or in fact; threads which are *tangled* or *entangled* hold and draw upon one another in a confusing and obstructive way; a knot is *intricate* when the strands are difficult to follow. An *abstruse* statement or conception is remote from the usual course of thought. *Antonyms:* clear, direct, homogeneous, obvious, plain, simple, uncombined, uncompounded, uniform, unraveled.

complex fraction See under FRACTION.

com·plex·ion (kəm·plek′shən) *n.* **1** The color and appearance of the skin, especially of the face. **2** General aspect; character; quality; hence, temperament; cast of mind or thought. **3** *Archaic* The combination of certain assumed qualities in a definite proportion supposed to control the nature of plants, bodies, etc.; also, the habit ascribed to such combination. [< F < L *complexio, -onis* the constitution of a body < *complectere.* See COMPLEX.] —**com·plex′ion·al** *adj.* —**com·plex′ioned** *adj.*

com·plex·i·ty (kəm·plek′sə·tē) *n. pl.* **·ties 1** The state of being complex. **2** Something complex.

complex sentence See under SENTENCE.

com·plex·us (kəm·plek′səs) *n.* **1** A complicated system; complex. **2** *Anat.* A large muscle of the back, which passes from the spine to the head. [< L < *complectere.* See COMPLEX.]

com·pli·a·ble (kəm·plī′ə·bəl) *adj.* Compliant. —**com·pli′a·ble·ness** *n.* —**com·pli′a·bly** *adv.*

com·pli·ance (kəm·plī′əns) *n.* **1** The act of complying, yielding, or acting in accord. **2** Complaisance. Also **com·pli′an·cy.**

com·pli·ant (kəm·plī′ənt) *adj.* Complying; yielding. See synonyms under DOCILE, OBSEQUIOUS, SUPPLE. [< COMPLY] —**com·pli′ant·ly** *adv.*

com·pli·ca·cy (kom′plə·kə·sē) *n. pl.* **·cies 1** The state of being complicated. **2** That which is complicated; complication.

com·pli·cate (kom′plə·kāt) *v.* **·cat·ed, ·cat·ing** *v.t.* **1** To make complex, difficult, or perplexing. **2** To twist or wind around; intertwine. —*v.i.* **3** To become complex or difficult. See synonyms under INVOLVE, PERPLEX. —*adj.* (kom′plə·kit) **1** Complicated; complex. **2** *Bot.* Folded lengthwise upon itself; conduplicate. **3** *Zool.* Folded longitudinally, as the wings of certain insects. [< L *complicatus,* pp. of *complicare* < *com-* together + *plicare* fold] —**com′pli·ca′tive** *adj.*

com·pli·cat·ed (kom′plə·kā′tid) *adj.* Containing or consisting of a combination of parts or elements difficult to separate, analyze, or understand; intricate. —**com′pli·cat′ed·ly** *adv.* —**com′pli·cat′ed·ness** *n.*

com·pli·ca·tion (kom′plə·kā′shən) *n.* **1** The act of complicating, or the state of being complicated; complexity. **2** Anything that complicates, as a disease coexisting with another disease.

com·plice (kom′plis) *n. Obs.* An accomplice or close associate. [< MF < LL *complex* closely connected]

com·plic·i·ty (kəm·plis′ə·tē) *n. pl.* **·ties 1** The act or state of being an accomplice. **2** Complexity.

com·pli·er (kəm·plī′ər) *n.* One who readily yields or complies.

com·pli·ment (kom′plə·mənt) *n.* **1** An expression of admiration, praise, congratulation, etc. **2** A formal greeting or remembrance: usually in the plural. **3** *Archaic* A gratuity; gift; favor. —*v.t.* (kom′plə·ment) **1** To pay a compliment to. **2** To show regard for, as by a gift or other favor. ◆ Homophone: *complement.* [< MF < Ital. *complimento* < Sp. *cumplimiento,* lit., completion of courtesy < L *complementum.* See COMPLEMENT.] —**com·pli·men·ta·ry** (kom′plə·men′tər·ē, -trē) *adj.* —**com′pli·men′ta·ri·ly** *adv.*

complimentary ticket A free ticket.

com·plin (kom′plin) *n.* The last of the canonical hours; also, the last service of common prayer for the day, generally just after vespers, held at this hour. Also **com·pline** (kom′plin, -plīn), **com′plines, com′plins.** [< OF *complie* < L *completa (hora)* finished (hour) < *complere* COMPLETE]

com·plot (kəm·plot′) *Archaic v.t. & v.i.* **·plot·ted, ·plot·ting** To combine in plotting; conspire. —*n.* (kom′plot) A concerted plot; conspiracy. [< F *comploter;* ult. origin uncertain] —**com·plot′·ter** *n.*

com·plu·vi·um (kom·plo͞o′vē·əm) *n. pl.* **·vi·a** (-vē·ə) A large opening for light and air in the roof of an ancient Roman house, through which rain water ran into the impluvium. [< L < *compluere* flow together (said of rain)]

com·ply (kəm·plī′) *v.i.* **·plied, ·ply·ing 1** To act in conformity; consent; obey: with *with.* **2** *Obs.* To be complaisant or courteous; observe civilities. See synonyms under AGREE, OBEY. [< Ital. *compire* < Sp. *cumplir* complete an act of courtesy < L *complere.* See COMPLETE.]

com·po (kom′pō) *n. pl.* **·pos 1** A compound or mixed substance of any kind, such as mortar, plaster, etc. **2** *Naut.* An instalment of wages paid to a ship's crew. [Short for COMPOSITION]

com·po·nent (kəm·pō′nənt) *n.* **1** A constituent part. **2** *Chem.* One of the ingredients of a mixture, in which it may exist in varying proportions and without loss of its own chemical properties, as salt in water: distinguished from *constituent.* **3** *Physics* **a** The smallest number of independently variable factors needed to establish equilibrium in a given system. Compare PHASE RULE. **b** One of two or more forces which, acting in fixed directions, are the equivalent of a given force. —*adj.* Forming a part or ingredient. [< L *componens, -entis,* ppr. of *componere.* See COMPOSE.]

com·po·ny (kəm·pō′nē) *adj. Her.* Composed of two tinctures, generally metal and color, in alternate squares in one row: said of an ordinary. Also **com·po′né.** [OF *componé,* prob. < L *componere.* See COMPOSE.]

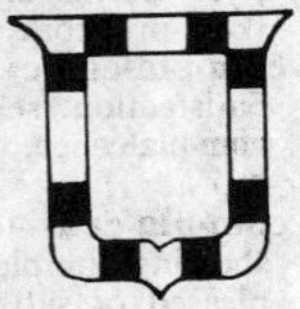

COMPONY

com·port (kəm·pôrt′, -pōrt′) *v.t.* To conduct (oneself). —*v.i.* To be compatible; agree. [< F *comporter* bear, behave < L *comportare* < *com-* together + *portare* carry]

com·port·ment (kəm·pôrt′mənt, -pōrt′-) *n.* Behavior; deportment.

com·pose (kəm·pōz′) *v.* **·posed, ·pos·ing** *v.t.* **1** To be the constituent elements or parts of; constitute; form. **2** *Obs.* To make up of elements or parts; construct. **3** To tranquilize; calm. **4** To reconcile, arrange, or settle, as differences. **5** To create artistically, as a literary or musical work. **6** To arrange (type) in lines; set. —*v.i.* **7** To engage in composition, as of a literary or musical work. **8** To set type. See synonyms under ALLAY, CONSTRUCT, MAKE, SETTLE. [< F *composer* < *com-* together + *poser.* See POSE[1].]

com·posed (kəm·pōzd′) *adj.* **1** Free from agitation; calm. **2** *Obs.* Artfully or well constructed. See synonyms under CALM. —**com·pos·ed·ly** (kəm·pō′zid·lē) *adv.* —**com·pos′ed·ness** *n.*

com·pos·er (kəm·pō′zər) *n.* **1** One who composes. **2** A writer of music.

com·pos·ing (kəm·pō′zing) *n.* **1** The act of one who composes. **2** Typesetting.

composing machine A machine that sets type for printing.

com·pos·ing-room (kəm·pō′zing·ro͞om′, -ro͝om′) *n.* A room where type is set.

com·pos·ing-stick (kəm·pō′zing·stik′) *n. Printing* A tray or receptacle, usually of metal, capable of adjustment so as to vary the length of a line as required, which the compositor holds in his hand, and in which he arranges in words and lines the type that he takes from the cases.

com·pos·ite (kəm·poz′it) *adj.* **1** Made up of separate parts or elements; combined or compounded. **2** *Bot.* Pertaining or belonging to a very large, cosmopolitan family (Compositae) of plants characterized by involucrate flower heads superficially resembling single flowers but typically composed of a central mass of disk florets surrounded by a fringe of ray florets. —*n.* **1** That which is composed or made up of parts; a compound. **2** *Bot.* A composite plant or flower, as a sunflower, daisy, etc. [< L *compositus,* pp. of *componere* < *com-* together + *ponere* put. Doublet of COMPOST.] —**com·pos′ite·ly** *adv.* —**com·pos′ite·ness** *n.*

composite number See under NUMBER.

Composite order *Archit.* A variant of the Corinthian order, having four volutes, like those of the Ionic order, above the acanthus leaves: used in Roman and in Renaissance architecture.

composite photograph A photograph formed by combining several photographs, either on the same plate, or on the same print from various negatives. Also **composite portrait.**

com·po·si·tion (kom′pə·zish′ən) *n.* **1** The act of composing, or the state or manner of being composed; specifically, the act, process, or art of inventing and producing a literary, musical, or artistic work or any part thereof. **2** The general structural arrangement or style of a work of art or a literary or musical production. **3** A literary, artistic, or musical production. **4** A compound or combination. **5** Typesetting. **6** An agreement or settlement; compromise. **7** The state or manner of being put together; also, that which is put together, or the components of which anything is made. **8** *Chem.* The structure of a compound as regards its different elements and the proportions in which they enter into the formation of the compound. See synonyms under PRODUCTION. [< F < L *compositio, -onis* < *componere.* See COMPOSITE.]

com·po·si·tion·al (kom′pə·zish′ə·nəl) *adj.* Of or pertaining to composition.

composition face The face or plane by which the parts of a twin crystal are united. Also **composition plane.**

composition of forces *Physics* The joining of two or more forces, exerted in the same or different directions, into one equivalent force, called the *resultant.*

com·pos·i·tive (kəm·poz′ə·tiv) *adj.* Having the power of compounding; synthetic.

com·pos·i·tor (kəm·poz′ə·tər) *n.* **1** A typesetter. **2** One who composes or sets in order.

com·pos men·tis (kom′pəs men′tis) *Law Latin* Of sound mind; mentally competent: opposed to *non compos mentis.*

com·post (kom′pōst) *n.* **1** A fertilizing mixture of decomposed vegetable matter. **2** A composition for plastering. **3** A mixture; compound. —*v.t.* To make into or cover with compost. [< OF < L *compositum,* var. of *compositum* < *componere.* Doublet of COMPOSITE.]

Com·po·ste·la (kōm′pō·stā′lä) See SANTIAGO DE COMPOSTELA.

com·po·sure (kəm·pō′zhər) *n.* **1** Tranquillity, as of manner or appearance; calmness; serenity. **2** Composition. See synonyms under APATHY, PATIENCE.

com·po·ta·tion (kom′pō·tā′shən) *n. Obs.* A drinking or tippling in company; carouse. [< L *compotatio, -onis* < *com-* together + *potare* drink]

com·pote (kom′pōt, *Fr.* kôn·pôt′) *n.* **1** Fruit stewed or preserved in sirup. **2** A dish for holding fruits, etc. [< F < OF *composte.* See COMPOST.]

com·pound[1] (kom′pound) *n.* **1** A combination of two or more elements, ingredients, or parts. **2** A compound engine. **3** A compound word. **4** *Chem.* A definite substance resulting from

the combination of specific elements or radicals in fixed proportions: distinguished from *mixture*. —*v.* (kom·pound′, kəm-) *v.t.* **1** To make by the combination of various elements or ingredients. **2** To mix elements or parts to form a compound substance; combine: to *compound* drugs. **3** To compromise; settle for less than the sum due: to *compound* a debt. **4** To cover up or condone (a crime) for a consideration: to *compound* a felony. **5** To compute, as interest, by geometric progression. **6** *Electr.* To place duplex windings on the field magnets of (a dynamo), one serving as a shunt and the other being in series with the main circuit, making the machine self-regulating. **7** *Obs.* To compose; form. —*v.i.* **8** To come to terms; take a compromise settlement. —*adj.* (kom′pound, kom·pound′) Composed of, or produced by the union of, two or more elements, ingredients, or parts; composite. See synonyms under COMPLEX. [< OF *compondre* < L *componere*. See COMPOSITE.] —**com·pound′a·ble** *adj.* —**com·pound′er** *n.*

com·pound² (kom′pound) *n.* In the Orient, the walled or fenced enclosure of a residence, cantonment, or factory; also, any similar enclosed place. [< Malay *kampong*]

compound E Cortisone.

compound engine A steam engine in which the exhaust steam from one or more cylinders enters and does work in one or more other cylinders.

compound flower *Bot.* The anthodium or head of the flower of a composite plant.

compound fraction See under FRACTION.

compound fracture See under FRACTURE.

compound interest Interest computed not only on the original principal but also on interest earned in succeeding periods.

compound leaf *Bot.* A leaf having several distinct blades on a common leafstalk. See illustrations under LEAF.

compound number See under NUMBER.

compound sentence See under SENTENCE.

compound triple time See under TIME.

compound word A word composed of two or more words united either with a hyphen (hypheme) or without (solideme), and usually distinguished from a phrase by a reduction of stress on one of the elements and a shortening of the pause between the words, as *green′ house′* and *a green′ house′*.

com·pra·dor (kom′prə·dôr′) *n.* In China and other Eastern countries, a native agent in a foreign business house, consulate, etc. Also **com′pra·dore′.** [< Pg., buyer]

com·preg (kom′preg) *n.* Resin-impregnated sheets of wood, bonded together by pressure and heat to impart special properties of strength, density, toughness, and finish. [< COM(PRESSED) +(IM)PREG(NATED)]

com·pre·hend (kom′pri·hend′) *v.t.* **1** To grasp mentally; understand fully. **2** To include, take in, or comprise. —*v.i.* **3** To understand. See synonyms under APPREHEND, CATCH, EMBRACE, KNOW, PERCEIVE. [< L *comprehendere* < *com-* together + *prehendere* seize] —**com′pre·hend′i·ble** *adj.*

com·pre·hen·si·ble (kom′pri·hen′sə·bəl) *adj.* **1** Capable of being comprehended or grasped by the mind; understandable; conceivable. **2** Capable of being comprised or included. —**com′·pre·hen′si·bil′i·ty, com′pre·hen′si·ble·ness** *n.* —**com′pre·hen′si·bly** *adv.*

com·pre·hen·sion (kom′pri·hen′shən) *n.* **1** The mental grasping of ideas, facts, etc., or the power of doing so; understanding. **2** The act or state of including, containing, or taking in; inclusion; comprehensiveness. **3** *Logic* The complete conception of a term, involving all the elements of its meaning and its correlations. See synonyms under KNOWLEDGE. [< L *comprehensio, -onis* < *comprehendere* COMPREHEND]

com·pre·hen·sive (kom′pri·hen′siv) *adj.* **1** Large in scope or content; including much; broad. **2** Having the power of fully understanding or comprehending. —**com′pre·hen′·sive·ly** *adv.* —**com′pre·hen′sive·ness** *n.*

com·press (kəm·pres′) *v.t.* To press together or into smaller space; condense; compact; concentrate. —*n.* (kom′pres) **1** A device for compressing. **2** *Med.* A soft pad for making local pressure on affected parts of the

body. **3** An apparatus for compressing bales of cotton, etc. [< OF *compresser* < LL *compressare*, freq. of *comprimere* < *com-* together + *premere* press] —**com·press′i·bil′i·ty, com·press′i·ble·ness** *n.* —**com·press′i·ble** *adj.* —**com·press′ive** *adj.* —**com·press′ive·ly** *adv.*

com·pressed (kəm·prest′) *adj.* **1** Flattened laterally. **2** *Biol.* Reduced in breadth, as the bodies of certain fishes or the leafstalks of some plants. **3** Pressed together or into smaller compass; made compact.

com·pres·sion (kəm·presh′ən) *n.* **1** The act of compressing or the state of being compressed. **2** The process by which a confined gas is reduced in volume through the application of pressure, as in the cylinder of an internal-combustion engine. Also **com·pres·sure** (kəm·presh′ər). [< L *compressio, -onis* < *comprimere* COMPRESS]

com·pres·sor (kəm·pres′ər) *n.* **1** One who or that which compresses. **2** *Anat.* A muscle that compresses a part of the body: the *compressor narium* of the nostrils. **3** *Surg.* An instrument for compressing a part of the body. **4** *Mech.* A power-driven machine for compressing a gas in order to utilize its expansion, as for refrigeration.

com·prise (kəm·prīz′) *v.t.* **·prised, ·pris·ing** To include and contain; consist of; embrace. [< F *compris,* pp. of *comprendre* < L *comprehendere* COMPREHEND] —**com·pri′sal** *n.*

com·pro·mis (kôn′prô·mē′) *n.* French The special agreement for an international arbitration, defining the subject of the dispute and establishing the procedure to be followed: derived from the French Civil Law relating to private arbitration. Also **compromis d'ar·bi·trage** (dár·bē·träzh′).

com·pro·mise (kom′prə·mīz) *n.* **1** An adjustment for settlement by arbitration and mutual concession, usually involving a partial surrender of purposes or principles. **2** *Law* An adjustment of a controversy by mutual consent in order to prevent or settle a lawsuit. **3** Anything that is the result of concessions; a medium between two conflicting courses; also, the habit or spirit of concession. **4** An imperiling or surrender, as of character or reputation. —*v.* **·mised, ·mis·ing** *v.t.* **1** To adjust by concessions. **2** To expose, as to suspicion, danger, or disrepute. **3** *Obs.* To bind or pledge mutually. —*v.i.* **4** To make a settlement by concessions. [< F *compromis* < L *compromissum* a mutual agreement to accept arbitration < *com-* together + *promittere* promise] —**com′pro·mis′er** *n.*

compt (kount) *n. Obs.* Account; reckoning. [< F *compte* account]

compte ren·du (kônt räṅ·dü′) *French* An official report; literally, account rendered.

compt·i·ble (koun′tə·bəl) *adj. Obs.* Accountable; tractable; sensitive.

Comp·tom·e·ter (komp·tom′ə·tər) *n.* A high-speed adding or calculating machine: a trade name.

Comp·ton (komp′tən), **Arthur Holly,** 1892–1962, U.S. physicist. —**Karl Taylor,** 1887–1954, U.S. physicist; brother of Arthur.

Compton effect *Physics* The phenomenon of the scattering of X-rays when subjected to bombardment by electrons of the lighter elements: the resulting radiation somewhat resembles fluorescence. [after A. H. *Compton*]

Compton shift *Physics* The shift in wavelength produced by the Compton effect.

comp·trol·ler (kən·trō′lər) *n.* A controller: the spelling sometimes employed to designate a city, State, or Federal officer in control of funds. [< Var. of CONTROLLER; infl. by COMPT] —**comp·trol′ler·ship** *n.*

com·pul·sion (kəm·pul′shən) *n.* **1** The act of compelling; coercion. **2** The state of being compelled. **3** *Psychol.* **a** The performance of an act contrary to the conscious will of the subject. **b** An act so performed. See synonyms under NECESSITY. [< MF < L *compulsio, -onis* < *compellere* COMPEL]

com·pul·sive (kəm·pul′siv) *adj.* **1** Compelling or tending to compel; compulsory. **2** *Psychol.* Pertaining to or describing acts or behavior independent of volition. —**com·pul′·sive·ly** *adv.* —**com·pul′sive·ness** *n.*

com·pul·so·ry (kəm·pul′sər·ē) *adj.* **1** Employing compulsion; compelling; coercive. **2** Re-

quired by law or other rule; enforced: *compulsory* education. See synonyms under NECESSARY. —**com·pul′so·ri·ly** *adv.* —**com·pul′·so·ri·ness** *n.*

com·punc·tion (kəm·pungk′shən) *n.* **1** Self-reproach for wrong-doing; a sense of guilt; remorseful feeling. **2** A feeling of slight regret. See synonyms under REPENTANCE. [< LL *compunctio, -onis* < *com-* greatly + *pungere* prick, sting] —**com·punc′tious** *adj.* —**com·punc′tious·ly** *adv.*

com·pur·ga·tion (kom′pər·gā′shən) *n.* The ancient practice of clearing an accused person by the oaths of several others, usually twelve, who swore to their belief in his innocence. [< LL *compurgatio, -onis* < *com-* thoroughly + *purgare* cleanse]

com·pur·ga·tor (kom′pər·gā′tər) *n.* One who testifies in favor of or vouches for another; especially, one of the twelve men called in cases of compurgation. [< Med. L < *com-* together + *purgare* cleanse]

com·pu·ta·tion (kom′pyə·tā′shən) *n.* **1** The act of computing; calculation. **2** A computed amount or number.

com·pute (kəm·pyōōt′) *v.t.* **·put·ed, ·put·ing** To estimate numerically; calculate; reckon. —*n.* Computation. [< L *computare* < *com-* together + *putare* reckon. Doublet of COUNT¹.] —**com·put′a·bil′i·ty** *n.* —**com·put′a·ble** *adj.* —**com·put′ist** *n.*

com·put·er (kəm·pyōō′tər) *n.* **1** One who or that which computes. **2** A power-driven machine equipped with keyboards, electronic circuits, storage compartments, and recording devices for the high-speed performance of mathematical operations.

com·rade (kom′rad, -rid) *n.* **1** A friend or intimate companion. **2** A partner, associate, or fellow member, as of a political party: used as a form of address, as in the Communist party. See synonyms under ASSOCIATE. [< MF *camarade* < Sp. *camarada* roommate < L *camera* room] —**com′rade·ship** *n.*

com·rade·ry (kom′rad·rē, -rid-) See CAMARADERIE.

COMSAT (kom′sat′) *adj. trademark/service mark* The services and apparatus utilized in satellite and microwave telecommunications, which are produced by COMSAT Corporation. [COM(MUNICATIONS) + SAT(ELLITE)]

Com·stock·er·y (kum′stok′ər·ē, kom′-) *n.* **1** Exaggerated censorship of immorality in literature, pictures, etc. **2** Prudishness.

Com·stock Lode (kum′stok, kom′-) A rich vein of silver and gold discovered in 1859 at Virginia City, Nevada. [after Henry *Comstock,* 1820–70, U.S. prospector]

comte (kônt) *n. French* A count².

Comte (kônt), **Auguste,** 1798–1857, French philosopher; founder of positivism. —**Com·ti·an** (kom′tē·ən, kôn′-) *adj.*

Com·tism (kom′tiz·əm, kôn′-) *n.* The philosophy of Comte; positivism. —**Com′tist** *adj.* & *n.*

Co·mus (kō′məs) **1** In Greek and Roman mythology, the young god of revelry, a companion of Dionysos. **2** A mask (1634) by John Milton.

con¹ (kon) *v.t.* **conned, con·ning** To study; peruse carefully; learn. [Var. of CAN¹] —**con′.ner** *n.*

con² (kon) *v.t.* **conned, con·ning** *Naut.* To direct the steering of (a vessel). Also **conn.** [Earlier cond < F *conduire* < L *conducere* CONDUCT]

con³ (kon) *Slang adj.* Shortened form of *confidence:* used in phrases: *con* man; *con* game. —*v.t.* **conned, con·ning** To defraud; dupe; swindle. —*n.* A confidence man.

con⁴ (kon) *n.* The contrary; the opposite side; the opponent, etc. —*adv.* Against. See PRO. [< L *contra* against]

con⁵ (kon) *n. Slang* A convict.

con— Assimilated var. of COM—.

Co·na·kry (kô·ná·krē′) A port in west Africa, the capital of Guinea: also *Konakri.*

con a·mo·re (kōn ä·mô′rā) **1** *Italian* With love. **2** *Music* Lovingly; with enthusiasm or tenderness: a direction to the performer.

Co·nant (kō′nənt), **James Bryant,** 1893–1978, U.S. chemist and educator.

co·na·tion (kō·nā′shən) *n. Psychol.* The element of conscious striving and activity con-

tained in every desire, impulse, aversion, etc. [< L *conatio, -onis* an attempt < *conari* try]

co·na·tive (kon′ə·tiv, kō′nə-) *adj.* **1** *Psychol.* Of or pertaining to conation. **2** *Gram.* Expressing endeavor: said of an aspect of certain Semitic verbs.

co·na·tus (kō·nā′təs) *n. pl.* **co·na·tus 1** An attempt or endeavor; effort. **2** *Biol.* An inherent tendency in plants and animals resembling effort in human beings. [< L < *conari* try]

con bri·o (kōn brē′ō) *Music* With spirit. [< Ital.]

con·cat·e·nate (kon·kat′ə·nāt) *v.t.* **·nat·ed, ·nat·ing** To join or link together; connect in a series. —*adj.* Joined together; connected in a series. [< L *concatenatus,* pp. of *concatenare* < *com-* together + *catena* chain]

con·cat·e·na·tion (kon·kat′ə·nā′shən) *n.* **1** The act of concatenating; union in a chainlike series. **2** A chainlike series, as of associated nerve cells or physiological reflexes. **3** *Mech.* A method of variable speed-control without undue loss of working energy: used on locomotives and motors.

con·cave (kon·kāv′, kon′kāv, kong′-) *adj.* **1** Hollow and rounded, as the interior of a sphere or circle; incurved: opposed to *convex.* **2** Hollow. —*n.* (kon′kāv, kong′-) A concave surface; vault. [< MF < L *concavus* < *com-* thoroughly + *cavus* hollow] **—con·cave′ly** *adv.* **—con·cave′ness** *n.*

con·cav·i·ty (kon·kav′ə·tē) *n. pl.* **·ties 1** The state of being concave. **2** A concave surface; hollow. See synonyms under HOLE.

con·ca·vo-con·cave (kon·kā′vō·kon·kāv′) *adj.* *Optics* Concave on both sides; doubly concave. See illustration under LENS.

con·ca·vo-con·vex (kon·kā′vō·kon·veks′) *adj.* **1** Concave on one side and convex on the other. **2** *Optics* Describing a lens in which the curvature of the concave side is greater than that of the convex; distinguished from *convexo-concave.* See illustration under LENS.

con·ceal (kən·sēl′) *v.t.* To hide; secrete; keep from sight, discovery, or knowledge. See synonyms under BURY, HIDE, MASK, PALLIATE. [< OF *conceler* < L *concelare* < *com-* thoroughly + *celare* hide] **—con·ceal′a·ble** *adj.*

con·ceal·ment (kən·sēl′mənt) *n.* **1** The act of concealing, or state of being concealed. **2** A hiding place.

con·cede (kən·sēd′) *v.* **·ced·ed, ·ced·ing** *v.t.* **1** To grant or yield, as a right or privilege. **2** To acknowledge as true, correct, or proper; admit. —*v.i.* **3** To make a concession. See synonyms under ACKNOWLEDGE, ALLOW, CONFESS. [< L *concedere* < *com-* thoroughly + *cedere* yield, go away] **—con·ced′er** *n.*

con·ceit (kən·sēt′) *n.* **1** Overweening self-esteem. **2 a** A fanciful idea; a quaint or humorous fancy; clever thought or expression. **b** An extended, flowery, strained metaphor. **3** Imagination. **4** A fancy or ingenious article or design. **5** Apprehension; understanding. **6** A conception or thought. See synonyms under EGOTISM, FANCY, IDEA, PRIDE. **—out of conceit with** Displeased with. —*v.t.* **1** *Obs.* To imagine or suppose; think. **2** *Dial.* To take a fancy to; regard favorably. **3** *Obs.* To form a conception or idea; conceive. [< CONCEIVE]

con·ceit·ed (kən·sē′tid) *adj.* **1** Having an excessively fine opinion of oneself; vain. **2** *Brit. Dial.* Fanciful; notional. **3** *Obs.* Intelligent; witty. **—con·ceit′ed·ly** *adv.* **—con·ceit′ed·ness** *n.*

con·ceive (kən·sēv′) *v.* **·ceived, ·ceiv·ing** *v.t.* **1** To procreate; beget or become pregnant with, as young. **2** To form an idea in the mind; think of; fancy. **3** To construct in the mind; formulate, as plans. **4** To believe or suppose; form an opinion. **5** To become possessed with: to *conceive* a hatred. **6** *Obs.* To understand. —*v.i.* **7** To form a mental image; think: with *of.* **8** To become pregnant. See synonyms under APPREHEND. [< OF *conceveir* < L *concipere* < *com-* thoroughly + *capere* take] **—con·ceiv′a·ble** *adj.* **—con·ceiv′a·bil′i·ty, con·ceiv′a·ble·ness** *n.* **—con·ceiv′a·bly** *adv.* **—con·ceiv′er** *n.*

con·cent (kən·sent′) *n. Obs.* Concord or harmony. [< L *concentus* < *concinere* < *com-* together + *canere* sing]

con·cen·ter (kon·sen′tər) *v.t.* To direct or bring to a common point or center; focus. —*v.i.* To come together at a common center; combine. Also **con·cen′tre.** [< F *concentrer* < L *com-* together + *centrum* center]

con·cen·trate (kon′sən·trāt) *v.* **·trat·ed, ·trat·ing** *v.t.* **1** To draw to a common center; concenter; focus. **2** To intensify in strength or to purify by the removal of certain constituents; condense. —*v.i.* **3** To converge toward a center; become compacted or intensified. —*n.* **1** A product of concentration. **2** *Usually pl. Metall.* The product of concentration processes whereby a mass of high metal content has been obtained from the ore or other raw materials. —*adj.* Concentrated. [< CONCENTER + -ATE[1]] **—con·cen·tra·tive** (kon′sən·trā′tiv, kən·sen′trə·tiv) *adj.* **—con′cen·tra′tive·ly** *adv.* **—con′cen·tra′tive·ness** *n.* **—con′cen·tra′tor** *n.*

con·cen·tra·tion (kon′sən·trā′shən) *n.* **1** The act of concentrating: said especially of focusing the attention upon a single object, problem, task, etc. **2** That which is concentrated. **3** A medicine strengthened by evaporation of inactive ingredients. **4** *Chem.* The amount of a substance per unit volume: in a solution it is the amount of the substance dissolved by a given quantity of the solvent.

concentration camp 1 A place of detention for prisoners of war, political prisoners, aliens, etc. **2** *Mil.* A place where troops are marshalled for redistribution.

con·cen·tric (kən·sen′trik) *adj.* Having a common center, as circles: opposed to *eccentric.* Also **con·cen′tri·cal. —con·cen′tri·cal·ly** *adv.* **—con·cen·tric·i·ty** (kon′sen·tris′ə·tē) *n.*

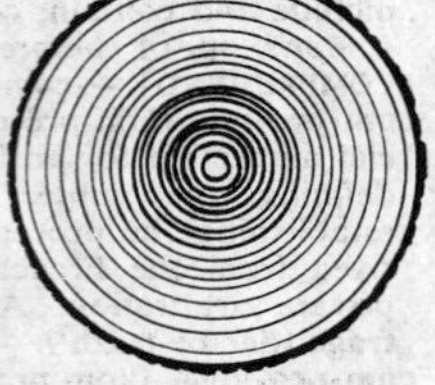
CONCENTRIC TREE RINGS

Con·cep·ción (kōn′sep·syōn′) A city in south central Chile.

con·cept (kon′sept) *n.* **1** An abstract notion or idea. **2** Any notion combining elements into the idea of one object. **3** A thought or opinion. See synonyms under IDEA. [< L *conceptus* a conceiving < *concipere* CONCEIVE]

con·cep·ta·cle (kən·sep′tə·kəl) *n. Bot.* A special cavity developed on the surface of many algae and fungi, for holding or enclosing reproductive organs. [< L *conceptaculum* a receptacle < *concipere.* See CONCEIVE.]

con·cep·tion (kən·sep′shən) *n.* **1** The act of conceiving or the state of being conceived. **2** The act, faculty, or power of conceiving or forming ideas or notions. **3** *Biol.* The impregnation of an ovum; act of becoming pregnant; also, an embryo; fetus. **4** A commencement; beginning; inception. **5** Anything that is conceived; a plan or invention of the mind; a product of the inventive or constructive faculty. See synonyms under FANCY, IDEA, IMAGE, THOUGHT. **—con·cep′tion·al** *adj.*

con·cep·tive (kən·sep′tiv) *adj.* Capable of conception.

con·cep·tu·al (kən·sep′chōō·əl) *adj.* Of or pertaining to conception or a concept. **—con·cep′tu·al·ly** *adv.*

con·cep·tu·al·ism (kən·sep′chōō·əl·iz′əm) *n.* The doctrine that general ideas, or universals, exist in the mind only, and that the mind is capable of forming abstract ideas independently of concrete existences: a theory devised as intermediate between the extremes of nominalism and realism. **—con·cep′tu·al·ist** *n.* **—con·cep′tu·al·is′tic** *adj.*

con·cern (kən·sûrn′) *v.t.* **1** To relate or belong to; be of interest or importance to. **2** To occupy, engage, or interest. **3** To affect with solicitude; trouble: usually in the passive. —*v.i.* **4** *Obs.* To be of importance. —*n.* **1** That which concerns one; something affecting one's interest or welfare; affair; business. **2** Solicitude; interest. **3** Relation; reference. **4** A business establishment. **5** *Colloq.* Any object or contrivance. See synonyms under ANXIETY, BUSINESS, CARE. [< MF *concerner* < Med. L *concernere* regard < *com-* thoroughly + *cernere* see, discern]

con·cerned (kən·sûrnd′) *adj.* **1** Having interest or involvement; involved. **2** Having anxiety or uneasiness.

con·cern·ing (kən·sûr′ning) *prep.* In relation to; regarding; about.

con·cern·ment (kən·sûrn′mənt) *n.* **1** The fact or condition of concerning; relation; bearing; importance. **2** Anxiety; solicitude. **3** Connection; participation. **4** Anything that relates to one; affair; concern; business.

con·cert (kon′sûrt) *n.* **1** A musical performance by a number of voices or instruments, or both; also, the combination of voices or instruments to produce harmony. **2** Harmony; agreement; accordance; unity. —*adj.* Of or for concerts. —*v.* (kən·sûrt′) *v.t.* **1** To arrange or contrive by mutual agreement. **2** To plan; contrive. —*v.i.* **3** To act or plan together. [< MF < Ital. *concerto* < *concertare* agree, be in accord]

con·cert·ed (kən·sûr′tid) *adj.* Arranged or agreed upon in concert or for a common purpose; especially, in music, arranged in parts: a *concerted* piece. **—con·cert′ed·ly** *adv.*

concert grand (piano) See under PIANO.

con·cer·ti·na (kon′sər·tē′nə) *n.* **1** A small musical instrument of the accordion type, with bellows and a keyboard at either end. **2** *Mil.* A portable, distensible barbed-wire entanglement, used to hinder the movements of enemy motorized equipment. [< Ital. < *concerto.* See CONCERT.]

con·cer·ti·no (kōn′cher·tē′nō) *n. pl.* **·ni** (-nē) *Music* A short or abridged concerto. [< Ital., dim. of *concerto.* See CONCERT.]

con·cert·mas·ter (kon′sərt·mas′tər, -mäs′-) *n.* The leader of the first violin section of an orchestra, who acts as assistant to the conductor. Also **con·cert·meis·ter** (kon′sərt·mīs′·tər, *Ger.* kôn·tsert′mīs′tər).

con·cer·to (kən·cher′tō) *n. pl.* **·tos,** *Ital.* **·ti** (-tē) *Music* A composition (usually of three movements) for performance by a solo instrument or instruments accompanied by an orchestra. [< Ital. See CONCERT.]

Concert of Europe 1 A tacit agreement of the great European powers, in the years following the Congress of Vienna (1815), to act together in matters concerning the peace of Europe. **2** Any agreement among the European powers. Also **Concert of Powers.**

concerto gros·so (grō′sō) An early form of concerto for a small group of solo instruments and a full orchestra. [< Ital., lit., big concerto]

con·ces·sion (kən·sesh′ən) *n.* **1** The act of conceding, or that which is conceded. **2** A subsidiary business, conducted by lease or by purchase of privilege, in office buildings, railroad stations, etc.: a coatroom *concession.* **3** A strip of land, as one adjoining a port, canal, etc., conceded to an alien government for its economic use, and in which self-government and extraterritorial rights are exercised. See synonyms under FAVOR. [< MF < L *concessio, -onis* < *concedere* CONCEDE]

con·ces·sion·ar·y (kən·sesh′ən·er′ē) *adj.* Bestowed by concession; of or pertaining to a concession. —*n. pl.* **·ar·ies** A concessioner.

con·ces·sion·er (kən·sesh′ən·ər) *n.* One who holds or seeks to secure a concession. Also **con·ces·sion·aire** (kən·sesh′ən·âr′), **con·ces′sion·naire′.**

concession road *Canadian* In Ontario and Quebec, a road following a survey line.

con·ces·sive (kən·ses′iv) *adj.* **1** Like or tending to concession. **2** *Gram.* Involving concession: said of the conjunctions *though, although,* etc., and of the subordinate adverbial clauses introduced by them.

conch (kongk, konch) *n. pl.* **conchs** (kongks) or **conch·es** (kon′chiz) **1** Any of various large marine gastropod mollusks (family Strombidae) having heavy, colorful, spiral shells. **2** The shell of such a mollusk, used to make cameos and other objects and as a crude trumpet. **3** In Roman mythology, such a shell blown as a horn by the Tritons. **4** *Archit.* A semidome, or the plain concave surface of a dome or vault. **5** *U.S. Dial.* One of a group of people native to the Florida Keys or the Bahamas. [< L *concha* < Gk. *konchē* shell]

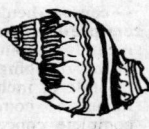

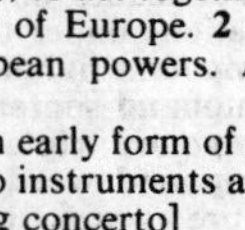
CONCH SHELL

con·cha (kong′kə) *n. pl.* **con·chae** (kong′kē) **1** *Anat.* A structure of shell-like appearance, as the external ear, or one of the turbinate bones. **2** *Archit.* A conch (def. 3). [< L See CONCH.]

con·chif·er·ous (kong·kif′ər·əs) *adj.* **1** Having or producing a shell; testaceous. **2** Of or pertaining to a former division of mollusks

(*Conchifera*). [<L *concha* shell + -FEROUS]
con·choid (kong′koid) *n. Math.* A curve traced by the locus of a point at the end of a straight line segment of fixed length rotating about the polar axis in such a way that the length of a perpendicular from the curve to a fixed straight line (its asymptote) is in constant proportion to the length of the segment, and so that the segment of the line intercepted by the curve and its asymptote is of constant length.

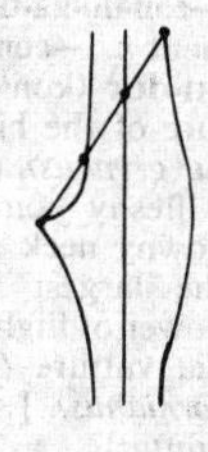
CONCHOID

con·choi·dal (kong·koid′l) *adj.* Having shell-shaped depressions and elevations. Also **con′·choid.**
con·chol·o·gy (kong·kol′ə·jē) *n.* The study of shells and mollusks. [<L *concha* shell + -LOGY] **—con·cho·log·i·cal** (kong′kə·loj′i·kəl) *adj.* **—con′cho·log′i·cal·ly** *adv.* **—con·chol′o·gist** *n.*
con·cho·scope (kong′kə·skōp) *n. Med.* A speculum used in examining the anterior and middle parts of the nasal passages. [<Gk. *konchē* shell + -SCOPE]
con·chy (kon′chē) *n. pl.* **·chies** *Slang* A conscientious objector.
con·ci·erge (kon′sē·ûrzh′, *Fr.* kôn·syârzh′) *n.* **1** A doorkeeper or porter. **2** A janitor. [<F]
con·cil·i·ate (kən·sil′ē·āt) *v.t.* **·at·ed, ·at·ing 1** To overcome the enmity or hostility of; obtain the friendship of; placate; mollify: to *conciliate* an enemy. **2** To secure or attract by reconciling measures; gain; win. [<L *conciliatus,* pp. of *conciliare* <*concilium* council] **—con·cil·i·a·ble** (kən·sil′ē·ə·bəl) *adj.* **—con·cil′i·a′tor** *n.* **—con·cil·i·a·to·ry** (kən·sil′ē·ə·tôr′ē, -tō′rē), **con·cil′i·a′tive** *adj.* **—con·cil′i·a·to′ri·ly** *adv.* **—con·cil′i·a·to′ri·ness** *n.*
con·cil·i·a·tion (kən·sil′ē·ā′shən) *n.* **1** The act of bringing into agreement. **2** The settlement or attempt to settle a labor dispute by the proposal of measures acceptable to the disputants. See ARBITRATION, MEDIATION.
con·cin·ni·ty (kən·sin′ə·tē) *n. pl.* **·ties** Fitness; harmony; elegance, as of rhetorical style. [<L *concinnitas, -tatis* <*concinnus* well adjusted]
con·cise (kən·sīs′) *adj.* Expressing much in brief form; compact; terse. See synonyms under TERSE. [<L *concisus,* pp. of *concidere* < *con-* thoroughly + *caedere* cut] **—con·cise′ly** *adv.* **—con·cise′ness** *n.*
con·ci·sion (kən·sizh′ən) *n.* **1** A cutting off or asunder; schism. **2** The quality or character of being concise. **3** *Obs.* Circumcision. [<L *concisio, -onis* <*concidere.* See CONCISE.]
con·cla·mant (kən·klā′mənt) *adj.* Calling out together, as in lamentation. [<L *conclamans, -antis,* ppr. of *conclamare* <*con-* together + *clamare* cry out]
con·cla·ma·tion (kon′klə·mā′shən) *n.* A calling out together; outcry of several voices.
con·clave (kon′klāv, kong′-) *n.* **1** A secret council or meeting. **2** In the Roman Catholic Church, the apartments in the Vatican in which the college of cardinals meets to choose a pope, and which is kept locked until the election is over; also, the assembly or meeting of the cardinals. See synonyms under ASSEMBLY, CABAL, COMPANY. [<F<L, a place which can be locked up <*com-* together + *clavis* key]
con·clav·ist (kon′klā·vist, kong′-) *n.* An ecclesiastic attendant upon a cardinal at an electoral conclave.
con·clude (kən·klōōd′) *v.* **·clud·ed, ·clud·ing** *v.t.* **1** To come to a decision about; decide or determine. **2** To infer or deduce as a result or effect. **3** To arrange or settle finally. **4** To terminate; bring to an end. **5** *Obs.* To shut in; enclose. *—v.i.* **6** To come to an end. **7** To infer or deduce a conclusion. See synonyms under CEASE, EFFECT, END. [<L *concludere* <*com-* thoroughly + *claudere* close, shut off] **—con·clud′er** *n.*
con·clu·sion (kən·klōō′zhən) *n.* **1** The act of concluding; termination; end. **2** A conviction reached in consequence of investigation, reasoning, inference, etc. **3** A practical determination; decision. **4** The closing part, as of a discourse. **5** *Logic* A proposition the truth of which is inferred from a premise or premises; especially, the third proposition of an Aristotelian syllogism. **6** *Law* An estoppel; a bar; also, the ending of a pleading or deed. See synonyms under DEMONSTRATION, END, INFERENCE, THOUGHT. [<F <L *conclusio, -onis* < *concludere* CONCLUDE]
con·clu·sive (kən·klōō′siv) *adj.* **1** Decisive; putting an end to doubt. **2** Leading to a conclusion; final. **—con·clu′s** *adv.* **—con·clu′·sive·ness** *n.*
con·coct (kon·kokt′, kən-) *v.t.* **1** To make by mixing ingredients, as a drink or soup. **2** To contrive; devise. [<L *concoctus,* pp. of *concoquere* <*com-* together + *coquere* cook, boil] **—con·coct′er, con·coc′tor** *n.* **—con·coc′·tive** *adj.*
con·coc·tion (kon·kok′shən, kən-) *n.* The act of concocting, or the thing concocted; contrivance; mixture.
con·col·or·ous (kon·kul′ər·əs) *adj.* Uniform in color; of one color. Also *Brit.* **con·col′our·ous.** [<L *concolor* <*com-* together + *color* color]
con·com·i·tant (kon·kom′ə·tənt, kən-) *adj.* Existing or occurring together; attendant. See synonyms under INCIDENTAL. *—n.* An attendant circumstance. See synonyms under APPENDAGE, CIRCUMSTANCE. [<L *concomitans, -antis,* ppr. of *concomitari* <*com-* with + *comitari* accompany <*comes* companion] **—con·com′i·tance, con·com′i·tan·cy** *n.* **—con·com′i·tant·ly** *adv.*
con·cord (kon′kôrd, kong′-) **1** Unity of feeling or interest; agreement; accord. **2** *Music* Consonance. **3** *Gram.* Agreement of words, as in gender, number, case, or person. See synonyms under HARMONY. [<F *concorde* <L *concordia* <*concors* agreeing <*com-* together + *cor, cordis* heart]
Con·cord (kong′kərd, kon′kôrd) *n.* A dark-blue to black, round American grape, grown extensively for market in New England and the NE United States: also **Concord grape.**
Con·cord (kong′kərd, kon′kôrd) **1** A town in NE Massachusetts; scene of a Revolutionary War battle, April 19, 1775. **2** The capital of New Hampshire.
con·cor·dance (kon·kôr′dəns, kən-) *n.* **1** An alphabetical index of words or topics in a book in their exact context; especially, such an index of the Bible. **2** Concord; agreement.
con·cor·dant (kon·kôr′dənt, kən-) *adj.* Existing in concord; consonant. [<L *concordans, -antis,* ppr. of *concordare* agree <*concors.* See CONCORD.] **—con·cor′dant·ly** *adv.*
con·cor·dan·tial (kon′kər·dan′shəl) *adj.* Of or pertaining to a Biblical concordance.
con·cor·dat (kon·kôr′dat) *n.* **1** In papal history, an agreement between the papal see and a secular power for the settlement and regulation of ecclesiastical affairs. **2** Any public act of agreement. [<Med. L *concordatum* thing agreed upon <*concordare.* See CONCORDANT.]
Con·corde (kon′kôrd, kong′-) *n.* A supersonic commercial aircraft, produced jointly by Great Britain and France.
Con·cor·di·a (kon·kôr′dē·ə) In Roman mythology, the goddess of concord or peace.
con·cor·po·rate (kon·kôr′pə·rāt) *v.t.* & *v.i.* **·rat·ed, ·rat·ing** *Obs.* To unite in one body or substance. [<L *concorporatus,* pp. of *concorporare* <*com-* together + *corpus* body]
con·cours (kôn·kōōr′) *n. French* **1** Concourse; meeting. **2** Competition; competitive examination.
con·course (kon′kôrs, -kōrs, kong′-)*n.* **1** An assembling or moving together; confluence. **2** An assembly; throng. **3** A large place, open or enclosed, for the passage of crowds; specifically, a boulevard or a long passageway in a railroad station, subway, etc. See synonyms under ASSEMBLY, COMPANY, THRONG. [<F *concours* <L *concursus* <*concurrere.* See CONCUR.]
con·cre·ma·tion (kon′krə·mā′shən) *n.* Cremation together or at the same time, as in the suttee ceremony in India. [<CON- + CREMATION]
con·cres·cence (kon·kres′əns) *n.* **1** *Anat.* A growing together of separate parts, as the roots of adjoining teeth. **2** *Biol.* A fusing together of the cells of an embryo during gastrulation. **3** Increase by addition of parts or particles; growth. [<L *concrescentia* < *concrescere.* See CONCRETE.]
con·crete (kon′krēt, kon·krēt′) *adj.* **1** Joined in or constituting a mass. **2** Embodied in actual existence: opposed to *abstract.* **3** Applied or relating to a particular case; individual; particular. **4** Made of concrete. *—n.* **1** A hardened mass; especially, one of sand and gravel or broken stone united by hydraulic cement. **2** A specific object or the conception of it. **3** Any mass of particles united and solidified. *—v.* (kon·krēt′ *for defs. 1, 2, 4;* kon′·krēt, kon·krēt′ *for def. 3)* **·cret·ed,·cret·ing** *v.t.* **1** To bring or unite together in one mass or body; cause to coalesce. **2** To bring into concrete or specific form; concretize. **3** To treat or cover with concrete. *—v.i.* **4** To coalesce; solidify. [<L *concretus,* pp. of *concrescere* < *com-* together + *crescere* grow] **—con·crete′ly** *adv.* **—con·crete′ness** *n.*
concrete number See under NUMBER.
con·cre·tion (kon·krē′shən) *n.* **1** The act of concreting; a concrete mass. **2** *Geol.* An aggregate of rounded masses found in sedimentary rocks and usually formed around a central core, which may be a fossil. **3** *Med.* **a** A calculus. **b** The abnormal joining of adjacent parts. **—con·cre·tion·ar·y** (kon·krē′shən·er′ē) *adj.* **—con·cre′tive** *adj.* **—con·cre′tive·ly** *adv.*
con·cre·tize (kon′kri·tīz, kong′-) *v.t.* **·tized, ·tiz·ing** To present in concrete terms; to render vivid or specific.
con·cre·tor (kon′krə·tər, kon·krē′tər) *n.* An apparatus for evaporating sugarcane juice and bringing it to a solid mass.
con·cu·bi·nage (kon·kyōō′bə·nij) *n.* **1** The state of being a concubine or of having concubines. **2** Habitual cohabitation without marriage.
con·cu·bine (kong′kyə·bīn, kon′-) *n.* **1** A woman who cohabits with a man without a marriage bond. **2** In certain polygamous societies, a secondary wife. **3** *Obs.* A paramour. [<F <L *concubina,* fem. of *concubinus* < *concumbere* <*com-* with + *cumbere* lie] **—con·cu·bi·nal** (kon·kyōō′bə·nəl), **con·cu′bi·nar′y** (-ner′ē) *adj.*
con·cu·bi·tant (kən·kyōō′bə·tənt) *n. Anthropol.* One whose status at birth carries with it marriage ability with another according to a degree of consanguinity. [<L *concubit-,* stem of *concumbere* lie together + -ANT]
con·cu·pis·cence (kon·kyōō′pə·səns) *n.* **1** Undue or illicit sexual desire; lust. **2** Any inordinate appetite or desire. See synonyms under DESIRE.
con·cu·pis·cent (kon·kyōō′pə·sənt) *adj.* Lustful; carnal; sensual. Also **con·cu·pis·ci·ble** (kon·kyōō′pi·sə·bəl). [<L *concupiscens, -entis,* ppr. of *concupiscere,* inceptive of *concupere* < *com-* thoroughly + *cupere* desire]
con·cur (kən·kûr′) *v.i.* **·curred, ·cur·ring 1** To agree, as in opinion or action; cooperate or combine. **2** To happen at the same time; coincide. **3** To converge to a point, as lines. See synonyms under AGREE, ASSENT. [<L *concurrere* <*com-* together + *currere* run]
con·cur·rence (kən·kûr′əns) *n.* **1** Combination or cooperation. **2** Agreement; approval. **3** A simultaneous occurrence; coincidence. **4** *Geom.* The point where three or more lines meet. **5** Competition; rivalry. **6** *Law* A power jointly held or a claim jointly shared. Also **con·cur′ren·cy.** See synonyms under HARMONY.
con·cur·rent (kən·kûr′ənt) *adj.* **1** Occurring or acting together; meeting in the same point. **2** United in action or application; coordinate; concomitant: *concurrent* remedies or jurisdiction. *—n.* **1** A person or thing that concurs. **2** One proceeding toward the same end or purpose. **3** A rival; competitor. See synonyms under INCIDENTAL. [<L *concurrens, -entis,* pp. of *concurrere.* See CONCUR.] **—con·cur′rent·ly** *adv.*
con·cuss (kən·kus′) *v.t.* **1** To affect or injure (the brain) by concussion. **2** *Scot.* To force or intimidate into action. **3** To agitate; shake. [<L *concussus,* pp. of *concutere* < *com-* together + *quatere* strike, beat]
con·cus·sion (kən·kush′ən) *n.* **1** A violent

shaking; shock; jar. **2** *Pathol.* A violent shock to some organ by a fall or sudden blow; also, the condition resulting from it. See synonyms under BLOW, COLLISION. [<L *concussio, -onis* <*concutere.* See CONCUSS.] **—con·cus′sion·al** *adj.* **—con·cus·sive** (kən·kus′iv) *adj.*

Con·dé (kôn·dā′), **Prince de,** 1621–86, Louis II de Bourbon, Prince d'Enghien, French general: called "the Great Condé."

con·demn (kən·dem′) *v.t.* **1** To express opinion against; hold or prove to be wrong; censure. **2** To pronounce judicial sentence against. **3** To forbid the use of, commonly by official order, as something unfit. **4** *U.S. Law* To appropriate for public use by judicial decree; declare forfeited. **5** To pronounce hopeless; give up as incurable. **6** To close up, or to withdraw from public use, as a door, gate, or road. **7** *Obs.* To convict. [<L *condemnare* <*com-* thoroughly + *damnare* condemn] **—con·dem·na·ble** (kən·dem′nə·bəl) *adj.* **—con·dem·na·to·ry** (kən·dem′nə·tôr′ē,-tō′rē) *adj.* **—con·demn·er** (kən·dem′ər) *n.*

Synonyms: blame, censure, convict, denounce, doom, reprobate, reprove, sentence. To *condemn* is to pass judicial sentence or render judgment or decision against. *Condemn* is more final than *blame* or *censure*; a *condemned* criminal has had his trial. A person is *convicted* when his guilt is made clearly manifest; in legal usage one is said to be *convicted* only by the verdict of a jury. To *denounce* is to make public or official declaration against, especially in a violent and threatening manner. Compare ARRAIGN, BLAME, REPROVE. *Antonyms*: absolve, acquit, applaud, approve, exonerate, justify, pardon.

con·dem·na·tion (kon′dem·nā′shən) *n.* **1** The act of condemning, or the state of being condemned. **2** The cause or occasion of condemnation. See synonyms under REPROOF. [<L *condemnatio, -onis* <*condemnare* CONDEMN]

con·den·sate (kən·den′sāt) *adj.* Condensed. *—n.* **1** A product of condensation. **2** *Physics* The liquid obtained by condensing the vapor in which it is suspended. [<L *condensatus,* pp. of *condensare.* See CONDENSE.]

con·den·sa·tion (kon′den·sā′shən) *n.* **1** The act of making dense or denser, or the state of being condensed. **2** Any product of condensing. **3** *Physics* The reduction of a vapor or gas to a liquid or a solid, or of a liquid to a solid or semisolid. **4** *Chem.* The rearrangement of atoms to form a molecule of greater weight, density, or complexity. **5** *Psychol.* A fusion of events, thoughts, elements of speech, individuals, pictures, etc., as in dreams. Compare CONDENSE. See synonyms under ABBREVIATION. **—con·dens′a·tive** *adj.*

con·den·sa·tor (kon′den·sā′tər) *n.* A condenser.

con·dense (kən·dens′) *v.* **·densed, ·dens·ing** *v.t.* **1** To compress or make dense; consolidate. **2** To abridge or make concise; epitomize, as an essay. **3** To change from the gaseous or vaporous to the liquid or solid state, as by cooling or compression. *—v.i.* **4** To become condensed. See synonyms under ABBREVIATE, REDUCE. [<L *condensare* <*condensus* thick <*com-* together + *densus* crowded, close] **—con·dens′a·bil′i·ty** *n.* **—con·dens′a·ble** or **con·dens′i·ble** *adj.*

condensed milk Cow's milk, sweetened, and thickened by evaporation of its water content.

con·dens·er (kən·den′sər) *n.* **1** One who or that which condenses. **2** Any device for reducing a vapor to liquid by removing from the vapor its heat of evaporation, as in a steam-power plant. **3** *Electr.* An arrangement of insulated conductors and dielectrics for the accumulation of an electric charge: used to block the flow of a direct current and to modify the capacity of an electric circuit. **4** *Optics* A combination of lenses for the effective condensation of light rays.

con·de·scend (kon′di·send′) *v.i.* **1** To stoop from a position of rank or dignity; come down to equal terms with an inferior. **2** To behave as if conscious of this stooping; patronize. **3** To lower or degrade oneself. **4** *Rare* To be gracious or affable. [<F *condescendre* <LL *condescendere* <*com-* together + *descendere* stoop. See DESCEND.]

con·de·scen·dence (kon′di·sen′dəns) *n.* **1** In Scots law, a plaintiff's statement of facts. **2** Condescension.

con·de·scend·ing (kon′di·sen′ding) *adj.* Showing condescension; especially, patronizing.

con·de·scen·sion (kon′di·sen′shən) *n.* **1** An act or instance of condescending. **2** Patronizing courtesy toward inferiors. See synonyms under FAVOR. [<LL *condescensio, -onis* <*condescendere.* See CONDESCEND.]

con·dign (kən·dīn′) *adj.* **1** Well-deserved; merited; deserved: said of punishment. **2** *Obs.* Deserving. [<F *condigne* <L *condignus* <*com-* thoroughly + *dignus* worthy] **—con·dign′ly** *adv.* **—con·dign′ness** *n.*

con·di·ment (kon′də·mənt) *n.* A sauce, relish, spice, etc. [<L *condimentum*]

con·di·tion (kən·dish′ən) *n.* **1** The state or mode in which a person or thing exists. **2** State of health; especially, a favorable or sound state of health. **3** A modifying circumstance. **4** An event, fact, or the like that is necessary to the occurrence of some other, though not its cause; a prerequisite. **5** Something required as prerequisite to a promise or to its fulfilment. **6** A grade or rank; especially, high social position. **7** *Gram.* That clause of a conditional sentence usually introduced by *if, unless,* etc. **8** A conditional proposition upon which another proposition depends as consequent. **9** *U.S.* **a** A requirement that a student who has not done satisfactory work in a college or university course do additional work to avoid failing the course. **b** A grade, often indicated by E, signifying this requirement. *—v.t.* **1** To place a stipulation or stipulations upon; prescribe. **2** To be the stipulation of or prerequisite to. **3** To specify as a stipulation or requirement. **4** To render fit. **5** *Psychol.* To train to a behavior pattern or conditioned response. **6** *U.S.* To subject (a student) to a condition. *—v.i.* **7** To stipulate. [<L *condicio, -onis* agreement <*condicere* <*com-* together + *dicere* say] **—con·di′tion·er** *n.*

con·di·tion·al (kən·dish′ən·əl) *adj.* **1** Expressing or imposing conditions: not absolute. **2** *Gram.* Expressing or implying a condition; a *conditional* clause. *—n. Gram.* A word, tense, clause, or mood expressive of a condition. **—con·di·tion·al·i·ty** (kən·dish′ən·al′ə·tē) *n.* **—con·di′tion·al·ly** *adv.*

con·di·tioned (kən·dish′ənd) *adj.* **1** Limited by or subjected to conditions or stipulations. **2** Circumstanced; placed. **3** *Psychol.* **a** Trained to give an identical response to a given stimulus. **b** Responsive to related stimuli. **4** Accustomed (to). **5** So treated or trained as to be in good condition for some task or contest.

conditioned response *Psychol.* A type of learned response elicited by a stimulus which, though originally ineffective, has fully replaced the normal or natural stimulus after a period of close and repeated juxtaposition with it. Also **conditioned reflex.**

con·di·ti·o si·ne qua non (kən·dish′ē·ō sī′nē kwā non′) *Latin* An indispensable condition.

con·do (kon′dō) *n. U.S. Colloq.* Condominium (def.3).

con·dole (kən·dōl′) *v.* **·doled, ·dol·ing** *v.i.* To grieve or express sympathy with one in affliction: with *with.* *—v.t. Rare* To grieve over with another; bewail. [<LL *condolere* <*com-* together + *dolere* grieve] **—con·do·la·to·ry** (kən·dō′lə·tôr′ē, -tō′rē) *adj.* **—con·dol′er** *n.*

con·do·lence (kən·dō′ləns) *n.* **1** Expression of sympathy with a person in pain, sorrow, or misfortune. **2** *Obs.* Lamentation. Also **con·dole′·ment.**

con do·lo·re (kōn dō·lō′rā) *Music* With sorrow; sadly. [Ital.]

con·dom (kon′dəm, kun′-) *n.* A membranous penile sheath of rubber or similar material, having an anti-venereal or contraceptive function: also spelled *cundum.* [? Alter. of *Conton,* an 18th c. English physician said to have invented it.]

con·do·min·i·um (kon′də·min′ē·əm) *n.* **1** Joint government; joint sovereignty, as over property. **2** *Law* A territory jointly governed by several states under international law. **3** *U.S.* An apartment house in which the units are owned separately by individuals and not by a corporation or cooperative; also, an apartment in such a building. [<NL <L *com-* together + *dominium* rule]

Con·don (kon′dən), **Edward U(hler),** 1902–74, U.S. physicist.

con·done (kən·dōn′) *v.t.* **·doned, ·don·ing** To treat (an offense) as overlooked or forgiven; forgive, See synonyms under PARDON. [<L *condonare* <*com-* thoroughly + *donare* give] **—con·do·na·tion** (kon′dō·nā′shən), **con·done′·ment** *n.* **—con·don′er** *n.*

con·dor (kon′dər) *n.* **1** A vulture of the high Andes *(Vultur gryphus),* characterized by a fleshy comb and a white downy neck ruff: it is one of the largest birds with the power of flight. **2** The California vulture *(Gymnogyps californianus).* [<Sp. <Quechua *cuntur*]

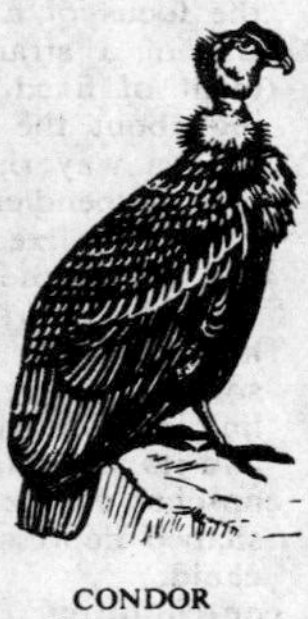

CONDOR (Wing spread 8 1/2 to 10 1/2 feet)

Con·dor·cet (kôn·dôr·se′), **Marquis de,** 1743–94, Marie Jean Caritat, French mathematician and philosopher.

con·dot·tie·re (kōn′dōt·tyâ′·rā) *n. pl.* **·ri** (-rē) **1** A hireling military chief of the14th and 15th centuries. **2** A freelance; adventurer. [<Ital. <*condotto* a mercenary <L *conductus* hired. See CONDUCT.]

con·duce (kən·do͞os′ -dyo͞os′) *v.i.* **·duced, ·duc·ing** To help or tend toward a result; contribute. [<L *conducere* bring together. See CONDUCT.] **—con·duc′er** *n.* **—con·du′ci·ble** *adj.* **—con·du′ci·bil′i·ty, con·du′ci·ble·ness** *n.* **—con·du′ci·bly** *adv.*

con·du·cive (kən·do͞o′siv, -dyo͞o′-) *adj.* Contributing; leading; helping: with *to.* Also **con·du·cent** (kən·do͞o′sənt, -dyo͞o′-). **—con·du′cive·ly** *adv.* **—con·du′cive·ness** *n.*

con·duct (kən·dukt′) *v.t.* **1** To accompany and show the way; guide; escort. **2** To manage or control. **3** To direct and lead the performance of. **4** To serve as a medium of transmission for; convey; transmit, as electricity. **5** To act or behave: reflexive *—v.i.* **6** To serve as a conductor. **7** To direct or lead. *—n.* (kon′dukt) **1** One's course of action; behavior. **2** The act of managing; direction; control; skilful management. **3** The action of leading; escort; convoy. [<L *conductus,* pp. of *conducere* <*com-* together + *ducere* lead] **—con·duct′i·bil′i·ty** *n.* **—con·duct′i·ble** *adj.*

con·duc·tance (kən·duk′təns) *n. Electr.* A measure of the ability of a circuit or circuit element to carry current that is effective in producing power, equal to the ratio of the resistance to the square of the magnitude of the impedance: expressed in mhos. Symbol *g, G*

con·duc·tion (kən·duk′shən) *n.* **1** *Physics* The transmission of heat, sound, or electricity through matter without bulk motion of the matter: distinguished from *convection.* **2** *Physiol.* The transference of a stimulus along the nerve fibers from the point of irritation to the nerve center. **3** Transmission or conveyance in general.

con·duc·ti·tious (kon′duk·tish′əs) *adj.* Employed for wages; kept for hire.

con·duc·tive (kən·duk′tiv) *adj.* **1** Having the power of conducting. **2** Proceeding by or resulting from conduction.

con·duc·tiv·i·ty (kon′duk·tiv′ə·tē) *n.* **1** *Physics* The capacity of a substance or body to transmit light, heat, or electricity. **2** *Electr.* The conductance between opposite parallel faces of a given material of unit length and cross-section. **3** *Physiol.* The property of nerve fibers by which they conduct stimuli.

con·duc·tor (kən·duk′tər) *n.* **1** One who or that which leads or shows the way; an escort; guide. **2** An officer of a railroad who has charge of a train or car and collects tickets and fares. **3** Any manager or director of a movement or operation; especially, the director of an orchestra or chorus. **4** Any conducting medium, material, or device; a conduit. **5** Any body or medium having sensible conductivity for electricity or heat. **6** A lightning rod. **—con·duc′tor·ship** *n.***—con·duc′tress** *n. fem.*

con·duit (kon′dit, -do͞o·it) *n.* **1** A means for conducting something, as a tube or pipe for a fluid; an aqueduct. **2** A passage or subway for electric wires, underground cables, gas and water pipes, or the like. **3** A fountain or a reservoir. [<F <*conduire* <L *conducere.* See CONDUCT.]

con·du·pli·cate (kon·do͞o′plə·kit, -dyo͞o′-) *adj. Bot.* Doubled together: said of leaves and coty-

con·dyle (kon′dil) *n. Anat.* **1** An enlarged, rounded prominence on the end of a bone, usually associated with a joint. **2** Any process by which an appendage is articulated in a depression or cavity, as the head to the base of the mandible. [<F <L *condylus* knuckle <Gk. *kondylos*] —**con·dy·lar** (kon′də·lər) *adj.*

con·dy·loid (kon′də·loid) *adj.* Resembling or connected with a condyle.

con·dy·lo·ma (kon′də·lō′mə) *n. pl.* **·ma·ta** (-mə·tə) *Pathol.* An indolent wartlike growth, sometimes syphilitic, usually near the anus and external genitals of either sex. —**con·dy·lom·a·tous** (kon′də·lom′ə·təs, -lō′mə·təs) *adj.*

cone (kōn) *n.* **1** A solid figure that tapers uniformly from a circular base to a point. **2** *Geom.* A solid whose surface is generated by the turning of a straight line on a fixed point, called the *vertex*, and intersecting a closed plane curve at all points on the circumference. **3** *Bot.* A dry multiple fruit, as of the pine, composed of scales arranged symmetrically around an axis and enclosing seeds. **4** *Mech.* Any of several conical instruments or parts as either of the two taper drums in the head stock of a spinning mule. **5** *Physiol.* One of the specialized, photosensitive cells in the retina of the eye concerned with the perception of color and with daylight vision. **6** A cone-shaped pastry shell used to hold a ball of ice-cream. —*v.t.* & *v.i.* **coned**, **con·ing** To shape or be shaped conically. [<L *conus* <Gk. *kōnos*]

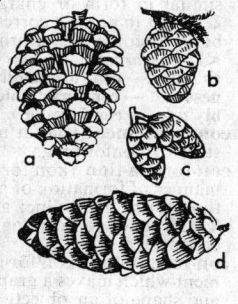

CONES
a. Stone pine.
b. California big tree.
c. Eastern hemlock.
d. Red spruce.

cone·flow·er (kōn′flou′ər) *n.* **1** Any of several hardy annual and perennial plants of the composite family, having a broadly conical disk of dark-brown chaff and flowers. **2** A rudbeckia.

con·el·rad (kon′əl·rad) *n. Aeron.* A technique for deliberately scrambling radio signals from separate stations so as to prevent enemy aircraft from using the signals of any one station as a navigation aid or for information: used in civil defense. [< *con(trol of) el(ectromagnetic) rad(iation)*]

cone-nose (kōn′nōz′) *n.* **1** A large hemipterous insect (genus *Triatoma*): the bloodsucking *cone-nose* (*T. sanguisuga*) of the United States. **2** An assassin bug.

cone of dispersion *Mil.* The conical pattern formed by the trajectories of several shots fired from one gun with the same sight setting: differences in the paths of flight are caused by gun vibration, discrepancies in ammunition, shifts in the wind, etc. Also **cone of fire.**

cone of silence *Telecom.* A small area resembling an inverted cone extending upward from a radio transmitting station, within the limits of which signals from that station are inaudible or blurred: also called *null.*

co·ne·pa·te (kō′nā·pä′tā) *n.* A white-backed, tropical American skunk (genus *Conepatus*); specifically, the hog-nosed skunk (*C. mesoleucus*) of South and Central America. Also **co·ne·pa·tl** (kō′nā·pät′l). [<Nahuatl *conepatl* < *conetl* small + *epatl* fox]

Con·es·to·ga wagon (kon′is·tō′gə) A covered wagon with broad wheels, used by American pioneers for prairie traveling. [from *Conestoga*, Pa., where first made]

co·ney (kō′nē, kun′ē) See CONY.

Co·ney Island (kō′nē) A seaside resort and amusement center in Brooklyn borough of New York City.

con·fab·u·late (kən·fab′yə·lāt) *v.i.* **·lat·ed**, **·lat·ing** **1** To chat; gossip, converse. **2** *Psychol.* To compensate for loss or impairment of memory by fabrication or invention of details. Also **con·fab** (kon′fab). [<L *confabulatus*, pp. of *confabulari* < *com-* together + *fabulari* chat <*fabula* story] —**con·fab′u·la′-**

tion, con′fab *n.* —**con·fab·u·la·to·ry** (kən·fab′yə·lə·tôr′ē, -tō′rē) *adj.*

con·far·re·a·tion (kon·far′ē·ā′shən) *n.* In ancient Rome, the patrician religious form of marriage, in which a cake of spelt was offered to Jupiter before the pontifex maximus and the flamens of Jupiter. [<L *confarreatio, -onis* < *confarreare* marry solemnly < *com-* together + *farreum* cake of spelt <*far* grain, wheat]

con·fect (kən·fekt′) *v.t.* **1** To make into a confection; preserve; prepare. **2** To construct or put together. —*n.* (kon′fekt) A confection. [<L *confectus*, pp. of *conficere* < *com-* together + *facere* make. Related to COMFIT.]

con·fec·tion (kən·fek′shən) *n.* **1** Any mixing or compounding; also, the article produced by either process. **2** An article of confectionery; a sweetmeat. **3** Any medicated conserve or sweetmeat; an electuary; also, any compound of drugs or spices. **4** An attractive, stylish article of dress for women. —*v.t.* To make up into a confection. [<F <L *confectio, -onis* < *conficere*. See CONFECT.]

con·fec·tion·ar·y (kən·fek′shən·er′ē) *adj.* Of, pertaining to, or like confections or confectionery. —*n. pl.* **·ies** **1** A confectioner. **2** A sweetmeat. **3** *Obs.* A room or shop where confections are prepared; a confectionery.

con·fec·tion·er (kən·fek′shən·ər) *n.* One who makes or deals in confectionery.

con·fec·tion·er·y (kən·fek′shən·er′ē) *n. pl.* **·er·ies** **1** Candies, sweetmeats, etc., collectively. **2** A confectioner's shop or the business or trade of a confectioner.

con·fed·er·a·cy (kən·fed′ər·ə·sē) *n. pl.* **·cies** **1** A number of states or persons in league with each other; league; confederation: the *Confederacy* of the Southern States. **2** *Law* An unlawful combination; conspiracy. See synonyms under ALLIANCE, ASSOCIATION, CABAL. —**Southern Confederacy** The Confederate States of America: also **the Confederacy.** [<AF *confederacie* <L *confoederatio* < *confoederare*. See CONFEDERATE.]

con·fed·er·ate (kən·fed′ər·it) *n.* One who is united with another or others in a league or plot; an associate; accomplice. See synonyms under ACCESSORY, AUXILIARY. —*adj.* Associated in a confederacy; united or allied by treaty. —*v.t.* & *v.i.* (kən·fed′ə·rāt) **·at·ed**, **·at·ing** To form together or join with in a league, confederacy, or conspiracy. [<LL *confoederatus*, pp. of *confoederare* join in a league < *com-* together + *foedus* league] —**con·fed′er·a·tive** *adj.*

Con·fed·er·ate (kən·fed′ər·it) *adj.* Pertaining to the **Confederate States of America**, a league of eleven southern States of the American Union that seceded from the United

THE CONFEDERATE STATES OF AMERICA

(map showing: VA., N.C., TENN., ARK., S.C., MISS., GA., ALA., ATLANTIC OCEAN, TEXAS, LA., FLA., MEXICO, GULF OF MEXICO)

States in 1860–61. They were South Carolina, Mississippi, Florida, Alabama, Georgia, Louisiana, Texas, Virginia, Arkansas, Tennessee, and North Carolina. —*n.* An adherent, soldier, or sailor of the Confederate States of America.

con·fed·er·a·tion (kən·fed′ə·rā′shən) *n.* **1** The act of confederating. **2** A confederacy. See synonyms under ALLIANCE, ASSOCIATION. —**the Confederation** The union of the American colonies, 1781–89, under the Articles of Confederation.

con·fer (kən·fûr′) *v.* **·ferred**, **·fer·ring** *v.t.* **1** To grant as a gift or benefit; bestow. **2** *Obs.* To collate; compare. —*v.i.* **3** To hold confer-

ence; consult. See synonyms under CONSULT, DELIBERATE, GIVE. [<L *conferre* < *com-* together + *ferre* bring, carry] —**con·fer′ment** *n.* —**con·fer′ra·ble** *adj.* —**con·fer′rer** *n.*

con·fer·ee (kon′fə·rē′) *n.* **1** A person with whom another confers. **2** A person upon whom some honor, degree, etc., is conferred.

con·fer·ence (kon′fər·əns, -frəns) *n.* **1** A formal meeting for counsel or discussion; an official council, as of two branches of a legislature. **2** Conversation; discourse. **3** *U.S.* One of several orders of assemblies of preachers and laymen of the Methodist Episcopal Church: the Annual *Conference*; the General *Conference*; the District *Conference*. **4** A local organization representing the Congregational churches of a district. **5** The act of bestowing; conferment. **6** A league or association, as of athletic teams. See synonyms under ASSEMBLY, COMPANY, CONVERSATION. [<MF *conférence* <Med. L *conferentia* <L *conferre*. See CONFER.] —**con·fer·en·tial** (kon′fə·ren′shəl) *adj.*

con·fer·va (kən·fûr′və) *n. pl.* **·vae** (-vē) or **·vas** *Bot.* Any member of a genus (*Tribonema*) of greenish, threadlike, fresh-water algae [<L] —**con·fer′val**, **con·fer′void**, **con·fer′vous** *adj.*

con·fer·vite (kən·fûr′vīt) *n. Bot.* A fossil plant allied to the aquatic confervae and found chiefly in the formations of the Cretaceous period.

con·fess (kən·fes′) *v.t.* **1** To acknowledge or admit, as a fault, guilt, or debt. **2** To acknowledge belief or faith in. **3** *Eccl.* **a** To admit or make known (one's sins), especially to a priest, to obtain absolution. **b** To hear the confession of: said of a priest. **4** To concede or admit to be true. **5** *Poetic* To demonstrate or make manifest. —*v.i.* **6** To make acknowledgment of, as a fault, crime, or error. **7** To make confession to a priest. [<F *confesser* <L *confessus*, pp. of *confiteri* < *com-* thoroughly + *fateri* own, declare]
Synonyms: accept, acknowledge, admit, allow, avow, certify, concede, disclose, endorse, grant, own, recognize. We *accept* another's statement; *admit* any point made against us; *acknowledge* what we have said or done, good or bad; *avow* our individual beliefs or feelings; *certify* to facts within our knowledge; *confess* our own faults; *endorse* a friend's note or statement; *grant* a request; *own* our faults or obligations; *recognize* lawful authority; *concede* a claim, demand, etc. The chief present use of *confess* is in the sense of making known to others one's own error or wrong-doing; as, to *confess* a crime. *Acknowledge* may be used as a milder word in this sense, but is more freely used of matters not involving error or fault: I *acknowledge* my signature, the receipt of a letter, a check, etc. *Own* commonly indicates a somewhat reluctant acknowledgment. *Admit* and *concede* have a similar suggestion of reluctance or of possible objection. See ACKNOWLEDGE, AVOW. Compare APOLOGY. *Antonyms:* cloak, conceal, cover, deny, disavow, disguise, disown, dissemble, dissimulate, hide, mask, repudiate, screen, secrete, veil.

con·fess·ed·ly (kən·fes′id·lē) *adv.* By admission or confession; indisputably.

con·fes·sion (kən·fesh′ən) *n.* **1** The act of confessing; the avowal or acknowledgment of an action, especially of one that is inculpatory or sinful; admission: a *confession* of crime. **2** An acknowledgment of belief (in another); recognition of a relation (to another): *confession* of Christ. **3** *Law* A voluntary declaration or acknowledgment by a party against whom some misdeed or default is alleged in respect of such allegation. **4** A formulary of faith: also called **confession of faith.** **5** A formulary of public worship embodying a general admission of common sinfulness, used in the Roman Catholic, Anglican, and other liturgies. **6** The contrite acknowledgment to a priest of any sins committed: a part of the sacrament of penance and a condition of absolution: called in full **sacramental** or **auricular confession.** **7** An organization, as a church or communion, using a confession of faith. **8** The tomb of a martyred Christian; also, an altar over such a tomb or the basilica in which the altar stood; an altar-tomb con-

fessionary. See synonyms under APOLOGY.
con·fes·sion·al (kən·fesh′ən·əl) *adj.* Pertaining to a confession. — *n.* **1** A cabinet in a church where a priest hears confessions. **2** The act, performance, or practice of confession before a priest.
con·fes·sion·ar·y (kən·fesh′ən·er′ē) *adj.* & *n. pl.* **·ar·ies** Confessional.
con·fes·sor (kən·fes′ər) *n.* **1** A priest who hears confessions; a spiritual adviser, as of a sovereign. **2** One who confesses or admits anything, as a crime. **3** One who confesses his faith in Christianity, especially in the face of persecution. Also **con·fess′er.** — **con·fes′·sor·ship** *n.*
con·fet·ti (kən·fet′ē) *n. pl.* **1** Small pieces of brightly colored paper thrown about at carnivals, weddings, etc. **2** Bonbons. [<Ital., pl. of *confetto* confection]
con·fi·dant (kon′fə·dant′, kon′fə·dant) *n.* A person to whom secrets are entrusted. [<F *confident* <Ital. *confidente* <L *confidens.* See CONFIDE.] — **con′fi·dante′** *n. fem.*
con·fide (kən·fīd′) *v.* **·fid·ed, ·fid·ing** *v.t.* **1** To reveal in trust or confidence. **2** To put into one's trust or keeping. — *v.i.* **3** To have faith or trust: often with *in.* See synonyms under COMMIT, TRUST. [<L *confidere* <*com-* thoroughly + *fidere* trust] — **con·fid′er** *n.*
con·fi·dence (kon′fə·dəns) *n.* **1** Trust in or reliance upon something or someone; belief in a person or thing. **2** Assurance; presumption. **3** Self-reliance; hence, courage or boldness. **4** Private conversation or communication; a secret. **5** *Obs.* That in which one confides. See synonyms under ASSURANCE, BELIEF, CERTAINTY, FAITH.
confidence game A swindle in which the swindler first wins the confidence of his victim and then defrauds him. Also **confidence trick,** *Colloq.* **con game.**
confidence man One who practices or promotes a confidence game.
con·fi·dent (kon′fə·dənt) *adj.* **1** Having confidence; assured; self-reliant. **2** *Obs.* Forward; impudent. See synonyms under SANGUINE, SECURE, SURE. — *n.* A confidant. [<L *confidens, -entis,* ppr. of *confidere.* See CONFIDE.] — **con′fi·dent·ly** *adv.*
con·fi·den·tial (kon′fə·den′shəl) *adj.* **1** Having secret or private relations; trusted; intimate: a *confidential* clerk. **2** Imparted in confidence; secret: *confidential* information. **3** Disposed to confide in another. **4** *U.S.* Denoting defense information classified next above "for official use only": the next lowest classification. Compare TOP-SECRET, SECRET (*adj.* def. 5). — **con·fi·den·ti·al·i·ty** (kon′fə·den′shē·al′ə·tē), **con′fi·den′tial·ness** *n.*
con·fi·den·tial·ly (kon′fə·den′shəl·ē) *adv.* **1** In a confidential manner: He spoke *confidentially.* **2** Regarding (the following or preceding statement) as a confidence: in function like an adverbial clause modifying a whole sentence: *Confidentially,* he's always late.
con·fid·ing (kən·fī′ding) *adj.* Unsuspicious; trustful. — **con·fid′ing·ly** *adv.* — **con·fid′ing·ness** *n.*
con·fig·u·rate (kən·fig′yə·rāt) *v.* **·rat·ed, ·rat·ing** *v.t.* To give shape or fashion to. — *v.i.* To be congruous. [<LL *configuratus,* pp. of *configurare.* See CONFIGURE.]
con·fig·u·ra·tion (kən·fig′yə·rā′shən) *n.* **1** Structural arrangement; conformation; contour. **2** *Psychol.* In the Gestalt theory, a static or dynamic aggregate of sensations, feelings, reflexes, and ideas so organized as to function as a unit in individual behavior. **3** *Physics* The spatial arrangement of atoms in a molecule or of nucleons and electrons in an atom. — **con·fig′u·ra′tion·ism** *n.*
con·fine (kən·fīn′) *v.* **·fined, ·fin·ing** *v.t.* **1** To shut within an enclosure; imprison. **2** To restrain or oblige to stay within doors. **3** To hold or keep within limits; restrict: to *confine* remarks. — *v.i.* **4** *Obs.* To border; abut. See synonyms under CIRCUMSCRIBE, LIMIT, RESTRAIN. — *n.* **1** *Usually pl.* A boundary; limit; border; frontier. **2** *Obs.* A prison. **3** *Obs.* Region, territory, or district. See synonyms under BOUNDARY, MARGIN. [<F *confiner* <Ital. *confinare* <L *confinis* bordering <*com-* together + *finis* border] — **con·fin′a·ble** *adj.* — **con·fin′er** *n.*
con·fined (kən·fīnd′) *adj.* **1** Limited; restricted. **2** In childbed.
con·fine·ment (kən·fīn′mənt) *n.* **1** The state of being confined; restriction; imprisonment. **2** Accouchement; the state of being in childbed.
con·firm (kən·fûrm′) *v.t.* **1** To assure by added proof; corroborate; verify; make certain. **2** To add firmness to; strengthen. **3** *Law* To ratify; sanction. **4** To establish in office. **5** To receive into the church by confirmation. [<OF *confermer* <L *confirmare* strengthen <*com-* thoroughly + *firmus* strong] — **con·firm′a·ble, con·firm′a·tive, con·firm·a·to·ry** (kən·fûr′mə·tôr′ē, -tō′rē) *adj.* — **con·firm′er** *n.*
Synonyms: assure, corroborate, establish, fix, prove, ratify, sanction, settle, strengthen, substantiate, sustain, uphold. *Confirm* means to add firmness or give stability to. Both *confirm* and *corroborate* presuppose something already existing to which the confirmation or corroboration is added. Testimony is *corroborated* by concurrent testimony or by circumstances; *confirmed* by *established* facts. That which is thoroughly *proved* is said to be *established*; so is that which is official and has adequate power behind it; as, the *established* government. The continents are *fixed.* A treaty is *ratified*; an appointment *confirmed.* An act is *sanctioned* by any person or authority that passes upon it approvingly. A statement is *substantiated*; a report *confirmed*; a controversy *settled*; the decision of a lower court *sustained* by a higher. Just government should be *upheld.* See RATIFY. *Antonyms*: abrogate, annul, cancel, destroy, overthrow, shake, shatter, unsettle, upset.
con·fir·ma·tion (kon′fər·mā′shən) *n.* **1** The act of confirming. **2** That which confirms; proof. **3** *Eccl.* A sacramental rite administered to baptized persons, confirming or strengthening their faith, and admitting them to all the privileges of the church. **4** *Law* An instrument that supplies some defect or omission in a former conveyance. See synonyms under PROOF.
con·firmed (kən·fûrmd′) *adj.* Fixed; firmly established; inveterate: a *confirmed* drunkard.
con·fir·mee (kon′fər·mē′) *n.* **1** *Law* One to whom anything is confirmed. **2** One who is confirmed.
con·fir·mor (kon′fər·môr′, kən·fûr′mər) *n. Law* The person who confirms anything, as a title, to a confirmee.
con·fis·cate (kon′fis·kāt) *v.t.* **·cat·ed, ·cat·ing** **1** To appropriate as forfeited to the public use or treasury, usually as a penalty. **2** To appropriate by or as by authority. — *adj.* Appropriated or forfeited. [<L *confiscatus,* pp. of *confiscare* <*com-* together + *fiscus* chest, treasury] — **con·fis·ca·ble** (kən·fis′kə·bəl), **con′fis·cat′a·ble** *adj.* — **con′fis·ca′tion** *n.* — **con′fis·ca′tor** *n.* — **con·fis·ca·to·ry** (kən·fis′kə·tôr′ē, -tō′rē) *adj.*
Con·fit·e·or (kən·fit′ē·ôr) *n.* The general confession said by the celebrant and servers at the beginning of the Roman Catholic mass. [<L, I confess: the first word]
con·fi·ture (kon′fi·chŏŏr) *n.* A confection; a sweet conserve. [<F]
con·fla·grant (kən·flā′grənt) *adj.* Burning fiercely. [<L *conflagrans, -antis,* ppr. of *conflagrare* <*com-* thoroughly + *flagrare* burn]
con·fla·gra·tion (kon′flə·grā′shən) *n.* A great or disastrous fire; destruction by burning. [<L *conflagratio, -onis* <*conflagrare.* See CONFLAGRANT.]
con·flate (kən·flāt′) *v.t.* **·flat·ed, ·flat·ing** **1** To combine from variant readings into a composite reading. **2** To blow together; bring together from diverse sources. — *adj.* **1** Composed of a variety of elements. **2** Blown together. [<L *conflatus,* pp. of *conflare* <*com-* together + *flare* blow] — **con·fla′tion** *n.*
con·flict (kon′flikt) *n.* **1** A struggle to resist or overcome; contest of opposing forces or powers; strife; battle. **2** A state or condition of opposition; antagonism; discord: the *conflict* of testimony. **3** Active antagonism; clash; collision. **4** *Psychoanal.* Painful tension set up by a clash between opposed and contradictory impulses in an individual; specifically, the antagonism existing between primitive desires and instincts and moral, religious, or ethical ideals. — *v.i.* (kən·flikt′) **1** To come into collision; be in mutual opposition; clash. **2** To engage in battle; struggle. [<L *conflictus,* pp. of *confligere* <*com-* together + *fligere* strike] — **con·flic′tion** *n.* — **con·flic′·tive** *adj.*
con·flu·ence (kon′flŏŏ·əns) *n.* **1** *Geog.* A junction of streams; the place where streams flow together. **2** A gathering and mingling. **3** A flocking together; concourse. Also **con·flux** (kon′fluks).
con·flu·ent (kon′flŏŏ·ənt) *adj.* Flowing together so as to form one; blended into one. — *n. Geog.* A stream that unites with another; a branch of a river. [<L *confluens, -entis,* ppr. of *confluere* <*com-* together + *fluere* flow]
con·fo·cal (kon·fō′kəl) *adj.* Having a common focus or common foci.
con·form (kən·fôrm′) *v.t.* **1** To make like or similar in form or character: with *to.* — *v.i.* **2** To act in accord; correspond; comply. **3** To be or become a conformist. [<F *conformer* <L *conformare* <*com-* together + *formare* shape] — **con·form′a·bil′i·ty, con·form′a·ble·ness** *n.* — **con·form′a·ble** *adj.* — **con·form′a·bly** *adv.* — **con·form′er** *n.*
con·form·ance (kən·fôr′məns) *n.* The act or state of conforming.
con·for·ma·tion (kon′fôr·mā′shən) *n.* **1** The manner of formation of a body; general structure, form, or outline; arrangement of parts. **2** The act of conforming, or the state of being conformed.
con·for·ma·tor (kon′fôr·mā′tər) *n.* An instrument which makes a graphic record of the size and shape of an object, as the head or bust.
con·form·ist (kən·fôr′mist) *n.* **1** One who conforms or complies. **2** In English history, one who adheres to the usages of the Established Church: opposed to *dissenter, nonconformist.*
con·form·i·ty (kən·fôr′mə·tē) *n. pl.* **·ties** **1** Correspondence in form, manner, or use; agreement; harmony; congruity. **2** The act or habit of conforming oneself; acquiescence. **3** In English history, adherence to the Church of England. See synonyms under HARMONY.
con·found (kon·found′, kən-) *v.t.* **1** To strike with confusion or amazement; perplex; overwhelm; abash. **2** To confuse with something else; mix. **3** To confuse or mingle (elements, things, or ideas) indistinguishably. **4** (kon′·found′) To imprecate ill upon: used as a mild oath. **5** *Obs.* To waste. **6** *Archaic* To defeat; overthrow; ruin, as an army or nation. See synonyms under ABASH, PERPLEX, REFUTE. [<OF *confondre* <L *confundere.* See CONFUSE.] — **con·found′er** *n.*
con·found·ed (kon·foun′did, kən-) *adj.* **1** Execrable; damned; outrageous: a mild oath. **2** Perplexed; discomfited; confused. — **con·found′ed·ly** *adv.*
con·fra·ter·ni·ty (kon′frə·tûr′nə·tē) *n. pl.* **·ties** **1** An association, brotherhood, or society of men united for a common object or purpose, especially in some profession; any body or class of men. **2** Specifically, a religious association in the Roman Catholic Church, usually of laymen, for some devotional, charitable, or educational object: called *archconfraternity* when composed of affiliated bodies. [<Med. L *confraternitas, -tatis* <LL *com-* with + *fraternitas* brotherhood]
con·frere (kon′frâr) *n.* A colleague; a fellow member of an association, or of a profession or calling. Also *French* **con·frère** (kôṅ·frâr′). [<MF <L *com-* with + *frater* brother]
con·front (kən·frunt′) *v.t.* **1** To stand face to face with; face defiantly. **2** To put face to face: with *with*: to *confront* the accused with the witnesses against him. **3** To compare. See synonyms under OPPOSE. [<F *confronter* <L *com-* together + *frons, frontis* face, forehead] — **con·front′er** *n.* — **con·front′ment** *n.*
con·fron·ta·tion (kon′frən·tā′shən) *n.* **1** The act of confronting, or the state of being confronted. **2** A direct challenge to the power of an opposing group or state, as by affirmation of policy, acts of protest, or acts or threats of violence. **3** A crisis or conflict between opposing political groups or states: events leading to a *confrontation* with China.
Con·fu·cian (kən·fyōō′shən) *adj.* Of or pertaining to Confucius, his teachings, or his followers. — *n.* An adherent of Confucius or his teachings. — **Con·fu′cian·ism** *n.* — **Con·fu′cian·ist** *n.*
Con·fu·cius (kən·fyōō′shəs), 551–478 B.C., Chinese philosopher and teacher, founder of an ethical system based on ancestor worship, devotion to family and friends, and the maintenance of justice and peace: *Chinese* K'ung Fu-tse.

con·fuse (kən·fyōōz′) v.t. ·fused, ·fus·ing 1 To perplex or perturb; confound; bewilder. 2 To throw into disorder; mix indiscriminately; derange: to *confuse* the colors of a picture. 3 To mix in such a way as to make distinction difficult or impossible: He *confused* the dates of the events. 4 *Obs.* To undo; ruin. See synonyms under ABASH, DISPLACE, EMBARRASS, MIX, PERPLEX. [< L *confusus*, pp. of *confundere* < *com-* together + *fundere* pour. Related to CONFOUND.] — **con·fus·ed·ly** (kən·fyōō′zid·lē) adv. — **con·fus′ed·ness** n. — **con·fus′ing·ly** adv.

con·fu·sion (kən·fyōō′zhən) n. 1 The act of confusing, or the state of being confused; perplexity; distraction. 2 Embarrassment; shame; intellectual discomfiture. 3 *Obs.* Destruction; ruin; overthrow. See synonyms under CHAGRIN, DISORDER, PERPLEXITY, TUMULT. — **con·fu′sion·al** adj.

con·fu·ta·tion (kon′fyōō·tā′shən) n. 1 The act of confuting; the process of showing to be false or illogical; disproof. 2 That which shows an argument, etc., to be false or invalid.

con·fute (kən·fyōōt′) v.t. ·fut·ed, ·fut·ing 1 To prove to be false or invalid; refute successfully. 2 To prove (a person) to be in the wrong. 3 To confound. See synonyms under REFUTE. [< L *confutare* check, restrain] — **con·fut′er** n.

con·ga (kong′gə) n. 1 A ballroom dance of Latin-American origin in which the dancers form a winding line. 2 The music for this dance, in fast 4/4 time, with a strongly accented fourth beat. [< Am. Sp.]

Con·ga·ree River (kong′gə·rē′) A river in central South Carolina, flowing SE 50 miles to the Santee River.

con·gé (kon′zhā, *Fr.* kôn·zhā) n. 1 Leave-taking; parting; especially, a formal leave-taking; also, permission to depart. 2 Dismissal. 3 *Obs.* A polite or formal bow. Also called *congee.* [OF *congié* < L *commeatus* leave of absence < *commeare* come and go < *com-* thoroughly + *ire* go]

con·geal (kən·jēl′) v.t. 1 To convert from a fluid to a solid condition, as by freezing or curdling. 2 To clot or coagulate, as blood. — v.i. 3 To become hard, stiff, or viscid. [< MF *congeler* < L *congelare* < *com-* together + *gelare* freeze < *gelum* frost] — **con·geal′a·ble** adj. — **con·geal′ment** n.

con·gee[1] (kon′jē) n. *Anglo-Indian* Rice water; rice gruel or any similar gruel; rice starch.

con·gee[2] (kon·jē′) n. *Rare* Congé. — v.i. ·geed, ·gee·ing To take formal leave; especially, to bow in leaving.

con·ge·la·tion (kon′jə·lā′shən) n. 1 A congealing. 2 A congealed state; clot; concretion. [< L *congelatio, -onis* < *congelare*. See CONGEAL.]

con·ge·ner (kon′jə·nər) n. A fellow member of the same genus, class, family, or kind. [< L, of the same race < *com-* together + *genus, generis* race, kind]

con·ge·ner·ic (kon′jə·ner′ik) adj. Of the same kind, class, or stock; generically allied. Also **con·ge·ner′i·cal, con·gen·er·ous** (kən·jen′ər·əs).

con·ge·net·ic (kon′jə·net′ik) adj. Alike in origin.

con·gen·ial (kən·jēn′yəl) adj. 1 Having similar character or tastes; sympathetic. 2 Suited to one's disposition; agreeable. See synonyms under DELIGHTFUL. [< CON- + GENIAL] — **con·ge·ni·al·i·ty** (kən·jē′nē·al′ə·tē) n. — **con·gen′ial·ly** adv.

con·gen·i·tal (kən·jen′ə·təl) adj. 1 Born with a person; existing at or from birth. 2 Acquired by an individual organism in the course of uterine development subsequent to action by the genes but prior to delivery from the womb: distinguished from *hereditary.* See synonyms under INHERENT. [< L *congenitus* < *com-* together + *genitus*, pp. of *gignere* bear, produce] — **con·gen′i·tal·ly** adv.

con·ger (kong′gər) n. A marine eel (*Conger conger*) from 4 to 10 feet long, used as a food fish. Also **conger eel.** [< OF *congre* < L *conger* < Gk. *gongros*]

con·ge·ries (kon′jə·rēz, kon·jir′ēz) n. pl. ·ge·ries A collection or aggregation of things; an assemblage of bodies; mass; heap. [< L < *congerere.* See CONGEST.]

con·gest (kən·jest′) v.t. 1 To collect or crowd together; overcrowd. 2 *Pathol.* To surcharge an organ or member with blood. 3 *Obs.* To collect; accumulate. — v.i. 4 To become congested. [< L *congestum*, pp. of *congerere* < *com-* together + *gerere* bear, carry] — **con·ges′tive** adj.

con·ges·tion (kən·jes′chən) n. 1 *Pathol.* An excessive accumulation, as of blood in the blood vessels. 2 An overcrowded condition.

con·gi·us (kon′jē·əs) n. pl. **con·gi·i** (kon′jē·ī) An ancient Roman liquid measure, containing 6 sextarii or about 0.75 U.S. gallon. [< L]

con·glo·bate (kon·glō′bāt, kong′glō·bāt) v.t. & v.i. ·bat·ed, ·bat·ing To gather or form into a globe: also **con·globe** (kon·glōb′). — adj. Globular. [< L *conglobatus*, pp. of *conglobare* < *com-* together + *globare* make a ball < *globus* ball]

con·glo·ba·tion (kong′glō·bā′shən) n. 1 The act of conglobating. 2 A spherical body or formation.

con·glom·er·ate (kən·glom′ər·it) adj. 1 Massed or clustered. 2 *Geol.* Consisting of loosely cemented heterogeneous material: *conglomerate* clay. See synonyms under COMPLEX, HETEROGENEOUS. — n. 1 A heterogeneous collection. 2 A large corporation formed by merging a number of separate companies, often in unrelated fields. 3 *Geol.* A rock composed of pebbles or fragments of rock loosely cemented together. — v.t. & v.i. (kən·glom′ə·rāt) ·at·ed, ·at·ing To gather into a cohering mass. [< L *conglomeratus*, pp. of *conglomerare* < *com-* together + *glomus, glomeris* ball] — **con·glom·er·at·ic** (kən·glom′ə·rat′ik) or **con·glom′er·it′ic** (-ə·rit′ik) adj.

con·glom·er·a·tion (kən·glom′ə·rā′shən) n. 1 A conglomerated mass. 2 The act of conglomerating.

con·glu·ti·nant (kən·glōō′tə·nənt) adj. 1 Causing to stick together. 2 *Med.* Healing by adhesion, as the edges of a wound. — n. *Med.* An application for wounds.

con·glu·ti·nate (kən·glōō′tə·nāt) v.t. & v.i. ·nat·ed, ·nat·ing 1 To glue or stick together; adhere. 2 *Med.* To reunite by adhesion, as wounds or fractures. — adj. 1 Glued together; united by adhesion. 2 *Bot.* United as if glued together, but not organically. [< L *conglutinatus*, pp. of *conglutinare* < *com-* together + *glutinare* stick < *gluten* glue] — **con·glu·ti·na′tion** n. — **con·glu·ti·na·tive** adj.

con·glu·ti·nous (kən·glōō′tə·nəs) adj. Causing adhesion; gluelike. — **con·glu′ti·nous·ly** adv.

con·go (kong′gō) n. 1 The congo snake. 2 The mud eel.

Con·go (kong′gō) n. A member of any of numerous Negro and Negroid tribes, mostly of Bantu linguistic stock, inhabiting equatorial and southern Africa. Also **Con·go·lese** (kong′gō·lēz′, -lēs′).

Con·go (kong′gō) One of the world's largest rivers, rising in SE Zaire Republic and flowing 2,900 miles to the South Atlantic.

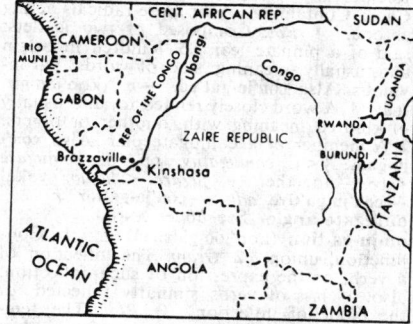

Congo, Democratic Republic of the See ZAIRE REPUBLIC.

Congo Free State A former name for REPUBLIC OF THE CONGO.

Congo group *Chem.* A class of direct dyes from benzidine or tolidine, mostly azo derivatives.

Con·go·lese (kong′gō·lēz′, -lēs′) adj. Pertaining to the region of the Congo or to the people inhabiting it. — n. A native or inhabitant of the Congo region.

Congo red *Chem.* A dye of the Congo group, used in dyeing cotton and wool, and in the making of **Congo paper**, which, used as an indicator, shows red in neutral or alkaline solutions and blue with acids.

Congo Republic An independent republic of the French Community in western equatorial Africa; 139,000 square miles; capital, Brazzaville; formerly *Middle Congo*, a French overseas territory. — **Con′go·lese′** adj. & n.

congo snake A tailed aquatic salamander (*Amphiuma means*) of the SE United States, of elongate eel-like form with rudimentary limbs. Also **congo eel.**

con·gou (kong′gōō) n. A grade of black tea from China, the third picking. Also **con·go** (kong′gō), **con′gu.** [< Chinese *kung-fu*(*ch′a*) labor (tea); tea on which labor has been spent]

con·grat·u·late (kən·grach′ōō·lāt) v.t. ·lat·ed, ·lat·ing 1 To express sympathetic pleasure in the joy, success, or good fortune of (another); felicitate. 2 *Obs.* To salute approvingly; welcome; hail. [< L *congratulatus*, pp. of *congratulari* < *com-* together + *gratulari* rejoice] — **con·grat′u·lant** adj. — **con·grat·u·la·to·ry** (kən·grach′ōō·lə·tôr′ē, -tō′rē) adj.

con·grat·u·la·tion (kən·grach′ōō·lā′shən) n. 1 The act of congratulating. 2 pl. Expressions of pleasure and good wishes on another's fortune or success; congratulatory speech or writing.

con·gre·gant (kong′grə·gənt) n. A member of a congregation; one who joins with others anywhere.

con·gre·gate (kong′grə·gāt) v.t. & v.i. ·gat·ed, ·gat·ing To bring or come together into a crowd; assemble. — adj. (kong′grə·git) 1 Relating to a congregation. 2 Gathered together; collected. [< L *congregatus*, pp. of *congregare* < *com-* together + *gregare* crowd, collect < *grex, gregis* flock] — **con′gre·ga′tive** adj. — **con′gre·ga′tive·ly** adv. — **con′gre·ga′tive·ness** n. — **con′gre·ga′tor** n.

con·gre·ga·tion (kong′grə·gā′shən) n. 1 The act of congregating; the collecting into one mass, body, or assembly; aggregation. 2 An assemblage of people or of things. 3 A group of people met together for worship; also, the body of persons who worship in a local church; a parish. 4 In the Old Testament, the whole body of Israel. 5 *Eccl.* A religious community or order bound by a common rule. 6 Any of several committees of cardinals who administer the departments of the papal government and assist the Pope. 7 In colonial New England, a town or settlement, considered as a religious community. See synonyms under ASSEMBLY, COMPANY. — **con′gre·ga′tion·al** adj.

Con·gre·ga·tion·al (kong′grə·gā′shən·əl) adj. Belonging or pertaining to the **Congregational Christian Churches**, an evangelical Protestant denomination, forming, since 1957, part of the *United Church of Christ.* See INDEPENDENT. — **Con′gre·ga′tion·al·ist** n.

con·gre·ga·tion·al·ism (kong′grə·gā′shən·əl·iz′əm) n. A form of church polity in which each local congregation is autonomous in all ecclesiastical matters.

Congregation of the Holy Office In the Roman Catholic Church, a department of the Curia which defends the faith and supervises morals. See INQUISITION.

con·gress (kong′gris) n. 1 An assembly or conference; a gathering. 2 A coming together; intercourse. 3 Sexual union. — v.i. (kən·gres′) To assemble; meet together. [< L *congressus* a coming together < *congredi* < *com-* together + *gredi* go, move] — **con·gres·sive** (kən·gres′iv) adj.

Con·gress (kong′gris) n. 1 The national legislative body of the United States, consisting of the Senate and the House of Representatives. 2 The legislative body of any of several Central and South American republics, usually consisting of a Senate and a Chamber of Deputies.

congress boot A half-shoe or gaiter, with elastic material in the sides. Also **congress gaiter.**

con·gres·sion·al (kən·gresh′ən·əl) adj. Pertaining to a congress, especially, *cap.*, the United States Congress.

Congressional district That section of a State, determined by population figures, entitled to one representative in Congress.
con·gres·sion·al·ist (kən·gresh′ən·əl·ist) *n.* A supporter or adherent of a congress. Also **con·gres′sion·ist.**
Congressional Medal of Honor See MEDAL OF HONOR.
Congressional Record The printed debates and proceedings of Congress: the official government publication since 1873, replacing the former **Congressional Globe.**
Con·gress·man (kong′gris·mən) *n.* *pl.* **·men** (-mən) A member of the U.S. Congress, particularly of the House of Representatives. — **Con′gress·wom′an** *n. fem.*
Congress of Confederation Continental Congress.
Congress of Industrial Organizations A former affiliation of trade unions founded in 1938: it was originally an offshoot of the American Federation of Labor, and, in 1955, merged with it to form the *AFL–CIO*.
Congress of Vienna A conference of European powers, 1814–15, held after the first exile of Napoleon, and aiming, under Metternich's leadership, at territorial readjustment and restoration of monarchical governments.
Con·greve (kon′grēv, kong′-) *n.* **1** A variety of friction match: short for **Congreve match. 2** A military rocket invented in 1808: short for **Congreve rocket.** [after Sir William *Congreve*, who invented both]
Con·greve (kon′grēv, kong′-), **William,** 1670–1729, English dramatist. — **Sir William,** 1772–1828, English engineer.
con·gru·ence (kong′gro͞o·əns) *n.* Harmony, conformity; agreement. Also **con′gru·en·cy.**
con·gru·ent (kong′gro͞o·ənt) *adj.* **1** Having mutual agreement or conformity; correspondent; appropriate. **2** *Math.* Describing two geometric figures which may be exactly superposed on each other, or two numbers which will give the same remainders when divided by a given quantity called the *modulus.* [<L *congruens, -entis,* ppr. of *congruere* agree] — **con′gru·ent·ly** *adv.*
congruent forms In crystallography, two forms which may be derived from each other by the rotation of the crystal.
con·gru·i·ty (kən·gro͞o′ə·tē) *n.* *pl.* **·ties 1** Agreement; harmoniousness; appropriateness. **2** An example or case of harmoniousness. **3** Geometrical agreement.
con·gru·ous (kong′gro͞o·əs) *adj.* **1** Harmoniously related or combined. **2** Appropriate; consistent. **3** *Math.* Having congruence. [<L *congruus* <*congruere* agree] — **con′gru·ous·ly** *adv.* — **con′gru·ous·ness** *n.*
con·ic (kon′ik) *adj.* **1** Cone-shaped. **2** Relating to or formed by or upon a cone. Also **con′i·cal.** — *n.* A conic section. [<Gk. *kōnikos* <*kōnos* cone] — **con′i·cal·ly** *adv.*
conic projection A type of map in which the terrain is plotted on a cone, the projection then being flattened out to a plane surface.
conic section *Math.* A curve formed by the intersection of a plane with a right circular cone: an ellipse, parabola, or hyperbola, according to the inclination of the cutting plane to the axis.
conic sections That branch of mathematics which treats of the ellipse, parabola, and hyperbola. Also **con′ics.**

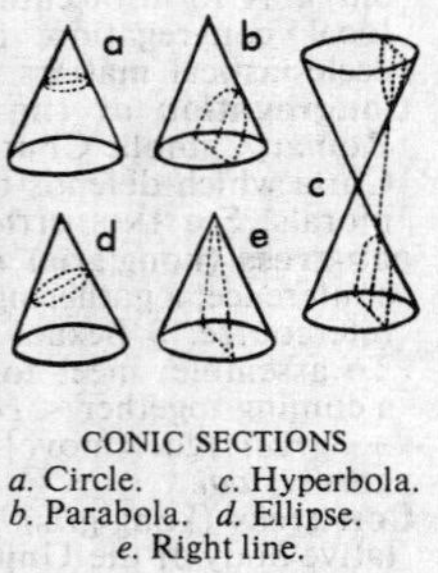

CONIC SECTIONS
a. Circle. *c.* Hyperbola.
b. Parabola. *d.* Ellipse.
e. Right line.

co·nid·i·if·er·ous (kō·nid′ē·if′ər·əs) *adj.* *Bot.* Bearing conidia. Also **co·nid′i·oph′o·rous** (-of′ər·əs). [<CONIDIUM + -FEROUS]
co·nid·i·o·phore (kō·nid′ē·ə·fôr′, -fōr′) *n.* *Bot.* A branch of the hypha in the mycelium of fungi which bears the conidia.
co·nid·i·um (kō·nid′ē·əm) *n.* *pl.* **co·nid·i·a** (kō·nid′ē·ə) *Bot.* A non-sexually produced propagative cell or spore borne upon special branches of the thallus in many species of fungi. Also **co·nid·i·o·spore** (kō·nid′ē·ə·spôr′, -spōr′). [<NL <Gk. *konis* dust] — **co·nid′i·al** *adj.*
con·i·fer (kon′ə·fər, kō′nə-) *n.* Any of an order of evergreen shrubs and trees *(Coniferales)* belonging to the Gymnosperm subdivision of plants, characterized by needle-shaped leaves, strobili or cones, and a resinous wood: includes the pines, spruces, firs, and junipers. [<L <*conus* cone + *ferre* bear]
co·nif·er·in (kō·nif′ər·in) *n.* *Chem.* A crystalline compound, $C_{16}H_{22}O_8 \cdot 2H_2O$, found in the sap of coniferous trees: used in the preparation of vanillin.
co·nif·er·ous (kō·nif′ər·əs) *adj.* **1** Cone-bearing. **2** Containing or composed of conifers: *coniferous* forests.
co·ni·ine (kō′ni·ēn, -nē·in) *n.* *Chem.* A yellowish, oily, volatile alkaloid, $C_8H_{17}N$, contained in poison hemlock *(Conium maculatum)*: a narcotic, sometimes used locally to relieve pain. Also **co·nin** (kō′nin), **co·nine** (kō′nēn). [<CONIUM]
co·ni·ol·o·gy (kō′nē·ol′ə·jē) *n.* The scientific study of dust, especially with reference to its effects upon plant and animal life: also spelled *koniology.* [<Gk. *konis* dust + -LOGY]
co·ni·ros·tral (kō′ni·ros′trəl) *adj.* *Ornithol.* Having a conical beak. [<L *conus* cone + *rostrum* beak]
co·ni·um (kō′nē·əm) *n.* Any of a genus *(Conium)* of tall, highly poisonous, biennial herbs of the parsley family; especially, *C. maculatum,* the poison hemlock. [<L <Gk. *kōneion* hemlock]
con·jec·tur·al (kən·jek′chər·əl) *adj.* **1** Of the nature of or dependent upon conjecture. **2** Given to conjecturing. — **con·jec′tur·al·ly** *adv.*
con·jec·ture (kən·jek′chər) *v.t.* **·tured, ·tur·ing** To conclude or suppose from incomplete evidence; guess; infer. — *v.i.* To make a conjecture. See synonyms under GUESS, SUPPOSE. — *n.* **1** An indecisive opinion; a guess; surmise. **2** The act of conjecturing. **3** *Obs.* Divination; prediction. See synonyms under GUESS, HYPOTHESIS. [<L *conjectura* <*conjicere* <*com-* together + *jacere* throw] — **con·jec′tur·a·ble** *adj.* — **con·jec′tur·a·bly** *adv.* — **con·jec′tur·er** *n.*
con·join (kən·join′) *v.t.* & *v.i.* To join together; associate; connect; unite. See synonyms under UNITE. [<F *conjoindre* <L *conjungere* <*com-* together + *jungere* join]
con·joint (kən·joint′) *adj.* **1** Associated; conjoined. **2** Joint. [<F, pp. of *conjoindre.* See CONJOIN.] — **con·joint′ly** *adv.*
con·ju·gal (kon′jo͞o·gəl) *adj.* Pertaining to marriage; connubial; matrimonial. [<F <L *conjugalis* <*conjunx, conjugis* spouse <*conjungere* join in marriage] — **con·ju·gal·i·ty** (kon′jo͞o·gal′ə·tē) *n.* — **con′ju·gal·ly** *adv.*
con·ju·gate (kon′jo͞o·gāt) *v.* **·gat·ed, ·gat·ing** *v.t.* **1** *Gram.* To give the inflections of: said of verbs. **2** *Rare* To unite or join together; couple, especially in marriage. — *v.i.* **3** *Biol.* To unite in conjugation. **4** *Rare* To unite in sexual intercourse. — *adj.* (kon′jo͞o·git, -gāt) **1** Joined in pairs; coupled; paired. **2** *Math.* Reciprocally related; interchangeable. **3** *Chem.* Containing two or more radicals acting as one. **4** *Bot.* Composed of two leaflets: said of a pinnate leaf. **5** Kindred in origin and, usually, meaning: said of words; paronymous. Also **con′ju·gat′ed.** — *n.* (kon′jo͞o·git, -gāt) **1** A word closely related to, and usually of kindred meaning with, another or others. **2** A member of a conjugate pair. Also **con′ju·gant.** [<L *conjugatus,* pp. of *conjugare* <*com-* together + *jugare* <*jugum* yoke] — **con′ju·ga′tive** *adj.* — **con′ju·ga′tor** *n.*
conjugate angle See under ANGLE.
con·ju·ga·tion (kon′jo͞o·gā′shən) *n.* **1** Conjunction; union. **2** *Gram.* The inflection of a verb, or the expression of such inflection; also, a class of verbs similarly inflected, or the mode of inflection. **3** *Biol.* The temporary fusion of two similar protozoans during which exchange of nuclear material takes place.
con·ju·ga·tion·al (kon′jo͞o·gā′shən·əl) *adj.* **1** Of or pertaining to conjugation. **2** *Anat.* Situated at the junction of two bones. — **con′ju·ga′tion·al·ly** *adv.*
con·junct (kən·jungkt′, kon′jungkt) *adj.* Joined together; conjoined. [<L *conjunctus,* pp. of *conjungere.* See CONJOIN.] — **con·junct′ly** *adv.*
con·junc·tion (kən·jungk′shən) *n.* **1** The state of being joined together, or the things so joined; combination; league. **2** *Astron.* The position of an inferior planet when it is on a direct line with the earth and the sun, or of a superior planet when the sun is on the direct line between it and the earth. **3** Simultaneous occurrence of events. **4** *Gram.* A word used to connect words, phrases, clauses, or sentences: one of the eight traditional parts of speech. See synonyms under ASSOCIATION, UNION. — **coordinate conjunction** A conjunction, as *and, but, or,* which joins words or groups of words of equal rank. — **subordinate conjunction** A conjunction, as *as, because, if, that, though,* which joins clauses of minor rank to principal clauses. — **con·junc′tion·al** *adj.* — **con·junc′tion·al·ly** *adv.*
con·junc·ti·va (kon′jungk·tī′və) *n.* *pl.* **·vas** or **·vae** (-vē) *Anat.* The mucous membrane lining the eyelids and covering the anterior part of the eyeball. See illustration under EYE. [<NL *(membrana) conjunctiva* connective (membrane)]
con·junc·ti·val (kon′jungk·tī′vəl) *adj.* **1** Serving to join or connect. **2** Of or pertaining to the conjunctiva.
con·junc·tive (kən·jungk′tiv) *adj.* **1** Joining; connective: *conjunctive* tissue. **2** Joined together. **3** *Gram.* **a** Serving to unite words, clauses, etc.; used as a conjunction: a *conjunctive* adverb. **b** Serving to unite both meaning and construction, as the conjunction *and.* — *n.* *Gram.* A conjunctive word. [<L *conjunctivus* <*conjungere.* See CONJOIN.] — **con·junc′tive·ly** *adv.*
con·junc·ti·vi·tis (kən·jungk′tə·vī′tis) *n.* *Pathol.* Inflammation of the conjunctiva; ophthalmia.
con·junc·ture (kən·jungk′chər) *n.* **1** A combination of circumstances; juncture; also, a crisis. **2** The act of joining; union.
con·ju·ra·tion (kon′jo͝o·rā′shən) *n.* **1** An enchantment; incantation; spell. **2** Magic or a magical expression used in an appeal for supernatural aid. **3** A solemn invocation; adjuration.
con·jure (kən·jo͝or′ *for v. defs. 1 and 6;* kon′jər, kun′- *for v. defs. 2–5*) *v.* **·jured, ·jur·ing** *v.t.* **1** To call on or appeal to solemnly; adjure. **2** To summon, bring, or drive away by incantation or spell, as a devil or spirit. **3** To accomplish or effect by or as by magic. — *v.i.* **4** To practice magic or legerdemain. **5** To summon a devil or spirit by incantation. **6** *Obs.* To conspire. — *adj.* (kon′jər, kun′-) *U.S. Dial.* Given to practicing magic or curing by magic: a *conjure* man. [<OF *conjurer* <L *conjurare* <*com-* together + *jurare* swear]
con·jur·er (kon′jər·ər, kun′- *for defs. 1 and 2,* kən·jo͝or′ər *for defs. 3 and 4*) *n.* **1** One who practices legerdemain; a juggler. **2** One who practices magic or works through supernatural powers; specifically, an Indian or Negro medicine man. **3** One who appeals or invokes solemnly. **4** *Obs.* A conspirator.
con·ju·ry (kon′jər·ē, kun′-) *n.* *pl.* **·ries** The practice of magic.
conk (kongk) *n.* *Slang* **1** The head. **2** *Brit.* The nose. — *v.t.* To hit on the head. — **to conk out** To stall or fail: said of a motor or engine. [? <CONCH]
con man (kon) *Slang* A confidence man.
conn (kon) See CON[2].
Con·nacht (kon′əkht, kon′ət) A province of western Ireland; 6,611 square miles. Also **Con·naught** (kon′ôt).
con·nate (kon′āt) *adj.* **1** Born in and with one; innate; congenital. **2** Born or existing together or with another; cognate. **3** *Biol.* Congenitally or firmly united, as the parts of an organism. [<L *connatus,* pp. of *connasci,* var. of *cognasci.* See COGNATE.] — **con′nate·ly** *adv.* — **con′nate·ness** *n.*
con·na·tion (kə·nā′shən) *n.* The state of being connate; congenital union.
con·nat·u·ral (kə·nach′ər·əl) *adj.* **1** Innate; congenital; inborn. **2** Allied; cognate. Also spelled *conatural.* [<Med. L *connaturalis* <*com-* together + *naturalis* NATURAL] — **con·nat′u·ral·ly** *adv.*
con·naught (kon′ôt) A cotton cloth used as a foundation for embroidery. [from *Connaught,* var. of *Connacht*]
con·nect (kə·nekt′) *v.t.* **1** To join together as by links or fastenings; unite or combine. **2** To bring into correlation; associate. **3** To think of as being similar or related; associate mentally. **4** To close or complete, as an electric circuit or telephone connection. — *v.i.* **5** To unite or join; be in close relation; be associated. **6** To meet as scheduled, as buses

or trains, for transference of passengers. 7 *U.S. Colloq.* In some sports, to hit the ball or mark. [<L *connectere*, var. of *conectere* <*com-* together + *nectere* bind]

Con·nect·i·cut (kə·net′ə·kət) A State of the NE United States: 5,009 square miles; capital, Hartford; entered the Union Jan. 9, 1788, one of the original thirteen States: nickname, *Nutmeg State*. Abbr. CT

Connecticut River The largest river of New England, flowing 345 miles between Vermont and New Hampshire, and through Massachusetts and Connecticut to Long Island Sound.

connecting rod *Mech.* A rod or bar in an engine, joining two or more moving parts.

con·nec·tion (kə·nek′shən) *n.* **1** The act or means of connecting or the state of being connected; union; combination. **2 a** Family relationship, especially by marriage. **b** A distant relative. **3** A company; denomination; a body of persons connected, or with whom one is connected, by relationship, belief, dealings, etc. **4** A direct transfer from one route to another, as in railway service. **5** Logical coherence or consistency, as the parts of an address. **6** That which connects or serves as a bond of union: There is no *connection* between the two. **7** A mechanism or apparatus which serves to form a union of parts; specifically, a connecting rod or a connecting passageway in a series of flues. Also *Brit.* **con·nex′ion.** See synonyms under ASSOCIATION, KINSMAN. —**con·nec′tion·al** *adj.*

con·nec·tive (kə·nek′tiv) *adj.* Capable of connecting, or serving to connect; causing or involving connection. —*n.* **1** That which connects. **2** *Gram.* A connecting word or particle, as a conjunction. **3** *Bot.* The portion of the filament of a stamen that unites the lobes of an anther. —**con·nec′tive·ly** *adv.*

connective tissue *Anat.* The fibrous tissue that pervades the whole body and serves to unite and support the various parts, as cartilage, bone, or tendon.

con·nec·tiv·i·ty (kon′ek·tiv′ə·tē) *n.* The property of being connective; order of connection.

con·nec·tor (kə·nek′tər) *n.* A person or thing that connects. Also **con·nect′er.**

Con·nel·ly (kon′əl·ē), **Marc,** born 1890, U.S. playwright: full name *Marcus Cook Connelly.*

con·ner[1] (kon′ər) *n.* **1** *Archaic* An inspector; a tester. **2** One who studies and peruses. [OE *cunnere* <*cunnian* test]

con·ner[2] (kon′ər) *n.* *Naut.* One who directs the steering of a ship from some point of observation. [<CON[2]]

con·ning–tow·er (kon′ing·tou′ər) *n.* **1** The armored pilothouse on the deck of a warship. **2** In submarines, an observation tower serving also as an entrance.

con·nip·tion (kə·nip′shən) *n. U.S. Colloq.* A fit of hysteria, rage, etc. Also **conniption fit.** [Cf. dial. E (Northern) *canapshus* ill–tempered]

con·ni·vance (kə·nī′vəns) *n.* **1** The act or fact of conniving. **2** Silent or indirect assent, especially to wrongdoing. **3** *Law* A guilty assent to or knowledge of a wrongful or criminal act during its occurrence. Also **con·ni′van·cy.**

con·nive (kə·nīv′) *v.i.* **·nived, ·niv·ing 1** To encourage or assent to a wrong by silence or feigned ignorance: with *at.* **2** To be in collusion: with *with.* [<L *connivere*, var. of *conivere* wink, shut the eyes] —**con·niv′er** *n.*

con·ni·vent (kə·nī′vənt) *adj. Biol.* Converging, as stamens or wings. [<L *connivens, -entis*, pp. of *connivere.* See CONNIVE.]

con·nois·seur (kon′ə·sûr′) *n.* A competent critical judge of anything, especially in matters of art and taste. [<F]

Con·nol·ly (kon′əl·ē), **James,** 1870–1916, Irish socialist; executed.

con·no·ta·tion (kon′ə·tā′shən) *n.* **1** The suggestive emotional content or significance of a word, additional to its explicit literal meaning; implication. **2** The act of connoting or connotating, and the quality or qualities connoted. [<Med. L *connotatio, -onis* < *connotare.* See CONNOTE.]

con·no·ta·tive (kon′ə·tā′tiv, kə·nō′tə·tiv) *adj.* **1** Having the quality of connoting. **2** Implying a correlative. —**con′no·ta′tive·ly** *adv.*

con·note (kə·nōt′) *v.t.* **·not·ed, ·not·ing** To indicate or imply along with the literal meaning; mention by implication. Also **con·no·tate** (kon′ə·tāt). [<Med. L *connotare* <*com-* together + *notare* mark]

con·nu·bi·al (kə·nōō′bē·əl, -nyōō′-) *adj.* Pertaining to matrimony; relating to husband or wife; matrimonial; conjugal; nuptial. [<L *connubialis* <*connubium* <*com-* together + *nubere* marry] —**con·nu·bi·al·i·ty** (kə·nōō′bē·al′ə·tē, -nyōō′-) *n.* —**con·nu′bi·al·ly** *adv.*

cono– *combining form* Cone; conical. Also, before vowels, **con–.** [<Gk. *kōnos* cone]

co·no·dont (kō′nə·dont, kon′ə-) *n. Paleontol.* A small toothlike fossil, found in Paleozoic rocks. [<CON(O)- + Gk. *odous, odontos* tooth]

co·noid (kō′noid) *adj.* Cone–shaped; conical. —*n.* Something having the form of a cone. [< Gk. *kōnoeides* conical] —**co·noi·dal** (kō·noid′l), **co·noi′dic** *adj.*

co·no·scen·te (kō′nō·shen′tā) See COGNOSCENTE.

co·no·scope (kō′nə·skōp, kon′ə-) *n.* A polariscope for examining crystals under converging light rays. [<CONO- + -SCOPE]

con·quer (kong′kər) *v.t.* **1** To overcome or subdue by force, as in war; vanquish. **2** To acquire or gain control of by or as by force of arms. **3** To overcome by mental or moral force; surmount. —*v.i.* **4** To be victorious. [<OF *conquerre* <L *conquirere* <*com-* thoroughly + *quaerere* seek] —**con′quer·a·ble** *adj.*

Synonyms: beat, checkmate, crush, defeat, discomfit, down, humble, master, overcome, overmaster, overmatch, overpower, overthrow, reduce, rout, subdue, subject, subjugate, surmount, triumph, vanquish, win, worst. A country is *conquered* when its armies are totally defeated and its territory is occupied by the enemy; it may be *subjected* to indemnity or to various disabilities; it is *subjugated* when it is held helplessly under military control; it is *subdued* when all resistance has died out. Any army is *defeated* when forcibly driven back; it is *routed* when it is converted into a mob of fugitives. Compare BAFFLE, BEAT, GAIN, HINDER, SUBDUE. *Antonyms*: capitulate, cede, fail, fall, fly, forfeit, lose, resign, retreat, submit, succumb, surrender, yield.

con·quer·ing (kong′kər·ing) *adj.* Overcoming; victorious. —**con′quer·ing·ly** *adv.*

con·quer·or (kong′kər·ər) *n.* One who conquers, subdues, or overcomes. —**the Conqueror** William, Duke of Normandy, who became William I of England when he won the battle of Hastings in 1066.

con·quest (kon′kwest, kong′-) *n.* **1** The act of conquering. **2** The thing conquered; that which is captured and taken forcibly, as territory, a person, or the favor of a person. See synonyms under VICTORY. —**the Conquest** The Norman Conquest. [<OF, pp. of *conquerre.* See CONQUER.]

con·qui·an (kong′kē·ən) *n.* A two–handed card game resembling rummy, requiring 40 cards: also spelled *cooncan.* [<Sp. *con quien* with whom]

con·quis·ta·dor (kon·kwis′tə·dôr, *Sp.* kōng·kes′·tä·thōr′) *n. pl.* **·dors,** *Sp.* **·do·res** (-thō′räs) A conqueror; specifically, any of the Spanish conquerors of Mexico and Peru in the 16th century. [<Sp. <*conquistar* conquer]

Con·rad (kon′rad) A masculine personal name. Also *Fr.* **Con·rade** (kôn·räd′), *Lat.* **Con·ra·dus** (kon·rä′dəs), *Sp.* **Con·ra·do** (kōn·rä′thō). [< Gmc., bold counsel]

Con·rad (kon′rad), **Joseph,** 1857–1924, English author born in Poland: real name *Teodor Józef Korzeniowski.*

con·san·guin·e·ous (kon′sang·gwin′ē·əs) *adj.* **1** Descended from the same parent or ancestor; akin. **2** Of or pertaining to consanguinity. Also **con·san·guine** (kon·sang′gwin), **con′san·guin′e·al.** [<L *consanguineus* <*com-* together + *sanguis* blood] —**con′san·guin′e·ous·ly** *adv.*

con·san·guin·i·ty (kon′sang·gwin′ə·tē) *n.* **1** The relationship that proceeds from a common ancestry; blood relationship. **2** Any near affinity or relationship. See synonyms under AFFINITY, KIN.

con·science (kon′shəns) *n.* **1** Moral consciousness in general; the activity or faculty by which distinctions are made between right and wrong in one's own conduct and character; the act or power of moral discrimination; ethical judgment or sensibility. **2** Conformity in conduct to one's conceptions of right and wrong. **3** *Obs.* Consciousness. —**in (all) conscience 1** In truth; in reason and honesty. **2** Certainly; assuredly. [<F <L *conscientia* <*com-* together + *scire* know] —**con′science·less** *adj.*

conscience clause A clause in a law which specially relieves persons who have conscientious scruples from performing acts enjoined therein: referring generally to laws relating to religious matters.

conscience money Money secretly paid to atone for some concealed act of dishonesty.

con·sci·en·tious (kon′shē·en′shəs) *adj.* Governed or dictated by conscience; scrupulous. —**con′sci·en′tious·ly** *adv.* —**con′sci·en′·tious·ness** *n.*

conscientious objector One who, on grounds of religious or moral convictions, objects to warfare and refuses to perform military service.

con·scion·a·ble (kon′shən·ə·bəl) *adj.* Conformable to conscience or right. —**con′scion·a·bly** *adv.*

con·scious (kon′shəs) *adj.* **1** Immediately aware of; mentally recognizing, to some degree and extent, one's own inner feeling and thought, or their objective reference. **2** Unjustifiably embarrassed by the sense of one's own individuality; self–conscious. **3** Mentally alert; well aware of some object, impression, or truth. **4** Present in the mind; recognized as belonging to oneself: *conscious* superiority. **5** Cognizant of guilt or fault. **6** Deliberate: a *conscious* lie. **7** Pertaining to consciousness. **8** Having the faculty and psychical attributes of consciousness. **9** *Obs.* Possessing knowledge in common with another; mutually informed. —*n.* *Psychoanal.* That part of mental life of which an individual is aware.[< L *conscius* <*com-* together + *scire* know] —**con′scious·ly** *adv.*

Synonyms (adj.): aware, cognizant, sensible. One is *aware* of that which exists without him; he is *conscious* of the inner workings of his own mind. *Sensible* may be used in the exact sense of *conscious,* or it may partake of both the senses mentioned above. One may be *sensible* of his own or another's error; he is *conscious* only of his own. A person may feel *assured* or *sure* of something false or non–existent; what he is *aware* of, still more what he is *conscious* of, must be fact. *Sensible* has often a reference to the emotions, where *conscious* might apply only to the intellect; to say a culprit is *sensible* of his degradation is more forcible than to say he is *conscious* of it. *Antonyms*: dead, deaf, ignorant, insensible, unaware, unconscious.

con·scious·ness (kon′shəs·nis) *n.* **1** The state of being conscious; sensation; knowledge. **2** The power of self–knowledge; internal perception. **3** The aggregate of the conscious states in an individual or a group of persons. **4** The awareness of some particular object, state, agency, or influence; an intuition. **5** Any form of intellectual activity or its product in direct and convincing knowledge, whether of external or internal objects. See synonyms under FEELING, MIND.

con·script (kon′skript) *adj.* **1** Registered; enrolled. **2** Compulsorily enlisted, as a soldier or an armed force. —*n.* One who is compulsorily enrolled for military service; a draftee. —*v.t.* (kən·skript′) To force into military service; draft. [<L *conscriptus,* pp. of *conscribere* enrol <*com-* together + *scribere* write]

conscript fathers 1 The senators of ancient Rome; also, the senators of medieval Venice. **2** The members of any legislative body.

con·scrip·tion (kən·skrip′shən) *n.* A compulsory enrolment of men for military service; draft.

con·se·crate (kon′sə·krāt) *v.t.* **·crat·ed, ·crat·ing 1** To set apart as sacred; dedicate to sacred uses with appointed ceremonies; to *consecrate* a church, a bishop, or the elements of the Eucharist. **2** To dedicate solemnly, as from emotions of gratitude or convictions of duty; devote: He *consecrated* his life to the cause. **3** To apotheosize; canonize. **4** To make

reverend or venerable; hallow: *consecrated* by time. —*adj.* Hallowed; consecrated. [<L *consecratus,* pp. of *consecrare* < *com-* thoroughly + *sacer* holy] —**con′se·cra′tor** *n.* —**con·se·cra·to·ry** (kon′sə·krə·tôr′ē, -tō′rē) *adj.*

con·se·cra·tion (kon′sə·krā′shən) *n.* **1** The act or ceremony of separating from a common to a sacred use; the state of being consecrated. **2** Canonization, as of a saint; apotheosis, as of a god.

con·se·cu·tion (kon′sə·kyōō′shən) *n.* **1** Actual, logical, or grammatical sequence. **2** *Music* A succession of similar intervals in harmony. **3** Any succession or series. [<L *consecutio, -onis* < *consequi.* See CONSEQUENT.]

con·sec·u·tive (kən·sek′yə·tiv) *adj.* **1** Following in uninterrupted succession; successive. **2** Characterized by logical sequence. **3** Following as a consequence or result; consequent. **4** *Gram.* Denoting result or consequence. [<L *consecutus,* pp. of *consequi.* See CONSEQUENT.] —**con·sec′u·tive·ly** *adv.* —**con·sec′·u·tive·ness** *n.*

consecutive fifths *Music* Progressions of perfect fifths or octaves, permissible for intentional emphasis. Also **consecutive octaves, con·sec′·u·tives.**

con·sen·su·al (kən·sen′shōō·əl) *adj.* **1** *Law* Existing merely by virtue of acquiescence. **2** *Physiol.* **a** Excited by sympathetic or reflex action. **b** Denoting instinctive and reflex actions and movements which are stimulated by conscious sensations. —**con·sen′su·al·ly** *adv.*

con·sen·sus (kən·sen′səs) *n.* A collective opinion; general agreement. [<L < *consentire* < *com-* together + *sentire* feel, think]

con·sent (kən·sent′) *v.i.* **1** To yield or accede, as to a proposal or request, when one has the right, power, or wish not to do so. **2** To give assent, as to a contract; agree. **3** *Obs.* To agree together; accord. See synonyms under AGREE, ASSENT. —*n.* **1** A voluntary yielding of the will, judgment, or inclination to what is proposed or desired by another; acquiescence; compliance. **2** Harmony in opinion or sentiment; agreement; concord. **3** *Law* A rational and voluntary concurrence in an act or contract. **4** *Obs.* Harmonious correspondence or operation. See synonyms under HARMONY, PERMISSION. [<OF *consentir* <L *consentire.* See CONSENSUS.] —**con·sent′er** *n.*

con·sen·ta·ne·ous (kon′sen·tā′nē·əs) *adj.* **1** Mutually consenting or agreeing; acquiescent. **2** Simultaneous. [<L *consentaneus* agreeing] —**con·sen·ta·ne·i·ty** (kən·sen′tə·nē′ə·tē), **con′·sen·ta′ne·ous·ness** *n.* —**con′sen·ta′ne·ous·ly** *adv.*

con·sent·i·ble (kən·sen′tə·bəl) *adj.* Capable of being established or fixed by consent of those interested.

con·sen·tience (kən·sen′shəns) *n.* **1** The state or quality of being in agreement or accord. **2** *Psychol.* The sensuous analog, in automatic or reflex action, of consciousness in conscious action. —**con·sen′tient** *adj.*

con·se·quence (kon′sə·kwens, -kwəns) *n.* **1** That which naturally follows from a preceding action or condition; the effect of a cause; result. **2** The conclusion of a syllogism; inference; deduction. **3** The relation between an antecedent and a consequent; causal or logical consecution; sequence. **4** Distinction; note: said of persons: a man of *consequence;* also, significance; moment: said of things: an event of no *consequence.* **5** Self-importance; consequentiality: used of persons.

Synonyms: consequent, effect, end, event, issue, outcome, outgrowth, result, sequel, upshot. Compare ACCIDENT, CAUSE, CIRCUMSTANCE, DEMONSTRATION, END, EVENT, INFERENCE.

con·se·quent (kon′sə·kwent, -kwənt) *adj.* **1** Following as a natural result or as a logical conclusion. **2** Characterized by correctness of reasoning; logical. —*n.* **1** The conclusion of an inference or syllogism; consequence. **2** That which follows something else, as in time, order, or relation, without causal connection: opposed to *antecedent.* **3** *Math.* **a** The second term of a ratio. **b** In a series of four proportionals, the second and fourth terms. **4** Having a course or direction depending on or resulting from the original slope of the surface. See synonyms under CONSEQUENCE. [<L *consequens, -entis,* ppr. of *consequi* < *com-* together + *sequi* follow]

con·se·quen·tial (kon′sə·kwen′shəl) *adj.* **1** Having or showing importance; self-important. **2** Following logically; consequent. —**con·se·quen·ti·al·i·ty** (kon′sə·kwen′shē·al′ə·tē), **con′·se·quen′tial·ness** *n.* —**con′se·quen′tial·ly** *adv.*

con·se·quent·ly (kon′sə·kwent′lē, -kwənt·lē) *adv.* As a result; therefore. See synonyms under THEREFORE.

con·ser·van·cy (kən·sûr′vən·sē) *n. pl.* **·cies** **1** The act of conserving. **2** A board or commission to conserve fisheries, waterways, etc. —**con·ser′vant** *adj.*

con·ser·va·tion (kon′sər·vā′shən) *n.* **1** The act of keeping or protecting from loss or injury: the *conservation* of health, or of social order. **2** The preservation of natural resources for economical use; specifically, the preservation of forests, fisheries, harbors, etc. [<L *conservatio, -onis* < *conservare.* See CONSERVE.] —**con′ser·va′tion·al** *adj.* —**con′ser·va′tion·al·ly** *adv.* —**con′ser·va′tion·ist** *n.*

conservation of energy *Physics* The principle that in any closed material system the total amount of energy remains constant, though it may assume different forms successively.

conservation of mass *Physics* The principle that the total mass of any material system remains constant through all changes taking place within the system.

con·ser·va·tism (kən·sûr′və·tiz′əm) *n.* Conservative principles and practices, as in criticism, theology, politics, etc.; disposition or tendency to be conservative.

con·ser·va·tive (kən·sûr′və·tiv) *adj.* **1** Adhering to and tending to preserve the existing order of things; opposed to change or progress. **2** Conserving; preservative. **3** Moderate; cautious; within a safe margin: a *conservative* estimate or statement. —*n.* A conservative person. —**con·ser′va·tive·ly** *adv.* —**con·ser′·va·tive·ness** *n.*

Con·ser·va·tive (kən·sûr′və·tiv) *adj.* In Great Britain or the British Commonwealth, of or pertaining to the Conservative party. —*n.* A member of this party.

Conservative Judaism Judaism as practiced especially in the U.S. by those who hold that both the Scriptures and the oral laws are divinely authoritative but that traditional rituals may be selectively observed or modified to accord with contemporary cultural conditions. Compare ORTHODOX JUDAISM, REFORM JUDAISM.

Conservative Party **1** In Great Britain, the name of the right-wing party since about 1832, opposed by the Labour party. See TORY. **2** In many dominions of the British Commonwealth, the political party of the right wing.

con·ser·va·tize (kən·sûr′və·tīz) *v.t.* & *v.i.* **·tized, ·tiz·ing** To convert to or adopt conservatism. Also *Brit.* **con·ser′va·tise.**

con·ser·va·tor (kon′sər·vā′tər, kən·sûr′və·tər) *n.* A protector; guardian; keeper.

con·ser·va·to·ry (kən·sûr′və·tôr′ē, -tō′rē) *n. pl.* **·ries** **1** A small greenhouse or glass-enclosed room in which plants are grown and displayed. **2** A school of art, especially of music. **3** *Obs.* A place for the preservation or protection of anything: also **con·ser·va·toire** (kən·sûr′və·twär′). —*adj.* Adapted to preserve.

con·serve (kən·sûrv′) *v.t.* **·served, ·serv·ing** **1** To keep from loss, decay, or depletion; supervise and protect. **2** To preserve with sugar. —*n.* (kon′sûrv, kən·sûrv′) **1** A kind of jam made of several fruits stewed together in sugar, often with nuts, raisins, etc. **2** A medicated confection of fresh vegetable substances and sugar. See synonyms under PRESERVE. [<F *conserver* <L *conservare* < *com-* thoroughly + *servare* keep, save] —**con·serv′a·ble** *adj.* —**con·serv′er** *n.*

con·sid·er (kən·sid′ər) *v.t.* **1** To think about or deliberate upon; examine mentally. **2** To look upon or regard as; think to be. **3** To hold as an opinion: with a clause as object. **4** To make allowance for; keep in mind. **5** To take into account; have a regard for: to *consider* the feelings of others. **6** *Archaic* To observe closely. **7** *Obs.* To fee; remunerate. —*v.i.* **8** To think closely; cogitate. [<F *considérer* <L *considerare,* ? < *com-* thoroughly + *sidus, sideris* star; with ref. to astrology]

Synonyms: contemplate, deliberate, examine, meditate, ponder, reflect, study, think, weigh. See CALCULATE, DELIBERATE, ESTEEM, EXAMINE, MUSE. *Antonyms:* disregard, forget, ignore, neglect, overlook, slight, trifle.

con·sid·er·a·ble (kən·sid′ər·ə·bəl) *adj.* **1** Somewhat large in amount, extent, etc. **2** Worthy of consideration by reason of size or quantity; a good deal of; a large part or portion of: He gave his friends *considerable* trouble; *Considerable* fruit has been spoiled. See synonyms under GOOD, LARGE. —*n.* A good deal; much; a pretty large amount. —**con·sid′er·a·bly** *adv.*

con·sid·er·ate (kən·sid′ər·it) *adj.* **1** Exhibiting or given to consideration. **2** Thoughtful; kind; prudent. See synonyms under CHARITABLE, THOUGHTFUL. —**con·sid′er·ate·ly** *adv.* —**con·sid′er·ate·ness** *n.*

con·sid·er·a·tion (kən·sid′ə·rā′shən) *n.* **1** The act of considering. **2** Thoughtful and kindly feeling or treatment. **3** A circumstance to be taken into account. **4** Something given in return for a service; remuneration. **5** Importance; consequence; standing. **6** *Law* The thing given or done, or to be given, done, or abstained from, by one party to a contract, in exchange for the act or promise of the other. Also *Obs.* **con·sid′er·ance.** See synonyms under FRIENDSHIP, PRUDENCE, REASON, REFLECTION, THOUGHT. [<F *considération* <L *consideratio, -onis* < *considerare.* See CONSIDER.]

con·sid·ered (kən·sid′ərd) *adj.* Premeditated; deliberated.

con·sid·er·ing (kən·sid′ər·ing) *prep.* In view of; taking into account the fact of: *Considering* his deafness, he takes a large part in the conversation. —*adv. Colloq.* Taking all the facts into account: He came out quite well, *considering.* —*conj.* In view of: *Considering* how I feel, you're lucky to see me at all.

con·sign (kən·sīn′) *v.t.* **1** To entrust or commit to the care of another. **2** To make over or relegate: They *consigned* his memory to oblivion. **3** To forward or deliver, as merchandise, for sale or disposal. **4** To set apart or devote, as for a specific purpose or use. **5** *Obs.* To impress, as with a seal; sign. —*v.i.* **6** *Obs.* To yield oneself; consent. See synonyms under COMMIT. [<F *consigner* <L *consignare* < *com-* with + *signum* a seal] —**con·sign′a·ble** *adj.* —**con·sign·or** (kən·sī′nər, kon′·sī·nôr′), **con·sign′er** *n.*

con·sig·na·tion (kon′sig·nā′shən) *n.* The act of consigning; consignment. [<LL *consignatio, -onis* < *consignare.* See CONSIGN.]

con·sig·na·to·ry (kən·sig′nə·tôr′ē, -tō′rē) *n. pl.* **·ries** One who signs jointly with another or others.

con·sign·ee (kon′sī·nē′) *n.* A person to whom property has been consigned; a factor.

con·sign·ment (kən·sīn′mənt) *n.* **1** The sending of property to a person for keeping, sale, or shipment. **2** The property consigned. **3** A written instrument by which something is consigned. **4** A method of wholesale or jobber selling whereby the retailer pays for goods only after he has sold them: usually in the phrase **on consignment.**

con·sist (kən·sist′) *v.i.* **1** To be made up or constituted: with *of.* **2** To have as substance, quality, or nature: with *in:* Her beauty *consists* in her virtue. **3** To be compatible; harmonize; exist in agreement: with *with:* His story *consists* with the evidence. [<L *consistere* < *com-* together + *sistere* stand]

con·sis·ten·cy (kən·sis′tən·sē) *n. pl.* **·cies** **1** Compatibility or harmony between things, acts, or statements; logical connection; agreement; also, agreement with what has been previously done, expressed, or agreed on. **2** The condition of holding together; firmness, nearness, or density. **3** Degree of firmness, thickness, or density. Also **con·sis′tence.** See synonyms under HARMONY.

con·sis·tent (kən·sis′tənt) *adj.* **1** Characterized by consistency; agreeing with itself; not self-contradictory. **2** Congruous; compatible. **3** Firmly united; solid. [<L *consistens, -entis* < *consistere.* See CONSIST.] —**con·sis′tent·ly** *adv.*

con·sis·to·ry (kən·sis′tər·ē) *n. pl.* **·ries** **1** *Eccl.* **a** The highest council of the Roman Catholic Church, composed of all the cardinals, and usually presided over by the Pope. **b** In many Reformed Churches, a local governing body consisting of the ministers and elders of a congregation. **c** A court of the Lutheran state churches, appointed by the government to oversee ecclesiastical affairs. **d** A diocesan court of the Church of England, presided over by the chancelor or commissary of the diocese. **2** The place where an ecclesiastical

court is held; a council house or hall of justice. **3** A council of dignitaries, as of Freemasons of the 32nd degree. [<LL *consistorium*] —**con·sis·to·ri·al** (kon′sis·tôr′ē·əl, -tō′·rē-), **con′sis·to′ri·an** *adj.*

con·so·ci·ate (kən·sō′shē·āt) *v.t.* & *v.i.* **·at·ed, ·at·ing** To bring or come into association; unite: said especially of pastors and organizations of Congregational churches. —*adj.* (kən·sō′shē·it, -āt) Associated with; united. —*n.* (kən·sō′shē·it) An associate; partner. [<L *consociatus*, pp. of *consociare* <*com-* together + *socius* ally, friend]

con·so·ci·a·tion (kən·sō′sē·ā′shən, -shē-) *n.* **1** The act of consociating. **2** An ecclesiastical court.

con·so·cies (kən·sō′shēz) *n. Ecol.* A plant or animal community marked by the dominance of one species belonging to the life forms typical of the given environment. [<NL <L *com-* together + *socius* ally]

con·sol (kon′sol, kən·sol′) Singular of CONSOLS.

con·so·la·tion (kon′sə·lā′shən) *n.* **1** The act of consoling, or the state of being consoled; solace. **2** A comforting thought, person, or fact. [<F <L *consolatio, -onis* <*consolari*. See CONSOLE.]

con·sol·a·to·ry (kən·sol′ə·tôr′ē, -tō′rē) *adj.* Providing comfort or solace.

con·sole¹ (kən·sōl′) *v.t.* **·soled, ·sol·ing** To comfort (a person) in grief or sorrow; solace; cheer. [<F *consoler* <L *consolari* <*com-* together + *solari* solace] —**con·sol′a·ble** *adj.*

Synonyms: comfort, condole, encourage, sympathize. One *condoles* with another by the expression of kindly sympathy in his trouble; he *consoles* him by considerations adapted to soothe and sustain the spirit; he *encourages* him by the hope of some relief or deliverance; he *comforts* him by whatever act or word tends to bring mind or body to a state of rest and cheer. We *sympathize* with others, not only in sorrow, but in joy. Compare ALLEVIATE, PITY. *Antonyms*: annoy, distress, disturb, grieve, hurt, sadden, trouble, wound.

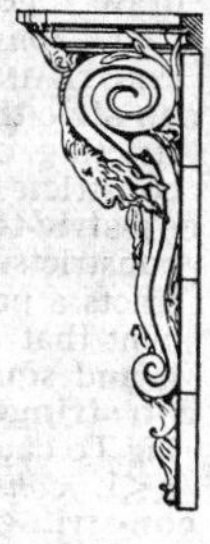
CONSOLE (*def. 1*)

con·sole² (kon′sōl) *n.* **1** A bracket of any kind, especially one used to support cornices or ornamental fixtures; a corbel. **2** A console table. **3** The portion of an organ containing the manuals and stops. **4** A cabinet for a radio, phonograph, or television set, designed to rest on the floor. [<F, a bracket; ult. origin uncertain]

console table A table supported wholly or in part by consoles, or whose legs have the appearance of consoles; a pier table.

con·sol·i·dant (kən·sol′ə·dənt) *adj.* **1** Having the power of consolidating. **2** Tending to heal wounds. —*n.* A medicine for wounds. [<F, ppr. of *consolider* <L *consolidare*. See CONSOLIDATE.]

con·sol·i·date (kən·sol′ə·dāt) *v.* **·dat·ed, ·dat·ing** *v.t.* **1** To make solid, firm, or coherent; strengthen. **2** *Mil.* To secure and strengthen, as a newly captured position. **3** To combine in one body or system; form a union of. —*v.i.* **4** To become united, solid, or firm. See synonyms under UNITE. [<L *consolidatus*, pp. of *consolidare* <*com-* together + *solidus* solid] —**con·sol′i·da′tor** *n.*

con·sol·i·dat·ed (kən·sol′ə·dā′tid) *adj.* Merged with one or more like concerns: a *consolidated* railroad.

Consolidated Fund A British public fund into which the main part of the revenue is paid, and out of which are paid interest on the national debt and other charges.

consolidated school See under SCHOOL.

con·sol·i·da·tion (kən·sol′ə·dā′shən) *n.* **1** The act of consolidating, or the state of being consolidated. **2** Combination; centralization.

con·sols (kon′solz, kən·solz′) *n. pl.* A British governmental security. [Short for *consolidated annuities*]

con·so·lute temperature (kon′sə·lo͞ot) Critical solution temperature.

con·som·mé (kon′sə·mā′, *Fr.* kôn·sô·mā′) *n.* A clear soup made of meat and sometimes vegetables boiled in water. [<F, pp. of *consommer* <L *consummare*. See CONSUMMATE.]

con·so·nance (kon′sə·nəns) *n.* **1** Agreement; accord; harmony. **2** *Physics* The induced vibration of one sonorous body acting in sympathy with another, as of one piano string with another; resonance. **3** *Music* A combination of tones regarded as pleasing and not requiring resolution. Also **con′so·nan·cy.** See synonyms under HARMONY.

con·so·nant (kon′sə·nənt) *adj.* **1** Being in agreement or harmony; consistent. **2** Consonantal. **3** *Music* Having the quality of consonance. Also **con′so·nous.** —*n.* **1** *Phonet.* A sound produced by a contact or constriction of the speech organs which results in complete or partial blockage of the breath stream. Distinguished from *vowels*, which are characterized primarily by the shape of the resonance cavity, consonants are described by their place of articulation (bilabial, alveolar, etc.), vibration or non–vibration of the vocal cords (voiced or voiceless), presence or absence of nasality, and manner of formation (stop, fricative, etc.). **2** A letter representing such a sound. [<MF <L *consonans, -antis*, ppr. of *consonare* <*com-* together + *sonare* sound] —**con′so·nant·ly** *adv.* —**con′so·nant·ness** *n.*

con·so·nan·tal (kon′sə·nan′təl) *adj.* **1** Of the nature of a consonant. **2** Having a consonant or consonants.

con·sort (kon′sôrt) *n.* **1** A companion or associate. **2** A husband or wife; mate. **3** An accompanying vessel. **4** Companionship; company. —*v.t.* (kən·sôrt′) **1** To join; associate. **2** *Obs.* To accompany; escort. —*v.i.* **3** To keep company; associate. **4** To be in agreement; harmonize. [<F <L *consors, consortis* <*com-* together + *sors* share, lot]

con·sor·ti·um (kən·sôr′shē·əm) *n. pl.* **·ti·a** (-shē·ə) **1** *Law* The right of a husband to the society and conjugal affection of his wife. **2** *Law* Coalition; union, as of incorporated companies. **3** *Bot.* The close association of certain algae and lichens. [<L, fellowship] —**con·sor·tial** (kən·sôr′shəl) *adj.*

con·spec·tus (kən·spek′təs) *n. pl.* **·tus·es** **1** A general view of a subject. **2** A digest or summary. See synonyms under ABRIDGMENT. [<L <*conspicere*. See CONSPICUOUS.]

con·sperse (kən·spûrs′) *adj.* **1** Sprinkled. **2** *Ornithol.* Irregularly dotted, as certain birds' eggs. [<L *conspersus*, pp. of *conspergere* sprinkle *com-* + *spargere* scatter]

con·spic·u·ous (kən·spik′yo͞o·əs) *adj.* **1** Clearly visible; prominent and distinct; obvious. **2** Readily attracting attention; unusual; striking. See synonyms under EMINENT, EVIDENT, MANIFEST. [<L *conspicuus* <*conspicere* <*com-* together + *specere* look at] —**con·spic′u·ous·ly** *adv.* —**con·spic′u·ous·ness** *n.*

con·spir·a·cy (kən·spir′ə·sē) *n. pl.* **·cies** **1** An agreement between two or more persons to do an evil act in concert; a plot; secret combination of men for an evil purpose. **2** *Law* A combination of two or more persons to commit any act punishable by law. **3** Any striking concurrence of persons, classes, or agencies. —**con·spir·a·tor** (kən·spir′ə·tər) *n.* —**con·spir·a·to·ri·al** (kən·spir′ə·tôr′ē·əl, -tō′rē-) *adj.* —**con·spir′a·tress** *n. fem.*

Synonyms: cabal, combination, conclave, crew, faction, gang. A *conspiracy* is a combination of persons for an evil purpose, or the act of so combining. A *faction* is more extensive than a *conspiracy*, less formal in organization, less definite in plan. *Faction* and its adjective, *factious*, have always an unfavorable sense. *Cabal* commonly denotes a *conspiracy* of leaders. A *gang* is a company of workmen all doing the same work under one leader; the word is used figuratively only of *combinations* which it is meant to stigmatize as rude and mercenary; *crew* is used in a closely similar sense. A *conclave* is secret, but of larger numbers, ordinarily, than a *cabal*, and may have honorable use; as, the *conclave* of cardinals. See CABAL.

con·spire (kən·spīr′) *v.* **·spired, ·spir·ing** *v.t.* **1** To plot; scheme for. —*v.i.* **2** To form a plot, especially secretly, for evil or unlawful purposes. **3** To concur in action or endeavor, as circumstances. [<F *conspirer* <L *conspirare* <*com-* together + *spirare* breathe] —**con·spir·ant** (kən·spī′rənt) *adj.* & *n.* —**con·spir′er** *n.*

con spi·ri·to (kōn spē′rē·tō) *Music* With spirit and vigor. [<Ital.]

con·sta·ble (kon′stə·bəl, kun′-) *n.* **1** An officer of the peace; a policeman. **2** A high military officer in medieval monarchies. **3** The keeper or governor of a castle. —**Lord High Constable of England** A former military and judicial officer of high rank. [<OF *conestable* <LL *comes stabuli* count of the stable, chief groom] —**con′sta·ble·ship′** *n.*

Con·sta·ble (kun′stə·bəl), **John**, 1776–1837, English landscape painter.

con·stab·u·lar·y (kən·stab′yə·ler′ē) *adj.* Pertaining to or consisting of constables. Also **con·stab′u·lar** (-lər). —*n. pl.* **·lar·ies** **1** Constables collectively. **2** A military police force.

Con·stance (kon′stəns, *Fr.* kôn·stäns′) A feminine personal name. Also *Lat.* **Con·stan·ti·a** (kon·stan′shē·ə, -shə), *Pg.* **Con·stan·ci·a** (kôn·stän′sē·ə), *Sp.* **Con·stan·za** (kōn·stän′thä). [<L, constant, firm]

Con·stance (kon′stəns) A city in southern Baden, Germany, on the Lake of Constance at the efflux of the Rhine: German *Konstanz.*

Constance, Lake of A lake between NE Switzerland, Austria, and southern Germany; 207 square miles: German *Bodensee.*

con·stan·cy (kon′stən·sē) *n.* **1** Steadiness in purpose or action; faithfulness in service or affection. **2** Stability. See synonyms under FIDELITY, INDUSTRY, PERSEVERANCE.

con·stant (kon′stənt) *adj.* **1** Steady in purpose; resolute; persevering; faithful. **2** Steady in movement. **3** Long–continuing, or continually recurring. **4** Invariable. **5** *Obs.* Firm; positive; consistent. —*n.* **1** That which is permanent or invariable. **2** *Math.* A quantity which retains a fixed value throughout a given discussion. **3** In the sciences, any characteristic of a substance, event, or phenomenon, numerically determined, that remains always the same under specified conditions, as gravitation, the velocity of light, the melting or freezing point, etc. See synonyms under CONTINUAL, PERPETUAL. [<L *constans, -antis*, ppr. of *constare* <*com-* thoroughly + *stare* stand] —**con′stant·ly** *adv.*

Con·stant (kon′stənt, *Fr.* kôn·stän′) A masculine personal name. Also *Lat.* **Con·stans** (kon′stənz), *Pg.*, *Sp.* **Con·stan·ci·o** (*Pg.* kôn·stän′sē·ō, *Sp.* kōn·stän′thē·ō). [<L, constant, firm]

Con·stant (kôn·stän′), **Jean Joseph Benjamin**, 1845–1902, French portrait painter.
—**Constant de Re·becque** (də rə·bek′), **Benjamin**, 1767–1830, French writer and statesman.

Con·stan·ţa (kôn·stän′tsä) A city in SE Rumania on the Black Sea. Also **Con·stan′tsa.**

con·stant·an (kon′stən·tan) *n.* A ductile, non-corrosive alloy of nickel and copper with high thermal and electrical resistance: used in rheostats and thermocouples. [Arbitrary coinage <CONSTANT]

Con·stan·tine (kon′stən·tēn, *Fr.* kôn·stän·tēn′) A city in NE Algeria.

Con·stan·tine (kon′stən·tēn, -tīn) A masculine personal name. Also *Du.* **Con·stan·tijn** (kōn′·stän·tīn), *Fr.* **Con·stan·tin** (kôn·stän·tan′), *Lat.* **Con·stan·ti·nus** (kon′stən·tī′nəs), *Pg.*, *Sp.* **Con·stan·ti·no** (*Pg.* kôn′stän·tē′no͞o, *Sp.* kōn′stän·tē′nō). [<L, constant, firm]
—**Constantine** The appellation of a number of early Christian emperors.
—**Constantine I, Flavius Valerius Aurelius**, 272–337, first Christian emperor of Rome: called "The Great."
—**Constantine VII**, 905–959, emperor of the East; as an author known as *Porphyrogenitus.*
—**Constantine XI** (erroneously **XIII**), 1394–1453, surnamed Palaeologus; last emperor of the East: known as *Dracoses.*

Con·stan·ti·no·ple (kon′stan·tə·nō′pəl) A former name for ISTANBUL.

Con·stan·tius II (kən·stan′shəs), 317–361, Roman emperor 337–361.

con·stel·late (kon′stə·lāt) *v.t.* & *v.i.* **·lat·ed, ·lat·ing** To group in constellations. —*adj.* Adorned or studded with constellations. [<LL *constellatus* studded with stars <*com-* together + *stella* star]

TABLE OF CONSTELLATIONS

Explanation: GROUP N includes all constellations within 45 degrees of the north pole. GROUP E includes all constellations within 45 degrees of each side of the equator. GROUP S includes all constellations within 45 degrees of the south pole.

NAME	Group	On the Meridian at 9 P. M.	NAME	Group	On the Meridian at 9 P. M.	NAME	Group	On the Meridian at 9 P. M.
Andromeda	E	Nov.	Delphinus	E	Sept.	Pegasus	E	Oct.
Antlia	E	April	Dorado	S	Jan.	Perseus	N	Dec.
Apus	S	July	Draco	N	June	Phœnix	S	Nov.
Aquarius	E	Oct.	Equuleus	E	Sept.	Pictor	S	Jan.
Aquila	E	Aug.	Eridanus	E	Dec.	Pisces	E	Nov.
Ara	S	July	Fornax	E	Dec.	Piscis Austrinus	E	Oct.
Aries	E	Dec.	Gemini	E	Feb.	Puppis	E	Feb.
Auriga	E	Feb.	Grus	S	Oct.	Pyxis	E	March
Boötes	E	June	Hercules	E	July	Reticulum	S	Jan.
Cælum	E	Jan.	Horologium	S	Dec.	Sagitta	E	Aug.
Camelopardalis	N	March	Hydra	E	April	Sagittarius	E	Aug.
Cancer	E	March	Hydrus	S	Dec.	Scorpius	E	July
Canes Venatici	E	May	Indus	S	Oct.	Sculptor	E	Nov.
Canis Major	E	Feb.	Lacerta	N	Oct.	Scutum	E	Aug.
Canis Minor	E	March	Leo	E	April	Serpens	E	July
Capricornus	E	Sept.	Leo Minor	E	April	Sextans	E	April
Carina	S	March	Lepus	E	Jan.	Taurus	E	Jan.
Cassiopeia	N	Nov.	Libra	E	June	Telescopium	S	Aug.
Centaurus	E	May	Lupus	E	June	Triangulum	E	Dec.
Cepheus	N	Nov.	Lynx	N	Feb.	Triangulum Australe	S	July
Cetus	E	Dec.	Lyra	E	Aug.	Tucana	S	Oct.
Chameleon	S	April	Mensa	S	Jan.	Ursa Major	N	April
Columba	E	Feb.	Microscopium	S	Sept.	Ursa Minor	N	....
Coma Berenices	E	May	Monoceros	E	March	Vela	S	March
Corona Australis	E	Aug.	Musca	S	May	Virgo	E	June
Corona Borealis	E	July	Norma	S	July	Volans	S	March
Corvus	E	May	Octans	S	....	Vulpecula	E	Sept.
Crater	E	April	Ophiuchus	E	July			
Crux	S	May	Orion	E	Jan.			
Cygnus	E	Sept.	Pavo	S	Aug.			

The four constellations Carina, Puppis, Pyxis, and Vela were formerly considered as a single one, called Argo Navis.

con·stel·la·tion (kon'stə·lā'shən) *n.* 1 *Astron.* An apparent group or cluster of stars, fortuitously associated on mythological or pictorial grounds. See table above. 2 An assemblage of brilliant things or persons. 3 In astrology, the aspect of the planets at the time of one's birth; hence, disposition or character as influenced by one's horoscope. 4 *Psychol.* A group of associated emotions, ideas, tendencies, etc., centering around a dominant element. — **con·stel·la·to·ry** (kən·stel'ə·tôr'ē, -tō'rē) *adj.*

con·ster·nate (kon'stər·nāt) *v.t.* **·nat·ed, ·nat·ing** *Rare* To overwhelm with terror and confusion; dismay. [<L *consternatus,* pp. of *consternare,* var. of *consternere* < *com-* thoroughly + *sternere* prostrate]

con·ster·na·tion (kon'stər·nā'shən) *n.* 1 Complete confusion; bafflement. 2 Sudden overwhelming fear; terror with confusion; dismay. See synonyms under ALARM, AMAZEMENT, FEAR.

con·sti·pate (kon'stə·pāt) *v.t.* **·pat·ed, ·pat·ing** To cause constipation in. [<L *constipatus,* pp. of *constipare* < *com-* together + *stipare* crowd] — **con'sti·pat'ed** *adj.*

con·sti·pa·tion (kon'stə·pā'shən) *n.* A morbid inactivity of the bowels; difficult evacuation.

con·stit·u·en·cy (kən·stich'ŏŏ·ən·sē) *n.* *pl.* **·cies** 1 A body of constituents. 2 The district from which a representative is elected to a legislative body.

con·stit·u·ent (kən·stich'ŏŏ·ənt) *adj.* 1 Serving to form or compose as a necessary part; constituting: Chlorine and sodium are the *constituent* elements of salt. 2 Entitled to vote for a public officer or representative. 3 Having the power to frame or modify a constitution. — *n.* 1 One represented politically or in business; a voter; client. 2 A necessary part of a chemical compound: distinguished from *component.* See synonyms under PART. [<L *constituens, -entis,* ppr. of *constituere.* See CONSTITUTE.]

con·sti·tute (kon'stə·tŏŏt, -tyŏŏt) *v.t.* **·tut·ed, ·tut·ing** 1 To form or be the substance of; compose; make up. 2 To impart a given character to. 3 To make or form, as of materials or elements; construct. 4 To establish or found, as a school. 5 To set up or enact, as a law. 6 To depute or appoint, as to an office or function. 7 To give legal or official form to, as a court or assembly. 8 *Obs.* To place or put in position. See synonyms under MAKE. [<L *constitutus,* pp. of *constituere* < *com-* together + *statuere* place, station] — **con'sti·tut'er** *n.* — **con'sti·tu'tive** *adj.* — **con'sti·tu'tive·ly** *adv.* — **con'sti·tu'tive·ness** *n.*

con·sti·tu·tion (kon'stə·tŏŏ'shən, -tyŏŏ'-) *n.* 1 The act of constituting. 2 A system of related parts; composition; specifically, bodily frame or temperament. 3 The fundamental laws and practices that normally govern the operation of a state or association; especially, **the Constitution** of the United States of America, which was framed and adopted by a convention called for that purpose (1787), subsequently ratified by each State separately, and went into operation Mar. 4, 1789. 4 *Archaic* An imperial ordinance or rescript. See synonyms under CHARACTER. — **rigid constitution** A constitution, like that of the United States, which can be amended only by special process of law. — **unitary constitution** A constitution that vests all or most of the power in the central organs of government.

Con·sti·tu·tion (kon'stə·tŏŏ'shən, -tyŏŏ'-) An American frigate active in the War of 1812: called *Old Ironsides.*

con·sti·tu·tion·al (kon'stə·tŏŏ'shən·əl, -tyŏŏ'-) *adj.* 1 Pertaining to, inherent in, or affecting the constitution of a person or of a state; consistent with the constitution of a state; lawful. 2 Acting under and controlled by a constitution: a *constitutional* monarchy. 3 Loyal to the constitution. 4 Framing or amending a constitution. See synonyms under RADICAL. — *n.* A walk taken for one's health. — **con·sti·tu·tion·al·i·ty** (kon'stə·tŏŏ'shən·al'ə·tē, -tyŏŏ'-) *n.* — **con'sti·tu'tion·al·ly** *adv.*

Constitutional amendment A legal alteration of or addition to the Constitution of the United States, ratified by three fourths of the States.

constitutional clergy In French history, that part of the clergy which accepted the civil constitution of the church established by the National Assembly at Paris in 1790.

con·sti·tu·tion·al·ism (kon'stə·tŏŏ'shən·əl·iz'-əm, -tyŏŏ-) *n.* 1 The theory or principle of constitutional government. 2 Adherence to this theory. 3 A constitutional form of government.

con·sti·tu·tion·al·ist (kon'stə·tŏŏ'shən·əl·ist, -tyŏŏ'-) *n.* 1 One who adheres to the constitution of the country. 2 One who advocates constitutionalism in opposition to absolutism, etc. 3 A student of constitutionalism.

con·strain (kən·strān') *v.t.* 1 To compel by physical or moral means; oblige. 2 To confine, as by bonds. 3 To restrain; compel to inaction. 4 *Obs.* To violate; force. See synonyms under COMPEL, MAKE, RESTRAIN. [<OF *constreindre* <L *constringere* < *com-* together + *stringere* bind tight. Doublet of CONSTRINGE.] — **con·strain'a·ble** *adj.* — **con·strain'er** *n.*

con·strained (kən·strānd') *adj.* Subjected to or resulting from constraint; compulsory; repressed. — **con·strain·ed·ly** (kən·strā'nid·lē) *adv.*

con·straint (kən·strānt') *n.* 1 The act of constraining, or the state of being constrained; compulsion. 2 Repression or embarrassment. 3 Anything that constrains. See synonyms under MODESTY, RESERVE. [<OF *constreinte* < *constreindre.* See CONSTRAIN.]

con·strict (kən·strikt') *v.t.* To compress or draw together at some point; bind; cramp. [<L *constrictus,* pp. of *constringere.* See CONSTRAIN.] — **con·stric'tive** *adj.*

con·stric·tion (kən·strik'shən) *n.* 1 A constricting, or a constricted part. 2 That which constricts or is constricted.

con·stric·tor (kən·strik'tər) *n.* 1 That which constricts. 2 *Anat.* A muscle which contracts a part or organ of the body. 3 A serpent that crushes its prey by coiling around it and squeezing.

con·stringe (kən·strinj') *v.t.* **·stringed, ·string·ing** To cause contraction in; shrink; compress. [<L *constringere.* Doublet of CONSTRAIN.]

con·strin·gent (kən·strin'jənt) *adj.* 1 Tending to constrict. 2 Causing constriction. [<L *constringens, -entis,* ppr. of *constringere.* See CONSTRAIN.] — **con·strin'gen·cy** *n.*

con·struct (kən·strukt') *v.t.* 1 To put together and set up; build; arrange. 2 To devise. — *n.* (kon'strukt) 1 Anything systematically constructed or composed. 2 *Psychol.* A complex of mental images and impressions, deliberately synthesized in a form to aid the imagination in further speculation. [<L *constructus,* pp. of *construere.* See CONSTRUE.] — **con·struct'er, con·struc'tor** *n.*

con·struc·tion (kən·struk'shən) *n.* 1 The act of constructing; also, that which is constructed. 2 Style of building or composing. 3 The act of construing, or the interpretation thereby arrived at. 4 *Gram.* a The putting together of forms syntactically, as in sentences, or morphologically, as in words; also, an example of this. b The syntactical relationship of words, clauses, and sentences to each other. — **con·struc'tion·al** *adj.*

con·struc·tion·ist (kən·struk'shən·ist) *n.* 1 One who construes laws, etc., or one who advocates a particular construction. 2 One who interprets literally a law or body of writings, especially the U.S. Constitution or the Bible.

con·struc·tive (kən·struk'tiv) *adj.* 1 Involving the act or possessing the power of constructing. 2 *Law* Assumed or inferred as being included within the intent or application of a law or a legal document. 3 Tending toward or resulting in positive conclusions; affirmative. — **con·struc'tive·ly** *adv.* — **con·struc'tive·ness** *n.*

con·strue (kən·strŏŏ') *v.* **·strued, ·stru·ing** *v.t.* 1 To analyze the grammatical structure of (a clause or sentence) so as to determine the use, interrelations, and function of each word; parse. 2 To translate orally. 3 To deduce by inference; interpret. 4 *Gram.* To combine (words, etc.) according to syntax: The noun *aerodynamics* is construed as a singular. — *v.i.* 5 To determine grammatical structure. 6 To infer; deduce. 7 To admit of grammatical analysis. — *n.* 1 A construction or act of construing. 2 A translation according to a given construction. [<L *construere* < *com-* together + *struere* build up] — **con·stru'a·ble** *adj.* — **con·stru'er** *n.*

con·sub·stan·tial (kon'səb·stan'shəl) *adj.* Having the same substance: The Son is *consubstantial* with the Father. See TRINITY.

— **con·sub·stan′tial·ly** *adv.* — **con·sub·stan·ti·al·i·ty** (kon′səb·stan′shē·al′ə·tē) *n.*
con·sub·stan·ti·ate (kon′səb·stan′shē·āt) *v.* **·at·ed, ·at·ing** *v.t.* 1 To unite in one common substance. 2 To regard as being so united. — *v.i.* 3 To become one in substance. 4 To believe in the doctrine of consubstantiation. [<Med. L *consubstantiatus*, pp. of *consubstantiare* < *com-* together + *substantia* SUBSTANCE]
con·sub·stan·ti·a·tion (kon′səb·stan′shē·ā′shən) *n. Theol.* The theory of the substantial presence of Christ in the consecrated eucharistic elements, together with the unchanged substance of bread and wine.
con·sue·tude (kon′swi·to͞od, -tyo͞od) *n.* Custom; association. [<OF <L *consuetudo* CUSTOM] — **con·sue·tu·di·nar·y** (kon′swi·to͞o′də·ner′ē, -tyo͞o′-), **con′sue·tu′di·nal** *adj.*
con·sul (kon′səl) *n.* 1 An officer appointed to reside in a foreign port or city, chiefly as the representative of his country's commercial interests. 2 Either of two chief magistrates ruling conjointly in the Roman republic. 3 Any of the three chief magistrates of the French republic, 1799–1804. [<L] — **con·su·lar** (kon′sə·lər) *adj.*
con·su·late (kon′sə·lit) *n.* 1 The office or term of office of a consul: also **con′sul·ship.** 2 Government by consuls. 3 The official place of business of a consul. [<L *consulatus* < *consul* consul]
consul general A consular officer of the highest rank stationed in an important foreign commercial city, who supervises the other consuls in his district.
con·sult (kən·sult′) *v.t.* 1 To ask advice or information of. 2 To have regard to, as interest or duty; consider. 3 *Obs.* To contrive or devise. — *v.i.* 4 To ask advice. 5 To compare views; take counsel: with *with.* [<L *consultare*, freq. of *consulere* seek advice] — **con·sult′er, con·sul′tor** *n.*
Synonyms: confer, deliberate. *Confer* suggests the interchange of counsel, advice, or information; *consult* indicates almost exclusively the receiving of it. A man *confers* with his associates, *consults* a physician or a dictionary. See DELIBERATE.
con·sult·ant (kən·sul′tənt) *n.* 1 A person referred to for expert or professional advice. 2 One who consults.
con·sul·ta·tion (kon′səl·tā′shən) *n.* 1 The act of consulting. 2 A meeting, as of physicians, for conference.
con·sult·a·to·ry (kən·sul′tə·tôr′ē, -tō′rē) *adj.* Proceeding from consultation; advisory.
con·sult·ing (kən·sul′ting) *adj.* Giving professional advice on consultation: a *consulting* physician.
con·sult·ive (kən·sul′tiv) *adj.* Involving consultation; deliberative. Also **con·sult·a·tive** (kən·sul′tə·tiv).
con·sume (kən·so͞om′) *v.* **·sumed, ·sum·ing** *v.t.* 1 To destroy, as by burning. 2 To eat or drink up. 3 To expend wastefully; squander; use up, as money or time. 4 To hold the interest of; engross. — *v.i.* 5 To be wasted or destroyed. See synonyms under ABSORB, BURN. [<L *consumere* < *com-* thoroughly + *sumere* take up, use] — **con·sum′a·ble** *adj.*
con·sum·ed·ly (kən·so͞o′mid·lē) *adv.* Excessively; unrestrainedly.
con·sum·er (kən·so͞o′mər) *n.* 1 One who or that which consumes. 2 One who uses up an article of exchangeable value; one of the buying public.
con·sum·er·ism (kən·so͞o′mər·iz′əm) *n.* The policy or program of protecting the interests of the consumer. [< CONSUMER + -ISM, on analogy with *capitalism*, etc.]
consumers' goods *Econ.* Products for satisfying people's needs rather than for producing other goods or services; goods sold for use: opposed to *producers' goods.*
con·sum·mate (kon′sə·māt) *v.t.* **·mat·ed, ·mat·ing** 1 To bring to completion or perfection; achieve. 2 To fulfil, as a marriage by cohabitation. See synonyms under ACCOMPLISH, EFFECT. — *adj.* (kən·sum′it) Of the highest degree; perfect; complete. [<L *consummatus*, pp. of *consummare* < *com-* together + *summa* sum, total] — **con·sum′mate·ly** *adv.* — **con′·sum·ma′tion** *n.* — **con′sum·ma′tive, con·sum·ma·to·ry** (kən·sum′ə·tôr′ē, -tō′rē) *adj.* — **con′·sum·ma′tor** *n.*
con·sump·ti·ble (kən·sump′tə·bəl) *adj.* Consumable, as by use. — *n.* Anything that can be consumed or used.
con·sump·tion (kən·sump′shən) *n.* 1 The act or process of consuming; gradual destruction, as by burning, etc. 2 *Pathol.* A wasting disease; specifically, pulmonary tuberculosis. 3 *Econ.* The use and consequent destruction of goods in the satisfying of people's needs. [<L *consumptio, -onis* < *consumere.* See CONSUME.]
con·sump·tive (kən·sump′tiv) *adj.* 1 Tending to, causing, or designed for consumption. 2 Connected with or affected by pulmonary tuberculosis. — *n.* A person affected with pulmonary tuberculosis. — **con·sump′tive·ly** *adv.* — **con·sump′tive·ness** *n.*
con·ta·bes·cence (kon′tə·bes′əns) *n. Bot.* A condition in which the stamens and pollen are abortive: often in hybridized plants. [<L *contabescens, -entis*, ppr. of *contabescere* < *com-* thoroughly + *tabes* a wasting away, dwindling] — **con′ta·bes′cent** *adj.*
con·tact (kon′takt) *n.* 1 The coming together, meeting, or touching of two bodies. 2 *Electr.* The touching or joining of points or surfaces of conductors, permitting the passage or flow of a current. 3 Immediate proximity or association. 4 Helpful vocational or social acquaintance. See synonyms under COLLISION. — *v.t.* 1 To bring or place in contact; touch. 2 *Colloq.* To get or be in touch with (a person); communicate with: I will *contact* you tomorrow. — *v.i.* 3 To be or come in contact; touch: with *with.* [<L *contactus*, pp. of *contingere* < *com-* together + *tangere* touch] — **con·tac·tu·al** (kən·tak′cho͞o·əl) *adj.*
contact flight *Aeron.* Control of the course of an aircraft by observing landmarks.
contact lens A thin corrective lens of hard or soft plastic that fits against the eyeball.
con·tac·tor (kon′tak·tər) *n. Electr.* A device for repeatedly opening and closing an electric circuit other than by hand.
contact print *Phot.* A positive print obtained by exposure of a photosensitive surface in direct contact with the negative.
contact process Catalysis.
contact twin A twin crystal, the two parts of which are united by some common crystal plane.
con·ta·gion (kən·tā′jən) *n.* 1 The communication of disease by contact, direct or indirect, or, figuratively, of mental states by suggestion or association. 2 Pestilential influence; pestilence; plague. 3 The medium of transmission of disease; contagium. [<F <L *contagio, -onis* < *contingere.* See CONTACT.]
Synonym: infection. The best usage limits *contagion* to diseases that are transmitted by contact with the diseased person, either directly by touch or indirectly by use of the same articles, by breath, effluvia, etc. *Infection* is applied to diseases produced chiefly by common climatic, malarious, or other wide-spread conditions believed to be chiefly instrumental.
con·ta·gious (kən·tā′jəs) *adj.* 1 Transmissible by contact, as a disease, or by sympathy, as emotions. 2 Catching; spreading. 3 Transmitting disease; pestilential. — **con·ta′gious·ly** *adv.* — **con·ta′gious·ness** *n.*
con·ta·gi·um (kən·tā′jē·əm) *n. pl.* **·gi·a** (-jē·ə) 1 The specific matter by which contagious disease is communicated: syphilitic *contagium.* 2 Contagion. [<L, var. of *contagio.* See CONTAGION.]
con·tain (kən·tān′) *v.t.* 1 To hold or enclose. 2 To include or comprise. 3 To be capable of containing; be able to hold. 4 To keep within bounds; restrain, as oneself or one's feelings. 5 *Math.* To be exactly divisible. 6 *Mil.* To hold, as an enemy, to a position or area, as by actual or feigned attacks. See synonyms under EMBRACE. [<OF *contenir* <L *continere* < *com-* together + *tenere* hold] — **con·tain′a·ble** *adj.* — **con·tain′er** *n.*
con·tain·er·i·za·tion (kən·tān′ər·i·zā′shən) *n.* The packing and shipping of freight in very large, sealed containers, thus facilitating loading and unloading. — **con·tain′er·ized** *adj.*
con·tain·er·ship (kən·tān′ər·ship′) *n.* A ship equipped to handle containerized cargo. Also **container ship.**
con·tain·ment (kən·tān′mənt) *n.* 1 *Mil.* The engagement of the enemy so that he is unable to extricate forces for use elsewhere. 2 In international politics, the forestalling or offsetting, by political and economic policy, of territorial or ideological extension by an inimical power.
con·tam·i·nate (kən·tam′ə·nāt) *v.t.* **·nat·ed, ·nat·ing** To make impure by contact or admixture; taint; defile; pollute. — *adj. Obs.* Contaminated. [<L *contaminatus*, pp. of *contaminare* < *contamen, contagmen* < *com-* together + *tag-*, root of *tangere* touch] — **con·tam′i·nant** *n.* — **con·tam′i·na′tive** *adj.* — **con·tam′i·na′tor** *n.*
con·tam·i·na·tion (kən·tam′ə·nā′shən) *n.* 1 The act of contaminating, or the state of being contaminated or polluted. 2 That which contaminates; defilement; taint.
con·tan·go (kən·tang′gō) *n. pl.* **·goes** *Brit.* 1 The putting off of payment due for stock till next settling day, on payment of a premium. 2 The premium or interest so paid. [? Alter. of CONTINGENT]
conte (kônt) *n. French* A short story, particularly one involving events of a humorous or startling nature.
con·temn (kən·tem′) *v.t.* To despise; scorn. [<OF *contemner* <L *contemnere* < *com-* thoroughly + *temnere* slight, scorn] — **con·temn·er** (kən·tem′ər, -tem′nər), **con·tem·nor** (kən·tem′nər) *n.*
con·tem·plate (kon′təm·plāt) *v.* **·plat·ed, ·plat·ing** *v.t.* 1 To look at attentively; gaze at. 2 To consider thoughtfully; ponder. 3 To intend or plan. 4 To treat of as contingent or possible: Secession was not *contemplated* in the Constitution. — *v.i.* 5 To meditate; muse. [<L *contemplatus*, pp. of *contemplari* < *com-* together + *templum* temple; with ref. to the art of divination] — **con·tem·pla·ble** (kən·tem′plə·bəl) *adj.* — **con′tem·pla′tor** *n.*
con·tem·pla·tion (kon′təm·plā′shən) *n.* 1 The act of keeping the eye or the mind fixed upon some object or subject. 2 Continued thought or abstraction in general; musing: *contemplation* of the heavens; absorbed in *contemplation.* 3 Expectation or intention of doing, or deliberation on something to be done, as of taking a journey. 4 Holy meditation; a life of prayer and meditation as practiced by certain Roman Catholic orders. See synonyms under REFLECTION, THOUGHT.
con·tem·pla·tive (kon′təm·plā′tiv, kən·tem′·plə-) *adj.* Of or given to contemplation; meditative. — **con′tem·pla′tive·ly** *adv.* — **con′·tem·pla′tive·ness** *n.*
con·tem·po·ra·ne·ous (kən·tem′pə·rā′nē·əs) *adj.* Living or occurring at the same time: also spelled *cotemporaneous.* [<L *contemporaneus* < *com-* together + *tempus, temporis* time] — **con·tem·po·ra·ne·i·ty** (kən·tem′pə·rə·nē′ə·tē), **con·tem′po·ra′ne·ous·ness** *n.* — **con·tem′po·ra′·ne·ous·ly** *adv.*
Synonym: contemporary. *Contemporaneous* is used chiefly of facts and events, *contemporary* of persons: *contemporary* writers; *contemporaneous* writings.
con·tem·po·rar·y (kən·tem′pə·rer′ē) *adj.* 1 Contemporaneous; living or existing at the same time. 2 Having the same age; coeval. — *n. pl.* **·rar·ies** A person or thing that is contemporary. Also spelled *cotemporary.* See synonym under CONTEMPORANEOUS.
con·tem·po·rize (kən·tem′pə·rīz) *v.t.* & *v.i.* **·rized, ·riz·ing** To make or be equal in respect of time; synchronize.
con·tempt (kən·tempt′) *n.* 1 The act of despising; disdain; scorn. 2 *Law* Wilful disregard of authority, as of a court. 3 The state of being despised; disgrace; shame. 4 An action implying contempt. See synonyms under SCORN. [<L *contemptus* < *contemnere* despise, disdain. See CONTEMN.]
con·tempt·i·ble (kən·temp′tə·bəl) *adj.* 1 Deserving of contempt; despicable; vile. 2 *Obs.* Contemptuous. See synonyms under BASE, LITTLE, PITIFUL. — **con·tempt′i·bil′i·ty, con·tempt′i·ble·ness** *n.* — **con·tempt′i·bly** *adv.*
con·temp·tu·ous (kən·temp′cho͞o·əs) *adj.* Disdainful. See synonyms under HAUGHTY.

— **con·temp′tu·ous·ly** *adv.* — **con·temp′tu·ous·ness** *n.*

con·tend (kən·tend′) *v.t.* **1** To maintain or assert in argument: with an objective clause. — *v.i.* **2** To debate earnestly; dispute. **3** To strive in competition or rivalry; vie: to *contend* for a prize. **4** To struggle or fight in opposition or combat. [<L *contendere* < *com-* together + *tendere* strive, strain] — **con·tend′er** *n.*

Synonyms: antagonize, argue, battle, combat, compete, contest, cope, dispute, fight, grapple, oppose, strive, vie, wrangle. See ARGUE, OPPOSE. *Antonyms*: see synonyms for AGREE, ALLOW.

con·tent[1] (kon′tent) *n.* **1** *Usually pl.* All that a thing contains. **2** The constituent elements of a conception, or meaning and relations involved; hence, significance or basic meaning. **3** Holding capacity; size. **4** Included area or space; extent. **5** The quantity of a specified part: the silver *content* of a ton of ore. — **latent content** *Psychoanal.* The underlying thoughts or repressed desires that motivate a dream. — **manifest content** *Psychoanal.* The incidents of a dream that are remembered and related by the dreamer. [<L *contentum*, pp. neut. of *continere*. See CONTAIN.]

con·tent[2] (kən·tent′) *n.* **1** Rest of mind; satisfaction; freedom from worry. **2** The means of contentment. — *adj.* Satisfied; not inclined to complain or desire something more or different than what one has. — *v.t.* To fulfil the hopes or expectations of; satisfy. See synonyms under INDULGE, SATISFY. [<L *contentus*, pp. of *continere*. See CONTAIN.]

con·tent·ed (kən·ten′tid) *adj.* Satisfied with things as they are; content; willing. See synonyms under COMFORTABLE. — **con·tent′ed·ly** *adv.* — **con·tent′ed·ness** *n.*

con·ten·tion (kən·ten′shən) *n.* **1** The act of contending; strife; conflict; struggle; dispute. **2** An object or point in debate or controversy. **3** A statement in support of an argument; also, the argument itself. See synonyms under ALTERCATION, FEUD, QUARREL. [<F <L *contentio, -onis* < *contendere*. See CONTEND.]

con·ten·tious (kən·ten′shəs) *adj.* Of, pertaining to, or fond of contention or strife; disputatious; quarrelsome: a *contentious* person. — **con·ten′tious·ly** *adv.* — **con·ten′tious·ness** *n.*

con·tent·ment (kən·tent′mənt) *n.* **1** The condition or fact of being content; satisfaction. **2** *Archaic* The act of satisfying or making content.

con·ter·mi·nous (kən·tûr′mə·nəs) *adj.* Having a common boundary line; coextensive: also *coterminous*. Also **con·ter′mi·nal.** See synonyms under ADJACENT. [<L *conterminus* < *com-* together + *terminus* limit] — **con·ter′mi·nous·ly** *adv.*

con·test (kon′test) *n.* **1** A struggle; competition; conflict. **2** Verbal conflict; controversy. See synonyms under BATTLE, COMPETITION, FEUD, QUARREL. [< *v.*] — *v.t.* (kən·test′) **1** To fight about; contend for; strive to take, keep, or control. **2** To strive to win, as a battle. **3** To argue about, especially in opposition; challenge; litigate: to *contest* an election. — *v.i.* **4** To contend, struggle, or vie: with *with* or *against*. [<F *contester* <L *contestari* bring legal action against < *com-* together + *testari* bear witness < *testis* witness] — **con·test′a·ble** *adj.* — **con·tes·ta·tion** (kon′tes·tā′shən) *n.* — **con·test′er** *n.*

con·test·ant (kən·tes′tənt) *n.* **1** One who enters a contest; a competitor. **2** A defeated political candidate who challenges election returns. [<F <L *contestans, -antis*, ppr. of *contestari*. See CONTEST.]

con·text (kon′tekst) *n.* The portions of a discourse, treatise, etc., that immediately precede and follow and are connected with a passage quoted or considered. [<L *contextus*, pp. of *contexere* < *com-* together + *texere* weave] — **con·tex·tu·al** (kən·teks′cho͞o·əl) *adj.* — **con·tex′tu·al·ly** *adv.*

con·tex·ture (kən·teks′chər, kon-) *n.* **1** A weaving together. **2** Something interwoven. **3** Style or manner of interweaving; texture. — **con·tex′tur·al** *adj.*

Con·ti (kōn′tē), **Niccolò de′**, 15th century Venetian traveler and writer.

con·ti·gu·i·ty (kon′tə·gyo͞o′ə·tē) *n.* **1** Nearness; proximity. **2** Uninterrupted connection; continuity. **3** An unbroken or continuous mass or series.

con·tig·u·ous (kən·tig′yo͞o·əs) *adj.* Touching or joining at the edge or boundary; adjacent. See synonyms under ADJACENT, IMMEDIATE. [<L *contiguus* < *contingere*. See CONTACT.] — **con·tig′u·ous·ly** *adv.* — **con·tig′u·ous·ness** *n.*

con·ti·nence (kon′tə·nəns) *n.* Self–restraint; moderation; especially, self–restraint in sexual passion; chastity. Also **con′ti·nen·cy.** See synonyms under ABSTINENCE.

con·ti·nent (kon′tə·nənt) *n.* **1** One of the great bodies of land on the globe, generally regarded as six in number: Africa, Asia, Australia, Europe, North America, and South America: Antarctica is sometimes regarded as the seventh continent. **2** *Obs.* That which contains; a boundary: also, that which is contained. — **the Continent** Europe, exclusive of the British Isles. — *adj.* **1** Self–restrained; abstinent; chaste. **2** *Obs.* Restraining; limiting. [<OF <L *continens, -entis*, ppr. of *continere*. See CONTAIN.] — **con·ti·nen·tal** (kon′tə·nen′təl) *adj.* — **con′ti·nent·ly** *adv.*

Con·ti·nen·tal (kon′tə·nen′təl) *adj.* **1** European; pertaining to the continent of Europe. **2** Pertaining to the United States during the Revolutionary War, or to the continental portion of the United States. — *n.* **1** A native or resident of the continent of Europe; European. **2** A soldier of the regular forces under the control of Congress in the Revolutionary War. **3** A note of the rapidly depreciated paper money issued by Congress during the Revolution. — **not worth a Continental** Practically valueless.

Continental Congress The legislative and governing body (1774–89) of the Revolutionary American colonies, at first merely *de facto* but later *de jure* under the Articles of Confederation, when it was also known as the *Congress of the Confederation.*

Continental Divide The great ridge of the Rocky Mountain summits separating west–flowing streams from east–flowing streams in North America: also *Great Divide.*

continental drift *Geol.* The theory that the continental land masses are subject to slow movement through the action of underlying magmatic material.

Continental Guinea See RÍO MUNI.

continental Morse code International Morse code.

continental shelf *Geog.* The submerged border of a continent, of varying width and degree of slope, which separates the land mass from the ocean depths.

con·tin·gen·cy (kən·tin′jən·sē) *n. pl.* **·cies** **1** Possibility of occurrence. **2** A fortuitous event; accident; casualty. **3** Something that is incidental. Also **con·tin′gence.** See synonyms under ACCIDENT, EVENT, HAZARD.

con·tin·gent (kən·tin′jənt) *adj.* **1** Likely to occur. **2** Fortuitous; possible. **3** *Law* Dependent upon an uncertain future event. — *n.* **1** A contingency. **2** A proportionate share; representation: the American *contingent* at the conference. **3** *Mil.* A quota of troops. See synonyms under INCIDENTAL. [<L *contingens, -entis*, ppr. of *contingere*. See CONTACT.] — **con·tin′gent·ly** *adv.*

con·tin·u·al (kən·tin′yo͞o·əl) *adj.* **1** Renewed in regular succession; often repeated. **2** Continuous (in time); uninterrupted. ◆ While *continual* is limited to continuity in time, and *continuous* refers to either space or time, usage now tends further to limit *continual* to the sense of "continuing after interruptions," in which sense it is not interchangeable with *continuous.* — **con·tin′u·al·ly** *adv.*

Synonyms: ceaseless, constant, continuous, incessant, invariable, perpetual, regular, unbroken, unceasing, uninterrupted, unremitting, unvarying. *Continuous* describes that which is absolutely without pause or break; *continual*, that which often intermits, but as regularly begins again. A similar distinction is made between *incessant* and *ceaseless*, but *ceaseless* may have the further meaning of unending, perpetual. *Constant* is sometimes used in the sense of *continual*; but its chief reference is to steadiness, as of purpose, sentiment, or movement; as, *constant* devotion; *constant* advance. See PERPETUAL.

con·tin·u·ance (kən·tin′yo͞o·əns) *n.* **1** The state of continuing; duration. **2** Uninterrupted succession; survival. **3** *Law* Postponement. **4** A continuation or sequel, as of a novel.

con·tin·u·ant (kən·tin′yo͞o·ənt) *n. Phonet.* A consonant whose sound may be prolonged on a single breath without a change in quality, as the fricatives (f) and (s): opposed to *stop.* [<L *continuans, -antis*, ppr. of *continuare.* See CONTINUE.]

con·tin·u·ate (kən·tin′yo͞o·āt) *adj.* **1** Closely joined together. **2** Unbroken; uninterrupted. [<L *continuatus*, pp. of *continuare.* See CONTINUE.]

con·tin·u·a·tion (kən·tin′yo͞o·ā′shən) *n.* **1** The act or state of continuing. **2** Something added which protracts, extends, or carries on; a sequel: the *continuation* of a novel. — **con·tin′u·a′tor** *n.*

con·tin·u·a·tive (kən·tin′yo͞o·ā′tiv) *adj.* Denoting or causing continuance or duration. — *n.* **1** That which causes continuation. **2** *Gram.* A conjunction which prolongs a sentence by introducing a subordinate clause at the end. — **con·tin′u·a′tive·ly** *adv.* — **con·tin′u·a′tive·ness** *n.*

con·tin·ue (kən·tin′yo͞o) *v.* **·tin·ued, ·tin·u·ing** *v.t.* **1** To extend or prolong in space or time. **2** To persist in or carry forward. **3** To cause to last or remain, as in a position or office. **4** To take up again, as a course of action or a narrative, after an interruption. **5** *Law* To postpone, as a judicial proceeding; grant a continuance of. — *v.i.* **6** To be durable; last; endure. **7** To keep on or persist. **8** To remain, as in a place or position; abide. **9** To resume after an interruption. See synonyms under ABIDE, LIVE, PERSEVERE, PERSIST, PROTRACT, STAND. [<L *continuare* < *continuus* < *continere.* See CONTAIN.] — **con·tin′u·a·ble** *adj.* — **con·tin′u·er** *n.*

con·tin·ued (kən·tin′yo͞od) *adj.* **1** Extended in space or time; uninterrupted. **2** Continual.

continued fraction See under FRACTION.

continued proportion *Math.* A series of three or more quantities in which the ratio is the same between each two adjacent terms; as, 2, 4, 8, 16, where 2 : 4 :: 4 : 8 :: 8 : 16.

con·ti·nu·i·ty (kon′tə·no͞o′ə·tē, -nyo͞o′-) *n.* **1** The state or quality of being continuous. **2** That which has or gives an orderly sequence, as a scenario for motion pictures or a radio script. **3** The close coordination of all details necessary to ensure smooth performance of a dramatic production, radio or television broadcast, etc.

con·tin·u·ous (kən·tin′yo͞o·əs) *adj.* **1** Connected, extended, or prolonged without a break; unbroken; uninterrupted. **2** Repeating, as a performance, without intermission: said of motion–picture showings, etc. See synonyms under CONTINUAL, GRADUAL, PERPETUAL. [<L *continuus* < *continere.* See CONTAIN.] — **con·tin′u·ous·ly** *adv.* — **con·tin′u·ous·ness** *n.*

con·tin·u·um (kən·tin′yo͞o·əm) *n. pl.* **·tin·u·a** (-tin′yo͞o·ə) **1** A total that is continuous and uninterrupted. **2** That which has perfect continuity: the *continuum* of space. **3** A basic, common character underlying a series or aggregation of indefinite variations. **4** *Math.* A set of numbers or points such that between any two of them a third may be interpolated. [<L, neut. of *continuus* CONTINUOUS]

con·to (kon′tō) *n. pl.* **·tos** A Portuguese money of account, formerly equal to 1,000,000 reis, now equal to 1,000 escudos in Portugal or 1,000 cruzeiros in Brazil.

con·tort (kən·tôrt′) *v.t.* To twist violently; wrench out of shape or place. See synonyms under TWIST. [<L *contortus*, pp. of *contorquere* < *com-* together + *torquere* twist] — **con·tor′tive** *adj.*

con·tor·tion (kən·tôr′shən) *n.* **1** The act of contorting. **2** Unnatural spasmodic writhing or wryness, as of the limbs.

con·tor·tion·ist (kən·tôr′shən·ist) *n.* An acrobat trained to distort his limbs.

con·tour (kon′to͝or) *n.* The line bounding a figure or body; outline. — *v.t.* **1** To make or draw in outline or contour; make contour lines on or determine the contour lines of. **2** To carry, as a road, around the contour of a ridge or hill. [<F <Ital. *contorno* < *contornare* <LL *com-* together + *tornare* round off, make round]

contour feathers The outer feathers that determine the outline of a bird; pennae.

contour line **1** The line, or one of the lines, constituting the boundary of a plane. **2** In maps, the line connecting points on the earth

which are at the same elevation above sea level.

contour map A map constructed to show the comparative elevation of topographic features by a series of contour lines, each separated from the next by a definite difference in height, called a **contour interval.**

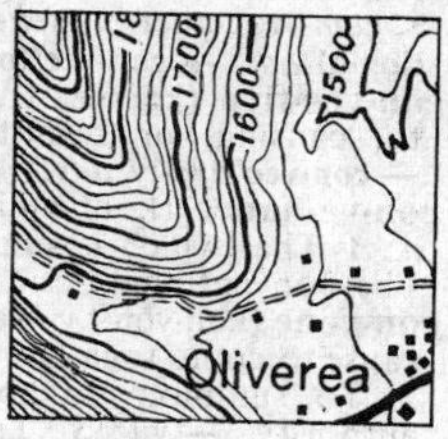

CONTOUR MAP WITH INTERVALS

contour plowing *Agric.* A method of cultivation in which the furrows follow the contours of uneven land in such a way as to minimize the destructive action of wind and erosion.

contra- *prefix* Against; opposite; contrary: *contradict.* [< L *contra* against]

con·tra (kon′trə) *n.* A rebel soldier in Central America, especially one in revolt during the 1980s against the Sandinistas in Nicaragua. [< Spanish, short for *contra-revolucionario* a counterrevolutionary]

con·tra·band (kon′trə·band) *adj.* Prohibited or excluded, as by military law; forbidden. —*n.* **1** Contraband goods or trade. **2** Any fugitive slave who took refuge within the Union lines during the Civil War. **3** Contraband of war. [< Sp. *contrabanda* a smuggling < Ital. *contrabando* < *contra* against + *bando* < LL *bannum* law, proclamation] —**con′tra·band′ist** *n.*

contraband of war Anything furnished by a neutral to a belligerent that is by the laws of war subject to seizure. Arms and military supplies are classed as **absolute contraband**; grain, horses, etc., as **occasional contraband**; goods consigned to a neutral country which may be transferred to a belligerent or to a belligerent country which may be used by the army or navy are **conditional contraband.**

con·tra·bass (kon′trə·bās) *n.* A double bass. —*adj.* Having its pitch an octave lower than another instrument of the same class; of deep range: a *contrabass* horn. [< Ital. *contrabasso*]

con·tra·bass·ist (kon′trə·bā′sist) *n.* One who performs on the contrabass.

con·tra·bas·soon (kon′trə·bə·so͞on′) *n.* The double-bassoon.

con·tra·cep·tion (kon′trə·sep′shən) *n.* The prevention of conception or fecundation. [< CONTRA- + (CON)CEPTION]

con·tra·cep·tive (kon′trə·sep′tiv) *adj.* **1** Serving or acting to prevent conception or impregnation. **2** Pertaining to contraception. —*n.* Any device or substance that inhibits conception.

con·tract (kən·trakt′ *for v. defs. 1, 2, 4–8;* kon′trakt, kən·trakt′ *for v. def. 3) v.t.* **1** To reduce in size; abridge in compass or duration; shrink; narrow. **2** To wrinkle; draw together, as the brow. **3** To arrange or settle by agreement; enter upon with reciprocal obligations. **4** To acquire or become affected with, as a disease or habit. **5** *Gram.* To shorten, as a word, by omitting or combining medial letters or sounds. **6** To betroth. —*v.i.* **7** To shrink; become reduced in size. **8** To make a contract. —*n.* (kon′trakt) **1** *Law* A formal agreement, or the writing containing it. **2** A betrothal or marriage. **3** The department of law dealing with contracts. **4** Contract bridge: see under BRIDGE^2. —**yellow dog contract** A contract whereby an employee agrees not to join a union. [< L *contractus,* pp. of *contrahere* < *com-* together + *trahere* pull, draw]

Synonyms (noun): agreement, arrangement, bargain, cartel, compact, convenant, engagement, promise, stipulation. An *agreement* or a *contract* may be oral or written, but a consideration or compensation is essential to a *contract.* A *covenant,* in law, is a written *contract* under seal. *Convenant* is frequent in religious usage, as *contract* is in law and business. *Compact* is essentially the same as *contract,* but is applied to international *agreements,* treaties, etc. A *bargain* is a mutual *agreement* for an exchange of values, without the formality of a *contract.* A *stipulation* is a single item in an *agreement* or *contract.* Compare SALE.

con·tract·ed (kən·trak′tid) *adj.* **1** Having undergone contraction; shrunken. **2** Not broad or liberal; narrow; mean; scanty. —**con·tract′ed·ly** *adv.* —**con·tract′ed·ness** *n.*

con·trac·tile (kən·trak′təl) *adj.* Having the power to contract or to induce a contraction. Also **con·tract′i·ble** or **con·tract′a·ble, con·trac′tive.** —**con·tract′i·bil′i·ty, con·tract′i·ble·ness, con·trac·til·i·ty** (kon′trak·til′ə·tē) *n.*

contractile tissue *Physiol.* Body tissue composed of smooth or striated muscle cells whose contraction aids in the production of movement.

con·trac·tion (kən·trak′shən) *n.* **1** The act of contracting or the state of being contracted. **2** That which is contracted, as a word by the omission of one or more medial letters or sounds. See synonyms under ABBREVIATION.

contract labor Laborers brought into a country under contract.

con·trac·tor (kon′trak·tər, kən·trak′tər *for defs. 1 and 2;* kən·trak′tər *for def. 3) n.* **1** One of the parties to a contract. **2** One who executes plans under contract; especially, one who agrees to supply labor or materials, or both, on a large scale. **3** *Anat.* A muscle that serves to contract.

con·trac·tu·al (kən·trak′cho͞o·əl) *adj.* Connected with or implying a contract.

con·trac·ture (kən·trak′chər) *n.* **1** *Med.* A permanent contraction and rigidity of muscles. **2** *Archit.* The narrowing of the higher part of a column.

con·tra·dance (kon′trə·dans′, -däns′) See CONTREDANSE. Also **con′tra·danse′.**

con·tra·dict (kon′trə·dikt′) *v.t. & v.i.* **1** To maintain the opposite of (a statement); refute or gainsay; deny. **2** To be inconsistent with or opposed to. See synonyms under OPPOSE. [< L *contradictus,* pp. of *contradicere* < *contra-* against + *dicere* say, speak] —**con′tra·dict′a·ble** *adj.* —**con′tra·dict′er** or **con′tra·dic′·tor** *n.* —**con′tra·dic′tion** *n.* —**con′tra·dic′tive** *adj.* —**con′tra·dic′·tive·ness** *n.*

con·tra·dic·to·ry (kon′trə·dik′tər·ē) *adj.* **1** Involving or of the nature of a contradiction; inconsistent; contrary. **2** Given or inclined to contradiction. See synonyms under ALIEN, CONTRARY, INCONGRUOUS, INIMICAL. —*n. pl.* **·ries** *Logic* A proposition by means of which another proposition is absolutely denied. —**con′tra·dic′to·ri·ly** *adv.* —**con′tra·dic′to·ri·ness** *n.*

con·tra·dis·tinct (kon′trə·dis·tingkt′) *adj.* Distinguished by contrary qualities or by contrast. —**con′tra·dis·tinct′ly** *adv.*

con·tra·dis·tinc·tion (kon′trə·dis·tingk′shən) *n.* Distinction by contrast or by contrasting qualities: a large corporation in *contradistinction* to a small business. —**con′tra·dis·tinc′·tive** *adj.* —**con′tra·dis·tinc′tive·ly** *adv.*

con·tra·dis·tin·guish (kon′trə·dis·ting′gwish) *v.t.* To discriminate by contrasting opposite qualities.

con·tra·fa·got·to (kon′trə·fə·got′ō) *n.* **1** A double-bassoon, an octave lower than the bassoon. **2** An organ stop made to imitate a contrafagotto. [< Ital.]

con·trail (kon′trāl) *n. Aeron.* The vapor trail which sometimes streams out in the wake of an airplane flying at high altitudes, caused by the condensation of moisture from exhaust gases of the engine. [< *con(densation) trail*]

con·tra·in·di·cate (kon′trə·in′də·kāt) *v.t. Med.* To indicate the danger or undesirability of (a given drug or method of treatment). —**con′·tra·in′di·cant** *adj. & n.* —**con′tra·in′di·ca′·tion** *n.*

con·tral·to (kən·tral′tō) *n. pl.* **·tos** or **·ti** (-tē) **1** The lowest female voice, intermediate between soprano and tenor: also called *alto.* **2** *Music* A part written for such a voice. **3** A singer with such a voice. [< Ital.]

con·tra·po·si·tion (kon′trə·pə·zish′ən) *n.* **1** *Logic* Conversion by negation, or by changing the quality of the judgment while the quantity remains unchanged; transposition. **2** A placing opposite.

con·trap·tion (kən·trap′shən) *n. Colloq.* A contrivance or gadget. [? < CONTRIVE] —**con·trap′tious** *adj.*

con·tra·pun·tal (kon′trə·pun′təl) *adj. Music* **1** Of or pertaining to counterpoint. **2** Characterized by the use of counterpoint; con-structed according to the principles of counterpoint. [< Ital. *contrapunto* counterpoint] —**con′tra·pun′tal·ly** *adv.* —**con′tra·pun′tal·ist, con′tra·pun′tist** *n.*

con·tra·ri·e·ty (kon′trə·rī′ə·tē) *n. pl.* **·ties** **1** The quality or state of being contrary. **2** A quality or a proposition contrary to another; an inconsistency; a contrary.

con·trar·i·ous (kən·trâr′ē·əs) *adj.* **1** Showing refractory opposition. **2** Harmful; vexatious: said of things. —**con·trar′i·ous·ly** *adv.* —**con·trar′i·ous·ness** *n.*

con·trar·i·wise (kon′trer·ē·wīz′; *for def. 3, also* kən·trâr′ē·wīz′) *adv.* **1** On the contrary; on the other hand. **2** In the reverse order; conversely. **3** Captiously; perversely.

con·trar·y (kon′trer·ē; *for adj. def. 4, also* kən·trâ·r′ē) *adj.* **1** Opposed in situation, direction, aim, purpose, or operation; antagonistic. **2** Adverse: *contrary* winds. **3** Opposite; opposing. **4** Characterized or swayed by perversity; inclined to opposition or contradiction; captious. —*n. pl.* **·trar·ies** **1** One of two opposing things. **2** The opposite. **3** *Logic* A statement whose truth is undetermined by the falsity of another, but which cannot be true if the latter is true: "The man is a perjurer" is the *contrary* of "The man is honest." —**by contraries** By way of opposition to anticipated procedure. —**on the contrary** Contrariwise; on the other hand. —**to the contrary** To the opposite effect. —*adv.* In a contrary manner; contrariwise. [< AF *contrarie* < L *contrarius* < *contra* against] —**con′trar·i·ly** *adv.* —**con′trar·i·ness** *n.*

Synonyms (adj.): antagonistic, conflicting, contradictory, contrasted, different, discordant, dissimilar, incompatible, incongruous, inconsistent, opposed, opposite, unlike. Things are *contradictory* which mutually exclude each other, so that both cannot exist in the same object at the same time, as life and death. Things are *contrary* when the highest degree of both cannot exist in the same object at the same time, but where a middle term is possible, partaking of the qualities of both, as wisdom and folly, or heat and cold. See ALIEN, INCONGRUOUS, INIMICAL, PERVERSE.

con·trast (kən·trast′) *v.t.* **1** To place or set in opposition so as to show dissimilarities. **2** To set off; afford a contrast to. —*v.i.* **3** To manifest dissimilarities when placed or set in opposition. —*n.* (kon′trast) **1** The unlikeness between two or more things or persons, as revealed by comparison. **2** A person or thing that shows unlikeness to another. [< OF *contraster* < Ital. *contrastare* < LL < L *contra-* against + *stare* stand] —**con·trast′a·ble** *adj.*

Synonyms (verb): compare, differentiate, discriminate, oppose. To *compare* is to place together in order to show likeness or unlikeness; to *contrast* is to set in opposition in order to show unlikeness. We *contrast* objects that have been already *compared.* We must *compare* them, at least momentarily, even to know that they are different. We *contrast* them when we observe their unlikeness in a general way; we *differentiate* them when we note the difference exactly and point by point. See DIFFERENCE.

con·tra·ter·rene (kon′trə·te·rēn′) *adj.* **1** Opposed to or destructive of the earth. **2** *Physics* Pertaining to or having the characteristics of antimatter. —*n.* Antiworld.

con·tra·val·la·tion (kon′trə·və·lā′shən) *n.* A chain of fortifications raised by besiegers round an invested place, to protect themselves from sallies of the garrison. [< F *contrevallation* < LL *contra-* against + *vallatio, -onis* rampart < *vallum* wall]

con·tra·vene (kon′trə·vēn′) *v.t.* **·vened, ·ven·ing** **1** To transgress; violate or infringe upon, as a law. **2** To deny or run counter to; oppose or be inconsistent with in principle. See synonyms under OPPOSE. [< F *contrevenir* < LL *contravenire* < L *contra-* against + *venire* come] —**con′tra·ven′er** *n.* —**con·tra·ven·tion** (kon′·trə·ven′shən) *n.*

con·tra·yer·va (kon′trə·yûr′və) *n.* **1** The stimulant and tonic root of a tropical American plant *(Dorstenia contrajerva)* of the mulberry family. **2** The plant. [< Sp. *contrayerba* antidote < *contra* against + *yerba* herb < L *herba*]

contre– *prefix* Counter; against; in opposition to. [<F <L *contra.* See CONTRA-.]

con·trec·ta·tion (kon′trek·tā′shən) *n.* The impulse to caress or fondle a person of the opposite sex. [<L *contrectatio, -onis* < *contrectare* <*com-* thoroughly + *tractare* touch, fondle]

con·tre·danse (kôṅ·trə·däns′) *n.* 1 A country dance. 2 One of the figures composing a quadrille. Also **con·tre·dance** (kon′trə·dans′, -däns′): also spelled *contradance, contradanse.* [<F, alter. of COUNTRY DANCE]

Con·tre·ras (kôn·trā′räs) A town in central Mexico; site of a battle of the Mexican War, 1847.

con·tre·temps (kôṅ·trə·täṅ′) *n. pl.* **·temps** (-täṅz′, *Fr.* -täṅ′) An embarrassing occurrence; awkward incident. [<F]

con·trib·ute (kən·trib′yo͞ot) *v.* **·ut·ed, ·ut·ing** *v.t.* 1 To give or furnish in common with others; give for a common purpose. 2 To submit, sell, or furnish, as an article or story, to a magazine or other publication. —*v.i.* 3 To share in effecting a result: These causes *contributed* to the king's downfall. 4 To make or give a contribution. [<L *contributus,* pp. of *contribuere* < *com-* together + *tribuere* grant, allot] —**con·trib′ut·a·ble** *adj.* —**con·trib′u·tive** *adj.* —**con·trib′u·tive·ly** *adv.* —**con·trib′u·tive·ness** *n.* —**con·trib′u·tor** *n.*

con·tri·bu·tion (kon′trə·byo͞o′shən) *n.* 1 The act of contributing, or that which is contributed. 2 A piece of writing furnished to a magazine, etc. 3 An impost; tax; levy. —**con′tri·bu′tion·al** *adj.*

con·trib·u·to·ry (kən·trib′yə·tôr′ē, -tō′rē) *adj.* 1 Contributing. 2 *Law* Casually sharing in some act. 3 Liable to an impost. —*n. pl.* **·ries** One who or that which contributes.

con·trite (kən·trīt′, kon′trīt) *adj.* 1 Broken in spirit because of a sense of sin; penitent; sorry. 2 Resulting from contrition. [<OF *contrit* <L *contritus,* pp. of *conterere* < *com-* together + *terere* rub] —**con·trite′ly** *adv.*

con·tri·tion (kən·trish′ən) *n.* 1 Deep and sincere sorrow for wrongdoing. 2 *Theol.* A feeling of repentance for sin, with an intention to amend, arising from love of God and consideration of His goodness (**perfect contrition**), or from inferior motives, as fear of punishment (**imperfect contrition**). Compare ATTRITION (def. 3). Also **con·trite′ness.** See synonyms under PENITENCE, REPENTANCE.

con·tri·vance (kən·trī′vəns) *n.* 1 The act of contriving or adapting something to a special purpose. 2 A device, tool, or implement. 3 A strategem, plan, or scheme. See synonyms under ARTIFICE.

con·trive (kən·trīv′) *v.* **·trived, ·triv·ing** *v.t.* 1 To scheme or plan; devise. 2 To plot or conspire. 3 To make ingeniously; improvise; invent: He *contrived* an extra sail. 4 To manage or carry through, as by some device or scheme. —*v.i.* 5 To form designs; plot. [<OF *controver* find, invent, ? <L *com-* together + *turbare* stir up, disclose, find] —**con·triv′a·ble** *adj.* —**con·triv′er** *n.*

con·trol (kən·trōl′) *v.t.* **·trolled, ·trol·ling** 1 To exercise a directing, restraining, or governing influence over. 2 To regulate or verify, as an experiment, by comparison with a parallel experiment or other relevant standard. 3 To check, as an account, by means of a duplicate register; verify or rectify. —*n.* 1 The act of controlling; restraining or directing influence; regulation; check; government. 2 One who or that which controls. 3 *Mech.* Any of variously designed and operated devices for the control of airplanes, motorcars, ships, machines, and the like. 4 *Meteorol.* An element, as atmospheric pressure, physical features, altitude, etc., serving as a determinant of climate. 5 A standard of comparison against which to check the results of an experiment, especially in the biological and medical sciences. 6 In spiritualism, a spirit presumed to act upon and through a medium in seances. [<MF *contrôler,* earlier *contreroller* keep a check list <Med. L *contrarotulus* a check list <L *contra-* against + *rotulus* list] —**con·trol′la·bil′i·ty, con·trol′la·ble·ness** *n.* —**con·trol′la·ble** *adj.* —**con·trol′ling** *adj.* —**con·trol′ment** *n.*

control chart *Stat.* A chart on which the numerical values of a series of observations are plotted in the order of their occurrence and checked to determine the extent of variation from designated standards of quality, quantity, performance, etc.

control day Any of various days whose weather is popularly believed to control the weather of a group of following days, as St. Swithin's Day.

control experiment An experiment designed to check the data in a series of related experiments by altering one of a group of specified factors and comparing the results with a view to exposing differences that might have causal significance.

con·trol·ler (kən·trō′lər) *n.* 1 One who or that which controls. 2 A magnet used in automatic regulation of an electric current. 3 An officer to examine and verify accounts: also spelled *comptroller.* —**con·trol′ler·ship** *n.*

control stick *Aeron.* The lever which operates the longitudinal and lateral control surfaces of an airplane: also called *joy-stick.*

control surface *Aeron.* Any movable device, as an airfoil, aileron, rudder, etc., operated to guide or control an aircraft, rocket, guided missile, etc.

con·tro·ver·sial (kon′trə·vûr′shəl) *adj.* 1 Debatable; open to argument; causing controversy; disputable. 2 Given to controversy; disputatious. —**con′tro·ver′sial·ist** *n.* —**con′tro·ver′sial·ly** *adv.*

con·tro·ver·sy (kon′trə·vûr′sē) *n. pl.* **·sies** 1 Debate or disputation; discussion as to schemes or opinions. 2 A quarrel or dispute. See synonyms under ALTERCATION, FEUD, QUARREL. [<L *controversia* < *controversus* < *contra-* against + *versus,* pp. of *vertere* turn]

con·tro·vert (kon′trə·vûrt, kon′trə·vûrt′) *v.t.* To endeavor to disprove; oppose in debate. See synonyms under DISPUTE. [<L *controversus,* on analogy with *convert, revert,* etc. See CONTROVERSY.] —**con′tro·vert′er** *n.* —**con′tro·vert′i·ble** *adj.* —**con′tro·vert′i·bly** *adv.*

con·tu·ma·cy (kon′to͞o·mə·sē, -tyo͞o-) *n. pl.* **·cies** Contemptuous disregard of the requirements of rightful authority; insolent and stubborn perverseness; incorrigible obstinacy. Also **con·tu·mac·i·ty** (kon′to͞o·mas′ə·tē, -tyo͞o-). [<L *contumacia* < *contumax* stubborn] —**con·tu·ma·cious** (kon′to͞o·mā′shəs, -tyo͞o-) *adj.* —**con′tu·ma′cious·ly** *adv.* —**con′tu·ma′cious·ness** *n.*

con·tu·me·ly (kon′to͞o·mə·lē, -tyo͞o-, -mē′lē; kən·to͞o′mə·lē, -tyo͞o′-) *n. pl.* **·lies** 1 Insulting rudeness in speech or manner; scornful insolence. 2 An act or statement exhibiting haughtiness and contempt. See synonyms under SCORN. [<OF *contumelie* <L *contumelia* reproach] —**con·tu·me·li·ous** (kon′to͞o·mē′lē·əs, -tyo͞o-) *adj.* —**con′tu·me′li·ous·ly** *adv.* —**con′tu·me′li·ous·ness** *n.*

con·tuse (kən·to͞oz′, -tyo͞oz′) *v.t.* **·tused, ·tus·ing** To bruise by a blow. [<L *contusus,* pp. of *contundere* < *com-* together + *tundere* beat] —**con·tu·sive** (kən·to͞o′siv, -tyo͞o′-) *adj.*

con·tu·sion (kən·to͞o′zhən, -tyo͞o′-) *n.* 1 The act of bruising, or the state of being bruised. 2 A bruise.

co·nun·drum (kə·nun′drəm) *n.* 1 A riddle, often depending on a pun. 2 Any perplexing question or thing. [Origin unknown]

con·ur·ba·tion (kon′ûr·bā′shən) *n.* A complex of towns, villages, and small cities closely associated with the needs and activities of a central metropolis. [<CON- + *urbs* city]

con·va·lesce (kon′və·les′) *v.i.* **·lesced ·lesc·ing** To recover from a sickness. [<L *convalescere* < *com-* thoroughly + *valescere,* inceptive of *valere* be strong]

con·va·les·cence (kon′və·les′əns) *n.* 1 Gradual recovery from illness. 2 The period of such recovery. Also **con′va·les′cen·cy.**

con·va·les·cent (kon′və·les′ənt) *adj.* Recovering health after sickness. —*n.* One who is convalescing. [<L *convalescens, -entis,* ppr. of *convalescere.* See CONVALESCE.]

Con·val·lar·i·a (kon′və·lâr′ē·ə) *n. pl.* A genus of monocotyledonous herbs of the lily family, with regular and perfect flowers and berrylike fruits. The only known species is the lily–of–the–valley.

con·vec·tion (kən·vek′shən) *n.* 1 The act of conveying. 2 *Physics* The diffusion of heat through a liquid or gas by motion of its parts: distinguished from *conduction.* 3 *Meteorol.* A thermal process whereby atmospheric circulation is maintained through the upward or downward transfer of air masses of different temperature. [<L *convectus,* pp. of *convehere* < *com-* together + *vehere* carry] —**con·vec′tion·al** *adj.* —**con·vec′tor** *n.*

con·vec·tive (kən·vek′tiv) *adj.* Of, pertaining to, causing, or resulting from convection. —**con·vec′tive·ly** *adv.*

con·ve·nance (kon′və·näns, *Fr.* kôṅ·və·näṅs′) *n.* 1 That which is suitable or proper. 2 *pl.* The conventionalities. [<F]

con·vene (kən·vēn′) *v.* **·vened, ·ven·ing** *v.t.* 1 To cause to come together or assemble; convoke. 2 To summon to appear, as by judicial authority. —*v.i.* 3 To come together; assemble. See synonyms under CONVOKE. [<L *convenire* < *com-* together + *venire* come] —**con·ven′a·ble** *adj.* —**con·ven′er** *n.*

con·ven·ience (kən·vēn′yəns) *n.* 1 The state, time, or quality of being convenient; suitableness; fitness. 2 Freedom from difficulty or discomfort; ease. 3 That which is convenient; that which gives ease or comfort; anything handy or labor–saving. 4 A convenient occasion. Also **con·ven′ien·cy.** See synonyms under OPPORTUNITY.

con·ven·ient (kən·vēn′yənt) *adj.* 1 Conducive to comfort or ease; serviceable; suitable; commodious; favorable; timely. 2 Near at hand; handy. 3 *Obs.* Of a fit character or quality. [<L *conveniens, -entis,* ppr. of *convenire.* See CONVENE.] —**con·ven′ient·ly** *adv.*

Synonyms: adapted, commodious, favorable, fit, fitted, handy, helpful, opportune, proper, seasonable, suitable, suited, useful. See COMFORTABLE, EXPEDIENT, GOOD. *Antonyms*: awkward, clumsy, inconvenient, superfluous, unhandy, unmanageable, unseasonable, useless.

con·vent (kon′vent, -vənt) *n.* 1 A religious community or association; a body of monks or nuns, especially the latter. 2 The building or buildings occupied by such a body. See synonyms under CLOISTER. [<L *conventus* meeting, assembly < *convenire.* See CONVENE.]

con·ven·ti·cle (kən·ven′ti·kəl) *n.* 1 A religious meeting, especially a secret one of Scottish Covenanters. 2 The building in which such meetings are held. 3 *Obs.* An assembly. [<L *conventiculum,* dim. of *conventus.* See CONVENT.] —**con·ven′ti·cler** *n.*

con·ven·tion (kən·ven′shən) *n.* 1 A formal or stated meeting of delegates or representatives, especially for legislative, political, religious, or professional purposes. 2 The act of coming together. 3 General consent, or something established by it; precedent; custom; specifically, a rule, principle, form, or technique in conduct or art; a conventionality. 4 A formal agreement or compact between two or more states relating usually to one specific subject: often used interchangeably with *treaty.* 5 *Law* An agreement or mutual engagement between persons. See synonyms under ASSEMBLY, COMPANY.

con·ven·tion·al (kən·ven′shən·əl) *adj.* 1 Established by convention or custom; agreed; stipulated; customary; formal. 2 Or or pertaining to a convention of delegates. 3 Represented according to artistic convention or rule, rather than to nature or fact. —**con·ven′tion·al·ism** *n.* —**con·ven′tion·al·ist** *n.* —**con·ven′tion·al·ly** *adv.*

con·ven·tion·al·i·ty (kən·ven′shən·al′ə·tē) *n. pl.* **·ties** 1 Adherence to established forms, customs, or usages; conformity to the accepted and traditional. 2 The state or quality of being in accord with convention. 3 A conventional act or utterance. —**the conventionalities** The accepted procedures and customs of social intercourse; the proprieties.

con·ven·tion·al·ize (kən·ven′shən·əl·īz) *v.t.* **·ized, ·iz·ing** 1 To make conventional. 2 *Art* To draw, design, or represent in a conventional manner. —**con·ven′tion·al·i·za′tion** *n.*

con·ven·tu·al (kən·ven′cho͞o·əl) *adj.* Belonging to a convent. —*n.* One who belongs to a convent. [<Med. L *conventualis* < *conventus.* See CONVENT.]

Con·ven·tu·al (kən·ven′cho͞o·əl) *n.* A member of a branch of the Franciscan order which follows a modified rule permitting the ownership of property in common.

con·verge (kən·vûrj′) *v.* **·verged, ·verg·ing** *v.t.* 1 To cause to tend toward one point. —*v.i.* To move toward one point; come together by gradual approach. 3 To tend toward the same conclusion or result. [<LL *convergere* < *com-* together + *vergere* bend]

con·ver·gence (kən·vûr′jəns) *n.* 1 The act or

process of converging. 2 State or quality of being convergent. 3 Degree or point of convergence. 4 *Meteorol.* The net horizontal inflow of air into a given layer of the atmosphere. 5 *Math.* The gradual approach of a series of values to a fixed limit as new values are added. 6 *Physiol.* The focusing of both eyes upon a near point. 7 *Biol.* The tendency of organisms of different types to develop similar functional and structural forms in response to the same environmental conditions. Also **con·ver′gen·cy** for defs. 1–3. —**con·ver′·gent** *adj.*

con·ver·sance (kon′vər·səns, kən·vûr′səns) *n.* The state or quality of being conversant; familiarity; acquaintanceship. Also **con′ver·san·cy.**

con·ver·sant (kon′vər·sənt, kən·vûr′sənt) *adj.* 1 Familiar, as a result of study, application, etc.: with *with* or, rarely, *in*: *Conversant* with the principles of a subject. 2 *Rare* Intimately acquainted, as with a person. [<OF, ppr. of *converser* <L *conversari.* See CONVERSE.] —**con′ver·sant·ly** *adv.*

con·ver·sa·tion (kon′vər·sā′shən) *n.* 1 The speaking together of two or more persons; informal exchange of ideas, information, etc.; colloquy. 2 Intimate association or intercourse. 3 *pl.* Diplomatic intercourse; specifically, an informal international conference on matters to be treated more officially later. 4 *Obs.* Deportment. 5 *Obs.* The act or condition of being or living anywhere, as in intimacy. —**criminal conversation** *Law* Unlawful sexual intercourse with a married person; adultery. [<OF <L *conversatio, -onis* < *conversari.* See CONVERSE[1].] —**con′·ver·sa′tion·al** *adj.* —**con′ver·sa′tion·al·ly** *adv.*

Synonyms: chat, colloquy, communication, communion, confabulation, conference, converse, dialog, discourse, intercourse, parley, talk. *Conversation* is, etymologically, an interchange of ideas with some other person or persons. *Talk* may be wholly one-sided. There may be *intercourse* without *conversation*, as by looks, signs, etc.; *communion* is of hearts, with or without words; *communication* is often by writing, and may be uninvited and unreciprocated. *Talk* may denote the mere utterance of words with little thought; thus, we say idle *talk*, empty *talk*, rather than idle or empty *conversation. Discourse* is applied chiefly to public addresses. A *conference* is more formal than a *conversation.* A *dialog* may be real and informal, but the word denotes ordinarily an artificial or imaginary *conversation*, strictly of two persons, but sometimes of more. A *colloquy* is indefinite as to number, and generally somewhat informal. See INTERCOURSE. Compare BEHAVIOR.

con·ver·sa·tion·al·ist (kon′vər·sā′shən·əl·ist) *n.* 1 One who converses. 2 An interesting talker. Also **con′ver·sa′tion·ist.**

conversation piece A type of genre painting popular in the 18th century, showing a group of people, usually of the upper classes, engaged in conversation; hence, any article of furniture, decoration, etc., that arouses comment, discussion, etc.

con·ver·sa·zi·o·ne (kon′vər·sat′sē·ō′nē, *Ital.* kōn′ver·sä·tsyō′nā) *n. pl.* **·nes** (-nēz), *Ital.* **·ni** (-nē) *Italian* A meeting for conversation, particularly on some special topic, as literature or art.

con·verse[1] (kən·vûrs′) *v.i.* **·versed, ·vers·ing** 1 To speak together informally and alternately; engage in familiar conversation or colloquy. 2 *Obs.* To associate; have intercourse; commune. —*n.* (kon′vûrs) 1 Conversation; interchange of thoughts. 2 Close intercourse; communion; fellowship. [<OF *converser* <L *conversari*, freq. of *convertere* < *com-* together + *vertere* turn] —**con·vers′·a·ble** *adj.* —**con·vers′a·bly** *adv.* —**con·vers′·er** *n.*

con·verse[2] (kən·vûrs′, kon′vûrs) *adj.* Turned about so that two parts are interchanged; transposed; reversed. —*n.* (kon′vûrs) 1 That which exists in a converse relation; opposite. 2 *Logic* A proposition that is the result of conversion. See CONVERSION BY LIMITATION. [<L *conversus*, pp. of *convertere* < *com-* thoroughly + *vertere* turn] —**con·verse·ly** (kən·vûrs′lē, kon′vûrs·lē) *adv.*

con·ver·sion (kən·vûr′zhən, -shən) *n.* 1 The act of converting, or the state of being converted, in any sense. 2 The act of turning or of being turned to religious belief. 3 *Law* **a** Wrongful appropriation to one's own use of the goods of another. **b** The exchange of real to personal property or the reverse, which is considered to have taken place where no actual exchange has been effected, as in settling the affairs of an estate. 4 *Logic* A form of immediate inference in which the subject and predicate or antecedent and consequent terms of a judgment change places in such a way that the converse or transposed form is a legitimate inference from the original judgment. 5 *Math.* The formation of a new proportion from four proportional terms by substituting for the second the difference between the first and second and for the fourth the difference between the third and fourth. 6 *Psychoanal.* The process by which a psychic conflict finds expression in motor or sensory disturbances associated with and partially satisfying the repressed emotion or desire: also **conversion hysteria;** see REPRESSION. See synonyms under CHANGE. —**con·ver′sion·al, con·ver·sion·ar·y** (kən·vûr′zhən·er′ē, -shən-) *adj.*

conversion by limitation *Logic* Conversion in which the quantity is changed from universal to particular while the quality remains unchanged.

con·vert (kən·vûrt′) *v.t.* 1 To change into another state, form, or substance; transform. 2 To apply or adapt to a new or different purpose or use. 3 To change from one belief, doctrine, creed, opinion, or course of action to another. 4 To turn from a sinful to a righteous life. 5 To exchange for an equivalent value, as goods for money. 6 To exchange for value of another form, as preferred for common stock. 7 *Chem.* To change chemically. 8 *Logic* To transpose the subject and predicate of (a proposition) by conversion. 9 *Law* To assume possession of illegally. —*v.i.* 10 To become changed in character. 11 In football, to score the extra point after touchdown, as by kicking a field goal. —*n.* (kon′vûrt) A person who has been converted, as from a sinful to a pious life, or from one opinion, creed, etc., to another. [<OF *convertir* <L *convertere.* See CONVERSE[2].]

Synonyms (noun): disciple, neophyte, proselyte. The name *disciple* is given to the follower of a certain faith, without reference to any previous belief or allegiance; a *convert* is a person who has come to one faith from a different belief or unbelief. A *proselyte* is one who has been led to accept a religious system, whether with or without true faith; a *convert* is always understood to be a believer. A *neophyte* is a new *convert*, not yet fully indoctrinated, or not admitted to full privileges. The antonyms *apostate, pervert*, and *renegade* are condemnatory names applied to the *convert* by those whose faith he forsakes.

con·vert·er (kən·vûr′tər) *n.* 1 One who or that which converts. 2 A vessel in which materials are changed from one condition into another. 3 A Bessemer converter. 4 *Electr.* An apparatus for converting direct into alternating current and vice versa. 5 One who converts raw textiles into finished products. Also **con·ver′tor.**

con·vert·i·ble (kən·vûr′tə·bəl) *adj.* Capable of being converted. —*n.* 1 A convertible thing. 2 An automobile with a retractable top. —**con·vert′i·bil′i·ty, con·vert′i·ble·ness** *n.* —**con·vert′i·bly** *adv.*

con·vert·i·plane (kən·vûr′tə·plān′) *n.* An aircraft combining the advantages of a helicopter with the ability to attain high speed in normal flight: also called *planicopter.* [< *converti(ble) (air)plane*]

con·vert·ite (kon′vər·tīt) *n. Archaic* A convert.

con·vex (kon·veks′, kon′veks) *adj.* Curving outward like a segment of a globe or of a circle viewed from outside; bulging out: opposed to *concave.* Compare illustration under LENS. —*n.* (kon′veks) A convex surface or body; convexity. [<L *convexus* vaulted, curved < *convehere* < *com-* together + *vehere* bring, carry] —**con·vex′ed·ly, con·vex′ly** *adv.*

con·vex·i·ty (kon·vek′sə·tē) *n. pl.* **·ties** 1 The state of being convex. 2 A convex surface. Also **con·vex′ed·ness, con·vex′ness.**

con·vex·o–con·cave (kon·vek′sō·kon·kāv′) *adj.* 1 Convex on one side and concave on the other. 2 *Optics* Describing a lens of which the convex surface has a greater curvature than the opposite concave surface: distinguished from *concavo–convex.* See illustration under LENS.

con·vex·o–con·vex (kon·vek′sō·kon·veks′) *adj.* Convex on both sides.

con·vex·o–plane (kon·vek′sō·plān′) *adj.* Plano-convex.

con·vey (kən·vā′) *v.t.* 1 To carry from one place to another; transport. 2 To serve as a medium or path for; transmit. 3 To make known or impart; communicate. 4 To transfer ownership of, as real estate. 5 *Obs.* To accompany; guide. [<AF *conveier* travel with <L *com-* together + *via* road, way. Doublet of CONVOY, *v.*] —**con·vey′a·ble** *adj.* —**con·vey′er, con·vey′or** *n.*

Synonyms: carry, change, give, move, remove, sell, shift, transfer, transmit, transport. *Convey, transmit*, and *transport* all imply delivery at a destination; *carry* does not necessarily imply delivery, and often does not admit of it. A man *carries* an appearance, *conveys* an impression, the appearance remaining his own, the impression being given to another; I will *transmit* the letter; *transport* the goods. *Transfer* may or may not imply delivery to another person; as, items may be *transferred* from one account to another or a word *transferred* to the following line. In law, real estate, which cannot be moved, is *conveyed* by simply *transferring* title and possession. *Transport* usually refers to material objects; *transfer, transmit*, and *convey* may refer to immaterial objects; we *transfer* possession, *transmit* intelligence; we *convey* ideas, but do not *transport* them. In the case of *convey* the figurative sense now predominates. Compare CARRY, LEAD. *Antonyms*: hold, keep, possess, preserve, retain.

con·vey·ance (kən·vā′əns) *n.* 1 The act of conveying. 2 That by which anything is conveyed. 3 A vehicle. 4 *Law* A document transferring title to property. 5 *Obs.* A device; artifice.

con·vey·anc·ing (kən·vā′ən·sing) *n. Law* The business of preparing conveyances of property, especially real estate, including the investigation of titles. —**con·vey′anc·er** *n.*

con·vict (kən·vikt′) *v.t.* 1 To prove guilty; find guilty after a judicial trial. 2 To awaken to a sense of sin. See synonyms under CONDEMN. —*adj. Obs.* Proved guilty. —*n.* (kon′vikt) One found guilty of or undergoing punishment for crime; a criminal. [<L *convictus*, pp. of *convincere.* See CONVINCE.] —**con·vic′tive** *adj.*

con·vic·tion (kən·vik′shən) *n.* 1 The act of convicting. 2 The fact or state of being convicted. 3 The state or condition of being convinced or fully awakened to awareness: under *conviction* of sin. 4 A doctrine or proposition which one firmly believes. 5 Fixed belief: He spoke with *conviction.* See synonyms under FAITH. —**con·vic′tion·al** *adj.*

con·vict·ism (kon′vik·tiz′əm) *n.* Convicts as a class.

con·vince (kən·vins′) *v.t.* **·vinced, ·vinc·ing** 1 To satisfy by evidence; persuade by argument. 2 *Obs.* To convict. [<L *convincere* < *com-* thoroughly + *vincere* overcome, conquer] —**con·vince′ment** *n.* —**con·vinc′er** *n.* —**con·vinc′i·ble** *adj.* —**con·vinc′ing** *adj.* —**con·vinc′ing·ly** *adv.* —**con·vinc′ing·ness** *n.*

Synonym: persuade. One is *convinced* by argument or evidence addressed to the intellect; he is *persuaded* by appeals addressed to the affections and the will. See PERSUADE.

con·viv·i·al (kən·viv′ē·əl) *adj.* Pertaining to a feast, especially a drinking feast; festive; jovial. [<L *convivialis* < *convivium* a feast, banquet < *convivere* < *com-* together + *vivere* live] —**con·viv′i·al·ist** *n.* —**con·viv·i·al·i·ty** (kən·viv′ē·al′ə·tē) *n.* —**con·viv′i·al·ly** *adv.*

con·vo·ca·tion (kon′vō·kā′shən) *n.* 1 The act of summoning together an assembly. 2 The assembly thus summoned. See synonyms under ASSEMBLY, COMPANY. [<L *convocatio*,

-*onis* <*convocare.* See CONVOKE.] **—con′vo·ca′tion·al** *adj.* **—con·voc·a·tive** (kən·vok′ə·tiv) *adj.* **—con′vo·ca′tor** *n.*

Con·vo·ca·tion (kon′vo·kā′shən) *n.* **1** An ecclesiastical body of the Church of England, similar to a synod, but meeting only at the call of some authority: the *Convocation* of Canterbury. **2** A voluntary convention of Protestant Episcopal clergy and laymen from a division of a diocese, meeting unofficially to discuss and promote church measures; also, the district thus organized.

con·voke (kən·vōk′) *v.t.* **·voked, ·vok·ing** To call together; summon. [<F *convoquer* <L *convocare* < *com-* together + *vocare* call, summon] — **con·vok′er** *n.*

Synonyms: assemble, call, collect, convene, gather, muster, summon. A convention is *called* by some officer or officers, as by its president, its executive committee, or some eminent leaders; the delegates are *assembled* or *convened* in a certain place, at a certain hour. *Convoke* implies an organized body and a superior authority; *assemble* and *convene* express more independent action; Parliament is *convoked*; Congress *assembles.* Troops are *mustered*; witnesses and jurymen are *summoned. Antonyms*: adjourn, disband, discharge, dismiss, disperse, dissolve, prorogue, scatter, separate.

con·vo·lute (kon′və·lōōt) *adj.* **1** Rolled one part on another or inward from one side. **2** *Bot.* Coiled longitudinally, as the petals of the wallflower. Also **con′vo·lut′ed, con′vo·lu′tive** [<L *convolutus,* pp. of *convolvere.* See CONVOLVE.] — **con′vo·lute′ly** *adv.*

con·vo·lu·tion (kon′və·lōō′shən) *n.* **1** The act of convolving. **2** The state of being convolved. **3** turn; fold. **4** *Anat.* One of the folds of the surface of the brain.

con·volve (kən·volv′) *v.* **·volved, ·volv·ing** *v.t.* To roll together; wind around something; twist; turn. —*v.i.* To turn or wind upon itself. [<L *convolvere* <*com-* together + *volvere* spin, twist]

con·vol·vu·la·ceous (kən·vol′vyə·lā′shəs) *adj. Bot.* Designating a family *(Convolvulaceae)* of gamopetalous, chiefly climbing herbs, shrubs, or trees with alternate leaves and showy flowers; the morning-glory family.

con·vol·vu·lar (kən·vol′vyə·lər) *adj.* **1** Winding in upon itself. **2** Twisted; wound together.

con·vol·vu·lus (kən·vol′vyə·ləs) *n.* Any of a genus *(Convolvulus)* of twining herbs with large, showy, trumpet-shaped flowers. [<L, bindweed]

con·voy (kon′voi) *n.* **1** A protecting force accompanying property in course of transportation, as a ship at sea or a military party by land. **2** The property so accompanied, as a ship or fleet at sea or a baggage train onland. **3** The act of convoying; the state of being convoyed, or the agency used in transportation or conveyance. [<MF *convoi* <*convoyer*] —*v.t.* (kən·voi′, kon′-) To escort and protect; guide; act as convoy to. <L *com-* together + *via* road. Doublet of CONVEY.]

con·vulse (kən·vuls′) *v.t.* **·vulsed, ·vuls·ing 1** To affect with violent movements; agitate violently. **2** To cause to laugh violently. [<L *convulsus,* pp. of *convellere* <*com-* together + *vellere* pull] **—con·vul·sive** (kən·vul′·siv) *adj.* **—con·vul′·sive·ly** *adv.* **—con·vul′sive·ness** *n.*

con·vul·sion (kən·vul′shən) *n.* **1** A violent and abnormal muscular contraction of the body; spasm; fit. **2** Any violent commotion or disturbance. **—con·vul·sion·ar·y** (kən·vul′·shən·er′e) *adj.* & *n.*

Con·vul·sion·ar·y (kən·vul′shən·er′e) *n. pl.* **·ar·ies** One of a group of religious fanatics of the 18th century. —*adj.* Of or pertaining to these fanatics. Also **Con·vul′sion·ist.**

co·ny (kō′ne, kun′e) *n. pl.* **co·nies 1** A rabbit, especially the European rabbit. **2** Rabbit fur. **3** In the Bible, the hyrax or daman. **4** The pika. **5** *Archaic* A dupe; one who is cheated. Also *coney.* [<OF *cony* <L *cuniculus* rabbit]

coo (kōō) *v.* **cooed, coo·ing** *v.t.* **1** To utter with the soft murmuring sound of a dove or pigeon. —*v.i.* **2** To utter the coo of a dove, or a similar sound. **3** To make love in low, murmuring tones: to bill and *coo.* —*n.* A murmuring note, as of a dove. [Imit.] **—coo′er** *n.* **—coo′ing·ly** *adv.*

Co·o (kô′ō) The Italian name for KOS.

Cooch Be·har (kōōch′ bi·här′) A district of NE West Bengal, India; 1,318 square miles; capital, Cooch Behar: formerly *Kooch Behar.*

coo·ee (kōō′e) *n.* A long, shrill cry of the Australian aborigines. Also **coo′ey. —within cooee** Within calling distance; close at hand. —*v.i.* **coo·eed, coo·ee·ing** To make this cry. [Imit.]

coof (kōōf) *n. Scot.* A lout; blockhead; coward.

cook (kŏŏk) *v.t.* **1** To prepare for consumption by the action of heat, as by roasting or boiling. **2** *Colloq.* To tamper with surreptitiously; garble; falsify. —*v.i.* **3** To do the work of a cook; act as a cook. **4** To undergo cooking. **—to cook (someone's) goose** To kill or ruin one; frustrate one's schemes or plans. **—to cook up** *Colloq.* To concoct or invent, as a plot. [<*n.*] —*n.* One who prepares food for eating. [OE *coc* <L *coquus*] — **cook′er** *n.*

Cook (kŏŏk), **James,** 1728–1779, English explorer: known as *Captain Cook.*

Cook, Mount 1 A mountain on the Yukon-Alaska border in the St. Elias range; 13,760 feet. **2** The highest peak in New Zealand, on South Island; 12,349 feet: also *Aorangi.*

cook·book (kŏŏk′bŏŏk′) *n.* A book containing recipes and instructions for cooking.

Cooke (kŏŏk), **Jay,** 1821–1905., U.S. financier and railroad magnate.

cook·er·y (kŏŏk′ər·ē) *n. pl.* **·er·ies 1** The art or practice of cooking. **2** A place for cooking.

Cook Inlet An inlet of the Gulf of Alaska in southern Alaska.

Cook Islands An archipelago comprising a New Zealand dependency SW of Samoa; total, 90 square miles; capital, Raratonga.

cook·out (kŏŏk′out′) *n. U.S. Colloq.* A picnic at which the meal is cooked out-of-doors.

Cook Strait The passage between North Island and South Island, New Zealand; narrowest point, 16 miles.

cook·y (kŏŏk′e) *n. pl.* **cook·ies 1** A small, sweet cake. **2** *Slang.* A person; also, a young woman or girl; sweetheart. Also **cook·ey, cook·ie.** [<Du. *koekje,* dim. of *koek* cake]

cool (kōōl) *adj.* **1** Moderate in temperature; not warm; some what cold. **2** Serving to produce or giving the effect of coolness. **3** Self-controlled; self-possessed. **4** Indifferent; chilling; slighting. **5** Audacious; impudent. **6** *Colloq.* Actual; absolute; not exaggerated: a *cool* million dollars. **7** *Art* Suggesting a sense of coolness: said of the colors blue, green, and violet. **8** *Slang* Very good; well done. See synonyms under CALM, FRESH. —*v.t.* **1** To lower the temperature of; make cooler or less hot. **2** To render less excited or excitable: allay, as passion; calm; moderate. —*v.i.* **3** To become cool or less hot. **4** To lose the heat of excitement or passion; become less ardent, angry, zealous, or affectionate. **—to cool it** *Slang* To calm down; take it easy. **—to cool one's heels** To wait long and wearily in attendance. —*n.* **1** A moderate temperature approaching cold: the *cool* of the day. **2** That which is cool. **3** *Slang* Calm detachment; composure. **—to blow one's cool** *Slang* To get excited; become emotional. [OE *col*] **—cool′ish** *adj.* **—cool′ly** *adv.* **—cool·ness** *n.*

cool·ant (kōō′lənt) *n.* Any substance of low freezing point used as a cooling medium, as for an internal combustion engine.

cool·er (kōō′lər) *n.* **1** That which cools, as a vessel to cool liquids. **2** A refreshing beverage. **3** *Slang* A jail.

Coo·ley's anemia (kōō′lez) A severe form of thalassemia developing in infants or young children who are homozygous for the causative genetic error. [after Thomas B. *Cooley,* 1871–1945, U.S. physician]

Coo·lidge (kōō′lij), **Calvin,** 1872–1933, thirtieth president of the United States 1923–1929. **—Julian Lowell,** 1873–1954. U.S. mathematician.

Coo·lidge tube An X-ray tube the temperature of whose spiral cathode can be closely controlled. [after W. D. *Coolidge,* 1873–1975. U.S. physicist]

coo·lie (kōō′le) *n.* **1** In the Orient, an unskilled laborer or menial. **2** Any such person doing heavy work, especially for low wages. Also **coo′ly.** [Prob. <*Kuli,* an aboriginal Gujarat tribe; infl. by Tamil *kuli* hire, wages]

coomb (kōōm) *n. Brit.* A bowl-shaped valley or hollow. Also spelled *comb, combe.* Also **coombe.** [OE *cumb.* ? <Celtic]

coon (kōōn) *n.* **1** The raccoon. **2** *Slang* A Negro: a derogatory use. [Short for RACCOON]

coon·can (kōōn′kan′) See CONQUIAN.

coon dog A dog used for hunting raccoons.

coon's age *U.S. Slang* A very long time.

coon·tie (kōōn′tē) *n.* A tropical American plant (genus *Zamia)* of the cycad family, whose stems and roots yield a starch. [<N. Am. Ind.]

coop (kōōp, kŏŏp) *n.* **1** An enclosure for small animals, as fowls or rabbits. **2** *Slang* A jail; prison. **—to fly the coop** *Slang* To decamp; quit. —*v.t.* To put into a coop; confine. [ME *cupe* <MLG. Cf. MDu. *kupe* cask]

co-op (kō′op, kō·op′) *n. Colloq.* A cooperative enterprise, as a store or market.

coop·er (kōō′pər, kŏŏp′ər) *n.* One whose business it is to make casks, barrels, etc. —*v.t.* & *v.i.* To make or mend (casks, barrels, etc.) [ME *couper* <LG. Cf. MDu. *kuper* < *kupe* a cask]

Coop·er (kōō′pər, kŏŏp′ər), **Hugh Lincoln,** 1865–1937, U.S. engineer. **—James Fenimore,** 1789–1851, U.S. novelist. **—Peter,** 1791–1883, U.S. manufacturer and philanthropist.

coop·er·age (kōō′pər·ij, kŏŏp′ər-) *n.* **1** The work of the cooper or the cost of such work. **2** A cooper's workshop.

co·op·er·ate (kō·op′ə·rat) *v.i.* **·at·ed, ·at·ing 1** To operate together for a common object: with *with.* **2** To practice economic cooperation. See synonyms under AID, HELP. [<L *cooperatus.* pp. of *cooperari* <*co-* together + *operari* <*opus* work] **—co·op′er·a′tor** *n.*

co·op·er·a·tion (kō·op′ə·rā′shən) *n.* **1** Joint action; profit-sharing. **2** A union of laborers or small capitalists for the purpose of advantageously manufacturing, buying, or selling goods, or of pursuing other modes of mutual benefit. — **co·op′er·a′tion·ist** *n.*

co·op·er·a·tive (kō·op′rə·tiv, -ə·rā′tiv) *n.* **1** An organization carrying on any of various economic activities for the mutual benefit of its members. **A consumers' cooperative,** buying and selling at market prices, distributes the savings over cost of operation to its members in proportion to their patronage. A **producers' cooperative** conducts marketing operations for the pooled output of primary producers, usually farmers. **2** An apartment house owned by an organization of tenants, with each tenant's share determined by the value of his own apartment; also, an apartment in such building. —*adj.* **1** Pertaining to or organized for economic cooperation: a *cooperative* store. **2** Working together for a common purpose. **—co·op′er·a·tive·ly** *adv.*

Cooperative Commonwealth Federation Former name of the NEW DEMOCRATIC PARTY.

coop·er·y (kōō′pər·ē, kŏŏp′ər·ē) *n. pl.* **·ies 1** The trade or workshop of a cooper; cooperage. **2** A cooper's wares, collectively.

co·opt (kō·opt′) *v.t.* **1** To choose by joint action; specifically, to elect to fill a vacant membership, as of a committee, board, etc. **2** To make ineffectual as an instrument for radical change by incorporating within the established order. Also **co·op′tate.** [<L *cooptare* <*co-* together + *optare* choose] **—co·op·ta·tive** (kō·op′tə·tiv) *adj.* — **co·op′tion, co′op·ta′tion** *n.*

co·or·di·nal (kō·ôr′də·nəl) *adj.* **1** *Biol.* Belonging to the same order, as in botany or zoology. **2** Having or defined by (a certain number of) coordinates.

co·or·di·nate (kō·ôr′də·nit, -nāt) *adj.* **1** Of the same order or rank; existing together in similar relation. **2** *Math.* Of or pertaining to coordinates. **3** Having separate colleges for men and women: a *coordinate* university. —*n.* **1** One who or that which is of the same order, rank, power, etc. **2** *Math.* Any of a set of magnitudes by means of which the position of a point, line, or angle is determined with reference to fixed elements. —*v.* (kō·ôr′·də·nāt) **·nat ·ed, ·nat·ing** *v.t.* **1** To put in the same rank, class, or order. **2** To harmonize or adjust; bring into harmonious relation or action. —*v.i.* **3** To be of the same order or rank. **4** To act in harmonious or reciprocal relation; come into adjustment. [<Med. L *coordinatus,* pp. of *coordinare* arrange <*co-* together + *ordinare* set in order <*ordo, -inis* rank] — **co·or′di·nate·ly** *adv.* **—co·or′di·nate·ness** *n.* — **co·or′di·na′tive** *adj.* **—co·or′di·na′tor** *n.*

co·or·di·na·tion (kō·ôr′də·nā′shən) *n.* **1** The act of coordinating. **2** The state of being

coordinate. **3** The harmonious, integrated action of the various parts and processes of a machine, organization, organism, etc.

Coorg (koorg) A chief commissioner's state in SW India; 1,593 square miles; capital, Mercara: sometimes *Kurg.*

Coo·sa River (kōō'sə) A river in NW Georgia and eastern Alabama, flowing 286 miles to the Alabama River.

coost (koost) *Scot.* Past tense of CAST.

coot (koot) *n.* **1** An aquatic bird of the genus *Fulica,* resembling the rails. **2** A sea duck, especially any of the North American scoters. **3** *Slang* A common or stupid fellow. [ME *cote* < LG. Cf. Du. *koet.*]

coot·er (koo'tər) *n.* **1** The Carolina box turtle *(Terrapene carolina).* **2** A turtle or tortoise of Florida *(Pseudemys floridana).* [Origin uncertain]

coot·ie[1] (koo'tē) *Slang* A body louse. [? < Indonesian *kutu,* a parasitic insect; orig. nautical slang]

coot·ie[2] (koo'tē) *n. Scot.* A small wooden basin or bowl for use in the kitchen.

co·own·er (kō-ō'nər) *n.* A joint owner. — **co·own·er·ship** *n.*

cop[1] (kop) *n.* **1** The top, as of a hill or the head of a thing. **2** The conical roll of thread formed on the spindle of a spinning machine; also, the tube on which this thread or yarn is wound. [OE *copp* summit]

cop[2] (kop) *Slang v.t.* **copped, cop·ping 1** To take; steal; appropriate. **2** To win: to *cop* a prize. **3** To catch or seize. —**to cop out** *U.S. Slang* To back down or turn away, as from one's responsibilities or ideals; renege. —*n.* A policeman: short for *copper*[2]. [? Var. of *cap* catch, take < OF *caper* < L *capere*]

co·pai·ba (kō-pā'bə, -pī'-) *n.* A viscous, aromatic South American balsam from some species of *Copaifera,* used in affections of the mucous membrane and in varnishes. Also **co·pai·va** (-və). [< Sp. < Tupian *cupauba*]

co·pal (kō'pəl) *n.* A hard, transparent resin exuded by various tropical trees, used for varnishes. [< Sp. < Nahuatl *copalli* incense]

co·palm (kō'päm) *n.* **1** The sweetgum tree. **2** The balsam obtained from it. [Origin uncertain]

Co·pán (kō-pän') A city of western Honduras; site of Mayan ruins.

co·par·ce·nar·y (kō-pär'sə-ner'ē) *n. pl.* **·nar·ies 1** *Law* An estate in lands inherited by coparceners. **2** Partnership. Also **co·par·ce·ny** (kō-pär'sə-nē).

co·par·ce·ner (kō-pär'sə-nər) *n. Law* One of two or more coheirs. [< CO-[1] + PARCENER]

co·part·ner (kō-pärt'nər) *n.* One who shares with another; specifically, an equal partner in a business. —**co·part'ner·ship** *n.*

co·pa·set·ic (kō'pə-set'ik) See COPESETIC.

cope[1] (kōp) *v.* **coped, cop·ing** *v.i.* **1** To contend or strive on equal terms; oppose successfully: often with *with.* **2** *Archaic* To meet or encounter: with *with.* **3** *Brit. Colloq.* To deal with a situation successfully. —*v.t.* **4** *Obs.* To deal with; meet in combat. **5** *Obs.* To requite. See synonyms under CONTEND. [< OF *couper* strike < *coup, colp* a blow < L *colaphus*]

cope[2] (kōp) *n.* **1** Anything that arches overhead: the *cope* of heaven. **2** A coping, as of a roof or over a window. **3** A semicircular mantle worn by priests or bishops on solemn or ceremonial occasions; also, a coronation, state, processional, or choral vestment often worn by laymen. —*v.t.* **coped, cop·ing 1** To dress in a cope or cloak. **2** To furnish with or form a coping, as a wall; bend or arch. **3** To form (a joint in a molding) without mitering, as in a sash frame. [< Med. L *cāpa* cape, cope, var. of LL *cappa.* See CAP.]

co·peck (kō'pek) See KOPECK.

Co·pen·ha·gen (kō'pən-hā'gən, -hä'-) A port on the east coast of Zealand Island, largest city and capital of Denmark: Danish *Köbenhavn.*

copenhagen blue A dusty, light blue.

co·pe·pod (kō'pə-pod) *n.* One of an order *(Copepoda)* of small, free-swimming, fresh-water and marine crustaceans. —*adj.* **1** Of, pertaining to, or belonging to this order. **2** Oar-footed, as a crustacean. Also **co·pep·o·dan** (kō-pep'ə-dən). [< NL < Gk. *kōpē* oar + *pous, podos* foot] —

co·pep'o·dous *adj.*

Co·per·ni·cus (kō-pûr'nə-kəs), **Nicholas,** 1473–1543, Polish astronomer who in 1543 declared that the planets revolve around the sun and that the earth rotates on its axis. —**Co·per'ni·can** *adj.*

co·pe·set·ic (kō'pə-set'ik) *adj. Slang.* Tip-top; first-rate; fine: also spelled *copasetic.* Also **co'pe·set'tic.** [U.S. coinage, c. 1930]

cope·stone (kōp'stōn') *n.* **1** The top stone of a wall. **2** One of the stones of a coping. **3** The final or crowning stroke; culmination.

cop·i·er (kop'ē·ər) *n.* **1** A copyist. **2** One who imitates closely the style of another.

co·pi·lot (kō'pī'lət) *n.* The assistant or relief pilot of an aircraft.

cop·ing (kō'ping) *n.* The top course of a wall, usually sloping to shed water.

coping saw A narrow-bladed saw set in a recessed frame and used for cutting small curved pieces from sections of wood.

co·pi·o·pi·a (kō'pē·ō'pē·ə) *n.* Eyestrain; asthenopia. [< Gk. *kopos* suffering + -OPIA]

co·pi·ous (kō'pē·əs) *adj.* **1** Possessing or showing abundance. **2** Ample; plenteous: large in quantity: *copious* notes. See synonyms under AMPLE. [< L *copiosus* < *copia* abundance] —**co'pi·ous·ly** *adv.* —**co'pi·ous·ness** *n.*

co·pla·nar (kō-plā'nər) *adj. Math.* In the same plane: said of figures.

Cop·land (kōp'lənd), **Aaron,** born 1900, U.S. composer.

Cop·ley (kop'lē), **John Singleton,** 1738–1815, U.S. portrait painter.

co·pol·y·mer (kō-pol'ə·mər) *n. Chem.* A compound formed by the polymerization of two or more unlike substances and having properties different from those of either component taken singly.

co·pol·y·mer·i·za·tion (kō-pol'ə·mər·ə·zā'shən) *n. Chem.* A process similar to polymerization, but involving the union of two or more distinct molecular species, each of which is capable of being polymerized alone, and yielding a copolymer.

co·pol·y·mer·ize (kō-pol'ə·mə·rīz') *v.t.* & *v.i.* **·ized, ·iz·ing** To subject to or undergo copolymerization.

cop·out (kop'out') *n. U.S. Slang* **1** A way of avoiding responsibility; especially, an easy or cowardly resolution of a problem; evasion. **2** One who cops out. [< criminal slang *cop out, cop a plea* to plead guilty]

copped (kopt) *adj.* Conical; pointed.

Cop·pée (kô-pā'), **François,** 1842–1908, French poet and novelist.

cop·per[1] (kop'ər) *n.* **1** A reddish, ductile, metallic element (symbol Cu, atomic number 29) occurring native and in combination, and a very good conductor of heat and electricity. See PERIODIC TABLE. **2** An article made of this metal; specifically, a vessel in which clothes are boiled. **3** A coin made of copper. **4** Any of several shades of rich, lustrous, reddish-brown, similar to the color of polished copper. —*v.t.* **1** To cover or coat with copper. **2** *Slang* To bet against. [OE *coper* < LL *cuprum* < L *(aes) cyprium* Cyprian (metal) < Gk. *kyprios* < *Kypros* Cyprus] — **cop'per·y** *adj.*

cop·per[2] (kop'ər) *n. Slang* A policeman; detective; cop. [< COP[2]]

cop·per·as (kop'ər·əs) *n.* A green, crystalline, astringent ferrous sulfate, $FeSO_4 \cdot 7H_2O$, used in dyeing, inkmaking, photography, etc.: also called *green vitriol.* [< MF *couperose* < Med. L *cuperosa, cuprosa* < *(aqua) cuprosa* copper (water) < LL *cuprum.* See COPPER.]

copper barilla A native copper mixed with sandstone, found in Bolivia.

copper glance Chalcocite.

cop·per·head (kop'ər·hed') *n.* A venomous North American crotaline snake *(Agkistrodon mokasen)* having reddish-brown markings on a buff-colored body: one of the pit vipers.

COPPERHEAD
(2 feet in length; rarely up to 3 feet)

Cop·per·head (kop'ər·hed') *n.* During the Civil War, a Northerner who sympathized with the Confederate States.

Cop·per·mine River (kop'ər·mīn') A river in Northwest Territories, Canada, flowing 525 miles NW to the Beaufort Sea.

copper nickel Niccolite.

cop·per·plate (kop'ər·plāt') *n.* An engraved plate of copper or an engraving or impression printed from it: often used adjectively.

copper pyrites See PYRITES.

cop·per·smith (kop'ər·smith') *n.* **1** One who makes utensils of copper. **2** The crimson-breasted barbet *(Xantholaena haematocephala),* common in India, Ceylon, Burma, and the Philippines.

copper sulfate Blue vitriol.

cop·pice (kop'is) *n.* & *v.* Copse.

cop·ple-crown (kop·əl·kroun') *n.* **1** A bird's crest. **2** A hen with a crest or topknot. [< dim. of COP[1] + CROWN] —**cop'ple-crowned'** *adj.*

cop·ra (kop'rə) *n.* The dried and broken kernel of the coconut, yielding coconut oil: also spelled *cobra.* Also **cop·per·ah** (kop'ər·ə), **cop'rah.** [< Pg. < Malayalam *koppara*]

co·pre·mi·a (kō-prē'mē·ə) *n. Pathol.* A poisoning of the blood from retained fecal matter in cases of obstruction of the bowels. Also **cop·rae'mi·a.** [< COPR(O)- + Gk. *haima* blood]—**cop·re'mic** *adj.*

copro- *combining form* Dung; feces; filth: *coprolite.* Also, before vowels, **copr-.** [< Gk. *kopros* dung]

cop·ro·la·li·a (kop'rō·lā'lē·ə) *n. Psychiatry* Abnormal indecency of speech, regarded as a sign of mental disorder. [< COPRO- + Gk. *lalein* speak]

cop·ro·lite (kop'rə·līt) *n.* The petrified dung of extinct vertebrates, in some localities forming, in part, a phosphatic rock which is mined for a fertilizer. —**cop'ro·lit'ic** (-lit'ik) *adj.*

cop·rol·o·gy (kop·rol'ə·jē) *n.* **1** A collection of filth. **2** Indecency or filth in art or literature; also, the study of this. [< COPRO- + -LOGY]

cop·roph·a·gous (kop·rof'ə·gəs) *adj.* Feeding upon dung, as scarabaeid beetles. [< NL < Gk. *koprophagos* < *kopros* dung + *phagein* eat]

cop·ro·phil·i·a (kop'rə·fil'ē·ə) *n. Psychiatry* Gratification derived from the contemplation or handling of filth. [< COPRO- + Gk. *philia* love] — **cop'ro·phil'ic** *adj.*

cop·roph·i·lous (kop·rof'ə·ləs) *adj.* **1** Growing readily on dung, as certain fungi. **2** Coprophagous. [< COPRO- + -PHILOUS]

cop·ro·phyte (kop'rə·fīt) *n.* A saprophyte found in dungheaps.

copse (kops) *n.* **1** A low-growing thicket. **2** Wood gathered from a copse; undergrowth. Also **copse'wood'.** —*v.t.* **copsed, cops·ing 1** To clip or turn down, as brushwood. **2** To plant or keep in growth, as underwood. —*v.i.* **3** To form a copse; grow up as a copse. [Earlier COPPICE < OF *copeiz* < *coper* cut]

Copt (kopt) *n.* **1** A native Egyptian descended from ancient Egyptian stock. **2** A member of the Coptic Church. [< Med. L *Coptus, Cophtus* < Arabic *quft* < Coptic *gyptios, kyptaios* < Gk. *Aigyptios* Egyptian]

Cop·tic (kop'tik) *adj.* Of or pertaining to the Copts, or to their language. —*n.* The Hamitic language of the Copts, the latest form of the ancient Egyptian: a dead language since 1500 but still the liturgical language of the Coptic Church.

Coptic Church The principal Christian sect of Egypt, which became a separate body in 451, adhering to the Monophysitic doctrine after this was rejected by the Council of Chalcedon. See MONOPHYSITE.

cop·u·la (kop'yə·lə) *n. pl.* **·las** or **·lae** (-lē) *Gram.* A verb that merely connects the subject and the predicate of a sentence without asserting action, particularly the verbs *be, appear, become, feel, look, seem, smell, sound,* and *taste*; a link verb. [< L, a link, band] —**cop'u·lar** *adj.*

cop·u·late (kop'yə·lāt) *v.i.* **·lat·ed, ·lat·ing** To unite in sexual intercourse. [< L *copulatus,* pp. of *copulare* fasten, link < *copula* a link] — **cop'u·la·tive** *adj.* & *n.* —**cop'u·la·tive·ly** *adv.* — **cop'u·la·to·ry** (kop'yə·lə·tôr'ē, -tō'rē) *adj.*

cop·u·la·tion (kop'yə·lā'shən) *n.* **1** The act

of coupling; also, the state of being coupled together. 2 Sexual intercourse.
copulative conjunction *Gram.* A coordinate conjunction, as *and.*
cop·y (kop′ē) *n. pl.* **cop·ies** 1 A reproduction or imitation; duplicate. 2 A single printed pamphlet, book, etc., of an edition or issue. 3 A pattern given for imitation. 4 Manuscript or other matter to be reproduced in type. 5 In journalism, someone or something that is newsworthy: He is good *copy.* — **certified copy** A copy attested by an officer having charge of the original. — *v.* **cop·ied, cop·y·ing** *v.t.* 1 To make a copy of; transcribe; reproduce; make in imitation, as in writing or painting. 2 To follow as a model; imitate, as in actions or opinions. — *v.i.* 3 To make a copy or reproduction. 4 To admit of being copied: That page *copies* well. 5 To do in imitation. [<F *copie* <Med. L *copia* transcript <L, supply, abundance]
cop·y·book (kop′ē·bo͝ok′) *n.* A book containing copies to be imitated in penmanship; a writing book.
cop·y–boy (kop′ē·boi′) *n.* An errand boy in a newspaper office who delivers copy to the editor, composing room, etc.
cop·y·cat (kop′ē·kat′) *n. Colloq.* An imitator: a child's term of derision.
cop·y–desk (kop′ē·desk′) *n.* A desk in a newspaper office where copy is edited and prepared for the typesetters.
cop·y·graph (kop′ē·graf, -gräf) *n.* A hectograph.
cop·y·hold[1] (kop′ē·hōld′) *n. Law* A tenure of lands evidenced by a copy of the court roll.
cop·y·hold[2] (kop′ē·hōld′) *v.i. Colloq.* To act as copyholder.
cop·y·hold·er (kop′ē·hōl′dər) *n.* 1 One who or that which holds copy; specifically, one who holds and reads copy so that a proofreader may detect errors in printed matter. 2 In English law, one who holds land by tenure of copyhold.
copying ink An ink containing sugar, glycerin, or some similarly acting substance, for use in any writing or printing to be reproduced in the copying press.
copying paper An unsized paper used in the copying press.
copying press A press for duplicating writing or printing done with copying ink.
cop·y·ist (kop′ē·ist) *n.* 1 One whose business it is to copy. 2 An imitator.
cop·y·read·er (kop′ē·rē′dər) *n.* A person in an editorial office, or by assignment elsewhere, who edits work intended for publication.
cop·y·right (kop′ē·rīt′) *n.* The exclusive statutory right of authors, composers, playwrights, artists, publishers, or distributors to publish and dispose of their works for a limited time; in the United States, for 28 years, with privilege of one renewal for an additional 28 years. The common–law property rights in unpublished works continue in effect until publication with or without copyright. — *v.t.* To secure copyright for, as a book or work of art. — **cop′y·right′a·ble** *adj.* — **cop′y·right′er** *n.*
cop·y–writ·er (kop′ē·rī′tər) *n.* One who writes copy for advertisements, including radio and television commercials.
coque·li·co (kōk′li·kō) *n.* 1 The English wild poppy *(Papaver rhoeas).* 2 The reddish–orange color of this flower. [<F]
Coque·lin (kôk·laṅ′), **Benoît Constant,** 1841–1909, French actor.
co·quet (kō·ket′) *v.* **co·quet·ted, co·quet·ting** *v.i.* 1 To flirt; play the coquette; trifle in love: said of women. 2 To act in a trifling, undecided manner; dally. — *v.t.* 3 *Obs.* To flirt with. [<F *coqueter* <*coquet,* dim. of *coq* a cock; with ref. to its strutting]
co·quet·ry (kō′kə·trē, kō·ket′rē) *n. pl.* **·ries** 1 Trifling in love, as a coquette; flirting. 2 The quality of being coquettish.
co·quette (kō·ket′) *n.* A woman or girl who endeavors to attract men's attention and admiration merely for the gratification of vanity; flirt. Also **co·quet′.** [<F, fem. dim. of *coq* a cock. See COQUET.] — **co·quet′tish** *adj.* — **co·quet′tish·ly** *adv.* — **co·quet′tish·ness** *n.*
co·quil·lage (kō·kē·yäzh′) *n.* A design made of or imitating shells, prevalent in the decorative arts of the rococo period. [<F <*coquille* shell]
co·quil·la nut (kō·kēl′yə, -kē′yə) The hard-shelled, oval nut of the Brazilian palm *Attalea funifera.* [<Sp. *coquillo,* dim. of *coco* coconut]
co·quille (kō·kēl′) *n.* 1 Any of various dishes, usually of sea food, baked in a shell. 2 Chill (*n.* def. 4). [<F, shell]
co·qui·na (kō·kē′nə) *n.* A soft, highly porous, limestone rock composed of fragments of marine shells: used as building material. [<Sp.]
co·qui·to (kō·kē′tō) *n. pl.* **·tos** 1 A tall, massive feather palm of Chile *(Jubaea spectabilis),* bearing a dense crown of foliage. 2 Its small, edible nut. [<Sp., dim. of *coco* coconut]
cor– Assimilated var. of COM–.
Co·ra (kôr′ə, kō′rə) A feminine personal name. [<Gk., maiden]
cor·a·ci·i·form (kôr′ə·sī′ə·fôrm) *adj.* Designating an order of non–passerine birds *(Coraciiformes),* including the rollers, kingfishers, hornbills, etc. [<NL <Gk. *korax, korakis* raven + -FORM]
cor·a·cle (kôr′ə·kəl, kor′-) *n.* A small fishing boat of hide or oilcloth on a wicker frame. [< Welsh *corwgl* < *corwg* boat]

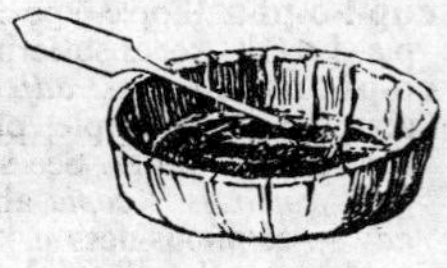

FRENCH CORACLE

cor·a·coid (kôr′ə·koid, kor′-) *adj.* 1 *Zool.* Designating the posterior inferior process of the shoulder girdle, a separate bone in many animals, as birds, reptiles, and monotremes, that unites with the scapula to form the glenoid cavity. 2 Shaped like a raven's beak. — *n.* 1 The coracoid process. 2 The chief bone of the shoulder girdle of a teleost fish. [<Gk. *korakoeidēs* < *korax, korakis* raven + *eidos* form]
cor·al (kôr′əl, kor′-) *n.* 1 The calcareous skeleton secreted in or by the tissues of various, usually compound marine coelenterates and deposited in various forms and colors. 2 These skeletons collectively. 3 An animal of this type. 4 A yellowish–red color. 5 An object, as a toy or a jewel, made of coral. 6 Lobster or crab roe: so called from its appearance when cooked. — *adj.* 1 Consisting of or like coral. 2 Colored like coral. [<OF <L *coralium* <Gk. *korallion*]

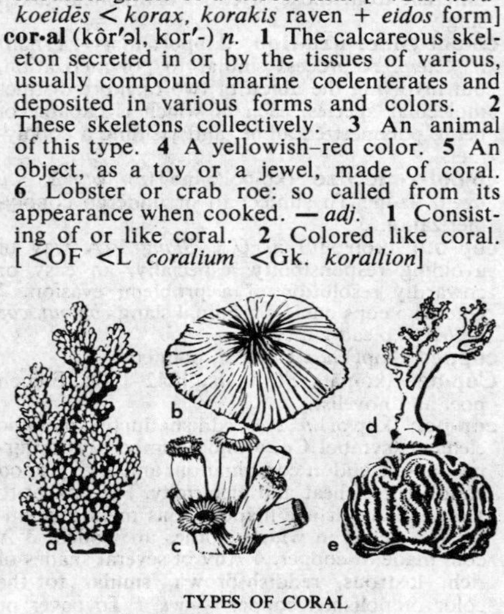

TYPES OF CORAL
a. Reef coral. *c.* Bud coral.
b. Mushroom coral. *d.* Red coral.
e. Brain coral.

cor·al·ber·ry (kôr′əl·ber′ē, kor′-) *n. pl.* **·ries** A bushy American shrub *(Symphoricarpos orbiculatus)* with dark berries somewhat resembling currants.
coralli– *combining form* Coral: *coralliferous.* Also, before vowels, **corall–.** [<Gk. *korallion* coral]
cor·al·lif·er·ous (kôr′ə·lif′ər·əs, kor′-) *adj.* Producing or containing coral. [<CORALLI- + -FEROUS]
cor·al·line (kôr′ə·lin, -līn, kor′-) *adj.* 1 Of, pertaining to, producing, or like coral. 2 Pinkish–red. — *n.* 1 A calcareous, coral-like seaweed. 2 A coral or coral–like animal.
cor·al·lite (kôr′ə·līt, kor′-) *n.* 1 An individual skeleton of coral polyp; a cup coral. 2 Fossil coral. — **cor′al·lit′ic** (-lit′ik) *adj.*
cor·al·loid (kôr′ə·loid, kor′-) *adj.* Coral–shaped; especially, branching like coral: also **cor′al·loi′dal.** — *n.* A polyzoan.
co·ral·lum (kə·ral′əm) *n. pl.* **co·ral·la** (kə·ral′ə) Coral, either as a compound mass or as the skeleton of a polyp. [<LL, var. of *coralium* CORAL]
coral reef A reef, often of great extent, formed by the gradual deposit of innumerable coral skeletons, found chiefly in tropical waters.
cor·al·root (kôr′əl·ro͞ot′, -ro͝ot′, kor′-) *n.* Any one of a small genus *(Corallorhiza)* of brownish, leafless orchids with much–branched coral–like rootstocks.
Coral Sea A SW area of the Pacific Ocean east of Australia and New Guinea; scene of Japanese naval defeat by U.S. forces in World War II, 1942.
coral snake Any of a genus *(Micrurus)* of venomous snakes of tropical America and the southern United States, noted for their brilliant red, black, and yellow rings; especially, *M. lemniscus* of South America and the harlequin snake *(M. fulvius)* of Mexico and the southern United States.
co·ram pop·u·lo (kō′ram pop′yə·lō) *Latin* In the presence of the people; publicly.
cor an·glais (kôr äṅ·gle′) *French* 1 The English horn. 2 A reed organ stop resembling the oboe in sound.
co·rant (kə·rant′), **co·ran·to** (kə·ran′tō, -rän′-) See COURANT.
Cor·an·tyn (kôr′ən·tīn, kor′-) See CORENTYN.
cor·ban (kôr′bən, kôr·bän′) *n.* An offering to God, as in fulfilment of a vow. *Mark* vii 11. [<Hebrew *qorbān*]
cor·beil (kôr′bəl) *n.* 1 *Obs.* A gabion. 2 *Archit.* A sculptured basket of fruit or flowers. [<F *corbeille* <L *corbicula,* dim. of *corbis* basket]
cor·bel[1] (kôr′bəl, -bel) *n. Archit.* **a** A projection from the face of a wall to support an overhanging weight; corbeling. **b** A short timber placed lengthwise upon a wall, etc., under a girder to increase its bearing. — *v.t.* **cor·beled** or **·belled, cor·bel·ing** or **·bel·ling** 1 To support by corbels. 2 To make in the form of corbels. [<OF <LL *corvellum,* dim. of *corvus* crow; from its shape]
cor·bel[2] (kôr′bəl, -bel) *n. Archit.* A piece serving as a cushion for a capital, as in a Corinthian column, that rests on the astragal. [<OF <L *corbis* basket]
cor·bel·ing (kôr′bəl·ing) *n. Archit.* An arrangement of stones or bricks in building a wall, in which successive courses project beyond those below them. Also **cor′bel·ling.**
cor·bel–steps (kôr′bəl·steps′) See CORBIE–STEPS.
cor·bie (kôr′bē) *n. Scot.* A crow; raven. Also **cor′by.**
corbie crow *Scot.* The carrion crow.
cor·bie–steps (kôr′bē·steps′) *n. pl. Scot.* Steps in the top of a gable wall, from the eaves to the apex of the roof, such as only a crow or cat could use: often called *crowsteps.*
Cor·co·va·do (*Pg.* kôr′kə·vä′tho͞o, *Sp.* kôr′kō·vä′thō) 1 A peak overlooking Río de Janeiro, Brazil; 2,310 feet. 2 A volcano in southern Chile; 7,550 feet.
Cor·cy·ra (kôr·sī′rə) Ancient name of CORFU.
cord (kôrd) *n.* 1 A string of several strands. 2 A measure for wood; in the United States a pile 4 x 4 x 8 feet, equal to 128 cubic feet, or 3.62 cubic meters. 3 A wale or rib in a fabric giving a raised effect. 4 A corded fabric. 5 *Pl. U.S.* Corduroy trousers. 6 *Anat.* A cordlike structure: the spinal *cord.* 7 *Often pl.* Any feeling that draws or restrains. 6 The rope used by a hangman. — *v.t.* 1 To bind or secure with cord; furnish with cords. 2 To pile (firewood) by the cord. ◆ Homophone: *chord.* [<F *corde* <L *chorda* <Gk. *chordē* string of a musical instrument. Doublet of CHORD.] — **cord′er** *n.*
cord·age (kôr′dij) *n.* 1 Ropes and cords collectively; especially, ropes in the rigging of a ship. 2 The amount in cords, as of wood, on a given area of land.
cor·date (kôr′dāt) *adj.* Heart–shaped, as a leaf. [<L *cordaius* < *cor* heart] — **cor′date·ly** *adv.*
Cor·day (kôr·dā′), **Charlotte,** 1768–93, French patriot; assassinated Marat: full name *Marie Anne Charlotte Corday d'Armont.*
cord·ed (kôr′did) *adj.* 1 Bound or fastened with cord or rope. 2 Striped or ribbed as if with cords: a *corded* fabric. 3 Piled in cord measure: *corded* firewood. 4 With the hair twisted or felted into strings or curls: said of dogs. 5 *Obs.* Made of cord or rope.
Cord·ed (kôr′did) *adj. Anthropol.* Designating a style of pottery decoration produced by the application of cords to the wet surface of the clay.
Corded people A Neolithic people of north central Europe who were named after corded pottery artifacts.

Cor·del·ia (kôr·dēl′yə, -dē′lē·ə; *Ger.* kôr·dā′·lē·ä) A feminine personal name. Also *Fr.* **Cor·dé·lie** (kôr·dā·lē′). [<Celtic, jewel of the sea]
— Cordelia The youngest of King Lear's three daughters, and the only one to remain faithful to him. See LEAR.

cor·de·lier (kôr′də·lir′) *n.* An early type of ropemaking machine. [<F]

Cor·de·lier (kôr′də·lir′) *n.* **1** A Franciscan friar who observes a very strict rule. **2** *pl.* A political club of the time of the French Revolution, whose meetings were held in an old Cordelier convent. [<F < *cordelle*, dim. of *corde* a cord; with ref. to the knotted cord worn by these friars]

cor·dial (kôr′jəl) *adj.* **1** Proceeding from the heart; exhibiting or expressing kindliness; imparting vigor or joy; cheering. See synonyms under AMICABLE. **—** *n.* **1** That which invigorates or exhilarates. **2** A sweet, aromatic alcoholic spirit; a liqueur. [<Med. L *cordialis* <L *cor, cordis* heart] **— cor·dial·i·ty** (kôr·jal′ə·tē, -jē·al′-, -dē·al′-), **cor′dial·ness** *n.* **— cor′dial·ly** *adv.*

cor·di·er·ite (kôr′dē·ə·rīt′) *n. Mineral.* A bluish silicate of magnesium, aluminum, and iron, crystallizing in the orthorhombic system: used as a gemstone: also called *iolite.* [after P. *Cordier,* 1777–1861, French geologist]

cor·di·form (kôr′də·fôrm) *adj.* Heart-shaped; cordate. [<L *cor, cordis* heart + -FORM]

cor·dil·le·ra (kôr′dil·yâr′ə, kôr·dil′ər·ə) *n. Geog.* The entire system of mountain ranges that borders a continent or occurs in the same general region. [<Sp. <OSp. *cordilla,* dim. of *cuerda* rope <L *chorda.* See CORD.] **— cor′·dil·le′ran** *adj.*

Cor·dil·le·ras (kôr′dil·yâr′əz, kôr·dil′ər·əz; *Sp.* kôr′thē·yä′räs) The Andes range in South America and its continuation in the Rocky Mountain system of North America.

cord·ite (kôr′dīt) *n.* A variety of smokeless powder consisting of cellulose nitrate or guncotton, nitroglycerin, and a mineral jelly, used chiefly as a propellant. [<CORD; with ref. to its appearance]

cor·do·ba (kôr′də·bə, *Sp.* kôr′thō·vä) *n.* The monetary unit of Nicaragua. [after Francisco de *Córdoba,* 16th c. Spanish explorer]

Cór·do·ba (kôr′thō·vä) **1** A province in Andalusia in southern Spain; 5,299 square miles; capital, Córdoba. **2** A province of central Argentina; 64,894 square miles; capital, Córdoba. Also **Cor·do·va** (kôr′də·və).

cor·don (kôr′dən) *n.* **1** An extended line, as of men, ships, forts, etc. **2** An ornamental lace, cord, or ribbon worn to secure something in place, as a badge of identification, or for adornment. **3** *Archit.* **a** A stringcourse. **b** A coping projecting from a scarp wall. [<F < *corde* cord]

cor·don bleu (kôr·dôn blœ′) *French* **1** The blue ribbon formerly worn by members of the order of the Holy Ghost, the highest order of the Bourbon monarchy. **2** Any high distinction. **3** One entitled to wear the cordon bleu. **4** Any person of distinction in his field.

cor·don·net (kôr′də·net′, *Fr.* kôr·dô·ne′) *n.* **1** The slightly raised edge of a point-lace pattern. **2** Edging made from piping. Also **cor′do·nette′.** [<F, dim. of *cordon.* See CORDON.]

cor·don sa·ni·taire (kôr·dôn′ sà·nē·târ′) *French* **1** A guarded line quarantining an infected area: also *sanitary cordon.* **2** A continuous line of countries cooperating to isolate another country in order to prevent the spread of its influence.

cor·do·van (kôr′də·vən) *n.* **1** Cordwain. **2** Fine horsehide leather.

Cor·do·van (kôr′də·vən) *adj.* Pertaining or belonging to Córdoba. **—** *n.* A native or resident of Córdoba.

cor·du·roy (kôr′də·roi, kôr′də·roi′) *n.* **1** A thick, corded or ribbed, durable fabric, usually of cotton. **2** *pl.* Trousers made of corduroy. **3** A corduroy road, or the materials used in construction. **—** *adj.* **1** Made of corduroy, as trousers. **2** Formed from logs laid transversely; a *corduroy* road. **—** *v.t.* To make into a corduroy road. [<F *corde du roi* fabric of the king]

corduroy road A road, as over miry ground, constructed with small logs laid together transversely.

cord·wain (kôrd′wān) *n. Archaic* Spanish leather: also *cordovan.* [<OF *cordoan* <OSp. *cordovan* of Córdoba]

cord·wood (kôrd′wo͝od′) *n.* Firewood sold by the cord.

cord·y (kôr′dē) *adj.* **1** In glassmaking, having stringlike imperfections due to impurities. **2** Full of cords; cordlike; having cordlike fibers or parts.

Cor·dy·ceps (kôr′di·seps) *n.* A genus of fungi parasitic on the larvae of insects or on certain subterranean fungi. [<NL <Gk. *kordylē* club + L *-ceps* < *caput* head]

core (kôr, kōr) *n.* **1** The central or innermost part of a thing. **2** The heart, as of an apple or pear, containing the seeds. **3** The most important part of anything; the pith of a subject. **4** A solid form placed in a mold, about which metal is poured, so as to be cast hollow. **5** *Electr.* **a** The insulated conducting wires of an electric cable. **b** The iron mass or bundle of iron rods, etc., around which the wire is coiled in an electromagnet or armature. **6** *Engin.* In submarine and geological investigations, a cylindrical mass of test material brought to the surface by a special hollow drill. **7** In fingerprint identification, the inner terminus or focal point which constitutes the approximate center of a pattern and is essential to its correct interpretation. **8** *Anthropol.* A type of Paleolithic stone implement consisting of a central mass of a rock, shaped for use in one of several standard forms, chiefly hand-axes. **—** *v.t.* **cored, cor·ing** To remove the core of. ◆ Homophone: *corps.* [Origin uncertain] **— core′less** *adj.* **— cor′er** *n.*

Cor·e·go·nus (kôr′i·gō′nəs, kor′-) *n.* A genus of salmonid fishes with small mouths and toothless jaws, including the whitefishes, many species of which inhabit inland waters in the northern hemisphere, and are among the most important of food fishes. [<NL < *korē* pupil of the eye + *gōnia* angle]

co·re·la·tion (kō′ri·lā′shən) See CORRELATION.

co–re·la·tion (kō′ri·lā′shən) *n.* **1** Joint or mutual relation. **2** Correlation.

co·re·lig·ion·ist (kō′ri·lij′ən·ist) *n.* An adherent of the same religion, church, or sect as another.

Co·rel·li (kō·rel′lē), **Arcangelo,** 1653–1713, Italian composer.

Co·rel·li (kə·rel′ē), **Marie,** 1864–1924, English novelist.

co·re·mi·um (kə·rē′mē·əm) *n. pl.* **·mi·a** (-mē·ə) *Bot.* A special form of non-sexual fruit body in the fungi in which spore-bearing hyphae are arranged in parallel order, side by side, to form an erect fascicle. [<Gk. *korēma* broom]

Cor·en·tyn (kôr′ən·tīn, kor′-) A river forming the boundary between British Guiana and Dutch Guiana, flowing 450 miles north to the Atlantic: also *Corantyn, Courantyne.* Also **Cor′en·tyne.**

co·re·op·sis (kôr′ē·op′sis, kō′rē-) *n.* A plant of a large genus (*Coreopsis*) of mainly North American herbs of the composite family, with heads of showy yellow or rose-colored flowers: also called *calliopsis.* [<NL <Gk. *koris* bug + *opsis* appearance; with ref. to the shape of the seed]

cor·e·plas·ty (kôr′ə·plas′tē, kor′-) *n. Surg.* Any plastic operation upon the iris. [<Gk. *korē* pupil of the eye + -PLASTY] **— cor′e·plas′tic** *adj.*

cor·er (kôr′ər, kō′rər) *n.* A utensil for removing the cores of apples and other fruit.

co·re·spon·dent (kō′ri·spon′dənt) *n. Law* A joint defendant; especially, in a suit for divorce, one charged with having committed adultery with the husband or wife from whom divorce is being sought. **— co′re·spon′den·cy** *n.*

corf (kôrf) *n. pl.* **corves** (kôrvz) **1** *Brit.* A small freight wagon, formerly a wicker basket, in which coal is carried from the working place to the shaft. **2** *Brit. Dial.* A floating receptacle for holding fish, etc. [ME <LG. Cf. MDu. *korf* basket.]

Cor·fi·ote (kôr′fē·ōt) *n.* A native or inhabitant of Corfu. Also **Cor·fute** (kôr′fyo͞ot).

Cor·fu (kôr·fo͞o′, kôr′fyo͞o) A Greek island in the Ionian group; 229 square miles; capital, Corfu: ancient *Corcyra*: Greek *Kerkyra.*

cor·gi (kôr′gē) *n.* A Welsh working dog. See WELSH CORGI.

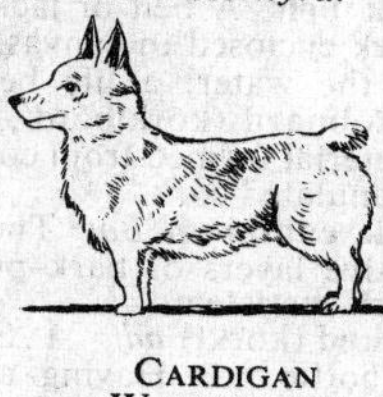
CARDIGAN WELSH CORGI
(12 inches high at the shoulder)

Co·ri (kô′rē), **Carl Ferdinand,** born 1896, and his wife **Gerty T.,** 1896–1957, *née* Radnitz, U.S. biochemists born in Czechoslovakia.

co·ri·a·ceous (kôr′·ē·ā′shəs, kō′rē-) *adj.* Of a rough leathery texture; like leather. [<L *corium* leather]

co·ri·an·der (kôr′ē·an′dər, kō′rē-) *n.* A plant of the parsley family (genus *Coriandrum*), bearing aromatic seeds used for seasoning and in medicine as a carminative. [<F *coriandre* <L *coriandrum* <Gk. *koriannon*]

Co·rin·na (kə·rin′ə) Diminutive of Cora. Also *Fr.* **Co·rinne** (kô·rin′).
— Corinna A Greek lyric poetess, about 490 B.C.

Cor·inth (kôr′inth, kor′-) **1** An ancient city in Argolis, Greece. **2** A modern city, three miles from the site of ancient Corinth, on the **Gulf of Corinth,** an arm of the Ionian Sea between the Peloponnesus and northern Greece: Italian *Gulf of Lepanto.* **— Isthmus of Corinth** An isthmus connecting the Peloponnesus with northern Greece; traversed by the **Corinth Canal,** connecting the Gulf of Corinth and the Saronic Gulf; 4 miles long; 72 feet wide.

Co·rinth (kō·rint′), **Lovis,** 1858–1925, German painter.

Co·rin·thi·an (kə·rin′thē·ən) *adj.* **1** Pertaining to Corinth. **2** *Archit.* Denoting an order marked by slender fluted columns with ornate, bell-shaped capitals decorated with a design of acanthus leaves. For illustration see CAPITAL. **3** Luxurious; licentious, as the people of Corinth were reputed to be. **—** *n.* **1** A native or inhabitant of Corinth. **2** A dissolute or profligate person. **3** *U.S.* A gentleman sportsman who sails his own yacht.
— Epistle to the Corinthians Either of two letters addressed by the apostle Paul to the Christians at Corinth, each forming a book of the New Testament.

Cor·i·o·la·nus (kôr′ē·ə·lā′nəs, kor′-) Roman patrician of the fifth century B.C. who led the Volscians against Rome; hero of Shakespeare's tragedy of the same name.

Cor·i·o·lis force (kôr′ē·ō′lis) *Meteorol.* The deflecting effect of the earth's rotation whereby freely moving air masses are deflected to the right in the northern hemisphere and to the left in the southern hemisphere (relatively, to an observer on the earth's surface). [after Gaspard Gustave de *Coriolis,* 1792–1843, French mathematician]

Co·ris·co (kō·ris′kō) An island of Spanish Guinea in the Bight of Biafra, Africa; 5 1/2 square miles.

co·ri·um (kôr′ē·əm, kō′rē-) *n. pl.* **·ri·a** (-ə) **1** *Anat.* The sentient and vascular portion of the skin beneath the epidermis. **2** *Entomol.* In certain insects (order *Heteroptera*), the elongated middle section or harder portion of the forewing. [<L, skin, hide]

cork[1] (kôrk) *n.* **1** A tough, elastic, light, and porous outer bark of an evergreen tree (*Quercus suber*), the cork oak, indigenous to southern Europe: it improves in quality with the age of the tree, and has many uses in industry and the arts. **2** A piece of this bark used as a bottle stopper. **3** Any stopper of other material: a rubber *cork.* **4** *Bot.* A protective tissue that forms in the stems beneath the epidermis of dicotyledons and replaces it. **—** *v.t.* **1** To stop with a cork, as a bottle. **2** To restrain or confine; check. **3** *U.S.* To blacken with burnt cork. **— to cork up** *U.S. Colloq.* To silence suddenly. [<OSp. *alcorque* a cork slipper <Arabic, ? <L *quercus* oak]

cork[2] (kôrk) See CALK: erroneous usage.

Cork (kôrk) The largest county in Ireland, in southern Munster province; 2,880 square miles; county seat, Cork.

cork·age (kôr′kij) *n.* A charge for serving

wine at a hotel, especially when the wine is the property of the guest.

cork belt A belt or jacket made of pieces of cork enclosed in canvas, to support a person in the water; a life belt. Also **cork jacket.**

cork·board (kôrk′bôrd′, -bōrd′) n. A building material formed from compressed and bonded granulated cork.

cork cambium Bot. The phellogen, or inner active layers of bark–producing tissue. Also **cork meristem.**

corked (kôrkt) adj. 1 Stopped with cork, as a bottle. 2 Having acquired the taste of cork: corked wine. 3 Slang Very drunk.

cork·er (kôr′kər) n. 1 One who or that which corks. 2 Slang An argument that puts a stop to discussion; anything that stops competition. 3 Slang Any unusual person or thing.

cork·ing (kôr′king) Slang adj. Fine; excellent; also, amazing. —adv. Fine; excellently.

cork oak An oak tree (Quercus suber) of southern Europe and North Africa, whose thick bark yields cork.

cork·screw (kôrk′skrōō′) n. 1 A spiral instrument for drawing corks from bottles. 2 A ringlet; curl. —v.t. & v.i. 1 To move or cause to move like a corkscrew; to twist. 2 Aeron. To fly in a spiral course in order to avoid enemy anti-aircraft fire. —adj. Shaped like a corkscrew; twisted; spiral.

cork·wood (kôrk′wŏŏd′) n. 1 The light, porous wood of several West Indian trees: specifically, of the custard-apple family (genus Annona), or of the balsa family, especially Ochroma pyramidale. 2 In the SE United States, a small tree (Leitneria floridana) with deciduous glossy leaves and a drupaceous fruit.

cork·y (kôr′kē) adj. ·i·er, ·i·est 1 Like cork; especially, shrunken; dried up. 2 Having the flavor or odor of cork: said especially of wines. 3 Of cork. —**cork′i·ness** n.

Cor Le·o·nis (kôr lē·ō′nis) See REGULUS.

Cor·liss (kôr′lis), **George Henry,** 1817–88, U.S. inventor and manufacturer.

corm (kôrm) n. Bot. A bulblike, solid, fleshy enlargement, usually of the underground stem in plants. [< Gk. kormos tree-trunk]

Cor·moph·y·ta (kôr·mof′i·tə) n. pl. A former primary division of the vegetable kingdom, embracing plants that possess a stem (axis) with leaves: distinguished from Thallophyta. [< NL < kormos trunk + phyton plant] —**cor·mo·phyte** (kôr′mə·fīt) n. —**cor′mo·phyt′ic** (-fit′ik) adj.

cor·mo·rant (kôr′mər·ənt) n. 1 A large, web–footed, voracious aquatic bird (genus Phalacrocorax) of wide distribution and gregarious habits, having a strongly hooked bill and large throat gular pouch. 2 Hence, a glutton or avaricious person. —adj. Like a cor-

CORMORANT
(Body size varies
from 1 1/2 to 3 feet)

morant; greedy; rapacious. [< F cormoran < L corvus marinus sea crow]

corn[1] (kôrn) n. 1 The edible seeds of cereal plants: in England, wheat, barley, rye, and oats collectively; in America, maize, or Indian corn. 2 The plants that produce corn when growing in the field; the stalks and ears, or the stalks, ears, and seeds, after harvesting. 3 Slang Anything regarded as trite, banal, sentimental, etc., especially popular music. 4 Colloq. Whisky distilled from corn. —v.t. 1 To preserve in salt or in brine: to corn beef. 2 U.S. To feed with corn. 3 Scot. To feed with oats. 4 To granulate. [OE] —Corn may appear as a combining form in hyphemes or solidemes, or as the first element in two-word phrases:

cornbin	corn crop	corn-growing
corn brandy	corn-eating	cornland
corncake	corn flour	cornloft
corn-colored	corn-grower	cornmill

corn[2] (kôrn) n. 1 A horny thickening of the cuticle, common on the feet. 2 A morbid condition of the forehoofs of horses caused by injuries to the tissue of the sole, producing inflammation of the horn. [< OF < L cornu. Akin to HORN.]

cor·na·ceous (kôr·nā′shəs) adj. Designating a

family (Cornaceae) of polypetalous shrubs or trees; the dogwood or cornel family.

corn borer The larva of certain insects which feeds on the ears and stalks of corn, especially the European corn borer (Pyrausta nubilalis).

corn·bread (kôrn′bred′) n. Bread made from the meal of maize or Indian corn. Also **corn bread.**

corn·cob (kôrn′kob′) n. The spike of maize round which the kernels grow. Also **corn cob.**

corncob pipe A pipe whose bowl is cut from a corncob.

corn-cock·le (kôrn′kok′əl) n. A tall purple-flowered weed of the pink family, especially Agrostemma githago: also called corn rose.

corn crake A European crake (Crex crex) frequenting cornfields: also called dakerhen.

corn-crib (kôrn′krib′) n. A building for storage of corn, usually raised on posts, with walls made of slats for ventilation.

corn-dodg·er (kôrn′doj′ər) n. A cake of corn-meal baked or fried hard.

cor·ne·a (kôr′nē·ə) n. Anat. The transparent anterior part of the outer coat of the eyeball, continuous with the sclera. See illustration under EYE. Also cornea lens. [< Med. L cornea horny < L cornu horn] —**cor′ne·al** adj.

corn·ear worm (kôrn′ir′) The bollworm.

corned (kôrnd) adj. 1 Preserved in coarse salt or in brine: corned beef. 2 U.S. Slang Drunk.

Cor·neille (kôr·nā′, Fr. kôr·nā′y′), **Pierre,** 1606–84, French dramatist and poet.

cor·nel (kôr′nəl) n. Any of a genus (Cornus) of shrubs and small trees with hard, compact wood, as the dogwood: also called cornus. [< G kornel(baum) < Med. L cornolius < MF cornoille, ult. < L cornus cornel tree] —**cor·nel·ian** (kôr·nēl′yən) adj.

Cor·nel·ia (kôr·nēl′yə, Ger. kôr·nā′lē·ä, Ital. kôr·nā′lyä) A feminine personal name. Also Fr. **Cor·né·lie** (kôr·nā·lē′). [< L, fem. of Cornelius]
— **Cornelia** Roman matron of the second century B.C.; mother of the Gracchi.
— **Cornelia** Wife of Julius Caesar; died 67? B.C.

cor·nel·ian (kôr·nēl′yən) See CARNELIAN.

Cor·nel·ius (kôr·nēl′yəs, Ger. kôr·nā′lē·ŏŏs) A masculine personal name. Also Fr. **Cor·né·li·us** (kôr·nā·lē·üs′); Ital., Sp. **Cor·ne·lio** (kôr·nā′lyō). [< L, ? war horn]

Cor·ne·li·us (kôr·nā′lē·ŏŏs, -ŏŏs), **Peter von,** 1783–1867, German painter.

Cor·nell (kôr·nel′), **Ezra,** 1807–74, U.S. philanthropist; founded Cornell University, 1865.
— **Katharine,** born 1898, U.S. actress.

cor·ne·ous (kôr′nē·əs) adj. Consisting of horn; of a hornlike texture; horny. [< L corneus horny]

cor·ner (kôr′nər) n. 1 The point formed by the intersection of two or more lines or surfaces, or the edge formed by the intersection of two surfaces; an angle. 2 The space or surface comprised between two converging walls or lines near their meeting. 3 A retired spot; nook: the chimney corner. 4 A position of embarrassment or difficulty, or one from which extrication is difficult. 5 A condition of a financial market when a commodity or security has been largely bought up with a view to forcing a higher price: a corner in cotton or stocks. 6 A part or spot, especially a remote or obscure part, of a particular place; also, any of the four directions: the four corners of the earth. 7 A tool used in decorating the corners of books: sometimes called corner-piece. 8 A metallic or other guard for the corner of a book, box, or other article. —to trim one's corners To take risks. —v.t. 1 To force or drive into a corner. 2 To place in a corner. 3 U.S. To place in a position of difficulty or embarrassment: to corner a witness. 4 To furnish with corners. 5 To acquire control of, as a commodity or stock, so as to demand a high price. —v.i. 6 U.S. To come together in a corner; be situated on a corner. 7 Colloq. To go round a corner, as in racing: The car corners beautifully. 8 To form a corner in a commodity or stock. —adj. 1 Located at a corner. 2 Designed for a corner. [< OF cornier < L cornu horn, point]

corner chair A small armchair having the back curved or placed at an angle around two sides of the seat, one leg supporting the front corner of the seat: also called round-about chair.

corner cupboard A cupboard, usually for household china, with curved or diagonal front, designed to fit into a corner.

cor·nered (kôr′nərd) adj. 1 Having corners. 2 Forced into a position of embarrassment or difficulty.

cor·ner·stone (kôr′nər·stōn′) n. 1 A stone uniting two walls at the corner of a building. 2 Such a stone, often inscribed and made into a repository, laid into the foundation of an edifice. 3 Something fundamental or of primary importance.

cor·ner·wise (kôr′nər·wīz′) adv. With the corner in front; diagonally.

cor·net[1] (kôr′net′ for def. 1; kôr′nit for defs. 2 and 3) 1 A small wind instrument of the trumpet class, in which the notes are determined by valves or pistons that open communication into auxiliary bands of tubing, thus varying the length of the vibrating air column. 2 A cone–shaped paper wrapper.

CORNET
(def. 3)

3 A portion of a woman's headdress, of varying shape, from the 14th to the 17th century; also, the headdress itself; also, the tall white headdress of the Sisters of Charity. [< OF, dim. of corn < L cornu a horn] —**cor·net′tist** or **cor·net′ist** n.

cor·net[2] (kôr′nit) n. 1 Formerly, the lowest commissioned cavalry officer in the British army, or a pennant carried by him. 2 A flag or standard; specifically, a signaling flag. [< F, dim. of corne < L cornu horn]

cor·net-à-pis·tons (kôr·net′ə·pis′tənz, Fr. kôr·ne′a·pē·stôn′) n. pl. **cor·nets-à-pis·tons** (kôr·nets′-, Fr. kôr·ne′zà·pē·stôn′) Cornet[1] (def. 1).

cor·net·cy (kôr′nit·sē) n. pl. ·cies The rank or commission of a cornet.

corn-fac·tor (kôrn′fak′tər) n. Brit. A wholesale dealer in grain.

corn-fed (kôrn′fed′) adj. U.S. 1 Nourished on corn. 2 Slang Strong and healthy, as if fed on an ample diet of corn, but rustic and unsophisticated.

corn·field (kôrn′fēld′) n. An area in which corn is grown: also **corn field.** —adj. 1 Of, from, or growing in a cornfield. 2 Rustic: cornfield philosophy.

corn·flow·er (kôrn′flou′ər) n. Any flower growing in grainfields; especially, the bluebottle or bachelor's–button.

corn·husk (kôrn′husk′) n. A corn shuck.

corn·husk·ing (kôrn′hus′king) n. U.S. 1 The husking of corn. 2 A social gathering for the purpose of husking corn, usually followed by refreshments, dancing, etc.; a husking bee. —**corn′husk′er** n.

cor·nice (kôr′nis) n. 1 Archit. a The horizontal molded projection at the top of a building or of a component part of a building, usually under the eaves. b The uppermost member of an entablature. See illustration under ENTABLATURE. 2 An ornamental molding around the walls of a room close to the ceiling; also, a light wooden molding around the

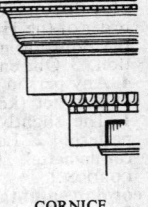

CORNICE

walls of a room, gallery, etc., at a convenient height for the support of pictures by hooks. 3 A frame, upholstered or of molding, fastened to a wall or window frame so as to cover the rods and hooks used for hanging curtains, etc. 4 A mass of snow projecting from a mountain ridge. —v.t. ·niced, ·nic·ing To provide or adorn with a cornice. [< Ital. < L coronis < Gk. korônis wreath, garland] —**cor′niced** adj.

cor·nic·u·late (kôr·nik′yə·lāt, -lit) adj. Having horns or hornlike processes. [< L corniculatus < corniculum, dim. of cornu horn]

Cor·ning (kôr′ning) A city in southern New York.

Cor·nish (kôr′nish) adj. Pertaining to Cornwall, in England, or its people. —n. The former language of Cornwall, belonging to the Brythonic branch of the Celtic languages: extinct since the early nineteenth century and replaced by a dialect of English.

Cor·nish·man (kôr'nish·mən) *n. pl.* **·men** (-mən) A native or inhabitant of Cornwall.

Corn Laws In English history, certain laws, the first dating from 1361, placing restrictions on the grain trade and especially the importation of grain: repealed in 1846.

corn lily 1 Either of two species of convolvulus, the greater or lesser bindweed. 2 Any bulbous plant of the genus *Ixia* of South Africa.

corn mayweed 1 The scentless wild camomile (*Matricaria inodora*): naturalized in parts of the United States. 2 The field camomile (*Anthemis arvensis*) of the eastern United States.

corn·meal (kôrn'mēl') *n.* 1 Meal made from corn; Indian meal. 2 *Scot.* Oatmeal. Also **corn meal.**

Cor·no (kôr'nō), **Mon·te** (môn'tā) The highest peak of the Apennines, in south central Italy; 9,560 feet. Also **Corno Gran·de** (grän'dā).

corn picker A machine for removing and husking ears of standing corn.

corn pit A section of a produce exchange devoted to business in corn.

corn pith The pith of Indian corn, used in the manufacture of paper, etc.

corn pone Bread made of cornmeal, water, and salt, usually without milk and eggs.

corn·pop·per (kôrn'pop'ər) *n.* A wire box or cylinder used for popping corn over a fire.

corn poppy A weed (*Papaver rhoeas*) growing in grain fields: also called *corn rose.*

corn rose See CORNCOCKLE, CORN POPPY.

corn salad Lamb lettuce (*Valerianella olitoria*), a European plant whose leaves are used for salad.

corn shock A conical bundle of stalks of Indian corn, often tied together at the top.

corn shuck The shuck or husk of an ear of maize: also *cornhusk.*

corn shucks scrub A scrubbing brush made out of corn shucks.

corn smut A widespread disease of corn, due to infection by the smut fungus, *Ustilago zeae*, and characterized by spore-containing tumor masses attached to the ears and other aerial parts of the plant.

corn snow In skiing, fallen snow which has melted slightly and refrozen, forming a coarse, granular surface which enables the skis to slide more easily.

corn spurry Beggarweed.

corn·stalk (kôrn'stôk') *n.* A stalk of Indian corn. Also **corn stalk.**

corn·starch (kôrn'stärch') *n.* 1 Starch made from corn. 2 A purified starchy meal used in making puddings.

corn sugar Glucose obtained from corn.

corn't (kôrnt) *adj. Scot.* Fed on oats.

cor·nu (kôr'nyōō) *n. pl.* **·nu·a** (-nyōō·ə) A horn, or anything shaped like a horn: applied to various anatomical structures: the superior and inferior *cornua* of the larynx. [<L, horn]

cor·nu·co·pi·a (kôr'nə·kō'pē·ə) *n.* 1 The horn of plenty, represented as overflowing with fruits and symbolizing peace and prosperity. See AMALTHEA. 2 A paper or cardboard horn for holding candies. 3 A superabundance. [<LL *cornucopia* <L *cornu copiae* horn of plenty] — **cor'nu·co'pi·an** *adj.*

cor·nus (kôr'nəs) See CORNEL.

cor·nute (kôr·nōōt', -nyōōt') *adj.* 1 Having horns or a hornlike process or appendage. 2 Shaped like a horn. Also **cor·nut'ed.** [<L *cornutus* <*cornu* horn]

cor·nu·to (kôr·nōō'tō, -nyōō'-) *n. pl.* **·tos** *Obs.* A cuckold. [<Ital.]

Corn·wall (kôrn'wôl, *Brit.* -wəl) A county of SW England; 1,357 square miles; county seat, Bodmin: a native of the country is known as a *Cornishman.*

Corn·wal·lis (kôrn·wôl'is, -wol'-), **Charles,** 1738–1805, first Marquis Cornwallis, English general and statesman.

Corn·wal·lis Island (kôrn·wôl'is, -wol'-) An island in the Northwest Territories, Canada; 2,592 square miles.

corn whisky Whisky distilled from corn.

corn·worm (kôrn'wûrm') *n.* The bollworm.

corn·y (kôr'nē) *adj.* **corn·i·er, corn·i·est** 1 Of, abounding in, or producing corn. 2 *Slang* Trite, banal, sentimental, or unsophisticated.

cor·o·dy (kôr'ə·dē, kor'-) *n. pl.* **·dies** In old

English law, a right pertaining to the king to send one of his chaplains to be maintained by a bishop; also, an allowance, as for food, granted for services: also spelled *corrody.* [<Med. L *corrodium*, var. of *corredium* provision]

co·rol·la (kə·rol'ə) *n. Bot.* The second series or inner circle of flower leaves, usually colored, forming the inner floral envelope or inner perianth, and serving mainly to attract insects; the petals of a flower collectively. Also **cor·ol** (kor'əl). [<L, dim. of *corona* crown] — **cor·ol·late** (kor'ə·lāt, kor'-), **cor'ol·lat'ed** *adj.*

cor·ol·lar·y (kôr'ə·ler'ē, kor'-; *Brit.* kə·rol'ər·ē) *n. pl.* **·lar·ies** 1 A proposition following so obviously from another that it requires little or no demonstration. 2 An inference; deduction. — *adj.* Like a corollary; deduced; resultant. [<L *corollarium* gift, orig. money paid for a garland <*corolla* garland]

Cor·o·man·del (kôr'ə·man'dəl, kor'-) The coast of SE India from the Kistna to Palk Strait.

Coromandel lacquer A type of Chinese lacquerwork in which the design is cut in intaglio and completed with varied colors and gold: so called because objects thus decorated were imported into western Europe by East India merchants with headquarters on the Coromandel Coast.

co·ro·na (kə·rō'nə) *n. pl.* **·nas** or **·nae** (-nē) 1 A garland or wreath given by the ancient Greeks and Romans as a reward for distinguished achievements. 2 *Archit.* The projecting brow of a cornice. 3 A crownlike part, structure, or process, as the crown of the head or the shell of a sea-urchin. 4 *Astron.* **a** A luminous circle around one of the heavenly bodies. **b** The luminous envelope of ionized gases surrounding the chromosphere of the sun and visible during a total eclipse. 5 Loosely, any halo. 6 *Electr.* The luminous discharge or process at the top of the tube of the corolla, as in jonquils. 8 *Geol.* A zone of minerals surrounding another mineral or at the junction of two minerals. [<L, crown]

CORONA
(*def. 4b*)

Corona Aus·tra·lis (ôs·trā'lis) The Southern Crown, a constellation south of Sagittarius: also called the *Wreath.* See CONSTELLATION.

Corona Bo·re·al·is (bôr'ē·al'is, -ā'lis, bō'rē-) The Northern Crown, a constellation between Hercules and Boötes. See CONSTELLATION.

cor·o·nach (kôr'ə·nəkh, kor'-) *n.* 1 *Scot.* A dirge, as for a chieftain. 2 In Ireland, a keening or wailing lament for the dead. [<Irish *coranach*]

Co·ro·na·do (kôr'ə·nä'dō, *Sp.* kō'rō·nä'thō), **Francisco Vasquez de,** 1510?–54, Spanish explorer.

co·ro·nal (kə·rō'nəl, kôr'ə·nəl, kor'-) *adj.* 1 Of or pertaining to a corona or halo, or to the crown of the head. 2 *Anat.* Having the direction of the coronal suture: a *coronal* plane. — **cor·o·nal** (kôr'ə·nəl, kor'-) *n.* A crown or garland.

coronal suture *Anat.* The suture between the frontal and the two parietal bones of the skull.

cor·o·nar·y (kôr'ə·ner'ē, kor'-) *adj.* 1 Pertaining to a crown or wreath. 2 *Anat.* Encircling, crowning: the *coronary* ligament of the liver; the two *coronary* arteries rising from the aorta. See illustration under HEART. — *n.* Coronary thrombosis. [<L *coronarius* <*corona* crown]

coronary thrombosis *Pathol.* The formation of a thrombus, or blood clot, in one of the coronary arteries, resulting in interruption of blood supply from the heart.

cor·o·na·tion (kôr'ə·nā'shən, kor'-) *n.* 1 The act or ceremony of crowning a monarch. 2 Accomplishment; fulfilment. [<OF *coronacion* <L *coronatus*, pp. of *coronare* crown]

Co·ro·nel (kō'rō·nel') A port of south central Chile; scene of a World War I German naval victory, 1914.

cor·o·ner (kôr'ə·nər, kor'-) *n.* A public officer who inquires into the cause of deaths not

clearly due to natural causes. [<AF *coruner* officer of the crown <*corune* crown <L *corona*] — **cor'o·ner·ship'** *n.*

coroner's jury See under JURY.

cor·o·net (kôr'ə·net, -nit, kor'-) *n.* 1 A small or inferior crown, denoting noble rank less

BRITISH CORONETS
a. H.R.H. Prince of Wales.
b. Younger son and brother of the Blood Royal.
c. Nephew, etc., of the Blood Royal.
d. Duke.
e. Marquis.
f. Earl.
g. Viscount.
h. Baron.

than sovereign. 2 Any chaplet or wreath for the head; especially, a semicircular band worn by women above the brow as a headdress. 3 The upper margin of a horse's hoof. [<OF *coronete*, dim. of *corone* crown <L *corona*]

co·ro·ni·form (kə·rō'nə·fôrm) *adj.* Having the form of a crown. [<L *corona* crown + -FORM]

Co·rot (kô·rō'), **Jean Baptiste Camille,** 1796–1875, French painter.

cor·po·ra (kôr'pər·ə) Plural of CORPUS.

cor·po·ral¹ (kôr'pər·əl) *adj.* 1 Belonging or relating to the body as opposed to the mind: *corporal* punishment. 2 Personal: *corporal* possession. 3 *Obs.* Having substance; corporeal; not spiritual. See synonyms under PHYSICAL. — *n.* The linen cloth on which the elements are placed during the celebration of the Eucharist: also **cor·po·ra·le** (kôr'pə·rā'lē) or **corporal cloth.** [<L *corporalis* <*corpus* body] — **cor·po·ral·i·ty** (kôr'pə·ral'ə·tē) *n.* — **cor'po·ral·ly** *adv.*

cor·po·ral² (kôr'pər·əl) *n.* 1 In the U.S. Army and Marine Corps, an enlisted man ranking next above a private first class and next below a sergeant. 2 In the British Navy; an assistant to the master at arms. 3 *U.S.* The fallfish (*Semotilus corporalis*). — **lance corporal** A private acting as corporal. [<MF *coporal*, var. of *caporal* <Ital. *caporale* <*capo* head <L *caput*]

corporal's guard *Mil.* The squad of men detailed for guard or other duty under a corporal; hence, any small number of persons, especially of attendants or adherents.

cor·po·rate (kôr'pər·it) *adj.* 1 Associated by legal enactment for the transaction of business; incorporated: a body politic and *corporate.* 2 Belonging to a corporation: *corporate* property. 3 Combined as a whole; considered as one; collective. 4 Having a visible body or form; corporeal; not spiritual. [<L *corporatus*, pp. of *corporare* assume a body <*corpus* body] — **cor'po·rate·ly** *adv.*

cor·po·ra·tion (kôr'pə·rā'shən) *n.* 1 An artificial person created by law, consisting of one or more natural persons united in one body under such grants as secure a succession of members without changing the identity of the body, and empowered to act in a certain capacity or to transact business of some designated form or nature like a natural person. 2 *Colloq.* A protuberant abdomen; paunch.

cor·po·ra·tive (kôr'pə·rā'tiv, -pər·ə·tiv') *adj.* 1 Of or pertaining to a corporation. 2 In political systems, regimenting the operation of the whole social and economic life through one or more corporate bodies selected from employers and employees of principal corporations and controlled by the government. — **cor'po·ra·tive·ly** *adv.*

cor·po·ra·tor (kôr'pə·rā'tər) *n.* A member of a corporation; especially, an original incorporator.

cor·po·re·al (kôr·pôr'ē·əl, -pō'rē·əl) *adj.* 1 Having a body; of a material nature; physical: distinguished from *immaterial, mental,* or

spiritual. **2** *Law* Perceivable by the bodily senses; substantial and permanent; opposed to *incorporeal: corporeal* hereditaments. See synonyms under PHYSICAL. [<L *corporeus* <*corpus* body] **—cor·po·re·al·i·ty** (kôr·pôr'·ē·al'ə·tē, -pō'rē-), **cor·po're·al·ness, cor·po·re·i·ty** (kôr'pə·rē'ə·tē) *n.* **—cor·po're·al·ly** *adv.*

cor·po·sant (kôr'pə·zant) *n.* A luminous discharge of atmospheric electricity from sharp points near the earth's surface, as from steeples, treetops, the masts of ships, etc.: also called *St. Elmo's fire.* [<Pg. *corpo santo* <L *corpus sanctus* holy body]

corps (kôr, kōr) *n. pl.* **corps** (kôrz, kōrz) **1** *Mil.* **a** A tactical unit, intermediate between a division and an army, and consisting of two or more divisions. **b** A special department or subdivision: the Quartermaster *Corps.* **2** A number of persons acting together. ◆ Homophone: *core.* [<F, var. of OF *cors.* See CORPSE.]

corps de bal·let (kôr' də ba·lā', *Fr.* bȧ·le') The ballet dancers who perform as a group in a performance and have no solo parts. [<F]

corps de garde (kôr də gȧrd') *French* **1** The sentry. **2** The guardroom.

corpse (kôrps) *n.* A dead body, usually of a human being. See synonyms under BODY. [ME *corps,* var. of *cors* <OF <L *corpus* body]

corpse fat Adipocere.

corps·man (kôr'mən, kōr'-) *n. pl.* **·men** (-mən) A member of a military corps. In the U.S. Navy, an enlisted man working as a pharmacist; in the U.S. Army, an enlisted man in the Medical Corps assigned to a combat area.

cor·pu·lent (kôr'pyə·lənt) *adj.* Having a great excess of fat; very fleshy. [<F <L *corpulentus* fleshy <*corpus* body] **—cor'pu·lence, cor'pu·len·cy, cor'pu·lent·ness** *n.*

Synonyms: adipose, burly, fat, fleshy, gross, obese, plethoric, portly, pursy, stout. *Antonyms*: bony, emaciated, gaunt, lean, poor, skinny, slight, spare, thin.

cor·pus (kôr'pəs) *n. pl.* **·po·ra** (-pər·ə) **1** A body of a man or animal. **2** The main body or substance of anything. **3** *Law* **a** A material object; especially, a corporeal property. **b** The elements or facts of a case considered collectively. **4** *Anat.* The main part or mass of an organ. [<L]

corpus cal·lo·sum (kə·lō'səm) *Anat.* A large band of commissural fibers connecting the two halves of the cerebral hemispheres. [<NL, hard body]

Cor·pus Chris·ti (kôr'pəs kris'tē, -tī) In the Roman Catholic Church, a festival held in honor of the Eucharist on the first Thursday following Trinity Sunday. [<L, body of Christ]

Cor·pus Chris·ti (kôr'pəs kris'tē) A port in Texas on **Corpus Christi Bay,** an arm of the Gulf of Mexico in southern Texas.

cor·pus·cle (kôr'pəs·əl, -pus·əl) *n.* **1** A minute particle of matter; molecule; atom; electron. **2** *Biol.* **a** Any protoplasmic granule of distinct shape or characteristic function. **b** One of the particles forming part of the blood of vertebrates, either a **red corpuscle** containing hemoglobin for oxygen transport, or a **white corpuscle,** known as a leukocyte. Also **cor·pus·cule** (kôr·pus'kyōōl). [<L *corpusculum,* dim. of *corpus* body] **—cor·pus·cu·lar** (kôr·pus'kyə·lər) *adj.*

corpus de·lic·ti (də·lik'tī) *Law Latin* The existence of the essential fact or facts which prove the commission of a crime, as the finding of stolen goods on the person of an alleged thief. [<L, the body of the offense]

corpus ju·ris (jŏŏr'is) *Latin* The body of law.

Corpus Juris Ca·non·i·ci (kə·non'ə·sī) *Latin* The collective title of the decrees and canons of the Roman Catholic Church, constituting the standard of canon law prior to 1918.

Corpus Juris Ci·vil·is (si·vil'is) *Latin* The collective title of the body of Roman law, comprising the Institutes, the Pandects or Digest, the Code, and the Novels or new laws, of Justinian: promulgated 528–534.

corpus lu·te·um (lōō'tē·əm) *pl.* **cor·po·ra lu·te·a** (-tē·ə) *Anat.* A yellow body formed by a Graafian follicle in the ovary, and appearing during menstruation and pregnancy: it secretes progesterone. [<L, yellow body]

corpus stri·a·tum (strī·ā'təm) *pl.* **cor·po·ra stri·a·ta** (-tə) *Anat.* One of two masses of ganglionic cells situated in front of the thalamus and at the base of either hemisphere of the brain. [<L, striped body]

cor·rach (kûr'əkh, kûr'ə) See CURRACH.

cor·rade (kə·rād') *v.t.* **·rad·ed, ·rad·ing** *Geol.* To disintegrate, as rocks, either by solution or by solution combined with mechanical wear: said of rivers. [<L *corradere* <*com-* together + *radere* scrape, rub]

cor·ra·di·ate (kə·rā'dē·āt) *v.i.* **·at·ed, ·at·ing** To converge to a focus, as rays of light. [<COR- + RADIATE]

Cor·ra·do (kôr·rä'dō) Italian form of CONRAD.

cor·ral (kə·ral') *n.* **1** An enclosed space or pen for livestock. **2** A space enclosed by wagons for protection against attack. —*v.t.* **·ralled, ·ral·ling** **1** To drive into and enclose in a corral; pen up. **2** To arrange in the form of a corral: to *corral* wagons. **3** *U.S. Colloq.* To seize or capture; secure. [<Sp., a yard, an enclosed space]

cor·ra·sion (kə·rā'zhən) *n. Geol.* The process of erosion by corrading; specifically, the vertical or lateral cutting performed by a river. Compare EROSION. [<L *corrasus,* pp. of *corradere.* See CORRADE.]

cor·rect (kə·rekt') *v.t.* **1** To rectify or remove error from; make right. **2** To point out the errors of; set right. **3** To rebuke or chastise. **4** To remedy or counteract, as a malfunction. **5** To make conformable to a standard: to *correct* a lens. See synonyms under AMEND, CHASTEN, RECLAIM. —*adj.* **1** Free from fault or mistake. **2** True, right, or proper; accurate; exact. [<L *correctus,* pp. of *corrigere* <*com-* together + *regere* make straight] **—cor·rect'a·ble** or **·i·ble** *adj.* **—cor·rec'tive** *adj.* & *n.* **—cor·rec'tive·ly** *adv.* **—cor·rect'ly** *adv.* **—cor·rect'ness** *n.* **—cor·rec'tor** *n.*

Synonyms (adj.): accurate, decorous, exact, faultless, perfect, precise, proper, right, true. See EXACT, PERFECT, PRECISE, RIGHT. *Antonyms*: erroneous, false, faulty, inaccurate, incorrect, wrong.

cor·rec·tion (kə·rek'shən) *n.* **1** The act of correcting or setting right; rectification; emendation. **2** That which is offered as an improvement. **3** The act or process of disciplining or chastening. **4** The act or process of neutralizing an undesired quality or condition. **—cor·rec'tion·al** *adj.*

cor·rec·ti·tude (kə·rek'tə·tōōd, -tyōōd) *n.* Freedom from impropriety; correctness.

Cor·reg·gio (kôr·red'jō), **Antonio Allegri da,** 1494–1534, Italian painter.

cor·reg·i·dor (kə·reg'ə·dôr, *Sp.* kôr·rā'hē·thôr') *n.* **1** The chief magistrate of a Spanish-American town. **2** A similar magistrate whose jurisdiction extends over part of a province. [<Sp. <*corregir* <L *corrigere.* See CORRECT.]

Cor·reg·i·dor (kə·reg'ə·dôr) An island in Manila Bay; 2 square miles; site of the surrender of the Philippines by United States forces to Japan, May, 1942, in World War II.

cor·re·late (kôr'ə·lāt, kor'-) *v.* **·lat·ed, ·lat·ing** *v.t.* **1** To place or put in reciprocal relation; establish a mutual relation between. **2** To show the mutual relation between. —*v.i.* **3** To have a correlation; be mutually or reciprocally related. —*adj.* Having mutual or reciprocal relations. —*n.* A correlative. [<COR- + RELATE]

cor·re·la·tion (kôr'ə·lā'shən, kor'-) *n.* **1** Mutual or reciprocal relation. **2** The act of bringing under relations of union or interaction. **3** *Physiol.* The combination of nervous impulses in sensory centers resulting in adaptive reactions. **4** *Math.* A statement of the kind and degree of relationship between two or more variables. Also spelled *corelation.* **—cor're·la'tion·al** *adj.*

correlation coefficient *Stat.* A numerical measure of the degree of correlation between two variables.

cor·rel·a·tive (kə·rel'ə·tiv) *adj.* **1** Having correlation; especially, mutually involving or implying one another: *correlative* structures. **2** Mutually related to grammatical or logical significance; referring to each other: *either* and *or* are *correlative* conjunctions. —*n.* **1** One of two or more persons or things united by reason of some natural relation or correspondence. **2** Either of two correlative terms. **—cor·rel'a·tive·ly** *adv.* **—cor·rel'a·tive·ness, cor·rel'a·tiv'i·ty** *n.*

cor·rep·tion (kə·rep'shən) *n.* In classical prosody, the treating of a metrically long syllable as short. Compare PROTRACTION. [<L *correptio, -onis* <*corripere* <*com-* thoroughly + *rapere* seize]

cor·re·spond (kôr'ə·spond', kor'-) *v.i.* **1** To agree or be conformable in respect to fitness; be proportional. **2** To be similar or analogous in character or in function. **3** To communicate by letters. [<Med. L *correspondere* <*com-* together + *respondere* answer] **—cor·re·spon·sive** (kôr'ə·spon'siv, kor'-) *adj.*

cor·re·spon·dence (kôr'ə·spon'dəns, kor'-) *n.* **1** The act, condition, or state of corresponding. **2** Mutual adaptation; congruity; agreement. **3** Communication by letters; also, the letters themselves. Also **cor're·spon'den·cy.** See synonyms under INTERCOURSE.

correspondence principle *Physics* The relation assumed to exist between the observed radiation characteristics of an electron orbit and those calculated by classical mechanics.

correspondence school A school which gives its courses of instruction in a series of written lessons and assignments exchanged by mail between teachers and students.

cor·re·spon·dent (kôr'ə·spon'dənt, kor'-) *n.* **1** One who communicates by means of letters; specifically, a newspaper or magazine employee who dispatches news and special reports from a seat of war or other place of public interest. **2** A person, partnership, firm, or corporation that carries on business transactions with another at a distance through letters or telegrams. **3** Anything that corresponds; a correlative. —*adj.* **1** Having correspondence; correlated in nature; adapted: with *to.* **2** *Obs.* Obedient.

cor·re·spond·ing (kôr'ə·spon'ding, kor'-) *adj.* **1** Correspondent; being similar and similarly placed: with *to.* **2** Carrying on a correspondence: with *with.* See synonyms under SYNONYMOUS. **—cor're·spond'ing·ly** *adv.*

cor·ri·dor (kôr'ə·dər, -dôr, kor'-) *n.* **1** A gallery or passage in a building, usually having various rooms opening upon it. **2** A strip of land across a foreign country by which a landlocked nation has access to the sea. **3** A strip of territory including two or more major cities, typically heavily traveled and as a region densely populated: the Northeast *Corridor* of the United States. [<F <Ital. *corridore* <*correre* run <L *currere*]

cor·rie (kôr'ē, kor'ē) *n. Scot.* A hollow in the side of a hill or at the head of a valley.

Cor·ri·en·tes (kôr'rē·än'tās) A province of NE Argentina; 33,544 square miles; capital, Corrientes.

cor·ri·gen·dum (kôr'ə·jen'dəm, kor'-) *n. pl.* **·da** (-də) **1** Something to be corrected: said of a printer's error. **2** *pl.* A list of corrected errors, as in a printed book. [<L, gerundive of *corrigere.* See CORRECT.]

cor·ri·gi·ble (kôr'ə·jə·bəl, kor'-) *adj.* Capable of being corrected or reformed. [<F <L *corrigere.* See CORRECT.] **—cor'ri·gi·bil'i·ty, cor'ri·gi·ble·ness** *n.* **—cor'ri·gi·bly** *adv.*

cor·rob·o·rant (kə·rob'ər·ənt) *adj.* Having the power to impart strength; invigorating. —*n.* Something that imparts strength or corroborates. [<L *corroborans, -antis,* ppr. of *corroborare.* See CORROBORATE.]

cor·rob·o·rate (kə·rob'ə·rāt) *v.t.* **·rat·ed, ·rat·ing** To strengthen, as conviction; confirm. See synonyms under CONFIRM, RATIFY. [<L *corroboratus,* pp. of *corroborare* <*com-* together + *robur* strength] **—cor·rob'o·rat'er, cor·rob'o·ra'tor** *n.* **—cor·rob'o·ra'tion** *n.* **—cor·rob·o·ra·tive** (kə·rob'ə·rā'tiv, -rob'ər·ə·tiv), **cor·rob·o·ra·to·ry** (kə·rob'ər·ə·tôr'ē, -tō'rē) *adj.* **—cor·rob'o·ra'tive·ly** *adv.*

cor·rob·o·ree (kə·rob'ər·ē) *n.* **1** A native Australian festival to celebrate tribal victories. **2** A noisy celebration. **3** A frog (*Pseudophryne corroboree*) of Australia, having brilliant orange and black stripes.

cor·rode (kə·rōd') *v.* **·rod·ed, ·rod·ing** *v.t.* To eat away gradually; rust; ruin or destroy little by little. —*v.i.* To be eaten or worn away. [<L *corrodere* <*com-* thoroughly + *rodere* gnaw] **—cor·ro'dent** *adj.* & *n.* **—cor·rod'i·ble, cor·ro·si·ble** (kə·rō'sə·bəl) *adj.*

Cor·ro·den·tia (kôr'ə·den'shə, kor'-) *n. pl.* An order of minute insects, including the book lice: also called *Psocoptera.*

cor·ro·dy (kôr'ə·dē, kor'-) See CORODY.

cor·ro·sion (kə·rō'zhən) *n.* **1** An eating or wearing away; gradual decay. **2** The destructive breaking down of metals into their oxides or metallic salts. **3** The product of corrosive

action. [<OF <LL *corrosio, -onis* <*corrodere.* See CORRODE.]

cor·ro·sive (kə·rō′siv) *adj.* Having the power of corroding: often used figuratively. —*n.* That which corrodes; a corroding agent. —**cor·ro′sive·ly** *adv.* —**cor·ro′sive·ness** *n.*

corrosive sublimate *Chem.* Mercuric chloride, a white, crystalline, poisonous compound, $HgCl_2$, formed by subliming a mixture of salt and mercuric sulfate: a strong disinfectant.

cor·ru·gant (kôr′ə·gant, -yə-, kor′-) *adj.* Having the power of corrugating. —*n.* A styptic or astringent. [<L *corrugans, -antis,* ppr. of *corrugare.* See CORRUGATE.]

cor·ru·gate (kôr′ə·gat, -yə-, kor′-) *v.t.* & *v.i.* **·gat·ed, ·gat·ing** To contract into alternate ridges and furrows; wrinkle. —*adj.* Contracted into ridges or folds; wrinkled: also **cor′ru·gat′ed.** [<L *corrugatus,* pp. of *corrugare* <*com-* together + *ruga* a wrinkle] —**cor′ru·ga′tion** *n.*

corrugated iron Sheets of iron or steel, usually galvanized, having a series of parallel, equally spaced curved ridges and hollows.

cor·rupt (kə·rupt′) *adj.* **1** In a state of decomposition; tainted; putrid. **2** Of a perverted character; depraved. **3** Dishonest; given to bribery. See synonyms under BAD, IMMORAL, ROTTEN. —*v.t.* **1** To cause to become putrescent or putrid; spoil. **2** To render impure; taint; contaminate. **3** To destroy the fidelity or integrity of; bribe: to *corrupt* a voter. **4** To destroy morally; pervert; ruin. **5** To debase or lower the quality or purity of by changes or errors: to *corrupt* a manuscript. **6** *Archaic* To waste; consume; corrode. —*v.i.* **7** To become rotten or corrupt; degenerate. [<OF <L *corruptus,* pp. of *corrumpere* <*com-* thoroughly + *rumpere* break] —**cor·rupt′er, cor·rup′tor** *n.* —**cor·rupt′i·bil′i·ty, cor·rupt′i·ble·ness** *n.* —**cor·rupt′i·ble** *adj.* —**cor·rupt′i·bly** *adv.* —**cor·rupt′ly** *adv.* —**cor·rupt′ness** *n.*

Synonyms (verb): contaminate, debase, defile, deprave, deteriorate, pollute, putrefy, spoil, vitiate. See DECAY, DEFILE, PERVERT, POLLUTE, PUTREFY.

cor·rup·tion (kə·rup′shən) *n.* **1** The act of corrupting, or the state of being corrupted. **2** A corrupting influence, as bribery. **3** A linguistic or orthographic change in a text, word, etc., to an incorrect form; also, an example of such a change: Porpentine is a *corruption* of porcupine.

cor·rup·tion·ist (kə·rup′shən·ist) *n.* **1** A bribe-giver or bribe-taker. **2** One who defends corruption. **3** One who is guilty of corrupt practices while holding public office.

corruption of blood *Law* An immediate consequence of a judgment of attainder of treason or felony whereby the guilty person was deprived of the right to receive or transmit property by inheritance: abolished in 1870.

cor·rup·tive (kə·rup′tiv) *adj.* Of a corrupting character.

cor·sac (kôr′sak) *n.* A small, yellowish Asiatic fox *(Vulpes corsac)*: also called *dog fox.* [<Turkic]

cor·sage (kôr·säzh′) *n.* **1** The bodice or waist of a woman's dress. **2** A small bouquet of fresh flowers for a woman to wear, as at the waist or bodice, [<OF <*cors* body <L *corpus*]

cor·sair (kôr′sâr) *n.* **1** A pirate; also, his vessel. **2** Specifically, a privateer, formerly authorized by the Turkish and Saracen governments to harry the coasts of Christian countries: Barbary *corsairs.* [<F *corsaire* <Med. L *cursarius* <*cursus* inroad, raid <L, a running <*currere* run. Doublet of HUSSAR.]

corse (kôrs) *n.* **1** *Archaic* A ribbon used for vestments. **2** *Poetic* A corpse. [<OF *cors.* See CORPSE.]

corse·let (kôrs′lit *for defs. 1, 2;* kôrs′sə·let′ *for def. 3)* **1** The complete armor of a soldier; also a breastplate. **2** *Zool.* The thorax of an arthropod. **3** A light corset, usually without stays, worn by women. Also **cors′let.** [<MF, double dim. of *cors* body. See CORPSE.]

cor·set (kôr′sit) *n.* **1** A close-fitting undergarment, usually tightened with laces and reinforced by stays, worn to give support or a desired shape to the body. **2** A medieval garment fitting closely to the body. —*v.t.* To enclose or dress in a corset. [<OF, dim. of *cors* body. See CORPSE.]

cor·se·tier (kôr·sə·tyā′) *n. French* A maker or fitter of corsets. —**cor·se·tière** (kôr·sə·tyâr′) *n. fem.*

Cor·si·ca (kôr′si·kə) An island in the Mediterranean, comprising a department of Metropolitan France; 3,367 square miles; capital, Ajaccio. *French* **Corse** (kôrs).

Cor·si·can (kôr′si·kən) *adj.* Of or pertaining to Corsica or to its inhabitants. —*n.* **1** A native of Corsica. **2** The Italian dialect spoken in Corsica. —**The Corsican** Napoleon Bonaparte.

cor·tège (kôr·tezh′, -tāzh′) *n.* **1** A train of attendants. **2** A ceremonial procession. See synonyms under PROCESSION. [<F <Ital. *corteggio* <*corte* court]

Cor·tes (kôr′tiz, *Sp.* kôr·tās′) *n.* The national legislature of Spain or of Portugal. [<Sp. <*corte* court]

Cor·tés (kôr·tez′, *Sp.* kôr·tās′), **Hernando,** 1485–1547, Spanish conqueror of Mexico. Also **Cor·tez′.**

cor·tex (kôr′teks) *n. pl.* **·ti·ces** (-tə·sēz) **1** *Bot.* The outer portion of the stem, thalli, or root in plants; specifically, the bark of trees or the rind of fruits. **2** *Zool.* In animals, the outer or investing layer of various organs. **3** *Anat.* **a** The external layer of gray matter of the cerebrum and cerebellum. **b** The external portion of the adrenal glands, enclosing the medullae and indispensable to proper glandular functioning. [<L, bark]

Cor·ti (kôr′tē), **Alfonso,** 1822–76, Italian anatomist.

cor·ti·cal (kôr′ti·kəl) *adj.* **1** Of, pertaining to, or consisting of a cortex, bark, or rind; hence, external. **2** *Physiol.* Designating a process, function, or condition caused by or associated with the cerebral cortex: *cortical* sensibility. [<NL *corticalis* <L *cortex* bark] —**cor′ti·cal·ly** *adv.*

cor·ti·cate (kôr′ti·kit, -kāt) *adj.* Sheathed in bark or in a cortex. Also **cor′ti·cat′ed.** [<L *corticatus* <*cortex* bark]

cor·ti·cose (kôr′ti·kōs) *adj.* Like or of the nature of bark. Also **cor′ti·cous** (-kəs). [<L *corticosus* with a thick bark <*cortex* bark]

cor·ti·co·ster·one (kôr′ti·kos′tə·rōn) *n. Biochem.* One of a group of steroids, $C_{21}H_{30}O_4$, occurring in, and closely associated with the proper functioning of, the adrenal cortex. [<*cortico-* (<L *cortex, -icis*) + STER(OID) + (HORM)ONE]

cor·ti·co·tro·pin (kor′ti·kō·trō′pin) *n.* A hormonal preparation having adrenocorticotropic activity, obtained from the anterior lobe of the pituitary gland of hogs and other domestic animals. [<*cortico-* (<L *cortex, -icis*) +TROP(IC) + -IN]—**cor′ti·co·tro′pic** *adj.*

cor·tin (kôr′tin) *n. Biochem.* A substance containing various hormones of the adrenal cortex: used in the treatment of certain disorders, as Addison's disease. [<CORT(EX) + -IN]

cor·ti·sone (kôr′tə·sōn, -zōn) *n.* A powerful hormone extracted from the outer part (cortex) of the adrenal gland and also made synthetically: in therapeutic doses it has a palliative effect upon some forms of rheumatoid arthritis and rheumatic fever. Formerly called *compound E.* [Short for CORTICOSTERONE]

Co·ru·ña (kō·rōō′nyä), **La** A province of NW Spain; 3,051 square miles; capital, La Coruña. Also **Co·run·na** (kō·run′ə).

co·run·dum (kə·run′dəm) *n.* A very hard native alumina, Al_2O_3, used in abrasives and represented in colored varieties by gemstones, as rubies, sapphires, etc. [<Tamil *kurundam* <Skt. *kuruvinda* ruby]

cor·us·cate (kôr′ə·skāt, kor′-) *v.i.* **·cat·ed, ·cat·ing** To give out sparkles of light. [<L *coruscatus.* pp. of *coruscare* glitter] —**cor′us·ca′tion** *n.*

cor·vée (kôr·vā′) *n.* **1** Formerly, an obligation to perform feudal service. **2** Any system of forced labor, particularly in repairing roads. [<F <OF *corovée* <L *corrogata (opera)* required (work), pp. of *corrogare* <*com-* together + *rogare* ask]

cor·vette (kôr·vet′) *n.* **1** A small, swift ship armed with depth charges and guns, and used chiefly as an anti-submarine escort vessel. **2** Formerly, a warship equipped with sails and a single tier of guns, and ranking next below a frigate. Also **cor·vet** (kôr·vet′, kôr′vet). [<F <Pg. *corveta* <L *corbita (navis)* cargo (ship) <*corbis* basket]

cor·vi·na (kôr·vi′nə) *n.* **1** A sciaenid food fish *(Micropogon undulatus)* found in Atlantic waters from Cape Cod to Texas. **2** A croaker (*Cynoscion parvipinnis*) of southern California, highly esteemed as a food fish. [<Sp.]

cor·vine (kôr′vin, -vin) *adj.* Of or pertaining to a crow; crowlike. [<L *corvinus* <*corvus* crow]

Cor·vus (kôr′vəs) **1** A southern constellation, the Crow or Raven. See CONSTELLATION. **2** A widely distributed genus of black- or dark-plumaged birds typical of the *Corvidae* family; the crows. [<L, raven]

Cor·y·bant (kôr′ə·bant, kor′-) *n. pl.* **Cor·y·bants** or **Cor·y·ban·tes** (kôr′ə·ban′tēz, kor′-) **1** A priest or attendant of the ancient Phrygian goddess Cybele, whose rites were celebrated with wild dances and revelry. **2** A reveler. [<F *Corybante* <L *Corybas, -antis* <Gk. *Korybas*] —**Cor·y·ban·tian** (kôr′ə·ban′shən, kor′-) or **·ban′tic** (-ban′tik) *adj.*

Co·ryd·a·lis (kə·rid′ə·lis) *n.* A large genus of erect or climbing herbs of the fumitory family, with divided leaves, fibrous or tuberous roots, and racemes of rose, white, or yellow flowers. [<NL <Gk. *korydallis, korydalos* a crested lark]

Co·ryd·a·lus (kə·rid′ə·ləs) *n.* An American genus of large insects (order *Megaloptera*), including the dobsonfly or hellgrammite. [<NL <L <Gk. *korydalos* a crested lark]

Cor·y·don (kôr′ə·dən, kor′ə·don) In pastoral poetry, a name for a shepherd or a rustic swain.

cor·ymb (kôr′imb, -im, kor′-) *n. Bot.* A flat-topped or convex open flower cluster of indeterminate inflorescence. [<L *corymbus* <Gk. *korymbos* flower cluster] —**co·rym·bose** (kə·rim′bōs), **co·rym·bous** (kə·rim′bəs) *adj.* —**co·rym′bose·ly** *adv.*

cor·y·phée (kôr′ə·fā′, kor′-) *n.* A ballet dancer who leads a movement of the corps de ballet.

cor·y·phe·us (kôr′ə·fē′əs, kor′-) *n. pl.* **·phe·i** (-fē′ī) **1** In ancient Greek drama, the leader of the chorus. **2** Any leader, as of a chorus, set, etc. Also **cor′y·phae′us.** [<L <Gk. *koryphaios* leader of the chorus <*koryphē* head, top <*korys* helmet]

co·ry·za (kə·rī′zə) *n.* **1** *Pathol.* Inflammation of the mucous membrane of the nose and connecting sinuses; nasal catarrh; cold in the head. **2** A contagious bacterial disease of the upper air passages of poultry, characterized by morbid secretions in the mouth, throat, and nasal cavities. [<L <Gk. *koryza* catarrh]

cos (kôs, kos) *n.* A kind of lettuce with a cylindrical head of erect, oblong leaves. [from island of *Kos,* where first grown]

Cos (kôs) See KOS.

Co·sa Nos·tra (kō′zə nōs′trə) A secret criminal organization in the U.S., associated with the Mafia. [Ital., our thing]

co·se·cant (kō·sē′kənt) *n. Trig.* The secant of the complement of an angle or an arc. [<CO-[2] + SECANT]

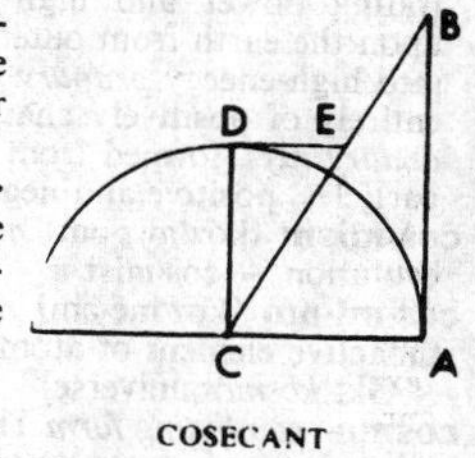

COSECANT

co·seis·mal (kō·siz′məl, -sis′-) *adj.* **1** Experiencing an earthquake shock simultaneously at all points: a *coseismal* line or zone. **2** Indicating the progress of an earthquake by a series of connected lines. Also **co·seis′·mic,** —*n.* A line on a map, usually forming a rough oval, and connecting the points at which simultaneous earthquake shocks are felt: often called *isoseismal.* [<CO-[1] + SEISMAL]

Co·sen·za (kō·zen′tsä) A town in Calabria, southern Italy.

co·sey (kō′zē) See COZY.

Cos·grave (koz′grāv), **William Thomas,** 1880–1965, Irish patriot.

cosh (kosh) *Brit. Slang n.* A small, loaded bludgeon; a blackjack. —*v.t.* To strike with or as with a cosh.

cosh·er[1] (kosh′ər) *v.t.* To pamper; treat fondly; coddle; pet. [? < dial. E (Northern) *cosh* snug, comfortable]

cosh·er[2] (kosh′ər) *v.i. Irish* To live or be entertained at another's expense. [< Irish *coisir* feast] **—cosh′er·er** *n.* **—cosh′er·ing** *n.*

co·si·ly (kō′zə·lē) See COZILY.

cos·in·age (kuz′ən·ij) *n.* Collateral relationship or kindred by blood; consanguinity: also spelled *cousinage.* [< OF *cousinage*]

co·sine (kō′sīn) *n. Trig.* The sine of the complement of a given angle or arc. [< CO-[2] + SINE]

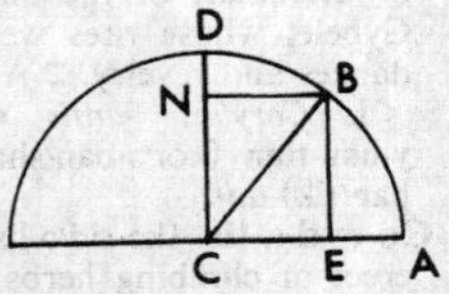

COSINE
Of the angle ACB, the ratio of EC to BC is the cosine; or, CD being unity, the line BN is the cosine.

cos·me·col·o·gy (koz′mə·kol′ə·jē) *n.* The investigation and study of the effects of cosmic phenomena on life. [< COSM(IC) + ECOLOGY]

cos·met·ic (koz·met′ik) *adj.* Pertaining to or used for beautifying, cleansing, or protecting, especially the skin, hair, nails, or other part of the human body, or of certain animals on exhibition. Also **cos·met′i·cal.** —*n.* **1** Any preparation intended to be applied to any part of the human body for cleansing, beautifying, promoting attractiveness, or altering its appearance, including bath salts, face and hand creams, etc., but excluding soaps other than shampoos and shaving soaps. **2** Any cologne or perfume. **3** A vanishing cream used as a protective barrier for the skin to prevent or correct skin irritations acquired in certain paint and chemical industries: also called *barrier cream.* [< Gk. *kosmetikos* < *kosmos* order, ornament] **—cos·met′i·cal·ly** *adv.*

cos·me·ti·cian (koz′mə·tish′ən) *n.* One who manufactures, sells, or applies cosmetics.

cos·me·tol·o·gy (koz′mə·tol′ə·jē) *n.* The study or art of cosmetics and their application. [< Gk. *kosmetikos* cosmetic + -OLOGY] **—cos′me·tol′o·gist** *n.*

cos·mic (koz′mik) *adj.* **1** Pertaining to the universe at large as a harmonious system. **2** Harmonious; orderly: opposed to *chaotic.* **3** Belonging to the material universe, especially that portion outside the solar system: *cosmic* changes. **4** Of a magnitude or extent in space or time suggesting those of the universe; of vast extent or duration. **5** Relating to cosmism. Also **cos′mi·cal.** [< Gk. *kosmikos* < *kosmos* the universe] **—cos′mi·cal·ly** *adv.*

cosmic dust Fine particles of extraterrestrial matter dispersed in space.

cosmic rays *Physics* Radiation of intense penetrating power and high frequency, impinging upon the earth from outer space and subdivided into high-energy *primary rays,* consisting almost entirely of positively charged particles, and *secondary rays,* formed from many types of atomic particles, positive and negative in charge.

cos·mism (koz′miz·əm) *n.* A doctrine of cosmic evolution. **—cos′mist** *n.*

cos·mi·um (koz′mē·əm) *n.* The hypothetical radioactive element of atomic number 137. [< NL < Gk. *kosmos* universe]

cosmo- *combining form* The universe: *cosmogony.* Also, before vowels, **cosm-.** [< Gk. *kosmos* the universe]

cos·mog·o·ny (koz·mog′ə·nē) *n. pl.* **·nies** A theory of creation, as of the world or of the universe. [< COSMO- + -GONY] **—cos·mo·gon·ic** (koz′mə·gon′ik) or **·i·cal, cos·mog′o·nal** *adj.* **—cos·mog′o·nist** *n.*

cos·mog·ra·phy (koz·mog′rə·fē) *n.* The science that describes the universe, including astronomy, geology, and geography. [< COSMO- + -GRAPHY] **—cos·mog′ra·pher, cos·mog′ra·phist** *n.* **—cos·mo·graph·ic** (koz′mə·graf′ik) or **·i·cal** *adj.*

Cos·mo·line (koz′mə·lēn) *n.* A heavy grade of petroleum or paraffin jelly, used as a rust preventive: a trade name.

cos·mol·o·gy (koz·mol′ə·jē) *n. pl.* **·gies** The general science or philosophy of the universe. [< COSMO- + -LOGY] **—cos·mo·log·ic** (koz′mə·loj′ik) or **·i·cal** *adj.* **—cos·mol′o·gist** *n.*

cos·mon (koz′mon) *n. Physics* The hypothetical particle from which the known universe developed, carrying a positive nucleonic charge in opposition to the negative charge attributed to the anticosmon. [< Gk. *kosmos* the universe]

cos·mo·naut (koz′mə·nôt) *n.* A traveler in outer space.

cos·mo·plas·tic (koz′mə·plas′tik) *adj.* Pertaining to the formation of the universe; cosmogonic.

cos·mop·o·lis (koz·mop′ə·lis) *n.* A city with a cosmopolitan population, where many cultures meet. [< COSMO- + Gk. *polis* city]

cos·mo·pol·i·tan (koz′mə·pol′ə·tən) *adj.* **1** Common to all the world; not local or limited. **2** At home in all parts of the world. **3** *Biol.* Widely distributed, as a plant or animal. —*n.* A citizen of the world. **—cos′mo·pol′i·tan·ism, cos′mo·pol′i·tism** *n.*

cos·mo·pol·i·tan·ize (koz′mə·pol′ə·tən·īz′) *v.t.* **·ized, ·iz·ing** To render cosmopolitan. **—cos′mo·pol′i·tan·i·za′tion** *n.*

cos·mop·o·lite (koz·mop′ə·līt) *n.* **1** One at home everywhere; a person of world-wide experience and travel. **2** One free from local prejudice or affection. **3** *Biol.* A plant or animal widely distributed over the world. —*adj.* World-wide in extent or existence; cosmopolitan. [< Gk. *kosmopolitēs* < *kosmos* world + *politēs* citizen < *polis* city] **—cos·mo·pol·it·i·cal** (koz′mō·pə·lit′i·kəl), **cos·mo·pol·i·tic** (koz′mō·pol′ə·tik) *adj.*

cos·mo·ra·ma (koz′mə·rä′mə, -ram′ə) *n.* An exhibition of scenes from different parts of the world. [< COSMO- + Gk. *horama* sight] **—cos′mo·ram′ic** *adj.*

cos·mos (koz′məs, -mos) *n.* **1** The world or universe considered as a system, perfect in order and arrangement: opposed to *chaos.* **2** Any harmonious and complete system evolved out of complex details. **3** Order; harmony. **4** *Bot.* Any member of a small genus *(Cosmos)* of the composite family of plants, related to the dahlia. [< Gk. *kosmos* order]

cos·mo·scope (koz′mə·skōp) *n.* An orrery.

cos·mo·tron (koz′mə·tron) *n.* A bevatron. [< *cosmo-* (< COSMIC RAYS) + (ELEC)TRON]

coss (kôs) *n.* In India, a unit of land measure, varying from one to three miles. [< Hind. *kos* < Skt. *krośa*]

Cos·sack (kos′ak, -ək) *n.* One of a people of the southern U.S.S.R. in Europe and adjoining regions of Asia, famous as cavalrymen. [< Russ. *kazak* < Turkic *quzzāq* guerrilla, freebooter]

cos·set (kos′it) *v.t.* To fondle; pet. [< *n.*] —*n.* **1** A pet lamb. **2** Any pet. [? OE *cot-sǣta* a dweller in a cottage]

Cos·sy·ra (kə·sī′rə) The ancient name of PANTELLERIA.

cost (kôst, kost) *v.* **cost** (*for def. 3, also* **cost·ed**), **cost·ing** *v.i.* **1** To be priced at; require as the price of possession, use, or accomplishment. **2** To cause sacrifice, loss, or suffering: It *cost* him his fortune. —*v.t.* **3** To estimate the cost of production of. —*n.* **1** The price paid for anything; outlay; expense; charge. **2** Loss; suffering; detriment. **3** *pl. Law* **a** The charges fixed by law or allowed by the court in a lawsuit; specifically, the charges payable to an attorney for the opposite side by an unsuccessful litigant. **b** *U.S.* The charges payable by a client to his attorney. See synonyms under EXPENSE, PRICE. [< OF *coster* < L *constare* < *com-* together + *stare* stand]

cos·ta (kos′tə) *n. pl.* **·tae** (-tē) **1** A rib or a riblike structure, part, or marking. **2** *Entomol.* A longitudinal vein along the anterior part of an insect's wing. [< L, rib] **—cos′tal** *adj.*

cost-ac·count·ant (kôst′ə·koun′tənt, kost′-) *n.* An accountant who keeps track of the costs of labor, materials, and overhead incurred in production and distribution. **—cost′-ac·count′ing** *n.*

Co·stan·za (kō·stän′tsä) Italian form of CONSTANCE.

Co·stan·zo (kō·stän′tsō) Italian form of CONSTANT. Also **Co·stan·te** (kō·stän′tä).

co-star (kō′stär′) *n.* An actor or actress given equal prominence with another or other players in a motion picture, play, etc. —*v.i.* & *v.t.* (kō′stär′) **co-starred, co-star·ring** To be or cause to be a co-star.

cos·tard (kos′tərd, kôs′-) *n.* **1** A variety of apple. **2** *Archaic* The head: a humorous usage. [< F *coste* rib]

Cos·ta Ri·ca (kos′tə rē′kə, kôs′tə) A republic of Central America; 19,650 square miles; capital, San José. **—Cos′ta Ri′can** *adj.* & *n.*

cos·tate (kos′tāt) *adj.* Having or bearing ribs. Also **cos′tat·ed.** [< L *costatus* < *costa* rib]

Cos·tel·lo (kos′tə·lō), **John Aloysius,** born 1891, prime minister of Ireland 1948–51, 1954–57.

Co·sten·za (kō·sten′thä) A Spanish form of CONSTANCE.

Cos·ter (kus′tər), **Laurens Janszoon,** 1370?–1450, Dutch inventor; reputed earliest inventor of movable types: also spelled *Koster.*

cos·ter·mon·ger (kos′tər·mung′gər, -mong′-, kôs′-) *n. Brit.* A street hawker of vegetables, etc., especially in the East End of London. Also **cos′tard·mon′ger, cos′ter.** [Earlier *costardmonger* < COSTARD + MONGER]

cos·tive (kos′tiv, kôs′-) *adj.* **1** Constipated. **2** Producing constipation. [< OF *costevé* < L *constipatus.* See CONSTIPATE.] **—cos′tive·ly** *adv.* **—cos′tive·ness** *n.*

cost·ly (kôst′lē, kost′-) *adj.* **·li·er, ·li·est 1** Of great cost; expensive. **2** Splendid; gorgeous. **3** *Obs.* Free-handed; lavish. See synonyms under CHOICE. **—cost′li·ness** *n.*

cost·mar·y (kost′mâr′ē, kôst′-) *n.* A fragrant southern European herb *(Chrysanthemum majus)*: used in salads. [< L *costum* an Eastern plant + *Maria* Mary]

costo- *combining form* Rib: used in anatomical, surgical, and zoological terms. Also, before vowels, **cost-.** [< L *costa* rib]

cost of living The average cost, as to an individual or family, of the necessities of life: food, clothing, shelter, etc.

cos·tot·o·my (kos·tot′ə·mē, kôs-) *n. Surg.* The operation of cutting or dividing a rib. [< COSTO- + -TOMY]

cost-plus (kôst′plus′, kost′-) *n.* The cost of production plus a percentage of that cost for profit: a term often used in contracts.

cos·tume (kos′tōōm, -tyōōm) *n.* **1** Dress or apparel, including all the garments worn at one time; external dress, especially that of a woman; hence, dress in general. **2** The dress belonging to a given country, time, class, calling, or the like. **3** Fancy dress: a *costume* ball. **4** Local color in art or literature; congruity and accuracy in the depicting of a given place or period in respect to details of dress, action, accessories, etc. —*v.t.* (kos·tōōm′, -tyōōm′) **·tumed, ·tum·ing** To furnish with costumes. See synonyms under DRESS. [< F < Ital. *costuma* fashion, guise < L *consuetudo* custom. Doublet of CUSTOM.]

cos·tum·er (kos·tōō′mər, -tyōō′-) *n.* **1** One who makes or furnishes costumes for stage wear or fancy dress. **2** A rack for clothing. Also **cos·tum·ier** (kos·tōōm′yər, -tyōōm′-; *Fr.* kôs·tü·myā′).

co·sy (kō′zē) See COZY.

cot[1] (kot) *n.* **1** A cottage. **2** A finger stall. See synonyms under HOUSE, HUT. [OE]

cot[2] (kot) *n.* A light, portable bedstead. [< Hind. *khāt* < Skt. *khatvā*]

co·tan·gent (kō·tan′jənt) *n. Trig.* The tangent of the complement of an angle. [< CO-[2] + TANGENT]

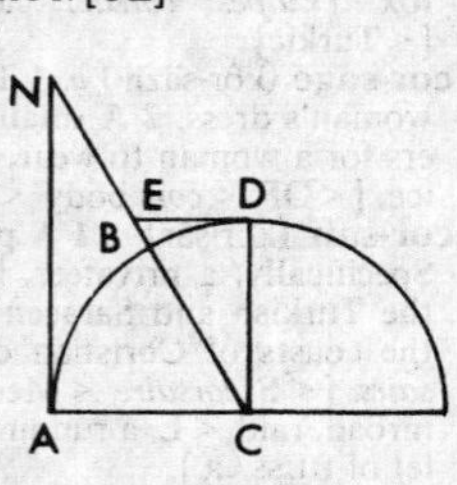

COTANGENT
Of the angle ACB, the ratio of DE to DC is the cotangent; or, DC being unity, the line DE is the cotangent.

co·tan·gen·tial (kō′tan·jen′shəl) *adj.* **1** Of or pertaining to a cotangent. **2** With the same tangent.

cote[1] (kōt) *n.* **1** A small place of shelter for sheep, birds, or chickens, used chiefly in compounds: *dovecote.* **2** *Dial.* A little house; hut. [OE]

cote[2] (kōt) *v.t.* **cot·ed, cot·ing** To go around by the side of; pass by. [? < F *côtoyer* < L *costa* rib, side]

co·teau (kô·tō′) *n. pl.* **co·teaux** (-tōz′, *Fr.* -tō′) **1** A hill or ridge. **2** A high plateau. [< F]

Côte d'A·zur (kōt dá·zür′) The eastern Mediterranean coast of France. See RIVIERA.

Côte d'I·voire (kōt dē·vwär′) The French name for IVORY COAST.

Côte d'Or (kōt dôr′) A department in east

central France; 3,391 square miles; capital, Dijon.

cô·te·lette (kō·tə·let′) *n. French* A cutlet

co·tem·po·ra·ne·ous (kō·tem′pə·rā′nē·əs), **co·tem·po·rar·y** (kō·tem′pə·rer′ē), etc. See CONTEMPORANEOUS, etc.

co·ten·ant (kō·ten′ənt) *n. Law* One of several holding the same property under the same title. — **co·ten′an·cy, co·ten·ure** (kō·ten′yər) *n.*

Co·ten·tin (kō·tän·tan′) A peninsula of lower Normandy, France, extending into the English Channel; scene of first landing (June 6, 1944) of Allied invasion troops in World War II: also *Cherbourg Peninsula.*

co·te·rie (kō′tə·rē) *n.* A set of persons who meet habitually; a clique. See synonyms under CLASS. [<F, earlier, an organization of tenants holding land from the same lord < *cotier* cotter < *cote* hut]

co·ter·mi·nous (kō·tûr′mə·nəs) See CONTERMINOUS.

co·thur·nus (kō·thûr′nəs) *n. pl.* **·ni** (-nī) A buskin, or high laced shoe, worn by actors in ancient Greek or Roman tragedies: regarded as a symbol of tragedy. Also **co·thurn** (kō′·thûrn, kō·thûrn′) [<L <Gk. *kothornos*] — **co·thur′nal** *adj.*

co·ti·dal (kō·tīd′l) *adj.* Indicating simultaneity in tides.

cotidal lines Lines on a chart, atlas, or sphere indicating the places at which high tide occurs simultaneously.

co·til·lion (kō·til′yən, kə-) *n.* 1 A square dance; quadrille. 2 The music for such a dance. 3 A series of round dances; the german. Also **co·til·lon** (kō·til′yən, kə-; *Fr.* kô·tē·yôn′). [<F *cotillon* petticoat, dim. of *cotte* coat]

Co·to·pax·i (kō′tō·pak′sē, *Sp.* kō′tō·pä′hē) A volcano in north central Ecuador; 19,344 feet: probably the world's highest active volcano.

cot·quean (kot′kwēn) *n. Archaic* 1 A low, vulgar woman. 2 A man who meddles with affairs regarded as belonging to women. [<COT¹ + QUEAN]

Cots·wold (kots′wōld, -wəld) *n.* A breed of sheep with long wool, originally bred in the Cotswold Hills.

Cotswold Hills A range of low hills in SW central England. Also **Cots′wolds.**

cot·ta (kot′ə) *n. pl.* **cot·tas** or **cot·tae** (kot′ē) 1 A short surplice, with short sleeves or none. 2 A very coarse blanket. [<Med. L *cota* coat]

cot·ta·bus (kot′ə·bəs) *n.* A game of the ancient Greeks which consisted of throwing wine from a cup into a basin. [<L <Gk. *kottabos*]

cot·tage (kot′ij) *n.* 1 A humble dwelling. 2 A small house in the suburbs or the country. 3 *U.S.* A temporary vacation residence at a resort. See synonyms under HOUSE, HUT. [<COT¹]

cottage cheese A soft, white cheese made of strained milk curds, usually seasoned with salt: also called *pot cheese.*

cottage pudding Cake without icing, served with a sweet sauce, whipped cream, etc.

cot·ter¹ (kot′ər) *n.* 1 *Scot.* A tenant occupying a plot of ground and a cottage under a system resembling cottier tenure. 2 *Irish* A cottier. 3 A cottager; farm tenant. Also **cot′tar.** [<Med. L *cotarius* < *cota* a cottage <Gmc.]

cot·ter² (kot′ər) *n.* A key or wedge, used to fasten parts of machinery together, as a wheel on its shaft. Also **cot·ter·el** (kot′ər·əl). [Origin uncertain]

cot·ter–pin (kot′ər·pin′) *n. Mech.* A split metal pin for insertion in a nut, bolt, etc., to hold it in place.

Cot·ti·an Alps (kot′ē·ən) A division of the western Alps on the French-Italian border.

cot·ti·er (kot′ē·ər) *n.* 1 Formerly, in Ireland, a tenant of a house and a plot of land at a rental fixed by public competition. 2 A peasant with a small farm. [<OF *cotier* <Med. L *cotarius* COTTER]

cot·tise (kot′is) *n. Her.* A small bend. [<MF *cotisse*] — **cot′tised** *adj.*

cot·ton (kot′n) *n.* 1 The soft, fibrous, white or yellowish material, of high cellulose content, appendant to the seeds of the cotton plant. It is graded chiefly in accordance with the length of the fibers (long-staple and short-staple) and is widely used as a textile, in

industry, chemistry, medicine, and the arts. 2 The cotton plant itself; also, cotton plants collectively. 3 Cotton cloth or thread. — *adj.* Woven or composed of cotton cloth or thread. — *v.t.* To wrap up in cotton; hence, to pet or coddle. — **to cotton to** *Colloq.* To become friendly with; take a liking to. — **to cotton up to** *Colloq.* To attempt to please or placate by friendly overtures or flattery. [<F *coton* <OSp. <Arabic *quṭun*]

Cot·ton (kot′n), **Charles,** 1630–87, English author and translator. — **John,** 1584–1642, English clergyman in America; grandfather of Cotton Mather.

cotton belt That region of the southern United States in which cotton is the chief crop.

cotton boll The seed capsule of the cotton plant.

cotton flannel Soft, warm cotton fabric, napped on one or both sides.

cotton gin A machine used to separate the seeds from the fiber of cotton. See GIN³.

cot·ton·grass (kot′n·gras′, -gräs′) *n.* One of various rushlike plants (genus *Eriophorum*) of the sedge family, growing in swampy places and bearing cottony spikes.

cot·ton–leaf worm (kot′n·lēf′) The larva of a lepidopterous insect (*Alabama argillacea*), injurious to the cotton plant. Also **cotton worm.**

cotton linters See LINTERS.

cot·ton·mouth (kot′n·mouth′) *n.* A venomous pit viper (*Agkistrodon piscivorus*) living along lakes and streams or in swamps of the southern United States; the water moccasin.

cotton picker A machine, usually driven by tractor, designed to remove the ripe cotton from the standing cotton plants.

cotton plant Any of various tropical shrubs or woody herbs (genus *Gossypium*) of the mallow family, widely cultivated for the cotton they produce; especially, in the United States, upland cotton (*G. hirsutum*) and Sea Island cotton (*G. barbadense*).

cot·ton·seed (kot′n·sēd′) *n.* The seed of the cotton plant. Also **cotton seed.**

cottonseed meal Cottonseed ground after the oil has been expressed: used in feeding cattle and as a fertilizer.

cottonseed oil A pale-yellow, viscid oil pressed from cottonseeds: used in cooking, paints, and as a lubricant.

cotton stainer Any of a genus (*Dysdercus*) of bugs that punctures the developing seeds of the cotton boll and stains them with its indelible yellow or red juices.

Cotton State Nickname of ALABAMA.

cot·ton·tail (kot′n·tāl′) *n.* The common American gray rabbit (genus *Sylvilagus*).

cotton tree 1 The cottonwood. 2 An East Indian tree (*Gossypium arboreum*) which produces the silk cotton used in cushions, etc.

cotton waste The refuse of cotton manufacture: used to clean machinery, as packing, etc.

cot·ton·weed (kot′n·wēd′) *n.* 1 A perennial herb (*Diotis candidissima*) of the composite family, grown in rock gardens. 2 The cudweed. 3 The everlasting. Also **cot′ton·rose′.**

cot·ton·wood (kot′n·wŏod′) *n.* 1 Any of several American species of poplar trees whose seeds discharge a cottony substance, especially *Populus deltoides.* 2 Its wood.

cotton wool Raw cotton.

cot·ton·y (kot′ən·ē) *adj.* 1 Made or consisting of cotton. 2 Like cotton; fluffy; soft.

Cot·tus (kot′əs) One of the Hecatoncheires.

cot·y·le·don (kot′ə·lēd′n) *n.* 1 *Bot.* A seed leaf, or one of a pair or whorl of the first leaves from a sprouting seed. 2 A genus (*Cotyledon*) of succulent, ornamental herbs native to the Old World. 3 *Anat.* A subdivision of the uterine surface of the placenta. [<L, navelwort <Gk. *kotylēdōn* socket < *kotyle* a hollow, cavity] — **cot′y·le′do·nous, cot′y·le′do·nal** *adj.*

cot·y·loid (kot′ə·loid) *adj.* 1 Cup-shaped. 2 *Anat.* Of or pertaining to a cotyloid cavity: the *cotyloid* ligament. Also **cot′y·loi′dal.** [<Gk. *kotyloeidēs* cup-shaped, hollow]

cotyloid cavity *Anat.* The acetabulum of the hip bone.

couch (kouch) *n.* 1 A structure on which to

rest or sleep, as a bed or other support. 2 A long seat or lounge. 3 Any place for repose, as the lair of a wild animal, etc. [<v.] — *v.t.* 1 To lay or cause to recline, as on a bed or cot. 2 To place upon a surface; deposit. 3 To embroider, as gold thread, laid flat on a surface. 4 To lower or depress, as a spear for attack: to *couch* a lance. 5 To phrase; put into words; also, to imply subtly: He *couched* a threat in his words. 6 *Surg.* To remove, as a cataract, by pushing down the opaque lens of the eye with a needle, until it lies below the line of vision. 7 In brewing, to spread out, as steeped barley, to germinate. — *v.i.* 8 To lie down; recline. 9 To lie in ambush; hide. 10 To lie in a heap or pile, as leaves. [<F *coucher* put to bed <OF *culcher* <L *collocare* set, place. See COLLOCATE.] — **couch′er** *n.*

couch·ant (kou′chənt) *adj.* 1 Lying down. 2 *Her.* Reclining with head uplifted. [<F, ppr. of *coucher.* See COUCH.]

cou·ché (kōō·shā′) *n. French* A late evening reception, as by a sovereign. Compare LEVEE². Also **cou·chée′.**

couch·grass (kouch′gras′, -gräs′) *n.* A perennial grass (*Agropyron repens*), multiplying injuriously in cultivated grounds by its long rootstocks: also called *cutch, quackgrass, quatchgrass, quickgrass.*

couch·ing (kou′ching) *n.* 1 *Surg.* The operation of removing a cataract. 2 Embroidery made by securing laid gold threads with minute stitches.

Cou·é (kōō·ā′), **Émile,** 1857–1926, French psychologist.

Cou·é·ism (kōō·ā′iz·əm) *n.* The principle of self-mastery by autosuggestion advocated by Émile Coué.

cou·gar (kōō′gər) *n.* The puma. [<F <Tupian]

cough (kôf, kof) *v.i.* 1 To expel air from the lungs in a noisy or spasmodic manner. — *v.t.* 2 To expel by a cough. 3 To utter or express by coughing. — **to cough down** To silence a speaker by continued coughing. — **to cough up** 1 To expel (phlegm, etc.) by a cough or coughs. 2 *Slang* To surrender; hand over, as money. — *n.* 1 A sudden, harsh expulsion of breath. 2 A disease productive of coughing. [ME *coghen, coughen.* Related to OE *cohhetan* cough.] — **cough′er** *n.*

cough–drop (kôf′drop′, kof′-) *n.* A small, medicated lozenge to ease a sore throat and relieve coughing.

could (kŏod) Past tense of CAN¹. [ME *coude,* OE *cuthe* knew how; *l* inserted on analogy with *should* and *would*]

could·na (kŏod′nə) *Scot.* Could not.

cou·lee (kōō′lē) *n.* 1 *Geol.* A sheet of solidified lava. 2 *U.S. Colloq.* A deep, usually dry gulch, distinguished by its inclined sides from a canyon. 3 A steep, trenchlike valley, as in the path of former glaciers. Also **cou·lée** (kōō·lā′). [<F < *couler* flow]

cou·leur de rose (kōō·lœr′ də rōz′) *French* Color of rose; idiomatically, in English, in an overly favorable light: to see the world *couleur de rose.*

cou·lisse (kōō·lēs′) *n.* 1 A grooved timber, as one in which the wings of a stage setting slide. 2 A side scene in a theater or one of the spaces between the side scenes. [<F, groove < *couler* slide]

cou·loir (kōō·lwàr′) *n.* 1 A deep gorge or gully, especially in rock, ice, or snow. 2 A dredging machine that employs iron buckets on an endless chain. [<F < *couler* flow]

cou·lomb (kōō·lom′) *n.* The practical unit of quantity in measuring electricity: the amount conveyed by one ampere in one second, equal to 6.3 x 10¹⁸ electrons. — **absolute coulomb** One tenth of an abcoulomb. — **international coulomb** The quantity of electricity passing any section of a circuit in one second when the current is one international ampere. [after C. A. de *Coulomb,* 1736–1806, French physicist]

cou·lom·e·ter (kōō·lom′ə·tər) *n.* An electrolytic cell for measuring the quantity of electricity by the chemical action produced: also called *voltameter.* Also **coulomb meter.**

coul·ter (kōl′tər) See COLTER.

Coul·ter (kōl′tər), **John Merle,** 1851–1928, U.S. botanist.

cou·mar·ic (ko͞o·mar′ik) *adj.* Of or pertaining to coumarin.

cou·ma·rin (ko͞o′mə·rin) *n. Chem.* A fragrant crystalline compound, $C_9H_6O_2$, contained in Tonka beans, sweet clover, and other plants, and also made synthetically: used as a flavor extract and in perfumery: also spelled *cumarin.* [<F *coumarine* <*coumarou* Tonka bean]

cou·ma·rou (ko͞o′mə·ro͞o) *n.* The Tonka bean or its seed. [<Tupian]

coun·cil (koun′səl) *n.* **1** An assembly of persons convened for consultation or deliberation: a *council* of physicians. **2** A body of men elected or appointed to assist in the administration of government, as of a city, or to legislate and advise, as in a territory or colony. **3** The deliberation or consultation that takes place in a council chamber: summoned from *council.* **4** A gathering of Roman Catholic ecclesiastical dignitaries and scholars, for the purpose of discussing and regulating matters of church doctrine and discipline: distinguished as **diocesan** (led by the bishop), **provincial** (led by the archbishop), **national** (led by the primate or patriarch), **general** (led by the Pope or papal legate), and **ecumenical** (world–wide) **councils. 5** The Sanhedrin. —**common council** A municipal, legislative body; also, a coordinate branch of such a body, called a **city council.** —**general council 1** A council made up of delegates representative of the whole of a certain territory or organization, as the British Parliament. **2** The deliberative body of a Scottish university. **3** The administrative board of Oxford University, properly known as the **Hebdomadal Council.** ◆ Homophone: *counsel.* [<OF *cuncile* <L *concilium* <*com-* together + *calare* call]

Council Bluffs A city in SW Iowa.

coun·cil·man (koun′səl·mən) *n. pl.* **·men** (-mən) A member of a council, especially the governing council of a city.

Council of Ten A secret legislative body of ten, later of seventeen, members which governed Venice from 1310 until 1797.

coun·cil·or (koun′səl·ər, -slər) *n.* A member of a council. Also **coun′cil·lor.** —**coun′cil·or·ship′** *n.*

coun·sel (koun′səl) *n.* **1** Mutual consultation or deliberation. **2** Opinion; advice. **3** Deliberate purpose. **4** Good judgment; prudence. **5** A lawyer or lawyers engaged in a cause in court; an advocate. —**to keep one's own counsel** To be reticent about one's opinions or affairs. —*v.* **·seled** or **·selled, ·sel·ing** or **·sel·ling** *v.t.* **1** To advise; give advice to. **2** To advise in favor of; recommend. —*v.i.* **3** To take counsel; deliberate. ◆ Homophone: *council.* [<OF *cunseil* <L *consilium* < *consulere* deliberate]

Synonyms (noun): admonition, advice, caution, dissuasion, hortation, persuasion, recommendation, suggestion, warning. *Advice* is an opinion suggesting or urging some course of action, on the ground of real or assumed superior knowledge. *Counsel* implies mutual conference. *Advice* may be unsought and even unwelcome; *counsel* is supposed to be desired. Yet the two words so far approach each other that one is said to seek *advice* from a lawyer, while a lawyer who is engaged to give *advice* or to act as an advocate in a legal proceeding is called the *counsel* of the person so employing him.

counsel of perfection An advisory declaration made by Christ or one of the Apostles as a guide to the highest morality.

coun·sel·or (koun′səl·ər, -slər) *n.* **1** One who gives counsel; an adviser. **2** An attorney at law; advocate. Also **coun′sel·lor.**

count[1] (kount) *v.t.* **1** To list or call off the units of (a group or collection) one by one to ascertain the total; number; enumerate: to *count* a flock. **2** To list numerals in a progressive sequence up to: to *count* ten. **3** To believe or consider to be; judge; think. **4** To determine by computation; reckon. **5** To take note of; include in a reckoning. **6** *Obs.* To place to the account of; ascribe. —*v.i.* **7** To list numbers in sequence. **8** To rely: with *on* or *upon.* **9** To be of (much, little, no) value: His testimony *counts* for naught. **10** *Mus.* To keep time by counting or beating. —**to count in 1** To include: *Count* me *in.* **2** To elect by fraud. —**to count out 1** In boxing, to reach a count of ten over (a downed boxer), thus declaring him defeated. **2** To prevent a fraudulently elected candidate from taking office; also, to ignore, as certain votes. **3** To exclude or excuse: *Count* me *out* on the picnic. —**to count the cost** To determine the risk beforehand. —*n.* **1** The act of counting; number. **2** Attention; heed; estimation. **3** An accounting, as of a stewardship or for an action. **4** *Law* A separate charge, as in an indictment. **5** In boxing, the counting from one to ten seconds, during which time the contestant who is down must get up or lose the fight. [<OF *conter* <L *computare.* Doublet of COMPUTE.]—**count′a·ble** *adj.*

count[2] (kount) *n.* In some European countries, a nobleman having a rank corresponding to that of an earl in England. [<AF *counte* <L *comes* an associate]

count–down (kount′doun′) *n.* A specified interval of time measured in a descending order of units, usually seconds, to zero, at which an intended action is to occur.

coun·te·nance (koun′tə·nəns) *n.* **1** The face or features. **2** Expression; appearance. **3** An encouraging aspect; hence, approval; support. See synonyms under FAVOR. —**out of countenance** Disconcerted; without ease or composure; abashed. —*v.t.* **·nanced, ·nanc·ing** To approve; encourage; abet. See synonyms under ABET, ENCOURAGE. [<OF *contenance* <L *continentia* behavior <*continere.* See CONTINENT.] —**coun′te·nanc·er** *n.*

count·er[1] (koun′tər) *n.* One who or that which counts, especially a machine for counting.

coun·ter[2] (koun′tər) *n.* **1** An opposite or that which is opposite; especially, a parry; counterblow; also, the act of delivering such a blow. **2** A piece of material encircling the heel of a shoe to stiffen and support the outer leather. **3** *Naut.* The portion of a ship between the water line and the knuckle of the stern. **4** A horse's breast. —*v.t.* **1** To return, as a blow, by another blow. **2** To oppose; contradict; controvert. **3** To put a new counter on, as a shoe. —*v.i.* **4** In boxing, to give a blow while receiving or parrying one. **5** In chess, to make a countermove. —*adj.* **1** Opposing; opposite; contrary. **2** Duplicate: a *counter* list. —*adv.* Contrary; in an opposite manner or direction: *counter* to etiquette. [<F *contre* against <L *contra*]

coun·ter[3] (koun′tər) *n.* **1** A piece of wood, ivory, etc., used in counting. **2** An imitation coin of inferior metal; counterfeit. **3** A table, board, etc., on which to count money or expose goods for sale. [<AF *counteour* <Med. L *computatorium* <L *computare* compute]

counter– *combining form* **1** Opposing; contrary; acting in opposition or response to the action of the main element (sometimes with the idea of outdoing or checking that action); as in:

counteraddress	**counterinfluence**
counteraffirmation	**counterlegislation**
counteragent	**countermeasure**
counteragitation	**counterorder**
counteralliance	**counterplan**
counterambush	**counterpoison**
counterappeal	**counterproject**
counterargue	**counterpropaganda**
counterargument	**counterproposal**
counterattraction	**counterreform**
counterbid	**counterreligion**
counterblow	**counterremonstrant**
counterconquest	**countersay**
countercry	**countersiege**
counterdeclaration	**counterstatement**
counterdemand	**countersuggestion**
counterdemonstration	**countertendency**
countereffort	**countertheory**
counterexercise	**counterthreat**
counterforce	**counterthrust**
countergambit	**counterview**
counterhypothesis	**countervote**
counterideal	**counterworking**

2 Done or acting in reciprocation or exchange; as in:

counterassurance	**counterquestion**
counterobligation	**countersignal**
counteroffer	**countertoken**

3 Complementing or corresponding; denoting the duplicate or parallel (often with the idea of balancing or sustaining); as in:

counterfugue	**counterstain**
counterseal	**countertally**
countersecure	**countertype**

4 Opposite in direction or position; as in:

counterapse	**counteropening**
counterarch	**counterposition**
countercurrent	**counterpressure**
counterflight	**counterpull**
counterflow	**counterstand**
countermigration	**counterstep**
countermovement	**counterturn**

coun·ter·act (koun′tər·akt′) *v.t.* To act contrary or in opposition to; check; frustrate; hinder. —**coun′ter·ac′tion** *n.* —**coun′ter·ac′·tive** *adj.* —**coun′ter·ac′tive·** *adv.*

coun·ter·at·tack (koun′tər·ə·tak′) *n.* An attack designed to counteract a previous hostile advance. —*v.t. & v.i.* (*usually* koun′tər·ə·tak′) To attack in order to frustrate or offset an enemy's previous attack.

coun·ter·bal·ance (koun′tər·bal′əns) *v.t.* **·anced, ·anc·ing** To oppose with an equal force; offset. —*n.* (koun′tər·bal′əns) **1** Any power equally opposing another. **2** A weight that balances another; counterpoise.

coun·ter·bar·rage (koun′tər·bə·räzh′) *n.* An artillery barrage answering or opposing an enemy barrage.

coun·ter·blast (koun′tər·blast′, -bläst′) *n.* **1** An opposing blast. **2** An answering argument; a denunciation.

coun·ter·bore (koun′tər·bôr′, -bōr′) *n. Mech.* **1** A cylindrical enlargement of the end of a cylinder bore or of a borehole. **2** A form of drill used for enlarging one end of a hole. —*v.t.* **·bored, ·bor·ing** To form a counterbore in; also, to enlarge.

coun·ter·change (koun′tər·chānj′) *v.t. & v.i.* **·changed, ·chang·ing 1** To exchange; interchange. **2** To diversify.

coun·ter·charge (koun′tər·chärj′) *n.* An opposing charge or accusation. —*v.t. & v.i.* (koun′·tər·chärj′) **·charged, ·charg·ing** To make rebuttal, as an opposing charge or accusation.

coun·ter·charm (koun′tər·chärm′) *v.t.* To counteract the effect of a charm upon; win by opposing charms. —*n.* (koun′tər·chärm′) An opposing charm.

coun·ter·check (koun′tər·chek′) *n.* **1** Something which checks or opposes a course of action. **2** Something which checks or thwarts another check. —*v.t.* (*usually* koun′tər·chek′) To check or thwart by counteraction.

coun·ter·claim (koun′tər·klām′) *n. Law* An opposing claim alleged by a defendant in his favor against the plaintiff. —*v.t. & v.i.* (*usually* koun′tər·klām′) To request or demand as a counterclaim; plead a counterclaim. —**coun′ter·claim′ant** *n.*

coun·ter·clock·wise (koun′tər·klok′wīz′) *adj. & adv.* Contrary to the direction taken by the hands of a clock around the dial; from right to left.

coun·ter·cul·ture (koun′tər·kul′chər) *n.* The special culture made up of those, chiefly of the younger generation, who reject the standards and values of established society.

coun·ter·cur·rent (koun′tər·kûr′ənt) *n.* An opposing current; a current opposed to another.

coun·ter·draw (koun′tər·drô′) *v.t.* **·drew, ·drawn, ·draw·ing** To trace in transparent material.

coun·ter·es·pi·o·nage (koun′tər·es′pē·ə·näzh′) *n.* Operations and measures intended to disrupt or counteract the effects of enemy spying.

coun·ter·ev·i·dence (koun′tər·ev′ə·dəns) *n.* Rebutting evidence.

coun·ter·feit (koun′tər·fit) *v.t.* **1** To make a copy of; imitate; hence, to feign; dissemble. **2** To make a spurious semblance of, as money or stamps, with the intent to deceive and defraud. —*v.i.* **3** To practice deception; feign. **4** To make counterfeits. [<*adj.*] See synonyms under IMITATE, PRETEND. —*adj.* Resembling or made to resemble some genuine thing, with intent to defraud; imitated; spurious. —*n.* **1** Something, as a coin, made fraudulently to resemble the genuine. **2** Any imitation, as a portrait or copy. **3** An impostor. [<OF *contrefet,* pp. of *contrefaire* <L *contra-* against + *facere* make] —**coun′ter·feit′er** *n.*

coun·ter·foil (koun′tər·foil′) *n.* A coupon containing a memorandum, as of a check or draft, to be retained by the drawer; stub.

coun·ter·fort (koun′tər·fôrt′, -fōrt′) *n.* **1** A pier or buttress. **2** A spur of a mountain.

coun·ter·glow (koun′tər·glō′) *n. Meteorol.* The gegenschein.

coun·ter·guard (koun′tər·gärd′) *n.* A small rampart in front of and parallel with the faces of a bastion.

coun·ter·in·sur·gen·cy (koun′tər·in·sûr′jən·sē) *n.* Measures, usually of a military nature, designed to combat guerrilla warfare or to suppress revolutionary activities.

coun·ter·ir·ri·tant (koun′tər·ir′ə·tənt) *n. Med.* An agent employed to excite irritation in one place so as to counteract irritation or inflammation existing elsewhere.

coun·ter–jump·er (koun′tər·jum′pər) *n. Slang* A salesman or clerk at a store counter: a derogatory term.

coun·ter·mand (koun′tər·mand′, -mänd′, koun′. tər·mänd) *v.t.* **1** To recall or revoke, as an order. **2** To contradict; oppose. —*n.* (koun′. tər·mand, -mänd) An order contrary to or revoking one previously issued. [<OF *contremander* <L *contra-* against + *mandare* order]

coun·ter·march (koun′tər·märch′, koun′tər. märch′) *v.t. & v.i.* To march back. —*n.* (koun′. tər·märch′) **1** A return march. **2** *Mil.* A reversal of front. **3** Any reversal of conduct or method.

coun·ter·mark (koun′tər·märk′) *n.* An added mark. —*v.t.* (*usually* koun′tər·märk′) To put an added mark on.

coun·ter·mine (koun′tər·mīn′) *v.t. & v.i.* **·mined, ·min·ing 1** To mine counter to (an enemy); hence, to baffle or obstruct by secret means. **2** To sow (an area) with mines in order to detonate enemy mines. —*n.* (koun′. tər·mīn′) **1** A mine or system of galleries run out to meet and destroy similar works of an enemy. **2** Hence, any stratagem to foil the designs of an opponent. **3** An underwater mine intended to detonate enemy mines.

coun·ter·move (koun′tər·mōōv′) *v.t.* **·moved, ·mov·ing** To move in a contrary direction. —*n.* (koun′tər·mōōv′) A move in the opposite direction.

coun·ter·mure (koun′tər·myōōr′) *n.* A wall raised before (and sometimes behind) a fortification wall to strengthen it. —*v.t.* (koun′tər. myōōr′) **·mured, ·mur·ing** To strengthen with a countermure. [<MF *contremur* <*contre* against + *mur* wall]

coun·ter·of·fen·sive (koun′tər·ə·fen′siv, koun′. tər·ə·fen′siv) *n.* A large–scale military action designed to stop the offensive of the enemy and to seize the initiative.

coun·ter·pane (koun′tər·pān′) *n.* A coverlet or quilt for a bed. [Alter. of COUNTERPOINT², after F *pan* quilt <L *pannus* rag, cloth]

coun·ter·part (koun′tər·pärt′) *n.* **1** A person precisely like another. **2** Anything closely resembling something else. **3** Something corresponding reversely, as the impression to the seal, or the right hand to the left; a complement; supplement; opposite. See synonyms under DUPLICATE.

coun·ter·plea (koun′tər·plē′) *n. Law* A replication; answering plea.

coun·ter·plot (koun′tər·plot′) *n.* One plot opposing another. —*v.t. & v.i.* (koun′tər·plot′) **·plot·ted, ·plot·ting** To oppose (a plot) by another plot.

coun·ter·point¹ (koun′tər·point′) *n.* **1** *Music* a The art of adding to a melody a part or parts that shall be related to but independent of it, according to the fixed rules of harmony. **b** The part or parts so arranged. **2** A point or position opposed to another. [<MF *contrepoint* <Med. L *(cantus) contrapunctus* (a melody) with contrasting notes <L *contra* against + *punctus* point, note]

coun·ter·point² (koun′tər·point′) *n. Obs.* A counterpane. [<MF *contrepoint*, alter. of OF *cuilte–pointe* <L *culcita puncta* a quilted coverlet]

coun·ter·poise (koun′tər·poiz′) *v.t.* **·poised, ·pois·ing 1** To bring to a poise by opposing with an equal weight; counterbalance. **2** To offset or frustrate. —*n.* (koun′tər·poiz) **1** A counterbalancing weight. **2** A counterbalancing force, power, or influence. **3** A state of equilibrium. [<OF *contrepeser* <L *contra* against + *pensare* weigh]

coun·ter·pro·duc·tive (koun′tər·prə·duk′tiv) *adj.* Producing an effect opposite from that in-

tended; harmful to a purpose: The slurs on his opponent proved *counterproductive.*

coun·ter–re·coil (koun′tər·ri·koil′) *n.* The return of a gun to firing position after its recoil.

coun·ter–re·con·nais·sance (koun′tər·ri·kon′ə·səns, -säns) The act of screening military operations from observation by the enemy.

coun·ter–ref·or·ma·tion (koun′tər·ref′ər·mā′. shən) *n.* A reformation aimed at counteracting and opposing a previous one.

Counter Reformation The movement within the Roman Catholic Church in the 16th century in reaction to the Protestant Reformation.

coun·ter·rev·o·lu·tion (koun′tər·rev′ə·lōō′shən) *n.* A revolution which aims at undoing the work of a previous revolution. —**coun′ter–rev′. o·lu′tion·ar′y** *adj. & n.* —**coun′ter–rev′o·lu′. tion·ist** *n.*

coun·ter·scarp (koun′tər·skärp′) *n.* The exterior slope of a ditch opposite the parapet of a fortification.

coun·ter·shaft (koun′tər·shaft′, -shäft′) *n. Mech.* An intermediate shaft driven by the main shaft and transmitting motion.

coun·ter·sign (koun′tər·sīn′, koun′tər·sīn′) *v.t.* To sign alongside of or in addition to (the signature of another); authenticate by an additional signature. —*n.* (koun′tər·sīn′) **1** A secret word or phrase to be given, as to a sentry; a watchword; password. **2** A countersignature.

coun·ter·sig·na·ture (koun′tər·sig′nə·chər) *n.* An additional, validating signature.

coun·ter·sink (koun′tər·singk′, koun′tər·singk′) *v.t.* **·sank** *or* **·sunk, ·sunk** (*Obs.* **·sunk·en**), **·sink·ing 1** To cut or shape (a depression), as for the head of a screw. **2** To sink, as a bolt or screw, into a corresponding depression. —*n.* (koun′tər·singk′) **1** A tool for countersinking. **2** A depression for a screwhead, bolt, etc.

coun·ter·stroke (koun′tər·strōk′) *n.* A return stroke.

coun·ter·ten·or (koun′tər·ten′ər) *n.* **1** A vocal part for a male voice higher than the tenor and lower than the treble. **2** A male voice of this kind. **3** A singer with such a voice.

coun·ter·vail (koun′tər·vāl′, koun′tər·vāl) *v.t.* To oppose with equal power; counteract; offset. —*v.i.* (<AF *countervaloir* <L *contra valere* avail against]

coun·ter·view (koun′tər·vyōō′) *n.* An opposing or opposite view.

coun·ter·weigh (koun′tər·wā′) *v.t. & v.i.* To weigh equivalently with; counterbalance.

coun·ter·weight (koun′tər·wāt′) *n.* Any counterbalancing weight, force, or influence. —**coun′ter·weight′ed** *adj.*

counter word A word widely used as a general term, without regard to its exact meaning, as *definitely, heavenly.*

coun·ter·work (koun′tər·wûrk′) *v.t. & v.i.* To work or act in opposition to (a person or thing). —*n.* (koun′tər·wûrk′) The act or effect of counterworking; a work in opposition; antagonism.

count·ess (koun′tis) *n.* **1** The wife or widow of a count, or, in Great Britain, of an earl. **2** A woman whose rank is equal to that of a count or earl. [<OF *contesse*, fem. of *conte.* See COUNT².]

count·ing–house (koun′ting·hous′) *n. Brit.* An office or building where the bookkeeping is done in a mercantile or other establishment. Also **coun′ting–room′.**

counting tube See GEIGER COUNTER.

count·less (kount′lis) *adj.* That cannot be counted; innumerable. See synonyms under INFINITE.

count palatine 1 Originally, a palsgrave, or count of the palace of the Holy Roman Empire, whose duties had to do with the royal tribunal, and who was selected from the emperor's comitatus; later, a provincial palsgrave who managed the royal lands, etc. **2** One of those who formerly exercised a king's prerogatives in various counties of England: also *county palatine.*

coun·tra (kun′trə) *Scot.* Country.

coun·tri·fied (kun′tri·fid) *adj.* Rural or rustic, as the manners of or attributed to country people, etc.

coun·try (kun′trē) *n. pl.* **·tries 1** A land under a particular sovereignty or government, inhabited by a certain people, or within definite geographical limits. **2** A particular nation, or the institutions peculiar to it; the land of one's nativity or allegiance. **3** A tract of land of indefinite extent; a region. **4** A rural region, or farming district, as opposed to the city: with *the:* a summer in the *country.* **5** The general public; the inhabitants of any region, collectively: with *the:* The whole *country* hated him. **6** *Law* A jury. Originally, a jury was summoned from the hundred in which the facts at issue were supposed to have occurred and the question was then said to be tried by the *country.* Litigants were said to put themselves **upon the country. 7** In cricket, that part of the field which is remote from the wicket. See synonyms under LAND. —*adj.* **1** Of or pertaining to, for, from, occurring in, or situated in the rural parts, as distinct from the city; rural; rustic. **2** Wanting in refinement or culture; rude; boorish; unpolished: *country* manners. **3** *Dial.* Relating to one's own country; national. [<OF *contrée* <LL *contrata* <L *contra* on the opposite side]

coun·try–and–west·ern (kun′trē·ənd·west′ərn) *n.* A stylized form of popular music, based on the folk music of the rural southern and western U.S. Abbr. *c–and–w* or *C–and–W.*

country club A club in the outskirts of a town or city, with a clubhouse, grounds, and facilities for outdoor sports.

country cousin A relative from the country, to whom city life is new or confusing.

country dance 1 A kind of quadrille in which the partners are ranged in opposite lines. **2** The music for this. See CONTREDANSE.

coun·try·folk (kun′trē·fōk′) *n. pl.* **1** People who live in the country, especially in a certain district. **2** Compatriots; fellow countrymen.

country gentleman A landed proprietor who lives on his estate.

coun·try·man (kun′trē·mən) *n. pl.* **·men** (-mən) **1** One living in the country; a rustic. **2** An inhabitant of a particular country; one of the same country with another.

coun·try·seat (kun′trē·sēt′) *n.* A dwelling or mansion in the country.

coun·try·side (kun′trē·sīd′) *n.* A section of country, or its inhabitants.

coun·try·wom·an (kun′trē·wŏŏm′ən) *n. pl.* **·wom·en** (-wim′ən) **1** A woman of a certain country, or of the same country with another. **2** A woman inhabiting a rural district.

count·ship (kount′ship) *n.* The dignity or position of a count.

coun·ty (koun′tē) *n. pl.* **·ties 1** A civil division of a state or kingdom, created for political, judicial, and administrative purposes. In the United States, it is the division next below a State with the exception of Louisiana, where it is called a *parish.* In England a county is sometimes called a *shire.* In some of the British Colonies a county is a division for administrative purposes. **2** The inhabitants of a county: Your *county* is noted for its intelligence. **3** *Obs.* The domain of an earl or count. **4** *Obs.* An earl or count. [<AF *counté* <L *comitatus* <*comes* count, companion]

county palatine See COUNT PALATINE.

county seat The seat of government of a county.

county town *Brit.* A county seat: also called *shire town.*

coup (kōō) *n. pl.* **coups** (kōōz, *Fr.* kōō) **1** A sudden, telling blow; a master stroke; stratagem. **2** Among North American Indians, the first wound or cut inflicted by hand on an enemy. **3** A coup d'état. —*v.t.* (koup) *Scot.* To turn upside down; upset. Also *cowp.* [<F, ult. <L *colaphus* a blow with the fist <Gk. *kolaphos*]

coup de grâce (kōō′ də gräs′) *French* The finishing or mortal stroke, as delivered to a sick or wounded animal; literally, stroke of mercy.

coup de main (kōō′ də maṅ′) *French* A sudden, vigorous stroke; surprise; literally, stroke of hand.

coup d'es·sai (kōō′ des·se′) *French* A first attempt; a trial.

coup d'é·tat (ko͞o' dā·tȧ') *French* An unexpected stroke of policy; a bold seizure of government, executed suddenly and often accompanied by violence; literally, stroke of state.
coup de thé·â·tre (ko͞o' də tā·ä'tr') *French* **1** A theatrical hit. **2** A theatrical or sensational trick.
coup d'oeil (ko͞o' dœ'y') *French* A quick, comprehensive glance; literally, stroke of eye.
coupe (ko͞op) *n. French* A cup of fresh fruit steeped in liqueur.
cou·pé[1] (ko͞o·pā'; *for def. 1, also* ko͞op) *n.* **1** A closed automobile shorter than a sedan, with a rumble seat or trunk compartment and a capacity of two or more persons. **2** A low, four-wheeled, two-seated closed carriage which seats from two to four persons. **3** The forward compartment of a French diligence, or a half-compartment of a Continental railway carriage. [<F, pp. of *couper* cut]
cou·pé[2] (ko͞o·pā') *n. French* A wine diluted with water.
cou·pee (ko͞o·pā') *n.* In dancing, a salute to a partner, made while resting on one foot and swinging the other backward or forward. —*v.i.* **·peed, ·pee·ing** To make such a salute. Also **cou·pé'.** [<F *coupé*, orig. pp. of *couper* cut]
Cou·pe·rin (ko͞o·pran'), **François,** 1668–1733, French composer.
Cou·pe·rus (ko͞o·pā'rəs), **Louis,** 1863–1923, Dutch novelist.
coup·le (kup'əl) *n.* **1** Two of a kind; a pair. **2** Two persons of opposite sex, wedded or otherwise paired; partners in a dance. **3** A coupler; bond; leash. **4** *Mech.* A pair of equal forces acting in opposite and parallel lines, thus tending to turn a body around without moving it from its place. **5** *Electr.* Two dissimilar metals joined to form a voltaic element in a battery; a voltaic couple. —*v.* **coup·led, coup·ling** *v.t.* **1** To join, as one thing to another; link; unite in pairs. **2** To join in wedlock; marry. **3** *Electr.* To connect (two electric currents or circuits) magnetically or directly. —*v.i.* **4** To copulate. **5** To form a pair or pairs. [<OF *cople* <L *copula* a band, a bond]
coup·ler (kup'lər) *n.* **1** One who or that which couples. **2** A mechanical device by which objects are connected. **3** *Telecom.* A device for transferring signals from one circuit to another, or through a condenser or transformer. —**automatic coupler** A contrivance for coupling railroad cars by means of interlocking jaws.
coup·let (kup'lit) *n.* **1** Two similar things taken or considered together. **2** Two lines of verse in immediate sequence, especially of the same length and riming together. [<F, dim. of *couple* a pair]
coup·ling (kup'ling) *n.* **1** The act of joining together; specifically, the act of joining in marriage or copulation. **2** A coupler, or that which couples: a car or carriage *coupling.* **3** The length between the tops of the shoulder blades and the tops of the hip joints in a dog. **4** The part of the body joining the hindquarters of a quadruped to the front part, as in a dog or a horse. See illustrations under DOG, HORSE. **5** *Mech.* A friction or jaw clutch to connect moving parts or break the connection. **6** *Electr.* A connection between two circuits permitting transfer of power from one to the other.
cou·pon (ko͞o'pon, kyo͞o'-) *n.* **1** One of a number of dated certificates attached, as to a bond, representing interest accrued and payable at stated periods. **2** A section or detachable portion of a ticket or form, serving as a certificate that the holder is entitled to something, as transportation for a certain number of miles, etc. [<F <*couper* cut]
coupon bond A bond to which are attached coupons representing interest due at fixed periods.
cour·age (kûr'ij) *n.* **1** That quality of mind which meets danger or opposition with intrepidity, calmness, and firmness; the quality of being fearless; bravery. **2** *Obs.* Heart; desire; disposition; condition. [<OF *corage* <L *cor* heart]
Synonyms: boldness, bravery, daring, fearlessness, fortitude, gallantry, hardihood, intrepidity, mettle, pluck, resolution, spirit, valor. See FORTITUDE, PROWESS. Compare BRAVE. *Antonyms*: cowardice, fear, fright, timidity, timorousness.
cou·ra·geous (kə·rā'jəs) *adj.* Possessing or characterized by courage; brave; daring: a *courageous* man; *courageous* words. —**cou·ra'geous·ly** *adv.* —**cou·ra'geous·ness** *n.*
cou·rant (ko͞o·ränt') *n.* **1** A newspaper; gazette: now used only in titles: the Hartford *Courant.* **2** An old, lively dance in triple measure. **3** The music for such a dance. Also spelled *corant.* Also **cou·rante** (ko͞o·ränt'), **cou·ran·to** (ko͞o·rän'tō). [<F, a runner <*courer* run]
Cour·an·tyne (kûr'ən·tīn) See CORENTYN.
Cour·bet (ko͞or·be'), **Gustave,** 1819–77, French painter.
Cour·be·voie (ko͞or·bə·vwȧ') A NW suburb of Paris, France.
cou·reur de bois (ko͞o·rœr' də bwä') *pl.* **cou·reurs des bois** (ko͞o·rœr' de bwä') *French* Formerly, a French or Canadian hunter or trader who traversed the American forests.
cou·ri·er (ko͞or'ē·ər, kûr'-) *n.* **1** A messenger. **2** A traveling attendant. See synonyms under HERALD. [<MF <Ital. *corriere* <*corre* run <L *currere*]
cour·lan (ko͞or'lən) *n.* A rail-like, tropical or subtropical American bird (genus *Aramus*) with stiff tail feathers: also called *limpkin.* [<F <native name]
Cour·land (ko͞or'land) A region of western and southern Latvia on the **Courland Lagoon,** a Baltic coastal lagoon: also *Kurland.*
course (kôrs, kōrs) *n.* **1** The act of moving onward; career. **2** The way passed over, or the direction taken. **3** A series of connected motions, acts, or events; customary sequence. **4** Line of conduct; manner of procedure; behavior. **5** The portion of a meal served at one time. **6** A row or layer. **7** *pl.* The menses. **8** *Naut.* **a** A sail bent to the lower yard of any square-rigged mast. **b** A point of the compass. **9** A charge or bout in a tournament. **10** A continuous horizontal range, as of stones in a wall. **11** *Mining* **a** An influx of water from one direction. **b** The direction of a lode or adit. **c** A corridor; passageway; the direction in which a mine is being worked. **12** *Music* A series of strings of uniform tone; also, a bell's chime. **13** A definite period of instruction and study in a certain subject: a *course* in French. **14** A series of studies undertaken to earn a degree: a college *course.* **15** In golf, links. **16** Racecourse. See synonyms under CAREER, DIRECTION, WAY. —**of course** As one might expect; naturally. —*v.* **coursed, cours·ing** *v.t.* **1** To hunt or pursue with hounds, as hares; chase. **2** To chase after; pursue. **3** To cause to run; urge to speed: to *course* horses. **4** To run through or over; traverse swiftly. —*v.i.* **5** To move swiftly; race. **6** To take a direction; follow a course. **7** To pursue game with hounds. **8** *Obs.* To engage in a hunt or joust. ◆ Homophone: *coarse.* [<OF *cours* <L *cursus* a running <*currere* run]
cours·er (kôr'sər, kōr'-) *n.* **1** A fleet and spirited horse. **2** One given to the chase. **3** A swift-footed plover (genus *Cursorius*) of arid regions in Asia, Africa, and occasionally Europe, as *C. cursor.* **4** The pratincole.
cours·ing (kôr'sing, kōr'-) *n.* The sport of chasing the hare or similar game with greyhounds, who follow by sight instead of by scent.
court (kôrt, kōrt) *n.* **1** A yard or space surrounded wholly by buildings or walls; a courtyard. **2** A building or group of buildings in a courtyard. **3** An imposing residence. **4** A space enclosed on three sides; a short street; a blind alley. **5** The actual residence of a sovereign, especially as the central seat of government and princely state; a palace. **6** The royal council, family, and retinue of a sovereign. **7** A sovereign and his retinue, considered as a body: the French *court.* **8** A formal assembly or reception held by a sovereign. **9** A place where justice is judicially administered. **10** A tribunal possessing civil, military, or ecclesiastical jurisdiction and duly constituted to administer justice. **11** A level space laid out for playing tennis, basketball, squash, or similar games; also, a subdivision of the ground so marked. **12** *Brit.* An official meeting of a corporation. **13** A local branch of certain fraternal orders; a lodge. **14** Flattery or homage paid to another to win favor. **15** Attention bestowed upon a woman to win her affection or love; wooing; courtship. —**Court of St. James's** The court of the monarch of Great Britain: so called from St. James's Palace. —*v.t.* **1** To make love to; woo. **2** To try to get in the good graces of; seek the favor of. **3** To solicit; attempt to gain: to *court* applause. **4** To lure; invite; entice into. —*v.i.* **5** To make love; act the courtier. —*adj.* Of or pertaining to a court: *court* customs. [<OF *cort* <L *cohors, cohortis* yard, troop of soldiers. Doublet of COHORT.]
—**admiralty court** See ADMIRALTY (def. 2).
—**Appeals, Circuit Court of** The highest U.S. court of appellate jurisdiction below the Supreme Court.
—**Appeals, Court of** A high court of justice to which cases from lower courts are taken for rehearing.
—**Arbitration, Permanent Court of** A tribunal established at The Hague in 1899 for the arbitration of disputes between nations, submission being voluntary: also called *Hague Tribunal.*
—**Assistants, Court of** A New England colonial court of supreme jurisdiction.
—**Assizes, Court of** A court held periodically in each English county. See ASSIZE.
—**chancery, court of** See CHANCERY.
—**circuit court 1** A Federal court of the United States superior to a district court: abolished, 1911. **2** A State court presided over by a circuit judge.
—**Claims, Court of** A court at Washington, D.C., having jurisdiction over questions relating to claims against the government.
—**Common Pleas, Court of 1** A common-law court of record, having original jurisdiction over civil and criminal matters. **2** Formerly, an English court with exclusive jurisdiction in various classes of civil cases.
—**district court** A U.S. court serving a Federal judicial district; also, a State court serving a State judicial district.
—**ecclesiastical court** In the United States, one of the courts established by the various churches for legislation and discipline, holding jurisdiction only within their own respective organizations; in England, a court instituted by the sovereign, having jurisdiction over matters pertaining to the established church.
—**equity, court of** See EQUITY (def. 3).
—**Exchequer, Court of** See EXCHEQUER.
—**hustings, court of** See HUSTING.
—**inquiry, court of** A tribunal for investigating matters pertaining to the military or naval service, with no power of trial or adjudication.
—**International Justice, Permanent Court of** An international tribunal established under the Covenant of the League of Nations (1921), empowered to interpret treaties and to give advisory opinions. Its functions, in general, were taken over (1945) by the International Court of Justice. Also called *World Court.*
—**Justice, International Court of** The principal judicial organ of the United Nations, functioning under a statute based on the Statute of the Permanent Court of International Justice as incorporated in the UN charter. All members of the UN are parties *ipso facto*; others join on recommendation of the Security Council.
—**juvenile court** A special court that deals with delinquents, neglected children, etc., under a fixed age.
—**King's** (or **Queen's**) **Bench, Court of** In England, the supreme court of common-law jurisdiction, consisting of a chief justice and four puisne or associate justices: now one of the divisions of the high courts of justice. Also *King's* (or *Queen's*) *Bench.*
—**last resort, court of** A tribunal from which there is no appeal.
—**municipal court** A local, city court having limited jurisdiction.
—**probate court** A court having jurisdiction of the proof of wills, of guardianships, and of the settlement of estates.
—**record, court of** A court keeping a record of its proceedings and having a clerk or prothonotary, a seal, and the power to fine and imprison.
—**Star Chamber, Court of 1** Formerly, in England, a court held, without the assistance of a jury, by members of the Privy Council, with the addition of two judges of the courts

of common law: abolished, because of abuses, 1641. **2** Any court engaging in arbitrary or illegal procedure.
— superior court In some States of the United States, a court between the inferior courts and those of last resort; in England, one of the principal courts at Westminster: King's Bench, Common Pleas, Exchequer.
— Supreme Court In the United States and in various States, a court of appellate jurisdiction and, in most cases, of last resort.

court–bar·on (kôrt′bar′ən, kōrt′-) *n.* Formerly, a court held by the steward of a manor for settling controversies between tenants, punishing misdemeanors, etc.

court bouillon A fish stock used primarily for poaching or boiling fish.

court card A king, queen, or jack in a deck of playing cards; a face card. [Alter. of *coat card*]

court cupboard A buffet of the 16th and 17th centuries, usually in two sections, the upper closed with a door or doors, the lower open or closed with doors or drawers.

courte é·chelle (ko͞or′ tā·shel′) *French* In mountaineering, the act of climbing over another climber, in order to reach an otherwise inaccessible spot.

cour·te·ous (kûr′tē·əs) *adj.* Showing courtesy; polite; affable. See synonyms under BLAND, POLITE. [<OF *curteis*] **— cour′te·ous·ly** *adv.* **— cour′te·ous·ness** *n.*

cour·te·san (kôr′tə·zən, kōr′-, kûr′-) *n.* A prostitute or woman of loose morals. Also **cour′te·zan.** [<F *courtisan* <Ital. *cortigiano* courtier < *corte* court]

cour·te·sy (kûr′tə·sē) *n. pl.* **·sies 1** Polite behavior; habitual politeness; courtliness. **2** A courteous favor or act. **3** A curtsy. [<OF *curteisie*]

courtesy of England See CURTESY OF ENGLAND.

courtesy title A title of address of no legal validity, given by social custom to the children of peers.

court hand The Gothic or Saxon handwriting formerly used in English public records. Compare ITALIAN HAND.

court·house (kôrt′hous′, kōrt′-) *n.* **1** A public building occupied by the judicial courts. **2** *U.S. Dial.* A county seat.

court·i·er (kôr′tē·ər, -tyər, kōr′-) *n.* **1** A member of the court circle. **2** One who seeks favor by flattery and complaisance. [<OF *cortoyer* be at court]

court·leet (kôrt·lēt′, kōrt-) See LEET.

court·like (kôrt′līk′, kōrt′-) *adj.* Polite; courtly.

court·ly (kôrt′lē, kōrt′-) *adj.* **·li·er, ·li·est 1** Pertaining to or befitting a court. **2** Elegant in manners. **—** *adv.* In a polite, stately, and refined manner. See synonyms under POLITE. **— court′li·ness** *n.*

court martial *pl.* **courts martial 1** A military court convened to try persons subject to military law. **2** A trial by such a court.
— drumhead court martial A court martial called for summary trial of a military offense committed on the line of march or in action: so called because a drumhead was sometimes used as a table on such occasions.
— general court martial The highest military court, consisting of five or more officers and enlisted men, convened to try the gravest offenses and empowered to deliver a death sentence, a dishonorable discharge, or any other punishment not barred by law.
— special court martial A court martial, consisting of three or more officers and enlisted men, which tries enlisted men for offenses not warranting a general court martial and delivers sentences of limited imprisonment, forfeiture of pay, or a bad conduct discharge.
— summary court martial The least formal court martial, presided over by one officer, which tries enlisted men for minor offenses and imposes limited penalties.

court–mar·tial (kôrt′mär′shəl, kōrt′-) *v.t.* **–mar·tialed** or **·tialled, –mar·tial·ing** or **·tial·ling** To try by court martial.

court plaster Sticking plaster; silk or other fabric coated with an adhesive material, used for covering slight cuts, etc.

Cour·trai (ko͞or·trā′) A town in NW Belgium. *Flemish* **Kort·rijk** (kôrt′rīk).

court·room (kôrt′ro͞om′, -ro͝om′, kōrt′-) *n.* A room in which judicial proceedings are held.

court·ship (kôrt′ship, kōrt′-) *n.* **1** The act or period of courting or wooing. **2** *Obs.* Courtly behavior.

court tennis See TENNIS.

court·yard (kôrt′yärd′, kōrt′-) *n.* An enclosed yard adjoining a building or surrounded by buildings to which it gives access; a court.

cous·in (kuz′ən) *n.* **1** One collaterally related by descent from a common ancestor, but not a brother or sister. Children of brothers and sisters are *first cousins*; children of first cousins are *second cousins* to each other. A *first cousin once removed* is the child of one's first cousin; a *first cousin twice removed* is the grandchild of one's first cousin, etc. *A second cousin once removed* is the child of one's second cousin, etc. **2** A noble of the king's council, or a fellow sovereign: a style of address used by a king. **3** One of a kindred race: our English *cousins.* **4** *Obs.* Any collateral relative more distant than a brother or sister. **—** *v.t.* To claim as a cousin or relative. [<OF *cosin* <L *consobrinus* child of a maternal aunt] **— cous′in·ly** *adj.* & *adv.*

Cou·sin (ko͞o·zaṅ′), **Victor,** 1792–1867, French philosopher.

cous·in·age (kuz′ən·ij) See COSINAGE.

cousin german A first or full cousin.

cous·in·hood (kuz′ən·ho͝od) *n.* **1** The state, condition, or relationship of cousins. **2** Cousins or kindred collectively. Also **cous′in·ship.**

cous·in·ry (kuz′ən·rē) *n. pl.* **·ries** Cousins collectively.

cou·teau (ko͞o·tō′) *n. pl.* **·teaux** (-tōz′, *Fr.* -tō′) *Obs.* A knife; especially, a long, straight, double–edged knife of the Middle Ages. Also **cou·tel** (ko͞o·tel′). [<F <OF *coutel, coltel* <L *culter* knife]

couteau de chasse (də shȧs′) *French* A hunting knife.

cou·thie (ko͞o′thē) *adj. Scot.* Snug; familiar; kind; agreeable. Also **couth** (ko͞oth).

cou·til (ko͞o′til, *Fr.* ko͞o·tē′) *n.* A linen or cotton canvas for mattresses and corsets. Also **cou·tille** (ko͞o·til′, *Fr.* ko͞o·tē′y′), **cou·telle** (ko͞o·tel′). [<F]

cou·tu·rier (ko͞o·tü·ryā′) *n. masc.* A dressmaker. [<F < *couture* sewing] **— cou·tu·rière** (ko͞o·tü·ryâr′) *n. fem.*

cou·vade (ko͞o·väd′) *n.* Among some primitive peoples, the practice of putting the father to bed as if in childbed while the mother is having the baby. [<F < *couver* brood <L *cubare* lie down]

co·va·lence (kō·vā′ləns) *n. Chem.* **1** A bond formed by the mutual sharing of electrons between the atoms of a compound. **2** The number of pairs of electrons which can be shared between the atoms of different elements. **— co′va′lent** *adj.*

Co·var·ru·bias (kō′vär·ro͞o′byäs), **Miguel,** 1902–57, Mexican artist and illustrator.

cove[1] (kōv) *n.* **1** A small bay or baylike recess. **2** A recess in a mountain. **3** A strip of grassland on the prairies, leading into a wood. **4** *Archit.* A concavity; the concave curved portion interposed in some ceilings between the flat ceiling proper and the wall. **—** *v.t.* & *v.i.* **coved, cov·ing** To arch over. [OE *cofa* chamber, cave]

cove[2] (kōv) *n. Brit. Slang* A boy or man; fellow. [<Romany *covo* that man]

co·vel·line (kō·vel′īn) *n.* A massive, submetallic, indigo–blue copper sulfide, CuS, crystallizing in the hexagonal system. Also **co·vel·lite** (kō·vel′īt). [after N. *Covelli,* 1790–1829, Italian chemist]

cov·en (kuv′ən) *n. Scot.* An assembly; meeting; especially, a gathering of witches.

cov·e·nant (kuv′ə·nənt) *n.* **1** An agreement entered into by two or more persons or parties; a compact. **2** God's promise of blessing to be fulfilled on the performance of a condition, as of obedience. **3** The solemn pledge by which members of a church bind themselves to maintain its faith, ordinances, etc. **4** *Law* A written agreement between parties under seal; a modifying agreement contained within a contract or deed; also, a form of action to recover damages for breach of contract. **— National Covenant** An agreement extensively signed by all classes of Presbyterians in Scotland, in 1638, to resist by force the introduction of episcopacy by Charles I. **— Solemn League and Covenant** An agreement between the English and the Scottish Parliaments, undertaken in 1643, to support Protestantism. **—** *v.t.* & *v.i.* To promise by or in covenant. [<OF < *covenir* agree <L *convenire* meet together, agree]

cov·e·nant·al (kuv′ə·nan′təl) *adj.* Of or pertaining to a covenant.

cov·e·nant·ee (kuv′ə·nən·tē′) *n.* The party to a covenant in which obligations are made to him.

cov·e·nant·er (kuv′ə·nən·tər) *n.* The party to a covenant assuming its obligations. Also **cov′e·nan·tor.**

Cov·e·nant·er (kuv′ə·nən·tər) *n.* One of the Scottish Presbyterians who adhered to the National Covenant.

cov·ent (kuv′ənt) *n. Obs.* A convent. [Var. of CONVENT]

Cov·ent Garden (kuv′ənt) A small district in central London; site of the city's chief markets, a theater, and the Royal Opera House.

Cov·en·try (kuv′ən·trē) A city in central Warwickshire, England. **— to send to** (or **put in**) **Coventry** To banish from society or social intercourse; ostracize.

Coventry blue A blue embroidery thread made at Coventry.

cov·er (kuv′ər) *v.t.* **1** To place something over or upon so as to protect or conceal. **2** To provide with a cover or covering; clothe; enwrap. **3** To hide or keep from view; conceal, as actions, facts, or crimes: often with *up.* **4** To provide shelter or protection for, as from evil or danger. **5** To occupy the surface of; overlay; serve as a cover or covering for. **6** To allow for or have provision for; treat of; include. **7** To be sufficient to pay, defray, or offset, as a debt, expense, or loss. **8** To incubate or sit on, as eggs. **9** To copulate with (a female): said of animals. **10** To travel over; traverse. **11** To aim directly at, as with a firearm. **12** *Mil.* **a** To have under command or protection. **b** To provide protective fire for (another person, unit, etc.). **c** To march in a position behind or in front of (another man). **13** In journalism, to report the details of, as an event or meeting. **14** In sports, to hinder the activity of (an opponent); also, to protect an area or position, as one temporarily left or vacated by another player: The shortstop *covered* second base. **15** To provide the equivalent of; equal, as the wager of an opponent. **16** In card games, to play a higher card than (the one previously played). **17** *Archaic* To pardon; put out of remembrance: in Biblical use. **18** *Rare* To don, or replace, as a hat, cap, or the like. **—** *v.i.* **19** To spread over so as to overlay or conceal something. **20** To put on a hat, cap, or the like. **21** In card games, to play a higher card than the one led. **—** *n.* **1** That which is spread or fitted over or which encloses anything. **2** A veil or disguise; pretext. **3** A shelter or defense; protection. **4** A thicket or underbrush, etc., sheltering game. **5** A setting of a cloth and articles for eating a meal for one person. **6** An envelope that has been marked at such time or place as to be of interest to philatelists. **7** A cover charge. **— to break cover** To come out from a hiding place. **— under cover** Secret; concealed; secretly. [<OF *covrir* <L *cooperire* < *co-* thoroughly + *operire* hide] **— cov′er·er** *n.* **— cov′er·ing** *n.*

cov·er·age (kuv′ər·ij) *n.* **1** The protection against risks extended by an insurance policy. **2** The amount of gold held in a national treasury as a basis for the issuance of paper currency. **3** In journalism, the extent to which a news story is covered.

cov·er·all (kuv′ər·ôl) *n.* One–piece overalls with sleeves, worn to protect the clothing. Also **cov′er·alls.**

cover charge A fixed charge added to the charge for food and drink at cabarets, hotels, etc., for the entertainment or service provided.

cover crop *Agric.* A crop sown to protect the ground through the winter and to enrich it when plowed under in the spring.

Cov·er·dale (kuv′ər·dāl), **Miles,** 1483?–1569,

English Augustinian monk; translated the Bible into English.

covered wagon A large, canvas-covered wagon; especially, one used by the American pioneers: also called *prairie schooner, Conestoga wagon.*

COVERED WAGON

cover girl A professional female model who poses for magazine cover illustrations.

cov·er·ing (kuv′ər·ing) *n.* Anything that serves to cover, protect, conceal, etc.

cov·er·let (kuv′ər·lit) *n.* The outer covering of a bed; a quilt. Also **cov′er·lid.**

Cov·er·ley (kuv′ər·lē), **Sir Roger de** The principal character in a series of sketches in *The Spectator* by Addison and Steele, represented as the typical country gentleman of the early 18th century.

co·versed sine (kō′vûrst) *Trig.* The versed sine of the complement of an angle or arc.

cov·ert (kuv′ərt) *adj.* **1** Concealed; secret. **2** Sheltered. **3** *Law* Under protection or authority, as a married woman. See synonyms under SECRET. — *n.* **1** Something that shelters, defends, or conceals. **2** A shady place or thicket. **3** *pl. Ornithol.* Feathers overlying the bases of the quills of a bird's wings and tail. See illustration under BIRD, FOWL. See synonyms under REFUGE. [<OF, pp. of *covrir* COVER] — **cov′ert·ly** *adv.*

co·vert cloth (kō′vərt, kuv′ərt) A fine, closely woven woolen cloth of double-twisted yarn both in warp and filling, used for suits, overcoats, etc.

covert coat A short riding or shooting coat made of covert cloth.

cov·er·ture (kuv′ər·chər) *n.* **1** *Law* Marriage; the legal state of a married woman. **2** A place, means, or condition of concealment; covering; hiding; disguise. [<OF]

cov·er-up (kuv′ər·up′) *n.* **1** An act or effort designed to prevent the facts or truth, as of an embarrassing or illegal activity, from becoming known. **2** A means of covering up or concealing something.

cov·et (kuv′it) *v.t. & v.i.* To have an inordinate desire for, especially for something belonging to another. [<OF *cuveiter* <L *cupiditas* eager desire <*cupere* desire] — **cov′et·a·ble** *adj.* — **cov′et·er** *n.*

cov·et·ous (kuv′ə·təs) *adj.* Inordinately desirous (of something); avaricious; greedy. See synonyms under AVARICIOUS. — **cov′et·ous·ly** *adv.* — **cov′et·ous·ness** *n.*

cov·ey (kuv′ē) *n. pl.* **·eys** **1** A flock of quails or partridges. **2** A company; set; bevy. See synonyms under FLOCK. [<OF *covée*, pp. of *cover* brood <L *cubare* lie down]

cov·ing (kō′ving) *n. Archit.* The projection of the upper stories over the lower. [<COVE¹]

Cov·ing·ton (kuv′ing·tən) A city in northern Kentucky on the Ohio River.

cow¹ (kou) *n. pl.* **cows** (*Archaic* **kine**) **1** The female of domestic cattle and of some other animals, as the elephant. **2** *Austral. Slang* An unpleasant person or event: also *fair cow.* [OE *cū*]

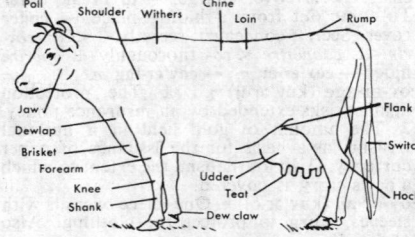

DAIRY COW
NOMENCLATURE OF ANATOMICAL PARTS

cow² (kou) *v.t.* To overawe; intimidate; daunt. See synonyms under FRIGHTEN. [<ON *kūga* tyrannize over]

cow³ (kou, kō) *v.t. Scot.* To remove the head or top of; clip; shear.

cow·age (kou′ij) See COWHAGE.

cow·ard (kou′ərd) *n.* One lacking in courage; a craven; poltroon. — *adj.* Of or pertaining

to a coward or cowardice; cowardly. [<OF *couard* <*coue* tail <L *cauda*; with ref. to a dog with its tail between its legs] — **cow′ard·ly** *adj. & adv.* — **cow′ard·li·ness** *n.*

Cow·ard (kou′ərd), **Noel,** 1899–1973, English playwright, actor, and composer.

cow·ard·ice (kou′ər·dis) *n.* Unworthy timidity; lack of courage; state of being easily frightened; pusillanimity.

cow·bane (kou′bān′) *n.* **1** The water hemlock. **2** An erect swamp plant (*Oxypolis rigidior*) of the eastern U.S., poisonous to cattle.

cow·bell (kou′bel′) *n.* **1** A wedge-shaped bell, usually of harsh and penetrating sound, hung by a strap around the neck of a cow. **2** The bladder campion.

cow·ber·ry (kou′ber′ē, -bər·ē) *n. pl.* **·ries** Any of a species (*Vaccinium vitis-idaea*) of trailing evergreen shrubs of the heath family, bearing acid red berries: also called *foxberry.*

cow·bind (kou′bīnd′) *n.* The white-berried bryony.

cow·bird (kou′bûrd′) *n.* An American blackbird (*Molothrus ater*), often found with cattle. Also **cow blackbird.**

cow·boy (kou′boi′) *n.* In the western United States, a man, usually working on horseback, who herds and tends cattle on a ranch: also *cowhand.*

cow bunting A cowbird.

cow camp The headquarters of the cowboys engaged in a roundup; also, any place where cowboys have gathered for working a herd.

cow·catch·er (kou′kach′ər) *n.* An iron frame on the front of a locomotive to throw obstructions from the track; pilot.

cow·er (kou′ər) *v.i.* **1** To crouch tremblingly. **2** To tremble; quail. [ME *couren*, prob. <Scand.]

Cowes (kouz) A port and resort center of the Isle of Wight, off Southampton.

cow·fish (kou′fish′) *n. pl.* **·fish** or **·fish·es** **1** One of various cetaceans, as a grampus, dolphin, etc. **2** A trunkfish. **3** A sirenian.

cow·hage (kou′ij) *n.* **1** The stinging hairs on the pods of a tropical climbing plant of the bean family (genus *Stizolobium* or *Mucuna*). **2** The pods themselves. **3** The plant. Also *cowage.* [Alter. of Hind. *kawāch*, short for *kawānch*]

cow·hand (kou′hand′) *n.* A cowboy.

cow·herb (kou′ûrb′, -hûrb′) *n.* A smooth-leaved Old World annual (*Saponaria vaccaria*): also *cow soapwort.*

cow·herd (kou′hûrd′) *n.* One who herds cattle.

cow·hide (kou′hīd′) *n.* **1** The skin of a cow, either before or after tanning. **2** A heavy, flexible whip made of braided leather and tapering from stock to lash. — *v.t.* **·hid·ed,** **·hid·ing** To whip with or as with a cowhide.

cow killer A large antlike wasp (*Dasymutilla occidentalis*) found in the SW United States.

cowl¹ (koul) *n.* **1** A monk's hood; also, any hooded garment. **2** A hood-shaped top for a chimney. **3** *Aeron.* A cowling. **4** That part of the body of an automobile to which the windshield, instrument board, and the rear end of the hood are attached. **5** *Scot.* A nightcap. — *v.t.* **1** To cloak with a cowl; make like or into a monk. **2** To cover with or as with a cowl. [OE *cugle, cuhle* <*cucullus* hood]

cowl² (koul) *n. Brit.* A large vessel for carrying water. [<OF *cuvel* <L *cupella*, dim. of *cupa* cask, vat]

cowled (kould) *adj.* **1** Wearing a cowl; hooded. **2** Shaped like a cowl.

Cow·ley (kou′lē, kōō′-), **Abraham,** 1618–67, English poet.

cow·lick (kou′lik′) *n.* A tuft of hair turned up over the forehead as if licked by a cow.

cowl·ing (kou′ling) *n. Aeron.* **1** A metal covering for an airplane engine and sometimes for part of the fuselage or a nacelle. See illustration under AIRPLANE. **2** The covering of an airplane cockpit.

cowl·staff (koul′staf′, -stäf′) *n. Brit.* A pole by which two persons carry a large water bucket or cowl.

cow·man (kou′mən) *n. pl.* **·men** (-mən) **1** One who owns cows; a rancher. **2** A cowboy.

co-work·er (kō′wûr′kər) *n.* **1** One engaged in the same work as another. **2** One who cooperates in an organization.

cowp (koup) See COUP.

cow-pars·nip (kou′pärs′nip) *n.* Any of a genus (*Heracleum*) of tall, stout, perennial herbs

of the parsley family. Also **cow parsnip.**

cow·pea (kou′pē′) *n.* **1** A twining herb of the bean family (*Vigna sinensis*), cultivated in the southern United States. **2** The edible pea of this herb.

Cow·per (kōō′pər, kŏŏp′ər, kou′pər), **William,** 1731–1800, English poet.

Cow·per's glands (kou′pərz, kōō′-) *Anat.* Two small glands near the base of the bladder that discharge into the male urethra. [after William *Cowper*, 1666–1709, English anatomist]

cow·pi·lot (kou′pī′lət) *n.* The pintano: so called from its supposed habit of accompanying the cowfish.

cow pony A small horse or pony used in herding cattle.

cow·pox (kou′poks′) *n.* An acute contagious disease of cows, forming pustules containing a virus which is the source of vaccine for smallpox.

cow·punch·er (kou′pun′chər) *n. U.S. Colloq.* A cowboy.

cow·rin (kōō′rin) *adj. Scot.* Cowering.

cow·ry (kou′rē) *n. pl.* **·ries** A shell with a high gloss, a small variety of which is used as money in Africa and southern Asia. Also **cow′rie.** [<Hind. *kaurī*]

cow shark A large shark (*Hexanchus griseus*) with six gill openings on each side, inhabiting European and West Indian waters.

cow·shed (kou′shed′) *n.* A shelter for cows.

cow·skin (kou′skin′) *n.* The hide of a cow.

cow·slip (kou′slip′) *n.* **1** An English wildflower (*Primula veris*) of the primrose family. **2** The marsh marigold of the United States. [OE *cūslyppe* <*cū* cow + *slyppe* dung; because it commonly grows in pastures]

cow soapwort Cowherb.

cow-tree (kou′trē′) *n.* **1** One of several trees yielding a milky juice which can be used as a food, especially the South American tree *Brosimum utile* of the mulberry family. **2** The bulytree. **3** Any of various other trees, as *Tabernaemontana utilis,* of the dogbane family, and certain members of the fig family.

cox (koks) *n. Colloq.* Coxswain. — *v.t. & v.i.* To serve or act as coxswain to (a boat).

cox·a (kok′sə) *n. pl.* **cox·ae** (-sē) **1** *Entomol.* The first joint or body joint of the leg in arthropods. **2** *Anat.* The hip or hip joint. [<L, hip] — **cox′al** *adj.*

cox·al·gi·a (kok·sal′jē·ə) *n. Pathol.* Pain in the hip. Also **cox′al·gy.** [<NL <L *coxa* hip + Gk. *algos* pain] — **cox·al′gic** *adj.*

cox·comb (koks′kōm′) *n.* **1** A pretentious and conceited fop: also spelled *cockscomb.* **2** Cockscomb (def. 1). **3** A piece of red cloth notched like a cock's comb, formerly worn in a jester's cap; also, the cap itself. **4** *Obs.* The top of the head, or the head itself. [Var. of *cockscomb*] — **cox·comb·i·cal, cox·com·i·cal** (koks·kom′i·kəl, -kō′mi-) *adj.* — **cox·comb′i·cal·ly** *adv.*

cox·comb·ry (koks′kōm′rē) *n.* **1** Coxcombs collectively. **2** Foppishness.

Cox·ey's Army (kok′sēz) A large group of unemployed people, led by "General" Jacob S. Coxey (1854–1951), U.S. political reformer, which marched on Washington to petition Federal aid during the depression of 1893.

cox·swain (kok′sən, kok′swān′) *n.* One who steers or has charge of a small boat or a racing shell: often spelled *cockswain.* [<COCK³ + SWAIN]

coy¹ (koi) *adj.* **1** Shrinking from notice, diffident; shy: said chiefly of women. **2** Simulating diffidence; coquettish. **3** *Obs.* Disdainful. [<F *coi* <OF *quei* <L *quietus.* Doublet of QUIET.] — **coy′ish** *adj.* — **coy′ly** *adv.* — **coy′ness** *n.*

coy² (koi) *n. Dial.* A decoy. [<Du. *kooi* berth, trap]

coy·o·te (kī·ō′tē, kī′ōt) *n.* The prairie wolf (*Canis latrans*) of the western United States. Also spelled *cayote.* [<Am. Sp. <Nahuatl]

Coyote State Nickname of SOUTH DAKOTA.

co·yo·til·lo (kō′yō·tēl′yō, kī′ō-) *n. pl.* **·los** A small shrub (*Karwinskia humboldtiana*) of the buckthorn family, producing poisonous fruit, native in northern Mexico and the SW United States. [<Am. Sp., dim. of *coyote* COYOTE]

coy·pu (koi′pōō) *n. pl.* **·pus** or **·pu** A South American aquatic, beaverlike rodent (*Myocastor coypus*), about 2 feet long, with webbed hind feet and round tail: it yields the fur

known as nutria. Also **coy′pou.** [<Am. Sp. <native name]

coz (kuz) *n. Colloq.* A cousin. [Short for COUSIN]

coz·en (kuz′ən) *v.t.* & *v.i.* To cheat in a petty way. [<F *cousiner* deceive by claiming kinship <*cousin* COUSIN] **—coz·en·age** (kuz′ən·ij) *n.* **—coz′en·er** *n.*

co·zy (kō′zē) *adj.* **co·zi·er, co·zi·est 1** Snugly and easily comfortable; contented. **2** Sociable. *—n.* A padded cap or cover for a teapot to prevent the heat from escaping after the tea is infused: also called *tea cozy.* Also spelled *cosy, cosey.* Also **co′zey.** [<dial. E (Scottish) *cosie,* prob. <Scand. Cf. Norw. *kose* comfortable.] **—co′zi·ly** *adv.* **—co′zi·ness** *n.*

CPR Cardiopulmonary resuscitation.

Cr *Chem.* Chromium (symbol Cr).

craal (kräl) See KRAAL.

crab[1] (krab) *n.* **1** Any of various species of ten-footed crustaceans of the suborder *Brachyura* in the order *Decapoda,* characterized by a small abdomen folded under the body, a flattened carapace, and short antennae. They can walk in any direction without turning, but usually move sideways. **2** The hermit crab. **3** The horseshoe crab. **4** A crab louse, *Phthirus pubis.* **5** *Aeron.* The lateral slant in an airplane needed to maintain a flight line in a cross-wind. **6** A form of windlass. **7** *pl.* The lowest throw of a pair of dice. **—to catch a crab.** In rowing, to sink an oar blade too deeply; also, to miss the water entirely or skim the surface in making a stroke, and thus fall backward. *—v.* **crabbed, crab·bing** *v.i.* **1** To take or fish for crabs. **2** *U.S. Colloq.* To back out: to *crab* out of an agreement. **3** *Naut.* To drift sideways, as a ship. *—v.t.* **4** *Aeron.* To head (an airplane) across a contrary wind so as to compensate for drift. [OE *crabba.* Akin to CRAB[3].]

crab[2] (krab) *n.* **1** A crab apple. **2** A crab-apple tree. **3** An ill-tempered, surly, or querulous person. *—v.* **crabbed, crab·bing** *v.t.* **1** *Colloq.* To disparage; belittle; complain about. **2** *Colloq.* To ruin or spoil: He *crabbed* the entire act. **3** *Obs.* To make surly or sour; irritate. **4** *Brit. Dial.* To cudgel or beat, as with a crabstick. *—v.i.* **5** To be ill-tempered. [? <Scand. Cf. dial. Sw. *scrabba* wild apple.]

crab[3] (krab) *v.i.* **crabbed, crab·bing** To seize each other fiercely, as hawks when fighting; claw. [<MDu. *crabben* scratch. Akin to CRAB[1].]

Crab A constellation and sign of the Zodiac; Cancer.

crab angle The angle between the direction of movement of an airplane, rocket or guided missile and the direction in which the nose points, resembling the sideways motion of a crab.

crab apple A kind of small, sour apple: also called *crab.*

crab-ap·ple tree (krab′ap′əl) A tree (genus *Malus*) bearing crab apples: also called *crab, crab tree.*

Crabbe (krab), **George,** 1754–1832, English poet.

crab·bed (krab′id) *adj.* **1** Sour-tempered. **2** Harsh; sour. **3** Hard to understand; abstruse. **4** Irregular in form; cramped. See synonyms under MOROSE. [<CRAB[1], *n.* (def. 1)] **—crab′bed·ly** *adv.* **—crab′bed·ness** *n.*

crab·ber (krab′ər) *n.* **1** One who fishes for or catches crabs. **2** A type of boat used by those who fish for crabs.

crab·bit (krab′it) *adj. Scot.* Crabbed.

crab·by (krab′ē) *adj.* **·bi·er, ·bi·est 1** Cross-grained; ill-tempered. **2** Like or pertaining to a crab.

crab·grass (krab′gras′, -gräs′) *n.* A low-growing or procumbent grass (genus *Digitaria*) with freely rooting stems, especially *D. sanguinalis;* a lawn pest.

crab·stick (krab′stik′) *n.* **1** A cudgel made of crab-tree wood; hence, any cudgel. **2** An ill-tempered person.

crab tree 1 A tree having a bitter bark, as the dogbane, that is used medicinally. **2** The crab-apple tree.

crack (krak) *v.t.* **1** To produce fissures or seams in; break open partially or completely. **2** To cause to give forth a short, sharp sound: to *crack* a whip. **3** To break with such a sound. **4** *Slang* To open in order to drink: to *crack* a bottle. **5** *Colloq.* To break into, as a safe or building, in order to rob. **6** To solve, as a puzzle, crime, or code. **7** *Slang* To tell (a joke). **8** To break or crush mentally, as with sorrow or torture: He *cracked* the man's spirit. **9** To cause (the voice) to become cracked or hoarse. **10** *Colloq.* To strike sharply or with a sharp sound: He *cracked* him on the jaw. **11** To reduce by distillation, as petroleum. **12** *Obs.* To make a boast. *—v.i.* **13** To split or break, especially with suddenness. **14** To make a sharp snapping sound, as a whip or pistol; break with such a sound. **15** Of the voice, to become hoarse or change tone. **16** To become impaired or broken, as the spirit or will. **17** *Slang* To fall back or behind; fail: said of racehorses. **18** *Archaic* To talk boastfully. **—cracked up to be** *Colloq.* Reputed or believed to be. **—to crack a book** *U.S. Slang* To open, as a textbook, and read or study. **—to crack a smile** *Slang* To smile. **—to crack down** *Colloq.* To take severe repressive measures: with *on* or *upon* **—to crack hardy** *Austral. Slang* To put on a bold front in the face of trouble. **—to crack on 1** *Naut.* To crowd on sail. **2** To travel at high speed. **—to crack up** *Colloq.* **1** To smash or destroy, as an airplane or automobile; also, to be in an automobile or airplane accident. **2** To have a breakdown, nervous or physical. **—to crack wise** *U.S. Slang* To wisecrack. *—n.* **1** An incomplete separation into two or more parts with or without a noticeable space between; a fissure; split; chink. **2** The narrow space between two boards, especially in a floor. **3** A sudden sharp or loud sound; report, as of a pistol or rifle. **4** A blow that resounds: He hit him a *crack.* **5** A mental or physical defect or imperfection; flaw. **6** *Colloq.* One of high skill or excellence in a certain line; the best: All the *cracks* were entered for that race. **7** A peculiar sound or tone of the voice, as when changing at puberty or weakened by age. **8** *Colloq.* A witty or sarcastic remark; a pun. **9** *Slang* A burglar; also, a burglary. **10** A moment; an exact instant; the duration of a crack: the *crack* of dawn. **11** *Scot.* A familiar chat. *—adj. Colloq.* Of superior excellence; first-class. [OE *cracian*]

crack·brain (krak′brān′) *n.* A weak-minded person. *—adj.* Weak-minded; crazy; odd: also **crack′-brained′.**

crack-down (krak′doun′) *n. U.S. Colloq.* Summary disciplinary or corrective action.

cracked (krakt) *adj.* **1** Having a crack or cracks; rent; split or broken into small pieces: *cracked* corn or ice. **2** Damaged or blemished. **3** *Colloq.* Crazy; mentally unsound.

crack·er (krak′ər) *n.* **1** A person or thing that cracks. **2** A firecracker. **3** A device consisting of two strips of paper with fulminating powder between them which explodes by friction when the strips are pulled apart, sometimes ornamented and combined with a motto, bonbon, paper cap, etc. **4** The snapper of a whip. **5** A thin brittle biscuit: an oyster *cracker.* **6** An impoverished white inhabitant of parts of the SE United States: a contemptuous term.

crack·er-bar·rel (krak′ər·bar′əl) *adj.* Denoting or characteristic of the informal, rambling discussions of those habitually gathered in a country store: *cracker-barrel* philosophy.

crack·er·jack (krak′ər·jak′) *Slang adj.* Of or pertaining to a person or thing of worth, merit, or the like. *—n.* A person or thing of exceptional value: Among salesman he is a *crackerjack.* Also **crack′a·jack′.**

Cracker State Nickname of GEORGIA.

crack·ing (krak′ing) *n. Chem.* A process by which the molecular structure of petroleum or other complex hydrocarbons is changed under pressure by heat or distillation so that fractions of high boiling point are broken down to those of low boiling point: important in the production of high-octane gasoline.

crack·le (krak′əl) *v.* **·led, ·ling** *v.i.* **1** To crack or snap repeatedly with light, sharp noises. *—v.t.* **2** To crush or crumple, as paper with such sounds. **3** To cover, as china, with a delicate network of cracks. *—n.* **1** A succession of light, cracking sounds; crepitation. **2** The appearance or condition produced in china, porcelain, glass, and the like, by the cracking of the glaze in all directions so as to form a fine network of cracks: also **crack′le·ware′.** [Freq. of CRACK, *v.*] **—crack′ly** *adj.*

crack·ling (krak′ling) *n.* **1** The action or process of giving out small sharp sounds in rapid succession. **2** The crisp browned skin of roasted pork. **3** *pl.* The crisp refuse of fat, as of the hog, after the removal of the lard or tallow. **4** *Brit.* A cake of beef scraps used as dogs' food.

crack·nel (krak′nəl) *n.* **1** A hard, brittle biscuit. **2** *pl.* Bits of crisply fried fat pork. [Alter. of F *craquelin*]

crack of doom 1 The signal announcing the dawn of Judgment Day. **2** Doomsday; the end of the world.

crack·pot (krak′pot′) *n. Slang* A weak-minded or eccentric person; a harmless fanatic; crank. *—adj.* Eccentric; foolish; insane.

crack shot *Colloq.* An excellent marksman.

cracks·man (kraks′mən) *n. pl.* **·men** (-mən) *Slang* A burglar; safe-robber.

crack-up (krak′up′) *n.* **1** *Aeron.* The partial or total destruction of an aircraft due to circumstances beyond the pilot's control. **2** Any sudden, unforseen breakdown.

crack·y (krak′ē) *interj.* An exclamation of surprise, astonishment, or delight. Also **by cracky.**

cra·co·vienne (krä·kō·vyen′) *n. French* A lively Polish dance or the music for it: also *krakowiak.*

Crac·ow (krak′ou, krā′kō) A city on the Vistula; a former capital of Poland: Polish *Kraków.*

-cracy *combining form* Government or authority: *democracy.* [<Gk. *-krateia* power <*krateein* rule]

Crad·dock (krad′ək), **Charles Egbert** Pseudonym of Mary Noailles Murfree, 1850–1922, U.S. novelist.

cra·dle (krād′l) *n.* **1** A rocking or swinging bed for an infant. **2** A place of birth; origin. **3** A scythe with fingers that catch the grain when cut. **4** An arch of thin wood or wire, to keep bedclothes from pressing on a tender part of the body; also a light case in which an injured limb can be swung. **5** *Engin.* **a** A frame, usually of heavy timber, for sustaining some heavy object or structure, as a ship on a marine railway or in drydock. **b** A scaffolding suspended by ropes. **6** A support for the frame or keel or an airship or dirigible under construction. **7** *Mining* A box on rockers, for washing auriferous dirt; a rocker; cradle-rocker. **8** *Brit.* A cage swung on gimbals in which miners ascend and descend a shaft. **9** A coarse ribbing on a vaulted surface that is to be plastered. **10** A currycomb-shaped tool for making mezzotint grounds on a metal plate; a rocker. **11** A life car or basket running on a line, to bring persons from a wreck to the shore. **12** *Mil.* The frame in a gun carriage in which the gun moves during a recoil. **13** The double-pronged, electrically connected holder for the operating unit of a handset telephone. *—v.* **·dled, ·dling** *v.t.* **1** To put into or rock in or as in a cradle; soothe. **2** To nurse in infancy; nurture. **3** To cut or reap, as grain, with a cradle. **4** To draw onto or transport in a cradle, as a ship. **5** *Mining* To wash, as gold-bearing gravel, in a cradle. *—v.i.* **6** To lie or rest in or as in a cradle. **7** To cut or reap. **—to rob the cradle** *Colloq.* To marry or take as a sweetheart one much younger than oneself. [OE *cradol*]

cra·dle-snatch·er (krād′l-snach′ər) *n. Slang* One who consorts with or marries a much younger person.

cra·dle·song (krād′l·sông′, -song′) *n.* A lullaby.

craft (kraft, kräft) *n.* **1** Cunning or skill, especially as used with ignoble motives; guile; artifice. **2** Skill or ingenuity in any calling, especially in a manual employment. **3** Occupation or employment; a trade. **4** The membership of a particular trade or organized society; a guild. **5** A vessel; ship; airplane: also used collectively. See synonyms under ARTIFICE, BUSINESS, DECEPTION. [OE *cræft* skill, art, strength, courage]

-craft *combining form* Skill; trade; art of: *wood-craft.* [<CRAFT]

crafts·man (krafts′mən, kräfts′-) *n. pl.* **·men** (-mən) **1** A member of a craft. **2** A skilled mechanic. **—crafts′man·ship** *n.*

craft union A labor union in which membership is limited to workers in a single trade. Compare INDUSTRIAL UNION.

craft·y (kraf′tē, kräf′-) *adj.* **craft·i·er, craft·i·est** Skilful in deceiving; cunning. See synonyms under ASTUTE, INSIDIOUS, POLITIC. **—craft′i·ly** *adv.* **—craft′i·ness** *n.*

crag (krag) *n.* A rough, steep, or broken rock rising or jutting out prominently. [ME *cragg* <Celtic. Cf. Irish *creag,* Welsh *craig.*]

crag·ged (krag′id) *adj.* Having numerous crags. Also **crag′gy. —crag′ged·ness, crag′gi·ness** *n.*

crags·man (krags′mən) *n. pl.* **·men** (-mən) One who climbs or is skilled in climbing crags or cliffs.

craig[1] (krāg) *n. Scot.* The neck or throat. Also **craig′ie.**

craig[2] (krāg) *n. Scot.* Crag.

Crai·gie (krā′gē), **Sir William Alexander,** 1867–1957, British lexicographer.

Craik (krāk), **Dinah Maria,** 1826–87, *née* Mulock, English novelist.

Cra·io·va (krä·yō′vä) A city in southern Rumania.

crake (krāk) *n.* A small, short-billed bird of the rail family, with a harsh cry; especially, the corn crake and the spotted crake. [<ON *kraka* crow]

cram (kram) *v.* **crammed, cram·ming** *v.t.* **1** To press tightly; pack together; crowd. **2** To feed to satiety. **3** To force, as a mass of knowledge or facts, into the mind, as in hurried preparation for an examination. *—v.i.* **4** To eat greedily; stuff oneself with food. **5** To force knowledge into the mind by hurried study. *—n.* **1** The act or process of cramming. **2** One who crams. **3** Hastily acquired knowledge gained by cramming. [OE *crammian* stuff]

Cram (kram), **Ralph Adams,** 1863–1942, U.S. architect.

cram·bo (kram′bō) *n.* **1** A word-riming game. **2** A word that rimes with another. [Alter. of L *crambe* cabbage (<Gk. *krambē*) in phrase *crambe repetita* an unpleasant repetition; lit., cabbage served over]

cram·mer (kram′ər) *n.* **1** One who prepares himself or others for examination by cramming. **2** A mechanical device for cramming poultry. **3** *Brit. Slang* A lie.

cram·oi·sy (kram′oi·zē, -ə·zē) *Obs. adj.* Crimson. *—n.* Crimson cloth. Also **cram′oi·sie.** [<OF *crameisi, cramoisi* <Ital. *cremesi* <Arabic *qirmazī* < *qirmiz* kermes]

cramp[1] (kramp) *n.* **1** A frame with one or more screws, in which pieces may be clamped or forced together, as in joinery; a clamp. **2** An adjustable device of wood or metal upon which vamps are stretched in shoe manufacturing. **3** A bench hook. **4** A narrow place in which it is necessary to deflect sharply the wheels of a vehicle in order to turn. **5** A cramp iron (def. 1).*—v.t.* **1** To restrain or confine the action of, as with a cramp; hamper; hinder. **2** To make fast; hold tightly, as with a cramp iron. **3** To shape over a cramp, as the upper of a boot. **4** To deflect, as the wheel of a vehicle, to one side in making a turn; also, to jam (a wheel) by turning too short. **—to cramp one's style** *Slang* To hamper one's customary skill or self-confidence.*—adj.* **1** Narrowed; straitened. **2** Contracted and irregular in form or action; cramped, as handwriting. [<MDu. *krampe* hook. Related to CRAMP[2].]

cramp[2] (kramp) *n.* **1** An involuntary, sudden, painful muscular contraction, occuring most frequently in the legs and often attacking swimmers; a tonic spasm, caused usually by strain or sudden chill. **2** A paralytic affection of local muscles caused by continued overexertion: writer's *cramp.* **3** Partial paralysis of the hindquarters, sometimes observed in animals during pregnancy. **4** *pl.* Acute abdominal pains. *—v.t.* **1** To affect with cramps. [<OF *crampe* <LG. Related to CRAMP[1].]

cramp·fish (kramp′fish′) *n. pl.* **·fish** or **·fish·es** The electric ray.

cramp iron 1 An iron with bent ends, serving to bind two pieces together more firmly, as in stonework: also called *cramp.* **2** A strip of metal on the side of a vehicle to prevent damage from scraping when the wheel is cramped.

cram·pon (kram′pən) *n.* **1** *Bot.* An aerial root for climbing, as in the ivy. **2** A pair of hooked pieces of iron for raising heavy stones, etc. **3** An iron attached to the shoe for walking on ice or to aid in climbing. Also **cram·poon** (kram·pōōn′). [<F <*crampe* CRAMP[2]]

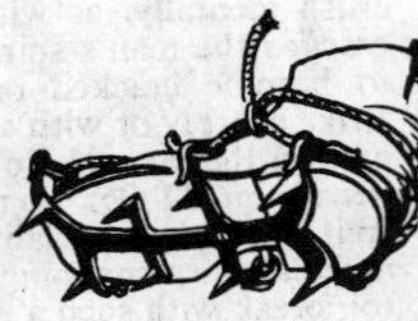

CRAMPON (*def.* 3)

Cra·nach (krä·näkh′), **Lucas,** 1472–1553, German painter and engraver: also spelled *Kranach.* **—Lucas,** 1515–86, German portrait painter; son of preceding: called "the younger."

cran·ber·ry (kran′ber′ē, -bər·ē) *n. pl.* **·ries 1** The edible, scarlet, acid berry of a plant *(Vaccinium macrocarpum)* growing in marshy land. **2** The plant itself. **—small cranberry** The common Old World cranberry *(V. oxycoccus).* [<Du. *kranebere*]

cranberry tree The guelder-rose. Also **cranberry bush.**

Cran·borne (kran′bôrn), **Viscount** See CECIL, ROBERT.

cran·dall (kran′dəl) *n.* A stonecutter's hammer for dressing ashlar. [Prob. <*Crandall,* a surname]

crane (krān) *n.* **1** One of a family *(Gruidae)* of large, long-necked, long-legged, heronlike birds allied to the rails; especially, the sandhill crane *(G. americana).* **2** A heron or cormorant. **3** A hoisting machine having the added capacity of moving a load in a horizontal or lateral direction. **4** An iron arm, swinging horizontally, attached to the back or side of a fireplace: used for suspending pots or kettles over a fire. *—v.t. & v.i.* **craned, cran·ing 1** To stretch out, as a crane stretches its neck; elongate or be elongated. **2** To halt and lean forward, as a horse hesitating at a leap; hence, to hesitate at anything. **3** To elevate or lift by or as if by a crane. [OE *cran*]

Crane (krān) The constellation Grus. See CONSTELLATION.

Crane (krān), **Bruce,** 1857–1937, U.S. painter. **—Hart,** 1899–1932, U.S. poet. **—Stephen,** 1871–1900, U.S. poet, novelist, and short-story writer. **—Walter,** 1845–1915, English painter and illustrator.

crane·fly (krān′flī′) *n. pl.* **·flies** A fly with very long, slender legs resembling a large mosquito (family *Tipulidae*): in England often called *daddy-long-legs.*

cranes·bill (kränz′bil′) *n.* Geranium (def. 1). Also **crane's-bill.**

cra·ni·al index (krā′nē·əl) Cephalic index.

cra·ni·ate (krā′nē·it, -āt) *adj.* Possessing a cranium. *—n.* Any of a primary division *(Craniata)* of the phylum *Chordata,* which includes all vertebrates having a skull, as fishes, reptiles, birds, and mammals. [<NL *craniata* <Med. L *cranium* CRANIUM]

cranio- *combining form* Cranium; cranial: *craniograph.* Also, before vowels, **crani-.** [<Med. L *cranium* skull <Gk. *kranion*]

cra·ni·og·no·my (krā′nē·og′nə·mē) *n.* The doctrine that regards the form and proportions of the skull as an index of the mental qualities or temperament. [<CRANIO- + -GNOMY]

cra·ni·o·graph (krā′nē·ə·graf′, -gräf′) *n.* An instrument for making a topographical chart of the skull. **—cra·ni·og·ra·phy** (krā′nē·og′rə·fē) *n.*

cra·ni·ol·o·gy (krā′nē·ol′ə·jē) *n.* The branch of anatomy and medicine that treats of the structure and characteristics of skulls. [<CRANIO- + -LOGY] **—cra·ni·o·log·i·cal** (krā′nē·ə·loj′i·kəl) *adj.* **—cra′ni·ol′o·gist** *n.*

cra·ni·om·e·ter (krā′nē·om′ə·tər) *n.* An instrument for measuring skulls. [<CRANIO- + -METER] **—cra·ni·o·met·ric** (krā′nē·ə·met′rik) or **·ri·cal** *adj.* **—cra′ni·o·met′ri·cal·ly** *adv.* **—cra′ni·om′e·try** *n.*

cra·ni·o·sa·cral (krā′nē·ō·sā′krəl) *adj.* Parasympathetic.

cra·ni·os·co·py (krā′nē·os′kə·pē) *n.* **1** Scientific examination of the configuration of the skull. **2** Formerly, phrenology. [<CRANIO- + -SCOPY] **—cra·ni·o·scop·ic** (krā′nē·ə·skop′ik) *adj.* **—cra′ni·os′co·pist** *n.*

cra·ni·ot·o·my (krā′nē·ot′ə·mē) *n. Surg.* **1** Any operation on the cranium. **2** An operation in which the fetal skull is perforated and the cranium compressed to facilitate delivery in difficult parturition. [<CRANIO- + -TOMY]

cra·ni·um (krā′nē·əm) *n. pl.* **·ni·ums** or **·ni·a** (-nē·ə) That part of the skull enclosing the brain; brainpan. [<Med. L <Gk. *kranion* skull] **—cra′ni·al** *adj.*

crank[1] (krangk) *n.* **1** A device for transmitting motion, as by the hand, or for converting rotary into reciprocating motion, as a handle attached at right angles to a shaft. **2** *Colloq.* One who lacks mental balance; a person given to caprices, crotchets, or vagaries. **3** A fantastic turn of speech; quip; conceit; also, a twist or perversion of judgment; whim. **4** An eccentric notion or action. **5** *Colloq.* A grouchy, ill-tempered person. **6** *Obs.* A bend. *—v.t.* **1** To bend into the shape of a crank. **2** To furnish with a crank. **3** To operate or start by a crank. *—v.i.* **4** To turn a crank, as in starting an internal-combustion engine. **5** *Obs.* To bend; twist. [OE *cranc,* as in *crancstæf* a weaving comb]

crank[2] (krangk) *adj.* **1** Ill-balanced; easily capsized: said of a boat. **2** Hence, shaky. Also *cranky.* [Earlier *crank-sided* <Du. *krengd* heeled over <*krengan* push]

crank[3] (krangk) *adj.* Spirited; lively. [Origin uncertain]

crank·case (krangk′kās′) *n. Mech.* The case enclosing an engine crankshaft, as of an automobile or the like.

cran·kle (krang′kəl) *n.* A bend; crinkle. *—v.t. & v.i.* **·kled, ·kling** To bend; crinkle. [Dim. of CRANK]

crank·ous (krang′kəs) *adj. Scot.* Irritable; cranky.

crank·pin (krangk′pin′) *n. Mech.* The round pin which joins reciprocating members of a connecting rod.

crank·shaft (krangk′shaft′, -shäft′) *n. Mech.* A shaft that bears one or more cranks.

crank·y[1] (krang′kē) *adj.* **crank·i·er, crank·i·est 1** Full of whims; irritable; easily exasperated; peevish. **2** Crooked; bent. **3** Loose and rickety. **—crank′i·ly** *adv.* **—crank′i·ness** *n.*

crank·y[2] (krang′kē) See CRANK[2].

Cran·mer (kran′mər), **Thomas,** 1489–1556, first Anglican archbishop of Canterbury; burnt at the stake by Mary Tudor.

cran·nog (kran′əg) *n.* In Scotland and Ireland, an ancient lake dwelling or village built on shallows or on palisaded islands. [<Irish <*crann* tree, timber]

cran·ny (kran′ē) *n. pl.* **·nies** A narrow opening; fissure. *—v.i.* **·nied, ·ny·ing 1** To become full of fissures or crevices. **2** To enter by crannies, as the wind. See synonyms under BREACH. [<OF *cran, cren* notch] **—cran′nied** *adj.*

crants (krants) *n. Obs.* A garland; wreath. [<G *kranz*]

crap (krap) *n. Scot.* **1** The top; summit. **2** A fowl's crop. **3** Scrap[1] (def. 3).

crape (krāp) *n.* **1** A sheer worsted fabric, usually black, used for funeral hangings and draperies. **2** A piece of this fabric, especially an armband or crêpe veil, worn or hung as a sign of mourning. *—v.t.* **craped, crap·ing 1** To produce crimps or a crinkled surface in; frizz. **2** To drape with crape; place crape upon as a sign of mourning. [Var. of CRÊPE]

crape·fish (krāp′fish′) *n. pl.* **·fish** or **·fish·es** Codfish salted and pressed.

crape·hang·er (krāp′hang′ər) *n. Slang* A gloomy or pessimistic person: so called in allusion to the hanging of black crape at funerals.

crap·pie (krap′ē) *n. pl.* **·pies** or **·pie** An edible fresh-water fish *(Pomoxis annularis)* of the central United States. [Cf. F *crape* crabfish]

craps (kraps) *n. U.S.* A game of chance, played with two dice. Also **crap game, crap′shoot′ing.** [<F *crabs, craps* <E *crabs,* the lowest throw (two aces) in hazard]

crap-shoot·er (krap′shōō′tər) *n. U.S.* One who plays the game of craps.

crap·u·lence (krap′yōō·ləns) *n.* **1** Sickness caused by intemperance in eating or drinking; surfeit. **2** Gross intemperance, as in drinking.

crap·u·lent (krap′yōō·lənt) *adj.* **1** Grossly

intemperate; drunken; gluttonous. 2 Sick from intemperance in drinking. Also **crap'u·lous.** [<LL *crapulentus* <*crapula* drunkenness <Gk. *kraipalē* drunken headache]

crap·y (krā'pē) *adj.* Crapelike; crimped; wavy, as hair.

crash[1] (krash) *v.t.* **1** To break or dash in pieces noisily and with violence. **2** To force or drive noisily and with violence: He *crashed* his way through the jungle. **3** *U.S. Colloq.* To intrude upon or enter uninvited or without paying admission: to *crash* a party or dance. **4** To cause, as an airplane, truck, or train, to fall to the earth or strike an obstacle. — *v.i.* **5** To break or fall in pieces with a violent, broken sound. **6** To make a noise of clashing or breaking. **7** To move with such a noise: The boulder *crashed* down the hillside. **8** To fall to the earth or strike an obstacle, as an airplane or automobile. **9** To fail or collapse; come to ruin: The stock market *crashed* suddenly. — *n.* **1** A loud noise, as of thunder. **2** Destruction; bankruptcy. **3** A destructive accident caused by collision: an airplane *crash.* [Imit.]

crash[2] (krash) *n.* A coarse fabric woven of thick, uneven yarns: used for towels, curtains, etc. [? <Russian *krashenina*]

Crash·aw (krash'ô), **Richard,** 1613?–49, English religious poet.

crash boat A speedy motorboat for rescuing personnel from forced landings or crashes of aircraft in the water.

crash dive *Nav.* The quick submergence of a submarine, usually to escape detection or attack.

crash helmet A heavy, padded helmet worn by the crew members of tanks and military aircraft.

crash pad Thick padding covering projections in tanks and military aircraft as protection for crew members.

crash program *U.S. Colloq.* An intensive emergency undertaking in government, science, etc., having priority over all others.

cra·sis (krā'sis) *n.* **1** The coalescence of two vowels into one long vowel or diphthong (as the final and initial vowels of two successive words); syneresis. **2** *Med.* A characteristic mixture of constituent elements, as of the blood. **3** Constitutional temperament [<Gk. *krasis* mixture]

cras·pe·do·mor·phol·o·gy (kras'pə·dō·môr·fol'ə·jē) *n.* That branch of photography which deals with the sharpness of images, clarity of detail, and the resolving power of camera lenses. [<Gk. *kraspedon* border, margin + MORPHOLOGY]

crass (kras) *adj.* Coarse in manner or feeling; insensitive; indelicate: *crass* indifference to human suffering. [<L *crassus* thick] — **crass'ly** *adv.* — **crass'ness** *n.*

cras·sa·men·tum (kras'ə·men'təm) *n. Med.* A coagulum or clot, as the semisolid portion of blood. [<L, dregs, sediment]

cras·su·la·ceous (kras'yo͞o·lā'shəs) *adj. Bot.* Of or pertaining to a family *(Crassulaceae)* of polypetalous, usually succulent herbs or shrubs, including the sedums and houseleeks. [<NL *Crassulaceae* <L *crassus* thick]

Cras·sus (kras'əs), **Marcus Licinius,** 115–53 B.C., Roman general and statesman; triumvir with Caesar and Pompey.

-crat *combining form* A supporter or member of a social class or of a type of government: *democrat, aristocrat.* See -CRACY. [<F *-crate* <Gk. *-kratēs* < *krateein* rule, govern]

crate (krāt) *n.* **1** A large wickerwork hamper or framework of slats, for protection in transporting various articles: also, its contents. **2** A packing box. **3** *Slang* An old or decrepit vehicle or airplane. — *v.t.* **crat·ed, crat·ing** To put in a crate; send or transport in a crate. [<L *cratis* wickerwork. Doublet of GRATE.] — **crat'er** *n.*

cra·ter (krā'tər) *n.* **1** The bowl-shaped depression forming the outlet of a volcano or of a hot spring. **2** Any large bowl or cavity. **3** In ancient Greece and Rome, a large bowl or vase in which wine was mixed with water before being served to guests. **4** The pit resulting from the explosion of a mine, bomb, or shell. [<L <Gk. *kratēr* bowl]

Cra·ter (krā'tər) A constellation of the southern hemisphere; the Cup. See CONSTELLATION.

Crater Lake National Park An area in SW Oregon; 251 square miles; established 1902; contains **Crater Lake,** a circular lake (20 square miles) in the crater of an extinct volcano.

crat·o·ma·ni·a (krat'ə·mā'nē·ə) *n. Psychiatry* A morbid desire for power and preeminence. [<Gk. *kratos* power + -MANIA]

cra·vat (krə·vat') *n.* A neckcloth or scarf; a necktie. [<F *cravate* < *Cravate* a Croatian <G *Krabate* <Croatian *Hrvat*; with ref. to the neckcloths worn by 17th c. Croatian soldiers]

crave (krāv) *v.* **craved, crav·ing** *v.t.* **1** To beg for humbly and earnestly. **2** To long for; desire greatly. **3** To be in need of; require: His body *craves* nourishment. — *v.i.* **4** To desire or long: with *for* or *after.* [OE *crafian*] — **crav'er** *n.*

cra·ven (krā'vən) *adj.* Lacking in courage; cowardly. — *n.* A base coward. [<OF *cravant* <L *crepans,* ppr. of *crepare* break] — **cra'ven·ly** *adv.* — **cra'ven·ness** *n.*

crav·ing (krā'ving) *n.* A yearning or appetite; intense longing. See synonyms under APPETITE, DESIRE, PETITION. — **crav'ing·ly** *adv.* — **crav'·ing·ness** *n.*

craw[1] (krô) *n.* **1** The first stomach or crop of a bird. **2** The stomach of any animal. [ME *crawe.* Akin to Du. *kraag* neck.]

craw[2] (krô) *n. Scot.* A rook or crow.

craw·dad (krô'dad') *n. Dial.* A crayfish.

craw·fish (krô'fish') *n. pl.* **·fish** or **·fish·es** A crayfish. — *v.i. U.S. Colloq.* To back out or retreat, as from a position or a promise. [Var. of CRAYFISH]

Craw·ford (krô'fərd), **Francis Marion,** 1854–1909, U.S. novelist. — **Thomas,** 1813?–57, U.S. sculptor.

crawl[1] (krôl) *v.i.* **1** To move by thrusting one part of the body forward upon a surface and drawing the other part after, as a worm; creep. **2** To move slowly, feebly, or cautiously: A sick person *crawls* about. **3** To move or make progress meanly and insinuatingly; seek influence by servility. **4** To have a sensation as of crawling things upon the body. **5** To progress or grow by extending branches, etc., as a vine or creeping plant. **6** To be filled with things that crawl, as a dead body. **7** *Colloq.* To back down from a declared position. — *n.* **1** The act of crawling; a creeping motion. **2** In swimming, a stroke made while lying face down, the arms being alternately thrust forward above the water. — **American crawl** A crawl stroke which combines a six-beat flutter kick with each stroke. — **Australian crawl** A crawl stroke which combines an eight-beat flutter kick with each stroke, the strokes being shorter than in the American crawl. [<ON *krafla* paw with the hands] — **crawl'er** *n.* — **crawl'ing·ly** *adv.*

crawl[2] (krôl) *n.* A pen or enclosure in the water for containing fish, turtles, etc. [Alter. of Du. *kraal.* See KRAAL.]

crawl space A shallow space beneath a floor, often to provide access to a building's ducts, electrical and plumbing fixtures, etc. Also **crawl·way** (crôl'wā').

crawl·y (krô'lē) *adj.* **crawl·i·er, crawl·i·est** *Colloq.* **1** Covered or filled with crawling things; crawling. **2** Having a sensation as of things crawling over the flesh.

cray·fish (krā'fish') *n. pl.* **·fish** or **·fish·es** **1** A spiny lobster. **2** A small, fresh-water crustacean (family *Astacidae*) resembling the lobster, especially the common American crayfish *(Cambarus affinis).* [Earlier *crevice* <OF <OHG *krebiz*; infl. in form by *fish*]

cray·on (krā'ən, -on) *n.* **1** A small cylinder of charcoal, prepared chalk, or other waxy material, as gypsum, and flour or pipe clay, especially colored, as with graphite, red ocher, etc., for drawing on paper. **2** An oily pencil, used in lithography. **3** A carbon point in an arc light. **4** A drawing made with crayons. **5** A piece of prepared chalk used for marking on blackboards. — *v.t.* To sketch or draw with a crayon or crayons. [<F, pencil < *craie* chalk <L *creta*] — **cray'on·ist** *n.*

craze (krāz) *v.* **crazed, craz·ing** *v.t.* **1** To cause to become insane or mentally ill. **2** To make full of minute intersecting cracks, as the glaze of pottery. **3** *Obs.* To impair or weaken; break down. — *v.i.* **4** To become insane. **5** To become full of minute cracks. — *n.* **1** Mental disorder. **2** A transient freak of fashion; a caprice or prejudice. **3** A flaw in the glaze of pottery. [ME *crasen* <Scand. Cf. Sw. *krasa* break.]

crazed (krāzd) *adj.* **1** Insane. **2** Cracked, as glaze.

cra·zy (krā'zē) *adj.* **cra·zi·er, cra·zi·est** **1** Insane; originating in or characterized by insanity. **2** Of or fit for an insane person. **3** Dilapidated; rickety. **4** *Colloq.* Inordinately eager; foolishly desirous. **5** *Colloq.* Inexplicable; odd or unconventional: a *crazy* driver. See synonyms under INSANE. — **cra'zi·ly** *adv.* — **cra'zi·ness** *n.*

crazy bone The funny bone.

crazy quilt A patchwork bed quilt made of pieces of various sizes, shapes, and colors.

cra·zy·weed (krā'zē·wēd') *n.* Loco or locoweed.

creak (krēk) *v.t.* & *v.i.* To make, or cause to make, a creak. — *n.* A sharp, squeaking sound, as from friction. [Imit.] — **creak'i·ly** *adv.* — **creak'i·ness** *n.* — **creak'y** *adj.*

cream (krēm) *n.* **1** A thick, oily, light-yellow substance composed chiefly of fatty globules that rise and gather on the surface of milk and combine into butter when churned. **2** Any substance formed in a similar manner. **3** A delicacy for the table resembling cream, or made in part from it; also, a candy containing a creamlike substance. **4** The part of something regarded as the choicest or most highly to be appreciated: the *cream* of fashion. **5** A soft, oily cosmetic for cleansing or protecting the skin. See COSMETIC. **6** A rich, sirupy cordial or liqueur. See CRÈME. **7** The lighter part of liquor which rises and gathers on the top. **8** The color of cream: a light-yellow color. — *v.t.* **1** To skim cream from. **2** To take the best part from. **3** To add cream to, as coffee. **4** To permit (milk) to form cream. **5** To beat, as milk and sugar, to a creamy consistency. **6** To cook or prepare (food) with cream or cream sauce. — *v.i.* **7** To be covered with cream; froth. **8** To form cream. [<F *crème* <OF *cresme* <LL *chrisma.* Doublet of CHRISM.] — **cream'i·ness** *n.* — **cream'y** *adj.*

cream cheese Soft, unripened cheese made of cream or a mixture of cream and milk.

cream-col·ored (krēm'kul'ərd) *adj.* Having the yellowish-white color of cream.

cream·cups (krēm'kups') *n.* An ornamental annual *(Platystemon californicus)* of the poppy family, with cream-colored flowers.

cream·er (krē'mər) *n.* **1** A cooler or other container in which milk is placed and the cream allowed to rise. **2** Any dish or machine in which cream is separated. **3** A cream pitcher.

cream·er·y (krē'mər·ē) *n. pl.* **·er·ies** **1** A place for collecting, keeping, or selling cream. **2** A place where butter and cheese are made, milk and cream are pasteurized, separated, bottled, etc.

cream-faced (krēm'fāst') *adj.* White; pale.

cream of tartar Potassium bitartrate, $HKC_4H_4O_6$, a white crystalline compound with an acidulous taste, made by purifying argol: an ingredient of baking powder.

cream puff **1** A shell of pastry filled with whipped cream or custard. **2** *Slang* A sissy; weakling.

crease[1] (krēs) *n.* **1** The mark of a wrinkle, fold, or the like. **2** In cricket, any of the lines limiting the position of the bowler or batsman. — *v.* **creased, creas·ing** *v.t.* **1** To make a crease, line, or fold in; wrinkle. **2** To stun or wound by a shot that grazes the flesh. — *v.i.* **3** To become wrinkled or fall into creases. [ME *creaste,* ? var. of *creste* a crest, ridge] — **creas'er** *n.* — **creas'y** *adj.*

crease[2] (krēs) See KRIS.

cre·ate (krē·āt') *v.* **·at·ed, ·at·ing** *v.t.* **1** To cause to come into existence; originate. **2** To be the cause of; occasion: The speech *created* much interest. **3** To produce, as a painting or poem, from thought and imagination. **4** To be the first to portray, as a character or part. **5** To invest with, as rank or office; appoint. — *v.i.* **6** *Brit. Slang* To make a fuss;

complain noisily. See synonyms under MAKE, PRODUCE. [<L *creatus*, pp. of *creare* produce, create]

cre·a·tine (krē'ə·tēn, -tin) *n. Biochem.* A nitrogenous compound, $C_4H_9N_3O_2$, found in the muscle tissue, brain, and blood of all vertebrate animals. It has been isolated in the form of white crystals, and is also made synthetically. Also **cre'a·tin** (-tin). [<Gk. *kreas, -atos* flesh + -INE[2]]

cre·at·i·nine (krē·at'ə·nēn, -nin) *n. Biochem.* The anhydride of creatine, $C_4H_7ON_3$, occurring normally in blood and urine: isolated as white or yellowish prismatic crystals. [<CREATINE + -INE[1]]

cre·a·tion (krē·ā'shən) *n.* **1** The act of creating; especially, in a theological sense, the original act of God in bringing the world or universe into existence. **2** The universe. **3** An act of construction; the combining or organizing of existing materials into new form: the *creation* of an empire. **4** That which is created; any product of the power of scientific, artistic, or practical construction: the *creations* of genius. **5** The act of investing with a new rank or character or of placing in a new office: the *creation* of two additional judges. **— all creation** Everybody; everything in the world. **— cre·a'tion·al** *adj.* **— cre·a'tion·al·ly** *adv.*

cre·a·tion·ism (krē·ā'shən·iz'əm) *n.* **1** The doctrine that the universe was originally brought into existence without preexistent material by the word of God, and also that new species or forms of being have been successively produced by the direct formative exercise of the Divine wisdom and power. **2** The doctrine that God creates a new soul whenever a human being begins to live: distinguished from *traducianism.* Also **cre·a'tion·al·ism. — cre·a'tion·ist** *n.* **— cre·a'tion·is'tic, cre·a'tion·al·is'tic** *adj.*

cre·a·tive (krē·ā'tiv) *adj.* **1** Having the power to create. **2** Productive; constructive. **— cre·a'tive·ly** *adv.* **— cre·a'tive·ness** *n.*

cre·a·tiv·i·ty (krē'ā·tiv'ə·tē) *n.* The quality of being able to produce original work or ideas in any field; creativeness.

cre·a·tor (krē·ā'tər) *n.* **1** One who creates or brings into being. **2** That which produces or causes; creative instrumentality. See synonyms under CAUSE. **— the Creator** God, as the maker of the universe. **— cre·a'tor·ship** *n.*

crea·ture (krē'chər) **1** That which has been created; a creation; a human being. **2** A domestic animal. **3** A person or thing considered as arising from, governed by, or conditioned upon something else: *creatures* of habit. **4** A person dependent upon the power or influence of another; dependent; tool. **— the creature** Strong drink; liquor: a drop of *the creature*: a humorous usage. **— crea'tur·al, crea'ture·ly** *adj.*

creature comforts Things that comfort or refresh the body: applied especially to food and drink.

Cré·bil·lon (krā·bē·yôṅ'), **Prosper Jolyot de,** 1674–1762, French dramatist. **— Claude Prosper Jolyot de,** 1707–77, French novelist; son of the preceding: known as *Crébillon fils.*

crèche (krāsh, kresh) *n.* **1** A public day-nursery. **2** A foundling asylum. **3** A modeled group representing the Nativity. [<F, crib, cradle]

Cré·cy (krā·sē') A village in northern France; scene of an English victory over French forces, August, 1346: also *Cressy.* Also **Cré·cy-en-Pon·thieu** (krā·sē'äṅ·pôṅ·tyœ').

cre·dence (krēd'ns) *n.* **1** Confidence based upon external evidence; belief. **2** That which serves to accredit; credentials. **3** *Eccl.* A small table or shelf near the altar to hold the eucharistic elements before they are consecrated. **4** A sideboard or serving table of medieval and Renaissance Europe. See synonyms under BELIEF, FAITH. [<F *crédence* <Med. L *credentia* < *credere* believe]

cre·den·dum (kri·den'dəm) *n. pl.* **·da** (-də) An article of faith; that which is to be believed: distinguished from *agendum.* [<L, gerundive of *credere* believe]

cre·dent (krēd'nt) *adj. Obs.* **1** Credible; to be believed. **2** Credulous.

cre·den·tial (kri·den'shəl) *n.* **1** That which certifies one's authority or claim to confidence. **2** *pl.* Certificate showing that a person is invested with certain authority or claim to confidence or consideration. **—** *adj.* Giving a title or claim to credit and confidence; accrediting.

cred·i·bil·i·ty (kred'ə·bil'ə·tē) *n.* **1** The capacity of being believed. **2** The capacity, as of a government or a public official, of maintaining the public's confidence that its report of the conduct of its affairs is worthy of belief.

credibility gap **1** A lessening or loss of credibility, as in a government or public official. **2** The extent or degree of a decline in credibility: The official statement only widened the *credibility gap.*

cred·i·ble (kred'ə·bəl) *adj.* Capable of being believed; worthy of credit, confidence, or acceptance. See synonyms under LIKELY, PROBABLE. [<L *credibilis* < *credere* believe] **— cred'i·ble·ness** *n.* **— cred'i·bly** *adv.*

cred·it (kred'it) *n.* **1** Belief in the truth of a statement or in the sincerity of a person; trust. **2** Reputation for trustworthiness; character; repute. **3** One who or that which adds honor or reputation: a student who is a *credit* to his class. **4** Influence derived from the good opinion or confidence of others: He has *credit* at court. **5** In bookkeeping, the entry in account of any amount paid by a debtor on account of his debt; the amount so entered; also, the right-hand side of an account, upon which are recorded values received: opposed to *debit.* **6** Transfer of property on promise of future payment. **7** Reputation for solvency and probity. **8** The amount to which a person, corporation, or business house may be financially trusted in a given case. **9** In an account, the balance in one's favor. **10** The time extended for the payment of a liability. **11** An amount placed by a bank at a customer's disposal against which he may draw. **12** In education, official certification that a course of study has been finished; also, a recognized unit of school or college work. **13** *Usually pl.* Acknowledgment of work done, as in the making of a motion picture. See synonyms under BELIEF, FAITH, FAME. **—** *v.t.* **1** To give credit for; accept as true. **2** To ascribe, as intelligence or honor, to: with *with.* **3** *Archaic* To reflect credit upon; bring into good repute. **4** In bookkeeping, to give credit for or enter as credit to. **5** In education, to give educational credits to (a student). [<F *crédit* <L *creditum* a loan < *credere* believe, trust] **— cred'it·a·bil'i·ty, cred'it·a·ble·ness** *n.* **— cred'it·a·ble** *adj.* **— cred'it·a·bly** *adv.*

cred·i·tor (kred'i·tər) *n.* **1** One to whom another is pecuniarily indebted. **2** In bookkeeping, that side of an account upon which are recorded values received or receivable.

credit standing Reputation for meeting financial obligations, paying bills, etc.

credit union A cooperative group for making loans to its members at low rates of interest.

cre·do (krē'dō, krā'-) *n. pl.* **·dos** **1** A creed, as the Apostles' or the Nicene Creed. **2** A musical setting for the creed. [<L, I believe; the opening word of the creed]

cre·du·li·ty (krə·dōō'lə·tē, -dyōō'-) *n.* **1** The state or quality of being credulous. **2** A proneness to believe the improbable or the marvelous. [<L *credulitas, -tatis* < *credulus* CREDULOUS]

cred·u·lous (krej'ōō·ləs) *adj.* **1** Apt or disposed to believe on slight evidence; easily deceived. **2** Arising from credulity. [<L *credulus* < *credere* believe] **— cred'u·lous·ly** *adv.* **— cred'u·lous·ness** *n.*

Cree (krē) *n. pl.* **Cree** or **Crees** **1** One of a tribe of the Algonquian stock of North American Indians formerly dwelling in Manitoba and Assiniboia between the Red River and the Saskatchewan. **2** The language of this tribe. **—** *adj.* Of or pertaining to this tribe or its language.

creed (krēd) *n.* **1** A formal summary of religious belief; an authoritative statement of doctrine; a confession of faith. **2** That which is believed; doctrine. See synonyms under BELIEF, FAITH. **— the Creed** The Apostles' Creed. [OE *creda* <L *credo* I believe. See CREDO.]

creek (krēk, krik) *n.* **1** A tidal or valley stream between a brook and a river in size: often written *crick.* **2** A small inlet, bay, or cove; a recess in the shore of the sea or of a river. **3** *Brit.* A small seaboard town. See synonyms under STREAM. **— up the creek** *U.S. Colloq.* **1** In a state of uncertainty or bewilderment. **2** Out of luck. [ME *creke, crike* <Scand. Cf. Sw. *krik* cove, inlet.]

Creek (krēk) *n.* **1** A confederacy of the Muskhogean tribes of North American Indians, once occupying a great portion of Georgia, Alabama, and northern Florida. **2** An Indian of any of the tribes in this confederacy. **3** Their Muskhogean language.

creel (krēl) *n.* **1** An angler's willow basket for carrying fish. **2** A cage of wickerwork for catching lobsters. **3** A frame in a spinning machine. **—** *v.t.* To put in a creel. [<OF *creil* <L *craticula*, dim. of *cratis* wickerwork. Doublet of GRILLE.]

creep (krēp) *v.i.* **crept, creep·ing** **1** To move like a serpent; crawl. **2** To move imperceptibly, slowly, secretly, or stealthily. **3** To exhibit servility; cringe. **4** To have a sensation as of contact with creeping things. **5** To grow along a surface or support: *creeping* plants. **6** To slip out of place: A sleeve *creeps* up the arm. **7** To move slightly along the line of length: said of railroad tracks. **—** *n.* **1** The act of creeping. **2** *pl.* A nervous sensation as of insects creeping under the flesh; hence, uneasy apprehensiveness. **3** *Metall.* A phenomenon associated with metals subjected to critical temperature and stresses, and characterized by a slow slipping or flow of the material. **4** *Geol.* The gradual movement of rock waste and soil down a slope from which it has been loosened by weathering. [OE *crēopan*]

creep·ie (krē'pē, krip'ē) *n. Scot.* A low stool. Also **creepie chair.**

creep·ie-peep·ie (krē'pē·pē'pē) *n.* A portable, one-man television camera transmitting pictures by wireless: analogous to a walkie-talkie.

creeping myrtle Periwinkle.

creep·y (krē'pē) *adj.* **creep·i·er, creep·i·est** **1** Feeling as if something were creeping over the skin; shivering; especially, chilled with fright. **2** Characterized by creeping. **— creep'i·ly** *adv.* **— creep'i·ness** *n.*

creese (krēs) See KRIS.

creesh (krēsh) *n. Scot.* Grease. **—** *v.t.* To grease. Also **creish. — creesh'y** *adj.*

cre·mate (krē'māt, kri·māt') *v.t.* **·mat·ed, ·mat·ing** To burn up; reduce, especially a dead body, to ashes. See synonyms under BURN. [<L *crematus*, pp. of *cremare* burn to ashes] **— cre'ma·tor** *n.*

cre·ma·tion (kri·mā'shən) *n.* The act or practice of burning, especially of burning the dead.

cre·ma·to·ry (krē'mə·tôr'ē, -tō'rē, krem'-) *adj.* Related to or connected with cremation. **—** *n. pl.* **·ries** A place for cremating dead bodies. Also **cre'ma·to'ri·um** (-tôr'ē·əm, -tō'rē-).

crème (krem) *n. French* Cream: used in names of sauces or liqueurs: *crème* de menthe.

crème de ca·ca·o (də kə·kā'ō, -kä'ō) *n.* A sweet, chocolate-flavored liqueur.

crème de la crème (də lä krem') *French* Literally, cream of the cream; the very best; most choice.

crème de menthe (də mänt) *French* A sweet, green or white cordial with a strong flavor of mint.

Crem·nitz white (krem'nits) A high-grade pigment made from litharge, or corroded white lead. Also *Kremnitz white.*

crem·o·carp (krem'ə·kärp, krē'mə-) *n. Bot.* The fruit of any plant of the parsley family, consisting of two one-seeded carpels, separating when ripe and hanging from the summit of the slender axis. Also **crem'o·car'pi·um** (-kär'pē·əm). [<Gk. *kremaein* hang + *karpos* fruit]

Cre·mo·na (kri·mō'nə, *Ital.* krā·mō'nä) *n.* Any violin made at Cremona, Italy, from the 16th to the 18th century, by the Amati family, by Antonio Stradivari, or by Josef Guarnerius.

Cre·mo·na (kri·mō'nə, *Ital.* krā·mō'nä) A province in Lombardy, northern Italy; 678 square miles; capital, Cremona.

cre·nate (krē'nāt) *adj. Bot.* Scalloped or toothed with even, rounded notches, as a leaf or margin. Also **cre'nat·ed.** [<NL *crenatus* < *crena* a notch]

cren·a·ture (kren'ə·chōōr, krē'nə-) *n.* **1** The rounded tooth of a crenate organ. **2** The state of being crenate. Also **cre·na·tion** (kri·nā'shən).

cren·el (kren′əl) *n.* 1 An embrasure of a battlement; an indentation. 2 A crenature. — *v.t.* **cren·el·ed** or **·el·led, cren·el·ing** or **·el·ling** To crenelate. Also **cre·nelle** (kri·nel′). [<OF, dim. of *cren* notch]

cren·e·late (kren′ə·lāt) *v.t.* **·lat·ed, ·lat·ing** To fortify or decorate with battlements. — *adj.* Crenulate. Also **cren′el·late. — cren′e·la′tion, cren′el·la′tion** *n.*

cren·u·late (kren′yə·lit, -lāt) *adj.* Finely notched or crenate. Also **cren′u·lat′ed.** [<NL *crenulatus* <*crenula,* dim. of *crena* notch]

cren·u·la·tion (kren′yə·lā′shən) *n.* 1 The state of being crenulate. 2 A small crenature.

cre·o·dont (krē′ə·dont) *n. Paleontol.* One of a suborder *(Creodonta)* of primitive Tertiary carnivora, having incisors with closed roots, distinct fibula, and developed otic bulla. [<NL *Creodonta* <Gk. *kreas* flesh + *odous, odontos* tooth]

Cre·ole (krē′ōl) *n.* 1 A native of Spanish America or the West Indies, of European parentage. 2 A descendant of French, Spanish, or Portuguese settlers of Louisiana and the Gulf States who retains his special speech or culture. 3 A Negro born in the Americas, as distinguished from one brought from Africa: also known as a **Creole Negro.** 4 The French patois of Louisiana: distinguished from *Cajun.* 5 Any person having both Creole and Negro blood and speaking the Creole patois. — *adj.* Relating or peculiar to the Creoles. [<F *créole* <Sp. *criollo* a native <*criar* produce, bring forth <L *creare* create]

cre·ole (krē′ōl) *n.* A creolized language. — *adj.* Cooked with a savory sauce including peppers, tomatoes, onions, etc.

Creole State Nickname of LOUISIANA.

Cre·o·lin (krē′ə·lin) *n.* Saponified creosote, a thick, black coal-tar liquid, used as an antiseptic, germicide, and deodorant: a trade name.

cre·o·lized language (krē′ə·lizd) An amalgamated language, such as Gullah, resulting from close and prolonged contact between two groups speaking dissimilar languages: it usually incorporates a simplified vocabulary from the dominant language with the grammatical system of the native language, and becomes the only language of the subject group. Compare PIDGIN.

Cre·on (krē′on) In Greek legend, the brother of Jocasta and successor to Oedipus on the throne of Thebes: he sentenced Antigone to death for burying her brother Polynices.

cre·o·sol (krē′ə·sōl, -sol) *n. Chem.* A colorless, aromatic, oily liquid compound, $C_8H_{10}O_2$, derived from beech tar or guaiac by distillation. [<CREOS(OTE) + -OL[2]]

cre·o·sote (krē′ə·sōt) *n. Chem.* 1 An oily liquid consisting principally of cresol and other phenols, obtained by the destructive distillation of wood and having a smoky odor and burning taste: it is an antiseptic, but a poor germicide, and is used to preserve timber, meat, etc. 2 A similar liquid distilled from coal tar: also **coal-tar creosote.** — *v.t.* **·sot·ed, ·sot·ing** To treat or impregnate with creosote, as shingles, etc. [<Gk. *kreas* flesh + *sōtēr* preserver <*sōzein* save]

creosote bush A shrub *(Larrea tridentata)* of the bean caltrop family of Mexico and the Colorado desert, having a resinous foliage that smells like creosote.

crêpe (krāp) *n.* A thin, light fabric, made of silk, cotton, wool, or synthetic fibers, generally with a crinkled, pebbled, or puckered surface: also spelled *crape.* Also **crepe.** [<F *(tissu) crêpe* crinkled cloth <L *crispus* curled]

crêpe de Chine (də shēn′) A soft, thin silk dress fabric, with a pebbly surface.

crêpe hair Artificial hair, used in theatrical make-up for beards and moustaches.

crêpe paper A tissue paper resembling crêpe, used for decorative purposes.

crêpe rubber Rubber prepared in crinkled texture for the soles of shoes.

crêpes su·zette (krāp′ sōō·zet′) Thin egg pancakes, rolled in a hot, orange-flavored sauce: usually served aflame in cognac or curaçao.

Cré·pin (krā·paṅ′) French form of CRISPIN.

crep·i·tate (krep′ə·tāt) *v.i.* **·tat·ed, ·tat·ing** To make a succession of quick snapping sounds; crackle; rattle. [<L *crepitatus,* pp. of *crepitare,* freq. of *crepare* creak] — **crep′i·tant** *adj.* — **crep′i·ta′tion** *n.*

crept (krept) Past tense of CREEP.

cre·pus·cu·lar (kri·pus′kyə·lər) *adj.* 1 Pertaining to twilight; like twilight; obscure. 2 Appearing or flying in the morning or evening twilight, as certain birds and insects. Also **cre·pus′cu·lous.**

cre·pus·cule (kri·pus′kyōōl) *n.* Twilight. Also **cre·pus·cle** (kri·pus′əl). [<L *crepusculum* <*creper* dark, dusky]

cre·scen·do (krə·shen′dō, -sen′-) *n. pl.* **·dos** *Music* 1 A gradual increase in the force of sound: expressed by the sign <— or the abbreviation *cres.* 2 A passage so performed. — *adj.* Slowly increasing in loudness or power. [<Ital. <*crescere* increase]

cres·cent (kres′ənt) *n.* 1 The visible part of the moon in its first quarter, having one concave edge and one convex edge; the new moon. 2 Something crescent-shaped, as the device on the Turkish standard; hence **The Crescent,** the Turkish or Mohammedan power. — *adj.* 1 Increasing: said of the moon in its first quarter. 2 Shaped like the moon in its first quarter. [<L *crescens, -entis,* ppr. of *crescere* increase] — **cres·cen·tic** (kre·sen′tik) *adj.*

cres·cive (kres′iv) *adj. Obs.* Growing; increasing. [<L *crescere* increase + -IVE]

cre·sol (krē′sōl, -sol) *n. Chem.* Any one of three isomeric liquid or crystalline compounds, C_7H_8O, obtained by the destructive distillation of coal, beechwood, or pinewood: used as an antiseptic. [Var. of CREOSOL]

cress (kres) *n.* One of various plants of the mustard family having a pungent taste and used in salads. [OE *cressa*] — **cress′y** *adj.*

cres·set (kres′it) *n.* An incombustible frame or vessel mounted to hold a torch, a beacon, or fuel for this. [<OF *craicet, craisset*]

Cres·si·da (kres′i·də) In medieval legend, in Chaucer's *Troilus and Criseyde,* and in Shakespeare's *Troilus and Cressida,* a Trojan girl unfaithful to her lover Troilus: also spelled *Criseyde.* Also **Cres′sid.** See PANDARUS.

Cres·sy (kres′ē) See CRÉCY.

crest (krest) *n.* 1 A comb or tuft on the head of an animal or bird. 2 The projection on the top of a helmet; a plume; tuft. 3 The ridge of a wave or of a mountain; the top of anything. 4 A heraldic device placed above the shield in a coat of arms. 5 *Archaic* Loftiness; pride; courage. 6 The ridge of the neck of a horse or a dog. 7 *Archit.* **a** The ridge of a roof. **b** Carved work or any continuous ornament on the ridge or other elevated parts of an edifice; a cresting. — *v.t.* 1 To serve as a crest for; cap. 2 To furnish with or as with a crest. 3 To reach the crest of. 4 To adorn with crestlike streaks or lines. — *v.i.* 5 To come to a crest, as a wave prior to breaking. [<OF *creste* <L *crista* tuft] — **crest′ed** *adj.*

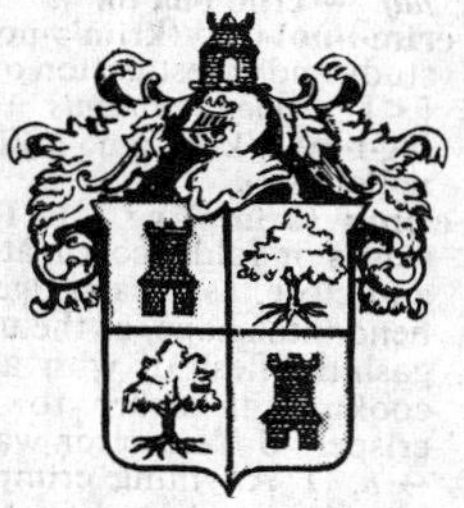
COAT OF ARMS WITH CREST

crested auklet A small, brownish-black diving bird *(Aethia cristatella),* abundant in Alaska and the North Pacific.

crested flycatcher Any flycatcher having a conspicuous crest, especially the great crested flycatcher *(Myiarchus crinitus)* of eastern North America.

crest·fall·en (krest′fô′lən) *adj.* 1 Having the crest or head lowered. 2 Dispirited; dejected.

crest·ing (kres′ting) *n. Archit.* An ornamental ridge surmounting a roof, wall, etc.

crest·less (krest′lis) *adj.* Having no crest.

cres·yl (kres′əl, krē′səl) *n. Chem* Tolyl. [<CRES(OL) + -YL]

cres·y·late (kres′ə·lāt) *n. Chem.* An ester derived from cresol.

cre·syl·ic (kri·sil′ik) *adj. Chem.* Of or derived from cresyl, cresol, or creosote.

cre·ta·ceous (kri·tā′shəs) *adj.* Consisting of or related to chalk; chalky. [<L *cretaceus* <*creta* chalk <*Creta* Cretan, of Crete (where large deposits of chalk occurred)]

Cre·ta·ceous (kri·tā′shəs) *n. Geol.* The third and last of the geologic periods of the Mesozoic era, preceded by the Jurassic and followed by the Tertiary period of the Cenozoic era. See chart under GEOLOGY. — *adj.* Pertaining to or characteristic of this period.

Crete (krēt) A Greek island 160 miles long in the Mediterranean SE of Greece; 3,207 square miles. *Greek* **Kre·te** (krē′tē). — **Cre′tan** *adj.* & *n.* — **Cre′tic** *adj.*

Cre·tic (krē′tik) *n.* In prosody, an amphimacer. [<Gk. *Krētikos* Cretan, a Cretic foot]

cre·tin (krē′tin) *n.* A person afflicted with cretinism. [<F *crétin,* var. of *chrétien* Christian, human being, i.e., not an animal] — **cre′tin·ous** *adj.*

cre·tin·ism (krē′tən·iz′əm) *n. Pathol.* A disease associated with prenatal thyroid deficiency and subsequent thyroid inactivity, marked by physical deformities, arrested development, goiter, and various forms of mental retardation, including imbecility: also called *hypothyroidism.*

cre·tonne (kri·ton′, krē′ton) *n.* A heavy, unglazed cotton, linen, or rayon fabric printed in colored patterns: used especially for draperies, chair coverings, etc. [from *Creton,* a village in Normandy]

Cre·u·sa (krē·ōō′sə) 1 In Greek legend, daughter of Creon and bride of Jason, killed by the jealous Medea. 2 In the *Aeneid,* wife of Aeneas, lost in the escape from Troy.

Creuse (krœz) A river of central France, flowing NW 160 miles to the Loire.

Creu·sot (krœ·zō′), **Le** See LE CREUSOT.

cre·vasse (krə·vas′) *n.* 1 A deep fissure, as in a glacier. 2 A breach in a levee. — *v.t.* **·vassed, ·vass·ing** To split with crevasses. [<F] — **cre·vassed′** *adj.*

Crève·coeur (krev·kœr′), **Michel-Guillaume Jean de,** 1735–1813, French author in America: pseudonym *J. Hector St. John.*

crev·ice (krev′is) *n.* A small fissure or crack. See synonyms under BREACH. [<OF *crevace* <LL *crepatia* <L *crepare* crack, creak] — **crev′iced** *adj.*

crew[1] (krōō) *n.* 1 *Naut.* **a** The company of seamen belonging to one ship or boat: sometimes including officers, and legally including both master and officers unless specifically excepted. **b** The gang of a boatswain, gunner, carpenter, or other petty officer. 2 A body of men organized or detailed for a particular work, as to run a train. 3 A group of students trained to handle a racing shell, consisting of oarsmen and coxswain. 4 A company of people in general; crowd: a motley *crew* of ne'er-do-wells and loafers. 5 Any band or troop of armed men. See synonyms under CABAL. [<OF *creue* an increase <*croistre* grow <L *crescere* increase]

crew[2] (krōō) Past tense of CROW.

crew cut A closely cropped haircut.

Crewe (krōō) A municipal borough in south central Cheshire, England.

crew·el (krōō′əl) *n.* A slackly twisted worsted yarn, used in fancywork. ◆ Homophone: *cruel.* [Origin uncertain]

crewel needle Any large-eyed needle, especially one used for crewel.

crew·el·work (krōō′əl·wûrk′) *n.* Embroidery with crewel.

crib (krib) *n.* 1 A rack or manger. 2 A stall for cattle. 3 A child's bedstead, with side railings. 4 A box, bin, or small building for grain, having slat or openwork sides. 5 A small raft. 6 A frame of wood or timber, used to retain a bank of earth. 7 *Colloq.* A petty theft, or the thing taken; plagiarism. 8 A translation or other unauthorized aid in study. 9 A house, cottage, lodging, etc. 10 In cribbage, the four discarded cards counted by the dealer. See CRIBBAGE. 11 A wickerwork basket. — *v.* **cribbed, crib·bing** *v.t.* 1 To enclose in or as in a crib; confine closely. 2 To line or bolster, as the walls of a pit, with timbers or planking. 3 *Colloq.* To take and pass off as one's own, as an answer or a piece of writing; copy; plagiarize. 4 *Colloq.* To steal; purloin. 5 In logging, to form (logs) into a raft, as for towing.

6 *Colloq.* To translate with the aid of a crib. —*v.i.* 7 *Colloq.* To use a crib in translating. 8 To crib-bite. [OE *cribb*] —**crib′ber** *n.*

crib·bage (krib′ij) *n.* A game of cards for two, three, or four players, in which the score is kept on a small board with rows of holes into which pegs are inserted. [<CRIB, *n.* (def. 10)]

crib-bite (krib′bīt′) *v.i.* **-bit, -bit·ten** or **-bit, -bit·ing** To bite a crib or manger, at the same time drawing in the breath with a peculiar sound: said of horses. —**crib′-bit′er** *n.* —**crib′-bit′ing** *n.*

crib·ble (krib′əl) *n.* 1 A coarse sieve. 2 Coarse flour or meal. —*v.t.* **·bled, ·bling** To separate with a coarse sieve or riddle; sift. Also **crib′le.** [<F *crible* <LL *cribellum,* dim. of L *cribrum* sieve]

crib·bled (krib′əld) *adj.* Covered with small punctures or dots, as in engraving or the decoration of wood or metal. [<F *criblé* <*crible* a sieve]

crib·ri·form (krib′rə·fôrm) *adj.* Having the form of a sieve; sievelike.

crib·work (krib′wûrk′) *n.* 1 A frame of logs filled in with stones: used to support wharves or to prevent water from washing out ground. 2 A crib, or anything constructed with cribs.

Crich·ton (krī′tən), **James,** 1560–82?, Scottish scholar and soldier: called "The Admirable Crichton."

crick[1] (krik) *n.* A spasmodic affection of the muscles, as of the neck; a cramp. —*v.t.* To turn or twist so as to produce a crick. [Origin uncertain]

crick[2] (krik) See CREEK (def. 1).

crick·et[1] (krik′it) *n.* A leaping orthopterous insect (family *Gryllidae*), with long antennae and three segments in each tarsus, the male of which makes a chirping sound by friction of the forewings. For illustration see under INSECT (injurious). [<OF *criquet* <LG]

crick·et[2] (krik′it) *n.* 1 An outdoor game played with bats, a ball, and wickets, between two opposing sides numbering eleven each: one of the most popular sports of England. 2 *Colloq.* Fair, gentlemanly behavior; sportsmanship. [<F *criquet* bat, stick <MDu. *cricke*] —**crick′et·er** *n.*

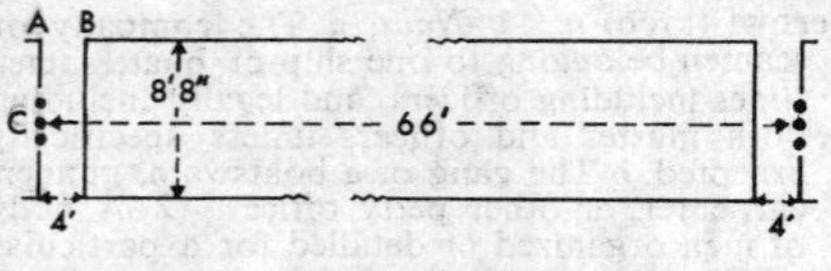

CRICKET FIELD
A. Bowling crease. *B.* Popping crease.
C. The wicket with its 3 stumps 8 inches apart.
The playing field is usually 150 x 100 yards.

crick·et[3] (krik′it) *n. Archit.* A small, sloping roof structure placed, for the purpose of diverting drainage, at the juncture of larger surfaces that meet at an angle. [Origin unknown]

crick·et[4] (krik′it) *n.* A footstool. [Origin unknown]

cri·coid (krī′koid) *Anat. adj.* Ringlike: designating a cartilage at the lowest part of the larynx. —*n.* The topmost cartilaginous ring of the trachea, whose posterior portion serves as a base for the arytenoids. [<Gk. *krikoeidēs* <*krikos* ring + *eidos* shape, form]

cri·co·thy·roid (krī′kō·thī′roid) *adj. Anat.* Of or pertaining to the cricoid and thyroid cartilages. See illustration under LARYNX.

cried (krīd) Past participle and past tense of CRY.

cri·er (krī′ər) *n.* One who publicly cries sales, lost articles, etc.

Crile (krīl), **George Washington,** 1864–1943, U.S. surgeon and scientist.

crime (krīm) *n.* 1 *Law* An act that subjects the doer to legal punishment; the commission or omission of an act specifically forbidden or enjoined by public law. 2 Any grave offense against morality or social order; wickedness; iniquity. See synonyms under ABOMINATION, OFFENSE, SIN. [<F <L *crimen* accusation, charge]

Cri·me·a A peninsula and autonomous republic of the Ukraine on the northern coast of the Black Sea; 10,400 square miles; capital, Simferopol; pop. 2,500,000. *Russian* **Krym (krim).** —*adj.* & *n* **Cri·me′an.**

Crimean War See table under WAR.

cri·men fal·si (krī′mən fal′sē) *Latin* The crime of perjury.

crim·i·nal (krim′ə·nəl) *adj.* 1 *Law* Relating to crime, or pertaining to the administration of penal as opposed to civil law. 2 Implying crime or heinous wickedness. 3 Guilty of crime: the *criminal* classes. —*n.* One who has committed an offense punishable by law. [<F *criminel* <L *criminalis*] —**crim·i·nal·i·ty** (krim′ə·nal′ə·tē), **crim′i·nal·ness** *n.* —**crim′·i·nal·ly** *adv.*

Synonyms (adj.): abominable, culpable, felonious, flagitious, guilty, illegal, immoral, iniquitous, nefarious, sinful, unlawful, vicious, vile, wicked, wrong. Every *criminal* act is *illegal* or *unlawful,* but *illegal* or *unlawful* acts may not be always *criminal.* Offenses against public law are *criminal,* offenses against private rights are *illegal* or *unlawful.* All acts punishable by fine or imprisonment or both are *criminal* in view of the law. It is *illegal* for a man to trespass on another's land, but it is not *criminal;* the trespasser is liable to civil suit for damages, but not to indictment, fine, or imprisonment. A *felonious* act is a *criminal* act punishable by imprisonment in the penitentiary or by death. A *flagitious* crime is one that brings public odium. *Vicious* refers to the indulgence of evil appetites, habits, or passions; *vicious* acts are not necessarily *criminal,* or even *illegal;* we speak of a *vicious* horse. That which is *iniquitous,* that is, contrary to equity, may sometimes be done under the forms of law. See IMMORAL. *Antonyms:* innocent, just, lawful, legal, meritorious, moral, right, virtuous.

criminal conversation See under CONVERSATION.

crim·i·nal·is·tics (krim′ə·nəl·is′tiks) *n.* That branch of criminology which deals especially with the scientific methods of crime detection.

crim·i·nate (krim′ə·nāt) *v.t.* **·nat·ed, ·nat·ing** To accuse of or implicate in crime; incriminate. [<L *criminatus,* pp. of *criminari* accuse of crime] —**crim′i·na′tion** *n.* —**crim′i·na′tive** *adj.* —**crim′i·na′tor** *n.*

crim·i·nol·o·gy (krim′ə·nol′ə·jē) *n.* The scientific study and investigation of crime and criminals. [<L *crimen, criminis* + -LOGY] —**crim·i·no·log·i·cal** (krim′ə·nə·loj′i·kəl) *adj.* —**crim′i·nol′o·gist** *n.*

crimp[1] (krimp) *v.t.* 1 To bend or press into ridges or folds; corrugate; flute. 2 To indent and close, as a cartridge case; crease. 3 To bend into shape, as the uppers of boots. 4 To gash the flesh of with a knife, as fish before cooking, in order to make it firmer and crisper. 5 To curl or wave: to *crimp* the hair. —*n.* 1 Anything crimped; especially, in the plural, waved or curled hair. 2 A crimping machine; crimper. 3 An offset in a piece of structural steel, used to fit one piece over another. 4 A collapse or breakdown of wood fibers, due to inherent weakness or a too rapid drying of timber. —*adj.* 1 Brittle and crisp; friable. 2 Inconsistent or contradictory. 3 Stiff, as if starched. [<MDu. *crimpen* wrinkle, draw together] —**crimp′age** *n.* —**crimp′er** *n.* —**crimp′y** *adj.*

crimp[2] (krimp) *n.* One who procures the impressment of sailors, soldiers, etc., by decoying or entrapping them. —*v.t.* To decoy or entrap into forced military or naval service. [Origin uncertain]

crim·son (krim′zən) *n.* A deep-red color having a tinge of blue, but lighter than purple. 1 Of a deep-red color. 2 Bloody. —*v.t.* & *v.i.* To make or become crimson; redden; blush. [<Sp. *cremesin,* var. of OSp. *carmesin, carmesi* <Arabic *qirmazi* <*qirmiz* kermes (insect used in making a red dye). Doublet of CARMINE.]

cringe (krinj) *v.i.* **cringed, cring·ing** 1 To bow in servility or cowardice; crouch. 2 To wince as with pain or fear. 3 To fawn. —*n.* A servile crouching. [ME *cringen, crengen;* related to OE *cringan* yield, fall] —**cring′er** *n.*

crin·gle (kring′gəl) *n. Naut.* An eye, loop, or grommet in a sail, on the side of a rope, etc. [<Du. *kringel* little ring]

cri·nite[1] (krī′nīt) *adj.* 1 *Bot.* Having hair or bearded with long weak hairs. 2 Resembling a tuft of hair. [<L *crinitus,* pp. of *crinire* cover with hair <*crinis* hair]

cri·nite[2] (krī′nīt, krin′īt) *n.* An encrinite. [<Gk. *krinon* lily]

crin·kle (kring′kəl) *v.t.* & *v.i.* **·kled, ·kling** 1 To form or cause to form, mold, or move with bends, turns, twists, or wrinkles. 2 To wind in and out; wave; corrugate. 3 To crackle metallically. —*n.* A wrinkle; ripple; twist; sinuosity. [ME *crenklen,* freq. of OE *crincan,* var. of *cringan* yield, fall] —**crin′kly** *adj.*

crin·kle·root (kring′kəl·ro͞ot′, -ro͝ot′) *n.* A toothwort (genus *Dentaria*) of the mustard family, especially *D. diphylla,* with small white or lilac flowers and a white-toothed rootstock with a pungent, aromatic taste: also called *pepperroot.*

crin·kum-cran·kum (kring′kəm·krang′kəm) *n.* 1 An odd, crooked figure or fanciful ornamentation; a zigzag. 2 A whimsy. [Varied reduplication of dial. *crink* a twisting]

cri·noid (krī′noid, krin′oid) *adj.* 1 Of or pertaining to the *Crinoidea.* 2 Containing crinoids: also **cri·noi·dal** (kri·noid′l). —*n.* One of the *Crinoidea.*

Cri·noi·de·a (krī·noi′dē·ə, kri-) *n. pl. Zool.* A class of echinoderms having jointed stems, attached by stalks to the sea bottom, and radial arms; the sea lilies. [NL <Gk. *krinoeidēs* <*krinon* lily + *eidos* form] —**cri·noi′·de·an** *n.* & *adj.*

crin·o·line (krin′ə·lin, -lēn) *n.* 1 A highly sized, stiff fabric, used in puffed sleeves, hems, interlinings, etc.: originally made of horsehair and linen. 2 A skirt stiffened with such fabric. 3 A hoop skirt. —*adj.* Resembling crinoline, or serving an analogous purpose. [<F <L *crinis* hair + *linum* flax, thread]

cri·num (krī′nəm) *n.* Any of a genus (*Crinum*) of frequently cultivated tropical herbs of the amaryllis family, with tunicate bulbs and a solid scape bearing numerous long, narrow leaves and showy, fragrant flowers. [<NL <Gk. *krinon* lily]

cri·o·sphinx (krī′ə·sfingks′) *n.* A sphinx with a ram's head. See SPHINX. [<Gk. *krios* ram + SPHINX]

crip·ple (krip′əl) *n.* 1 A maimed or lamed person or animal; one lacking the natural use of a limb or the body. 2 *U.S. Dial.* A piece of low, marshy land, partly covered by the tide and partly overgrown with trees and brush. 3 A staging used in cleaning windows. —*v.t.* **·pled, ·pling** To lame; impair or disable. [OE *crypel.* Akin to CREEP.]

Cripple Creek A city of central Colorado; center of one of the world's richest gold-producing areas in former years.

crip·pler (krip′lər) *n.* 1 A crimping board or graining board for leather. 2 One who or that which cripples.

Cripps (krips), **Sir (Richard) Stafford,** 1889–1952, English statesman and diplomat.

cris (krēs) See KRIS.

Cri·sey·de (kri·sā′də) See CRESSIDA.

cri·sis (krī′sis) *n. pl.* **cri·ses** (-sēz) 1 A turning point in the progress of an affair or of a series of events; a critical moment. 2 *Pathol.* Any sudden or decisive change in the course of a disease, favorable or unfavorable. [<L <Gk. *krisis* <*krinein* decide]

crisp (krisp) *adj.* 1 Firm and brittle; also, crumbling readily, as pastry. 2 Terse or pithy; curt. 3 Fresh; bracing. 4 Having curls or waves; crinkled; crisped. —*v.t.* & *v.i.* To make or become crisp. [OE <L *crispus* curled] —**crisp′er** *n.* —**crisp′ly** *adv.* —**crisp′ness** *n.* —**crisp′y** *adj.*

cris·pate (kris′pāt) *adj.* Having a crisped or curled appearance. Also **cris′pat·ed.** [<L *crispatus,* pp. of *crispare* curl <*crispus* curled]

cris·pa·tion (kris·pā′shən) *n.* 1 A slight contraction or spasmodic constriction. 2 A minute ripple of a liquid's surface, caused by vibration. Also **crisp·a·ture** (kris′pə·cho͝or).

Cris·pi (krēs′pē), **Francesco,** 1819–1901, Italian statesman.

Cris·pin (kris′pin) A masculine personal name. Also *Ger.* **Cris·pus** (kris′po͞os), *Ital.* **Cris·pi·no** (krēs·pē′nō), **Cris·po** (krēs′pō), *Lat.* **Cris·pi·nus** (kris·pī′nəs), **Cris·pus** (kris′pəs), *Sp.* **Cris·po** (krēs′pō). [<L, curly]

—**Crispin, Saint** A Roman Christian martyr of the late third century; patron saint of shoemakers; hence, **Crispin,** a shoemaker.

cris·sal (kris′əl) *adj.* 1 Of or pertaining to the crissum. 2 Having a bright-colored crissum.

criss-cross (kris′krôs′, -kros′) *v.t.* To cross with interlacing lines. —*v.i.* To move in criss-

crosses. —*adj.* Crossing one another in different directions; said of lines or the like. —*n.* **1** The cross of one who cannot write. **2** A congeries of intersecting lines. **3** A game played by children. —*adv.* In different cross-directions; crosswise. [Alter. of CHRIST-CROSS]
criss-cross-row (kris′krôs′rō′, -kros′-) See CHRIST-CROSS-ROW.
cris·sum (kris′əm) *n. Ornithol.* The undertail coverts of a bird; the region or feathers about the anus. [<NL <L *crissare* move the haunches]
cris·tate (kris′tāt) *adj.* **1** Crested. **2** Carinate. Also **cris′tat·ed.** [<L *cristatus < crista* crest]
Cris·tia·no (krēs·tyä′nō) Italian and Spanish form of CHRISTIAN, personal name.
Cris·ti·na (krēs·tē′nä) Italian and Spanish form of CHRISTINA.
Cris·tó·bal (krēs·tō′väl) Spanish form of CHRISTOPHER.
Cris·tó·bal (krēs·tō′bəl, *Sp.* krēs·tō′väl) A port in Panama at the Atlantic entrance to the Panama Canal.
Cris·to·fo·ro (krēs·tô′fō·rō) Italian form of CHRISTOPHER.
cri·te·ri·on (krī·tir′ē·ən) *n. pl.* **·te·ri·a** (-tir′ē·ə) or **·te·ri·ons** **1** A standard by which a correct judgment can be made; a model or example. **2** A test, rule, or measure for distinguishing between the true or false, perfect or imperfect, etc. [<Gk. *kritērion < kritēs* a judge < *krinein* decide]
crit·ic (krit′ik) *n.* **1** One who judges anything by some standard or criterion, particularly one who so judges literary or artistic productions. **2** One who judges severely; a caviler. **3** *Obs.* A critique or review. —*adj.* Pertaining to criticism; critical. [<L *criticus* <Gk. *kritikos < kritēs* a judge. See CRITERION.]
crit·i·cal (krit′i·kəl) *adj.* **1** Of, pertaining to, or characteristic of a critic or criticism. **2** Disposed to judge or discriminate with care and precision. **3** Given to severe judgment; faultfinding; carping. **4** Based upon principles or methods of criticism; analytical. **5** Of doubtful result; risky; perilous. **6** Contributing to a decisive judgment: *critical evidence.* **7** *Pathol.* Pertaining to a crisis in the course of a disease. **8** *Math.* Relating to the coalescence of different values. **9** *Physics* Designating a constant value or point indicating a decisive change in a specified condition, as temperature, pressure, speed, etc. **10** Necessary for the prosecution of a war: said of any material for which there is no substitute and of which there is an insufficient supply. See synonyms under CAPTIOUS, MINUTE. —**crit′i·cal·ly** *adv.* —**crit′i·cal·ness** *n.*
critical angle See under ANGLE.
critical point *Physics* The point at which the densities and other physical properties of the liquid and gaseous states of a substance are indistinguishable from each other.
critical solution temperature *Physics* The temperature above which any substance is soluble in any proportion in its solvent: also called *consolute temperature.*
critical speed *Physics* The speed at which a rotating shaft becomes dynamically unstable, and which, if maintained, will result in serious vibration and resonance effects.
critical temperature *Physics* A temperature which is characterized by a change or transition; specifically, the temperature above which a substance can exist only in the gaseous state, no matter what pressure may be applied.
crit·ic·as·ter (krit′ik·as′tər) *n.* A petty critic: a term of contempt. [<CRITIC + -ASTER] —**crit′ic·as′try** *n.*
crit·i·cism (krit′ə·siz′əm) *n.* **1** The act or art of criticizing. **2** A discriminating judgment; an evaluation. **3** A severe or unfavorable judgment. **4** The principles or rules for judging anything, especially works of literature or art. **5** A review, article, etc., expressing a critical judgment. See synonyms under ANIMADVERSION.
crit·i·cize (krit′ə·sīz) *v.t. & v.i.* **·cized,** **·ciz·ing** **1** To examine and judge as a critic. **2** To judge severely; censure. Also *Brit.* **crit′i·cise.** —**crit′i·ciz′a·ble** *adj.* —**crit′i·ciz′er** *n.*
cri·tique (kri·tēk′) *n.* **1** A criticism; critical review. **2** The art of criticism. [<F]
Crit·ten·den (krit′ən·dən), **Eugene Casson,**

born 1880, U.S. physicist; assistant director of the National Bureau of Standards.
crit·ter (krit′ər) *n. U.S. Dial.* **1** A domestic animal. **2** Any living creature. [Var. of CREATURE]
crizz·ling (kriz′ling) *n.* The fine cracks which appear in or on the surface of glass as a result of local chilling in the process of manufacture. [? <CRAZE, *v.* (def. 5)]
croak (krōk) *v.i.* **1** To utter a hoarse, low-pitched cry, as a frog or raven. **2** To speak in a low, hoarse voice. **3** To talk in a doleful tone; forbode evil; grumble. **4** *Slang* To die. —*v.t.* **5** To utter with a croak. **6** *Slang* To kill. —*n.* A hoarse vocal sound, as of a frog or raven. [Imit. Cf. OE *cracethan* croak.] —**croak′y** *adj.*
croak·er (krō′kər) *n.* **1** Any of various animals that croak; especially, one of a class of marine fishes, the grunts. **2** One who speaks dismally or forebodes evil; an alarmist.
Cro·at (krō′at, -ət) *n.* **1** A Slavic native of Croatia. **2** The Croatian language.
Croa·tan Sound (krō′tan) A strait between eastern North Carolina and Roanoke Island.
Cro·a·tia A republic founded from Yugoslavia; 21,611 square miles; capital, Zagreb; formerly an independent kingdom; *Serbo-Croatian: Hr·vat·ska.*
Cro·a·tian *adj.* Pertaining to Croatia or the Croats. —*n.* **1** A Croat. **2** The South Slavic language of the Croats.
Croatoan The word found in 1591 carved on a tree on Roanoke Island, the only clue to the vanished colonists, including Virginia Dare, settled there in 1587 by Sir Walter Raleigh.
Cro·ce (krō′chā), **Benedetto,** 1866–1952, Italian philosopher, critic, historian, and statesman.
cro·ce·in (krō′sē·in) *n. Chem.* One of many artificially produced yellow and bright-red dyes, generally formed of diazo and sulfonic acid derivatives of benzene and naphthol. [<L *croceus* yellow + -IN]
cro·chet (krō·shā′) *v.t. & v.i.* **·cheted** (-shād′), **·chet·ing** (-shā′ing) To form or ornament (a fabric) by interlacing thread with a hooked needle. [<n.] —*n.* A kind of fancywork produced by crocheting: now chiefly attributive, as in *crochet hook.* [<F, dim. of *croche* a hook]
cro·cid·o·lite (krə·sid′ə·līt) *n.* **1** A fibrous, silky, blue or green hydrous silicate; blue asbestos. **2** A yellow alteration product of this silicate used as a gemstone; tiger's-eye. [<Gk. *krokis, -idos* nap of cloth + -LITE]
cro·cin (krō′sin) *n.* A vivid red powder, $C_{44}H_{66}O_{28}$, obtained from saffron and from the fruit of a Chinese gardenia (*Gardenia jasminoides*): used as a dye. [<L *crocus* saffron (<Gk. *krokos*) + -IN]
cro·cine (krō′sin, -sēn) *adj.* Of or pertaining to the crocus.
crock[1] (krok) *n.* **1** An earthenware pot or jar. **2** A fragment of earthenware. —*v.t.* To store in a crock, as butter. [OE *crocca*]
crock[2] (krok) *n.* **1** The black product of combustion; soot. **2** The coloring matter that rubs off from cloth; smut. —*v.t.* To stain; soil. [Origin uncertain]
crock[3] (krok) *n. Brit. Dial.* **1** An old ewe. **2** A broken-down horse. **3** *Slang* A worthless, decrepit, or disabled person. **4** *Slang* One who is not expert at a game or sport; a duffer. —*v.i.* To become weak or sick. [ME *crocke* <Scand. Cf. Sw. *krake* a decrepit horse.]
Crock·er (krok′ər), **Charles,** 1822–88, U.S. financier.
crock·er·y (krok′ər·ē) *n.* Earthenware; earthen vessels collectively.
crock·et (krok′it) *n.* **1** A projecting ornament usually terminating in a curve or roll of foliage and flowers: used to decorate pastoral staffs and the angles of pinnacles, spires, gables, and cornices. **2** A terminal tine of a deer's antler. [<AF *croquet,* OF *crocket,* dim. of *croche* hook]
Crock·ett (krok′it), **David,** 1786–1836, U.S. frontiersman and congressman, killed defending the Alamo: called *Davy Crockett.* — **Samuel Rutherford,** 1860–1914, Scottish clergyman and novelist.

croc·o·dile (krok′ə·dīl) *n.* **1** A large, lizardlike, amphibious reptile (order *Crocodilia*) widely distributed in tropical regions, with long jaws, armored skin, and webbed feet; especially, the Nile crocodile (*Crocodylus niloticus*), and the American crocodile (*C. americanus*). The head is longer and narrower than that of an alligator, and the lower molars shut into marginal notches instead of pits. **2** A gavial. [Earlier *cocodrille* <OF <Med. L *cocodrillus,* alter. of L *crocodilus* <Gk. *krokodilos* lizard, crocodile.]

CROCODILE
(Nile: to 18 feet long; American: to 14 feet)

Croc·o·dile (krok′ə·dīl) See LIMPOPO.
crocodile bird A small black-headed plover (*Pluvianus aegyptius*) of northern Africa, that often perches on crocodiles and devours their insect parasites.
crocodile tears Simulated or pretended weeping; hypocritical grief: from the ancient tale that the crocodile weeps over those he devours.
croc·o·dil·i·an (krok′ə·dil′ē·ən) *adj.* **1** Of, pertaining to, or like a crocodile. **2** Of an order (*Crocodilia*) of crocodiles, alligators, and similar reptiles. —*n.* One of the *Crocodilia.* Also **croc′o·dil′e·an.**
cro·co·ite (krō′kō·it) *n.* An adamantine to vitreous, hyacinth-red, translucent lead chromate, $PbCrO_4$, crystallizing in the monoclinic system: often called *red-lead ore.* Also **cro·coi·site** (krō·kō′ə·sīt). [<Gk. *krokoeis* saffron-colored]
cro·cus (krō′kəs) *n. pl.* **cro·cus·es** or **cro·ci** (krō′sī) **1** Any of a genus (*Crocus*) of plants of the iris family, with long grasslike leaves and large flowers. **2** The flower of this plant. **3** A red or yellow polishing powder of iron oxide. [<L <Gk. *krokos* saffron]
Croe·sus (krē′səs) A wealthy, sixth century B.C. king of Lydia; hence, any very wealthy man.
croft (krôft, kroft) *n.* A small field near a house. —*v.t.* To bleach (fabrics or clothes) on the grass in the sun. [OE, a field]
croft·er (krôf′tər, krof′-) *n.* A tenant cultivating a croft.
crois·sant (krwä·sän′) *n. French* A small, crescent-shaped yeast dough roll.
Croix de Guerre (krwä də gâr′) A French decoration for bravery, awarded to officers, non-commissioned officers, and enlisted men; literally, cross of war.
cro·jik (krō′jik) *n.* A crossjack: altered form.
Cro·ker (krō′kər), **John Wilson,** 1780–1857, English essayist and politician. — **Richard,** 1841–1922, U.S. politician: known as *Boss Croker.*
Cro-Mag·non (krō·mag′non, *Fr.* krō·mà·nyôn′) A member of a prehistoric race of tall, erect men: so called from the name of a cave in the Dordogne department, France, where their remains have been found. The Cro-Magnons are associated with Aurignacian culture, and are considered to belong to the same species (*Homo sapiens*) as modern man. —*adj.* Pertaining or relating to the Cro-Magnon race.
Cro·mer (krō′mər), **Earl of,** 1841–1917. Evelyn Baring, British colonial administrator and diplomat.
crom·lech (krom′lek) *n.* **1** An ancient sepulchral structure consisting of a large flat stone resting on upright unhewn stones. **2** An ancient monument of standing stones arranged in a circle. [<Welsh <*crom* bent + *llech* flat stone]
cro·mor·na (krə·môr′nə) *n.* A clarinetlike reed-stop in an organ. [<F *cromorne,* alter. of G *krummhorn* crooked horn]

Cromp·ton (kromp′tən), **Samuel,** 1753–1827, English inventor of the spinning mule.

Crom·well (krom′wel, -wəl, krum′-), **Oliver,** 1599–1658, English general and statesman; lord protector of England 1653–58. —**Richard,** 1626–1712, son of the preceding; lord protector of England 1658–59. —**Thomas,** 1485?–1540, English statesman.

Cromwell Current A long, swift Pacific equatorial current running eastward just beneath the surface and terminating at the Galapagos Islands. [after Townsend *Cromwell,* 1922–58, U. S. oceanographer]

Crom·wel·li·an (krom·wel′ē·ən, krum-) *adj.* **1** Of or pertaining to Oliver Cromwell or his times. **2** Pertaining to or naming a severe, angular style of furniture prevalent in England under the Protectorate.

crone (krōn) *n.* **1** A withered old woman. **2** *Rare* A senile man. —*v.i.* **croned, cron·ing** To talk like a crone. [<Du. *kronye* an old ewe <OF *carogne* carcass]

Cron·je (krōn′yə), **Piet Arnoldus,** 1840?–1911, Boer general.

Cro·nus (krō′nəs) See KRONOS.

cro·ny (krō′nē) *n. pl.* **·nies** A familiar friend. [<Gk. *chronios* contemporary; orig. university slang]

croo (kro͞o) *v.i. Brit. Dial.* To coo. Also **crood** (kro͞od). [Imit.]

croo·dle (kro͞od′l) *v.i. Scot.* To coo; coax.

crook (kro͝ok) *n.* **1** A bend or curve; also, something bent or crooked. **2** The curved or bent part of a thing: the *crook* of a branch. **3** A genuflection. **4** A device; scheme; artifice. **5** An implement with a crook in it: a shepherd's *crook.* **6** *Scot.* A pothook. **7** *Colloq.* A criminal; swindler; cheat. **8** *Austral. Slang* Ill; out of sorts; also, angry; annoyed. —**to go crook at** *Austral. Slang* To be angry at. —*v.t.* To bend; make crooked. —*v.i.* To grow crooked. See synonyms under BEND, TWIST. [<ON *krōkr*]

crook·back (kro͝ok′bak′) *n.* A person with a crooked back; a hunchback: also *crouchback.* —**crook′–backed′** *adj.*

crook·ed (kro͝ok′id) *adj.* **1** Not straight; having angles or curves. **2** Not straightforward in conduct. **3** Tricky; dishonest. —**to be** (or **go**) **crooked on** *Austral. Slang* To be ill-disposed toward. See synonyms under IRREGULAR. —**crook′ed·ly** *adv.* —**crook′ed·ness** *n.*

Crookes (kro͝oks), **Sir William,** 1832–1919, English physicist and chemist.

Crookes' space *Physics* A non–luminous region in a vacuum tube containing a gas at low pressure, through which an electric discharge is passing. [after Sir William *Crookes*]

Crookes' tube *Physics* A vacuum tube in which the gases are exhausted to a high degree, permitting the free movement of molecules.

crook·neck (kro͝ok′nek′) *n.* One of several varieties of squash with a long, curved neck.

crool (kro͞ol) *v.i.* To gurgle. [Imit.]

croon (kro͞on) *v.t. & v.i.* **1** To sing or hum in a low, monotonous manner; specifically, to sing (popular songs) with exaggerated sentiment or pathos. **2** *Rare* To bellow in a muffled tone. —*n.* **1** A low, mournful humming or singing; the sound made in crooning. **2** A crooning song. [<MDu. *kronen* sing softly, lament] —**croon′er** *n.*

croon song A song of exaggerated sentiment and pathos, adapted for crooning or humming.

crop (krop) *n.* **1** Cultivated plants or grains collectively. **2** The soil product of a particular kind, place, or season. **3** The yield or seasonal product of things other than plants or grains: a *crop* of lambs or calves; the entire yield of anything. **4** The act of cutting; also, the result of cutting; specifically, a short haircut. **5** The first stomach of a bird: a large, pouch-like reservoir at the base of the distensible gullet, serving for preliminary maceration of food; a craw. **6** A growth of hair or beard, especially when short and stiff. **7** A hunting or riding whip with a leather loop for a lash. **8** A collection of things produced: a *crop* of lies. **9** An earmark. **10** The hollow behind a cow's shoulders. **11** An entire hide prepared for sole leather. —*v.* **cropped, crop·ping** *v.t.* **1** To cut or eat off the stems or ends of, as grass or vegetables. **2** To pluck or reap. **3** To cut off closely, as hair; trim, as a dog's ears or tail; formerly, to trim (the ears) of a criminal for punishment. **4** To raise a crop or crops on; cause to bear crops. —*v.i.* **5** To appear above the surface; sprout: with *up* or *out.* **6** To develop or come up unexpectedly: with *up* or *out.* **7** To bear or yield a crop or crops. [OE *cropp*]

crop–eared (krop′ird′) *adj.* **1** Having the ears cropped. **2** With the hair cut short above the ears: said of the Roundheads.

crop·per[1] (krop′ər) *n.* **1** One who raises crops on shares. **2** A tool or machine that crops. **3** A plant that produces a crop: generally with *good, bad, heavy,* etc.: Corn is a heavy *cropper* in Kansas.

crop·per[2] (krop′ər) *n.* A fall, as from a horse when one is thrown over the horse's head. —**to come a cropper 1** To fall headlong, as from a horse. **2** To fail disastrously in an undertaking. [? < *neck and crop* completely, thoroughly]

crop rotation A method of conserving soil productivity by planting dissimilar crops in successive seasons, thereby in one season replenishing the soil nutrients expended in a previous season, checking a disease cycle, etc.

cro·quet (krō·kā′) *n.* **1** An outdoor game played by knocking wooden balls through a series of wire arches by means of mallets. **2** The act of croqueting. —*v.i.* **cro·queted** (krō·kād′), **cro·quet·ing** (krō·kā′ing) In croquet, to drive one's opponent's ball away from its objective by placing one's own ball in contact with it and striking the latter sharply, keeping it in position with the foot. [<AF *croquet,* var. of *crochet.* See CROCHET.]

cro·quette (krō·ket′) *n.* A ball or cake of previously cooked, minced food, fried in deep fat or baked. [<F < *croquer* crunch]

cro·qui·gnole (krō′kə·nōl, -kin·yōl) *n.* A kind of permanent wave in which the hair is wound from the ends toward the scalp, after which it is treated with chemical heat. Also **croquignole wave.** [<F, a fillip < dial. F *croquer* < *crocher* hook < *croc* a hook]

cro·quis (krô·kē′) *n. French* A rough likeness or quick sketch, especially of a fashion design.

crore (krôr, krōr) *n.* In India, ten millions or one hundred lakhs: a *crore* of rupees. [< Hind. *karōr*]

cro·sier (krō′zhər) *n.* **1** A staff surmounted by a crook or cross, borne by or before a bishop or archbishop on occasions of ceremony. **2** *Bot.* A circinate or coiled young fern frond. Also spelled *crozier.* [<OF *crocier* staff-bearer <Med. L *crociarius* < *crocia* bishop's crook]

Cro·sier (krō′zhər) The Southern Cross constellation; Crux. See CONSTELLATION.

cross (krôs, kros) *n.* **1** A sacred or mystic symbol in many ancient religions, consisting of two intersecting lines, supposed to have been originally emblematic of the union of the active and passive elements in nature. **2** That

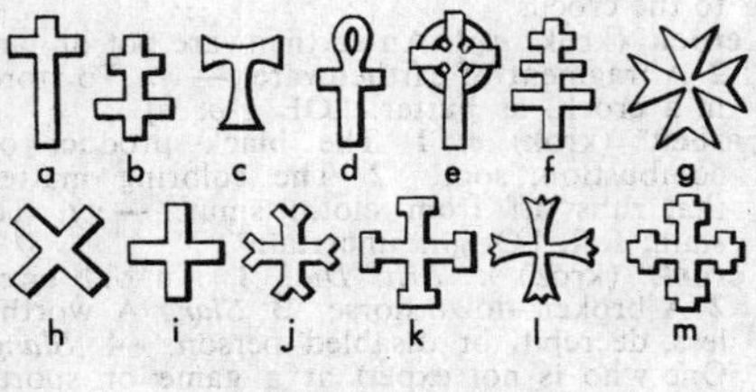

TYPES OF CROSSES

a. Latin cross.
b. Cross of Lorraine.
c. Tau cross.
d. Ansate cross.
e. Celtic cross.
f. Papal cross.
g. Maltese cross.
h. St. Andrew's cross.
i. Greek cross or cross of St. George.
j. Cross fourchée.
k. Jerusalem cross.
l. Cross fleury.
m. Cross crosslet.

which resembles a cross: to mark a ballot with a *cross.* **3** An ancient instrument of torture in the form of a cross, on which criminals were fastened and exposed until they died from exhaustion. **4** Any suffering borne patiently for Christ's sake; a trial; tribulation. **5** A structure in the form of or surmounted by a cross, erected in some public place for devotional or memorial purposes. **6** *Biol.* **a** A mixing of varieties or breeds of plants or animals. **b** The product of any intermingling of strains; a hybrid or mongrel. **7** Anything that resembles or is intermediate between two other things: a *cross* between prose and poetry. **8** An old English coin stamped with a cross. **9** *Her.* A figure used as a bearing. **10** An ornament, in some form of the cross, worn as a distinction by knights of various orders and by persons honored for exceptional merit or bravery. **11** *Electr.* The accidental contact of two wires so that a portion of the current from one flows to the other. **12** The geometric mean of two formulas: used in index numbers. —**to take the cross** To turn crusader. —*v.t.* **1** To pass, move or extend from side to side of; traverse; span. **2** To cancel, as by marking with crossed lines: with *off* or *out.* **3** To lay or place over or across: to *cross* the legs. **4** To intersect, as streets or lines. **5** To draw a line across. **6** To meet and pass: Your letter *crossed* mine. **7** To transport across: He *crossed* his army yesterday. **8** To make the sign of the cross upon or over. **9** To obstruct or hinder; thwart. **10** To cause, as plants or animals, to interbreed; hybridize; crossbreed. **11** *Naut.* To put (a yard) in place across a mast. —*v.i.* **12** To intersect; lie athwart. **13** To pass, move, or extend from side to side; traverse; span. **14** To meet and pass. **15** To breed together; interbreed. —**to cross one's mind** To occur to one. —**to cross one's palm 1** To pay a fortune–teller by marking crosses on his or her palm with a coin and then laying the coin in the fortune–teller's hand. **2** To pay someone money; make a bribe. —**to cross swords** To fight with swords; hence, to contest with. —**to cross up** *Colloq.* To play the traitor to; betray: He *crossed* me *up.* —*adj.* **1** Resulting from or expressive of peevishness or ill–humor; out of humor; disagreeable; peevish. **2** Transverse; crossing; intersecting. **3** Hybrid. **4** Contrary. See synonyms under CAPTIOUS, FRETFUL. —*adv.* **1** Across; crosswise; transversely. **2** Adversely; contrarily; counter. [OE *cros* <ON *kross* <L *crux*] —**cross′ly** *adv.* —**cross′ness** *n.*

—**ansate cross** The tau cross with a loop at the top: also called *crux ansata.* Also **ansated cross.** See ANKH.

—**Calvary cross** *Her.* A Latin cross set on three graduated steps.

—**Celtic cross** An upright cross having a circle behind the crossbeam.

—**cross crosslet** A cross having a small cross near the end of each arm.

—**cross fleu·ry** (flo͞o′rē) A cross whose arms end in fleurs–de–lis.

—**cross for·mée** (fôr·mā′) A cross having arms that gradually expand from the central crossing and nearly form a square. The Maltese cross is a modification of this.

—**cross four·chée** (fo͞or·shā′) A cross proportioned like the Greek cross but having each extremity forked.

—**fiery cross** A cross of light wood whose ends were set on fire, formerly used as a call to arms in Scotland.

—**Geneva cross** A red St. George's or Greek cross on a white ground, worn by members of the Red Cross Society as a badge of neutrality.

—**Greek cross** A cross formed by an upright crossing the middle of a beam of equal length. See also *gammadion.*

—**Iron Cross** A Maltese cross awarded by Germany for conspicuous military service: instituted by Prussia in 1813.

—**Jerusalem cross** A cross having four arms, each ending in a crossbar: also **cross potent.**

—**Latin cross** A cross in which the upright is longer than the beam which crosses it near the top: the cross used by the ancient Romans for crucifixions: also called *crux immissa.*

—**Lorraine cross** A cross having two horizontal arms, the lower one longer than the other: also **cross of Lorraine.**

—**Maltese cross** An eight–pointed cross formed by four arrowheads joining at their points: the badge of the Knights of Malta, worn as an order of chivalry: also **Cross of Malta.**

—**Papal cross** A cross having three crossbars or transoms, the top one the shortest and the bottom one the longest.

—**Patriarchal cross** A cross having two horizontal arms like those of the Lorraine cross but placed nearer together.

— St. Andrew's cross An oblique cross in the form of the letter X: also called *crux decussata.* See SALTIRE.
— St. George's cross The cross of St. George, the patron saint of England: same shape as the Greek cross.
— St. Patrick's cross A cross like the diagonal St. Andrew's cross.
— tau cross A cross in the form of a T: also called *crux commissa.* Also **St. Anthony's cross.** See TAU.
— Victoria Cross A Maltese cross awarded for conspicuous bravery to members of the British army or navy and the Royal Air Force: instituted in 1856.

Cross (krôs, kros) *n.* **1** The emblem of Christianity, a symbolical representation of the instrument of punishment on which Christ died. **2** The crucifixion of Christ; the atonement. **3** The Christian religion; Christianity.

Cross (krôs, kros) A river in SE Nigeria, flowing 300 miles west to the Gulf of Guinea.

Cross (krôs, kros), **Wilbur Lucius,** 1862–1948, U.S. educator and politician.

cross·band (krôs′band′, kros′-) *v.t.* To arrange (plywood) so that the grain in each layer is at right angles to the grain of the adjoining layers. **— cross′band′ing** *n.*

cross·bar (krôs′bär′, kros′-) *n.* A transverse bar or line used in any structure. **—** *v.t.* To secure or mark with transverse bars. **— cross′-barred′** *adj.*

cross-bed·ded (krôs′bed′id, kros′-) *adj. Geol.* Characterized by subsidiary beds or layers of rock cutting across the main stratification.

cross·bill (krôs′bil′, kros′-) *n.* A finchlike bird (genus *Loxia),* the points of whose mandibles cross each other when the beak is closed.

cross·birth (krôs′bûrth′, kros′-) *n. Med.* Any abnormal presentation of a fetus before delivery which requires a manual turning in the womb.

cross·bones (krôs′bōnz′, kros′-) *n.* A representation of two bones crossing each other, usually surmounted by a skull, as a symbol of death.

cross·bow (krôs′bō′, kros′-) *n.* A medieval missile weapon consisting of a bow fixed transversely on a grooved stock. **— cross′·bow′man** *n.*

cross·breed (krôs′brēd′, kros′-) *v.t.* & *v.i.* **·bred, ·breed·ing** *Biol.* To produce a strain or animal by interbreeding or blending two varieties; mix together; hybridize. **—** *n.* A strain or animal produced by crossbreeding; a hybrid; mongrel. **— cross′bred′** *adj.*

cross bun A hot cross bun.

cross·but·tock (krôs′but′ək, kros′-) *n.* **1** A throw in wrestling in which the wrestler, having his back to his opponent, throws him over his hip. **2** Any unexpected setback.

cross-coun·try (krôs′kun′trē, kros′-) *adj.* Of or pertaining to a route across the country fields and lots, regardless of roads.

cross-cut (krôs′kut′, kros′-) *v.t.* **-cut, -cut·ting** To cut crosswise or through; run across; intersect. **—** *adj.* Used or made for the purpose of cutting something across: a *cross-cut* saw. **—** *n.* A cut across or a shortcut.

crosse (krôs, kros) *n.* A lacrosse stick.

cross-ex·am·ine (krôs′ig·zam′in, kros′-) *v.t.* **·ined, ·in·ing 1** To question anew (a witness called by the opposing party) for the purpose of testing the reliability of his previous testimony. **2** To cross-question generally. **— cross′-ex·am′i·na′tion** *n.* **— cross′-ex·am′·in·er** *n.*

cross-eye (krôs′ī′, kros′-) *n.* Strabismus. **— cross′-eyed′** *adj.*

cross-fer·ti·li·za·tion (krôs′fûr′tə·lə·zā′shən, kros′-) *n.* **1** *Biol.* The fertilization of an organism by the union of sexually differentiated reproductive cells or gametes, one from the ovum and one from the sperm. **2** *Bot.* The fertilization of one plant or flower by the pollen from another.

cross-fer·ti·lize (krôs′fûr′tə·līz, kros′-) *v.t.* **·lized, ·liz·ing** To fertilize (a plant or animal) by cross-fertilization.

cross-fig·ure (krôs′fig′yər, kros′-) *n.* A style of pattern in veneer consisting of a roll or dip of the grain approximately at right angles to the long axis of the tree.

cross·fire (krôs′fīr′, kros′-) *n.* **1** *Mil.* The intersection of two lines of fire; a shooting from two different points so that the lines of fire cross. **2** Any like situation: a *crossfire* of congratulations. **3** *Electr.* The interference in a telegraph or telephone circuit of impulse currents from another communication channel. **—** *v.i.* **·fired, ·fir·ing** To shoot from different points so that the lines of fire intersect.

Cross-Florida Waterway A system of linked canals, rivers, and lakes extending 155 miles across the Florida peninsula: also *Okeechobee Waterway.*

cross·foot (krôs′fŏŏt′, kros′-) *n.* A form of clubfoot which compels walking on the outer border of the foot, with the sole turned inward.

cross-grained (krôs′grānd′, kros′-) *adj.* **1** Having the grain gnarled and hard to cut: a *cross-grained* board. **2** Hard to please or persuade; stubborn; perverse: a *cross-grained* man.

cross-hair (krôs′hâr′, kros′-) *n.* One of two fine threads or strands, as of a spider's web, crossed in the center of the focal plane of an optical instrument, to define the exact point to which the readings of the circle or micrometer refer: also called *cross-wire.*

cross-hatch (krôs′hach′, kros′-) *v.t.* To shade, as a picture, by crossed lines, either diagonal or rectangular. **— cross′-hatch′ing** *n.*

cross-head (krôs′hed′, kros′-) *n. Mech.* **1** A beam across the top of something; specifically, a block sliding upon one guide bar, or between two or more bars, to move a piston in a straight line, axial with the cylinder. **2** The connection between the piston and the connecting rods of a reciprocating engine.

cross-in·dex (krôs′in′deks, kros′-) *v.t.* & *v.i.* To insert cross-references in (an index, etc.).

cross·ing (krôs′ing, kros′-) *n.* **1** The place where something, as a roadway or waterway, may be crossed; a ford. **2** Intersection, as of threads or roads. **3** The act of crossing.

cross·jack (krôs′jak′, kros′-) *n. Naut.* The sail carried on the lower yard on the mizzenmast of a full-rigged ship: commonly altered to *crojik.*

cross·let (krôs′lit, kros′-) *n. Her.* A small cross. [<AF *croiselette,* dim. of OF *crois* cross]

cross·light (krôs′līt′, kros′-) *n.* A light whose rays cross other rays, lighting up what these left dark.

cros·sop·te·ryg·i·an (kro·sop′tə·rij′ē·ən) *n. Zool.* Any of a group *(Crossopterygii)* of bony fishes abundant in the Devonian period, having paddle-shaped, lobate fins: they are regarded as the direct ancestors of amphibians. [<NL *Crossopterygii* <Gk. *krossoi* fringe + *pterygia* fins of a fish, pl. dim. of *pteryx* wing]

cross-o·ver (krôs′ō′vər, kros′-) *n.* **1** A place at which one traverses a road, river, etc.; intersection; passageway. **2** The intersection of two electric lines. **3** A part of a woman's coat, dress, or wrap which crosses from one side to the other. **4** *Genetics* An interchange of parts between two homologous chromosomes in meiosis: known also as *recombination.*

cross·patch (krôs′pach′, kros′-) *n.* A cranky, ill-tempered person.

cross-peen (krôs′pēn′, kros′-) *n.* A chisel-like peen on a hammer head, with a blunted edge parallel to the shaft.

cross·piece (krôs′pēs′, kros′-) *n.* A piece of material of any kind crossing another.

cross-pol·li·nate (krôs′pol′ə·nāt, kros′-) *v.t.* **·nat·ed, ·nat·ing** To cross-fertilize.

cross-pol·li·na·tion (krôs′pol′ə·nā′shən, kros′-) *n. Bot.* **1** Cross-fertilization of flowering plants. **2** Hybridization.

cross-pur·pose (krôs′pûr′pəs, kros′-) *n.* **1** A purpose which antagonizes another; a conflicting aim. **2** *pl.* A conversational game in which questions and answers having no natural connection are brought together.

cross-ques·tion (krôs′kwes′chən, kros′-) *v.t.* To question minutely or in different ways, especially to elicit facts. **—** *n.* A question asked in a cross-examination. **— cross′-ques′·tion·ing** *n.*

cross-re·fer (krôs′ri·fûr′, kros′-) *v.* **·ferred, ·fer·ring** *v.t.* To refer to another passage or part. **—** *v.i.* To make a cross-reference.

cross-ref·er·ence (krôs′ref′rəns, kros′-) *n.* **1** A reference from one passage in a book or treatise to another passage in the same work. **2** In a library catalog, and in research and documentation, reference from one subject to another.

cross·road (krôs′rōd′, kros′-) *n.* A road that crosses another, or that crosses from one main road to another. Also **cross′way′.**

cross·roads (krôs′rōdz′, kros′-) *n.* A place where roads cross.

cross·ruff (krôs′ruf′, kros′-) *n.* In card games, a condition in which each of two partners alternately trumps the other's lead: also called *see-saw.*

cross-sec·tion (krôs′sek′shən, kros′-) *n.* **1** A plane section of any object cut at right angles to the longitudinal axis. **2** Any specimen, figure, or diagram presenting a representation typical of the whole.

cross-stitch (krôs′stich′, kros′-) *n.* **1** A double stitch in the form of a cross. **2** Needlework made with this stitch. **—** *v.t.* To make or mark with a cross-stitch.

cross-talk (krôs′tôk′, kros′-) *n.* The garbled sounds heard in a telephone receiver or on the radio as a result of interfering currents from another channel.

cross-thread (krôs′thred′, kros′-) *n.* In hemstitching, one of those threads remaining in a fabric across the space from which a number of parallel threads have been drawn, and which are divided and fastened into clusters in the process of hemstitching. See illustration under HEMSTITCH.

cross-tie (krôs′tī′, kros′-) *n.* A tie or sleeper connecting and supporting the parallel rails of a railroad track. **— cross′-tied′** *adj.*

cross-town (krôs′toun′, kros′-) *adj.* Going across a town or city: a *cross-town* bus. **—** *adv.* Across a town or city: They headed *cross-town.*

cross·tree (krôs′trē′, kros′-) *n. Naut. Usually pl.* One of the pieces of wood or iron set crosswise at the head of a mast to extend the shrouds.

cross·walk (krôs′wôk′, kros′-) *n.* Any lane marked off, usually by white lines, to be used by pedestrians in crossing a street.

cross-wind (krôs′wind′, kros′-) *n.* **1** A wind blowing across the take-off or flight path of an aircraft or the course of a ship. **2** Any wind at right angles to a given course or direction.

cross-wire (krôs′wīr′, kros′-) *n.* **1** One wire crossing another. **2** Cross-hair.

cross·wise (krôs′wīz′, kros′-) *adv.* **1** Across. **2** In the form of a cross. **3** Contrarily; at cross-purposes. Also **cross′ways′.**

cross-word puzzle (krôs′wûrd′, kros′-) See under PUZZLE.

crot·a·lus (krot′ə·ləs, krō′tə-) *n. pl.* **·li** (-lī) Any snake of a genus *(Crotalus)* typical of the rattlesnake family *(Crotalidae).* [<NL <Gk. *krotalon* rattle] **— crot′a·line** (-lin, -līn) *adj.*

crotch (kroch) *n.* **1** A point of division or divergence; a separation into two parts or branches; bifurcation; fork: the *crotch* of a tree. **2** A forked support for a swinging boom when not in use. **3** The region of the human body where the legs separate from the pelvis. [Prob. <AF *croche* crook]

crotched (krocht) *adj.* **1** Having a crotch; forked. **2** Ill-tempered; cross; peevish; crotchety.

crotch·et (kroch′it) *n.* **1** A whimsical notion; a conceit; an eccentricity. **2** *Music* A quarter note. **3** A small hook. See synonyms under WHIM. [<F *crochet.* See CROCHET.]

crotch·et·y (kroch′ə·tē) *adj.* **1** Whimsical; eccentric. **2** Like a crotchet. See synonyms under FICKLE, QUEER. **— crotch′et·i·ness** *n.*

crotch·wood (kroch′wŏŏd′) *n.* An elaborately patterned veneer obtained from the portion of a tree where two limbs join.

cro·ton (krōt′n) *n.* **1** Any member of a genus *(Croton)* of widely dispersed trees and shrubs of the spurge family. **2** An ornamental tropical shrub *(Codiaeum variegatum)* grown for its foliage. [<NL <Gk. *krotōn* a tick; so called from the appearance of the seeds]

Croton bug A small, light-colored, winged,

cosmopolitan cockroach (*Blattella germanica*): also called *German cockroach, water bug.* For illustration see INSECT (injurious). [from *Croton Aqueduct*; so called because the first serious infestation in New York City occurred shortly after Croton aqueduct was opened in 1842]

cro·ton·ic acid (krō-ton'ik, -tŏn'ik) *Chem.* A compound, $C_4H_6O_2$, obtained from croton oil: used in organic synthesis and as a stabilizer in volatile organic solvents.

Cro·ton Lake (krōt'n) An artificial lake formed by damming the **Croton River,** flowing through SE New York: a source of water supply for New York City.

croton oil A pale-yellow or brownish-yellow viscid oil obtained from the seeds of a small East Indian tree (*Croton tiglium*): used as a purgative and rubefacient.

crouch (krouch) *v.i.* 1 To stoop or bend low with the limbs pressed to the body, as a person in fear or an animal ready to spring. 2 To cringe; abase oneself; cower. —*v.t.* 3 To bend low. —*n.* A crouching or the position taken in crouching. [< OF *crochir* be bent < *croc* a hook]

crouch·back (krouch'bak') See CROOKBACK.

crouch·ie (krōō'chē) *adj. Scot.* Round-shouldered; hunch-backed.

croup[1] (krōōp) *n. Pathol.* 1 A disease of the throat characterized by hoarse coughing, laryngeal spasm, and the formation of a false membrane. 2 Loosely, inflammation of the larynx. [Imit.] —**croup'ous, croup'y** *adj.*

croup[2] (krōōp) *n.* The rump; portion of a horse's back behind the saddle. Also **croupe.** [< F *croupe*]

crou·pi·er (krōō'pē-ər, *Fr.* krōō-pyā') *n.* 1 A clerk in charge of a gaming table, collecting winnings and paying losses. 2 The assistant chairman at a public dinner. [< F, lit., one who rides on the croup, an assistant]

crouse (krōōs) *adj. Scot.* Contented and jolly; frisky; saucy. —**crouse'ly** *adv.*

crou·stade (krōō·städ') *n. French.* A small pastry shell filled with custard, mince, oysters, etc.

crou·ton (krōō'ton, krōō·ton'; *Fr.* krōō·tôn') *n.* One of the small crusts or bits of bread fried in butter or oil, often served in soups, etc. [< F *croûton* < *croûte* crust]

crow (krō) *n.* 1 Any of various raucous, oscine birds of the genus *Corvus,* with glossy black plumage; specifically, *C. corone,* the European carrion crow; also, the rook, the raven, and the American species, *C. brachyrhynchos.* ◆Collateral adjective: **corvine.** 2 A crowbar. 3 The cry of a cock, or any like sound. —**as the crow flies** In a straight line. —**to eat crow** *Colloq.* To recant a statement; back down; to humiliate oneself. —*v.i.* 1 To utter the cry of a cock. 2 To exult; boast. 3 To utter sounds expressive of delight, as an infant. —*v.t.* 4 To announce by crowing. [OE *crāwe*]

Crow (krō) *n.* 1 A North American Indian of a Siouan tribe which formerly inhabited the region between the Platte and the Yellowstone. 2 The language of this tribe.

Crow (krō) The constellation Corvus. See CONSTELLATION.

crow·bar (krō'bär') *n.* A straight iron or steel bar, with the point flattened and sometimes set at an angle: used as a lever.

crow·ber·ry (krō'ber'ē, -bər·ē) *n. pl.* **·ries** 1 The black berrylike drupe of a low shrubby evergreen (*Empetrum nigrum*) of the family *Emperaceae*: usually called **black crowberry.** 2 This plant. 3 The bearberry. [Prob. trans. of G *krähenbeeri*]

crow blackbird A large crowlike bird; especially, the purple grackle.

crowd[1] (kroud) *n.* 1 A numerous collection of persons gathered closely together; multitude; throng. 2 A collection of things. 3 The populace mob. 4 *Colloq.* A particular set of people; a clique. See synonyms under ASSEMBLY, COMPANY, MOB, THRONG. [< v.] —*v.t.* 1 To shove or push. 2 To fill to overflowing, as with a crowd; fill to excess. 3 To cram together; force into a confined space. 4 *Colloq.* To put moral pressure upon; press annoyingly. —*v.i.* 5 To gather in large numbers; throng together. 6 To push forward force one's way. 7 To shove or push. See synonyms under HUSTLE, JAM. —**to crowd off** *Naut.* To work a vessel off from the shore

under heavy press of sail. —**to crowd out** To drive out or exclude by pushing or pressing, morally or physically; eliminate by pressure: The press of business has *crowded out* this matter. —**to crowd on sail** *Naut.* To spread a very great amount of sail in proportion to the strength of the wind. [OE *crūdan*] —**crowd'er** *n.*

crowd[2] (kroud) *n.* An ancient violinlike instrument, used in Ireland and Wales: also spelled *cruth, crwth.* Also **croud, crowth.** [< Welsh *crwth* violin]

crow·die (krōō'dē, krōōd'ē) *n. Scot.* 1 Porridge. 2 Pressed curds prepared with butter. Also **crow'dy.**

crow·foot (krō'fŏŏt') *n. pl.* **·foots** for def. 1, **·feet** for defs. 2–6. 1 Any plant of the genus *Ranunculus* (family *Ranunculaceae*); especially, the common meadow or bulb crowfoot (*R. bulbosus*) of the eastern United States. 2 *Naut.* A number of lines or small divergent cords rove through a euphroe to support an awning. 3 Caltrop (def. 1). 4 An arbitrary mark on drawings as for indicating limits of measurement. 5 *Electr.* A form of battery zinc used in a gravity cell. 6 *Aeron.* Crow's-foot.

crow·hop (krō'hop') *n.* 1 A short hop. 2 *U.S.* The bucking of a horse with its back arched and legs stiffened.

crown (kroun) *n.* 1 A decorative circlet or covering for the head, especially as a mark of sovereign power. 2 A sovereign ruler: with *the.* 3 Sovereignty. 4 A wreath or garland

HISTORIC CROWNS
a. Imperial crown of all the Russias.
b. Crown of the German Empire.
c. Iron Crown of Lombardy.
d. Imperial crown of Charlemagne.

for the head. 5 A reward; prize. 6 A complete or perfect state or type; acme. 7 The top or summit; crest; the *crown* of a hill. 8 The top of the head: a bald *crown.* 9 The head itself: Jack fell down and broke his *crown.* 10 The upper portion of a hat. 11 *Dent.* **a** The part of a tooth exposed beyond the gum; especially, the grinding surface of a molar. **b** An artificial substitute for a crown. 12 A clerical tonsure. 13 A coin stamped with a crown or crowned head; in England, a five-shilling piece. 14 A knot made with the strands at the end of a rope. 15 *Naut.* The outer point of junction of the two arms of an anchor. 16 *Archit.* **a** The upper projecting part of a cornice; the corona. **b** A lantern or spire formed by converging flying buttresses. 17 A halo. 18 A circlet for candles. 19 A crown lens. See under LENS. 20 The upper part of a tree, including the living branches with their foliage. 21 *Bot.* The point where stem and root unite in a seed plant. 22 *Her.* A bearing representing a crown. 23 The part of a cut gemstone above the girdle. See also CORONA. —*v.t.* 1 To place a crown or garland on the head of. 2 To enthrone; make a monarch of. 3 To surmount; be the topmost part of. 4 To form the ultimate ornament to or aspect of. 5 To endow with honor or dignity. 6 To finish or bring to completion; consummate. 7 To cause to round upward; make convex, as a road. 8 *Colloq.* To hit, as a person, on the head. 9 In checkers, to make into a king. [< AF *coroune* < L *corona*] —**crown'er** *n.* —**crown'less** *adj.*

crown colony A colonial dependency of Great Britain in which the crown retains control of legislation: usually administered by a governor, with executive and legislative councils.

crown·er (krou'nər) *n. Brit. Dial.* A coroner.

crown·et (krou'nit) *n. Obs.* A coronet.

crown glass See under GLASS.

crown gold Gold 3.9166 fineness, especially as used in British coinage. Compare STERLING.

crown-im·pe·ri·al (kroun'im·pir'ē·əl) *n.* An ornamental plant (*Fritillaria imperialis*) of the lily family, from Persia, bearing a cluster

of large, bell-shaped flowers beneath a crown of leaves.

crown land The real estate belonging hereditarily to the English sovereign: now nearly all surrendered for a fixed annual allowance. Also **crown'lands** (kroun'landz') *n.*

crown lens See under LENS.

crown·let (kroun'lit) *n.* A small crown.

crown·piece (kroun'pēs') *n.* 1 A piece forming the top or crown of anything. 2 The strap in a bridle that goes over the horse's head and is buckled with the cheek straps. See illustration under HARNESS.

Crown Point A village in NE New York; site of two colonial forts, strategic in the French and Indian War and captured from the British in the Revolutionary War.

crown prince The heir apparent to a crown, a monarch's oldest living son.

crown princess 1 The wife of a crown prince. 2 The female heir apparent to a sovereign throne.

crown saw A ring-shaped saw with teeth at right angles to its plane, mounted on a cylinder, and operated with a rotary motion.

crown·vetch (kroun'vech') *n.* Axseed.

crown wheel *Mech.* A wheel with cogs at right angles to its plane, as the wheel that drives the balance in a watch.

crown·work (kroun'wûrk') *n.* 1 A fortification running into the field, designed to cover some advantageous position and to protect other works. 2 *Dent.* The placing of artificial crowns upon teeth; also, the work so done.

crow·quill (krō'kwil') *n.* 1 The quill of a crow. 2 A pen made from a crow's quill: used formerly for the finest kind of writing. 3 A fine metallic pen adapted for similar work.

crow's-foot (krōz'fŏŏt') *n. pl.* **·feet** 1 One of the wrinkles diverging from the outer corner of the eye. 2 A three-pointed embroidery stitch. 3 *Aeron.* An arrangement of short ropes diverging from a main rope: used to distribute strain in the handling of lighter-than-air craft; also *crowfoot.*

crow's-nest (krōz'nest') *n.* 1 *Naut.* A small sheltered platform at a ship's masthead, used by the lookout. 2 Any similar lookout station, as one ashore.

Croy·don (kroid'n) A county borough of NE Surrey, a residential suburb of London and site of a major airport.

croze (krōz) *n.* 1 The groove in the staves of a cask in which the edge of the head is set. 2 A crozer. [? < OF *croz* groove]

croz·er (krō'zər) *n.* A coopers' tool for making a croze.

cro·zier (krō'zhər) See CROSIER.

croz·zle (kroz'əl) *Brit. Dial. v.i.* To burn to coal; char. —*n.* A partially charred coal, as coke.

cru·ces (krōō'sēz) A plural of CRUX.

cru·cial (krōō'shəl) *adj.* 1 Determining absolutely the truth or falsity of a view or theory; decisive; searching. 2 Having the form of a cross. 3 Severe; excruciating. [< F < L *crux, crucis* cross, torture] —**cru'cial·ly** *adv.* —**cru·ci·al·i·ty** (krōō'shē·al'ə·tē) *n.*

cru·ci·ate (krōō'shē·it, -āt) *adj.* 1 Cross-shaped. 2 *Entomol.* Having the wings crossing. 3 *Bot.* Having the parts arranged in the form of a cross with equal arms. [< L *cruciatus,* pp. of *cruciare* crucify < *crux* cross]

cru·ci·ble (krōō'sə·bəl) *n.* 1 A pot or vessel made of a substance that will stand extreme heat, as clay, sand, graphite, platinum, etc., for melting metals or minerals. 2 The hollow place in the bottom of a furnace. 3 A trying and purifying test. [< Med. L *crucibulum* earthen pot]

crucible steel *Metall.* A high-grade steel made by reheating small batches of wrought iron with charcoal, ferromanganese, or other special steels in crucibles placed in specially designed furnaces.

cru·ci·fer (krōō'sə·fər) *n.* 1 Any plant of a large family (Cruciferae) of annual and perennial herbs characterized by pungent, watery juice and regular flowers with four petals in the form of a cross, as mustard, cress, etc. 2 One who bears a cross in a religious procession. [< LL < L *crux* cross + *ferre* bear] —**cru·cif·er·ous** (krōō·sif'ər·əs) *adj.*

cross. 2 *Bot.* Having cruciate flowers; pertaining to or resembling the *Cruciferae.*

cru·ci·fix (kro͞o′sə·fiks) *n.* 1 A cross bearing an effigy of Christ crucified. 2 The cross as a Christian emblem. [< OF *crucefix* < L *cruci fixus* one hanged on a cross < *crux* cross + *figere* fasten]

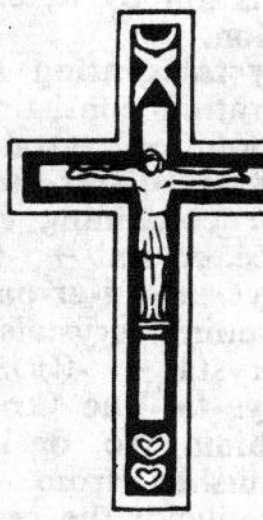

CRUCIFIX (*def. 1*)

cru·ci·fix·ion (kro͞o′sə·fik′·shən) *n.* 1 The act of putting to death by nailing or binding to a cross. 2 Death upon the cross; especially, **the Crucifixion** of Christ on Mount Calvary. 3 Any pictorial representation of Christ's death.

cru·ci·form (kro͞o′sə·fôrm) *adj.* Cross-shaped; cruciate. [< L *crux* cross + -FORM]

cru·ci·fy (kro͞o′sə·fī) *v.t.* **·fied, ·fy·ing** 1 To put to death by fastening to a cross. 2 Figuratively, to mortify; subdue, as impulses or desires: to *crucify* the lusts of the flesh. 3 To torture; torment. [< OF *crucifier,* ult. < L *cruci figere* fasten to a cross] **—cru′ci·fi′er** *n.*

crud (krud) *n.* 1 *Brit. Dial.* Curd. 2 *Slang* Worthless rubbish. [ME *crud* curd; origin uncertain]

crude (kro͞od) *adj.* **crud·er, crud·est** 1 In a state needing preparation for use; not refined; raw; uncooked. 2 Not having reached its complete or mature form; unripe; immature. 3 Lacking in completeness of form or arrangement; exhibiting roughness; incomplete. 4 Characterized by lack of knowledge or skill; imperfect; superficial: a *crude* effort. 5 Not disguised; bare: *crude* statements. 6 Lacking in tact or good taste; uncultured: a *crude* joke. *—n.* Petroleum as it comes from the well; unrefined petroleum and hydrocarbons. [< L *crudus* immature. Akin to CRUEL.] **—crude′ly** *adv.* **—crude′ness** *n.*

Cru·den (kro͞o′dən), **Alexander,** 1701–70, Scottish compiler of a Biblical concordance.

cru·di·ty (kro͞o′də·tē) *n. pl.* **·ties** 1 The state or quality of being crude. 2 A crude act, remark, etc.

cru·el (kro͞o′əl) *adj.* 1 Disposed to inflict suffering; indifferent to others' suffering; pitiless. 2 Unreasonably severe; harsh; distressing. See synonyms under BARBAROUS, HARD, IMPLACABLE. ◆ Homophone: *crewel.* [< F < L *crudelis* severe. Akin to CRUDE.] **—cru′el·ly** *adv.*

cru·el·ty (kro͞o′əl·tē) *n. pl.* **·ties** 1 The disposition to inflict pain. 2 Indifference to the suffering of other beings; inhumanity. 3 The act of inflicting suffering. 4 An inhuman or brutal act.

cru·et (kro͞o′it) *n.* 1 A small glass bottle, as for vinegar. 2 *Brit.* A caster. [< AF, dim. of OF *crue* pot]

Cruik·shank (kro͝ok′shangk), **George,** 1792–1878, English artist and caricaturist.

cruise (kro͞oz) *v.* **cruised, cruis·ing** *v.i.* 1 To sail about on the ocean with no set destination, as for pleasure or in search of plunder. 2 *Colloq.* To wander about; roam. 3 To move or proceed at a moderate speed, or at the optimum speed for sustained travel: This car *cruises* at 50 miles per hour. *—v.t.* 4 To sail over or about. 5 To proceed aimlessly through or across; wander. *—n.* 1 A voyage at sea; a sailing to and fro or from place to place. 2 A cruse. [< Du. *kruisen* < *kruis* cross < L *crux* cross]

cruise missile A guided missile that flies like an airplane at low altitudes.

cruis·er (kro͞o′zər) *n.* 1 A person, vehicle, or ship that cruises. 2 A fast, maneuverable warship, having long cruising radius, with medium tonnage and armament. 3 A small power vessel equipped with complete living arrangements: also called **cabin cruiser.**

cruising radius The longest round trip a ship or airplane can make without refueling.

crul·ler (krul′ər) *n.* A small, twisted cake of sweetened dough, fried brown in deep fat: also spelled *kruller.* [< Du. < *krullen* curl]

crumb (krum) *n.* 1 A small bit, as of crumbled bread. 2 A morsel. 3 The soft inner part of a loaf, as distinguished from the crust. *—v.t.* 1 To break into small pieces with the fingers; crumble. 2 In cooking, to dress or cover with bread crumbs. 3 *Colloq.* To brush crumbs from. Also **crum.** [OE *cruma; b* added on analogy with *dumb, lamb,* etc.]

crum·ble (krum′bəl) *v.t. & v.i.* **·bled, ·bling** To fall or cause to fall to small pieces; disintegrate; decay. *—n.* 1 A crumb. 2 Any crumbly material. [Freq. of CRUMB, *v.*] **—crum′bly** *adj.*

crumb·y (krum′ē) *adj.* **crumb·i·er, crumb·i·est** 1 Having crumbs. 2 Soft, like the crumb of bread. 3 *U.S. Slang* Inferior; shoddy; lousy. Also **crum′my.**

crum·mie (krum′ē, kro͞om′ē) *Scot. adj.* Crooked; bent. *—n.* A cow with crooked horns: often used as a name for any cow.

crum·mock (krum′ək, kro͞om′ək) *n. Scot.* A staff with a crooked head or stem. Also **crum′muk.**

crump (krump, kro͞omp) *adj. Scot. & Brit. Dial.* Crisp; crusty; brittle.

crum·pet (krum′pit) *n.* A thin, leavened batter cake baked on a gridiron and usually toasted and buttered. [Short for *crumpet cake,* ME *crompid cake,* pp. of *crompen* curl up]

crum·ple (krum′pəl) *v.t. & v.i.* **·pled, ·pling** 1 To become or cause to become wrinkled; rumple. 2 *Colloq.* To collapse. *—n.* A wrinkle, as in cloth or the earth; anything crumpled. [Freq. of obs. *crump,* var. of CRIMP] **—crum′pled** *adj.*

crunch (krunch) *v.t.* 1 To chew with a brittle, crushing sound; crush with the teeth. 2 To crush or grind noisily. *—v.i.* 3 To chew noisily. 4 To move or advance with a crushing sound. *—n.* 1 The act or sound of crunching. 2 *U.S. Slang* A critical time, as the moment of decision. [Imit.]

cru·node (kro͞o′nōd) *n. Math.* A point at which a curve crosses itself and therefore has two tangents. [< L *crux* cross + NODE] **—cru·no′dal** *adj.*

cru·or (kro͞o′ôr) *n.* Clotted blood; gore. [< L, gore]

crup·per (krup′ər) *n.* 1 The looped strap that goes under a horse's tail. 2 The rump of a horse; croup. [< F *croupière* < *croupe* CROUP[2]]

cru·ra (kro͞or′ə) Plural of CRUS.

cru·ral (kro͞or′əl) *adj.* Of or pertaining to the leg or the thigh. [< L *cruralis* < *crus* leg]

crus (krus) *n. pl.* **cru·ra** (kro͞or′ə) 1 *Anat.* **a** That part of the leg between the knee and the ankle. **b** *Usually pl.* A stalk or peduncle: applied to compact masses of fibers which connect different parts of the brains. 2 Any part resembling or likened to a leg. [< L, leg]

cru·sade (kro͞o·sād′) *n.* 1 Any of the military expeditions undertaken by European Christians from the 11th through the 13th century to recover the Holy Land from the Moslems. 2 Any expedition under papal sanction against heathens or heretics. 3 Any vigorous concerted movement or cause, especially against public evil. *—v.i.* **·sad·ed, ·sad·ing** To go on or engage in a crusade. [< Sp. *cruzada* < Med. L *cruciata* a crossing < *cruciare* mark with a cross < L *crux* a cross; infl. in form by related F *croisade*] **—cru·sad′er** *n.*

cru·sa·do (kro͞o·sā′dō) *n. pl.* **·does** or **·dos** A former Portuguese gold coin: also spelled *cruzado.* [< Pg., lit., marked with a cross]

cruse (kro͞oz, kro͞os) *n.* A small bottle, flask, or jug; cruet: also spelled *cruise.* [? < ON *krūs* jar, pot]

cru·set kro͞o′sit) *n.* A goldsmith's melting pot. [< F *creuset*]

crush (krush) *v.t.* 1 To press or squeeze out of shape; mash. 2 To smash or grind into fine fragments or particles. 3 To obtain or extract by pressure. 4 To press upon; crowd. 5 To rumple or press out of shape. 6 To put down; subdue; conquer. 7 *Archaic* To burden or oppress. 8 *Rare* To drink. *—v.i.* 9 To become broken or misshapen by pressure. See synonyms under BREAK, CONQUER, JAM, REPRESS, SUBDUE. *—n.* 1 A violent colliding; breaking, bruising, or deforming by violent pressure. 2 A pressing or crowding together; a crowd; jam. 3 *Colloq.* A sudden romantic attachment; infatuation. [< OF *croissir* break < Gmc.] **—crush′er** *n.*

crush hat 1 A soft felt hat that can be folded without injury. 2 A collapsible high hat; opera hat.

Cru·soe (kro͞o′sō), **Robinson** See ROBINSON CRUSOE.

crust (krust) *n.* 1 A hard, thin coating, usually over something softer. 2 The outer part of bread; a bit of bread, especially if stale and hard. 3 The pastry envelope of a pie or the like. 4 An incrustation, especially from wine, on the interior of bottles. 5 A coating, as of coagulated blood or other solidified exudate of the body. 6 The cold, exterior portion or zone of the earth. 7 The part of a horse's hoof on which the shoe is nailed. 8 A crisp firm surface upon snow. 9 *Slang* Insolence; impertinence. *—v.t. & v.i.* To cover with or acquire a crust. [< L *crusta* crust] **—crust′al** *adj.* **—crust′ed** *adj.*

crus·ta·cean (krus·tā′shən) *n.* One of a class of arthropods *(Crustacea)* having crustlike shells, and generally aquatic, including lobsters, crabs, barnacles, sow-bugs, etc. *—adj.* Of or pertaining to the *Crustacea.* [< NL *Crustacea* < L *crusta* crust; with ref. to the shell]

crus·ta·ceous (krus·tā′shəs) *adj.* 1 Having, or pertaining to, a crustlike shell. 2 Crustacean.

crust·er (krus′tər) *n. U.S.* One who hunts game, especially deer or moose, in deep snow when the ice crust will hold the weight of a man but not the quarry: a term of contempt. Also **crust′·hunt′er.**

crus·tose (krus′tōs) *adj.* Crustlike: crustaceous.

crust·y (krus′tē) *adj.* **crust·i·er, crust·i·est** 1 Crustlike. 2 Having or hard as a crust. 3 Morosely curt in manner or speech; surly. See synonyms under MOROSE. **—crust′i·ly** *adv.* **—crust′i·ness** *n.*

crutch (kruch) *n.* 1 A staff with a crosspiece fitting under the armpit, used as a support in walking. 2 Any one of various mechanical devices involving the principle or use of such a support. 3 *Naut.* A forked support for a swinging boom when not in use. 4 The horn on a woman's saddle. 5 A rack. 6 A hooked rod used to immerse sheep while washing. 7 The crotch of a human body. *—v.t.* To prop up, as on crutches. [OE *crycc*]

crutched (krucht) *adj.* Bearing the sign of the cross: The *Crutched* Friars. [Earlier *crouched,* pp. of obs. *crouch* mark with a cross]

cruth, crwth (kro͞oth) See CROWD[2].

crux (kruks) *n. pl.* **crux·es** or **cru·ces** (kro͞o′sēz) 1 A pivotal, fundamental, or vital point. 2 A cross. 3 A tormenting or baffling problem; a perplexing difficulty. [< L, a cross]

Crux (kruks) The Southern Cross. See CONSTELLATION.

crux an·sa·ta (an·sā′tə) See ANSATE CROSS under CROSS.

crux com·mis·sa (kə·mis′ə) See TAU CROSS under CROSS.

crux de·cus·sa·ta (dē′kə·sā′tə) See ST. ANDREW'S CROSS under CROSS.

crux im·mis·sa (i·mis′ə) See LATIN CROSS under CROSS.

cru·za·do (kro͞o·sā′dō) *n.* A crusado. [Var. of CRUSADO]

Cru·zan (kro͞o′zən) *n.* A native or inhabitant of St. Croix. *—adj.* Relating to St. Croix.

cru·zei·ro (kro͞o·zā′rō, *Pg.* -ro͞o) *n.* The gold monetary unit of Brazil, equivalent to 100 centavos. [< Pg. < *cruz* cross < L *crux*]

cry (krī) *v.* **cried, cry·ing** *v.t.* 1 To utter loudly or shout out; exclaim. 2 To proclaim loudly and publicly; advertise loudly, as goods or services. 3 *Archaic* To beg or implore: I *cry* you mercy. 4 To affect (one) in some specified way by weeping: to *cry* oneself to sleep. *—v.i.* 5 To speak, call, or appeal loudly; shout; yell. 6 To utter sounds of grief and lamentation; weep; sob. 7 To weep or shed tears inaudibly. 8 To make characteristic calls: said of animals. See synonyms under CALL, ROAR. **—to cry down** 1 To disparage. 2 To silence or put down by cries. **—to cry quits** To declare to be even, or that neither has the advantage. *—n. pl.* **cries** 1 A loud or passionate utterance; a call; shout; yell. 2 The act of weeping. 3 An earnest appeal; entreaty. 4 Advertisement by outcry; proclamation: the hawker's *cry.* 5 General report or rumor; common saying; public opinion. 6 A pack of dogs; hence, in contempt, a company of per-

sons; party. **7** A subject or topic made temporarily important for political purposes; watchword; party phrase. **8** A word or phrase to rally men in battle; war cry. **9** Demand; requisition: a *cry* for clean streets. **10** The characteristic call of a bird or an animal. **—a far cry** The farthest distance over which a cry can be heard; hence, a long way. **—in full cry** In full pursuit, as hunting dogs when baying in chorus. [< F *crier* < L *quiritare* call out]

cry·ba·by (krī'bā'bē) *n. pl.* **·bies** A person, especially a child, given to crying or complaining over his circumstances.

cry·ing (krī'ing) *adj.* Calling for immediate action or redress; self-proclaiming; notorious: a *crying* shame.

cryo- *combining form* Cold; frost: *cryogenic.* [< Gk. *kryos* frost]

cry·o·bi·ol·o·gy (krī'ō·bī·ol'ə·j) *n.* The study of the effects of freezing and low temperatures on living organisms.

cry·o·gen (krī'ə·jən) *n.* A freezing mixture.

cry·o·gen·ic (krī'ə·jen'ik) *adj.* Pertaining to the study of, or experiments in, low temperatures.

cry·o·gen·ics (krī'ə·jen'iks) *n.* The branch of physics dealing with the phenomena of extreme cold.

cry·o·hy·drate (krī'ə·hī'drāt) *n.* A crystalline eutectic mixture of constant composition and melting point, as of salt with water, which forms below the freezing point of water.

cry·o·lite (krī'ə·līt) *n.* A vitreous, snow-white, translucent fluoride of sodium and aluminum, occurring in Greenland: used in the production of aluminum, soda, and glass, to which it gives a milky hue. Also spelled *kryolite, kryolith.*

cry·om·e·ter (krī·om'ə·tər) *n.* An instrument for measuring a lower temperature than the ordinary mercury thermometer will indicate, as an alcohol thermometer. [< CRYO- + -METER]

cry·oph·o·rus (krī·of'ər·əs) *n.* An instrument for showing the decrease of temperature in water through evaporation: socalled because such decrease may freeze the water. [< CRYO- +-PHOROUS]

cry·o·scope (krī'ə·skōp) *n.* An instrument used for determining the freezing point of liquids and other substances.

cry·os·co·py (krī·os'kə·pē) *n.* The study of the freezing points of solutions, especially in relation to the lowered freezing point of the solute.

cry·o·stat (krī'ə·stat) *n.* A receptacle, constructed on the principle of the Dewar flask, for containing substances studied in low-temperature research; a heat regulator for low temperatures.

cry·o·ther·a·py (krī'ə·ther'ə·pē) *n. Med.* The use of low or freezing temperatures as a therapeutic measure.

cry·o·tron (krī'ə·tron) *n. Electronics* A device for utilizing the superconductivity of certain metals at temperatures approaching that of liquid helium. [< CRYO- + (ELEC)TRON]

crypt (kript) *n.* **1** A secret recess or vault; especially, one used, as in the catacombs, for interment. **2** A vault under some churches, used as a chapel, cemetery, etc. **3** *Physiol.* A minute follicle or secreting cavity of the skin or mucous membrane. [< L *crypta* < Gk. *kryptē* < *kryptos* hidden. Doublet of GROTTO.]

cryp·ta·nal·y·sis (krip'tə·nal'ə·sis) *n. pl.* **·ses** (-sēz) The scientific study and conversion into plain text of cryptograms, ciphers, codes, and other forms of secret communication to which the key is not known. [< CRYPTO- + ANALYSIS] **—cryp·tan·a·lyst** (krip·tan'ə·list) *n.* **—cryp'·tan·a·lyt'ic** *adj.*

cryp·tes·the·sia (krip'təs·thē'zhə, -zhē·ə) *n. Psychol.* Any of various modes of supernormal sensibility, as clairvoyance, telepathy, extrasensory perception, etc. [< CRYPTO- + ESTHESIA]

cryp·tic (krip'tik) *adj.* **1** Secret; occult; arcane. **2** Tending to concealment; puzzling; mysterious. Also **cryp'ti·cal.** [< LL *crypticus* < Gk. *kryptikos* < *kryptos* hidden]

cryp·to- *combining form* Hidden; secret: *cryptogram.* Also, before vowels, **crypt-.** [< Gk. *kryptos* hidden]

cryp·to·clas·tic (krip'tō·klas'tik) *adj. Geol.* Composed of microscopic fragmental grains, derived from preexisting rocks, as shale. [< CRYPTO- + CLASTIC]

cryp·to·cli·mate (krip'tō·klī'mit) *n.* The range of climatic conditions found within a house, building, or other enclosed structure, especially as compared with the *microclimate* of the local area and the *macroclimate* of the entire region.

cryp·to·crys·tal·line (krip'tō·kris'tə·lin, -lēn) *adj. Mineral.* Possessing a crystalline structure which cannot be resolved into distinct individuals even under the microscope: opposed to *phanerocrystalline.*

cryp·to·gam (krip'tə·gam) *n. Bot.* **1** Any of a former division of plants (*Cryptogamia*) that have no true flowers, but propagate by spores, as algae, fungi, lichens, and mosses. **2** A plant lacking true seeds: opposed to *phanerogam.* Also **cryp'to·phyte** (-fīt). [< CRYPTO- + Gk. *gamos* marriage] **—cryp'to·gam'ic** *adj.* **—cryp·tog·a·mous** (krip·tog'ə·məs) *adj.*

cryp·tog·a·my (krip·tog'ə·mē) *n. Bot.* The state or condition of being cryptogamic or having concealed fructification. [< CRYPTO- + -GAMY]

cryp·tog·e·nous (krip·toj'ə·nəs) *adj.* Of obscure origin. Also **cryp·to·ge·net·ic** (krip'tō·jə·net'ik), **cryp·to·gen·ic** (krip'tə·jen'ik). [< CRYPTO- + -GENOUS]

cryp·to·gram (krip'tə·gram) *n.* A written communication in the form of symbols chosen arbitrarily but according to a system permitting reconversion to the original plain text, as a cipher or code.

cryp·to·graph (krip'tə·graf, -gräf) *n.* **1** A cryptogram. **2** A system of cipher-writing; a cipher. **—cryp·tog·ra·pher** (krip·tog'rə·fər), **cryp·tog'ra·phist** *n.* **—cryp'to·graph'ic** *adj.*

cryp·tog·ra·phy (krip·tog'rə·fē) *n.* **1** The art and process of writing in cipher. **2** Any system of writing in secret characters.

cryp·tol·o·gy (krip·tol'ə·jē) *n.* Enigmatic language; cryptography. [CRYPTO- + -LOGY]

cryp·tom·ne·sia (krip'təm·nē'zhə, -zhē·ə) *n. Psychol.* A form of memory which causes experiences to appear to the subject as new, without conscious recognition of or identification with their original source. [< CRYPTO- + Gk. *mnasthai* remember]

cryp·to·nym (krip'tə·nim) *n.* A secret name. [< CRYPTO- + Gk. *onoma, onyma* name] **—cryp·ton·y·mous** (krip·ton'ə·məs) *adj.*

cryp·to·psy·chics (krip'tə·sī'kiks) *n.* Metapsychics.

cryp·to·zo·ic (krip'tə·zō'ik) *adj. Zool.* Of, pertaining to, or designating animals which live in dark and hidden places.

crys·tal (kris'təl) *n.* **1** The solid form assumed by many minerals; specifically, colorless transparent quartz, or rock crystal. **2** *Physics* A homogeneous solid body, exhibiting a definite and symmetrical internal structure, with geometrically arranged cleavage planes and external faces that assume any of a group of patterns associated with peculiarities of atomic structure. **3** Flint glass, or any fine glass, especially as made into high-grade tableware and decorative pieces. **4** A watchglass. **5** A clear, white diamond. **6** A specially shaped and ground piece of quartz or similar material, used to improve radio reception. **—adj.** Composed of or like crystal; extremely clear; limpid. [< OF *cristal* < L *crystallum* clear ice < Gk. *krystallos* < *krystainein* freeze < *kryos* frost] **—crys·tal·lic** (kris·tal'ik) *adj.*

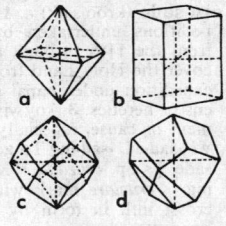

TYPES OF CRYSTALS
a. Tetragonal pyramid.
b. Tetragonal prism.
c. Dodecahedron.
d. Deltahedron.

crystal analysis *Physics* The study of the molecular, atomic, and ionic configuration in crystals, aided by X-ray methods.

crystal ball A ball of crystal or glass used in crystal-gazing.

crystal control *Telecom.* The maintenance of prescribed frequency operation of a radio station by the use of a quartz crystal.

crystal detector *Telecom.* A device consisting of metal electrodes in contact with suitable crystal materials: used to rectify incoming radio signals in a crystal set.

crys·tal·gaz·ing (kris'təl·gā'zing) *n.* The act

of looking into a ball of crystal and pretending to see pictures within it or to exercise divination by it; crystallomancy: also **crystal vision.**

crystal grating *Physics* A very fine diffraction grating consisting of a suitably prepared and mounted crystal: used in X-ray work.

crys·tal·lif·er·ous (kris'tə·lif'ər·əs) *adj.* Bearing or containing crystals. [< L *crystallum* clear ice, crystal + -(I)FEROUS]

crys·tal·lig·er·ous (kris'tə·lij'ər·əs) *adj.* Containing crystals. [< L *crystallum* clear ice, crystal + -(I)GEROUS]

crys·tal·line (kris'tə·lin, -lēn) *adj.* **1** Of, pertaining to, or like crystal or crystals: distinguished from *clastic.* **2** Transparent; pure; pellucid: the *crystalline* lens of the eye. **—n.** A crystallized or partly crystallized substance. [< F *cristallin* < L *crystallinus* < Gk. *krystallinos* < *krystallos.* See CRYSTAL.]

crystalline boron See under BORON.

crystalline lens *Anat.* A transparent, biconvex, lentiform body situated between the iris and the vitreous body of the eye, serving to focus an image upon the retina. Also **crystalline humor.**

crys·tal·lite (kris'tə·līt) *n. Mineral.* One of certain minute, spherical, rod-shaped or hairlike bodies without the true properties of a crystal, but resulting from a crystallizing tendency, observable in thin sections of igneous rock and in slags. [< L *crystallum* clear ice, crystal + -ITE[1]] **—crys·tal·lit·ic** (kris'tə·lit'ik) *adj.*

crys·tal·li·tis (kris'tə·lī'təs) *n. Pathol.* Inflammation of the crystalline lens. [< NL < Gk. *krystallos* crystal + -ITIS]

crys·tal·lize (kris'tə·līz) *v.* **·lized, ·liz·ing** *v.t.* **1** To cause to form crystals or become crystalline. **2** To bring to definite and permanent form. **—v.i. 3** To assume the form of crystals. **4** To assume definite and permanent form. **—crys'tal·liz'a·ble** *adj.* **—crys'·tal·li·za'tion** *n.*

crystallo- *combining form* Crystal: *crystallography.* Also, before vowels, **crystall-.** [< Gk. *krystallos* crystal]

crys·tal·lo·graph·ic (kris'tə·lə·graf'ik) *adj.* Of or pertaining to crystallography. Also **crys'·tal·lo·graph'i·cal.** **—crys'tal·lo·graph'i·cal·ly** *adv.*

crystallographic axes Imaginary lines within a crystal, to which its faces can be referred.

crystallographic indices A series of numbers indicating the relative intercepts of a crystal face upon the crystal axes.

crys·tal·log·ra·phy (kris'tə·log'rə·fē) *n.* The science of crystals, including the study of their geometrical, physical, and chemical structure.

crys·tal·loid (kris'tə·loid) *adj.* Like a crystal; of or pertaining to the crystal state of matter. **—n. 1** *Chem.* One of a class of substances, usually crystallizable, whose solutions are readily diffusible: distinguished from *colloid.* **2** *Bot.* A crystal-like protein body found in plant cells: a protein crystal. [< Gk. *krystalloeidēs* like crystal] **—crys'tal·loi'dal** *adj.*

crys·tal·lo·man·cy (kris'tə·lə·man'sē) *n.* Divination by gazing into a crystal globe. [< CRYSTALLO- + -MANCY]

crys·tal·lon (kris'tə·lon) *n.* A crystal fragment dropped into a saturated solution to provide a nucleus around which the solution may crystallize: also called *seed crystal.* [< Gk., neut. of *krystallos* of crystal]

crys·tal·lose (kris'tə·lōs) *n.* Soluble saccharin: a sweetening compound. [< CRYSTALL(O)- + -OSE]

crystal set A radio receiving set operating with a crystal detector but without vacuum tubes.

crystal system Any of the variously named and classified fundamental patterns by which all crystals may be identified: determined on the basis of the imaginary axes drawn from each face or edge through the center of the crystal. Six major systems are generally recognized. See following table.

CRYSTAL SYSTEMS

	Name	No. of axes	Type example
I	Isometric	3	fluorite, garnet
II	Tetragonal	3	cassiterite, zircon
III	Hexagonal	4	calcite, quartz
IV	Orthorhombic	3	sulfur, topaz
V	Monoclinic	3	gypsum, augite
VI	Triclinic	3	rhodonite

crystal violet A derivative of rosaniline,

used as an indicator in medicine and bacteriology.

Cs *Chem.* Cesium (symbol Cs).

Csa·ba (cho'bo) See BÉKÉSCSABA.

cte·nid·i·um (tə·nid'ē·əm) *n. pl.* **·nid·i·a** (-nid'-ē·ə) *Zool.* **1** One of the respiratory organs of mollusks, resembling a comb. **2** One of the comblike structures situated on the toes of some birds. [< NL < Gk. *ktenidion*, dim. of *kteis* comb]

cteno- *combining form* Comb: *ctenophore.* Also, before vowels, **cten-.** [< Gk. *kteis, ktenos* comb]

cten·oid (ten'oid, tē'noid) *adj. Biol.* Having a comblike margin, as certain plants, and the scales in ctenophores. [< Gk. *ktenoeidēs* like a comb]

cten·o·phore (ten'ə·fôr, -fōr, tē'nə-) *n.* One of the *Ctenophora,* a subphylum or phylum of coelenterates which includes the marine comb jellies. [< NL *Ctenophora* < Gk. *kteis, ktenos* comb + *pherein* bear]

Ctes·i·phon (tes'ə·fon) A ruined ancient city on the Tigris in central Iraq; capital of the Sassanides.

Cu *Chem.* Copper (symbol Cu). [L *cuprum*]

Cuan·za (kwän'zə) A river in central Angola, SW Africa, flowing 600 miles to the Atlantic.

cua·ren·ta (kwä·ren'tä) *n.* A silver coin of Cuba, equal in value to forty centavos. [< Sp., forty]

cub (kub) *n.* **1** The young of the bear, fox, wolf, and certain other carnivores; a whelp. **2** A rough, awkward, uncouth, or ill-mannered youth. **3** A beginner or learner; an apprentice. — *adj.* Young; inexperienced: a *cub* reporter; *cub* pilot. [Origin uncertain] —**cub'bish** *adj.* —**cub'bish·ly** *adv.*

Cu·ba (kyōo'bə) The largest island of the West Indies, comprising a republic; 44,164 square miles; capital, Havana. —**Cu'ban** *adj. & n.*

Cuba li·bre (lē'brə) An alcoholic drink made of rum, lemon juice, and a cola beverage. [< Sp., free Cuba]

Cuban eight *Aeron.* An airplane flight maneuver made up of a 3/4-normal loop, a half-roll, another 3/4-normal loop, and ending with another half-roll.

Cu·ban·go (kōo·vaŋg'gōo) The Portuguese name for the OKOVANGGO.

cu·ba·ture (kyōo'bə·chŏor) *n.* **1** The process of determining the cubical contents of a solid. **2** Cubical contents. Also **cu·bage** (kyōo'bij). [< L *cubus* cube]

cub·by·hole (kub'ē·hōl) *n.* A small, enclosed, space. [< *cubby,* dim. of dial. E *cub* shed + HOLE]

cube¹ (kyōob) *n.* **1** *Geom.* A solid bounded by six equal squares and having all its angles right angles. **2** *Math.* The third power of a quantity; the product of three equal factors. — *v.t.* **cubed, cub·ing** **1** To raise (a number or quantity) to the third power. **2** To find the cubic capacity of. **3** To form or cut into cubes or cubelike shapes; dice: to *cube* potatoes. [< MF < LL *cubus* < Gk. *kybos* cube, die²]

cu·be² (kōo'bā) *n.* A substance extracted from the roots of *Lonchocarpus nicou,* a leguminous plant native to Peru: it contains rotenone and tephrosin and is used as a fish poison. [< Sp. *quibey* < native name]

cu·beb (kyōo'beb) *n.* A berry of an East Indian shrub (*Piper cubeba*) of the pepper family: used in treating urinary and bronchial diseases and often smoked in the form of cigarettes. [< MF *cubèbe* < Med.L *cubeba* < Arabic *kabābah*]

cube root The number which, taken three times as a factor, produces a given number called its cube: 4 is the *cube root* of 64.

cu·bic (kyōo'bik) *adj.* **1** Formed like a cube. **2** Being, or equal to, a cube whose edge is a given unit: a *cubic* foot. **3** *Math.* Of the third power or degree. Also **cu'bi·cal.** [< F *cubique* < L *cubicus* < Gk. *kybikos* < *kybos* cube] —**cu'bi·cal·ly** *adv.* —**cu'bi·cal·ness** *n.*

cu·bi·cle (kyōo'bi·kəl) *n.* **1** A bedroom. **2** A partially enclosed section of a dormitory. **3** Hence, any small room. [< L *cubiculum* bedroom < *cubare* lie down]

cubic measure A unit or system of units for measuring volume, or the amount of space occupied in three dimensions. The principal customary units are given in the table below. See also METRIC SYSTEM.

144 cubic inches (cu. in.)	= 1 board foot (bd. ft.)
1728 cubic inches	= 1 cubic foot (cu. ft.; ft.³)
27 cubic feet	= 1 cubic yard (cu. yd.; yd.³)
128 cubic feet	= 1 cord (cd.)

cu·bic·u·lar (kyōo·bik'yə·lər) *adj.* Of or pertaining to a bedchamber; private. Also **cu·bic'u·lar'y** (-ler'ē). [< L *cubicularis* < *cubiculum.* See CUBICLE.]

cu·bic·u·lum (kyōo·bik'yə·ləm) *n. pl.* **·la** (-lə) **1** A small bedchamber; cubicle. **2** A burial chamber with recesses in the walls for dead bodies, as in the Roman catacombs. Also *Obs.* **cu·bic'u·lo** (-lō). [< L]

cu·bi·form (kyōo'bə·fôrm) *adj.* Shaped like a cube.

cu·bism (kyōo'biz·əm) *n.* A school of modern art concerned with the analysis of form by means of abstract and geometric representation, rather than with a realistic interpretation of nature. —**cu'bist** *adj. & n.*

cu·bit (kyōo'bit) *n.* An ancient measure of length, originally represented by the length of the forearm: about 18 to 20 inches. [< L *cubitum* elbow]

cu·bi·tal (kyōo'bə·təl) *adj.* **1** Of or pertaining to the ulna or to the forearm. **2** Of the measure of a cubit.

cu·bi·tus (kyōo'bə·təs) *n. pl.* **·ti** (-tī) **1** A cubit. **2** *Entomol.* **a** The fifth longitudinal vein of an insect's wing. **b** The tibia of the anterior leg. **c** The radial or stigmal vein in the Hemiptera. **3** *Anat.* The forearm. [< L, var. of *cubitum.* See CUBIT.]

cu·boid (kyōo'boid) *n.* **1** *Anat.* The outer distal bone of the tarsus or ankle. **2** *Geom.* A rectangular parallelepiped. — *adj.* Shaped like a cube: also **cu·boi'dal.** [< Gk. *kyboeidēs* like a cube]

cub scout A member of a subdivision of the Boy Scouts, comprising boys eight to eleven years of age.

Cu·chu·lain (kōo·khōo'lən) A legendary Irish hero, supposed to have defended his country single-handed against invaders.

cuck·ing stool (kuk'ing) A chair in which disorderly women, scolds, and dishonest tradesmen were tied, left to public derision, and sometimes ducked. [< obs. *cuck* defecate]

cuck·old (kuk'əld) *n.* The husband of an unfaithful wife. — *v.t.* To make a cuckold of. [< OF *cucuault* < *cucu* cuckoo; with ref. to the cuckoo's habit of laying its eggs in another bird's nest.] —**cuck'old·ly, cuck'old·y** *adj.*

cuck·old·ry (kuk'əl·drē) *n.* The cuckolding of a husband.

cuck·oo (kōok'ōo) *n.* **1** A bird belonging to a large family (*Cuculidae*), many species of which, as the common European cuckoo (*Cuculus canorus*), deposit their eggs in the nests of other birds to be hatched and cared for. **2** Any of various birds similar to the English cuckoo, as the Australasian small owl, or the American yellow-billed cuckoo (*Coccyzus americanus*) and the black-billed cuckoo (*C. erythrophthalmus*). **3** One who repeats the saying of another or follows slavishly, as in politics; a fool; ninny. **4** A cuckoo's cry. **5** One who commits adultery. —*v.* **·ooed, ·oo·ing** *v.t.* To repeat without cessation. —*v.i.* To utter or imitate the cry of the cuckoo. —*adj.* (also kōo'kōo) *Slang* Slightly deranged mentally; crazy; silly. [< OF *cucu, coucou;* imit.]

cuckoo bud A buttercup or kingcup.

cuckoo clock A clock in which a mechanical cuckoo announces the hours.

cuckoo flower 1 A species of bittercress (*Cardamine pratensis*) with showy flowers: also called *lady's-smock.* **2** Ragged robin.

cuckoo pint A tuberous herb (*Arum maculatum*) of the arum family, with long leaves and erect, purple-spotted spathes: also called *Bobbin-and-Joan, lords-and-ladies, wake robin.*

cuckoo spit 1 A frothy secretion exuded upon plants by the larvae of certain insects, as froghoppers: also called *frog spit.* **2** An insect that secretes froth; a froghopper.

cu·cu·ba·no (kōo·kōo·bä'nō) *n.* The West Indian fire beetle. [< Sp.]

cu·cu·li·form (kyōo·kyōo'lə·fôrm) *adj. Ornithol.* Of or pertaining to an order of birds (*Cuculiformes*) including the cuckoos and roadrunners. [< NL *Cuculiformis* < L *cuculus* cuckoo]

cu·cul·late (kyōo'kə·lāt, kyōo·kul'āt) *adj.* **1** Hood-shaped. **2** *Bot.* Having a hoodlike part, as

certain leaves. Also **cu·cul·lat·ed** (kyōo'kə·lā'tid, kyōo·kul'ā·tid). [< LL *cucullatus* < L *cucullus* hood]

cu·cul·li·form (kyōo·kul'ə·fôrm) *adj.* Having the form of a hood; cucullate. [< L *cucullus* hood + -FORM]

cu·cum·ber (kyōo'kum·bər) *n.* **1** The oblong, hard-rinded fruit of a creeping plant of the gourd family (*Cucumis sativus*), cultivated as a vegetable. **2** The plant. [< OF *cocombre* < L *cucumis, -eris*]

cucumber tree 1 A straight, tall tree (*Magnolia acuminata*) of the eastern United States, bearing a fruit resembling a small cucumber. **2** An East Indian tree (*Averrhoa bilimbi*) cultivated for its edible acid berries and its flowers.

cu·cu·mi·form (kyōo·kyōo'mə·fôrm) *adj.* Having the form of a cucumber. [< L *cucumis* cucumber + -FORM]

cu·cur·bit (kyōo·kûr'bit) *n.* **1** The body of an alembic, originally gourd-shaped. **2** Any similar vessel, as the cucurbitula. **3** Any plant of the gourd family. [< F *cucurbite* < L *cucurbita* gourd] —**cu·cur·bi·ta·ceous** (kyōo·kûr'bə·tā'shəs) *adj.*

cu·cur·bit·u·la (kyōo'kər·bit'yōo·lə) *n.* A cupping glass. [< L, dim. of *cucurbita* gourd, cupping glass]

cud (kud) *n.* **1** Food forced up into the mouth from the first stomach of a ruminant and chewed over again. **2** The rumen. [OE *cudu, cwida* cud]

Cud·a·hy (kud'ə·hē), **Michael,** 1841–1910, U.S. meat packer.

cud·bear (kud'bâr) *n.* **1** A purplish-red dyestuff, similar to archil, made from lichens and used as a coloring for foods and drugs. **2** The lichen (genus *Lecanora*) that furnishes the dye. [Coined from his first name by Dr. *Cuthbert* Gordon, who first made it]

cud·die (kud'ē, kud'ē) *n. Scot.* A donkey.

cud·dle (kud'l) *v.* **·dled, ·dling** *v.t.* To protect and caress fondly within a close embrace; hug. —*v.i.* To lie close; hug one another; nestle together. —*n.* An embrace; caress. [? < dial. E (Northern) *couth* snug, cozy] —**cud'dle·some** *adj.* —**cud'dly** *adj.*

cud·dy (kud'ē) *n. pl.* **·dies 1** *Naut.* A small cabin; a cook's galley. **2** Any small cupboard or pantry. [Origin unknown]

cudg·el (kuj'əl) *n.* A short, thick stick used as a club. —**to take up the cudgels** To enter into a contest or controversy. —*v.t.* **·eled** or **·elled, ·el·ing** or **·el·ling** To beat with a cudgel. See synonyms under BEAT. —**to cudgel one's brains** To think hard; puzzle. [OE *cycgel*] —**cudg'el·er** or **cudg'el·ler** *n.*

cudg·el·play (kuj'əl·plā') *n.* The art of using quarterstaves, singlesticks, or similar weapons, or a contest in which they are used.

cud·weed (kud'wēd') *n.* Any one of various plants of the composite family (genus *Gnaphalium* or *Helichrysum*), as the everlasting. [< CUD + WEED; because given to cattle]

Cud·worth (kud'wûrth, -wərth), **Ralph,** 1617–1688, English philosopher.

cue¹ (kyōo) *n.* **1** A long, tapering rod, used in billiards, pool, etc., to strike the cue ball. **2** A queue of hair. **3** A queue or line of persons. —*v.t.* **cued, cu·ing 1** To twist, braid, or tie into a cue: to *cue* the hair. **2** In billiards, etc., to hit with a cue. [F *queue* tail]

cue² (kyōo) *n.* **1** The closing words in an actor's speech, serving as a signal for his successor; hence, a catchword; hint; suggestion. **2** A part to be performed by an actor. **3** State of mind; humor. —*v.t.* **cued, cu·ing** To call a cue to (an actor); prompt. [Earlier *Q, qu,* said to have been an abbreviation of L *quando* when, written in actors' copies of plays to mark their entrances.]

cue³ (kyōo) *n.* The letter Q.

cue ball A white or whitish-yellow ball struck by the cue in billiards or pool.

cue drawing One of the master drawings pre-

pared as a basis for the succession of action drawings to be filmed as an animated cartoon.

Cuen·ca (kweng′kä) **1** A province in east central Spain; 6,588 square miles; capital, Cuenca. **2** A city in south central Ecuador.

Cuer·na·va·ca (kwâr′nä·vä′kä) A resort city in central Mexico.

cue sheet An instruction sheet for stage technicians giving exact details on the character and timing of all changes in lighting, sound effects, etc., during a performance.

cues·ta (kwes′tə) *n. SW U.S.* A ridge or hill that has a steep descent on one side and a gentle slope on the other. [< Sp.]

cuff[1] (kuf) *n.* **1** A band about the wrist. **2** The lower part of a sleeve. **3** The portion of a long glove or gauntlet covering the wrist. **4** The turned-up hem on a trouser leg. **5** A handcuff. — **on the cuff** *U.S. Slang* On credit; with payment postponed. [ME *cuffe, coffe;* origin unknown]

cuff[2] (kuf) *v.t.* To strike, as with the open hand; buffet. —*v.i.* To scuffle or fight; box. —*n.* A blow, especially with the open hand. [? < Scand. Cf. Sw. *kuffa* push.]

cuff links A pair of linked buttons, etc., used to fasten shirt cuffs.

Cu·fic (kyōō′fik) See KUFIC.

Cu·i (kü·ē′), **César Antonovich,** 1835–1918, Russian composer.

Cu·ia·bá (kōō′yä·bä′) A city in western Brazil, capital of Mato Grosso. Formerly **Cu′ya·bá′.**

cui bo·no (kwē′ bō′nō, kī′) *Latin* For whose benefit? Also, inaccurately, for what purpose?

cui·rass (kwi·ras′) *n.* **1** A piece of defensive armor covering the entire upper part of the trunk, and consisting of a breastplate and backplate; also, the breastplate alone. **2** A cuirasslike covering, as the bony plates of a mailed fish, the armor of a ship, etc. —*v.t.* To cover, as with a cuirass. [< F *cuirasse*]

cui·ras·sier (kwi′rə·sir′) *n.* A mounted soldier wearing a cuirass.

cuir-bouil·li (kwēr′bōō·yē′) *n.* Leather made extremely hard by boiling or soaking in hot water and drying, usually shaping in a mold. Also **cuir′-bouil·ly′.** [< F, boiled leather]

cuish (kwish) *n.* Armor, especially plate armor, for the thigh: sometimes written *quish.* Also **cuisse** (kwis). [< OF *cuissel* < *cuisse* thigh < L *coxa* hip]

cui·sine (kwi·zēn′) *n.* **1** Style or quality of cooking. **2** The food prepared. [< F]

culch (kulch) *n.* Refuse; stuff; rubbish: also spelled *cultch.* [? < OF *culche* bed, layer]

Cul·dee (kul′dē) *n.* One of an order of ecclesiastics, with monasteries in Scotland and Ireland, existing from the 9th to the 14th century. [< Irish *cēle dē* < *cēle* servant + *dē* of God] — **Cul·de′an** *adj.*

cul-de-sac (kul′də·sak′, kōōl′-; *Fr.* kü′də·sák′) *n. pl.* **cul·de·sacs,** *Fr.* **culs·de·sac** (kü′-) **1** A passage open only at one end; blind alley; trap. **2** *Anat. & Zool.* A saclike cavity or part open only at one end. **3** *Mil.* The position of a force surrounded by hostile lines. [< F, bottom of the bag]

-cule *suffix of nouns* Small; little: *animalcule.* [< F < L *-culus,* dim. suffix]

Cu·le·bra Cut (kōō·lā′brə) A former name for the GAILLARD CUT.

cu·let (kyōō′lit) *n. pl.* **·lets** or **·lettes 1** The small lower terminus of a brilliant-cut gem, parallel to the table: also called *collet.* **2** One of the plates of armor for the lower part of the back: often used in the plural. [< OF, dim. of *cul* bottom < L *culus* a buttock]

cu·lex (kyōō′leks) *n.* Any of a large, cosmopolitan genus *(Culex)* of mosquitoes including the common pests of North America and Europe as well as some species that transmit viral diseases of birds, horses, and humans. —**cu·li·cine** (kyōō′lə·sēn) *adj.* & *n.*

cul·gee (kul·gē′) *n. Anglo-Indian* **1** A jeweled aigret or plume, as worn on turbans in India. **2** A figured silk fabric of Indian origin. [< Hind. *kalghī* < Persian *kalagī, kalakī* of a festive company]

Cu·lia·cán (kōō′lyä·kän′) A city in western Mexico, capital of Sinaloa state.

cu·li·cid (kyōō·lis′id) *n.* A member of any genus (family Culicidae).

cu·li·cide (kyōō′lə·sīd) *n.* Any agent that destroys mosquitoes. —**cu′li·cid′al** *adj.*

cu·li·nar·y (kyōō′lə·ner′ē) *adj.* Of or pertaining to cooking or the kitchen. [< L *culinarius* < *culina* kitchen]

cull (kul) *v.t.* **culled, cull·ing 1** To pick or sort out; collect apart. **2** To select and gather: to *cull* a bouquet. See synonyms under CHOOSE. —*n.* Something picked or sorted out; hence, something rejected. [< OF *cuillir* < L *colligere* collect] —**cull′er** *n.*

cul·lay (kə·lī′) See QUILLAI.

Cul·len (kul′ən), **Coun·tée** (koun·tā′), 1903–1946, U.S. Negro poet.

cul·len·der (kul′ən·dər) See COLANDER.

cul·let (kul′it) *n.* Glass waste, variously used as a powder or in melted state. [< F *collet,* dim. of *col* neck < L *collum;* with ref. to the neck of glass left on the pipe after blowing.]

cul·lion (kul′yən) *n.* **1** A bulblike root; an orchid. **2** A poltroon. [< F *couillon* testicle] —**cul′lion·ly** *adj.*

cul·lis (kul′is) *n.* **1** *Archit.* A gutter in a roof. **2** A groove, as for a theatrical side scene. [< F *coulisse*]

Cul·lo·den Moor (kə·lō′dən) A tract in Inverness, Scotland; scene of decisive defeat of Scottish Highlanders by British forces, 1746. Also **Colloden Muir.**

cul·ly (kul′ē) *n. pl.* **·lies 1** *Colloq.* One who is tricked; a dupe. **2** *Brit. Slang* Fellow; pal. —*v.t.* **·lied, ·ly·ing** *Obs.* To impose upon; gull. [? < *cullion* def. 2)]

culm[1] (kulm) *n. Bot.* The jointed, usually hollow, stem or straw of grasses. —*v.i.* To form a culm. [< L *culmus* stalk] —**cul·mif·er·ous** (kul·mif′ər·əs) *adj.*

culm[2] (kulm) *n.* **1** Anthracite refuse, or carbonaceous shale. **2** An inferior anthracite coal. [Var. of dial. *coom* soot] —**cul·mif·er·ous** (kul·mif′ər·əs) *adj.*

cul·men (kul′mən) *n.* **1** A summit or eminence. **2** *Ornithol.* The ridge or central longitudinal line of the upper mandible of bird's bill. **3** *Anat.* A small eminence on the upper surface of the cerebellum: also **culmen mon·tic·u·li** (mon·tik′yə·lī). [< L]

cul·mi·nate (kul′mə·nāt) *v.i.* **·nat·ed, ·nat·ing 1** To attain the highest point or degree. **2** *Astron.* To reach the meridian, or the point of greatest or least altitude. **3** To come to a complete result; reach a final effect. [< LL *culminatus,* pp. of *culminare* mature < *culmen* top, highest point] — **cul′mi·nal** *adj.*

cul·mi·na·tion (kul′mə·nā′shən) *n.* **1** The highest point, condition, or degree. **2** *Astron.* The passage of a heavenly body over the meridian.

culm measures *Geol.* A rock formation belonging to the Lower Carboniferous era, alterloting marine-fossil beds with plant-fossil beds.

cu·lottes (kyōō·lots′, kōō-) *n. pl.* A woman's sportswear garment having knee-length trouser legs cut full to resemble a skirt. [< F]

cul·pa (kul′pə) *n. Law* A fault, especially of negligence. [< L]

cul·pa·ble (kul′pə·bəl) *adj.* Deserving of blame or censure. See synonyms under CRIMINAL. [< OF < L *culpabilis* < *culpa* fault] — **cul′pa·bil′i·ty, cul′pa·ble·ness** *n.* —**cul′pa·bly** *adv.*

Cul·pep·er (kul′pep′ər), **Lord Thomas,** 1635–1689, English colonial governor of Virginia 1680–83.

cul·prit (kul′prit) *n.* **1** A guilty person; criminal. **2** In old English law, one charged with crime, but not yet convicted. [< AF *cul prit,* short for *culpable* guilty (< L *culpabilis*) + *prit* ready for trial < OF *prist, prest* < L *praesto* at hand; orig., prosecutor's reply to plea of "not guilty"]

cult (kult) *n.* **1** Worship or religious devotion; especially, a form of religion. **2** A system of religious observances. **3** Extravagant devotion to a person, cause, or thing; also, the object of such devotion. [< F *culte* < L *cultus* < *colere* worship]

cultch (kulch) *n.* **1** Culch. **2** Gravel, empty shells, etc., used to form a bed to which the spawn of oysters may adhere. **3** Oyster spawn: also spelled *cutch.* [Var. of CULCH]

cul·ti·gen (kul′tə·jən) *n. Bot.* A domesticated plant species of unknown or obscure origin, distinct in its characteristics from known natural species: distinguished from *indigen.* [< CULTI(VATE) + -GEN]

cul·ti·va·ble (kul′tə·və·bəl) *adj.* Capable of cultivation. Also **cul′ti·vat′a·ble.** [< F < *cultiver* cultivate] —**cul′ti·va·bil′i·ty, cul′ti·vat′a·bil′i·ty** *n.*

cul·ti·var (kul′tə·vär) *n. Bot.* A specially cultivated horticultural or garden variety of plant, flower, etc. [< CULTI(VATED) + VAR(IETY)]

cul·ti·vate (kul′tə·vāt) *v.t.* **·vat·ed, ·vat·ing 1** To work by stirring, fertilizing, sowing, and reaping; raise crops from. **2** To bestow labor and care upon for the purpose of aiding and improving growth. **3** To loosen the soil about (growing plants) with a cultivator, hoe, etc.: to *cultivate* potatoes twice. **4** To improve or develop by study, exercise, or training; refine; civilize. **5** To study carefully; pay special attention to; endeavor to acquire, improve, or develop by study and effort; cherish: to *cultivate* philosophy. **6** To cherish carefully the friendship or society of: to *cultivate* one's relatives. **7** To prepare a culture of bacteria. [< Med. L *cultivatus,* pp. of *cultivare* < *cultivus* tilled < L *cultus,* pp. of *cultivare* < *cultivus* tilled < L *cultus,* pp. of *colere* care for, worship] —**cul′ti·vat′ed** *adj.*

cul·ti·va·tion (kul′tə·vā′shən) *n.* **1** The act of cultivating. **2** Improvement; development; culture. See synonyms under AGRICULTURE, EDUCATION, REFINEMENT.

cul·ti·va·tor (kul′tə·vā′tər) *n.* **1** One who cultivates. **2** *Agric.* A machine for cultivating, commonly having several shares which loosen the ground and destroy weeds.

cul·trate (kul′trāt) *adj.* **1** *Bot.* Sharp-edged and pointed, as a leaf. **2** Shaped like a pruning knife, as the beak of a bird. Also **cul′trat·ed.** [< L *cultratus* < *culter* knife]

cul·tur·al (kul′chər·əl) *adj.* **1** Of, pertaining to, or developing culture: *cultural* books. **2** Resulting from breeding or artificial cultivation, as certain varieties of fruits or plants. —**cul′tur·al·ly** *adv.*

cultural lag *Sociol.* A marked retardation in the rate of development of certain features of a culture as compared with others.

cul·ture (kul′chər) *n.* **1** Cultivation of plants or animals, especially with a view to improvement. **2** The training, improvement, and refinement of mind, morals, or taste. **3** Tillage of the soil. **4** *Bacteriol.* **a** The development of micro-organisms, as in gelatin, beef tea, etc. **b** The organisms so developed. **5** Enlightenment or civilization: Greek *culture.* **6** *Anthropol.* The sum total of the attainments and activities of any specific period, race, or people, including their implements, handicrafts, agriculture, economics, music, art, religious beliefs, traditions, language, and story. **7** Those physical features of a terrain which are of human origin or construction, as roads, trails, canals, buildings, boundary lines; also, their symbolic representation on a map. —*v.t.* **·tured, ·tur·ing 1** To cultivate (plants or animals). **2** *Bacteriol.* **a** To develop or grow (micro-organisms) in a gelatin or other medium. **b** To inoculate with a prepared culture. **3** *Obs.* To educate or refine. [< F < L *cultura* < *colere* care for] **cul′tur·ist** *n.*

culture area *Sociol.* A region characterized by similar cultural patterns among the different social and ethnic groups inhabiting it.

culture center *Sociol.* The focal district of a culture area, inhabited by communities regarded as being most typical in respect to the cultural features prevailing in the area.

culture complex *Sociol.* An aggregate of culture traits functionally integrated with some dominant community activity, such as that based on the use of horses among the North American Plains Indians.

cul·tured (kul′chərd) *adj.* **1** Possessing manifest education and refinement. **2** Cultivated. **3** Artificially propagated, as a culture of bacteria. **4** Describing a variety of pearl artificially cultivated by inserting a suitable core within the shell or mantle of a mollusk, promoting the growth of nacre around it. See synonyms under POLITE.

culture medium See under MEDIUM.

culture trait *Sociol.* Any socially transmitted element or feature within a culture.

cul·tus (kul′təs) *n.* **1** A cult. **2** State of religious, ethical, or esthetic development. [< L. See CULT.]

cul·ver (kul′vər) *n.* A pigeon or dove. [OE *culfer*]

cul·ver·in (kul′vər·in) *n.* A long cannon used in the 16th century. [< F *coulevrin* < *couleuvre* serpent]

Cul·ver's-phys·ic (kul′vərz·fiz′ik) *n.* A weed (*Veronicastrum virginicum*) from three to

eight feet high, with from one to five long terminal racemes of flowers: used as an aperient and tonic. Also **Cul'ver's-root'.**

cul·vert (kul'vərt) n. An artificial, covered channel for water, as under a road. [Origin uncertain]

Cu·mae (kyōo'mē) An ancient city on the coast of Campania, Italy; the earliest Greek colony in Italy. Also **Cu'mæ.**

Cu·mae·an (kyōo·mē'ən) adj. Of or pertaining to Cumae: the *Cumaean* sibyl.

Cu·ma·ná (kōō'mä·nä') A city in NE Venezuela.

cu·ma·rin (kōō'mə·rin) See COUMARIN.

cum·ber (kum'bər) v.t. 1 To hinder by or as by a weight or burden; obstruct. 2 To weigh down; oppress; perplex. 3 *Obs.* To overwhelm; prostrate; destroy. See synonyms under LOAD. — n. *Obs.* 1 Perplexity; distress. 2 An encumbrance. [Cf. OF *encombrer* hinder]

Cum·ber·land (kum'bər·lənd) 1 A county in NW England on the Scottish border; 1,520 square miles; county seat, Carlisle. 2 A city on the Potomac River in western Maryland.

Cum·ber·land (kum'bər·lənd), **Duke of,** 1721–1765, William Augustus, English general; third son of George II.

Cumberland Gap A natural passage through the Cumberland Mountains between Virginia and Tennessee.

Cumberland Mountains The SW division of the Appalachian Mountains, extending from SW West Virginia to NW Alabama. Also **Cumberland Plateau.**

Cumberland River A river in Kentucky and Tennessee, flowing 693 miles west to the Ohio River.

Cumberland Road A national highway, first constructed in the early 19th century from Cumberland, Maryland, westward to the Ohio River: also *National Road.*

cum·ber·some (kum'bər·səm) adj. 1 Moving or working heavily or with difficulty; unwieldy. 2 Vexatious; burdensome. — **cum'ber·some·ly** adv. — **cum'ber·some·ness** n.

cum·brance (kum'brəns) n. 1 An encumbrance. 2 A burdened condition; trouble.

Cum·bre (kōōm'brā), **La** See USPALLATA.

cum·brous (kum'brəs) adj. Cumbersome. See synonyms under HEAVY. — **cum'brous·ly** adv. — **cum'brous·ness** n.

cum gra·no sa·lis (kum grā'nō sā'lis) *Latin* With a grain of salt; with some reservation; not literally.

cum·in (kum'in) n. 1 An annual (*Cuminum cyminum*) of the carrot family, with fennel-like leaves. 2 Its seeds, used in Eastern countries as a condiment. Also **cum'min.** [OE *cymen* <L *cuminum* <Gk. *kyminon* <Semitic]

cum lau·de (kum lô'dē, kōōm lou'de) *Latin* With praise: used on diplomas to denote the special merit of the recipient's work. — **magna cum laude** With high praise. — **summa cum laude** With highest praise.

cum·mer·bund (kum'ər·bund) n. A shawl or broad sash worn as a waistband; also, a girdle; a belt: sometimes spelled *kummerbund.* [<Persian *kamar-band* <*kamar* loin + *band* band]

Cum·mings (kum'ingz), **Edward Estlin,** 1894–1962, U.S. poet, author, and artist: usually written by him as **e. e. cummings.**

cum·quat (kum'kwot) See KUMQUAT.

cum·shaw (kum'shô) n. Something given as a present; a tip; baksheesh. — v.t. To give baksheesh to; to tip. [<Chinese *kan hsieh* grateful thanks]

cu·mu·late (kyōo'myə·lāt) v.i. ·lat·ed, ·lat·ing To collect into a heap; accumulate. — adj. (also kyōo'myə·lit) Massed; heaped; accumulated. [<L *cumulatus,* pp. of *cumulare* heap up < *cumulus* a heap] — **cu'mu·la'tion** n.

cu·mu·la·tive (kyōo'myə·lā'tiv) adj. 1 Gathering volume, strength, or value by addition or repetition; steadily increasing. 2 Consisting of portions gathered or collected one after another. 3 Increasing or accruing, as unpaid interest or dividends, to be paid in the future. 4 *Law* Reinforcing or proving previous evidence. — **cu'mu·la'tive·ly** adv.

cu·mu·li·form (kyōo'myə·lə·fôrm') adj. *Meteorol.* Denoting clouds with dome-shaped upper surfaces and generally horizontal under

surfaces, usually separated by clear spaces. [<L *cumulus* heap + -FORM¹]

cumulo– *combining form* Cumulus: *cumulonimbus.*

cu·mu·lo·cir·rus (kyōo'myə·lō-sir'əs) See ALTOCUMULUS.

cu·mu·lo·nim·bus (kyōo'myə·lō-nim'bəs) n. *Meteorol.* Heavy, massive clouds rising vertically in the shape of mountains, turrets, or anvils, with accompanying sheets of fibrous appearance; thunder and shower clouds. See table under CLOUD.

cumulonimbus mam·ma·tus (mə-mā'təs) *Meteorol.* A variation of cumulonimbus having pouchlike protuberances on the lower surface.

cu·mu·lo·stra·tus (kyōo'myə·lō-strā'təs) See STRATOCUMULUS.

cu·mu·lo·vol·ca·no (kyōo'myə·lō-vol·kā'nō) n. A volcano characterized by the formation of steep, cumulous masses of lava near the crater.

cu·mu·lus (kyōo'myə·ləs) n. pl. ·li (-lī) 1 A mass; pile; top of a heap; summit. 2 *Meteorol.* Dense clouds with dome-shaped upper surfaces and horizontal bases, seen in fair weather. See table under CLOUD. [<L] — **cu'mu·lous** adj.

Cu·nax·a (kyōo·nak'sə) A town in Babylonia near the Euphrates; scene of a battle between Cyrus the Younger and Artaxerxes II, 401 B.C.

cunc·ta·tion (kungk·tā'shən) n. Delay; cautious slowness. [<L *cunctatio, -onis* < *cunctari* delay] — **cunc·ta·tive** (kungk'tə·tiv) adj.

cunc·ta·tor (kungk·tā'tər) n. One who delays or procrastinates.

cun·dum (kun'dəm) See CONDOM.

cu·ne·al (kyōo'nē·əl) adj. Of or pertaining to a wedge-shaped part; cuneiform. [<Med. L *cunealis* <L *cuneus* wedge]

cu·ne·ate (kyōo'nē·it, -āt) adj. Wedge-shaped. Also **cu'ne·at'ed, cu'ne·at'ic** (kyōo'nē·at'ik). [<L *cuneatus,* pp. of *cuneare* make wedge-shaped < *cuneus* wedge] — **cu'ne·ate·ly** adv.

cuneate lobule *Anat.* A wedge-shaped portion of the median surface of the occipital lobe of the brain. Also **cu·ne·us** (kyōo'nē·əs).

cu·ne·i·form (kyōo·nē'ə·fôrm, kyōo'nē-ə·fôrm') adj. 1 Of a wedge shape, as noted in the characters in some ancient Assyrian, Babylonian and Persian inscriptions. 2 *Anat.* Designating a wedge-shaped bone in the wrist, or one of three in the human foot. See illustration under FOOT. — n. Cuneiform writing. Also **cu·ni·form** (kyōo'nə·fôrm). [<L *cuneus* wedge + -FORM]

CUNEIFORM (n.)

Cu·ne·ne (kōō·nā'nə) A river in west central Angola, SW Africa, flowing about 650 miles SW to the Atlantic: also *Kunene.*

Cun·ha (kōō'nyə), **Tristão da,** 1460?–1540, Portuguese navigator and explorer.

cu·nic·u·lus (kyōo·nik'yə·ləs) n. pl. ·li (-lī) 1 A small underground passage or drain. 2 The track or burrow of a skin parasite. [<L, rabbit, burrow]

cun·ner (kun'ər) n. A small, edible fish (*Tautogolabrus adspersus*), abundant along the North Atlantic shores of America. [Origin uncertain]

cun·ning (kun'ing) n. 1 Skill in deception; guile; artifice. 2 Knowledge combined with skill; dexterity. See synonyms under ARTIFICE, DECEPTION. — adj. 1 Crafty or shrewd; artful; guileful. 2 Attractive; bright; amusing; cute. 3 Ingenious; dexterous; made with skill: a *cunning* design. 4 *Obs.* Learned; knowing. See synonyms under ACUTE, ASTUTE, INSIDIOUS, KNOWING, POLITIC. [OE *cunning* knowledge < *cunnan.* Related to CAN¹.] — **cun'ning·ly** adv. — **cun'ning·ness** n.

Cun·ning·ham (kun'ing·ham, -əm), **Sir Andrew Browne,** 1883–1963, British admiral.

cup (kup) n. 1 A small open vessel of glass, porcelain, wood, waxed paper, metal, etc., used chiefly for drinking. 2 A cupful; a measure of capacity equal to 8 fluid ounces or 16 tablespoons. 3 The ornamental vessel used in administering the sacramental wine; also, the wine itself. 4 Figuratively, one's lot in life; portion. 5 Intoxicating drink, or the habit of drinking: pleasures of the *cup.* 6 A prize, usually a vase, or a cup-shaped vessel, contended for in races: the Ascot *cup.* 7 *Med.* A cupping glass or vessel for drawing blood. 8 A small hole or cuplike depression in a course; also, a hole especially made in the putting green into which the golf ball is played. 9 Any cup-shaped object: the *cup* of a flower, an oil *cup,* etc. 10 The concave part of any drinking vessel having a base and stem. 11 A beverage made of wine, generally iced, with herbs, fruits, and vegetables: claret *cup.* 12 That curvature of a board or other flat piece of lumber which runs transversely against the grain. — **in one's cups** Intoxicated; also, in the act of drinking. — v.t. **cupped, cup·ping** 1 To bleed, as by scarification and bringing the blood to the surface under an exhausted cup. 2 To shape like or place in a cup. [OE *cuppe* <LL *cuppa* cup, var. of L *cupa* tub]

Cu·par (kōō'pär, -pər) County town of Fifeshire, Scotland.

cup-bear·er (kup'bâr'ər) n. One who serves wine and other drinks to guests.

cup·board (kub'ərd) n. 1 A closet or cabinet with shelves, as for tableware. 2 Any small cabinet or closet.

cup-cake (kup'kāk') n. A cake baked in cup-shaped receptacles: formerly, most of the ingredients were measured by cupfuls.

cu·pel (kyōo'pəl, kyōo·pel') v.t. ·peled or ·pelled, ·pel·ing or ·pel·ling To separate from base metals by cupellation. [<n.] — n. A shallow, absorbent vessel, generally of bone ash: used in assaying gold and silver ores. [<MF *coupelle* <Med. L *cupella,* dim. of *cuppa* cup]

cu·pel·la·tion (kyōo'pə·lā'shən) n. The process of refining gold or silver by the use of a cupel, or in a muffle furnace. [<F]

cup·ful (kup'fool) n. pl. ·fuls The quantity held or measured by a cup; half a pint.

Cu·pid (kyōo'pid) 1 In Roman mythology, the god of love: identified with the Greek *Eros.* 2 A representation of the god of love as a naked, winged boy with a bow and arrow. [<L *Cupido* <*cupido* passion, desire]

cu·pid·i·ty (kyōo·pid'ə·tē) n. An inordinate wish for possession, especially of wealth; avarice. [<L *cupiditas, -tatis* < *cupidus* desirous]

cup of tea *Brit. Colloq.* That which suits one; a favorite or preferred object, activity, etc.

cu·po·la (kyōo'pə·lə) n. 1 A dome; hemispherical roof. 2 *Archit.* Any small structure above the roof of a building. 3 A turret on an armored ship. 4 The small hatch in the turret of certain military tanks. 5 *Metall.* A shaft furnace used for melting iron, especially that for foundry use. 6 *Geol.* The domelike protuberance on the roof of a batholith, a possible reservoir for magma. — v.t. ·laed, ·la·ing To provide with a cupola. [<Ital. <L *cupula,* dim. of *cupa* tub, cask]

cupped (kupt) adj. Cup-shaped; concave.

cup·per (kup'ər) n. One who carries out the operation of cupping.

cup·ping (kup'ing) n. *Med.* The process of drawing blood to another part by creating a vacuum at that point, as by means of a cupping glass, with or without scarification.

cupping glass *Med.* A cup, generally of glass, applied to the skin in the operation of cupping. also called *cucurbitula.*

cup plant A stout herb (*Silphium perfoliatum*) of the composite family, from 4 to 8 feet high, of the western and southern United States: named from the cup formed around the stem by the upper pair of perfoliate leaves.

cup·py (kup'ē) adj. 1 Cup-shaped; having hollows like cups. 2 Marred, as timber, by cupshakes.

cu·pram (kyōo'prəm) n. A fungicide formed of ammoniacal copper carbonate. [Short for CUPRAMMONIA]

cu·pram·mo·nia (kyōō′prə·mōn′yə, -mō′nē·ə) *n. Chem.* Schweitzer's reagent. [< CUPR(O)- + AMMONIA]
cu·pram·mo·ni·um process (kyōō′prə·mō′·nē·əm) *Chem.* A process for making rayon by treating cellulose with Schweitzer's reagent.
cu·pre·ous (kyōō′prē·əs) *adj.* Of, pertaining to, containing, or like copper. [< LL *cupreus* < *cuprum* copper]
cu·pric (kyōō′prick) *adj. Chem.* Of or pertaining to copper, especially copper in its highest valence: *cupric* oxide.
cupric acetate *Chem.* Verdigris.
cupric oxide A compound, CuO, occurring in nature as the mineral tenorite and prepared by heating copper in oxygen and also by heating certain copper compounds.
cupric sulfate A white compound, $CuSO_4$, which forms blue vitriol or bluestone.
cu·prif·er·ous (kyōō·prif′ər·əs) *adj.* Yielding or containing copper. [< CUPR(O)- + -(I)FEROUS]
cu·prite (kyōō′prīt) *n.* A red, translucent cuprous oxide found in isometric crystals, and also massive, granular, or earthy: an important ore of copper.
cupro- *combining form* Copper: *cupronickel.* Also, before vowels, **cupr-**. [< L *cuprum* copper]
cu·pro·nick·el (kyōō′prō·nik′əl) *n.* Any of several alloys of copper and nickel, sometimes combined with other elements, as manganese and iron.
cu·prous (kyōō′prəs) *adj. Chem.* Of or derived from copper, especially copper in its lowest valence: *cuprous* oxide, Cu_2O.
cu·prum (kyōō′prəm) *n.* Copper. [< L]
cup·shake (kup′shāk) *n.* A division or shrinkage between the annual rings of timber: also called *ringshake.* [< CUP (def. 12) + SHAKE (def. 5)]
cu·pule (kyōō′pyōōl) *n.* **1** A concave or cup-shaped depression. **2** *Bot.* **a** A cup-shaped part, as the involucre of the fruit of the oak, chestnut, beech, etc. **b** The receptacle of certain fungi, mosses, and liverworts. [< LL *cupula.* See CUPOLA.]
Cu·que·nán (kōō′kə·nän′) See KUKENAAM.
cur (kûr) *n.* **1** A mongrel dog. **2** A mean or malicious person. [Short for earlier *kur-dogge.* Cf. dial. Sw. *kurre* dog.] **—cur′rish** *adj.* **—cur′rish·ly** *adv.* **—cur′rish·ness** *n.*
cur·a·ble (kyŏŏr′ə·bəl) *adj.* Capable of being cured. **—cur′a·bil′i·ty, cur′a·ble·ness** *n.* **—cur′·a·bly** *adv.*
cu·ra·çao (kyŏŏr′ə·sō′) *n.* A liqueur made by distilling spirits with macerated bitter orange peel. [from *Curaçao*]
Cu·ra·çao (kyŏŏr′ə·sō′, kōō′rä·sou′) The largest island in the western group of the Netherlands West Indies; 173 square miles; capital, Willemstad.
cu·ra·cy (kyŏŏr′ə·sē) *n. pl.* **·cies** The position, duties, or term of office of a curate.
cu·ra·re (kyōō·rä′rē) *n.* **1** A blackish, brittle, resinous extract of certain South American trees of the genus *Strychnos,* especially *S. toxifera,* used as an arrow poison, in pharmacological research, and as an adjunct in general anesthesia. **2** The plant from which this extract is abstracted: sometimes written *woorali* or *urare.* Also **cu·ra·ra** (kyōō·rä′rə), **cu·ra′ri.** [< Sp. *curaré* < Tupian]
cu·ra·rine (kyōō·rä′rēn, -rin) *n. Chem.* A poisonous alkaloid, $C_{19}H_{26}ON_2$, obtained from curare. [< CURARE + -INE[2]]
cu·ra·rize (kyŏŏr′ə·rīz, kyōō·rä′rīz) *v.t.* **·rized, ·riz·ing 1** To poison by the use of curare. **2** To administer curare to, as for paralyzing the motor nerves in vivisection. **—cu′ra·ri·za′tion** *n.*
cu·ras·sow (kyŏŏr′ə·sō, kyōō·ras′ō) *n.* A large turkeylike South American bird (family *Cracidae*) with naked cere and tarsi: also spelled *carassow.* [from *Curaçao*]
cu·rate (kyŏŏr′it) *n.* A clergyman assisting a parish priest, rector, or vicar. [< Med. L *curatus* < *cura* care, a cure] **—cu′rate·ship** *n.*
cur·a·tive (kyŏŏr′ə·tiv) *adj.* **1** Possessing power or tendency to cure. **2** Relating to the cure of diseases. —*n.* A remedy. **—cur′a·tive·ly** *adv.* **—cur′a·tive·ness** *n.*
cu·ra·tor (kyōō·rā′tər) *n.* **1** A person having charge, as of a museum or library; a superintendent. **2** *Law* A guardian appointed to take charge of the property of a person not legally qualified to act for himself. **3** In some European universities, a member of a board of managers. [< L < *curare* care for < *cura* care] **—cu·ra·to·ri·al** (kyŏŏr′ə·tôr′ē·əl, -tō′rē-) *adj.*
cu·ra·tor·ship (kyōō·rā′tər·ship) *n.* **1** A curator's office or position. **2** A body of curators collectively.
curb (kûrb) *n.* **1** A chain or strap to brace a bit against a horse's lower jaw: used to check the horse when the reins are pulled; also, a bit so arranged. **2** Anything that restrains or controls. **3** A curbstone. **4** The framework at the top of a well. **5** Originally, the street as a market for selling securities out of hours or securities not listed on the regular stock exchanges: also *curb exchange.* **6** A hard swelling on a horse's hind leg, especially back of the hock and below its point. —*v.t.* **1** To hold in subjection; control, as with reins and curb. **2** To protect with a curb. **3** To shorten and sharpen (telegraphic signals) in order to obtain more rapid transmission. Also *Brit. kerb.* See synonyms under GOVERN, REPRESS, RESTRAIN. [< F *courbe,* orig. adj., curved < L *curvus*]
curb broker A broker who buys and sells securities traded on the curb exchange.
curb exchange 1 An organization for the sale of securities not listed on the stock exchange, wheat exchange, etc. **2** The building in which this market operates.
curb·ing (kûr′bing) *n.* **1** Curbstones collectively. **2** Material for making a curb. **3** A curb or a part of a curb.
curb roof *Archit.* A roof having two sets of rafters, of which the upper slopes less than the lower.
curb·stone (kûrb′stōn′) *n.* A stone, or a row of stones, on the outer edge of a sidewalk: also *Brit. kerbstone.*
curch (kûrch) *n. Scot.* A woman's headkerchief or cap.
cur·chie (kûr′chē) *n. Scot.* A curtsy; courtesy.
cur·cu·li·o (kûr·kyōō′lē·ō) *n. pl.* **·os** One of a family *(Curculionidae)* of beetles, characterized by a prolongation of the head into a beak: many species are injurious to fruits and nuts: also called *snout beetle, weevil.* For illustration see under INSECT (injurious). [< L, weevil]
cur·cu·ma (kûr′kyōō·mə) *n.* Any of several plants (genus *Curcuma*) of the ginger family: the perennial rootstocks of *C. longa* yield turmeric, and those of *C. angustifolia* the East Indian arrowroot. [< NL < Arabic *kurkum* saffron]
curcuma paper See TURMERIC PAPER.
cur·cu·min (kûr′kyōō·mən) *n.* **1** The yellow compound, $C_{21}H_{20}O_6$, contained in the turmeric or curcuma root, of which it is the coloring substance. **2** An artificial acid dye. Also **cur′cu·mine** (-mīn). [< CURCUMA + -IN]
curd (kûrd) *n.* The coagulated portion of milk, of which cheese is made, as distinct from the watery portion or whey. —*v.t.* & *v.i.* To form into or become curd; curdle. [Metathetic var. of CRUD] **—curd′i·ness** *n.* **—curd′ly, curd′y** *adj.*
cur·dle (kûrd′l) *v.t.* & *v.i.* **·dled, ·dling 1** To change or turn to curd; coagulate; congeal. **2** To thicken. Also *Dial. cruddle.* [Freq. of CURD, *v.*]
cure (kyŏŏr) *n.* **1** A restoration or return to a sound or healthy condition. **2** That which restores health or abolishes an evil. **3** Spiritual care; a curacy: the *cure* of souls. **4** A mode or manner of curing anything, as hams, fish, etc. —*v.* **cured, cur·ing** *v.t.* **1** To restore to a healthy or sound condition. **2** To remedy or eradicate, as a disease or bad habit. **3** To preserve, as by salting or smoking. **4** To vulcanize, as rubber. —*v.i.* **5** To bring about recovery. **6** To be preserved, as meat, by salting or drying. [< OF < L *cura* care] **—cure′less** *adj.*
cu·ré (kyōō·rā′) *n.* In France, a parish priest. [< F, curate]
cure-all (kyŏŏr′ôl′) *n.* That which is asserted to cure all diseases or evils; a panacea.
cure of souls The care for the spiritual needs of the faithful, which devolves upon the clergy of the Anglican and Roman Catholic Churches.
cu·ret·tage (kyōō·ret′ij, kyŏŏr′ə·täzh′) *n.* The use or application of the curette.
cu·rette (kyōō·ret′) *n. Med.* A small instrument, usually resembling a spoon or scoop, used for removing morbid matter by scraping from a cavity, as the ear or throat. —*v.t.* **·ret·ted, ·ret·ting** To apply a curette to. [< F < *curer* cure, restore]
cur·few (kûr′fyōō) *n.* **1** An ancient police regulation requiring fires and lights to be put out at the tolling of a bell. **2** The bell itself. **3** The hour of ringing such a bell. **4** The ringing of a bell at a certain hour in the evening, still prevailing locally, as in parts of the United States and France. **5** A police or military regulation that civilians keep off the streets after a designated hour; also, a municipal order of the same tenor applying to children only. [< AF *coeverfu,* OF *cuevrefu* < *couvrir* cover + *feu* fire]
cu·ri·a (kyŏŏr′ē·ə) *n. pl.* **·ae** (-ē) **1** A court of justice. **2** The collective body of officials of the papal government; also **Curia Romana. 3** The court or family residence of a medieval monarch or feudal lord. **4** A tribal division made by Romulus, or its meeting place. **5** The Roman senate house or the senate of any Italian city. [< L] **—cu′ri·al** *adj.*
cu·ri·al·ism (kyŏŏr′ē·əl·iz′əm) *n.* The political principles and policy of the papal see, especially in their exclusive tendencies; ultramontanism. **—cu′ri·al·ist** *n.* **—cu′ri·al·is′tic** *adj.*
Cu·ri·a·ti·i (kyŏŏr′ē·ā′shē·ī) See HORATII.
cu·rie (kyŏŏr′ē, kyōō·rē′) *n. Physics* **1** The unit of radioactivity, equal to 3.70×10^{10} disintegrations per second, of any radioactive nuclide. **2** The quantity of radon emanation in equilibrium with one gram of radium: also called **cu′rie·gram.** [after Marie *Curie*]
Cu·rie (kyŏŏr′ē, kyōō·rē′; *Fr.* kü·rē′), **Eve,** born 1904, French journalist; daughter of Marie and Pierre. **—Irène** See JOLIOT-CURIE. **—Marie,** 1867–1934, French physicist and chemist, born in Poland; discoverer, with her husband, of radium. **—Pierre,** 1859–1906, French scientist; husband of Marie.
Curie point *Physics* The temperature at which the transformation of ferromagnetism into paramagnetism takes place.
Curie's law *Physics* The statement that paramagnetic substances are magnetically susceptible in inverse proportion to the absolute temperature.
cur·ing (kyŏŏr′ing) *n.* **1** Any method of treating for preservation: said of meats, vegetables, etc. **2** A method of treating raw hides and skins so as to prevent deterioration during transport or in storage. **3** The transition of a heat-molded plastic from the liquid to the solid state without lowering the temperature.
cu·ri·o (kyŏŏr′ē·ō) *n. pl.* **·os** A curiosity; a rare or curious article of virtu. [Short for CURIOSITY]
cu·ri·o·log·ic (kyŏŏr′ē·ə·loj′ik) *adj.* Relating to pictorial hieroglyphics: also spelled *kyriologic.* Also **cu′ri·o·log′i·cal.** [< Gk. *kyriologikos* < *kyrios* literal + *logos* word] **—cu′ri·o·log′i·cal·ly** *adv.*
cu·ri·o·sa (kyŏŏr′ē·ō′sə) *n. pl.* Books, papers, etc., on unusual, especially pornographic, subjects. [< L, neut. pl. of *curiosus* curious, prying]
cu·ri·os·i·ty (kyŏŏr′ē·os′ə·tē) *n. pl.* **·ties 1** Desire for knowledge of something. **2** Inquisitive interest in the private affairs of others. **3** An interesting or strange quality. **4** Any object adapted to excite interest or inquiry. **5** *Obs.* Fastidiousness; nicety. [< L *curiositas, -tatis* < *curiosus* CURIOUS]
cu·ri·ous (kyŏŏr′ē·əs) *adj.* **1** Eager for information; inquistive; prying. **2** Adapted to attract attention or excite interest; novel; odd; strange; mysterious. **3** Involving ingenuity or skill. **4** *Obs.* Fastidious; delicate; scrupulous. See synonyms under INQUISITIVE, QUEER, RARE[1]. [< OF *curios, curius* < L *curiosus* < *cura* care] **—cu′ri·ous·ly** *adv.* **—cu′ri·ous·ness** *n.*
Cu·ri·ti·ba (kōō′rē·tē′və) A city in southern Brazil, capital of Paraná state.
cu·ri·um (kyōō′rē·əm) *n.* An artificially created, intensely radioactive metallic element (symbol Cm, atomic number 96) produced by bombardment of plutonium in nuclear reactors. See PERIODIC TABLE. [after Marie and Pierre *Curie*]
curl (kûrl) *v.t.* **1** To twist into ringlets or curves, as the hair. **2** To form into a curved or spiralshape. **3** *Obs.* To adorn with curls. —*v.i.* **4** To become curved; take a spiral shape. **5** To play at the game of curling. —*n.* **1** Anything coiled or spiral, as a ringlet. **2**

Sinuosity. **3** A circling or wavelike marking. **4** *Bot.* A disease of plants, especially of peach trees. **5** *Physics* A vector differential operator used in studying phenomena of spin or rotation. [Metathetic var. of ME *crollid, crulled* curled < *crull* curly < MLG] —**curl′i·ness** *n.* —**curl′y** *adj.*

curled toe A disease of growing chicks caused by a vitamin deficiency and characterized by a twisted or flexed condition of the toes.

curl·er (kûr′lər) *n.* **1** A person or thing that curls. **2** One who plays the game of curling.

cur·lew (kûr′lyoo) *n.* **1** A shore bird (family *Scolopacidae*), with long bill and legs, as the European curlew (*Numenius arquatus*) and the Hudsonian curlew (*Phaeopus hudsonicus*). **2** Any bird superficially resembling the curlew. [< OF *corlieu, courlieus*; orig. imit., infl. in form by OF *courlieu* messenger]

curl·i·cue (kûr′li·kyoo) *n.* **1** Anything oddly curled or twisted, as in flourishes with a pen: *curlicues* made in skating. **2** A frolicsome trick; caper. Also **curl′y·cue.** [< CURLY + CUE¹]

curl·ing (kûr′ling) *n.* A game in which the opposing players slide large, smooth, circular stones along the ice toward a goal or tee at either end.

curling iron An implement of metal, used when heated for curling or waving the hair. Also **curling tongs.**

curling stone One of the heavy stones, provided with a handle, with which the game of curling is played.

cur·mudg·eon (kər·muj′ən) *n.* A miserly or churlish person. [Origin unknown] —**cur·mudg′eon·ly** *adj.*

cur·mur·ring (kər·mûr′ing) *n. Scot.* A low murmuring or grumbling sound.

SCOTTISH CURLING STONE

cur·ple (kûr′pəl) *n. Scot.* Buttocks; crupper.

curr (kûr) *v.i. Scot. & Brit. Dial.* To coo, purr, or hoot like an owl. [< ON *kurra* murmur]

cur·rach (kûr′əkh, kûr′ə) *n. Scot. & Irish* A coracle: sometimes spelled *corrach*. Also **cur′ragh.**

Cur·ragh (kûr′ə) A plain in central County Kildare, Ireland; 8 square miles.

cur·ra·jong (kûr′ə·jong) See KURRAJONG.

cur·rant (kûr′ənt) *n.* **1** A small, round, acid berry, used for making jelly. **2** The bush (genus *Ribes*) producing it; especially, the red or white currant (*R. sativum*) and the black currant (*R. nigrum*). **3** A small seedless raisin from the Levant. ♦ Homophone: *current*. [Back formation < *Coraunz* taken as pl. in AF (*raisins de*) *Coraunz* (raisins from) Corinth]

cur·ren·cy (kûr′ən·sē) *n. pl.* **·cies 1** The current medium of exchange; coin or bank notes. **2** The state of being current. **3** Current value or estimation; general esteem or standing: to gain *currency* without desert. See synonyms under MONEY. —**blocked currency** Currency subject to abnormal administrative restrictions, usually in the interests of controlling foreign exchange. —**flexible currency** Currency which is regulated by existing business requirements, and increased or decreased with their demands. —**managed currency** A theoretical financial arrangement intended to stabilize currency by regulation of the standard monetary unit.

cur·rent (kûr′ənt) *adj.* **1** Circulating freely. **2** Generally accepted. **3** In actual progress, or belonging to the immediate present. **4** *Math.* Differing from point to point. **5** *Rare* Moving; running; flowing. See synonyms under AUTHENTIC. —*n.* **1** A continuous onward movement, as of a stream; also, a fluid thus flowing. **2** That part of any body of water which has a more or less steady flow in a definite direction: an ocean *current.* See list of OCEAN CURRENTS below. **3** *Electr.* **a** A movement or flow of electricity passing through a conductor. **b** The rate at which it flows. **4** Any connected onward movement;

course. —**alternating current** *Electr.* A current which periodically reverses its direction of flow, each complete cycle having the same value. — **direct current** *Electr.* A current flowing in one direction continuously, with negligible or zero changes in value. —**eddy current** *Electr.* A current produced in a solid conductor, such as the armature or polepiece of a dynamo or motor, which is wasted by conversion into heat: also called **Foucault current.** ♦Homophone: *currant.* [< OF *curant,* ppr. of *corre* < L *currere* run; infl. in form by L *currens, -entis,* ppr. of *currere*] —**cur′rent·ly** *adv.* —**cur′rent·ness** *n.*

OCEAN CURRENTS

—**Agulhas current** A southern branch of the Equatorial Current, which skirts the east coast of South Africa.

—**Australia Current** A southern branch of the Equatorial Current, which flows south and east after passing along the eastern coast of Australia.

—**Brazil Current** A southern branch of the Equatorial Current, flowing southward along the coast of Brazil.

—**California Current** A broad, cold ocean current flowing southward along the Pacific coast of North America from about 50° N. to the mouth of the Gulf of California.

—**Equatorial Current** A great drift of ocean waters north and south of the Equator, set in motion by the trade winds and having a general westerly direction except when diverted by coastal features.

—**Guinea Current** An ocean current moving eastward along the upper coast of Guinea toward the Equatorial Current of the Atlantic.

—**Japan Current** A warm ocean current flowing northeastwards across the Pacific from Japan to the southern coast of Alaska: also called *Japan Stream, Kuroshiwo.* Also **Black Current.**

—**Kamchatka Current** The northern branch of the Japan Current, which flows northeast in the direction of the Aleutian Islands.

—**Labrador Current** An ocean current originating in Davis Strait and flowing southward along the coasts of Labrador and Newfoundland. Also called **Arctic Current.**

—**Peruvian Current** A cold ocean current flowing north and east along the shores of Chile and Peru. Also called **Chilean Current, Humboldt Current.**

current density See under DENSITY.

Cur·rer Bell (kûr′ər) The pen name of *Charlotte Brontë.*

cur·ri·cle (kûr′i·kəl) *n.* A two-wheeled, two-horse carriage with a pole. [< L *curriculum* race < *currere* run]

cur·ric·u·lum (kə·rik′yə·ləm) *n. pl.* **·lums** or **·la** (-lə) **1** A regular or particular course of study, as in a college. **2** All such courses of study, collectively. [< L, a race < *currere* run] —**cur·ric′u·lar** *adj.*

cur·ric·u·lum vi·tae (kə·rik′yə·ləm vī′tē) *Latin* **1** Course of life; career. **2** A short biographical statement giving information such as one's date of birth, schooling, marital status, record of employment, etc.

cur·ri·er (kûr′ē·ər) *n.* **1** One who curries leather. **2** One who curries horses.

Cur·ri·er and Ives (kûr′ē·ər; īvz) **1** A U.S. firm of lithographers, founded in 1835 by Nathanael Currier, 1813–88, later joined by James Merritt Ives, 1824–95. **2** Any print issued by the firm, the subjects of which were scenes of American life, manners, and history.

cur·ri·er·y (kûr′ē·ər·ē) *n. pl.* **·er·ies** The trade or occupation of a currier, or a currier's shop.

cur·rish (kûr′ish) *adj.* Like a cur; snarling; mean; nasty. —**cur′rish·ly** *adv.* —**cur′rish·ness** *n.*

cur·ry¹ (kûr′ē) *v.t.* **·ried, ·ry·ing 1** To clean with a currycomb; groom (a horse, dog, etc.). **2** To dress (tanned hides) for use. **3** To beat or pummel. —**to curry favor** To seek favor by adulation and subserviency. [< OF *carreier, conreder* make ready, prepare]

cur·ry² (kûr′ē) *n. pl.* **·ries 1** A cooked dish consisting of meats, fish, rice, etc., seasoned with curry powder or curry sauce. **2** A pungent sauce of Indian origin, made of vegetables, spices, and

strong condiments: also **curry sauce. 3** Curry powder. —*v.t.* **·ried, ·ry·ing** To flavor with curry. [< Tamil *kari* sauce]

cur·ry·comb (kûr′ē·kōm′) *n.* A comb consisting of a series of upright serrated ridges, for grooming horses. —*v.t.* To comb with a currycomb.

curry powder A powdered condiment, prepared from the dried leaves of an Indian plant (*Murraya koenigi*), together with other pungent spices, turmeric, etc.: used in making curry sauce and curried dishes.

curse (kûrs) *v.* **cursed** or **curst, curs·ing** *v.t.* **1** To invoke evil or injury upon; anathematize; damn. **2** To swear at; execrate. **3** To cause evil or injury to. —*v.i.* **4** To utter imprecations; swear; blaspheme. —*n.* **1** An imprecation of evil; any profane oath. **2** Calamity invoked or threatened. **3** A source of calamity or evil; also, the evil which comes as a result of invocation or as punishment. **4** An object of execration. See synonyms under ABOMINATION, IMPRECATION, OATH. [OE *cursian* < OIrish *cursagim* blame]

curs·ed (kûr′sid, kûrst) *adj.* **1** Under a curse. **2** Deserving a curse; execrable; detestable. — **curs·ed·ly** (kûr′sid·lē) *adv.*

cur·sive (kûr′siv) *adj.* Running; flowing: said of writing in which the letters are joined. —*n.* A letter or character used in cursive writing. [< Med. L *cursivus* < L *cursus* < *currere* run] — **cur′sive·ly** *adv.*

cur·sor (kûr′sər) *n.* A pointer on a computer screen that shows the position where an operation is taking place.

cur·so·ri·al (kûr·sôr′ē·əl, -sō′rē-) *adj.* **1** Fitted for running or walking, as distinguished from other modes of progression. **2** Having, or executed by means of, limbs of such a character.

cur·so·ry (kûr′sər·ē) *adj.* Rapid and superficial; hasty. Also *Obs.* **cur·so·rar·y** (kûr′sə·rer′ē). [< LL *cursorius* pertaining to running < *cursor* a runner < *currere* run] —**cur′so·ri·ly** *adv.* — **cur′so·ri·ness** *n.*

Synonyms: careless, desultory, hasty, slight, superficial. *Antonyms:* careful, critical, elaborate, exhaustive, minute, painstaking, thorough.

curst (kûrst) A past tense and past participle of CURSE. —*adj.* Of a hateful disposition; vicious.

curt (kûrt) *adj.* **1** Concise and abrupt in act or expression. **2** Short and sharp in manner; brusk. [< L *curtus* shortened] —**curt′ly** *adv.* —**curt′ness** *n.*

cur·tail (kər·tāl′) *v.t.* To cut off or cut short; abbreviate; lessen; reduce. See synonyms under ABBREVIATE, RETRENCH. —*n.* The scrollshaped end of an architectural member. [< CURTAL; infl. in form by TAIL] —**cur·tail′er** *n.* — **cur·tail′ment** *n.*

cur·tain (kûr′tən) *n.* **1** A piece of fabric, often adjustable, hung for decoration, concealment, or to shut out light, as before a wall, window, doorway, etc. **2** Something that conceals, covers or separates like a curtain. **3** Part of a rampart that connects the flanks of two bastions or towers. **4** *Archit.* That portion of a wall between two towers. **5** In the theater: **a** The drapery hanging at the front of a stage, drawn up or aside to reveal the stage. **b** The speech or situation in a play occurring immediately before the fall of the curtain. —*v.t.* **1** To supply or adorn with or as with a curtain or curtains. **2** To conceal or shut off as with a curtain; cover. [< OF *curtine* < LL *cortina*]

curtain call The prolonged applause which a performer acknowledges by appearing on the stage after the end of a play, scene, etc.

curtain lecture A private chiding or faultfinding, as administered by a wife to her husband: supposedly given in an old-fashioned curtained bed.

cur·tain-rais·er (kûr′tən·rā′zər) *n.* A short play or sketch presented before a longer or more important play.

curtain speech In the theater, a speech, as made by one of the actors, from in front of the curtain at the end of a performance.

curtain wall *Archit.* An outside wall that encloses but gives no structural support.

cur·tal (kûr′təl) *Obs. adj.* Cut off; short; curt;

brief. —*n.* An animal with a docked tail. [<OF *curtald*]

cur·tal-ax (kûr′təl·aks′) *n. Obs.* A cutlass. [Alter. of CUTLASS]

curtal friar *Obs.* A short-frocked friar attendant at the gate of a monastery court.

cur·tate (kûr′tāt) *adj.* Shortened. [<L *curtatus,* pp. of *curtare* shorten < *curtus* shortened]

cur·te·sy (kûr′tə·sē) *n. pl.* **·sies** Courtesy.

curtesy of England In English law, the tenure by which a man holds for life the estates of his deceased wife inheritable by their children.

cur·ti·lage (kûr′tə·lij) *n. Law* The ground adjacent to a dwelling house, and used in connection with it. [<AF, var. of OF *cortillage* < *cortil,* dim. of *cortis, cort* COURT]

Cur·tin (kûr′tin), **Jeremiah,** 1838–1906, U.S. ethnologist. —**John,** 1885–1945, Australian politician; premier 1941–45.

Cur·tis (kûr′tis), **Charles,** 1860–1936, U.S. statesman, vice president of the United States 1929–33. —**Cyrus Hermann,** 1850–1933, U.S. publisher.

Cur·tiss (kûr′tis), **Glenn Hammond,** 1878–1930, U.S. pioneer aviator and inventor.

Cur·ti·us (kōōr′tsē·ōōs), **Ernst,** 1814–96, German archeologist and educator.

curt·sy (kûrt′sē) *n. pl.* **·sies** A gesture of civility or respect, consisting of a slight bending of the knees, and performed chiefly by women: sometimes spelled *courtesy.* —*v.i.* **·sied, ·sy·ing** To bend the knees and lower the body slightly, as a gesture of civility, reverence, or respect. Also **curt′sey.** [Var. of COURTESY]

cu·rule (kyōōr′ōōl) *adj.* **1** Of or pertaining to an ancient Roman magisterial chair reserved for state dignitaries. **2** Privileged to sit in the curule chair; hence, magisterial; official. [<L *curulis* < *currus* chariot]

curule chair The official seat of Roman magistrates of the highest rank: also **curule seat.**

curule dignity The right to sit in the curule chair.

cur·va·ceous (kûr·vā′shəs) *adj. Colloq.* Having voluptuous curves; shapely in form: said of a woman.

cur·vate (kûr′vāt) *adj.* Evenly bent; curved. Also **cur′vat·ed.** [<L *curvatus,* pp. of *curvare* bend] —**cur·va′tion** *n.*

cur·va·ture (kûr′və·chər) *n.* **1** The act of bending, or the state of being curved; amount or rate of bending. **2** Any deviation from a normal or expected rectilinear course: a lateral *curvature* of the spine. [<L *curvatura* < *curvare* bend]

curve (kûrv) *n.* **1** A line continuously bent so that no portion of it is straight, as the arc of a circle. **2** A bending, or something bent. **3** An instrument for drawing curves: used by draftsmen. **4** *Math.* The locus of a point moving in such a way that its course can be defined by an equation. **5** *Physics* A line representing variations in force, quantity, temperature, etc. **6** In baseball, the course given to a ball by the pitcher, causing it to curve to one side or the other before crossing the plate. —*v.* **curved, curv·ing** *v.t.* **1** To cause to assume the form of a curve. —*v.i.* **2** To assume the form of a curve. **3** To move in a curve, as a projectile or ball; bend. —*adj.* Curved. [<L *curvum* < *curvus* bent]

curved (kûrvd) *adj.* Having a different direction at every point; bent. —**curv·ed·ly** (kûr′vid·lē) *adv.* —**curv′ed·ness** *n.*

cur·vet (kər·vet′, kûr′vit) *v.t. & v.i.* **·vet·ted** or **·vet·ed, ·vet·ting** or **·vet·ing 1** To prance or cause to prance. **2** To frisk about. —*n.* (kûr′vit) A light, low leap of a horse, made so that at one movement all four legs are off the ground. [<Ital. *corvettare* < *corvetta,* dim. of *corva* bent <L *curvus*]

curvi– *combining form* Curved. [<L *curvus* curved]

cur·vi·fo·li·ate (kûr′və·fō′lē·it, -āt) *adj. Bot.* Having curved leaves.

cur·vi·lin·e·ar (kûr′və·lin′ē·ər) *adj.* Formed by curved lines. Also **cur′vi·lin′e·al.** See synonyms under ROUND.

cur·vi·ty (kûr′və·tē) *n.* The state of being curved; curvature.

Cur·zon (kûr′zən), **George Nathaniel,** 1859–1925, First Marquess Curzon of Kedleston, English statesman; viceroy of India 1899–1905.

Curzon Line The demarcation line between Poland and the U.S.S.R., anchored in its center on the Western Bug: first proposed by George Nathaniel *Curzon* in 1919, altered in 1945 and again in 1951.

Cus·co (kōōs′kō) See CUZCO.

cus·cus (kōōs′kōōs) *n.* Any of various arboreal phalangers (genus *Phalanger*) of Australia and New Zealand, as the **brown cuscus** (*P. orientalis*) or the **spotted cuscus** (*P. maculatus*), having long prehensile tails.

cu·sec (kyōō′sek) *n.* A cubic foot per second: a unit for measuring the rate of flow of a liquid. [<CU(BIC) + SEC(OND)]

Cush (kush) A son of Ham. *Gen.* x 6.

Cush (kush) A region referred to in the Bible as settled by the descendants of Cush, identified as Ethiopia: also *Kush.*

cush·at (kush′ət, kōōsh′-) *n.* The European ring dove (*Columba palumbus*), having the neck partly encircled with a cream-colored mark. [OE *cūscote*]

cu·shaw (kə·shô′) *n.* A variety of the crookneck squash: also called *cashaw, China squash.* [<N. Am. Ind.]

Cush·ing (kōōsh′ing), **Caleb,** 1800–79, U.S. jurist and diplomat. —**Harvey Williams,** 1869–1939, U.S. surgeon.

cush·ion (kōōsh′ən) *n.* **1** A flexible bag or casing filled with some soft or elastic material, as feathers, air, etc. **2** Anything resembling a cushion in appearance, construction, or application; especially, any device to deaden the jar or impact of parts, as padding or inserted rubber. **3** The elastic rim of a billiard table. **4** A pincushion. **5** A pillow used in making lace. **6** The motive fluid remaining in the cylinder of a reciprocating engine after the closing of the exhaust port. **7** The fleshy part of the hind quarter of a hog, horse, etc. —*v.t.* **1** To place, seat, or arrange on or as on a cushion; prop up. **2** To provide with a cushion. **3** To cover or hide as with a cushion. **4** To pad, as with a cushion; absorb the shock or effect of. **5** *Mech.* To compress, as exhaust steam or other motive fluid, by closing the exhaust outlet of a cylinder. —*v.i.* **6** In billiards, to cause the cue ball to strike the cushion before contact with the second object ball, either before or after striking the first. [<F *coussin,* ? var. of OF *coissin,* ult. <L *coxa* hip, thigh] —**cush′ion·y** *adj.*

Cush·it·ic (kōōsh·it′ik) *n.* A group of Hamitic languages spoken in Ethiopia and Somaliland. —*adj.* Pertaining to this group of languages. Also spelled *Kushitic.*

Cush·man (kōōsh′mən), **Charlotte,** 1816–76, U.S. actress.

cush·y (kōōsh′ē) *adj. Slang* **cush·i·er, cush·i·est** Comfortable; agreeable. [<CUSHION; orig. Brit. slang]

cusk (kusk) *n. pl.* **cusks** or **cusk 1** An edible codlike fish (*Brosmius brosme*) of northern seas. **2** The burbot. [Origin unknown]

cusp (kusp) *n.* **1** A point or pointed end. **2** *Astron.* Either point of a crescent moon. **3** *Geom.* A point at which two branches of a curve meet and end, with a common tangent. **4** *Archit.* A projecting point between small arcs, as in medieval tracery. **5** *Anat.* **a** A prominence or point, as on the crown of a tooth. **b** The pointed fold forming a segment of the cardiac valves. **6** *Bot.* A sharp, stiff point, as of a leaf. **7** In astrology, the first entrance of a house in the determination of nativities. **8** *Geol.* An angular, projecting beach or portion of a beach, formed by the interaction of conflicting currents. [<L *cuspis, -idis* a point]

cus·pate (kus′pāt) *adj.* **1** Having a cusp or cusps. **2** Cusp-shaped. Also **cus′pat·ed, cusped** (kuspt).

cus·pid (kus′pid) *n.* A canine tooth. —*adj.* Cuspidate.

cus·pi·date (kus′pə·dāt) *adj.* **1** Having a cusp or cusps. **2** *Bot.* Ending in a cusp, as a leaf. Also **cus′pi·dat′ed, cus·pi·dal** (kus′pə·dəl).

cus·pi·da·tion (kus′pə·dā′shən) *n. Archit.* Decoration with cusps.

cus·pi·dor (kus′pə·dôr) *n.* A spittoon. Also **cus′pi·dore.** [<Pg., spitter < *cuspir* spit <L *conspuere* < *com-* thoroughly + *spuere* spit]

cus·pis (kus′pis) *n. pl.* **·pi·des** (-pə·dēz) *Latin* A cusp.

cuss (kus) *U.S. Colloq. v.t. & v.i.* To curse. —*n.* **1** A curse. **2** A worthless or disagreeable person: a humorous or contemptuous term. [Var. of CURSE]

cuss·ed (kus′id) *adj. U.S. Colloq.* **1** Cursed. **2** Mean; perverse. —**cuss′ed·ly** *adv.* —**cuss′ed·ness** *n.*

cus·so (kus′ō) *n.* **1** An Abyssinian tree (*Hagenia abyssinica*) of the rose family. **2** The flowers of this tree, used by natives as a vermifuge; brayera: also spelled *kousso, kusso.* [<native name]

cus·ta·lo·rum (kus′tə·lôr′əm, -lō′rəm) *n. Obs.* Custos rotulorum: a corruption.

cus·tard (kus′tərd) *n.* A mixture of milk, eggs, sugar, and flavoring, either boiled or baked. [Alter. of earlier *crustarde, crustade* <F *croustade,* a type of pie <L *crusta* crust]

custard apple 1 The papaw: also called **custard tree. 2** A tropical American tree (*Annona reticulata*). **3** Its soft, edible fruit.

Cus·ter (kus′tər), **George Armstrong,** 1839–1876, U.S. general and Indian fighter, killed in a battle with Indians at Little Bighorn.

cus·tock (kus′tək) *n. Scot.* The core of a cabbage; a cabbage stalk.

cus·to·di·an (kus·tō′dē·ən) *n.* A guardian; caretaker. —**cus·to′di·an·ship′** *n.*

cus·to·dy (kus′tə·dē) *n. pl.* **·dies 1** A keeping; guardianship. **2** The state of being held in keeping or under guard; restraint of liberty; imprisonment. See synonyms under FETTER. —**to take into custody** To arrest. [<L *custodia* guard < *custos* guardian] —**cus·to·di·al** (kus·tō′dē·əl) *adj.*

cus·tom (kus′təm) *n.* **1** An ordinary or usual manner of doing or acting. **2** The habitual practice of a community or people; common usage. **3** *Law* An old and general usage that has obtained the force of law. **4** Customary frequenting, as of a hotel, or habitual purchase, as of goods, staple commodities, etc., at a particular place; business support; patronage. **5** A tariff or duty assessed by law, levied upon goods imported or exported; hence, any regular toll or tax: in the first of these senses always plural. **6** *pl.* The former ritual sacrifice of human victims in Ashanti and Dahomey, on the death of a chief or king. **7** Customary rent, tribute, or service due from a feudal tenant to his lord. —*adj.* **1** Made to order: also **cus′tom-built′, cus′tom-made. 2** Specializing in made-to-order goods: a *custom* tailor. **3** From or for customers: *custom* ore; a *custom* smelter. [<OF *custume* <L *consuetudo* < *com-* thoroughly + *suescere* become used to. Doublet of COSTUME.]

Synonyms (*noun*): fashion, habit, manner, practice, style, use. See HABIT, TAX.

cus·tom·a·ble (kus′təm·ə·bəl) *adj.* Liable or subject to duty or customs; dutiable.

cus·tom·ar·y (kus′tə·mer′ē) *adj.* **1** Conforming to or established by custom. **2** In English law, holding, or held by custom, as a tenant or his tenancy. See synonyms under COMMON, GENERAL, HABITUAL, USUAL. —*n. pl.* **·ar·ies** A written or printed statement of laws and customs. —**cus·tom·ar·i·ly** (kus′tə·mer′ə·lē, kus′tə·mer′ə·lē) *adv.* —**cus′tom·ar′i·ness** *n.*

cus·tom·er (kus′təm·ər) *n.* **1** One who gives his custom or trade; a purchaser. **2** *Colloq.* A person to be dealt with; a fellow: a queer *customer*; an ugly *customer.*

cus·tom·house (kus′təm·hous′) *n.* The place where entries of imports are made, vessels cleared, and duties collected; the department of customs.

customs union An association of nations that remove tariff restrictions among themselves and conduct a common tariff policy toward other nations.

cus·tos (kus′tos) *n. pl.* **cus·to·des** (kus·tō′dēz) **1** A custodian; keeper. **2** *Music* A direct. **3** The superior in certain religious houses. [<L, guardian]

custos mo·rum (môr′əm, mō′rəm) *Latin* Guardian of morals.

custos ro·tu·lo·rum (rō′tə·lôr′əm, -lō′rəm) A principal justice of an English county, who keeps the rolls or records of the sessions of the justices' court. [<L, keeper of the records]

cus·tu·mal (kus′chōō·məl, -tyōō-) *adj.* Belonging to the customs of a city. —*n.* A written collection of the customs of a city.

cut (kut) *v.* **cut, cut·ting** *v.t.* **1** To pierce, gash, or pass through with or as with a sharp edge. **2** To strike sharply, as with a whip. **3** To affect deeply; hurt the feelings of. **4** To divide, sever, or carve into parts or segments. **5** To fell, hew, or chop down, as a tree or timber: often with *down.* **6** To mow or reap,

as grain. **7** To shape, prepare, or make, as gems or carvings. **8** To hollow out, excavate. **9** To trim, shear, or pare. **10** To excise; edit out. **11** To reduce or lessen: to *cut* prices. **12** To dilute or weaken: to *cut* whisky. **13** To dissolve or break down, as fat globules: to *cut* grease. **14** To cross or intersect. **15** To castrate; geld. **16** *Colloq.* **a** To ignore socially, snub. **b** To stay away from wilfully, as work or classes. **17** To divide, as a pack of cards before dealing. **18** In racket sports, to chop (the ball) so it will spin and bound sharply and irregularly. **19** To turn the wheels of, as an automobile, so as to make the vehicle turn sharply. **20** To perform; present: to *cut* a caper. **21** To grow or acquire: to *cut* a tooth. — *v.i.* **22** To cut, cleave, or make an incision; do the work of a sharp edge. **23** To admit of being severed or cut. **24** To use an instrument for cutting. **25** To grow out through the gums: said of teeth. **26** To divide a card pack before dealing. **27** In sports, to chop the ball; also, to veer sharply while running. **28** To move or proceed by the shortest or most direct route: The boys *cut* across the field. — **to cut a figure** **1** To make a fine appearance. **2** To be of importance. **3** To make an impression: to *cut a* poor *figure* in scholarship. — **to cut a melon** To divide, as large profits or gains, with one's associates. — **to cut and run** Formerly, to cut the moorings of a vessel and set sail hastily; hence, to dash off without notice. — **to cut back** **1** To shorten by removing the end. **2** To curtail or cancel, as a contract, before fulfilment. **3** In sports, to run or dash erratically; change direction suddenly. — **to cut corners** To eliminate all but the most necessary items, as clothing for a trip, expenses, etc. — **to cut down** **1** To reduce the length or amount of; shorten; curtail. **2** To kill, as with a sword. — **to cut no ice** *Colloq.* To make no impression; have no significance. — **to cut in** **1** To interrupt a dancing couple in order to take the place of one partner. **2** To interrupt, as a conversation. **3** To move into (a line or queue) out of turn. — **to cut it fine** To arrange or estimate to the narrowest degree of tolerance: He *cut it fine* when he passed that car. — **to cut loose** **1** To release. **2** To speak or behave without restraint. — **to cut off** **1** To put an end to; destroy. **2** To interrupt. **3** To intercept. — **to cut out** **1** *Colloq.* To start away with haste. **2** To displace (another); supplant, as a rival. **3** To quit or renounce, as smoking. **4** To separate from the herd, as a horse or steer. **5** *Austral. Colloq.* To complete wool shearing; to complete any task. — **to cut up** **1** To slice or cut into pieces. **2** *Slang* To behave in an unruly manner. — *n.* **1** The opening, cleft, or wound made by an edged instrument; a gash; slit. **2** A cutting motion or stroke. **3** The part cut off. **4** That which cuts or hurts the feelings. **5** A cutting; excavated passage; groove; a road made through rock or a mountain for a railroad, canal, etc. **6** A direct way, as across an angle. **7** Fashion, form, style; also, number of arrangements of facets: the *cut* of a diamond. **8** An engraved block, or an impression from it. **9** A reduction, as in rates or of written matter; also, the part thus removed. **10** A refusal to recognize an acquaintance. **11** *Colloq.* An intentional failure in attendance, as at classes in college. **12** One of the bits of material used in drawing lots: to draw *cuts.* **13** The act of cutting in card playing. **14** A stroke imparting spin to a ball, in lawn tennis and cricket; also, the spin so imparted. **15** A fancy dancing step. **16** In a strip of motion-picture film, the narrow band separating one frame or exposure from the next. **17** *Chem.* **a** The quantity of resin added to each gallon of solvent. **b** A fraction of petroleum. **18** The output or seasonal yield of anything to be cut, as grain, timber, etc. **19** A group of animals, as cows or steers, separated from a herd to be driven elsewhere. **20** *U.S. Colloq.* A share. — *adj.* **1** Formed or affected by cutting; wounded; severed. **2** Dressed or finished by a tool, as stone or glass. **3** Castrated. **4** Reduced. **5** *Bot.* Incised or cleft. **6** Diluted. [ME *cutten, kytten* <Scand.]

Synonyms (verb): carve, chop, cleave, dissect, gash, hack, hew, sever, shear, slice, sunder, whittle. See RETRENCH.

cut-and-dried (kut′ən·drīd′) *adj.* **1** Prepared and arranged beforehand. **2** Lacking suspense; uninteresting; routine.

cut-and-thrust (kut′ən·thrust′) *adj.* Intended for cutting and thrusting: said of a sword.

cu·ta·ne·ous (kyōō·tā′nē·əs) *adj.* Consisting of, pertaining to, affecting, or of the nature of skin: a *cutaneous* covering; a *cutaneous* disease. [<Med. L *cutaneus* < *cutis* skin]

cut·a·way (kut′ə·wā′) *n.* A man's coat with the front corners cut slopingly away from the waist down to the back: also **cutaway coat.**

cut·back (kut′bak′) *n.* A sharp cut in the scheduled production of raw materials or manufactured goods, due to a sudden or unforeseen lessening of demand.

cutch[1] (kuch) *n.* Couchgrass.

cutch[2] (kuch) *n. Anglo-Indian* Catechu.

Cutch (kuch) A chief commissioner's state in western India; 8,461 square miles; capital, Bhuj; on the NE border lies the **Rann of Cutch,** a vast salt waste. Also *Kutch.*

cut·cher·ry (kə·cher′ē) *n. Anglo-Indian* A hall of justice; also, any public administrative office. Also **cutch·er·y** (kuch′ər·ē).

cute (kyōōt) *adj.* **1** *U.S. Colloq.* Pretty or dainty; attractive. **2** *Dial.* Clever or sharp, especially in looking out for one's own advantage in petty ways. [Var. of ACUTE] — **cute′ly** *adv.* — **cute′ness** *n.*

cut glass See under GLASS.

cut·grass (kut′gras′, -gräs′) *n.* A swamp grass *(Leersia oryzoides)* with flat, rough-edged leaves that cut the flesh when drawn against it.

Cuth·bert (kuth′bərt), **Saint,** died 687, English monk.

cu·ti·cle (kyōō′ti·kəl) *n.* **1** The outer layer of cells that protect the true skin; epidermis; scarfskin. **2** Any superficial covering. **3** *Zool.* A thick lining membrane, as the cell integument of protozoa. **4** The crescent of toughened skin around the base of a fingernail or toenail. **5** *Bot.* A continuous hyaline film covering the surface of a plant, derived from the layers of epidermal cells. Also **cu·tic·u·la** (kyōō·tik′yə·lə). [<L *cuticula,* dim. of *cutis* skin] — **cu·tic′u·lar** *adj.*

cu·tie (kyōō′tē) *n. U.S. Slang* A pretty young woman. Also **cu′tey.** [<CUTE]

cu·ti·fy (kyōō′ti·fī) *v.i.* To form new skin [<L *cutis* skin + -FY]

cu·tin (kyōō′tin) *n.* **1** *Bot.* A variety of fatty or waxy protective cuticle of leaves, stems, etc., of plants. **2** *Med.* A substitute for catgut or silk used in suturing wounds: it is prepared from the gut of an ox. [<L *cutis* skin + -IN]

cut-in (kut′in′) *n.* **1** The coordination of an automatic train-control system with the moving train so as to ensure application of the brakes. **2** *Printing* An insert in the text matter of a page.

cu·tin·i·za·tion (kyōō′tən·ə·zā′shən, -ī·zā′-) *n. Bot.* The modification of cell walls by the presence of cutin, making them waterproof.

cu·tin·ize (kyōō′tən·īz) *v.t.* & *v.i.* **·ized, ·iz·ing** To make or become cuticular.

cu·tis (kyōō′tis) *n.* The derma or true skin; also, the corium. Also **cutis ve·ra** (vir′ə). [<L]

cut·las (kut′ləs) *n.* A short, swordlike weapon, often curved, formerly used chiefly by sailors in hand-to-hand fighting. Also **cut′lass.** [<F *coutelas,* aug. of *couteau* knife <L *culter*]

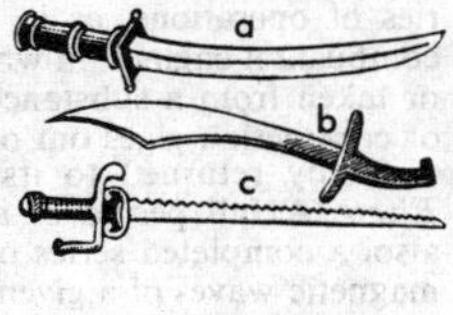

CUTLASES
a. British, 10th century.
b. German, 15th century.
c. Mariner's, 17th century.

cutlas fish Scabbard fish.

cut·ler (kut′lər) *n.* One who manufactures or deals in cutlery. [<F *coutelier* <Med. L *cultellarius* maker of knives <L *cultellus,* dim. of *culter* knife]

cut·ler·y (kut′lər·ē) *n.* **1** Cutting instruments collectively; especially, those for use at the dinner table. **2** The occupation of a cutler. [<OF *coutelerie* < *coutelier* CUTLER]

cut·let (kut′lit) *n.* **1** A thin piece of meat from the ribs or leg, for broiling or frying. **2** A flat croquette of chopped meat, fish, etc. [<F *côtelette,* double dim. of *côte* side <L *costa* rib; infl. in form by *cut*]

cut-line (kut′līn′) *n.* The title of an illustration.

cut money Money made by cutting gold and silver coins into pieces: used in the early Spanish colonies.

cut-off (kut′ôf′, -of′) *n.* **1** A short cut. **2** A mechanism that cuts off the flow of a fuel or fluid, as of steam to a boiler. **3** The point at which flow is thus cut off; the act of so doing. **4** A channel, natural or artificial, that diverts the course of a stream.

cut-out (kut′out′) *n.* **1** *Electr.* A switchlike arrangement, as for cutting a light out from a circuit. **2** A device to let the exhaust gases from an internal-combustion engine pass direct to the air without passing through the muffler. **3** The severing of the automatic train-control system from a moving train so as to prevent application of brakes.

cut-o·ver (kut′ō′vər) *adj.* Having the timber cut off: *cut-over* land.

cut-price (kut′prīs′) *adj.* Sharply reduced in price; below the usual rate.

cut·purse (kut′pûrs′) *n.* A pickpocket.

cut rate A reduced price.

cut-rate (kut′rāt′) *adj.* Sold for, or selling goods for, reduced prices: a *cut-rate* ticket, a *cut-rate* store.

Cut·tack (ku·tak′) A city in NE India; former capital of Orissa.

cut·ter (kut′ər) *n.* **1** One who cuts, shapes, or fits anything by cutting. **2** That which cuts, as a tool or a machine. **3** *Naut.* **a** A sloop-rigged, fast-sailing vessel of narrow beam and deep draft, with bow and stern lines of the hull almost perpendicular. **b** A small, swift, armed, engined vessel, as in the revenue marine service. **c** A medium-sized boat used by a man-of-war. **4** A small sleigh usually drawn by one horse.

CUTTER *(def. 4)*

cut-throat (kut′thrōt′) *adj.* **1** Ruffianly; bloodthirsty. **2** Played by three single players: said of poker and other card games. **3** Profitless: *cut-throat* stock. **4** Ruinous; merciless: *cut-throat* competition. — *n.* **1** A bloodthirsty ruffian. **2** A cut-throat card game.

cut·tie (kut′ē) *n.* An auk: also called *black guillemot.*

cut·ting (kut′ing) *adj.* **1** Adapted to cut; edged. **2** Disagreeably penetrating; sharp; chilling. **3** Tending to wound the feelings; sarcastic; bitter. See synonyms under BITTER[1], BLEAK[1]. — *n.* **1** The act of severing. **2** Something obtained or made by cutting; a piece cut off or out. **3** *Bot.* A young plant shoot cut off for rooting or vegetative propagation. **4** An excavation, as for a railroad track. **5** *Chem.* In the making of soap, the separation of the final product from glycerol and aqueous products.

cut·tle (kut′l) *n.* **1** A cuttlefish. **2** Cuttlebone. [OE *cudele*]

cut·tle·bone (kut′l·bōn′) *n.* The internal calcareous plate of a cuttlefish: used as a dietary supplement for birds and, when powdered, as a polishing agent.

cut·tle·fish (kut′l·fish′) *n. pl.* **·fish** or **·fish·es** A carnivorous marine cephalopod (genus *Sepia*), with lateral fins, ten sucker-bearing arms, and an internal calcareous skeleton: it conceals itself by ejecting an inky fluid.

cut·ty (kut′ē, kōōt′ē) *Scot. adj.* Short; hasty; quick. — *n. pl.* **·ties** **1** Anything cut short, as a spoon or tobacco pipe. **2** A hare. **3** A thick-set girl. **4** A slattern.

cutty sark (särk) *Scot.* A short chemise.

cutty stool *Scot.* **1** A little stool. **2** A seat in church where offenders sat to receive public rebuke.

cut-up (kut′up′) *n. Colloq.* A person who tries to seem funny to others; a practical joker.

cut·wa·ter (kut′wô′tər, -wot′ər) *n.* **1** The forward part of the prow of a vessel. **2** The sharp edge on the up-stream side of a bridge pier.

cut·worm (kut′wûrm′) *n.* The larva of a moth (family *Noctuidae*) that cuts off young plants, usually at or near the surface of the ground. For illustration see under INSECT (injurious).

cu·vée (kü·vā′) *n. French* **1** The contents of a wine vat or cask; also, a vintage. **2** A blend of wines used in making champagne.

Cu·vi·er (ko͞o′vē·ā, kyo͞o′-; *Fr.* kü·vyā′), **Baron Georges,** 1769–1832, French naturalist.

Cux·ha·ven (ko͝oks′hä·fən) A port at the mouth of the Elbe in NW Germany: also *Kuxhaven.*

Cu·yu·ni (ko͞o·yo͞o′nē) A river in British Guiana and Venezuela, flowing 150 miles NE to the Mazaruni.

Cuz·co (ko͞os′kō) A department of southern Peru; 55,731 square miles; capital, Cuzco, formerly capital of the Inca Empire: also *Cusco.*

Cwm·ry (ko͞om′rē) See CYMRY.

-cy *suffix* Forming nouns: **1** *(from adjectives)* Quality, state, or condition of: *secrecy, bankruptcy.* **2** *(from nouns)* Rank, order, or condition of: *chaplaincy, baronetcy.* [<F *-cie, -tie* <L *-cia, -tia* <Gk. *-kia, -keia, -tia, -teia*; or directly <L or <Gk.]

cyan- Var. of CYANO-.

cy·an·a·mide (sī·an′ə·mīd, -mid, sī′ə·nam′īd, -id) *n. Chem.* A white crystalline compound, CH_2N_2, formed from calcium cyanamide or by the action of cyanogen chloride on ammonia. Also **cy·an·a·mid** (sī·an′ə·mid, sī′ə·nam′id). [<CYAN- + AMIDE]

cyanamide process *Chem.* A method for the fixation of atmospheric nitrogen by passing a current of the gas over superheated calcium carbide and treating with high-pressure steam to yield ammonia.

cy·a·nate (sī′ə·nāt) *n. Chem.* A salt or ester of cyanic acid. [<CYAN- + -ATE[3]]

cy·an·ic (sī·an′ik) *adj.* **1** Of, pertaining to, or containing cyanogen. **2** Of or pertaining to blue.

cyanic acid *Chem.* A volatile liquid compound, HCNO, with a penetrating pungent odor and caustic properties, that is stable at low temperatures only. It is prepared by heating anhydrous cyanuric acid in carbonic acid gas.

cy·a·nide (sī′ə·nīd) *n. Chem.* A compound of cyanogen with a metallic element or radical: potassium *cyanide.* —*v.t.* **·nid·ed, ·nid·ing** *Metall.* To subject to the action of cyanide: to extract gold by *cyaniding* the ore. [<CYAN- + -IDE] — **cy′a·ni·da′tion** *n.*

cyanide process *Metall.* A process of extracting metal (chiefly gold) from ores by means of a dilute potassium-cyanide or sodium-cyanide solution which, assisted by the action of oxygen, dissolves the metal.

cy·a·nin (sī·ə·nin) *n. Biochem.* Any of a group of blue pigments obtained from certain flowers, as the iris, violet, and cornflower: also called *anthocyanin.* [<CYAN- + -IN]

cy·a·nine (sī′ə·nēn, -nin) *n. Chem.* A bluish-green, crystalline derivative, $C_{29}H_{35}N_2I$, of quinoline, used in photography as a sensitizer and indicator. [<CYAN- + -INE[1]]

cy·a·nite (sī′ə·nīt) *n.* A blue, gray, or black aluminum silicate, occurring in long, bladelike, triclinic crystals, and also found columnar to fibrous in structure: often spelled *kyanite.* [<CYAN- + -ITE[1]]

cyano- *combining form* **1** *Chem.* Cyanogen: *cyanogenesis.* **2** *Med.* Characterized by bluish coloring: *cyanosis.* **3** Dark-blue; blue: *cyanometer.* Also, before vowels, **cyan-.** [<Gk. *kyanos* dark-blue]

cy·an·o·gen (sī·an′ə·jən) *n. Chem.* **1** A colorless, intensely poisonous, liquefiable gas, C_2N_2, having an almondlike odor and burning with a purple flame. **2** The univalent radical, CN.

cy·a·no·gen·e·sis (sī′ə·nō·jen′ə·sis) *n. Chem.* **1** The making of hydrocyanic acid. **2** The process by which a glucoside through hydrolysis yields hydrocyanic (prussic) acid as one of its products.

cy·a·nom·e·ter (sī′ə·nom′ə·tər) *n. Meteorol.* An instrument for measuring the intensity of blue, as in the sky. [<CYANO- + -METER] **—cy·a·no·met·ric** (sī′ə·nō·met′rik) *adj.* **—cy′a·nom′e·try** *n.*

cy·a·nop·a·thy (sī′ə·nop′ə·thē) *n.* Cyanosis. [<CYANO- + -PATHY] **—cy·a·no·path·ic** (sī′ə·nō·path′ik) *adj.*

cy·a·noph·i·lous (sī′ə·nof′ə·ləs) *adj.* Stainable with blue dyes. [<CYANO- + -PHILOUS]

cy·a·no·pi·a (sī′ə·nō′pē·ə) *n. Pathol.* A diseased condition in which all things seem appear blue or bluish. Also **cy·a·nop·si·a** (sī′ə·nop′sē·ə). [<CYAN- + -OPIA].

cy·a·no·sis (sī′ə·nō′sis) *n. Pathol.* A disordered condition of the circulation due to inadequate airing of the blood and causing a livid bluish color of the skin. Also **cy·a·no·chroi·a** (sī′ə·nō·kroi′ə), **cy′a·no·der′ma** (-dûr′mə). [<CYAN- + -OSIS] **—cy·a·not·ic** (sī′ə·not′ik) *adj.*

cy·an·o·type (sī·an′ə·tīp′) *n.* A photographic picture, as a blueprint, made with the use of a cyanide.

cy·a·nu·ric (sī′ə·nyo͝or′ik) *adj. Chem.* **1** Of or pertaining to cyanogen and urea. **2** Designating a crystalline acid, $C_3H_3O_3N_3$, obtained variously, as by the dry distillation of uric acid. [<CYAN- + URIC]

Cyb·e·le (sib′ə·lē) In Phrygian mythology, the goddess of nature: identified with the Greek *Rhea*: also called *Great Mother.*

cy·ber·net·ics (sī′bər·net′iks) *n.* The science which treats of the principles underlying the common elements in the functioning of automatic machines and of the human nervous system; the theory of control and communication in machines and organisms. [<Gk. *kybernētēs* steersman + -ICS]

cy·bo·tax·is (sī′bə·tak′sis) *n. Physics* The arrangement of molecules in a liquid in such a manner as to suggest crystal structure, but without permanence or stability at any point. [<Gk. *kybos* cube + *taxis* arrangement] **—cy′bo·tac′tic** (-tak′tik) *adj.*

cy·cad (sī′kad) *n.* Any of a small family *(Cycadaceae)* of primitive, seed-bearing, mostly tropical plants of fernlike or palmlike appearance. [<NL *Cycas, -adis* <Gk. *kykas,* a copyist's error for *koïkas,* accusative pl. of *koïx* a palm tree] **—cyc·a·da·ceous** (sik′ə·dā′shəs) *adj.*

Cyc·la·des (sik′lə·dēz) A Greek island group in the southern Aegean; total, 1,023 square miles. *Greek* **Ki·kla·dhes** (kē·klä′thes).

cyc·la·men (sik′lə·mən, -men) *n.* An Old World bulbous flowering herb (genus *Cyclamen*) of the primrose family, with white, pink, or crimson flowers: also called *sowbread.* [<NL <L *cyclaminos* <Gk. *kyklaminos, kyklamis,* ? <*kyklos* a circle; with ref. to the shape of the root]

cyc·las (sik′ləs, sī′kləs) *n. pl.* **cyc·la·des** (sik′lə·dēz) A close-fitting, often sleeveless tunic or surcoat worn during the Middle Ages. [<L <Gk. *kyklas,* a woman's garment]

cy·cle (sī′kəl) *n.* **1** *Astron.* **a** A period of time, at the end of which certain aspects or motions of the heavenly bodies repeat themselves. **b** An orbit or circle in the heavens. **2** A round of years or of ages; a vast period; eon. **3** *Bot.* An entire turn or circle, as of a spiral leaf-structure. **4** A body of legends, poems, or romances relating to one period, person, etc.; also, a series of miracle plays: the Chester *cycle.* **5** A bicycle, tricycle, etc. **6** *Math.* A closed path in a diagram; loop. **7** A series that repeats itself. **8** *Physics* A recurring series of operations, as in gas or other internal-combustion engines, in which heat is imparted to or taken from a substance, which by expansion or contraction gives out or stores up energy and is finally returned to its original condition. **9** *Electr.* A full period of an alternating current; also, a completed series of variations in electromagnetic waves of a given frequency, as in radio transmission. —*v.i.* **cy·cled, cy·cling** **1** To pass through cycles. **2** To ride a bicycle, tricycle, or the like. [<F <LL *cyclus* <Gk. *kyklos* circle]

cycle car A light automobile with three or four wheels, tires, and engine of similar type and size to those of a motorcycle.

cy·clic (sī′klik, sik′lik) *adj.* **1** Pertaining to or characterized by cycles; recurring in cycles. **2** *Chem.* Of, pertaining to, or characterized by a closed chain or ring formation, as benzene, naphthalene, anthracene, etc. **3** *Bot.* Having parts arranged in whorls, as a flower. Also **cy′cli·cal.**

cyclic AMP A cyclic isomer of adenosine monophosphate.

cy·cling (sī′kling) *n.* The sport of riding the bicycle, tricycle, etc.; the art or skill of a cyclist.

cy·clist (sī′klist) *n.* One who rides a bicycle, tricycle, etc. Also **cy′cler.**

cyclo- *combining form* **1** Circular: *cyclograph.* **2** *Chem.* A saturated cyclic hydrocarbon compound: *cyclopropane.* Also, before vowels, **cycl-.** [<Gk. *kyklos* circle]

cy·clo·gen·e·sis (sī′klō·jen′ə·sis) *n. Meteorol.* The conditions which create a new cyclone or intensify the actions of a preexisting one. [<CYCLO(NE) + GENESIS]

cy·clo·gi·ro (sī′klō·jī′rō) *n. Aeron.* An aircraft equipped with airfoils designed to give support by rotating about an axis perpendicular to the longitudinal axis of the plane. Also **cy′clo·gy′ro.** [<CYCLO- + (AUTO)GIRO]

cy·clo·graph (sī′klə·graf, -gräf) *n.* **1** An instrument for drawing arcs of circles by means of two wheels of different diameters. **2** An arcograph. **3** A camera with which a panoramic view of an object may be taken.

cy·clo·hex·ane (sī′klō·hek′sān) *n. Chem.* A saturated hydrocarbon, C_6H_{12}, made by the hydrogenation of benzene and occurring in petroleum: it is composed of six methylene radicals arranged in cyclic form.

cy·cloid (sī′kloid) *adj.* **1** Resembling a circle or somewhat circular: specifically said of fish scales with concentric rings and smooth edges. **2** *Psychiatry* Of or pertaining to a personality type exhibiting marked alternations of mood. —*n. Geom.* The curve described by a point on the circumference of a circle that rolls, without slipping, along a straight line in a single plane. [<Gk. *kykloeidēs* circular] **—cy·cloi′dal** *adj.* **—cy′cloid·ism** *n.*

CYCLOID
As the circle *c* rolls along the straight line *bd,* point *a* on its circumference traces the cycloid *bad.*

cy·clom·e·ter (sī·klom′ə·tər) *n.* **1** An instrument for recording the rotations of a wheel to show speed and distance traveled; a speedometer. **2** A device for measuring circular arcs. [<CYCLO- + -METER]

cy·clom·e·try (sī·klom′ə·trē) *n.* The art of measuring circles. **—cy·clo·met·ric** (sī′klō·met′rik) *adj.*

cy·clone (sī′klōn) *n.* **1** *Meteorol.* A system of winds circulating about a center of relatively low barometric pressure, and, at the earth's surface, advancing with clockwise rotation in the southern hemisphere, counterclockwise in the northern. **2** Loosely, any violent and destructive whirling windstorm. [<Gk. *kyklōn,* ppr. of *kykloein* move in a circle <*kyklos*] **—cy·clo·nal** (sī·klō′nəl), **cy·clon·ic** (sī·klon′ik) or **·i·cal** *adj.* **—cy·clon′i·cal·ly** *adv.*

cyclone cellar An underground shelter adapted for use during cyclones and tornadoes. Also **storm cellar.**

cy·clon·o·scope (sī·klon′ə·skōp) *n. Meteorol.* An apparatus for detecting the approach of a cyclone or tornado. [<*cyclono-* (<CYCLONE) + -SCOPE]

Cy·clo·pe·an (sī′klə·pē′ən) *adj.* Of or pertaining to the Cyclopes or their work; gigantic; colossal.

cy·clo·pe·di·a (sī′klə·pē′dē·ə) *n.* **1** A work giving a summary of some branch of knowledge. **2** An encyclopedia. Also **cy′clo·pae′di·a.** [Short for ENCYCLOPEDIA]

cy·clo·pe·dic (sī′klə·pē′dik) *adj.* **1** Of or pertaining to a cyclopedia. **2** Like a cyclopedia; embracing a wide range of knowledge. Also **cy′clo·pae′dic, cy′clo·pe′di·cal, cy′clo·pae′di·cal.** **—cy′clo·pe′di·cal·ly** *adv.*

cy·clo·pe·dist (sī′klə·pē′dist) *n.* One who makes or contributes to a cyclopedia. Also **cy′clo·pae′dist.**

cy·clo·pen·tane (sī′klə·pen′tān) *n. Chem.* A relatively inert liquid compound, C_5H_{10}, obtained from some American and Caucasian mineral oils.

cy·clo·phon (sī′klə·fon) *n. Electronics* A type of vacuum tube in which a beam of electrons serves as a switching or commutating element. [<CYCLO- + Gk. *phōnē* a sound]

cy·clo·ple·gi·a (sī′klə·plē′jē·ə) *n. Pathol.* Paralysis of the ciliary muscle of the eye. **—cy′clo·ple′gic** *adj.*

cy·clo·pro·pane (sī′klə·prō′pān) *n. Chem.* A colorless, pungent, inflammable gas, C_3H_6, used as an inhalation anesthetic.

Cy·clops (sī′klops) *n. pl.* **Cy·clo·pes** (sī·klō′·pēz) **1** In Homeric legend, any of a race of one-eyed giants in Sicily, of whom Polyphemus was chief. **2** In Hesiodic legend, any of the three Titans who forged Zeus's thunderbolts.

cy·clo·ram·a (sī′klə·ram′ə, -rä′mə) *n.* **1** A panorama on the interior of a cylindrical surface, appearing as in natural perspective, the spectator standing in the center. **2** A backdrop curtain, often concave, used on theater stages to give the illusion of perspective; a concave plaster structure, sometimes merely a dome, used in the same way. [< CYCLO- + Gk. *horama* a view] —**cy·clo·ram·ic** (sī′klə·ram′ik) *adj.*

cy·clo·sis (sī·klō′sis) *n. Biol.* The streaming cyclical movement of protoplasm within a cell. [< Gk. *kyklōsis* a going around]

cy·clo·spor·ine (sī′klō·spôr′ēn) *n.* A drug of fungal origin, valuable for its suppressive influence on the body's natural inclination to reject organ transplants.

cy·clo·stome (sī′klə·stōm, sik′lə-) *n.* Any of a class *(Cyclostomata)* of primitive, carnivorous, aquatic vertebrates, having round, suctorial mouths devoid of jaws, and a single nostril; the lampreys and hagfishes. —*adj.* Having a round mouth; also, pertaining to the cyclostomes: also **cy·clos·to·mate** (sī·klos′tə·māt), **cy·clo·stom·a·tous** (sī′klə·stom′ə·təs).

cy·clo·stroph·ic (sī′klə·strof′ik, -strō′fik, sik′·lə-) *adj. Meteorol.* Designating the centrifugal tendency of an air mass or wind current due to the curvature of its path over the earth's surface. Compare GEOSTROPHIC. [< CYCLO- + Gk. *strophē* a turning, a twisting]

cy·clo·style (sī′klə·stīl, sik′lə-) *n.* An apparatus for manifolding manuscript. [< Gk. *kyklos* circle, wheel + STYLE (def. 7)]

cy·clo·thy·mi·a (sī′klə·thī′mē·ə) *n. Psychiatry* Manic-depressive psychosis, especially as characterized by fluctuations of mood from gaiety to depression at frequent intervals. [< CYCLO- + -THYMIA] —**cy′clo·thy′mic** *adj.*

cy·clo·tron (sī′klə·tron) *n. Physics* An apparatus which obtains high-energy deuterons by whirling a stream of electrons or ions at immense speeds in a strong magnetic field alternating in synchronism with their accelerated motion; an atom smasher. [< CYCLO- + (ELEC)TRON]

Cyd·nus (sid′nəs) The ancient name for the TARSUS.

Cy·do·ni·a (sī·dō′nē·ə) The ancient name for CANEA, Crete.

cy·e·sis (sī·ē′sis) *n.* Pregnancy. [< Gk. *kyēsis < kyeein conceive, be pregnant]*

cyg·net (sig′nit) *n.* A young swan. ◆ Homophone: *signet.* [< F *cygne* < L *cycnus* < Gk. *kyknos* + -ET]

Cyg·nus (sig′nəs) The Swan, a northern constellation. See CONSTELLATION.

cyl·in·der (sil′in·dər) *n.* **1** *Geom.* **a** A solid described by the circumference of a circle as its center moves along a straight line: the ends of the solid are parallel, equal circles. It is called a *right cylinder* when the line along which the center moves is at right angles to the plane of the circle, and *oblique cylinder* when the line is not at right angles. **b** Any curved surface generated by the motion of a straight line remaining parallel to itself and constantly intersecting a curve. **2** Any cylindrical portion of a machine, especially if hollow, and proportioned so that the length exceeds the diameter. **3** *Mech.* A cylindrical member of a motor in which a piston moves and receives direct impact from the steam or other motive fluid. **4** A rotating cylindrical portion of a printing press. **5** The rotating chamber that holds the cartridges of a revolver. **6** A cylindrical stone bearing an inscription; especially, an inscribed clay tablet, found buried under the corners of edifices in Babylonia and Assyria. —*v.t.* To press or fit with a cylinder. [< L *cylindrus* < Gk. *kylindros* < *kylindein* roll]

cylinder head The detachable end cover of an internal-combustion engine, comprising a portion of the combustion chamber.

cyl·in·der-stop (sil′in·dər·stop′) *n.* The mechanism that locks each chamber in the cylinder of a revolver in alinement with the barrel. See illustration under REVOLVER.

cy·lin·dri·cal (si·lin′dri·kəl) *adj.* **1** Of or pertaining to a cylinder. **2** Having the form or shape of a cylinder. Also **cy·lin′dric.** —**cy·lin′·dri·cal·ly** *adv.* —**cy·lin·dri·cal·i·ty** (si·lin′dri·kal′ə·tē) *n.*

cyl·in·droid (sil′in·droid) *n.* A solid body resembling a cylinder but having elliptical bases equal and parallel. [< Gk. *kylindroeidēs*]

cy·lix (sī′liks, sil′iks) See KYLIX.

Cyl·le·ne (si·lē′nē), **Mount** A mountain group in northern Peloponnesus, Greece; highest point, 7,792 feet; traditionally regarded as Hermes' birthplace.

Cyl·le·ni·an (si·lē′nē·ən) *adj.* Of or pertaining to Hermes, who was said to have been born on Mount Cyllene; hence, relating to any of the arts or practices of which he was the patron. —**the Cyllenian art** Thievery.

cy·ma (sī′mə) *n. pl.* **·mae** (-mē) **1** *Archit.* A curved molding with a reversed curve as its profile: frequently placed above a cornice in Greek and Greco-Roman art. **2** *Bot.* A cyme. [< NL < Gk. *kyma* a wave]

cyma rec·ta (rek′tə) *Archit.* A cyma with the convex part nearest the wall.

cyma re·ver·sa (ri·vûr′sə) *Archit.* A cyma with the concave part nearest the wall.

cy·ma·ti·um (si·mā′shē·əm) *n. pl.* **·ti·a** (-shē·ə) *Archit.* A cyma; hence, any molding that caps a division of an entablature, separating it from the next. [< L < Gk. *kymation*, dim of *kyma* a wave]

cym·bal (sim′bəl) *n.* One of a pair of platelike metallic musical instruments played by being clashed together. ◆ Homophone: *symbol.* [OE and < OF *cymbale*, both < L *cymbalum* < Gk. *kymbalon* < *kymbē* cup, hollow of a vessel] —**cym′bal·ist, cym′bal·er** *n.*

Cym·be·line (sim′bə·lēn) Title of a drama by Shakespeare (1609).

cyme (sīm) *n. Bot.* A flat-topped flower cluster in which the central flowers bloom first. [< F < L *cyma* a wave, a sprout < Gk. *kyma*]

cy·mene (sī′mēn) *n. Chem.* One of three isomeric liquid compounds, $C_{10}H_{14}$, with lemonlike odor, contained in several volatile oils, as cumin, wild thyme, etc., and obtained by distilling camphor with phosphoric anhydride: sometimes called *camphogen.* Also **cy·mol** (sī′mōl, -mol). [< Gk. *kyminon* + -ENE]

cym·lin (sim′lin) *n.* A kind of squash: sometimes spelled *simlin.* Also **cym′bling, cym′ling.** [Var. of *simlin*, an alter. of SIMNEL]

cymo- *combining form* Wave: *cymometer.* [< Gk. *kymos* wave]

cy·mo·gene (sī′mə·jēn) *n. Chem.* A volatile, inflammable distillate of petroleum, consisting of hydrocarbons with a high butane content. [< Gk. *kyminon* cumin + -GENE]

cy·mo·graph (sī′mə·graf, -gräf) *n.* **1** An instrument for tracing in profile the outlines of architectural moldings. **2** Kymograph. —**cy′mo·graph′ic** *adj.*

cy·moid (sī′moid) *adj.* Of the form of a cyme.

cy·mom·e·ter (sī·mom′ə·tər) *n.* An instrument for the measurement of wavelengths and of small electrical capacities. [< CYMO- + -METER]

cy·mo·phane (sī′mə·fān) *n.* A variety of chrysoberyl with a changeable luster; the Oriental cat's-eye.

cy·mo·scope (sī′mə·skōp) *n.* An instrument for detecting the presence of electromagnetic waves.

cy·mose (sī′mōs, sī·mōs′) *adj. Bot.* Bearing, pertaining to, or like a cyme. Also **cy·mous** (sī′məs). —**cy′mose·ly** *adv.*

Cym·ric (kim′rik, sim′-) *adj.* Relating to the Cymry; Brythonic. —*n.* **1** The Welsh language. **2** The Brythonic branch of the Celtic languages. Also spelled *Kymric.*

Cym·ry (kim′rē, sim′-) *n.* A collective name for the Welsh and their Cornish and Breton kin: also spelled *Cwmry, Kymry.* Also **Cym′ri.** [< Welsh *Cymry* the Welsh, pl. of *Cymro* a Welshman]

Cyn·e·wulf (kin′ə·wo͝olf) Anglo-Saxon poet of the eighth century: also *Kynewulf.*

cyn·ic (sin′ik) *n.* A sneering, captious person; a misanthrope; pessimist. —*adj.* **1** Pertaining to Sirius, the Dog Star. **2** *Rare* Of or like a dog. **3** Cynical. [< Gk. *kynikos* doglike]

Cyn·ic (sin′ik) *n.* One of a sect of Greek philosophers of the fifth and fourth centuries B.C., who held that virtue, rather than intellectual or sensual pleasure, was the ultimate goal of life: their doctrine gradually came to symbolize insolent self-righteousness. —*adj.* Belonging to or like the Cynics: also **Cyn′i·cal.**

cyn·i·cal (sin′i·kəl) *adj.* **1** Given to distrusting evidences of virtue and disinterested motives; inclined to moral skepticism; pessimistic. **2** Currish; sneering. See synonyms under CAPTIOUS. —**cyn′i·cal·ly** *adv.*

cyn·i·cism (sin′ə·siz′əm) *n.* The state or quality of being cynical; contempt for the virtues or generous sentiments of others. Also **cyn′·i·cal·ness.**

cy·no·pho·bi·a (sī′nə·fō′bē·ə, sin′ə-) *n.* An abnormal fear of dogs. [< Gk. *kyōn, kynos* dog + -PHOBIA] —**cy′no·phobe** *n.*

cy·no·sure (sī′nə·sho͝or, sin′ə-) *n.* An object of general interest or attention. [< MF < L *cynosura* < Gk. *kynosoura* the constellation Ursa Minor < *kyōn, kynos* dog + *oura* tail]

Cy·no·sure (sī′nə·sho͝or, sin′ə-) **1** The constellation of the Little Bear, which contains the North Star. **2** The North Star itself.

Cyn·thi·a (sin′thē·ə) A feminine personal name. [< L, fem. of *Cynthius* < Gk. *Kynthios* from Mt. Cynthus, birthplace of Artemis and Apollo] —**Cynthia** Artemis or Diana; hence, the moon.

Cyn·thus (sin′thəs), **Mount** In ancient geography, a mountain in Delos, Greece, regarded as sacred to Artemis and Apollo.

cy·per·a·ceous (sī′pə·rā′shəs, sip′ə-) *adj. Bot.* Designating a family *(Cyperaceae)* of glasslike or rushlike monocotyledonous herbs, the sedge family, with solid stems and closed sheaths. [< NL *Cyperaceae*, the sedge family < Gk. *kypeiros* sedge]

cy·pher (sī′fər) See CIPHER.

cy pres (sē′prā′) *Law* **1** As nearly as possible: applied in interpreting the principle whereby a gift legal in form which cannot be administered just as the testator directed, or which is not specified in a definite manner, may be applied as nearly as possible according to the donor's intentions. [< OF *si pres* as near as]

cy·press[1] (sī′prəs) *n.* **1** An evergreen tree (family *Cupressaceae*) of southern Europe and western Asia, having durable timber; especially, *C. funebris*, having pendulous branches like a weeping willow. **2** Any of various other trees of kindred genera, as the evergreen American cypress or white cedar (genus *Chamaecyparis*), and the bald cypress *(Taxodium distichum)* of the southern United States. **3** The wood of these trees. [< OF *cypres* < LL *cypressus* < Gk. *kyparissos* cypress]

cy·press[2] (sī′prəs) *n. Obs.* A transparent, black lawn fabric: also spelled *cyprus.* [< OF *Cipre, Cypres* Cyprus, whence the cloth was first imported into Europe]

cypress knee A hollow, knee-shaped growth which aerates the roots of the bald cypress.

cypress vine An annual, twining plant *(Quamoclit pennata)* with leaves pinnately parted into linear, parallel lobes, and bearing narrow, funnel-shaped, scarlet, and sometimes white flowers.

Cyp·ri·an (sip′rē·ən) *adj.* **1** Of or pertaining to Cyprus. **2** Of or pertaining to Aphrodite; hence, lewd. —*n.* **1** Cypriote. **2** A prostitute; courtesan. [< L *Cyprius* < Gk. *Kyprios* < *Kypros* Cyprus]

Cyp·ri·an (sip′rē·ən), **Saint,** 200–258, Latin church father, bishop of Carthage; martyred under Valerian.

cy·pri·nid (si·prī′nid, sip′rə·nid) *n.* A cyprinoid fish. —*adj.* Of, like, or pertaining to cyprinoids. [< NL *Cyprinidae*, the carp genus]

cyprino- *combining form* Carp: *cyprinodont.* Also, before vowels, **cyprin-.** [< Gk. *kyprinos* carp]

cy·prin·o·dont (si·prin′ə·dont, si·prī′nə-) *n.* Any of a family *(Cyprinidae)* of fishes with flattish, scaly heads; killifishes, guppies, minnows, etc. [< CYPRIN(O)- + Gk. *odous, odontos* tooth]

cyp·ri·noid (sip′rə·noid, si·prī′-) *adj.* Carp-

like. — *n*. A fish of the carp family, including barbels, breams, goldfishes, and many of the fresh-water minnows. [<Gk. *kyprinos* carp]

Cyp·ri·ote (sip'rē·ōt) *n*. **1** A native or inhabitant of Cyprus. **2** The ancient or modern Greek dialect of Cyprus. — *adj*. Of or pertaining to Cyprus. Also **Cyp·ri·ot** (sip'rē·ət).

cyp·ri·pe·di·um (sip'rə·pē'dē·əm) *n*. Any of a genus (*Cypripedium*) of orchids, mainly terrestrial, with fibrous roots, plaited leaves, and large flowers with pouchlike lip: called *ladyslipper* and *moccasin flower*. [<NL <Gk. *Kypris* Aphrodite + *podion* a slipper, dim. of *pous, podos* a foot]

cy·prus (sī'prəs) See CYPRESS².

Cy·prus (sī'prəs) An island in the Mediterranean, south of Asia Minor, comprising an independent republic; 3,572 square miles; capital, Nicosia: a native of Cyprus is known as a *Cypriote.*

cyp·se·la (sip'sə·lə) *n*. *pl*. **·lae** (-lē) *Bot*. An achenium in plants of the sunflower family. [<NL <Gk. *kypselē* hollow vessel]

Cyr·a·no de Ber·ge·rac (sir'ə·nō) də bûr'zhə·rak), **Savinien de**, 1619-55, French poet and soldier, celebrated for his large nose.

Cyr·e·na·ic (sir'ə·nā'ik, sī'rə-) *adj*. **1** Of or relating to Cyrene. **2** Belonging to or characteristic of the Cyrenaics. — *n*. **1** A disciple of the hedonistic school of post-Socratic philosophy founded by Aristippus of Cyrene. **2** A native or inhabitant of Cyrenaica. Also **Cy·re·ni·an** (sī·rē'nē·ən).

Cyr·e·na·i·ca (sir'ə·nā'i·kə, sī'rə-) The eastern division of Libya on the Mediterranean; 300,000 square miles; capital, Benghazi: also *Barca*: Italian *Cirenaica*.

Cy·re·ne (sī·rē'nē) A town in western Cyrenaica; formerly a Greek colony and capital of Cyrenaica: Italian *Cirene*.

Cyr·il (sir'əl) A masculine personal name. Also *Fr.* **Cy·rille** (sē·rēl'), *Ger.* **Cyrill** (tsü·ril'), *Lat.* **Cy·ril·lus** (si·ril·əs). [<Gk., lordly]
— **Cyril, Saint**, 376?-444, Latin church father, archbishop of Alexandria.
— **Cyril, Saint**, 827-869: called "Apostle of the Slavs."

Cy·ril·lic (si·ril'ik) *adj*. Of or pertaining to Saint Cyril.

Cyrillic alphabet An old Slavic alphabet, based mainly on that of the Greeks, said to have been devised by Saint Cyril, the "Apostle of the Slavs," in the ninth century: in its modern forms, used in Bulgaria, Serbia, and the Soviet Union. See Table of Foreign Alphabets, page 42.

Cy·rus (sī'rəs; *Fr.* sē·rü', *Ger.* tsē'rōōs) A masculine personal name. [<Persian, the sun]
— **Cyrus the Great**, died 529 B.C., founder of the Persian Empire.
— **Cyrus the Younger**, 424?-401 B.C., second son of Darius Notus, king of Persia, who led 10,000 Greeks against his brother, Artaxerxes II. See ANABASIS.

Cy·rus (sī'rəs) The ancient name for KURA.

cyst¹ (sist) *n*. **1** Any membranous sac or vesicle containing liquid or semisolid material: the biliary *cyst*, the urinary *cyst*. **2** *Pathol*. Any abnormal sac or vesicle in which morbid matter may be collected and retained. **3** *Zool*. A bladderlike sac, as that with which an embryonic tapeworm surrounds itself; also, a bladderworm. **4** *Bot*. **a** A receptacle for oil in the rind of the orange and like fruits. **b** A cell or cavity containing reproductive bodies in certain cryptogams. **c** The spore case of a seaweed. [<Gk. *kystis* bladder <*kyein* contain]

cyst² (sist) *n*. A chest; cist. [Var. of CIST]

cys·tec·to·my (sis·tek'tə·mē) *n*. *pl*. **·mies** *Surg*. **1** An operation to remove a cyst. **2** Removal of the gall bladder. [<Gk. *kystis* bladder + *ektemnein* excise]

cys·te·ine (sis'ti·ēn, -in) *n*. An amino acid, H₇C₃SO₂, derived from cystine. Also **cys'te·in** (-in). [<CYSTINE]

cysti– Var. of CYSTO–.

cys·tic (sis'tik) *adj*. **1** Encysted. **2** Having cysts. **3** Of or pertaining to a cyst or to the bladder. **4** Cystlike. Also **cys'tous.**

cys·ti·cer·cus (sis'tə·sûr'kəs) *n*. *pl*. **·ci** (-sī) *Zool*. A hydatid cyst which develops from the larva of a tapeworm and gives rise to the head and neck (scolex) of the future tapeworm: formerly regarded as a distinct genus. [<CYSTI- + Gk. *kerkos* tail] — **cys'ti·cer'coid** *adj*.

cys·tid·i·um (sis·tid'ē·əm) *n*. *pl*. **·tid·i·a** (-tid'·ē·ə) *Bot*. A sterile, spherical cell projecting among the basidia in fleshy fungi. [<NL <Gk. *kystis* cyst + *-idion*, dim. suffix]

cys·tine (sis'tēn, -tin) *n*. *Biochem*. One of the amino acids, C₆H₁₂O₄N₂S₂, produced by the digestion or hydrolysis of proteins in the body, and isolated from the urine in the form of white hexagonal crystals. It is an important factor in nutrition. [<CYST(O) + -INE]

cys·ti·tis (sis·tī'tis) *n*. *Pathol*. Inflammation of the bladder. [<CYST(O)- + -ITIS¹]

cys·ti·tome (sis'tə·tōm) *n*. *Surg*. An instrument used in opening the capsule of the crystalline lens.

cysto– *combining form* Bladder, cyst: *cystoscope*. Also, before vowels, **cyst–**. [<Gk. *kystis* bladder]

cys·to·carp (sis'tə·kärp) *n*. *Bot*. The fructification from an archicarp or procarp in fungi and red algae; a sporocarp. — **cys'to·car'pic** *adj*.

cys·to·cele (sis'tə·sēl) *n*. *Pathol*. A hernia or rupture involving the protrusion of the urinary bladder.

cys·toid (sis'toid) *adj*. Shaped like a cyst; encysted. — *n*. A cystoid growth.

cys·to·lith (sis'tə·lith) *n*. *Bot*. A mineral and usually somewhat crystalline concretion in the epidermal or subjacent cells of the leaf in some plants, especially of the nettle family.

cys·to·scope (sis'tə·skōp) *n*. *Med*. A catheter with a device for introducing light into the bladder to permit of ocular examination. — **cys·to·scop·ic** (sis'tə·skop'ik) *adj*. — **cys·tos·co·py** (sis·tos'kə·pē) *n*.

cys·tos·to·my (sis·tos'tə·mē) *n*. *pl*. **·mies** *Surg*. The making of an artificial outlet from the bladder. [<CYSTO- + Gk. *stoma* mouth]

cys·tot·o·my (sis·tot'ə·mē) *n*. *pl*. **·mies** *Surg*. A cutting into the bladder; also, the operation of puncturing an encysted tumor. [<CYSTO- + -TOMY]

cy·tase (sī'tās) *n*. *Biochem*. A digestive enzyme found in the seeds of certain plants and aiding in the formation of mannose and galactose sugars. [<CYT(O) + -ASE]

cy·tas·ter (sī·tas'tər, sī'tas'-) *n*. *Biol*. A star-like form assumed by the nucleus of a cell undergoing division; specifically, an aster not associated with the chromosomes. [CYT(O)- + Gk. *astēr* star]

–cyte *combining form* Cell: *phagocyte*. [<Gk. *kytos* hollow vessel]

Cy·the·ra (si·thir'ə) The Latin name for KYTHERA.

Cyth·e·re·a (sith'ə·rē'ə) Aphrodite; Venus: so called from the island of Kythera, near which she is fabled to have risen from the sea. Also **Cy·the·ra** (si·thir'ə).

cyto– *combining form* Cell: *cytochrome*. Also, before vowels, **cyt–**. [<Gk. *kytos* hollow vessel < *kyein* contain, be pregnant with]

cy·to·chrome (sī'tə·krōm) *n*. *Biochem*. A pigment found in the respiratory cells of plants and animals, as chlorophyll, hemoglobin, and also in certain aerobic bacteria.

cy·to·di·ag·no·sis (sī'tō·dī'əg·nō'sis) *n*. *Med*. A diagnosis from the examination of cells in body fluids.

cy·to·gen·e·sis (sī'tō·jen'ə·sis) *n*. *Biol*. The formation of cells. Also **cy·to·gen·e·sis** (sis'tō·jen'ə·sis), **cy·tog·e·ny** (sī·toj'ə·nē). — **cy·to·ge·net·ic** (sī'tō·jə·net'ik), **cy·to·gen·ic** (sī'tō·jen'ik) *adj*.

cy·to·ge·net·ics (sī'tō·jə·net'iks) *n*. The scientific investigation of the role of cells in the phenomena of heredity and evolution.

cy·to·ki·ne·sis (sī'tō·ki·nē'sis, -kī-) *n*. *Biol*. The changes which take place in the cytoplasm of the cell during mitosis, meiosis, and fertilization. [<CYTO- + Gk. *kinēsis* motion]

cy·tol·o·gy (sī·tol'ə·jē) *n*. The scientific study of the structure, organization, and function of cells. [<CYTO- + -LOGY] — **cy·to·log·ic** (sī'tə·loj'ik) or **·i·cal** *adj*. — **cy'to·log'i·cal·ly** *adv*. — **cy·tol'o·gist** *n*.

cy·tol·y·sis (sī·tol'ə·sis) *n*. *Biol*. The dissolution or breaking up of cells. [<CYTO- + Gk. *lysis* a loosing] — **cy·to·lyt·ic** (-lit'ik) *adj*.

cy·tom·e·ter (sī·tom'ə·tər) *n*. A device for measuring and counting organic cells. [< CYTO- + -METER]

cy·to·mi·cro·some (sī'tō·mī'krə·sōm) *n*. *Biol*. A cytoplasmic microsome, as differentiated from a nuclear one.

cy·to·mi·tome (sī'tō·mī'tōm, sī·tom'ə·tōm) *n*. *Biol*. The cytoplasmic threads as opposed to those of the nuclear threadwork. [<CYTO- + Gk. *mitos* thread + -OME]

cy·toph·a·gy (sī·tof'ə·jē) *n*. *Biol*. The destruction of cells by other cells; phagocytosis. [<CYTO- + -PHAGY]

cy·to·phar·ynx (sī'tō·far'ingks) *n*. *Zool*. The esophageal tube of a protozoan.

cy·to·plasm (sī'tə·plaz'əm) *n*. *Biol*. All the protoplasm of a cell except that in the nucleus. — **cy'to·plas'mic** *adj*.

cy·to·plast (sī'tə·plast) *n*. Cytoplasm. — **cy'to·plas'tic** *adj*.

Cyz·i·cus (siz'i·kəs) **1** An ancient city at the southern end of Kapidaǧi Peninsula, Turkey. **2** The ancient name for the KAPIDAǦI PENINSULA.

czar (zär) *n*. **1** An emperor or absolute monarch; especially, one of the former emperors of Russia: often spelled *tsar*. **2** An absolute ruler; despot. [<Russian *tsare*, ult. <L *Caesar* Caesar, a family name later used as a title of the imperial heirs]

czar·das (chär'däsh) *n*. A Hungarian dance consisting of a slow, melancholy section followed by a quick, fiery one. [<Hungarian *csárdás*]

czar·dom (zär'dəm) *n*. **1** The territory ruled by a czar. **2** The position or power of a czar: also spelled *tsardom*.

czar·e·vitch (zär'ə·vich) *n*. The eldest son of a czar of Russia: also written *cesarevitch, tsarevitch*. [<Russian *tsarevich*]

cza·rev·na (zä·rev'nə) *n*. **1** The wife of the czarevitch. **2** Formerly the title of any daughter of the czar. Also spelled *tsarevna*. [<Russian *tsarevna*]

cza·ri·na (zä·rē'nə) *n*. The wife of a czar of Russia. Also **cza·rit·za** (zä·rit'sə). [<Russian <G *czarin*]

Czech *n*. **1** A member of the Czech Republic, descended from the people of Bohemia, Moravia, and northern Silesia. **2** The language of the Czech: formerly called Bohemian. *adj*. —**Czech'ic, Czech'ish.**

Czech Republic A republic of east Central Europe; 30,449 square miles, pop. 10,300,000; capital Prague. The Czech Republic separated from the Slovak Republic in 1993, dividing Czechoslovakia into the Czech and Slovac Republics. Formerly known as **Bohemia, Czechoslovakia** (1918–1993).

Czech·o·slo·va·ki·a A former republic of east central Europe (1918–1993): in 1918, the Austro-Hungarian Empire separated into Austria, Hungary, and Czechoslovakia: Czechoslovakia divided January 1, 1993, into two separate republics, the Czech Republic and the Slovak Republic.

Czech·o·slo·va·ki·an *n*. **1** a resident of the former Czechoslovakia. **2** The West Slavic language of the Czechoslovaks, including the Czech, Moravian, and Slovak dialects. —*adj*. Of or pertaining to the former Czechoslovakia, its inhabitants, or their language.

Cze·sto·cho·wa (chaṅ'stô·hô'vä) A city in southern Poland.

D

d, D (dē) *n. pl.* **d's, D's** or **Ds, ds, dees** (dēz)
1 The fourth letter of the English alphabet, from Phoenician *daleth*, through the Hebrew *daleth*, Greek *delta*, Roman *D.* **2** The sound of the letter *d*, usually a voiced alveolar stop. See ALPHABET. — *symbol* **1** In Roman notation, the numeral 500. See under NUMERAL. **2** *Music* **a** The second note in the natural scale of C; *re.* **b** The pitch of this tone, or the written note representing it. **c** The scale built upon D. **3** Differentiation or, in algebra, a known quantity. **4** Anything shaped like a D or a half circle, as the iron loop on a saddle to which articles are attached. **5** Pence (*d.*, from Latin *denarii*) in English money. **6** *Chem.* Deuterium.

dab¹ (dab) *n.* **1** One of various flounders, especially the American **sand dab** (*Limanda ferruginea*) of the Atlantic and Pacific coasts. **2** Any flatfish. [Origin uncertain]

dab² (dab) *n. Brit. Colloq.* A skilful person; an adept. [Origin uncertain]

dab³ (dab) *n.* **1** A gentle blow; a pat. **2** A quick stroke or thrust; a peck. **3** A small lump or patch of soft substance, as butter or paint; hence, a little bit. — *v.t.* & *v.i.* **dabbed, dab·bing** **1** To strike softly; tap. **2** To peck. **3** To pat with something soft and damp. **4** To apply (paint, etc.) with light strokes. [ME *dabben.* Cf. G *tappe* footprint, MDu. *dabben* fumble, dabble.]

dab·ber (dab′ər) *n.* **1** One who or that which dabs. **2** A printers' inking ball; an engravers' pad, etc.; a dauber.

dab·bing (dab′ing) *n.* The process of indenting, as with a sharp hammer, the surface of a stone.

dab·ble (dab′əl) *v.* **·bled, ·bling** *v.i.* **1** To play, as with the hands, in a liquid; splash gently. **2** To engage in superficially or without serious involvement: to *dabble* in art. — *v.t.* **3** To wet slightly; bespatter, as with water or mud. [Freq. of DAB³, *v.*] — **dab′bler** *n.*

dab·chick (dab′chik) *n.* **1** A fledgling; hence, an immature or delicate person. **2** A small grebe of Europe (*Podiceps ruficollis*) or the pied-billed grebe of North America (*Podilymbus podiceps*): often called *helldiver.* [< DAB³ + CHICK]

dab·ster (dab′stər) *n.* **1** *Brit. Dial.* A handy person; an adept. **2** *Colloq.* A dabbler or bungler.

da ca·po (dä kä′pō) *Music* From the beginning: a direction to repeat a passage or return to the beginning of a movement. [<Ital.]

Dac·ca (dä′kä) The capital of Bangla Desh.

d'ac·cord (dà-kôr′) *French* Agreed; in accord.

dace (dās) *n. pl.* **dac·es** or **dace 1** A small cyprinoid fresh-water fish of Europe (*Leuciscus leuciscus*). **2** A fresh-water fish of North America (*Semotilus atromaculatus*). [< OF *darz, dars,* nominative sing. of *dart,* a small fish]

Da·chau (dä′khou) A town in Upper Bavaria, Germany; site of a Nazi concentration camp.

dachs·hund (däks′- hŏont′, daks′hŏond′, dash′-) *n.* A breed of dog native to Germany, of medium size, with long, compact body and short legs, short coat, usually of red or tan or black and tan. [< G < *dachs* badger + *hund* dog]

DACHSHUND
(From 7 to 9 inches in height at the shoulder)

Da·cia (dä′shə) A region of SE Europe, corresponding roughly to modern Rumania, comprising a province of the ancient Roman empire. — **Da′cian** *adj.* & *n.*

da·cite (dä′sīt) *n.* An igneous rock, usually volcanic, composed of plagioclase and quartz, commonly mixed with hornblende, biotite, or both. [from *Dacia*]

dack·er (dak′ər) *Scot.* & *Brit. Dial. v.i.* **1** To

waver. **2** To saunter. — *n.* **1** A saunter. **2** A contest. Also spelled *daiker.*

da·coit (də-koit′) *n.* A member of a robber band in India or Burma: also spelled *dakoit.* [<Hind. *dakait* < *dākā* robbery by a gang]

da·coit·y (də-koi′tē) *n.* Robbery by dacoits.

Da·cron (dā′kron, dak′ron) *n.* A synthetic polyester fiber of high tensile strength, having great resistance to stretching and wrinkling when woven into fabrics: a trade name.

dac·ry·o·gen·ic (dak′rē·ō·jen′ik) *adj. Med.* Capable of producing tears. [<Gk. *dakryon* a tear + -GENIC]

dac·ry·on (dak′rē·on) *n. pl.* **·ry·a** (-rē-ə) *Anat.* The point near the root of the nose indicating the junction of the frontal, lacrimal, and superior maxillary bones. [<Gk. *dakryon* tear]

dac·tyl (dak′təl) *n.* **1** In prosody, a three-syllable measure consisting of one long or accented syllable followed by two short or unaccented ones (‒ ◡ ◡). **2** A finger or toe; digit. [<Gk. *daktylos* finger, dactyl]

dac·ty·late (dak′tə·lāt) *adj.* Having fingerlike organs or processes.

dac·tyl·ic (dak·til′ik) *adj.* Of or pertaining to dactyls. — *n.* A dactylic verse.

dac·tyl·i·og·ra·phy (dak·til′ē·og′rə·fē) *n.* The engraving of gems for rings. [<Gk. *daktylios* finger ring + -GRAPHY]

dac·tyl·i·on (dak·til′ē·on) *n. pl.* **·tyl·i·a** (-til′ē·ə) **1** The extreme tip or end of the middle finger when the hand is fully extended: a measuring point in anthropometry. **2** The joining or webbing together of fingers; syndactylism. Also **dac·tyl′i·um** (-əm). [<NL <Gk. *daktylos* finger]

dactylo– *combining form* Finger; toe: *dactylology.* Also, before vowels, **dactyl–**. [<Gk. *daktylos* finger]

dac·tyl·o·gram (dak·til′ə·gram) *n.* A fingerprint.

dac·ty·log·ra·phy (dak′tə·log′rə·fē) *n.* The scientific study of fingerprints. [<DACTYLO- + -GRAPHY] — **dac·ty·lo·graph·ic** (dak′tə·lə·graf′ik) *adj.*

dac·ty·lol·o·gy (dak′tə·lol′ə·jē) *n.* The use of the fingers in communicating ideas, as in the deaf-and-dumb alphabet. [<DACTYLO- + -LOGY]

dac·ty·los·co·py (dak′tə·los′kə·pē) *n.* The examination of fingerprints as a means of identification. [<DACTYLO- + -SCOPY] — **dac·ty·lo·scop·ic** (dak′tə·lə·skop′ik) *adj.*

dad (dad) *n. Colloq.* Father: used familiarly, as by children. Also **dad′dy.**

Da·da (dä′dä, -də) *n.* A movement in art and literature, about 1916-20, that declared a program of protest against civilization, rejecting all previous art by means of violent satire and incongruous humor: several of its chief exponents were later associated with surrealism. Also **Da′da·ism.** [<F *dada,* a nonsense word] — **Da′da·ist** *n.*

dad·dle (dad′l) See DIDDLE¹.

dad·dy-long-legs (dad′ē·lông′legz′, -long′-) *n.* **1** A long-legged, insect-eating arachnid of the order *Phalangida,* resembling a spider; the harvestman. **2** *Brit.* The cranefly. **3** A very long-legged person.

da·do (dā′dō) *n. pl.* **da·does** *Archit.* **1** A plain, flat surface at the base of a wall, as of a room: often decorated. **2** One of the faces of a pedestal. [<Ital., a die, a cube <L *datum.* See DIE².]

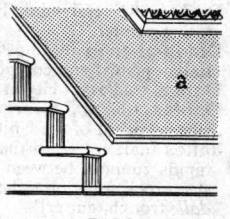
DADO
Area (*a*) between baseboard and wall decoration.

spelled *dedal.* [<L *daedalus* <Gk. *daidalos* skilful, cunning]

Daed·a·lus (ded′ə·ləs, *Brit.* dē′də-) In Greek mythology, an Athenian architect and inventor who devised the Cretan Labyrinth in which he was later imprisoned with his son Icarus and from which they escaped by means of artificial wings. Also **Dæd′a·lus.** — **Dae·da·li·an, Dae·da·le·an** (di-dā′lē·ən, -dāl′yən) *adj.* **dae·mon** (dē′mən), **dae·mon·ic** (dē-mon′ik), etc. See DEMON, etc.

daff¹ (daf, däf) *v.t. Obs.* **1** To toss away; thrust aside; discard. **2** To doff; take off. [Var. of DOFF]

daff² (daf, däf) *Scot. v.i.* To play the fool; talk foolishly. — *n. Obs.* A blockhead; idiot. [? Var. of DAFT]

daff·ing (daf′ing, däf′-) *n. Scot.* Foolery; play. Also **daff′in.**

daf·fo·dil (daf′ə·dil) *n.* A plant (*Narcissus pseudo-narcissus*) of the amaryllis family, with solitary yellow flowers, Also **daf′fa·down·dil′ly, daf′fy·down·dil′ly.** [Var. of ME *affodille* <Med. L *affodillus* <L *asphodelus.* Doublet of ASPHODEL.]

daf·fy (daf′ē) *adj.* **·fi·er, ·fi·est** *Colloq.* Crazy; daft. [<DAFF²]

daft (daft, däft) *adj.* **1** Silly; imbecile; insane. **2** Frolicsome. [OE *gedæfte* mild, meek] — **daft′ly** *adv.* — **daft′ness** *n.*

daft days *Scot.* The festive holidays at Christmas and the New Year.

dag¹ (dag) *n.* A loose-hanging point, lock, or shred. [ME *dagge*; origin uncertain]

dag² (dag) *v.i. Brit. Dial.* To drizzle.

Da·gan (dä′gän) The Babylonian god of the earth.

Dag·da (däg′thə) The chief god of ancient Irish mythology.

Dag·en·ham (dag′nəm) A municipal borough of SW Essex, England, 12 miles NE of London.

dag·ger (dag′ər) *n.* **1** A short, edged, and pointed weapon, for stabbing. **2** *Printing* A reference mark (†): the second in a series. — **double dagger** A mark of reference (‡) used in printing; a diesis: the third in a series. — *v.t.* **1** To pierce with a dagger; stab. **2** *Printing* To mark with a dagger. [ME *dag* pierce, stab. Cf. F *dague* dagger]

dag·gle (dag′əl) *v.t.* & *v.i.* **·gled, ·gling** To trail or draggle in the mud or wet. [Freq. of dial. *dag* dampen, bemire]

TYPES OF DAGGERS

Da·ghe·stan (dä′gə·stän′) An autonomous Soviet Socialist Republic in southeastern U.S.S.R.: 14,750 square miles; capital, Makhachkala. Also **Da′ge·stan′.**

dag·lock (dag′lok′) *n.* A dirty or tangled lock, as of wool on a sheep: also called *taglock.* [< dial. *dag* bemire + LOCK²]

da·go (dä′gō) *n. pl.* **·gos** or **·goes** *U.S. Slang* An Italian, or, less commonly, a Spaniard or Portuguese: a contemptuous usage. [Alter. of Sp. *Diego,* a personal name]

da·go·ba (dä′gə·bə) *n.* A dome-shaped Buddhist monument or shrine, built on a mound, and containing sacred relics. [<Singhalese *dāgaba*]

Da·gon (dā′gon) A national god of the Philistines and later of the Phoenicians, represented as half man and half fish.

da·guer·re·an (də-ger′ē·ən) *adj.* Pertaining to the daguerreotype. Also **da·guer′ri·an.**

da·guerre·o·type (də-ger′ə-tīp′, -ē·ə-tīp′) *n.* **1** An early photographic process using silver-coated, light-sensitive metallic plates developed by mercury vapor. **2** A picture made by this process. [after Louis Jacques Mandé *Daguerre,* 1789-1851, French inventor, +

TYPE] —**da·guerre′o·typ′er**, **da·guerre′o·typ′ist** *n.* —**da·guerre′o·typ′y** *n.*

da·ha·be·ah (dä′hə·bē′ə) *n.* A passenger boat of the Nile, having a sharp prow and a broad stern, originally equipped with lateen sails, and now generally propelled by engines. Also **da′ha·bi′eh**, **da′ha·biy′eh**. [< Arabic *dhahabiyah* golden < *dhahab* gold; with ref. to the gilded royal Egyptian barges]

DAHABEAH

Da·ha·na (dä′hə·nä) A desert area of the Arabian Peninsula, comprising a region of east central Arabia. Also **Dah′na**.

Dahl·gren (dal′grən), **John A.**, 1809–70, U.S. rear admiral; inventor of a smooth-bored gun used by the Union navy in the Civil War.

dahl·ia (dal′yə, däl′-) *n.* **1** A tender perennial herb (genus *Dahlia*) of the composite family, having tuberous roots and showy red, purple, yellow, or white flowers. **2** The flower or root of this herb. [after Anders *Dahl*, 18th c. Swedish botanist]

Da·ho·mey (də·hō′mē) See BENIN.

da·hoon (də·hōōn′) *n.* A small evergreen tree (*Ilex cassine*) of the holly family, found in the southern United States. [Origin uncertain]

dail (dāl) *n. Scot.* Deal[1].

Dail Ei·reann (dôl âr′ən) The lower house of the legislature of Ireland.

dai·ly (dā′lē) *adj.* Occurring, appearing, or pertaining to every day; diurnal. —*n. pl.* **·lies** A daily publication. —*adv.* Day after day; on every day. [OE *dæglic* < *dæg* day]

Synonym (adj.): diurnal. *Daily* is the native English and popular term, *diurnal* the Latin and scientific term. In strict usage, *daily* is the antonym of *nightly* as *diurnal* is of *nocturnal*. *Daily* is not, however, held strictly to this use; a physician makes *daily* visits if he calls at some time within each period of twenty-four hours. *Diurnal* is more exact in all its uses; a *diurnal* flower opens or blooms only in daylight; a *diurnal* bird or animal flies or ranges only by day: in contradistinction to *nocturnal* flowers, birds, etc. A *diurnal* motion exactly fills an astronomical day or the time of one rotation of a planet on its axis, while a *daily* motion is much less definite. *Antonyms:* nightly, nocturnal.

daily double In horse racing, a single bet, the winning of which depends upon choosing the winner in two specified races.

dai·men (dā′min) *adj. Scot.* Occasional; scattered.

dai·mio (dī′myō) *n.* **1** The former class of hereditary feudal barons in Japan. **2** A member of this class. Also **dai′myo**. [< Japanese < Chinese *dai* great + *mio, myo* name] —**dai·mi·ate** (dī′mē·āt) *n.*

dai·mon (dī′mōn), **dai·mon·ic** (dī·mon′ik), etc. See DEMON, etc.

Dai Nip·pon (dī nēp·pōn) A Japanese name for JAPAN.

dain·ty (dān′tē) *adj.* **·ti·er**, **·ti·est** **1** Refined or delicate in taste. **2** Delicious; agreeable to the taste. **3** Charming in appearance; pretty. **4** Overly nice; fastidious. [< *n.*] —*n. pl.* **·ties** Something choice, delicate, or delicious. See synonyms under CHOICE, DELICIOUS, ELEGANT, FINE, SQUEAMISH. [< OF *daintié* < L *dignitas, -tatis.* Doublet of DIGNITY.] —**dain′ti·ly** *adv.* —**dain′ti·ness** *n.*

dai·qui·ri (dī′kər·ē, dak′ər·ē) *n.* A cocktail made of rum, lime or lemon juice, and sugar, mixed and chilled. [from *Daiquirí*, Cuba, where the rum originally used for the drink was made]

Dai·ren (dī′ren′) A port at the southern tip of Liaotung Peninsula, Southern Manchuria: Russian *Dalny*, Chinese *Talien*.

dair·y (dâr′ē) *n. pl.* **dair·ies 1** A place where milk and cream are kept and made into butter and cheese. **2** A place for the sale of milk products. **3** A dairy farm. **4** A herd of milk cattle. **5** The business of dealing in such products. [ME *deierie* < *deie* dairymaid < OE *dæge*]

dairy cattle Cows of a breed specially adapted for milk production. Also **dairy cows**.

dairy farm A farm devoted to producing dairy products.

dair·y·ing (dâr′ē·ing) *n.* The business of conducting a dairy farm or a dairy.

dair·y·maid (dâr′ē·mād′) *n.* A woman or girl who works in a dairy.

dair·y·man (dâr′ē·mən) *n. pl.* **·men** (-mən) A man who works in, or for, or keeps a dairy.

da·is (dā′is, dās) *n.* **1** A raised platform in a room. **2** A seat on a dais or against a wall. [< OF *deis* < LL *discus.* Doublet of DESK, DISH, DISK.]

dai·sy (dā′zē) *n. pl.* **dai·sies 1** A low European herb (*Bellis perennis*) of the composite family, having a yellow disk with white or rose-colored rays; the English daisy. **2** A common American field flower, the oxeye daisy (*Chrysanthemum leucanthemum*): also called *whiteweed*. **3** *Slang* Any very fine, excellent person or thing. [OE *dæges ēage* day's eye] —**dai′sied** *adj.*

Dai·sy (dā′zē) A feminine personal name.

Daisy Millerism Unconventional behavior on the part of women. [after *Daisy Miller*, the unconventional heroine and title character of a novel (1879) by Henry James]

dak (dôk, däk) *n. Anglo-Indian* The East Indian post or inland mail: a relay of palanquin-bearers, running footmen, or horses for the service of travelers: also spelled **dawk**. [< Hind. *dāk*]

Da·kar (dä·kär′, də-) The capital of the Republic of Senegal; a port on Cape Verde.

da·ker·hen (dā′kər·hen′) *n.* The corn crake.

dakh·ma (däk′mə) See TOWER OF SILENCE.

Da·kin's solution (dā′kinz) *Med.* An antiseptic of sodium carbonate dissolved in water, to which chlorinated lime and boric acid are added, forming a neutral sodium hypochlorite solution. [after Henry Drysdale *Dakin*, 1880–1952, U.S. chemist]

da·koit (də·koit′) See DACOIT.

Da·ko·ta (də·kō′tə) A former territory of the United States, comprising what is now North and South Dakota.

Da·ko·ta (də·kō′tə) *n.* **1** A member of the largest division of the Siouan linguistic stock of North American Indians; a Sioux; one of the Plains Indians: now on reservations in North and South Dakota, Minnesota, and Montana. **2** The Siouan language of the Dakotas. —**Da·ko′tan** *adj. & n.*

Dakota River See JAMES RIVER (def. 2).

Da·la·dier (dä·lä·dyā′), **Edouard**, 1884–1970, French politician and statesman, premier 1938–40.

Da·lai La·ma (dä·lī′ lä′mə) The principal one of the two major lamas of Tibet and Mongolia, the other being known as the *Tesho Lama*: often called *Grand Lama*. Also **da·lai′**.

dale (dāl) *n.* A small valley. [OE *dæl.* Akin to DELL.]

Dale (dāl), **Sir Henry Hallett**, 1875–1968, English physiologist. —**Sir Thomas**, died 1619, English governor of Virginia.

Da·lén (dä·lān′), **Nils Gustaf**, 1869–1937, Swedish engineer.

dales·man (dālz′mən) *n. pl.* **·men** (-mən) One living in a dale, especially in the north of England.

da·leth (dä′ləth) *n.* The fourth Hebrew letter. See ALPHABET.

Dal·hou·sie (dal·hōō′zē), **Earl of**, 1770–1838, George Ramsay, Scottish general; colonial governor of Canada 1819–28. —**Marquis of**, 1812–60, James Andrew Ramsay, British governor general of India 1848–56; son of the preceding.

Da·li (dä′lē), **Salvador**, born 1904, Spanish surrealist painter.

Dal·la·pic·co·la (däl′ä·pē′kō·lä), **Luigi**, 1904–75, Italian pianist and composer.

Dal·las (dal′əs) A city in northern Texas.

Dal·las (dal′əs), **George Mifflin**, 1792–1864, vice president of the United States 1845–49.

dalles (dalz) *n. pl.* In the western United States, rapids running between steep rock walls; also, steep rock walls on either side of a ravine. [< F *dalle* trough, gutter]

dal·li·ance (dal′ē·əns) *n.* The act of dallying; frivolous or flirtatious action.

dal·ly (dal′ē) *v.* **dal·lied**, **dal·ly·ing** *v.i.* **1** To make love sportively; frolic. **2** To toy with; trifle; flirt: to *dally* with death. **3** To waste time. —*v.t.* **4** To waste (time): with *away*.

[< OF *dalier* converse, chat] —**dal′li·er** *n.*

Dal·ma·tia (dal·mā′shə) A region of Croatia, between the Adriatic Sea and Bosnia and Herzegovina; formerly a titular kingdom under Austrian control. *Serbo-Croatian* **Dal·ma·ci·ja** (däl·mä′tsē·yä). —**Dal·ma′tian** *adj. & n.*

Dal·ma·tian (dal·mā′shən) *n.* A large, short-haired dog, white with black spots: also called *carriage dog, coach dog, English coach dog.*

dal·mat·ic (dal·mat′ik) *n.* **1** A wide-sleeved tunic, worn over the alb and cassock by the deacon at high mass. **2** A medieval state robe. [< OF *dalmatique* < L *dalmatica (vestis)* Dalmatian (robe) < *Dalmatia* Dalmatia]

Dal·ny (däl′y·nyi) The Russian name for DAIREN.

Dal·rym·ple (dal·rim′pəl, dal′rim·pəl), **James**, 1619–95, Viscount Stair, Scottish jurist and historian. —**John**, 1673–1747, second Earl of Stair, English general and diplomat.

dal se·gno (däl sā′nyō) *Music* From the sign: a direction to return and repeat to the end from the sign ⸭: Abbr. *D.S.* [< Ital., from the sign]

dal·ton (dôl′tən) *n. Physics* The unit of atomic mass, equal to 1/12 of the mass of an atom of carbon of mass number 12, or approximately 1.6604×10^{-24} gram. [after John *Dalton*]

Dal·ton (dôl′tən), **John**, 1766–1844, English chemist and physicist; discoverer of colorblindness; originator of the modern atomic theory.

Dal·to·ni·an (dôl·tō′nē·ən) *adj.* Of or pertaining to John Dalton or his atomic theory.

dal·ton·ism (dôl′tən·iz′əm) *n.* Colorblindness, especially to the colors red and green. [after John *Dalton*]

Dalton plan In elementary and secondary education, a system of individual instruction in which a student organizes his own assignments and advances as fast as his ability allows. [from *Dalton*, Mass., where it was first used]

Dalton's law 1 *Chem.* The statement that the elements forming more than one compound unite in amounts which bear a simple multiple relationship to each other. **2** *Physics* The statement that the total pressure of a mixture of gases equals the sum of the partial pressures of each constituent regarded as occupying alone the same volume at the same temperature.

Da·ly (dā′lē), **John Augustin**, 1838–99, U.S. playwright and theatrical manager.

dam[1] (dam) *n.* **1** A barrier to check the flow of a stream. **2** The water held up by a dam. **3** Any barrier for preventing the passage of water, air, or gas. **4** Figuratively, any obstruction. —*v.t.* **dammed, dam·ming 1** To erect a dam in; stop or obstruct by a dam. **2** To keep back; restrain: with *up* or *in.* [< MDu. *damm*]

dam[2] (dam) *n.* A female parent: said of animals. [Var. of *dame*]

Dam (däm), **(Carl Peter) Henrik**, 1895–1976, Danish biochemist.

dam·age (dam′ij) *n.* **1** Destruction or impairment of value; injury; harm. **2** *pl. Law* Money recoverable for a wrong or an injury. See synonyms under INJURY, LOSS. —*v.* **dam·aged**, **dam·ag·ing** *v.t.* To cause damage to; impair the usefulness or value of. —*v.i.* To be susceptible to damage. See synonyms under ABUSE, HURT. [< OF < *dam* loss < L *damnum*] —**dam′age·a·ble** *adj.*

dam·an (dam′ən) *n.* A small, hyracoidean, hoofed mammal (genus *Procavia*) with rhinoceros-like molar teeth, especially *P. syriaca* of Asia Minor. [< Arabic *damān isrāil* sheep of Israel]

Da·man·hur (dä′män·hōōr′) A town in Lower Egypt.

Da·mão (də·moun′) A district of Portuguese India, comprising the region of Damão on the NW coast of India, with the dependent territories of **Da·drá** (də·drä′) and **Na·gar·A·ve·li** (nu·gûr′ä·vä′lē); total 176 square miles; capital, Damão. Also **Da·man** (də·man′).

Da·ma·ra (dä·mä′rə, də-) *n.* A native of Damaraland.

Da·ma·ra·land (dä·mä′rə·land′, də-) A region in central South-West Africa.

dam·as·cene (dam′ə·sēn, dam′ə·sēn′) *v.t.* **·cened**, **·cen·ing** To ornament (metal, iron,

steel, etc.) with wavy or variegated patterns. Also **dam·as·keen** (dam'ə·skēn, dam'ə·skēn'). — *adj.* Relating to damascening. — *n.* Work ornamented by damascening.

Dam·a·sce·nus (dam'ə·sē'nəs), **Johannes** See JOHN OF DAMASCUS.

Da·mas·cus (də·mas'kəs) An ancient city, capital of Syria. *Arabic* **Es Sham** (ash sham'), *French* **Da·mas** (dà·mäs'). — **Dam·as·cene** (dam'ə·sēn, dam'ə·sēn') *adj. & n.*

Damascus blade A sword or dagger blade made in Damascus, or like those once made there, celebrated for the excellence of its steel, and distinguished by wavy and variegated ornamentation.

Damascus steel The steel formerly used in making swords at Damascus; also, any steel having damascene markings.

dam·ask (dam'əsk) *n.* 1 A rich silk, linen, or wool fabric woven in elaborate patterns. 2 A fine table linen, so woven that two sets of parallel threads on the surface give the pattern different aspects from different points of view. 3 Damascus steel or Damascus work. 4 A deep pink or rose color. — *adj.* 1 Of, pertaining to, or from Damascus. 2 Made of damask steel or fabric. 3 Of the color of damask. — *v.t.* 1 To damascene. 2 To weave or ornament with rich patterns. 3 To make deep pink or rose in color. [from *Damascus*]

damask rose A large pink rose (*Rosa damascena*) of the Near East, noted for its fragrance.

dam·bo·nite (dam'bə·nīt) *n.* A white crystalline compound, $C_8H_{16}O_6$, contained in certain forms of caoutchouc. Also **dam·bon·i·tol** (dam·bon'ə·tōl, -tōl). [< native African *n'dambo*, the tree which produces it + -ITE[1]]

dame (dām) *n.* 1 A woman of high social position; a lady. 2 A married or mature woman; matron. 3 *Archaic* A schoolmistress. 4 A title of address for the lady recipients of the Grand Cross (suffix, G.B.E.), or for the Dames Commanders (suffix, D.B.E.) of the Order of the British Empire, created in 1917. See under ORDER (*n.* def. 9). 5 A female parent or ancestress. 6 *Slang* Any woman. [< OF < L *domina* lady, fem. of *dominus* master. Doublet of DUENNA.]

dame·wort (dām'wûrt') *n.* A coarse herb of the mustard family (*Hesperis matronalis*), with lanceolate, toothed leaves and fragrant lilac to deep-mauve flowers: also called *dame violet, dame rocket*.

dam·i·an·a (dam'ē·an'ə, -ē·ä'nə) *n.* The leaves of a Mexican plant (*Turnera diffusa*), used as a nerve tonic. [< NL < Sp. < native Mexican name]

Da·mien de Veus·ter (dà·myan' də vœs·târ'), **Joseph**, 1840–89, Belgian Roman Catholic missionary to the lepers in Molokai: known as *Father Damien* (dā'mē·ən).

Dam·i·et·ta (dam'ē·et'ə) A city in NE Egypt, in the Nile Delta: Arabic *Dumyat*.

dam·mar (dam'ər) *n.* 1 An oleoresinous gum yielded by various evergreen trees (genus *Agathis*) of Australia, India, and Asia: used as a colorless varnish in photography, etc. 2 A similar resin from other plant sources, as *Vateria indica, Shorea wiesneri*, etc. Also **dam'ar, dam'mer.** [< Malay *damar*]

damn (dam) *v.t.* 1 To pronounce worthless, unfit, bad, a failure, etc.: to *damn* the opposition or a play. 2 To curse or swear at. 3 *Theol.* To condemn to eternal punishment. 4 To pronounce guilty; bring ruin upon: His words *damned* him. 5 *Obs.* To adjudge guilty; doom. — *v.i.* 6 To swear; curse. — **to damn with faint praise** To praise so reluctantly as to imply adverse criticism. — *n.* 1 A curse; an oath. 2 Anything as valueless as an oath. [< OF *damner* < L *damnare* condemn to punishment]

dam·na·ble (dam'nə·bəl) *adj.* Meriting or causing damnation; detestable; outrageous. [< OF < L *damnabilis* < *damnare* condemn] — **dam'·na·ble·ness** *n.* — **dam'na·bly** *adv.*

dam·na·tion (dam·nā'shən) *n.* 1 Condemnation to future punishment or perdition. 2 The act of damning or the state of the damned. 3 Ruinous adverse criticism or public disapproval, as of a book or play. 4 Cause or occasion of eternal punishment; a mortal

sin. 5 *Obs.* Condemnation. [< F < L *damnatio, -onis* < *damnare* condemn]

dam·na·to·ry (dam'nə·tôr'ē, -tō'rē) *adj.* Tending to convict or condemn; consigning to damnation.

damned (damd, *poetic or rhetorical* dam'nid) *adj.* 1 Judicially reprobated and condemned; sentenced to eternal punishment. 2 Damnable; execrably bad; detestable. — *adv. Colloq.* Very; extremely: *damned* funny; *damned* irritating.

damned·est (dam'dist) *Colloq. adj.* Utmost: superlative of *damned.* — *n.* The utmost.

damned Yankee See DAMYANKEE.

dam·ni·fy (dam'nə·fī) *v.t.* **·fied, ·fy·ing** *Law* To cause injury, hurt, or damage to, in person or estate. [< OF *damnifier* < L *damnificare* injure]

damn·ing (dam'ing, dam'ning) *adj.* That damns or condemns; inculpating: *damning* evidence. — **damn'ing·ly** *adv.*

Dam·o·cles (dam'ə·klēz) In Greek legend, a courtier who, having overpraised the happiness of the tyrant Dionysius the Elder, was placed by him at a banquet, with a sword suspended over his head by a single hair to show him the perilous nature of that happiness. — **sword of Damocles** The sword hung over Damocles' head; hence, any impending danger or calamity. — **Dam·o·cle·an** (dam'ə·klē'ən) *adj.*

Da·mo·dar (dä'mə·där) A river in NE India, flowing 340 miles SE to the Hooghly.

Da·mon and Pyth·i·as (dā'mən; pith'ē·əs) In Roman legend, two Syracusan philosophers celebrated for their friendship. When Pythias was sentenced to death by Dionysius the Elder and wished to visit his home before dying, Damon volunteered to remain as hostage; Pythias returned and the loyalty of the two friends moved Dionysius to pardon the offender.

dam·o·sel (dam'ə·zel) *n. Archaic* A damsel. Also **dam·oi·selle** (dam'ə·zel'), **dam·o·sel'la** (-zel'ə), **dam·oy·sele,** **dam'o·zel.** [Var. of DAMSEL]

damp (damp) *n.* 1 A moderate degree of moisture; dampness; fog; mist. 2 Foul air; poisonous gas, occurring especially in coal mines. 3 Depression of spirits, or that which produces it. — *adj.* 1 Somewhat wet; moist. 2 Dejected. — *v.t.* 1 To moisten; make damp. 2 To check or discourage (energy, ardor, etc.). 3 *Music* To check the vibrations of (a string, etc.); deaden. 4 To bank, as a fire. 5 *Physics* To reduce the amplitude of (a series of waves). [< MDu., vapor, steam] — **damp'ly** *adv.* — **damp'ness** *n.*

damp·en (dam'pən) *v.t.* 1 To make or become damp; moisten. 2 To check; depress, as ardor or spirits. — *v.i.* 3 To become damp. — **damp'en·er** *n.*

damp·er (dam'pər) *n.* 1 One who or that which damps or checks. 2 A device to check the draft, as of a stove, or to stop vibration, as in a piano. 3 *Electr.* A device to check oscillation of a magnetic needle, or to control movement in an electrical mechanism. 4 *Eng.* A shock absorber.

Damp·ier (damp'yər, dam'pē·ər, -pir), **William**, 1652–1715, English privateer, explorer, and author.

damp·ish (dam'pish) *adj.* Slightly damp.

Dam·rosch (dam'rosh), **Walter Johannes**, 1862–1950, U.S. musician and conductor born in Germany.

dam·sel (dam'zəl) *n. Archaic* A young unmarried woman; maiden. [< OF *dameisele* gentlewoman, ult. < L *domina*. See DAME.]

damsel fly A slender-bodied dragonfly (order *Odonata*) with four similar elongate wings that are folded together over the back when at rest. For illustration see under INSECT (beneficial).

dam·son (dam'zən) *n.* 1 An oval purple plum of Syrian origin (*Prunus insititia*). 2 The tree producing it. Also **damson plum.** [ME *damascene* < L (*Prunum*) *Damascenum* plum from Damascus]

dam·yan·kee (dam'yang'kē, dam'-) *n. U.S. Colloq.* A Northerner: a contemptuous term used by Southerners since the Civil War: now chiefly jocular. Also *damned Yankee.*

dan (dan) *n. Obs.* Don; sir: a title of honor.

Dan (dan) A masculine personal name. [< Hebrew, judge]

— **Dan** One of the twelve tribes of Israel; descended from **Dan**, fifth son of Jacob and first of Bilhah. *Gen.* xxx 6.

Dan (dan) A city at the northern extremity of Palestine. Compare BEERSHEBA. — **from Dan to Beersheba** From end to end; throughout: Dan and Beersheba being respectively the extreme northern and southern cities of Palestine.

Da·na (dā'nə), **Charles Anderson**, 1819–97, U.S. editor. — **Edward Salisbury**, 1849–1935, U.S. mineralogist. — **James Dwight**, 1813–1895, U.S. geologist. — **Richard Henry**, 1815–82, U.S. lawyer and writer.

Dan·a·e (dan'i·ē) In Greek mythology, a maiden loved by Zeus in the form of a shower of gold: their son was Perseus.

Dan·a·id (dan'ē·id) *n.* One of the Danaides.

Da·na·i·des (də·nā'ə·dēz) In Greek mythology, the fifty daughters of Danaus who, with the exception of Hypermnestra, murdered their husbands, the sons of Aegyptus, on their bridal night at their father's command: these forty-nine were punished in Hades by having to draw water in a sieve forever. — **Dan·a·id·e·an** (dan'ē·id'ē·ən) *adj.*

Dan·a·us (dan'ē·əs) In Greek mythology, a king of Argos, father of the Danaides.

Dan·bur·y (dan'ber·ē, dan'bər·ē) A city in SW Connecticut.

dance (dans, däns) *v.* **danced, danc·ing** *v.i.* 1 To move the body and feet rhythmically, especially to music. 2 To move or skip excitedly; quiver, as from excitement or emotion. 3 To bob up and down; move about lightly and quickly. — *v.t.* 4 To perform or take part in the steps or figures of (a dance). 5 To effect or bring about by dancing: to *dance* the night away. 6 To cause to dance. 7 To dandle. See synonyms under FRISK, LEAP. — *n.* 1 A series of rhythmic concerted movements and steps timed to music. 2 A dancing party; ball. 3 A tune to dance by. 4 The intricate gyrations of swarming insects. [< OF *danser*] — **danc'er** *n.*

dance fly A small or medium-sized, slender, predacious fly (genus *Empis*, family *Empididae*) which mates in dancing swarms over the surface of land and water. For illustration see under INSECT (beneficial).

dance of death An allegory, often found in medieval art, representing Death as a skeleton leading men of all estates and conditions to the grave: also *danse macabre.*

dance·script (dans'skript', däns'-) *n.* Choroscript.

dan·de·li·on (dan'də·lī'ən) *n.* A wide-spread plant of the composite family (*Taraxacum officinale*), having yellow flower heads and deeply toothed, edible leaves. [< F *dent de lion* lion's tooth; with ref. to the shape of the leaves]

dan·der[1] (dan'dər) *U.S. Colloq.* Ruffled temper; anger. — **to get one's dander up** *Colloq.* To become angry. [? Var. of Scottish *dunder* ferment]

dan·der[2] (dan'dər) *v.i. Scot.* To saunter about: also spelled *daunder.*

Dan·die Din·mont (dan'dē din'mont) A short-legged, long-bodied, grayish or mustard-colored terrier with drooping ears. Also **Dandie Dinmont terrier.** [after a Scottish farmer who claimed to have started the breed, portrayed in Scott's *Guy Mannering*]

dan·di·fy (dan'də·fī) *v.t.* **·fied, ·fy·ing** To cause to resemble a dandy. — **dan'di·fi·ca'tion** *n.*

dan·di·prat (dan'dē·prat) *n. Obs.* 1 A little fellow. 2 A silver coin issued by Henry VII. Also **dan'dy·prat.** [Origin unknown]

dan·dle (dan'dəl) *v.t.* **·dled, ·dling** 1 To move up and down lightly on the knees or in the arms, as an infant or child. 2 To fondle; caress. [Cf. Ital. *dandolare*] — **dan'dler** *n.*

dan·druff (dan'drəf) *n.* A fine scurf forming on the scalp. Also **dan·driff** (dan'drif). [Origin unknown]

dan·dy[1] (dan'dē) *n. pl.* **·dies** 1 A man excessively and ostentatiously refined in dress and affected in manner; a fop; coxcomb. 2 *Colloq.* A particularly fine specimen of its kind. 3 A dandy roll. 4 A two-wheeled hand cart used about furnaces and mills for carrying fuel,

etc. 5 A yawl. — *adj.* 1 Like a dandy. 2 *U.S. Colloq.* Excellent; very fine. [Alter. of *Andy* <*Andrew*, a personal name. Cf. MERRY-ANDREW.]

dan·dy[2] (dan′dē) *n.* *pl.* **·dies** *Anglo-Indian* 1 A Ganges boatman. 2 A cloth hammock slung on a bamboo staff to be carried by bearers. 3 A Sivaistic ascetic who carries a small wand. Also **dan′dee, dan′di.** [<Hind. *ḍāṇḍī* <*ḍāṇḍ* a staff, oar]

dan·dy[3] (dan′dē) *n.* In the West Indies, dengue. Also **dandy fever.** [Alter. of DENGUE]

dan·dy·ish (dan′dē·ish) *adj.* Having the appearance or disposition of a dandy; foppish. — **dan′dy·ism** *n.*

dandy roll A cylinder of wire gauze by which a web of paper pulp is given a watermark. Also **dan′dy.**

Dane (dān) *n.* A native or citizen of Denmark. [<ON *Danir* the Danes]

dane·flow·er (dān′flou′ər) See PASQUEFLOWER.

Dane·geld (dān′geld′) *n.* An annual tax imposed about the end of the tenth century in Britain, originally to pay for protection against the Danes, but later continued by the Normans as a land tax. Also **Dane′gelt′** (-gelt′). [<Scand. Cf. ODan. *Danegjeld.*]

Dane·law (dān′lô′) *n.* A code of laws established by the Danes in England; also, the territory ruled under it. Also **Dane′lagh′** (-lô′). [OE *Dena-lagu* Danes' law]

dane·wort (dān′wûrt′) *n.* The European dwarf elder (*Sambucus ebulus*): also called **Dane's′-blood′, dane′weed′.**

dang (dang) *v.t.* Damn: a euphemism.

dan·ger (dān′jər) *n.* 1 Exposure to chance of evil, injury, or loss; peril; risk; also, a cause of peril or risk. 2 *Obs.* Power; control; ability to injure. [<OF, power of a lord, power to harm <L *dominium* lordship <*dominus* lord]

Synonyms: hazard, insecurity, jeopardy, peril, risk. *Danger* is exposure to injury or evil; *peril* is exposure to imminent, threatening injury or evil. *Jeopardy* involves, like *risk*, more of the element of chance or uncertainty; a man tried upon a capital charge is said to be put in *jeopardy* of life. *Insecurity* is a feeble word, but exceedingly broad, applying to the placing of a dish, or the possibilities of a life, a fortune, or a government. Compare HAZARD. *Antonyms*: defense, immunity, protection, safeguard, safety, security, shelter.

dan·ger·ous (dān′jər·əs) *adj.* Attended with danger; hazardous; perilous; unsafe. See synonyms under FORMIDABLE, SERIOUS. — **dan′ger·ous·ly** *adv.* — **dan′ger·ous·ness** *n.*

dan·gle (dang′gəl) *v.* **·gled, ·gling** *v.i.* 1 To hang loosely; swing to-and-fro. 2 To follow or hover near someone as a suitor or hanger-on. 3 To be hanged. — *v.t.* 4 To hold so as to swing loosely to-and-fro. 5 To hang (someone). — *n.* 1 Manner or act of dangling. 2 Something which dangles. [<Scand. Cf. Dan. *dangle.*] — **dan′gler** *n.*

dan·gle·ber·ry (dang′gəl·ber′ē) See TANGLEBERRY.

Dan·iel (dan′yəl; *Fr.* dà·nyel′; *Ger.* dä′nē·el) A masculine personal name. Also *Ital.* **Da·niel·le** (dä·nyel′lā). [<Hebrew, God is my judge]

— **Daniel** One of the greater Hebrew prophets, captive in Babylon in the sixth century B.C.; also, the book of the Old Testament attributed to him.

Dan·iel (dan′yəl), **Samuel,** 1562–1619, English poet; poet laureate 1599–1619.

Dan·iels (dan′yəlz), **Farrington,** born 1889, U.S. electro-chemist. — **Josephus,** 1862–1948, U.S. journalist and statesman.

Dan·ish (dā′nish) *adj.* Of or pertaining to Denmark, the Danes, or their language. — *n.* The North Germanic language of the Danes. Abbr. *Dan.* [OE *Denisc*]

Danish pastry A rich, flaky pastry made with raised dough, often filled with cheese or jam.

Danish West Indies A former name for the VIRGIN ISLANDS OF THE UNITED STATES.

Dan·ite (dan′īt) *adj.* Of or pertaining to the tribe of Dan. — *n.* 1 A descendant of Dan. 2 One of a reputed Mormon band or secret brotherhood (called also *Destroying Angels*): said to have been organized in the early history of the Mormons to support their cause at any cost.

dank (dangk) *adj.* Unpleasantly damp; moist; wet. — *n.* Disagreeable humidity; wetness. [ME *danke* <Scand. Cf. Sw. *dank* marshy ground.] — **dank′ish** *adj.* — **dank′ish·ness** *n.* — **dank′ly** *adv.*

Dan·ne·brog (dan′ə·brôg) *n.* 1 The Danish national flag. 2 A Danish order of knighthood. [<Dan. <*Dane-* Danish + *brog* cloth]

D'An·nun·zio (dän·nōōn′tsyō), **Gabriele,** 1863–1938, Italian author and soldier.

Da·no-Nor·we·gian (dā′nō·nôr·wē′jən) *n.* Riksmål.

danse ma·ca·bre (däns mà·kä′br′) *French* Dance of death.

dan·seuse (dän·sœz′) *n.* *pl.* **·seus·es** (-sœ′ziz, *Fr.* -sœz′) A female ballet dancer; a ballerina. [<F]

Dan·te A·li·ghie·ri (dän′tā ä′lē·gyâ′rē, dan′tē) 1265–1321, Italian poet; author of the *Divine Comedy.* Also *Durante Alighieri.*

Dan·tesque (dan·tesk′) *adj.* Pertaining to, resembling, or in the style of Dante Alighieri; especially, characterized by solemn and impassioned sublimity. Also **Dan·te·an** (dan′tē·ən, dan·tē′ən). [<Ital. *dantesco* <*Dante*]

Dan·tist (dan′tist) *n.* One versed in the works of Dante.

Dan·ton (dän·tôn′), **Georges Jacques,** 1759–1794, French Revolutionary leader; guillotined.

Dan·u (thän′ōō) In ancient Irish mythology, the goddess of death and mother of all the gods.

Dan·ube (dan′yōōb) A river in central and SE Europe, flowing 1,750 miles eastward from Baden, Germany, to the Black Sea: German *Donau,* Hungarian *Duna,* Rumanian *Dunărea.*

Da·nu·bi·an (dan·yōō′bē·ən, də·nōō′-) *adj.* Pertaining to the Danube or the regions and peoples near it.

Dan·zig (dan′sig, *Ger.* dän′tsikh) A port of northern Poland on the **Gulf of Danzig,** an inlet of the Baltic Sea between Poland and the U.S.S.R.; former capital of the territory of the **Free City of Danzig** (731 square miles) as constituted by the Treaty of Versailles (1919). Polish *Gdańsk.*

dap (dap) *v.i.* **dapped, dap·ping** 1 To dip lightly or suddenly into water, as a bird. 2 To fish by dropping a baited hook gently on the water. 3 To bounce or skip. [Prob. var. of DAB[3]]

daph·ne (daf′nē) *n.* 1 The laurel (*Laurus nobilis*) of southern Europe. 2 Any of a genus (*Daphne*) of shrubs, some deciduous, some evergreen, with fragrant flowers. [<NL <Gk. *daphnē*]

Daph·ne (daf′nē) In Greek mythology, a nymph who became a laurel tree in order to escape from Apollo.

Daph·nis (daf′nis) In Greek mythology, a Sicilian shepherd, son of Hermes and inventor of bucolic poetry.

Daphnis and Chloe A pair of lovers in a Greek pastoral romance attributed to Longus.

dap·per (dap′ər) *adj.* 1 Trim; neat; natty; smartly dressed. 2 Small and active. [<MDu., strong, energetic]

dap·ple (dap′əl) *v.t.* **·pled, ·pling** To make spotted or variegated in color. — *adj.* Spotted; variegated: also **dap′pled.** — *n.* 1 A spot or dot, as on the skin of a horse. 2 An animal marked with spots. [Origin uncertain]

Dap·sang (dup′sung) See K2.

Dar·bhan·ga (dûr·bung′gə) A city in Bihar, India.

dar·bies (där′bēz) *n. pl. Brit. Slang* Handcuffs. [? <*Darby,* a surname]

d'Ar·blay (där′blā, *Fr.* dàr·blā′) See BURNEY, FANNY.

Dar·by and Joan (där′bē; jōn) John Darby and his wife Joan, popularized in an English ballad, about 1735; hence, types of conjugal felicity.

Dar·dan (där′dən) *adj.* & *n.* Trojan. Also **Dar·da·ni·an** (där·dā′nē·ən).

Dar·da·nelles (där′də·nelz′) A narrow strait in NW Turkey connecting the Sea of Marmara with the Aegean; length, 37 miles: ancient *Hellespont. Turkish* **Ça·nak·ka·le Bo·ğa·zi** (chä′näk·kä·le′ bō′ä·zi′).

Dar·da·nus (där′də·nəs) In Greek mythology, a son of Zeus and ancestor of the Trojans.

dare[1] (dâr) *v.* **dared** (*Archaic* **durst**), **dar·ing** *v.t.* 1 To have the courage or boldness to undertake; venture on. 2 To challenge to attempt something as proof of courage, etc. 3 To defy; oppose and challenge. — *v.i.* 4 To have the courage or boldness to do or attempt something; venture. — **I dare say** I am reasonably certain. — *n.* 1 The act of daring; a challenge: to do something on a *dare.* 2 Daring; bravery. [OE *durran*] — **dar′er** *n.*

dare[2] (dâr) *v.* **dared, dar·ing** *Obs. v.t.* 1 To daunt; scare. 2 To dazzle; paralyze. — *v.i.* 3 To be in fear. [OE *darian* lurk]

Dare (dâr), **Virginia,** born 1587, first child of English parents born in America, on Roanoke Island.

dare·dev·il (dâr′dev′əl) *n.* One who is recklessly bold. — *adj.* Venturesome; reckless. — **dare′dev′il·try** *n.*

dare·ful (dâr′fəl) *adj.* Defiant; full of daring.

Dar-el-Bei·da (där′el·bī·dä′, -bā·dä′) The Arabic name for CASABLANCA.

Dar-es-Sa·laam (där′es·sə·läm′) A port on the Indian Ocean, capital of Tanganyika.

Dar·fur (där·fōōr′) A province of western Sudan; 138,150 square miles; capital, El Fasher.

dar·ic (dar′ik) *n.* An ancient Persian gold coin; also, a silver coin of the same design, worth one twentieth of the gold daric. [<Gk. *Dareikos* coin of Darius]

Dar·i·en (dâr′ē·en′, dâr′ē·en′; *Sp.* dä·ryān′) The eastern part of Panama between the Gulf of San Miguel and the **Gulf of Darien,** a bight of the Caribbean Sea in the east coast of Panama. — **Isthmus of Darien** A former name of the ISTHMUS OF PANAMA.

dar·ing (dâr′ing) *adj.* 1 Possessing courage; bold; brave; venturesome. 2 Audacious; presuming. See synonyms under BRAVE. — *n.* Heroic courage; bravery. See synonyms under COURAGE. — **dar′ing·ly** *adv.* — **dar′ing·ness** *n.*

Da·rí·o (dä·rē′ō), **Rubén,** pen name of Félix Rubén García-Sarmiento, 1867–1916, Nicaraguan poet.

Da·ri·us (də·rī′əs) A masculine personal name.

— **Darius I, Hys·tas·pes** (his·tas′pēz), 558?–485 B.C.; king of Persia 521–485 B.C.; invaded Scythia and Greece, defeated at Marathon: called "Darius the Great."

— **Darius III, Co·do·man·nus** (kō·dō·man′əs), king of Persia 336–330 B.C., conquered by Alexander the Great.

Dar·jee·ling (där·jē′ling) A resort town in northern West Bengal.

dark (därk) *adj.* 1 Lacking light. 2 Of a deep shade; black, or approaching black. 3 Obscure; mysterious; not understandable. 4 Gloomy; disheartening. 5 Unenlightened. 6 Atrocious; dastardly; wicked. 7 Of brunette complexion. 8 Blind; unknowing. 9 Secretive; reticent. — *n.* 1 Lack of light. 2 A place, position, or state where there is little or no light. 3 Night. 4 Obscurity; secrecy. 5 Ignorance: especially in the phrase *in the dark.* 6 A heavy shade or shadow in a drawing or painting. — *v.t.* & *v.i. Obs.* To make or become dark; darken. [OE *deorc*]

Synonyms (*adj.*): black, dim, dismal, dusky, gloomy, murky, mysterious, obscure, opaque, sable, shadowy, shady, somber, swart, swarthy. Strictly, that which is *black* is absolutely destitute of color; that which is *dark* is absolutely destitute of light. In common speech, however, a coat is *black,* though not optically colorless; the night is *dark,* though the stars shine. That is *obscure, shadowy,* or *shady* from which the light is more or less cut off. *Dusky* is applied to objects which appear as if viewed in fading light; the word is often used, as are *swart* and *swarthy,* of the human skin when quite *dark,* or even verging on *black. Dim* refers to imperfection of outline, from distance, darkness, mist, etc., or from some defect of vision. *Opaque* objects are impervious to light. *Murky* is said of that which is at once *dark, obscure,* and *gloomy*; as, a *murky* den; a *murky* sky. Figuratively, *dark* is emblematic of sadness, agreeing with *somber, dismal, gloomy,* also of moral evil:

as, a *dark* deed. Of intellectual matters, *dark* is now rarely used in the old sense of a *dark* saying, etc. See MYSTERIOUS, OBSCURE. *Antonyms*: bright, brilliant, clear, crystalline, dazzling, gleaming, glowing, illumined, light, lucid, luminous, radiant, shining, transparent, white. Compare synonyms for LIGHT.

Dark Ages 1 The period in European history between the fall of the Western Roman Empire (A.D. 476) and the Italian Renaissance. **2** The early part of the Middle Ages, to the end of the tenth century: so called because the period was considered to be characterized by a waning of Roman civilization and a retardation in social, political, and intellectual development.

Dark and Bloody Ground Kentucky: so called because of the numerous Indian wars in the territory now included within the State.

dark conduction *Electr.* Conductive of residual electricity in a photosensitive substance when not illuminated.

Dark Continent Africa: so called because it was little known until the 19th century.

dark current *Electr.* The current set up in a photoelectric cell when the light beam is interrupted.

dark·en (där′kən) *v.t.* **1** To make dark or darker; deprive of light. **2** To make dark in color; make black. **3** To fill with gloom; sadden. **4** To blind. **5** To obscure; confuse. — *v.i.* **6** To grow dark or darker. **7** To become sad or gloomy; grow dark or flushed, as the face with anger or hatred. **8** To become blind. — **dark′en·er** *n.*

dark–field illumination (därk′fēld′) *Optics* The lighting of the field of a microscope from the side instead of from below, so as to reveal the specimen against a dark background.

dark horse 1 An unknown or little talked-of horse that unexpectedly wins a race. **2** A little-known political candidate unexpectedly nominated.

dark·ish (där′kish) *adj.* Somewhat dark.

dark lantern A lantern having a case with one transparent side, which can be covered by a shield to hide the light.

dar·kle (där′kəl) *v.i.* **·kled, ·kling 1** To appear darkly or indistinctly; be in darkness. **2** To grow gloomy or dark; darken. [Back formation <DARKLING, DARKLE]

dar·kling (därk′ling) *adj. Poetic* Dim; obscure; occurring or being in the dark. — *adv.* In the dark; blindly; mysteriously.

dark·ly (därk′lē) *adv.* **1** In a dark manner. **2** Obscurely; mysteriously.

dark·ness (därk′nis) *n.* **1** Total or partial absence of light; gloom. **2** Physical, mental, or moral blindness. **3** Want of clearness; obscurity; secrecy. **4** The quality of being dark in color or shade.

dark·room (därk′rōōm′, -rōōm′) *n. Phot.* A room equipped to exclude actinic rays, for treating plates, films, etc.

dark·some (därk′səm) *adj. Poetic* Dark; darkish.

dark star See under STAR.

dark·y (där′kē) *n. pl.* **dark·ies** *Colloq.* A Negro: a contemptuous term. Also **dark′ey, dark′ie.**

Dar·lan (där·län′), **Jean François,** 1881–1942, French admiral and politician; assassinated.

dar·ling (där′ling) *n.* One tenderly beloved: often a term of direct address. — *adj.* Tenderly beloved; very dear. [OE *dēorling*, dim. of *dēor* dear]

Darling Range A mountain system of Western Australia: highest peak, 1,910 feet.

Dar·ling River (där′ling) A river in SE Australia, flowing SW 1,910 miles to the Murray River.

Dar·ling·ton (där′ling·tən) A county borough in south Durham, England.

Dar·ling·ton (där′ling·tən), **Cyril Dean,** born 1903, English geneticist.

Darm·stadt (därm′shtät) A city in southern Hesse, Germany.

darn¹ (därn) *v.t. & v.i.* To repair (a garment or a hole or rent) by filling the gap with interlacing stitches. — *n.* A place mended by darning; also, the act of darning. [Earlier *dern*, prob. <OE *dernan* conceal <*derne* hidden]

darn² (därn) *v.t., adj., n., & interj. Colloq.* Damn: a euphemism.

darn·dest (därn′dist) *n. & adj. Colloq.* Damnedest: a euphemism.

dar·nel (där′nəl) *n.* A grass (*Lolium temulentum*); ryegrass; an annual weed often found in grain fields. [<dial. F *darnelle*]

darn·er (där′nər) *n.* **1** One who or that which darns. **2** A darning needle.

darning needle 1 A large-eyed needle used in darning. **2** A dragonfly: also devil's-darning-needle. **3** The Venus's-comb.

Darn·ley (därn′lē), **Lord,** 1546–67, Henry Stuart, second husband of Mary Queen of Scots; murdered.

Dar·row (dar′ō), **Clarence Seward,** 1857–1938, U.S. lawyer.

d′Ar·son·val (där·sôn·väl′), **Jacques Arsène,** 1851–1940, French physicist.

DARNEL
A. Spikelet.

dart (därt) *n.* **1** A pointed missile weapon, as a javelin; also, something like an arrow or having the effect of one. **2** A sudden and rapid motion. **3** A tapering tuck made in a garment by stitching or cutting so as to fit it to the figure. **4** An insect's sting. — *v.t. & v.i.* **1** To emit swiftly or suddenly; shoot out. **2** To move swiftly and suddenly. See synonyms under THROW. [<OF <Gmc.]

dart·er (där′tər) *n.* **1** A small American perchlike fish (subfamily *Estheostomatinae*). **2** The American snakebird.

dar·tle (där′təl) *v.t. & v.i.* **·tled, ·tling** To dart or shoot out repeatedly.

Dart·moor (därt′mōōr′) **1** A wild upland in south Devonshire, England; 350 square miles. **2** A famous prison in this region.

darts (därts) *n.* A game of skill in which small darts are thrown at a bull's-eye target.

Dar·win (där′win) A port, capital of Northern Territory, Australia; formerly *Palmerston.*

Dar·win (där′win), **Charles Robert,** 1809–82, English naturalist; formulated the theory of evolution by natural selection. — **Erasmus,** 1731–1802, English physician and poet; grandfather of the preceding.

Dar·win·i·an (där·win′ē·ən) *adj.* Pertaining to Charles Darwin, or to Darwinism. — *n.* An advocate of Darwinism.

Dar·win·ism (där′win·iz′əm) *n.* **1** The biological doctrine of descent by natural selection with variation, advocated by Charles Darwin. **2** The evolutionary theory of Charles Darwin: also **Darwinian theory. — Dar′win·ist** *n. & adj. —* **Dar′win·is′tic** *adj. —* **Dar′win·ite** (-īt) *n.*

Dar·yal Gorge (dür′yal′) A defile in the central Caucasus north of Tiflis; 5,900 feet deep.

dash¹ (dash) *v.t.* **1** To strike with violence, especially so as to break or shatter. **2** To throw, thrust, or knock suddenly and violently: usually with *away, out, down,* etc. **3** To splash; bespatter. **4** To do, write, etc., hastily: with *off* or *down.* **5** To frustrate; confound: to *dash* hopes. **6** To daunt or discourage. **7** To put to shame; abash. **8** To adulterate; mix: with *with.* **9** *Brit.* To damn: a euphemism. — *v.i.* **10** To strike; hit: The waves *dashed* against the shore. **11** To rush or move impetuously. See synonyms under THROW. — *n.* **1** A sudden advance or onset; short, spirited rush or race. **2** Impetuosity; spirit; vigor. **3** Ostentatious display, especially in the phrase *to cut a dash.* **4** A check or hindrance; discomfiture. **5** A slight admixture; a tinge; a small addition of some other ingredient. **6** A collision or concussion; also, its sound. **7** A horizontal line (—), as a mark of punctuation, etc. **8** The long sound in the Morse code, used in combination with dots to represent letters. **9** A dashboard. **10** The dasher of a churn. [ME *daschen* <Scand. Cf. Dan. *daske* a slap.]

dash² (dash) *v.t.* In West Africa, to bribe; also, offer as a bribe. — *n.* A bribe. [Earlier *dashee,* alter. of Pg. *Que das me?* What do you give me?]

dash·board (dash′bôrd′, -bōrd′) *n.* **1** An upright screen on the front of a vehicle to intercept mud, etc., thrown up by a horse. **2** A sprayboard at

the bow of a vessel. **3** The instrument board of an automobile.

da·sheen (da·shēn′) *n.* A tropical plant (*Colocasia esculenta*) related to the taro, the root of which is a staple food of the tropics. [<F *de Chine* of China]

dash·er (dash′ər) *n.* **1** One who or that which dashes, plunges, or cuts a dash. **2** The plunger of a churn. **3** A dashboard.

da·shi·ki (dä·shē′kē) *n. pl.* **·kis** A loose-fitting, sleeved garment of varying length, often with a print design or embroidery, worn by men and women in West Africa and elsewhere. [< Yoruba]

dash·ing (dash′ing) *adj.* **1** Spirited; bold; impetuous. **2** Ostentatiously showy or gay. — **dash′ing·ly** *adv.*

Dasht-i-Ka·vir (däsht′ē·kä·vēr′) A salt desert of the central Iranian plateau; 200 miles wide.

Dasht-i-Lut (däsht′ē·lōōt′) A desert of eastern Iran; 200 miles long, 100 miles wide.

dash·y (dash′ē) *adj.* **dash·i·er, dash·i·est** Stylish.

das·tard (das′tərd) *n.* A base coward; a sneak. — *adj.* Dastardly. [? ME *dased, dast,* pp. of *dasen* daze, stupefy + -ARD]

das·tard·ly (das′tərd·lē) *adj.* Base; cowardly. — **das′tard·li·ness, das′tard·y** *n.*

das·y·ure (das′ē·ōōr) *n.* **1** An arboreal marsupial; especially, a small, spotted, civetlike marsupial, as the **spotted dasyure** (*Dasyurus maculatus*) of Tasmania and southern Australia. **2** The Tasmanian devil. [<Gk. *dasys* hairy + *oura* tail]

DASYURE
(Body length: 1 to 1 1/2 feet)

da·ta (dā′tə, dat′ə, dä′tə) *n. pl.* of DATUM Facts or figures from which conclusions may be drawn: often construed as a singular. [<L, neut. pl. of *datus,* pp. of *dare* give]

data bank An extensive body of information organized and stored in a computer's memory for the quick retrieval of data in response to particular queries.

data processing The operation of digital or analog computers.

da·ta·ry (dā′tə·rē) *n. pl.* **·ries 1** A papal official, usually a bishop, having charge of grants and dispensations and the dating and registration of all important documents. **2** The office or employment of this official. [<Med. L *datarius* <L *dare* give, grant]

date¹ (dāt) *n.* **1** That part of a writing, inscription, coin, etc., which tells when, or when and where, it was written, published, etc. **2** The time of some event; a point of time. **3** Duration; age. **4** *U.S. Colloq.* An engagement; appointment. **— down to date** Covering the current day. **— out of date** Obsolete. — **up to date** Having modern knowledge, style, etc. — *v.* **dat·ed, dat·ing** *v.t.* **1** To furnish or mark with a date. **2** To ascertain the time or era of; assign a date to. **3** *U.S. Colloq.* To make an appointment with, as a member of the opposite sex. — *v.i.* **4** To have origin in or be in existence since an era or time: usually with *from*: This coin *dates* from the Renaissance. **5** To reckon time. [<F <L *data,* fem. sing. of *datus,* pp. of *dare* give; from first word of Latin formula giving a letter's date and place of writing] — **dat′er** *n.*

date² (dāt) *n.* **1** An oblong, sweet, fleshy fruit of the date palm, enclosing a single hard seed. **2** A lofty palm bearing this fruit (*Phoenix dactylifera* and varieties): also called **date palm.** [<OF <L *dactylus* <Gk. *daktylos* finger; with ref. to its shape]

dat·ed (dā′tid) *adj.* **1** Marked with a date. **2** Antiquated; old-fashioned.

date·less (dāt′lis) *adj.* **1** Bearing no date. **2** Without end or limit. **3** Immemorial; of permanent interest.

date line 1 The line containing the date of publication of a periodical or of any contribution, dispatch, etc., printed in it. **2** An imaginary line approximately congruent with 180° longitude from Greenwich, internationally agreed upon as determining those points on the earth's surface where a day is dropped on crossing it from west to east and added on crossing from east to west: also called **International Date Line.**

da·tive (dā′tiv) *n. Gram.* **1** In inflected Indo-European languages, that case of a noun, pronoun, or adjective denoting the remoter, or indirect object: expressed in English by *to* or *for* with the objective or by word order, as in *I told the story to him, I told him the story.* **2** A word in this case. —*adj.* **1** *Gram.* Pertaining to or designating the dative case or a word in this case. **2** *Law* That may be disposed of at will; also, that may be removed; removable as opposed to perpetual: a *dative* officer. [< L *dativus,* trans. of Gk. *(ptōsis) dotikē* (the case of) giving < *didonai* give] —**da′tive·ly** *adv.*

dat·o·lite (dat′ō-līt) *n.* A vitreous, translucent, brittle calcium borosilicate occurring in massive monoclinic crystals. [< Gk. *dateesthai* divide + -LITE]

dat·to (dä′tō) *n. pl.* **·tos 1** In the Philippines, a chief of a Moslem Moro tribe. **2** The headman of a barrio or Malay tribe. Also **da′to.** [< Malay *datôq*]

da·tum (dā′təm, dat′əm, dä′təm) *n. pl.* **da·ta 1** A known, assumed, or conceded fact from which an inference is made. **2** The point from which any reckoning or scale starts. [< L, neut. sing. of *datus.* See DATA.]

datum plane *Engin.* The horizontal plane from which heights and depths are measured: also **datum level.**

da·tu·ra (də-tŏor′ə, -tyŏor′ə) *n.* One of a genus (*Datura*) of rank-smelling, poisonous plants of the nightshade family, with large funnel-shaped flowers and a prickly capsule, of which the jimsonweed is the best-known species. [< NL < Hind. *dhātūrā,* a plant]

DATURA
a. Fruit.
b. Grain.

daub (dôb) *v.t. & v.i.* **1** To smear or coat (something), as with plaster, grease, mud, etc. **2** To paint without skill or taste. —*n.* **1** Mud, plaster, clay, etc.; any sticky application. **2** A smear or spot. **3** A poor, coarse painting. **4** An instance or act of daubing. See synonyms under BLEMISH. [< OF *dauber* < L *dealbare* whitewash]

daub·er (dô′bər) *n.* **1** One who or that which daubs. **2** One who paints coarsely or cheaply. **3** A brush to put blacking on shoes; a dabber. **4** *Obs.* A flatterer. —**daub′er·y, daub′ry** *n.* —**daub′ing** *n.*

Dau·bi·gny (dō-bē·nyē′), **Charles François,** 1817–78, French painter.

daub·y (dô′bē) *adj.* **1** Pertaining to or like daub; sticky. **2** Unskilfully done, as a painting; also, smeary.

daud (dôd, däd) *v.t. & v.i. Scot.* To thump; beat.

Dau·det (dō-de′), **Alphonse,** 1840–97, French novelist. —**Léon,** 1867–1942, French journalist and novelist; son of the preceding.

Dau·ga·va (dou′gä·vä) The Latvian name for the WESTERN DVINA.

daugh·ter (dô′tər) *n.* **1** A female child or descendant. **2** Any person or thing in a relation analogous to that of a female child, regarded with reference to her, or its, origin. **3** *Obs.* A maiden. [OE *dohtor*] —**daugh′ter·ly** *adj.*

daughter cell *Biol.* Either of the two cells resulting from a mitotic division of a cell.

daugh·ter-in-law (dô′tər-in-lô′) *n. pl.* **daugh·ters-in-law** The wife of one's son.

Daughters of the American Revolution A patriotic society of women who are lineal descendants of patriots in the American Revolution, organized in Washington, D.C., in 1890.

Dau·mier (dō-myä′), **Honoré,** 1808–79, French painter and caricaturist.

daun·der (dôn′dər, dän′-) See DANDER[2].

daunt (dônt, dänt) *v.t.* **1** To dishearten or intimidate; cow. **2** To pack into a barrel with a daunt. See synonyms under ABASH, FRIGHTEN. —*n.* **1** A fright. **2** A wooden disk with which to press salted fish, especially herring, into barrels. [< OF *danter, donter* < L *domitare,* freq. of *domare* tame]

daunt·less (dônt′lis, dänt′-) *adj.* Fearless; intrepid. See synonyms under BRAVE. —**daunt′less·ly** *adv.* —**daunt′less·ness** *n.*

dau·phin (dô′fin, *Fr.* dō·faṅ′) *n.* The eldest son of a king of France: a title used from 1349 to 1830.

[< F, a dolphin; used as a personal name and title]

Dau·phi·né (dō·fē·nā′) A region and former province of SE France.

dau·phin·ess (dô′fin-is) *n.* The wife of a dauphin. Also **dau′phine** (-fēn).

daur (dôr) *v.t. Scot.* To dare.

daur·na (dôr′nə) *Scot.* Dare not.

daut (dôt, dät) *v.t. Scot.* To fondle: also spelled **dawt.**

daut·ie (dô′tē) *n. Scot.* A little pet: also spelled **dawtie.**

Da·vaine (də-vān′), **Casimir Joseph,** 1812–82, French physician and bacteriologist.

Da·vao (dä′vou) A port on Davao Gulf, an inlet on the SE coast of Mindanao, Philippines.

Dav·e·nant (dav′ə-nənt), **Sir William,** 1606–1668, English poet and dramatist; poet laureate 1638–68. Also **D'Av′e·nant.**

dav·en·port (dav′ən-pôrt, -pōrt) *n.* **1** A large, upholstered sofa, often one that can be used as a bed. **2** A small writing desk. [Prob. after the name of the first manufacturer]

Dav·en·port (dav′ən-pôrt, -pōrt) A city on the Mississippi in eastern Iowa.

Dav·en·port (dav′ən-pôrt, -pōrt), **Charles Benedict,** 1866–1944, U.S. zoologist. —**John,** 1597–1670, English clergyman; one of the founders of New Haven.

Da·vid (dā′vid, *Ger.* dä′vēt) A masculine personal name; familiarly **Dave, Da′vie, Da′vy.** Also *Fr.* **Da·vide** (dà·vēd′), *Ital.* **Da·vid** (dä·vēd′), **Da·vi·de** (dä·vē′dä). [< Hebrew, beloved] —**David,** 1000?–960? B.C., second king of Israel; reputed writer of *Psalms.* —**David I,** 1084–1153, king of Scotland 1124–1153. —**David, Saint,** died 601?, patron of Wales.

Da·vid (dà·vēd′), **Gerard,** 1450?–1523, Flemish painter. —**Jacques Louis,** 1748–1825, French painter. —**Pierre Jean,** 1788–1856, French sculptor: also called **"David d'An·gers"** (däṅ·zhā′).

David, Star of See MOGEN DAVID.

Da·vid·son (dā′vid·sən), **Jo,** 1883–1952, U.S. sculptor.

da Vin·ci (dä vēn′chē), **Leonardo** See LEONARDO DA VINCI.

Davis (dā′vis), **Jefferson,** 1808–89, U.S. statesman; president of the Confederacy 1862–1865. —**John,** 1550?–1605, English navigator. —**Norman Hezekiah,** 1878–1944, U.S. financier and diplomat. —**Owen,** 1874–1956, U.S. dramatist. —**Richard Harding,** 1864–1916, U.S. journalist and novelist. —**Stuart,** born 1894, U.S. painter. —**William Stearns,** 1877–1930, U.S. educator and historian.

Davis Cup A trophy cup presented to that nation whose team wins the International Lawn Tennis Championship, commonly called the Davis Cup matches. [after Dwight F. *Davis,* 1879–1945, who instituted the tournament in 1900]

Da·vis·son (dā′vis·ən), **Clinton Joseph,** 1881–1958, U.S. physicist.

Davis Strait An arm of the Atlantic between Baffin Island and SW Greenland.

dav·it (dav′it, dā′vit) *n. Naut.* **1** One of a pair of small cranes on a ship's side for hoisting its boats, stores, etc. **2** A curved piece of timber or iron for hoisting the flukes of an anchor. [from *David,* proper name]

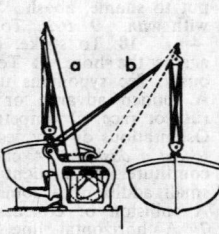

DAVIT
a. Position on deck.
b. Position when lowering lifeboat.

Da·vos (dä·vōs′) A resort town in eastern Switzerland.

Da·vout (dà·vōō′), **Louis Nicolas,** 1770–1823, duke of Auerstadt and prince of Eckmühl; French marshal.

da·vy (dā′vē) *n. pl.* **·vies** A safety lamp.

Da·vy (dā′vē), **Sir Humphry,** 1778–1829, English chemist; inventor of the safety lamp, the electrolytic method of preparing potassium, etc.

Da·vy Jones (dā′vē jōnz′) Sailors' name for the spirit of the sea.

Davy Jones's locker The bottom of the ocean, especially as the grave of the drowned.

daw[1] (dô) *n.* **1** A jackdaw. **2** A simpleton. [ME *dawe*]

daw[2] (dô) *n. & v.i. Scot.* Dawn.

daw·dle (dôd′l) *v.t. & v.i.* **·dled, ·dling** To waste (time) in slow trifling; loiter: often with *away.* See synonyms under LINGER. [Prob. var. of DADDLE] —**daw′dler** *n.*

Dawes (dôz), **Charles Gates,** 1865–1951, U.S. financier and statesman; vice president of the United States 1925–29.

dawk (dôk, däk) See DAK.

dawn (dôn) *v.i.* **1** To begin to grow light. **2** To begin to be understood: with *on* or *upon.* **3** To begin to expand or develop. —*n.* **1** The first appearance of light in the morning; daybreak. ◆Collateral adjective: *auroral.* **2** An awakening; beginning or unfolding. [Back formation < *dawning,* earlier *dawenyng* daybreak < Scand. Cf. Sw. *dagning.*]

Dawn man Eoanthropus.

Daw·son (dô′sən) A city in western Yukon, Canada; formerly the capital of the territory.

Daw·son (dô′sən), **Sir John William,** 1820–99, Canadian geologist.

Dawson Creek A village in eastern British Columbia; the southern terminal of the Alaska Highway.

dawt (dôt, dät) See DAUT.

Dax (däks) A resort town of SW France.

day (dā) *n.* **1** The period from dawn to dark; hence, daylight or sunlight. **2** The interval represented by one revolution of the earth upon its axis; twenty-four hours; also, this period as a unit in computing time. ◆Collateral adjective: *diurnal.* See under TIME. **3** The hours appointed for labor. **4** A day's journey. **5** The period of rotation about its axis of any heavenly body. **6** A time or period; an age. **7** A contest or battle, or its result: The liberals won the *day.* **8** A specified epoch: in Caesar's *day.* **9** A specified date: Independence *Day.* —**day after day** Every day. —**day by day** Each day. —**day in, day out** Every day. —**(from) day to day** From one day to the next; not long-range. —**the day** *Scot.* Today: How are ye *the day?* [OE *dæg*]

Day (dā), **Edmund Ezra,** 1883–1951, U.S. educator; president of Cornell University 1937–49. —**Thomas,** 1748–89, English author. —**William Rufus,** 1849–1923, U.S. statesman and jurist.

Day·ak (dī′ak) See DYAK.

day-bed (dā′bed′) *n.* A lounge or couch, usually with back and sides, that can be converted into a bed at night.

day blindness Hemeralopia.

day·book (dā′bŏok′) *n.* **1** In bookkeeping, the book in which transactions are recorded in the order of their occurrence. **2** A diary.

day·break (dā′brāk′) *n.* Dawn; the time when the sun rises.

day camp A camp where children spend the day in supervised activities, returning home each evening.

day-care center (dā′kâr′) A place for the care of young children during the day, especially while their mothers are at work: also called *day nursery.*

day coach A railroad car equipped for daytime travel only, as opposed to a sleeping-car, dining-car, etc.

day·dream (dā′drēm′) *n.* **1** An exercise of the fancy or imagination; a reverie. **2** A delusion of happiness. —*v.i.* To indulge the mind idly in wishful thinking. —**day′dream′er** *n.*

day flower Any species of the genus *Commelina* whose flowers last only a day.

day-fly (dā′flī′) *n.* A mayfly or ephemerid insect.

day labor Labor hired and paid for by the day.

day laborer One who works for pay by the day, as at unskilled manual tasks.

day letter A lettergram sent during the day.

day·light (dā′līt′) *n.* **1** The light received from the sun; the light of day. **2** The period of light during the day. **3** Insight into or understanding of something formerly puzzling. **4** Exposure to view; publicity.

day·lights (dā′līts′) *n. Slang.* **1** Vital organs; life itself: The mule worked his *daylights* out. **2** Consciousness; wits: to shake the *daylights* out of one.

day·light-sav·ing time (dā′līt′sā′ving) Time in which more daylight for the working day is

obtained by setting clocks one or more hours ahead of standard time, especially during the summer months.

day·lil·y (dā′lil′ē) n. pl. ·lil·ies 1 Any of several lyworts (genus *Hemerocallis*), with lanceolate leaves, and large flowers on a round thick scape, usually lasting one day. Two species, *H. fulva*, tawny red, and *H. flava*, bright yellow, are commonly cultivated. 2 A common cultivated lyiwort (genus *Hosta*) of Asian origin, with large, broad, ovate or oblong leaves, and generally white flowers.

day·long (dā′lông′, -long′) adj. & adv. All day; lasting through the entire day.

day nursery A day-care center.

Day of Atonement Yom Kippur.

Day of Judgment The day of the Last Judgment; the last day of the world.

day school 1 A school that holds classes during the daytime: distinguished from *night school*. 2 A private school attended by pupils living outside the school: distinguished from *boarding school*.

days of grace Days (usually three) allowed for the payment of a note or bill of exchange after the date of payment expressed in the instrument itself.

day·spring (dā′spring′) n. *Poetic* The early dawn.

day·star (dā′stär′) n. 1 The morning star. 2 *Poetic* The sun.

day·time (dā′tīm′) n. The time of daylight; the time between sunrise and sunset.

Day·ton (dā′tən) A city on the Miami River in SW Ohio.

Day·to·na Beach (dā-tō′nə) A resort city on the NE coast of Florida.

daze (dāz) v.t. dazed, daz·ing To stupefy or bewilder, as by a glare of light or by a physical or mental shock; stun. —n. The state of being dazed. [ME *dasen*. Related to ON *dasask* become weary.] —daz·ed·ly (dā′zid·lē) adv.

daz·zle (daz′əl) v. ·zled, ·zling v.t. 1 To blind or dim the vision of by excess of light. 2 To bewilder or charm, as with brilliant display. —v.i. 3 To be blinded by lights or glare. 4 To excite admiration. —n. 1 The act of dazzling; dazzled condition. 2 Something that dazzles; brightness. [Freq. of DAZE] —daz′zling·ly adv.

D-day (dē′dā′) n. In military operations, the day or date of the launching of an attack: used especially in the planning of operations before a specific date is set or is disclosed.

DDT A powerful insecticide effective on contact. [<D(ICHLORO-)D(IPHENYL-)T(RICHLORO-ETHANE)]

de (də) prep. *French* Of; from: used in names and phrases, as in Cyrano de Bergerac; coup de main. *De* combines with the masculine singular article *le* to form *du*, and with the plural article *les* to form *des*; before vowels and silent *h* the *e* is elided, as in coup d'état.

de- prefix 1 Away; off: *deflect, decapitate.* 2 Down: *decline, descend.* 3 Completely; utterly: *derelict, denude.* 4 The undoing, reversing, or ridding of (the action or condition expressed by the main element): *decoding, decentralization, decarbonization.* [<L *de* from, away, down; also <F *dé-* <L *de-*, or <OF *des-* <L *dis-* (see DIS-)]

De- may appear as a prefix in hyphemes or solidemes, with the sense of definition 4; as in:

de-anglicize	deconsecrate
de-arm	decrustation
de-armed	decrystallization
de-arming	de-emphasis
debarbarize	de-emphasize
debrutalize	de-energize
decanonize	deflocculate
decapitalize	dehydrogenize
decarbonize	dehypnotize
decharm	de-idealize
de–Christianize	de-ionize
decivilize	depeople
declass	depersonalize
declassed	depolish
declassify	depopularize
deconcentrate	desilver

dea·con (dē′kən) n. 1 A lay church officer or subordinate minister. 2 In the Anglican, Greek, and Roman Catholic Churches, a clergyman ranking next below a priest. 3 Any

---

cleric, as a bishop or priest, acting as chief assistant at a high mass; a gospeler. —v.t. *U.S. Colloq.* 1 To read aloud a line or two of (a hymn) at a time, as an aid to congregational singing: an office of the deacon when hymn books were scarce. 2 To arrange (garden or orchard produce) for sale with only the best showing. 3 To do dishonestly; alter; adulterate. [OE <L *diaconus* <Gk. *diakonos* servant, minister] —dea′con·ry, dea′con·ship n.

dea·con·ess (dē′kən·is) n. A woman appointed or chosen as a lay church worker or officer.

de·ac·ti·vate (dē-ak′tə·vāt) v.t. ·vat·ed, ·vat·ing *Mil.* To release (a military unit, ship, etc.) from active duty; demobilize. —de·ac′ti·va′tion n.

dead (ded) adj. 1 Having ceased to live; lifeless. 2 In a state or condition resembling death; temporarily disabled; lacking in vitality; numb; motionless. 3 Inanimate; inorganic. 4 Complete; utter; absolute; exact: a *dead* stop, a *dead* level. 5 Unfailing; certain; sure; complete or perfect: a *dead* shot. 6 Not productively employed; also, dull or slow: *dead* capital; also, ineffective; inoperative. 7 Without break or variation; flat; unvaried: a *dead* wall. 8 Dull; uninteresting; lusterless; unburnished. 9 Without elasticity or resilience; non-resonant: a *dead* floor. 10 Extinct; obsolete: a *dead* language. 11 *Colloq.* Exhausted; worn-out. 12 Deprived of civil life, as a life-prisoner. 13 Not fresh or invigorating; lifeless; unresponsive, insensible: usually with *to*. 14 In games, not to be counted: a *dead* ball. 15 Giving no light or heat: *dead* cinders. 16 Not imparting motion; spent; also, unsupported, unrelieved, as of strains or weights. 17 Muffled, as a sound. 18 Not transmitting an electric current. 19 Bringing death; deadly. 20 Past the active point of ferment; also, tasteless, as a beverage. 21 Not required for further use, as composed type, etc. 22 Lying so near the hole that the putt is a certainty: said of a golf ball. —n. 1 The most lifeless or inactive period: the *dead* of night. 2 Dead persons collectively: with *the*. —adv. To the last degree; wholly; absolutely; exactly: *dead* right, *dead* straight. [OE *dēad*] —dead′ness n.

Synonyms (adj.): deceased, defunct, departed, inanimate, lifeless. See LIFELESS. *Antonyms:* alive, animate, living.

dead air *Telecom.* A silent interval due to a failure in transmission or a breakdown in the scheduled broadcast.

dead·beat¹ (ded′bēt′) adj. 1 Beating without recoil, as a watch escapement. 2 *Mech.* Coming to rest without oscillation. —n. A movement without recoil; a deadbeat escapement.

dead·beat² (ded′bēt′) n. 1 *U.S. Colloq.* One who is notorious for not paying his bills. 2 *Slang* A sponger.

dead beat *Colloq.* Utterly exhausted: I was *dead beat.* ◆ In attributive use, **dead′-beat′**: a *dead-beat* horse.

dead center *Mech.* That position of a crank or crank motion in which the crank axle, crank pin, and connecting rod centers are all in alinement; the point where a connecting rod has no power to turn a crank. It occurs at each end of the stroke. Also *dead point.* —dead′-cen′ter adj.

dead drunk So intoxicated as to be close to unconsciousness. ◆ In attributive use, **dead′-drunk′**.

dead duck *Slang* A person or thing whose career, power, influence, etc., is ruined or spent.

dead·en (ded′n) v.t. 1 To diminish the sensitivity, force, or intensity of. 2 To lessen or impede the velocity of; retard. 3 To render soundproof. 4 To make dull or less brilliant in color. —v.i. 5 To become dead. —dead′en·er n.

dead-end (ded′end′) n. An end of a passage, street, road, etc., having no outlet; a blind alley.

dead·en·ing (ded′n·ing) n. 1 The act or agent by which something is deadened. 2 Any material used for dulling or shutting out sound, as in walls. 3 The act of killing trees by girdling. 4 A clearing made by girdling trees.

dead·eye (ded′ī′) n. *Naut.* A sheaveless block

---

having scores to receive the lanyard: used to set up shrouds, stays, etc., in rigging a vessel.

dead·fall (ded′fôl′) n. 1 A trap operated by a weight that, when its support is removed, falls upon and kills or holds an animal. 2 Fallen trees and rubbish matted together.

dead·hand (ded′hand′) See under MORTMAIN.

dead·head (ded′hed′) n. 1 One who receives gratis any service or accommodation for which the general public is expected to pay. 2 A wooden buoy. 3 A sunken or partly sunken log. —v.t. & v.i. 1 To treat or act as a deadhead. 2 In railroading, to travel with empty cars or with no cars at all: said of locomotives.

dead heat A race in which two or more competitors finish together and there is no one winner.

dead horse *U.S. Colloq.* A debt for something already used up or worn out: so called from the old expression *to pay for a dead horse.*

dead·house (ded′hous′) n. A morgue.

dead letter 1 A letter which, after lying undelivered for a certain length of time, has been sent to the **dead-letter office,** the department of the general post office where unclaimed letters are examined and returned to their writers or destroyed. 2 Something, as a law, that exists in verbal form, but is not enforced or active.

dead lift 1 A lift made without help, leverage, pulleys, etc. 2 A task or effort accomplished under thankless and discouraging conditions.

dead·light (ded′līt′) n. 1 *Naut.* a A strong shutter, usually of iron, to protect a cabin window or porthole in stormy weather. b Round thick glass windows in the side or deck of a ship. 2 A skylight that does not open. 3 *Scot.* A will-o′-the-wisp; ignis fatuus.

dead·line (ded′līn′) n. 1 A bounding line, as within the limits of a military prison, the crossing of which by a prisoner incurs the penalty of being fired upon by the guard. 2 The time limit before or by which one must complete news copy or other work.

dead load The fixed and permanent load of a structure, as the weight of a building or bridge.

dead·lock (ded′lok′) n. 1 A lock worked from the outside by a key and from the inside by a handle or the like. 2 A lock in which the bolt has to be turned in each direction by a key: opposed to *springlock.* 3 A block or stoppage of business, as in a legislative or other body, caused by the refusal of opposing parties to cooperate. —v.t. & v.i. To cause or come to a deadlock.

dead·ly (ded′lē) adj. ·li·er, ·li·est 1 Liable or certain to cause death; fatal. 2 Aiming or tending to kill; mortal; implacable. 3 Resembling death; deathly. See synonyms under NOISOME, PERNICIOUS. —adv. *Obs.* So as to cause death. —dead′li·ly adv. —dead′li·ness n.

deadly nightshade Belladonna.

deadly sins See SEVEN DEADLY SINS. Compare VENIAL SIN.

dead·man (ded′man) n. pl. ·men (-men) *Naut.* A log, concrete block, or other heavy mass, usually buried and serving as anchorage for a guy line.

deadman's handle The control mechanism or brake valve of a traction motor equipped with a safety device automatically to cut off the current or apply the brake should the operator's hand relax its pressure for any reason. Also **deadman control.**

dead·march (ded′märch′) n. A piece of solemn music played at a funeral, especially a military one; music written for a funeral procession.

dead·net·tle (ded′net′l) n. Any of several herbs of the mint family (genus *Lamium*) having stingless, nettlelike leaves.

dead pan *U.S. Slang* A completely expressionless face. —dead′-pan′ adj. & adv.

dead point See DEAD CENTER.

dead reckoning *Naut.* 1 The computation of a vessel's place at sea by log and compass without astronomical observations. 2 The position of a ship so computed.

Dead Sea A salt lake on the border of Jordan and Israel; 49 miles long; 405 square miles; 1,292 feet below sea level.

Dead Sea fruit Apple of Sodom.

Dead Sea Scrolls A number of scrolls of leather or copper, dating from about 100 B.C. to A.D. 100, containing Hebrew and Aramaic texts of Biblical works and liturgical and communal writings earlier than any such manuscripts extant, found in clay jars in Wadi Qumrân caves, 1947, and later at other sites near the Dead Sea.

dead set *Colloq.* Determined: with *on* or *against.*

dead shot 1 A true shot, one that exactly hits the mark. **2** A person who never misses.

dead soldier *Slang* **1** An empty bottle; especially, an empty liquor bottle: also **dead man.** **2** An old cigar or cigarette stub: also called *old soldier.* **3** A dull companion; a bore.

dead storage Storage of vehicles, equipment, etc., for an indefinite period.

dead time *Physics* An interval during which a Geiger counter or similar instrument gives no indication of radioactivity.

dead water 1 Still water. **2** The water that eddies about the stern of a moving vessel.

dead·weight (ded′wāt′) *n.* **1** A burden borne without aid; an oppressive weight or load. **2** In shipping, freight charged for by weight instead of by bulk. **3** In railway transportation, weight of rolling stock as distinguished from its load.

dead·wood (ded′wo͝od′) *n. Naut.* **1** A mass of timber built up above the keel of a vessel at either end to support the cant timbers. **2** Worthless material; a profitless or burdensome person or thing. **3** Wood dead upon the tree. **4** In bowling, a fallen pin lying in front of the standing pins, and giving, if not removed, the next ball a great advantage. —**to have the deadwood on** *U.S. Colloq.* To have superiority or power ver.

deaf (def) *adj.* **1** Lacking or deficient in the sense of hearing. **2** Determined not to hear or be persuaded. **3** *Cap* The community of deaf people who use American Sign Language to communicate. [OE *dēaf*] —**deaf′ly** *adv.* —**deaf′ness** *n.*

deaf·en (def′ən) *v.t.* **1** To make deaf. **2** To confuse, stupefy, or overwhelm, as with noise: The noise of the jets taking off was *deafening.* **3** To drown (a sound) by a louder sound. **4** To make soundproof.

deaf-mute (def′myo͞ot′) *n.* A deaf-and-dumb person. Taken to be offensive. Also **deaf mute.**

De·ák (dä-äk′), **Fe·rencz** (fe′rents), 1803–76, Hungarian statesman.

deal¹ (dēl) *n.* A board or plank, or the wood, either fir or pine, of which it is made. [<MDu. *dele* board, plank]

deal² (dēl) *v.* **dealt** (delt), **deal·ing** *v.t.* **1** To distribute among a number of persons; meteout, as playing cards. **2** To apportion to (one person) as his or her share. **3** To deliver or inflict, as a blow. —*v.i.* **4** To conduct oneself; behave towards: with *with:* to *deal* effectively with a matter. **5** To be concerned or occupied: with *in* or *with:* I *deal* in facts. **6** To consider, discuss, or administer; take action: with *with:* The court will *deal* with him. **7** To trade; do business: with *in, with,* or *at.* **8** In card games, to act as dealer. See synonyms under APPORTION. —*n.* **1** Distribution; apportionment. **2** The act of distributing; especially, the distribution of, or right to distribute cards; a single round of play; also, the hand dealt. **3** *Colloq.* A secret bargain in politics or commerce. **4** A transaction or bargain. **5** Treatment given or received: a square *deal.* **6** An indefinite quantity, degree, or extent: a great *deal* of trouble. [OE *dǣlan.* Related to DOLE¹.]

Deal (dēl) A port and resort town in eastern Kent, England.

deal·er (dē′lər) *n.* **1** A trader. **2** The player who distributes the cards.

deal·fish (dēl′fish′) *n. pl.* **·fish** or **·fish·es** A ribbonfish (*Trachypterus arcticus*) of northern seas.

deal·ing (dē′ling) *n.* **1** *Usually pl.* Any transaction or dealings with others. **2** The act of one who deals. **3** The method or manner of treatment: honest *dealing.*

de·am·i·na·tion (dē-am′ə-nā′shən) *n. Biochem.* The splitting off of the amino radical, NH_2, from the amino acid molecule in the body, as a stage in the formation of fatty acids from proteins. Also **de·am′i·ni·za′tion.**

dean (dēn) *n.* **1** The chief ecclesiastical officer of a cathedral or of a collegiate church. **2** *Chiefly Brit.* An ecclesiastical officer, often acting as a deputy of a bishop or archdeacon in the administration of part of a diocese: also called *rural dean.* **3** An executive officer of a college or university, having jurisdiction over a particular class or group of students, or acting as head of a faculty: *dean* of men, *dean* of the law school. **4** The senior member, in length of service, of an association or body of men: the *dean* of American composers. [<OF *deien* <LL *decanus* head of ten men <L *decem* ten]

Dean (dēn), **Forest of** A wooded district of western Gloucester, England.

Deane (dēn), **Silas,** 1737–89, American Revolutionary patriot and diplomat.

dean·er·y (dē′nər-ē) *n. pl.* **·er·ies** The office, revenue, jurisdiction, or place of residence of a dean.

dean·ship (dēn′ship) *n.* The office, rank, or title of a dean.

dear¹ (dir) *adj.* **1** Beloved; precious. **2** Highly esteemed; used in letter salutations: *Dear Sir.* **3** Held at a high price, or rate; costly. **4** Characterized by high prices. **5** Intense; earnest: our *dearest* wish. **6** *Obs.* Noble; glorious. —*n.* One who is much beloved; a darling. —*adv.* Dearly. —*interj.* An exclamation of regret, surprise, etc. ◆Homophone: *deer.* [OE *dēore*] —**dear′ness** *n.*

dear² (dir) *adj. Obs.* Severe; dire; difficult. Also **dere.** ◆Homophone: *deer.* [OE *dēor* wild]

Dear·born (dir′bôrn′, -bərn) A city in SE Michigan near Detroit.

dear·ly (dir′lē) *adv.* **1** With much affection; fondly; tenderly. **2** At a high price or rate; at great cost. **3** Earnestly; deeply.

dearth (dûrth) *n.* **1** Scarcity; lack; famine. **2** *Obs.* Dearness; costliness. See synonyms under WANT. [ME *derthe*]

death (deth) *n.* **1** Cessation of physical life. **2** Extinction of anything; destruction. **3** Something likely to produce death; a cause or occasion of death. **4** Something considered as terrible as death. **5** The cessation, absence, or opposite of spiritual life; spiritual and eternal ruin. **6** A fatal plague. **7** A personification, type, or representation of mortality, generally a skeleton holding a scythe. **8** Slaughter; bloodshed. **9** The condition of being dead. ◆Collateral adjectives: *lethal, mortal.* —**at death's door** Almost dead. —**to be death on** *Colloq.* **1** To dislike intensely enough to kill. **2** To have a special talent for; be very fond of. —**to death** Very much: He frightened me *to death.* —**to put to death** To kill; execute. [OE *dēath*]

death·bed (deth′bed′) *n.* The bed on which one dies; the last hours of life: also used attributively.

death bell 1 A bell announcing death; a passing bell. **2** A ringing in the ears like a tolling bell: thought by some to presage the news of a death.

death·blow (deth′blō′) *n.* A fatal blow or shock.

death camas Any of several herbaceous plants of the lily family (genus *Zygadenus*) common in the western United States and poisonous to men and animals: often confused with the edible camas.

death camp A concentration camp established for the purpose of eliminating part of the population of a country or minority group by systematic mass executions: also called *extermination camp.*

death chair The electric chair.

death·cup (deth′kup′) *n.* A common, poisonous mushroom (*Amanita phalloides*) having bright-red caps dotted with white.

death duty Inheritance taxes; a tax on property inherited.

death·ful (deth′fəl) *adj.* **1** Deadly; murderous; full of slaughter. **2** Mortal; liable to die. **3** Having the appearance of death. —**death′·ful·ness** *n.*

death house That part of a prison, as a block of cells, in which prisoners condemned to death are confined.

death·less (deth′lis) *adj.* Not liable to die; undying; unending; perpetual. See synonyms under ETERNAL, IMMORTAL. —**death′less·ly** *adv.* —**death′less·ness** *n.*

death·ly (deth′lē) *adj.* **1** Having the semblance or suggestion of death: also **death′like′.** **2** Pertaining to death. **3** Deadly. See synonyms under GHASTLY. —*adv.* So as to be as one dead or dying. —**death′li·ness** *n.*

death mask A cast of the face taken just after death.

death point *Bacteriol.* The critical upper and lower temperatures beyond which microorganisms cannot live.

death rate The number of persons per thousand of population dying in a given unit of time.

death rattle The rattling sound caused by the breath passing through mucus in the throat of one dying.

death's-head (deths′hed′) *n.* A human skull or a representation of it, as a symbol of death.

death's-head moth A large, Old World sphinx

DEATH'S-HEAD MOTH

moth (genus *Acherontia*), with markings like a death's-head on the upper surface of the thorax.

deaths·man (deths′mən) *n. pl.* **·men** (-mən) *Archaic* The hangman.

death·trap (deth′trap′) *n.* A building or structure where the risk of death, particularly from fire, is great.

Death Valley A deep and desert basin in SE California; site of **Death Valley National Monument**; 2,906 square miles; established 1933.

death warrant 1 *Law* An official order for the execution of a person. **2** That which insures destruction or puts an end to hope.

death·watch (deth′woch′, -wôch′) *n.* **1** The last vigil with the dying or with the body of one dead. **2** A guard set over a condemned man before his execution. **3** A small, European, wood-boring beetle. (*Xestobium rufovillosum*) that makes a ticking noise, superstitiously thought to presage death.

death whisper Sound waves of such high frequency as to be inaudible to human ears, and having the power to kill small animals, as fish in water, under certain conditions.

death·y (deth′ē) *adj. adv. Rare* Deathly.

Deau·ville (dō′vil, *Fr.* dō·vēl′)A resort town of NW France on the English Channel.

deave (dēv) *v.t. Scot. Brit. Dial.* To deafen or bewilder with noise. [OE *dē afian* in *adēafian* grow deaf]

de·ba·cle (dā-bä′kəl, -bak′əl, di-) *n.* **1** A sudden and disastrous breakdown, overthrow, or collapse, as of a government; ruin; rout. **2** The breaking up of ice in a river, etc. **3** A violent flood carrying great masses of rock and other debris. [<F *débâ cle* <*débâcler* unbar, set free]

de·bar (di-bär′) *v.t.* · **barred**, **·bar·ring 1** To bar or shut out; exclude: usually with *from.* **2** To prohibit; hinder. See synonyms under PROHIBIT, SUSPEND. [<F *débarrer* <*dé-* away (<L *dis-*) + *barrer* bar]

de·bark (di·bärk′) *v.t.* To put ashore or unload from a ship. — *v.i.* To go ashore; disembark. Compare DISEMBARK. [<F *débarquer* < *dé-* away, from + *barque* a ship] — **de·bar·ka·tion** (dē′bär·kā′shən) *n.*

de·bar·ment (di·bär′mənt) *n.* The act of debarring; exclusion; obstruction.

de·base (di·bās′) *v.t.* **de·based, de·bas·ing** To lower in character, purity, or value; degrade. See synonyms under ABASE, CORRUPT, IMPAIR. [<DE- + obs. *base*, var. of ABASE] — **de·base′·ment** *n.* — **de·bas′er** *n.*

de·bate (di·bāt′) *v.* **de·bat·ed, de·bat·ing** *v.t.* **1** To discuss or argue about, as in a public meeting. **2** To discuss in formal argument. **3** To consider; deliberate upon in the mind, as alternatives. **4** *Obs.* To fight or contend for or over. — *v.i.* **5** To argue; discuss. **6** To engage in formal argument. **7** To deliberate mentally; consider. See synonyms under DELIBERATE, DISPUTE. — *n.* **1** The discussing of any question; argumentation; dispute; controversy. **2** A formal argument conducted systematically to test the reasoning skill of two persons or teams taking opposing sides of a specific question (the resolution). **3** *Obs.* Combat; strife. See synonyms under ALTERCATION, REASONING. [<OF *debatre* < *de-* down (<L *de-*) + *batre* <L *batuere* strike] — **de·bat′a·ble** *adj.* — **de·bat′er** *n.*

de·bauch (di·bôch′) *v.t.* **1** To corrupt in morals; seduce; deprave. **2** *Obs.* To cause to forsake allegiance; disaffect. — *v.i.* **3** To indulge in lechery, gluttony, or drunkenness; dissipate. See synonyms under POLLUTE, VIOLATE. — *n.* **1** An act or occasion of debauchery; a carouse. **2** Excess; intemperance; lewdness. [<F *débaucher* lure from work <OF *desbaucher*]

de·bauched (di·bôcht′) *adj.* **1** Corrupted. **2** Characterized by debauchery. — **de·bauch·ed·ly** (di·bô′chid·lē) *adv.* — **de·bauch′ed·ness** *n.*

deb·au·chee (deb′ô·chē′, -shē′) *n.* One habitually profligate, drunken, or lewd; a libertine.

de·bauch·er (di·bô′chər) *n.* One who debauches; a seducer.

de·bauch·er·y (di·bô′chər·ē) *n.* *pl.* **·er·ies** **1** Licentiousness; drunkenness. **2** Seduction from virtue, purity, or fidelity. Also **de·bauch′ment.**

Deb·by (deb′ē) Diminutive of DEBORAH.

de Beau·voir (də bō·vwär′) See BEAUVOIR, SIMONE DE.

de·ben·ture (di·ben′chər) *n.* **1** An instrument in the nature of a bond, given as an acknowledgment of debt, and providing for repayment out of some specified fund or source of income: as, a mortgage *debenture*, one secured by a mortgage. **2** A customhouse certificate providing for a drawback. **3** A government pay order. See under BOND, STOCK. [<L *debentur* there are owing < *debere* owe]

debenture bond See under BOND.

De·bierne (də·byârn′), **André Louis,** 1874–1949, French chemist.

de·bil·i·tate (di·bil′ə·tāt) *v.t.* **·tat·ed, ·tat·ing** To make feeble or languid; weaken. [<L *debilitatus*, pp. of *debilitare* < *debilis* weak] — **de·bil′i·tant** *adj.* & *n.* — **de·bil′i·tat′ed** *adj.* — **de·bil′i·ta′tion** *n.* — **de·bil′i·ta′tive** *adj.*

de·bil·i·ty (di·bil′ə·tē) *n.* *pl.* **·ties** Abnormal weakness; languor; feebleness. [<F *débilité* <L *debilitas, -tatis* < *debilis* weak]

deb·it (deb′it) *v.t.* **1** To enter on the debit side of an account. **2** To charge (a customer) for goods. — *n.* The debit side of an account; a debt or debts recorded; something owed. Compare CREDIT. [<L *debitum*, pp. of *debere* owe. Doublet of DEBT.]

deb·o·nair (deb′ə·nâr′) *adj.* Gentle or courteous; affable; complaisant; gay. Also **deb′·o·naire′, deb′on·naire′.** [<F *debonnaire* <OF *de bon aire* of good mien] — **deb′o·nair′ly** *adv.* — **deb′o·nair′ness** *n.*

de bo·nis non (ad·min·i·stra·tis) (dē bō′nis non ad·min′ə·strā′tis) *Law Latin* Of the goods not (administered): said of unadministered property transferred from an administrator to his successor.

de bonne grâce (də bôn gräs′) *French* With good grace; cheerfully.

Deb·o·rah (deb′ər·ə, deb′rə) A feminine personal name. Also *Fr.* **Dé·bo·ra** (dā·bô·rá′), *Ital.* **De·bo·ra** (dā′bō·rä). [<Hebrew, a bee] — **Deborah** A prophetess of Mount Ephraim, who judged Israel, and who, with Barak, defeated Sisera about 1285 B.C. *Judges* iv 4.

de·bouch (di·bo͞osh′) *v.i.* **1** *Mil.* To come forth or issue from a defile or a wood into the open. **2** To come forth; emerge. — *v.t.* **3** To cause to emerge. — *n.* **1** An opening, especially in military works, for the passage of troops. **2** An outlet for commerce; market. Also *French* **dé·bou·ché** (dā·bo͞o·shā′) *n.* [<F *déboucher* < *dé-* from (<L *dis-*) + *bouche* a mouth]

de·bouch·ment (di·bo͞osh′mənt) *n.* **1** *Geog.* The opening out of a valley, stream, etc. **2** The act of debouching. Also *French* **dé·bou·chure** (dā·bo͞o·shür′).

De·bre·cen (de′bre·tsen) A city in eastern Hungary. Formerly **De′bre·czen.**

dé·bride·ment (dā·brēd·mäṅ′, di·brēd′mənt) *n.* *Surg.* The excision of tissues and dead matter from the interior of wounds, to prevent septic infection. [<F *débrider* unbridle]

de·brief (dē′brēf′) *v.t.* *Mil.* To question or instruct (a pilot, agent, etc.) at the end of a mission or period of service.

de·bris (də·brē′, dā′brē; *Brit.* deb′rē) *n.* **1** Accumulated fragments; ruins; rubbish. **2** *Geol.* An aggregation of detached fragments of rocks. Also **dé·bris′.** See synonyms under WASTE. [<F *débris* <OF *débriser* < *des-* away (<L *dis-*) + *brisier* break]

de Bro·glie (də·brœ′y′) A family, originally of Piedmont, distinguished in French history: especially **Duc Achille Charles Léonce Victor,** 1785–1870, statesman; **Maurice,** 1875–1960, and **Louis Victor,** born 1892, physicists.

de Broglie wave *Physics* A wave or group of waves thought to be associated with elementary particles, as electrons, protons, etc. [after Louis Victor *de Broglie*]

Debs (debz), **Eugene Victor,** 1855–1926, U.S. labor leader; Socialist candidate for president 1900–12, 1920.

debt (det) *n.* **1** That which one owes. **2** An obligation. **3** The state of being indebted. **4** *Theol.* A sin; trespass. [<OF *dette* <L *debitum*. Doublet of DEBIT.]

debt·or (det′ər) *n.* **1** One who is in debt; one who is under obligation to another, as for money or goods, or for service, benefit, or help. **2** The left–hand or debit side of an account in bookkeeping. [<OF *dettor* <L *debitor* < *debere* owe]

de·bunk (di·bungk′) *v.t.* *Colloq.* To reveal the sham, false pretensions, etc., of. [<BUNK[2]]

De·bus·sy (də·byo͞o′sē, *Fr.* də·bü·sē′), **Claude Achille,** 1862–1918, French composer.

de·but (di·byo͞o′, dā-, dā′byo͞o) *n.* A first appearance, as in society or on the stage; first attempt; beginning. Also **dé·but′.** [<F *début* < *débuter* begin, lead off]

deb·u·tante (deb′yo͞o·tänt′, deb′yo͞o·tant) *n.* *fem.* A young girl or woman who makes a debut, especially into society. Also **dé′bu·tante′.** [<F *débutante*, fem. ppr. of *débuter* begin] — **deb′u·tant′** *n.* *masc.*

deca– *combining form* **1** Ten: *decapod.* **2** In the metric system, deka–. Also, before vowels, **dec–.**

dec·ade (dek′ād, de·kād′) *n.* **1** A period of ten years. **2** A group or set of ten. [<MF <L *decas, decadis* a group of ten <Gk. *dekas* < *deka* ten]

de·ca·dence (di·kād′ns, dek′ə·dəns) *n.* A process of deterioration; decay; a condition or period of decline, as in literature, art, morals, etc. [<F *décadence* <Med. L *decadentia* <L *decadere* < *de-* down + *cadere* fall]

de·ca·dent (di·kād′nt, dek′ə·dənt) *adj.* Falling into ruin or decay. — *n.* **1** One who has fallen from a high social position. **2** One in a state or process of mental or moral decay; a decadent person. **3** Specifically, a member of a school of French writers of the late 19th century characterized by their cultivation of subtle, refined, artificial qualities in subject and treatment. — **de·ca′dent·ly** *adv.*

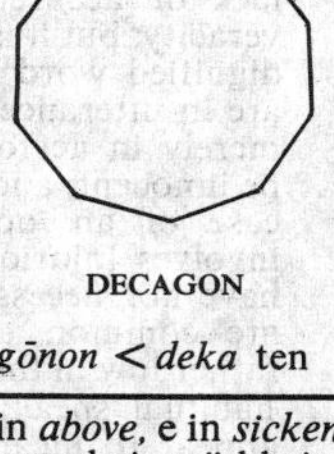
DECAGON

dec·a·gon (dek′ə·gon) *n.* A plane figure with ten sides and ten angles. [<Gk. *dekagōnon* < *deka* ten + *gōnia* angle] — **de·cag·o·nal** (di·kag′ə·nəl) *adj.* — **de·cag′o·nal·ly** *adv.*

dec·a·gram (dek′ə·gram) See DEKAGRAM.

dec·a·he·dron (dek′ə·hē′drən) *n.* A solid bounded by ten plane faces. [<DECA- + Gk. *hedra* seat] — **dec′a·he′dral** *adj.*

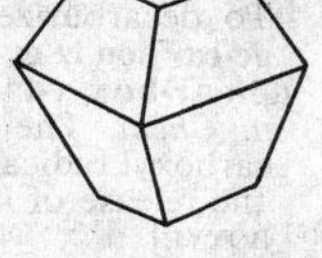
DECAHEDRON

dé·ca·lage (dā·kä·läzh′) *n.* *Aeron.* The variance in angle of incidence between two sustaining surfaces of an airplane. [<F < *décaler* shift, set at an angle]

de·cal·ci·fi·ca·tion (dē·kal′sə·fə·kā′shən) *n.* **1** The action of decalcifying. **2** *Dent.* The removal of calcareous matter from the teeth.

de·cal·ci·fy (dē·kal′sə·fī) *v.t.* **·fied, ·fy·ing** To deprive of lime.

de·cal·co·ma·ni·a (di·kal′kə·mā′nē·ə, -mān′yə) *n.* **1** A process of transferring decorative pictures or designs from paper to glass, porcelain, etc. **2** Such a print to be transferred. **3** The decoration of glassware by gumming pictures upon it. Also **de·cal′.** [<F *décalcomanie* < *décalquer* transfer a tracing + *-manie* -MANIA]

de·ca·les·cence (dē′kə·les′əns) *n.* *Physics* The sudden absorption of heat by metals when the temperature passes a certain critical point, indicating internal structural changes: opposed to *recalescence.* — **de′ca·les′cent** *adj.* [<L *decalescens, -entis*, ppr. of *decalescere* < *de-* not + *calescere* grow hot]

dec·a·li·ter (dek′ə·lē′tər) See DEKALITER.

Dec·a·log (dek′ə·lôg, -log) *n.* The Ten Commandments. *Exod.* xx 2–17. Also **Dec′a·logue.** [<Gk. *dekalogos* < *deka* ten + *logos* word]

De·cam·er·on (di·kam′ər·ən) A collection of 100 stories by Boccaccio (published 1353), told by ten Florentines who secluded themselves for ten days from their plague–striken city. [<Ital. *decamerone* <Gk. *deka* ten + *hēmera* day]

dec·a·me·ter (dek′ə·mē′tər) *n.* **1** A dekameter. **2** Verse consisting of ten rhythmical feet. Also **dec′a·me′tre.** [<F *décamètre* <Gk. *dekametron* < *deka* ten + *metron* measure]

de·camp (di·kamp′) *v.i.* **1** To break camp or leave camp. **2** To leave suddenly or secretly; run away. See synonyms under ESCAPE. — **de·camp′ment** *n.*

De·camps (də·käṅ′), **Alexandre Gabriel,** 1803–60, French painter.

dec·a·nal (dek′ə·nəl, di·kā′nəl) *adj.* Of or pertaining to a dean or deanery. [<LL *decanus.* See DEAN.] — **dec′a·nal·ly** *adv.*

de·can·drous (di·kan′drəs) *adj.* *Bot.* Having ten stamens. [<DEC(A)- + Gk. *anēr, andros* man]

dec·ane (dek′ān) *n.* *Chem.* Any of several isomeric hydrocarbons, $C_{10}H_{22}$, of the methane series, variously derived, from coal tar, etc. [<DEC(A)- + -ANE[2]]

de·cant (di·kant′) *v.t.* **1** To pour off gently so as not to disturb the sediment. **2** To pour from one container into another. [<F *décanter* <Med. L *decanthare* < *de-* from + *canthus* lip of a jug <Gk. *kanthos*] — **de·can·ta·tion** (dē′kan·tā′shən) *n.*

de·cant·er (di·kan′tər) *n.* An ornamental bottle for wine, etc.

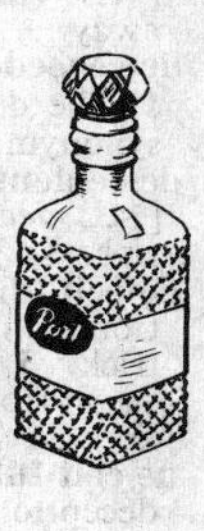
DECANTER

de·cap·i·tate (di·kap′ə·tāt) *v.t.* **·tat·ed, ·tat·ing** To behead. [<Med. L *decapitare* < *de-* down + *caput* head] — **de·cap′i·ta′tion** *n.* — **de·cap′i·ta′tor** *n.*

dec·a·pod (dek′ə·pod) *adj.* **1** Ten-footed or ten–armed. **2** *Zool.* Of or pertaining to the *Decapoda*, an order of crustaceans with five pairs of legs, including the crabs, lobsters, shrimps, etc. — *n.* A ten–legged crustacean; also, a ten-armed cephalopod, as a cuttlefish or squid. [<Gk. *dekapous, -podos* < *deka* ten + *pous* foot] — **de·cap·o·dal** (di·kap′ə·dəl), **de·cap′o·dous** *adj.*

dec·a·pod·i·form (dek′ə·pod′ə·fôrm) *adj.* Shaped like a decapod.

De·cap·o·lis (di·kap′ə·lis) A region in the north of ancient Palestine containing a confederacy of ten cities. *Matt.* iv 25.

de·cap·su·la·tion (di·kap′sə·lā′shən) *n.* *Surg.*

The removal of the enveloping membrane of an organ, especially the capsule of the kidney.

de·car·bon·ate (di·kär′bə·nāt) *v.t.* **·at·ed, ·at·ing** To free from carbon dioxide. — **de·car′bon·a′tor** *n.*

de·car·bon·ize (di·kär′bə·nīz) *v.t.* **·ized, ·iz·ing** To decarburize. — **de·car′bon·i·za′tion** *n.* — **de·car′bon·iz′er** *n.*

de·car·box·y·la·tion (dē′kär·bok′sə·lā′shən) *n. Chem.* The elimination of one or more carboxyl radicals from an organic acid, with the release of carbon dioxide. [<DE- + CARBOXYL]

de·car·bu·rize (dē·kär′byə·rīz) *v.t.* **·rized, ·riz·ing** **1** To deprive wholly or in part of carbon. **2** To remove carbon from (molten steel or the cylinders of an internal-combustion engine). — **de·car′bu·ri·za′tion** *n.*

dec·are (dek′âr, dek·âr′) See DEKARE.

dec·a·stere (dek′ə·stir) See DEKASTERE.

dec·a·syl·la·ble (dek′ə·sil′ə·bəl) *n.* A line of verse having ten syllables. — **dec·a·syl·lab·ic** (dek′ə·si·lab′ik) *adj.*

de·cath·lon (di·kath′lon) *n.* An athletic contest consisting of ten different track and field events in which each contestant participates. [<DEC(A)- + Gk. *athlon* a contest]

dec·at·ing (dek′āt·ing) *n.* A method for the application of heat, moisture, and pressure to fabrics in order to set the nap, add luster, and control shrinkage. Also **dec·a·tiz·ing** (dek′ə·tī′zing). [<F *dicatir* sponge (a fabric) to set the gloss]

De·ca·tur (di·kā′tər) A city in central Illinois.

De·ca·tur (di·kā′tər), **Stephen,** 1779–1820, U.S. naval officer.

de·cay (di·kā′) *v.i.* **1** To fail slowly in health, beauty, quality, or any form of excellence. **2** To rot; decompose. — *v.t.* **3** To cause to decay. — *n.* **1** A passing into a feeble or reduced condition tending toward dissolution. **2** A gradual decline in health, size or quality; deterioration. **3** Decomposition; corruption; rottenness. **4** *Physics* The disintegration of a radioactive element. See synonyms under RUIN. [<OF *decair,* var. of *decaoir* <L *decidere* < *de-* down + *cadere* fall] — **de·cay′a·ble** *adj.* — **de·cay·ed·ness** (di·kā′id·nis) *n.*

Synonyms (verb): corrupt, decompose, molder, putrefy, rot, spoil. *Rot* is a strong and direct word. To say that a thing is *decayed* may denote only a partial result, but to say it is *decomposed* ordinarily implies that the change is complete or nearly so. *Putrefy* and the adjectives *putrid* and *putrescent,* and the nouns *putridity* and *putrescence,* are used almost exclusively of animal matter in a state of decomposition, the more general word *decay* being used of either animal or vegetable substances. *Decay* may also be extended to any process of decline or breaking down, physical, mental, social, etc. See PUTREFY.

Dec·can Plateau (dek′ən) A triangular tableland covering most of peninsular India.

Deccan States A group of former princely states within south and central Bombay state, India.

de·cease (di·sēs′) *v.i.* **de·ceased, de·ceas·ing** To die. [< *n.*] — *n.* Departure from life; death. [<OF *déces* <L *decessus* < *decedere* < *de-* away + *cedere* go]

de·ceased (di·sēst′) *adj.* Dead. — **the deceased** **1** The dead person. **2** Dead persons. See synonyms under LIFELESS.

de·ce·dent (di·sēd′nt) *n.* A person deceased. [<L *decedens, -entis,* ppr. of *decedere.* See DECEASE.]

de·ceit (di·sēt′) *n.* The act of deceiving; deception; lying. **2** A lie or other dishonest action; trick. **3** Deceptiveness. See synonyms under DECEPTION, FRAUD, LIE. [<OF *deceite* < *deceveir* DECEIVE]

de·ceit·ful (di·sēt′fəl) *adj.* Characterized by deception; false; tricky; fraudulent. See synonyms under BAD, DECEPTIVE, INSIDIOUS, PERFIDIOUS, ROTTEN, VAIN. — **de·ceit′ful·ly** *adv.* — **de·ceit′ful·ness** *n.*

de·ceiv·a·ble (di·sē′və·bəl) *adj.* Capable of being deceived; liable to imposition. — **de·ceiv′a·ble·ness** *n.* — **de·ceiv′a·bly** *adv.*

de·ceive (di·sēv′) *v.* **de·ceived, de·ceiv·ing** *v.t.* **1** To mislead by or as by falsehood; impose upon; delude. **2** *Obs.* To while away (time). — *v.i.* **3** To practice deceit. [<OF *deceveir* <L *decipere* < *de-* away, down + *capere* take] — **de·ceiv′ing·ly** *adv.*

Synonyms: beguile, betray, cheat, circumvent, defraud, delude, dupe, ensnare, entrap, mislead, outwit, overreach, trick. See MISLEAD. Compare DECEPTION.

de·ceiv·er (di·sē′vər) *n.* One who deceives. See synonyms under HYPOCRITE.

de·cel·er·ate (dē·sel′ə·rāt) *v.t.* & *v.i.* **·at·ed, ·at·ing** To diminish in velocity. [<DE- + L *celeratus,* pp. of *celerare* hasten < *celer* quick] — **de·cel′er·a′tor** *n.*

de·cel·er·a·tion (dē·sel′ə·rā′shən) *n.* Negative acceleration. See under ACCELERATION (def. 2).

De·cem·ber (di·sem′bər) The twelfth month of the year, having 31 days. [<L < *decem* ten; because December was the tenth month in the old Roman calendar]

De·cem·brist (di·sem′brist) *n.* One of those who conspired against Czar Nicholas I, on his accession, Dec., 1825.

de·cem·vir (di·sem′vər) *n. pl.* **·virs** or **·vi·ri** (-və·rī) A member of any body of ten magistrates; specifically, one commissioned to codify the laws of Rome in 451 B.C. [<L < *decem* ten + *vir* man] — **de·cem′vi·ral** *adj.*

de·cem·vi·rate (di·sem′və·rit, -rāt) *n.* **1** A body of ten men in authority. **2** The office of such a body.

de·cen·cy (dē′sən·sē) *n. pl.* **·cies** **1** Propriety in conduct, speech, or dress; modesty. **2** That which is decent, proper, or seemly. **3** *pl.* Things required for a proper or comfortable manner of life. [<L *decentia* < *decens.* See DECENT.]

de·cen·na·ry (di·sen′ər·ē) *adj.* Consisting of or pertaining to ten; pertaining to ten years or to a tithing: also **de·cen′a·ry.** — *n. pl.* **·ries** **1** In old English law, a tithing or group of ten freeholders and their families. **2** A period of ten years. [<L *decennis* < *decem* ten + *annus* year]

de·cen·ni·al (di·sen′ē·əl) *adj.* Continuing for or consisting of ten years; occurring every ten years. — *n.* An anniversary observed at periods of ten years. — **de·cen′ni·al·ly** *adv.*

de·cen·ni·um (di·sen′ē·əm) *n. pl.* **·cen·ni·ums** or **·cen·ni·a** (-sen′ē·ə) A period of ten years; decade. [<L < *decem* ten + *annus* year]

de·cent (dē′sənt) *adj.* **1** Characterized by propriety of conduct, speech, manners, or dress; proper; decorous; respectable. **2** Free from indelicacy; modest; chaste. **3** Sufficient; passable; moderate. **4** *Obs.* Appropriate; also, symmetrical; comely. See synonyms under BECOMING, MODEST. [<L *decens, -entis,* ppr. of *decere* be fitting, be proper] — **de′cent·ly** *adv.* — **de′cent·ness** *n.*

de·cen·ter (dē·sen′tər) *v.t.* **1** To put out of center; make eccentric. **2** *Optics* To cut, as a lens for an eyeglass, so that the physical center and the optical center of the lens surfaces do not coincide. Also **de·cen′tre.**

de·cen·tral·ize (dē·sen′trəl·īz) *v.t.* **·ized, ·iz·ing** **1** To remove from a center; distribute: used especially of government or other authority. **2** *Econ.* To reorganize (a large enterprise, industry, or corporation) into smaller and more dispersed units in order to permit more efficient management and control. — **de·cen′tral·i·za′tion** *n.*

de·cep·tion (di·sep′shən) *n.* **1** The act of deceiving. **2** The state of being deceived. **3** Anything that deceives or is meant to deceive; a delusion. [<L *deceptio, -onis* < *decipere.* See DECEIVE.]

Synonyms: craft, cunning, deceit, deceitfulness, delusion, dissimulation, double-dealing, duplicity, fabrication, falsehood, finesse, fraud, guile, hypocrisy, imposition, lie, lying, prevarication, trickery, untruth. *Deceit* is especially applied to the habit, *deception* to the act; *guile* applies to the disposition out of which *deceit* and *deception* grow, and also to their actual practice. A *lie, lying,* or *falsehood* is the uttering of what one knows to be false with intent to deceive. *Untruth* is more than lack of accuracy, implying always lack of veracity; but it is a somewhat milder and more dignified word than *lie. Falsehood* and *lying* are in utterance; *deceit* and *deception* may be merely in act or implication. *Deception* may be innocent, and even unintentional, as in the case of an optical illusion; *deceit* always involves injurious intent. *Craft* and *cunning* have not necessarily any moral quality; they are common traits of animals, but stand rather low in the human scale. *Duplicity* is the habitual speaking or acting with intent to appear to mean what one does not. *Dissimulation* is rather a concealing of what is than a pretense of what is not. *Finesse* is simply an adroit and delicate management of a matter for one's own side, not necessarily involving *deceit.* Compare FRAUD, LIE. *Antonyms*: candor, frankness, guilelessness, honesty, openness, simplicity, sincerity, truth, veracity.

de·cep·tive (di·sep′tiv) *adj.* Having power or tendency to deceive. — **de·cep′tive·ly** *adv.* — **de·cep′tive·ness** *n.*

Synonyms: deceitful, delusive, illusive, illusory. Persons are *deceitful*: things are *deceptive.* We speak of a *deceitful,* but not of a *deceptive* man. We speak, however, of *deceitful* promises, as involving personal intent to deceive. It is more accurate to say *deceptive* than *deceitful* appearances. See BAD, COUNTERFEIT. *Antonyms*: fair, frank, genuine, honest.

de·cer·e·brate (dē·ser′ə·brāt) *v.t.* **·brat·ed, ·brat·ing** To remove the brain from, as in certain operations and laboratory experiments. — *adj.* (-brit) Having the brain removed. [<DE- + L *cerebrum* brain] — **de·cer′e·bra′tion** *n.*

de·cer·e·brize (dē·ser′ə·brīz) *v.t.* **·brized, ·briz·ing** To remove the cerebrum or brain from, as in vivisection.

de·cern (di·sûrn′) *v.t.* **1** In Scots law, to decree. **2** To discern. [<F *décerner* <L *decernere* decide < *de-* down + *cernere* decide]

deci- *combining form* A tenth. See METRIC SYSTEM. [<L *decimus* tenth < *decem* ten]

dec·i·are (des′ē·âr) *n.* One tenth of an are. See METRIC SYSTEM. [<F *déciare*]

dec·i·bel (des′ə·bel) *n. Physics* One tenth of a bel: the common unit of measure of loudness of sounds.

de·cide (di·sīd′) *v.* **·cid·ed, ·cid·ing** *v.t.* **1** To determine; settle, as a controversy, dispute, contest, etc.; arbitrate: to *decide* who is right. **2** To cause the outcome of; settle: The charge *decided* the battle. **3** To bring (someone) to a decision. — *v.i.* **4** To give a decision. **5** To make a decision. See synonyms under SETTLE. [<MF *décider* <L *decidere* < *de-* down, away + *caedere* cut] — **de·cid′a·ble** *adj.*

de·cid·ed (di·sī′did) *adj.* **1** Free from uncertainty; unquestionable; unmistakable. **2** Determined; resolute; emphatic. See synonyms under FIRM. — **de·cid′ed·ly** *adv.* — **de·cid′ed·ness** *n.*

de·cid·u·a (di·sij′o͞o·ə) *n. Physiol.* The thickened mucous membrane of the uterus cast off and expelled either during menstruation (*decidua menstrualis*) or at parturition (*decidua graviditatis*). [<NL (*membrana*) *decidua* (membrane) that is cast off < *deciduus.* See DECIDUOUS.] — **de·cid′u·al** *adj.*

de·cid·u·ous (di·sij′o͞o·əs) *adj.* **1** *Bot.* Falling off or shed at maturity or at specific seasons, as petals, fruit, or leaves; also, characterized by such a falling off; not evergreen. **2** *Zool.* Liable to be shed at periodical times, as antlers, hair, teeth, wings of insects, etc. **3** Not enduring; evanescent; short-lived. Compare PERSISTENT. [<L *deciduus* < *decidere* < *de-* down, away + *cadere* fall] — **de·cid′u·ous·ly** *adv.* — **de·cid′u·ous·ness** *n.*

dec·i·gram (des′ə·gram) *n.* The tenth part of a gram. See METRIC SYSTEM. Also **dec′i·gramme.**

dec·ile (des′il) *n. Stat.* One of the parts or intervals of a frequency distribution, each of which contains one tenth of the observations or cases in the complete series. [<F *décile* <L *decem* ten]

dec·i·li·ter (des′ə·lē′tər) *n.* The tenth part of a liter. See METRIC SYSTEM. Also **dec′i·li′tre.**

de·cil·lion (de·sil′yən) *n.* The numeral 1 followed by thirty-three ciphers according to American and French notation, or by sixty ciphers in English notation. [<DEC(A)- + (M)ILLION] — **de·cil′lionth** *adj.*

dec·i·mal (des′ə·məl) *adj.* **1** Pertaining to or founded on the number 10. **2** Proceeding by powers of 10 or of one tenth. — *n.* A decimal fraction or one of its digits. [<Med. L *decimalis* of tenths < *decimus* tenth < *decem* ten]

decimal fraction See under FRACTION.

dec·i·mal·i·za·tion (des′ə·məl·i·zā′shən) *n.* The process or program of adopting the decimal system, as in currency.

dec·i·mal·ize (des′ə·məl·īz′) *v.t.* **·ized, ·iz·ing** To reduce to a decimal system.

decimal point A dot or period used before a decimal fraction.

decimal system A system of reckoning by tens or tenths.

dec·i·mate (des′ə·māt) v.t. ·mat·ed, ·mat·ing 1 To destroy or kill a large proportion of. 2 To select by lot and kill one out of every ten of. 3 Obs. To exact a tithe from; take a tenth part of. [< L decimatus, pp. of decimare take a tenth part from < decem ten] —dec′i·ma′tion n. —dec′i·ma′tor n.

dec·i·me·ter (des′ə·mē′tər) n. The tenth part of a meter. See METRIC SYSTEM. Also dec′i·me′tre.

de·ci·pher (di·sī′fər) v.t. 1 To determine the meaning of, as hieroglyphics or illegible writing. 2 To translate from cipher into ordinary characters. 3 To determine the meaning of (anything obscure). See synonyms under INTERPRET. —de·ci′pher·a·ble adj. —de·ci′pher·er n. —de·ci′pher·ment n.

de·ci·sion (di·sizh′ən) n. 1 The act of deciding or making up one's mind. 2 Decisive result; settlement; judgment, as of a court. 3 The quality of being positive and firm; determination. See synonyms under DETERMINATION, WILL. [< F décision < L decisio, -onis < decidere. See DE-CIDE]

de·ci·sion-making (di·sizh′ən·mā′king) n. 1 The process by which decisions are made, especially important decisions affecting others and made by virtue of one's office or position. 2 The power or ability to make decisions of consequence. —adj. Of, relating to, or requiring decision-making. —de·ci′sion-mak′er n.

de·ci·sive (di·sī′siv) adj. 1 Putting an end to uncertainty, debate, or question; conclusive. 2 Prompt; positive; decided. —de·ci′sive·ly adv. —de·ci′sive·ness n.

dec·i·stere (des′ə·stir) n. A cubic decimeter, or the tenth part of a stere. See METRIC SYSTEM.

De·ci·us (dē′shəs, desh′əs) , **Gaius Messius**, 201–51, Roman emperor 249–51.

deck (dek) n. 1 Naut. a A platform covering or extending horizontally across a vessel. b The space between two such platforms. 2 Any similar flat surface. 3 A car roof. 4 A covering or shelter. 5 A pack of cards. 6 In journalism, lines under a headline; bank. —to hit the deck Slang 1 To rise from bed quickly; get up. 2 Slang To prepare or start to work. 3 Slang To drop to a prone position. —on deck 1 Present; alive and able-bodied. 2 Next at bat in a baseball game. —v.t. 1 To array; dress elegantly; adorn; decorate. 2 Naut. To put a deck on. 3 Obs. To cover, clothe. See synonyms under GARNISH. [< MDu. dek roof, covering]

deck·er (dek′ər) n. 1 One who decks. 2 A vessel, car, etc., with one or more decks: a double-decker.

deck hand A sailor employed about the deck.

deck·house (dek′hous′) n. A compartment built on an upper deck of a ship.

deck·le (dek′əl) n. 1 In papermaking by hand, a rectangular frame laid upon a wire mold to confine the paper pulp to a definite area, thus limiting the size of the sheet. 2 A raw or ragged edge of paper: also deckle edge. [< G deckel, dim. of decke cover]

deck·le-edged (dek′əl·ejd′) adj. Uncut; rough-edged.

de·claim (di·klām′) v.i. 1 To speak loudly and in a rhetorical manner. 2 To give a recitation. 3 To condemn or attack verbally and vehemently: with against. —v.t. 4 To utter aloud in a rhetorical manner. See synonyms under SPEAK. [< L declamare < de- completely + clamare shout] —de·claim′er n.

dec·la·ma·tion (dek′lə·mā′shən) n. 1 The act of declaiming. 2 A speech or selection recited or to be recited from memory.

de·clam·a·to·ry (di·klam′ə·tôr′ē, -tō′rē) adj. 1 Using, characterized by, or pertaining to declamation. 2 In a noisy, empty rhetorical style. —de·clam′a·to′ri·ly adv.

dec·la·ra·tion (dek′lə·rā′shən) n. 1 A formal or explicit statement; the act of declaring, or that which is declared. 2 In common-law pleading, the paper filed by the plaintiff in which he alleges the facts constituting his cause of action and demands judgment; also, a solemn declaration made by a witness under the penalties of perjury, equivalent to an oath. 3 In bridge, the naming of the trump suit and the tricks, above six, to be taken: also called make.

Declaration of Independence 1 The resolution of the Continental Congress, adopted June 7, 1776, declaring that "these United Colonies are, and of right ought to be, free and independent States." 2 The manifesto of the Continental Congress adopted July 4, 1776, and entitled "A Declaration by the Representatives of the United States of America" (popularly known as the Declaration of Independence), giving the reasons why the colonies had declared their independence.

de·clar·a·tive (di·klar′ə·tiv) adj. Making a declaration or statement; affirmative: a declarative sentence. Also de·clar·a·to·ry (di·klar′ə·tôr′ē, -tō′rē).

de·clare (di·klâr′) v. ·clared, ·clar·ing v.t. 1 To assert positively; aver. 2 To announce or state formally and solemnly: to declare war or a dividend. 3 To manifest; make known: His actions declare him a saint. 4 To make full statement of, as goods liable to duty or tax. 5 In card games, to name (a suit) trumps. —v.i. 6 To make a declaration. 7 To proclaim a choice or decision. See synonyms under AFFIRM, ALLEGE, ANNOUNCE, ASSERT, AVOW, PUBLISH, SPEAK. [< L declarare < de- completely + clarare make clear < clarus clear] —de·clar·ed·ly (di·klâr′id·lē) adv. —de·clar′ed·ness n. —de·clar′er n.

dé·clas·sé (dā·klä·sā′) adj. French Fallen in social status; lowered in class, rank, etc.

de·clen·sion (di·klen′shən) n. 1 Gram. a The inflection of nouns, pronouns, and adjectives to indicate case, number, and gender. b A class of words similarly inflected: Stella and nauta are Latin nouns of the first declension. 2 Decline: deterioration. 3 The act of declining. 4 A slope; incline. [< L declinatio, -onis < declinare. See DE-CLINE.] —de·clen′sion·al adj.

dec·li·na·tion (dek′lə·nā′shən) n. 1 The act of declining; inclination; descent; slope. 2 Deterioration; decay. 3 Refusal; non-acceptance. 4 Deviation. 5 Astron. The angular distance of a heavenly body north or south from the celestial equator; celestial latitude. 6 The angle between the direction in which the magnetic needle points and the true meridian: often called magnetic declination. 7 Obs. Grammatical declension; inflection.

de·cline (di·klīn′) v. ·clined, ·clin·ing v.i. 1 To refuse to accept, comply with, or do something, especially politely. 2 To lessen or fail, as in value, health, or force; wane. 3 To bend or incline downward or aside. 4 Poetic To fall off morally. —v.t. 5 To refuse to accept, comply with, or do, especially politely. 6 To cause to bend or incline downward or aside. 7 Gram. To give the inflected forms of (a noun, pronoun, or adjective). See synonyms under ABATE, DIE, FALL. —n. 1 The act or result of declining; deterioration; decay. 2 The period of such decay. 3 That stage of a disease during which the symptoms decrease in violence. 4 Any enfeebling disease, as tabes. 5 A declivity; a slope. [< OF decliner < L declinare lean down] —de·clin′a·ble adj. —de·clin′er n.

dec·li·nom·e·ter (dek′lə·nom′ə·tər) n. An instrument, often self-registering, for measuring or recording the declination of the magnetic needle. [< DECLINE + -(O)METER]

de·cliv·i·tous (di·kliv′ə·təs) adj. Sloping downward; somewhat steep. Also de·cli·vous (di·klī′vəs).

de·cliv·i·ty (di·kliv′ə·tē) n. pl. ·ties A downward slope; descending surface of a hill or mountain: opposed to acclivity. [< L declivitas, -tatis < declivis < de- down + clivus hill, slope]

de·coct (di·kokt′) v.t. To extract by boiling; boil down; condense. [< L decoctus, pp. of decoquere < de- down + coquere cook]

de·coc·tion (di·kok′shən) n. 1 The act of boiling anything, especially in water, to extract its soluble properties: distinguished from infusion. 2 An aqueous preparation made by boiling an animal or vegetable substance; an essence or extract.

de·code (dē·kōd′) v.t. ·cod·ed, ·cod·ing To convert (a coded message) into plain language. —de·cod′er n.

de·co·here (dē′kō·hir′) v.t. & v.i. ·hered, ·her·ing To cease or cause to cease cohering. —de′co·her′ence n.

de·co·her·er (dē′kō·hir′ər) n. An electromagnetic device for restoring a coherer to its normal condition after the passing of an electric wave: also called anticoherer. See COHERER.

de·co·he·sion (dē′kō·hē′zhən) n. The act or state of decohering.

de·col·late (di·kol′āt) v.t. ·lat·ed, ·lat·ing To behead. [< L decollatus, pp. of decollare < de-down, from + collum neck] —de·col′la·tor n.

dé·colle·tage (dā·kôl·täzh′) n. French 1 The outline of the bodice of a dress cut low in the neck and shoulders. 2 A dress so cut.

dé·colle·té (dā′kol·tā′, Fr. dā·kôl·tā′) adj. 1 Cut low in the neck, as a gown. 2 Having the neck and shoulders bare; wearing a low-necked gown. [< F, pp. of décolleter bare the neck < dé- from (< L de-) + collet, dim. of col neck, shoulder < L collum]

de·col·or (dē·kul′ər) v.t. To deprive of color; bleach. Also Brit. de·col′our. —de·col′or·a′tion n.

de·col·or·ant (dē·kul′ər·ənt) adj. Bleaching. —n. A bleaching substance.

de·col·or·ize (dē·kul′ə·rīz) v.t. ·ized, ·iz·ing To decolor. Also Brit. de·col′our·ise. —de·col′or·i·za′tion n. —de·col′or·iz′er n.

de·com·mis·sion (dē′kə·mish′ən) v.t. To take out of active service, as a ship.

de·com·pose (dē′kəm·pōz′) v.t. & v.i. ·posed, ·pos·ing 1 To separate into constituent parts or elements. 2 To decay; putrefy. —de′com·pos′·a·ble adj. —de′com·pos′er n.

de·com·pos·ite (dē′kəm·poz′it) adj. 1 Compounded of compounds, as a word. 2 Bot. Decompound, as a leaf.

de·com·po·si·tion (dē′kom·pə·zish′ən) n. The act, process, or result of decomposing by chemical action or by natural decay. —double decomposition Chem. The formation of two compounds by the union of the radicals formed by the decomposition of two other compounds; metathesis.

de·com·pound (dē·kom′pound′, dē′kəm·pound′) adj. Bot. Several times divided or compounded, as a leaf. [< DE- (def. 3) + COMPOUND]

de·com·press (dē′kəm·pres′) v.t. 1 To free of pressure. 2 To remove the pressure on (caisson workers, etc.), as in an airlock.

de·com·pres·sion (dē′kəm·presh′ən) n. The reduction or removal of pressure, especially in connection with work in caissons or under high atmospheric pressure.

decompression chamber An enclosed chamber equipped for the decompression of bodies subjected to high pressure, or for reducing normal pressure in simulation of or preparatory to high altitude flying.

decompression sickness A painful and potentially fatal syndrome due to the release of bubbles of nitrogen from solution in the blood and tissues following a too-rapid transition from high pressure to atmospheric pressure, such as may occur in high-altitude flying, underwater diving, and tunnel construction. Also called aeroembolism, the bends, caisson disease, tunnel disease.

de·con·tam·i·nate (dē′kən·tam′ə·nāt) v.t. ·nat·ed, ·nat·ing 1 To rid of contamination. 2 To prepare (a contaminated object or area) for normal use by destroying or neutralizing noxious chemicals or radioactivity.

de·con·trol (dē′kən·trōl′) v.t. ·trolled, ·trol·ling To remove from control, specifically, from government controls. —n. The removal of controls.

dé·cor (dā′kôr, dā·kôr′) n. 1 The plan or arrangement of furnishings and colors in an interior space, as a home or office. 2 In the theater, scenery. [< F décorer decorate]

dec·o·rate (dek′ə·rāt) v.t. ·rat·ed, ·rat·ing 1 To adorn; ornament. 2 To confer a decoration or medal upon. See synonyms under ADORN, GAR-NISH. [< L decoratus, pp. of decorare < decus, decoris grace, embellishment]

decorated architecture A style of English Gothic architecture prevailing from the end of the 13th to the last part of the 14th century.

dec·o·ra·tion (dek′ə·rā′shən) n. 1 The act, process, or art of decorating. 2 Ornamentation; an ornament. 3 A badge or emblem conferred as a mark of honor; a medal.

Decoration Day A day first set apart for decorating the graves of those who fell in the Civil War, now for the dead of any American war: observed as a legal holiday on May 30

in most States: also called *Memorial Day.*

dec·o·ra·tive (dek′rə·tiv, dek′ə·rā′tiv) *adj.* Of, pertaining to, or suitable for decoration; ornamental. – **dec′o·ra·tive·ly** *adv.* — **dec′o·ra·tive·ness** *n.*

dec·o·ra·tor (dek′ə·rā′tər) *n.* One who decorates; especially, an interior decorator.

dec·o·rous (dek′ər·əs, di·kôr′əs, -kō′rəs) *adj.* Proper; becoming; suitable. See synonyms under BECOMING, CORRECT, MODEST. [<L *decorus* < *decus, decoris* grace] — **dec′o·rous·ly** *adv.* — **dec′o·rous·ness** *n.*

de·cor·ti·cate (di·kôr′tə·kāt) *v.t.* **·cat·ed, ·cat·ing 1** To strip off the bark or outer coat of; peel; husk; hull. **2** To strip off a portion of the cortical substance of (the brain, kidney, etc.). [<L *decorticatus,* pp. of *decorticare* < *de-* down + *cortex, corticis* bark] — **de·cor′·ti·ca′tion** *n.* — **de·cor′ti·ca′tor** *n.*

de·co·rum (di·kôr′əm, -kō′rəm) *n. pl.* **·co·rums** or **·co·ra** (-kôr′ə, -kō′rə) **1** Propriety, as in manner, conduct, etc.; politeness. **2** An act demanded by social custom. [<L, neut. of *decorus* DECOROUS]

de·cou·page (dā′kōō·päzh′) *n.* **1** The art of using pieces cut from paper, etc., to decorate an entire surface. **2** A work produced by such means. Also **dé′cou·page′.** [<F]

de·coy (di·koi′, dē′·koi) *n.* **1** One who or that which allures or is intended to allure into danger or temptation. **2** A swindler's accomplice. **3** A lure; a bird or animal, or the likeness of one, used to lure game into a snare or net or within gunshot.

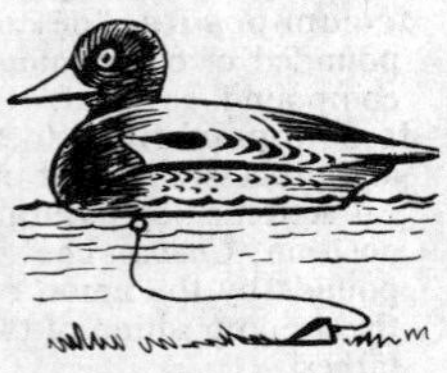

DECOY

4 An enclosed place into which game may be lured for capture. **5** *Mil.* A dummy military installation designed to distract enemy fire from a real position or installation, or to delude the foe as to the point of one's own attack. — *v.t.* & *v.i.* (dē′koi) To lure or be lured into danger, a snare, etc. [Earlier *coy* <Du. *kooi* a cage < L *cavea* < *cavus* hollow] — **de·coy′er** *n.*

de·crease (di·krēs′) *v.t.* & *v.i.* **·creased, ·creas·ing** To grow, or cause to grow, less or smaller; diminish, especially by a gradual process; abate; reduce. — *n.* (*usually* dē′krēs) **1** The act, process, or state of decreasing. **2** The amount or degree of loss; diminution. See synonyms under ABATE, IMPAIR, RETRENCH. [<OF *decreiss-,* stem of *decreistre* <L *decrescere* < *de-* down + *crescere* grow] — **de·creas′ing·ly** *adv.*

de·cree (di·krē′) *n.* **1** A formal order determining what is to be done or not to be done in a particular matter; a law or ordinance of either a civil or an ecclesiastical ruler, council, or legislative body. **2** *Theol.* A foreordaining, eternal purpose of God. See synonyms under LAW. — *v.t.* To order, adjudge, ordain, or appoint by law or edict. — *v.i.* To issue an edict or decree. See synonyms under DICTATE. [<OF *decre, decret* <L *decretum,* neut. pp. of *decernere.* See DECERN.]

dec·re·ment (dek′rə·mənt) *n.* **1** A decreasing; waning. **2** Amount of loss by decrease or waste. **3** *Math.* A decrease in value of a variable quantity; negative increment. [<L *decrementum* < *decrescere.* See DECREASE.]

dec·re·me·ter (dek′rə·mē′tər, di·krim′ə·tər) *n.* *Electr.* An instrument used for measuring the proportional reduction of an electrical oscillation. [<DECRE(MENT) + -METER]

de·crep·it (di·krep′it) *adj.* Enfeebled by old age; broken down. [<L *decrepitus* < *de-* completely + *crepare* creak] — **de·crep′it·ly** *adv.*

de·crep·i·tate (di·krep′ə·tāt) *v.* **·tat·ed, ·tat·ing** *v.t.* To heat (salt, minerals, etc.) so as to cause to crepitate or crackle. — *v.i.* To crackle when heated, as salt. [<NL *decrepitatus,* pp. of *decrepitare* < *de-* completely + *crepitare,* freq. of *crepare* creak]

de·crep·i·ta·tion (di·krep′ə·tā′shən) *n.* **1** The act of decrepitating. **2** The crackling sound produced by certain salts when heated.

de·crep·i·tude (di·krep′ə·tōōd, -tyōōd) *n.* Enfeeblement through infirmity or old age.

de·cre·scen·do (dē′krə·shen′dō) See DIMINUENDO.

de·cres·cent (di·kres′ənt) *adj.* Decreasing; waning. [<L *decrescens, -entis,* ppr. of *decrescere.* See DECREASE.] — **de·cres′cence** *n.*

de·cre·tal (di·krēt′l) *n.* **1** An authoritative decree, or a letter containing such a decree; especially, a letter or rescript of the Pope determining some point in ecclesiastical law. **2** A book or compilation of decrees, orders, or laws. [<F *décrétale* <Med. L *decretale* <L *decretum.* See DECREE.]

De·cre·tals (di·krēt′lz) *n. pl.* The collection of papal laws and decisions published by authority of Gregory IX in 1234, forming part of the canonical laws of the Church.

de·cre·tist (di·krē′tist) *n.* One versed in the Decretals.

de·cre·tive (di·krē′tiv) *adj.* Pertaining to or having the force or nature of a decree. — **de·cre′tive·ly** *adv.*

dec·re·to·ry (dek′rə·tôr′ē, -tō′rē) *adj.* **1** Pertaining to, resulting from, or announcing a decree; judicial. **2** Definitive.

de·crim·i·nal·ize (dē·krim′ə·nəl·īz) *v.t.* **·ized, ·iz·ing** To abstain from applying criminal penalties to; regard as non–punishable. — **de·crim′i·nal·i·za′tion** *n.*

de·cru·des·cence (dē′krōō·des′əns) *n. Med.* A lessening in the intensity of the symptoms of a disease. [<DE- (def. 4) + L *crudescens, -entis,* ppr. of *crudescere* grow harsh < *crudus* harsh] — **de′cru·des′cent** *adj.*

de·cry (di·krī′) *v.t.* **·cried, ·cry·ing 1** To condemn or disparage openly; traduce. **2** To depreciate or condemn officially, as foreign or obsolete coins. See synonyms under ASPERSE, DISPARAGE. [<F *décrier* <*dé-* down (<L *de-*) + *crier* cry] — **de·cri′al** *n.* — **de·cri′er** *n.*

de·cryp·to·graph (dē·krip′tə·graf, -gräf) *v.t.* To convert a cryptogram into plain text by decoding or deciphering or by the use of a combined cipher–code key. Also **de·crypt′.**

dec·u·ba·tion (dek′yōō·bā′shən) *n. Med.* The period of convalescence from an infectious disease, ending with the disappearance of the micro–organisms from the body. [<DE- (def. 4) + L *cubatio, -onis* a lying down < *cubare* recline]

dec·u·man (dek′yōō·mən) *adj.* **1** Principal; chief; large. **2** Of or pertaining to the tenth or hypothetically largest recurrent ocean wave. — *n.* A great wave. [<L *decumanus,* var. of *decimanus* of the tenth part, large < *decimus* tenth]

de·cum·bence (di·kum′bəns) *n.* A decumbent or prostrate state or position. Also **de·cum′·ben·cy.**

de·cum·bent (di·kum′bənt) *adj.* **1** Lying down; recumbent. **2** *Bot.* Prostrate: said of stems, shoots, etc., growing along the ground. [<L *decumbens, -entis,* ppr. of *decumbere* < *de-* down + *cumbere* lie, recline]

dec·u·ple (dek′yōō·pəl) *v.t.* **·pled, ·pling** To increase tenfold. — *adj.* Tenfold. — *n.* A number or quantity ten times as large as another or ten times repeated. [<F *décuple* <L *decuplus* < *decem* ten]

de·cu·pli·cate (dek·yōō′plə·kit) *adj.* **1** Tenfold. **2** Raised to the tenth power. — *v.t.* (-kāt) **·cat·ed, ·cat·ing** To decuple. — *n.* One of ten like things. [<DECUPLE, on analogy with *duplicate, triplicate,* etc.] — **de·cu′·pli·cate·ly** *adv.* — **de·cu′pli·ca′tion** *n.*

de·cu·ri·on (di·kyōōr′ē·ən) *n.* **1** An officer who commanded ten soldiers: the lowest military officer of ancient Rome; also, a member of the Roman Senate in a colony or municipal town. **2** Any person having command over or responsibility for ten others. [<L *decurio, -onis* < *decem* ten]

de·cur·rent (di·kûr′ənt) *adj. Bot.* Extending or running downward into another structure, as leaves along a plant stem. [<L *decurrens, -entis,* ppr. of *decurrere* < *de-* down + *currere* run] — **de·cur′rent·ly** *adv.*

de·cur·sive (di·kûr′siv) *adj.* Decurrent. [<L *decursus,* pp. of *decurrere.* See DECURRENT.] — **de·cur′sive·ly** *adv.*

de·curve (di·kûrv′) *v.t.* & *v.i.* **·curved, ·curv·ing** To curve downward.

dec·u·ry (dek′yōō·rē) *n. pl.* **·ries 1** A body of ten men. **2** In ancient Rome, the ten soldiers commanded by a decurion; also, a division of the curiae, of the hundred senators, and of the judges and corporations. [<L *decuria* < *decem* ten]

de·cus·sate (di·kus′āt, dek′ə·sāt) *v.i.* **·sat·ed, ·sat·ing** To intersect; cross in the form of the letter X; interlace. — *adj.* (di·kus′āt, -it) **1** Crossed; intersected. **2** *Bot.* Having each pair of leaves at right angles with the pair next below or above: also **de·cus′sat·ed.** [<L *decussatus,* pp. of *decussare* mark with an X < *decussis* the number ten, X] — **de·cus′·sate·ly** *adv.*

dec·us·sa·tion (dek′ə·sā′shən) *n.* **1** The act or state of decussating; that which decussates. **2** *Anat.* A crossing over of symmetrical parts, as nerve fibers intersecting the median plane of the central nervous system to connect centers on either side.

de·dal (dēd′l) See DAEDAL.

ded·a·lous (ded′ə·ləs) *adj.* Pertaining to or like a labyrinth; involved; intricately and skilfully made. [<L *daedalus* skilfully made <Gk. *daidalos*]

de·dans (dē′dəns) *n.* **1** In court tennis, the gallery, screened off for spectators. **2** The spectators. [<F < *dedans* inside]

De·de·a·gach (de′de′ä·gäch′) A former name for ALEXANDROUPOLIS.

ded·i·cate (ded′ə·kāt) *v.t.* **·cat·ed, ·cat·ing 1** To set apart for sacred uses; consecrate. **2** To set apart for or devote to any special use, duty, or purpose. **3** To preface with a dedication, as a work of literature. See synonyms under INSCRIBE. — *adj.* Dedicated; devoted. [<L *dedicatus,* pp. of *dedicare* < *de-* down + *dicare* proclaim] — **ded′i·ca′tive** *adj.* — **ded′·i·ca′tor** *n.* — **ded′i·ca·to′ry** (-kə·tôr′ē, -tō′rē) *adj.* — **ded′i·ca·to′ri·ly** *adv.*

ded·i·ca·tion (ded′ə·kā′shən) *n.* **1** A dedicating or being dedicated. **2** An inscription in a book, etc., as to a friend or cause.

de·duce (di·dōōs′, -dyōōs′) *v.t.* **·duced, ·duc·ing 1** To derive as a conclusion; infer; conclude. **2** To trace, as derivation or origin. [<L *deducere* < *de-* down + *ducere* lead] — **de·duce′ment** *n.* — **de·duc′i·ble** *adj.*

de·duct (di·dukt′) *v.t.* To subtract; take away. [<L *deductus,* pp. of *deducere.* See DEDUCE.] — **de·duct′i·ble** *adj.*

de·duc·tion (di·duk′shən) *n.* **1** The act of deducing. **2** *Logic* Reasoning from stated premises to the formally valid conclusion; reasoning from the general to the particular. **3** An inference; conclusion. **4** The act of deducting. **5** A subtraction; abatement. See synonyms under DEMONSTRATION, INFERENCE. Compare INDUCTION.

de·duc·tive (di·duk′tiv) *adj.* **1** Of or proceeding by deduction. **2** Inferential; deducible. — **de·duc′tive·ly** *adv.*

dee[1] (dē) *n.* **1** The sound or the shape of the letter D. **2** A metal loop for connecting parts of harness. **3** One of a pair of D–shaped half–hollow cylinder units of a cyclotron in which the stream of entering electrons is continuously accelerated in an electromagnetic field.

dee[2] (dē) *v.i. Scot.* To die.

Dee (dē) **1** A river in NE Scotland, flowing east 87 miles to the North Sea at Aberdeen. **2** A river and lake in SW Scotland. **3** A river in northern Wales and England, flowing NE 70 miles to the Irish Sea.

deed (dēd) *n.* **1** Anything done; an act. **2** An exploit, a notable achievement. **3** Fact; truth; reality. **4** Action performed, as opposed to words. **5** *Law* A written instrument containing a grant signed and sealed by the grantor; an instrument of conveyance under seal: a *deed* for land. Any instrument in writing under seal, whether a bond, agreement, or contract of any kind, is a *deed,* but the word is more frequently used in regard to the conveyance of real estate. See synonyms under ACT, TRANSACTION, WORK. — **in deed** In fact; actually. — *v.t.* To convey or transfer by deed. [OE *dǣd*] — **deed′ful** *adj.* — **deed′·less** *adj.*

deed·ed (dē′did) *adj. Law* Conveyed by a deed.

deem (dēm) *v.t.* & *v.i.* To judge; think; regard; believe. See synonyms under CALCULATE, ESTEEM, SUPPOSE. [OE *dēman,* judge]

de–em·pha·size (dē·em′fə·sīz) *v.t.* **·sized, ·siz·ing** To place less emphasis on. — **de·em′pha·sis** (-sis) *n.*

deem·ster (dēm′stər) *n.* **1** One who deems or dooms; a judge. **2** Either of the two highest judicial officers in the Isle of Man. [ME *demestre*] — **deem′ster·ship** *n.*

deep (dēp) *adj.* **1** Extending or situated far, or comparatively far, below the surface. **2** Extending or entering far back, in, or away from the spectator's point of view. **3** Having

a depth, thickness, dimension, or quantity measured from above downward, from before backward, or from without inward. **4** Profound in nature, reach, or degree. **5** Hard to understand or fathom because abstruse, complex, or well concealed. **6** Of great and well–trained or far–reaching intellectual powers; sagacious; penetrating. **7** Of great intensity; great in degree; extreme; hence, heartfelt and earnest. **8** Artful in the concealment of plans or schemes; insidious; scheming; designing. **9** Of low, sonorous, or heavy tone; grave. **10** Of intense or dark hue. **11** Immersed; absorbed: *deep* in a book. **—*n.*** **1** A place or thing that has great depth; deep water; an abyss; especially, the sea or ocean. **2** Something too profound, vast, or abstruse to be easily comprehended; a mystery. **3** The most profound part; culmination: the *deep* of night. **4** *Naut.* The interval between two successive marked fathoms on a lead line or sounding line of a vessel. **—*adv.*** **1** Deeply. **2** Far on, in reference to time. [OE *dēop.* Akin to DIP.] **—deep′ness** *n.*

deep-dish pie (dēp′dish′) A pie baked in a deep dish and having only a top crust.

deep–dyed (dēp′dīd′) *adj.* Thoroughgoing; absolute: a *deep–dyed* villain.

deep·en (dē′pən) *v.t.* & *v.i.* To make or become deep or deeper.

deep–freeze (dēp′frēz′) *n.* A refrigerator in which foods may be kept for long periods of time at temperatures approximating 0° F. **—*v.t.* –froze** or **–freezed, –fro·zen** or **–freezed, –freez·ing** To place or store in such a refrigerator.

deep–fry (dēp′frī′) *v.t.* **·fried, ·fry·ing** To fry in deep fat or oil.

deep–laid (dēp′lād′) *adj.* Made with extreme care and cleverness, usually in secret: *deep–laid* plans.

deep·ly (dēp′lē) *adv.* **1** At or to a great depth. **2** To a great extent or degree; intensely; profoundly; thoroughly. **3** At a low pitch or tone. **4** With deep color. **5** Artfully; intricately.

deep reflex *Physiol.* Any reflex affecting a deep–lying muscle or other internal structure, as produced by tapping an adjacent tendon or bone.

deep–root·ed (dēp′rōō′tid, -rŏŏt′id) *adj.* **1** Having roots that reach far below the surface. **2** Firmly held: said of beliefs, prejudices, etc.

deep–sea (dēp′sē′) *adj.* Of, in, or pertaining to the depths of the sea.

deep–seat·ed (dēp′sē′tid) *adj.* So far in as to be ineradicable or almost ineradicable: said of emotions, diseases, etc.

Deep South The southernmost parts of Alabama, Georgia, Louisiana, and Mississippi, conventionally regarded as typifying Southern culture and traditions.

deer (dir) *n. pl.* **deer 1** A ruminant (family *Cervidae*) having deciduous antlers, usually in the male only, as the moose, elk, and reindeer. Popularly, *deer* is used mainly of the smaller species. ◆ Collateral adjective: *cervine.* See FALLOW DEER, VENISON. **2** A deerlike animal. **3** Formerly, any quadruped; a wild animal. ◆ Homophone: *dear.* [OE *dēor* beast]

deer·ber·ry (dir′ber′ē) *n. pl.* **·ries 1** The buckberry (def. 2). **2** The wintergreen. **3** The partridgeberry.

deer·fly (dir′flī′) *n. pl.* **·flies** A bloodsucking fly (genus *Chrysops*), similar to a horsefly but smaller and with banded wings. For illustration see INSECT (injurious).

deer·grass (dir′gras′, -gräs′) *n.* **1** Meadow–beauty. **2** A forage grass (*Muhlenbergia rigens*) of Mexico and the SW United States.

deer·hound (dir′hound′) *n.* A breed of sporting dog, having a long, flat head, pointed muzzle, and a shaggy, dark–gray, or brindle coat: also called *staghound.* Also **Scottish deerhound.**

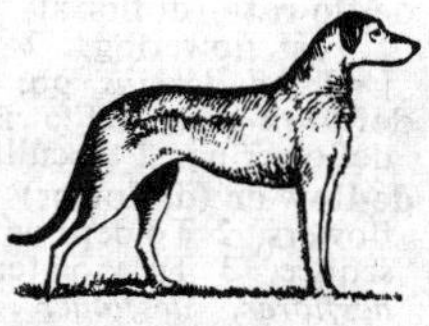

DEERHOUND
(28 to 32 inches high at the shoulder)

deer·let (dir′lət) *n.* A pigmy deer.

deer–lick (dir′lik′) *n.* A place, naturally or artificially salted, where deer come to lick the saline earth.

deer mouse A small, long–tailed, furry mouse (*Peromyscus maniculatus*), many varieties of which are widely distributed in North America; the white–footed mouse.

deer·skin (dir′skin′) *n.* A deer's hide, or leather made from it; buckskin.

deer·stalk·er (dir′stô′kər) *n.* **1** One who hunts deer by stalking. **2** A helmet–shaped cloth cap, usually red, commonly worn by deer hunters.

deer·weed (dir′wēd′) *n.* A branching, leguminous herb (*Lotus scoparius*) found in parts of Arizona and southern California: sometimes utilized for cattle food. Also **deer′vetch′.**

de–es·ca·late (dē-es′kə·lāt) *v.t.* & *v.i.* **·lat·ed, ·lat·ing** To decrease or be decreased gradually, as in scope, effect, or intensity: to *de–escalate* a war. **—de–es′ca·la′tion** *n.*

dee·wan (di·wän′) See DEWAN.

de·face (di·fās′) *v.t.* **·faced, ·fac·ing 1** To mar or disfigure the face or surface of. **2** To obliterate wholly or partially, as an inscription; efface. [<obs. F *defacer* <OF *desfacier* <*des-* down, away + *face* face <L *facies*] **—de·face′a·ble** *adj.* **—de·fac′er** *n.* **—de·fac′ing** *adj.* **—de·fac′ing·ly** *adv.*

de·face·ment (di·fās′mənt) *n.* **1** The act of defacing. **2** Anything that disfigures.

de fac·to (dē fak′tō) Actually or really existing, with or without legal sanction, as a government: distinguished from *de jure.* [<L]

de·fal·cate (di·fal′kāt) *v.i.* **·cat·ed, ·cat·ing** To commit defalcation; embezzle money. [<Med. L *defalcatus,* pp. of *defalcare* lop off <*de-* down, away + *falx, falcis* scythe] **—de·fal′ca·tor** *n.*

de·fal·ca·tion (dē′fal·kā′shən) *n.* **1** A fraudulent appropriation of money held in trust; embezzlement; also, the amount embezzled. **2** A deducting; an abatement. **3** The amount deducted.

def·a·ma·tion (def′ə·mā′shən) *n.* The act of defaming; aspersion; calumny. See synonyms under SCANDAL. [<L *diffamatio, -onis* a speaking against <*diffamare.* See DEFAME.]

de·fam·a·to·ry (di·fam′ə·tôr′ē, -tō′rē) *adj.* Slanderous.

de·fame (di·fām′) *v.t.* **·famed, ·fam·ing 1** To attack the good name or reputation of; slander; libel. **2** *Obs.* To indict; accuse. See synonyms under ABUSE, ASPERSE, REVILE. [<L *diffamare* <*dis-* away, from + *fama* a report, reputation]

de·fam·er (di·fā′mər) *n.* One who slanders or dishonors another.

de·fault (di·fôlt′) *n.* **1** A failure in or neglect of an obligation or duty; failure to appear or plead in a suit; failure to pay a sum due. **2** Want or deficiency; absence; lack: in *default* of evidence. **3** *Obs.* A fault; transgression. **4** The failure to appear for an athletic contest, race, etc.; failure to finish a contest. See synonyms under NEGLECT, WANT. **—in default of** Owing to lack or failure of. **—judgment by default** A judgment in a civil action rendered for failure to prosecute or defend. **—*v.i.*** **1** To fail or neglect to fulfil or do a duty, obligation, etc. **2** To fail to meet financial obligations. **3** *Law* To fail to appear in court; also, to lose by default. **4** In sports, to fail to compete or complete a game, etc.; also, to lose or forfeit a game, etc., by default. **—*v.t.*** **5** To fail to perform or pay. **6** To declare in default, especially legally. **7** In sports, to fail to compete in, as a game; also, to forfeit by default. [<OF *defaut* <*defaillir* <*de-* down + *fallere* deceive]

de·fault·er (di·fôl′tər) *n.* **1** One who defaults; especially, one who fails to appear in court. **2** One who fails to account for trust money; a delinquent; embezzler; also, one who fails to pay debts. **3** *Brit.* A soldier who has committed an offense against military law.

de·fea·sance (di·fē′zəns) *n.* **1** A making null or void; an annulment. **2** *Law* A condition in a deed or collateral instrument by the performance of which the principal deed is rendered void. [<OF *defesance* an undoing <*defaire.* See DEFEAT.]

de·fea·si·ble (di·fē′zə·bəl) *adj.* Capable of being rendered void. **—de·fea′si·ble·ness, de·fea′·si·bil′i·ty** *n.*

de·feat (di·fēt′) *v.t.* **1** To overcome in any contest; vanquish. **2** To baffle; circumvent, as plans; frustrate. **3** *Law* To make void; annul. **4** *Obs.* To destroy; ruin. See synonyms under BAFFLE, BEAT, CONQUER. **—*n.*** **1** The act or result of defeating; an overthrow; a failure to win or succeed. **2** Prevention; frustration. **3** *Law* An annulment. **4** *Obs.* Destruction. See synonyms under LOSS, RUIN. [<OF *defeit,* pp. of *defaire* <*de-* not (<L *dis-*) + *faire* do <L *facere*]

de·feat·ism (di·fē′tiz·əm) *n.* **1** Acknowledgment or acceptance of defeat, usually on grounds of the futility of resistance. **2** The conduct, state of mind, or propaganda that makes for this. **—de·feat′ist** *n.* & *adj.*

de·fea·ture (di·fē′chər) *n. Obs.* **1** Defeat. **2** A defect or injury.

def·e·cate (def′ə·kāt) *v.* **·cat·ed, ·cat·ing** *v.t.* **1** To clear of dregs or impurities, refine; purify. **—*v.i.*** **2** To become free of dregs. **3** To discharge excrement. **—*adj.*** Clarified; refined. [<L *defaecatus,* pp. of *defaecare* <*de-* down, away + *faex* dregs] **—def′e·ca′·tion** *n.*

def·e·ca·tor (def′ə·kā′tər) *n.* **1** One who or that which clarifies or purifies. **2** In sugar–making, an apparatus for clearing sirups, juices, etc., of impurities.

de·fect (di·fekt′, dē′fekt) *n.* **1** Lack or absence of something essential; imperfection. **2** A blemish; failing; fault. See synonyms under BLEMISH, FOIBLE, WANT. **—*v.i.*** (di·fekt′) To desert; go over to the enemy or opposition. [<L *defectus,* pp. of *deficere* fail <*de-* not + *facere* do]

de·fec·tion (di·fek′shən) *n.* **1** Abandonment of allegiance or duty; failure. **2** Apostasy; desertion.

de·fec·tive (di·fek′tiv) *adj.* **1** Incomplete or imperfect; faulty. **2** *Gram.* Lacking one or more of the declensional or conjugational forms normal for its class: Can is a *defective* verb. **3** *Psychol.* Having less than normal intelligence. **—*n.*** One who or that which is incomplete or imperfect; specifically, a mentally defective person. **—de·fec′tive·ly** *adv.* **—de·fec′tive·ness** *n.*

defective number See under NUMBER.

de·fec·tor (di·fek′tər) *n.* One who deserts an allegiance, army, etc.

de·fence (di·fens′), **de·fence·less** (di·fens′lis), etc. See DEFENSE, etc.

de·fend (di·fend′) *v.t.* **1** To shield from attack or injury; protect. **2** To justify or vindicate; support. **3** *Law* **a** To act in behalf of (an accused). **b** To contest, as a claim, charge, or suit. **4** *Obs.* To forbid. **—*v.i.*** **5** To make a defense. See synonyms under JUSTIFY, KEEP, PRESERVE, SHELTER. [<L *defendere* <*de-* down, away + *fendere* strike] **—de·fend′a·ble** *adj.*

de·fen·dant (di·fen′dənt) *adj.* **1** Sustaining defense. **2** *Obs.* Defensive. **—*n.*** **1** *Law* A person against whom an action is brought. **2** One who defends; a defender. [<F *défendant,* ppr. of *défendre* defend]

de·fend·er (di·fen′dər) *n.* One who defends or protects; a champion.

Defender of the Faith A hereditary title given in 1521 by Pope Leo X to Henry VIII of England for writing in defense of the seven sacraments against Luther: revoked later, but restored by Parliament and still used by English sovereigns.

de·fen·es·tra·tion (dē·fen′ə·strā′shən) *n.* The act of throwing out of a window, or the result of or subjection to such an act: used specifically with reference to a mode of executing popular vengeance practiced in Bohemia in the later Middle Ages. [<L *de* out of, down + *fenestra* window]

de·fense (di·fens′) *n.* **1** The act of defending; protection; the state of being defended. **2** Anything that defends. **3** A plea in justification; excuse; apology. **4** *Law* An opposing or denying of the truth, validity, or sufficiency of a plaintiff's complaint; also, whatever is alleged, pleaded, or offered in evidence as sufficient to defeat an action either wholly or in part. **5** The art or science of defending by force of arms; skilfulness in defending oneself, as in fencing or boxing. **6** *Obs.* A prohibitory decree. Also *defence.* **—Department of Defense** An executive department of the U.S.

government (established in 1947), headed by the Secretary of Defense and composed of the Department of the Army, the Department of the Navy, the Department of the Air Force, and various military agencies and staffs: from 1947 to 1949 called the National Military Establishment. [<OF <L *defensus,* pp. of *defendere.* See DEFEND.]

Synonyms: apology, bulwark, exculpation, fortress, guard, justification, protection, rampart, resistance, safeguard, shelter, shield, vindication. The weak may speak or act in *defense* of the strong; none but the powerful can assure others of *protection.* A *defense* is ordinarily against actual attack; *protection* is against possible as well as actual dangers. We speak of *defense* against an assault, *protection* from the cold. *Vindication* is a triumphant *defense* of character and conduct against charges of error or wrong. Compare APOLOGY, RAMPART. *Antonyms*: abandonment, betrayal, capitulation, desertion, flight, surrender.

de·fense·less (di·fens′lis) *adj.* Having no defense or means of defense; unprotected. **— de·fense′less·ly** *adv.* **— de·fense′less·ness** *n.*

defense mechanism 1 *Psychoanal.* An unconscious adjustment of behavior or mental attitude directed toward protection of the personality against unpleasant emotions or realities: also called **defense dynamism, defense reaction.** 2 *Physiol.* Any self-protective reaction, as the resistance of an organism to bacteria.

de·fen·si·ble (di·fen′sə·bəl) *adj.* Capable of being defended, maintained, or justified. **— de·fen′si·bil′i·ty, de·fen′si·ble·ness** *n.* **— de·fen′si·bly** *adv.*

de·fen·sive (di·fen′siv) *adj.* 1 Intended or suitable for defense. 2 Carried on in defense: distinguished from *offensive.* 3 Making defense. **—** *n.* An attitude or condition of defense: means of defense; safeguard. **— de·fen′sive·ly** *adv.*

de·fen·sor (di·fen′sər) *n. Latin* 1 One who defends; a defender. 2 *Law* One who appears for and defends another in an action in court.

de·fer[1] (di·fûr′) *v.t.* & *v.i.* **·ferred, ·fer·ring** To delay or put off to some other time; postpone. See synonyms under PROCRASTINATE, SUSPEND. [<OF *différer* <L *differre.* Doublet of DIFFER.] **— de·fer′ra·ble** *adj.* **— de·fer′·ment** *n.*

de·fer[2] (di·fûr′) *v.i.* **·ferred, ·fer·ring** To yield to the opinions or decisions of another: with *to.* [<MF *déférer* <L *deferre* <*de-* down + *ferre* bear, carry] **— de·fer′rer** *n.*

Synonyms: respect, revere, submit, venerate, yield. We *defer* to recognized superiors in position, ability, or attainments; we *respect* power and worth wherever found. A military officer must *defer* to the views or authority of a superior whom he may not personally *respect*; a discoverer sure of his facts may not *defer to* the incredulity of those whom on other grounds he *respects* most highly. See OBEY. *Antonyms*: defy, despise, disregard, scorn, slight.

def·er·ence (def′ər·əns) *n.* Respectful yielding; respect; regard.

def·er·ent (def′ər·ənt) *adj.* 1 Carrying off; bearing away; adapted to carry or convey. 2 *Anat.* Pertaining to certain ducts, as the vas deferens: opposed to *afferent.* 3 Characterized by deference; deferential. **—** *n.* In the Ptolemaic astronomy, the circle around the earth, as a center, on the circumference of which the center of the epicycle was supposed to move. See under EPICYCLE. [<L *deferens, -entis,* ppr. of *deferre.* See DEFER[2].]

def·er·en·tial (def′ə·ren′shəl) *adj.* Marked by deference; respectful; courteous. See synonyms under OBSEQUIOUS. **— def′er·en′tial·ly** *adv.*

de·ferred (di·fûrd′) *adj.* 1 Postponed. 2 With benefits or payments held back until a later date.

def·er·ves·cence (def′ər·ves′əns) *n.* 1 The cessation of boiling. 2 *Med.* The fall of temperature, indicating the disappearance of fever. [<L *defervescens, -entis,* ppr. of *defervescere* cool down] **— def′er·ves′cent** *adj.*

Def·fand (de·fäṅ′), **Marquise du,** 1698–1780, *née* Marie de Vichy-Chamrond, a leader in French literary circles.

de·fi·ance (di·fī′əns) *n.* 1 The act of defying; a challenge. 2 Bold opposition; disposition to oppose or resist; contemptuous disregard of authority or opposition.

de·fi·ant (di·fī′ənt) *adj.* Showing or characterized by defiance. [<OF ppr. of *defier.* See DEFY.] **— de·fi′ant·ly** *adv.*

de·fib·ril·late (dē·fib′rə·lāt, dē·fī′brə-) *v.t.* **·lat·ed, ·lat·ing** *Pathol.* To stop fibrillation of (the heart muscle), as by jolting with an electric current. **— de·fib′ril·la′tion, de·fib′ril·la′tor** *n.*

de·fi·bri·na·tion (dē·fī′brə·nā′shən) *n.* The removal of fibrin from the blood or lymph in order to prevent coagulation and facilitate study of the blood cells in liquid form.

de·fi·cien·cy (di·fish′ən·sē) *n. pl.* **·cies** 1 The state of being deficient. 2 That which is deficient; lack; insufficiency; defect. Also **de·fi′cience.** See synonyms under WANT.

deficiency disease *Pathol.* 1 A disease, such as pellagra, rickets, scurvy, etc., caused by insufficiency or lack of some necessary element in the body. 2 Avitaminosis.

deficiency judgment *Law* A judgment in favor of a creditor for that amount of a debt, secured by a mortgage, not satisfied by foreclosure and sale.

de·fi·cient (di·fish′ənt) *adj.* 1 Lacking an adequate or proper supply; insufficient. 2 Lacking in some essential; incomplete; imperfect; defective. See synonyms under SCANTY. [<L *deficiens, -entis,* ppr. of *deficere.* See DEFECT.] **— de·fi′cient·ly** *adv.*

def·i·cit (def′ə·sit) *n.* A deficiency, or falling short in amount; shortage, especially of revenue. [<L, it is lacking]

de fi·de (dē fī′dē) *Latin* Of the faith; specifically, in the Roman Catholic Church, denoting a truth revealed to and taught by the Church.

de·fi·er (di·fī′ər) *n.* One who defies.

def·i·lade (def′ə·lād′) *v.t.* **·lad·ed, lad·ing** To plan or construct so as to protect from enfilading and from reverse fire: said of a fortification. [<*n.*] **—** *n.* 1 The act of defilading. 2 The protection afforded by natural cover or object, or other shield against enemy fire or observation: also **de·file′ment.** [<F *défilade* <*défiler* unthread <*dé-* away (<L *dis-*) + *fil* thread <L *filum*]

de·file[1] (di·fīl′) *v.t.* **·filed, ·fil·ing** 1 To make foul or dirty; pollute. 2 To tarnish or sully the brightness of; corrupt the purity of. 3 To sully; profane (a name, reputation, etc.). 4 To render ceremonially unclean. 5 To corrupt the chastity of. [<OF *defouler* <*de-* down (<L *de-*) + *fouler* trample; infl. in form by ME *filen* soil, OE *fȳlan* <*fūl* foul] **— de·file′ment** *n.* **— de·fil′er** *n.*

Synonyms: befoul, contaminate, corrupt, infect, pollute, soil, spoil, stain, sully, taint, tarnish, vitiate. The hand may be *defiled* by a touch of pitch; swine that have been wallowing in the mud are *befouled. Contaminate* and *infect* refer to something evil that deeply pervades and permeates, as the human body or mind. *Pollute* is used chiefly of liquids; as, water *polluted* with sewage. *Tainted* meat is repulsive; *infected* meat contains germs of disease. A *soiled* garment may be cleansed by washing; a *spoiled* garment is beyond cleansing or repair. Bright metal is *tarnished* by exposure; a fair sheet is *sullied* by a dirty hand. We speak of a *vitiated* taste or style; fraud *vitiates* a title or a contract. See ABUSE, CORRUPT, POLLUTE, VIOLATE. *Antonyms:* clean, cleanse, disinfect, hallow, purify, sanctify.

de·file[2] (di·fīl′, dē′fīl) *v.i.* **·filed, ·fil·ing** To march in a line or by files; file off. **—** *n.* 1 A long narrow pass; a gorge between mountains. 2 A marching in file. [<MF *défiler* <*dé-* down (<L *de-*) + *file* FILE[1] (def. 3)]

de·fine (di·fīn′) *v.t.* **·fined, ·fin·ing** 1 To state the meaning of (a word or phrase). 2 To determine the limits of and specify exactly. 3 To determine and fix the boundaries of. 4 To show or bring out the form or outline of. 5 To constitute the definition of. See synonyms under INTERPRET. [<OF *definer* <L *definire* <*de-* down + *finire* finish <*finis* end] **— de·fin′a·ble** *adj.* **— de·fin′er** *n.*

def·i·nite (def′ə·nit) *adj.* 1 Having precise limits; known with exactness; determined; clear; precise. 2 *Gram.* Limiting; particularizing: The *definite* article in English is *the.* See synonyms under PARTICULAR, PRECISE. [<L *definitus,* pp. of *definire.* See DEFINE.] **— def′·i·nite·ly** *adv.* **— def′i·nite·ness** *n.*

def·i·ni·tion (def′ə·nish′ən) *n.* 1 A description or explanation of a word or thing, by its attributes, properties, or relations, that distinguishes it from all other things. 2 The act of stating or showing what a word means, what a thing is, or what the content of a conception is; the act of defining. 3 The state of being definite; fixed shape; definitiveness. 4 The determining of the outline or limits of anything. 5 The state of being clearly outlined or determined. 6 *Optics* The power of a lens to give a distinct image at whatever magnification. 7 In television, the clarity of detail in a transmitted image, reckoned in terms of the number of picture elements or scanning lines in each image or frame. 8 In radio, the clearness of sounds received.

Synonyms: comment, commentary, description, explanation, exposition, interpretation, rendering, translation. A *definition* is formal and exact, an *explanation* general; a *description* pictorial. A *definition* must include all that belongs to the object defined, and exclude all that does not; a *description* may include only some general features: an *explanation* may simply throw light upon some point of special difficulty. An *exposition* explains a subject in detail. *Interpretation* may translate from other languages, or give the plain meaning of difficult passages, or render the thought and emotion of worthy literature by adequate written or oral expression. *Definition, explanation, exposition,* and *interpretation* are ordinarily blended in a *commentary,* which may also include *description.* A *comment* is upon a single passage; a *commentary* may be the same, but is usually understood to be a volume of *comments.*

de·fin·i·tive (di·fin′ə·tiv) *adj.* 1 Sharply defining or limiting; determinate; explicit; positive. 2 Bringing to an end; conclusive and unalterable. 3 *Biol.* Completely formed; fully developed. 4 Most nearly accurate, complete, etc. **—** *n.* A word that defines or limits. **— de·fin′i·tive·ly** *adv.* **— de·fin′i·tive·ness** *n.*

def·la·grate (def′lə·grāt) *v.t.* & *v.i.* **·grat·ed, ·grat·ing** To burn quickly and with dazzling light. [<L *deflagratus,* pp. of *deflagrare* <*de-* completely + *flagrare* burn] **— def·la·gra·ble** (def′lə·grə·bəl) *adj.*

def·la·gra·tion (def′lə·grā′shən) *n.* A quick and violent combustion, with or without explosion: distinguished from the instantaneous decomposition of an entire compound in a *detonation.*

def·la·gra·tor (def′lə·grā′tər) *n.* That which induces or produces very rapid combustion.

de·flate (di·flāt′) *v.t.* & *v.i.* **·flat·ed, ·flat·ing** 1 To collapse or cause to collapse by the removal of contained air or gas. 2 To take the conceit, confidence, or self-esteem out of. 3 To devaluate; lessen (currency or prices). [<L *deflatus,* pp. of *deflare* <*de-* down + *flare* blow] **— de·fla′tor** *n.*

de·fla·tion (di·flā′shən) *n.* 1 The act or condition of being deflated or reduced in volume. 2 A decrease in the amount of currency in a country. **— de·fla·tion·ar·y** (di·flā′shən·er′ē) *adj.* **— de·fla′tion·ist** *n.* & *adj.*

de·flect (di·flekt′) *v.t.* & *v.i.* To turn aside; swerve or cause to swerve from a course. See synonyms under BEND. [<L *deflectere* <*de-* down + *flectere* bend] **— de·flec′tive** *adj.* **— de·flec′tor** *n.*

de·flec·tion (di·flek′shən) *n.* 1 A turning aside; deviation. 2 A bending of light rays; see DIFFRACTION. 3 The deviation of a galvanometer or magnetic needle from its normal position or from zero. Also *Brit.* **de·flex′ion.**

de·flex (di·fleks′) *v.t.* To bend downward. [<L *deflexus,* pp. of *deflectere.* See DEFLECT.] **— de·flex·ure** (di·flek′shər) *n.*

de·flo·rate (di·flôr′āt, -it, -flō′rāt) *adj. Bot.* 1 Past flowering. 2 Having cast its pollen. [<LL *defloratus,* pp. of *deflorare* DEFLOWER]

def·lo·ra·tion (def′lə·rā′shən) *n.* 1 The act of deflowering. 2 A culling of the choicest part.

de·flow·er (di·flou′ər) *v.t.* 1 To despoil of flowers. 2 To deprive (a woman) of virginity; seduce. 3 To violate; rob of beauty. [<OF *desflorer, desflouer* <LL *deflorare* <*de-* down, away + *flos, floris* flower; infl. in form by flower]

de·flux·ion (di·fluk′shən) *n. Pathol.* The flowing off of fluids, as in catarrh. [<LL *defluxio, -onis* <*defluere* <*de-* down + *fluere* flow]

De·foe (di·fō′), **Daniel,** 1661?–1731, English novelist and essayist.

de·fo·li·ate (dē·fō'lē·āt) v. ·at·ed, ·at·ing v.t. To deprive or strip of leaves. — v.i. To lose leaves. [<Med. L *defoliatus*, pp. of *defoliare* <*de-* down + *folium* leaf] — **de·fo'li·a'tion** n. — **de·fo'li·a'tor** n.

de·force (di·fôrs', -fōrs') v.t. ·forced, ·forc·ing Law 1 To withhold, as an estate, from lawful possession. 2 To keep (someone) from lawful possession by force. [<AF *deforcer*, var. of OF *deforcier* <*de-* down, away (<L *de-*) + *forcier* FORCE] — **de·force'ment** n.

de·for·ciant (di·fôr'shənt, -fōr'-) n. A person chargeable with deforcement.

de·for·est (dē·fôr'ist, -for'-) v.t. To clear of forests or trees. — **de·for'es·ta'tion** n. — **de·for'est·er** n.

De For·est (di·fôr'ist, -for'-), **Lee**, 1873–1961, U.S. inventor: called "the father of radio."

de·form (di·fôrm') v.t. 1 To mar or distort the form of; disfigure. 2 To spoil the beauty of; make ugly or dishonorable. 3 Mech. To change in form. — v.i. 4 To become deformed or disfigured. [<L *deformare* <*de-* away, down + *forma* figure, form] — **de·form'a·bil'i·ty** n. — **de·form'a·ble** adj. — **de·form'er** n.

def·or·ma·tion (def'ər·mā'shən) n. 1 The act of deforming; state of being deformed; misshapenness. 2 Change in form for the worse. 3 Mech. An alteration in the form of a body subjected to sudden or prolonged stress. 4 An altered form or shape.

de·formed (di·fôrmd') adj. Misshapen. — **de·form·ed·ly** (di·fôr'mid·lē) adv. — **de·form'ed·ness** n.

de·form·i·ty (di·fôr'mə·tē) n. pl. ·ties 1 Pathol. a A deformed or misshapen condition. b A deformed part; that which causes disfigurement. 2 Unsightliness; lack of symmetry. 3 Moral depravity. 4 One who or that which is deformed. See synonyms under BLEMISH. [<OF *deformité* <L *deformitas, -tatis* <*deformis* <*de-* down + *forma* form]

de·foul (di·foul') v.t. Obs. To make foul; defile. [<OF *defouler*. See DEFILE.]

de·fraud (di·frôd') v.t. To take or withhold property, etc., from by fraud; cheat; swindle. See synonyms under DECEIVE. [<OF *defrauder* <L *defraudare* <*de-* completely + *fraus, fraudis* a cheat] — **de·fraud·a·tion** (dē'frô·dā'shən) n. — **de·fraud'er** n.

de·fray (di·frā') v.t. 1 To pay for; bear the expense of. 2 To disburse; spend. [<F *défrayer* <OF *defraier* <*de-* away (<L *de-*) + *fraier* spend <*frai* cost, charge] — **de·fray'a·ble** adj. — **de·fray'al, de·fray'ment** n. — **de·fray'er** n.

de·frock (dē·frok') v.t. To unfrock.

de·frost (dē·frôst', -frost') v.t. To remove ice or frost from.

de·frost·er (dē·frôs'tər, -fros'-) n. A device for removing the formation of ice or frost, as from an exposed surface.

deft (deft) adj. Neat and skilful in action; handy; apt; dexterous; clever. [OE *gedæfte* meek, gentle. Related to DAFT.] — **deft'ly** adv. — **deft'ness** n.

de·funct (di·fungkt') adj. Dead; deceased; extinct. — n. A dead person: with the. See synonyms under DEAD, LIFELESS. [<L *defunctus*, pp. of *defungi* <*de-* not + *fungi* perform]

de·fy (di·fī') v.t. ·fied, ·fy·ing 1 To resist or disregard openly or boldly. 2 To challenge: I defy you to cross this line. 3 To resist successfully; baffle; obstruct: to defy definition. 4 Archaic To invite to combat. See synonyms under OPPOSE. — n. pl. ·fies U.S. Slang A challenge. [<OF *defier* <Med. L *diffidare* <*dis-* not + *fidare* be faithful <*fidus* loyal]

dé·ga·gé (dā·gà·zhā') adj. French Free in manner; unconstrained.

de·ga·me (də·gä'mə) n. Lemonwood. [<Sp. *dagame* <native name]

de·gas (dē·gas') v.t. ·gassed, ·gas·sing 1 To remove noxious and poisonous gases from (contaminated areas or affected persons). 2 To exhaust the gases from (vacuum tubes or thermionic valves).

De·gas (də·gä'), **Edgar Hilaire Germain**, 1834–1917, French painter.

De Gas·pe·ri (dā gäs'pe·rē), **Alcide**, 1881–1954, Italian statesman.

de Gaulle (də·gôl', Fr. də·gōl'), **Charles An-** dré **Joseph Marie**, 1890–1970, French general and statesman; president 1944–45, 1959–69.

de·gauss (dē·gous') v.t. To make (a ship) safe against the action of magnetic mines, especially by the use of a **degaussing cable,** fitted around the hull to neutralize the magnetic field set up by the ship. [<DE- + GAUSS]

de·gen·er·ate (di·jen'ə·rāt) v.i. ·at·ed, ·at·ing 1 To become worse or inferior. 2 Biol. To revert to a lower type; decline; deteriorate. — adj. (di·jen'ər·it) 1 Having become worse or inferior; deteriorated; degraded. 2 Physics Having a common value of energy but differing in other dynamical properties. — n. (-it) 1 A deteriorated or degraded individual, animal or human. 2 A morally degraded person. [<L *degeneratus*, pp. of *degenerare* <*de-* down, away + *generare* create] — **de·gen'er·ate·ly** adv. — **de·gen'er·a'tive** adj. — **de·gen'er·ate·ness** n.

de·gen·er·a·tion (di·jen'ə·rā'shən) n. 1 The process of degenerating; also, a degenerate condition. 2 Biol. Progressive deterioration of an organ, tissue, or part, especially as caused by chemical and metabolic changes in the body. 3 Electronics A reduction of radio signal strength by feedback.

de·glu·ti·nate (dē·gloo'tə·nāt) v.t. ·nat·ed, ·nat·ing To remove the gluten from, as from wheat. — **de·glu'ti·na'tion** n.

de·glu·ti·tion (dē'gloo·tish'ən) n. Physiol. The act, process, or power of swallowing. [<F *déglutition* <L *deglutitio, -onis* <*de-* down + *glutire* swallow]

de·grad·a·ble (di·grā'də·bəl) adj. Chem. Capable of being degraded, as a compound.

deg·ra·da·tion (deg'rə·dā'shən) n. 1 The act of degrading. 2 The state of being reduced in rank or disgraced. 3 Geol. Disintegration, especially of rocks by erosion and wind. 4 The degeneration of the physiological body or an organ. — **deg'ra·da'tion·al** adj.

de·grade (di·grād') v. ·grad·ed, ·grad·ing v.t. 1 To reduce in rank; remove from office, dignity, etc.; disgrace. 2 To debase or lower in character, morals, etc. 3 To bring into contempt; dishonor. 4 To reduce in quality, intensity, etc. 5 Biol. To reduce from a higher to a lower type. 6 Geol. To reduce the height of by erosion. 7 Chem. To break down (a compound) into less complex parts; decompose. — v.i. 8. To degenerate; become of a lower type. See synonyms under ABASE. [<OF *degrader* <LL *degradi* <*de-* down + *gradi* step]

de·grad·ed (di·grā'did) adj. Deteriorated; debased. — **de·grad'ed·ly** adv. — **de·grad'ed·ness** n.

de·grad·ing (di·grā'ding) adj. Debasing; humiliating. — **de·grad'ing·ly** adv.

dé·gras (də·grä', deg'rəs) n. 1 A by-product of the tannage of chamois leather with fish oils, consisting of a mixture of fish oil and nitric acid: also called *moellon*. 2 Wool grease obtained by washing sheep's wool; sod oil: used to dress leather, beltings, etc., and to produce lanolin. [<F *dégras* <*dégraisser* remove grease <*dé-* away (<L *de*) + *graisser* <*graisse* grease]

de·gree (di·grē') n. 1 One of a succession of steps, grades, or stages. 2 Relative rank in life; attainment; station. 3 Relative extent, amount, or intensity. 4 Gram. One of the three forms in which an adjective or adverb is compared: the positive, comparative, and superlative *degrees*. 5 An academic rank or title conferred by an institution of learning. 6 One remove in the chain of relationship between persons in the line of descent. 7 A subdivision or unit, as in a thermometric scale. 8 The 360th part of a circle, as of longitude or latitude; the 90th part of a right angle; the unit divisions marked accordingly on various instruments. 9 Math. The power to which an algebraic quantity, equation, or number is raised. 10 In notation, a group of three figures in a number; a period. 11 Music A line or space of a staff. 12 A grade of seriousness: said of crimes: murder in the first *degree*. — **by degrees** Little by little; gradually. — **to a degree** 1 Brit. Extremely. 2 Somewhat. [<OF *degre* <*de-* down (<L *de-*) + *gre* <L *gradus* a step]

de·gree-day (di·grē'dā') n. A unit for estimat- ing the fuel requirements of buildings during the heating season: equivalent to a declination in the mean outside temperature for one day of one degree from a standard temperature of (about) 65° F. A decline of 20° in one day would be 20 degree–days.

degree of freedom Chem. The particular state of a substance, compound, or body with respect to the arrangement of its parts and the number of variables, as pressure, temperature, volume, etc., required to define the system.

de·gres·sion (di·gresh'ən) n. 1 Decrease by steps; descent. 2 Stated decrease in tax rates on sums below a certain amount. [<LL *degressio, -onis* <*degradi*. See DEGRADE.] — **de·gres·sive** (di·gres'iv) adj. — **de·gres'sive·ly** adv.

de·gum (dē·gum') v.t. ·gummed, ·gum·ming To remove excess of gum filling from: said of silk.

de·gust (di·gust') v.t. & v.i. Rare To taste, especially with care. Also **de·gus'tate.** [<L *degustare* <*de-* completely + *gustare* taste] — **de·gus·ta'tion** n.

de gus·ti·bus non est dis·pu·tan·dum (dē gus'ti·bəs non est dis'pyoo·tan'dəm) Latin There is no disputing about tastes.

de·hisce (di·his') v.i. ·hisced, ·hisc·ing Biol. To burst open, as the cocoon of a larva or the capsule of a plant. [<L *dehiscere* <*de-* down + *hiscere*, inceptive of *hiare* gape, yawn] — **de·his'cent** adj.

de·his·cence (di·his'əns) n. 1 A gape or gaping. 2 Biol. The opening or manner of opening, as of the cocoon of a larva or of a capsule when discharging seeds.

de·horn (dē·hôrn') v.t. To remove the horns of (cattle).

de·hort (di·hôrt') v.t. Obs. To try to divert by persuasion; deter. [<L *dehortari* <*de-* away + *hortari* entreat, urge] — **de·hort'er** n.

de·hor·ta·tion (dē'hôr·tā'shən) n. Rare Advice against or dissuasion from anything. — **de·hor·ta·to·ry** (dē·hôr'tə·tôr'ē, -tō'rē), **de·hor'ta·tive** adj.

de·hu·man·ize (dē·hyoo'mən·īz) v.t. ·ized, ·iz·ing To divest or deprive of human qualities or attributes. — **de·hu'man·i·za'tion** n.

de·hu·mid·i·fi·er (dē'hyoo·mid'ə·fī'ər) n. An apparatus for removing moisture from the air.

de·hu·mid·i·fy (dē'hyoo·mid'ə·fī) v.t. ·fied, ·fy·ing To render less humid; remove moisture from. — **de'hu·mid'i·fi·ca'tion** n.

de·hy·drate (dē·hī'drāt) v. ·drat·ed, ·drat·ing v.t. 1 To deprive of water; anhydrate: to *dehydrate* alcohol. 2 To remove water from, as vegetables, so as to preserve. — v.i. 3 To suffer loss of water.

de·hy·dra·tion (dē'hī·drā'shən) n. 1 The process of removing water from a substance or body, as by heat, distillation, or chemicals. 2 The artificial drying of food products to reduce weight and preserve them for future use.

de·hy·dro·gen·ize (dē·hī'drə·jən·īz') v.t. ·ized, ·iz·ing Chem. To free from hydrogen; remove hydrogen from (a compound).

de·hyp·no·tize (dē·hip'nə·tīz) v.t. ·tized, ·tiz·ing To awaken (a person) from the hypnotic state.

De·ia·ni·ra (dē'yə·nī'rə) In Greek mythology, the wife of Hercules, who killed herself because she caused his death. See NESSUS. Also **De'ja·ni'ra.**

de·ice (dē·īs') v.t. & v.i. –iced, –ic·ing To remove (ice) by means of a de–icer.

de·ic·er (dē·ī'sər) n. A mechanical or thermal device which breaks up formations of ice, as on an airplane wing.

de·i·cide (dē'ə·sīd) n. 1 The killing of a god; especially, the crucifixion of Christ. 2 The slayer of a god. [<L *deus* god + -CIDE]

deic·tic (dīk'tik) adj. 1 Logic Proving by direct argument; direct: distinguished from *elenchic, refutative,* or *indirect.* 2 Gram. Demonstrative: a *deictic* pronoun. [<Gk. *deiktikos* able to show <*deiknynai* show, prove] — **deic'ti·cal·ly** adv.

de·if·ic (dē·if'ik) adj. 1 Making, or tending to make, divine. 2 Divine. Also **de·if'i·cal.**

de·i·form (dē'ə·fôrm) adj. In the form of a god; like a god. [<Med. L *deiformis* <L *deus* god + *forma* form]

de·i·fy (dē'ə·fī) v.t. ·fied, ·fy·ing 1 To make

a god of; rank as a deity. **2** To regard or worship as a god. [<F *déifier* <LL *deificare* <L *deus* god + *facere* make] —**de′i·fi·ca′tion** *n.* —**de′i·fi′er** *n.*

deign (dān) *v.t.* **1** To stoop so far as to grant or allow; condescend. **2** *Obs.* To deem worthy of notice or acceptance. —*v.i* **3** To think it befitting oneself (to do something). [<OF *deignier* <L *dignari* <*dignus* worthy]

De·i gra·ti·a (dē′ī grā′shē·ə, dā′ē grä′tē·ä) *Latin* By the grace of God.

deil (dēl) *n. Scot.* **1** The devil. **2** A mischievous fellow.

de·in·sti·tu·tion·al·ize (dē′in·sti·to͞o′shə·nə·līz, -tyo͞o′-) *v.t.* **·ized, ·iz·ing** **1** To remove the institutional character from. **2** *U.S. Colloq.* To remove (someone) from an institution (def. 2).

De·iph·o·bus (dē·if′ə·bəs) In greek mythology, the son of Priam, who married Helen after Paris was killed; slain by Menelaus.

deip·nos·o·phist (dīp·nos′ə·fist) *n.* One who talks learnedly at the table. [<Gk. *deipnosophistēs* <*deipnon* dinner + *sophistēs* a wise man <*sophia* wisdom] —**deip·nos′o·phism** *n.* —**dep·nos′o·phis′tic** *adj.*

de·ip·o·tent (dē·ip′ə·tənt) *adj.* Having divine power. [<L *deus* god + *potens* powerful]

De·i·ra (dē′i·rə) An Anglian kingdom of the sixth century between the Humber and the Tyne; later, a part of Northumbria.

de·ism (dēīz·əm) *n.* **1** The belief in the existence of a personal God, based solely on the testimony of reason and rejecting any supernatural revelation; natural religion. **2** The belief that God created the world and set it in motion, subject to natural laws, but take no interest in it. **3** The belief in a first cause which is not intrinsically perfect or complete, and therefore not a proper object for worship. [<L *deus* a god + -ISM] —**de·is′tic** or **·ti·cal** *adj.* —**de·is′ti·cal·ly** *adv.*

de·ist (dē′ist) *n.* One who subscribes to or professes deism.

de·i·ty (dē′ə·tē) *n. pl.* **·ties** **1** A god, goddess, or divine person. **2** Divine nature or status; godhead; divinity. —**the Deity** God. [<F *déité* <LL *deitas, -tatis* <L *deus* a god]

dē·jà vu (dā·zha vü′) *Psychol.* A distortion of memory in which a new situation or experience is regarded as having happened before: a form of paramnesia. [<F, lit., already seen]

de·ject (di·jekt′) *v.t.* **1** To depress or cast down in spirit. **2** *Obs.* To throw down. —*adj.* Dejected: cast down. [<L, *dejectus*, pp. of *dejicere* <*de*-down + *jacere* throw]

de·jec·ta (di·jek′tə) *n. pl.* Excrements. [<L, neut. pl. of *dejectus*. See DEJECT.]

de·ject·ed (di·jek′tid) *adj.* Having low or depressed spirits; disheartened. —**de·ject′ed·ly** *adv.* —**de·ject′ed·ness** *n.*

de·ject·tion (di·jek′shən) *n.* **1** A state or condition of being dejected; depression. **2** *Med.* **a** Evacuation of the bowels. **b** Excrement.

dé·jeu·ner (dé·zhœ·nā′) *n.* **1** A late breakfast. **2** Luncheon. [<F, breakfast <*dé-* away (<L *de-*) - *jeun* fasting <L *jejunus*]

de ju·re (dē jo͝or′ē) *Latin* By right; rightfully or legally: distinguished from *de facto*.

deka- *combining form* Ten: used in the metric system, as a *dekagram, dekaliter.* Also, before vowels, **dek-**. [Gk. *deka* ten]

dek·a·gram (dek′ə·gram) *n.* A measure of weight equal to 10 grams. See METRIC SYSTEM. Also **dek′a·gramme.**

De Kalb (di kalb′), **Baron Johann,** 1721–80, German major general under Washington in the American Revolution.

dek·a·li·ter (dek′ə·lē′tər) *n.* A measure of capacity equal to 10 liters: also spelled *decaliter*. See METRIC SYSTEM. Also **dek′a·li′tre.**

dek·a·me·ter (dek′ə·mē′tər) *n.* A measure of length equal to 10 meters. See METRIC SYSTEM. Also **dek′a·me′tre.**

dek·are (dek′âr) *n.* In the metric system, 1,000 square meters or 10 ares: also spelled *decare*. See METRIC SYSTEM.

dek·a·stere (dek′ə·stir) *n.* A measure of volume equal to 10 steres. See METRIC SYSTEM.

Dek·ker (dek′ər), **Thomas,** 1572?–1632? English 1572?–1632? English dramatist: also spelled *Decker*.

de Klerk (də·klark′) **Frederik Wilhelm,** 1936–, president of Republic of South Africa (1989–1994).

De·la·croix (də·lä·krwä′), **Ferdinand Victor Eugène,** 1799–1863, French painter.

Del·a·go·a Bay (del′ə·gô′ə) An inlet of the Indian Ocean in the south cost of Mozambique.

de·laine (də·lān′) *n.* A light, untwilled wool, or cotton and wool, dress material. [<F *(mousse-line) de laine* (muslin) of wool]

De la Mare (də lə mâr′, del′ə·mâr), **Walter,** 1973–1956, English poet and novelist.

de·lam·i·nate (dē·lam′ə·nāt) *v.t.* & *v.i.* **·nat·ed, ·nat·ing** To split into thin layers.

de·lam·i·na·tion (dē·lam′ə·nā′shən) *n.* A splitting into layers: said especially of the cells of plant or animal tissue.

De·land (də·land′), **Margaret,** 1857–1945, *née* Margaretta Campbell, U.S. novelist.

de la Roche (də lä rôsh′), **Mazo,** 1885–1961, Canadian novelist.

de·late (di·lāt′) *v.t.* **·lat·ed, ·lat·ing** **1** *Scot.* To bring a charge against; accuse; denounce. **2** To publish or spread abroad. [<L *delatus*, pp. to *deferre* bring down, denounce. See DEFER².] —**de·la′tion** *n.*

de·la·tor (di·lā′tər) *n.* An informer; accuser; spy.

De·la·vigne (də·là·vēn′y′), **Jean François Casimir,** 1793–1843, French poet and dramatist.

Del·a·ware (del′ə·wâr) *n.* A confederacy of Algonquian tribes of North American Indians; the Lenapes: formerly occupying the whole Delaware River valley, now in Oklahoma. —**Del′a·war′e·an** *adj.*

Del·a·ware (del′ə·wâr) *n.* A small, sweet, reddish, hybrid grape. [from *Delaware*]

Del·a·ware (del′ə·wâr) *n.* A Middle Atlantic State of the United States: 1,978 square miles; capital, Dover; entered the Union Dec. 7, 1787, on of the original thirteen States: nickname *Diamond State:* abbr. *Del.*

Delaware Bay An inlet of the Atlantic Ocean between Delaware and New Jersey.

Delaware River A river separating Pennsylvania and Delaware from New York and New Jersey, flowing SE 350 miles to Delaware Bay.

Delaware Water Gap A resort borough in eastern Pennsylvania, in a narrow cut of the same name through the Kittatinny Mountains, through which the Delaware River flows.

De La Warr (del′ə·wâr, *Brit.* ·wər) **Lord,** 1577–1618, Thomas West, English administrator; first colonial governor of Virginia. Also **Del′a·ware.**

de·lay (di·lā′) *v.t.* **1** To put off to a future time; postpone; defer. **2** To cause to be late; detain. —*v.i.* **3** to linger; procrastinate. See synonyms under HINDER, PROCRASTINATE, PROTRACT SUSPEND. —*n.* **1** A putting off; postponement; procrastination. **2** A temporary stoppage or stay; also, a loitering or lingering. See synonyms under RESPITE [<OF *delaier*] —**de·lay′er** *n.*

de·layed-ac·tion di·lād′ak′shən *adj.* Designating a kind of bomb, fuze, or mine designed to explode at a set time after it has been armed or put into action

Del·cas·sé (del·kà·sā′), **Théophile,** 1852–1923, French statesman.

de·le (dē′lē) *v.t.* **de·led, de·le·ing** *Printing* To take out; delete: usually an imperative represented by a sign. (   ) Compare STET. [<L, imperative of *delere* erase]

del·e·ble (del′ə·bəl) *adj.* Capable of being erased. Also **del′i·ble.**

de·lec·ta·ble (di·lek′tə·bəl) *adj.* Giving pleasure; delightful; charming. see synonyms under LOVELY. [<OF <L *delectabilis* <*delectare*. See DELIGHT.] —**de·lec′ta·ble·ness** *n.* —**de·lec′·ta·bly** *adv.*

Delectable Mountains In Bunyan's *Pilgrim's Progress*, the mountains from which the Celestial City is seen.

de·lec·tate (di·lek′tāt) *v.t.* **·tat·ed, ·tat·ing** To charm; delight. [<L *delectatus*, pp. of *delectare*. See DELIGHT.]

de·lec·ta·tion (dē′lek·tā′shən) *n.* **1** Delight; enjoyment. **2** Amusement; entertainment.

De·led·da (dā·led′dä), **Grazia,** 1879–1936, Italian novelist.

de·leer·it (də·lir′it) *adj. Scot.* Delirious; demented. Also **de·lier′et.**

del·e·ga·cy (del′ə·gə·sē) *n. pl.* **·cies** **1** The action or system of delegating; authority given to act as a delegate. **2** A body of delegates. **3** The condition of being delegated.

del·e·gant (del′ə·gənt) *n.* **1** One that delegates. **2** One that assigns a debt due him to a creditor.

del·e·gate (del′ə·gāt, ·git) *n* **1** A person appointed and sent by another, with power to transact business as his representative; deputy; representative, commissioner. **2** *U.S.* A person elected or appointed to represent a Territory in the House of Representatives where he has the right to participate in debates, but not to vote. **3** A member of the House of Delegates. Compare BURGESS. **4** A person sent as a representative to a convention of any kind, take part in the transaction of business. —**walking delegate** A member of a trade union, commissioned to visit other labor organizations and to secure the united action of employees in the advancement of common interests. —*v.t.* (-gāt) **·gat·ed, ·gat·ing** **1** To send as a representative, with authority to act; depute. **2** To commit or entrust (powers, authority, etc.) to another as an agent or representative. **3** To assign (a debtor) to one's creditor to satisfy a claim. —*adj.* (-gāt, -git) Sent as a deputy. [<L *delegatus*, pp. of *delegare* <*de-* down + *legare* send]

Synonyms (noun): deputy, legate, proxy, representative, substitute. These words agree in designating one who acts in the place of some other or others. The *legate* is an ecclesiastical officer representing the pope. In strict usage the *deputy* or *delegate* is more limited in functions and more closely bound by instructions than a *representative*. A single officer may have a *deputy:* many persons combine to choose a *delegate* or *representative*. In the United States informal assemblies send *delegates* to nominating conventions with no legislative authority; *representatives* are legally elected to Congress and the various lawmaking assemblies.

del·e·ga·tion (del′ə·gā′shən) *n.* **1** the act of delegating: a *delegation* of powers or authority. **2** A person or persons appointed to act for another or others; delegates collectively.

del·len·da est Car·tha·go (di·len′də est kär·thā′gō) *Latin* Carthage must be destroyed: a saying ascribed to Cato the Elder.

de·lete (di·lēt′) *v.t.* **·let·ed, ·let·ing** To blot out; erase, cancel; dele. [L *deletus*, pp. of *delere* erase, destroy]

del·e·te·ri·ous (del′ə·tir′ē·əs) *adj.* Causing moral or physical injury; hurtful; pernicious. See synonyms under BAD, NOISOME. [<NL *deleterius* <GK. *dēlētērios* harmful <*deleesthai* hurt] —**del′e·te′ri·ous·ly** *adv.* —**del′e·te′ri·our·ness** *n.*

de·le·tion (di·lē′shən) *n.* The act of deleting; erasure; also, matter erased or canceled.

delft (delft) *n.* **1** A colored glazed earthenware. made first a Delft about 1310. **2** Any tableware resembling this. Also **delf** (delf), delft′ ware′. [from DELFT]

Delft (delft) A town in western Netherlands.

Del·ga·do (del·gä′dō), **Cape** A headland of northernmost Mozambique.

Del·hi (del′ē) **1** A Union Territory of NE central India containing New Delhi; 578 square miles. **2** Its capital: formerly capital of India (1912–31): also **Old Delhi**. See NEW DELHI.

del·i (del′ē) *n. pl.* **del·is** *U.S. Colloq.* A delicatessen.

Del·ia (dēl′yə) A feminine personal name. [Gk. *Dēlia*, fem. of *Dēlios* of Delos] —**Delia** A name of Artemis.

De·li·an (dē′lē·ən) *adj.* Of or pertaining to Delos. —*n.* A native or inhabitant of Delos.

de·lib·er·ate (di·lib′ə·rāt) *v.* **·t·ed, ·at·ing** *v.i.* **1** To think or consider carefully and at length. **2** To consider reasons or arguments for and against something so as to reach a conclusion or decision. **3** To pause to think. —*v.t.* **4** To think about or consider carefully; weigh. —*adj.* (di·lib′ər·it) **1** Acting with deliberation; carefully thought out; not hasty. **2** Done after deliberation; intentional. [<L *deliberatus*, pp. of *deliberare* <*de-* completely + *librare* weigh <*libra* a scale] —**de·lib′er·ate·ly** *adv.* —**de·lib′er·ate·ness** *n.*

Synonyms (verb): confer, consider, consult, debate, meditate, ponder, reflect, weigh. An individual *considers, meditates, ponders, reflects* by himself. *Consult* and *confer* always imply two or more persons, as does *debate*, except in rare reflexive use. *Deliberate,* which can be applied to a single individual, is also

the word for a great number, while *consult* is ordinarily limited to a few; a committee *consults*; an assembly *deliberates. Deliberating* always carries the idea of slowness; a *consultation* may be hasty. We *consider* or *deliberate* with a view to action; *meditation* may be purposeless. See CONSIDER, CONSULT, MUSE.

de·lib·er·a·tion (di·lib′ə·rā′shən) *n.* **1** The act of deliberating. **2** Thoughtfulness and care in deciding or acting. **3** Forethought or intention. See synonyms under REFLECTION, THOUGHT[1].

de·lib·er·a·tive (di·lib′ə·rā′tiv) *adj.* **1** Pertaining to or of the nature of deliberation. **2** Characterized by or existing for deliberation. — **de·lib′er·a′tive·ly** *adv.* — **de·lib′er·a′tive·ness** *n.*

De·libes (də·lēb′), **Léo,** 1836–91, French composer.

del·i·ca·cy (del′ə·kə·sē) *n. pl.* **·cies** **1** The quality or state of being delicate; fineness; daintiness. **2** Sensitiveness of touch or perception. **3** Fragility; frailty. **4** A luxury; dainty. **5** Need of careful treatment; subtlety; nicety. **6** Refinement of feeling; fastidiousness; consideration for others. **7** *Obs.* Voluptuousness; luxuriousness.

del·i·cate (del′ə·kit) *adj.* **1** Fine and light, as in texture or color. **2** Daintily pleasing; delightful. **3** Nicely constructed or adjusted; accurate; sensitive, as an instrument. **4** Easily injured; tender; frail; fragile. **5** Requiring cautious or subtle treatment. **6** Refined and considerate. **7** Pure; chaste. **8** Fastidious; dainty. **9** Nice in discrimination; sensitive. **10** *Obs.* Voluptuous; luxurious. See synonyms under FINE, FRAGILE. — *n. Obs.* **1** A delicacy; luxury. **2** An effeminate or luxurious person. [<L *delicatus* pleasing] — **del′i·cate·ly** *adv.* — **del′i·cate·ness** *n.*

del·i·ca·tes·sen (del′ə·kə·tes′ən) *n. pl.* **1** Cooked or preserved foods; cooked meats, canned goods, salads, cheeses, pickles, etc.: often construed as singular. **2** A store that sells such foods. [<G, pl. of *delicatesse* dainty food]

de·li·cious (di·lish′əs) *adj.* Extremely pleasant or enjoyable; affording great pleasure, especially to the taste. [<OF <LL *deliciosus* < *delicia* a delight] — **de·li′cious·ly** *adv.* — **de·li′cious·ness** *n.*

Synonyms: dainty, delightful, exquisite, luscious, savory. That is *delicious* which affords a gratification at once vivid and delicate to the senses, especially to those of taste and smell; as, *delicious* fruit; a *delicious* odor; *luscious* has a kindred but more fulsome meaning, inclining toward a cloying excess of sweetness or richness. *Savory* is applied chiefly to cooked food made palatable by spices and condiments. *Delightful* may be applied to the higher gratifications of sense, as *delightful* music, but is chiefly used for that which is mental and spiritual. *Delicious* has a limited use in this way; as, a *delicious* bit of poetry; the word is sometimes used ironically for some pleasing absurdity; as, this is *delicious.* Compare DELIGHTFUL. *Antonyms*: acrid, bitter, nauseous, unpalatable, unsavory.

De·li·cious (di·lish′əs) *n.* A cultivated North American variety of red apple, esteemed for its sweet flavor.

de·lict (di·likt′) *n.* In civil and Scots law, an offense; a misdemeanor: corresponds to *tort* in English and French law. [<L *delictum* < *delinquere.* See DELINQUENT.]

del·i·ga·tion (del′ə·gā′shən) *n.* **1** The act of binding or bandaging. **2** The application of ligatures. [<L *deligatus,* pp. of *deligare* < *de-* completely + *ligare* bind]

de·light (di·līt′) *n.* **1** Great pleasure; gratification; joyful satisfaction. **2** That which affords extreme enjoyment. **3** The quality of delighting; charm. See synonyms under ENTERTAINMENT, HAPPINESS. — *v.i.* **1** To take great pleasure; rejoice: with *in* or the infinitive. **2** To give great enjoyment. — *v.t.* **3** To please or gratify highly. See synonyms under CHARM, ENTERTAIN, RAPTURE, RAVISH, REJOICE. [<OF *delit* < *deliter* <L *delectare,* freq. of *delicere* < *de-* away + *lacere* entice]

de·light·ed (di·lī′tid) *adj.* **1** Highly pleased; joyfully gratified. **2** *Obs.* Affording delight; charming. See synonyms under HAPPY. — **de·light′ed·ly** *adv.*

de·light·ful (di·līt′fəl) *adj.* Affording delight; extremely gratifying; charming. — **de·light′ful·ly** *adv.* — **de·light′ful·ness** *n.*

Synonyms: acceptable, agreeable, congenial, delicious, grateful, gratifying, pleasant, pleasing, pleasurable, refreshing, satisfying, welcome. *Agreeable* refers to whatever gives a mild degree of pleasure; as, an *agreeable* perfume. *Acceptable* indicates a thing worthy of acceptance; as, an *acceptable* offer. *Grateful* is stronger than *agreeable* or *gratifying,* indicating whatever awakens a feeling akin to gratitude. A *pleasant* face and *pleasing* manners arouse *pleasurable* sensations, and make the possessor an *agreeable* companion; if possessed of intelligence, vivacity, and goodness, such a person's society will be *delightful* and *congenial. Satisfying* denotes anything that is received with acquiescence, as substantial food, or established truth. That is *welcome* which is received with heartiness; as, *welcome* tidings. See BEAUTIFUL, CHARMING, DELICIOUS, GRATEFUL, HAPPY, LOVELY. *Antonyms*: depressing, disappointing, distressing, hateful, horrible, melancholy, miserable, mournful, painful, saddening, woeful, wretched.

de·light·some (di·līt′səm) *adj.* Delightful. — **de·light′some·ly** *adv.* — **de·light′some·ness** *n.*

De·li·lah (di·lī′lə) **1** A Philistine woman, the mistress of Samson, who betrayed him to the Philistines by cutting off his hair while he was asleep, thus depriving him of his strength. *Judges* xvi 4–20. **2** A temptress.

de·lim·it (di·lim′it) *v.t.* To prescribe the limits of; bound. Also **de·lim′i·tate.** [<F *délimiter* <L *delimitare* < *de-* completely + *limitare* bound < *limes* a boundary] — **de·lim′i·ta′tion** *n.* — **de·lim′i·ta′tive** *adj.*

de·lin·e·ate (di·lin′ē·āt) *v.t.* **·at·ed, ·at·ing** **1** To draw in outline; trace out. **2** To portray pictorially. **3** To describe verbally. See synonyms under CIRCUMSCRIBE. [<L *delineatus,* pp. of *delineare* < *de-* completely + *lineare* draw a line < *linea* a line] — **de·lin′e·a′tive** *adj.*

de·lin·e·a·tion (di·lin′ē·ā′shən) *n.* **1** The act or art of delineating. **2** A representation either by word or pictorial image. Also **de·lin·e·a·ment** (di·lin′ē·ə·mənt), **de·lin′e·a·ture** (-chŏŏr). See synonyms under PICTURE, SKETCH.

de·lin·e·a·tor (di·lin′ē·ā′tər) *n.* **1** One who sketches or delineates. **2** A tailor's expansible pattern for cutting garments of various sizes.

de·lin·quen·cy (di·ling′kwən·sē) *n. pl.* **·cies** **1** Neglect of duty; failure to do what is required. **2** A fault; offense; misdemeanor. See synonyms under OFFENSE, SIN.

de·lin·quent (di·ling′kwənt) *adj.* **1** Neglectful of or failing in duty or obligation; faulty. **2** Due and unpaid, as taxes. — *n.* One who fails to perform a duty or who commits a fault. [<L *delinquens, -entis,* pp. of *delinquere* < *de-* down, away + *linquere* leave] — **de·lin′quent·ly** *adv.*

del·i·quesce (del′ə·kwes′) *v.i.* **·quesced, ·quesc·ing** **1** To become liquid by absorption of moisture from the air, as certain salts. **2** To melt or pass away gradually. **3** *Bot.* **a** To become lost by repeated branching, as stems. **b** To become fluid, as a ripe agaric. [<L *deliquescere* < *de-* completely + *liquescere* melt]

del·i·ques·cence (del′ə·kwes′əns) *n.* **1** The act or process of deliquescing. **2** The condition of being deliquescent; also, the resultant liquid.

del·i·ques·cent (del′ə·kwes′ənt) *adj.* **1** Liquefying in the air. **2** *Bot.* **a** Dividing; ramifying; forming many small branches, as an elm tree. **b** Becoming liquid at maturity, as certain mushrooms.

de·liq·ui·um (di·lik′wē·əm) *n.* **1** *Rare* A fainting spell. **2** A softened, impaired, and weakened condition of mind. [<L < *delinquere.* See DELINQUENT.]

del·i·ra·tion (del′ə·rā′shən) *n.* Delirium; irrationality.

de·lir·i·ant (di·lir′ē·ənt) *n.* **1** A poison that induces delirium, as cannabis or hyoscyamine. **2** A delirious person. [<L *delirium* madness + -ANT]

de·lir·i·ous (di·lir′ē·əs) *adj.* Suffering from delirium; light-headed; raving. See synonyms under INSANE. — **de·lir′i·ous·ly** *adv.* — **de·lir′i·ous·ness** *n.*

de·lir·i·um (di·lir′ē·əm) *n.* **1** A sporadic or temporary mental disturbance associated with fever, intoxication, shock, or injury and marked by restlessness, excitement, hallucinations, and general incoherence. **2** Intense excitement; frenzy; rapture. See synonyms under INSANITY. [<L < *delirare* < *de-* down, away + *lira* a furrow, track]

delirium tre·mens (trē′mənz) A violent form of delirium caused especially by excessive use of alcoholic liquors and narcotic drugs, and characterized by tremblings, acute mental distress, and delusions of the senses. [<NL, trembling delirium]

del·i·tes·cence (del′ə·tes′əns) *n.* **1** *Med.* **a** A sudden subsidence of the symptoms of a disease. **b** The latent period of an infection or a poison. **2** The state of being concealed; retirement; seclusion. Also **del′i·tes′cen·cy.** [<L *delitescens, -entis,* ppr. of *delitescere* < *de-* away + *litescere,* inceptive of *latere* lie hidden] — **del′i·tes′cent** *adj.*

De·li·us (dē′lē·əs, dēl′yəs), **Frederick,** 1863?–1934, English composer.

de·liv·er (di·liv′ər) *v.t.* **1** To hand over; surrender; transfer possession of. **2** To carry and distribute. **3** To utter; give forth in words. **4** To relieve of a child in childbirth; also, to assist in the birth of (a child). **5** To free from restraint, evil, danger, etc.; set free; rescue. **6** To send forth; discharge, as a broadside. **7** To give; strike, as a blow. **8** To throw or pitch, as a ball. — *adj. Obs.* Nimble; active. [<F *délivrer* <LL *deliberare* < *de-* down, away + *liberare* set free < *liber* free] — **de·liv′er·a·ble** *adj.* — **deliv′er·er** *n.*

Synonyms (verb): discharge, emancipate, free, liberate, ransom, redeem, rescue, save. See GIVE, RELEASE. *Antonyms*: betray, capture, confine, enslave, imprison, incarcerate.

de·liv·er·ance (di·liv′ər·əns) *n.* **1** The act of delivering or state of being delivered; rescue; release. **2** An expression of opinion; utterance. **3** *Obs.* Parturition.

de·liv·er·y (di·liv′ər·ē) *n. pl.* **·er·ies** **1** The act of delivering; liberation; release; transference; surrender. **2** Parturition. **3** Mode of utterance, as in public speaking or singing. **4** Mode of projecting or discharging. **5** That which is or has been delivered: a mail *delivery.*

de·liv·er·y·man (di·liv′ər·ē·mən) *n. pl.* **·men** (-mən) A man who delivers parcels, bulky articles, or the like.

dell (del) *n.* A small, secluded valley; glen; dale. [OE. Akin to DALE.]

Del·la-Crus·can (del′ə·krus′kən) *adj.* Relating to or resembling the Accademia della Crusca (literally, the Academy of Chaff, from its object of sifting or purifying the Italian language) established at Florence in 1582. — *n.* **1** A member of the Accademia della Crusca. **2** Any of the Della-Cruscan school of 18th century English poets living in Florence, whose affected style and extravagant praises of each other exposed them to public ridicule.

dells (delz) See DALLES.

Del·mar·va Peninsula (del·mär′və) A peninsula between Chesapeake and Delaware Bays, including Delaware and parts of Maryland and Virginia.

de·lo·cal·ize (dē·lō′kəl·īz) *v.t.* **·ized, ·iz·ing** To remove from place or free from local relations; enlarge the scope of; broaden. — **de·lo′cal·i·za′tion** *n.*

De Long (də lông), **George Washington,** 1844–81, U.S. arctic explorer.

De·lorme (də·lôrm′), **Marion,** 1612?–50, French courtesan: also spelled **de Lorme.** — **Philibert,** 1518?–70, French architect: also spelled **de l'Orme.**

De·los (dē′los) The smallest island of the Cyclades, Greece; traditionally regarded as the birthplace of Apollo and Artemis. *Modern Greek* **Dhí·los** (thē′lôs). — **De′li·an** *adj.* & *n.*

de·louse (dē·lous′) *v.t.* **·loused, ·lous·ing** To remove lice or other insect vermin from.

Del·phi (del′fī) An ancient city in Phocis, Greece; famous for its oracle of Apollo. Also **Del′fi.** —**Del·phi·an** (del′fē·ən) *adj.* & *n.*

Del·phic (del′fik) *adj.* **1** Relating to Delphi or to Apollo's oracle there. **2** Oracular; ambiguous.

Delphic oracle The oracle of Apollo at Delphi: the sayings of its priestess, the Pythia, were enigmatic and ambiguous.

del·phin (del′fin) *adj.* Of or pertaining to a dolphin or to a family of cetaceans *(Delphinidae),* including dolphins, porpoises, etc. —*n.* **1** *Obs.* A dolphin. **2** A neutral fat contained in the oil of certain dolphins. [< L *delphinus* < Gk. *delphis, delphinos* dolphin]

Del·phin (del′fin) *adj.* Pertaining to the Dauphins of France: The *Delphin* classics were prepared for the use of the son of Louis XIV.

del·phin·ic (del·fin′ik) *adj.* **1** Of, pertaining to, or derived from a dolphin. **2** Of, pertaining to, or derived from the larkspur *(Delphinium).*

del·phi·nine (del′fə·nēn, -nin) *n.* A poisonous crystalline alkaloid, $C_{34}H_{47}NO_9$, found in the seeds of stavesacre: used in medicine. Also **del′phi·nin** (-nin). [< DELPHIN(IUM) + -INE[2]]

del·phin·i·um (del·fin′ē·əm) *n.* Any of a genus *(Delphinium)* of perennial plants of the crowfoot family, having large, spurred flowers, usually blue; the larkspur. [< NL < Gk. *delphinion* larkspur, dim. of *delphis* dolphin; so called from the shape of the nectary]

Del·phi·nus (del·fī′nəs) The Dolphin: a northern constellation. See CONSTELLATION.

Del·sarte system (del·särt′) A system of exercises for the development of bodily grace, voice, and dramatic expression. [after François Alexandre *Delsarte,* 1811–71, French singer and elocutionist]

del·ta (del′tə) *n.* **1** The fourth letter in the Greek alphabet (Δ, δ): corresponding to English *d.* As a numeral it denotes 4. **2** *Geog.* An alluvial, typically triangular-shaped, silt deposit at or in the mouth of a river. **3** Anything triangular. —**del·ta·ic** (del·tā′ik) *adj.*

delta rays *Physics* The fringe of secondary ionization along tracks formed by the impact of primary cosmic rays upon heavy atomic nuclei.

delta wing A triangular, swept-back aircraft wing that provides speed and lift.

del·ti·ol·o·gy (del′tē·ol′ə·jē) *n.* The collecting of postcards as a hobby. [< Gk. *deltion,* dim. of *deltos* writing tablet + -LOGY]

del·toid (del′toid) *n.* **1** *Anat.* A triangular muscle of the shoulder and upper arm. **2** *Geom.* A quadrilateral formed by two unequal isosceles triangles set base to base. —*adj.* **1** Shaped like a delta; triangular. **2** Of or pertaining to the deltoid. [< Gk. *deltoeidēs* triangular < *delta* the letter Δ + *eidos* form]

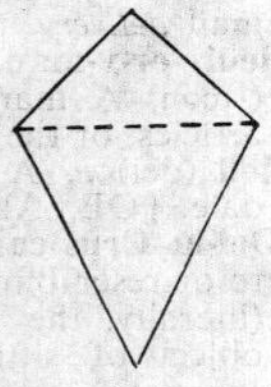
DELTOID

de·lude (di·lōōd′) *v.t.* **·lud·ed, ·lud·ing 1** To mislead the mind or judgment of; beguile; deceive. **2** *Obs.* To evade; elude. **3** *Obs.* To frustrate. See synonyms under DECEIVE. [< L *deludere* < *de-* down, away + *ludere* play] —**de·lud′er** *n.* —**de·lud′ing·ly** *adv.*

del·uge (del′yōōj) *v.t.* **·uged, ·ug·ing** To flood with water; inundate; submerge. **2** To overwhelm; destroy. [< *n.*] —*n.* **1** A great flood; inundation. **2** Anything that comes like a flood. —**the Deluge** The flood in the time of Noah. *Gen.* vii. [< F *déluge* < L *diluvium* < *diluere* wash away < *dis-* away + *luere* wash]

de·lu·sion (di·lōō′zhən) *n.* **1** The state of being deluded; a false belief, especially when persistent. **2** The act of deluding; deception. **3** The error thus conveyed or believed. **4** *Psychiatry* False belief about the self, often present in paranoia and dementia precox. [< L *delusio, -onis* < *deludere.* See DELUDE.]

Synonyms: error, fallacy, fantasm, hallucination, illusion. A *delusion* is a mistaken conviction, an *illusion* a mistaken perception or inference. An *illusion* may be wholly of the senses; a *delusion* always involves some mental error. We speak of the *illusions* of fancy or of hope, but of the *delusions* of the insane. A *hallucination* is a false image or belief which has nothing, outside of the disordered mind, to suggest it; as, the *hallucinations* of delirium tremens. Compare DECEPTION. *Antonyms*: actuality, certainty, fact, reality, truth, verity.

de·lu·sion·al (di·lōō′zhən·əl) *adj.* Consisting of, marked by, or subject to, delusions.

de·lu·sive (di·lōō′siv) *adj.* Tending to delude; misleading; deceptive. Also **de·lu·so·ry** (di·lōō′sər·ē). See synonyms under DECEPTIVE, VAIN. —**de·lu′sive·ly** *adv.* —**de·lu′sive·ness** *n.*

de·lus·ter·ing (dē·lus′tər·ing) *n.* The treatment of synthetic yarns and fabrics by special pigments or other chemicals in order to reduce their natural luster.

de luxe (di lŏŏks′, di luks′; *Fr.* də lüks′) Elaborate and expensive; of superfine quality. [< F, of luxury]

delve (delv) *v.* **delved, delv·ing** *v.i.* **1** To make careful investigation for facts, knowledge, etc.: to *delve* into a crime. **2** To slope down; descend, as a road or hill. **3** *Archaic* & *Dial.* To engage in digging. —*v.t.* **4** *Archaic* & *Dial.* To turn over or dig (ground). —*n.* An excavation; pit; depression in a surface. [OE *delfan*] —**delv′er** *n.*

de·mag·net·ize (dē·mag′nə·tīz) *v.t.* **·ized, ·iz·ing** To deprive (a substance) of magnetism. —**de·mag′net·i·za′tion** *n.* —**de·mag′net·iz′er** *n.*

dem·a·gog (dem′ə·gôg, -gog) *n.* **1** One who leads the populace by pandering to their prejudices and passions; an unprincipled politician. **2** Anciently, any popular leader or orator. Also **dem′a·gogue.** [< Gk. *dēmagōgos* < *dēmos* people + *agein* lead] —**dem′a·gog′ic** (-goj′ik) or **·i·cal** *adj.* —**dem′a·gog′ism** (-gog′iz·əm) or **dem′a·gogu′ism, dem′a·gogu′er·y** (-gog′ər·ē), **dem·a·go·gy** (dem′ə·gō′jē, -gôg′ē, -gog′ē) *n.*

de mal en pis (də mál än pē′) *French* From bad to worse.

de·mand (di·mand′, -mänd′) *v.t.* **1** To ask for boldly or peremptorily; insist upon. **2** To claim as due; ask for authoritatively. **3** To ask to know; inquire formally. **4** To have need for; require. **5** *Law* **a** To summon to court. **b** To make formal claim to (property). —*v.i.* **6** To make a demand. —*n.* **1** The act of demanding, or that which is demanded; requirement; claim; need. **2** A desire to obtain; call. **3** An actionable legal claim; also, that act of requesting payment or performance of what is due. **4** The desire to possess combined with the ability to purchase; also, the totality of such effectual desire in a given market with reference to a given commodity at a certain price. **5** An inquiry. See synonyms under TAX. —**in demand** Desired; sought after. —**on demand** On presentation: a note payable *on demand.* [< F *demander* < L *demandare* < *de-* down, away + *mandare* command; order] —**de·mand′a·ble** *adj.* —**de·mand′er** *n.*

Synonyms (verb): ask, challenge, claim, exact, request, require. *Demand* is a determined and often an arrogant word; one may rightfully *demand* what is his own or his due, when it is withheld or denied; or he may wrongfully *demand* that to which he has no claim but power. *Require* is less arrogant and obtrusive than *demand,* but is exceedingly strenuous; as, the court *requires* the attendance of witnesses. *Request* is milder than *demand* or *require*: a creditor may *demand* or *require* payment; a friend *requests* a favor. We may speak of a humble *request,* but not of a humble *demand.* Compare ASK. *Antonyms*: decline, deny, refuse, reject, repudiate.

de·man·dant (di·man′dənt, -män′-) *n. Law* The plaintiff in a real action; any plaintiff.

demand bill A bill or draft payable on demand.

demand deposit A deposit available to the depositor without advance notice.

demand loan A loan that can be paid, or demanded to be paid, at any time.

demand note A note payable on demand.

de·man·toid (di·man′toid) *n.* An emerald-green garnet. [< G *demant* diamond + -OID]

de·mar·cate (di·mär′kāt, dē′mär·kāt) *v.t.* **·cat·ed, ·cat·ing 1** To mark the bounds or limits of; delimit. **2** To distinguish; discriminate; separate. [Back formation < DEMARCATION]

de·mar·ca·tion (dē′mär·kā′shən) *n.* **1** The fixing of boundaries or limits. **2** Limitation; discrimination. **3** The limit or line fixed. Also **de′mar·ka′tion.** —**Line of Demarcation** The line established, chiefly in modern Brazil, by Pope Alexander VI in 1493 to prevent disputes between Spain and Portugal in regard to their discoveries in the New World. [< Sp. *demarcación* < *demarcar* < *de-* down (< L *de-*) + *marcar* mark a boundary < Gmc.]

De·mar·çay (də·mȧr·sā′), **Eugène,** 1852–1903, French chemist.

de·march (dē′märk) *n.* **1** The chief executive head of an Attic deme. **2** The mayor of a modern Greek town. [< Gk. *dēmarchos* < *dēmos,* district, people + *archein* rule]

dé·marche (dā·mȧrsh′) *n. French* **1** A manner of approach or mode of procedure. **2** In diplomacy, a change in plan of action.

de·ma·te·ri·al·ize (dē′mə·tir′ē·əl·īz′) *v.t.* & *v.i.* **·ized, ·iz·ing** To lose or cause to lose material attributes. —**de′ma·te′ri·al·i·za′tion** *n.*

Dem·a·vend (dem′ə·vend′) A peak, the highest in Iran, of the Elburz Mountains, 18,603 feet.

deme (dēm) *n.* **1** One of the districts into which the ten tribes of Attica were divided by Cleisthenes. **2** A commune. **3** A local group of organisms whose members freely interbreed only within the group. [< Gk. *dēmos*]

de·mean[1] (di·mēn′) *v.t.* **1** To behave; conduct: always used reflexively. **2** *Obs.* To direct; control. —*n. Obs.* Behavior; conduct; bearing. [< OF *demener* < *de-* down (< L *de-*) + *mener* lead < LL *minare* threaten, drive]

de·mean[2] (di·mēn′) *v.t.* To degrade; debase in dignity or reputation. [< DE- + MEAN[2]]

de·mean·or (di·mē′nər) *n.* Behavior; bearing; deportment; mien. Also *Brit.* **de·mean′our.** See synonyms under AIR[1], BEHAVIOR, MANNER.

de·ment (di·ment′) *v.t.* To deprive of mental powers; make insane. [< L *dementare* < *de-* away + *mens, mentis* mind]

de·ment·ed (di·men′tid) *adj.* Deprived of reason; insane. —**de·ment′ed·ly** *adv.* —**de·ment′·ed·ness** *n.*

de·men·tia (di·men′shə, -shē·ə) *n. Psychiatry* Unsoundness of mind resulting from organic or functional disorders, and leading to total loss or serious impairment of the faculty of coherent thought. See synonyms under INSANITY. [< L, madness]

dementia praecox (prē′koks) *Obs.* Schizophrenia.

dementia se·ni·lis (si·nī′lis) Senile dementia.

Dem·e·rar·a (dem′ə·rȧr′ə, -rā′rə) A river in British Guiana, flowing north 200 miles to the Atlantic Ocean.

de·mer·it (di·mer′it) *n.* **1** In schools, a mark for failure or misconduct. **2** Censurable conduct. [< Med. L *demeritum* a fault < L, pp. of *demerere* < *de-* down, away + *merere* deserve]

Dem·e·rol (dem′ə·rōl, -rôl) *n.* Proprietary name for a brand of meperidine hydrochloride.

de·mer·sal (di·mûr′səl) *adj. Ecol.* Found in deep water or on the bottom of streams, pools, or the ocean: said especially of certain fish eggs.

de·mersed (di·mûrst′) *adj. Bot.* Situated or growing under water, as leaves of aquatic plants; submersed. [< obs. *demerse* plunge down < L *demersus,* pp. of *demergere* < *de-* down + *mergere* plunge]

de·mes·mer·ize (dē·mes′mə·rīz, -mez′-) *v.t.* **·ized, ·iz·ing** To release from mesmeric influence; dehypnotize.

de·mesne (di·mān′, -mēn′) *n.* **1** In feudal law, lands held in one's own power, as distinguished from feudal lands which were held (by permission) of a superior. **2** A manor house and the adjoining lands in the immediate use and occupation of the owner of an estate. **3** The grounds appertaining to any residence, or any landed estate. **4** Any region over which sovereignty is exercised; domain. Also **de·main, de·maine** (di·mān′). [< AF *demeyne,* OF *demeine, demaine.* Doublet of DOMAIN.]

De·me·ter (di·mē′tər) In Greek mythology, the goddess of agriculture, marriage, and fertility: identified with the Roman *Ceres.*

De·me·tri·us (di·mē′trē·əs) A masculine personal name. Also *Ital.* **De·me·tri·o** (dā·mā′·trē·ō), *Ger.* **De·me·tri·us** (dā·mā′trē·ōōs), *Fr.* **Dé·mé·tri·us** (dā·mā·trē·üs′), *Russ.* **Dmi·tri** (dmē′trē). [< Gk., of Demeter]

demi- *prefix* **1** Half; intermediate: *demitint, demilune.* **2** Inferior or less in size, quality, etc.; partial: *demigod.* [< F *demi* < L *dimidius* half < *dis-* from, apart + *medius* middle]

dem·i·god (dem′ē·god′) *n.* **1** An inferior or lesser deity; a hero, supposed to be the offspring of a god and a mortal. **2** A man with the attributes of a god. — **dem′i·god′dess** *n. fem.*

dem·i·john (dem′ē·jon′) *n.* A large, juglike glass or crockery vessel enclosed in wickerwork. [<F *dame-jeanne*, lit., Lady Jane]

de·mil·i·ta·rize (dē·mil′ə·tə·rīz′) *v.t.* **·rized**, **·riz·ing** **1** To remove the military form of; free from militarism. **2** To transfer from military to civilian control. **3** To remove military equipment and troops from and declare neutral, as an area or zone. — **de·mil′i·ta·ri·za′tion** *n.*

De Mille (də mil′), **Cecil B(lount)**, 1881–1959, U.S. motion-picture producer.

dem·i·lune (dem′ē·lōōn′) *n.* **1** The moon in its first or last quarter. **2** A crescent. **3** A crescent-shaped outwork, having two faces and two small flanks, covering the shoulders and curtain of the bastion. [<F *demi* half + *lune* moon]

dem·i·mon·daine (dem′ē·mon·dān′) *n.* A woman of the demimonde. [<F]

dem·i·monde (dem′ē·mond, dem′ē·mond′) *n.* The class of women who have lost social position and repute as a result of equivocal or scandalous behavior. [<F <*demi-* half, partial + *monde* world; coined by A. Dumas *fils*]

dem·i·pique (dem′ē·pēk) *n. Obs.* A saddle with a pommel half the height of a military saddle. [<DEMI- + PEAK; infl. in form by F *pique* pike]

dem·i·qua·ver (dem′ē·kwā′vər) *n. Music* A sixteenth note; semiquaver.

dem·i·re·lief (dem′ē·ri·lēf′) *n.* Mezzo-relievo. *Italian* de·mi·ri·lie·vo (dām′ē·rē·lyä′vō).

dem·i·rep (dem′ē·rep) *n.* A woman of questionable chastity. [<DEMI- + REP(UTATION)]

de·mise (di·mīz′) *n.* **1** Death; decease. **2** *Law* **a** Decease involving as a result the transfer of an estate. **b** A transfer or conveyance of rights or estate. **3** The immediate transfer of a sovereign's rights at his death or abdication to his successor. — *v.* **·mised**, **·mis·ing** *v.t.* **1** To bestow by will; bequeath: said especially of sovereignty on the death or abdication of a king, etc. **2** *Law* To lease (an estate) for life or for a term of years. — *v.i.* **3** To pass by will or inheritance. [<OF, fem. of *demis*, pp. of *demettre* send away <L *demittere*. See DEMIT.] — **de·mis′a·ble** *adj.*

dem·i·sem·i (dem′ē·sem′ē) *adj.* Half-half; quarter.

dem·i·sem·i·qua·ver (dem′ē·sem′ē·kwā′vər) *n. Music* A note of the value of 1/4 of a quaver; a thirty-second note.

de·mis·sion (di·mish′ən) *n.* A giving up or relinquishment, as of an office; resignation. [<L *demissio, -onis* <*demittere*. See DEMIT.]

de·mit (di·mit′) *v.* **·mit·ted**, **·mit·ting** *v.t.* **1** To resign (an office or dignity). **2** *Obs.* To release; dismiss. — *v.i.* **3** To resign. — *n.* A letter of dismissal or one attesting honorable resignation; a recommendation. [<L *demittere* <*de-* down, away + *mittere* send]

dem·i·tasse (dem′ē·tas′, -täs′) *n.* **1** A small cup in which after-dinner coffee is served; literally, a half cup. **2** The coffee served in such a cup. [<F]

dem·i·tint (dem′ē·tint′) *n.* **1** A half-tint; a tint intermediate between the extremes of dark and light coloring in a painting. **2** Broken tints or tertiary shades of color. **3** The portion of a work of art so tinted.

dem·i·urge (dem′ē·ûrj) *n.* **1** In Plato's philosophy, the creator of the material universe. **2** In the Gnostic systems, Jehovah as an emanation of the Supreme Being; creator of the material world: sometimes also regarded as the creator of evil. **3** One of a class of public officers or magistrates in several ancient Peloponnesian states. Also **dem′i·ur′gus** (-ûr′gəs), **dem′i·ur′gos**. [<Gk. *demiourgos* skilled or public worker <*demos* people + *ergein* work] — **dem′i·ur′geous** (-jəs), **dem′i·ur′gic**, **dem′i·ur′gi·cal** *adj.*

dem·i·volt (dem′ē·vōlt′) *n.* In horseback riding, a movement of the horse, consisting of a half turn with the forelegs raised. Also **dem′i·volte**. [<F *demi-volte* <*demi-* half + *volte* a leap]

dem·i·wolf (dem′ē·wŏŏlf′) *n.* A mongrel, half wolf and half dog.

de·mob (dē·mob′) *v.t.* **·mobbed**, **·mob·bing** *Brit. Slang* To demobilize.

de·mo·bil·ize (dē·mō′bəl·īz′) *v.t.* **·ized**, **·iz·ing** **1** To disband, as troops that have been mobilized. **2** To change, as an army, from a war to a peacetime basis. — **de·mo′bil·i·za′tion** *n.*

de·moc·ra·cy (di·mok′rə·sē) *n. pl.* **·cies** **1** A theory of government which, in its purest form, holds that the state should be controlled by all the people, each sharing equally in privileges, duties, and responsibilities and each participating in person in the government, as in the city-states of ancient Greece. In practice, control is vested in elective officers as representatives who may be upheld or removed by the people. **2** A government so conducted; a state so governed; the mass of the people. **3** Political, legal, or social equality. [<F *démocratie* <Med. L *democratia* <Gk. *dēmokratia* <*dēmos* people + *kratein* rule]

De·moc·ra·cy (di·mok′rə·sē) *n.* The principles of the Democratic party; also, the party, or its members collectively.

dem·o·crat (dem′ə·krat) *n.* **1** One who favors a democracy. **2** One who believes in political and social equality.

Dem·o·crat (dem′ə·krat) *n.* A member of the Democratic party in the United States.

dem·o·crat·ic (dem′ə·krat′ik) *adj.* **1** Of or pertaining to democracy or a democracy; characterized by the fact, spirit, or principles of popular government. **2** Pertaining to or characteristic of any democratic party. **3** Tending to level social distinctions; practicing social equality; not snobbish. — **dem′o·crat′i·cal·ly** *adv.*

Democratic party One of the two major political parties in the United States, dating from 1828.

de·moc·ra·tize (di·mok′rə·tīz) *v.t. & v.i.* **·tized**, **·tiz·ing** To make or become democratic. — **de·moc′ra·ti·za′tion** *n.*

De·moc·ri·tus (di·mok′rə·təs) 460?–352? B.C., Greek philosopher; propounded the theory that all substance is composed of moving atoms. — **De·moc·ri·te·an** (di·mok′rə·tē′ən), **Dem·o·crit·i·cal** (dem′ə·krit′i·kəl) *adj.*

dé·mo·dé (dā·mô·dā′) *adj. French* Old-fashioned; outmoded; out of style.

de·mod·ed (dē·mō′did) *adj.* Out of fashion.

de·mod·u·late (dē·moj′ŏŏ·lāt) *v.t.* **·lat·ed**, **·lat·ing** *Electronics* To detect. — **de·mod′u·la′tion** *n.*

De·mo·gor·gon (dē′mə·gôr′gən, dem′ə-) The genius of the earth or underworld: regarded by later classical and medieval writers as a mysterious and dreaded infernal deity or magician.

de·mog·ra·phy (di·mog′rə·fē) *n.* The study of vital and social statistics in their application to ethnology, anthropology, and public health. [<Gk. *dēmos* people + -GRAPHY] — **de·mog′ra·pher**, **de·mog′ra·phist** *n.* — **dem·o·graph·ic** (dem′ə·graf′ik) or **·i·cal** *adj.* — **dem′o·graph′i·cal·ly** *adv.*

dem·oi·selle (dem′·wä·zel′) *n.* **1** An unmarried woman; a damsel. **2** An Old World crane (Numidian crane, family *Gruidae*) of graceful form and carriage. **3** A dragonfly (family *Agriidae*). [<F, var. of *damoiselle* <OF *dameisele*. See DAMSEL.]

DEMOISELLE
(About 4 feet erect)

de·mol·ish (di·mol′ish) *v.t.* **1** To tear down; raze, as a building. **2** To destroy utterly; ruin; lay waste to. [<F *démoliss-*, stem of *démolir* <L *demoliri* <*de-* down + *moliri* build <*moles* heap, mass] — **de·mol′ish·er** *n.* *Synonyms:* destroy, overthrow, overturn, raze, ruin. A building, monument, or other structure is *demolished* when reduced to a shapeless mass; it is *razed* when level with the ground; it is *destroyed* when its structural unity is gone, whether or not its component

parts remain. An edifice is *destroyed* by fire or earthquake; it is *demolished* by bombardment; it is *ruined* when, by violence or neglect, it has become unfit for human habitation. Compare ABOLISH, BREAK. *Antonyms:* build, construct, create, make, repair, restore.

dem·o·li·tion (dem′ə·lish′ən) *n.* The act or result of demolishing; destruction. Also **de·mol′ish·ment.** — **dem·o·li′tion·ist** *n.*

demolition bomb See under BOMB.

de·mon (dē′mən) *n.* **1** An evil spirit; devil. **2** A wicked or cruel person. **3** In ancient Greek religion, a supernatural intelligence; a guardian spirit; genius. **4** A person of great energy, skill, etc. — *adj.* Being or possessed of a demon. Also spelled *daemon, daimon.* [<L *daemon* evil spirit (orig., spirit, god) <Gk. *daimōn*] — **de·mon·i·an** (di·mō′nē·ən), **de·mon·ic** (di·mon′ik) *adj.*

de·mon·a·chize (dē·mon′ə·kīz) *v.t.* **·chized**, **·chiz·ing** To remove monks from. [<DE- + L *monachus* monk]

de·mon·e·ti·za·tion (dē·mon′ə·tə·zā′shən) *n.* The act of demonetizing, or the condition of being demonetized.

de·mon·e·tize (dē·mon′ə·tīz) *v.t.* **·tized**, **·tiz·ing** **1** To deprive (currency) of standard value. **2** To withdraw from use as currency.

de·mo·ni·ac (di·mō′nē·ak) *adj.* **1** Of, like, or befitting a demon or evil spirit; devilish. **2** Influenced or produced by or as by demons; mad; violent; frenzied. Also **de·mo·ni·a·cal** (dē′mə·nī′ə·kəl) — *n.* One possessed of a demon or evil spirit; a lunatic. — **de·mo·ni′·a·cal·ly** *adv.*

de·mon·ism (dē′mən·iz′əm) *n.* Belief in the existence and power of demons. — **de′mon·ist** *n.*

de·mon·ize (dē′mən·īz) *v.t.* **·ized**, **·iz·ing** **1** To make a demon of. **2** To bring under demonic influence.

demono- *combining form* Demon: *demonology.* Also, before vowels, **demon-.** [<Gk. *daimōn* spirit, god]

de·mon·ol·a·try (dē′mən·ol′ə·trē) *n.* The worship of demons. [<DEMONO- + Gk. *latreia* worship] — **de·mon·ol′a·ter** *n.*

de·mon·ol·o·gy (dē′mən·ol′ə·jē) *n.* The study of or belief in demons or demonism. [<DEMONO- + -LOGY] — **de·mon·ol′o·gist** *n.*

de·mon·stra·ble (di·mon′strə·bəl, dem′ən-) *adj.* Capable of being proved. — **de·mon′stra·ble·ness, de·mon′stra·bil′i·ty** *n.* — **de·mon′stra·bly** *adv.*

de·mon·strance (di·mon′strəns) *n.* Demonstration.

de·mon·strant (di·mon′strənt) *n.* One who makes, furthers, or takes part in a public demonstration.

dem·on·strate (dem′ən·strāt) *v.* **·strat·ed**, **·strat·ing** *v.t.* **1** To explain or describe by use of experiments, examples, etc. **2** To explain the operation or use of. **3** To prove or show to be by logic; make evident. **4** To exhibit; make clear, as emotions. — *v.i.* **5** To take part in a public demonstration. **6** To make a show of military force. [<L *demonstratus,* pp. of *demonstrare* <*de-* completely + *monstrare* show, point out]

dem·on·stra·tion (dem′ən·strā′shən) *n.* **1** A pointing out; the act of making known. **2** An exhibition or expression; manifestation. **3** Proof by such evidence of facts, principles, and arguments as precludes denial or reasonable doubt. **4** The exhibition and description of examples in teaching an art or science. **5** A public exhibition of welcome, approval, or condemnation, as by a mass meeting or procession. **6** *Logic* A system of reasoning showing how, from given premises, such as definitions, axioms, postulates, a certain result must follow. **7** A show of military force or of aggressive movement, especially when intended as a feint, or in time of peace as a menace. **8** An exhibition and explanation of the fine points and workability of an article or commodity to be sold. *Synonyms:* certainty, conclusion, consequence, deduction, evidence, induction, inference, proof. *Demonstration,* in the strict and proper sense, is the highest form of *proof* and gives the most absolute *certainty,* but cannot be applied outside of pure mathematics or other strictly deductive reasoning:

there can be *proof* and *certainty,* however, in matters that do not admit of *demonstration.* A *conclusion* is the absolute and necessary result of the admission of certain premises; an *inference* is a probable *conclusion* toward which known facts, statements, or admissions point, but which they do not absolutely establish; sound premises, together with their necessary *conclusion,* constitute a *demonstration. Evidence* is that which tends to show a thing to be true. *Proof* in the strict sense is complete, irresistible *evidence*; as, there was much *evidence* against the accused, but not amounting to *proof* of guilt. Moral *certainty* is a conviction resting on such *evidence* as puts a matter beyond reasonable doubt, while not so irresistible as *demonstration.* Compare CERTAINTY, INDUCTION, INFERENCE, PROOF.

de·mon·stra·tive (di·mon′strə·tiv) *adj.* **1** Having the power of demonstrating or pointing out; convincing and conclusive. **2** Inclined to strong expression of feeling or opinions. **3** *Gram.* Serving to indicate the person or object referred to or intended. —*n.* A demonstrative pronoun. **—de·mon′stra·tive·ly** *adv.* **—de·mon′stra·tive·ness** *n.*

demonstrative pronoun See under PRONOUN.

dem·on·stra·tor (dem′ən·strā′tər) *n.* **1** One who demonstrates. **2** One who exhibits and explains, as in an anatomy class. **3** A salesman who demonstrates the desirability and workability of some article or product to the public. **4** The article used for demonstration, as a vacuum cleaner or automobile. Also **dem′on·strat′er.**

dem·o·pho·bi·a (dem′ə·fō′bē·ə) *n. Psychol.* Morbid fear of crowds; also called *ochlophobia.* [< Gk. *dēmos* people + -PHOBIA] **—dem′o·pho′bic** *adj.*

de·mor·al·ize (di·môr′əl·īz, -mor′-) *v.t.* **·ized, ·iz·ing 1** To corrupt or deprave. **2** To dishearten; undermine discipline among, as troops. **3** To throw into disorder. **—de·mor′al·i·za′tion** *n.* **—de·mor′al·iz′er** *n.*

de mor·tu·is nil ni·si bo·num (dē môr′chōō·is nil nī′sī bō′nəm) *Latin* Of the dead (say) nothing but good.

de·mos (dē′mos) *n.* **1** The people of an ancient Greek state. **2** The common people; the masses. [< Gk. *dēmos*]

De·mos·the·nes (di·mos′thə·nēz), 384?–322 B.C., Athenian orator and patriot.

de·mote (di·mōt′) *v.t.* **·mot·ed, ·mot·ing** To reduce to a lower grade or rank: opposed to *promote.* [< DE- + (PRO)MOTE] **—de·mo′tion** *n.*

de·mot·ic (di·mot′ik) *adj.* **1** Of or pertaining to the people or to the population of a region, country, locality, etc.; popular. **2** Pertaining to the simplified form of the hieratic alphabet of ancient Egypt. [< Gk. *dēmotikos* < *dēmos* people]

de·mot·ics (di·mot′iks) *n.* Sociology in its most inclusive sense.

de·mount (dē·mount′) *v.t.* To remove, as a motor, from its mounting, setting, or place of support.

de·mount·a·ble (dē·moun′tə·bəl) *adj.* That may be easily taken apart, or removed from its position, as an automobile wheel.

demp·ster (demp′stər) *n.* **1** A deemster. **2** In old Scots law, a doomster. Also **dem′ster.** [Var. of DEEMSTER]

de·mul·cent (di·mul′sənt) *adj.* Soothing. —*n. Med.* A soothing application, especially one to relieve irritated mucous membranes. [< L *demulcens, -entis,* ppr. of *demulcere* < *de-* down + *mulcere* soothe]

de·mur (di·mûr′) *v.i.* **murred, ·mur·ring 1** To offer objections; take exception. **2** To delay; hesitate. **3** *Law* To interpose a demurrer. —*n.* **1** A suspension of decision or action; a delay. **2** An objection. **3** *Obs.* A demurrer. [< OF *demeurer* < L *demorari* < *de-* completely + *morari* delay < *mora* a delay] **—de·mur′ra·ble** *adj.*

de·mure (di·myŏŏr′) *adj.* **1** Having a sedate or modest demeanor. **2** Affecting modesty; prim; coy. See synonyms under SERIOUS. [ME *mure* < OF *meur* < L *maturus* mature, discreet] **—de·mure′ly** *adv.* **—de·mure′ness** *n.*

de·mur·rage (di·mûr′ij) *n.* **1** The detention of a vessel or conveyance by a consigner or consignee beyond the specified time. **2** Compensation for such delay. [< OF *demourage* < *demourer* < L *demorare.* See DEMUR.]

de·mur·ral (di·mûr′əl) *n.* Hesitation; delay; demur.

de·mur·rer (di·mûr′ər) *n.* **1** *Law* A pleading that admits the facts stated in the pleading to which it replies, but denies that they are sufficient to constitute a good cause of action or defense in law. **2** Any objection or exception taken. **3** One who demurs.

de·my (di·mī′) *n. pl.* **de·mies 1** A size of paper, in the United States about 16 × 21 inches. **2** A foundation scholar of Magdalen College, Oxford. [< DEMI-]

de·myth·ol·o·gize (dē′mi·thol′ə·jīz) *v.t.* **-gized, -giz·ing** To divest of mythological elements.

den (den) *n.* **1** A cavern occupied by animals; a lair. **2** A low haunt. **3** A room for privacy; sanctum. See synonyms under HOLE. —*v.i.* **denned, den·ning** To dwell in, or as in, a den. [OE *denn*]

de·nar·i·us (di·nâr′ē·əs) *n. pl.* **·nar·i·i** (-nâr′ē·ī) **1** The most important coin of ancient Rome, made of silver and weighing, under Augustus, 1/84 of a pound; the penny of the New Testament. **2** Later, a small copper coin. **3** A gold coin, the **denarius aureus,** worth 25 silver denarii. *Denarius* was the Latin name of the English penny, the initial of which (*d.*) is preserved in monetary notation. [< L *denarius (nummus)* denary (coin); because it was worth ten asses]

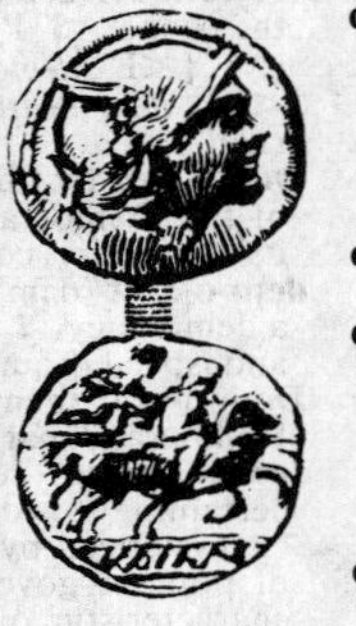

ROMAN DENARIUS

den·a·ry (den′ə·rē, dē′nə-) *adj.* Containing ten; decimal. —*n. pl.* **·ries 1** The number 10. **2** A tithing. [< L *denarius* < *deni* by tens < *decem* ten]

de·na·tion·al·ize (dē·nash′ən·əl·īz′) *v.t.* **·ized, ·iz·ing 1** To deprive of national character, status, or rights. **2** To change the nationality of. **—de·na′tion·al·i·za′tion** *n.*

de·nat·u·ral·ize (dē·nach′ər·əl·īz′) *v.t.* **·ized, ·iz·ing 1** To render unnatural. **2** To deprive of naturalization or citizenship; denationalize. **—de·nat′u·ral·i·za′tion** *n.*

de·na·ture (dē·nā′chər) *v.t.* **·tured, ·tur·ing 1** To alter the natural properties of (a substance) by adding an adulterant. **2** *Biochem.* To modify the molecular structure of (a protein or nucleic acid) by physical or chemical means. Also **de·na′tur·ize. —de·na′tur·ant** *n.* **—de·na′tur·a′tion** *n.*

denatured alcohol Ethyl alcohol made unfit for drinking purposes by the addition of a toxic or distasteful substance.

de·na·zi·fy (dē·nät′sə·fī, -nat′-) *v.t.* **·fied, ·fy·ing** To rid of Nazi influences or of Nazism. **—de·na′zi·fi·ca′tion** *n.*

Den·bigh (den′bē) A county in NE Wales; 669 square miles; capital, Denbigh. Also **Den′bigh·shire** (-shir).

den·dri·form (den′drə·fôrm) *adj.* Like a tree in structure; tree-shaped.

den·drite (den′drīt) *n.* **1** *Mineral.* Any mineral crystallizing in a branching, treelike form; a rock or mineral with treelike markings. **2** *Physiol.* A filamentous, arborescent process of a nerve cell which conducts impulses toward the cell body. [< Gk. *dendritēs* of a tree]

den·drit·ic (den·drit′ik) *adj.* **1** Resembling a tree; dendriform. **2** Of or pertaining to a dendrite. Also **den·drit′i·cal. —den·drit′i·cal·ly** *adv.*

dendro- *combining form* Tree: *dendrochore.* Also, before vowels, **dendr-.** Also **dendri-.** [< Gk. *dendron* tree]

den·dro·chore (den′drə·kôr, -kōr) *n. Ecol.* The region of trees and forests: a major division of the biochore. **—den′dro·chor′ic** *adj.*

den·dro·chro·nol·o·gy (den′drə·krə·nol′ə·jē) *n.* The determination of the approximate dates of past events and of periods of time by a study of the growth rings on trees.

den·droid (den′droid) *adj.* Like a tree; dendritic. Also **den·droi′dal.** [< Gk. *dendroeidēs*]

den·dro·lite (den′drə·līt) *n. Bot.* A petrified or fossil shrub, plant, or part of a plant.

den·drol·o·gy (den·drol′ə·jē) *n.* That branch of botany and forestry that deals with trees. [< DENDRO- + -LOGY] **—den·drol′o·gist** *n.*

den·dron (den′dron) *n. Physiol.* A nerve dendrite. [< Gk., tree]

-dendron *combining form* Tree: *philodendron.* [< Gk. *dendron* tree]

dene (dēn) *n. Brit.* A sandy stretch of land or a low, sandy hill near the sea. [Origin uncertain]

Den·eb (den′eb) A star of the first magnitude; Alpha in the constellation Cygnus.

De·neb·o·la (di·neb′ə·lə) The star Beta in the constellation Leo; magnitude, 2.2.

den·e·gate (den′ə·gāt) *v.t.* **·gat·ed, ·gat·ing** *Obs.* To deny; refuse. [< DE- + NEGATE]

den·e·ga·tion (den′ə·gā′shən) *n.* A denial or refusal.

dene·hole (dēn′hōl′) *n. Archeol.* One of a class of ancient excavations found in the chalk formation of southern England.

den·gue (deng′gē, -gā) *n. Pathol.* An acute, tropical, frequently epidemic virus disease transmitted by the bite of the mosquito *Aëdes aegypti* and characterized by fever, eruptions, and severe pains in the joints: also known as *breakbone fever.* [< Sp., ult. < Swahili]

de·ni·a·ble (di·nī′ə·bəl) *adj.* That can be denied. **—de·ni′a·bly** *adv.*

de·ni·al (di·nī′əl) *n.* **1** The act of denying; declaration that a statement made is untrue; contradiction: opposed to *affirmation.* **2** Refusal to acknowledge or admit; a disowning or disavowal; rejection. **3** Refusal to grant, indulge, or agree; non-compliance, as with something urged.

de·nic·o·tin·ize (dē·nik′ə·tin·īz′) *v.t.* **·ized, ·iz·ing** To remove nicotine from.

de·ni·er[1] (di·nī′ər) *n.* One who makes denial.

den·ier[2] (den′yər, də·nir′ *for def. 1,* də·nir′ *for def. 2; Fr.* də·nyā′) *n.* **1** A unit of rayon or silk yarn size, based on a standard weight of five centigrams per 450 meters of silk. **2** A silver coin, introduced by Pepin the Short in 755, which was for centuries the chief silver coin in Europe. [< F < L *denarius* DENARIUS.]

den·i·grate (den′ə·grāt) *v.t.* **·grat·ed, ·grat·ing 1** To make black; blacken. **2** To slander. [< L *denigratus,* pp. of *denigrare* < *de-* completely + *nigrare* blacken < *niger* black] **—den′i·gra′tion** *n.* **—den′i·gra′tor** *n.* **—den·i·gra·to·ry** (den′ə·grə·tôr′ē, -tō′rē) *adj.*

De·ni·ker (dā·nē·kâr′), **Joseph,** 1852–1918; French anthropologist and ethnographer.

den·im (den′əm) *n.* A twilled cotton used for overalls, uniforms, etc. [< F *(serge) de Nîmes* (serge) of Nîmes, where first made]

Den·is (den′is) A masculine personal name. See DIONYSIUS, its original, uncontracted form. Also **Den′nis,** *Fr.* **De·nis** or **De·nys** (də·nē′).
—**Denis, Saint,** died 280? patron saint of France and first bishop of Paris: also spelled *Denys.*

de·ni·trate (dē·nī′trāt) *v.t.* **·trat·ed, ·trat·ing** *Chem.* To remove nitrogen, nitric or nitrous acid, nitrates, or nitrogen oxide from. **—de′ni·tra′tion** *n.*

de·ni·tri·fy (dē·nī′trə·fī) *v.t.* **·fied, ·fy·ing 1** *Chem.* To remove nitrogen or its compounds from. **2** *Bacteriol.* To reduce (nitrates) to nitrites, nitrogen, or ammonia, as by certain bacteria. Also **de·ni′trize. —de·ni′tri·fi·ca′tion** *n.*

den·i·zen (den′ə·zən) *n.* **1** One who lives in a place; a citizen; inhabitant. **2** *Brit.* An alien who has been admitted to residence and to certain privileges of citizenship. **3** A person, animal, or thing at home in any region, although not a native. —*v.t. Brit.* **1** To admit to the rights of citizenship. **2** To populate with denizens. [< AF *deinzein* < *deinz* inside < L *de intus* from within] **—den′i·zen·a′tion** *n.*

Den·mark (den′märk) A kingdom in NW Europe; 16,575 square miles; capital, Copenhagen. *Danish* **Dan·mark** (dän′märk).

Denmark Strait A channel between Greenland and Iceland, connecting the Atlantic with the Greenland Sea.

de·nom·i·nate (di·nom′ə·nāt) *v.t.* **·nat·ed, ·nat·ing** To give a name to; call: to *denominate* him a thief. —*adj.* (-nit) Made up of units of a designated kind: opposed to *abstract.* [< L *denominatus,* pp. of *denominare* < *de-* down + *nomen* name] **—de·nom′i·na·ble** (-ə·nə·bəl) *adj.*

denominate number See under NUMBER.

de·nom·i·na·tion (di-nom′ə-nā′shən) *n.* **1** The act of naming. **2** A class designation; name; epithet; appellation. **3** A body of Christians having a distinguishing name; sect. **4** A class of arithmetical units of one kind and name. **5** A unit of value: said of money: bills of all *denominations* from $1.00 to $500.00. See synonyms under NAME, SECT. — **de·nom′i·na′tion·al** *adj.* — **de·nom′i·na·tion·al·ism** *n.* — **de·nom′i·na·tion·al·ist** *n.* — **de·nom′i·na·tion·al·ly** *adv.*

de·nom·i·na·tive (di-nom′ə-nā′tiv, -nə·tiv) *adj.* **1** That gives or constitutes a name; appellative. **2** *Gram.* Derived from a noun or adjective. — *n.* **1** That which describes or denominates. **2** *Gram.* A word, especially a verb, derived from a noun or adjective, as the verb *to garden.* — **de·nom′i·na′tive·ly** *adv.*

de·nom·i·na·tor (di-nom′ə-nā′tər) *n.* **1** One who or that which names. **2** *Math.* That term of a fraction below or to the right of the line which expresses the number of equal parts into which the unit is divided; divisor. — **common denominator** Any common multiple of the denominators of a series of fractions.

de·no·ta·tion (dē′nō·tā′shən) *n.* **1** The act of denoting or distinguishing by name; a marking off; designation or separation. **2** The object or objects denoted by a word, as distinguished from the marks or qualities which it suggests: contrasted with *connotation.* **3** That which indicates; a sign. **4** That which is signified; meaning.

de·no·ta·tive (di-nō′tə·tiv, dē′nō·tā′tiv) *adj.* Having power to denote; significant. — **de·no′ta·tive·ly** *adv.*

de·note (di-nōt′) *v.t.* **·not·ed, ·not·ing** **1** To mark; point out or make known. **2** To serve as a symbol for; signify; indicate. **3** To designate; mean: said of words, symbols, etc. See synonyms under IMPORT. [< L *denotare* < *de-* down + *notare* mark] — **de·not′a·ble** *adj.*

dé·noue·ment (dā·nōō·män′) *n.* **1** The final unraveling or solution of the plot of a play, novel, or short story; issue; outcome. **2** The point in the plot where this occurs. **3** Any final issue or solution. See synonyms under CATASTROPHE. [< F < *dénouer* < *dé-* away (< L *dis-*) + *nouer* knot < L *nodare* < *nodus* a knot]

de·nounce (di-nouns′) *v.t.* **·nounced, ·nounc·ing** **1** To attack or condemn openly and vehemently; inveigh against. **2** To inform against; accuse. **3** To threaten, as evil or vengeance; menace. **4** To give formal notice of, specifically, of the termination of a treaty or convention. **5** *Obs.* To announce; foretell. See synonyms under CONDEMN. [< OF *denoncer* < L *denuntiare* < *de-* down + *nuntiare* proclaim, announce] — **de·nounce′ment** *n.* — **de·nounc′er** *n.*

de no·vo (dē nō′vō) *Latin* From the beginning; anew.

dense (dens) *adj.* **dens·er, dens·est** **1** Having its parts crowded closely together; compact in structure; thick; close. **2** Hard to penetrate; obtuse; stupid; dull. **3** *Phot.* Opaque when developed, and consequently strongly contrasted in lights and shades; intense: said of a negative. See synonyms under HARD, IMPENETRABLE. [< L *densus*] — **dense′ly** *adv.* — **dense′ness** *n.*

den·sim·e·ter (den·sim′ə·tər) *n.* A hydrometer. [< L *densus* thick + -METER]

den·si·tom·e·ter (den′sə·tom′ə·tər) *n. Phot.* An apparatus for determining the density of silver deposits on a plate or film. [< DENSITY + -METER]

den·si·ty (den′sə·tē) *n. pl.* **·ties** **1** Compactness; the closeness of any space distribution. **2** *Physics* The mass of a substance per unit of its volume. In the metric system the unit of density is the mass of a cubic centimeter of water at 4°C. **3** *Sociol.* The number of specified units, as persons, families, or dwellings, per acre or square mile. **4** *Electr.* The quantity of current flowing through a given cross–section of a conductor: usually expressed in terms of amperes per square centimeter or square inch: also **current density. 5** *Ecol.* The relative thickness of the vegetative cover in forests, on prairies, etc., scaled

in 10ths with 1 as the maximum growth. [< MF *densité* < L *densitas, -tatis* < *densus* thick]

dent¹ (dent) *n.* A small depression made by striking or pressing; indentation. See synonyms under BLEMISH, HOLE. — *v.t.* To make a dent in. — *v.i.* To become dented. [Var. of DINT]

dent² (dent) *n.* **1** The space between two wires in the reed of a loom. **2** A tooth, as of a comb, gear wheel, etc. [< F < L *dens, dentis* tooth]

den·tal (den′təl) *adj.* **1** Of or pertaining to the teeth. **2** Of or pertaining to dentistry. **3** *Phonet.* Describing a consonant produced with the tip of the tongue against or near the upper front teeth, as French *t* and *d.* The English alveolars (t) and (d) are sometimes, inaccurately, called dentals. — *n. Phonet.* A dental consonant. [< NL *dentalis* < L *dens, dentis* a tooth]

dental floss A strong, silky filament for cleaning between the teeth.

dental plate A denture.

den·tate (den′tāt) *adj.* **1** Having teeth or toothlike processes; toothed. **2** *Bot.* Having a notched edge resembling teeth, as certain leaves. [< L *dentatus* having teeth] — **den′tate·ly** *adv.*

den·ta·tion (den·tā′shən) *n.* **1** A toothed formation or condition. **2** The state or quality of being dentate.

denti– *combining form* Tooth: *dentiform.* Also, before vowels, **dent-**. [< L *dens, dentis* tooth]

den·ti·cle (den′ti·kəl) *n.* **1** A small tooth or toothlike projection. **2** *Dent.* A small, calcified mass in the pulp cavity of a tooth. **3** *Archit.* Dentil. [< L *denticulus,* dim. of *dens, dentis* tooth]

den·tic·u·late (den·tik′yə·lit, -lāt) *adj.* **1** Finely dentate or toothed. **2** *Archit.* Formed into dentils. Also **den·tic′u·lat·ed.** — **den·tic′u·late·ly** *adv.* — **den·tic′u·la′tion** *n.*

den·ti·fi·ca·tion (den′tə·fə·kā′shən) *n.* The formation of teeth. [< DENTI- + L *facere* make]

den·ti·form (den′tə·fôrm) *adj.* Tooth-shaped.

den·ti·frice (den′tə·fris) *n.* A preparation for cleaning the teeth. [< MF < L *dentifricium* < *dens, dentis* tooth + *fricare* rub]

den·til (den′til) *n. Archit.* A small, square projecting block in a cornice: also *denticle.* **2** *Her.* An indentation or notch. Also **den′tel.** [< MF *dentille,* dim. of *dent* a tooth]

DENTILS

den·ti·la·bi·al (den′ti·lā′bē·əl) *adj. & n. Phonet.* Labiodental.

den·ti·lin·gual (den′ti·ling′gwəl) *adj. & n. Phonet.* Interdental.

den·tine (den′tēn, -tin) *n.* The hard calcified substance forming the body of a tooth just beneath the enamel and cementum. Also **den′tin** (-tin). — **den′tin·al** *adj.*

den·ti·phone (den′tə·fōn) *n.* An instrument for hearing sounds by means of vibrations transmitted through the teeth to the auditory nerve. Also **den′ta·phone.**

den·tist (den′tist) *n.* One who practices dentistry. [< F *dentiste* < *dent* a tooth]

den·tist·ry (den′tis·trē) *n.* **1** The branch of medicine which is concerned with the diagnosis, prevention, and treatment of diseases affecting the teeth and their associated structures, including the extraction, filling, and crowning of teeth, the construction of bridges and dentures, and general oral prophylaxis. **2** The work of a dentist.

den·ti·tion (den·tish′ən) *n.* **1** The process or period of cutting teeth; teething. **2** *Biol.* The kind and number of teeth characteristic of an animal, and the manner in which they are arranged in the jaws. [< L *dentitio, -onis* teething < *dentire* cut teeth < *dens, dentis* teeth]

dento– *combining form* Dental. [< L *dens, dentis* tooth]

den·toid (den′toid) *adj.* Like a tooth. [< DENT(I)- + -OID]

D'En·tre·cas·teaux Islands (dän·trə·kás·tō′) A Papuan island group SE of New Guinea; total, 1,200 square miles.

den·ture (den′chər) *n.* **1** The teeth of an animal collectively. **2** A block or set of teeth. **3** *Dent.* A frame of plastic or other material adapted to fit the upper or lower jaw and containing a partial or complete set of artificial teeth. [< F *dent* tooth]

den·ty (den′tē) *adj. Scot.* Dainty: also spelled *dentie.*

de·nu·date (di-nōō′dāt, -nyōō′-, den′yōō·dāt) *adj.* Naked; stripped of foliage or other covering. — **den·u·date** (den′yōō·dāt, di·nōō′. dāt, -nyōō′-) *v.t.* **·dat·ed, ·dat·ing** To denude; lay bare. [< L *denudatus,* pp. of *denudare.* See DENUDE.]

de·nu·da·tion (den′yōō·dā′shən, dē′nōō-, -nyōō-) *n.* **1** The act of denuding or state of being stripped bare. **2** *Geol.* **a** The laying bare of land, especially by erosion. **b** The slow disintegration of rock surfaces by weathering; a wearing down of hills and mountains.

de·nude (di-nōōd′, -nyōōd′) *v.t.* **·nud·ed, ·nud·ing** **1** To strip the covering from; make naked. **2** *Geol.* To wear away or remove overlying matter from, and so expose to view. [< L *denudare* < *de-* down, completely + *nudare* strip < *nudus* bare, naked]

de·nu·mer·a·ble (di-nōō′mər·ə·bəl, -nyōō′-) *adj. Math.* Capable of being put in a one-to-one correspondence with positive integers, as a set of rational numbers. — **de·nu′mer·a·bly** *adv.*

de·nun·ci·ate (di-nun′sē·āt, -shē-) *v.t. & v.i.* **·at·ed, ·at·ing** To denounce. [< L *denuntiatus,* pp. of *denuntiare.* See DENOUNCE.] — **de·nun′ci·a′tor** *n.*

de·nun·ci·a·tion (di-nun′sē·ā′shən, -shē-) *n.* **1** The act of declaring an action or person worthy of reprobation or punishment; arraignment. **2** The declaration of a threatening purpose; the proclamation of impending and deserved evil; a menace. **3** The denouncing of a treaty. **4** *Obs.* A formal announcement; proclamation. See synonyms under OATH, REPROOF. — **de·nun′ci·a·tive** *adj.* — **de·nun′ci·a′tive·ly** *adv.*

de·nun·ci·a·to·ry (di-nun′sē·ə·tôr′ē, -tō′rē, -shē-) *adj.* Containing or bearing denunciation; threatening.

Den·ver (den′vər) The capital of Colorado.

de·ny (di-nī′) *v.t.* **·nied, ·ny·ing** **1** To declare to be untrue; contradict. **2** To reject as false; declare to be unfounded or not real, as a doctrine. **3** To refuse to give; withhold. **4** To refuse (someone) a request. **5** To refuse to acknowledge; disown; repudiate. **6** To refuse access to. **7** *Obs.* To decline; refuse to accept. See synonyms under RENOUNCE. — **to deny oneself** To refuse oneself a gratification. [< OF *denier* < L *denegare* < *de-* completely + *negare* say no, refuse]

de·ob·stru·ent (dē-ob′strōō·ənt) *adj.* Having the power to remove obstructions. — *n.* A medicine for removing obstructions; an aperient. [< NL *deobstruens, -entis* < L *de-* away + *obstruens, -entis,* ppr. of *obstruere.* See OBSTRUCT.]

de·o·dand (dē′ə·dand) *n.* **1** A thing given or forfeited to God. **2** In early English law, any personal chattel that had been immediately instrumental in causing the death of a person, and was therefore forfeited to the crown for pious uses: abolished in 1846. [< LL *deodandum* < L *deus* god + *dandum,* gerundive of *dare* give]

de·o·dar (dē′ə·där) *n.* **1** The East Indian cedar (*Cedrus deodara*), prized for its light–red wood. **2** This wood. [< Hind. < Skt. *devadāru* divine tree]

de·o·dor·ant (dē-ō′dər·ənt) *adj.* Destroying, absorbing, or disguising bad odors. — *n.* A deodorizer; specifically, any cosmetic cream, spray, or powder used to absorb or counteract body odors. [< DE- (def. 4) + L *odorans, -antis,* ppr. of *odorare* have an odor]

de·o·dor·ize (dē-ō′dər·īz) *v.t.* **·ized, ·iz·ing** To modify, destroy, or disguise the odor of. — **de·o′dor·i·za′tion** *n.* — **de·o′dor·iz′er** *n.*

De·o fa·ven·te (dē′ō fə·ven′tē) *Latin* With God's favor.

De·o gra·ti·as (dē′ō grā′shē·əs) *Latin* Thanks to God.

De·o ju·van·te (dē′ō jōō·van′tē) *Latin* With God's help.

de·on·tol·o·gy (dē′on·tol′ə·jē) *n.* The science of moral obligation or duty; ethics. [<Gk. *deon, deontos* necessary, orig. ppr. neut. of *deein* lack, need + -LOGY] —**de·on·to·log·i·cal** (dē·on′tə·loj′i·kəl) *adj.* —**de′on·tol′o·gist** *n.*

De·o vo·len·te (dē′ō vō·len′tē) *Latin* God willing; by God's will.

de·ox·i·dize (dē·ok′sə·dīz) *v.t.* **·dized, ·diz·ing** 1 To remove oxygen from. 2 To reduce from the state of an oxide. Also **de·ox′i·date.** —**de·ox′i·di·za′tion, de·ox′i·da′tion** *n.* —**de·ox′i·diz′er** *n.*

de·ox·y·gen·ate (dē·ok′sə·jə·nāt′) *v.t.* **·at·ed, ·at·ing** To remove oxygen from. Also **de·ox′·y·gen·ize′.** —**de·ox′y·gen·a′tion** *n.*

de·ox·y·ri·bo·nu·cle·ic acid (dē·ok′sē·rī·bō·no͞o·klē′ik, -nyo͞o-) *Biochem.* A nucleic acid of complex molecular structure forming a principal constituent of the genes and known to play an important role in the genetic action of the chromosomes. Abbr. **DNA.**

de·part (di·pärt′) *v.i.* 1 To go away; leave: opposed to *arrive.* 2 To deviate; differ; vary: with *from.* 3 To die. —*v.t.* 4 *Rare* To leave: to *depart* this life. See synonyms under DIE[1], ESCAPE. —*n. Obs.* Departure; death. [<OF *departir* <*de-* away (<L *dis-*) + *partir* divide <L *partire* <*pars, partis* a part]

de·part·ment (di·pärt′mənt) *n.* 1 A distinct part; a division or subdivision of an organization, business, etc. 2 A division in a secondary school, college, or university devoted to teaching courses in a certain subject: French *department, department* of sociology. 3 A subdivision of a U.S. Territory for military purposes: also **territorial department.** 4 A subdivision of a governmental organization: the State *Department, Department* of Labor, etc. 5 In France, a government administrative district. [<OF <*departir.* See DEPART.]

de·part·men·tal (dē′pärt·men′təl) *adj.* 1 Pertaining to a department or to departments. 2 Organized on a system of departments. —**de′part·men′tal·ism** *n.*

de·part·men·tal·ize (dē′pärt·men′təl·īz) *v.t.* & *v.i.* **·ized, ·iz·ing** To divide into departments.

department store See under STORE.

de·par·ture (di·pär′chər) *n.* 1 The act of departing. 2 The act of deviating from a method, course of action, set of ideas, etc.; divergence. 3 The act of leaving this world; death. 4 *Naut.* **a** Distance east or west of a given meridian. **b** The position of a ship taken at the commencement of a voyage as a basis for calculations by dead reckoning.

de·pas·ture (dē·pas′chər, -päs′-) *v.* **·tured, ·tur·ing** *v.t.* 1 To denude (land) of herbage by grazing. 2 To pasture (cattle). —*v.i.* 3 To graze.

de·pau·per·ate (dē·pô′pə·rāt) *v.t.* **·at·ed, ·at·ing** To deprive of fertility or richness; impoverish; exhaust. —*adj.* (-rit) 1 *Bot.* Diminutive or imperfectly developed, as if starved: said of plants grown in poor soil. 2 *Obs.* Impoverished. [<Med. L *depauperatus,* pp. of *depauperare* <L *de-* down + *pauperare* make poor <*pauper* poor]

de·pe·gram (dē′pi·gram) *n. Meteorol.* A graphic curve relating the dew point to pressure changes at a given atmospheric level. [<DE(W)P(OINT) + E(NTROPY) + -GRAM]

de·pend (di·pend′) *v.i.* 1 To trust; have full reliance: with *on* or *upon.* 2 To be conditioned or determined; be contingent: with *on* or *upon.* 3 To rely for maintenance, support, etc.: with *on* or *upon.* 4 To hang down: with *from.* 5 To be pending, undecided, or in suspension. See synonyms under LEAN[1]. [<OF *dependre* <L *dependere* <*de-* down + *pendere* hang]

de·pend·a·ble (di·pen′da·bəl) *adj.* That can be depended upon; trustworthy. —**de·pend′a·bil′·i·ty, de·pend′a·ble·ness** *n.* —**de·pend′a·bly** *adv.*

de·pen·dence (di·pen′dəns) *n.* 1 The act or relation of depending, or the state of being dependent on or determined by some one or something else. 2 Reliance; trust. 3 Reciprocal reliance. 4 Subordination; subjection; that which is subordinate to or contingent on something else. 5 That on which one relies. Also **de·pen′dance.**

de·pen·den·cy (di·pen′dən·sē) *n. pl.* **·cies** 1 That which is dependent. 2 A subject or tributary state. 3 Dependence. Also **de·pen′dan·cy.**

de·pen·dent (di·pen′dənt) *adj.* 1 Depending upon something exterior; subordinate; contingent: often with *on* or *upon.* 2 Needing support or aid; needy. 3 Hanging down; pendent: often with *from.* 4 *Gram.* Subordinate. See SUBORDINATE CLAUSE under CLAUSE. See synonyms under SUBJECT. —*n.* 1 One who looks to another for support or favor; a retainer. 2 A consequence; corollary. Also **de·pen′dant.** —**de·pen′dent·ly** *adv.*

De·pew (də·pyo͞o′), **Chauncey Mitchell,** 1834–1928, U.S. senator and orator.

de·phleg·ma·tor (dē·fleg′mā·tər) *n. Chem.* A fractionating column. [<NL <L *dephlegmare* <*de-* away + *phlegma* phlegm <Gk.]

de·pict (di·pikt′) *v.t.* 1 To portray or represent by drawing, sculpturing, painting, etc. 2 To describe verbally. [<L *depictus,* pp. of *depingere* <*de-* down + *pingere* paint] —**de·pic′tion** *n.*

dep·i·late (dep′ə·lāt) *v.t.* **·lat·ed, ·lat·ing** To remove hair from. [<L *depilatus,* pp. of *depilare* <*de-* away + *pilus* hair] —**dep′i·la′·tion** *n.* —**dep′i·la′tor** *n.*

de·pil·a·to·ry (di·pil′ə·tôr′ē, -tō′rē) *adj.* Having the power to remove hair. —*n.* A preparation for removing hair from the human skin.

de·plane (di·plān′) *v.i.* **·planed, ·plan·ing** To disembark from an aircraft.

de·plete (di·plēt′) *v.t.* **·plet·ed, ·plet·ing** 1 To reduce or lessen, as by use, exhaustion, or waste. 2 To empty, or partially empty: to *deplete* the treasury. 3 *Med.* To lessen or remove the contents of (an overcharged organ or vessel), as by purging or bloodletting. [<L *depletus,* pp. of *deplere* <*de-* not + *plere* fill]

de·ple·tion (di·plē′shən) *n.* 1 The act of depleting. 2 The state of being depleted. 3 Reduction of capital. —**de·ple′tive, de·ple·to·ry** (di·plē′tər·ē) *adj.* & *n.*

de·plor·a·ble (di·plôr′ə·bəl, -plō′rə-) *adj.* Lamentable; pitiable; sad. —**de·plor′a·bil′·i·ty** *n.* —**de·plor′a·bly** *adv.*

de·plore (di·plôr′, -plōr′) *v.t.* **·plored, ·plor·ing** To feel or express deep regret or concern for; lament. See synonyms under MOURN. [<L *deplorare* <*de-* completely + *plorare* bewail]

de·ploy (di·ploi′) *v.t.* & *v.i.* To spread out in line of battle, as troops. [<F *déployer* <OF *desployer, despleier* <LL *displicare* <*dis-* from + *plicare* fold. Doublet of DISPLAY.]

de·ploy·ment (di·ploi′mənt) *n. Mil.* Extension of a battle front from close order to battle formation in lines of skirmishers, foragers, etc., after development has been effected.

de·plu·mate (di·plo͞o′mit) *adj. Ornithol.* Bare of feathers.

de·plu·ma·tion (dē′plo͞o·mā′shən) *n. Ornithol.* The falling or stripping off of feathers; molting.

de·plume (dē·plo͞om′) *v.t.* **·plumed, ·plum·ing** 1 To strip the plumage or feathers from. 2 To strip; despoil, as of honors or wealth. [<F *déplumer* <*dé-* away (<L *dis-*) + *plume* feather <L *pluma*]

de·po·lar·ize (dē·pō′lə·rīz) *v.t.* **·ized, ·iz·ing** 1 *Electr.* To break up or remove the polarization of, as by separating the electrodes of an electric cell. 2 To deprive of polarity. —**de·po′lar·i·za′tion** *n.* —**de·po′lar·iz′er** *n.*

de·pone (di·pōn′) *v.t.* & *v.i.* **·poned, ·pon·ing** 1 To testify, especially under oath; depose. 2 *Obs.* To deposit, as a pledge or wager. [<L *deponere* <*de-* down + *ponere* place]

de·po·nent (di·pō′nənt) *adj.* In Latin and Greek grammar, denoting a verb that has the form of the passive or middle voice but is active in meaning. —*n.* 1 A deponent verb. 2 *Law* One who gives sworn testimony, especially in writing.

de·pop·u·late (dē·pop′yə·lāt) *v.t.* **·lat·ed, ·lat·ing** To remove the inhabitants from, by massacre, famine, epidemics, etc. —*adj.* (-lit, -lāt) *Obs.* Depopulated. [<L *depopulatus,* pp. of *depopulari* <*de-* down + *populari* lay waste <*populus* people] —**de·pop′u·la′·tor** *n.*

de·pop·u·la·tion (dē·pop′yə·lā′shən) *n.* 1 The act of depopulating, or the state of being depopulated. 2 That condition of a country in which the birth rate does not compensate for losses by the death rate.

de·port (di·pôrt′, -pōrt′) *v.t.* 1 To transport forcibly; banish. 2 To behave or conduct (oneself). [<OF *deporter* <L *deportare* <*de-* away + *portare* carry]

de·por·ta·tion (dē′pôr·tā′shən, -pōr-) *n.* 1 The act of deporting; the state of being deported; exile. 2 The sending back of an undesirable alien to the country from which he came.

de·por·tee (dē′pôr·tē′, -pōr-) *n.* A person banished from a country as undesirable or as having entered illegally. [<F *déporté* a banished person; orig., pp. of *déporter* banish]

de·port·ment (di·pôrt′mənt, -pōrt′-) *n.* Conduct or behavior; demeanor; bearing. See synonyms under BEHAVIOR, MANNER.

de·pos·al (di·pō′zəl) *n.* The act of deposing, especially removal from office or sovereignty.

de·pose (di·pōz′) *v.* **·posed, ·pos·ing** *v.t.* 1 To deprive of official rank or office; oust, as a king. 2 To state on oath; give testimony of. 3 To take the deposition of. —*v.i.* 4 To bear witness. See synonyms under AFFIRM. [<OF *deposer* <*de-* down (<L *de-*) + *poser.* See POSE[1].] —**de·pos′a·ble** *adj.*

de·pos·it (di·poz′it) *v.t.* 1 To give in trust or for safekeeping. 2 To give as part payment or as security. 3 To put or lay on or in some place or receptacle. 4 To cause, as sediment, to form a layer or deposit. —*n.* 1 That which is or has been deposited or precipitated; especially, sediment; precipitate. 2 Money or property deposited, as in a bank for safekeeping, or as security. 3 The act of depositing, or the state of being deposited. 4 A place where anything is deposited. 5 The condition of being placed to one's order, as in a bank, in trust, or for safekeeping: on *deposit.* 6 *Geol.* An accumulated mass of iron, oil, salt, etc. 7 A layer of metal deposited by electrolytic action. [<L *depositus,* pp. of *deponere.* See DEPONE.]

de·pos·i·tar·y (di·poz′ə·ter′ē) *n. pl.* **·tar·ies** 1 A person entrusted with anything for safekeeping; a trustee. 2 A depository.

dep·o·si·tion (dep′ə·zish′ən, dē′pə-) *n.* 1 The act of depositing. 2 That which is deposited; especially, an accumulation or sediment. 3 The written testimony of a sworn witness; hence, allegation; evidence. 4 The act of deposing, as from office. —**the Deposition** The taking down of Christ's body from the Cross; also, in art, a representation of this. See synonyms under TESTIMONY.

de·pos·i·tor (di·poz′ə·tər) *n.* One who makes a deposit.

de·pos·i·to·ry (di·poz′ə·tôr′ē, -tō′rē) *n. pl.* **·ries** 1 A place where anything is deposited. 2 A person or body of persons to whom something is entrusted for safekeeping.

de·pot (dē′pō, *Mil.* & *Brit.* dep′ō) *n.* 1 A warehouse or storehouse. 2 *U.S.* A railroad station. 3 *Mil.* A storehouse or collecting station for personnel or materiel. [<F *dépôt* <OF *depost* <L *depositum* a pledge <*deponere.* See DEPONE.]

dep·ra·va·tion (dep′rə·vā′shən) *n.* 1 The act of depraving, or the state of being depraved or deteriorated. 2 A corrupt tendency; a depravity.

de·prave (di·prāv′) *v.t.* **·praved, ·prav·ing** 1 To render bad or worse, especially in morals; corrupt; pervert. 2 *Obs.* To vilify; slander. See synonyms under CORRUPT, POLLUTE. [<L *depravare* <*de-* completely + *pravus* corrupt, wicked] —**de·prav′er** *n.*

de·praved (di·prāvd′) *adj.* Having a corrupt or vicious character.

de·prav·i·ty (di·prav′ə·tē) *n. pl.* **·ties** 1 The state of being depraved; wickedness. 2 A depraved act or habit. See synonyms under SIN[1].

dep·re·cate (dep′rə·kāt) *v.t.* **·cat·ed, ·cat·ing** 1 To express disapproval of or regret for; plead earnestly against. 2 To disparage or belittle; depreciate. 3 *Archaic* To desire or pray for deliverance from, as threatened evil. [<L *deprecatus,* pp. of *deprecari* <*de-* away + *precari* pray] —**dep·re·ca·ble** (dep′rə·kə·bəl) *adj.* —**dep′re·cat′ing·ly** *adv.* —**dep′re·ca′·tion** *n.* —**dep′re·ca′tive** *adj.* —**dep′re·ca′tive·ly** *adv.* —**dep′re·ca′tor** *n.*

dep·re·ca·to·ry (dep′rə·kə·tôr′ē, -tō′rē) *adj.* Apologetic; disparaging.

de·pre·ci·ate (di·prē′shē·āt) *v.* **·at·ed, ·at·ing** *v.t.* 1 To lessen the worth of; lower the price or rate of. 2 To disparage; belittle. —*v.i.* 3 To become less in value, etc. See synonyms under ASPERSE, DISPARAGE. [<L *depretiatus,* pp. of *depretiare* <*de-* down + *pretium* price] —**de·pre′ci·a′tor** *n.*

de·pre·ci·a·tion (di·prē′shē·ā′shən) *n.* 1 The act of depreciating, or the state of being depreciated. 2 The wear and tear of equipment,

machinery, plant, etc. **3** A diminished value; also, the amount estimated or written off to offset such loss of value.

de·pre·ci·a·to·ry (di·prē′shē·ə·tôr′ē, -tō′rē) *adj.* Tending to depreciate. Also **de·pre′ci·a′tive.**

dep·re·date (dep′rə·dāt) *v.t.* & *v.i.* **—dat·ed, ·dat·ing** To prey upon; pillage; plunder. [< LL *depraedatus,* pp. of *depraedari* < *de-* completely + *praeda* booty, prey] **—dep′re·da′tor** *n.* **— dep·re·da·to·ry** (dep′rə·dā′tər·ē) *adj.*

dep·re·da·tion (dep′rə·dā′shən) *n.* A plundering; robbery.

de·press (di·pres′) *v.t.* **1** To lower the spirits of; make gloomy; sadden. **2** To lessen in vigor, force, or energy; weaken; make dull. **3** To lessen the price or value of. **4** To press or push down; lower. **5** *Music* To lower the pitch of. **6** *Obs.* To subjugate; suppress. See synonyms under ABASE. [< OF *depresser* < L *depressus,* pp. of *deprimere* < *de-* down + *primere* press]

de·pres·sant (di·pres′ənt) *Med. adj.* Lessening functional activity or depressing vital force. —*n.* A drug or other substance which reduces vital functions.

de·pressed (di·prest′) *adj.* **1** Sad; dejected. **2** Lowered in position; pressed or kept down. **3** Flattened from above; sunk below the general surface, as the solid part of a plant body. **4** *Ornithol.* Broader than high, as the bill of a flycatcher.

depressed area A region characterized by economic depression, unemployment, a low standard of living, etc.

de·press·ing (di·pres′ing) *adj.* Disheartening; causing sadness or low spirits; sad. **— de·press′ing·ly** *adv.*

de·pres·sion (di·presh′ən) *n.* **1** The act of depressing, or the state of being depressed; low spirits or vitality; dejection; melancholy. **2** That which is depressed; a low or hollow place. **3** A decline in business or trade; also, the period of time during which this inactivity prevails. **4** *Meteorol.* Low atmospheric pressure; also, a region of low atmospheric pressure. **5** *Astron.* The vertical angular distance of a heavenly body below the horizon: opposed to *altitude.* **6** The angular distance of an object below the horizontal plane through the point of observation: the opposite of *elevation.* **7** *Psychiatry* A lowering of vital powers; melancholy; especially, psychopathic melancholy leading to mental disorders. **8** *Music* Flatting of a tone.

de·pres·sive (di·pres′iv) *adj.* Tending to or causing depression. **—de·pres′sive·ly** *adv.* **— de·pres′sive·ness** *n.*

de·pres·so·mo·tor (di·pres′ō·mō′tər) *adj. Physiol.* Diminishing the capacity for movement; retarding motor activity. —*n. Med.* An agent that lowers the activity of the motor centers, as a bromide.

de·pres·sor (di·pres′ər) *n.* **1** One who or that which depresses. **2** *Physiol.* A depressor nerve. **3** *Anat.* One of several muscles which depress or contract a part. **4** *Surg.* An instrument for pressing down a part.

depressor nerve *Physiol.* An afferent nerve connected with the heart, which controls blood pressure.

dep·ri·va·tion (dep′rə·vā′shən) *n.* The act of depriving, or the state of being deprived; loss; want. Also **de·priv·al** (di·prī′vəl). See synonyms under LOSS.

de·prive (di·prīv′) *v.t.* **·prived, ·priv·ing 1** To take something away from; dispossess; divest. **2** To keep from acquiring, using, or enjoying. **3** *Obs.* To put an end to. [< OF *depriver* < L *de-* completely + *privare* strip, remove] **—de·priv′a·ble** *adj.*

De Pro·fun·dis (dē prō·fun′dis) The 130th Psalm: so called from the first words of the Latin version. [< L, out of the depths]

de·pro·gram (dē·prō′gram) *v.t.* **-gramed** or **-grammed, -gram·ing** or **-gram·ming** To try to convince (a person) to forsake something learned well or accepted, esp. a religious belief.

de pro·pri·o mo·tu (dē prō′prē·ō mō′tōō) *Latin* Of its own accord.

dep·side (dep′sīd, -sid) *n. Chem.* One of a group of aromatic compounds formed from phenol carboxylic acids: found chiefly in lichens or made synthetically. [< Gk. *depsein* soften, tan + -IDE]

Dept·ford (det′fərd) A metropolitan borough of SE London.

depth (depth) *n.* **1** The state or degree of being deep; extent or distance downward, inward, or backward. **2** A deep place. **3** The innermost part. **4** Profundity of thought or feeling; utmost extent; immensity; extremity. **5** The quality of being deep, crafty, or scheming. **6** The quality of being dark in shade, or rich in color. **7** The quality of being low-pitched in tone. [ME *depthe*]

depth bomb or **charge** See under BOMB.

depth-sound·er (depth′soun′dər) *n.* An instrument for measuring the depth of water by sending sound waves and receiving their echoes from the bottom.

dep·u·rate (dep′yə·rāt) *v.t.* & *v.i.* **·rat·ed, ·rat·ing** To free or become free from morbid matter or impurities. [< Med. L *depuratus,* pp. of *depurare* < *de-* completely + *purus* pure] **—dep′u·ra′tion** *n.* **—dep′u·ra′tor** *n.*

dep·u·ra·tive (dep′yə·rā′tiv) *adj.* Purifying; purgative. —*n.* A purifying agent. Also **dep·u·rant** (dep′yə·rənt).

dep·u·ta·tion (dep′yə·tā′shən) *n.* **1** A person or persons acting for another; a delegation. **2** The act of deputing, or the state of being deputed. **3** *Brit.* A forestry license granted to a gamekeeper.

de·pute (di·pyōōt′) *v.t.* **·put·ed, ·put·ing 1** To appoint as an agent, deputy, or delegation; send with authority. **2** To transfer, as authority, to another. [< OF *deputer* < LL *deputare* < *de-* away + *putare* think]

dep·u·tize (dep′yə·tīz) *v.* **·tized, ·tiz·ing** *v.t.* To appoint as a deputy. —*v.i.* To act as a deputy.

dep·u·ty (dep′yə·tē) *n. pl.* **·ties 1** One appointed to act for another; representative agent. **2** A member of a legislative assembly in certain countries. See synonyms under DELEGATE. [< F *député,* pp. of *députer* < OF *deputer* DEPUTE]

De Quin·cey (di kwin′sē), **Thomas,** 1785–1859, English essayist.

de·rac·i·nate (di·ras′ə·nāt) *v.t.* **·nat·ed, ·nat·ing** To pull up by the roots; eradicate. [< F *déraciner* < *dé-* away (< L *dis-*) + *racine* a root < L *radix*] **—de·rac′i·na′tion** *n.*

de·raign (di·rān′) *v.t. Obs.* To determine or maintain (a claim, right, etc.) by judicial argument or wager of battle. [< OF *deraisnier* < *de-* down (< L *de-*) + *raisnier* reason < L *ratio, -onis* reason] **—de·raign′ment** *n.*

de·rail (dē·rāl′) *v.t.* To cause to leave the rails, as a train. —*v.i.* To leave the rails. [< F *dérailler* < *dé-* from + *rail* a rail] **—de·rail′ment** *n.*

de·range (di·rānj′) *v.t.* **·ranged, ·rang·ing 1** To disturb the arrangement or order of; disarrange; disorder. **2** To unbalance the reason of; craze. **3** To disturb the condition, action, or functions of. See synonyms under DISPLACE. [< F *déranger* < *dé-* away (< L *dis-*) + *ranger* RANGE, *v.*]

de·ranged (di·rānjd′) *adj.* **1** Insane. **2** Disordered.

de·range·ment (di·rānj′mənt) *n.* **1** The act of deranging, or state of being deranged. **2** Any severe mental disorder; insanity. See synonyms under INSANITY.

de·ray (di·rā′) *n. Obs.* Confusion; disorder; boisterous revelry. [< OF *desrei* < *desreer* disorder < *des-* away (< L *dis-*) + *rei* order]

der·by (dûr′bē) *n. pl.* **·bies** A stiff, felt hat with curved brim and round crown: in England called a *bowler.* [< DERBY]

Der·by (dûr′bē, *Brit.* där′bē) **1** An annual horse race for three-year-olds run at Epsom Downs in Surrey, England: named for the founder, the 12th Earl of Derby (1780). **2** Any horse race of similar importance; especially, the Kentucky Derby.

Der·by (dûr′bē, *Brit.* där′be) A county in central England; 1,006 square miles; its county seat, Derby. Also **Der′by·shire** (-shir).

Der·by (dûr′bē, *Brit.* där′bē), **Earl of** English title traditionally dating from 1138; held by the Stanley family from the 15th century to the present.

de rè·gle (də re′gl′) *French* According to rule; in proper form.

de·reg·u·late (di·reg′yə·lāt) *v.t.* **-lat·ed, -lat·ing** To remove regulations or restrictions from.

de·re·ism (dir′ē·iz′əm) *n. Psychol.* Mental activity freed of ordinary logic, the facts of experience, or the realities of the external world: common in dreams and in certain mental disorders. [< DE- + L *res* thing + -ISM] **—de′re·is′tic** *adj.* **— de′re·is′ti·cal·ly** *adv.*

der·e·lict (der′ə·likt) *adj.* **1** Neglectful of obligation; unfaithful; remiss. **2** Deserted or abandoned. —*n.* **1** That which is deserted or abandoned. **2** Any property which is abandoned at sea, as a deserted wreck. **3** Land exposed or gained by receding of the sea. **4** One who betrays a trust. **5** A person outside the pale of respectability. [< L *derelictus,* pp. of *derelinquere* < *de-* completely + *relinquere* abandon]

der·e·lic·tion (der′ə·lik′shən) *n.* **1** Neglect or wilful omission; failure in duty. **2** Voluntary abandonment of a charge or property. **3** The state or fact of being abandoned. **4** *Law* **a** A gain of land by a permanent receding of water. **b** The land thus gained.

de re·rum na·tu·ra (dē rir′əm nə·tōōr′ə, nə·tyōōr′ə) *Latin* Concerning the nature of things.

de re·tour (də rə·tōōr′) *French* Back again; returned.

de·ride (di·rīd′) *v.t.* **·rid·ed, ·rid·ing** To treat with scornful mirth; ridicule. See synonyms under MOCK, RIDICULE. [< L *deridere* < *de-* completely + *ridere* laugh, mock] **—de·rid′er** *n.* **— de·rid′ing·ly** *adv.*

de ri·gueur (də rē·gœr′) *French* Necessary according to etiquette; required by good form.

de·ris·i·ble (di·riz′ə·bəl) *adj.* Open to derision.

de·ri·sion (di·rizh′ən) *n.* **1** The act of deriding; ridicule; mockery; scornful laughter. **2** An object of ridicule or scorn. See synonyms under BANTER, RIDICULE, SCORN. [< L *derisio, -onis* < *deridere.* See DERIDE.]

de·ri·sive (di·rī′siv) *adj.* Expressive of or characterized by derision. Also **de·ri·so·ry** (di·rī′sər·ē). **—de·ri′sive·ly** *adv.* **—de·ri′sive·ness** *n.*

der·i·va·tion (der′ə·vā′shən) *n.* **1** The act of deriving, or the condition of being derived. **2** The tracing of a word from its original form and meaning; also, a statement of the information thus obtained. **3** Origin; descent; extraction. **4** *Math.* **a** The process of forming a derivative. **b** The act of deriving an equation or reaching a conclusion expressed as an equation. **— der′i·va′tion·al** *adj.*

de·riv·a·tive (di·riv′ə·tiv) *adj.* Coming or acquiring by derivation; of or pertaining to derivation or evolution; derived; not original or basic. —*n.* **1** That which is derived. **2** *Gram.* A word developed from a basic word, as by the addition of a prefix or suffix or by phonetic change: "Functional" is a *derivative* of "function." **3** *Chem.* **a** A compound formed or regarded as being formed from another, usually by partial replacement. **b** Any organic compound containing a specified radical: a benzene *derivative.* **4** *Music* A chord derived from another by inversion, or from the harmonics of an assumed root: often used in the plural. **5** *Math.* The instantaneous rate of change of a function with reference to a variable. **— de·riv′a·tive·ly** *adv.*

de·rive (di·rīv′) *v.* **·rived, ·riv·ing** *v.t.* **1** To draw or receive, as from a source, principle, or root; be descended from. **2** To deduce, as from a premise; draw, as a conclusion. **3** To trace the derivation of (a word). **4** *Chem.* To obtain (a compound) from another as by partial replacement. **5** *Obs.* To cause to come; bring: with *on, to,* or *upon.* — *v.i.* **6** To have derivation; originate. [< L *derivare* < *de-* from + *rivus* stream] **—de·riv′a·ble** *adj.* **— de·riv′er** *n.*

de·rived unit (di·rīvd′) *Physics* A unit based on or derived from any primary unit of mass, length, time, etc.

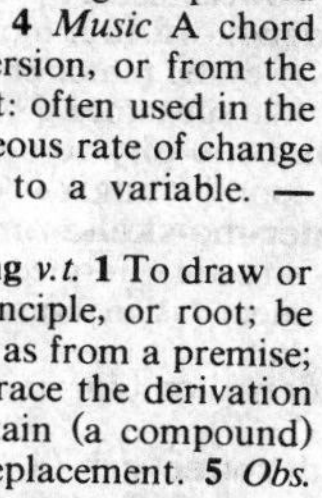

DERM
a. The true derm.

derm (dûrm) *n.* **1** *Anat.* The sensitive and vascular or true skin. **2** The skin in general: also **dermis.** Also **der·ma** (dûr′mə). [< Gk. *derma* skin]

-derm suffix Skin: *endoderm.* [< Gk. *derma* skin]

der·mal (dûr′məl) *adj.* Of or pertaining to the skin or

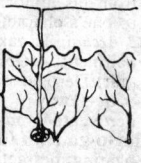

epidermis, or, properly, to the corium; cutaneous: *dermal* affections. Also **der′mic.**

dermal body *Zool.* Any of the structures characterized by a glandular or sensory function which are present in the dermis and partly in the epidermis of some marine worms.

dermal layer *Zool.* A single layer of cells covering the outer surface of a sponge, through which the calcareous needle-shaped spicules project.

der·map·ter·ous (dər·map′tər·əs) *adj. Entomol.* Of or pertaining to an order *(Dermaptera)* of small, elongate, terrestrial, and mostly nocturnal insects with a pair of large, forcepslike, caudal appendages and chewing mouth parts: they are wingless or with one or two pairs of inconspicuous wings; the earwigs. [< DERM(O)- + Gk. *a-* without + *pteron* wing]

der·ma·ti·tis (dûr′mə·tī′tis) *n. Pathol.* Inflammation of the skin. [< DERMAT(O) + -ITIS]

dermato- *combining form* Skin: *dermatology.* Also, before vowels, **dermat-.** [< Gk. *derma, dermatos* skin]

Der·ma·to·bi·a (dûr′mə·tō′bē·ə) *n.* A genus of insects (family *Oestridae*) whose larvae live under the skin of animals, causing painful swellings; gadflies; botflies. [< NL < Gk. *derma, dermatos* skin + *bios* life]

der·ma·to·bi·a·sis (dûr′mə·tō·bī′ə·sis) *n.* Infection by the larva of *Dermatobia.* [< DERMATOB(IA) + -IASIS]

der·mat·o·gen (dər·mat′ə·jən, dûr′mə·tō′jən) *n. Bot.* The outermost layer of cells in plants, forming the permanent epidermal tissue: also called *protoderm.*

der·ma·to·glyph·ics (dûr′mə·tō·glif′iks) *n.* **1** The study of the surface ridges of the skin, especially of the palm and the sole. **2** Ink impressions of such ridges taken for identification purposes. [< DERMATO- + Gk. *glyphein* carve]

der·ma·toid (dûr′mə·toid) *adj.* Dermoid.

der·ma·tol·o·gist (dûr′mə·tol′ə·jist) *n.* One who studies or is skilled in dermatology.

der·ma·tol·o·gy (dûr′mə·tol′ə·jē) *n.* The branch of medical science that relates to the skin and its diseases. [< DERMATO- + -LOGY] **—der·ma·to·log·i·cal** (dûr′mə·tə·loj′i·kəl) *adj.*

der·ma·top·a·thy (dûr′mə·top′ə·thē) *n.* Any skin disease.

der·ma·to·phyte (dûr′mə·tō·fīt′) *n. Bot.* A plant living parasitically upon the skin, as certain fungi which produce ringworm, favus, etc. **—der′ma·to·phyt′ic** (-fit′ik) *adj.*

der·ma·to·plas·ty (dûr′mə·tō·plas′tē) *n. Surg.* The replacement of destroyed skin by flaps or skin grafts.

der·mis (dûr′mis) See DERM.

dermo- *combining form* Dermato-. Also, before vowels, **derm-.** [< Gk. *derma* skin]

der·moid (dûr′moid) *adj.* Like skin. *—n. Pathol.* A cystic tumor enclosing skin tissue or any skinlike substance. [< DERM(O)- + -OID]

der·mo·phy·to·sis (dûr′mō·fī·tō′sis) *n.* Athlete's foot. [< DERMO- + -PHYTE + -OSIS]

der·mo·skel·e·ton (dûr′mō·skel′ə·tən) *n. Zool.* A structure formed by the hardening of integument, as in crustaceans, insects, etc.; exoskeleton.

der·ni·er (dûr′nē·ər, *Fr.* der·nyā′) *adj.* Last; final. [< F]

der·nier cri (der·nyā′ krē′) *French* **1** The last word. **2** The latest fashion.

der·nier res·sort (der·nyā′ rə·sôr′) *French* Last resort.

der·o·gate (der′ə·gāt) *v.* **·gat·ed, ·gat·ing** *v.i.* **1** To take away; detract, as from reputation, honor, or powers: with *from:* The charge cannot *derogate* from his honor. **2** To do something derogatory to one's character or position; degenerate. *—v.t.* **3** *Archaic* To take away so as to cause loss or impairment. **4** *Obs.* To disparage. *—adj.* (der′ə·git, -gāt) Derogated. [< L *derogatus,* pp. of *derogare* < *de-* away + *rogare* ask, propose a law] **—der′o·gate·ly** *adv.*

der·o·ga·tion (der′ə·gā′shən) *n.* **1** The act of derogating; detraction; disparagement. **2** The act of limiting in application, as a law, authority, etc.

de·rog·a·tive (di·rog′ə·tiv) *adj.* Tending to derogate or detract; derogatory. **—de·rog′a·tive·ly** *adv.*

de·rog·a·to·ry (di·rog′ə·tôr′ē, -tō′rē) *adj.* Lessening in good repute; detracting in estimation; disparaging. **—de·rog′a·to′ri·ly** *adv.* **—de·rog′a·to′ri·ness** *n.*

der·rick (der′ik) *n.* **1** An apparatus, as a mast with a hinged boom, or a framework, for hoisting and swinging heavy weights into place. **2** The framework over the mouth of an oil well or similar drill hole. [after *Derrick,* 17th c. London hangman]

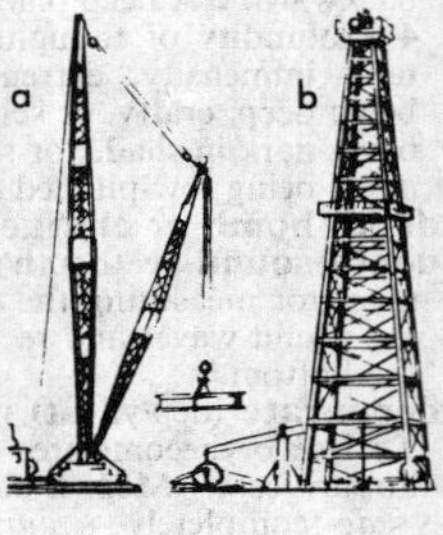

DERRICKS
a. Hoisting derrick.
b. Oil well derrick.

der·rid (der′id) *n.* An extremely toxic, resinous alkaloid obtained from a species of derris *(Derris elliptica):* used as an arrow poison by the Malays. Also **derride** (der′īd).

der·ri·ère (der′ē·er′, *Fr.* de·ryâr′) *n. French* The rear; hind parts; buttocks.

der·ring-do (der′ing·dōō′) *n.* Courageous deeds; daring action. [ME *dorryng don* daring to do; mistaken for a noun phrase by Spenser]

der·rin·ger (der′in·jər) *n.* A pistol having a short barrel and a large bore. [after Henry *Derringer,* 19th c. U.S. gunsmith, who invented it]

der·ris (der′is) *n.* Any plant of a genus *(Derris)* of woody, climbing plants of the East Indies; especially, *D. tripliata* and *D. elliptica,* whose roots yield rotenone. Also **derris root.** [< NL < Gk., a covering]

der·ry (der′ē) *n. pl.* **·ries** A meaningless word used as a refrain in old songs; hence, a set of verses; a ballad. Also **der′ry-down′.**

Der·ry (der′ē) See LONDONDERRY.

der Tag (der täk′) *German* The day: signifying the day Germany begins to establish her supremacy; hence, any important moment.

der·vish (dûr′vish) *n.* **1** A Mohammedan mendicant friar; a fakir. **2** A member of certain fanatical tribes of Upper Egypt. [< Turkish < Persian *darvish*]

Der·went (dûr′wənt) **1** A river in Yorkshire, England, flowing 60 miles NW to the Ouse River. **2** A river in Derbyshire, England, flowing 60 miles SE to the Trent River. **3** A river in Cumberland, England, flowing 35 miles NW to Solway Firth. **4** A river in southern Tasmania, flowing 120 miles SE to the Tasman Sea.

Der·went·wa·ter (dûr′wənt·wô′tər) A lake in south Cumberland, England. Also **Der′went Wa′ter.**

DES Diethylstilbestrol.

Des·a·gua·de·ro (des′ä·gwä·thā′rō) A river in western Bolivia, flowing 200 miles SE to Lake Poopó.

de·salt (dē·sôlt′) *v.t.* To remove the salt from, as sea water, to make potable. **—de·salt′er** *n.*

des·cant (des′kant) *n.* **1** The act of discussing; a series of remarks. **2** *Music* **a** A varied melody or song. **b** Formerly, an ornamental variation of the main subject or song. **c** A counterpoint above the plain song. **d** The composition or singing of such counterpoint or variations. **e** The upper part in part music, especially the soprano. *—v.t.* (des·kant′, dis-) **1** To discourse at length; hold forth: with *on* or *upon.* **2** To make a descant; sing. Also spelled *discant.* [< AF < Med. L *discantus* < L *dis-* away + *cantus* a song < *canere* sing]

Des·cartes (dā·kärt′), **René,** 1596–1650, French mathematician and philosopher.

de·scend (di·send′) *v.i.* **1** To move from a higher to a lower point; go or come down; sink. **2** To slope or incline downward, as a path. **3** To stoop; lower oneself. **4** To come down by inheritance; be inherited. **5** To be derived by heredity: with *from.* **6** To come or arrive in an overwhelming manner, as from above; attack: with *on* or *upon.* **7** To pass, as from the general to the particular. **8** *Astron.* To move southward or toward the horizon, as a star. *—v.t.* **9** To move from an upper to a lower part of; go down, as a ladder. See synonyms under FALL. [< OF *descendre* < L *descendere* < *de-* down + *scandere* climb]

de·scen·dant (di·sen′dənt) *n.* One who is descended lineally from another; offspring. *—adj.* Descendent. [< F, ppr. of *descendre.* See DESCEND.]

de·scen·dent (di·sen′dənt) *adj.* **1** Proceeding downward; descending. **2** Issuing by descent, as from an ancestor. [< L *descendens, -entis,* ppr. of *descendere.* See DESCEND.]

de·scend·er (di·sen′dər) *n.* **1** One who or that which descends. **2** *Printing* **a** The part of a letter that reaches into the bottom of the body of the type. **b** Any of such letters, as *j, g, q,* etc.

de·scend·i·ble (di·sen′də·bəl) *adj.* **1** That can be descended. **2** That can pass by descent; inheritable. Also **de·scend′a·ble.**

de·scen·sive (di·sen′siv) *adj.* Inclined to descend.

de·scent (di·sent′) *n.* **1** The act of descending. **2** Decline; deterioration; fall. **3** A descending way; declivity; slope. **4** Lineage; birth; extraction. **5** Descendants; issue. **6** A hostile visitation; invasion. **7** The transmission of an estate by inheritance. **8** A generation in the scale of genealogy. See synonyms under AFFINITY, KIN. [< F *descente* < *descendre.* See DESCEND.]

Des·chutes River (dā·shōōt′) A river in central Oregon, flowing NE 240 miles to the Columbia River.

de·scribe (di·skrīb′) *v.t.* **·scribed, ·scrib·ing** **1** To give an account of; represent, with spoken or written words. **2** To draw the figure of; delineate; outline. **3** To descry: an erroneous form. See synonyms under CIRCUMSCRIBE, RELATE. [< L *describere* < *de-* down + *scribere* write] **—de·scrib′a·ble** *adj.* **—de·scrib′er** *n.*

de·scrip·tion (di·skrip′shən) *n.* **1** The act of describing; a portrayal or explanation; a drawing or tracing. **2** A group of attributes constituting a class; sort; kind; nature. See synonyms under DEFINITION, REPORT. [< OF *description* < L *descriptio, -onis* < *describere.* See DESCRIBE.]

de·scrip·tive (di·skrip′tiv) *adj.* **1** Characterized by or containing description; serving to describe. **2** Designating a science or branch of a science concerned with the classification of material; taxonomical. **3** *Gram.* Having the function of describing: a *descriptive* adjective. See synonyms under GRAPHIC. **—de·scrip′tive·ly** *adv.* **—de·scrip′tive·ness** *n.*

descriptive geometry That application of geometry in which the representation of solids is projected upon two planes so that their metrical properties can be accurately deduced.

descriptive linguistics See under LINGUISTICS.

descriptive science Any science in which the emphasis is placed upon the classification and description of the material with which it deals: distinguished from *exact science* and *normative science.*

de·scry (di·skrī′) *v.t.* **·scried, ·scry·ing** **1** To discover with the eye, as in the distance or through obscurity; discern; detect. **2** To discover or find out by observation or investigation. See synonyms under DISCERN, DISCOVER, LOOK. [< OF *descrier* < *des-* away (< L *dis-*) + *crier* cry] **—de·scri′er** *n.*

Des·de·mo·na (dez′də·mō′nə) The heroine of Shakespeare's *Othello.*

des·e·crate (des′ə·krāt) *v.t.* **·crat·ed, ·crat·ing** To divert from a sacred to a common use; profane. See synonyms under VIOLATE. [< DE- (def. 4) + L *sacratus,* pp. of *sacrare* make holy < *sacer* holy] **—des′e·crat′er** or **des′e·cra′tor** *n.*

des·e·cra·tion (des′ə·krā′shən) *n.* The act of profanation; condition of being desecrated; violation.

de·seg·re·gate (dē·seg′rə·gāt) *v.t.* **·gat·ed, ·gat·ing** To eliminate racial segregation in (schools, armed forces, public transportation, etc.).

de·seg·re·ga·tion (dē′seg·rə·gā′shən) *n.* **1** The act of ending segregation of races, as of Negroes and whites, in schools and public facilities. **2** The condition resulting from such action.

de·sen·si·tize (dē·sen′sə·tīz) *v.t.* **·tized, ·tiz·ing** **1** To make less sensitive. **2** *Phot.* To reduce the sensitiveness to light. **3** *Physiol.* To lessen the reactive power of (an organ or tissue) to a stimulus, as an allergen, serum, etc. **—de·sen′si·ti·za′tion** *n.* **—de·sen′si·tiz′er** *n.*

des·e·ret (dez′ə·ret′) *n.* The honey bee: used as a mystic word in the *Book of Mormon.*

Des·e·ret (dez′ə·ret′) A proposed State of the United States, organized in 1849 by a con-

vention of Mormons: refused recognition by Congress, which instead set up Utah Territory in 1850.

de·sert[1] (dez′ərt) *n.* **1** A region so lacking in rainfall, moisture, and vegetation as to be uninhabitable by any considerable population. **2** Any region which is uncultivated and desolate because of deficient moisture, barren soil, or permanent frost. —*adj.* **1** Of or like a desert; barren; waste. **2** *Obs.* Deserted; forsaken. [<OF *deserte* <LL *desertum* <L, pp. neut. of *deserere* <*de-* away + *serere* join]

de·sert[2] (di·zûrt′) *n.* **1** The state of deserving reward or punishment; merit or demerit. **2** *Often pl.* That which is deserved or merited. **3** A meritorious or worthy act; meritoriousness. [<OF <*deservir.* See DESERVE.]

de·sert[3] (di·zûrt′) *v.t.* **1** To forsake or abandon, with or without right. **2** To forsake in violation of one's oath or orders, as a service, post, etc. —*v.i.* **3** To abandon one's post, duty, etc. See synonyms under ABANDON. [<F *déserter* <LL *desertare,* freq. of *deserere.* See DESERT[1].]

de·sert·er (di·zûr′tər) *n.* One who forsakes a service, duty, party, or friends; especially, an absconding soldier or sailor.

des·ert·i·fi·ca·tion (dez′ər·tə·fə·kā′shən) *n.* The process of becoming a desert.

de·ser·tion (di·zûr′shən) *n.* **1** The act of deserting. **2** The state of being deserted; desolation.

desert rat *Slang* **1** In the western United States, a person who has spent a long time in the desert. **2** In World War II, a soldier of the Seventh British Armored Division, which fought in the North African campaigns of 1941–42.

de·serve (di·zûrv′) *v.* **·served, serv·ing** *v.t.* To be entitled to or worthy of, by either merit or demerit.—*v.i.* To be worthy. [<OF *deservir* <L *deservire* <*de-* completely + *servire* serve] —**de·serv′er** *n.*

de·served (di·zûrvd′) *adj.* Earned; merited; suited to one's efforts or shortcomings. —**de·serv·ed·ness** (di·zûr′vid·nis) *n.*

de·serv·ed·ly (di·zûr′vid·lē) *adv.* According to desert; justly.

de·serv·ing (di·zûr′ving) *adj.* Worthy; meritorious. —*n.* Desert; merit or demerit. —**de·serv′ing·ly** *adv.* —**de·serv′ing·ness** *n.*

de·sex (dē seks′) *v.t.* Desexualize.

de·sex·u·al·ize (dē sek′shōō·ə·līz) *v.t.* **·ized, ·iz·ing 1** to remove sexual characteristics from. **2** to remove the reproductive organs from. —**de·sex′u·al·i·za′tion** *n.*

des·ha·bille (dez′ə·bēl′) See DISHABILLE.

des·ic·cant (des′ə·kənt) *adj.* Producing dryness; desiccating, as a medicine or chemical agent. —*n.* A desiccant agent or substance.

des·ic·cate (des′ə·kāt) *v.* **·cat·ed, ·cat·ing** *v.t.* **1** To exhaust or remove the moisture from, as for preserving. **2** To dry thoroughly. —*v.i.* **3** To become dry. [<L *desiccatus,* pp. of *desiccare* <*de-* completely + *siccare* dry out <*siccus* dry] —**des′ic·ca′tion** *n.*

des·ic·cat·ed (des′ə·kā′tid) *adj.* **1** *Brit.* Dehydrated: *desiccated* soup. **2** Shriveled; dried up.

des·ic·ca·tive (des′ə·kā′tiv) *adj.* Drying. —*n.* A drying agent for external application.

des·ic·ca·tor (des′ə·kā′tər) *n.* **1** One who or that which desiccates. **2** An apparatus for drying meat, vegetables, etc. **3** A tightly covered glass or porcelain vessel having a device for absorbing moisture: used to hold substances to be dried.

de·sid·er·ate (di·sid′ə·rāt) *v.t.* **·at·ed, ·at·ing** To feel desire or need for; feel the lack of. [<L *desideratus,* pp. of *desiderare.* See DESIRE.] —**de·sid′er·a′tion** *n.*

de·sid·er·a·tive (di·sid′ə·rā′tiv) *adj.* Having, implying, or expressing desire. —*n.* **1** A desideratum. **2** *Ling.* A verb derived from another verb and indicating desire to perform the action expressed in the original verb, as Latin *esurio* I wish to eat, I am hungry, from *edo* I eat.

de·sid·er·a·tum (di·sid′ə·rā′təm) *n. pl.* **·ta** (-tə) Something not possessed, but needed or regarded as desirable; a want felt. [<L]

de·sign (di·zīn′) *v.t.* **1** To make, draw, or prepare preliminary plans or sketches of. **2** To plan and make with art or skill, as a structure or work of art. **3** To form or make (plans, schemes, etc.) in the mind; conceive; invent. **4** To intend; purpose. **5** *Archaic* To mark out; designate. —*v.i.* **6** To make drawings or plans; be a designer. **7** To plan mentally; conceive. —*n.* **1** An arrangement of forms or colors, or both, intended to be wrought out for use or ornament in or on various materials; a pattern; preliminary sketch; coordination of details. **2** The art of designing; artistic invention; the artistic idea as executed; original work in the graphic or plastic arts. **3** A fixed purpose or intention; plot; scheme. **4** The adaptation of means to an end; plan; contrivance. **5** The object or reason; final purpose. [<MF *désigner* designate <L *designare.* See DESIGNATE.] —**de·sign′a·ble** *adj.*

Synonyms (noun): aim, device, end, intent, intention, object, plan, project, proposal, purpose, scheme. *Design* refers to the adaptation of means to an *end,* the correspondence and coordination of parts, or of separate acts, to produce a result; *intent* and *purpose* overleap all particulars, and fasten on the *end* itself. *Intention* is simply the more familiar form of the legal and philosophical *intent. Plan* relates to details of form, structure, and action, in themselves; *design* considers these same details all as a means to an *end.* The *plan* of a campaign may be for a series of sharp attacks, with the *design* of thus surprising and overpowering the enemy. A man comes to a fixed *intention* to kill his enemy; he forms a *plan* to entrap him into his power, with the *design* of then compassing his death; as the law cannot read the heart, it can only infer the *intent* from the evidences of *design. Intent* denotes a straining, stretching forth toward an *object, purpose* simply the placing it before oneself. *Intention* contemplates the possibility of failure; *purpose* looks to assured success, *intent* or *intention* refers especially to the state of mind of the actor, *purpose* to the result of the action. Compare AIM, END, IDEA, MODEL, PROJECT, PURPOSE, REASON.

des·ig·nate (dez′ig·nāt) *v.t.* **·nat·ed, ·nat·ing 1** To indicate or make recognizable by some mark, sign, or name. **2** To name or entitle; characterize. **3** To select or appoint for a specific purpose, duty, office, etc. See synonyms under CIRCUMSCRIBE. —*adj.* (dez′ig·nit, -nāt) Designated; selected. [<L *designatus,* pp. of *designare* <*de-* completely + *signare* mark <*signum* a sign] —**des′ig·na′tive** *adj.* —**des′ig·na′tor** *n.*

designated hitter In baseball, a batter designated to bat in the place of the pitcher, who pitches throughout the game but does not bat.

des·ig·na·tion (dez′ig·nā′shən) *n.* **1** The act of designating. **2** A distinctive mark, name, or title. **3** Import, as of a word; character; description. See synonyms under NAME.

de·sign·ed·ly (di·zī′nid·lē) *adv.* By design; purposely; intentionally.

des·ig·nee (dez′ig·nē′) *n.* A person designated. [<F *désigné,* pp. of *désigner* DESIGN]

de·sign·er (di·zī′nər) *n.* **1** One who forms designs; a contriver; schemer. **2** One who invents and prepares useful, decorative, or artistic designs. See synonyms under CAUSE.

de·sign·ing (di·zī′ning) *n.* **1** The act or art of making designs or sketches. **2** The act of plotting or scheming. —*adj.* Artful; scheming. See synonyms under INSIDIOUS. —**de·sign′ing·ly** *adv.*

de·sil·ver·ize (dē·sil′və·rīz) *v.t.* **·ized, ·iz·ing** To remove the silver from.

des·i·nence (des′i·nəns) *n.* **1** A termination or ending. **2** *Gram.* A formative suffix. [<MF *désinence* <L *desinentia* <*desinere* <*de-* away + *sinere* leave]

de·sip·i·ence (di·sip′ē·əns) *n.* Silliness; foolishness; trifling. Also **de·sip′i·en·cy.**

de·sip·i·ent (di·sip′ē·ənt) *adj.* Nonsensical; foolish. [<L *desipiens, -entis,* ppr. of *desipere* <*de-* away + *sapere* know, be wise]

de·sir·a·ble (di·zīr′ə·bəl) *adj.* Worthy or likely to be desired or wanted; worth having. See synonyms under PROFITABLE. —**de·sir′a·bil′i·ty, de·sir′a·ble·ness** *n.* —**de·sir′a·bly** *adv.*

de·sire (di·zīr′) *v.t.* **·sired, ·sir·ing 1** To wish or long for; covet; crave. **2** To express a wish for; ask for; request. —*n.* **1** An earnest wishing for something; longing; craving; yearning. **2** A request; wish; prayer. **3** An object desired. **4** Appetite; passion; lust. [<OF *desirer* <L *desiderare,* ? <*de-* from + *sidus, sideris* star; with ref. to astrology] —**de·sir′er** *n.*

Synonyms (noun): appetency, appetite, aspiration, concupiscence, coveting, craving, hankering, inclination, longing, proclivity, propensity, wish. *Inclination* is the mildest of these terms; it is a quiet, or even a vague or unconscious, tendency. Even when we speak of a strong or decided *inclination* we do not express the intensity of *desire. Desire* has a wide range, from the highest objects to the lowest; *desire* is for an object near at hand, or near in thought, and viewed as attainable; a *wish* may be for what is remote or uncertain; or even for what is recognized as impossible. *Craving* is stronger than *hankering; hankering* may be the result of a fitful and capricious *appetite; craving* may be the imperious and reasonable demand of the whole nature. *Longing* is a reaching out with deep and persistent demand for that which is viewed as now distant but at some time attainable; as, the captive's *longing* for release. *Coveting* ordinarily denotes wrong *desire* for that which is another's. Compare APPETITE, FANCY, INCLINATION. *Antonyms:* see synonyms for ANTIPATHY.

de·sir·ous (di·zīr′əs) *adj.* **1** Having desire; experiencing a wish or craving; eager. **2** *Obs.* Exciting desire; desirable.

de·sist (di·zist′) *v.i.* To cease, as from an action or proceeding; forbear; stop: often with *from.* See synonyms under CEASE, END, REST. [<L *desistere* <*de-* from + *sistere* stop, cease] —**de·sis′tance** *n.*

desk (desk) *n.* **1** A table or case specially adapted for writing or studying. **2** A stand for public reading or preaching; pulpit. [<Med. L *desca* <LL *discus.* Doublet of DAIS, DISH, DISK.]

des·man (des′mən) *n. pl.* **·mans** (-mənz) An aquatic, shrew-like, insectivorous mammal (family *Talpidae*), having musk-secreting glands and valued for its fur; especially, *Desmana moschata* of SE Russia and *D. pyrenaica* of the Pyrenees. [<Sw. *desman* musk]

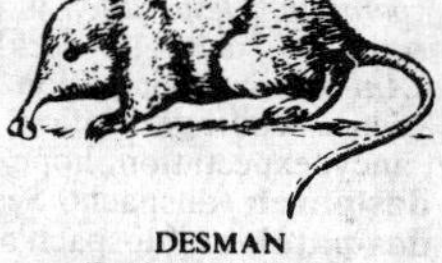

DESMAN
(Body to 10 inches: tail about 6 inches)

des·mid (des′mid) *n.* Any of a family *(Desmidiaceae)* of minute, bright-green, unicellular, mainly solitary, fresh-water algae. The individual is usually divided into symmetrical halves or semi-cells connected by an isthmus. [<NL *desmidium,* the typical genus <Gk. *desmos* a band, chain] —**des·mid·i·a·ceous** (des·mid′ē·ā′shəs) *adj.* —**des·mid′i·an** *adj.*

des·moid (des′moid) *adj. Anat.* Resembling a ligament; ligamentous; also, fibrous: a *desmoid* tumor. —*n. Pathol.* A tough, very hard fibroma. [<Gk. *desmos* band + -OID]

Des Moines (də moin′, -moinz′) The capital of Iowa.

Des Moines River A river in Minnesota and Iowa, flowing 500 miles SE to the Mississippi.

des·mot·ro·pism (des·mot′rə·piz′əm) *n. Chem.* A form of tautomerism in organic compounds in which two molecules may have atoms of the same number, kind, and valence, and arranged in the same position, but with the shifting double bond permitting the independent existence of two types of the compound. [<Gk. *desmos* band + *tropos* turning] —**des·mo·trop·ic** (des′mə·trop′ik, -trō′pik) *adj.*

Des·mou·lins (dā·mōō·laṅ′), **Camille Benoît,** 1760-94, French revolutionist.

Des·na (dyis′nä) A river in western European U.S.S.R., flowing 737 miles SW to the Dnieper.

des·o·late (des′ə·lit) *adj.* **1** Destitute of inhabitants, dwellings, etc.; laid waste; deserted; abandoned. **2** Lonely; solitary. **3** Without friends; forlorn; sorrowful; afflicted; gloomy. See synonyms under BLEAK[1], SAD. —*v.t.* (des′ə·lāt) **·lat·ed, ·lat·ing 1** To deprive of inhabitants. **2** To lay waste, devastate. **3** To

make sorrowful, wretched, or forlorn. **4** To forsake; abandon. [<L *desolatus,* pp. of *desolare* <*de-* completely + *solus* alone] **—des′o·late·ly** *adv.* **—des′o·late·ness** *n.* **—des′o·lat′er, des′o·la′tor** *n.*

des·o·la·tion (des′ə·lā′shən) *n.* **1** The state or condition of being desolate; loneliness; dreariness; sadness; affliction; grief. **2** A desolate region; a waste. **3** The act of making desolate; devastation.

Desolation Island See KERGUELEN ISLANDS.

de·sorp·tion (dē·sôrp′shən) *n. Chem.* The liberation or removal of a substance, usually gaseous, from the surface of adsorbing material: opposed to *adsorption.*

De So·to (də sō′tō), **Hernando,** 1499?–1542, Spanish explorer; discovered the Mississippi River 1541.

de·spair (di·spâr′) *v.i.* To lose or abandon hope; be or become hopeless: with *of.* —*v.t. Obs.* To lose hope or faith in. —*n.* **1** Utter hopelessness and discouragement. **2** That which causes despair or which is despaired of. [<OF *desperer* <L *desperare* <*de-* away + *sperare* hope <*spes* hope] **—de·spair′ing** *adj.* **—de·spair′ing·ly** *adv.*

Synonyms (noun): desperation, despondency, discouragement, hopelessness. *Discouragement* is the result of so much repulse or failure as wears out courage. *Discouragements* too frequent and long continued may produce a settled *hopelessness. Hopelessness* is negative, and may result from simple apathy; *despondency* and *despair* are more emphatic and decided. *Despondency* is an incapacity for the present exercise of hope; *despair* is the utter abandonment of hope. *Despondency* relaxes energy and effort and is always attended with sadness or distress; *despair* may produce a stony calmness, or it may lead to *desperation. Desperation* is energized *despair,* vigorous in action, reckless of consequences. *Antonyms:* anticipation, assurance, cheer, confidence, courage, elation, encouragement, expectancy, expectation, hope, hopefulness, trust.

des·patch (di·spach′) See DISPATCH.

des·patch·er (di·spach′ər) See DISPATCHER.

des·per·a·do (des′pə·rā′dō, -rä′dō) *n. pl.* **·does** or **·dos** A desperate character; a ruffian. [<OSp., pp. of *desperar* <L *desperare.* See DESPAIR.]

des·per·ate (des′pər·it) *adj.* **1** Without care for danger; reckless, as from despair. **2** Resorted to in a last extremity; instigated by or denoting despair; hazardous; frantic; furious. **3** Regarded as almost irremediable; despaired of. **4** Utterly, hopelessly bad; outrageous. **5** Hopeless of recovery; irrecoverable: said especially of a money claim. **6** *Obs.* Despairing. [<L *desperatus,* pp. of *desperare.* See DESPAIR.] **—des′per·ate·ly** *adv.* **—des′per·ate·ness** *n.*

des·per·a·tion (des′pə·rā′shən) *n.* **1** The state of being desperate. **2** The act of despairing. **3** The recklessness of despair; blind fury. See synonyms under DESPAIR.

Des·piau (des·pyō′), **Charles,** 1874–1946, French sculptor.

des·pi·ca·ble (des′pi·kə·bəl, di·spik′ə·bəl) *adj.* Capable of being, or deserving to be, despised; contemptible; mean; vile. See synonyms under BASE[2], PITIFUL. [<LL *despicabilis* <*despicere.* See DESPISE.] **—des′pi·ca·bil′i·ty, des′pi·ca·ble·ness** *n.* **—des′pi·ca·bly** *adv.*

de·spise (di·spīz′) *v.t.* **·spised, ·spis·ing** To regard as contemptible or worthless; disdain; scorn. See synonyms under ABHOR. [<OF *despis-,* stem of *despire* <L *despicere* <*de-* down + *specere* look at] **—de·spis′a·ble** *adj.* **—de·spis′er** *n.*

de·spite (di·spīt′) *n.* **1** An act of defiance, malice, or injury. **2** Extreme malice; hatred; spite. **3** *Obs.* Defiance. See synonyms under SCORN *n.* **—in despite of** Notwithstanding; in opposition or contradiction to: He seized my hand *in despite of* my efforts to the contrary. —*prep.* In spite of; notwithstanding: They will fight on, *despite* impediments. See synonyms under NOTWITHSTANDING. Also **de·spight′.** —*v.t.* **·spit·ed, ·spit·ing** *Obs.* **1** To despise. **2** To offend. [<OF *despit* <L *despectus* a looking down, contempt <*despicere.* See DESPISE.]

de·spite·ful (di·spīt′fəl) *adj. Archaic* Full of spite; malicious; malignant; offensive. **—de·spite′ful·ly** *adv.* **—de·spite′ful·ness** *n.*

des·pit·e·ous (des·pit′ē·əs) *adj. Archaic* Stirred with malicious scorn or hate; despiteful. **—des·pit′e·ous·ly** *adv.*

Des Plaines River (des plānz′) A river in Wisconsin and Illinois, flowing 110 miles SW to the Illinois River.

de·spoil (di·spoil′) *v.t.* To strip or deprive of something by or as by force; plunder. [<OF *despoillier* <L *despoliare* <*de-* completely + *spoliare* rob <*spolium* plunder] **—de·spoil′er** *n.* **—de·spoil′ment** *n.*

de·spo·li·a·tion (di·spō′lē·ā′shən) *n.* The act of despoiling, or state of being despoiled or plundered. [<LL *despoliatio, -onis* <*despoliare.* See DESPOIL.]

de·spond (di·spond′) *v.i.* To lose spirit, courage, or hope; be depressed. —*n. Obs.* Despondency. [<L *despondere* <*de-* away + *spondere* promise] **—de·spond′ing·ly** *adv.*

de·spon·dent (di·spon′dənt) *adj.* Dejected in spirit; disheartened. Also **de·spond′ing.** See synonyms under SAD. **—de·spon′den·cy, de·spon′dence** *n.* **—de·spon′dent·ly** *adv.*

des·pot (des′pət, -pot) *n.* **1** An absolute monarch; autocrat; a hard master; tyrant. **2** In Oriental countries a title, originally of a Byzantine emperor; later, of various subordinate rulers: applied also to the bishops and patriarchs of the Greek Church. See synonyms under MASTER. [<OF <Gk. *despotēs* a master]

des·pot·ic (di·spot′ik) *adj.* Of or like a despot or despotism; tyrannical. See synonyms under ABSOLUTE, ARBITRARY, IMPERIOUS. **—des·pot′i·cal** *adj.* **—des·pot′i·cal·ly** *adv.* **—des·pot′i·cal·ness** *n.*

des·pot·ism (des′pə·tiz′əm) *n.* **1** Absolute power; autocracy. **2** Any tyrannical control.

des·pot·ize (des′pə·tīz) *v.i.* **·ized, ·iz·ing** To be despotic; play the tyrant.

des·pu·mate (des′pyōō·māt, di·spyōō′māt) *v.* **·mat·ed, ·mat·ing** *v.t.* **1** To skim. **2** To throw off as scum. —*v.i.* **3** To throw or work off impurities in froth or scum. [<L *despumatus,* pp. of *despumare* <*de-* away + *spumare* skim <*spuma* scum] **—des′pu·ma′tion** *n.*

des·qua·mate (des′kwə·māt) *v.i.* **·mat·ed, ·mat·ing** *Pathol.* To peel or scale off, as the epithelial cells in certain skin ailments. [<L *desquamatus,* pp. of *desquamare* <*de-* away + *squama* a scale]

des·qua·ma·tion (des′kwə·mā′shən) *n. Pathol.* The scaling off of the cuticle, as in measles and scarlatina.

Des·sa·lines (des·sȧ·lēn′), **Jean Jacques,** 1758–1806, emperor of Haiti 1804–06: called "Jacques I."

Des·sau (des′ou) A city in Saxony-Anhalt, Germany.

des·sert (di·zûrt′) *n.* A service of something sweet, as pie, cake, pudding, fruit, etc., at the close of lunch or dinner. [<F <*desservir* clear a table <*des-* away + *servir* serve]

des·sert·spoon (di·zûrt′spōōn′) *n.* A spoon intermediate in size between a teaspoon and a tablespoon, holding about 8 cubic centimeters. **—des·sert′spoon′ful** *n.*

des·sia·tine (des′yə·tēn) *n.* A Russian unit of area, equal to 2.698 acres. [<Russian *desyatina*]

des·ti·na·tion (des′tə·nā′shən) *n.* **1** A predetermined end. **2** The point to which a journey, or the course of anything, is directed; goal. **3** A destining; appointment.

des·tine (des′tin) *v.t.* **·tined, ·tin·ing** **1** To design for or appoint to a distinct purpose or end. **2** To determine the future of, as by destiny or fate. See synonyms under ALLOT. [<F *destiner* <L *destinare* make fast, ult. <*de-* completely + *stare* stand]

des·tined (des′tind) *adj.* Bound for an appointed place; assigned to go to a place designated.

Des·ti·nies (des′tə·nēz) In classical mythology, the Fates or Parcae.

Des·tinn (des′tin), **Emmy,** 1878–1930, Czech operatic soprano: real name *Kittl.*

des·ti·ny (des′tə·nē) *n. pl.* **·nies** **1** That to which any person or thing is destined; fortune; doom. **2** Inevitable necessity; divine decree; fate. See synonyms under NECESSITY. [<OF *destinée* <*destiner.* See DESTINE.]

des·ti·tute (des′tə·tōōt, -tyōōt) *adj.* **1** Not having or possessing; entirely lacking: with *of.* **2** Being in want; extremely poor. **3** *Obs.* Desolate; forsaken. [<L *destitutus,* pp. of *destituere* abandon <*de-* down + *statuere* set, place]

des·ti·tu·tion (des′tə·tōō′shən, -tyōō′-) *n.* The state or condition of being destitute; extreme poverty. See synonyms under POVERTY.

des·tri·er (des′trē·ər, des·trir′) *n. Archaic* A war horse. [<AF *destrer,* OF *destrier* <LL *(equus) dextrarius* (horse) led by the right hand <L *dexter* right]

de·stroy (di·stroi′) *v.t.* **1** To ruin utterly; consume; dissolve. **2** To demolish; raze; tear down. **3** To put an end to; do away with. **4** To kill. **5** To make ineffective; counteract. See synonyms under ABOLISH, ANNUL, BREAK, DEMOLISH, EXTERMINATE, SUBVERT. [<OF *destruire,* ult. <L *destruere* <*de-* down + *struere* build]

de·stroy·er (di·stroi′ər) *n.* **1** One who or that which destroys. **2** A speedy war vessel, smaller than a cruiser, and equipped with guns, torpedo tubes, depth bombs, and anti-aircraft batteries: widely used as an escort

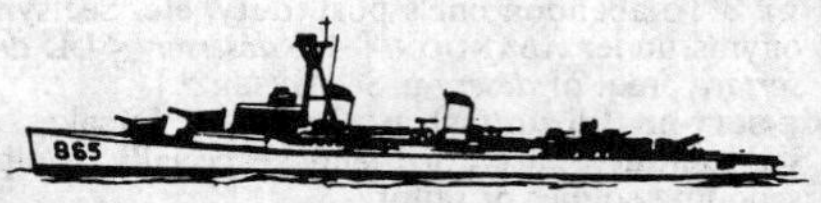

DESTROYER, U.S. NAVY, WORLD WAR II

vessel. **3** A self-propelled anti-tank gun: also **tank destroyer.**

destroyer escort A U.S. Navy vessel smaller and slower than a destroyer and equipped for anti-submarine warfare.

de·struct (di·strukt′) *Aerospace n.* The act of destroying a defective missile or rocket after launch. —*v.t.* & *v.i.* To destroy a defective missile or rocket after launch.

de·struc·ti·ble (di·struk′tə·bəl) *adj.* Liable to destruction; capable of being destroyed. **—de·struc′ti·bil′i·ty** *n.* **—de·struc′ti·ble·ness** *n.*

de·struc·tion (di·struk′shən) *n.* **1** The act of destroying, or state of being destroyed; demolition; ruin. **2** That which destroys. See synonyms under LOSS, RUIN. [<OF <L *destructio, -onis* <destruere. See DESTROY.]

de·struc·tion·ist (di·struk′shən·ist) *n.* **1** One who favors destruction, or the overthrow of existing conditions. **2** An anarchist.

de·struc·tive (di·struk′tiv) *adj.* **1** Tending or fitted to destroy; causing destruction. **2** Pernicious; ruinous. See synonyms under NOISOME, PERNICIOUS. **—de·struc′tive·ly** *adv.* **—de·struc′tive·ness** *n.*

destructive distillation A process in which a complex organic substance such as wood or coal is decomposed by heat in the absence of air and the volatile components are recovered by condensation.

de·struc·tiv·i·ty (dē′struk·tiv′ə·tē) *n.* The state or quality of being destructive.

de·struc·tor (di·struk′tər) *n.* A furnace or retort for burning refuse.

des·ue·tude (des′wə·tōōd, -tyōōd) *n.* **1** The cessation of use. **2** A condition of disuse. [<MF *désuétude* <L *desuetudo* <*desuescere* <*de-* away + *suescere* be used]

de·sul·fur·ize (dē·sul′fə·rīz) *v.t.* **·ized, ·iz·ing** To remove sulfur from. Also **de·sul′fur, de·sul′fur·ate, de·sul′phur·ize.** **—de·sul′fur·i·za′tion** *n.* **—de·sul′fur·iz′er** *n.*

des·ul·to·ry (des′əl·tôr′ē, -tō′rē) *adj.* **1** Passing abruptly and irregularly from one thing to another; fitful; changeable; unmethodical. **2** Starting suddenly as if by a leap; not connected with what precedes. See synonyms under CURSORY, IRREGULAR. [<L *desultorius* <*desultor* a leaper <*de-* down + *salire* leap, jump] **—des′ul·to′ri·ly** *adv.* **—des′ul·to′ri·ness** *n.*

de·tach (di·tach′) *v.t.* **1** To unfasten and make separate; disconnect; disunite. **2** To separate and send off for a special service, duty, etc., as a regiment or a ship. See synonyms under ABSTRACT. [<F *détacher* <*dé-* away (<L *dis-*) + OF *tache* nail <Gmc.] **—de·tach′a·bil′i·ty** *n.* **—de·tach′a·ble** *adj.* **—de·tach′er** *n.*

de·tached (di·tacht′) *adj.* **1** Separated from others; disconnected; disunited. **2** *Mil.* Designated to special duty elsewhere than with the unit to which assigned, with or without transfer of administration. **3** Pertaining to relief from assignment or attachment and assumption of another status. **4** In painting, standing alone in the foreground or distinctly separate from other objects. **5** Aloof; hence, unbiased.

detached retina *Pathol.* A disconnection of the inner layers of the retina from the pigment layer.

de·tach·ment (di·tach′mənt) *n.* **1** A detaching; separation. **2** Something detached, as a body of troops for special service. **3** Dissociation from surroundings or worldly interest; aloofness.

de·tail (di·tāl′, dē′tāl) *n.* **1** A separately considered particular or item; minor part; accessory. **2** *Mil.* A small detachment assigned to some subordinate service; also, the person or persons assigned. **3** In art and architecture, a minor part essential to the completeness and finish of a work, yet secondary and accessory. See synonyms under CIRCUMSTANCE. —**in detail** Item by item; with particularity. [<*v.*] —*v.t.* (di·tāl′) **1** To report or narrate minutely; enter into or give the details of. **2** *Mil.* (often dē′tāl) To select and send off for a special service, duty, etc. See synonyms under RELATE. [<F *détailler* cut into pieces <*dé-* completely + *tailler* cut up]

detail drawing Drawing of special or typical parts or features of a structure, machine, or design, made to a large scale or of full size.

de·tain (di·tān′) *v.t.* **1** To restrain from proceeding; stop; delay. **2** To keep back; withhold. **3** To hold in custody. See synonyms under RETAIN. [<OF *detenir* <L *detinere* <*de-* away + *tenere* hold] —**de·tain′ment** *n.*

de·tain·er (di·tā′nər) *n.* **1** One who detains, stops, or withholds. **2** *Law* **a** A process for recovering possession of lands or goods wrongfully held. **b** A writ directing the continued holding of a prisoner in custody pending an additional action. —**forcible detainer** The seizure by violence, or keeping possession of by threats, force, or the display of arms, of lands or tenements without authority of law.

de·tect (di·tekt′) *v.t.* **1** To discover, perceive, or find, as something obscure: to *detect* an error in spelling. **2** To expose or uncover, as a crime, fault, or a criminal. **3** *Telecom.* To rectify (a high-frequency carrier wave) to the desired lower frequency; to demodulate. See synonyms under DISCOVER. [<L *detectus*, pp. of *detegere* <*de-* away + *tegere* cover] —**de·tect′a·ble** or **·i·ble** *adj.* —**de·tect′er** *n.*

de·tec·ta·phone (di·tek′tə·fōn) *n.* A wiretapping device for the interception and transmission of telephone messages.

de·tec·tion (di·tek′shən) *n.* **1** The act of detecting; discovery. **2** *Telecom.* Any method of operating on a modulated signal wave so as to obtain the signal imparted to it: a process of demodulation of incoming electrical signals.

de·tec·tive (di·tek′tiv) *adj.* **1** Skilled in or fitted for detection; employed to detect. **2** Belonging or pertaining to detectives and their work. —*n.* A person, often a policeman, whose work is to investigate crimes, discover evidence, capture criminals, etc.

de·tec·tor (di·tek′tər) *n.* **1** One who or that which detects. **2** A device for detecting, as for showing low water in a boiler, indicating the presence of torpedoes under water, etc. **3** *Electr.* A device for discovering the presence of electric waves, as a coherer; also, a portable galvanometer. **4** *Telecom.* A demodulator or a device for obtaining the signal from a modulated carrier.

de·tent (di·tent′) *n. Mech.* A stop or checking device, as a pin, lever, etc., on a ratchet wheel or the like. [<F *détente* <*détendre* slacken <*dé-* away (<L *dis-*) + *tendre* stretch <L *tendere*]

dé·tente (dā·tänt′) *n. French* An easing, as of discord between nations.

de·ten·tion (di·ten′shən) *n.* **1** The act of detaining. **2** The state of being detained; restraint; custody; delay. [<L *detentio, -onis* <*detinere.* See DETAIN.] —**de·ten′tive** *adj.*

detention camp A camp at which recruits or prisoners of war are held to determine whether they have communicable diseases.

de·ter (di·tûr′) *v.t.* **·terred, ·ter·ring** To prevent or restrain by fear, difficulty, danger, etc., from acting or proceeding. [<L *deterrere* <*de-* away + *terrere* frighten] —**de·ter′ment** *n.*

de·terge (di·tûrj′) *v.t.* **·terged, ·terg·ing** **1** To cleanse of morbid or dead matter, as a wound. **2** To wipe off; purge away. [<L *detergere* <*de-* away + *tergere* wipe]

de·ter·gent (di·tûr′jənt) *adj.* Having cleansing qualities; purging. —*n.* **1** A cleansing substance, as soap or an antiseptic. **2** *Chem.* Any of a class of surface-active compounds having strong cleansing effects. —**de·ter′gence, de·ter′gen·cy** *n.*

de·te·ri·o·rate (di·tir′ē·ə·rāt′) *v.t.* & *v.i.* **·rat·ed, ·rat·ing** To make or become worse; reduce in quality, value, etc.; degenerate. See synonyms under CORRUPT, IMPAIR. [<L *deterioratus*, pp. of *deteriorare* <*deterior* worse] —**de·te′ri·o·ra′tion** *n.* —**de·te′ri·o·ra′tive** *adj.*

de·ter·mi·na·ble (di·tûr′mi·nə·bəl) *adj.* **1** That may be accurately found out, settled, or decided. **2** *Law* Liable to be put an end to; terminable.

de·ter·mi·nant (di·tûr′mə·nənt) *adj.* Determinative. —*n.* **1** That which influences to determine. **2** *Math.* A set of algebraic quantities arranged in a square matrix and operated upon according to special rules for the solution of various linear systems of equations. **3** *Biol.* A former name introduced by Weismann for one of the hypothetical secondary units of germ plasm or hereditary substance regulating the origin and the development of cells and systems of cells.

de·ter·mi·nate (di·tûr′mə·nit) *adj.* **1** Definitely limited or fixed; specific; distinct. **2** Predetermined; positive. **3** Known or fixed, as a mathematical quantity. **4** *Bot.* Limited in extent, as an inflorescence or cyme. **5** Determined; intended; determining; decisive. —**de·ter′mi·nate·ly** *adv.* —**de·ter′mi·nate·ness** *n.*

de·ter·mi·na·tion (di·tûr′mə·nā′shən) *n.* **1** The act of determining; a firm resolve. **2** The quality of being earnest and decided; firmness. **3** Judicial decision; authoritative opinion or conclusion. **4** The ascertaining exactly of the character, amount, dimensions, or proportion of a thing; the result of such investigation. **5** *Logic* The making of a notion definite or more definite by the addition of a qualifying or limiting idea; specification; also, an attribute which determines. **6** *Biol.* **a** The classification of plants and animals. **b** The process whereby the cells of a developing organism become differentiated in structure and function: sex *determination.* **7** *Physiol.* Tendency or increased flow, as of blood, to a part. **8** The exercise of decisive force or power: *determination* of the will toward an object. **9** *Obs.* A limiting or putting an end to.

Synonyms: decision, resolution, resolve. *Decision* is literally a cutting off, or cutting short, of debate or questioning; *determination* is a setting of the limits within which one must act; *resolve* is a separating of the essential act from all that might cause doubt or hesitation. *Resolve* always refers to a single act; *resolution* may have the same meaning, or it may refer to the habit of mind which readily forms and adheres to a *resolve. Decision* and *determination* especially mark the beginning of action; *resolution* holds out to the end. See AIM, PURPOSE. Compare synonyms for DESIGN. *Antonyms*: doubt, faltering, fickleness, hesitancy, hesitation, indecision, instability, irresolution, vacillation, wavering.

de·ter·mi·na·tive (di·tûr′mə·nā′tiv, -mə·nə·tiv) *adj.* Tending or having power to determine or fix; deciding; shaping. —*n.* **1** That which determines. **2** *Gram.* A demonstrative pronoun. **3** *Ling.* In certain languages, an element affixed to a word which modifies or determines its meaning, as *-sc-* in Latin *calesco* I grow warm, from *caleo* I am warm. —**de·ter′mi·na′tive·ly** *adv.* —**de·ter′mi·na′tive·ness** *n.*

de·ter·mine (di·tûr′min) *v.* **·mined, ·min·ing** *v.t.* **1** To settle or decide, as an argument, question, or debate. **2** To ascertain or fix, as after thought or observation. **3** To cause to reach a decision. **4** To regulate; fix or decide causally: Demand *determines* supply. **5** To give aim, purpose, or direction to. **6** To set bounds to; limit in extent, variety, etc. **7** *Logic* To limit or define by adding differences. **8** To limit; terminate: usually in legal usage. —*v.i.* **9** To come to a decision; resolve. **10** To come to an end: usually in legal usage. See synonyms under PURPOSE. [<OF *determiner* <L *determinare* <*de-* completely + *terminare* end <*terminum* a limit]

de·ter·mined (di·tûr′mind) *adj.* Resolute; settled; determinate. See synonyms under FIRM, OBSTINATE. —**de·ter′mined·ly** *adv.* —**de·ter′mined·ness** *n.*

de·ter·min·er (di·tûr′mə·nər) *n.* **1** A person or thing that determines. **2** *Gram.* Any of a class of words, including articles and possessive adjectives, whose presence in a phrase, often before a descriptive adjective, indicates that the head word is a noun or substantive. In *his old coat,* "his" is a determiner.

de·ter·min·ism (di·tûr′mə·niz′əm) *n. Philos.* The doctrine that man's choices, decisions, and actions are decided by antecedent causes, inherited or environmental, acting upon his character: opposed to *free will.* —**de·ter′min·ist** *adj.* & *n.* —**de·ter′min·is′tic** *adj.*

de·ter·rent (di·tûr′ənt) *adj.* Tending or serving to deter. —*n.* Something that deters. —**de·ter′rence** *n.*

de·ter·sion (di·tûr′zhən) *n.* A cleansing, as of a wound. [<LL *detersio, -onis* <*detergere.* See DETERGE.]

de·ter·sive (di·tûr′siv) *adj.* Cleansing; detergent. —*n.* A cleansing or purging medicine or agent.

de·test (di·test′) *v.t.* To hate; dislike with intensity; abhor. See synonyms under ABHOR. [<MF *détester* <L *detestari* denounce <*de-* away + *testis* a witness] —**de·test′er** *n.* —**de·test′a·bil′i·ty** *n.* —**de·test′a·ble** *adj.* —**de·test′a·ble·ness** *n.* —**de·test′a·bly** *adv.*

de·tes·ta·tion (dē′tes·tā′shən) *n.* **1** Extreme dislike; hatred; abhorrence. **2** An act or thing detested. See synonyms under ABOMINATION, ANTIPATHY, HATRED.

de·throne (dē·thrōn′) *v.t.* **·throned, ·thron·ing** To remove from the throne; depose. —**de·throne′ment** *n.* —**de·thron′er** *n.*

det·i·nue (det′i·nyōō) *n. Law* An action to recover personal property wrongfully detained; the writ used in such action; also, the act of detaining wrongfully. [<OF *detenue*, pp. of *detenir.* See DETAIN.]

Det·mold (det′mōlt) A city in North Rhine-Westphalia, Germany; former capital of Lippe.

det·o·nate (det′ə·nāt, dē′tə-) *v.* **·nat·ed, ·nat·ing** *v.t.* To cause to explode suddenly and with violence. —*v.i.* To explode suddenly with a loud report. [<L *detonatus*, pp. of *detonare* <*de-* down + *tonare* thunder]

detonating powder A powder, chiefly of the mercury fulminates, which explodes violently when heated or struck: used chiefly to fire other explosives.

det·o·na·tion (det′ə·nā′shən, dē′tə-) *n.* A violent and sudden explosion resulting from the instantaneous combustion of a mixture, compound, or substance.

det·o·na·tor (det′ə·nā′tər, dē′tə-) *n.* Any contrivance, as a primer or fuze, for detonating the main charge of a projectile, bomb, etc.

de·tor·sion (dē·tôr′shən) *n.* The act of twisting back or removing torsion. [<DE- + TORSION]

de·tort (dē·tôrt′) *v.t. Obs.* To pervert; distort. [<L *detortus*, pp. of *detorquere* <*de-* away + *torquere* twist]

de·tour (dē′tŏŏr, di·tŏŏr′) *n.* A roundabout way; any turning aside from a direct route or course of action; specifically, a byroad substituted for part of a main road temporarily impassable. —*v.t.* & *v.i.* To go or cause to go by a roundabout way. [<F *détour* <*détourner* <*dé-* away + *tourner* turn]

de·tox·i·cate (dē·tok′sə·kāt) *v.t.* **·cat·ed, ·cat·ing** To reduce or destroy the toxic properties of (a substance). [<DE- + (IN)TOXICATE] —**de·tox′i·ca′tion** *n.* —**de·tox′i·cant** (-kənt) *n.*

de·tract (di·trakt′) *v.t.* **1** To take away; withdraw. **2** *Obs.* To disparage. —*v.i.* **3** To take away a part, especially from a reputation, enjoyment, honor, etc. [<L *detractus*, pp. of *detrahere* <*de-* away + *trahere* draw, pull] —**de·trac′tive** *adj.* —**de·tract′ing·ly** *adv.* —**de·trac′tor, de·trac′ter** *n.*

de·trac·tion (di·trak′shən) *n.* The act of detracting; slander; defamation. See synonyms under SCANDAL.

de·trac·to·ry (di·trak′tər·ē) *adj.* Defamatory.

de·train (dē·trān′) *v.t.* & *v.i.* To leave or cause to leave a railway train. **—de·train′ment** *n.*
det·ri·ment (det′rə·mənt) *n.* **1** Something that impairs or injures, or causes damage or loss. **2** Injury or loss. See synonyms under INJURY, LOSS. [<L *detrimentum* <*deterere* <*de-* away + *terere* rub]
det·ri·men·tal (det′rə·men′təl) *adj.* Injurious; hurtful. See synonyms under BAD, NOISOME. **—det′ri·men′tal·ly** *adv.*
de·tri·tion (di·trish′ən) *n.* The act of rubbing or wearing off particles.
de·tri·tus (di·trī′təs) *n.* **1** *Geol.* Loose fragments or particles separated from masses of rock by erosion, glacial action, and other mechanical forces. **2** Any mass of disintegrated material; debris. [<L <*deterere.* See DETRIMENT.] **—de·tri′tal** *adj.*
De·troit (di·troit′) A port on the Detroit River in SE Michigan.
Detroit River A river 31 miles long, connecting Lake St. Clair with Lake Erie and forming part of the boundary between the United States and Canada.
de trop (də trō′) *French* Too much; not wanted; superfluous.
de·trude (di·trōōd′) *v.t.* **·trud·ed, ·trud·ing 1** To thrust down or out. **2** To push down forcibly. [<L *detrudere* <*de-* away + *trudere* thrust] **—de·tru′sion** *n.* **—de·tru′sive** *adj.*
de·trun·cate (di·trung′kāt) *v.t.* **·cat·ed, ·cat·ing** To shorten by cutting off a part; cut off. [<L *detruncatus,* pp. of *detruncare* <*de-* from + *truncare* lop] **—de′trun·ca′tion** *n.*
Det·ting·en (det′ing·ən) A village in NW Bavaria; scene of a French defeat by English and German forces, 1743.
de·tu·mes·cence (dē′tōō·mes′əns, -tyōō-) *n.* *Physiol.* **1** The subsidence of any swelling in an organ or part. **2** Subsidence of the erectile tissue of the genitals following the orgasm. **—de′tu·mes′cent** *adj.*
Deu·ca·li·on (dōō·kā′lē·ən, dyōō-) In Greek mythology, a son of Prometheus who, with his wife Pyrrha, was the only survivor of a deluge sent by Zeus to punish the world's wickedness: they renewed the human race by throwing stones behind them, those thrown by Deucalion becoming men, those by Pyrrha, women.
deuce[1] (dōōs, dyōōs) *n.* **1** Two; especially, a card or side of a die having two spots. **2** In tennis, a condition of the score when it is tied at 40 or at five games each and either side must win two successive points for the game or two successive games for the set. [<F *deux* <L *duo* two]
deuce[2] (dōōs, dyōōs) *n.* The devil; plague: a mild oath used with or without the article in exclamation, signifying disgust or surprise at an unpleasant occurrence. [Prob. <LG *de duus* the deuce (lowest throw at dice)]
deuce-ace (dōōs′ās′, dyōōs′-) *n.* A low throw at dice (ace and deuce); hence, poor luck.
deu·ced (dōō′sid, dyōō′-, dōōst, dyōōst) *adj.* Devilish; confounded; exceeding. *—adv.* Deucedly.
deu·ced·ly (dōō′sid·lē, dyōō′-) *adv.* Extremely; devilishly; confoundedly.
De·us (dē′əs, dā′ōōs) *n. Lat.* God.
de·us ex mach·i·na (dē′əs eks mak′ə·nə) **1** In classical drama, a god brought to the stage in a mechanical device to intervene in the action. **2** Any unexpected event, person, or circumstance worked into a play or novel to resolve a problem. **3** Contrived or providential salvation. [<L, a god from a machine]
De·us vo·bis·cum (dē′əs vō·bis′kəm) *Latin* God be with you.
De·us vult (dē′əs vult′) *Latin* God wills it: the battle cry of the First Crusade.
deu·ter·ag·o·nist (dōō′tər·ag′ə·nist, dyōō′-) *n.* The actor next in importance to the protagonist in the ancient Greek drama. [<Gk. *deuteragōnistēs* <*deuteros* second + *agōnistēs* actor]
deu·ter·a·no·pi·a (dōō′tər·ə·nō′pē·ə, dyōō′-) *n.* *Pathol.* An eye defect which results in an inability to see the color green. Also **deu′ter·a·nop′si·a** (-nop′sē·ə). [<DEUTER(O)- + Gk. *an-* without + *ops* eye]
deu·te·ric (dōō·tir′ik, dyōō-) *adj. Chem.* Pertaining to an acid containing deuterium.
deu·ter·ide (dōō′tə·rīd, dyōō′-) *n. Chem.* Any compound of deuterium with an element or radical.
deu·te·ri·um (dōō·tir′ē·əm, dyōō-) *n.* The isotope of hydrogen having twice the mass of ordinary hydrogen. Symbol, D or ^{2}H: also called *heavy hydrogen.* [<NL <Gk. *deuteros* second]
deuterium oxide Heavy water.
deutero- *combining form* Second; secondary: *deuterogamy.* Also, before vowels, **deuter-**. [<Gk. *deuteros* second]
deu·ter·o·ca·non·i·cal (dōō′tər·ō·kə·non′i·kəl, dyōō′-) *adj.* Pertaining to or constituting a second canon: applied to the books or parts of books of the Old and New Testament whose authenticity and inspiration were at first contested and afterward admitted by the Roman Catholic Church; in Protestant churches, the contested parts of the Old Testament are considered extracanonical. See APOCRYPHA.
deu·ter·og·a·mist (dōō′tər·og′ə·mist, dyōō′-) *n.* One who marries a second time.
deu·ter·og·a·my (dōō′tər·og′ə·mē, dyōō′-) *n.* A second marriage. [<DEUTERO- + Gk. *gamos* marriage]
Deu·ter·o-I·sa·iah (dōō′tər·ō·ī·zā′ə, dyōō′-) The presumed author of *Isaiah* xl-lxvi, a post-exilian Hebrew writer.
deu·ter·on (dōō′tər·on, dyōō′-) *n. Physics* The nucleus of a deuterium atom. [<NL <Gk., neut. sing. of *deuteros* second]
Deu·ter·on·o·my (dōō′tər·on′ə·mē, dyōō′-) The fifth book of the Pentateuch, which contains a second statement of the Mosaic law. [<Gk. *deuteronomion* <*deuteros* second + *nomos* law]
deu·ter·op·a·thy (dōō′tər·op′ə·thē, dyōō′-) *n.* *Med.* A disease associated with but secondary to another disease. [<DEUTERO- + -PATHY] **—deu·ter·o·path·ic** (dōō′tər·ō·path′ik, dyōō′-) *adj.*
deuto- *combining form* Deutero-.
deu·to·plasm (dōō′tə·plaz′əm, dyōō′-) *n. Biol.* The nutritive material formed within the cytoplasm of a cell; the food yolk of an ovum or egg cell. Also **deu·ter·o·plasm** (dōō′tər·ō·plaz′əm, dyōō′-). **—deu′to·plas′mic** or **·plas′tic** *adj.*
Deutsch·land (doich′länt) The German name for GERMANY.
Deutsch·land ü·ber al·les (doich′länt ü′bər ä′les) *German* Germany above all: a nationalist song and slogan.
deut·zi·a (dōōt′sē·ə, doit′-) *n.* Any of a genus (*Deutzia*) of ornamental shrubs having clusters of pink or white flowers. [<NL <Johann van der *Deutz,* 1743–1784, Dutch horticulturist]
de·va (dā′və) *n.* In Hindu mythology, a god or good spirit. Also **dev** (dāv). [<Skt.]
de Va·le·ra (dev′ə·lâr′ə, dā′və·lir′ə), **Éamon,** 1882–1975, Irish statesman born in the United States; prime minister 1937–48, 1951–54, 1957–59; president 1959–73.
de·val·u·ate (dē·val′yōō·āt) *v.t.* **·at·ed, ·at·ing 1** To reduce or annul the value or worth of. **2** To establish the value of (a currency) at some point below par. Also **de·val′ue. —de·val′u·a′tion** *n.*
De·va·na·ga·ri (dā′və·nä′gə·rē) *n.* The script of the educated classes in northern, western, and central India, in which Sanskrit and much of the literature of the modern Indic languages are written: also called *Nagari.*
dev·as·tate (dev′ə·stāt) *v.t.* **·tat·ed, ·tat·ing** To lay waste, as by war, fire, flood, etc.; destroy; ravage. [<L *devastatus,* pp. of *devastare* <*de-* completely + *vastare* lay waste <*vastus* waste] **—dev′as·tat′ing** *adj.* **—dev′as·tat′ing·ly** *adv.* **—dev′as·ta′tor** *n.*
dev·as·ta·tion (dev′ə·stā′shən) *n.* The act of devastating or condition of having been devastated; waste; desolation; ravage.
deve (dēv) *v.i. Brit. Dial.* To dive.
dev·el (dev′əl) *v.t. Scot.* To strike with a heavy blow. *—n.* A stunning blow.
de·vel·op (di·vel′əp) *v.t.* **1** To expand or bring out the potentialities, capabilities, etc., of; cause to come to completeness or perfection. **2** To expand; enlarge upon, as an idea. **3** To make more extensive or productive, as atomic power. **4** *Phot.* **a** To bring to view by means of a developer (the latent image) produced on a sensitized surface by means of light. **b** To subject (a plate or film) to a developer. **5** *Biol.* To cause to evolve to a higher stage, as in function or structure. **6** *Music* To elaborate on (a theme). **7** *Math.* To expand (an expression) in the form of a series. **8** *Geom.* To change the form of (a surface) as if by bending or unbending. **9** *Obs.* To disclose; reveal. *—v.i.* **10** To increase in capabilities, maturity, etc. **11** To advance from a lower to a higher state; grow; evolve. **12** To disclose itself; become apparent: The plot of a novel *develops.* Also **de·vel′ope.** See synonyms under AMPLIFY. [<F *développer* <*de-* away (<L *dis-*) + OF *voluper* fold] **—de·vel′op·a·ble** *adj.*
de·vel·op·er (di·vel′əp·ər) *n.* **1** One who or that which develops. **2** One who builds housing, shopping centers, etc., on a speculative basis. **3** *Phot.* A chemical bath or reagent used for making a latent image visible on a photographic plate.
de·vel·op·ment (di·vel′əp·mənt) *n.* **1** Gradual evolution or completion; also, the result of such an evolution or completion. **2** *Biol.* The series of changes by which an individual plant or animal passes from a lower to a higher state of being or from an embryonic condition to maturity. See synonyms under EDUCATION, PROGRESS. **—de·vel·op·men·tal** (di·vel′əp·men′təl) *adj.* **—de·vel′op·men′tal·ly** *adv.* **—de·vel′op·men′ta·ry** (-tər·ē) *adj.*
Dev·e·reux (dev′ə·rōō), **Robert** See ESSEX, EARL OF.
de·vest (di·vest′) *v.t.* **1** *Law* To take away, as a title or estate. **2** *Obs.* To remove vesture from; divest; strip. [<OF *devester, desvestir* <*de-* from (<L *dis-*) + *vestir* clothe <L *vestire* <*vestis* a garment]
De·vi (dā′vē) The Hindu goddess Shakti, consort of Siva. [<Skt., goddess]
de·vi·ate (dē′vē·āt) *v.* **·at·ed, ·at·ing** *v.i.* **1** To turn aside from a straight or appointed way or course; wander; diverge. **2** To differ, as in thought or belief. *—v.t.* **3** To cause to turn aside. See synonyms under BEND[1], WANDER. [<LL *deviatus,* pp. of *deviare* <*de-* from + *via* a road] **—de′vi·a′tor** *n.* **—de·vi·a·to·ry** (dē′vē·ə·tôr′ē, -tō′rē) *adj.*
de·vi·a·tion (dē′vē·ā′shən) *n.* **1** The act of deviating, or its result. **2** Variation or deflection from a straight line, from a prescribed course, or from a customary method or standard. **3** *Stat.* The difference between one value in a series of observations and the arithmetic mean of the series.
de·vi·a·tion·ism (dē′vē·ā′shən·iz′əm) *n.* In Communist ideology, departure from currently established party doctrine or policy. **—de′vi·a′tion·ist** *n.*
de·vice (di·vīs′) *n.* **1** Something invented and constructed for a special purpose; contrivance. **2** A plan or scheme; an artifice; stratagem; plot. **3** A fanciful design or pattern, as in embroidery or ornamentation. **4** A motto or emblem, as on a shield. **5** The act, state, or power of devising; inventive skill. **6** Expressed desire; inclination: now only in the phrase *left to one's own devices.* **7** *Obs.* Design or style of anything; cast of mind. **8** *Obs.* A spectacle; show; masque. See synonyms under ARTIFICE, DESIGN, PROJECT. [<OF *devis* intention, will <*diviser,* infl. by OF *devise* emblem, design. See DEVISE.]
dev·il (dev′əl) *n.* **1** *Sometimes cap.* In Jewish and Christian theology, the prince and ruler of the kingdom of evil; Satan. **2** Any subordinate evil spirit; a demon. **3** In Christian Science usage, Evil; a lie; error; neither corporeality nor mind; opposite of Truth; a belief in sin, sickness, and death; animal magnetism or hypnotism. **4** A wicked or malignant person. **5** A wretched fellow: poor *devil.* **6** A person of great energy, daring, or effrontery. **7** A machine for any of various purposes, as for cutting or tearing up rags. **8** A printer's apprentice or errand boy: also **printer's devil. 9** An expletive used profanely or humorously: with *the.* **10** In English law, a junior barrister who prepares a case for a senior, receiving little or no pay. **—between the devil and the deep blue sea** Between equally bad alternatives; in a dilemma. **—the devil to pay** Trouble to be expected as a consequence. **—to give the devil his due** To acknowledge the ability or success of even a bad or disliked person, antagonist, etc. *—v.t.* **dev·iled** or **·illed, dev·il·ing** or **·il·ling 1** To prepare for eating by seasoning highly and sometimes broiling or frying. **2** To make fiendish. **3** To cut up, as cloth, in a devil. **4** To annoy or harass excessively; tease. [OE

dēofol < LL *diabolus* < Gk. *diabolos* a slanderer; later, the devil < *diaballein* slander < *dia-* across + *ballein* throw]

dev·il·fish (dev′əl·fish′) *n. pl.* **·fish** or **·fish·es** 1 Any of a family *(Mobulidae)* of very large top-swimming rays having a pair of fins projecting from the head with which they sweep small prey into the mouth. Also called *devil ray, manta, manta ray.* 2 The octopus.

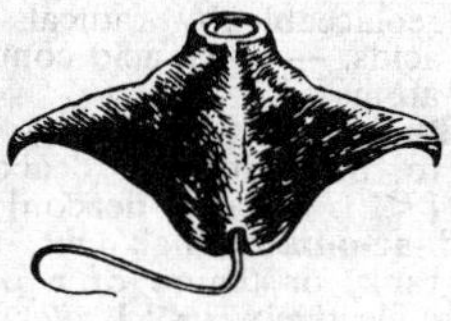

DEVILFISH (Often 20 feet in breadth)

devil grass Any of the several spreading, injurious grasses.

dev·il·ish (dev′əl·ish, dev′lish) *adj.* 1 Having the qualities of the devil; diabolical; malicious. 2 *Colloq.* Excessive; enormous. —*adv. Colloq.* Excessively; very. See synonyms under INFERNAL. —**dev′il·ish·ly** *adv.* —**dev′il·ish·ness** *n.*

dev·il·kin (dev′əl·kin) *n.* An imp; a little devil.

dev·il-may-care (dev′əl·mā·kâr′) *adj.* Careless; reckless; rollicking.

dev·il·ment (dev′əl·mənt) *n.* Mischief; impish action or tricks.

dev·il-on-two-sticks (dev′əl·on·to͞o′stiks′) *n.* The spool or top used in the game diabolo.

dev·il·ry (dev′əl·rē) *n. pl.* **·ries** 1 Malicious mischief; deviltry. 2 Evil magic or art; demonology.

devil's advocate 1 A Roman Catholic official whose duty is to raise objections to a candidate for beatification or canonization. 2 One who argues perversely or for a bad cause.

dev·il's-darn·ing-nee·dle (dev′əlz·där′ning·nēd′l) *n.* 1 A dragonfly. 2 The Venus's-comb. Also **dev′il-darn′ing-nee′dle.**

dev·il's-food cake (dev′əlz·fo͞od′) A rich, reddish-brown chocolate cake.

Devil's Island A rocky island off the Atlantic coast of northern French Guiana; formerly a French penal colony: French *Île du Diable.*

devil's tattoo A drumming or pounding with the feet or hands.

dev·il·try (dev′əl·trē) *n. pl.* **·tries** 1 Wanton and malicious mischief, or the spirit inciting it 2 Devilry.

dev·il·wood (dev′əl·wo͝od′) *n.* The American olive *(Osmanthus americanus),* a small tree of the southern Atlantic states, with a fine-grained, hard wood.

de·vi·ous (dē′vē·əs) *adj.* 1 Winding or leading away from a straight course; rambling. 2 Straying from the way of duty. See synonyms under IRREGULAR. [< L *devius* < *de-* from + *via* way] —**de′vi·ous·ly** *adv.* —**de′vi·ous·ness** *n.*

de·vis·a·ble (di·vī′zə·bəl) *adj.* 1 *Law* That can be devised, or given by will. 2 That can be contrived or invented.

de·vi·sal (di·vī′zəl) *n.* The act of contriving or of bequeathing; a devising.

de·vise (di·vīz′) *v.* **·vised, ·vis·ing** *v.t.* 1 To form in the mind; invent; contrive; plan. 2 *Law* To transmit (real estate) by will. 3 *Obs.* To separate; distribute. 4 *Obs.* To imagine; guess. —*v.i.* 5 To form a plan. —*n. Law* 1 A gift of lands by will. 2 The act of bequeathing lands. 3 A will, or a clause in a will conveying real estate. [< OF *deviser* divide, distinguish, contrive < L *dividere* < *dis-* apart + *videre* see] —**de·vis′er** *n.*

de·vi·see (di·vī′zē′, dev′ə·zē′) *n. Law* The person to whom a devise is made.

de·vi·sor (di·vī′zər, -zôr) *n. Law* One who gives by will.

de·vi·tal·ize (dē·vī′təl·īz) *v.t.* **·ized, ·iz·ing** 1 To deprive of vital power or of the power to sustain life. 2 To destroy the vitality of; make weak. —**de·vi′tal·i·za′tion** *n.*

de·vi·ta·min·ize (dē·vī′tə·min·īz′) *v.t.* **·ized, ·iz·ing** To deprive of vitamins.

de·vit·ri·fi·ca·tion (dē·vit′rə·fi·kā′shən) *n.* The conversion of glassy to crystalline or lithoidal texture by slow crystallization after solidification.

de·vit·ri·fy (dē·vit′rə·fī) *v.t.* **·fied, ·fy·ing** 1 To remove the glassy quality of. 2 To render opaque and hard like porcelain by long-continued great heat: said of glass. [< DE- from + VITRIFY]

de·vo·cal·ize (dē·vō′kəl·īz) *v.t.* **·ized, ·iz·ing** *Phonet.* To deprive of voice or of vocal quality. —**de·vo′cal·i·za′tion** *n.*

de·voiced (dē·voist′) *adj. Phonet.* Unvoiced.

de·void (di·void′) *adj.* Not possessing; destitute: with *of.* [ME *devoided,* pp. of obs. *devoid* empty out < OF *devoidier* < *de-* down (< L *de-*) + *voidier* VOID]

de·voir (də·vwär′, dev′wär) *n.* 1 Service or duty. 2 *pl.* Respectful attentions: to pay one's *devoirs* to. [< OF *deveir* < L *debere* owe]

dev·o·lu·tion (dev′ə·lo͞o′shən) *n.* 1 The act of delivering to another; a passing to a successor. 2 *Biol.* a Degeneration: opposed to *evolution.* b Involution. c Catabolism. 3 The delegation or surrender of the powers of a central government to local authorities. [< Med. L *devolutio, -onis* < *devolvere.* See DEVOLVE.]

de·volve (di·volv′) *v.* **·volved, ·volv·ing** *v.t.* 1 To cause to pass to a successor or substitute. 2 *Archaic* To roll down. —*v.i.* 3 To pass from a possessor to a successor or substitute: with *to, on,* or *upon.* [< L *devolvere* < *de-* down + *volvere* roll] —**de·volve′ment** *n.*

Dev·on (dev′ən) *n.* A valuable breed of small, hardy cattle originating in Devon, England.

Dev·on (dev′ən) A county in SW England; 2,611 square miles; county seat, Exeter. Also **Dev′on·shire** (-shir).

De·vo·ni·an (di·vō′nē·ən) *adj.* 1 Of or pertaining to Devon or Devonshire in England. 2 *Geol.* Of or pertaining to the Devonian period. —*n.* 1 A person born or residing in Devonshire. 2 The Devonian period or its characteristic rock system.

Devonian period *Geol.* The fourth of the periods in the Paleozoic era, following the Silurian, and succeeded by the Mississippian, or Lower Carboniferous, period. See chart under GEOLOGY. [from *Devon,* England; with ref. to rocks and fossils first found there]

Dev·on Island (dev′ən) An island of the Northwest Territories, Canada, in Baffin Bay; 21,606 square miles.

de·vote (di·vōt′) *v.t.* **·vot·ed, ·vot·ing** 1 To give or apply (attention, time, or oneself) completely to some activity, purpose, etc. 2 To set apart; dedicate; consecrate. 3 *Obs.* To doom. [< L *devotus,* pp. of *devovere* < *de-* away + *vovere* vow] —**de·vote′ment** *n.*

de·vot·ed (di·vō′tid) *adj.* 1 Feeling or showing devotion; ardent; zealous; devout. 2 Set apart, as by a vow; consecrated. 3 *Obs.* Doomed. See synonyms under ADDICTED, FAITHFUL, HOLY. —**de·vot′ed·ly** *adv.* —**de·vot′ed·ness** *n.*

dev·o·tee (dev′ə·tē′) *n.* One zealously devoted, especially to religious observances; a votary; zealot. —**dev′o·tee′ism** *n.*

de·vo·tion (di·vō′shən) *n.* 1 The state of being devoted, as to religious faith or duty; zeal. 2 Strong attachment or affection expressing itself in earnest service. 3 *Usually pl.* An act of worship; prayer. 4 The act of devoting. See synonyms under ALLEGIANCE, ATTACHMENT, ENTHUSIASM, FIDELITY, FRIENDSHIP, LOVE, PRAYER, RELIGION. —**de·vo′tion·al** *adj.* —**de·vo′tion·al·ism** *n.* —**de·vo′tion·al·ly** *adv.*

De Vo·to (də vō′tō), **Bernard Augustine,** 1897–1956, U.S. author and critic.

de·vour (di·vour′) *v.t.* 1 To eat up greedily and voraciously. 2 To destroy; waste: The disease *devoured* him. 3 To take in greedily with the senses: He *devoured* the book. 4 To engross the attention of. 5 To engulf; absorb. [< OF *devorer* < L *devorare* < *de-* down + *vorare* gulp, swallow]. —**de·vour′er** *n.* —**de·vour′ing** *adj.* —**de·vour′ing·ly** *adv.* —**de·vour′ing·ness** *n.*

de·vout (di·vout′) *adj.* 1 Earnestly religious; pious; reverent. 2 Warmly devoted; heart-felt; sincere. 3 Containing or expressing devotion, especially religious devotion. [< OF *devot* < L *devotus.* See DEVOTE.] —**de·vout′ly** *adv.* —**de·vout′ness** *n.*

De Vries (də vrēs′), **Hugo,** 1848–1935, Dutch botanist.

dew (do͞o, dyo͞o) *n.* 1 Moisture condensed from the atmosphere in small drops upon the cool surfaces of plants and other bodies. 2 Anything moist, gentle, or refreshing as dew or suggesting the freshness of dewy morning: the *dew* of sleep, the *dew* of youth. 3 Moisture generally, especially that which appears in minute drops, as perspiration, tears, etc. —*v.t.* To wet with or as with dew; bedew. ◆ Homophone: *due.* [OE *dēaw*] —**dew′less** *adj.*

de·wan (di·wän′, -wôn′) *n.* In India and Moslem countries, any of various government officials: also spelled *deewan, diwan.* [< Persian *dīwān.* See DIVAN.]

Dew·ar (dyo͞o′ər), **Sir James,** 1842–1923, Scottish chemist; invented the **Dewar vessel** or **flask,** a double-walled glass vessel for holding liquid air, etc.

dew·ber·ry (do͞o′ber′ē, -bər·ē, dyo͞o′-) *n. pl.* **·ries** 1 The fruit of the low blackberry (genus *Rubus*). 2 The plant bearing it.

dew·claw (do͞o′klô′, dyo͞o′-) *n.* 1 A rudimentary toe in some dogs. 2 The false rudimentary hoof above the true hoof of hogs, deer, etc. —**dew′clawed′** *adj.*

dew·drop (do͞o′drop′, dyo͞o′-) *n.* A drop of dew.

De Wet (də vet′), **Christian Rudolph,** 1854–1922, Boer general and statesman.

Dew·ey (do͞o′ē, dyo͞o′ē), **George,** 1837–1917, U.S. admiral. —**John,** 1859–1952, U.S. philosopher, psychologist, and educator. —**Melvil,** 1851–1931, U.S. librarian. —**Thomas Edmund,** 1902–1971, governor of New York 1943–54.

dew·fall (do͞o′fôl′, dyo͞o′-) *n.* 1 The formation of dew. 2 The time of evening when dew appears.

De Witt (di wit′), **Cornelius,** 1623–72, Dutch statesman and naval officer. —**Jan,** 1625–1672, Dutch statesman; brother of the preceding.

dew·lap (do͞o′lap′, dyo͞o′-) *n.* 1 The pendulous skin under the throat of cattle. 2 Something likened to a dewlap, as the wattles of a turkey, or the flaccid skin sometimes seen under the chin of an aged person. [ME *dewlappe* < *dew,* origin uncertain + *lappe,* OE *læppe* lobe, fold] —**dew′lapped′** *adj.*

Dew line A chain of radar stations in North America at about the 70th parallel, maintained by the United States in cooperation with Canada. Also DEW line. [< *D(istant) E(arly) W(arning)*]

dew point *Meteorol.* 1 The temperature at which dew forms or condensation occurs. 2 The temperature at which a given mass of air will have a relative humidity of 100.

dew pond *Brit.* A pond especially built to hold water in dry weather: replenished by the condensation of dew and mist.

Dews·bur·y (dyo͞oz′bər·ē) A county borough of Southern Yorkshire, England.

dew·worm (do͞o′wûrm′, dyo͞o′-) *n. Canadian* A nightcrawler.

dew·y (do͞o′ē, dyo͞o′ē) *adj.* **dew·i·er, dew·i·est** 1 Moist, as with dew. 2 Of, like, or yielding dew. 3 Appearing as if covered with dewdrops. —**dew′i·ness** *n.*

dex·ter (dek′stər) *adj.* 1 Right-hand; right. 2 *Her.* On the wearer's right, the spectator's left. 3 Auspicious; favorable; propitious. [< L, right]

Dex·ter (dek′stər) A masculine personal name.

dex·ter·i·ty (dek·ster′ə·tē) *n.* 1 Readiness and skill in using the hands; expertness. 2 Mental quickness, adroitness, or skill. [< L *dexteritas, -tatis* skill, aptness < *dexter* on the right]

Synonyms: adroitness, aptitude, cleverness, expertness, readiness, skill. *Adroitness* and *dexterity* might each be rendered "right-handedness"; but *adroitness* carries more of the idea of eluding, parrying, or checking some hostile movement, or taking advantage of another in controversy; *dexterity* conveys the idea of doing, accomplishing something readily and well, without reference to any action of others. We speak of *adroitness* in fencing, boxing, or debate; of *dexterity* in horsemanship, in the use of tools, weapons, etc. *Aptitude* is a natural *readiness,* which by practice may be developed into *dexterity. Skill* is more exact to line, rule, and method than *dexterity. Dexterity* can not be communicated; *skill* to a very great extent can be imparted. Compare ABILITY, ADDRESS, INGENUITY, POWER.

dex·ter·ous (dek′strəs, -stər·əs) *adj.* 1 Possessing dexterity; skilful or adroit; artful. 2 Done with dexterity. Also **dex·trous** (dek′-

strəs). See synonyms under CLEVER, GOOD, HAPPY. —**dex′ter·ous·ly, dex′trous·ly** *adv.* —**dex′ter·ous·ness, dex′trous·ness** *n.*

dex·trad (dek′strad) *adv. Anat.* On or toward the right hand or side. [<L *dexter* right + *ad* to]

dex·tral (dek′strəl) *adj.* **1** Of, pertaining to, or situated on the right side; right–hand or right–handed. **2** Propitious; favorable: said of omens. —**dex′tral·ly** *adv.* —**dex·tral·i·ty** (dek·stral′ə·tē) *n.*

dex·tran (dek′stran) *n. Biochem.* A white, gumlike substance produced by bacterial action in milk, molasses, beet juice, etc.: used as a substitute for blood plasma in the treatment of severe burns and shock. [<DEXTR(O)- + -AN(E)]

dex·trin (dek′strin) *n. Biochem.* An amorphous, colorless, water–soluble, dextrorotatory carbohydrate formed by the action of acids, heat, or diastase on starch: used as a substitute for gum arabic. Also **dex·trine** (dek′strin, -strēn). [<DEXTR(O)- + IN]

dextro– *combining form* Turned or turning to the right: used especially in chemistry and physics, as in *dextrorotatory.* Also, before vowels, **dextr–.** [<L *dexter* right]

dex·tro·ro·ta·tion (dek′strə·rō·tā′shən) *n. Optics* Clockwise rotation of the plane of polarization of light.

dex·tro·ro·ta·to·ry (dek′strə·rō′tə·tôr′ē, -tō′·rē) *adj. Chem.* Causing the plane of polarization of light to rotate to the right or clockwise: said of certain crystals and compounds: opposed to *levorotatory.* Also **dex·tro·gy·rate** (dek′strə·jī′rāt), **dex·tro·ro·ta·ry** (dek′strə·rō′·tər·ē).

dex·trorse (dek′strôrs, dek·strôrs′) *adj. Bot.* Rising spirally toward the right: opposed to *sinistrorse*; said of the morning–glory. Also **dex·tror′sal.** [<L *dextrorsum, dextrovorsum* <*dexter* right + *vertere* turn] —**dex′·trorse·ly** *adv.*

dex·trose (dek′strōs) *n. Biochem.* The dextrorotatory form of glucose. Also called **dex·tro·glu·cose** (dek′strə·glōō′kōs) [<DEXTR(O)- + (GLUC)OSE]

dey (dā) *n.* **1** The title of a governor of Algiers before the French conquest of 1830. **2** Formerly, the title of a ruler of Tunis or Tripoli. [<F <Turkish *dāī,* orig. uncle]

Dezh·nev (dyezh′nif), **Cape** The northeasternmost point of Asia, on Chukchi Peninsula in the Bering Strait: also *East Cape.*

de·zinc·i·fi·ca·tion (dē·zing′kə·fi·kā′shən) *n. Metall.* The removal of zinc by corrosive action from the surface of an alloy of zinc and copper.

Dhah·ran (dä·rän′) An oil town in eastern Saudi Arabia: also *Zahran.*

dhak (däk, dôk) *n.* A tree of India and Burma (*Butea monosperma*) having trifoliolate leaves and bright orange–red flowers. [<Hind.]

dhar·ma (där′mə, dûr′-) *n.* **1** In Hinduism and Buddhism, right behavior; conformity to law; hence, truth and righteousness. **2** In Buddhism, the law which, together with Buddha and Sangha, forms the three Ratnas or treasures of Buddhism. [<Skt., law]

Dhar·ma (där′mə, dûr′-) In Hindu mythology, a wise man whose numerous offspring personify the virtues and certain religious practices.

dhar·na (där′nə, dûr′-) *n.* In India, a method of claiming justice by refusing food or starving to death while sitting before the gate or door of the oppressor, to the end that the death shall be upon the oppressor's head. Also **dhur′na.** [<Hind. *dharnā*]

Dhau·la·gi·ri (dou′lə·gir′ē) A peak in the central Nepal Himalayas; 26,810 feet.

Dhi·ban (thē·bän′, dē-) A village in central Jordan where the Moabite Stone was discovered. Also **Di·ban′.**

dhole (dōl) *n.* A red–coated wild dog of SE Asia (genus *Cuon*) that hunts in packs and attacks even large game. [Origin uncertain]

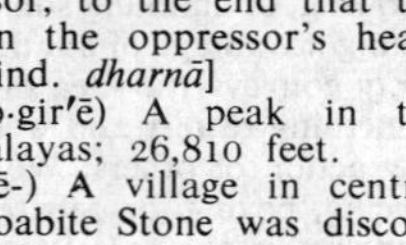

DHOLE
(About 30 inches high at the shoulder)

dho·ti (dō′tē) *n. pl.* **·tis** A loincloth worn by Hindu men; also the cloth for this. Also **dhoo·ti** (dōō′tē). [<Hind. *dhotī* a loincloth]

dhour·ra, dhoo·ra (dōōr′ə) See DURRA.

dhow (dou) *n.* An Arabian coasting vessel with a sharp prow and high poop, usually having one mast and lateen rigging. [<Arabic *dāw*]

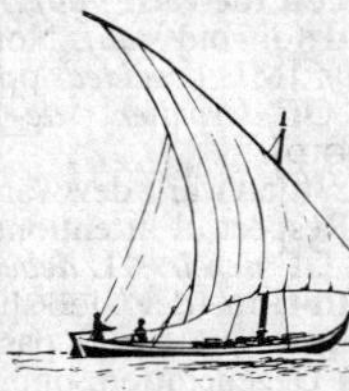

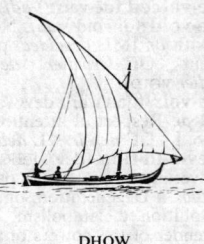

DHOW

dhu (dōō) *adj.* Black: used in Celtic names of places and persons: Roderick *Dhu* (black Roderick). [<Irish *dubh* black]

di–[1] Reduced var. of DIS–[1].

di–[2] *prefix* **1** Twice; double: *digraph.* **2** *Chem.* Containing two atoms, molecules, radicals, etc.: *dichloride.* Also, before *s, dis–,* as in *dissyllable.* [Gk. *di–* <*dis* twice]

dia– *prefix* Through; across; between: *diagonal.* Also, before vowels, **di–.** [<Gk. *dia–* through]

di·a·base (dī′ə·bās) *n. Geol.* A granular igneous rock, composed essentially of plagioclase, and characterized by the feldspar having crystallized before the augite: sometimes called *dolerite.* [<Gk. *diabasis* a crossing over <*dia-* across + *bainein* go] —**di′a·ba′sic** *adj.*

di·a·be·tes (dī′ə·bē′tis, -tēz) *n. Pathol.* A disease associated with inadequate production of insulin by the pancreas and ordinarily characterized by excessive urinary secretion containing an abnormal quantity of sugar. In the form distinguished as **diabetes mel·li·tus** (mə·lī′təs), there is also emaciation with excessive hunger and thirst. [<NL <Gk. *diabētēs* a passer through <*dia-* through + *bainein* go]

di·a·bet·ic (dī′ə·bet′ik, -bē′tik) *adj. Med.* Of, pertaining to, or affected by diabetes. Also **di′a·bet′i·cal.** —*n.* One who has diabetes.

di·a·ble·rie (dē·ä′blə·rē, *Fr.* dyȧ·blə·rē′) *n.* **1** Demonology. **2** Fantastic and perverse behavior; deviltry; impishness. **3** Sorcery. Also **di·a′ble·ry.** [<F <*diable* devil]

Di·a·blo Crater (dē·ä′blō) See METEOR CRATER.

di·a·bol·ic (dī′ə·bol′ik) *adj.* Of, pertaining to, or like the devil; satanic; fiendish; infernal. Also **di′a·bol′i·cal.** [<Gk. *diabolikos* <*diabolos.* See DEVIL.] —**di′a·bol′i·cal·ly** *adv.* —**di′a·bol′i·cal·ness** *n.*

di·ab·o·lism (dī·ab′ə·liz′əm) *n.* **1** Conduct befitting or inspired by the devil; devilishness. **2** Possession by the devil or devils. **3** In occultism, the conjuration or raising of evil spirits; sorcery. **4** A system of belief or doctrine in which devils are worshiped. **5** A devilish nature or disposition. —**di·ab′·o·list** *n.*

di·ab·o·lize (dī·ab′ə·līz) *v.t.* **·lized, ·liz·ing 1** To render devilish or diabolical. **2** To bring under diabolical influence. **3** To represent as devilish.

di·ab·o·lo (dē·ab′ə·lō) *n.* A game played with a spool or top (called *devil–on–two–sticks*) which is spun on a cord tied to two sticks, thrown into the air, and caught again on the cord. [<Ital. <LL *diabolus.* See DEVIL.]

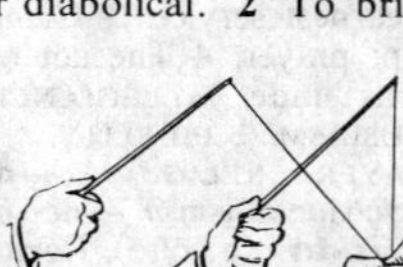

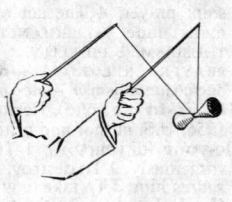

DIABOLO

di·a·caus·tic (dī′ə·kôs′tik) *adj. Optics* Denoting a caustic curve formed by refracted rays: opposed to *catacaustic.* —*n.* **1** A diacaustic curve. **2** Formerly, a burning glass for cauterization. [<DIA- + CAUSTIC (def. 3)]

di·ac·e·tyl·mor·phine (dī·as′ə·təl·môr′fēn) *n.* Heroin.

di·a·chron·ic (dī′ə·kron′ik) *adj.* **1** Existing through time. **2** *Ling.* Pertaining to the study of the historical development of a language in any of its aspects. See SYNCHRONIC.

di·ach·y·lon (dī·ak′ə·lon) *n. Med.* **1** A plaster formed by combining lead oxide, olive oil, and water; lead or litharge plaster. **2** A mixture of mucilaginous vegetable juices, gums, etc., formerly used in making plasters and salves. Also **diachylon plaster, di·ach′·y·lum** (-ə·ləm). [<Med. L *diachylum* <L *diachylon* <Gk. *dia chylōn* made of juices; orig. referring to an ointment made of vegetable juices]

di·ac·id (dī·as′id) *adj. Chem.* **1** Capable of combining with two molecules of a monoacid or with one of a diacid: said of bases and alcohols. **2** Having two hydrogen atoms replaceable by radicals or atoms: said of acids. —*n.* An acid containing two hydrogen atoms.

di·ac·o·nal (dī·ak′ə·nəl) *adj.* Of, pertaining to, or befitting a deacon or the diaconate. [<LL *diaconus* deacon]

di·ac·o·nate (dī·ak′ə·nit, -nāt) *n.* **1** The office, rank, or tenure of a deacon. **2** Deacons collectively. [<LL *diaconatus*]

di·a·crit·ic (dī′ə·krit′ik) *n.* **1** A mark, point, or sign attached to a letter to indicate its exact phonetic value, or to distinguish it from another letter: also **diacritical mark.** For a complete listing of the diacritics used in this book, see page xx. **2** A differential diagnosis. —*adj.* Of or pertaining to a diacritic. [<Gk. *diakritikos* distinguishing <*diakrinein* <*dia-* between + *krinein* distinguish]

di·a·crit·i·cal (dī′ə·krit′i·kəl) *adj.* **1** Marking a difference; distinguishing; distinctive. **2** Indicating certain variations of sounds or of form. **3** *Electr.* Denoting a current sufficient to magnetize a solenoid core to half–saturation. —**di′a·crit′i·cal·ly** *adv.*

di·ac·tin·ic (dī′ak·tin′ik) *adj.* Capable of transmitting actinic or chemical rays: said of a body or substance. —**di·ac′tin·ism** *n.*

di·a·del·phous (dī′ə·del′fəs) *adj. Bot.* Having the stamens combined by their filaments so as to form two sets or bundles. Also **di′a·del′phi·an.** [<Gk. *di-* two + *adelphos* brother]

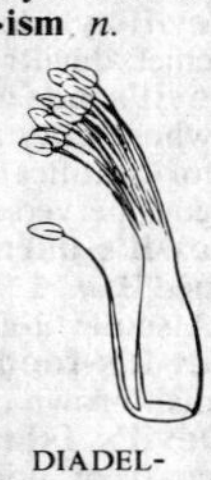

DIADELPHOUS STAMENS
Common in papilionaceous flowers in this arrangement.

di·a·dem (dī′ə·dem) *n.* **1** A symbol of royalty worn upon the head; a crown. **2** Regal power; sovereignty. —*v.t.* To decorate with or as with a diadem; crown. [<OF *diademe* <L *diadema* <Gk. *diadēma* <*dia-* across + *deein* bind]

di·aer·e·sis (dī·er′ə·sis), **di·ae·ret·ic** (dī′ə·ret′ik) See DIERESIS, etc.

di·a·ge·ot·ro·pism (dī′ə·jē·ot′rə·piz′əm) *n. Bot.* Transverse or oblique geotropism: an arrangement of plant organs at right angles to the direction of gravitation. [<DIA- + GEOTROPISM] —**di·a·ge·o·trop·ic** (dī′ə·jē′ə·trop′ik, -trō′pik) *adj.*

Dia·ghi·lev (dyä′gi·lef), **Sergei Pavlovich,** 1872–1929, Russian ballet producer.

di·ag·nose (dī′əg·nōs′, -nōz′) *v.* **·nosed, ·nos·ing** *v.t.* To examine or distinguish by diagnosis. —*v.i.* To make a diagnosis of a person, disease, etc.

di·ag·no·sis (dī′əg·nō′sis) *n.* **1** *Med.* **a** The art or act of discriminating between diseases and of distinguishing them by their characteristic symptoms. **b** A summary of symptoms and the conclusion arrived at. **2** *Biol.* Scientific discrimination between similar or related things or conditions for the purpose of accurate classification. [<Gk. *diagnōsis* <*diagignōskein* <*dia-* between + *gignōskein* know] —**di·ag·nos·tic** (dī′əg·nos′tik) *adj.* —**di′ag·nos′ti·cal·ly** *adv.*

di·ag·nos·ti·cian (dī′əg·nos·tish′ən) *n.* One who is versed in diagnosis.

di·ag·nos·tics (dī′əg·nos′tiks) *n.* The science or recognized principles of diagnosis.

di·ag·o·nal (dī·ag′ə·nəl) *adj.* **1** Crossing obliquely; oblique. **2** Marked by oblique lines or the like. **3** *Geom.* **a** Joining two nonadjacent or reentering angles of a figure: a *diagonal* line. **b** Joining, as a plane, two nonadjacent edges of a solid. —*n.* **1** *Geom.* A straight line or plane passing from one angle, as of a square, to any other angle not adjacent. **2** A fabric woven with diagonal ridges or lines: also **diagonal cloth. 3** Anything running diagonally. [<L *diagonalis* <*diagonios* <*dia-* across + *gonia* angle] —**di·ag′o·nal·ly** *adv.*

Di·ag·o·ras (dī·ag′ə·rəs) Greek poet and philosopher of the fifth century B.C.: called "the Atheist."

di·a·gram (dī′ə·gram) *n.* **1** A line drawing, mechanical plan, or outline, as distinguished from a perspective drawing. **2** A rough projection, map, chart, etc. **3** A figure drawn to aid in demonstrating a geometrical propo-

sition or to illustrate geometrical relations. **4** An outline figure intended to represent any object or area, or to show the relation between parts or places, or to illustrate the value or relations of quantities, forces, etc. **5** A graph. — *v.t.* **·gramed** or **·grammed**, **·gram·ing** or **·gram·ming** **1** To represent by diagram. **2** To illustrate by a diagram. [<Gk. *diagramma* <*dia-* across + *graphein* write] — **di·a·gram·mat·ic** (dī′ə·grə·mat′ik) or **·i·cal** *adj.* — **di′a·gram·mat′i·cal·ly** *adv.*

diagram factor *Mech.* In the cylinder of a steam engine, the ratio between the actual average pressure and the ideal pressure as shown on an indicator diagram.

di·a·graph (dī′ə·graf, -gräf) *n.* A protractor and scale combined for drawing diagrams. [<DIA- + -GRAPH]

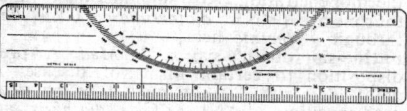

DIAGRAPH

di·a·he·li·o·tro·pism (dī′ə·hē′lē·ot′rə·piz′əm) *n. Bot.* A turning of plant organs so as to assume a position transverse to the light; transverse heliotropism. — **di·a·he·li·o·trop·ic** (dī′ə·hē′lē·ə·trop′ik, -trō′pik) *adj.*

di·al (dī′əl, dīl) *n.* **1** Any graduated circular plate or face, as of a watch, clock, gage, mariner's compass, or radio receiving set. **2** A plate bearing letters and numbers, used to make connections in an automatic telephone system. **3** A device for indicating time by means of the shadow of a gnomon or style thrown upon a graduated plate; a sundial. **4** A compass; especially, a miner's compass for underground surveying. **5** *Obs.* Any timepiece. — *v.t.* & *v.i.* **di·aled** or **di·alled**, **di·al·ing** or **di·al·ling** **1** To measure or survey with a dial. **2** To turn or adjust a dial; indicate on a dial. **3** To call by means of a telephone. **4** To adjust a radio or television set to (a station, program, etc.). [<Med. L *dialis* daily <L *dies* day] — **di′al·er**, **di′al·ler** *n.* — **di′al·ist**, **di′al·list** *n.*

di·a·lect (dī′ə·lekt) *n.* **1** A variety of speech distinguished from the standard or literary language by variations of idiom, vocabulary, phonology, and morphology peculiar to a particular geographical location: the Southern *dialect* of American English. **2** A manner of speech adopted by the members of a class, trade, or profession; jargon; cant: the *dialect* of the cultured. **3** An imperfect use of the standard language by those to whom another language is native. **4** A language developed from a root language, retaining recognizable elements of the parent but having distinctive vocabulary, pronunciation, forms, and idiom; a linguistic branch: The Romance languages are *dialects* of Latin. See synonyms under LANGUAGE. [<MF *dialecte* <L *dialectus* <Gk. *dialektos* discourse, way of speaking <*dialegesthai* <*dia-* across + *legesthai* speak] — **di·a·lec·tal** (dī′ə·lek′təl) *adj.* Of or characterized by a dialect. Abbr. *dial.*

dialect atlas A collection of linguistic maps marking areas showing a uniformity of dialectal characteristics of pronunciation, vocabulary, syntax, etc.: also called *linguistic atlas.*

di·a·lec·tic (dī′ə·lek′tik) *adj.* **1** Formerly, dialectal. **2** Pertaining to dialectics; logical; argumentative. Also **di′a·lec′ti·cal.** — *n.* **1** *Usually pl.* The art or practice of examining logically, as by a method of question and answer. **2** A specific mode of argument. [<OF *dialectique* <L *dialectica* <Gk. *dialektika (technē)* (art) of discourse <*dialektos.* See DIALECT.]

dialectical materialism A socio-economic theory introduced by Karl Marx and Friedrich Engels, according to which history and the forms of society are interpreted as the result of conflicts between social classes arising from their relations to the means of production.

di·a·lec·ti·cian (dī′ə·lek·tish′ən) *n.* **1** A logician. **2** One who specializes in the study of dialects.

di·a·lec·ti·cism (dī′ə·lek′tə·siz′əm) *n.* **1** The character or nature distinguishing a dialect. **2** A dialectal word or peculiarity. **3** The practice of dialectics.

di·a·lec·tol·o·gy (dī′ə·lek·tol′ə·jē) *n.* The study of dialects.

di·al·ing (dī′əl·ing) *n.* **1** The act of using a dial. **2** The measurement of time by sundials; the art of making sundials. **3** Underground surveying with a dial, especially in mines. Also **di′al·ling.**

di·al·lage (dī′ə·lij) *n.* A brown, gray, or green, thin-foliated variety of pyroxene, crystallizing in the monoclinic system. [<F <Gk. *diallagē* an interchange <*dia-* across + *allassein* change]

di·al·o·gism (dī·al′ə·jiz′əm) *n.* **1** A dialogue or discussion; especially, a discourse with oneself. **2** *Logic* An inference with a single premise and disjunctive conclusion.

di·al·o·gist (dī·al′ə·jist) *n.* One who writes or takes part in a dialogue. — **di·a·lo·gis·tic** (dī′ə·lō·jis′tik) or **·ti·cal** *adj.*

di·al·o·gize (dī·al′ə·jīz) *v.i.* **·gized**, **·giz·ing** To carry on a dialogue.

di·a·logue (dī′ə·lôg, -log) *n.* **1** A conversation in which two or more take part. **2** A literary work in which two or more characters are represented as conversing. **3** An exchange of opinions or ideas; free interchange of different points of view; discussion: to propose a *dialogue* among the Christian churches. See synonyms under CONVERSATION. — *v.* **·logued**, **·logu·ing** *v.t.* To express in dialogue form. — *v.i.* To carry on a dialogue. Also **di′a·log.** [<F <*dialogus* <Gk. *dialogos* <*dialegesthai.* Related to DIALECT.] — **di′a·logu′er**, **di′a·log′er** *n.* — **di·a·log·ic** (dī′ə·loj′ik) or **·i·cal** *adj.*

dial telephone A telephone on which a required number may be called by manipulation of a dial bearing letters and numbers.

dial tone The low, steady, humming tone indicating to the user of a dial telephone that a call may be put through, or that a connection has been broken. Compare BUSY SIGNAL.

di·al·y·sis (dī·al′ə·sis) *n.* *pl.* **·ses** (-sēz) **1** *Bot.* Separation of parts previously or normally joined together. **2** *Chem.* The separating of solutions of mixed substances of unequal diffusibility by means of moist membranes or septa; specifically, the separation of a colloid from a substance in true solution. See OSMOSIS. [<Gk. *dialysis* <*dialyein* <*dia-* completely + *lyein* loosen] — **di·a·lyt·ic** (dī′ə·lit′ik) *adj.* — **di′a·lyt′i·cal·ly** *adv.*

di·a·lyze (dī′ə·līz) *v.t.* **·lyzed**, **·lyz·ing** *Chem.* To subject to or prepare by dialysis; separate by dialysis.

di·a·lyz·er (dī′ə·lī′zər) *n. Chem.* An apparatus used for dialysis, especially a membranous septum stretched over a gutta-percha ring.

di·a·mag·net·ic (dī′ə·mag·net′ik) *adj. Physics* **1** Pertaining to or designating the property of substances tending to lie at right angles to the poles of a magnet. **2** Having a negative magnetic susceptibility, or a permeability less than that of a vacuum; as bismuth or copper. — *n.* A substance that possesses such properties. — **di′a·mag′net·ism** *n.* — **di′a·mag·net′i·cal·ly** *adv.*

Di·a·man·ti·na (dē′ə·mann·tē′nə) A city in eastern Brazil. Formerly **Te·ju·co** (te·hōō′kō).

Di·a·man·ti·na River (dē′ə·mən·tē′nə) A river in east central Australia, flowing 468 mi. SW.

di·am·e·ter (dī·am′ə·tər) *n.* **1** A straight line passing through the center of a figure or body and terminated by the boundaries thereof. **2** The length of such a line. **3** The thickness of an object as measured by such a line. [<OF *diametre* <L *diametrus* <Gk. *diametros* <*dia-* through + *metron* measure]

di·a·met·ri·cal (dī′ə·met′ri·kəl) *adj.* **1** Of or pertaining to a diameter; coinciding with a diameter: also **di·am·e·tral** (dī·am′ə·trəl). **2** Of or pertaining to the ends of a diameter; directly opposite, and as far removed as possible: also **di′a·met′ric.**

di·a·met·ri·cal·ly (dī′ə·met′rik·lē) *adv.* **1** In the manner of a diameter. **2** Irreconcilably: diametrically opposed.

di·a·mine (dī·am′ēn, -in, dī′ə·mēn, -min) *n. Chem.* Any of a group of compounds containing two amino radicals; a double amine. Also **di·am·in** (dī·am′in, dī′ə·min).

dia·mond (dī′mənd, dī′ə·) *n.* **1** A mineral of great hardness and refractive power, consisting of carbon crystallized in the isometric system under great pressure and temperature. When pure it is a valuable gem with a beautiful display of prismatic colors, especially when cut. See list below. **2** A natural crystal face of this stone, used in cutting glass, etc. **3** *Geom.* A figure bounded by four equal straight lines, and having two of the angles acute and two obtuse; a rhomb or lozenge. **4** *Printing* A size of type next above brilliant; 4- or 4 1/2-point. **5** A lozenge-shaped spot on a playing card, or a card or (in the plural) suit so marked. **6** The square enclosed by the lines between the bases on a baseball field. — *v.t.* To adorn with or as with diamonds. [<OF *diamant* <LL *diamas*, *-antis*, alter. of L *adamas.* Doublet of ADAMANT.] — **dia′mond·ed** *adj.*

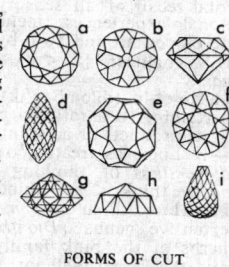

FORMS OF CUT DIAMONDS
a.b.c. Brilliant cut.
d. Marquise cut.
e. Pitt or regent cut.
f. Kohinor cut.
g. Double rose (side view)
h. Rose cut.
i. Briolette cut.

— **Cullinan diamond** The world's largest diamond, 3,106 metric carats, discovered in South Africa, 1905, and named for Sir T. M. Cullinan: cut into several pieces, one set in the British scepter, one in the crown: presented to King Edward VII and renamed by King George V the **Star of Africa.**

— **Great Mogul diamond** An Indian diamond found about 1650 and said to have weighed 787 carats: named when the diamond was part of the treasure of the Mogul court. The second largest diamond, it has since disappeared.

— **Hope diamond** A blue diamond, the largest and most celebrated of the colored diamonds, 44.5 carats: named for Sir H. T. Hope, one of its owners.

— **Jonker diamond** The world's fourth largest diamond, 726 metric carats, found in South Africa in 1934 by Jacobus Jonker.

— **Koh-i-nor diamond** One of the British crown jewels, 186 carats in original cutting, dating back earlier than the 14th century: from the Persian meaning "mountain of light."

— **Vargas diamond** The world's third largest diamond, 726.6 metric carats, found in Brazil in 1938: named for President G. D. Vargas of Brazil.

dia·mond-back (dī′mənd·bak′, dī′ə-) *n.* **1** An edible turtle (*Malaclemys centrata*) inhabiting salt marshes of the southern United States, having diamond-shaped markings on the shell: also **diamond-back terrapin.** **2** A large rattlesnake (*Crotalus adamanteus*) of the SE United States, having diamond-shaped markings on the back: also **dia′mond-rat′tler.**

Diamond, Cape A promontory on the Saint Lawrence River in the city of Quebec, Canada.

Diamond Head A promontory on the SE shore of Oahu, Hawaii.

Diamond Mountains A mountain range of central Korea; highest peak, 5,374 feet. *Korean* **Kum·gang-San** (kōōm·gäng·sän).

Diamond State Nickname of DELAWARE.

Di·an·a (dī·an′ə) A feminine personal name. Also **Di·an** (dī′an), **Di·ane** (dī·an′, *Fr.* dyȧn′). [<L]

— **Diana** In Roman mythology, goddess of the hunt, virginity, and the moon: identified with the Greek *Artemis.* Hence, the moon.

— **Diana of Poitiers**, 1499–1566, mistress of Henry II of France.

— **Diana of the Ephesians** An Asiatic goddess of fertility, confused with the Roman Diana. *Acts* xix 21.

di·an·drous (dī·an′drəs) *adj. Bot.* Having two stamens. [<NL *diandrus* <Gk. *di-* two + *anēr, andros* man, male]

di·a·net·ics (dī′ə·net′iks) *n.* A system and technique of psychotherapy based on the total recall of all sensory, motor and emotional experiences, including the prenatal: developed around 1950 by L. Ron Hubbard, U.S. engineer. [? <DIANOETIC] — **di′a·net′ic** *adj.*

di·a·no·et·ic (dī′ə·nō·et′ik) *adj. Logic* Of or pertaining to a rational or discursive faculty or its products or acts; intellectual; discursive. — *n.* Logic as treating of reasoning. [<Gk. *dianoētikos* of thinking < *dia-* through + *noeein* think < *nous* mind]

di·an·thus (dī·an′thəs) *n.* Any plant of an extensive genus (*Dianthus*) of ornamental herbs of the pink family, as the carnation and the sweet william. [<NL <Gk. *Dios* of Zeus + *anthos* flower]

di·a·pa·son (dī′ə·pā′zən, -sən) *n.* **1** The basal melodic tone of a pipe organ; also, the stop producing it. In the **open diapason** the pipes are of metal and open at the top; in the **stopped diapason** the pipes are of wood and closed at the top. **2** A tuning fork, or the standard pitch given by a tuning fork. **3** In old Greek music, an octave. **4** *Archaic* Comprehensive or fundamental harmony; universal concord. [<L <Gk. *dia pasōn (chordōn)* through all (the notes)]

di·a·pe·de·sis (dī′ə·pə·dē′sis) *n. Pathol.* The passing of leucocytes through intact blood vessels into the adjoining tissue: noted especially during inflammation. [<NL <Gk. *diapēdēsis* < *dia-* through + *pedaein* leap, throb] — **di′a·pe·det′ic** (-det′ik) *adj.*

di·a·per (dī′ə·pər) *n.* **1** In the Middle Ages, a fine figured silken or linen cloth. **2** In art and architecture, a form of surface decoration, consisting of a system of reticulations, each of which contains a flower pattern, geometric design, etc., either carved or painted. **3** A soft, absorbent, bleached cotton fabric, of plain or birdseye weave: used for toweling, babies' breechcloths, etc. **4** A baby's breechcloth; waistcloth. — *v.t.* **1** To decorate with a repeated figure or similar figures. **2** To put a diaper on. [<OF *diapre,* earlier *diaspre* <Med. Gk. *diaspros* < *dia-* completely + *aspros* white]

A DIAPER PATTERN (*def. 2*)

di·a·pha·ne·i·ty (dī′ə·fə·nē′ə·tē) *n.* Translucency.

di·a·pha·nom·e·ter (dī′ə·fə·nom′ə·tər) *n.* An instrument for observing and measuring the transparency of materials, as fluids, paper, milk, etc., by means of transmitted light. [<Gk. *diaphanēs* transparent + -METER]

di·aph·a·no·scope (dī·af′ə·nə·skōp′) *n. Med.* A device for illuminating cavities of the body to facilitate medical examination and treatment. [<Gk. *diaphanēs* transparent + -SCOPE] — **di·aph·a·nos·co·py** (dī·af′ə·nos′kə·pē) *n.* — **di·aph·a·no·scop·ic** (dī·af′ə·nə·skop′ik) *adj.*

di·aph·a·nous (dī·af′ə·nəs) *adj.* Showing light through its substance; transparent; translucent. See synonyms under CLEAR. [<Med. L *diaphanus* <Gk. *diaphanēs* < *dia-* through + *phainein* show] — **di·aph′a·nous·ly** *adv.* — **di·aph′a·nous·ness** *n.*

di·aph·o·ny (dī·af′ə·nē) *n. pl.* **·nies** **1** *Music* The parallel movement of voices at definite intervals from one another. **2** Anciently, dissonance: opposed to *symphony.* [<LL *diaphonia* dissonance <Gk. *diaphōnia* < *dia-* across + *phoneein* sound < *phonē* a sound] — **di·a·phon·ic** (dī′ə·fon′ik) *adj.* — **di′a·phon′·ics** *n.*

di·a·pho·re·sis (dī′ə·fə·rē′sis) *n. Med.* Copious perspiration. [<LL <Gk. *diaphorēsis* < *diaphorein* perspire < *dia-* across, through + *phorein* carry]

di·a·pho·ret·ic (dī′ə·fə·ret′ik) *adj. Med.* Producing perspiration. — *n.* Any drug or agent that causes or increases perspiration. Also **di′a·pho·ret′i·cal.**

di·a·phragm (dī′ə·fram) *n.* **1** *Anat.* An important muscle used in respiration, situated between the thoracic and abdominal cavities; the midriff. **2** Any dividing membrane or partition. **3** Any device supposed to resemble a diaphragm in shape, appearance, or elasticity, as the thin vibrating disk of a telephone or phonograph, or the flexible rubber sheet of a vacuum brake. **4** The porous cup of a voltaic cell. **5** *Optics* A perforated disk whose aperture may be reduced in order to cut off marginal rays in a camera or telescope. — *v.t.* To act upon or furnish with a diaphragm. [<L *diaphragma* <Gk. < *dia-* across + *phragma* a fence] — **di·a·phrag·mat·ic** (dī′ə·frag·mat′ik) *adj.* — **di′a·phrag·mat′i·cal·ly** *adv.*

di·aph·y·sis (dī·af′ə·sis) *n. pl.* **·ses** (-sēz) *Anat.* **1** The shaft of a long bone or the part that ossifies from the center. **2** Any prominent part of a bony process, or a ligament, of the knee joint. [<NL <Gk., a growing through < *dia-* through + *phyein* grow, produce] — **di·a·phys·i·al** (dī′ə·fiz′ē·əl) *adj.*

di·a·poph·y·sis (dī′ə·pof′ə·sis) *n. pl.* **·ses** (-sēz) *Anat.* The superior or articular part of the transverse process of a vertebra. [<DI(A) + APOPHYSIS] — **di·ap·o·phys·i·al** (dī′ap·ə·fiz′ē·əl) *adj.*

Di·ar·bekr (dē·är′bek′ər) See DIYARBEKIR.

di·ar·chy (dī′är·kē) *n. pl.* **·chies** A form of government in which two persons are jointly invested with supreme power, as William and Mary in England: also spelled *dyarchy.* [<DI-[2] + -ARCHY]

di·a·rist (dī′ə·rist) *n.* One who keeps a diary.

di·ar·rhe·a (dī′ə·rē′ə) *n. Pathol.* Morbidly frequent and fluid evacuation of the bowels. Also **di′ar·rhoe′a.** [<L *diarrhoea* <Gk. *diarrhoia* < *dia-* through + *rheein* flow] — **di′ar·rhe′·al** or **·rhoe′al, di′ar·rhe′ic** or **·rhoe′ic, di′ar·rhet′ic** or **·rhoet′ic** (-ret′ik) *adj.*

di·ar·thro·sis (dī′är·thrō′sis) *n. pl.* **·ses** (-sēz) *Anat.* A freely movable joint in which the ends of the bones are surrounded by a capsule and covered by cartilage. [<NL <Gk. *diarthrosis* < *dia-* completely + *arthrosis* an articulation < *arthron* a joint] — **di′ar·thro′·di·al** (-dē·əl) *adj.*

di·a·ry (dī′ə·rē) *n. pl.* **·ries** **1** A record of daily events; especially, a personal record of one's activities, experiences, or observations; a journal. **2** A book for keeping such record. [<LL *diarium* <L *dies* a day]

Di·as (dē′əs), **Bartholomeu,** 1445?–1500, Portuguese navigator; discovered Cape of Good Hope: also *Diaz.*

Di·as·po·ra (dī·as′pər·ə) *n.* **1** The dispersion of the Jews among the Gentiles after the Babylonian exile. **2** The Jews or Jewish communities so dispersed. **3** In the New Testament, the Jewish Christians living outside Palestine. I *Pet.* i 1. [<Gk., a dispersion < *dia-* completely + *speirein* sow, scatter]

di·a·spore (dī′ə·spôr, -spōr) *n.* A variously colored, translucent to subtranslucent aluminum hydroxide, AlO·OH. [<Gk. *diaspora* a dispersion (see DIASPORA); so called from its rapid decrepitation and dispersion when heated]

di·a·stal·sis (dī′ə·stal′sis) *n. pl.* **·ses** (-sēz) *Physiol.* A downward-thrusting contraction wave forming part of the peristaltic action of the digestive tube. [<NL <Gk. *dia-* through + *stellein* place, send] — **di′a·stal′·tic** *adj.*

di·a·stase (dī′ə·stās) *n. Biochem.* A white, amorphous enzyme that converts starch and glycogen into dextrin and sugar (chiefly maltose): found in germinating grain and in various parts of plants and in animal fluids, as saliva, pancreatic juice, etc.; an amylase. [<F <Gk. *diastasis* a separation < *dia-* apart + *histanai* set, cause to stand] — **di′a·sta′sic, di′a·stat′ic** (-stat′ik) *adj.*

di·as·ter (dī·as′tər) *n. Biol.* **1** That stage of cell division in which the chromosomes have separated to form two groups of starlike radiations at the poles. **2** One of the groups of radiations so formed. [<DI-[2] + Gk. *aster* star]

di·as·to·le (dī·as′tə·lē) *n.* **1** *Physiol.* The regular expansion or dilatation of the heart and of the arteries: opposed to *systole.* **2** *Zool.* A corresponding motion in protozoans and in parts of other animal organisms. **3** In Greek and Latin prosody, the lengthening of a syllable naturally short. Compare SYSTOLE. [<LL <Gk. *diastolē* a separation, lengthening < *dia-* apart + *stellein* send, put] — **di·as·tol·ic** (dī′ə·stol′ik) *adj.*

di·as·tro·phism (dī·as′trə·fiz′əm) *n. Geol.* **1** The process of deformation of the earth's crust, producing continents and ocean beds, plateaus, mountains, valleys, folds, and faults. **2** Any deformation so caused. [<Gk. *diastrophē* < *dia-* across + *strephein* turn] — **di·a·stroph·ic** (dī′ə·strof′ik) *adj.*

di·a·tes·sa·ron (dī′ə·tes′ə·ron) *n.* **1** In ancient music, a perfect fourth. **2** A harmony of the four Gospels arranged to make one continuous narrative. [<OF <L <Gk. *dia tessarōn* made of four]

di·a·ther·man·cy (dī′ə·thûr′mən·sē) *n. Physics* The property of being transparent to infrared rays, or of transmitting them. Also **di′a·ther′·mance, di′a·ther′ma·cy** (-mə·sē). [<F *diathermansie* <Gk. *dia-* through + *thermansis* a heating] — **di·a·ther·ma·nous** (dī′ə·thûr′mə·nəs) *adj.*

di·a·ther·mize (dī′ə·thûr′mīz) *v.t.* **·mized, ·miz·ing** To apply diathermy to.

di·a·ther·my (dī′ə·thûr′mē) *n. Med.* Application of heat to the deeper tissues of the body by means of high-frequency electric currents; thermopenetration. Also **di·a·ther·mi·a** (dī′ə·thûr′mē·ə). [<NL *diathermia* <Gk. *dia-* through + *thermē* heat]

di·ath·e·sis (dī·ath′ə·sis) *n.* **1** *Med.* A predisposition to certain forms of disease: a gouty *diathesis.* **2** Any mental or physical predisposition. [<NL <Gk. *diathēsis* an arrangement, disposition < *dia-* apart + *tithenai* place] — **di·a·thet·ic** (dī′ə·thet′ik) *adj.* — **di′a·thet′i·cal·ly** *adv.*

di·a·tom (dī′ə·təm, -tom) *n.* A marine and fresh-water plankton, unicellular or colonial, belonging to the family *Chlorophyceae* of microscopic green algae, characterized by bivalve walls containing silica. [<NL *diatoma* <Gk. *dia-* through + *temnein* cut] — **di·a·to·ma·ceous** (dī′ə·tə·mā′shəs) *adj.*

diatomaceous earth The siliceous skeletons of diatoms, dried and used in the manufacture of dynamite, pottery, abrasives, glaze, etc.; kieselguhr. Also **di·at·o·mite** (dī·at′ə·mīt).

di·a·tom·ic (dī′ə·tom′ik) *adj. Chem.* **1** Containing only two atoms: a *diatomic* molecule. **2** Containing two replaceable univalent atoms. **3** Bivalent.

di·a·ton·ic (dī′ə·ton′ik) *adj. Music* Designating the regular tones of a major or minor key (or scale), in distinction from chromatic or occasional tones; having eight tones to an octave. [<MF *diatonique* <LL *diatonicus* <Gk. *diatonikos* < *dia-* through + *teinein* stretch] — **di·a·ton′i·cal·ly** *adv.*

di·a·tribe (dī′ə·trīb) *n.* An abusive discourse; denunciation; invective. [<F <L *diatriba* <Gk. *diatribē* a wearing away of time < *dia-* through + *tribein* rub]

di·at·ro·pism (dī·at′rə·piz′əm) *n. Bot.* The propensity of some plant organs to arrange themselves transversely to the line of action of an external stimulus. [<DIA- + TROPISM] — **di·a·trop·ic** (dī′ə·trop′ik) *adj.*

Dí·az (dē′äts), **Armando,** 1861–1928, Italian general; commander in chief of the Italian Army in World War I.

Di·az (dē′əs), **Bartholomeu** See DIAS.

Dí·az (dē′äs), **Porfirio,** 1830–1915, president of Mexico 1877–80, 1884–1911; overthrown by revolution.

Dí·az de Bi·var (dē′äth thā bē·vär′) See CID.

Diaz de la Pe·ña (dyàz də là pā·nyà′), **Narcisse Virgile,** 1808–76, French painter.

di·a·zine (dī′ə·zēn, -zin, dī·az′in) *n. Chem.* One of three isomeric cyclic hydrocarbon compounds, the ring of which contains two nitrogen and four carbon atoms. Also **di·a·zin** (dī′ə·zin, dī·az′in). [<DIAZ(O)- + -IN]

di·az·o (dī·az′ō, dī·ā′zō) *adj. Chem.* Pertaining to or designating any of a group of very reactive compounds in which two nitrogen atoms are united to a hydrocarbon radical: used in dyestuff manufacture. In compounds, **diazo-** or, before vowels, **diaz-,** as in *diazomethane, diazine.* [<DI-[2] + AZO(TE)]

di·a·zole (dī′ə·zōl, dī·az′ōl) *n. Chem.* Any member of a class of heterocyclic hydrocarbon compounds, the ring of which contains two nitrogen and three carbon atoms. [<DIAZ(O)- + -OLE[1]]

di·az·o·meth·ane (dī·az′ō·meth′ān, dī·ā′zō-) *n. Chem.* An odorless, poisonous, yellow gas, CH_2N_2, used in organic syntheses.

di·a·zo·ni·um (dī′ə·zō′nē·əm) *n. Chem.* A basic organic radical which forms aromatic nitrogen compounds. [<DIAZ(O)- + (AMM)ONIUM]

diazonium salt *Chem.* Any of a group of salts formed by the action of nitrous acid at low temperature upon a salt of a primary aromatic amine.

di·az·o-re·ac·tion (dī·az′ō·rē·ak′shən, dī·ā′zō-)

n. Med. A reaction, especially in typhoid fever, in which the urine becomes deep red in color when treated with certain reagents.

di·az·o·tize (dī·az′ə·tīz) *v.t.* **·tized, ·tiz·ing** *Chem.* To bring about chemical reactions or changes that form a diazo compound or derivative. **— di·az′o·ti·za′tion** *n.*

di·ba·sic (dī·bā′sik) *adj. Chem.* **1** Containing two atoms of hydrogen replaceable by a base or basic radical, as sulfuric acid. **2** Of or derived from such an acid: said of salts. **— di·ba·sic·i·ty** (dī′bā·sis′ə·tē) *n.*

dib·ble[1] (dib′əl) *n.* A gardeners' pointed tool for planting seeds, setting slips, etc. **—** *v.t.* **·bled ·bling 1** To make holes in (soil) with a dibble. **2** To plant or set (seeds, etc.) with a dibble. Also **dib·ber** (dib′ər). [? < *dib,* var. of DAB[3]]

dib·ble[2] (dib′əl) *v.i. Brit. Dial.* **1** In angling, to dip the bait gently into the water. **2** To dabble; tamper. Also **dib.** [Freq. of *dib,* var. of DAB[3]]

di·bran·chi·ate (dī·brang′kē·it, -āt) *n.* Any of an order *(Dibranchiata)* of cephalopods including the squids and octopuses, with 8 or 10 sucker-bearing arms surrounding the mouth, 2 internal gills, and a sac and siphon for emitting an inky liquid. **—** *adj.* Of or pertaining to the *Dibranchiata.* [<NL *dibranchiata* <Gk. *di-* two + *branchia* gills]

di·bro·mide (dī·brō′mīd, -mid) *n. Chem.* A compound containing two atoms of bromine.

di·bro·mo·gal·lic acid (dī′brō·mə·gal′ik) Gallobromal.

di·car·box·yl·ic acid (dī·kär′bok·sil′ik) *Chem.* An organic compound having two carboxyl radicals.

di·cast (dī′kast, dik′ast) *n.* In ancient Athens, one of the citizens selected annually to serve as a judge of the high court: also called *heliast.* [<Gk. *dikastēs* < *dikē* justice] **— di·cas′tic** *adj.*

dice (dīs) *n. pl. of* **die 1** Small cubes of bone, ivory, or composition, having the sides marked with spots from one to six. **2** A game played with such cubes. **— poker dice** Dice marked with card faces from nine to ace inclusive. **—** *v.* **diced, dic·ing** *v.t.* **1** To cut into small cubes. **2** To decorate with a dice-like pattern. **3** To gamble away or win with dice. **—** *v.i.* **4** To play at dice. [See DIE[2]] **— dic′er** *n.* **— dic′ing** *n.*

dice box A box used for shaking and throwing dice.

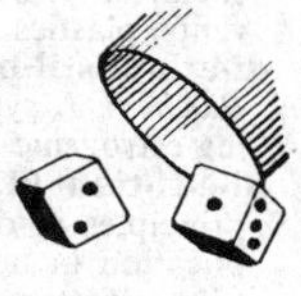
DICE *(def. 1)*

di·cen·tra (dī·sen′trə) *n.* **1** Any plant of a genus *(Dicentra)* of low, delicate, perennial herbs, with a raceme of nodding, rose-colored or yellow, heart-shaped flowers, as the bleeding heart and dutchman's-breeches. [<NL < Gk. *dikentros* < *di-* two + *kentron* a spur]

di·ceph·a·lous (dī·sef′ə·ləs) *adj.* Having two heads.

dic·er·ous (dis′ər·əs) *adj.* Having two horns or antennae. [<Gk. *dikeros* < *di-* two + *keras* horn]

di·cha·si·um (dī·kā′zhē·əm, -zē·əm) *n. pl.* **·si·a** (-zhē·ə, -zē·ə) *Bot.* A cymose inflorescence in which two lateral branches grow from the primary axis below the flower, each branch repeating the division; a two-parted cyme. [<NL <Gk. *dichasis* a division < *dicha* in two] **— di·cha′si·al** *adj.*

di·chlor·a·mine (dī·klôr′ə·mēn) *n. Chem.* A yellowish-white, crystalline compound, $C_7H_7SO_2NCl_2$, used as an antiseptic in treating wound infection. [<DI-[2] + CHLOR- + -AMINE]

di·chlor·eth·yl sulfide (dī′klôr·eth′əl) See MUSTARD GAS.

di·chlo·ride (dī·klôr′id, -id, -klō′rid, -rid) *n. Chem.* A compound having two atoms of chlorine combined with an element or radical; a bichloride. Also **di·chlo·rid** (dī·klôr′id, -klō′rid).

di·chlor·o·di·phen·yl·tri·chlor·o·eth·ane (dī·klôr′ō·dī·fen′il·trī·klôr′ō·eth′ān) *n.* DDT.

dicho- *combining form* In two; in pairs: *dichotomy.* Also, before vowels, **dich-.** [<Gk. < *dicha* in two < *dis* twice]

di·chog·a·my (dī·kog′ə·mē) *n. Bot.* A condition, brought about by the maturity at different times of the anthers and stigmas, for promoting intercrossing between hermaphrodite flowers: distinguished from *homogamy.* [<DICHO- + -GAMY] **— di·chog′a·mous** *adj.*

di·chot·o·mize (dī·kot′ə·mīz) *v.* **·mized, ·miz·ing** *v.t.* **1** To cut or part into two sections; subdivide or separate and classify into pairs. **2** *Astron.* To exhibit as a half disk, as the moon. **—** *v.i.* To be or become separated into two parts. **— di·chot′o·mi·za′tion** *n.*

di·chot·o·mous (dī·kot′ə·məs) *adj.* **1** Pertaining to or involving dichotomy. **2** Dividing into two parts or branches. Also **di·cho·tom·ic** (dī′kə·tom′ik). **— di·chot′o·mous·ly, di′cho·tom′i·cal·ly** *adv.*

di·chot·o·my (dī·kot′ə·mē) *n. pl.* **·mies 1** The state of being divided in two; division into two parts or into two branches; division by pairs. **2** *Logic* The division of a class into two mutually exclusive subclasses, one positive and the other negative, as minerals into gold and not-gold. **3** *Astron.* The aspect of the moon, Mercury, or Venus, at first and last quarter, when half the apparent disk is illuminated. **4** *Bot.* **a** A forking in pairs, as the stem of a plant; successive bifurcation. **b** A system of branching in which each successive axis forks or bifurcates into two equally developed branches. [<Gk. *dichotomia* < *dicho-* in two + *temnein* cut]

di·chro·ic (dī·krō′ik) *adj.* **1** Of, pertaining to, or exhibiting dichroism. **2** Dichromatic. Also **di·chro·it·ic** (dī′krō·it′ik).

di·chro·ism (dī′krō·iz′əm) *n.* **1** *Physics* The property of showing different colors when viewed in different directions, exhibited by doubly refracting crystals. **2** *Chem.* The property of being differently colored in different degrees of concentration: shown by some solutions. [<Gk. *dichroos* two-colored < *di-* two + *chrōs* color]

di·chro·ite (dī′krō·īt) *n.* The mineral iolite. [<Gk. *dichroos* two-colored + -ITE[1]]

di·chro·mate (dī·krō′māt) *n. Chem.* A compound containing two chromium atoms: potassium *dichromate.*

di·chro·mat·ic (dī′krō·mat′ik) *adj.* **1** Having either of two colors. **2** *Zool.* Having two color phases: said of certain birds and insects, etc., that, apart from changes due to age or sex, exhibit a coloration differing from the normal. **3** *Pathol.* Affected with blue-, green-, or red-blindness; able to see only two of the three primary colors.

di·chro·ma·tism (dī·krō′mə·tiz′əm) *n.* The state of being dichromatic, especially with reference to colorblindness. Also **di·chro′mism.**

di·chro·mic (dī·krō′mik) *adj.* **1** Containing two atoms of chromium, or their equivalents. **2** Dichromatic.

dichromic acid *Chem.* A dibasic acid, $H_2Cr_2O_7$, known only through its salts, the dichromates or bichromates.

Dich·tung und Wahr·heit (dikh′to͝ong o͝ont vär′hīt) *Ger.* "Poetry and Truth": the title of Goethe's autobiography.

di·chro·scope (dī′krə·skōp) *n.* An instrument for examining or exhibiting dichroism, as of crystals. Also **di·chro·o·scope** (dī·krō′ə·skōp). [<Gk. *dichroos* two-colored + -SCOPE] **— di·chro·scop·ic** (dī′krə·skop′ik) *adj.*

dick (dik) *n. U.S. Slang* A detective.

Dick (dik) A masculine nickname: diminutive of RICHARD.

Dick (dik), **George Frederick,** born 1881, and his wife, **Gladys,** born 1881, U.S. physiologists.

dick·cis·sel (dik·sis′əl) *n.* A bunting *(Spiza americana)* of the Mississippi region, distinguished by its black throat and lively call. Also **dick·sis′sel.** [Imit.]

dick·ens (dik′ənz) *n. Colloq.* The devil: a euphemistic expletive.

Dick·ens (dik′ənz), **Charles,** 1812–70, English novelist.

Dick·en·si·an (di·ken′zē·ən) *adj.* Of or characteristic of Charles Dickens, his writing, or his style; especially, denoting a literary style in which odd characters from ordinary life are portrayed humorously and kindly.

dick·er (dik′ər) *n. U.S.* **1** A petty trade; a bargain. **2** A political deal. **—** *v.t. & v.i.* **1** To trade by haggling or bartering, especially on a small scale. **2** In politics, to bargain; work toward a deal. [ME *dyker,* OE (unrecorded) *dicor* a lot of ten, esp. skins or hides, ult. <L *decuria* a group of ten]

dick·ey (dik′ē) *n.* **1** A detachable article of clothing, as a false shirt front, or sweater front; also, a bib; pinafore. **2** A driver's outside seat on a carriage; also, one behind the body, for servants. **3** A donkey. **4** *Colloq.* Any small bird. Also **dick′y.** [<*Dicky,* double dim. of RICHARD]

Dick·in·son (dik′ən·sən), **Emily Elizabeth,** 1830–86, U.S. poet. **— John,** 1732–1808, American statesman.

Dick test *Med.* A test of susceptibility to or immunity from scarlet fever, consisting of subcutaneous injections of streptococcus toxins of the disease. [after George and Gladys *Dick*]

di·cli·nous (dī′kli·nəs, dī·klī′-) *adj. Bot.* Having stamens in one flower and pistils in another; unisexual. [<DI-[2] + Gk. *klinē* bed]

di·cli·ny (dī′kli·nē, dī·klī′nē) *n. Bot.* The condition of being diclinous.

di·cot·y·le·don (dī′kot·ə·lēd′n, dī·kot′-) *n. Bot.* **1** A plant having two cotyledons or seed leaves. **2** A member of the class *Dicotyledones.*

di·cot·y·le·do·nous (dī′kot·ə·lē′də·nəs, dī·kot′-) *adj. Bot.* Belonging or pertaining to the largest, most important subclass *(Dicotyledones)* of angiosperms or flowering plants, characterized by having seeds with two cotyledons. It embraces the majority of deciduous trees and of herbs and shrubs.

di·crot·ic (dī·krot′ik) *adj. Physiol.* Having an abnormal heartbeat, with a double pulse beat to each systole of the heart. Also **di·cro·tal** (dī·krō′təl), **di·cro·tous** (dī′krə·təs). [<Gk. *dikrotos* < *di-* two + *krotos* beat] **— di·cro·tism** (dī′krə·tiz′əm) *n.*

dic·ta (dik′tə) Plural of DICTUM.

Dic·ta·phone (dik′tə·fōn) *n.* A type of phonographic instrument that records and reproduces words spoken into its mouthpiece, as for transcription by a stenographer: a trade name.

dic·tate (dik′tāt, dik·tāt′) *v.* **·tat·ed, ·tat·ing** *v.t.* **1** To utter or read aloud (something) to be recorded by another, as by writing. **2** To give, impose, or prescribe authoritatively, as commands, terms, rules, etc. **—** *v.i.* **3** To utter aloud something to be recorded by another. **4** To give orders. **—** *n.* (dik′tāt) **1** An authoritative suggestion or prompting; a rule, precept, or maxim. **2** A positive order. [<L *dictatus,* pp. of *dictare,* freq. of *dicere* say, speak]

Synonyms (verb): command, decree, direct, enjoin, order, prescribe, require. See SPEAK. *Antonyms*: accept, follow, obey, submit, yield.

dic·ta·tion (dik·tā′shən) *n.* **1** The act of dictating. **2** The matter or material dictated. **3** Arbitrary control. **— dic·ta′tion·al** *adj.*

dic·ta·tor (dik′tā·tər, dik·tā′tər) *n.* **1** One invested with absolute power, especially in a state in time of emergency. **2** One who dictates or prescribes. **3** In ancient Rome, a chief magistrate with supreme authority, appointed by the Senate in cases of emergency for a term of about six months. **— dic′ta·tor·ship′** *n.* **— dic·ta′tress** *n. fem.*

dic·ta·to·ri·al (dik′tə·tôr′ē·əl, -tō′rē-) *adj.* Given to dictating; overbearing. See synonyms under ARBITRARY, DOGMATIC, IMPERIOUS. **— dic′ta·to′ri·al·ly** *adv.* **— dic′ta·to′ri·al·ness** *n.*

dic·tion (dik′shən) *n.* **1** The use, choice, and arrangement of words and modes of expression. **2** The manner of speaking or of any vocal expression; enunciation. [<L *dictio,* *-onis* speech < *dicere* say, speak]

Synonyms: expression, language, phrase, phraseology, style, verbiage, vocabulary, wording, words. An author's *diction* is strictly his choice and use of words, with no special reference to thought; *expression* regards the words simply as the vehicle of the thought. *Phrase* and *phraseology* apply to words or combinations of words which are somewhat technical; as, in legal *phraseology*; in military *phrase. Diction* is general; *wording* is limited; we speak of the *diction* of an author or of a work, the *wording* of a proposition, of a resolution, etc. *Verbiage* is wordiness. *Style* includes *diction, expression,* rhetorical figures such as metaphor and simile, the effect of an author's prevailing tone of thought, of his

personal traits—in short, all that makes up the clothing of thought in words. Compare LANGUAGE.

dic·tion·ar·y (dik′shən·er′ē) *n. pl.* **·ar·ies** **1** A book containing the words of a language, or of a department of knowledge, arranged alphabetically, usually with their syllabication, pronunciation, definition, and etymology; lexicon; wordbook. **2** A similar work having definitions or equivalents in another language: a German-English *dictionary.* [< Med. L *dictionarium* a collection of words and phrases < *dictio.* See DICTION.]

Dic·to·graph (dik′tə·graf, -gräf) *n.* A sensitive telephonic device used to transmit or overhear conversations: a trade name.

dic·tum (dik′təm) *n. pl.* **dic·ta** (-tə) **1** An authoritative, dogmatic, or positive utterance; a pronouncement. **2** *Law* An opinion by a judge on a point not essential to the decision on the main question in the case on trial. **3** A popular saying; a maxim. See synonyms under ADAGE. [< L < *dicere* say]

dic·ty·nid (dik′tə·nid) *n.* One of a family (*Dictynidae*) of spiders that build their webs of a curled thread and in irregular forms. [< NL < Gk. *diktyon* a net]

Di·cu·ma·rol (dī·ko͞o′mə·rôl, -rol, -kyo͞o′-) *n.* Proprietary name for a derivative of coumarin: used to delay the coagulation of blood.

did (did) Past tense of DO[1].

Did·a·che (did′ə·kē) *n.* The teaching of the Twelve Apostles: the title of the oldest church manual, written in the second century. [< Gk., a teaching]

di·dac·tic (dī·dak′tik, di-) *adj.* **1** Pertaining to or of the nature of teaching; intended to instruct; expository. **2** Morally instructive; preceptive. **3** Overly inclined to teach; pedantic. Also **di·dac′ti·cal.** [< Gk. *didaktikos* apt to teach < *didaskein* teach] **—di·dac′ti·cal·ly** *adv.* **—di·dac′ti·cism** *n.*

di·dac·tics (dī·dak′tiks, di-) *n.* The science or art of instruction or education.

di·dap·per (dī′dap′ər) *n.* A dabchick. [Short for *divedapper*]

did·dle[1] (did′l) *v. Colloq.* **·dled, ·dling** *v.t.* To cheat. —*v.i.* To dawdle; pass time idly. Also *daddle.* [? < DIDDLE[2]] **—did′dler** *n.*

did·dle[2] (did′l) *v.i.* **·dled, ·dling** To jerk up and down or back and forth; jiggle. [Var. of dial. *didder,* ME *diddiren* quiver, shake, tremble]

Di·de·rot (dē·drō′), **Denis** 1713–84, French philosopher, critic, and encyclopedist.

didg·er·i·du (dij′ər·ē·do͞o′) *n. Austral.* An aboriginal musical instrument, a foot to eight feet long, that amplifies a nasal whine. [< native Australian]

did·na (did′nə) *Scot.* Did not.

did·n't (did′nt) Did not: a contraction.

di·do (dī·dō) *n. pl.* **·dos** or **·does** *Colloq.* An extravagant action; caper; antic. [Origin unknown]

Di·do (dī′dō) In Roman legend, a Tyrian princess, founder and queen of Carthage. In the *Aeneid,* she falls in love with Aeneas when he lands in Carthage after his flight from Troy, and kills herself when he leaves her.

di·drach·ma (dī·drak′mə) *n. pl.* **·mas** or **mae** (-mē) **1** A double drachma in ancient Greece. **2** The earliest Roman silver coin. [< Gk. < *di-* two + *drachma* a drachma]

didst (didst) *Archaic* Second person singular past tense of DO[1]: used with *thou.*

di·dy (dī′dē) *n. pl.* **·dies** *Colloq.* A baby's diaper. [< DIAPER]

di·dym·i·um (dī·dim′ē·əm, di-) *n.* A mixture of the elements neodymium and praseodymium of the lanthanide series, found in cerite and formerly regarded as one of the elements. [< NL < Gk. *didymos* double]

did·y·mous (did′ə·məs) *adj.* **1** *Bot.* Twin; formed in pairs; growing double, as umbelliferous fruits. **2** Double, as markings. [< Gk. *didymos* double]

die[1] (dī) *v.i.* **died, dy·ing** **1** To suffer death; pass from life; expire. **2** To suffer the pains of death: The coward *dies* a thousand deaths. **3** To lose energy or power; pass: with *away: down,* or *out.* **4** To cease to exist; fade away, The smile *died* on his lips. **5** To become extinct: with *out* or *off.* **6** To become indifferent or insensible: with *to*: to *die* to the world. **7** To desire exceedingly, as if to death: He's *dying* to meet her. **8** To stop functioning, as an engine. **9** To faint or swoon. **10** *Theol.* To suffer spiritual death. **—to die game** To die fighting. ◆ Homophone: *dye.* [< ON *deyja*]

Synonyms: cease, decease, decline, depart, expire, perish, wither. *Die* is applied to anything which has the appearance of life; an echo, a strain of music, a tempest, a topic, an issue, *dies. Expire* is a softer word for *die;* it is used figuratively of things that *cease* to exist by reaching a natural limit; as, a lease *expires;* the time has *expired.* To *perish* is oftenest used of death by privation or exposure; sometimes, of death by violence. Knowledge and fame, art and empires, may be said to *perish;* the word denotes destruction and decay. *Antonyms*: begin, exist, flourish, grow, live, survive.

die[2] (dī) *n. pl.* **dice** *for defs.* **1** *and* **2 dies** *for defs.* **3** *to* **6. 1** A small cube used in games. See DICE. **2** A cast, as in playing dice; stake; hazard. **3** *Mech.* **a** A hard metal pattern for stamping or cutting out some object; specifically, one of a pair between which a metal blank is forced or forged into a special shape, as a spoon. **b** One of a pair of such patterns, one cameo and the other intaglio, between which a sheet of metal is embossed. **c** A block or counter having an orifice through which a punch passes. Also **die plate. 4** A tool for cutting screw threads on a nut, bolt, etc. **5** The cubical part of a pedestal. **6** Any small cubical block or body. **—the die is cast** The choice is made that commits one to an irrevocable course of action —*v.t.* To cut or stamp with or as with a die. ◆ Homophone: *dye.* [< OF *de* < L *datum* something given]

die·back (dī′bak′) *n.* Arrested or retarded development in the twigs of certain woody plants, due to parasites or to being winter-killed: also called *twig blight.*

Di·e·go (dē·ā′gō) A Spanish form of JAMES.

die-hard (dī′härd′) *n.* **1** One who fights to the last. **2** One who obstinately refuses to abandon or modify his views; especially, a political conservative who obstinately opposes a winning liberal measure.

di·el·drin (dī·el′drin) *n.* A toxic chlorinated hydrocarbon, $C_{12}H_8Cl_6O$, stereoisomeric with endrin and likewise used as a pesticide.

di·e·lec·tric (dī′ə·lek′trik) *Electr. adj.* **1** Non-conducting. **2** Capable of sustaining an electric field, as by induction. Also **di′e·lec′tri·cal. —***n.* A dielectric substance, medium or material. **—di′e·lec′tri·cal·ly** *adv.*

Dien Bien Phu (dyen byen fo͞o) A town in North Vietnam; besieged and captured from the French by Vietnamese forces in 1954.

di·en·ceph·a·lon (dī′en·sef′ə·lon) *n. Anat.* That part of the brain forming the posterior part of the prosencephalon, from which are developed the pineal body, the pituitary, and other structures of the third ventricle; the interbrain or middle brain: also called *thalamencephalon.* [< NL < Gk. *di(a)-* between + *enkephalos* brain]

-diene *suffix Chem.* Denoting an open-chain unsaturated hydrocarbon compound having two double bonds: *butadiene.* [< DI-[2] + -ENE]

Di·eppe (dē·ep′, *Fr.* dyep) A port on the English Channel in northern France.

di·er·e·sis (dī·er′ə·sis) *n. pl.* **·ses** (-sēz) **1** Two dots (¨) placed over the second of two adjacent vowels that are to be pronounced separately. **2** The separation of syllables or vowels by dots. **3** In the pronunciations in this book, a diacritic used over *a* to indicate the vowel sound in *palm* (päm). See also ü, Foreign Sounds page xx. **4** The coincidence of the end of a metrical foot with the end of a word in a verse. Also spelled *diaeresis.* Compare SYNERESIS. [< LL *diaeresis* < Gk. *diairesis* a division < *diaireein* < *dia-* apart + *haireein* seize] **—di·e·ret·ic** (dī′ə·ret′ik) *adj.*

di·es (dī′ēz) *n. pl.* **di·es** (dī′ēz) *Latin* Day.

die·sel engine (dē′zəl) An internal-combustion engine, in which crude oil, used as fuel, is ignited by the heat resulting from the high compression of air drawn into the cylinder. Also **Diesel engine.** [after Rudolf *Diesel,* 1858–1913, German inventor]

Di·es I·rae (dī′ēz ī′rē) The name of a famous medieval Latin hymn on the Day of Judgment, used as the sequence in masses for the dead: so called from its opening words; literally, Day of Wrath. [< L]

di·e·sis (dī′ə·sis) *n.* **1** *Music* The difference in tone between a major and a minor semitone, represented by the ratio of vibrations 125:128; also, an interval smaller than a half-step. **2** In Greek music, one of several intervals varying from a semitone to a quartertone. **3** *Printing* The double dagger (‡): a reference mark for the third in a series. [< L < Gk. < *diienai* < *dia-* through + *hienai* send]

di·es non ju·rid·i·cus (dī′ēz non′ jo͝o·rid′ə·kəs) *Latin Law* A day on which courts are not in session. Also **di′es non′.**

Diest (dēst) A town in north central Belgium.

die·stock (dī′stok′) *n. Mech.* A double-handled holder for a die used to cut threads on screws, bolts, etc.

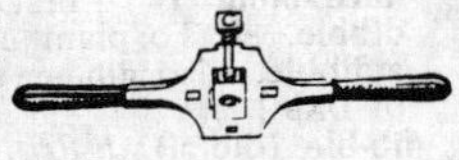
DIESTOCK

di·et[1] (dī′ət) *n.* **1** A regulated course of eating and drinking; a specially prescribed regimen. **2** The daily fare; victuals. **3** *Obs.* Allowance of food; ration. See synonyms under FOOD. —*v.t.* **1** To regulate or restrict the food and drink of. —*v.i.* **2** To take food and drink according to a regimen; eat discriminatingly. **3** To take food; eat. [< OF *diete* < L *diaeta* < Gk. *diaita* a way of living] **—di′et·er** *n.*

di·et[2] (dī′ət) *n.* **1** A legislative assembly. **2** *Scot.* A single session, as of a court; a day appointed for a session. [< Med. L *dieta* < L *dies* a day]

Di·et (dī′ət) *n.* **1** The legislature of certain countries. **2** The semiannual meeting of the estates of the Holy Roman Empire: often distinguished by the name of the city where it was held: the *Diet* of Worms.

di·e·tar·y (dī′ə·ter′ē) *n. pl.* **·tar·ies** **1** A system or regimen of dieting. **2** A standard or regulated allowance of food. —*adj.* Pertaining or relating to diet: also **di·e·tet·ic** (dī′ə·tet′ik), **di′e·tet′i·cal. —di′e·tet′i·cal·ly** *adv.*

Diet·bold (dēt′bōlt) A German form of THEOBALD.

di·e·tet·ics (dī′ə·tet′iks) *n.* The branch of hygiene that treats of diet and dieting and the feeding of individuals or of great numbers.

di·eth·y·lene glycol (dī·eth′ə·lēn) *Chem.* An organic compound, $O(CH_2CH_2OH)_2$, used as an anti-freeze mixture and as an agent in many chemical processes for the production of solvents, plastics, explosives, etc.

di·eth·yl·stil·bes·trol (dī·eth′əl·stil·bes′trōl) *n. Biochem.* A synthetic compound, $C_{18}H_{20}O_2$, having estrogenic and carcinogenic properties.

di·e·ti·tian (dī′ə·tish′ən) *n.* One skilled in the principles of dietetics and in their practical application in health and disease. Also **di·e·tet·ist** (dī′ə·tet′ist), **di′e·ti′cian.**

diet kitchen **1** An institution, usually connected with a dispensary or hospital, that provides food for the invalid poor. **2** A kitchen where special diets are prepared and from which they are served under the supervision of a dietitian who gives student nurses dietetic training.

Dieu a·vec nous (dyœ′ à·vek′ no͞o′) *French* God with us.

Dieu et mon droit (dyœ′ ā môn′ drwà′) *French* God and my right: motto of the royal arms of Great Britain.

Dieu vous garde (dyœ′ vo͞o′ gàrd′) *French* God protect you.

dif- Assimilated var. of DIS-.

dif·fer (dif′ər) *v.i.* **1** To be unlike in quality, degree, form, etc.; often with *from.* **2** To disagree; dissent: often with *with.* **3** To quarrel: sometimes with *over* or *about.* [< OF *differer* < L *differre* < *dis-* apart + *ferre* carry. Doublet of DEFER[1].]

dif·fer·ence (dif′ər·əns, dif′rəns) *n.* **1** The state or quality of being other or unlike, or that in which two things are unlike; dissimilarity; variation. **2** A mark or peculiarity which distinguishes. **3** A disagreement in sentiment or opinion; controversy; quarrel. **4** A separate treatment; discrimination. **5** *Math.* The result obtained by subtracting one number from another. **6** *Logic* The specific difference; differentia. **7** In commerce, a margin that has become payable. **8** *Her.* A device in blazons to distinguish persons bearing the same arms. —*v.t.* **·enced, ·enc·ing** **1** To make or mark as different; distinguish; discriminate. **2** *Her.* To add a mark of difference to.

Synonyms (noun): contrariety, contrast, disagreement, discrepancy, discrimination, disparity, dissimilarity, dissimilitude, distinction, divergence, diversity, inconsistency, inequality, unlikeness, variation. A *difference* is in the things compared; a *discrimination* is in our judgment of them; a *distinction* is in our definition or description or mental image of them. Careful *discrimination* of real *differences* results in clear *distinctions*. *Disparity* is stronger than *inequality*, implying that one thing falls far below another; as, the *disparity* of our achievements when compared with our ideals. *Dissimilarity* is between things sharply contrasted; there may be a *difference* between those almost alike. There is a *discrepancy* in accounts that fail to balance. *Diversity* involves more than two objects; *variation* is a *difference* in the condition or action of the same object at different times. *Antonyms*: agreement, consonance, harmony, identity, likeness, resemblance, sameness, similarity, uniformity, unity.

dif·fer·ent (dif′ər·ənt, dif′rənt) *adj.* **1** Not the same; distinct; other: A *different* clerk is there now. **2** Marked by a difference; completely or partly unlike; dissimilar. **3** Unusual. See synonyms under CONTRARY. [<F *différent* <L *differens, -entis,* ppr. of *differre.* See DIFFER.] **—dif′fer·ent·ly** *adv.* **—dif′fer·ent·ness** *n.* ◆ **different from, than, to** In American usage, *from* is established as the idiomatic preposition to follow *different*; when, however, a clause follows the connective, *than* is gaining increasing acceptance: a result *different than* (= *from that which* or *from what*) had been expected. This last is established British usage, which also accepts *to* on a par with *from*: She is *different to* her sister.

dif·fer·en·ti·a (dif′ə·ren′shē·ə) *n. pl.* **·ti·ae** (-shi·ē) *Logic* A specific difference; a characteristic attribute distinguishing a species from others of the same genus. [<L, neut. pl. of *differens.* See DIFFERENT.]

dif·fer·en·ti·a·ble (dif′ə·ren′shē·ə·bəl) *adj.* **1** That can be differentiated. **2** *Math.* Belonging to or having a differential coefficient. **—dif′fer·en′ti·a·bil′i·ty** *n.*

dif·fer·en·tial (dif′ə·ren′shəl) *adj.* **1** Relating to, making, or marked by a difference. **2** Distinctive; discriminative. **3** *Math.* Pertaining to or involving differentials or differentiation. **4** *Mech.* Characterized by a construction in which a movement is obtained by the difference in two motions in the same direction. See DIFFERENTIAL GEAR. **—***n.* **1** *Math.* **a** An infinitesimal increment of a quantity: indicated by the symbol Δ. **b** The derivative of a function multiplied by the increment of the independent variable. **2** A differential rate. **3** *Mech.* A differential gear. **4** *Electr.* One of two resistance coils the current of which flows in a direction opposite to that of the other. **—dif′fer·en′tial·ly** *adv.*

differential calculus See under CALCULUS.

differential coefficient *Math.* The ratio of the infinitesimal increase of a function to that of a variable on which the function depends; a derivative. Also **differential quotient.**

differential equation *Math.* An equation in which derivatives or differentials of an unknown function appear.

differential gear or **gearing** *Mech.* A coupling consisting of an epicyclic train used to connect shafts, as in the driving axle of an automobile, so that a rigid union is effected when moving in a straight line, but permitting of independent motion when describing a curve.

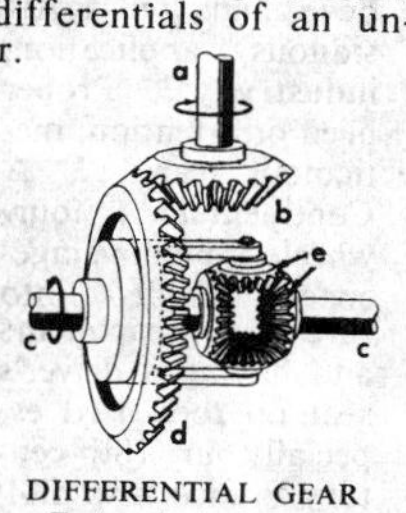

DIFFERENTIAL GEAR
a. Drive shaft. *b.* Drive-shaft gear. *c.* Axles. *d.* Ring gear. *e.* Epicyclic train of gears.

differential windlass See under WINDLASS.

dif·fer·en·ti·ate (dif′ə·ren′shē·āt) *v.* **·at·ed, ·at·ing** *v.t.* **1** To constitute a difference between; mark off. **2** To perceive and indicate the differences of or between. **3** *Biol.* To cause to be unlike; develop differences in. **4** *Math.* To derive the differential of (a function). **—***v.i.* **5** To discriminate; perceive a difference. **6** To become specialized; acquire a distinct character. See synonyms under CONTRAST.

dif·fer·en·ti·a·tion (dif′ə·ren′shē·ā′shən) *n.* **1** The process of making or becoming different. **2** *Biol.* **a** Progressive change from the general to the special, as in all organs and tissues in course of development. **b** The setting apart of special organs for special work: distinguished from ordinary cellular growth in that the cells produced by division are dissimilar to the parent cells. **3** *Logic* Distinction on grounds of difference; discrimination. **4** *Math.* The finding of a differential.

dif·fi·cile (dif′ə·sēl′, *Fr.* dē·fē·sēl′) *adj. French* Difficult; especially, difficult to deal with or please.

dif·fi·cult (dif′ə·kult, -kəlt) *adj.* **1** Hard to do or be done; arduous; troublesome to understand; perplexing. **2** Hard to persuade, overcome, or satisfy; intractable; exacting. [Back formation <DIFFICULTY] **—dif′fi·cult·ly** *adv.*

Synonyms: arduous, exhausting, hard, laborious, onerous, severe, toilsome, trying. *Arduous* applies to that which involves great and sustained exertion; great learning can only be won by *arduous* toil. Anything is *hard* that involves tax and strain whether of the physical or mental powers. *Difficult* is not used of that which merely taxes physical force; a dead lift is called *hard* rather than *difficult*; that is *difficult* which involves skill, sagacity, or address, with or without a considerable expenditure of physical force; a geometrical problem may be *difficult* to solve, a mountain *difficult* to ascend. *Hard* may be active or passive; a thing may be *hard* to do or *hard* to bear. *Arduous* is always active. That which is *laborious* or *toilsome* requires the steady application of labor or toil till accomplished; *toilsome* is the stronger word. That which is *onerous* is mentally burdensome or oppressive. See ARDUOUS, HARD, OBSCURE, SQUEAMISH, TROUBLESOME. *Antonyms*: easy, facile, light, pleasant, slight, trifling, trivial.

dif·fi·cul·ty (dif′ə·kul′tē, -kəl-) *n. pl.* **·ties** **1** The state or quality of being difficult or of presenting or constituting an obstacle to achievement or mastery. **2** An obstacle; hindrance; something difficult to effect or to understand. **3** Reluctance; objection. **4** A quarrel. **5** *Usually pl.* Financial embarrassment; a strait; trouble: generally in the plural. See synonyms under IMPEDIMENT. [<L *difficultas, -tatis* <*difficilis* <*dis-* away, not + *facilis* easy <*facere* do, make]

dif·fi·dence (dif′ə·dəns) *n.* Self-distrust; shyness; modesty.

dif·fi·dent (dif′ə·dənt) *adj.* **1** Affected or possessed with self-distrust; timid; shy; modest. **2** *Obs.* Distrustful of others; doubtful. [<L *diffidens, -entis,* ppr. of *diffidere* <*dis-* away + *fidere* trust <*fides* faith] **—dif′fi·dent·ly** *adv.*

dif·fract (di·frakt′) *v.t.* **1** To separate into parts. **2** To subject to diffraction. [<L *diffractus,* pp. of *diffringere* <*dis-* away + *frangere* break] **—dif·frac′tive** *adj.* **—dif·frac′tive·ly** *adv.* **—dif·frac′tive·ness** *n.*

dif·frac·tion (di·frak′shən) *n. Physics* **1** A deviation of rays of light from a straight course when partially cut off by any obstacle or passing near the edges of an opening, or through a minute hole, generally accompanied by prismatic colors due to interference. Diffraction is a phenomenon accompanying all forms of wave motion, its effect being more marked as the wavelength increases. It is best shown by **diffraction gratings,** plates of glass or polished metal ruled closely with parallel lines, by means of which **diffraction spectra** are obtained. **2** A similar deviation of sound waves in passing the angle or edge of a large body.

dif·fuse (di·fyōōz′) *v.t.* & *v.i.* **·fused, ·fus·ing** **1** To pour or send out so as to spread in all directions; spread abroad; circulate; permeate. **2** To subject to or spread by diffusion. See synonyms under SPREAD. **—***adj.* (di·fyōōs′) **1** Characterized by redundance; prolix; verbose. **2** Widely spread out; extended. [<L *diffusus,* pp. of *diffundere* <*dis-* away, from + *fundere* pour] **—dif·fuse·ly** (di·fyōōz′lē) *adv.* **—dif·fuse·ness** (di·fyōōs′nis) *n.*

dif·fus·er (di·fyōō′zər) *n.* **1** One who or that which diffuses. **2** A device for diffusing the heat of a thermoelectric battery, or changing the characteristics of a liquid flow. **3** A reflector placed above an arc lamp to aid in the uniform distribution of the light. Also **dif·fu′sor.**

dif·fus·i·ble (di·fyōō′zə·bəl) *adj.* Capable of being diffused. **—dif·fus′i·bil′i·ty, dif·fus′i·ble·ness** *n.*

dif·fu·sion (di·fyōō′zhən) *n.* **1** The act or process of diffusing, or the state of being diffused; a scattering; dissemination; dispersion; circulation. **2** Prolixity; diffuseness of verbal expression. **3** The scattering and criss-crossing of light rays, producing general illumination rather than direct radiation. **4** *Physics* The intermingling by thermal agitation of the atoms or molecules of two substances initially unmixed but in contact. **5** *Anthropol.* The transmission of culture traits from one area, group, or people to another.

dif·fu·sive (di·fyōō′siv) *adj.* Having the property of diffusing; tending to diffuse; spreading abroad. **—dif·fu′sive·ly** *adv.* **—dif·fu′sive·ness** *n.*

dig (dig) *v.* **dug** (*Archaic* **digged**), **dig·ging** *v.t.* **1** To break up, turn up, or remove (earth, etc.), as with a spade, claws, or the hands. **2** To make or form by or as by digging. **3** To take out or obtain by digging: to *dig* clams. **4** To thrust or force into or against, as a tool, heel, or elbow. **5** To discover or bring out by careful effort or study: often with *up* or *out:* to *dig* up evidence of political corruption. **6** *U.S. Slang* To understand. **—***v.i.* **7** To break or turn up earth, etc. **8** To force or make a way by or as by digging. **9** *U.S. Colloq.* To work hard and steadily; plod. **—to dig in** **1** To dig trenches. **2** To entrench (oneself). **3** *Colloq.* To begin to work intensively. **—***n. Colloq.* **1** A thrust; poke. **2** A sarcastic remark; jibe; slur. **3** An archeological excavation. **4** *U.S.* A hard-working student. [<OF *diguer* <Gmc. Akin to DIKE.]

di·gam·ma (dī·gam′ə) *n.* The original, but early disused, sixth letter in the Greek alphabet [Ϝ], equivalent in sound to *W,* but in form to *F.* [<Gk. <*di-* two + *gamma* the letter G] **—di·gam·mat·ed** (dī·gam′ā·tid) *adj.*

dig·a·my (dig′ə·mē) *n.* A second, legal marriage. [<LL *digamia* <Gk. <*di-* two + *gamos* a marriage] **—dig′a·mist** *n.* **—dig′a·mous** *adj.*

di·gas·tric (dī·gas′trik) *adj. Anat.* **1** Having fleshy ends and a central tendon, as one of the muscles that depress the lower jaw. **2** Having two bellies. [<DI-[2] + Gk. *gastēr* belly]

Dig·by (dig′bē), **Sir Kenelm,** 1603–65, English naval commander, diplomat, and philosopher.

di·gen·e·sis (dī·jen′ə·sis) *n. Biol.* Reproduction by two methods, a sexual followed by an asexual; alternation of generations. [<DI-[2] + GENESIS] **—di·ge·net·ic** (dī′jə·net′ik) *adj.*

di·gest (di·jest′, dī-) *v.t.* **1** To convert (food) into chyme in the stomach and intestines; prepare for assimilation. **2** To take in or assimilate mentally. **3** To arrange in systematic form, usually by condensing; summarize and classify. **4** To tolerate patiently; endure. **5** *Chem.* **a** To expose to heat or moisture so as to become softened or decomposed. **b** To treat, as wood, etc., with chemical agents under pressure so as to obtain a desired result. **6** *Obs.* To distribute; disperse. **—***v.i.* **7** To be assimilated, as food. **8** To assimilate food. **9** To be subjected to heat, moisture, chemical agents, or pressure. **—***n.* (dī′jest) **1** A systematic arrangement, as of writings; classified and abridged summary, as of news; compilation. **2** *Law* A compilation of statutes systematically arranged under proper heads and titles; a brief synopsis of the adjudications of courts as recorded in the original reports. See synonyms under ABRIDGEMENT. [<L *digestus,* pp. of *digerere* <*dis-* away + *gerere* carry]

Digest, The The body of Roman laws collected by order of Justinian; the Pandects.

di·ges·tant (di·jes′tənt, dī-) *n.* Any drug which assists digestion. **—***adj.* Digestive.

di·gest·er (dī·jes′tər, di-) *n.* **1** One who makes

a digest, analysis, or summary. 2 A digestant. 3 A strong, closed vessel in which substances may be exposed to the action of water or other liquids at temperatures above their boiling points, to soften or decompose them or to extract some ingredient.

di·gest·i·ble (di·jes′tə·bəl, dī-) *adj.* Capable of being digested or assimilated. **—di·gest′i·bil′i·ty** *n.* **—di·gest′i·bly** *adv.*

di·ges·tion (di·jes′chən, dī-) *n.* **1** *Physiol.* **a** The process of dissolving and chemically changing food in the stomach, so that it can be assimilated by the blood and furnish nutriment to the body. **b** The power to digest; the digestive functions. **2** Mental reception and assimilation. **3** Exposure of a substance to heat and moisture preparatory to a chemical or other operation; solution. **4** Any absorption and assimilation, as of carbon dioxide, or of insects and other animal matter, by plants.

di·ges·tive (di·jes′tiv, dī-) *adj.* Pertaining or conducing to digestion. *—n.* A medicine to aid digestion.

dig·ger (dig′ər) *n.* **1** One who or that which digs. **2** A digger wasp. **3** Any implement or part of a machine for lifting and turning the soil or excavating. **4** *Colloq.* A soldier from Australia or New Zealand.

Dig·ger (dig′ər) *n.* Originally, one of a tribe of agricultural North American Indians of Utah; later, an Indian of any tribe of the American Northwest known to subsist chiefly on roots; hence, applied to various tribes of different linguistic stocks.

digger wasp A wasp (family *Sphecidae*) which digs a hole in the ground for its nest, especially the common American genera, *Sphex* or *Ammophila,* and *Bembidula.* For illustration see INSECT (beneficial).

dig·ging (dig′ing) *n.* **1** The act of one who or that which digs. **2** A shallow excavation made by a miner in search for ore.

diggings (dig′ingz) *n. pl.* **1** A mining region; especially a mining region having many exploratory excavations. **2** The materials dug out of such a region. **3** *Brit. Colloq.* Quarters; lodgings.

dight (dīt) *v.t.* **dight** or **dight·ed, dight·ing** *Obs.* **1** To dress, adorn; equip. **2** To prepare. **3** *Dial.* To cleanse; winnow. *—n.* A rub or wipe in order to dry or clean. [OE *dihtan* arrange, prepare <L *dictare.* See DICTATE.]

dig·it (dij′it) *n.* **1** A finger or toe. **2** Any one of the ten Arabic numeral symbols, 0 to 9: so named from counting upon the fingers. **3** *Astron.* The twelfth part of the diameter of the sun or moon. **4** An old English measure of length, equal to about three fourths of an inch. [<L *digitus* finger]

dig·i·tal (dij′ə·təl) *adj.* **1** Of, pertaining to, or like the fingers or digits. **2** Digitate. **3** Showing information, such as numerals, by means of electronics: *digital* watches. *—n.* A key of the piano or organ. **—dig′i·tal·ly** *adv.*

digital computer An electronic computing machine which receives problems and processes the answers in numerical form, especially one using the binary system. Compare *analog computer.*

dig·i·tal·in (dij′ə·tal′in, -tā′lin) *n.* **1** A crystalline, poisonous glucoside, $C_{36}H_{56}O_{14}$, contained in the leaves of the foxglove, of which it is the active principle. **2** Any of several different extracts of foxglove.

dig·i·tal·is (dij′ə·tal′is, -tā′lis) *n.* **1** Any of a genus *(Digitalis)* of tall, Old World herbs of the figwort family, including *D. purpurea,* the foxglove, often cultivated: sometimes called *fairy gloves.* **2** The dried leaves of foxglove, containing several glucosides, some of which are used as a heart tonic. [<NL <L, finger-shaped <*digitus* finger]

dig·i·tal·ism (dij′ə·təl·iz′əm) *n. Pathol.* The effect on the body resulting from the excessive administration of digitalis.

dig·i·tate (dij′ə·tāt) *adj.* **1** *Bot.* Having parts, as leaflets, arranged like the fingers of a hand. **2** *Zool.* Having fingerlike processes. [<L *digitatus* <*digitus* finger] **—dig′i·tat·ed** *adj.* **—dig′i·tate·ly** *adv.*

dig·i·ta·tion (dij′ə·tā′shən) *n.* **1** The state of being digitate. **2** A fingerlike process.

digiti- *combining form* Finger; toe: *digitiform.* [<L *digitus* finger, toe]

dig·i·ti·form (dij′ə·tə·fôrm′) *adj.* Having the form or arrangement of a finger or fingers.

dig·i·ti·grade (dij′ə·tə·grād′) *adj. Zool.* Walking on the toes, without resting on the whole sole of the foot, as dogs, cats: opposed to *plantigrade.*

dig·i·tox·in (dij′ə·tok′sin) *n.* A powerful form of digitalin. [<DIGI(TALIS) + TOXIN]

di·glot (dī′glot) *adj.* **1** Composed in two languages. **2** Speaking or writing two languages; bilingual. *—n.* A diglot version or book. [<Gk. *diglōttos* <*di-* two + *glōtta* tongue]

dig·ni·fied (dig′nə·fīd) *adj.* **1** Characterized by or invested with dignity; stately. **2** Invested with dignities; promoted in rank; honored. See synonyms under GRAND. **—dig′ni·fied·ly** *adv.*

dig·ni·fy (dig′nə·fī) *v.t.* **·fied, ·fy·ing 1** To impart or add dignity to; honor; ennoble. **2** To give a high-sounding name to. [<OF *dignefier* <Med. L *dignificare* <*dignus* worthy + *facere* make]

dig·ni·tar·y (dig′nə·ter′ē) *n. pl.* **·tar·ies** One having high official position; especially, a churchman of rank above a canon or priest.

dig·ni·ty (dig′nə·tē) *n. pl.* **·ties 1** Grave or stately bearing: stateliness. **2** High rank; title, office, or position; distinction, especially in the church. **3** A dignitary; persons of high rank collectively. **4** The state or quality of being excellent, worthy, or honorable. **5** Grade of elevation; rank. [<OF *digneté* <L *dignitas, -tatis* <*dignus* worthy]

di·graph (dī′graf, -gräf) *adj.* Consisting of two letters which represent only one sound. *—n.* A union of two characters representing a single sound, as *oa* in *boat, sh* in *she.* Compare LIGATURE, DIPHTHONG.

di·graph·ic (dī·graf′ik) *adj.* **1** Pertaining to a digraph. **2** Written in two different alphabets or characters.

di·gress (di·gres′, dī-) *v.i.* To turn aside from the main subject in speaking or writing; ramble; wander. See synonyms under WANDER. [<L *digressus,* pp. of *digredi* <*di-* away, apart + *gradi* go, step]

di·gres·sion (di·gresh′ən, dī-) *n.* **1** The act of digressing. **2** That which digresses; any part of a discourse or writing that deviates from the main subject. **3** Deviation; divergence. **—di·gres′sion·al** *adj.*

di·gres·sive (di·gres′iv, dī-) *adj.* Given to or marked by digression. **—di·gres′sive·ly** *adv.* **—di·gres′sive·ness** *n.*

Di·gul (dē′gŏŏl) A river in Netherlands New Guinea, flowing 400 miles SW to the Arafura Sea. Also **Di′goel.**

di·he·dral (dī·hē′drəl) *adj.* **1** Two-sided; formed by or having two plane faces. **2** *Aeron.* Having two or more plane faces: said of an airplane. [<DI-[2] + Gk. *hedra* base]

dihedral angle See under ANGLE.

di·hy·dro·mor·phi·none hydrochloride (dī·hī′drō·môr′fə·nōn) A white, crystalline derivative of morphine, $C_{17}H_{19}O_3N{\cdot}HCl$, a narcotic and analgesic of great potency: sometimes used as a substitute for morphine.

Di·jon (dē·zhôn′) A city in eastern France.

dik-dik (dik′dik′) *n.* A small NE African antelope (genera *Madoqua* and *Rhynchotragus*) about a foot tall. [<native name]

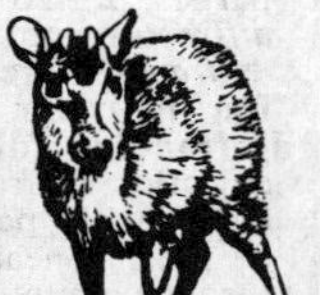

DIK–DIK

dike (dīk) *n.* **1** An embankment to protect low land from inundation. **2** A bank formed by the excavation of a ditch; a causeway. **3** A low wall of stone or turf for dividing or enclosing land. **4** *Mining* A fissure which has been filled with solid material other than the ore through which it cuts. **5** *Geol.* A mass of igneous rock filling a fissure in other rocks, into which it has been intruded. *—v.t.* **diked, dik·ing 1** To surround or furnish with a dike. **2** To drain by ditching. Also spelled *dyke.* [OE *dīc.* Related to DITCH.] **—dik·ing, dik′er** *n.*

di·lac·er·ate (di·las′ə·rāt, dī-) *v.t.* **·at·ed, ·at·ing** To tear asunder; rip to pieces. [<L *dilaceratus,* pp. of *dilacerare* <*dis-* apart + *lacerare* tear, rip] **—di·lac′er·a′tion** *n.*

Di·lan·tin (dī·lan′tin) *n.* Proprietary name for a brand of diphenylhydantoin sodium.

di·lap·i·date (di·lap′ədāt) *v.t.* & *v.i.* **·dat·ed, ·dat·ing** To fall or cause to fall into partial ruin or decay. [<L *dilapidatus,* pp. of *dilapidare* <*dis-* away + *lapidare* throw stones <*lapis, idis* stone] **—di·lap′i·dat·ed** *adj.* **—di·lap′i·da′tion** *n.*

di·la·tant (dī·lā′tənt, di-) *adj.* Having the property of increasing in volume when changed in shape; dilating. *—n.* A dilating substance or instrument. **—di·la′tan·cy** *n.*

di·la·tate (dī·lā′tit, di-) Dilated.

di·la·ta·tion (dī′lə·tā′shən, dil′ə-) *n.* **1** The act or process of dilating. **2** The state of being dilated. **3** That which is dilated. **4** *Pathol.* An excessive enlargement of an organ, orifice, or part. **5** *Med.* A restoration to normal functioning of a small passageway, as in the throat or rectum.

di·late (dī·lāt′, di-) *v.* **·lat·ed, ·lat·ing** *v.t.* **1** To make wider, larger or expanded; cause to swell or spread. *—v.i.* **2** To expand, become larger or wider. **3** To speak or write diffusely; enlarge; expatiate: with *on* or *upon.* See synonyms under AMPLIFY. [<L *dilatare* spread out <*dis-* apart + *latus* wide] **—di·lat′a·ble** *adj.* **—di·lat′a·ble·ness, di·lat′a·bil′i·ty** *n.* **—di·lat′a·bly** *adv.*

di·la·tive (dī·lā′tiv, di-) *adj.* Tending to dilate; causing expansion or distention.

dil·a·tom·e·ter (dil′ə·tom′ə·tər) *n.* An apparatus for measuring the expansion of substances, whether due to mechanical or chemical action. [<DILATE + -(O)METER] **—dil′a·tom′e·try** *n.*

di·la·tor (dī·lā′tər, di-) *n.* **1** One who or that which dilates. **2** *Med.* An instrument for opening or expanding a wound, aperture, or cavity. Also **di·la·ta·tor** (dī′lə·tā′tər, dil′ə-), **di·lat′er.**

dil·a·to·ry (dil′ə·tôr′ē, -tō′rē) *adj.* **1** Given to or characterized by delay; tardy; slow. **2** Tending to cause delay. See synonyms under SLOW, TEDIOUS. **—dil′a·to′ri·ly** *adv.* **—dil′a·to′ri·ness** *n.*

Di·lau·did (dī·lô′did) *n.* Proprietary name for a brand of dihydromorphinone hydrochloride.

dil·do (dil′dō) *n. Archaic* A meaningless refrain or burden in old ballads and songs; also, a ballad or song. [? <obs. *dildoe* a phallus]

di·lem·ma (di·lem′ə) *n.* **1** A necessary choice between equally undesirable alternatives, a perplexing predicament. **2** *Logic* A syllogistic argument which presents an antagonist with two (or more) alternatives, but is equally conclusive against him, whichever alternative he chooses. **—the horns of a dilemma** The equally undesirable alternatives between which a choice must be made. [<LL <GK. *dilēmma* <*di-* two + *lēmma* a premise] **—dil·em·mat·ic** (dil′ə·mat′ik) *adj.*

dil·et·tan·te (dil′ə·tan′tē, dil′ə·tänt′) *n. pl.* **·ti** or **·tes 1** A person who interests himself in a subject merely for amusement or superficially. **2** A person who loves the arts. *—adj.* Pertaining to or like a dilettante. [<Ital., ppr. of *dilettare* delight <L *delectare*] **—dil′et·tan′tish, dil′et·tan′ŏŏ·te·ish** *adj.*

dil·et·tan·te·ism (dil′ə·tan′tē·iz′əm, dil′ə·tän′·tiz·əm) *n.* The attitude or characteristics of a dilettante; a superficial approach or interest. Also **dil′et·tan′tism.**

Di·li (dil′ē) The capital of Portuguese Timor. Also **Dil′ly.**

dil·i·gence (dil′ə·jəns, *for def. 3 also Fr.* dē·lē·zhäns′) *n.* **1** Assiduous application; industry. **2** Proper heed or attention; meticulous care. **3** A Continental, four-wheeled, public stagecoach, divided into three compartments and having a driver's seat on top: used especially in 18th-century France: also **dil·ly** (dil′ē). See synonyms under INDUSTRY.

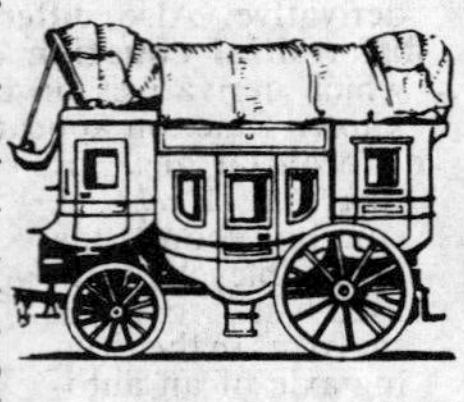

DILIGENCE

dil·i·gent (dil′ə·jənt) *adj.* **1** Possessed of or showing diligence; industrious. **2** Done or pursued diligently; painstaking: *diligent* search. See synonyms under ACTIVE, BUSY, INDUSTRIOUS. [<OF <L *diligens, -entis* attentive; orig. ppr. of *diligere* choose] **—dil′i·gent·ly** *adv.*

dill (dil) *n.* **1** An Old World annual of the parsley family (genus *Anethum*) with long-stalked umbels of yellow flowers and aromatic, pungent, medicinal seeds: referred to as *anise* in the Bible. **2** The seeds or leaves of this plant. [OE *dile*]

dill pickle A cucumber pickled in vinegar and flavored with dill.

dil·ly (dil'ē) *n.* **1** The daffodil. **2** *Colloq.* A good one; lulu. [Short for DAFFODIL]

dil·ly·bag (dil'ē·bag') *n. Austral.* **1** An aborigine's string bag. **2** Any small bag for general carrying purposes.

dil·ly–dal·ly (dil'ē·dal'ē) *v.i.* **–dal·lied, –dal·ly·ing** To waste time, especially in indecision or vacillation; loiter or trifle. [Varied reduplication of DALLY]

dil·u·ent (dil'yo͞o·ənt) *adj.* **1** Serving to dilute, weaken, or thin by admixture; diluting. **2** Having the property of dissolving, solvent. —*n.* That which dilutes. [<L *diluens, -entis,* ppr. of *diluere.* See DILUTE.]

di·lute (di·lo͞ot', dī-) *v.t.* **·lut·ed, ·lut·ing** **1** To make weaker or more fluid by admixture. **2** To weaken; to reduce the intensity, strength, or purity of (a color, drug, etc.) by admixture. —*adj.* (*also* dī'lo͞ot, -lyo͞ot) Weak; diluted. [<L *dilutus,* pp. of *diluere* < *dis-* away + *luere* wash]

di·lu·tion (di·lo͞o'shən, dī·lyo͞o'shən) *n.* **1** The act of diluting or weakening by admixture. **2** The state of being diluted. **3** Something diluted.

di·lu·vi·al (di·lo͞o'vē·əl) *adj.* **1** Of or pertaining to a flood, especially the Noachian deluge. **2** *Geol.* Produced by a deluge or by floods; consisting of or related to diluvium. Also **di·lu'vi·an.**

di·lu·vi·um (di·lo͞o'vē·əm) *n. Geol.* Coarse rock material transported and deposited by glaciers; glacial drift. [<NL <L, a flood < *diluere* wash away. See DILUTE.]

dim (dim) *adj.* **dim·mer, dim·mest** **1** Obscure from faintness of light or from lack of visual or mental perception; indistinct; shadowy; misty; also, faint, as a sound. **2** Not seeing or perceiving clearly; purblind; obtuse. **3** Lacking luster; tarnished. See synonyms under DARK, FAINT, OBSCURE. —*v.t.* & *v.i.* **dimmed, dim·ming** To render or grow dim; fade. [OE *dim(m)*] —**dim'ly** *adv.* —**dim'ness** *n.*

dime (dīm) *n.* A silver coin, one tenth of a dollar. [<OF *disme* <L *decima* a tenth part < *decem*]

di·men·hy·drin·ate (dī'mən·hī'drə·nāt) *n. Chem.* A white, crystalline, odorless compound, $C_{17}H_{22}NO$, resembling the antihistamines in action.

dime novel A cheap, sensational novel, usually paper–backed, originally costing a dime.

di·men·sion (di·men'shən) *n.* **1** Any measurable extent or magnitude, as length, breadth, or thickness. **2** Importance; extent; bulk. **3** *pl.* Material parts, as of the human body; proportions. **4** *Math.* A factor used to characterize a term: $a^2\ b^3\ c^4$ is a term of nine *dimensions,* counting all the exponents. See synonyms under MAGNITUDE. [<MF <L *dimensio, -onis* < *dis-* apart + *metiri* measure] —**di·men'sion·al** *adj.*

di·mer (dī'mər) *n. Chem.* A compound formed by the polymerization of two molecules of the same substance. [<DI-[2] + Gk. *meros* part]

di·mer·cap·rol (dī'mər·kap'rol) *n. Chem.* A colorless liquid compound, $C_3H_8OS_2$, containing two sulfhydryl radicals: used in medicine for the treatment of poisoning by arsenic, gold, and mercury. Also called *BAL.* [<DI-[2] + MERCAP(TAN) + PR(OPANE) + -OL[1]]

dim·er·ous (dim'ər·əs) *adj.* **1** Composed of two members or parts. **2** *Bot.* Composed of two members in each circle or whorl: frequently written *2–merous.* **3** *Entomol.* Having two–jointed tarsi. —**dim'er·ism** *n.*

dime store A five– and ten–cent store.

dim·e·ter (dim'ə·tər) *n.* In prosody, a verse of two metrical feet. [<DI-[2] + -METER]

di·meth·yl (dī·meth'əl) *n. Chem.* An alkyl radical, $(CH_3)_2$, generally occurring in combination with other compounds: used in the making of drugs, dyestuffs, solvents, etc.

di·met·ric (dī·met'rik) *adj.* Tetragonal.

di·mid·i·ate (di·mid'ē·āt) *adj. Bot.* Divided in half; lop–sided: said of plants appearing to lack half of a member, or with halves functionally or structurally different. —*v.t.* **·at·ed, ·at·ing** To cut in half. [<L *dimidiatus,* pp. of *dimidiare* halve < *dimidium* a half < *dis-* apart + *medius* middle] —**di·mid'i·a'tion** *n.*

di·min·ish (di·min'ish) *v.t.* **1** To make smaller or less; lessen; decrease. **2** *Music* To lessen (an interval) by a half–step. —*v.i.* **3** To grow or become smaller or less; dwindle; decrease. See synonyms under ABATE, IMPAIR, RETRENCH. [Fusion of ME *diminuen* lessen (<OF *diminuer* <L *diminuere* < *de-* down + *minuere* lessen < *minus* less) and ME *menusen* <OF *menusier* MINISH] —**di·min'ish·a·ble** *adj.*

di·min·ish·ing return (di·min'ish·ing) *Econ.* The theory that an added increment of capital or labor, exceeding a fixed amount, causes a proportionately lower increase in production.

di·min·u·en·do (di·min'yo͞o·en'dō) *Music adj.* & *adv.* Gradually lessening in volume of sound: expressed by *dim., dimin.,* or the sign ⟩. —*n. pl.* **·dos** Diminution, as in force; a diminuendo passage in music. Also called *decrescendo.* [<Ital., ppr. of *diminuire* lessen <L *diminuere.* See DIMINISH.]

dim·i·nu·tion (dim'ə·no͞o'shən, -nyo͞o'-) *n.* **1** The act of diminishing, or the condition of being diminished: reduction. **2** *Music* The repetition of a theme in notes of one half or one quarter the time value of those first used: opposite of *augmentation.* [<AF *diminuciun* <L *diminutio, deminutio, -onis* < *diminuere.* See DIMINISH.]

di·min·u·tive (di·min'yə·tiv) *adj.* **1** Of relatively small size; small; little. **2** Diminishing or tending to diminish. **3** Expressing diminished size: said of certain suffixes. —*n.* **1** A word formed from another to express diminished size, or familiarity, affection, etc.: Johnny is a *diminutive* of John, Tom of Thomas, etc. Abbr. *dim.* **2** Anything very small; a very small variety or form of anything. See synonyms under LITTLE, MINUTE.

dim·is·so·ry (dim'ə·sôr'ē, -sō'rē, də·mis'ər·ē) *adj.* **1** Sending away; dismissing to another jurisdiction: said of episcopal letters. **2** Granting leave to go away. [<LL *dimissorius* <L *dimittere* DISMISS]

Di·mi·trov (dē·mē'trôf), **Georgi,** 1882–1949, Bulgarian Communist leader.

dim·i·ty (dim'ə·tē) *n. pl.* **·ties** A sheer cotton fabric woven with stripes, cords, or checks: used for dresses, curtains, etc. [<Ital. *dimito* <Gk. *dimitos* having a double thread < *di-* two + *mitos* thread]

dim·mer (dim'ər) *n.* **1** Anything that dims. **2** *Electr.* An adjustable rheostat used for varying the intensity of illumination in a lamp system.

Dim·net (dēm·ne'), **Ernest,** 1866–1954, French writer: known as *Abbé Dimnet.*

di·morph (dī'môrf) *n.* A form exhibiting dimorphism.

di·mor·phism (dī·môr'fiz·əm) *n.* **1** The quality of existing in two different forms. **2** *Bot.* The existence of two distinct forms of the same organ on the same plant, or on the same species of plant. **3** *Zool.* A difference in form, color, etc., between individuals of the same species, characterizing two distinct types. **4** *Physics* Crystallization of the same substance in two forms. **5** *Ling.* The existence of a word in two different forms in the same language, as *dent* and *dint, card* and *chart;* a doublet. [<Gk. *dimorphos* < *di-* two + *morphē* form] —**di·mor'phic, di·mor'phous** *adj.*

dim–out (dim'out') *n.* A form of modified lighting in a city or throughout a certain area to prevent or eliminate night–glow: used as a military safety measure. Compare BLACK–OUT.

dim·ple (dim'pəl) *n.* A slight depression on the cheek or chin, or on any smooth surface. —*v.t.* & *v.i.* **dim·pled, dim·pling** To mark with dimples; form dimples. [ME *dympull*; origin uncertain] —**dim'ply** *adj.*

dim·wit (dim'wit') *n. Slang.* A stupid or simple–minded person. —**dim'wit'ted** *adj.*

din[1] (din) *n.* A loud continuous noise or clamor; a rattling or clattering sound. See synonyms under NOISE. —*v.* **dinned, din·ning** *v.t.* **1** To assail with confusing noise. **2** To urge or press with repetition or insistence. —*v.i.* **3** To make a din. [OE *dyne*]

din[2] (din) *adj. Scot.* Dun.

Di·nah (dī'nə) A feminine personal name. [<Hebrew, judgment]

di·nar (di·när') *n.* **1** A gold coin of medieval Arabia, especially one issued by the caliphs of Damascus. **2** An Iranian money of account. **3** A silver coin of Yugoslavia. [<Arabic *dīnār* <LGk. *dēnarion* <L *denarius* DENARIUS]

Di·nar·ic Alps (di·nar'ik) The SE division of the eastern Alps, in Yugoslavia along the eastern coast of the Adriatic; highest peak, 8,174 feet.

Dinaric race A tall, brachycephalic people inhabiting the regions along the northern Adriatic: also called *Adriatic race.*

Din·dings (din'dingz) The coastal district of western Perak, Malaya, with adjoining islands; formerly a British possession; 190 square miles.

din·dle (din'dəl, din'əl) *v.t.* & *v.i.* **din·dled, din·dling** *Scot.* & *Brit Dial.* To tingle with pain, as from cold; vibrate. —*n.* A tingling; thrill.

d'In·dy (daṅ·dē'), **(Paul Marie Théodore) Vincent,** 1851–1931, French composer.

dine (dīn) *v.* **dined, din·ing** *v.i.* **1** To eat dinner. **2** To eat any meal. —*v.t.* **3** To entertain at dinner. —**to dine out** To take a meal away from home. [<F *dîner* <OF *disner* <L *dis-* away + *jejunus* fast] —**din'ing** *adj.* & *n.*

din·er (dī'nər) *n.* **1** One who dines. **2** A railroad dining–car. **3** A restaurant built in the form of a railroad car.

di·ner·ic (dī·ner'ik) *adj. Chem.* Of or relating to the surface separating two contiguous liquids in the same container. [DI-[2] + Gk. *nēros* liquid]

di·ne·ro (dē·nā'rō) *n. pl.* **·ros** **1** A Peruvian silver coin, one tenth of a sol. **2** *U.S. Slang* Money. [Sp., penny <L *denarius* DENARIUS]

di·nette (dī·net') *n.* **1** An alcove where meals are served. **2** A little dinner. [<F]

di·neu·tron (dī·no͞o'tron, -nyo͞o'-) *n. Physics* A transitory atomic particle believed to consist of two neutrons produced by tritons in a nuclear reaction and acting as a unit under certain special conditions.

ding (ding) *v.t.* **1** To ring; sound, as a bell. **2** *Colloq.* To instill by constant iteration; din. **3** *U.S. Slang* & *Brit. Dial.* To beat; strike. —*v.i.* **4** To ring or sound. **5** *Colloq.* To speak with constant iteration. —*n.* The sound of a bell or a sound like it. [Imit. Cf. ON *dengja* hammer, Dan. *dænge* bang, beat]

ding·bat (ding'bat') *n. Colloq.* **1** Any small object, especially one hurled at another object. **2** A small thing, the name of which is unknown or unrecalled. **3** *Printing* An ornament. [< dial. *ding* knock, dash + BAT[1]]

DINGBATS (*def. 3*)

ding–dong (ding'dong', -dông') *n.* **1** The peal of a bell. **2** Any monotonous repetition. **3** A device in a clock for striking the quarter–hours. —*adj.* **1** Characterized by successive blows. **2** *Colloq.* Energetically and closely contested, as a race. [Imit.]

din·ghy (ding'gē, ding'ē) *n. pl.* **·ghies** **1** Any of various kinds of small rowing boats, as a small, clinker–built skiff, a ship's boat, etc. **2** A sleeping car for railway employees. Also **din'gey, din'ghy, din'gy.** [<Hind. *dīngī,* boat]

din·gle (ding'gəl) *n.* **1** A narrow valley; glen. **2** *U.S. Dial.* The enclosed weather porch of a house. See synonyms under VALLEY. [ME *dingel*; origin unknown]

din·go (ding'gō) *n. pl.* **din·goes** The native wild dog (*Canis dingo*) of Australia, having a foxlike face, bushy tail, and reddish–brown color. [< native name]

ding·us (ding'əs) *n. Slang* A thing or device: said of something the name of which is unknown or forgotten. [<Afrikaans < *ding* a thing]

Ding·wall (ding'wôl, -wəl) The county town of Ross and Cromarty county, Scotland.

din·gy (din'jē) *adj.* **din·gi·er, din·gi·est** Of a dusky color, as if soiled; dull; tarnished; grimy; shabby. [Origin uncertain] —**din'gi·ly** *adv.* —**din'gi·ness** *n.*

din·ing–car (dī'ning·kär') *n.* A railway car in which meals are served en route.

din·ing–room (dī'ning·ro͞om', -ro͝om') *n.* A room in which meals are served.

dinitro– *combining form Chem.* Having two

nitro groups, NO_2, as certain isomeric compounds.

di·ni·tro·ben·zene (dī·nī′trō·ben′zēn) *n. Chem.* One of three isomeric compounds, $C_6H_4(NO_2)_2$, that crystallizes in colorless flexible needles, formed by heating benzene with a mixture of nitric and sulfuric acids.

di·ni·tro·cre·sol (dī·nī′trō·krē′sōl) *n. Chem.* A poisonous, orange, coal-tar dye, $C_7H_6O_5N_2$: sometimes used as a substitute for true saffron and in insecticides and rat-killers.

di·ni·tro·phe·nol (dī·nī′trō·fē′nōl) *n. Chem.* Any of six isomeric nitrogen compounds, $C_6H_4O_5N_2$: used in the manufacture of dyes.

dink (dingk) *Scot. v.t.* To dress; array. —*adj.* Neat; trim; tidy. [Origin uncertain]

Din·ka (ding′kä) *n.* **1** A member of a Negroid tribe of the southern Sudan. **2** The Sudanic language of this tribe.

dink·ey (ding′kē) *n. Colloq.* A small engine used for shunting freight. [< DINKY]

dink·um (ding′kəm) *adj. Austral. Colloq.* True; vouched for; honest. Also **dink·y·die** (-kē·dī′).

dink·y (ding′kē) *adj.* **dink·i·er, dink·i·est** *Colloq.* Tiny; insignificant. [< DINK + -Y]

din·mont (din′mənt) *n. Brit. Dial.* A wether between its first and second shearings. [Origin uncertain]

Din·mont (din′mənt) See DANDIE DINMONT.

din·na (din′nə) *Scot.* Do not.

din·ner (din′ər) *n.* **1** The principal meal of the day. **2** A banquet in honor of a notable person or event. **3** A formal feast. [< F *dîner.* See DINE.]

dinner coat or **jacket** A tuxedo jacket.

din·ner·ware (din′ər·wâr′) *n.* The dishes used in a household for serving food.

dino- *combining form* Terrible; huge: *dinosaur.* [< Gk. *deinos* terrible]

di·noc·er·as (dī·nos′ər·əs) *n. Paleontol.* A gigantic, extinct, herbivorous mammal of the Tertiary period (order *Amblypoda*), having three pairs of protuberances on the upper surface of the head. [< DINO- + Gk. *keras* horn]

di·no·saur (dī′nə·sôr) *n. Paleontol.* One of a group of reptiles (orders *Saurischia* and *Ornithischia*) existing on all the continents, but extinct by the end of the Mesozoic period. They varied in size from small, two-footed, pigeonlike carnivores to gigantic, four-footed, aquatic and terrestrial forms, many of them heavily armored, of both herbivorous and carnivorous habits. [< DINO- + Gk. *sauros* lizard] —**di′no·sau′ri·an** *adj.* & *n.*

di·no·there (dī′nə·thir) *n. Paleontol.* One of an extinct Miocene genus (*Dinotherium*) of elephantlike mammals having a pair of huge tusks extending downward from the lower jaw. [< DINO- + Gk. *thēr* wildbeast]

dint (dint) *n.* **1** A small depression made by a blow; a dent. **2** Active agency; force; efficacy: by *dint* of. —*v.t.* To make a dent or dint in; to drive in forcibly. [OE *dynt* blow]

Din·wid·die (din′wid·ē), **Robert,** 1690?–1770, English colonial governor of Virginia.

di·o·bol (dī·ō′bəl) *n.* A silver coin of ancient Greece equal to two obols. See OBOLUS. Also **di·ob·o·lon** (dī·ob′ə·lon). [< Gk. *diōbolon* < *di-* two + *obolos* an obol]

di·oc·e·san (dī·os′ə·sən, dī′ə·sē′sən) *adj.* Of or pertaining to a diocese. —*n.* A bishop in charge of a diocese.

di·o·cese (dī′ə·sēs, -sis) *n.* The territory or the churches under a bishop's jurisdiction. [< OF *diocise* < Med. L *diocesis* < L *dioecesis* a district < Gk. *dioikēsis,* orig. management of a house < *dia-* completely + *oikeein* dwell, manage]

Di·o·cle·tian (dī′ə·klē′shən), **Gaius Aurelius Valerius,** 245–313, Roman emperor, 284–305.

di·ode (dī′ōd) *n. Electronics* A vacuum tube which permits the stream of electrons to pass in one direction only, from the cathode to the anode; a rectifier. [< DI(A)- + Gk. *hodos* a road, way]

di·oe·cious (dī·ē′shəs) *adj. Bot.* Having the male and female organs borne by different individuals, as a plant with stamens and pistils in separate individuals: also spelled *diecious.* Also **di·oi·cous** (dī·oi′kəs). [< DI-[2] + Gk. *oikia* house, dwelling] —**di·oe′cious·ly** *adv.* —**di·oe′cious·ness** *n.*

di·oes·trum (dī·es′trəm, -ēs′-) *n. Zool.* The period of calm in the estrus or mating cycle of animals. [< NL < Gk. *dia-* between + *oistros* passion, frenzy] —**di·oes′trous** *adj.*

Di·og·e·nes (dī·oj′ə·nēz), 412–323 B.C., Greek Cynic philosopher, reputed to have lived in a tub to show his austerity and to have sought for an honest man at midday with a lantern.

Di·o·mede Islands (dī′ə·mēd) Two small islands, one Russian, one American, in the Bering Strait midway between Siberia and Alaska.

Di·o·me·des (dī′ə·mē′dēz) **1** In Greek legend, a king of Argos at the siege of Troy who aided Odysseus in the theft of the Palladium. **2** In Greek mythology, a Thracian king who was fed to his own man-eating horses by Hercules.

di·o·nae·a (dī′ə·nē′ə) *n.* The Venus flytrap. [< NL < Gk. *Diōnē* Dione]

Di·o·ne (dī·ō′nē) In Greek mythology, one of the Oceanids, mother of Aphrodite by Zeus.

di·o·nism (dī′ə·niz′əm) *n.* Normal love between the sexes; heterosexuality: opposed to *uranism.* [< Gk. *Diōnē* Dione]

Di·o·nys·i·a (dī′ə·nish′ē·ə, -nis′-) *n. pl.* Any of the Greek festivals in honor of Dionysus, especially those at Athens connected with the origins of Greek drama. Also **Di′o·nys′i·acs.** —**Di′o·nys′i·ac, Di·o·ny·si·a·cal** (dī′ə·nə·sī′·ə·kəl), **Di′o·nys′ian** *adj.* —**Di′o·ny·si′a·cal·ly** *adv.*

Di·o·nys·ian era or **period** (dī′ə·nish′ən, -nis′ē·ən) A period of 532 Julian years, employed to compute the date of Easter. [after *Dionysius Exiguus*]

Di·o·nys·i·us (dī′ə·nish′ē·əs, -nis′-) A masculine personal name. Also *Ital.* **Di·o·ni′gio** (dē′ō·nē′jō), *Ger.* **Di·o·nys** (dē′ə·nēs′), *Pg., Sp.* **Di·o·ny·si·o** (dē′ō·nē′sē·ō), *Gk.* **Di·o·ny·si·os** (dē′ō·nē′sē·ôs). [< Gk., belonging to Dionysus]

—**Dionysius** Name of two tyrants of Syracuse: **The Elder,** 430–367 B.C., and **The Younger,** 395?–343? B.C.

—**Dionysius Exiguus,** died 545?, Christian theologian; calculated traditional date of Christ's birth. See CHRISTIAN ERA.

—**Dionysius of Alexandria, Saint,** theologian of the third century.

—**Dionysius of Halicarnassus,** 68–7 B.C., Greek historian and rhetorician.

Di·o·ny·sus (dī′ə·nī′səs) In Greek mythology, son of Zeus and Semele, a fertility god especially associated with the vine: identified with the Roman *Bacchus.* See DIONYSIA. Also **Di′o·ny′sos.**

Di·o·phan·tus of Alexandria (dī′ə·fan′təs) Third century A.D., Greek mathematician, inventor of **Diophantine analysis** and **Diophantine equations,** algebraic processes for finding integers that satisfy equations with unknown quantities.

di·op·side (dī·op′sīd, -sid) *n.* A grayish-white or grayish-green variety of pyroxene. [< F < Gk. *di-* two + *opsis* view]

di·op·tase (dī·op′tās) *n.* A vitreous, emerald-green, transparent to translucent, hydrous copper silicate, crystallizing in the hexagonal system. [< F < Gk. *dia-* through + *optos* visible]

di·op·ter (dī·op′tər) *n. Optics* The unit for measuring the refractive power of a lens, expressed as the reciprocal of its focal length in meters: a convergent lens of 1 meter focal length has a power of +1 diopter; a divergent lens, of −1 diopter. Also **di·op′tre, di·op′try.** [< MF *dioptre* < L *dioptra* < Gk., an optical instrument]

di·op·tom·e·ter (dī′op·tom′ə·tər) *n.* An optical instrument for measuring refraction and accommodation of the eye. [< DI(A)- + OPTOMETER] —**di′op·tom′e·try** *n.*

di·op·tric (dī·op′trik) *adj. Optics* **1** Aiding the vision by refraction, as a lens. **2** Of or pertaining to dioptrics. **3** Of or pertaining to a diopter, or the system of numbering optical glasses metrically. Also **di·op′tri·cal.** [< Gk. *dioptrikos* belonging to the use of the dioptra < *dioptra* diopter]

di·op·trics (dī·op′triks) *n.* The branch of optics treating of light-refraction by transparent media.

di·o·ra·ma (dī′ə·rä′mə, -ram′ə) *n.* **1** A painting, or a series of paintings, for exhibition, in which, by the use of cloth transparencies and arrangements of lights, alterations in the pictures are produced in view of the spectators. **2** A group of modeled figures, for exhibition, set in a naturalistic foreground blended into a painted background. **3** A building in which such a picture or group is exhibited. [< Gk. *dia-* through + *horama* a sight] —**di·o·ram·ic** (dī′ə·ram′ik) *adj.*

di·o·rite (dī′ə·rīt) *n.* A granular, crystallized, igneous rock composed of feldspar and hornblende. Also **di′o·ryte.** [< F < Gk. *diorizein* divide < *dia-* through + *horos* limit] —**di·o·rit·ic** (dī′ə·rit′ik) *adj.*

Di·os·cu·ri (dī′ə·skyŏŏr′ī) *n. pl.* Castor and Pollux. [< Gk. *Dioskouroi* < *Dios* of Zeus + *kouros* boy, son]

di·os·mo·sis (dī′os·mō′sis, -oz-) *n.* Osmosis.

Di·os·po·lis (dī·os′pə·lis) A Greek name for THEBES, Egypt.

di·ox·ane (dī·ok′sān) *n. Chem.* A colorless liquid derivative of glycol, $C_4H_8O_2$, having a pleasant, faint odor: used as a solvent for resins, oils, waxes, and organic compounds. [< DI-[2] + OX(A)- + -ANE[2]]

di·ox·ide (dī·ok′sīd, -sid) *n. Chem.* An oxide containing two atoms of oxygen to the molecule. Also **di·ox·id** (dī·ok′sid).

di·ox·in (dī·ok′sən) *n.* An extremely toxic and mutagenic, fat-soluble compound produced inadvertently in the large-scale manufacture of polychlorinated biphenyls.

dip (dip) *v.* **dipped, dip·ping** *v.t.* **1** To put or let down into a liquid momentarily and then take out. **2** To obtain or lift up and out by scooping, bailing, etc.: to *dip* crackers from a barrel, or water from a boat. **3** To lower and then raise, as a flag in salute. **4** To baptize by immersion. **5** To plunge (animals) into a disinfectant so as to rid of insects, germs, etc. **6** To dye by immersion. **7** *Chem.* to coat (a metallic surface) by immersion in a solution of readily decomposed salt. **8** To make (candles) by repeatedly immersing wicks in wax or tallow. **9** *Obs.* To wet. **10** *U.S. Colloq.* To apply snuff to the gums and teeth. —*v.i.* **11** To plunge into and come out of water or other liquid, especially briefly and quickly. **12** To plunge one's hand or a receptacle into water, etc., or into a container, especially so as to take something out. **13** To sink or go down suddenly. **14** To incline downward; go down; decline. **15** *Geol.* To lie at an angle to the horizon, as rock strata. **16** *Aeron.* To drop rapidly and then climb. **17** To engage in or inquire into something slightly or superficially; dabble. **18** To read here and there, as in a book or magazine; browse. —**to dip into** To take a part of (something held in reserve, saved, etc.): to *dip into* one's savings account. See synonyms under IMMERSE. —*n.* **1** The act of dipping; a plunge; bath; depression. **2** A liquid into which something is to be dipped. **3** Inclination, as of the magnetic needle. **4** A candle made by dipping a wick repeatedly into melted tallow. **5** Magnetic dip. **6** *Geol.* Position, other than horizontal, or rock strata; also, the angle between strata and the horizontal plane. **7** *Aeron.* A rapid drop of an airplane followed by a climb. **8** *Colloq.* A pickpocket. **9** A small amount of snuff taken into the mouth on a moistened brush. **10** An antiseptic solution in which sheep are dipped to kill parasites: also called *sheep dip.* [OE *dyppan.* Related to DEEP.]

di·pet·al·ous (dī·pet′əl·əs) *adj. Bot.* Having two petals: also *bipetalous.*

di·phase (dī′fāz′) *adj. Electr.* **1** Having two phases: said of a current compounded of two alternating currents, the maxima and minima of which differ from one another by 90 degrees. **2** The circuit carrying such a current or the generator producing it. Also **di·phas·ic** (dī·fā′zik).

di·phen·yl (dī·fen′əl, dī·fē′nəl) *n.* Biphenyl.

di·phen·yl·a·mine (dī·fen′əl·ə·mēn′, -am′in, -fē′nəl-) *n. Chem.* A crystalline aromatic amine, $(C_6H_5)_2NH$, obtained by heating aniline hydrochloride with aniline: used as a stabilizer and in the manufacture of dyestuffs. Also **di·phen′·yl·am′in** (-am′in).

di·phen·yl·am·ine·chlor·ar·sine (dī·fen′əl·am′·in·klôr′är′sēn, -sin, -fē′nəl-) *n.* Adamsite.

di·phen·yl·cy·an·ar·sine (dī·fen′əl·sī′ə·när′sēn, -sin, -fē′nəl-) *n. Chem.* A lung irritant compound, $(C_6H_5)_2AsCN$, with an odor of garlic and bitter almonds: used in chemical warfare.

di·phen·yl·hy·dan·to·in sodium (dī·fen′əl·hī·dan′tō·in, -fē′nəl-) *Chem.* A white, odorless, slightly bitter compound, $C_{15}H_{11}N_2O_2Na$: used in the treatment of epileptic convulsions. Also called *Dilantin.*

di·pho·ni·a (dī·fō′nē·ə, -fōn′yə, di-) *n.* A speech condition in which the same voice produces two distinct tones; double voice. [<NL <Gk. *di-* two + *phonē* sound]

di·phos·gene (dī·fos′jēn) *n. Chem.* A chemical warfare agent, $C_2O_2Cl_4$, an oily liquid with a suffocating odor and a destructive effect on the lungs.

diph·the·ri·a (dif·thir′ē·ə, dip-) *n. Pathol.* An acute contagious disease, caused by the Klebs–Loeffler bacillus (*Corynebacterium diphtheriae*) and characterized by inflammation, usually of the pharynx, the formation of a false membrane on mucous surfaces, and toxemia. [<NL <F *diphthérie* <Gk. *diphthera* leather, membrane]

diph·ther·it·ic (dif′thə·rit′ik, dip-) *adj. Pathol.* 1 Pertaining to diphtheria. 2 Resembling, or having symptoms characteristic of diphtheria. Also **diph·the′ri·al, diph·the′ric.**

diph·thong (dif′thông, -thong, dip′-) *n.* 1 *Phonet.* A combination of two vowels in one syllable, whether written with two letters, as *oi* in *coil* and *ou* in *doubt*, or with a single letter, as *i* in *fine* and *a* in *bate.* 2 In popular usage, either of the ligatures æ, œ, pronounced as a single sound, but which were true diphthongs in classical Latin. See DIGRAPH, TRIGRAPH. [<F *diphthongue* <LL *diphthongus* <Gk. *diphthongos* <*di-* two + *phthongos* sound] — **diph·thon′gal** *adj.* — **diph·thong′ic** *adj.*

diph·thong·ize (dif′thông·īz, -thong-, dip′-) *v.* **·ized, ·iz·ing** *v.t.* 1 To make a diphthong of; combine with another sound in a diphthong. 2 To pronounce as a diphthong. — *v.i.* 3 To become a diphthong. — **diph′thong·i·za′tion, diph′thong·a′tion** *n.*

di·phyl·lous (dī·fil′əs) *adj. Bot.* Two-leaved. [<DI- + Gk. *phyllon* leaf]

diph·y·o·dont (dif′ē·ō·dont) *adj. Zool.* Having two sets of teeth, one deciduous, the second permanent. [<Gk. *diphyēs* double + *odous, odontos* tooth]

di·plex (dī′pleks) *adj. Telecom.* 1 Pertaining to the transmission of two simultaneous telegraph messages over one wire in the same direction. 2 Designating a method for the simultaneous transmission or reception of two radio signals. Compare DUPLEX. [<DI-² + (DU)PLEX]

diplo– *combining form* Double: *diplococcus.* Also, before vowels, **dipl–.** [<Gk. *diploos* double]

di·lo·car·di·a (dip′lə·kär′dē·ə) *n. Anat.* A condition in which the right and left sides of the heart are distinctly separated, as by a fissure. [<DIPLO- + Gk. *kardia* heart] — **dip′lo·car′·di·ac** (-ak) *adj.*

di·plo·coc·cus (dip′lə·kok′əs) *n.* *pl.* **·coc·ci** (-kok′sī) 1 A cell or micro-organism consisting of two cells united. 2 *Bacteriol.* Any of a genus (*Diplococcus*) of parasitic bacteria, Gram-positive, usually encapsulated and occurring in pairs or chains, including *D. pneumoniae*, the infective agent of lobar pneumonia. See illustration under BACTERIA.

Di·plo·doc·i·dae (dip′lə·dos′ə·dē) *n. pl. Paleontol.* A family of sauropod, herbivorous dinosaurs of huge size, fossil in the Upper Jurassic rocks of Wyoming and Colorado. The family has but a single genus, **Di·plod·o·cus** (di·plod′ə·kəs), a mounted skeleton of which is 84 1/2 feet long and 14 feet high. [<NL <Gk. *diploos* double + *dokos* a beam]

dip·lo·e (dip′lō·ē) *n. Anat.* The reticulate bony tissue between the two walls of the cranial bones. [<NL <Gk., a fold]

dip·loid (dip′loid) *adj.* 1 Twofold or doubled. 2 *Biol.* Having two sets of chromosomes in the somatic cells, as of all higher organisms. — *n.* 1 A cell having double the haploid number of chromosomes. 2 An isometric crystal with 24 trapezoidal planes.

di·plo·ma (di·plō′mə) *n.* 1 A writing, usually under seal, granting some privilege or authority, or bestowing some honor; especially, the official certificate of graduation in arts, medicine, law, etc., bestowed by a college or university. 2 An instrument authorizing a person to practice a profession. 3 An official document; charter. [<L <Gk. *diplōma* paper folded double, a letter]

di·plo·ma·cy (di·plō′mə·sē) *n. pl.* **·cies** 1 The art, science, or practice of conducting negotiations between nations. 2 Tact, shrewdness, or skill in conducting any affair. [<F *diplomatie* <*diplomate* DIPLOMAT]

dip·lo·mat (dip′lə·mat) *n.* One employed or skilled in diplomacy. [<F *diplomate* <*diplomatique* <NL *diplomaticus* <L *diploma* DIPLOMA]

dip·lo·mat·ic (dip′lə·mat′ik) *adj.* 1 Of or pertaining to diplomacy. 2 Characterized by special tact in negotiation; wary; adroit; tactful. 3 Pertaining to diplomatics. Also **dip′lo·mat′i·cal.** See synonyms under POLITIC. — **dip′lo·mat′i·cal·ly** *adv.*

diplomatic agent 1 Any person who carries on the diplomatic relations of the state he represents in the country to which he has been appointed. See also AMBASSADOR, PLENIPOTENTIARY, MINISTER RESIDENT under RESIDENT, CHARGÉ D'AFFAIRES. 2 A diplomatic representative of the lowest rank, accredited to a country that does not have full sovereignty. 3 An agent who represents a sovereign or head of state for some special purpose.

diplomatic corps Collectively, the heads of foreign diplomatic missions and their staffs at the capital of any country.

diplomatic immunity Exemption of diplomatic agents or representatives, their staffs and premises, from the ordinary processes of local law.

dip·lo·mat·ics (dip′lə·mat′iks) *n.* 1 The science of deciphering ancient documents, charters, etc. 2 Diplomacy.

di·plo·ma·tist (di·plō′mə·tist) *n.* 1 A diplomat. 2 One remarkable for tact and shrewd management.

di·plo·pi·a (di·plō′pē·ə) *n. Pathol.* A derangement of the visual axes whereby two distinct impressions are received from a single object; double vision. Also **dip·lo·py** (dip′lə·pē). [<NL <Gk. *diploos* double + *ops* eye] — **di·plop·ic** (di·plop′ik) *adj.*

dip·lo·pod (dip′lə·pod) *n. Zool.* Any of a class (*Diplopoda*) of segmented terrestrial arthropods; the millipedes. [<NL *Diplopoda* <Gk. *diploos* double + *pous, podos* foot]

di·plo·sis (di·plō′sis) *n. Genetics* The union of two haploid sets of chromosomes by syngamy of the male and female gametes. [<DIPL(O)- + -OSIS]

dip·lo·some (dip′lə·sōm) *n. Biol.* A small, paired body in the cell, as a double centriole within the centrosome.

dip·lo·so·mi·a (dip′lə·sō′mē·ə, -sōm′yə) *n. Pathol.* An abnormal joining of two bodies. Also **dip·lo·so·ma·tia** (dip′lə·sō·mā′shə, -shē·ə). [<NL <Gk. *diploos* double + *sōma* body]

dip·lo·ste·mo·nous (dip′lə·stē′mə·nəs) *adj. Bot.* Having twice as many stamens as petals. [<DIPLO- + Gk. *stēmōn* thread (used for *stēma* a stamen)]

dip needle An inclinometer (def. 2), used in magnetic compasses.

dip·no·an (dip′nō·ən) *n.* Any of a group (*Dipnoi*) of fishes with regular gills, a single or double lung, and nostrils inside as well as outside the mouth; a lungfish. — *adj.* Of or pertaining to the *Dipnoi.* [<NL <Gk. *dipnoos* <*dis-* two + *pnoē* breath]

dip·o·dy (dip′ə·dē) *n. pl.* **·dies** In prosody, a dimeter. [<L *dipodia* <Gk. <*dis-* two + *pous, podos* foot]

di·pole (dī′pōl) *n.* 1 *Physics* Any material system having two electric charges, equal in magnitude but of unlike sign, as the proton and electron of a hydrogen atom, or two equal but opposite magnetic poles. 2 *Chem.* A molecule exhibiting polar separation of positive and negative charges.

dip·per (dip′ər) *n.* 1 A long-handled, bowl-shaped utensil, used principally for dipping water, as from a larger vessel into a smaller one. 2 Any of several American birds, so called because they are quick divers; specifically, the dabchick or pied-billed grebe, the small bufflehead duck of North America, and the water ouzel.

Dip·per (dip′ər) *n.* 1 *Astron.* The Big Dipper. 2 A Dunker or member of any other immersionist religious sect: a contemptuous use.

dip·py (dip′ē) *adj. Slang.* Insane; queer; eccentric.

dip·sas (dip′səs) *n. pl.* **dip·sa·des** (dip′sə·dēz) 1 A serpent whose bite was fabled to produce extreme thirst. 2 Any of several tropical colubrine snakes (subfamily *Dipsadomorphinae*). [<L <Gk. *dipsa* thirst]

dip·sey (dip′sē) *adj.* Deep-sea. — *n. pl.* **·sies** 1 A sinker for a fishing line. 2 A line equipped with a number of hooks and sinkers used for bottom fishing. Also **dip′sie, dip′sy.** [Alter. of DEEP–SEA]

dip·so·ma·ni·a (dip′sə·mā′nē·ə) *n.* An uncontrollable craving for alcoholic drink. [<Gk. *dipsa* thirst + -MANIA]

dip·so·ma·ni·ac (dip′sə·mā′nē·ak) *adj.* Pertaining to or affected by dipsomania: a *dipsomaniac* diathesis: also **dip·so·ma·ni·a·cal** (dip′sə·mə·nī′ə·kəl) — *n.* A person affected with dipsomania; a confirmed drunkard.

dip·ter·al (dip′tər·əl) *adj. Archit.* Having or resembling a double peristyle or colonnade. 2 Dipterous. [<L *dipteros* <Gk. *dipteros.* See DIPTEROUS.]

dip·ter·an (dip′tər·ən) *n.* A dipterous insect. Also **dip′ter·on** (-on).

dip·ter·ous (dip′tər·əs) *adj.* 1 *Entomol.* Of or pertaining to an order (*Diptera*) of insects having a single pair of membranous wings with a posterior pair of balancers and a sucking proboscis, including the flies, gnats, mosquitoes, etc. 2 *Bot.* Two-winged, as a seed or fruit. [<Gk. *dipteros* two-winged <*di-* twice + *pteron* wing]

dip·tych (dip′tik) *n.*  1 A double tablet; especially, two tablets of wood, metal, or ivory, hinged together and covered on the inside with wax, on which the ancient Greeks and Romans wrote with a stylus. 2 A cover for a book, resembling this. 3 A double picture or design on a pair of hinged tablets or panels. [<LL *diptycha* <Gk., pair of tablets; orig. neut. pl. of *diptychos* folded <*di-* twice + *ptyssein* fold]

DIPTYCH (def. 3)

Di·rac (di·rak′), **Paul Adrien Maurice,** born 1902, British physicist.

Dirac electron *Physics* The positively charged electron as conceived in terms of the wave mechanics formulated by P. A. M. Dirac: now identified as the positron.

dire (dīr) *adj.* **dir·er, dir·est** Extremely calamitous; dreadful; terrible. See synonyms under AWFUL. [<L *dirus* fearful] — **dire′ful** *adj.* — **dire′ly** *adv.* — **dire′ness** *n.*

di·rect (di·rekt′, dī-) *v.t.* 1 To control or conduct the affairs of; manage; govern. 2 To order or instruct with authority; command: often with a clause as object. 3 *Music* To lead as a conductor. 4 To tell (someone) the way. 5 To cause to move, face, or go in a desired direction; aim: He *directed* his gaze toward her. 6 To indicate the destination of, as a letter. 7 To intend, as remarks or insults, to be heard by a person; address: Did you *direct* that remark at me? — *v.i.* 8 To give commands or guidance. 9 To lead performances, musicians, etc. See synonyms under DICTATE, GOVERN, LEAD, REGULATE. — *adj.* 1 Having or being the straightest course; straight; shortest; nearest. 2 Free from intervening agencies or conditions; immediate; exact; in the speaker's words: *direct* discourse. 3 Straightforward, as in meaning, statement or intention; unambiguous; candid; plain. 4 Of succession, lineal: opposed to *collateral.* 5 *Electr.* a Continuous as opposed to alternating, as a current. b Having the same direction as the primary: said of an induced current: opposed to *inverse.* 6 *Astron.* Designating motion on the celestial sphere from west toward east, in the direction of the sun's movement among the stars: opposed to *retrograde.* 7 *Chem.* Of or pertaining to dyes applied to fabrics without the use of mordants; substantive. See synonyms under IMMEDIATE, RIGHT. — *adv.* By direct course: directly. — *n.* 1 *Music* A mark (∧ or ∿) at the end of a line or page of music indicating the position of

the first note on the next. [<L *directus,* pp. of *dirigere* <*dis-* apart + *regere* set straight]

di·rect-ac·tion (di·rekt′ak′shən, dī-) *adj. Mech.* Having no transmitting mechanism, such as gearwheels, between the part driven and the power that drives it.

direct action An attempt by labor to enforce the granting of its demands by means of demonstrations, strikes, sabotage, or the like.

direct current See under CURRENT.

direct discourse See under DISCOURSE.

direct dye See under DYE.

di·rec·tion (di·rek′shən, dī-) *n.* **1** The position of one point in relation to another without reference to the intervening distance. **2** The trend of a line or of a course of motion, as determined by its spatial relation with some fixed standard of reference; loosely, the trend of a line or course as determined by its extremity. **3** Tendency; aim. **4** The act of directing, governing, or ordering; superintendence; administration. **5** Instruction; command; order. **6** The name and residence of a person; address. **7** *Music* A sign, phrase, or word, in a score designating the proper mood, intensity, etc., of a passage.

Synonyms: aim, bearing, course, inclination, tendency, way. The *direction* of an object is the line of motion or of vision toward it, or the line in which the object is moving, considered from one's own standpoint. *Way,* literally the road or path, comes naturally to mean the *direction* of the road or path. *Bearing* is direction with reference to another object or to the points of the compass. *Course* is the direction of a moving object; *inclination,* that toward which an object leans; *tendency,* that toward which anything stretches or reaches out; *tendency* is stronger and more active than *inclination.* See AIM, CARE, INCLINATION, ORDER, OVERSIGHT.

di·rec·tion·al (di·rek′shən·əl, dī-) *adj.* **1** Pertaining to direction in space. **2** *Telecom.* **a** Adapted for indicating from which of several directions signals are received. **b** Describing an antenna which radiates or receives radio waves more effectively in or from some directions than from others.

di·rec·tion-find·er (di·rek′shən·fīn′dər, dī-) *n. Telecom.* A receiving device with which, by the use of a loop antenna, the direction of radio signals may be determined.

di·rec·tive (di·rek′tiv, dī-) *n.* **1** An order or regulation. **2** The document or the vehicle through which the order is transmitted: applied especially to governmental and military pronouncements. — *adj.* **1** That directs or points out, rules, or governs. **2** Responsive to direction.

di·rect·ly (di·rekt′lē, dī-) *adv.* **1** In a direct line or manner. **2** Without medium, agent, or go-between. **3** Immediately; as soon as possible. **4** Exactly; precisely. See synonyms under IMMEDIATELY. — *conj. Brit.* As soon as.

direct mail Mail sent directly to individuals that promotes the sale of merchandise or services or solicits contributions.

di·rect·ness (di·rekt′nis, dī-) *n.* The quality of being direct; straightness; straightforwardness.

direct object See under OBJECT.

Di·rec·toire (dē·rek·twär′) *n.* The Directory. — *adj.* Of the time, modes, or fashions of the French Directory (1795–99): A *Directoire* gown is characterized by a high waist, low rounded neckline, and puffed sleeves.

di·rec·tor (di·rek′tər, dī-) *n.* **1** One who or that which directs; specifically, a member of a governing body, as of a club or corporation. **2** A conductor of an orchestra. **3** One who supervises a dramatic production. **4** In the Roman Catholic Church, a spiritual guide. **5** *Mil.* An apparatus that systematically computes firing data for use against moving enemy targets. Also **di·rect′er.** See synonyms under MASTER. — **di·rec′tress** *n. fem.*

di·rec·tor·ate (di·rek′tər·it, dī-) *n.* **1** A body of directors. **2** The office or power of a director. Also **di·rec′tor·ship.**

di·rec·to·ri·al (di·rek′tôr′ē·əl, -tō′rē-, dī-) *adj.* **1** That directs; directive. **2** Pertaining to a director or directorate.

di·rec·to·ry (di·rek′tər·ē, dī-) *n. pl.* **·ries** **1** An alphabetical or classified list, as of the names and addresses of the inhabitants or business houses of a city. **2** A collection of rules; especially a book of directions for church worship, as the ordinal of the Roman Catholic Church, or the rules adopted by the Scottish General Assembly in 1645, still observed in the Presbyterian Church. **3** A body of directors. — *adj.* Containing directions.

Di·rec·to·ry (di·rek′tər·ē, dī-) *n.* The five men who were the executives of the French government after the downfall of the Convention, October 26, 1795, to November 9, 1799.

di·rec·trix (di·rek′triks, dī-) *n. pl.* **·tri·ces** (-tri·sēz) or **·trix·es** **1** *Mil.* In gunnery, the median line in the plane of fire. **2** *Geom.* A line which so determines the motion of another line, or of a point, that the latter shall describe some surface or curve.

dire·ful (dīr′fəl) *adj.* Most dire; dreadful; terrible. See synonyms under AWFUL, FRIGHTFUL. — **dire′ful·ly** *adv.* — **dire′ful·ness** *n.*

dirge (dûrj) *n.* **1** A song, tune, lament, or wail expressing grief and mourning. **2** A hymn or choral service at a funeral. [<L *dirige* (imperative of *dirigere* DIRECT), the first word of the antiphon (*Psalms* v 8) of matins in the Latin burial office] — **dirge′ful** *adj.*

dir·i·ga·tion (dir′ə·gā′shən) *n.* **1** The power of controlling or modifying involuntary bodily functions, such as the pulse, temperature, or digestion. **2** The exercise of that power. [<L *dirigere* DIRECT + -ATION]

dir·i·gi·ble (dir′ə·jə·bəl) *adj.* **1** That may be directed or controlled: a *dirigible* balloon.

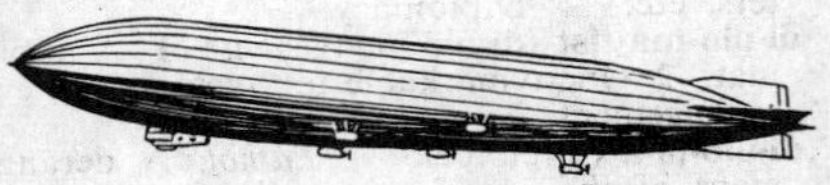

A RIGID TYPE OF DIRIGIBLE

2 *Aeron.* Designating an airship, the outer envelope of which is of elongated form, provided with a propelling system, cars, rudders, and stabilizing surfaces. The form of the envelope may be **nonrigid,** by the pressure of the contained gases assisted by the car-suspension system; **rigid,** by a framework contained within the envelope; or **semirigid,** by means of attachment to an exterior girder construction containing the cars. — *n.* An airship. [<L *dirigere* DIRECT + -IBLE] — **dir′i·gi·bil′i·ty** *n.*

dir·i·go (dir′i·gō) *Latin* I direct: motto of the State of Maine.

dir·i·ment (dir′ə·mənt) *adj.* Rendering absolutely void; nullifying. [<L *dirimens, -entis,* ppr. of *dirimere* <*dis-* apart + *emere* take]

diriment impediment of marriage A sufficient cause for rendering a marriage null and void: a Roman Catholic usage.

dirk (dûrk) *n.* A dagger or poniard. — *v.t.* To stab with a dirk. [Origin unknown]

dirl (dirl, dûrl) *v.t.* & *v.i. Scot.* To tingle; vibrate.

dirn·dl (dûrn′dəl) *n.* **1** A woman's dress with a full skirt gathered to a tight bodice. **2** Such a skirt without the bodice: also **dirndl skirt.** [<G *dirndl* girl]

dirt (dûrt) *n.* **1** Any foul or filthy substance; refuse; trash. **2** Loose earth; garden loam. **3** Uncleanness in action or speech; abuse or obscenity. **4** In placer mining, washed-down material or detritus containing precious metal: called **pay dirt** when it yields more than enough to compensate for working. — *adj.* Made of earth: a *dirt* road. [Metathetical var. of earlier *drit* <ON, dirt, bird droppings]

dirt-cheap (dûrt′chēp′) *adj.* & *adv. U.S. Colloq.* Very inexpensive; as cheap as dirt.

dirt-eat·ing (dûrt′ē′ting) *n.* Geophagy.

dirt farmer *U.S. Colloq.* A farmer who does his own work: opposed to *gentleman farmer.*

dirt·y (dûr′tē) *adj.* **dirt·i·er, dirt·i·est** **1** Unclean; foul; imparting dirt; filthy. **2** Base; despicable; contemptible; also, mean or unkind. **3** Impure; not clear: said of colors. **4** Uncomfortable or disagreeable to the traveler, as weather or roads. **5** Obscene. See synonyms under FOUL. — *v.t.* & *v.i.* **dirt·ied, dirt·y·ing** To make or become dirty or soiled. — **dirt′i·ly** *adv.* — **dirt′i·ness** *n.*

dirty work **1** *Colloq.* Trickery; deceit; foul play. **2** A difficult job or the most difficult part of a job.

Dis (dis) **1** In Roman mythology, god of the lower world: identified with *Pluto.* **2** The kingdom of the dead: identified with the Greek *Hades.*

dis-[1] *prefix* **1** Apart; away from: *disembody, dislodge, dismiss, dissolve.* **2** The reverse of or the undoing of (what is expressed in the rest of the word): *disarm, disband, disconnect, disrobe, disown.* **3** Deprivation of some quality, power, rank, etc.: *disable, disbar, discolor, disenfranchise.* **4** Not: *disadvantageous, disloyal, distasteful.* **5** Completely; thoroughly (simple intensive with an already negative word): *disannul.* Also: *di-* before *b, d, l, m, n, r, s, v,* and usually before *g,* as in *digress, direct, diverge* (in Late Latin this was often changed back to the full form, as in *dismiss, disrupt*); *dif-* before *f,* as in *differ.* The living English prefix is always in the form *dis-.* [<L *dis-,* sometimes replacing OF *des-* (see DE-)]

dis-[2] *prefix* Var. of DI-[2]. [<Gk. *dis* twice]

dis·a·bil·i·ty (dis′ə·bil′ə·tē) *n. pl.* **·ties** **1** That which disables. **2** Lack of ability; inability. **3** Legal incapacity or inability to act.

disability clause In insurance policies, a clause waiving premiums upon certain disabilities of the policyholders.

dis·a·ble (dis·ā′bəl) *v.t.* **·a·bled, ·a·bling** **1** To render incapable or unable; cripple; impair. **2** To render legally incapable, as of inheriting property, etc. — **dis·a′ble·ment** *n.*

dis·a·bled (dis·ā′bəld) *adj.* Incapacitated.

dis·a·buse (dis′ə·byōōz′) *v.t.* **·a·bused, ·a·bus·ing** To rid of a false notion or impression.

di·sac·cha·ride (dī·sak′ə·rīd, -rid) *n. Biochem.* One of a series of carbohydrates, as lactose and maltose, constituting the chief ingredients of sugarcane and milk: on hydrolysis, they yield two monosaccharides. Also **di·sac′cha·rid** (-rid). [<DI-[2] + SACCHARIDE]

dis·ac·cord (dis′ə·kôrd′) *n.* The state of being inharmonious; disagreement; incongruity. — *v.t.* To disagree; refuse assent. [<OF *desacorder* <*des-* away + *acorder* ACCORD]

dis·ac·cus·tom (dis′ə·kus′təm) *v.t.* To free of a habit or of anything to which one has been habituated. — **dis′ac·cus′tomed** *adj.* — **dis′ac·cus′tomed·ness** *n.*

dis·ad·van·tage (dis′əd·van′tij, -vän′-) *n.* **1** That which hinders, prevents, or is prejudicial to success. **2** Prejudice to interest, reputation, credit, or other good; loss; drawback; injury. **3** A state of inferiority; unfavorable condition: The army was at a *disadvantage.* See synonyms under INJURY, LOSS. — *v.t.* **·taged, ·tag·ing** To injure the interest of; prejudice; hinder. [<OF *désavauntage* <*dés-* away (<L *dis-*) + *avauntage* ADVANTAGE]

dis·ad·van·taged (dis′əd·van′təjd) *adj.* Having less than what is regarded as basic or minimal for decent living, as money, social position, etc.; underprivileged.

dis·ad·van·ta·geous (dis·ad′vən·tā′jəs) *adj.* Attended with disadvantage; detrimental; inconvenient. — **dis·ad′van·ta′geous·ly** *adv.* — **dis·ad′van·ta′geous·ness** *n.*

dis·af·fect (dis′ə·fekt′) *v.t.* To destroy or weaken the affection or loyalty of; alienate.

dis·af·fect·ed (dis′ə·fek′tid) *adj.* Alienated in feeling or loyalty; estranged. See synonyms under INIMICAL. — **dis′af·fect′ed·ly** *adv.*

dis·af·fec·tion (dis′ə·fek′shən) *n.* Discontent; disloyalty; estrangement.

dis·af·fil·i·ate (dis′ə·fil′ē·āt) *v.t.* & *v.i.* **·at·ed, ·at·ing** To sever affiliation (with).

dis·af·firm (dis′ə·fûrm′) *v.t.* **1** To deny; contradict. **2** *Law* **a** To reverse; set aside, as a decision. **b** To repudiate; disclaim, as a contract. — **dis′af·firm′ance, dis·af·fir·ma·tion** (dis·af′ər·mā′shən) *n.*

dis·af·for·est (dis′ə·fôr′ist, -for′-) *v.t.* **1** In English law, to reduce from the privileges of a forest to common ground. Compare AFFOREST. **2** To clear of forests. [<Med. L *disafforestare* <*dis-* away + *afforestare* AFFOREST]

dis·a·gree (dis′ə·grē′) *v.i.* **·a·greed, ·a·gree·ing** **1** To vary in opinion; differ; dissent. **2** To quarrel. **3** To fail to agree or harmonize, as facts. **4** To be unfavorable or injurious in action or effect, as food or climate: with *with.* [<OF *desagreer* <*des-* away (<L *dis-*) + *agreer* AGREE]

dis·a·gree·a·ble (dis′ə·grē′ə·bəl) *adj.* **1** Repugnant to taste, sentiment, opinion, or the senses; not agreeable; displeasing; unpleasant. — **dis′a·gree′a·ble·ness, dis′a·gree′a·bil′i·ty** *n.* — **dis′a·gree′a·bly** *adv.*

dis·a·gree·ment (dis′ə·grē′mənt) *n.* Failure to agree; dissimilarity; variance; unsuitableness; incongruity; altercation; quarrel. See synonyms under DIFFERENCE, QUARREL.

dis·al·low (dis′ə·lou′) *v.t.* **1** To refuse to allow or permit. **2** To reject as untrue or invalid. See synonyms under PROHIBIT. [<OF *desalouer* <*des-* away (<L *dis-*) + *alouer* ALLOW] — **dis′al·low′a·ble** *adj.* — **dis′al·low′ance** *n.*

dis·an·nul (dis′ə·nul′) *v.t.* To annul completely. — **dis′an·nul′ment** *n.*

dis·a·noint (dis′ə·noint′) *v.t.* To invalidate the consecration of.

dis·ap·pear (dis′ə·pir′) *v.i.* **1** To pass from sight or view; fade away; vanish. **2** To cease to exist. — **dis′ap·pear′ance** *n.*

disappearing carriage *Mil.* A mechanism by which coastal artillery of large caliber is raised above a protective embankment before firing and automatically lowered behind it after the discharge.

dis·ap·point (dis′ə·point′) *v.t.* **1** To fail to fulfil the expectation, hope, or desire of (a person). **2** To prevent the fulfilment of (a hope or plan); frustrate. [<OF *desappointer* <*des-* away (<L *dis-*) + *appointer* APPOINT] — **dis′ap·point′ed** *adj.* — **dis′ap·point′ed·ly** *adv.*

dis·ap·point·ment (dis′ə·point′mənt) *n.* **1** The state, condition, or sense of being disappointed. **2** That which disappoints: failure; frustration. See synonyms under CHAGRIN, MISFORTUNE.

dis·ap·pro·ba·tion (dis·ap′rə·bā′shən) *n.* Disapproval; unfavorable judgment. — **dis·ap·pro·ba·to·ry** (dis·ap′rə·bə·tôr′ē, -tō′rē) *adj.*

dis·ap·prov·al (dis′ə·pro͞o′vəl) *n.* The act of disapproving; the withholding of approval; disapprobation. See synonyms under ANIMADVERSION.

dis·ap·prove (dis′ə·pro͞ov′) *v.* **·proved, ·prov·ing** *v.t.* **1** To regard with disfavor or censure; condemn. **2** To refuse assent to; decline to approve. — *v.i.* **3** To have or express an unfavorable opinion: often with *of.* — **dis′ap·prov′ing** *adj.* — **dis′ap·prov′ing·ly** *adv.*

dis·arm (dis·ärm′) *v.t.* **1** To deprive of weapons. **2** To render harmless; make unable to do damage, attack, or defend. **3** To allay or reduce, as suspicion or antagonism. — *v.i.* **4** To lay down arms. **5** To reduce or restrict the size of armed forces. [<OF *desarmer* <*des-* away (<L *dis-*) + *armer* arm <L *armare* <*arma* arms]

dis·ar·ma·ment (dis·är′mə·mənt) *n.* **1** The act of disarming. **2** The reduction or limitation of armed forces or of certain types of weapons.

dis·arm·ing (dis·är′ming) *adj.* Removing suspicion or anger.

dis·ar·range (dis′ə·rānj′) *v.t.* **·ranged, ·rang·ing** To disturb the arrangement of. See synonyms under DISPLACE. — **dis′ar·range′ment** *n.*

dis·ar·ray (dis′ə·rā′) *n.* **1** Want of array or regular order; disorder; confusion. **2** Scantiness of dress; negligent or disordered dress. — *v.t.* **1** To impair the order of; throw into disorder, as an army. **2** To undress.

dis·ar·tic·u·late (dis′är·tik′yə·lāt) *v.* **·lat·ed, ·lat·ing** *v.t.* To separate the joints of. — *v.i.* To become separated or unjointed. — **dis′ar·tic′u·la′tion** *n.* — **dis′ar·tic′u·la′tor** *n.*

dis·as·sem·ble (dis′ə·sem′bəl) *v.t.* **·bled, ·bling** To take apart.

dis·as·sem·bly (dis′ə·sem′blē) *n.* A state of being separated into component parts; a disassembling.

dis·as·so·ci·ate (dis′ə·sō′shē·āt) *v.t.* **·at·ed, ·at·ing** To dissociate. — **dis′as·so′ci·a′tion** *n.*

dis·as·ter (di·zas′tər, -zäs′-) *n.* **1** Crushing misfortune; a calamity; a terrible accident. **2** *Obs.* An evil portent; especially, in astrology, the inimical aspect or action of a star or planet. See synonyms under ACCIDENT, BLOW, MISFORTUNE. [<MF *désastre* <*des-* away + *astre* a star <L *astrum* <Gk. *astron*]

dis·as·trous (di·zas′trəs, -zäs′-) *adj.* **1** Occasioning or accompanied by disaster; calamitous. **2** Threatening disaster; ill-boding; gloomy; dismal; ill-starred. — **dis·as′trous·ly** *adv.* — **dis·as′trous·ness** *n.*

dis·a·vow (dis′ə·vou′) *v.t.* To refuse to acknowledge; disclaim responsibility for or approval of; disown; repudiate. See synonyms under RENOUNCE. [<OF *desavouer* <*des-* away (<L *dis-*) + *vouer* AVOW]

dis·a·vow·al (dis′ə·vou′əl) *n.* A disowning; denial; repudiation.

dis·band (dis·band′) *v.t.* To break up the organization of; remove from military service. — *v.i.* To break up; scatter; cease to be an organization. [<MF *desbander* <*des-* away (<L *dis-*) + *bander* tie <*bande* a band] — **dis·band′ment** *n.*

dis·bar (dis·bär′) *v.t.* **·barred, ·bar·ring** To deprive of the status of a lawyer; expel from the bar. — **dis·bar′ment** *n.*

dis·be·lief (dis′bi·lēf′) *n.* A conviction that a statement is untrue; positive unbelief. See synonyms under DOUBT.

dis·be·lieve (dis′bi·lēv′) *v.t.* & *v.i.* **·lieved, ·liev·ing** To refuse to believe; deem false. — **dis′be·liev′er** *n.*

dis·bos·om (dis·bo͝oz′əm) *v.t.* To reveal, as a secret; unbosom; confess.

dis·branch (dis·branch′, -bränch′) *v.t.* **1** To deprive of branches, as a tree; prune; trim. **2** To cut off, as a branch.

dis·bur·den (dis·bûr′dən) *v.t.* **1** To relieve (someone or something) of a burden; unload. **2** To unload or get rid of (a burden). — *v.i.* **3** To put off a load or burden; unburden. Also *Obs.* **dis·bur′then** (-thən). — **dis·bur′den·ment** *n.*

dis·burse (dis·bûrs′) *v.t.* **·bursed, ·burs·ing** To pay out; expend. [<OF *desbourser* <*des-* away (<L *dis-*) + *bourse* a purse] — **dis·burs′a·ble** *adj.* — **dis·burs′er** *n.*

dis·burse·ment (dis·bûrs′mənt) *n.* **1** The act of disbursing. **2** That which is expended; money paid out.

disc (disk) *n.* **1** A phonograph record. **2** *Biol.* A disk (def. 2). [Var. of DISK]

disc·al (dis′kəl) *adj.* Of, pertaining to, or like a disk.

dis·calced (dis·kalst′) *adj.* Having the shoes off; bare-footed: applied especially to those religious orders whose members go unshod or wear sandals. [<L *discalceatus* <*dis-* not + *calceatus* a shoe, orig. pp. of *calceare* shoe]

dis·cant (dis′kant, dis·kant′) See DESCANT.

dis·card (dis·kärd′) *v.t.* **1** To cast aside as useless or undesirable; reject; dismiss. **2** In card games, to throw out (a card or cards) from one's hand; also, to play (a card, other than a trump, of a different suit from the suit led). — *v.i.* **3** In card games, to throw out a card or cards from one's hand. See synonyms under RENOUNCE. — *n.* (dis′kärd) **1** The act of discarding. **2** A card or cards discarded. **3** A person or thing cast off or dismissed.

dis·case (dis·kās′) *v.t.* **·cased, ·cas·ing** To remove the case or covering of; unsheathe.

dis·cept (di·sept′) *v.i.* To dispute or debate. [<L *disceptare* <*dis-* away + *ceptare,* freq. of *capere* take] — **dis′cep·ta′tion** *n.*

dis·cern (di·zûrn′, di·sûrn′) *v.t.* **1** To perceive, as with sight or mind; recognize; apprehend. **2** To discriminate mentally; recognize as separate and different. — *v.i.* **3** To distinguish; discriminate. [<OF *discerner* <L *discernere* <*dis-* apart + *cernere* separate] — **dis·cern′er** *n.*

Synonyms: descry, discriminate, distinguish, perceive, recognize. What we *discern* we see apart from all other objects; what we *discriminate* we judge apart; what we *distinguish* we mark apart, or *recognize* by some special mark or manifest difference. We *descry* (originally *espy*) what is difficult to discover. Compare DISCOVER, KNOW, LOOK.

dis·cern·i·ble (di·zûr′nə·bəl, -sûr′-) *adj.* Capable of being discerned; perceivable. See synonyms under EVIDENT. — **dis·cern′i·ble·ness** *n.* — **dis·cern′i·bly** *adv.*

dis·cern·ing (di·zûr′ning, -sûr′-) *adj.* Quick to discern; discriminating; penetrating. See synonyms under ACUTE, ASTUTE, INTELLIGENT, KNOWING, SAGACIOUS. — **dis·cern′ing·ly** *adv.*

dis·cern·ment (di·zûrn′mənt, -sûrn′-) *n.* **1** The act or process of discerning. **2** The mental power of discerning; keenness of judgment; insight. See synonyms under ACUMEN, UNDERSTANDING, WISDOM.

dis·cerp (di·sûrp′) *v.t. Obs.* **1** To tear or pluck to pieces. **2** To disjoin; separate; divide. [<L *discerpere* <*dis-* apart + *cerpere* pluck] — **dis·cerp′ti·ble** *adj.* — **dis·cerp′tion** *n.*

dis·charge (dis·chärj′) *v.* **·charged, ·charg·ing** *v.t.* **1** To unload; remove the contents of: to *discharge* a ship. **2** To remove or send forth: to *discharge* passengers or cargo. **3** To send forth; emit (fluid). **4** To shoot or fire, as a gun, bow, shot, or arrow. **5** To dismiss from office; fire. **6** To release; set at liberty, as a prisoner, soldier, or patient. **7** To relieve of duty or obligation: to *discharge* a jury. **8** To perform or fulfil the functions and duties of (a trust, office, etc.). **9** To pay (a debt) or meet and satisfy (an obligation or duty). **10** In dyeing, to remove (color) from textiles. **11** *Obs.* To free of blame or accusation. **12** *Electr.* To free of an electrical charge. — *v.i.* **13** To get rid of a load, burden, etc. **14** To go off, as a cannon. **15** To give or send forth contents: The wound *discharges* constantly. **16** *Electr.* To lose a charge of electricity. See synonyms under ABSOLVE, ACCOMPLISH, BANISH, CANCEL, DELIVER, PAY, RELEASE. — *n.* (*also* dis′chärj) **1** The act of removing a load or charge. **2** A firing of a weapon; a release of a missile. **3** An emission; ejection; an issuing forth. **4** The rate or amount of outflow. **5** That which is discharged or released, as blood from a wound. **6** A relieving or freeing from burden or obligation. **7** The payment of a debt. **8** Fulfilment; execution: the *discharge* of one's duty. **9** Release or dismissal from service, employment, or custody. **10** Something which releases or dismisses, as a certificate separating one from military service. **11** *Electr.* **a** The equalization of difference of potential between terminals of a condenser or of a current source, when connected by a conductor, or placed in very near contact. **b** The removal of an electrostatic charge, as from a Leyden jar, a battery, etc. [<OF *deschargier* <*des-* away (<L *dis-*) + *chargier* CHARGE] — **dis·charge′a·ble** *adj.* — **dis·charg′er** *n.*

dis·ci·ple (di·sī′pəl) *n.* One who accepts and follows a teacher or a doctrine; a pupil or learner. **2** One of **the disciples,** the twelve chosen companions and apostles of Jesus. See synonyms under ADHERENT, CONVERT. — *v.t.* **·pled, ·pling 1** To cause to become a disciple; convert. **2** *Obs.* To train; teach. [OE *discipul* <L *discipulus* <*discere* teach; infl. in form by OF *diciple, disciple* <L *discipulus*] — **dis·ci′ple·ship** *n.*

Disciples of Christ A religious body that originated in Pennsylvania in 1809, in connection with the labors of Thomas and Alexander Campbell, holding to Christian union on the basis of the Bible alone, rejecting creeds and party names, and practicing immersion and weekly communion: also called *Christians.*

dis·ci·pli·nal (dis′ə·plī′nəl, dis′ə·plin·əl) *adj.* Of or pertaining to discipline.

Dis·ci·plin·ant (dis′ə·plin·ənt) *n.* One of a former Spanish religious order whose members publicly scourged and otherwise tortured themselves; a Flagellant.

dis·ci·pli·nar·i·an (dis′ə·plə·nâr′ē·ən) *n.* One who disciplines; one strict in discipline; a martinet. — *adj.* Disciplinary.

dis·ci·pli·nar·y (dis′ə·plə·ner′ē) *adj.* Of, relating to, or having the nature of discipline; employed in discipline.

dis·ci·pline (dis′ə·plin) *n.* **1** Systematic training or subjection to authority; especially, the training of the mental, moral, and physical powers by instruction and exercise. **2** The result of this; subjection; habit of obedience. **3** Training resulting from misfortune, troubles, etc. **4** Punishment for the sake of training; correction; chastisement. **5** A system of rules, or method of practice, as of a church. **6** The studies collectively embraced in a course of learning. **7** The self-scourging of some ascetics of the Roman Catholic Church; also, a scourge. See synonyms under EDUCATION. — *v.t.* **·plined, ·plin·ing 1** To train to obedience or subjection. **2** To drill; educate. **3** To punish or chastise. See synonyms under CHASTEN, TEACH. [<OF <L *disciplina* instruction <*discipulus* DISCIPLE] — **dis′ci·plin·a·ble** *adj.* — **dis′ci·plin·er** *n.*

dis·cis·sion (di·sish′ən, -sizh′-) *n.* **1** A cutting into a part. **2** *Surg.* An operation to relieve a soft cataract by lacerating the capsule of the lens. [<LL *discissio, -onis* <*dis-* apart + *scindere* cleave, cut]

disc jockey An announcer on a radio program that presents recorded music, usually interspersed with comments and commercials.

dis·claim (dis·klām′) *v.t.* **1** To disavow any claim to, connection with, or responsibility for; disown; reject. **2** To reject or deny the claim or authority of; deny. **3** *Law* To renounce a right or claim to. —*v.i.* **4** *Law* To renounce or repudiate a legal claim. See synonyms under RENOUNCE. [< AF *desclamer* < *des-* away (< L *dis-*) + *clamare* cry]

dis·claim·er (dis·klā′mər) *n.* **1** One who disclaims. **2** A disclaiming act, notice, or instrument.

dis·cla·ma·tion (dis′klə·mā′shən) *n.* A disavowal.

dis·close (dis·klōz′) *v.t.* **·closed, ·clos·ing 1** To expose to view; lay bare; uncover. **2** To make known; divulge; open. **3** *Obs.* To open. See synonyms under CONFESS, DISCOVER, INFORM, PUBLISH. [< OF *desclos-*, stem of *desclore* close] — **dis·clos′er** *n.*

dis·clo·sure (dis·klō′zhər) *n.* **1** The act or process of disclosing. **2** Anything disclosed.

dis·co (dis′kō) *n.* A discothèque. —*v.i.* **·coed, ·co·ing** To dance to music at a disco.

dis·cob·o·lus (dis·kob′ə·ləs) *n.* A discus thrower. Also **dis·cob′o·los. —the Discobolus** A famous Greek statue of a discus thrower, attributed to Myron. [< L < Gk. *diskobolos* < *diskos* a discus + *ballein* throw]

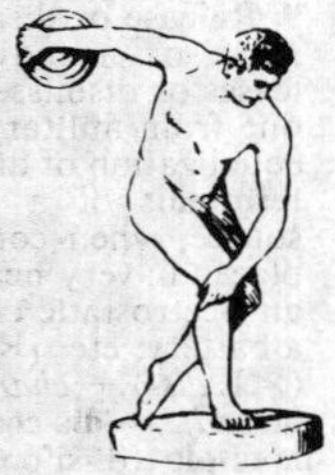

DISCOBOLUS
After statue by Myron in the Vatican.

dis·coid (dis′koid) *adj.* **1** *Zool.* Having the form of a disk, as certain univalve shells with the whorls coiled in one plane. **2** Pertaining to, like, or forming a disk or disks. **3** *Bot.* Disk-shaped; rayless, as the tubular central florets of a composite flower, such as the sunflower: also **dis·coi′dal.** — *n.* A disk or disklike object. [< L *discoïdes* < Gk. *diskoeidēs* < *diskos* a discus + *eidos* form]

dis·col·or (dis·kul′ər) *v.t.* To give an unnatural color to; stain. —*v.i.* To become stained, faded, or of a changed color. Also *Brit.* **dis·col′our.** [< OF *descolorer* < *des-* away (< L *dis-*) + *colorer* color < L *colorare* < *color* a color]

dis·col·or·a·tion (dis·kul′ə·rā′shən) *n.* **1** The act or process of discoloring; a discolored state or appearance; changed hue or aspect. **2** A stain or discolored spot or part. Also **dis·col′or·ment.**

dis·com·fit (dis·kum′fit) *v.t.* **1** To defeat the plans or purposes of; frustrate. **2** To rout; vanquish. See synonyms under CONQUER. —*n. Obs.* Rout. [< OF *desconfit*, pp. of *desconfire* < *des-* away (< L *dis-*) + *confire* < L *conficere.* See CONFECT.]

dis·com·fi·ture (dis·kum′fi·chər) *n.* The act of discomfiting or the state of being discomfited: defeat. See synonyms under RUIN.

dis·com·fort (dis·kum′fərt) *n.* **1** The state of being positively uncomfortable; disturbance; disquietude. **2** That which causes an uncomfortable condition. See synonyms under PAIN. —*v.t.* **1** To make uneasy; trouble. **2** *Obs.* To dishearten; dismay. [< OF *desconfort* < *desconforter* < *des-* away (< L *dis-*) + *conforter* COMFORT]

dis·com·fort·a·ble (dis·kum′fər·tə·bəl) *adj.* **1** Uncomfortable. **2** *Archaic* Producing discomfort.

dis·com·mend (dis′kə·mend′) *v.t.* **1** To express disapproval of. **2** To speak of dissuasively. **3** *Obs.* To cause to be regarded unfavorably. — **dis′com·mend′a·ble** *adj.* **—dis′com·men·da′·tion** *n.*

dis·com·mode (dis′kə·mōd′) *v.t.* **·mod·ed, ·mod·ing** To cause inconvenience to; trouble; disturb. [< DIS-[1] + L *commodus* convenient]

dis·com·mod·i·ty (dis′kə·mod′ə·tē) *n. pl.* **·ties 1** The state, fact, or quality of being inconvenient, troublesome, or injurious. **2** Something that causes annoyance, inconvenience, trouble, or loss.

dis·com·mon (dis·kom′ən) *v.t.* *Law* To change from the condition of a common, as land; make private property of.

dis·com·pose (dis′kəm·pōz′) *v.t.* **·posed, ·pos·ing 1** To disturb the composure of; make uneasy; ruffle; agitate. **2** To disorder or disarrange; derange. See synonyms under ABASH.

dis·com·po·sure (dis′kəm·pō′zhər) *n.* Agitation; disorder; perturbation.

dis·co·my·cete (dis′kə·mī·sēt′) *n. pl.* **·cetes** (-sēts) *Bot.* Any of a group *(Discomycetes)* of fungi belonging to the *Ascomycetes;* a cup fungus. [< NL < Gk. *diskos* disk + *mykēs, mykētos* fungus]

dis·con·cert (dis′kən·sûrt′) *v.t.* **1** To disturb the self-possession or composure of; confuse; upset. **2** To throw into confusion; frustrate, as a plan. See synonyms under ABASH. [< MF *disconcerter* < *dis-* apart + *concerter* agree] **—dis′con·cert′ing** *adj.* **—dis′con·cert′ing·ly** *adv.* **—dis′con·cer′tion, dis′con·cert′ment** *n.*

dis·con·cert·ed (dis′kən·sûr′tid) *adj.* Confused; perturbed; discomposed. **—dis′con·cert′ed·ly** *adv.* **—dis′con·cert′ed·ness** *n.*

dis·con·form·i·ty (dis′kən·fôr′mə·tē) *n. pl.* **·ties** Lack of conformity; nonconformity.

dis·con·nect (dis′kə·nekt′) *v.t.* To undo or dissolve the connection of; disunite; separate. — **dis′con·nec′tion,** *Brit.* **dis′con·nex′ion** *n.*

dis·con·nect·ed (dis′kə·nek′tid) *adj.* **1** Not connected; disjointed. **2** Incoherent; rambling. — **dis′con·nect′ed·ly** *adv.* **—dis′con·nect′ed·ness** *n.*

dis·con·so·late (dis·kon′sə·lit) *adj.* **1** Destitute of consolation; inconsolable; sad. **2** Marked by gloominess; cheerless; saddening. See synonyms under SAD. [< Med. L *disconsolatus* < *dis-* not + *consolatus,* pp. of *consolari* CONSOLE[1]] — **dis·con′so·late·ly** *adv.* **—dis·con′so·late·ness** *n.*

dis·con·so·la·tion (dis·kon′sə·lā′shən) *n.* The state of being disconsolate.

dis·con·tent (dis′kən·tent′) *n.* Lack of content; dissatisfaction; uneasiness: also **dis′con·tent′ed·ness, dis′con·tent′ment.** —*v.t.* To render discontented; dissatisfy. **—dis′con·tent′ing** *adj.*

dis·con·tent·ed (dis′kən·ten′tid) *adj.* Ill at ease; dissatisfied. **—dis′con·tent′ed·ly** *adv.*

dis·con·tin·u·ance (dis′kən·tin′yōō·əns) *n.* **1** The act of discontinuing, or state of being discontinued; interruption or intermission. **2** Discontinuity. **3** *Law* The interruption of a suit, as by failure of the plaintiff to follow it up: distinguished from *dismissal.*

dis·con·tin·ue (dis′kən·tin′yōō) *v.* **·tin·ued, ·tin·u·ing** *v.t.* **1** To break off or cease from; stop. **2** To cease using, receiving, etc.: to *discontinue* a newspaper. **3** *Law* To abandon (a suit, etc.) by discontinuance. —*v.i.* **4** To come to an end; stop. See synonyms under ABANDON, CEASE, SUSPEND. [< OF *discontinuer* < Med. L *discontinuare* < *dis-* not + L *continuare* CONTINUE] — **dis′con·tin′u·a′tion** *n.* **—dis′con·tin′u·er,** *Law* **dis′con·tin′u·or** *n.*

dis·con·ti·nu·i·ty (dis′kon·tə·nōō′ə·tē, -nyōō′-) *n.* **1** Lack of continuity. **2** A gap, as in a structure or electric current.

dis·con·tin·u·ous (dis′kən·tin′yōō·əs) *adj.* Not continuous; characterized by interruptions or breaks. **—dis′con·tin′u·ous·ly** *adv.* **—dis′con·tin′u·ous·ness** *n.*

disc·o·phile (dis′kə·fīl) *n.* A collector, student, and connoisseur of phonograph recordings. [< L *discus* a plate, disk + -PHILE]

dis·cord (dis′kôrd) *n.* **1** Variance or strife; lack of agreement; contention. **2** *Music* A combination of dissonant sounds; lack of harmony. **3** A harsh or disagreeable medley of noises; dissonance. — *v.i.* To be out of accord or harmony; disagree; clash. [< OF *descord* < *descorder* disagree < L *discordare* < *discors* at variance < *dis-* away + *cor, cordis* heart]

dis·cor·dance (dis·kôr′dəns) *n.* **1** A discordant state or quality. **2** A discord. Also **dis·cor′dan·cy.**

dis·cor·dant (dis·kôr′dənt) *adj.* **1** Contradictory; inconsistent. **2** Quarrelsome. **3** Not harmonious; dissonant. **4** *Geol.* Lacking in conformity, as in the direction or sequence of rock strata. See synonyms under CONTRARY, HETEROGENEOUS, INCONGRUOUS. [< OF *descordant,* ppr. of *descorder.* See DISCORD.] **—dis·cor′dant·ly** *adv.*

Dis·cor·di·a (dis·kôr′dē·ə) The Roman goddess of discord.

dis·co·thèque (dis·kə·tek′) *n.* A night club offering recorded music for dancing instead of music played by a band of live musicians. [< F, lit., record library]

dis·count (dis′kount) *n.* **1** An amount counted off or deducted from a sum owing or to be paid: ten per cent *discount* for cash. **2** The interest allowed and deducted from the face amount for advancing money on negotiable paper. **3** The act of discounting. **4** The rate of discount. **—at a discount** At less than the face value; below par; hence, not in esteem. **—true** or **arithmetical discount** That interest at a given rate and term which, added to the principal received, gives the face value of the discounted paper. —*v.t.* (dis′kount, dis·kount′) **1** To set aside or deduct, as a portion of an amount owed; make an allowance of. **2** To buy or sell (a bill or note) for face value less the amount of interest to be accumulated before maturity. **3** To disregard; take no account of. **4** To believe only part of; allow for exaggeration in. **5** To take into account beforehand; diminish by anticipation, especially so as to lessen value, effect, enjoyment, etc. —*v.i.* **6** To lend money, deducting the interest beforehand. [< MF *descompte, desconte* < OF *descompter* < Med. L *discomputare* < *dis-* away + *computare* COMPUTE] **—dis′count·a·ble** *adj.* **—dis′count·er** *n.*

dis·coun·te·nance (dis·koun′tə·nəns) *v.t.* **·nanced, ·nanc·ing 1** To look upon with disfavor; disapprove or discourage. **2** To abash; disconcert. —*n. Obs.* Disapprobation; abashment. [< MF *descontenancer* < *des-* away (< L *dis-*) + *contenancer* favor < *contenance* COUNTENANCE]

dis·cour·age (dis·kûr′ij) *v.t.* **·aged, ·ag·ing 1** To deprive of courage; dispirit; dishearten. **2** To deter or dissuade with *from.* **3** To obstruct; hinder: Malnutrition *discourages* growth. **4** To attempt to repress or prevent by disapproval. [< OF *descoragier* < *des-* away (< L *dis-*) + *corage* courage] **—dis·cour′ag·er** *n.* **—dis·cour′ag·ing** *adj.* **—dis·cour′ag·ing·ly** *adv.*

dis·cour·age·ment (dis·kûr′ij·mənt) *n.* **1** The act of discouraging, or the state of being discouraged. **2** That which discourages. See synonyms under DESPAIR.

dis·course (dis′kôrs, dis·kôrs′) *n.* **1** Connected communication of thought sequence; continuous expression or exchange of ideas. **2** Familiar conversation; talk. **3** Formal expression of thought, oral or written; a long treatise or dissertation; a sermon. **Direct discourse** is spoken or written language quoted in the exact words of the speaker or writer, as in *I will go,* and is contrasted with **indirect discourse,** in which his words are reported with change of person or tense, as in *he said he would go.* **4** An act, the exercise, or the power of analytical and consecutive thought; ratiocination. See synonyms under CONVERSATION, SPEECH. —*v.* (dis·kôrs′) **·coursed, ·cours·ing** *v.i.* **1** To set forth one's thoughts and conclusions concerning a subject: with *on* or *upon.* **2** To converse; confer. —*v.t.* **3** *Obs.* To discuss. [< OF *discours* < L *discursus* < *dis-* apart + *cursus* a running < *currere* run] **—dis·cours′er** *n.*

dis·cour·te·ous (dis·kûr′tē·əs) *adj.* Showing discourtesy; rude. See synonyms under BLUFF[2]. — **dis·cour′te·ous·ly** *adv.* **—dis·cour′te·ous·ness** *n.*

dis·cour·te·sy (dis·kûr′tə·sē) *n. pl.* **·sies** Rude behavior; impoliteness.

dis·cov·er (dis·kuv′ər) *v.t.* **1** To find or gain knowledge of, especially for the first time. **2** *Archaic* To act or speak so as to expose or betray, especially unwittingly. **3** *Archaic* To remove the covering of; reveal; disclose. **4** *Obs.* To distinguish, as black from white. [< OF *descovrir* < *des-* away (< L *dis-*) + *covrir* COVER] — **dis·cov′er·a·bil′i·ty** *n.* **—dis·cov′er·a·ble** *adj.* — **dis·cov′er·er** *n.*

Synonyms: ascertain, descry, detect, discern, disclose, expose, find, invent. Of human actions or character, *detect* is used almost without exception of what is evil; *discover* may be used in either the good or the bad sense, oftener in the good; he was *detected* in a fraud; real merit is sure to be *discovered.* In scientific language, *detect* is used of delicate indications that appear in course of careful watching; as, a slight fluttering of the pulse could be *detected.* We *discover* what has existed but has not been known to us; we *invent* combinations or arrangements not before in use. *Find* is the most general word for every means of coming to know what was not before certainly known. Compare CATCH, KNOW. *Antonyms*: see synonyms for HIDE.

dis·cov·ert (dis·kuv′ərt) *adj.* **1** *Law* Not under

the bonds of matrimony; not covert; unmarried: said of a widow, divorcée, or spinster. 2 *Obs.* Uncovered; revealed. [<OF *descovert,* pp. of *descovrir* DISCOVER]

dis·cov·er·y (dis·kuv′ər·ē) *n. pl.* **·er·ies** 1 The act of discovering; disclosure. 2 Something discovered.

Discovery Bay An inlet of the Indian Ocean in SE Australia.

Discovery Day Columbus Day.

dis·cre·ate (dis′krē·āt′) *v.t.* **·at·ed, ·at·ing** To undo (what has been created); destroy; annihilate. — **dis′cre·a′tion** *n.*

dis·cred·it (dis·kred′it) *v.t.* 1 To disbelieve. 2 To injure the credit or reputation of; dishonor. 3 To show to be unworthy of belief or confidence. — *n.* 1 The act of discrediting. 2 The state of being discredited or disbelieved. 3 Lack of credit; impaired reputation; dishonor. See synonyms under ABASE, DISPARAGE.

dis·cred·it·a·ble (dis·kred′it·ə·bəl) *adj.* Hurtful to credit or reputation; disreputable. — **dis·cred′it·a·bly** *adv.*

dis·creet (dis·krēt′) *adj.* 1 Wise in avoiding errors or in selecting the best means to accomplish a purpose. 2 Judicious; prudent; careful. See synonyms under POLITIC. ◆ Homophone: *discrete.* [<OF *discret* <LL *discretus* learned, orig. pp. of *discernere* discern] — **dis·creet′ly** *adv.* — **dis·creet′ness** *n.*

dis·crep·an·cy (dis·krep′ən·sē) *n. pl.* **·cies** A disagreement or difference; state or point of variance; inconsistency. Also **dis·crep′ance.** See synonyms under DIFFERENCE.

dis·crep·ant (dis·krep′ənt) *adj.* Inharmoniously different; opposite; inconsistent; contrary; discordant. See synonyms under INCONGRUOUS. [<OF <L *discrepans, -antis* < *dis-* away + *crepare* creak, make a noise]

dis·crete (dis·krēt′) *adj.* 1 Disconnected from others; distinct or separate. 2 Made up of distinct parts or separate units; discontinuous. 3 Denoting opposition or contrariety. 4 *Bot.* Separate; not coalescent, as leaves; distinct; segregate: opposed to *confluent.* ◆ Homophone: *discreet.* [Var. of DISCREET] — **dis·crete′ly** *adv.* — **dis·crete′ness** *n.*

dis·cre·tion (dis·kresh′ən) *n.* 1 Cautious and correct judgment; prudence; sagacity; the quality of being discreet. 2 Liberty of action; freedom in the exercise of judgment. 3 *Law* The act or the liberty of deciding according to justice and propriety, and one's idea of what is right and proper under the circumstances, without wilfulness or favor. 4 *Obs.* Distinction or separation; disjunction. See synonyms under ADDRESS, PRUDENCE, WISDOM. — **at discretion** At will; according to one's own judgment. [<OF <L *discretio, -onis* < *discretus* discrete]

dis·cre·tion·al (dis·kresh′ən·əl) *adj.* Discretionary. — **dis·cre′tion·al·ly** *adv.*

dis·cre·tion·ar·y (dis·kresh′ə·ner′ē) *adj.* 1 Exercisable at or left to discretion. 2 Uncontrolled legally except by discretion.

dis·crim·i·nate (dis·krim′ə·nāt) *v.* **·nat·ed, ·nat·ing** *v.i.* 1 To treat someone or something with partiality: with *against* or *in favor of*: to *discriminate* against a group or in favor of a relative. 2 To observe a difference; make a distinction: with *between.* — *v.t.* 3 To discern the difference in or between. 4 To make or constitute a difference in or between: The meter *discriminates* one poem from the other. See synonyms under CONTRAST, DISCERN, KNOW. — *adj.* (-nit) 1 Noting differences; discriminating. 2 Discriminated. [<L *discriminatus,* pp. of *discriminare* < *discrimen, -inis* < *dis-* apart + *crimen* a judgment] — **dis·crim′i·nate·ly** *adv.* — **dis·crim′i·nate·ness** *n.*

dis·crim·i·nat·ing (dis·krim′ə·nā′ting) *adj.* 1 Having power to distinguish keenly: a *discriminating* intellect. 2 Serving to distinguish: a *discriminating* mark. 3 Establishing distinction or inequality. See synonyms under ASTUTE. — **dis·crim′i·nat′ing·ly** *adv.*

dis·crim·i·na·tion (dis·krim′ə·nā′shən) *n.* 1 The act or power of discriminating; the discernment of distinctions. 2 Differential treatment; bias: *discrimination* against minorities. 3 The state or condition of being discriminated; distinction; sometimes, unjust distinction. See synonyms under DIFFERENCE.

dis·crim·i·na·tive (dis·krim′ə·nā′tiv) *adj.* 1 Discriminating. 2 Distinctive or characteristic. Also **dis·crim′i·na·to′ry** (-nə·tôr′ē, -tō′rē). — **dis·crim′i·na′tive·ly** *adv.*

dis·crown (dis·kroun′) *v.t.* To deprive of a crown; dethrone.

dis·cur·sive (dis·kûr′siv) *adj.* Passing from one subject to another; wandering away from the point or theme; digressive. [<L *discursus.* See DISCOURSE.] — **dis·cur′sive·ly** *adv.* — **dis·cur′sive·ness** *n.*

dis·cus (dis′kəs) *n. pl.* **dis·cus·es** or **dis·ci** (dis′ī) 1 A heavy circular plate thrown in athletic contests: originally, in Greek and Roman games, of stone or metal; quoit. 2 The exercise of throwing this plate. For illustration see DISCOBOLUS. 3 *Biol.* A disc. [<L <Gk. *diskos*]

dis·cuss (dis·kus′) *v.t.* 1 To treat of in conversation or in writing; talk about; argue the faults and merits of. 2 *Colloq.* To test by eating or drinking, as a meal. 3 In civil law, to exhaust proceedings against (the principal debtor) before proceeding against the surety or sureties. See synonyms under DISPUTE, EXAMINE. [<L *discussus,* pp. of *discutere* discuss, orig. < *dis-* apart + *quatere* shake] — **dis·cuss′i·ble** *adj.*

dis·cus·sant (dis·kus′ənt) *n.* One who takes part in a discussion; an active participant in a symposium.

dis·cus·sion (dis·kush′ən) *n.* 1 The act of discussing; argumentative examination; debate. See synonyms under ALTERCATION, QUARREL, SPEECH. 2 *Obs.* The scattering or dispersion of any effusion, tumor, or swelling in the body. [<OF <LL *discussio, -onis* < *discutere.* See DISCUSS.]

dis·cus·sive (dis·kus′iv) *Obs. adj.* Possessing the property of dispersing tumors and the like. — *n.* A medicine that disperses tumors. Also **dis·cu·tient** (dis·kyōō′shənt).

dis·dain (dis·dān′) *v.t.* 1 To consider unworthy of one's regard or notice; treat with contempt or scorn. 2 To reject as beneath oneself; scorn. — *n.* A feeling of superiority and dislike; proud contempt. See synonyms under ARROGANCE, SCORN. [<OF *desdeignier* < *des-* away (<L *dis-*) + *deignier* DEIGN]

dis·dain·ful (dis·dān′fəl) *adj.* Filled with or expressing disdain; scornful. See synonyms under HAUGHTY. — **dis·dain′ful·ly** *adv.* — **dis·dain′ful·ness** *n.*

dis·ease (di·zēz′) *n.* 1 Disturbed or abnormal structure or physiological action in the living organism as a whole, or in any of its parts. 2 A morbid condition resulting from such disturbance. 3 Any disturbed or abnormal condition in organic substances, as wines, liquors, etc.; a taint. 4 *Obs.* Uneasiness; inconvenience; discomfort; discontent. — *v.t.* **·eased, ·eas·ing** 1 To cause disease in; disorder; derange. 2 *Obs.* To make uneasy; distress. [<AF, OF *desaise* < *des-* away (<L *dis-*) + *aise* EASE] — **dis·eased′** *adj.*

Synonyms (noun): affection, ailment, complaint, disorder, distemper, illness, indisposition, infirmity, malady, sickness, unhealthiness, unsoundness. *Disease* is the general term for deviation from health; in a more limited sense it denotes some definite morbid condition; *disorder* and *affection* are rather partial and limited; as, a nervous *affection*; a *disorder* of the digestive system. Although *sickness* was generally used in English speech and literature, till the close of the eighteenth century at least, for every form of physical *disorder,* there is now a tendency to restrict the words *sick* and *sickness* to nausea, and to hold *ill* and *illness* as the proper words to use in a general sense. We speak of trifling *ailments,* a slight *indisposition,* a serious or a deadly *disease*; a slight or severe *illness*; an insidious, serious, severe, or deadly *disease. Complaint* is a popular term, which may be applied to any degree of ill health, slight or severe. *Infirmity* denotes a chronic or lingering weakness or disability, as blindness or lameness. See ILLNESS. *Antonyms*: health, robustness, sanity, soundness, strength, sturdiness, vigor.

dis·em·bark (dis′em·bärk′) *v.t.* & *v.i.* To put or go ashore from a ship; land; unload. [<MF *desembarquer* < *des-* away (<L *dis-*) + *embarquer* EMBARK] — **dis·em′bar·ka′tion, dis′em·bark′ment** *n.*

dis·em·bar·rass (dis′em·bar′əs) *v.t.* To free from embarrassment. — **dis′em·bar′rass·ment** *n.*

dis·em·bed (dis′em·bed′) *v.t.* **·bed·ded, ·bed·ding** To extract (a thing embedded).

dis·em·bel·lish (dis′em·bel′ish) *v.t.* To strip of embellishment.

dis·em·bod·y (dis′em·bod′ē) *v.t.* **·bod·ied, ·bod·y·ing** To free from the body; free from physical existence. — **dis′em·bod′i·ment** *n.*

dis·em·bogue (dis′em·bōg′) *v.t.* & *v.i.* **·bogued, ·bo·guing** 1 To pour out or discharge (waters) at the mouth; empty: said of rivers, streams, etc. 2 *Obs.* To sail out of a river, bay, or harbor. [<Sp. *desembocar* < *des-* out (<L *dis-*) + *embocar* put into the mouth <L *in-* into + *bucca* mouth] — **dis′em·bogue′ment** *n.*

dis·em·bos·om (dis′em·bŏŏz′əm) *v.t.* & *v.i.* To reveal (a secret); to disburden (oneself) of a secret.

dis·em·bow·el (dis′em·bou′əl, -boul′) *v.t.* **·bow·eled** or **·bow·elled, ·bow·el·ing** or **·bow·el·ling** 1 To take out the bowels of; eviscerate. 2 To remove the contents of. — **dis′em·bow′el·ment** *n.*

dis·en·a·ble (dis′en·ā′bəl) *v.t.* **·bled, ·bling** To disable; make unfit.

dis·en·chant (dis′en·chant′, -chänt′) *v.t.* To free from enchantment; disillusion. [<OF *desenchanter* < *des-* away (<L *dis-*) + *enchanter* ENCHANT] — **dis′en·chant′er** *n.* — **dis′en·chant′ment** *n.*

dis·en·cum·ber (dis′en·kum′bər) *v.t.* To free from encumbrance or burden. [<OF *desencombre, desencombrer* < *des-* away (<L *dis-*) + *encombrer* ENCUMBER] — **dis′en·cum′berment, dis′en·cum′brance** *n.*

dis·en·dow (dis′en·dou′) *v.t.* To take away an endowment or endowments from. — **dis′en·dow′er** *n.* — **dis′en·dow′ment** *n.*

dis·en·fran·chise (dis′en·fran′chīz) *v.t.* **·chised, ·chis·ing** To disfranchise. — **dis′en·fran′chise·ment** (-chiz·mənt) *n.*

dis·en·gage (dis′en·gāj′) *v.t.* & *v.i.* **·gaged, ·gag·ing** To set or be free from engagement, entanglement, or occupation; become detached; withdraw. See synonyms under RELEASE. — **dis′en·gaged′** *adj.* — **dis′en·gag′ed·ness** *n.*

dis·en·gage·ment (dis′en·gāj′mənt) *n.* 1 The act of disengaging, or the state of being disengaged; extrication. 2 Freedom from toil or care; leisure; ease.

dis·en·tail (dis′en·tāl′) *v.t. Law* To free from or break the entail of, as an estate. — **dis′en·tail′ment** *n.*

dis·en·tan·gle (dis′en·tang′gəl) *v.t.* **·gled, ·gling** To free or relieve of entanglement or perplexity; unravel. — **dis′en·tan′gle·ment** *n.*

dis·en·thral (dis′en·thrôl′) *v.t.* **·thralled, ·thral·ling** To release from or as from thraldom; set free: also spelled *disinthral.* Also **dis′en·thrall′.** — **dis′en·thral′ment** or **dis′en·thrall′ment** *n.*

dis·en·throne (dis′en·thrōn′) *v.t.* To dethrone; depose. — **dis′en·throne′ment** *n.*

dis·en·ti·tle (dis′en·tī′tl) *v.t.* **·tled, ·tling** To take away the title from; deprive of a right.

dis·en·tomb (dis′en·tōōm′) *v.t.* To exhume; disinter. — **dis′en·tomb′ment** *n.*

dis·en·train (dis′en·trān′) *v.t.* & *v.i.* To detrain, as troops.

dis·en·trance (dis′en·trans′, -träns′) *v.t.* **·tranced, ·tranc·ing** To arouse from a trance.

dis·en·twine (dis′en·twīn′) *v.t.* & *v.i.* **·twined, ·twin·ing** To untwine; disentangle.

di·sep·a·lous (dī·sep′ə·ləs) *adj. Bot.* Having two sepals. [<DI-[2] + SEPALOUS]

dis·es·tab·lish (dis′es·tab′lish) *v.t.* 1 To deprive of established character. 2 To withdraw state patronage from: to *disestablish* a church. — **dis′es·tab′lish·ment** *n.*

dis·es·teem (dis′es·tēm′) *v.t.* To feel a lack of esteem for; regard slightingly or with dislike; disapprove of. — *n.* Lack of esteem.

di·seuse (dē·zœz′) *n. French* A woman entertainer performing dramatic impersonations, monologs, etc.

dis·fa·vor (dis·fā′vər) *n.* 1 Lack of favor; disapproval; dislike. 2 The state of being discountenanced, disliked, or opposed; odium. 3 An unkind act. 4 *Obs.* Ugliness; homeliness. — *v.t.* To treat or regard without favor;

discountenance; oppose. Also *Brit.* **dis·fa′vour.**

dis·fea·ture (dis·fē′chər) *v.t.* **·tured, ·tur·ing** To mar the features of; disfigure; deface.

dis·fig·ure (dis·fig′yər) *v.t.* **·ured, ·ur·ing** To mar or destroy the figure or beauty of; render unsightly; deform. [<OF *desfigurer* <*des-* away (<L *dis-*) + *figurer* <L *figurare* form, fashion <*figura* a shape] **—dis·fig′ur·er** *n.* **—dis·fig′ured** *adj.* **—dis·fig′ure·ment, dis·fig′u·ra′tion** *n.*

dis·for·est (dis·fôr′ist, -for′-) *v.t.* **1** To clear of forest; deforest. **2** *Law* To disafforest. **—dis·for′es·ta′tion** *n.*

dis·fran·chise (dis·fran′chīz) *v.t.* **·chised, ·chis·ing 1** To deprive of a privilege, right, or grant. **2** To dispossess of a citizen's privileges, as of the ballot. **—dis·fran′chis·er** *n.* **—dis·fran′chise·ment** (-chiz·mənt) *n.*

dis·frock (dis·frok′) *v.t.* To unfrock.

dis·fur·nish (dis·fûr′nish) *v.t. Obs.* To strip of furniture, equipment, or belongings. [<OF *desfourniss-*, stem of *desfournir* <*des-* away (<L *dis-*) + *fournir* FURNISH] **—dis·fur′nish·ment** *n.*

dis·gorge (dis·gôrj′) *v.t.* **·gorged, ·gorg·ing 1** To throw out, as from the throat or stomach; eject; vomit. **2** To give up unwillingly, especially something wrongfully obtained. —*v.i.* **3** To throw up; vomit. [<OF *desgorger* <*des-* from (<L *dis-*) + *gorge* throat]

dis·grace (dis·grās′) *v.t.* **·graced, ·grac·ing 1** To bring reproach or shame upon. **2** To dismiss from favor; treat with dishonor. —*n.* **1** Disfavor. **2** Infamy; ignominy. **3** That which disgraces. See synonyms under ABASE, BLEMISH, STAIN. [<MF *disgracier* <Ital. *disgraziare* <*disgrazia* <*dis-* away (<L *dis-*) + *grazia* <L *gratia* favor] **—dis·grac′er** *n.*

dis·grace·ful (dis·grās′fəl) *adj.* Characterized by or causing disgrace; shameful. See synonyms under FLAGRANT, INFAMOUS. **—dis·grace′ful·ly** *adv.* **—dis·grace′ful·ness** *n.*

dis·grun·tle (dis·grun′təl) *v.t.* **·grun·tled, ·grun·tling** To disappoint and make discontented; cause to sulk.

dis·guise (dis·gīz′) *v.t.* **·guised, ·guis·ing 1** To change the appearance of; hide or conceal the identity of, as by a mask. **2** To obscure or cover up the actual nature or character of by false representation; dissemble; misrepresent. See synonyms under HIDE[1], MASK[1]. —*n.* **1** The act of disguising, or the state of being disguised. **2** Something that disguises, alters the appearance of, or renders difficult of recognition. See synonyms under PRETENSE. [<OF *desguisier* <*des-* down (<L *de-*) + *guise* GUISE] **—dis·guis′ed·ly** (-id·lē) *adv.* **—dis·guis′er** *n.*

dis·gust (dis·gust′) *v.t.* **1** To affect with physical nausea; offend the senses of. **2** To offend the sensibilities of; affect with loathing or aversion. —*n.* Strong aversion or repugnance. See synonyms under ABOMINATION, ANTIPATHY. [<MF *desgouster* <*des-* away (<L *dis-*) + *gouster* taste <L *gustare*]

dis·gust·ed (dis·gus′tid) *adj.* Affected with loathing or disgust. **—dis·gust′ed·ly** *adv.* **—dis·gust′ed·ness** *n.*

dis·gust·ful (dis·gust′fəl) *adj.* **1** Disgusting. **2** Full of or characterized by disgust. **—dis·gust′ful·ly** *adv.* **—dis·gust′ful·ness** *n.*

dis·gust·ing (dis·gus′ting) *adj.* Serving or fitted to provoke disgust; odious; revolting. **—dis·gust′ing·ly** *adv.*

dish (dish) *n.* **1** A concave or hollow vessel for serving food at meals; anything of similar shape. **2** The amount of food served in a dish: also **dish′ful. 3** Food prepared in a special way. **4** Concavity. —*v.t.* **1** To place in a dish or dishes; serve as food: often with *up* or *out.* **2** To make concave. **3** *Slang* To ruin; cheat. —*v.i.* **4** To become concave; sink in. [<OE *disc* <L *discus.* Doublet of DAIS, DESK, DISK.]

dis·ha·bille (dis′ə·bēl′) *n.* **1** A state of being partially or negligently dressed, as in night clothes. **2** The clothes or garments worn in this state. Also spelled *deshabille.* [<F *déshabillé,* pp. of *deshabiller* undress <*des-* away (<L *dis-*) + *habiller* dress]

dis·hal·low (dis·hal′ō) *v.t.* To render unhallowed; profane; desecrate.

dis·har·mo·nize (dis·här′mə·nīz) *v.t.* & *v.i.* **·nized, ·niz·ing** To render or be discordant; make or be inharmonious. **—dis·har′mo·nism** *n.*

dis·har·mo·ny (dis·här′mə·nē) *n. pl.* **·nies** Lack of harmony; incongruity; discord. **—dis·har·mo·ni·ous** (dis′här·mō′nē·əs) *adj.* **—dis′·har·mo′ni·ous·ly** *adv.*

dish·cloth (dish′klôth′, -kloth′) *n.* A cloth used in washing dishes. Also **dish′clout′** (-klout′), **dish′rag′** (-rag′).

dishcloth gourd A loofah.

dis·heart·en (dis·här′tən) *v.t.* To weaken the spirit or courage of; dispirit; discourage. See synonyms under ABASH. **—dis·heart′en·ing** *adj.* **—dis·heart′en·ing·ly** *adv.* **—dis·heart′en·ment** *n.*

dished (disht) *adj.* **1** Shaped like a dish; concave. **2** Of wheels, slanted inward at the bottom. **3** *Slang* Worn out; exhausted.

dis·her·i·son (dis·her′ə·zən) *Obs. n.* The act of depriving of an inheritance. —*v.t.* To disinherit. [<OF *desheriteisun* <L *dis-* away + *hereditas* inheritance]

dis·her·it (dis·her′it) *v.t. Obs.* To disinherit. [<OF *desheriter* <LL *dis-* away + *hereditare* inherit <L *heres, -edis* an heir]

di·shev·el (di·shev′əl) *v.t.* **·eled** or **·elled, ·el·ing** or **·el·ling** To disorder (the hair); disarrange (the dress) [<MF *descheveler* <*des-* away (<L *dis-*) + *chevel* hair <L *capillus*] **—di·shev′el·ment** *n.*

dish-faced (dish′fāst′) *adj.* Having a round, flat face.

dis·hon·est (dis·on′ist) *adj.* **1** Lacking in honesty; untrustworthy. **2** Characterized by dishonesty; fraudulent; See synonyms under BAD[1], IMMORAL. [<OF *deshoneste* <LL *dis-* away + *honestus* honest] **—dis·hon′est·ly** *adv.*

dis·hon·es·ty (dis·on′is·tē) *n. pl.* **·ties 1** The quality of being dishonest. **2** Fraud or violation of trust; a dishonest action.

dis·hon·or (dis·on′ər) *v.t.* **1** To deprive of honor; disgrace; insult. **2** To violate the chastity of; seduce. **3** To decline or fail to pay, as a note. See synonyms under ABASE, BLEMISH, DISPARAGE, POLLUTE, STAIN. —*n.* **1** Lack of honor or of honorable character. **2** Degradation. **3** Insult; reproach; stain. **4** Refusal or failure to pay a note, etc., when due. Also *Brit.* **dis·hon′our.** See synonyms under SCORN. [<OF *deshonor* <L *dis-* away + *honor* HONOR] **—dis·hon′or·er** *n.*

dis·hon·or·a·ble (dis·on′ər·ə·bəl) *adj.* **1** Characterized by or bringing dishonor or reproach; discreditable; mean; ignoble: a *dishonorable* motive or act. **2** Lacking honor or honorableness: a *dishonorable* lawyer. **3** In a state of dishonor or disesteem; dishonored: a *dishonorable* grave. See synonyms under INFAMOUS. **—dis·hon′or·a·ble·ness** *n.* **—dis·hon′or·a·bly** *adv.*

dish·pan (dish′pan′) *n.* A pan for washing dishes.

dish·wash·er (dish′wosh′ər, -wôsh′-) *n.* A person or machine that washes dishes.

dish·wa·ter (dish′wô′tər, -wot′-) *n.* Water in which dishes are to be or have been washed.

dis·il·lu·sion (dis′i·lōō′zhən) *v.t.* To free from illusion or delusion; disenchant. Also **dis′il·lu′sion·ize.** —*n.* The act of freeing or state of being freed from illusion. Also **dis′il·lu′sion·ment.**

dis·il·lu·sive (dis′i·lōō′siv) *adj.* Tending to dispel an illusion.

dis·im·pris·on (dis′im·priz′ən) *v.t.* To free from prison or imprisonment. **—dis′im·pris′on·ment** *n.*

dis·in·cen·tive (dis′in sen′tiv) *n.* Something that deters, or reduces incentive.

dis·in·cli·na·tion (dis·in′klə·nā′shən) *n.* Distaste; aversion; unwillingness.

dis·in·cline (dis′in·klīn′) *v.t.* & *v.i.* **·clined, ·clin·ing** To make or be unwilling or averse.

dis·in·cor·po·rate (dis′in·kôr′pə·rāt) *v.t.* **·rat·ed, ·rat·ing 1** To free from incorporation; deprive of chartered rights or character, as a company. **2** To separate from a corporation.

dis·in·fect (dis′in·fekt′) *v.t.* **1** To purify from infection. **2** To free from morbid or pathogenic matter, as a wound, clothing, etc. See synonyms under CLEANSE.

dis·in·fec·tant (dis′in·fek′tənt) *adj.* Disinfecting. —*n.* A substance used to disinfect or to destroy the germs of infectious and contagious diseases, as chlorine, carbolic acid, etc.

dis·in·fec·tion (dis′in·fek′shən) *n.* The act of disinfecting; fact or state of being disinfected.

dis·in·fest (dis′in·fest′) *v.t.* To exterminate vermin from; delouse. **—dis·in′fes·ta′tion** *n.*

dis·in·fla·tion (dis′in·flā′shən) *n. Econ.* The process, usually governmental, of attempting to reduce the price level, or to hold it steady, through restrictions of credit and other monetary measures, resulting in a decline in industrial production and reduced pressure on foreign exchange reserves: distinguished from *deflation* by a lesser depressant effect in the economy.

dis·in·for·ma·tion (dis·in′fər·mā′shən) *n.* False, misleading information deliberately disseminated.

dis·in·gen·u·ous (dis′in·jen′yōō·əs) *adj.* Not sincere or ingenuous; artful; deceitful. **—dis′in·gen′u·ous·ly** *adv.* **—dis′in·gen′u·ous·ness** *n.*

dis·in·her·it (dis′in·her′it) *v.t.* To deprive of an inheritance. **—dis′in·her′i·tance** *n.*

dis·in·hume (dis′in·hyōōm′) *v.t.* **·humed, ·hum·ing** To exhume; disinter.

dis·in·te·grate (dis·in′tə·grāt) *v.* **·grat·ed,·grat·ing** *v.t.* To break or reduce into component parts or particles; destroy the wholeness of. —*v.i.* To become reduced to fragments or particles; crumble. **—dis·in′te·gra·ble** (-grə·bəl) *adj.* **—dis·in′te·gra′tor** *n.*

dis·in·te·gra·tion (dis·in′tə·grā′shən) *n.* **1** The act of disintegrating, or the state of being disintegrated; a crumbling away. **2** *Geol.* The gradual decay and wasting, as of rocks under elemental action. **3** *Physics* The disappearance of an initial quantity of any radioactive element due to its conversion into another element as a result of the changes in nuclear properties attendant on the emission of alpha or beta particles.

dis·in·ter (dis′in·tûr′) *v.t.* **·terred, ·ter·ring 1** To dig up, as from a grave; exhume. **2** To bring to light or life as if from a grave. [<MF *désenterrer* <*des-* away + *enterrer* INTER] **—dis′in·ter′ment** *n.*

dis·in·ter·est (dis·in′tər·ist, -trist) *n.* **1** Lack of interest; indifference. **2** Freedom from bias; impartiality.

dis·in·ter·est·ed (dis·in′tər·is·tid, -tris·tid, -tə·res′-) *adj.* **1** Free from self-interest or bias; unselfish; impartial. **2** Loosely, uninterested. See synonyms under GENEROUS. **—dis·in′ter·est·ed·ly** *adv.* **—dis·in′ter·est·ed·ness** *n.*

dis·in·thral, dis·in·thrall (dis′in·thrôl′) See DISENTHRAL, etc.

dis·ject (dis·jekt′) *v.t.* To split apart forcibly; separate; break asunder. [<L *disjectus,* pp. of *disjicere* <*dis-* apart + *jacere* throw]

dis·join (dis·join′) *v.t.* To keep apart; undo or prevent the joining of; separate. —*v.i.* To become divided or separated. [<OF *desjoindre* <*des-* away (<L *dis-*) + *joindre* JOIN]

dis·joint (dis·joint′) *v.t.* **1** To put out of joint; dislocate. **2** To take apart; disconnect the pieces of. **3** To destroy the coherence, connections, or sequence of; disorder. —*v.i.* **4** To break into parts; become out of joint. —*adj. Obs.* Out of joint; disconnected. [<OF *desjoint,* pp. of *desjoindre.* See DISJOIN.] **—dis·joint′ly** *adv.*

dis·joint·ed (dis·join′tid) *adj.* Dislocated; disconnected; incoherent. **—dis·joint′ed·ly** *adv.* **—dis·joint′ed·ness** *n.*

dis·junct (dis·jungkt′) *adj.* **1** *Entomol.* Having the head, thorax, and abdomen separated by constrictions. **2** Not connected; detached. Compare illustrations under INSECT. [<L *disjunctus,* pp. of *disjungere* <*dis-* away + *jungere* join]

dis·junc·tion (dis·jungk′shən) *n.* **1** Sundering; separation: also **dis·junc′ture. 2** *Biol.* The moving apart of each pair of homologous chromosomes during the anaphase of cell mitosis.

dis·junc·tive (dis·jungk′tiv) *adj.* **1** Helping or serving to disjoin. **2** *Gram.* Expressing separation or disjoining, as certain conjunctions, as *either—or, else, otherwise,* etc. —*n.* **1** That which disjoins. **2** *Gram.* A disjunctive conjunction. **3** A Hebrew character used to separate words and clauses in sentences. **4** *Logic* A disjunctive proposition. **—dis·junc′tive·ly** *adv.*

disk (disk) *n.* **1** A flat plate of any material that is circular, or approximately circular; also, any surface that is flat and circular, or apparently so: the *disk* of a planet. **2** *Biol.* Any approximately flat circular outgrowth, organ, or structure of a planet or animal: in this sense usually spelled *disc.* **3** In the Roman Catholic Church, a paten or plate for the eucharistic bread. **4** A quoit or discus. See Illustration under DISCOBOLUS. **5** *Agric.*

A disk harrow. 6 *Astron.* The figure of a heavenly body, irrespective of its actual form. 7 A disc (def. 1). **—winged disk** In Egyptian art, the disk or symbol of the sun, supported by

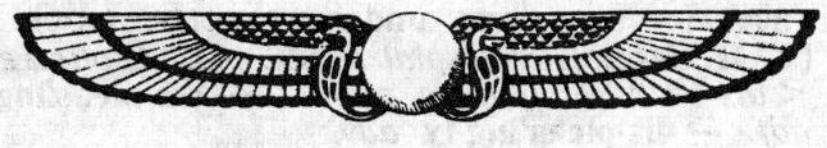

EGYPTIAN WINGED DISK

two uraei and the expanded wings of a vulture: also **sun disk.** [<L *discus* <Gk. *diskos* disk, platter. Doublet of DAIS, DESK, DISH.]

disk brake A brake in which a pad of durable, heat-resistant material is pressed against a metal disk: also called *spot brake.*

disk flower Any of the small, tubular florets, usually containing both stamens and pistil, that make up the central disk of a composite flower head. Also **disk floret.**

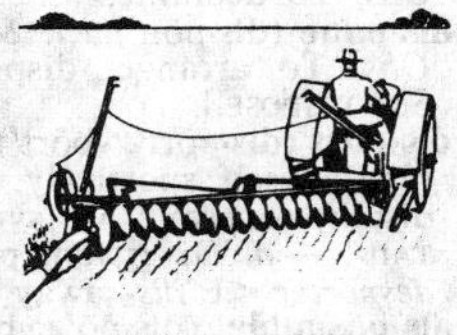

DISK HARROW
Number and type of disks may be varied for different types of plowing.

disk harrow *Agric.* A harrow consisting of a series of rolling, saucer-shaped disks set on edge and at an angle along one or more axles.

Dis·ko (dis′kō) A Danish island in Davis Strait, west of Greenland; 3,312 square miles. Also **Dis′co.**

disk wheel A wheel with a continuous, flat, convex, or concave outer surface from hub to rim, used on many automobiles.

dis·like (dis·līk′) *v.t.* **·liked, ·lik·ing** To regard with aversion or antipathy. See synonyms under ABHOR. *—n.* Distaste; repugnance; aversion. See synonyms under ANTIPATHY, HATRED. **—dis·lik′a·ble** *adj.* **—dis·lik′er** *n.*

dis·lo·cate (dis′lō·kāt, dis·lō′kāt) *v.t.* **·cat·ed, ·cat·ing 1** *Anat.* To put out of joint, as a bone. **2** To put out of proper place or order; displace; disarrange. [<Med. L *dislocatus,* pp. of *dislocare* <*dis-* away + L *locare* set, place <*locus* a place]

dis·lo·ca·tion (dis′lō·kā′shən) *n.* **1** *Anat.* The partial or complete displacement of one or more of the bones of a joint. **2** The act of displacing or disarranging, or the resulting condition; disarrangement; disorder. **3** *Geol.* A fault in or a shifting of rocks, generally followed by a displacement on either side. **4** *Physics* A disturbance of the normal atomic or molecular configuration in a crystal, revealed by changes in crystal properties.

dis·lodge (dis·loj′) *v.* **·lodged, ·lodg·ing** *v.t.* To remove or drive out, as from an abode, hiding place, or fortification. *—v.i.* To leave a place of abode; move. See synonyms under BANISH. [<OF *desloger, deslogier* <*dis-* away + *loger* LODGE] **—dis·lodg′ment,** *Brit.* **dis·lodge′ment** *n.*

dis·loy·al (dis·loi′əl) *adj.* False to one's allegiance or obligations; faithless. See synonyms under PERFIDIOUS. [<OF *desloial* <*des-* not (<L *dis-*) + *loial* LOYAL] **—dis·loy′al·ly** *adv.*

dis·loy·al·ty (dis·loi′əl·tē) *n. pl.* **·ties 1** The state of being disloyal; unfaithfulness; inconstancy. **2** A disloyal action.

dis·mal (diz′məl) *adj.* **1** Producing or expressing depression or gloom of feeling; cheerless; mournful. **2** Relating to adversity or trouble; direful; horrible. **3** Calamitous; ill-omened. See synonyms under DARK, SAD. *—n.* **1** *Colloq.* Usually *pl.* Gloomy feelings; depression. **2** *U.S.* A piece of swampy land along or near the southern Atlantic coast. Also **dismal swamp.** [<L *dies mali* evil or unpropitious days] **—dis′mal·ly** *adv.* **—dis′mal·ness** *n.*

Dismal Swamp A coastal swamp in SE Virginia and NE North Carolina; 20 miles long.

dis·man·tle (dis·man′təl) *v.t.* **·tled, ·tling 1** To strip of furniture, equipments, or defenses. **2** To take apart; reduce to pieces. **3** *Obs.* To divest of clothing. [<MF *desmanteller* <*des-* away + *manteller* cover with a cloak <*mantel* a cloak] **—dis·man′tle·ment** *n.*

dis·mast (dis·mast′, -mäst′) *v.t. Naut.* To destroy or bring down the masts of; deprive of masts.

dis·may (dis·mā′) *v.t.* To paralyze with fear; deprive of courage and the ability to act; daunt utterly. See synonyms under FRIGHTEN. *—n.* A state of overwhelming embarrassment and fright; consternation; terror. See synonyms under ALARM, CHAGRIN, FEAR, FRIGHT. [ME *dismayen,* prob. <OF. Cf. OF *dismayé* dismayed.]

disme (dēm) *n. Obs.* A tenth part; a tithe. [<OF. See DIME.]

dis·mem·ber (dis·mem′bər) *v.t.* **1** To cut or pull limb from limb or part from part. **2** To divide; separate into parts and distribute, as an empire. [<OF *desmembrer* <L *dis-* apart + *membrum* a limb, member] **—dis·mem′ber·ment** *n.*

dis·miss (dis·mis′) *v.t.* **1** To put out of office or service by an act of authority; discharge. **2** To cause or allow to depart; send away. **3** To put away or aside; reject; put beyond consideration. **4** *Law* To send out of court; reject without further hearing: The case was *dismissed.* See synonyms under BANISH. [<LL *dismissus* <*dis-* away + *missus,* pp. of *mittere* send] **—dis·miss′i·ble** *adj.* **—dis·mis′so·ry, dis·mis′sive** *adj.*

dis·mis·sal (dis·mis′əl) *n.* **1** Removal from office; a dismissing; discharge. **2** A notice of discharge. Also **dis·mis′sion** (-mish′ən).

dis·mount (dis·mount′) *v.i.* **1** To get off or alight from a horse, etc. *—v.t.* **2** To remove from a mounting, as a cannon or a jewel. **3** To come down; descend. **4** To take (a machine) to pieces. **5** To remove from or deprive of horses. *—n.* The act or manner of dismounting. **—dis·mount′a·ble** *adj.*

dis·na (diz′nə) *Scot.* Does not.

Disney (diz′nē), **Walt,** 1901–1966, U.S. producer of animated cartoons: full name Walter Elias Disney.

Dis·ney·land (diz′nē·land′) *n.* **1** A large amusement park near Los Angeles, California. **2** Any fantastic or unreal place. [after Walt *Disney*]

dis·o·be·di·ent (dis′ə·bē′dē·ənt) *adj.* Neglecting or refusing to obey; refractory. See synonyms under REBELLIOUS. [<OF *desobedient* <L *dis-* not + *obediens, -entis* OBEDIENT] **—dis′o·be′di·ence** *n.* **—dis′o·be′di·ent·ly** *adv.*

dis·o·bey (dis′ə·bā′) *v.t.* & *v.i.* To refuse or fail to obey. [<OF *desobeir* <LL *dis-* away + *obedire* OBEY] **—dis′o·bey′er** *n.*

dis·o·blige (dis′ə·blīj′) *v.t.* **1** To neglect or refuse to oblige. **2** *Colloq.* To discommode or inconvenience. **3** To slight; affront. [<OF *desobliger* <L *dis-* not + *obligare* OBLIGE] **—dis·ob′li·ga′tion** *n.*

dis·o·blig·ing (dis′ə·blī′jing) *adj.* Not disposed to oblige; unaccommodating. **—dis′o·blig′ing·ly** *adv.* **—dis′o·blig′ing·ness** *n.*

di·so·di·um (dī·sō′dē·əm) *adj. Chem.* Characterized by the presence of two sodium atoms in one molecule. **—di·so′dic** *adj.*

dis·or·der (dis·ôr′dər) *n.* **1** The state of being disarranged; disorderliness. **2** Hence, disregard or neglect of orderliness. **3** A disturbance of the peace; an infraction of law or discipline; minor uprising or tumult. **4** Derangement of the bodily or mental functions; disease. **5** *Obs.* Agitation. *—v.t.* **1** To throw out of order; disarrange. **2** To disturb the natural functions of, as body or mind; unsettle; derange. **3** *Obs.* To agitate. [<OF *desordre* <L *dis-* away from, out of + *ordo* order]

Synonyms (noun): anarchy, clutter, confusion, disturbance, irregularity. See DISEASE, ILLNESS, TUMULT. *Antonyms*: method, order, regularity, system.

dis·or·dered (dis·ôr′dərd) *adj.* **1** Having no order or arrangement; confused. **2** Mentally deranged.

dis·or·der·ly (dis·ôr′dər·lē) *adj.* & *adv.* **1** Being in or causing disorder; not orderly; without order. **2** Lawless; disreputable. See synonyms under IRREGULAR, TURBULENT. *—n. pl.* **·lies** A disorderly person; offender against public order: a term used in police courts. **—dis·or′der·li·ness** *n.*

disorderly conduct *Law* A minor offense against public peace and order.

disorderly house An establishment run for illegal purposes, as prostitution, gambling, etc.

dis·or·di·nate (dis·ôr′də·nit) *adj. Obs.* Inordinate; without moderation. [<OF *desordené,* pp. of *desordener* <*des-* away (<L *dis-*) + *ordener* ORDAIN]

dis·o·ri·ent (dis·ôr′ē·ənt, -ō′rē-) *v.t.* **1** To cause to lose the sense of direction. **2** *Psychol.* To cause to lose appreciation of spatial, temporal, or human relationships. [<F *désorienter* <*des-* away (<L *dis-*) + *orienter* ORIENT] **—dis·o′ri·en·ta′tion** *n.*

dis·own (dis·ōn′) *v.t.* To refuse to acknowledge or to admit responsibility for or ownership of; deny; repudiate. See synonyms under RENOUNCE.

dis·par·age (dis·par′ij) *v.t.* **·aged, ·ag·ing 1** To speak of slightingly; undervalue. **2** To bring discredit or dishonor upon. [<OF *desparagier* match unequally <*des-* down, away (<L *dis-*) + *parage* equality, rank] **—dis·par′ag·er** *n.* **—dis·par′ag·ing·ly** *adv.*

Synonyms: belittle, decry, depreciate, discredit, dishonor, lower, underestimate, underrate, undervalue. To *decry* is to cry down, in some noisy, public, or conspicuous manner. A witness or a statement is *discredited*; the currency is *depreciated*; a good name is *dishonored* by unworthy conduct; we *underestimate* in our own minds; we may *underrate* or *undervalue* in statement to others. To *disparage* is to *belittle* by damaging comparison or suggestion. These words are used, with few exceptions, of things such as qualities, merits, attainments, etc. See ASPERSE. *Antonyms*: see synonyms for PRAISE.

dis·par·age·ment (dis·par′ij·mənt) *n.* **1** The act of depreciating, aspersing, slighting, or undervaluing; derogation. **2** A condition of low estimation or valuation; a reproach; disgrace. **3** An unjust classing or comparison with that which is of less worth; degradation.

dis·pa·rate (dis′pə·rit) *adj.* That cannot be compared; dissimilar; radically different; different in essential qualities. [<L *disparatus,* pp. of *disparare* <*dis-* apart + *parare* make ready; infl. in meaning by L *dispars, -partis* unequal] **—dis′pa·rate·ly** *adv.* **—dis′pa·rate·ness** *n.*

dis·pa·ra·tion (dis′pə·rā′shən) *n. Pathol.* An optical distortion, consisting of double images of objects within or beyond the focal point of the eyes.

dis·par·i·ty (dis·par′ə·tē) *n. pl.* **·ties** The state of being dissimilar; inequality; difference. [<MF *disparité* <L *dis-* apart + *paritas* equality]

dis·park (dis·pärk′) *v.t. Obs.* **1** To throw open, as a private park; convert to other uses. **2** To release from enclosure.

dis·part[1] (dis·pärt′) *v.t.* & *v.i.* To divide; separate into pieces or parts. [<Ital. *dispartire* <L *dis-* away + *partire* divide <*pars, partis* a part, share]

dis·part[2] (dis·pärt′) *n. Mil.* **1** The difference between the semidiameters of the base ring and the muzzle of a cannon. **2** A piece upon the top of a cannon's muzzle to raise the line of sight parallel with the axis of the bore; a muzzle sight: also **dis·part′-sight′.** [Origin uncertain]

dis·part·ment (dis·pärt′mənt) *n.* The act of disparting; also, a division; separation.

dis·pas·sion (dis·pash′ən) *n.* Freedom from passion or emotion; lack of bias.

dis·pas·sion·ate (dis·pash′ən·it) *adj.* Free from passion; unprejudiced. See synonyms under CALM, SOBER. **—dis·pas′sion·ate·ly** *adv.* **—dis·pas′sion·ate·ness** *n.*

dis·patch (dis·pach′) *v.t.* **1** To send off, especially on official business or for special purposes. **2** To transact with promptness; finish quickly. **3** To execute; kill summarily. *—v.i.* **4** *Obs.* To make haste. See synonyms under KILL. *—n.* **1** The act of dispatching; a forwarding to some destination: usually with the implication of promptness or celerity: the *dispatch* of a messenger. **2** A message sent by special means and with haste, as by telegraph; especially, a communication on public matters sent by one official to another. **3** Quick transaction, as of business; the prompt performance and completion of work; expedition; speed. **4** The act of killing; a putting to death. **5** An organi-

zation or conveyance for the speedy transmission of money, goods, or messages: I will send it by *dispatch*. **6** *Obs*. Dismissal; deliverance; riddance. Also, in diplomatic use, spelled *despatch*. [<Ital. *dispacciare*, ? ult. <LL *dis*- away, not + *pactare* fasten, fix] — **dis·patch'ful** *adj*.

dispatch boat A fast vessel for carrying government dispatches.

dis·patch·er (dis·pach'ər) *n*. **1** One who dispatches. **2** One who directs the movement of trains, trucks, etc., and maintains records of such movement: also spelled *despatcher*.

dis·pel (dis·pel') *v.t.* **·pelled, ·pel·ling** To scatter in various directions; break up and drive away; disperse. [<L *dispellere* <*dis*- away + *pellere* drive]

dis·pend (dis·pend') *v.t. Obs*. To spend; also, to spend lavishly; squander. [<OF *despendre* <L *dispendere*. See DISPENSE.]

dis·pen·sa·ble (dis·pen'sə·bəl) *adj*. **1** That can be dispensed with. **2** That can be distributed or administered to others. **3** That can be removed by or made the subject of dispensation; pardonable. — **dis·pen'sa·bil'i·ty, dis·pen'sa·ble·ness** *n*.

dis·pen·sa·ry (dis·pen'sər·ē) *n. pl.* **·ries** A place or establishment, often public, where medicines are compounded and dispensed gratis or at a nominal price.

dis·pen·sa·tion (dis'pən·sā'shən) *n*. **1** The act of dispensing; a dealing out; distribution. **2** That which is bestowed on or appointed to one from a higher power. **3** The divine arrangement and administration of the affairs of the world: the *dispensation* of Providence. **4** A specific plan: a special *dispensation* of nature. **5** Special exemption granted from the requirements of a law, rule, or obligation; specifically, in the Roman Catholic Church, exemption by express ecclesiastical authority from an obligation incurred at the free will of the individual. Compare INDULGENCE. **6** *Theol*. One of the several systems or bodies of law in which at different times God has revealed his mind and will to man, or the continued state of things resulting from the operation of one of these systems: the Mosaic *dispensation*; also, the period during which a particular revelation of God's mind and will has been directly operative on mankind: during the Christian *dispensation*. [<OF <L *dispensatio, -onis* <*dispensare*. See DISPENSE.] — **dis'pen·sa'tion·al** *adj*.

dis·pen·sa·tor (dis'pen·sā'tər) *n*. One who dispenses or distributes; a dispenser.

dis·pen·sa·to·ry (dis·pen'sə·tôr'ē, -tō'rē) *adj*. Of or pertaining to dispensing or dispensation: also **dis·pen'sa·tive**. — *n. pl.* **·ries** A book in which medicinal substances are described; a pharmacopoeia.

dis·pense (dis·pens') *v.* **·pensed, ·pens·ing** *v.t.* **1** To give or deal out in portions; distribute. **2** To compound and give out (medicines). **3** To administer, as laws. **4** To relieve or excuse; absolve. — *v.i.* **5** To grant exemption or dispensation. See synonyms under APPORTION. — **to dispense with** To waive the observance of; relinquish; forgo. [OF *despenser* <L *dispensare*, freq. of *dispendere* <*dis*- away + *pendere* weigh]

dis·pens·er (dis·pen'sər) *n*. One who dispenses, manages, or administers.

dis·peo·ple (dis·pē'pəl) *v.t.* **·pled, ·pling** To depopulate. — **dis·peo'ple·ment** *n*. — **dis·peo'·pler** *n*.

di·sper·mous (dī·spûr'məs) *adj. Bot*. Two-seeded. [<DI-² + Gk. *sperma* seed]

di·sper·my (dī·spûr'mē) *n. Biol*. The fecundation of one egg with two spermatozoa. — **di·sper'mic** *adj*.

dis·per·sal (dis·pûr'səl) *n*. The act or fact of scattering or dispersing; dispersion.

dis·perse (dis·pûrs') *v.* **·persed, ·pers·ing** *v.t.* **1** To cause to scatter and go off in various directions. **2** To dispel; dissipate: The sun *dispersed* the mists. **3** To spread abroad; diffuse. **4** To separate (light) into its component spectral colors. — *v.i.* **5** To scatter and go off in various directions; dissipate. See synonyms under SPREAD. [<MF *disperser* <L *dispersus*, pp. of *dispergere* <*dis*-away + *spargere* scatter] — **dis·pers'i·ble** *adj*. — **dis·per'sive** *adj*.

dis·persed (dis·pûrst') *adj*. **1** Scattered; dissipated. **2** Placed ·near together but in a random manner. — **dis·pers'ed·ly** (-id·lē) *adv*.

disperse phase *Chem*. In a colloid system, that constituent which is dispersed in · the medium: gold particles are the *disperse phase* of colloidal gold. See COLLOID. Also **dispersed phase**.

dis·pers·er (dis·pûr'sər) *n*. One who or that which disperses.

dis·per·sion (dis·pûr'zhən, -shən) *n*. **1** The act of dispersing; the state or result of being dispersed; also **dis·per'sal**. **2** *Mil*. The dispersed pattern of hits made by bombs dropped under the same conditions, or by bullets or shells shot from one gun with the same firing data. **3** *Physics* **a** The separation of light rays of different colors by the action of a prism or lens. **b** The process of sorting out emissions, as of electrons, in accordance with the values or magnitudes of selected properties, physical, chemical, electrical, etc. **4** *Chem*. The condition of the components making up a colloid system: distinguished from *solution*. **5** *Stat*. The arrangement of a series of values around the median or mean of a distribution.

dis·per·soid (dis·pûr'soid) *n. Chem*. A colloid system.

dis·pir·it (dis·pir'it) *v.t.* To render cheerless or hopeless; depress; dishearten. — **dis·pir'it·ed·ly** *adv*. — **dis·pir'it·ed·ness** *n*. — **dis·pir'it·ing·ly** *adv*.

dis·pir·it·ment (dis·pir'it·mənt) *n*. **1** The act of dispiriting, or the state of being dispirited; dejection. **2** That which dispirits, as a sorrow.

dis·pit·e·ous (dis·pit'ē·əs) *adj*. Remorseless; without pity.

dis·place (dis·plās') *v.t.* **·placed, ·plac·ing** **1** To remove or shift from the proper place. **2** To take the place of; supplant. **3** To remove from a position or office; discharge. **4** *Chem*. To release from combination: Zinc *displaces* the hydrogen of an acid. **5** *Obs*. To banish. [<OF *desplacer* <*des*- away (<L *dis*-) + *placer* place]

Synonyms: confuse, derange, disarrange, disturb, jumble, mislay, misplace, remove, unsettle. Objects are *displaced* when moved out of the place they have occupied; they are *misplaced* when they are put into a place where they should not be. One may know where to find what he has *misplaced*; what he has *mislaid* he cannot locate. *Antonyms*: adjust, array, assort, classify, dispose, group, order, place, sort.

dis·placed person (dis·plāst') Any inhabitant forced by military action or calamity to flee his country or leave his home. Abbr. *DP*

dis·place·ment (dis·plās'mənt) *n*. **1** The act of displacing, or the state of being displaced. **2** *Astron*. An apparent change of position, as of a star. **3** *Physics* **a** The weight of water displaced by a body floating in it, this weight being equal to the weight of the body. **b** The quantity of air displaced by an airplane, balloon, etc. **4** The relation between the position of a moving object at any time and its original position. **5** Electric displacement. **6** *Geol*. A fault. **7** *Psychoanal*. Substitution of a secondary, harmless, or unimportant element for a primary and significant one, as in a dream, for purposes of concealment.

displacement law *Physics* **1** The principle that an atom deprived of one of its electrons acquires the physicochemical properties of the element preceding it in the periodic table. See ELECTROMOTIVE SERIES. **2** The statement that radioactive emission of an alpha particle lowers the atomic number of the element by 2, while emission of a beta particle raises the atomic number by 1.

displacement ton See under TON.

dis·plant (dis·plant', -plänt') *v.t.* **1** To take (a plant) from the ground; uproot. **2** *Obs*. To dislodge; displace. [<OF *desplanter* <L *dis*- away + *plantare* plant] — **dis·plan·ta'·tion** *n*.

dis·play (dis·plā') *v.t.* **1** To show; make apparent to the eye or the mind. **2** To show off; exhibit ostentatiously. **3** To unfold; unfurl, as a flag or sail. **4** In printing, to give special prominence to, as by size, style, or spacing of type. See synonyms under FLAUNT. — *n*. **1** The act of spreading out, unfolding, exhibiting, or bringing to the view or to the mind. **2** Ostentatious show. **3** *Printing* A style of type calculated to attract attention. **4** The matter so displayed. See synonyms under OSTENTA-

TION, SPECTACLE. [<OF *despleier* <LL *displicare*. Doublet of DEPLOY.]

dis·please (dis·plēz') *v.* **·pleased, ·pleas·ing** *v.t.* To cause displeasure in or annoyance to; vex; offend. — *v.i.* To cause displeasure or annoyance. See synonyms under AFFRONT, PIQUE¹. [<OF *desplaisir, desplaire*, ult. <L *displicere* <*dis*- not + *placere* please] — **dis·pleas'ing** *adj*. — **dis·pleas'ing·ly** *adv*.

dis·pleas·ure (dis·plezh'ər) *n*. **1** The state of being displeased; dissatisfaction; vexation; indignant disapproval. **2** An annoyance; offense. See synonyms under ANGER, OFFENSE, PIQUE¹.

dis·plode (dis·plōd') *v.t.* & *v.i.* **·plod·ed, ·plod·ing** *Obs*. To explode. [<L *displodere* <*dis*-apart + *plaudere* clap, burst] — **dis·plo'sion** *n*.

dis·plume (dis·plōōm') *v.t.* **·plumed, ·plum·ing** *Obs*. To deplume.

dis·pone (dis·pōn') *v.t.* & *v.i.* **·poned, ·pon·ing** *Obs*. To arrange; dispose. [<L *disponere*. See DISPOSE.]

dis·port (dis·pôrt', -pōrt') *v.i.* To gambol; display oneself sportively. — *v.t.* To amuse or display (oneself). See synonyms under ENTERTAIN. — *n*. Diversion; pastime; sport. [<OF *desporter* <L *dis*- away + *portare* carry]

dis·pos·a·ble (dis·pō'zə·bəl) *adj*. Subject to disposal; free to be used as occasion may require.

dis·po·sal (dis·pō'zəl) *n*. **1** The act of disposing; arrangement; order; distribution. **2** A getting rid of, a transfer, as by gift or sale. **3** Power of control, outlay, management, or distribution.

dis·pose (dis·pōz') *v.* **·posed, ·pos·ing** *v.t.* **1** To put in order; arrange properly by sequence or interrelation. **2** To incline or influence the mind of; give a tendency to. **3** To put or set in a particular place or location. **4** *Archaic* To prepare; make ready. — *v.i.* **5** To arrange or settle something. — **to dispose of 1** To settle; finish. **2** To throw away. **3** To get rid of by selling or giving. — *n. Obs*. **1** Disposal. **2** Order; arrangement. **3** Disposition; deportment. [<OF *disposer* <*dis*- apart (<L *dis*-) + *poser*. See POSE.] — **dis·posed'** *adj*.

dis·pos·er (dis·pō'zər) *n*. One who disposes or orders.

dis·po·si·tion (dis'pə·zish'ən) *n*. **1** The act of disposing; arrangement, as of troops. **2** Distribution; state or manner of disposal; final settlement. **3** Control; power: usually with *at*: at his *disposition*. **4** Natural tendency; temper or temperament; characteristic spirit; bent; propensity. **5** Natural tendency of animate or inanimate things. **6** *Archit*. Arrangement, as of plan, perspective, etc.: distinguished from *distribution*. See synonyms under APPETITE, CHARACTER, INCLINATION, MIND, WILL¹. [<F <L *dispositio, -onis* <*dis*- away + *ponere* place] — **dis·pos·i·tive** (dis·poz'ə·tiv) *adj*.

dis·pos·sess (dis'pə·zes') *v.t.* To deprive (someone) of possession, as of a house or land; eject; oust. [<OF *despossesser* <*des*- away (<L *dis*-) + *possesser* POSSESS] — **dis'pos·ses'sion** (-zesh'ən) *n*. — **dis'pos·ses'sor** *n*.

dis·pos·ses·so·ry (dis'pə·zes'ər·ē) *adj*. Referring to or partaking of dispossession.

dis·po·sure (dis·pō'zhər) *n. Obs*. **1** Disposal; direction. **2** Disposition; arrangement. **3** Nature; temperament.

dis·praise (dis·prāz') *v.t.* **·praised, ·prais·ing** To speak of with disapproval or censure; disparage. — *n*. The expression of unfavorable opinion; disparagement; censure. [<OF *despreisier* <*dis*- not (<L *dis*-) + *preisier* PRAISE] — **dis·prais'er** *n*. — **dis·prais'ing·ly** *adv*.

dis·pread (dis·pred') *v.t.* & *v.i.* **·pread, ·pread·ing** To spread out or abroad; diffuse; expand: also spelled *disspread*.

dis·prize (dis·prīz') *v.t.* **·prized, ·priz·ing** *Obs*. To think of little value; hold in low esteem. [OF *despriser*, var. of *despreisier*. See DESPRAISE.] — **dis·priz'ing·ly** *adv*.

dis·proof (dis·prōōf') *n*. Refutation; confutation.

dis·prop·er·ty (dis·prop'ər·tē) *v.t. Obs*. To dispossess.

dis·pro·por·tion (dis'prə·pôr'shən, -pōr'-) *n*. Want of due relative proportion; lack of symmetry; also, inadequacy. — *v.t.* To make of unsuitable size or proportions. [<F]

dis·pro·por·tion·a·ble (dis'prə·pôr'shən·ə·bəl, -pōr'-) *adj*. Unsuitable; inadequate.

dis·pro·por·tion·ate (dis'prə·pôr'shən·it, -pōr'-) *adj*. Out of proportion with regard to size,

form, or value; disproportioned. Also **dis′·pro·por′tion·al.** **—dis′pro·por′tion·ate·ly, dis′·pro·por′tion·al·ly** *adv.* **—dis′pro·por′tion·ate·ness** *n.*
dis·prove (dis·prōōv′) *v.t.* **·proved, ·prov·ing** To prove (a statement, claim, etc.) to be false or erroneous; refute. [<OF *desprouver* < *des-* not (<L *dis-*) + *prouver* prove] **—dis·prov′·a·ble** *adj.* **—dis·prov′al** *n.*
dis·put·a·ble (dis·pyōō′tə·bəl, dis′pyŏŏ·tə·bəl) *adj.* That can be disputed; controvertible; doubtful. **—dis·put′a·bil′i·ty** *n.* **—dis·put′a·bly** *adv.*
dis·pu·tant (dis′pyŏŏ·tənt, dis·pyōō′tənt) *adj.* Engaged in controversy; disputing. —*n.* One who disputes. [<L *disputans, -antis,* ppr. of *disputare.* See DISPUTE.]
dis·pu·ta·tion (dis′pyŏŏ·tā′shən) *n.* **1** The act of disputing; controversy; discussion; argumentation. **2** A rhetorical or logical exercise; a scholastic debate. See synonyms under ALTERCATION. [<L *disputatio, -onis* < *disputare.* See DISPUTE.]
dis·pu·ta·tious (dis′pyŏŏ·tā′shəs) *adj.* Characterized by or pertaining to dispute. **—dis′·pu·ta′tious·ly** *adv.* **—dis′pu·ta′tious·ness** *n.*
dis·put·a·tive (dis·pyōō′tə·tiv) *adj.* Disputatious. **—dis·put′a·tive·ly** *adv.*
dis·pute (dis·pyōōt′) *v.* **·put·ed, ·put·ing** *v.t.* **1** To argue about; discuss. **2** To question the validity, genuineness, etc., of; controvert. **3** To strive for; contest for, as a prize. **4** To resist; oppose. —*v.i.* **5** To argue. **6** To quarrel; wrangle. —*n.* **1** A controversial discussion; a verbal contest. **2** An altercation; wrangle; quarrel. See synonyms under ALTERCATION, FEUD, QUARREL. [<OF *desputer* <L *disputare* < *dis-* away + *putare* think] **—dis·put′er** *n.*
Synonyms (verb): antagonize, argue, battle, combat, contend, contest, controvert, debate, discuss, oppose, quarrel, question, reason, wrangle. Persons may *contend* either from mere ill will or self-interest, or from the highest motives; "that ye should earnestly *contend* for the faith which was once delivered to the saints," *Jude* 3. To *controvert* is to *argue* wholly on the negative side, urging considerations against an opinion, proposition, or the like. One may *argue* and *discuss* without an opponent. We may *question* or *discuss* a proposition without reference to any one's advocacy of it, but to *contend, debate,* or *dispute* implies an opponent. A *dispute* may be personal, fractious, and petty; a *debate* is formal and orderly; if otherwise, it becomes a mere *wrangle.* Compare ARGUE, CONTEND, QUESTION, REASON.
dis·qual·i·fi·ca·tion (dis·kwol′ə·fə·kā′shən) *n.* **1** The act of debarring a person from participation in a contest or enterprise, or from sharing in the prizes or rewards, due to an infraction of rules or other irregularity. **2** The state of being disqualified; lack of requisite qualities or training. **3** That which disqualifies.
dis·qual·i·fy (dis·kwol′ə·fī) *v.t.* **·fied, ·fy·ing** **1** To render unqualified or unfit; incapacitate; disable. **2** To pronounce unqualified or ineligible; especially, in sports, to deprive (a competitor) of a prize for rule infractions; also, to debar from further competition for such infractions.
dis·qui·et (dis·kwī′ət) *n.* An unsettled or disturbed condition; lack of quiet; restlessness; uneasiness: also **dis·qui′et·ness, dis·qui′e·tude** (-tōōd, -tyōōd). See synonyms under ALARM, ANXIETY, FEAR. —*v.t.* To make anxious or uneasy; disturb; alarm. —*adj. Rare* Restless; uneasy; impatient. **—dis·qui′et·ly** *adv.*
dis·qui·et·ing (dis·kwī′ət·ing) *adj.* Causing disquiet; making uneasy.
dis·qui·si·tion (dis′kwi·zish′ən) *n.* A systematic treatise or discourse; dissertation. [<L *disquisitio, -onis* an investigation < *dis-* from + *quaerere* seek, ask]
dis·quis·i·tor (dis·kwiz′ə·tər) *n.* One who makes disquisitions: an investigator.
Dis·rae·li (diz·rā′lē), **Benjamin,** 1804–81, Earl of Beaconsfield, English statesman and novelist; prime minister 1867, 1874–80. **—Isaac,** 1766–1848, English writer; father of the preceding.
dis·rate (dis·rāt′) *v.t.* **·rat·ed, ·rat·ing** To lower in rating or rank, as a petty officer; degrade.
dis·re·gard (dis′ri·gärd′) *v.t.* **1** To pay no attention to; ignore. **2** To treat as undeserving of consideration, respect, or attention; slight. —*n.* Want of regard; neglect; slight. See synonyms under NEGLECT, SLIGHT. **—dis′re·gard′er** *n.* **—dis′re·gard′ful** *adj.*
dis·rel·ish (dis·rel′ish) *v.t.* To dislike; have a distaste for. —*n.* **1** A feeling of slight repugnance; distaste or dislike. **2** Lack of palatableness; the quality of being displeasing or distasteful.
dis·re·mem·ber (dis′ri·mem′bər) *v.t. U.S. Dial.* To be unable to recall; forget.
dis·re·pair (dis′ri·pâr′) *n.* The state of being out of repair.
dis·rep·u·ta·ble (dis·rep′yə·tə·bəl) *adj.* Being in or causing ill repute; disgraceful. See synonyms under INFAMOUS. **—dis·rep′u·ta·ble·ness** *n.* **—dis·rep′u·ta·bly** *adv.*
dis·re·pute (dis′ri·pyōōt′) *n.* Lack or loss of reputation; ill repute. Also *Obs.* **dis·rep′u·ta′·tion.**
dis·re·spect (dis′ri·spekt′) *n.* Lack of respect; discourtesy. —*v.t.* To treat or regard with lack of respect.
dis·re·spect·a·ble (dis′ri·spek′tə·bəl) *adj.* Wanting respectability; disreputable. **—dis′re·spect′a·bil′i·ty** *n.*
dis·re·spect·ful (dis′ri·spekt′fəl) *adj.* Wanting in respect; discourteous. **—dis′re·spect′ful·ly** *adv.* **—dis′re·spect′ful·ness** *n.*
dis·robe (dis·rōb′) *v.t.* & *v.i.* **·robed, ·rob·ing** To undress. **—dis·robe′ment** *n.*
dis·root (dis·rōōt′, -rŏŏt′) *v.t.* **1** To tear up by the roots. **2** To tear from the foundation.
dis·rupt (dis·rupt′) *v.t.* & *v.i.* To burst or break asunder. —*adj. Obs.* Burst asunder; rent. [<L *disruptus,* pp. of *disrumpere* < *dis-* apart + *rumpere* burst] **—dis·rupt′er, dis·rup′tor** *n.*
dis·rup·tion (dis·rup′shən) *n.* **1** The act of bursting or tearing asunder. **2** The state of being so torn. See synonyms under RUPTURE.
dis·rup·tive (dis·rup′tiv) *adj.* Producing, resulting from, or attending disruption; rending; bursting. **—dis·rup′tive·ly** *adv.*
disruptive discharge *Electr.* A strong discharge in an insulating medium caused by breakdown under electrostatic stress.
diss (dis) *n.* The fibrous stems of a reedlike Mediterranean plant (*Ampelodesma mauritanicus*): used for making hats, paper, cordage, etc. [<Arabic *dīs*]
dis·sat·is·fac·tion (dis′sat·is·fak′shən) *n.* A dissatisfied state or feeling; discontent.
dis·sat·is·fac·to·ry (dis′sat·is·fak′tər·ē) *adj.* Giving dissatisfaction or discontent; unsatisfactory. **—dis′sat·is·fac′to·ri·ness** *n.*
dis·sat·is·fy (dis·sat′is·fī) *v.t.* **·fied, ·fy·ing** To fail to satisfy; disappoint; displease.
dis·seat (dis·sēt′) *v.t.* To unseat.
dis·sect (di·sekt′) *v.t.* **1** To cut apart or divide, as an animal body or a plant, in order to examine the structure; anatomize. **2** To analyze critically; examine. See synonyms under CUT. [<L *dissectus,* pp. of *dissecare* < *dis-* apart + *secare* cut]
dis·sect·ed (di·sek′tid) *adj.* **1** Cut in pieces; separated at the joints. **2** *Geol.* Cut into ridges, as a plateau. **3** *Bot.* Deeply cut into lobes or segments, as a leaf.
dis·sec·tion (di·sek′shən) *n.* **1** The act of dissecting. **2** A dissected object; an anatomical preparation. **3** A critical analysis.
dis·sec·tor (di·sek′tər) *n.* **1** One who dissects. **2** An instrument used in dissecting.
dis·seize (dis·sēz′) *v.t.* **–seized, –seiz·ing** *Law* To oust from the possession of an estate in freehold, usually unlawfully. Also **dis–seise′.** [<AF *disseisir,* OF *dessaisir* < *des-* away (<L *dis-*) + *saisir* SEIZE] **—dis–sei′zor** (-zər, -zôr), **dis–sei′sor** *n.*
dis–sei·zee (dis′sē·zē′, dis·sē′zē′) *n.* One who is dis–seized. Also **dis′–seis·ee′.**
dis–sei·zin (dis·sē′zin) *n. Law* The unlawful entry upon the freehold of another and wrongful ouster of him from possession. Also **dis–sei′sin, dis–seiz·ure** (dis·sē′zhər). [<AF *disseisine* < *disseisir.* See DIS–SEIZE.]
dis·sem·blance (di·sem′bləns) *n. Obs.* **1** Dissimilarity. **2** Dissimulation.
dis·sem·ble (di·sem′bəl) *v.* **·bled, ·bling** *v.t.* **1** To conceal or disguise the true nature of (intentions, feelings, etc.) so as to deceive; dissimulate. **2** To pretend not to notice; ignore. **3** *Obs.* To feign. —*v.i.* **4** To conceal one's true nature, intentions, etc.; act hypocritically. See synonyms under HIDE[1], MASK[1]. [Earlier *dissimule* <OF *dissimuler* <L *dissimulare* < *dis-* not, away + *similis* alike; infl. in form by RESEMBLE] **—dis·sem′·bler** *n.* **—dis·sem′bling·ly** *adv.*
dis·sem·i·nate (di·sem′ə·nāt) *v.t.* **·nat·ed, ·nat·ing** To spread about; scatter, as seed in sowing; promulgate. See synonyms under SPREAD. [<L *disseminatus,* pp. of *disseminare* < *dis-* away + *seminare* sow < *semen* seed] **—dis·sem′i·na′tion** *n.* **—dis·sem′i·na′tive** *adj.* **—dis·sem′i·na′tor** *n.*
dis·sem·i·nule (di·sem′ə·nyōōl) *n. Bot.* A seed fruit modified for migration. [<DISSEMIN(ATE) + -ULE]
dis·sen·sion (di·sen′shən) *n.* Angry or violent difference of opinion; discord; strife. See synonyms under ALTERCATION, QUARREL.
dis·sent (di·sent′) *v.i.* **1** To differ in thought or opinion; disagree; to withhold approval or consent. **2** To refuse adherence to an established church. —*n.* **1** The act or state of dissenting; disagreement. **2** Refusal to conform to an established church; nonconformity. [<L *dissentire* < *dis-* apart + *sentire* think, feel]
dis·sent·er (di·sen′tər) *n.* **1** One who dissents or disagrees; one who declares his disapproval or disagreement. **2** *Often cap.* A Protestant who refuses assent to the doctrines, or compliance with the usages, of an established or state church, especially the Church of England: opposed to *conformist.* See synonyms under HERETIC.
dis·sen·tient (di·sen′shənt) *adj.* Dissenting; expressing disagreement. —*n.* A dissenter. [<L *dissentiens, -entis,* ppr. of *dissentire.* See DISSENT.]
dis·sent·ing (di·sen′ting) *adj.* Disagreeing; avowing or expressing disagreement or dissent. **—dis·sent′ing·ly** *adv.*
dis·sen·tious (di·sen′shəs) *adj. Rare* Contentious; quarrelsome. **—dis·sen′tious·ly** *adv.*
dis·sep·i·ment (di·sep′ə·mənt) *n.* **1** *Bot.* A partition, as one of those that divide a compound pericarp into two or more cells. **2** *Zool.* A horizontal plate between the vertical septa in corals. [<L *dissaepimentum* < *dis-* apart + *saepire* fence in < *saepes* a fence, a hedge]
dis·ser·tate (dis′ər·tāt) *v.i.* **·tat·ed, ·tat·ing** *Obs.* To discourse or write in a learned or formal manner. Also *Obs.* **dis·sert′.** [<L *dissertatus,* pp. of *dissertare,* freq. of *dissere* < *dis-* apart + *serere* join, connect] **—dis′ser·ta′tive** *adj.* **—dis′ser·ta′tor** *n.*
dis·ser·ta·tion (dis′ər·tā′shən) *n.* An extended and argumentative treatise or discourse; disquisition; thesis. See synonyms under SPEECH.
dis·serve (dis·sûrv′) *v.t.* **·served, ·serv·ing** To serve or to treat badly; do an ill turn to.
dis·serv·ice (dis·sûr′vis) *n.* Ill service; an ill turn.
dis·serv·ice·a·ble (dis·sûr′vis·ə·bəl) *adj.* Disadvantageous; detrimental; unserviceable.
dis·sev·er (di·sev′ər) *v.t.* **1** To divide; separate. **2** To separate into parts. —*v.i.* **3** To separate; part. [<AF *deseverer,* OF *dessevrer* <L *disseparare* < *dis-* apart + *separare* SEPARATE] **—dis·sev′er·ance, dis·sev′er·ment** *n.*
dis·si·dence (dis′ə·dəns) *n.* Disagreement; dissent.
dis·si·dent (dis′ə·dənt) *adj.* Dissenting; differing. —*n.* A dissenter. [<L *dissidens, -entis,* ppr. of *dissidere* < *dis-* apart + *sedere* sit]
dis·sil·i·ent (di·sil′ē·ənt) *adj.* **1** Springing or flying open. **2** *Bot.* Bursting asunder, as the dry pod of the jewelweed. [<L *dissiliens, -entis,* ppr. of *dissilire* < *dis-* apart + *salire* leap] **—dis·sil′i·ence** or **dis·sil′i·en·cy** *n.*
dis·sim·i·lar (di·sim′ə·lər) *adj.* Unlike, different: often with *to.* See synonyms under CONTRARY, HETEROGENEOUS. **—dis·sim′i·lar·ly** *adv.*
dis·sim·i·lar·i·ty (di·sim′ə·lar′ə·tē) *n. pl.* **·ties** Unlikeness; difference. See synonyms under DIFFERENCE.
dis·sim·i·late (di·sim′ə·lāt) *v.t.* & *v.i.* **·lat·ed, ·lat·ing** **1** To make or become unlike. **2**

Phonet. To undergo or cause to undergo dissimilation. [<DIS-[1] + L *similis* alike]

dis·sim·i·la·tion (di·sim′ə·lā′shən) *n.* **1** The act or process of making or becoming dissimilar. **2** *Phonet.* The process whereby one of two or more identical or similar sounds in a word is changed or omitted, as in the pronunciation (lī′ber′ē) for *library,* or the English form *turtle* from Latin *turtur.*

dis·si·mil·i·tude (dis′si·mil′ə·tōōd, -tyōōd) *n.* Lack of resemblance; unlikeness. [<L *dissimilitudo* <*dissimilis* <*dis-* not + *similis* alike]

dis·sim·u·late (di·sim′yə·lāt) *v.t.* & *v.i.* **·lat·ed, ·lat·ing** To conceal (intentions, feelings, etc.) by pretense; dissemble. [<L *dissimulatus,* pp. of *dissimulare.* See DISSEMBLE.] **—dis·sim′u·la′tive** *adj.* **—dis·sim′u·la′tor** *n.*

dis·sim·u·la·tion (di·sim′yə·lā′shən) *n.* False pretense; hypocrisy. See synonyms under DECEPTION, HYPOCRISY, PRETENSE.

dis·si·pate (dis′ə·pāt) *v.* **·pat·ed, ·pat·ing** *v.t.* **1** To disperse or drive away; dispel. **2** To disintegrate; destroy or dissolve utterly. **3** To squander; spend lavishly and wastefully. —*v.i.* **4** To become dispersed; scatter. **5** To engage in excessive or dissolute pleasures. See synonyms under SQUANDER. [<L *dissipatus,* pp. of *dissipare* <*dis-* away + *supare* throw]

dis·si·pat·ed (dis′ə·pā′tid) *adj.* **1** Wasted; scattered. **2** Pursuing pleasure to excess; dissolute. **—dis′si·pat′ed·ly** *adv.* **—dis′si·pat′ed·ness** *n.*

dis·si·pa·tion (dis′ə·pā′shən) *n.* **1** The act of dissipating or state of being dissipated. **2** Excessive indulgence, especially in vicious pleasures. **3** Distraction, as of the mind, or anything that distracts. See synonyms under EXCESS.

dis·si·pa·tive (dis′ə·pā′tiv) *adj.* **1** Having a tendency to dissipate or disperse, or pertaining to such a tendency. **2** Of or pertaining to dissipation. **3** Tending to a dissipated life.

dis·so·cia·ble (di·sō′shə·bəl, -shē·ə-) *adj.* **1** Not well assorted or associated; incongruous; unsociable. **2** Capable of being separated or dissociated. **3** Unsociable. **—dis·so′cia·bil′i·ty, dis·so′cia·ble·ness** *n.* **—dis·so′cia·bly** *adv.*

dis·so·cial (di·sō′shəl) *adj.* Unsocial; unfriendly.

dis·so·cial·ize (di·sō′shəl·īz) *v.t.* **·ized, ·iz·ing** To make dissocial.

dis·so·ci·ate (di·sō′shē·āt) *v.* **·at·ed, ·at·ing** *v.t.* **1** To break the association of; disconnect; separate. **2** To regard as separate in concept or nature. **3** *Chem.* To resolve by dissociation. —*v.i.* **4** To break an association. **5** *Chem.* To undergo dissociation. [<L *dissociatus,* pp. of *dissociare* <*dis-* apart + *sociare* join together <*socius* a companion] **—dis·so′ci·a′tive** *adj.*

dis·so·ci·a·tion (di·sō′sē·ā′shən, -shē·ā′-) *n.* **1** The act of dissociating; state of separation. **2** *Chem.* **a** The resolution of a compound into simpler constituents by a change in physical state, as by heat or pressure, with recombination when the original conditions are restored. **b** Electrolytic dissolution. **3** *Psychiatry* A mental disorder in which one or several groups of ideas become split off from the main body of the personality and are not accessible to conscious control: contrasted with *association.*

dis·sol·u·ble (di·sol′yə·bəl) *adj.* **1** Separable into parts. **2** Capable of being dissolved or decomposed. [<L *dissolubilis* <*dissolvere.* See DISSOLVE.] **—dis′sol·u·bil′i·ty, dis·sol′u·ble·ness** *n.*

dis·so·lute (dis′ə·lōōt) *adj.* Abandoned; profligate. See synonyms under IMMORAL, IRREGULAR. [<L *dissolutus,* pp. of *dissolvere.* See DISSOLVE.] **—dis′so·lute·ly** *adv.* **—dis′so·lute·ness** *n.*

dis·so·lu·tion (dis′ə·lōō′shən) *n.* **1** The act or state of dissolving; disintegration. **2** *Chem.* Decomposition; separation into elements or components. **3** Liquefaction. **4** Separation; breaking up, as of an assembly or corporation, or of a partnership, in accordance with the articles of co–partnership, or by the death or incompetence of a partner, or by the decree of a court. **5** Death, the separation of soul and body.

dis·so·lu·tive (dis′ə·lōō′tiv) *adj.* **1** Dissolving. **2** Pertaining to or characterized by physical or mental dissolution.

dis·solve (di·zolv′) *v.* **·solved, ·solv·ing** *v.t.* **1** To change (a substance) from a solid to a fluid condition. **2** To cause to pass into or combine with a solution; melt; liquefy. **3** To end the existence, functions, or meetings of: to *dissolve* Parliament. **4** To end or conclude (a relationship or association): to *dissolve* a partnership or a marriage. **5** *Law* To set aside; annul, as an injunction. **6** To disunite. —*v.i.* **7** To pass into or as into a liquid state; melt; become fluid. **8** To come to an end; disperse, as a meeting. **9** To fade away; vanish, as an image. **10** In motion pictures, to change gradually from one picture or scene to another, the two overlapping in the process. See synonyms under MELT. —*n.* In motion pictures and television, the slow emergence of one scene out of another, caused by the lapping of a fade–in over a fade–out; a lap–dissolve. [<L *dissolvere* <*dis-* apart + *solvere* loosen] **—dis·solv′a·ble** *adj.* **—dis·sol′vent** *adj.* & *n.*

dis·solv·er (di·zol′vər) *n.* One who or that which dissolves; specifically, a device for producing a dissolving view.

dissolving view A series of magic–lantern slides, each of which appears to fade gradually into the next when successively projected on a screen.

dis·so·nance (dis′ə·nəns) *n.* **1** A discordant mingling of sounds; discord. **2** *Music* A combination of tones regarded as displeasing and requiring resolution. **3** Harsh disagreement; incongruity; discord. Also **dis′so·nan·cy.**

dis·so·nant (dis′ə·nənt) *adj.* **1** Harsh in sound; inharmonious. **2** Naturally hostile; incongruous. **3** *Music* Having the quality of dissonance. [<L *dissonans, -antis,* ppr. of *dissonare* <*dis-* away + *sonare* sound] **—dis′so·nant·ly** *adv.*

dis·spread (dis·pred′) See DISPREAD.

dis·suade (di·swād′) *v.t.* **·suad·ed, ·suad·ing** **1** To change or alter the plans of (a person) by persuasion or advice: with *from.* **2** *Obs.* To advise against (a course of action). See synonyms under ADMONISH. [<L *dissuadere* <*dis-* away + *suadere* persuade] **—dis·suad′er** *n.*

dis·sua·sion (di·swā′zhən) *n.* **1** The act of dissuading. **2** A dissuasive. See synonyms under COUNSEL. [<L *dissuasio, -onis* <*dissuadere.* See DISSUADE.]

dis·sua·sive (di·swā′siv) *adj.* Tending or intended to dissuade. —*n.* A dissuading argument, fact, or consideration. **—dis·sua′sive·ly** *adv.* **—dis·sua′sive·ness** *n.*

dis·syl·lab·i·fy (dis′i·lab′ə·fī, dis′si-) *v.t.* **·fied, ·fy·ing** To make dissyllabic: also spelled *disyllabify.* Also **dis·syl·la·bize** (di·sil′ə·bīz, dis·sil′-).

dis·syl·la·ble (di·sil′ə·bəl, dis′sil′ə·bəl) *n.* A word of two syllables: also spelled *disyllable.* [<F <L *disyllabus* <Gk. *disyllabos* <*dis-* twofold + *syllabos* SYLLABLE] **—dis′syl·lab′ic** *adj.* **—dis′syl·lab′i·fi·ca′tion** *n.*

dis·sym·me·try (dis·sim′ə·trē) *n.* Lack of symmetry. **—dis′sym·met′ric** or **·ri·cal** *adj.* **—dis′sym·met′ri·cal·ly** *adv.*

dis·taff (dis′taf, -täf) *n.* *pl.* **dis·taffs** or *Rare* **dis·taves** (dis′tāvz) **1** A rotating vertical staff that holds the bunch of flax or wool for use in spinning by hand. **2** Figuratively, woman, as the holder of a distaff; also, woman's work or domain. [OE *distæf* <*dis* bundle of flax + *stæf* staff]

distaff side **1** The maternal branch of a family. **2** Women collectively. Compare SPINDLE SIDE, SPEAR SIDE.

dis·tain (dis·tān′) *v.t. Archaic* **1** To stain; dye. **2** To sully, disgrace. [<OF *desteindre* <*des-* completely (<L *dis-*) + *teindre* <L *tingere* stain, dye]

dis·tal (dis′təl) *adj. Biol.* Relatively remote from the center of the body or the point of attachment; peripheral: opposed to *proximal.* [<DIST(ANT) + -AL[1]] **—dis′tal·ly** *adv.*

dis·tance (dis′təns) *n.* **1** Length of separation in space, or, by extension, in time. **2** The state of being distant; separation; remoteness; a remote point. **3** Reserve; haughtiness; coldness. **4** Separation in rank, relationship, or succession. **5** In art, the part of a picture that represents distant objects. **6** *Music* The interval between two notes. **7** In horse racing, an interval measured back from the winning post to a point on the course marked by a flag or post, called the **distance post.** To be allowed to run in succeeding heats of the race, a horse must reach the distance post before the winning horse reaches the finish line. —*v.t.* **·tanced, ·tanc·ing** **1** To leave behind, as in a race; outstrip; excel. **2** To separate by a space. **3** To cause to appear distant.

dis·tant (dis′tənt) *adj.* **1** Separated in space or time; far apart; not closely related in qualities or in position; far away; remote. **2** Reserved or unapproachable; formal. **3** Indistinct; faint. **4** Not obvious or plain; indirect. See synonyms under ALIEN, HAUGHTY. [<F <L *distans, -antis,* ppr. of *distare* <*dis-* apart + *stare* stand] **—dis′tant·ly** *adv.*

dis·taste (dis·tāst′) *n.* **1** Aversion to food or drink; disrelish. **2** Alienation; disapproval; dislike. See synonyms under ANTIPATHY. —*v.t.* *Rare* **1** To dislike. **2** To displease; cause the dislike of.

dis·taste·ful (dis·tāst′fəl) *adj.* **1** Causing distaste; disagreeable. **2** Denoting distaste: a *distasteful* glance. **—dis·taste′ful·ly** *adv.* **—dis·taste′ful·ness** *n.*

dis·tel·fink (dis′təl·fingk) *n.* A highly stylized bird design, used on Pennsylvania Dutch furniture, fabrics, etc. Also **dis′tle·fink.** [<G, a goldfinch]

dis·tem·per[1] (dis·tem′pər) *n.* **1** Any of several infectious diseases of animals, especially a catarrhal affection of puppies associated with a filtrable virus. **2** An improper or disordered temper; ill humor. **3** Political or civil disturbance; riot; disorder. [<*v.*] —*v.t.* **1** To disturb or derange the faculties or functions of; disorder. **2** To ruffle; disturb. [<Med. L *distemperare* <*dis-* away + *temperare* regulate, mix]

dis·tem·per[2] (dis·tem′pər) *n.* **1** A pigment mixed with a vehicle (as yolk of eggs or glue) soluble in water, used chiefly for mural decoration and scene painting. **2** The art or process of painting with such materials, or a painting executed in them. —*v.t.* **1** To mix, as colors, for distemper painting. **2** To color or paint with distemper. —*adj.* Of or pertaining to internal decoration done with distemper. [<OF *destemprer* <Med. L *distemperare* <*dis-* apart + *temperare* mix, mingle, soak]

dis·tem·per·a·ture (dis·tem′pər·ə·chər) *n.* **1** Disorder; sickness. **2** Disarrangement; perturbation.

dis·tend (dis·tend′) *v.t.* & *v.i.* To expand; swell; dilate, as from or by pressure from within. [<L *distendere* <*dis-* apart + *tendere* stretch]

dis·ten·si·ble (dis·ten′sə·bəl) *adj.* Capable of being distended. **—dis·ten′si·bil′i·ty** *n.*

dis·tent (dis·tent′) *adj. Obs.* Distended.

dis·ten·tion (dis·ten′shən) *n.* **1** The act of distending. **2** The state of being distended. Also **dis·ten′sion.** [<L *distentio, -onis* <*distendere.* See DISTEND.]

dis·tich (dis′tik) *n.* In prosody, a couplet; a two–line stanza considered as a unit. [<L *distichon* <Gk., neut. sing. of *distichos* <*di-* two + *stichos* row, line]

dis·ti·chous (dis′ti·kəs) *adj. Bot.* Disposed in two longitudinal rows on opposite sides of a common axis, as leaves. [<L *distichus* <Gk. *distichos.* See DISTICH.] **—dis′ti·chous·ly** *adv.*

dis·til (di·stil′) *v.* **·tilled, ·til·ling** *v.t.* **1** To subject to or as to distillation, so as to purify, concentrate, or refine. **2** To extract volatile substances from by distillation: to *distil* corn. **3** To extract or produce by distillation: to *distil* whisky. **4** To give forth or send down in drops: The clouds *distil* rain. —*v.i.* **5** To undergo distillation. **6** To exude in drops; trickle; drip. Also **dis·till′.** [<L *distillare,* var. of *destillare* <*de-* down + *stillare* drop, trickle] **—dis·til′la·ble** *adj.*

dis·til·late (dis′tə·lit, -lāt) *n.* The condensed product separated by distillation. [<L *distillatus,* pp. of *distillare.* See DISTILL.]

dis·til·la·tion (dis′tə·lā′shən) *n.* **1** The act of distilling; separation of the more volatile parts of a substance from those less volatile by vaporizing and subsequently condensing, as by heating in a retort or still and cooling in a retort or worm. **2** The purification or rectification of a substance by this process. **3** The substance separated by distilling; a distillate. **4** The essential or abstract quality of anything.

dis·til·ler (dis·til′ər) *n.* **1** One who distils; a maker and seller of distilled liquors. **2** A condenser used in distilling.

dis·til·ler·y (di·stil′ər·ē) *n.* *pl.* **·ler·ies** An establishment for distilling, especially for producing alcoholic liquors by distillation.

dis·til·ment (di·stil′mənt) *n.* Distillation. Also **dis·till′ment.**

dis·tinct (dis·tingkt′) *adj.* **1** Clear to the senses or mind; plain; unmistakable. **2** Clearly standing apart, as in space or thought, from other objects; evidently not identical; observably or decidedly different. **3** Standing apart by itself; disjoined; unconnected. **4** Using or marked by clear vision and understanding; not obscure nor confused: a man of *distinct* ideas. **5** *Poetic* Adorned; variegated. See synonyms under CLEAR, EVIDENT, MANIFEST, PARTICULAR, PLAIN[1]. [<L *distinctus,* pp. of *distinguere.* See DISTINGUISH.] **—dis·tinct′ly** *adv.* **—dis·tinct′ness** *n.*

dis·tinc·tion (dis·tingk′shən) *n.* **1** A distinguishing mark or quality; a characteristic difference; also, the relation of difference between objects having distinguishing marks or qualities. **2** The act of distinguishing; discrimination. **3** Heed or regard to differences, as of rank or character. **4** A mark of honor; superiority; honorable position. See synonyms under CHARACTERISTIC, DIFFERENCE, FAME.

dis·tinc·tive (dis·tingk′tiv) *adj.* **1** Characteristic; distinguishing. See synonyms under PARTICULAR. **2** *Ling.* Relevant. **—dis·tinc′·tive·ly** *adv.* **—dis·tinc′tive·ness** *n.*

dis·tin·gué (dis′tang·gā′, *Fr.* dēs·taṅ·gā′) *adj.* Distinguished; having an air of distinction [< F, pp. of *distinguer.* See DISTINGUISH.] **—dis′·tin·guée′** *adj. fem.*

dis·tin·guish (di·sting′gwish) *v.t.* **1** To mark as different; indicate or constitute the differences of or between. **2** To recognize as separate or distinct; discriminate. **3** To divide into classes or categories classify. **4** To bring fame, celebrity, or credit upon. **5** To apperceive by one of the physical senses. *—v.i.* **6** To make or discern differences; discriminate: often with *among* or *between.* See synonyms under DISCERN, KNOW. [<F *distinguer* (<L *distinguere* separate) + -ISH[2]] **—dis·tin′·guish·a·ble** *adj.* **—dis·tin′guish·a·bly** *adv.* **—dis·tin′·guish·er** *n.*

dis·tin·guished (di·sting′gwisht) *adj.* Conspicuous; eminent. See synonyms under EMINENT, ILLUSTRIOUS.

Distinguished Flying Cross *U.S.* A military decoration in the form of a bronze cross on which is superimposed a four-bladed propeller: awarded to members of the Air Force for exceptional heroism while participating in an aerial flight. Abbr. *D.F.C.*

Distinguished Service Cross *U.S.* A decoration in the form of a bronze cross with an eagle on the center and "For Valor" on a scroll below: awarded to members of the armed forces who display extraordinary heroism in connection with military operations against an armed enemy. Abbr. *D.S.C.*

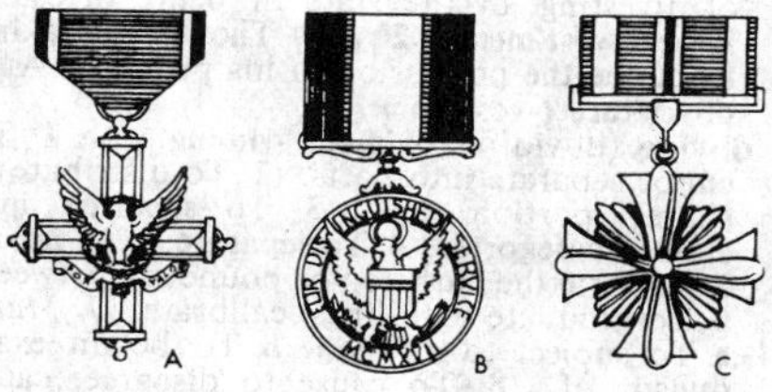

A Distinguished Service Cross — B Distinguished Service Medal — C Distinguished Flying Cross

Distinguished Service Medal *U.S.* A decoration in the form of a bronze, gold, and blue enamel medal, awarded to members of the Army, Navy, Air Force, or merchant marine for exceptionally meritorious service involving responsibility. Abbr. *D.S.M.*

dis·tin·guish·ing (di·sting′gwish·ing) *adj.* Constituting difference or distinction; characteristic.

dis·tin·guish·ment (di·sting′gwish·mənt) *n. Obs.* Observation of difference.

dis·tome (dis′tōm) *n.* One of a genus *(Distoma)* of trematode, parasitic worms: also called *flukes.* [<NL<Gk. *di-* two + *stoma* mouth]

dis·tort (dis·tôrt′) *v.t.* **1** To twist or bend out of shape; make crooked or misshapen. **2** To twist the meaning of; misrepresent; pervert. See synonyms under PERVERT. [<L *distortus,* pp. of *distorquere* <*dis-* apart + *torquere* twist] **—dis·tort′er** *n.* **—dis·tort′ed** *adj.* **—dis·tort′ed·ly** *adv.* **—dis·tort′ed·ness** *n.*

dis·tor·tion (dis·tôr′shən) *n.* **1** The act of distorting. **2** A deformity; perversion. **3** *Optics* An imperfect image due to a defective lens or retina. **4** *Telecom.* A change in the wave form of a signal caused by non-uniform transmission at different frequencies. **5** *Psychoanal.* The process whereby certain objectionable elements of the mental life are altered so as to make them acceptable to the conscious ego. Compare CENSORSHIP (def. 2). **—dis·tor′tion·al** *adj.*

dis·tract (dis·trakt′) *v.t.* **1** To draw or divert (the mind, etc.) in a different direction. **2** To turn or draw (the mind or attention) in various directions; bewilder; confuse. **3** To make frantic; craze. See synonyms under PERPLEX. [<L *distractus,* pp. of *distrahere* <*dis-* away + *trahere* draw] **—dis·tract′i·ble** *adj.* **—dis·tract′ing, dis·trac′tive** *adj.*

dis·tract·ed (dis·trak′tid) *adj.* **1** Bewildered or harassed. **2** Mentally deranged; mad. See synonyms under INSANE. **—dis·tract′ed·ly** *adv.*

dis·trac·tion (dis·trak′shən) *n.* **1** A drawing off or diversion of the mind, as from some object or from troubles or cares. **2** Mental disturbance or confusion; perplexity. **3** Strong agitation, excitement, or distress; wild or violent grief. **4** Mental aberration; frenzy; madness. **5** Anything that distracts; a disturbing or diverting object or cause; an interruption or diversion. See synonyms under PERPLEXITY.

dis·train (dis·trān′) *v.t. Law* **1** To take and detain (personal property) by distress as security for a debt, claim, etc. **2** To subject (a person) to distress. *—v.i.* **3** To impose a distress. [<OF *destreindre* <L *distringere* < *dis-* completely + *stringere* draw tight, compress] **—dis·train′a·ble** *adj.* **—dis·train′er** or **dis·train′or** *n.* **—dis·train′ment** *n.*

dis·train·ee (dis′trā·nē′) *n. Law* A person whose property has been distrained.

dis·traint (dis·trānt′) *n. Law* The act or process of distraining.

dis·trait (dis·trā′, *Fr.* dēs·tre′) *adj.* Absent-minded. [<F, pp. of *distraire* <L *distrahere.* See DISTRACT.] **—dis·traite** (dis·trāt′, *Fr.* dēs·tret′) *adj. fem.*

dis·traught (dis·trôt′) *adj.* In a state of distraction. [Var. of earlier *distract,* pp. of DISTRACT]

dis·tress (dis·tres′) *v.t.* **1** To inflict suffering upon; cause agony, anxiety, or worry to; afflict. **2** To constrain by suffering or pain. **3** *Law* To distrain. See synonyms under PERSECUTE. *—n.* **1** Acute or extreme suffering or its cause; pain; trouble. **2** An afflicted, wretched, or exhausted condition; dangerous situation. **3** *Law* Distraint; goods taken by distraint. See synonyms under AGONY, GRIEF, MISFORTUNE, PAIN, POVERTY. [<AF *destresser,* OF *destrecier* <LL *districtiare* <L *distringere.* See DISTRAIN.] **—dis·tress′ful** *adj.* **—dis·tress′·ful·ly** *adv.* **—dis·tress′ful·ness** *n.* **—dis·tress′·ing·ly** *adv.*

dis·trib·u·tar·y (dis·trib′yoo·ter′ē) *n. pl.* **·tar·ies** A river branch flowing away from the main branch and not returning to it: opposed to *tributary.*

dis·trib·ute (dis·trib′yoot) *v.t.* **·ut·ed, ·ut·ing** **1** To divide and deal out in shares; apportion; allot. **2** To divide and classify; categorize: to *distribute* plants into orders. **3** To scatter or spread out, as in an area or over a surface. **4** To divide and arrange into distinctive parts or functions. **5** *Logic* To use (a term) in its full extension, so as to include all members of the class which it names. **6** *Printing* To separate (type) and return the letters to the proper boxes. See synonyms under ALLOT, APPORTION, SPREAD. [<L *distributus,* pp. of *distribuere* <*dis-* away + *tribuere* give, allot] **—dis·trib′ut·a·ble** *adj.*

dis·trib·ut·er (dis·trib′yə·tər) *n.* **1** One who or that which distributes; specifically, a marketing agent. **2** A device used in distribution, as in an automobile or a Linotype machine. Also **dis·trib′u·tor** (-tər, -tôr).

dis·tri·bu·tion (dis′trə·byoo′shən) *n.* **1** The act of distributing; apportionment; arrangement; disposition. **2** That which is distributed. **3** The state or manner of being distributed. **4** *Archit.* The arrangement and interdependence of interior subdivisions, etc., as distinguished from *disposition.* **5** In commerce, the total of all steps involved in the delivery of goods from producer to consumer, including such items as sales methods, transport, storage, financing, accounting, etc.

distribution curve A frequency curve.

dis·trib·u·tive (dis·trib′yə·tiv) *adj.* **1** Serving or tending to distribute; pertaining to distribution. **2** Denoting individual action or consideration. **3** *Gram.* Denoting objects or groups composed of individuals acting individually: The *distributive* pronouns "each," "every," "either," and "neither" are called *distributive* adjectives when they modify nouns. **4** Expressing the act of taking singly: the Latin *distributive* numeral "bini" (two by two). **5** *Logic* Indicating or effecting the distribution of a term. *—n.* A distributive pronoun, adjective, or numeral, as *each, every,* etc. **—dis·trib′u·tive·ly** *adv.* **—dis·trib′·u·tive·ness** *n.*

dis·trict (dis′trikt) *n.* **1** A portion of territory specially set off or defined, as for judicial, political, educational, or other purposes. **2** A subdivision of the United States or of one State having its own Federal or State court. **3** Any region of space; a tract. See synonyms under LAND. *—v.t.* To divide into districts. [<MF <Med. L *districtus* jurisdiction <L *distringere.* See DISTRAIN.]

district attorney The prosecuting officer of a Federal or State judicial district. See PROSECUTING ATTORNEY under ATTORNEY.

district judge A judge who presides over a Federal or State district court.

District of Columbia A Federal district, capital of the United States, coextensive with the city of Washington on the Potomac River; 69 square miles: abbr. DC

Dis·tri·to Fe·de·ral (dēs·trē′tō fā′th ā·räl′) The Spanish form of FEDERAL DISTRICT (Mexico City).

dis·trust (dis·trust′) *v.t.* To feel no trust for or confidence in; doubt; suspect. *—n.* Doubt; suspicion; discredit. See synonyms under DOUBT.

dis·trust·ful (dis·trust′fəl) *adj.* **1** Entertaining doubt or distrust. **2** Wanting in confidence; diffident; modest. **—dis·trust′ful·ly** *adv.* **—dis·trust′ful·ness** *n.*

dis·turb (dis·tûrb′) *v.t.* **1** To destroy or interfere with the repose, tranquility, or peace of. **2** To agitate the mind of; disquiet; trouble. **3** To upset the order, system, or progression of: She has *disturbed* the rhythm of my days. **4** To interrupt; break in on. **5** To cause inconvenience to. See synonyms under DISPLACE. [<OF *destorber* <L *disturbare* <*dis-* completely + *turbare* disorder] **—dis·turb′er** *n.*

dis·tur·bance (dis·tûr′bəns) *n.* **1** A change, or alteration, whether as the result of internal or external action, from a condition of order, repose, or peace to one of agitation or disorder. **2** The act of effecting this change. **3** A tumult or commotion by which the public peace is disturbed. **4** A disordered condition of the mind; mental agitation, distraction, or confusion. See synonyms under ALTERCATION, ANXIETY, DISORDER, TUMULT. [<OF *destorbance* <*destorber.* See DISTURB.]

dis·tyle (dis′tīl) *adj. Archit.* Having two columns; specifically, referring to a portico in antes. See ANTA. *—n.* A building so constructed. [<DI-[2] + Gk. *stylos* pillar]

di·sul·fate (dī·sul′fāt) *n. Chem.* **1** A pyrosulfate. **2** A bisulfate. Also **di·sul′phate.**

di·sul·fide (dī·sul′fīd) *n. Chem.* A sulfide containing two atoms of sulfur to the molecule: also *bisulfide.* Also **di·sul′fid** (-fid), **di·sul′·phide.**

di·sul·fu·ric (dī′sul·fyoor′ik) *adj. Chem.* Pyrosulfuric.

disulfuric acid *Chem.* Pyrosulfuric acid.

dis·un·ion (dis·yoon′yən) *n.* **1** The state of being disunited; severance; rupture. **2** A condition of disagreement; breach of concord.

dis·un·ion·ist (dis·yoon′yən·ist) *n.* **1** An advocate of disunion. **2** In U.S. history, one who, before and during Civil War of 1861, favored the dissolution of the Union.

3 In English history, an opponent of the Act of Union with Ireland of 1801. Compare UNIONIST. — **dis·un′ion·ism** *n.*

dis·u·nite (dis′yōō·nīt′) *v.* **·nit·ed, ·nit·ing** *v.t.* 1 To break the union of; separate; disjoin; part. 2 To alienate; estrange, as friends. — *v.i.* 3 To come apart. [<L *dis-* apart + *unus* one]

dis·use (dis·yōōs′) *n.* The state of being excluded or retired from use; desuetude: also **dis·us′age** (-ij). — *v.t.* (dis·yōōz′) **·used, ·us·ing** To cease to use or practice; discontinue.

dis·u·til·i·ty (dis′yōō·til′ə·tē) *n.* Injuriousness; harmfulness.

dis·u·til·ize (dis·yōō′təl·īz) *v.t. Rare* **·ized, ·iz·ing** To destroy the usefulness of.

dis·val·ue (dis·val′yōō) *v.t.* **·val·ued, ·val·u·ing** To treat as of little value; disparage.

di·syl·lab·i·fy (dī′si·lab′ə·fī) See DISSYLLABIFY.

di·syl·la·ble (di·sil′ə·bəl) See DISSYLLABLE.

dis·yoke (dis·yōk′) *v.t.* **·yoked, ·yok·ing** To unyoke.

di·ta (dē′tə) *n.* A Philippine forest tree *(Alstonia scholaris)* of the dogbane family. The wood is used in making furniture, and a substitute for quinine is obtained from the bark. Also **di′taa.** [< native name]

di·tat De·us (dī′tat dē′əs) *Latin* God enriches: motto of Arizona.

ditch (dich) *n.* A narrow trench in the ground, as for drainage; an irrigation trench. — *v.t.* 1 To dig or lay a ditch or ditches in. 2 To run or throw into a ditch; derail. 3 *U.S. Slang* To abandon; get rid of. — *v.i.* 4 To make a ditch or ditches. [OE *dīc.* Related to DIKE.]

ditch·er (dich′ər) *n.* 1 One who digs ditches. 2 A machine for digging ditches.

di·the·ism (dī′thē·iz′əm) *n. Theol.* The doctrine that maintains the existence of two coequal gods or powers of good and evil; Manicheism. [<DI-^{2} + Gk. *theos* god] — **di′·the·ist** *n.* — **di′the·is′tic** *adj.*

dith·er (dith′ər) *v.i.* To tremble; shake; vibrate. — *n.* 1 A trembling; vibration; state of nervousness or anxiety. 2 *pl. Colloq.* An attack of nerves. [Var. of earlier *didder* tremble, shake; origin uncertain] — **dith′er·y** *adj.*

di·thi·on·ic (dī′thī·on′ik, dith′ē-) *adj. Chem.* Hyposulfuric. [<DI-^{2} + Gk. *theion* sulfur]

dith·y·ramb (dith′ə·ram, -ramb) *n.* 1 In ancient Greece, a wild, passionate choric hymn sung in honor of Dionysus. 2 A metrical composition resembling this. 3 A wild or vehement speech or writing. Also **dith′y·ram′·bus.** [<L *dithyrambus* <Gk. *dithyrambos*] — **dith′y·ram′bic** (-ram′bik) *adj.*

Dit·mars (dit′märz), **Raymond Lee,** 1876–1942, U.S. herpetologist.

dit·ta·ny (dit′ə·nē) *n. pl.* **·nies** 1 A perennial American herb of the mint family *(Cunila origanoides)*, with small, purplish or lilac blossoms; the stonemint. 2 Any of various plants of the mint family, as the **Cretan dittany** *(Origanum dictamnus)*. 3 Fraxinella. [<OF *ditan, dictamne* <L *dictamnus* <Gk. *diktamon,* ? from *Diktē,* a mountain in Crete where it grew]

dit·to (dit′ō) *n. pl.* **·tos** The same thing repeated; the aforesaid: often written *do.,* or expressed by two inverted commas, called **ditto marks,** beneath the word intended to be duplicated. — *adv.* As before; likewise. — *v.t.* **·toed, ·to·ing** To copy; duplicate. [<Ital. *detto, ditto* aforesaid <L *dictum.* See DICTUM.]

dit·to·gram (dit′ō·gram) *n.* One letter or more unconsciously repeated in the copying of a manuscript. Also **dit′to·graph** (-graf, -gräf). [<Gk. *dittos* double + -GRAM]

dit·tog·ra·phy (di·tog′rə·fē) *n.* 1 The absent-minded repetition of letters or words by a copyist. 2 A passage or reading resulting from such repetition. [<Gk. *dittos* double + -GRAPHY] — **dit′to·graph′ic** *adj.*

dit·ty (dit′ē) *n. pl.* **·ties** 1 A short, simple song; lay. 2 *Obs.* A refrain. [<OF *dittié, ditié* <L *dictatum* a thing said < *dictare.* See DICTATE.]

dit·ty–bag (dit′ē·bag′) *n.* A sailor's bag for needles, thread, personal belongings, etc. [Origin uncertain]

dit·ty–box (dit′ē·boks′) *n.* 1 A small box used in place of a ditty–bag. 2 A motion–picture cameraman's repair kit.

Di·u (dē′ōō) A district of Portuguese India, comprising the island of Diu off the coast of NW India, with the continental dependencies of Gogola and Simbor; total, 14 square miles. See PORTUGUESE INDIA.

di·u·re·sis (dī′yōō·rē′sis) *n. Pathol.* Excessive excretion of urine. [<NL <Gk. *dia-* thoroughly + *ourēsis* urination]

di·u·ret·ic (dī′yōō·ret′ik) *adj.* Stimulating the secretion and flow of urine: also **di′u·ret′i·cal.** — *n.* A diuretic medicine.

di·ur·nal (dī·ûr′nəl) *adj.* 1 Happening every day; daily; also, performed in a day: a planet's *diurnal* revolution. 2 Done in or pertaining to the daytime: opposed to *nocturnal.* 3 *Med.* Increasing in violence by day, as the symptoms of a disease. 4 *Bot.* Expanding by day and closing at night, as certain flowers. 5 Lasting only one day; ephemeral. See synonyms under DAILY. — *n.* 1 *Eccl.* A service book containing the offices for prime, tierce, sext, nones, vespers, and compline. 2 A diurnal bird or insect. 3 *Obs.* A journal; diary. 4 *Obs.* A daily newspaper. [<L *diurnalis* < *diurnus* daily < *dies* day. Doublet of JOURNAL.] — **di·ur′nal·ly** *adv.*

div (div) *v. Scot.* A corruption of the auxiliary verb *do.*

di·va (dē′və) *n. pl.* **·vas** or **·ve** (-vā) A celebrated female operatic singer; a prima donna. [<Ital., fem. of *divo* divine <L *divus*]

di·va·gate (dī′və·gāt) *v.i.* **·gat·ed, ·gat·ing** 1 To wander or stray aimlessly. 2 To digress. [<L *divagatus,* pp. of *divagari* < *dis-* away + *vagari* wander] — **di′va·ga′tion** *n.*

di·va·lent (dī·vā′lənt, div′ə-) See BIVALENT.

di·van (di·van′, dī′van) *n.* 1 A cushioned or pillowed place for reclining; a couch. 2 A café; smoking–room. 3 An Oriental governmental council; a council chamber. 4 A collection of poems usually written by one man: also spelled *diwan.* [<Turkish *dīvān* <Persian *dēvān,* orig. a collection of poems, a register; later, a council, a chamber, a bench]

di·var·i·cate (di·var′ə·kāt, dī-) *v.t.* & *v.i.* **·cat·ed, ·cat·ing** To branch off or cause to branch off; diverge. — *adj.* (di·var′ə·kit, -kāt, dī-) Branching off; widely diverging. [<L *divaricatus,* pp. of *divaricare* < *dis-* apart + *varicare* straddle < *varicus* straddling] — **di·var′i·cate·ly** *adv.* — **di·var′i·ca′tor** *n.*

di·var·i·ca·tion (di·var′ə·kā′shən, dī-) *n.* 1 The act of branching off or diverging; a forking. 2 *Biol.* A crossing or intersection of fibers at different angles. 3 *Obs.* A divergence of opinion.

dive (dīv) *v.* **dived** (*U.S. Colloq.* **dove**), **dived, div·ing** *v.i.* 1 To plunge, usually headfirst, into water, etc. 2 To submerge, as a submarine. 3 To plunge the body, hand, or an object into something, usually so as to obtain a part: He *dived* into the candy. 4 To enter suddenly or abruptly: He *dived* into the forest. 5 To descend at a steep angle and at high speed: The hawk *dived* toward the earth. 6 To work under water as a diver. 7 To become engrossed or deeply involved: to *dive* into politics. — *v.t.* 8 To thrust or plunge (the body, hand, or an object) into something. 9 To cause (an airplane) to descend at a steep angle. — *n.* 1 A plunge headforemost into or as into water. 2 A steep downward plunge of an airplane. 3 *Colloq.* A disreputable resort; den. [Blend of OE *dūfan* dive and *dȳfan* immerse]

dive bomber See BOMBER.

div·er (dī′vər) *n.* 1 One who dives. 2 One whose work is to explore, or gather objects under water. 3 A bird that dives, especially any of several species of loon. 4 In the West Indies, a grebe.

di·verge (di·vûrj′, dī-) *v.* **·verged, ·verg·ing** *v.i.* 1 To extend or lie in different directions from the same point: opposed to *converge.* 2 To vary from a typical form; differ. 3 *Math.* To fail to converge toward a limit: said of an infinite series, the sum of whose terms has no limit. — *v.t.* 4. To make divergent, cause to fork. See synonyms under BEND, WANDER. [<NL *divergere* < *dis-* apart + *vergere* incline]

di·ver·gence (di·vûr′jəns, dī-) *n.* 1 The act of diverging. 2 *Meteorol.* An atmospheric condition in which there is a net outflow of air from a given region. — **di·ver′gen·cy** *n.*

di·ver·gent (di·vûr′jənt, dī-) *adj.* 1 Ever going farther apart. 2 Varying. 3 Differing; conflicting; deviating. 4 Producing divergence. Also **di·verg′ing.** [<NL *divergens, -entis* ppr. of *divergere* DIVERGE] — **di·ver′gent·ly** *adv.*

di·vers (dī′vərz) *adj.* 1 More than one, but not a great number; several; sundry. 2 *Archaic* Of different kinds; various. See synonyms under MANY. [<OF <L *diversus* different; orig. pp. of *divertere.* See DIVERT.]

◆ *Divers* implies severalty; *diverse,* difference. Hence we say: "The Evangelists narrate events in *divers* manners" but "The views of the two parties were quite *diverse.*"

di·verse (di·vûrs′, dī-, dī′vûrs) *adj.* 1 Differing essentially; distinct. 2 *Obs.* Capable of various forms; multiform. [<L *diversus.* See DIVERS.] — **di·verse′ly** *adv.*

di·ver·si·fi·ca·tion (di·vûr′sə·fə·kā′shən, dī-) *n.* 1 Variation; variety. 2 The act of branching out into diverse lines of activity: product *diversification.*

di·ver·si·form (di·vûr′sə·fôrm, dī-) *adj.* Of different forms.

di·ver·si·fy (di·vûr′sə·fī, dī-) *v.t.* **·fied, ·fy·ing** To make diverse; impart variety to.

di·ver·sion (di·vûr′zhən, -shən, dī-) *n.* 1 The act of diverting. 2 *Mil.* An attack or feint intended to divert enemy troops from the point where a full–scale attack is to be made. 3 That which diverts; amusement; recreation. See synonyms under ENTERTAINMENT, SPORT.

di·ver·si·ty (di·vûr′sə·tē, dī-) *n. pl.* **·ties** 1 The state of being diverse; dissimilitude. 2 Variety: a *diversity* of interests. See synonyms under CHANGE, DIFFERENCE.

diver's palsy See CAISSON DISEASE.

di·vert (di·vûrt′, dī-) *v.t.* 1 To turn aside; deflect, as in direction, course, interest, or purpose. 2 To draw off the attention of. 3 To amuse; entertain. See synonyms under ENTERTAIN, RELAX. [<L *divertere* < *dis-* apart + *vertere* turn] — **di·vert′er** *n.* — **di·vert′ing** *adj.* — **di·vert′ing·ly** *adv.*

di·ver·tic·u·lum (dī′vər·tik′yə·ləm) *n. pl.* **·la** (-lə) *Anat.* A blind pouch or structure which has arisen or developed from another larger one, as the cecum, the air bladder of a fish, or the lungs of a vertebrate, all of which arise from the intestinal canal. [<L *diverticulum, deverticulum* a by–path < *divertere.* See DIVERT.] — **di′ver·tic′u·lar** *adj.*

di·ver·ti·men·to (di·ver′ti·men′tō) *n. pl.* **·ti** (-tē) *Music* 1 A light and graceful instrumental composition in several movements. 2 A potpourri. [<Ital., diversion]

di·ver·tisse·ment (dē·ver·tēs·män′) *n.* 1 A brief performance, often a ballet, between the acts of a play. 2 *Music* A divertimento. 3 A diversion; amusement. [<F, diversion]

Di·ves (dī′vēz) 1 A rich man in a parable. *Luke* xvi 19–31; hence, in general, a rich, worldly man. 2 Crassus. [<L, rich]

di·vest (di·vest′, dī-) *v.t.* 1 To strip, as of clothes, ornaments, or equipment. 2 To dispossess; deprive, as of office, rights, or honors. [<Med. L *divestire, disvestire* <OF *desvestir.* See DEVEST.]

di·vest·i·ture (di·ves′tə·chər, dī-) *n.* 1 The act of divesting, or the state of being divested. Also **di·vest′ment.** 2 *Law* The act of taking from one the possession of his property. Also **di·ves′ture** (-ves′chər).

di·vide (di·vīd′) *v.* **·vid·ed, ·vid·ing** *v.t.* 1 To cut or separate into parts. 2 To distribute in shares; portion out. 3 To separate into classes; categorize. 4 To separate; keep apart. 5 To form the partition or boundary between. 6 To graduate with lines; calibrate. 7 *Math.* **a** To subject to division. **b** To be an exact divisor of. 8 To cause to disagree; cause discord among. — *v.i.* 9 To be or come apart; separate. 10 To differ in opinion; disagree. 11 *Brit. Govt.* To vote in two groups, one for and one against a measure. 12 To share. See synonyms under ALLOT, APPORTION. — *n.* 1 *Geol.* A mountain range or area of high land separating one drainage system from another; a watershed. 2 The boundary line between life and death. 3 *Colloq.* The division of profits, booty or spoils. [<L *dividere* separate] — **di·vid′a·ble** *adj.*

di·vid·ed (di·vī′did) *adj.* 1 Parted; disunited. 2 *Bot.* Having incisions or indentations extending to the base or the midrib, as in certain leaves.

di·vi·de et im·pe·ra (div′ə·dē et im′pər·ə) *Latin* Divide and rule.

div·i·dend (div′ə·dend) *n.* 1 A quantity divided, or to be divided, into equal parts. 2 A sum of money to be distributed according to some fixed scheme, as profit on shares, share of surplus or assets, etc. [<L *dividendum*

thing to be divided < *dividere* separate, divide]

di·vid·er (di·vī′dər) *n.* **1** One who or that which divides, separates, or apportions. **2** *pl.* Compasses for measuring or setting off distances.

div·i-div·i (div′ē·div′ē) *n.* **1** A small tropical American tree (*Caesalpinia coriaria*). **2** Its astringent, reddish-brown, curved pods, used for dyeing and tanning. **3** A prickly shrub or small tree of tropical America (*Caesalpinia spinosa*) whose pods are similarly used. [<Sp. <Tupian]

di·vid·u·al (di·vij′o͞o·əl) *adj. Obs.* **1** Shared with others; divided. **2** Separate; fragmentary. [<L *dividuus* divisible < *dividere* divide] — **di·vid′u·al·ism** *n.* — **di·vid′u·al·ly** *adv.*

div·i·na·tion (div′ə·nā′shən) *n.* **1** The act or art of trying to foretell the future or the unknown. **2** A forecast; augury. **3** A successful or clever guess.

di·vin·a·to·ry (di·vin′ə·tôr′ē, -tō′rē) *adj.* Of or pertaining to divination; conjectural.

di·vine (di·vīn′) *adj.* **1** Pertaining to, proceeding from, or of the nature of God or of a god; sacred. **2** Addressed or offered up to God in service or adoration; religious; holy. **3** Altogether excellent or admirable; godlike. **4** Pertaining to a deity or to divinity or theology. —*n.* One versed in divinity; a theologian; clergyman. —*v.* **·vined, ·vin·ing** *v.t.* **1** To foretell or prophesy, supposedly with supernatural aid. **2** To surmise or conjecture intuitively; guess. **3** *Obs.* To portend; presage. —*v.i.* **4** To practice divination. See synonyms under AUGUR, GUESS, PROPHESY. [<OF *devin, divin* <L *divinus* < *deus* a god] — **di·vine′ly** *adv.* — **di·vine′ness** *n.* — **di·vin′er** *n.*

Divine Comedy A narrative poem in 100 cantos, written (1307–1321) in Italian by Dante Alighieri and dealing with the poet's imaginary journey through HELL, PURGATORY, and PARADISE. *Italian* **Di·vi·na Com·me·dia** (dē·vē′nä kōm·mā′dyä).

divine right of kings Royal authority considered as God-given.

diving beetle Any aquatic, predacious beetle of the family *Dytiscidae*: the larva is called *water tiger.*

diving bell A hollow, watertight vessel, open below and supplied with air under pressure, in which divers may be lowered into and work under water.

diving board A springboard.

diving rudder See ELEVATOR (def. 5).

diving suit A waterproof garment with detachable helmet worn by divers doing underwater work, supplied with air from the surface or from portable tanks.

divining rod A forked twig, usually of witch hazel, held by the tips and believed to bend downward when carried over unrevealed sources of water, mineral deposits, etc.: so called for its assumed supernatural power. See RHABDOMANCY.

di·vin·i·ty (di·vin′ə·tē) *n. pl.* **·ties** **1** The quality or character of being divine. **2** A lesser deity. **3** Theology. **4** An attribute, virtue, or quality assumed to be divine. **5** A being who partakes of the divine nature or qualities. — **the Divinity** The Deity; God. [<OF *devinité* theology <L *divinitas, -tatis* godhead, deity < *divinus* DIVINE]

divinity school A college or school of theology.

div·i·nize (div′ə·nīz) *v.t.* **·nized, ·niz·ing** To make or treat as divine. — **div′i·ni·za′tion** *n.*

di·vis·i·ble (di·viz′ə·bəl) *adj.* **1** Capable of being divided. **2** *Math.* Admitting of division without a remainder. — **di·vis′i·bil′i·ty, di·vis′i·ble·ness** *n.* — **di·vis′i·bly** *adv.*

di·vi·sion (di·vizh′ən) *n.* **1** The act of dividing. **2** A part; section. **3** Separation; disagreement; discord. **4** That which separates, divides, or makes different. **5** *Math.* The operation of finding how often one quantity is contained in another, or the ratio of one to another: opposed to *multiplication.* **6** *Mil.* A large tactical and administrative unit. In the U.S. Army it is larger than a brigade and smaller than a corps and is under the command of a major general. **7** In the U.S. Navy, a group of three battleships, four cruisers, or two aircraft-carriers, under the command of a rear admiral; or four destroyers, commanded by a captain; also, a portion of a ship's company. **8** A voting of a legislative body, specifically by going into affirmative and negative lobbies, as in the British Parliament. **9** *Music* A series of notes sung to one syllable as a showy or brilliant passage. **10** *Zool.* A category of animals having common characters but of no established rank in taxonomy. **11** *Bot.* A category of plants analogous to a phylum in zoology. See synonyms under PART. [<OF <L *divisio, -onis* < *dividere* divide]

di·vi·sion·al (di·vizh′ən·əl) *adj.* Pertaining to dividing or to a division. Also **di·vi′sion·ar′y.**

di·vi·sive (di·vī′siv) *adj.* **1** Causing or expressing division. **2** Causing discord.

di·vi·sor (di·vī′zər) *n. Math.* That by which a number or quantity is divided. — **common divisor** A number or quantity that is contained in another number or quantity without leaving a remainder.

di·vorce (di·vôrs′, -vōrs′) *n.* **1** Legal dissolution of a marriage relation. **2** Hence, severance; separation. **3** A decree dissolving a marriage. —*v.* **·vorced, ·vorc·ing** *v.t.* **1** To free by legal process from the relationship of husband and wife. **2** To sunder; sever; separate. **3** To obtain a legal divorce from. —*v.i.* **4** To get a divorce. [<F <L *divortium* < *divertere* divert] — **di·vorce′ment** *n.* — **di·vorc′er** *n.*

di·vor·cé (di·vôr′sā′, -vōr′-, di·vôr′sā, -vōr′-) *n.* A divorced man. — **di·vor′cée′** *n. fem.* [<F, pp. of *divorcer* divorce]

di·vor·cee (di·vôr′sē′, -vōr′-) *n.* A divorced person.

div·ot (div′ət) *n.* **1** A piece of turf cut from the sod by the stroke of a golf club. **2** *Scot.* An oblong piece of turf or sod used for thatching, etc.

di·vul·gate (di·vul′gāt) *v.t.* **·gat·ed, ·gat·ing** To make known; publish. [<L *divulgatus,* pp. of *divulgare.* See DIVULGE.] — **di·vul′gat·er** *n.* — **di·vul·ga·tion** (div′əl·gā′shən) *n.*

di·vulge (di·vulj′) *v.t.* **·vulged, ·vulg·ing** **1** To tell, as a secret; disclose; reveal. **2** *Obs.* To proclaim publicly. See synonyms under INFORM[1], PUBLISH, SPREAD. [<L *divulgare* < *dis-* away + *vulgare* make public] — **di·vulge′ment** *n.* — **di·vulg′er** *n.*

di·vul·gence (di·vul′jəns) *n.* A revelation; disclosure.

di·vul·sion (di·vul′shən) *n.* **1** The act of plucking or pulling apart. **2** A rupturing or dilating. [<L *divulsio, -onis* < *dis-* apart + *vellere* pull] — **di·vul′sive** *adj.*

div·vy (div′ē) *Slang n. pl.* **·vies** A share; dividend. —*v.t.* **·vied, ·vy·ing** To divide. Also **divvy up.** [Short for DIVIDE]

di·wan[1] (di·wän′, -wôn′) See DEWAN.

di·wan[2] (di·wän′, -wôn′) *n.* Divan (def. 4).

Dix (diks), **John Adams,** 1798–1879, U.S. general and statesman. — **Dorothy** Pseudonym of *Elizabeth Meriwether Gilmer,* 1870–1951, U.S. journalist.

Dix·ie (dik′sē) **1** Traditionally, those States which comprised the southern Confederacy during the Civil War; hence, the southern United States: also **Dixie Land.** **2** A song composed by D. D. Emmett in 1859, adopted by the Confederate Army as a marching song.

Dix·ie·crat (dik′sē·krat) *n.* A member of the U.S. Democratic party who rejected the plank of civil liberties of the party platform and its candidate for the presidency, especially one from the southern States who voted for the States' Rights party candidates. [<DIXIE + (DEMO)CRAT; coined during the 1948 presidential campaign]

Dix·ie·land (dik′sē·land′) *n.* A style of jazz in two-beat or four-beat rhythm, originally played in New Orleans and other cities in the South.

dix·it (dik′sit) *n.* A statement or a declaration made upon personal authority. [<L, he has said]

Dix·on (dik′sən), **Thomas,** 1864–1946, U.S. novelist.

Di·yar·be·kir (dē·yär′be·kir′) A city on the Tigris in eastern Turkey: also *Diarbekr.*

diz·en (diz′ən, dī′zən) *v.t.* To deck out; bedizen. [<MDu. *disen* put flax on a distaff] — **diz′en·ment** *n.*

diz·zy (diz′ē) *adj.* **·zi·er, ·zi·est** **1** Having a feeling of whirling and confusion, with a tendency to fall; giddy. **2** Causing or caused by giddiness; having vertigo. **3** *Colloq.* Thoughtless; capricious; silly; stupid. —*v.t.* **·zied, ·zy·ing** To make giddy; confuse. [OE *dysig* foolish] — **diz′zi·ly** *adv.* — **diz′zi·ness** *n.*

Djai·lo·lo (jī·lō′lō) See HALMAHERA.

Dja·kar·ta (jä·kär′tä) See JAKARTA.

Dja·ko·vi·ca (dyä·kō′vit·sä) A town in SW Serbia, Yugoslavia: also *Dyakovitsa.* Formerly **Dja·ko·va** (dyä′kô·vä).

djeb·el (jeb′əl) See JEBEL.

Dji·bou·ti (ji·bo͞o′tē) A port on the Gulf of Aden, capital of French Somaliland: also *Jibuti.*

djin·ni (ji·nē′) See JINNI, etc.

Djok·ja·kar·ta (jōk′yə·kär′tə) See JOGJAKARTA.

D-lay·er (dē′lā′ər) *n.* A region of the atmosphere lying just below the Heaviside layer and capable of reflecting very long radio waves.

D-line (dē′līn′) *n. Physics* One of the two closely associated yellow lines in the emission spectrum of sodium.

Dmi·tri (dmē′trē) Russian form of DEMETRIUS.

Dne·pro·dzer·zhinsk (dnye′prə·dzer·zhinsk′) A city on the Dnieper in Ukrainian S.S.R. Formerly **Ka·men·sko·ye** (kä′myin·sko͞o′yə).

Dne·pro·ges (dnye·prô·ges′) A village in Ukrainian S.S.R. on the Dnieper, site of the largest dam (200 feet high, 1/2 mile long) and hydroelectric power station in Europe: formerly *Dneprostroi.*

Dne·pro·pe·trovsk (dnye′prə·pə·trôfsk′) A city in SW Ukrainian S.S.R., on the Dnieper: formerly *Ekaterinoslav.* Also **Dnie′pro·pe·trovsk′.**

Dne·pro·stroi (dnye′prə·stroi′) A former name for DNEPROGES.

Dnie·per (dnye′pər, nē′pər) A river in western U.S.S.R., flowing 1,420 miles SW to the Black Sea. Also **Dne′pr.**

Dnies·ter (dnyes′tər, nēs′tər) A river in western U.S.S.R., flowing 876 miles SE to the Black Sea: Rumanian *Nistru.* Also **Dnes′tr.**

do[1] (do͞o) *v.* Present: *sing.* **do, do** (*Archaic* **thou do·est** or **dost), does** (*Archaic* **do·eth** or **doth),** *pl.* **do;** past: **did** (*Archaic* **thou didst);** *pp.* **done;** *ppr.* **do·ing** *v.t.* **1** To perform, as an action; execute or fabricate, as a piece of work. **2** To finish; complete. **3** To deal with or take care of: to *do* chores. **4** To cause or produce; bring about: to *do* good or evil. **5** To exert; put forth: He *did* his best. **6** To work at as one's occupation. **7** To translate. **8** To present (a play, etc.): They are *doing* Hamlet tonight. **9** To play the part of: to *do* Ophelia. **10** To cover; travel: to *do* a mile in four minutes. **11** To visit; make a tour of: to *do* the Louvre. **12** To serve; be sufficient for: Five dollars will *do* me. **13** To extend; render: to *do* homage. **14** To solve; work out, as a problem. **15** To serve, as a term in prison. **16** *Colloq.* To cheat; swindle. —*v.i.* **17** To exert oneself; be active; strive: to *do* or die. **18** To conduct or behave oneself. **19** To fare; get along: I *did* badly in the race. **20** To suffice; serve the purpose. — **to do away with** **1** To throw away; discard. **2** To kill; destroy. — **to do by** To act toward. — **to do for** **1** To provide for; care for. **2** *Colloq.* To ruin; kill. — **to do in** *Slang* To kill. — **to do over** *Colloq.* To redecorate. — **to do to death** To execute; kill. — **to do up** **1** To wrap or tie up, as a parcel. **2** To roll up or arrange, as the hair. **3** To clean; repair. **4** To tire out. — **to make do** To get along with whatever is available. — *auxiliary* As an auxiliary, *do* is used: **1** Without specific meaning in negative, interrogative, and inverted constructions: I *do* not want it; *Do* you want to leave?; Little *did* he know. **2** To add force to imperatives: *Do* hurry. **3** To express emphasis: I *do* believe you. **4** As a substitute for another verb to avoid repetition: I will not affirm, as some *do*; Did he come? Yes, he *did.* —*n.* **1** *Colloq.* A trick; cheat: It is a regular *do.* **2** Deed; duty: chiefly in the phrase *to do one's do.* **3** *Colloq.* Festivity. **4** *Obs.* Bustle; stir. [OE *dōn*]

Synonyms (verb): accomplish, achieve, actualize, commit, complete, consummate, discharge, effect, execute, finish, fulfil, perform, perpetrate, realize, transact. *Do* is the one comprehensive word which includes this whole list. We may say of the least item of daily

work, "It is *done*," and of the grandest human achievement, "Well *done*!" To *discharge* is to *do* what is given in charge, expected, or required; we may say to *do* or to *discharge* one's duty, the duty or duties of one's office, station, position, etc., where *discharge* is the more formal and technical word, signifying to *perform* to the last and utmost all that is required. *Commit*, as applied to actions, is used only of those that are bad, whether grave or trivial; *perpetrate* is used chiefly of aggravated crimes, or, somewhat humorously, of blunders. A man may *commit* a sin, a trespass, or a murder; *perpetrate* an outrage or a felony. *Perform* is used generally in a good sense; as, to *perform* a task, a duty, a service, etc. Compare PERFORM, under ACCOMPLISH. We *finish* a garment or a letter, *complete* an edifice or a life work, *consummate* a bargain or a crime, *discharge* a duty, *effect* a purpose, *execute* a command, *fulfil* a promise, *perform* our daily tasks, *realize* an ideal, *accomplish* a design, *achieve* a victory. Compare ACCOMPLISH, MAKE, TRANSACTION. *Antonyms*: baffle, defeat, destroy, fail, frustrate, mar, miscarry, miss, neglect, ruin, spoil.

do[2] (dō) *n. Music* The first of the syllables commonly used in solmization; the keynote of any key. [< Ital.]

do·a·ble (do͞o′ə·bəl) *adj.* Capable of being done.

do-all (do͞o′ôl′) *n.* A general helper; factotum.

doat·y (dō′tē) *adj.* Stained by decay: *doaty* birch. Also spelled *doty.* [Var. of DOTY] **—doat′i·ness** *n.*

dob·ber[1] (dob′ər) *n.* A dabchick. [Origin uncertain]

dob·ber[2] (dob′ər) *n. U.S.Dial.* A float on a fishing line. [< Du., float, cork]

dob·bin (dob′in) *n.* A horse, especially a plodding or patient one; a workhorse. [from *Dobbin,* var. of *Robin* < Robert]

dob·by (dob′ē) *n. pl.* **·bies** A mechanical attachment on a loom for weaving small designs, known as **dobby weave.** [Dim. of *Dobbin.* See DOBBIN.]

Do·bell's solution (dō′belz) A solution of phenol, borax, sodium bicarbonate, and glycerin, used as a spray for throat and nasal infections. [after H. B. *Dobell,* 1828–1917, English physician]

Dö·be·rei·ner (dœ′bə·rī′nər), **Johann Wolfgang,** 1780–1849, German chemist.

Do·ber·man pin·scher (dō′bər·mən pin′shər) See PINSCHER.

do·bie (dō′bē) *n. pl.* **·bies** *SW U.S.* Adobe. Also **do′by.** [Aphetic var. of ADOBE]

Do·bie (dō′bē), **James Frank,** 1888–1964, U.S. writer and folklorist.

do·bla (dō′blä) *n.* An ancient Spanish gold coin. [< Sp. < *doble* double < L *duplus*]

do·blon (də·blōn′) *n. pl.* **·blo·nes** (-blō′nās) A former Spanish and Spanish-American gold coin. See also DOUBLOON. [< Sp. *doblón*]

do·bra (dō′brə) *n.* Any of several former Portuguese gold coins. [< Pg. < *dobre* double < L *duplus*]

Do·bru·ja (dô′bro͞o·jä) A region of SE Rumania and NE Bulgaria along the Black Sea; 9,000 square miles. Also **Do′bru·dja,** *Rumanian* **Do·bro·gea** (dô′brô·jä), *Bulgarian* **Do·bru·dzha** (dô′bro͞o·jä).

dob·son (dob′sən) *n.* The hellgrammite. [? from *Dobson,* a surname]

Dob·son (dob′sən), **(Henry) Austin,** 1840–1921, English poet.

dobson fly A large, North American, megalopterous insect *(Corydalis cornutus),* the adult of the hellgrammite or dobson.

Dob·zhan·sky (dôb·zhän′skē), **Theodosius,** 1900–1975, U.S. geneticist, born in Russia.

do·cent (dō′sənt) *n.* A person licensed to teach in a university, but without regular faculty rank; a tutor. [< G *(Privat)dozent* < L *docens, -entis,* ppr. of *docere* teach] **—do′cent·ship** *n.*

doch-an-dor·is (dôkh′ən·dor′is) *n. Scot.* A stirrup-cup. Also **doch′-an-dor′ach** (-əkh) or **-dor′och.**

doch·ter (dôkh′tər) *n. Scot.* Daughter.

doc·ile (dos′əl, *Brit.* dō′sīl) *adj.* **1** Amenable to training; easy to manage; tractable. **2** Easily worked or handled. [< MF < L *docilis* able to be taught < *docere* teach] **—doc′ile·ly** *adv.* **—do·cil·i·ty** (dō·sil′ə·tē, do-) *n.*

Synonyms: amenable, compliant, gentle, manageable, obedient, pliable, pliant, submissive, tame, teachable, tractable, yielding. One who is *docile* is easily taught; one who is *tractable* is easily led; one who is *pliant* is easily bent in any direction; *compliant* represents one as inclined or persuaded to agreement with another's will. Compare DUTY. *Antonyms*: determined, dogged, firm, inflexible, intractable, obstinate, opinionated, resolute, self-willed, stubborn, unyielding, wilful.

dock[1] (dok) *n.* **1** An artificial basin for vessels. **2** The space between two adjoining piers or wharves; also, the piers themselves; hence, a wharf. **3** The front portion of a theater beneath the stage. —*v.t.* To bring (a vessel) into a dock. —*v.i.* To come into a dock. [< MDu. *docke*]

dock[2] (dok) *n.* **1** The stump of a tail. **2** A leather case to cover a horse's tail when doubled. —*v.t.* **1** To cut off the end of (a tail, etc.); clip. **2** To take a part from (wages, etc.). **3** To clip short the tail of. **4** To take a part from the wages of. [Cf. LG *dokke* bundle]

dock[3] (dok) *n.* An enclosed space for prisoners on trial in a criminal court. [< Flemish *dok* cage]

dock[4] (dok) *n.* **1** Any of various plants of the sorrel or buckwheat family (genus *Rumex*) or the **sour dock** *(R. acetosa),* a troublesome weed. **2** Any plant resembling these. [OE *docce*]

dock·age[1] (dok′ij) *n.* **1** A charge for docking. **2** Provision for docking a vessel. **3** The act of docking.

dock·age[2] (dok′ij) *n.* **1** Curtailment, as of wages; reduction. **2** Waste matter in grain, easily separated by cleaning.

dock·er (dok′ər) *n.* A dock laborer; a longshoreman.

dock·et (dok′it) *n.* **1** A condensed statement of a document, generally minuted upon the back of the same; summary; abstract. **2** *Law* An entry on the records of a court of the principal steps taken in a case; the registry of judgments of a court; also, the book in which such entries are made or such judgments registered. **3** A calendar of the cases to be called at any time of the court; a trial docket; hence, any calendar of business, as in an ecclesiastical assembly. **4** A tag or label attached to a parcel ready for delivery. —*v.t.* **1** To place, as a cause or announcement, on a calendar or program to determine order of precedence or a routine of procedure. **2** To make an abstract of (a case) and keep for record. **3** To make a minute on the back of; endorse. **4** To attach a docket, tag, or label to. [Origin uncertain]

dock·mack·ie (dok′mak·ē) *n.* A shrub *(Viburnum acerifolium)* of the United States and Canada, with slender cymes of white flowers and crimson fruit. [< N. Am. Ind.]

dock·wal·lop·er (dok′wol′əp·ər) *n. Slang* A worker on docks or wharves.

dock·yard (dok′yärd′) *n.* **1** A place for collecting and storing naval material, and for building or repairing ships. **2** *Brit.* A navy yard.

doc·tor (dok′tər) *n.* **1** A qualified practitioner of medicine or surgery in any of its branches. **2** A person who has received a diploma of the highest degree in a faculty, as of divinity, law, literature, etc. **3** *Mech.* A device in a machine, for doing some special work; specifically, an auxiliary or donkey engine. **4** A long knife for distributing and removing color on a printing roller. **5** A steel edge on a calender roll to scrape off dirt. **6** On sailing vessels, the steward or the cook. **7** *Colloq.* The cook in a logging camp or on shipboard. **8** Among primitive people, a medicine man, wizard, or conjurer. **9** Any of several varieties of brightly colored, artificial flies, used for fishing. **10** *Obs.* A person of great learning qualified to instruct. —*v.t. Colloq.* **1** To prescribe for or treat medicinally. **2** To repair. **3** To alter; falsify, as evidence. —*v.i. Colloq.* **4** To practice medicine. **5** To take medicine or undergo medicinal treatment. [< L, a teacher < *docere* teach] **—doc′tor·al** *adj.*

doc·tor·ate (dok′tər·it) *n.* The degree, status, or title of a doctor.

doc·tri·naire (dok′trə·nâr′) *adj.* Theoretical; visionary. —*n.* One whose views are derived from theories rather than from facts; a scholastic or impractical theorist. **—doc′tri·nair′ism** *n.*

doc·tri·nal (dok′trə·nəl, *also Brit.* dok·trī′nəl) *adj.* **1** Pertaining to or characterized by doctrine. **2** Having to do with teaching; instructive. See synonyms under DOGMATIC. **—doc′tri·nal·ly** *adv.*

doc·tri·nar·i·an (dok′trə·nâr′ē·ən) *n.* A doctrinaire. **—doc′tri·nar′i·an·ism** *n.*

doc·trine (dok′trin) *n.* **1** That which is taught or set forth for acceptance or belief; that which is held to be true by any person, sect, or school; especially, in religion, a tenet, or body of tenets; belief; dogma. **2** *Obs.* Instruction; teaching. [< OF < L *doctrina* teaching < *docere* teach]

Synonyms: article, belief, dogma, precept, principle, teaching, tenet. *Doctrine* primarily signifies that which is taught; *principle,* the fundamental basis on which the *teaching* rests. A *doctrine* is reasoned out, and may be defended by reasoning; a *dogma* rests on authority, as of the decision of the church, etc. A *doctrine* or *dogma* is a statement of some one item of *belief*; a *creed* is a summary of *doctrines* or *dogmas. Dogma* has commonly the signification of a *belief* arrogantly asserted. *Tenet* is simply that which is held, and is applied to a single item of *belief.* Compare FAITH, LAW.

doc·u·dra·ma (dok′yə·drä′mə, -dra′-) *n.* A television drama or series based on fact but presented in the style of a documentary.

doc·u·ment (dok′yə·mənt) *n.* **1** An original piece of written or printed matter conveying authoritative information or evidence. **2** One of the several papers affixed to a documentary bill and testifying to or effecting the transfer of goods, as a bill of lading, certificate of insurance, etc. **3** A documentary. **4** *Obs.* A cautionary example. **5** *Obs.* Instruction. **6** *Obs.* Evidence. See synonyms under RECORD. —*v.t.* **1** To furnish with documents. **2** To prove by documentary evidence. **3** To supply with references and notes to authoritative material: to *document* a text. [< OF < L *documentum* a lesson < *docere* teach] **—doc′u·men′tal** *adj.*

doc·u·men·tal·ist (dok′yə·men′təl·ist) *n.* A specialist in the assembling, classifying, and organizing of documents; an archivist with special training in the field of documentation.

doc·u·men·tar·i·an (dok′yə·men·târ′ē·ən) *n.* **1** One who believes in the importance and value of documents. **2** An advocate of the documentary treatment of the subject of motion pictures, television, etc.

doc·u·men·ta·ry (dok′yə·men′tər·ē) *adj.* Of, pertaining to, supported by, or based upon documents: also **doc′u·men′tal.** —*n. pl.* **·ries** A motion-picture film that records or exhibits a phase of regional, social, or cultural life without fictionalization.

doc·u·men·ta·tion (dok′yə·men·tā′shən) *n.* **1** The preparation or supplying of documents, references, records, etc. **2** The documents thus furnished. **3** The act of citing sources in a literary work.

dod·der[1] (dod′ər) *v.i.* To tremble or totter, as from age. [Cf. ME *didder* tremble]

dod·der[2] (dod′ər) *n.* Any of several leafless, twining herbs of the genus *Cuscuta,* parasitic on various plants to which they adhere by suckers. [ME *doder*]

dod·dered (dod′ərd) *adj.* **1** Having lost the top or branches through age or decay: said of trees. **2** Shattered; infirm. [ME *dodden* clip]

dod·der·ing (dod′ər·ing) *adj.* Shaky; infirm; hence, senile.

dodeca- *combining form* Twelve; of or having twelve: *dodecagon.* Also, before vowels, **dodec-.** [< Gk. *dōdeka* twelve]

do·dec·a·gon (dō·dek′ə·gon) *n. Geom.* A figure, especially a plane figure, with twelve sides and twelve angles. [< Gk. *dōdekagōnon*] **—do·de·cag·o·nal** (dō′de·kag′ə·nəl) *adj.*

do·dec·a·he·dron (dō′dek·ə·hē′drən) *n. pl.* **·drons** or **·dra** (-drə) A solid bounded by twelve regular faces. [< Gk. *dōdekaedron,* neut. sing. of *dōdekadros* < *dōdeka* twelve + *hedra* seat] **—do′·dec·a·he′dral** *adj.*

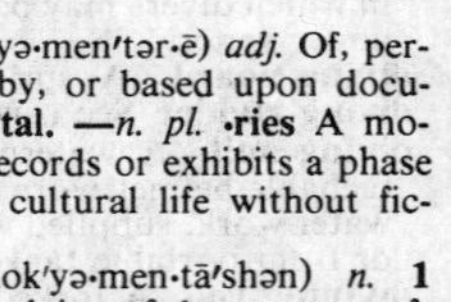

DODECAHEDRON *A.* Simple. *B.* Pentagonal.

Do·dec·a·nese (dō·dek′ə·nēs′, -nēz′, dō′dek·ə-) A Greek island group in the SE Aegean; total, 1,044 square miles; capital, Rhodes. *Greek* **Do·de·ka·ne·sos** (thō′the·kä′nē·sôs).

do·dec·a·phon·ic (dō′dek·ə·fon′ik) *adj. Music* Twelve–tone.

dodge (doj) *v.* **dodged, dodg·ing** *v.t.* **1** To avoid, as a blow, by a sudden turn or twist. **2** To evade, as a duty or issue, by cunning or trickery. —*v.i.* **3** To move quickly to one side or change position suddenly, as to avoid a blow. **4** To practice trickery; be deceitful. —*n.* An act of dodging; evasion; hence, a trick to deceive or cheat; any trick. See synonyms under ARTIFICE. [Origin unknown]

Dodge (doj), **Mary Elizabeth,** 1838–1905, *née* Mapes, U.S. author and editor.

dodg·er (doj′ər) *n.* **1** One who dodges; a tricky fellow. **2** A small handbill. **3** A cooked cake of Indian meal; corn dodger.

Dodg·son (doj′sən), **Charles Lutwidge,** 1832–1898, English mathematician and author of *Alice in Wonderland*: pseudonym, *Lewis Carroll.*

do·do (dō′dō) *n. pl.* **·does** or **·dos** A large, extinct bird (genus *Rapheco*) of Mauritius and Réunion, about the size of a turkey, with rudimentary, functionless wings. [<Pg. *doudo* foolish]

Do·do·na (dō-dō′nə) An ancient town in Epirus, Greece; seat of a temple of Zeus and of the oldest of Greek oracles. —**Do·do·nae·an** or **Do·do·ne·an** (dō′də-nē′ən), **Do·do′ni·an** *adj.*

Dods·ley (dodz′lē), **Robert.** 1703–64, English author and bookseller.

doe (dō) *n.* The female of the deer, antelope, hare, rabbit, or kangaroo. ◆ Homophone: *dough.* [OE *dā*]

Doe·nitz (dœ′nits), **Karl,** born 1891, German admiral; successor to Hitler at the fall of the Third Reich in 1945.

do·er (dōō′ər) *n.* One who acts, does, or performs; an agent. See synonyms under AGENT.

does (duz) Present tense, third person singular, of DO.

doe·skin (dō′skin′) *n.* **1** The skin of a doe, especially when dressed. **2** A heavy, twilled, cotton fabric napped on one side; also, a heavy, short–napped, woolen fabric resembling doeskin.

does·n't (duz′ənt) Does not: a contraction.

doff (dof, dôf) *v.t.* **1** To take off or remove, as clothing. **2** To take off (the hat) in salutation. **3** To throw away; discard. [Contraction of DO OFF] —**doff′er** *n.*

dog (dôg, dog) *n.* **1** A domesticated carnivorous mammal (*Canis familiaris*), of world–wide distribution and many varieties, noted for its adaptability and its devotion to man. ◆ Collateral adjective: *canine.* **2** One of

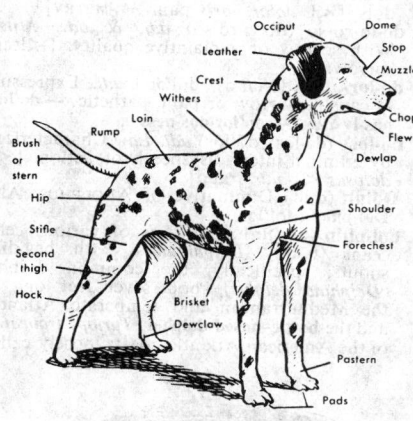

DOG
Nomenclature for anatomical parts

various other species of the family *Canidae*, as the dingo, etc. **3** The male of the dog and various other animals of the *Canidae*: a *dog* fox. **4** In the western United States, a prairie dog. **5** *Mech.* Any small device that holds or grips; a catch, detent, or pawl. **6** The hammer of a firearm. **7** An andiron. **8** *Meteorol.* A sundog or fog dog. **9** A fellow; man–about–town: a gay *dog.* **10** A scoundrel; rascal. **11** *U.S. Slang* A hot dog. **12** *pl. Slang* Feet. — **dead dog** *Slang* A person or thing of no use

or value. —**to put on the dog** *U.S. Slang* To make a pretentious display. —*adv.* Very; utterly: used in combination: *dog–tired.* —*v.t.* **dogged, dog·ging 1** To follow persistently; hound; hunt. **2** To fasten with or as with a dog or catch. [OE *dogga*]

Dog (dôg, dog) **1** Either of two southern constellations, called *Canis Major* and *Canis Minor.* See CONSTELLATION. **2** Sirius, the Dog Star.

dog–ape (dôg′āp′, dog′–) *n.* A baboon or similar ape.

dog·bane (dôg′bān′, dog′–) *n.* Any of a genus (*Apocynum,* family *Apocynaceae*) of smooth, reddish–stemmed herbs about 3 feet high, having an acrid, milky juice; especially, the hemp dogbane (*A. cannabinum*), used in medicine as a cardiac tonic, and the **spreading dogbane** (*A. androsaemifolium*) of North America.

dog·ber·ry (dôg′ber′ē, dog′–) *n. pl.* **·ries 1** The European dogwood (*Cornus sanguinea*). **2** Its fruit. **3** The chokeberry. **4** The bearberry (genus *Arctostaphylos*). **5** The English dog rose.

Dog·ber·ry (dôg′ber′ē, dog′–) In Shakespeare's *Much Ado About Nothing,* a smug, egotistical constable.

dog biscuit A hard biscuit made with meat scraps, ground bones, etc., for feeding dogs.

dog·bri·er (dôg′brī′ər, dog′–) *n.* The dog rose.

dog–cart (dôg′kärt′, dog′–) *n.* **1** A one–horse vehicle, usually two–wheeled, with two seats set back to back and, originally, an enclosed space for dogs beneath the rear seat. **2** A cart hauled by one or more dogs.

dog–catch·er (dôg′kach′ər, dog′–) *n.* A person licensed by a town or city to pick up and impound stray dogs.

dog–cheap (dôg′chēp′, dog′–) *adj.* Absurdly or exceedingly cheap.

dog days The hot, sultry season in July and August, when the Dog Star (*Sirius*) rises with the sun.

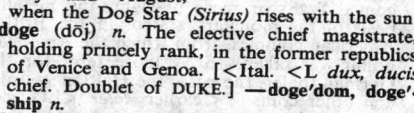

DOG–CART

doge (dōj) *n.* The elective chief magistrate, holding princely rank, in the former republics of Venice and Genoa. [<Ital. <L *dux, ducis* chief. Doublet of DUKE.] —**doge′dom, doge′·ship** *n.*

dog–ear (dôg′ir′, dog′–) *n.* The corner of a page of a book, turned down to mark a place or by careless use. —*v.t.* To turn or fold down the corner of (a page). Also **dog's–ear.** —**dog′–eared′** *adj.*

dog·face (dôg′fās′, dog′–) *n. U.S. Slang* A soldier in the U.S. Army; especially, a private.

dog–fen·nel (dôg′fen′əl, dog′–) *n.* **1** Mayweed. **2** The heath aster.

dog·fight (dôg′fīt′, dog′–) *n.* **1** A fight between or as between dogs. **2** *Mil.* Combat at close quarters between aircraft or tanks.

dog·fish (dôg′fish′, dog′–) *n. pl.* **·fish** or **·fish·es** One of various small, littoral sharks, as the common spiny dogfish (*Squalus acanthias*) of North American waters, and the smooth dogfish (genus *Mustelus*).

dog fox 1 A male fox. **2** The corsac.

dog·ged (dôg′id, dog′–) *adj.* Silently or sullenly persistent; stubborn; obdurate. See synonyms under MOROSE, OBSTINATE. —**dog′ged·ly** *adv.* —**dog′ged·ness** *n.*

dog·ger (dôg′ər, dog′–) *n. Naut.* A two–masted fishing vessel, broad of beam and having a fish–well in the center, used in the North Sea. [ME *doggere*; origin uncertain]

Dogger Bank A submerged sand shoal in the North Sea between Denmark and England; scene of a German naval defeat of World War I (1915).

dog·ger·el (dôg′ər·əl, dog′–) *n.* Trivial, awkwardly written verse, usually comic or burlesque in effect. —*adj.* Of or composed of such verse. Also **dog′grel.** [ME; origin unknown] —**dog′ger·el·ist** *n.*

dog·ger·el·ize (dôg′ər·əl·īz, dog′–) *v.i.* **·ized, ·iz·ing** To write doggerel.

dog·ger·y (dôg′ər·ē, dog′–) *n. pl.* **·ger·ies 1** Dogs collectively. **2** Canaille; the mob; riff-

raff. **3** Doglike conduct.

dog·gish (dôg′ish, dog′–) *adj.* **1** Like a dog; snappish. **2** *Colloq.* Showily fashionable; pretentious. —**dog′gish·ly** *adv.* —**dog′gish·ness** *n.*

dog·go (dôg′ō, dog′–) *adv. Slang* In a place of concealment; in hiding: to lie *doggo.*

dog–gone (dôg′gôn′, dog′gon′) *U.S. Colloq. v.t.* **–goned, –gon·ing** To damn: a euphemism. —*interj.* Damn!; darn!: a mild oath. [? Alter. of *God damn*]

dog·gy (dôg′ē, dog′–) *adj.* **·gi·er, ·gi·est 1** Of or pertaining to dogs; doglike: a *doggy* smell. **2** *Colloq.* Admirable; fashionable; attractive. —*n. pl.* **·gies** A dog, especially a little or pet dog. Also **dog′gie.**

doggy bag A bag containing leftover food which a restaurant customer may carry home for his dog.

dog house 1 A kennel. **2** The caboose on a freight train. —**in the dog house** *Slang* Out of favor.

do·gie (dō′gē) *n.* In the western United States, a stray or motherless calf: also spelled *dogy.* [Origin unknown]

dog in the manger One who will neither enjoy a thing himself nor permit others to.

dog Latin 1 Barbarous or incorrect Latin. **2** A schoolboy jargon imitating Latin.

dog–leg·ged (dôg′leg′id, -legd′, dog′–) *adj.* Having a bend like a dog's hind leg: said of stairs, etc. Also **dog′–leg′.**

dog·ma (dôg′mə, dog′–) *n. pl.* **·mas** or **·ma·ta** (-mə·tə) **1** *Theol.* A doctrine or system of teachings of religious truth as maintained by the Christian church or any portion of it; hence, a statement of religious faith or duty formulated by a body possessing or claiming authority to decree or decide. **2** Doctrine asserted and adopted on authority, as distinguished from that which is the result of one's own reasoning or experience; a dictum. **3** Any settled opinion or conviction; an accepted principle, maxim, or tenet. See synonyms under DOCTRINE. [<L <Gk. *dogma, -atos* opinion, tenet <*dokeein* think]

dog·mat·ic (dôg·mat′ik, dog–) *adj.* **1** Marked by positive and authoritative assertion; stating opinions without evidence. **2** Hence, arrogant. **3** Like or pertaining to dogma. Also **dog·mat′i·cal.** —**dog·mat′i·cal·ly** *adv.* —**dog·mat′i·cal·ness** *n.*

Synonyms: arrogant, authoritative, dictatorial, doctrinal, domineering, imperious, magisterial, opinionated, overbearing, positive, self–opinionated, systematic. *Dogmatic* is technically applied to that which is formally enunciated by adequate authority; *doctrinal* to that which is stated in the form of doctrine to be taught or defended. Outside of theology, *dogmatic* has generally an offensive sense; a *dogmatic* statement is one for which the author does not trouble himself to give a reason, either because of the strength of his convictions, or because of his contempt for those whom he addresses; thus *dogmatic* is, in common use, allied with *arrogant* and kindred words. See IMPERIOUS.

dog·mat·ics (dôg·mat′iks, dog–) *n. pl.* (construed as singular) *Theol.* The systematic exposition of religious dogmas. Also **dogmatic theology.**

dog·ma·tism (dôg′mə·tiz′əm, dog′–) *n.* **1** Positive or arrogant assertion, as of belief, without proof. **2** *Philos.* An uncritical faith in the presumptions of reason or a priori principles: opposed to *scepticism.*

dog·ma·tize (dôg′mə·tīz, dog′–) *v.* **·tized, ·tiz·ing** *v.i.* To express oneself dogmatically. —*v.t.* To declare or assert as a dogma. —**dog′ma·tist** *n.* —**dog′ma·ti·za′tion** *n.* —**dog′ma·tiz′er** *n.*

do–good·er (dōō′gŏŏd′ər) *n.* An idealistic philanthropist or reformer: a derisive term.

dog rose The wild brier (*Rosa canina*) of European hedges and thickets, bearing single pink flowers and fruits known as *hips.*

dog's–ear (dôgz′ir′, dogz′–) See DOG–EAR.

dog sled A sled drawn by one or more dogs. Also **dog sledge.**

dog's–let·ter (dôgz′let′ər, dogz′–) *n.* A name for the letter *r,* especially when pronounced with a trill. [Trans. of L *litera canina,* so called because it resembles a dog's growl]

dog's life *Colloq.* A wretched existence.

dog's–tail (dôgz′tāl′, dogz′–) *n.* An Old World perennial grass (genus *Cynosurus*) with flat

leaves and spikelets in dense clusters, especially the **crested dog's-tail** *(C. cristatus)*, naturalized in eastern North America: also *dogtail.*

Dog's Tail The constellation Ursa Minor.

Dog Star The star Sirius (Alpha of the constellation Canis Major).

dog's-tongue (dôgz′tung′, dogz′-) *n.* Hound's-tongue.

dog's-tooth violet (dôgz′tōōth′, dogz′-) *n.* **1** A spring-flowering European herb of the lily family *(Erythronium dens-canis)* bearing yellow, purple, or white flowers: also called *adder's-tongue.* **2** One of various American plants, as *Erythronium albidum*, bearing pinkish flowers, and the yellow-flowered *E. americanum.* Also **dogtooth violet.**

dog tag 1 A pendant or small metal plate for the collar of a dog, usually indicating ownership. **2** *Colloq.* A soldier's identification tag, worn around the neck.

dog·tail (dôg′tāl′, dog′-) See DOG'S-TAIL.

dog-tired (dôg′tīrd′, dog′-) *adj. Colloq.* Very tired.

dog·tooth (dôg′tōōth′, dog′-) *n.* **1** A human canine tooth or eyetooth. **2** An English architectural ornament, popular in the 13th century, generally composed of four radiating leaves, suggesting a dog's tooth. Also **dog tooth.**

dog-town (dôg′toun′, dog′-) *n.* In the western U.S., a colony of prairie dogs; also, land occupied by prairie dogs.

dog-trot (dôg′trot′, dog′-) *n.* A regular and easy trot.

dog-vane (dôg′vān′, dog′-) *n. Naut.* A small vane of bunting, cork, and feathers placed on the weather gunwale of a vessel to indicate direction of wind.

dog-watch (dôg′woch′, -wôch′, dog′-) *n. Naut.* One of two watches aboard ship, each of two hours, between 4 to 6 and 6 to 8 p.m.

dog·wood (dôg′wŏŏd′, dog′-) *n.* Any of certain trees or shrubs (family *Cornaceae*); specifically, the European **red dogwood** *(Cornus sanguinea)* and the **flowering** or **Virginia dogwood** *(C. florida)* of the United States, with large decorative pinkish-white flowers.

do·gy (dō′gē) See DOGIE.

Do·ha (dō′hə) Capital of Qatar sheikdom.

Doh·na·nyi (dō′nä·nyē), **Ernst von,** born 1877, Hungarian composer.

doiled (doild) *adj. Brit. Dial.* Stunned; dazed; confused. [Var. of ME *dold*, orig. pp. of *dollen* make dull]

doi·ly (doi′lē) *n. pl.* **·lies** A small, matlike, ornamental napkin, used under dishes, as a decoration, etc.: also spelled *doyley, doyly.* [after *Doily* or *Doyley*, 17th c. English draper]

do·ings (dōō′ingz) *n. pl.* Proceedings; acts; course of conduct. See synonyms under ACT, TRANSACTION, WORK.

Doi·sy (doi′zē), **Edward Adelbert,** born 1893, U.S. biochemist.

doit (doit) *n.* Formerly, a small copper coin of the Netherlands; a trifle. [<Du. *duit* coin]

doit·ed (doi′tid, -tit) *adj. Scot.* Foolish from or as from dotage; senile.

dokh·ma (dok′mə) *n.* See TOWER OF SILENCE.

dol (dol) *n.* A unit of pain intensity, corresponding to a barely perceptible sensation from the application of heat rays to the skin, with a maximum for any given subject of about 10 dols. [<L *dolor* pain]

do·lab·ri·form (dō·lab′rə·fôrm) *adj. Bot.* Ax- or hatchet-shaped, as leaves, etc. [<L *dolabra* ax + (I)FORM]

dol·ce (dōl′chā) *adj. Music* Smooth and sweet in performance. —*adv. Music* Sweetly; softly. —*n.* A soft-toned organ stop. [<Ital. <L *dulcis* sweet]

dol·ce far nien·te (dōl′chā fär nyen′te) *Italian* Pleasant idleness; literally, (it is) sweet to do nothing.

Dol·ci (dōl′chē), **Carlo,** 1616–86, Italian painter.

dol·drums (dol′drəmz) *n. pl.* **1** Those parts of the ocean near the equator where calms or baffling winds prevail. **2** A becalmed state. **3** A dull, depressed, or bored condition of mind; the dumps. [Cf. ME *dold*, pp. of *dollen* make dull]

dole[1] (dōl) *n.* **1** That which is doled out; a small portion; a gratuity. **2** Specifically, a sum of money officially paid to an unemployed person for sustenance; in Great Britain, government relief for the unemployed, instituted 1911, consisting of weekly payments from a special fund contributed by workers, employers, and government: so called since 1918. **3** *Obs.* Lot; portion. —*v.t.* **doled, dol·ing** To dispense in small quantities; distribute: usually with *out.* [OE *dāl.* Related to DEAL[2].]

dole[2] (dōl) *n. Obs.* Grief; mourning. [<OF *dol* <LL *dolium* grief <*dolere* feel pain]

Dole (dōl), **Sanford Ballard,** 1844–1926, U.S. jurist; president of the republic of Hawaii 1894–98; first governor of the Territory of Hawaii 1900–03.

dole·ful (dōl′fəl) *adj.* Melancholy; mournful. Also **dole′some.** [<DOLE[2]] —**dole′ful·ly** *adv.* —**dole′ful·ness** *n.*

dol·er·ite (dol′ə·rīt) *n.* **1** A coarse, crystalline basalt, containing labradorite and augite: sometimes used interchangeably with *diabase.* **2** *U.S.* Any dark, greenish igneous rock not readily identified by visual examination. [<Gk. *doleros* deceptive <*dolos* deceit + -ITE[1]; so called because not easily identified] —**dol′er·it′ic** (-rit′ik) *adj.*

Dol·gel·ly (dol·geth′lē, -gel′ē) The county town of Merioneth, Wales.

dol·i·cho·ce·phal·ic (dol′i·kō·sə·fal′ik) *adj.* Having a long skull, the breadth less than one third of the length, the cephalic index being 75.9 or less: distinguished from *brachycephalic.* Also **dol′i·cho·ceph′a·lous** (-sef′ə·ləs). [<Gk. *dolichos* long + *kephalē* head] —**dol′·i·cho·ceph′al** *adj. & n.* —**dol′i·cho·ceph′a·lism, dol′i·cho·ceph′a·ly** *n.*

dol·i·cho·mor·phic (dol′i·kō·môr′fik) *adj.* Longilineal.

doll (dol) *n.* **1** A child's toy representing a person; a puppet. **2** A pretty but superficial woman. **3** A pretty child. **4** *Slang* Any girl or woman. Also *dolly.* —*v.t. & v.i. Slang* To dress up; dress elaborately: with *up.* [from *Doll*, a nickname for Dorothy.] —**doll′ish** *adj.* —**doll′ish·ly** *adv.* —**doll′ish·ness** *n.*

dol·lar (dol′ər) *n.* **1** The standard monetary unit of the United States and of various other countries which use the $ sign for their coinage, as Canada and Argentina. Specifically, a U.S. silver coin, of the legal value of 100 cents, authorized in 1792 by Congress. **2** A U.S. gold piece, coined 1849–90. **3** A U.S. legal tender note, either a greenback or a silver certificate. **4** The Spanish milled dollar (first coined 1728) or piece-of-eight, the metallic basis of the monetary system in the British American colonies, from which the American dollar was taken. **5** A loose term for the German thaler, the peso, the Haitian gourde, and other coins. [<earlier *daler* <LG <G *taler, thaler*, contraction of *Joachimstaler* money of Joachimstal, Bohemian city where first coined]

—**Hong Kong dollar, British dollar, Straits Settlements dollar** Coins issued by the British for use in parts of the Commonwealth.

—**Levant dollar** or **Maria Theresa dollar** A silver coin issued for trade purposes by Austria since 1780.

—**trade dollar** A U.S. special silver dollar, heavier than normal and of special composition, used in Oriental trade, 1885–87.

dol·lar-a-year man (dol′ər·ə·yir′) One who serves as a government employee for the minimum legal salary.

dollar diplomacy 1 The policy of utilizing the financial interests or power of a country as a means of strengthening its foreign relations. **2** A policy of subordinating all other considerations to the foreign trade and financial interests of a country.

dol·lar·fish (dol′ər·fish′) *n. pl.* **·fish** or **·fish·es** **1** A spiny-finned butterfish of oval, compressed form (genus *Poronatus*), common on the Atlantic coast of the United States. **2** The moonfish.

dollar mark or **sign** The sign ($) meaning dollar or dollars when placed before a number.

Doll·fuss (dôl′fōōs), **Engelbert,** 1892–1934, Austrian premier 1932–34; assassinated.

Döl·ling·er (dœl′ing·ər), **Johann Joseph Ignaz von,** 1799–1890, German Roman Catholic theologian; excommunicated for opposition to certain dogmatic teachings.

dol·ly (dol′ē) *n. pl.* **·lies** **1** A doll: child's word. **2** *Mining* A contrivance for stirring ore while it is being washed. **3** *Austral.* A rude ore-crushing device. **4** *Mech.* A block or other extension placed on a pile to lengthen it while being driven. **5** A tool for holding one end of a rivet while a head is formed at the other. **6** A small narrow-gage locomotive for use in switching. **7** A light hand truck, with wheels or rollers, used for moving heavy loads, as books, boxes, lumber, etc. **8** *Brit. Dial.* A wooden instrument for beating or stirring clothes while washing. **9** A low, wheeled platform on which a motion-picture or television camera is set. —*v.t.* **·lied, ·ly·ing 1** To crush or concentrate (ore) with a dolly. **2** *Brit. Dial.* To stir or wash (clothes) with a dolly. —*v.i.* **3** To move a television or motion-picture camera toward a scene or subject: with *in.* [from *Dolly*, a nickname for Dorothy]

Dolly Var·den (vär′dən) **1** A dress with a printed or figured design, worn over a petticoat of a plain color. **2** A woman's large, flower-trimmed hat. **3** A salmonoid fish *(Salvelinus malma)* of the Rocky Mountain streams, having red spots on the back and sides and resembling the eastern brook trout: also **Dolly Varden trout.** [after *Dolly Varden*, a character in Dickens' *Barnaby Rudge*]

dol·man (dol′mən) *n. pl.* **dol·mans 1** A long Turkish outer garment. **2** A woman's coat with dolman sleeves or capelike arm pieces. **3** The capelike uniform jacket of a hussar. [<F *doliman* <Turkish *dōlāmān* long robe]

dolman sleeve A sleeve on a coat or dress, tapering from a wide opening at the armhole to a narrow one at the wrist.

dol·men (dol′men) *n.* A megalithic, sepulchral monument of large unhewn stones set on end and covered with a single huge stone or several stones, so as to form a small chamber and often covered with earth. Compare CROMLECH. [<F, prob. <Cornish *tolmen* hole of stone]

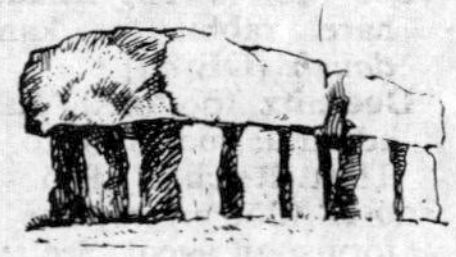

DOLMEN

dol·o·mite (dol′ə·mīt) *n.* A brittle calcium magnesium carbonate, occurring abundantly in white to pale-pink rhombohedral crystals. Many so-called marbles are dolomites. [after D. de *Dolomieu*, 1750–1801, French geologist] —**dol′o·mit′ic** (-mit′ik) *adj.*

Dol·o·mites (dol′ə·mīts) An eastern division of the Alps in northern Italy; highest peak, 10,964 feet. Also **Dolomite Alps.**

do·lor (dō′lər) *n. Poetic* Sorrow; anguish. Also *Brit.* **do′lour.** [<L, pain]

dol·or·im·e·try (dol′ə·rim′ə·trē) *n.* The measurement of the intensity of pain in terms of dols. [<L *dolor, -oris* pain + -METRY]

do·lo·ro·so (dō′lə·rō′sō) *adj. & adv. Music* With sorrow or a plaintive quality. [<Ital., sorrowful]

do·lor·ous (dō′lər·əs, dol′ər-) *adj.* Expressing or causing sorrow or pain; pathetic. —**do′lor·ous·ly** *adv.* —**do′lor·ous·ness** *n.*

do·lose (də·lōs′, dō′lōs) *adj. Law* Characterized by criminal intent, as speech or action. [<L *dolosus* <*dolus* fraud]

Dolph (dolf) Diminutive of ADOLPHUS. Also **Dol·phus** (dol′fəs).

dol·phin (dol′fin) *n.* **1** Any of various cetaceans (family *Delphinidae*), with beaklike snouts; specifically, the common dolphin *(Delphinus delphis)*, about seven feet long, of the Mediterranean and temperate Atlantic; and the **bottle-nosed dolphin** *(Turiops truncatus)* of the American Atlantic coast: loosely called *porpoise.* **2** Either of two fish of the genus *Coryphaena* of southern waters; especially, the edible *C. hippurus*: also called *dorado.* **3** *Naut.* **a** A spar or block of wood attached to an anchor and used for small boats to ride by. **b** A mooring post or buffer, or a series of such posts contiguous to each other. **c** A group of protective rope fenders just beneath the gunwale of a boat. —*adj.* Of or pertaining to devices having a fancied resemblance to the dolphin. [<OF *daulphin* <L *delphinus* <Gk. *delphis, -inos*]

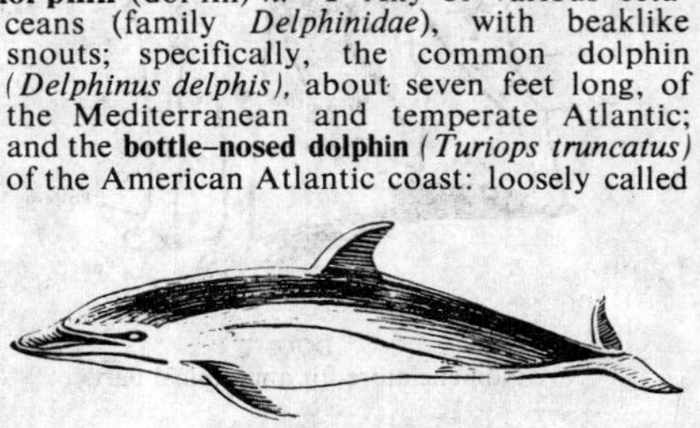

THE COMMON DOLPHIN

Dol·phin (dol′fin) The constellation Delphinus. See CONSTELLATION.
dol·phin–strik·er (dol′fin·strī′kər) *n. Naut.* **1** The spearlike point of the martingale boom. **2** The martingale boom.
dolt (dōlt) *n.* A stupid person; blockhead; dunce. [ME *dold* dulled, stupid] **— dolt′ish** *adj.* **— dolt′ish·ly** *adv.* **— dolt′ish·ness** *n.*
Dom (dom) *n.* **1** In Portugal and Brazil, a title of respect given to a gentleman: used with the given name. **2** A title given to certain Roman Catholic monks and other church dignitaries. [<Pg. <L *dominus* master]
-dom *suffix of nouns* **1** State or condition of being: *freedom.* **2** Rank of; domain of: *kingdom.* **3** The totality of those having a certain rank, state or condition: *Christendom.* [OE *-dōm* < *dōm* state]
Do·magk (dō′mäk), **Gerhard,** 1895–1964, German chemist.
do·main (dō·mān′) *n.* **1** A territory over which dominion is exercised; commonwealth; province. **2** A department, as of knowledge; range; scope. **3** A manor. **4** Absolute proprietorship in land. **5** Dominion; empire; rule. [<MF *domaine* <OF *demeine, demaine* <L *dominicum,* neut. sing. of *dominicus* of a lord < *dominus* lord. Doublet of DEMESNE.] **— do·ma·ni·al** (dō·mā′nē·əl) *adj.*
dome (dōm) *n.* **1** *Archit.* The vaulted roof of a rotunda; a cupola. **2** Any cuplike covering, vertical extension, or dome-shaped top. **3** A majestic building; specifically, following Italian and German usage, a cathedral. **4** In the orthorhombic, monoclinic, and triclinic crystal systems, a form whose faces intersect the vertical axis and one lateral axis. When the face is parallel to the shorter axis, it is called a *brachydome*; when parallel to the longer axis, a macrodome. **— *v.* domed, dom·ing** *v.t.* **1** To furnish or cover with a dome. **2** To shape like a dome. **—** *v.i.* **3** To rise or swell upward like a dome. [<F *dôme* <Ital. *duomo* cupola <L *domus* house]
Do·me·ni·chi·no (dō·mā′nē·kē′nō), 1581–1641, Italian painter: original name *Domenico Zampieri.*
domes·day (do͞omz′dā′) *n.* Doomsday.
Domesday Book A book containing the record of the statistical survey of England, made in 1085–86 by order of William the Conqueror: also spelled *Doomsday Book.*
do·mes·tic (də·mes′tik) *adj.* **1** Belonging to the house or household; concerning or relating to the home or family. **2** Given to the concerns of home; fond of or adapted to family life, duties, or employments; devoted to housekeeping. **3** Domesticated; tame. **4** Of or pertaining to one's own state or country; produced at home; not foreign; home-made. **—** *n.* **1** A family servant. **2** *pl.* Home-made fabrics or cloth: sometimes restricted to cotton goods. [<L *domesticus* < *domus* house] **— do·mes′ti·cal·ly** *adv.*
do·mes·ti·cate (də·mes′tə·kāt) *v.* **·cat·ed, ·cat·ing** *v.t.* **1** To train for domestic use; tame. **2** To civilize. **3** To cause to feel at ease or at home, make domestic. **—** *v.i.* **4** To become domestic. Also **do·mes′ti·cize.** [<Med. L *domesticatus,* pp. of *domesticare* live in a house <L *domus* house] **— do·mes′ti·ca′tion** *n.*
do·mes·tic·i·ty (dō′mes·tis′ə·tē) *n. pl.* **·ties 1** The state of being domestic; fondness of home and family. **2** A household habit or affair.
domestic science Home economics.
do·mi·cal (dō′mi·kəl, dom′i-) *adj.* Of or like a dome, or characterized by a dome or domes. **— do′mi·cal·ly** *adv.*
dom·i·cile (dom′ə·səl, -sīl) *n.* **1** A settled place of abode; home, house, or dwelling. **2** The place where a person has his legal abode. See synonyms under HOME, HOUSE. **— *v.* ·ciled, ·cil·ing** *v.t.* To establish in a place of abode. **—** *v.i.* To have one's abode; dwell: also **dom′·i·cil′i·ate.** Also **dom′i·cil.** [<F <L *domicilium* < *domus* house]
dom·i·cil·i·ar·y (dom′ə·sil′ē·er′ē) *adj.* Pertaining to a fixed or a private residence.
dom·i·nance (dom′ə·nəns) *n.* **1** Control; ascendancy. **2** *Genetics* The condition of having or exhibiting only one of a pair of contrasting genetic characteristics. Also **dom′i·nan·cy.**
dom·i·nant (dom′ə·nənt) *adj.* **1** Ruling; governing; predominant. **2** *Genetics* Designating a character transmitted by one parent of a hybrid offspring, in which it appears to the masking of the contrasted character transmitted by the other parent: opposed to *recessive.* **—** *n. Music* The fifth tone of a diatonic scale. [<F <L *dominans, -antis,* ppr. of *dominare* DOMINATE]
dom·i·nate (dom′ə·nāt) *v.* **·nat·ed, ·nat·ing** *v.t.* **1** To exercise control over; govern. **2** To tower above; loom over: The city *dominates* the plain. **—** *v.i.* **3** To have control; hold sway. [<L *dominatus,* pp. of *dominare* rule, dominate < *dominus* lord] **— dom′i·na′tive** *adj.* **— dom′i·na′tor** *n.*
dom·i·na·tion (dom′ə·nā′shən) *n.* **1** Control; dominion. **2** *pl. Theol.* The fourth order in the hierarchy of heavenly beings: also called *dominions.*
dom·i·ne (dom′ə·nē, dō′mə-) *n. Obs.* A title of address meaning lord or master. [<L, vocative of *dominus* lord]
dom·i·neer (dom′ə·nir′) *v.t.* & *v.i.* **1** To rule arrogantly or insolently; tyrannize; bully. **2** To tower or loom (over or above). [<Du. *domineren* <F *dominer* <L *dominus* lord]
dom·i·neer·ing (dom′ə·nir′ing) *adj.* Overbearing. See synonyms under ARBITRARY, DOGMATIC, IMPERIOUS. **— dom′i·neer′ing·ly** *adv.*
Dom·i·nic (dom′ə·nik) A masculine personal name. Also **Dom′i·nick.** [<L, of the Lord]
Dom·i·nic (dom′ə·nik), **Saint,** 1170–1221, Spanish friar; founded the Dominican Order: original name *Domingo de Guzmán.*
Dom·i·ni·ca (dom′ə·nē′kə, də·min′i·kə) A British colony in the Windward Islands; 305 square miles; capital, Roseau.
do·min·i·cal (də·min′i·kəl) *adj.* **1** Relating to Christ as the Lord. **2** Relating to Sunday as the Lord's day. **—** *n.* **1** A church edifice. **2** A dominical letter. **3** One who celebrates the Christian Sunday: opposed to *Sabbatarian.* **4** *Obs.* The veil worn by women when attending divine service in the Roman Catholic Church; also, a Sunday dress. [<LL *dominicalis* of the Lord <L *dominicus* < *dominus* lord]
dominical letter One of the first seven letters of the alphabet, used in the ecclesiastical calendar to designate the Sundays in a given year, and to aid in determining the date of Easter.
Do·min·i·can (də·min′i·kən) *adj.* **1** Of or pertaining to St. Dominic. **2** Belonging to a monastic order or institution following the rule of St. Dominic. **3** Of the Dominican Republic. **—** *n.* **1** A member of a mendicant monastic order *(Black Friars)* founded in 1216 by St. Dominic: officially called *Fratres Praedicatores* or *Preaching Friars.* **2** A native of the Dominican Republic.

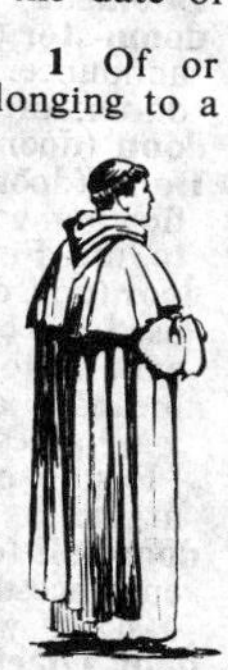

DOMINICAN FRIAR

Dominican Republic A republic occupying the eastern part of Hispaniola; 19,129 square miles; capital, Santo Domingo· formerly *Ciudad Trujillo. Spanish* **Re·pú·bli·ca Do·mi·ni·ca·na** (rā·po͞o′blē·kä dō·mē′nē·kä′nä).
dom·i·nie (dom′ə·nē) *n.* **1** *Scot.* A schoolmaster. **2** *U.S.* A minister of the Dutch Reformed Church. **3** *Colloq.* Any minister. [Var. of DOMINE]
do·min·ion (də·min′yən) *n.* **1** Sovereign authority; sway. **2** *Law* The right of absolute possession and use; ownership; dominium. **3** A country under a particular government. **4** Formerly, a self-governing member of the Commonwealth of Nations. **5** *pl.* Domination (def. 2). [<F <L *dominium* < *dominus* lord]
Dominion Day In Canada, the anniversary of the federation of Canada into a dominion (July 1, 1867): a legal holiday.
Dom·i·nique (dom′ə·nēk′) *n.* An American breed of domestic fowls, with gray-barred plumage, yellow legs, and rose comb. Also **Dom′i·nick.** [<F, Dominica]
do·min·i·um (də·min′ē·əm) *n. Law* The absolute right of ownership and control of property, especially of land: *dominium* in fee simple. [<L < *dominus* lord]
dom·i·no[1] (dom′ə·nō) *n. pl.* **·noes** or **·nos 1** A small mask for the eyes. **2** A loose robe, hood and mask worn at masquerades. **3** A person wearing this. **4** A hooded garment forming an outer ecclesiastical vestment. [<MF, a clerical garment <L *dominus* lord]
dom·i·no[2] (dom′ə·nō) *n. pl.* **·noes** or **·nos 1** A small, flat block, as of wood or plastic, divided on one side into halves, each left blank or marked with usually one to six dots. **2** *pl.* A game played with a set (usually 28) of such pieces, the object being to match the halves having the same number of dots: construed as singular. **—** *adj.* Describing the view or political theory that a series of events is unavoidably contingent on the occurrence of an initial event, as a row of dominoes collapses when the first is toppled: the *domino* theory of Communist aggrandizement.
dom·i·nus (dom′ə·nəs) *n. pl.* **·ni** (-nī) *Latin* Master; sir: a title formerly given to a clergyman, knight, or lord of a manor. Compare DOMINE.
Dom·i·nus (dom′ə·nəs) *n. Latin* The Lord.
Dom·i·nus vo·bis·cum (dom′ə·nəs vō·bis′kəm) *Latin* The Lord be with you.
Do·mi·tian (də·mish′ən), A.D. 51–96, Roman emperor 81–96: full name *Titus Flavius Domitianus Augustus.*
Dom·re·my (dôn·rə·mē′) A village in NE France; birthplace of Joan of Arc. Also **Dom·re·my′–la–Pu·celle′** (-la·pü·sel′).
don[1] (don) *n.* **1** A Spanish gentleman or nobleman. **2** An important personage. **3** *Colloq.* In English universities a head, residential fellow, or tutor of a college. [<Sp. <L *dominus* lord]
don[2] (don) *v.t.* **donned, don·ning** To put on, as a garment. [Contraction of *do on*]
Don (don) *n.* Seignior; sir: a title of respect or address, used with the given name in Spain and Spanish-speaking countries.
Don (don) Short for DONALD.
Don (don) **1** A river in south central Russian S.F.S.R., flowing 1,222 miles south to the Sea of Azov: ancient *Tanais.* **2** A river in Aberdeenshire, Scotland, flowing 82 miles east to the North Sea. **3** A river in southern Yorkshire, England, flowing 70 miles to the Ouse.
do·na (dō′nə) *n.* A Portuguese lady.
do·ña (dō′nyä) *n.* A Spanish lady.
Do·na (dô′nə) *n.* The Portuguese form of DOÑA.
Do·ña (dō′nyä) *n.* Lady; madam: the feminine title corresponding to *Don.* [<Sp. <L *domina* mistress]
Don·ald (don′əld) A masculine personal name. [<Celtic, proud chief]
Do·nar (dō′när) In Teutonic mythology, the god of thunder: identified with the Norse *Thor.*
do·nate (dō′nāt) *v.t.* **·nat·ed, ·nat·ing** To bestow as a gift, especially to a cause; present; contribute. [<L *donatus,* pp. of *donare* give < *donum* a gift] **— do′na·tor** *n.*
Do·na·tel·lo (dō′nä·tel′lō), 1386–1466, Italian sculptor: original name *Donato di Niccolò di Betto Bardi.*
do·na·tion (dō·nā′shən) *n.* **1** The act of donating. **2** That which is donated; a gift; grant; offering. See synonyms under GIFT.
Don·a·tism (don′ə·tiz′əm) *n.* The principles of the Donatists.
Don·a·tist (don′ə·tist) *n.* One of a fourth-century, schismatic sect of North Africa. [<Med. L *Donatista,* after *Donatus,* North African bishop and founder of the sect] **— Don′a·tis′tic** or **·ti·cal** *adj.*
don·a·tive (don′ə·tiv, dō′nə·tiv) *adj.* Belonging by deed of gift. **—** *n.* A donation; gift.
Do·nau (dō′nou) The German name for the DANUBE.
Don·cas·ter (dong′kas·tər, *Brit.* -kəs-) A county borough in south Yorkshire.
done (dun) Past participle of DO[1]. **—** *adj.* **1** Completed; finished; ended; agreed. **2** Cooked sufficiently.
do·nee (dō·nē′) *n.* One who receives a gift. [<DON(OR) + -EE]
done for 1 Tired; exhausted. **2** Finished; put out of the running; ruined. **3** Dead or about to die.
Don·e·gal (don′i·gôl, don′i·gôl′) A county in Ulster province, Ireland; 1,865 square miles; county seat, Lifford.

add, āce, câre, pälm; end, ēven; it, īce; odd, ōpen, ôrder; to͝ok, po͞ol; up, bûrn; ə = a in *above,* e in *sicken,* i in *clarity,* o in *melon,* u in *focus;* yo͞o = u in *fuse;* oi, oil; ou, pout; ch, check; g, go; ng, ring; th, thin; th, this; zh, vision. Foreign sounds à, œ, ü, kh, ṅ; and ◆: see page xx. < from; + plus; ? possibly.

Do·nets (do·nets', *Russian* dô·nyets') A river in SW European U.S.S.R., flowing 631 miles SE to the Don.

Donets Basin A principal industrial region of the U.S.S.R., SW of the lower Donets; 10,000 square miles. Also **Don·bas** (don·bäs'), **Don·bass'**.

don·ga (dong'gə) *n. Afrikaans* The dry bed of a stream.

don·go·la (dong'gə·lə) *n.* Sheepskin, goatskin, or calfskin tanned by the use of mineral and vegetable substances (called the **dongola process**), producing a finish resembling kid. Also **Dongola kid**, **Dongola leather**. [from DON·GOLA, where originally made]

Don·go·la (dong'gə·lə) A town on the Nile in Northern Province, Sudan; former capital of the **Christian Kingdom of Dongola** (6th to 14th centuries).

Do·ni·zet·ti (don'ə·zet'ē, *Ital.* dô'nē·dzet'tē), **Gaetano**, 1797–1848, Italian operatic composer.

don·jon (dun'jən, don'-) *n.* The principal tower or keep of a medieval castle. Also **don'jon·keep'**. [Archaic var. of DUNGEON]

Don Juan (don jōō'·ən, *Sp.* dôn hwän') 1 A legendary Spanish nobleman and seducer of women, the hero of many poems, operas, plays, etc. 2 Any rake or seducer.

DONJON
Chateau de Viviennes, France

don·key (dong'kē, dung'-) *n.* 1 An ass. 2 A stupid or stubborn person. [? from DUNCAN]

donkey engine A small subsidiary engine for pumping, hoisting, etc.

don·na (don'ə, *Ital.* dôn'nä) *n.* An Italian lady. [<Ital. <L *domina* lady]

Don·na (don'ə, *Ital.* dôn'nä) *n.* Lady; madam: a title of respect or address, used with the given name in Italy and Italian-speaking countries.

Don·nan (don'ən), **Frederick George**, 1870–1956, English chemist.

Donne (dun), **John**, 1573?–1631, English poet and clergyman.

don·nerd (don'ərd) *adj. Scot.* 1 Stupid; dunderheaded. 2 Dazed; stunned. Also **don'nered**, **don'nert** (-ərt).

don·nish (don'ish) *adj.* 1 Of, characteristic of, or pertaining to the dons or a English university. 2 Formal; distant; pedantic. — **don'nish·ness** *n.*

Don·ny·brook Fair (don'ē·brŏŏk') 1 An annual fair formerly held at Donnybrook, Ireland: abolished in 1855 because of its disorder. 2 Any disorderly gathering or free-for-all fight.

do·nor (dō'nər) *n.* 1 A giver; donator. 2 One who gives his blood for transfusion, or tissue, skin, etc., for surgical grafting, for another. [<AF *donour*, OF *doneur* <L *donator* <*donare* give]

do–noth·ing (dōō'nuth'ing) *n.* An idler; procrastinator. — *adj.* Idle; indolent, procrastinating.

Don·o·van (don'ə·vən), **William Joseph**, 1883–1959, U.S. lawyer and general: known as **Wild Bill Donovan.**

Don Quix·ote (don kwik'sət, ki·hō'tē; *Sp.* dôn kē·hō'tä) 1 The hero of Cervantes' romance of that name, a satire on chivalry, written in 1605 and followed by a continuation in 1615. 2 Anyone who naively undertakes to do extravagantly romantic things. Also **Don Qui·jo'te.** See QUIXOTIC.

don·sie (don'sē) *adj. Scot.* 1 Neat; trim: a *donsie* lass. 2 Sickly; feeble. 3 Unfortunate; unlucky. Also **don'cie.**

don't (dōnt) Do not: a contraction.

don·zel (don'zəl) *n. Obs.* A young attendant, page, or gallant. [<Ital. *donzello* <LL *domnicellus*, dim. of *dominus* lord]

doo·dad (dōō'dad) *n. Colloq.* 1 A doo-hickey. 2 A small ornament; bauble.

doo·dle¹ (dōō'd'l) *v.t.* **·dled, ·dling** To play (the bagpipe). [<G *dudeln*]

doo·dle² (dōō'd'l) *v.i. Colloq.* To draw pictures, symbols, etc., abstractedly, on whatever material comes to hand, while the mind is otherwise occupied. — *n.* The drawings or symbols so made. [Cf. dial. E *doodle* be idle, trifle]

doo·dle–bug (dōō'd'l·bug') *n.* 1 Any device supposed to be able to detect the location of minerals, water, etc. 2 *Entomol.* The larva of the ant–lion. For illustration see under INSECT (beneficial). 3 Loosely, any droning insect, as the tumblebug. 4 *Colloq.* A robot plane. See under BOMB. [? <dial.E *doodle* an idler, a fool + BUG]

doo·dle·sack (dōō'd'l·sak') *n.* A bagpipe. [<G *dudelsack*]

doo–hick·ey (dōō'hik'ē) *n. Colloq.* Any contrivance or device, the name of which is not known or immediately recalled; doodad. Also, **doo'–hick'us, doo'hink'ey.**

dook (dōōk) *v.t. & v.i. Scot.* To plunge; bathe; duck.

dool (dōōl) *n. Scot.* Dole; sorrow; grief.

doo·lee (dōō'lē) *n. Anglo–Indian* A light litter; a palanquin. Also **doo'lie, doo'ly.** [<Hind. *dōlī,* dim. of *dōla* litter <Skt.]

Doo·lit·tle (dōō'lit'l), **Hilda**, 1886–1961, U.S. poet: pen name *H. D.* — **James Harold,** born 1896, U.S. general.

doom (dōōm) *v.t.* 1 To pronounce judgment or sentence upon; condemn. 2 To destine to a disastrous fate. 3 To decree as a penalty. See synonyms under CONDEMN. [<*n.*] — *n.* 1 The act of dooming, or the state of being doomed. 2 Death; ruin; sad or evil destiny. 3 Judicial decision; condemnation; sentence. 4 The Last Judgment. 5 *Obs.* An enactment; decree. — **crack of doom** The signal for the Last Judgment: also **day of doom** [OE *dōm*]

doom palm A palm of northern Africa (*Hyphaene thebaica*), the fruit of which has the flavor of gingerbread: also called *gingerbread tree:* also spelled **doum palm.** [<F *doum* <Arabic *dawm*]

dooms·day (dōōmz'dā') *n.* The day of the Last Judgment, or of any final judgment: also spelled **domesday.** [OE *domesdæg* judgment day < *dōm* doom + *dæg* day]

Doomsday Book See DOMESDAY BOOK.

doom·ster (dōōm'stər) *n. Scot. Law* The court announcer, who announced the judgment, or doom, of the court.

doon (dōōn) *adv. & prep. Scot.* Down.

Doon (dōōn) A river in Ayrshire, Scotland, flowing 27 miles NW through **Loch Doon** to the Firth of Clyde.

door (dôr, dōr) *n.* 1 A hinged or sliding frame used for closing or opening an entrance or exit, as to a house. 2 Doorway. 3 Any means or avenue of exit or entrance; passageway; access. See synonyms under ENTRANCE. [Fusion of OE *duru* pair of doors and *dor* a gate]

door·bell (dôr'bel', dōr'-) *n.* A device at the entrance to a building or apartment to sound a signal within.

door check A device, usually operated by compressed air, for closing a door automatically and for preventing it from being slammed.

door·jamb (dôr'jam', dōr'-) *n.* The vertical piece at the side of a doorway supporting the lintel.

door·keep·er (dôr'kē'pər, dōr'-) *n.* A guardian or keeper of a door; a minor official of an organized meeting or assembly.

door·knob (dôr'nob', dōr'-) *n.* The handle for turning the catch to open a door.

door·man (dôr'man', -mən, dōr'-) *n. pl.* **·men** (-men', -mən) An attendant at the door of a hotel, apartment house, etc., who assists persons entering and leaving the building.

door·mat (dôr'mat', dōr'-) *n.* A mat placed at an entrance for wiping off mud and moisture from the shoes.

Doorn (dōrn) A village in central Netherlands; residence of William II of Germany, 1919–41.

door·nail (dôr'nāl', dōr'-) *n.* A nail or stud against which a knocker is struck. — **dead as a doornail** Quite dead.

door·plate (dôr'plāt', dōr'-) *n.* A metal plate on a door, with the occupant's name, address, etc. Also **door plate.**

door·post (dôr'pōst', dōr'-) *n.* The post on either side of a doorway: also **door post.**

door·sill (dôr'sil', dōr'-) *n.* The sill or threshold of a door: also **door sill.**

door·step (dôr'step', dōr'-) *n.* A step or one of a series of steps leading to a door.

door·stop (dôr'stop', dōr'-) *n.* A device to keep a door open or to prevent it from slamming.

door·way (dôr'wā', dōr'-) *n.* The passage for entrance and exit into and out of a building, room, etc.

door·yard (dôr'yärd', dōr'-) *n.* A yard around, or especially in front of, a house.

doot (dōōt) *v. & n. Scot.* Doubt.

dop (dop) *n.* A small metal cup on a long stem or holder in which a gemstone is held while being cut or polished. [<Du., lit., shell]

dope (dōp) *n.* 1 *Slang* Any potentially harmful narcotic used for inducing euphoria. 2 *Slang* A dope fiend. 3 A drug given to a race horse to influence its speed. 4 *Slang* Information as to the condition, past performance, etc., of a race horse. 5 *Slang* Any information; also, a calculation or forecast based on it; hence, confidential or inside information. 6 Any thick liquid or semifluid, as an article of food, a lubricant, etc.; specifically, axle grease. 7 An absorbent material for holding a thick liquid, as cotton waste, or a substance for holding nitroglycerin, as in dynamite. 8 *Aeron.* Any material used in treating cloth surface of airplane members to increase strength or produce or maintain tautness. 9 *Slang* A stupid person. — *v.t.* 1 To give or administer dope to (a race horse). 2 *Slang* To stupefy or exhilarate as by a drug: often with *up.* — **to dope out** *U.S. Slang* 1 To plan, as a course of action. 2 To figure out; solve. [<Du. *doop* dipping sauce <*doopen* dip]

dope fiend *Slang* A habitual user of a narcotic drug.

dope ring A combination of persons trafficking illegally in narcotics.

dope sheet *Slang* An information sheet on horses in the day's races, giving their pedigree, past performance, etc.

do·pey (dō'pē) *adj.* **·pi·er, ·pi·est** *Slang* Stupid from or as if from narcotics; dull; heavy.

Dop·pel·gäng·er (dôp'əl·geng'ər) *n. German* 1 A person exactly like another; a double. 2 A wraith, especially of a person not yet dead. Also *doubleganger.*

Dop·pler (dôp'lər), **Christian Johann**, 1803–1853, Austrian physicist and mathematician.

Doppler effect *Physics* The change in the frequency of a sound, light, or radio wave due to the motion of the observer or of the source toward or away from one another. Also **Doppler shift.** [after C. J. *Doppler*]

dor¹ (dôr) *n.* 1 A black European dung beetle (genus *Geotrupes*), known by its droning flight. 2 The June beetle. For illustration see under INSECT (injurious). Also **dor beetle, dor bug, dorr, dorr beetle.** [OE *dora* bumblebee]

dor² (dôr) *n. Obs.* A trick; deception; humbug. [? <ON *dār* scoff]

Do·ra (dôr'ə, dō'rə) Short for DOROTHY, EUDORA, or THEODORA.

do·ra·do (də·rä'dō) *n.* A fish of the genus *Coryphaena.* See DOLPHIN. [<Sp., gilded <LL *deauratus,* pp. of *deaurare* <*de-* completely + *aurum* gold]

Do·ra·do (də·rä'dō) *n.* A southern constellation, the Swordfish. See CONSTELLATION.

Dor·cas society (dôr'kəs) A women's society, usually connected with a church, for supplying garments to the poor. [after *Dorcas,* a female disciple. See *Acts* ix 36.]

Dor·ches·ter (dôr'ches·tər, -chis-) A municipal borough, capital of Dorset, England.

Dor·dogne (dôr·dôn'y') A river in central and SW France, flowing 305 miles SW to the Garonne.

Dor·drecht (dôr'drekht) A town in SW Netherlands: also *Dort.*

Dore (dôr), **Monts** (môn) The highest range of the Auvergne Mountains in central France. Also **Mas·sif du Mont–Dore** (mä·sēf' dü môn·dôr').

Do·ré (dô·rā'), **(Paul) Gustave**, 1833–83, French painter, illustrator, and engraver.

do·ri·a (dôr'ē·ə, dō'rē·ə) *n.* An East Indian cotton fabric with stripes of varying widths. [<Hind. *doriyā* <*dor* thread, stripe]

Do·ri·an (dôr'ē·ən, dō'rē-) *n.* A member of one of the four major tribes of ancient Greece. The Dorians settled in the Peloponnesus about 1100 B.C. — *adj.* Doric.

Dor·ic (dôr′ik, dor′-) *adj.* **1** Relating to or characteristic of Doris or its inhabitants: also **Dorian. 2** *Archit.* Constructed in accordance with the earliest and simplest of the three orders of Greek architecture: called the **Doric order.** For illustration see under ARCHITECTURE, CAPITAL. — *n.* **1** A dialect of ancient Greek, spoken by the Dorians in northern Greece, the Peloponnesus, Crete, Sicily, etc.: used by Pindar and many other lyric poets. **2** A rustic dialect of English.

Dor·i·cism (dôr′ə·siz′əm, dor′-) *n.* A Doric idiom or peculiarity of speech. Also **Do·rism** (dôr′iz·əm, dō′riz-).

Do·rin·da (də·rin′də) A feminine personal name. [<Gk., gift]

Dor·is (dôr′is, dor′-) A feminine personal name. [<Gk., the Dorian girl] — **Doris** In Greek mythology, wife of Nereus and mother of the Nereids.

Dor·is (dôr′is, dor′-) **1** A small mountainous district of west central Greece, traditionally the home of the Dorians. **2** An ancient district on the coast of SW Asia Minor, consisting of Dorian settlements.

Dor·king (dôr′king) *n.* One of a breed of domestic fowls, characterized by five toes on each foot and a large, heavy body. [from *Dorking,* a town in Surrey, England]

dorm (dôrm) *n. Colloq.* A dormitory (def. 2). [Short for DORMITORY]

dor·man·cy (dôr′mən·sē) *n.* A state of torpidity; lethargy; inactivity.

dor·mant (dôr′mənt) *adj.* **1** Being in a state of, or resembling, sleep; torpid. **2** *Bot.* Resting, as plants or parts of plants in winter. **3** *Geol.* Quiescent; not erupting: said of a volcano. **4** Inactive; unused. **5** Not asserted or enforced, as claims. **6** *Her.* In the attitude of sleep. Compare COUCHANT, RAMPANT. [< OF, ppr. of *dormir* <L *dormire* sleep]

dor·mer (dôr′mər) *n.* **1** *Archit.* **a** A vertical window in a small gable rising from a sloping roof: also **dormer window. b** The roofed projection or gable in which this window is set. **c** A sleeper or beam. **2** *Archaic* A sleeping room. [<OF *dormeor* <L *dormitorium.* See DORMITORY.]

DORMER WINDOW

dor·mi·to·ry (dôr′mə·tôr′ē, -tō′rē) *n. pl.* **·ries 1** A large room in which many persons sleep. **2** A building providing sleeping and living accommodations, especially at a school, college, or resort. [<L *dormitorium* <*dormire* sleep]

dor·mouse (dôr′mous′) *n. pl.* **·mice** One of the various small, arboreal, Old World, squirrel–like rodents (family *Gliridae*). [? <F *dormir* sleep <L *dormire* + MOUSE]

dor·my (dôr′mē) *adj.* In golf, being as many holes ahead of an opponent as there are holes still to play. Also **dor′mie.** [<dial. E *dorm* doze, ult. <L *dormire* sleep; so called because no further effort is needed]

DORMOUSE (2 to 3 inches long)

dor·nick (dôr′nik) *n.* A heavy damask cloth, used for hangings, carpets, etc. Also **dor′nock** (-nək). [<Flemish *Doornik* Tournai, where originally made]

Dor·noch (dôr′nokh, -nəkh) The county seat of Sutherlandshire, Scotland.

Dor·o·thy (dôr′ə·thē, dor′-) A feminine personal name. Also **Dor·o·the·a** (dôr′ə·thē′ə, dor′-; *Dan., Du., Ger., Sw.* dô′rō·tā′ä), *Fr.* **Do·ro·thée** (dô·rə·tā′), *Ital. Sp.* **Do·ro·te·a** (dō′rō·tā′ä). [<Gk., gift of God]

dorp (dôrp) *n.* A village. [<Du. Akin to THORP.]

Dor·pat (dôr′pät) The German name for TARTU.

dorr (dôr) See DOR[1].

Dorr (dôr), **Thomas Wilson,** 1805–54, U.S. politician; instigated **Dorr's Rebellion** to set up a government in Rhode Island in 1842.

dor·sad (dôr′sad) *adv. Anat.* Toward the back. [<L *dorsum* back + *ad* toward]

dor·sal (dôr′səl) *adj.* **1** *Zool.* Of, pertaining to, on, or near the back: opposed to *ventral.* **2** *Bot.* Pertaining to the under surface, as of a leaf. **3** *Phonet.* Describing those consonants produced with the back of the tongue, as (k) in *cool.* — *n.* Dossal. [<Med.L *salis* <L *dorsum* back] — **dor′sal·ly** *adv.*

dorsal fin The long, unpaired fin along the backbone of fish and other aquatic vertebrates. For illustration see FISH.

Dor·set (dôr′sit) A county in SW England; 973 square miles; capital, Dorchester. Also **Dor′set·shire** (-shir).

Dor·set (dôr′sit), **Earl of** See SACKVILLE.

Dorset Horn A large–horned breed of English sheep, having a tightly textured fleece of medium length.

dorsi– *combining form* **1** On, to, or of the back: *dorsiferous.* **2** Dorso–. [<L *dorsum* back]

dor·sif·er·ous (dôr′sif′ər·əs) *adj. Bot.* Borne on the back, as the sori of ferns. [<DORSI- + -FEROUS]

dor·si·ven·tral (dôr′si·ven′trəl) *adj.* **1** *Bot.* Having distinct surfaces on both sides, as most leaves. **2** Dorsoventral.

dorso– *combining form* Dorsal; dorsal and: *dorsoventral.* [<L *dorsum* back]

dor·so·ven·tral (dôr′sō·ven′trəl) *adj. Zool.* Extending from the back to the ventral side. — **dor′so·ven′tral·ly** *adv.*

dor·sum (dôr′səm) *n. pl.* **·sa** (-sə) *Anat.* **1** The back. **2** Any part of an organ corresponding to or resembling a back. See illustration under BIRD. **3** *Phonet.* The back of the tongue. [<L]

Dort (dôrt) A shortened form of DORDRECHT. Also **Dordt.**

Dort·mund (dôrt′mənd, *Ger.* dôrt′mо̄ont) A city in North Rhine–Westphalia, West Germany, in the Ruhr valley.

dort·y (dôr′tē) *adj. Scot.* Sulky; haughty.

Do·rus (dō′rəs) In Greek legend, son of Hellen and ancestor of the Dorians.

do·ry[1] (dôr′ē, dō′rē) *n. pl.* **·ries** A deep, flat-bottomed rowboat with a sharp prow and flat

DORY

triangular stern, adapted for rough weather: used especially by North Atlantic fishermen. [<native Honduran name]

do·ry[2] (dôr′e, dō′rē) *n. pl.* **·ries 1** The wall-eyed pike. **2** The john dory. [<F *dorée,* pp. fem. of *dorer* gild <LL *deaurare.* See DORADO.]

dor·y·line ant (dôr′ē·līn′, dō′rē-) The driver ant.

dos–à–dos (dō·zà·dō′) *adv. French* Back to back. — *n. pl.* **dos–à–dos** (-dōz′, *Fr.* -dō′) **1** An open vehicle, sofa, etc., made so the occupants sit back to back. **2** (dō′sē·dō′) In square dances, a call directing the dancers to pass each other back to back.

dos·age (dō′sij) *n.* **1** The administering of medicine in prescribed quantity. **2** The total amount to be given. **3** The process of adding sugar, liqueur, etc., to wines to improve quality and flavor or to increase strength.

dose (dōs) *n.* **1** The quantity of medicine prescribed to be taken at one time; also, the quantity and strength of X–rays or other radiation to be taken in a certain period of time. **2** Anything disagreeable given as a prescription or infliction. **3** A determinate quantity or portion of whatever tends to benefit or reform individuals or society. — *v.* **dosed, dos·ing** *v.t.* **1** To give medicine to in a dose or doses. **2** To give, as medicine or drugs, in doses. **3** To perform the process of dosage upon: said of wines. — *v.i.* **4** To take medicines. [<MF <L *dosis* <Gk., orig., a giving] — **dos′er** *n.*

do·sim·e·ter (dō·sim′ə·tər) *n. Med.* An instrument for measuring the dosage of X–rays; also called quantimeter. [<Gk. *dosis* a dose + -METER]

do·sim·e·try (dō·sim′ə·trē) *n. Med.* **1** The accurate measurement of doses. **2** A method for the regular administration of alkaloids of definite strength, usually in granular form. — **do·si·met·ric** (dō′si·met′rik) *adj.*

Dos Pas·sos (dōs pas′ōs), **John,** 1896–1970, U.S. novelist.

doss (dos) *n. Brit. Slang* **1** A sleeping place; a bed; especially, a bed in a cheap lodging house (**doss house**). **2** Sleep. [<F *dos* back <L *dorsum*] — **doss′er** *n.*

dos·sal (dos′əl) *n.* A hanging of silk, etc., for the back of an altar, throne, etc.: also spelled *dorsal.* Also **dos′sel.** [<Med.L *dossalis,* var. of *dorsalis* of the back <L *dorsum*]

dos·ser (dos′ar) *n.* **1** A rich hanging for a hall or church. **2** A pannier. [<OF *dossier* <*dos* back <L *dorsum*]

dos·si·er (dos′ē·ā, dos′ē·ər; *Fr.* dô·syā′) *n.* A collection of memoranda, papers, documents, etc., relating to a particular matter or person. [<F, bundle of papers]

dos·sil (dos′əl) *n.* **1** A plug or spigot. **2** *Printing* A cloth roll for wiping ink from an engraved plate. **3** A soft pledget for cleaning out a wound. [<OF *dosil* <LL *duciculus,* dim. of *dux, ducis* a leader]

Dos·so Dos·si (dôs′sō dôs′sē), 1479?–1542, Italian painter: original name *Giovanni de Luteri.*

dost (dust) Do: obsolescent or poetic second person singular, present tense of DO: used with *thou.*

Dos·to·ev·ski (dôs′tô·yef′skē), **Feodor Mikhailovich,** 1821–81, Russian novelist. Also **Dos·to·yev′sky.**

dot[1] (dot) *n.* **1** A minute, round, or nearly round mark; a speck, spot, or point. **2** In writing and printing, a small spot used as a part of a letter, in punctuation, etc. **3** *Music* A point, written after a note or rest, which lengthens its value by half. **4** A little lump; clot. **5** A precise moment of time: on the *dot.* **6** *Telecom.* A signal of shorter duration than the dash, with which it is combined in the transmission of messages in the Morse or any similar code. — *v.* **dot·ted, dot·ting** *v.t.* **1** To mark with a dot or dots. **2** To spread or scatter like dots. **3** To diversify with, or delineate by means of, dots. — *v.i.* **4** To make a dot or dots. — **to dot one's i's and cross one's t's** To be or to make one's work perfect in every detail. [OE *dott* head of a boil]

dot[2] (dot) *n.* A woman's marriage portion; dowry. [<F <L *dos, dotis*] — **do·tal** (dōt′l) *adj.*

Dot (dot), **Dot·ty** (dot′ē) Diminutives of DOROTHY.

do·tage (dō′tij) *n.* **1** Feebleness of mind, as a result of old age; senility. **2** Foolish and extravagant affection; also, any object of it. **3** A feeble or foolish fancy of a dotard. [<DOTE + -AGE]

do·tard (dō′tərd) *n.* One in his dotage. Also **do′tant.**

do·ta·tion (dō·tā′shən) *n.* **1** The act of making or apportioning a dowry. **2** An endowment, as of a public institution. [<OF <L *dotatio, -onis* <*dotare* endow]

dote[1] (dōt) *v.i.* **dot·ed, dot·ing 1** To lavish extreme fondness: with *on* or *upon.* **2** To be in one's dotage. [ME *doten.* Cf. MDu. *doten* be silly.] — **dot′er** *n.*

dote[2] (dōt) *n.* A form of decay in wood fibers. [<DOTE[1]]

doth (duth) Do: obsolescent or poetic third person singular, present tense of DO.

dot·ing (dō′ting) *adj.* **1** Extravagantly or foolishly fond. **2** Feeble–minded; driveling. **3** Decaying from age: said of plants. — **dot′ing·ly** *adv.* — **dot′ing·ness** *n.*

dot–se·quen·tial (dot′si·kwen′shəl) *adj.* Pertaining to a system of color television in which the three primary colors are dissected, projected, transmitted, and received in sequence as a series of dots interwoven to produce the image in its original form. Compare FIELD–SEQUENTIAL, LINE–SEQUENTIAL.

dot·ted (dot′id) *adj.* **1** Marked or flecked with dots; spotted. **2** Distinguished by a dot or dots.

dotted line On a document, the line to carry the signature: to sign on the *dotted line.*

dotted swiss A sheer, crisp, cotton fabric, having either lappet or swivel dots.

dot·ter (dot′ər) *n.* One who or that which makes dots.

dot·ter·el (dot′ər·əl) *n.* **1** A migratory plover (genus *Eudromias*) of northern Europe and Asia, noted for the ease with which it can be taken. **2** A person easily deceived; dupe. Also **dot′trel** (-rəl). [< ME *dotrelle.* Related to DOTE[1].]

dot·tle (dot′l) *n.* The unconsumed tobacco left in a pipe after smoking. Also **dot′tel.** [? Dim. of DOT]

dot·ty (dot′ē) *adj.* **·ti·er, ·ti·est 1** Consisting of or marked with dots. **2** *Colloq.* Of unsteady or feeble gait; hence, slightly demented; imbecile.

do·ty (dō′tē) *adj.* **·ti·er, ·ti·est** Decayed: said of trees, etc. Compare DOATY. [< DOTE[2]]

Dou (dou), **Gerard** See DOW, GERARD.

Dou·ai (dōō·ā′, *Fr.* dwā) A town in northern France. Formerly **Dou·ay′.**

Douay Bible See under BIBLE.

doub·le (dub′əl) *adj.* **1** Having two of a sort together; being in pairs; coupled. **2** Twice as large, much, strong, heavy, valuable, or many. **3** Twofold; hence, ambiguous, deceitful, or two-faced. **4** Doubled; folded. **5** *Bot.* Having the petals increased in number: said of flowers. **6** In musical instruments, making tones an octave lower. —*n.* **1** Something that is twice as much. **2** A fold or plait. **3** A person or thing that closely resembles another; hence, an apparition or wraith. **4** A backward turn, as of a hunted fox; a trick or stratagem. **5** A player or singer who understudies the part of a principal artist, so as to be able to supply his or her place in case of illness, etc.; an understudy. **6** *pl.* A tennis game between two pairs of players; also, two successive faults in tennis. **7** *Eccl.* A feast at which the antiphon is said both before and after the psalms. **8** In baseball, a two-base hit. **9** A domino piece bearing the same number of pips on each half. **10** In card playing, the act of doubling. See DOUBLE (*v.* def. 13). **11** A double star. **—on** (or **at**) **the double** In double-quick time: a military command. —*v.* **doub·led, doub·ling** *v.t.* **1** To make twice as great in number, size, value, force, etc.; increase by adding an equal amount. **2** To fold or bend one part of upon another; make of two thicknesses: usually with *over, up, back,* etc. **3** To do over again; repeat. **4** To be twice the quantity or number of. **5** To act or be the double of. **6** In baseball, to advance (a base runner) by hitting a double: He *doubled* him home. **7** *Naut.* To sail around: to *double* a cape. **8** *Music* To add the upper or lower octave to. —*v.i.* **9** To become double; increase by an equal amount. **10** To turn and go back on a course: often with *back.* **11** To act or perform in two capacities. **12** In baseball, to hit a double. **13** In bridge, to declare each trick in the suit last bid by an opponent to be of twice the normal value in points: done in the expectation of defeating the hand and thereby exacting an increased penalty. **—to double in brass** *U.S. Slang* To take more than one part in anything, as in addition to one's specialty: originally said of musicians. **—to double up 1** To bend over or cause to bend over, as from pain or laughter. **2** To fold or clench, as a fist. **3** To share one's quarters, bed, etc., with another. **4** In baseball, to complete a double play upon. —*adv.* **1** In twofold degree; twice. **2** In twice the quantity. **3** Deceitfully. Also **doub′ly** *adv.* [< OF *duble* < L *duplus* double]

Double, meaning two, twofold, or twice, may appear as a combining form in hyphemes, as in:

double-action	**double-rivet**
double-barrel	**double-riveted**
double-bitt	**double-shot**
double-bitted	**double-space**
double-handed	**double-spacing**
double-leaded	**double-thread**
double-leaf	**double-tooth**
double-lock	**double-track**
double-locking	**double-voiced**

doub·le-banked (dub′əl·bangkt′) *adj. Naut.* **1** Having two men at each oar. **2** Having two tiers of oars: said of oar-propelled boats or ships.

double bar *Music* A double vertical line on a staff, indicating the end of a piece of music or of a section of it.

doub·le-bar·reled (dub′əl·bar′əld) *adj.* **1** Having two barrels, as a shotgun. **2** Doubly powerful or effective: *double-barreled* oratory. **3** Ambiguous as to meaning.

doub·le-bass (dub′əl·bās′) *n. Music* The largest and deepest toned of the stringed instruments played with a bow: also called *bass viol, contrabass, string bass.* —*adj.* Contrabass.

doub·le-bas·soon (dub′əl·bə·sōōn′) *n.* An instrument of the oboe family, an octave below the ordinary bassoon in pitch.

double bed A bed wide enough for two people: usually about 54 inches across.

doub·le-blind (dub′əl·blīnd′) *adj.* Describing a method of minimizing bias in conducting experiments with human subjects by concealing from both researchers and subjects the identity of those receiving the treatment under investigation and those acting as a control, who receive a superficially similar treatment.

double boiler A cooking utensil consisting of two pots, one fitting into the other so that food placed in the upper pot is cooked by boiling water in the lower one.

doub·le-breast·ed (dub′əl·bres′tid) *adj.* Having two rows of buttons and fastening so as to provide a double thickness of cloth across the breast: said of a coat or vest.

double chin A fat, fleshy fold under the chin.

double coconut The sea coconut.

double concave Concavo-concave.

double convex Convexo-convex.

doub·le-cross (dub′əl·krôs′, -kros′) *Slang v.t.* To betray by not acting, or by failing to act, as promised; be treacherous to; cheat. —*n.* (-krôs, -kros′) The act of or an instance of cheating or betraying an associate. **—doub′le-cross′er** *n.*

double dagger See under DAGGER.

double date *Colloq.* An appointment made by two couples.

doub·le-date (dub′əl·dāt′) *v.t.* & *v.i.* **-dat·ed, -dat·ing** To make or go out on a double date (with).

doub·le-deal·er (dub′əl·dē′lər) *n.* One who acts with duplicity.

doub·le-deal·ing (dub′əl·dē′ling) *adj.* Treacherous; deceitful. —*n.* Treachery; duplicity. See synonyms under DECEPTION.

doub·le-deck·er (dub′əl·dek′ər) *n.* **1** *Naut.* A vessel with two decks above the water line. **2** A vehicle with an upper deck. **3** A bed containing two decks. **4** A sandwich made with three slices of bread and two layers of filling.

dou·ble-dig·it (dub′əl·dij′it) *adj.* Being at least 10 percent: *double-digit* inflation.

double drum A bass drum.

doub·le-du·ty (dub′əl·dōō′tē, -dyōō′-) *adj.* **1** Built to stand twice as much wear or use. **2** Serving a dual function.

double eagle A gold coin of the United States with a face value of $20: withdrawn from circulation in 1934.

doub·le-edged (dub′əl·ejd′) *adj.* **1** Having two cutting edges. **2** Applicable both for as well as against.

dou·ble-en·ten·dre (dōō·blän·tän′dr′) *n.* A word or phrase of double meaning, the less obvious one often of doubtful propriety. [Alter. of F *double entente*]

dou·ble en·tente (dōō·blän·tänt′) *French* Double meaning; equivocal sense.

double entry A method of bookkeeping in which every transaction is made to appear as both debtor and creditor. **—doub′le-en′try** *adj.*

doub·le-faced (dub′əl·fāst′) *adj.* **1** Having two faces. **2** Having a pattern on each side: said of a fabric. **3** Deceitful; hypocritical: a *double-faced* friend.

double feature A program of two full-length motion pictures.

doub·le-first (dub′əl·fûrst′) *n.* In British universities, a degree with the highest honors in two subjects; also, a student who obtains such a degree.

doub·le-gang·er (dub′əl·gang′ər) *n.* A Doppelgänger.

doub·le-head·er (dub′əl·hed′ər) *n.* **1** A long, heavy train pulled by two engines. **2** Two games, especially of baseball, played in succession on the same day by the same two teams.

double indemnity A clause in a life insurance policy by which a payment of double the face value of the policy is made in the event of accidental death.

doub·le-joint·ed (dub′əl·join′tid) *adj. Anat.* Characterized by a form of diarthrosis in which the bones move freely backward and forward.

doub·le-mind·ed (dub′əl·mīn′did) *adj.* **1** Unsettled; wavering. **2** Deceitful.

doub·le·ness (dub′əl·nis) *n.* **1** The state or quality of being double. **2** Duplicity.

doub·le-park (dub′əl·pärk′) *v.t.* & *v.i.* To park (a motor vehicle) alongside another already parked along the curb. **—doub′le-park′ing** *n.*

double play In baseball, a play in which two base runners are put out.

double pneumonia Pneumonia affecting both lungs.

doub·le-quick (dub′əl·kwik′) *n.* In the U.S. Army, a rate of march of 180 steps a minute: now usually called *double-time.* —*v.t.* & *v.i.* To march or cause to march at this pace.

doub·le-reed (dub′əl·rēd′) *n. Music* A wind instrument with a reed consisting of two segments united at the lower end and separated at the upper end. —*adj.* **1** Having such a reed. **2** Designating a group of instruments having such a reed, as the oboe, bassoon, etc.

doub·le-rip·per (dub′əl·rip′ər) *n.* A coasting sled composed of two small bobs or pairs of runners connected lengthwise by a long seat or board. Also **doub′le-run′ner.**

double salt *Chem.* **1** Any salt which yields two different anions or cations when hydrolyzed. **2** A molecular combination of two simple salts.

double standard A standard of conduct permitting greater sexual liberty to men than to women.

double star See under STAR.

doub·le-sur·faced (dub′əl·sûr′fist) *adj.* Having two surfaces.

doub·let (dub′lit) *n.* **1** One of a pair of like things; a pair or couple. **2** A short, close-fitting, outer garment, with or without sleeves, worn by men from the 15th to 17th centuries. **3** An imitation gem consisting of a real stone cemented to a piece of glass colored to simulate the imitated gem; also, a paste jewel mounted with a thin face of a genuine jewel. **4** *Ling.* One of a pair of words derived from the same original but entering a language through different routes, as *regal* and *royal.* **5** *Usually pl.* A pair of dice that, when thrown, show on the upper surface the same number of spots: He threw *doublets.* **6** *Optics* A pair of lenses joined so as to eliminate the distortion caused by either lens used alone. [< OF, something folded, orig. dim. of DOUBLE]

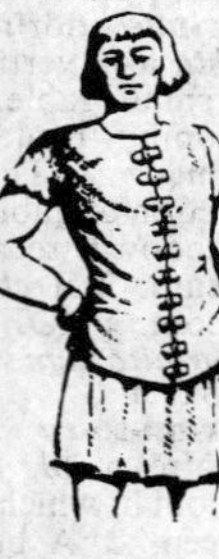

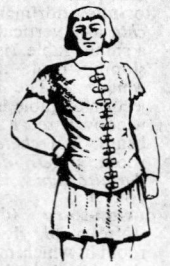

DOUBLET (*def. 2*)

doub·le-take (dub′əl·tāk′) *n.* A delayed reaction, with visible evidence of surprise, to a joke or situation.

double talk 1 A manner of speech, adopted to confuse the listener, in which meaningless syllable combinations are substituted for expected words. **2** Ambiguous talk meant to deceive.

doub·le-think (dub′əl·thingk′) *n.* **1** The capacity to hold contradictory opinions in full knowledge of their contradiction. **2** Confused thought. Also **dou′ble·think′.**

doub·le-time (dub′əl·tīm′) See DOUBLE-QUICK.

doub·le-tongue (dub′əl·tung′) *v.i.* **-tongued, -tongu·ing** To apply the tongue rapidly to the teeth and hard palate alternately, as in executing a staccato passage for the flute or cornet.

doub·le-tongued (dub′əl·tungd′) *adj.* Characterized by duplicity of speech.

doub·le-tree (dub′əl·trē′) *n.* The bar or cross piece to the ends of which two swingletrees are fastened.

doub·ling (dub′ling) *n.* **1** The act of one who or that which doubles. **2** Something doubled over or together; a fold; plait. **3** *Her.* The fur lining of a mantle or robe.

doub·loon (du·blōōn′) *n.* A former Spanish gold coin worth about $16. See DOBLA, DOBLON. [< Sp. *doblón,* aug. of *doble* double; orig. worth two pistoles]

doub·ly (dub′lē) See DOUBLE *adv.*

Doubs (dōō) A river in eastern France, flowing 270 miles NE to the Saône.

doubt (dout) *v.t.* **1** To hesitate to accept as true; hold as uncertain; disbelieve. **2** *Obs.* To be apprehensive of; fear. — *v.i.* **3** To be in doubt; be uncertain. **4** To be mistrustful. — *n.* **1** Lack of certain knowledge; uncertainty regarding the truth or reality of something. **2** A matter or case of dubitation; indecision. **3** A question requiring settlement, an objection. **4** *Obs.* Fear; dread. [<OF *duter, douter* <L *dubitare*; spelling refashioned after L] — **doubt'a·ble** *adj.* — **doubt'er** *n.*

Synonyms (verb): distrust, mistrust, surmise, suspect. To *doubt* is to lack conviction. Incompleteness of evidence may compel one to *doubt*, or some perverse bias of mind may so incline him. *Distrust* may express simply a lack of confidence. *Mistrust* and *suspect* imply that one is almost assured of positive evil; one may *distrust* himself or others; he *suspects* others. *Mistrust* is rarely used of persons, but only of motives, intentions, etc. *Distrust* is always serious: *mistrust* is often used playfully. Compare DOUBT *n.*, QUESTION, SUPPOSE. *Antonyms*: believe, trust.

Synonyms (noun): disbelief, distrust, hesitancy, hesitation, incredulity, indecision, irresolution, misgiving, perplexity, question, scruple, suspense, suspicion, uncertainty. *Doubt* is lack of conviction; *disbelief* is conviction to the contrary; *unbelief* refers to a settled state of mind. *Perplexity* seeks a solution; *doubt* may be content to linger unresolved. Any improbable statement awakens *incredulity*. As regards practical matters, *uncertainty* applies to the unknown or undecided; *doubt* implies some negative evidence. *Suspense* regards the future, and is eager and anxious; *uncertainty* may relate to any period, and be quite indifferent. *Misgiving* is ordinarily in regard to the outcome of something already done or decided; *hesitation, indecision,* and *irresolution* have reference to something that remains to be decided or done and are due oftener to infirmity of will than to lack of knowledge. *Distrust* and *suspicion* apply especially to the motives, character, etc., of others, and are more decidedly adverse than *doubt*. *Scruple* relates to matters of conscience and duty. See PERPLEXITY, QUESTION. *Antonyms*: assurance, belief, certainty, confidence, conviction, decision, determination, persuasion, reliance, resolution, resolve, trust.

doubt·ful (dout'fəl) *adj.* **1** Subject to, entertaining, or admitting of doubt. **2** Uncertain; undecided; contingent. **3** Indistinct; vague; ambiguous. **4** Questionable; dubious. See synonyms under EQUIVOCAL, IRRESOLUTE, PRECARIOUS. — **doubt'ful·ly** *adv.* — **doubt'ful·ness** *n.*

Doubting Thomas A confirmed or habitual skeptic. *John* xx 25.

doubt·less (dout'lis) *adj.* **1** Confident; fearless. **2** Indubitable; certain. — *adv.* Without doubt; unquestionably: also **doubt'less·ly.**

douce (do͞os) *adj. Scot.* Sober; sedate; not frivolous. — **douce'ly** *adv.* — **douce'ness** *n.*

dou·cet (do͞o'sit) *n. Obs.* **1** A sweet pastry. **2** A dowcet. [<F, dim. of *douce* sweet <L *dulcis*]

dou·ceur (do͞o·sœr') *n.* **1** A small present; bribe; tip. **2** Sweetness of manners. **3** *Obs.* A compliment. [<F <L *dulcor, -oris* sweetness < *dulcis* sweet]

douche (do͞osh) *n.* **1** A jet of water or vapor sprayed on or into the body for medicinal or hygienic reasons. **2** The instrument for administering it. **3** A bath taken by making use of these facilities. — *v.t. & v.i.* **douched, douch·ing** To give or take a douche. [<F <Ital. *doccia* a water pipe, ult. <L *ducere* lead]

dough (dō) *n.* **1** A soft mass of moistened flour or meal, mixed for cooking into bread, cake, etc. **2** Any soft pasty mass. **3** *Slang* Money. ◆ Homophone: *doe*. [OE *dāh*] — **dough'y** *adj.*

dough·boy (dō'boi') *n.* **1** A dumpling of raised dough. **2** *U.S. Colloq.* An infantry soldier: also **dough'foot'** (-fo͝ot').

dough·face (dō'fās') *n. U.S.* **1** A mask or false face. **2** In American history, a Northern politician who was accused of truckling to the slave power during the period of anti-slavery agitation.

dough·nut (dō'nut) *n.* A small cake made of dough raised by baking powder or yeast and fried in deep fat; a fried cake: usually cut with a hole in the center before frying.

dought (dout) *Scot.* Past tense of DOW.

dough·ty (dou'tē) *adj.* **·ti·er, ·ti·est** *Archaic* Brave; valiant; redoubtable: now chiefly in humorous use. See synonyms under BRAVE. [OE *dohtig*] — **dough'ti·ly** *adv.* — **dough'ti·ness** *n.*

Dough·ty (dou'tē), **Charles Montagu,** 1843–1926, English traveler and author.

Doug·las (dug'ləs) Capital of the Isle of Man.

Doug·las (dug'ləs) Name of a family prominent in Scottish history; especially, **Sir William the Hardy,** first Lord of Douglas, died 1298?, a follower of Wallace; his son, **Sir James the Good,** 1286–1330: known as *Black Douglas,* follower of Robert the Bruce; **James,** 1358–1388, second Earl of Douglas and Mar; **Gawin,** 1474?–1522, Scottish poet.
— **Lewis Williams,** born 1894, U.S. diplomat.
— **Stephen Arnold,** 1813–61, U.S. senator; opposed Lincoln in a series of debates, 1858.
— **William Orville,** born 1898, U.S. jurist, associate Supreme Court justice 1939–75.

Douglas fir A large timber tree (*Pseudotsuga taxifolia*) of the pine family, growing on the Pacific Coast of the United States: often called *red fir, Oregon fir.* Also called **Douglas hemlock, Douglas pine, Douglas spruce.** [after David *Douglas,* 1798–1834, Scottish botanist]

Doug·las–Home (dug'ləs·hyo͞om'), **Sir Alec (Frederick),** former Earl of Home, born 1903, British statesman; prime minister, 1963–1964.

Doug·lass (dug'ləs), **Frederick,** 1817–95, U.S. Negro abolitionist and diplomat.

Dou·kho·bors (do͞o'kə·bôrz') See DUKHOBORS.

dou·kit (do͞o'kit) *adj. Scot.* Ducked. Also spelled *dookit*.

Dou·ma (do͞o'mä) See DUMA.

Dou·mergue (do͞o·merg'), **Gaston,** 1863–1937, French statesman; president 1924–31.

doum palm (do͞om) The doom palm.

doun (do͞on) *adv. Scot.* Down.

doup (doup, do͞op) *Scot.* The end; butt end.

dou·pi·on (do͞o'pē·ən) *n.* **1** Silk thread of uneven weight and thickness, spun from two cocoons in close contact with each other. **2** A fabric made from such thread, as pongee, nankeen, or shantung. Also **doup·pi·on·i** (do͞o'pē·on'ē, -ō'nē). Also *dupion, dupioni.* [<F <Ital. *doppione,* aug. of *doppio* double <L *duplus*]

dour (do͝or) *adj. Scot.* Hard; unyielding; sullen. [<L *durus*] — **dour'ly** *adv.* — **dour'ness** *n.*

dou·ra (do͝or·ə) See DURRA.

dou·ri·cou·li (do͝or'i·ko͞o'lē) *n.* A small, bushy-tailed, arboreal monkey (genus *Aotes*) of South America, having large eyes adapted for nocturnal vision. [<S. Am. Ind.]

dou·rine (do͞o·rēn') *n.* An infectious disease of horses and asses transmitted through sexual contact by a parasitic micro-organism (*Trypanosoma equiperdum*): also called *equine syphilis.* [<F <Arabic *darin* unclean]

Dou·ro (dō'ro͞o) A river in Spain and Portugal, flowing 475 miles west to the Atlantic: Spanish *Duero.*

douse[1] (dous) *v.* **doused, dous·ing** *v.t.* **1** To plunge into water or other liquid; dip suddenly; duck. **2** To drench with water or other liquid. — *v.i.* **3** To become drenched or immersed. See synonyms under IMMERSE. — *n.* A ducking or drenching. Also spelled *dowse.* [Origin unknown]

douse[2] (dous) See DOWSE[2].

douse[3] (dous) *v.t.* **doused, dous·ing** **1** To strike; give a blow to. **2** *Naut.* To take in or haul down quickly, especially a sail. **3** *Colloq.* To take off, as clothes. **4** *Colloq.* To put out; extinguish. [Cf. MDu. *dossen* beat, strike]

douse[4] (do͞os) *Scot.* See DOUCE.

d'ou·tre mer (do͞o'tr' mâr') *French* From beyond the sea.

douze·pers (do͞oz'pârz') *n. pl. sing.* **·par** (-pâr') **1** In medieval legend, the twelve knights of Charlemagne. **2** In French history, the twelve chief spiritual and temporal peers. [<OF *douze pers* twelve peers]

DO·VAP (dō'vap) *n.* A method for determining the course and velocity of high-altitude, long-range rockets by radio waves whose return frequencies are interpreted on the principle of the Doppler effect. [Do(PPLER) V(ELOCITY) A(ND) P(OSITION)]

dove[1] (duv) *n.* **1** A pigeon; especially, the mourning dove, turtledove, etc. **2** *Eccl.* A symbol of the Holy Spirit. **3** A symbol of peace. **4** One who seeks to resolve a war primarily by means of limited military action, negotiation, or unilateral withdrawal: opposed to *hawk*[1] (def. 4). **5** Any gentle, innocent creature. [Cf. ON *dūfa*]

dove[2] (dōv) *U.S. Colloq. & Brit. Dial.* Past tense of DIVE.

dove·cot (duv'kot') *n.* A house for tame pigeons; generally, a houselike box set on a pole or on the roof or side of a building. Also **dove'cote'** (-kōt', -kot').

dove hawk The goshawk.

dove·kie (duv'kē) *n.* **1** The little auk (*Alle alle*), an arctic bird about 7 1/2 inches long, black above, white below. **2** The black guillemot. Also **dove'key.**

Do·ver (dō'vər) **1** A port in eastern Kent, England, on the **Strait of Dover** (French *Pas de Calais*), a strait 21 miles wide at the eastern end of the English Channel. **2** The capital of Delaware.

Dover's powder *Med.* An anodyne diaphoretic compounded of ipecacuanha, opium, and sugar of milk. [after Thomas *Dover,* 1660–1742, English physician]

dove·tail (duv'tāl') *n.* **1** A manner of joining boards, timbers, etc., by interlocking wedge-shaped tenons and spaces. **2** The joint so made. — *v.t. & v.i.* **1** To join by means of a dovetail or dovetails. **2** To fit in closely or aptly.

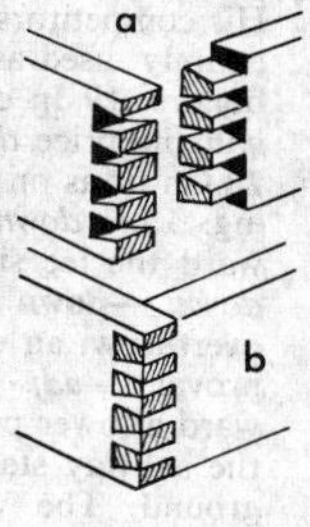

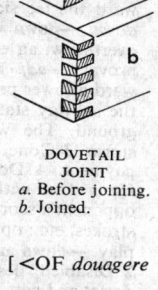

DOVETAIL JOINT
a. Before joining.
b. Joined.

dov·ish (duv'ish) *adj.* Disposed to rely on conciliation to resolve a war: opposed to *hawkish.*

Dow (dou), **Gerard,** 1613–1675, Dutch painter. Also spelled *Dou.*

dow·a·ger (dou'ə·jər) *n.* **1** In English law, a widow holding property or title derived from her late husband. **2** *Colloq.* Any elderly lady of dignified bearing. [<OF *douagere* < *douage* a dower]

dow·cet (dou'sit) *n. Obs.* A testicle of a deer: also spelled *doucet.* [Var. of DOUCET]

Dow·den (dou'dən), **Edward,** 1843–1913, Irish critic and Shakespearean scholar.

dow·dy (dou'dē) *adj.* **·di·er, ·di·est** Ill-dressed; not neat or fashionable; in bad taste; shabby. Also **dow'dy·ish.** — *n. pl.* **·dies** **1** A slatternly woman. **2** A fruit pie baked in a deep dish. [ME *doude* a slut; origin unknown] — **dow'·di·ly** *adv.* — **dow'di·ness** *n.*

dow·el (dou'əl) *n.* **1** A pin or peg, usually cylindrical, for joining together two adjacent pieces, as parts of a barrelhead: distinguished from a *tenon.* **2** A piece of wood built or driven into a wall, to which to nail finishings: also **dowel pin.** — *v.t.* **·eled** or **·elled, ·el·ing** or **·el·ling** To fasten or furnish with dowels. [<MLG *dovel* plug]

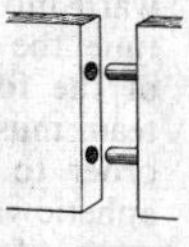
DOWELS

dow·er (dou'ər) *n.* **1** A widow's life portion (usually a third) of her husband's lands and tenements. **2** The sum of one's natural gifts; endowment. — *v.t.* **1** To provide with a dower. **2** To endow, as with a talent or quality. [OF *douaire* <LL *dotarium* <L *dos, dotis* a dowery] — **dow'er·less** *adj.*

dow·er·y (dou'ər·ē) See DOWRY.

dowf (douf, do͞of) *adj. Scot.* Dull; stupid.

dow·ie (dou'ē, dō'ē) *adj. Scot.* Dull; spiritless; mournful; in poor health. Also **dow'y.**

Do·wie (dou'ē), **John Alexander,** 1847–1907, Scottish religious leader in America.

dow·itch·er (dou'ich·ər) *n.* **1** The gray snipe (*Limnodromus griseus*) of eastern North America. **2** A related bird, the long-billed *dowitcher* (*L. griseus scolopaceus*). [<N. Am. Ind.]

dowl (doul) *n.* **1** A filament of a feather. **2** Down or a fiber of down. Also **dowle.** [Origin uncertain]

down[1] (doun) *adv.* **1** From a higher to a lower place, level, position, etc.: Come *down*

from that ladder! 2 In or into a lower place, position, etc.: The cattle put their heads *down.* 3 On or to the ground: The house burned *down.* 4 To or toward the south: Come *down* to Florida this winter. 5 To or in an outlying or distant place: life *down* on the farm. 6 Below the horizon: The sun went *down.* 7 From an upright to a prone or prostrate position: to knock a man *down.* 8 From a former or earlier time or owner: This necklace came *down* to me from my ancestors. 9 To or toward the end; away from the start: Read from the beginning *down* to chapter five. 10 To a smaller bulk, greater density, heavier consistency, etc.: The mixture boiled *down* to a hard crust. 11 To or into a less active or violent state: The tumult died *down.* 12 To a diminished pitch or volume: Turn the radio *down!* 13 To a lower rate, price, demand or amount: The market has gone *down.* 14 Into or in an attitude or state of close application, intensity, earnestness, etc.: to get *down* to work; to track *down* a clue. 15 In a depressed mental or emotional state: His troubles had him *down.* 16 In or into ill health: He came *down* with a fever. 17 In or into a degraded, inferior, or helpless state; in subjection: His competitors kept him *down.* 18 Completely; entirely: used as an intensive: loaded *down* with honors. 19 In cash, as at the time of purchase: half the price *down* and the rest in instalments. 20 On or as on paper or other material for writing: Take *down* his words. 21 *Naut.* To or toward the lee side of a vessel: to put the helm *down.* **—down with** (Let us) do away with or overthrow: an exclamation of disfavor or disapproval. *—adj.* 1 Going, facing, or directed toward a lower position or place: the *down* side of the subway station. 2 In a lower place; on the ground: The wires are *down* because of the storm. 3 Gone, brought, or paid down: a *down* payment. 4 Downcast; dejected. 5 Bedridden: He is *down* with a cold. 6 In games, behind an opponent's score by (a number of) points, goals, strokes, etc.: opposed to *up.* 7 In football, not in play. **—down and out** 1 In boxing, knocked out. 2 Disabled, destitute, or socially outcast. Also **down′-and-out′. —down on** Opposed to as from anger, ill will, or enmity. *—v.t.* 1 To knock, throw, or put *down*; subdue. 2 To swallow; gulp *down.* *—v.i.* 3 *Rare* To go, fall, or sink *down.* See synonyms under CONQUER. *—prep.* 1 In a descending direction along, upon, or in: The logs floated *down* the river. 2 From an earlier to a later period in the duration of: The story has remained the same *down* the ages. *—n.* 1 A downward movement; a descent. 2 A reverse of fortune: the ups and *downs* of life. 3 In football, any of the four consecutive plays during which a team must advance the ball at least ten yards in order to maintain possession of it. [OE *dūne,* aphetic var. of *adūne* <*of dune* from the hill]

down[2] (doun) *n.* 1 The fine, soft plumage of birds under the feathers, especially that on the breast of water birds. 2 The first feathering of a bird. 3 The soft hairs that first appear on the human face. 4 *Bot.* Soft, short hairs; pubescence, as on plants or fruits. 5 Any feathery, fluffy substance. [<ON *dunn*]

down[3] (doun) *n.* 1 A hill having a broad, treeless, grass-grown top; also, the open space on its top. 2 *pl.* Turf-covered, undulating tracts of upland. 3 A dune. [OE *dūn.* Akin to DUNE.]

Down (doun) A county of eastern Ulster province, Ireland; 952 square miles; county seat, Downpatrick.

dow·na (dou′nə) *Scot.* Cannot. See DOW.

down·beat (down′bēt′) *n. Music* 1 The first accent of each measure. 2 The downward gesture made by the conductor to indicate this accent.

down-bow (doun′bō′) *n.* In stringed instruments, a downward stroke of the bow across the strings: opposite of *up-bow.*

down·cast (doun′kast′, -käst′) *adj.* 1 Directed downward or to the ground: a *downcast* look. 2 Low in spirits; dejected; depressed. See synonyms under SAD. *—n.* A shaft down which a ventilating air current passes.

down·come (doun′kum′) *n.* 1 A downfall, especially a sudden one. 2 A downcomer.

down·com·er (doun′kum′ər) *n.* 1 The pipe which receives the outpourings from the eaves of a roof; leader. 2 A pipe in a mine which conveys combustible gases downward. 3 A circulating tube in water-tube boilers.

Down East New England, especially Maine. **—down′-east′** *adj.*

down·er (doun′ər) *n. Slang* Any of various drugs that depress the central nervous system, as barbiturates.

Downes (dounz), **(Edwin) Olin,** 1886–1955, U.S. music critic.

down·fall (doun′fôl′) *n.* 1 A falling or flowing downward. 2 A sudden, heavy fall of rain. 3 A fall; disgrace. 4 A trap operating as by the descent of a weight; a deadfall. See synonyms under RUIN.

down·fallen (doun′fô′lən) *adj.* Fallen; ruined.

down·grade (doun′grād′) *n.* A descending slope, as of a hill or road. **—on the down·grade** Declining in health, reputation, status, etc. *—adj.* Downhill. *—v.t.* **·grad·ed, ·grad·ing** To reduce in status, salary, etc.

down·haul (doun′hôl′) *n. Naut.* A rope for hauling down certain sails, as a jib, staysail, etc.

down·heart·ed (doun′här′tid) *adj.* Dejected, discouraged; low-spirited. **—down′heart′ed·ly** *adv.* **—down′heart′ed·ness** *n.*

down·hill (doun′hil′, doun′hil′) *adj.* Descending; sloping. *—adv.* With a downward direction; toward the bottom of a hill. **—to go downhill** To decline, as in success.

Down·ing Street (dou′ning) 1 A street in Westminster, London; site of the official residence of the Prime Minister (No. 10). 2 The British Government or cabinet.

down-lead (doun′lēd′) *n. Brit.* A lead-in.

down payment In instalment buying, the initial payment on a purchase.

down·play (doun′plā′) *v.t.* To play down.

down·pour (doun′pôr′, -pōr′) *n.* A copious and heavy fall of rain.

down·right (doun′rīt′) *adj.* 1 Straight to the point; unequivocal; plain; outspoken. 2 Directed downward. 3 Thorough; utter; absolute. *—adv.* 1 Directly downward. 2 Without doubt or qualification. 3 In the extreme; utterly. See synonyms under FLAT[1]. **—down′right′ly** *adv.* **—down′right′ness** *n.*

Downs (dounz), **The** 1 A sheltered roadstead in the English Channel off the SE coast of Kent. 2 Two parallel ranges of low chalk hills in southern England.

down·spout (doun′spout′) *n.* A pipe for draining rain water, etc., from a roof or from a gutter along a roof.

Down's syndrome (dounz) *Pathol.* Congenital mental and physical retardation due to a chromosomal anomaly, accompanied by variable signs including a flat face and pronounced epicanthic folds: also called *Mongolism.* [<J.L.H. *Down,* 1828–96, Eng. physician]

down·stage (doun′stāj′) *n.* The half of a stage, from left to right, that is nearest to the audience. *—adj.* Belonging or pertaining to the front half of a stage. *—adv.* Toward, near, or on the front half of a stage.

down·stairs (doun′stârz′) *adj.* Below the stairs; on a lower floor. *—n.* The downstairs region of a building. *—adv.* Down the stairs; toward a lower floor.

down·stream (doun′strēm′) *adj.* & *adv.* In the direction of the current; down the stream.

down·take (doun′tāk′) *n.* A downward air passage: the *downtake* to the blowers of a boiler.

down·throw (doun′thrō′) *n.* The act of throwing down, or the state of being overthrown or prostrated.

down·time (doun′tīm′) *n.* The time during working hours when a machine, computer, section, or entire factory is not functioning.

down·town (doun′toun′) *adj.* 1 Of or in the part of a city or town geographically lower than the other parts: opposed to *uptown.* 2 Of, in, or characteristic of the chief business section of a city or town. *—adv.* To, toward, or in the geographically lower or chief business part of a town or city. *—n.* The downtown section of a town or city.

down-trod·den (doun′trod′n) *adj.* Trodden under foot; oppressed. Also **down′-trod.**

down·turn (doun′tûrn′) *n.* A downward turn or decline, as in popularity or in a state's economy.

down under Australia or in New Zealand.

down·ward (doun′wərd) *adj.* 1 Descending or tending from a higher to a lower level (literally or figuratively). 2 Descending from that which is more remote. *—adv.* 1 From a higher to a lower position. 2 From that which is more remote, as in place or time. 3 Toward the extremities. Also **down′ward·ly, down′wards** *adv.*

down·y (doun′ē) *adj.* **down·i·er, down·i·est** 1 Of, pertaining to, like, or covered with down. 2 Soft; quiet; soothing. **—down′i·ness** *n.*

downy mildew Grape rot.

dow·ry (dou′rē) *n. pl.* **·ries** 1 The property a wife brings to her husband in marriage. 2 *Archaic* A reward paid for a wife. *Gen.* xxxiv 12. 3 Any endowment or gift. Also spelled *dowery.* [<AF *dowarie,* var. of OF *douaire* DOWER]

dowse[1] (dous) See DOUSE[1].

dowse[2] (douz) *v.i.* **dowsed, dows·ing** To search for water, minerals, etc., with a dowsing-rod: also spelled *douse.* [Origin uncertain] **—dows′er** *n.*

dows·ing-rod (dou′zing·rod′) *n.* A divining-rod.

dox·ol·o·gy (dok·sol′ə·jē) *n. pl.* **·gies** 1 A hymn or verse of praise to God: specifically applied to a stanza beginning "Praise God, from whom all blessings flow." 2 A formula of praise, used as the closing words of a sermon. **—greater doxology** The Gloria in excelsis. **—lesser doxology** The Gloria Patri. [<Med. L *doxologia* <Gk. <*doxa* praise + *legein* speak] **—dox·o·log·i·cal** (dok′sə·loj′i·kəl) *adj.* **—dox′o·log′i·cal·ly** *adv.*

dox·y[1] (dok′sē) *n. pl.* **dox·ies** *Slang* A mistress or paramour; a prostitute. Also **dox′ie.** [<MDu. *docke* a doll]

dox·y[2] (dok′sē) *n.* A doctrine; belief, especially a religious one. [<*-doxy,* as in *orthodoxy, heterodoxy*]

doy·en (doi′ən, *Fr.* dwä·yaṅ′) *n.* The eldest or senior member of a group. [<F <L *decanus.* See DEAN.] **—doy·enne** (doi′en, *Fr.* dwä·yen′) *n. fem.*

Doyle (doil), **Sir Arthur Conan,** 1859–1930, English physician and novelist; known for his *Sherlock Holmes* stories.

doy·ley, doy·ly (doi′lē) See DOILY.

D'Oy·ly Carte (doi′lē kärt′) See CARTE.

doze (dōz) *v.* **dozed, doz·ing** *v.t.* To spend or pass (time) listlessly or in a doze: to *doze* one's hours away. *—v.i.* To sleep unsoundly or lightly; nap; be drowsy. *—n.* A light, unsound sleep. [<Scand. Cf. Dan. *döse* make dull.] **—doz′er** *n.*

doz·en[1] (duz′ən) *n.* Twelve things of a kind, collectively. **—a long dozen** Thirteen. [<OF *dozeine* <*douze* twelve <L *duodecim* <*duo* two + *decim* ten] **—doz′enth** *adj.*

doz·en[2] (dō′zən) *v.t.* & *v.i. Scot.* To stun; daze; make or become torpid.

do·zy (dō′zē) *adj.* **·zi·er, ·zi·est** Drowsy; soporific. **—do′zi·ly** *adv.* **—do′zi·ness** *n.*

drab[1] (drab) *adj.* 1 Dull; colorless. 2 Of the color drab. 3 Made of drab. [<*n.*] *—n.* 1 A yellow-gray color. 2 A special kind of cloth so colored. [<F *drap* cloth <LL *drappus,* ? <Gmc.] **—drab′ly** *adv.* **—drab′ness** *n.*

drab[2] (drab) *n.* A slattern; a slut. *—v.i.* **drabbed, drab·bing** To associate with drabs. [Cf. Irish *drabog* a slattern]

drab[3] (drab) *n.* In the manufacture of salt, a box for draining salt. [Origin unknown]

drab·bet (drab′it) *n. Brit.* A coarse linen fabric of drab color.

drab·ble (drab′əl) *v.t.* & *v.i.* **·bled, ·bling** To draggle. [<LG *drabbeln* walk in water or mud, splash]

dra·cae·na (drə·sē′nə) *n.* One of various tropical shrubs and small trees (genera *Dracaena* and *Cordyline*) of the lily family, widely distributed in the Old World and grown as an ornamental plant. [<NL <Gk. *drakaina,* fem. of *drakōn* a dragon]

drachm (dram) *n. Brit.* 1 A dram. 2 A drachma. [<F *drachme* <L *drachma* DRACHMA]

drach·ma (drak′mə) *n. pl.* **·mas** or **·mae** (-mē) 1 The modern gold monetary unit of Greece, equivalent to 100 lepta. 2 An ancient Greek silver coin. 3 An ancient Greek unit of weight. [<L *drachma* <Gk. *drachmē* a handful. Doublet of DRAM.]

Dra·co (drā′kō) A northern constellation, the Dragon. See CONSTELLATION.

Dra·co (drā′kō) An archon of Athens about 621 B.C.; reputed author of the first Athenian written code of laws.

Dra·co·ni·an (drā·kō′nē·ən) *adj.* Pertaining to Draco or his laws; hence, inflexible; severe.
dra·con·ic (drā·kon′ik) *adj.* Of or resembling a dragon. [<L *draco, -onis* <Gk. *drakōn* + -IC]
Dra·con·ic (drā·kon′ik) *adj.* **1** Draconian. **2** Pertaining to the constellation Draco. Also **Dra·con′i·cal.** — **Dra·con′i·cal·ly** *adv.*
draff (draf) *n.* Refuse grain from breweries and distilleries; also, lees or dregs. [Prob. <ON *draf*]
draff·ish (draf′ish) *adj.* Worthless. Also **draff′y, draft′y.**
draft (draft, dräft) *n.* **1** A current of air. **2** The act of drinking or inhaling, as a liquid or air; also, that which is so drawn into the mouth or throat in one drink or gulp. **3** *Naut.* The depth to which a vessel sinks in the water. **4** The act of drawing or drawing out, or the fact of being drawn; also, that which is drawn or drawn out, or its weight or resistance; a haul; pull; drag; a load. **5** The result of a drawing, as of a net in fishing. **6** A plan; outline; sketch. See synonyms under SKETCH. **7** A writing of articles or propositions as framed or drawn up, but not adopted or enacted. **8** An order drawn by one party or person on another for the payment of money to a third. **9** An order for money drawn by one bank and payable at another to the person designated in the order; a bill of exchange. **10** A damper, door, or other device for controlling the airflow in a furnace, stove, etc. **11** A military or naval conscription; levy. **12** That which tends to reduce or exhaust by drawing away a part: a *draft* on one's time, strength, etc. **13** An allowance on the invoices of goods for samples drawn from the packages. **14** *Metall.* The bevel given to the pattern for a casting so that it may be drawn from the mold without injuring the latter; in general, a taper given to an article or part. **15** The total sectional area of the openings in a turbine wheel, or the area of the opening of a sluicegate. **16** A line or border chiseled on a stone to guide in its dressing. **17** A ravine; a gully. **18** *pl.* Draughts. — **on draft** Ready to be drawn, as beer, etc., from a cask or the like. — *v.t.* **1** To outline in writing; sketch; delineate. **2** To select and draw off, as for military service; conscript. **3** In weaving, to pull through the heddles. **4** To draw off or away. **5** To cut a draft on (a stone). — *adj.* **1** Suitable or used for pulling heavy loads: a *draft* animal. **2** Not bottled, as beer; drawn from a cask. Also *(esp. for n. defs. 1, 2, 3, 5, 10, and adj. 2) draught.* [ME *draht* <OE *dragan* draw] — **draft′er** *n.* — **draft′i·ness** *n.*
draft board An official, local board of civilians which selects qualified men for compulsory service in the armed forces.
draft dodger One who avoids or attempts to avoid conscription into military service.
draft·ee (draf·tē′, dräf-) *n.* A person drafted for service in the armed forces.
drafts·man (drafts′mən, dräfts′-) *n. pl.* **·men** (-mən) **1** One who draws or prepares plans, designs, deeds, conveyances, etc.: also spelled *draughtsman.* **2** A draughtsman. — **drafts′·man·ship** *n.*
draft·y (draf′tē, dräf′-) *adj.* **draft·i·er, draft·i·est** Having or exposed to drafts. Also spelled *draughty.* — **draft′i·ly** *adv.* — **draft′i·ness** *n.*
drag (drag) *v.* **dragged, drag·ging** *v.t.* **1** To pull along by main force; haul. **2** To sweep or search the bottom of, as with a net or grapnel; dredge. **3** To catch or recover, as with a grapnel or net. **4** To draw along heavily and wearily. **5** To harrow (land). **6** To protract; continue tediously: often with *on* or *out.* **7** To introduce (an irrelevant subject or matter) into a discussion, argument, etc. — *v.i.* **8** To be pulled or hauled along; trail to or as to the ground. **9** To move heavily or slowly: The procession *dragged* along. **10** To lag behind: The tenor *dragged* in his part. **11** To pass slowly, as time. **12** To operate a dredge. **13** To cause a feeling of clutching or tugging: Worry *dragged* at him. See synonyms under DRAW. — **to drag one's feet** *U.S. Colloq.* To act or work with deliberate slowness. — *n.* **1** The act of dragging or that which drags or is dragged, as a grapple, a dredge, a dragnet; a brake or shoe for causing a carriage wheel to drag, as in going down a hill; a runnerless sled; a dragrope, as of a gun; hence, any clog or impediment. **2** A long, high, four-wheeled carriage; a four-in-hand coach. **3** A slow or difficult movement: to walk with a *drag.* **4** An artificial scent used in hunting, as an aniseed bag. **5** The scent or trail of a fox before it is found and started by the hounds: so called because originally the fox was hunted by the line of scent left by it on its return from a predatory expedition. **6** A draghunt. **7** *Aeron.* That component of the total air force acting on a body which is parallel to the relative wind: said of aircraft in flight. **8** The last of a herd of cattle; the stragglers. **9** *Slang* Influence resulting in special favors; pull. **10** *Slang* A puff of a cigarette. **11** *U.S. Slang* A dull, boring person or thing. **12** *U.S. Slang* Women's clothing worn by a man. [OE *dragan;* infl. in form by ON *draga.* Related to DRAW.]

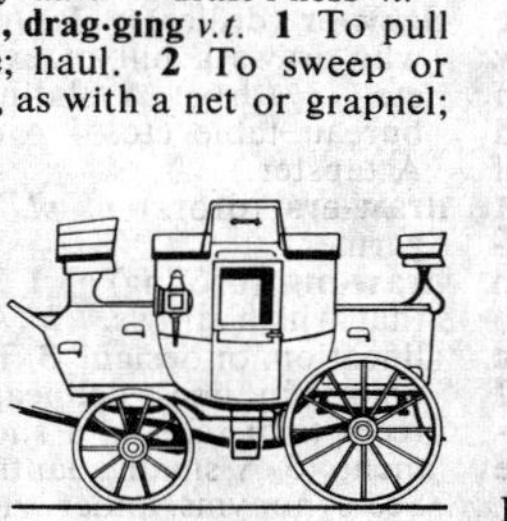
DRAG
One type of drag; others are open-topped; usually drawn by four horses.

drag-driv·er (drag′drī′vər) *n.* The cowboy who drives the stragglers at the end of a herd.
drag·gle (drag′əl) *v.* **·gled, ·gling** *v.t.* **1** To make soiled or wet by dragging in mud or over damp ground; muddy. — *v.i.* **2** To become wet or soiled; drag in the mud. **3** To follow slowly; lag. [Freq. of DRAG]
drag·gle·tail (drag′əl·tāl′) *n.* An untidy person.
drag·gle·tailed (drag′əl·tāld′) *adj.* Bedraggled from or as if from having the garments trailing in the wet or mud.
drag·hound (drag′hound′) *n.* A hound trained to follow an artificial scent.
drag·hunt (drag′hunt′) *n.* A hunt in which an artificial scent is used.
drag·line (drag′līn′) *n.* A guiderope; dragrope.
drag·link (drag′lingk′) *n. Mech.* A link for connecting crankshafts, as a main-shaft crank with an inner paddle shaft in a marine engine.
drag·net (drag′net′) *n.* **1** A net to be drawn along the bottom of the water or along the ground, for taking fish or small animals. **2** Any device or plan by which a criminal can be caught.
Dra·go doctrine (drä′gō) A doctrine proposed in 1902, stating that an international debt does not justify armed intervention by the creditor power. [after Luis M. *Drago,* 1859–1921, Argentine statesman]
drag·o·man (drag′ə·mən) *n. pl.* **·mans** (-mənz) or **·men** (-mən) An interpreter or agent for travelers in the Near East. [<F <LGk. *dragoumanos* <Arabic *tarjumān* translator]
drag·on (drag′ən) *n.* **1** A fabulous, serpentlike, winged monster. **2** In the Authorized Version, a word variously understood as a large reptile, a marine monster, a jackal, etc. **3** A fierce or overbearing person; especially, a duenna. **4** *Bot.* A plant of the arum family. **5** A short, large-bored firearm of the 17th century. **6** *Zool.* A small, arboreal, Asian lizard (genus *Draco*) capable of making long glides between trees by means of winglike expansions of the skin which are supported by the elongated and extensible hind ribs; a flying lizard. [<F <L *draco, -onis* <Gk. *drakōn* serpent]

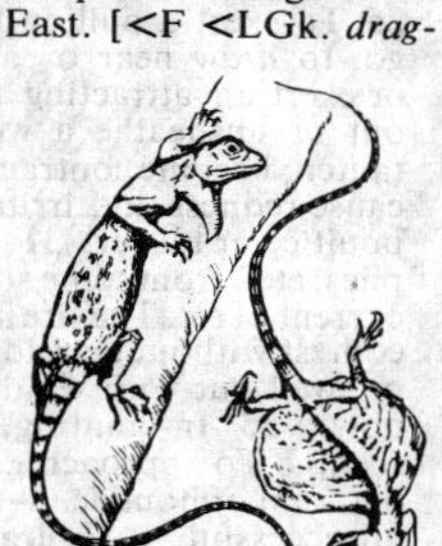
DRAGON LIZARD
(From 12 to 15 inches long)

Drag·on (drag′ən) A northern constellation, Draco. See CONSTELLATION.
drag·on·et (drag′ən·it) *n.* **1** The yellow gurnard. **2** A small dragon. [<OF, dim. of *dragon* a dragon]
drag·on·fly (drag′ən·flī′) *n. pl.* **·flies** A predatory insect (order *Odonata*), having a slender body, four finely veined wings, large eyes, and strong jaws: also called *darning needle, devil's-darning-needle.* For illustration see under INSECT (beneficial).
drag·on·head (drag′ən·hed′) *n.* Any of a genus (*Dracocephalum*) of hardy annual or perennial herbs of the mint family.
drag·on·nade (drag′ə·nād′) *n.* **1** In French history, the quartering of dragoons on French Protestant families by Louis XIV as a means of persecution. **2** Any military persecution. [<F <*dragon* dragoon]
drag·on·root (drag′ən·ro͞ot′, -ro͝ot′-) *n.* The green dragon.
drag·on's-blood (drag′ənz·blud′) *n.* One of various reddish-brown resins used as a pigment, especially those obtained from the fruit of a Malayan rattan palm *(Daemonorops draco)* and from the dragon tree.
drag·on's-head (drag′ənz·hed′) *n.* **1** A dragonhead. **2** *Astron.* One of the two points where the ecliptic is intersected by the moon's or planet's orbit. The symbol of the first is ☊; that of the second, which is called **dragon's-tail,** is ☋, and is used only in astrology.
dragon tree *n.* A gigantic tree of the Canary Islands *(Dracaena draco),* yielding dragon's-blood.
dragon withe A West Indian climbing plant (genus *Banisteriopsis* or *Heteropteris*], bearing winged fruit: the roots of some species have been used as an adulterant of ipecac.
dra·goon (drə·go͞on′) *n.* **1** In some European armies, a cavalryman. **2** *Obs.* A soldier who served on horseback or on foot as occasion required. **3** *Obs.* Dragon (def. 5). — *v.t.* **1** To harass by dragoons. **2** To coerce; browbeat. [<F *dragon* dragon (def. 5)]
drag race In racing hot-rod automobiles, a timed test of acceleration over a straight, measured course, usually one kilometer in length.
drag·rope (drag′rōp′) *n.* **1** A rope with chain and hook attached, used as a brake on a gun carriage. **2** A guiderope. **3** A rope dragged by a balloon over the ground to check speed and control height of ascent.
drag·sail (drag′sāl′) *n. Naut.* A driftsail or sea anchor made from a sail. Also **drag′sheet′** (-shēt′).
drai·gle (drā′gəl) *v.t.* & *v.i. Scot.* To draggle.
drain (drān) *v.t.* **1** To draw off gradually, as a fluid; cause to run off. **2** To draw water or any fluid from: to *drain* a swamp. **3** To empty; drink completely. **4** To filter. **5** To exhaust; use up: to *drain* one's vitality; to *drain* a region of resources. — *v.i.* **6** To flow off or leak away gradually. **7** To become empty. — *n.* **1** The act of draining. **2** Continuous strain, leak, or outflow. **3** A pipe or trench for draining; a drainpipe. **4** *Surg.* An appliance to facilitate the discharge of matter from a wound. **5** *pl.* Draff. [OE *drēahnian* strain out] — **drain′er** *n.*
drain·age (drā′nij) *n.* **1** The act or means of draining; a system of drains. **2** That which is drained off; waste water. **3** The area drained; drainage basin. **4** *Surg.* The gradual drawing off of morbid fluids from deep-seated wounds or abscesses.
drainage basin A large surface area whose waters are drained off into a principal river system.
drain·pipe (drān′pīp′) *n.* Pipe used for draining.
drake[1] (drāk) *n.* **1** A male duck. **2** A flat stone used in the game of ducks and drakes. [Cf. dial. G *draak*]
drake[2] (drāk) *n.* **1** A mayfly, used as bait in angling: also **drake′fly′.** **2** A small brass cannon of the 17th and 18th centuries. **3** *Obs.* A dragon, or an ancient standard bearing a dragon for its emblem. [OE *draca* <L *draco.* See DRAGON.]

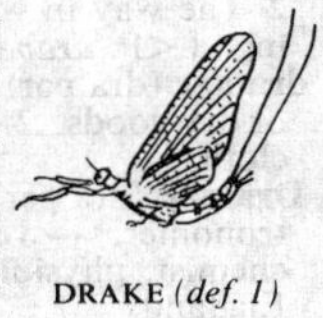
DRAKE *(def. 1)*

Drake (drāk), **Sir Francis,** 1540–96, English admiral and circumnavigator of the globe.
Dra·kens·berg (drä′kənz·bûrg) A mountain range in South Africa; highest peak, 11,425 feet: also *Quathlamba.*
Drake Passage (drāk) A strait joining the South Pacific and the South Atlantic between Cape Horn and the South Shetland Islands.
dram (dram) *n.* **1** An apothecaries' weight equal to 60 grains, 3.88 grams, or one eighth

of an ounce. **2** An avoirdupois measure equal to 27.34 grains, 1.77 grams, or one sixteenth of an ounce. **3** A drachma. **4** A drink of spirits: a *dram* of whisky. **5** In pharmacy, a fluid dram. **6** A small portion; a bit. **— fluid dram** A measure of capacity equal to one eighth of an ounce, 60 minims, or 3.69 cubic centimeters. Also **fluid drachm**: sometimes spelled *fluidram, fluidrachm.* — *v.t.* & *v.i.* **drammed, dram·ming** To use intoxicants freely; to treat to liquor. [<OF *drame* <L *drachma.* Doublet of DRACHMA.]

dra·ma (drä′mə, dram′ə) *n.* **1** A literary composition that tells a story, usually representing human conflict by means of dialog and action to be performed upon the stage; a play. **2** Stage representations collectively; the art or profession of writing, acting, or producing plays; the institution of the theater: often with *the.* **3** A series of actions, events, or purposes, considered collectively as possessing dramatic quality. [<LL, a play <Gk., a deed, an action < *draein* act, do]

Dra·ma (drä′mə) A town in Macedonia, NE Greece. Ancient **Dra·bes·cus** (drä·bes′kəs).

Dram·a·mine (dram′ə·mēn) *n.* Proprietary name of a brand of dimenhydrinate.

dra·mat·ic (drə·mat′ik) *adj.* Of, connected with, or like the drama; especially, involving conflict. Compare LYRIC. Also **dra·mat′i·cal.** — **dra·mat′i·cal·ly** *adv.*

dra·mat·ics (drə·mat′iks) *n. pl.* **1** Dramatic performance, especially by amateurs: construed as plural. **2** The art of staging or acting plays: construed as singular or plural.

dram·a·tis per·so·nae (dram′ə·tis pər·sō′nē) *Latin* The characters of a play; also, a list of these.

dram·a·tist (dram′ə·tist) *n.* One who writes plays.

dram·a·ti·za·tion (dram′ə·tə·zā′shən, -tī·zā′-) *n.* **1** The act or process of dramatizing. **2** A dramatized version.

dram·a·tize (dram′ə·tīz) *v.t.* **·tized, ·tiz·ing** **1** To present in dramatic form; convert for stage use. **2** To tell, represent, or interpret (events, one's personality, etc.) in a theatrical manner. Also *Brit.* **dram′a·tise.**

dram·a·turge (dram′ə·tûrj) *n.* The author of a drama, especially one who also directs and oversees the performance of it; a playwright. Also **dram′a·tur′gist.** [<F <Gk. *dramatourgos* < *drama, -atos* a play + *ergein* work]

dram·a·tur·gic (dram′ə·tûr′jik) *adj.* Of or pertaining to dramaturgy; histrionic; befitting the stage. Also **dram′a·tur′gi·cal.**

dram·a·tur·gy (dram′ə·tûr′jē) *n.* The art of making dramas and placing them properly on the stage; dramatic composition and representation.

dram·shop (dram′shop′) *n.* A saloon; bar.

Drang nach Ost·en (dräng näkh ôs′tən) *German* The policy of extending German political, cultural, and economic influence southeastward through the Balkans into the Near East; literally, drive to the east.

drank (drangk) Past tense of DRINK.

drant (dränt, drônt) *Scot.* & *Brit. Dial. v.t.* & *v.i.* To drawl or drone in speaking or singing; also, to spend time tediously. — *n.* A drawl. Also DRAUNT.

drap (drap) *v.* & *n. Scot.* Drop.

drape (drāp) *v.* **draped, drap·ing** *v.t.* **1** To cover or adorn in a graceful fashion, as with drapery or clothing. **2** To arrange (drapery, etc.) in graceful folds. — *v.i.* **3** To hang in folds. — *n.* **1** *Usually pl.* Drapery; curtain. **2** The way in which cloth hangs, as in clothing. [<F *draper* weave < *drap* cloth]

drap·er (drā′pər) *n.* **1** *Brit.* A dealer in cloth or dry goods. **2** Originally, a manufacturer of cloth.

Dra·per (drā′pər), **Henry,** 1837–82, U.S. astronomer. — **John William,** 1811–82, U.S. chemist, physiologist, and historian; born in England.

drap·er·y (drā′pər·ē) *n. pl.* **·er·ies** **1** Loosely hanging attire or its arrangement, especially on figures in art. **2** Hangings; curtains, tapestry, etc. **3** *Brit.* The business of a draper. **4** Cloth in general.

drap·pie (drap′ē) *n. Scot.* A little drop. Also **drap′py.**

dras·tic (dras′tik) *adj.* Acting vigorously; extreme; violently effective. — *n.* A powerful medicine; a strong purgative. [<Gk. *drastikos* effective < *draein* act, do] — **dras′ti·cal·ly** *adv.*

drat (drat) *interj.* An exclamation of anger or annoyance. — *v.t.* Confound; damn: *Drat* him! [Alter. of *God rot*] — **drat′ted** *adj.*

draught (draft, dräft), etc. See DRAFT, etc.

draught·board (draft′bôrd′, -bōrd′, dräft′-) A checkerboard.

draughts (drafts, dräfts) *n. pl. Brit.* The game of checkers: also spelled *drafts.* See CHECKERS.

draughts·man (drafts′mən, dräfts′-) *n. pl.* **·men** (-mən) **1** A piece in the game of draughts. **2** Draftsman.

draunt (dränt, drônt) See DRANT.

Dra·va (drä′vä) A river in south central Europe, flowing 450 miles SE to the Danube: *German* **Drau** (drou). Also **Dra′ve** (drä′və).

drave (drāv) Obsolete past tense of DRIVE.

Dra·vid·i·an (drə·vid′ē·ən) *n.* **1** One belonging to the most ancient indigenous race of southern India. **2** A non–Indo–European family of agglutinative languages spoken primarily in southern India and northern Ceylon, including Tamil, Malayalam, Kanarese, and Telugu. — *adj.* Of the Dravidians or their languages: also **Dra·vid′ic.**

draw (drô) *v.* **drew, drawn, draw·ing** *v.t.* **1** To cause to move to or with the mover by means of strength, force, etc.; pull; haul. **2** To acquire or obtain, as from a receptacle: to *draw* water. **3** To cause to flow forth: to *draw* blood or tears. **4** To cause to come forth; induce: to *draw* praise, laughter, criticism, etc. **5** To take or pull off, on, or out, as gloves or a sword: She *drew* off her gloves. **6** To get or receive; earn, as a salary or interest. **7** To take out; remove, as money from a bank. **8** To deduce; extract by mental process; formulate: to *draw* a conclusion or comparison. **9** To attract; allure: Honey *draws* flies. **10** To close, as against light; shut, as curtains, a bag, etc. **11** To elicit; bring out, as truth or information. **12** To stretch out; manufacture by stretching or hammering, as wire or dies. **13** To disembowel: to *draw* a chicken. **14** To take in; inhale, as breath. **15** To drain of contents, as a pond. **16** To win (a prize) in a lottery; to obtain, as by chance. **17** *Naut.* To require (a specified depth) to float: said of vessels. **18** To depict, as a sketch or diagram; to describe pictorially or verbally; delineate. **19** To write out; draft, as a check or deed: often with *up.* **20** In card games, **a** To ask for or take an additional card or cards. **b** To force (a card or cards) to be played: to *draw* trumps. **21** In billiards, to cause (the cue ball) to recoil after contact. **22** In cricket, to deflect (the ball) by a slight turn of the bat. **23** In curling, to play (the stone) gently. **24** To leave undecided, as a game or contest. — *v.i.* **25** To exert a pulling force. **26** To come or go: to *draw* near or away. **27** To exercise or exert an attracting influence. **28** To pull out or unsheathe a weapon. **29** To shrink; tauten; become contracted, as a wound. **30** To cause redness and irritation of the skin, as a poultice or blister. **31** To obtain money, supplies, etc., from some source. **32** To produce a current of air: The fire *draws* well. **33** To end a contest without decision; tie. **34** *Naut.* To fill or swell out with wind: The sails are *drawing* now. **35** In hunting, **a** To track game by scent. **b** To approach game slowly after pointing: said of hounds. **— to draw a blank** To be unsuccessful. **— to draw a (or the) long bow** To exaggerate. **— to draw and quarter** In medieval executions: **a** To disembowel and dismember after hanging. **b** To tie each of the victim's arms and legs to a different horse and whip the horses in different directions. **— to draw back** To recoil, as from an unfavorable situation. **— to draw fire** To be a target of attack. **— to draw first blood** **1** In dueling, to inflict the first wound. **2** To score first in any contest or competition. **— to draw on** **1** To rely upon or make requirements of: He *drew on* his reputation. **2** To lure or entice. **3** To approach its end: The evening is *drawing on.* **— to draw out** **1** To protract; prolong. **2** To cause (someone) to give information or express opinions. **— to draw the line** To fix the limit; refuse to go further. **— to draw up** **1** To put in required legal form, as a will or deed. **2** To overtake: He *drew up* with the leader. **3** To form in ranks; marshal, as troops. **4** To straighten (oneself); stiffen, as in anger or resentment. — *n.* **1** An act of drawing or state of being drawn; also, that which is drawn. **2** An indecisive contest; a tie game. **3** The movable section of a drawbridge. **4** Anything that draws; specifically, an exhibition that attracts a crowd. **5** A drawn chance or ticket, as in a lottery. **6** A quantity drawn. **7** The act of drawing a revolver or knife: quick on the *draw.* **8** In various card games, cards dealt or drawn after the discard. **9** A ravine or coulee. [OE *dragan*]

Synonyms (verb): allure, attract, drag, entice, haul, incline, induce, lead, lure, pull, tow, tug. One object *draws* another when it moves it toward itself or in the direction of its own motion by the exertion of adequate force, whether slight or powerful. To *attract* is to exert a force that tends to *draw,* while it may produce no actual motion; all objects are *attracted* toward the earth, but they may be sustained from falling. To *drag* is to *draw* against strong resistance; as, to *drag* a sled over bare ground, or a carriage up a steep hill. To *pull* is to exert a *drawing* force, whether adequate or inadequate; as, the fish *pulls* on the line; a dentist *pulls* a tooth. To *tug* is to *draw,* or try to *draw,* a resisting object with a continuous straining motion. To *haul* is to *draw* somewhat slowly a heavy object; as, to *haul* a seine; to *haul* logs. One vessel *tows* another. In the figurative sense, *attract* is more nearly akin to *incline, draw* to *induce.* We are *attracted* by one's appearance, *drawn* to his side. See ACTUATE, ALLURE, INFLUENCE. *Antonyms*: alienate, estrange, push, rebuff, reject, repel, repulse. See synonyms for DRIVE.

draw·back (drô′bak′) *n.* **1** Anything that checks or hinders progress, success, prosperity, enjoyment, contentment, etc.; a disadvantage. **2** An allowance, consisting in a total or partial paying back, as of duties previously paid on imported articles on their being exported, or as of freight paid to a railway company; rebate.

draw·bar (drô′bär′) *n.* A projecting bar or heavy beam beneath the body of a locomotive, railway car, or tractor, and used as a coupling.

draw·bore (drô′bôr′, -bōr′) *n.* In carpentry, a hole passing through a tenon and the cheeks of its mortise, to enable the former to be drawn up to its shoulder by driving in a pin (called a **drawbore pin**).

draw·bridge (drô′brij′) *n.* A bridge of which the whole or a part may be raised, let down, or drawn aside.

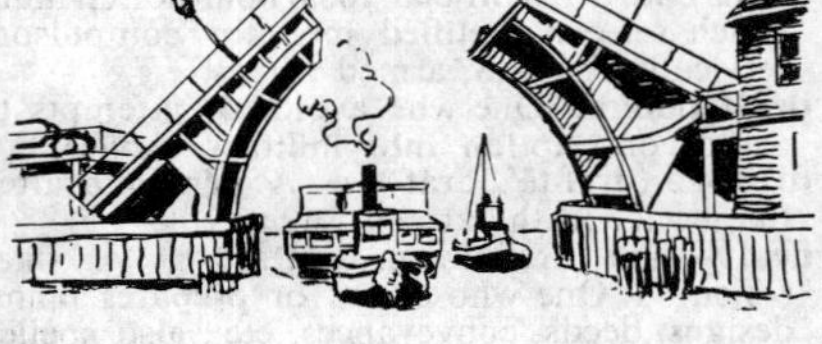

DRAWBRIDGE

draw·ee (drô′ē′) *n.* One on whom an order for the payment of money is drawn.

draw·er (drô′ər) *n.* **1** One who draws. **2** One who draws a bill of exchange, money order, etc. **3** (drôr) A sliding receptacle, as in a bureau, table, etc. **4** A draftsman. **5** *Archaic* A tapster.

draw·ers (drôrz) *n. pl.* A trouserlike undergarment.

draw·ing (drô′ing) *n.* **1** The act of one who or that which draws. **2** A picture, sketch, delineation, or design. **3** The art of representing objects by lines; delineation. **4** *pl. Brit.* The receipts of sales in a shop or other establishment. **5** A small quantity of tea for steeping. See synonyms under PICTURE, SKETCH.

drawing account An account, by a business firm, which shows the payments to a partner, employee, or salesman advanced against his expected income, salary or commission.

drawing board A smooth, flat board to which paper or canvas is attached for drawing.

draw·ing–card (drô′ing·kärd′) *n.* Any feature that attracts a crowd.

draw·ing–room (drô′ing·ro͞om′, -ro͝om′) *n.* **1** A room for reception of company. **2** A reception held or the company assembled in such

a room. 3 *Brit.* A court reception. 4 *U.S.* A small private room in a sleeping-car on a train. [Short for WITHDRAWING ROOM]

draw·knife (drô′nīf′) *n. pl.* **·knives** (-nīvz′) A knife with a handle at each end, used for cutting with a drawing motion. Also **draw′·ing–knife′.**

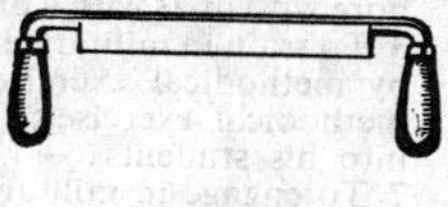

DRAWKNIFE

drawl (drôl) *v.t.* & *v.i.* To speak or pronounce slowly; to lengthen speech sounds, especially vowels. — *n.* The act of drawling; the attenuation of sounds giving an impression of slowness of speech: said of the patterns of speech in part of the southern United States. [Cf. Du. *dralen* loiter] — **drawl′er** *n.* — **drawl′ing·ly** *adv.* — **drawl′y** *adj.*

drawn (drôn) *adj.* 1 Equally contested; undecided, as a game. 2 Eviscerated: a *drawn* fowl. 3 Having all iron removed by magnets: said of brass filings. 4 Subjected to a process of elongation: hard-*drawn* wire. 5 Haggard: His face looked *drawn.*

drawn butter Butter melted and prepared as a sauce.

drawn work Ornamental openwork made by pulling out threads of fabric and embroidering or hemstitching the edges of the openings thus made. For illustration see HEMSTITCH.

draw·plate (drô′plāt′) *n.* 1 The plate on a locomotive to which the drawbar is attached. 2 *Mech.* A hard plate with holes of successively diminishing diameters for drawing out metal rods or wire.

draw·shave (drô′shāv′) *n.* A drawknife.

draw·string (drô′string′) *n.* A string, ribbon, or cord run through a casing or hem, which pulls together, contracts the size of, or closes an opening. Also **drawing string.**

draw·tube (drô′to͞ob′, -tyo͞ob′) *n. Optics* The tube, consisting of two sliding parts, containing the lenses of a microscope.

dray (drā) *n.* 1 A strong, heavy vehicle, usually low for convenience in loading heavy articles. 2 A rude sledge. — *v.t.* To transport by means of a dray. [Cf. OE *dræge* dragnet < *dragan* draw]

dray·age (drā′ij) *n.* 1 The act of conveying in a dray. 2 The charge for draying.

dray horse A horse for drawing a dray; a cart horse.

dray·man (drā′mən) *n. pl.* **·men** (-mən) A man who drives a dray.

Dray·ton (drā′tən), **Michael,** 1563–1631, English poet.

dread (dred) *v.t.* & *v.i.* 1 To anticipate with great fear or anxiety. 2 *Obs.* To be in awe (of). — *adj.* 1 Causing great fear; terrible. 2 Exciting awe or reverential fear. See synonyms under AWFUL. — *n.* 1 Unconquerable fright; shrinking horror; terrifying anticipation. 2 Fear joined to deep respect; awe. See synonyms under ALARM, ANXIETY, FEAR, FRIGHT, VENERATION. [ME *dreden* <OE *andrædan* < *and* against + *drædan* fear] — **dread′less** *adj.*

dread·ful (dred′fəl) *adj.* 1 Inspiring dread or awe; terrible. 2 Awful. See synonyms under AWFUL, FRIGHTFUL. — *n.* A sensational novelette, or a periodical that prints melodramatic stories: a penny *dreadful.* Compare DIME NOVEL. — **dread′ful·ly** *adv.* — **dread′ful·ness** *n.*

dread·nought (dred′nôt′) *n.* 1 One of a class of heavily armed battleships formerly used in the British navy, typified by the *Dreadnought,* of 17,900 tons and carrying an armament of 10 12-inch guns and 24 quick-firing guns. 2 Any battleship of great size carrying large-caliber guns. 3 A heavy cloth or a garment made of it. 4 One who fears nothing. Also **dread′naught′.**

dream (drēm) *n.* 1 A train of thoughts or images passing through the mind in sleep. 2 A mental condition similar to that of one sleeping; abstracted imagining; daydreaming. 3 A visionary idea, anticipation, or fancy; also, anything real having a dreamlike quality. 4 *Psychoanal.* A medium for the expression during sleep of various aspects of the ego and superego typically withdrawn from consciousness but, when recorded and analyzed, having some value in the diagnosis, interpretation, and treatment of certain maladjustments of the personality. — *v.* **dreamed** or **dreamt** (dremt), **dream·ing** *v.t.* 1 To see or imagine in a dream. 2 To imagine or envision as in a dream. 3 To while away, as in idle reverie. — *v.i.* 4 To have a dream or dreams. 5 To have a vague idea or conception of something. — **to dream up** *Colloq.* To concoct or create, especially by artistic invention or unbridled fancy. See synonyms under MUSE. [OE *drēam;* infl. in meaning by ON *draum* a dream] — **dream′ful** *adj.* — **dream′ful·ly** *adv.* — **dream′·less** *adj.* — **dream′less·ly** *adv.*

Synonyms (noun): daydream, fancy, fantasy, hallucination, illusion, reverie, romance, trance, vision. A *dream* is strictly a train of thoughts, fantasies, and images passing through the mind during sleep; a *vision* may occur when one is awake and in clear exercise of the senses and mental powers; *vision* is often applied to something seen by the mind through supernatural agency, whether in sleep or wakefulness, conceived as more real and authoritative than a *dream;* a *trance* is an abnormal state, which is different from normal sleep or wakefulness. A *reverie* is a purposeless drifting of the mind when awake, under the influence of mental images; a *daydream* that which passes before the mind in such condition. A *fancy* is some image presented to the mind, often in the fullest exercise of its powers. *Hallucination* is the seeming perception of non-existent objects, as in insanity or delirium. In the figurative sense, we speak of *dreams* of fortune, *visions* of glory, with little difference of meaning except that the *vision* is thought of as fuller and more vivid. We speak of a *trance* of delight when the emotion almost sweeps one away from the normal exercise of the faculties. Compare DELUSION. *Antonyms:* certainty, fact, reality, realization, substance, verity.

dream·er (drē′mər) *n.* 1 One who dreams. 2 A visionary.

dream·ing (drē′ming) *n. Austral.* An aboriginal totemic site; also, a totem.

dream·land (drēm′land′) *n.* The realm of dreams.

dream·time (drēm′tīm′) *n. Austral.* The aboriginal concept of Creation; the beginning.

dream world A world of illusions.

dream·y (drē′mē) *adj.* **dream·i·er, dream·i·est** 1 Of, causing, pertaining to, or given to dreams. 2 Appropriate to dreams; shadowy; vague; also, soothing; soft. 3 Filled with dreams; visionary. See synonyms under IMAGINARY, ROMANTIC, VAIN. — **dream′i·ly** *adv.* — **dream′i·ness** *n.*

drear (drir) *adj. Poetic* Dreary.

drear·y (drir′ē) *adj.* **drear·i·er, drear·i·est** 1 Causing or manifesting sadness, loneliness, or gloom; dismal. 2 Causing or showing weariness; monotonous; lifeless; dull. 3 Sorrowful. See synonyms under BLEAK[1], SAD, TEDIOUS. [OE *drēorig* sad, bloody < *drēor* gore] — **drear′i·ly** *adv.* — **drear′i·ness** *n.* — **drear′i·some** *adj.*

dredge[1] (drej) *n.* An appliance for bringing up mud, silt, etc., from under water; a dredging machine. — *v.* **dredged, dredg·ing** *v.t.* 1 To clear or widen by means of a dredge. 2 To remove, catch, or gather by a dredge. — *v.i.* 3 To use a dredge. [ME *dreg.* Akin to DRAW.]

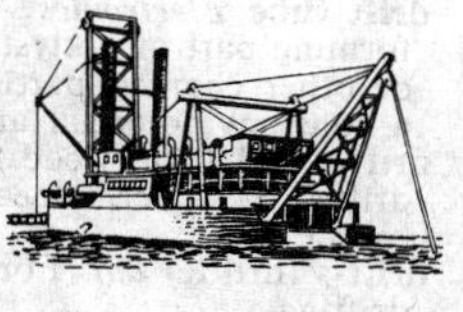

FLOATING DREDGE

dredge[2] (drej) *v.t.* 1 To sprinkle or dust with flour before cooking. 2 To sift; sprinkle. [< earlier *dragie* a sweetmeat <OF ? ult. <Gk. *tragema, -atos* a condiment]

dredg·er[1] (drej′ər) *n.* 1 One who dredges. 2 A dredging machine. 3 A boat engaged in dredging.

dredg·er[2] (drej′ər) *n.* In cookery, a box with a perforated lid used for sprinkling flour, etc.: also called **dredging box.**

dredg·ing (drej′ing) *n.* 1 The act of using a dredge. 2 That which is dredged.

dree (drē) *v.t.* & *v.i. Scot.* To suffer; endure: also spelled *driech.* — **to dree one's weird** *Scot* To endure one's fate.

dreel (drēl) *v.t. Scot.* To drill.

dreep (drēp) *v.i. Brit. Dial.* 1 To drip. 2 To droop; lose heart or courage. Also **drepe.** [Var. of DRIP]

dreg·gy (dreg′ē) *adj.* **·gi·er, ·gi·est** Containing dregs; full of dregs; foul. — **dreg′gi·ness** *n.* — **dreg′gish** *adj.*

dregs (dregz) *n. pl.* 1 The sediment of liquids, especially of beverages. 2 Worthless residuum; the coarse part: the *dregs* of society. 3 *sing.* The remaining part; residuum. See synonyms under WASTE. [<ON *dreggjar*]

Drei·bund (drī′bo͝ont) *n.* A triple alliance; specifically, that of Germany, Austria-Hungary, and Italy (1882–1915). [<G < *drei* three + *bund* alliance]

Drei·ser (drī′sər, -zər), **Theodore,** 1871–1945, U. S. novelist.

drench (drench) *v.t.* 1 To wet thoroughly; soak. 2 In veterinary medicine, to administer a potion to; force to swallow a draft. — *n.* 1 A liquid medicine, administered by compulsion, as to a horse. 2 A large draft or quantity of fluid. 3 A water solution for drenching. 4 The act of drenching; also, that which drenches. [OE *drencan* cause to drink] — **drench′er** *n.*

Drep·a·num (drep′ə·nəm) The ancient name for TRAPANI.

Dres·den (drez′dən, *Ger.* drās′dən) *n.* A fine china made in Dresden, Germany.

Dres·den (drez′dən, *Ger.* drās′dən) The capital of Saxony, east central Germany, on the Elbe.

dress (dres) *v.* **dressed** or **drest, dress·ing** *v.t.* 1 To clothe; supply with clothing. 2 To trim or decorate; adorn, as a Christmas tree or a store window. 3 To treat medicinally, as a wound or sore. 4 To comb and arrange (hair). 5 To curry (a horse). 6 To prepare (stone, timber, fabrics, etc.) for use or sale. 7 To clean (fowl, game, fish, etc.) for cooking. 8 To till, trim, or prune. 9 To put in proper alinement, as troops. 10 *Colloq.* To scold; reprove severely: usually with *down.* — *v.i.* 11 To put on or wear clothing, especially formal clothing. 12 To come into proper alinement. — **to dress ship** To display the national colors, all signal flags, and bunting, as in honor of an individual or event. — **to dress up** To put on or wear formal attire or clothing more elaborate than usually worn. — *n.* 1 Covering for the body; clothes collectively; especially, elegant or fashionable attire. 2 The art of dressing correctly. 3 A gown or frock of a woman or child. 4 Full dress as opposed to business attire, etc. 5 External appearance; guise. 6 Dressing or size, as of leather. — *adj.* 1 Of, pertaining to, or suitable for making dresses: *dress* goods. 2 To be worn on formal occasions: a *dress* suit, *dress* uniform. [<OF *dresser,* ult. <L *directus.* See DIRECT.]

Synonyms (noun): apparel, array, attire, clothes, clothing, costume, garb, garments, habiliments, habit, raiment, robes, uniform, vestments, vesture. *Clothing* denotes the entire covering of the body, taken as a whole; *clothes* and *garments* view it as composed of separate parts. *Clothes, clothing,* and *garments* may be used of inner or outer covering; all the other words in the list (with possible rare exceptions in the case of *raiment*) refer to the outer *garments. Array, raiment,* and *vesture* are archaic or poetic; so, too, is *habit,* except in technical use to denote a lady's riding *dress.* The word *vestments* is now rare, except in ecclesiastical use. *Apparel* and *attire* are most frequently used of somewhat complete and elegant outer *clothing. Dress* may be used, specifically, for a woman's gown, and in that sense may be either rich or shabby; but in the general sense it denotes outer *clothing* which is meant to be elegant, complete, and appropriate to some social or public occasion; as, full *dress,* court *dress,* evening *dress,* etc. *Dress* has now largely displaced *apparel* and *attire. Garb* denotes the *clothing* characteristic of some class, profession, or the like; as, the *garb* of a priest. *Costume* is chiefly used for that which befits an assumed character; as, a theatrical *costume;* we sometimes speak of a national *costume,* etc. See HABIT. *Antonyms:* bareness, disarray, dishabille, exposure, nakedness, nudity, undress.

add,āce,câre,pälm; end, ēven; it,īce; odd,ōpen,ôrder; to͝ok,po͞ol; up,bûrn; ə = a in *above,* e in *sicken,* i in *clarity,* o in *melon,* u in *focus;* yo͞o = u in *fuse;* oi,oil; ou,pout; ch,check; g,go; ng,ring; th,thin; th,this; zh,vision. Foreign sounds à,œ,ü,kh,ṅ; and ◆: see page xx. < from; + plus; ? possibly.

dres·sage (dres′ij, *Fr.* dre·säzh′) *n.* **1** In equitation, the act of guiding a mount through a set of paces or maneuvers by imperceptible movements on the part of the rider, usually for exhibition purposes. **2** The technique of training a horse to respond to such movements.

dress circle A section of seats in a theater or concert hall, usually comprising the first gallery behind and above the orchestra: so called because originally reserved for patrons in evening dress.

dress coat The coat of a man's dress suit.

dressed (drest) *adj.* **1** Prepared, as animal skins, for use; tanned, dyed, softened, etc. **2** Prepared for use, as lumber or stone. **3** Prepared for cooking, as fowl. **4** Clothed; especially, wearing formal dress.

dress·er[1] (dres′ər) *n.* **1** One who dresses something, as shop windows, leather, etc. **2** One who assists another to dress. **3** One who dresses well or in a particular way: a fancy *dresser.* **4** *Brit.* A surgical assistant assigned to dress and bandage wounds.

dress·er[2] (dres′ər) *n.* **1** A chest of drawers supporting a swinging mirror, useful in a dressing-room. **2** A cupboard for dishes. **3** *Obs.* A table on which meat is dressed. [OF *dresseur* < *dresser* dress]

dress goods Fabrics for dresses.

dress·ing (dres′ing) *n.* **1** The act of dressing. **2** That with which anything, as a wound, is dressed. **3** A seasoned sauce served with salads and vegetables; also, a stuffing for fowl or meats. **4** *pl. Archit.* Moldings around the wall openings in a brick building. **5** The mechanical preparation of ore for smelting. **6** *Colloq.* A beating or scolding. **7** The preparation for use of skins, lumber, stone, etc. **8** Fertilizer.

dress·ing-down (dres′ing·doun′) *n. U.S. Colloq.* **1** A reprimand. **2** A beating.

dressing gown A loose gown worn while dressing or in undress.

dress·ing-room (dres′ing·ro͞om′, -ro͝om′) *n.* A room used for dressing, as backstage in a theater.

dressing station *Mil.* A medical field station for giving immediate aid to the wounded.

dress·ing-ta·ble (dres′ing·tā′bəl) *n.* A small table equipped with a mirror and used in making one's toilet; a vanity.

dress·mak·er (dres′mā′kər) *n.* One who makes women's dresses, etc. — *adj.* Not severely tailored, but having soft, dressy, or feminine lines: a *dressmaker* suit.

dress parade A formal military parade in dress uniform.

dress rehearsal The last rehearsal of a play before the public performance, in full costume and using all properties.

dress shield A crescent-shaped piece of fabric with waterproof lining, worn to protect clothes from underarm perspiration.

dress suit A man's suit, usually black, for formal evening wear, characterized by a low-cut vest and an open coat with long, wide lapels, cut to the hips in front, curving into a bifurcated tail, extending almost to the knee: also called *full-dress suit.*

dress·y (dres′ē) *adj.* **dress·i·er, dress·i·est** *Colloq.* **1** Fond of dress. **2** Showy; elegant. — **dress′i·ness** *n.*

drew (dro͞o) Past tense of DRAW.

Drew (dro͞o), **John,** 1853–1927, U.S. actor.

Drex·el (drek′səl), **Anthony Joseph,** 1826–1893, U.S. banker and philanthropist.

Drey·fus (drā′fəs, drī′-; *Fr.* dre·füs′), **Alfred,** 1859–1935, French army officer falsely accused and convicted of treason, 1894 and 1899; his innocence was fully established on retrial in 1906.

drib (drib) *v.t.* **dribbed, drib·bing** *Obs.* **1** To let fall in drops. **2** To do or say (something) little by little. [Var. of DRIP]

drib·ble (drib′əl) *v.t.* & *v.i.* **·bled, ·bling 1** To fall or let fall in drops; drip. **2** To drool; drivel. **3** In basketball, to propel (the ball) by bouncing with the hands. **4** In soccer, to propel (the ball) by successive pushes or kicks with the feet. — *n.* **1** A small quantity of a liquid falling in drops or flowing in a scanty and broken stream. **2** *Scot.* Showery or drizzly weather. **3** In basketball and soccer, the act of dribbling. [Freq. of DRIB] — **drib′·bler** *n.*

drib·let (drib′lit) *n.* **1** A small piece, part, or sum. **2** A drop or clot formed as if by dribbling: money paid in *driblets.* Also **drib′·blet.**

drid·dle (drid′l) *v.i. Scot.* To waste time and strength to no purpose; dawdle; loiter.

driech (drēkh) See DREE.

dried (drīd) Past tense and past participle of DRY.

dri·er (drī′ər) *n.* **1** One who or that which dries. **2** A substance added to paint, etc., to make it dry more quickly. **3** A mechanical device for drying: also spelled *dryer.*

dri·er (drī′ər), **dri·est** (drī′ist) Comparative and superlative of DRY.

Driesch (drēsh), **Hans Adolf Eduard,** 1867–1941, German biologist.

drift (drift) *n.* **1** That which is driven or carried onward by a current: a *drift* of clouds across the sky. **2** A heap of any matter piled up by wind or sea. **3** A course along which or an end toward which anything moves on; tendency; meaning: the *drift* of a discourse. **4** A driving; an urgent force; hence, controlling power or influence. **5** A number of objects moving onward by one force; especially, anything floating or moving with the current of a river or stream, as logs, trees, etc.; driftwood. **6** A ford. **7** The fact or condition of being driven; the action of drifting. **8** A boring tool. **9** *Geol.* Material which has been transported by moving masses of ice or by running water created by glaciers, and deposited over portions of the earth's surface. **10** *Mining* A horizontal or nearly horizontal passage in a mine; also, the direction of a passage or gallery. **11** The direction of a current. **12** *Naut.* Leeway; the distance which a vessel is driven from her direct course by wind or sea or other causes. **13** A fishing net that drifts with the tide; a drift net. **14** *Aeron.* The angular difference between the long axis of an aircraft and the line of its flight path: also **drift angle. 15** The movement of a herd of cattle, as before a storm. See synonyms under HEAP, INCLINATION, PURPOSE, STREAM. — *v.t.* **1** To carry along, as on a current. **2** To cause to pile up in heaps, as snow or sand. — *v.i.* **3** To float or be carried along, as by a current. **4** To wander. **5** To accumulate in heaps. [ME <OE *drīfan* drive]

drift·age (drif′tij) *n.* **1** The operation or process of drifting. **2** Anything carried by currents of wind or sea.

drift anchor A sea anchor.

drift·bolt (drift′bōlt′) *n.* A drivebolt.

drift·er (drif′tər) *n.* **1** One who or that which drifts. **2** A fishing boat used for fishing with drift nets. **3** *Colloq.* A person having no settled home or occupation.

drift fence A fence to halt the drifting of cattle.

drift-me·ter (drift′mē′tər) *n. Aeron.* An instrument for measuring the drift of an aircraft and also for taking bearings from ground objects. Also **drift′-in′di·ca′tor** (-in′də·kā′tər).

drift sail *Naut.* A drag sail.

drift tube *Electronics* A cylindrical enclosure forming part of a klystron in which electrons or other charged particles are maintained at a constant potential and velocity.

drift·wood (drift′wo͝od′) *n.* Wood floated or drifted by water, especially that cast ashore by the sea.

drift·y (drif′tē) *adj.* Forming or full of drifts; drifting.

drill[1] (dril) *n.* **1** A boring tool for metal or other hard substance. **2** The art or action of training in military exercises; hence, thorough and regular discipline in any branch of knowledge, activity, or industry. See synonyms under PRACTICE. **3** *Zool.* A mollusk (*Urosalpinx cinereus*) which kills oysters by drilling holes in their shells. — *v.t.* **1** To pierce or bore with or as with a drill. **2** To bore (a hole). **3** To train in military exercises. **4** To instruct by methodical exercises. **5** To impart by methodical exercises: He *drilled* the lessons into his students. — *v.i.* **6** To use a drill. **7** To engage in military exercises. **8** To engage in methodical exercises. See synonyms under PIERCE, TEACH. [<Du. *dril, drille* < *drillen* bore]

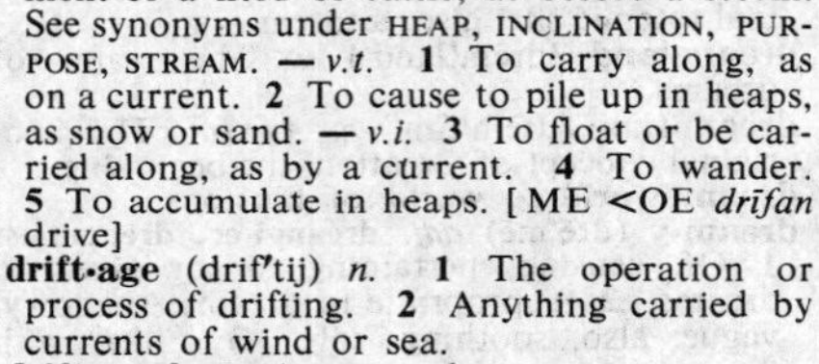

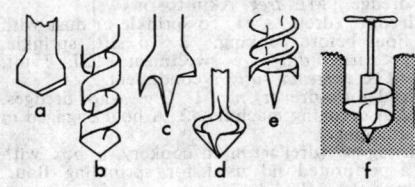

DRILLS

a. V-drill (metal). *b.* Twist drill (metal). *c.* Center bit (wood). *d.* Countersink (wood or metal). *e.* Twist bit (wood). *f.* Earth borer.

drill[2] (dril) *Agric. n.* **1** A machine for planting seeds in rows. **2** A small furrow in which seeds are sown. **3** A row of seeds so planted. — *v.t.* To plant in rows: to *drill* a field; to *drill* seeds. — *v.i.* To sow or plant in drills. [Origin uncertain]

drill[3] (dril) *n.* Heavy, twilled linen or cotton cloth. Also **drill′ing.** [Short for *drilling* <G *drilich* cloth with three threads <L *trilix* < *tres* three + *licium* thread]

drill[4] (dril) *n.* A black-faced baboon of West Africa (genus *Papio*), similar to the mandrill. For illustration see MANDRILL. [? < native name]

drill·er (dril′ər) *n.* **1** One who or that which drills. **2** A drilling machine.

drill·ing (dril′ing) *n.* **1** Material excavated by a drill. **2** The act of one who drills; the act of using a drill.

drill·mas·ter (dril′mas′tər, -mäs′tər) *n.* A trainer in military or gymnastic exercises.

drill·press (dril′pres′) *n.* An upright drilling machine for working in metal.

drill·stock (dril′stok′) *n.* A holder for a drill. See DRILL[1] (def. 1).

dri·ly (drī′lē) See DRYLY.

Drin (drēn) A river in Albania, flowing 65 miles west into the Adriatic: ancient **Dri·lo** (drī′lō). *Albanian* **Dri·ni** (drē′nē).

Dri·na (drē′nä) A river in east Bosnia, Yugoslavia, flowing 285 miles north to the Sava.

drink (dringk) *v.* **drank** (*Obs.* **drunk**), **drunk** (*Obs.* **drunk·en**), **drink·ing** *v.t.* **1** To take into the mouth and swallow, as water. **2** To soak up or absorb (a liquid or moisture). **3** To take in eagerly through the senses or the mind: often with *in.* **4** To drink the health of; toast. **5** To swallow the contents of. — *v.i.* **6** To swallow a liquid. **7** To drink alcoholic liquors, especially to excess or habitually; tope. **8** To drink a toast: with *to.* — *n.* **1** Any liquid that is or may be swallowed; a beverage. **2** Alcoholic liquor. **3** The practice of drinking to excess. **4** As much as is or may be taken at one time; a draft. — **in drink** Overcome by liquor. [OE *drincan*]

drink·a·ble (dringk′ə·bəl) *adj.* Capable of or suitable for use as a drink; potable. — *n. Usually pl.* A beverage.

drink·er (dringk′ər) *n.* **1** One who drinks. **2** One who drinks alcoholic liquors habitually.

Drinker respirator An iron lung. [after Philip *Drinker,* born 1894, U.S. Public Health engineer]

Drink·wa·ter (dringk′wô′tər, -wot′ər), **John,** 1882–1937, English poet and playwright.

drip (drip) *n.* **1** A falling, or letting fall, in drops. **2** Dripping; that which drips. **3** *Archit.* A projecting molding over an opening for a window or a door. **4** Condensed moisture, as in gas pipes. **5** *U.S. Slang* A person regarded as socially inept. — *v.t.* & *v.i.* **dripped, drip·ping** To fall or let fall in drops. [OE *dryppan*]

drip coffee Coffee made by letting boiling water seep slowly through a strainer containing finely ground coffee beans.

drip-dry (drip′drī′) *adj.* Designating or pertaining to a garment or fabric that is treated to dry quickly after being hung while dripping wet, to retain its shape, and to require little or no ironing. — *v.i.* **-dried, -dry·ing** To dry after being hung while dripping wet: said especially of drip-dry garments or fabrics.

drip·ping (drip′ing) *n.* **1** That which falls in drops. **2** *Usually pl.* Fat exuded from meat in cooking. **3** The act of falling in drops; also, the sound so produced.

dripping pan A pan for receiving drippings or holding meat in roasting.

drip·stone (drip′stōn′) *n. Archit.* A label or projecting molding over a window or door.

drive (drīv) *v.* **drove, driv·en, driv·ing** *v.t.* **1** To

push or propel onward with force; urge or press forward; impel. **2** To force to act or work; urge on by or as by coercion: He *drives* his workers too hard. **3** To bring to a state or condition as if by coercion: Failure *drove* him to despair. **4** To cause to penetrate or pass through: often with *in*: to *drive* in a nail. **5** To form by penetrating or passing through: to *drive* a well. **6** To control the movements or direction of: to *drive* an automobile. **7** To transport in a vehicle. **8** To carry on or complete (trade, a bargain, etc.) with energy. **9** In sports, to strike and propel (a ball) with force. **10** *Mech.* To provide power for: The wind *drives* the generator. **11** In hunting, **a** To chase (game) from cover or into traps, nets, etc. **b** To search (an area) in such a manner. **12** *Mining* To excavate (a tunnel) horizontally. — *v.i.* **13** To move forward or onward rapidly or with force: The ship *drove* before the wind. **14** To operate or travel in a vehicle: We all *drove* together into town. **15** To have an object or intention: with *at*: What are you *driving* at? **16** To aim a blow: with *at*. — **to drive home 1** To force in all the way, as a nail. **2** To make clear or evident; complete. — **to let drive at** To aim or discharge a shot, blow, missile, etc. — *n.* **1** The act of driving. **2** A road for driving; also, an approach for vehicles to a private house or other building. **3** A journey or excursion in an automobile or other vehicle. **4** Urgent pressure, as of business. **5** A hunt by driving; a drove or drift, as of cattle; a round-up; also, any objects driven, collectively. **6** A special sale at reduced price. **7** *Mil.* An advance of troops in mass against an enemy so as to break through defenses and drive back the defenders. **8** In golf, a stroke from the tee made with a wooden club; the distance traveled by the ball. **9** In certain games, as baseball, cricket, croquet, etc., the act of driving the ball, or the stroke by which the ball is driven; also, the flight of the ball. **10** *Mining* A driven tunnel. **11** *Mech.* A driving gear; a means of transmitting power, as from the motor of an automobile to the wheels. **12** Energy; vitality; also, aggressiveness. **13** Logs felled in the winter to be floated downstream in the spring. **14** The mass of logs floating down a river or stream. **15** An organized money-raising campaign: a Red Cross *drive*. See synonyms under WAY. [OE *drīfan*]

Synonyms (verb): compel, impel, propel, push, repel, repulse, resist, ride, thrust. To *drive* is to move an object with some force or violence before or away from oneself; it is the direct reverse of *draw, lead,* etc. A man leads a horse by the halter, *drives* him with whip and rein. One may be *driven* to a thing or from it; hence, *drive* is a synonym equally for *compel* or for *repel* or *repulse*. *Repulse* is stronger and more conclusive than *repel*; one may be *repelled* by the very aspect of the person whose favor he seeks, but is not *repulsed* except by the direct refusal or ignoring of his suit. It is common to speak of *driving* in a car, *riding* upon a horse; though many good authorities use *ride* in the older and broader sense as signifying to be supported and borne along by any means of conveyance. Compare ACTUATE, BANISH, COMPEL, INFLUENCE, PUSH. *Antonyms*: see synonyms for DRAW.

drive·bolt (drīv′bōlt′) *n.* **1** A tool for driving bolts home. **2** A bolt used to drive out another bolt: also called *driftbolt*.

drive-in (drīv′in′) *n.* A restaurant, shop, motion-picture theater, etc., serving patrons seated in their automobiles. — *adj.* So constructed as to allow service to the occupants of automobiles.

driv·el (driv′əl) *v.* **driv·eled** or **driv·elled, driv·el·ing** or **driv·el·ling** *v.i.* **1** To let saliva flow from the mouth; slobber. **2** To flow like saliva. **3** To talk or act in a foolish or stupid manner. — *v.t.* **4** To let flow from the mouth. **5** To say in a foolish manner. — *n.* **1** An involuntary flow of saliva from the mouth. **2** Senseless talk; twaddle. [OE *dreflian*] — **driv′el·er** or **driv′el·ler** *n.*

driv·en (driv′ən) Past participle of DRIVE.

driven well A well made by driving a pipe into the ground until the perforated tip reaches a stratum where water is found. Compare illustration under ARTESIAN WELL. Also **drive·well** (drīv′wel′).

driv·er (drī′vər) *n.* **1** One who or that which drives; a coachman; locomotive engineer; the operator of any motor vehicle. **2** *Mech.* Any of various machine parts which communicate motion; especially, the driving wheel of a locomotive; also, in power transmission, any wheel which moves another, as distinguished from the follower; a driving wheel. See illustration under ECCENTRIC. **3** *Naut.* A four-cornered fore-and-aft sail; a spanker. **4** A wooden-headed golf club with full-length shaft, somewhat supple, for driving the greatest distances from the tee. See illustration under GOLF CLUB. **5** The overseer of a group of laborers. **6** One who works on a log drive. **7** A carriage horse.

Dri·ver (drī′vər), **Samuel Rolles,** 1846–1914, English Hebraic and Biblical scholar and critic.

driver ant Any of a subfamily *(Dorylinae)* of carnivorous, stinging ants of tropical Africa and South America (genera *Dorylus* and *Eciton*), which live in temporary nests and raid the countryside in huge armies: also called *legionary ant, doryline ant.*

drive shaft *Mech.* A shaft for transmitting power from an engine to the working parts of machinery, especially one connecting the transmission with the rear axle of an automobile.

drive train A mechanical system for transmitting motion from the source of power to its point of application, as the engine, transmission, drive shaft, differential gearing, axles, and driving wheels of an automobile: also called *power train.*

drive·way (drīv′wā′) *n.* **1** A private road providing access to a building or house. **2** A road.

driv·ing (drī′ving) *adj.* **1** Transmitting power: a *driving* wheel. **2** Active and energetic: a *driving* personality.

driving wheel 1 One of the large wheels of a locomotive which converts the energy of steam into motion. **2** Any wheel used to communicate motion to any part of a machine.

driz·zle (driz′əl) *v.t.* & *v.i.* **·zled, ·zling** To rain steadily in fine drops. — *n.* A light rain. [? Freq. of ME *dresen,* OE *drēosan* fall] — **driz′zly** *adj.*

drod·dum (drod′əm) *n. Scot.* The breech.

dro·ger (drō′gər) *n.* **1** A small, West Indian coasting vessel, with long masts and lateen sails. **2** Any clumsy coasting vessel. [<MF *drogueur* <MDu. *drogher* < *droogen* dry; orig. a ship which caught and dried fish]

Dro·ghe·da (drô′ə·də, dro′hē·də) A port on the Boyne river, county town of County Louth, Ireland; Cromwell massacred its inhabitants in 1649.

Dro·go·byez (drô′gə·bich) A city in SE Poland. *Polish* **Dro·ho′bycz** (drô·hô′bēch).

drogue (drōg) *n.* **1** *Naut.* A floating anchor, usually made of spars and strong canvas, dragged from the stern to reduce yawing. **2** The drag attached to the end of a harpoon line. **3** *Meteorol.* A tapered fabric bag, open at both ends, to show the direction of the wind: also called *windsock.* **4** *Aeron.* A parachute or similar device used to slow down or stabilize an aircraft in flight. [? Related to DRAG]

droit (droit, *Fr.* drwà) *n.* **1** A legal right or claim of ownership, as distinguished from possession; also, that to which one has a legal claim. **2** Right in general; law; justice; equity. **3** *pl.* Customs duties. [<F, a right <LL *directum* <L *dirigere* set straight]

droit des gens (drwà dā zhäṅ′) *French* Law of nations; international law.

droits of Admiralty (droits) Rights to the property of an enemy, once belonging to the office of admiral of England. These droits now go into the public treasury.

droit·u·ral (droi′chər·əl) *adj.* Relating to a right of ownership as distinguished from possession.

droll (drōl) *adj.* Facetiously or humorously odd; comical; ludicrous; funny; queer. See synonyms under HUMOROUS, JOCOSE, ODD, QUEER, RIDICULOUS. — *n.* **1** A jester; a funny fellow. **2** A farce. **3** A comical tale. — *v.i.* To jest; play the jester. [<MF *drôle* a jester] — **drol′ly** *adv.*

droll·er·y (drō′lər·ē) *n. pl.* **·er·ies 1** Comical speech or manners; buffoonery; oddity. **2** The quality of being droll; facetiousness; humor. **3** A jest; a facetious or amusing story. **4** *Obs.* A comic picture, drawing, performance, or exhibition. See synonyms under WIT[1].

Drôme (drōm) A river in SE France, flowing 63 miles NW to the Rhône.

-drome *combining form* Racecourse; place for running: *hippodrome.* [<Gk. *dromos* a running]

drom·e·dar·y (drom′ə·der′ē) *n. pl.* **·dar·ies 1** The swift, one-humped Arabian camel *(Camelus dromedarius)* trained for riding. For illustration see CAMEL. [<OF *dromedaire* <LL *dromedarius* <L *dromas* <Gk., a running]

dro·mo·ma·ni·a (drō′mə·mā′nē·ə, mān′yə, drom′ə-) *n. Psychiatry* An abnormal desire to travel: also called *periomania.* [<Gk. *dromos* a running + -MANIA]

drom·on (drom′ən, drum′-) *n.* A swift medieval warship propelled by both oars and sails. Also **drom·ond** (drom′ənd, drum′-). [<AF *dromund,* OF *dromon* <LL *dromon* <LGk. *dromōn* < *dromos* a running]

dro·mo·pho·bi·a (drō′mə·fō′bē·ə, -fōb′yə, drom′ə-) *n. Psychiatry* A morbid fear of crossing streets. [<Gk. *dromos* a running + -PHOBIA] — **dro′mo·pho′bic** *adj.*

dro·mos (drō′məs) *n. pl.* **dro·moi** (-moi) **1** In ancient Greece and Rome, a racecourse. **2** An entrance passage or avenue, as the walled passages leading to the tombs at Mycenae. [<Gk., a running]

-dromous *combining form* Running: *catadromous.* [<-DROME + -OUS]

drone[1] (drōn) *v.* **droned, dron·ing** *v.i.* **1** To make a dull, monotonous, humming sound; hum. **2** To speak in a slow, dull, tone. — *v.t.* **3** To say in a slow, dull tone. — *n.* **1** A dull, monotonous, humming sound, as of a bee. **2** One of the single-note reed pipes of the bagpipe: distinguished from *chanter*; also, a bagpipe or similar instrument. See illustration under BAGPIPE. **3** *Music* A sustained bass commonly of one note. **4** A drawling speaker. [ME *dronen* < *drone* a male bee]

drone[2] (drōn) *n.* **1** A stingless male bee, that gathers no honey. **2** Hence, an idler. **3** *Aeron.* An unmanned airplane piloted by remote control. — *v.* **droned, dron·ing** *v.t.* To spend idly. — *v.i.* To live in idleness; be indolent. [OE *drān*] — **dron′ism** *adj.*

dron·go (drong′gō) *n.* A crowlike, insectivorous bird *(Dicrurus forficatus)* of the East Indies and Africa, with a long, forked tail and dark plumage. Also **drongo shrike.** [<Malagasy]

drool (dro͞ol) *v.t.* & *v.i.* To drivel; slaver. — *n.* **1** Spittle. **2** *Colloq.* Foolish talk; stuff and nonsense. [Contraction of DRIVEL]

droop (dro͞op) *v.i.* **1** To sink down; hang downward. **2** To lose vigor or vitality. **3** To become dejected; lose spirit. — *v.t.* **4** To allow to hang or sink down. See synonyms under FALL. — *n.* A sinking or hanging down; specifically, the bending under its own weight of the long barrel of an artillery gun. [<ON *drūpa*] — **droop′ing** *adj.* — **droop′ing·ly** *adv.*

droop·y (dro͞o′pē) *adj.* **droop·i·er, droop·i·est** Forlorn; drooping; tending to droop. — **droop′·i·ness** *n.*

drop (drop) *n.* **1** A globule of liquid; also, a very small quantity of anything, as of a beverage. **2** Anything that resembles or hangs like a drop of liquid, or that is made in drops or by dropping; a pendant earring, small piece of candy, etc. **3** A fall; the distance fallen; a sudden change of level; descent. **4** Any one of various contrivances that drop or depend, or are employed in lowering, as the drop curtain of a theater; also, in the theater, a drop scene. **5** *Mech.* **a** A forging machine. **b** A press used for forging, stamping, etc. **6** A trap door; especially, the platform of a gallows. **7** *pl.* Any liquid medicine given by the drop. **8** *Naut.* The vertical depth of a course on its central line. **9** A letter-drop. **10** A fall in prices: Stocks took a *drop.* — **at the drop of a** (or **the**) **hat** At

once; with little or no hesitation or provocation. **— to have the drop on** To have the advantage over; specifically, to have (a person) covered with a gun before he can draw his. — *v.* **dropped, drop·ping** *v.t.* **1** To let fall in drops. **2** To let fall in any way; release and let fall; lower. **3** To give birth to: said of animals. **4** To say as if casually or incidentally: to *drop* a hint. **5** To write and send (a note, etc.) hastily and informally. **6** To bring down or cause to fall, as by tackling, striking, or shooting. **7** To stop treating of or associating with: to *drop* a subject or a friend. **8** To leave at a specific place, as from a ship or vehicle. **9** To omit (a syllable, letter, or word): He *dropped* the *von* from his name. **10** To sprinkle with drops. **11** *Slang* To lose (money or the like), as in gambling. **12** *U.S.* To discharge (an employee); to dismiss (a student). **13** *Naut.* To outdistance; sail away from. — *v.i.* **14** To fall in drops, as a liquid. **15** To fall rapidly; come down. **16** To fall down exhausted, injured, or dead. **17** To crouch, as a hunting dog at sight of game. **18** To come to an end; cease; stop. **19** To fall into some state or condition: to *drop* into a habit. **20** To fall behind or to the rear: often with *behind* or *back.* See synonyms under FALL. **— to drop down** To move down a stream or along a coast, as a vessel. **— to drop in** To happen in, as for a call. **— to drop out** To leave; withdraw from. [OE *dropa*]

drop curtain A theater curtain lowered in front of the stage between the acts.

drop·forge (drop′fôrj′) *v.t.* **·forged, ·forg·ing** To forge (metal) between dies by a machine employing the mechanical force of a dropped weight. **— drop′forg′ing** *n.*

drop hammer A machine for forging, stamping, etc., in which a heavy weight sliding between vertical guides strikes blows at regular intervals or at the will of the operator.

drop·kick (drop′kik′) *n.* In football, a kick given the ball just as it is rebounding after being dropped. **— drop′kick′er** *n.*

drop–kick (drop′kik′) *v.t.* & *v.i.* To kick (a football) in the manner of a dropkick.

drop leaf A hinged section of a table that may be folded down when not in use. **— drop′–leaf′** *adj.*

drop·let (drop′lit) *n.* A little drop.

drop–let·ter (drop′let′ər) *n.* A letter delivered by the same office in which it is posted.

drop·light (drop′līt′) *n.* **1** An attachment to a side fixture or an overhead chandelier by which a lamp can be raised or lowered at will. **2** The light thus raised or lowered.

drop·out (drop′out′) *n.* **1** A student who leaves school or college after attendance is no longer compulsory, or before graduation. **2** One who abandons any undertaking before completing it.

drop·per (drop′ər) *n.* **1** One who or that which drops. **2** *Agric.* A machine that cuts grain and drops it in bundles at intervals. **3** A glass tube with a suction bulb at one end and a narrow orifice at the other, for dispensing a liquid in drops.

drop·ping (drop′ing) *n.* **1** The act of falling or letting fall in drops. **2** *Usually pl.* Falling drops, or that which has fallen in drops. **3** *pl.* The dung of animals.

drop press A drop hammer.

drop scene A scene, usually across the entire stage, dropped like a curtain.

drop shot Gunshot made by dropping molten metal from a height into water.

drop·si·cal (drop′si·kəl) *adj.* Resembling, relating to, or affected with dropsy. **— drop′·si·cal·ly** *adv.*

drop·sied (drop′sēd) *adj.* Afflicted with dropsy; swollen.

drop·sonde (drop′sond′) *n. Meteorol.* A radiosonde dropped by parachute from an airplane above terrain not suitable for ground stations. [<DROP + F *sonde* a sounding]

drop·sy (drop′sē) *n.* **1** *Pathol.* An abnormal accumulation of serous fluid in cellular tissue as in some body cavity. **2** A disease of certain plants, due to an excess of water. [Short for HYDROPSY]

drop·wort (drop′wûrt′) *n.* **1** A perennial plant (*Filipendula hexapetala*) of the rose family, with interruptedly pinnate leaves and white or reddish, odorless flowers. **2** Any of a genus (*Oenanthe*), of apiaceous plants, as the hemlock dropwort. **3** A North American marsh plant (*Oxypolis rigidior*) of the parsley family.

drosh·ky (drosh′kē, drôsh′kē) *n. pl.* **·kies** **1** A light, open, four-wheeled Russian carriage. **2** Any of several similar carriages. Also **dros′·ky.** [<Russian *drozhki,* dim. of *drogi* wagon]

DROSHKY

dro·soph·i·la (drō·sof′ə·lə, drə-) *n. pl.* **·lae** (-lē) Any of a genus (*Drosophila*) of fruit flies, especially *D. melanogaster,* used for research in genetics and heredity. See FRUIT FLY. [<NL <Gk. *drosos* dew + *phileein* love]

dross (drôs, dros) *n.* **1** *Metall.* Refuse or impurity in melted metal; slag; cinders. **2** Waste matter; refuse. See synonyms under WASTE. [OE *drōs*] **— dross′i·ness** *n.* **— dross′y** *adj.*

drought (drout) *n.* **1** Long-continued dry weather; want of rain. **2** Scarcity; dearth. **3** Thirst. Also **drouth** (drouth). [OE *drugoth.* Related to DRY.]

drought·y (drou′tē) *adj.* Marked by or suffering from drought or thirst; thirsty. Also **drouth·y** (drou′thē). **— drought′i·ness, drouth′·i·ness** *n.*

drouk (drōōk) *v.t. Scot.* **1** To wet through and through; saturate; soak. **2** To overcome.

drouk·it (drōō′kit) *adj. Scot.* Drenched.

drove[1] (drōv) Past tense of DRIVE.

drove[2] (drōv) *n.* **1** A number of animals driven or herded for driving. **2** A moving crowd of human beings. **3** A stone mason's broad-edged chisel: also called **drove chisel.** **4** The surface of stone smoothed by a drove: also called **drove′work′.** See synonyms under FLOCK[1]. — *v.t.* **·droved, drov·ing** **1** To drive (cows, etc.) for some distance; work as a drover. **2** To dress (stone) with a broad-edged chisel. [OE *drāf.* Related to DRIVE.]

drov·er (drō′vər) *n.* **1** One who drives animals in droves to market; a cattle-dealer. **2** A small fishing boat equipped with a drift net.

drown (droun) *v.t.* **1** To kill by immersion and suffocation in water or other liquid. **2** To flood; deluge. **3** To overwhelm; overpower; extinguish. — *v.i.* To die by immersion and suffocation in water or other liquid. [ME *drūnen, drounen*; origin uncertain]

drowse (drouz) *v.* **drowsed, drows·ing** *v.i.* **1** To be sleepy; doze; be listless. — *v.t.* **2** To make sleepy. **3** To pass (time) in drowsing. — *n.* The state of being half asleep; a doze. [OE *drūsian* become sluggish]

drow·sy (drou′zē) *adj.* **·si·er, ·si·est** **1** Heavy with sleepiness; dull. **2** Lulling; soporific. See synonyms under SLOW. **— drow′si·ly** *adv.* **— drow′si·ness** *n.*

drow·sy·head (drou′zē·hed′) *n. Obs.* Drowsiness; sleepiness. Also **drow′si·head′.**

drub (drub) *v.t.* **drubbed, drub·bing** **1** To beat, as with a stick; cudgel; thrash. **2** To vanquish; overcome. **3** To stamp (the feet). — *n.* A blow; thump. [? <Arabic *ḍarb* a beating < *ḍaraba* beat] **— drub′ber** *n.*

drub·bing (drub′ing) *n.* **1** A thrashing; a beating. **2** Defeat.

drudge (druj) *v.i.* **drudged, drudg·ing** To toil; work hard and slavishly at menial tasks. — *n.* One who toils at menial tasks. [Prob. related to OE *drēogan* work, labor]

drudg·er·y (druj′ər·ē) *n. pl.* **·er·ies** Dull, wearisome, or menial work. See synonyms under TOIL, WORK.

drug (drug) *n.* **1** Any substance, other than food, intended for use in the diagnosis, cure, mitigation, treatment, or prevention of disease in man or other animals. **2** Any article or substance recognized in the U.S. pharmacopoeia. **3** Any narcotic; also, any substance or chemical agent, exclusive of food, employed for other than medical reasons to obtain a given physiological effect or to satisfy a craving. **4** A commodity that is overabundant or in excess of demand: a *drug* on the market. — *v.t.* **drugged, drug·ging** **1** To mix drugs with (food, drink, etc.), especially narcotic or poisonous drugs. **2** To administer drugs to. **3** To stupefy or poison with or as with drugs; overcome: *drugged* with sleep. [<MF *drogue*; ult. origin unknown]

drug addict One addicted to a habit-forming drug.

drug·get (drug′it) *n.* **1** A coarse woolen or wool and cotton fabric for rugs, etc. **2** A rug made of such material. **3** A kind of dress fabric; woolen rep. [<MF *droguet*]

drug·gist (drug′ist) *n.* **1** One who compounds prescriptions and sells drugs; a pharmacist. **2** A dealer in drugs.

drug·store (drug′stôr′, -stōr′) *n.* A place where prescriptions are compounded, and drugs and miscellaneous merchandise are sold; a pharmacy.

dru·id (drōō′id) *n.* One of an order of priests or teachers of religion in ancient Gaul, Britain, and Ireland. [<MF *druide* <L *druidae, druides* <Celtic] **— dru′id·ess** (-is) *n. fem.*

dru·id·i·cal (drōō·id′i·kəl) *adj.* Of or pertaining to the druids. Also **dru·id′ic.**

dru·id·ism (drōō′id·iz′əm) *n.* The religious system of ancient Gaul, Britain, and Ireland, administered by the druids; also, its ceremonies, rites, and philosophy. Also **dru′id·ry** (-rē).

drum[1] (drum) *n.* **1** A hollow cylinder of wood or metal, with skin or vellum stretched upon ringlike frames fitted over each end, kept taut with hoops and cords, and played by beating the head or the heads with drumsticks; also, the sound produced by beating this instrument. **2** The body of a banjo, tambourine, etc. **3** *Anat.* The tympanum, or middle ear. **4** A drummer. **5** Anything resembling a drum in shape, as a cylindrical receptacle for oil, fruit, fish, etc. **6** The drumfish. **7** Any mechanical construction or device shaped like a drum. **8** *Obs.* A social gathering; formerly, a crowded and noisy fashionable card party at a private house. — *v.* **drummed, drum·ming** *v.t.* **1** To perform on or as on a drum. **2** To expel in disgrace: usually with *out.* **3** To summon by beating a drum. **4** To force into the mind or upon the attention by constant repetition. — *v.i.* **5** To beat a drum. **6** To beat on anything continuously or rhythmically. **7** To make a loud, beating noise: said especially of the wings of certain birds, as partridge or grouse. **— to drum up** To seek or solicit: to *drum* up trade. [Prob. <MDu. *tromme*]

HOISTING DRUM

drum[2] (drum) *n.* **1** *Scot.* & *Irish* A hill or elevation. **2** A drumlin.

drum·beat (drum′bēt′) *n.* The sound of a drum; also, the action of beating a drum.

drum·ble (drum′bəl) *v.i. Obs.* To move sluggishly. [< obs. *drumble,* var. of *dummel* stupid <DUMB]

drum brake A brake in which a shoe lined with a durable, heat-resistant material is pressed outward against the inner rim of a drum.

drum·fire (drum′fīr′) *n.* Gunfire so rapid and continuous as to sound like drums; continuous firing.

drum·fish (drum′fish′) *n. pl.* **·fish** or **·fishes** **1** A sciaenoid fish (*Pogonias cromis*) of the North American Atlantic coast which makes a drumming sound, especially in the breeding season. **2** Any of similar fishes, as the fresh-water drum (*Aplodinotus grunniens*) of the Great Lakes and the Mississippi.

drum·head (drum′hed′) *n.* **1** The membrane stretched over the end of a drum, especially the end that is beaten. **2** *Naut.* The circular top of a capstan. See illustration under CAPSTAN. **3** *Anat.* The tympanic membrane; the eardrum. See illustration under EAR. **4** An Australian grasstree.

drumhead court martial See under COURT MARTIAL.

drum·lin (drum′lin) *n. Geol.* A compact, elongated, oval mound of glacial drift, usually unstratified and having its longer axis in the direction of the local glacial movement. [<Irish *druim*]

drum major One who instructs or leads a band or drum corps.

drum ma·jor·ette (mā′jə·ret′) A woman who leads or precedes a marching band or accompanies such a band while twirling a baton.

drum·mer (drum′ər) *n.* **1** One who or that which drums. **2** *U.S.* A traveling salesman.

drum·mock (drum′ək) *n. Scot.* Raw oatmeal and water.

Drum·mond (drum′ənd), **Henry**, 1851–97, Scottish evangelical author and lecturer. **— William**, 1585–1649, Scottish poet. **— William Henry**, 1854–1907, Canadian physician and poet, born in Ireland.

Drummond light 1 The calcium light. 2 A type of heliostat. [after T. *Drummond*, 1797–1840, Scottish engineer, who invented it]

drum·stick (drum′stik′) *n.* 1 A stick for beating a drum. 2 The lower joint of the leg of a cooked fowl.

drunk (drungk) Past participle of DRINK; former past tense. **— adj.** 1 Inebriated; intoxicated; figuratively, saturated; satiated; glutted: *drunk* with slaughter. 2 *Obs.* Drenched. **— n. Colloq.** 1 A spree; fit of drunkenness. 2 A drunken person; a case of drunkenness.

drunk·ard (drungk′ərd) *n.* One who habitually drinks to intoxication; a sot.

drunk·en (drungk′ən) *adj.* 1 Given to, resulting from, or characterized by drunkenness; drunk; tipsy. 2 Saturated. **— drunk′en·ly** *adv.* **— drunk′en·ness** *n.*

drunt (drunt) *n. Scot.* Pettishness; a huff; ill humor.

dru·pa·ceous (droo·pā′shəs) *adj. Bot.* Of, like, or bearing drupes.

drupe (droop) *n. Bot.* A soft, fleshy fruit enclosing a hard-shelled stone or seed, as in the peach or cherry. See illustration under FRUIT. [<NL *drupa* <L *drupa (oliva)* an overripe (olive) <Gk. *druppa*]

drupe·let (droop′lit) *n. Bot.* A little drupe, as in a)raspberry or blackberry. Also **drupel** (droo′pəl), **dru·pe·ole** (droo′pē·ōl).

Dru·ry Lane (droor′ē) A street in London, known in the 17th and 18th centuries for its theaters.

druse (drooz) *n. Geol.* A cavity lined with crystals of the same minerals as the rock enclosing them: distinguished from *geode*. [<G] **— drus′y, drused** *adj.*

Druse (drooz) *n.* One of a fanatical religious sect of Syrians. [<Arabic *Duruz*, pl., after Ismail al–*Darazi*, who founded the sect] **— Dru·si·an** (droo′zē·ən), **Dru′se·an** *adj.*

Dru·sus (droo′səs) Name of two Roman generals: **Nero Claudius Drusus Germanicus**, 38–9 B.C., brother of the Emperor Tiberius; and **Drusus Caesar**, 15? B.C.–A.D. 23, son of the Emperor Tiberius.

dry (drī) *adj.* **dri·er, dri·est** 1 Lacking moisture; not wet or damp; not fresh; not green, as wood; also, lacking lubrication, as bearings. 2 Thirsty. 3 Lacking interest; lifeless; dull. 4 Slyly jocose or satirical; shrewd, as wit. 5 Free from sweetness: said of wines; also, denoting any wine having 14 percent or less of alcohol. 6 Subject to or in favor of a prohibitory liquor law: a *dry* town. 7 Not giving milk: a *dry* cow. 8 Not liquid; solid: said of merchandise, etc. 9 Tearless: said of the eyes. 10 Characterized by absence of bloodshed. 11 Without butter: said of toast. 12 Wanting in cordiality; not genial. **— v. dried, dry·ing** *v.t.* 1 To make dry; rid of moisture. 2 To cure or preserve, as meat, fish, etc., by evaporation or desiccation. **— v.i.** 3 To become dry. **— to dry up** 1 To cease or cause to cease flowing. 2 *Colloq.* To stop talking. **— n. pl. dries** 1 A state or condition of dryness; especially, a drought. 2 *Often cap. Colloq.* A prohibitionist. [OE *drȳge*] **— dry′ly, dri′ly** *adv.* **— dry′ness** *n.*

dry·ad (drī′əd, -ad) *n.* In Greek mythology a wood nymph. [<L *dryas, -adis* <Gk. *drys, dryos* an oak tree] **— dry·ad′ic** *adj.*

dry·as·dust (drī′əz·dust′) *adj.* An uninteresting, pedantic writer or speaker; a dull pedant. **— dry′–as·dust′** *n.*

dry battery See under BATTERY.

dry·bone ore (drī′bōn′) Smithsonite.

dry cell See under CELL.

dry·clean (drī′klēn′) *v.t.* To clean (clothing, etc.) with solvents other than water, such as carbon tetrachloride, etc. Also **dry′cleanse′**. **— dry′clean′er** *n.* **— dry′clean′ing** *n.*

Dry·den (drīd′n), **John**, 1631–1700, English poet, critic, and dramatist; poet laureate 1670–88.

dry distillation See under DISTILLATION.

dry·dock (drī′dok′) *n.* A structure, either floating or stationary, into which a ship is floated for repairs or cleaning. Gates and pumps operate to remove the enclosed water for convenience in working. **— v.t. & v.i.** To put in or go into drydock.

FLOATING DRYDOCK
a. Water line at the time ship is floated into dock.
b. Water line after water is pumped out of dock.
c. Block supports for ship.
d. Shoring for side support.
e. Watertight compartments.

dry·er (drī′ər), **dry·est** (drī′ist) See DRIER, DRIEST.

dry–eyed (drī′īd′) *adj.* Tearless; not weeping.

dry–farm·ing (drī′fär′ming) *n.* In an arid or dry country, the raising of crops without irrigation, mainly by saving the moisture of the soil and by raising drought–resisting crops. **— dry′farm′er** *n.*

dry fog *Meteorol.* Haze formed from a suspension of fine dust or smoke particles in the atmosphere.

dry·foot (drī′foot′) *adv.* 1 With dry feet. 2 *Obs.* By scent of the foot.

dry–goods (drī′goodz′) *n. pl.* Textile fabrics, as distinguished from groceries, hardware, etc.

Dry Ice Solid carbon dioxide used as a refrigerant: a trade name.

dry·ing (drī′ing) *adj.* 1 Able to draw out or absorb moisture; causing evaporation; absorbent. 2 Becoming dry rapidly, as certain oils.

dry kiln A heated oven or chamber for drying and seasoning lumber.

dry law A law prohibiting the sale of spirituous liquors.

dry measure A unit or system of units for measuring the volume of dry commodities, as fruits, grain, etc. The principal customary U.S. units are as in the table below. See also METRIC SYSTEM.

2 pints (pt., pts.)	= 1 quart (qt., qts.)
8 quarts	= 1 peck (pk., pks.)
4 pecks	= 1 bushel (bu.)

dry·nurse (drī′nûrs′) *v.t.* **·nursed, ·nurs·ing** 1 To nurse without suckling. 2 To coach or give hints to, as in or concerning the duties of an office. **— n.** 1 A nurse who nourishes and rears a child without suckling it. 2 One who cares for another; particularly, one who instructs his superior in the latter's duties.

Dry·o·pi·the·cus (drī′ō·pi·thē′kəs) *Paleontol. n.* Any of a genus of extinct apes of the Miocene and Pliocene epochs: closely related types are *Sivapithecus* and *Proconsul*. [NL <Gk. *drys, dryos* an oak tree + *pithēkos* a monkey, ape]

dry·point (drī′point′) *n.* 1 A fine etching needle used to incise copperplate in fine lines, without the use of acid or etching ground. 2 A line or work thus engraved, or the method thus used.

dry·rot (drī′rot′) *n.* 1 A fungous disease of timber, causing it to crumble into powder. 2 A disease of potato tubers and other vegetables. 3 Inward and gradual corruption, as of morals.

dry–run (drī′run′) *n.* 1 *Mil.* Practice in aiming and firing weapons without using live ammunition. 2 Any rehearsal or practice exercise.

dry·salt (drī′sôlt′) *v.t.* To preserve (food) by salting and removing moisture.

dry·salt·er (drī′sôl′tər) *n.* 1 One who deals in dried and salted meats, pickles, etc. 2 *Brit.* A dealer in chemical preparations, dyestuffs, etc. **— dry′salt′er·y** *n.*

dry–shod (drī′shod′) *adj. & adv.* Having the shoes or feet dry; without getting the feet wet: to cross a ford *dry–shod.*

dry socket *Dent.* A morbid condition of a tooth socket after extraction of a tooth, resulting from the disintegration of a blood clot without the formation of pus and accompanied by a foul odor and severe pain.

Dry Tor·tu·gas (tôr·too′gəz) A group of Florida islets west of the Marquesas Keys.

dry wash 1 Laundry which has been washed and dried, but not ironed. 2 *U.S.* A gully or arroyo which contains water only after a heavy rain.

du·ad (doo′ad, dyoo′-) *n.* A pair of units. [<Gk. *dyas, -ados* the number two]

du·al (doo′əl, dyoo′-) *adj.* 1 Denoting or relating to two. 2 Composed of two, as of two natures; twofold; binary. **— n. Gram.** In some languages, as Sanskrit and Greek, the form of the noun or verb indicating its application to two persons or things: the dual number: distinguished from *singular* and *plural.* ◆ Homophone: *duel.* [<L *dualis* <*duo* two] **— du·al·i·ty** (doo·al′ə·tē, dyoo-) *n.*

Du·a·la (doo·ä′lä) *n.* 1 One of a Bantu people inhabiting the Cameroons, West Africa. 2 Their language.

Dual Alliance An alliance (1879) between Germany and Austria–Hungary against Russia.

du·al·ism (doo′əl·iz′əm, dyoo′-) *n.* 1 The state of being twofold; duality. 2 A system or theory which asserts a twofoldness of nature, being, or operation; specifically, **theological dualism**, or the doctrine that there are two eternal and opposing principles, or beings, one good and the other evil; **philosophical dualism**, or the theory that the nature of the universe is twofold, *i.e.*, comprised of mind and matter, as opposed either to idealistic or materialistic monism; **psychological** or **psychophysical dualism**, the theory that the body and mind of man are two different existences but are placed by the order of nature in a most intimate system of correlations or interactions; or **ethical dualism**, the system of morals which demands and justifies one kind of conduct toward one's fellows in the same social group and another kind of conduct toward other men. 3 *Gram.* The expression of the condition of duality.

du·al·ist (doo′əl·ist, dyoo′-) *n.* A believer in some form of dualism.

du·al·is·tic (doo′əl·is′tik, dyoo′-) *adj.* 1 Of or pertaining to dualism. 2 Having a dual nature. **— du′al·is′ti·cal·ly** *adv.*

du·al–pur·pose (doo′əl·pûr′pəs, dyoo′-) *adj.* Having two functions or uses.

Du·ar·te (dwer′tā) Portuguese form of EDWARD.

dub¹ (dub) *v.t.* **dubbed, dub·bing** 1 To confer knighthood upon by tapping on the shoulder with a sword. 2 To name or style; entitle. 3 To smooth or rub; dress, as timber. [OE *dubbian*]

dub² (dub) *v.t. & v.i.* **dubbed, dub·bing** 1 To push or thrust. 2 To beat (a drum). **— n.** 1 A blow. 2 A beat of a drum. [Prob. imit.]

dub³ (dub) *Slang n.* A clumsy, blundering person; a poor or second-rate player in any game. **— v.t. dubbed, dub·bing** To bungle. [? <DUB²]

dub⁴ (dub) *n. Scot.* A pool; puddle.

dub⁵ (dub) *v.t.* **dubbed, dub·bing** To re-record (a sound record) in order to change volume or frequency. **— to dub in** 1 In motion pictures, to insert (a new sound track) into a film. 2 To blend (new sounds, music, etc.) into the sound track of a film, or into a radio or television broadcast. [Short for DOUBLE]

dub–a–dub (dub′ə·dub′) *n.* 1 Drumbeating, or a similar sound. 2 A drummer. [Imit.]

du Bar·ry (doo bär′ē, *Fr.* dü bà·rē′), **Comtesse**, 1746?–93, Jeanne Bécu, mistress of Louis XV; guillotined.

Du·bawnt River (doo·bônt′) A river in north central Canada, flowing 580 miles NE through **Dubawnt Lake** (1,600 square miles) to the Thelon River.

dub·bing¹ (dub′ing) *n.* 1 Material for softening leather and making it waterproof. 2 Pieces of wood, etc., for filling up deep depressions or interstices in a wall before plastering. 3 The material of the body of a fishing fly. [<DUB¹]

dub·bing² (dub′ing) *n.* The re-recording of a sound record, in whole or in part, where a change in volume levels or frequency characteristics is necessary; especially, the synchronized conversion of a motion-picture sound track from the language of the original cast into some other language. [<DUB⁵]

Dub·he (doob′he) The star Alpha in the constellation Ursa Major: the larger of the two

stars which together make the Pointer toward the Pole Star.

du·bi·e·ty (dōō·bī′ə·tē, dyōō-) *n.* The state of being doubtful or dubious; doubt; doubtfulness. Also **du·bi·os·i·ty** (dōō′bē·os′ə·tē, dyōō′-). [<LL *dubietas, -tatis* <*dubius* doubtful]

du·bi·ous (dōō′bē·əs, dyōō′-) *adj.* 1 Unsettled in judgment or opinion; in a state of doubt; doubtful. 2 Being a subject or matter of doubt; causing doubt. 3 Of uncertain result; not yet settled; problematic. 4 Of questionable propriety; open to objections, especially of a moral kind, or to suspicion; questionable. 5 Being the occasion of doubt; difficult of explanation; equivocal. See synonyms under EQUIVOCAL, PRECARIOUS. [<L *dubiosus* <*dubium* doubt] — **du′bi·ous·ly** *adv.* — **du′bi·ous·ness** *n.*

du·bi·ta·ble (dōō′bə·tə·bəl, dyōō′-) *adj.* Doubtful; debatable. — **du′bi·ta·bly** *adv.*

du·bi·tate (dōō′bə·tāt, dyōō′-) *v.i.* **·tat·ed, ·tat·ing** *Rare* To doubt. [<L *dubitatus*, pp. of *dubitare* doubt]

du·bi·ta·tive (dōō′bə·tā′tiv, dyōō′-) *adj.* Tending to or expressing doubt; also, hesitating. — **du′bi·ta′tive·ly** *adv.*

Dub·lin (dub′lin) 1 The capital of Ireland, a port on the Liffey river at **Dublin Bay**, an inlet of the Irish Sea on the eastern coast of Ireland: Irish *Baile Atha Cliath.* 2 A county of Leinster province, eastern Ireland: 356 square miles; county seat, Dublin.

Dub·no (dōōb′nô) A city in Ukrainian S.S.R.

Du·bois (dü·bwä′), **Théodore,** 1837–1924, French composer.

Du Bois (dōō bois′), **William Edward Burghardt,** 1868–1963, U.S. educator and writer.

Du Bois-Rey·mond (dü bwä′rā·môn′), **Emil,** 1818–96, German physiologist.

du·bon·net (dōō′bə·nā′) *n.* A reddish purple, the color of Dubonnet.

Du·bon·net (dōō′bô·nā′, *Fr.* dü·bô·ne′) *n.* A fortified French red wine: a trade name.

Du·brov·nik (dōō′brôv·nik) A port on the Adriatic in SW Yugoslavia: Italian *Ragusa.*

Du·buque (də·byōōk′) A city in eastern Iowa on the Mississippi.

du·cal (dōō′kəl, dyōō′-) *adj.* Of or pertaining to a duke or a duchy. [<MF <LL *ducalis* <*dux* leader] — **du′cal·ly** *adv.*

Du Cange (dü känzh′), **Charles du Fresne,** 1610–88, French historian and philologist.

duc·at (duk′ət) *n.* 1 One of several European coins of varying value, the first struck by Roger II of Sicily. 2 A former coin of Venice and Holland. 3 *Slang* A ticket, usually for the theater or a sports event. [<MF <Ital. *ducato* <LL *ducatus*, orig. a duchy <*dux* leader]

Duc·cio di Buo·nin·se·gna (dōōt′chô dē bwô′nēn·sā′nyä), 1260?–1339?, Italian painter.

du·ce (dōō′chā) *n. Ital.* A leader; commander. — **il Duce** The title assumed by Benito Mussolini as leader of the Italian Fascists.

Du Chail·lu (dü shà·yü′), **Paul Belloni,** 1835–1903, U.S. explorer in Africa, born in France.

Du·champ (dü·shän′), **Marcel,** 1887–1968, French painter.

duch·ess (duch′is) *n.* 1 The wife or widow of a duke. 2 The female sovereign of a duchy. [<OF *duchesse* <LL *ducissa* <L *dux* leader]

duch·y (duch′ē) *n. pl.* **duch·ies** The territory or dominion of a duke; a dukedom. [<OF *duché* <L *dux* leader]

duck¹ (duk) *n.* 1 A web-footed, short-legged, broad-billed water bird of the *Anatidae* family comprising fresh-water and wood ducks (*Anatinae*), the sea and bay ducks (*Fuligulinae*), and the mergansers (*Merginae*). ◆ Collateral adjective: *anatine.* 2 The female of this bird: distinguished from *drake.* 3 The flesh of this bird. 4 *Colloq.* A dear; darling. 5 *Slang* A person; a fellow. [OE *duce*, lit. "diver"]

AMERICAN MALLARD DUCK
(About 23 inches in length)

duck² (duk) *v.t. & v.i.* 1 To plunge suddenly under water; dive. 2 To lower quickly; bob, as the head. 3 To dodge; evade (a blow or punishment). 4 To avoid (a duty, person, etc.). 5 To move quickly and abruptly: He *ducked* through the crowd. See synonyms un-

der IMMERSE. — *n.* A sudden downward movement, as of the head; a bob or nod; also, a quick plunge under water. [ME *duken, douken* dive, ult. <Gmc.]

duck³ (duk) *n.* 1 A strong tightly woven linen or cotton fabric with a plain weave, similar to canvas; sailcloth: heavier weights are used for tents, sails, and military and naval equipment; light weights for trousers, middy blouses, etc. 2 *pl.* Trousers made of this fabric. [<Du. *doek* cloth]

duck⁴ (duk) *n. Mil.* An amphibious military vehicle of World War II, having a watertight body and equipped with a propeller and a rudder for use when traveling on water. [<DUKW, code word for this type of vehicle]

duck·bill (duk′bil′) *n.* The platypus.

duck·board (duk′bôrd′, -bōrd′) *n.* A board or section of boarding laid over a wet floor or muddy ground to form a raised surface for walking.

duck·er¹ (duk′ər) *n.* 1 One who or that which ducks. 2 A diving bird.

duck·er² (duk′ər) *n.* 1 A duck hunter. 2 One who rears ducks.

duck-foot·ed (duk′fŏŏt′id) *adj.* With the back toe pointing nearly forward: applied to poultry.

duck hawk The American peregrine falcon.

duck·ing (duk′ing) *n.* 1 The act of plunging into water; a wetting. 2 The act of dodging or bobbing down, as to escape a blow. 3 Duck hunting.

ducking stool A stool on which the culprit was tied and plunged into water; a cucking stool: formerly used as a punishment in New England, especially for quarrelsome women.

duck·ling (duk′ling) *n.* A young duck.

duck·mole (duk′mōl′) *n.* The platypus.

duck·pin (duk′pin′) *n.* A pin 9 inches high and 3 1/2 inches in diameter at the body: used in the game of tenpins called **duckpins.**

ducks and drakes A game in which one skims or skips flat stones, shells, etc., along the surface of water. — **to make (or play) ducks and drakes** To throw away or squander: with *of* or *with.*

duck·weed (duk′wēd′) *n.* 1 Any of several small, disk-shaped, aquatic plants (genus *Lemna*) common in streams and ponds in the United States. 2 A somewhat larger plant of the same family, the large duckweed (*Spirodela polyrhiza*). Also **duck′meat′.**

duck·y (duk′ē) *adj. Slang* Delightful; darling; dear.

duct (dukt) *n.* 1 Any tube, canal, or passage by which a fluid is conveyed. 2 *Anat.* A tubular passage for fluid, especially one by which a secretion is carried away from a gland: the nasal *duct.* 3 *Electr.* A tubular channel for carrying electric power, telegraph or telephone cables. [<L *ductus* a leading <*ducere* lead]

duc·tile (duk′til) *adj.* 1 Capable of being hammered into thin layers or of being drawn out into wire, as certain metals. 2 Easily led; tractable; pliant. [<F <L *ductilis* <*ducere* lead] — **duc·til′i·ty, duc′tile·ness** *n.*

duct·less gland (dukt′lis) See ENDOCRINE GLAND.

dud¹ (dud) *n. Colloq.* 1 A garment. 2 *pl.* Clothing; especially, old clothes. 3 *pl.* Belongings in general. [ME *dudde* a cloak; origin uncertain]

dud² (dud) *n.* 1 *Mil.* A shell that fails to explode. 2 *Colloq.* Any person or thing that is inadequate or fails to operate. [<Du. *dood* dead]

dud·die (dud′ē) *adj. Scot.* Clothed in duds; poor; ragged; torn. Also **dud′dy.**

dude (dōōd, dyōōd) *n.* 1 *U.S.* A fop; an affected man. 2 A city person, especially one from the eastern United States who is vacationing on a ranch. [Coined 1883, ? <*duds* clothing] — **dud′ish** *adj.* — **dud′ism, dud′ish·ness** *n.*

du·deen (dōō·dēn′) *n. Irish* A short-stemmed tobacco pipe. [<Irish *dúidín*, diminutive of *dúd* a smoking pipe]

dude ranch A ranch operated as a resort for tourists.

Dude·vant (düd·vän′), **Baroness** See SAND, GEORGE.

dudg·eon¹ (duj′ən) *n.* Sullen displeasure; resentment. [Origin unknown]

dudg·eon² (duj′ən) *n.* 1 The root of the box-wood tree, formerly used for dagger hilts. 2 Any mottled or veined wood. 3 *Obs.* A

wooden hilt of a dagger; a dudgeon dagger. [<AF *digeon*; ult. origin unknown]

Dud·ley (dud′lē), **Joseph,** 1647–1720, American colonial governor. — **Robert** See LEICESTER. — **Thomas,** 1576–1653, administrator in Massachusetts Bay colony; father of Joseph.

Dud·ley (dud′lē) A county borough of Worcestershire, England.

due (dōō, dyōō) *adj.* 1 Owing and demandable; owed; especially, payable because of the arrival of the time set or agreed upon. 2 That should be rendered or given; justly claimable; appropriate. 3 Suitable; lawful; sufficient; regular. 4 Appointed or expected to arrive; having had time to arrive. 5 That may be charged or attributed; ascribable; owing: with *to:* The delay was *due* to rain. ◆ *Due to* as a preposition, though widely used, is still questioned by some, who would substitute for it *because of* or *on account of: Because of* (not *due to*) rain, we were delayed. — *n.* 1 That which is owed or rightfully required; a debt or obligation. 2 Legal charge or fee: club *dues.* — *adv.* 1 Directly; exactly: *due* east. 2 Duly. ◆ Homophone: *dew.* [<OF *deü*, pp. of *devoir* owe <L *debere*]

due bill A written acknowledgment of indebtedness.

du·el (dōō′əl, dyōō′-) *n.* 1 A prearranged combat between two persons, usually fought with deadly weapons in the presence of witnesses or seconds. 2 A struggle between two contending parties. — *v.t. & v.i.* **du·eled** or **·elled, du·el·ing** or **·el·ling** To fight or fight with, in a duel. ◆ Homophone: *dual.* [<F <Ital. *duello* <L *duellum*, var. of *bellum* war] — **du′el·er, du′el·ler** *n.* — **du′el·ist, du′el·list** *n.*

du·el·ing (dōō′əl·ing, dyōō′-) *n.* The act of fighting a duel. Also **du′el·ling.**

du·en·na (dōō·en′ə, dyōō-) *n.* An elderly woman who watches over a young woman in Spanish and Portuguese families; hence, a chaperon. [<Sp. <L *domina* lady. Doublet of DAME.]

Due·ro (dwā′rō) The Spanish name for DOURO.

du·et (dōō·et′, dyōō-) *n.* A musical composition for two voices or performers. [<Ital. *duetto*, dim. of *duo* a duet <L *duo* two]

duff¹ (duf) *v.t.* 1 *Brit. Colloq.* To fix or change so as to give the appearance of truth or right to; to fake or cheat. — *v.i.* 2 *Austral.* To steal cattle or horses, especially in large numbers. [? Back formation from *duffer*]

duff² (duf) *n.* 1 A thick flour pudding boiled in a bag. 2 The litter of dead leaves, broken branches, etc., accumulated in a forest. 3 Small or fine coal. [Var. of DOUGH]

duf·fel (duf′əl) *n.* 1 A woolen fabric; a heavyweight kersey. 2 Outfit; supplies; especially, camping outfit. Also **duf′fle.** [from *Duffel*, a town near Antwerp]

duffel bag A sack, usually of canvas or duck, used to carry clothing and personal possessions.

duf·fer (duf′ər) *n.* 1 *Colloq.* One who performs in an incompetent or perfunctory manner. 2 *Brit. Dial.* A peddler or hawker; especially, one who sells spurious or flashy articles. 3 *Slang* Any counterfeit or sham. 4 *Austral.* A stealer of horses or cattle. [Origin uncertain]

duf·fle coat (duf′əl) A heavy woolen outer coat, usually knee-length and hooded. Also **duf′fel coat.** [Var. of DUFFEL]

Du·fy (dü·fē′), **Raoul,** 1877–1953, French painter.

dug¹ (dug) Past tense and past participle of DIG.

dug² (dug) *n.* A teat or udder. [Cf. Dan. *dægge* suckle]

Du Gard (dü gàr′), **Roger Martin,** 1881–1958, French novelist.

du·gong (dōō′gong) *n.* An aquatic, herbivorous mammal (genus *Dugong*) of the East Indies

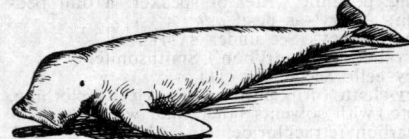

DUGONG
(From 9 to 12 feet in length; 450 to 2000 pounds)

and Australia, having flippers in front, a paddlelike tail, and tusks which in the male grow to large size: also called *sea cow.* [<Malay *duyong*]

dug-out (dug′out′) *n.* **1** A canoe formed of a hollowed log. See illustration under CANOE. **2** A rude dwelling excavated in a hillside; a cave. **3** An underground shelter against bombs and shells, or for protection from tornadoes, etc. **4** A low, boxlike structure facing a baseball diamond, to shelter the players when not at bat or in the field.

Du Gues·clin (dü ge·klaṅ′), **Bertrand,** 1320?–1380, French soldier; constable of France.

Du·ha·mel (dü·ȧ·mel′), **Georges,** 1884–1966, French author.

dui·ker·bok (dī′kər·bok′) *n.* A small antelope (genus *Cephalophus*) widely distributed over southern and tropical Africa, with short conical horns set far back, a tufted head, and very short tail. Also **dui′ker, dui′ker·buck′.** [<Du. < *duiker* ducker, diver + *bok* buck; from its habit of plunging through thickets]

Duis·burg (düs′bŏŏrkh) A city on the Rhine in North Rhine–Westphalia, West Germany. Formerly **Duis′burg–Ham′born** (-häm′bôrn).

Du·kas (dü·kä′), **Paul,** 1865–1935, French composer.

duke (dōōk, dyōōk) *n.* **1** An English temporal peer of the highest rank, yielding precedence to a prince of the blood or an archbishop, and ranking above a marquis or a bishop. **2** A Continental noble or prince of corresponding rank. **3** A reigning prince of less importance than a king ruling over a duchy or a small state. **4** Formerly, a powerful semi–independent vassal. — *v.i.* **duked, duk·ing** To play the duke. [<F *duc* <L *dux* leader]

Duke (dōōk, dyōōk), **Benjamin Newton,** 1855–1929, and his brother **James Buchanan,** 1856–1925, U.S. tobacco magnates.

duke·dom (dōōk′dəm, dyōōk′-) *n.* **1** A duchy. **2** The dignity or title of a duke.

dukes (dōōks, dyōōks) *n. pl. Slang* The fists. [Short for *Duke of Yorks,* orig. riming slang for forks; later fingers, hands, fists]

Du·kho·bors (dōō′kō·bôrz) *n. pl.* A religious sect of Russian peasants who emigrated from Russia in 1895 to escape persecution, and settled in western Canada and Cyprus. Also spelled *Doukhobors.* [<Russian *dukhobortsy* < *dukh* spirit + *bortsy* wrestlers]

Du·la·wan (dōō·lä′wän) A municipality in south central Mindanao, Philippines. Also **Du·la′uan.**

dul·cet (dul′sit) *adj.* **1** *Obs.* Sweet to the taste. **2** Sweet or melodious to the ear; soothing. — *n.* An organ stop resembling the dulciana, but an octave higher in tone. [<DOUCET, refashioned after L *dulcis* sweet]

dul·ci·an·a (dul′sē·an′ə) *n.* An organ stop of soft and delicate tone. [<Med. L *dulciana* <L *dulcis* sweet]

dul·ci·fy (dul′sə·fī) *v.t.* **·fied, ·fy·ing 1** *Obs.* To make sweet. **2** To please; mollify. — **dul′ci·fi·ca′tion** *n.*

dul·ci·mer (dul′sə·mər) *n.* **1** A stringed instrument played with two padded hammers. **2** A wind instrument. *Dan.* iii 10. [<OF *doulcemer, doulcemele* ? <L *dulcemelos* <*dulcis* sweet + *melos* a song <Gk.]

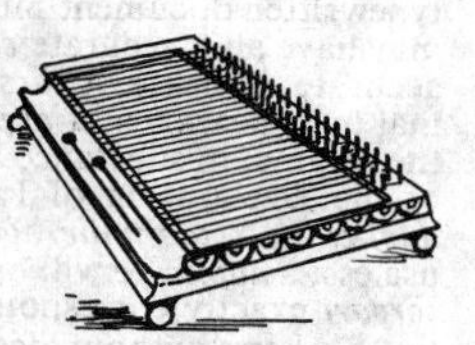

DULCIMER

dul·cin·e·a (dul·sin′ē·ə, dul′sə·nē′ə) *n.* A sweetheart; ladylove. [after *Dulcinea* del Toboso, character in *Don Quixote*]

Dul·heg·gia (dul·hej′ə) See CALENDAR (Mohammedan).

du·li·a (dōō·lī′ə, dyōō-) *n. Theol.* A secondary kind of worship, as distinguished from *latria,* or supreme worship: used in the sense of *veneration* of the saints and angels. [<Gk. *douleia* service < *doulos* slave]

Dul·kaa·da (dul·kä′də) See CALENDAR (Mohammedan).

dull (dul) *adj.* **1** Not sharp or keen; having a blunt edge or point. **2** Not acute or intense: *dull* pain. **3** Not quick, as in thought; sluggish; listless; stupid; lacking in perception, sensibility, or responsiveness. **4** Not brisk or active. **5** Not bright or spirited; wearisome; boring; sad. **6** Lacking luster; cloudy; dim. **7** Of sounds, indistinct; heavily muffled. See synonyms under BLUNT, FLAT, HEAVY, LIFELESS, NUMB, SAD, SLOW, TEDIOUS. — *v.t.* & *v.i.* To make or become dull. [ME *dul.* Akin to OE *dol* foolish.] — **dull′ish** *adj.* — **dul′ly** *adv.* — **dul′ness, dull′ness** *n.*

dull·ard (dul′ərd) *n.* A dull or stupid person.

Dul·les (dul′əs), **John Foster,** 1888–1959, U.S. lawyer and statesman; secretary of state 1952–1959.

Du·long and Pe·tit's law (dü·lôṅ′, pe·tēz′) *Physics* A statement that the specific heat of any solid element, multiplied by the atomic weight is nearly a constant (approximately, 6.4). [after P. L. *Dulong,* 1785–1838; A. T. *Petit,* 1791–1820, French physicists]

du·lo·sis (dōō·lō′sis, dyōō-) *n. Entomol.* A form of slavery practiced by certain genera of ants. [<NL <Gk. *doulōsis* enslavement] — **du·lot′·ic** (-lot′ik) *adj.*

dulse (duls) *n.* A reddish–brown seaweed (*Rhodymenia palmata*) eaten in Ireland, Scotland, and elsewhere as a vegetable. Also **dulce.** [<Irish *duileasg*]

Du·luth (də·lōōth′, dōō-) A port on Lake Superior in NE Minnesota.

du·ly (dōō′lē, dyōō′-) *adv.* In accordance with what is due; fitly; becomingly; regularly; in due time or manner.

Du·ma (dōō′mä) *n.* The former Russian national assembly elected indirectly by the people; created by an imperial ukase in 1905: also spelled *Douma.* [<Russian]

Du·mas (dōō·mä′, dōō′mä; *Fr.* dü·mȧ′), **Alexandre** Name of two French writers: **Dumas père,** 1803–70, novelist and dramatist, and his son **Dumas fils,** 1824–95, dramatist and novelist.

Du Mau·ri·er (dōō′môr′ē·ā, dyōō′-), **Daphne,** born 1907, English novelist. — **George,** 1834–1896, English illustrator and novelist born in France; grandfather of the preceding.

dumb (dum) *adj.* **1** Unable to make articulate sounds; having no power of speech: deaf and *dumb.* **2** Refraining from speaking; not using words or sounds; mute; silent. **3** Not having usual characteristics, symptoms, accompaniments, or powers; latent: *dumb* ague or chill. **4** *U.S. Colloq.* Stupid. **5** *Naut.* Having no sails: a *dumb* barge. See synonyms under TACITURN. [OE; in def. 4, infl. by cognate G *dumm* stupid] — **dumb′ly** *adv.* — **dumb′ness** *n.*

dumb ague A form of chills and fever in which the symptoms of the disease are concealed or obscure.

Dum·bar·ton (dum·bär′tən) A county of western Scotland; 240 square miles; county seat, Dumbarton. Also **Dum·bar′ton·shire** (-shir).

Dum·bar·ton Oaks (dum′bär·tən, dum·bär′·tən) An estate near Washington, D.C., at which conferences leading to proposals for an international organization were held, August–October 1944.

dumb·bell (dum′bel′) *n.* **1** A gymnastic implement consisting of a handle with a weighted ball at each end. **2** *U.S. Slang* A stupid person.

dumb·found (dum′found′) *v.t.* To strike dumb, confuse; confound. Also **dumb′found′er.** [Blend of DUMB and CONFOUND]

dumb show 1 Gestures and signs without words; pantomime. **2** In early English drama, pantomime representation of part of the action of a play.

dumb·wait·er (dum′wā′tər) *n.* A movable serving table or elevator for carrying things from one room or floor to another.

dum·dum bullet (dum′dum′) A small–arms bullet having a soft point or a jacket which has been cut across at the point so that it will mushroom on impact and tear a gaping wound. [from *Dumdum,* a town near Calcutta, India, where first made]

Dum·fries (dum·frēs′) A county in southern Scotland; 1,073 square miles; capital, Dumfries. Also **Dum·fries′shire** (-shir).

dum·my (dum′ē) *n. pl.* **dum·mies 1** *Colloq.* One who is dumb; a mute; hence, a stupid person; dolt. **2** A silent person, as an actor without a speaking part. **3** A figure used by a ventriloquist. **4** A comparatively noiseless steam locomotive without a blast pipe. **5** A dumbwaiter. **6** A thing made to represent something else; a model; a figure on which clothes can be displayed. **7** A figure stuffed with straw or sawdust, used in bayonet practice; also, a similar figure used by football players in tackling practice. **8** In certain card games, an exposed hand played by the opposite player; also, the player to whom that hand has been dealt. **9** A person who represents another in a transaction, but who poses as acting for himself; a straw man. **10** *Printing* A model book, usually blank, made up as a pattern. — **double dummy** Whist or bridge as played by two persons, each playing two hands, one of which is exposed. — *adj.* **1** Sham; counterfeit. **2** Silent. **3** Having no explosive charge: *dummy* ammunition. **4** Made to resemble some object, but having no real use; artificial: a *dummy* door. — *v.t.* **dum·mied, ·my·ing** To lay out (printed matter) as a guide for making up. — **to dummy up** *U.S. Slang* To become silent. [<DUMB]

du·mor·ti·er·ite (dōō·môr′tē·ə·rīt′, dyōō-) *n.* An aluminum borosilicate mineral resembling lapis lazuli: used in the making of refractories and high–grade porcelain dielectrics and sometimes cut as a gemstone. [after E. *Dumortier,* French paleontologist]

dump[1] (dump) *v.t.* **1** To drop or throw down abruptly or heavily. **2** To empty out, as from a container. **3** To empty (a container), as by overturning. **4** To throw (goods or commodities) on a market, especially a foreign market, in quantity and at low prices. **5** To get rid of; throw away. — *v.i.* **6** To fall or drop. **7** To unload goods or commodities. **8** To unload. — *n.* **1** A dumping ground; especially, a place where city refuse is dumped. **2** That which is dumped. **3** A place where ammunition, stores, or supplies are held for rapid distribution. **4** *U.S. Slang* A poor, ill–kept dwelling or place; also, lodgings. **5** A leaden counter used by boys in various games. **6** Something short, thick, and heavy. **7** *Brit.* A large globular sweetmeat; a bull's–eye. **8** A coin more or less thick and shapeless. [ME <Scand. Cf. Norw. *dumpa* fall suddenly.] — **dump′er** *n.*

dump[2] (dump) *n.* **1** *pl.* A gloomy state of mind; melancholy. **2** *Obs.* A slow, melancholy dance, or the music for it. [Cf. MD *domp* mental haze]

dump·ish (dump′ish) *adj.* Depressed in spirits; sad; morose. — **dump′ish·ly** *adv.* — **dump′ish·ness** *n.*

dump·ling (dump′ling) *n.* **1** A small piece of pie crust or biscuit dough filled with fruit and baked or steamed. **2** A small mass of dough dropped into boiling soup or stew. **3** A short, stocky person or animal.

dump truck A truck for hauling gravel, coal, etc., which unloads by tilting back the cargo bin and opening the tailboard.

dump·y[1] (dump′ē) *adj.* **dump·i·er, dump·i·est** Sullen or discontented; sulky; gloomy or cast down.

dump·y[2] (dump′ē) *adj.* **dump·i·er, dump·i·est** Short and thick; stocky. — **dump′i·ly** *adv.* — **dump′i·ness** *n.*

dumpy level A surveyor's level consisting of a short telescope rigidly attached to the spindle connecting it with the horizontally rotating table.

Dum·yat (dŏŏm·yät′) The Arabic name for DAMIETTA.

dun[1] (dun) *v.t.* & *v.i.* **dunned, dun·ning** To press (a debtor) for payment; importune; pester. — *n.* **1** One who duns. **2** A demand for payment. [Prob. var. of DIN[1]]

dun[2] (dun) *adj.* Of a grayish–brown or reddish–brown color. — *n.* **1** Dun color. **2** A dun–colored horse. **3** *Obs.* A nickname for an old horse; a jade. **4** A dun fly. — *v.t.* **dunned, dun·ning 1** To make dun–colored. **2** *U.S.* To cure (fish) by salting and packing in a dark place. [OE *dunn*]

dun[3] (dun) *n.* In ancient Ireland and Scotland, a fort or fortified dwelling, encircled by earthworks or mounds: surviving in place names, as *Dundalk, Dundee,* etc. [<Irish *dūn* hill]

Dü·na (dü′nä) The German name for the DVINA.

Dü·na·burg (dü′nä·bŏŏrkh) The German name for DAUGAVPILS.

Du·na·jec (dōō·nä′yets) A river in south Poland, flowing 128 miles east to the Vistula.

Du·nant (dü·näṅ′), **Jean Henri,** 1828–1910, Swiss author; founded the International Red Cross Society, 1864.

Du·nă·rea (do͞o'nə·ryä) The Rumanian name for the Danube.
Dun·bar (dun·bär') A burgh on the North Sea, Scotland; scene of Cromwell's victory over the Scots, 1650.
Dun·bar (dun'bär), **Paul Laurence,** 1872–1906, U.S. Negro poet. — **William,** 1465?–1530?, Scottish monk and poet.
Dun·can (dung'kən) A masculine personal name. [<Scottish Gaelic, brown chief] — **Duncan,** died 1040, king of Scotland murdered by Macbeth; portrayed in Shakespeare's *Macbeth.*
Dun·can (dung'kən), **Isadora,** 1878–1927, U.S. dancer.
Duncan Phyfe See PHYFE, DUNCAN.
dunce (duns) *n.* A stupid or ignorant person. [after Johannes *Duns* Scotus]
dunce cap A conical paper cap formerly placed on the head of a dull-witted pupil.
dunch (dunch, do͝onch) *v.t. Scot.* To nudge or shove with the elbow; jog. — *n.* A push with the elbow; a jog; a powerful blow.
Dun·ci·ad (dun'sē·ad) *n.* A satirical poem (Books I–III published in 1728, Book IV in 1742) by Alexander Pope.
Dun·dee (dun·dē') A port on the Firth of Tay, a burgh of south Angus county, Scotland.
Dun·dee (dun·dē'), **Viscount,** 1649?–89, John Graham of Claverhouse, Scottish soldier; foe of the Covenanters.
dun·der·head (dun'dər·hed') *n.* A blockhead; dunce. Also **dun'der·pate'** (-pāt'). [< dial. E (Scottish) *dunder* rumble, boom + HEAD] — **dun'der·head'ed** *adj.*
dune (do͞on, dyo͞on) *n.* A hill of loose sand heaped up by the wind: usually near a shore; a down. [<F <MDu. Akin to DOWN³.]
Dun·e·din (dun·ē'din) **1** A port in SE South Island, New Zealand. **2** The Gaelic name for EDINBURGH.
Dun·ferm·line (dun·fûrm'lin) A burgh in SW Fifeshire, Scotland.
dun·fish (dun'fish') *n. U.S.* Codfish cured by dunning.
dun fly An artificial fly variously imitative of the mayfly, used in angling.
dung¹ (dung) *n.* **1** Animal excrement; feces; manure. **2** Anything foul. — *v.t.* To cover or enrich with or as with dung. [OE] — **dung'y** *adj.*
dung² (dung, do͝ong) *adj. Scot.* Knocked; beaten; hence, finished; exhausted.
dun·ga·ree (dung'gə·rē') *n.* **1** A coarse cotton cloth, originally from the East Indies, used for sailors' working clothes, tents, sails, etc. **2** *pl.* Working clothes made of this fabric. [<Hind. *dungrī*]
dung beetle Any of various scarabaeid beetles that breed in dung, as the tumblebug and the sacred scarab of Egypt. Also **dung chafer.**
dun·geon (dun'jən) *n.* **1** A dark underground prison. **2** A donjon. For illustration see DONJON. See synonyms under HOLE. [<OF *donjon* <Gmc.]
dung·hill (dung'hil') *n.* **1** A heap of manure. **2** Figuratively, a vile abode or condition. — *adj.* From or of the dunghill; ignoble.
dun·ie·was·sal (do͞o'nē·wos'əl) *n. Scot.* **1** A yeoman; contemptuously, a farmer of the lower class. **2** A gentleman; especially, a younger son of a family of rank. Also **dun'nie·was'sal.**
dun·ite (dun'īt) *n.* A variety of peridotite either wholly composed of olivine or with a small amount of chromite or ilmenite. [from *Dun* Mountain, New Zealand]
dunk (dungk) *v.t. & v.i.* To dip or sop (bread, doughnuts, etc.) into tea, coffee, soup, etc., while eating. [<G *tunken* dip] — **dunk'er** *n.*
Dun·ker (dung'kər) *n.* One of a body of German-American Baptists, practising triple immersion and opposed to military service and the taking of legal oaths: officially called *German Baptist Brethren.* Also **Dun'kard.** [<G *tunker* < *tunken* dip]
Dun·kirk (dun'kûrk) A port on the North Sea in northern France; scene of evacuation of British forces (more than 300,000 men) to Britain, May 26–June 4, 1940, World War II. *French* **Dun·kerque** (dœ̃·kerk').
Dun Laoghai·re (dun lâr'ē) The principal port for Dublin. Formerly **Dun·lea'ry** (dun·lir'ē) or **King'ston.**
dun·lin (dun'lin) *n.* The red-backed sandpiper (*Pelidna alpina*) of the northern hemisphere.
Dun·lop (dun'lop, dun·lop'), **John Boyd,** 1840–1921, Scottish inventor.
dun·nage (dun'ij) *n.* **1** *Naut.* Mats and battens used to protect cargo on board ship. **2** A layer of planks placed under stored goods to protect them from contact with the ground. **3** Sailors' baggage. **4** Camp equipment. [Origin uncertain]
Dunne (dun), **Finley Peter,** 1867–1936, U.S. journalist and humorist.
dun·nite (dun'īt) *n.* A shock-resistant explosive composed largely of ammonium picrate: used in armor-piercing projectiles: also called *explosive D.* [after Major B. W. *Dunn,* 1860–1936, U.S. inventor]
Du·nois (dü·nwà'), **Jean,** 1403–68, French commander under Joan of Arc, natural son of the Duke of Orléans: called the "Bastard of Orléans."
Dun·sa·ny (dun·sā'nē), **Lord,** 1878–1957, Edward John Moreton Drax Plunkett, 18th Baron Dunsany, Irish writer.
Dun·si·nane (dun'sə·nān', dun'sə·nān) A hill in SE Perthshire, Scotland: reputed scene of Macbeth's defeat, 1054.
Duns Sco·tus (dunz skō'təs), **Johannes,** 1265–1308, Franciscan monk; scholastic philosopher: called also "the Subtile Doctor."
Dun·stan (dun'stən), **Saint,** 924?–988, English Benedictine monk and statesman; abbot of Glastonbury; archbishop of Canterbury 959–988.
dunt (dunt, do͝ont) *n.* **1** *Scot. Dial.* A blow or thwack. **2** An injury from such a blow.
du·o (do͞o'ō, dyo͞o'ō) *n. pl.* **du·os** or **du·i** (-ē) *Music* An instrumental duet. [<Ital.]
duo- *combining form* Two: *duogravure.* [<L *duo* two]
du·o·dec·i·mal (do͞o'ō·des'ə·məl, dyo͞o'-) *adj.* Pertaining to twelve; reckoning by twelves. — *n.* **1** One of the numbers used in duodecimal arithmetic; a twelfth. **2** *pl.* A method of computing by twelves instead of by tens. [<L *duodecimus* twelfth < *duodecim* twelve]
du·o·dec·i·mo (do͞o'ō·des'ə·mō, dyo͞o'-) *adj.* **1** Having twelve pages or leaves to one sheet of printing paper. **2** Being about 4 1/2 by 7 1/2 inches in size: said of a page or book. Written also *12 mo, 12°.* — *n. pl.* **·mos** **1** The size of a page folded twelve to a sheet; also, a page or a book of this size. **2** *Music* An interval of a twelfth. [<L *(in) duodecimo* (in) twelfth]
du·o·dec·u·ple (do͞o'ō·dek'yo͞o·pəl, dyo͞o'-) *adj.* Consisting of twelve; having twelve parts or members; twelvefold; also, taken by twelves. — *n.* A number or sum twelve times as great as another. [<L *duodecim* twelve; infl. in form by DECUPLE]
du·o·de·cu·pli·cate (do͞o'ō·de·kyo͞o'plə·kit, dyo͞o'-) *adj.* **1** Twelvefold. **2** Raised to the twelfth power. — *v.t.* (-kāt) **·cat·ed, ·cat·ing** To multiply by twelve. — *n.* One of twelve like things. — **du'o·de·cu'pli·cate·ly** *adv.*
du·o·den·a·ry (do͞o'ō·den'ər·ē, -dē'nər·ē, dyo͞o'-) *adj.* **1** Pertaining to or determined by the number twelve. **2** Denoting or belonging to a system of arithmetical numeration of which the base is twelve. [<L *duodenarius* containing twelve]
du·o·de·ni·tis (do͞o'ə·də·nī'tis, dyo͞o'-) *n. Pathol.* Inflammation of the duodenum. [<DUODEN(O)- + -ITIS]
duodeno- *combining form* Of or pertaining to the duodenum. Also, before vowels, **duoden-.** [<Med. L *duodenum* the duodenum]
du·o·de·num (do͞o'ə·dē'nəm, dyo͞o'-, do͞o·od'ə·nəm) *n. pl.* **·na** (-nə) *Anat.* That part of the small intestine extending from the pylorus to the jejunum. [<Med. L *duodenum (digitorum)* of twelve (fingers) < *duodecim* twelve; with ref. to its length] — **du'o·de'nal** *adj.*
du·o·gra·vure (do͞o'ō·grə·vyo͞or', -grā'vyər, dyo͞o'-) *n.* **1** A process in photoengraving in which two plates are used to produce a print in two shades of one color. **2** A print made by this process. Also **du·o·graph** (do͞o'ə·graf, -gräf, dyo͞o'-).
du·o·log (do͞o'ə·lôg, -log, dyo͞o'-) *n.* A literary composition for two speakers; dialog. Also **du'o·logue.** [<DUO- + (MONO)LOG]
duo·mo (dwô'mō) *n. pl.* **·mi** (-mē) *Italian* A cathedral.
du·o·tone (do͞o'ə·tōn', dyo͞o'-) *n.* A duogravure; any illustration in two tones of the same color.
du·o·type (do͞o'ə·tīp', dyo͞o'-) *n.* A picture produced from two halftones, the plates being from one negative, but dissimilar in etching.
dup (dup) *v.t. Obs.* To open. [Contraction of *do up*]
dupe¹ (do͞op, dyo͞op) *n.* One misled through credulity; a victim of deception. — *v.t.* **duped, dup·ing** To make a dupe of; impose upon; deceive; trick. See synonyms under DECEIVE. [<OF <L *upupa* a hoopoe (a bird thought to be stupid)] — **dup'a·bil'i·ty** *n.* — **dup'a·ble** *adj.* — **dup'er** *n.*
dupe² (do͞op, dyo͞op) *n.* In motion pictures, a negative film made from the positive, as a source for further positives. [Short for DUPLICATE]
dup·er·y (do͞o'pər·ē, dyo͞o'-) *n. pl.* **·er·ies** The act or practice of duping; the condition of being deceived.
du·pi·on (do͞o'pē·ən), **du·pi·on·i** (do͞o'pē·on'ē, -ō'nē) See DOUPION.
du·ple (do͞o'pəl, dyo͞o'-) *adj.* **1** Double; twofold. **2** Having two beats to a measure, as 2-2 or 2-4 time. [<L *duplus.* See DOUBLE]
Du·pleix (dü·pleks'), **Joseph François,** 1697–1763, Marquis Dupleix, governor of early French settlements in India.
Du·ples·sis-Mor·nay (dü·ple·sē'môr·nā') See MORNAY.
duple time See under TIME.
du·plex (do͞o'pleks, dyo͞o'-) *adj.* **1** Having two parts; double; twofold. **2** Having different faces, as some kinds of paper. **3** *Mech.* Working mechanically in two ways, whether in opposite directions along the same line, upon two things, by two similar parts, or by two separate operations at once. **4** *Biol.* Double, or with twice the number of parts; twinned. — *n.* A duplex house or apartment. [<L < *duo* two + stem of *plicare* fold] — **du·plex'i·ty** *n.*
duplex apartment An apartment having rooms on two floors instead of on one.
duplex house A house having two one-family units.
duplex telegraphy Telegraphy adapted to the sending of two messages simultaneously over a single wire and in opposite directions.
du·pli·cate (do͞o'plə·kit, dyo͞o'-) *adj.* **1** Made or done exactly like an original. **2** Growing in pairs; double. **3** Replayed by other players with the same cards as originally dealt: *duplicate* whist. See also DUPLICATE BRIDGE under BRIDGE². — *n.* A double or counterpart; something that exactly corresponds to an original from which it is made; a copy: originally one of two, now one of any number of like objects considered in their relation to the original and not to one another. — *v.t.* (do͞o'plə·kāt, dyo͞o'-) **·cat·ed, ·cat·ing** **1** To make an exact copy of; reproduce exactly. **2** To double; make twofold. **3** To repeat, as an action or effort; do a second time. See synonyms under IMITATE. [<L *duplicatus,* pp. of *duplicare* double < *duplex* twofold] — **du'pli·cate·ly** *adv.*

Synonyms (noun): copy, counterpart, facsimile, imitation, likeness, replica, reproduction, transcript. A *copy* is as nearly like the original as the copyist has power to make it; a *duplicate* is exactly like the original; a carbon *copy* of a typewritten document must be a *duplicate;* we may have an inaccurate *copy,* but never an inaccurate *duplicate.* A *facsimile* is like the original in appearance; a *duplicate* is the same as the original in substance and effect; a *facsimile* of the Declaration of Independence is not a *duplicate.* A *facsimile* of a key might be quite useless; a *duplicate* will open the lock. A *counterpart* exactly corresponds to another object, but perhaps without design, while a *copy* is intentional. An *imitation* is always thought of as inferior to the original; as, an *imitation* of Milton. A *replica* is a *copy* of a work of art by the maker of the original. In law, a *transcript* is an official *copy,* authenticated by the signature of the proper officer, and by the seal of the appropriate court. *Antonyms*: archetype, model, original, pattern, prototype.

du·pli·ca·tion (do͞o'plə·kā'shən, dyo͞o'-) *n.* The act of duplicating, or the state of being duplicated; doubling. — **du'pli·ca'tive** *adj.*
du·pli·ca·tor (do͞o'plə·kā'tər, dyo͞o'-) *n.* **1** One who makes anything in duplicate. **2** A contrivance or device for making duplicates, as written or typewritten matter or a drawing.
du·pli·ca·ture (do͞o'plə·kā'chər, dyo͞o'-) *n. Biol.* A doubling or folding, as of a membrane.
du·plic·i·ty (do͞o·plis'ə·tē, dyo͞o-) *n. pl.* **·ties** **1** Tricky deceitfulness; double-dealing. **2** *Obs.* The state of being two; doubleness. See synonyms under DECEPTION, FRAUD. [<OF *duplicité* <LL *duplicitas, -tatis* doubleness < *duplex* twofold] — **du·plic'i·tous** *adj.*

du Pont (do͞o·pont′, dyo͞o-; *Fr.* dü pô:nf′) Family of U.S. industrialists, founded by **Éleuthère Irénée**, 1771–1834, who established the E.I. Du Pont de Nemours Company. —**Samuel Francis**, 1803–65, rear admiral, nephew of the preceding.

du Pont de Ne·mours (do͞o pont′ də nə·mo͞or′, dyo͞o pôn′ də nə·mo͞or′; *Fr.* dü pôn′ də nə·mo͞or′), **Pierre Samuel**, 1739–1817, French economist and statesman.

Du·que de Ca·xi·as (do͞o′kə thə kə·shē′əs) A city in SE Brazil: also *Caxias*.

Du·quesne (do͞o·kān′, dyo͞o-), **Fort** A French fort, taken by the English and renamed FORT PITT, on present site of Pittsburgh.

du·ra[1] (do͞or′ə, dyo͞or′ə) *n.* **1** Duramen. **2** The dura mater.

du·ra[2] (do͞or′ə) See DURRA.

du·ra·bil·i·ty (do͞or′ə·bil′ə·tē, dyo͞or′-) *n.* **1** The quality of being durable. **2** The power of long resistance to decay or change. Also **du′ra·ble·ness.** —**du′ra·bly** *adv.*

du·ra·ble (do͞or′ə·bəl, dyo͞or′-) *adj.* Able to continue long in the same state; lasting. See synonyms under PERMANENT. [<OF <L *durabilis* <*durare* endure <*durus* hard]

du·rain (do͞o·rān′, dyo͞o-) *n. Geol.* Bituminous coal having bands of a dense, hard, granular structure, often flecked with thin streaks of brighter material. [<L *durus* hard + (FUS-AIN)]

du·ral (do͞or′əl, dyo͞or′-) *adj.* Of, pertaining to, or derived from the dura mater.

Du·ral·u·min (do͞o·ral′yə·min, dyo͞o-) *n.* A light, strong alloy of aluminum and copper, with addition of magnesium and manganese: a trade name.

du·ra ma·ter (do͞or′ə mā′tər, dyo͞or′ə) *Anat.* The tough fibrous membrane forming the outermost covering of the brain and spinal cord. [<Med. L <L *dura* hard + *mater* mother, trans. form Arabic]

du·ra·men (do͞o·rā′min, dyo͞o-) *n. Bot.* The heartwood of an exogenous stem or tree trunk; the darker central portion of the wood, comprised of dead tissue, surrounded by the alburnum. See illustration under EXOGEN. [<L, a ligenous vine branch]

dur·ance (do͞or′əns, dyo͞or′-) *n.* **1** Personal restraint; imprisonment. **2** *Obs.* Duration; continuance. [<OF, duration <*durer* last <L *durare*.]

Du·ran·go (do͞o·räng′gō) A state in northern Mexico; 47,691 square miles; capital, Durango.

Du·ran·te (do͞o·rän′tā) See DANTE.

du·ra·tion (do͞o·rā′shən, dyo͞o-) *n.* **1** The period of time during which anything lasts. **2** Continuance; time in general. [<LL *duratio, -onis* <*durare* endure]

du·ra·tive (do͞or′ə·tiv, dyo͞or′-) *adj. Gram.* Designating an aspect of the verb that expresses the action as incomplete or continuing; imperfective. —*n.* The durative aspect, or a verb in this spect.

Du·raz·zo (do͞o·rät′tsō) The chief port of Albania, on the Adriatic; ancient *Dyrrhachium.* Albanian *Durres.*

Dur·ban (dûr′bən) A port and the largest city of KwaZulu/Natal province, Republic of South Africa.

dur·bar (dûr′bär) *n.* Anglo-Indian **1** Formerly a reception or levee given by a native ruler or officer of rank in British India; a state levee. **2** The room in which such a levee is held; court; hall of audience. **3** Formerly, the executive officer or government of a native state, as distinguished from the British resident officials. [<Hind. <Persian *darbār* court <*dar* door + *bār* assembly]

dure (do͞or, dyo͞or) *Obs. v.t. & v.i.* To endure. —*adj.* Severe; hard; rough. [<L *durare* <*durus* hard]

Dü·rer (dü′rər, Albrecht, 1471–1528, German painter and engraver.

du·ress (do͞or′is, dyo͞or′-, do͞o·res′, dyo͞o-) *n.* Constraint by force or fear; compulsion; imprisonment. Also **du·resse′.** See synonyms under *fetter.* [<OF *duresse* hardness, constraint <L *duritia* <*durus* hard]

D'Ur·fey (dûr′fē), **Thomas**, 1653–1723, English dramatist and humorous song writer.

Dur·ham (do͞or′əm) *n.* One of a breed of hort-horned beef cattle. [from *Durham*, England]

Dur·ham (do͞or′əm) **1** A county in NE England; 1,015 square miles; county seat, Durham. **2** A city in north central North Carolina.

du·ri·an (do͞or′ē·ən) *n.* **1** A tall forest tree (*Durio zibethinus*) cultivated throughout the Malay Peninsula. **2** The fruit of this tree, often ten inches in length with thick, spiny rind, and custard-like pulp having a fetid odor. The seeds are eaten roasted like chestnuts. Also **du′ri·on.** [<Malay <*duri* a thorn]

DURIAN FRUIT AND BLOSSOM (The tree about 80 feet in height)

dur·ing (do͞or′ing, dyo͞or′-) *prep.* **1** Throughout the time, existence, or action of: The noise continued *during* the night. **2** In the course of; at some period in: He interrupted *during* the speech. [Orig. ppr. of DURE]

durk (dûrk) *n. Scot.* Dirk. Also **durke.**

dur·mast (dûr′mast, -mäst) *n.* **1** The valuable dark, tough, elastic wood of the European oak (*Quercus petraea*). **2** The tree itself. [Origin uncertain]

du·ro (do͞or′rō) *n. pl.* **·ros** The Spanish and Spanish-American silver dollar. [< Sp. (*peso*) *duro* hard (peso) <L *durus* hard]

Du·roc (dü·rôk′), **Géraud Christophe Michel**, 1772–1813, Duc de Friuli, French general under Napoleon.

dur·ra (do͞or′ə) *n.* A grain sorghum of southern Asia and northern Africa; Indian millet: also spelled *dhoura, doura, dura.* Also **durr** (do͞or). [<Arabic *dhura*]

Dur·res (do͞or′rəs) Albanian name for DURAZZO.

durst (dûrst) Archaic past tense of DARE.

du·rum (do͞or′əm, dyo͞or′-) *n.* A species of wheat (*Triticum durum*) widely grown for macaroni and spaghetti products; introduced into the United States from southern Russia and the Mediterranean. [<L, neut. sing. of *durus* hard]

Du·ru·y (dü·rü·ē′) **Victor**, 1811–94, French historian.

Du·se (do͞o′ze), **Eleonora**, 1859–1924, Italian actress.

dusk (dusk) *n.* **1** A state between darkness and light; twilight. **2** Swarthiness; shadowiness. —*adj.* **1** Somewhat dark or obscure by reason of failing or feeble light; dim. **2** Dark in color; swarthy. —*v.t. v.i.* To make, grow, or appear shadowy or dim; darken. [OE *dox*]

dusk·i·ness (dus′kē·nis) *n.* Moderate darkness.

dusk·y (dus′kē) *adj.* **dusk·i·er, dusk·i·est** **1** Somewhat dark; dim; obscure; swarthy. **2** Gloomy; dejected. Also **dusk′ish.** See synonyms under DARK. —**dusk′i·ly** *adv.*

dusky glider The greater glider.

dusky grouse A blue grouse (*Dendrogapus obscurus*).

Düs·sel·dorf (düs′əl·dôrf) A city on the Rhine in North Rhine-Westphalia.

dust (dust) *n.* **1** Any substance, as earth, reduced to powder. **2** A cloud of pulverized earth; hence, figuratively, a bewildering cloud of words, arguments, etc.; confusion; controversy. **3** Gold dust. **4** A dead body; remains. **5** The earth; the grave; figuratively, downfall or humiliation. **6** *Brit.* Rubbish; anything worthless; ashes and household sweepings. See synonyms under BODY. —**to bite the dust** To fall wounded or dead. — **to make the dust fly 1** To act or go with energy and speed. **2** To create a fuss. —**to throw dust in one's eyes** To deceive; mislead. —*v.t.* **1** To wipe or brush dust from. **2** To sprinkle with powder, etc. **3** To soil with dust. —*v.i.* **4** To wipe or brush dust from furniture, etc. **5** *Slang* To hurry away: often with *off* or *out.* See synonyms under CLEANSE. [OE *dūst*] —**dust′·less** *adj.*

dust·bin (dust′bin′) *n. Brit.* A container for trash, garbage, or ashes.

Dust Bowl A desert region in the south central United States where the eroded topsoil of fallow lands has been blown away by dust storms. Also **dust bowl.**

dust devil *Meteorol.* A small whirlwind, often of great intensity, which lifts dust, leaves, straw, and other light material to heights of two or three hundred feet in dry or desert areas.

dust·er (dus′tər) *n.* **1** One who or that which dusts. **2** A cloth or brush for removing dust; a receptacle for sprinkling a powder. **3** A garment or covering to protect from dust.

dust jacket A removable covering for a book, usually of paper, and often bearing printed matter.

dust·man (dust′mən) *n. pl.* **·men** (-mən) **1** *Brit.* One whose business is the removal of ashes, refuse, etc., from yards and houses. **2** The sandman.

dust·pan (dust′pan′) *n.* An implement, resembling a short-handled shovel, into which dust from a floor is swept.

dust·proof (dust′pro͞of′) *adj.* Capable of excluding dust.

dust·storm (dust′stôrm′) *n.* A windstorm carrying clouds of dust along with it. Also **dust storm.**

dust·y (dus′tē) *adj.* **dust·i·er, dust·i·st 1** Covered with or as with dust. **2** Of the color of dust. **3** Powdered, like dust. —**dust′i·ly** *adv.* —**dust′i·ness** *n.*

dusty pink A very light dull red.

Dutch (duch) *adj.* **1** Belonging or relating to, or characteristic of the Netherlands or its people. **2** *Archaic* Belonging or relating to the Teutonic or German peoples. **3** *Slang* German: A humorous or derogatory use. —*n.* **1** The people of the Netherlands: with *the.* **2** *Slang* The Germans: with *the.* **3** The Low German, West Germanic language of the Netherlands. Abbr. *Du.* —**Middle Dutch** The pre-Reformation, literary language of Flanders, Brabant, and Limburg. Abbr. *MDu.* —**to beat the Dutch** *Slang* **1** To exceed in causing surprise; surpass in strangeness. **2** To overcome stubborn resistance. **3** Excessively; extremely: adverbial use. —**to get in Dutch** *Slang* To incur disapproval. —**to go Dutch** *U.S. Colloq.* To have each participant pay his own expenses. —**to talk like a Dutch uncle** To talk with severity and kindness at the same time. [<MDu. *dutsch* Germanic, Dutch]

Dutch Belted A breed of dairy cattle originating in the Netherlands and characterized by a wide white band around the middle of the body.

Dutch Borneo See BORNEO.

Dutch cheese 1 A hard, round, skim-milk cheese; also, cottage cheese. **2** The common mallow.

Dutch courage Temporary courage inspired by or as by intoxicating drink; also, the drink itself.

Dutch door A door divided horizontally in the middle, thus allowing the opening of one half or of both.

Dutch East Indies See NETHERLANDS EAST INDIES.

Dutch elm disease A fungus disease of elms which attacks the leaves, causing defoliation, decay, and death.

DUTCH DOOR

Dutch foil, Dutch gold, Dutch leaf See DUTCH METAL.

Dutch Guiana See SURINAM.

Dutch Harbor A village and United States naval base on a small island off Unalaska Island, Aleutian Islands.

dutch·man (du ch′mən) *n. pl.* **·men** (-mən) **1** A piece inserted in a crevice to fill it or hide bad fitting, or to take the place of a defective piece cut out or a piece broken. **2** A shim. **3** A stick placed transversely in a load of logs to serve as a brace. **4** A buried log, or the like, serving as an anchor; a deadman.

Dutch·man (duch′mən) *n. pl.* **·men** (-mən) **1** A native of the Netherlands. **2** A Dutch ship. **3** *Slang* A German.

dutch·man's-breech·es (duch′mənz-brich′iz) *n.* A low woodland herb (*Dicentra cucullaria*) of the fumitory family, with widely spreading spurs suggesting the name. Also **dutch′ mans-breech′es.**

dutch·man's-pipe (duch′mənz·pīp′) *n.* A climbing shrub *(Aristolochia durior)* of the Mississippi Valley, which has a calyx tube shaped like the bowl of a meerschaum pipe.

Dutch metal A malleable alloy of copper, tin, and zinc, used in the form of thin leaves as a substitute for gold leaf in bookbinding, toymaking, etc.; tombac.

Dutch New Guinea See NETHERLANDS NEW GUINEA.

Dutch oven **1** A brick oven heated by fire within it and cooking by the heat retained when the embers are removed. **2** A shallow, iron, lidded baking pot, heated by surrounding or covering it with coals. **3** A tin or sheet-steel oven used in front of an open fire, cooking by reflected heat.

Dutch treat *U.S. Colloq.* Entertainment at which each person pays his own bill.

Dutch uncle A very frank and severe critic or advisor.

Dutch West Indies See NETHERLANDS WEST INDIES.

du·te·ous (do͞o′tē·əs, dyo͞o′-) *adj.* Rendering due respect and obedience; dutiful. **—du′te·ous·ly** *adv.* **—du′te·ous·ness** *n.*

du·ti·a·ble (do͞o′tē·ə·bəl, dyo͞o′-) *adj.* Subject to impost duty.

du·tied (do͞o′tēd, dyo͞o′-) *adj. U.S.* Subjected to taxes or customs duties.

du·ti·ful (do͞o′ti·fəl, dyo͞o′-) *adj.* **1** Performing the duties of one's position; submissive to superiors; obedient. **2** Expressive of respect or of a sense of duty; respectful. See synonyms under GOOD, MORAL. **—du′ti·ful·ly** *adv.* **—du′ti·ful·ness** *n.*

Du·tra (do͞o′trə), **Eurico Gaspar,** born 1885, Brazilian general; president of Brazil 1946–1951.

du·ty (do͞o′tē, dyo͞o′-) *n. pl.* **·ties** **1** That which one is bound, by any natural, legal, or moral obligation, to pay, do, or perform. **2** Specific obligatory service or function, as of a soldier, sailor, etc.: He is on sea *duty.* **3** The obligation to do that which is prescribed or required, especially by the moral law; moral obligation; right action. **4** An impost or customs tax, as upon goods imported, exported, or consumed. **5** *Agric.* **a** The quantity of water necessary, in artificial irrigation, to supply adequately a definite surface of land. **b** The acreage which a stated amount of water will adequately serve: called **duty of water.** **6** *Mech.* **a** The efficiency of or useful work done by an engine or motor under stated conditions. **b** The efficiency of a steam engine expressed in terms of its capacity to lift a definite weight one foot high while consuming a certain quantity of coal. **7** A formal expression of respect. **—customs duty** A tax levied on imports (or exports) for purposes of revenue or, more commonly, for the protection of domestic manufacturers. [<AF *duete* <*du* DUE]

Synonyms: accountability, business, function, obligation, office, responsibility, right, righteousness. Etymologically, *duty* is that which is owed or due; *obligation,* that to or by which one is bound; *right,* that which is correct, straight, or in the direct line of truth and goodness; *responsibility,* that for which one must answer. *Duty* and *responsibility* are thought of as to some person or persons; *right* is impersonal. One's *duty* may be to others or to himself; his *obligations* and *responsibilities* are to others. *Duty* arises from the nature of things; *obligation* and *responsibility* may be created by circumstances, as by one's own promise, or by the acceptance of a trust, etc. We speak of a parent's *duty,* a debtor's *obligation*; or of a child's *duty* of obedience, and a parent's *responsibility* for the child's welfare. *Right* is that which accords with the moral system of the universe. *Righteousness* is *right* incarnated in action. In a more limited sense, *right* may be used of what one may rightly claim, and so be the converse of *duty.* It is the creditor's *right* to demand payment, and the debtor's *duty* to pay. Compare BUSINESS, TAX, VIRTUE.

du·ty-free (do͞o′tē·frē′, dyo͞o′-) *adj.* & *adv.* Free from customs duties.

du·um·vir (do͞o·um′vər, dyo͞o-) *n. pl.* **·virs** or **·vi·ri** (vi·rī) One of two ancient Roman magistrates holding an office jointly. [<L <*duo* two + *vir* man] **—du·um′vi·ral** *adj.*

du·um·vi·rate (do͞o·um′və·rit, dyo͞o-) *n.* **1** The joint office of duumviri. **2** A combination of two men; government by a pair of associated officials.

Du·veen (do͞o·vēn′), **Joseph,** 1869–1939, first Baron Duveen of Millbank, English art dealer.

Du·ve·neck (do͞o′və·nek), **Frank,** 1848–1919, U.S. painter, sculptor, and art instructor.

du·ve·tyn (do͞o′və·tēn, do͞o′və·tēn′) *n.* Twill-weave fabric with a napped surface, made of wool, rayon, cotton, or silk, or combinations of fibers. Also **du′ve·tine, du′ve·tyne.** [<F *duvet* down]

dux (duks) *n. pl.* **du·ces** (do͞o′sēz, dyo͞o′-) or **dux·es** **1** *Scot.* The head or leader of a class in a school. **2** *Music* The subject or principal melody of a fugue. [<L, leader]

Dvi·na (dvē′nə) **1** A river in northern European Russian S.F.S.R., flowing 455 miles NW to **Dvina Bay** (also *Archangel Bay*), an inlet of the White Sea; also *Northern Dvina.* **2** A river in west European U.S.S.R. and Latvia, flowing 633 miles SW to the Gulf of Riga: German **Dü·va** (dü′vä): also *Western Dvina.*

Dvinsk (dvēnsk) The Russian name for DAUGAVPILS.

Dvoř·ák (dvôr′zhäk), **Antonín,** 1841–1904, Czech composer.

dwarf (dwôrf) *n.* A person, animal, or plant that is unnaturally small; especially, an adult human being less than four feet tall. *—v.t.* **1** To prevent the natural development of; stunt. **2** To cause to appear small by comparison. *—v.i.* **3** To become stunted; grow smaller. *—adj.* Smaller than others of its kind; diminutive; stunted. [OE *dweorh*]

dwarf alder The smaller alder-leafed buckthorn *(Rhamnus alnifolia).*

dwarf chestnut The chinkapin.

dwarf cornel A woody perennial herb (genus *Cornus*) of the dogwood family, especially the bunchberry.

dwarf·ish (dwôr′fish) *adj.* Like a dwarf; diminutive; stunted. **—dwarf′ish·ly** *adv.* **—dwarf′·ish·ness** *n.*

dwarf mallow See under MALLOW.

dwarf star See under STAR.

dwell (dwel) *v.i.* **dwelt** or **dwelled, dwell·ing** **1** To have a fixed abode; reside. **2** To linger, as on a subject; pause, expatiate: with *on* or *upon.* **3** To remain; continue in a state or place. See synonyms under ABIDE. *—n.* **1** The short cessation of motion of a part of a machine to effect its allotted service. **2** *Obs.* Stoppage; delay; pause. [OE *dwellan* mislead, hinder, stay] **—dwell′er** *n.*

dwell·ing (dwel′ing) *n.* A residence; domicile; abode. See synonyms under HOME, HOUSE.

dwelling house A house built for habitation; a domicile. In law it may embrace the dwelling itself and such buildings as are used in connection with it.

Dwight (dwīt), **Timothy,** 1752–1817, American author and educator; president of Yale University 1795–1817.

dwin·dle (dwin′dəl) *v.t.* & *v.i.* **·dled, ·dling** To diminish or become less; make or become smaller; decline. [Freq. of DWINE]

dwine (dwīn) *v.i. Scot.* or *Obs.* To pine or waste away; languish. [OE *dwinan* waste away] **—dwin′ing** *adj.*

Dy *Chem.* Dysprosium (symbol Dy).

dy·ad (dī′ad) *adj.* **1** *Chem.* Having a combining power of two; bivalent. **2** Dyadic. *—n.* **1** A pair of units; duad. **2** *Chem.* An atom, radical, or element that has a combining power of two. See VALENCE. **3** *Biol.* **a** One of a pair of chromosomes, especially in the prophases of the second division in the formation of gametes. See TETRAD. **b** A secondary unit made up of an aggregate of monads. [<L *dyas, dyadis* <Gk. *dyas* the number two]

dy·ad·ic (dī·ad′ik) *adj.* **1** Of or pertaining to a dyad. **2** Based on or relating to the number 2; binary.

Dy·ak (dī′ak) *n.* **1** One of the aboriginal people of Borneo, linguistically akin to the Malays, but differing from them in stature, type, and culture. **2** The Indonesian language of these people. Also spelled *Dayak.*

Dya·ko·vit·sa (dyä·kō′vit·sä) See DJAKOVICA.

dy·ar·chy (dī′är·kē) See DIARCHY.

Dyce (dīs), **Alexander,** 1798–1869, Scottish editor.

dye (dī) *v.* **dyed, dye·ing** *v.t.* **1** To fix a color by soaking in liquid coloring matter. **2** To stain; tinge. *—v.i.* **3** To take or give color: This cloth *dyes* badly. See synonyms under STAIN. *—n.* A fluid or coloring matter used for dyeing; also, the color or hue so produced. According to the method of application, dyes are classified as *substantive,* or *direct,* when they color by simple immersion; *adjective,* or *mordant,* when a fixing agent is used; *ingrain,* or *ice,* when deposited by chemical reaction; *vat,* when applied in an alkali-soluble state and oxidized; and *sulfur,* when used in a sodium sulfide bath followed by oxidation. ◆ Homophone: *die.* [OE *dēagian* <*deag* dye, color]

dye·house (dī′hous′) *n.* A building in which dyeing is done.

dyed-in-the-wool (dīd′in·thə·wo͝ol′) *adj.* **1** Dyed before being woven. **2** Thoroughgoing; complete.

dye·ing (dī′ing) *n.* The act, process, or trade of fixing colors in cloth or the like.

dy·er (dī′ər) *n.* One who or that which dyes; especially, a person engaged in the business of dyeing.

Dy·er (dī′ər), **John,** 1700?–58, English poet.

dy·er's-broom (dī′ərz·bro͞om′, -bro͝om′) *n.* A shrubby plant *(Genista tinctoria)* yielding a yellow dye which with woad becomes a permanent green; woadwaxen: also called *dyeweed.* Also **dyer's-green·weed** (dī′ərz·grēn′·wēd′).

dy·er's-weed (dī′ərz·wēd′) *n.* Any of several plants that yield dyeing matter, such as dyer's woad *(Isatis tinctoria).*

dye·stuff (dī′stuf′) *n.* Any material used for dyeing.

dye·weed (dī′wēd′) *n.* Dyer's-broom.

dye·wood (dī′wo͝od′) *n.* A wood that yields dyestuff, such as logwood.

dy·ing (dī′ing) *adj.* **1** Becoming dead; near to death; expiring; closing. **2** Destined to die; mortal; perishable. **3** Relating to death; given, uttered, or manifested just before death.

dyke (dīk) See DIKE.

dyna- *combining form* Power: *dynameter.* Also, before vowels, **dyn-.**

dy·nam·e·ter (dī·nam′ə·tər) *n. Optics* A device for measuring the magnifying power of telescopes. [<DYNA- + METER]

dy·nam·ic (dī·nam′ik) *adj.* **1** Of or pertaining to forces not in equilibrium, or to motion as the result of force: opposed to *static.* **2** Pertaining to or characterized by mechanical force. **3** Producing or involving activity or action of any kind; motive; efficient; causal. **4** Mentally or spiritually energetic, forceful, or powerful: a *dynamic* leader. **5** Of or pertaining to musical dynamics. Also **dy·nam′i·cal.** [<Gk. *dynamikos* powerful <*dynamis* power] **—dy·nam′i·cal·ly** *adv.*

dy·nam·ics (dī·nam′iks) *n. pl.* *(construed as singular in defs. 1,2, and 4)* **1** The branch of physics that treats of the motion of bodies and the effects of forces in producing motion, and of the laws of the motion thus produced *(kinetics)*: opposed to *statics.* **2** The science that treats of the action of forces, whether producing equilibrium or motion; in this sense including both statics and kinetics. **3** The forces producing or governing activity or movement of any kind; also, the methods of such activity: spiritual *dynamics.* **4** *Music* **a** The words, symbols, etc., used to indicate degrees of loudness: also **dynamic marks.** **b** The act or technique of producing varying degrees of loudness.

dy·na·mism (dī′nə·miz′əm) *n.* **1** *Philos.* One of various doctrines that endeavor to explain the phenomena of the universe, chiefly or wholly, in terms of force or energy. **2** *Psychol.* Any of various psychic forces, as repression, sublimation, etc., acting to produce certain effects upon behavior or the personality: also called *mechanism.* **—dy′na·mist** *n.* **—dy′na·mis′tic** *adj.*

dy·na·mite (dī′nə·mīt) *n.* **1** An explosive composed of nitroglycerin held in an absorbent substance. **2** *Slang* Anything wonderful or spectacular: The news was *dynamite!* *—v.t.* **·mit·ed, ·mit·ing** **1** To blow up or shatter with or as with dynamite. **2** To charge with dynamite; as a mine. [<Gk. *dynamis* power]

dy·na·mit·er (dī′nə·mī′tər) *n.* **1** An expert user of dynamite. **2** One who uses or advocates the destructive use of dynamite, especially for political or revolutionary purposes. Also **dy′na·mit′ist.**

dy·na·mo (dī′nə·mō) *n. pl.* **·mos** A machine for the conversion of mechanical energy into

DYNAMO

electrical energy through the agency of electro-magnetic induction. Compare GENERATOR and ELECTRIC MOTOR. [Short for DYNAMOELEC-TRIC MACHINE]

dynamo- *combining form* Force; power: *dyna-mograph.* [< Gk. *dynamis* power]

dy·na·mo·e·lec·tric (dī′nə·mō·i·lek′trik) *adj.* Pertaining to the relation between electricity and mechanical force. Also **dy′na·mo·e·lec′tri·cal.**

dy·na·mog·e·ny (dī′nə·moj′ə·nē) *n. Physiol.* Pro-duction of increased nervous activity; the rein-forcing effect of sensorial stimuli upon muscular action. [< DYNAMO- + -GENY]

dy·nam·o·graph (dī·nam′ə·graf, -gräf) *n.* A re-cording dynamometer; specifically, one used to register muscular power. Also **dy′no·graph.**

dy·na·mom·e·ter (dī′nə·mom′ə·tər) *n.* An in-strument for measuring force exerted or power expended, as by a machine. [< DYNAMO- + -METER] —**dy·na·mo·met·ric** (dī′nə·mō·met′rik) or **·ri·cal** *adj.*

dy·na·mom·e·try (dī′nə·mom′ə·trē) *n.* The act or art of measuring the expenditure of power.

dy·na·mo·path·ic (dī′nə·mō·path′ik) *adj. Med.* Having an effect upon the character or course of bodily functions.

dy·na·mo·tor (dī′nə·mō′tər) *n.* A dynamoelectric machine having one field magnet, one armature core, and two armature windings, each having a commutator and being insulated from the other.

dy·nast (dī′nast, -nəst) *n.* A monarch; ruler. [< L *dynastes* < Gk. *dynastēs* < *dynasthai* be power-ful]

dy·nas·ty (dī′nəs·tē) *n. pl.* **·ties** A succession of sovereigns in one line of family descent govern-ing the same country; also, the length of time during which one family is in power. —**dy·nas·tic** (dī·nas′tik) or **·ti·cal** *adj.* —**dy·nas′ti·cal·ly** *adv.*

dy·na·tron (dī′nə·tron) *n. Electronics* A four-electrode vacuum tube designed to utilize the secondary emission of electrons to decrease the plate current as the plate voltage increases; used as an oscillator in radio. [< DYNA- + (ELEC)TRON]

dyne (dīn) *n. Physics* The fundamental unit of force in the cgs system that, if applied to a mass

of one gram, would give it an acceleration of one centimeter per second per second. *Abbr. d., D.* [< F < Gk. *dynamis* power]

Dyr·ra·chi·um (di·rā′kē·əm) Ancient name for DURAZZO.

dys- *combining form* Bad; defective; difficult; hard: *dysphasia, dyspnea:* opposed to *eu-.* [< Gk. *dys-* bad, difficult]

dys·cra·si·a (dis·krā′zhē·ə, -zhə) *n. Pathol.* **1** A depraved condition of the system and especially of the blood, due to constitutional disease. **2** General bad health. [< Med. L < Gk. *dyskrasia* bad temperament < *dys-* bad + *krasia* mixture] —**dys·cra′si·al, dys·cras·ic** (dis·kraz′ik, -kras′-) *adj.*

dys·cra·site (dis′krə·sīt) *n.* A silver-white, opaque silver antimonide, Ag₃Sb, found massive and in orthorhombic crystals. [< Gk. *dyskrasia* bad mixture + -ITE¹]

dys·e·mi·a (dis·ē′mē·ə) *n. Pathol.* A morbid or vitiated condition of the blood, especially as due to mineral poisoning. Also **dys·ae′mi·a.** [< NL < Gk. *dys-* hard + *haima* blood]

dys·en·ter·y (dis′ən·ter′ē) *n. Pathol.* A severe in-flammation of the mucous membrane of the large intestine, attended with bloody evacua-tions, griping pains, and some fever; bloody flux. [< OF *dysenterie* < L *dysenteria* < Gk. *dys-* bad + *enteron* intestine] —**dys′en·ter′ic** or **·i·cal** *adj.*

dys·es·the·si·a (dis′əs·thē′zhē·ə, -zhə) *n. Pathol.* Loss of sensation, partial or complete; numb-ness. Also **dys′aes·the′si·a.**

dys·func·tion (dis·fungk′shən) *n.* Deterioration of the natural action of (anything); malfunction.

dys·gen·ic (dis·jen′ik) *adj.* Relating to or causing the biological impairment or deterioration of a strain or race, especially man: opposite of *eu-genic.*

dys·gen·ics (dis·jen′iks) *n. pl.* (*construed as sin-gular*) The science dealing with the factors oper-ating to produce biological, and especially ge-netic, deterioration in the offspring of animals.

dys·ge·og·e·nous (dis′jē·oj′ə·nəs) *adj. Bot.* Growing on soils, such as granite or hard rocks generally, which do not readily yield a detritus: said of plants. [< DYS- + Gk. *gē* earth, soil + -GENOUS]

dys·ki·ne·si·a (dis′ki·nē′zhē·ə, -zhə) *n. Pathol.* Loss or impairment of the power of voluntary movement. [< Gk. *dyskinēsia* < *dys-* hard + *ki-nesis* movement] —**dys′ki·net′ic** *adj.*

dys·lex·i·a (dis·lek′sē·ə) *n. Pathol.* Loss of the ability to read due to a central brain lesion. [< NL < Gk. *dys-* hard + *lexis* speech, word]

dys·lo·gis·tic (dis′lō·jis′tik) *adj.* Conveying dis-approval or censure: opposed to *eulogistic.* [< DYS- + (EU)LOGISTIC] —**dys′lo·gis′ti·cal·ly** *adv.*

dys·men·or·rhe·a (dis·men′ə·rē′ə) *n. Pathol.* Dif-ficult or painful menstruation. Also **dys·men′or·rhoe′a.** [< NL < Gk. *dys-* hard + *mēn, mēnos* month + *rhein* flow]

dys·pep·sia (dis·pep′shə, -sē·ə) *n.* Difficult or painful digestion, generally chronic. [< L < Gk. < *dys-* hard + *peptein* cook, digest]

dys·pep·tic (dis·pep′tik) *adj.* **1** Relating to, of the nature of, or suffering from dyspepsia; hence, morbid; querulous. **2** Tending to produce dys-

pepsia; indigestible. Also **dys·pep′ti·cal.** —*n.* A dyspeptic person. —**dys·pep′ti·cal·ly** *adv.*

dys·pha·gi·a (dis·fā′jē·ə) *n. Pathol.* Great diffi-culty in swallowing due to some constriction of the muscles of the throat. [< NL < Gk. *dys-* hard + *phagein* eat] —**dys·phag′ic** (-faj′·ik) *adj.*

dys·pha·sia (dis·fā′zhə, -zhē·ə) *n.* Partial aphasia or incoherent speech due to a brain lesion. —**dys·pha′sic** *adj.* [< NL < Gk. *dys-* hard + *phasis* utterance]

dys·pho·ni·a (dis·fō′nē·ə) *n. Psychiatry* Difficulty in uttering articulate sounds; harsh, abnormal, or indistinct vocalization. [< NL < Gk. *dysphōnia* roughness of sound < *dys-* hard + *phōnē* sound] —**dys·phon′ic** (-fon′ik) *adj.*

dys·pho·ri·a (dis·fôr′ē·ə, -fō′rē·ə) *n. Pathol.* A chronic feeling of illness and discontent: oppo-site of *euphoria.* [< NL < Gk. *dysphoria* < *dys-* hard + *phoreein* suffer]

dys·phot·ic (dis·fot′ik, -fō′tik) *adj.* Dimly illu-mined, as the bottom of a deep canyon or the sea depths. —*n.* Any plant or animal adapted to such surroundings. [< Gk. *dys-* hard, defective + *phōs, phōtos* light]

dysp·noe·a (disp·nē′ə) *n. Pathol.* Labored, diffi-cult breathing. Also **dysp·ne′a.** [< NL < L *dy-spnoea* < Gk. *dyspnoia* < *dys-* hard + *pneein* breathe] —**dysp·noe′al** or **·ic, dysp·ne′al** or **·ic** *adj.*

dys·pro·si·um (dis·prō′sē·əm, -shē-) *n.* A rare-earth element (symbol Dy, atomic number 66) difficult to separate from its oxide. See PERIODIC TABLE. [< NL < Gk. *dysprositos* < *dys-* hard + *prosienai* approach]

dys·tax·i·a (dis·tak′sē·ə) *n. Pathol.* Muscular tremor, resulting from disorder of the spinal cord. [< NL < Gk. *dys-* hard, defective + *taxis* arrangement]

dys·tel·e·ol·o·gy (dis·tel′ē·ol′ə·jē, -tē′lē-) *n.* The doctrine of purposelessness or of the absence of a final cause: opposed to *teleology.* —**dys·tel′e·o·log′i·cal** (-ē·ə·loj′i·kəl) *adj.*

dys·tro·phy (dis′trə·fē) *n.* Defective or per-verted nutrition. Also **dys·tro·phi·a** (dis·trō′-fē·ə). [< NL *dystrophia* < Gk. *dys-* hard, defec-tive + *trophē* nourishment]

dys·tro·py (dis′trə·pē) *n. Psychiatry* Abnormal behavior, however caused. [< DYS- + Gk. *tropē* turning, change] —**dys·trop′ic** (-trop′·ik) *adj.*

dys·u·ri·a (dis·yōōr′ē·ə) *n. Pathol.* Difficult, pain-ful, or incomplete urination. [< LL < Gk. *dy-souria* < *dys-* hard + *ouron* urine] —**dys·u′ric** *adj.*

Dyu·sham·be (dyōō·shäm′bə) The former name for STALINABAD.

dy·vour (dē′vər) *n. Scot.* A bankrupt or insolvent debtor; specifically, one who assigns all his prop-erty to his creditors.

Dzaoud·zi (dzoud′zē) Capital of the Comoro Is-lands.

Dzau·dzhi·kau (dzou·jē′kou) A city on the Terek, capital of North Ossetian Autonomous S.S.R.: formerly *Ordzhonikidze.*

Dzer·dzhinsk (dyer·zhinsk′) A city on the Oka in European Russian S.F.S.R.

Dzhu·ga·shvi·li (jōō′gä·shvē′lē), **Iosif** See STA-LIN.

dzig·ge·tai (dzig′ə·tī) *n.* A species of Mongolian wild ass: also spelled *chigetai.* [< Mongolian *dschiggetai* long-eared]

E

e, E (ē) *n. pl.* **e's, E's** or **es, Es, ees** (ēz) **1** The fifth letter of the English alphabet: from Phoen-ician *he,* through Hebrew *he,* Greek *epsilon,* and Roman *E.* **2** Any sound of the letter *e.* See AL-PHABET.
—*symbol* **1** *Music* **a** The third tone in the natu-ral scale of C, *mi;* the pitch of this tone, or the note representing it. **b** The scale built upon E. **2** *Math.* The limit of the expression $(1 + 1/n)^n$, as

n increases without limit: 2.7182818284+: the base to which Napierian logarithms are calcu-lated: written *e.*

e- Reduced var. of EX-.

E·a (ā′ä) In Babylonian mythology, one of the supreme deities and god of the waters. He was the bestower of the arts and sciences, healer of the sick, and the supposed creator of mankind.

each (ēch) *adj.* Being one of two or more indi-

viduals that together form an aggregate; every. —*pron.* Every one of any number or aggrega-tion considered individually; each one. See syn-onyms under EVERY. —*adv.* For or to each per-son, article, etc.; apiece: one dollar *each.* [OE *ælc* < *a* ever + *gelic* alike]

each other A compound reciprocal pronoun used in oblique cases: They saw *each other.*

that is, Each saw the other. The possessive case is *each other's.*

Ead·mund (ēd′mənd), **Ead·ward** (ed′wərd) See EDMUND, etc.

Eads (ēdz), **James Buchanan,** 1820–87, U.S. civil engineer.

ea·ger[1] (ē′gər) *adj.* **1** Impatiently anxious for something. **2** Showing insistent or intense feeling or desire. **3** *Obs.* Sour; tart; pungent. [< OF *aigre* < L *acer* sharp] —**ea′ger·ly** *adv.* —**ea′ger·ness** *n.*
Synonyms: animated, anxious, ardent, avid, burning, desirous, earnest, enthusiastic, fervent, glowing, hot, impatient, impetuous, importunate, intense, intent, keen, longing, vehement, yearning, zealous. One is *eager* who impatiently desires to accomplish some end; one is *earnest* with a desire that is less impatient, but more deep, resolute, and constant; one is *anxious* with a desire that foresees rather than the pain of disappointment than the delight of attainment. One is *eager* for the gratification of any appetite or passion; he is *earnest* in conviction, purpose, or character. *Eager* usually refers to some specific and immediate satisfaction, *earnest,* to something permanent and enduring; the patriotic soldier is *earnest* in his devotion to his country, *eager* for a decisive battle. See ARDENT, HOT. Compare ENTHUSIASM. *Antonyms:* apathetic, calm, careless, cold, cool, dispassionate, frigid, heedless, indifferent, negligent, phlegmatic, purposeless, regardless, stolid, stony, stupid, unconcerned, uninterested, unmindful, unmoved.

ea·ger[2] (ē′gər, ā′-) *n.* A sudden flood of the tide in an estuary: also *eagre.* See BORE[2]. [Prob. OE *ēa* river + *gār* storm]

eager beaver *Slang* A person exceedingly zealous or diligent.

ea·gle (ē′gəl) *n.* **1** Any of various species of very large diurnal predatory birds of the family Accipitridae of worldwide distribution, notable for keen sight and strong flight. ◆ Collateral adjective: *aquiline.* **2** A gold coin of the United States, value $10, weight 258 grains: withdrawn from circulation 1934. **3** A Roman military standard, bearing the image of an eagle; also adopted as a standard by France during the two empires. **4** Any article in the design of which an eagle is prominent. **5** In golf, two strokes less than par in playing a hole. [< OF *egle, aigle* < L *aquila*]

Ea·gle (ē′gəl) The constellation Aquila. See CONSTELLATION.

ea·gle-eyed (ē′gəl-īd′) *adj.* Keen-sighted like an eagle.

eagle owl A large predatory European owl (*Bubo bubo*).

eagle ray Any of a family (Myliobatidae) of rays having the eyes and spiracles at the sides of the head and usually bearing a single dorsal spine on the long, whiplike tail.

Eagle Scout A Boy Scout of the highest rank.

ea·gle·stone (ē′gəl-stōn′) *n.* A yellow clay iron-stone occurring as hollow nodules.

ea·glet (ē′glit) *n.* A young eagle.

ea·gle·wood (ē′gəl-wŏod′) See AGALLOCH.

ea·gre (ē′gər, ā′-) See EAGER[2].

Ea·ker (ā′kər), **Ira Clarence,** born 1896, U.S. aviator and general.

Ea·kins (ā′kinz), **Thomas,** 1844–1916, U.S. painter.

eal·dor·man (ôl′dər·mən) *n.* The chief officer of a shire in pre-Norman England. Also **eal′·der·man.** [Var. of ALDERMAN.]

Ealh·wi·ne (alkh′wī·ne) See ALCUIN.

Eal·ing (ē′ling) A municipal borough of Middlesex, England, west of London.

EAM In World War II, a Greek underground organization formed to resist German domination, consisting of leftist groups. [< Modern Gk. *E(thniko) A(peleftherotiko) M(etopo)* National Liberation Front]

Eames (āmz), **Emma,** 1865–1952, U.S. prima donna.

ear[1] (ir) *n.* **1** The organ of hearing: in man and other mammals it consists of an *auricle* and external auditory *meatus* for collecting sounds, a *tympanum,* containing the *ossicles* for transmitting them, and a *labyrinth* that includes the *cochlea* for delivering them to the end organs of the auditory nerve. ◆ Collateral adjective: *aural.* **2** The sense of hearing; especially, nice perception of musical

sounds. **3** Attentive consideration; heed. **4** Anything like the external ear, as a projecting

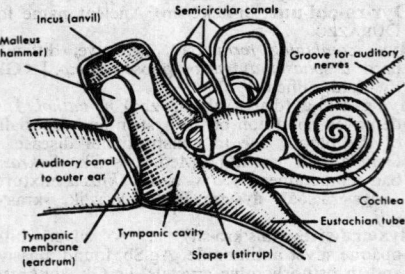

NOMENCLATURE: FRONTAL SECTION OF HUMAN EAR

piece, handle, etc. **5** The external ear alone. **6** *pl.* Spiritual understanding. —**about one's ears** Surrounding one on all sides, as falling objects. —**by the ears** In close struggle or conflict; at variance; as in **to set by the ears,** to cause discord between. —**up to the ears** *Colloq.* Almost covered, as one sinking; almost at the end of one's resources. [OE *ēare*] —**ear′less** *adj.*

ear[2] (ir) *n.* The fruit-bearing part of a cereal plant; the head. —**in** (or on) **the ear** On the cob, as corn; unhusked, as grain. —*v.i.* To form ears, as grain. [OE *ēar*]

ear[3] (ir) *v.t. Obs.* To till with a plow. [OE *erian*]

ear·ache (ir′āk′) *n.* Pain in the middle or internal ear; otalgia.

ear·cap (ir′kap′) *n.* A cap with tabs that cover the ears.

ear cup A device, fitted over the ear in a sound-proof military helmet, to detect sounds, as of enemy aircraft.

ear·drop (ir′drop′) *n.* An earring with a pendant.

ear·drum (ir′drum′) *n.* The tympanum or the tympanic membrane.

ear dust *Anat.* Otoconia.

eared (ird) *adj.* Having ears or earlike appendages; auriculate.

eared seal Any of a family (*Otariidae*) of seals; the sea lion and the fur seals.

ear·flap (ir′flap′) *n.* One of a pair of adjustable earmuffs permanently attached to a cap.

ear·ful (ir′fŏol′) *n. U.S. Colloq.* **1** Something heard or overheard and considered enough or too much: Did you get an *earful*? **2** Surprising or important news. **3** A scolding.

Ear·hart (âr′härt), **Amelia,** 1898–1937, U.S. aviatrix; wife of George P. Putnam.

ear·ing (ir′ing) *n. Naut.* A small line used to fasten the corners of a sail to a yard. [< EAR[1]]

earl (ûrl) *n.* A member of the British nobility next above a viscount. *Earl* is the equivalent of the Norman *count,* in Norman French, and the wife of an earl is still called *countess.* [OE *eorl* nobleman]

Earl (ûrl) A masculine personal name.

ear·lap (ir′lap′) *n.* **1** The external ear; especially, the lobes. **2** An earflap.

earl·dom (ûrl′dəm) *n.* The dignity, prerogative, or territory of an earl.

earl marshal A British officer of state, originally *marshal of England,* who attends the sovereign when Parliament is opened or closed, etc.

ear·lobe (ir′lōb′) *n.* The soft fleshy protuberance at the lower part of the external ear.

ear·lock (ir′lok′) *n.* A lock of hair curling over or near the ear; a lovelock.

ear·ly (ûr′lē) *adj.* **·li·er, ·li·est** **1** Being near the beginning of any stated period of time or definite course of existence; being or occurring among the first in a series; ancient. **2** Being or occurring sooner than is usual or necessary. **3** About to be or happen; soon to occur. [< *adv.*] —*adv.* **1** At or near the beginning of a period of time. **2** In good time or season. —**early on** Near the beginning. [OE *ærlīce* < *ær* sooner + *-līce* -ly] —**ear′li·ness** *n.*

Ear·ly (ûr′lē), **Jubal Anderson,** 1816–94, Confederate general.

early bird *Colloq.* **1** One who arrives early. **2** An early morning riser.

ear·mark (ir′märk′) *v.t.* **1** To make a mark of identification on. **2** To mark an animal's ear. **3** To set aside for special purposes, as money. —*n.* An owner's mark on an animal's ear; any mark of identification.

ear·mind·ed (ir′mīn′did) *adj.* Having a marked preference for auditory images in the various mental processes. —**ear′·mind′ed·ness** *n.*

ear·mold (ir′mōld′) *n.* A plastic mold to be worn in the ear as a means of conducting sound from the earphone of a hearing aid.

ear·muff (ir′muf′) *n.* One of a pair of adjustable coverings for the ears, worn as a protection against cold.

earn[1] (ûrn) *v.t.* **1** To receive, as salary or wages, for labor or exertion. **2** To merit as a result, reward, or punishment; deserve: He *earned* our condemnation. **3** To bring in (interest, etc.) as gain or profit. See synonyms under GAIN[1], GET, OBTAIN. ◆ Homophones: *erne, urn.* [OE *earnian*] —**earn′er** *n.*

earn[2] (ûrn) *v.t. & v.i. Brit. Dial.* To curdle, as milk. ◆ Homophones: *erne, urn.*

ear·nest[1] (ûr′nist) *adj.* **1** Intent and direct in purpose; zealous; fervent: of persons. **2** Marked by deep feeling or conviction; heart-felt; hearty: of words or acts. **3** Requiring careful consideration; serious; important. See synonyms under EAGER, SERIOUS. —*n.* Seriousness; reality, as opposed to pretense or trifling. —**in earnest** With full and serious intent; real and intended. [OE *eorneste*] —**ear′nest·ly** *adv.* —**ear′nest·ness** *n.*

ear·nest[2] (ûr′nist) *n.* **1** Money paid in advance to bind a bargain. **2** An assurance of something to come; pledge. See synonyms under SECURITY. [Prob. < OF *erres* < L *arra, arrhabo* < Gk. *arrhabōn* < Hebrew *'ērābōn;* infl. by EARNEST[1]]

earn·ing (ûr′ning) *n.* Usually *pl.* That which is earned; compensation; wages; salary.

ear·phone (ir′fōn′) *n.* **1** A headphone. **2** That part of an electronic hearing aid which transmits sound by air conduction through the earmold.

ear·plug (ir′plug′) *n.* A wax or plastic mold inserted into the ear to exclude water or noise, as in swimming or sleeping.

ear·ring (ir′ring′) *n.* A ring or hook usually with a pendant, worn at the ear.

ear shell An ear-shaped shell. See ABALONE.

ear·shot (ir′shot′) *n.* The distance at which sounds may be heard.

ear·split·ting (ir′split′ing) *adj.* Painfully loud or high-pitched; deafening.

ear·stone (ir′stōn′) *n.* An otolith.

earth (ûrth) *n.* **1** The solid portion or surface of the globe; ground. **2** Soil as distinguished from rock. **3** Those who inhabit the globe; the world at large. **4** The hole of a burrowing animal. **5** *Electr.* **a** The ground that forms part of an electric circuit. **b** A fault in a telegraphic or telephonic line, caused by connection of the conductor with the ground; also such connection. **6** Any natural soft soil, as clay and ocher. **7** *Chem.* A rare earth. **8** Temporal and transient interests and pursuits as contrasted with those that are spiritual; material things; worldly matters. **9** *Obs.* A locality upon the earth; country. See synonyms under LAND. —**down to earth** Realistic; unfanciful. —**to run to earth** To hunt down and find, as a fox. —*v.t.* **1** To bank up or protect with earth, as plants, flowers, etc. **2** To chase, as a fox, into a burrow or hole. **3** *Electr.* To ground. —*v.i.* **4** To burrow or hide in the earth, as a fox. [OE *eorthe*]

Earth (ûrth) **1** The third planet in order of distance from the sun and fifth in order of size among the planets. It has an area of 196,400,000 square miles, a mass of 6.57 sextillion tons (6.57 × 10²¹), a mean diameter of 7,918 miles, and a mean solar distance of 93,000,000 miles. ◆ Collateral adjectives: *telluric, terrestrial.* **2** The abode of man, considered as distinct from Heaven and Hell.

earth-bor·er (ûrth′bôr′ər, -bō′rər) *n.* An auger for boring into the ground.

earth-born (ûrth′bôrn′) *adj.* **1** Born out of the earth; of earthly origin. **2** Of terrestrial birth, as distinguished from celestial origin. **3** Springing from earthly or temporal considerations; mean or ignoble.

earth-bound (ûrth′bound′) *adj.* **1** Having only material interests. **2** Firmly fixed in or on the earth.

earth color Any of several pigments or paints

prepared from naturally occurring earth materials, as umber, ocher, chalk.

earth current 1 *Electr.* A direct current induced in the earth by grounded currents near powerhouses and thought responsible for the corrosion of the lead sheaths of cables, etc. **2** An electrical current, variable in strength, duration, and direction, which circulates within the earth's crust.

earth·en (ûr′thən) *adj.* Made of earth or baked clay; earthly.

earth·en·ware (ûr′thən·wâr′) *n.* Pottery, especially of inferior grade, as distinguished from porcelain and stoneware.

earth flax 1 Asbestos. **2** Amianthus.

earth inductor *Electr.* An induction coil which may be sharply rotated in the earth's magnetic field in order to determine the intensity of the field by the strength of the induced current as read on a galvanometer.

earth inductor compass A form of earth inductor designed to aid the pilot of an aircraft in maintaining a correct flight path with reference to the earth's magnetic field.

earth·i·ness (ûr′thē·nis) *n.* The quality of being earthy or like earth.

earth·light (ûrth′līt′) *n.* **1** Light sometimes visible at night, not directly attributable to sun, moon, or stars. **2** Earthshine.

earth·ling (ûrth′ling) *n.* A worldling or mortal.

earth·ly (ûrth′lē) *adj.* **1** Pertaining to the earth or the world of the present; material; secular; worldly; carnal. **2** *Colloq.* Possible; imaginable: of no *earthly* use. —**earth′li·ness** *n.*

earth·nut (ûrth′nut′) *n.* **1** The tuber of any one of several sedges. **2** The peanut. **3** Either of two European herbs (genus *Carum*) of the parsley family, as the caraway. **4** A truffle.

earth pea The hog peanut.

earth plate *Electr.* A ground plate.

earth·quake (ûrth′kwāk′) *n.* A vibration or sudden undulation of a portion of the earth's crust, caused by the splitting or faulting of a mass of rock or by volcanic or other disturbances. ◆Collateral adjective: *seismic.*

earth return *Electr.* The return path through the earth of an electric circuit which is completed by it: also called *ground-return circuit.*

earth·shine (ûrth′shīn′) *n. Astron.* Sunlight reflected from the earth so as to illuminate slightly those parts of the moon not in the direct rays of the sun.

earth·star (ûrth′stär′) *n.* A fungus (genus *Geaster*) having the outer coat distinct from the inner and split into several reflexed divisions suggestive of a star.

earth·ward (ûrth′wərd) *adv.* Toward the earth: also **earth′wards.** —*adj.* Moving toward the earth.

earth wax Ozocerite.

earth·work (ûrth′wûrk′) *n.* **1** *Mil.* An offensive or defensive fortification made largely or wholly of earth. **2** *Engin.* An operation or work, as a cutting or an embankment, requiring the removal of or filling in with earth. **3** Anything similar to a military earthwork.

earth·worm (ûrth′wûrm′) *n.* **1** A burrowing terrestrial annelid (family *Lumbricidae*), useful for enriching the soil. **2** A weak and insignificant or sordid person.

earth·y (ûr′thē) *adj.* **earth·i·er, earth·i·est 1** Of, pertaining to, or like earth or soil; made of earth. **2** Unrefined; coarse.

ear trumpet An instrument made to collect and concentrate sound. Compare HEARING AID.

ear·wax (ir′waks′) *n.* A waxy substance secreted by the glands lining the passages of the external ear; cerumen.

ear·wig (ir′wig′) *n.* **1** An insect (family *Forficulidae*) with horny, short (or absent) forewings and a caudal pair of forceps: erroneously believed to enter the human ear. For illustration see under INSECT(injurious). **2** Loosely, in the United States, a small centipede. **3** *Obs.* A secret informer. —*v.t.* **·wigged, ·wig·ging** To influence by secret and stealthy counsel; to insinuate against by or as by whispering in the ear. [OE *earwicga*]

ease (ēz) *n.* **1** Freedom from pain, agitation, or perplexity; comfort. **2** Freedom from or absence of apparent effort; facility. **3** Freedom from affectation or constraint. —*v.* **eased, easing** *v.t.* **1** To relieve the mentalor physical

pain or oppression of; comfort. **2** To make less painful or oppressive: This will *ease* your pain. **3** To lessen the pressure, weight, tension, etc., of: to *ease* an axle. **4** To move, lower, or put in place gradually and with care. **5** *Colloq.* To rob: with *of*: a humorous usage: He was *eased* of his wallet. **6** *Rare* To facilitate. —*v.i.* **7** To diminish in severity, speed, etc.: often with *up* or *off*: The pain *eased.* —**to ease away** (or **off**) To move away slightly, as one ship from another. —**to ease the helm** *Naut.* To put the helm a trifle to midships so as to reduce the strain on the rudder. [<OF *aise* <LL *adjacens, -entis* neighboring. See ADJACENT.] —**ease′ful·ly** *adv.* —**ease′fulness** *n.*

Synonyms (noun) : easiness, expertness, facility, knack, readiness. *Ease* may be either of condition or of action; *facility* is always of action; *readiness* is of action or of expected action. One lives at *ease* who has no pressing cares; one stands at *ease*, moves or speaks with *ease*, when wholly without restraint. *Facility* is always active; *readiness* may be active or passive; the speaker has *facility* of expression, *readiness* of wit. *Ease* of action may imply merely the possession of ample power; *facility* always implies practice and skill. *Readiness* in the active sense includes much of the meaning of *ease* with the added idea of promptness or alertness. *Easiness* applies to the thing done, rather than to the doer. *Expertness* applies to the more mechanical processes of body and mind; we speak of the *readiness* of an orator, but of the *expertness* of a gymnast. Compare COMFORTABLE, DEXTERITY, POWER. *Antonyms*: annoyance, awkwardness, constraint, difficulty, discomfort, disquiet, trouble, uneasiness, vexation, worry.

ease·ful (ēz′fəl) *adj.* Causing or promoting ease or quiet; comfortable; peaceful.

ea·sel (ē′zəl) *n.* A folding frame for supporting a picture, panel, etc. [<Du. *ezel* easel, orig. an ass]

ease·ment (ēz′mənt) *n.* **1** *Law* The incorporeal privilege or right of making limited use of another's adjacent property, as for access over a road or path, or for a telephone line, water pipe, or the like. **2** Relief. **3** Anything that gives ease or relief.

eas·i·ly (ē′zə·lē) *adv.* In an easy manner; readily; quietly.

eas·i·ness (ē′zi·nis) *n.* The state of being at ease, or of being easy to do or accomplish.

east (ēst) *n.* **1** The point of the compass at which the sun rises at the equinox, directly opposite *west.* See COMPASSCARD. **2** Any direction, region, or part of the horizon near that point. —**Far East** Eastern Asia, including China, Japan, and adjacent islands. —**Middle East 1** The region generally including the countries of SW Asia lying west of Pakistan and India. **2** *Brit.* This region with the exception of Turkey and including India, Pakistan, Burma, Tibet, Libya, Ethiopia, and Somaliland. —**Near East 1** The countries lying east of the Mediterranean, mostly in SW Asia, including Turkey, Syria, Lebanon, Israel, Jordan, Saudi Arabia, etc., and sometimes the Balkans and Egypt. **2** *Brit.* The Balkans. —**the East 1** The part of the earth including Asia and the adjacent islands; the Orient. **2** In the United States: **a** The region eastward of the Mississippi and north of the Ohio. **b** The region east of the Allegheny Mountains and north of Maryland. —*adj.* **1** To, toward, facing, or placed in the east; eastern. **2** Coming from the east: the *east* wind. **3** Near the altar of a church as seen from the nave. —*adv.* In or toward the east; in an easterly direction. —*v.i.* To go or turn toward the east; proceed in an easterly direction. [OE]

East (ēst), **Edward Murray**, 1879–1938, U.S. biologist.

East Africa Protectorate A former name of KENYA.

East An·gli·a (ang′glē·ə) An old Anglo-Saxon kingdom in SE England, comprising Norfolk and Suffolk counties.

East Bengal See under BENGAL.

east-bound (ēst′bound′) *adj.* Going eastward. Also **east′bound′.**

East·bourne (ēst′bôrn, -bərn) A seaside borough in SE Sussex, England.

east by north One point north of east on the mariner's compass. See COMPASS CARD.

east by south One point south of east on the mariner's compass. See COMPASS CARD.

East Cape See DEZHNEV, CAPE.

East China Sea The NE part of the China Sea, bounded by Korea, Japan, Taiwan, and China.

east·er (ēs′tər) *v.i. Obs.* To shift to the east, as the wind.

East·er (ēs′tər) *n.* **1** A Christian festival commemorating the resurrection of Christ. **2** The day on which this festival is celebrated, the Sunday immediately after the first full moon that occurs on or after March 21: also **Easter Day.** [OE *Eastre* goddess of spring]

Easter egg A decorated egg, or imitation of an egg, given as a present at Easter.

Easter Island A Chilean island in the South Pacific; 45 1/2 square miles; known for its numerous stone monuments of undetermined origin: native name *Rapa Nui.* Spanish **Is·la de Pas·cua** (ēs′lä thä päs′kwä).

east·er·ling (ēs′tər·ling) *n. Obs.* A native of the East; an Oriental.

east·er·ly (ēs′tər·lē) *adj.* **1** Situated, moving, or directed toward the east; eastward. **2** Coming from the east: said of winds. —*adv.* Toward the east: also **east′ern·ly.**

Easter Monday The day following Easter.

east·ern (ēs′tərn) *adj.* **1** Of, pertaining to, from or situated in the east. **2** *Usually cap.* Pertaining to the East. **3** Moving to or from the east; easterly.

Eastern Church See GREEKCHURCH.

Eastern Empire The Byzantine Empire.

East·ern·er (ēs′tərn·ər) *n. U.S.* One who dwells in the eastern part of the United States.

Eastern Ghats See GHATS.

eastern hemisphere See under HEMISPHERE.

east·ern·most (ēs′tərn·mōst′) *adj.* Farthest east.

Eastern (Roman) Empire The Byzantine Empire.

Eastern Samoa See SAMOA.

Eastern Shore The eastern coast of Chesapeake Bay; especially, the tidewater region of Maryland.

Eastern Standard Time See STANDARD TIME. Abbr. *E.S.T.*

Eastern Turkestan See under TURKESTAN.

East·er·tide (ēs′tər·tīd′) *n.* **1** The season of Easter; a period extending in various churches from Easter to Ascension Day, Whitsunday, or Trinity Sunday. **2** The week beginning with and immediately following Easter [<EASTER + TIDE[1] (def. 4)]

East Flanders A province of NW Belgium; 1,147 square miles; capital, Ghent. *Flemish* **Oost-Vlaan·de·ren** (ōst′vlän′də·rən).

East Germanic See under GERMANIC.

East Germany See under GERMANY.

East Ham A county borough in SW Essex, England.

East India Company The name of various mercantile associations organized in the 17th and 18th centuries by Europeans to carry on trade with the East Indies: notably the British, Dutch, and French companies.

East Indies 1 The islands of the Malay Archipelago. **2** SE Asia. **3** *Archaic* India. Also **East India.** —**East Indian.**

east·ing (ēs′ting) *n.* **1** *Naut.* The distance traversed by a ship running on an easterly course. **2** The distance eastward from a given meridian. **3** A shifting or moving toward the east.

East Liverpool A city on the Ohio River in eastern Ohio.

East London A port in Eastern Cape Province, Republic of South Africa. *Afrikaans* **Oos-Lon·den** (ōs′lôn′də).

East Lo·thi·an (lō′thē·ən) A county of SE Scotland; 267 square miles; county seat, Haddington. Formerly **Had·ding·ton·shire** (had′-ing·tən·shir′).

East·man (ēst′mən), **George**, 1854–1932, U.S. pioneer in photography. —**Max**, 1883–1969, U.S. editor and writer.

East Midland See under MIDLAND.

east-north·east (ēst′nôrth′ēst′) *adj., adv., n.*

Midway between east and northeast. See COMPASS CARD.
Eas·ton (ēs′tən) A city on the Delaware River in eastern Pennsylvania.
East Orange A city in NE New Jersey.
East Pakistan See PAKISTAN.
East Prussia A former province of Prussia in NE Germany; capital, Königsberg: German *Ostpreussen.*
East Riding An administrative division of SE Yorkshire, England; 1,172 square miles.
East River A navigable tidal strait in SE New York, connecting Long Island Sound and New York Bay and separating Manhattan Island from Long Island; 16 miles long.
East Semitic See under SEMITIC.
east-south·east (ēst′south′ēst′) *adj., adv., & n.* Midway between east and southeast. See COMPASS CARD.
East St. Louis A city in SW Illinois on the Mississippi River.
east·ward (ēst′wərd) *adj.* Running, tending, or situated in an easterly direction. — *adv.* Toward the east: also **east′wards.** Also **east′·ward·ly.**
eas·y (ē′zē) *adj.* **eas·i·er, eas·i·est** 1 Not involving great exertion, discomfort, or difficulty. 2 Free from discomfort or anxiety; comfortable. 3 Possessed of a sufficient competence. 4 Free from embarrassment or affectation; natural. 5 Yielding; indulgent. 6 Gentle; tractable. 7 Causing no disquiet or discomfort; not burdensome. 8 Self-indulgent. 9 Not straitened or tight, as money. 10 To be paid in small instalments: *easy* terms. 11 Not having much current: *easy* water. — **to go easy on** To be moderate in the use of; also, to be tactful about. — **to live on easy street** To be in good financial circumstances. [<OF *aisé,* pp. of *aiser, aisier* put at ease]
easy chair A large, comfortable chair, usually padded or stuffed.
eas·y-go·ing (ē′zē·gō′ing) *adj.* 1 Not inclined to effort or worry; complacently unconcerned. 2 Moving at an easy pace, as a horse.
easy mark *Colloq.* A person easily fooled or victimized.
eat (ēt) *v.* **ate** or *Brit.* **eat** (et), **eat·en, eat·ing** *v.t.* 1 To take (food) into the mouth and swallow. 2 To consume or destroy by or as by eating: often with *away* or *up.* 3 To wear into or away; corrode; rust. 4 To make (a way or hole) by or as by gnawing or chewing. — *v.i.* 5 To take in food; have a meal. 6 To bore into or corrode something: with *through* or *into.* — **to eat crow** To accept what one had been against; submit to humiliation. — **to eat humble pie** To make humble apologies. — **to eat one's words** To retract what one has said. — **to eat up** 1 To consume completely. 2 To pass over rapidly: to *eat up* the miles. [OE *etan*] — **eat′er** *n.*
eat·a·ble (ē′tə·bəl) *n.* Something edible: often in the plural. — *adj.* Fit to be eaten; edible.
eat·age (ē′tij) *n. Brit.* Pasturage, especially that obtained from aftermath. Compare EDDISH.
eat·er·y (ē′tər·ē) *n. U.S. Slang* An eating house.
eat·ing (ē′ting) *n.* 1 The act of taking food. 2 Food: Brook trout are good *eating.*
Ea·ton (ē′tən), **Theophilus,** 1590–1658, English colonial administrator in America; first governor of New Haven Colony 1636–58.
eats (ēts) *n. pl. U.S. Slang* Food.
eau (ō) *n. pl.* **eaux** (ō) Water: a word designating various perfumes, cordials, medicinal waters, etc. [<F <L *aqua* water]
Eau Claire (ō klâr′) A city in west central Wisconsin.
eau de Co·logne (ō′ də kə·lōn′) See COLOGNE.
eau de vie (de vē′) *French* Brandy; literally, water of life.
eaves (ēvz) *n. pl.* The projecting edge of a roof. [OE *efes* edge]
eaves·drip (ēvz′drip′) *n.* An ancient law forbidding the erection of a building so close to a boundary line that the eaves would drip on the land of another.
eaves·drop (ēvz′drop′) *v.i.* **·dropped, ·drop·ping** To listen, or try to listen, secretly, as to a private conversation. — *n.* 1 Water that drops from the eaves. 2 The line near the wall of a house made by such droppings. Also **eave′·drop′.** [< *eavesdrop, n.*; with ref. to one who listens within the eavesdrop] — **eaves′drop′per** *n.* — **eaves′drop′ping** *n.*

ebb (eb) *v.i.* 1 To recede, as the tide. 2 To decline; fail. — *n.* 1 The reflux of tidewater to the ocean; low tide: opposed to *flood*: also **ebb tide.** 2 Decrease; condition or period of decline. See synonyms under ABATE. [OE *ebbian*]
Eb·e·ne·zer (eb′ə·nē′zər) *n.* 1 In the Bible, a stone set up by Samuel to commemorate a victory of the Israelites: 1 *Sam.* vii 12. 2 Any memorial of divine help and deliverance. 3 A masculine personal name. [<Hebrew *eben ha-'ēzer* stone of help]
E·bers (ā′bərz), **Georg,** 1837–98, German novelist and Egyptologist.
E·bert (ā′bərt), **Friedrich,** 1871–1925, first president of the German republic 1919–25.
E·bi·o·nite (ē′bē·ə·nīt′) *n.* One of a party in the early church, second to fourth century, chiefly made up of Pharisees and Essenes. Compare NAZARENE. [<L *ebionita* <Hebrew *'ebyōn* poor] — **E′bi·o·nit′ic** (-nit′ik) *adj.*
Eb·lis (eb′lis) In Moslem mythology, the chief of the evil jinn, who, refusing to worship Adam, were cast out of heaven: also called *Iblees.* [<Arabic *Iblis* <Gk. *Diabolos* devil]
E-boat (ē′bōt′) *Brit.* A fast German torpedo boat. [< *e(nemy) boat*]
eb·on (eb′ən) *adj.* 1 Of ebony. 2 Very black. — *n.* Ebony.
eb·on·ite (eb′ən·īt) *n.* Black vulcanite, or hard rubber.
eb·on·ize (eb′ən·īz) *v.t.* **·ized, ·iz·ing** To stain or polish, as wood, in imitation of ebony.
eb·on·y (eb′ən·ē) *n. pl.* **·on·ies** 1 A hard, heavy wood, usually black, used for cabinetwork, etc. It is furnished by various species of a tropical genus (*Diospyros*) of hardwood trees. 2 Any tree of this genus, especially *D. ebenum* of Ceylon and Southern India. — *adj.* Made of ebony; ebonylike. [<L *hebeninus* <Gk. *hebeninos* of ebony < *ebenos* ebony <Egyptian *hebni*]
Eb·or·a·cum (eb′ə·rā′kəm) Ancient Roman name for York, England.
e·brac·te·ate (ē·brak′tē·āt) *adj. Bot.* Without bracts. [<NL *ebracteatus* <L *ex-* without + *bractea* plate, bract]
e·bri·e·ty (i·brī′ə·tē) *n. Obs.* Drunkenness; inebriety. [<F *ébrieté* <L *ebrietas, -tatis* < *ebrius* drunken]
e·bri·os·i·ty (ē′brē·os′ə·tē) *n. Obs.* Habitual intoxication.
E·bro (ē′brō, *Sp.* ā′brō) A river in NE Spain, flowing over 500 miles SE to the Mediterranean.
e·bul·lient (i·bul′yənt) *adj.* 1 Bubbling over with enthusiasm. 2 In a boiling condition; boiling. [<L *ebulliens, -entis,* ppr. of *ebullire* < *ex-* out + *bullire* boil] — **e·bul′lient·ly** *adv.* — **e·bul′lience, e·bul′lien·cy** *n.*
eb·ul·lism (eb′ə·liz′əm) *n. Pathol.* The bubbling out or vaporizing of body fluids when their boiling point drops below the normal temperature of 98°F.: a condition associated with high-altitude space travel. [<L *ebullire* boil out]
eb·ul·li·tion (eb′ə·lish′ən) *n.* 1 The bubbling of a liquid; boiling. 2 Any sudden or violent agitation. [<L *ebullitio, -onis* < *ebullire.* See EBULLIENT.]
eb·ur·nat·ed (eb′ər·nā′tid) *adj.* Condensed and hardened like bone.
eb·ur·na·tion (eb′ər·nā′shən) *n. Pathol.* 1 Ossification of joint cartilage. 2 Condensation of a bone structure to the hardness of ivory. [<L *eburnus* ivory + -ATION]
e·bur·ne·an (ē·bûr′nē·ən) *adj.* Of or pertaining to ivory. Also **e·bur′ni·an.** [<L *eburnus* ivory]
ec- Var. of EX-².
e·cad (ē′kad) *n. Ecol.* A habitat plant form or modification due to non-inherited adaptation to unusual environment. [<EC(OLOGY) + -AD]
E·car·di·nes (ē·kär′də·nēz) *n. pl.* An order of brachiopods with hornlike or calcareous shells joined only by muscles: formerly called *Inarticulata.* [<NL <L *e-* away + *cardo, cardinis* hinge]
é·car·té (ā′kär·tā′) *n.* A game of cards for two persons. [<F, pp. of *écarter* discard]
Ec·bat·a·na (ek·bat′ə·nə) The capital of ancient Media, on the present site of HAMADAN, Iran.
ec·bol·ic (ek·bol′ik) *adj. Med.* Causing contraction of the uterus and thus inducing abortion or promoting parturition. — *n.* An ecbolic drug. [<Gk. *ekbolē* a casting out (< *ex-* out + *ballein* throw) + -IC]

Ec·ce Ho·mo (ek′sē hō′mō, ek′e) 1 Behold the Man!: the words of Pilate (*John* xix 5). 2 An artistic or other representation of Christ crowned with thorns.
ec·cen·tric (ek·sen′·trik) *adj.* 1 Departing from the usual custom or practice; peculiar; erratic. 2 Not in the center. 3 *Math.* Not having the same center: said of circles, ellipses, spheres, etc.: opposed to *concentric.* 4 Not being a perfect circle, as an ellipse. 5 Of or pertaining to an eccentric. 6 Not holding to an identical purpose. 7 Removed or apart from a nerve center. 8 *Colloq.* Odd or unconventional to a degree short of mental unbalance: said of persons whose actions are considered peculiar to a marked degree. See synonyms under IRREGULAR, ODD, QUEER. — *n.* 1 *Mech.* A disk mounted out of center on a driving shaft, bound to it by a key, and surrounded by a collar or strap connected with a rod, effecting a crank motion. 2 One who or that which is eccentric. 3 *Math.* A circle not having the same center as another that partly coincides with it: also spelled *excentric.* [<LL *eccentricus* <Gk. *ekkentros* < *ek-* out, away + *kentron* center] — **ec·cen′tri·cal** *adj.* — **ec·cen′tri·cal·ly** *adv.*

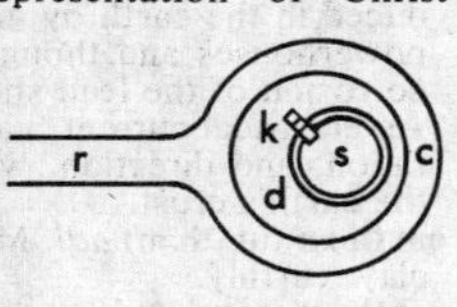

ECCENTRIC
r. Driving shaft, eccentric to center of disk *d. k.* Key binding disk to shaft. *c.* Collar connecting with rod *r.*

ec·cen·tric·i·ty (ek′sen·tris′ə·tē) *n. pl.* **·ties** 1 The state or quality of being eccentric; oddity. 2 An odd or capricious act. 3 The distance between the centers of two eccentric circles or objects. 4 The condition or quality of being eccentric. 5 *Math.* The ratio of the distance between the focus and the center of a conic to half of its transverse axis; formerly, the distance itself. Also spelled *excentricity.*
ec·chy·mosed (ek′i·mōzd) *adj. Med.* Discolored by reason of a contusion, as in the case of a black eye.
ec·chy·mo·sis (ek′i·mō′sis) *n. pl.* **·ses** (-sēz) *Med.* A discoloration, as a black-and-blue spot, resulting from the rupture of small blood vessels by a blow or contusion. [<NL <Gk. *ekchymōsis* < *ek-* out + *chymos* humor (def. 4)] — **ec′chy·mot′ic** (-mot′ik) *adj.*
Ec·cles (ek′əlz), **Marriner Stoddard,** born 1890, U.S. banker and economist.
ec·cle·si·a (i·klē′zhē·ə, -zē·ə) *n. pl.* **·si·ae** (-ē) 1 The popular or legislative assembly in Athens and other ancient Greek states in which every free citizen could vote. 2 A body of Christians organized for worship and religious work; a church; congregation. [<L <Gk. *ekklēsia* < *ekkaleein* < *ek-* out + *kaleein* call]
ec·cle·si·arch (i·klē′zē·ärk) *n.* A church ruler, especially one in high authority. [<ECCLESIA + Gk. *archos* chief]
Ec·cle·si·as·tes (i·klē′zē·as′tēz) One of the books of the Old Testament, formerly attributed to King Solomon. [<Gk. *ekklēsiastēs,* trans. of Hebrew *qōhēleth* a preacher]
ec·cle·si·as·tic (i·klē′zē·as′tik) *adj.* Ecclesiastical. — *n.* 1 One officially set apart for the service of the church; a cleric; a churchman: used chiefly in episcopal communions. 2 In early church history, a member of the established or orthodox church, as distinguished from heretics and unbelievers. [<Gk. *ekklēsiastikos* for the assembly < *ekklēsia* assembly]
ec·cle·si·as·ti·cal (i·klē′zē·as′ti·kəl) *adj.* Of or pertaining to the church, especially considered as an organized and governing power: distinguished from *civil.* Abbr. *Eccl.* — **ec·cle′si·as′ti·cal·ly** *adv.*
ec·cle·si·as·ti·cism (i·klē′zē·as′tə·siz′əm) *n.* 1 Devotion to the principles of the church or to its privileges and forms. 2 The spirit that leads to such devotion. 3 Systematically exercised ecclesiastical authority.
Ec·cle·si·as·ti·cus (i·klē′zē·as′ti·kəs) One of the books of the Old Testament Apocrypha, resembling in form the Proverbs of Solomon: accepted as canonical by the Roman Catholic Church: called also *The Wisdom of Jesus, the Son of Sirach.*
ec·cle·si·ol·a·try (i·klē′zē·ol′ə·trē) *n.* Worship of the church; extreme veneration for the authority, forms, and traditions of the church.

[< Gk. *ekklēsia* church + *latreia* worship] — **ec·cle·si·ol·a·ter** *n.*

ec·cle·si·ol·o·gy (i·klē·zē·ol′ə·jē) *n.* **1** The study of the organization, government, liturgy, and ritual of the Christian church. **2** The study of church architecture and decoration. —**ec·cle′·si·o·log′ic** (-zē·ō·loj′ik) or **·i·cal** *adj.*

ec·dem·ic (ek·dem′ik) *adj. Med.* Of or pertaining to diseases originating at a distance: opposed to *endemic.* [< EC- + Gk. *dēmos* people]

ec·de·mo·ma·ni·a (ek·dē′mə·mā′nē·ə, -mān′yə) *n. Psychiatry* A morbid compulsion to wander away from home. Also **ec·de′mo·no·ma′ni·a.** [< EC- + Gk. *dēmos* folk, people + -MANIA]

ec·dys·i·ast (ek·diz′ē·ast, -əst) *n.* A strip-teaser. Also **ek·dys′i·ast.** [< Gk. *ekdysis* a shedding of the skin; coined by H. L. Mencken in 1940]

ec·dy·sis (ek′di·sis) *n. pl.* **·ses** (-sēz) The act of casting off an integument, as in serpents and insects. [< NL < Gk. < *ek-* off + *dyein* dress, clothe]

e·ce·sis (i·sē′sis) *n. Ecol.* The adjustment of a plant to a new habitat; the establishment of a migrant organism. [< NL < Gk. *oikēsis* a dwelling]

ec·go·nine (ek′gə·nēn, -nin) *n. Chem.* A white, bitter crystalline alkaloid, $C_9H_{15}O_3N·H_2O$, resulting from the decomposition of cocaine by hydrochloric acid. [< Gk. *ekgonos* born of, sprung from + -INE²]

ec·hard (ek′härd) *n. Ecol.* The non-available water of the soil: opposed to *chresard.* [Gk. *echthos* outside + *ardeia* irrigation]

eche (ēch) *v.t. Obs.* To increase or enlarge. [OE *ēcan*]

E·che·ga·ray y Ei·za·guir·re (ā′chä·gä·rī′ ē ā′thä·gir′rā), **José,** 1832–1916, Spanish dramatist.

ech·e·lon (esh′ə·lon) *n.* **1** A staggered troop, fleet, or airplane formation, one rank, ship, or airplane behind the other, but extending farther toward one flank than the preceding rank, ship, or airplane: often V-shaped. **2** *Mil.* **a** One of the different fractions of a command arranged from front to rear, to which a particular combat mission is assigned: assault *echelon,* support *echelon.* **b** One of the various subdivisions from front to rear of a military headquarters: forward *echelon,* rear *echelon.* **c** A military unit regarded as having a distinct function: command *echelon,* first *echelon* maintenance, etc. **3** *Optics* A diffraction grating made of glass plates so constructed that each overlaps the one below, forming a stairlike pattern. —*v.t. & v.i.* To form in echelon. [< F *échelon* < *échelle* ladder < L *scala*]

ECHELON (def. 1)

ech·e·lon·ment (esh′ə·lon·mənt) *n.* The act of forming or the state of being formed into echelons, including those of formation, position, or function.

e·chid·na (i·kid′nə) *n. pl.* **·nae** (-nē) An egg-laying monotreme of Australia, etc. (*Echidna aculeata*), having a vermiform tongue, tubular snout with nostrils near the tip, fossorial feet, and strong spines intermixed with fur; a spiny ant-eater. [< NL < Gk., adder]

ECHIDNA
(About 15 inches in body length)

ech·i·na·ce·a (ek′ə·nā′shē·ə) *n.* A genus of hardy perennial plants of the composite family native in the United States; the root of *E. angustifolia* has medicinal properties. [< NL < Gk. *echinos* hedgehog]

ech·i·nate (ek′ə·nāt) *adj.* Set or armed thickly with prickles; bristly; spiny. Also **ech′i·nat′ed.**

e·chi·ni·form (i·kī′nə·fôrm) *adj.* Having the form of a sea urchin.

echino- *combining form* Spiny; prickly: *echinoderm:* also, before vowels, **echin-.** Also **echini-.** [< Gk. *echinos* hedgehog]

e·chi·no·derm (i·kī′nə·dûrm) *n.* Any of a phylum (Echinodermata) of coelomate, bottom-dwelling marine animals, as starfishes, sea cucumbers, etc., characterized by pentamerous radial symmetry, a skeleton of calcite plates just beneath the skin, and a water-vascular system which serves primarily for locomotion. —**e·chi′no·der′ma·tous** (-dûr′mə·təs), **e·chi′no·der′mal** *adj.*

e·chi·noid (i·kī′noid) *n.* Any of a class (*Echinoidea*) of echinoderms, including sea urchins, sand dollars, etc. —*adj.* Echiniform. —**ech·i·noi·de·an** (ek′i·noi′dē·ən) *adj. & n.*

ech·i·nop·sine (ek′ə·nop′sēn, -sin) *n.* An alkaloid, $C_{10}H_9ON$, obtained from the globe thistle (genus *Echinops*) and similar in action to strychnine. [< NL *Echinops,* genus of the globe thistle + -INE]

e·chi·nus (i·kī′nəs) *n. pl.* **·ni** (-nī) **1** *Archit.* The cushion of the capital of a Doric column, or the corresponding part in some other order. For illustration see under CAPITAL. **2** A sea urchin or echinoid. **3** A hedgehog. [< L < Gk. *echinos* hedgehog, sea urchin]

Ech·mi·a·dzin (ech′mē·ä·dzēn′) A city of central Armenian S.S.R.; former capital of Armenia: also *Ejmiadzin, Etchmiadzine.*

ech·o (ek′ō) *n. pl.* **·oes 1** The sound produced by the reflection of sound waves from an opposing surface. **2** Reproduction of another's views or thoughts; a close imitation. **3** Prompt response. **4** The repetition of a musical phrase in soft tone; an echo-stop; an echo-organ. **5** A verse construction wherein one line repeats the last syllable or syllables of the line preceding. **6** *Telecom.* A retarded sound wave in radio reception; a signal received in addition to or later than the expected one. **7** In bridge, the play of a conventional card after a lead, to inform one's partner. —*v.t.* **1** To repeat or send back (sound) by echo: The walls *echoed* the shot. **2** To repeat the words, opinions, etc., of. **3** To repeat (words, opinions, etc.) in imitation of another. —*v.i.* **4** To give back sound; reverberate. **5** To be repeated or given back; resound. [< L < Gk. *ēchō*] —**ech′o·er** *n.*

Ech·o (ek′ō) In Greek mythology, a nymph who, because of her unrequited love for Narcissus, pined away until only her voice was left.

ech·o·gram (ek′ō·gram) *n.* A pictorial representation, as of an organ or other structure within the body, of objects under water, etc., detected by means of reflected ultrasound. Also called *sonogram.*

e·cho·ic (e·kō′ik) *adj.* Pertaining to echoism or onomatopoeia.

ech·o·ism (ek′ō·iz′əm) *n.* Word-making by the repetition or imitation of a sound heard; onomatopoeia.

ech·o·la·li·a (ek′ō·lā′lē·ə) *n. Psychiatry* The senseless repetition of words. [< NL < Gk. *ēchō* echo + *laleein* babble]

ech·o·lo·ca·tion (ek′ō·lō·kā′shən) *n.* The determination of the distance and position of objects by the interpretation of sound waves transmitted to and returned from them. Compare RADAR, SONAR.

ech·o·or·gan (ek′ō·ôr′gən) *n.* A group of pipes or stops of a pipe organ, set apart from the main instrument, and intended for echo effects.

ech·o·stop (ek′ō·stop′) *n.* On a pipe organ, a stop with pipes enclosed so as to echo the tones produced.

Eck (ek), **Johann,** 1486–1543, German Roman Catholic theologian: original name *Johann Mayer.*

Eck·er·mann (ek′ər·man), **Johann Peter,** 1792–1854, German writer.

Eck·hart (ek′härt), **Johannes,** 1260–1327?, German Dominican mystic and pantheist: known as *Meister Eckhart.* Also **Eck′ardt.**

é·clair (ā·klâr′, i·klâr′) *n.* A small oblong pastry shell filled with custard or whipped cream and usually iced with chocolate. [< F, lit., flash of lightning]

é·clair·cisse·ment (ā·klâr·sēs·män′) *n. French* The clearing up of something obscure; a full explanation.

ec·lamp·si·a (ek·lamp′sē·ə) *n. Pathol.* A sudden convulsive seizure, without loss of consciousness, especially during pregnancy or childbirth.

[< NL < Gk. *eklampsis* < *ek-* forth + *lampein* shine]

é·clat (ā·klä′, i·klä′) *n.* **1** Showiness of achievement; brilliancy; splendor. **2** Renown; celebrity; glory. [< F < *éclater* burst out]

ec·lec·tic (ek·lek′tik, ik-) *adj.* **1** Selecting or made by selection from different systems or sources. **2** Having broad views; liberal. **3** Composed of selections: an *eclectic* review. Also **ec·lec′ti·cal.** —*n.* One who practices selection from all systems or sources, as in philosophy or medicine. [< Gk. *eklektikos* < *ek-* out + *legein* select] —**ec·lec′ti·cal·ly** *adv.*

ec·lec·ti·cism (ek·lek′tə·siz′əm, ik-) *n.* **1** An eclectic method or system. **2** A system of philosophy composed of doctrines selected from different sources. **3** That which is conceived or formed eclectically.

e·clipse (i·klips′) *n.* **1** *Astron.* The dimming or elimination of light reaching an observer from a heavenly body. A **lunar eclipse** is caused by the passage of the moon through the earth's shadow; a **solar eclipse** by the passage of the moon between the sun and the observer. **2** Any hiding or obscuring. See ANNULAR ECLIPSE.

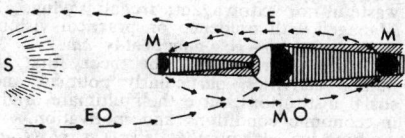
ECLIPSE
S. Sun. *E.* Earth. *M.* Moon. *EO.* Earth's orbit.
MO. Moon's orbit.

When the moon passes between the sun and the earth, it causes an eclipse of the sun, this solar eclipse being total to observers within the umbra (darker shaded portions) of the moon's shadow and partial to those within the penumbra (lighter portions). When the moon passes through the earth's shadow, earth observers witness a total or partial lunar eclipse.

—*v.t.* **e·clipsed, e·clips·ing 1** To cause an eclipse of; darken. **2** To obscure the beauty, fame, worth, etc., of; overshadow. [< OF < L *eclipsis* < Gk. *ekleipsis* < *ek-* out + *leipein* leave]

eclipsing variable See under STAR.

e·clip·sis (i·klip′sis) *n.* **1** Ellipsis. **2** In the Celtic languages, a phonetic change undergone by the initial consonant of a word under the influence of a preceding word or form. [< L. See ECLIPSE.]

e·clip·tic (i·klip′tik, ē-) *n.* **1** *Astron.* **a** That plane, passing through the center of the sun, which contains the orbit of the earth: also **plane of the ecliptic. b** The great circle in which this plane intersects the celestial sphere; the apparent path of the sun around the celestial sphere. **2** A great circle on a terrestrial globe drawn tangent to the tropics, used when a terrestrial globe is employed for a celestial. —**fixed ecliptic** A fixed plane in the position of the ecliptic at some standard epoch. —*adj.* Pertaining to eclipses or to the ecliptic. —**e·clip′ti·cal·ly** *adv.*

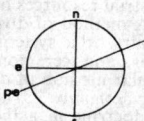
PLANES OF THE ECLIPTIC
n. s. North, south poles.
e. Equator. *pe.* Plane.
ns. Greenwich meridian.

ec·lo·gite (ek′lə·jīt) *n.* A rock consisting of red garnet, greenish pyroxene, and emerald-green smaragdite. [< Gk. *eklogē* selection < *ek-* out + *legein* select]

ec·logue (ek′lôg, -log) *n.* **1** A poem containing discourses or dialogs, with shepherds as principal speakers. **2** A short pastoral poem; bucolic. Also **ec′log.** [< F *éclogue* < L *ecloga* < Gk. *eklogē.* See ECLOGITE.]

e·clo·sion (i·klō′zhən) *n.* **1** *Biol.* The process of hatching from an egg. **2** *Entomol.* The emergence of the mature insect from the pupa. [< F *éclosion* < *éclore* be hatched]

ec·o·cide (ek′ō·sīd) *n.* The disruption of an ecosystem, as by the reckless introduction of an agent or process that destroys some key element in the system. —**ec′o·cid′al** *adj.*

é·cole (ā·kôl′) *n. French* School.

e·col·o·gy (i·kol′ə·jē) *n.* **1** That division of

biology which treats of the relations between organisms and their environment; bionomics. **2** The study of human populations and of their reciprocal relations in terms of physical environment, spatial distribution, and cultural characteristics. [<Gk. *oikos* home + -LOGY] **— ec′o·log′ic** (ek′ə·loj′ik) or **·i·cal** *adj.* **— ec′·o·log′i·cal·ly** *adv.* **— e·col′o·gist** *n.*

e·con·o·met·ric (i·kon′ə·met′rik) *adj.* Pertaining to a system of analysis of economic affairs using a specialized statistical technique for large masses of assembled data.

e·con·o·met·rics (i·kon′ə·met′riks) *n.* The application of the principles of mathematical analysis to economic problems, specifically those pertaining to business and finance. [<ECONOMY + -METRICS] **— e·con′o·met′ric** *adj.*

ec·o·nom·ic (ek′ə·nom′ik, ē′kə-) *adj.* **1** Relating to the science of economics; pertaining to money matters or wealth. **2** Economical. **3** Of practical utility: *economic* botany. **4** *Obs.* Pertaining to the management of household affairs. [<L *oeconomicus* <Gk. *oikonomia.* See ECONOMY.]

ec·o·nom·i·cal (ek′ə·nom′i·kəl, ē′kə-) *adj.* **1** Careful and provident in management; not wasteful nor extravagant; frugal; saving. **2** Managed with prudence or practical vision. **3** Economic. **— ec′o·nom′i·cal·ly** *adv.*

economic determinism The theory that all human activities, particularly political and social institutions, have their ultimate origin in economic conditions and motivation.

ec·o·nom·ics (ek′ə·nom′iks, ē′kə-) *n. pl.* (*Construed as singular*) The science that treats of the production and distribution of wealth.

e·con·o·mist (i·kon′ə·mist) *n.* **1** One who is proficient in economics. **2** A manager of domestic or pecuniary resources. **3** One who is careful and thrifty in management.

e·con·o·mize (i·kon′ə·mīz) *v.* **·mized, ·miz·ing** *v.t.* To use thriftily. **—** *v.i.* To be frugal or economical. Also *Brit.* **e·con′o·mise.** See synonyms under RETRENCH. **— e·con′o·miz′er** *n.*

e·con·o·my (i·kon′ə·mē) *n. pl.* **·mies** **1** Disposition to save or spare; carefulness in outlay; freedom from extravagance or waste; frugality: *economy* of words, *economy* in dress. **2** Cheapness of operation, relative or absolute, as expressed in steam, fuel, or money. **3** The management of household matters: usually with a qualifying adjective: domestic *economy.* **4** Any practical system in which means are adjusted to ends, especially in the natural world: the *economy* of nature, the animal *economy,* the *economy* of a plant. **5** The practical adjustment, organization, or administration of affairs or resources, especially of industrial resources of a state: political *economy.* **6** A method of divine management of human affairs or a system of laws and regulations, rites, and ceremonies; specifically, any particular method of divine government: the Mosaic *economy.* **7** The handling and presentation of doctrine in a judicious manner. See synonyms under FRUGALITY, LEGISLATION. [<L *oeconomia* <Gk. *oikonomia* < *oikos* house + *nemein* manage]

e·con·o·my-sized (i·kon′ə·mē·sīzd′) *adj.* Large-sized: a term used in consumer advertising. Also **e·con′o·my-size′.**

e·co·spe·cies (ē′kə·spē′shēz, ek′ə-) *n. Ecol.* A species of plant, natural or cultivated, highly adapted to its habitat. [<Gk. *oikos* home, habitat + SPECIES]

ec·o·sys·tem (ek′ō·sis′təm) *n. Ecol.* A community of organisms and their nonliving environment. [<Gk. *oikos* habitat + SYSTEM]

e·co·tone (ē′kə·tōn, ek′ə-) *n. Ecol.* A zone where two different forms of vegetable life compete. [<Gk. *oikos* habitat + *tonos* stress]

e·co·tope (ē′kə·tōp, ek′ə-) *n. Ecol.* A specialized habitat within a larger region. [<Gk. *oikos* habitat + *topos* place]

e·co·type (ē′kə·tīp, ek′ə-) *n. Ecol.* A biotype adapted for life in a particular kind of habitat. [<Gk. *oikos* habitat + TYPE]

é·cra·seur (ā·krä·zœr′) *n. Surg.* An instrument in the form of a fine chain, wire, or cord, for tightening around a tumor, etc., as a means of removal. [<F < *écraser* crush]

ec·ru (ek′rōō, ā′krōō) *adj.* **1** Unbleached. **2** Having the color of unbleached linen or of hemp. **—** *n.* **1** The color of unbleached linen; a light-yellowish brown. **2** Goods made of unbleached linen. Also **é′cru.** [<F <OF *escru* <L *ex-* thoroughly + *crudus* raw]

ec·sta·size (ek′stə·sīz) *v.t.* & *v.i.* **·sized, ·siz·ing** To fill with, or go into, a feeling of ecstasy; enrapture.

ec·sta·sy (ek′stə·sē) *n. pl.* **·sies** **1** The state of being beside oneself through some extravagant and overpowering emotion or mental exaltation: an *ecstasy* of joy. **2** An enrapturing or transporting influence; a rapture. **3** In mysticism, the state of trance supposed to accompany inspiration. **4** Religious rapture. **5** *Obs.* Madness. See synonyms under ENTHUSIASM, HAPPINESS, RAPTURE. [<OF *extasie* <LL *ecstasis* <Gk. *ekstasis* distraction < *ek-* out + *histanai* place]

ec·stat·ic (ek·stat′ik) *adj.* Pertaining to or of the nature of ecstasy; transporting; enraptured: also **ec·stat′i·cal.** **—** *n.* **1** A person subject to ecstasies or trances; an enthusiast. **2** *pl.* Rapturous emotions. **— ec·stat′i·cal·ly** *adv.*

ec·thy·ma (ek·thī′mə) *n. pl.* **·thym·a·ta** (-thim′·ə·tə) *Pathol.* A virus disease characterized by the formation on the skin of ulcerating pustules whose discharge produces vesicular lesions. [<Gk. *ekthyma* pustule < *ek-* out + *thuein* seethe]

ecto- *combining form* Without; outside; external: *ectoderm.* Also, before vowels, **ect-.** [<Gk. *ekto-* < *ektos* outside]

ec·to·blast (ek′tə·blast) *n. Biol.* The embryonic stage of the ectoderm. **— ec′to·blas′tic** *adj.*

ec·to·derm (ek′tə·dûrm) *n. Biol.* **1** The outer layer of the integument of a multicellular organism. **2** The outer germ layer of the embryo, from which the epithelial structures of the surface of the body and the nervous system develop by the process of gastrulation: often called *exoderm.* **— ec′to·der′mal, ec′to·der′mic** *adj.*

ec·to·en·zyme (ek′tō·en′zīm, -zim) *n. Biochem.* An enzyme which functions outside of the cell and acts directly upon the surrounding blood or tissue: opposed to *endoenzyme,* and often spelled *exoenzyme.* Also **ec′to·en′zym** (-zim).

ec·tog·e·nous (ek·toj′ə·nəs) *adj. Biol.* Having the power of development without a host: said of certain parasitic organisms, as bacteria. Also **ec·to·gen·ic** (ek′tə·jen′ik).

ec·tog·o·ny (ek·tog′ə·nē) *n.* The influence supposed to be exerted upon the mother by a developing embryo. [<ECTO- + Gk. *gonē* child]

ec·to·mere (ek′tə·mir) *n. Biol.* One of the blastomeres derived from the segmentation of the ovum during the development of the ectoderm. **— ec′to·mer′ic** (-mer′ik) *adj.*

ec·to·mor·phic (ek′tə·môr′fik) *adj.* Denoting a physical and personality type associated with the body structure as developed from the ectodermal layer of the embryo, and characterized by predominance of the nervous system. Compare ENDOMORPHIC and MESOMORPHIC.

-ectomy *combining form* Removal of a part by cutting out: used in surgical terms to indicate certain kinds of operations; as, *appendectomy.* [<Gk. *ektomē* < *ek-* out + *temnein* cut]

ec·to·par·a·site (ek′tə·par′ə·sīt) *n. Biol.* A parasite that lives upon the exterior of its host, as a louse.

ec·to·phyte (ek′tə·fīt) *n.* An ectoparasite which attacks plants.

ec·to·pi·a (ek·tō′pē·ə) *n. Pathol.* Displacement of parts or organs, especially when congenital. [<NL <Gk. *ek-* out, from + *topos* place] **— ec·top′ic** (-top′ik) *adj.*

ec·to·plasm (ek′tə·plaz′əm) *n.* **1** *Biol.* The firm outer layer of the cytoplasm of a unicellular organism or of a plant cell. **2** The substance alleged to emanate from the body of a spiritualist medium during a trance: also called *teleplasm.* **— ec′to·plas′mic** *adj.*

ec·to·sarc (ek′tə·särk) *n. Biol.* The ectoplasm of protozoans. [<ECTO- + Gk. *sarx* flesh]

ec·tos·to·sis (ek′tos·tō′sis) *n. Pathol.* Ossification around the exterior of a cartilage. [<ECT(O)- + OST(EO)- + -OSIS]

ec·to·troph·ic (ek′tə·trof′ik, -trō′fik) *adj. Bot.* Nourished by the outside (of roots): said of certain fungi. [<ECTO- + Gk. *trophikos* < *trephein* grow, nourish]

ec·trog·e·ny (ek·troj′ə·nē) *n. Pathol.* The loss or absence, usually congenital, of an organ or part of the body. [< *ectro-* absence (<Gk. *ektrōsis* an abortion) + -GENY] **— ec·tro·gen·ic** (ek′trə·jen′ik) *adj.*

ec·tro·pi·um (ek·trō′pē·əm) *n. Anat.* A turning outward, partial or complete, of a part, as an eyelid, or the lips of the neck of the womb. Also **ec·tro′pi·on.** [<NL <Gk. *ektropion* < *ektropos* < *ek-* out + *trepein* turn]

ec·type (ek′tīp) *n.* **1** An imitation or reproduction of an original: opposed to *prototype* and distinguished from *replica.* **2** *Archit.* A figure or other work in relief. **3** A reproduction, in a world of time and sense, of an eternal and non-sensuous idea: contrasted with *archetype.* **4** *Psychiatry* A physical or mental constitution that varies markedly from the average. [<Gk. *ektypos* < *ek-* out + *typos* < *typtein* stamp] **— ec′ty·pal** *adj.*

é·cu (ā·kü′) *n. pl.* **é·cus** (ā·kü′) *French* A former coin and monetary unit of European countries, commonly called a crown, and having a wide range of values.

Ec·ua·dor (ek′wə·dôr) A republic in NW South America; 108,478 square miles; capital, Quito. **— Ec′ua·do′re·an, Ec′ua·do′ri·an** *adj.* & *n.*

ec·u·men·i·cal (ek′yōō·men′i·kəl) *adj.* **1** Of or pertaining to the habitable world; general; universal. **2** Belonging to or accepted by the Christian church throughout the world: an *ecumenical* council. Also spelled *oecumenical.* Also **ec′u·men′ic.** [<LL *oecumenicus* <Gk. *oikoumenikos* < *oikoumenē* (*gē*) the inhabited (world) < *oikeein* dwell] **— ec′u·men′i·cal·ly** *adv.*

ec·u·men·ism (ek′yōō·men′iz·əm) *n.* The beliefs, principles, or practices of those who desire and work for world-wide unity and co-operation among all Christian churches. Also **ec·u·men·i·cal·ism** (ek′yōō·men′ə·kəl·iz·əm), **ec·u·men·i·cism** (ek′yōō·men′ə·siz′əm).

ec·ze·ma (ek′sə·mə, eg′zə·mə, eg·zē′mə) *n. Pathol.* An inflammatory disease of the skin attended by itching, watery discharge, and the appearance of lesions. [<Gk. *ekzema* < *ek-* out + *zeein* boil] **— ec·zem′a·tous** (-zem′ə·təs) *adj.*

Ed (ed) Diminutive of EDGAR, EDMUND, EDWARD, EDWIN.

-ed[1] *suffix* Used in the past tense of regular verbs: *walked, killed, played.* [OE *-ede, -ode, -ade*]

-ed[2] *suffix* **1** Used in the past participles of regular verbs: *clothed, washed.* **2** Forming adjectives from adjectives in *-ate,* with the same general meaning: *bipinnated.* [OE *-ed, -ad, -od*]

-ed[3] *suffix* **1** Having; possessing; characterized by: *toothed, green-eyed.* **2** Like; resembling: *bigoted.* [OE *-ede*]

e·da·cious (i·dā′shəs) *adj.* Given to eating; voracious; devouring. [<L *edax, edacis* < *edere* eat] **— e·da′cious·ly** *adv.*

e·dac·i·ty (i·das′ə·tē) *n.* Excess in eating; gluttony. Also **e·da′cious·ness.**

E·dam (ē′dəm, ē′dam) A town in NW Netherlands.

Edam cheese A mild curd cheese, originally produced in Edam, made in a round, flattened mold and usually coated with red paraffin.

e·daph·ic (i·daf′ik) *adj. Ecol.* Of, pertaining to, or affected by the state or condition of the soil rather than by climate; indigenous; local. [<Gk. *edaphos* ground]

Ed·da (ed′ə) Either of two collections of Old Icelandic or Old Norse literature: the **Elder Edda,** also called the **Poetic Edda,** containing mythological and heroic poetry of the 10th–13th centuries; and the **Younger Edda** or **Prose Edda,** a commentary on Norse mythology and composition by Snorri Sturluson (1178–1241). [<ON] **— Ed·da·ic** (e·dā′ik), **Ed′dic** *adj.*

ed·der (ed′ər) *Brit. Dial. n.* **1** A hedge. **2** Light, supple wood used to bind together the tops of hedges. **—** *v.t.* To fasten or bind with edders. [OE *eodor* a hedge]

Ed·die (ed′ē) Diminutive of EDGAR, EDMUND, EDWARD, EDWIN.

Ed·ding·ton (ed′ing·tən), **Sir Arthur Stanley,** 1882–1944, English astronomer, astrophysicist, and author.

ed·dy (ed′ē) *n. pl.* **·dies** **1** A whirl or backward-circling current of water or air; a whirlpool. **2** Figuratively, a turning aside or departure from the main current of thought or life. See synonyms under STREAM. **—** *v.t.* & *v.i.* **·died, ·dy·ing** To move, or cause to move, in or as in an eddy. [Prob. <ON *idha*]

Ed·dy (ed′ē), **Mary Baker,** 1821–1910, U.S. religious leader; founder of the Church of Christ, Scientist.

eddy current See under CURRENT.

Ed·dy·stone Rocks (ed′i·stōn′) A dangerous

reef in the English Channel, 14 miles SSW of Plymouth; site of **Eddystone Lighthouse.**

E·de (ā'dā) A town of SW Nigeria.

e·del·weiss (ā'dəl·vīs) *n.* A small perennial alpine herb of the composite family *(Leontopodium alpinum),* with white woolly leaves suggesting a flower, and dense terminal cymes. [<G <*edel* noble + *weiss* white]

EDELWEISS (Plant about 4 inches high over all)

e·de·ma (i·dē'mə) *n. pl.* **·ma·ta** (-mə·tə) *Pathol.* A morbid accumulation of serous fluid in various organs or tissues of the body, as the pleural cavity or the retina: also spelled *oedema.* [<NL < Gk. *oidēma* a tumor < *oidein* swell] **—e·dem·a·tous** (i·dem'ə·təs), **e·dem'a·tose** (-tōs) *adj.*

E·den (ēd'n) **1** In the Bible, the garden that was the first home of Adam and Eve: often *Paradise.* **2** Any delightful region or abode; a paradise.

E·den (ēd'n), **Sir (Robert) Anthony,** 1897–1977, English statesman; prime minister 1955–1957.

e·den·tate (ē·den'tāt, i·den'-) *adj.* **1** Toothless. **2** Of or pertaining to an order of placental mammals *(Edentata* or *Xenarthra),* some of which lack teeth, including sloths, ant–eaters, and armadillos. **—***n.* **1** One of the *Edentata.* **2** A creature without teeth. [<L *edentatus* <*ex-* without + *dens, dentis* tooth]

e·den·tu·lous (ē·den'chōō·ləs, i·den'-) *adj.* Having no teeth. Also **e·den'tu·late** (-lit, -lāt).

E·des·sa (i·des'ə) Ancient name for URFA. **—E·des'san** *adj.*

e·des·tin (i·des'tin) *n. Biochem.* A crystalline protein found in the castor–oil bean, hemp seed, and other seeds. [<Gk. *edestos* edible + -IN]

Ed·fu (ed'fōō) A town on the Nile in Upper Egypt; site of several temples and ruins: also *Idfu.*

Ed·gar (ed'gər, *Ger.* et'gär) A masculine personal name. Also *Ital.* **Ed·ga·ro** (ed·gä'rō), *Lat.* **Ed·ga·rus** (ed·gä'rōōs).

edge (ej) *n.* **1** The thin, sharp cutting part of a blade. **2** Sharpness; acuteness. **3** An abrupt border or margin; verge, brink; rim: the *edge* of a cliff. **4** A bounding or dividing line: the *edge* of a plain. See synonyms under BANK[1], BOUNDARY, MARGIN. **—on edge 1** Nervous; irritable. **2** Keenly eager. **—***v.* **edged, edg·ing** *v.t.* **1** To put a cutting edge on; sharpen. **2** To put an edging or border on. **3** To move cautiously sidewise: to *edge* one's way through a mob. **4** To move by degrees; inch: to *edge* one's chair closer. **5** *U.S. Colloq.* To defeat by a slight margin: The home team just *edged* the visitors. **—***v.i.* **6** To move sidewise. **7** To move by degrees: to *edge* away. [OE *ecg*] **—edged** *adj.* **—edge'·less** *adj.*

Edge·hill (ej'hil') A ridge in southern Warwickshire, England; site of a battle between Charles I and Parliamentary forces, 1642.

edge tool 1 Any sharp, cutting tool. **2** A tool for making an edging, or finishing an edge.

edge·wise (ej'wīz') *adv.* With the edge forward; on, by, with, along, or in the direction of the edge. Also **edge'ways'.**

Edge·worth (ej'wərth), **Maria,** 1767–1849, English novelist.

edg·ing (ej'ing) *n.* **1** Anything serving as or attached to an edge; trimming. **2** The making, dressing, or ornamenting of edges.

edg·y (ej'ē) *adj.* **1** Brought out too sharply; edgelike, as the outlines of a sculptured figure. **2** Irritable; sharp–tempered; eager. **—edg'i·ness** *n.*

edh (eth) *n.* The name of the letter ð, capital Đ, used in Old English to represent both voiceless and voiced *th,* as in *thin, then;* and in Icelandic and in phonetic writing to represent voiced *th,* as in *then:* also spelled *eth.* Compare THORN (*n.* def. 5).

ed·i·ble (ed'ə·bəl) *adj.* Fit to eat. **—***n. Usually pl.* Something suitable for food. [<LL *edibilis*< L *edere* eat] **—ed'i·bil'i·ty** *n.***—ed'i·ble·ness** *n.*

e·dict (ē'dikt) *n.* **1** That which is uttered or proclaimed by authority as a rule of action; a public ordinance emanating from a sovereign and having the force of law. **2** Any proclamation of command or prohibition. See synonyms under LAW. [<L *edictum,* pp. neut. of *edicere* <*ex-* out + *dicere* say] **—e·dic'tal** *adj.* **—e·dic'tal·ly** *adv.*

ed·i·fice (ed'ə·fis) *n.* A large structure of impressive architecture; a building. See synonyms under HOUSE. [<F *édifice* <L *aedificium* <*aedes* building + *facere* make] **—ed·i·fi·cial** (ed'ə·fish'əl) *adj.*

ed·i·fy (ed'ə·fī) *v.t.* **fied, fy·ing** To build up or strengthen, especially in morals or religion; instruct; improve; enlighten. [<OF *edifier* <L *aedificare* <*aedes* building + *facere* make] **—ed'i·fi·ca'tion** *n.* **—ed'i·fi'er** *n.* **—ed'i·fy'ing** *adj.* **—ed'i·fy'ing·ly** *adv.*

e·dile (ē'dīl) See AEDILE.

Ed·in·burgh (ed'ən·bûr'ə) The capital of Scotland on the Firth of Forth: Gaelic *Dunedin.*

E·dir·ne (e·dir'ne) See ADRIANOPLE.

Ed·i·son (ed'ə·sən), **Thomas Alva,** 1847–1931, U.S. inventor.

ed·it (ed'it) *v.t.* **1** To manage the preparation and publication of (a newspaper, etc.). **2** To compile, arrange and emend for publication: to *edit* memoirs or letters. **3** To correct and prepare (a manuscript, copy, etc.) for publication. [<L *editus,* pp. of *edere* <*ex-* out + *dare* give]

E·dith (ē'dith) A feminine personal name. Also *Ital.* **E·di·ta** (ā'dē·tä), *Lat.* **Ed·i·tha** (ed'i·tä). [OE, rich war]

E·dith Cav·ell Mountain (ē'dith kav'əl) A mountain in Jasper National Park, Alberta, Canada; 11,033 feet.

e·di·tion (i·dish'ən) *n.* **1** A published form of a literary work, or a copy of the form so published. **2** The total number of copies of a book, magazine, newspaper, etc., issued at one time.

é·di·tion de luxe (ā·dē·syôn' də lüks') *French* An elaborate and costly edition, often limited.

e·di·ti·o prin·ceps (i·dish'ē·ō prin'seps) *Latin* First edition, especially of a work printed from manuscript for the first time in the early years of printing.

ed·i·tor (ed'i·tər) *n.* **1** One who prepares manuscripts, copy, etc., for publication. **2** One having charge of a publication.

ed·i·to·ri·al (ed'i·tôr'ē·əl, -tō'rē-) *adj.* Of or pertaining to or emanating from an editor. **—***n.* An article in a journal, or periodical, presumably written by the editor or by his subordinate, and published as an official argument or expression of opinion; a leading article. **—ed'i·to'ri·al·ly** *adv.*

ed·i·to·ri·al·ize (ed'i·tôr'ē·əl·īz', -tō'rē-) *v.t. & v.i.* **·ized, iz·ing 1** To express opinions on (a subject) editorially. **2** To insert editorial opinions into (a news item, etc.).

editorial plural The editorial "we": the first person plural substituted for the first person singular in editorial writing.

editor in chief *pl.* **editors in chief** The chief editor of a publication; the one responsible for carrying out policies.

ed·i·tor·ship (ed'i·tər·ship') *n.* The office and duties of an editor.

Ed·mon·ton (ed'mən·tən) **1** A northern suburb of London. **2** The capital of Alberta province, Canada.

Ed·mund (ed'mənd, *Ger.* et'mōōnt) A masculine personal name. Also *Du.* **Ed·mond** (et'·mônt), *Fr.* **Ed·mond** (ed·môṅ'), *Ital.* **Ed·mon·do** (ed·mōn'dō), *Pg., Sp.* **Ed·mun·do** *(Pg.* ed·mōōn'dōō, *Sp.* -dō). [OE, rich protector]

—Edmund II, 989–1016; king of England 1016: known as *Ironside.* Also spelled *Eadmund.*

Ed·na (ed'nə) A feminine personal name. [< Hebrew, rejuvenation]

E·do (e·dō) A former name for TOKYO.

E·dom (ē'dəm) See IDUMAEA.

E·dom·ite (ē'dəm·īt) *n.* A descendant of Esau, or an inhabitant of Edom. **—E'dom·it'ish** *adj.*

É·douard (ā·dwàr') French form of EDWARD. Also *Ital.* **E·doar·do** (ā·dwär'dō).

ed·u·ca·ble (ej'oo·kə·bəl) *adj.* Capable of being educated.

ed·u·cate (ej'oo·kāt) *v.t.* **·cat·ed, ·cat·ing 1** To develop or train the mind, capabilities, and character of by or as by formal schooling or instruction; teach. **2** To train for some special purpose: He was *educated* for the ministry. **3** To develop and train (taste, special ability, etc.). **4** To provide schooling for. See synonyms under TEACH. [<L *educatus,* pp. of *educare* bring up <*educere.* See EDUCE.] **—ed'u·cat'a·ble** *adj.*

ed·u·cat·ed (ej'ōō·kā'tid) *adj.* **1** Developed and informed by education; instructed; trained. **2** Having a cultivated mind, speech, manner, etc. See synonyms under INTELLIGENT.

ed·u·ca·tion (ej'ōō·kā'shən) *n.* **1** The systematic development and cultivation of the natural powers, by inculcation, example, etc. **2** Instruction and training in an institution of learning. **3** The knowledge and skills resulting from such instruction and training. **4** Teaching as a system, science, or art; pedagogy. **5** The training of animals. **6** The culture of bees, bacteria, etc. **—Education, Office of** See UNITED STATES OFFICE OF EDUCATION. **—ed'u·ca'tion·al** *adj.* **—ed'u·ca'tion·al·ly** *adv.* **—ed'u·ca'tion·ar'y** *adj.*

Synonyms: breeding, cultivation, culture, development, discipline, information, instruction, knowledge, learning, nurture, reading, schooling, study, teaching, training, tuition. *Education* (L. *educere,* to lead or draw out) is the systematic *development* and *cultivation* of the mind and other natural powers. It begins in the nursery, continues through school, and also through life, whether we will or not. *Instruction,* the impartation of *knowledge* by others is but a part of education. *Teaching* is the more familiar and less formal word for *instruction. Training* refers not merely to the impartation of *knowledge,* but to the exercising of one in actions with the design to form habits. *Discipline* is systematic and rigorous *training,* with the idea of subjection to authority and perhaps of punishment. *Tuition* is the technical term for *teaching* as the business of an instructor or as in the routine of a school. We speak of the *teaching, training,* or *discipline,* rather than of the *education* or *tuition* of a dog or a horse. Compare KNOWLEDGE, LEARNING, NURTURE, REFINEMENT, WISDOM. *Antonyms:* ignorance, illiteracy. Compare synonyms for IGNORANT.

ed·u·ca·tion·al·ist (ej'ōō·kā'shən·əl·ist) *n.* **1** One interested in educational forms or methods; one employed in educational pursuits; a practical educator. **2** One versed in educational theories or devoted to educational interests: also **ed'u·ca'tion·ist.**

ed·u·ca·tive (ej'ōō·kā'tiv) *adj.* Instructive; developing; educating.

ed·u·ca·tor (ej'ōō·kā'tər) *n.* A teacher. **—ed'u·ca·to'ry** (-tôr'ē, -tō'rē) *adj.*

e·duce (i·dōōs', i·dyōōs') *v.t.* **e·duced, e·duc·ing 1** To call forth; draw out; evoke. **2** To develop or formulate, as from data or experimentation. [<L *educere* <*ex-* out + *ducere* lead] **—e·duc'i·ble** *adj.* **—e·duc·tive** (i·duk'·tiv) *adj.* **—e·duc'tor** *n.*

e·duct (ē'dukt) *n.* **1** That which is educed; something brought out or developed from another. **2** *Chem.* A substance or body derived from another body in which it originally existed, as opposed to a *product* resulting from chemical change.

e·duc·tion (i·duk'shən) *n.* **1** The act or process of educing. **2** An educt. **3** The act of exhausting, as an engine cylinder, of steam: used in various self–explaining compounds, as **eduction pipe:** now superseded by *exhaust.*

E·dui·no (ā·dwē'nō) Italian form of EDWIN.

e·dul·co·rate (i·dul'kə·rāt) *v.t.* **·rat·ed, ·rat·ing 1** To correct the acidity or acridity of; soften; sweeten. **2** *Chem.* To cleanse or free from soluble acids, salts, etc., by washing with water. [<L *edulcoratus,* pp. of *edulcorare* <*ex-* out + *dulcis* sweet] **—e·dul'co·ra'tion** *n.* **—e·dul'co·ra'tive** *adj.*

Ed·ward (ed'wərd) A masculine personal name. Also *Du., Ger.* **E·duard** (ā'dwärt), *Ital., Pg., Sp.* **E·duar·do** (ā·dwär'dō, *Pg.* -dōō), *Dan.* **Ed·vard** (ed'värth). [OE, rich guardian]

—Edward, 1330–76, prince of Wales; fought at Crécy and Poitiers; son of Edward III: called the "Black Prince."

—Edward, 1004?–66, king of England 1042–1066: known as *Edward the Confessor.*

— **Edward I,** 1239–1307, king of England 1272–1307: known as *Edward Longshanks.*
— **Edward II,** 1284–1327, king of England 1307–27; defeated by Bruce at Bannockburn, 1314; murdered.
— **Edward III,** 1312–77, king of England 1327–77; defeated the Scots and French.
— **Edward IV,** 1442–83, king of England 1461–70, 1471–83; overthrew the Lancastrians.
— **Edward V,** 1470?–83, king of England 1483; murdered in the Tower.
— **Edward VI,** 1537–53, king of England 1547–53; son of Henry VIII and Jane Seymour.
— **Edward VII,** 1841–1910, king of England 1901–10.
— **Edward VIII,** 1894–1972, succeeded his father George V as king of England, Jan. 20, 1936; abdicated Dec. 10, 1936; became the Duke of Windsor.

Edward, Lake A lake in Africa, situated between Uganda and Belgian Congo; 830 square miles: also *Albert Lake.*

Ed·ward·i·an (ed·wär′dē·ən) *adj.* **1** *Law* Relating to Edward I as regards the writs founded on the statute of Gloucester, which enforced the law that a grant in fee simple by a tenant for life, or in dower, caused forfeiture of the entire estate. **2** *Archit.* Indicating the style of the time of the first three Edwards. **3** *Eccl.* Pertaining to the adoption of a new ritual and important changes in church management, under Edward VI. **4** Relating to Edward VII, his reign and especially the literature, manners, and decorative styles characterizing this period.

Ed·wards (ed′wərdz), **Jonathan,** 1703–58, American theologian and preacher.

Edwards Plateau A SE extension of the Great Plains in SW Texas; elevation, 2,500 feet.

Ed·win (ed′win; *Dan.* ed′vin, *Ger.* et′vin) A masculine personal name. Also *Lat.* **Ed·wi·nus** (ed·vī′nəs). [OE, rich friend]
— **Edwin,** 583?–633, king of Northumbria.

ee (ē) *n. Scot.* An eye.

-ee *Suffix of nouns* **1** A person who undergoes the action or receives the benefit of the main element: *payee*: often used in legal terms and opposed to *-er, -or,* as in *grantor, grantee.* **2** A person who is described by the main element: *absentee.* [AF *-é,* suffix of pp. <L *-atus*]

eel (ēl) *n. pl.* **eels** or **eel 1** A voracious teleost fish belonging to the order *Apodes,* having an elongated snakelike body, usually without scales or pelvic fins, and of both marine and fresh-water habitat; especially the **American eel** *(Anguilla bastoniensis)* and the **European eel** *(A. anguilla).* **2** Any of certain other eel-like fishes, as the lamprey, frequently called the lamprey eel, electric eel, etc. **3** An eelworm. [OE *æl*] — **eel′y** *adj.*

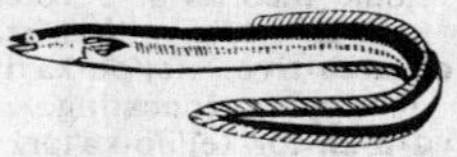

AMERICAN EEL
(Average length under 3 feet, maximum 4 feet)

eel·grass (ēl′gras′, -gräs′) *n.* An herb *(Zostera marina)* of the pondweed family, of grass-like appearance, and growing wholly under water: used as a sound insulator, for packing, etc.

eel·pot (ēl′pot′) *n.* A form of basket for trapping eels.

eel·pout (ēl′pout′) *n. pl.* **·pouts** or **·pout** A marine fish with an eel-like body tapering backward. *Zoarces anguillaris* is the American and *Z. viviparus* the European eelpout. [OE *ælepute*]

eel·worm (ēl′wûrm′) *n.* **1** A threadworm or nematode, especially *Ascaris lumbricoides,* parasitic in the human digestive tract. **2** The vinegar eel.

een (ēn) *n. Scot.* Eyes.

e'en (ēn) *adv. Poetic* Even. — *n. Poetic & Dial.* Evening.

-eer *suffix of nouns and verbs* **1** One who is concerned with, works with, or produces: *engineer*: now often used disdainfully, as in *pamphleteer.* **2** Be concerned with: *electioneer.* [<F *-ier* <L *-arius*]

e'er (âr) *adv. Poetic* Ever.

ee·rie (ē′rē, ir′ē) *adj.* **1** Inspiring fear or awe; weird. **2** Affected by fear; awed. Also **ee′ry.** [ME *eri* timid, var. of *erg* <OE *earg*] — **ee′ri·ly** *adv.* — **ee′ri·ness** *n.*

Ees·ti (ās′tē) The Estonian name for ESTONIA.

ef- Assimilated var. of EX-[1].

E·fa·te (e·fä′tē) A central island of the New Hebrides group; 200 square miles: also *Vaté.*

ef·fa·ble (ef′ə·bəl) *adj.* That can be uttered or explained. [<L *effabilis* <*ex-* out + *fari* speak]

ef·face (i·fās′) *v.t.* **·faced, ·fac·ing 1** To rub out, as written characters; erase; cancel. **2** To obliterate or destroy, as a memory. **3** To make (oneself) inconspicuous or insignificant. See synonyms under CANCEL. [<F *effacer* <L *ex-* out + *facies* face] — **ef·face′a·ble** *adj.* — **ef·face′ment** *n.* — **ef·fac′er** *n.* — **ef·fa′cive** *adj.*

ef·fect (i·fekt′) *n.* **1** A result or product of some cause or agency; a consequence. **2** Practical efficiency. **3** The substance of a statement; gist. **4** Active operation; execution. **5** Fact or reality: following *in.* **6** *pl.* Movable goods. **7** Useful work performed by a machine. **8** A mental state or attitude resulting from observation or external impression: the *effect* of a picture. See synonyms under ACT, CONSEQUENCE, END, OPERATION, PRODUCT. — *v.t.* **1** To bring about; produce as a result; cause. **2** To achieve; accomplish. [<L *effectus,* pp. of *efficere* <*ex-* out + *facere* do, make] — **ef·fect′er** *n.* — **ef·fect′i·ble** *adj.*

Synonyms (verb): accomplish, achieve, close, complete, conclude, consummate, do, end, execute, finish, fulfil, perform, produce, realize. *Effect, execute, consummate,* and *realize* all signify to embody in fact what was before in thought. One may *realize* that which he has done nothing to *bring about*; he may *realize* the dreams of youth by inheriting a fortune; but he cannot *effect* his early designs except by *doing* the utmost that is necessary to make them fact. *Effect* includes all that is *done* to *accomplish* the intent; *execute* refers rather to the formal steps; *consummate* is limited quite sharply to the concluding act. Care must be taken to distinguish between *effect* and *affect.* An officer *executes* the law when he proceeds against its violators; a purchase is *consummated* when the money is paid and the property delivered. *Execute* refers more commonly to the commands of another, *effect* and *consummate* to one's own designs; as, The commander *effected* the capture of the fort, because his officers and men promptly *executed* his commands. See ACCOMPLISH, DO[1], MAKE.

ef·fec·tive (i·fek′tiv) *adj.* **1** Producing, or adapted to produce, an effect; efficient. **2** Impressive; moving, as oratory. **3** In force, as a law. **4** Ready, as an army. — *n.* **1** One who is fit for duty. **2** The number of men available for active service: a war *effective* of 250,000. **3** That which effects; a cause. **4** Silver or gold currency, as distinguished from paper; coin. See synonyms under EFFICIENT, POWERFUL. — **ef·fec′tive·ly** *adv.* — **ef·fec′tive·ness** *n.*

ef·fec·tor (i·fek′tər) *n. Physiol.* A specialized structure at the periphery of a motor nerve, as a muscle or gland, serving to transform efferent nerve impulses into physical action, or to innervate them. Compare RECEPTOR.

ef·fec·tu·al (i·fek′chōō·əl) *adj.* **1** Possessing or exercising adequate power to produce a designed effect; completely efficient; efficacious: *effectual* measures. **2** In force; legal, as a rule or law. See synonyms under POWERFUL. [<OF *effectuel* <LL *effectualis* <*effectus.* See EFFECT.] — **ef·fec′tu·al′i·ty** (-al′ə·tē) *n.* — **ef·fec′tu·al·ness** *n.*

ef·fec·tu·al·ly (i·fek′chōō·əl·ē) *adv.* With effect; actually; truly.

ef·fec·tu·ate (i·fek′chōō·āt) *v.t.* **·at·ed, ·at·ing** To make effectual; effect. [<F *effectuer* <L *effectus.* See EFFECT.] — **ef·fec′tu·a′tion** *n.*

ef·fem·i·na·cy (i·fem′ə·nə·sē) *n.* The quality of being effeminate; womanishness.

ef·fem·i·nate (i·fem′ə·nit) *adj.* Having womanish traits or qualities; unmanly; voluptuous; delicate. See synonyms under FEMININE. [<L *effeminatus,* pp. of *effeminare* <*ex-* out + *femina* a woman] — **ef·fem′i·nate·ly** *adv.* — **ef·fem′i·nate·ness** *n.*

ef·fen·di (i·fen′dē) *n.* A title of respect in Turkey: sir; master. [<Turkish *efendi,* ult. <Gk. *authentēs* master]

ef·fer·ent (ef′ər·ənt) *adj. Physiol.* Carrying or carried outward, as impulses from the central nervous system to muscles, the cells of glands, etc.; discharging: opposed to *afferent.* — *n.* **1** An efferent duct, vessel, or nerve. **2** A stream carrying off water, as from a pond. [<L *efferens, -entis,* ppr. of *efferre* <*ex-* out + *ferre* carry]

ef·fer·vesce (ef′ər·ves′) *v.i.* **·vesced, ·vesc·ing 1** To bubble up; give off bubbles of gas, as water charged with carbon dioxide. **2** To come away in bubbles, as a gas. **3** To show exhilaration or lively spirits. [<L *effervescere* <*ex-* out + *fervescere* boil, inceptive of *fervere* be hot]

ef·fer·ves·cence (ef′ər·ves′əns) *n.* **1** The escape of bubbles of gas from a liquid otherwise than by boiling, or the condition of a substance resulting therefrom. **2** A bubbling up: the *effervescence* of a carbonate with an acid. **3** Irrepressible excitement or emotion. Also **ef′fer·ves′cen·cy.** [<L *effervescens, -entis,* ppr. of *effervescere.* See EFFERVESCE.]

ef·fer·ves·cent (ef′ər·ves′ənt) *adj.* **1** Giving off bubbles of gas; coming off in bubbles, as gas from a liquid. **2** Effervescing, or having the property of effervescing. — **ef′fer·ves′ci·ble** *adj.* — **ef′fer·ves′cive** *adj.*

ef·fete (i·fēt′) *adj.* Worn out and incapable of further production, as an animal, a plant, or soil; exhausted; barren. [<L *effetus* <*ex-* out + *fetus* a breeding] — **ef·fete′ness** *n.*

ef·fi·ca·cious (ef′ə·kā′shəs) *adj.* Producing or capable of producing an intended effect; having efficacy. See synonyms under EFFICIENT, POWERFUL. [<L *efficax, -cacis* <*efficere.* See EFFECT.] — **ef′fi·ca′cious·ly** *adv.* — **ef′fi·ca′cious·ness** *n.*

ef·fi·ca·cy (ef′ə·kə·sē) *n. pl.* **·cies** Power to produce an effect; effective energy. See synonyms under POWER, WEIGHT.

ef·fi·cien·cy (i·fish′ən·sē) *n. pl.* **·cies 1** The character of being efficient; effectiveness. **2** The ratio of the work done or energy expended by an organism or machine to the energy supplied in the form of food or fuel. Also **ef·fi′cience.** See synonyms under ABILITY, POWER.

ef·fi·cient (i·fish′ənt) *adj.* **1** Acting or having power to act effectually; competent: an *efficient* leader. **2** Productive of effects; causative. — *n.* **1** A qualified person; specifically, in the British Army, a volunteer certified for his qualifications. **2** An efficient cause. [<L *efficiens, -entis,* ppr. of *efficere.* See EFFECT.] — **ef·fi′cient·ly** *adv.*

Synonyms (adj.): effective, effectual, efficacious. That is *effective* which accomplishes an intended effect with emphasis, decision, and certainty; that is *effectual* which acts with such finality as to leave no more to be done. A person may be said to be *efficient* in general character or action; as, an *efficient* businessman; he may be called *effective* in some special relation; as, an *effective* speaker; the *efficient* person is habitually energetic, industrious, sagacious, and alert; a man may be an *effective* speaker on occasion who is not *efficient* in ordinary life. *Efficacious* and *effectual* are not used of persons. *Antonyms*: awkward, dull, feckless, feeble, fruitless, idle, ineffective, ineffectual, inefficacious, inefficient, inoperative, negligent, powerless, remiss, unavailing, useless, vain.

efficient cause The immediate force or agent in the performance of work.

ef·fi·gy (ef′ə·jē) *n. pl.* **·gies 1** A figure representing a person, as in sculpture or numismatics. **2** A representation of a person who has incurred odium. — **to burn** (or **hang**) **in effigy** To burn or hang publicly an image of a person who is hated. [<F *effigie* <L *effigies* <*ex-* out + *fingere* fashion] — **ef·fig·i·al** (e·fij′ē·əl) *adj.*

ef·fla·tion (i·flā′shən) *n.* That which is blown or breathed forth; an emanation. [<L *efflatus* <*ex-* out + *flare* blow]

ef·fleu·rage (e·flœ·räzh′) *n. French* A gentle rubbing with the palm of the hand; massage.

ef·flo·resce (ef′lô·res′, -lō-) *v.i.* **·resced, ·resc·ing 1** *Bot.* To blossom, bloom, or flower. **2** *Chem.* **a** To become powdery, wholly or in part, and lose crystalline structure through loss of water of crystallization on exposure to the air. **b** To become covered with a crust of saline particles left by evaporation, as the ground. [<L *efflorescere* <*ex-* thoroughly + *florescere* bloom <*flos, floris* a flower]

ef·flo·res·cence (ef′lô·res′əns, -lō-) *n.* **1** *Bot.* The time or act of flowering. **2** *Pathol.* A rash on the skin. **3** The process, act, or result of efflorescing. **4** A crystalline deposit on the

surface of a mineral or on the face of a stone wall. Also **ef′flo·res′cen·cy.**

ef·flo·res·cent (ef′lô·res′ənt, -lo-) adj. **1** Bot. Blossoming out; blooming. **2** Tending or liable to effloresce. **3** Chem. **a** Forming into white threads or powder. **b** Covered with efflorescence. [<L efflorescens, -entis, ppr. of efflorescere. See EFFLORESCE.]

ef·flu·ence (ef′lŏŏ·əns) n. A flowing out; emanation. Also **ef′flu·en·cy.**

ef·flu·ent (ef′lŏŏ·ənt) adj. Flowing out. —n. **1** Sewage after purification treatment. **2** An outflow, as of water from a lake or stream. [<L effluens, -entis, ppr. of effluere < ex- out + fluere flow]

ef·flu·vi·um (i·flŏŏ′vē·əm) n. pl. ·vi·a (-vē·ə) **1** An invisible emanation. **2** A noxious or ill-smelling exhalation from decaying matter: commonly in the plural, the effluvia from foul drains. **3** A theoretic imponderable agent formerly regarded as the source of the electric and magnetic forces of certain substances. [<L, a flowing out] —**ef·flu′vi·al, ef·flu′vi·ous** adj.

ef·flux (ef′luks) n. An outflow; effluence; emanation; effluvium. [<L effluxus <ex- out + fluere flow]

ef·flux·ion (i·fluk′shən) n. **1** A flowing forth; hence, lapse, as of time. **2** That which flows forth; emanation, outpouring.

ef·fort (ef′ərt) n. **1** A voluntary exertion of power; strenuous endeavor; attempt. **2** A result or display of consciously directed power; an achievement. **3** Mech. Force exerted against the inertia of a body. See synonyms under ENDEAVOR, INDUSTRY. [<F < efforcer <L ex- out + fortis strong]

ef·fort·less (ef′ərt·lis) adj. Showing or making no effort; easy. —**ef′fort·less·ly** adv.

ef·front·er·y (i·frun′tər·ē) n. pl. ·er·ies Insolent assurance; audacity; impudence. [<F effronterie <OF esfront shameless <LL effrons <ex- out + frons, frontis forehead, face]

Synonyms: assurance, audacity, boldness, brass, hardihood, impudence, insolence, shamelessness. *Audacity*, in the sense here considered, is a reckless defiance of law, decency, public opinion, or personal rights, claims, or views, approaching the meaning of *impudence* or *shamelessness*, but always carrying the thought of the personal risk that one disregards in such defiance; the merely *impudent* or *shameless* person may take no thought of consequences; the *audacious* person recognizes and recklessly braves them. *Hardihood* defies and disregards the rational judgment of men. *Effrontery* (L effrons bare-faced, shameless) adds to *audacity* and *hardihood* the special element of defiance of considerations of propriety, duty, and respect for others, yet not to the extent implied in *impudence* or *shamelessness*. Impudence disregards what is due to superiors: *shamelessness* defies decency. *Boldness* is forward-stepping courage, spoken of with reference to the presence and observation of others; *boldness*, in the good sense, is courage viewed from the outside; but the word is frequently used in an unfavorable sense to indicate a lack of proper sensitiveness and modesty. Compare ASSURANCE, BRAVE, IMPUDENCE. *Antonyms:* bashfulness, coyness, diffidence, modesty, sensitiveness, shrinking, shyness, timidity.

ef·fulge (i·fulj′) v.t. & v.i. **·fulged, ·fulg·ing** To shine forth; radiate. [<L effulgere < ex- out + fulgere shine]

ef·ful·gence (i·ful′jəns) n. A shining forth brilliantly; beaming brightness; splendor. [<L effulgens, -entis, ppr. of effulgere. See EFFULGE.] —**ef·ful′gent** adj. —**ef·ful′gent·ly** adv.

ef·fuse (i·fyŏŏs′) adj. **1** Bot. Spreading loosely, as the panicle of the common rush, or spreading flat, as the plant body of some thallophytic epiphytes. **2** Bacteriol. Profuse, as a thin spreading film of bacteria in a culture. **3** Entomol. Composed of loosely joined parts; not compact, as an insect's body. **4** Zool. Having the lips separated by a groove, as a shell; expanded. **5** Obs. Poured out freely; profuse. —v. (i·fyŏŏz′) **·fused, ·fus·ing** v.t. **1** To pour forth; shed. —v.i. **2** To emanate; exude. **3** Physics To flow through a porous diaphragm or aperture under pressure: said

of gases. [<L effusus, pp. of effundere < ex- out + fundere pour]

ef·fu·sion (i·fyŏŏ′zhən) n. **1** The act or process of pouring forth, or that which is poured forth. **2** An outpouring, as of fancy or sentiment: applied ironically to literary compositions. **3** Sentimental demonstration. **4** Pathol. The pouring out of the blood or other fluid, as into the cellular tissue. **5** Physics The flow of gases under pressure through openings in the container.

ef·fu·sive (i·fyŏŏ′siv) adj. **1** Overflowing with sentiment; demonstrative; gushing. **2** Pouring forth; shedding abroad: with of. —**ef·fu′sive·ly** adv. —**ef·fu′sive·ness** n.

effusive rocks Geol. Volcanic material poured out and solidified on the surface of the earth.

Ef·ik (ef′ik) n. pl. **Ef·ik 1** One of a Negro people inhabiting Nigeria. **2** The language of these people, showing Sudanic characteristics.

eft[1] (eft) n. **1** A newt. **2** Formerly, a small lizard. [OE efeta]

eft[2] (eft) adv. Obs. Again; afterwards. [OE]

eft·soon (eft′sŏŏn′) adv. Obs. Soon afterward or again; hence, speedily; quickly; also, often. Also **eft′soons′.** [OE eftsona immediately afterwards]

e·gad (i·gad′, ē·gad′) interj. By God!: a mild oath. [Prob. alter. of ah, God!]

Eg·a·di Islands (eg′ə·dē) An island group in the Mediterranean off western Sicily; total, 15 square miles: ancient Aegates: also Aegadian Islands, Aegaedean Islands.

e·gal (ē′gəl) Obs. adj. Equal. —n. An equal. [<F égal]

e·gal·i·tar·i·an (i·gal′ə·târ′ē·ən) n. One who believes in or works for equal rights. —adj. Equalitarian. [<F égalitaire] —**e·gal′i·tar′i·an·ism** n.

é·ga·li·té (ā·gà·lē·tā′) n. French Equality.

Eg·bert (eg′bərt) A masculine personal name. Also Ital. **Eg·ber·to** (eg·ber′tō), Lat. **Eg·ber·tus** (eg·bûr′təs). [OE, bright sword] — **Egbert,** 775?-839; king of Wessex 802-839; king of England 827-839.

E·ger (ā′gər) A river in Bavaria and western Bohemia, flowing 159 miles east to the Elbe: Czech Ohře.

E·ge·ri·a (i·jir′ē·ə) **1** In Roman legend, an Italian nymph who was the wife and adviser of Numa, second king of Rome. **2** Any woman adviser.

e·gest (ē·jest′) v.t. To eject or void, as feces or perspiration; excrete. [<L egestus, pp. of egerere < ex- out + gerere carry]

e·ges·ta (ē·jes′tə) n. Excreta: opposed to ingesta. [<L, neut. pl. of egestus. See EGEST.]

e·ges·tion (ē·jes′chən) n. The expulsion or voiding of digested matter; defecation.

e·ges·tive (ē·jes′tiv) adj. Excretory: opposed to ingestive.

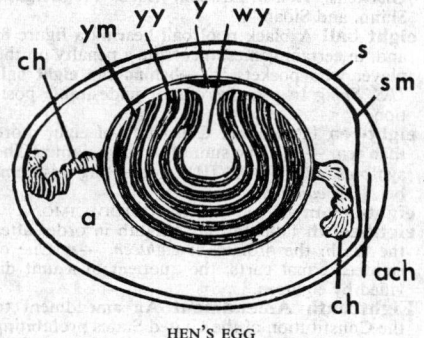

HEN'S EGG

ch. Chalazae.	s.	Shell.
ym. Yolk membrane.	sm.	Shell membrane.
yy. Yellow food yolk.	ach.	Air chamber.
y. Germinal vesicle.	a.	Albumin, or white of the egg.
wy. White yolk.		

egg[1] (eg) n. **1** A reproductive body containing the germ and the food yolk of birds, insects,

reptiles, or fishes, enclosed in a membranous or shell-like covering. **2** In common usage, such a body, especially that of the domestic fowl. See also illustration under EMBRYOLOGY, FROG. **3** The female reproductive cell of animals which, when fertilized, becomes a zygote; an ovum or germ cell. **4** Something like or likened to an egg. **5** Figuratively, that which contains a germ. —v.t. **1** To mix or cover with eggs. **2** U.S. To pelt with eggs. —v.i. **3** To collect birds' eggs. —**lay an egg** U.S. Slang To fail: said of a play, joke, etc. [<OE æg]

egg[2] (eg) v.t. To instigate or incite; urge: usually with on. [<ON eggja]

egg-and-an·chor (eg′ənd·ang′kər) n. Archit. An ornamental molding carved with series of alternate egg-shaped and anchor-shaped, or dart- or tongue-shaped figures. Also **egg′-and-dart′, egg′-and-tongue′.**

EGG-AND-ANCHOR MOLDING

egg-beat·er (eg′bē′tər) n. A kitchen utensil for beating an egg after it has been removed from the shell.

eg·ger (eg′ər) n. **1** Any of several European moths (genera Lasiocampa and Eriogaster). **2** The tent caterpillar. Also called **eg′ger moth.** Also spelled **eg′gar.** [Prob. <EGG, with ref. to the shape of the cocoon]

egg·head (eg′hed′) n. U.S. Slang An intellectual; a highbrow: usually slightly derisive.

egg-lay·ing (eg′lā′ing) adj. Oviparous.

Eg·gle·ston (eg′əl·stən), **Edward,** 1837-1902, U.S. clergyman and novelist. — **George Cary,** 1839-1911, U.S. writer; brother of preceding.

Egg·mühl (ek′mül) See ECKMÜHL.

egg·nog (eg′nog′) n. A drink made of beaten eggs and milk with sugar and nutmeg and sometimes with brandy, rum, or other liquor. [<EGG + NOG (def. 1)]

egg·plant (eg′plant′, -plänt′) n. **1** A widely cultivated herb (Solanum melongena) of the nightshade family, with large egg-shaped edible fruit. **2** The fruit, used as a vegetable. **3** A very dark blackish-purple; the color of the skin of the eggplant.

egg·shell (eg′shel′) n. **1** The hard, brittle, outer envelope of an egg. **2** A light ivory shade; the color commonly associated with that of a hen's egg. **2** A very thin and delicate porcelain: also **eggshell china, eggshell porcelain.**

egg tray A tray to hold eggs in an incubator. See illustration under INCUBATOR.

egg white The albumen of an egg as distinguished from the yolk: also white of egg.

E·gi·di·us (i·jid′ē·əs, Du., Ger. ā·gē′ē·dŏŏs) Dutch and German form of GILES. Also Fr. **É·gide** (ā·zhēd′), Ital. **E·gi·dio** (ā·jē′dyō).

e·gis (ē′jis) See AEGIS.

eg·lan·tine (eg′lən·tīn, -tēn) n. Either of two roselike plants, the sweetbrier, and the dog rose. Also Obs. **eg·la·tere** (eg′lə·tir′). [<F églantine <OF aiglent, ult. <L acus needle]

Eg·mont (eg′mont) An extinct volcano on North Island, New Zealand; 8,260 feet: Maori Taranaki.

Eg·mont (eg′mont, Flemish ekh′mônt), **Lamoral,** 1522-68, Count of Egmont, Flemish general and statesman.

e·go (ē′gō, eg′ō) n. pl. **e·gos 1** Self, considered as the seat of consciousness. **2** In philosophy, the entire man, body and mind. **3** Psychol. The self, considered as the aggregate of all conscious acts and states, whether organized or sporadic, but having a unity and continuity differentiating it from all others. **4** Psychoanal. The superficial conscious part of the id, developed in response to the physical and social environment. **5** In metaphysics, the permanent real being to whom all the conscious states and attributes belong. **6** Colloq. Self-centeredness; egotism; conceit. [<L, I]

e·go·cen·tric (ē′gō·sen′trik, eg′ō-) adj. **1** Self-centered; reacting to all things from a personal point of view; caring only for self or personal interests. **2** Philos. Proceeding from self as the center, as one's knowledge of the nature of the outside world. —**e′go·cen′tric·i·ty** (-sen·tris′ə·tē) n.

e·go·ism (ē′gō·iz′əm, eg′ō-) *n.* **1** In ethics, the doctrine that the supreme end of human conduct is the perfection or happiness of the ego, or self, and that all virtue consists in the pursuit of self-interest; also, that part of the theory or practice of conduct or duty that has reference to oneself, as distinguished from *altruism.* **2** Selfishness. **3** Egotism. See synonyms under EGOTISM.

e·go·ist (ē′gō·ist, eg′ō-) *n.* One who advocates or practices egoism.

e·go·is·tic (ē′gō·is′tik, eg′ō-) *adj.* **1** Characterized by inordinate regard for self. **2** Of or pertaining to self. **3** Egotistic. Also **e′go·is′ti·cal.** —**e′go·is′ti·cal·ly** *adv.*

e·go·ma·ni·a (ē′gō·mā′nē·ə, -mān′yə, eg′ō-) *n.* Abnormal or excessive egotism. —**e′go·ma′·ni·ac** *n.* & adj.

E·gor·evsk (yi·gôr′yifsk) See YEGORYEVSK.

e·go·tism (ē′gə·tiz′əm, eg′ə-) *n.* The habit or practice of thinking and talking much of oneself, or the spirit that leads to this practice; self-exaltation.

Synonyms: conceit, egoism, self-assertion, self-conceit, self-confidence, self-consciousness, self-esteem, vanity. *Egoism* is the giving the "I" undue supremacy in thought; *egotism* is giving the "I" undue prominence in speech and action. *Self-assertion* is the claim of what one believes to be his due; *self-conceit* is an overestimate of one's own powers or deserts. *Self-consciousness* (as here considered) is the keeping of one's thoughts upon oneself, with the constant anxious question of what others will think. *Vanity* is an overweening admiration of self, craving equal admiration from others. *Self-esteem* is more solid and better founded than *self-conceit*; but is ordinarily a weakness, and never has the worthy sense of *self-confidence.* Compare ASSURANCE, PRIDE. *Antonyms*: bashfulness, deference, diffidence, humility, modesty, self-distrust, self-forgetfulness, shyness, unobtrusiveness, unostentatiousness.

e·go·tist (ē′gə·tist, eg′ə-) *n.* One characterized by egotism. —**e′go·tis′ti·cal** *adj.* —**e′go·tis′·ti·cal·ly** *adv.*

e·gre·gious (i·grē′jəs, -jē·əs) *adj.* **1** Flagrant; outstanding in bad or evil qualities. **2** *Obs.* Prominent; protuberant. See synonyms under EXTRAORDINARY, NOTORIOUS. [<L *egregius*, outstanding <*ex-* out + *grex, gregis* herd] —**e·gre′gious·ly** *adv.* —**e·gre′gious·ness** *n.*

e·gress (ē′gres) *n.* **1** A going out; passing forth, as from a building. **2** A place of exit. **3** *Astron.* The end of the apparent passage of a small body over the face of a larger one, as the end of an eclipse. Also **e·gres′sion.** [<L *egressus* <*ex-* out + *gradi* go]

e·gret (ē′grit) *n.* **1** A heron characterized, in the breeding season, by long and loose plumes drooping over the tail, and usually white plumage; especially, the American egret (*Casmerodius albus*), and the snowy egret (*Egretta thula*). **2** A plume or tuft of its feathers, called an *aigrette.* [Var. of AIGRET]

SNOWY EGRET
(Length of body about 2 feet)

E·gypt (ē′jipt) A republic of NE Africa; 386,186 square miles, of which about 12,000 square miles are cultivated; capital, Cairo; divided into **Lower Egypt,** the Nile Delta, and **Upper Egypt,** the Nile Valley between a point a few miles south of Cairo and the Sudan. Officially *Arab Republic of Egypt.*

E·gyp·tian (i·jip′shən) *adj.* Of or pertaining to Egypt, its people, or their culture. —*n.* **1** One of the people of Egypt, ancient or modern. **2** The Hamitic language of Egypt, in its final stage called Coptic, and superseded, about 1500, by Arabic. **3** *Obs.* A gipsy.

Egyptian blue A blue pigment made from a mixture of copper silicates and widely used by the early Egyptians, Cretans, and Romans: now imitated by coal-tar colors.

Egyptian hallel See HALLEL.

E·gyp·tian·ize (i·jip′shən·īz) *v.t.* & *v.i.* **·ized, ·iz·ing** To make or act like an Egyptian or the Egyptians.

Egyptian lily See under CALLA.

E·gyp·tol·o·gist (ē′jip·tol′ə·jist) *n.* A student of or one versed in Egyptology. Also **E′gyp·tol′o·ger.**

E·gyp·tol·o·gy (ē′jip·tol′ə·jē) *n.* The science or scientific investigation or study of the antiquities of Egypt. —**E·gyp·to·log·ic** (ē·jip′tə·loj′ik), or **·i·cal** *adj.*

eh (ā, e) *interj.* What: used as an interrogative.

Eh·ren·breit·stein (ā′rən·brīt′shtīn) A fortress on the Rhine opposite Coblenz, Germany: called *Gibraltar of the Rhine.*

Eh·ren·burg (ā′rən·bŏŏrkh), **Ilya Grigorievich,** 1891–1967, U.S.S.R. writer.

Ehr·lich (âr′likh), **Paul,** 1854–1915, German bacteriologist.

ei·dent (ī′dənt) *adj. Scot.* Diligent; industrious. Also spelled *eydent.*

ei·der (ī′dər) *n.* A large sea duck of northern regions (genus *Somateria*), having plumage mostly white above and black below. Also **eider duck.** [<ON *ædhr-* in *ædhar-dūn* eider down; infl. in form by Sw. *eider* eider]

Ei·der (ī′dər) A river in NW Germany, flowing 117 miles NE to the North Sea.

eider down **1** The down of the eider used for stuffing pillows and quilts. **2** A warm, lightweight cotton or woolen fabric with a woolen nap. [<ON *ædhar-dūn*]

ei·det·ic (ī·det′ik) *adj. Psychol.* Of or pertaining to the faculty, voluntary or otherwise, of clearly visualizing objects previously seen. [<Gk. *eidētikos* pertaining to images]

eidetic imagery *Psychol.* The phenomenon of visual reproduction of previously seen objects: usually associated with pre-adolescent children.

ei·do·graph (ī′də·graf, -gräf) *n.* An instrument for copying drawings, usually on a reduced scale. [<Gk. *eidos* form + -GRAPH]

ei·do·lon (ī·dō′lən) *n. pl.* **·la** (-lə) **1** A representation; image. **2** A phantom. [<Gk. *eidōlon* image]

Ei·fel (ī′fəl) A desolate plateau region of western Germany between the Rhine, the Moselle, and the Ardennes; 2,447 feet high.

Eif·fel (ī′fəl, *Fr.* ā·fel′), **Alexandre Gustave,** 1832–1923, French engineer; pioneer in aerodynamics.

Eiffel Tower An iron tower in Paris, 984.25 feet high: designed for the Exposition of 1889 by A. G. Eiffel.

eight (āt) *n.* **1** The cardinal number following seven and preceding nine, or any of the symbols (8, viii, VIII) used to represent it. ◆ Collateral adjective: *octonary.* **2** Anything made up of eight units or members, as the crew of a racing shell, or a playing card with eight pips. —*adj.* Being or consisting of one more than seven; twice four. [OE *eahta*]

Eight, The A group of U.S. painters who opposed sentimentalism and academicism, but who varied widely in their individual work. The group, organized in 1908, included Davies, Glackens, Henri, Lawson, Luks, Prendergast, Shinn, and Sloan.

eight ball A black pool ball bearing a figure 8, and, in certain games, incurring a penalty on the player who pockets it. —**behind the eight ball** *U.S. Slang* In a dangerous or undesirable position.

eight·een (ā′tēn′) *adj.* Consisting of eight more than ten. —*n.* **1** The sum of ten and eight. **2** The symbols (18, xviii, XVIII) representing this number. [OE *eahtatēne*]

eight·een·mo (ā′tēn′mō′) See OCTODECIMO.

eight·eenth (ā′tēnth′) *adj.* Eighth in order after the tenth: the ordinal of *eighteen.* —*n.* One of eighteen equal parts; the quotient of a unit divided by eighteen.

Eighteenth Amendment An amendment to the Constitution of the United States prohibiting the manufacture, sale, and transportation of intoxicating liquors for beverage purposes: ratified in 1919 and put into effect, January, 1920: repealed in 1933 by the Twenty-first Amendment.

eight·fold (āt′fōld′) *adv.* So as to be eight times as many or as great; octuplicate. —*adj.* **1** Consisting of eight parts. **2** Eight times as many or as great.

eighth (ātth, āth) *adj.* **1** Next in order after the seventh. **2** Being one of eight equal parts. —*adv.* In the eighth order, place, or rank: also, in formal discourse, **eighth′ly.** —*n.* An eighth number or part.

eighth note *Music* A quaver.

eight·i·eth (ā′tē·ith) *adj.* **1** Tenth in order after the seventieth. **2** Being one of eighty equal parts. —*n.* **1** One of eighty equal parts. **2** That which follows the seventy-ninth.

eight·score (āt′skôr′, -skōr′) *adj.* & *n.* Eight times twenty.

eight·y (ā′tē) *adj.* Consisting of ten more than seventy. —*n.* **1** Eight times ten. **2** The symbols (80, lxxx, LXXX) representing this number. [OE *eahtatig*]

eight·y-nin·er (ā′tē·nī′nər) *n.* One of the Oklahoma homestead settlers of 1889.

ei·gon (ī′gon) *n. Med.* A compound of iodine with certain protein substances: used as an antiseptic.

Eijk·man (īk′män), **Christian,** 1858–1930, Dutch physician; pioneer in nutrition.

ei·kon (ī′kon) See ICON.

eild (ēld) *n. Scot.* Eld; old age.

eild·ing (ēl′ding) *n. Scot.* Elding; fuel; rubbish.

Ei·leen (ī·lēn′) Irish form of HELEN.

-ein Var. of -IN.

Eind·ho·ven (īnt′hō·vən) A city in south Netherlands.

ein·korn (īn′kôrn) *n.* A variety of wheat (*Triticum monococcum*) with narrow, slender curved spikelets usually bearing only one fertile floret; one-grained wheat: cultivated especially in central Europe. [<G; trans. of NL *monococcum*, species name <Gk. *monos* one + *kokkos* grain]

Ein·stein (īn′stīn), **Albert,** 1878–1955, mathematical physicist, developed the theory of relativity; born in Germany, active in Switzerland and the United States.

ein·stein·i·um (īn·stīn′ē·əm) *n.* A synthetic transuranium element (symbol Es, atomic number 99) originally detected in the debris of a thermonuclear explosion, the most stable isotope having a half-life of 276 days. See PERIODIC TABLE. [after Albert *Einstein*]

Eint·ho·ven (īnt′hō·vən), **Willem,** 1860–1927, Dutch physiologist.

Eir·e (âr′ə) A former name for the REPUBLIC OF IRELAND.

Eire·ann (âr′ən) *adj. Irish* Of Ireland.

Ei·re·ne (ī·rā′nə) Greek form of Irene.

Ei·sen·ach (ī′zə·näkh) A city in Thuringia, central Germany.

Ei·sen·how·er (ī′zən·hou′ər), **Dwight David,** 1890–1969, president of the United States 1953–61; supreme commander of Allied forces in invasion of Europe, World War II.

Ei·sen·stadt (ī′zən·shtät) The capital of Burgenland, Austria.

Ei·ser·nes Tor (ī′zer·nəs tôr′) The German name for IRON GATE.

eis·tedd·fod (ā·steth′vod, es·teth′-) *n. pl.* **·fods** or **·fod·au** (-vod′ī) An annual assembly of bards, in Wales, to foster national, musical, and literary interests. Also **eis′tedd′vod.** [<Welsh, session <*eistedd* sit] —**eis′tedd·fod′ic** *adj.*

ei·ther (ē′thər, ī′-) *adj.* **1** One or the other of two: Use *either* foot on the pedal. **2** Each of two; one and the other: on *either* side. See synonyms under EVERY. —*pron.* One of two; one or the other. —*conj.* In one of two or more cases, indeterminately or indifferently: used as a disjunctive correlative introducing a first alternative, the second and any other being preceded by *or*: *Either* I shall go *or* he will come. —*adv.* At all; any more so: used after the denial of an alternative: He could not speak, and I could not *either.* [OE *ægther*]

ei·ther-or (ē′thər·ôr′, ī′thər-) *adj.* Offering a choice between two alternatives, with other possibilities excluded.

e·jac·u·late (i·jak′yə·lāt) *v.* **·lat·ed, ·lat·ing** *v.t.* **1** To say vehemently and suddenly. **2** To throw out suddenly; eject, as fluids from the body. —*v.i.* **3** To exclaim. See synonyms under CALL, EXCLAIM. [<L *ejaculatus*, pp. of *ejaculari* <*ex-* out + *jaculari* throw] —**e·jac′u·la′tive** *adj.* —**e·jac′u·la′tor** *n.*

e·jac·u·la·tion (i·jak′yə·lā′shən) *n.* **1** The uttering of brief, sudden exclamations; an exclamation. **2** *Eccl.* A brief prayer; a short, pious utterance. **3** *Physiol.* The forceful expulsion of semen during the orgasm; an emission.

e·jac·u·la·to·ry (i·jak′yə·lə·tôr′ē, -tō′rē) *adj.* **1** In the form or of the nature of an ejaculation; exclamatory. **2** Pertaining to or using ejaculation, in any sense.

e·ject (i·jekt′) *v.t.* **1** To throw or drive out by sudden force; expel. **2** To evict. See synonyms under BANISH. —*n.* (ē′jekt) *Psychol.* A

perception, mental state, etc. (of another) inferred as an entity by one's own consciousness, but which is essentially inaccessible to consciousness. [< L *ejectus*, pp. of *ejicere* < *ex-* out + *jacere* throw] **—e·jec′tor** *n.*

e·jec·ta (i·jek′tə) *n. pl.* Matter or refuse that has been cast out, as by a volcano or the body. Also **e·jec·ta·men·ta** (i·jek′tə·men′tə). [< L, neut. pl. of *ejectus*. See EJECT.]

e·jec·ta·ble (i·jek′tə·bəl) *adj.* Capable of being ejected.

e·jec·tion (i·jek′shən) *n.* **1** The act of ejecting; expulsion. **2** Matter ejected. **—e·jec′tive** *adj.* **—e·jec′tive·ly** *adv.*

e·ject·ment (i·jekt′mənt) *n.* **1** A casting out; eviction. **2** *Law* An action to recover posession of real estate, with damages for wrongful withholding; also, the writ by which this action is instituted.

ejector seat A pilot's seat which can be catapulted from an aircraft, thus enabling the pilot to bail out at high speeds.

e·ji·do (ā·hē′thō) *n.* A communal farm, specifically in Mexico. [< Sp.]

Ej·mi·a·dzin (ech′mē·ä·dzēn′) See ECHMIADZIN.

E·ka·te·ri·na (ä′kä·tə·rē′nə) Russian form of CATHERINE.

E·ka·te·rin·burg (ye·kä′tye·rin·bo͝orkh′) A former name for SVERDLOVSK.

E·ka·te·ri·no·dar (ye·kä′tye·rē′nô·där) A former name for KRASNODAR.

E·ka·te·ri·no·slav (ye·kä′tye·rē′nô·släf) A former name for DNEPROPETROVSK.

eke[1] (ēk) *v.t.* **eked, ek·ing 1** To supplement; make small additions to; piece out: usually with *out.* **2** To obtain or produce (a living) with difficulty. **3** *Obs.* To protract; lengthen; increase. *—n. Obs.* An addition, as to a bell rope; postscript; appendix. [Var. of ECHE]

eke[2] (ēk) *adv. & cong. Archaic* Likewise; also. [OE *ēac*]

e·kis·tics (i·kis′tiks) *n. pl.* (*construed as sing.*) The study of human settlements, including area planning and the relationship between communities. [< Gk. *oikos* habitat + -ICS] **—e·kis′tic** *adj.*

ek·ka (ek′ə) *n.* A one-horse vehicle used in India. [< Hind. *ekkā* < *ek* one]

El (el) *n.* An elevated railroad. Also *L.* [Short for ELEVATED]

el- Assimilated var. of EN-[2].

e·lab·o·rate (i·lab′ə·rāt) *v.* **·rat·ed, ·rat·ing** *v.t.* **1** To create and work out with care and in detail: to *elaborate* a system. **2** To produce by labor; make. *—v.i.* **3** To speak or write so as to embellish a matter, subject, etc., with additional details; be more specific: with *on* or *upon.* *—adj.* (-ər·it) Developed in detail with care or painstaking; carefully wrought out; done with thoroughness or exactness. [< L *elaboratus*, pp. of *elaborare* < *e-* out + *laborare* work] **—e·lab′o·rate·ly** *adv.* **—e·lab′o·rate·ness** *n.* **—e·lab′o·ra′tion** *n.* **—e·lab′o·ra′tive** *adj.* **—e·lab′o·ra′tor** *n.*

e·lae·o·lite (i·lē′ə·līt) *n.* A coarsely crystallized or massive opaque variety of nephelite with a resinous luster: also spelled *eleolite.* [< Gk. *elaion* oil + -LITE]

el·ae·op·tene (el′ē·op′tēn) *n. Chem.* The liquid hydrocarbon or terpene constituent of an essential oil: distinguished from *stearoptene.* [< Gk. *elaion* oil + *ptenos* flying]

El·a·gab·a·lus (el′ə·gab′ə·ləs) See HELIOGABALUS.

e·la·in (i·lā′ən) See OLEIN.

E·laine (i·lān′) A feminine personal name. [See HELEN]

—Elaine In Arthurian legend, any of several ladies; especially, the mother of Sir Galahad.

elaio- *combining form* Oil: *elaioplast.* Also **elaeo-.** [< Gk. *elaion* olive oil]

el·ai·o·plast (el′ē·ō·plast) *n. Bot.* One of the highly refractive oil-secreting protoplasmic granules found near the nuclei of plant cells: also spelled *eleoplast.*

E·lam (ē′ləm) An ancient country of SW Asia between the Persian Gulf and the Caspian Sea. *Gen.* x 22: also *Susiana.*

E·lam·ite (ē′ləm·īt) *n.* **1** One of the ancient inhabitants of Elam. **2** An extinct, unrelated, agglutinative language, or group of languages, spoken in Elam: also **E·lam·it·ic** (ē′ləm·it′ik): also called *Susian.* *—adj.* Of or pertaining to Elam, its inhabitants or their language: also **E′lam·it′ic, E′lam·it′ish** (-ī′tish).

é·lan (ā·läṅ′) *n.* Ardor; dash; vivacity. [< F < *élancer* < *é-* out + *lancer* dart, throw]

e·land (ē′lənd) *n.* A large oxlike African antelope with twisted horns (genus *Taurotragus*); especially; the common eland (*T. oryx*), of SE Africa. [< Du., elk]

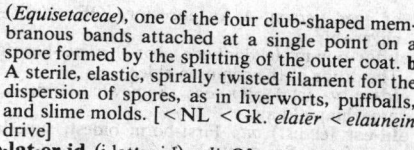

ELAND

élan vi·tal (vē·tȧl′) *French* Literally, life force; vital energy; in Bergson's philosophy, the creative life impulse of all evolution. Compare VITALISM.

el·a·phine (el′ə·fīn, -fin) *adj.* **1** Of or pertaining to a genus (*Elaphodus*) of deer native in China. **2** Describing the antlers characteristic of this genus. [< L *elaphus* < Gk. *elaphos* a stag]

el·a·pine (el′ə·pīn, -pin) *adj. Zool.* Of or pertaining to a subfamily (*Elipinae*) of tropical snakes, including many of the most venomous species, as the coral snake, cobra, and harlequin snake. [< NL < Gk. *elaps*, var. of *ellops*, a kind of serpent]

e·lapse (i·laps′) *v.i.* **e·lapsed, e·laps·ing** To slip by; pass away: said of time. [< L *elapsus*, pp. of *elabi* < *e-* out, away + *labi* glide]

El A·raish (el ä·rīsh′) The Arabic name for LARACHE.

e·las·mo·branch (i·las′mō·brangk, i·laz′-) *n.* Any of a subclass (Elasmobranchii) of fishes having cartilaginous skeletons and lamellate gills, including sharks and rays. *—adj.* Pertaining to or belonging to the subclass Elasmobranchii. [< NL < Gk. *elasmos* metal plate + *branchia* gills]

e·las·tance (i·las′təns) *n. Electr.* The reciprocal of capacitance. [< ELAST(ICITY) + -ANCE]

e·las·tic (i·las′tik) *adj.* **1** Spontaneously returning to a former size, shape, or configuration after being altered from it; springy; accommodating. **2** Capable of quick recovery, as from misfortune or depression; buoyant. **3** Increasing or diminishing readily in response to a changing stimulus, demand, or other causative influence: an *elastic* price, one that soars or drops quickly owing to sudden variations in demand. **4** Capable of expansion and contraction, as a gas; flexible. *—n.* A strip, cord, or piece of india rubber or of webbing made elastic by india-rubber threads woven therein, used as a band, suspender, etc.; specifically, a garter. [< NL *elasticus* < Gk. *elastikos* driving, propulsive < *elaunein* drive] **—e·las′ti·cal·ly** *adv.*

e·las·tic·i·ty (i·las′tis′ə·tē, ē′las-) *n.* **1** *Physics* That property of matter by virtue of which a body tends to resist deformation, returning to a former or normal size, shape, or configuration, after being deflected, compressed, expanded, twisted or drawn. **2** The rebounding quality of bodies; resilience; springiness: the *elasticity* of the air. **3** The tendency to recover from depression or misfortune; buoyancy.

e·las·tin (i·las′tin) *n. Biochem.* The protein substance, of high glycine and leucine content, which is found in tendons, cartilage, connective tissue, and bone.

e·las·to·mer (i·las′tə·mər) *n. Chem.* One of a class of polymerized compounds characterized by elastic, rubberlike properties, as the synthetic rubbers and various plastics. [< ELAST(IC) + -o- + Gk. *meros* part]

e·late (i·lāt′) *v.t.* **·lat·ed, ·lat·ing** To raise the spirits of; excite. *—adj.* Exalted or triumphant; exultant. [< L *elatus*, pp. for *efferre* < *ex-* out + *ferre* bear] **—e·lat′ed** *adj.* **—e·lat′ed·ly** *adv.* **—e·lat′ed·ness** *n.*

El·a·te·a (el′ə·tē′ə) An ancient city of Phocis, Greece.

el·a·ter (el′ə·tər) *n.* **1** *Entomol.* **a** A click beetle or elaterid. **b** A spring or terminal bristlelike abdominal appendage of a springtail or podurid insect. **2** *Bot.* **a** In the horsetail family of plants (*Equisetaceae*), one of the four club-shaped membranous bands attached at a single point on a spore formed by the splitting of the outer coat. **b** A sterile, elastic, spirally twisted filament for the dispersion of spores, as in liverworts, puffballs, and slime molds. [< NL < Gk. *elatēr* < *elaunein* drive]

e·lat·er·id (i·lat′ər·id) *adj.* Of or pertaining to a family (*Elateridae*) of beetles with serrate antennae, including the click beetles or snapping beetles. *—n.* An elaterid beetle. [< NL < Gk. *elatēr.* See ELATER.]

e·lat·er·in (i·lat′ər·in) *n. Chem.* A bitter crystalline compound, $C_{20}H_{28}O_5$, contained in elaterium and having a powerful cathartic effect. [< ELATER(IUM) + -IN]

e·lat·er·ite (i·lat′ə·rīt) *n.* An elastic, resinous, dark-brown, subtranslucent mineral hydrocarbon, found in soft masses. [< obs. *elater* elasticity (< Gk. < *elaunein* drive) + -ITE[1]]

el·a·te·ri·um (el′ə·tir′ē·əm) *n.* **1** The squirting cucumber (*Ecballium elaterium*). **2** A purgative derived from its juice. **3** A greenish to gray strongly cathartic substance contained in the juice of the fruit of the squirting cucumber. [< L < Gk. *elatērion* a purgative < *elaunein* drive]

E·lath (ē′lath) **1** A port at the southern extremity of Israel on the Gulf of Aqaba. **2** The ancient name for AQABA.

e·la·tion (i·lā′shən) *n.* Exalted feeling, as from pride or joy; exultation.

E·lay·er (ē′lā′ər) *n.* The Heaviside layer.

El·ba (el′bə) The largest island of the Tuscan Archipelago; 86 square miles; a sovereign principality under the exiled Napoleon I, 1814–15.

El·be (el′bə) A river of central Europe, flowing 691 miles NW to the North Sea near Hamburg. *Czechoslovakian* **La·be** (la′be).

El Be·kaa (el bē·kä′) Bekaa. Also **El Bi·ka′, El Bi·qa′.**

El·ber·feld (el′bər·felt) See WUPPERTAL.

El·bert (el′bərt) A masculine personal name. Also *Lat.* **El·ber·tus** (el·bûr′təs).

Elbert, Mount A peak in central Colorado, highest in the United States Rockies; 14,431 feet.

El·bing (el′bing) A port in northern Poland on the Vistula estuary. *Polish* **El′blag** (el′blôṅgk).

el·bow (el′bō) *n.* **1** The joint at the bend of the arm; also, the joint resembling an elbow in the shoulder or hock of a quadruped. Compare illustration under HORSE. **2** Any outward bend resembling an elbow, as a short angular pipe fitting, or a projection on the side of a chair or sofa on which to rest the arm. *—v.t.* **1** To push or jostle with or as with the elbows. **2** To make (one's way) by such pushing. *—v.i.* **3** To make one's way by pushing or jostling. [OE *elboga*]

elbow grease *Colloq.* Steady application; hard work.

elbow room Ample room; scope for activity or occupation.

El·brus (el′bro͞os) A peak in the Caucasus Mountains in NW Georgian S.S.R. and the highest peak in Europe; 18,481 feet.

el·buck (el′buk) *n. Scot.* Elbow.

El·burz (el·bo͝orz′) A mountain range in northern Iran; highest peak, 18,603 feet.

El Ca·ney (el kä·nā′) A town in east Cuba; scene of an American victory over Cuban forces (1898) in the Spanish-American War: also *Caney.*

El Cap·i·tan (el kap·i·tan′) A peak in the Yosemite Valley, California; 7,564 feet.

El·che (el′chā) A city in eastern Spain.

eld (eld) *n. Archaic* Old times; antiquity; old age. [OE *eldo* old age]

el·der[1] (el′dər) *n.* **1** A shrub (genus *Sambucus*) of the honeysuckle family, with white flowers and purple-black or red berries; the roots of some species contain a very poisonous alkaloid, but the flowers and berries are often used in medicine. **2** Any one of various trees or plants resembling elder: the poison *elder* (*Rhus vernix*). [OE *ellærn*]

eld·er[2] (el′dər) *adj.* **1** Having lived longer; earlier born. **2** Senior: alternative comparative of *old.* **3** Earlier in time. **4** Prior in rank. *—n.* **1** A prince or head of a tribe or family. **2** A church officer or minister. **3** An older

or aged person. **4** An ancestor. [OE *eldra*] — **eld′er·ship** *n.*

el·der·ber·ry (el′dər·ber′ē, -bər·ē) *n. pl.* **·ber·ries** The drupe of the common elder.

eld·er·ly (el′dər·lē) *adj.* Somewhat old; approaching old age.

eld·est (el′dist) *adj.* First-born; oldest; superlative of OLD. See ELDER².

eldest hand The first player in a card game; the player on the dealer's left; in poker, the age: opposed to *younger hand.*

el·ding (el′ding) *n. Scot.* Firewood; fuel.

El Do·ra·do (el də·rä′dō) **1** A legendary South American realm rich in gold and jewels: the object of the early Spanish conquerors and of many European explorers. **2** Any region of the western United States conceived of as promising wealth and opportunity to the adventurous, particularly California during and after the gold rush of 1848–49. **3** Any region rich in gold or opportunity. **4** A golden opportunity. Also **El′do·ra′do.**

E·le·a (ē′lē·ə) An ancient town in Lucania, Italy, where the Eleatic school of philosophy was founded.

El·ea·nor (el′ə·nər, -nôr) A feminine personal name. Also *Lat.* **El·e·a·no·ra** (el′ē·ə·nôr′ə, -nō′rə), *Dan., Ger.* **E·le·o·no·re** (ā·lā′ə·nō′rə), *Ital.* **E·le·o·no·ra** (ā·lā′ə·nō′rä). [See HELEN] — **Eleanor of Aquitaine,** 1122–1204, divorced wife of Louis VII of France; married Henry II of England: also **Eleanor of Guienne. —Eleanor of Castile,** died 1290, wife of Edward I of England. **—Eleanor of Provence,** died 1291, wife of Henry III of England.

El·e·at·ic (el′ē·at′ik) *adj.* Pertaining to or characteristic of Elea or the school of philosophy founded there by Xenophanes and Parmenides. —*n.* **1** A native of Elea. **2** A disciple of the Eleatic school of philosophy, which developed the conception of the universal unity of being. [<L *Eleaticus* <*Elea* ELEA] **—El′e·at′i·cism** *n.*

El·e·a·zar (el′ē·ā′zər, *Du.* ā′lā·ä′zär) A masculine personal name. Also **El′e·a′zer,** *Fr.,* **É·lé·a·zar** (ā·lā·ä·zär′), *Ital.* **E·le·a·za·ro** (ā·lā·äd′zä·rō), *Sp.* **E·le·á·za·ro** (ā′lā·ä′thä·rō). [<Hebrew, God's help, or God is helper]

el·e·cam·pane (el′i·kam·pān′) *n.* **1** A tall perennial herb of the composite family (*Inula helenium*), having large leaves, yellow flowers, and a mucilaginous root yielding a tonic. **2** A coarse candy flavored with an extract made from the root of this herb. [<Med. L *enula* elecampane + *campana* of the field]

a **e·lect** (i·lekt′) *v.t.* **1** To choose for an office by vote. **2** To take by choice or selection. **3** *Theol.* To choose or set aside for eternal life. —*v.i.* **4** To make a choice. —*adj.* **1** Elected to office, but not yet in charge: used as the second element in compounds, as president-*elect.* **2** *Theol.* Chosen of God for salvation; of saintly or divine character. **3** Selected; chosen; picked out. —*n.* **1** *Theol.* A person, or body of persons, chosen of God for salvation or for special service. **2** One who is favored or preferred. [<L *electus,* pp. of *eligere* <*ex-* out + *legere* choose]

e·lec·tion (i·lek′shən) *n.* **1** The selecting of a person or persons for office, as by ballot. **2** A popular vote on any question. **3** A choice, as between alternatives; choice in general. **4** In Calvinism, the predestination of some individuals to be saved from God's wrath and punishment. See synonyms under ALTERNATIVE.

e·lec·tion·eer (i·lek′shən·ir′) *v.i.* **1** To endeavor to win an election. **2** To canvass for votes.

e·lec·tive (i·lek′tiv) *adj.* **1** Of or pertaining to a choice by vote. **2** Obtained or bestowed by election. **3** Exerting the privilege of choice. **4** Subject to choice; optional. **5** *Chem.* Having a tendency to attract and combine with some substances and not with others: *elective* absorption. —*n.* An optional study in a fixed college curriculum. — **e·lec′·tive·ly** *adv.* **—e·lec′tive·ness** *n.*

e·lec·tor (i·lek′tər) *n.* **1** One who elects; a person qualified to vote at an election. **2** *U.S.* A presidential elector. **3** One of the great princes who formerly (12th to 18th century) had the right of electing the Holy Roman Emperor. **—presidential electors** The persons chosen by the several States and the District of Columbia to elect the president and vice president of the United States. The District of Columbia has three electors; each State sends a number equal to its total of senators and representatives.

e·lec·tor·al (i·lek′tər·əl) *adj.* Pertaining to, of, or comprising electors.

electoral college The whole corporate body of the presidential electors chosen at one election, although they never meet as a body; also, those of a single State, which do meet: a popular, unofficial term, first used informally in 1821.

e·lec·tor·ate (i·lek′tər·it) *n.* **1** Those who elect; the mass of voters. **2** The rank or territory of an elector in the Holy Roman Empire.

e·lec·tor·ess (i·lek′tər·is) *n.* **1** A woman qualified to vote at an election. **2** The wife or widow of an elector of the Holy Roman Empire. Also **e·lec′tress** (-tris).

E·lec·tra (i·lek′trə) **1** In Greek legend, a daughter of Agamemnon and Clytemnestra who persuaded her brother Orestes to kill their mother and their mother's lover Aegisthus to avenge their father's murder. **2** One of the Pleiades. Also *Elektra.*

Electra complex *Psychoanal.* A compulsive, strongly repressed sexual attachment of the daughter to her father: the female analog of the *Oedipus complex.*

e·lec·tret (i·lek′trit) *n.* A dielectric, usually rod-shaped, which may be strongly charged with positive electricity at one pole and with negative electricity at the other: it is the electrical analog of the magnet. [<ELECTR(ICITY) + (MAGN)ET]

e·lec·tric (i·lek′trik) *adj.* **1** Relating to, derived from, produced, or operated by electricity. **2** Containing, producing, or carrying electricity. **3** Spirited; magnetic; thrilling. Also **e·lec′tri·cal.** — *n.* **1** A street car, train, or other vehicle run by electricity. **2** Any substance or material, as amber or resin, which can be given an electric charge by rubbing. [<NL *electricus* <L *electrum* amber <Gk. *ēlektron*] **—e·lec′tri·cal·ly** *adv.*

electrical transcription See under TRANSCRIPTION (def. 3).

electric breeze **1** A stream of ions repelled from an electrified point. **2** A brush discharge as used in therapeutics.

electric calamine Hemimorphite

electric cell Any of a large variety of devices consisting of two dissimilar metals or materials immersed in an electrolyte, capable of generating an electric charge by chemical action.

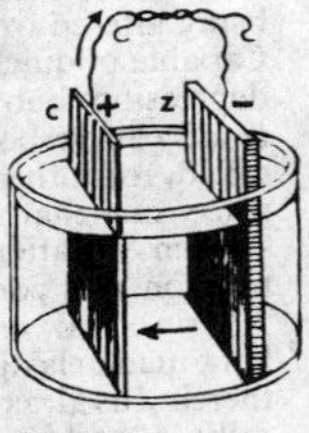

ELECTRIC CELL
c. Carbon (positive pole).
z. Zinc (negative pole).

electric chair **1** A chair used for electrocuting criminals by sending a high voltage of electricity through the body of the person fastened into it. **2** Hence, the death penalty.

electric clock Any of variously designed clocks which are actuated by electricity in any way; especially, a clock operated by plugging in on an alternating current transmitting electromagnetic impulses from a master clock.

electric current A stream of electrons flowing through a conducting body; it is usually measured and expressed in terms of amperes, coulombs, and volts. See ELECTRON.

electric displacement The theoretical movement of the electricity in a dielectric as a result of changes in the electric field where the latter is located.

electric eel A cyprinoid, eel-like fish (*Electrophorus electricus*) of tropical America, which sometimes reaches a length of six feet, carrying in its tail organs capable of delivering powerful electric shocks.

electric energy The capacity possessed by electricity for doing work.

electric eye A photoelectric cell.

electric field A field of force surrounding a charged object or a moving magnet.

electric fish Any fish having organs capable of imparting an electric shock.

electric furnace **1** A furnace in which high temperatures are obtained by the use of an electric arc or by induction from a central power station. **2** A smelting furnace in which the heat is produced by an electric current.

e·lec·tri·cian (i·lek′trish′ən, ē′lek-) *n.* **1** One versed in the science of electricity. **2** An inventor, maker, or repairer of electrical apparatus.

e·lec·tric·i·ty (i·lek′tris′ə·tē, ē′lek-) *n.* **1** A fundamental property of matter, associated with atomic particles whose movements, free or controlled, lead to the development of fields of force and the generation of kinetic or potential energy. The electron is the basic unit of *negative* electricity, and the proton of *positive* electricity. Any accumulation of one kind of electricity in excess of an equivalent of the opposite kind is called a *charge* and is measured in appropriate units. A charge fixed at one point or within a circumscribed field of force, as a Leyden jar, is *static* electricity; a charge which flows through a conductor is *current* electricity. **2** The property of many substances, as amber, fur, glass, etc., mutually to attract or repel each other when subjected to friction. **3** The science which deals with the phenomena, laws, theory, and application of this property.

electric light **1** Illumination produced by electricity. **2** The lamp, tower, or other device used for electric illumination, especially the bulb.

electric machine **1** An apparatus for generating static electricity, as by friction. **2** A dynamo.

electric motor A machine for transforming electric energy into mechanical power: distinguished from *dynamo.*

Electric Peak The highest peak in the Gallatin Range, SW Montana; 11,155 feet.

electric ray Any of a family (Torpedinidae) of rays with usually round bodies and short tails having an organ in each winglike fin that delivers an electric shock as a means of stunning prey or of defense against predators. Also called *crampfish, numbfish, torpedo.*

e·lec·tri·fy (i·lek′trə·fī) *v.t.* **·fied, ·fy·ing** **1** To act upon, charge with, or subject to electricity. **2** To equip, as a house, for the use of electricity. **3** To adapt for operation by electric power, as a railroad. **4** To arouse; startle; thrill. — **e·lec′tri·fi′a·ble** *adj.* **—e·lec′tri·fi·ca′·tion** *n.* — **e·lec′tri·fi′er** *n.*

e·lec·trine (i·lek′trin) *adj.* **1** Made of electrum. **2** Made of or related to amber. —*n.* An imaginary substance, supposed by some to be the basis of electricity. [<Gk. *ēlektrinos* <*ēlektron* amber]

e·lec·trize (i·lek′trīz) *v.t.* **·trized, ·triz·ing** To electrify. **—e·lec′tri·za′tion** *n.*

e·lec·triz·er (i·lek′trī·zər) *n.* One who or that which electrizes.

e·lec·tro (i·lek′trō) *n. pl.* **·tros** **1** An electrotype. **2** Electroplating. —*v.t.* **·troed, ·tro·ing** To make an electrotype of; electroplate. [Short for ELECTROTYPE]

electro- *combining form* **1** Electric; by, with, or of electricity: *electrocardiogram.* **2** Electrolytic: *electroanalysis.* Also, before vowels, sometimes **electr-.** [<Gk. *ēlektron* amber]

e·lec·tro·a·cous·tics (i·lek′trō·ə·kōō′stiks) *n.* The branch of acoustics which studies the design, operation, and efficiency of equipment used in the electrical and electronic transmission of sound, as microphones, loudspeakers, soundtrack apparatus, tape-recorders, etc. — **e·lec′tro·a·cous′tic** *adj.*

e·lec·tro·a·nal·y·sis (i·lek′trō·ə·nal′ə·sis) *n.* An analysis by and in accordance with the methods of electrolysis.

e·lec·tro·bi·ol·o·gy (i·lek′trō·bi·ol′ə·jē) *n.* The study of electrical phenomena associated with the functioning and behavior of living organisms.

e·lec·tro·bi·os·co·py (i·lek′trō·bī·os′kə·pē) *n.* The determination of the presence of absence of life in an organism by means of suitably applied electric currents. **—e·lec′tro·bi′o·scop′·ic** (-bī′ə·skop′ik) *adj.*

e·lec·tro·cap·il·lar·i·ty (i·lek′trō·kap′i·lar′ə·tē) *n.* That change in the surface tension between two conducting liquids in contact which occurs when an electric current is passed between them.

e·lec·tro·car·di·o·gram (i·lek′trō·kär′dē·ə·gram′) *n. Med.* A graph indicating electromotive variations in the action of the heart.

e·lec·tro·car·di·o·graph (i·lek′trō·kä′dē·ə·graf′, -gräf′) *n. Med.* An instrument for recording the electric current produced by the action of the heart muscle: used in the diagnosis of

diseases affecting the heart. **—e·lec·tro·car·di·og·ra·phy** (i·lek′trō·kär′dē·og′rə·fē) *n.*

e·lec·tro·chem·is·try (i·lek′trō·kem′is·trē) *n.* The branch of chemistry that treats of electricity as active in effecting chemical change. —**e·lec′tro·chem′i·cal** *adj.* **—e·lec′tro·chem′i·cal·ly** *adv.* **—e·lec′tro·chem′ist** *n.*

e·lec·tro·co·ag·u·la·tion (i·lek′trō·kō·ag′yə·lā′·shən) *n.* The destructive coagulation of protoplasmic material or of living tissue, healthy or morbid, by the passage through it of an electric current.

e·lec·tro·co·ma (i·lek′trō·kō′mə) *n.* Coma induced by electroshock therapy.

e·lec·tro·cul·ture (i·lek′trō·kul′chər) *n.* The stimulation of the growth, development, and maturing of plants by electrical means, especially by static electricity and fields of force in the atmosphere.

e·lec·tro·cute (i·lek′trə·kyo͞ot) *v.t.* **·cut·ed, ·cut·ing 1** To execute in the electric chair. **2** To kill by electricity. [< ELECTRO- + (EXE)CUTE] — **e·lec′tro·cu′tion** *n.*

e·lec·trode (i·lek′trōd) *n. Electr.* Either of the two conducting elements through which a current leaves or enters an electrolytic cell, vacuum tube, electric arc or furnace, or any non-metallic conductor; an anode or cathode. Compare illustration under ELECTRIC CELL. [< ELECTR(O) + -ODE[1]]

e·lec·tro·de·pos·it (i·lek′trō·di·poz′it) *v.i.* To deposit chemically, as metal from a solution, by means of an electric current. —*n.* That which is so deposited. **—e·lec′tro·dep′o·si′tion** (-dep′ə·zish′ən, -dē′pə-) *n.*

e·lec·tro·des·ic·ca·tion (i·lek′trō·des′ə·kā′·shən) *n.* The destruction of animal tissues by means of controlled high-frequency electric-spark discharges: also called *fulguration.*

e·lec·tro·dy·nam·ic (i·lek′trō·dī·nam′ik) *adj.* Relating to the forces of attraction and repulsion produced by electric currents. **—e·lec′tro·dy·nam′i·cal·ly** *adv.*

e·lec·tro·dy·nam·ics (i·lek′trō·dī·nam′iks) *n.* The branch of physics which deals with the forces of electrical attraction and repulsion and with the energy transformations of magnetic fields and electric currents.

e·lec·tro·dy·na·mom·e·ter (i·lek′trō·dī′nə·mom′ə·tər) *n.* An instrument for measuring electrical current, voltage, or power, in which the deflecting force arises from the interaction of two wire coils carrying currents.

e·lec·tro·en·ceph·a·lo·gram (i·lek′trō·en·sef′ə·lə·gram′) *n.* A record of electrical impulses and changes in the brain: important in the diagnosis of certain diseases, as epilepsy. **—e·lec′tro·en·ceph′a·lo·graph′** (-graf′,-gräf′) *n.*

e·lec·tro·en·ceph·a·log·ra·phy (i·lek′trō·en·sef′ə·log′rə·fē) *n.* **1** The art and technique of recording electrical changes in the brain. **2** The science of interpreting these changes in the diagnosis of epilepsy and other incapacitating brain diseases.

e·lec·tro·en·dos·mo·sis (i·lek′trō·en′dos·mō′·sis) *n.* The diffusion of fluids through permeable membranes or diaphragms by the application of an electrical potential.

e·lec·tro·form (i·lek′trō·fôrm′) *v.t.* To produce (shaped objects) by the electrolytic deposition of metal upon a mold.

e·lec·tro·form·ing (i·lek′trō·fôr′ming) *n.* The production of metal tubing, medals, and the like by the electrolytic deposition of metal upon a mold of the desired shape or pattern.

e·lec·tro·gas·tro·gram (i·lek′trō·gas′trə·gram) *n. Med.* The record of an electrogastrograph.

e·lec·tro·gas·tro·graph (i·lek′trō·gas′trə·graf, -gräf) *n. Med.* A device for indicating electrical changes caused by muscular contractions of the stomach.

e·lec·tro·graph (i·lek′trə·graf, -gräf) *n.* **1** The linear record of an electrometer. **2** An apparatus for tracing a design to be etched for use in printing wallpaper, calico, etc. **3** A roentgenogram. **—e·lec′tro·graph′ic** *adj.* **—e·lec·trog·ra·phy** (i·lek′trog′rə·fē, ē′lek-) *n.*

e·lec·tro·ki·net·ic (i·lek′trō·ki·net′ik) *adj.* Pertaining to or caused by electricity in motion.

e·lec·tro·ki·net·ics (i·lek′trō·ki·net′iks) *n.* That branch of electrical science which treats of the motion of electricity and the forces producing or regulating it: opposed to *electrostatics.*

e·lec·tro·ky·mo·gram (i·lek′trō·kī′mə·gram) *n.* The record made by an electrokymograph.

e·lec·tro·ky·mo·graph (i·lek′trō·kī′mə·graf, -gräf) *n. Med.* An instrument for measuring the action of the heart by means of X-rays which project the heart shadow upon a fluorescent screen used in conjunction with a photocell.

e·lec·tro·lier (i·lek′trə·lir′) *n.* A fixture, usually ornamental, for holding electric lamps. [< ELECTRO- + (CHANDE)LIER]

e·lec·tro·lu·mi·nes·cence (i·lek′trō·lo͞o′mə·nes′·əns) *n.* **1** Light produced by the agency of electricity. **2** The emission of a soft, uniformly diffused light from phosphor powders embedded in the surface of a panel of glass or other insulating material which is directly subjected to the action of an alternating electric field. — **e·lec′tro·lu′mi·nes′cent** *adj.*

e·lec·trol·y·sis (i·lek′trol′ə·sis) *n.* **1** The decomposing of a chemical compound by passing an electric current through it. **2** The use of an electrified needle to destroy the roots of unwanted body hair. [< ELECTRO- + -LYSIS]

e·lec·tro·lyte (i·lek′trə·līt) *n.* **1** A substance, usually in solution, which will transmit an electric current by the formation of ions. **2** A solution which conducts an electric current between the electrodes of a cell, accompanied by the release of a gas or the deposition of a solid. [< ELECTRO- + Gk. *lytos* loosed < *luein* loosen] — **e·lec·tro·lyt·ic** (i·lek′trə·lit′ik) or **·i·cal** *adj.* — **e·lec′tro·lyt′i·cal·ly** *adv.*

e·lec·tro·lyze (i·lek′trə·līz) *v.t.* **·lyzed, ·lyz·ing** To decompose by electric current. **—e·lec′·tro·ly·za′tion** *n.* **—e·lec′tro·lyz′er** *n.*

e·lec·tro·mag·net (i·lek′trō·mag′nit) *n.* A core of soft iron or the like, which temporarily becomes a magnet during the passage of an electric current through a coil of wire surrounding it. — **e·lec′tro·mag·net′ic** (-mag·net′ik) or **·i·cal** *adj.* — **e·lec′tro·mag·net′i·cal·ly** *adv.*

e·lec·tro·mag·net·ism (i·lek′trō·mag′nə·tiz′əm) *n.* **1** Magnetism developed by electricity. **2** That science which treats of the relations between electricity and magnetism and the phenomena due to these relations. Also **e·lec′tro·mag·net′ics.**

e·lec·tro·met·al·lur·gy (i·lek′trō·met′ə·lûr′jē, -mə·tal′ər·jē) *n.* The art or science of electrolytically depositing metals, or of separating them from their ores or alloys by electrolysis or the electric furnace. **—e·lec′tro·met′al·lur′gi·cal** *adj.*

e·lec·trom·e·ter (i·lek′trom′ə·tər, ē′lek-) *n.* An instrument for measuring the voltage in an electric circuit by the electrostatic forces exerted between two charged bodies.

e·lec·trom·e·try (i·lek′trom′ə·trē, ē′lek-) *n.* The science or art of making electrical measurements. **—e·lec·tro·met·ric** (i·lek′trō·met′rik) or **·ri·cal** *adj.*

e·lec·tro·mo·tion (i·lek′trə·mō′shən) *n.* **1** The passage of an electric current in a voltaic circuit. **2** Motion produced by electricity employed as power.

e·lec·tro·mo·tive (i·lek′trə·mō′tiv) *adj.* Producing, or tending to produce an electric current; distinguished from *magnetomotive.*

electromotive force That which tends to produce the flow of electricity from one point to another; difference of potential between the terminals of an electrolyte, voltaic cell, or other conducting medium; voltage.

electromotive series An arrangement of the elements in a series such that each will, in general and under suitable conditions, replace from its compounds any element listed after it. See table below for the series of metals, from the most active to the least active. Also called *displacement, activity,* or *electrochemical series.*

ELECTROMOTIVE SERIES OF THE METALS

1. Potassium	10. Chromium	19. Arsenic
2. Barium	11. Iron	20. Bismuth
3. Strontium	12. Cadmium	21. Antimony
4. Calcium	13. Cobalt	22. Mercury
5. Sodium	14. Nickel	23. Silver
6. Magnesium	15. Tin	24. Gold
7. Aluminum	16. Lead	25. Platinum
8. Manganese	17. Hydrogen	
9. Zinc	18. Copper	

e·lec·tro·mo·tor (i·lek′trə·mō′tər) *n.* **1** An electric motor. **2** Any electric source, as a voltaic cell.

e·lec·tro·my·o·gram (i·lek′trō·mī′ə·gram) *n.* The tracing made by an electromyograph.

e·lec·tro·my·o·graph (i·lek′trō·mī′ə·graf, -gräf) *n. Med.* An instrument for determining the location and extent of nerve lesions by the application of an electric stimulus to muscles whose responses are converted into both sound and visual records. **—e·lec′tro·my·og′ra·phy** (-mī·og′rə·fē) *n.* **e·lec′tro·my′o·graph′i·cal** *adj.*

e·lec·tron (i·lek′tron) *n.* An electrically charged particle of the atom: it carries the unit charge of negative electricity, estimated at 4.8×10^{-10} cgs electrostatic units, and has a mass approximately one eighteen-hundredth (more exactly 1/1837) of that of the proton. Electrons are emitted in the form of beta particles and cathode rays. **—free electron** An electron not permanently bound to any atom and free to move within the limits of a given substance or material, as in a galvanic current. [< Gk. *ēlektron* amber]

e·lec·tro·nar·co·sis (i·lek′trō·när·kō′sis) *n. Psychiatry* Narcosis induced by the passing of a very mild electric current between two electrodes attached to the sides of the head: used in the treatment of schizophrenia and related mental disorders.

e·lec·tro·neg·a·tive (i·lek′trō·neg′ə·tiv) *adj.* **1** Appearing, as an element in electrolysis, at the positive electrode. **2** Having the property of becoming negatively electrified by contact with or the chemical action of another element.

electron gun An apparatus, usually in the form of a slender tube with thermionic filaments and focusing and accelerating electrodes, used in television for directing a steady stream of electrons in a given direction.

e·lec·tron·ic (i·lek′tron′ik, ē′lek-) *adj.* **1** Of or pertaining to electrons. **2** Operating or produced by the movement of free electrons or other carriers of electric charge, as in an electron tube. **3** Pertaining to electronics. — **e·lec′tron′i·cal·ly** *adv.*

e·lec·tron·ics (i·lek′tron′iks, ē′lek-) *n. pl. (Construed as singular)* The study of the properties and behavior of electrons under all conditions, especially with reference to technical and industrial applications.

electron lens A distribution of an electric field surrounding the path of an electron beam such that the beam may be concentrated in a focus similar to that of an optical lens.

electron microscope A microscope which uses high-voltage streams of electrons in order to bring into visibility objects not accessible to the relatively large wavelengths of visible light used by the most powerful optical microscopes.

electronic music Music based on an arrangement of electronically produced, organized, or altered sounds, recorded on tape.

e·lec·tro·nog·ra·phy (i·lek′trō·nog′rə·fē) *n.* A method of printing without pressure between paper and the inked surface, by means of an applied electric charge which ionizes the ink particles, causing them to migrate to the oppositely charged printing surface. [< ELECTRON + -(O)GRAPHY]

electron optics A method for the control of electron beams or rays by properly adjusted magnetic or electric fields so that the flow of electrons will simulate the effect of light rays in an optical instrument.

electron shell *Physics* The orbital arrangement of electrons outside the nucleus of an atom.

electron tube A high vacuum tube in which a stream of electrons is emitted from a heated cathode and subjected to the controlling action of a grid which amplifies and directs the current.

electron volt A unit of energy equal to that acquired by an electron which passes through a potential difference of one volt: equal to 1.602×10^{-12} erg: also called *equivalent volt.*

e·lec·tro·op·tics (i·lek′trō·op′tiks) *n. Physics* The study of the modification of optical phenomena by the application of an electric field.

e·lec·trop·a·thy (i·lek′trop′ə·thē, ē′lek-) *n. Med.* The treatment of disease by means of electricity. **—e·lec′tro·path′ic** (-trə·path′ik) *adj.* **—e·lec′tro·path′i·cal·ly** *adv.*

e·lec·tro·pho·re·sis (i·lek′trō·fə·rē′sis) *n. Chem.*

The slow movement of colloidal particles suspended in a fluid, when under the influence of an electric field.

e·lec·troph·o·rus (i·lek′trof′ər·əs, ē′lek-) *n. pl.* **·ri** (-rī) An instrument for generating static electricity by induction: commonly a flat disk of resin, to which may be applied another of wood coated with tinfoil. Also **e·lec·tro·phore** (i·lek′trə·fôr, -fōr).

e·lec·tro·phren·ic (i·lek′trə·fren′ik) *adj. Med.* Describing a method of artificial respiration by the electrical stimulation of one or both of the phrenic nerves.

e·lec·tro·phys·i·ol·o·gy (i·lek′trō·fiz′ē·ol′ə·jē) *n.* The study of the electric phenomena of living organs. — **e·lec′tro·phys′i·o·log′i·cal** (-fiz′ē·ə·loj′i·kəl) *adj.*

e·lec·tro·plate (i·lek′trə·plāt′) *v.t.* **·plat·ed, ·plat·ing** To coat with metal by electrolysis, the object being immersed in a solution of a salt of the metal in connection with the negative pole of a battery or dynamo. — *n.* An electroplated article. — **e·lec′tro·plat′er** *n.*

e·lec·tro·plat·ing (i·lek′trə·plā′ting) *n.* 1 The act or process of depositing metal by electric means. 2 The coat of metal so deposited.

e·lec·tro·pos·i·tive (i·lek′trō·poz′ə·tiv) *adj.* 1 Appearing at the negative electrode: said of an element in electrolysis. 2 Having the property of becoming positively electrified by contact or chemical action.

e·lec·tro·scis·sion (i·lek′trō·sizh′ən) *n. Surg.* The cutting or division of tissues by an electrically operated knife.

e·lec·tro·scope (i·lek′trə·skōp) *n.* An instrument for detecting the presence of electricity upon a conductor by the attraction or repulsion of pith balls or strips of gold leaf. See illustration. — **e·lec′tro·scop′ic** (-skop′ik) *adj.*

ELECTROSCOPE
Metallic pole (*m*), electrically charged by (*e*), conducts the impulse to strips (*s*) that acquire the charge and move apart in electrostatic repulsion.

e·lec·tro·shock (i·lek′trō·shok′) *n. Psychiatry* A shock to the nervous system of a mental patient, produced by a carefully regulated electric current passed through the head.

e·lec·tro·stat·ics (i·lek′trō·stat′iks) *n.* That branch of electrical science which treats of the phenomena of electricity at rest or of frictional electricity: opposed to *electrokinetics*. — **e·lec′tro·stat′ic** or **·i·cal** *adj.* — **e·lec′tro·stat′i·cal·ly** *adv.*

electrostatic unit An electric charge which, concentrated at one point in a vacuum, would repel with a force of 1 dyne an equal and like charge placed 1 centimeter away.

e·lec·tro·ste·nol·y·sis (i·lek′trō·sti·nol′ə·sis) *n.* The depositing of metallic particles in the pores of a high–resistance membrane by electrolysis.

e·lec·tro·tax·is (i·lek′trō·tak′sis) *n. Biol.* 1 That property of protoplasm which makes it susceptible to the influence of an electric stimulus, as shown by the direction of movements. 2 Any similar property in simple organisms. Also **e·lec′trot′ro·pism** (i·lek′trot′rə·piz′əm, ē′lek-). — **e·lec′tro·tac′tic** (-tak′tik) *adj.*

e·lec·tro·tech·nics (i·lek′trō·tek′niks) *n.* The science of the methods, processes, and operations by which electricity is applied in the industrial arts. — **e·lec′tro·tech′nic** (-nik) or **·ni·cal** *adj.*

e·lec·tro·ther·a·peu·tics (i·lek′trō·ther′ə·pyoo′tiks) *n.* The treatment of disease by electricity, or the laws, etc., of such treatment. Also **e·lec′tro·ther′a·py** (-ə·pē) — **e·lec′tro·ther′a·peu′tic** (-tik) or **·ti·cal** *adj.*

e·lec·tro·ther·a·pist (i·lek′trō·ther′ə·pist) *n.* A practitioner of electrotherapeutics. Also **e·lec′·tro·ther′a·peu′tist.**

e·lec·trot·o·nus (i·lek′trot′ə·nəs, ē′lek-) *n. Physiol.* The change in the activity of a nerve or muscle induced by a voltaic current. [<NL <ELECTRO- + Gk. *tonos* tension] — **e·lec·tro·ton·ic** (i·lek′trō·ton′ik) *adj.*

e·lec·tro·type (i·lek′trō·tīp′) *n.* 1 A metallic copy of any surface, as a coin, made by electric deposition, especially one of a page of type for printing. 2 An impression from an electrotyped cut. 3 The process of electrotyping; electrotypy. — *v.t.* **·typed, ·typ·ing** To make an electrotype of.

e·lec·tro·typ·er (i·lek′trō·tī′pər) *n.* One who electrotypes. Also **e·lec′tro·typ′ist.**

e·lec·tro·typ·ic (i·lek′trō·tip′ik) *adj.* Pertaining to or made by electrotyping.

e·lec·tro·typ·ing (i·lek′trō·tī′ping) *n.* The act or business of forming electrotypes. Also **e·lec′tro·typ′y** (-tī′pē).

e·lec·tro·va·lence (i·lek′trō·vā′ləns) *n. Chem.* A bond formed by the complete transfer of electrons from the atoms of one element of a compound to the atoms of another element: distinguished from *covalence.*

e·lec·tro·va·lent (i·lek′trō·vā′lənt) *adj. Chem.* Designating a compound formed by electrovalence.

e·lec·trum (i·lek′trəm) *n.* 1 German silver or other like alloy. 2 Anciently, amber. 3 Native gold containing a large percentage of silver. [<L <Gk. *ēlektron* amber]

e·lec·tu·ar·y (i·lek′choo·er′ē) *n. pl.* **·ar·ies** A medicine mixed with honey or sirup to form a paste. [<LL *electuarium* <Gk. *ekleikton* < *ek* out + *leichein* lick]

el·ee·mos·y·nar (el′ə·mos′ə·nər, el′ē·ə-). *n.* 1 One who gives charity. 2 The supervisor of the distribution of papal charities. 3 *Obs.* Almoner.

el·ee·mos·y·nar·y (el′ə·mos′ə·ner′ē, el′ē·ə-) *adj.* 1 Of or pertaining to charity or alms; existing for the relief of the poor. 2 Charitable; nonprofit: *eleemosynary* institutions. 3 Aided by or dependent upon charity: the *eleemosynary* classes. — *n. pl.* **·nar·ies** A recipient of charity. [<Med. L *eleemosynarius* < *eleemosyna* ALMS]

el·e·gance (el′ə·gəns) *n.* 1 The state or quality of being elegant or refined. 2 Anything elegant. Also **el′e·gan·cy.**

el·e·gant (el′ə·gənt) *adj.* 1 Marked by refinement, grace, or symmetry, as of action, form or structure; also, possessing or exhibiting refined taste. 2 Possessing a fine sense of beauty or fitness. 3 *Colloq.* Excellent; capital. 4 Marked by completeness and simplicity; appropriate: an *elegant* solution. [<F *élégant* <L *elegans, -antis* fastidious] — **el′e·gant·ly** *adv.*

Synonyms: dainty, exquisite. *Elegant* (Latin *elegans*, select) refers to the lighter, finer elements of beauty in form or motion, but is often misused as a general term of approval. *Exquisite* denotes the utmost perfection of the elegant in minute details; we speak of an *elegant* garment, and *exquisite* lace. *Exquisite* is also applied to intense keenness of any feeling; as, *exquisite* delight; *exquisite* pain. *Dainty,* at its best, applies to what is at once slight, delicate, and pleasing; in its extreme use, it may apply to sensibilities or feelings too delicate for the demands of practical life, overnice, squeamish. See BEAUTIFUL, CHOICE, FINE[1], POLITE. *Antonyms:* common, coarse, harsh, rude.

el·e·gi·ac (el′ə·jī′ək, i·lē′jē·ak) *adj.* 1 Pertaining to elegies. 2 Of the nature of an elegy; sad; plaintive. 3 In ancient prosody, written in distichs consisting of hexameter and pentameter. Also **el′e·gi′a·cal.** — *n.* 1 A poet who writes in the tone or in the meter of the elegy. 2 *pl.* Verse composed in the elegiac spirit or form.

el·e·gist (el′ə·jist) *n.* A writer of funeral songs; one who writes in elegiac verse. Also **e·le·gi·ast** (i·lē′jē·ast), **el·e·gi·og·ra·pher** (el′ə·jē·og′rə·fər).

el·e·git (i·lē′jit) *n. Law* 1 A writ of execution, issued on the election of a judgment creditor, directing the sheriff to turn over to him the debtor's attachable goods, and, if these be insufficient, half the debtor's land, the latter to be held till the rents and profits shall extinguish the debt. 2 The right secured by this writ. [<L]

el·e·gize (el′ə·jīz) *v.t. & v.i.* **·gized, ·giz·ing** To mourn or commemorate in elegiac form.

el·e·gy (el′ə·jē) *n. pl.* **·gies** 1 A funeral song. 2 A meditative poem with sorrowful theme. 3 A classical poem written in elegiac verse. [<F *élégie* <L *elegia* <Gk. *elegeia* < *elegos* a song]

E·lek·tra (i·lek′trə) See ELECTRA.

el·e·ment (el′ə·mənt) *n.* 1 A component or essential part; especially, a simple part of anything complex; a constituent; ingredient. 2 *pl.* First principles or fundamental ideas; rudiments. 3 *Eccl.* The bread and wine of the Lord's Supper. 4 An ultimate and essential principle in the make–up of anything; essential constituent; anciently, one of the substances —earth, air, fire, and water—supposed to make up all things: still in popular use: the fury of the *elements,* the devouring *element.* 5 The natural sphere or environment: The *element* of fishes is water. 6 *Physics* One of a limited number of substances each of which is com-

TABLE OF CHEMICAL ELEMENTS
(See also PERIODIC TABLE OF ELEMENTS.)

Name	Symbol	Atomic No.	Name	Symbol	Atomic No.	Name	Symbol	Atomic No.
Actinium	Ac	89	Gold (*aurum*)	Au	79	Polonium	Po	84
Aluminum	Al	13	Hafnium	Hf	72	Potassium (*kalium*)	K	19
Americium	Am	95	Helium	He	2	Praseodymium	Pr	59
Antimony (*stibium*)	Sb	51	Holmium	Ho	67	Promethium	Pm	61
Argon	A	18	Hydrogen	H	1	Protactinium	Pa	91
Arsenic	As	33	Indium	In	49	Radium	Ra	88
Astatine	At	85	Iodine	I	53	Radon	Rn	86
Barium	Ba	56	Iridium	Ir	77	Rhenium	Re	75
Berkelium	Bk	97	Iron (*ferrum*)	Fe	26	Rhodium	Rh	45
Beryllium	Be	4	Krypton	Kr	36	Rubidium	Rb	37
Bismuth	Bi	83	Lanthanum	La	57	Ruthenium	Ru	44
Boron	B	5	Lawrencium	Lw	103	Samarium	Sm	62
Bromine	Br	35	Lead (*plumbum*)	Pb	82	Scandium	Sc	21
Cadmium	Cd	48	Lithium	Li	3	Selenium	Se	34
Calcium	Ca	20	Lutetium	Lu	71	Silicon	Si	14
Californium	Cf	98	Magnesium	Mg	12	Silver (*argentum*)	Ag	47
Carbon	C	6	Manganese	Mn	25	Sodium (*natrium*)	Na	11
Cerium	Ce	58	Mendelevium	Md	101	Strontium	Sr	38
Cesium	Cs	55	Mercury			Sulfur	S	16
Chlorine	Cl	17	(*hydrargyrum*)	Hg	80	Tantalum	Ta	73
Chromium	Cr	24	Molybdenum	Mo	42	Technetium	Tc	43
Cobalt	Co	27	Neodymium	Nd	60	Tellurium	Te	52
Columbium	(Cb)		Neon	Ne	10	Terbium	Tb	65
See NIOBIUM			Neoytterbium			Thallium	Tl	81
Copper (*cuprum*)	Cu	29	See YTTERBIUM			Thorium	Th	90
Curium	Cm	96	Neptunium	Np	93	Thulium	Tm	69
Dysprosium	Dy	66	Nickel	Ni	28	Tin (*stannum*)	Sn	50
Einsteinium	Es	99	Niobium	Nb	41	Titanium	Ti	22
Erbium	Er	68	Niton See RADON			Tungsten		
Europium	Eu	63	Nitrogen	N	7	See WOLFRAM		
Fermium	Fm	100	Nobelium	No	102	Uranium	U	92
Fluorine	F	9	Osmium	Os	76	Vanadium	V	23
Francium	Fr	87	Oxygen	O	8	Wolfram	W	74
Gadolinium	Gd	64	Palladium	Pd	46	Xenon	Xe	54
Gallium	Ga	31	Phosphorus	P	15	Ytterbium	Yb	70
Germanium	Ge	32	Platinum	Pt	78	Yttrium	Yt	39
Glucinum See BERYLLIUM			Plutonium	Pu	94	Zinc	Zn	30
						Zirconium	Zr	40

posed entirely of atoms having an invariant nuclear charge and none of which may be decomposed by ordinary chemical means, as gold, carbon, sodium, etc. See Table, page 408. **7** One of the primary parts of an organism; also, a cell or morphological unit. **8** One of a number of parts composing a symmetrical whole. **9** *Geom.* One of the forms or data which together compose a figure, as a line, a point, a plane, a space. **10** *Math.* **a** An infinitely small portion of a magnitude; a generatrix. **b** A term in an algebraic expression. **11** One of the dissimilar substances in a voltaic cell or battery, etc. **12** A group or class of people distinguished from a larger group to which it belongs by its own peculiar beliefs, attitudes, behavior, etc.: the conservative *element* in the party; a rowdy *element* in the crowd. See synonyms under PART, PARTICLE. **— to be in one's element** To be in pleasing surroundings or be engaged in activities in which one excels. [<L *elementum* first principle]

el·e·men·tal (el'ə·men'təl) *adj.* **1** Pertaining to the fundamental or basic constituent of anything; primary; simple. **2** Having to do with rudiments or first principles. **3** Pertaining to or like one of the four elements of ancient physics, fire, air, earth, and water. **4** Pertaining to the forces, phenomena, or powers of physical nature, often as personified: *elemental* spirits. **5** Comparable to the great primal powers of nature: *elemental* storms. **6** Of or pertaining to chemical elements, or one of the chemical elements; uncompounded. **— el'e·men'tal·ly** *adv.*

el·e·men·ta·ry (el'ə·men'tər·ē) *adj.* **1** Of, pertaining to, or being an element or elements, in any sense. **2** Treating of the first principles of anything; rudimentary: an *elementary* analysis. **3** Having the nature of an infinitesimal part of a quantity or magnitude. **— el'e·men'ta·ri·ly** *adv.* **— el'e·men'ta·ri·ness** *n.*

elementary education Public school and private education beyond kindergarten and preceding secondary school, from six to eight years in length, dealing with the fundamentals of education.

elementary school See under SCHOOL.

el·e·mi (el'ə·mē) *n.* Any one of several gum resins obtained from tropical trees of various genera, especially Manila elemi, from the pili tree of the Philippines: used in drugs and varnishes. [<Sp. *elemi,* ? <Arabic *al-lāmī*]

E·le·na (*Sp., Ital.* ā·lā'nä) See HELEN.

e·len·chus (i·leng'kəs) *n. pl.* **·chi** (-kī) **1** The contradictory opposite of a proposition; hence, a refuting argument; a refutation. **2** A false refutation; sophism. Also **e·lench** (i·lengk'). [<L <Gk. *elenchos* a cross-examination] **— e·len'chic** or **·chi·cal, e·lenc'tic** or **·ti·cal** *adj.*

e·le·o·lite (i·lē'ə·līt) See ELAEOLITE.

el·e·o·plast (el'ē·ə·plast') See ELAIOPLAST.

el·e·phant (el'ə·fənt) *n.* **1** A massively built, almost hairless ungulate mammal of Asia and Africa (family *Elephantidae*), the largest of existing land animals, having a flexible proboscis or trunk, and the upper incisors developed as tusks valued as the chief source of ivory. There are two genera: the small-eared Asian elephant, *Elephas Maximus* and the African elephant, *Loxodonta africana,* with large flapping ears. **2** Something unwieldy, burdensome, or hard to dispose of. See WHITE ELEPHANT. **3** A size of paper, 23 by 38 inches. [<OF *olifant* <L *elephantus* <Gk. *elephas, -antos* ivory; ult. origin unknown]

AFRICAN ELEPHANT
(Height at the shoulder rarely above 11 feet; the Indian elephant slightly smaller; the cows, 7 to 9 feet)

El·e·phan·ta (el'ə·fan'tə) An island in Bombay Harbor; site of Brahmanic caves carved in hillside (main hall, eighth century) and statues.

Elephant Butte Dam The main unit of the Rio Grande reclamation project in SW New Mexico; 306 feet high; 1,674 feet long; impounding **Elephant Butte Reservoir.**

elephant ear The taro.

elephant foot A South African twining vine (*Testudinaria elephantipes*) of the yam family, having a conical, cormlike stem covered with a barky substance which, becoming deeply cracked, forms large angular protuberances like those on the shell of a tortoise (whence the name *tortoise plant*): often cultivated in greenhouses. Also called *Hottentot bread.* Also **el'e·phant's-foot'.**

el·e·phan·ti·a·sis (el'ə·fən·tī'ə·sis) *n. Pathol.* The final chronic stage of a filariasis caused by the presence in the blood and lymph of a parasitic nematode worm (*Wuchereria bancrofti*). It is characterized by a thickening and hardening of the skin, together with an enormous enlargement of the part affected, usually the lower extremities. [<L <Gk. <*elephas* elephant]

el·e·phan·tine (el'ə·fan'tēn, -tin, -tīn) *adj.* **1** Pertaining to an elephant. **2** Enormous; unwieldy.

El·eu·sin·i·a (el'yo͞o·sin'ē·ə) *n. pl.* The Athenian festival and mysteries in honor of Demeter and Persephone, formerly held at Eleusis. [<Gk.]

El·eu·sin·i·an (el'yo͞o·sin'ē·ən) *adj.* Of or pertaining to Eleusis or the Eleusinia.

Eleusinian mysteries The secret religious rites, which were probably originated by the Thracians at Eleusis and later absorbed by the Athenian state religion.

E·leu·sis (i·lo͞o'sis) In Greek mythology, the son of Mercury.

E·leu·sis (i·lo͞o'sis) A port on the **Bay of Eleusis** in east central Greece, on the site of an ancient Attic city. See ELEUSINIA. Modern Greek **E·lev·sis** (â'lâf·sēs').

El·eu·the·ri·a (el'yo͞o·thir'ē·ə) *n.* A quadrennial festival kept by the Greeks after the battle of Plataea in honor of Zeus Eleutherios (the Deliverer). [<Gk.]

el·e·vate (el'ə·vāt) *v.t.* **·vat·ed, ·vat·ing** **1** To raise; lift up. **2** To raise in rank, status, position, etc.; promote. **3** To raise the spirits of; cheer; inspire. **4** To raise the pitch or loudness of. **5** To raise the moral character or intellectual nature of, as a conversation. See synonyms under HEIGHTEN, PROMOTE, RAISE. [<L *elevatus,* pp. of *elevare* <*ex-* out + *levare* lighten]

el·e·vat·ed (el'ə·vā'tid) *adj.* **1** Lofty in situation; high: an *elevated* plateau. **2** Lofty in character; sublime: *elevated* sentiments. See synonyms under GRAND, HIGH. **—** *n. Colloq.* An overhead railroad.

el·e·va·tion (el'ə·vā'shən) *n.* **1** The act of elevation; exaltation. **2** An elevated place. **3** *Archit.* A geometrical drawing of the upright parts of a structure, as shown in blueprints and scale drawings. **4** *Eccl.* **a** The raising of the eucharistic elements: also **elevation of the Host. b** The music of voice or instrument that accompanies the elevation of the Host. **5** Height above the sea level. **6** *Astron.* The angular distance of a celestial body above the horizon. See synonyms under HEIGHT, RAMPART.

el·e·va·tor (el'ə·vā'tər) *n.* **1** One who or that which elevates. **2** A hoisting mechanism for grain. **3** A warehouse where grain is elevated and distributed. **4** A movable platform or cage in a building, for carrying freight or passengers up or down. **5** *Aeron.* An auxiliary airfoil, by the tilting or dipping of which the ascent or descent of the airplane is regulated: also called *diving rudder.* See illustration under AIRPLANE.

é·lève (ā·lev') *n. French* Pupil; scholar.

e·lev·en (i·lev'ən) *adj.* Consisting of one more than ten. **—** *n.* **1** The cardinal number preceding twelve and following ten. **2** Any of the symbols (11, xi, XI) representing this number. **3** A team or side of eleven players, as in cricket or football. [OE *endleofan*]

e·lev·en·fold (i·lev'ən·fōld') *adj.* Consisting of eleven; eleven times as great or as much; undecuplicate.

e·lev·enth (i·lev'ənth) *adj.* **1** Next in order after the tenth. **2** Being one of eleven equal parts. **—** *n.* **1** One of eleven equal parts. **2** The quotient of a unit divided by eleven: five is one *eleventh* of fifty-five. **3** In a series, the unit or thing after the tenth.

eleventh hour The latest possible time; the last opportunity.

el·e·von (el'ə·von) *n. Aeron.* A combined aileron and elevator, used in certain types of airplanes. [<ELEV(ATOR) + (AILER)ON]

elf (elf) *n. pl.* **elves** (elvz) **1** In folklore, a dwarfish, mischievous sprite. **2** A dwarf or diminutive person: a pet name for a lively child. [OE *ælf.* Akin to OAF.]

El Fai·yum (el fī·o͞om') See FAIYUM.

elf·child (elf'chīld') *n.* A child believed to have been left by elves in place of one that they have stolen; a changeling.

El Fer·rol del Cau·di·llo (el fer·rōl' thel kou·thē'lyō) A port in NW Spain. Formerly **El Fer·rol'.**

elf·in (el'fin) *adj.* Relating or belonging to elves. **—** *n.* **1** An elf. **2** A sportive child.

elf·ish (el'fish) *adj.* Relating to elves; mischievous. **— elf'ish·ly** *adv.* **— elf'ish·ness** *n.*

elf-land (elf'land') *n.* The supposed home of the elves; fairyland.

elf-lock (elf'lok') *n.* A lock of hair tangled as if by elves; a straggling lock.

El·gar (el'gär), **Sir Edward,** 1857–1934, English composer.

El·gin (el'gin) **1** A burgh, county town of Morayshire, Scotland. **2** A former name for MORAYSHIRE: also **El'gin·shire** (-shir). **3** (el'·jin) A city in NE Illinois.

Elgin marbles A collection of Greek sculpture in the British Museum, formerly on the Acropolis at Athens. [after the Earl of *Elgin,* who had the collection brought to England, 1803–12]

El Gi·zeh (el gē'zə) See GIZA.

El·gon (el'gon), **Mount** An extinct volcano on the Uganda-Kenya border NE of Lake Victoria; 14,178 feet.

El Gre·co (el grā'kō, grek'ō) See under GRECO.

El Ha·sa (el hä'sə) See HASA, EL.

E·li (ē'lī) A Biblical high priest and judge. 1 *Sam.* iv 13–18. [<Hebrew, the highest]

E·li·a (ē'lē·ə) Pen name of Charles Lamb.

E·li·as (i·lī'əs) See ELIJAH.

e·lic·it (i·lis'it) *v.t.* To draw out or forth, as by some attraction or inducement; bring to light: to *elicit* truth. [<L *elicitus,* pp. of *elicere* <*ex-* out + *lacere* entice] **— e·lic'i·ta'tion** *n.* **— e·lic'i·tor** *n.*

e·lide (i·līd') *v.t.* **e·lid·ed, e·lid·ing** **1** To omit (a vowel or syllable) in writing or pronouncing a word. **2** To suppress; omit; ignore. **3** *Law* To annul. [<L *elidere* <*ex-* out + *laedere* strike] **— e·lid'i·ble** *adj.*

el·i·gi·ble (el'ə·jə·bəl) *adj.* Capable of being chosen or elected; worthy of acceptance. **—***n.* One who is eligible in any sense. [<F *éligible* <L *eligere.* See ELECT.] **— el'i·gi·bil'i·ty, el'i·gi·ble·ness** *n.* **— el'i·gi·bly** *adv.*

E·li·hu (el'ə·hyo͞o) A masculine personal name. [See ELIJAH]
— Elihu A young man who visits Job. *Job* xxxii–xxxvii.

E·li·jah (i·lī'jə) A masculine personal name. Also **E·li'as.** [<Hebrew, Jehovah is my God]
— Elijah A prophet of Jehovah in the time of Ahab, ninth century B.C.

e·lim·i·nate (i·lim'ə·nāt) *v.t.* **·nat·ed, ·nat·ing** **1** To expel; get rid of. **2** To disregard as irrelevant or incorrect; ignore. **3** *Physiol.* To void; excrete. **4** *Math.* To remove (a quantity) from a system of algebraic equations. [<L *eliminatus,* pp. of *eliminare* <*ex-* out + *limen* a threshold]

e·lim·i·na·tion (i·lim'ə·nā'shən) *n.* **1** The act of eliminating. **2** The state of being cast out or expelled. **— e·lim'i·na'tive** *adj.* **— e·lim'i·na·tor** *n.* **— e·lim'i·na·to'ry** (-tôr'ē, -tō'rē) *adj.*

El·i·nor (el'ə·nər, -nor) See ELEANOR.

El·i·ot (el'ē·ət), **Charles William,** 1834–1926, U.S. educator; president of Harvard 1869–1909. **— George** Pen name of Mary Ann Evans, 1819–80, English novelist. **— John,** 1604–90, American clergyman; apostle to the Indians. **— Sir John,** 1592–1632, English statesman and champion of liberty. **— T(homas) S(tearns),** 1888–1965, U.S. poet, dramatist and essayist; became a British subject.

E·liph·a·let (i·lif'ə·lit) A masculine personal name. Also **E·liph'a·lat** (-lat). [<Hebrew, God delivers]

E·lis (ē′lis) A nome of west central Greece; 1,178 square miles, in part the ancient country and city of Elis. Modern Greek **I·li·a** (ē·lyē′ä).

E·lis·a·beth (i·liz′ə·bəth) See ELIZABETH.

E·lis·a·beth·ville (i·liz′ə·bəth·vil′) A former name for LUBUMBASHI.

E·li·sha (i·lī′shə) A masculine personal name. [<Hebrew, God is salvation]
— **Elisha**, ninth century B.C., a Jewish prophet of Jehovah; successor of Elijah.

e·li·sion (i·lizh′ən) n. 1 The eliding or striking out of a part of a word, as in "o'er" for "over." 2 A suppression of a part. [<L *elisio, -onis* < *elidere*. See ELIDE.]

e·lite (ā·lēt′, i·lēt′) n. 1 The choicest part, as of a society, army, etc.; the pick. 2 A size of typewriter type, equivalent to 10–point, with 12 characters to the inch. Also **é·lite**. [<F *élite* <Med. L *electa* choice <L *eligere*. See ELECT.]

Élite Guard The Schutzstaffel.

e·lix·ir (i·lik′sər) n. 1 A sweetened alcoholic medicinal preparation; a cordial; formerly a compound tincture. 2 An imaginary liquid or soluble substance by means of which alchemists once hoped to change base metals into gold. 3 An imaginary cordial supposed to be capable of sustaining life indefinitely: also *Obs.* **elixir vi·tae** (vī′tē). 4 The essential principle; concentrated essence. [<Med. L <Arabic *al-iksir* <Gk. *xerion* medicated powder < *xeros* dry]

E·liz·a·beth (i·liz′ə·bəth) A feminine personal name. Also **E·li·za** (i·lī′zə), **E·lis·a·beth** (i·liz′ə·bəth, *Dan., Du., Ger.* ā·lē′zä·bet), *Fr.* **É·li·sa·beth** (ā·lē·zä·bet′), *Ital.* **E·li·sa·bet·ta** (ā·lē′zä·bet′tä). [<Hebrew, God has sworn]
— **Elizabeth**, the mother of John the Baptist. *Luke* ii 5–14.
— **Elizabeth**, born 1900, Elizabeth Angela Marguerite Bowes-Lyon, wife of George VI of England, king 1937–52.
— **Elizabeth**, pseudonym of Countess Elizabeth Mary Russell. See RUSSELL.
— **Elizabeth, Saint**, 1207–31, Hungarian princess; queen of Thuringia 1221–27.
— **Elizabeth I**, 1533–1603, queen of England 1558–1603; daughter of Henry VIII and Anne Boleyn.
— **Elizabeth II**, born 1926, Elizabeth Alexandra Mary, queen of Great Britain 1952– ; daughter of George VI; married to Prince Philip.
— **Elizabeth Pe·trov·na** (pe·trôv′nə), 1709–62, empress of Russia 1741–62.

E·liz·a·beth (i·liz′ə·bəth) A port in NE New Jersey.

E·liz·a·be·than (i·liz′ə·bē′thən, -beth′ən) adj. Relating to Elizabeth I of England, or to her era. — n. 1 An Englishman who lived during the reign of Elizabeth. 2 An author who wrote during her reign or during the reign of James I.

Elizabethan sonnet See under SONNET.

Elizabeth River A short, branching river of SE Virginia.

E·liz·a·beth·ville (i·liz′ə·bəth·vil′) See ELISABETHVILLE.

E·li·za·vet·pol (ye·lē′sä·vet·pôl′y′) Former name of KIROVABAD.

elk (elk) n. pl. **elks** or **elk** 1 A large deer of northern Europe and Asia (genus *Alces*), with palmated antlers and the upper lip forming a proboscis for browsing upon trees. 2 The American wap·iti. [ME *elke* <OE *elh*]

Elk (elk) A town in NE Poland. *German* Lyck (lēk).

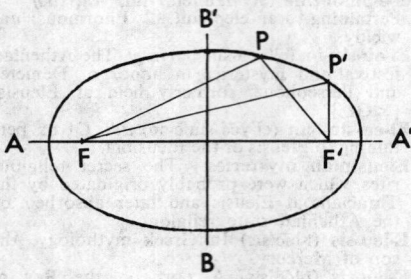
ELK
(Height at the shoulder up to 7 feet)

El Kha·lil (el kä·lēl′, khä-) The Arabic name for HEBRON.

elk·hound (elk′hound′) n. A sporting dog of Norwegian origin, of medium size, with a short, robust body and thick gray coat.

Elk Mountains A range of the Rocky Mountains in west central Colorado; highest peak, 14,259 feet.

ell¹ (el) n. A measure of length now rarely used; in England, 45 inches, or 1.114 meters. [OE *eln* an arm's length]

ell² (el) n. Anything shaped like the letter L, as an addition at right angles to one side of a house. Also **el**.

El·las (el′əs) The modern Greek name for GREECE.

El·len (el′ən) A feminine personal name. [See HELEN]

El·ler·y (el′ər·ē), **William**, 1727–1820, American lawyer; signer, for Rhode Island, of the Declaration of Independence.

Elles·mere Island (elz′mir) An island in NE Franklin District, Northwest Territories, Canada; 77,392 square miles.

El·lice Islands (el′is) An island group SE of the Gilbert Islands, comprising a district of the Gilbert and Ellice Islands colony; total, 9 1/2 square miles: formerly **Lagoon Islands**.

El·lick (el′ik) Diminutive of ALEXANDER.

El·li·ott (el′ē·ət), **Maxine**, 1871–1940, stage name of the U.S. actress *Jessie Dermot*.

el·lipse (i·lips′) n. *Geom.* 1 A plane curve such that the sum of the distances from any

ELLIPSE
A–A′ Major axis. *B–B′* Minor axis.
F, F′ Foci. *P, P′* Points on curve.
FP + PF′ = FP′ + P′F′

point of the curve to two fixed points, called *foci*, is a constant. 2 A conic section. [<L *ellipsis*. See ELLIPSIS.]

el·lip·sis (i·lip′sis) n. pl. **·ses** (-sēz) 1 The omission of a word or words necessary to complete a sentence or expression. 2 Marks indicating omission, such as . . . or * * *. Also **eclipsis**. [<L <Gk. *elleipsis* <*en-* in + *leipsis* a leaving <*leipein* leave]

el·lip·soid (i·lip′soid) n. *Geom.* A solid of which every plane section is an ellipse or a circle. — adj. Resembling a compressed sphere or ellipsoid: also **el·lip·soi·dal** (ē′lip·soi′dl).

el·lip·tic (i·lip′tik) adj. 1 Of, pertaining to, or shaped like an ellipse; oblong with rounded ends. 2 Characterized by ellipsis; shortened. Also **el·lip′ti·cal**. — **el·lip′ti·cal·ly** adv.

el·lip·tic·i·ty (el′ip·tis′ə·tē, i·lip′-) n. 1 The state of being elliptic. 2 The degree of deviation of an ellipse from a circle.

El·lis (el′is), **Alexander John**, 1814–90, English philologist and phoneticist. — **(Henry) Havelock**, 1859–1939, English psychologist and author.

Ellis Island (el′is) An island in upper New York Bay; formerly site of the chief United States immigration station.

el·lit·or·al (i·lit′ər·əl) adj. Of or pertaining to that part of the ocean from a depth of below 120 feet to as far as the light will penetrate.

Ells·worth (elz′wərth), **Lincoln**, 1880–1951, U.S. polar explorer. — **Oliver**, 1745–1807, American jurist.

ell·wand (el′wänd) n. A measuring stick one ell in length.

elm (elm) n. 1 A deciduous shade tree of America, Europe, and Asia (genus *Ulmus*), with a broad, spreading, or overarching top: *U. americana* is the American elm and *U. fulva* the slippery elm. 2 The wood of this tree.

El·man (el′mən), **Mischa**, 1891–1967, U.S. violinist born in Russia.

elm–bark beetle (elm′bärk′) Any of various beetles (family *Scolytidae*) destructive of elm trees, especially a European species (*Scolytus multistratus*) introduced into America, which acts as the carrier of a parasitic fungus.

El Mis·ti (el mēs′tē) A volcano in southern Peru; 19,110 feet.

elm–leaf beetle (elm′lēf′) A coleopterous insect (*Galerucella xanthomelaena* or *luteola*), yellowish–green with dark lateral spots: introduced from Europe. Both larvae and adults are injurious to elm trees.

elm·y (el′mē) adj. Consisting of or abounding in elm trees.

E·lo·bey (ā′lō·bā′), **Great** and **Little** Two islands in the Bight of Biafra, comprising part of Spanish Guinea; total, 1 1/2 square miles.

el·o·cu·tion (el′ə·kyōō′shən) n. 1 The art of correct intonation, and inflection, in public speaking or reading. 2 Manner of utterance. [<L *elocutio, -onis* < *eloqui* < *ex-* out + *loqui* speak] — **el′o·cu′tion·ar′y** adj.

el·o·cu·tion·ist (el′ə·kyōō′shən·ist) n. One who is skilled in or teaches elocution; especially, one who gives public elocutionary readings.

é·loge (ā·lōzh′, *Fr.* ā·lôzh′) n. A biographical and eulogistic memoir or panegyric. Also **el·o·gy** (el′ō·jē). [<F <Med. L *eulogium* a eulogy; infl. in form by L *elogium* an inscription]

E·lo·him (e·lō·him′, -lō′him) God: Hebrew name used in the Old Testament. [<Hebrew *'Elōhīm*, pl. of *'Eloah* God]

E·lo·hist (e·lō′hist) n. The author of those portions of the Hexateuch that are characterized by the use of *Elohim* for God instead of *Yahweh* or *Jehovah*. Compare YAHWIST.

E·lo·his·tic (el′ō·his′tik) adj. 1 Of or pertaining to those portions of the Hexateuch where *Elohim* occurs in the Hebrew text and not *Yahweh* or *Jehovah*. 2 Written by the Elohist.

e·loin (i·loin′) v.t. *Law* To remove beyond the jurisdiction of; carry away, as property. Also **e·loign′**. [<OF *esloignier* carry off <LL *elongare*. See ELONGATE.] — **e·loin′er, e·loign′er** n. — **e·loin′ment, e·loign′ment** n.

E·lo·i·sa (ā′lō·ē′zä) Italian form of LOUISE.

e·lon·gate (i·lông′gāt, i·long′-) v.t. & v.i. **·gat·ed, ·gat·ing** To make or grow longer; lengthen. — adj. Elongated. See synonyms under PROTRACT. [<LL *elongatus*, pp. of *elongare* <*ex-* away + *longe* far off]

e·lon·ga·tion (ē′lông·gā′shən, ē′long-) n. 1 The act of elongating, or the state of being elongated. 2 An addition or appendage that adds to the length of something. 3 An extension or continuation.

e·lope (i·lōp′) v.i. **e·loped, e·lop·ing** 1 To run away with a lover, usually to get married. 2 To abscond; run off. [<AF *aloper*. Cf. OE *ahleapen* flee] — **e·lope′ment** n. — **e·lop′er** n.

el·o·quence (el′ə·kwəns) n. 1 Lofty, impassioned, and convincing utterance. 2 The quality of being eloquent, moving, forceful, or persuasive. See synonyms under SPEECH.

el·o·quent (el′ə·kwənt) adj. 1 Possessed of or manifesting eloquence. 2 Persuasive; convincing. 3 Visibly expressive of emotion. [<L *eloquens, -entis* ppr. of *eloqui*. See ELOCUTION.] — **el′o·quent·ly** adv.

El Pas·o (el pas′ō) A city on the Rio Grande in western Texas.

El Pa·so del Nor·te (el pä′sō thel nôr′tä) A former name of CIUDAD JUÁREZ.

El·phin·stone (el′fin·stōn, -stən), **Mountstuart**, 1779–1859, British historian and statesman. — **William**, 1431–1514, Scottish prelate; founded Aberdeen University.

El·sa (el′sə) A feminine personal name. Also *Dan., Ger.* **El·se** (el′zə), *Du.* **Els·ye** (els′yə). [See ALICE]
— **Elsa** The heroine of Wagner's opera *Lohengrin*.

El Sal·va·dor (el sal′və·dôr, *Sp.* el säl′vä·thôr′) A republic in western Central America; 13,176 square miles; capital, San Salvador. — **Sal·va·dor′an, Sal′va·do′ri·an**, adj. & n.

El·sass (el′zäs) The German name for ALSACE.

El·sass–Lo·thring·en (el′zäs·lō′tring·ən) The German name for ALSACE–LORRAINE.

else (els) adv. 1 In a different place, time, or way; elsewhere. 2 If the case or facts were different; otherwise; besides; instead. — adj. Additional; different; somebody *else*: What *else* can I do? — conj. If not; under other conditions. [OE *elles*]
◆ The expressions *someone else, anyone else, everyone else, somebody else*, etc., are in good usage treated as substantive phrases and have the possessive inflection upon the *else*: *somebody else's* umbrella.

else·where (els′hwâr′) adv. In or to another place or places; somewhere or anywhere else.

El·sie (el′sē) A feminine personal name. [See ALICE]

El·si·nore (el′sə·nôr, -nōr) A port on Zealand Island, Denmark; scene of Shakespeare's *Hamlet*: Danish *Helsingør*.

e·lu·ci·date (i·lōō′sə·dāt) *v.t.* **·dat·ed, ·dat·ing** To throw light upon; clear up; make plain. See synonyms under INTERPRET. [<LL *elucidatus,* pp. of *elucidare* <*ex-* out + *lucidus* clear] — **e·lu′ci·da′tive, e·lu′ci·da·to′ry** (-də·tôr′ē, -tō′rē) *adj.* — **e·lu′ci·da′tor** *n.*

e·lu·ci·da·tion (i·lōō′sə·dā′shən) *n.* The act of of elucidating; an illustration.

e·lude (i·lōōd′) *v.t.* **e·lud·ed, e·lud·ing 1** To avoid or escape from by dexterity or artifice. **2** To escape the notice or understanding of: Your meaning *eludes* me. See synonyms under ESCAPE. [<L *eludere* <*ex-* out + *ludere* play] — **e·lud′i·ble** *adj.*

E·lul (e·lōōl′, *Hebrew* el′ōōl) A Jewish month nearly corresponding to September. See CALENDAR (Hebrew).

e·lu·sion (i·lōō′zhən) *n.* The act of eluding or escaping; evasion. [<Med. L *elusio, -onis* <L *eludere.* See ELUDE.]

e·lu·sive (i·lōō′siv) *adj.* **1** Tending to slip away or escape; hard to understand; baffling. **2** Hard to grasp or keep: the *elusive* dream of wealth. Also **e·lu′so·ry** (-sər·ē). — **e·lu′sive·ly** *adv.* — **e·lu′sive·ness** *n.*

e·lute (i·lōōt′) *adj. Entomol.* Having indistinct or barely visible markings: said especially of insects. [<L *elutus,* pp. of *eluere* <*ex-* away + *luere* wash]

e·lu·tri·ate (i·lōō′trē·āt) *v.t.* **·at·ed, ·at·ing 1** To purify by washing. **2** To separate, as finer from coarser powder, by washing and straining or decanting. [<L *elutriatus,* pp. of *elutriare* wash off] — **e·lu′tri·a′tion** *n.*

e·lu·vi·a·tion (i·lōō′vē·ā′shən) *n.* The process, mechanical or chemical, of removing the fine particles of soil from an area. [<L *eluvies* a washing away + -ATION]

e·lu·vi·um (i·lōō′vē·əm) *n. Geol.* A deposit of soil and dust particles remaining where they were formed by the decomposition of rock masses. [<NL <L *eluvies* <*eluere.* See ELUTE.] — **e·lu′vi·al** *adj.*

El·ve·hjem (el·vā′əm), **Conrad Arnold,** born 1901, U. S. physiologist and biochemist.

el·ver (el′vər) *n.* A young eel. [Var. of *eelfare* the journey of young eels upstream <EEL + FARE]

elves (elvz) Plural of ELF.

elv·et (el′vit) *n. Rare* A little elf.

elv·ish (el′vish) *adj.* Elfish; prankish. Also **elv′an.** — **elv′ish·ly** *adv.*

E·ly (ē′lē) An urban district in the **Isle of Ely,** an administrative county of Cambridgeshire, England; site of a 12th century cathedral.

El·y·ot (el′ē·ət, el′yət), **Sir Thomas,** 1490?–1546, English scholar, diplomat, and lexicographer.

É·ly·sée (ā·lē·zā′) *n.* The residence in Paris of the president of France.

E·ly·sian (i·lizh′ən, -ē·ən) *adj.* **1** Belonging to, or like, Elysium. **2** Supremely blessed or happy.

E·ly·si·um (i·lizh′ē·əm, i·liz′-) **1** In Greek mythology, the abode of the blessed dead, represented as in Hades, or in the Islands of the Blest in the Western Ocean; also **Elysian Fields. 2** A place or a condition of supreme delight; a paradise. [<L <Gk. *ēlysion (pedion)* the Elysian (field)]

el·y·tra (el′ə·trə) Plural of ELYTRON.

el·y·troid (el′ə·troid) *adj.* Sheathlike; like an elytron.

el·y·tron (el′ə·tron) *n. pl.* **·tra** *Entomol.* One of the thickened forewings of certain insects, as beetles; a wing cover: usually in the plural for the wing pair. Also **el′y·trum** (-trəm). [<Gk. *elytron* case <*eiluein* wrap up]

El·ze·vir (el′zə·vir) *adj.* **1** Belonging or related to Louis Elzevir, his successors, or their firm. **2** Denoting the type face used by the Elzevirs in their books. — *n.* **1** A book printed by the Elzevirs. **2** A compact, modern printing type.

El·ze·vir (el′zə·vir), **Louis,** 1540?–1617, Dutch printer; founder of a 17th century publishing house celebrated for fine editions of the classics.

El·ze·vir·an (el′zə·vir′ən) *adj.* Of or pertaining to the Elzevirs. — *n.* A collector of Elzevirs. Also **El′ze·vir′i·an.**

em (em) *n.* **1** The name of the thirteenth letter in the English alphabet, written M or m. **2** *Printing* The square of the body size of a type; especially, a pica *em,* about 1/6 of an inch, used as a standard unit of measurement: originally, the space occupied by the letter M in a font.

em–[1] *prefix* Var. of EN–[1], used before the labials *b, p,* and *m,* as in *embody, empower,* etc.

em–[2] Assimilated var. of EN–[2].

'em (əm, m) *pron. Colloq.* Them. [OE *heom* dative pl. of *he* he]

E·ma (ā′mä) Spanish form of EMMA.

e·ma·ci·ate (i·mā′shē·āt) *v.t.* **·at·ed, ·at·ing** To make abnormally lean; cause to lose flesh. [<L *emaciatus,* pp. of *emaciare* waste away <*ex-* out + *macies* leanness] — **e·ma′ci·a′tion** *n.*

e·ma·ci·at·ed (i·mā′shē·ā′tid) *adj.* Very thin; wasted away.

em·a·nant (em′ə·nənt) *adj.* Issuing from a source; emanating. [<L *emanans, -antis,* ppr. of *emanare.* See EMANATE.]

em·a·nate (em′ə·nāt) *v.i.* **·nat·ed, ·nat·ing 1** To come or flow forth, as from a source. **2** to take rise; originate; emerge. [<L *emanatus,* pp. of *emanare* <*ex-* out + *manare* flow]

em·a·na·tion (em′ə·nā′shən) *n.* **1** The act of issuing or flowing forth from some origin or source. **2** That which proceeds from an origin or source; efflux; effluence. **3** The pantheistic doctrine that all existing things have been created as effluxes of the Divine Essence; hence, an outcome or product of such a process. **4** *Physics* An inert gaseous product of disintegration in certain radioactive substances, as radon and thoron. — **em′a·na′tive** *adj.* — **em′a·na′tive·ly** *adv.*

e·man·ci·pate (i·man′sə·pāt) *v.t.* **·pat·ed, ·pat·ing 1** To release from bondage or slavery, or any physical or spiritual oppression or authority; liberate; set free. **2** In Roman law, to free (a child) from its father's control. [<L *emancipatus,* pp. of *emancipare* <*ex-* out + *manus* hand + *capere* taken] — **e·man′ci·pa·to′ry** (-pə·tôr′ē, -tō′rē) *adj.* — **e·man′ci·pa′tive** *adj.* — **e·man′ci·pa′tor** *n.*

e·man·ci·pa·tion (i·man′sə·pā′shən) *n.* **1** The act of emancipating, or the state of being emancipated. **2** Liberation from bondage, disability, or dependence, or from any injurious or undue restraint or influence: *emancipation* from evil associations. **3** In Roman law, the enfranchisement of a minor by his father. See synonyms under LIBERTY.

Emancipation Proclamation A proclamation issued by President Abraham Lincoln on January 1, 1863, declaring free all Negro slaves in the seceded States: reinforced by the 13th Amendment (1865), which freed the slaves in eight other States.

E·man·u·el (i·man′yōō·əl, -el; *Ger.* ā·mä′nōō·el) See EMMANUEL. Also *Ital.* **E·ma·nu·e·le** (ā·mä′nōō·ā′lā).

e·mar·gi·nate (i·mär′jə·nit, -nāt) *adj. Bot.* Having the margin interrupted or notched; specifically, notched at the summit: said of leaves, petals, etc. Also **e·mar′gi·nat′ed.** [<L *emarginatus,* pp. of *emarginare* <*ex-* off, away + *margo, -inis* border, edge]

e·mas·cu·late (i·mas′kyə·lāt) *v.t.* **·lat·ed, ·lat·ing 1** To deprive of procreative power; castrate; geld. **2** To deprive of strength; weaken; make effeminate. **3** To impair by cutting down or censoring, as a literary work. — *adj.* (i·mas′kyə·lit) Emasculated; weakened. [<L *emasculatus,* pp. of *emasculare* <*ex-* away + *masculus* male] — **e·mas′cu·la′tion** *n.* — **e·mas′cu·la′tive** *adj.* — **e·mas′cu·la′tor** *n.* — **e·mas′cu·la·to′ry** (-tôr′ē, -tō′rē) *adj.*

em·ball (im·bôl′) *v.t. Obs.* To ensphere.

em·balm (im·bäm′) *v.t.* **1** To preserve from decay, as a dead body, by treatment with balsams, antiseptic preparations, drugs, and chemicals. **2** To perfume. **3** To preserve from oblivion. Also spelled *imbalm.* [<F *embaumer* <*em-* in (<L *in-*) + *baume* <OF *basme* BALM]

em·balm·er (im·bä′mər) *n.* **1** One who embalms the dead. **2** Anything that preserves from decay.

em·balm·ment (im·bäm′mənt) *n.* The act of embalming.

em·bank (im·bangk′) *v.t.* To confine or protect by a bank, dike, or the like.

em·bank·ment (im·bangk′mənt) *n.* **1** A protecting or supporting bank. **2** The process of strengthening by a bank. See synonyms under RAMPART.

em·bar (im·bär′) *v.t.* **·barred, ·bar·ring 1** To enclose within bars; fasten in. **2** To stop; check, as by a bar. — **em·bar′ment** *n.*

em·bar·ca·de·ro (im·bär′kə·dâr′ō) *n. SW U.S.* A wharf or landing place. [<Sp. <*embarcar* embark]

em·bar·ca·tion (em′bär·kā′shən) See EMBARKATION.

em·bar·go (im·bär′gō) *n. pl.* **·goes 1** A prohibition by the sovereign power of a nation temporarily restraining vessels from leaving or entering its ports. **2** Authoritative stoppage of foreign commerce or of any special trade. **3** Any imposed impediment; a check or hindrance; specifically, in railroad operation, a notice forbidding massing of cars at specified places. — *v.t.* **·goed, ·go·ing** To lay an embargo upon. [<Sp. <*embargar* <*em-* in (<L *in-*) + *bargar* <LL *barra* a bar]

em·bark (im·bärk′) *v.t.* **1** To put or take aboard a vessel. **2** To invest (money) or involve (a person) in a venture. — *v.i.* **3** To go aboard a vessel, as for a voyage. **4** To engage in a venture. [<F *embarquer* <LL *imbarcare* <*in-* in + *barca* boat] — **em·bark′ment** *n.*

em·bar·ka·tion (em′bär·kā′shən) *n.* The act of embarking. Also spelled *embarcation.*

embarkation center A military establishment near a port for the care of troops about to embark.

em·bar·ras des ri·chesses (äṅ·bȧ·rä′ dā rē·shes′) *French* An encumbrance of wealth; hence, the burden of obligations and circumstances that accompany wealth.

em·bar·rass (im·bar′əs) *v.t.* **1** To make ill at ease, self-conscious, and uncomfortable; abash; disconcert. **2** To involve in difficulties, especially in business. **3** To hamper; encumber. **4** To render difficult; complicate. [<F *embarrasser* <*em-* in (<L *in-*) + *barre* <OF BAR] — **em·bar′rass·ing** *adj.* — **em·bar′rass·ing·ly** *adv.*

Synonyms: abash, confuse, discomfit, disconcert, faze, hamper, hinder, impede, rattle. *Embarrass* implies some influence which impedes freedom of thought, speech, or action and refers to persons and things they plan to do. One is *embarrassed* in the presence of others, and because of their presence. *Confusion* is of the intellect, *embarrassment* of the feelings. A witness may be *embarrassed* by annoying personalities, so as to become *confused* in statements. As applied to mental action, a solitary thinker may be *confused* by some difficulty in a subject, or by some mental defect. *Rattle* is a colloquialism which implies a disorganization of one's mental processes. *Faze* is an Americanism usually found in negative expressions, but sometimes carries the implications of *abash* and *rattle*; as, Nothing can *faze* him. *Hamper* is used either literally or figuratively; as, *hampered* by debt; encumbered. *Hinder* is used in the sense of obstruction; as, Adverse winds *hindered* the ship. Compare ABASH, HINDER, INVOLVE, OBSTRUCT, PERPLEX. *Antonyms*: assure, cheer, compose, embolden, encourage, help, relieve, sustain.

em·bar·rass·ment (im·bar′əs·mənt) *n.* **1** The state of being embarrassed. **2** That which embarrasses.

em·bas·sa·dor (im·bas′ə·dər, -dôr) See AMBASSADOR.

em·bas·sage (em′bə·sij) *n. Obs.* **1** The sending, business, office, or message of an ambassador or an embassy. **2** The body of ambassadors or embassy itself.

em·bas·sy (em′bə·sē) *n. pl.* **·sies 1** An ambassador together with his suite; the person or body of persons deputed for a mission from one government to another. **2** The mission or office of an envoy or ambassador. **3** The official residence of an ambassador and his suite. [Var. of earlier *ambassy* <OF *ambassé* <Med. L *ambactia,* ult. <Celtic]

em·bathe (em·bāth′) *v.t.* **·bathed, ·bath·ing** To bathe; drench; immerse: also spelled *imbathe.*

em·bat·tle[1] (em·bat′l) *v.t.* **·tled, ·tling** To form in line of battle; prepare or equip for battle. [<OF *embataillier* <*en-* in (<L *in-*) + *bataille* BATTLE]

em·bat·tle[2] (em·bat′l) *v.t.* **·tled, ·tling** To furnish with battlements. [<EM-[1] + BATTLE in obs. sense of "fortify" <OF *bastiller* build]

em·bat·tled (em·bat′ld) *adj.* **1** Drawn up in battle array; ready for battle. **2** Made the scene of a muster or battle. **3** Having battlements.

em·bat·tle·ment (em·bat′l·mənt) *n.* **1** A battlement. **2** The fortifying, as of a wall, with battlements. For illustrations see BATTLEMENT.

em·bay (em·bā′) *v.t.* **1** To put or force into a bay, as a ship. **2** To shut in by arms of land.

em·bay·ment (em·bā′mənt) *n.* **1** A bay or large inlet. **2** The process of forming a bay.

em·bed (im·bed′) *v.t.* **·bed·ded, ·bed·ding 1** To place in or as in a bed. **2** To set firmly in surrounding matter. **3** To hold in the mind; keep in memory. Also spelled *imbed.* **—em·bed′ment** *n.*

em·bel·lish (im·bel′ish) *v.t.* **1** To beautify by adding ornamental features; decorate. **2** To heighten the interest of, as a story, by adding fictitious details. See synonyms under ADORN, GARNISH. [<OF *embelliss-*, stem of *embellir* beautify <*em-* in (<L *in-*) + *bel* beautiful <L *bellus*]

em·bel·lish·ment (im·bel′ish·mənt) *n.* **1** The act of adorning. **2** An ornament; ornamentation.

em·ber (em′bər) *n.* **1** A live coal or an unextinguished brand. **2** *pl.* A dying fire. [OE *ǣmerge*]

Ember days *Eccl.* A three-day period of fasting and prayer observed quarterly on the Wednesday, Friday, and Saturday after the first Sunday in Lent, after Whitsunday, after September 14, and after December 13. [OE *ymbrene, ymbryne* circuit, cycle <*ymb* around + *ryne* a running]

Ember week A week including Ember days.

em·bez·zle (im·bez′əl) *v.t.* **·zled ·zling 1** To appropriate fraudulently to one's own use. **2** *Obs.* To misappropriate secretly; make off with. See synonyms under STEAL. [<AF *embesiler* <*em-* in + *besiler* destroy] **—em·bez′·zle·ment** *n.* **—em·bez′zler** *n.*

em·bit·ter (im·bit′ər) *v.t.* To render bitter, unhappy, or resentful. **—em·bit′ter·ment** *n.*

em·blaze (em·blāz′) *v.t.* **·blazed, ·blaz·ing** To emblazon. [EM- + BLAZE[3]] **—em·blaz′er** *n.*

em·bla·zon (em·blā′zən) *v.t.* **1** To adorn with or as with heraldic designs; decorate. **2** To adorn magnificently; set off in resplendent colors. **3** To extol; celebrate the fame or virtues of. **—em·bla′zon·er** *n.* **—em·bla′zon·ment** *n.*

em·bla·zon·ry (em·blā′zən·rē) *n.* *pl.* **·ries 1** The act or art of emblazoning. **2** Heraldic devices, collectively; any brilliantly colored representation or embellishment. See under ESCUTCHEON.

em·blem (em′bləm) *n.* **1** An object suggesting something which it does not directly represent; a figurative representation; symbol. **2** A distinctive badge; ensign. **3** An allegorical picture, usually having a motto. **4** *Obs.* An inlaid or inserted ornament. **—***v.t. Rare* To emblematize. [<L *emblema* inlaid work <Gk. *emblēma* an insertion <*em-* in + *ballein* throw]

Synonyms: attribute, figure, sign, symbol, token, type. An *emblem* has some natural fitness to suggest that for which it stands; a *symbol* has been chosen or agreed upon to suggest something else, with or without natural fitness; a *sign* does actually suggest the thing with or without reason, and with or without intention or choice. A *symbol* may be also an *emblem*. On the other hand, the same thing may be both a *sign* and a *symbol*; a letter of the alphabet is a *sign* which indicates a sound; but letters are often used as mathematical, chemical, or astronomical *symbols*. A *token* is some object given or act done as a pledge or expression of feeling or intent; a ring, the natural *emblem* of eternity, and also its accepted *symbol*, is frequently given as a *token* of friendship or love. Compare FIGURE, IMAGE, LETTER, SIGN.

em·blem·at·ic (em′blə·mat′ik) *adj.* Of, pertaining to, or serving as an emblem; symbolic. Also **em′blem·at′i·cal.** **—em′blem·at′i·cal·ly** *adv.*

em·blem·a·tize (em·blem′ə·tīz) *v.t.* **·tized, ·tiz·ing 1** To serve as an emblem of. **2** To represent by a symbol or emblem.

em·ble·ments (em′blə·mənts) *n. pl. Law* **1** Growing crops produced by the labor of the cultivator of the soil. **2** The right to or profits from such crops. [<OF *emblaement* <*emblaer*, sow with grain <LL *imbladare* <*in-* in + *bladum* grain]

em·blem·ize (em′blə·mīz) *v.t.* **·ized, ·iz·ing** To represent by an emblem; make into an emblem.

em·bod·i·ment (im·bod′i·mənt) *n.* **1** The act or process of embodying, the state of being embodied, or that which embodies; incarnation. **2** A concrete example: She is the *embodiment* of wit.

em·bod·y (im·bod′ē) *v.t.* **·bod·ied, ·bod·y·ing 1** To invest with or as with a body; incarnate; make corporeal. **2** To collect into one whole; incorporate. **3** To express concretely.

em·bold·en (im·bōl′dən) *v.t.* To make bold; give courage to. See synonyms under ABET, ENCOURAGE.

em·bo·lec·to·my (em′bə·lek′tə·mē) *n. Surg.* Removal of an embolus. [<EMBOL(US) + -ECTOMY]

em·bol·ic (em·bol′ik) *adj.* **1** *Pathol.* Of, pertaining to, or caused by embolism or an embolus: *embolic* abscesses. **2** Embolismic. **3** *Biol.* Growing or pushing inward: *embolic* invagination.

em·bo·lism (em′bə·liz′əm) *n.* **1** *Pathol.* The stopping up of a vein or artery, as by a blood clot or foreign particle. **2** Intercalation, as of days, for the adjustment of the calendar. [<LL *embolismus* <Gk. *embolismos* intercalary <*embolos.* See EMBOLUS.]

em·bo·lis·mic (em′bə·liz′mik) *adj.* **1** Of or pertaining to embolism or intercalation. **2** Adjusted by intercalation; intercalated.

embolismic year The period covered by 13 lunar months or 384 days; the year in which there is an intercalation.

em·bo·lo·la·li·a (em′bə·lō·lā′lē·ə) *Psychiatry* The interspersing of speech or writing with meaningless words or phrases. Also **em′bo·lo·pha′si·a** (-fā′zhē·ə). [<NL <Gk. *embolos* peg + *lalia* talk, speech]

em·bo·lus (em′bə·ləs) *n.* *pl.* **·li** (-lī) **1** Anything inserted or shaped for insertion, as a wedge, sucker of a pump, plunger, or piston. **2** *Pathol.* Any solid body (as a piece of fibrin or a blood clot) that forms an obstruction in a blood vessel. [<L <Gk. *embolos* peg <*en-* in + *ballein* throw]

em·bon·point (äṅ·bôṅ·pwaṅ′) *n. French* Marked corpulence; plumpness; stoutness.

em·bor·der (em·bôr′dər) *v.t.* To furnish with a border.

em·bos·om (em·bo͝oz′əm, -bo͞o′zəm) *v.t.* **1** To take to the bosom; embrace. **2** To cherish. **3** To shelter; enclose.

em·boss[1] (im·bôs′, -bos′) *v.t.* **1** To cover or adorn (a surface) with raised figures, designs, etc. **2** To raise or represent (designs, figures, etc.) from or upon a surface. **3** To decorate sumptuously. [<OF *embocer* <*em-* in + *boce* a boss] **—em·boss′er** *n.* **—em·boss′ment** *n.*

em·boss[2] (im·bôs′, -bos′) *v.t. Obs.* **1** To cover with foam; fleck. **2** To drive, as a hunted animal, into a thicket; press to extremity; tire out. **3** To conceal. [ME *embose,* ? <EN-[1] + OF *bois* woods, thicket]

em·bossed (im·bôst′, -bost′) *adj.* **1** Ornamented with raised figures. **2** *Obs.* Swollen; puffed up.

em·boss·ing (im·bôs′ing, -bos′-) *n.* In textiles, the process of raising design from the surface, so that it stands out in relief: usually done, in making embossed damask, seersucker, etc., by passing a resin-impregnated fabric between hot, engraved metal rollers, but for velvet and plush effected by shearing high pile to different levels or by pressing parts flat.

em·bou·chure (äm·bo͞o·sho͝or′, *Fr.* äṅ·bo͞o·shür′) *n.* **1** The mouth, as of a river or stream; point of discharge. **2** Any opening resembling a mouth: the *embouchure* of a cannon or embrasure. **3** A mouthpiece, or the place where the mouth is applied. **4** Position or adjustment of the lips, tongue, and other organs in playing a wind instrument or in vocalization. [<F <*emboucher* <*em-* in (<L *in-*) + *bouche* mouth <L *bucca* cheek]

em·bow (em·bō′) *v.t.* To bend or curve like a bow; arch. **—em·bow′ment** *n.*

em·bowed (em·bōd′) *adj.* Bent like a bow; curved outward; arched: an *embowed* window.

em·bow·el (em·bou′əl, -boul′) *v.t.* **·eled** or **·elled, ·el·ing** or **·el·ling 1** To disembowel; figuratively, to rend. **2** To embed deeply: *emboweled* in the earth. [Def. 1 <OF *enboweler*, alter. of *esboueler* <*es-* out (<L *ex-*) + *boel* BOWEL; def. 2 <EN-[1] + BOWEL]

em·bow·er (em·bou′ər) *v.t.* & *v.i.* To cover, shelter, or rest in or as in a bower.

em·brace[1] (im·brās′) *v.* **·braced, ·brac·ing** *v.t.* **1** To take or infold in the arms; hug. **2** To accept willingly; adopt, as a religion or doctrine. **3** To avail oneself of: to *embrace* an offer. **4** To surround; encircle. **5** To include; contain. **6** To take in visually or mentally. **7** To have sexual intercourse with. **—***v.i.* **8** To hug each other. **—***n.* The act of embracing; a clasping in the arms; a hug. [<OF *embracer* <LL *in-* in + *bracchia* arm] **—em·brace′ment** *n.* **—em·brac′er** *n.*

Synonyms (verb): adopt, clasp, comprehend, comprise, contain, encircle, enclose, encompass, entwine, environ, espouse, grasp, hold, hug, surround. See CARESS. *Antonyms*: disown, exclude, refuse, reject, repel, repulse.

em·brace[2] (em·brās′) *v.t.* **·braced, ·brac·ing** *Law* To influence, or attempt to influence, corruptly. [Back formation from EMBRACER]

em·brac·er (em·brā′sər) *n. Law* One guilty of embracery. Also **em·brace′or.** [<OF *embraceor* <*embraser* kindle, incite <*em-* in + *braise* charcoal]

em·brac·er·y (em·brā′sər·ē) *n. Law* The act of influencing or trying to influence, corrupt, or bribe a jury, judge, etc.

em·branch·ment (em·branch′mənt, -bränch′-) *n.* A branching out or off, as of an arm of a river; a branch, ramification, or division.

em·bran·gle (em·brang′gəl) *v.t.* **·gled, ·gling** To entangle; complicate; confuse. [<EM-[2] + dial. *brangle* brawl] **—em·bran′gle·ment** *n.*

em·bra·sure (em·brā′zhər) *n.* **1** An opening in a wall, as for a cannon. **2** *Archit.* **a** The sloping or beveling of an opening in a wall, as of a window or door, so as to enlarge its interior profile. **b** The opening itself, or the space within it. For illustrations see BASTION, BATTLEMENT. [<F <*embraser* widen <*em-* in (<L *in-*) + *braser* bevel]

em·brit·tle (em·brit′l) *v.t.* **·tled, ·tling** To make brittle, as steel by sudden cooling.

em·brit·tle·ment (em·brit′l·mənt) *n.* A deterioration of the lining metal of steam boilers, due to the presence of excess sodium carbonate in the water.

em·bro·cate (em′brō·kāt) *v.t.* **·cat·ed, ·cat·ing** To moisten and rub, as with liniment or oil. [<Med. L *embrocatus,* pp. of *embrocare* <*embrocha* an ointment <Gk. *embrochē*]

em·bro·ca·tion (em′brō·kā′shən) *n.* **1** The application of a soothing liniment to any part of the body. **2** The liniment or preparation so used.

em·broi·der (im·broi′dər) *v.t.* **1** To ornament with designs in needlework. **2** To execute in needlework. **3** To embellish or adorn; exaggerate, as a narrative with fictitious details. **—***v.i.* **4** To make embroidery. [<EN-[1] + BROIDER] **—em·broi′der·er** *n.*

em·broi·der·y (im·broi′dər·ē) *n.* *pl.* **·der·ies 1** Ornamental needlework, or the art of producing such work. **2** Any variegated or elaborate decoration or ornamentation; embellishment.

em·broil (em·broil′) *v.t.* **1** To involve in dissension or strife. **2** To throw into uproar or tumult. **3** To render complicated or confused; entangle. See synonyms under INVOLVE. [<F *embrouiller* <*em-* in (<L *in-*) + *brouiller* confuse]

em·broil·ment (em·broil′mənt) *n.* The act or result of embroiling; strife.

em·brown (em·broun′) *v.t.* & *v.i.* **1** To make or become brown or dusky. **2** To darken.

em·bry·ec·to·my (em′brē·ek′tə·mē) *n. Surg.* An operation for removing an embryo through an incision in the abdomen.

em·bry·o (em′brē·ō) *n.* *pl.* **·os 1** The germ or rudimentary form of anything in its earliest stage; specifically, the germ of an organism before it has developed its distinctive form. **2** The germ of a viviparous animal in the first stages of its existence (in the human species the first two months). **3** *Bot.* The rudimentary plant within the seed, which makes its appearance soon after fertilization of the ovule by the pollen and then passes through a period of rest until the germination or sprouting of the seed. Also **em′bry·on** (-on). **—in embryo** In an undeveloped or incipient

stage or state; not yet developed or advanced, as a project or undertaking. For illustrations see under EGG, EMBRYOLOGY, FROG. — *adj.* Pertaining to an embryo; rudimentary: also **em′bry·al.** [<Gk. *embryon* <*en-* in + *bryein* swell]

embryo– *combining form* Embryo; embryonic: *embryogenesis.* Also, before vowels, **embry–.** [<Gk. *embryon* embryo]

em·bry·o·gen·e·sis (em′brē·ō·jen′ə·sis) *n.* The development of an organism from its embryonic stage. Also **em·bry·og·e·ny** (em′brē·oj′ə·nē) — **em′bry·o·gen′ic** or **-ge·net′ic** (-jə·net′ik) *adj.*

em·bry·ol·o·gy (em′brē·ol′ə·jē) *n.* The science which deals with the origin, structure, and

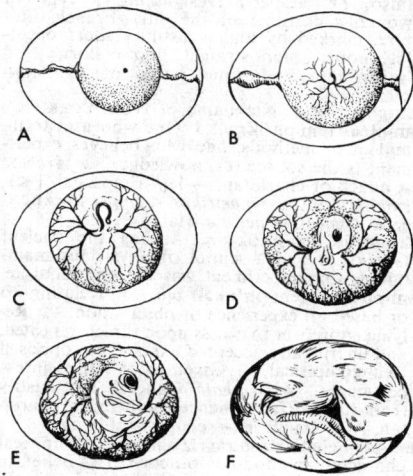

EMBRYOLOGY OF A CHICKEN
A. Before incubation, a germinal disk shown by small black spot. *B.* Three-day-old embryo, showing blood vessels radiating from heart. *C.* The fourth day. *D.* The fifth day. *E.* The seventh day. *F.* The nineteenth day, when chick absorbs remaining yolk. The chick hatches on the twenty-first day.

development of the embryo. — **em′bry·o·log′i·cal** (-ə·loj′i·kəl) *adj.* — **em′bry·o·log′i·cal·ly** *adv.* — **em′bry·ol′o·gist** *n.*

em·bry·o·nal (em′brē·ə·nəl) *adj.* Of or pertaining to an embryo or embryonic stage; embryonic.

em·bry·on·ic (em′brē·on′ik) *adj.* **1** Of, pertaining to, or like an embryo. **2** Undeveloped.

embryo sac *Bot.* The sac, formed of one cell, rarely more, within the nucleus of the ovule of flowering, seed-producing plants, containing the embryonal· vesicle.

em·bry·o·scope (em′brē·ə·skōp′) *n.* A device for observing embryonic development, especially in the eggs of birds. — **em·bry·os·co·py** (em′brē·os′kə·pē) *n.*

em·cee (em′sē′) *Colloq. n.* Master of ceremonies. — *v.i. & v.t.* **em·ceed, em·cee·ing** To act or direct as master of ceremonies. [<*M(aster of)* C(*eremonies*)]

Em·den (em′dən) A port on the Ems at the North Sea, Lower Saxony, Germany.

eme (ēm) *n. Brit. Dial.* An uncle; also, a friend, or neighbor. [OE *ēam*]

e·meer (ə·mir′) See EMIR.

Em·e·line (em′ə·lin, -lēn) A feminine personal name. [<Gmc., industrious ruler]

e·mend (i·mend′) *v.t.* **1** To make corrections or changes in the form or wording of (a literary work, etc.), especially after scholarly study. **2** To free from faults; correct. Also **e·men·date** (ē′men·dāt). [<L *emendare* <*ex-* out + *menda* a fault] — **e·mend′a·ble** *adj.*

Synonyms: amend, correct, rectify, redress, reform, remedy, revise. *Amend, emend, correct,* and *mend* all imply the *correction* of an evil. To *amend* is to *rectify* defects by positive means, generally by adding or altering, as to *amend* a law. *Emend* means negatively to remove particular faults in a literary work by alteration of letters, single words, or passages.

e·men·da·tion (ē′men·dā′shən, em′ən-) *n.* A correction or alteration. [<L *emendatio,*

-onis <*emendare.* See EMEND.] — **e′men·da′tor** *n.* — **e·mend·a·to·ry** (i·men′də·tôr′ē, -tō′rē) *adj.*

em·er·ald (em′ər·əld, em′rəld) *n.* **1** A bright-green variety of beryl, which when clear and nearly flawless is one of the most highly valued gems. **2** In the Bible, an unidentified precious stone. **3** A rich and vivid green. **4** One of various green moths. **5** *Printing* A size of type intermediate between minion and nonpareil. — **Oriental emerald** A valuable transparent variety of corundum. — *adj.* **1** Pertaining to or like the emerald. **2** Of a rich green color. [<OF *emeraude, esmeralda* <L *smaragdus.* Doublet of SMARAGD.]

emerald green A brilliant green, highly poisonous pigment made from copper and arsenic.

Emerald Isle Ireland: probably so called because of the rich green of its landscape.

emerald nickel Zaratite.

e·merge (i·mûrj′) *v.i.* **e·merged, e·merg·ing** **1** To rise, as from a fluid. **2** To come forth into view or existence; become noticeable or apparent. [<L *emergere* <*ex-* out + *mergere* dip]

e·mer·gence (i·mûr′jəns) *n.* **1** The process or result of emerging. **2** *Bot.* An outgrowth, as a prickle or hair growing from the tissue under the epidermis of a plant.

e·mer·gen·cy (i·mûr′jən·sē) *n. pl.* **·cies** A sudden condition or state of affairs calling for immediate action.

e·mer·gent (i·mûr′jənt) *adj.* **1** Rising or emerging, as from a fluid or from concealment. **2** Coming unexpectedly; urgent. **3** *Biol.* New and unforeseen in the evolution of plant and animal organisms. — *n.* That which emerges; the result of a natural process. [<L *emergens, -entis,* ppr. of *emergere* EMERGE]

emergent evolution A philosophical theory stated by C. Lloyd Morgan and S. Alexander differentiating between two types of evolutionary products: *resultants,* which are predictable from previously existing conditions; and *emergents,* such as new species and new manifestations of life which are not predictable from the known laws of matter.

e·mer·i·tus (i·mer′ə·təs) *adj.* Retired from active service (as on account of age), but retained in an honorary position: pastor *emeritus.* [<L, pp. of *emerere* <*ex-* out + *merere* deserve]

em·er·od (em′ər·od) *n. Obs.* **1** A tumor; boil; hemorrhoid. **2** In the Bible, an infectious disease, probably bubonic plague. 1 *Sam.* v 6. Also **em′er·oid.** [Var. of HEMORRHOID]

e·mersed (ē·mûrst′) *adj. Bot.* Standing above and out of water, as the stems and leaves of aquatic plants. [<L *emersus,* pp. of *emergere* EMERGE]

e·mer·sion (ē·mûr′shən, -zhən) *n.* **1** The act or process of emerging. **2** *Astron.* The rising out of or from behind something, as the moon from the earth's shadow during an eclipse.

Em·er·son (em′ər·sən), **Haven,** 1874–1957. U.S. physician; public health administrator. — **Ralph Waldo,** 1803–82, U.S. essayist, philosopher, and poet.

em·er·y (em′ər·ē, em′rē) *n.* A very hard, black or grayish-black variety of corundum mixed with magnesite and other minerals; used as an abrasive. [F *émeri* <OF *esmeril* <LL *smericulum* <Gk. *smēris* emery powder]

Em·er·y (em′ər·ē) A masculine personal name. Also *Fr.* **É·me·ri** (ām·rē′). [<Gmc., work ruler]

emery bag A small bag, often the size and shape of a strawberry, filled with emery powder: used to keep needles clean of rust.

emery board A small, flat board covered with powdered emery, used in manicuring.

emery cloth Cloth coated with powdered emery, used for fine abrading and polishing.

Em·e·sa (em′ə·sə) Ancient name for HOMS.

em·e·sis (em′ə·sis) *n. Pathol.* Vomiting. [<NL <Gk. <*emeein* vomit]

e·met·ic (i·met′ik) *adj.* Tending to produce vomiting. — *n.* A medicine used to induce vomiting. [<Gk. *emetikos* <*emeein* vomit]

em·e·tine (em′ə·tēn, -tin) *n. Chem.* A white crystalline alkaloid, $C_{29}H_{40}O_4N_2$, from the ipecacuanha root, used in certain conditions of amebic dysentery. Also **em′e·tin** (-tin). [<Gk. *emetos* vomiting + -INE[2]]

e·meu, e·mew (ē′myōō) See EMU.

é·meute (ā·mœt′) *n. French* A seditious or mutinous outbreak; riot; tumult.

–emia *combining form Med.* Blood; condition of the blood: used in names of diseases: *leukemia.* Also spelled *–aemia.* [<Gk. *haima* blood]

em·i·grant (em′ə·grənt) *adj.* Moving from one place or country for the purpose of settling in another: opposed to *immigrant.* — *n.* **1** A person who leaves one country, or section of a country, to settle in another. **2** A person from the eastern United States who went west to settle new lands. [<L *emigrans, -antis,* ppr. of *emigrare.* See EMIGRATE.]

emigrant trail A road made by the constant travel of emigrants to the West.

em·i·grate (em′ə·grāt) *v.i.* **·grat·ed, ·grat·ing** To go from one country, or section of a country, to settle in another. [<L *emigratus,* pp. of *emigrare* <*ex-* out + *migrare* move]

Synonyms: immigrate, migrate. To *migrate* is to change one's dwelling place, usually with the idea of repeated change, or of periodical return; it applies to wandering tribes of men, and to many birds and animals. *Emigrate* and *immigrate* carry the idea of a permanent change of residence to some other country or some distant region; the two words are used distinctively of human beings, and apply to the same person and the same act, according to the side from which the action is viewed. A person *emigrates from* the land he leaves, and *immigrates to* the land where he takes up his abode.

em·i·gra·tion (em′ə·grā′shən) *n.* **1** The act of emigrating. **2** Emigrants collectively.

Emigration Road The Oregon Trail.

é·mi·gré (em′ə·grā, *Fr.* ā·mē·grā′) An emigrant; especially one who fled during the French or Russian revolutions. [<F, pp. of *émigrer* <L *emigrare* EMIGRATE]

E·mil (ā′məl, ē′məl, em′əl) A masculine personal name. Also **E·mile** (ā·mēl′), *Fr.* **É·mile** (ā·mēl′). [<L, ? <Gmc., labor]

E·mi·lia–Ro·ma·gna (ā·mē′lyä·rō·mä′nyä) A region of north central Italy; 8,542 square miles; capital, Bologna. Formerly **E·mi′lia.**

Em·i·ly (em′ə·lē) A feminine personal name. Also *Fr.* **É·mi·lie** (ā·mē·lē′), *Ger.* **E·mi·li·e** (e·mē′lē·ə), *Ital., Pg., Sp.* **E·mi·lia** (ā·mē′lyä). [<L, ? <Gmc., labor]

é·min·cé (ā·maṅ·sā′) *n. French* Meat cut into thin slices, cooked, and served with a sauce.

em·i·nence (em′ə·nəns) *n.* **1** A lofty place; a hill. **2** An exalted rank, condition, or degree. **3** A title of honor applied to cardinals of the Roman Catholic Church. Also **em′i·nen·cy.** See synonyms under FAME, HEIGHT. [<L *eminentia* <*e-* forth + *minere* project]

em·i·nent (em′ə·nənt) *adj.* **1** High in station, merit, or esteem; distinguished; prominent; conspicuous: an *eminent* scholar. **2** Rising above other things; high in relative position; lofty: an *eminent* tower. [<L *eminens, -entis,* ppr. of *eminere* project] — **em′i·nent·ly** *adv.*

Synonyms: conspicuous, distinguished, famed, famous, known, lofty, noted, prominent, remarkable, signal. See CELEBRATED, HIGH, ILLUSTRIOUS, PARAMOUNT. *Antonyms:* common, commonplace, inferior, low, mean, ordinary.

eminent domain *Law* The right or power of the state to take private property for public use or to control its use, usually at an adequate compensation.

e·mir (ə·mir′) *n.* **1** Any independent prince or commander in the Moslem East, especially in Arabia. **2** A descendant of Mohammed through Fatima, his favorite daughter. **3** A high Turkish official. Also spelled *emeer.* [<Arabic *amīr* ruler]

e·mir·ate (ə·mir′it) *n.* The jurisdiction of an emir.

em·is·sar·y (em′ə·ser′ē) *n. pl.* **·sar·ies 1** A person sent on a mission as an agent or representative of a government, as to negotiate or gather information. **2** A secret agent; spy. **3** *Archaic* A channel, as for water: also **em·is·sa·ri·um** (em′ə·sâr′ē·əm). **4** *Archaic* An excretory or connecting canal in the body. See synonyms under SPY. — *adj.* Sent forth or out. [<L *emissarius* <*emittere.* See EMIT.]

e·mis·sion (i·mish′ən) *n.* **1** The act of emitting or that which is emitted. **2** *Electronics* The ejection of electrons from the heated cathode or filament of a vacuum tube. **3** *Med.* A discharge of body fluids, especially semen.

[<L *emissio, -onis* <*emittere*. See EMIT.]

emission spectrum *Physics* The spectrum of a substance indicating the type of radiation which it emits: distinguished from *absorption spectrum*.

e·mis·sive (i·mis′iv) *adj.* Sending or sent out or forth; emitting.

emissive power *Physics* The rate at which a body at a given temperature will radiate energy per unit of surface area.

em·is·siv·i·ty (em′ə·siv′ə·tē) *n. Physics* Emissive power or rate; specifically, the total emissive power of a radiating surface, expressed as a ratio to that of a black body of identical area and temperature.

e·mit (i·mit′) *v.t.* **e·mit·ted, e·mit·ting** **1** To send or give out; discharge. **2** To utter (sounds, oaths, etc.). **3** To promulgate, as a law or decree. **4** To put into circulation, as paper money. [<L *emittere* <*ex-* out + *mittere* send] —**e·mit′ter** *n.*

Em·ma (em′ə; *Fr.* e·mà′, *Ger.* em′ä, *Ital.* em′mä) A feminine personal name. [<Gmc., grandmother]
—**Emma, Queen,** 982–1052, wife of Ethelred the Unready; after his death she married Canute; mother of Edward the Confessor.

Em·man·u·el (i·man′yōō·əl, *Fr.* ā·mà·nü·el′) A masculine personal name. See also EMANUEL, IMMANUEL. [<Hebrew, God with us]

Em·me·line (em′ə·līn, -lēn) See EMELINE.

em·men·a·gog (i·men′ə·gôg, -gog) *n.* Any medicine or substance that stimulates or renews the menstrual flow. Also **em·men′a·gogue.** [<Gk. *emmēna* the menses < *agōgos* leading <*agein* lead]

em·mer (em′ər) *n.* Amelcorn. [< dial. G]

em·met (em′it) *n. Archaic* An ant. [OE *ǣmete*. Related to ANT.]

Em·met (em′it), **Robert,** 1778–1803, Irish patriot; hanged by the British.

em·me·tro·pi·a (em′ə·trō′pē·ə) *n.* The normal state of the eye as regards the power of accommodation or refraction. [<NL <Gk. *emmetros* <*en-* in + *metron* measure + *ōps* eye] —**em′me·trop′ic** (-trop′ik) *adj.*

Em·my (em′ē) *n.* A gold-plated statuette awarded annually since 1949 by the Academy of Television Arts and Sciences for exceptional performances and productions on television. [Alter. of *immy,* short for *image* orthicon tube. See under ORTHICON.]

em·o·din (em′ə·din) *n. Chem.* An orange-red crystalline glucoside, $C_{15}H_{10}O_5$, obtained from rhubarb, senna, aloes, and various other related plants: used as a cathartic. [<NL *(Rheum) emodi,* a species of rhubarb (<Gk. *ēmōdos* Himalaya) + -IN]

em·ol·les·cence (em′ə·les′əns) *n.* The state or degree of softness in which a body begins to lose its shape, as in melting; incipient fusion. [<E- + L *mollescere* become soft + -ENCE]

e·mol·li·ate (i·mol′ē·āt) *v.t.* **·at·ed, ·at·ing** *Obs.* To render soft; make effeminate.

e·mol·lient (i·mol′yənt, -ē·ənt) *adj.* Softening or relaxing; soothing. —*n. Med.* A softening or soothing external application. Also *mollient.* [<L *emolliens, -entis,* ppr. of *emollire* <*ex-* thoroughly + *mollire* soften <*mollis* soft]

e·mol·u·ment (i·mol′yə·mənt) *n.* **1** The compensation, salary, fees, perquisites, advantage, gain, or profit arising from an office or employment. **2** General advantage; gain; profit. See synonyms under PROFIT. [<L *emolumentum* <*emolere* <*ex-* out + *molere* grind]

e·mote (i·mōt′) *v.i.* **e·mot·ed, e·mot·ing** *Colloq.* To exhibit an exaggerated emotion, as in acting a melodramatic role: a humorous use. [Back formation <EMOTION]

e·mo·tion (i·mō′shən) *n.* **1** Any strong manifestation or disturbance of the conscious or the unconscious mind, typically involuntary and often leading to complex bodily changes and forms of behavior; an act or state of excited feeling: *emotions* of fear. **2** The power of feeling, with or without a corresponding trend of activities; sensibility; sentiment. **3** *Obs.* Unusual or disturbed motion. See synonyms under FEELING, SENSATION, WARMTH. [<L *emotio, -onis* <*emovere* <*ex-* out + *movere* move]

e·mo·tion·al (i·mō′shən·əl) *adj.* **1** Of, pertaining to, or expressive of emotion. **2** Having capacity for emotion. **3** Moving or suited to move the feelings or passions: an *emotional* poem. —**e·mo′tion·al·ly** *adv.*

e·mo·tion·al·ism (i·mō′shən·əl·iz′əm) *n.* **1** The expression of emotion. **2** The disposition or tendency to see and judge all things from an emotional point of view. **3** The act or habit of appealing to the emotions.

e·mo·tion·al·ist (i·mō′shən·əl·ist) *n.* **1** One whose feelings are easily excited or wrought upon. **2** One who aims to influence others through the emotions. **3** In ethics, one who bases his theory of conduct on the emotions, as in making pleasure or happiness the supreme end. **4** One who uses emotional methods in art, in religion, or in the promotion of any project.

e·mo·tion·al·i·ty (i·mō′shən·al′ə·tē) *n.* The state or quality of being emotional.

e·mo·tion·al·ize (i·mō′shən·əl·īz′) *v.t.* **·ized, ·iz·ing** To make emotional; treat in an emotional manner. —**e·mo′tion·al·i·za′tion** *n.*

e·mo·tive (i·mō′tiv) *adj.* **1** Tending to excite emotion. **2** Expressing or characterized by or inducing emotion: *emotive* eloquence. —**e·mo′tive·ly** *adv.* —**e·mo′tive·ness, e·mo·tiv·i·ty** (ē′mō·tiv′ə·tē) *n.*

em·pale (im·pāl′) See IMPALE.

em·pan·el (im·pan′əl), etc. See IMPANEL, etc.

em·path·ic (em·path′ik) *adj.* Characterized by or pertaining to empathy. —**em·path′i·cal·ly** *adv.*

em·pa·thize (em′pə·thīz) *v.t.* & *v.i.* **·thized, ·thiz·ing** To regard with or feel empathy.

em·pa·thy (em′pə·thē) *n.* **1** *Psychol.* A strong imaginative or emotional projection of one's self into a work of art; esthetic appreciation. **2** *Psychoanal.* The mental identification of the ego with the character and experiences of another person. [<Gk. *empatheia* <*en-* in + *pathos* feeling; trans. of G *Einfühlung*]

Em·ped·o·cles (em·ped′ə·klēz) Greek poet and philosopher of the fifth century B.C.

em·pen·nage (em′pi·nij, *Fr.* äṅ·pe·näzh′) *n. Aeron.* The tail parts of an airplane, used to steer or steady it. See illustration under AIRPLANE. [<F <*empenner* provide with feathers <*em-* in (<L *in-*) + *penne* <L *pinna* feather]

em·per·or (em′pər·ər) *n.* **1** The sovereign of an empire. **2** One of various moths, as the **emperor moth** *(Samia cecropia),* or butterflies, as the **purple emperor** *(Apatura iris),* or the **tawny emperor** *(Asterocampa clyton),* etc. [<OF *empereor* <L *imperator* commander <*imperare* order]

emperor goose A small goose of the Alaskan coasts *(Philacte canagica)* with barred plumage, a short neck, and short wings.

em·per·y (em′pər·ē) *n. pl.* **·per·ies** *Poetic* **1** Sovereignty; dominion. **2** The domain of an emperor. [OF *emperie* <L *imperium* empire]

em·pha·sis (em′fə·sis) *n. pl.* **·ses** (-sēz) **1** A stress laid upon some word or words in speaking or reading: indicated in print or writing by underscoring or underlining, by italics, or by accent marks. **2** The act of emphasizing; distinctiveness; stress of thought or importance; significance. [<L <Gk. *en-* in + *phainein* show]

em·pha·size (em′fə·sīz) *v.t.* **·sized, ·siz·ing** To make especially distinct or prominent; put stress on; give emphasis to.

em·phat·ic (im·fat′ik) *adj.* **1** Speaking or spoken with emphasis or stress. **2** Conveying or expressing emphasis; habitually forceful and decisive; striking; forcible; positive. Also **em·phat′i·cal.** [<Gk. *emphatikos,* var. of *emphantikos* <*emphainein.* See EMPHASIS.] —**em·phat′·i·cal·ly** *adv.*

em·phy·se·ma (em′fə·sē′mə, -zē′mə) *n. Pathol.* A puffed condition of body tissues or organs caused by the infiltration of air; especially, a condition of the lungs marked by difficulty in breathing because of enlargement and consequent loss of elasticity of the alveoli, or air sacs. [<NL <Gk. *emphysēma* an inflation <*en-* in + *physaein* blow] —**em′phy·sem′a·tous** (-sēm′ə·təs, -zēm′ə·təs) *adj.*

em·phy·teu·sis (em′fə·tyōō′sis) *n.* In ancient Roman law, a perpetual lease of lands and tenements in consideration of annual rent and improvements thereon; an improving lease. [<LL <Gk. <*en-* in + *phyteuein* plant]

em·piece·ment (em·pēs′mənt) *n.* In sewing, an insertion.

em·pire (em′pīr) *n.* **1** A state, or union of states, governed by an emperor. **2** A union of dispersed territories, dominions, colonies, states, and unrelated peoples under one sovereign rule. **3** Wide and supreme dominion.
—**Holy Roman Empire** Certain portions of the old Roman Empire of the West together with the Frankish possessions of Charlemagne, who was crowned emperor by Pope Leo III at Rome in 800. In 962 the real Holy Roman-German Empire began. It became extinct in 1806, when Francis II resigned the elective imperial crown for the hereditary one of Austria. [<F <L *imperium* rule, authority]

Em·pire (em′pīr) *adj.* **1** Of, belonging to, or characterizing an empire, especially the French Empire, 1804–15, under Napoleon I. **2** Designating a simple and dignified type of furniture introduced at the time of the first French Empire by Percier, Fontaine, and others. **3** (also, *Fr.* äṅ·pēr′) Designating a type of woman's costume of the first French Empire, marked by high waistline, short décolleté bodice, and straight, loose skirt.

Empire Day Former name of COMMONWEALTH DAY.

Empire State Nickname of NEW YORK.

em·pir·ic (em·pir′ik) *n.* **1** One who uses trial-and-error methods; one who believes experiment is the source of knowledge. **2** *Archaic* A quack or charlatan. —*adj.* Empirical. [<L *empiricus* <Gk. *empeirikos* <*empeiria* experience <*en-* in + *peira* a trial]

Em·pir·ic (em·pir′ik) *n.* Among the ancient Greeks, one of a school of physicians maintaining that experiment was the one requisite.

em·pir·i·cal (em·pir′i·kəl) *adj.* **1** Relating to or based on experience or observation. **2** Relying entirely or to excess upon direct, repeated, and uncritically accepted experience: opposed to metempirical. **3** Given to or skilled in experiments. **4** *Archaic* Generalizing hastily from limited facts; hence, befitting a charlatan. Also **em·pir′ic.** —**em·pir′i·cal·ly** *adv.*

em·pir·i·cism (em·pir′ə·siz′əm) *n.* **1** Empirical character, method, or practice. **2** Belief in experiment and repudiation of theory; quackery. **3** *Philos.* The doctrine that all knowledge is derived from experience through the senses. —**em·pir′i·cist** *n.*

em·place·ment (im·plās′mənt) *n.* **1** The position assigned to guns or to a battery within a fortification; also, a gun platform or the like. **2** A setting in place; location. [<F]

em·plane (im·plān′) *v.t.* & *v.i.* To board or put aboard an airplane.

em·plas·tic (im·plas′tik) *adj.* Glutinous. —*n.* **1** A constipating medicine. **2** An adhesive substance. [<Gk. *emplastikos* <*em-* in + *plassein* mold, form]

em·ploy (im·ploi′) *v.t.* **1** To hire; engage the services of. **2** To provide work and livelihood for; have as employees. **3** To make use of as a means or instrument: to *employ* cunning. **4** To devote or apply: to *employ* one's energies in research. —*n.* The state of being employed; service. [<F *employer* <L *in-* in + *plicare* fold. Doublet of IMPLY.] —**em·ploy′a·ble** *adj.* —**em·ployed′** *adj.*

Synonyms (verb): engage, engross, hire, use. In general terms it may be said that to *employ* is to devote to one's purpose, to *use* is to render subservient to one's purpose; what is *used* is viewed as more absolutely an instrument than what is *employed*; a merchant *employs* a clerk; he *uses* pen and paper; hence, *use,* as applied to persons, inclines to the derogatory sense; as, The conspirators *used* him as a go-between. That which is *used* is often consumed in the *using*; as, We *used* twenty tons of coal last winter; in such cases we could not substitute *employ.* A person may be *employed* in his own work or in that of another; in the latter case the service is always understood to be for pay. In this connection *employ* is a word of more dignity than *hire*; a general is *employed* in his country's service; a mercenary adventurer is *hired* to fight; *hire* now implies that the one *hired* works directly and primarily for the pay. See OCCUPY, RETAIN.

em·ploy·ee (im·ploi′ē, em′ploi·ē′) *n.* One who works for another in return for a salary, wages, or other consideration. Also **em·ploy′e.**

em·ploy·er (im·ploi′ər) *n.* **1** One who employs. **2** A person or business firm that employs workmen, servants, etc., for wages.

em·ploy·ment (im·ploi′mənt) *n.* **1** The act of employing, or the state of being employed. **2** The work upon which one is or may be engaged; occupation; trade. See synonyms under BUSINESS, EXERCISE, WORK.

employment agency An office or bureau that puts employers in contact with people seeking work: also **employment bureau.**

em·poi·son (em·poi′zən) *v.t.* **1** To envenom; corrupt. **2** *Obs.* To poison. **—em·poi′son·ment** *n.*

Em·po·ri·a (em·pôr′ē·ə, -pō′rē·ə) A city in eastern Kansas.

em·po·ri·um (em·pôr′ē·əm, -pō′rē-) *n. pl.* **·ri·ums** or **·ri·a** (-ē·ə) **1** A store carrying general merchandise. **2** The chief mart of a wide territory. **3** A bazaar. [<L <Gk. *emporion* a market <*emporos* merchant, traveler <*en-* in + *poros* journey]

em·pov·er·ish (im·pov′ər·ish) See IMPOVERISH.

em·pow·er (im·pou′ər) *v.t.* **1** To authorize; delegate authority to. **2** To enable; permit. See synonyms under PERMIT.

em·press (em′pris) *n.* **1** A woman who rules an empire. **2** The wife or widow of an emperor. [<OF *emperesse,* fem. of *emperere,* var. of *empereor* EMPEROR]

Empress Augusta Bay An inlet of the South Pacific in SW Bougainville, Solomon Islands.

em·presse·ment (äṅ·pres·mäṅ′) *n. French* Animated earnestness; demonstrative cordiality.

em·prise (em·prīz′) *n. Archaic* **1** Enterprise; adventure. **2** Chivalric or martial prowess. Also **em·prize′.** [<OF, orig. pp. of *emprendre* undertake <L *in-* in + *prehendere* take]

emp·tings (emp′tingz) *n. pl. U.S.* The lees of beer, etc., used as yeast. Also **emp′tins.** [<obs. *empt* empty]

emp·ty (emp′tē) *adj.* **·ti·er, ·ti·est 1** Having nothing within; containing nothing; void; vacant: often with reference to particular, usual, or proper contents, as food or inhabitants: an *empty* pitcher. **2** Without force, weight, value, or meaning: *empty* protestations, *empty* promises. **3** Without substance or significance; hollow; unreal; unsubstantial. **4** Destitute of intelligence, ideas, manners, etc.; senseless; inane; frivolous; contemptible: *empty* talk. **5** Being without supplies, etc.; unsupplied; unsatisfied; unfed. **6** Not carrying or drawing anything: *empty* hands. **7** Having no fruit; barren. **8** *Colloq.* Hungry. See synonyms under BLANK, FLAT[1], VACANT, VAIN. —*v.* **emp·tied, emp·ty·ing** *v.t.* **1** To make empty. **2** To transfer the contents of as if to another place or container: He *emptied* the bucket onto the fire. **3** To transfer (the contents) as if to another place or container: He *emptied* the milk into the street. **4** To remove (the contents): often with *out*: He *emptied* out the water. —*v.i.* **5** To become empty. **6** To discharge or pour out: The river *empties* into the bay. —*n. pl.* **emp·ties** A boat, barge, freight car, tank, etc., containing or transporting nothing. [OE *ǣmetig* <*ǣmetta* leisure] **—emp′ti·ly** *adv.* **—emp′ti·ness** *n.*

emp·ty-hand·ed (emp′tē·han′did) *adj.* Having or carrying nothing.

emp·ty-head·ed (emp′tē·hed′id) *adj.* Without sense or discretion; foolish; brainless.

Empty Quarter The English name for the RUB AL KHALI.

em·pur·ple (em·pûr′pəl) *v.t.* **·pled, ·pling** To tinge or color with purple: also spelled *impurple.*

em·py·e·ma (em′pi·ē′mə, -pī-) *n. Pathol.* A collection or formation of pus, especially in the pleural cavity, often associated with various bacterial infections. [<NL <Gk. *empyēma* suppuration <*en-* in + *pyon* pus]

em·pyr·e·al (em·pir′ē·əl, em′pə·rē′əl, -pī-) *adj.* **1** Of or pertaining to the highest region of heaven; celestial. **2** Most highly refined; originally, formed of light or fire. —*n.* The empyrean. [<Med. L *empyreus* <Gk. *empyros* in the fire <*en-* in + *pyr* fire]

em·py·re·an (em′pə·rē′ən, -pī-) *n.* **1** The ancient supposed region of pure fire; the highest heaven. **2** Hence, the abode of God and the angels. **3** The upper sky. Also **em′py·rae′um.** —*adj.* Empyreal.

em·py·reu·ma (em′pə·rōō′mə, -pī-) *n.* The disagreeable odor produced when organic substances are decomposed by heat in a closed vessel. [<Gk. *empyreuma* covered live coal <*empyros.* See EMPYREAL.] **—em·py·reu·mat·ic** (em′pə·rōō·mat′ik) or **·i·cal** *adj.*

Ems (emz, *Ger.* āms) **1** A resort town in Rhineland-Palatinate, western Germany: also **Bad Ems. 2** A river of NW Germany, flowing 250 miles NE to the North Sea.

e·mu (ē′myōō) *n.* A large ostrichlike Australian bird (genus *Dromiceius*), with neck and most of the head feathered: also spelled *emeu, emew.* [Prob. <Pg. *ema* ostrich]

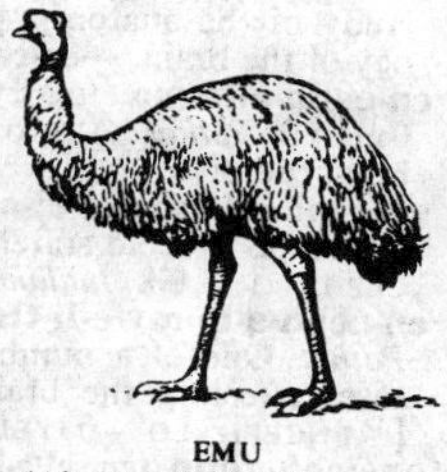

EMU
(About 5 feet tall; second largest living bird)

em·u·late (em′yə·lāt) *v.t.* **·lat·ed, ·lat·ing 1** To try to equal or surpass. **2** To rival with some success. [<L *aemulatus,* pp. of *aemulari* rival <*aemulus* jealous] **—em′u·la′tive** *adj.* **—em′u·la′tive·ly** *adv.* **—em′u·la′tor** *n.*

em·u·la·tion (em′yə·lā′shən) *n.* **1** Effort or ambition to equal or excel another in any act or quality. **2** *Obs.* Selfish rivalry and strife.

Synonyms: ambition, competition, opposition, rivalry. We speak of *competition* in business, *emulation* in scholarship, *rivalry* in love, politics, etc.; *emulation* of excellence, success, achievement; *competition* for a prize. *Competition* may be friendly; *rivalry* is commonly hostile. See AMBITION, COMPETITION.

e·mul·gent (i·mul′jənt) *adj.* Milking out or straining. —*n.* Any preparation to aid an excretory organ or duct. [<L *emulgens, -entis,* ppr. of *emulgere* <*ex-* out + *mulgere* milk]

em·u·lous (em′yə·ləs) *adj.* **1** Eager or striving to equal or excel another; competitive. **2** *Obs.* Envious; jealous. **—em′u·lous·ly** *adv.* **—em′u·lous·ness** *n.*

e·mul·si·fy (i·mul′sə·fī) *v.t.* **·fied, ·fy·ing** To make or convert into an emulsion. **—e·mul′si·fi·ca′tion** *n.* **—e·mul′si·fi′er** *n.*

e·mul·sion (i·mul′shən) *n.* **1** A liquid mixture in which a fatty or resinous substance is suspended in minute globules, as butter in milk. **2** Any milky liquid. **3** *Phot.* A substance, as a silver salt, held in suspension in collodion or gelatin, and used to coat dry plates. **4** *Physics* A colloid system, consisting of the globules or particles of one liquid finely dispersed in another. See COLLOID. [<LL *emulsio, -onis* <L *emulgere.* See EMULGENT.]

e·mul·sive (i·mul′siv) *adj.* **1** Capable of emulsifying. **2** Of the nature of an emulsion; softening. **3** Producing oil on being pressed.

e·munc·to·ry (i·mungk′tər·ē) *adj.* Serving to discharge excrementitious matter. —*n. pl.* **·ries** An organ for removing waste matter, as the kidneys, intestines, etc. [<NL *emunctorius* <L *emunctorium* a snuffer <*emungere* <*ex-* out + *mungere* blow the nose]

em·yd (em′id) *n.* A fresh-water tortoise of North America *(Emys blandingii)* having a black carapace covered with pale yellow spots. Also called *Blanding's turtle.* Also **em·yde** (em′id). [<Gk. *emys, emydos*]

en (en) *n.* **1** The name of the fourteenth letter in the English alphabet, written N or n. **2** *Printing* A space half the width of an em.

en-[1] *prefix* Forming transitive verbs: **1** (from nouns) To cover or surround with; to place into or upon: *encircle.* **2** (from adjectives and nouns) To make; cause to be or to resemble: *enable, enfeeble.* **3** (from verbs) Often with simple intensive force, or used to form transitive verbs from intransitives: *enact, encompass.* Also, **em-** before *b, p,* and sometimes *m,* as in *embark.* Many words in *en-* have variant forms in *in-* because of the confusion between Old French *en-,* Latin *in-,* and native English *in-.* Compare IN-[2] and IN-[3]. [<OF <L *in-* <*in* in, into]

en-[2] *prefix* In, into; on: *endemic.* Also: *el-* before *l,* as in *ellipse; em-* before *b, m, p, ph,* as in *embolism, empathy; er-* before *r,* as in *errhine.* [<Gk. *en-* <*en* in, into]

-en[1] *suffix* Forming verbs: **1** (from adjectives) Cause to be; become: *deepen, harden.* **2** (from nouns) Cause to have; gain: *hearten, strengthen.* [OE *-nian*]

-en[2] *suffix of adjectives* Made of; resembling: *woolen, brazen.* [OE]

-en[3] *suffix* Used in the past participles of many strong verbs: *broken, beaten.* [OE]

-en[4] *suffix* Used in the plural of certain nouns: *oxen, children.* [OE *-an,* plural ending of the weak declension]

-en[5] *suffix* Small; little: *chicken, kitten.* [OE]

en·a·ble (in·ā′bəl) *v.t.* **·bled, ·bling 1** To make able; give means or power to. **2** To make possible or more easy.

en·a·bling act (in·ā′bling) *Law* **1** An act enabling persons or corporations to do what before was not allowed. **2** *U.S.* A Congressional act allowing the people of a territory to prepare a constitution for statehood.

en·act (in·akt′) *v.t.* **1** To make into a law. **2** To carry out in action; perform. **3** To represent in or as in a play. **—en·act′a·ble** *adj.* **—en·ac′tor** *n.*

en·ac·tive (in·ak′tiv) *adj.* Tending or having efficacy to enact or establish; enacting: the *enactive* clause of a bill.

en·act·ment (in·akt′mənt) *n.* **1** A law enacted; a statute. **2** The act of establishing a law. See synonyms under LAW.

en·ac·to·ry (in·ak′tər·ē) *adj.* Connected with the enactment of law: sometimes opposed to *declaratory,* and then meaning that the law does not simply interpret another law.

en·ac·ture (in·ak′chər) *n. Obs.* An action; effect; fulfilment.

en·a·lid (en′ə·lid) *n. Bot.* A plant growing on the sea bottom, as eelgrass. [<Gk. *enalios* (<*en-* in + *hals, halos* the sea) + ID[1]]

en·al·la·ge (en·al′ə·jē) *n.* In rhetoric, the use of one part of speech, gender, etc., for another. [<L <Gk. *enallagē* exchange <*en-* in + *allassein* change]

en·am·el (in·am′əl) *n.* **1** A semi-opaque, vitreous material that is applied by fusion to gold, silver, copper, or other metals, or to porcelain, either as a decoration in colors or to form a surface for encaustic painting; also, as a lining for culinary and chemical vessels. **2** A work executed in such material: a fine cloisonné *enamel.* **3** One of various glossy lacquers or varnishes used for leather, paper, etc. **4** A kind of cosmetic or paint for the face, supposed to imitate exactly the natural gloss of the complexion. **5** *Anat.* The layer of hard, glossy, calcareous material forming the exposed outer covering of the teeth and protecting the dentine. —*v.t.* **·eled** or **·elled, ·el·ing** or **·el·ling 1** To cover or inlay, with enamel. **2** To surface with or as with enamel. **3** To adorn with different colors, as if with enamel. [<AF *enamyller* <*en-* on + *amayl,* OF *esmail* enamel <Gmc.] **—en·am′el·er, en·am′el·ler** *n.* **—en·am′el·ist, en·am′el·list** *n.*

en·am·el·ing (in·am′əl·ing) *n.* **1** The art or occupation of one who enamels. **2** The ornamentation or coating of enamel. Also **en·am′el·ling.**

en·am·el·ware (in·am′əl·wâr′) *n.* Enameled kitchen utensils.

en·am·or (in·am′ər) *v.t.* To inspire with ardent love: used chiefly in the past participle, and followed by *of* or *with.* Also *Brit.* **en·am′our.** [<OF *enamourer* <*en-* in (<L *in-*) + *amour* love <L *amor*] **—en·am′ored** *adj.*

en·an·ti·o·mer (en·an′tē·ə·mər) *n.* Enantiomorph. **—en·an·ti·o·mer·ic** (en·an′tē·ə·mer′ik) *adj.*

en·an·ti·o·morph (en·an′tē·ə·môrf′) *n.* Either of a pair of molecular or crystalline forms which are mirror images of each other. **—en·an′ti·o·morph′ism** *n.* **—en·an′ti·o·mor′phous** *adj.* [<Gk. *enantios* opposite + *morphē* form]

en·an·ti·op·a·thy (en·an′tē·op′ə·thē) *n.* **1** *Pathol.* A morbid condition or disease which is hostile to or preventive of another. **2** The curing of one disease by inducing another. Also **en·an·ti·o·path·i·a** (en·an′tē·ə·path′ē·ə). [<Gk. *enantios* opposite + -PATHY] **—en·an′ti·o·path′ic** (-tē·ə·path′ik) *adj.*

en ar·rière (äṅ ná·ryâr′) *French* In the rear; behind.

en·ar·thro·sis (en′är·thrō′sis) *n. Anat.* An articulation in which the rounded head of a bone is received into a corresponding cavity; a ball-and-socket joint, as the hip joint. [<NL <Gk. *enarthrōsis* <*enarthros* jointed <*en-* in + *arthron* a joint] **—en′ar·thro′di·al** (-dē·əl) *adj.*

e·nate (ē′nāt, i·nāt′) *adj.* **1** Growing out. **2** Related on the mother's side: distinguished from *agnate.* —*n.* A relative on the mother's

side. [< L *enatus,* pp. of *enasci* < *ex-* out + *nasci* be born] **—e·nat·ic** (i·nat′ik) *adj.*
e·na·tion (i·nā′shən) *n. Bot.* An excessive development in plants, consisting in the formation of supplementary lobes or excrescences, usually on the upper surface of other organs, as scales on petals.
en a·vant (äṅ nȧ·väṅ′) *French* Forward; onward.
en bloc (äṅ blôk′) *French* In one piece; as a whole; in the lump.
en broche (äṅ brôsh′) *French* Served on skewers: quail *en broche.*
en·cae·ni·a (en·sē′nē·ə, -sēn′yə) See ENCENIA.
en·cage (in·kāj′) *v.t.* **·caged, ·cag·ing** To shut up in a cage: also spelled *incage.*
en·camp (in·kamp′) *v.i.* To go into camp; live in a camp. —*v.t.* To place in a camp.
en·camp·ment (in·kamp′mənt) *n.* **1** The act of pitching a camp. **2** A camp, or the persons occupying it.
en·car·nal·ize (in·kär′nəl·īz) *v.t.* **·ized, ·iz·ing 1** To invest with flesh and blood; to embody. **2** To make gross or sensual.
en·case (in·kās′) See INCASE.
en casse·role (äṅ kȧs·rôl′) *French* Prepared and served in a casserole.
en·caus·tic (en·kôs′tik) *adj.* **1** Painted and having the hues fixed by heat. **2** Painted in wax and burnt in. —*n.* The art of encaustic painting. [< L *encausticus* < Gk. *enkaustikos* < *en-* in + *kaiein* burn]
encaustic painting A method of painting statues or architectural details with hot, colored wax or with cold, colored wax later fused with hot irons.
en·cave (in·kāv′) *v.t.* **·caved, ·cav·ing** To put in or as in a cave.
-ence *suffix of nouns* Forming nouns of action, quality, state or condition from adjectives in *-ent,* as in *diffidence, prominence.* Compare -ENCY. See note under -ANCE. [< F *-ence* < L *-entia,* a suffix used to form nouns from present participles; or directly < L]
en·ceinte[1] (en·sānt′, *Fr.* äṅ·saṅt′) *adj.* With child; pregnant. [< F < LL *incincta,* pp. of *incingere* unbind < *in-* not + *cingere* bind]
en·ceinte[2] (en·sānt′, *Fr.* äṅ·saṅt′) *n.* **1** A girdle of works encircling a fortified place. **2** The place they encircle. **3** A close or precinct, as of an abbey or cathedral. [< F < *enceindre* < L *incingere* < *in-* on + *cingere* bind]
En·cel·a·dus (en·sel′ə·dəs) In Greek mythology, a giant who revolted against the gods; buried under Mt. Etna.
en·ce·ni·a (en·sē′nē·ə, -sēn′yə) *n. pl. (sometimes sing.)* **1** A ceremony at Oxford University, held every year in June, in commemoration of founders and benefactors. **2** A yearly celebration to commemorate the dedication of a temple or church, particularly of the Temple at Jerusalem. Also spelled *encaenia.* [< L *encaenia* < Gk. *enkainia* a feast of dedication < *en-* in + *kainos* new]
en·ce·phal·ic (en′sə·fal′ik) *adj.* **1** Of or pertaining to the encephalon. **2** Situated within the cranial cavity.
en·ceph·a·li·tis (en′sef·ə·lī′tis, en·sef′-) *n. Pathol.* Inflammation of the brain; brain fever. **—en′ceph·a·lit′ic** (-lit′ik) *adj.*
encephalitis le·thar·gi·ca (li·thär′ji·kə) *Pathol.* An acute, frequently epidemic, viral encephalitis, deeply involving the central nervous system, and accompanied by widely varying symptoms, including fever, lethargy, and numerous sensory disturbances. Also called *sleeping sickness.*
en·ceph·a·li·za·tion (en·sef′ə·lə·zā′shən, -lī·zā′-) *n. Biol.* **1** The developmental processes resulting in the formation of the head. **2** The gradual association of various physiological functions, sensory and motor, with localized areas in the brain.
encephalo- *combining form* Brain: *encephalogram.* Also, before vowels, **encephal-.** [< Gk. *enkephalos* brain < *en-* in + *kephalē* head]
en·ceph·a·lo·cele (en·sef′ə·lə·sēl′) *n. Pathol.* Hernia of the brain, usually through a traumatic or congenital fissure in the skull.
en·ceph·a·lo·di·al·y·sis (en·sef′ə·lō·dī·al′ə·sis) *n. Pathol.* Softening of the brain. [< ENCEPHALO- + Gk. *dialysis* dissolution]
en·ceph·a·lo·gram (en·sef′ə·lə·gram′) *n.* An X-ray photograph of the brain, obtained by replacing the cerebral fluid by air, oxygen, or helium. **—en·ceph′a·log′ra·phy** (-log′rə·fē) *n.*
en·ceph·a·lol·o·gy (en·sef′ə·lol′ə·jē) *n.* The study of the anatomy, physiology, and pathology of the brain. **—en·ceph′a·lol′o·gist** *n.*
en·ceph·a·lo·ma (en·sef′ə·lō′mə) *n. pl.* **·ma·ta** (-mə·tə) *Pathol.* A growth upon the brain; a brain tumor.
en·ceph·a·lo·ma·la·ci·a (en·sef′ə·lō·mə·lā′shē·ə) *n. Pathol.* Morbid softening of the brain. [< ENCEPHALO- + Gk. *malakos* soft]
en·ceph·a·lo·my·e·li·tis (en·sef′ə·lō·mī′ə·lī′tis) *n. Pathol.* One of a number of inflammatory diseases affecting the brain and the spinal cord. [< ENCEPHALO- + MYEL(O)- + -ITIS]
en·ceph·a·lon (en·sef′ə·lon) *n. pl.* **·la** (-lə) *Anat.* The brain. Also **en·ceph′a·los.** [< NL < Gk. *enkephalos*] **—en·ceph′a·lous** *adj.*
en·ceph·a·lop·a·thy (en·sef′ə·lop′ə·thē) *n. Pathol.* Any degenerative disease of the brain. **—en·ceph·a·lo·path·ic** (en·sef′ə·lə·path′ik) *adj.*
en·chafe (in·chāf′) *v.t. Obs.* **1** To heat. **2** To irritate; stir up.
en·chain (in·chān′) *v.t.* **1** To bind with or as with a chain. **2** To hold fast or captive, as attention.
en·chain·ment (in·chān′mənt) *n.* The act of enchaining, or the state of being enchained.
en·chant (in·chant′, -chänt′) *v.t.* **1** To put a magic spell upon; bewitch. **2** To delight; charm completely. **3** *Obs.* To mislead; delude. See synonyms under CHARM[1], RAVISH. [< F *enchanter* < L *incantare* < *in-* in + *cantare* sing] **—en·chant′ing** *adj.* **—en·chant′ing·ly** *adv.*
en·chant·er (in·chan′tər, -chän′-) *n.* One who enchants; a magician.
en·chant·ment (in·chant′mənt, -chänt′-) *n.* **1** The act of enchanting, or the state of being enchanted. **2** Illusive charm.
en·chant·ress (in·chan′tris, -chän′-) *n.* **1** A sorceress. **2** An attractive or fascinating woman.
en·chase (en·chās′) *v.t.* **·chased, ·chas·ing 1** To incase in a setting, as a jewel in gold. **2** To enrich or decorate with engraved, chased, or inlaid work. **3** To engrave or work (figures, designs, etc.). [< F *enchâsser* < *en-* in (< L *in-*) + *châsse* case < L *capsa*]
en·chi·la·da (en′chi·lä′də) *n. SW U.S.* A Mexican dish composed of a rolled tortilla stuffed with meat or cheese and flavored with chile. [< Sp.]
en·chi·rid·i·on (en′kī·rid′ē·ən, -kə-) *n. pl.* **·i·ons** or **·i·a** (-ē·ə) A handbook; specifically, a manual of devotions. [< Gk. *encheiridion* < *en-* in + *cheir* hand + *-idion,* dim. suffix]
en·chon·dro·ma (en′kon·drō′mə) *n. pl.* **·ma·ta** (-mə·tə) or **·mas** *Pathol.* A cartilaginous tumor; chondroma. [< NL < Gk. *en-* in + CHONDR(O) + -OMA] **—en·chon·drom·a·tous** (en′kon·drom′ə·təs, -drō′mə-) *adj.*
en·cho·ri·al (en·kôr′ē·əl, -kō′rē-) *adj.* Peculiar to a country; native; popular; indigenous. Also **en·chor·ic** (en·kôr′ik, -kor′-), **en·cho′ri·ous, en′cho·ris′tic.** [< Gk. *enchorios* native < *en-* in + *chōra* country]
en·chy·ma (eng′kə·mə) *n. Physiol.* The formative juice of tissues elaborated from chyme. [< NL < Gk. *enchyma* infusion < *en-* in + *chyma* fluid < *cheein* pour]
en·ci·na (en·sē′nə) *n.* **1** The California live oak *(Quercus agrifolia).* **2** The live or holm oak *(Q. virginiana).* [< Sp. < LL *ilicina* < L *ilex, ilicis* an oak] **—en·ci′nal** (-sī′nəl) *adj.*
en·ci·pher (en·sī′fər) *v.t.* To convert (a message, report, etc.) from plain text into cipher.
en·cir·cle (en·sûr′kəl) *v.t.* **·cled, ·cling 1** To form a circle around. **2** To go around; make a circuit of. See synonyms under EMBRACE[1], TWIST. **—en·cir′cle·ment** *n.*
en·clasp (en·klasp′, -kläsp′) *v.t.* To hold in or as in a clasp; embrace.
en·clave (en′klāv) *n.* **1** Part of a country surrounded by the territory or possessions of a foreign government, as East Prussia after World War I. **2** A substance removed from its normal place in the body and enclosed in another organ or tissue. Also **en·cla·vure** (-klā′vyər). —*v.t.* **·claved, ·clav·ing** To surround, as a region or country, with the territories of another country. [< F < *enclaver* enclose < LL *inclavare* < *in-* in + *clavis* key]
en·clit·ic (en·klit′ik) *adj.* **1** *Gram.* Attached to and dependent on a preceding word in stress and accent, as *ge* in Greek and *-que* in Latin. Such forms yield their own accent and generally change that of the word to which they are attached, usually causing a secondary accent to be laid on the final syllable of the latter. The particles *de, ge,* and *te* in Greek and *-que, -ne,* and *-ve* in Latin are examples. **2** *Anat.* Having the planes of the fetal head inclined to those of the maternal pelvis: opposed to *synclitic.* —*n.* An unaccented word attached to a preceding accented word. [< LL *encliticus* < Gk. *enklitikos* < *en-* on + *klinein* lean]
en·close (in·klōz′) *v.t.* **·closed, ·clos·ing 1** To close in; fence in. **2** To place in a cover, envelope, etc. **3** To place, as a check, in a cover, envelope, etc., with a letter or message. **4** To surround; trap. Also spelled *inclose.* See synonyms under CIRCUMSCRIBE, EMBRACE[1]. [< EN-[1] + CLOSE, after OF *enclos,* pp. of *enclore* shut in] **—en·clos′er** *n.*
en·clo·sure (in·klō′zhər) *n.* **1** The act of enclosing, or the state of being enclosed. **2** An enclosed object or space. **3** That which encompasses, encloses, or shuts in, as a fence, wall, case, or wrapper. **4** The fencing in of land. **5** Clausura. Also spelled *inclosure.* See synonyms under BOUNDARY.
en·code (en·kōd′) *v.t.* **·cod·ed, ·cod·ing** To transform a message, document, etc., from plain text into code. **—en·cod′ing** *n.*
en·co·mi·ast (en·kō′mē·ast) *n.* A eulogist; panegyrist. **—en·co′mi·as′tic** or **·ti·cal** *adj.*
en·co·mi·um (en·kō′mē·əm) *n. pl.* **·mi·ums** or **·mi·a** (-me·ə) A formal expression of praise; a eulogy. See synonyms under EULOGY, PRAISE. [< L < Gk. *enkōmion* a eulogy]
en·com·pass (in·kum′pəs) *v.t.* **1** To form a circle around; encircle. **2** To surround, either protectively or hostilely; shut in. **3** *Obs.* To outwit. See synonyms under EMBRACE[1]. **—en·com′pass·ment** *n.*
en·core (äng′kôr, -kōr, än′-) *v.t.* **·cored, ·cor·ing** To call for a repetition of (a performance) or by (a performer). —*n.* **1** The call for a repetition, as of some part of a performance. **2** The repetition itself. —*adv.* Again; once more. [< F]
en·coun·ter (in·koun′tər) *n.* **1** A coming together, especially when casual or unexpected. **2** A hostile meeting, contest; battle. **3** *Obs.* Manner of meeting; address. See synonyms under BATTLE, COLLISION. —*v.t.* **1** To meet accidentally; come upon. **2** To meet in conflict; face in battle. **3** To be faced with (opposition, difficulties, etc.). —*v.i.* **4** To meet accidentally or in battle. See synonyms under ATTACK. [< OF *encontrer* < LL *incontrare* < *in-* in + *contra* against]
en·cour·age (in·kûr′ij) *v.t.* **·aged, ·ag·ing 1** To inspire with courage, hope, or resolution. **2** To help or foster; be favorable toward. [< OF *encoragier* < *en-* in (< L *in-*) + *corage* COURAGE] **—en·cour′ag·er** *n.*
Synonyms: animate, arouse, cheer, countenance, embolden, excite, forward, hearten, impel, inspire, inspirit, instigate, promote, prompt, rally, reassure, stimulate. See ABET, AID, CHERISH, CONSOLE[1], HELP, PROMOTE.
en·cour·age·ment (in·kûr′ij·mənt) *n.* **1** The act of encouraging, or the state of being encouraged; incitement; stimulation. **2** That which encourages.
en·cour·ag·ing (in·kûr′ij·ing) *adj.* Giving, or tending to give, courage or confidence. See synonyms under AUSPICIOUS. **—en·cour′ag·ing·ly** *adv.*
en·crim·son (en·krim′zən) *v.t.* To make crimson; redden.
en·cri·nite (en′krə·nīt) *n. Paleontol.* A fossil crinoid, especially one with cylindrical stem and developed arms. Also *crinite.* [< NL *Encrinus,* name of the genus (< Gk. *en-* in + *krinon* lily) + -ITE[1]]
en·croach (in·krōch′) *v.i.* **1** To intrude upon the possessions or rights of another by or as by stealth; trespass: with *on* or *upon.* **2** To advance or make inroads beyond the proper or usual limits, extent, etc.: The water is *encroaching* on the land. [< OF *encrochier* < *en-* in + *croc* a hook] **—en·croach′er** *n.*
en·croach·ment (in·krōch′mənt) *n.* **1** Entrance upon the rights or domain of another; especially, gradual intrusion. **2** That which is gained or seized by encroaching. See synonyms under AGGRESSION, ATTACK, INVASION.
en·crust (in·krust′), etc. See INCRUST, etc.
en·crypt (en·kript′) *v.t.* To convert (a message) from plain text into a cryptogram. **—en·cryp·tion** (en·krip′shən) *n.*
en·cul·tu·ra·tion (in·kul′chə·rā′shən) *n. Sociol.* The processes whereby individuals are conditioned by, adjusted to, and integrated with the

cultural norms prevalent in the society of which they are members. — **en·cul'tu·ra'tive** *adj.*
en·cum·ber (in·kum'bər) *v.t.* **1** To obstruct or hinder in action or movement, as with a burden; impede. **2** To obstruct or make hard to use; block: The decks were *encumbered* with fallen spars. **3** To weigh down or burden with a duty, financial obligations, mortgages, etc. Also spelled *incumber.* See synonyms under HINDER[1]. [<OF *encombrer* <LL *incombrare* < *in-* in + *combrus* an obstacle]
en·cum·brance (in·kum'brəns) *n.* **1** That which encumbers. **2** *Law* Any lien or liability attached to real property. **3** One's wife, child, or dependent. Also spelled *incumbrance.* See synonyms under IMPEDIMENT, LOAD. [<OF *encombrance* < *encombrer.* See ENCUMBER.]
en·cum·branc·er (in·kum'brən·sər) *n.* One who holds a legal claim or burden on an estate: also spelled *incumbrancer.*
-ency *suffix of nouns* A variant of -ENCE, as in *decency, urgency,* used to form words expressing quality, state or condition, the earlier form being reserved largely for nouns of action. [<L *-entia*]
en·cyc·li·cal (en·sik'li·kəl, -sī'kli-) *adj.* Intended for general circulation; circular: said of letters: also **en·cyc'lic.** —*n. Eccl.* A circular letter addressed by the pope to all the bishops, dealing with matters affecting the church in general. [<LL *encyclicus* <Gk. *enkyklios* general, common < *en-* in + *kyklos* circle]
en·cy·clo·pe·di·a (en·sī'klə·pē'dē·ə) *n.* **1** A work containing information on all subjects, or exhaustive of one subject; a cyclopedia. **2** A work of this kind by some of the intellectual leaders of the French Revolution, the French Encyclopedists. **3** The entire circle of knowledge. Also **en·cy'clo·pae'di·a.** [<NL *encyclopaedia* <Gk. *enkyklopaideia,* a misreading for *enkyklios paideia* a general education]
en·cy·clo·pe·dic (en·sī'klə·pē'dik) *adj.* Pertaining to, of the character of, or proper to an encyclopedia; comprehending a wide range of topics. Also **en·cy'clo·pae'dic, en·cy'clo·pe'di·ac** or **en·cy·clo·pe·di·a·cal** (en·sī'klə·pi·dī'ə·kəl), **en·cy'clo·pe'di·al, en·cy'clo·pe'di·an.**
en·cy·clo·pe·dism (en·sī'klə·pē'diz·əm) *n.* **1** The work or art of compiling encyclopedias; an encyclopedic quality. **2** The doctrines of the French Encyclopedists. Also **en·cy'clo·pae'·dism.**
en·cy·clo·pe·dist (en·sī'klə·pē'dist) *n.* **1** A writer for or compiler of an encyclopedia. **2** One whose studies embrace all sciences. Also **en·cy'clo·pae'dist.** — **French Encyclopedist** One of the writers of the *Encyclopédie ou Dictionnaire raisonné des sciences, des arts, et des métiers* (1751–65): among these were the two editors, Diderot and D'Alembert, and a number of contributors, of whom Voltaire and Rousseau are the best known.
en·cyst (en·sist') *v.t.* & *v.i. Biol.* To envelop or become enclosed in a cyst, sac, etc. — **en·cyst'ed** *adj.*
en·cyst·ment (en·sist'mənt) *n. Biol.* A process by which certain protozoans, after retraction of the pseudopodia or other processes, become enclosed in a cyst, usually preparatory to reproduction, but also for protection against desiccation or putrefaction, in hibernation, etc. Also **en'cys·ta'tion.**
end (end) *n.* **1** The terminal point or part of any material object that has length. **2** The part of an object that is near either extremity. **3** The point in time at which some process ceases; hence, the conclusion of any work or operation. **4** The farthest limit of the space occupied by any extended object. **5** The purpose in view. **6** An inevitable or natural consequence. **7** The close of life. **8** A fragment; remnant. **9** A player stationed at the end of a line, as in football. **10** In archery, a unit of shooting toward a butt; in England, three arrows; in the United States, six. — **at loose ends** In an unsettled or confused state. — **in the end** At last. — **to the end that** In order that. —*v.t.* **1** To bring to a finish or termination; conclude. **2** To be the end of. **3** To cause the death of; kill. —*v.i.* **4** To come to an end. **5** To die. [OE *ende*]
Synonyms (noun): accomplishment, achievement, bound, boundary, cessation, close, completion, conclusion, consequence, consummation, design, effect, expiration, extent, extremity, finale, finis, finish, fulfilment, goal, intent, issue, limit, outcome, period, point, purpose, result, termination, terminus, tip, utmost, uttermost. The *end* is the terminal part of a material object that has length; the *extremity* is distinctively the terminal *point,* and may thus be but part of the *end* in the general sense of that word; the *extremity* is viewed as that which is most remote from some center, or some mean or standard position; the southern *end* of South America includes all Patagonia, the southern *extremity* or *point* is Cape Horn. *Tip* has nearly the same meaning as *extremity,* but is said of small or slight and tapering objects; as, the *tip* of the finger; *point* in such connections is said of that which is drawn out to exceeding fineness or sharpness, as the *point* of a needle, a fork, or a sword; *extremity* is said of something considerable; we do not speak of the *extremity* of a needle. A *goal* is an *end* sought or striven for, as in a race. For the figurative senses of *end* and its associated words, compare the synonyms for the verb END; also for AIM, CONSEQUENCE, DESIGN, EVENT, PURPOSE, REASON. *Antonyms*: see synonyms for BEGINNING.
Synonyms (verb): cease, close, complete, conclude, desist, expire, finish, quit, terminate, top. That *ends,* or is *ended,* of which there is no more, whether or not more was intended or needed; that is *closed, completed, concluded,* or *finished* which has come to an expected or appropriate end. A tumult in the audience may cause a speech to be *ended* when it is neither *closed, completed,* nor *finished,* nor, in the strict sense, *concluded.* An argument may be *closed* with nothing proved; when an argument is *concluded* all that is deemed necessary to prove the point has been stated. To *finish* is to do the last thing there is to do. To *terminate* may be to bring either to an arbitrary or to an appropriate end; as, He *terminated* his remarks abruptly; The spire *terminates* in a cross. A thing *stops* that comes to rest from motion; or the motion *stops* or *ceases* when the object comes to rest; *stop* frequently signifies to bring or come to a sudden and decided cessation of motion, progress, or action of any kind. Compare ABOLISH, CEASE, EFFECT, FINISH, TRANSACT. *Antonyms*: commence, found, inaugurate, initiate, institute, open, originate, start, undertake. Compare INSTITUTE *(verb).*
end-all (end'ôl') *n.* The end of everything or that which ends everything.
en·dam·age (en·dam'ij) *v.t.* **·aged, ·ag·ing** To cause damage to; injure.
en·dam·age·ment (en·dam'ij·mənt) *n. Obs.* Injury.
en·da·me·ba (en'də·mē'bə) *n.* Any of a genus *(Endamoeba)* of protozoan organisms, some species of which are parasitic on man, especially *E. histolytica,* a causative agent in dysentery and liver abscess: also spelled *entamoeba.* Also **en'da·moe'ba.** [<END(O)- + AMEBA]
en·dan·ger (en·dān'jər) *v.t.* To expose to danger.
en·dar·te·ri·tis (en·där'tə·rī'tis) *n. Pathol.* Inflammation of the endarterium.
en·dar·te·ri·um (en'där·tir'ē·əm) *n. Anat.* The innermost coat of an artery. [<NL <Gk. *endo-* within + *artēria* an artery]
end·brain (end'brān') *n.* The telencephalon.
end·brush (end'brush') *n. Physiol.* The tufted branching fibrils forming the termination of many nerve cells.
en·dear (in·dir') *v.t.* **1** To make dear or beloved. **2** *Obs.* To win or secure the affection of.
en·dear·ing (in·dir'ing) *adj.* **1** Making dear or beloved. **2** Manifesting affection; caressing. — **en·dear'ing·ly** *adv.*
en·dear·ment (in·dir'mənt) *n.* **1** Something, as an act, that expresses or attracts affection; an utterance of fondness; a caress. **2** The act of endearing, or the state of being endeared; hence, affection; love.
en·deav·or (in·dev'ər) *n.* An attempt or effort to do or attain something; earnest exertion for an end. —*v.t.* To make an effort to do or effect; try: usually with an infinitive as object. —*v.i.* To make an effort; strive: usually with *at, after,* or *for.* Also *Brit.* **en·deav'our.** [ME *endeveren* <EN[1] + DEVOIR. Cf. F *se mettre en devoir* make it one's duty, set about]
Synonyms (noun): attempt, effort, essay, exertion, struggle, trial. *Effort* denotes the voluntary putting forth of power to attain or accomplish some specific thing; it reaches toward a definite end; *exertion* is a putting forth of power without special reference to an object. Every *effort* is an *exertion,* but not every *exertion* is an *effort. Attempt* is more experimental than *effort, endeavor* less strenuous but more continuous. An *effort* is a single act, an *endeavor* a continued series of acts. A *struggle* is a violent *effort* or strenuous *exertion.* An *essay* is an *attempt, effort,* or *endeavor* made as a test of the powers of the one who makes it. See AIM, ATTEMPT.
Synonyms (verb): attempt, essay, strive, try, undertake. To *attempt* is to take action somewhat experimentally with the hope and purpose of accomplishing a certain result; to *endeavor* is to *attempt* strenuously and with firm and enduring purpose. To *attempt* expresses a single act; to *endeavor,* a continuous exertion; we say, I will *endeavor* (not I will *attempt*) while I live. To *attempt* is with the view of accomplishing; to *essay* with a view of testing our own powers. To *undertake* is to accept or take upon oneself as an obligation, as some business, labor, or trust; the word often implies complete assurance of success: as, I will *undertake* to produce the witness. To *strive* suggests little of the result, much of toil, strain, and contest, in seeking it; I will *strive* to fulfil your wishes, that is, I will spare no labor and exertion to do it. *Try* is the most comprehensive of these words. The original idea of testing or experimenting is not thought of when a man says "I will *try.*" To *attempt* suggests giving up, if the thing is not accomplished at a stroke; to *try* implies using other means and studying out other ways if not at first successful. *Try* is more earnest; *endeavor* is more mild and formal. *Antonyms*: abandon, dismiss, drop, neglect, omit, overlook.
en·deav·or·er (in·dev'ər·ər) *n.* One who endeavors.
en·dec·a·gon (en·dek'ə·gon), etc. See HENDECAGON, etc.
En·de·cott (en'di·kot, -kət), **John,** 1589–1665, English colonial governor of Massachusetts. Also spelled **En'di·cott.**
en·dem·ic (en·dem'ik) *adj.* **1** Peculiar to or prevailing in or among some (specified) country or people. **2** *Ecol.* Indigenous or native to a restricted area: said of plants and animals: opposed to *ecdemic.* **3** *Pathol.* Pertaining to a disease confined to or characteristic of a given locality, as distinguished from an epidemic or sporadic disease. Also **en·de·mi·al** (en·dē'mē·əl), **en·dem'i·cal.** [<Gk. *endēmos* native < *en-* in + *dēmos* people]
en·de·mic·i·ty (en'də·mis'ə·tē) *n. Ecol.* The condition of growing in only one natural area, or of being restricted in distribution to a given locality. Also **en'de·mism.**
end·er (en'dər) *n.* One who or that which brings something to an end.
En·der·bur·y Island (en'dər·ber'ē) One of the Phoenix Islands, comprising a condominium (1939) of Great Britain and the United States; 2 square miles.
En·der·by Land (en'dər·bē) A region on the coast of Antarctica south of the continent of Africa.
en·der·mic (en·dûr'mik) *adj. Med.* Acting by being absorbed in or through the skin. [<EN-[2] + Gk. *derma* skin] — **en'der·mism** *n.*
en dés·ha·bil·lé (äṅ dā·zà·bē·yā') *French* In dishabille.
En·di·an·dra (en'dē·an'drə) *n.* A genus of close-grained, straight-fibered hardwood trees of the laurel family native to Australia, bearing large globular fruit, especially *E. glauca,* with an aromatic teaklike wood.
end·ing (en'ding) *n.* **1** The act of bringing or coming to an end; also, an end; extremity. **2** One or more letters or syllables added to the base of a word, especially to indicate an inflection.

en·dive (en′dīv, än′dēv) *n.* **1** An herb *(Cichorium endivia)* allied to chicory. There are many varieties, divided into two groups, the **curled** or **narrow-leaved endive** (variety *crispa*) and the **broad-leaved endive** (variety *latifolia*). **2** The blanched leaves of this herb, used as a salad. [< F < L *intibus* endive]

end·less (end′lis) *adj.* **1** Enduring everlastingly; eternal. **2** Having no end in space; boundless; infinite. **3** Continually recurring; incessant. **4** Forming a closed loop or circle; continuous. See synonyms under ETERNAL, IMMORTAL, PERPETUAL. —**end′less·ly** *adv.* —**end′less·ness** *n.*

end·long (end′lông′, -long′) *adv.* **1** Lengthwise; at full length. **2** Continuously. **3** On end; perpendicularly.

end man In a minstrel troupe, one who sits at either end of the company as grouped upon the stage, and who engages in comic dialogs with the interlocutor.

end·most (end′mōst′) *adj.* Placed or being at the extreme end; most remote; farthest.

endo- *combining form* Within; inside: *endocarp.* Also, before vowels, **end-**. [< Gk. < *endon* within]

en·do·blast (en′dō·blast) *n. Biol.* The hypoblast: also spelled *entoblast.* —**en′do·blas′tic** *adj.*

en·do·car·di·ac (en′dō·kär′dē·ak) *adj. Anat.* **1** Situated or being within the heart. **2** Of or pertaining to the endocardium. Also **en′do·car′di·al.**

en·do·car·di·tis (en′dō·kär·dī′tis) *n. Pathol.* Inflammation of the endocardium. —**en′do·car·dit′ic** (-dit′ik) *adj.*

en·do·car·di·um (en′dō·kär′dē·əm) *n. Anat.* The delicate endothelial membrane lining the chambers of the heart. [< NL < Gk. *endo-* within + *kardia* heart]

en·do·carp (en′dō·kärp) *n. Bot.* The inner layer of a pericarp, as the hard inner part of a cherry stone.

en·do·cen·tric (en′dō·sen′trik) *adj. Ling.* Denoting a syntactic construction which as a unit has the same function as any one of its component parts, as the phrase *healthy boys and girls* in *healthy boys and girls eat well*: opposed to *exocentric.*

en·do·cho·ri·on (en′dō·kôr′ē·ən, -kō′rē-) *n.* **1** *Anat.* The inner chorion associated with the fetal membrane. **2** *Entomol.* The inner layer of the chorion or shell, covering an insect egg.

en·do·crine (en′dō·krin, -krīn) *adj.* **1** Producing an internal secretion. **2** Pertaining to or produced by an endocrine gland or glands. **3** Hormonal. Also **en′do·cri′nal** (-krī′nəl), **en·doc·ri·nous** (en·dok′rə·nəs), **en′do·crin′ic** (-krin′ik). —*n.* The secretion of an endocrine gland; a hormone. [< ENDO- + Gk. *krinein* separate]

endocrine gland Any of numerous ductless, hormone-secreting structures in various sites in the body which release secretions into surrounding tissue and thence into the bloodstream, either directly or through the lymphatic system.

ENDOCRINE GLANDS

Name	*Location*
Adrenals (2)	Anterior to the kidneys
Gonads	Sex glands collectively
Ovaries (2)	Paired sex glands of the female
Pancreas	Upper abdominal cavity
Parathyroids	In pairs, near the thyroid
Pineal	Attached to the brain, near the pituitary
Pituitary	In the floor of the skull
Testes (2)	Paired sex glands of the male
Thymus	Above the heart
Thyroid	Paired lobes, one on each side of the trachea

en·do·cri·nol·o·gy (en′dō·kri·nol′ə·jē, -krī-) *n.* That branch of medicine which treats of the anatomy, physiology, and pathology of the endocrine glands and the properties and functions of the various internal secretions. —**en′do·cri·nol′o·gist** *n.*

en·do·cyte (en′dō·sīt) *n. Biol.* A foreign substance found inside a cell.

en·do·cyt·ic (en′dō·sit′ik) *adj. Biol.* Pertaining to the contents of a cell.

en·do·derm (en′dō·dûrm) *n. Biol.* **1** The innermost of the germ layers of the embryo. **2** The inner layer of the integument of an organism. Also spelled *entoderm.*

en·do·der·mis (en′dō·dûr′mis) *n. Bot.* A sheath of one or more layers of modified parenchymatous cells between the cortex and the central zone of the stem or root in plants: also spelled *entoderm.* [< ENDODERM, on analogy with *epidermis*] —**en′do·der′mal, en′do·der′mic** *adj.*

en·do·don·tics (en′dō·don′tiks) *n.* The branch of dentistry which is concerned with the prevention, diagnosis, and treatment of diseases of the tooth pulp, as root canal work. Also **en′do·don′tia** (-don′shə), **en′do·don′tol′o·gy** (-don′tol′ə·jē). [< ENDO- + Gk. *odous, odontos* a tooth + -ICS] —**en′do·don′tist** *n.*

en·do·en·zyme (en′dō·en′zīm, -zim) *n. Biochem.* An enzyme or ferment acting from within the cell, as zymase: opposed to *ectoenzyme.* Also **en′do·en′zym** (-zim).

en·dog·a·my (en·dog′ə·mē) *n.* **1** *Anthropol.* The custom of marriage within the group, class, caste, or tribe; inbreeding: opposed to *exogamy.* **2** *Bot.* The fertilization of plants by pollination between two flowers on the same plant. —**en·dog′a·mous, en·do·gam·ic** (en′dō·gam′ik) *adj.*

en·do·gen (en′dō·jen) *n. Bot.* A plant that increases by the growth of new vascular and cellular tissue among that already formed; a monocotyledon: opposed to *exogen.*

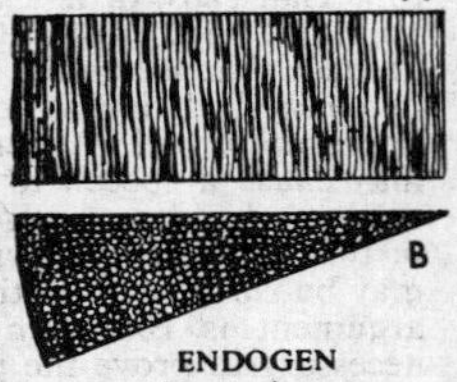

ENDOGEN
A. Vertical section.
B. Cross-section.

en·dog·e·nous (en·doj′ə·nəs) *adj.* Originating or produced internally; due to internal causes. —**en·dog′e·nous·ly** *adv.*

en·dog·e·ny (en·doj′ə·nē) *n.* **1** Growth from within; specifically, endogenous cell formation. **2** Endogamy.

en·do·lymph (en′dō·limf) *n. Anat.* The serous fluid that fills the membranous labyrinth of the ear.

en·do·me·tri·um (en′dō·mē′trē·əm) *n. Anat.* The mucous membrane which lines the uterus. [< NL < Gk. *endo-* within + *mētra* womb] —**en′do·me′tri·al** *adj.*

en·dom·e·try (en·dom′ə·trē) *n.* The measurement of cavities; specifically of the interior of body organs, as the cranium. —**en·do·met·ric** (en′dō·met′rik) or **·ri·cal** *adj.*

en·do·mix·is (en′dō·mik′sis) *n. Biol.* The periodic reorganization of the nucleus in certain unicellular organisms which reproduce asexually, as paramecium; a form of parthenogenesis: distinguished from *amphimixis.* [< ENDO- + Gk. *mixis* intercourse]

en·do·morph (en′dō·môrf) *n. Mineral.* A mineral enclosed within another, as a crystal of tourmaline in quartz.

en·do·mor·phic (en′dō·môr′fik) *adj.* **1** *Mineral.* **a** Of or pertaining to an endomorph. **b** Occurring on the inside; produced by endomorphism. **2** Pertaining to a physical and personality type associated with the development of the endodermal layer of the embryo, and characterized by predominance of the abdominal system. Compare ECTOMORPHIC and MESOMORPHIC.

en·do·morph·ism (en′dō·môr′fiz·əm) *n. Geol.* The changes produced in igneous rocks by the action upon them of underlying and intrusive magmatic material.

en·do·par·a·site (en′dō·par′ə·sīt) *n. Biol.* A parasite that lives in the internal parts of its host, as an intestinal worm. —**en′do·par′a·sit′ic** (-sit′ik) *adj.*

en·do·path·ic (en′dō·path′ik) *adj. Pathol.* Pertaining to those diseases originating from within the organism. —**en·dop·a·thy** (en·dop′ə·thē) *n.*

en·do·phyte (en′dō·fīt) *n. Bot.* A plant living within another organism, usually as a parasite, as certain algae and fungi. Also spelled *entophyte.* —**en′do·phy′tal** *adj.* —**en′do·phyt′ic** (-fit′ik) *adj.* —**en′do·phyt′i·cal·ly** *adv.*

en·doph·y·tous (en·dof′ə·təs) *adj.* Living within wood, as the larvae of certain insects.

en·do·plasm (en′dō·plaz′əm) *n. Biol.* The inner granular portion of the cytoplasm of the cell, enclosing the nucleus. Also **en·do·sarc** (en′dō·särk). —**en′do·plas′mic** *adj.*

en·dop·o·dite (en·dop′ə·dīt) *n. Biol.* The inner, variously modified branch of the shaft or stem of an appendage, as in the thoracic region of a lobster, crab, or other decapod. [< ENDO- + Gk. *pous, podos* foot + -ITE[1]]

end organ *Physiol.* Any organ adapted for the reception or delivery of nervous stimuli.

en·dor·phin (en·dôr′fin) *n.* Any of several peptides produced by the brain and having a morphinelike effect. [< ENDO- + (M)ORPHIN(E)]

en·dorse (in·dôrs′) *v.t.* **·dorsed, ·dors·ing 1** To write upon the back of; especially, to write one's name on the back of (a check, draft, etc.) to assign it or to guarantee its payment; to write one's name on the back of (a check, etc.) in exchanging the document for the cash it represents. **2** To indicate receipt of (a sum) by signing one's name. **3** To give sanction to. See synonyms under ACKNOWLEDGE, AFFIRM, CONFESS, JUSTIFY, RATIFY. Also spelled *indorse.* [< OF *endosser* < Med.L *indorsare* < L *in-* on + *dorsum* back; partially refashioned after L] —**en·dors′a·ble** *adj.* —**en·dors′er, en·dor′sor** *n.*

en·dor·see (en′dôr·sē′, in·dôr′sē) *n.* One to whom transference by endorsement is made.

en·dorse·ment (in·dôrs′mənt) *n.* **1** The writing of one's name on the back of a note, check, etc. **2** The act of ratification; approval. **3** The act or method by which bills, notes, and other negotiable instruments are transferred. **4** Any writing on the back of a document. **5** A rider attached to an insurance policy to modify the original contract. Also spelled *indorsement.*

en·do·scope (en′də·skōp) *n. Med.* An instrument for viewing the inside of a body cavity or hollow organ, especially the womb, rectum, urethra, and bladder. —**en·dos·co·py** (en·dos′kə·pē) *n.*

en·do·skel·e·ton (en′dō·skel′ə·tən) *n. Zool.* The internal supporting structure of an animal, characteristic of all vertebrates; all of the skeleton not of dermal origin: opposed to *exoskeleton.* —**en′do·skel′e·tal** *adj.*

en·dos·mo·sis (en′dos·mō′sis, -doz-) *n. Chem.* **1** Osmosis in that direction in which the fluid traverses the septum most rapidly. **2** Osmosis from an outer vessel to one within it. Also **en′dos·mose′** (-mōz′). —**en′dos·mot′ic** (-mot′ik) *adj.*

en·do·sperm (en′dō·spûrm) *n. Bot.* The albumen of a seed; nutritive substance within the embryo sac of an ovule.

en·do·spore (en′dō·spôr, -spōr) *n. Bot.* **1** A spore formed within the membrane of a cell. **2** The delicate inner layer of the wall of a spore: also **en′do·spo′ri·um.** **3** An asexual spore produced by certain bacteria: opposed to *arthrospore.* —**en·dos·po·rous** (en·dos′pər·əs) *adj.*

en·dos·te·um (en·dos′tē·əm) *n. pl.* **·te·a** (-tē·ə) *Anat.* The thin, vascular membrane lining the medullary cavity of a bone. [< NL < Gk. *endo-* within + *osteon* bone]

en·dos·to·sis (en′dos·tō′sis) *n. Biol.* Ossification that takes place between cartilage cells.

en·do·style (en′dō·stīl) *n. Zool.* In ascidians, a longitudinal fold of the endoderm of the pharyngeal cavity, projecting into the blood cavity. [< ENDO- + -STYLE[2]]

en·do·sym·bi·o·sis (en′dō·sim′bē·ō′sis) *n.* Symbiosis in which one of the symbiontic partners lives within the body of the other.

en·do·the·ci·um (en′dō·thē′sē·əm) *n. pl.* **·ci·a** (-sē·ə) *Bot.* **1** The inner lining of the cell of an anther. **2** The internal lining of the capsule of mosses. [< NL < Gk. *endo-* within + *thēkion* a small case]

en·do·the·li·o·ma (en′dō·thē′lē·ō′mə) *n. pl.* **·ma·ta** (-mə·tə) or **·mas** *Pathol.* A tumorous growth developed in or from the endothelium.

en·do·the·li·um (en′dō·thē′lē·əm) *n. pl.* **·li·a** (-lē·ə) *Anat.* A membrane, composed of flat, thin cells, that lines blood vessels, lymphatic tubes, and cavities. [< NL < Gk. *endo-* within + *thēlē* nipple] —**en′do·the′li·al** *adj.* —**en′do·the′li·oid, en·doth·e·loid** (en·doth′loid) *adj.*

en·do·therm (en′də·thûrm) *n.* An animal that maintains a uniform temperature independent of and usually higher than the ambient temperature; a warm-blooded animal.

en·do·ther·mic (en′dō·thûr′mik) *adj.* **1** *Chem.* Pertaining to, attended by, or produced from

the absorption of heat; heat-absorbing: *endothermic* combination or reaction: opposed to *exothermic.* 2 *Zool.* Warm-blooded. Also **en·do·ther′mal.**

en·do·tox·in (en′dō·tok′sin) *n. Bacteriol.* A toxic product liberated by the disintegration of certain bacteria which fails to induce the formation of an antitoxin in an animal organism. —**en′do·tox′ic** *adj.*

en·do·troph·ic (en′dō·trof′ik, -trō′fik) *adj. Bot.* Relating to the condition of fungi which live in and feed upon the internal cells of plant parts, such as roots.

en·dow (in·dou′) *v.t.* 1 To bestow a permanent fund or income upon. 2 To furnish or equip, as with talents or natural gifts: usually with *with.* 3 *Obs.* To provide with a dower. Also spelled *indow.* [<OF *endouer* <*en-* in (<L *in-*) + *douer* <L *dotare* give]

en·dow·ment (in·dou′mənt) *n.* 1 Money or property given for the permanent use of an institution, person, or object. 2 Any natural gift, as talent or beauty. 3 The act of endowing. Also spelled *indowment.*

endowment insurance See under INSURANCE.

end papers In bookbinding, those papers, plain or variously colored and decorated, placed at the front and back of a book, one leaf being pasted to the binding or cover, the others acting as flyleaves.

end·plate (end′plāt′) *n.* 1 *Electronics* One of the electrodes of a vacuum tube, carrying a negative potential to prevent the escape of electrons at the anode. 2 *Physiol.* The termination of a motor nerve, usually embedded in muscle fiber.

end product The final product, result, or outcome of any rocess.

en·drin (en′drin) *n.* A toxic chlorinated hydrocarbon, $C_{12}H_8OCl_6$, used as a pesticide and tending to persist in fats in the food chain.

end table A small table to be placed beside chairs, at the end of a sofa, etc.

en·due (in·do͞o′, -dyo͞o′) *v.t.* **·dued, ·du·ing** 1 To provide or endow, as with some quality or power: with *with.* 2 To put on; don. 3 To clothe; garb. Also spelled *indue.* [Fusion of OF *enduire* introduce <L *inducere* (see INDUCE) and OF *enduire* clothe <L *induere*; infl. in meaning by ENDOW]

en·dur·a·ble (in·do͝or′ə·bəl, -dyo͝or′-) *adj.* That can be endured; bearable.

en·dur·ance (in·do͝or′əns, -dyo͝or′-) *n.* 1 The capacity or power to endure; ability to suffer pain, distress, hardship, or any very prolonged stress without succumbing; patient fortitude. 2 The act or experience of enduring or suffering. 3 *Obs.* Hardship. See synonyms under FORTITUDE.

en·dure (in·do͝or′, -dyo͝or′) *v.* **·dured, ·dur·ing** *v.t.* 1 To bear or undergo, as pain, grief, or injury, especially without yielding; withstand; suffer. 2 To tolerate; put up with. —*v.i.* 3 To last; continue to be. 4 To suffer without yielding; hold out. [<OF *endurer* <L *indurare* <*in-* in + *durare* harden <*durus* hard]

Synonyms: abide, afford, allow, bear, brook, permit, suffer, support, sustain, tolerate, undergo. *Bear* is the most general of these words; it is metaphorically to hold up or keep up a burden of care, pain, grief, annoyance, or the like, without sinking, lamenting, or repining. *Allow* and *permit* involve large concession of the will; whispering is *allowed* by the schoolteacher who does not forbid nor censure it; a state *tolerates* a religion which it would be glad to suppress. To *endure* is to *bear* with strain and resistance, but with conscious power; *endure* conveys a fuller suggestion of contest and conquest than *bear.* One may choose to *endure* the pain of a surgical operation rather than take anesthetics; he *permits* the thing to come which he must brace himself to *endure* when it comes. To *afford* is to be equal to a pecuniary demand, that is, to be able to *bear* it. *Abide* combines the senses of await and *endure*; as, I will *abide* the result. Compare ABIDE, LIVE, PERSEVERE, PERSIST, STAND, SUPPORT. *Antonyms*: break, despair, droop, fail, faint, fall, falter, sink, succumb, surrender, yield.

en·dur·ing (in·do͝or′ing, -dyo͝or′-) *adj.* 1 Lasting; permanent. 2 Long-suffering. See synonymsunder PERMANENT, PERPETUAL. —**en·dur′ing·ly** *adv.* —**en·dur′ing·ness** *n.*

end·wise (end′wīz′) *adv.* 1 With the end foremost or uppermost. 2 On end; so as to present the end toward the spectator or some object. 3 Lengthwise; from end to end. Also **end′ways′** (-wāz′).

En·dym·i·on (en·dim′ē·ən) In Greek legend, a beautiful young shepherd loved by Selene and granted eternal youth and sleep at her request.

-ene *suffix Chem.* 1 Denoting an open-chain, unsaturated, hydrocarbon compound having one double-bond: *ethylene.* 2 Denoting an aromatic compound of the benzene series.

E·ne·as (i·nē′əs) A masculine personal name. Also *Fr.* **E·née** (ā·nā′), See AENEAS. [<Gk., praiseworthy]

en ef·fet (äṅ nef·fe′) *French* In effect; consequently; substantially.

en·e·ma (en′ə·mə) *n. pl.* **·mas** or **e·nem·a·ta** (e·nem′ə·tə) *Med.* 1 A liquid injected into the rectum for cleansing or nutritive purposes. 2 The injection of such a liquid. 3 The apparatus for such an injection. [<Gk. <*enienai* <*en-* in + *hienai* send]

en·e·my (en′ə·mē) *n. pl.* **·mies** 1 One who cherishes resentment or malicious purpose toward another; an adversary; foe. 2 One of a hostile army or nation. 3 A hostile nation or military force collectively. —*adj.* 1 Of or pertaining to a hostile army or power. 2 *Obs.* Unfriendly; hostile. [<OF *enemi* <L *inimicus* <*in-* not + *amicus* friend]

Synonyms (noun): adversary, antagonist, competitor, foe, opponent, rival. An *enemy* in private life is one who is moved by hostile feeling with active disposition to injure; but in military language all who fight on the opposite side are called *enemies* or collectively "the *enemy,*" where no personal animosity may be implied; *foe,* which is rather a poetical and literary word, implies intensely hostile spirit and purpose. An *antagonist* is one who opposes and is opposed actively and with intensity of effort; an *opponent,* one in whom the attitude of resistance is the more prominent; a *competitor,* one who seeks the same object for which another is striving; *antagonists* in wrestling, *competitors* in business, *opponents* in debate may contend with no personal ill will; *rivals* in love, ambition, etc., rarely avoid inimical feeling. *Adversary* now commonly denotes one who not only opposes another in fact, but does so with hostile spirit or perhaps out of pure malignity. Compare synonyms for AMBITION. *Antonyms*: abettor, accessory, accomplice, ally, friend, helper, supporter.

enemy alien An alien living or interned in a country which is at war with his own country.

en·er·ge·sis (en′ər·jē′sis) *n. Bot.* The chemical and physical changes which set free the energy produced by the respiratory processes in plant cells. [<NL <Gk. *energeein* be active]

en·er·get·ic (en′ər·jet′ik) *adj.* 1 Having or displaying energy. 2 Acting with prompt, rapid, and effective force; forceful and efficient; strenuous. Also **en′er·get′i·cal.** [<Gk. *energētikos* <*energeein* be active] —**en′er·get′i·cal·ly** *adv.*

en·er·get·ics (en′ər·jet′iks) *n. pl. (construed as singular)* 1 The science of the laws and phenomena of energy in all its forms. 2 The philosophic doctrine which attributes all natural phenomena to the action of energy.

en·er·gid (i·nûr′jid) *n. Biol.* The cytoplasm and nucleus of a cell considered as a unit. [<Gk. *energos* active + -ID[1]]

en·er·gize (en′ər·jīz) *v.* **·gized, ·giz·ing** *v.t.* To give energy, force, or strength to; activate. —*v.i.* To be in operation; be active. —**en′er·giz′er** *n.*

en·er·gu·men (en′ər·gyo͞o′mən) *n.* One who is supposed to be possessed by evil spirits; a demoniac; hence, a fanatical enthusiast. [<LL *energumenus* <Gk. *energoumenos,* ppr. of *energeein* be active]

en·er·gy (en′ər·jē) *n. pl.* **·gies** 1 The power by which anything acts effectively to move or change other things or accomplish any result. 2 Habitual tendency to and readiness for effective action. 3 Power in active exercise; force in operation. 4 *Physics* The capacity of doing work and of overcoming inertia, as by heat, light, radiation, or mechanical and chemical forces. **Potential energy** is that due to the position of one body relative to another; **kinetic energy** is manifested by bodies in motion. The units of energy and work are mutually convertible, and energy itself is regarded as functionally related to the mass and velocity of a material system. See QUANTUM. 5 Vigor and forcefulness of style or expression. See synonyms under POWER, WARMTH. [<LL *energia* <Gk. *energeia* <*energēs* <*en-* on + *ergon* work]

energy level *Physics* Any of several discrete states which an electron may assume within an atom, transition between which is associated with the emission of quanta: also called *quantum state.*

en·er·vate (en′ər·vāt) *v.t.* **·vat·ed, ·vat·ing** To deprive of nerve, energy, or strength; weaken. —*adj.* (i·nûr′vit) Rendered feeble or effeminate; weakened. [<L *enervatus,* pp. of *enervare* weaken <*ex-* out + *nervus* a sinew] —**en′er·va′tor** *n.*

en·er·va·tion (en′ər·vā′shən) *n.* The act of enervating, or the state of being enervated; debility.

en·face (en·fās′) *v.t.* **·faced, ·fac·ing** To write or print on the face of. —**en·face′ment** *n.*

en fa·mille (äṅ fà·mē′y′) *French* Within the family; at home; informally.

en·fant per·du (äṅ·fäṅ′ per·dü′) *French* A soldier assigned to a position of extreme danger; literally, a lost child.

en·fant ter·ri·ble (äṅ·fäṅ′ te·rē′bl′) *French* A precocious child given to disconcerting remarks; literally, a terrible child.

en·fee·ble (en·fē′bəl) *v.t.* **·bled, ·bling** To render feeble. See synonyms under IMPAIR. —**en·fee′ble·ment** *n.* —**en·fee′bler** *n.*

en·feoff (en·fēf′, -fef′) *v.t.* 1 *Law* To invest with a fee or fief. 2 *Obs.* To surrender, as a vassal; give over, as oneself. Also spelled *infeoff.* [<OF *enfeoffer* <*en-* in + *fief* FIEF]

en·feoff·ment (en·fēf′mənt, -fef′-) *n.* The act or instrument by which an estate in fee is transferred: also spelled *infeoffment.*

en·fet·ter (en·fet′ər) *v.t.* To enchain.

En·field (en′fēld) A town in northern Middlesex, England.

Enfield rifle A .30-caliber, bolt-action, breech-loading magazine rifle used by the U.S. Army and by the British: officially, Lee Enfield. [from *Enfield,* England, where it was first manufactured]

en·fi·lade (en′fə·lād′) *Mil. v.t.* **·lad·ed, ·lad·ing** To fire or be in a position to fire down the length of, as a trench or column of troops. [<*n.*] —*n.* 1 Gunfire that can rake lengthwise a line of troops, etc. 2 A position exposed to a raking fire. [<F <*enfiler* thread <*en-* in + *fil* thread]

en·fin (äṅ·faṅ′) *adv. French* Finally; in conclusion.

en·fleu·rage (äṅ′flœ·räzh′) *n.* The extraction of perfumes by exposing odorless fats to the exhalations of the more delicate flowers. [<F <*enfleurer* <*en-* in + *fleur* flower]

en·fold (in·fōld′), etc. See INFOLD, etc.

en·force (in·fôrs′, -fōrs′) *v.t.* **·forced, ·forc·ing** 1 To compel obedience to, as laws. 2 To compel (performance, obedience, etc.) by physical or moral force. 3 To make convincing; give weight to, as an argument. 4 *Obs.* To force; coerce. See synonyms under EXECUTE. [<OF *enforcier* <LL *infortiare* <*in-* in + *fortis* strong] —**en·force′a·ble** *adj.* —**en·forc′er** *n.*

en·force·ment (in·fôrs′mənt, -fōrs′-) *n.* The act of enforcing, or the state of being enforced; compulsory execution; compulsion.

en·frame (in·frām′) *v.t.* **·framed, ·fram·ing** To enclose in or as in a border or a frame. **·en·frame′ment** *n.*

en·fran·chise (en·fran′chīz) *v.t.* **—chised, ·chis·ing** 1 To endow with a franchise, as the right to vote. 2 To set free, as from bondage. 3 *Law* In England, to convert (a copyhold estate) into a freehold, either by payment in gross or by setting a fixed annual rent charge. [<OF *enfranchiss-,* stem of *enfranchir* <*en-* in + *franc* free. See FRANK.]

en·fran·chise·ment (en·fran′chiz·mənt) *n.* The act of enfranchising, or the state of being enfranchised.

En·ga·dine (eng′gə-dēn) The valley of the Inn in eastern Switzerland; a resort center; 60 miles long.

en·gage (in-gāj′) v. ·gaged, ·gag·ing v.t. 1 To bind by a promise, pledge, etc. 2 To promise to marry; betroth: usually in the passive. 3 To hire, as a lawyer, or his services; secure the use of, as a room. 4 To hold the interest or attention of. 5 To hold (interest or attention); occupy. 6 To occupy or take up the extent, energies, etc., of: How do you *engage* your time? 7 To win over; attract: to *engage* affections. 8 To begin a battle with: We *engaged* the enemy. 9 *Mech.* To mesh or interlock. — v.i. 10 To bind oneself by a promise, pledge, etc. 11 To devote or occupy oneself: to *engage* in research. 12 To begin a battle. 13 *Mech.* To mesh. See synonyms under BIND, EMPLOY, INTEREST, OCCUPY, RETAIN. [<F *engager* < en- in + *gager* pledge]

en·gaged (in-gājd′) adj. 1 Affianced. 2 Occupied or busy. 3 Partially sunk or built into another part of a structure, or so appearing. 4 *Mech.* Geared together; driven by gearing. 5 Involved in a contest or conflict. See synonyms under BUSY, INDUSTRIOUS.

en·gage·ment (in-gāj′mənt) n. 1 The act of engaging. 2 The condition of being engaged; a betrothal. 3 Something that engages or binds; an obligation; agreement; promise; contract. 4 An entering into or being in battle; a battle. 5 *Mech.* The state of being in gear. 6 *pl.* Pecuniary obligations. 7 A salaried position. See synonyms under BATTLE, CONTRACT.

en·gag·ing (in-gā′jing) adj. Attracting interest; winning. See synonyms under AMIABLE. — **en·gag′ing·ly** adv.

en·gar·çon (än gàr-sôn′) *French* In bachelorhood.

en garde (än gärd′) *French* On guard. See under GUARD.

en·gar·land (en-gär′lənd) v.t. To encircle with or as with garlands; wreathe.

Eng·els (eng′əls), Friedrich, 1820–95, German socialist and author; associate of Karl Marx.

en·gen·der (in-jen′dər) v.t. 1 To cause to exist; produce. 2 *Rare* To beget. — v.i. 3 To come into being. See synonyms under PRODUCE, PROPAGATE. [<OF *engendrer* <L *ingenerare* < in- in + *genus, generis* race]

en·gild (en-gild′) v.t. To gild or brighten.

en·gine (en′jin) n. 1 A machine by which energy is applied to the doing of work, notably one that converts heat energy into mechanical work: a steam *engine,* gas *engine,* etc. 2 A locomotive, taken as a whole. 3 Any large mechanism or material contrivance for producing some effect, especially of destruction or disintegration: an *engine* of war. 4 Any agency or instrumentality designedly employed. [<OF *engin* <L *ingenium* < in- in + *gen-,* root of *gignere* beget]

en·gine–driv·er (en′jin-drī′vər) n. *Brit.* A locomotive engineer.

en·gi·neer (en′jə-nir′) n. 1 One versed in or practicing any branch of engineering. 2 One who runs or manages an engine; engine-driver. 3 A manager; inventor; plotter. 4 A member of the division of an army which constructs forts and bridges, clears and builds roads, etc. Also *Obs.* **en′gin·er.** — v.t. 1 To put through or manage by contrivance: to *engineer* a scheme. 2 To plan and superintend as engineer: to *engineer* an aqueduct.

en·gi·neer·ing (en′jə-nir′ing) n. 1 The art of designing, building, or using engines and machines, or of designating and constructing public works or the like. The general art is now subdivided into numerous branches, dealing chiefly with the application of scientific knowledge for purposes useful to man: chemical *engineering,* civil *engineering,* electrical *engineering,* hydraulic *engineering,* mining *engineering.* 2 Painstaking management; maneuvering.

en·gine·ry (en′jin-rē) n. 1 *Mil.* a Engines of war. b Their management. 2 Engines collectively. 3 An artful scheme. 4 Any powerful agency.

en·gi·nous (en′jə-nəs) adj. *Obs.* Tricky; crafty; deceitful. [<OF *engineus* <L *ingeniosus* INGENIOUS]

en·gird (en-gûrd′) v.t. ·girt or ·gird·ed, ·gird·ing To gird about; encompass; surround.

en·gir·dle (en-gûr′dəl) v.t., ·dled, ·dling To encircle; girdle.

en·gla·cial (en-glā′shəl) adj. 1 Embedded within glacier ice. 2 Occurring in a glacier.

Eng·land (ing′glənd) The southern part and largest political division of Great Britain, south of Scotland and east of Wales; 50,874 square miles; capital, London: Latin *Anglia.* See COMMONWEALTH OF NATIONS, GREAT BRITAIN, UNITED KINGDOM.

gion, time, or person: Chaucerian *English,* American *English.* 5 *Printing* A size of type between pica and great primer: about 14 points; also, a type face resembling German text: more commonly called **Old English.** 6 In billiards, a horizontal twist or spin given to the cue ball by striking it on one side; by the British called *side:* also applied in

SOVEREIGNS OF ENGLAND, GREAT BRITAIN, AND THE UNITED KINGDOM

	Began to reign		Began to reign
SOVEREIGNS OF ENGLAND[1]		**HOUSE OF TUDOR**	
ANGLO–SAXON LINE	A.D.	Henry VII (great-great-great-	A.D.
Egbert	800	grandson of Edward III)	1485
Ethelwulf (son)	836	Henry VIII (son)	1509
Ethelbald (son)	857	Edward VI (son)	1547
Ethelbert (brother)	860	Mary I (half-sister)	1553
Ethelred I (brother)	866	Elizabeth I (half-sister)	1558
Alfred *the Great* (brother)	871		
Edward *the Elder* (son)	901	**SOVEREIGNS OF GREAT BRITAIN**	
Athelstan (son)	925	**STUART LINE**	
Edmund I (brother)	940	James I of England or VI of Scotland	
Edred (brother)	946	(son of Mary Queen of Scots, great-	
Edwy (nephew)	955	granddaughter of Henry VII)	1603
Edgar (brother)	957	Charles I (son)	1625
Edward *the Martyr* (son)	975	**COMMONWEALTH** (during which Oliver	
Ethelred II, *the Unready*		Cromwell ruled as Lord Protector	
(half-brother)	979	1653–58, being succeeded by Rich-	
Edmund II, *Ironside* (son)	1016	ard Cromwell, his son, 1658–59; a	
DANISH LINE		year of anarchy followed)	
Canute (son of Sweyn, a Viking)	1017	**STUART LINE** (RESTORED)	
Harold I, *Harefoot* (son)	1036	Charles II (son of Charles I)	1660
Hardicanute (half-brother)	1039	James II (brother)	1685
SAXON LINE (RESTORED)		**HOUSE OF ORANGE**	
Edward *the Confessor*		William III (nephew) and Mary II	
(son of Ethelred II)	1041	(daughter of James II)	1688
Harold II (son of Earl Godwin)	1066	**STUART LINE**	
NORMAN LINE		Anne (daughter of James II)	1702
William I	1066	**HOUSE OF HANOVER**	
William II (son)	1087	George I (great-grandson of James I)	1714
Henry I (brother)	1100	George II (son)	1727
Stephen (nephew)	1135	**SOVEREIGNS OF THE UNITED KINGDOM**[2]	
PLANTAGENET LINE		George III (grandson)[3]	1760
Henry II (grandson of Henry I)	1154	George IV (son)	1820
Richard I (son)	1189	William IV (brother)	1830
John (brother)	1199	Victoria (niece of William IV)	1837
Henry III (son)	1216	**SAXE–COBURG LINE**	
Edward I (son)	1272	Edward VII (son)	1901
Edward II (son)	1307	**HOUSE OF WINDSOR**[4]	
Edward III (son)	1327	George V (son)	1910
Richard II (grandson)	1377	Edward VIII (son): abdicated	1936
HOUSE OF LANCASTER		George VI (brother)	1936
Henry IV (grandson of Edward III)	1399	Elizabeth II (daughter)	1952
Henry V (son)	1413		
Henry VI (son)	1422		
HOUSE OF YORK			
Edward IV (great-great-grandson			
of Edward III)	1461		
Edward V (son)	1483		
Richard III (uncle)	1483		

The British Sovereign has, from Norman times, been advised in the conduct of the government by a Committee of his *Privy Council,* known later as the *Cabinet.* See these words. [2]United, 1801. [3]Son of Frederick, Prince of Wales, who died 1751. [4]Created by Royal Proclamation July 17, 1917. Relationship is to previous sovereign, unless otherwise stated.

Eng·land·er (ing′glən-dər) n. A native of England.

Eng·lish (ing′glish) adj. 1 Of, pertaining to, or derived from England or its people. 2 Expressed in or belonging to the English language. — n. 1 The people of England collectively: with *the.* 2 The Low German, West Germanic language spoken by the people of the British Isles and most of the British Commonwealth, and of the United States, its territories, and possessions. — **Old English** or **Anglo–Saxon,** the English language from about A.D. 450 to A.D. 1150, consisting of the Kentish, West Saxon, Mercian, and Northumbrian dialects: represented by the epic poem *Beowulf* and the writings of Alfred the Great. The language in this period is synthetic in form and consists of an almost purely Germanic vocabulary. Abbr. *OE* — **Middle English,** the language of England after the Norman Conquest, from about 1150 to 1500: represented by the works of Chaucer. The characteristics of this period are the gradual loss of inflections accompanied by a stabilizing of word order, extensive borrowings from Latin, French, and the Low German languages, and the rise of the East Midland dialect as the standard. Abbr. *ME* — **Modern English,** the English language after 1500. 3 An English rendering or equivalent: "John" is the *English* of the French "Jean." 4 The English pronunciation, style, syntax, vocabulary, etc., of a particular re-

other games to the spin given to a ball. — **king's English** Spoken or written English considered as correct by official (or the king's) authority: also **queen's English.** — **plain English** A direct simple statement: This is the *plain English* of it. — v.t. 1 To translate into English. 2 To make English; Anglicize; as, a foreign word. 3 In billiards and other games, to apply English to (a ball). [OE *Englisc* <*Engle* the Angles]

English bulldog See under BULLDOG.

English Channel An arm of the Atlantic between England and France, connecting the North Sea with the Atlantic Ocean: French *La Manche.*

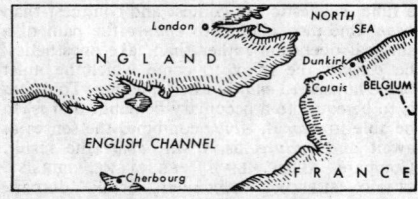

English coach dog A Dalmatian.

English daisy See under DAISY.

English horn A woodwind instrument, with a pitch a fifth lower than an oboe: also called *cor anglais.*

Eng·lish·ism (ing′glish·iz′əm) n. 1 An English

peculiarity or idiom; Briticism. **2** Devotion to what is English in speech, manners, customs, etc.

Eng·lish·man (ing′glish·mən) *n. pl.* **·men** (-mən) **1** A native or citizen of England. **2** An English ship. Also **Eng′lish·er.**

Eng·lish·man's tie *Naut.* A strong knot for heavy ropes.

English Revolution See under REVOLUTION.

Eng·lish·ry (ing′glish·rē) *n.* **1** People of English birth or descent collectively: applied especially to the English in Ireland. **2** The condition or fact of being an Englishman.

English setter See under SETTER.

English sonnet See under SONNET.

English sparrow See under SPARROW (def. 1).

English springer spaniel See under SPANIEL.

Eng·lish·wom·an (ing′glish·wo͝om′ən) *n. pl.* **·wom·en** (-wim′in) A woman of English birth; also, one who is English by naturalization, marriage, or domicile.

en·globe (en·glōb′) *v.t.* **·globed, ·glob·ing 1** To ensphere. **2** To take up or assimilate within a globular body: An ameba *englobes* nutriment.

en·glut (en·glut′) *v.t. Obs.* **1** To swallow up; gulp down. **2** To satiate; glut.

en·gorge (en·gôrj′) *v.t.* **·gorged, ·gorg·ing 1** To fill with blood, as an artery. **2** To devour or swallow greedily. [<F *engorger* <*en-* in + *gorge* throat]

en·gorge·ment (en·gôrj′mənt) *n.* **1** The act of feeding voraciously or swallowing greedily. **2** The condition of being engorged, as an organ with blood. **3** *Pathol.* Excessive fullness of an organ, passage, or tissue; congestion.

en·graft (en·graft′, -gräft′) *v.t.* **1** To graft (a cion) to another type of tree or plant for propagation. **2** To implant; set firmly. Also spelled *ingraft.* —**en·graft′ment** *n.*

en·grail (en·grāl′) *v.t.* To ornament the edge of with a series of concave notches; indent the edge of. [<OF *engresler* indent as by hailstones <*en-* in + *gresle* hail] —**en·grailed′** *adj.*

en·grain (in·grān′) *v.t.* **1** To ingrain. **2** To grain in imitation of wood.

en·gram (en′gram) *n. Psychol.* **1** A memory picture latent in consciousness. **2** The trace or impression assumed in a certain theory of mnemonics to be left in cells subjected to a constantly repeated stimulus. [<EN-[2] + -GRAM]

en·grave (in·grāv′) *v.t.* **·graved, ·grav·ing 1** To carve or etch figures, letters, etc., into (a surface). **2** To impress deeply. **3** To cut (pictures, lettering, etc.) into metal, stone, or wood, for printing. **4** To print from plates made by such a process. See synonyms under INSCRIBE. [<EN-[1] + GRAVE[3]; cf. F *engraver*]

en·grav·er (in·grā′vər) *n.* **1** A person who engraves. **2** One whose occupation is to make engravings.

en·grav·ing (in·grā′ving) *n.* **1** The act or art of cutting designs on a plate. **2** An engraved design on a plate. **3** A picture or design printed from an engraved plate; a print. See synonyms under PICTURE.

en·gross (in·grōs′) *v.t.* **1** To occupy completely; absorb. **2** To copy legibly; make a formal transcript of. **3** To monopolize, as the supply of a marketable product. See synonyms under ABSORB, EMPLOY. [<AF *engrosser* <LL *ingrossare* write large <*in-* in + *grossus* large] —**en·gross′ing** *adj.* —**en·gross′ing·ly** *adv.*

en·gross·ment (in·grōs′mənt) *n.* **1** The act of engrossing. **2** Something engrossed, as a deed or charter. **3** The state of being wholly occupied with something.

en·gulf (in·gulf′) *v.t.* **1** To swallow up in or as in a gulf. **2** To bury or overwhelm completely.

en·hance (in·hans′, -häns′) *v.t.* **·hanced, ·hanc·ing** To make higher or greater, as in reputation, cost, beauty, quality, etc. See synonyms under AGGRAVATE, HEIGHTEN, INCREASE. [<AF *enhaucer,* prob. var. of OF *enhaucer* <*en-* in, on + *haucer* lift, ult. <L *altus* high]

en·hance·ment (in·hans′mənt, -häns′-) *n.* Increase; advance.

en·har·mon·ic (en′här·mon′ik) *Music adj.* **1** Having intervals less than a half-step. **2** Pertaining to that perfectly true intonation which is violated on keyed instruments to avoid complexity: C-sharp and D-flat are not the same in the *enharmonic* scale, though they are on the pianoforte. **3** Relating to that Greek scale whose intervals were quartertones and major thirds: distinguished from the *diatonic* and *chromatic* tetrachords. —*n.* **1** An enharmonic chord or note. **2** *pl.* Music distinguished by enharmonic intervals. [<L *enharmonicus* <Gk. *enharmonikos* <*en-* in + *harmonia* HARMONY] —**en′har·mon′i·cal** *adj.* —**en′har·mon′i·cal·ly** *adv.*

e·ni·ac (ē′nē·ak) *n.* An electronically operated calculating machine designed to solve complicated mathematical problems at high speed: a trade name. [<E(LECTRONIC) N(UMERICAL) I(NTEGRATOR) A(ND) C(OMPUTER)]

E·nid (ē′nid) A feminine personal name. [<Celtic, soul]

—**Enid** In Arthurian legend and Tennyson's *Idylls of the King,* a lady of Arthur's court, the wife of Geraint.

e·nig·ma (i·nig′mə) *n.* **1** An obscure or ambiguous saying; a riddle. **2** Anything that puzzles or baffles. See synonyms under RIDDLE. [<L *aenigma* <Gk. *ainigma* <*ainissesthai* speak in riddles <*ainos* tale]

en·ig·mat·ic (en′ig·mat′ik) *adj.* Of or like an enigma; ambiguous; puzzling. Also **en′ig·mat′i·cal.** See synonyms under EQUIVOCAL, MYSTERIOUS. —**en′ig·mat′i·cal·ly** *adv.*

e·nig·ma·tist (i·nig′mə·tist) *n.* A maker or propounder of riddles.

e·nig·ma·tize (i·nig′mə·tīz) *v.i.* **·tized, ·tiz·ing** To make or propound riddles; speak enigmatically.

E·ni·sei (yen·i·sā′) See YENISEI.

en·isle (en·īl′) *v.t.* **·isled, ·isl·ing** *Poetic* **1** To place on an island; isolate. **2** To make an island of.

E·ni·we·tok (en′i·wē′tok, i·nē′wi·tôk) An atoll in the Marshall Islands; U.S. proving grounds (1948) for atomic weapons.

en·jambe·ment (in·jam′mənt, -jamb′-; *Fr.* äṅ·zhäṅb·mäṅ′) *n.* In prosody, the running over of a sentence or thought from one couplet or line to the next, without a pause at the end of the line or verse division. Also **en·jamb′ment.** [<F *enjamber* encroach <*en-* in + *jambe* leg]

en·join (in·join′) *v.t.* **1** To order authoritatively and emphatically; direct (a person or group) to a course of action, conduct, etc. **2** To impose (a condition, course of action, etc.) on a person or group. **3** To forbid or prohibit, especially by judicial order or injunction. See synonyms under DICTATE. [<OF *enjoindre* <L *injungere* <*in-* on + *jungere* join] —**en·join′er** *n.*

en·joy (in·joi′) *v.t.* **1** To experience joy or pleasure in; receive pleasure from the possession or use of. **2** To have the use or benefit of. —**to enjoy oneself** To be happy; receive pleasure from an experience, party, etc. See synonyms under ADMIRE, REJOICE. [<OF *enjoir* <*en-* in (<L *in-*) + *joir* <L *gaudere* rejoice] —**en·joy′a·ble** *adj.* —**en·joy′a·ble·ness** *n.* —**en·joy′a·bly** *adv.* —**en·joy′er** *n.*

en·joy·ment (in·joi′mənt) *n.* **1** The act or state of enjoying; pleasure. **2** Something that gives joy or satisfaction. See synonyms under COMFORT, ENTERTAINMENT, HAPPINESS, SATISFACTION.

en·keph·a·lin (en·kef′ə·lin) *n.* A neurohormone elaborated by the pituitary and acting as an endogenous opiate.

en·keph·a·lin·er·gic (en·kef′ə·li·nûr′jik) *adj.* Effecting the release or activation of enkephalin.

en·kin·dle (en·kin′dəl) *v.t.* **·dled, ·dling 1** To set on fire; kindle. **2** To stir to action; excite; inflame. —**en·kin′dler** *n.*

en·lace (in·lās′) *v.t.* **·laced, ·lac·ing 1** To bind or wrap with or as with laces. **2** To intertwine; entangle. Also spelled *inlace.* [<F *enlacer* <*en-* in + *lacer* <OF *las* LACE] —**en·lace′ment** *n.*

en·large (in·lärj′) *v.* **·larged, ·larg·ing** *v.t.* **1** To make greater or larger; increase the amount or extent of; expand. **2** *Phot.* To increase the size of (a photograph) by projection printing. —*v.i.* **3** To become greater or larger; increase; widen. **4** To express oneself in greater detail or at greater length; expatiate: with *on* or *upon.* See synonyms under ADD, AMPLIFY, INCREASE. [<OF *enlarger* <*en-* in + *large* large] —**en·larg′er** *n.*

en·large·ment (in·lärj′mənt) *n.* **1** The act of making or growing larger; also, the state of being enlarged; an addition or extension. **2** Increase of range or capacity; expansion; dilatation: *enlargement* of the mind. **3** A photograph made larger than its original negative. **4** *Obs.* A setting at liberty. **5** Fullness of statement. See synonyms under ACCESSION, INCREASE.

en·light·en (in·līt′n) *v.t.* **1** To impart intellectual or spiritual knowledge to; cause to know or understand; teach. **2** *Obs.* To light up. See synonyms under TEACH. —**en·light′en·er** *n.*

en·light·ened (in·līt′nd) *adj.* **1** Having or exhibiting enlightenment. **2** Having reached the highest stage of civilization.

en·light·en·ment (in·līt′n·mənt) *n.* **1** The act or result of enlightening, or the state of being enlightened. **2** Great moral and intellectual advancement. See synonyms under WISDOM.

En·light·en·ment (in·līt′n·mənt) *n.* A philosophical movement of the 18th century, characterized by rationalistic methods and skepticism of established dogmas.

en·link (en·lingk′) *v.t.* To unite by or as by links; connect closely. —**en·link′ment** *n.*

en·list (in·list′) *v.t.* **1** To engage for service, as in the army or navy. **2** To gain the help or interest of (a person or his services). —*v.i.* **3** To enter military or naval services voluntarily. **4** To join in some venture, cause, etc. See synonyms under ENROL, RECRUIT.

en·list·ed man (in·lis′tid) Any member of the armed forces who is not a commissioned officer or warrant officer; a private, seaman, or a noncommissioned officer.

en·list·ment (in·list′mənt) *n.* **1** The act of enlisting or the state of being enlisted; voluntary enrolment. **2** The document binding one enlisted. **3** The term for which one enlists.

en·li·ven (in·lī′vən) *v.t.* **1** To make lively, cheerful, or sprightly. **2** To make active or vigorous; stimulate. See synonyms under ENTERTAIN. —**en·li′ven·er** *n.*

en masse (en mas′, *Fr.* äṅ mȧs′) In a mass or body; all together. [<F]

en·mesh (en·mesh′) *v.t.* To ensnare or entangle in or as in a net: also spelled *inmesh.*

en·mi·ty (en′mə·tē) *n. pl.* **·ties 1** The spirit of an enemy; hostility. **2** The state of being an enemy; a hostile condition. [<OF *enemistié,* ult. <L *inimicus* hostile <*in-* not + *amicus* a friend]

Synonyms: acrimony, animosity, antagonism, bitterness, hatred, hostility, malevolence, malice, malignity, rancor, spite. *Enmity* is the state of being an enemy or the feeling and disposition characterizing an enemy (compare ENEMY). *Animosity* denotes a feeling more active and vehement, but often less enduring and determined, than *enmity. Hostility* is *enmity* in action; the term *hostilities* between nations denotes actual armed collision. *Bitterness* is a resentful feeling arising from a belief that one has been wronged; *acrimony* is a kindred feeling, but deeper and more persistent, and may arise from the crossing of one's wishes or plans by another, where no injustice or wrong is felt. *Antagonism* does not necessarily imply *enmity,* but ordinarily suggests a shade, at least, of hostile feeling. *Malice* is a disposition or intent to injure others, for the gratification of some evil passion; *malignity* is intense and violent *enmity, hatred,* or *malice.* Compare synonyms for ACRIMONY, ANGER, FEUD, HATRED. *Antonyms:* agreement, alliance, amity, concord, friendship, harmony, kindliness, kindness, regard, sympathy.

ennea- *combining form* Nine: *enneagon.* [<Gk. *ennea* nine]

en·ne·ad (en′ē·ad) *n.* The number nine; any system or group containing nine objects. [<Gk. *enneas, enneados*]

en·ne·a·gon (en′ē·ə·gon) *n. Geom.* A figure, especially a plane figure, with nine sides and nine angles.

en·ne·a·he·dron (en′ē·ə·hē′drən) *n. pl.* **·drons** or **·dra** (-drə) *Geom.* A solid bounded by nine surfaces. —**en′ne·a·he′dral** *adj.*

en·ne·an·drous (en′ē·an′drəs) *adj. Bot.* Having nine stamens.

en·ne·a·style (en′ē·ə·stīl′) *adj. Archit.* Having nine columns. [<ENNEA- + Gk. *stylos* a pillar]

En·nis·kil·len (en′is·kil′ən) County town of Fermanagh, Ireland.

En·ni·us (en'ē·əs), **Quintus**, 239–169 B.C., Roman epic poet.

en·no·ble (i·nō'bəl, en-) v.t. **·bled, ·bling** 1 To make honorable or noble in nature, quality, etc. 2 To confer a title of nobility upon. [<F *ennoblir* < *en-* in (<L *in-*) + *noble* NOBLE] — **en·no'bler** n.

en·no·ble·ment (i·nō'bəl·mənt, en-) n. 1 The act of ennobling; also, elevation to the rank of a noble. 2 Anything that ennobles or exalts.

Enns (enz, *Ger.* ens) A river in central Austria, flowing 160 miles NE to the Danube.

en·nui (än'wē, än·nwē') n. A feeling of listless weariness resulting from satiety, boredom, inactivity, etc. — v.t. **en·nuied, en·nuy·ing** To oppress with tedium and lack of interest; bore. [<F <OF *enui* <L *in odio*. See ANNOY.]

en·nuy·é (än·nwē·ā') *French adj.* Oppressed with ennui; mentally satiated, wearied, or bored. — n. A person afflicted with ennui. — **en·nuy·ée'** adj. & n. fem.

E·noch (ē'nək, *Fr.* e·nôk') A masculine personal name. Also *Lat.* **E·no·chus** (i·nō'kəs). Also *Henoch.* [<Hebrew, dedicated]
— **Enoch** The eldest son of Cain. *Gen.* iv 17.
— **Enoch** The father of Methuselah. *Gen.* v 21.

e·nol (ē'nōl, -nol) n. *Chem.* An organic compound in which a hydroxyl group is joined with a doubly linked carbon atom. [Prob. <Gk. *en*, neut. of *heis* one + -OL[1]]

e·nol·o·gy (i·nol'ə·jē) n. The science or study of wines. Also *oenology, oinology.* [<Gk. *oinos* wine + -LOGY] — **e·no·log·i·cal** (ē'nə·loj'i·kəl) adj.

e·norm (i·nôrm') adj. *Obs.* Enormous; huge. [<F <L *enormis* < *ex-* out + *norma* a pattern]

e·nor·mi·ty (i·nôr'mə·tē) n. pl. **·ties** 1 The state of being outrageous or extremely wicked. 2 A great or flagrant instance of wickedness or depravity; an outrageous offense; atrocity.

e·nor·mous (i·nôr'məs) adj. 1 Excessive or extraordinary in size, amount, or degree. 2 Wicked above measure; atrocious. See synonyms under FLAGRANT, IMMENSE, LARGE. — **e·nor'mous·ly** adv. — **e·nor'mous·ness** n.

E·nos (ē'nəs) A masculine personal name. [< Hebrew, man]
— **Enos** A son of Seth. *Gen.* iv 26.

e·no·sis (e·nō'sis) n. Union, especially as proposed between Cyprus and Greece. [<Gk. *enôsis* union]

e·nough (i·nuf') adj. Adequate for any demand or need; sufficient. — n. An ample supply; a sufficiency. — adv. So as to be sufficient; sufficiently. — *interj.* It is enough; stop. [OE *genoh, genog*]
Synonyms (adj.): ample, sufficient. *Enough* is relative, denoting a supply equal to a given demand. A temperature of 70° Fahrenheit is *enough* for a living-room; of 212° *enough* to boil water; neither is *enough* to melt iron. *Sufficient* is an equivalent of the Saxon *enough*, with no perceptible difference of meaning, but only of usage, *enough* being the more blunt, homely, and forcible word, while *sufficient* is in many cases the more elegant or polite. *Sufficient* usually precedes its noun; *enough* preferably follows. See AMPLE.

e·nounce (i·nouns') v.t. **e·nounced, e·nounc·ing** 1 To make a formal statement of; announce. 2 To give verbal expression to; utter; enunciate. [<F *énoncer* <L *enuntiare*. See ENUNCIATE.] — **e·nounce'ment** n.

e·now[1] (i·nou') adj., n., & adv. *Archaic* Enough. [Var. of ENOUGH]

e·now[2] (ē·nō') adv. *Brit. Dial.* Presently; by and by. [? Short for *even now*]

en pas·sant (än pä·sän') 1 By the way; in passing. 2 In chess, applied to the taking of a pawn that, in its first move, passes over a square commanded by a hostile pawn. [<F]

en·phy·tot·ic (en'fī·tot'ik) adj. *Bot.* Of regular occurrence in a locality: said of certain fungus diseases of plants. [<Gk. *en-* in + *phyton* plant]

en·plane (en·plān') v.i. **·planed, ·plan·ing** To board an airplane.

en·quire (in·kwīr'), **en·quir·y** (in·kwīr'ē), etc. See INQUIRE, etc.

en·rage (in·rāj') v.t. **·raged, ·rag·ing** To throw into a rage; infuriate. See synonyms under INCENSE. [<OF *enrager* < *en-* in + *rage* RAGE]

en rap·port (än ră·pôr') *French* In sympathetic relation; in accord.

en·rapt (in·rapt') adj. Overpowered by emotion.

en·rap·ture (in·rap'chər) v.t. **·tured, ·tur·ing** To bring into a state of rapture; delight extrava-

gantly. See synonyms under CHARM[1], RAVISH, REJOICE.

en·rav·ish (en·rav'ish) v.t. To enrapture.

en·reg·is·ter (en·rej'is·tər) v.t. To put on record; enrol; register. [<F *enregistrer*]

en re·gle (än re'gl') *French* According to rule; in due order.

en re·vanche (än rə·vänsh') *French* In return; by way of compensation; in revenge.

en·rich (in·rich') v.t. 1 To make rich; increase the wealth of. 2 To make fertile, as soil. 3 To increase or enhance the level, quality, etc., of: to *enrich* a poem with images. 4 To increase the food value of, as bread. 5 To increase the beauty of; adorn. [<OF *enricher* < *en-* in + *riche* rich] — **en·rich'er** n.

en·rich·ment (in·rich'mənt) n. 1 The act or process of making rich or richer. 2 That which enriches. 3 A decoration; ornament.

En·ri·ghet·ta (än'rē·get'tä) Italian form of HENRIETTA. Also *Sp.* **En·ri·que·ta** (än'rē·kā'tä).

en·ring (en·ring') v.t. 1 To enclose with or as with a ring; encircle. 2 To adorn with rings; put a ring on.

en·robe (en·rōb') v.t. **·robed, ·rob·ing** To put a robe on; attire.

en·rob·er (en·rō'bər) n. An automatic machine for applying icing to cakes, cookies, etc.

en·rol (in·rōl') v. **·rolled, ·rol·ling** v.t. 1 To write or record (a name) in a roll; register; list. 2 To enlist. 3 To place on record; record, as a document or decree. 4 To roll up; wrap. — v.i. 5 To place one's name on a list; register oneself. Also **en·roll'**. [<OF *enroller* < *en-* in + *rolle* ROLL]
Synonyms: enlist, enter, incorporate, initiate, list, register. Compare RECORD *(noun)*. *Antonyms:* disband, dismiss, expel, refuse, reject.

en·rol·ment (en·rōl'mənt) n. 1 The act of enrolling. 2 An enrolled entry; a record. Also **en·roll'ment**.

en·root (en·rōōt', -rŏŏt') v.t. To cause to take root; implant deeply: used chiefly in the past participle.

en route (än rōōt', *Fr.* än rōōt') On the road; on the way.

ens (enz) n. pl. **en·ti·a** (en'shē·ə) In scholastic philosophy, the abstract conception of being, or being as absolute, without regard to any question of actual existence. [<LL, orig. ppr. formed from *esse* be]

en·sam·ple (en·sam'pəl, -säm'-) *Archaic v. & n.* Example.

en·san·guine (en·sang'gwin) v.t. **·guined, ·guin·ing** To cover or stain with or as with blood.

En·sche·de (en'skhe·dā') A town in eastern Netherlands.

en·sconce (en·skons') v.t. **·sconced, ·sconc·ing** 1 To fix securely or comfortably in some place; settle snugly. 2 To shelter; hide.

en·seal (en·sēl') v.t. *Obs.* To seal up; put a seal upon. [<OF *enseeler* < *en-* in + *seel* SEAL]

en·sem·ble (än·säm'bəl, *Fr.* än·sän'bl') n. 1 The parts of a thing viewed as a whole; general effect. 2 A combination of clothing and accessories that match or harmonize in color. 3 *Music* The union of soloists and chorus in a concerted number. 4 The scene in a play, usually the last, that includes the entire cast. [<F <L *insimul* < *in-* in + *simul* at the same time]

en·sep·ul·cher (en·sep'əl·kər) v.t. **·chered, ·cher·ing** To put into or as into a sepulchre; entomb. Also **en·sep'ul·chre.**

en·shrine (in·shrīn') v.t. **·shrined, ·shrin·ing** 1 To place in or as in a shrine. 2 To cherish devoutly; hold sacred. — **en·shrine'ment** n.

en·shroud (en·shroud') v.t. To cover as with a shroud; conceal.

en·si·form (en'sə·fôrm) adj. *Bot.* Sword-shaped, as certain leaves. [<L *ensis* sword + -FORM]

en·sign (en'sīn) n. 1 A distinguished flag or banner; especially, a national standard or naval flag. 2 (en'sən) In the U.S. Navy or Coast Guard, a commissioned officer of the lowest grade, ranking with a second lieutenant in the U.S. Army, Air Force, or Marine Corps. 3 In the British Army, until 1871, a commissioned officer who carried the flag of a regiment or company. 4 A badge or symbol, as of office. 5 *Obs.* A signal. [<F *enseigne* <L *insignia* < *in-* in + *signum* mark]

en·sign·cy (en'sən·sē) n. pl. **·cies** The function, rank, or commission of an ensign. Also **en'sign·ship.**

en·si·lage (en'sə·lij) n. 1 The process of preserving succulent fodder in closed pits or silos. 2 The fodder thus preserved: also called *silage.* — v.t. **·laged, ·lag·ing** To store in a silo for preservation: also **en·sile** (en·sīl'). [<F <ensiler < *en-* in + *silo* SILO]

en·sky (en·skī') v.t. **·skied, ·sky·ing** To fix or place in the sky or in heaven: used in the passive.

en·slave (in·slāv') v.t. **·slaved, ·slav·ing** To make a slave of; dominate. — **en·slave'ment** n. — **en·slav'er** n.

en·snare (en·snâr') v.t. **·snared, ·snar·ing** To catch in a snare; trick. Also spelled *insnare.* See synonyms under CATCH, DECEIVE.

en·sor·cel (en·sôr'səl) v.t. *Obs.* To bewitch. Also **en·sor'cell.** [<OF *ensorceler*]

en·soul (en·sōl') v.t. 1 To endow with a soul. 2 To receive or put into the soul. Also spelled *insoul.*

en·sphere (en·sfir') v.t. **·sphered, ·spher·ing** 1 To enclose in a sphere. 2 To give the form of a sphere to.

en·sta·tite (en'stə·tīt) n. *Mineral.* A variety of orthorhombic pyroxene low in iron oxide: a constituent of many basic igneous rocks. [<Gk. *enstatēs* adversary + -ITE[1]; so called from its refractory nature]

en·steep (en·stēp') v.t. *Obs.* To steep; plunge under water.

en·sue (en·sōō') v.i. **·sued, ·su·ing** 1 To follow; occur afterward or subsequently. 2 To follow as a consequence; result. [<OF *ensu-*, stem of *ensuivre* <L *insequor* < *in-* on, in + *sequi* follow]

en suite (än swēt') *French* In a series, set, or succession.

en·sure (in·shoor') See INSURE.

en·swathe (en·swāth') v.t. **·swathed, ·swath·ing** To enwrap, as in swaddling clothes; swathe: also spelled *inswathe.* — **en·swathe'ment** n.

-ent suffix of nouns and adjectives 1 Having the quality, or performing the action of (the main element): *potent.* 2 One who or that which performs the action of (the main element): *superintendent.* Compare –ANT. [<F *-ent* <L *-ens, -entis,* suffix of present participle]

ent- See ENTO-.

en·tab·la·ture (en·tab'lə·chər) n. *Archit.* 1 The uppermost member of a classical order or columnar system, consisting of the architrave, frieze, and cornice. 2 A projecting frieze or cornice of several members, as on the front of an edifice. 3 A platform. [< MF <Ital. *intavolatura* < *in-* in + *tavola* base, table <L *tabula*]

ENTABLATURE
A. Cornice. B. Frieze. C. Architrave. D. Capital on shaft. a, b, c. Fasciae.

en·ta·ble·ment (en·tā'bəl·mənt) n. *Archit.* 1 An entablature. 2 The series of platforms supporting a statue above the dado and base. [<F < *en-* in, on + *table* TABLE]

en·tail (in·tāl') v.t. 1 To impose or result in (labor, concentration, etc.) as a necessary consequence. 2 *Law* To restrict the inheritance of (real property) to an unalterable succession of heirs. 3 To leave (anything) to an unalterable succession of heirs. — n. 1 Anything transmitted as an inalienable inheritance. 2 An estate in fee limited to a particular class of heirs, as eldest sons. 3 The act or custom of thus limiting inheritance. [<EN-[1] + TAIL[2]] — **en·tail'ment** n.

en·tame (en·tām') v.t. *Obs.* To tame.

en·ta·moe·ba (en'tə·mē'bə) See ENDAMEBA.

en·tan·gle (in·tang'gəl) v.t. **·gled, ·gling** 1 To catch in or as in a snare; hamper. 2 To make tangled; snarl; interlace; complicate. 3 To involve in difficulties; perplex; embarrass. See synonyms under INVOLVE, PERPLEX. — **en·tan'gled** adj. — **en·tan'gler** n.

en·tan·gle·ment (in·tang'gəl·mənt) n. 1 Something that entangles; a snare; complication. 2 The act of entangling, or the state of being entangled.

en·ta·sis (en′tə·sis) *n.* **1** *Archit.* A slight convex curve in the vertical outlines of the shaft of a pilaster or of a column. **2** *Physiol.* Spasmodic contraction of a muscle; a tonic spasm: also **en·ta·si·a** (en·tā′zhē·ə). [<NL <Gk. *entasis* a stretching < *enteinein* < *en-* in + *teinein* stretch] — **en·tas·tic** (en·tas′tik) *adj.*

En·teb·be (en·teb′ē) A city in central Uganda, on Lake Victoria.

en·tel·e·chy (en·tel′ə·kē) *n. pl.* **·chies** *Philos.* **1** In Aristotle's metaphysics, completed realization, as distinguished from potentiality. **2** In the philosophy of Driesch, Bergson, etc., the non-physicochemical principle, or vital force, assumed to be responsible for life and growth. [<L *entelechia* <Gk. *entelecheia* actuality < *en telei echein* be complete]

en·tel·lus (en·tel′əs) *n.* The hanuman or East Indian bearded monkey (genus *Presbytis*). [<NL, appar. after a character in the *Aeneid*]

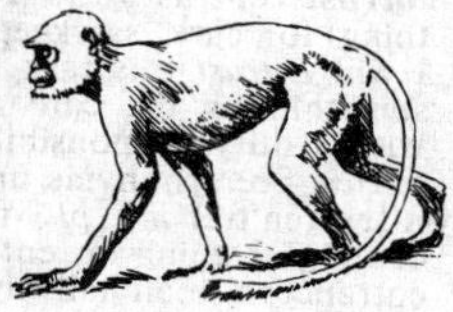

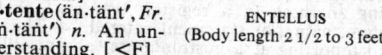

ENTELLUS
(Body length 2 1/2 to 3 feet)

en·tente (än·tänt′, *Fr.* äṅ·täṅt′) *n.* An understanding. [<F]

entente cor·diale (kôr·dyȧl′) Cordial understanding; in politics, friendliness between governments; especially, **Entente Cordiale,** the alliance between France and England, formed in 1904; enlarged to include Russia in 1907, and then called the **Triple Entente.** [<F]

en·ter (en′tər) *v.t.* **1** To come or go into. **2** To make a way into; penetrate; pierce. **3** To set or insert in: to *enter* a wedge. **4** To become a member of; join. **5** To begin; pass within the limits of; start: to *enter* middle age. **6** To obtain admission; enrol, as in a school or competition. **7** To write or record, as in a list, book, etc. **8** To report (goods, a vessel, etc.) to the customhouse. **9** *Law* **a** To place on the records of a court, as evidence, a plea, or an appearance. **b** To go upon or into feloniously or as a trespasser. **c** To file for title to (public lands). — *v.i.* **10** To come or go inward; make an entrance. **11** To come onto the stage: *Enter* the queen, weeping. — **to enter into 1** To begin; start. **2** To become a party to; engage in: to *enter into* a discussion. **3** To take an interest in; join in: to *enter into* the plans for a party. **4** To form a part of; be a constituent of: Oxygen *enters into* many compound bodies. **5** To consider or discuss: to *enter into* the particulars. — **to enter on** (or **upon**) To begin; set out on: to *enter upon* a career of dissipation. [<F *entrer* <L *intrare* < *intra* within]

en·ter·al·gi·a (en′tə·ral′jē·ə) *n. Pathol.* Intestinal neuralgia.

en·ter·ec·to·my (en′tə·rek′tə·mē) *n. Surg.* Excision of a portion of an intestine.

en·ter·ic (en·ter′ik) *adj.* **1** Of or pertaining to the intestine. **2** Having an intestine. [<Gk. *enterikos* < *enteron* intestine < *entos* within]

enteric fever Typhoid fever.

entering edge *Aeron.* The forward or leading edge of an airplane wing.

en·ter·i·tis (en′tə·rī′tis) *n. Pathol.* Inflammation of the intestines, particularly of the small intestine.

entero– *combining form* Intestine. Also, before vowels, **enter–.** [<Gk. *enteron* intestine]

en·ter·o·cep·tor (en′tə·rō·sep′tər) See INTEROCEPTOR.

en·ter·o·gas·trone (en′tə·rō·gas′trōn) *n. Biochem.* A hormone obtained from the mucous lining of the upper intestine and having the power to inhibit the action of the gastric juices. [<ENTERO- + GASTR(O)- + (HORM)ONE]

en·ter·o·ci·ne·sia (en′tə·rō·si·nē′zhə) *n. Physiol.* Peristalsis. [<ENTERO- + Gk. *kinēsis* movement] — **en′ter·o·ci·net′ic** (-si·net′ik) *adj.*

en·ter·o·ki·nase (en′tə·rō·kī′nās, -kin′ās) *n. Biochem.* An intestinal enzyme which converts trypsinogen into trypsin.

en·ter·o·lith (en′tə·rō·lith′) *n. Pathol.* An intestinal concretion; a bezoar.

en·ter·ol·o·gy (en′tə·rol′ə·jē) *n.* The study of the intestines.

en·ter·on (en′tə·ron) *n. pl.* **·ter·a** (-tər·ə) *Anat.* The entire intestine or alimentary canal; the gut. [<NL <Gk.]

en·ter·op·to·sis (en′tə·rop·tō′sis) *n. Pathol.* Prolapse of the intestines. [<NL <Gk. *enteron* intestine + *ptosis* < *piptein* fall] — **en′ter·op′·tic** *adj.*

en·ter·o·scope (en′tər·ə·skōp′) *n. Med.* An instrument equipped with an electric light for examining the intestines. — **en·ter·os·co·py** (en′tə·ros′kə·pē) *n.*

en·ter·o·sta·sis (en′tə·rō·stā′sis) *n. Pathol.* A stoppage of food in the intestinal passages; intestinal stasis.

en·ter·o·stax·is (en′tə·rō·stak′sis) *n. Pathol.* Gradual hemorrhage through the mucous membrane of the intestine. [<ENTERO- + Gk. *staxis* < *stazein* drip]

en·ter·os·to·my (en′tə·ros′tə·mē) *n. Surg.* The formation of a permanent artificial opening through the abdominal wall into the intestine.

en·ter·ot·o·my (en′tə·rot′ə·mē) *n. Surg.* Any cutting operation upon the intestines.

en·ter·o·tox·e·mi·a (en′tə·rō·tok·sē′mē·ə) *n.* Severe intestinal poisoning of sheep caused by the toxins of certain bacteria, especially *Clostridium perfringens.*

en·ter·prise (en′tər·prīz) *n.* **1** Any projected task or work; an undertaking. **2** Boldness, energy, and invention in practical affairs. [<F *enterprise* < *entreprendre* < *entre-* between (<L *inter-*) + *prendre* take <L *prehendere*]

en·ter·pris·ing (en′tər·prī′zing) *adj.* Energetic and progressive. — **en′ter·pris′ing·ly** *adv.*

en·ter·tain (en′tər·tān′) *v.t.* **1** To hold the attention of; amuse; divert. **2** To extend hospitality to; receive as a guest. **3** To take into consideration, as a proposal. **4** To keep or bear in mind; maintain: to *entertain* a grudge. **5** *Obs.* To keep up; maintain. — *v.i.* **6** To receive and care for guests: to *entertain* lavishly. [<F *entretenir* < *entre-* between (<L *inter-*) + *tenir* < *tenere* hold] — **en′ter·tain′·a·ble** *adj.* — **en′ter·tain′er** *n.*

Synonyms: amuse, beguile, cheer, delight, disport, divert, enliven, gratify, interest, occupy, please, recreate. To *entertain,* in the sense here considered, is to engage and pleasantly occupy the attention; to *amuse* is to occupy the attention in an especially bright and cheerful way, often with that which excites merriment or laughter; as, He *entertained* us with an *amusing* story. To *divert* is to turn from serious thoughts or laborious pursuits to something that lightly and agreeably occupies the mind; one may be *entertained* or *amused* who has nothing serious or laborious from which to be *diverted.* To *recreate,* literally to re-create, is to engage mind or body in some pleasing activity that restores strength and energy for serious work. To *beguile* is, as it were, to cheat into cheer and comfort by something that insensibly draws thought or feeling away from pain or disquiet. We *beguile* a weary hour, *cheer* the despondent, *divert* the preoccupied, *enliven* a dull evening or company, *gratify* our friends' wishes, *entertain, interest, please* a listening audience, *occupy* idle time, *disport* ourselves when merry, *recreate* when worn with toil; we *amuse* ourselves or others with whatever pleasantly passes the time without special exertion, each according to his taste. See ACCOMMODATE, CHERISH, INTEREST. *Antonyms*: annoy, bore, busy, disquiet, distract, disturb, tire, weary.

en·ter·tain·ing (en′tər·tā′ning) *adj.* Of a character to entertain; amusing; diverting. — **en′·ter·tain′ing·ly** *adv.* — **en′ter·tain′ing·ness** *n.*

en·ter·tain·ment (en′tər·tān′mənt) *n.* **1** The act of receiving and caring for guests; hospitable accommodation in the inn or dwelling of a host; the furnishing of food, lodging, and service to a guest. **2** A source or means of amusement; a diverting performance, especially a public performance, as a concert, drama, or the like. **3** Pleasure afforded by an amusing act or spectacle; amusement. **4** A social party; also, the refreshments provided for guests. **5** *Obs.* Maintenance; employment; service.

Synonyms: amusement, cheer, delight, diversion, enjoyment, frolic, fun, merriment, pastime, pleasure, recreation, sport. *Entertainment* and *recreation* imply thought and mental occupation, but in an agreeable, refreshing way; they are therefore words of a high order. *Entertainment* is used of somewhat mirthful, mental delight; *recreation* may, and usually does, combine the mental with the physical. *Amusement* and *pastime* are nearly equivalent, the latter probably the lighter word; many slight things may be *pastimes* which we should hardly dignify by the name of *amusements. Sports* are almost wholly on the physical plane, while involving a certain grade of mental action. *Cheer* may be very quiet, as the *cheer* of a bright fire to an aged traveler; *merriment* suggests liveliness and laughter; *fun* and *frolic* are apt to be boisterous. Compare ENTERTAIN, FROLIC, SPORT. *Antonyms*: ennui, fatigue, labor, lassitude, toil, weariness, work.

en·thal·py (en·thal′pē, en′thəl·pē) *n. Physics* The quantity of heat in a substance or physical system per unit of mass; heat content. [<Gk. *enthalpein* < *en-* in + *thalpein* warm]

en·thet·ic (en·thet′ik) *adj.* **1** Introduced from without. **2** *Med.* Communicated by inoculation: said of infectious diseases. [<Gk. *enthetikos* fit for implanting < *en-* in + *tithenai* put]

en·thral (in·thrôl′) *v.t.* **·thralled, ·thral·ling 1** To keep spellbound; fascinate; charm. **2** To put or keep in thraldom; enslave. Also spelled *inthral.* Also **en·thrall′.** — **en·thral′·ment, en·thrall′ment** *n.*

en·throne (in·thrōn′) *v.t.* **·throned, thron·ing 1** To put upon a throne. **2** To invest with sovereign or ecclesiastical power. **3** To exalt; revere. Also spelled *inthrone.* — **en·throne′·ment** *n.*

en·thuse (in·thōōz′) *v.t.* & *v.i.* **·thused, ·thus·ing** *U.S. Colloq.* To make enthusiastic; yield to or display enthusiasm. [Back formation from ENTHUSIASM]

en·thu·si·asm (in·thōō′zē·az′əm) *n.* **1** Earnest and fervent feeling; ardent zeal for a person or cause. **2** *Archaic* Exalted or ecstatic feeling; also, irrational religious ecstasy; divine fury or frenzy; possession. **3** An object of great interest to a person. [<LL *enthusiasmus* <Gk. *enthusiasmos,* ult. < *entheos, enthous* inspired < *en-* in + *theos* god]

Synonyms: ardor, devotion, eagerness, earnestness, ecstasy, excitement, extravagance, fanaticism, fervency, fervor, frenzy, inspiration, intensity, passion, rapture, transport, vehemence, warmth, zeal. The old meaning of *enthusiasm* implies a pseudo-*inspiration,* an almost frantic *extravagance* in behalf of something supposed to be an expression of the divine will. This sense remains as the controlling one in the kindred noun *enthusiast. Enthusiasm* has now chiefly the meaning of an earnest and commendable *devotion,* an intense and eager interest. *Zeal* is burning *earnestness,* always tending to vigorous action with all the *devotion* of *enthusiasm,* but often without its hopefulness. Compare WARMTH. *Antonyms*: calculation, calmness, caution, coldness, deadness, dulness, indifference, lukewarmness, policy, prudence, timidity, wariness.

en·thu·si·ast (in·thōō′zē·ast) *n.* One prone to or moved by enthusiasm; an ardent adherent; zealot.

en·thu·si·as·tic (in·thōō′zē·as′tik) *adj.* Given to enthusiasm; ardent; zealous. Also **en·thu′·si·as′ti·cal.** See synonyms under EAGER, SANGUINE. — **en·thu′si·as′ti·cal·ly** *adv.*

en·thy·meme (en′thə·mēm) *n. Logic* An argument in which one of the premises of the syllogism is not stated. [<L *enthymema* <Gk. *enthymēma* < *enthymeesthai* think < *en-* in + *thymos* mind]

en·tice (in·tīs′) *v.t.* **·ticed, ·tic·ing** To lead on or attract by arousing hope of pleasure, profit, etc.; allure. See synonyms under ALLURE, CHARM[1], DRAW, PERSUADE. [<OF *enticier* arouse <L *in-* in + *titio* a firebrand] — **en·tic′er** *n.* — **en·tic′ing** *adj.* — **en·tic′ing·ly** *adv.*

en·tice·ment (in·tīs′mənt) *n.* **1** The act of enticing. **2** State of being enticed. **3** That which entices; allurement.

en·tire (in·tīr′) *adj.* **1** Complete in all its parts; undivided; whole. **2** Free from admixture; unalloyed; pure. **3** *Bot.* Having the margin of a leaf not serrated, as a tiger lily. **4** Consisting of only one piece. **5** Uncastrated: an *entire* horse. See synonyms under PERFECT, RADICAL. —*n.* The whole; the entirety. [<OF *entier* <L *integer.* See INTEGER.] — **en·tire′ly** *adv.* — **en·tire′ness** *n.*

en·tire·ty (in·tīr′tē) *n. pl.* **·ties** **1** The state or condition of being entire; completeness. **2** That which is entire; a whole. See synonyms under AGGREGATE.

en·ti·tle (in·tīt′l) *v.t.* **·tled, ·tling** **1** To give a right to demand or expect; authorize or qualify: His position *entitles* him to do it. **2** To give a name or designation to. **3** To give (a person) a title designating rank, honor, etc. Also spelled *intitle.* [<AF *entitler,* OF *entituler* <LL *intitulare* < *in-* in + *titulus* a title]

en·ti·ty (en′tə·tē) *n. pl.* **·ties** **1** Anything that exists or may be supposed to exist· being. **2** A fact or conception regarded as complete in itself. [<L *entitas, -tatis* < *ens,* ppr. of *esse* be]

ento– *combining form* Within, interior: *entozoic.* Also, before vowels, *ent–*

en·to·blast (en′tō·blast), **en·to·blas·tic** (en′tō·blas′tik) See ENDOBLAST, etc.

en·to·derm (en′tō·dûrm) See ENDODERM.

en·toil (in·toil′) *v.t. Obs.* To ensnare.

en·tomb (in·to͞om′) *v.t.* **1** To place in or as in a tomb; bury. **2** To serve as a tomb for. Also spelled *intomb.* See synonyms under BURY, HIDE. [<OF *entoumber* < *en-* in + *tombe* a tomb] — **en·tomb′er** *n.* — **en·tomb′ment** *n.*

entomo– *combining form* Insect: *entomogenous.* Also, before vowels, **entom–.** [<Gk. *entoma* insects, orig. neut. pl. of *entomos* cut up < *en-* in + *temnein* cut; with ref. to their body structure]

en·to·mog·e·nous (en′tə·moj′ə·nəs) *adj. Bot.* Growing in or upon insects, as certain fungi.

en·to·mol·o·gist (en′tə·mol′ə·jist) *n.* A student of or one versed in entomology.

en·to·mol·o·gize (en′tə·mol′ə·jīz) *v.i.* **·gized, ·giz·ing** **1** To study insects. **2** To collect insects for scientific study.

en·to·mol·o·gy (en′tə·mol′ə·jē) *n.* The branch of zoology that treats of insects. — **en·to·mo·log·i·cal** (en′tə·mə·loj′i·kəl) or **·log′ic** *adj.* — **en′to·mo·log′i·cal·ly** *adv.*

en·to·moph·a·gous (en′tə·mof′ə·gəs) *adj.* Feeding on insects.

en·to·moph·i·lous (en′tə·mof′ə·ləs) *adj. Bot.* Insect-loving: said of those flowers that are especially adapted for pollination by the agency of insects.

en·to·moph·i·ly (en′tə·mof′ə·lē) *n. Bot.* The condition or state of being pollinated by insects. [<ENTOMO- + Gk. *philos* loving]

en·to·mos·tra·can (en′tə·mos′trə·kan) *adj.* Designating a subclass *(Entomostraca)* of crustaceans, chiefly marine, including the branchiopods, copepods, etc. — *n.* A member of this subclass. [<ENTOM(O) + Gk. *ostrakon* shell]

en·to·phyte (en′tō·fīt) See ENDOPHYTE.

en·top·ic (en·top′ik) *adj. Med.* Situated or occurring in its normal place: opposed to *ectopic.* [<Gk. *entopos* in a place < *en-* in + *topos* place]

en·top·tic (en·top′tik) *adj. Med.* **1** Of or pertaining to the interior of the eye. **2** Describing visual perception dependent on the eye itself, and not on anything external to it: *entoptic* phenomena. [<ENT- + Gk. *optikos* optic] — **en·top′ti·cal·ly** *adv.*

en·top·tics (en·top′tiks) *n.* The science of the eye with reference to its interior functions and the phenomena of visual perception.

en·to·sarc (en′tō·särk) See ENDOPLASM.

en·tot·ic (en·tot′ik) *adj. Med.* Of or pertaining to the interior of the ear. Compare illustration under EAR. [<ENT- + Gk. *ous, otos* ear]

en·tou·rage (än′to͞o·räzh′, *Fr.* äṅ·to͞o·räzh′) *n.* **1** Associates, companions, or attendants collectively, especially of a person of rank. **2** Environment. [<F < *entourer* surround < *entour* around]

en·to·zo·an (en′tə·zō′ən) *n.* Any of a branch *(Entozoa)* of metazoans, chiefly parasitic worms, characterized by the possession of a gut cavity and a two-layered cell arrangement. — *adj.* Entozoic. [<ENTO- + Gk. *zōon* animal]

en·to·zo·ic (en′tə·zō′ik) *adj. Biol.* **1** Living within another animal. **2** Of, pertaining to, or caused by entozoans. Also **en′to·zo′al, en′·to·zo′i·cal.**

en·tr'acte (än·trakt′, *Fr.* äṅ·träkt′) *n.* **1** The time between any two acts of a play or opera. **2** A musical interlude, dance, or the like, performed between acts. [<F]

en·trails (en′trālz, -trəlz) *n. pl.* The internal parts, especially the intestines, of an animal. [<F *entrailles* <LL *intralia* intestines]

en·train[1] (en·trān′) *v.t. Physics* To draw along after itself: Steam *entrains* water. [<F *entraîner* < *en-* away (<L *inde*) + *trainer* drag]

en·train[2] (en·trān′) *v.t.* & *v.i.* To put or go aboard a railway train. — **en·train′ment** *n.*

en·tram·mel (en·tram′əl) See TRAMMEL.

en·trance[1] (en′trəns) *n.* **1** The act of entering, in any sense. **2** A passage into a house or other enclosed space. **3** The right or power of entering; entrée. **4** The entry of a vessel at a port. **5** The point or moment at which an actor first enters a scene. **6** *Obs.* Commencement; beginning. [<OF < *entrer* ENTER]

Synonyms: access, accession, adit, admission, admittance, door, doorway, entry, gate, gateway, ingress, inlet, introduction, opening, penetration, portal. *Entrance* refers merely to the fact of passing from without to within some enclosure; *admission* and *admittance* refer to entering by consent given or opportunity allowed. We may effect or force an *entrance,* but not *admittance* or *admission*; those we gain, procure, obtain, secure, win. *Admittance* refers to place; *admission* refers also to position, privilege, favor, friendship, etc. *Entrance* is also used figuratively for setting out upon some career, or becoming a member of some organization, profession, etc. *Antonyms*: departure, egress, ejection, exclusion, exit, expulsion, refusal, rejection, withdrawal.

en·trance[2] (in·trans′, -träns′) *v.t.* **·tranced, ·tranc·ing** **1** To fill with rapture or wonder; delight; charm. **2** To put into a trance. See synonyms under CHARM[1], RAVISH. — **en·trance′·ment** *n.* — **en·tranc′ing** *adj.* — **en·tranc′ing·ly** *adv.*

en·trant (en′trənt) *adj.* Entering; admitting. — *n.* **1** One who enters; a beginner. **2** One who competes in a contest.

en·trap (in·trap′) *v.t.* **·trapped, ·trap·ping** **1** To catch in or as in a trap. **2** To trick into danger or difficulty; deceive; ensnare. See synonyms under CATCH, DECEIVE. — **en·trap′ment** *n.*

en·treas·ure (in·trezh′ər) *v.t.* **·ured, ·ur·ing** To store in a treasury; treasure up.

en·treat (in·trēt′) *v.t.* **1** To beg of abjectly; beseech; implore. **2** To ask for earnestly. **3** *Obs.* To act toward; treat. — *v.i.* **4** To ask earnestly. See synonyms under ASK, PLEAD, PRAY. [<OF *entraiter* <*en-* in + *traiter* TREAT] — **en·treat′ing·ly** *adv.* — **en·treat′ment** *n.*

en·treat·y (in·trē′tē) *n. pl.* **·treat·ies** An earnest request; supplication. See synonyms under PETITION.

en·tre·chat (äṅ·trə·shä′) *n. French* In ballet, a leap upward in which the dancer repeatedly crosses his feet while in the air.

en·tre·côte (äṅ·trə·kōt′) *n. French* Rib steak.

en·trée (än′trā, *Fr.* äṅ·trā′) *n.* **1** The act or privilege of entering; entrance; admission. **2** The principal course at a dinner or luncheon. **3** Formerly, a subordinate dish served between the fish and meat courses or directly before the main course. [<F, orig. pp. of *entrer* ENTER]

en·tre·mets (än′trə·mā, *Fr.* äṅ·trə·me′) *n. pl.* **·mets** (-māz, *Fr.* -me′) *French* A dish served between the main courses of a meal or as a side dish.

en·trench (in·trench′) *v.t.* **1** To fortify or protect with or as with a trench or trenches. **2** To establish firmly: The idea was *entrenched* in his mind. — *v.i.* **3** To encroach or trespass: with *on* or *upon.* Also spelled *intrench.*

en·trench·ment (in·trench′mənt) *n.* **1** A breastwork of earth, especially one with a ditch. **2** Any defense or protection. **3** The act of entrenching, or the state of being entrenched. **4** Encroachment. Also spelled *intrenchment.*

en·tre nous (äṅ′tr′ no͞o′) *French* Between ourselves; confidentially.

en·tre·pôt (än′trə·pō, *Fr.* äṅ·trə·pō′) *n.* A depot or storehouse. [<F < *entreposer* < *entre-* between (<L *inter-*) + *poser.* See POSE[1].]

en·tre·pre·neur (än′trə·prə·nûr′, *Fr.* äṅ·trə·prə·nœr′) *n.* **1** One who undertakes to start and conduct an enterprise or business, assuming full control and risk. **2** One who originates and manages entertainments, especially musical productions; an impresario. [<F < *entreprendre.* See ENTERPRISE.]

En·tre Ri·os (en′trā rē′ōs) A province of eastern Argentina; 28,487 square miles; capital, Paraná.

en·tre·sol (en′tər·sol, *Fr.* äṅ·trə·sôl′) *n.* A half story or mezzanine, especially one next above the ground floor. [<F]

en·tro·pi·on (en·trō′pē·on) *n. Anat.* A turning inward of the edge of the eyelid or of any similar structure. [<NL <Gk. *entropē.* See ENTROPY.]

en·tro·py (en′trə·pē) *n.* **1** *Physics* An index of the degree in which the total energy of a thermodynamic system is uniformly distributed and is thus unavailable for conversion into work. **2** In information theory, a measure of the uncertainty of our knowledge. [<Gk. *entropia,* var. of *entropē* a turning < *en-* in + *trepein* turn]

en·truck (en·truk′) *v.i.* To board a truck.

en·trust (in·trust′) *v.t.* **1** To give over (something) for care, safekeeping, or performance: I will *entrust* this task to you. **2** To place something in the care or trust of; trust, as with a duty, responsibility, etc. Also spelled *intrust.* See synonyms under COMMIT.

en·try (en′trē) *n. pl.* **·tries** **1** The act of coming or going in; entrance. **2** A place of entrance; a small hallway. **3** The act of entering anything in a register, list, etc., or the item, name, or statement entered. **4** The act of reporting at a customhouse, as prescribed by law, the arrival of a ship in port and the nature of her cargo. **5** The act of assuming actual possession of lands or tenements by entering upon them. **6** A contestant listed for a race, prize competition, etc. See synonyms under ENTRANCE[1], RECORD. [<F *entrée* < *entrer.* See ENTER.]

en·try·man (en′trē·mən) *n. pl.* **·men** (-mən) *U.S.* One who takes action for an entry upon, that is, for legal possession of, a portion of the public land; a homesteader.

en·try·way (en′trē·wā′) *n.* A way of entrance; entry.

en·twine (in·twīn′) *v.t.* & *v.i.* **·twined, ·twin·ing** To twine around; twine or twist together: also spelled *intwine.* See synonyms under EMBRACE[1], TWIST.

en·twist (in·twist′) *v.t.* To twist; intertwine: also spelled *intwist.*

e·nu·cle·ate (i·no͞o′klē·āt, -nyo͞o′-) *v.t.* **·at·ed, ·at·ing** **1** To shell, as a kernel. **2** *Surg.* To extract, as a tumor, eyeball, etc.; to extract from a sac without cutting. **3** To explain clearly; disclose. **4** *Biol.* To remove the nucleus from, as a cell. — *adj.* (-it, -āt) Without a nucleus. [<L *enucleatus,* pp. of *enucleare* < *ex-* out + *nucleus* kernel] — **e·nu′·cle·a′tor** *n.*

e·nu·cle·a·tion (i·no͞o′klē·ā′shən, -nyo͞o′-) *n. Surg.* The operation of extracting a tumor in its entirety.

e·nu·mer·ate (i·no͞o′mə·rāt, -nyo͞o′-) *v.t.* **·at·ed, ·at·ing** **1** To name one by one; list. **2** To count or ascertain the number of. See synonyms under CALCULATE. [<L *enumeratus,* pp. of *enumerare* < *ex-* out + *numerare* count] — **e·nu′mer·a′tive** *adj.*

e·nu·mer·a·tion (i·no͞o′mə·rā′shən, -nyo͞o′-) *n.* **1** Detailed mention of things in succession; a catalog; a census. **2** The act of ascertaining a number by counting. See synonyms under RECORD.

e·nu·mer·a·tor (i·no͞o′mə·rā′tər, -nyo͞o′-) *n.* One who enumerates; specifically, one of the minor officials employed in taking a census.

e·nun·ci·a·ble (i·nun′sē·ə·bəl, -shē-) *adj.* That may be enunciated, in any sense. — **e·nun′ci·a·bil′i·ty** *n.*

e·nun·ci·ate (i·nun′sē·āt, -shē-) *v.* **·at·ed, ·at·ing** *v.t.* **1** To pronounce or articulate (words), especially clearly and distinctly. **2** To state with exactness, as a theory or dogma. **3** To announce or proclaim. — *v.i.* **4** To utter or pronounce words. See synonyms under ANNOUNCE, SPEAK. [<L *enunciatus,* pp. of *enunciare* < *ex-* out + *nunciare* announce < *nuntius* a messenger] — **e·nun′ci·a′tive, e·nun′ci·a·to′ry** (-ə·tôr′ē, -tō′rē) *adj.* — **e·nun′ci·a′tive·ly** *adv.* — **e·nun′ci·a′tor** *n.*

e·nun·ci·a·tion (i·nun′sē·ā′shən, -shē-) *n.* **1** The utterance or mode of utterance of vocal sounds. **2** Definite statement.

en·ure (in·yo͝or′) See INURE.

en·u·re·sis (en′yə·rē′sis) *n. Pathol.* Incontinence of urine. [<NL <Gk. *enoureein* < *en-* in + *oureein* urinate]

en·vel·op (in·vel′əp) *v.t.* **·oped, ·op·ing** **1** To wrap; enclose. **2** To hide from sight or understanding; obscure. **3** To surround. Also

en·vel′ope. [<OF *enveloper* <*en-* in + *voluper* fold] —**en·vel′op·er** *n.*

en·ve·lope (en′və·lōp, än′-) *n.* **1** A case or wrapper of paper with gummed edges, for enclosing a letter or the like. **2** Any enclosing covering; a wrapper. **3** *Aeron.* The outer fabric covering of an aerostat. **4** *Biol.* The enclosing membrane of an organ. **5** *Electronics* The glass or metal casing of a vacuum tube. **6** *Geom.* A curve or surface to which another curve or surface, varying or moving according to any law, is invariably tangent. **7** *Astron.* A curved sheet of nebulous matter rising and expanding from the nucleus of a comet on the side toward the sun. Also **en′ve·lop.** [<F *enveloppe* <*envelopper* <OF *enveloper* ENVELOP]

en·vel·op·ment (in·vel′əp·mənt) *n.* **1** The act of enveloping, or the state of being enveloped. **2** That which envelops; a covering; envelope: the seed and its *envelopment.*

en·ven·om (en·ven′əm) *v.t.* **1** To impregnate with venom; poison. **2** To render vindictive; embitter. [<OF *envenimer* <*en-* in + *venim* venom]

en vé·ri·té (än vā·rē·tā′) *French* In truth; verily.

En·ver Pa·sha (en·ver′ pä·shä′), 1881–1922, Turkish general.

en·vi·a·ble (en′vē·ə·bəl) *adj.* Adapted to excite envy; covetable. —**en′vi·a·bly** *adv.*

en·vi·ous (en′vē·əs) *adj.* **1** Having, showing, or cherishing envy; characterized or caused by envy; grudging: an *envious* feeling. **2** *Obs.* Jealous; emulous. **3** *Obs.* Spiteful. [<AF <OF *envieus* <L *invidiosus.* Doublet of INVIDIOUS.] —**en′vi·ous·ly** *adv.* —**en′vi·ous·ness** *n.*

Synonyms: jealous, suspicious. One is *envious* who cherishes selfish ill will toward another because of his superior success, endowments, possessions, or the like. A person is *envious* of that which is another's, and to which he himself has no right or claim; he is *jealous* of intrusion upon that which is his own, or to which he maintains a right or claim. An *envious* spirit is always bad; a *jealous* spirit may be good or bad, according to its object and tendency. A free people must be *jealous* of their liberties if they would retain them. One is *suspicious* of another from unfavorable indications or from a knowledge of wrong in his previous conduct, or even without reason. Compare DOUBT. *Antonyms*: contented, friendly, kindly, satisfied, trustful.

en·vi·ron (in·vī′rən) *v.t.* To be or extend around; encircle; surround. See synonyms under EMBRACE[1]. [<F *environner* <*environ* about]

en·vi·ron·ment (in·vī′rən·mənt, -ərn-) *n.* **1** Whatever encompasses. **2** *Biol.* The aggregate of all external and internal conditions affecting the existence, growth, and welfare of organisms. **3** One's surroundings or external circumstances collectively. **4** The act of environing, or the state of being environed. —**en·vi′ron·men′tal** *adj.*

en·vi·ron·ment·al·ist (in·vī′rən·men′təl·ist) *n.* **1** One who advocates preservation of the environment, as from commercial exploitation. **2** One who attaches more importance to environment than to heredity as a determinant in the development of a person or a group. —**en·vi′ron·men′tal·ism** *n.*

en·vi·rons (in·vī′rəns) *n. pl.* The surrounding region; outskirts; suburbs. [<F <*environ* about]

en·vis·age (en·viz′ij) *v.t.* **·aged, ·ag·ing 1** To face; look into the face of. **2** To form a mental image of; visualize. —**en·vis′age·ment** *n.*

en·vi·sion (en·vizh′ən) *v.t.* To see or foresee in the imagination: to *envision* the future.

en·voi (än·vwä′) See ENVOY[1].

en·voy[1] (en′voi) *n.* **1** A diplomatic agent. See PLENIPOTENTIARY. **2** A diplomat dispatched on a special mission. **3** Any one entrusted with a mission; a commissioner. [<F *envoyé,* pp. of *envoyer* send <OF *envoiier* <*en voie* on the way]

en·voy[2] (en′voi) *n.* **1** A postscript to or the closing lines of a poem: generally printed *l'envoi.* **2** *Obs.* The act of sending a message. [<OF *envoye* <*envoiier.* See ENVOY[1].]

en·vy (en′vē) *v.* **·vied, ·vy·ing** *v.t.* **1** To regard enviously. **2** To feel envy because of; begrudge. **3** To covet; desire; want. —*v.i.* **4** To feel or show envy. —*n. pl.* **·vies 1** Selfish and unfriendly grudging of what another enjoys; in a mild sense, the longing for a good possessed by another, without ill will toward the possessor. **2** An object of envy. **3** *Obs.* Hatred; ill will. [<F *envie* <L *invidia* <*in-* on + *videre* see, look] —**en′vi·er** *n.* —**en′vy·ing·ly** *adv.*

en·wind (en·wind′) *v.t.* To wind or coil around.

en·womb (en·wōōm′) *v.t.* To hold in the womb; conceal as in a womb.

en·wrap (en·rap′) *v.t.* **·wrapped, ·wrap·ping** To wrap in a cover; hence, to envelop: also spelled *inwrap.* —**en·wrap′ment** *n.*

en·wreathe (en·rēth′) *v.t.* **·wreathed, ·wreath·ing** To wrap or encircle with or as with a wreath: also spelled *inwreathe.*

E·ny·o (ē·nī′ō) **1** In Greek mythology, the goddess of war: later identified with the Roman *Bellona.* **2** One of the Graeae.

en·zo·ot·ic (en′zō·ot′ik) *adj.* Endemic among animals, as a disease. [<Gk. *en-* in + *zōon* animal]

en·zyme (en′zīm, -zim) *n. Biochem.* A complex organic substance, usually a protein, produced by cells and having the power to initiate or accelerate specific chemical reactions in the metabolism of plants and animals; a ferment; an organic catalyst: also called *biocatalyst.* Also **en′zym** (-zim). [<L <Gk. *enzymos* leavened <*en-* in + *zymē* leaven] —**en·zy·mat·ic** (en′zī·mat′ik, -zi-) *adj.*

en·zy·mol·o·gy (en′zī·mol′ə·jē) *n.* The branch of biochemistry which treats of the structure, properties, and functions of enzymes.

en·zy·mol·y·sis (en′zī·mol′ə·sis) *n.* The chemical change induced by the action of enzymes. Also **en′zy·mo′sis** (-mō′sis).

eo- *combining form* Earliest; early part of: used in geology, paleontology, archeology, etc. [<Gk. *ēōs* dawn, daybreak]

E·o·an·thro·pus (ē′ō·an·thrō′pəs, -an′thrə-) *n.* A spurious type of early man (*E. dawsoni*) based on incompatible skull fragments found by Charles Dawson and others in Pleistocene gravel beds near Piltdown, England, between 1909 and 1915; exposed in 1953 as a fossil artifact combining a modern skull with the jaw of an orangutan. Also called *Dawn man, Piltdown man.* [<NL <Gk. *ēōs* dawn + *anthropos* man]

e·o·bi·ont (ē′ō·bī′ənt) *n.* A living organism; specifically, one produced by biopoesis. [<EO- + Gk. *biōn, biontos* ppr. of *bioein* live]

E·o·cene (ē′ə·sēn) *Geol. adj.* Of, pertaining to, or existing in the Lower Tertiary period of the Cenozoic era, following the Paleocene and succeeded by the Oligocene. —*n.* The second epoch of the Cenozoic era, associated with a warm climate and the rise of mammals. See chart under GEOLOGY. [<EO- + Gk. *kainos* new]

e·o·cli·max (ē′ō·klī′maks) *n. Ecol.* The climax of the period of dominance of a given plant population. See EOSERE.

E·o·gene (ē′ə·jēn) *adj. Geol.* Of or pertaining to the Paleocene, Eocene, and Oligocene epochs of the Cenozoic era; Paleogene.

E·o·hip·pus (ē′ō·hip′əs) *n. Paleontol.* A genus of primitive, now extinct, small, four-toed horses, connected through a complete series of succeeding types with the present horse; associated with the lower Eocene of the western United States. [<EO- + Gk. *hippos* horse]

e·o·li·an (ē·ō′lē·ən) See AEOLIAN.

E·o·li·an (ē·ō′lē·ən), **E·ol·ic** (ē·ol′ik), etc. See AEOLIAN, etc.

e·ol·i·pile (ē·ol′ə·pīl) *n.* **1** A reaction engine consisting of a hollow sphere upon trunnions, usually above a boiler connected with it. At right angles to its trunnions, two or more radial pipes project from the sphere, their openings so disposed that the forcible ejection of steam rotates the sphere in the opposite direction. **2** One of various devices working on the same principle, as for operating toys, etc. Also **e·ol′o·pile**: often spelled *aeol-* or *-pyle.* [<L *aeolipilae* an instrument for investigating the nature of the wind <*Aeolus* god of the winds + *pila* a ball]

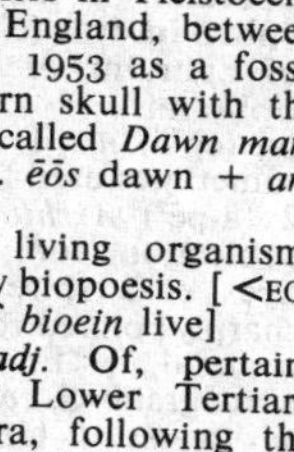

EOLIPILE

e·o·lith (ē′ə·lith) *n.* A stone tool of the earliest form; a celt. For illustration see CELT. [<EO- + Gk. *lithos* stone]

E·o·lith·ic (ē′ə·lith′ik) *adj. Anthropol.* Of or pertaining to a period of protohuman culture extending from the late Pliocene to the first glacial epoch of the Pleistocene and followed by the Paleolithic period: known only by the rudest implements of bone and chipped stone.

e·o·li·trop·ic (ē′ə·lə·trop′ik) See ANISOTROPIC.

e·on (ē′on) *n.* **1** An incalculable period of time; an age; eternity. **2** *Geol.* A time interval including two or more eras. Also spelled *aeon.* [<L *aeon* <Gk. *aiōn* age]

e·o·ni·an (ē·ō′nē·ən) *adj.* Pertaining to or lasting for eons; everlasting: also spelled *aeonian.*

e·o·nism (ē′ə·niz′əm) *n.* The adoption by a male of female habits, clothing, etc.; transvestitism. [after Chevalier Charles *d'Éon,* 1728–1810, French diplomat]

E·os (ē′əs) In Greek mythology, the goddess of the dawn, daughter of Hyperion: identified with the Roman *Aurora.*

e·o·sere (ē′ə·sir) *n. Ecol.* The total development of a particular vegetation, such as ferns, conifers, etc., throughout a geological period that was dominated by plant population.

e·o·sin (ē′ə·sin) *n. Chem.* **1** A reddish coloring matter, $C_{20}H_8Br_4O_5$, derived from coal tar: used for dyeing, for making red ink and pink lakes, and as a stain in microscopical work. **2** Any of several analogous dyes derived from coal tar. Also **e′o·sine** (-sin, -sēn). [<Gk. *eos* dawn + -IN] —**e′o·sin′ic** *adj.*

e·o·sin·o·phile (ē′ə·sin′ə·fīl, -fil) *n. Biol.* A micro-organism, cell, or cell substance with a special affinity for eosin stains or acid stains in general. —**e·o·si·noph·i·lous** (ē′ō·si·nof′ə·ləs), **e′o·sin′o·phil′ic** (-fil′ik) *adj.*

Eöt·vös balance (œt′vœsh) *Physics* An extremely sensitive torsion balance designed to detect and measure local irregularities in gravity: used in geophysics research. [after Roland von *Eötvös,* 1848–1919, Hungarian physicist]

-eous *suffix* Of the nature of: *vitreous.* [<L *-eus*]

E·o·zo·ic (ē′ə·zō′ik) *adj. Geol.* Of or pertaining to the upper portion of the Pre-Cambrian period, immediately underlying the Paleozoic, and showing the first signs of invertebrate life. [<EO- + Gk. *zōē* life]

ep- Var. of EPI-.

e·pact (ē′pakt) *n. Astron.* **1** The excess of the solar year over 12 lunar months, generally about 11 days. **2** The number of days in the age of the moon on the first day of any particular year. [<LL *epacta* <Gk. *epaktē,* fem. sing., added <*epi-* upon + *agein* lead]

E·pam·i·non·das (i·pam′ə·non′dəs), 418?–362 B.C., Theban general and statesman.

ep·arch (ep′ärk) *n.* **1** The chief administrator of a Grecian eparchy. **2** In the Greek Church, a metropolitan or bishop. —**ep·ar′chi·al** *adj.*

ep·ar·chy (ep′är·kē) *n. pl.* **·chies 1** In ancient Greece, a district corresponding to a Roman province, under the jurisdiction of an eparch. **2** In modern Greece, a governmental subdivision of the country. **3** In the Greek Church, an ecclesiastical province or diocese. [<Gk. *eparcheia* <*eparchos* <*epi-* on + *archein* rule]

ep·au·let (ep′ə·let) *n.* **1** *Mil.* A fringed shoulder ornament of commissioned officers: no longer used in the British Army; used in the U. S. Army and Navy with full dress. **2** A shoulder ornament of women's dresses designed to give the effect of width to the shoulder line. Also **ep′au·lette.** [<F *épaulette,* dim. of *épaule* shoulder, OF *espale* <L *spatula*; from its having been used as a device to hold a shoulder belt or protect the shoulder bearing a musket. See SPATULA.]

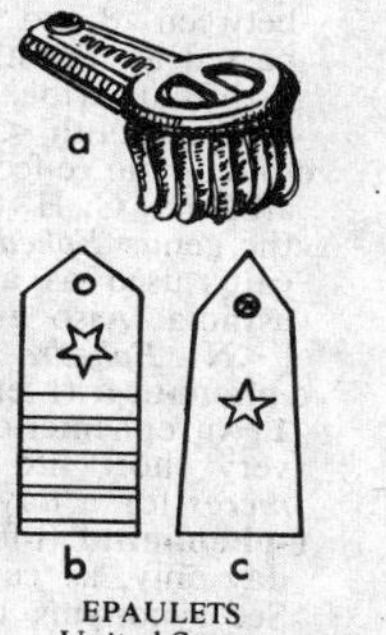

EPAULETS
United States
a. Full dress, 1812.
b. Captain, Navy.
c. Brigadier General, Army.

é·pée (ā·pā′) *n.* A dueling sword with a sharp point and no cutting edge. [<F <OF *espee* <L *spatha* a broad, flat blade <Gk. *spathē*]

é·pée·ist (ā·pā′ist) *n.* A skilled or expert swordsman or fencer.

e·pei·ro·gen·ic (i·pī′rō·jen′ik) *adj. Geol.* Of, pertaining to, or designating continent-making movements of the earth's crust, or the rising and sinking of vast areas: also spelled *epirogenic.* Also **e·pei′ro·ge·net′ic** (-jə·net′ik). [<Gk. *ēpeiros* mainland + -GENIC]

ep·ei·rog·e·ny (ep′ī·roj′ə·nē) *n. Geol.* The process of the formation of a continent or of the greater masses that compose a continent: also spelled *epirogeny.* See DIASTROPHISM.

ep·en·ceph·a·lon (ep′en·sef′ə·lon) *n. pl.* **·la** (-lə) *Anat.* **1** The hind brain. **2** The cerebellum. — **ep·en·ce·phal·ic** (ep′en·si·fal′ik) *adj.*

ep·en·dy·ma (ep·en′di·mə) *n. Anat.* The tissue lining the central cavities of the brain and spinal cord and derived from the original epithelium of the neural tube. [<NL <Gk. < *epi-* upon + *endyma* a garment] — **ep·en′dy·mal** *adj.*

ep·en·the·sis (ep·en′thə·sis) *n. pl.* **·ses** (-sēz) **1** The intrusion of a letter or syllable within a word, as the *d* in *thunder* (Old English *thunor*). **2** The phonetic change resulting from the transference of a semivowel to the syllable preceding, as (in the Greek) in changing *karjo* to *kairo.* [<LL <Gk. < *epi-* upon + *en-* in + *tithenai* place] — **ep·en·thet·ic** (ep′·en·thet′ik) *adj.*

e·pergne (i·pûrn′, ā·pârn′) *n.* An ornamental centerpiece for a dinner table, often consisting of several grouped dishes for fruit, sweets, flowers, etc. [? <F *épargne* economy, thrift]

É·per·nay (ā·per·nā′) A town on the Marne in northern France.

E·pe·us (i·pē′əs) In Greek mythology, the builder of the wooden horse, used by the Greeks to enter and destroy Troy. See TROJAN HORSE.

ep·ex·e·ge·sis (ep·ek′sə·jē′sis) *n.* Something added by way of further elucidation; fuller statement or explanation. [<Gk. *epexēgēsis* < *epi-* upon + *exēgēsis.* See EXEGESIS.]

ep·ex·e·get·ic (ep·ek′sə·jet′ik) *adj.* Explanatory of or additional to a preceding explanation; of the nature of epexegesis. Also **ep·ex′e·get′i·cal.** — **ep·ex′e·get′i·cal·ly** *adv.*

eph- Var. of EPI-.

e·phah (ē′fə) *n.* An ancient Jewish measure of capacity, a little over a bushel, dry measure. Also **e′pha.** [<Hebrew]

ep·har·mone (ep·här′mōn) *n. Ecol.* A plant form differing from the normal through influences of the environment in which it lives. [<EPHARMONY]

ep·har·mo·ny (ep·här′mə·nē) *n. Ecol.* The growth and form of plants as determined by their adaptability to environmental influences, or the harmony between the structure of a plant and the external factor. Also **ep′har·mo′sis** (-mō′sis). [<EP(H)- outside + HARMONY]

e·phe·bic (e·fē′bik) *adj.* **1** Of or pertaining to an ephebus. **2** Of or relating to the adult stages of an organism.

e·phe·bus (e·fē′bəs) *n. pl.* **·bi** (-bī) In ancient Greece, especially Attica, a free-born youth between 18 and 20 years of age, who, having passed an examination, was entered on the list of his tribe. Also **e·phe′bos.** [<L <Gk. *ephēbos* youth < *epi-* upon + *hēbē* youth]

e·phed·rine (e·fed′rin, ef′ə·drēn) *n. Chem.* An alkaloid, $C_{10}H_{15}ON$, isolated from plants of the genus *Ephedra,* and also made synthetically; used as a cardiac depressant and for asthma. Also **e·phed·rin** (i·fed′rin, ef′ə·drin). [<NL *Ephedra,* a genus of plants + -INE[2]]

e·phem·er·a (i·fem′ər·ə) *n. pl.* **·as** or **·ae** (-ē) **1** An ephemerid or mayfly. **2** Anything of very short life or duration. [<Gk. *ephēmeros* for a day < *epi-* on + *hēmera* day]

e·phem·er·al (i·fem′ər·əl) *adj.* **1** Living one day only, as certain insects. **2** Transitory. See synonyms under TRANSIENT. — *n.* Anything lasting for a very short time. — **e·phem′·er·al·ly** *adv.*

e·phem·er·id (i·fem′ər·id) *n.* Any of a widespread order *(Ephemerida)* of insects with aquatic early stages and a very short-lived adult stage; of fragile build, with two or three long caudal filaments, hind wings reduced in size, and vestigial mouth parts; a mayfly, dayfly, or shadfly. [<NL *Ephemeridae* <Gk. *ephēmeros.* See EPHEMERA.]

e·phem·er·is (i·fem′ər·is) *n. pl.* **eph·e·mer·i·des** (ef′ə·mer′ə·dēz) **1** A table showing the calculated positions and motions of a heavenly body, or of several such bodies, from day to day or at regular intervals. **2** A collection of such tables, or an annual publication giving such tables: an astronomical almanac. **3** Ephemera. **4** *Obs.* A diary or other diurnal record of events. [<L, a diary <Gk. *ephēmeris* < *ephēmeros.* See EPHEMERA.]

e·phem·er·on (i·fem′ər·on) *n. pl.* **·er·a** (-ər·ə) **1** An ephemerid, or ephemera. **2** Anything short-lived.

E·phe·sian (i·fē′zhən) *adj.* Of or pertaining to Ephesus. — *n.* **1** A citizen of Ephesus. **2** *Rare* A jovial comrade; boon companion.

E·phe·sians (i·fē′zhənz) **1** The people of Ephesus. **2** The New Testament epistle to the church at Ephesus.

Eph·e·sus (ef′ə·səs) An ancient Greek city in western Asia Minor; site of a great temple of Diana.

Eph·i·al·tes (ef′ē·al′tēz) *n.* In Greek mythology, the demon supposed to inflict nightmares; hence, any nightmare.

eph·od (ef′od, ē′fod) *n.* A Jewish priestly vestment. *Ex.* xxviii 31. [<Hebrew *ēphōd* < *āphad* clothe]

eph·or (ef′ôr, -ər) *n. pl.* **·ors** or **·o·ri** (-ə·rī) **1** In ancient Greece, one of a body of supervising magistrates at Sparta and other Doric towns. **2** In modern Greece, a supervisor of public works. [<L *ephorus* <Gk. *ephoros* < *epi-* over + *hor-,* root of *horaein* see]

E·phra·im (ē′frē·əm, ē′frəm) **1** In the Old Testament, Joseph's second son, who obtained the birthright. *Gen.* xlvi 20. **2** The tribe descended from him. *Josh.* xiv 4.

E·phra·im (ē′frē·əm, ē′frəm) **1** A hilly region of Palestine between the Mediterranean and the Plain of Jezreel, occupied by the Ephraimites: also **Mount Ephraim, the Hills of Ephraim.** **2** The kingdom of Israel.

E·phra·im·ite (ē′frē·əm·īt) *n.* A descendant of Ephraim or a member of the tribe of Ephraim.

ep·i (ep′ē) *n.* **1** A short spur of a railroad, sometimes used for mounting coastal artillery. **2** (ā·pē′) *Archit.* A protection for the apex of a spire or sharply pointed roof; a finial. [<F, lit., ear of grain <L *spica*]

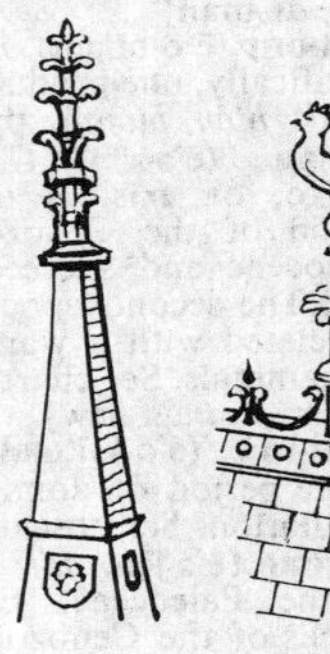

EPI

epi- *prefix* **1** Upon; above; among; outside: *epidermis.* **2** Besides; over; in addition to: *epilog.* **3** Near; close to; beside: *epifocal.* Also: *ep-,* before vowels, as in *eponym; eph-,* before an aspirate, as in *ephemeral.* [<Gk. *epi-, ep-, eph-* <*epi* upon, on]

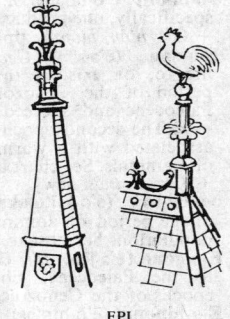

ep·i·blast (ep′ə·blast) *n.* **1** *Biol.* The outermost of the germ layers of the embryo; the ectoderm. **2** *Bot.* A small scalelike appendage in front of the embryo in the seed of certain grasses. — **ep′i·blas′tic** *adj.*

ep·i·bol·ic (ep′ə·bol′ik) *adj. Biol.* Of, pertaining to, or exhibiting epiboly: *epibolic* invagination.

e·pib·o·ly (e·pib′ə·lē) *n. Biol.* The inclusion of one set of segmenting cells within another by means of the more rapid division of the latter. Also **e·pib′o·lism.** [<Gk. *epibolē* < *epi-* upon + *ballein* throw]

ep·ic (ep′ik) *n.* A poem celebrating in stately, formal verse the achievements of heroes, gods, and demigods: also **heroic epic.** Homer's *Iliad* and *Odyssey,* Vergil's *Aeneid* are famous classical epics; the Hindu *Mahabharata* and *Ramayana,* and the Babylonian *Creation Epic* are among the world's greatest, as are also the medieval French *Chanson de Roland* and the 12th century Spanish *Poema del Cid.* The conscious **art epic** is typified by Milton's *Paradise Lost.* — *adj.* Of, pertaining to, or like an epic; grand; noble; heroic: also **ep′i·cal.** [<Gk. *epikos* < *epos* word] — **ep′i·cal·ly** *adv.*

ep·i·ca·lyx (ep′ə·kā′liks, -kal′iks) *n. pl.* **·ca·lyx·es** or **·ca·ly·ces** (-kā′lə·sēz, -kal′ə-) *Bot.* An external involucel or accessory calyx outside the true calyx of a flower. Compare illustration under INVOLUCEL.

ep·i·can·thic fold (ep′ə·kan′thik) *Anat.* A vertical fold of skin on the nasal side of the eyelid whose presence gives the slant-eyed effect noted chiefly in certain Mongoloid peoples. Also **ep′i·can′thus.** [<NL *epicanthus* <Gk. *epi-* upon + *kanthos* corner of the eye]

ep·i·car·di·um (ep′ə·kär′dē·əm) *n. pl.* **·di·a** (-dē·ə) *Anat.* The portion of the pericardium that is directly united with the substance of the heart. [<NL <Gk. *epi-* upon + *kardia* heart] — **ep′i·car′di·ac** (-ak), **ep′i·car′di·al** *adj.*

ep·i·carp (ep′ə·kärp) *n. Bot.* The outer layer of a pericarp. Compare illustration under FRUIT.

ep·i·ce·di·um (ep′ə·sē′dē·əm) *n. pl.* **·di·a** (-dē·ə) A dirge; funeral hymn; lament. [<L <Gk. *epikēdeion,* neut. sing. of *epikēdeios* funereal < *epi-* upon + *kēdos* care, funeral]

ep·i·cene (ep′ə·sēn) *adj.* **1** Of common gender. **2** Belonging to or partaking of the characteristics of both sexes. **3** Loosely, sexless. — *n.* **1** A noun that includes both sexes, as *bird, rat.* **2** A person who exhibits characteristics of both sexes. Also **ep′i·coene.** [<L *epicoenus* <Gk. *epikoinos* < *epi-* upon + *koinos* common] — **ep′i·cen′ism** *n.*

ep·i·cen·ter (ep′ə·sen′tər) *n. Geol.* The point or area on the earth's surface vertically above the focus or point of origin of an earthquake. Also **ep′i·cen′trum.** — **ep′i·cen′tral** *adj.*

ep·i·cot·yl (ep′ə·kot′l) *n. Bot.* That part of the young stem of a plant seedling above the cotyledons. [<EPI- + COTYL(EDON)]

e·pic·ri·sis[1] (i·pik′rə·sis) *n. pl.* **·ses** (-sēz) **1** An elaborate or detailed literary criticism. **2** *Med.* Critical discussion and analysis of a disease subsequent to its termination. [< Gk. *epikrisis* < *epi-* upon + *krinein* judge]

ep·i·cri·sis[2] (ep′ə·krī′sis) *n. pl.* **·ses** (-sēz) *Med.* A supplementary crisis in a disease. [<EPI- + CRISIS]

ep·i·crit·ic (ep′ə·krit′ik) *adj. Physiol.* Of or pertaining to nerve fibers in the skin which are responsive to very delicate variations in touch and temperature stimuli: opposed to *protopathic.* [<Gk. *epikritikos* < *epikrisis.* See EPICRISIS[1].]

Ep·ic·te·tus (ep′ik·tē′təs) Greek Stoic philosopher, first century A.D.

ep·i·cure (ep′ə·kyŏŏr) *n.* One given to refined indulgence in the pleasures of the table; originally, a sensualist. [after *Epicurus*] — **ep′·i·cu·re′an** (-kyŏŏ·rē′ən) *adj.* & *n.* — **ep′i·cu·re′·an·ism** *n.* — **ep′i·cur·ism** *n.*

Ep·i·cu·re·an (ep′ə·kyŏŏ·rē′ən) *adj.* Pertaining to the Greek philosopher Epicurus or to his doctrine. — *n.* A follower of Epicurus.

Ep·i·cu·re·an·ism (ep′ə·kyŏŏ·rē′ən·iz′əm) *n.* The doctrine or spirit of the philosophy of Epicurus.

Ep·i·cu·rus (ep′ə·kyŏŏr′əs), 342?–270? B.C., Greek philosopher who maintained that freedom from pain and peace of mind constitute the chief good, to be gained by self-control and the pursuit of virtue: mistakenly regarded as the philosopher of pleasure and indulgence of the senses.

ep·i·cy·cle (ep′ə·sī′kəl) *n.* **1** In the Ptolemaic cosmogony, a small circle whose center moves on the circumference of a larger circle (the deferent) concentric with the earth, while its own circumference forms the orbit of a planet. **2** *Geom.* A circle that rolls upon the exterior or interior of the circumference of another circle. [<L *epicyclus* <Gk. *epikyklos* < *epi-* upon + *kyklos* a circle] — **ep′i·cy′clic** (-sī′klik, -sik′lik), **ep′i·cy′cli·cal** *adj.*

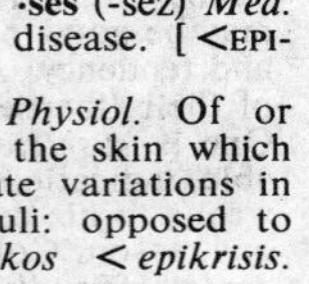

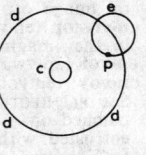

EPICYCLE
c. Earth.
e. Epicycle.
d.d.d. Deferent.
p. Planet.

epicyclic train *Mech.* A train of gear wheels in which, in addition to the motions of the wheels about their respective axes, one has a fixed axis about which the other axes revolve.

ep·i·cy·cloid (ep′ə·sī′kloid) *n. Math.* The curve traced by a point on the circumference of a circle which rolls without slipping upon the outside of the circumference of a fixed circle.

ep·i·cy·cloi·dal (ep′ə·sī·kloid′l) *adj.* Having the form of part of an epicycloid; tracing an epicycloid.

epicycloidal wheel One of the wheels in an epicyclic train.

ep·i·dem·ic (ep′ə·dem′ik) *adj.* Affecting many in a community at once: also **ep′i·dem′i·cal.** —*n.* **1** *Med.* A disease temporarily prevalent in a community or throughout a large area. **2** Any widespread excitement, influence, etc. [<F *épidémique* <*épidémie* a plague <LL *epidemia* <Gk. *epidēmia* <*epi-* upon + *dēmos* people] — **ep′i·dem′i·cal·ly** *adv.* —**ep·i·de·mic·i·ty** (ep′ə·də·mis′ə·tē) *n.*

ep·i·de·mi·ol·o·gist (ep′ə·dē′mē·ol′ə·jist, -dem′·ē-) *n.* A specialist in epidemic diseases.

ep·i·de·mi·ol·o·gy (ep′ə·dē′mē·ol′ə·jē, -dem′ē-) *n.* That branch of medicine which treats of the origin, nature, pathology, and prevention of epidemic diseases. —**ep′i·de′mi·o·log′ic** (-dē′·mē·ə·loj′ik) or **·i·cal** *adj.*

ep·i·der·mis (ep′ə·dûr′mis) *n.* **1** *Anat.* The outer, non-vascular covering of the skin, overlying the corium; the cuticle. **2** Any integument or tegumentary covering. **3** *Bot.* The outermost layer of cells covering the surface of a plant when there are several layers of tissue. Also **ep′i·derm.** [<NL <Gk. <*epi-* upon + *derma* skin] — **ep′i·der′mal, ep′i·der′mic** *adj.*

ep·i·der·moid (ep′ə·dûr′moid) *adj.* Resembling epidermis. Also **ep′i·der·moi′dal.**

ep·i·di·a·scope (ep′ə·dī′ə·skōp) *n.* A device for projecting the images of opaque or transparent objects upon a screen: also called *aphengoscope.* [<EPI- + DIA- + -SCOPE]

ep·i·did·y·mec·to·my (ep′ə·did′ə·mek′tə·mē) *n.* *Surg.* Removal of the epididymis.

ep·i·did·y·mis (ep′ə·did′ə·mis) *n.* *pl.* **ep·i·di·dym·i·des** (ep′ə·di·dim′ə·dēz) *Anat.* An oblong body composed of the convoluted efferent duct of the testis, at the posterior part of that organ. [<NL <Gk. <*epi-* upon + *didymos* testicle] — **ep′i·did′y·mal** *adj.*

ep·i·dote (ep′ə·dōt) *n.* A monoclinic, greenish-to-black, aluminum calcium silicate. [<F *épidote* <Gk. *epididonai* <*epi-* upon + *didonai* give; from the large base of its crystals] —**ep′i·dot′ic** (-dot′ik) *adj.*

ep·i·do·ti·za·tion (ep′ə·dō′tə·zā′shən, -tī·zā′-) *n.* Metamorphic alteration into epidote.

ep·i·fo·cal (ep′ə·fō′kəl) *adj.* *Geol.* Of, pertaining to, or situated near the focus of an earthquake; epicentral.

ep·i·gam·ic (ep′ə·gam′ik) *adj.* *Biol.* Attractive to the opposite sex, especially during the mating season: said of animal coloration.

ep·i·gas·tric (ep′ə·gas′trik) *adj.* *Anat.* **1** Relating to the anterior walls of the abdomen. **2** Of or pertaining to the epigastrium or the abdomen generally. Also **ep′i·gas′tri·al.**

ep·i·gas·tri·um (ep′ə·gas′trē·əm) *n.* *pl.* **·tri·a** (-trē·ə) *Anat.* The upper part of the abdomen, especially the region over the stomach and its walls. See illustration under ABDOMINAL. [<NL <Gk. *epigastrion,* neut. sing. of *epigastrios* <*epi-* upon + *gastēr* stomach]

ep·i·ge·al (ep′ə·jē′əl) *adj.* **1** *Bot.* Epigeous. **2** *Zool.* Keeping close to ground, as certain insects. Also **ep′i·ge′an.**

ep·i·gene (ep′ə·jēn) *adj.* *Geol.* **1** Produced or occurring at the surface of the earth: *epigene* disintegration, *epigene* rocks: contrasted with *hypogene.* **2** Pseudomorphous; irregular; changed from its original formation: said of crystals. [<F *épigène* <Gk. *epigenēs* <*epi-* on, upon + *gen-,* root of *gignesthai* be born]

ep·i·gen·e·sis (ep′ə·jen′ə·sis) *n.* **1** *Biol.* The theory that the structure, organization, and development of new organisms, as in embryos, is the result of the successive interactions between male and female cells subsequent to fertilization: opposed to the doctrines of *preformation* and *syngenesis.* **2** *Geol.* An alteration in the character of rocks due to external forces or agents. **3** *Med.* An accessory or secondary symptom of a disease. —**ep′i·ge·net′ic** (-jə·net′ik) *adj.*

e·pig·e·nous (i·pij′ə·nəs) *adj.* *Bot.* Growing on the surface, especially the upper surface, as fungi on leaves. [<EPIGENE + -OUS]

ep·i·ge·ous (ep′ə·jē′əs) *adj.* *Bot.* Related or pertaining to plants or plant parts which appear above the surface of the ground, especially applied to cotyledons. [<Gk. *epigeios* <*epi-* upon + *gē* earth]

ep·i·glot·tis (ep′ə·glot′is) *n.* *Anat.* The leaf-shaped cartilaginous lid, at the base of the tongue, that covers the trachea, or windpipe, during the act of swallowing. [<NL <Gk. *epiglōttis* <*epi-* upon + *glōtta* tongue] —**ep′·i·glot′tal** *adj.*

E·pig·o·ni (i·pig′ə·nī) *n. pl.* In Greek legend, the descendants of the Seven against Thebes, who attacked Thebes successfully ten years later.

ep·i·gram (ep′ə·gram) *n.* **1** A pithy, caustic, or thought-provoking saying. **2** A short, pithy poem, especially one ending with a caustic point. [<L *epigramma* <Gk., an inscription <*epi-* upon + *graphein* write] —**ep′·i·gram′ma·tism** *n.* —**ep′i·gram′ma·tist** *n.*

ep·i·gram·mat·ic (ep′ə·grə·mat′ik) *adj.* Pertaining to or marked by epigram; witty; pointed; antithetical. Also **ep′i·gram·mat′i·cal.** —**ep′i·gram·mat′i·cal·ly** *adv.*

ep·i·gram·ma·tize (ep′ə·gram′ə·tīz) *v.* **·tized, ·tiz·ing** *v.t.* To make an epigram of; express in an epigram. —*v.i.* To write or speak in epigrams; make an epigram.

ep·i·graph (ep′ə·graf, -gräf) *n.* **1** A carved inscription on a monument, tomb, etc. **2** The superscription prefixed to a book or chapter. [<Gk. *epigraphē* <*epi-* upon + *graphein* write] —**ep′i·graph′ic** or **·i·cal** *adj.* —**ep′i·graph′i·cal·ly** *adv.*

e·pig·ra·phy (i·pig′rə·fē) *n.* The science that treats of the study, interpretation, etc., of inscriptions or epitaphs. —**e·pig′ra·pher, e·pig′·ra·phist** *n.*

e·pig·y·nous (i·pij′ə·nəs) *adj.* *Bot.* Having floral organs adnate to and near the summit of the ovary. [<EPI- + -GYNOUS] —**e·pig′y·ny** *n.*

ep·i·lep·sy (ep′ə·lep′sē) *n.* *Pathol.* A chronic nervous affection characterized by sudden loss of consciousness, sometimes accompanied by paroxysmic seizures of varying intensity and duration: primarily a symptom complex associated with various neuropsychiatric disorders. See also GRAND MAL, PETIT MAL. Also **ep′i·lep′si·a.** [<OF *epilepsie* <LL *epilepsia* <Gk. *epilēpsia* <*epi-* upon + *lambanein* seize]

ep·i·lep·tic (ep′ə·lep′tik) *adj.* Pertaining to or affected with epilepsy. —*n.* One affected with epilepsy. —**ep′i·lep′ti·cal·ly** *adv.*

ep·i·lep·toid (ep′ə·lep′toid) *adj.* Having the character of or resembling epilepsy. —*n.* One affected with a disorder resembling epilepsy.

ep·i·log (ep′ə·lôg, -log) *n.* **1** The conclusion of a discourse. **2** A short poem or speech to the audience delivered by an actor after the conclusion of a play. **3** The close of a novel or a narrative or dramatic poem. Also **ep′i·logue.** [<F *epilogue* <L *epilogus* <Gk. *epilogos* a peroration <*epi-* upon, in addition + *legein* say] —**ep′i·log′ic** (-loj′ik) or **·i·cal** *adj.* —**ep′i·lo·gis′tic** (-lō·jis′tik) *adj.*

e·pil·o·gize (i·pil′ə·jīz) *v.* **·gized, ·giz·ing** *v.i.* To utter an epilog, as to a play. —*v.t.* To give an epilog to. Also **ep′i·log,** *Brit.* **e·pil′·o·gise.**

ep·i·me·ron (ep′ə·mē′ron) *n.* *pl.* **·ra** (-rə) *Entomol.* The posterior division of the pleuron in the thorax of an insect. Also **ep′i·me′rum.** [<NL <Gk. *epi-* upon, besides + *mēros* thigh] — **ep′i·me′ral** *adj.*

Ep·i·me·the·us (ep′ə·mē′thē·əs) In Greek mythology, a Titan, the brother of Prometheus and husband of Pandora.

ep·i·mor·pha (ep′ə·môr′fə) *n. pl.* *Zool.* Larvae having all their segments fully formed before hatching. [<NL <Gk. *epi-* on, upon + *morphē* form]

ep·i·mor·pho·sis (ep′ə·môr·fō′sis) *n.* *Biol.* The proliferation of new tissue preceding the regeneration of a part, as in many invertebrate animals.

É·pi·nal (ā·pē·nàl′) A town on the Moselle in eastern France.

ep·i·nas·ty (ep′ə·nas′tē) *n.* *Bot.* Downward curvature of a plant member, induced by a more active growth on its upper side. [<EPI- + Gk. *nastos* compact] —**ep′i·nas′tic** *adj.*

ep·i·neph·rine (ep′ə·nef′rin, -rēn) *n.* A hormone, $C_9H_{13}NO_3$, secreted by the adrenal medulla, which stimulates heart action and causes constriction of blood vessels, thus increasing blood pressure. Also *Brit. adrenaline.* [<EPI- + Gk. *nephros* kidney]

ep·i·neu·ri·um (ep′ə·nŏŏr′ē·əm, -nyŏŏr′-) *n.* *pl.* **·ri·a** (-ē·ə) *Anat.* The sheath of connective tissue that surrounds a nerve trunk. [<NL <Gk. *epi-* upon + *neuron* nerve, sinew] —**ep′i·neu′ri·al** *adj.*

ep·i·no·sis (ep′ə·nō′sis) *n.* **1** *Pathol.* A morbid condition subordinate to an original and primary illness. **2** *Psychoanal.* A secondary illness or disorder exploited by the patient to gain relief from the primary affliction and to obtain further sympathy. [<EPI- + Gk. *nosos* illness] —**ep′i·no′sic** *adj.*

ep·i·on·tol·o·gy (ep′ē·on·tol′ə·jē) *n.* The study of the geographic distribution of plants. [<Gk. *epiōn, -ontos,* ppr. of *epienai* (<*epi-* upon + *ienai* go) + -LOGY] —**ep′i·on′to·log′i·cal** (-tə·loj′·i·kəl) *adj.* —**ep′i·on·tol′o·gist** *n.*

Ep·i·pa·le·o·lith·ic (ep′ə·pā′lē·ə·lith′ik) *adj.* *Anthropol.* Mesolithic.

ep·i·pet·a·lous (ep′ə·pet′ə·ləs) *adj.* *Bot.* Inserted or growing on a petal, as a stamen.

e·piph·a·ny (i·pif′ə·nē) *n.* *pl.* **·nies** A bodily manifestation, as of a deity. [<OF *epiphanie* <Gk. *epiphainein* manifest <*epi-* upon + *phainein* show]

E·piph·a·ny (i·pif′ə·nē) *n.* *Eccl.* A festival, observed on January 6, commemorating the manifestation of Christ to the Gentiles, represented by the Magi: also called *Twelfth Day.*

ep·i·phe·nom·e·non (ep′ə·fə·nom′ə·non) *n.* *pl.* **·nom·e·na** (-nə) A phenomenon which is secondary to or a by-product of one or more other phenomena; one which is a mere accompaniment of some effect and exerts no causal influence on the effect.

ep·i·phyl·lous (ep′ə·fil′əs) *adj.* *Bot.* Situated or growing upon a leaf, especially with reference to stamens inserted on a perigonium. Also **ep′i·phyl′line** (-īn, -ēn). [<EPI- + Gk. *phyllon* leaf]

e·piph·y·sis (i·pif′ə·sis) *n.* *pl.* **·ses** (-sēz) *Anat.* **1** The extremity of a long bone, originally separated from it by cartilage but later consolidated with it by ossification. **2** The pineal body. [<NL <Gk., an outgrowth <*epi-* upon + *phyein* grow] —**ep·i·phys·i·al** (ep′ə·fiz′ē·əl), **ep′i·phys′e·al** *adj.*

ep·i·phyte (ep′ə·fīt) *n.* *Bot.* **1** A plant growing nonparasitically upon another plant or on a nonliving support and deriving nutrients and moisture from the air; also called *air plant, aerophyte.* **2** A plant, as a fungus, parasitic upon the exterior surface of an animal. —**ep′i·phyt′ic** (-fit′ik) or **·i·cal** *adj.*

ep·i·phy·tot·ic (ep′ə·fī·tot′ik) *adj.* Having or characterized by a wide-spreading plant disease. Compare EPIDEMIC, EPIZOOTIC.

ep·i·po·di·um (ep′ə·pō′dē·əm) *n.* *pl.* **·di·a** (-dē·ə) *Zool.* A lateral part of the foot in certain mollusks. [<NL <Gk. *epipodios* on the feet <*epi-* upon + *pous, podos* foot]

E·pi·rus (i·pī′rəs) A region of NW Greece on the Ionian Sea, formerly an independent kingdom and republic. Also **E·pei′rus.**

e·pis·co·pa·cy (i·pis′kə·pə·sē) *n.* *pl.* **·cies** **1** Government of a church by bishops. **2** A bishop's state or office. **3** The body of bishops collectively. [<LL *episcopatus* <*episcopus* BISHOP]

e·pis·co·pal (i·pis′kə·pəl) *adj.* **1** Of or pertaining to bishops. **2** Having a government vested in bishops; characterized by episcopacy. **3** Advocating or supporting episcopacy. [<LL *episcopalis* <*episcopus* BISHOP] —**e·pis′co·pal·ly** *adv.*

E·pis·co·pal (i·pis′kə·pəl) *adj.* Belonging or pertaining to the Protestant Episcopal Church, or to any church in the Anglican communion.

Episcopal Church See PROTESTANT EPISCOPAL CHURCH.

e·pis·co·pa·li·an (i·pis′kə·pā′lē·ən, -pāl′yən) *n.* An advocate of episcopacy. —*adj.* Pertaining to or favoring episcopal government.

E·pis·co·pa·li·an (i·pis′kə·pā′lē·ən, -pāl′yən) *n.* A member of the Protestant Episcopal Church. —*adj.* Episcopal. —**E·pis′co·pa′li·an·ism** *n.*

e·pis·co·pal·ism (i·pis′kə·pəl·iz′əm) *n.* That view of the constitution of the church that places the supreme power in the hands of a body of bishops, and recognizes no single supreme

head, as the pope, with ordinary jurisdiction over the whole church.
e·pis·co·pate (i·pis′kə·pit, -pāt) *n.* 1 The office, dignity, or term of office of a bishop. 2 A bishopric. 3 Bishops collectively.
ep·i·sode (ep′ə·sōd) *n.* 1 An incident or story in a literary work, separable from, yet related to it. 2 A notable incident or action occurring as a break in the regular course of events. 3 An intermediate passage in a musical composition whereby the development of the subject is for a time suspended for the sake of variety and relief. 4 A portion of a Greek tragedy occurring between two choric songs. See synonyms under EVENT. [<Gk. *epeisodion* < *epeisodios* coming in besides < *epi-* upon + *eisodos* entrance < *eis-* into + *hodos* way, road] — **ep′i·sod′ic** (-sod′ik) or **·i·cal, ep′i·so′·dal** or **·di·al** *adj.* — **ep′i·sod′i·cal·ly** *adv.*
ep·i·spas·tic (ep′ə·spas′tik) *adj.* Raising blisters; blistering. — *n.* A blistering medicament. [<NL *epispasticus* <Gk. *epispastikos* < *epi-* on + *spaein* draw]
ep·i·sperm (ep′ə·spûrm) *n. Bot.* The outer covering of a seed. — **ep′i·sper′mic** *adj.*
ep·i·spore (ep′ə·spôr, -spōr) *n. Bot.* The outer integument or coat of a spore.
e·pis·ta·sis (i·pis′tə·sis) *n.* 1 *Genetics* The masking of one factor in Mendelian inheritance by another not allelomorphic to it. 2 *Med.* The stoppage of a hemorrhage or other fluid discharge of the body. [<NL <Gk., a stoppage < *epi-* upon + *histanai* stand]
ep·i·stat·ic (ep′ə·stat′ik) *adj. Genetics* 1 Pertaining to the dominance of one factor over another not of the same allelomorphic pair. 2 Possessing such a factor: opposed to *hypostatic.*
ep·i·stax·is (ep′ə·stak′sis) *n. Pathol.* Nosebleed. [<NL <Gk. *epistaxis* < *epi-* upon + *stazein* drop, drip]
e·pis·te·mol·o·gy (i·pis′tə·mol′ə·jē) *n.* That department of philosophy which investigates critically the nature, grounds, limits, and criteria, or validity, of human knowledge; theory of cognition. [<Gk. *epistēmē* knowledge + -LOGY] — **e·pis·te·mo·log·i·cal** (i·pis′·tə·mə·loj′i·kəl) *adj.* — **e·pis′te·mo·log′i·cal·ly** *adv.* — **e·pis′te·mol′o·gist** *n.*
e·pis·tle (i·pis′əl) *n.* 1 A written message; communication; letter: more formal than *letter,* and especially applied to ancient epistolary writings of sacred character or of literary excellence: the Pauline *epistles.* 2 *Eccl. Usually cap.* A selection, usually from an apostolic epistle, read in the communion service of the Greek, Roman, and Anglican churches. [OE *epistol* <L *epistola* <Gk. *epistolē* < *epi-* on + *stellein* send]
e·pis·tler (i·pis′lər) *n.* 1 One who writes epistles. 2 *Eccl.* The reader of the Epistle at the Eucharist; the subdeacon. Also **e·pis′to·ler** (-tə·lər).
e·pis·to·lar·y (i·pis′tə·ler′ē) *adj.* Belonging or suitable to correspondence by letter; included in or maintained by letters: also **ep·is·tol·ic** (ep′is·tol′ik), **ep′is·tol′i·cal.** — *n. pl.* **·lar·ies** A book containing the epistles of a liturgy.
e·pis·tro·phe (i·pis′trə·fē) *n.* 1 In rhetoric, that form of repetition in which successive clauses or sentences end with the same word. 2 A musical refrain. 3 *Bot.* The arrangement of chlorophyll granules (as on the upper and under walls of leaf cells) when exposed to diffused light. [<EPI- + Gk. *strophe* turning about]
ep·i·style (ep′ə·stīl) *n. Archit.* An architrave.
ep·i·taph (ep′ə·taf, -täf) *n.* 1 An inscription on a tomb or monument in honor or in memory of the dead. See EPIGRAPH. 2 A sentiment in prose or verse written as for inscription on a tomb. [<L *epitaphium* a eulogy <Gk. *epitaphios* at a tomb < *epi-* upon, at + *taphos* a tomb] — **ep′i·taph′ic** (-taf′ik), **ep′i·taph′i·al** *adj.*
e·pit·a·sis (i·pit′ə·sis) *n.* In Greek drama, the main action of a play, wherein the plot develops, leading on to the catastrophe: opposed to *protasis.* [<NL <Gk., an intensifying < *epiteinein* intensify < *epi-* in addition + *teinein* stretch]
ep·i·tha·la·mi·um (ep′ə·thə·lā′mē·əm) *n. pl.* **·mi·a** (-mē·ə) A nuptial poem or song. Also **ep′i·tha·la′mi·on.** [<L <Gk. *epithalamion* < *epi-* at + *thalamos* a bridal chamber]
ep·i·the·li·oid (ep′ə·thē′lē·oid) *adj. Biol.* Resembling epithelium or epithelial tissue.
ep·i·the·li·o·ma (ep′ə·thē′lē·ō′mə) *n. pl.* **·o·ma·ta** (-ō′mə·tə) or **·o·mas** *Pathol.* A tumor originating in or affecting epithelial tissue; specifically, cancer of the skin. — **ep·i·the·li·om·a·tous** (ep′ə·thē′lē·om′ə·təs) *adj.*
ep·i·the·li·um (ep′ə·thē′lē·əm) *n. pl.* **·li·ums** or **·li·a** (-lē·ə) *Biol.* A membranous tissue consisting of one or more layers of cells of various types and sizes, compactly joined and serving to line the canals, cavities, and ducts of the body as well as all free surfaces exposed to the air. [<NL <Gk. *epi-* upon + *thēlē* nipple]
ep·i·thet (ep′ə·thet) *n.* 1 A phrase or word used adjectively to express some characteristic attribute or quality. 2 An expressive surname or nickname, as Harry *Hotspur, Old Hickory.* Also **e·pith·e·ton** (i·pith′ə·ton). See synonyms under NAME. [<L *epitheton* <Gk. < *epitithenai* attribute < *epi-* upon + *tithenai* place] — **ep′i·thet′ic** or **·i·cal** *adj.*
e·pit·o·me (i·pit′ə·mē) *n.* 1 A typical example; embodiment: the *epitome* of arrogance. 2 An extreme example; climax or culmination. 3 A concise summary; abridgement. See synonyms under ABBREVIATION, ABRIDGMENT. [<L <Gk. *epitomē* < *epi-* upon + *temnein* cut] — **ep·i·tom·ic** (ep′ə·tom′ik) or **·i·cal** *adj.* — **e·pit′o·mist** or **e·pit′o·miz′er** or *Brit.* **e·pit′o·mis′er** *n.*
e·pit·o·mize (i·pit′ə·mīz) *v.t.* **·mized, ·miz·ing** 1 To abridge. 2 To be an epitome of. Also *Brit.* **e·pit′o·mise.** See synonyms under ABBREVIATE.
ep·i·trite (ep′ə·trīt) *n.* In ancient prosody, a foot of three long syllables and one short. [<LL *epitritos* <Gk. *epitritos* containing one and one third < *epi-* upon + *tritos* third]
ep·i·troch·le·a (ep′ə·trok′lē·ə) *n. Anat.* The bony prominence on the inner side of the humerus at its lower end; the inner condyle.
ep·i·zeux·is (ep′ə·zo͞ok′sis) *n.* That form of figurative repetition in which a word is repeated without any intervening words or clauses. Example: He is brave—brave beyond measure. [<LL <Gk. < *epizeugnunai* < *epi-* upon + *zeugnunai* yoke, join]
ep·i·zo·on (ep′ə·zō′on) *n. pl.* **·zo·a** (-zō′ə) An animal parasite living on the outside of the body.
ep·i·zo·ot·ic (ep′ə·zō·ot′ik) *adj.* Common to or affecting many animals at the same time: said especially of diseases. — *n.* An epizootic disease: also **ep′i·zo′o·ty** (-zō′ə·tē).
e plu·ri·bus u·num (ē plo͝or′ə·bəs yo͞o′nəm) *Latin* One out of many; motto of the United States.
ep·och (ep′ək, *Brit.* ē′pok) *n.* 1 A point in the onward course of history from which succeeding years are counted: Atomic energy marks an *epoch* in history. 2 An interval of time or a series of years, regarded as a whole, memorable for extraordinary events and far-reaching results; any definite period of history. 3 *Geol.* A minor subdivision of time; a time interval less than a period: the Pleistocene *epoch.* See chart under GEOLOGY. 4 *Astron.* A moment of time when a planet reaches a certain known position with reference to the sun. [<Gk. *epochē* a stoppage, point of time < *epi-* upon + *echein* have]
ep·och·al (ep′ə·kəl) *adj.* Creating or marking an epoch.
ep·och–mak·ing (ep′ək·mā′king, *Brit.* ē′pok-) *adj.* Opening up a new era, as in history, science, culture, etc.
ep·ode (ep′ōd) *n.* 1 That part of a Pindaric ode following the strophe and antistrophe. 2 A species of lyric poem, in which a longer verse is followed by a shorter one. [<F *épode* <L *epodos* <Gk. *epōidos* an incantation < *epi-* in addition + *aidein* sing]
ep·o·nym (ep′ə·nim) *n.* 1 A personage assumed as the founder and name–giver of a race, state, or city; also, the name of that personage. 2 A name or phrase formed from the name of a person to designate a people, period, scientific theory, disease, etc. 3 A high official in ancient Assyria, whose name was given to the year during which he held office. [<Gk. *epōnymos* < *epi-* upon + *onyma* name]
e·pon·y·mist (i·pon′ə·mist) *n.* One from whom an eponym is derived.
e·pon·y·mous (i·pon′ə·məs) *adj.* Pertaining to an eponym. Also **ep·o·nym·ic** (ep′ə·nim′ik).
e·pon·y·my (i·pon′ə·mē) *n.* 1 The year or period of office of an eponym. 2 Eponymic nomenclature.
ep·o·pee (ep′ə·pē, ep′ə·pē′) *n.* 1 An epic poem. 2 Epic poetry in general. Also **ep′o·poe′ia.** [<F *épopée* <Gk. *epopoiia* epic poetry < *epos* word, song + *poieein* make]
ep·opt (ep′opt) *n.* In ancient Greece, one of the initiated; hence, one to whom all the secrets of any body of mysteries have been revealed. [<LL *epopta* <Gk. *epoptes* < *epi-* upon + *op-*, stem of *horaein* see, look] — **ep·op′tic** *adj.*
ep·os (ep′os) *n.* 1 An epopee. 2 Unwritten narrative poetry; a series of heroic events. [<L <Gk., word, song]
e·pox·y (i·pok′sē) *n. Chem.* The radical –O–, especially as bonded to different atoms already joined in different ways to form the durable **epoxy resins** much used for varnishes and adhesives.
Ep·ping (ep′ing) An urban district of western Essex, England, on the edge of **Epping Forest** which once included all Essex, now a public park of 5,600 acres.
ep·si·lon (ep′sə·lon) *n.* The fifth letter and second vowel of the Greek alphabet (E, ϵ), equivalent to English short *e.* As a numeral it denotes 5. [<Gk. *epsilon* < *e* e + *psilon* simple]
Ep·som (ep′səm) A town in north central Surrey, England, famous for its racecourse on **Epsom Downs** where the Derby and other races are run.
Epsom salts A hydrous magnesium sulfate, used as a purge or to reduce inflammation. Also **Epsom salt.**
Ep·stein (ep′stīn), **Sir Jacob,** 1880–1959, English sculptor born in the United States.
Ep·worth League (ep′wərth) An American youth organization in the Methodist Church.
eq·ua·bil·i·ty (ek′wə·bil′ə·tē, ē′kwə-) *n.* Evenness, as of temper or action. Also **eq′ua·ble·ness.**
eq·ua·ble (ek′wə·bəl, ē′kwə-) *adj.* Of uniform condition or movement; steady; even; not readily disturbed: an *equable* disposition. [<L *aequabilis* < *aequare* make equal] — **eq′·ua·bly** *adv.*
e·qual (ē′kwəl) *adj.* 1 Of the same degree with another or with each other, as in magnitude or value; neither greater nor less. 2 Equable. 3 Adequate for the purpose; commensurate. 4 *Archaic* Equitable; just. 5 Having the same rank, rights, or importance. 6 Level. 7 Uniform in operation: *equal* laws. See synonyms under ADEQUATE, ALIKE. — *v.t.* **e·qualed** or **e·qualled, e·qual·ing** or **e·qual·ling** 1 To be or become equal to. 2 To do or produce something equal to. 3 To recompense in full. 4 *Obs.* To make equal; equalize. — *n.* A person or thing equal to another; a person of the same rank or condition. [<L *aequalis* < *aequus* even] — **e′qual·ly** *adv.* — **e′qual·ness** *n.*
e·qual·i·tar·i·an (i·kwol′ə·târ′ē·ən) *adj.* Of or pertaining to the doctrine that all men are equal. — *n.* A believer in this doctrine.
e·qual·i·ty (i·kwol′ə·tē) *n. pl.* **·ties** 1 The state of being equal. 2 Exact agreement; uniformity.
Equality State Nickname of WYOMING.
e·qual·i·za·tion (ē′kwəl·ə·zā′shən, -ī·zā′-) *n.* 1 The act of equalizing. 2 An equal state.
equalization fund A fund established for the purpose of equalizing payments, income, taxes, etc., of different economic classes.
e·qual·ize (ē′kwəl·īz) *v.t.* **·ized, ·iz·ing** 1 To make equal. 2 To render uniform. Also *Brit.* **e′qual·ise.**
e·qual·iz·er (ē′kwəl·ī′zər) *n.* 1 One who or that which equalizes. 2 *Mech.* A device for equalizing pressure or strain between parts of a structure, as the springs and wheels of a locomotive. 3 *Electr.* **a** A conductor of low resistance used to join the currents of two generators and equalize their voltage. **b** Any contrivance for equalizing the pull of electromagnets. 4 *U.S. Slang* A revolver.
equal rights Equality of rights, especially between men and women.
e·quan·gu·lar (i·kwang′gyə·lər) *adj.* Equiangular.
e·qua·nim·i·ty (ē′kwə·nim′ə·tē, ek′wə-) *n.* Evenness of mind or temper; composure; calmness. [<L *aequanimitas, -tatis* < *aequus* even + *animus* mind]
e·quan·i·mous (i·kwan′ə·məs) *adj.* Even–tempered.
e·quate (i·kwāt′) *v.t.* **e·quat·ed, e·quat·ing** 1 To make equal; treat or consider as equivalent. 2 *Math.* To indicate the equality of; express as an equation. 3 To reduce to an average;

correct so as to reduce to a common standard [<L *aequatus*, pp. of *aequare* make even < *aequus* even]

e·qua·tion (i·kwā′zhən, -shən) *n.* **1** The process or act of making equal; equal division; equality. **2** *Math.* A statement expressing (usually by the symbol =) the equality of two quantities. **3** *Chem.* A symbolic representation of a chemical reaction, as $Na_2CO_3 + H_2SO_4 = Na_2SO_4 + CO_2 + H_2O$. The first member includes the substances reacting; the second, the products. The sum of the quantities of the two members must be equal. — **e·qua′tion·al** *adj.* — **e·qua′tion·al·ly** *adv.*

equation of payments The determination of the time at which several sums of money, due at various times, should be due, if all are paid at once.

e·qua·tor (i·kwā′tər) *n.* **1** A great circle of the earth, a planet, etc., lying at right angles to its axis and equidistant from the poles. **2** Any similar circle, as of the sun, a planet, etc. **3** The celestial equator. [<LL (*circulus*) *aequator* (*equalizer* (circle); so called because day and night are equal when the sun crosses the equator]

e·qua·to·ri·al (ē′kwə·tôr′ē·əl, -tō′rē-) *adj.* Relating to, near, or determined by an equator: *equatorial* climate. — *n. Astron.* A telescope turning on two axes at right angles to each other, the principal one being parallel to the axis of the earth.

Equatorial Islands See LINE ISLANDS.

equatorial plate *Biol.* In cell division, the group of chromosomes collected into a disk midway between the centrosomes, just prior to the anaphase: also called *nuclear plate.* See MITOSIS, also illustration under CELL.

eq·uer·ry (ek′wə·rē) *n. pl.* **·ries 1** An officer having charge of the horses of a prince or nobleman. **2** An officer of the royal household of England, who occasionally attends upon the sovereign or a royal prince. Also **eq′uer·y.** [<F *écurie* stable <OF *escurie*, ult. <Gmc.; infl. by L *equus* a horse]

e·ques·tri·an (i·kwes′trē·ən) *adj.* **1** Pertaining to horses or horsemanship; skilled in horsemanship. **2** Representing as on horseback. **3** Composed of or pertaining to knights. — *n.* One skilled in horsemanship. [<L *equester, -tris* < *eques* a horseman < *equus* a horse]

e·ques·tri·an·ism (i·kwes′trē·ən·iz′əm) *n.* Horsemanship.

e·ques·tri·enne (i·kwes′trē·en′) *n.* A woman skilled in horsemanship.

equi– *combining form* Equal; equally: *equidistant.* [<L *aequus* equal]

e·qui·an·gu·lar (ē′kwē·ang′gyə·lər) *adj.* Having equal angles.

equiangular spiral Logarithmic spiral.

e·qui·dis·tant (ē′kwə·dis′tənt) *adj.* Equally distant. — **e′qui·dis′tance** *n.*

e·qui·lat·er·al (ē′kwə·lat′ər·əl) *n.* A side of equal length with another, or a figure with equal sides. — *adj.* Having all the sides equal. — **e′qui·lat′er·al·ly** *adv.*

equilateral hyperbola *Math.* A rectangular hyperbola.

e·qui·len·in (ē′kwə·len′in) *n. Biochem.* A sex hormone obtained from the urine of pregnant mares: a derivative of estrone. [<L *equus* horse]

e·quil·i·brant (i·kwil′ə·brənt) *n. Physics* A force or system of forces which, applied to a body, counteracts another force or system and produces equilibrium. [<F *équilibrant*, ppr. of *équilibrer* balance < *équilibre* <L *aequilibrium* equilibrium]

e·qui·li·brate (ē′kwə·lī′brāt, i·kwil′ə-) *v.t. & v.i.* **·brat·ed, ·brat·ing 1** To bring into or be in a state of equilibrium. **2** To counterpoise. [<L *aequilibratus* level < *aequus* equal + *libratus* level < *libra* a balance] — **e′qui·li·bra′tion** *n.*

e·qui·li·bra·tor (ē′kwə·lī′brā·tər, i·kwil′ə-) *n.* A device for establishing equilibrium.

e·quil·i·brist (i·kwil′ə·brist) *n.* One skilled in balancing, as a rope-walker. — **e·quil′i·bris′tic** *adj.*

e·qui·lib·ri·um (ē′kwə·lib′rē·əm) *n.* **1** A state of balance produced by the counteraction of two or more forces; equipoise. **2** *Physics* A condition of balance among forces acting within or upon a body or material system such that there is no change in the state of rest or motion of the system. **3** *Chem.*

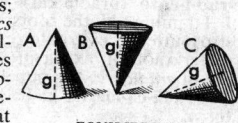

EQUILIBRIUM
A. Stable. B. Unstable.
C. Neutral.
g. Center of gravity.

The state in a chemical process when the components no longer react among themselves or react in such a way as to maintain a balanced condition. **4** Equal balance of the mind between conflicting or differing motives or reasons; hence, fairness of judgment; well-balanced state. Also **e′qui·lib′ri·ty.** [<L *aequilibrium* < *aequus* equal + *libra* a balance]

e·qui·mul·ti·ple (ē′kwə·mul′tə·pəl) *adj.* Produced by multiplying by the same number. — *n.* One of two or more products of different quantities by the same multiplier.

e·quine (ē′kwīn) *adj.* Of, pertaining to, or like a horse. — *n.* A horse, or a related animal. [<L *equinus* < *equus* horse]

equine syphilis Dourine.

e·qui·noc·tial (ē′kwə·nok′shəl) *adj.* **1** Occurring at or near the time when the sun crosses the celestial equator. **2** Of or pertaining to the equinox, or equality of day and night. **3** *Bot.* Opening and closing at regular hours: said of certain flowers, as the four-o'clock. **4** Of or pertaining to the equator or equatorial regions. — *n.* **1** *Meteorol.* A severe storm occurring usually at or near the equinox: also called, locally, *line storm.* **2** The equator. See EQUINOX. [<L *aequinoctialis* < *aequinox* EQUINOX]

equinoctial line The celestial equator.

equinoctial points The points of intersection of the equator and the ecliptic; the equinoxes.

equinoctial time Time reckoned from the moment at which the sun passes the vernal equinox.

e·qui·nox (ē′kwə·noks) *n.* One of two opposite points at which the sun crosses the celestial equator, when the days and nights are equal; also, the time of this crossing (about Mar. 21, the **vernal** or **spring equinox**, and Sept. 21, the **autumnal equinox**). [<L *aequinox* < *aequus* equal + *nox* night]

e·quip (i·kwip′) *v.t.* **e·quipped, e·quip·ping 1** To furnish or fit out with whatever is needed for any purpose or undertaking. **2** To dress or attire; array. [<F *équiper* <OF *esquiper*, prob. <ON *skipa* outfit a vessel < *skip* a ship]

eq·ui·page (ek′wə·pij) *n.* **1** The equipment for a camp, army, etc. **2** A carriage, with its horses, attendants, etc. **3** Imposing display; retinue. **4** *Archaic* A complete set, as of toilet articles, silverware, etc.; also, a case containing such a set. [<F *équiper* EQUIP]

e·qui·par·ti·tion (ē′kwə·pär·tish′ən) *n. Physics* **1** The balanced arrangement of atoms, as in a crystal. **2** That state of the molecules in a gas where they keep the same average distance apart under the same pressure. Also **equipartition of energy.**

e·quip·ment (i·kwip′mənt) *n.* **1** The act or process of equipping. **2** The state of being equipped or furnished. **3** Whatever constitutes an outfit for some special purpose or service. **4** Personal acquirements, as of an instructor, a diplomatist, etc. **5** The rolling stock and apparatus for operating a railroad or other transportation system, as distinguished from stations, trackage, and personnel.

equipment bond A railroad bond for which the rolling stock only is pledged.

equipment note A note issued to a railroad for the sole purpose of purchasing equipment, as locomotives, etc.

equipment trust The deed of trust securing an equipment bond.

e·qui·poise (ē′kwə·poiz, ek′wə-) *n.* **1** Equality or equal distribution, as of weight and power; equilibrium. **2** A counterpoise.

e·qui·pol·lence (ē′kwə·pol′əns) *n.* The state or quality of being equipollent. Also **e′qui·pol′len·cy.**

e·qui·pol·lent (ē′kwə·pol′ənt) *adj.* **1** Equal in weight, power, effect, etc.; equivalent. **2** Equivalent in meaning and force. **3** Equal and parallel. — *n.* An equivalent. [<F *équipollent* <L *aequipollens, -entis* < *aequus* equal + *pollere* be strong]

e·qui·pon·der·ance (ē′kwə·pon′dər·əns) *n.* Equality of weight; equipoise. — **e′qui·pon′der·ant** *adj.*

e·qui·pon·der·ate (ē′kwə·pon′də·rāt) *v.t.* **·at·ed, ·at·ing 1** To counterbalance. **2** To make balanced. [<Med. L *aequiponderatus*, pp. of *aequiponderare* <L *aequus* equal + *ponderare* weigh]

e·qui·po·ten·tial (ē′kwə·pō·ten′shəl) *adj.* **1** Having equal power or influence. **2** *Electr.* Of equal potential at all points.

e·qui·prob·a·ble (ē′kwə·prob′ə·bəl) *adj.* Having an equal chance of occurring or being selected, as any one of a group of numbers, objects, events, etc., forming part of a random array. Compare CHANCIFY. — **e′qui·prob·a·bil′i·ty** *n.*

eq·ui·se·tum (ek′wə·sē′təm) *n. pl.* **·se·ta** (-sē′tə) Any of a widely distributed genus (*Equisetum*) of rushlike, non-seed-bearing plants; the horsetail. [<NL <L *equus* horse + *saeta* bristle]

e·qui·so·nance (ē′kwə·sō′nəns) *n. Music* The consonance which exists between octaves.

e·qui·so·nant (ē′kwə·sō′nənt) *adj.* In ancient and medieval music, of like or equal sound, as a tone and its octave.

eq·ui·ta·ble (ek′wə·tə·bəl) *adj.* **1** Characterized by equity, or fairness and just dealing; impartial. **2** *Law* Of or pertaining to the principles of right and justice as administered by courts of equity, having relation to the system of rules and remedies enforced by those courts, as distinguished from courts of common law. **3** Within the cognizance of a court of equity. See synonyms under HONEST, JUST, RIGHT. [<F *équitable* < *équité* EQUITY] — **eq′ui·ta·ble·ness** *n.* — **eq′ui·ta·bly** *adv.*

eq·ui·tant (ek′wə·tənt) *adj. Bot.* Overlapping or riding, as leaves folded forward. [<L *equitans, -antis*, pp. of *equitare* ride on horseback < *eques, -itis* horseman < *equus* horse]

eq·ui·ta·tion (ek′wə·tā′shən) *n.* **1** Horsemanship. **2** The art of riding on horseback. [<L *equitatio, -onis* < *equitare.* See EQUITANT.]

eq·ui·tes (ek′wə·tēz) *n. pl.* The equestrian order of knights in ancient Rome, consisting originally of the mounted soldiers. [<L, pl. of *eques* horseman]

eq·ui·ty (ek′wə·tē) *n. pl.* **·ties 1** Fairness or impartiality; justness. **2** Something that is fair or equitable. **3** *Law* **a** Justice administered between litigants which is based on natural reason or ethical judgment. **b** That field of jurisprudence superseding the legal remedies of statute law and common law when these are considered inadequate or inflexible for the purposes of justice to the parties concerned. **c** A right recognized by a court of equity. **4** Value in excess of mortgage or other liens. See synonyms under JUSTICE. [<F *équité* <L *aequitas, -tatis* < *aequus* equal]

equity of redemption The equitable right accorded to a mortgagor to redeem his mortgaged premises on payment of the sum due, notwithstanding that the time appointed for payment has passed.

e·quiv·a·lence (i·kwiv′ə·ləns) *n.* **1** The state of being equivalent or of having equal values. **2** *Chem.* The property of having equal valences. **3** Valence. Also **e·quiv′a·len·cy.**

e·quiv·a·lent (i·kwiv′ə·lənt) *adj.* **1** Equal in value, force, meaning, or the like. **2** Equal in area or volume. **3** *Chem.* Having the same valence or the same combining weight. See synonyms under ALIKE, IDENTICAL, SYNONYMOUS. — *n.* **1** That which is equivalent; something equal in value, power, or effect. **2** *Chem.* **a** A number or amount representing one of the relative weights in which elements unite with each other to form compounds, or replace other elements in compounds. **b** The combining weight of an element, compound, or radical, or that weight which combines with or displaces

8 parts of oxygen or 1.008 parts of hydrogen. [<LL *aequivalens, -entis* ppr. of *aequivalere* < *aequus* equal + *valere* be worth] — **e·quiv′a·lent·ly** *adv.*

equivalent volt An electron volt.

e·quiv·o·cal (i·kwiv′ə·kəl) *adj.* 1 Having a doubtful meaning; susceptible of different interpretations. 2 Of uncertain significance, origin, character, or value; questionable. [<LL *aequivocus* ambiguous < *aequus* equal + *vox* voice] — **e·quiv′o·cal·ly** *adv.* — **e·quiv′o·cal·ness** *n.*

Synonyms: ambiguous, doubtful, dubious, enigmatic, enigmatical, indefinite, indeterminate, indistinct, obscure, perplexing, questionable, suspicious, uncertain. *Ambiguous* is applied only to spoken or written statements; *equivocal* has other applications. A statement is *ambiguous* when it causes the mind of the reader or hearer to fluctuate between two meanings, which would fit the language equally well; it is *equivocal* when it would naturally be understood in one way, but is capable of a different interpretation; an *equivocal* expression is, as a rule, intentionally deceptive, while an *ambiguous* utterance may result merely from a lack of clear thought or of adequate expression. That which is *enigmatical* must be guessed like a riddle. That is *doubtful* which is fairly open to doubt; that is *dubious* which has become the subject of doubts so grave as scarcely to fall short of condemnation; as a *dubious* reputation. *Questionable* may be used nearly in the sense either of *dubious* or of *doubtful*; a *questionable* statement is one that must be proved before it can be accepted. A *suspicious* character gives reason to be suspected; a *suspicious* temper is inclined to suspect the others, with or without reason. Compare CLEAR, PRECARIOUS. *Antonyms*: certain, clear, distinct, evident, indisputable, indubitable, lucid, manifest, obvious, perspicuous, plain, unambiguous, unequivocal, unquestionable, unquestioned.

e·quiv·o·cate (i·kwiv′ə·kāt) *v.i.* **·cat·ed, ·cat·ing** To use ambiguous language with intent to deceive. [<LL *aequivocatus*, pp. of *aequivocare* call by the same name < *aequivocus*. See EQUIVOCAL.]

e·quiv·o·ca·tion (i·kwiv′ə·kā′shən) *n.* 1 The act of equivocating. 2 A fallacy arising from the employment of a word of doubtful meaning. — **e·quiv′o·ca′tor** *n.* — **e·quiv′o·ca·to′ry** (-kə·tôr′ē, -tō′rē) *adj.*

eq·ui·voke (ek′wə·vōk) *n.* 1 An ambiguous term or expression; an equivocal word or phrase. 2 An equivocation. 3 A play upon words; pun. Also **eq′ui·voque.**

E·quu·le·us (i·kwōō′lē·əs) A southern constellation, near Aquarius. See CONSTELLATION.

er– Assimilated var. of EN–².

–er¹ *suffix of nouns* 1 A person or thing that performs the action of the root verb: *checker*. 2 A person concerned with or practicing a trade or profession: *glover*. 3 One who lives in or comes from: *New Yorker*. 4 A person, thing, or action related to or characterized by: *three-decker*. ◆ Nouns of agency are generally formed in English by adding **–er** to a verb, as in *leader*, but some such nouns, on analogy with those from French or Latin, are formed with **–or.** There is no definite rule regarding the use of these suffixes. [OE *-ere, -are*]

–er² *suffix of nouns* A person or thing concerned with, or related to: *jailer*. [<AF *-er*, OF *-ier* <L *-arius, -arium*]

–er³ *suffix* More: used in the comparative degree of adjectives and adverbs: *harder, later*. [OE *-ra, -or*]

–er⁴ *suffix* Repeatedly: used in frequentative verbs: *stutter*. [OE *-rian*]

–er⁵ *suffix* Denoting the action expressed by the root word: *waiver*: used mostly in legal terms. [<F *-er*, infinitive ending]

e·ra (ir′ə, ē′rə) *n.* 1 A historical period or reckoning of years, dating from some important event or fixed point of time; a period running from a fixed epoch established as the basis of a chronology. 2 A period of time characterized by some coextensive phenomenon or order of things, or social, intellectual, or physical conditions, etc. 3 A date or event from which time is reckoned; a time or age marked by a remarkable event; the beginning of a period; an epoch: the Christian *era*. 4 *Geol.* A division of geological history of highest rank: the Cenozoic *era*. See chart under GEOLOGY. [<LL *aera* counters; orig. pl. of *aes* brass, money]

e·ra·di·ate (i·rā′dē·āt) *v.t.* & *v.i.* **·at·ed, ·at·ing** To radiate. — **e·ra′di·a′tion** *n.*

e·rad·i·cate (i·rad′ə·kāt) *v.t.* **·cat·ed, ·cat·ing** 1 To pull up by the roots; root out. 2 To destroy utterly; extirpate; erase. See synonyms under ABOLISH, EXTERMINATE. [<L *eradicatus*, pp. of *eradicare* < *e-* out + *radix, -icis* a root] — **e·rad′i·ca·ble** (-ə·kə·bəl) *adj.* — **e·rad′i·ca′tor** *n.*

e·rad·i·ca·tion (i·rad′ə·kā′shən) *n.* Extirpation; extermination.

e·rad·i·ca·tive (i·rad′ə·kā′tiv) *adj.* Serving or tending to eradicate.

Era of Good Feeling The period of President Monroe's administration (1817–24), characterized by an absence of political dissension

e·rase (i·rās′) *v.t.* **e·rased, e·ras·ing** 1 To obliterate, as by scraping or rubbing out; efface. 2 *U.S. Slang* To kill. See synonyms under CANCEL. [<L *erasus*, pp. of *eradere* < *e-* out + *radere* scrape] — **e·ras′a·ble** *adj.*

e·ras·er (i·rā′sər) *n.* 1 One who or that which erases. 2 A sharp tool or a rubber for removing pencil or ink marks. 3 An oblong device of wood, felt, etc., for removing chalk marks.

e·ra·sion (i·rā′zhən) *n.* 1 The act of erasing; erasure. 2 *Surg.* The operation of scraping away diseased material; specifically, that of laying open a diseased joint and removing morbid tissue by scraping.

E·ras·mus (i·raz′məs, *Dan., Du., Ger.* ā·räs′mōōs; *Lat.* e·räs′məs) A masculine personal name. Also *Fr.* **É·rasme** (ā·rásm′), *Ital., Sp.* **E·ras·mo** (*Ital.* ā·räz′mō, *Sp.* ā·räs′mō). [< Greek, lovely]

E·ras·mus (i·raz′məs), **Desiderius,** 1466?–1536, Dutch scholar: original name *Geert Geerts.*

E·ras·tian·ism (i·ras′chən·iz′əm, -tē·ən-) *n.* The doctrine that the church is entirely subservient to the authority of the state. [after Thomas *Erastus*, to whom this doctrine is improperly attributed] — **E·ras′tian** *adj.* & *n.*

E·ras·tus (i·ras′təs), **Thomas,** 1524–83, Swiss Protestant theologian.

e·ra·sure (i·rā′shər, -zhər) *n.* 1 The act of erasing or the state of being erased. 2 Anything erased.

Er·a·to (er′ə·tō) The Muse of lyric and love poetry.

Er·a·tos·the·nes (er′ə·tos′thə·nēz), 276?–195? B.C., Greek astronomer and geographer.

Er·ber·to (er·ber′tō) Italian form of HERBERT.

Er·bil (ir′bil) A town in northern Iraq on the site of ancient Arbela. Also **Ar·bil** (ir′bil).

er·bi·um (ûr′bē·əm) *n.* A metallic element (symbol Er) of the lanthanide series, first isolated in crude form by C. G. Mosander in 1843. It is found in gadolinite and some other minerals. See ELEMENT. [<NL < *(Ytt)erby*, town in Sweden where first found]

Er·ci·yas Da·ği (er′jē·yäs′ dä·ē′) A mountain in central Turkey; 12,848 feet: ancient *Argaeus*. Formerly **Er′ji·as′.**

Erck·mann–Cha·tri·an (erk·màn′shà·trē·äṅ′) Joint pseudonym of **Émile Erckmann,** 1826–1899, and **Alexandre Chatrian,** 1826–90, French literary collaborators.

ere (âr) *Archaic & Poetic prep.* Prior to; before in time. — *conj.* 1 Earlier than; before. 2 Sooner than; rather than. [OE *ǣr*]

Er·e·bus (er′ə·bəs) In Greek mythology, a dark region under the earth through which the shades of the dead pass on their way to Hades.

Er·e·bus (er′ə·bəs), **Mount** A volcano on Ross Island, Antarctica; 13,200 feet.

Er·ech·the·um (er′ək·thē′əm) A temple to the tutelary deities of Athens on the Acropolis, completed about 407 B.C. and famous as an example of Ionic architecture. *Greek* **Er′ech·thei′on** (-thī′on).

E·rech·theus (i·rek′thyōōs, -thē·əs) A legendary king of Athens, honored at the Erechtheum.

e·rect (i·rekt′) *v.t.* 1 To construct, as a house; build. 2 To assemble the parts of; set up. 3 To set upright; lift up: to *erect* a flagpole. 4 To construct or establish; formulate, as a theory. 5 *Geom.* To draw upon a given base, as a geometrical figure. 6 *Optics* To cause (an inverted image) to become upright. 7 *Obs.* To raise to a higher position; exalt. See synonyms under CONSTRUCT, INSTITUTE, RAISE. — *adj.* 1 Upright in position, form, or person; vertical. 2 Directed upward. 3 Free from depression or humiliation. 4 Attentive; alert. [<L *erectus*, pp. of *erigere* < *e-* out + *regere* make straight] — **e·rect′ly** *adv.* — **e·rect′ness** *n.*

e·rec·tile (i·rek′təl, -til) *adj.* Susceptible of erection: *erectile* feathers. Also **e·rect′a·ble.** — **e′rec·til′i·ty** *n.*

e·rec·tion (i·rek′shən) *n.* 1 The act or process of building or constructing; also, the state of being erected. 2 A raising to and fixing in an upright position; a setting up. 3 A building or structure. 4 *Physiol.* **a** The raising up or stiffening of a part through the accumulation of blood in erectile tissue. **b** The state of being so raised and stiffened.

e·rec·tive (i·rek′tiv) *adj.* Tending to erect or raise.

e·rec·tor (i·rek′tər) *n.* 1 One who or that which erects. 2 *Anat.* Any of various muscles which stiffen or hold up a part of the body.

ere·long (âr′lông′, -long′) *adv.* Before much time has passed; soon.

er·e·ma·cau·sis (er′ə·mə·kô′sis) *n. Biochem.* The process of gradual decay by oxidation in animal or vegetable matter when in contact with air and moisture. [<NL <Gk. *ērema* slightly + *kausis* a burning < *kaiein* burn]

e·re·mic (i·rē′mik) *adj. Ecol.* Designating plant communities adapted to deserts and steppes. [<Gk. *erēmos* deserted]

er·e·mite (er′ə·mīt) *n.* A hermit. [<LL *eremita* <LGk. *erēmitēs* < *erēmia* a desert < *erēmos* deserted] — **er·e·mit·ic** (er′ə·mit′ik) or **·i·cal, er′e·mit′ish** (-mī′tish) *adj.*

er·e·mo·phil·i·a (er′ə·mō·fil′ē·ə, -fēl′yə) *n. Psychiatry* A morbid craving for solitude. [<NL <Gk. *erēmos* deserted + -PHILIA]

er·e·mo·phyte (er′ə·mō·fīt′) *n. Ecol.* Any individual of a society of desert plants. [<Gk. *erēmos* deserted + -PHYTE]

ere·now (âr′nou′) *adv.* Before this time; heretofore.

e·rep·sin (i·rep′sin) *n. Biochem.* An enzyme or group of associated enzymes found in the intestinal and pancreatic juices of animals: it splits peptones into amino acids and ammonia. Also **e·rep′tase** (-tās). [<L *ereptus*, pp. of *eripere* set free + *-sin*, as in *pepsin*] — **e·rep′tic** *adj.*

er·e·thism (er′ə·thiz′əm) *n. Physiol.* Abnormal excitability or irritability in any part of the body. [<Gk. *erethismos* < *erethizein* irritate] — **er′e·this′mic** *adj.*

ere·while (âr′hwīl′) *adv. Archaic* Some time ago; heretofore. Also **ere′whiles′.**

Er·furt (er′fōōrt) A city in Thuringia, central Germany.

erg (ûrg) *n. Physics* In the cgs system, the unit of work and of energy, being the work done in moving a body one centimeter against the force of one dyne. See UNIT. Also **er·gon** (ûr′gon). [<Gk. *ergon* work]

er·gas·the·ni·a (ûr′gəs·thē′nē·ə, -thēn′yə) *n.* A condition of debility and exhaustion from overwork. — **er′gas·then′ic** (-then′ik) *adj.*

er·ga·tes (ûr′gə·tēz) *n. Entomol.* A worker ant. [<Gk. *ergatēs* workman]

er·go (ûr′gō) *conj.* & *adv. Latin* Hence; therefore. [<L]

ergo– *combining form* Work; of or related to work: *ergometer*. Also, before vowels, **erg–.** [<Gk. *ergon* work]

er·go·gen·ic (ûr′gō·jen′ik) *adj.* Tending to increase the quantity of work done under given conditions.

er·go·graph (ûr′gō·graf, -gräf) *n. Physiol.* An instrument for registering on a moving drum the movement of a finger or a contracting muscle in doing work: used as an index of mental excitement, fatigue, etc.

er·gom·e·ter (ûr·gom′ə·tər) *n. Physiol.* An apparatus, as a geared bicycle wheel, for measuring the metabolism rate or the amount of energy expended in doing work.

er·go·nom·ics (ûr′gə·nom′iks) *n.* The study of the relationship between man and his working environment, with special reference to anatomical, physiological, and psychological factors; human engineering. [<ERGO- + (ECO)NOMICS] — **er′go·nom′ic** *adj.*

er·go·phile (ûr′gō·fīl, -fil) *n.* A lover of work.

er·gos·ter·ol (ûr·gos′tə·rōl) *n. Biochem.* An inert sterol, $C_{28}H_{44}O$, obtained from ergot, yeast, and certain other plants: irradiation by sunlight or ultraviolet light converts it into vitamin D_2. [<ERGO(T) + STEROL]

er·got (ûr′gət) *n.* 1 A fungus *(Claviceps purpurea)* that sometimes takes the place of the grain in rye and other grasses; it yields several

alkaloids which are used medicinally in parturition. **2** The disease of rye and other cereal grasses caused by this growth. **3** The dried sclerotia of rye ergot, used in medicine to contract muscle fibers, especially those of the uterus, in order to check hemorrhage. [<F <OF *argot* spur of a cock] **—er'got·ed** *adj.*

er·got·in·ine (ûr·got'ə·nēn, -nin) *n. Chem.* A crystalline alkaloid, $C_{35}H_{39}N_5O_5$, obtained from ergot; used in medicine.

er·got·ism (ûr'gə·tiz'əm) *n.* **1** *Pathol.* A morbid condition produced by excessive doses of ergot; poisoning from ergotized grain. **2** The formation of ergot in grasses.

Er·hard (er'härt), **Ludwig,** 1897–1977, German statesman; chancellor of the West German Republic, 1963–66.

Er·ic (er'ik) A masculine personal name. [< Scand., ever king]

—Eric the Red Scandinavian navigator; discovered and colonized Greenland around 983.

er·i·ca·ceous (er'ə·kā'shəs) *adj. Bot.* Of or relating to the heath family *(Ericaceae)* of trees, shrubs, or herbs, natives of temperate or cold climates, including the azalea, rhododendron, wintergreen, mountain laurel, etc. [<NL *Ericaceae* <*Erica*, name of a genus <L *erica* heath <Gk. *ereikē*]

Er·ic·son (er'ik·sən), **Leif** Norse rover; son of Eric the Red; probable discoverer of North America about A.D. 1000. Also **Er'ics·son.**

Er·ics·son (er'ik·sən), **John,** 1803–89, U.S. engineer born in Sweden; invented the screw propeller.

E·rid·a·nus (i·rid'ə·nəs) A southern constellation, containing the bright star Achernar. See CONSTELLATION. [<L, the Po river]

E·rie (ir'ē) A port in Pennsylvania on Lake Erie.

E·rie (ir'ē) *n. pl.* **E·rie** or **E·ries** One of a tribe of North American Indians of Iroquoian stock, formerly inhabiting the southern shores of Lake Erie.

Erie, Lake The southernmost and fourth largest of the Great Lakes; 241 by 57 miles; 9,940 square miles.

Erie Canal A historic waterway in New York, extending 350 miles from Buffalo on Lake Erie to Albany on the Hudson River; now part of the *New York State Barge Canal.*

E·rig·e·na (i·rij'ə·nə), **Johannes Scotus** Irish philosopher of the ninth century.

e·rig·er·on (i·rij'ə·ron) *n.* Any plant of a large genus *(Erigeron)* of mainly North American weedy herbs of the composite family, usually bearing solitary heads with numerous violet, purple, or white ray flowers. Certain species, as *E. canadensis,* yield **oil of erigeron,** used as a hemostatic drug. [<L, groundsel <Gk. *ērigerōn* <*ēri* early + *gerōn* old man; with ref. to a hoary growth on some species]

Er·in (âr'in, ir'in) *Poetic* Ireland.

er·i·na·ceous (er'ə·nā'shəs) *adj.* Of or like a hedgehog. [<L *erinaceus* hedgehog]

e·rin·go (i·ring'gō) See ERYNGO.

E·rin·y·es (i·rin'i·ēz) *pl. of* **E·rin·ys** (i·rin'is, i·rī'nis) In Greek mythology, the Furies. [<L <Gk. *Erinys*]

er·i·om·e·ter (er'ē·om'ə·tər) *n.* An instrument for measuring by diffraction the diameters of very small objects. [<Gk. *erion* wool, fibre + -METER] **—er'i·om'e·try** *n.*

E·ris (ir'is, er'is) In Greek mythology, the sister of Ares, and goddess of discord.

e·ris·tic (e·ris'tik) *adj.* **1** Relating to controversy. **2** Prone to dispute: also **e·ris'ti·cal.** **—***n.* **1** A person given to controversy. **2** A scholar of Euclid's Eristic or Megarian school of philosophy. [<Gk. *eristikos* <*eris* strife]

E·ri·tre·a (er'i·trē'ə) An autonomous state in eastern Africa on the Red Sea, federated with Ethiopia; formerly an Italian colony; 45,754 square miles; capital, Asmara. **—Er'i·tre'an** *adj. & n.*

Er·i·van (er'i·vän'y') The capital of Armenian S.S.R.: Armenian *Yerevan.*

Er·land·er (er'län·dər), **Tage Fritiof,** born 1901, Swedish political leader.

Er·lang·en (er'läng·ən) A city in north central Bavaria, Germany.

Er·lan·ger (der·län·zhā'), **Baron Frederic d',** 1868–1943, British composer born in France.

Er·lang·er (ûr'lang·ər), **Joseph,** 1874–1965, U.S. physiologist.

Er·len·mey·er flask (ûr'lən·mī'ər) A conical glass flask with a narrow neck and very broad base, extensively used in laboratory work in chemistry, physiology, and medicine. [after Emil *Erlenmeyer,* 1825–1909, German chemist]

erl·king (ûrl'king') *n.* In Teutonic folklore, the king of the elves, malicious toward children.

Er·man·no (er·män'nō) The Italian form of HERMAN.

er·mine (ûr'min) *n.* **1** A long-bodied, slender, voracious weasel (genus *Mustela)* of the northern hemisphere; the stoat, especially in its winter dress, which is white, with a black tail tip. **2** Its fur, used in Europe for the facings of official robes, as of judges. **3** The judicial office or its ideal purity. [<OF *(h)ermine,* ? <Gmc.] **—er'mined** *adj.*

ERMINE
(Body: 9 to 12 inches; tail: 3 to 3 1/2 inches)

ermine moth A moth *(Yponomeuta padella),* whose larvae destroy the foliage of apple and related trees.

er·myte (er'mit) *n. Obs.* A hermit.

erne (ûrn) *n.* A sea eagle (genus *Haliaetus*). Also **ern.** ◆ Homophones: *earn, urn.* [OE *earn*]

Er·nest (ûr'nist, *Fr.* er·nest') A masculine personal name. Also *Dan., Ger., Sw.* **Ernst** (ernst), *Du.* **Er·nes·tus** (er·nes'to͝os), *Ital., Sp.* **Er·nes·to** (er·nes'tō). [<Gmc., serious]

Ernst (ûrnst; *Ger.* ernst), **Max,** born 1891, German painter, in the U.S. since 1941.

e·rode (i·rōd') *v.* **e·rod·ed, e·rod·ing** *v.t.* **1** To eat or wear into or away. **2** *Geol.* To wear down, as rocks, soil, etc., by the action of wind, water, and other agencies; also, to form, as a canyon, by such action. **—***v.i.* **3** To become eroded. [<L *erodere* <*e-* off + *rodere* gnaw]

e·ro·dent (i·rōd'nt) *adj.* **1** Causing erosion. **2** Caustic, as certain drugs. **—***n.* A caustic drug; that which erodes or burns away. [<L *erodens, -entis,* ppr. of *erodere.* See ERODE.]

e·rog·e·nous (i·roj'ə·nəs) *adj.* Producing erotic feeling; exciting sexual desire. Also **er·o·gen·ic** (er'ə·jen'ik). [<Gk. *erōs* love, + -GENOUS]

Er·os (ir'os, er'os) **1** In Greek mythology, the god of love, youngest of the gods, son of Aphrodite and Zeus, Ares, or Hermes; identified with the Roman *Cupid.* **2** *Astron.* An asteroid of the sixth magnitude, discovered in 1898, and used in determination of the distance of the sun from the earth. **3** *Psychoanal.* **a** The libido. **b** The sum total of the life-preserving and self-preserving instincts: opposed to *Thanatos.*

e·rose (i·rōs') *adj.* **1** Appearing as if gnawed. **2** *Bot.* Having an irregularly toothed margin, as some leaves. [<L *erosus,* pp. of *erodere.* See ERODE.]

e·ro·sion (i·rō'zhən) *n.* **1** *Geol.* The wearing away of materials, as rocks by wind and water; denudation. **2** *Med.* The eating away of body tissue, bone, etc.

e·ro·sive (i·rō'siv) *adj.* **1** Having the power or property of gnawing or wearing away. **2** Acting by erosion: an *erosive* acid.

e·rot·ic (i·rot'ik) *adj.* Of or pertaining to passionate love; amorous; amatory: also **e·rot'i·cal.** **—***n.* **1** An amatory poem. **2** A theory or science of love: also **e·rot'ics. 3** An erotic person. [<Gk. *erōtikos*<*erōs* love] **—e·rot'i·cal·ly** *adv.*

e·rot·i·ca (i·rot'i·kə) *n. pl.* Erotic pictures, books, etc. [<Gk. *erōtika,* neut. pl. of *erōtikos* EROTIC]

e·rot·i·cism (i·rot'ə·siz'əm) *n.* Erotic tendency or character.

er·o·tism (er'ə·tiz'əm) *n.* **1** Eroticism. **2** *Psychoanal.* Sexual life in all its phases of physical and mental development and manifestations.

e·ro·to·ma·ni·a (i·rō'tə·mā'nē·ə, i·rot'ə-) *n.* **1** *Psychiatry* A morbid propensity to love or make love; uncontrollable sexual desire. **2** Melancholia caused by love.

err (ûr) *v.i.* **erred, err·ing 1** To make a mistake; be wrong. **2** To go astray morally; sin. **3** *Obs.* To wander; stray. See synonyms under WANDER. [<OF *errer* <L *errare* wander]

er·ran·cy (er'ən·sē) *n.* **1** The condition of erring or of containing errors. **2** Liability to err.

er·rand (er'ənd) *n.* **1** A trip or journey made to carry a message or do a commission. **2** The object of a going or coming; the business or commission to be done or message to be given by a messenger. [OE *ǣrende* message, news]

er·rant (er'ənt) *adj.* **1** Roving or wandering. **2** Erring; erratic. **3** *Obs.* See ARRANT. [<OF *errant,* ppr. of *errer* travel <L *iter* a journey; infl. by OF *errant* <*errer* wander. See ERR.] **—er'rant·ly** *adv.*

er·rant·ry (er'ənt·rē) *n.* The vocation, conduct, or career of a knight errant; knight-errantry.

er·ra·re hu·ma·num est (e·rā'rē hyo͞o·mā'·nəm est) *Latin* To err is human.

er·ra·ta (i·rā'tə, e·rä'tə) Plural of ERRATUM.

er·rat·ic (i·rat'ik) *adj.* **1** Not conforming to rules or standards; irregular; eccentric. **2** Wandering; straying. **3** *Geol.* Transported from the original site by natural agencies: *erratic* rocks or gravel. Also **er·rat'i·cal.** See synonyms under IRREGULAR, QUEER. [<L *erraticus* <*errare* wander] **—er·rat'i·cal·ly** *adv.*

er·ra·tum (i·rā'təm, e·rä'-) *n. pl.* **·ra·ta** (-rā'tə, -rä'tə) An error, as in writing or printing. [< L]

er·rhine (er'in, -in) *adj. Med.* Promotive of sneezing and nasal discharges. **—***n.* A medicine to be snuffed; a sternutatory. [<NL *errhinum* <Gk. *errhinon* <*en-* in + *rhis, rhinos* nose]

err·ing (ûr'ing, er'ing) *adj.* **1** Sinning; doing wrong. **2** In error; wrong. **—err'ing·ly** *adv.*

er·ro·ne·ous (ə·rō'nē·əs, e·rō'-) *adj.* Marked by error; incorrect; mistaken. **—er·ro'ne·ous·ly** *adv.* **—er·ro'ne·ous·ness** *n.*

er·ror (er'ər) *n.* **1** The condition of erring, or going astray from the truth, especially in matters of opinion or belief; also, deviation from a right standard of judgment or conduct, as through ignorance or inadvertence; mistake. **2** Something done, said, or believed wrongly; a deviation from correctness or accuracy, or from truth. **3** Any misplay in baseball which prolongs the batsman's time at bat or permits a base runner to make one or more bases. Misplays, as a passed ball or a wild pitch, made by catcher or pitcher, are not scored as *errors.* **4** A violation or neglect of duty; transgression; sin. **5** *Math.* **a** The difference between the observed value of a magnitude and the true or mean value as determined by a series of measurements of the same quantity. **b** Any deviation from the true or mean value not due to gross blunders of observation and measurement. **6** In Christian Science, the contradiction of truth; a belief without understanding; that which seems and is not. [<OF <L < *errare* wander]

Synonyms: balk, blunder, fallacy, falsity, fault, hallucination, mistake, omission, oversight, unsoundness. See DELUSION, FOIBLE.

ers (ûrs) *n.* See under VETCH. [<F <L *ervum*]

er·satz (er·zäts') *n.* A substitute; equivalent; replacement, usually inferior to the original product or material. **—***adj.* Substitute. [<G <*ersetzen* replace]

Erse (ûrs) *n.* **1** Scottish Gaelic. **2** Irish Gaelic. [Var. of IRISH]

Er·skine (ûr'skin), **John,** 1695–1768, Scottish jurist. **—John,** 1879–1951, U.S. educator and writer. **—Lord Thomas,** 1750–1823, first Baron of Restormel, lord chancellor of England.

erst (ûrst) *Archaic adv.* **1** Formerly; long ago; once. **2** In the beginning. **—***adj.* First. [OE *ǣrest*]

erst·while (ûrst'hwīl') *adj.* Former. **—***adv. Archaic* Formerly.

er·u·bes·cence (er'o͞o·bes'əns) *n. Med.* The process or condition of growing red; redness; blush. Also **er'u·bes'cen·cy.** [<LL *erubescentia* <L *erubescere* blush] **—er'u·bes'cent** *adj.*

e·ruct (i·rukt') *v.t. & v.i.* To belch. Also **e·ruc'·** [<L *eructare* <*e-* out + *ructare* belch]

e·ruc·ta·tion (i·ruk'tā'shən, ē'ruk-, er'ək-) *n.* **1** The act of belching. **2** That which is thrown off in belching. [<L *eructatus,* pp. of

eructare. See ERUCT.] **—e·ruc·ta·tive** (i·ruk′·tə·tiv) *adj.*

er·u·dite (er′yōō·dīt, er′ōō-) *adj.* Very learned; scholarly. [< L *eruditus,* pp. of *erudire* instruct < *e-* out + *rudis* untrained] **—er′u·dite·ly** *adv.* **—er′u·dite·ness** *n.*

er·u·di·tion (er′yōō·dish′ən, -ōō-) *n.* **1** Extensive knowledge of history, literature, languages, etc.; accomplished scholarship. **2** *Obs.* The act of instructing. See synonyms under KNOWLEDGE, LEARNING, WISDOM. **—er′u·di′tion·al** *adj.*

e·ru·gi·nous (i·rōō′jə·nəs) *adj.* See AERUGINOUS. [< L *aeruginosus* < *aerugo, -inis* copper rust < *aes* copper]

e·rum·pent (i·rum′pənt) *adj. Bot.* Bursting forth, as if through the epidermis, as the spore clusters of certain fungi. [< L *erumpens, -entis,* ppr. of *erumpere.* See ERUPT.]

e·rupt (i·rupt′) *v.i.* **1** To cast forth smoke, lava, etc., suddenly and with violence: The volcano *erupted.* **2** To be thrown forth: Steam is *erupting* from the volcano. **3** *Dent.* To become visible in the mouth, as teeth. *—v.t.* **4** To cause to burst forth. [< L *eruptus,* pp. of *erumpere* < *e-* out + *rumpere* burst]

e·rup·tion (i·rup′shən) *n.* **1** A breaking forth with violence; bursting out. **2** That which bursts forth, as lava from a volcano. **3** A breaking out, as in a rash. **4** Any sudden outbreak, as of armed forces.

e·rup·tive (i·rup′tive) *adj.* Pertaining or tending to eruption. **—e·rup′tive·ly** *adv.* **—e·rup′·tive·ness** *n.*

Er·vine (ûr′vin), **St. John Greer,** 1883–1971, Irish novelist and playwright.

-ery *suffix of nouns* **1** A business, place of business, or place where something is done: *brewery.* **2** A place or residence for: *nunnery.* **3** A collection of goods, wares, etc.: *pottery*; or things pertaining to: *popery.* **4** The qualities, principles, or practices of: *snobbery.* **5** An art, trade, or profession: *cookery.* **6** A state, or condition of being: *slavery.* Also *-ry,* as in *jewelry.* [< OF *-erie* < *-ier* (< L *-arius*) + *-ie* < L *-ia.* See -ARY, -Y[2].]

Er·y·man·thi·an Boar (er′ə·man′thē·ən) In Greek mythology, a savage boar captured alive by Hercules.

Er·y·man·thus (er′ə·man′thəs), **Mount** A mountain between Arcadia and Achaea in Greece. **—Er′y·man′thi·an** *adj.*

e·ryn·go (i·ring′gō) *n.* **1** Any of various coarse herbs of the genus *Eryngium*: the roots are used in medicine. **2** *Obs.* The candied root of sea eryngo *(E. maritimum),* formerly deemed an aphrodisiac. Also spelled *eringo.* [? Alter. of Ital. *eringio* < L *eryngion* < Gk. *eryngion* < *eryngos*]

er·y·sip·e·las (er′ə·sip′ə·ləs, ir′ə-) *n. Pathol.* An acute inflammatory disease of the skin, due to infection by various strains of streptococcus and accompanied by fever. [< NL < Gk., ? < *erysis* a reddening + *pella* skin] **—er·y·si·pel·a·tous** (er′ə·si·pel′ə·təs, ir′ə-), **er′y·sip′·e·lat′ic** (-lat′ik), **er′y·sip′e·lous** *adj.*

er·y·sip·e·loid (er′ə·sip′ə·loid, ir′ə-) *n. Pathol.* A localized dermatitis caused by infection with a bacterium (genus *Erysipelothrix*).

Er·y·thei·a (er′ə·thē′ə) **1** In classical geography, the westernmost point of the known world: an island beyond the pillars of Hercules. **2** One of the Hesperides.

er·y·the·ma (er′ə·thē′mə) *n. Pathol.* **1** A superficial skin disease characterized by abnormal redness, but without swelling or fever. **2** Abnormal redness of the cheek in hectic fever. [< NL < Gk. *erythēma* redness < *erythros* red] **—er′y·them′a·tous** (-them′ə·təs, -thē′mə-), **er′y·the·mat′ic** (-thi·mat′ik), **er′y·the′mic** *adj.*

Er·y·thrae (er′i·thrē) An ancient Ionian city in Asia Minor. Also **Er′y·thræ. —Er′y·thrae′an** *adj.* & *n.*

Er·y·thrae·an Sea (er′i·thrē′ən) An ancient name for the RED SEA.

er·y·thre·an (er′i·thrē′ən) *adj.* Red. Also **er′y·thrae′an.** [< L *erythraeus* < Gk. *erythraios* < *erythros* red]

e·ryth·rin (i·rith′rin) *n. Chem.* A crystalline compound, $C_{20}H_{22}O_{10}$, contained in various lichens, as *Rocella tinctoria,* from which it is extracted by milk of lime. Also **e·ryth′rine.**

e·ryth·rism (i·rith′riz·əm) *n.* **1** Morbid fondness for red. **2** Abnormal or excessive redness, especially when exhibited by certain dichromatic birds, as the screech owl, which has two distinct plumage phases, one grayish and the other red. **—er·y·thris·mal** (er′ə·thriz′məl), **er′y·thris′tic** *adj.*

e·ryth·rite (i·rith′rīt) *n.* **1** A crimson and peach-red transparent, hydrous cobalt arsenate, found amorphous and also crystallized in the monoclinic system; cobalt bloom. **2** Erythritol.

e·ryth·ri·tol (i·rith′rə·tōl, -tol) *n. Chem.* Any of three isomeric compounds, $C_4H_{10}O_4$, contained in certain algae and lichens, especially one occurring as a white, crystalline saccharide alcohol.

erythro- *combining form* Red: *erythrocyte.* Also, before vowels, **erythr-.** [< Gk. *erythros* red]

e·ryth·ro·blast (i·rith′rō·blast) *n. Anat.* One of the colored ameboid cells from which the red corpuscles of the blood are believed to be developed: found in the red marrow of bones.

e·ryth·ro·ca·tal·y·sis (i·rith′rō·kə·tal′ə·sis) *n.* Destruction of red blood corpuscles by phagocytes.

e·ryth·ro·chlo·ro·pi·a (i·rith′rō·klôr′ə·pē′ə, -klō′·rə-) *n. Pathol.* A visual defect which allows correct perception only of red and green. Also **e·ryth′ro·chlo·rop′si·a** (-klô·rop′sē·ə, -klō·rop′-). [< ERYTHRO- + CHLOR(O)- + -OPIA]

e·ryth·ro·cyte (i·rith′rō·sīt) *n. Anat.* A red blood cell, formed in the red bone marrow and, in all mammals, lacking a nucleus: it contains hemoglobin and transports oxygen to all tissues of the body. **—e·ryth′ro·cyt′ic** (-sit′ik) *adj.*

e·ryth·ro·cy·tom·e·ter (i·rith′rō·sī·tom′ə·tər) *n.* A device for counting erythrocytes.

e·ryth·ro·cy·to·sis (i·rith′rō·sī·tō′sis) *n. Pathol.* An excessive increase in the number of red blood corpuscles in the circulatory system.

e·ryth·ro·dex·trin (i·rith′rō·dek′strin) *n. Biochem.* A dextrin produced by the action of saliva on starch: it turns red on contact with iodine.

er·y·throl (er′ə·thrōl, -thrôl) *n.* A crystalline alkaloid, $C_4H_{10}O_4$, found in certain lichens: the compound **erythrol tetranitrate** is used medicinally as a substitute for amyl nitrite and nitroglycerin in heart ailments, and also in explosives as a detonator.

e·ryth·ro·me·lal·gi·a (i·rith′rō·mə·lal′jē·ə) *n. Pathol.* A nervous disease of the extremities, characterized by persistent redness on the soles of the feet or palms of the hands, with burning pain. [< ERYTHRO- + Gk. *melos* limb + -ALGIA]

er·y·throph·i·lous (er′ə·throf′ə·ləs) *adj. Biol.* Having an affinity for red coloring matter.

e·ryth·ro·pho·bi·a (i·rith′rō·fō′bē·ə) *n.* A morbid fear of the color red; specifically, fear of blushing. **—e·ryth′ro·pho′bic** *adj.*

e·ryth·ro·phyll (i·rith′rō·fil) See ANTHOCYANIN.

Erz·ber·ger (erts′ber·gər), **Matthias,** 1875–1921, German political leader; signer of the armistice at Compiègne, 1918.

Erz·ge·bir·ge (erts′gə·bir′gə) A mountain range on the Bohemia-Saxony border; highest peak, 4,080 feet: English *Ore Mountains.*

Er·zu·rum (er′zə·rōōm) A province of NE Turkey; 9,244 square miles; capital, Erzurum. Also **Er′ze·rum.**

Es *Chem.* Einsteinium (symbol Es).

es- *prefix* Out: used in words borrowed into English from Old French: *escape, escheat.* It was often later refashioned to *ex-* after Latin, as in *exchange,* formerly *eschange.* [< OF < L *ex-.* See EX-[1].]

-es[1] An inflectional ending used to form the plural of nouns ending in a sibilant *(glasses, fuses, fishes)* or an affricate *(witches, judges).* After such consonants it is pronounced as a separate syllable; after vowels, as in *potatoes,* it merely extends the syllable. [OE *-as*]

-es[2] An inflectional ending used to form the third person singular present indicative of verbs ending in a sibilant, affricate, or vowel: *goes, kisses, poaches.* [ME *-es*]

E·sai·as (*Lat.* e·sä′yəs; *Dan.* ā·sī′äs; *Ger.* ā·zä′·yäs) See ISAIAH.

E·sau (ē′sô) A masculine personal name. Also *Fr.* **E·sa·u** (ā·zä·ü′), *Lat.* **E·sa·vus** (e·sä′vəs). [< Hebrew, hairy]

—Esau Eldest son of Isaac; sold his birthright to his brother Jacob. *Gen.* xxv 25.

es·ca·drille (es′kə·dril′, *Fr.* es·kȧ·drē′y′) *n.* **1** In France, a unit of six military airplanes. **2** A squadron of naval vessels. [< F, dim. of *escadre* a squadron; infl. by Sp. *escuadrilla,* dim. of *escuadra* a squadron; both ult. < L *ex-* completely + *quadrare* make square < *quattuor* four]

es·ca·lade (es′kə·lād′) *v.t.* **·lad·ed, ·lad·ing** To attack and force a way into or over (a fort, rampart, etc.) by means of ladders. *—n.* An attack by escalading. [< F < Sp. *escalada* < *escalar* climb < L *scala* a ladder]

Es·ca·lan·te (ās′kä·län′tā) A municipality in NE Negros island, Philippines.

es·ca·late (es′kə·lāt) *v.t.* & *v.i.* **·lat·ed, ·lat·ing 1** To ascend or raise on an escalator. **2** To increase or be increased in a gradual manner. **3** To determine the upward trend of material and labor costs in adjusting (price contracts). [Back formation from ESCALATOR] **—es′ca·la′tion** *n.*

Es·ca·la·tor (es′kə·lā′tər) *n.* A moving stairway, built on the endless-chain principle, used in stores, railroad stations, etc.: a trade name. [< ESCAL(ADE) + (ELEV)ATOR]

escalator clause A clause in a contract stipulating an increase or decrease in wages, prices, etc., under certain specified conditions.

es·cal·lop (e·skol′əp, -skal′-), **es·cal·op** See SCALLOP.

es·ca·pade (es′kə·pād) *n.* **1** An act in reckless disregard of propriety; a mischievous prank. **2** An escape from restraint. **3** *Obs.* A plunging or kicking, as of a horse. [< F < Sp. *escapada* < *escapar* escape]

es·cape (ə·skāp′, e·skāp′) *v.* **es·caped, es·cap·ing** *v.t.* **1** To get away from; flee from, as guards or prison. **2** To avoid, as harm or evil. **3** To be uttered involuntarily; slip from: No cry *escaped* him. **4** To slip away from or elude (notice or recollection); fail to be understood or remembered. *—v.i.* **5** To get free from or avoid arrest, custody, danger, etc. **6** To elude notice or recollection. **7** To come forth; emerge; leak: Gas is *escaping* from the stove. **8** *Bot.* To grow wild, as a newly introduced plant. *—n.* **1** A successful flight from, or evasion of, custody, pursuit, danger, injury, or annoyance. **2** Mental relief from monotony, anxiety, etc.: literature of *escape.* **3** Issue, as of a fluid; leakage. **4** *Bot.* Any plant formerly cultivated that now grows wild in fields. **5** *Obs.* An outburst; sally. **6** *Obs.* An inadvertence; act of transgression. [< AF *escaper* < L *ex-* out + *cappa* a cloak] **—es·cap′er** *n.*

Synonyms (verb): abscond, avoid, decamp, depart, elude, evade, flee, fly, shun. To *escape* is to get away clear; to *flee* or *fly* is to attempt it, with or without success; to *abscond* is both to *flee* and to hide, or at least to seek concealment and obscurity. To *escape* may be noble and worthy; to *abscond* is ordinarily an act of cowardice and guilt. See AVOID.

escape cock *Mech.* **1** A cock or bearing in a watch to support the escape wheel. **2** A cock or faucet in an engine cylinder to draw off condensed steam.

escape hatch A means of exit, as from an aircraft, submarine, etc., for use in emergencies.

escape lung A respiratory device for underwater breathing, especially in escaping from submarines: it consists of a tightly fitting mask with a nose clamp, connected with an oxygen-filled rubber chamber and a canister of powdered charcoal or other adsorbent material.

escape mechanism *Psychol.* The process whereby the mind evades its problems, anxieties, responsibilities, etc.

es·cape·ment (ə·skāp′mənt, e·skāp′-) *n.* **1** *Mech.* A device used in timepieces for securing a uniform movement, consisting of an escape wheel and a detent or lock, through which periodical impulses are imparted to the balance wheel, to keep it in oscillation, and to which, in turn, motion is imparted by the return movement of the balance wheel actuated by a mainspring or a weight. **2** *Obs.* The act of escaping; an escape or a means of escape; a vent.

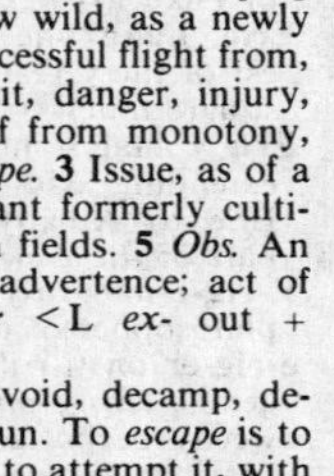

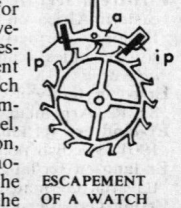

ESCAPEMENT OF A WATCH
a. Anchor.
l. Lever or fork.
ip. Impulse pallet.
lp. Locking pallet.
r. Roller.

escape wheel A toothed wheel in an escape-

ment: also called *scape wheel*. See illustration under PENDULUM.

es·cap·ist (ə·skā′pist, e·skā′-) *adj.* Offering or intended to offer relief from unpleasant or monotonous realities of life: *escapist* drama; *escapist* novels. — *n.* One who seeks to avoid the realities of life. — **es·cap′ism** *n.*

es·car·got (es·kär·gō′) *n. French* A snail, especially one of an edible variety.

es·carp (es·kärp′) *n.* The inner wall or side of the ditch at the foot of a rampart: distinguished from *counterscarp*, the further or outer side. See illustration under BASTION. — *v.t.* 1 To cause to slope steeply. 2 To provide with a scarp. [<F <Ital. *scarpa* a scarp]

es·carp·ment (es·kärp′mənt) *n.* 1 A precipitous artificial slope about a fortification or position. 2 A steep slope; the precipitous face of a more or less extended line of cliffs: sometimes called *scarp*.

Es·caut (es·kō′) The French name for the SCHELDT.

-esce *suffix of verbs* To become or grow; begin to be or do (what is indicated by the main element): *phosphoresce*. [<L *-escere,* suffix of inceptive verbs]

-escence *suffix of nouns* Forming nouns of state or quality corresponding to adjectives in *-escent*: *effervescence.* [<L *-escentia*]

-escent *suffix of adjectives* Beginning to be, have, or do (what is indicated by the main element): *effervescent.* [<L *-escens, -escentis,* suffix of ppr. of inceptive verbs]

esch·a·lot (esh′ə·lot, esh′ə·lot′) *n. Rare* A shallot. [<F *eschalotte,* dim. of *eschaloigne* an onion]

es·char (es′kär) *n. Med.* The dry crust produced by mortification or cauterization; a slough or scab. [<L *eschara* <Gk. *eschara* a hearth]

es·cha·rot·ic (es′kə·rot′ik) *adj. Med.* Able to destroy living tissue and form an eschar; caustic. — *n.* A powerful caustic.

es·cha·tol·o·gy (es′kə·tol′ə·jē) *n.* The branch of theology that treats of death, resurrection, immortality, the end of the world, final judgment, and the future state. [<Gk. *eschatos* last + -LOGY] — **es′cha·to·log′ic** (-tə·loj′ik) or **-i·cal** *adj.* — **es′cha·tol′o·gist** *n.*

es·cheat (es·chēt′) *Law v.t. & v.i.* To revert, or cause to revert, to the state or crown. — *n.* 1 The reversion of lands, in the United States to the state, in England to the crown, in default of heirs or devisees. 2 In feudal law, reversion of an estate to the lord of the fee on failure of heirs or service. 3 Forfeiture of property, real or personal, for default; confiscation. [<OF *eschete, escheoite* <*escheoir* <*es-* out <(L *ex-*) + *cheoir* <*cadere* fall] — **es·cheat′a·ble** *adj.* — **es·cheat′age** *n.*

Esch·en·bach (esh′ən·bäkh), **Wolfram von** See WOLFRAM VON ESCHENBACH.

es·chew (es·chōo′) *v.t.* To shun, as something unworthy or injurious. [<OF *eschiver,* ult. <Gmc. Akin to SHY[1].] — **es·chew′al** *n.*

Esch·scholt·zi·a (e·shōlt′sē·ə, e·sholt′-, esh·kolt′-) *n.* A genus of smooth herbs of the poppy family with dissected leaves and long–peduncled yellow flowers of western North America. The California poppy is the best known. [<NL, after J. F. von *Eschscholtz,* 1793–1831, German naturalist]

es·co·pette (es′kō·pet′) *n. SW U.S.* A short carbine. Also **es·co·pe′ta** (-pā′tə), **es′co·pet′, es′co·pate′** (-pāt′). [<Sp. *escopeta;* infl. in form by F *escopette* a musket]

Es·co·ri·al (es·kôr′ē·əl, -kō′rē·əl; *Sp.* es′kō·ryäl′) *n.* A monastery, church, and royal residence built by Philip II in the 16th century, 27 miles NW of Madrid. Also **Es·cu·ri·al** (es·kyōor′ē·əl).

es·cort (es·kôrt′) *v.t.* To accompany; go with, as from courtesy or to protect; conduct; convoy. See synonyms under LEAD. [< *n.*] — *n.* (es′kôrt) 1 A guard accompanying a person or property in transit, for protection, surveillance, as compulsion, or as a mark of respect. 2 Safeguard; protection. 3 A companion at a social affair. [<F *escorte* <Ital. *scorta* <*scorgere* lead <L *ex-* out + *corrigere.* See CORRECT.]

es·cri·toire (es′kri·twär′) *n.* A secretary; writing desk. [<OF <LL *scriptorium* place for

writing <*scribere* write] — **es′cri·to′ri·al** (-tôr′ē·əl, -tō′rē-) *adj.*

es·croll (es·krōl′) *n.* 1 *Her.* A scroll. 2 *Obs.* An escrow. Also **es·crol′.** [<OF *escroele,* dim. of *escroe.* See ESCROW.]

es·crow (es′krō, es·krō′) *n. Law* An instrument, under seal, placed in the hands of a third person for delivery to the grantee on some condition, the instrument being of no effect until delivery. [<AF *escrowe,* OF *escroe* a scroll <Gmc.]

es·cu·age (es′kyōo·ij) *n.* In feudal law, a military tax paid in lieu of knight service; originally, shield service or personal military duty, a form of feudal tenure. [<AF <OF *escu* <L *scutum* a shield]

es·cu·do (es·kōo′dō; *Pg.* es·kōo′thōo, *Sp.* es·kōo′thō) *n. pl.* **·dos** 1 The monetary unit of Portugal, containing 100 centavos. 2 An obsolete Spanish silver coin equal to ten reals. [<Pg. <L *scutum* shield]

Es·cu·la·pi·an (es′kyōo·lā′pē·ən) See AESCULAPIAN.

es·cu·lent (es′kyə·lənt) *adj.* Suitable for food; edible. — *n.* Anything suitable for food, especially a plant that is edible. [<L *esculentus* <*esca* food]

es·cutch·eon (i·skuch′ən) *n.* 1 *Her.* The surface, usually shield–shaped, upon which armorial bearings are displayed; a heraldic shield. See under FIELD. 2 Any shield–shaped surface or device. 3 *Entomol.* The scutum of the mesothorax in certain insects. 4 An ornamented plate about a keyhole, or one to which a door knocker is attached. 5 *Naut.* That part of a ship's stern on which her name is inscribed. [<AF *escuchon* <L *scutum* shield]

ESCUTCHEON
Divisions of shield:
a. Dexter chief.
b. Middle chief.
c. Sinister chief.
d. Dexter flank.
e. Fess point.
f. Sinister flank.
g. Dexter base.
h. Middle base.
i. Sinister base.
j. Honor point.
k. Nombril point.

Es·dra·e·lon (ez′drə·ē′lən) See JEZREEL, PLAIN OF.

Es·dras (ez′drəs, *Fr.* ez·dräs′) 1 Variant of EZRA. 2 The name of the first two books of the Old Testament Apocrypha.

-ese *suffix of nouns and adjectives* 1 A native or inhabitant of: *Milanese.* 2 The language or dialect of: *Chinese.* 3 Originating in; denoting the inhabitants or language of: *Tirolese.* 4 In the manner or style of: *journalese.* [<OF *-ese* <L *-ensis*]

E·se·nin (yi·syā′nyin), **Sergei Aleksandrovich,** 1895–1925, Russian poet.

es·er·ine (es′ə·rēn, -rin) See PHYSOSTIGMINE.

Es·fa·han (is′fə·hän′) See ISFAHAN.

E·sher (ē′shər) An urban district of NE Surrey, England.

es·ker (es′kər) *n. Geol.* A ridge of glacial gravel, deposited by a subglacial stream between banks of ice. Also **es′kar.** [<Irish *escir* ridge]

E·skils·tu·na (ā′shils·tōo′nä) A city in eastern Sweden.

Es·ki·mo (es′kə·mō) *n. pl.* **·mos** 1 One of a Mongoloid people indigenous to the Arctic coasts of North America, Greenland, and NE Siberia. 2 The language of the Eskimos, belonging to the Eskimo–Aleut family. Also spelled *Esquimau.* [<Dan. <F *Esquimaux* <N. Am. Ind., eaters of raw flesh]

Es·ki·mo-Al·e·ut (es′kə·mō·al′ē·ōot) *n.* A family of polysynthetic languages spoken along the shores of Greenland, the coasts of Labrador, in the Hudson Bay area, along the entire Arctic coast of North America, in western and northern Alaska, the Chukchi peninsula of NE Siberia, and the Aleutian Islands: possibly related to the Altaic languages.

Es·ki·mo·an (es′kə·mō′ən) *adj.* Of, pertaining to, or designating the Eskimo people or their language. Also **Es′ki·mau·an.**

Eskimo dog One of a breed of large, sturdy, broad–chested dogs used by the Eskimos to draw sledges.

Es·ki·se·hir (es′kē·she·hir′) A province of west central Turkey; 5,245 square miles; capital, Eskisehir. Also **Es′ki·she·hir′.**

es·ne (es′nē) *n. Obs.* An Anglo-Saxon domestic slave. [OE]

e·soph·a·gos·to·my (i·sof′ə·gos′tə·mē) *n. Surg.* The forming of an artificial opening into the esophagus. [<ESOPHAGUS + -STOMY]

e·soph·a·gus (i·sof′ə·gəs) *n. pl.* **·gi** (-jī) *Zool.* The tube in vertebrate and invertebrate animals through which food passes from the mouth to the stomach: also *oesophagus.* [<NL <Gk. *oisophagos*] — **e·so·phag·e·al** (ē′sō·faj′ē·əl, i·sof′ə·jē′əl), **e·soph′a·gal** (-ə·gəl) *adj.*

E·so·pi·an (i·sō′pē·ən) See AESOPIAN.

es·o·ter·ic (es′ə·ter′ik) *adj.* 1 Confined to a select circle; confidential. 2 Adapted exclusively for the initiated and enlightened few; abstruse; profound: opposed to *exoteric.* [<Gk. *esōterikos* inner <*esō* inside] — **es′o·ter′i·cal·ly** *adv.*

ESP Extrasensory perception.

es·pa·drille (es′pə·dril′, *Fr.* es·pȧ·drē′y′) *n.* A canvas shoe soled with rope: used in sports and in mountain–climbing. [<F]

es·pal·ier (es·pal′yər) *n.* 1 A trellis on which small fruit trees, shrubs, etc., are trained to grow flattened out. 2 A tree or row of plants

ESPALIER
A tree espaliered against a wall.

trained on a wall or framework. — *v.t.* To train on or furnish with an espalier, as small trees. [<F <Ital. *spalliera* <*spalla* a shoulder]

Es·pa·ña (es·pä′nyä) The Spanish name for SPAIN.

es·par·cet (es′pär′set, es′pär·set′) *n. Obs.* Sainfoin. Also **es·par′cette, es′par·sette.** [<F]

Es·par·te·ro (es·pär·tā′rō), **Baldomero,** 1792–1879, Spanish statesman and general.

es·par·to (es·pär′tō) *n.* A hardy perennial rush-like grass (genera *Lygeum* and *Stipa*) of sandy regions in northern Africa and southern Spain: used for weaving and for making a grade of paper. Also **esparto grass.** [<Sp. <L *spartum* <Gk. *sparton* a fiber rope < *spartos* esparto]

es·pe·cial (es·pesh′əl) *adj.* 1 Exceptional; noteworthy. 2 Particular or individual; special. [<OF <L *specialis* <*species* kind, type]

es·pe·cial·ly (es·pesh′əl·ē) *adv.* Preeminently; particularly.

es·per·ance (es′pər·əns) *n. Obs.* Hope. [<F *espérance*]

Es·pe·ran·to (es′pə·rän′tō) *n.* An artificial language designed for universal use, invented by Ludwig Zamenhof, a Russian scholar, and published in 1887. Its vocabulary, as far as was found practicable, consists of words common to every important European language, spelled more or less phonetically. [after Dr. *Esperanto* (Dr. Hopeful), pen name of inventor] — **Es′pe·ran′tism** *n.* — **Es′pe·ran′tist** *n.*

es·pi·al (es·pī′əl) *n.* 1 The action of a spy. 2 A watching in secret; concealed observation. 3 *Obs.* A company of spies, or a spy. 4 The catching or being caught sight of.

es·piè·gle (es·pye′gl′) *adj. French* Roguish; playful.

es·piè·gle·rie (es·pye·glə·rē′) *n. French* Roguishness; bantering.

es·pi·o·nage (es′pē·ə·nij, -näzh; *Fr.* es·pyō·näzh′) *n.* 1 The practice of spying; excessive or offensive surveillance. 2 The employment and activities of spies and secret agents in time of war. [<F *espionnage* <espier spy]

Es·pí·ri·to San·to (is·pē′rē·tŏŏ sun′tŏŏ) A coastal state in eastern Brazil; 15,780 square miles; capital, Vitória.

Es·pí·ri·tu San·to (es·pē′rē·tŏŏ sän′tō) The largest island of the New Hebrides group; 1,875 square miles: also *Marina.*

es·pla·nade (es′plə·nād′, -näd′) *n.* A level open space, as before a fortress or along a waterside, for promenading, driving, etc. [<F <Sp.

esplanada <*explanar* <L *explanare* <*ex-* out + *planus* level]

es·pon·toon (es·pon′to͞on) See SPONTOON.

es·pou·sal (es·pou′zəl) *adj.* Of or pertaining to a betrothal or marriage. —*n.* **1** The act of espousing; plighting of troths; betrothal; marriage. **2** The adoption, as of a cause or principle.

es·pouse (es·pouz′) *v.t.* **·poused, ·pous·ing 1** To take as a spouse; marry. **2** To promise or give in marriage. **3** To make one's own; adopt, as a cause or doctrine. **4** *Obs.* To pledge; commit. See synonyms under EMBRACE. [<OF *espouser* <L *sponsare* <*sponsus.* See SPOUSE.] **—es·pous′er** *n.*

es·prin·gal (es·pring′gəl) *Obs.* See SPRINGAL[1].

es·prit (es·prē′) *n.* Spirit; wit. [<F <L *spiritus*]

esprit de corps (də kôr) *French* The spirit of the group; morale; especially, common devotion of members to a group.

es·py (es·pī′) *v.t.* **es·pied, es·py·ing 1** To catch sight of (something distant or hidden); see; descry. **2** *Obs.* To observe closely; explore; spy. [<OF *espier* <Gmc.]

-esque *suffix of adjectives* Like; in the manner or style of: *picturesque, arabesque.* [<F <Ital. *-esco* <Gmc.]

Es·qui·line (es′kwə·līn) *n.* One of the seven hills on which Rome is built.

Es·qui·malt (es·kwī′môlt) A naval base and port at the SE end of Vancouver Island, British Columbia, Canada.

Es·qui·mau (es′kə·mō) *n. pl.* **·maux** (mōz) See ESKIMO.

es·quire (es·kwīr′, es′kwīr) *n.* **1** A title of dignity, office, or courtesy ranking below that of *knight.* In the United States, the title is given specially to lawyers and justices of the peace, but occasionally to any man as a mark of respect. **2** In England, a landed proprietor; squire. **3** A gentleman who escorts a lady in public. —*v.t.* (es·kwīr′) **es·quired, es·quir·ing 1** *Rare* To squire. **2** To address as or raise to the title of esquire. [<OF *esquier* <LL *scutarius* shield-bearer <*scutum* a shield]

ess (es) *n. pl.* **ess·es 1** The letter *S, s.* **2** Anything shaped like an *S.* [<L *es* letter *s*]

-ess *suffix* Female: *goddess, lioness*: used to form the feminine of many nouns. [<F *-esse* <LL *-issa* <Gk.]

es·say (e·sā′) *v.t.* **1** To try to do or accomplish; attempt. **2** To test the nature, quality, etc., of. See synonyms under ENDEAVOR. [Var. of ASSAY, *v.*] —*n.* (e·sā′, es′ā) **1** (es′ā) A literary composition on some special subject, analytical, expository, critical, or reflective and personal, commonly briefer and less complete and formal than a *treatise*; latterly, any dissertation on a particular subject, a form of pure representative discourse. **2** An endeavor; attempt; effort. **3** *Obs.* An assay. **4** In philately, a rejected or unused design for a stamp. See synonyms under ENDEAVOR, PROOF. [<OF *essai.* Doublet of ASSAY, *n.*]

es·say·ist (es′ā·ist) *n.* **1** A writer of essays. **2** *Rare* One who makes an attempt.

Es·sen (es′ən) A city in North Rhine-Westphalia, Germany, in the Ruhr valley.

es·sence (es′əns) *n.* **1** The intrinsic nature of anything; that which makes a thing what it is. **2** Being or existence in the abstract. **3** A being, especially a spiritual being. **4** A solution, as of an essential oil in alcohol. **5** The active principle of a plant or medicinal substance. **6** Perfume; scent. [<F <L *essentia* <*esse* be]

Es·sene (es′ēn) *n.* One of an ascetic sect of Jews formed about the second century B.C.: their beliefs in voluntary poverty, community of property, celibacy, and a high degree of personal holiness influenced early Christianity. [<L *Esseni* the Essenes <Gk. *Essēnoi*] **—Es·se′ni·an, Es·sen·ic** (e·sen′ik) *adj.*

es·sen·tial (ə·sen′shəl) *adj.* **1** Of or pertaining to the essence or intrinsic nature of anything; substantial; basal; characteristic. **2** Indispensable, necessary, or highly important, as to success or completeness; absolutely requisite; cardinal. **3** Constituting, containing, or derived from the essence or any distinguishing constituent, as of a plant; constitutive: *essential* oils. **4** Having real existence; real; actual: distinguished from *accidental.* **5** Having the appearance or properties of an essence. See synonyms under INHERENT, NECESSARY, RADICAL. —*n.* **1** That which is essential or characteristic. **2** A necessary element, organ, or part. See synonyms under NECESSITY. [<LL *essentialis* <*essentia.* See ESSENCE.] **—es·sen′ti·al′i·ty** (-shē·al′ə·tē) *n.* **—es·sen′tial·ly** *adv.* **—es·sen′tial·ness** *n.*

essential amino acid Any of some eight amino acids that must be present in the human diet because they are required for protein synthesis but are not themselves synthesized in the human body.

essential oil Any of a group of volatile oils which give to plants their characteristic odors and are used in the making of perfumes and flavors.

Es·se·qui·bo (es′ə·kwē′bō) The largest river of British Guiana, flowing 600 miles north to the Atlantic.

Es·sex (es′iks), **Earl of,** 1567?–1601, Robert Devereux, English courtier; favorite of Elizabeth I; beheaded for treason.

Es·sex (es′iks) A county of SE England north of the Thames estuary; 1,528 square miles; county seat, Chelmsford.

Es·sie (es′ē) Diminutive of ESTHER.

Ess·ling (es′ling) A town east of Vienna, Austria; site of Napoleon's defeat by Austrian forces, 1809.

Ess·ling·en (es′ling·ən) A city in Baden-Württemberg, Germany. Also **Ess·ling·en-am-Neck·ar** (-äm·nek′är).

es·soin (i·soin′) *n.* **1** In English law, an excuse for non-appearance in court, or the allegation of such excuse. **2** The person so excused. **3** *Obs.* Excuse; delay. —*v.t.* To excuse for not appearing at court. Also **es·soign′.** [<OF *essoine, essoigne* <*essoignier* <Med. L *exsoniare* <*ex-* out + *soniare* <*sonia* excuse]

es·so·nite (es′ə·nīt) *n.* Cinnamon stone: also called *hessonite.* [<Gk. *hēssōn* lesser, inferior + -ITE[1]; because softer than similar minerals]

-est[1] *suffix* Most: used in the superlative degree of adjectives and adverbs: *hardest, latest.* [OE *-ast, -est, -ost*]

-est[2] An archaic inflectional ending used in the second person singular present and past indicative, with *thou: eatest, walkest.* Also, in contracted forms, *-st,* as in *hast, didst.*

es·tab·lish (es·tab′lish) *v.t.* **1** To settle or fix firmly; make stable or permanent. **2** To set up; found, as an institution or business. **3** To set up; install (oneself or someone else) in business, a position, etc.: to *establish* oneself in an apartment. **4** To make firm; build up securely: to *establish* a reputation. **5** To put into effect permanently; ordain, as laws. **6** To gain acceptance for; prove, as a theory or argument. **7** To appoint (a church) as a national or state institution. **8** In card games, to gain command of (a suit). See synonyms under CONFIRM, INSTITUTE, MAKE, RATIFY, SET, SETTLE. [<OF *establiss-*, stem of *establir* <L *stabilire* <*stabilis* STABLE[1]] **—es·tab′lish·er** *n.*

established church A church maintained by the state and receiving financial support out of public funds, as the Church of England or the Presbyterian Church of Scotland.

es·tab·lish·ment (es·tab′lish·mənt) *n.* **1** The act of establishing. **2** The state of being established, in any sense of the word. **3** Anything established. **4** A household; a family residence, with its grounds and equipment. **5** An organized staff of servants or employees, together with the building in which they are located. **6** A place of business, together with its equipment. **7** An organized civil, military, or navel force. **8** The act of recognizing a church as a state church. **9** A church so recognized. **10** A settlement in life; particularly, a fixed allowance or income. **—the Establishment** Those collectively who occupy positions of influence and status in a society.

es·ta·cade (es′tə·kād′, -käd′) *n. Mil.* A stockade or dike of piles in a morass, sea, or river, to prevent any enemy's approach; also, any defensive work of stakes or piles. Also **es′ta·ca′do** (-kä′dō). [<F <Sp. *estacada* <*estaca* stake, post]

E·sta·cio (e·stä′syo͞o) Portuguese form of EUSTACE.

es·ta·fette (es′tə·fet′) *n.* A mounted courier. [<F *estafette* <Ital. *staffetta,* dim. of *staffa* stirrup <OHG *stapho* step]

Es·taing (des·taṅ′), **Charles Hector, Count d',** 1729–94, French admiral.

es·ta·mi·net (es·tà·mē·nā′) *n. French* A drinking place; wineshop; a café.

es·tan·cia (es·tän′syä) *n. SW U.S.* A large estate or cattle ranch. [<Sp.]

es·tate (es·tāt′) *n.* **1** One's entire property; a tract of land. **2** Property left after death. **3** Condition or state; social standing; rank; dignity. **4** A class or order of persons in a state. **5** *Brit.* The lords spiritual, lords temporal, and commons. **6** *Law* The degree, nature, and amount of one's lawful interest in any property. **7** *Obs.* Pomp; display. See synonyms under PROPERTY. **—third estate** The commons, as distinguished from the clergy and the nobles, the **first** and the **second estates.** —*v.t. Obs.* To set up in or as in an estate. [<OF *estat* <L *status* STATE]

es·tate-bot·tled (es·tāt′bot′ld) *adj.* Referring to wine bottled by the vineyard owner or producer.

Estates of the Realm 1 The Parliament of Scotland: so called before the union with England in 1707. **2** Throughout feudal Europe, the three estates: clergy, nobility and commons.

Es·te (es′tā) Italian princely family of Ferrara, notably **Alfonso d'Este I,** 1476–1534, his brother **Ipollito I, Cardinal d'Este,** 1479–1520, and their sisters, **Isabella d'Este,** 1474–1539, Marchioness of Mantua, and **Beatrice d'Este,** 1475–97, Duchess of Milan, patronesses of the arts.

Es·te·ban (es·tā′bän) Spanish form of STEPHEN. Also *Pg.* **Es·te·vão** (es·te·vouṅ′).

es·teem (es·tēm′) *n.* **1** Favorable opinion or estimation on the basis of worth, especially that based on moral characteristics; respect; regard. **2** Character that commands respect or consideration; estimableness: a person of *esteem.* **3** *Obs.* Estimation or judgment of merit or demerit; opinion; estimation. [<*v.*] —*v.t.* **1** To value highly; regard as having worth or excellence. **2** To think to be; deem; consider: to *esteem* one fortunate. [<F *estimer* <L *aestimare* value]

Synonyms (noun): estimate, estimation, favor, regard, respect. *Esteem* for a person is a favorable opinion on the basis of worth, especially of moral worth, joined with a feeling of interest in and attraction toward the person. *Regard* for a person is the mental view or feeling that springs from a sense of his excellence, with a cordial and hearty friendliness. *Regard* is more personal and less distant than *esteem,* and adds a special kindliness; *respect* is a more distant word than *esteem. Respect* may be wholly on one side, while *regard* is commonly mutual; *respect* in the fullest sense is given to what is lofty, worthy, and honorable, or to a person of such qualities; but we may pay *respect* to station or office, regardless of the person holding it. *Estimate* has more of calculation; as, My *estimate* of the man, or of his abilities, is very high. *Estimation* involves the idea of appraisal, and is especially used of the feeling entertained by numbers of people; as, He stood high in public *estimation.* Compare ESTEEM *verb,* ATTACHMENT, FRIENDSHIP, LOVE, REGARD. *Antonyms*: abhorrence, antipathy, aversion, contempt, dislike, hatred, loathing, repugnance.

Synonyms (verb): appreciate, calculate, consider, deem, estimate, hold, prize, regard, think, value. *Esteem* and *estimate* alike imply to set a certain mental value upon, but *esteem* is less precise and mercantile than *calculate* or *estimate.* We *esteem* a jewel precious; we *estimate* it to be worth so much money. In popular usage *esteem,* as said of persons, denotes a union of respect and kindly feeling and, in the highest sense, of moral approbation; as, one whom I highly *esteem.* To *appreciate* anything is to be deeply or keenly sensible of or sensitive to its qualities or influence; as, to *appreciate* beauty or harmony; to *appreciate* one's services. To *prize* is to set a high value on for something more than merely commercial reasons. To *regard* (F *regarder* look at, observe) is to have a certain mental view favorable or unfavorable; as, I *regard* him as a friend; or, I *regard* him as a villain; *regard* has a distinctively favorable sense as applied to institutions, proprieties, duties, etc., but does not share the use of the noun *regard* as applied to persons; we *regard* the Sabbath; we *regard* a person's feelings; we have a *regard* for the person. See ADMIRE, APPRECIATE, LIKE. Compare ESTEEM *noun. Antonyms*: see synonyms for ABHOR.

Es·telle (es·tel′) See STELLA. Also *Sp.* **Es·tel·la** (es·tel′lä). [<L, star]

es·ter (es′tər) *n. Chem.* Any of a class of organic compounds formed by the reaction of an acid with an alcohol: they include oils, natural fats, and waxes, and are important in the manufacture of explosives, plastics, rayon, etc. [Coined by Leopold Gmelin, 1788–1853, German chemist]
es·ter·ase (es′tə·rās) *n. Biochem.* A hydrolytic enzyme having the power of accelerating the breakdown of esters, as the lipases.
Es·ter·ha·zy (es·ter·á·zē′), **Marie Charles Ferdinand,** 1847–1923, French army officer; forger of the documents in the Dreyfus case.
es·ter·i·fi·ca·tion (es·ter′ə·fə·kā′shən) *n. Chem.* The formation of an ester by the direct action of an acid on an alcohol in the presence of hydrogen ions, and accompanied by the removal of water.
es·ter·i·fy (es·ter′ə·fī) *v.t.* & *v.i.* **·fied, ·fy·ing** To make or change into an ester.
Es·ther (es′tər; *Fr.* es·târ′, *Ger.* es′tər) A feminine personal name. Also *Ital., Sp.* **Es·ter** (*Ital.* es′tər, *Sp.* es·târ′), *Ital.* **Es·ter·re** (es·ter′·rā), *Lat.* **Es·the·ra** (es·thē′rə). [<Persian, star] — **Esther** Queen of Ahasuerus (Xerxes); heroine of the Old Testament book of Esther.
es·the·sia (es·thē′zhə, -zhē·ə) *n. Physiol.* The capacity or state of feeling or sensation; sensibility: also *aesthesia, aesthesis.* Also **es·the′·sis** (-sis). [<NL <Gk. *aisthēsis* a feeling, sensation]
es·the·si·om·e·ter (es·thē′zē·om′ə·tər) *n.* An instrument for measuring the degrees of discriminative sensitiveness to touch.
es·thete (es′thēt) *n.* A votary of the beautiful; a possessor of or a pretender to fine taste and artistic culture: also spelled *aesthete.* [<Gk. *aisthetēs* one who feels]
es·thet·ic (es·thet′ik) *adj.* **1** Pertaining to beauty, taste, or the fine arts; artistic. **2** Appreciating or loving the beautiful. Also **es·thet′i·cal.** —*n.* **1** The philosophy of the beautiful; the principles underlying beauty. **2** Esthetics. Also spelled *aesthetic.* [<Gk. *aisthētikos* perceptive] — **es·thet′i·cal·ly** *adv.*
es·the·ti·cian (es′thə·tish′ən) *n.* One devoted to esthetics; an expert in matters of taste.
es·thet·i·cism (es·thet′ə·siz′əm) *n.* Devotion to beauty in its sensuous forms; also, the principles or spirit of those devoted to beauty in its sensuous forms.
es·thet·ics (es·thet′iks) *n. pl.* (*construed as singular*) **1** The science of beauty and taste. **2** Knowledge of the fine arts and art criticism. Also spelled *aesthetics.*
Es·tho·ni·a (es·thō′nē·ə) See ESTONIA.
Es·tienne (es·tyen′) A French family of printers and scholars, especially **Henri,** 1528–98, and **Robert,** 1503–59.
es·ti·ma·ble (es′tə·mə·bəl) *adj.* **1** Deserving of esteem. **2** That may be estimated or calculated. **3** Valuable. — **es′ti·ma·ble·ness** *n.* — **es′ti·ma·bly** *adv.*
es·ti·mate (es′tə·māt) *v.* **·mat·ed, ·mat·ing** *v.t.* **1** To form an approximate opinion of (size, amount, number, etc.); calculate roughly. **2** To form an opinion about; judge, as character. —*v.i.* **3** To make or submit an estimate. See synonyms under APPRECIATE, CALCULATE, ESTEEM. —*n.* (es′tə·mit) **1** A valuation based on opinion or roughly made from imperfect or incomplete data; a calculation not professedly exact; appraisement; also, a statement, as by a builder, in regard to the cost of certain work. **2** Carefully weighed judgment; formal opinion: an *estimate* of a person's character. [<L *aestimatus,* pp. of *aestimare* value] — **es′ti·ma′tive** *adj.* — **es′ti·ma′tor** *n.* — **es′ti·ma·to′ry** (-mə·tôr′ē, -tō′rē) *adj.*
es·ti·ma·tion (es′tə·mā′shən) *n.* **1** The act of estimating. **2** The conclusion arrived at; an estimate. **3** Esteem; regard. See synonyms under ATTACHMENT, ESTEEM.
Es·ti·mé (es·tē·mā′), **Dumarsais,** 1900–1953, president of Haiti 1946–50.
e·stip·u·late (ē·stip′yə·lit) See EXSTIPULATE.
es·ti·val (es′tə·vəl, es·tī′-) *adj.* Of or pertaining to summer; appearing in summer: also spelled *aestival.* [<LL *aestivalis* <L *aestas* summer]
es·ti·vate (es′tə·vāt) *v.i.* **·vat·ed, ·vat·ing** **1** To pass the summer. **2** To pass the summer in torpor: said of certain animals. Compare HIBERNATE. Also spelled *aestivate.* [<L *aestivatus,* pp. of *aestivare* < *aestas* summer] — **es′·ti·va′tor** *n.*
es·ti·va·tion (es′tə·vā′shən) *n.* **1** The act of spending the summer. **2** *Zool.* The dormancy in summer of certain animals. **3** *Bot.* The disposition of the parts of a flower in the bud; prefloration. Also spelled *aestivation.*
es·toile (es·toil′, -twäl′) *n.* A heraldic star, having six, eight, or more points. [<OF <L *stella* star]
Es·to·ni·a A republic, northern-most of the Baltic states of NE Europe; 17,400 square miles; capital, Tallinn; pop. 1,600,000. Formerly the **Estonian Soviet Socialist Republic** (1940–1991). Estonia separated from the Soviet Union on August 20, 1991. It received a seat in the United Nations on September 17, 1991.
Es·to·ni·an (es·tō′nē·ən) *adj.* Of or pertaining to Estonia. —*n.* **1** One of a Finnish people inhabiting Estonia and other districts. **2** The Finno-Ugric language of this people.
es·top (es·top′) *v.t.* **·topped, ·top·ping** **1** *Law* To prevent by estoppel. **2** *Obs.* To bar; plug. [<AF *estopper,* OF *estoper* <OF *estoupe* tow <L *stuppa*] — **es·top′page** (-ij) *n.*
es·top·pel (es·top′əl) *n.* **1** *Law* An impediment to a right of action, whereby one is forbidden to contradict or deny one's own previous statement or act. **2** Prohibition.
es·to·vers (es·tō′vərz) *n. pl. Law* **1** Necessaries or supplies allowed by law, as wood taken by a tenant for his own use. **2** Alimony allowed to a wife separated from her husband; also, a widow's allowance. [<OF *estover* < *estovoir* be necessary]
es·trange (es·trānj′) *v.t.* **·tranged, ·trang·ing** **1** To make (someone previously friendly or affectionate) indifferent or hostile; alienate, as affections. **2** To remove or dissociate (oneself, etc.): to *estrange* oneself from society. [<OF *estranger* <L *extraneare* < *extraneus.* See STRANGE.]
es·trange·ment (es·trānj′mənt) *n.* The act of estranging, or the condition of being estranged.
es·tray (es·trā′) *n.* **1** *Law* A stray or unclaimed domestic animal. **2** Something which has gone astray. —*v.t.* To go astray. [<OF *estraié,* pp. of *estraier.* See STRAY.]
es·treat (es·trēt′) *Brit. Law n.* An exact copy of a record or writing, especially of fines and amercements on court rolls. —*v.t.* **1** To copy from the records of a court for prosecution. **2** To levy (a fine, etc.) under estreat of record; exact, as a fine. [<AF *estrete,* OF *estrait,* pp. of *estraire* <L *extrahere.* See EXTRACT.]
Es·tre·ma·du·ra (es′trə·mə·do͝or′ə) **1** (esh′trə·mə·do͞o′rə) A province of central Portugal; 2,064 square miles; capital, Lisbon. **2** (*Sp.* es′trā·mä·tho͞o′rä) A historic region of western Spain bordering on Portugal, comprising Cáceres (**Upper Estremadura**) and Badajoz (**Lower Estremadura**) provinces; 16,059 square miles: Spanish *Extremadura.*
es·tridge (es′trij) *n. Obs.* Ostrich.
es·tri·ol (es′trē·ōl, -ol) *n. Biochem.* An estrogen, $C_{18}H_{24}O_3$, found in the urine of pregnant women: also *oestriol.* [<ESTRUS + -OL[1]]
es·tro·gen (es′trə·jən) *n. Biochem.* Any of several hormones found in the ovarian fluids of the mammalian female and exercising a more or less specific and critical influence on the sexual cycle: also called *oestrin.* [<ESTRUS + -GEN] — **es′tro·gen′ic** *adj.*
Es·tron (es′tron) *n. Chem.* A synthetic fiber made of cellulose acetate: used to distinguish from the regenerated cellulose products known as rayon: a trade name.
es·trone (es′trōn) *n. Biochem.* An estrogen, $C_{18}H_{22}O_2$, present in the ovary, adrenal glands, urine and placental tissue: also *oestrone.* [<ESTRUS + -ONE]
es·trus (es′trəs, ēs′-) *n.* **1** *Zool.* The peak of the sexual cycle in animals, culminating in ovulation; heat or rut, especially in female mammals. **2** A violent or passionate impulse, craving, or stimulus; specifically, erotic desire. Also spelled *oestrus, oestrum.* [<L *oestrus* frenzy, passion <Gk. *oistros* a gadfly] — **es′tru·al** *adj.*
es·tu·ar·y (es′cho͞o·er′ē) *n. pl.* **·ar·ies** The wide mouth of a river where it is met and invaded by the sea, especially in a depression of the coast. [<L *aestuarium* < *aestus* tide] — **es′·tu·ar′i·al** (-âr′ē·əl), **es′tu·ar′i·an, es·tu·a·rine** (es′cho͞o·ə·rin, -rīn) *adj.*
es·tu·fa (es·to͞o′fä) *n. SW U.S.* **1** A council chamber and religious meeting place in Pueblo villages, wholly or partly underground and containing a perpetual religious fire. **2** A stove. [<Sp., stove]
e·su·ri·ent (i·so͝or′ē·ənt) *adj.* Hungry; greedy; eager for food. [<L *esuriens, -entis,* ppr. of *esurire* be greedy < *edere* eat] — **e·su′ri·ence, e·su′ri·en·cy** *n.* — **e·su′ri·ent·ly** *adv.*
-et *suffix* Small; little: *islet*: often without appreciable force, as in *sonnet.* [<F]
e·ta (ā′tə, ē′-) *n.* **1** The seventh letter and third vowel of the Greek alphabet (H,η): corresponding to English *e* long. As a numeral it denotes 8. **2** Symbol for the viscosity of fluids. [<Gk. *eta* <Phoenician *hēth*]
e·taer·i·o (i·tē′rē·ō) *n. pl.* **·ri·os** *Bot.* An aggregate fruit, such as the strawberry. Also **e·tae′ri·um.** [<Gk. *hetairia* society < *hetairos* companion]
é·ta·gère (ā·tà·zhâr′) *n.* An ornamental stand with shelves; a what-not. [<F < *étage* stage]
et a·li·i (et ā′lē·ī) *Latin* And others: abbreviated *et al.*
et·a·lon (et′ə·lon) *n. Physics* An interferometer for studying the fine lines of a spectrum by means of multiple reflection between parallel, half-silvered plates of glass or quartz arranged at fixed distances. [<F *étalon* a standard (def. 4)]
et·a·mine (et′ə·mēn) *n.* A loosely woven, buntinglike fabric. Also **et′a·min** (-min). [<F *étamine*]
é·tape (ā·tàp′) *n.* **1** A public warehouse. **2** A halting place. **3** Supplies allotted to troops during a march. **4** The distance marched in one day. [<F <OF *estaple* <MDu. *stapel* a warehouse]
et cet·er·a (et set′ər·ə, set′rə) And other things; and the rest; and so forth. Also **et caet′er·a.** Abbr. *etc.* and *&c.* [<L]
etch (ech) *v.t.* **1** To engrave by means of acid or other corrosive fluid, especially for making a design on a plate for printing. **2** To outline or sketch by scratching lines with a pointed instrument. [<Du. *etsen* <G *ätzen* <MHG *etzen,* causative of *ezzen* eat] — **etch′·er** *n.*
etch figure *Physics* The pattern etched on a crystal or metal surface by a reagent, valuable in indicating molecular structure.
etch·ing (ech′ing) *n.* **1** A process of engraving in which lines are scratched with a needle on a plate covered with wax or other coating, and the parts exposed are subjected to the biting of an acid. **2** A figure or design formed by etching. **3** An impression from an etched plate.
Etch·mi·a·dzin (ech′mē·ə·dzēn′) See ECHMIADZIN.
E·te·o·cles (i·tē′ə·klēz) In Greek legend, a son of Oedipus and Jocasta. See SEVEN AGAINST THEBES.
e·ter·nal (i·tûr′nəl) *adj.* **1** Having neither beginning nor end of existence; infinite in duration. **2** Having no end; everlasting. **3** Continued without interruption; perpetual. **4** Independent of time or its conditions, or of the things that are perishable; unchangeable; immutable. **5** Of or pertaining to eternity. **6** Appearing interminable; perpetual; incessant: often implying weariness or disgust: George and his *eternal* jokes. —*n.* One who or that which is everlasting: usually in the plural. — **the Eternal** God. [<OF <LL *aeternalis* < *aeternus* < *aevum* an age] — **e·ter′·nal·ly** *adv.* — **e·ter′nal·ness, e·ter·nal·i·ty** (ē′tər·nal′ə·tē) *n.*

Synonyms (*adj.*): deathless, endless, eonian, everlasting, everliving, fadeless, immortal, imperishable, interminable, never-ending, never-failing, perennial, perpetual, timeless, unceasing, undying, unending, unfading, unfailing. *Eternal* strictly signifies without beginning or end; *everlasting* applies to that which may or may not have beginning, but can never cease; *endless,* without end, in its utmost reach, is not distinguishable from *everlasting,* but is constantly used in inferior senses, especially in mechanics, as in the phrases "an *endless* screw," "an *endless* chain." *Everlasting, endless,* and *interminable*

are used in a limited sense of protracted, indefinite, but not infinite duration; as, the *everlasting* hills; *endless* debates; *interminable* quarrels. *Immortal* applies to that which now has life and is forever exempt from death. *Timeless* carries the fullest idea of *eternal,* as above and beyond time, and not to be measured by it. See IMMORTAL, INFINITE, PERPETUAL.

Eternal City Rome.

e·terne (i·tûrn′) *adj. Archaic* or *Poetic* Eternal.

e·ter·ni·ty (i·tûr′nə·tē) *n. pl.* **·ties 1** Infinite duration or existence. **2** An endless or limitless time. **3** Immortality. **4** That which is eternal or immortal. [< OF *eternité* < L *aeternitas, -tatis*]

Eternity Cape A mountainous headland on the Saguenay River, Quebec, Canada; 1,700 feet high.

e·ter·nize (i·tûr′niz) *v.t.* **·nized, ·niz·ing 1** To make eternal. **2** To perpetuate the fame of; immortalize. Also *Brit.* **e·ter′nise.** **—e·ter′·ni·za′tion** *n.*

e·te·sian (i·tē′zhən) *adj. Meteorol.* Annually periodic, as certain northerly Mediterranean summer winds. [< L *etesius* < Gk. *etēsios* < *etos* a year]

eth (eth) See EDH.

-eth[1] An archaic inflectional ending used in the third person singular present indicative of some verbs: *eateth, drinketh.* Also, in contracted forms, *-th,* as in *hath, doth.* [OE *-ath, -eth, -oth*]

-eth[2] *suffix* Var. of -TH[2].

E·than (ē′thən) A masculine personal name. [< Hebrew, firmness]

eth·ane (eth′ān) *n. Chem.* A colorless, odorless, gaseous compound, C_2H_6, of the paraffin series contained in the gases given off by petroleum and in illuminating gas; an alkane or saturated hydrocarbon of the methane series. [< ETHER]

eth·a·nol (eth′ə·nōl, -nol) *n.* Alcohol (def. 1); an organic compound, C_2H_5OH, representing the second member of the homologous series of alcohols of the general formula $C_nH_{2n+1}OH$. Also called *ethyl alcohol, grain alcohol.*

Eth·el (eth′əl) A feminine personal name. [< Gmc., noble]

Eth·el·bert (eth′əl·bûrt), 552–616, king of Kent, converted by Augustine in 597. Also spelled *Æthelbert.*

Eth·el·dre·da (eth′əl·drā′də), **Saint** A British abbess of the seventh century: also called *Saint Audrey.*

Eth·el·red II (eth′əl·red), 968–1016, king of England 979?–1016: called "Ethelred the Unready." Also spelled *Æthelred.*

eth·ene (eth′ēn) *n.* Ethylene.

e·ther (ē′thər) *n.* **1** *Chem.* **a** A colorless, mobile, volatile, aromatic liquid compound, ethyl oxide, $(C_2H_5)_2O$, made by the action of sulfuric acid on alcohol: used as an anesthetic and solvent. **b** Any of a group of organic compounds in which an oxygen atom is joined with two organic radicals. **2** A solid or semisolid, perfectly elastic medium formerly assumed to pervade all of space and to be responsible for the transmission of light, heat, gravitational effects, and all forms of energy and radiation. **3** The upper air. Also spelled *aether* (for defs. 2 and 3). [< L *aether* sky < Gk. *aithēr* < *aithein* burn, shine]

e·the·re·al (i·thir′ē·əl) *adj.* **1** Having the nature of ether or air. **2** Light; airy; fine; subtle; exquisite. **3** Existing in or belonging to the ether or upper air; aerial; heavenly. **4** Of or pertaining to ether. See synonyms under AIRY. **—e·the·re·al′i·ty, e·the′re·al·ness** *n.* **—e·the′re·al·ly** *adv.* **—e·the′re·ous** *adj.*

e·the·re·al·ize (i·thir′ē·əl·īz) *v.t.* & *v.i.* **·ized, ·iz·ing** To make or become ethereal; spiritualize. **—e·the′re·al·i·za′tion** *n.*

Eth·er·ege (eth′ə·rij), **Sir George,** 1635–91, English dramatist.

e·ther·i·fy (i·ther′ə·fī) *v.t.* **·fied, ·fy·ing** *Chem.* To form ether from (an alcohol). **—e·ther′i·fi·ca′tion** *n.*

e·ther·ize (ē′thə·rīz) *v.t.* **·ized, ·iz·ing 1** To subject to the influence of ether; anesthetize. **2** To change into ether. **—e′ther·i·za′tion** *n.* **—e′ther·iz′er** *n.*

eth·ic (eth′ik) *adj.* Ethical; moral. —*n.* **1** The philosophy of morals; ethics: now in revived use by some philosophical writers instead of *ethics.* **2** The standard of character set up by any race or nation. [< L *ethicus* < Gk. *ēthikos* < *ethos* character]

eth·i·cal (eth′i·kəl) *adj.* **1** Pertaining or relating to ethics. **2** Treating of morals. **3** In accordance with right principles, as defined by a given system of ethics or professional conduct. See synonyms under MORAL. **—eth′i·cal′i·ty, eth′i·cal·ness** *n.* **—eth′i·cal·ly** *adv.*

eth·i·cize (eth′ə·sīz) *v.t.* **·cized, ·ciz·ing** To make ethical; treat ethically.

eth·ics (eth′iks) *n. pl. (construed as singular in defs.* 1 and *3)* **1** The study and philosophy of human conduct, with emphasis on the determination of right and wrong: one of the normative sciences. **2** The basic principles of right action. **3** A work or treatise on morals.

E·thi·op (ē′thē·op) *Archaic adj.* Ethiopian; Negro; black. —*n.* An Ethiopian. [< L *Aethiops* < Gk. *Aithiops,* ? < *aithein* burn + *ops* face]

E·thi·o·pi·a (ē′thē·ō′pē·ə) **1** A native empire in eastern Africa; 350,000 square miles; capital, Addis Ababa; annexed by Italy, 1936; recovered by British forces, 1941: also *Abyssinia.* **2** An ancient country south of Egypt.

E·thi·o·pi·an (ē′thē·ō′pē·ən) *adj.* **1** Of or pertaining to Ethiopia, or to the Ethiopians. **2** Of or pertaining to a group of Hamitic languages spoken in Abyssinia and regions to the south. **3** *Ecol.* Designating a zoogeographical region including Africa south of the Sahara, southern Arabia, and Madagascar. —*n.* **1** A native of modern Abyssinia. **2** A member of the Ethiopian race. **3** A blackamoor. **4 a** The Hamitic language of Abyssinia and the regions to the south; Cushitic. **b** Ethiopic.

Ethiopian race An old designation of a division of mankind, applied to all the African Negro and Negrito peoples.

E·thi·op·ic (ē′thē·op′ik) *n.* The ancient Semitic language of Abyssinia, developed by Arabian invaders and still used in the services and records of the Christian Abyssinian Church: also called *Geez.* —*adj.* Ethiopian.

eth·moid (eth′moid) *n. Anat.* A bone, cubical in man, composed of thin plates and situated at the base of the skull, behind the nose. —*adj.* Of or pertaining to the ethmoid; sievelike. [< Gk. *ēthmoeidēs* < *ēthmos* sieve + *eidos* form] **—eth·moi′dal** *adj.*

eth·narch (eth′närk) *n.* In ancient Rome, a governor of a nation or people; viceroy. [< Gk. *ethnarchēs* < *ethnos* nation + *archein* rule]

eth·nar·chy (eth′när·kē) *n. pl.* **·chies 1** The office or jurisdiction of an ethnarch. **2** The territory ruled by him.

eth·nic (eth′nik) *adj.* **1** Of or pertaining to race, races, or peoples. **2** Pertaining to groups or stocks of mankind as having certain physical, mental, or cultural characteristics in common, and usually but not necessarily living within a given geographic area; ethnological. **3** Belonging distinctively to a race. **4** Pertaining to peoples neither Jewish nor Christian; gentile; heathen; pagan. Also **eth′ni·cal.** —*n. Colloq.* A member of a minority ethnic group, esp., in the U.S., a non-black minority. [< Gk. *ethnikos* < *ethnos* nation] **—eth′ni·cal·ly** *adv.*

ethno- *combining form* Race, nation; peoples: *ethnogenic, ethnozoology.* Also, before vowels, **ethn-.**

eth·no·bi·ol·o·gy (eth′nō·bi·ol′ə·jē) *n.* The study of human societies in relation to their biological environment, especially as regards plant life and food supply; human ecology.

eth·no·bot·a·ny (eth′nō·bot′ə·nē) *n.* The study of plants in relation to the needs and customs of a given ethnic group or people. **—eth′no·bo·tan′i·cal** (-bə·tan′i·kəl) *adj.* **—eth′no·bot′a·nist** *n.*

eth·no·cen·trism (eth′nō·sen′triz·əm) *n. Sociol.* The concept, formulated by W. G. Sumner, that the attitudes, beliefs, and customs of one's own group, nation, or people are of central importance and a basis for judging all other groups. **—eth′no·cen′tric** *adj.*

eth·no·gen·ic (eth′nō·jen′ik) *adj.* **1** Of or pertaining to the origin of races and ethnic groups. **2** Producing races or peoples.

eth·nog·e·ny (eth·noj′ə·nē) *n.* The department of ethnology that deals with the origin of races and ethnic groups.

eth·nog·ra·pher (eth·nog′rə·fər) *n.* One who studies or is proficient in ethnography. Also **eth·nog′ra·phist.**

eth·no·graph·ic (eth′nō·graf′ik) *adj.* Of or pertaining to ethnography; descriptive of races and peoples. Also **eth′no·graph′i·cal.** **—eth′no·graph′i·cal·ly** *adv.*

eth·nog·ra·phy (eth·nog′rə·fē) *n.* **1** The branch of anthropology that considers man geographically and descriptively, treating of the subdivision of races and peoples, the causes of migration, etc. **2** Formerly, ethnology.

eth·no·lin·guis·tics (eth′nō·ling·gwis′tiks) *n.* The study, through linguistic methodology, of the relation between language and ethnology.

eth·nol·o·gist (eth·nol′ə·jist) *n.* A student of or an expert in ethnology.

eth·nol·o·gy (eth·nol′ə·jē) *n.* The science of the subdivisions and families of men, their origins, characteristics, distribution, and physical and linguistic classification. **—eth·no·log·i·cal** (eth′·nō·loj′i·kəl) or **eth′no·log′ic** *adj.* **—eth′no·log′·i·cal·ly** *adv.*

eth·no·zo·ol·o·gy (eth′nō·zō·ol′ə·jē) *n.* The study of a regional fauna in relation to the needs, uses, and customs of a given people or ethnic community. **—eth′no·zo′o·log′i·cal** (-zō′·ə·loj′i·kəl) *adj.* **—eth′no·zo·ol′o·gist** *n.*

e·thog·ra·phy (i·thog′rə·fē) *n.* A description of the moral attributes and customs of mankind. [< Gk. *ēthos* character + -GRAPHY]

e·thol·o·gy (i·thol′e·jē) *n.* **1** The scientific study of animal behavior. **2** The science of the formation of human character. [< Gk. *ēthos* character + -LOGY] **—e·tho·log·ic** (ē′thə·loj′ik) or **·i·cal** *adj.*

e·thos (ē′thos) *n.* **1** The characteristic spirit, disposition, or tendency of a people or community regarded as an endowment and as expressed in their customs. **2** The genius or spirit of an institution or a system. **3** The essential characteristics, or ideal attributes, of a work, or period in art or literature, or the type to which the art or period corresponds, as opposed to what is merely emotional, incidental, and transient. Compare PATHOS. [< Gk. *ēthos* character]

eth·yl (eth′il) *n. Chem.* **1** A univalent hydrocarbon radical, C_2H_5, of the paraffin series, denoting the presence of the radical in any of numerous compounds widely used in industry, medicine, and the arts: *ethyl* acetate, *ethyl* cellulose, etc. **2** Any gasoline treated with tetraethyl lead to reduce knock. [< ETHER + -YL] **—eth·yl′ic** *adj.*

Eth·yl (eth′il) *n.* An anti-knock motor fuel containing tetraethyl lead ethylene dibromide: a trade name.

ethyl alcohol Ethanol.

eth·y·late (eth′ə·lāt) *v.t.* **·lat·ed, ·lat·ing** To treat or combine so as to cause the introduction of ethyl or its compounds. **—eth′y·la′tion** *n.* **—eth′y·lat′ed** *adj.*

eth·yl·di·chlor·ar·sine (eth′əl·dī′klôr·är′sēn) *n. Chem.* A colorless, pungent, liquid compound, $C_2H_5AsCl_2$, used in chemical warfare as a lung irritant and vesicant.

eth·y·lene (eth′ə·lēn) *n.* A flammable, unsaturated gaseous compound, C_2H_4, used in manufacturing numerous organic chemicals and in medicine. Also called *ethene, olefiant gas.*

ethylene dibromide *Chem.* A volatile liquid hydrocarbon, $C_2H_4Br_2$, having an odor resembling that of chloroform: used in the making of ethyl gas.

ethylene glycol See GLYCOL.

eth·yl·u·re·thane (eth′əl·yŏŏr′ə·thān) *n. Chem.* Urethan.

eth·yne (eth′īn) *n.* Acetylene.

É·tienne (ā·tyen′) French form of STEPHEN.

e·ti·o·late (ē′tē·ə·lāt′) *v.t.* & *v.i.* **·lat·ed, ·lat·ing** To whiten, or become white, as a plant or person kept from sunlight. [< F *étioler* < OF *estieuler* grow up in stalks, ? ult. < L *stipula* straw]

e·ti·o·la·tion (ē′tē·ə·lā′shən) *n.* A blanching or yellowing, specifically in plants deprived of light or deficient in chlorophyll.

e·ti·ol·o·gy (ē′tē·ol′ə·jē) *n.* **1** The science of efficient, as distinguished from final, causes. **2** That department of medicine that treats of the causes of disease. **3** The giving of a cause or reason for anything; also, the reason itself. Also spelled *aetiology.* [< LL *aetiologia* < Gk. *aitiologia* < *aitia* cause + *logos* word, study] **—e·ti·o·log·i·cal** (ē′tē·ə·loj′i·kəl) *adj.* **—e′ti·o·log′i·cal·ly** *adv.* **—e′ti·ol′o·gist** *n.*

et·i·quette (et′ə·ket, -kət) *n.* The usages of polite society or professional intercourse. [< F < OF *estiquette.* Doublet of TICKET.]

Et·na (et′nə) A volcano in eastern Sicily; 10,740 feet: ancient *Aetna.* — **Et·ne·an** (et·nē′·ən) *adj.*

é·toile (ā·twäl′) *n.* A lustrous satin fabric with plain or changeable surface. [<F, star]

E·ton (ēt′n) An urban district opposite Windsor on the Thames river, England: seat of **Eton College,** a public school.

E·to·ni·an (i·tō′nē·ən) *n.* One who is or has been a student at Eton College.

Eton jacket 1 A short black broadcloth jacket cut off square at the hips and generally worn with a wide overlapping stiff collar, the **Eton collar**: originally used by the boys of Eton College. 2 A jacket, similar in cut, worn by women. Also **Eton coat.**

E·tru·ri·a (i·trŏŏr′ē·ə) An ancient country of west central Italy. — **E·tru′ri·an** *adj.* & *n.*

E·trus·can (i·trus′kən) *adj.* Belonging or relating to ancient Etruria or to its people, or their language, civilization, or art. — *n.* 1 One of the ancient people of Etruria. 2 The extinct language of the Etruscans, as yet unclassified, but apparently not of the Indo-European family.

et se·quens (et sē′kwənz) *pl.* **et se·quen·ti·a** (si·kwen′shē·ə) *Latin* And the following. Abbr. *et seq.*

-ette *suffix* 1 Little, small: *kitchenette.* 2 Resembling; like; imitating: *leatherette.* 3 Feminine: *farmerette.* [<F *-ette,* fem. of *-et,* dim. suffix]

et·tle (et′l) *Scot. v.t* & *v.i.* To aim; intend. — *n.* 1 Intention; aim. 2 Opportunity.

Et·trick Forest (et′rik) A grazing area including Selkirk, Scotland, formerly part of the forest covering SE Scotland.

et tu, Bru·te (et tōō brōō′tā) *Latin* And thou, Brutus!: exclamation attributed to Caesar when he saw his friend Brutus among his assassins.

é·tude (ā′tōōd, -tyōōd; *Fr.* ā·tüd′) *n. Music* 1 A composition designed to illustrate some phase of technique. 2 A composition meant to be played for its esthetic effect, but also exemplifying some aspect of technical virtuosity. [<F. See STUDY.]

é·tui (ā·twē′) *n. pl.* **é·tuis** A case for carrying small articles. Also **et·wee′.** [<F]

et·y·mo·log·i·cal (et′ə·mə·loj′i·kəl) *adj.* Relating to or based upon the study of etymology. Also **et′y·mo·log′ic.** —**et′y·mo·log′i·cal·ly** *adv.*

et·y·mo·log·i·con (et′ə·mə·loj′i·kon) *n. pl.* **·ca** (-kə) An etymological dictionary or a treatise on the derivation of words. [<LL <Gk. *etymologikon* of an etymologist]

et·y·mol·o·gist (et′ə·mol′ə·jist) *n.* A student of or one versed in the derivations, form changes, and meanings of words.

et·y·mol·o·gize (et′ə·mol′ə·jīz) *v.t.* & *v.i.* **·gized, ·giz·ing** To trace or give the derivation of (a word or words).

et·y·mol·o·gy (et′ə·mol′ə·jē) *n. pl.* **·gies** 1 The history of a word as indicated by breaking it down into basic elements, or by tracing it back to the earliest known form or root, with all its changes in form and meaning; also, a statement of this. 2 The study of the derivation of words. See FOLK ETYMOLOGY. [<F *etymologie* <L *etymologia* <Gk. < *etymon* original meaning + *logos* word, study]

et·y·mon (et′ə·mon, -mən) *n. pl.* **·mons** or **·ma** (-mə) 1 The radical or root form of a word. 2 The primitive signification of a word. [<L <Gk., original meaning; orig. neut. sing. of *etymos* true, genuine]

Et·zel (et′səl) In the *Nibelungenlied,* the king of the Huns who married Kriemhild after Siegfried's death: identified with *Attila.*

eu- *prefix* Good; well; easy; agreeable: *euphony, eupnea*: opposed to *dys-.* [<Gk. *eu-* < *eus* well]

Eu·bac·te·ri·a·les (yōō′bak·tir′ē·ā′lēz) *n. pl.* A large and highly diversified order of bacteria, including many of the disease-producing genera, as the cholera, typhoid, anthrax, and dysentery groups. See illustration under BACTERIA. [<NL *Eubacterium,* one of an order of bacteria <Gk. *eu-* good, typical + *bacterium* BACTERIUM]

Eu·boe·a (yōō·bē′ə) The largest Greek island in the Aegean, off central Greece; 1,457 square miles; capital, Chalcis: Greek *Evvoia,* Italian *Negroponte.* Also **Eu·bœ′a.**

eu·caine (yōō·kān′, yōō′kə·in) *n. Chem.* Either of two important compounds similar in effect to cocaine, but less toxic, used for local anesthesia, known as **eucaine A** and **eucaine B.** [<EU- + (CO)CAINE]

eu·ca·lypt (yōō′kə·lipt) *n.* A tree of the genus *Eucalyptus.* — **eu′ca·lyp′tic** *adj.*

eu·ca·lyp·te·ol (yōō′kə·lip′tē·ōl, -ol) *n. Chem.* A crystalline compound, $C_{10}H_{16}\cdot 2HCl$, with a camphorlike odor, derived from eucalyptol. Also **eucalyptene hydrochloride.**

eu·ca·lyp·tol (yōō′kə·lip′tōl, -tol) *n.* A colorless camphoraceous liquid compound, $C_{10}H_{18}O$, contained in eucalyptus oil: used as an antiseptic and expectorant: also called *cineol.* [<EUCALYPT(US) + -OL[2]]

eu·ca·lyp·tus (yōō′kə·lip′təs) *n. pl.* **·lyp·ti** (-tī) or **·lyp·tus·es** Any of a genus *(Eucalyptus)* of large, chiefly Australian evergreen trees of the myrtle family: widely used as timber, for ornamental purposes, and in the preparation of drugs, especially the volatile, pungent, essential **oil of eucalyptus.** [<NL <Gk. *eu-* well + *kalyptos* covered < *kalyptein* cover; from the covering of the buds]

eu·cha·ris (yōō′kə·ris) *n.* Any plant of a small genus *(Eucharis)* of bulbous South American plants of the amaryllis family, with elliptic or ovate leaves and white, fragrant flowers in umbels. [<NL <Gk. *eucharis* agreeable < *eu-* good + *charis* grace]

Eu·cha·rist (yōō′kə·rist) *n.* 1 A Christian sacrament in which bread and wine are consecrated, distributed, and consumed in commemoration of the passion and death of Christ. 2 The consecrated bread and wine of this sacrament. See synonyms under SACRAMENT. [<OF *eucariste* <LL *eucharistia* <Gk. < *eu-* well + *charizesthai* give thanks] — **eu′cha·ris′tic** or **·ti·cal** *adj.*

eu·char·is·tial (yōō′kə·ris′chəl) *n.* A pyx (def. 1).

eu·chre (yōō′kər) *n.* 1 A card game for two to four players, played with 32 cards, one side in choosing trumps being required to take three to five tricks to win. See BOWER[2]. 2 An instance of euchring an opponent or of being euchred. — *v.t.* **eu·chred** (-kərd), **eu·chring** 1 In the game of euchre, to defeat (the trump-making side) by taking three tricks. 2 *Colloq.* To outwit or defeat. [Origin uncertain]

Eu·cken (oi′kən), **Rudolf Christoph,** 1846–1926, German philosopher.

eu·clase (yōō′klās) *n.* A very brittle pale-green silicate of beryllium and aluminum, used rarely as a gem. [<EU- + Gk. *klasis* breaking < *klaein* break]

Eu·clid (yōō′klid) 1 An Athenian geometer who lived about 300 B.C. 2 The work on geometry written by him. 3 An elementary textbook of geometry. 4 Impersonally, the science of geometry or its principles.

Eu·clid·e·an (yōō·klid′ē·ən) *adj.* Of or pertaining to Euclid; accordant with the axioms and postulates of his geometry. Also **Eu·clid′i·an.**

eu·de·mon (yōō·dē′mən) *n.* A benevolent spirit or genius. Also **eu·dae′mon.** [<Gk. *eudaimōn* fortunate < *eu-* well + *daimōn* spirit]

eu·de·mo·ni·a (yōō′də·mō′nē·ə) *n.* A state of complete well-being, as defined by the philosophy of Aristotle; good fortune; true happiness, as arising from a rational satisfaction. Also **eu′dae·mo′ni·a, eu·de′mo·ny.** [<Gk. *eudaimonia* <*eudaimōn.* See EUDEMON.]

eu·de·mon·ic (yōō′də·mon′ik) *adj.* Of, pertaining to, or tending to produce happiness; conceived or done for the sake of happiness: *eudemonic* morals. Also **eu′de·mon′i·cal.**

eu·de·mon·ics (yōō′də·mon′iks) *n.* 1 The branch of ethics that discusses happiness. 2 Means of comfort or happiness. 3 Eudemonism.

eu·de·mon·ism (yōō·dē′mən·iz′əm) *n.* Any of several philosophical theories which maintain that man's greatest good exists in some form of mental or spiritual happiness. See HEDONISM. — **eu·de′mon·ist** *n.* — **eu·de′mon·is′tic** or **·ti·cal** *adj.* — **eu·de′mon·is′ti·cal·ly** *adv.*

eu·di·om·e·ter (yōō′dē·om′ə·tər) *n. Chem.* A graduated glass vessel used in the volumetric analysis of gases. [<Gk. *eudios* clear, fine + -METER; orig. used to measure the amount of oxygen in the air] — **eu·di·o·met·ric** (yōō′·dē·ə·met′rik) or **·ri·cal** *adj.* — **eu′di·o·met′ri·cal·ly** *adv.* — **eu′di·om′e·try** *n.*

Eu·dist (yōō′dist) *n.* One of a French missionary order founded in 1643 by Jean Eudes.

Eu·do·ra (yōō·dôr′ə, -dō′rə) A feminine personal name. Also *Fr.* **Eu·dore** (œ·dôr′). [<Gk., good gift]

Eu·ga·ne·an Hills (yōō·gā′nē·ən) A range in northern Italy; highest point 1,978 feet. *Italian* **Col·li E·u·ga·ne·i** (kôl′lē ā′ōō·gä·nā′ē).

Eu·gene (yōō·jēn′) A masculine personal name. Also *Fr.* **Eu·gène** (œ·zhen′), *Ger.* **Eu·gen** (oi′·gān, oi·gān′), *Ital., Pg., Sp.* **E·u·ge·nio** (*Ital.* ā′ōō·jā′nyō, *Pg.* ā′ōō·zhe′nyōō, *Sp.* ā′ōō hā′·nyō), *Du., Sw.* **Eu·ge·ni·us** (*Du.* œ·kā′nē·əs, *Sw.* ā′ōō·gā′nē·əs). [<Gk., well-born]

Eu·gène of Savoy (œ·zhen′), **Prince,** 1663–1736, François Eugène de Savoie-Carignan, Austrian general.

Eu·ge·ni·a (yōō·jē′nē·ə; *Ger.* oi·gā′nē·ä, *Ital.* ā′ōō·jā′nyä; *Sp.* ā′ōō·hā′nyä) A feminine personal name. Also **Eu·ge·nie** (yōō·jē′nē), *Fr.* **Eu·gé·nie** (œ·zhā·nē′). See EUGENE.
— **Eugénie,** 1826–1920, Eugénie Marie de Montijo de Guzmán, empress of France 1853–70, wife of Napoleon III.

eu·gen·ic (yōō·jen′ik) *adj.* 1 Relating to the development and improvement of human stocks. 2 Well-born. Also **eu·gen′i·cal.** [<Gk. *eugenēs* well-born (< *eu-* well + *genos* race) + -IC] — **eu·gen′i·cal·ly** *adv.*

eu·gen·ics (yōō·jen′iks) *n. pl. (construed as singular)* The science and art of improving human breeds by so applying the ascertained principles of genetics and inheritance as to secure a desirable combination of physical characteristics and mental traits in the offspring of suitably mated parents. [Coined by Sir Francis Galton in 1883]

eu·ge·nist (yōō′jə·nist, yōō·jen′ist) *n.* A student or advocate of eugenics. Also **eu·gen·i·cist** (yōō·jen′ə·sist).

eu·ge·nol (yōō′jə·nōl, -nol) *n. Chem.* A colorless oil, $C_{10}H_{12}O_2$, of spicy odor and burning taste contained in oil of cloves, oil of bay, and other oils: used medicinally and in the manufacture of vanillin. [<EUGEN(IA) + -OL[2]]

Eu·gle·na (yōō·glē′nə) *n. Zool.* A genus of microscopic fresh-water protozoans (class *Mastigophora*) having one flagellum and a red eyespot or stigma, especially *E. viridis,* noted for its green chromatophores. [<NL <Gk. *eu-* well + *glēnē* eyeball]

eu·he·mer·ism (yōō·hē′mə·riz′əm, -hem′ə-) *n.* The rationalistic system of **Euhemerus,** a Sicilian philosopher of the fourth century B.C., who explained mythology as the deification of earth-born kings and heroes, and denied the existence of divine beings. — **eu·he′mer·ist** *n.* — **eu·he′mer·is′tic** *adj.* — **eu·he′mer·is′ti·cal·ly** *adv.*

eu·he·mer·ize (yōō·hē′mə·rīz, -hem′ə-) *v.t.* **·ized, ·iz·ing** To explain (myths) by euhemerism.

Eu·la·li·a (yōō·lā′lē·ə, *Ital., Sp.* ā′ōō·lä′lyä) A feminine personal name. Also *Fr.* **Eu·la·lie** (œ·là·lē′). [<Gk., fair speech]

Eu·ler (oi′lər), **Leonhard,** 1707–83, Swiss mathematician and physicist. — **Eu·le·ri·an** (oi·lir′ē·ən) *adj.*

Eu·ler-Chel·pin (oi′lər·kel′pin), **Hans August von,** born 1873, Swedish chemist born in Germany.

eu·lo·gi·a (yōō·lō′jē·ə) *n.* 1 In the Greek Church, unconsecrated bread which is blessed and distributed to non-communicants after the Eucharist. 2 In patristic writings, the Eucharist itself. [<LL <Gk. See EULOGY.]

eu·lo·gist (yōō′lə·jist) *n.* One who speaks in high or extravagant praise; the author of a eulogy. Also **eu′lo·giz′er.**

eu·lo·gize (yōō′lə·jīz) *v.t.* **·gized, ·giz·ing** To speak or write a eulogy about; to praise highly. Also *Brit.* **eu′lo·gise.** See synonyms under PRAISE. — **eu·lo·gis·tic** (yōō′lə·jis′tik) or **·ti·cal, eu·lo·gi·ous** (yōō·lō′jē·əs) *adj.* —**eu′lo·gis′ti·cal·ly** *adv.*

eu·lo·gy (yōō′lə·jē) *n. pl.* **·gies** A spoken or written laudation of a person's life or character; praise. Also **eu′lo·gism, eu·lo·gi·um** (yōō·lō′jē·əm). [<Gk. *eulogia* praise < *eu-* well + *legein* speak] — **eu·log·ic** (yōō·loj′ik) *adj.* — **eu·log′i·cal·ly** *adv.*

Synonyms: applause, commendation, encomium, laudation, panegyric, praise. *Panegyric* is *commendation* expressed *to* an assembly, and *applause* is *commendation* expressed *by* an

assembly. *Eulogy* is now used almost in the very sense of *panegyric,* a laudatory address before an audience; as Blaine's *eulogy* on Garfield; *eulogy,* however, is regarded as more discriminating than *panegyric,* which is unstinted *praise.* Compare APPLAUSE, PRAISE. *Antonyms:* abuse, calumny, denunciation, detraction, invective, obloquy, philippic, slander, vilification, vituperation.

Eu·men·i·des (yōō·men·ə·dēz) *n. pl.* The Furies. [< Gk., the kind ones]

Eu·nice (yōō′nis) A feminine personal name. Also *Lat.* **Eu·ni·ce** (yōō·nī′sē). [< Gk., happy victory]

Eu·no·mi·an (yōō·nō′mē·ən) *n.* A follower of **Eunomius,** a fourth century heretic who held that Christ was created by God, and a wholly subordinate being.

eu·nuch (yōō′nək) *n.* An emasculated man, formerly employed as a harem attendant or an Oriental palace official. [< L *eunuchus* < Gk. *eunouchos* chamber attendant < *eunē* bed + *echein* keep, guard]

eu·nuch·oid (yōō′nək·oid) *adj.* Having the appearance of a eunuch.

eu·on·y·mus (yōō·on′ə·məs) *n.* Any of a widely distributed genus *(Euonymus)* of shrubs or small trees having inconspicuous flowers and many-colored fruits; especially, the wahoo: also spelled *evonymus.* [< L *euonymos* < Gk. *euōnymos* < *eu-* well + *onyma* name]

eu·pa·to·ri·um (yōō′pə·tôr′ē·əm, -tō′rē-) *n.* Any plant of the large, principally American genus *(Eupatorium)* of herbaceous or shrubby plants of the composite family, the thoroughworts, with mainly aromatic or bitter leaves and numerous corymbose heads of small flowers, as the joe-pye-weed, the boneset, the white snakeroot, and hemp agrimony. [< NL < Gk. *eupatorion* agrimony; named after Mithridates VI, called *Eupator* < *eu-* good + *patēr* father]

eu·pat·rid (yōō·pat′rid, yōō′pə·trid) *adj.* Of or pertaining to the eupatridae; of patrician birth. —*n.* One of the eupatridae; a patrician.

eu·pat·ri·dae (yōō·pat′rə·dē) *n. pl.* The hereditary aristocracy of early Attica. [< Gk. *eupatridēs* of noble father < *eu-* good + *patēr* father]

Eu·pen (oi′pən) A town on the Belgian-German frontier; ceded to Belgium under the Treaty of Versailles.

eu·pep·si·a (yōō·pep′sē·ə, -shə) *n.* Healthy digestion: opposed to *dyspepsia.* Also **eu·pep·sy** (yōō′pep·sē, yōō·pep′-). [< NL < Gk. < *eu-* good + *pepsia* digestion]

eu·pep·tic (yōō·pep′tik) *adj.* **1** Pertaining to good digestion. **2** Promoting digestion. **3** Optimistic; sanguine.

Eu·phe·mi·a (yōō·fē′mē·ə; *Ger.* oi·fā′mē·ä; *Ital., Sp.* ā′ōō·fā′myä) A feminine personal name. Also *Fr.* **Eu·phé·mie** (œ·fā·mē′). [< Gk., of good report]

eu·phe·mism (yōō′fə·miz′əm) *n.* A mild or agreeable expression substituted for a realistic description of something disagreeable. [< Gk. *euphēmismos* < *euphēmizein* < *eu-* well + *phēmizein* < *phanai* speak] —**eu′phe·mist** *n.* —**eu′phe·mis′tic** or **·ti·cal** *adj.* —**eu′phe·mis′ti·cal·ly** *adv.*

eu·phe·mize (yōō′fə·mīz) *v.t.* & *v.i.* **·mized, ·miz·ing** To say in euphemistic form; express oneself euphemistically. —**eu′phe·miz′er** *n.*

eu·phon·ic (yōō·fon′ik) *adj.* Agreeable in sound; pertaining to euphony; euphonious. Also **eu·phon′i·cal.** —**eu·phon′i·cal·ly** *adv.* —**eu·phon′i·cal·ness** *n.*

eu·pho·ni·ous (yōō·fō′nē·əs) *adj.* Pleasant in sound, as a word; characterized by euphony. —**eu·pho′ni·ous·ly** *adv.* —**eu·pho′ni·ous·ness** *n.*

eu·pho·ni·um (yōō·fō′nē·əm) *n. Music* **1** A bass and tenor brass wind instrument, producing a mellower tone than the baritone saxhorn, and having the same range (E to B flat). **2** A musical instrument consisting of glass tubes connected by steel bars. [< NL < Gk. *euphōnos.* See EUPHONY.]

eu·pho·nize (yōō′fə·nīz) *v.t.* **·nized, ·niz·ing** To make euphonious. —**eu′pho·nism** *n.*

eu·pho·ny (yōō′fə·nē) *n. pl.* **·nies 1** Agreeableness of sound. **2** Pleasant-sounding combination or arrangement of words. See synonyms under METER. [< Gk. *euphōnia* < *euphōnos* < *eu-* good + *phōnē* sound]

eu·phor·bi·a (yōō·fôr′bē·ə) *n.* Any plant of a large and widely distributed genus *(Euphorbia)* of herbs of the spurge family, characterized by their milky juice and various medicinal properties. [< NL < L *euphorbea* < Gk. *euphorbion*; named after *Euphorbos,* a Greek physician] —**eu·phor′bi·a′ceous, eu·phor′bi·al** *adj.*

eu·pho·ri·a (yōō·fôr′ē·ə, -fō′rē-) *n.* **1** Physical comfort or well-being. **2** *Psychiatry* An exaggerated buoyancy and sense of bodily health. [< NL < Gk. *euphoria* < *eupherein* be well] —**eu·phor·ic** (yōō·fôr′ik, -for′-) *adj.*

eu·pho·ri·ant (yōō·fôr′ē·ənt, -fō′rē-) *n. Med.* A drug or other agent which induces euphoria.

eu·phot·ic (yōō·fot′ik) *adj. Ecol.* Of or pertaining to the receipt of the maximum amount of sunlight: The *euphotic* zone. [< Gk. *eu-* well + *phōs, photos* light]

eu·phra·sy (yōō′frə·sē) *n.* Eyebright. [< Med. L *euphrasia* < Gk, delight < *eu-* well + *phrēn* mind]

Eu·phra·tes (yōō·frā′tēz) A river of SW Asia, rising in eastern Turkey and flowing 1,700 miles SW to the Persian Gulf.

eu·phroe (yōō′frō, -vrō) *n. Naut.* A long wooden block having several holes through which to reeve a cord: used in adjusting an awning on shipboard, also sometimes in tightening tent ropes: also spelled *uphroe.* [< Du. *juffrouw,* orig., a maiden]

Eu·phros·y·ne (yōō·fros′ə·nē, -froz′-) One of the Graces.

eu·phu·ism (yōō′fyōō·iz′əm) *n.* **1** An affectation of elegance in writing; a high-flown periphrastic style, such as that of John Lyly. **2** An instance of such a style. **3** Affected elegance in dress, etc. [after *Euphues,* character created by John Lyly] —**eu′phu·ist** *n.* —**eu′phu·is′tic** or **·ti·cal** *adj.* —**eu′phu·is′ti·cal·ly** *adv.*

eu·phu·ize (yōō′fyōō·īz) *v.t.* **·ized, ·iz·ing** To speak or write in an affected style.

eu·plas·tic (yōō·plas′tik) *adj. Biol.* Readily transformable into organic tissue. —*n.* Matter thus transformable. [< Gk. *euplastos* easily molded < *eu-* well + *plassein* form]

eu·ploid (yōō′ploid) *adj. Genetics.* Having a number of chromosomes that is an exact multiple of the haploid number. —*n.* A euploid cell or organism. —**eu·ploid·y** *n.*

eup·ne·a (yōōp·nē′ə) *n. Med.* Easy, natural breathing, normal respiration: opposed to *dyspnea.* Also **eup·noe′a.** [< EU- + Gk. *pnoia* breath < *pneein* breathe]

Eur·a·sia (yōō·rā′zhə, -shə) The land mass comprising the continents of Europe and Asia.

Eur·a·sian (yōō·rā′zhən, -shən) *adj.* **1** Pertaining to both Europe and Asia. **2** Of European and Asian descent. —*n.* A half-caste of mixed European and Asian parentage. Also **Eur·a·si·at·ic** (yōō·rā′zhē·at′ik, -shē-), **Eu·ro·pa·sian** (yōōr′ō·pā′zhən, -shən).

eu·re·ka (yōō·rē′kə) *interj.* I have found (it): attributed to Archimedes on his discovery of a method of determining the ratio of weight to volume: the motto of the State of California. [< Gk. *heurēka*]

Eure (œr) A river in NW France, flowing 112 miles to the Seine.

eu·rhyth·mics (yōō·rith′miks) See EURYTHMICS.

eu·rhyth·my (yōō·rith′mē) See EURYTHMY.

Eu·rip·i·des (yōō·rip′ə·dēz), 480–406 B.C., Greek tragic dramatist.

eu·ri·pus (yōō·rī′pəs) *n. pl.* **·pi** (-pī) **1** An arm of the sea where the tide rushes in strong, shifting currents. **2** A scene or occasion of violent changes. [< L < Gk. *euripos* a strait < *eu-* well + *rhipē* rush]

Eu·ro·com·mu·nism (yōōr′ō·kom′yə·niz·əm) *n.* A form of Communism practiced in some West-ern European countries that emphasizes the importance of democratic methods.

Eu·ro·dol·lar (yōōr′ō·dol′ər) *n. Econ.* A U.S. dollar on deposit outside the United States, especially in one of the western European countries. [< EUR(OPE) + DOLLAR]

Eu·ro·pa (yōō·rō′pə) **1** In Greek mythology, a Phoenician princess abducted to Crete by Zeus in the guise of a bull, where she bore Minos, Rhadamanthus, and Sarpedon. **2** A female figure representing Europe.

Eu·rope (yōōr′əp) A continent comprising a vast western peninsula of the Eurasian land mass; about 3,800,000 square miles, or excluding European U.S.S.R. and Turkey about 1,902,600 square miles.

Eu·ro·pe·an (yōōr′ə·pē′ən) *adj.* Relating to or derived from Europe or its inhabitants. —*n.* A native of Europe.

European Economic Community A customs union of France, Italy, West Germany, and the Benelux nations. Also **European Common Market.**

Eu·ro·pe·an·ize (yōōr′ə·pē′ən·īz) *v.t.* **·ized, ·iz·ing** To make European in characteristics, views, culture, etc. —**Eu′ro·pe′an·i·za′tion** *n.*

European plan The system of hotel-keeping by which lodging and service are charged for separately from meals, these being furnished to order. Compare AMERICAN PLAN.

eu·ro·pi·um (yōō·rō′pē·əm) *n.* A rare metallic element (symbol Eu, atomic number 63) of the lanthanide series. See PERIODIC TABLE. [< NL < L *Europa* Europe]

Eu·rus (yōōr′əs) In Greek mythology, the god of the east or southeast wind. [< L < Gk. *Euros* east wind]

eury- *combining form* Wide; broad: *eurychoric.* [< Gk. *eurys* wide]

Eu·ry·a·le (yōō·rī′ə·lē) One of the Gorgons.

eu·ry·ce·phal·ic (yōōr′i·sə·fal′ik) *adj. Anat.* Broad-headed. Also **eu′ry·ceph′a·lous** (-sef′ə·ləs).

eu·ry·cho·ric (yōōr′i·kôr′ik, -kō′rik) *adj. Ecol.* Of or pertaining to a wide distribution in varying climates, as plant species. [< EURY- + Gk. *chōros* country]

Eu·ryd·i·ce (yōō·rid′ə·sē) In Greek mythology, the wife of Orpheus. See ORPHEUS.

eu·ryg·na·thous (yōōr′ig·nā′thəs) *adj. Anat.* Having a wide upper jaw. Also **eu′ryg·na′thic.** [< EURY- + Gk. *gnathos* jaw]

eu·ry·on (yōōr′ē·on) *n. Anat.* The point on either side of the head above the ear having the greatest lateral projection: the distance between the two euryons is a measure of the head width. [< Gk. *eurys* broad]

eu·ryp·ter·id (yōō·rip′tər·id) *n. Paleontol.* Any member of an extinct Silurian order *(Eurypterida)* of very large aquatic arthropods related to the *Arachnida* and to the king crab. —*adj.* Belonging to this order. [< NL *Eurypterida* < Gk. eurys broad + *pteron* wing]

Eu·rys·the·us (yōō·ris′thē·əs) In Greek legend, a king of Argos who imposed the twelve labors upon Hercules.

eu·ry·ther·mic (yōōr′i·thûr′mik) *adj. Biol.* Designating plant or animal organisms capable of withstanding a wide range of temperature conditions, as bacteria. [< EURY- + Gk. *thermē* heat]

eu·ryth·mics (yōō·rith′miks) *n.* A method of free-style rhythmical bodily movements in interpretation of musical compositions: devised by Émile Jaques-Dalcroze (1860–1950), Swiss composer. Also spelled *eurhythmics.*

eu·ryth·my (yōō·rith′mē) *n.* Harmony and just proportion. Also spelled *eurhythmy.* [< L < Gk. *eurythmia* harmony < *eu-* well + *rhythmos* rhythm] —**eu·ryth′mic** or **·mi·cal** *adj.*

Eus·den (yōōz′dən), **Laurence,** 1688–1730, English poet; poet laureate 1718–30.

Eu·se·bi·an (yōō·sē′bē·ən) *adj.* **1** Of or pertaining to Eusebius Pamphili, bishop of Caesarea: the *Eusebian* canons. **2** Of or pertaining to Eusebius, bishop of Constantinople, a leader of the Arians. —*n.* A follower of Eusebius.

Eu·se·bi·us (yōō·sē′bē·əs), 264?–340?, bishop of Caesarea: called "the father of church history": surnamed *Pamphili.*

Eu·se·bi·us (yōō·sē′bē·əs), died A.D. 341, Arian bishop of Nicomedia and Constantinople.

eu·sol (yōō′sōl, -sol) *n.* A chlorinated antiseptic solution for wound treatment. [< E(DINBURGH) U(NIVERSITY) SOL(UTION)]

eu·spo·ran·gi·ate (yōō′spə·ran′jē·āt) *adj. Bot.* Having sporangia developed from a group of cells, instead of from a single cell. [< EU- + SPORANGIA]

Eus·tace (yōōs′tis) A masculine personal name. Also *Du.* **Eu·sta·ti·us** (oi·stä′sē·əs), *Fr.* **Eu·stache** (œ·stäsh′), *Ger.* **Eu·sta·thi·us** (oi·stä′tē·ōōs), *Ital.* **E·u·sta·zi·o** (ā′ōō·stä′dzē·ō), *Lat.* **Eu·sta·chi·us** (yōō·stā′kē·əs), *Sp.* **E·u·sta·quio** (ā′ōō·stä′kyō), *Pg.* **E·sta·cio** (e·stä′syōō). [< Gk., happy in harvest]

Eu·sta·chi·an (yōō·stā′kē·ən, -shē·ən, -shən) *adj.* Of, pertaining to, or named for Eustachio.

Eustachian tube *Anat.* A passage between the pharynx and the inner ear; it forms the auditory canal and serves to equalize air pressure between the inner ear, the tympanic cavity of the middle ear, and the external air.

See illustration under EAR. [after Bartolommeo *Eustachio*]

E·u·sta·chio (ā'o͞o'stä'kyō), **Bartolommeo,** 1520–74, Italian anatomist.

eu·tax·it·ic (yo͞o'tak·sit'ik) Of or pertaining to ore deposits occurring in stratified form: opposed to *ataxitic.*

eu·tax·y (yo͞o·tak'sē) *n.* Good arrangement; orderly disposition. [<Gk. *eutaxia* <*eu-* good + *taxis* arrangement <*tassein* arrange]

eu·tec·tic (yo͞o·tek'tik) *adj. Chem.* Melting readily or at a low temperature: said of an alloy or a solution that has the lowest possible fusing point, usually below that of any of the components taken separately. —*n.* A eutectic substance, as an alloy. [<GK. *eutēktos* <*eu-* well, easily + *tēkein* fuse]

eu·tec·toid (yo͞o·tek'toid) *adj. Chem.* Like a eutectic; formed at the lowest temperature.

eu·tel·e·gen·e·sis (yo͞o·tel'ə·jen'ə·sis) *n. Biol.* Artificial insemination. [<EU- + TELE- + GENESIS] **—eu·tel'e·gen'ic, eu·tel'e·ge·net'ic** *adj.*

Eu·ter·pe (yo͞o·tûr'pē) The Muse of lyric song and music. **—Eu·ter'pe·an** *adj.*

eu·tha·na·si·a (yo͞o'thə·nā'zhē·ə, -zhə) *n.* **1** Painless, peaceful death. **2** The deliberate putting to death of a person suffering from a painful and incurable disease; mercy killing. Also called *active euthanasia.* **3** Death resulting from the cessation of heroic measures to prolong a life. Also called *passive euthanasia.* [<Gk. <*eu-* easy + *thanatos* death]

eu·then·ics (yo͞o·then'iks) *n. pl. (construed as singular)* **1** The science of improving the human race by external influences, apart from considerations of heredity. **2** The science which aims at securing the most favorable environmental conditions for the growth of plants and animals. Compare EUGENICS. [<GK. *euthenia* well-being] **—eu'the·nist** *n.*

Eu·the·ri·a (yo͞o·thir'ē·ə) *n.* A subclass of mammals characterized by a highly developed placenta and lengthy prenatal development of offspring: includes man and most of the mammalian types: formerly called *Monodelphia.* [<NL <Gk. *eu-* good, typical + *thērion* animal]

eu·troph·ic (yo͞o·trof'ik, -trō'fik) *adj. Ecol.* Of a lake or other body of water, characterized by an advanced stage of eutrophication; rich in nutrients; mature. [<Gk. *eutrophos* well-nourished]

eu·troph·i·ca·tion (yo͞o·trof'ə·kā'shən, -trō'fə-) *n. Ecol.* The process by which a body of water, as a lake, matures and ages, characterized by an environment growing progressively richer in mineral and organic nutrients, resulting in a seasonally recurring depletion in oxygen that is ultimately incompatible with animal life. [<EUTROPHIC + -ATION]

eux·e·nite (yo͞ok'sə·nīt) *n.* A brilliant, metallic-vitreous, brownish-black mineral crystallizing in the orthorhombic system and valuable as a source of certain rare elements, as titanium, germanium, cerium. [<Gk. *euxenos* hospitable + -ITE[1], because it often contains rare elements]

Eux·ine Sea (yo͞ok'sin, -sīn) See BLACK SEA.

E·va (ē'və; *Du., Ger., Ital., Pg., Sp.* ā'vä; *Sw.* e'vä) A feminine personal name. Also **Eve** (ēv), *Fr.* **Ève** (ev). [See EVE]

e·vac·u·ant (i·vak'yo͞o·ənt) *adj. Med.* Producing evacuation; cathartic, diuretic, or emetic. —*n.* Something that assists evacuation.

e·vac·u·ate (i·vak'yo͞o·āt) *v.* **·at·ed, ·at·ing** *v.t.* **1** *Mil.* **a** To give up or abandon possession of; withdraw from, as a fortress or city. **b** To withdraw (troops, inhabitants, etc.) from a threatened area or place. **2** To make empty; vacate. **3** To remove the contents of. **4** *Physiol.* To discharge or eject, as from the bowels. —*v.i.* **5** To withdraw, as from a threatened area or place. [<L *evacuatus,* pp. of *evacuare* <*e-* out + *vacuare* make empty <*vacuus* empty] **—e·vac'u·a'tive, e·vac'u·a·to'ry** (-tôr'ē, -tō'rē) *adj.* **—e·vac'u·a'tor** *n.*

e·vac·u·a·tion (i·vak'yo͞o·ā'shən) *n.* **1** The act of evacuating or making empty: the *evacuation* of a fort. **2** *Physiol.* That which is evacuated or ejected by excretory passages, especially by the bowels. **3** The act of making void or null, as a contract.

e·vac·u·ee (i·vak'yo͞o·ē') *n.* One who has been removed from or has abandoned his home.

e·vade (i·vād') *v.* **e·vad·ed, e·vad·ing** *v.t.* **1** To escape or get away from by tricks or cleverness; save oneself from: to *evade* pursuers or a crisis. **2** To avoid or get out of; get around: to *evade* a question or a duty. **3** To baffle; elude: The facts *evade* explanation. —*v.i.* **4** To practice evasion. **5** *Rare* To escape; get away. See synonyms under ESCAPE. [<L *evadere* <*e-* out + *vadere* go] **—e·vad'a·ble, e·vad'i·ble** *adj.* **—e·vad'er** *n.*

e·vag·i·nate (i·vaj'ə·nāt) *v.t.* **·nat·ed, ·nat·ing** *Biol.* To turn inside out, as a tubular organ; protrude by eversion; unsheathe. [<LL *evaginatus,* pp. of *evaginare* <*e-* out + *vagina* a sheath] **—e·vag'i·na'tion** *n.*

e·val·u·ate (i·val'yo͞o·āt) *v.t.* **·at·ed, ·at·ing** **1** To find or determine the amount, worth, etc., of; appraise. **2** *Math.* To determine the numerical value of. [<F *évaluer* <*e-* out (<L *ex*) + *valuer* <OF *valoir.* See VALUE.]

e·val·u·a·tion (i·val'yo͞o·ā'shən) *n.* Accurate appraisal of value.

Ev·an (ev'ən) A masculine personal name. [<Celtic, young warrior]

ev·a·nesce (ev'ə·nes') *v.t.* **·nesced, ·nesc·ing** To disappear by degrees; vanish gradually. [<L *evanescere* <*e-* out + *vanescere* vanish <*vanus* empty] **—ev'a·nes'ci·ble** *adj.*

ev·a·nes·cent (ev'ə·nes'ənt) *adj.* Passing away, or liable to pass away, gradually or imperceptibly. See synonyms under TRANSIENT. [<F *évanescent* <L *evanescens, -entis,* ppr. of *evanescere.* See EVANESCE.] **—ev'a·nes'cence** *n.* **—ev'a·nes'cent·ly** *adv.*

e·van·gel[1] (i·van'jəl) *n.* **1** The message of redemption through Jesus Christ; the Christian gospel. **2** *Usually cap.* One of the four Gospels of the New Testament. **3** Any good news or glad tidings. [<OF *evangile* <LL *evangelium* <Gk. *euangelion* good news <*eu-* good + *angellein* announce]

e·van·gel[2] (i·van'jəl) An evangelist. [<MGk. *euangelos* <*eu-* good + *angelos* messenger]

e·van·gel·i·cal (ē'van·jel'i·kəl, ev'ən-) *adj.* **1** In or agreeing with the four Gospels or the teachings of the New Testament. **2** Denoting the adherents of a school of Protestant theology stressing the divine inspiration, authority, and sufficiency of the Scriptures, the fallen state of man, salvation by faith in the redeeming work of Christ, and spiritual regeneration, and denying in whole or in part the efficacy of the sacraments and the authority of the church. **3** *U.S.* Loosely, orthodox; Trinitarian in belief. **4** Zealous or fervent: *evangelical* preaching. **5** Pertaining to the work of an evangelist; evangelistic: *evangelical* labors. —*n.* A member of an evangelical church, or of an evangelical party within a church, as of the Low Church party in Anglicanism. Also **e'van·gel'ic.** [<LL *evangelicus* <Gk. *euangelikos* <*euangelion.* See EVANGEL[1].] **—e'van·gel'i·cal·ism, e'van·gel'i·cism** *n.* **—e'van·gel'i·cal·ly** *adv.* **—e'van·gel'i·cal·ness, e·van·ge·lic·i·ty** (i·van'jə·lis'ə·tē) *n.*

Evangelical and Reformed Church A presbyterial Protestant denomination, first organized in 1934, and, since 1957, a part of the *United Church of Christ.*

Evangelical Counsel See COUNSEL OF PERFECTION.

E·van·ge·line (i·van'jə·lin, -līn, -lēn) A feminine personal name. [<Gk., bearer of glad tidings] **—Evangeline** The heroine of Longfellow's poem of this name.

e·van·gel·ism (i·van'jə·liz'əm) *n.* **1** The zealous preaching or spreading of the gospel. **2** The work of an evangelist.

e·van·gel·ist (i·van'jə·list) *n.* **1** *Usually cap.* One of the four writers of the New Testament Gospels; Matthew, Mark, Luke, or John. **2** An itinerant or missionary preacher; a revivalist. **3** In the Mormon Church, a patriarch.

e·van·gel·is·tic (i·van'jə·lis'tik) *adj.* **1** Pertaining to an evangelist. **2** Evangelical. **3** Seeking or suited to evangelize. **—e·van'gel·is'ti·cal·ly** *adv.*

e·van·gel·ize (i·van'jəl·īz) *v.* **·ized, ·iz·ing** *v.t.* **1** To preach the gospel to. **2** To convert to Christianity. —*v.t.* **3** To preach as an evangelist. **—e·van'gel·i·za'tion** *n.* **—e·van'gel·iz'er** *n.*

Ev·ans (ev'ənz), **Sir Arthur John,** 1851–1941, English archeologist. **—Herbert McLean, 1882–1971, U.S.** anatomist and embryologist. **—Maurice,** born 1901, English actor. **—Robley Dunglison,** 1846–1912, U.S. admiral. **—Rudulph,** 1878–1960, U.S. sculptor.

Ev·ans·ton (ev'ən·stən, -ənz·tən) A city on Lake Michigan, Illinois; a northern suburb of Chicago.

Ev·ans·ville (ev'ənz·vil') A city on the Ohio River in SW Indiana.

e·vap·o·ra·ble (i·vap'ər·ə·bəl) *adj.* Capable of being converted into vapor. **—e·vap'o·ra·bil'i·ty** *n.*

e·vap·o·rate (i·vap'ə·rāt) *v.* **·rat·ed, ·rat·ing** *v.t.* **1** To convert into vapor, usually by application of heat; vaporize. **2** To remove moisture from by a drying or heating process; to concentrate (fruit, milk, etc.) by evaporation. —*v.i.* **3** To become vapor; pass off as vapor. **4** To yield vapor. **5** To vanish; disappear. [<LL *evaporatus,* pp. of *evaporare* <*e-* out, away + *vapor.* See VAPOR.] **—e·vap'o·ra'tive** *adj.*

evaporated milk Cow's milk, unsweetened, with much of its water content removed.

e·vap·o·ra·tion (i·vap'ə·rā'shən) *n.* **1** The act or process of changing or being changed into vapor, specifically, at temperatures below the boiling point. **2** A rising of or passing off in vapor. **3** The act of drying or concentrating. **4** The result of evaporation; vapor.

e·vap·o·ra·tor (i·vap'ə·rā'tər) *n.* An apparatus for drying substances, as fruits, by evaporation.

e·vap·o·rim·e·ter (i·vap'ə·rim'ə·tər) *n.* An apparatus for testing the rate of evaporation of a liquid; an atmometer. Also **e·vap'o·rom'e·ter.**

Ev·arts (ev'ərts), **William Maxwell,** 1818–1901, U.S. lawyer and statesman.

e·va·sion (i·vā'zhən) *n.* The act, means, or result of evading; equivocation; subterfuge. [<LL *evasio, -onis* <*evadere.* See EVADE.]

e·va·sive (i·vā'siv) *adj.* Tending or seeking to evade; marked by evasion; elusive. **—e·va'·sive·ly** *adv.* **—e·va'sive·ness** *n.*

eve (ēv) *n.* **1** *Poetic* Evening. **2** The evening before a church festival or saint's day: Christmas *Eve.* **3** The time immediately preceding some event. [Var. of EVEN[2]]

Eve (ēv) A feminine personal name. [<Hebrew, life]
—Eve The wife of Adam and the mother of all mankind. *Gen.* iii 20.

e·vec·tics (i·vek'tiks) *n. pl (construed as singular)* **1** The art of developing health, physical vigor, strength, and energy. **2** Hygiene. [<Gk. *euektikē* (*technē*) (skill) of good health <*eu echein* be well]

e·vec·tion (i·vek'shən) *n. Astron.* The largest inequality in the motion of the moon, due to the action of the sun, which causes periodic changes in the eccentricity of the moon's orbit. [<LL *evectio, -onis* <*evehere* <*e-* out + *vehere* carry] **—e·vec'tion·al** *adj.*

Ev·e·li·na (ev'ə·lī'nə, -lē'-) A feminine personal name. Also **Ev'e·line** (-līn, -lēn, -lin). [<Celtic, pleasant]

Ev·e·lyn (ev'ə·lin, ēv'lin) A feminine, or (especially British) masculine, personal name. [<L, hazelnut]

Eve·lyn (ēv'lin), **John,** 1620–1706, English diarist; one of the founders of the Royal Society.

e·ven[1] (ē'vən) *adj.* **1** Free from inequalities or irregularities; level; uniform. **2** Divisible by 2 without remainder: said of numbers. **3** On the same level or line. **4** Without advantage on either side; of the same character; equal; fair; impartial. **5** Unvarying in disposition, action, or quality. **6** Whole or entire: said of money, numbers, etc.: *even* dollars. See synonyms under FLAT, HORIZONTAL, JUST, LEVEL, SMOOTH. **—of even date** *Law* Of identical date. **—on an even keel** Smoothly: from a nautical phrase applied to a ship with the same draft of water forward and aft. **—to get even** To get revenge; retaliate. —*adv.* **1** To a like degree; at the very time; so far or so much as; exactly; precisely; fully; quite: used to express emphasis, surprise, concession, or extension to what might not be expected: *even* to the end, intelligible *even* to a child. **2** As much as; yet: They would not believe the report, nor *even* the evidence. **3** Smoothly; regularly;

evenly: His verses ran *even*. **4** *Obs.* Exactly. — *v.t.* & *v.i.* **1** To make or become even or level; balance: often with *up*. **2** To make or become equal; equalize. [OE *efen* level] — **e'ven·ly** *adv.* — **e'ven·ness** *n.*

e·ven² (ē'vən) *n. Archaic* **1** Evening. **2** The eve before a church festival, an event, etc. [OE *æfen*]

e·ven·fall (ē'vən·fôl') *n.* Early evening; twilight; dusk.

e·ven-hand·ed (ē'vən·han'did) *adj.* Treating all alike; impartial. — **e'ven-hand'ed·ly** *adv.* — **e'ven-hand'ed·ness** *n.*

even if Although; notwithstanding.

eve·ning (ēv'ning) *n.* **1** The closing part of the day and beginning of the night; in a strict sense, from sunset till dark; in common speech, the latter part of the day and the earlier part of the night, until bedtime: used also adjectively: *evening* prayer. ◆ Collateral adjective: *vesperal*. **2** *U.S. Dial.* Afternoon until dark. **3** A closing or declining part of any state or period: the *evening* of life. [OE *æfnung* < *æfnian* grow to evening]

evening dress Formal evening wear, especially of men.

evening gown A woman's formal dress for evening wear.

Evening Prayer In the Anglican Church, an order of worship prescribed for use in the evening: also called *evensong, vespers.*

evening primrose **1** A stout, erect American biennial herb (*Oenothera biennis*), with conspicuous yellow flowers opening in the evening. **2** Any other species of this genus.

eve·nings (ēv'ningz) *adv.* During the evening: They played bridge *evenings*.

evening star A bright planet when visible in the west just after sunset: especially applied to Venus: also called *Hesperus* and *Vesper*.

e·ven-mind·ed (ē'vən·mīn'did) *adj.* Characterized by equanimity; fair; just.

e·ven·song (ē'vən·sông', -song') *n.* **1** *Eccl.* The service of Evening Prayer, or the time, usually near sunset, of saying it. **2** A song or hymn sung at evening. [OE *æfensang*]

e·vent (i·vent') *n.* **1** Anything that happens or comes to pass. **2** The result or outcome of any action. **3** A contingent occurrence or state of things. **4** One incident in a series, as of games. **5** *Philos.* Anything that occurs, usually manifesting changes and lasting only a relatively short time: thus opposed to *object*, which endures. [< OF < L *eventus* < *e-* out + *venire* come] — **e·vent'less** *adj.*

Synonyms: case, chance, circumstance, consequence, contingency, end, episode, fact, fortune, incident, issue, occurrence, outcome, possibility, result, sequel. Etymologically, the *incident* is that which falls in, the *event* that which comes out; *event* is thus greater and more signal than *incident*; we speak of trifling *incidents*, great *events*; *incidents* of daily life, *events* of history. *Circumstance* agrees with *incident* in denoting a matter of relatively slight importance, but implies a more direct connection with the principal matter as indicated in the phrase "circumstantial evidence." An *occurrence* is, etymologically, that which we run against, without thought of its origin, connection, or tendency. An *episode* is connected with the main course of *events*, like an *incident* or *circumstance*, but is of more independent interest and importance. *Outcome* is the Saxon, and *event* the Latin for expressing the same original idea. *Consequence* and *result* express more of logical connection. and are more comprehensive. The *end* may be simple cessation; the *event* is what has been accomplished; the *event* of a war is victory or defeat; the *end* of the war is reached when a treaty of peace is signed. Since the future is contingent, *event* comes to have the meaning of a *contingency*; as, In the *event* of his death, the policy will at once fall due. Compare CIRCUMSTANCE, CONSEQUENCE, END.

e·vent·ful (i·vent'fəl) *adj.* Attended or characterized by important or noteworthy events; also, momentous. — **e·vent'ful·ly** *adv.* — **e·vent'ful·ness** *n.*

e·ven·tide (ē'vən·tīd') *n. Poetic* Evening time.

e·ven·tu·al (i·ven'chōō·əl) *adj.* **1** Pertaining to or being a result; consequential; ultimate. **2** Dependent upon a final contingency. — **e·ven'tu·al·ly** *adv.*

e·ven·tu·al·i·ty (i·ven'chōō·al'ə·tē) *n. pl.* **·ties** **1** The character of happening contingently

or as a result. **2** A consequential event or issue.

e·ven·tu·ate (i·ven'chōō·āt) *v.t.* **·at·ed**, **·at·ing** **1** To have a particular event or issue; result. **2** To be the event or issue; happen. — **e·ven'tu·a'tion** *n.*

ev·er (ev'ər) *adv.* **1** At any time; in any case: better than *ever*. **2** In any degree: Run as fast as *ever* you can. **3** Under all circumstances; invariably; always. [OE *æfre*]

Ever may appear as a combining form in hyphemes or solidemes; as in:

ever-abiding	ever-growing
ever-active	ever-increasing
ever-admiring	everliving
everbearing	ever-loving
ever-blazing	ever-moving
ever-blessed	ever-new
everblooming	ever-present
ever-burning	ever-ready
ever-celebrated	ever-recurrent
ever-changeful	ever-renewed
ever-changing	ever-renewing
ever-circling	ever-strong
ever-constant	ever-varying
ever-deepening	ever-widening
ever-dying	ever-willing
ever-esteemed	ever-winding
ever-expanding	ever-wise
ever-faithful	ever-young

ever and anon Now and then; at one time and at another; repeatedly.

Ev·er·est (ev'ər·ist), **Mount** A peak of the Himalayas in eastern Nepal, the highest recorded point of the earth's surface; 29,002 feet. *Tibetan* **Cho·mo·lung·ma** (chō'mō·lōong'· mä).

Ev·er·ett (ev'ər·it), **Edward**, 1794–1865, U.S. scholar, statesman, and orator.

Ev·er·ett (ev'ər·it) A port on Puget Sound in NW Washington.

ev·er·glade (ev'ər·glād) *n.* A tract of low swampy land covered with tall grass. — **The Everglades** A swampy subtropical region of southern Florida; 100 miles long, 50–75 miles wide.

Everglades National Park A government reservation in the southern part of the Everglades; 1,719 square miles; established 1947.

Everglade State Nickname of FLORIDA.

ev·er·green (ev'ər·grēn') *adj.* Retaining verdure throughout the year: opposite of *deciduous*. — *n.* **1** A tree or other plant which retains its foliage throughout the year, as the pine, fir, hemlock, laurel, etc. **2** A branch or twig of an evergreen plant or tree, or the plant, used for decoration: Christmas *evergreens*.

evergreen oak Any of various live oaks of the United States; especially, *Quercus nigra* of the South, and encina.

Evergreen State Nickname of WASHINGTON.

ev·er·last·ing (ev'ər·las'ting, -läs'-) *adj.* **1** Lasting forever; eternal. **2** Interminable; incessant. — *n.* **1** Past or future endless duration; eternity. **2** A plant, the flowers of which retain their form and color when dried, as the cudweed. **3** Prunella, a durable woolen material. **4** A game of cards. See synonyms under ETERNAL, IMMORTAL. — **the Everlasting** The Eternal; God. — **ev'er·last'ing·ly** *adv.* — **ev'er·last'ing·ness** *n.*

ev·er·more (ev'ər·môr', -mōr') *adv.* During all time; always.

e·ver·si·ble (i·vûr'sə·bəl) *adj.* Capable of being everted.

e·ver·sion (i·vûr'zhən) *n.* A turning outward or inside out. [< L *eversio, -onis* < *evertere*. See EVERT.]

ever so Exceedingly, very: He is *ever so* strong. See NEVER SO.

e·vert (i·vûrt') *v.t.* To turn inside out; turn outward. [< L *evertere* < *e-* out + *vertere* turn] — **e·ver·tile** (i·vûr'til) *adj.*

e·ver·tor (i·vûr'tər) *n. Anat.* A muscle which serves to rotate an organ or a part outward.

eve·ry (ev'rē, ev'ər·ē) *adj.* **1** Each individual or part, as of an aggregate whole; all taken one by one. **2** All possible; very great: Show him *every* consideration. **3** *Obs.* All: with plural noun. — *pron. Law* Every one; each. [ME < OE *æfre* ever + *ælc* each]

Synonyms (adj.): all, any, both, each, either. *Any* makes no selection and may not reach to the full limits of *all*; *each* and *every* make no exception or omission, and must extend to

all; *all* sweeps in the units as part of a total, each and every proceed through the units to the total. A promise made to *all* omits none; a promise made to *any* may not reach *all*; a promise made to *every* one is so made that no individual shall fail to be aware of it; a promise made to *each* is made to the individuals personally, one by one. *Each* divides, both unites; if a certain sum is given to *each* of two persons, *both* (together) receive twice the amount; a man may fire *both* barrels of a gun by a single movement; if he fires *each* barrel, he discharges them separately. *Either* denotes one of two, indefinitely to the exclusion of the other; *either* is also in good, but somewhat rare, use, in the sense of *each* or *both* of two, taken separately and indifferently; as, on *either* side of the river.

eve·ry·bod·y (ev'rē·bod'ē, -bud'ē) *pron.* Every person; everyone.

◆ **everybody, everyone** *Everybody*, like *everyone*, calls for a singular verb and singular pronouns of reference: *Everybody* here *has* had *his* turn.

eve·ry·day (ev'rē·dā', -dā') *adj.* **1** Suitable for every day; ordinary; *everyday* clothes. **2** Happening every day. **3** Having general utility; practicable. See synonyms under GENERAL, USUAL.

every now and then Occasionally; intermittently. Also **every now and again.**

every once in a while Every now and then.

eve·ry·one (ev'rē·wun', -wən) *pron.* Everybody; every person: *Everyone* likes ice-cream. See note under EVERYBODY.

every one Each individual person or thing out of the whole number, excepting none: *Every one* of the men is ill.

every so often At more or less regular intervals.

eve·ry·thing (ev'rē·thing') *pron.* Each one in a collection or number of things, none being omitted; whatever exists; whatever pertains to some specified person, thing, place, condition, etc. — *n.* That which is of the highest importance or which includes all things: Health is *everything* to the worker.

eve·ry·where (ev'rē·hwâr') *adv.* **1** At or in every place. **2** Wherever.

every which way *U.S. Colloq.* In every way; in all directions.

Eve's-cup (ēvz'kup') *n.* An insectivorous American pitcherplant (*Sarracenia flava*) with trumpet leaves, crimson throat, and yellow flowers.

Eve·sham (ēv'shəm, ē'shəm, ē'səm) A municipal borough in SE Worcester, England; scene of Edward I's victory over Simon de Montfort, 1265.

e·vict (i·vikt') *v.t.* **1** To expel (a tenant) by legal process; dispossess; put out. **2** To recover, as property, by legal process. See synonyms under BANISH. [< L *evictus*, pp. of *evincere* < *e-* out + *vincere* conquer] — **e·vic'tion** *n.* — **e·vic'tor** *n.*

ev·i·dence (ev'ə·dəns) *n.* **1** That which makes evident or clear, whether taken singly or collectively. **2** Any ground or reason for knowledge or certitude in knowledge. **3** Proof, whether immediate or derived by inference. **4** A fact or body of facts on which a proof, belief, or judgment is based. **5** *Law* That by means of which a fact is established: distinguished from *proof*, which is the result of evidence, and *testimony*, which is evidence given orally. **6** Evidentness; clearness. See synonyms under CERTAINTY, DEMONSTRATION, PROOF, TESTIMONY. — **circumstantial evidence** Evidence consisting of circumstances which furnish reasonable ground for believing or deciding as to the existence of fact, or the guilt or innocence of an accused person. — **in evidence** Present; at hand; to be seen; conspicuous. — *v.t.* **·denced, ·denc·ing 1** To make evident; show clearly; display. **2** To support by one's testimony; attest.

ev·i·dent (ev'ə·dənt) *adj.* Plain, manifest, or clear, as to the mind or the senses; obvious. [< L *evidens, -entis*, ppr. of *evidere* < *e-* out + *videre* see] — **ev'i·dent·ly** *adv.*

Synonyms: apparent, clear, conspicuous, discernible, distinct, glaring, indubitable, manifest, obvious, open, overt, palpable, patent, perceptible, plain, tangible, transparent, unmistakable, visible. That is *apparent* which clearly appears to the senses or to the mind as soon as the attention is directed toward it;

that is *evident* of which the mind is made sure by some inference that supplements the facts of perception: The marks of a struggle were *apparent* in broken shrubbery and trampled ground, and the finding of a mutilated body and a rifled purse made it *evident* that robbery and murder had been committed. That is *manifest* which we can lay the hand upon; *manifest* is thus stronger than *evident*, as touch is more absolute than sight. That is *obvious* which is directly in the way so that it cannot be missed; as, The application of the remark was *obvious*. *Visible* applies to all that can be perceived by the sense of sight, whether the noonday sun, a ship on the horizon, or a microscopic object. *Discernible* applies to that which is dimly or faintly *visible*, requiring strain and effort in order to be seen; as, The ship was *discernible* through the mist. That is *conspicuous* which stands out and attracts the attention. *Palpable* and *tangible* express more emphatically the thought of *manifest*. See APPARENT, CLEAR, MANIFEST, NOTORIOUS. *Antonyms*: concealed, covert, dark, hidden, impalpable, impenetrable, imperceptible, invisible, latent, obscure, occult, secret, undiscovered, unimagined, unknown, unseen, unsuspected, veiled.

ev·i·den·tial (ev′ə·den′shəl) *adj.* **1** Of the nature of or furnishing evidence. **2** Based or relying on evidence. **— ev′i·den′tial·ly** *adv.*

e·vil (ē′vəl) *adj.* **1** Morally bad; contrary to divine or righteous law; wrong or wicked; sinful or depraved. **2** Possessing injurious nature or qualities; unwholesome; noxious. **3** Characterized by calamity, trouble, or sorrow. **4** Of ill repute. See synonyms under BAD[1], IMMORAL, PERNICIOUS. — *n.* **1** Wicked conduct or disposition as showing depravity or as being destructive of good; sinfulness as injurious; moral depravity. **2** Something that harms or hurts; that which hinders prosperity, diminishes welfare, or prevents the enjoyment of a good; affliction. **3** King's evil. See synonyms under ABOMINATION, INJURY, SIN. — *adv.* In an evil manner. [OE *yfel*] **— e′vil·ly** *adv.* **— e′vil·ness** *n.*

e·vil-do·er (ē′vəl·dōō′ər) *n.* A wicked person. **— e′vil-do′ing** *n.*

evil eye In folklore, an eye having the power to cast an evil spell on a person or animal, or able to blight or cause the death of anything on which its glance falls, with or without the intent and ill will of the possessor. **— e′vil-eyed′** *adj.*

Ev·ill (ev′il), **Sir Douglas Claude Strathern,** born 1892, British air marshal.

e·vil-mind·ed (ē′vəl·mīn′did) *adj.* **1** Having an evil disposition; malicious. **2** Apt to interpret actions, language, intentions, etc., in the worst sense. See synonyms under MALICIOUS. **— e′vil-mind′ed·ly** *adv.* **— e′vil-mind′ed·ness** *n.*

Evil One Satan.

e·vince (i·vins′) *v.t.* **e·vinced, e·vinc·ing** **1** To show plainly or certainly; make evident; display. **2** *Obs.* To conquer. [<L *evincere.* See EVICT.] **— e·vin′ci·ble** *adj.* **— e·vin′ci·bly** *adv.*

e·vin·cive (i·vin′siv) *adj.* Capable of proving; convincing.

ev·i·ra·tion (ev′i·rā′shən) *n.* **1** Castration. **2** *Psychiatry* A paranoid condition in which a man develops the conviction that he is a woman, especially in relation to sexual behavior and personality traits. [<L *e-* out + *vir* man + -ATION]

e·vis·cer·ate (i·vis′ə·rāt) *v.t.* **·at·ed, ·at·ing** **1** To disembowel. **2** To remove the essential or vital parts of (anything). — *adj.* (i·vis′ə·rit) *Surg.* Disemboweled: an *eviscerate* abdomen. [<L *evisceratus*, pp. of *eviscerare* < *e-* out + *viscera* entrails]

ev·i·ta·ble (ev′ə·tə·bəl) *adj.* That may be escaped, avoided, or shunned; avoidable. [<L *evitabilis* < *evitare* < *e-* out + *vitare* shun]

e·vite (i·vīt′) *v.t. Obs.* To avoid. [<L *evitare.* See EVITABLE.]

ev·o·ca·ble (ev′ə·kə·bəl) *adj.* Capable of being evoked or called forth.

ev·o·ca·tion (ev′ə·kā′shən) *n.* **1** A calling forth or out; summoning, as of memories, etc. **2** Specifically, the summoning of a spirit, or of the dead, from a grave. **3** The formula used in such a summons. **4** In civil law, the transference of a suit from a lower to a higher court. [<L *evocatio, -onis* < *evocare.* See EVOKE.]

e·voc·a·tive (i·vok′ə·tiv, -vō′kə-) *adj.* Evoking; calling forth; fitted or calculated to evoke or call forth.

ev·o·ca·tor (ev′ə·kā′tər) *n.* One who summons up spirits.

ev·o·e (ev′ō·ē) *interj.* A cry of Bacchanals. Also **ev′o·he.** [<L <Gk. *euoi*]

e·voke (i·vōk′) *v.t.* **e·voked, e·vok·ing** **1** To call or summon forth; elicit, as an emotion or reply. **2** To summon up (spirits) by or as by spells. [<L *evocare* < *e-* out + *vocare* call]

ev·o·lute (ev′ə·lōōt) *n. Math.* A curve which is the locus of the center of curvature of another curve, its *involute*, and therefore tangent to all its normals; a curve that is the envelope of all the normals of another curve. [<L *evolutus*, pp. of *evolvere.* See EVOLVE.]

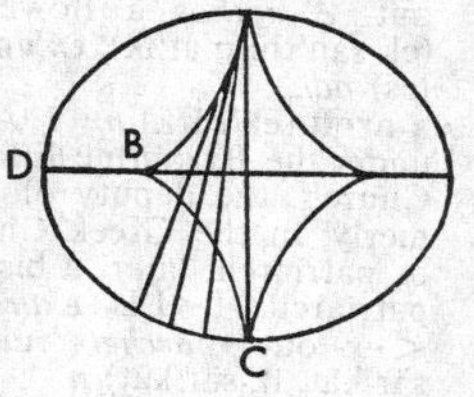

EVOLUTE OF AN ELLIPSE

ABC is the evolute of ellipse *ADC*. Cord *AC*, if fastened at *A* and swung so as to encompass *AB*, will describe arc *CD* of the ellipse.

ev·o·lu·tion (ev′ə·lōō′shən) *n.* **1** The act or process of unfolding; development or growth, usually in slow stages and from simpler forms to those which are more complex: the *evolution* of the telephone. **2** *Biol.* **a** The doctrine that all forms of life originated by descent, with gradual or abrupt modifications, from preexisting forms which themselves trace backward in a continuing series to the most rudimentary organisms. **b** The series of changes by which a given type of organism has acquired the physiological and structural characteristics differentiating it from other types; phylogeny. **3** The old theory of preformation, that the germ contains all the parts of the mature organism in minute form; development from such a germ: opposed to *epigenesis*. **4** *Math.* The operation of extracting a root. **5** A move or maneuver, as of troops. **6** *Philos.* The cosmological theory that accounts for the universe and its contents by the combination of separate and diffused atoms existing originally in a condition of absolute homogeneity. **7** A movement forming one of a series of complex motions; hence, any intricate or involved form: the *evolutions* of the labyrinth. **8** Anything evolved; also, a series unfolded. **— ev′o·lu′tion·al** *adj.* **— ev′o·lu′tion·al·ly** *adv.* **— ev′o·lu′tion·ism** *n.* **— ev′o·lu′tion·ist** *adj.* & *n.*

ev·o·lu·tion·ar·y (ev′ə·lōō′shən·er′ē) *adj.* Pertaining or relating to evolution, in any sense.

e·volve (i·volv′) *v.* **e·volved, e·volv·ing** *v.t.* **1** To unfold or expand. **2** To work out; develop: to *evolve* a plan. **3** *Biol.* To develop, as by a differentiation of parts or functions, to a more highly organized condition. **4** To give or throw off (vapor, heat, etc.); emit. — *v.i.* **5** To undergo the process of evolution. **6** To open out; develop. [<L *evolvere* unroll < *e-* out + *volvere* roll] **— e·volv′a·ble** *adj.* **— e·volv′ent** *adj.* & *n.* **— e·volve′ment** *n.* **— e·volv′er** *n.*

e·von·y·mus (i·von′ə·məs) See EUONYMUS.

e·vul·sion (i·vul′shən) *n.* A plucking out; forcible extraction. [<L *evulsio, -onis* < *e-* out + *vellere* pluck]

Ev·voia (ev·vyä′) The Greek name for EUBOEA.

ev·zone (ev′zōn) *n.* A modern Greek soldier, one of a corps picked from the mountainous regions. [<Modern Gk. *euzōnoi* <Gk. *euzōnos* well-girdled < *eu-* well + *zōnē* belt]

E·wald (i′väl), **Johannes,** 1743–81, Danish poet and dramatist: also *Evald*.

ewe (yōō, *Dial.* yō) *n.* A female sheep. ◆ Homophone: *yew*. [OE *eowu*]

E·we (ā′wā, ā′vā) *n.* **1** One of a tribe of African Negroes of the Slave Coast. **2** The Sudanic language of this tribe.

ewe lamb The one highly valued possession of a person who has little else; a beloved or an only child.

Ew·ell (yōō′əl), **Richard Stoddert,** 1817–72, American Confederate general.

ewe-neck (yōō′nek′) *n.* A neck, as of some horses, thin and bowed backward, like that of a ewe. **— ewe′-necked′** *adj.*

ew·er (yōō′ər) *n.* A wide-mouthed pitcher, sometimes with a lid. [<OF *aiguier* <L *aquaria* vessel for water < *aqua* water]

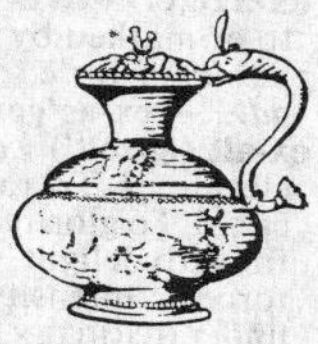

PERSIAN EWER

E·wig·keit (ā′vikh·kīt) *n. German* Eternity.

E·wig-Weib·li·che, das (däs ā′vikh·vīp′likh·ə) *n. German* The eternal feminine.

Ew·ing (yōō′ing), **Sir James Alfred,** 1855–1935, Scottish physicist and engineer. **— Juliana Horatia,** 1841–85, *née* Gatty, English author of juvenile literature.

ex[1] (eks) *prep.* **1** In finance, without the right to have or to participate in; excluding: said of stocks, as *ex* bonus, *ex* dividend, etc. **2** In commerce, free out of; not subject to charge until taken out of, as *ex* elevator, *ex* ship, *ex* store, etc. **3** *U.S.* From, but not having graduated with a given class: *ex* '54. [<L *ex-* out]

ex[2] (eks) *n. pl.* **ex·es** The letter X, x.

ex-[1] *prefix* **1** Out; out of: *exit, exhale.* **2** Remove from; free from: *exonerate.* **3** Thoroughly: *exasperate, excruciate.* **4** Without; not having: *excaudate.* **5** Once; formerly (hyphenated): *ex-president.* Also: *e-* before consonants except *c, f, p, q, s, t*, as in *edentate, erode, evade; ef-* before *f*, as in *efferent.* [<L *ex-* < *ex* from, out of]

ex-[2] *prefix* Out of; from; forth: *exodus.* Also, before consonants, *ec-*, as in *eclipse.* [<Gk. *ex-, ek-* < *ex* out]

ex-[3] Var. of EXO-.

ex·ac·er·bate (ig·zas′ər·bāt) *v.t.* **·bat·ed, ·bat·ing** **1** To make more sharp or severe; aggravate (feelings, a disease, pain, etc.). **2** To embitter or irritate (someone). [<L *exacerbatus*, pp. of *exacerbare* < *ex-* completely + *acerbus* bitter, harsh]

ex·ac·er·ba·tion (ig·zas′ər·bā′shən) *n.* **1** The act of exacerbating, or the state of being exacerbated. **2** *Pathol.* Increased severity, as in the symptoms of a disease.

ex·act (ig·zakt′) *adj.* **1** Perfectly conformed to a standard; nicely adjusted; strictly accurate or correct. **2** Precise: the *exact* sum. **3** Accurately or precisely conceived or expressed; characterized by definite knowledge or principles; rigorously determined; definite: *exact* thinking. **4** Capable of yielding results of high precision and accuracy: an *exact* instrument. See synonyms under CORRECT, JUST, MINUTE, PARTICULAR, PRECISE. — *v.t.* **1** To compel the yielding or payment of; extort. **2** To demand; insist upon as a right. **3** To require; call for: The task will *exact* great effort. See synonyms under DEMAND. [<L *exactus*, pp. of *exigere* determine < *ex-* out + *agere* drive. Related to EXAMINE.] **— ex·act′a·ble** *adj.* **— ex·act′er, ex·ac′tor** *n.*

ex·act·ing (ig·zak′ting) *adj.* Making unreasonable or inconsiderate demands; taxing; arduous. See synonyms under HARD, IMPERIOUS. **— ex·act′ing·ly** *adv.* **— ex·act′ing·ness** *n.*

ex·ac·tion (ig·zak′shən) *n.* **1** The act of exacting; extortion. **2** Something exacted; a compulsory levy. See synonyms under TAX.

ex·act·ly (ig·zakt′lē) *adv.* **1** In an exact manner; precisely. **2** Yes indeed; quite so.

ex·act·ness (ig·zakt′nis) *n.* The condition or quality of being accurate and precise. Also **ex·act′i·tude** (-tōōd, -tyōōd).

exact science A science the data of which are susceptible to precise formulation and rigorous mathematical analysis, especially one that permits accurate prediction of future events within its prescribed field, as physics or astronomy: distinguished from *descriptive science, normative science.*

ex·ag·ger·ate (ig·zaj′ə·rāt) *v.* **·at·ed, ·at·ing** *v.t.* **1** To describe or represent beyond the bounds of truth; overstate. **2** To increase or enlarge immoderately. — *v.i.* **3** To use exaggeration. See synonyms under INCREASE. [<L *exaggeratus*, pp. of *exaggerare* < *ex-* out + *agger* mound, heap] **— ex·ag′ger·at′ed** *adj.* **— ex·ag′ger·at′ed·ly** *adv.* **— ex·ag′ger·at′ing·ly** *adv.* **— ex·ag′ger·a′tor** *n.*

ex·ag·ger·a·tion (ig·zaj′ə·rā′shən) *n.* The act

of exaggerating; overstatement; hyperbole. See synonyms under CARICATURE.

ex·ag·ger·a·tive (ig·zaj′ə·rā′tiv) *adj.* Tending to or marked by exaggeration. Also **ex·ag′ger·a·to′ry** (-tôr′ē, -tō′rē). — **ex·ag′ger·a′tive·ly** *adv.* — **ex·ag′ger·a′tive·ness** *n.*

ex·alt (ig·zôlt′) *v.t.* **1** To raise on high; lift up; elevate. **2** To raise in rank, character, honor, etc. **3** To glorify or praise; pay honor to. **4** To fill with delight, pride, etc. **5** To increase the force or intensity of, as colors. See synonyms under HEIGHTEN, PROMOTE, RAISE. [<L *exaltare* < *ex-* out + *altus* high] — **ex·alt′er** *n.*

ex·al·ta·tion (eg′zôl·tā′shən) *n.* **1** The act of exalting. **2** The state of being exalted. **3** Promotion; elevation, political, social, or spiritual: used specifically of promotion to the papal office. **4** Intensification. **5** A mental state distinguished by ecstatic joy, abnormal optimism, or delusions of grandeur. See synonyms under HEIGHT. [<F <LL *exaltatio, -onis* < *exaltare.* See EXALT.]

ex·alt·ed (ig·zôl′tid) *adj.* **1** Raised up or aloft; elevated. **2** Raised in rank, position, or dignity. **3** Dignified; sublime: *exalted* poetry. **4** Intensely joyous or abnormally elated. — **ex·alt′ed·ly** *adv.* — **ex·alt′ed·ness** *n.*

ex·am (ig·zam′) *n. Colloq.* An examination.

ex·a·men (ig·zā′men) *n.* **1** A scrutiny or searching of conscience. **2** *Eccl.* An examination, as for ordination. [<L. See EXAMINE.]

ex·am·i·nant (ig·zam′ə·nənt) *n.* An examiner.

ex·am·i·na·tion (ig·zam′ə·nā′shən) *n.* **1** The act or process of examining or being examined; careful scrutiny or inquiry; investigation; inspection. **2** A testing of knowledge, progress, skill, qualifications, etc: an *examination* in history, civil service *examination.* **3** *Law* Inquiry by means of interrogation or testimony; the result of such inquiry; testimony reduced to writing. See synonyms under INQUIRY. [<F <L *examinatio, -onis* < *examinare.* See EXAMINE.] — **ex·am′i·na′tion·al** *adj.*

ex·am·ine (ig·zam′in) *v.t.* **·ined, ·in·ing** **1** To inspect or scrutinize with care; investigate critically. **2** To test by questions or exercises as to qualifications, fitness, etc., as a pupil. **3** To question in order to elicit facts, etc. **4** To assay; analyze. [<OF *examiner* <L *examinare* < *examen* a testing < *ex-* out + *ag-*, root of *agere* drive. Related to EXACT.] — **ex·am′in·a·ble** *adj.* — **ex·am′i·na·to′ri·al** (-tôr′ē·əl, -tō′rē-) *adj.* — **ex·am′i·nee′** *n.* — **ex·am′in·er** *n.*

Synonyms: canvass, consider, criticize, discuss, explore, inspect, interrogate, investigate, observe, overhaul, ponder, question, ransack, scrutinize, search, study, test, try, view, weigh. See CONSIDER, INQUIRE, REVIEW. Compare synonyms for DELIBERATE.

ex·am·ple (ig·zam′pəl, -zäm′-) *n.* **1** A thing or person suitable to be used as a model. **2** An instance of something to be avoided; an act, especially a punishment, serving or designed to serve as a warning. **3** A sample; specimen. **4** An instance serving to illustrate a rule. **5** A problem to be solved. **6** That with which something may be compared; precedent; parallel. — *v.t. Obs.* **1** To exemplify. **2** To teach by example. [<OF, earlier *essample* <L *exemplum* something taken out < *eximere* < *ex-* out + *emere* buy. Doublet of SAMPLE.]

Synonyms (noun): archetype, exemplar, exemplification, ideal, model, pattern, precedent, prototype, sample, specimen, standard, type, warning. From its original sense of *sample* or *specimen* (L *exemplum*), *example* derives the seemingly contradictory meanings, on the one hand of a *pattern* or *model,* and on the other hand of a *warning*—a *sample* or *specimen* of what is to be followed, or of what is to be shunned. An *example,* however, may be more than a *sample* or *specimen* of any class; it may be the very *archetype* or *prototype* to which the whole class must conform. *Example* comes nearer to *model* than to the necessary exactness of the *pattern.* In its application to a person or thing, *exemplar* can scarcely be distinguished from *example*; but *example* is most frequently used for an act, or course of action, for which *exemplar* is not used; as, one sets a good (or a bad) *example.* An *exemplification* is an illustrative working out in action of a principle or law, without any reference to its being copied or repeated; an *example* guides, an *exemplification* illustrates or explains. Compare ARCHETYPE, MODEL, PRECEDENT, SAMPLE.

ex·an·i·mate (ig·zan′ə·mit, -māt) *adj.* **1** Deprived of life; inanimate. **2** Having no animation; dispirited; spiritless. [<L *exanimatus,* pp. of *exanimare* kill < *ex-* out + *animus* breath, life]

ex·an·i·ma·tion (ig·zan′ə·mā′shən) *n.* Real or apparent death; swooning.

ex an·i·mo (eks an′i·mō) *Latin* From the heart; sincerely.

ex·an·the·ma (ek′san·thē′mə) *n. pl.* **·them·a·ta** (-them′ə·tə, -thē′mə·tə) *Pathol.* A breaking out upon the skin; a rash, or a disease accompanied by rash, as smallpox or measles; specifically, usually in the plural, the eruptive fevers. [<LL <Gk. *exanthēma* a blossoming < *ex-* out + *anthos* a flower] — **ex·an·the·mat·ic** (ek·san′thi·mat′ik), **ex′an·them′a·tous** (-them′ə·təs) *adj.*

ex·arch (ek′särk) *n.* **1** A provincial governor under the Byzantine Empire. **2** In the Greek Church, the deputy of a patriarch. **3** Formerly, in the Greek Church, a metropolitan or patriarch; later, a bishop ranking below a patriarch. [<LL *exarchus* <Gk. *exarchos* < *ex-* out + *archein* rule] — **ex·ar·chate** (ek′·sär·kāt, ik·sär′kāt) *n.*

ex·as·per·ate (ig·zas′pə·rāt) *v.t.* **·at·ed, ·at·ing** **1** To irritate exceedingly; enrage. **2** To make worse; intensify; inflame. See synonyms under AFFRONT, INCENSE. [<L *exasperatus,* pp. of *exasperare* < *ex-* out + *asper* rough] — **ex·as′per·at′er** *n.* — **ex·as′per·at′ing** *adj.* — **ex·as′per·at′ing·ly** *adv.*

ex·as·per·a·tion (ig·zas′pə·rā′shən) *n.* **1** The act of exasperating, in any sense; especially, provocation of extreme anger. **2** The state of being exasperated; extreme anger; rage. **3** Aggravation, as of a disease. See synonyms under ANGER.

Ex·cal·i·bur (eks·kal′ə·bər) In Arthurian legend, the sword of King Arthur: also called *Caliburn.* Also **Ex·cal′i·bar.** [<OF *Escalibor* <Med. L *Caliburnus* <Celtic]

ex cap·i·te (eks kap′i·tē) *Latin* Out of the head; from memory; by heart.

ex ca·the·dra (eks kə·thē′drə, kath′i-) *Latin* Officially; with authority. See CATHEDRA.

ex·cau·date (eks·kô′dāt) *adj. Zool.* Having no tail.

ex·ca·vate (eks′kə·vāt) *v.t.* **·vat·ed, ·vat·ing** **1** To make a hole or cavity in; hollow or dig out. **2** To form or make by hollowing, digging out, or scooping. **3** To remove by digging or scooping out, as soil. **4** To uncover by digging, as ruins. [<L *excavatus,* pp. of *excavare* < *ex-* out + *cavus* hollow]

ex·ca·va·tion (eks′kə·vā′shən) *n.* **1** A digging out. **2** A cavity or hollow formed by excavating. See synonyms under HOLE.

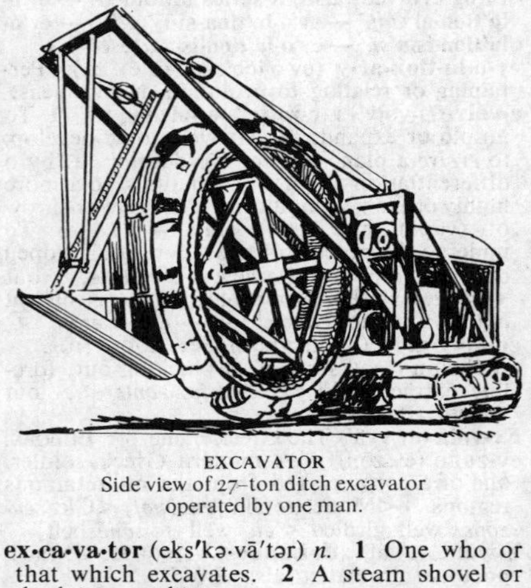

EXCAVATOR
Side view of 27–ton ditch excavator operated by one man.

ex·ca·va·tor (eks′kə·vā′tər) *n.* **1** One who or that which excavates. **2** A steam shovel or dredging machine.

ex·ceed (ik·sēd′) *v.t.* **1** To go or be beyond; surpass, as in quantity, quality, measure, or value. **2** To go beyond the limit or extent of: to *exceed* one's income. — *v.i.* **3** To be superior; surpass others. [<F *excéder* <L *excedere* < *ex-* out, beyond + *cedere* go]

ex·ceed·ing (ik·sē′ding) *adj.* Greater than usual; surpassing; extraordinary. — *adv. Obs.* Exceedingly.

ex·ceed·ing·ly (ik·sē′ding·lē) *adv.* To a greater degree than usual; extremely.

ex·cel (ik·sel′) *v.t.* & *v.i.* **·celled, ·cel·ling** To go beyond or above; outdo; surpass (another or others). See synonyms under LEAD. [<OF *exceller* <L *excellere* rise]

ex·cel·lence (ek′sə·ləns) *n.* **1** Possession of eminently good qualities; great merit, virtue, or goodness. **2** A superior trait. See synonyms under VIRTUE. Also **ex′cel·len·cy.**

Ex·cel·len·cy (ek′sə·lən·sē) *n. pl.* **·cies** An honorary title of various high officials, specifically used of the governors of Massachusetts and New Hampshire: also used to address a foreign president or minister of foreign affairs or a foreign ambassador.

ex·cel·lent (ek′sə·lənt) *adj.* **1** Having good qualities in a high degree; superior in worth or value. **2** *Obs.* Eminent; excelling. [<OF <L *excellens, -entis,* ppr. of *excellere* rise]

Synonyms: admirable, capital, choice, fine, first–class, first–rate, precious, prime, select, superior, transcendent, valuable, worthy. That which is *excellent* excels, but an object that is *valuable* or a man who is *worthy* so far excels the majority of persons or things that these words have become close synonyms for *excellent.* See CHOICE, FINE, GOOD, MORAL. *Antonyms*: bad, base, defective, deficient, good–for–nothing, imperfect, inferior, mean, poor, unworthy, useless, valueless, vile, worthless.

ex·cel·lent·ly (ek′sə·lənt·lē) *adv.* Surpassingly.

ex·cel·si·or (ik·sel′sē·ər) *n.* **1** A packing material composed of long, fine, wood shavings. **2** *Printing* An old size of type, equivalent to 3 points. [< a trade name]

Ex·cel·si·or (ek·sel′sē·ôr) Upward: motto of the State of New York. [Compar. of L *excelsus* high]

ex·cen·tric (ek·sen′trik) See ECCENTRIC.

ex·cept (ik·sept′) *v.t.* To leave or take out; exclude; omit. — *v.i.* To object; take exception: with *to.* — *prep.* With the exception of; excluding; leaving out; save; but: Tell no one *except* me. — *conj. Archaic* If not that; unless: *except* a man be born again. [<F *excepter* <L *exceptare,* freq. of *excipere* < *ex-* out + *capere* take] — **ex·cep′tor** *n.*

ex·cept·ing (ik·sep′ting) *prep.* Except; excluding. — *conj. Archaic* Unless.

ex·cep·tion (ik·sep′shən) *n.* **1** That which is excluded, as from a list. **2** The act of excepting; exclusion. **3** A captious objection, complaint, or quibble. **4** *Law* A formal objection to the decision of a court during trial. — **to take exception** To take offense; object.

ex·cep·tion·a·ble (ik·sep′shən·ə·bəl) *adj.* Open to exception or objection. — **ex·cep′tion·a·bly** *adv.*

ex·cep·tion·al (ik·sep′shən·əl) *adj.* Unusual or uncommon; superior. See synonyms under IRREGULAR. — **ex·cep′tion·al·ly** *adv.*

ex·cep·tive (ik·sep′tiv) *adj.* **1** Of the nature of an exception. **2** Captious.

ex·cerpt (ek′sûrpt) *n.* An extract from written or printed matter. — *v.t.* (ik·sûrpt′) To take out, as a passage or quotation; extract. See synonyms under QUOTE. [<L *excerptus,* pp. of *excerpere* < *ex-* out + *carpere* pluck, seize] — **ex·cerp′tion** *n.* — **ex·cerp′tive** *adj.* — **ex·cerp′tor** *n.*

ex·cess (ik·ses′) *n.* **1** That which passes the ordinary, reasonable, or required limit. **2** Inordinate gratification of appetite. **3** The amount by which one thing is greater than another; overplus. — *adj.* (*also* ek′ses) Being above a stipulated amount; extra. [<OF *exces* <L *excessus* a departure < *excedere.* See EXCEED.]

Synonyms (noun): dissipation, exorbitance, extravagance, intemperance, lavishness, overplus, prodigality, profusion, redundance, redundancy, superabundance, superfluity, surplus, waste, wastefulness. *Excess* is more than enough of anything, and, since this in many cases indicates a lack either of judgment or of self–control, the word is used frequently in an unfavorable sense. Careless expenditure in *excess* of income is *extravagance*; we may have also *extravagance* of language, professions, etc. As *extravagance* is *excess* in outlay, *exorbitance* is *excess* in demands, especially in pecuniary demands. *Overplus* and *superabundance* denote in the main a satisfactory, and *superfluity* an undesirable, *excess*; *lavishness* and *profusion,* a generous or bountiful *excess. Surplus* has none of the unfavorable meaning that often attaches to *excess*; a *surplus* is that which remains over

after all demands are met. *Redundance* or *redundancy* refers chiefly to literary style, denoting an *excess* of words or matter. *Excess* in the moral sense is expressed by *dissipation, prodigality, intemperance,* etc. *Antonyms*: dearth, defect, deficiency, destitution, economy, failure, frugality, inadequacy, insufficiency, lack, need, poverty, scantiness, shortcoming, want.

ex·ces·sive (ik·ses′iv) *adj.* Being in, tending to, marked by excess; immoderate; extreme. See synonyms under IMMODERATE, REDUNDANT. **— ex·ces′sive·ly** *adv.* **— ex·ces′sive·ness** *n.*

excess profits Net profits beyond the normal average for a period of years.

ex·change (iks·chānj′) *n.* **1** The act of giving or receiving one thing as an equivalent for another; a trade; a bartering: an *exchange* of prisoners. **2** Interchange: an *exchange* of wit, remarks, etc. **3** The mutual giving and receiving of equivalents in money, goods, or labor. **4** The system by which titles to commodities in distant localities are transferred by means of credits, drafts, etc. **5** The rate of exchange. **6** The percentage of difference between currencies of values at two given places. **7** Bills, drafts, etc., presented to a clearing house for settlement. **8** A transition from one experience or condition to another. **9** That which is given or received by interchange, as a periodical or an advertisement exchanged for another. **10** A place where merchants or brokers effect exchanges: a stock *exchange.* See CURB[1]. **11** A central telephone office. **12** *Physics* The mutual interaction between the electrons, protons, and other components of the same or different atoms. **13** *Brit.* A labor exchange. See synonyms under INTERCOURSE. **— bill of exchange** A written order or request from one person to another for the payment of money to a third, the amount to be charged to the drawer of the bill. **— par of exchange** The comparison of value in gold of the monetary units of two different countries. **— rate of exchange** The price at which a bill drawn in one country upon a drawee in another country may be sold where drawn. **—** *v.* **·changed, ·chang·ing** *v.t.* **1** To give or part with for something regarded as of equal value, etc.: to *exchange* francs for dollars. **2** To give and receive in turn; reciprocate. **3** To replace by or give up for something else: to *exchange* poverty for wealth. **—** *v.i.* **4** To be given or taken in exchange: American money *exchanges* well. **5** To make an exchange. See synonyms under CHANGE. [<AF *eschaunge* <LL *excambium* < *excambiare* < *ex-* out + *cambiare* exchange] **— ex·change′a·bil′i·ty** *n.* **— ex·change′a·ble** *adj.* **— ex·change′a·bly** *adv.*

ex·cheq·uer (iks·chek′ər, eks′chek·ər) *n.* **1** The treasury of a state. **2** *Colloq.* Finances; pecuniary resources. [<OF *eschequier.* See CHECKER.]

Ex·cheq·uer (iks·chek′ər, eks′chek·ər) *n.* **1** The administrative department of the British government having the management of the public revenue. **2** In England, an ancient common law court taking cognizance of matters connected with the public revenue. In 1873, this **Court of Exchequer** was made a division of the High Court of Justice, and in 1881 this division was merged in the Queen's Bench division.

ex·cip·i·ent (ik·sip′ē·ənt) *n. Med.* Any inert substance used to give drug preparations a suitable form or pleasant taste. [<L *excipiens, -entis,* ppr. of *excipere.* See EXCEPT.]

ex·cise[1] (ik·sīz′, ek′sīz) *n.* **1** An indirect tax on commodities manufactured, produced, sold, used, or transported within a country, including license fees for various sports, trades, or occupations. **2** *Brit.* A branch of the department of the civil service having charge of the inland revenue taxes and duties. See synonyms under TAX. **—** *v.t.* (ik·sīz′) **·cised, ·cis·ing** To levy an excise upon. [<MDu. *excijs, accijs* <OF *acceis* <L *ad-* to + *census* a tax] **— ex·cis′a·ble** *adj.*

ex·cise[2] (ik·sīz′) *v.t.* **·cised, ·cis·ing** To cut out or off; remove; extirpate; expunge. [<L *excisus,* pp. of *excidere* < *ex-* out + *caedere* cut] **— ex·ci·sion** (ik·sizh′ən) *n.*

ex·cise·man (ik·sīz′mən) *n. pl.* **·men** (-mən) *Brit.* A revenue officer.

ex·cit·a·bil·i·ty (ik·sī′tə·bil′ə·tē) *n.* **1** The quality of being excitable; susceptibility to excitement. **2** *Physiol.* Sensitiveness to stimuli.

ex·cit·a·ble (ik·sī′tə·bəl) *adj.* **1** Easily excited; high-strung. **2** *Physiol.* Susceptible to stimuli. See synonyms under ARDENT, IMPETUOUS. **— ex·cit′a·ble·ness** *n.* **— ex·cit′a·bly** *adv.*

ex·ci·tant (ik·sī′tənt, ek′sə·tənt) *n.* A drug that excites or stimulates. **—** *adj.* Adapted or tending to excite or stimulate: also **ex·ci′ta·tive, ex·ci′ta·to′ry** (-tôr′ē, -tō′rē). [<L *excitans, -antis,* ppr. of *excitare.* See EXCITE.]

ex·ci·ta·tion (ek′sī·tā′shən) *n.* **1** A state of disturbance or agitation; excitement. **2** *Physics* **a** The deflection of an electron from its normal orbit in an atom to one of higher energy content: also called *activation.* **b** The electrification or magnetization of a substance. **3** *Biol.* The action of a stimulus on a plant or animal organism. [<F <L *excitatio, -onis* < *excitare.* See EXCITE.]

ex·cite (ik·sīt′) *v.t.* **·cit·ed, ·cit·ing 1** To arouse (a feeling, interest, etc.) into being or activity; evoke: to *excite* admiration or jealousy. **2** To arouse feeling in; stimulate the emotions of: to *excite* someone to hatred. **3** To cause action in; stir to activity or motion: Wine *excites* the tongue. **4** To bring about; stir up: to *excite* a riot. **5** *Physiol.* To cause increased activity in; stimulate (muscles or nerves). **6** *Electr.* To initiate or develop a magnetic field in, as a dynamo. **7** *Physics* To raise an atom or molecule to a higher energy or quantum state, as by heat, radiation, or electron bombardment. See synonyms under ACTUATE, ENCOURAGE, INFLUENCE, INTEREST, PROMOTE, STIR. [<OF *exciter* <L *excitare,* freq. of *exciere* < *ex-* out + *ciere* arouse, stir up] **— ex·cit′ed** *adj.* **— ex·cit′ed·ly** *adv.*

ex·cite·ment (ik·sīt′mənt) *n.* **1** The act of exciting; stimulation. **2** That which excites. **3** The state of being excited, agitated, or aroused; disturbance; agitation. Also *excitation.* See synonyms under ENTHUSIASM, WARMTH.

ex·cit·er (ik·sī′tər) *n.* **1** One who or that which excites, stimulates, or rouses: an *exciter* of the people. **2** *Electr.* **a** An auxiliary generator which supplies energy for the field magnets of a dynamo. **b** A machine which generates electric waves of definite length by means of sparks.

ex·cit·ing (ik·sī′ting) *adj.* Of a nature to excite; stirring; rousing. **— ex·cit′ing·ly** *adv.*

ex·ci·to·mo·tor (ik·sī′tə·mō′tər) *n.* Any agent or drug which increases the activity of the motor centers. **—** *adj.* Exciting motion, but without sensation or volition: also **ex·ci′to·mo′to·ry** (-mō′tər·ē). [< *excito-* stimulating (<EXCITE) + MOTOR]

ex·ci·tor (ik·sī′tər) *n. Physiol.* An afferent nerve connected with the spinal division of the nervous system. Also **ex·cit′er.**

ex·claim (iks·klām′) *v.t. & v.i.* To say or cry out abruptly; speak vehemently, as in surprise or anger. [<F *exclamer* <L *exclamare* < *ex-* out + *clamare* cry] **— ex·claim′er** *n.*

Synonyms (verb): call, ejaculate. We may *exclaim* by mere interjections, or by connected words. To *ejaculate* is to throw out brief, disconnected, but coherent utterances of joy, regret, and of appeal, petition, prayer; such devotional utterances are named "ejaculatory prayer." See CALL.

ex·cla·ma·tion (eks′klə·mā′shən) *n.* **1** Clamorous or passionate outcry. **2** An abrupt or emphatic expression; an interjection. **3** An exclamation mark.

exclamation mark A point, note, or mark (!) placed after an interjection or exclamation to indicate its character. Also **exclamation point.**

ex·clam·a·tive (iks·klam′ə·tiv) *adj.* Exclamatory. **—** *n.* A word, phrase, or sound uttered under emotional stress; an ejaculation.

ex·clam·a·to·ry (iks·klam′ə·tôr′ē, -tō′rē) *adj.* **1** Of the nature of exclamation. **2** Given to or characterized by the use of exclamation.

ex·clave (eks′klāv) *n.* A minor part of a country disjoined from the main part and lying within an alien territory. Compare ENCLAVE. [<EX- + (EN)CLAVE]

ex·clo·sure (iks·klō′zhər) *n. Ecol.* An area set apart from its surroundings as a means of studying the characteristics of a region under controlled conditions. [<EX- + (EN)CLOSURE]

ex·clude (iks·klōōd′) *v.t.* **·clud·ed, ·clud·ing 1** To keep from entering; shut out, as from a place or group. **2** To refuse to notice, consider, or allow for; leave out: opposed to *include.* **3** To put out; eject. [<L *excludere* < *ex-* out + *claudere* close] **— ex·clud′a·ble** *adj.* **— ex·clud′er** *n.*

ex·clu·sion (iks·klōō′zhən) *n.* **1** The act of excluding. **2** The state of being excluded. **3** That which is excluded. [<L *exclusio, -onis* < *excludere.* See EXCLUDE.] **— ex·clu′sion·ism** *n.* **— ex·clu′sion·ist** *n.*

exclusion principle *Physics* The principle, discovered by W. Pauli, which states that no two electrons in a molecular or atomic system can simultaneously have all four quantum numbers identical.

ex·clu·sive (iks·klōō′siv) *adj.* **1** Intended for or possessed by a single group or individual; not shared: *exclusive* fishing rights; *exclusive* information. **2** Restricting membership or patronage; fastidiously reluctant to accept outsiders; hence, snobbish: an *exclusive* club. **3** Singly devoted; undivided: *exclusive* attention to music. **4** Not including; not comprising: usually followed by *of*: *exclusive* of fees. **5** Not counting the specified terminal points: 20 to 30 *exclusive* (including 21 through 29 and excluding 20 and 30): opposed to *inclusive.* **— ex·clu′sive·ly** *adv.* **— ex·clu′sive·ness** *n.*

ex·cog·i·tate (iks·koj′ə·tāt) *v.t.* **·tat·ed, ·tat·ing** To think out carefully; invent; devise. [<L *excogitatus,* pp. of *excogitare* < *ex-* out + *cogitare* think]

ex·cog·i·ta·tion (iks·koj′ə·tā′shən) *n.* **1** The act of excogitating; invention. **2** That which is thought out. **— ex·cog′i·ta′tive** *adj.*

ex·com·mu·ni·ca·ble (eks′kə·myōō′ni·kə·bəl) *adj.* Punishable by or deserving excommunication.

ex·com·mu·ni·cate (eks′kə·myōō′nə·kāt) *v.t.* **·cat·ed, ·cat·ing 1** To punish by an ecclesiastical sentence of exclusion from the sacraments and communion of the church. **2** To expel in disgrace from any organization. **—** *adj.* Excommunicated. **—** *n.* An excommunicated person. [<LL *excommunicatus,* pp. of *excommunicare* < *ex-* out + *communicare* share < *communis* common] **— ex′com·mu′ni·ca′tor** *n.*

ex·com·mu·ni·ca·tion (eks′kə·myōō′nə·kā′shən) *n.* The act of excommunicating, or the state of having been excommunicated; a cutting off of an offender from all privileges of church membership.

ex·com·mu·ni·ca·tive (eks′kə·myōō′nə·kā′tiv, -kə·tiv) *adj.* Favoring or decreeing excommunication.

ex·com·mu·ni·ca·to·ry (eks′kə·myōō′ni·kə·tôr′ē, -tō′rē) *adj.* Causing or of the nature of excommunication.

ex·co·ri·ate (ik·skôr′ē·āt, -skō′rē-) *v.t.* **·at·ed, ·at·ing 1** *Physiol.* To strip off the skin or covering of; flay; abrade; gall. **2** To denounce scathingly. [<L *excoriatus,* pp. of *excoriare* < *ex-* out, off + *corium* skin] **— ex·co′ri·a′tion** *n.*

ex·cre·ment (eks′krə·mənt) *n.* Refuse matter discharged from an animal body; feces. [<L *excrementum* < *excernere.* See EXCRETE.] **— ex′cre·men′tal, ex′cre·men′ta·ry, ex′cre·men·ti′tial** (-tish′əl), **ex′cre·men·ti′tious** (-tish′əs) *adj.*

ex·cres·cence (iks·kres′əns) *n.* **1** An unnatural or disfiguring outgrowth, as a wart on the human body or a nutgall on the oak. **2** Any unnatural addition, outgrowth, or development. **3** A natural outgrowth, as hair.

ex·cres·cen·cy (iks·kres′ən·sē) *n. pl.* **·cies** Excrescence; especially, an abnormal outgrowth.

ex·cres·cent (iks·kres′ənt) *adj.* **1** Of the nature of or pertaining to an excrescence; superfluous. **2** *Phonet.* Intrusive. [<L *excrescens, -entis,* ppr. of *excrescere* < *ex-* out + *crescere* grow]

ex·cre·ta (iks·krē′tə) *n. pl.* **1** *Physiol.* All useless matter eliminated from the bodily system, especially that which has entered into the constitution of the body and is removed in urine or sweat. **2** Noxious or worthless matter generated in a plant body by destructive

metabolism. [<NL <L <*excernere.* See EXCRETE.] — **ex·cre′tal** *adj.*

ex·crete (iks·krēt′) *v.t.* **·cret·ed, ·cret·ing** To throw off or eliminate, as waste matter, by normal discharge from an organism or any of its tissues. [<L *excretus,* pp. of *excernere* <*ex-* out + *cernere* separate]

ex·cre·tion (iks·krē′shən) *n.* **1** The act of excreting. **2** Matter excreted, particularly sweat, urine, and the juices exuded from certain plants: distinguished from *secretion.*

ex·cre·tive (iks·krē′tiv) *adj.* Having the function or power to excrete. Also **ex·cre·to·ry** (eks′krə·tôr′ē, -tō′rē).

ex·cru·ci·ate (iks·kro͞o′shē·āt) *v.t.* **·at·ed, ·at·ing** To inflict extreme pain or agony upon; torture. [<L *excruciatus,* pp. of *excruciare* <*ex-* completely + *cruciare* torture <*crux, crucis* cross] — **ex·cru′ci·a′tion** *n.*

ex·cru·ci·at·ing (iks·kro͞o′shē·ā′ting) *adj.* Causing or inflicting intense pain; agonizing. — **ex·cru′ci·at′ing·ly** *adv.*

ex·cul·pate (eks′kəl·pāt, ik·skul′-) *v.t.* **·pat·ed, ·pat·ing** To declare free from blame; prove innocent of guilt or fault; exonerate. See synonyms under JUSTIFY. [<EX-[1] + L *culpatus,* pp. of *culpare* blame <*culpa* a fault] — **ex·culp′a·ble** *adj.*

ex·cul·pa·tion (eks′kəl·pā′shən) *n.* **1** The act of freeing, or of attempting to free, from blame; vindication. **2** The state of being freed from blame.

ex·cul·pa·to·ry (ik·skul′pə·tôr′ē, -tō′rē) *adj.* Tending to or resulting in exculpation; vindicatory.

ex cu·ri·a (eks kyo͝or′ē·ə) *Latin* Out of court.

ex·cur·rent (ik·skûr′ənt) *adj.* **1** Running or passing out. **2** *Biol.* Running through to the surface, summit, or tip, as the midrib of a leaf, or the canal of a sponge. [<L *excurrens, -entis,* ppr. of *excurrere* <*ex-* out + *currere* run]

ex·cur·sion (ik·skûr′zhən, -shən) *n.* **1** A short journey, usually for pleasure. **2** A boat or train trip at reduced rates, accommodating groups of excursionists to specified points. **3** A body of excursionists collectively. **4** A digression; deviation. **5** A running out or going forth. **6** *Physics* Half the amplitude of vibration; the movement of a vibrating or oscillating body from its mean to either of its extreme states or positions. **7** *Astron.* The apparent movement to and fro of a heavenly body, as of a satellite about its primary. See synonyms under JOURNEY. [<L *excursio, -onis* <*excurrere.* See EXCURRENT.]

ex·cur·sion·ist (ik·skûr′zhən·ist, -shən-) *n.* One who makes an excursion.

excursion ticket A round-trip ticket at a reduced rate.

ex·cur·sive (ik·skûr′siv) *adj.* **1** Given to making excursions; wandering. **2** Desultory; erratic; digressive. — **ex·cur′sive·ly** *adv.* — **ex·cur′sive·ness** *n.*

ex·cur·sus (eks·kûr′səs) *n. pl.* **·sus·es** or **·sus** **1** A supplemental dissertation added to a work. **2** A wandering off; digression. [<L, a going out <*excurrere.* See EXCURRENT.]

ex·cus·al (ik·skyo͞o′zəl) *n. Rare* The act of excusing.

ex·cuse (ik·skyo͞oz′) *v.t.* **·cused, ·cus·ing** **1** To pardon and overlook (a fault, offense, etc.); regard as unimportant. **2** To try to free (someone) from blame; seek to remove blame from: I *excused* myself to him. **3** To offer a reason or apology for (an error, fault, etc.); try to obtain pardon for or minimize. **4** To be or serve as a reason for; justify: His energy does not *excuse* his lateness. **5** To release from attendance, a duty, promise, etc. **6** To refrain from exacting or enforcing, as a demand or claim. See synonyms under JUSTIFY, PALLIATE, PARDON. — *n.* (ik·skyo͞os′) **1** A plea in extenuation of an offense, neglect, or failure. **2** The act of excusing. **3** A reason for excusing. See synonyms under APOLOGY, PRETENSE. [<OF *excuser* <L *excusare* <*ex-* out, away + *causa* charge, accusation] — **ex·cus′a·ble** *adj.* — **ex·cus′a·ble·ness** *n.* — **ex·cus′a·bly** *adv.* — **ex·cus′er** *n.*

ex de·lic·to (eks di·lik′tō) *Latin* From the crime.

ex·e·cra·ble (ek′sə·krə·bəl) *adj.* Worthy of execration; abominable; accursed; appallingly bad. — **ex′e·cra·bly** *adv.*

ex·e·crate (ek′sə·krāt) *v.* **·crat·ed, ·crat·ing** *v.t.* **1** To curse, or call down evil upon. **2** To detest; abhor. — *v.i.* **3** To utter curses. [<L *execratus,* pp. of *execrari* curse <*ex-* out + *sacrare* devote to a god <*sacer* holy, accursed] — **ex′e·cra′tor** *n.*

ex·e·cra·tion (ek′sə·krā′shən) *n.* **1** The act of execrating. **2** An imprecation; malediction; a curse. **3** An accursed thing. See synonyms under ABOMINATION, IMPRECATION, OATH. — **ex′e·cra′tive** *adj.*

ex·ec·u·tant (ig·zek′yə·tənt) *n.* One who executes or performs; specifically, a skilled musical performer.

ex·e·cute (ek′sə·kyo͞ot) *v.t.* **·cut·ed, ·cut·ing** **1** To do or carry out fully: to *execute* an order. **2** To put in force; administer, as a law. **3** To put to death by legal sentence. **4** *Law* To make legal or valid by fulfilling all requirements of law. **5** To do or perform, as a maneuver or a musical work. **6** To produce, as according to a preconceived plan or design: to *execute* a portrait in oils. [<L *executus,* var. of *exsecutus,* pp. of *exsequi* <*ex-* out + *sequi* follow] — **ex′e·cut′a·ble** *adj.* — **ex′e·cut′er** *n.*

Synonyms: administer, do, enforce, perform. To *execute,* is to follow through to the end, put into absolute and final effect in action; to *administer* is to conduct as one holding a trust, as a minister and not an originator; the sheriff *executes* a writ; the trustee *administers* an estate, a charity, etc.; to *enforce* is to put into effect by force, actual or potential. To *administer* the laws is the province of a court of justice; to *execute* or *enforce* the laws is the province of a sheriff, marshal, constable, or other executive officer; to *administer* the law is to declare or apply it; to *execute* the law is to put it in force; for this *enforce* is the more general word, *execute* the more specific. *Administer* passes by a natural transition to signify *inflict, dispense,* and blows, medicine, etc., are said to be *administered. Enforce* signifies also to present and urge home by intellectual and moral force; as, to *enforce* a precept or a duty. Compare ACCOMPLISH, EFFECT, KILL, MAKE.

ex·e·cu·tion (ek′sə·kyo͞o′shən) *n.* **1** The act of executing. **2** *Law* A judicial writ, as for the seizure of goods, etc. **3** The act of carrying into effect or enforcing any legislative or judicial act or decree. **4** The signing, as of a deed. **5** The infliction of capital punishment. **6** Style of performance; technical skill, as in music or art. **7** Effective work: said especially of warlike operations. See synonyms under ACT, OPERATION.

ex·e·cu·tion·er (ek′sə·kyo͞o′shən·ər) *n.* One who executes a death sentence.

ex·ec·u·tive (ig·zek′yə·tiv) *adj.* **1** Having the function, power, or skill of executing or performing. **2** Having ability or aptitude for directing or controlling. **3** Connected with or pertaining to direction or control; carrying into effect; administrative, as distinguished from *judicial* and *legislative*: an *executive* department of the government. Compare JUDICIAL, LEGISLATIVE. **4** Adroit or dexterous in execution. — *n.* **1** An official personage or body charged with the administration of a government: applied in the United States to the president and to governors. **2** The executive branch of government. **3** A director of a business or other organization.

executive agreement *U.S.* An international agreement concluded by the president and not requiring Senate ratification.

Executive Mansion **1** The White House, Washington, D.C.: the official residence of the president of the United States. **2** The residence of the governor of a State.

executive officer *U.S.* The principal officer assisting a commanding officer. Compare CHIEF OF STAFF (def. 2).

executive session A session of the U.S. Senate, closed to the public and convened to consider confidential business.

ex·ec·u·tor (ig·zek′yə·tər) *n.* **1** *Law* A person nominated by the will of another to execute the will. **2** One who executes, in any sense.

ex·ec·u·to·ri·al (ig·zek′yə·tôr′ē·əl, -tō′rē-) *adj.* **1** Executive. **2** In Scots law, of or pertaining to the execution of a judicial writ.

ex·ec·u·to·ry (ig·zek′yə·tôr′ē, -tō′rē) *adj.* **1** Pertaining to execution; executive; administrative. **2** *Law* That is to be executed or put into effect; especially, becoming operative on a future contingency: an *executory* consideration, contract, or devise.

ex·ec·u·trix (ig·zek′yə·triks) *n. fem. pl.* **ex·ec·u·trix·es** or **ex·ec·u·tri·ces** (-trī′sēz) *Law* A female executor.

ex·e·dra (ek′sə·drə, ik·sē′drə) *n. pl.* **·drae** (-drē) *Archit.* **1** In classical antiquity, a range of permanent seats, or a platform with seats, by the roadside, in a court, or otherwise placed, built of masonry and often curved in plan, intended for rest and conversation. **2** A curved seat, accommodating several persons, for use in the open air. **3** An apse, niche, window recess, or the like. [<L <Gk. *exedra* <*ex-* out + *hedra* a seat]

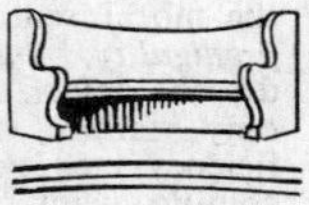

EXEDRA

ex·e·ge·sis (ek′sə·jē′sis) *n. pl.* **·ses** (-sēz) Explanation of the language and thought of a literary work; especially, Biblical exposition or interpretation. [<Gk. *exēgēsis* <*exegeesthai* explain <*ex-* out <*hegeesthai* <*agein* lead]

ex·e·gete (ek′sə·jēt) *n.* One skilled in interpretation, as of the Bible. Also **ex′e·ge′tist.**

ex·e·get·ic (ek′sə·jet′ik) *adj.* Pertaining to exegesis; expository; explanatory. [<Gk. *exēgētikos* <*exēgēsis.* See EXEGESIS.] — **ex′e·get′i·cal·ly** *adv.*

ex·e·get·ics (ek′sə·jet′iks) *n. pl. (construed as singular)* **1** The science of exegesis. **2** The science of the interpretation of the Bible.

ex·em·plar (ig·zem′plər, -plär) *n.* **1** A model, pattern, or original, to be copied or imitated. **2** The mental conception or image of something to be produced. **3** A specimen or transcript; especially, a specimen copy of a book or writing. **4** A typical example; archetype. See synonyms under EXAMPLE. [<OF *exemplaire* <L *exemplarium* <*exemplum* EXAMPLE; infl. in form by L *exemplar* typical <*exemplum*]

ex·em·pla·ry (ig·zem′plər·ē) *adj.* **1** Serving or fitted to serve as a model or example worthy of imitation; commendable: *exemplary* conduct. **2** Serving as or furnishing a warning example: *exemplary* damages; a most *exemplary* punishment. **3** Serving to exemplify; illustrative. — **ex·em′pla·ri·ly** *adv.* — **ex·em′pla·ri·ness** *n.*

ex·em·pli·fi·ca·tion (ig·zem′plə·fə·kā′shən) *n.* **1** The act of exemplifying. **2** An example. **3** *Law* A certified copy. See synonyms under EXAMPLE, SAMPLE.

ex·em·pli·fy (ig·zem′plə·fī) *v.t.* **·fied, ·fy·ing** **1** To show by example; illustrate. **2** *Law* **a** To prove by an attested copy. **b** To make an authenticated transcript from, as a public record. [<Med. L *exemplificare* <*exemplum* EXAMPLE + *facere* make] — **ex·em′pli·fi·ca′tive** *adj.*

ex·em·pli gra·ti·a (ig·zem′plē grā′shē·ə) *Latin* By way of example: abbreviated *e.g.* or *ex. gr.*

ex·empt (ig·zempt′) *v.t.* **1** To free or excuse from some obligation to which others are subject; grant immunity to: to *exempt* one from military service. **2** *Obs.* To take or put away; remove. See synonyms under ABSOLVE, RELEASE. — *adj.* **1** Free, clear, or excused, as from some liability, restriction, or burden. **2** *Obs.* Remote; separated. See synonyms under FREE. — *n.* A person who is exempted, as from military service. [<L *exemptus,* pp. of *eximere* <*ex-* out + *emere* buy, take] — **ex·empt′i·ble** *adj.*

ex·emp·tion (ig·zemp′shən) *n.* **1** The act of exempting. **2** The state of being exempt; a dispensation giving freedom from duty or penalty; freedom or immunity from some liability, requirement, or evil: *exemption* from punishment. See synonyms under RIGHT.

ex·en·ter·ate (eks·en′tə·rāt) *v.t.* **·at·ed, ·at·ing** *Surg.* To eviscerate. [<L *exenteratus,* pp. of *exenterare* <*ex-* out + Gk. *enteron* intestine] — **ex·en′ter·a′tion** *n.*

ex·e·qua·tur (ek′sə·kwā′tər) *n.* In international law, the official recognition given to a consul or commercial agent by the government of the country in which he is to exercise his functions. [<L, let him perform]

ex·e·quy (ek′sə·kwē) *n. pl.* **·quies** **1** *pl.* Funeral ceremonies; obsequies. **2** A funeral procession. [<OF *exequies* <L *exequiae* <*exequi, exsequi.* See EXECUTE.]

ex·er·cise (ek′sər·sīz) *v.* **·cised, ·cis·ing** *v.t.* **1** To subject to drills, systematic movements, etc., so as to train or develop (troops, muscles, the mind, etc.). **2** To make use of; employ: to

exercise caution or a right. **3** To perform or execute, as the duties of an office. **4** To wield; exert, as influence or authority. **5** To do habitually; make a habit of: used reflexively or in the passive: to be *exercised* in good works. **6** To occupy the mind of; especially, to make anxious; worry. — *v.i.* **7** To take exercise. **8** To undergo training. [< *n.*] — *n.* **1** A putting into use, action, or practice. **2** Activity for health, development, or training. **3** An act of speaking, reading, etc., as at a school exhibition or religious meeting: usually in the plural. **4** An act of worship; a religious service. **5** A lesson assigned to a student; also, the written or oral fulfilment of that assignment. [<OF *exercice* <L *exercitium* < *exercere* practice < *ex-* out, away + *arcere* restrain] — **ex′er·cis′a·ble** *adj.*

Synonyms (noun): act, action, activity, application, employment, exertion, occupation, operation, performance, practice, use. See ACT, PRACTICE. *Antonyms*: idleness, inaction, inactivity, relaxation, rest.

ex·er·cised (ek′sər·sīzd) *adj.* Harassed; agitated, excited.

ex·er·cis·er (ek′sər·sī′zər) *n.* **1** One who exercises. **2** An apparatus for the exercise of the body.

ex·er·ci·ta·tion (ig·zûr′sə·tā′shən) *n.* **1** An exercise, as a disciplinary mental act. **2** Exercise or practice. [<OF <L *exercitatio, -onis* < *exercitare,* freq. of *exercere.* See EXERCISE.]

ex·ergue (ig·zûrg′, ek′sûrg) *n.* The space beneath the principal design on the reverse of a coin or medal, with date, place of coining, etc. [<F <Gk. *ex* out + *ergon* work]

ex·ert (ig·zûrt′) *v.t.* **1** To put forth or put in action, as strength, force, or faculty; bring into strong or vigorous action. **2** *Obs.* To push or thrust forth. —**to exert oneself** To put forth effort. [<L *exertus,* var. of *exsertus,* pp. of *exserere* thrust out < *ex-* out + *serere* bind] — **ex·er′tive** *adj.*

ex·er·tion (ig·zûr′shən) *n.* The act of putting some power or faculty into vigorous action; a strong effort. See synonyms under ACT, ENDEAVOR, EXERCISE, INDUSTRY, WORK.

ex·e·sion (ig·zē′zhən, -shən) *n. Pathol.* The slow superficial destruction of organic tissues, especially bone, by the action of abscesses and other agencies. [<L *exesus,* pp. of *edere* eat + -ION]

Ex·e·ter (ek′sə·tər) The county seat of Devonshire, England. A native of Exeter is known as an *Exonian.*

ex·e·unt (ek′sē·ənt, -o͝ont) They go out: a stage direction. [<L]

exeunt om·nes (om′nēz) All go out: a stage direction. [<L]

ex fac·to jus (eks fak′tō jo͞os) *Latin* The law arises out of the fact.

ex·fo·li·ate (eks·fō′lē·āt) *v.t.* & *v.i.* **·at·ed, ·at·ing** **1** To remove scales or splinters (from). **2** To peel or scale off in thin flakes, as the bark of a tree. **3** *Geol.* To split off in scales or sheets, as a heated mineral or weathered rock. [<LL *exfoliatus,* pp. of *exfoliare* < *ex-* off + *folium* a leaf] — **ex·fo′li·a′tive** *adj.*

ex·fo·li·a·tion (eks·fō′lē·ā′shən) *n.* **1** A scaling or peeling off, as of bark, skin, bone, or flakes of mineral. **2** Matter scaled off or exfoliated.

ex·ha·lant (eks·hā′lənt, ig·zā′-) *adj.* Having the property of exhaling. — *n.* Anything exhaled or which exhales; specifically, a duct used for exhaling. [<F <L *exhalans, -antis,* pp. of *exhalare* EXHALE]

ex·ha·la·tion (eks′hə·lā′shən, eg′zə-) *n.* **1** A breathing out; anything exhaled. **2** An emitted vapor or fume; evaporation; expiration. [<L *exhalatio, -onis* < *exhalare* EXHALE]

ex·hale (eks·hāl′, ig·zāl′) *v.* **·haled, ·hal·ing** *v.i.* **1** To expel air or vapor; breathe out. **2** To pass off or rise as a vapor or effluence; evaporate. — *v.t.* **3** To breathe forth or give off, as gas, vapor, or an aroma. **4** To draw off; cause to evaporate: Heat *exhales* the earth's moisture. [<F *exhaler* <L *exhalare* < *ex-* out + *halare* breathe] — **ex·hal′a·ble** *adj.*

ex·haust (ig·zôst′) *v.t.* **1** To make tired; wear out completely. **2** To drain of resources, strength, etc.; use up. **3** To draw off, as gas, steam, etc., from or as from a container. **4** To empty (a container) of contents; drain. **5** To study, treat of, or develop thoroughly and completely: to *exhaust* a subject. **6** In pharmacy, to remove the essential principles of by means of a solvent, thus leaving an inert remainder. — *v.i.* **7** To pass out as the exhaust: The steam *exhausts* from the pipe. See synonyms under ABSORB. — *n.* **1** The fluid discharged or escaping from the cylinder of a steam engine after expansion. **2** The formation of air currents by creating a partial vacuum. **3** The device used in flour mills to conduct dust particles away by means of air currents. **4** The escape of the waste gases from the cylinders of an internal-combustion engine; also, more loosely, the muffler which regulates this escape. **5** Foul air escaping from an apartment by a special register or pipe. **6** Emission. [<L *exhaustus,* pp. of *exhaurire* < *ex-* out + *haurire* draw] — **ex·haust′er** *n.* — **ex·haust′i·bil′i·ty** *n.* — **ex·haust′i·ble** *adj.*

ex·haust·ed (ig·zôs′tid) *adj.* **1** Used up; consumed; spent. **2** Emptied: an *exhausted* cask. **3** Depleted of essential ingredients: said specifically of soil. **4** Deprived of air; having a vacuum. **5** Weakened; tired out. — **ex·haust′ed·ly** *adv.*

ex·haust·ing (ig·zôs′ting) *adj.* Producing or tending to produce exhaustion; wearying; weakening.

ex·haus·tion (ig·zôs′chən) *n.* **1** The act or process of exhausting. **2** The state of being exhausted. **3** Deprivation of strength or energy.

ex·haus·tive (ig·zôs′tiv) *adj.* **1** Having the effect or tendency to exhaust, as by thorough and complete discussion. **2** Covering all points or items, as in an investigation or discussion. — **ex·haus′tive·ly** *adv.* — **ex·haus′tive·ness** *n.*

ex·haust·less (ig·zôst′lis) *adj.* Inexhaustible. — **ex·haust′less·ly** *adv.* — **ex·haust′less·ness** *n.*

exhaust steam Steam which has already performed work: distinguished from *live steam.*

exhaust velocity The velocity of exhaust gases at the moment of their expulsion from an internal-combustion engine, jet engine, rocket motor, or the like.

ex·hib·it (ig·zib′it) *v.t.* **1** To present to view; display. **2** To show or reveal: to *exhibit* ill will. **3** To present for public inspection or entertainment, as a product, play, etc. **4** *Law* To present formally or officially, as evidence. **5** *Med.* To administer, as a remedy. — *v.i.* **6** To place something on display. See synonyms under FLAUNT. — *n.* **1** Any object or objects exhibited. **2** *Law* A document or object marked for use as evidence. **3** A showing or manifestation; especially, a written statement of the condition of anything. [<L *exhibitus,* pp. of *exhibere* < *ex-* out + *habere* hold, have] — **ex·hib′i·tor, ex·hib′it·er** *n.*

ex·hi·bi·tion (ek′sə·bish′ən) *n.* **1** The act of exhibiting; display. **2** Anything exhibited; a show; especially, a public showing of works of art, athletic prowess, cattle, agricultural or manufactured products, etc. **3** An examination of students before an audience. **4** A display of student work. **5** *Brit.* A bursary. See synonyms under SPECTACLE. [<OF *exhibicion* <L *exhibitio, -onis* < *exhibere.* See EXHIBIT.]

ex·hi·bi·tion·er (ek′sə·bish′ən·ər) *n.* **1** *Brit.* A student maintained in a university by a donated allowance. **2** An exhibitor.

ex·hi·bi·tion·ism (ek′sə·bish′ən·iz′əm) *n.* **1** The tendency to display one's personal qualities in a manner that will attract attention. **2** *Psychiatry* The tendency, usually compulsive, to obtain sexual gratification by public exposure of one's body or genitalia. — **ex′hi·bi′tion·ist** *n.*

ex·hib·i·tive (ig·zib′ə·tiv) *adj.* **1** Representative. **2** Serving for exhibition.

ex·hib·i·to·ry (ig·zib′ə·tôr′ē, -tō′rē) *adj.* Pertaining to exhibition; exhibiting; tending to exhibit.

ex·hil·a·rant (ig·zil′ər·ənt) *adj.* Causing exhilaration. — *n.* Something that exhilarates. [<F <L *exhilarans, -antis,* ppr. of *exhilarare.* See EXHILARATE.]

ex·hil·a·rate (ig·zil′ə·rāt) *v.t.* **·rat·ed, ·rat·ing** To induce a lively or enlivening feeling in; enliven; cheer; stimulate. See synonyms under REJOICE. [<L *exhilaratus,* pp. of *exhilarare* gladden < *ex-* completely + *hilarare* < *hilaris* glad] — **ex·hil′a·rat′ing** *adj.* — **ex·hil′a·rat′ing·ly** *adv.* — **ex·hil′a·ra′tor** *n.*

ex·hil·a·ra·tion (ig·zil′ə·rā′shən) *n.* The act of exhilarating, or the state of being exhilarated; animation; enlivenment; stimulation. — **ex·hil′a·ra′tive, ex·hil′a·ra·to′ry** (-tôr′ē, -tō′rē) *adj.*

ex·hort (ig·zôrt′) *v.t.* To urge by earnest appeal or argument; advise or caution strongly. — *v.i.* To utter exhortation. [<L *exhortari* < *ex-* completely + *hortari* urge]

ex·hor·ta·tion (eg′zôr·tā′shən, ek′sər-) *n.* **1** The act or practice of exhorting; attempt to arouse or incite, as by appeal, argument, or admonition. **2** That which is spoken in exhorting; admonition; earnest advice. See synonyms under COUNSEL. [<L *exhortatio, -onis* < *exhortari.* See EXHORT.]

ex·hort·a·tive (ig·zôr′tə·tiv) *adj.* Containing or serving for exhortation. Also **ex·hort′a·to′ry** (-tôr′ē, -tō′rē).

ex·hort·er (ig·zôr′tər) *n.* One who exhorts; especially, a sensational religious speaker.

ex·hu·ma·tion (eks′hyo͞o·mā′shən) *n.* The digging up of that which has been buried; disinterring; especially, the disinterring of a human body.

ex·hume (ig·zyo͞om′, iks·hyo͞om′) *v.t.* **·humed, ·hum·ing** To dig out of the earth, as a dead body; disinter. [<F *exhumer* <Med. L *exhumare* <L *ex-* out + *humus* ground]

ex·i·gen·cy (ek′sə·jən·sē) *n. pl.* **·cies** **1** The state of being urgent or exigent; pressing need or demand. **2** A case requiring immediate attention, assistance, or remedy. **3** A critical period or condition; a pressing necessity. Also **ex′i·gence.** See synonyms under NECESSITY.

ex·i·gent (ek′sə·jənt) *adj.* **1** Demanding immediate aid or action; urgent. **2** Feeling the need; requiring; exacting. [<L *exigens, -entis,* ppr. of *exigere.* See EXACT.]

ex·i·gi·ble (ek′sə·jə·bəl) *adj.* That may be exacted, demanded, or required; demandable.

ex·ig·u·ous (ig·zig′yo͞o·əs, ik·sig′-) *adj.* Small; slender; diminutive. [<L *exiguus* scanty] — **ex·i·gu·i·ty** (ek′sə·gyo͞o′ə·tē), **ex·ig′u·ous·ness** *n.*

ex·ile (eg′zīl, ek′sīl) *n.* **1** Banishment from one's home or native land; expatriation. **2** One driven or wandering away from country or home; an expatriate. — **the Exile** The Babylonian captivity of the Jews. — *v.t.* **ex·iled, ex·il·ing** To expel from and forbid to return to a native land or home; banish. See synonyms under BANISH. [<OF *exil, essil* <L *exsilium* < *ex-* out + *sal-,* root of *salire* leap] — **ex·il·ic** (eg·zil′ik, ek·sil′ik) *adj.*

ex·ist (ig·zist′) *v.i.* **1** To have actual being or reality; be. **2** To continue to live or be: Animal life cannot *exist* without oxygen. **3** To be present; occur: This species now *exists* only in Australia. See synonyms under LIVE. [<F *exister* <L *existere* < *ex-* out + *sistere* be located < *stare* stand]

ex·is·tence (ig·zis′təns) *n.* **1** Being; the state or fact of being, or continuing to be, whether as substance, essence, personality, or consciousness: a brief or an endless *existence,* real or idle *existence.* **2** Possession or continuance of animate or vital being; life: a fight for *existence.* **3** Anything that exists or has the quality of objectivity; an entity; actuality.

ex·is·tent (ig·zis′tənt) *adj.* Having being or existence. — *n.* That which exists. See synonyms under ALIVE. [<L *existens, -entis,* ppr. of *existere.* See EXIST.]

ex·is·ten·tial (eg′zis·ten′shəl) *adj.* **1** Of or pertaining to existence. **2** Expressing or stating the fact of existence. — **ex′is·ten′tial·ly** *adv.*

ex·is·ten·tial·ism (eg′zis·ten′shəl·iz′əm) *n.* **1** A movement in 20th century philosophy, influenced in its development by Kierkegaard and Nietzsche and popularized in France by Sartre, emphasizing the active participation of the will, rather than the reason, in confronting the problems of a non-moral or absurd universe. Man is defined in existentialism as the sum total of his acts rather than his intentions or potentialities, and exists in order to will himself to act. **2** A cult of nihilism and pessimism popularized in France after World War II, supposedly based on the doctrines of Sartre and other existentialist writers. — **ex′is·ten′tial·ist** *adj.* & *n.*

ex·it (eg′zit, ek′sit) *n.* **1** A way or passage

out; egress. 2 The departure of an actor from the stage. 3 Any departure, as that from the scenes of life; death. —*v.i.* 1 To go out. 2 (He or she) goes out: a stage direction. [< L *exitus* < *exire* < *ex-* out + *ire* go]

ex li·bris (eks lī′bris, lē′-) *Latin* From the books (of): used as an inscription or label on a book, followed by the owner's name; hence, a bookplate.

Ex·moor (eks′mo͝or) A plateau in west Somersetshire and NE Devonshire, England, 30 square miles.

ex mo·re (eks mō′rē) *Latin* According to custom.

Ex·mouth (eks′məth) A channel port in SE Devonshire, England.

ex ne·ces·si·ta·te re·i (eks ni·ses′ə·tā′tē rē′ī) *Latin* From the necessity of the case; the case demands.

exo- *combining form* Out; outside; external: *exocarp.* Also, before vowels, *ex-*. [< Gk. *exo-*, *ex-* < *exō* outside]

ex·o·bi·ol·o·gy (ek′sō·bī·ol′ə·jē) *n.* 1 The scientific investigation of extraterrestrial life. 2 The study of the effects of space travel on terrestrial organisms. —**ex′o·bi·o·log′i·cal** *adj.*

ex·o·car·di·a (ek′sō·kär′dē·ə) *n. Pathol.* A displacement of the heart from its normal position. [< NL < Gk. *exo-* out + *kardia* heart]

ex·o·car·di·ac (ek′sō·kär′dē·ak) *adj.* Situated outside the heart. Also **ex′o·car′di·al.**

ex·o·carp (ek′sō·kärp) *n. Bot.* The outer wall of a fruit covering, when it is possible to distinguish more than one; epicarp. Compare ENDOCARP and illustrations under FRUIT.

ex·o·cen·tric (ek′sō·sen′trik) *adj. Ling.* Denoting a syntactic construction which as a unit functions differently from any of its component parts, as *Jim works hard* is an *exocentric* construction: opposed to *endocentric.*

ex·o·derm (ek′sō·dûrm) *n.* The ectoderm.

ex·od·ic (ek·sod′ik) *adj.* 1 Of or pertaining to an exodus. 2 Efferent.

ex·o·don·tia (ek′sō·don′shə, -shē·ə) *n.* The branch of dentistry concerned with the extraction of teeth. [< NL < Gk. *ex-* out + *odōn, odontos* a tooth] —**ex′o·dont′ist** *n.*

ex·o·dus (ek′sə·dəs) *n.* A going forth, or departure, as of a multitude, from a place or country. —**the Exodus** The departure of the Israelites from Egypt under the guidance of Moses, described in **Exodus,** the second book of the Old Testament. [< L < Gk. *exodos* < *ex-* out + *hodos* way]

ex·o·en·zyme (ek′sō·en′zīm, -zim) See ECTOENZYME.

ex of·fi·ci·o (eks ə·fish′ē·ō) *Latin* by virtue of or because of office or position.

ex·og·a·my (eks·og′ə·mē) *n.* 1 The custom of certain peoples forbidding any man to marry within his own tribe or clan. 2 Marriage outside of one's tribe, clan, or family: opposed to *endogamy.* 3 *Biol.* The union of two protozoans of different ancestry, with fusion of nuclei, as the commencement of a new cycle of growth. —**ex·og′a·mous, ex·o·gam·ic** (ek′·sō·gam′ik) *adj.*

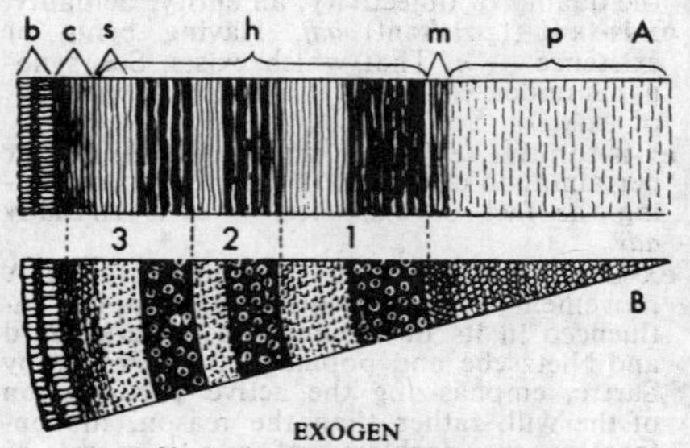

EXOGEN

A. Vertical section; *B.* Cross-section; showing growth rings for three successive years at *1, 2, 3.*

b. Bark. *s.* Sapwood (alburnum). *m.* Medullary sheath.
c. Cambium layer. *h.* Heartwood (duramen). *p.* Pith.

ex·o·gen (ek′sə·jən) *n. Bot.* A plant which increases in size by successive concentric additions or rings beneath the bark and outside the previous growth; a dicotyledon: opposed to *endogen.*

ex·og·e·nous (eks·oj′ə·nəs) *adj.* 1 Originating outside the organism. 2 Due to external causes. 3 Growing by addition at the outer surface. —**ex·og′e·nous·ly** *adv.*

ex·on·er·ate (ig·zon′ə·rāt) *v.t.* **·at·ed, ·at·ing** 1 To free from accusation or blame; acquit; exculpate. 2 To relieve or free from a responsibility or the like. See synonyms under ABSOLVE, JUSTIFY. [< L *exoneratus,* pp. of *exonerare* < *ex-* out, away + *onus, oneris* burden] —**ex·on′er·a′tion** *n.* —**ex·on′er·a′tive** *adj.*

Ex·o·ni·an (ek·sō′nē·ən) *n.* A native or inhabitant of Exeter. —*adj.* Of or pertaining to Exeter.

ex·o·path·ic (ek′sō·path′ik) *adj. Pathol.* Of or resulting from causes external to the organism: an *exopathic* disease.

ex·oph·thal·mic (ek′sof·thal′mik) *adj.* Pertaining to, of the nature of, accompanied by, or affected with exophathlmos.

exophthalmic goiter *Pathol.* A disease characterized by enlargement of the thyroid gland, protrusion of the eyeballs, anemia, and palpitation of the heart; Basedow's disease: also called *Graves' disease.*

ex·oph·thal·mos (ek′sof·thal′məs) *n. Pathol.* Undue protrusion of the eyeball. Also **ex′oph·thal′mus.** [< NL < Gk., with prominent eyes < *ex-* out + *ophthalmos* eye]

ex·o·ra·ble (ek′sər·ə·bəl) *adj.* Capable of being persuaded or moved by entreaty; capable of relenting. [< L *exorabilis* < *ex-* out, away + *orare* pray] —**ex′o·ra·bil′i·ty** *n.*

ex·or·bi·tance (ig·zôr′bə·təns) *n.* Excessiveness in degree or amount; extravagance; a tendency to be exorbitant. Also **ex·or′bi·tan·cy.** See synonyms under EXCESS.

ex·or·bi·tant (ig·zôr′bə·tənt) *adj.* 1 Going beyond usual and proper limits, as in price or demand; excessive; extravagant. 2 Out of the realm of the law; illegal. See synonyms under IMMODERATE. [< LL *exorbitans, -antis,* ppr. of *exorbitare* go astray < *ex-* out + *orbita* a track] —**ex·or′bi·tant·ly** *adv.*

ex·or·cise (ek′sôr·sīz) *v.t.* **·cised, ·cis·ing** 1 To cast out (an evil spirit) by prayers or incantations. 2 To free of an evil spirit. 3 *Obs.* To summon or conjure up, as a demon. Also **ex′or·cize.** [< OF *exorciser* < LL *exorcizare* < Gk. *exorkizein* < *ex-* out + *horkos* an oath]—**ex′or·cis′er** or **·ciz′er** *n.*

ex·or·cism (ek′sôr·siz′əm) *n.* 1 The act of casting out or exorcising evil spirits. 2 *Obs.* The act or formula of calling or conjuring up the devil or a spirit. —**ex′or·cis′mal** *adj.* —**ex′or·cist** *n.*

ex·or·di·um (ig·zôr′dē·əm, ik·sôr′-) *n. pl.* **·di·ums** or **·di·a** (-dē·ə) The introductory part, as of a discourse; a prelude. [< L < *exordiri* < *ex-* out + *ordiri* begin] —**ex·or′di·al** *adj.*

ex·o·re·ic (ek′sə·rē′ik) *adj.* Pertaining to or designating a region whose surface drainage reaches the oceans, as the greater part of North and South America. [< EXO- + Gk. *rheein* flow]

ex·o·skel·e·ton (ek′sō·skel′ə·tən) *n. Biol.* An external skeleton; any bony or horny external covering, armor, or structure of hardened integument, especially in invertebrates; dermoskeleton: opposed to *endoskeleton.*

ex·os·mo·sis (ek′sos·mō′sis, -soz-) *n. Chem.* 1 Osmosis in that direction in which the fluid crosses the septum most slowly. 2 Osmosis from an inner to an outer vessel; opposed to *endosmosis.* Also **ex′os·mose.** —**ex′os·mot′ic** (-mot′ik) *adj.* —**ex·os′mic** *adj.*

ex·o·sphere (ek′sō·sfir) *n.* The outermost region of the earth's atmosphere, beginning at a height of about 400 miles.

ex·o·spore (ek′sō·spôr, -spōr) *n. Bot.* 1 The outer wall of a spore. 2 An outer coat of the spores of certain fungi.

ex·os·to·sis (ek′sos·tō′sis) *n. pl.* **·ses** (-sēz) *Pathol.* An excessive bony outgrowth or tumor formed on either the outer or the inner surface of a bone or on a cartilage. [< NL < Gk. < *ex-* out + *osteon* bone]

ex·o·ter·ic (ek′sə·ter′ik) *adj.* 1 Adapted or intelligible, as a doctrine, to those outside the inner circle of disciples, or to the uninitiated; suitable for popular comprehension: opposed to *esoteric.* 2 External. Also **ex′o·ter′i·cal.** [< LL *exotericus* < Gk. *exōterikos* < *exōterō,* comparative of *exō* outside] —**ex′o·ter′i·cal·ly** *adv.* —**ex′o·ter′i·cism** *n.*

ex·o·ther·mic (ek′sō·thûr′mik) *adj. Chem.* Designating those reactions which are accompanied by the liberation of heat: opposed to *endothermic.* Also **ex·o·ther′mal.** [< EXO- + Gk. *thermē* heat]

ex·ot·ic (ig·zot′ik) *adj.* Belonging by nature or origin to another part of the world; brought in from abroad; foreign; strange: an *exotic* flower. —*n.* Something not native, as a plant, person, word, etc. [< L *exoticus* < Gk. *exōtikos* foreign < *exō* outside] —**ex·ot′i·cal·ly** *adv.* —**ex·ot′i·cism** *n.*

ex·o·tox·in (ek′sō·tok′sin) *n. Biochem.* A toxin formed within and excreted by an organism which is not itself toxic: distinguished from *endotoxin.* —**ex′o·tox′ic** *adj.*

ex·pand (ik·spand′) *v.t.* 1 To increase the range, scope, volume, size, etc., of: to *expand* a business. 2 To spread out by unfolding or extending; open: The peacock *expands* his tail. 3 To write or develop in full the details or form of, as a thought, argument, etc. —*v.i.* 4 To grow larger, wider, etc.; unfold; increase. See synonyms under AMPLIFY, SPREAD. [< L *expandere* < *ex-* out + *pandere* spread. Doublet of SPAWN.] —**ex·pand′er** *n.*

expanding bit *Mech.* A bit which can be adjusted to bore holes of varying size.

ex·panse (ik·spans′) *n.* That which lies spread out; a vast continuous area or stretch: the blue *expanse* of heaven. [< L *expansum* < *expandere.* See EXPAND.]

ex·pan·si·ble (ik·span′sə·bəl) *adj.* Capable of being expanded; expansile. —**ex·pan′si·bil′·i·ty** *n.*

ex·pan·sile (ik·span′səl) *adj.* 1 Capable of expanding or of causing expansion. 2 Capable of being expanded.

ex·pan·sion (ik·span′shən) *n.* 1 The act of expanding, in any sense. 2 The condition or state of being expanded. 3 The amount of increase in size, scope, or the like. 4 That which is expanded; an expanded continuation or result; an extended surface; an expanded part; an enlargement. 5 The extent or space over or through which a thing expands; hence, extent in general; unlimited space; expanse; immensity. 6 *Physics* Increase of volume, as of steam in an engine cylinder when cut off from connection with the supply of pressure, or of the exploding gas in an internal-combustion engine. 7 *Math.* Development of a mathematical function into a series; also, the full expression as developed: the *expansion* of $(a + b)^3$ into $a^3 + 3a^2b + 3ab^2 + b^3$.

expansion bolt *Mech.* A bolt fitted with a split sleeve or other expansible member, by which it may be secured in a hole in masonry and the like.

ex·pan·sion·ism (ik·span′shən·iz′əm) *n.* Belief in or advocacy of a policy of expansion, as of commerce, currency, or territory. —**ex·pan′·sion·ist** *n.*

ex·pan·sive (ik·span′siv) *adj.* 1 Capable of enlarging or being expanded; tending to expand; causing or characterized by expansion. 2 Presenting an expanse; extending; extensive. 3 Comprehensive; broad in mind or sympathies; liberal. 4 Amiable and effusive: an *expansive* personality. —**ex·pan′sive·ly** *adv.* —**ex·pan′sive·ness** *n.*

expansive delusion *Psychiatry* A delusion of wealth, power, etc., accompanied by euphoria.

ex par·te (eks pär′tē) *Latin* Emanating from or in the interest of one side only. [< L]

ex·pa·ti·ate (ik·spā′shē·āt) *v.i.* **·at·ed, ·at·ing** 1 To speak or write in a lengthy manner; elaborate: with *on* or *upon.* 2 *Rare* To roam at large; range widely or unrestrainedly. See synonyms under AMPLIFY. [< L *ex(s)patiatus,* pp. of *ex(s)patiari* < *ex-* out + *spatiari* walk < *spatium* space] —**ex·pa′ti·a′tion** *n.* —**ex·pa′ti·a′tor** *n.* —**ex·pa′ti·a·to′ry** (-tôr′ē, -tō′rē) *adj.*

ex·pa·tri·ate (eks·pā′trē·āt) *v.t.* **·at·ed, ·at·ing** 1 To drive (a person) from his native land; exile; banish. 2 To withdraw (oneself) from one's native land. —*n.* (-it, -āt) One exiled. —*adj.* Banished; exiled. [< Med. L *expatriatus,* pp. of *expatriare* < *ex-* out + *patria* native land] —**ex·pa′tri·a′tion** *n.*

ex·pect (ik·spekt′) *v.t.* 1 To look forward to as certain or probable; anticipate in thought. 2 To look for as right, proper, or necessary; require. 3 *Colloq.* To presume; suppose. 4 *Obs.* To wait for. See synonyms under ABIDE, ANTICIPATE. [< L *ex(s)pectare* < *ex-* out + *spectare* look at]

ex·pec·tan·cy (ik·spek′tən·sē) *n. pl.* **·cies** 1

The act or state of expecting; expectation. 2 An object of expectation. 3 *Law* The state of being expected; abeyance: an estate in *expectancy*. See synonyms under ANTICIPATION. Also **ex·pec′tance.**

ex·pec·tant (ik·spek′tənt) *adj.* 1 Waiting or looking forward in expectation. 2 Awaiting the birth of a child: an *expectant* mother. —*n.* One who is anticipating confidently. [<OF <L *ex(s)pectans, -antis,* ppr. of *ex(s)pectare.* See EXPECT.] —**ex·pec′tant·ly** *adv.*

ex·pec·ta·tion (ek′spek·tā′shən) *n.* 1 The act of looking confidently for something; expectancy. 2 Anticipation; prospect of good to come, as of wealth: often plural. 3 Something expected. 4 The present value of a probability. See synonyms under ANTICIPATION. [<L *ex(s)pectatio, -onis* < *ex(s)pectare.* See EXPECT.]

ex·pec·ta·tive (ik·spek′tə·tiv) *adj.* Contingent.

ex·pect·ing (ik·spek′ting) *adj.* Pregnant; also, due to give birth.

ex·pec·to·rant (ik·spek′tər·ənt) *adj.* Relating to or promotive of expectoration. —*n.* A medicine to promote expectoration. [<L *expectorans, -antis,* ppr. of *expectorare.* See EXPECTORATE.]

ex·pec·to·rate (ik·spek′tə·rāt) *v.t.* & *v.i.* **·rat·ed, ·rat·ing** 1 To discharge, as phlegm, by hawking or coughing up and spitting from the mouth. 2 To spit. [<L *expectoratus,* pp. of *expectorare* < *ex-* out + *pectus, -oris* breast]

ex·pec·to·ra·tion (ik·spek′tə·rā′shən) *n.* The act of expectorating; also, matter expectorated.

ex·pe·di·en·cy (ik·spē′dē·ən·sē) *n. pl.* **·cies** 1 The quality of being proper, suitable, and advantageous under given circumstances; advantageousness; fitness. 2 That which is most practicable, all things considered. 3 In ethics, the doing of what is useful, politic, or advantageous, regardless of justice or right. See synonyms under PROFIT, UTILITY. Also **ex·pe′di·ence.**

ex·pe·di·ent (ik·spē′dē·ənt) *adj.* 1 Serving to promote a desired end; suitable under the circumstances; contributing to personal advantage; advisable. 2 Pertaining to utility or advantage rather than principle. 3 *Obs.* Speedy; expeditious. —*n.* 1 That which furthers or promotes an end. 2 A device; shift. [<OF <L *expediens, -entis,* ppr. of *expedire.* See EXPEDITE.] —**ex·pe′di·ent·ly** *adv.*

Synonyms (adj.): advantageous, beneficial, convenient, favorable, paying, profitable, sensible, suitable, useful, wise, worthwhile. See PROFITABLE. Compare synonyms for PROFIT, UTILITY. *Antonyms*: absurd, ill-adapted, ill-considered, ill-devised, ill-judged, inexpedient, irrational, reckless, unsuitable, unwise.

ex·pe·di·en·tial (ik·spē′dē·en′shəl) *adj.* Of or pertaining to expediency.

ex·pe·dite (ek′spə·dīt) *v.t.* **·dit·ed, ·dit·ing** 1 To speed up the process or progress of; facilitate. 2 To do quickly. 3 To send or issue officially; dispatch. See synonyms under PUSH. —*adj.* Prompt; expeditious. [<L *expeditus,* pp. of *expedire* < *ex-* out + *pes, pedis* foot]

ex·pe·dit·er (ek′spə·dī′tər) *n.* One who or that which expedites; especially, one who facilitates the delivery of goods. Also **ex′pe·di′tor.**

ex·pe·di·tion (ek′spə·dish′ən) *n.* 1 A journey, march or voyage, generally of several or many persons, for a definite purpose: an Arctic *expedition.* 2 The body of persons engaged in such a journey, march, or voyage, together with their equipment. 3 The quality of being expeditious; speed; dispatch. See synonyms under JOURNEY.

ex·pe·di·tion·ar·y (ek′spə·dish′ən·er′ē) *adj.* Of the nature of, for the purpose of, or constituting an expedition.

expeditionary force A force of men equipped for military service abroad.

ex·pe·di·tious (ek′spə·dish′əs) *adj.* Accomplished with energy and dispatch; quick; speedy. See synonyms under ACTIVE. —**ex′pe·di′tious·ly** *adv.* —**ex′pe·di′tious·ness** *n.*

ex·pel (ik·spel′) *v.t.* **·pelled, ·pel·ling** 1 To drive out by force or authority; force out. 2 To dismiss, as a pupil from a school; eject. See synonyms under BANISH, EXTERMINATE. [<L *expellere* < *ex-* out + *pellere* drive, thrust] —**ex·pel′la·ble** *adj.*

ex·pel·lant (ik·spel′ənt) *adj.* Of a nature or having the power to expel: expelling: *expellant* treatment in medicine. —*n.* That which expels, as a purgative. Also **ex·pel′lent.** [<OF <L *expellens, -entis,* ppr. of *expellere.* See EXPEL.]

ex·pel·lee (ek′spel·ē′) *n.* One who has been expelled.

ex·pend (ik·spend′) *v.t.* To pay out or spend; use up. [<L *expendere* < *ex-* out + *pendere* weigh]

ex·pend·a·ble (ik·spen′də·bəl) *adj.* That may be expended; capable of being, or to be, consumed, used, or sacrificed, as men and materiel in warfare.

ex·pen·di·ture (ik·spen′də·chər) *n.* 1 The act of expending; outlay; disbursement. 2 That which is expended; expense. See synonyms under EXPENSE, PRICE. [<Med. L *expenditus,* irreg. pp. of *expendere.* See EXPEND.]

ex·pense (ik·spens′) *n.* 1 The laying out or expending, as of money or other resources; expenditure. 2 Loss: at the *expense* of health. 3 Money expended; outlay. 4 Anything requiring expenditure. [<AF <LL *expensa* < *expendere.* See EXPEND.]

Synonyms: cost, expenditure, outgo, outlay. The *cost* of a thing is whatever one surrenders or gives up for it, intentionally or unintentionally, or even unconsciously; *expense* is what is laid out by calculation or intention. We say, "He won his fame at the *cost* of his life"; "I know it to my *cost*"; we speak of a joke at another's *expense*; at another's *cost* would seem to make it a more serious matter. There is a tendency to use *cost* of what we pay for a possession, *expense* of what we pay for a service; we speak of the *cost* of goods, the *expense* of manufacture. *Outlay* is used of some definite *expenditure,* as for the purchase of supplies; *outgo* of a steady drain or of incidental *expenses.* See PRICE. *Antonyms*: gain, income, proceeds, product, profit, profits, receipt, receipts, return, returns.

ex·pen·sive (ik·spen′siv) *adj.* Causing or involving much expense; costly. —**ex·pen′sive·ly** *adv.* —**ex·pen′sive·ness** *n.*

ex·pe·ri·ence (ik·spir′ē·əns) *n.* 1 Knowledge derived from one's own action, practice, perception, enjoyment, or suffering; experimental knowledge; especially, the state of such knowledge in an individual as an index of wisdom or skill: He is a lawyer of *experience.* 2 Something undergone, enjoyed, etc. 3 Spiritual exercise of mind; conversion. 4 Every form of knowledge due to one's immediate observation; also, the sum total of such knowledge in the life of an individual. 5 Length, duration, or state of occupation with or employment in a particular study, business, or work. See synonyms under ACQUAINTANCE, KNOWLEDGE. —*v.t.* **·enced, ·enc·ing** To undergo personally; feel. See synonyms under KNOW. —**to experience religion** To undergo a change of heart; be converted. [<OF <L *experientia* < *experiri* try out]

ex·pe·ri·enced (ik·spir′ē·ənst) *adj.* Taught by experience; practiced; skilled.

experience meeting A religious meeting for prayer and the relation of personal religious experiences.

experience table In life insurance, a mortality table based on the records and reports of one or more companies.

ex·pe·ri·en·tial (ik·spir′ē·en′shəl) *adj.* Pertaining to or acquired by experience; empirical. —**ex·pe′ri·en′tial·ly** *adv.*

ex·per·i·ment (ik·sper′ə·mənt) *n.* 1 An act or operation designed to discover, test, or illustrate a truth, principle, or effect; a test, especially one intended to confirm or disprove something which is still in doubt. 2 The conducting of such operations or tests. 3 Something undergoing the test of actual experience, as opposed to that whose practicability or usefulness has been fully demonstrated: often used depreciatively: Your boasted institutions are but an *experiment.* 4 *Obs.* Experience. —*v.i.* (-ment) To make experiments; make a test or trial. [<OF <L *experimentum* < *experiri* try out] —**ex·per′i·ment′er** *n.*

ex·per·i·men·tal (ik·sper′ə·men′təl) *adj.* 1 Pertaining to, growing out of, or known by methods of controlled testing and direct observation under stated conditions: *experimental* science: opposed to *speculative.* 2 Designating or pertaining to that which is learned by experience: distinguished from *theoretical.* —**ex·per′i·men′tal·ism** *n.* —**ex·per′i·men′tal·ist** *n.* —**ex·per′i·men′tal·ly** *adv.*

ex·per·i·men·ta·tion (ik·sper′ə·men·tā′shən) *n.* The act or practice of experimenting. —**ex·per′i·men′ta·tive** (-men′tə·tiv) *adj.*

experiment station A place where agricultural experiments are developed and conducted with a view to improvement in methods and products.

ex·pert (ek′spûrt) *n.* 1 One who has special skill or knowledge; a specialist. 2 In the U.S. Army, the highest of three grades for skill in the use of small arms. 3 A soldier having this grade. Compare MARKSMAN, SHARPSHOOTER. —*adj.* (*also* ik·spûrt′) 1 Skilful as the result of practice; dexterous; marked by skill. 2 Proceeding from an expert. See synonyms under CLEVER, GOOD. [<L *expertus,* pp. of *experiri* try out] —**ex·pert′ly** *adv.* —**ex·pert′ness** *n.*

ex·per·tise (ek′spər·tēz′) *n. French* An evaluation or assessment by an expert.

ex·pi·a·ble (ek′spē·ə·bəl) *adj.* That may be expiated or atoned for.

ex·pi·ate (ek′spē·āt) *v.t.* **·at·ed, ·at·ing** To atone for; make amends for. [<L *expiatus,* pp. of *expiare* < *ex-* completely + *piare* appease < *pius* pious] —**ex′pi·a′tor** *n.*

ex·pi·a·tion (ek′spē·ā′shən) *n.* 1 The active means of expiating, or of making reparation or satisfaction, as for offense or sin. 2 The removing of guilt by suffering punishment; atonement. ◆ Collateral adjective: *piacular.* See synonyms under PROPITIATION. —**ex′pi·a·to′ry** (-tôr′ē, -tō′rē) *adj.*

ex·pi·ra·tion (ek′spə·rā′shən) *n.* 1 The natural termination of anything, as of a lease or a period of time. 2 The act of breathing out, as air from the lungs: opposed to *inspiration.* 3 The outbreathing of life; death. 4 That which is expired. 5 The sound made in respiration. See synonyms under END. [<L *expiratio, -onis* < *expirare.* See EXPIRE.]

ex·pir·a·to·ry (ik·spī′rə·tôr′ē, -tō′rē) *adj.* Pertaining to, or used for, the expiration of breath.

ex·pire (ik·spīr′) *v.* **·pired, ·pir·ing** *v.i.* 1 To exhale one's last breath; die. 2 To die out, as the embers of a fire. 3 To come to an end; terminate, as a contract or magazine subscription. 4 To breathe out air from the lungs; exhale. —*v.t.* 5 To breathe out from the lungs. 6 *Obs.* To emit (a vapor or odor). See synonyms under DIE, END. [<L *ex(s)pirare* < *ex-* out + *spirare* breathe] —**ex·pir′er** *n.*

ex·pi·ry (ik·spī′rē) *n. pl.* **·ries** 1 End; termination. 2 *Archaic* Death.

ex·plain (ik·splān′) *v.t.* 1 To make plain or clear; make understandable. 2 To give a meaning to; interpret. 3 To give reasons for; state the cause or purpose of. —*v.i.* 4 To give an explanation. See synonyms under INTERPRET. [<L *explanare* < *ex-* out + *planare* make level < *planus* flat] —**ex·plain′a·ble** *adj.*

ex·pla·na·tion (ek′splə·nā′shən) *n.* 1 The act or means of explaining; elucidation. 2 Meaning; significance; sense. 3 The process of settling a disagreement, or reconciling a difference, by explaining the circumstances; reconciliation. See synonyms under DEFINITION. [<L *explanatio, -onis* < *explanare.* See EXPLAIN.]

ex·plan·a·to·ry (ik·splan′ə·tôr′ē, -tō′rē) *adj.* Serving or tending to explain. Also **ex·plan′a·tive.** —**ex·plan′a·to′ri·ly** *adv.*

ex·plant (iks·plant′, -plänt′) *v.t.* To place outside its habitat, as an organ of the body or bacteria in a medium, for purposes of observation and study.

ex·ple·tive (eks′plə·tiv) *n.* 1 An interjection, often profane. 2 A word or syllable employed for rhetorical or rhythmical effect. 3 Something serving to fill out. —*adj.* Added for emphasis; redundant: also **ex′ple·to′ry** (-tôr′ē, -tō′rē). [<LL *expletivus* <L *expletus,* pp. of *explere* < *ex-* completely + *plere* fill]

ex·pli·ca·ble (eks′pli·kə·bəl, *frequently* iks·plik′ə·bəl) *adj.* Capable of explanation.

ex·pli·cate (eks′plə·kāt) *v.t.* **·cat·ed, ·cat·ing** To clear from obscurity; explain. See synonyms under INTERPRET. [<L *explicatus,* pp. of

explicare < *ex-* out + *plicare* fold] — **ex′pli·ca′tor** *n.*
ex·pli·ca·tion (eks′plə·kā′shən) *n.* **1** Explanation, especially of a passage in any text, or definition, as of a word, by unfolding what is implied in it. **2** The act or process of explicating. **3** A detailed description.
ex·pli·ca·tive (eks′plə·kā′tiv) *adj.* **1** Serving to unfold or explain. **2** Analytic. Also **ex′pli·ca·to′ry** (-tôr′ē, -tō′rē).
ex·plic·it (ik·splis′it) *adj.* **1** Plainly expressed, or that plainly expresses. **2** Having no disguised meaning or reservation; definite; open; unreserved. **3** *Logic* Brought out definitely in words; not merely implied: opposed to *implicit.* [<L *explicitus,* var. of *explicatus.* See EXPLICATE.] — **ex·plic′it·ly** *adv.* — **ex·plic′·it·ness** *n.*
Synonym: express. Both *explicit* and *express* are opposed to what is merely implicit or implied. See IMPLICIT. That which is *explicit* is unfolded, so that it may not be obscure, doubtful, or ambiguous; that which is *express* is uttered or stated so decidedly that it may not be forgotten nor overlooked. An *explicit* statement is too clear to be misunderstood; an *express* command is too emphatic to be disregarded. Compare CLEAR, PLAIN, PRECISE. *Antonyms*: ambiguous, doubtful, implicit, implied, indefinite, indeterminate, uncertain.
ex·plode (ik·splōd′) *v.* **·plod·ed, ·plod·ing** *v.t.* **1** To cause to expand violently or pass suddenly from a solid to a gaseous state: to *explode* gunpowder. **2** To cause to burst or blow up violently and with noise: to *explode* a bomb. **3** To disprove utterly; refute: to *explode* a theory. **4** *Phonet.* To pronounce with an explosion. **5** *Obs.* To drive from the stage, as an actor. — *v.i.* **6** To be exploded, as gunpowder. **7** To burst into pieces or fragments; blow up. **8** To make a noise as if bursting: to *explode* with laughter. [<L *explodere,* orig. drive off the stage, hiss < *ex-* out + *plaudere* clap] — **ex·plod′er** *n.*
ex·plo·dent (ik·splōd′nt) *n. Phonet.* A plosive.
ex·ploit (eks′ploit, ik·sploit′) *n.* A deed or act, especially one marked by heroism, daring, skill, or brilliancy. See synonyms under ACT. — *v.t.* (ik·sploit′) **1** To use for one's own advantage; take advantage of: Rulers often *exploit* the people. **2** To put to use; make use of: to *exploit* water power. [<OF *esploit* <L *explicitum,* neut. sing. of *explicitus.* See EXPLICIT.] — **ex·ploit′a·ble** *adj.*
ex·ploi·ta·tion (eks′ploi·tā′shən) *n.* **1** The act of exploiting. **2** Selfish employment for one's own use or advantage.
ex·ploit·a·tive (ik·sploi′tə·tiv) *adj.* Tending or serving to exploit.
ex·ploi·ter (ik·sploi′tər) *v.t.* To turn to one's use or advantage illegitimately; exploit. — *n.* One who exploits.
ex·plo·ra·tion (eks′plə·rā′shən) *n.* **1** The act of exploring; especially, geographical research in unknown regions. **2** The examination of internal organs or parts. [<L *exploratio, -onis* < *explorare.* See EXPLORE.]
ex·plor·a·to·ry (ik·splôr′ə·tôr′ē, ik·splō′rə·tō′·rē) *adj.* Of, for, or relating to exploration. Also **ex·plor′a·tive.**
ex·plore (ik·splôr′, -splōr′) *v.* **·plored, ·plor·ing** *v.t.* **1** To search through or travel in or over, as new lands, for discovery. **2** To look into carefully; scrutinize. **3** *Med.* To examine: to *explore* a wound with a probe. —*v.i.* **4** To make explorations. See synonyms under EXAMINE. [<L *explorare* investigate < *ex-* out + *plorare* cry out]
ex·plor·er (ik·splôr′ər, -splō′rər) *n.* **1** One who explores; especially, one who travels in a new or strange region. **2** Any device with which to explore or examine; a probe.
Ex·plor·er The first U. S. artificial satellite, launched from Cape Canaveral, Fla., Jan. 31, 1958; maximum height about 1600 miles; weight, 30.8 lbs.; orbital velocity, 18,000 mph.
ex·plo·sion (ik·splō′zhən) *n.* **1** The act of exploding; rapid combustion or other similar process, usually causing a loud report. **2** The power stroke of an internal-combustion engine. **3** *Physiol.* The sudden discharge of a neural cell or group of cells. **4** A sudden and violent outbreak as of physical forces or of human emotion. **5** *Phonet.* Plosion. [<L *explosio, -onis* < *explodere.* See EXPLODE.]
ex·plo·sive (ik·splō′siv) *adj.* **1** Pertaining to explosion. **2** Liable to explode or to cause explosion. **3** *Phonet.* Plosive. — *n.* **1** *Physics* Any substance or mixture of substances which, on impact or by ignition, reacts by a violent rearrangement of its molecules accompanied by the sudden expansion of gases and the liberation of relatively large amounts of thermal energy. **2** *Phonet.* A plosive consonant. — **ex·plo′sive·ly** *adv.* — **ex·plo′sive·ness** *n.*
explosive D Dunnite.
ex·po·nent (ik·spō′nənt) *n.* **1** One who or that which explains, interprets, or expounds. **2** *Logic* An illustrative example of a general proposition. **3** *Math.* Any number or symbol placed as a superscript to the right of a quantity to indicate a power or the reciprocal or root of a power: thus, $3^2 = 3 \times 3$; $3^{-2} = 1/3^2$; $3^{\frac{1}{2}} = \sqrt{3}$. **4** Any person or thing that represents the character or principles of something: Franklin was the *exponent* of American principles in France. [<L *exponens, -entis,* ppr. of *exponere* indicate < *ex-* out + *ponere* place] — **ex·po·nen·tial** (ek′spō·nen′shəl) *adj.* — **ex′po·nen′tial·ly** *adv.*
ex·po·ni·ble (ik·spō′nə·bəl) *adj.* Needing explanation, as in logic, when propositions must be restated to be intelligible. — *n.* An exponible statement.
ex·port (ik·spôrt′, -spōrt′, eks′pôrt, -pōrt) *v.t.* To carry or send, as merchandise or raw materials, to other countries for sale or trade. — *n.* (eks′pôrt, -pōrt) **1** The act of exporting; exportation. **2** That which is exported; especially, merchandise sent from one country to another: usually in the plural. — *adj.* Of or pertaining to exports or exportation. [<L *exportare* < *ex-* out + *portare* carry] — **ex·port′a·ble** *adj.* — **ex·port′a·bil′i·ty** *n.* — **ex·port′er** *n.*
ex·por·ta·tion (ek′spôr·tā′shən, -spōr-) *n.* **1** The act or practice of exporting. **2** An export commodity.
ex·pose (ik·spōz′) *v.t.* **·posed, ·pos·ing** **1** To lay open, as to harm, attack, ridicule, censure, etc. **2** To leave open to the action of a force or influence. **3** To present to view; show; display: The dress *exposed* her shoulders. **4** To cause to be known; make public, as a conspiracy or crime. **5** To lay open or make known the crimes, faults, etc., of (a person): to *expose* a traitor. **6** To abandon so as to cause the death of: to *expose* an unwanted child. **7** *Phot.* To admit light to (a sensitized film or plate). **8** In the Roman Catholic Church, to show for adoration or worship, as the Host. See synonyms under DISCOVER. [<MF *exposer* < *ex-* out + *poser.* See POSE[1].] — **ex·po′sal** *n.* — **ex·pos′er** *n.*
ex·po·sé (ek′spō·zā′) *n.* **1** An undesirable or embarrassing disclosure or exposure. **2** A revelation or disclosure of something to the public, as corruption, political graft, social injustice, etc. — *adj.* Given to exposing discreditable things: an *exposé* magazine. [<F, pp. of *exposer.* See EXPOSE.]
ex·posed (ik·spōzd′) *adj.* **1** In plain view. **2** Uncovered; open to or unprotected from, as the elements.
ex·po·si·tion (eks′pə·zish′ən) *n.* **1** A public exhibition of the arts, products, achievements, etc., of a specific region, country, or group, as a world's fair. **2** An explanation; commentary. **3** Rhetorical analysis. **4** The part of a dramatic composition that unfolds the plot. **5** In the Roman Catholic Church, a service in which the blessed sacrament is exposed for adoration. **6** *Music* The initial presentation or statement of the themes of a movement; especially, in a fugue, the introduction of the several parts or voices. See synonyms under DEFINITION. [<OF <L *expositio, -onis* < *exponere.* See EXPONENT.]
ex·pos·i·tor (ik·spoz′ə·tər) *n.* One who expounds.
ex·pos·i·to·ry (ik·spoz′ə·tôr′ē, -tō′rē) *adj.* Conveying, containing, or pertaining to exposition. Also **ex·pos′i·tive.**
ex post fac·to (eks pōst fak′tō) Arising or enacted after the fact but retroacting upon it; retroactive; retrospective. [<L]
ex·pos·tu·late (ik·spos′chə·lāt) *v.i.* **·lat·ed, ·lat·ing** To reason earnestly with a person, against some action: usually with *with.* [<L *expostulatus,* pp. of *expostulare* < *ex-* out + *postulare* demand] — **ex·pos′tu·la′tor** *n.*
ex·pos·tu·la·tion (ik·spos′chə·lā′shən) *n.* The act of expostulating; dissuasion. — **ex·pos′tu·la′tive** *adj.* — **ex·pos′tu·la′tive·ly** *adv.*
ex·pos·tu·la·to·ry (ik·spos′chə·lə·tôr′ē, -tō′rē) *adj.* Conveying, containing, or pertaining to expostulation.
ex·po·sure (ik·spō′zhər) *n.* **1** The act or process of exposing, or the state of being exposed in any sense; disclosure of the hitherto hidden truth, usually discreditable, about a person or situation. **2** An open situation or position in relation to the sun, elements, or points of the compass; outlook; aspect: The house had a southern *exposure.* **3** In ancient Greece and Rome, the practice of abandoning sickly and deformed (and often female) infants. **4** *Phot.* The act of submitting a sensitized plate or film to the action of actinic rays. **5** *Geol.* The portion of a rock mass exposed to view. **6** *Law* Offensive public display of one's body.
exposure meter *Phot.* An instrument which shows the correct film exposure required for best results.
ex·pound (ik·spound′) *v.t.* **1** To set forth in detail; state; declare, as a doctrine or theory. **2** To explain the meaning or significance of; interpret. See synonyms under INTERPRET. [<OF *espondre* <L *exponere.* See EXPONENT.] — **ex·pound′er** *n.*
ex·press (ik·spres′) *v.t.* **1** To put (thought or opinion) into spoken or written words. **2** To make apparent; reveal: His actions *express* his anger. **3** To represent in art, poetry, etc.; depict by symbols: The rose *expresses* love. **4** *Math.* To represent by a figure, symbol, letter, etc. **5** *U.S.* To send by express. **6** To press out; squeeze out, as juice or moisture. **7** To force out by or as by pressure. **8** To send or cause to be sent by express, as a package. — **to express oneself** **1** To make known one's thoughts. **2** To give expression to one's imagination or emotions, especially in artistic activity. See synonyms under SPEAK. — *adj.* **1** Set forth distinctly; explicit; plain; direct. **2** Specially prepared; adapted to a specific purpose: There was *express* provision for strangers. **3** Done, traveling, or carried with speed or in haste: an *express* train. **4** Exactly resembling an original: an *express* likeness. **5** Of or pertaining to an express company. See synonyms under EXPLICIT. — *adv.* With speed; not stopping at local stations: This train runs *express.* — *n.* **1** A system of transportation for trunks, small parcels, packages, etc., by organized corporations. **2** The packages, parcels, etc., sent by this system. **3** Any means of rapid transmission. **4** A message; dispatch; special communication sent with speed. **5** A messenger bearing dispatches; a courier. **6** An express rifle. **7** An express train. [<OF *expresser* <L *ex-* out + *pressare* < *premere* press]
ex·press·age (ik·spres′ij) *n.* **1** The transportation of goods by special system. **2** Amount charged for carrying by express.
express company A business company that operates a system for the rapid transportation of trunks, packages, and other articles.
ex·press·er (ik·spres′ər) *n.* **1** One who sends anything by express. **2** One who or that which presses out a juice or the like.
ex·press·i·ble (ik·spres′ə·bəl) *adj.* Capable of being expressed. — **ex·press′i·bly** *adv.*
ex·pres·sion (ik·spresh′ən) *n.* **1** The act or mode of uttering or representing, as by language or gesture. **2** Any act or object by which some truth or idea is conveyed: the *expression* of pleasure. **3** That which is uttered; a saying; any embodiment of a thought: a common *expression* among doctors. **4** Outward aspect; especially, the ensemble of the face as indicating the feelings, etc.; look. **5** The quality of having proper expressive methods; the effective utterance of thought or feeling; expressiveness. **6** The development or revelation of character and sentiment in art, music, etc., by shadings, nuances, variations in style. **7** A pressing out. **8** *Math.* A group of characters, numbers, and symbols composing a statement. Also *Obs.* **ex·pres′sure.** See synonyms under AIR, DICTION, LANGUAGE, TERM. [<F <L *expressio, -onis* < *exprimere* < *ex-* out + *premere* press] — **ex·pres′sion·less** *adj.*
Ex·pres·sion·ism (ik·spresh′ən·iz′əm) *n.* A movement in the arts, originating in Europe at about the time of World War I, which had as its object the free expression of the inner experience of the artist rather than the realistic representation of appearances. — **ex·pres′·sion·ist** *n.* & *adj.* — **ex·pres′sion·is′tic** *adj.*

ex·pres·sis ver·bis (ek·spres′is vûr′bis) *Latin* In express terms.

ex·pres·sive (ik·spres′iv) *adj.* **1** Of, pertaining to, or characterized by expression. **2** Conveying or containing expression, in any sense of the word. **3** Manifesting special significance or force. See synonyms under MOBILE. — **ex·pres′sive·ly** *adv.* — **ex·pres′sive·ness** *n.*

express letter *Brit.* A special delivery letter.

ex·press·ly (ik·spres′lē) *adv.* With definitely stated intent or application; exactly and unmistakably; in direct terms: The condition was *expressly* named.

ex·press·man (ik·spres′mən) *n. pl.* **·men** (-mən) An employee of an express company; a driver or deliveryman on an express truck.

express money order A money order issued by an express company.

express rifle A modern sporting rifle with a large charge of powder and a light bullet of large caliber, for use at close range.

express train A train operated at high speed with few stops.

ex·press·way (ik·spres′wā′) *n.* A road designed for rapid travel.

ex pro·fes·so (eks prō·fes′ō) *Latin* Openly; avowedly; professedly.

ex·pro·pri·ate (eks·prō′prē·āt) *v.t.* **·at·ed, ·at·ing 1** To take from the owner, especially for public use. **2** To deprive of ownership or property. [<LL *expropriatus,* pp. of *expropriare* < *ex-* out + *proprium* property < *proprius* one's own] — **ex·pro′pri·a′tor** *n.*

ex·pro·pri·a·tion (eks·prō′prē·ā′shən) *n.* **1** The act, process, or result of expropriating. **2** The act of taking land for public use by right of eminent domain.

ex pro·pri·is (eks prō′prē·is) *Latin* From one's own resources.

ex pro·pri·o mo·tu (eks prō′prē·ō mō′tōō) *Latin* Of its (or his) own accord; voluntarily.

ex·pul·sion (ik·spul′shən) *n.* **1** The act of expelling; forcible ejection. **2** The state of being expelled. [<L *expulsio, -onis* < *expellere.* See EXPEL.] — **ex·pul′sive** *adj.*

ex·punc·tion (ik·spungk′shən) *n.* The act of expunging; erasure. [<L *expunctio, -onis* < *expungere.* See EXPUNGE.]

ex·punge (ik·spunj′) *v.t.* **·punged, ·pung·ing** To blot or scratch out, as from a record or list; obliterate; efface. See synonyms under CANCEL. [<L *expungere* < *ex-* out + *pungere* prick] — **ex·pung′er** *n.*

ex·pur·gate (eks′pər·gāt) *v.t.* **·gat·ed, ·gat·ing** To clear, as a book, of whatever is considered objectionable, immoral, etc. [<L *expurgatus,* pp. of *expurgare* < *ex-* out + *purgare* cleanse] — **ex′pur·ga′tion** *n.* — **ex′pur·ga′tor** *n.* — **ex·pur·ga·to·ry** (ik·spûr′gə·tôr′ē, -tō′rē) *adj.*

ex·pur·ga·to·ri·al (ik·spûr′gə·tôr′ē·əl, -tō′rē-) *adj.* Pertaining to expurgation; purifying.

ex·qui·site (eks′kwi·zit, ik·skwiz′it) *adj.* **1** Characterized by fineness and delicacy; dainty in make or quality; satisfying to the esthetic faculties; refined; delicately beautiful. **2** Having unusually refined perception or judgment; delicately sensitive and accurate; of keen esthetic discrimination; nice; fastidious: *exquisite* taste. **3** Causing or marked by intense or extreme emotion; exciting or fitted to excite extreme pleasure or pain; intense or poignant: *exquisite* rapture or pain. **4** *Obs.* Very careful; curious. **5** *Obs.* Particular; choice. See synonyms under BEAUTIFUL, CHOICE, DELICIOUS, ELEGANT, FINE. —*n.* A person very dainty in dress or manners; a fop; dandy; dude. [<L *exquisitus,* pp. of *exquirere* < *ex-* out + *quarere* seek] — **ex′qui·site·ly** *adv.* — **ex′qui·site·ness** *n.*

ex·san·guine (eks·sang′gwin) *adj.* Having no blood; anemic.

ex·scind (ek·sind′) *v.t.* To cut out; sever. [<L *exscindere* < *ex-* out + *scindere* cut]

ex·se·cant (eks′sē′kənt, -kant) *n. Trig.* A function of an angle expressible as the secant of the angle minus one. See TRIGONOMETRICAL FUNCTIONS. [<EX(TERIOR) SECANT]

ex·sect (ek·sekt′) *v.t.* To cut out. [<L *exsectus,* pp. of *exsecare* < *ex-* out + *secare* cut] — **ex·sec′tion** *n.*

ex·sert (ek·sûrt′) *v.t.* To push out; protrude. [<L *exsertus.* See EXERT.] — **ex·ser′tile** (-til) *adj.* — **ex·ser′tion** *n.*

ex·sert·ed (ek·sûr′tid) *adj. Bot.* Protruding from surrounding parts, as the stamens or style beyond the mouth of some tubular corollas; thrust out; unsheathed.

ex·sic·ca·tae (ek′sə·kā′tē) *n. pl.* Dried specimens of plants, especially in numbered sets for herbariums. [<L, fem. pl. of *exsiccatus.* See EXSICCATE.]

ex·sic·cate (ek′sə·kāt) *v.t.* & *v.i.* **·cat·ed, ·cat·ing** To dry up or out. [<L *exsiccatus,* pp. of *exsiccare* < *ex-* out + *siccus* dry] — **ex·sic·cant** (ek·sik′ənt) *adj.* & *n.* — **ex′sic·ca′tion** *n.* — **ex′sic·ca′tive** *adj.* — **ex′sic·ca′tor** *n.*

ex·sic·ca·ti (ek′sə·kā′tī) *n. pl.* Dried specimens of fungi, especially in numbered sets for herbariums. [<L, masc. pl. of *exsiccatus.* See EXSICCATE.]

ex·stip·u·late (eks·stip′yə·lit, -lāt) *adj. Bot.* Destitute of stipules: also *estipulate.*

ex·stro·phy (ek′strə·fē) *n. Pathol.* The turning of an inner part outward, as the bladder. [<Gk. *ex-* out + *strephein* turn]

ex·suf·fli·cate (eks·suf′lə·kit, -kāt) *adj. Obs.* Inflated; empty; frivolous. [Cf. L *exsufflare* blow on]

ex·tant (ek′stənt, ik·stant′) *adj.* **1** Still existing and known; living. **2** *Obs.* Standing out; manifest; conspicuous. [<L *ex(s)tans, -antis,* ppr. of *exstare* < *ex-* out + *stare* stand]

ex·tem·po·ral (ik·stem′pər·əl) *adj. Obs.* or *Archaic* Extemporaneous; extemporary. — **ex·tem′po·ral·ly** *adv.*

ex·tem·po·ra·ne·ous (ik·stem′pə·rā′nē·əs) *adj.* **1** Done or made with little or no preparation; composed or uttered on the spur of the moment; unpremeditated. **2** Given to speaking without notes. [<LL *extemporaneus* < *ex-* out + *tempus, temporis* time] — **ex·tem′po·ra′ne·ous·ly** *adv.* — **ex·tem′po·ra′ne·ous·ness** *n.*

Synonyms: extemporary, extempore, impromptu, improvised, offhand, unpremeditated. *Extemporaneous,* originally signifying *of* or *from the time* or *occasion,* has come to mean done or made with but little (if any) preparation, and is now chiefly applied to addresses of which the thought has been prepared, and only the language and incidental treatment left to the suggestion of the moment, so that an *extemporaneous* speech is understood to be one that is not read or recited; *impromptu* keeps its original sense, denoting something that springs from the instant. *Offhand* is still more emphatic as to the readiness and freedom of the utterance. *Unpremeditated* is graver and more formal, denoting absolute want of preparation, but is too heavy a word to be applied to such apt, ready utterance as is generally designated by *impromptu.* *Antonyms*: elaborated, premeditated, prepared, read, recited, studied, written.

ex·tem·po·rar·y (ik·stem′pə·rer′ē) *adj.* **1** Extemporaneous. **2** Made for the occasion; extemporized: an *extemporary* shelter. — **ex·tem′po·rar′i·ly** *adv.* — **ex·tem′po·rar′i·ness** *n.*

ex·tem·po·re (ik·stem′pər·ē) *adj.* Done on the spur of the moment; extemporaneous; unstudied; offhand. —*adv.* Without special preparation; extemporaneously. See synonyms under EXTEMPORANEOUS. [<L *ex tempore* out of the time]

ex·tem·po·rize (ik·stem′pə·rīz) *v.t.* & *v.i.* **·rized, ·riz·ing** To do, make, or compose without preparation; improvise. — **ex·tem′po·ri·za′tion** *n.* — **ex·tem′po·riz′er** *n.*

ex·tend (ik·stend′) *v.t.* **1** To open or stretch to full length. **2** To cause to stretch to a specified point, in a given direction, or for a given distance; make longer. **3** To cause to last until or for a specified time; continue. **4** To widen or enlarge the range, area, scope, meaning, etc., of: to *extend* the duties of an office. **5** To hold out or put forth, as the hand. **6** To give or offer to give: to *extend* hospitality. **7** To straighten, as a leg or arm. **8** In business, to put off the date of completion or payment of, as a contract or debt, beyond that originally set. **9** *Law* **a** *Brit.* To assess; appraise. **b** To seize under a writ of extent. —*v.i.* **10** To be extended; stretch. **11** To reach, as in a specified direction: This road *extends* west. — **to extend oneself** To put forth great effort. See synonyms under ADD, AMPLIFY, INCREASE, PROTRACT, SPREAD. [<L *extendere* < *ex-* out + *tendere* stretch] — **ex·tend′i·ble** *adj.*

ex·tend·ed (ik·sten′did) *adj.* **1** Covering a great extent of time or space. **2** Pulled or stretched out. **3** Broad in proportion to height: said of type: an *extended* letter. — **ex·tend′ed·ly** *adv.*

ex·ten·si·ble (ik·sten′sə·bəl) *adj.* That may be extended. — **ex·ten′si·bil′i·ty, ex·ten′si·ble·ness** *n.*

ex·ten·sile (ik·sten′sil) *adj.* Extensible.

ex·ten·sion (ik·sten′shən) *n.* **1** The act or process of extending. **2** An annex; addition. **3** That property of matter by virtue of which it occupies space. **4** *Logic* The capacity of a general concept to cover the specific classes or individual things connoted by it; the degree of applicability belonging to a notion. **5** *Surg.* Traction of a fractured or dislocated limb in order to replace its parts. **6** *Anat.* The straightening of a limb: opposed to *flexion.* **7** The act of a creditor allowing to a debtor further time in which to pay a debt. See synonyms under ACCESSION, APPENDAGE, INCREASE. [<L *extensio, -onis* < *extendere.* See EXTEND.]

ex·ten·si·ty (ik·sten′sə·tē) *n.* **1** The quality of extension; extensiveness. **2** *Psychol.* An element of sensation yielding the spatial qualities of perception.

ex·ten·sive (ik·sten′siv) *adj.* **1** Extended widely in space, time, or scope; great; wide. **2** Designating a method of land cultivation in which the crop depends on the area treated rather than (as in *intensive* agriculture) on the fertilization and care of a restricted area. **3** Of or pertaining to extension. See synonyms under LARGE. — **ex·ten′sive·ly** *adv.* — **ex·ten′sive·ness** *n.*

ex·ten·som·e·ter (eks′ten·som′ə·tər) *n. Mech.* A micrometer by which to measure the expansion of a body, as a bar of metal. Also **ex′ten·sim′e·ter.**

ex·ten·sor (ik·sten′sər, -sôr) *n. Anat.* A muscle that causes extension. Compare FLEXOR.

ex·tent (ik·stent′) *n.* **1** The dimension or degree to which anything is extended; compass; reach; size; range; also, the limit to which anything reaches. **2** Size within given bounds: the *extent* of his power. **3** *Law* A writ directing the appraisal of lands at their yearly value, and their delivery to a creditor for a limited time to satisfy his claim. **4** *Logic* Extension (def. 4). **5** Any continuous magnitude, as of a line, surface, or solid. See synonyms under END, MAGNITUDE. [<L *extentus,* pp. of *extendere.* See EXTEND.]

ex·ten·u·ate (ik·sten′yōō·āt) *v.t.* **·at·ed, ·at·ing 1** To represent as less blameworthy; make excuses for. **2** To cause to seem less serious or blameworthy. **3** *Rare* To make thin or weak; attenuate. **4** *Obs.* To diminish in estimation; depreciate; detract from. [<L *extenuatus,* pp. of *extenuare* weaken < *ex-* out + *tenuis* thin] — **ex·ten′u·at′ing** *adj.* — **ex·ten′u·a′tor** *n.*

ex·ten·u·a·tion (ik·sten′yōō·ā′shən) *n.* The act of extenuating, in any sense; palliation; excuse. — **ex·ten′u·a′tive** *adj.* & *n.* — **ex·ten′u·a·to′ry** (-tôr′ē, -tō′rē) *adj.*

ex·te·ri·or (ik·stir′ē·ər) *adj.* **1** External; outlying. **2** Manifest to the senses. **3** Acting from without. **4** Pertaining to foreign countries; foreign. —*n.* **1** That which is outside; external features or qualities. **2** Hence, the sum of observable qualities or traits: one's physiognomy, demeanor, general appearance, or outward conduct. [<L *exterior,* compar. of *exterus* outside] — **ex·te′ri·or·ly** *adv.*

exterior angle See under ANGLE.

ex·te·ri·or·i·za·tion (ik·stir′ē·ər·ə·zā′shən) *n.* *Psychiatry* The act or process of turning the thoughts and emotions away from the self and toward the external world: used in the treatment of schizophrenia and related mental disorders.

ex·ter·mi·nate (ik·stûr′mə·nāt) *v.t.* **·nat·ed, ·nat·ing** To destroy entirely; annihilate. Also *Obs.* **ex·ter·mine.** [<L *exterminatus,* pp. of *exterminare* < *ex-* out + *terminus* a boundary] — **ex·ter′mi·na·ble** *adj.* — **ex·ter′mi·na′tive, ex·ter′mi·na·to′ry** (-tôr′ē, -tō′rē) *adj.*

Synonyms: annihilate, banish, demolish, destroy, eradicate, expel, extirpate, overthrow, remove, uproot. The word *exterminate* is applied to groups or masses of men or animals; individuals are said to be *banished, expelled,*

destroyed, etc. *Eradicate* is primarily applied to numbers or groups of plants; a single tree may be *uprooted,* but is not said to be *eradicated.* To *extirpate* is to *destroy* the very stock, so that the race can never be restored; we speak of *eradicating* a disease, of *extirpating* a cancer, *exterminating* wild beasts or hostile tribes; we seek to *eradicate* or *extirpate* vice. See ABOLISH. *Antonyms*: augment, beget, cherish, colonize, develop, foster, increase, plant, populate, propagate, replenish, settle.

ex·ter·mi·na·tion (ik·stur′mə·nā′shən) *n.* The act or process of exterminating; annihilation.

extermination camp A death camp.

ex·ter·mi·na·tor (ik·stûr′mə·nā′tər) *n.* **1** Someone or something that exterminates. **2** A person whose business is destroying rodents, insects, etc. **3** A chemical preparation used to destroy rodents, insects, etc.

ex·tern (eks′tûrn) *n.* **1** *Brit.* A pupil who does not live at the school he attends; a day scholar. **2** A member of the house staff of a hospital who does not reside in the institution; opposed to *intern.* Also **ex′terne.** — *adj.* (ik·stûrn′) *Obs.* External. [<F *externe* <L *externus* outer < *ex* out]

ex·ter·nal (ik·stûr′nəl) *adj.* **1** Situated or occurring outside of the subject; being on or relating to the exterior. **2** Visible from the outside; hence, often, superficial: *external* polish. **3** Belonging to the material or phenomenal world as distinguished from the mind that perceives it; objective. **4** Relating to the surface of the body: an *external* disease. **5** Pertaining to or coming from foreign lands or people; foreign: *external* traffic. **6** Extraneous; extrinsic. —*n.* **1** An exterior or outer part. **2** *pl.* Outward symbols, as of religion. [<L *externus* outer < *ex* out] —**ex·ter′nal·ly** *adv.*

ex·ter·nal–com·bus·tion (ik·stûr′nəl·kəm·bus′chən) *adj.* Pertaining to or designating a type of engine in which ignition of the fuel–air mixture takes place outside the engine cylinder.

ex·ter·nal·ism (ik·stûr′nəl·iz′əm) *n.* **1** *Philos.* The doctrine that only things which are the objects of sense perception have reality, or can be known to have it; phenomenalism. **2** Devotion to externals, especially in matters of religion.

ex·ter·nal·i·ty (ek′stər·nal′ə·tē) *n.* **1** Location on the outside, or as on a surface outside. **2** Regard for or devotion to externals.

ex·ter·nal·ize (ik·stûr′nəl·īz) *v.t.* **·ized, ·iz·ing** **1** To give shape to; embody. **2** To make outwardly real. —**ex·ter′nal·i·za′tion** *n.*

ex·ter·o·cep·tor (ek′stər·ō·sep′tər) *n. Physiol.* A peripheral sense organ that responds to stimulation from external agents, as in sight, hearing, touch, etc. Compare INTEROCEPTOR. [<L *exterus* external + (RE)CEPTOR] —**ex′ter·o·cep′tive** *adj.*

ex·ter·ri·to·ri·al (eks′ter·ə·tôr′ē·əl, -tō′rē-) *adj.* Extraterritorial. —**ex′ter·ri·to′ri·al′i·ty** *n.* —**ex′ter·ri·to′ri·al·ly** *adv.*

ex·tinct (ik·stingkt′) *adj.* **1** Extinguished; inactive; quenched: an *extinct* volcano. **2** Exterminated; no longer existing: an *extinct* animal or species. **3** Void; lapsed: an *extinct* title. See synonyms under LIFELESS. [<L *ex(s)tinctus,* pp. of *ex(s)tinguere* EXTINGUISH]

ex·tinc·tion (ik·stingk′shən) *n.* **1** The act of extinguishing or state of being extinguished; extinguishment. **2** A putting an end to something; a destroying; complete destruction; annihilation. **3** A quenching or slaking, as of quicklime with water. **4** *Physics* A diminution in the intensity of radiation due to absorption by or scattering in the medium; also, the stopping of incident X–rays by the outer layers of atoms in a crystal.

ex·tinc·tive (ik·stingk′tiv) *adj.* Calculated to extinguish; extinguishing.

ex·tin·guish (ik·sting′gwish) *v.t.* **1** To put out; quench, as a fire. **2** To make extinct; wipe out. **3** To obscure or throw into the shade; eclipse. **4** *Law* To cause to end and become extinct; pay off and satisfy in full. See synonyms under ANNUL, SUBVERT. [<L *ex(s)tinguere* < *ex-* completely + *stinguere* quench] —**ex·tin′guish·a·ble** *adj.* —**ex·tin′guish·er** *n.* —**ex·tin′guish·ment** *n.*

ex·tir·pate (ek′stər·pāt, ik·stûr′-) *v.t.* **·pat·ed, ·pat·ing** To root out or up; eradicate; destroy wholly. See synonyms under ABOLISH, EXTERMINATE. [<L *ex(s)tirpatus,* pp. of *ex(s)tirpare* < *ex-* out + *stirps* stem, root] —**ex·tir′pa·ble** *adj.* —**ex′tir·pa′tion** *n.* —**ex′tir·pa′tive** *adj.* —**ex′tir·pa′tor** *n.* —**ex·tir·pa·to·ry** (ik·stûr′pə·tôr′ē, -tō′rē) *adj.*

ex·tol (ik·stōl′, -stol′) *v.t.* **·tolled, ·tol·ling** To praise in the highest terms; magnify. See synonyms under ADMIRE, PRAISE. Also **ex·toll′.** [<L *extollere* < *ex-* out, up + *tollere* raise] —**ex·tol′ler** *n.* —**ex·tol′ment** or **ex·toll′ment** *n.*

ex·tort (ik·stôrt′) *v.t.* To obtain from a person by violence, threat, oppression, or abuse of authority; wring; wrest. See synonyms under STEAL. [<L *extortus,* pp. of *extorquere* < *ex-* out + *torquere* twist] —**ex·tort′er** *n.* —**ex·tor′tive** *adj.*

ex·tor·tion (ik·stôr′shən) *n.* **1** The act or practice of extorting. **2** That which has been extorted. **3** *Law* The offense, committed by an official, of taking money under color of his office, with the consent of the victim, either where none is due, in excess of what is due, or before it is due. —**ex·tor′tion·er** or **·ist** *n.*

ex·tor·tion·ar·y (ik·stôr′shən·er′ē) *adj.* Practicing extortion.

ex·tor·tion·ate (ik·stôr′shən·it) *adj.* Characterized by extortion; oppressive. —**ex·tor′tion·ate·ly** *adv.*

ex·tra (eks′trə) *adj.* Being over and above what is required; additional. —*n.* **1** Something beyond what is usual or required. **2** A copy or an edition of a newspaper issued for some special purpose, or at a time different from that of the regular edition. **3** In cricket, any run resulting from a by, leg–by, no–ball, or wide. **4** Something of a special quality. **5** An actor, not a member of the regular cast, hired for a special scene, as a mob scene, or for a small part. —*adv.* Unusually. [<L, outside, beyond]

extra- *prefix* Beyond; outside; outside the scope of: *extraordinary* beyond the ordinary; *extra–oral* outside the mouth. [<L *extra-* < *extra* < *exter* on the outside < *ex* out]

Extra– may appear as a prefix in hyphemes or solidemes, as in:

extra–alimentary	extra–insular
extra–American	extra–intellectual
extra–analogical	extra–Judaical
extra–articular	extrajugal
extra–artistic	extrajural
extra–atmospheric	extralegal
extra–axillar	extraligamentous
extra–axillary	extralimitary
extra–Britannic	extralogical
extrabuccal	extramanorial
extrabureau	extramarine
extracapsular	extramarital
extracarpal	extramatrimonial
extracathedral	extramedial
extracellular	extramental
extracerebral	extrametaphysical
extra–Christian	extrametropolitan
extracivic	extramodal
extraclassroom	extramolecular
extraclaustral	extramoral
extracloacal	extramoralist
extracollegiate	extramusical
extraconscious	extranational
extraconstellated	extranatural
extraconstitutional	extranormal
extracorporeal	extranuclear
extracorpuscular	extra–ocular
extracosmic	extra–official
extracosmical	extra–oral
extracranial	extra–orbital
extracultural	extra–organismal
extracurial	extra–ovate
extracutaneous	extra–ovular
extradecretal	extraparental
extradialectal	extraparliamentary
extradural	extraparochial
extra–embryonic	extrapatriarchal
extra–European	extrapelvic
extrafascicular	extraperiodic
extrafloral	extraperiosteal
extrafocal	extraperitoneal
extrafoliaceous	extraphenomenal
extraformal	extraphysiological
extragastric	extrapituitary
extragenital	extraplanetary
extraglacial	extrapleural
extragovernmental	extraprostatic
extragrammatical	extrapulmonary
extrahepatic	extrarenal
extrahistoric	extraretinal
extrahistorical	extrasacerdotal
extrahuman	extrascholastic
extra–industrial	extrascriptural
extra–Scriptural	extratellurian
extrasensible	extratemporal
extrasocial	extraterrene
extrasolar	extraterrestrial
extrasomatic	extrathoracic
extraspectral	extratracheal
extraspherical	extratropical
extraspinal	extra–university
extrastate	extra–urban
extrasyllabic	extravaginal
extrasyllogistic	extravisceral
extratabular	extrazodiacal

ex·tra-bold (eks′trə·bōld′) *adj. Printing* Denoting a very heavy face of type.

ex·tra–ca·non·i·cal (eks′trə·kə·non′i·kəl) *adj.* Being outside the canon; non–canonical: *extra–canonical* writings.

ex·tra–con·densed (eks′trə·kən·denst′) *adj. Printing* Extremely narrow in proportion to the height: said of type.

ex·tract (ik·strakt′) *v.t.* **1** To draw or pull out by force: to *extract* a tooth. **2** To obtain from a substance by pressing, treatment with chemicals, etc. **3** To draw out or obtain as if by such process; derive, as instruction or pleasure. **4** To copy out; select for quotation. **5** *Math.* To calculate (the root of a number). See synonyms under QUOTE. —*n.* (eks′trakt) **1** Something extracted or drawn out. **2** A selection from a book; a passage quoted. **3** The portion of a plant or substance removed by solvents and used in drug preparations in solid, powdered, or liquid form. [<L *extractus,* pp. of *extrahere* < *ex-* out + *trahere* draw, pull] —**ex·tract′a·ble** or **ex·tract′i·ble** *adj.*

ex·trac·tion (ik·strak′shən) *n.* **1** The act of extracting. **2** That which is extracted. **3** Lineage; descent.

ex·trac·tive (ik·strak′tiv) *adj.* **1** That extracts or tends to extract. **2** Capable of extraction. —*n.* **1** Something capable of being extracted. **2** That portion of an extract which becomes insoluble.

ex·trac·tor (ik·strak′tər) *n.* **1** One who or that which extracts. **2** The device in a firearm or cannon which withdraws a spent round of ammunition from the chamber prior to ejection.

ex·tra–cur·ric·u·lar (eks′trə·kə·rik′yə·lər) *adj.* Of or pertaining to those activities which are not a part of the curriculum, but which form an important part of school or college life, as athletics, fraternities, campus publications, etc. Also **ex′tra–cur·ric′u·lum.**

ex·tra·dit·a·ble (eks′trə·dī′tə·bəl) *adj.* Liable to or warranting extradition.

ex·tra·dite (eks′trə·dīt) *v.t.* **·dit·ed, ·dit·ing** **1** To deliver up, as to another state or nation. **2** To obtain the extradition of. [Back formation from EXTRADITION]

ex·tra·di·tion (eks′trə·dish′ən) *n.* The surrender of an accused person by a government to the justice of another government, or of a prisoner by one authority to another. [<F <L *extraditio, -onis* < *ex-* out + *traditio* a surrender. See TRADITION.]

ex·tra·dos (eks·trā′dos) *n. Archit.* The exterior curve of an arch. For illustration see under ARCH. [<F < *extra-* EXTRA- + *dos* the back <L *dorsum*]

ex·tra·ga·lac·tic (eks′trə·gə·lak′tik) *adj. Astron.* Beyond the Galaxy.

ex·tra–ju·di·cial (eks′trə·jōō·dish′əl) *adj.* Happening out of court; out of the jurisdiction of the proper court. —**ex′tra·ju·di′cial·ly** *adv.*

ex·tra·mun·dane (eks′trə·mun′dān, -mun·dān′) *adj.* Existing outside of our world or beyond the limits of the material universe.

ex·tra·mu·ral (eks′trə·myŏŏr′əl) *adj.* **1** Situated without or beyond the walls, as of a fortified city. **2** Beyond the boundaries of an educational institution: *extramural* games: opposed to *intramural.*

ex·tra·ne·ous (ik·strā′nē·əs) *adj.* Not intrinsic or essential to matter under consideration; foreign. [<L *extraneus* foreign. Doublet of STRANGE.] —**ex·tra′ne·ous·ly** *adv.* —**ex·tra′ne·ous·ness** *n.*

ex·traor·di·nar·y (ik·strôr′də·ner′ē; *esp. for def. 3,* eks′trə·ôr′də·ner′ē) *adj.* **1** Being beyond or out of the common order, course, or method. **2** Exceeding the ordinary degree; not ordinary; unusual; remarkable: an *extraordinary* accident. **3** Employed for a special purpose or on an exceptional occasion; special: an envoy *extraordinary.* **4** *Optics* Designating that component of a plane–

polarized ray of light which, on passing through a doubly refracting crystal, has different speeds in different directions. [<L *extraordinarius* <*extra* beyond + *ordo, ordinis* order] — **ex·traor′di·nar′i·ly** *adv.*

Synonyms: amazing, egregious, marvelous, monstrous, peculiar, preposterous, prodigious, remarkable, signal, singular, strange, striking, uncommon, unprecedented, unusual, unwonted, wonderful. See ODD, RARE[1]. *Antonyms*: common, commonplace, frequent, natural, ordinary, unimportant, usual.

extraordinary session A special session of the U. S. Congress.

ex·trap·o·late (eks·trap′ə·lāt, eks′trə·pə·lāt′) *v.t.* & *v.i.* **·lat·ed, ·lat·ing** 1 *Math.* To estimate those values of a magnitude or a function which lie beyond the range of known or determined values: distinguished from *interpolate.* 2 To infer (a possibility) beyond the strict evidence of a series of facts, events, observations, etc. [<EXTRA- + (INTER)POLATE]

ex·trap·o·la·tion (eks·trap′ə·lā′shən, eks′trə·pə·lā′shən) *n.* 1 *Math.* The assignment of values beyond either limit of the known range of values of a function or quantity. 2 Conjecture based on but not strictly validated by a given range of facts, events, etc. 3 Any instance of extrapolating.

ex·tra–pro·fes·sion·al (eks′trə·prə·fesh′ən·əl) *adj.* Being outside the usual limits of professional duty or interest.

ex·tra·sen·so·ry (eks′trə·sen′sər·ē) *adj. Psychol.* 1 Of or pertaining to phenomena outside of or beyond normal sensory perception. 2 Designating those powers of perception not yet scientifically explained in relation to any of the senses, as telepathy, clairvoyance, etc. Compare PARAPSYCHOLOGY.

ex·tra·ter·ri·to·ri·al (eks′trə·ter′ə·tôr′ē·əl, -tō′rē-) *adj.* 1 Exempt from territorial jurisdiction; not subject to the laws of one's abode: the *extraterritorial* rights of an ambassador. 2 Of or pertaining to things beyond the national territory: *extraterritorial* possessions. — **ex′tra·ter′ri·to′ri·al·ly** *adv.*

ex·tra·ter·ri·to·ri·al·i·ty (eks′trə·ter′ə·tôr′ē·al′ə·tē, -tō′rē-) *n.* In international law, the state or privilege of freedom from (local) territorial jurisdiction, accorded to foreign sovereigns, to diplomatic representatives, their suites, and to a certain extent their dwellings.

ex·traught (eks·trôt′) *adj. Obs.* 1 Extracted. 2 Distraught. [Var. of EXTRACT]

ex·tra–u·ter·ine (eks′trə·yōō′tər·in, -tə·rīn) *adj.* Situated or occurring externally to the uterus.

ex·trav·a·gance (ik·strav′ə·gəns) *n.* 1 An extravagant act or group of such acts; especially, undue expenditure of money; lavishness: prodigality; excess. 2 Overly exaggerated statement or language. 3 Ridiculous action. Also **ex·trav′a·gan·cy.** See synonyms under ENTHUSIASM, EXCESS.

ex·trav·a·gant (ik·strav′ə·gənt) *adj.* 1 Exceeding ordinary limits; needlessly free or lavish in expenditure. 2 Immoderate; fantastic; unrestrained, as language or behavior. 3 Excessive; exorbitant. 4 *Obs.* Straying beyond bounds; wandering abroad. See synonyms under IMMODERATE, ROMANTIC. [<MF <Med. L *extravagans, -antis,* ppr. of *extravagari* <L *extra-* outside + *vagari* wander] — **ex·trav′a·gant·ly** *adv.* — **ex·trav′a·gant·ness** *n.*

ex·trav·a·gan·za (ik·strav′ə·gan′zə) *n.* 1 A lavish or fantastic composition in literature, music, or the drama; especially, a spectacular musical comedy. 2 Any extravagant utterance or act. See synonyms under CARICATURE. [<Ital. *estravaganza* extravagance, ult. <Med. L *extravagari.* See EXTRAVAGANT.]

ex·trav·a·gate (ik·strav′ə·gāt) *v.i.* **·gat·ed, ·gat·ing** 1 To roam at will. 2 To exceed proper bounds. [<Med. L *extravagatus,* pp. of *extravagari.* See EXTRAVAGANT.]

ex·trav·a·sate (ik·strav′ə·sāt) *v.* **·sat·ed, ·sat·ing** *v.t.* 1 *Pathol.* To cause or allow the escape of from the proper vessels, as blood or air. 2 *Geol.* To gush out, as lava. — *v.i.* 3 *Pathol.* To filter or ooze into surrounding tissues, as blood from an artery or vein following a bruise. [<EXTRA- + L *vas* a vessel + -ATE[2]]

ex·trav·a·sa·tion (ik·strav′ə·sā′shən) *n.* 1 The state or process of being extravasated. 2 The substances extravasated.

ex·tra·vas·cu·lar (eks′trə·vas′kyə·lər) *adj. Anat.* 1 Situated outside the vascular system. 2 Having no blood vessels; non-vascular.

ex·tra·ver·sion (eks′trə·vûr′zhən, -shən), **ex·tra·vert** (eks′trə·vûrt) See EXTROVERSION, EXTROVERT.

Ex·tre·ma·du·ra (es′trā·mä·thōō′rä) The Spanish name for ESTREMADURA.

ex·treme (ik·strēm′) *adj.* 1 At or to the farthest limit; outermost; utmost. 2 Last; final. 3 In the utmost degree; far removed from the normal or average: *extreme* joy; *extreme* poverty. 4 Immoderate or radical: *extreme* opinions. — *n.* 1 The utmost or highest degree: the *extreme* of cruelty. 2 Either of two ends (of a line, series, scale, etc.): *extremes* of temperature. 3 *Math.* The first or last term of a proportion or series. 4 *Logic* **a** Either the subject or predicate of a proposition, distinguished from the copula. **b** Either of the two terms of a syllogism which, separated in the premises, are joined in the conclusion. [<OF <L *extremus,* superl. of *exterus* outside] — **ex·treme′ly** *adv.* — **ex·treme′ness** *n.*

extreme unction See under UNCTION.

ex·trem·ism (ik·strē′miz·əm) *n.* A tendency to extremes.

ex·trem·ist (ik·strē′mist) *n.* One who supports or advocates extreme measures or holds extreme views.

ex·trem·i·ty (ik·strem′ə·tē) *n. pl.* **·ties** 1 The utmost or farthest point; termination, end, or edge. 2 The greatest degree. 3 Desperate distress or need. 4 *pl.* Extreme measures. 5 *Usually pl.* The end part of a limb or appendage. See synonyms under END, NECESSITY.

ex·tri·cate (eks′trə·kāt) *v.t.* **·cat·ed, ·cat·ing** 1 To free from hindrance, difficulties, etc.; disentangle. 2 To cause to be given off; evolve, as gas or moisture. See synonyms under RELEASE. [<L *extricatus,* pp. of *extricare* <*ex-* out + *tricae* troubles] — **ex·tri·ca·ble** (eks′tri·kə·bəl) *adj.* — **ex′tri·ca·bly** *adv.*

ex·tri·ca·tion (eks′trə·kā′shən) *n.* 1 The act or process of extricating. 2 The act of evolving; disengagement.

ex·trin·sic (ek·strin′sik) *adj.* 1 Being outside of the nature of an object or case; not inherent or included in a thing; not essential: opposed to *intrinsic.* 2 *Anat.* Originating beyond the limits of a body or limb: *extrinsic* muscles. 3 Irrelevant; extraneous. Also **ex·trin′si·cal.** [<F *extrinsèque* <L *extrinsecus* outwardly <*exter* outside + *secus* besides] — **ex·trin′si·cal·ly** *adv.* — **ex·trin′si·cal·ness** *n.*

ex·trorse (eks·trôrs′) *adj. Bot.* Turned outward, as an anther from the axis of a flower. Also **ex·tror′sal.** [<F <LL *extrorsus* outwards <*extra* outside + *versus* towards]

ex·tro·ver·sion (eks′trō·vûr′zhən, -shən) *n.* 1 *Psychol.* The turning of one's interests toward the outside world or toward persons other than oneself; the quality of finding interest and pleasure in outside interests; opposed to *introversion.* Also *extraversion.* 2 *Anat.* Exstrophy. [<*extro-* outwards (<EXTRA-) + L *versio, -onis* a turning <*vertere* turn]

ex·tro·vert (eks′trō·vûrt) *n.* A person highly adapted to living in and deriving satisfaction from the external world: opposed to *introvert.* Also *extravert.*

ex·trude (ik·strōōd′) *v.* **·trud·ed, ·trud·ing** *v.t.* 1 To force, thrust, or push out; expel. 2 To force (a plastic, metal, or other substance) through a shaped opening in order to give it a desired cross-section. — *v.i.* 3 To protrude. [<L *extrudere* <*ex-* out + *trudere* thrust]

ex·tru·sion (ik·strōō′zhən) *n.* 1 The act or process of extruding; expulsion. 2 *Geol.* An overflow of lava upon the earth's surface through conduits or fissures in the rocks; effusion.

ex·tru·sive (ik·strōō′siv) *adj.* 1 Tending to extrude. 2 *Geol.* Extruded, as outflows of igneous rocks.

ex·u·ber·ance (ig·zōō′bər·əns) *n.* 1 Abounding variety or copiousness. 2 Superabundance: an *exuberance* of imagination. Also **ex·u′ber·an·cy.**

ex·u·ber·ant (ig·zōō′bər·ənt) *adj.* 1 Effusive; overflowing; lavish. 2 Marked by plentifulness; producing copiously. See synonyms under FERTILE, REDUNDANT. [<L *exuberans, -antis* <*ex-* completely + *uberare* be fruitful <*uber* rich] — **ex·u′ber·ant·ly** *adv.*

ex·u·ber·ate (ig·zōō′bə·rāt) *v.i.* **·rat·ed, ·rat·ing** *Rare* To be exuberant.

ex·u·date (eks′yōō·dāt) *n. Biol.* Any substance which filters through the walls of living cellular tissue and is available for removal or extraction, as gums and resins. [<L *ex(s)udatus,* pp. of *ex(s)udare.* See EXUDE.]

ex·u·da·tion (eks′yōō·dā′shən) *n.* 1 The act or process of exuding. 2 That which is exuded.

ex·ude (ig·zōōd′, ik·sōōd′) *v.t.* & *v.i.* **·ud·ed, ·ud·ing** To give off or come forth gradually; ooze or trickle forth, as sweat. [<L *ex(s)udare* <*ex-* out + *sudare* sweat]

ex·ult (ig·zult′) *v.i.* To rejoice in or as in triumph; take great delight. [<F *exulter* <L *ex(s)ultare,* freq. of *exsilire* leap up <*ex-* out + *salire* leap] — **ex·ult′ing·ly** *adv.*

ex·ul·tant (ig·zul′tənt) *adj.* 1 Rejoicing triumphantly. 2 Denoting great joy. [<L *ex(s)ultans, -antis,* ppr. of *ex(s)ultare.* See EXULT.] — **ex·ul′tant·ly** *adv.*

ex·ul·ta·tion (eg′zul·tā′shən, ek′sul-) *n.* The act or state of exulting; triumphant joy. Also **ex·ul′tance, ex·ul′tan·cy.** [<L *ex(s)ultatio, -onis* <*ex(s)ultare.* See EXULT.]

ex·urb (eks′ûrb′) *n.* A residential area outside a city beyond the suburbs, usually characterized by relative affluence. [<EX- + *-urb* (on analogy with *suburb*) <L *urbs* city] — **ex·urb·an** (eks·ûr′bən) *adj.*

ex·ur·ban·ite (eks·ûr′bən·īt) *n.* One living outside a city in a usually affluent residential area beyond the suburbs, and who commutes to work in the city.

ex·ur·bi·a (eks·ûr′bē·ə) *n.* Exurbs collectively.

ex·u·vi·ae (ig·zōō′vi·ē, ik·sōō′-) *n. pl.* Parts cast off or shed by animals. [<L <*exuere* cast off, undress] — **ex·u′vi·al** *adj.*

ex·u·vi·ate (ig·zōō′vē·āt, ik·sōō′-) *v.t.* & *v.i.* **·at·ed, ·at·ing** To cast off or shed (skin, shell, etc.); slough; molt. — **ex·u′vi·a′tion** *n.*

ex vi ter·mi·ni (eks vī tûr′mə·nī) *Latin* By force of the term.

ey·as (ī′əs) *n.* A young hawk; nestling. [ME *nyas* <F *niais* <L *nidus* a nest; in ME *a nyas* became *an eyas*]

Eyck (īk), **Hubert van,** 1366?–1426, and **Jan van,** 1385?–1440, Flemish painters, brothers; traditional inventors of oil painting.

-ey Var. of -Y[1].

ey·dent (ī′dənt) See EIDENT.

eye[1] (ī) *n.* 1 The organ of vision in animals; especially, the human eye, a nearly spherical mass set in a cavity of the skull and consisting

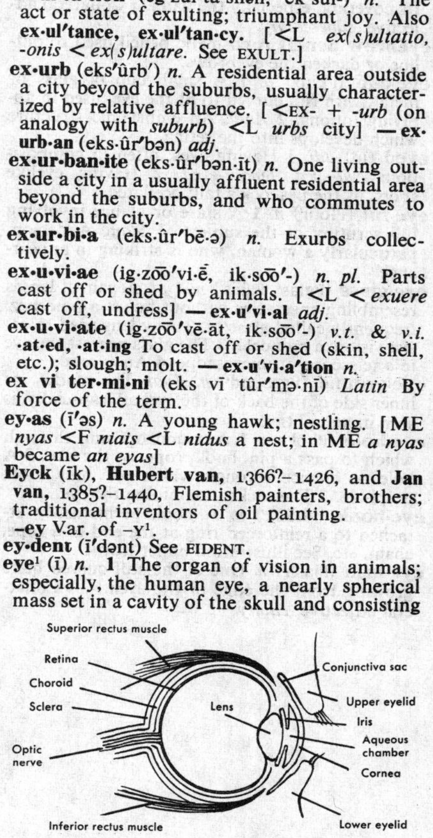
Superior rectus muscle
Retina
Choroid
Sclera
Lens
Conjunctiva sac
Upper eyelid
Iris
Aqueous chamber
Cornea
Optic nerve
Inferior rectus muscle
Lower eyelid

CROSS–SECTION OF THE HUMAN EYE

of the cornea, iris, pupil, lens, with associated muscles and optic nerve, also the eyelids, eyelashes, and eyebrows. 2 Ocular perception; sight. 3 Capacity for seeing or discerning. 4 Attentive observation; watchful care. 5 A particular look or expression; mien. 6 Mental or moral vision; estimation; also, regard; desire. 7 Anything that resembles the human organ of sight, or its socket, in shape, place, or office: the *eye* of a needle, the *eye* of a potato, apple, gooseberry, dahlia, etc. 8 *Meteorol.* The calm central area of an advancing hurricane or cyclone: also **eye of the storm.** — **to keep an eye out** or **peeled** To watch for; keep alert. — **to lay eyes on** To see. — *v.t.* **eyed, ey·ing** or **eye·ing** 1 To look at carefully; scrutinize. 2 To make a hole in, like the eye of a needle. ◆ Homophones: *aye, I.* [OE *ēage*]

eye[2] (ī) *n.* A brood, as of pheasants. ◆ Homophones: *aye, I.* [ME *nye* <OF *ni* <L *nidus* a nest: in ME *a nye* was altered to *an eye*]

eye agate A variety of agate with concentric banding which, on cutting and polishing, resembles an eye.

eye·ball (ī′bôl′) n. The globe or ball of the eye.

eye bank Med. A collection of healthy corneas stored at very low temperatures, for use in transplanting on eyes which have been seriously injured by accident or disease.

eye·bar (ī′bär′) n. Engin. A heat-treated steel bar of high tensile strength, usually rectangular in cross-section, with holes punched in the terminal heads for attachment to other structural members, as suspension cables, trusses, etc.

eye·beam (ī′bēm′) n. A quick look or glance of the eye.

eye·bolt (ī′bōlt′) n. Mech. Any of various forms of bolt having, in place of a head, an eye or ring to receive a rope, hook, etc.

eye·bright (ī′brīt′) n. 1 A low annual herb of the figwort family (Euphrasia officinalis), formerly used in eye lotions. 2 The red or scarlet pimpernel.

eye·brow (ī′brou′) n. 1 The arch over the eye. 2 Its covering, especially the hairs. ◆ Collateral adjective: superciliary.

eyebrow pencil A cosmetic pencil used to outline or darken the eyebrows.

eye·cup (ī′kup′) n. 1 A small cup of glass or metal, with rim curved to fit the eye, used in applying lotions. 2 Anat. An embryonic structure which develops into the retina.

eyed (īd) adj. 1 Having eyes: often in composition: evil-eyed, tender-eyed. 2 Having eyelike spots, as the peacock's tail; ocellated.

eye·ful (ī′fŏŏl′) n. 1 A stare or glance involving full scrutiny of the subject. 2 Slang A person, particularly a woman, who is striking in appearance.

eye·glass (ī′glas′, ī′gläs′) n. 1 pl. A pair of lenses resembling spectacles but without bows; a pincenez: frequently called glass′es. 2 Any lens used to assist vision; a monocle. 3 The glass nearest the eye in a telescope or microscope. 4 An eyecup.

eye·ground (ī′ground′) n. Anat. The fundus, or inner side of the back of the eyeball, especially as seen in an ophthalmoscope.

eye·hole (ī′hōl′) n. 1 A round opening through which to pass a pin, hook, rope, or the like. 2 A hole or crevice through which one may look; peephole. 3 The socket containing the eye.

eye·hook (ī′hŏŏk′) n. A hook permanently attached to a reinforced ring at the end of a rope, chain, etc. See illustration under HOOK.

eye·lash (ī′lash′) n. One of the stiff curved hairs growing from the edge of the eyelids. ◆ Collateral adjective: ciliary.

eye·less (ī′lis) adj. Lacking eyes; deprived of sight.

eye·let (ī′lit) n. 1 A small hole or opening; a little eye or aperture. 2 A hole made in canvas, leather, paper, or the like, either bushed with metal or worked around with buttonhole stitch. 3 A metal ring for protecting such a perforation: also **eye′let-ring′**. 4 Entomol. An ocellus. —v.t. To make eyelets in. [< F oeillet, dim. of oeil an eye]

eye·let·eer (ī′lə-tir′) n. An instrument for making eyelet holes; a stiletto.

eye·lid (ī′lid′) n. One of the curtains of loose integument that cover the eyeballs in front. ◆ Collateral adjective: palpebral.

eye-o·pen·er (ī′ō′pən-ər) n. U.S. 1 Anything that opens the eyes, actually or figuratively. 2 An incredible tale or piece of news. 3 Colloq. Something enabling one to comprehend what was before a mystery or unheeded. 4 Colloq. A drink of liquor, especially one taken early in the morning.

eye·piece (ī′pēs′) n. Optics The lens or combination of lenses nearest the eye in a telescope or microscope.

eye rime A rime not phonetically correct, but composed of words similar in spelling: as in good, flood; move, love.

eye·ser·vant (ī′sûr′vənt) n. One who does his duty only when watched. Also **eye′serv′er**.

eye·ser·vice (ī′sûr′vis) n. 1 Duty performed only when the worker is being watched. 2 Admiring glances.

eye shadow A cosmetic preparation, tinted blue, green, black, etc., applied to the eyelids to enhance the eyes.

eye·shot (ī′shot′) n. Reach or scope of the eye; view; sight.

eye·sight (ī′sīt′) n. 1 The power or sense of sight. 2 Extent of vision; view.

eye·some (ī′səm) adj. Pleasant to look at.

eye·sore (ī′sôr′, ī′sōr′) n. 1 A diseased place on or near the eye. 2 Anything that offends the sight.

eye speculum An instrument for retracting the eyelids and holding them apart.

eye·splice (ī′splīs′) n. Naut. A loop formed by bending back the end of a rope and splicing it into the rope.

eye·spot (ī′spot′) n. Biol. 1 One of the rudimentary visual organs of many invertebrates, consisting of a few pigment cells overlaying a nerve filament sensitive to light. 2 The rudimentary eye in an embryo. 3 An ocellus. 4 An eyelike marking.

eye·stalk (ī′stôk′) n. Zool. A stalk or peduncle that supports an eye, as in lobsters and crabs.

eye·stone (ī′stōn′) n. A small smooth calcareous disk with one side convex, used to remove foreign substances from the eye.

eye·strain (ī′strān′) n. An affection caused by excessive or improper use of the eyes.

eye·string (ī′string′) n. Anat. A muscle or tendon that holds or moves the eye.

eye·tooth (ī′tōōth′) n. pl. **eye·teeth** One of the upper canine teeth. —**to cut one's eyeteeth** To grow old enough to gain wisdom by experience.

eye·wash (ī′wosh′, ī′wôsh′) n. 1 A medicinal wash for the eye. 2 Slang Nonsense; bunk.

eye·wa·ter (ī′wô′tər, ī′wot′ər) n. 1 The natural water that forms in the eye; tears. 2 A medicated lotion for the eyes.

eye·wink·er (ī′wingk′ər) n. An eyelash.

eye·wit·ness (ī′wit′nis) n. One who has seen a thing or an occurrence with his own eyes and hence can give testimony about it.

eye worm A nematode worm (Thelazia californiensis), whitish in color and about half an inch long, which lives underneath the eyelids and in the tear ducts, causing inflammation and discomfort: parasitic on dogs, sheep, cats, and man.

Ey·lau (ī′lou) A former name for BAGRATIONOVSK. German **Preuss·isch Ey·lau** (proi′sish ī′lou).

ey·ra (ī′rə) n. The jaguarundi. [< Tupian]

eyre (âr) n. Obs. 1 A circuit or journey. 2 A court of circuit judges. —**justices in eyre** Judges who prior to the time of Edward III rode a circuit periodically to hold court in the English shires. [< OF erre < L iter journey]

Eyre (âr), **Lake** A salt lake in northern South Australia, often dry; 3,430 square miles.

Eyre Peninsula (âr) A peninsula of southern South Australia, between Spencer's Gulf and the Great Australian Bight. Also **Eyre's Peninsula**.

ey·ry, ey·rie (âr′ē, ir′ē) See AERIE.

Eysk (āsk) See EISK.

E·zé·chias (ā-zā-kyäs′) French form of HEZEKIAH. Also Ital. **E·ze·chia** (ā-dzā′kyä), Sp. **E·ze·qui·as** (ā′thä-kē′äs).

E·ze·ki·el (i-zē′kē-əl, -kyəl; Du., Ger. ā-sā′kē-äl) A masculine personal name. Also spelled Heseikel. Also Fr. **É·zé·chiel** (ā-zā-kyel′), Sp. **E·ze·quiel** (ā′thä-kyel′). [< Hebrew, strength of God] —**Ezekiel** A major Hebrew prophet of the sixth century B.C.; also, a book of the Old Testament written by him.

E·ze·ki·el (i-zē′kē-əl, -kyəl)′, **Moses Jacob,** 1844–1917, U.S. sculptor and musician.

Ez·ra (ez′rə) A masculine personal name. [< Hebrew, rising light or helper] —**Ezra** Hebrew high priest of the fifth century B.C., who originated public preaching, and who wrote, in part, the Old Testament **book of Ezra**. Also Esdras.

F

f, F (ef) pl. **f's, F's** or **fs, Fs, effs** (efs) n. 1 The sixth letter of the English alphabet, from Phoenician vau, through Hebrew vau, Greek digamma, which was early dropped from the Greek alphabet, but was restored by the Romans. 2 The sound of the letter f, usually a voiceless labiodental fricative. See ALPHABET. —symbol 1 Music a The fourth tone in the musical scale of C; the pitch of this tone, or the note representing it. b The scale built upon F. c The bass clef in musical notation. 2 Chem. Fluorine (symbol F). 3 Genetics A filial generation, usually followed by a subscript numeral, as F_1, F_2, for the first, second, etc., filial generation offspring of a given mating. 4 In education, a grade meaning failure, or, sometimes, fair.

fa (fä) n. The fourth tone of any key in music, or of the so-called natural key. [< Ital.]

fa' (fô) n. Scot. 1 Lot; luck. 2 Share. 3 Fall. Also spelled faw.

fa·ba·ceous (fə-bā′shəs) adj. Bot. Designating a very large family (Leguminosae; formerly Fabaceae) of herbs, shrubs, and trees, characterized by stipulate leaves, irregular flowers,

and fruits that are true pods or legumes; the bean or pea family. [< L fabaceus leguminous < faba a bean]

Fa·bi·an (fā′bē-ən) adj. Designating a policy like that of Quintus Fabius Maximus Verrucosus (died 203 B.C.), who, in the Second Punic War with Hannibal, acquired the nickname Cunctator or Delayer, because he avoided direct engagements and used dilatory tactics, thereby foiling his antagonist; hence, practicing the policy of delay. —n. A member of the Fabian Society. —**Fa′bi·an·ism** n. —**Fa′·bi·an·ist** n. & adj.

Fabian Society An English association of socialists, formed in 1884, including many able writers on economics, having as their object the achievement of socialism by easy stages.

fa·ble (fā′bəl) n. 1 A brief story or tale embodying a moral and introducing persons, animals, or inanimate things as speakers or actors. 2 A foolish or improbable story; fabrication. 3 Archaic The plot of an epic or dramatic poem. 4 Common talk. See synonyms under ALLEGORY, FICTION. —v.t. & v.i.

fa·bled, fa·bling To invent or tell (fables or stories); fabricate; lie. [< OF < L fabula < fari say, speak] —**fa′bler** n.

fa·bled (fā′bəld) adj. 1 Recorded in fable; made famous by fable. 2 Existing only in fable; mythical.

fab·li·au (fab′lē-ō, Fr. fȧ-blē-ō′) n. pl. **·aux** (-ōz, Fr. -ō′) A short, comic or gay tale, usually in eight-syllable verse: the genre which arose in France in the 12th and 13th centuries. [< F, ult. < OF fable. See FABLE.]

Fabre (fä′bər, Fr. fȧ′br′), **Jean Henri,** 1823–1915, French entomologist.

fab·ric (fab′rik) n. 1 A woven, felted, or knitted material, as cloth, felt, hosiery, or lace; also, the material used in its making. 2 Something that has been fabricated, constructed, or put together; any complex construction. 3 An edifice: St. Paul's, that noble fabric. 4 The manner of construction; workmanship; texture: cloth of a very intricate fabric. 5 Geol. The texture or structure of igneous rock. See synonyms under FRAME. [< OF fabrique < L fabrica a workshop < faber a workman. Doublet of FORGE.]

fab·ri·cant (fab′rə·kənt) *n.* A manufacturer; maker. [<F <L *fabricans, -antis,* ppr. of *fabricare.* See FABRICATE.]

fab·ri·cate (fab′rə·kāt) *v.t.* **·cat·ed, ·cat·ing** **1** To make or manufacture; build. **2** To make by combining parts; assemble. **3** To invent, as lies or reasons; concoct. See synonyms under CONSTRUCT, MAKE. [<L *fabricatus,* pp. of *fabricare* construct <*faber* a workman] — **fab′ri·ca′tor** *n.*

fab·ri·ca·tion (fab′rə·kā′shən) *n.* **1** The art of fabricating. **2** Something fabricated, as a structure or contrivance. **3** A contrived or trumped-up story; a falsehood. See synonyms under DECEPTION, FICTION, LIE.

Fab·ri·koid (fab′rə·koid) *n.* A fabric with cloth base but pyroxylin surface, impervious to water or other fluid: a trade name.

fab·u·list (fab′yə·list) *n.* **1** A composer of fables. **2** One who falsifies or fabricates.

fab·u·lize (fab′yə·līz) *v.i.* **·lized, ·liz·ing** To compose or relate fables or stories. Also *Brit.* **fab′·u·lise.** [<L *fabula* a fable + -IZE]

fab·u·lous (fab′yə·ləs) *adj.* **1** Belonging to fable; fictitious; mythical. **2** Passing the limits of belief; incredible. — **fab′u·lous·ly** *adv.* — **fab′u·lous·ness** *n.*

fa·çade (fə·säd′, fa-; *Fr.* fà·såd′) *n.* **1** *Archit.* The front or chief face of a building. **2** The front, visible part, or most conspicuous part of an institution, often designed to convey a favorable impression of the whole. [<F <*face* a face, on analogy with Ital. *facciata,* both ult. <L *facies* a face]

face (fās) *n.* **1** The anterior portion of the head, in which the eyes, nose, and mouth are situated, comprising in man the surface between the top of the forehead and the bottom of the chin, and extending laterally from ear to ear. **2** The surface, or most important surface, of anything; a front or working surface; that side or edge presented to view, or to any particular adjustment for operating; a side or surface of a solid: the *face* of a dam, one of the *faces* of a crystal, the *face* of a playing card, the *face* of a molar tooth. **3** The façade. **4** The flat portion of a propeller blade. **5** The flat or rounded striking surface of a hammer. **6** The long outer slope of a bastion; also, that part of the line of defense ending with the curtain and the angle of the shoulder. **7** *Mining* **a** The end of a drift or tunnel. **b** The sharply defined and more important joint in coal running at right angles to the plane of stratification. **8** *Printing* **a** The impression surface of a type body or of a printing plate. **b** The letter or other character cut on the type, or the size or style of the character cut on the type. **9** The dial of a clock or watch. **10** The obverse of a coin, or medal, which bears the effigy; occasionally the reverse side. **11** The inscribed side of a document, or printed side of a sheet. **12** One of the sides of any military formation, as of a square. **13** The external aspect or appearance; look; show; outward effect or impression: He put a bold *face* on the matter. **14** Personal force, influence, opinion, or will, as if expressed in the countenance: He set his *face* steadily against it. **15** Personal presence; immediate cognizance; sight: before the *face* of, to one's *face.* **16** *Colloq.* Effrontery; audacity; assurance. **17** The value as expressed on the written or printed surface: said of any commercial paper, as a note or bond. **18** In golf, the striking side of a club head; the side or slope of a hillock or bunker. — **in the face of** **1** In the presence of; confronting. **2** In opposition to; in defiance of; in spite of. — **to save face** To save one's reputation or standing; protect one's dignity in the opinion of others. — **to lose face** To lose standing or reputation. — **to make faces** To grimace. — *v.* **faced, fac·ing** *v.t.* **1** To bear or turn the face toward; front upon: The house *faces* the street. **2** To cause to turn in a given direction, as soldiers. **3** To meet face to face; confront, as with courage or boldness: to *face* great odds. **4** To realize or be aware of: to *face* facts. **5** To cover with a layer or surface of another material: to *face* brick with stucco or a garment with silk. **6** To make smooth the surface of; dress: to *face* stone. **7** To turn face upward, as a playing card. — *v.i.* **8** To be turned or placed with the face in a given direction: The house *faces* west. **9** To turn in a given direction: The soldiers *faced* right. See synonyms under OPPOSE. — **to face down** To abash or disconcert by a bold stare or audacious manner. — **to face out** To see to completion or endure, as by a persevering manner. — **to face the music** *U.S. Slang* To accept the consequences. — **to face up to** **1** To meet with courage; confront. **2** To realize: become aware of. [<F, ult. <L *facies* a face] — **face′a·ble** *adj.*

face card A playing card bearing the picture of a king, queen, or knave.

face·hard·en (fās′här′dən) *v.t.* *Metall.* To harden the surface of (steel, iron, etc.), by the addition of carbon in conjunction with great heat.

face-height (fās′hīt′) *n.* *Anat.* The distance between the gnathion and the nasion. Also **face′-length′.**

face-lift·ing (fās′lif′ting) *n.* An operation that removes or tightens sagging tissues or muscles in the face; plastic surgery of the face.

face pack A cosmetic paste having a mud, clay, or meal base compounded with certain astringents, bleaches, etc., applied thickly to the face and allowed to dry like a mask: also called *beauty pack, facial mask.*

face·plate (fās′plāt′) *n.* *Mech.* A disk that holds and rotates work, as on a lathe or boring mill.

face powder A cosmetic powder usually having a talc or rice-starch base, applied to the face to dull shiny skin, cover blemishes, etc.

fac·er (fā′sər) *n.* **1** *Colloq.* A blow in the face, as in boxing; hence, any stunning check. **2** *Colloq.* A difficult, challenging, or elusive problem; a poser. **3** *Mech.* An attachment to a machine tool to hold a cutter in facing or surfacing.

fac·et (fas′it) *n.* **1** One of the small plane surfaces cut upon a diamond or other gem. For illustration see DIAMOND. **2** *Archit.* A flat projecting fillet between the flutes of a column. **3** *Zool.* A unit of a compound eye in insects and crustaceans; also, the surface or cornea of such an eye. **4** One side, view, or phase of a subject or of a person's mind or character. **5** *Anat.* A small flat surface on a bone. **6** *Dent.* A flat abraded spot on a tooth: also **fac′ette.** — *v.t.* **fac·et·ed** or **·et·ted, fac·et·ing** or **·et·ting** To cut or work a facet or facets upon. [<F *facette,* dim. of *face* FACE]

fa·cete (fə·sēt′) *adj.* *Archaic* Clever; witty; humorous. [<L *facetus* splendid, facetious]

fa·ce·ti·ae (fə·sē′shi·ē) *n. pl.* **1** Facetious sayings collectively. **2** Coarsely witty books. [<L]

fa·ce·tious (fə·sē′shəs) *adj.* Indulging in, characterized by, or marked by wit or humor; jocular; jocose; waggish; witty; funny; humorous. See synonyms under HUMOROUS, JOCOSE, MERRY. [<L *facetia* wit + -OUS] — **fa·ce′tious·ly** *adv.* — **fa·ce′tious·ness** *n.*

face value See under VALUE.

fa·cial (fā′shəl) *adj.* Of, near, or affecting the face. — *n.* *Colloq.* A massage or other treatment of the face for the purpose of enhancing health and beauty of facial skin.

facial angle *Anat.* The angle, subtended between the line representing the face-height and the axis of the skull from the edge of central incisors to the auricular point.

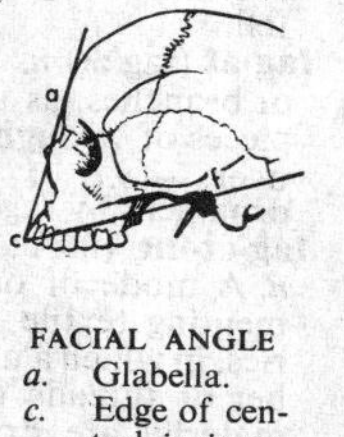

FACIAL ANGLE
a. Glabella.
c. Edge of central incisors.
f. Auricular point.
acf. Facial angle.

facial index A number expressing the ratio of the breadth to the length of the face.

facial mask A face pack.

facial nerve *Anat.* The seventh cranial nerve, one of a pair which actuate the muscles controlling facial expression.

fa·ci·end (fā′shē·end) *n.* *Math.* An operand. [<L *faciendum,* neut. gerundive of *facere* do]

-facient *suffix* Causing; making: *sorbefacient.* [<L *faciens, -entis,* ppr. of *facere* do]

fa·ci·es (fā′shi·ēz) *n.* **1** The general aspect or external appearance of anything. **2** *Geol.* The aggregate of the characteristics which determine the origin, composition, and mode of formation of rock deposits. **3** *Med.* The expression of the face in a given disease. **4** A surface. [<L, face, appearance]

fac·ile (fas′il) *adj.* **1** Easy of performance. **2** Easily gained; readily mastered. **3** Easily moved or persuaded; pliant; yielding. **4** Ready or quick in performance; dexterous; skilful. [<F <L *facilis* easy to do <*facere* do] — **fac′ile·ly** *adv.* — **fac′ile·ness** *n.*

fa·ci·le prin·ceps (fas′ə·lē prin′seps) *Latin* Unquestionably first or foremost.

fa·ci·lis de·scen·sus A·ver·no (fas′ə·lis di·sen′səs ə·vûr′nō) or **A·ver·ni** (ə·vûr′nī) *Latin* Easy is the descent into Avernus (hell).

fa·cil·i·tate (fə·sil′ə·tāt) *v.t.* **·tat·ed, ·tat·ing** To make easier or more convenient. — **fa·cil′i·ta′tion** *n.*

fa·cil·i·ty (fə·sil′ə·tē) *n. pl.* **·ties** **1** Ease or readiness in doing; dexterity. **2** Readiness of compliance; pliancy. **3** *pl.* Any aid or convenience: *facilities* for travel. **4** A place or office equipped to fulfill a special function: a government *facility.* [<L *facilitas, -tatis* ability <*facere* do]

fac·ing (fā′sing) *n.* **1** A covering in front serving any purpose. **2** A covering plate or layer in front, for ornament or protection against wear or corrosion, or to alter the contour. **3** The lining of a garment on parts exposed by being turned back, as the lapel of a coat or a hem, cuff, etc. **4** Any heavy, durable fabric used for this. **5** An improvement to the appearance of a food product, as by the addition of coloring matter. **6** *Mech.* A smooth, machined surface for attachment to another part. **7** *pl.* The different-colored collars and cuffs on a military uniform, often indicative of the branch of the service.

fac·sim·i·le (fak·sim′ə·lē) *n.* An exact copy or reproduction, often differing in scale but always identical or closely imitative in detail, material, etc. See synonyms under DUPLICATE. — *adj.* **1** Exactly copied or reproduced; exactly similar or corresponding: a *facsimile* autograph. **2** Producing exact copies or facsimiles. [<L *fac simile* make like]

facsimile telegraph An apparatus for telegraphing messages, designs, drawings, etc., in facsimile. Compare TELAUTOGRAPH.

fact (fakt) *n.* **1** Anything that is done or happens, as an act or deed. **2** Anything actually existent. **3** Any statement strictly true; truth; reality. **4** *pl.* *Law* The issues raised by the pleadings and evidence in an action and upon which the jury must base their verdict. **5** *Obs.* A thing done; a deed; performance. See synonyms under CIRCUMSTANCE, EVENT, PROOF. [<L *factum* <*facere* do. Doublet of FEAT.]

fact-find·ing (fakt′fīn′ding) *n.* The ascertainment of facts or conditions. —*adj.* Collecting facts and information: a *fact-finding* commission.

fac·tice (fak′tis) *n.* A fluffy, rubberlike material obtained by vulcanizing linseed oil with sulfur or sulfur chloride. [<F <L *factitius.* See FACTITIOUS.]

fac·tion (fak′shən) *n.* **1** A number of persons combined for a common purpose. **2** A party within a party; an irregular association of partisans; a cabal. **3** Violent opposition, as to a government; turbulence; dissension. See synonyms under CABAL. [<F <L *factio, -onis* <*facere* do. Doublet of FASHION.] — **fac′tion·ist,** *Obs.* **fac′tion·ar′y** *n.*

fac·tion·al (fak′shən·əl) *adj.* Of or pertaining to a faction. — **fac′tion·al·ism** *n.*

fac·tious (fak′shəs) *adj.* Given to, characterized by, or promoting faction; turbulent; partisan. See synonyms under PERVERSE. — **fac′tious·ly** *adv.* — **fac′tious·ness** *n.*

fac·ti·tious (fak·tish′əs) *adj.* **1** Artificial; conventional; affected; unnatural. **2** Proceeding from or created by art as opposed to nature. [<L *factitius* artificial <*facere* do] — **fac·ti′tious·ly** *adv.* — **fac·ti′tious·ness** *n.*

Synonyms: affected, artificial, manufactured, pretended, sham, simulated, spurious.

fac·ti·tive (fak′tə·tiv) *adj.* *Gram.* Pertaining to or designating a verb which takes, in addition to an object, a characterizing complement. Examples: They elected *him president;* He called *John* a *villain.* [<NL *factitivus*

<*factitare*, freq. of *facere* do] **—fac′ti·tive·ly** *adv.*
fac·tor (fak′tər) *n.* **1** *Math.* One of two or more quantities that, when multiplied together, produce a given quantity. **2** One of several elements or causes that produce a result. **3** *Brit.* A commission merchant; agent. **4** *Scot.* A bailiff or steward; also, a person legally appointed to care for forfeited property. **5** *U.S.* In some States, a garnishee. **6** A specialized commercial banker who finances manufacturers and dealers, accepting receivables as collateral. **7** The unit of heredity. See GENE. **8** *Physiol.* An element important in metabolism and nutrition, as a vitamin, enzyme, or hormone. **9** The agent controlling one of the remaining posts of the Hudson's Bay Company. See synonyms under AGENT. **—***v.t.* **1** To manage as a factor. **2** *Math.* To resolve into factors; factorize. [<L, maker <*facere* make]
fac·tor·age (fak′tər·ij) *n.* **1** A factor's commission. **2** The conduct of a factor's business.
fac·to·ri·al (fak·tôr′ē·əl, -tō′rē-) *n. Math.* The product of a series of consecutive positive integers from 1 to a given number; thus, *factorial* four (written 4! or |4) = 1 × 2 × 3 × 4 = 24. **—***adj.* Pertaining to a factor or a factorial.
fac·tor·ize (fak′tə·rīz) *v.t.* **·ized, ·iz·ing 1** *Law* To garnishee. **2** *Math.* To convert into factors. **—fac′tor·i·za′tion** *n.*
fac·tor·ship (fak′tər·ship) *n.* **1** The business of a factor or a factory. **2** A body of factors.
fac·to·ry (fak′tər·ē) *n. pl.* **·ries 1** An establishment devoted to the manufacture of something, including the building or buildings and machinery necessary to such manufacture; a manufactory. **2** A business establishment in charge of factors or agents in a foreign country.
fac·to·tum (fak·tō′təm) *n.* An employee hired to do all kinds of work. [<Med. L <*fac*, sing. imperative of *facere* do + *totum* everything]
fac·tu·al (fak′chōō·əl) *adj.* Pertaining to, containing, or consisting of facts; literal and exact; genuine.
fac·tu·al·ly (fak′chōō·əl·ē) *adv.* In factual form; actually.
fac·u·la (fak′yə·lə) *n. pl.* **·lae** (-lē) *Astron.* A small spot on the sun brighter than the rest of the photosphere. [<L, dim. of *fax* torch]
fac·ul·ta·tive (fak′əl·tā′tiv) *adj.* **1** Producing or imparting faculty or power; enabling; qualifying. **2** Endowing with authority or power, but allowing the use of it at option or contingently. **3** Empowering but not requiring one to perform some act; providing, as a law, for optional action: distinguished from *obligative*. **4** *Biol.* Having the power to exist in and become adapted to changed conditions, as aerobic bacteria, which may become anaerobic: distinguished from *obligate*. **5** Related or pertaining to a faculty or faculties.
fac·ul·ty (fak′əl·tē) *n. pl.* **·ties 1** Any mode of bodily or mental behavior regarded as implying a natural endowment or acquired power: the *faculty* of seeing, feeling, reasoning. **2** Any special form of skill, or unusual ability, whether natural or acquired; knack; turn; native facility. **3** One of the native complex capacities or powers into which the older psychology analyzed, and to which it ascribed, the phenomena of conscious mental life: the *faculty* of perception, memory, thought, etc. **4** The members of any one of the learned professions, collectively: the *faculty* of law or medicine. **5** The body of instructors in a university, college, or higher educational institution. **6** A department of learning or instruction at a university: the English *faculty*. **7** In the Roman Catholic Church, the right to perform certain ecclesiastical functions, bestowed by a prelate upon a subordinate; formerly, also, power or privilege in general bestowed or otherwise obtained: chiefly in the plural. **8** Ability to do or manage: executive skill and efficiency, especially in domestic matters: a housekeeper of notable *faculty*. **9** Pecuniary resources; means. See synonyms under ABILITY. [<OF *faculté* <L *facultas, -tatis* <*facilis*. See FACILE.]
fad (fad) *n.* A passing fancy or fashion; hobby. [Cf. dial. E *fad* be busy with trifles] **—fad′·dist** *n.*
fad·dle (fad′l) *Brit. Dial. v.t.* & *v.i.* **·dled, ·dling** To dandle; toy; trifle. **—***n.* A toy; trifle; fad.
fad·dom (fad′əm) *v.t. Scot.* To fathom; measure.
fad·dy (fad′ē) *adj.* **·di·er, ·di·est** *Colloq.* Full of, given to, or like fads. Also **fad′dish.**
fade (fād) *v.* **fad·ed, fad·ing** *v.i.* **1** To lose brightness or clearness; become indistinct; dim. **2** To lose freshness, vigor, youth, etc.; wither; wane. **—***v.t.* **3** To cause to fade. **4** *U.S. Slang* In dice, to cover (a bet). **—to fade in** In motion pictures, to come into view gradually. **—to fade out** In motion pictures, to disappear gradually. See synonyms under DIE[1]. [<OF *fader* <*fade* pale, insipid]
fade-a·way (fād′ə·wā′) *n.* In baseball, a slow, curved ball, seemingly pitched fast, that breaks inward toward the batter.
fade-in (fād′in′) *n.* A gradual appearance of a motion-picture sequence on the screen, often, as by double exposure, etc., replacing a preceding sequence.
fade·less (fād′lis) *adj.* Unfading. See synonyms under ETERNAL. **—fade′less·ly** *adv.*
fade-out (fād′out′) *n.* A gradual disappearance of a motion-picture sequence on the screen.
fad·er (fā′dər) *n.* In motion pictures, a potentiometer for the control of sound volume in reproduction, or for controlling the amount of light in developing the film.
fad·ing (fā′ding) *n. Telecom.* A lessening in the strength of electromagnetic signals owing to increased distance from the transmitting station, atmospheric condition, or mechanical defect.
fae·ces (fē′sēz), **fae·cal** (fē′kəl), etc. See FECES, etc.
Fa·en·za (fä·en′zə, *Ital.* fä·en′dzä) A city in north central Italy: ancient *Faventia.*
fa·er·ie (fā′ə·rē, fâr′ē) *n.* **1** The imaginary world inhabited by fairies. **2** *Archaic* A fairy. **—***adj. Archaic* Of or pertaining to fairies or fairyland. [See FAIRY]
Faerie Queene An allegorical romance of chivalry by Edmund Spenser, planned in twelve books, of which only six were published (1590–96).
Faer·oe Islands (fâr′ō) A group of 21 Danish Islands in the North Atlantic; 540 square miles; capital, Thorshavn: also *Faroe Islands.* Also **Faer′oes,** *Danish* **Faer·ö·er·ne** (fer·œ′er·nə).
Faf·nir (fäv′nir, fäf′-) In Norse mythology, the dragon who guards the hoard of the Nibelungs; slain by Sigurd. Also **Faf′ner.**
fag (fag) *v.* **fagged, fag·ging** *v.i.* **1** To weary oneself by working. **2** To work or serve as a fag. **—***v.t.* **3** To tire out by hard work. **4** To make a fag of. **—***n.* **1** One who does menial service for another, as in English public schools. **2** A piece of drudgery. **3** *Slang* A cigarette. **4** *Slang* A male homosexual. [? Alter. of *flag*[3]] **—fag′ger** *n.*
fa·ga·ceous (fə·gā′shəs) *adj. Bot.* Of or pertaining to a large family *(Fagaceae)* of trees and shrubs having alternate simple leaves, sterile flowers, and one-celled, one-seeded nuts; the beech family. [<NL *Fagaceae,* the beech family <L *fagus* a beech]
fag-end (fag′end′) *n.* **1** The frayed end, as of a rope. **2** A remnant or last part, usually of slight utility.
fag·got (fag′ət) *n.* **1** See FAGOT. **2** *Slang* A male homosexual. [Origin unknown]
Fa·gin (fā′gin) In Dickens's *Oliver Twist,* an old thief-trainer into whose hands Oliver fell.
fag·ot (fag′ət) *n.* **1** A bundle of sticks, twigs, or branches, as used for fuel. **2** A bundle of pieces of wrought iron or steel to be worked over. **—***v.t.* **1** To make a fagot of. **2** To ornament by fagoting. Also *faggot.* [<F]
fag·ot·ing (fag′ət·ing) *n.* A mode of ornamenting textile fabrics, in which a number of threads of a material are drawn out and the cross-threads tied together in the middle; in basketry, hemstitching. Also **fag′got·ing.**

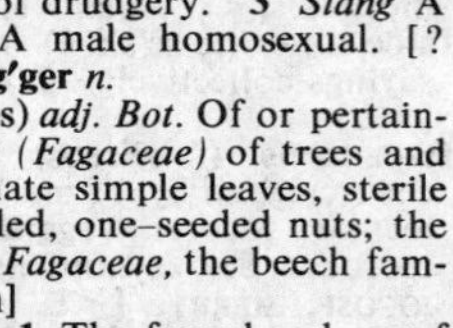

FAGOTING
Hemstitch Drawn work

fahl·band (fäl′band′, *Ger.* fäl′bänt′) *n. Geol.* A band or stratum of rock containing metallic sulfides. [<G <*fahl* pale + *band* band]
Fahr·en·heit (far′ən·hīt, *Ger.* fär′ən·hīt) *adj.* **1** Designating a temperature scale in which zero is the temperature of a mixture of equal weights of snow and common salt; the freezing point of water is 32° and the boiling point 212°, all under standard atmospheric pressure. **2** Noting a thermometer graduated to this scale. Abbr. *F.* or *Fahr.* See TEMPERATURE. [after Gabriel Daniel *Fahrenheit,* 1686–1736, German physicist]
fa·ïence (fī·äns′, fā-; *Fr.* fà·yäns′) *n.* A variety of majolica, usually highly decorated. [<F, pottery from Faenza]
fail (fāl) *v.i.* **1** To be unsuccessful; be unable. **2** To be deficient or wanting, as in ability, faithfulness, etc.; prove disappointing: He *failed* in his duty. **3** To give out: His strength *failed.* **4** To become extinct; die out. **5** To fade away; disappear: The light *failed* rapidly. **6** To weaken gradually, as in illness or death. **7** To become insolvent; go bankrupt. **8** To receive a failing grade. **—***v.t.* **9** To prove to be inadequate or of no help to; abandon; forsake: My courage *fails* me. **10** To leave undone or unfulfilled; neglect: with infinitive as object: He *failed* to carry out orders. **11** In education: **a** To receive a failing grade in (a course or test). **b** To assign a failing grade to (a pupil). See synonyms under FALL, SUSPEND. **—***n.* Failure: in the phrase *without fail.* [<OF *faillir* <L *fallere* to deceive]
fail·ing (fā′ling) *n.* A minor fault; foible; infirmity. See synonyms under FOIBLE. **—***adj.* **1** Characterized by failure. **2** Diminishing; weakening. **—fail′ing·ly** *adv.*
faille (fāl, fīl; *Fr.* fà′y′) *n.* An untwilled silk dress fabric having a light grain or cord. [<F]
fail-safe (fāl′sāf′) *adj.* **1** Utilizing a system that makes automatic adjustments in the event of operational failure to assure satisfactory performance. **2** *Mil.* Describing a system that automatically prevents a nation's own military aircraft from carrying out planned bombing missions without specific confirming authority.
fail·ure (fāl′yər) *n.* **1** The act of failing, cessation of supply, power, etc.: *failure* of sight. **2** A becoming bankrupt or proving unsuccessful in business or in any profession or trade. **3** Neglect or non-performance. **4** That which fails; anything unsuccessful. **5** One who fails conspicuously or in some specific effort. See synonyms under LOSS, MISFORTUNE, NEGLECT. [Earlier *failer* <AF, orig. var. of OF *faillir.* See FAIL.]
fain (fān) *adj. Archaic* & *Poetic* **1** Reluctantly willing; content. **2** Glad; rejoiced. **3** Eager; desirous. **—***adv.* Gladly: with *would* and infinitive: He would *fain* depart. ◆ Homophones: *fane, feign.* [OE *fægen*]
fai·naigue (fə·nāg′) *v.t.* & *v.i.* **·naigued, ·naiguing** *Dial.* To finagle; revoke; cheat. [? <FEIGN] **—fai·nai′guer** *n.*
fai·né·ant (fā′nē·ənt, *Fr.* fe·nā·än′) *adj.* Ineffective; lazy; useless. **—***n.* An idler; a do-nothing. [<F <*faire* do + *néant* nothing]
faint (fānt) *v.i.* **1** To lose consciousness; swoon: often with *away.* **2** *Archaic* To fail in courage or hope. **3** *Obs.* To become weak. See synonyms under FALL. [<*adj.*] **—***adj.* **1** Lacking in purpose, courage, or energy; timid. **2** Ready to faint; weak. **3** Evincive of weakness, feebleness, or lack of purpose; slight. **4** Indistinct; feeble; dim. **—***n.* A swoon; syncope: also **faint′·ing.** ◆ Homophone: *feint.* [<OF, pp. of *faindre* FEIGN] **—faint′er** *n.* **—faint′ish** *adj.* **—faint′·ish·ness** *n.* **—faint′ly** *adv.* **—faint′ness** *n.*

Synonyms (adj.): dim, exhausted, faded, faint-hearted, faltering, fatigued, feeble, half-hearted, ill-defined, indistinct, irresolute, languid, listless, purposeless, timid, weak, wearied, worn. *Faint,* with the general sense of lacking strength or effectiveness, covers a wide range of meaning, signifying overcome by physical weakness or exhaustion, or lacking in purpose, courage, or energy, as said of persons; or lacking definiteness or distinctness of color or sound, as said of written characters, voices, or musical notes. A person may be *faint* when physically *wearied,* or when overcome by fear; he may be a *faint* adherent because naturally *feeble* or *purposeless,* or because *half-hearted* in the cause; he may be a *faltering* supporter because naturally *irresolute* or because *faint-hearted* and *timid* in view of perils that threaten, a *listless* worker, through want of mental energy and purpose. Written characters may be *faint* or *dim,* either because originally written with poor ink, or because they have become *faded* by time and exposure. *Antonyms*: bright, brilliant, clear, conspicuous, daring, energetic, fresh, hearty, resolute, strong, sturdy, vigorous.
faint-heart·ed (fānt′här′tid) *adj.* Timorous;

cowardly. — **faint′-heart′ed·ly** *adv.* — **faint′-heart′ed·ness** *n.*

faints (fānts) *n. pl.* The dilute and impure spirit produced during the first and last stages of the distillation of whisky: also spelled *feints.*

fair[1] (fâr) *adj.* **1** Free from clouds; not obscure; sunshiny; clear. Compare def. 13. **2** Open; distinct. **3** Free from spot or blemish. **4** Showing no partiality, prejudice, or favoritism; hence, just, upright; honest. **5** Having light or clear color or hue; not dark or sallow: *fair* hair or complexion. **6** Pleasing to the eye or the mind; comely; beautiful. **7** Nearly or fully up to the average; moderately satisfactory or excellent; passably good or large: a *fair* crop. **8** Easily legible; well-formed and distinct: a *fair* print; a *fair* handwriting. **9** Apparently good and plausible, but not sincere: *fair* promises. **10** Accurately trimmed; even; regular; flowing: said of timbers, lines, or the like. **11** In games and sports, according to rule: a *fair* tackle, *fair* walking. **12** In a favorable direction: *fair* wind. **13** *Meteorol.* Having the sky cloudless to half covered with clouds; no aspect of rain, snow, or hail; fine; bright; sunny. **14** Properly open to attack: He is *fair* game. See synonyms under BEAUTIFUL, CANDID, GOOD, HONEST, JUST[1], PURE, RIGHT. — *adv.* **1** In a spirit of justice and reason: fairly, justly; honestly: deal *fair* with me. **2** In clear view; distinctly: *fair* in sight. **3** Favorably; fortunately; happily; to bid *fair.* **4** Politely; kindly; plausibly: to speak *fair.* **5** *Obs.* Deliberately; quietly. — *v.t.* To make smooth, as timbers. — *v.i. Dial.* To become fair or clear: said of weather. — *n.* **1** A fair one; sweetheart. **2** Women: with *the*: also *the fair sex.* **3** *Obs.* Good fortune; good luck. **4** *Obs.* Beauty. — **for fair** For sure. ◆ Homophone: *fare.* [OE *fæger*] — **fair′ness** *n.*

fair[2] (fâr) *n.* **1** An exhibit and sale of fancywork, etc., for the especial benefit of some object. **2** An occasional or periodical exhibit of agricultural products, manufactures, or other articles of value or interest: a county *fair,* an industrial *fair.* **3** A stated or regular market; a gathering of buyers and sellers. ◆ Homophone: *fare.* [<OF *feire* <L *feria* a holiday]

fair-and-square (fâr′ənd·skwâr′) *adj.* Thoroughly fair-dealing and honest. — *adv.* In a straightforward way; honestly.

Fair·banks (fâr′bangks), **Douglas,** 1883–1939, U.S. film actor.

Fair·banks (fâr′bangks) A town in east central Alaska, the northern terminus of the Alaska Highway.

fair catch **1** In football, the catch of a kicked ball by a defensive player who has signaled that he will not attempt a runback, and who therefore may not be tackled or interfered with without penalty. **2** In Rugby football, a ball caught in a manner that entitles the catching team to an extra kick.

fair copy **1** The copy of a document made after final corrections and revisions. **2** The state of such a copy.

fair cow *Austral. Slang.* Cow (def. 2).

Fair Deal The domestic program and policies of the administration of President Truman, as set forth in his State of the Union message to the U.S. Congress, January 5, 1949.

fair fa′ (faw) *Scot.* Good luck to.

fair-faced (fâr′fāst′) *adj.* **1** Having a fair face. **2** Specious.

Fair·fax (fâr′faks), **Thomas,** 1612–71, third Baron Fairfax, English Parliamentary leader.

fair green In golf, a fairway.

fair·ground (fâr′ground′) *n.* The ground or enclosure in which a fair is held.

fair-haired (fâr′hârd′) *adj.* **1** Flaxen-haired. **2** Favorite.

fair·ing[1] (fâr′ing) *n. Aeron.* **1** In airplanes, an auxiliary structure designed to reduce drag, or head resistance, of the part to which it is attached. Also called *fillet.* **2** The operation of shaping the contour of a part to obtain maximum aerodynamic efficiency. [<FAIR[1] (def. 10) + -ING[3]]

fair·ing[2] (fâr′ing) *n. Archaic* A present bought at a fair; reward. Also *Scot.* **fair′in.**

fair·ish (fâr′ish) *adj.* Moderately good, well, or large; passable.

fair lead *Naut.* **1** Such direction of a rope as will prevent it from chafing or fouling. **2** A protective guide for a rope, usually a ring or a perforated board through which rigging is passed.

fair-lead·er (fâr′lē′dər) *n. Naut.* A perforated block or a cringle for giving a rope a fair lead.

fair·ly (fâr′lē) *adv.* **1** In a just manner; equitably; properly. **2** Moderately; tolerably: a *fairly* tall building. **3** Positively; completely: The crowd *fairly* roared. **4** Clearly; distinctly. **5** *Obs.* Handsomely; courteously. **6** *Obs.* Softly; gently.

fair-mind·ed (fâr′mīn′did) *adj.* Free from bias or bigotry; open to reason; honest-minded. — **fair′mind′ed·ness** *n.*

Fair Oaks A locality east of Richmond, Virginia; scene of an indecisive Civil War battle, 1862: also *Seven Pines.*

fair play **1** Fairness in playing, contending, debating, etc. **2** The ideal and practice of justice, unaffected by prejudice or partiality.

fair sex Women.

fair shake *Slang* A fair chance or treatment.

fair-spo·ken (fâr′spō′kən) *adj.* Having grace of speech; plausible.

fair-trade (fâr′trād′) *v.t.* **-trad·ed, -trad·ing** To set a price no less than the manufacturer's minimum price on (a branded or trademarked product). — *adj.* Of or pertaining to such a price.

fair·wa·ter (fâr′wô′tər, -wot′ər) *n.* A streamlined covering of metal or plastic shaped to fit over the superstructures of a submarine as a protection against the mechanical and chemical action of sea water.

fair·way (fâr′wā′) *n.* **1** The proper course through a channel or harbor. **2** That part of a links or golf course, between the several tees and putting greens, on which the grass is constantly kept short: also called *fair green.*

fair-weath·er (fâr′weth′ər) *adj.* **1** Suitable for or restricted to fair weather, as a racetrack. **2** Useful or dependable only in favorable circumstances; not helpful in adversity: *fair-weather* friends.

Fair·weath·er (fâr′weth′ər), **Mount** Highest peak (15,300 feet) of the **Fairweather Range** in SE Alaska.

fair·y (fâr′ē) *n. pl.* **fair·ies** **1** An imaginary being, ordinarily of small and graceful human form, capable of working good or ill to mankind. **2** *Slang* A male homosexual. — *adj.* **1** Of or pertaining to fairies. **2** Resembling fairies. Also *Obs. faery* or *faerie.* [<OF *faerie* enchantment <*fae.* See FAY[2].] — **fair′y-like′** *adj.*

fairy gloves Digitalis; foxglove.

fair·y·hood (fâr′ē·hŏŏd) *n.* **1** Enchantment by fairies. **2** Fairy nature or characteristics. **3** The race of fairies.

fair·y·ism (fâr′ē·iz′əm) *n.* **1** Belief in fairies; fairy lore. **2** Resemblance to fairies or to their supposed habitations, customs, or characteristics.

fair·y·land (fâr′ē·land′) *n.* The fancied abode of the fairies.

fairy rings Circles in lawns or pastures, usually caused by the spreading of the mycelia of certain fungi, but popularly said to be made by fairies.

fairy stone **1** A fossil sea urchin or echinite. **2** A stone arrowhead. **3** A variously shaped concretion found in alluvial clays in Scotland.

fairy tale **1** A tale about fairies; an imaginative or legendary story. **2** An incredible statement.

fairy wand Blazing star (def. 1).

Fai·sal (fī′səl) See FEISAL.

fait ac·com·pli (fe·tȧ·kôṅ·plē′) *French* A thing done beyond recall or opposition; literally, an accomplished fact.

faith (fāth) *n.* **1** Belief without evidence. **2** Confidence in or dependence on a person, statement, or thing as trustworthy. ◆ Collateral adjective: *fiducial.* **3** Belief in God or the testimony of God as revealed in Scripture. **4** A doctrine or system of doctrines, propositions, etc., held to be true: the Christian *faith.* **5** Anything given adherence or credence: a man's political *faith.* **6** Allegiance or loyal adherence to something; faithfulness: to pledge *faith* in a venture. — **bad faith** Deceit; dishonesty. — **in faith** Indeed; truly. — **in good faith** Honestly; with honorable intentions. — **to break faith** **1** To betray one's principles or beliefs. **2** To fail to keep a promise. — **to keep faith** **1** To adhere to one's principles or beliefs. **2** To keep a promise. — *interj.* In truth; indeed. [<OF *feit, feid* <L *fides* < *fidere* trust]

Synonyms (noun): assent, assurance, belief, confidence, conviction, credence, credit, creed, doctrine, opinion, reliance, trust. *Belief,* as an intellectual process, is the acceptance of something as true on other grounds than personal observation and experience. We give *credence* to a report, *assent* to a proposition or to a proposal. *Belief* is stronger than *credence*; *credence* might be described as a prima-facie *belief*; *credence* is a more formal word than *belief,* and seems to imply somewhat more of volition; we speak of giving *credence* to a report, but not of giving *belief.* Goods are sold on *credit*; we give one *credit* for good intentions. *Conviction* is a *belief* established by argument or evidence; *assurance* is *belief* beyond the reach of argument; as, the Christian's *assurance* of salvation. *Faith* is a union of *belief* and *trust. Faith* is often personal; *belief* may be quite impersonal, but as soon as a *belief* is strong enough to be followed by definite action, the *belief* becomes *faith.* In religion it is common to distinguish between intellectual *belief* of religious truth, as any other truth might be believed, and *belief* of the heart, or saving *faith.* Compare FIDELITY, OPINION, RELIGION, TRUST. *Antonyms*: denial, disbelief, dissent, distrust, doubt, incredulity, infidelity, misgiving, rejection, skepticism, suspicion, unbelief.

faith cure **1** The alleged cure of disease by virtue of prayer, with faith in its efficacy. **2** The procedure, prescribed acts, etc., to effect such cure.

faith·ful (fāth′fəl) *adj.* **1** True or trustworthy in the performance of duty, especially in the fulfilment of promises, obligations, vows, and the like: a *faithful* servant, *faithful* to one's agreement. **2** True in detail; accurate in correspondence, or exact in description: a *faithful* copy. **3** Truthful; worthy of belief or confidence: a *faithful* witness, a *faithful* saying. **4** Full of faith; strong or firm in faith: *faithful* convictions. — **the faithful** **1** In the early church, all true believers in God. **2** The members in good standing of the Christian church, or any part of it. **3** In Islam, the followers of Mohammed. **4** The devoted members of a group or organization. — **faith′ful·ly** *adv.* — **faith′ful·ness** *n.*

Synonyms: devoted, firm, incorruptible, loyal, staunch, sure, true, trustworthy, trusty, unwavering. A person is *faithful* who will keep faith, whether with or without power to aid or serve; a person or thing is *trusty* that possesses such qualities as to justify the fullest confidence and dependence. We may speak of a *faithful* but feeble friend; we say a *trusty* agent, a *trusty* steed, a *trusty* sword. See HONEST, MORAL. *Antonyms*: capricious, faithless, false, fickle, unfaithful, untrue, untrustworthy.

faith healer One who heals by faith cures.

faith·less (fāth′lis) *adj.* **1** Untrue to promise or obligation; unfaithful; disloyal. **2** Tending or calculated to delude; deceptive and unreliable. **3** Lacking in or devoid of faith, especially in the Christian religion. See synonyms under PERFIDIOUS. — **faith′less·ly** *adv.* — **faith′less·ness** *n.*

fai·tor (fā′tər) *n. Obs.* A deceiver or rogue; an impostor. Also **fai′tour.** [<AF *faitour* <L *factor* a doer. See FACTOR.]

Fai·yum (fī·yōōm′) A province of Upper Egypt; 686 square miles; capital, Faiyum: also *Fayum, El Faiyum.*

Fai·za·bad (fī′zə·bad, fī′zä·bäd′) **1** A town in NE Afghanistan. **2** A city in east central Uttar Pradesh, India: formerly *Fyzabad.*

Fa·ka·ra·va (fä′kə·rä′və) The second largest of the Tuamotu islands, French Oceania. Formerly *Wittgenstein Island.*

fake[1] (fāk) *n. Colloq.* Anything or any person not genuine; a counterfeit. — *adj.* Spurious. — *v.* **faked, fak·ing** *v.t.* **1** To make up and attempt to pass off as genuine: to *fake* a pedigree. **2** To simulate; feign: to *fake* gratitude. **3** To improvise, as in music or a play. — *v.i.* **4** To practice faking. [? Var.

of obs. *feague, feak* <Du. *vegen* beat, dust off]

fake[2] (fāk) *n. Naut.* A single coil or turn of a rope or cable. — *v.t.* **faked, fak·ing** To coil, as a rope. [Origin uncertain]

fak·er (fā′kər) *n. Colloq.* **1** A street vendor or other person who sells fakes or notions. **2** One who originates a fake, humbug, or swindling contrivance.

fak·er·y (fā′kər·ē) *n. pl.* **·er·ies** *Colloq.* The practice of faking; a deceptive imitation.

fa·kir (fə·kir′, fā′kər) *n.* **1** A Mohammedan ascetic, religious mendicant, or mendicant priest. **2** Loosely, a Hindu Yogi or mendicant devotee. Also **fa·keer** (fə·kir′). [<Arabic *faqīr* poor]

fa–la (fä′lä, fə·lä′) *n.* **1** A refrain in old songs. **2** An old simple style of part song. Also spelled *fal-la.*

Fa·laise (fâ·lez′) A town in NW France, ancient seat of the Dukes of Normandy; scene of heavy fighting (1944) in World War II.

Fa·lange (fā′lanj, fə·lanj′; *Sp.* fä·läng′hā) The official fascist party of Spain. [<Sp., a phalanx]

Fa·lan·gist (fə·lan′jist) *n.* A member of the fascist party in Spain.

fal·ba·la (fal′bə·lə) *n. Obs.* A furbelow; flounce. [<F; ult. origin uncertain]

fal·cate (fal′kāt) *adj.* Sickle– or scythe–shaped: also **fal′cat·ed.** — *n.* A sickle–shaped figure. [<L *falcatus* <*falx, falcis* sickle] — **fal·ca′·tion** *n.*

fal·chion (fôl′chən, -shən) *n.* A sword of the Middle Ages with a broad and slightly curved blade; hence, poetically, any sword. [<OF *fauchon,* ult. <L *falx, falcis* a sickle]

fal·ci·form (fal′sə·fôrm) *adj.* Curved like a sickle; falcate.

fal·con (fôl′kən, fô′-, fal′-) *n.* **1** A diurnal bird of prey (genus *Falco*) used by falconers; especially, the peregrine falcon (*F. peregrinus*), with long, pointed wings, the hobby, merlin, or gerfalcon. **2** A falconine bird, whether used in falconry or not, having the upper mandible toothed, and circular nostrils, as a kestrel, duck hawk, prairie falcon (*F. mexicanus*), or sparrow hawk. **3** A small cannon of the 15th–17th centuries, firing a shot of around six pounds. [<OF *faucon, falcun* <LL *falco, -onis* <L *falx, falcis* a sickle]

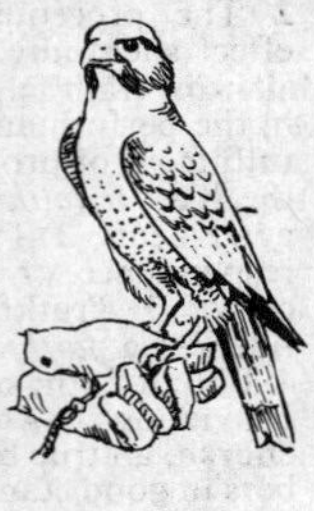
FALCON

fal·con·er (fôl′kən·ər, fô′-, fal′-) *n.* One who breeds, trains or hunts with falcons for sport.

fal·co·net (fôl′kə·net, fô′-, fal′-) *n.* **1** A little falcon. **2** A small cannon of the 16th century.

fal·con–gen·tle (fôl′kən·jen′təl, fô′-, fal′-) *n.* **1** The European goshawk. **2** A female falcon. Also **fal′con–gen′til.**

fal·co·ni·form (fal·kō′nə·fôrm) *adj. Ornithol.* Belonging to the order of birds (*Falconiformes*) which includes the vultures, hawks, falcons, and eagles.

fal·co·nine (fal′kə·nīn, -nin) *adj.* Falconlike.

fal·con·ry (fôl′kən·rē, fô′-, fal′-) *n.* The training or using of falcons for sport.

fal·cu·la (fal′kyə·lə) *n.* **1** A sharp, curved claw, as in birds of prey. **2** *Anat.* A sickle–shaped process of the dura mater between the lobes of the cerebellum: also called *falx cerebelli.* [<L, dim. of *falx* a sickle]

fal·de·ral (fal′də·ral) *n.* **1** Any trifling fancy or conceit; foolish nonsense. **2** A gew–gaw; a trifling ornament. **3** A meaningless refrain used in old English songs. Also *Scot. folderol.*

fald·stool (fôld′stōōl′) *n.* **1** A desk at which the litany is read, as in the Church of England. **2** A folding seat, stool, or chair, especially one used by a king, or by a bishop when performing pontifical acts away from his cathedral, or in the presence of a superior. **3** A camp stool. [<Med. L *faldistolium* <OHG *faldstuol* a folding stool]

Fa·lie·ri (fä·lyā′rē), **Marino,** 1278?–1355, doge of Venice 1354–55: also **Fa·lie·ro** (fä·lyā′rō).

Fa·lis·can (fə·lis′kən) *adj.* Of or pertaining to the **Fa·lis·ci** (fə·lis′ī), an ancient people of southern Etruria. — *n.* **1** One of the Falisci. **2** Their Italic language, closely related to Latin.

Fa·lis·co–La·tin·i·an (fə·lis′kō·lə·tin′ē·ən) *n.* A branch of the Italic subfamily of Indo–European languages, including Latin and its modern descendants (French, Italian, Spanish, Portuguese, Rumanian, etc.), and ancient Faliscan.

Fal·ken·hayn (fäl′kən·hīn), **Erich von,** 1861–1922, German chief of staff 1914–16.

Fal·kirk (fôl′kûrk, fô′-) A town in Stirlingshire, Scotland; scene of English defeat of Scottish forces under Wallace, 1298.

Falk·land Island Dependencies (fôk′lənd) The territories in the South Atlantic administered by Great Britain along with the Falkland Islands, including South Georgia, the South Shetland, South Orkney, and South Sandwich islands, and Palmer Peninsula in Antarctica.

Falk·land Islands (fôk′lənd) A British crown colony in the South Atlantic, 4,618 square miles; capital, Stanley. *Spanish* **Is·las Mal·vi·nas** (ēs′läs mäl·vē′näs).

Falk·ner (fôk′nər), **William** See FAULKNER.

fall (fôl) *v.* **fell, fall·en, fall·ing** *v.i.* **1** To drop from a higher to a lower place or position because of removal of support or loss of hold or attachment. **2** To drop from an erect to a less erect or prone position: He *fell* to his knees. **3** To collapse; come down: The bridge *fell.* **4** To become less in height, number, force, volume, value, etc. **5** To descend or become less in rank, estimation, importance, etc. **6** To be wounded or slain, as in battle. **7** To be overthrown; lose power, as a government. **8** To be taken or captured: The fort *fell.* **9** To yield to temptation; sin. **10** To hit; land: The bombs *fell* short. **11** To slope downward: The road *falls* into the valley. **12** To hang down; droop. **13** To begin and continue: Night *fell.* **14** To pass into a state or condition: to *fall* asleep. **15** To experience or show dejection: His face *fell.* **16** To come or happen by chance or lot: Suspicion *fell* on him. **17** To happen; occur: Hallowe'en *falls* on Tuesday. **18** To pass by right or inheritance, as an estate. **19** To be uttered as if accidentally: An oath *fell* from his lips. **20** To be born, as a lamb. **21** To happen or come at a specific place: The accent *falls* on the last syllable. **22** To be classified or divided: with *into.* — *v.t.* **23** *U.S.* To fell or cut down, as a tree. — **to fall afoul (or foul) of 1** To collide with, as a vessel. **2** To quarrel or argue with. — **to fall away 1** To become lean or emaciated. **2** To die; decline. — **to fall away from** To renounce allegiance to. — **to fall back** To recede; retreat. — **to fall back on** (or **upon**) **1** *Mil.* To retreat to. **2** To resort to; have recourse to. — **to fall behind 1** To drop back; lose ground. **2** To be in arrears. — **to fall down on** *U.S. Slang* To fail in. — **to fall flat** To fail to produce the intended effect or result. — **to fall for** *U.S. Colloq.* **1** To be deceived by. **2** To fall in love with. — **to fall in** *Mil.* To take proper place in a formation or group. — **to fall in with 1** To meet and accompany. **2** To agree with; conform to. — **to fall off 1** To leave or withdraw. **2** To become less: Attendance is *falling off.* **3** *Naut.* To veer to leeward from the former course. — **to fall on** (or **upon**) **1** To attack; assail. **2** To find; discover. — **to fall out 1** To quarrel. **2** To happen; result. **3** *Mil.* To leave ranks. — **to fall through** To come to nothing; fail. — *adj.* **1** Of or pertaining to autumn; happening, or for use in, the fall of the year: *fall* weather, *fall* planting, a *fall* coat. **2** *Slang* Easily duped: a *fall* guy. — *n.* **1** The act, process, or result of falling, in any sense of the word: the *fall* of Adam, a *fall* in price, the *fall* of Rome. **2** *Usually pl.* A waterfall; cataract; cascade. **3** A flowing or discharge, as of one stream or body of water into another. **4** That which falls or is caused to fall; also, the amount of descent. **5** *Often cap.* The season coming between summer and winter; autumn. **6** A falling band or ruff for the neck; also, a veil. **7** In wrestling, the throwing of or being thrown by one's opponent, or the method of doing it. **8** That which acts by falling, as a *deadfall.* **9** In music and oratory, a cadence; a sinking of tone or decrease of volume of sound. **10** A hoisting rope, or the part of a hoisting rope or tackle to which power is applied or by which power is exerted; the rope of a tackle or purchase. **11** The birth of animals. See synonyms under RUIN. — **the fall of man** The disobedience of Adam and Eve. [OE *feallan*]

Synonyms (verb): decline, descend, droop, drop, fail, faint, lapse, set, sink, subside. See HAPPEN. *Antonyms*: ascend, climb, mount, rise, soar.

fal–la (fä′lä, fə·lä′) See FA–LA.

Fal·la (fä′lyä), **Manuel de,** 1876–1946, Spanish composer.

fal·la·ci·a (fə·lā′shē·ə, -shə) *n. Psychiatry* An illusion or hallucination: *fallacia* optica, an optical illusion. [<L. See FALLACY.]

fal·la·cious (fə·lā′shəs) *adj.* Of, pertaining to, embodying, or involving a fallacy; deceptive; misleading; delusive. — **fal·la′cious·ly** *adv.* — **fal·la′cious·ness** *n.*

fal·la·cy (fal′ə·sē) *n. pl.* **·cies 1** Anything that deceives the mind or eye; deception. **2** A flaw in reasoning; fallaciousness. **3** *Logic.* Any reasoning, exposition, argument, etc., contravening the canons of logic. See synonyms under DELUSION, ERROR. [<L *fallacia* <*fallax, fallacis* deceptive <*fallere* deceive]

fal·lal (fal·lal′) *n.* **1** An ornament or trinket; gew–gaw. **2** Pretentiousness. Also **fal·lal′er·y.** [Cf. FALBALA]

fall dandelion An herb (*Leontodon autumnalis*) of the composite family having yellow flowers.

fall·en (fô′lən) *adj.* **1** Having come down by falling. **2** Overthrown; disgraced; ruined.

fall·er (fô′lər) *n.* **1** One who or that which falls. **2** A machine or part that acts by falling.

fall·fish (fôl′fish′) *n. pl.* **·fish** or **·fish·es 1** A fresh–water cyprinoid fish (genus *Semotilus*) of eastern North America, about 18 inches long, bluish above, with silvery sides. **2** One of various other cyprinoids, as the **red fallfish** (*Notropis rubricroceus*).

fall guy *Slang* A dupe; gullible person.

fal·li·ble (fal′ə·bəl) *adj.* **1** Liable to error or mistake. **2** Liable to be misled or deceived. **3** Liable to be erroneous, incorrect, or false. [<Med. L *fallibilis* <*fallere* deceive] — **fal′·li·bil′i·ty, fal′li·ble·ness** *n.* — **fal′li·bly** *adv.*

falling band A 16th or 17th century broad linen or lace collar or ruff worn over the shoulders; Vandyke.

fall·ing–leaf (fô′ling·lēf′) *n. Aeron.* A flight maneuver in which an airplane loses altitude by a series of lateral oscillations resembling those of a falling leaf.

fall·ing–sick·ness (fô′ling·sik′nis) *n. Rare* Epilepsy. Also **fall′ing–e′vil.**

falling star A shooting star; a meteor. Also **falling stone.**

fall line The brink of a plateau, as indicated by waterfalls.

Fal·lo·pi·an tube (fə·lō′pē·ən) *Anat.* One of a pair of long, slender ducts in mammals, serving as a passage for the ovum from the ovary to the uterus.

Fal·lo·pi·o (fä·lō′pē·ō), **Gabriello,** 1523?–62, Italian anatomist.

fall–out (fôl′out′) *n. Physics* **1** The descent of minute particles of radioactive material resulting from the explosion of an atomic or thermonuclear bomb. **2** The particles themselves. **3** Any incidental result; unplanned or unpredictable consequences. Also **fall′out′.**

fal·low[1] (fal′ō) *adj.* Left unseeded after being plowed; uncultivated. — *n.* **1** Land left unseeded after plowing; also, cleared woodland. **2** The act or system of plowing or working land and leaving it unseeded for a time. — *v.t.* & *v.i.* To make, keep, or become fallow. [OE *fealga* fallow land] — **fal′low·ness** *n.*

fal·low[2] (fal′ō) *adj.* Pale–yellow or pale–red. [OE *fealu* tawny]

fallow crop A crop alternated with the main crop to nourish the soil.

fallow deer A European deer (genus *Dama*), about 3 feet high at the shoulders and spotted white in the summer.

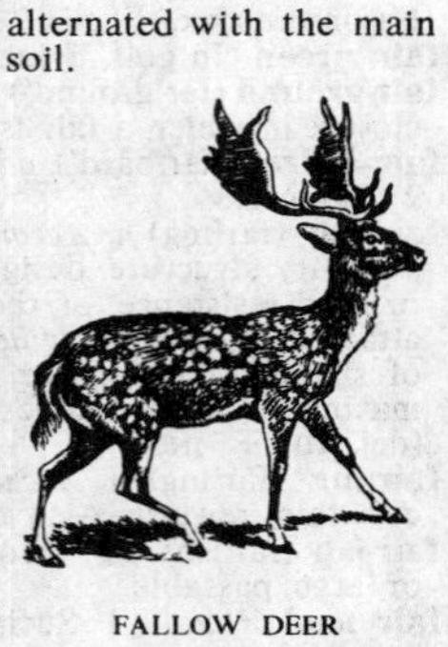
FALLOW DEER

Fall River A city in SE Massachusetts.

fall term 1 A court session beginning in the fall. **2** A school session beginning in the fall.

fall·way (fôl′wā′) *n.* A hoistway through several floors, as of a warehouse.

Fal·mouth (fal′məth) A port in SW Cornwall, England.

false (fôls) *adj.* **1** Contrary to truth or fact. **2** Deceptive; counterfeit; artificial; not real or genuine. **3** Incorrect; irregular. **4** Lying; dishonest; faithless; treacherous. **5** Supplementary; substitutive. **6** Out of tune. See synonyms under BAD, COUNTERFEIT, PERFIDIOUS. —*adv. Obs.* Falsely. [<OF *fals, faus* <L *falsus,* orig. pp. of *fallere* deceive] **—false′ly** *adv.* **—false′ness** *n.*

False Bay (fôls) An inlet of the Atlantic in Western Cape Province, Republic of South Africa.

false bottom **1** A partition that appears to be the bottom, as of a trunk, drawer, etc., forming a secret compartment beneath it. **2** The base of a drinking glass formed in such a way as to give a deceptive notion of the capacity of the glass.

false cirrus *Meteorol.* Cirrus formed from the upper frozen parts of a cumulonimbus cloud, often spreading out from the summit of a thundercloud.

false colors **1** The flag of a country not one's own. **2** Deceptive presentation of fact; pretense.

false face A covering for the face; mask.

false foxglove Any of several widely distributed plants of the figwort family (genus *Aureolaria)* bearing bright yellow flowers.

false glottis The space between the false vocal cords. See VOCAL CORD.

false-heart·ed (fôls′här′tid) *adj.* Having a false heart; treacherous; deceitful.

false hellebore See under HELLEBORE.

false·hood (fôls′o͝od) *n.* **1** Lack of accord to fact or truth; untruthfulness. **2** An intentional untruth; a lie. **3** Act of lying; falsification, **4** An untrue belief or idea. See synonyms under DECEPTION, FICTION, LIE.

false imprisonment The forcible detention of a person contrary to law.

false keel *Naut.* A supplementary keel attached to the bottom of the true keel of a vessel.

false pretenses Wilful misrepresentations made to cheat and defraud; swindling.

false ribs *Anat.* Ribs that do not unite directly with the sternum; in man, there are five on each side. See RIB.

false step **1** A stumble. **2** An error or blunder in behavior. See FAUX PAS.

fal·set·tist (fôl·set′ist) *n.* One who speaks or sings in falsetto.

fal·set·to (fôl·set′ō) *n. pl.* **·tos** **1** The artificial tones of the voice, higher than the chest voice or natural voice. **2** A singer possessing such a voice. —*adj.* Having the quality of the falsetto; shrill; artificial. [<Ital., dim. of *falso* false]

false vampire Any of a group of large Old World bats (families *Nycteridae* and *Megadermidae)* wrongly supposed to suck blood.

false·work (fôls′wûrk′) *n.* **1** A temporary scaffolding to facilitate the erection of a permanent structure. **2** That part of a structure designed to improve its shape or increase its efficiency, but without carrying any of the fundamental stresses, as an airplane fairing.

fals·ies (fôl′sēz) *n. pl. Colloq.* Pads worn within a brassière to give the breasts a fuller appearance.

fal·si·fi·ca·tion (fôl′sə·fə·kā′shən) *n.* **1** The act or process of falsifying. **2** *Law* The intentional alteration of a record, an account, or any document, so as to render it untrue. Compare SURCHARGE.

fal·si·fy (fôl′sə·fī) *v.* **·fied, ·fy·ing** *v.t.* **1** To misrepresent; tell lies about. **2** To prove to be false; disprove; **3** *Law* To tamper with, as a document. **4** In prosody, to alter (an accent in a poem) from the usual form or rule. —*v.i.* **5** To tell falsehoods; lie. See synonyms under PERVERT. [<F *falsifier* <LL *falsificare* <L *falsificus* making false <*falsus* FALSE + *facere* make] **—fal′si·fi′er** *n.*

fal·si·ty (fôl′sə·tē) *n. pl.* **·ties** **1** The quality of being false. **2** A false statement, thing, or appearance. See synonyms under ERROR.

Fal·staff (fô′staf, -stäf), **Sir John** A jovial, witty solider, fat, boastful, and mendacious, in Shakespeare's *Henry IV* and *The Merry Wives of Windsor.* **—Fal·staff′i·an.**

Fal·ster (fäl′sər) A Danish island in the Baltic Sea; 198 square miles.

falt·boat (fält′bōt′) *n.* A collapsible, kayaklike boat, seating one person, propelled by a double-bladed paddle; used chiefly on rivers: also *foldboat.* [<G *faltboot* folding boat]

fal·ter (fôl′tər) *v.i* **1** To be hesitant or uncertain; waver; give way. **2** To stumble; move unsteadily. **3** To speak haltingly; stammer. —*v.t.* **4** To utter haltingly. —*n.* A faltering hesitation; a trembling. [? <ON *faltrask* be encumbered] **—fal′ter·er** *n.* **—fal′ter·ing** *adj.* **—fal′ter·ing·ly** *adv.*

falx cer·e·bel·li (falks ser′ə·bel′ī) See FALCULA.

Fa·ma·gu·sta (fä′mä·go͞os′tä) A port of **Famagusta Bay,** an inlet of the Mediterranean in eastern Cyprus.

fame (fām) *n.* **1** Public or general reputation; renown. **2** *Obs.* Report; rumor. —*v.t.* **famed, fam·ing** **1** To speak of widely; celebrate. **2** To make famous. [<F <L *fama* report, reputation <*fari* speak]

Synonyms (noun): celebrity, credit, distinction, eminence, glory, honor, laurels, notoriety, renown, reputation, repute. *Fame* is the widely disseminated report of a person's character, deeds, or ability, and is oftenest used in the favorable sense. *Reputation* and *repute* are more limited than *fame,* and may be either good or bad. *Notoriety* is evil *repute* or a dishonorable counterfeit of *fame. Eminence* and *distinction* may result from rank, station, or character. *Celebrity* is limited in range; we speak of local *celebrity,* or world-wide *fame. Fame* in its best sense may be defined as the applause of numbers; *renown,* as such applause worthily won: we speak of the conqueror's *fame,* the patriot's *renown. Glory* and *honor* are of good import; *honor* may be given for qualities or acts that should not win it, but it is always given as for something good and worthy; we speak of an evil *fame,* but not of evil *honor; glory* has a more exalted and often a sacred sense. *Antonyms:* contempt, contumely, discredit, disgrace, dishonor, disrepute, humiliation, ignominy, infamy, oblivion, obscurity, shame.

Fa·meuse (fə·myo͞oz′, *Fr.* fä·mœz′) *n.* An early winter apple, striped with deep red, and having tender white flesh; also called *snow apple.* [<F, famous]

fa·mil′ial (fə·mil′yəl) *adj.* **1** Of, pertaining to, involving, or associated with the family. **2** *Genetics* Transmitted within the family, as certain hereditary diseases. [<L *familia* family]

fa·mil·iar (fə·mil′yər) *adj.* **1** Having close knowledge; well acquainted; thoroughly versed; followed by *with.* **2** Having the relation of an intimate or near friend; arising from or characterized by close acquaintance; not distant; informal. **3** Exercising undue intimacy; forward; intrusive. **4** Well known, as from habitual use or long acquaintance; common; frequent; customary. **5** Domesticated; attached: said of animals. See synonyms under COMMON, GENERAL, HABITUAL, USUAL. —*n.* **1** An intimate friend. **2** A person with whom one frequently associates. **3** A spirit supposed to attend and obey a sorcerer: also **familiar spirit.** **4** A servant of a prelate of the Roman Catholic Church, or the inquisition. [<L *familiaris* of the family <*familia* family] **—fa·mil′iar·ly** *adv.*

fa·mil·i·ar·i·ty (fə·mil′ē·ar′ə·tē, -mil′yar′-) *n. pl.* **·ties** **1** The state or condition of being familiar; intimacy; intimate knowledge or acquaintance, as with a subject. **2** Conduct implying familiar intimacy. **3** *Often pl.* Offensively familiar conduct. See synonym under ACQUAINTANCE, ASSOCIATION.

fa·mil·iar·ize (fə·mil′yə·rīz) *v.t.* **·ized, ·iz·ing** **1** To make (oneself or someone) accustomed or familiar. **2** To cause to be well known or familiar. **—fa·mil′iar·i·za′tion** *n.*

fam·i·lis·ter·y (fam′ə·lis′tər·ē) *n. pl.* **·ter·ies** **1** A communal dwelling. **2** A group of families living together in one building and sharing facilities. [<F *familistère* <*familie* family + *(phalan)stère* PHALANSTERY]

fam·i·ly (fam′ə·lē, fam′lē) *n. pl.* **·lies** **1** A group of persons, consisting of parents and their children. **2** The children as distinguished from the parents. **3** A group of persons forming a household, including servants, etc.; a household. **4** A succession of persons connected by blood, name, etc.; a house, line; clan, tribe; race. **5** Distinguished or ancient lineage with its traditions; descent. **6** *Biol.* A taxonomic category higher than a genus; for animals, family names end in *-idae,* for plants, in *-aceae.* **7** Any class or group of like or related things. **8** *Ling.* A grouping of languages, such as Indo-European, assumed from certain shared characteristics, to be descended from a common parent: often subdivided into *subfamily, branch,* and *group.* —*adj.* Of, belonging to, or suitable for a family. [<L *familia* family <*famulus* servant]

family circle The members of a family.

fam·i·ly-cir·cle (fam′ə·lē·sûr′kəl, fam′lē) *n.* The upper balcony in a theater, containing inexpensive seats.

family name A surname, as distinguished from a *personal* or *Christian name.*

family planning Control by means of contraceptive measures of the timing and number of births in a family.

family tree **1** A relational diagram of a family showing its ancestors and various branches of descendants. **2** The ancestors and descendants of a family, collectively.

fam·ine (fam′in) *n.* **1** A wide-spread scarcity of food; dearth. **2** A great scarcity of anything: a water *famine.* **3** Starvation. [<OF <L *fames* hunger]

famine fever Typhus.

fam·ish (fam′ish) *v.t.* & *v.i.* To suffer or die, or to cause to suffer or die, from lack of nourishment; starve. [Earlier *fame* <F *afamer;* refashioned after verbs in *-ish,* as *banish, finish,* etc.] **—fam′ish·ment** *n.*

fa·mous (fā′məs) *adj.* **1** Having fame or celebrity; renowned. **2** *Colloq.* Admirable, excellent. See synonyms under EMINENT, ILLUSTRIOUS. **—fa′mous·ly** *adv.* **—fa′mous·ness** *n.*

fam·u·lus (fam′yə·ləs) *n. pl.* **·li** (-lī) An assistant or servant; specifically, the assistant or amanuensis of a scholar or the familiar of a magician. [<L, servant]

fan[1] (fan) *n.* **1** An implement or device for agitating the air; specifically, a light, flat implement, often collapsible, spreading a wedge-shaped sheet from a stem or point, with a stock or handle. **2** One of various implements or machines for stirring up currents of air or doing something similar. **3** A kind of basket formerly used for winnowing grain, by tossing the grain in the air. **4** A winnowing machine. **5** A small sail or vane to keep the sails of a windmill at right angles to the wind. **6** A propeller; also, one of its blades. **7** Something that excites or stimulates. —*v.* **fanned, fan·ning** *v.t.* **1** To move or stir (air) with or as with a fan. **2** To direct air upon; cool or refresh with or as with a fan. **3** To move or stir to action; excite, as fire or rage. **4** To winnow (grain or chaff). **5** To spread like a fan. **6** In baseball, to cause (a batter) to strike out —*v.i.* **7** To spread out like a fan. **8** In baseball, to strike out. [OE *fann* <L *vannus* winnowing fan]

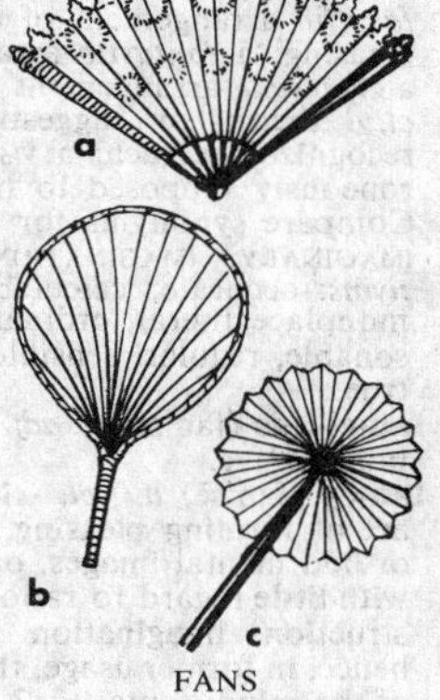

FANS
a. Folding. *b.* leaf. *c.* Collapsible.

fan[2] (fan) *n. Colloq.* **1** An enthusiastic devotee of any sport or diversion, as of baseball or of motion pictures; a fanatic. **2** An ardent admirer, usually of a public character, writer, artist, etc. [? <*the fancy* (see under FANCY)]

fa'n (fän) *adj. Scot.* Fallen.

Fan·ar (fan′ər) PHANAR.

fa·nat·ic (fə·nat′ik) *adj.* Actuated by extravagant or intemperate zeal; inordinately and unreasonably enthusiastic: also **fa·nat′i·cal.** —*n.* One who is motivated by intemperate zeal; one who is moved by a frenzy of enthusiasm; especially, a religious zealot. [<L *fanaticus* inspired <*fanum* a temple] **—fa·nat′i·cal·ly** *adv.*

fa·nat·i·cism (fə·nat′ə·siz′əm) *n.* The spirit or conduct of a fanatic; unreasonable zeal. Also **fa·nat′i·cal·ness.**
Synonyms: bigotry, credulity, intolerance, superstition. *Fanaticism* is extravagant or even frenzied zeal; *bigotry* is obstinate and unreasoning attachment to a cause or creed; *fanaticism* and *bigotry* usually include *intolerance*, which is unwillingness to tolerate beliefs or opinions contrary to one's own; *superstition* is ignorant and irrational religious belief. *Credulity* is not distinctively religious, but is a general readiness to believe without sufficient evidence, with a proneness to accept the marvelous. *Bigotry* has not the capacity to reason fairly, *fanaticism* has not the patience, *superstition* has not the knowledge and mental discipline, *intolerance* has not the disposition. *Bigotry, fanaticism,* and *superstition* are perversions of the religious sentiment; *credulity* and *intolerance* often accompany skepticism or atheism. Compare ENTHUSIASM, FRENZY. *Antonyms*: cynicism, free-thinking, indifference, latitudinarianism.
fa·nat·i·cize (fə·nat′ə·sīz) *v.t.* & *v.i.* **·cized, ·ciz·ing** To make or to become fanatical; act like a fanatic.
fan·ci·er (fan′sē·ər) *n.* **1** A breeder and seller of birds or animals. **2** One having a taste for special objects; an amateur. **3** A dreamer; visionary.
fan·ci·ful (fan′si·fəl) *adj.* **1** Proceeding from or produced by fancy; ideal; odd; curious in appearance. **2** Existing only in the fancy; unreal; visionary. **3** Whimsical. **— fan′ci·ful·ly** *adv.* **— fan′ci·ful·ness** *n.*
Synonyms: chimerical, fantastic, grotesque, imaginative, visionary. That is *fanciful* which is dictated or suggested by fancy independently of more serious considerations; the *fantastic* is the *fanciful* with the added elements of whimsicalness and extravagance. The *fanciful* swings away from the real or the ordinary lightly and pleasantly, the *fantastic* extravagantly, the *grotesque* ridiculously. A *fanciful* arrangement of objects is commonly pleasing, a *fantastic* arrangement is striking, a *grotesque* arrangement is laughable. A *fanciful* theory or suggestion may be clearly recognized as such; a *visionary* scheme is erroneously supposed to have a basis in fact. Compare synonyms for DREAM, IDEA, IDEAL, IMAGINARY, IMAGINATION, ROMANTIC. *Antonyms*: accurate, calculable, calculated, commonplace, literal, ordinary, prosaic, real, reasonable, regular, sensible, solid, sound, sure, true.
fan·ci·less (fan′si·lis) *adj.* Lacking fancy; unimaginative.
fan·cy (fan′sē) *n. pl.* **·cies 1** The power or act of forming pleasing, graceful, whimsical, or odd mental images, or of combining them with little regard to rational processes of construction; imagination in its lower form; hence, in former usage, the re-imaging faculty of the mind; fantasy. **2** Any product of the exercise of this faculty; an imaginary notion, representation, or image; whimsical notion; vagary. **3** A baseless or visionary idea; notion; illusion. **4** An unreasoned liking or fondness, resulting from caprice; preference. **5** A pet pursuit; an object sought after to gratify the taste or a whim without regard to utility; a hobby; fad. **6** Taste exhibited in production; artistic invention; design: The edifice showed a cultivated *fancy.* **7** *Obs.* A specter; phantom. **8** *Obs.* Love. **— the fancy** The votaries collectively of any special art, sport, or amusement. **—** *adj.* **·ci·er, ·ci·est 1** Adapted to please the fancy; ornamental; decorative: *fancy* embroidery. **2** Evolved from the fancy; imaginary; ideal. **3** Capricious; whimsical; fanciful. **4** In commerce, of higher grade than the average; choice; characterized by variety, excellence, or special request: *fancy* fruits. **5** Extravagant; exorbitant: *fancy* prices. **6** Selectively bred to a type, as an animal. **7** Performed with exceptional grace and skill: the *fancy* bowing of a violinist. **—** *v.t.* **·cied, ·cy·ing 1** To imagine; picture. **2** To take a fancy to; like. **3** To believe without proof or conviction; suppose. **4** To breed, as animals, for conventional points of symmetry or beauty. [Short for FANTASY]
Synonyms (noun): belief, caprice, conceit, conception, desire, humor, idea, image, imagination, inclination, liking, mood, predilection, supposition, vagary, whim. An intellectual *fancy* is a mental *image* or picture founded upon slight or whimsical association or resemblance; a *conceit* has less of the picturesque and more of the theoretic than a *fancy*. An intellectual *fancy* or *conceit* may be pleasing or amusing, but is never worth serious discussion. An emotional or personal *fancy* is a capricious *belief, idea,* or *liking* formed with slight reason or judgment, and liable to fade as lightly as it was formed. Compare synonyms for DREAM, IDEA, IMAGINATION, INCLINATION, THOUGHT[1], WHIM. *Antonyms*: actuality, certainty, fact, reality, truth, verity.
fancy ball A ball at which fancy dress is worn. Also **fan′cy-dress′ ball.**
fancy dress Masquerade costume. **— fan′cy-dress′** *adj.*
fan·cy-free (fan′sē·frē′) *adj.* Not in love.
fancy man *Slang* A man supported by a woman, especially by a prostitute.
fancy woman A mistress or a prostitute.
fan·cy·work (fan′sē·wûrk′) *n.* Embroidery, tatting, crocheting, lacework, etc.
fan·dan·go (fan·dang′gō) *n. pl.* **·gos 1** A Spanish dance in triple time, usually accompanied by castanets. **2** The music for this dance. **3** A dancing party or ball. [<Sp.]
fan delta An alluvial cone.
fane (fān) *n.* A sanctuary; temple. ◆ Homophones: *fain, feign.* [<L *fanum* temple]
fa·ne·ga (fä·nā′gä) *n.* A Spanish dry measure equal to a little more than 1 1/2 bushels, but variable in Latin-American countries. Also **fan·ga** (fäng′gä). [<Sp.]
fa·ne·ga·da (fä′nā·gä′thä) *n.* A Spanish unit of area, equal to 6.92 acres or 7,449 square feet.
Fan·euil Hall (fan′əl, fan′yəl) A public hall and market house built in Boston, Mass., by **Peter Faneuil,** 1700–43, a merchant. Called the "Cradle of American Liberty" because it was used by Revolutionary patriots.
fan·fare (fan′fâr′) *n.* A flourish, as of trumpets; a noisy parade or demonstration. [<F]
fan·fa·ron (fan′fə·ron) *n. Obs.* **1** A swaggering boaster; a bully. **2** A fanfare. [<F <Sp. *fanfarrón* <Arabic *farfār* talkative]
fan·fa·ron·ade (fan′fə·rə·nād′) *n.* A blustering, ranting, or vainglorious speech or style; a boastful or bullying manner; rodomontade. **—** *v.i.* **·ad·ed, ·ad·ing** To swagger; bluster. [<F <Sp. *fanfarronada* <*fanfarrón.* See FANFARON.]
fang (fang) *n.* **1** A long pointed tooth or tusk by which an animal seizes, holds, or tears its prey, as the canine tooth of a boar or dog. **2** One of the long, curved, hollow or grooved, usually erectile teeth with which a venomous serpent injects its poison into its victim. **3**

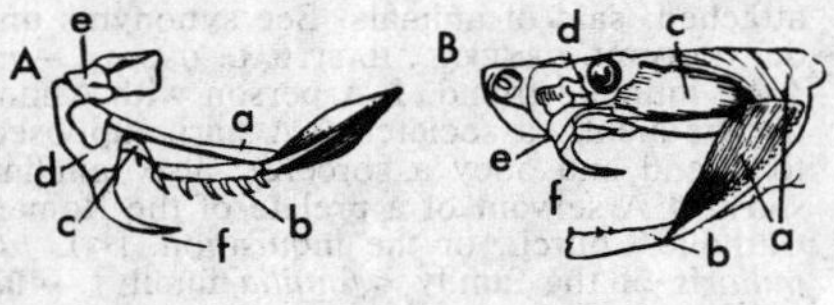

FANGS OF THE RATTLESNAKE
A. Fang and accompanying bones: *f.* fang; *a.* external pterygoid; *b.* internal pterygoid; *c.* palatal; *d.* superior maxillary; *e.* lacrimal. *B.* Muscles related to the venom gland and fang: *f.* fang; *a.* anterior temporal muscles; *b.* internal pterygoid; *c.* venom gland; *d.* the fang, half erected; *e.* point where the venom enters the channel of the fang.

One of various pointed or incurved objects, organs, or devices, especially for clutching or holding fast, as the root of a tooth or the claw or talon of a bird. **—** *v.t.* **1** *Obs.* To seize or take hold of. **2** To sink fangs into. [OE *fang* catching, seizing] **— fanged** (fangd) *adj.* **— fang′less** *adj.* **— fang′like′** *adj.*
fan·gle (fang′gəl) *n. Rare* A fashion; novelty: new fads and *fangles.* [<NEWFANGLED, incorrectly taken as *new* + *fangle*]
fan·ion (fan′yən) *n. Archaic* A small flag. [<OF, var. of *fanon.* See FANON.]
fan·jet (fan′jet′) *n.* A turbofan (def. 2).
fan·light (fan′līt′) *n.* **1** A fan window. **2** *Brit.* A transom.
fan mail Complimentary letters to public performers, as actors, musicians, and the like.
fan·nel (fan′əl) *n.* A fanon. [<Med. L *fanula,* dim. of *fano.* See FANON.]
fan·ner (fan′ər) *n.* **1** One who or that which fans. **2** A ventilating fan or fan blower.
Fan·ning Island (fan′ing) Headquarters of the Line Islands district of the Gilbert and Ellice Islands colony; 12 square miles.
fan·ny (fan′ē) *n. U.S. Slang* The buttocks.
Fan·ny (fan′ē) Diminutive of FRANCES.
fan·on (fan′ən) *n. Eccl.* **1** A maniple or napkin used by a celebrant at mass. **2** A cape worn only by the pope, as he presides at solemn pontifical mass. Also **fan·o** (fan′ō), **fan·um** (fan′əm). [<OF *fanon* <Med. L *fano, -onis* a banner, napkin <Gmc.]
fan palm Any palm with fan-shaped leaves; especially, the talipot palm of Ceylon and the Malabar Coast, having immense leaves; the palmetto of Florida; and the California or Washington fan palm *(Washingtonia filifera)*, occurring in California and Lower California.
fan·tail (fan′tāl′) *n.* **1** A variety of domestic pigeon having fanlike tail feathers. **2** An Australian or Oriental flycatcher (genus *Rhipidura*) having fanlike tail feathers. **3** A fan-shaped joint or mortise. **4** Any end or tail shaped like a fan. **5** Any of certain species of fancy-bred goldfish, having double anal and dorsal fins. **6** *Naut.* The overhanging stern of some vessels.

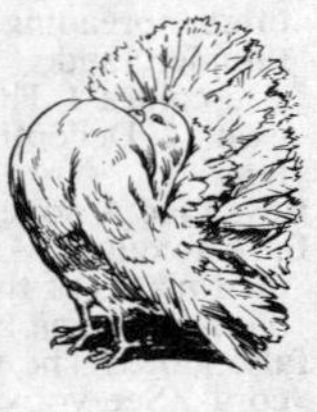

FANTAIL PIGEON

fan-tailed (fan′tāld′) *adj.* Having the tail feathers arranged like a fan or capable of expansion like a fan, as the flycatcher.
fan-tan (fan′tan′) *n.* **1** A Chinese gambling game, played with coins or other small objects, which the players cover, and then bet on what the remainder will be when the pile has been divided by four. **2** A game of cards played in sequence, the winner being the person who gets rid of his cards first. [<Chinese *fan t'an* repeated divisions]
fan·ta·si·a (fan·tā′zē·ə, -zhə, fan′tə·zē′ə) *n.* **1** A fanciful, irregular, fantastic composition, not observing strict musical forms. **2** A piece of orchestral music less formal than an overture; also, a prelude to an organ fugue. [<Ital., a fancy]
fan·ta·size (fan′tə·sīz) *v.* **·sized, ·siz·ing** *v.i.* **1** To imagine or daydream about fantastic events. **—** *v.t.* **2** To create in fantasy, as in daydreaming. **— fan′ta·sist** *n.*
fan·tasm (fan′taz·əm) *n.* **1** An imaginary appearance; a phantom. **2** A mental image; fancy. Also spelled *phantasm.* See synonyms under DELUSION. [<Gk. *phantasma.* Doublet of PHANTOM.]
fan·tas·ma·go·ri·a (fan·taz′mə·gôr′ē·ə, -gō′rē·ə) *n.* **1** A changing, incoherent series of apparitions or fantasms. **2** An exhibition of pictures projected on a screen and made to increase or diminish in size rapidly while continually in focus. Also **fan·tas′ma·go′ry:** also spelled *phantasmagoria.* [<NL <Gk. *phantasma* an apparition + prob. *agora* assembly, crowd] **— fan·tas′ma·go′ri·al, fan·tas′ma·gor′ic** (-gôr′ik, -gor′-) or **·i·cal** *adj.*
fan·tas·mal (fan·taz′məl) *adj.* Of or like a fantasm; unreal or illusive. Also **fan·tas′mic.**
fan·tast (fan′tast) *n.* **1** One who believes in or advocates a fantastic delusion as a true doctrine. **2** A dreamer or visionary. [<Med. L *phantasta* <Gk. *phantastēs* a boaster <*phantazein* boast]
fan·tas·tic (fan·tas′tik) *adj.* **1** Of an odd appearance; grotesque. **2** Capricious; whimsical: a *fantastic* imagination. **3** Of the nature of fantasy; fanciful; illusory. See synonyms under FANCIFUL, ODD, QUEER, ROMANTIC. **—** *n.* One who is fantastic in conduct or appearance: also *Obs.* **fan·tas′ti·co.** Also **fan·tas′ti·cal.** [<Med. L *fantasticus* <L *phantasticus* <Gk. *phantastikos* <*phantastēs.* See FANTAST.] **— fan·tas′ti·cal·ly** *adv.* **— fan·tas′ti·cal·ness** *n.*
fan·tas·ti·cal·i·ty (fan·tas′ti·kal′ə·tē) *n.* **1** The quality of being fantastic. **2** Anything which is fantastic or grotesque.
fan·ta·sy (fan′tə·sē, -zē) *n. pl.* **·sies 1** A fantastic notion or mental image; fancy. **2** A fantastic design, as in embroidery. **3** *Psychol.* The form of representation that brings before the mind a sequence of images serving to fulfil a need not gratified in the real world; a daydream. **4** *Music* A fantasia. **5** A capricious mood. See synonyms under

DREAM, IDEA, IMAGINATION. — *v.t.* **·sied, ·sy·ing** To imagine; conceive. Also spelled *phantasy.* [<F *fantasie* <L *phantasia* <Gk., appearance <*phainein* show]

Fan·tin-La·tour (fäṅ·taṅ′lȧ·to͝or′), **Henri,** 1836–1904, French painter.

fan·toc·ci·ni (fan′tə·chē′nē) *n. pl.* **1** Marionettes. **2** A puppet show. [<Ital. <*fantoccio* puppet <*fante* child]

fan·tom (fan′təm) See PHANTOM.

fan tracery *Archit.* Bar tracery, diverging like a fan to form a section of fan vaulting rising from a capital or corbel, as in Henry VII's chapel, Westminster.

fan vaulting *Archit.* A system of vaulting in which the ribs spread out like a fan: used in later English Gothic.

fan window *Archit.* A semicircular window containing a sash with bars radiating from the middle of its base.

fan·wort (fan′wûrt′) *n.* An American aquatic plant *(Cabomba caroliniana)* which occurs in the southern United States; one of the water-lily family: also called *fishgrass.*

far (fär) *adv.* **1** At a remote or distant point or place; so as to be a long way off: *far* distant. **2** To a great distance; so as to reach to a point a long way off; so as to occupy or cover an extent of time or space: How *far* did Caesar march? **3** To a great degree; by much; very greatly: *far* wiser than their ancestors. **4** From afar; from a long distance: a *far*-traveled guest. — **by far** In a great degree; by much. — *adj.* **far·ther** or **fur·ther, far·thest** or **fur·thest**: see FARTHER. **1** Situated at a great distance in space or time; being a long way off; remote: He went into a *far* country. **2** Extending widely or at length; reaching a long way. **3** Being the more distant of two: the *far* end of the garden. **4** Advanced; progressed, as in age. [OE *feor*]

far·ad (far′əd, -ad) *n. Electr.* The unit of capacitance; the capacitance of a condenser that retains one coulomb of charge with one volt difference of potential. [after Michael *Faraday*]

far·a·day (far′ə·dā) *n. Electr.* The quantity of electricity required in electrolysis to liberate one unit equivalent weight of an element, equal to 96,500 coulombs per gram equivalent. [after Michael *Faraday*]

Far·a·day (far′ə·dā), **Michael,** 1791–1867, English chemist and physicist; discovered electromagnetic induction.

fa·rad·ic (fə·rad′ik) *adj.* Pertaining to or caused by induced electric currents. Also **far·a·da·ic** (far′ə·dā′ik).

far·a·dism (far′ə·diz′əm) *n.* **1** The electricity of an induced current. **2** *Med.* The treatment of a nerve or muscle with a faradic current.

far·a·dize (far′ə·dīz) *v.t.* **·dized, ·diz·ing** To stimulate (a nerve, muscle, etc.) by faradic currents. — **far′a·di·za′tion** *n.* — **far′a·diz′er** *n.*

far·ad·me·ter (far′əd·mē′tər, -ad-) *n.* An instrument, usually graded in microfarads, for measuring the strength of an induced electric current.

far and away By a great deal; emphatically.

far·an·dine (far′ən·dīn) *n.* A fabric of silk mixed with hair or wool, used during the 17th century. [<F *ferrandine,* after Ferrand de Lyon, its inventor]

far·an·dole (far′ən·dōl, *Fr.* fȧ·räṅ·dôl′) *n.* A rapid dance in which the participants whirl in a circle, alternately facing in and out.

far and wide Everywhere; in every place. Also **far and near.**

far-a·way (fär′ə·wā′) *adj.* **1** Distant: a *far-away* town. **2** Absent-minded; abstracted.

farce (färs) *n.* **1** A short comedy with exaggerated effects and incidents. **2** A ridiculous proceeding; an absurd failure. — *v.t.* **farced, farc·ing 1** To fill out with witticisms, jibes, etc., as a play. **2** *Obs.* To fill with dressing; stuff, as a fowl. [<F, orig. stuffing <*farcer* stuff <L *farcire*] — **far·cial** (fär′shəl) *adj.*

far·ceur (fär·sœr′) *n.* One who writes or acts a farce; a jester; wag. Also **farc·er** (fär′sər). [<F]

far·ci·cal (fär′si·kəl) *adj.* Of, pertaining to, or of the nature of a farce; absurd. See synonyms under RIDICULOUS. — **far′ci·cal·ly** *adv.* — **far′ci·cal·ness, far′ci·cal′i·ty** *n.*

far·cy (fär′sē) *n.* A contagious disease, primarily of the horse, characterized by pustular eruptions; glanders. [Var. of obs. *farcin* <F <L *farcimimum,* a disease of horses]

far·cy-bud (fär′sē·bud′) *n.* A swollen gland, as in glanders.

far·del (fär′dəl) *n. Archaic* A bundle; pack; burden. [<OF, dim. of *farde* <Arabic *fardah* a bundle]

fare (fâr) *v.i.* **fared, far·ing 1** To be in a specified state; get on. **2** To turn out; happen. **3** To eat; be supplied with food. **4** *Archaic* To go; travel. — *n.* **1** Passage money. **2** A passenger carried for hire. **3** Food and drink; diet; eatables. See synonyms under FOOD. ◆ Homophone: *fair.* [OE *faran* go, travel]

Far East See under EAST.

fare·box (fâr′boks′) *n.* A box into which passengers boarding a street car or bus deposit their fares.

far·er (fâr′ər) *n.* One who travels: most commonly in compounds, as *wayfarer,* etc.

fare·well (fâr′wel′) *n.* **1** A parting salutation; a good-by; adieu. **2** The act of taking leave; parting. — *inter.* (fâr′wel′) May you fare well; may you prosper: now used only at parting. — *adj.* Parting; closing; valedictory. — *v.t. Poetic* To take leave of. — **to a fare-you-well** *U.S. Colloq.* Completely; with finality: beaten *to a fare-you-well*: also **to a fare-thee-well.** [Earlier *fare well.* See FARE.]

Synonyms (noun): adieu, congé, good-by, leave-taking, valediction, valedictory. *Good-by* is the homely and hearty parting salutation, *farewell* the formal, English word at parting. *Adieu,* from the French, is still more ceremonious than *farewell*; *congé,* also from the French, is commonly contemptuous or supercilious, and equivalent to dismissal. *Valediction* is a learned word never in popular use. A *valedictory* is a public farewell to a company or assembly.

Farewell, Cape The most southerly point of Greenland.

far-fetched (fär′fecht′) *adj.* **1** Brought in only by laborious or strained effort. **2** Neither natural nor obvious.

far-flung (fär′flung′) *adj.* Having great range; extending over great distances.

Far·go (fär′gō) A city on the Red River in SE North Dakota.

fa·ri·na (fə·rē′nə) *n.* **1** A meal or flour obtained chiefly from cereals, nuts, potatoes, or Indian corn, and used as a breakfast food. **2** Starch. **3** A mealy powder found on certain insects. [<L <*far* spelt]

Fa·ri·na (fä·rē′nä), **Salvatore,** 1846–1918, Italian novelist.

far·i·na·ceous (far′ə·nā′shəs) *adj.* **1** Consisting or made of farina. **2** Containing or yielding starch. **3** Mealy.

far·i·nose (far′ə·nōs) *adj.* **1** Yielding farina: *farinose* plants. **2** *Bot.* Covered with or as if with a white meal-like powder, as the under side of the leaves of certain primroses.

far·kle·ber·ry (fär′kəl·ber′ē) *n. pl.* **·ries** A shrub or small tree *(Vaccinium arboreum)* of the heath family, with globose black berries. [Origin uncertain]

farl (färl) *n. Scot.* A fourth part, as of a cake. Also **farle.**

Far·ley (fär′lē), **James Aloysius,** born 1888, U.S. political leader.

farm (färm) *n.* **1** A tract of land forming a single property and devoted to agriculture, stock-raising, dairying, or some allied activity. **2** A tract of water used for the cultivation of marine life: an oyster *farm.* **3** *Obs.* **a** The system of farming out revenues or taxes. **b** A fixed annual sum paid as a rent or tax. **4** In baseball, a minor-league club used by a major-league club for training its recruits. — *v.t.* **1** To cultivate (land). **2** To take a lease of, as the use of a business or the collection of taxes, for a fixed rental, retaining the profits. **3** To let at a fixed rental, as lands, collection of taxes, etc.: usually with *out*: to *farm* out taxes. **4** To let out the services of (a person) for hire. **5** To agree to maintain or care for at a fixed price, as paupers. **6** To arrange for (work) to be performed by persons or a firm not in the main organization; subcontract: with *out.* **7** In baseball, to place (a player) with a minor-league team for training: often with *out.* — *v.i.* **8** To practice farming; be a farmer. [<F *ferme* <Med. L *firma* a fixed payment <L *firmare* fix, settle <*firmus* firm]

Far·man (fär·mäṅ′), **Henri,** 1874?–1934, French airplane manufacturer and pioneer aviator.

Farm Bureau A local organization of farmers in the United States, forming a unit in the **American Farm Bureau Federation,** dealing with farm problems.

farm·er (fär′mər) *n.* **1** One who follows the occupation of farming; an agriculturist. **2** One who collects revenues for a percentage or commission.

Far·mer (fär′mər), **Fannie Merritt,** 1857–1915, U.S. cookery expert.

farm·er·ette (fär′mə·ret′) *n. Colloq.* A woman or girl who farms.

farmer general *pl.* **farmers general** A member of a privileged class in France before the revolution of 1789, who farmed or leased the public revenues. — **farm′er-gen′er·al·ship** *n.*

Farm·er-La·bor party (fär′mər·lā′bər) A minor U.S. political party, 1919–23: active since 1923 in Minnesota.

farm·er·y (fär′mər·ē) *n. Brit.* The buildings, yards, etc., of a farm.

farm·hand (färm′hand′) *n.* One who works for wages on a farm. Also **farm laborer.**

farm·house (färm′hous′) *n.* The homestead on a farm, commonly occupied by the farmer's family.

farm·ing (fär′ming) *n.* The act of one who farms; the management of or labor on a farm; agriculture. See synonyms under AGRICULTURE. — *adj.* Engaged in, suitable for, or used for, agriculture: a *farming* region, *farming* implements.

farm·stead (färm′sted) *n.* A farm and the buildings on it. Also **farm′stead·ing.**

farm·yard (färm′yärd′) *n.* A space surrounded by farm buildings, and enclosed for confining stock, etc.

Far·ne·se (fär·nā′sā) The name of an old Italian family. — **Alessandro** See Paul III. — **Alessandro,** 1545–92, general; governor of the Netherlands.

far·ne·sol (fär′nə·sōl, -sol) *n. Chem.* An alcohol with a delicate fragrance, $C_{15}H_{25}O$, extracted from the flowers of the acacia and from various essential oils: used in perfumery. [<NL *(Acacia) farnesiana,* a species of acacia + -OL[1]]

far·o (fâr′ō) *n.* A game of cards in which the players bet against the dealer as to the order in which certain cards will appear. [alter. of *Pharaoh,* ? from a picture originally on one of the cards]

Fa·ro (fä′ro͞o) The southernmost city of Portugal, capital of Algarve province.

faro bank 1 A house or establishment for playing faro. **2** The proprietor's fund risked in the game.

Far·oe Islands (fâr′ō) See FAEROE ISLANDS.

Far·o·ese (fâr′ō·ēz′, -ēs′) *n.* **1** A native or the natives of the Faeroe Islands. **2** The North Germanic language spoken in these islands: also **Far′o·ish.**

far-off (fär′ôf′, -of′) *adj.* Situated at a great distance; remote.

fa·rouche (fȧ·ro͞osh′) *adj. French* **1** Fierce. **2** Sullen. **3** Shy.

Fa·rouk I (fə·ro͞ok′), 1920–1965, king of Egypt 1936–52; abdicated. Also *Faruk.*

far-out (fär′out′) *adj.* **far·ther-out, far·thest-out** *Slang* Advanced, unconventional, or avant-garde.

far-point (fär′point′) *n. Physiol.* The farthest point at which the eye, under conditions of relaxation, can see objects distinctly: greatest in normal and hypermetropic vision.

Far·quhar (fär′kwər, -kər), **George,** 1678–1707, British dramatist.

far·ra·go (fə·rā′gō, -rä′-) *n. pl.* **·goes** A confused mixture; medley: a *farrago* of nonsense. [<L, salad, mixture <*far* spelt] — **far·rag·i·nous** (fə·raj′ə·nəs) *adj.*

Far·ra·gut (far′ə·gət), **David Glasgow,** 1801–1870, U.S. naval officer; Union admiral in the Civil War.

Far·rar (fə·rär′), **Geraldine,** 1882–1967, U.S. operatic soprano.

far-reach·ing (fär′rē′ching) *adj.* **1** Producing effects that extend far; having profound consequences: a *far-reaching* decision. **2** Reaching far either in time or in space.

Far·rell (far′əl), **James Thomas,** 1904–1979, U. S. novelist.

far·ri·er (far′ē·ər) *n. Brit.* **1** One who shoes horses. **2** A veterinary surgeon. [<OF *ferrier* <L *ferrarius* <*ferrum* iron]

far·ri·er·y (far′ē·ə·rē) *n. pl.* **·er·ies** The business or shop of a farrier.

far·row[1] (far′ō) *n.* **1** A litter of pigs. **2** *Obs.* A little pig. —*v.t.* & *v.i.* To give birth to (young): said of swine. [OE *fearh* young pig]

far·row[2] (far′ō) *adj.* Not producing young during a given year, as a cow. [Cf. Flemish *varvekoe* cow no longer fertile]

Fars (färs) A former province of southern Iran on the Persian Gulf, coextensive with ancient Persis. Also **Far·si·stan** (fär′sē·stän′).

Far·sa·la (fär′sä·lä) See PHARSALA.

far–see·ing (fär′sē′ing) *adj.* **1** Seeing afar. **2** Having foresight.

far–sight·ed (fär′sī′tid) *adj.* **1** Able to see things at a distance more clearly than things near at hand; hypermetropic. **2** Far–seeing; prescient, as a statesman. —**far′–sight′ed·ly** *adv.* —**far′–sight′ed·ness** *n.*

fart (färt) *n.* An anal emission of intestinal gases, especially when audible: now a vulgar term. [<*v.*] —*v.i.* To emit gas in such a way. [ME *farten.* Cf. OHG *ferzan*]

far·ther (fär′thər) Comparative of FAR. —*adj.* More distant in space; more advanced. —*adv.* **1** To or at a more forward or distant point in space. **2** At a more forward stage; more fully or completely. [Var. of FURTHER; infl. in form by *far*]

◆ **farther, further** *Farther* is used only with reference to literal, spatial distance; *further* is employed in figurative senses involving time, degree, or quantity: *further* in the future; *further* (=additional) damage. Because it is often hard to tell whether the meaning is spatial or figurative, *further* is also used where some might prefer *farther*: We drove no *further* that day.

Farther India See INDOCHINA.

far·ther·most (fär′thər·mōst′) *adj.* Farthest.

far·thest (fär′thist) Superlative of FAR. —*adj.* & *adv.* Most distant or advanced in space. [Var. of FURTHEST; infl. by *far*]

far·thing (fär′thing) *n.* **1** One fourth of an English penny, at par value, about one half of a cent. **2** A small trifle. [OE *feorthing* < *feortha* a fourth]

far·thin·gale (fär′thing·gāl) *n.* A woman's hoop skirt of the 16th and 17th centuries: so called because distended by hoops of green osier, willow, or rattan. [<OF *verdugale,* alter. of Sp. *verdugado* <*verdugo* a rod, hoop]

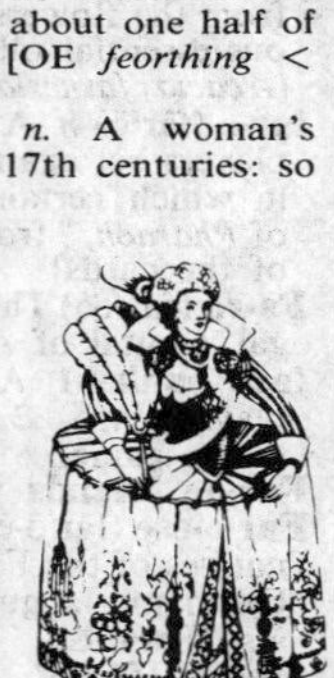
FARTHINGALE

Faruk (fə·ro͝ok′) See FAROUK.

Fas (fäs) The Arabic name for FEZ.

fas·ces (fas′ēz) *n. pl.* In ancient Rome, a bundle of rods enclosing an ax, borne by lictors before consuls and other magistrates as a symbol of power. [<L] —**fas·ci·al** (fash′ē·əl) *adj.*

fas·ci·a (fash′ē·ə) *n. pl.* **·ci·ae** (-i.ē) **1** *Anat.* Condensed connective tissue forming sheets or layers, for the investment of organs or the insertion of muscles. **2** *Archit.* A flat member or broad volute; a jutting brick course in any story of a building except the uppermost. See illustration under ENTABLATURE. **3** Something that binds together, as a fillet; a band. **4** A bandage. **5** A distinct band of color, as in certain plants and animals. [<L, a band] —**fas′·ci·al** *adj.*

fas·ci·ate (fash′ē·āt) *adj.* **1** Bound with a fascia or belt. **2** Characterized by fasciation. **3** Marked with transverse bands: said of insects. Also **fas′ci·at′ed.** [<L *fasciatus* <*fascia* a band] —**fas′ci·ate′ly** *adv.*

fas·ci·a·tion (fash′ē·ā′shən) *n.* **1** The act of securing or fastening by fasciae. **2** The state of being fasciate or of bearing fasciate marking. **3** *Bot.* A flat, ribbonlike malformation in plants, sometimes due to an accumulated surplus of food materials.

fas·ci·cle (fas′i·kəl) *n.* **1** A small collection; bundle; cluster; group. **2** *Anat.* A bundle of fibers in the body; a fasciculus. **3** *Bot.* A cluster or bundle, as of leaves, flowers, or stalks, which proceed from a common point. **4** A number of sheets of printed work bound together. [<L *fasciculus,* dim. of *fascia* a bundle]

fas·cic·u·lar (fə·sik′yə·lər) *adj.* Of or pertaining to a fascicle.

fas·cic·u·late (fə·sik′yə·lit) *adj.* Composed of or growing in bundles. Also **fas′ci·cled, fas·cic′u·lat′ed** —**fas·cic′u·late′ly** *adv.* —**fas·cic′·u·la′tion** *n.*

fas·cic·u·lus (fə·sik′yə·ləs) *n. pl.* **·li** (-lī) A fascicle; especially, a bundle of nerve fibers.

fas·ci·nate (fas′ə·nāt) *v.* **·nat·ed, ·nat·ing** *v.t.* **1** To attract irresistibly, as by beauty or other qualities; captivate. **2** To hold spellbound, as by terror or awe. **3** *Obs.* To bewitch. —*v.i.* **4** To be fascinating. See synonyms under CHARM. [<L *fascinatus,* pp. of *fascinare* charm <*fascinum* a spell] —**fas′ci·nat′ing** *adj.* —**fas′ci·nat′ing·ly** *adv.*

fas·ci·na·tion (fas′ə·nā′shən) *n.* **1** The act of fascinating. **2** The state of being fascinated. **3** Enchantment; charm.

fas·ci·na·tor (fas′ə·nā′tər) *n.* **1** A person who fascinates. **2** A covering for the head of silk, lace, or crocheted net worn by women.

fas·cine (fas·ēn′, fə·sēn′) *n.* A bundle of sticks tied together and used in building earthworks and fortifications, filling ditches, etc. [<F <L *fascina* <*fascis* bundle]

fas·cism (fash′iz·əm) *n.* Any authoritarian, antidemocratic, anti–communist system of government in which economic control by the state, militaristic nationalism, propaganda, and the crushing of opposition by means of secret police emphasize the supremacy of the state over the individual. [<Ital. *fascismo* < *fascio* political club <L *fascis* a bundle] —**fas′cist** *n.* —**fa·scis′tic** *adj.* —**fa·scis′ti·cal·ly** *adv.*

Fas·cism (fash′iz·əm) *n.* The system of one–party government, developed by the Fascisti in Italy, which exercised a centralized autocratic control over the activities of all individuals, especially through the economic agency of state corporations.

Fas·cist (fash′ist) *n.* One of the Fascisti.

Fa·scis·ti (fə·shis′tē, *Ital.* fä·shē′stē) *n. pl. of* **Fa·scis′ta** The members of a totalitarian, syndicalist society in Italy, formed in 1919 under Benito Mussolini to oppose socialism and communism: in control of the government, 1922–43. [<Ital. <*fascio* a political club; meaning infl. by L *fasces* a bundle of rods. See FASCES.] —**Fas′cism,** *Italian* **Fa·scis·mo** (fä·shēs′mō) *n.*

fash (fash) *v.t.* & *v.i. Scot.* To worry; fret: to *fash* one's wits. —*n.* Worry; annoyance; vexation.

fash·ion (fash′ən) *n.* **1** The prevailing mode, especially in dress; the usage of polite society. **2** Manner of doing a thing; method; way. **3** The make or shape of a thing; external appearance; form. **4** Fashionable people, collectively. **5** Common practice or custom; usage. **6** A thing that is fashionable. See synonyms under AIR, CUSTOM, HABIT. —**after a fashion** In a way; not thoroughly, well, or enthusiastically: also **in a fashion.** —*v.t.* **1** To give shape or form to; frame; mold; make. **2** To conform; accommodate; fit. See synonyms under ADAPT, MAKE. [<AF *fachon,* var. of OF *façon* <L *factio, -onis.* Doublet of FACTION.]

fash·ion·a·ble (fash′ən·ə·bəl) *adj.* **1** Conforming to the current edicts of fashion. **2** Established and approved by the prevailing custom or polite usage. **3** Of, pertaining to, or like persons of fashion. —*n.* A person of fashion. —**fash′ion·a·ble·ness** *n.* —**fash′ion·a·bly** *adv.*

fash·ioned (fash′ənd) *adj.* **1** Made; shaped; formed: carefully *fashioned.* **2** Of a certain style or fashion: usually compounded, as old–*fashioned.*

fash·ion·er (fash′ən·ər) *n.* One who forms, molds, or puts together anything, according to a pattern or model.

fash·ion·mon·ger (fash′ən·mung′gər, -mong′-) *n.* **1** One whose life is devoted to following and spreading modes and fashions. **2** An exquisite; a dandy. —**fash′ion·mon′ger·ing, fash′·ion·mon′ging** *adj.* & *n.*

fashion plate **1** A picture representing the prevailing fashions in wearing apparel. **2** *Colloq.* One whose attire is perfect, according to the current mode.

Fa·sho·da (fə·shō′də) A town in south central Sudan, on the White Nile; scene of an encounter that led to an Anglo–French diplomatic crisis, the **Fashoda Incident** (1898): modern *Kodok.*

fasht (fasht) *Scot.* Troubled; wearied.

fast[1] (fast, fäst) *adj.* **1** Firm in place; not easily moved. **2** Firmly secured or bound. **3** Constant; steadfast. **4** Unfadable: said of colors. **5** Resistant: *acid–fast.* **6** Sound or deep, as sleep. **7** Acting or moving quickly; swift. **8** Performed quickly: *fast* work. **9** Adapted to, or suitable for, quick movement: a *fast* track. **10** Requiring rapidity of action or motion: a *fast* schedule. **11** Indicating a time in advance of the true time: The clock is *fast.* **12** Given to dissipation or moral laxity: *fast* living. **13** *Phot.* Intended for short exposure, as a high–velocity shutter or a highly sensitive film. —*adv.* **1** Firmly; fixedly; securely. **2** Soundly: *fast* asleep. **3** Quickly; rapidly; swiftly. **4** In quick succession: His thoughts came *fast.* **5** Dissipatedly; recklessly: to live *fast.* **6** *Archaic* Near: *fast* by. —*n.* **1** Something which is firm or fixed, as shore ice. **2** A mooring line. [OE *fæst*]

fast[2] (fast, fäst) *v.i.* **1** To abstain from food. **2** To go without food, wholly or in part, as in observance of a religious duty. —*n.* **1** Abstinence from food, partial or total, or from prescribed kinds of food, particularly as a religious duty. **2** A period prescribed for religious fasting and other observances: opposed to *feast.* [OE *fæstan*]

fast and loose Originally, a cheating game; hence, **to play fast and loose,** to act in a tricky or untrustworthy fashion.

fast·back (fast′bak′, fäst′-) *n.* **1** An automobile's continuous, downward–sloping roof from windshield to rear bumper. **2** An automobile having such a design.

fast day A day set apart for religious fasting appointed by civil or ecclesiastical authority.

fast·en (fas′ən, fäs′-) *v.t.* **1** To attach or secure to something else; connect. **2** To make fast; secure: to *fasten* a door. **3** To direct, as attention or the eyes, steadily. **4** To cause to cling or be attributed: to *fasten* blame. —*v.i.* **5** To take fast hold; cling: usually with *on.* **6** To become firm or attached. See synonyms under BIND. [OE *fæstnian* <*fæst* fixed] —**fast′en·er** *n.*

fast·en·ing (fas′ən·ing, fäs′-) *n.* **1** The act of making fast. **2** That which fastens, as a bolt. See synonyms under LOCK.

fast–food (fast′fo͞od′) *adj.* Serving quickly prepared foods, such as hamburgers, frankfurters, french–fried potatoes, etc.

fas·tid·i·ous (fas·tid′ē·əs) *adj.* Hard to please; overnice; squeamish. See synonyms under SQUEAMISH. [<L *fastidiosus* <*fastidium* disgust] —**fas·tid′i·ous·ly** *adv.* —**fas·tid′i·ous·ness** *n.*

fas·tig·i·ate (fas·tij′ē·it, -āt) *adj.* **1** Tapering toward a point. **2** *Zool.* Forming a conical bundle. **3** *Bot.* Nearly parallel and pointing upward, as the branches of a Lombardy poplar. [<L *fastigium* top + -ATE[1]]

fast·ness (fast′nis, fäst′-) *n.* **1** A fortress; stronghold. **2** The state of being firm or fixed; security. **3** Rapidity. **4** Dissipation. See synonyms under FORTIFICATION.

fat (fat) *adj.* **fat·ter, fat·test** **1** Having much or superfluous flesh; corpulent; obese. **2** Containing much oil, grease, etc. **3** Broad: said of a ship's quarter, of type bodies, etc. **4** *Printing* Profitable, because containing a large proportion of open space, illustrations, etc.: said of type matter or copy for it: also spelled *phat.* **5** Stupid; sluggish; dull. **6** Prosperous; thriving; flourishing. **7** Rich in products or in profits; rewarding: *fat* lands, a *fat* office. **8** Resinous; as *fat* wood. **9** Well–filled: a *fat* larder. **10** Plump, well–nourished, and healthy, as cattle. See synonyms under CORPULENT. —*n.* **1** *Biochem.* A gray to white, greasy, easily melted compound contained in certain specialized cells of plants and animals, and forming an important food reserve as well as a source of hormones, vitamins, and other products essential in metabolism. **2** The richest or most desirable part of anything: the *fat* of the land. **3** *Chem.* Any of various compounds of carbon, oxygen, and hydrogen which are glycerol esters of certain acids, as stearic, palmitic, etc.; they include waxes, lipids, and sterols, are insoluble in water, and in the pure state are generally colorless, odor-

less, and tasteless. — **the fat is in the fire** The mischief is done. — *v.t.* & *v.i.* **fat·ted, fat·ting** To fatten. [OE *fæt*] — **fat′ly** *adv.* — **fat′ness** *n.*

fa·tal (fāt′l) *adj.* **1** Bringing or connected with death or ruin; destructive; deadly. **2** Portentous; ominous. **3** Fraught with or determining fate or destiny; fateful. **4** *Obs.* That must be; inevitable. [<L *fatalis* <*fatum* FATE]

fa·tal·ism (fā′təl·iz′əm) *n.* **1** *Philos.* The doctrine that every event is predetermined by fate and inevitable. **2** A disposition to accept every event as preordained.

fa·tal·ist (fā′təl·ist) *n.* A believer in fatalism. — **fa′tal·is′tic** *adj.* — **fa′tal·is′ti·cal·ly** *adv.*

fa·tal·i·ty (fā·tal′ə·tē, fə-) *n. pl.* **·ties 1** A state of being fated. **2** Destiny; a decree of fate. **3** A disastrous or fatal event; death. **4** Tendency to danger or disaster. See synonyms under NECESSITY.

fa·tal·ly (fā′təl·ē) *adv.* **1** In a disastrous manner; ruinously; mortally. **2** According to the decrees of fate.

fa·ta mor·ga·na (fä′tə môr·gä′nə) A mirage, especially as observed on the coast of Sicily, poetically attributed to the fairy, **Fata Morgana.** See MORGAN LE FAY.

fat·back (fat′bak′) *n.* **1** The menhaden. **2** The American striped mullet. **3** Unsmoked salt pork.

fat·bird (fat′bûrd′) *n.* **1** The pectoral sandpiper (*Pisobia melanota*). **2** The guacharo.

fat–body (fat′bod′ē) *n. Entomol.* The tissue of oily cells closely associated with the nutritive and metabolic functions of insects.

fat cat *U.S. Slang* A wealthy individual who is considered a potential source for large political campaign contributions.

fat–cell (fat′sel′) *n. Biol.* One of a class of nucleated cells filled with fatty matter. See illustration under HAIR.

fat chance *U.S. Slang* Not much chance.

fate (fāt) *n.* **1** Predetermined and inevitable necessity; that power which is thought to determine one's future, success or failure, etc. **2** Destiny; fortune; lot. **3** Evil destiny; doom; destruction; death. **4** Outcome; final result. See synonyms under NECESSITY. — *v.t.* **fat·ed, fat·ing** To predestine: obsolete except in passive. [<L *fatum,* orig. neut. sing. of *fatus,* pp. of *fari* speak]

fat·ed (fā′tid) *adj.* Determined by fate; destined; doomed.

fate·ful (fāt′fəl) *adj.* **1** Fraught with fate. **2** Fatal. **3** Controlled by fate. — **fate′ful·ly** *adv.* — **fate′ful·ness** *n.*

Fates (fāts) In Greek mythology, three goddesses who control human destiny: Clotho spins the thread of life, Lachesis decides its length, and Atropos severs it: identified with the Roman *Parcae*: also *Destinies.*

fat·head (fat′hed′) *n. U.S. Slang* A dullard; dunce. — **fat′–head′ed** *adj.*

fa·ther (fä′thər) *n.* **1** The male human parent. **2** Any male ancestor; forefather. **3** A patriarch; an aged and reverend man or honored official. **4 a** In the Roman Catholic and, sometimes, in the Anglican Church, a priest: often used as a title and capitalized when preceding a name. **b** A church dignitary, as a bishop or abbot. **5** *Eccl.* Any one of the early historical or doctrinal writers of the Christian Church. **6** An author; founder. **7** *Brit.* The oldest member of a class or body; doyen. **8** One who bears a paternal relationship toward another. **9** A member of the ancient Roman Senate. **10** *pl.* The chiefs of a city or assembly. — *v.t.* **1** To beget as a father. **2** To found, create, or make. **3** To acknowledge as one's offspring. **4** To act as a father to. **5** To take or accept the responsibility of. [OE *fæder*] — **fa′ther·like′** *adj.* & *adv.*

Fa·ther (fä′thər) *n.* The Deity; God; the first person in the Trinity.

father confessor A priest of the Roman Catholic Church or of any other church to whom the members confess their faults and sins; hence, any one in whom one confides.

fa·ther·hood (fä′thər·hŏŏd) *n.* The state of being a father.

fa·ther–in–law (fä′thər·in·lô′) *n. pl.* **fa·thers–in–law** The father of one's husband or wife.

fa·ther·land (fä′thər·land′) *n.* The land of one's birth.

fa·ther·less (fä′thər·lis) *adj.* Not having a living father.

father–long–legs (fä′thər·lông′legz′, -long′-) *n.* **1** A daddy–long–legs. **2** The crane fly.

fa·ther·ly (fä′thər·lē) *adj.* **1** Of, pertaining to, or like a father. **2** Manifesting the affection of a father; paternal. — **fa′ther·li·ness** *n.*

Father of History Herodotus.

Father of Medicine Hippocrates.

Father of the Constitution James Madison.

Father's Day A memorial day, observed in honor of fathers, on the third Sunday in June.

Fathers of the Church The teachers and defenders of Christianity during its first seven centuries.

fath·om (fath′əm) *n. pl.* **·oms** or **·om** A measure of length, 6 feet, or 1.829 meters: used principally in marine and mining measurements. — *v.t.* **1** To find the depth of; sound. **2** To get to the bottom of; understand; interpret. [OE *fæthm* the span of two arms outstretched] — **fath′om·a·ble** *adj.*

fa·thom·e·ter (fə·thom′ə·tər) *n.* A device for registering ocean depths by measuring the time required for the transmission and reflection of sound waves.

fath·om·less (fath′əm·lis) *adj.* Unfathomable.

fa·tid·ic (fə·tid′ik) *adj.* Able to prophesy; oracular. Also **fa·tid′i·cal.** [<L *fatidicus* <*fatum* FATE + *dicere* speak]

fat·i·ga·ble (fat′ə·gə·bəl) *adj.* Capable of causing or experiencing fatigue; tiring; wearying.

fat·i·gate (fat′ə·gāt) *adj. Obs.* Fatigued; exhausted. [<L *fatigatus,* pp. of *fatigare* tire]

fa·tigue (fə·tēg′) *n.* **1** Exhaustion of strength by toil; weariness. **2** Wearing toil. **3** *Physiol.* **a** A condition of lessened activity of an organism or any of its parts, resulting from prolonged exertion. **b** A diminished susceptibility to stimulation of the central nervous system, affecting primarily the junction between nerve and muscle fibers. **4** *Metall.* The failure of metals under prolonged or repeated stress, characterized by local deformation of structure. **5** Fatigue duty. **6** *pl.* Strong, durable clothes worn on fatigue duty. — *v.t.* & *v.i.* **·tigued, ·ti·guing** To weary; tire out. [<F <*fatiguer* tire <L *fatigare*]

fatigue duty Common labor done by soldiers.

Fat·i·ma (fat′i·mə, fə·tē′mə), 606?–632, the only daughter of Mohammed.

Fat·i·ma (fat′i·mə, fə·tē′mə) The seventh wife and widow of Bluebeard.

Fát·i·ma (fat′ē·mə) A village in central Portugal, a Roman Catholic pilgrimage center since 1917.

Fat·i·mid (fat′i·mid) *n.* **1** A descendant of Fatima, daughter of Mohammed. **2** One of a North African Arab dynasty (909–1171). — *adj.* **1** Pertaining to or descended from Fatima. **2** Of or pertaining to the Fatimid dynasty. Also **Fat′i·mite** (-mīt).

fat·ling (fat′ling) *adj.* Fat; plump. — *n.* A young animal fattened for slaughter.

Fat·shan (fät′shän′) A former name for NAMHOI. Also **Fa·chan** (fä′shän′).

fat–sol·u·ble (fat′sol′yə·bəl) *adj. Biochem.* That may be dissolved in fat, as certain vitamins.

fat·ten (fat′n) *v.* **fat·tened, fat·ten·ing** *v.t.* **1** To make fat or plump. **2** To make (land) fertile or productive. **3** To make rich or richer. — *v.i.* **4** To become fat. — **fat′ten·er** *n.*

fat·tish (fat′ish) *adj.* Somewhat fat. — **fat′tish·ness** *n.*

fat·trels (fat′rəlz) *n. pl. Scot.* The ends of a ribbon; gathers in dressmaking.

fat·ty (fat′ē) *adj.* **fat·ti·er, fat·ti·est** Fat; unctuous. — **fat′ti·ly** *adv.* — **fat′ti·ness** *n.*

fatty acid *Chem.* A derivative of the paraffin series formed by oxidizing one of the monatomic alcohols. The physical characteristics of the higher complex fatty acids, as palmitic and stearic acids, give the name to the group.

fatty degeneration *Pathol.* A condition in which the efficient cells in an organ are enveloped in or replaced by fat.

fa·tu·i·ty (fə·tōō′ə·tē, -tyōō′-) *n.* **1** Obstinate or conceited folly. **2** Imbecility; idiocy; feeble–mindedness. [<F *fatuité* <L *fatuitas, -tatis* <*fatuus* foolish] — **fa·tu′i·tous** *adj.*

fat·u·oid (fach′ōō·oid) *n.* A species of wild oat (*Avena fatua*) resembling the cultivated variety; it is frequently a troublesome weed.

fat·u·ous (fach′ōō·əs) *adj.* **1** Stubbornly blind or foolish; idiotic. **2** Baseless; illusory, like the will–o'–the–wisp. [<L *fatuus* foolish] — **fat′u·ous·ly** *adv.* — **fat′u·ous·ness** *n.*

fat–witt·ed (fat′wit′id) *adj.* Of a dull wit; stupid.

fau·bourg (fō′bŏŏrg, *Fr.* fō·bōōr′) *n.* A suburb; originally, a quarter of a city outside the old wall. [<F]

fau·cal (fô′kəl) *adj. Anat.* Of or pertaining to the fauces; produced in the fauces; deeply guttural. Also **fau·cial** (fô′shəl).

fau·ces (fô′sēz) *n. pl. Anat.* The parts bordering on the opening between the back of the mouth and the pharynx. [<L]

fau·cet (fô′sit) *n.* A spout fitted with a valve, for drawing liquids through a pipe. [<OF *fausset,* prob. <*fausser* break into, damage <L *falsare* <*falsus* FALSE]

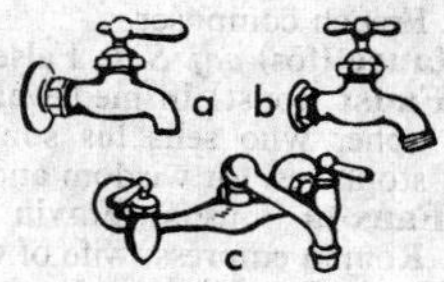

TYPES OF FAUCETS
a. Sink. *b.* Hose. *c.* Mixing.

faugh (fô) *interj.* An exclamation of disgust, contempt, or rejection.

fauld (fôld, fäd) *v.t. Scot.* To fold. — *n.* **1** The working arch of a furnace; a tymp arch. **2** *Scot.* Fold.

Faulk·ner (fôk′nər), **William,** 1897–1962, U.S. novelist: also spelled *Falkner.*

fault (fôlt) *n.* **1** A slight offense; failure; negligence. **2** Whatever impairs excellence; an imperfection or defect in a person or thing; failure; blemish. **3** *Geol.* **a** A dislocation of a stratum or vein of ore which breaks its continuity. **b** A displacement or break in the continuity of rock masses, caused by disturbances of the earth's crust and resulting in a wide variety of surface features. **4** A missing or losing of the trail or scent: said of hunting dogs. **5** *Electr.* A deflection or leak in a current, due to abnormal connection of circuits or defective insulation of a conductor. **6** In tennis, rackets, etc., a failure by the server to drive the ball into the proper part of his opponent's court; also, a failure by the server to have both feet on the ground behind the service line in serving: usually called **foot fault.** **7** *Obs.* Default; lack. See synonyms under BLEMISH, ERROR, OFFENSE. — **at fault 1** In the wrong. **2** Worthy of blame. **3** Off the scent. **4** Hence, at a loss; in a quandary. — **in fault** Blameworthy. — **to a fault** Exceedingly; excessively: generous *to a fault.* — *v.t.* **1** *Rare* To find fault with; blame. **2** *Geol.* To cause a fault in. — *v.i.* **3** *Archaic* To commit a fault; err. **4** *Geol.* To crack or fracture so as to produce a fault. [<OF *faute,* ult. <L *fallere* deceive] — **fault′ful·ly** *adv.* — **fault′ful·ness** *n.*

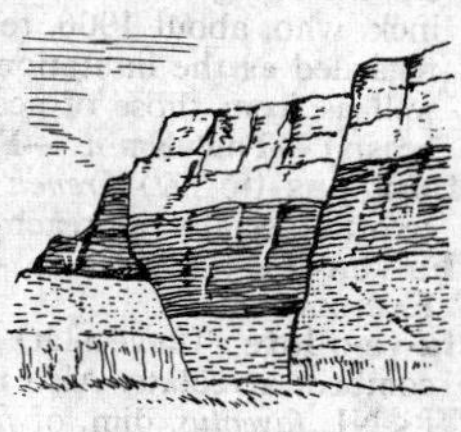

FAULT (*def.* 3)

fault–current (fôlt′kûr′ənt) *n. Electr.* A current flowing from conductor to ground or to another conductor because of faulty connections.

fault·find·er (fôlt′fīnd′dər) *n.* **1** A person given to complaining or finding fault; one who is excessively critical. **2** An instrument designed to locate leaks in electric current. — **fault′find′ing** *adj.* & *n.*

fault·less (fôlt′lis) *adj.* Without fault; flawless. See synonyms under CORRECT, INNOCENT, PERFECT. — **fault′less·ly** *adv.* — **fault′less·ness** *n.*

fault plane *Geol.* The fracture along which faulting occurs, commonly a curved surface.

fault·y (fôl′tē) *adj.* **fault·i·er, fault·i·est 1** Having faults or blemishes. **2** Characterized by faults of conduct. **3** *Obs.* Guilty of faults; blamable. — **fault′i·ly** *adv.* — **fault′i·ness** *n.*

faun[1] (fôn) *n.* In Roman mythology, a deity of the woods and herds, half–human, with pointed ears and goat's feet; a satyr. ◆ Homophone: *fawn.* [<L *Faunus,* a rural god]

faun[2] (fôn, fän) *Scot.* Fallen.

fau·na (fô′nə) *n. pl.* **fau·nas** or **fau·nae** (-nē) **1** The animals living within a given area or environment or during a stated period: distinguished from *flora.* **2** A treatise upon a fauna. See synonyms under ANIMAL. [< NL, after L *Fauna,* a rural goddess] **—fau′nal** *adj.* **—fau′nal·ly** *adv.*

Fau·na (fô′nə) See BONA DEA.

Fau·nus (fô′nəs) In Roman mythology, a god of nature, patron of agriculture: identified with the Greek *Pan.*

Faure (fôr), **Élie,** 1873–1937, French art critic and historian.

Fau·ré (fô·rā′), **Gabriel Urban,** 1845–1924, French composer.

fause (fôs) *adj. Scot.* False.

Faust (foust) In medieval legend, an old philosopher who sells his soul to the devil, Mephistopheles, for wisdom and power. Also **Faust′us.**

Faus·ta (fous′tə), **Flavia Maximiana,** 289?–326, Roman empress; wife of Constantine the Great.

Faus·tine (fôs′tēn, *Fr.* fôs·tēn′; *Ger.* fous·tē′nə) A feminine personal name. Also **Faus·ti·na** (fôs·tē′nə, *Ital.* fous·tē′nä). [< L, lucky]

Faus·tus (fôs′təs, *Ger.* fous′to͞os) A masculine personal name. [< L. See FAUSTA.]

faut (fôt, fät) *v.* & *n. Scot.* Fault. Also **faute.**

fau·teuil (fō′til, *Fr.* fō·tœ′y′) *n.* An upholstered armchair. [< F < OF *faudeteuil* < Med. L *faldistolium* FALDSTOOL]

Fauves (fōv), **Les** (lā) A group of French painters, including Derain, Dufy, Matisse, and Vlaminck, who, about 1906, revolted from what they regarded as the limitations of Impressionism as well as from those of academic art. [< F, wild beasts] **—Fau′vism** *n.* **—Fau′vist** *n.*

faux pas (fō pä′) *French* A false step; mistake; error; especially, a breach of etiquette.

Fa·ven·ti·a (fə·ven′shē·ə, -shə) Ancient name for FAENZA.

fa·ve·o·late (fə·vē′ə·lāt) *adj.* Pitted; honeycombed; alveolate. Also **fa·vose** (fā′vōs, fə·vōs′). [< NL *faveolus,* dim. of *favus* a honeycomb < L + -ATE[1]]

fa·vo·ni·an (fə·vō′nē·ən) adj. **1** Of or pertaining to Favonius, the west wind, promoter of vegetation. **2** Auspicious.

fa·vor (fā′vər) *n.* **1** An act or course of generosity; kind and favorable feeling; privilege granted. **2** The state or condition of being favored or approved. **3** Favoritism; bias; partiality. **4** Kind permission. **5** Convenience; facility. **6** Something given as a token; a gage. **7** A letter, especially a business letter. **8** That which is favored. **—in favor of 1** On the side of. **2** To the benefit of; payable to. *—v.t.* **1** To look upon with favor or kindness; like. **2** To treat with partiality; show preference for. **3** To make easier; facilitate. **4** To be in favor of; support; help. **5** To do a favor for; oblige. **6** To use carefully; spare, as a lame foot. **7** *Colloq.* To look like; resemble. See synonyms under INDULGE. Also *Brit.* **fa′vour.** [< L *favere* favor] **—fa′vor·er** *n.*

Synonyms (noun): benefit, blessing, boon, civility, concession, condescension, countenance, gift, grace, kindness, patronage, predilection, preference, regard. A *favor* is a *benefit* or *kindness* that one is glad to receive, but cannot demand or claim, hence always indicating good will or *regard* on the part of the person by whom it is conferred. See ESTEEM, FRIENDSHIP, GIFT, MERCY. *Antonyms*: disapproval, disfavor, dislike, harm, hostility, hurt, injury, insult, repulse.

fa·vor·a·ble (fā′vər·ə·bəl) *adj.* **1** Convenient; advantageous. **2** Friendly; propitious. Also *Brit.* **fa′vour·able.** See synonyms under AMICABLE, AUSPICIOUS, CONVENIENT, EXPEDIENT, FRIENDLY, GOOD, PROPITIOUS. **—fa′vor·a·ble·ness** *n.* **—fa′vor·a·bly** *adv.*

fa·vored (fā′vərd) *adj.* **1** Having an aspect or appearance; in compounds: ill-*favored.* **2** Wearing a favor. **3** Befriended; aided; privileged. See synonyms under FORTUNATE.

fa·vor·ite (fā′vər·it) *adj.* Regarded with special favor; preferred. *—n.* **1** A person or animal that is considered to have the best chance of success in a race or other contest. **2** A person or thing particularly liked or favored. Also *Brit.* **fa′vour·ite.** [< OF *favorit* < Ital. *favorito,* pp. of *favorire* favor < L *favor*]

favorite son A man favored by his native State; especially, a political leader honored by receiving from his constituents a nomination for high office, as the presidency.

fa·vor·it·ism (fā′vər·ə·tiz′əm) *n.* **1** A disposition to favor unfairly or unreasonably. **2** The state or condition of being a favorite. Also *Brit.* **fa′vour·it·ism.**

fa·vus (fā′vəs) *n. Pathol.* A contagious disease as of the scalp, caused by a parasitic fungus *(Achorion schönleinii)* and producing yellow flattened scabs and baldness; scaldhead. [< L, honeycomb]

Fawkes (fôks), **Guy** See under GUY FAWKES DAY.

fawn[1] (fôn) *v.i.* **1** To show cringing fondness, as a dog: often with *on* or *upon.* **2** To show affection or seek favor by or as by cringing. ◆ Homophone: *faun.* [OE *fahnian,* var. of *fægnian* rejoice] **—fawn′er** *n.* **—fawn′ing** *adj.* & *n.* **—fawn′ing·ly** *adv.* **—fawn′ing·ness** *n.*

fawn[2] (fôn) *n.* **1** A young deer; a buck or doe in its first year. **2** The color of a fawn. *—adj.* Fawn-colored. ◆ Homophone: *faun.* [< OF *faon,* ult. < L *fetus* offspring]

fawn-col·ored (fôn′kul′ərd) *adj.* Light-yellowish brown.

faw·sont (fô′sənt) *adj. Scot.* Proper; decent: also spelled *fausant.*

fay[1] (fā) *v.t.* & *v.i.* To fit or join closely; lie closely together, as two timbers. *—n.* A fitting smoothly, as of one plank to another. [OE *fegan*]

fay[2] (fā) *n.* A fairy. [< OF *fae* < L *fata* the Fates, pl. of *fatum* fate]

fay[3] (fā) *n. Obs.* Faith: by my *fay.* [< OF *fei,* var. of *feid* FAITH]

Fay (fā) A feminine personal name. Also **Faye.** [< OF, faith]

Fa·yal (fə·yäl′) An island of the central Azores; 64 square miles; chief town Horta.

fay·al·ite (fā′əl·īt, fī·äl′īt) *n.* A black magnetic iron silicate crystallizing in the orthorhombic system. [from *Fayal* + -ITE[1]]

Fa·yûm (fī·yo͞om′) See FAIYUM.

faze (fāz) *v.t.* **fazed, faz·ing** *U.S. Colloq.* To worry; disturb; disconcert. Also *fease, feaze, feeze.* ◆ Homophone: *phase.* [Var. of dial. E *fease,* OE *fēsian* frighten]

fa·zen·da (fä·zen′dä) *n.* In Brazil: **1** A hacienda. **2** An industrial enterprise for the production of coffee, cotton, or sugarcane. [< Pg. < *fazer* do]

Fe *Chem.* Iron (symbol Fe). [L *Ferrum*]

feal (fēl) *adj. Archaic* Faithful. [< OF, var. of *feeil* < L *fidelis* loyal]

fe·al·ty (fē′əl·tē) *n. pl.* **·ties 1** Fidelity, as of a vassal to his lord. **2** Devoted faithfulness; loyalty. See synonyms under ALLEGIANCE, FIDELITY. [< OF *feaute, feaulte* < L *fidelitas.* Doublet of FIDELITY.]

fear (fir) *n.* **1** An emotion excited by threatening evil or impending pain, accompanied by a desire to avoid or escape it; apprehension; dread. **2** Uneasiness about a thing; solicitude accompanied with dread. **3** That which causes fear. **4** Alarming character; formidableness. **5** Reverence for constituted authority, especially when accompanied by obedience thereto: the *fear* of God. *—v.t.* **1** To be afraid of; be fearful of. **2** To look upon with awe or reverence; venerate: to *fear* God. **3** To be anxious about; be apprehensive about. *—v.i.* **4** To be afraid; feel fear. **5** To be anxious or doubtful. [OE *fǣr* peril, sudden attack] **—fear′er** *n.*

Synonyms (noun): affright, apprehension, awe, consternation, dismay, disquiet, dread, fright, horror, misgiving, panic, terror, timidity, trembling, tremor, trepidation. *Fear* is the generic term denoting an emotion excited by threatening evil with a desire to avoid or escape it; *fear* may be sudden or lingering, in view of present, of imminent, or of distant and only possible danger; in the latter sense *dread* is oftener used. *Horror* (etymologically a shivering or shuddering) denotes a shuddering *fear* accompanied by abhorrence, or such a shock to the feelings and sensibilities as may exist without *fear,* as when one suddenly encounters some ghastly spectacle; we say of a desperate but fettered criminal, "I looked upon him with *horror.*" Where *horror* includes *fear,* it is *fear* mingled with abhorrence. (See ABHOR.) *Timidity* is a quality, habit, or condition, a readiness to be affected with *fear.* A person of great *timidity* is constantly liable to needless *alarm* and even *terror. Dread* is terrifying anticipation of evil, and is lingering and oppressive. *Dismay* is a helpless sinking of heart in view of some overwhelming peril or sorrow, actual or prospective. *Dismay* is more reflective, enduring, and despairing than *fright*; a horse is subject to *fright* or *terror,* but not to *dismay. Awe* is a reverential *fear.* Compare ALARM, ANXIETY, FRIGHT. *Antonyms*: see synonyms for FORTITUDE. Compare BRAVE.

Fear (fir), **Cape** A promontory in North Carolina near the mouth of the **Cape Fear River,** flowing 200 miles south to the Atlantic Ocean.

fear·ful (fir′fəl) *adj.* **1** Experiencing fear; afraid; apprehensive. **2** Timid; timorous. **3** Inspiring fear; terrible. **4** Caused by fear: *fearful* tremblings. **5** Full of awe and reverential fear. **6** *Colloq.* Very bad; appalling. See synonyms under AWFUL, FRIGHTFUL. **—fear′ful·ly** *adv.* **—fear′ful·ness** *n.*

fear·less (fir′lis) *adj.* Being without fear. See synonyms under BRAVE. **—fear′less·ly** *adv.* **—fear′less·ness** *n.*

fear·naught (fir′nôt′) *n.* **1** A fearless individual. **2** A heavy shaggy woolen goods; dreadnaught. Also **fear′nought′.**

fear·some (fir′səm) *adj.* **1** Causing fear; alarming. **2** Timid; frightened. **—fear′some·ly** *adv.* **—fear′some·ness** *n.*

fea·sance (fē′zəns) *n. Law* Performance of a duty; fulfilling a condition. [< AF *fesance* < *faire* do < L *facere*]

fease (fāz) See FAZE.

fea·si·ble (fē′zə·bəl) *adj.* **1** That may be done; practicable. **2** Open to being dealt with successfully. [< OF *faisable* < *faire* do < L *facere*] **—fea′si·bil′i·ty, fea′si·ble·ness** *n.* **—fea′si·bly** *adv.*

fea·sor (fē′zər) *n. Law* A doer; one who does a tort or wrong. See TORT. [< OF]

feast (fēst) *n.* **1** A sumptuous repast. **2** Anything affording great pleasure or enjoyment. **3** A day set aside for the commemoration of some person or event with rejoicing; a festival or joyous anniversary: opposed to *fast. —v.t.* **1** To give a feast for; entertain lavishly. **2** To delight; gratify: He *feasted* his eyes on her beauty. *—v.i.* **3** To partake of a feast; eat heartily. **4** To dwell delightedly, as on beauty. [< OF *feste* < L *festa,* neut. pl. of *festus* joyful] **—feast′er** *n.*

feast·ful (fēst′fəl) *adj.* Festive; sumptuous.

Feast of Dedication See HANUKKAH.

Feast of Lanterns 1 A Chinese festival held at the first full moon of every year (January–February): so called from the practice of hanging colored lanterns at every door and every grave. **2** The Japanese festival, Bon.

feat (fēt) *n.* **1** A notable act or performance, as one displaying skill, endurance, or daring; an achievement. **2** *Obs.* An act of any kind. See synonyms under ACT. *—adj. Obs.* **1** Dexterous; neat; ingenious. **2** Fit; befitting. [< OF *fait* < L *factum.* See FACT.]

feath·er (feth′ər) *n.* **1** One of the horny, elongated structures which form the body covering of birds and provide the flight surface for their wings. It consists of a central *shaft* composed of a hollow part near the body called the *quill* and a distal solid part, the *rachis,* along each side of which is a series of processes, the *barbs.* The barbs are provided with a fringe of smaller processes, the *barbules,* which in turn are equipped with *barbicels,* or hooklets, the whole composing the *vane* of the feather. **2** Something resembling a feather, as in mechanisms; a tongue, wedge, or fin. **3** Kind; class or species: birds of a *feather.* **4** Frame of mind; mood; spirits. **5** In rowing, the act of feathering. **6** The wake of the periscope of a submarine. **7** An irregular flaw in a gem. **8** The hairy fringe on the backs of the legs and on

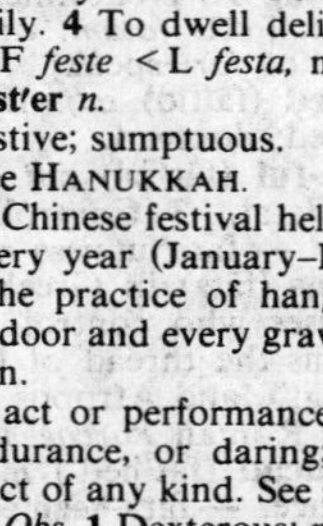

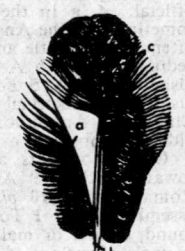

FEATHER
a. Aftershaft.
b. Shaft.
c. Barbs.

the tail of some dogs. 9 *pl.* Plumage; by extension, dress or attire. 10 A fin or guide on the shaft of an arrow. 11 Anything light or trivial: A *feather* would upset him. — **a feather in one's cap** An achievement to be proud of; a thing to one's credit. — **in full feather** In full force; fully equipped. — **in high, fine,** or **good feather** In a cheerful or confident frame of mind. — *v.t.* 1 To fit with a feather, as an arrow. 2 To cover, adorn, or fringe with feathers. 3 To join by a tongue and groove. 4 In rowing, to turn (the oar blade) as it comes from the water until it is horizontal or nearly horizontal, thus offering the least resistance while reaching for a new stroke. 5 *Aeron.* To turn one edge of (the propeller blade) into the wind, thus minimizing drag. — *v.i.* 6 To grow or become covered with feathers. 7 To move, spread, or expand like feathers. 8 To feather an oar or propeller blade. — **to feather one's nest** To provide well for one's own future while acting as the agent of another. [OE *fether*]

feath·er·bed (feth′ər·bed′) *v.i.* **·bed·ded, ·bed·ding** To force the employment of unneeded workmen or the slowing of work so as to reduce unemployment: said of labor unions. — **feath′er·bed′ding** *n.*

feath·er·bone (feth′ər·bōn′) *n.* A substitute for whalebone, prepared from the quills of feathers of turkeys and chickens.

feath·er·brain (feth′ər·brān′) *n.* A light-headed or weak-minded person. — **feath′er-brained** *adj.*

feath·ered (feth′ərd) *adj.* 1 Provided with feathers or featherlike appendages. 2 Winged; swift.

feath·er-edge (feth′ər·ej′) *n.* A very thin edge, as in a wedge-shaped board or on a millstone. — **feath′er-edged′** *adj.*

feather grass 1 An ornamental grass (*Stipa pennata*) of southern Europe, having a feathered beard. 2 A related species (*S. comata*) of the western United States, sometimes called *needle grass.*

feath·er·head (feth′ər·hed′) *n.* A giddy, frivolous person. — **feath′er-head′ed** *adj.*

feath·er·less (feth′ər·lis) *adj.* Without feathers.

feather palm Any of various palms having feather-shaped or pinnate leaves.

feather star One of a genus (*Comatula*) of free-swimming crinoids with plumelike arms.

feath·er·stitch (feth′ər·stich′) *n.* A kind of decorative stitch, resembling a feather, made by taking one or more short stitches alternately on either side of a straight line. — **feath′er·stitch′ing** *n.*

feath·er-veined (feth′ər·vānd′) *adj. Bot.* Having the veins all proceeding from opposite sides of a midrib.

feath·er·weight (feth′ər·wāt′) *n.* 1 A boxer or wrestler weighing from 118 to 126 pounds. 2 The least weight allowed to a race horse in a handicap. 3 A person weighing very little; hence, anyone of little ability or importance. — *adj.* Of little weight; insignificant; unimportant.

feath·er·wood (feth′ər·wood′) *n.* A hickorylike, hardwood timber tree of Australia (*Polyosma cunninghami*).

feath·er·y (feth′ər·ē) *adj.* Covered with or resembling feathers; light, soft, or fluffy. — **feath′er·i·ness** *n.*

fea·ture (fē′chər) *n.* 1 Any part of the human face. 2 *pl.* The whole face. 3 A salient point. 4 A magazine or newspaper article or story on a special subject. 5 A full-length motion picture. 6 *Archaic* Make; shape; form. See synonyms under CHARACTERISTIC, CIRCUMSTANCE. — *v.t.* **fea·tured, fea·tur·ing** 1 To make a feature of, as in a newspaper story. 2 To be a feature of. 3 To portray or outline the features of. 4 *U.S. Slang* To imagine; fancy. 5 *Colloq.* To resemble; favor. [<OF *faiture* <L *factura* <*facere* do] — **fea′ture·less** *adj.*

fea·tured (fē′chərd) *adj.* 1 Chiseled; shaped or fashioned. 2 Having or exhibiting features. 3 Given special prominence.

fea·ture-length (fē′chər·length′) *adj.* Full-length: said especially of a motion picture.

feaze (fāz) See FAZE.

Fe·be (fē′bē) The Italian form of PHOEBE.

Fe·bold Fe·bold·son (fē′bōld fē′bəld·sən) In American folklore, a Swedish pioneer plainsman, defier of tornadoes, Indians, politicians, and extreme heat or cold.

febri- *combining form* Fever: *febrifuge.* Also, before vowels, **febr-.** [<L *febris* fever]

fe·bric·i·ty (fə·bris′ə·tē) *n.* The condition of being feverish.

fe·bric·u·la (fə·brik′yə·lə) *n.* A light and passing fever. [<L, little fever]

feb·ri·fa·cient (feb′rə·fā′shənt) *n.* A substance that produces fever. — *adj.* Producing or promoting fever.

fe·brif·ic (fə·brif′ik) *adj.* 1 Causing fever. 2 Feverish. Also **fe·brif′er·ous.**

feb·ri·fuge (feb′rə·fyōōj) *n.* A medicine efficacious in reducing or removing fever. [<FEBRI- + L *fugere* flee] — **fe·brif·u·gal** (fə·brif′yə·gəl) *adj.*

fe·brile (fē′brəl, feb′rəl) *adj.* Pertaining to fever; caused by or indicating fever; feverish. [<F *fébrile* <L *febrilis* <*febris* fever]

Feb·ru·ar·y (feb′rōō·er′ē) The second month of the year, having twenty-eight, or, in leap years, twenty-nine days. See LEAP YEAR. [<F *Februarius (mensis)* (month) of purification <*februa,* a Roman purificatory festival, celebrated on Feb. 15]

fe·ces (fē′sēz) *n. pl.* 1 Animal excrement; ordure. 2 Any foul refuse matter or sediment. Also spelled *faeces.* [<L *faex, faecis* sediment] — **fe·cal** (fē′kəl) *adj.*

Fech·ner (fekh′nər), **Gustav Theodor,** 1801–1887, German scientist and psychophysicist.

fecht (fekht) *v.* & *n. Scot.* Fight.

fe·cial (fē′shəl) See FETIAL.

feck (fek) *Scot. adj.* Hardy; vigorous. — *n.* 1 Power; strength; vigor. 2 Amount, quantity, number, or value. 3 The main part: also called **maist feck.** [Aphetic var. of EFFECT]

feck·et (fek′it) *n. Scot.* An undervest or sleeveless shirt.

feck·less (fek′lis) *adj.* Feeble; good-for-nothing; irresponsible. — **feck′less·ly** *adv.* — **feck′less·ness** *n.*

feck·ly (fek′lē) *adv. Scot.* For the most part; mostly.

fec·u·la (fek′yə·lə) *n. pl.* **·lae** (-lē) 1 Starch, especially as extracted by washing farinaceous pulp; also called **amylaceous fecula.** 2 The sediment or dregs precipitated from an infusion. [<L *faecula* crust of wine, orig. dim. of *faex* dregs]

fec·u·lence (fek′yə·ləns) *n.* 1 The condition or quality of being feculent; foulness; muddiness. 2 That which is feculent; dregs. Also **fec′u·len·cy.**

fec·u·lent (fek′yə·lənt) *adj.* Turbid or foul from impurities; fecal. [<L *faeculentus* <*faecula.* See FECULA.]

fe·cund (fē′kund, fek′und) *adj.* Fruitful; fertile; prolific. [<OF *fecond* <L *fecundus*]

fe·cun·date (fē′kən·dāt, fek′ən-) *v.t.* **·dat·ed, ·dat·ing** 1 To make fruitful or fecund. 2 To impregnate; fertilize. [<L *fecundatus,* pp. of *fecundare* fertilize <*fecundus* fruitful] — **fe′cun·da′tion** *n.*

fe·cun·di·ty (fi·kun′də·tē) *n.* Productiveness; fruitfulness.

fed (fed) Past tense and past participle of FEED.

Fe·da·la (fə·dä′lə) A city in NW Morocco.

Fe·da·yeen (fe·dä′yēn) *n.* In Arab states, a commando. [<Arabic *fidayim,* pl. of *fidayi* one who ransoms or redeems his country < *fida* redemption <*faday* redeem]

fed·er·a·cy (fed′ər·ə·sē) *n. pl.* **·cies** A confederacy.

fed·er·al (fed′ər·əl) *adj.* 1 *Govt.* Of or pertaining to a form of government in which certain states agree by compact to grant control of common affairs to a central authority but retain individual control over internal affairs. 2 Of or pertaining to a union or central authority so established. 3 Favoring or supporting a government formed by a union of several states. 4 Relating to, arising from, or founded upon a league or covenant. — *n.* An advocate of federalism. [<F *fédéral* <L *foedus, -eris* a compact, league] — **fed′er·al·ly** *adv.*

Fed·er·al (fed′ər·əl) *adj.* 1 Of, pertaining to, owned or used by, or representing the United States of America: a *Federal* building, the *Federal* Bureau of Investigation. 2 Supporting the Union cause in the American Civil War of 1861–65: the *Federal* forces. — *n.* One who favored or fought for the Union cause in the American Civil War.

Federal Bureau of Investigation A branch of the Department of Justice which investigates all violations of Federal laws other than those specifically assigned to other agencies: popularly the FBI.

Federal Capital Territory A former name for the AUSTRALIAN CAPITAL TERRITORY.

Federal Communications Commission An agency of the U.S. government which supervises wire, radio, and television communication in the interest of maximum efficiency and public service.

Federal District A district reserved by a country for the location of the national government; in Argentina, including Buenos Aires, 74 square miles; in Brazil, including Rio de Janeiro, 154 square miles; in Mexico, including Mexico City, 573 square miles; in Venezuela, including Caracas, 745 square miles; in the United States, the District of Columbia, including Washington, 61 square miles. Spanish and Portugese *Distrito Federal.*

fed·er·al·ism (fed′ər·əl·iz′əm) *n.* 1 The doctrine of federal union in government. 2 *Cap.* The principles of the Federal party.

fed·er·al·ist (fed′ər·əl·ist) *n.* An advocate of federalism.

Fed·er·al·ist (fed′ər·əl·ist) *n.* One who supported the federal union of the American colonies and the adoption of the Constitution of the United States; a member of the Federal party. — **The Federalist** A series of 85 essays by Alexander Hamilton, John Jay, and James Madison, explaining, and recommending for ratification, the Constitution of the United States.

fed·er·al·is·tic (fed′ər·əl·is′tik) *adj.* Of or pertaining to federalists or federalism.

fed·er·al·ize (fed′ər·əl·īz) *v.t.* **·ized, ·iz·ing** To bring together under federal compact or government. — **fed′er·al·i·za′tion** *n.*

Federal party A political party (1787–1830) originally under the leadership of Alexander Hamilton, which advocated the adoption of the United States Constitution and the formation of a strong national government.

Federal Power Commission An agency of the U.S. government which supervises the development and utilization of power resources on Federal property, regulates the activities of public utilities engaged in interstate commerce, and provides for a uniform system of accounts in the management of electric power enterprises.

Federal Republic of Germany See under GERMANY.

Federal Reserve System A banking system created by the **Federal Reserve Act** (1913) and controlled by a **Federal Reserve Board** of eight members, established to provide an elastic currency and to concentrate the national banking resources in a system of twelve **Federal reserve banks,** each designed to regulate and aid the member banks in its respective **Federal reserve district.** The **Federal reserve cities** are Boston, New York, Philadelphia, Cleveland, Richmond, Atlanta, Chicago, St. Louis, Minneapolis, Kansas City, Dallas, and San Francisco.

Federal Territory A former name for the AUSTRALIAN CAPITAL TERRITORY.

Federal Trade Commission An agency of the U.S. government which enforces Federal laws against unfair trade practices, as price-fixing, false advertising claims, etc.

fed·er·ate (fed′ə·rāt) *v.t.* & *v.i.* **·at·ed, ·at·ing** To unite in a federation. — *adj.* Leagued; confederate; federal. [<L *foederatus,* pp. of L *foederare* <*foedus, -eris* a league]

Federated Malay States Former collective name for the states of Negri Sembilan, Pahang, Perak, and Selangor, now incorporated in Malaysia.

fed·er·a·tion (fed′ə·rā′shən) *n.* 1 The act of uniting under a federal government. 2 A federated body; league. 3 A national union. See synonyms under ALLIANCE, ASSOCIATION.

Federation of Malaya See MALAYA, FEDERATION OF

Federation of Rhodesia and Nyasaland See RHODESIA.

fed·er·a·tive (fed′ər·ə·tiv, fed′ə·rā′tiv) *adj.* Pertaining to federation; federal. **—fed′er·a′tive·ly** *adv.*

Fe·de·ri·ca (fā′dā·rē′kä) Italian form of FREDERICA.

Fe·de·ri·co (fā′dā·rē′kō) Italian, Portuguese, and Spanish forms of FREDERICK. Also *Ital.* **Fe·de·ri·go** (fā′dā·rē′gō).

fe·do·ra (fə·dôr′ə, -dō′rə) *n.* A low hat, usually of soft felt, with the crown creased lengthwise. [after *Fédora,* a play by V. Sardou]

fee (fē) *n.* **1** A payment, as for professional service. **2** A charge for a special privilege, as admission to an entertainment or membership in a society or club. **3** A gratuity. **4** *Law* An estate of inheritance, either in *fee-simple,* in which the heir has unqualified ownership and power of disposition, or in *fee-tail,* in which inheritance is limited to a man and his heirs or to certain classes of heirs. **5** In feudal law, a fief. **6** Ownership; property. See synonyms under SALARY. *—v.t.* **feed, fee·ing 1** To give a fee to; tip, as a waiter. **2** *Scot.* To hire. **3** *Obs.* To bribe. [< AF, var. of OF *fé, fief* < Med. L *feudum* FEUD[2]]

fee·ble (fē′bəl) *adj.* **fee·bler, fee·blest 1** Lacking muscular power; frail; infirm. **2** Lacking strength for support or resistance; weak: a *feeble* barrier. **3** Lacking force, energy, or vigor. See synonyms under FAINT, LITTLE, MEAGER, PUSILLANIMOUS. [< OF *feble* < *fleible* weak < L *flebilis* tearful < *flere* weep. Related to FOIBLE.] **—fee′ble·ness** *n.* **—fee′blish** *adj.* **—fee′bly** *adv.*

fee·ble-mind·ed (fē′bəl·mīn′did) *adj.* **1** Deficient in will or understanding; irresolute; imbecile. **2** *Psychol.* In the United States, designating all grades of mental deficiency and backwardness, from the moron to the idiot. **—fee′ble-mind′ed·ly** *adv.* **—fee′ble-mind′ed·ness** *n.*

feed (fēd) *n.* **1** Anything that is used for food; especially, food for domestic animals; fodder, such as hay and grain. **2** The amount of food given to an animal at one time. **3** The motion that carries material into a machine or work toward a tool. **4** The machinery by which motion of the work toward the tool or of the tool toward the work is produced. **5** The material supplied to a machine to be operated upon or consumed, as wool to a carding engine or water to a boiler. **6** *Colloq.* A meal. See synonyms under FOOD. [< *v.*] *—v.* **fed, feed·ing** *v.t.* **1** To give food to; supply with food. **2** To give as food. **3** To furnish with what is necessary for the continuance, growth, or operation of: to *feed* a furnace. **4** To supply (what is necessary) for operation, manufacture, etc.: to *feed* steel to a factory. **5** To enlarge; increase, as if by causing to grow: Compliments *feed* his vanity. **6** To cue an actor with (lines). **7** In sports, to hand or throw (the ball or puck) to a player who will try for a goal, etc. *—v.i.* **8** To take food; eat: said of animals. **9** To subsist; depend: usually with *on:* to *feed* on hopes. [OE *fēdan*]

feed·back (fēd′bak′) *n.* **1** *Electronics* The transfer of a portion of the energy from the output circuit of an electronic system to the input circuit; when properly controlled and in correct phase, it is positive or regenerative; reversed or improper forms anywhere in the system are negative or degenerative. **2** A similar energy transfer occurring in certain biological processes, as in the transmission of stimuli along an interconnected system of nerve fibers.

feed·bag (fēd′bag′) *n.* A bag for feeding horses, hung over the muzzle.

feed·er (fē′dər) *n.* **1** One who or that which feeds, as a person or appliance for supplying material to a machine. **2** A person, animal, or plant that takes in nourishment. **3** Anything that supplies the wants, or increases the importance, of something else, as a tributary stream, a branch railroad, a small vein in a mine, running into a main lode. **4** One who fattens livestock for market. **5** An animal intended for intensive feeding in preparation for slaughter, or an animal that is on such feed. **6** A plant root. **7** A large box or container for feed for animals. **8** *Electr.* A conductor or group of conductors between different generating or distributing units of a power system.

feed·lift (fēd′lift′) *n.* The emergency feeding of stranded livestock by supplies dropped from airplanes in regions isolated from ground assistance by storms, blizzards, and extreme cold.

feed·lot (fēd′lot′) *n.* An area where cattle are penned and fattened up prior to their being shipped to market.

feed pipe A pipe for the distribution of liquid or gas.

feed pump A device for forcing water into a steam boiler.

feed·stock (fēd′stok′) *n.* Any raw material supplied to a machine or factory that processes it into manufactured products.

feed·stuff (fēd′stuf′) *n.* Fodder, as grain (corn, oats, etc.) or alfalfa for domestic animals.

fee-fi-fo-fum (fē′fī′fō′fum′) *n.* **1** Nonsense words of a giant in the tale of *Jack the Giant-Killer.* **2** Any jargon or mummery.

feel (fēl) *v.* **felt, feel·ing** *v.t.* **1** To touch; examine by touching or handling. **2** To perceive or become aware of by the senses: to *feel* the prick of a pin. **3** To be conscious of the effects of: to *feel* the weight of a storm. **4** To be conscious of mentally; experience: to *feel* joy. **5** To have the emotions stirred by; be affected by: to *feel* a slight. **6** To be convinced of intellectually; believe in: to *feel* the need for reform. *—v.i.* **7** To have perception as if by the sense of touch: I *feel* cold. **8** To seem; appear: The air *feels* humid to me. **9** To have the emotions or opinions stirred: I *feel* strongly about the matter. **10** To make examination with or as with the hands; grope: to *feel* around a room. **—to feel like** *Colloq.* To have a desire or inclination for: to *feel like* a swim. **—to feel one's oats** *Colloq.* To act in a high-spirited manner. **—to feel out 1** To examine the possibilities of (a situation). **2** To talk to (a person) so as to determine opinions, ideas, etc. **—to feel up to** To feel able to do. *—n.* **1** The sense of touch. **2** Sensation; perception by touch. **3** Perception in general as accompanied with feeling: the *feel* of joy. **4** The quality of a thing that is perceived by the touch: Fur has a soft *feel.* [OE *fēlan*]

feel·er (fē′lər) *n.* **1** One who or that which feels. **2** *Zool.* An antenna; tentacle. **3** *Bot.* A tendril of a vine. **4** An indirect approach; a trial venture.

feel·ing (fē′ling) *n.* **1** The sense of touch or immediate contact, as aroused by stimulating receptors in the skin, muscles, or internal organs. **2** The fact or the power of perceiving the qualities of the objects arousing the sensations: the *feeling* of a glassy or metallic surface. **3** The collective state or general tone of consciousness due to more or less complex and obscure combinations of classes of sensations: a rested *feeling,* etc. **4** Any emotion as apart from the body; mental stirring; emotion; sentiment; presentiment: to express *feelings* of sympathy: The *feeling* of the meeting was hostile. **5** Sensitiveness, or the capacity to feel deeply; refined sensibility shown in tenderness or ready sympathy; by extension, sentimentality: a woman of *feeling,* to hurt one's *feelings.* **6** *Psychol.* The affective, emotional aspect of all mental life and its phenomena, as distinguished from the intellectual and voluntary, or active, aspects. **7** That quality by which expression is given to the emotions, and which should actuate a painter in the conception and execution of his design; sympathetic expression in art. *—adj.* **1** Possessed of warm sensibilities; sympathetic. **2** Marked by, or indicating deep sensibility or fervor and earnestness; hence, affecting. **—feel′ing·ly** *adv.*

Synonyms (noun): consciousness, emotion, impression, passion, pathos, sensation, sense, sensibility, sensitiveness, sentiment, tenderness. See IMPULSE, LOVE, SENSATION.

fee-sim·ple (fē′sim′pəl) *n. Law* An estate of inheritance free from condition.

feet (fēt) Plural of FOOT. **—feet′less** *adj.*

fee-tail (fē′tāl′) *n. Law* An estate limited to a person and the heirs of his body, or to a particular class of them.

feeze (fēz, fāz) See FAZE.

feign (fān) *v.t.* **1** To make a false show of; simulate; pretend. **2** To invent deceptively, as excuses. **3** To make up or imagine, as myths or stories. *—v.t.* **4** To pretend; dissimulate. See synonyms under ASSUME, PRETEND. ◆ Homophones: *fain, fane.* [< OF *feindre* < L *fingere* shape] **—feign·ed·ly** (fā′nid·lē), **—feign′ing·ly** *adv.* **—feign′er** *n.*

feint (fānt) *n.* **1** A deceptive appearance or movement; a ruse or pretense. **2** In boxing, fencing, war, etc., an apparent or pretended blow or attack meant to divert attention from an attack to be made on another part. **3** *pl.* Faints. *—v.i.* To make a feint. *—adj. Obs.* Feigned; pretended. ◆ Homophone: *faint.* [< F *feinte* < *feindre.* See FEIGN.]

Fei·sal I (fī′səl), 1885–1933, king of Iraq 1921–1933. **—Feisal II,** 1935–58, king of Iraq 1939–58. Also spelled *Faisal.*

feist (fīst) *n.* A fice.

feis·ty (fīs′tē) *adj. U.S. Colloq.* Frisky; meddlesome; spunky.

feld·spar (feld′spär, fel′-) *n.* Any one of a group of crystalline rock-forming materials which consist of silicates of aluminum with potassium, sodium, or calcium: sometimes spelled *felspar.* Also **feld′spath** (-spath). [Partial trans. of G *feldspat* < *feld* field + *spat* spar[3]] **—feld·spath′ic, feld·spath′ose** *adj.*

feld·spath·oid (feld·spath′oid) *n.* One of a group of rock-forming minerals, as leucite, nepheline, sodalite, etc.; in general, silicates of aluminum and potassium or sodium, which act like the feldspars in the formation of igneous rocks.

Fel·ci·a (fə·lish′ē·ə, -lish′ə; *Ital.* fä·lē′chē·ä) A feminine personal name. Also **Fel·li′ci·ty,** *Fr.* **Fé·li·cie** (fā·lē·sē′) or **Fé·li·ci·té** (fā·lē·sē·tā′), *Sp.* **Fe·li·ci·dad** (fā·lē′thē·thäth′). [< L, happy]

fe·li·cif·ic (fē′lə·sif′ik) *adj.* Producing happiness. [< L *felix* happy + -FIC]

fe·lic·i·tate (fə·lis′ə·tāt) *v.t.* **·tat·ed, ·tat·ing 1** To wish joy or happiness to; congratulate. **2** *Rare* To make happy. *—adj.* Made happy. [< L *felicitatus,* pp. of *felicitare* < *felix* happy]

fe·lic·i·ta·tion (fə·lis′ə·tā′shən) *n.* **1** The act of felicitating. **2** Congratulation.

fe·lic·i·tous (fə·lis′ə·təs) *adj.* **1** Marked by or producing felicity. **2** Happy in operation or effect; appropriate; apt. See synonyms under HAPPY. **—fe·lic′i·tous·ly** *adv.* **—fe·lic′i·tous·ness** *n.*

fe·lic·i·ty (fə·lis′ə·tē) *n. pl.* **·ties 1** A state of great and well-founded happiness, comfort, and content; good fortune; blissfulness. **2** Something causing happiness; a source of content or satisfaction. **3** Happy faculty or turn; tact or knack. **4** A clever, happy, or apt expression. See synonyms under HAPPINESS. [< L *felicitas, -tatis* < *felix* happy]

fe·lid (fē′lid) *n.* Any member of a family of carnivores *(Felidae),* the cat family, including the lion, tiger, leopard, puma, lynx, etc., and the domestic cat. [< NL < L *felis* a cat]

fe·line (fē′līn) *adj.* **1** Of or pertaining to cats or catlike animals. **2** Catlike; sly. *—n.* A cat; one of the cat family. [< L *felinus* < *felis* cat] **—fe′line·ly** *adv.* **—fe′line·ness, fe·lin·i·ty** (fə·lin′ə·tē) *n.*

Fe·li·pa (fā·lē′pä) Spanish and Portuguese form of PHILIPPA.

Fe·li·pe (fā·lē′pā) Spanish form of PHILIP. Also *Pg.* **Fe·lip·pe** (fə·lē′pe).

Fe·lix (fē′liks, *Dan., Du., Ger., Sp.* fā′lēks) A masculine personal name. Also *Fr.* **Fé·lix** (fā·lēks′), *Ital.* **Fe·li·ce** (fā·lē′chā), *Pg.* **Fe·liz** (fe·lēs′). [< L, happy, fortunate, prosperous]

fell[1] (fel) *v.t.* **1** To cause to fall; cut down. **2** In sewing, to finish with a flat seam. *—n.* **1** A seam made by joining edges, folding them under, and stitching flat. **2** The end of the web in weaving. **3** The timber cut down during one season. [OE *fellan*] **—fell′a·ble** *adj.*

fell[2] (fel) Past tense of FALL.

fell[3] (fel) *adj.* **1** Characterized by fierceness or cruelty; inhuman; barbarous. **2** Hideous. **3** *Scot.* Strong; sharp; heroic: *fell* liquor. **4** *Scot.* Huge; immense. [< OF, cruel, orig. nominative of *felon.* See FELON.]

fell[4] (fel) *n.* **1** Hair; a growth of hair. **2** A hide or pelt. [OE, hide]

fell[5] (fel) *n. Scot. & Brit. Dial.* **1** A tract of waste land; a moor. **2** A barren hill or upland level.

fel·lah (fel′ə) *n. pl.* **fel·lahs** or **fel·la·heen** or **·hin** (fel′ə·hēn′) A peasant; laborer, as in Egypt. [< Arabic *fellāh*]

fell·er (fel′ər) *n.* **1** One who or that which fells. **2** A sewing machine attachment for the felling of seams.

fell field An area of scattered dwarf plants,

chiefly cryptogams, usually in very cold zones or on mountains above the timber line.

fell·mon·ger (fel′mung′gər, -mong′-) *n.* A dealer in fells, or skins and furs. — **fell′mon′·ger·ing, fell′mon′ger·y** *n.*

fell·ness (fel′nis) *n.* Great cruelty; ruthlessness.

fel·loe (fel′ō) *n.* A felly. ◆ Homophone: *fellow.*

fel·low (fel′ō) *n.* **1** A man; boy. **2** A person or individual; one: A *fellow* can't work day and night. **3** A companion; mate; a counterpart or one of a pair; an equal. **4** An inferior or worthless person. **5** A trustee or member of the corporation in some educational institutions. **6** A member of a society. **7** A graduate or student of a university holding a fellowship or stipend awarded for excellence in and the further pursuit of a special field of study. See FELLOWSHIP. **8** *Colloq.* A girl's beau. See synonyms under ASSOCIATE. — *v.t.* **1** To make or proclaim an equal to another. **2** To produce an equal to; match. — *adj.* Joined or associated; associate; having the same relation to something. ◆ Homophone: *felloe.* [OE *fēolaga* business partner <*feoh* property + *lag-*, stem of *lecgan* lay]

Fellow may appear as the first element in two-word phrases, with the adjectival meaning.

fellow Christian	**fellow passenger**
fellow citizen	**fellow prisoner**
fellow conspirator	**fellow soldier**
fellow countryman	**fellow student**
fellow employee	**fellow townsman**
fellow man	**fellow worker**

fellow creature A being of the same kind; any person or animal created by the same creator.

fellow feeling A sympathetic understanding.

fellow servant **1** One of a group of servants hired by the same master. **2** *Law* One of a group in common employment, in such relationship to each other that each accepts the liability of safety or danger to himself as depending upon the care or negligence of every other.

fel·low·ship (fel′ō-ship) *n.* **1** The state of being a companion or fellow; association; communion; friendly intercourse: the *fellowship* of students. **2** The condition of being sharers or partakers; community of interest, condition, or feeling; joint interest or experience: *fellowship* in prosperity or adversity. **3** A body of persons associated by reason of a community of taste, views, or interests; a company. **4** A position to which graduate members of a college may be elected, carrying with it certain privileges. **5** A foundation, as in a college or university, the income of which is bestowed upon a student, to aid him in pursuing further studies. **6** The rules for determining the shares of partners in the gains or losses of a business; partnership. See synonyms under ACQUAINTANCE, ASSOCIATION, INTERCOURSE. — *v.* **·shiped** or **·shipped, ·ship·ing** or **·ship·ping** *v.t.* To admit to religious fellowship. — *v.i. U.S.* To unite with others in fellowship.

fellow traveler A person who favors the ideology or program of a political party (specifically, the Communist party) without membership in the party.

fel·ly[1] (fel′ē) *n. pl.* **fel·lies** A segment of the rim of a wooden wheel, in which the spokes are inserted; also, sometimes, the entire rim: also spelled *felloe.* [OE *felg*]

fel·ly[2] (fel′ē) *adv. Archaic* Harshly; fiercely.

fe·lo de se (fē′lō də sē, fel′ō) *pl.* **fe·lo·nes de se** (fel′ō-nēz) or **fe·los de se** *Law Latin* **1** A suicide; self-murderer. **2** The act of suicide. [<Med. L *felo* felon + *de* of + *se* self]

fel·on[1] (fel′ən) *n.* **1** One who has committed a felony. **2** *Obs.* A criminal or depraved person. — *adj.* **1** Obtained by felony. **2** Wicked; criminal; treacherous. [<OF, base, ult. <L *fellare* suck (in obscene sense)]

fel·on[2] (fel′ən) *n. Pathol.* Inflammation of the cellular tissue and periosteum, as on a finger; a whitlow. [Origin uncertain]

fe·lo·ni·ous (fə-lō′nē-əs) *adj.* **1** Showing criminal purpose; malicious; villainous. **2** Like or involving legal felony. See synonyms under CRIMINAL. — **fe·lo′ni·ous·ly** *adv.* — **fe·lo′ni·ous·ness** *n.*

fel·on·ry (fel′ən-rē) *n.* A body of felons; a convict population, as of a penal colony.

fel·o·ny (fel′ə-nē) *Law n. pl.* **·nies** **1** In common law, an offense the punishment of which carried with it the forfeiture of lands or goods, or both. **2** One of the highest class of offenses, variously limited by common law or by statute, and punishable by imprisonment or death. Included are treason, murder, rape, robbery, arson, etc., and punishment is in a State prison.

In modern usage, and especially in American law, forfeiture of estate for crime being generally abolished, the word is used, as defined above, as distinct from *misdemeanor,* an offense of minor degree, punishable by fine or imprisonment in a county jail. Hence, *felony* is now a generic term that denotes a general class or grade of offenses, usually those of greater enormity.

felony murder A murder perpetrated during the commission of a crime of arson, rape, robbery, or burglary.

fel·site (fel′sīt) *n.* A cryptocrystalline mixture of quartz and feldspar: the groundmass of the quartz porphyries, and often the product of devitrification. Also **fel′stone** (-stōn). [<G. *fels* rock] — **fel·sit·ic** (fel-sit′ik) *adj.*

fel·spar (fel′spär) see FELDSPAR.

felt[1] (felt) Past tense and past participle of FEEL.

felt[2] (felt) *n.* **1** A fabric made by compacting wool, fur, or hair, or a mixture thereof, by mechanical or chemical action, moisture, and heat. **2** A piece of material so made; also, some article manufactured therefrom. **3** A thick fabric made of asbestos by weaving or other process. **4** In papermaking, one of two woolen or cotton blankets on which the sheet is carried and between which it is pressed on passing through the rolls of the machine. — *adj.* Made of felt. — *v.t.* **1** To make into felt. **2** To overlay with felt. — *v.i.* **3** To become matted together. [OE]

felt·ing (fel′ting) *n.* **1** The process by which, or the materials of which, felt is made. **2** Felt in quantity.

fe·luc·ca (fə-luk′ə, fe-) *n.* A small, swift Mediterranean vessel propelled by lateen sails and by oars. [<Ital. <Arabic *falūkah*]

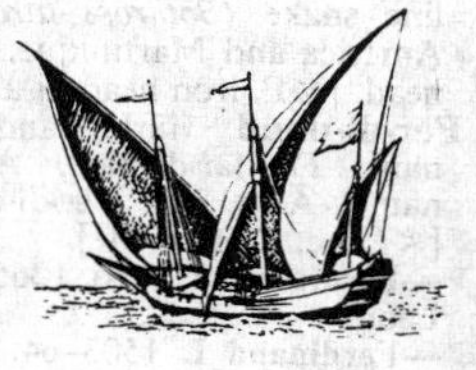

FELUCCA

fe·male (fē′māl) *adj.* **1** Of or pertaining to the sex that brings forth young or produces ova. **2** Characteristic of a woman; feminine. **3** *Bot.* Designating a plant which has a pistil but no stamen; pistillate; capable of being fertilized and producing fruit. **4** *Mech.* Denoting some object having a correlative known as the male; specifically, a part having a hollow or bore into which the correlative may enter. **5** *Obs.* Effeminate. See synonyms under FEMININE. — *n.* **1** A person or animal of the female sex. ◆ The use of the word to mean a woman is a survival of an old English usage now regarded with disfavor by good speakers and writers. But *female* is correctly used as the correlative of *male,* whether the latter be expressed or not: "Statistics of population show that there is an excess of *females* in many cities." **2** A pistillate plant. [<OF *femelle* <L *femella,* dim. of *femina* woman]

female rime A feminine rime.

female suffrage See under SUFFRAGE.

feme (fem) *n. Law* **1** A wife: a baron and *feme.* **2** *Obs.* A woman. [<OF]

feme cov·ert (kuv′ərt) *Law* A married woman.

feme sole (sōl) *Law* **1** A single woman, unmarried, widowed, or divorced. **2** A married woman who is independent of her husband in controlling her property.

feme–sole trader (fem′sōl′) *Law* A married woman in business on her own account, independently of her husband. Also **feme–sole merchant.**

fem·i·na·cy (fem′ə-nə-sē) *n. pl.* **·cies** Feminine qualities; female nature. [<L *femina* woman]

fem·i·nal·i·ty (fem′ə-nal′ə-tē) *n.* The quality of being female; womanliness. Also **fem′i·ne′i·ty** (-nē′ə-tē). [<OF *feminal* <L *femina* a woman]

fem·i·nie (fem′ə-nē) *n. Archaic* Women collectively; womankind; also, the Amazons. [<OF]

Fem·i·nie (fem′ə-nē) *Archaic* The country of the Amazons.

fem·i·nine (fem′ə-nin) *adj.* **1** Belonging to or characteristic of womankind; having qualities, as modesty, delicacy, tenderness, tact, etc., normally characteristic of women. **2** Lacking in manly qualities; effeminate. **3** *Gram.* Applicable to females only or to objects classified with them. — *n.* **1** Women, or a woman. **2** *Gram.* A word belonging to the feminine gender. [<L *femininus* <*femina* a woman] — **fem′i·nine·ly** *adv.* — **fem′i·nine·ness** *n.*

Synonyms (adj.): effeminate, female, womanish, womanly. We apply *female* to the sex, *feminine* to the qualities, especially the finer physical or mental qualities that distinguish the *female* sex in the human family, or to the objects appropriate for or especially employed by them. A *female* voice is the voice of a woman; a *feminine* voice may belong to a man. *Womanish* denotes the undesirable, *womanly* the admirable or lovely qualities of woman. *Womanly* tears would suggest respect and sympathy, *womanish* tears a touch of contempt. The word *effeminate* is always used reproachfully, and only of men as possessing *womanish* traits such as are inconsistent with true manliness. *Antonyms*: See synonyms for MASCULINE.

feminine ending **1** The termination of an iambic verse (line of poetry) with an unaccented final syllable. **2** *Gram.* A termination or final syllable indicating feminine gender.

feminine rime Rime of the two final syllables of two or more verses in which the accent falls on the next to the last syllable, as in Keats's *Endymion,*

A thing of beauty is a joy forever:
Its loveliness increases; it will never . . .

fem·i·nin·i·ty (fem′ə-nin′ə-tē) *n.* **1** The quality or state of being feminine. **2** Women collectively. Also **fe·min′i·ty.**

fem·i·nism (fem′ə-niz′əm) *n.* **1** The doctrine which declares the equality of the sexes and advocates equal social, political, and economic rights for women. **2** *Med.* The existence of female characteristics in the male. — **fem′i·nist** *n.* — **fem′i·nis′tic** *adj.*

fem·i·nize (fem′ə-nīz) *v.t.* & *v.i.* **·nized, ·niz·ing** To make or become effeminate or feminine. — **fem′i·ni·za′tion** *n.*

femme (fâm) *n. French* **1** A woman; wife. **2** *Law* Feme.

femme de cham·bre (də shäṅ′br′) *French* A chambermaid.

fem·o·ral (fem′ər-əl) *adj. Anat.* Pertaining to the femur or thigh: the *femoral* artery.

fe·mur (fē′mər) *n. pl.* **fe·murs** or **fem·o·ra** (fem′·ər-ə) **1** *Anat.* The long bone that forms the chief support of the thigh; thigh bone; thigh. **2** *Entomol.* The third, strongest, and most prominent segment of the leg in insects, situated between the trochanter and the tibia. Compare illustration under KNEE JOINT. [<L, thigh]

fen[1] (fen) *n.* A marsh; bog. — **The Fens** A low, flat district in Cambridgeshire, Norfolk, Huntingdonshire, and Lincolnshire, England. [OE *fenn*]

fen[2] (fen) *Scot. v.t.* & *v.i.* To defend; work hard to exist; struggle to live. — *n.* A struggle for one's self; a shift.

fence (fens) *n.* **1** An enclosing structure of rails, pickets, wires, or the like. **2** A defense; shield; bulwark. **3** The art of using weapons in self-defense; especially, the skilful use of the épée, rapier, or saber; hence, skill in repartee or debate. **4** *Mech.* A guard, guide, or gage. **5** A receiver of stolen goods, or the place where such goods are received. See synonyms under RAMPART. — **on the fence** Undecided or non-committal as to opposing opinions, parties, etc. — **worm fence** A zigzag fence of rails crossed at their ends: varieties of this fence are known as *panel, serpent, snake,* and *Virginia rail fence.* — *v.* **fenced, fenc·ing** *v.t.* **1** To enclose with or as with a fence. **2** To separate with or as with a fence. **3** *Archaic* To protect; shield. **4** *Obs.* To keep out; ward off. — *v.i.* **5** To engage in the art of fencing. **6** To attempt to avoid giving direct answers; parry. **7** To deal in stolen goods. See synonyms under CIRCUMSCRIBE. [Aphetic var. of DEFENSE]

fence·less (fens′lis) *adj.* Having no fence; unenclosed or unguarded; hence, defenseless. — **fence′less·ness** *n.*

fenc·er (fen′sər) *n.* 1 One who fences, as with foil or sword. 2 A horse good at leaping fences. 3 One who builds or mends fences.

fence-rid·er (fens′rī′dər) *n.* One who rides along fences on a cattle ranch to find and repair breaks: also called a *line-rider*.

fence-sit·ter (fens′sit′ər) *n. Colloq.* A person remaining neutral, usually waiting to see which side will win.

fence-view·er (fens′vyoo′ər) *n.* In New England, a township official in charge of the inspection and erecting of fences, and the settling of line disputes.

fenc·i·ble (fen′sə·bəl) *adj. Scot.* Capable of defending or of being defended. —*n. Archaic* A soldier enlisted for home service only.

fenc·ing (fen′sing) *n.* 1 The art of attacking and defending as with a foil or sword. 2 Skilful debate or the parrying of prying questions. 3 Material for fences; fences collectively.

fend (fend) *v.t.* 1 To ward off; parry: usually with *off.* 2 *Archaic* To defend. —*v.i.* 3 To offer resistance; parry. 4 *Colloq.* To provide or get along: with *for:* to *fend for* oneself. [Aphetic var. of DEFEND]

fend·er (fen′dər) *n.* 1 One who or that which fends or wards off. 2 A metal guard before an open fire, to keep burning coals from falling onto the floor. 3 *Naut.* Any timber, rope plaiting, or other device hanging against or lying along a vessel's side as a protection from injury. 4 A plate of pressed steel over the wheels of a motor vehicle; a mudguard.

Fé·ne·lon (fā·nə·lôn′), **François de Salignac de la Mothe,** 1651–1715, French ecclesiastic and writer.

fen·es·tel·la (fen′is·tel′ə) *n. pl.* **·lae** (-ē) *Archit.* 1 A small window. 2 A niche in the wall to the side of the altar of a Roman Catholic church, containing a piscina and often the credence. [< L, dim. of *fenestra* window]

fe·nes·tra (fə·nes′trə) *n. pl.* **·trae** (-trē) 1 *Anat.* A windowlike aperture in the body: the **fenestra ovalis,** the opening between the tympanum and the vestibule of the middle ear, closed by the foot of the stapes. See illustration under EAR. 2 *Entomol.* A transparent, glassy spot, as in the wings of some insects. [< L] —**fe·nes′tral** *adj.*

fe·nes·trate (fə·nes′trit, -trāt) *adj.* 1 Having windows or windowlike openings. 2 Having transparent spots. Also **fe·nes′trat·ed.** [< L *fenestratus,* pp. of *fenestrare* furnish with windows < *fenestra* window]

fen·es·tra·tion (fen′is·trā′shən) *n.* 1 The design or arrangement of the windows of a building. 2 A fenestral or fenestrated state. 3 *Surg.* The operation of perforating: *fenestration* of the semicircular canals.

Feng·kieh (fung′jye′) A city on the Yangtze in south central China. Formerly **Kwei·chow** (gwā′jō′).

Feng·tien (fung′tyen′) The former name for MUKDEN.

Fe·ni·an (fē′nē·ən, fēn′yən) *n.* 1 A member of an Irish society called the Fenian Brotherhood, formed in New York in 1857 to seek independence for Ireland. 2 One sympathizing with the Fenian Brotherhood. 3 One of the Fianna, the warriors of Fionn MacCumal, Irish chieftain of the second and third centuries. —*adj.* Of or belonging to, composed of, or characteristic of the Fenians or the Fianna. [< Irish *Fiann,* a legendary Irish warrior; infl. by OIrish *fene* an Irishman] —**Fe′ni·an·ism** *n.*

Fenian cycle A body of Old Irish tales dealing with the expoits of Fionn MacCumal and his warriors, called the Fianna, in the second and third centuries A.D.

fen·land (fen′land′) *n.* Low, boggy land; marsh.

fen·nec (fen′ek) *n.* A small, fawn-colored African fox (*Vulpes zenda*) having very large, pointed ears. [< Arabic *fanak*]

fen·nel (fen′əl) *n.* 1 A tall, stout European herb (*Foeniculum vulgare*) of the parsley family, with finely dissected leaves and yellow flowers: cultivated in the United States for use in sauces and for its aromatic seeds. 2 The seeds of this plant. —**giant fennel** An Old World herb (*Ferula communis*) of the parsley family, sometimes attaining a height of 15 feet. [OE *fenugl, fenol* < L *faeniculum* fennel, dim. of *faenum* hay]

fen·nel·flow·er (fen′əl·flou′ər) *n.* 1 An ornamental annual herb (genus *Nigella*) of the crowfoot family; ragged lady. 2 The nutmeg flower (*N. sativa*), the seeds of which are used as seasoning.

fen·ny (fen′ē) *adj.* Marshy; boggy. Also **fen′nish.**

Fen·rir (fen′rir) In Norse mythology, a monster wolf, the son of Loki. He is kept chained by the gods, but will break loose at Ragnarok, swallow Odin, and be killed by Vidar, Odin's son. Also **Fen′rer, Fen·ris·wolf** (fen′ris·wŏŏlf′).

fent (fent) *n. Brit.* 1 A remnant or flawed piece of fabric. 2 *Dial.* A slit or vent in a garment. [< F *fente* < *fendre* split < L *findere*]

fen·u·greek (fen′yŏŏ·grēk′) *n.* 1 An Old World herb (*Trigonella foenum-graecum*) of the pea family, having strong-scented leaves and mucilaginous seeds. 2 The seeds, used in medicine and as curry powder. [OE *feno-graecum* < L *faenum Graecum* Greek hay]

feod (fyōod) *n.* **feo·dal** (fyōod′l), etc. See FEUD, etc.

Fe·o·dor (fā′ə·dôr) Polish and Russian form of THEODORE.

feoff (fef, fēf) *Law v.t.* **feoffed, feoff·ing** To give or grant a fief to; enfeoff. —*n.* A fief; fee. [< AF *feoffer,* OF *fieffer* < *fief* FIEF]

feoff·ee (fef·ē′, fēf·ē′) *n. Law* One to whom a feoffment is made.

feof·fer (fef′ər, fēf′-) *n.* One who grants a feoffment. Also **feof′for.**

feoff·ment (fef′mənt, fēf′-) *n.* 1 A grant of lands in fee by deed with delivery. 2 The accompanying deed.

-fer *combining form* One who or that which bears: *conifer.* [< L < *ferre* bear]

fe·ra·cious (fə·rā′shəs) *adj.* Fruitful; fertile. [< L *ferax, feracis* < *ferre* bear] —**fe·rac·i·ty** (fə·ras′ə·tē) *n.*

fe·ral (fir′əl) *adj.* 1 Undomesticated; existing in a wild state; savage. 2 Pertaining to or characteristic of the wild state. Also *ferine.*

Fer·ber (fûr′bər), **Edna,** 1887–1968, U.S. novelist and playwright.

fer-de-lance (fâr′də·läns′) *n.* A venomous crotaline snake (*Bothrops atrox*) of tropical South America and Martinique, related to the copperhead. [< F, iron head of a lance]

Fer·di·nand (fûr′di·nand, *Du., Ger.* fer′dē·nänt; *Fr.* fâr·dē·nän′) A masculine personal name. Also *Ital.* **Fer·di·nan·do** (fer′dē·nän′dō). [< Gmc., ? brave life]

—**Ferdinand I,** died 1065, king of Castile and Leon.

—**Ferdinand I,** 1503–64, king of Bohemia and Hungary; Holy Roman Emperor 1556–64.

—**Ferdinand II,** 1578–1637, king of Bohemia and Hungary; Holy Roman Emperor 1619–1637; grandson of preceding; involved in the Thirty Years' War.

—**Ferdinand III,** 1608–57, king of Bohemia and Hungary; Holy Roman Emperor 1637–57; son of Ferdinand II; signed Peace of Westphalia, 1648.

—**Ferdinand V,** 1452–1516, king of Castile and Aragon; established the Inquisition at Seville; expelled the Jews and Moors; promoted the expeditions of Columbus and Vespucci. Known as *Ferdinand the Catholic.*

—**Ferdinand VII,** 1784–1833, king of Spain 1808, 1814–33.

fere[1] (fir) *adj. Obs.* Able; strong; healthy. [< ON *foer(r)*]

fere[2] (fir) *n. Obs.* A companion: also spelled *feer.* [ME, OE *gefera.* Related to FARE.]

Fer·en·czi (fer′ən·tsē), **Sandor,** 1873–1933, Hungarian psychoanalyst.

fer·e·to·ry (fer′ə·tôr′ē, -tō′rē) *n. pl.* **·ries** 1 A portable shrine for the relics of saints; a reliquary. 2 The place in a church where the shrine is kept; a fixed shrine. [Alter. of earlier *fertre* < OF *fiertre* < L *feretrum* < Gk. *pheretron* < *pherein* bear]

FERETORY (def. 1)

Fer·ga·na (fer·gä′nə) A city in Uzbek S.S.R.

Fer·gus (fûr′gəs) A masculine personal name. [< Celtic, man's strength]

Fer·gu·son (fûr′gə·sən), **Samuel,** 1810–86, Irish poet and antiquary.

fe·ri·a (fir′ē·ə) *n. pl.* **·ri·ae** (-ē) 1 Any day of the week except Sunday, if not a church feast day. 2 *pl.* Holidays; festivals. [< L, holiday] —**fe′ri·al** *adj.*

fe·rine (fir′īn, -in) *adj.* Feral. [< L *ferinus* < *fera* wild beast] —**fe′rine·ly** *adv.*

Fe·ring·gi (fə·ring′gē) *n.* In the Orient, a European: among the Hindus, a European, usually in a disparaging sense, or specifically, an Indianborn Portuguese. Also **Fe·ren′ghi, Fe·rin′gee, Fe·rin′ghee, Fe·rin′ghi.** [< Persian *farangi* < Arabic *faranji* a Frank]

fer·i·ty (fer′ə·tē) *n.* Wildness; fierceness; cruelty. [< L *feritas, -tatis* < *ferus* wild, fierce]

fer·ly (fûr′lē) *adj. Obs.* Fearful or wonderful; surprising; sudden. —*n. pl.* **·lies** 1 *Scot. & Brit. Dial.* A wonder or marvel; also, wonder; surprise. 2 A fault or weakness. —*v.t. & v.i.* **fer·lied, fer·ly·ing** *Scot. & Brit. Dial.* To surprise, wonder. Also **fer′lie.** [OE *færlic* sudden < *fær* sudden danger]

Fer·man·agh (fər·man′ə) A county in SW Northern Ireland, once in Ulster; 653 square miles; county town, Enniskillen.

fer·ma·ta (fer·mä′tä) *n. Music* A pause of indeterminate length. Also *German* **fer·ma·te** (fer·mä′te). [< Ital.]

Fer·ma·tian (fər·mä′shən) *adj.* Of or pertaining to **Pierre de Fer·mat** (fer·mä′), 1601–65, French mathematician, or to the method of mathematical induction used by him.

Fer·mat's spiral (fûr′mats) A parabolic spiral.

fer·ment (fûr′ment) *n.* 1 A substance productive of fermentation, as yeast; an enzyme. 2 Fermentation. 3 Excitement or agitation. —*v.t. & v.i.* (fər·ment′) 1 To undergo fermentation or produce fermentation in; work. 2 To stir with anger; agitate or be agitated by emotions or passions. [< F < L *fermentum* < *fervere* boil] —**fer·ment′a·ble** or **·i·ble** *adj.* —**fer·ment′a·bil′i·ty** *n.*

fer·men·ta·tion (fûr′mən·tā′shən) *n.* 1 *Chem.* The gradual decomposition of organic compounds induced by the action of living organisms, by enzymes, or by chemical agents; specifically, the conversion of glucose into ethyl alcohol through the action of zymase. 2 Commotion, agitation, or excitement.

fer·ment·a·tive (fər·men′tə·tiv) *adj.* Causing, capable of causing, or caused by fermentation; fermenting.

fer·mi (fer′mē, fûr′-) *n. Physics* A unit for the measurement of the radii of atomic particles, equal to 10^{-13} centimeter. [after E. Fermi]

Fer·mi (fer′mē), **Enrico,** 1901–54, Italian nuclear physicist active in the United States.

fer·mi·um (fer′mē·əm, fûr′-) *n.* A synthetic radioactive element (symbol Fm, atomic number 100) produced by neutron bombardment of plutonium and by other nuclear reactions, first identified in residue from a thermonuclear explosion. See PERIODIC TABLE. [after E. Fermi]

fern[1] (fûrn) *n.* Any of a widely distributed class (*Filicineae*) of flowerless, seedless pteridophytic plants, having roots and stems and feathery leaves (fronds) which carry the reproductive spores in clusters of sporangia called *sori*: related to the horsetails and clubmosses. See SORUS. [OE *fearn*] —**fern′like** *adj.*

fern[2] (fûrn) *Obs. adj.* Former. —*adv.* Formerly; in olden times. [OE *fyrn*]

Fer·nán·dez (fer·nän′dāth), **Juan,** 1536?–1602?, Spanish navigator.

Fer·nan·do (fer·nän′·dō) Italian and Spanish form of FERDINAND. Also *Pg.* **Fer·não** (fer·noun′).

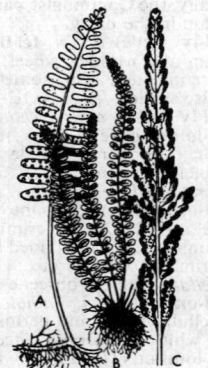

FERNS

A. Polypodium: rootstock and frond.
B. Asplenium trichomanes: fronds.
C. Osmunda cinnamomea: fertile frond.

Fer·nan·do de No·ro·nha (fer·nän′dōō de nō·rō′nyə) An island in the South Atlantic comprising a federal territory of Brazil; 7 square miles.
Fernando Po (pō) An island in the Bight of Biafra, comprising a district of Spanish Guinea; 779 square miles; capital, Santa Isabel. *Spanish* **Fer·nan′do Pó·o** (pō′ō).
fern·er·y (fûr′nər·ē) *n.* *pl.* **·er·ies** A place in which ferns are grown.
fern seed The reproductive spores of the fern which were formerly supposed to render one carrying them invisible.
fern·wort (fûrn′wûrt′) *n.* Any pteridophyte or fern.
fern·y (fûr′nē) *adj.* Of, pertaining to, abounding in, or resembling ferns.
fe·ro·cious (fə·rō′shəs) *adj.* **1** Of a fierce and savage nature; rapacious. **2** Very intense: *ferocious* heat. See synonyms under FIERCE, GRIM. [<L *ferox, ferocis* <*ferus* wild beast] — **fe·ro′cious·ly** *adv.* — **fe·ro′cious·ness** *n.*
fe·roc·i·ty (fə·ros′ə·tē) *n.* *pl.* **·ties** The state or quality of being ferocious or savage; fierce cruelty.
-ferous *combining form* Bearing or producing: *coniferous.* [<-FER + -OUS]
fer·ral·i·um (fə·ral′ē·əm) *n.* A medicine or drug containing iron; a chalybeate. [Erroneous sing. of NL *ferralia* <L *ferralis* containing iron <*ferrum* iron]
Fer·rand (fe·räṅ′) French form of FERDINAND. Also *Ital.* **Fer·ran·do** (fer·rän′dō).
Fer·ra·ra (fə·rä′rə, *Ital.* fer·rä′rä) A city in north central Italy in the Po delta. — **Fer·ra·rese** (fer′ə·rēz′, -rēs′) *adj.* & *n.*
fer·rate (fer′āt) *n.* *Chem.* A salt of the hypothetical ferric acid, especially **sodium ferrate,** Na_2FeO_4, a deep-red or purple, unstable solution.
fer·re·ous (fer′ē·əs) See FERROUS.
Fer·re·ro (fer·rā′rō), **Guglielmo,** 1871–1942, Italian historian.
fer·ret[1] (fer′it) *n.* **1** A small, red-eyed domesticated polecat of Europe (genus *Mustela*), about 14 inches long: used to hunt rodents and other vermin. **2** A black-footed weasel of the western United States (*M. nigripes*), which preys on prairie dogs. — *adj.* Ferret-like; red, like the eyes of a ferret. — *v.t.* **1** To drive out of hiding with a ferret. **2** To search out by careful investigation: with *out.* **3** To hunt with ferrets. — *v.i.* **4** To hunt by means of ferrets. **5** To search. [<OF *fuiret,* dim. of *fuiron* <LL *furon* robber <*fur* a thief] — **fer′ret·er** *n.* — **fer′ret·y** *adj.*

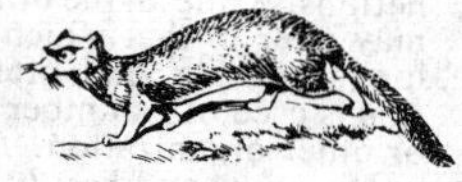

FERRET

fer·ret[2] (fer′it) *n.* A narrow ribbon or tape, used for binding fabrics, etc. Also **fer′ret·ing.** [<Ital. *fioretto,* dim. of *fiore* a flower <L *flos, floris*]
fer·ret[3] (fer′it) *n.* A glassmaker's iron rod for trying the melted material. [<F, dim. of *fer* iron <L *ferrum*]
ferret badger A stout-bodied carnivore (genus *Helictis*) of SE Asia.
ferri- *combining form Chem.* Containing iron in the ferric condition: *ferricyanide.* [Var. of FERRO-]
fer·ri·age (fer′ē·ij) *n.* **1** The act of ferrying; conveyance by ferry. **2** The toll charged for ferrying.
fer·ric (fer′ik) *adj. Chem.* **1** Pertaining to iron. **2** Pertaining to or designating compounds of iron in its higher valence. [<L *ferrum* iron + -IC]
ferric acetate *Chem.* A reddish-brown powder, $FeO_5H_7C_4$, widely used as an ingredient in many chemicals as a mordant, and in certain drug preparations.
ferric oxide Hematite.
ferric sulfate *Chem.* A compound of iron, $Fe_2(SO_4)_3$, uniting with water in the form of colorless crystals: used alone or as iron alum in tanning and dyeing.
fer·ri·cy·an·ic (fer′ə·sī·an′ik) *adj. Chem.* Of or pertaining to a compound of iron in its higher valence and cyanogen: *ferricyanic* acid, $H_3Fe(CN)_6$.
fer·ri·cy·a·nide (fer′ə·sī′ə·nīd, -nid) *n.* *Chem.* A salt containing the trivalent negative ion radical $Fe(CN)_6$, as potassium ferricyanide, $K_3Fe(CN)_6$.
fer·rif·er·ous (fə·rif′ər·əs) *adj.* Yielding iron, as rocks.
Fer·ris wheel (fer′is) A giant, vertical, power-driven wheel that revolves on a stationary axle and bears swinging observation cars for passengers. Also **ferris wheel.** [after G. W. G. *Ferris,* 1859–96, U.S. engineer]
fer·rite (fer′īt) *n.* **1** *Geol.* Indeterminable reddish decomposition products in altered igneous rocks, presumably containing iron. **2** *Chem.* Any compound, such as franklinite (zinc ferrite), considered as a derivative of the ferric hydroxide, $Fe(OH)_3$. **3** *Metall.* The pure metallic constituent in iron and steel. [<L *ferrum* iron + -ITE[1]]
Fer·ro (fer′rō) A former name for HIERRO.
ferro- *combining form* **1** Derived from, containing, or alloyed with iron: *ferromanganese.* **2** *Chem.* Containing iron in the ferrous condition: *ferrocyanide.* [<L *ferrum* iron]
fer·ro·al·loy (fer′ō·al′oi, -ə·loi′) *n.* *Metall.* An alloy of iron with certain other metals used in the making of special steels, as nickel, manganese, chromium, etc.
fer·ro·cal·cite (fer′ō·kal′sīt) *n.* A variety of calcite containing ferrous carbonate.
fer·ro·chrome (fer′ō·krōm′) *n.* *Metall.* An alloy of iron and chromium: used in the production of especially hard steel. Also **fer′ro·chro′mi·um.**
fer·ro·con·crete (fer′ō·kon′krēt, -kon·krēt′) *n.* Concrete containing metal bars or rods disposed through the mass in such a way as to increase its tensile strength and durability: also called *reinforced concrete.*
fer·ro·cy·an·ic (fer′ō·sī·an′ik) *adj. Chem.* Designating a compound obtained by the treatment of ferrocyanide with acid: *hydroferrocyanic* acid, $H_4Fe(CN)_6$.
fer·ro·cy·a·nide (fer′ō·sī′ə·nīd, -nid) *n.* *Chem.* A compound containing the tetravalent radical $Fe(CN)_6$: potassium *ferrocyanide,* $K_4Fe(CN)_6$.
Fer·rol (fer·rōl′) See EL FERROL DEL CAUDILLO.
fer·ro·mag·ne·sian (fer′ō·mag·nē′shən) *adj.* *Geol.* Relating to rocks rich in iron and magnesium, as pyroxene.
fer·ro·mag·net·ic (fer′ō·mag·net′ik) *adj.* *Physics* **1** Acting in a magnetic field as or like iron; also, extremely magnetic. **2** Formerly, paramagnetic. — **fer′ro·mag′ne·tism** *n.*
fer·ro·man·ga·nese (fer′ō·mang′gə·nēs, -nēz) *n.* An alloy of iron, containing 50 percent or more of manganese and being rich in carbon: used in making tough steel.
fer·ro·mo·lyb·de·num (fer′ō·mə·lib′də·nəm) *n.* An alloy of iron and molybdenum: used in the manufacture of a special steel.
fer·ro·nick·el (fer′ō·nik′əl) *n.* An alloy of iron containing at least 25 percent of nickel and practically free from carbon.
fer·ro·sil·i·con (fer′ō·sil′ə·kən) *n.* An alloy of silicon and iron added to iron when molten, to increase the proportion of silicon.
fer·ro·tung·sten (fer′ō·tung′stən) *n.* An alloy of iron and tungsten: used in the manufacture of high-speed tool steel.
fer·ro·type (fer′ō·tīp′) *n.* A tintype.
fer·rous (fer′əs) *adj. Chem.* Of or pertaining to bivalent iron, where its combining value is lowest: *ferrous* chloride, $FeCl_2$: also spelled *ferreous.* [<L *ferrum* iron + -OUS]
ferrous carbonate A compound, $FeCO_3$, precipitated as a white solid, uniting readily with the free oxygen of the air; also found as a mineral, which is an important iron ore.
ferrous sulfate A compound, $FeSO_4 \cdot H_2O$, which unites with free oxygen to form ferric sulfate. See COPPERAS.
ferrous sulfide A compound, FeS, formed either as a black solid precipitated by the action of an iron salt solution with an alkaline sulfide, or as a brittle solid from the union of sulfur and iron under heat: a source of hydrogen sulfide.
fer·ro·va·na·di·um (fer′ō·və·nā′dē·əm) *n.* An alloy of iron and vanadium: used in the manufacture of a special steel.
fer·ru·gi·nous (fə·rōō′jə·nəs) *adj.* **1** Of or like iron. **2** Rust-colored. [<L *ferruginus* <*ferrugo, -inis,* iron rust <*ferrum* iron]
ferruginous thrush The brown thrasher.
fer·rule (fer′əl, -ōōl, -ool) *n.* **1** A metal ring or cap, as on the end of a cane or around the handle of a tool. **2** A bushing or thimble. **3** The frame of a slate. **4** A ferule. — *v.t.* **·ruled, ·rul·ing** To furnish with a ferrule. [Earlier *verrel* <OF *virelle* <L *viriola,* dim. of *viriae* bracelets; infl. in form by L *ferrum* iron]
fer·ry (fer′ē) *n.* *pl.* **·ries** **1** Transportation by boat or airplane across a body of water. **2** The place of crossing a river, bay, strait, or the like by boat. **3** The legal right to run a ferry and to charge toll for transporting passengers and goods. **4** A boat for such transportation; a ferryboat. — **trail ferry** A raft connected with a cable crossing a stream and so adjusted as to utilize the force of the current for motive power. [< *v.*] — *v.* **fer·ried, fer·ry·ing** *v.t.* **1** To carry across a body of water in a boat. **2** To cross (a river, bay, etc.) in a boat. **3** To bring or take (an airplane or vehicle) to a point of delivery under its own power. — *v.i.* **4** To cross a body of water in a boat or by ferry. [OE *ferian* carry, convey]
fer·ry·boat (fer′ē·bōt′) *n.* A boat, often double-ended, used to transport passengers, vehicles, goods, etc., across a river, bay, strait, etc.
fer·ry·man (fer′ē·mən) *n.* *pl.* **·men** (-mən) **1** One who has charge of a ferry: also **fer′ry·mas′ter.** **2** A member of the crew of a ferry.
ferry slip A landing dock for a ferryboat.
fer·tile (fûr′təl) *adj.* **1** Producing or capable of producing abundantly; fruitful or prolific; rich; productive; inventive. **2** Reproducing or capable of reproducing. **3** *Bot.* **a** Bearing or capable of producing fruit; capable of fertilizing or of being fertilized, as perfect anthers and pistils. **b** Productive of spore-bearing organs: said of ferns, etc. **4** *Biol.* Capable of growth or development; productive: said of seeds or eggs. **5** Causing or imparting productiveness: *fertile* rains. **6** Produced abundantly; plentiful. [<OF *fertil* <L *fertilis* <*ferre* bear] — **fer′tile·ly** *adv.*
Synonyms: exuberant, fecund, fruitful, luxuriant, productive, prolific, rich, teeming.
Fertile Crescent **1** Originally, the arc-shaped area in the Near and Middle East in which agriculture was supposedly first practiced. **2** A similar region extending from the Levant to modern Iraq.
fer·til·i·ty (fər·til′ə·tē) *n.* **1** The state or quality of being fertile. **2** Procreative capacity; fruitfulness. **3** Quickness; readiness. Also **fer′tile·ness.**
fer·til·i·za·tion (fûr′təl·ə·zā′shən) *n.* **1** The act or process of fertilizing or rendering productive. **2** *Biol.* The fusion of two gametes or of the sperm or male cell with an egg, to form a new individual, the zygote. **3** *Bot.* Pollination. **4** The treatment of soils to increase their crop productivity.
fer·til·ize (fûr′təl·īz) *v.t.* **·ized, ·iz·ing** **1** To render fertile or fruitful. **2** To impregnate an egg, ovum, or seed. **3** To enrich, as soil. — **fer′til·iz′a·ble** *adj.*
fer·til·iz·er (fûr′təl·īz′ər) *n.* **1** One who or that which fertilizes. **2** A fertilizing material applied to soil, as guano, manure, etc.
fer·u·la (fer′yōō·lə, -ōō·lə) *n.* *pl.* **·lae** (-lē) or **·las** **1** Any of a large genus (*Ferula*) of chiefly Mediterranean herbs of the parsley family, with dissected leaves and umbels of yellow flowers. Several species supply important medicinal products, as asafetida, galbanum, and sumbul or muskroot. **2** A ferule; rod. **3** A scepter, especially that of the Byzantine emperors. [<L, giant fennel, whip, rod]
fer·u·la·ceous (fer′yōō·lā′shəs, -ōō-) *adj.* Pertaining to reeds or canes; having a stalk like a reed.
fer·ule (fer′əl, -ōōl) *n.* **1** A flat stick or ruler sometimes used for punishing children. **2** Punishment; discipline. — *v.t.* **fer·uled, fer·ul·ing** To punish with a ferule. [<L *ferula* FERULA]
fer·vent (fûr′vənt) *adj.* **1** Ardent in feeling; fervid. **2** Burning, or very hot. See synonyms under ARDENT, EAGER, HOT. [<L *fervens, -entis,* pp. of *fervere* be hot] — **fer′ven·cy** *n.* — **fer′vent·ly** *adv.* — **fer′vent·ness** *n.*
fer·vid (fûr′vid) *adj.* **1** Burning with zeal or eagerness; vehement. **2** Hot; glowing; fiery. [<L *fervidus* hot, violent <*fervere* be hot]

— fer·vid′i·ty, fer′vid·ness *n.* **— fer′vid·ly** *adv.*
Fer·vi·dor (fûr′vi·dôr, *Fr.* fer·vē·dôr′) See under CALENDAR (Republican).
fer·vor (fûr′vər) *n.* **1** Ardor, or intensity of feeling; zeal. **2** Heat; warmth. Also *Brit.* **fer′vour.** See synonyms under ENTHUSIASM, WARMTH. [<OF <L, heat, passion <*fervere* be hot]
Fès (fes) See FEZ.
Fes·cen·nine (fes′ə·nīn, -nin) *adj.* Relating to the ancient festivals attributed to Fescennium, a town in Etruria, and to the rude jests and licentious verses that characterized the festivals; hence, obscene; indelicate.
fes·cue (fes′kyo͞o) *n.* **1** Any of a genus *(Festuca)* of slender, tough grasses, valuable for pasturage. **2** A twig or straw formerly used to point out the letters to children learning to read. [<OF *festu* <L *festuca* a stalk, straw]
fess (fes) *n. Her.* A horizontal band across the middle of the shield and having a breadth equal to one third of the field. Compare illustration under ESCUTCHEON. Also **fesse.** [<OF *fesse* <L *fascia* band]

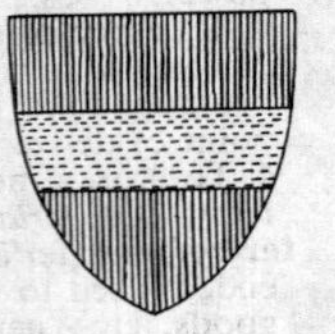
FESS

Fes·sen·den (fes′ən·dən), **William Pitt,** 1806–1869, U.S. statesman.
fess·wise (fes′wīz′) *adv. Her.* Horizontally. Also **fesse′wise′.**
fes·tal (fes′təl) *adj.* Pertaining to a festival, feast, or holiday; festive. [<OF <L *festum* a feast] **— fes′tal·ly** *adv.*
fes·ter (fes′tər) *v.i.* **1** To generate morbid matter; ulcerate. **2** To become embittered; rankle. **3** To decay; rot. **—** *v.t.* **4** To cause to fester or rankle. [<*n.*] **—** *n.* **1** The act of festering; rankling. **2** An ulcerous sore. [<OF *festre* <L *fistula* ulcer]
fes·ti·na len·te (fes·tī′nə len′tē) *Latin* Make haste slowly.
fes·ti·nate (fes′tə·nāt) *Obs. v.t. & v.i.* **fes·ti·nat·ed, fes·ti·nat·ing** To hasten. **—** *adj.* Quick; speedy. [<L *festinatus,* pp. of *festinare* hasten] **— fes′ti·nate·ly** *adv.*
fes·ti·na·tion (fes′tə·nā′shən) *n.* **1** *Psychiatry* Involuntary haste in walking, as in certain nervous diseases. **2** Haste.
fes·ti·val (fes′tə·vəl) *adj.* **1** Of, pertaining to, or suitable to a feast. **2** *Obs.* Joyous; merry. **—** *n.* **1** A period of feasting or celebration, as an anniversary. **2** A season devoted periodically to some form of entertainment. **3** An entertainment, as a supper, bazaar, etc., to raise funds for some charitable or other purpose: a church *festival.* [<OF <Med. L *festivalis* <L *festivus* FESTIVE]
fes·tive (fes′tiv) *adj.* Pertaining or suited to a feast; gay; joyful. [<L *festivus* <*festum* feast] **— fes′tive·ly** *adv.* **— fes′tive·ness** *n.*
fes·tiv·i·ty (fes·tiv′ə·tē) *n. pl.* **·ties** A festive celebration; social enjoyment or merriment; gaiety; merrymaking. See synonyms under FROLIC, REVEL.
fes·toon (fes·to͞on′) *n.* **1** A decorative garland or band hanging in a curve between two points. **2** An ornamental carving resembling a wreath or garland. **—** *v.t.* **1** To decorate with festoons. **2** To fashion into festoons. **3** To link together by festoons. [<F *feston* <Ital. *festone* <*festa* a feast <L *festus*] **— fes·toon′y** *adj.*
fes·toon·er·y (fes·to͞on′ər·ē) *n.* A system, method, or arrangement of festoons.
fet (fet) *v.t. Obs.* **fet·ted, fet·ting** To fetch. [OE *fetian*]
fe·tal (fēt′l) *adj.* Pertaining to the fetus: also spelled *foetal.*
fetal rickets Achondroplasia.
fe·ta·tion (fē·tā′shən) *n.* Pregnancy: also spelled *foetation.*
fetch¹ (fech) *v.t.* **1** To go after and bring back. **2** To cause to come; draw; bring, as a reply. **3** To heave (a sigh); to utter (a groan). **4** To bring as a price; sell for. **5** To execute; perform, as a leap or other movement. **6** *Colloq.* To captivate; charm. **7** *Naut.* To reach or arrive at. **8** *Colloq.* To strike or deliver, as a blow. **—** *v.i.* **9** To go after and bring things back. **10** In hunting, to retrieve game. **11** *Naut.* **a** To take a course. **b** To reach or get. **— to fetch and carry** To perform menial tasks; be a servant. **— to fetch up** To rear; bring up. **—** *n.* **1** The act of fetching. **2** The distance something is brought. **3** A stratagem. [OE *feccan,* var. of *fetian.* See FET.]
fetch² (fech) *v.t. Scot.* To pull by fits and starts.
fetch³ (fech) *n.* The apparition of one still living; a wraith. [Origin uncertain]
fetch·er (fech′ər) *n.* One who or that which goes and brings.
fetch·ing (fech′ing) *adj. Colloq.* Calculated to attract; taking; fascinating. **— fetch′ing·ly** *adv.*
fête (fāt) *n.* A festival; holiday. **—** *v.t.* **fêt·ed, fêt·ing** To honor with festivities; give a feast or celebration for. [<F <OF *feste.* See FEAST.]
fête cham·pê·tre (fet shäṅ·pe′tr′) *French* An open-air festival.
fet·e·ri·ta (fet′ə·rē′tə) *n.* A variety of sorghum introduced as fodder in the United States: also called *Sudan durra.* [< native Sudanese name]
fe·tial (fē′shəl) *adj.* Pertaining to the fetiales or to their office. **—** *n.* One of the fetiales. Also spelled *fecial.*
fe·ti·a·les (fē′shē·ā′lēz) *n. pl.* A college of twenty priests or heralds in ancient Rome who conducted the negotiations and the ceremonies attending declarations of war and peace. [<L; ult. origin unknown]
fe·ti·cide (fē′tə·sīd) *n.* **1** *Law* The felonious killing of an unborn child. **2** The intentional production of abortion. Also spelled *foeticide.* [<L *fetus* fetus + -CIDE] **— fe′ti·ci′dal** *adj.*
fet·id (fet′id) *adj.* Emitting an offensive odor: also spelled *foetid.* See synonyms under NOISOME, ROTTEN. [<L *fetidus* <*fetere* stink] **— fet′id·ly** *adv.* **— fet′id·ness** *n.*
fetid hellebore Helleboraster.
fe·tip·a·rous (fə·tip′ər·əs) *adj.* Bringing forth undeveloped young, as marsupials: also spelled *foetiparous.* [<L *fetus* fetus + -PAROUS]
fe·tish (fē′tish, fet′ish) *n.* **1** A natural object believed to be the dwelling of a spirit, or to represent a spirit that may be induced or compelled magically to help and safeguard the possessor, and to protect him from harm or disease: an object of worship among savages. **2** Any object of devotion or blind affection. Also **fe′tich.** [<F *fétiche* <Pg. *feitiço* a charm, orig. an adj. <L *factitius* artificial]
fe·tish·ism (fē′tish·iz′əm, fet′ish-) *n.* **1** The belief in, devotion to, or worship of fetishes, or rites used in fetish-worship. **2** The mental state which characterizes such worship; superstition. **3** *Psychiatry* Sensual or sexual pleasure derived from fixing the attention on a part of the body or on a piece of wearing apparel belonging to a person. Also **fe′tich·ism.** **— fe′tish·ist** *n.* **— fe′tish·is′tic** *adj.*
fet·lock (fet′lok′) *n.* **1** The tuft of hair above a horse's hoof. **2** The projection and the joint at this place. See illustration under HORSE. [ME *fitlok, fetlak,* prob. <LG. Cf. Du. *vitlok.*]
fe·tor (fē′tər, -tôr) *n.* A stench: also spelled *foetor.* [<L]
fet·ter (fet′ər) *n.* A shackle for the ankles or a rope that binds, etc.; hence, anything that confines. **—** *v.t.* **1** To fasten fetters upon; shackle. **2** To prevent the activity of; restrain. [OE *feter, fetor.* Related to FOOT.]
Synonyms (noun): bondage, bonds, chains, custody, durance, duress, gyves, handcuffs, imprisonment, irons, manacles, shackles. *Bonds* may be of cord, leather, or any other substance that can bind; *chains* are of linked metal. *Manacles* and *handcuffs* are for the hands, *fetters* are primarily chains or jointed iron fastenings for the ankles; *gyves* may be for either. A *shackle* is a metallic ring, clasp, or braceletlike fastening for encircling and restraining a limb: commonly one of a pair, used either for hands or feet. *Bonds, fetters,* and *chains* are used in a general way for almost any form of restraint. *Gyves* is now wholly poetic, and the other words are mostly restricted to the literary style; *handcuffs* is the specific and *irons* the general term in popular usage; as, The prisoner was put in *irons. Bonds, chains,* and *shackles* are frequently used in the metaphorical sense of restraint.
fetter bone The first phalanx or great pastern of a horse's foot, just below the fetlock. See illustration under HORSE.
fet·ter·bush (fet′ər·bo͝osh′) *n.* **1** An evergreen shrub *(Lyonia lucida)* of the heath family, with alternate leaves and fragrant white flowers, of the southern United States. **2** A related shrub *(Pieris floribunda),* with white, bell-shaped flowers.
fet·ter·lock (fet′ər·lok′) *n.* A fetlock.
fet·tle (fet′l) *v.t.* **fet·tled, fet·tling** **1** *Metall.* To line or cover with a refractory material: to *fettle* the hearth of a puddling furnace. **2** *Brit. Dial.* To put in repair or good condition. **3** To beat; thrash. **—** *n.* **1** State of repair; condition. **2** The fettling used in a furnace. **— fine fettle** Good condition; high spirits. [ME *fetlen* prepare, lit., gird up <OE *fetel* a belt]
fet·tling (fet′ling) *n. Metall.* Iron ore, cinder, or other oxidizing agents, used to cover the hearth of a puddling furnace before charging it.
fet·tuc·ci·ne (fet′ə·chē′nē) *n.pl. (construed as sing. or pl.)* Flat noodles, often prepared with butter, cheese, heavy cream, etc. Also **fet′tu·ci′ne, fet′tu·ci′ni.** [<Ital., lit., dim. of *fettucia* ribbon]
fe·tus (fē′təs) *n. pl.* **fe·tus·es** The young in the womb of viviparous animals in the later stages of development; specifically, in women, from the end of the second month, prior to which it is called the *embryo*; unborn offspring: also spelled *foetus.* [<L]
feu (fyo͞o) *n.* **1** Tenure of lands based on agricultural service, or rent in grain or money: distinguished from *ward-holding,* the military tenure of the country; also, a perpetual lease at a stipulated rent. **2** The ground so held. **3** A piece of land held in fee. **—** *v.t.* In Scots law, to grant (land) upon feu. [<OF, var. of *fé.* See FEE.]
feud¹ (fyo͞od) *n.* **1** Vindictive strife or hostility between families or clans, commonly hereditary. **2** Any quarrel or conflict. **—** *v.i.* To engage in a feud; quarrel bitterly. [ME *fede* <OF <OHG *fehida* hatred, revenge] **— feud′·ist** *n.*
Synonyms: animosity, bitterness, contention, contest, controversy, dispute, dissension, enmity, hostility, quarrel, strife. A *feud* is *enmity* between families, clans, or parties, with acts of *hostility* mutually retaliated and avenged; *feud* is rarely used of individuals, never of nations. While all the other words of the group may refer to that which is transient, a *feud* is long-enduring, and often hereditary. *Dissension* is used of a number of persons, of a party or other organization. *Bitterness* is in feeling only; *enmity* and *hostility* involve will and purpose to oppose or injure. Compare QUARREL.
feud² (fyo͞od) *n. Law* Land held of a superior on condition of rendering service; a fief: also spelled *feod.* [<Med. L *feudum* <Gmc.]
feu·dal (fyo͞o′dəl) *adj.* **1** Pertaining to the relation of lord and vassal, or to the feudal system. **2** Relating to or of the nature of a feud or fee. **— feu′dal·ly** *adv.*
feu·dal·ism (fyo͞o′dəl·iz′əm) *n.* The medieval European system of land tenure on condition of military aid and other services. **— feu′dal·is′tic** *adj.*
feu·dal·ist (fyo͞o′dəl·ist) *n.* One learned in the laws of feudalism.
feu·dal·i·ty (fyo͞o·dal′ə·tē) *n.* **1** The condition or quality of being feudal; the practice and principles of feudalism. **2** A fief.
feu·dal·ize (fyo͞o′dəl·īz) *v.t.* **·ized, ·iz·ing** To bring under the feudal system; render feudal. **— feu′dal·i·za′tion** *n.*
feudal system A politico-social system in force throughout Europe from the 9th to the 15th century, founded on the tenure of feuds, or fiefs, given as compensation for military services rendered by chiefs and by them sublet by allotments to their subordinates and vassals.
feu·da·ry (fyo͞o′dər·ē) *adj.* Relating to a feudal tenure. **—** *n. pl.* **·ries** One holding land by feudal tenure; a vassal.
feu·da·to·ry (fyo͞o′də·tôr′ē, -tō′rē) *adj.* Holding or held by feudal tenure. **—** *n. pl.* **·ries** **1** A feud or fief. **2** A vassal.
feud·ist¹ (fyo͞o′dist) *n.* **1** One versed in feudal law; a writer on feudalism. **2** One subject to feudal law. **3** The holder of a feud.
feud·ist² (fyo͞o′dist) *n. U.S.* One who takes part in a feud or quarrel.
Feu·er·mann (foi′ər·män), **Emanuel,** 1902–42, Austrian violoncellist active in the United States.
Feu·illant (fœ·yäṅ′) *n.* **1** A reformed Cistercian of the order instituted by Jean de la Barrière and approved by the pope in 1586: so called from the monastery of Feuillants in Languedoc. **2** A member of a club of conservative royalists in the French Revolution of 1789: named from the convent of the Feuillants, where it met.

Feuil·let (fœ·ye′), **Octave,** 1821–90, French novelist and dramatist.
feuil·le·ton (fœ·yə·tôṅ′) *n.* **1** The part of a French newspaper devoted to light literature, criticism, etc.: usually a space across the foot of the page. **2** An article or critique. **3** A serialized article or story. [<F <*feuillet,* dim. of *feuille* a leaf <L *folium*] **— feuil′le·ton·ism** *n.* **— feuil′le·ton·ist** *n.* **— feuil′le·ton·is′·tic** *adj.*
feu·ter·er (fyōō′tər·ər) See FEWTERER.
fe·ver (fē′vər) *n.* **1** Body temperature above the normal; pyrexia. **2** A disorder marked by high temperature, rapid pulse, increased tissue-destruction, loss of appetite, restlessness, and delirium. ◆ Collateral adjective: *febrile.* **3** Emotional excitement; great interest, enthusiasm, or urge. **—** *v.t.* To affect with fever. [OE *fēfer* <L *febris* <*fervere* be hot] **— fe′·vered** *adj.*
fever blister A form of herpes affecting the lips. Also **fever sore.**
fe·ver·bush (fē′vər·bŏŏsh′) *n.* **1** The benjamin-bush. **2** The winterberry.
fe·ver·few (fē′vər·fyōō′) *n.* An erect bushy herb (*Chrysanthemum parthenium*) of the composite family, bearing white-rayed flowers, once used to make a medicinal tea. [OE *feferfuge* <LL *febrifugia* <L *febris* fever + *fugare* put to flight]

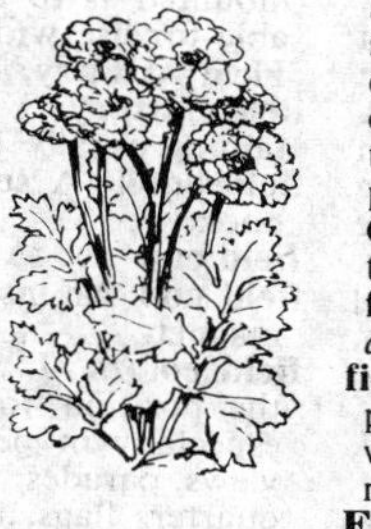
FEVERFEW (Plants from 1 1/2 to 3 feet tall)

fever heat 1 Body temperature in excess of the normal; in man, above 98.6 degrees Fahrenheit. **2** A condition of great excitement or interest.
fe·ver·ish (fē′vər·ish) *adj.* **1** Affected with fever. **2** Eager; hot; impatient. **— fe′ver·ish·ly** *adv.* **— fe′ver·ish·ness** *n.*
fe·ver·ous (fē′vər·əs) *adj.* Feverish. **— fe′ver·ous·ly** *adv.*
fever therapy Pyretotherapy.
fever tree 1 The bluegum tree (*Eucalyptus globulus*) from which eucalyptol is obtained. **2** An American tree (*Pinckneya pubens*), with a bark of tonic and febrifugal properties.
fe·ver·weed (fē′vər·wēd′) *n.* Any of a genus (*Eryngium*) of herbs of the parsley family having medicinal uses.
fe·ver·wort (fē′vər·wûrt′) *n.* A perennial weedy herb (*Triosteum perfoliatum*) of the honeysuckle family having brownish-purple flowers and a nauseous odor. Its root is a purgative and emetic. Also **fe′ver·root′** (-rōōt′, -rŏŏt′).
few (fyōō) *adj.* Small or limited in number; not many. **—** *n.* A small number; some: Give me a *few.* **— the few** The minority. **— quite a few** An appreciable number. ◆ **fewer, less** See LESS (def. 3). [OE *fēawe*]
few·ness (fyōō′nis) *n.* The state of being few; scarcity.
few·ter·er (fyōō′tər·ər) *n. Obs.* A keeper of hounds, especially greyhounds: also spelled *feuterer.* [Alter. of AF *veutrier,* OF *veutre,* ult. <L *vertragum* a greyhound <Celtic]
few·trils (fyōō′trilz) *n. pl. Brit. Dial.* Trifling or unimportant things, as small articles of furniture.
fey[1] (fā) *adj. Scot.* **1** Fated or foredoomed to death, particularly to a sudden death. **2** Seeming to be fated or doomed.
fey[2] (fā) *adj.* **1** Affected by association with the fairies; enchanted, under a spell; hence, out of touch with reality. **2** Visionary; touched in the head. [<F *fé,* pp. of *féer* enchant <*fee,* *fae.* See FAY[2].]
fez (fez) *n.* A brimless felt cap, usually red with a black tassel, formerly worn by the Turks. [<F <Turkish *fes,* after *Fez* in Morocco, where these caps were formerly manufactured] **— fezzed** *adj.*
Fez (fez) A city in NE Morocco: also *Fès*: Arabic *Fas.*
Fez·zan (fe·zan′) The SW district of Libya; 280,000 square miles; capital, Sebha.
fi·a·cre (fē·ä′kər, *Fr.* fyà′kr′) *n.* A small four-wheeled public carriage; a French hackney coach. [<F, after Hotel St. *Fiacre,* a Parisian inn]
fi·an·cé (fē′än·sā′, fē·än′sā; *Fr.* fē·äṅ·sā′) *n. masc.* An affianced or betrothed person. [<F] **— fi′an·cée′** *n. fem.*
Fi·an·na Eir·eann (fē′ə·nə âr′in) The Fenians of Ireland.
fi·ar (fē′ər) *n.* In Scots law, one who holds the fee-simple to land or an estate.
fi·as·co (fē·as′kō) *n. pl.* **·cos** or **·coes** A complete or humiliating failure. [<Ital., a flask; semantic development uncertain]
fi·at (fē′at, -ət) *n.* **1** A positive and authoritative command that something be done; an order or decree. **2** Authorization. [<L, let it be done]
fi·at lux (fī′ət luks′) *Latin* Let there be light.
fiat money Irredeemable paper money made legal tender by law.
fib (fib) *n.* A petty falsehood. **—** *v.i.* **fibbed, fib·bing** To tell a fib. [? Alter. of FABLE] **— fib′ber** *n.*
fi·ber (fī′bər) *n.* **1** A fine filament. **2** A slender or threadlike component of a substance, as of wood, or spun glass. **3** An individual filament, as of wool or cotton. **4** A structure composed of filaments; especially, any natural or synthetic material that may be separated into threads for spinning, weaving, etc.: the *fiber* of hemp, flax, rayon, or wool, etc. **5** *Bot.* **a** A slender, elongated, and thickened cell in the strengthening tissue of plants. **b** A filamentous wool; also, a rootlet. **6** The texture of anything. **7** Character; nature; make-up: a woman of strong *fiber.* Also **fi′bre.** [<F *fibre* <L *fibra* fiber] **— fi′bered** *adj.* **— fi′ber·less** *adj.*
fi·ber·board (fī′bər·bôrd′, -bōrd′) *n.* A tough, pliable, water-resistant material made of wood or other plant fibers compressed and rolled into sheets of varying thickness.
Fi·ber·glas (fī′bər·glas′, -gläs′) *n.* A flexible, non-flammable, moisture- and rot-proof material made of glass spun into filaments: it is widely used for textiles, insulators, mats, filters, etc.: a trade name.
fiber leather Leatherboard.
fiber optics A branch of optics concerned with optical fibers and their applications.
fiber silk An imitation of silk woven from the fibrils of cellulose.
fi·bri·form (fī′brə·fôrm) *adj.* **1** Having a fibrous form or structure. **2** Resembling fiber.
fi·bril (fī′brəl) *n.* **1** A minute fiber, especially a nerve or muscle filament. **2** *Bot.* A root hair. [<NL *fibrilla,* dim. of L *fibra* fiber]
fi·bril·la (fī·bril′ə) *n. pl.* **·lae** (-ē) *Biol.* One of the filamentous structures found in the cytoplasm of cells and thought to be essential in cell development and function. [<NL, dim. of L *fibra* a fiber]
fi·bril·lar (fī′brə·lər) *adj.* Of, pertaining to, resembling, or composed of fibers or fibrils. Also **fi′bril·lar′y.**
fi·bril·late (fib′rə·lāt, fī′brə-) *v.i.* **·lat·ed, ·lat·ing** *Pathol.* To undergo fibrillation.
fi·bril·la·tion (fī′brə·lā′shən, fī′brə-) *n.* **1** The formation of fibers. **2** *Physiol.* A localized twitching of certain muscle fibers. **3** *Pathol.* Rapid, irregular, uncoordinated contractions of the muscle fibers of the heart.
fi·bril·lif·er·ous (fī′brə·lif′ər·əs) *adj.* Fibril-bearing.
fi·bril·li·form (fī·bril′ə·fôrm) *adj.* Having the form of fibrils.
fi·bril·lose (fī′brə·lōs) *adj.* Composed of fibers or fibrils.
fi·brin (fī′brin) *n.* **1** *Biochem.* An insoluble protein which forms an interlacing network of fibers in clotting blood, with resulting coagulation of the plasma and separation of the serum. **2** The fibrous portion of flesh. **3** *Bot.* Gluten, or vegetable fibrin.
fi·brin·o·gen (fī·brin′ə·jən) *n. Biochem.* A complex protein of the globulin group, found in blood plasma and in other body fluids. It is associated with a ferment, thrombin, in the formation of fibrin during the process of coagulation. **— fi′brin·o·gen′ic, fi·bri·nog·e·nous** (fī′brə·noj′ə·nəs) *adj.*
fi·bri·no·ly·sin (fī′brə·nō·lī′sin) *n. Biochem.* A toxic substance having the power to liquefy human fibrin. It is formed by the action of certain pathogenic bacteria, as staphylococci.
fi·bri·no·sis (fī′brə·nō′sis) *n. Pathol.* A condition of excess fibrin in the blood.
fi·bri·nous (fī′brə·nəs) *adj.* Possessed of the properties, characteristics, or nature of fibrin.
fibro– *combining form* Related to or composed of fibrous tissue; having a fibrous structure: *fibrovascular.* Also, before vowels, **fibr–.** [<L *fibra* fiber]
fi·broid (fī′broid) *adj.* Of the nature of fiber; fibrous: as a *fibroid* tumor.
fi·bro·in (fī′brō·in) *n. Biochem.* A white, lustrous protein, forming the principal ingredient in natural silk and spider webs.
fi·bro·ma (fī·brō′mə) *n. pl.* **·ma·ta** (-mə·tə) *Pathol.* A fibrous tumor. **— fi·bro′ma·tous** *adj.*
fi·bro·sis (fī·brō′sis) *n. Pathol.* Morbid increase of fibrous tissue in the body; fibroid degeneration, as of the blood capillaries.
fi·brous (fī′brəs) *adj.* Composed of, or having the character of fibers.
fi·bro·vas·cu·lar (fī′brə·vas′kyə·lər) *adj. Bot.* Composed or consisting of woody fibers and vessels, as **fibrovascular tissue,** a tissue composed of elongated, thick-walled, and generally fusiform elements, as wood and bast.
fib·u·la (fib′yōō·lə) *n. pl.* **·lae** (-lē) **1** *Anat.* The outer of the two bones forming the lower part of the leg or hind limb; the calf bone. ◆ Collateral adjective: *peroneal.* **2** An ancient type of ornamental brooch, fastening somewhat like a safety pin. [<L, a clasp <*figere* fasten] **— fib′u·lar** *adj.*
-fic *suffix* Making, rendering, or causing: *beatific, scientific.* [<L *-ficus* <*facere* make, render]
-fication *suffix* The making, rendering, or causing to be of a certain sort of character: *beatification, glorification.* [<L *-ficatio, -onis* <*-ficare* <*facere* make]
fice (fīs) *n.* A small dog of mixed breed, but usually terrierlike: also spelled *feist, fist.* [Short for *fisting dog* <obs. *fist* break wind]
fiche (fēsh) *n.* Microfiche.
Fich·te (fikh′tə), **Johann Gottlieb,** 1762–1814, German philosopher. **— Fich′te·an** *adj.* & *n.*
Fich·te·an·ism (fikh′tē·ə·niz′əm) *n.* The philosophy of J. G. Fichte, a pure idealism, based upon the self or ego as the only reality.
fi·chu (fish′ōō, *Fr.* fē·shü′) *n.* **1** A triangular piece of light material worn about the neck. **2** A three-cornered cape worn with the ends crossed or tied in front. [<F <*ficher* put on hastily]
fick·le (fik′əl) *adj.* Inconstant in feeling or purpose; changeful; capricious. [OE *ficol* crafty] **— fick′le·ness** *n.*
Synonyms: capricious, changeable, changeful, crotchety, fitful, inconstant, irresolute, mutable, shifting, unstable, unsteady, vacillating, variable, veering, wavering, whimsical. See IRRESOLUTE, MOBILE. *Antonyms*: constant, decided, determined, firm, fixed, immutable, invariable, reliable, resolute, steadfast.
fi·co (fē′kō) *n. pl.* **·coes 1** *Archaic* A trifle; a fig's worth. **2** *Obs.* A gesture of contempt made by thrusting the thumb between two fingers or into the mouth. [<Ital. <L *ficus* a fig]
fic·tile (fik′til) *adj.* **1** Made of molded earth or clay; pertaining to pottery. **2** Capable of being molded; plastic. [<L *fictilis* <*fingere* form]
fic·tion (fik′shən) *n.* **1** The act of feigning or imagining that which does not exist or is not actual. **2** That which is feigned or imagined, as opposed to that which is actual. **3** The department of literature that embraces fictitious narrative, including romances, novels, short stories, art epics, etc. See NOVEL. **4** A legal assumption, for the furtherance of justice, that a certain thing which is or may be false is true. **5** *Obs.* The act of fashioning; also, a device; fabric. **6** *Obs.* Pretense; deceit. [<F <L *fictio, -onis* a making <*fingere* form]
Synonyms: allegory, apolog, fable, fabrication, falsehood, figment, invention, legend, myth, novel, romance, story. *Fiction* is now chiefly used of a prose work in narrative form in which the characters are partly or wholly imaginary, and which is designed to portray human life, with or without a practical lesson; a *romance* portrays what is picturesque or striking, as a mere *fiction* may not do; *novel* is a general name for any continuous fictitious narrative, especially a love story. The moral of the *fable* is expressed formally; the lesson of

the *fiction,* if any, is inwrought. A *fiction* is studied; a *myth* grows up without intent. A *legend* may be true, but cannot be historically verified; a *myth* has been received as true at some time. A *fabrication* is designed to deceive; it is a less odious word than *falsehood,* but is really stronger, as a *falsehood* may be a sudden unpremeditated statement, while a *fabrication* is a series of statements carefully studied and fitted together in order to deceive; the *falsehood* is all false; the *fabrication* may mingle the true with the false. A *figment* is something imaginary which the one who utters it may or may not believe to be true; we say, "That statement is a *figment* of his imagination." The *story* may be either true or false, and covers the various senses of all the words in the group. *Apolog,* a word simply transferred from Greek into English, is the same as *fable.* Compare ALLEGORY. *Antonyms*: certainty, fact, history, literalness, reality, truth, verity.

fic·tion·al (fik′shən·əl) *adj.* Belonging to fiction; ideal. — **fic′tion·al·ly** *adv.*

fic·tion·ist (fik′shən·ist) *n.* One who writes fiction.

fic·ti·tious (fik·tish′əs) *adj.* **1** Belonging to or of the nature of fiction. **2** Counterfeit; false; assumed. See synonyms under COUNTERFEIT, ROMANTIC. — **fic·ti′tious·ly** *adv.* — **fic·ti′tious·ness** *n.*

fic·tive (fik′tiv) *adj.* **1** Of the nature of a figment; imaginary. **2** Having to do with the creation of fiction: *fictive* ability. — **fic′tive·ly** *adv.*

Fi·cus (fī′kəs) *n.* A large genus of plants, mostly tropical trees, shrubs, and vines, belonging to the mulberry family and including the fig, banyan, and rubber plant. [<L, a fig tree]

fid (fid) *n. Naut.* **1** A supporting bar; a crosspiece to hold a topmast in place. **2** A large tapering wooden pin used for stretching eyes in rigging, opening ropes when splicing, etc. [Origin uncertain]

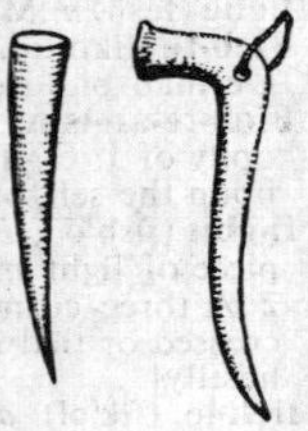

FIDS

-fid *combining form Bot.* Divided into; split: *pinnatifid.* [<L *-fidus* <*findere* split]

fid·dle (fid′l) *n.* **1** A violin. **2** *Naut.* A rack or frame used at table on board ship in rough weather to keep the dishes in place. — *v.* **fid·dled, fid·dling** *v.i.* **1** To play on a fiddle. **2** To pass the time in trifling matters. **3** To toy with an object. — *v.t.* **4** To play (an air, tune, etc.) on a fiddle. **5** To trifle; fritter: to *fiddle* time away. [OE *fithele,* found in *fithelere* a fiddler. Akin to VIOL.]

fiddle block *Mech.* A pulley block with two sheaves, the larger one above the smaller.

fiddle bow A bow[3] (def. 4).

fid·dle-de-dee (fid′l·dē·dē′) *interj.* & *n.* Nonsense. [Fanciful var. of FIDDLE]

fid·dle-fad·dle (fid′l·fad′l) *v.i.* **-fad·dled, -fad·dling** **1** To trifle. **2** To talk nonsense. — *n.* Idle talk; nonsense. [Varied reduplication of FIDDLE]

fid·dle·head (fid′l·hed′) *n.* **1** *Naut.* An ornament just above a ship's cutwater, resembling the convoluted head of a fiddle. **2** *Canadian* An edible fern shoot. Also **fid′dle·neck′** (-nek′).

fid·dler (fid′lər) *n.* **1** One who plays a fiddle. **2** A fiddler crab. — **to pay the fiddler** To suffer the consequences.

fiddler crab A small burrowing crab (genus *Uca*) the male of which flourishes its enlarged claw as if fiddling: found on the Atlantic coast of the United States.

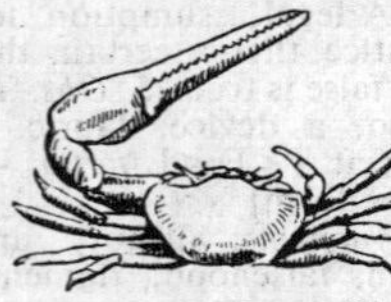

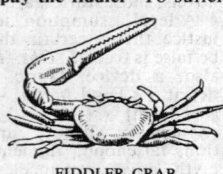

FIDDLER CRAB
(Carapace about 1/2 to 1 inch in width)

fid·dle·stick (fid′l·stik′) *n.* **1** A fiddle bow. **2** A trifling or absurd thing.

fid·dle·sticks (fid′l·stiks′) *interj.* Nonsense!

fid·dle·wood (fid′l·wŏŏd′) *n.* Any one of several species of trees of the vervain family (*Citharexylum* and allied genera): used in tropical America for building.

fi·de·i·com·mis·sar·y (fī′de·ī·kom′ə·ser′ē) *n. Law* A beneficiary in a trust estate, or one for whose benefit a trust has been created. [<L *fidei commissarius*] — **fi′de·i·com′mis·sar′i·ly** *adv.* — **fi′de·i·com·mis′sion** *n.* — **fi′de·i·com·mis′sion·er** *n.*

fi·de·i·com·mis·sum (fī′de·ī·kə·mis′əm) *n. pl.* **·sa** In Roman and civil law, a devise or bequest coupled with a request to the party named to give the property to a third party who could not hold directly under the will; a trust estate. [<L <*fidei,* dat. of *fides* faith + *commissum,* pp. neut. sing of *committere* entrust to]

Fi·de·i De·fen·sor (fī′dē·ī di·fen′sôr) *Latin* Defender of the Faith: a title of the British sovereign.

fi·de·jus·sion (fī′də·jush′ən) *n. Law* The condition of being bound as surety for another; suretyship. [<L *fideiussio, -onis* <*fideiubere* <*fide,* ablative sing. of *fides* faith + *iubere* order] — **fi′de·jus′so·ry** (-jus′ər·ē) *adj.*

Fi·de·li·a (fi·dē′lē·ə, -dēl′yə) A feminine personal name. [<L, faithful]

fi·del·i·ty (fī·del′ə·tē, fə-) *n. pl.* **·ties** **1** Faithfulness in the discharge of duty or of obligation. **2** Hearty allegiance to those to whom one is bound in affection or honor; loyalty; devotion: matrimonial *fidelity, fidelity* to a father or friend. **3** Strict adherence to truth or fact; reliability; veracity. **4** *Electronics* A measure of the accuracy and freedom from distortion with which a sound-reproducing system, as radio, will receive and transmit the input signals; it may be high, medium, or low. [<F *fidelité* <L *fidelitas, -tatis* <*fides* faith] *Synonyms*: allegiance, constancy, devotion, faith, faithfulness, fealty, honesty, integrity, loyalty, truth, truthfulness. See ALLEGIANCE. *Antonyms*: disloyalty, infidelity, treachery, treason.

fidg·et (fij′it) *v.i.* **1** To move about restlessly. **2** To toy with something nervously. — *v.t.* **3** To make restless; worry. — *n.* **1** Nervous restlessness: often in the plural: to have the *fidgets.* **2** A restless person; one who fidgets. [<obs. *fidge* move about; ultimate origin unknown] — **fidg′et·y** *adj.* — **fidg′et·i·ness** *n.*

fi·du·cial (fi·dōō′shəl, -dyōō′-) *adj.* **1** Of the nature of or indicating faith or practical confidence. **2** Of the nature of a trust; fiduciary. **3** *Physics* Fixed as a basis of measurement or reference: the *fiducial* point of a scale. [<L *fiducialis* <*fiducia* trust] — **fi·du′cial·ly** *adv.*

fi·du·ci·ar·y (fi·dōō′shē·er′ē, -shə·rē, -dyōō′-) *adj.* **1** Pertaining to a position of trust or confidence; confidential: a *fiduciary* relation, as that of an attorney, guardian, or trustee. **2** Unwavering; trustful; undoubting. **3** Relying on the confidence of the public as for paper currency or value. **4** Held in trust. — *n. pl.* **·ar·ies** *Law* A person who holds a thing in trust; a trustee.

Fi·dus A·cha·tes (fī′dəs ə·kā′tēz) See ACHATES.

fie (fī) *interj.* An expression of impatience or disapproval. [<OF *fi, fy* <L *fi,* an expression of disgust]

fief (fēf) *n.* A landed estate held under feudal tenure; a fee: also spelled *feoff.* [<OF <Med. L *feudum* FEUD[2]]

fiel (fēl) *adj. Scot.* Snug; comfortable.

field[1] (fēld) *n.* **1** A piece of cleared land set apart and enclosed for tillage or pasture. ◆ Collateral adjective: *campestral.* **2** A plot of land set apart for a particular use: the potter's *field.* **3** A region of the countryside considered as yielding some natural product: the *coalfields* of Pennsylvania. **4** *Mil.* **a** A sphere of action or place of contest. **b** A battleground. **c** A battle: a hard-fought *field.* **5** Open or unenclosed countryside: the beast of the *field.* **6** Any wide or open expanse: the *fields* of ocean. **7** Sphere of study, investigation or practice. **8** In painting, the surface of canvas upon which the figures of a composition are set. **9** That portion of the face of a coin or medal which is not occupied by the type or principal figure. **10** The ground of each section of a flag: a blue *field* with white stars. **11** In games, the plot of ground on which the game is played; especially, in baseball, the outfield, or part outside the diamond; in baseball and cricket, the fielders collectively. For illustration see BASEBALL. **12** *Her.* The whole surface of the escutcheon upon which the charges and bearings are depicted, or of each separate coat when the shield contains quarterings or impalements. See illustration under ESCUTCHEON. **13** *Physics* **a** A portion of space at every point of which force is exerted. **b** The force exerted therein: the magnetic *field,* a *field* of force. **14** *Optics* The space or apparent surface within which objects are seen in a telescope or other optical instrument. **15** The participants in a hunt; all the competitors in a contest or race; also, the contestants exclusive of the favorites in the betting. — **to keep the field** **1** To hold one's ground against all opposers. **2** To continue active operations. — *adj.* **1** Of, pertaining to, or found in the fields: *field* flowers. **2** Used in, or for use in, the fields: a *field* gun. **3** Played on a field: *field* sports. — *v.t.* In baseball, cricket, etc. **1** To catch and return (a ball in play). **2** To put (a player or team) on the field. — *v.i.* **3** In baseball, cricket, etc., to play as a fielder. [OE *feld*]

field[2] (fyeld) See FJELD.

Field (fēld), **Cyrus West,** 1819–92, U.S. merchant; laid the first transatlantic cable, 1858, and a second in 1866. — **Eugene,** 1850–95, U.S. poet and journalist. — **Marshall,** 1834–1906, U.S. merchant.

field artillery Light or heavy artillery so mounted as to be freely movable, and suitable for use with troops in the field. Hence, **Field Artillery,** a branch of the U.S. Army.

field battery A battery of field artillery, containing usually four or six guns.

field book A surveyor's or naturalist's notebook.

field cap See OVERSEAS CAP.

field coil An insulated coil for exciting a field magnet.

field colors **1** Small flags used for marking the position for companies and regiments, especially in peacetime field maneuvers, reviews, parades, etc. **2** Any regimental headquarters flags, used in field service.

field corn Any of several kinds of Indian corn used for feeding livestock.

field day **1** A day when army troops are taken to the field for exercise and maneuvers. **2** In the navy, a day for general cleaning up. **3** A school holiday devoted to athletic sports. **4** Any day of display, excitement, celebration, or success. **5** A day of outdoor scientific excursion.

field·er (fēl′dər) *n.* In baseball, cricket, etc., a player stationed in the field to stop, or catch, and return the balls. Compare illustration under BASEBALL.

fielder's choice In baseball, the decision by a player to attempt to retire a base runner rather than the batter, the latter being credited with a time at bat but not with a hit.

field events The jumping, vaulting, and casting contests at an athletic meet: distinguished from *track events.*

field·fare (fēld′fâr′) *n.* A European thrush (*Turdus pilaris*), deep brown above, with a pearl-gray head and black tail, streaked on the breast and throat with blackish-brown. [OE *feldeware,* ? misspelling of *feldefare* (<*feld* field + *faran* go); or <*feld* field + *warian* dwell]

field glass **1** A small, portable, terrestrial telescope, monocular or binocular; a spyglass. **2** A field lens.

field goal **1** In football, a goal scored from scrimmage by means of a dropkick or placement kick. **2** In basketball, a goal scored with the ball in active play.

field gun A cannon mounted on wheels for rapid movement in operations by troops in the field; a fieldpiece.

field hand An agricultural laborer.

field hockey See under HOCKEY.

field hospital A hospital established on a field of battle; also, its medical officers and attendants, with their equipment for service.

field ice Ice formed in fields or floes: distinguished from *icebergs.*

Field·ing (fēl′ding), **Henry,** 1707–54, English novelist and playwright.

field intensity *Electr.* A measure of the direction and magnitude of the force exerted upon a unit charge at a given point.

field jacket A lightweight, cotton, waterproof jacket of olive-drab worn by soldiers in the field.

field kitchen A portable unit used to cook food for soldiers in the field; also, the site at which the unit is set.

field lark **1** The American meadowlark. **2** The English skylark. **3** Any of various larklike birds, as the pipit.

field lens *Optics* The anterior of the two lenses in the eyepiece of a telescope or microscope, whose purpose is to enlarge the field of view.
field magnet **1** The magnet of a magneto-electric or dynamoelectric machine, which produces the *magnetic field.* **2** A small magnet, commonly of horseshoe shape, used in determining the existence of iron ore in minerals.
field marshal A general officer of high rank in the armies of several European nations.
field martin The kingbird.
field mouse A mouse inhabiting fields and meadows, as the common European vole *(Microtus agrestis)* and the small short-tailed vole of North America *(M. pennsylvanicus)*: also called *meadow mouse.*
field music **1** The drummers, buglers, fifers, etc., who play for military troops on the march, sound regimental calls, etc. **2** The music produced by them.
field notes **1** A surveyor's notes detailing a survey. **2** A naturalist's notes taken in the field.
field officer An officer intermediate between a company and a general officer; a major, lieutenant colonel, or colonel.
field of force See FIELD[1] (def. 13).
field of honor **1** The ground where a duel is fought. **2** A battlefield.
field·piece (fēld′pēs′) *n.* A cannon mounted on wheels, for use in field battles.
field plover **1** The upland plover. **2** The golden plover.
fields·man (fēldz′mən) *n. pl.* **·men** (-mən) In cricket, a fielder.
field spaniel See under SPANIEL.
field sparrow A small light-breasted American sparrow *(Spizella pusilla).*
field sports **1** Outdoor sports, especially hunting, shooting, and racing. **2** Athletic games played on the field, as opposed to races, hurdles, etc., on the track.
field·stone (fēld′stōn′) *n.* Loose stone found near a construction site and used in building. — *adj.* Consisting of or having the appearance of fieldstone: a *fieldstone* house.
field stop An opening in an opaque screen, generally circular, for determining the size of the field of view of an optical instrument.
field strength *Electr.* The magnitude of a field, expressed as a vector quantity in volts per unit length at a given point.
field trial A trial or test of hunting dogs in field performance.
field trip A trip outside the classroom for purposes of first-hand observation and study.
field winding *Electr.* The winding of the field-magnet coils of a dynamoelectric machine.
field·work (fēld′wûrk′) *n.* A temporary fortification thrown up in the field.
field work Observations or performance in the field, as by scientists, surveyors, etc.
fiend (fēnd) *n.* **1** An evil spirit; a devil; demon. **2** An intensely malicious or wicked person; one having a cruel, diabolical spirit. **3** *Colloq.* One unduly devoted to some theory or occupation; one exceptionally interested in and clever or talented in a certain subject: an algebra *fiend*; a crank; monomaniac: a fresh-air *fiend.* **4** *Colloq.* One morbidly addicted to the use of a narcotic drug or some deleterious habit: a cocaine *fiend.* **5** An implacable enemy; foe. — **the Fiend** Satan; the devil. [OE *fēond* enemy, devil]
fiend·ish (fēn′dish) *adj.* Of, pertaining to, or resembling a fiend or his conduct; diabolical. — **fiend′ish·ly** *adv.* — **fiend′ish·ness** *n.*
fient (fēnt) *n. Scot.* Fiend.
fient a haet (ə hāt) *Scot.* Devil a bit; nothing at all.
fier (fir) *adj. Scot.* Sound; healthy: also spelled *fere.*
fierce (firs) *adj.* **1** Having a violent and cruel nature or temper; savage; ferocious. **2** Violent in action; furious. **3** Vehement; passionate; extreme. **4** *Slang* Very bad; atrocious. [<OF *fers, fiers,* nominative sing. of *fier* proud <L *ferus* wild] — **fierce′ly** *adv.* — **fierce′·ness** *n.*
Synonyms: ferocious, fiery, furious, impetuous, raging, savage, uncultivated, untrained, violent, wild. *Fierce* signifies having a *furious* and cruel nature, or being in a *furious* and cruel mood. It applies to that which is intensely excited at the moment, or liable to intense and sudden excitement. *Ferocious* refers to a state or disposition; that which is *fierce* flashes or blazes; that which is *ferocious* steadily burns; we speak of a *ferocious* animal, a *fierce* passion. A *fiery* spirit with a good disposition is quickly excitable in a good cause, but may not be *fierce* or *ferocious. Savage* signifies *untrained, uncultivated. Ferocious* always denotes a tendency to violence; it is more distinctly bloodthirsty than the other words; a person may be deeply, intensely cruel, and not at all *ferocious*: a *ferocious* countenance expresses habitual ferocity; a *fierce* countenance may express habitual fierceness, or only the sudden anger of the moment. That which is *wild* is simply unrestrained; the word may imply no anger or harshness; as *wild* delight, *wild* alarm. See ARDENT, GRIM. *Antonyms*: affectionate, docile, gentle, harmless, kind, mild, patient, peaceful, submissive, tame, tender.
fi·e·ri fa·ci·as (fī′ə·rī fā′shē·əs) *Law* A writ of execution commanding a levy on goods, etc., to satisfy a judgment; literally, that you cause to be done. [<L]
fier·y (fīr′ē, fī′ər·ē) *adj.* **fier·i·er, fier·i·est** **1** Of or pertaining to fire; having the appearance of or containing fire; glowing; glaring; burning; hot: a *fiery* furnace. **2** Of the nature of ardor, rage, or animation; passionate; impetuous; fervid; spirited: a *fiery* disposition. **3** Inflammable: a *fiery* gas in a coal mine. See synonyms under ARDENT, FIERCE, HOT, IMPETUOUS. — **fier′i·ly** *adv.* — **fier′i·ness** *n.*
fiery cross See under CROSS *n.*
fiery hunter A large, black ground beetle of the United States *(Calosoma calidum)* with small coppery spots on the wing covers. For illustration see under INSECT (beneficial).
Fie·so·le (fye′zō·lā), **Fra Giovanni da** See ANGELICO, FRA.
Fie·so·le (fye′zō·lā) A town in central Italy near Florence. Ancient **Fae·su·lae** (fē′zyŏŏ·lē).
fi·es·ta (fē·es′tə, *Sp.* fyes′tä) *n.* A feast day; holiday. [<Sp. <L *festa.* See FEAST.]
fife (fif) *n.* A small, shrill-toned, flute-like, martial wind instrument. — *v.t.* & *v.i.* **fifed, fif·ing** To play on a fife. [<G *pfeife* pipe <OHG *pfifa* < (assumed) LL *pipa* <L *pipare* peep, chirp. Doublet of PIPE.] — **fif′er** *n.*

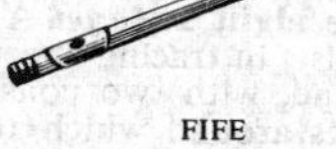
FIFE

Fife (fif) A county in eastern Scotland; 505 square miles; county seat, Cupar. Also **Fife′·shire** (-shir).
fife rail *Naut.* A railing around a mast for holding belaying pins, etc.
fif·teen (fif′tēn′) *adj.* Consisting of five more than ten; quindecimal. — *n.* **1** The sum of ten and five: a cardinal number. **2** Any of the symbols (15, xv, XV) representing this number. [OE *fiftēne*]
fif·teenth (fif′tēnth′) *adj.* **1** Fifth in order after the tenth: the ordinal of *fifteen.* **2** Being one of fifteen equal parts: a *fifteenth* share. — *n.* **1** One of the fifteen equal parts of anything. **2** The quotient of a unit divided by fifteen.
Fifteenth Amendment An amendment to the Constitution of the United States, providing that the right of citizens to vote shall not be denied or abridged on account of "race, color, or previous condition of servitude. . . ."
fifth (fifth) *adj.* **1** Next in order after the fourth: the ordinal of *five.* **2** Being one of five equal parts: a *fifth* part. — *n.* **1** One of five equal parts of anything. **2** The quotient of a unit divided by five. **3** *Music* **a** The interval between any note and the fifth note above it in the diatonic scale, counting the starting point as one (see SCALE[2]). **b** A note separated by this interval from any other, considered in relation to that other; specifically, the fifth above the keynote; the dominant. **4** One fifth of a U.S. gallon used as a measure of spirituous liquors. — *adv.* In the fifth order, place, or rank: also, in formal discourse, **fifth′ly.**
Fifth Amendment An amendment to the Constitution of the United States, providing that no person "shall be compelled in any criminal case to be a witness against himself. . . ."
Fifth Avenue A street running north and south in Manhattan borough of New York City, famous for the elegance of its shopping district and its wealthy residential sections.
fifth column A group, within a city or country, of civilian sympathizers with an enemy, who act as spies, saboteurs, and propagandists: first applied to Franco agents and sympathizers in Madrid by Gen. Emilio Mola (1887–1937), who led four armed columns against that city in 1936.
fifth-col·um·nist (fifth′kol′əm·nist) *n.* A member of a fifth column.
fifth wheel **1** A horizontal metallic circle or segment of a circle attached to the upper side of the fore axle of a carriage or wagon to give support to the body in turning; a circle iron. **2** An additional wheel carried with a vehicle as a replacement in case of accidents. **3** A superfluous thing or person.
fif·ti·eth (fif′tē·ith) *adj.* **1** Tenth in order after the fortieth: the ordinal of *fifty.* **2** Being one of fifty equal parts of a thing. — *n.* **1** One of fifty equal parts. **2** The quotient of a unit divided by fifty.
fif·ty (fif′tē) *adj.* Consisting of ten more than forty or five times ten. — *n. pl.* **fif·ties** **1** The sum of ten and forty; five times ten. **2** Any of the symbols (50, l, L) representing this number. [OE *fiftig*]
fif·ty-fif·ty (fif′tē·fif′tē) *adj. Colloq.* Sharing equally, as benefits: *fifty-fifty* partners in business.
fig[1] (fig) *n.* **1** The small, edible, pear-shaped fruit of a tree (genus *Ficus*), cultivated in warm climates. **2** The tree *(F. carica)* that bears the fruit. **3** Any tree or plant bearing a fruit somewhat like the fig, or the fruit of such a tree or plant. **4** One of several Australian trees and shrubs of the fig family, as *F. macrophylla,* used as fodder for cattle. **5** A petty matter; trifle. **6** An insulting gesture; a fico. — *v.t. Obs.* To make a fico at; insult. [<OF *fige, figue* <L *ficus* a fig]
fig[2] (fig) *v.t.* **figged, fig·ging** *Colloq.* To dress; deck; rig. — *n.* **1** Figure; dress; array: in full *fig.* **2** Condition. [Var. of obs. *feague* whip <G *fegen* polish]
fig·eat·er (fig′ē′tər) *n.* **1** A large velvety-green scarabaeid beetle *(Cotinis nitida)* common in the southern United States, injurious to ripe fruits. **2** The beccafico. **3** The grape-eater.
fight (fīt) *v.* **fought, fight·ing** *v.t.* **1** To struggle against in battle or physical combat. **2** To struggle against in any manner. **3** To carry on or engage in (a battle, duel, court action, etc.). **4** To make (one's way) by struggling. **5** To maneuver or handle, as troops or a gun, in battle. **6** To cause to fight, as dogs or game-cocks. — *v.i.* **7** To take part in battle or physical combat. **8** To struggle in any manner. See synonyms under CONTEND. — **to fight shy of** To avoid meeting (an opponent or an issue) squarely. — **to fight it out** To fight until a final decision is reached. — *n.* **1** Strife or struggle between adversaries; battle; conflict; combat. **2** Strife to attain an object in spite of difficulties or opposition. **3** Power or disposition to fight; pugnacity. **4** *Obs.* A temporary bulwark or screen on a ship when in action, to conceal the men. See synonyms under BATTLE. [OE *feohtan*]
fight·er (fī′tər) *n.* **1** One who fights; a combatant; warrior. **2** A pugnacious or spirited person. **3** *Mil.* A fast, highly maneuverable airplane designed to hunt out and destroy enemy planes in the air.
fight·er-bomb·er (fī′tər·bom′ər) *n. Mil.* An aircraft which combines the functions of the fighter and the bomber.
fighter command A division of the U.S. Air Force intermediate between a wing and an air force, used for interception of enemy aircraft and for support of air and ground offensive forces.
fighter plane A pursuit plane.
fight·ing (fī′ting) *adj.* **1** Qualified, equipped, trained, or ready to fight; active in war or battle. **2** Of, pertaining to, suitable for, engaged in, or used for conflict. — *n.* Strife; struggle; battle; conflict.
fighting chance A bare possibility of success, contingent on a hard struggle.

fighting cock A gamecock.
fighting fish A brightly colored Siamese aquarium fish (*Betta splendens*), the males of which are noted for their nesting habits and pugnacity.
fighting top On war vessels, a platform at the lower masthead for the fire-control lookout, or for light anti-aircraft guns.
Figl (fē′gəl), **Leopold,** 1902–1965, Austrian agrarian and politician; acting president of Austria 1950–51.
fig marigold Any of several species of a South African genus of herbs (*Mesembryanthemum*) yielding a fig-shaped fruit.
fig·ment (fig′mənt) *n.* **1** Something imagined or feigned; a fiction. **2** *Obs.* An object molded or shaped. [<L *figmentum* anything made, <*fingere* form]
Fi·gue·ro·a (fē·gā·rō′ä), **Francisco de,** 1536?–1620, Spanish poet.
fig·u·line (fig′yo͞o·lin, -līn) *adj.* **1** Capable of being used in the manufacture of porcelain or earthenware. **2** Made or molded as in potter's clay. — *n.* **1** Fictile ware; any object made of potter's clay, especially if decorated. **2** Potter's clay. [<L *figulinus* <*figulus* potter <*fingere* form]
fig·ur·a·ble (fig′yər·ə·bəl) *adj.* Capable of being brought to or retained in a fixed form or shape.
fig·ur·al (fig′yər·əl) *adj.* **1** Represented by or consisting of figures or delineation. **2** *Music* Figurate.
fig·u·rant (fig′yo͞o·rant, *Fr.* fē·gü·rän′) *n.* **1** An accessory character on the stage. **2** A non-featured ballet dancer. [<F, ppr. of *figurer* figure] — **fig·u·rante** (fig′yo͞o·rant′, -ränt′; *Fr.* fē·gü·ränt′) *n. fem.*
fig·ur·ate (fig′yər·it) *adj.* **1** Having a definite or characteristic figure or shape; resembling anything of definite form. **2** *Music* Florid; figured. [<L *figuratus*, pp. of *figurare* form <*figura*. See FIGURE.]
fig·ur·a·tion (fig′yə·rā′shən) *n.* **1** The act or process of shaping something or of marking with a figure or figures. **2** External form or shape. **3** *Music* Ornamentation or variation, as by addition of passing notes; also, the preparation of a figured bass. **4** *Obs.* A type or symbol.
fig·ur·a·tive (fig′yər·ə·tiv) *adj.* **1** Not literal; metaphorical; symbolic. **2** Ornate; florid. **3** Of or pertaining to the representation of form or figure. **4** Representing by means of a form or figure; emblematic. — **fig′ur·a·tive·ly** *adv.* — **fig′ur·a·tive·ness** *n.*
fig·ure (fig′yər, *Brit.* fig′ər) *n.* **1** The visible form of any person or thing; fashion; shape; outline; appearance; hence, any visible object thus recognized. **2** The representation or likeness of the form of a person or other object, as in wax or marble, in a painting or drawing, upon a fabric, or as embodied in a diagram or illustration; a cut. **3** A combination of lines, points, surfaces, or solids representing an object or illustrating a condition or relation, or simply for decoration; a diagram, drawing, or pattern. **4** *Geom.* **a** A surface enclosed by lines, as a square, triangle, etc.: called a **plane figure. b** A space enclosed by planes or surfaces, as a cube, sphere, etc.: called a **solid figure. 5** Any person, thing, or act that figures or prefigures, or is a type of some other or future thing or person. **6** Any personage or character, especially one who is active or conspicuous; one who plays a prominent part. **7** The appearance that a person or his conduct makes: to make a sorry *figure*. **8** A character representing a number: the *figure* 5; hence, amount stated in numbers; price; value: to sell goods at a high *figure*. **9** One of the regular movements or divisions of a dance, in which a certain set of steps or evolutions is completed. **10** Something conjured up by the imagination; a fancy; fantasm; imagination; idea. **11** A form of expression that deviates intentionally from the ordinary mode of speech for the sake of more powerful, pleasing, or distinctive effect; pictorial or poetic language. **12** An intentional deviation from ordinary form or construction, as in syntax, euphony, or prosody. **13** *Logic* The character of a syllogism with reference to the places occupied by the middle term in the major and minor premises. **14** *Music* **a** Any short succession of notes, either as melody or a group of chords, which produces a single, complete, and distinct impression; a musical phrase. **b** A theme or melody repeated throughout a whole movement as an accompaniment or bond of connection. **c** A numeral written in connection with the bass to show the unwritten harmony of a piece. **15** A horoscope; the diagram of the aspects of the astrological houses. — *v.* **fig·ured, fig·ur·ing** *v.t.* **1** To make an image, picture, or other representation of; depict. **2** To form an idea or mental image of; imagine. **3** To ornament or mark with a design. **4** To compute numerically; calculate. **5** To express metaphorically; symbolize. **6** *Colloq.* To think; believe; predict. **7** *Music* **a** To embellish, as by adding passing notes. **b** To mark with figures above or below the staff, indicating accompanying chords. — *v.i.* **8** To be conspicuous; appear prominently. **9** To make computations; do arithmetic. — **to figure on** (or **upon**) **1** To think over; consider. **2** To plan; expect. — **to figure out** To reckon; ascertain; solve. [<F <L *figura* <*fingere* form] — **fig′ur·er** *n.*

Synonyms (noun): appearance, aspect, attribute, comparison, delineation, diagram, drawing, emblem, form, illustration, image, likeness, metaphor, simile, similitude, shape, symbol, type. *Figure* is the general term, including all representation of *form* to the eye, as in drawing, painting, or sculpture, and also the *form* itself that may be so represented. *Figure* is also the general word for representation of anything to the mind, as by *illustration, metaphor,* or *symbol.* An *image* is a visible representation, especially in sculpture, having or supposed to have a close resemblance to that which it represents. We speak of one object as the *type* of the class whose characteristics it exhibits, as in the case of animal or vegetable *types.* An *attribute* in art is some accessory used to characterize a *figure* or scene; the *attribute* is often an emblem or symbol; thus the eagle is the *attribute* of St. John as an *emblem* of lofty spiritual vision. Compare ALLEGORY, ATTRIBUTE, EMBLEM, FORM, IMAGE, SIGN, SIMILE.

fig·ured (fig′yərd) *adj.* **1** Adorned or marked with figures or designs: *figured* cottons. **2** Represented by figures; pictured. **3** *Music* **a** Figurate. **b** Indicated by figures, as a bass.
figure eight **1** *Aeron.* A flight maneuver which consists in tracing the figure eight above the ground, with two conspicuous points as the pivots around which to describe each loop. **2** A similar maneuver in ice skating. **3** A style of knot. See illustration under KNOT.
fig·ure·head (fig′yər·hed′) *n.* **1** *Naut.* A carved or ornamental figure on the prow of a vessel. **2** A person having nominal leadership but without real power, responsibility, or authority.

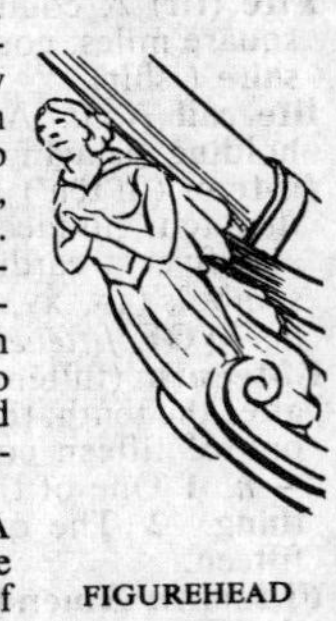
FIGUREHEAD

figure of speech An expression, usually within a sentence, which deviates from simple, normal speech to produce a fanciful or vivid impression, as simile, metaphor, personification, etc.
fig·u·rine (fig′yə·rēn′) *n.* A small, painted, single figure or an attached group of figures, especially in terra cotta or ivory; a statuette. [<F <Ital. *figurina*, dim. of *figura* <L. See FIGURE.]
fig·wort (fig′wûrt′) *n.* **1** A plant (genus *Scrophularia*) with small, dark-colored flowers, formerly supposed to cure scrofula. **2** Any plant of the figwort family (*Scrophulariaceae*).
Fi·ji (fē′jē) A British colony in the South Pacific SW of Samoa, comprising the **Fiji Islands,** 7,056 square miles: capital, Suva; and the dependency of Rotuma.
Fi·ji (fē′jē) *n.* **1** One of the native people of the Fiji Islands, mostly Melanesian with Polynesian admixture. **2** The Melanesian language of the Fijis.
Fi·ji·an (fē′jē·ən) *adj.* Of Fiji, its people, or their language. — *n.* A Fiji.
fike (fīk) See FYKE[1].
fil·a·gree (fil′ə·grē) See FILIGREE.
fil·a·ment (fil′ə·mənt) *n.* **1** A fine thread, fiber, or fibril. **2** Any threadlike structure or appendage. **3** *Bot.* The stalk or support of an anther. **4** *Electr.* The slender wire of tungsten, carbon, or other material, which, when an electric current is passed through it in a vacuum, is heated to a brilliant glow and produces light. See illustration under INCANDESCENT LAMP. **5** *Electronics* A similar wire, forming the cathode of a vacuum tube, from which electrons are emitted under the action of heat. **6** *Ornithol.* The barb of a feather. [<F <LL *filamentum* <*filare* spin <*filum* a thread]
fil·a·men·tous (fil′ə·men′təs) *adj.* Like, consisting of, or bearing filaments; threadlike. Also **fil′a·men′ta·ry.**
fi·lar (fī′lər) *adj.* **1** Of, pertaining to, or characterized by a thread or threads; threadlike. **2** *Optics* Having fine threads across the field of view, as in a microscope equipped with a *filar* micrometer for measuring the sizes of objects under examination. [<L *filum* a thread + -AR[1]]
fi·lar·i·a (fi·lâr′ē·ə) *n. pl.* **·i·ae** (-i·ē) A nematode or threadworm (family *Filariidae*) parasitic in the blood and intestines of man and other animals; especially *Wuchereria bancrofti*, the causative agent of elephantiasis, and the Guinea worm. [<NL <L *filum* a thread] — **fi·lar′i·al, fi·lar′i·an** *adj.*
fil·a·ri·a·sis (fil′ə·rī′ə·sis) *n. Pathol.* **1** Infection with nematode worms. **2** The disease so caused, affecting chiefly the lymph glands and connective tissues.
fil·a·ture (fil′ə·chər) *n.* **1** The act or process of forming threads or of reeling off raw silk from cocoons. **2** An apparatus, machine, or establishment for reeling silk, etc. [<F <L *filare* spin <*filum* a thread]
fil·bert (fil′bərt) *n.* **1** The edible nut of the European or the Oriental hazel (*Corylus avellana*); and also, sometimes, of the American hazel (*C. americana* and *C. cornuta*). **2** The bushy shrub or small tree that bears the nut. [Earlier *filbert nut* <dial. F *noix de filbert* nut of Philibert, after St. *Philibert*, near whose feast (Aug. 22) these nuts ripen]
filch (filch) *v.t.* To steal slyly and in small amounts; pilfer. See synonyms under STEAL. [Origin uncertain] — **filch′er** *n.*
file[1] (fīl) *n.* **1** Any device, as a pointed wire, to keep papers in order for reference; also, a cabinet, drawer, or the like, in which papers are filed. **2** A collection of papers or documents arranged systematically for reference. **3** Any orderly succession or line of men or things; especially a line or row of men standing or marching one behind another: distinguished from *rank*; a small detachment; corporal's guard. **4** Place or standing on a list for advancement, as in the army. **5** A roll; list. **6** A vertical row of squares running directly across a chessboard from one player to the other. — **single file** An arrangement of persons or things one behind another in a single line: also *Indian file.* — *v.* **filed, fil·ing** *v.t.* **1** To put on file in systematic order, as papers for reference. — *v.i.* **2** To march in file, as soldiers. **3** To make an application, as for a job. [Fusion of F *fil* thread and *file* a row, both ult. <L *filum* a thread] — **fil′er** *n.*
file[2] (fīl) *n.* **1** A hard steel abrading or smoothing instrument with ridged cutting surfaces. **2** Figuratively, anything used to abrade, smooth, or polish. **3** *Brit. Slang* A shrewd or artful person. — *v.t.* **filed, fil·ing** **1** To cut, smooth, or sharpen with a file. **2** To remove with a file: with *away* or *off*: to *file away* rust. [OE *fil*] — **fil′er** *n.*
file[3] (fīl) *v.t. Archaic* To defile; sully. [OE *-fȳlan*, found in *befȳlan* befoul]
file card A wire brush for cleaning the teeth of files.
file clerk An employee who maintains files and records.
file-clos·er (fīl′klō′zər) *n.* In close order drill, a non-commissioned officer at the rear of a rank who sees that the leader's commands are executed.
file·fish (fīl′fish′) *n.* **·fish** or **·fish·es** **1** Any of certain fish (family *Balistidae*) with roughly granulated skin, especially the triggerfish. **2** Any of certain fish (family *Monacanthidae*) with prickly scales.
file-lead·er (fīl′lē′dər) *n.* The front man in a military file; hence, any recognized or official leader.
Fi·le·mo·na (fē′lā·mō′nä) Italian feminine form of PHILEMON.
fil·e·mot (fil′ə·mot) *adj. Archaic* Having the

color of a dead or faded leaf. —*n. Obs.* The color of a dead or faded leaf. [Alter. of F *feuillemorte* dead leaf]

fi·lé powder (fi·lā′) A sassafras seasoning and thickening for sauces and gravies.

fi·let (fi·lā′, fil′ā; *Fr.* fē·le′) *n.* 1 Net lace having a square mesh. 2 Fillet (def. 2 and 3). [< F. See FILLET.]

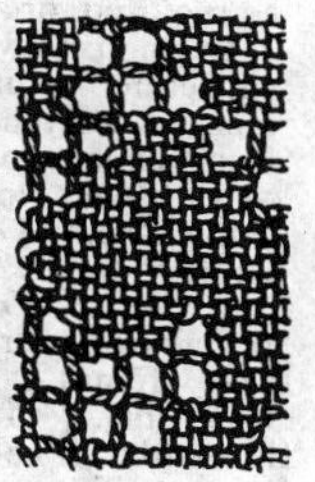

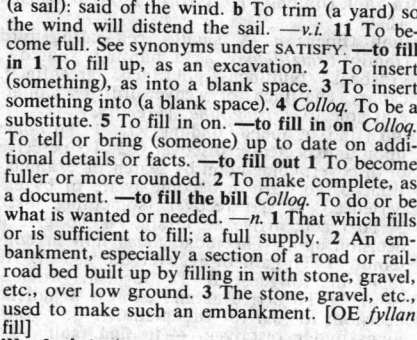

LACE FILET

filet de sole (də sôl′) *French* Fillet of sole.

fi·let mi·gnon (fi·lā′min·yon′) A small fillet of beef cooked with a garnish of bacon. [< F]

fil·i·al (fil′ē·əl, fil′yəl) *adj.* 1 Of, pertaining to, or befitting a son or daughter; due to parents. 2 *Genetics* Pertaining to a generation following the parental. The first filial generation is designated F_1, the second F_2, etc. [< LL *filialis* < L *filius* a son] —**fil′i·al·ly** *adv.*

fil·i·ate (fil′ē·āt) *v.t.* **·at·ed, ·at·ing** To affiliate. [< LL *filiatus,* pp. of *filiare* have a son < *filius* son]

fil·i·a·tion (fil′ē·ā′shən) *n.* 1 The relation of a child to a parent. 2 *Law* The judicial determination of parentage; affiliation. 3 Causal connection or relationship; descent. 4 The formation of offshoots, as of a language.

fil·i·beg (fil′ə·beg) *n.* A kilt of the modern fashion, as distinguished from the earlier great kilt, which covered the body: also spelled *philabeg, philibeg.* [< Scottish Gaelic *feileadh* kilt + *beag* little]

fil·i·bus·ter (fil′ə·bus′tər) *n.* 1 *U.S.* A member of a legislative body who attempts to obstruct legislation by prolonged speaking to consume time; hence, any such prolonged speech. 2 A freebooter or buccaneer; pirate. 3 An adventurer who takes part in an unlawful military expedition into a foreign country. —*v.i.* 1 *U.S.* To obstruct legislation by long speeches and constant delay. 2 To act as a freebooter or adventurer. —*v.t.* 3 *U.S.* To block passage of (legislation) by constant delay. [< Sp. *filibustero* < Du. *vrijbuiter* freebooter] —**fil′i·bus′ter·er** *n.* —**fil′i·bus′trous** *adj.*

fil·i·cide (fil′ə·sīd) *n.* 1 One who kills his child. 2 The act of killing one's child. [< L *filius* a son + -CIDE] —**fil′i·ci′dal** *adj.*

Fil·i·cin·e·ae (fil′ə·sin′i·ē) *n. pl.* A large class of pteridophyte plants; the ferns. [< NL *filicineus* < *Filicales,* an order of ferns < L *filix, filicis* a fern]

fil·i·coid (fil′ə·koid) *adj.* Resembling a fern; fernlike: a *filicoid* pattern. See illustration under FROST. [< L *filix, filicis* a fern + -OID]

Fi·li·de (fē′lē·dā) Italian form of PHYLLIS.

fil·i·form (fil′ə·fôrm) *adj.* Threadlike; filamentous; thready. [< L *filum* thread + -FORM]

fil·i·gree (fil′ə·grē) *n.* 1 Delicate ornamental work formed of intertwisted gold or silver wire. 2 Anything fanciful and delicate, but purely ornate. —*adj.* Made of or adorned with filigree; fanciful; ornate. —*v.t.* **·greed, ·gree·ing** To adorn with filigree; work in filigree. Sometimes spelled *filagree* or *fillagree.* Also *Obs.* **fil′i·grain.** [Short for *filigreen,* var. of *filigrane* < F < Ital. *filigrana* < L *filum* thread + *granum* a grain]

fil·ing (fī′ling) *n.* 1 The act or process of using a file. 2 A particle removed by a file.

Fi·lip (*Pol.* fē′lēp; *Rus.* fē·lēp′; *Sw.* fil′ip) Polish, Russian, and Swedish form of PHILIP. Also *Ital.* **Fi·lip·po** (fē·lēp′pō).

Fil·i·pi·no (fil′ə·pē′nō) *n. pl.* **·nos** A native or inhabitant of the Philippines. —*adj.* Of or pertaining to the Philippines.

Fi·lip·pa (fē·lēp′pä) Italian form of PHILIPPA. Also **Fi·lip·pi·na** (fē′lēp·pē′nä).

fill (fil) *v.t.* 1 To make full; put as much in as possible. 2 To occupy to capacity; pack. 3 To abound in. 4 To stop up or plug: to *fill* a tooth. 5 To supply with what is necessary or ordered: to *fill* a prescription. 6 To occupy (an office or position). 7 To put someone into (an office or position): to *fill* the governorship with a good man. 8 To feed to fullness; to satisfy; glut. 9 *Engin.* To build up or make full, as an embankment or a ravine, by adding fill. 10 *Naut.* **a** To distend (a sail): said of the wind. **b** To trim (a yard) so the wind will distend the sail. —*v.i.* 11 To become full. See synonyms under SATISFY. —**to fill in** 1 To fill up, as an excavation. 2 To insert (something), as into a blank space. 3 To insert something into (a blank space). 4 *Colloq.* To be a substitute. 5 To fill in on. —**to fill in on** *Colloq.* To tell or bring (someone) up to date on additional details or facts. —**to fill out** 1 To become fuller or more rounded. 2 To make complete, as a document. —**to fill the bill** *Colloq.* To do or be what is wanted or needed. —*n.* 1 That which fills or is sufficient to fill; a full supply. 2 An embankment, especially a section of a road or railroad bed built up by filling in with stone, gravel, etc., over low ground. 3 The stone, gravel, etc., used to make such an embankment. [OE *fyllan* fill]

fille de joie (fē′y′ də zhwä′) *French* A prostitute.

filled gold (fild) A layer of gold rolled upon base metal and not merely electroplated on it.

filled milk Milk in which vegetable oils replace the normal cream content.

fill·er[1] (fil′ər) *n.* 1 One who or that which fills. 2 Any substance used for filling. 3 A composition for filling pores or holes in wood, before painting or varnishing. 4 Tobacco used for the inside of cigars and for plug tobacco. 5 Any device which conducts a substance into a receptacle, as a funnel or a conduit to a reservoir. 6 A brief piece of writing, usually an unimportant item, used to fill space in a newspaper or magazine.

fil·lér[2] (fēl′lâr) *n. sing. & pl.* A Hungarian coin, the hundredth part of a forint. [< Hungarian]

fil·let (fil·lit, *usually for defs. 2 and 3* fil′ā) *n.* 1 A narrow band or ribbon for binding the hair. 2 A strip of lean meat. 3 A flat slice of fish without the bone. 4 A thin band, strip, or engraved line. 5 *Archit.* **a** A small band or molding, usually rectangular, narrow, and flat, used to separate or ornament larger moldings or members. **b** The narrow ridge or strip between the flutes of a column or filling any similar function; a facet. **c** A strip or molding fastened to a wall or the like. 6 *Physiol.* An important nerve tract by which sensory impressions are conveyed to the higher cerebral centers. 7 *Her.* A diminutive ordinary occupying the lower fourth part of the chief. 8 The loins of a horse. 9 Fairing[1] (def. 1). —*v.t.* 1 To bind or adorn with a fillet or band. 2 (also fil′ā, fi·lā′) To slice into fillets; cook as a fillet. [< F *filet,* dim. of *fil* a thread < L *filum*]

fill-in (fil′in′) *n.* 1 A person or thing included to fill a gap or omission. 2 *Colloq.* A summary of facts given to complete one's understanding of a situation.

fill·ing (fil′ing) *n.* 1 The act of making or becoming full. 2 Something used to fill a cavity or vacant space: a *filling* of gold for a tooth. 3 In weaving, the weft or woof, which crosses the warp. 4 A custard, jelly, or fruit-and-nut mixture placed between layers of a cake.

filling station A station for supplying gasoline, oil, and other necessaries to automobiles.

fil·lip (fil′əp) *n.* 1 A sudden flip of a finger from contact with the thumb; a quick snap or blow with the end of a finger. 2 Anything which serves as an incitement or gives impulse, as to an ambition. —*v.t.* 1 To strike by or as by a fillip; snap with the finger. 2 To project or impel, as by a fillip. —*v.i.* To make a fillip. [Var. of FLIP]

fil·li·peen (fil′ə·pēn′) See PHILOPENA.

fil·lis·ter (fil′is·tər) *n. Mech.* 1 A plane for making grooves. 2 A rabbet on a sash bar, for receiving the edge of the glass and the putty. 3 A type of screw with a round head. [Origin unknown]

Fill·more (fil′môr), **Millard,** 1800–74, president of the United States 1850–53.

fil·ly (fil′ē) *n. pl.* **fil·lies** A young mare. [< ON *fylja* < *fōli* foal]

film (film) *n.* 1 A thin coating, layer, or membrane. 2 *Phot.* **a** A thin coating of a light-sensitive emulsion laid on a glass plate or on a flexible base, for making photographs. **b** The base itself. 3 A motion picture. 4 A delicate filament, as of a cobweb. 5 *Pathol.* A morbid growth on the cornea of the eye. —*v.t.* 1 To cover or obscure by or as by a film. 2 To photograph on a film; especially, to take motion pictures of. —*v.i.* 3 To become covered or obscured by a film. 4 To take motion pictures. [OE *filmen* membrane]

film pack *Phot.* A set of films so packaged that it may be safely handled in daylight, each individual film being exposed in turn.

film·strip (film′strip′) *n.* A length of film containing frames of still pictures which are projected on a screen, usually as a visual aid in lectures.

film·y (fil′mē) *adj.* **film·i·er, film·i·est** Like a film; cloudy; obscure; also, gauzy; thin; unsubstantial. —**film′i·ly** *adv.* —**film′i·ness** *n.*

fil·o·plume (fil′ə·ploōm′, fī′lə-) *n. Ornithol.* A thread feather. [< L *filum* thread + *pluma* plume]

fi·lose (fī′lōs) *adj.* Having a threadlike appendage. [< L *filum* thread + -OSE[1]]

fils (fēs) *n. French* Son: used after a surname to distinguish father (*père*) from son: Dumas *fils.*

fil·ter (fil′tər) *n.* 1 Any device or porous substance, as paper, cloth, fine clay, or charcoal, used as a strainer for clearing or purifying fluids. Compare illustration under FUNNEL. 2 *Electr.* A device which permits the passage of currents of certain frequencies and limits the flow of certain others, such as a **band filter,** which passes currents neither above nor below a given range, a **high-pass filter,** which selects certain high-frequency currents and a **low-pass filter,** which permits the flow of certain low-frequency currents; also used in power transmission. 3 *Phot.* A colored screen of glass, or of other translucent material, placed in front of a camera lens to control the kind and relative intensity of light waves in an exposure. —*v.t.* 1 To pass (liquids) through a filter; strain. 2 To separate (solid matter) from liquid by a filter. —*v.i.* 3 To pass through a filter. 4 To move slowly; leak out, as news. See synonyms under PURIFY. ◆ Homophone: *philter.* [< OF *filtre* < Med. L *fēltrum.* Related to FELT[2].] —**fil′ter·a·bil′i·ty, fil·tra·bil·i·ty** (fil′trə·bil′ə·tē), **fil′ter·a·ble·ness** *n.* —**fil′ter·a·ble, fil·tra·ble** (fil′·trə·bəl) *adj.*

filter bed A reservoir with a sand or gravel bottom for purifying large quantities of water.

filter feeder Any aquatic organism that feeds on small organisms which are strained out of the surrounding water as it is channeled through a specialized sieve or filtering system.

filter paper A soft porous paper suitable for filtering.

filth (filth) *n.* 1 Anything that soils, or makes foul; that which is foul or dirty. 2 Moral defilement; obscenity. [OE *fӯlth*]

filth·y (fil′thē) *adj.* **filth·i·er, filth·i·est** Of the nature of or containing filth; foul; obscene. See synonyms under FOUL. —**filth′i·ly** *adv.* —**filth′·i·ness** *n.*

filtrable virus See under VIRUS.

fil·trate (fil′trāt) *v.t.* **·trat·ed, ·trat·ing** To filter. —*n.* The liquid or other substance separated by filtration. [< NL *filtratus,* pp. of *filtrare* < Med. L *filtrum* a filter]

fil·tra·tion (fil·trā′shən) *n.* 1 The act or process of filtering. 2 The separation of liquids from solids. 3 The sterilization of liquids by the mechanical removal of bacteria and other impurities.

filtration plant A place equipped with large filters, through which the water supply of a city passes to be purified.

fi·lum (fī′ləm) *n. pl.* **·la** (-lə) *Anat.* A thread or threadlike structure. [< NL < L]

fim·ble (fim′bəl) *n.* The male hemp plant, which is generally harvested before the female plant. [< Du. *femel* < F *(chanvre) femelle* female (hemp)]

fim·bri·a (fim′brē·ə) *n. Zool.* A fringe or fringelike structure, as around the mouth of a tube or duct in certain animals. [< NL < L, a fringe]

fim·bri·ate (fim′brē·āt) *v.t.* **·at·ed, ·at·ing** *Biol.* To furnish with a fringe or border; fringe. —*adj.* (-it) Having such a fringe or border. —**fim′bri·a′tion** *n.*

fim·bri·at·ed (fim′brē·ā′tid) *adj.* Having a fringe or fringelike processes; fimbriate.

fim·bril·late (fim·bril′it) *adj. Biol.* Having a fine fringe or border. [<NL *fimbrilla,* dim. of *fimbra* a fringe]
fin[1] (fin) *n.* **1** A membranous extension from the body of a fish or other aquatic animal, serving to propel, balance, or steer it in the water. For illustrations see FISH, RORQUAL. **2** Any finlike or projecting part, appendage, or attachment. **3** *Naut.* A finlike appendage to a submarine boat or the like; a fin keel. **4** *Aeron.* A fixed supplementary surface of an aircraft, usually vertical: a tail *fin.* See illustration under AIRPLANE. **5** A projecting rib on a radiator or on the cylinder of an internal-combustion engine. **6** Any finlike part, as on a rocket, bomb, etc. **7** A flipper (def. 2). **8** *Mech.* The projecting ridge of a metal casting at the line of junction with the mold. — *v.* **finned, fin·ning** *v.t.* To cut up or trim off the fins of (a fish). — *v.i.* To beat the water with the fins, as a whale when dying. [OE *finn*]
fin[2] (fīn) *v.t.* & *v.i. Scot.* To find.
fin·a·ble (fī′nə·bəl) *adj.* **1** Liable to or involving a fine. **2** Capable of being refined or purified. Also *fineable.*
fi·na·gle (fi·nā′gəl) *v.* **·gled, ·gling** *Colloq. v.t.* **1** To get (something) by trickery or deceit. **2** To cheat or trick (someone). — *v.i.* **3** To use trickery or deceit; be sly. **4** In card games, to renege. [Var. of FAINAIGUE] — **fi·na′gler** *n.*
fi·nal (fī′nəl) *adj.* **1** Pertaining to, or coming at or as, the end; ultimate; last. **2** Precluding, or making unnecessary, further action or controversy; conclusive; decisive. **3** Relating to or consisting in the end or purpose aimed at: a *final* cause. — *n.* **1** Something that is terminal, last, or final; that which makes an end; a finale. **2** The last, deciding match in a tournament or series of games. **3** The last examination of a term in a school or college. [<F <L *finalis* <*finis* end]
final cause The object or end to be reached by an action or process; purpose.
fi·na·le (fi·nä′lē, -nal′ē; *Ital.* fē·nä′lā) *n.* **1** The last act, part, or scene; end. **2** The last movement in a musical composition. See synonyms under END. [<Ital., final]
fi·nal·ist (fī′nəl·ist) *n.* In athletics, a contestant who takes part in the final round, as of a tournament, race, etc.
fi·nal·i·ty (fi·nal′ə·tē) *n. pl.* **·ties** **1** The state or quality of being final. **2** A final, conclusive, or decisive act, determination, offer, etc. **3** *Philos.* The doctrine of final causes, that design actuates the universe; teleology. **4** The belief that there can be no progress or change.
fi·nal·ize (fī′nəl·īz) *v.t.* **·ized, ·iz·ing** **1** To bring to a state of completion, as a transaction, sale, or agreement. **2** To put into final or complete form.
fi·nal·ly (fī′nəl·ē) *adv.* **1** At or in the end; ultimately. **2** Lastly. **3** Completely; irrecoverably.
fi·nance (fi·nans′, fī′nans) *n.* **1** The science of monetary affairs. **2** *pl.* Monetary affairs; pecuniary resources; funds; revenue; income. — *v.t.* **·nanced, ·nanc·ing** **1** To manage the finances of. **2** To supply the money for. [<OF, payment <*finer* settle <*fin* end. See FINE[2].]
finance bill Legislation to raise revenue for the government.
fi·nan·cial (fi·nan′shəl, fī-) *adj.* **1** Of or pertaining to finance; monetary. **2** Of or pertaining to those dealing professionally with money and credit. — **fi·nan′cial·ly** *adv.*
Synonyms: fiscal, monetary, pecuniary. These words all relate to money, receipts, or expenditures. *Monetary* relates to actual money, coin, currency; as, the *monetary* system; a *monetary* transaction is one in which money is transferred. *Pecuniary* refers to that in which money is involved, but less directly; we speak of one's *pecuniary* affairs or interests, with no special reference to the handling of cash. *Financial* applies especially to governmental revenues or expenditures, or to private transactions of considerable moment; we speak of a *pecuniary* reward, a *financial* enterprise; we give a needy person *pecuniary* (not *financial*) assistance. *Fiscal* applies to the state treasury or public finances or accounts; it is common to speak of the *fiscal* rather than the *financial* year.
fin·an·cier (fin′ən·sir′) *n.* One skilled in or occupied with financial affairs; a capitalist. — *v.t.* & *v.i.* To finance.
fin·back (fin′bak′) *n.* A rorqual. Also **finback whale.**
finch (finch) *n.* A small, seed-eating bird (family *Fringillidae*), as a bunting, sparrow, grosbeak, bullfinch, goldfinch, greenfinch, canary, chaffinch, or weaverbird. ◆ Collateral adjective: *fringilline.* [OE *finc*]
find (fīnd) *v.* **found, find·ing** *v.t.* **1** To come upon unexpectedly; discover. **2** To perceive or discover; come upon by search or examination. **3** To learn or become aware of by experience. **4** To recover (something lost). **5** To reach; arrive at; attain. **6** To give a decision upon: The judge *found* him in contempt. **7** To gain or recover the use of: He *found* his tongue. **8** To furnish; provide. — *v.i.* **9** To arrive at and express a judicial decision: to *find* for the plaintiff. See synonyms under DISCOVER. — **to find fault** To complain of some defect or deficiency. — **to find oneself** **1** To become aware of one's special ability or vocation. **2** To fare in health; feel. — **to find out** To detect or discover, as a thief. — **to find out about** To learn the truth concerning. — *n.* A finding; a thing found or discovered; especially, a valuable discovery. [OE *findan*]
find·er (fīn′dər) *n.* **1** One who or that which finds. **2** *Astron.* A small telescope by the side of a large one, used to locate a particular object for astronomical observation. **3** *Phot.* A supplementary lens attached to a camera, to locate the object in the field of view.
fin de siè·cle (fan̐ də sye′kl′) *French* End of the century; specifically, the close of the 19th century, viewed as a period of transition in social and moral values.
fin-de-siè·cle (fan̐·də·sye′kl′) *adj. French* Decadent.
find·ing (fīn′ding) *n.* **1** The act of finding; that which is found; discovery. **2** *Law* A conclusion arrived at before an official or a court. **3** Support; expense.
find·ings (fīn′dingz) *n. pl.* **1** Small tools and supplies which a workman provides for himself. **2** Sewing essentials, as thread, needles, tape, buttons, etc.; notions. **3** *Law* Conclusions as to matters of fact arrived at through testimony heard before an official or a court.
fine[1] (fīn) *adj.* **fin·er, fin·est** **1** Excellent in quality; admirable; superior. **2** Suggesting lightness; light or delicate; not coarse, gross, or dull; subtle; thin; keen. **3** Showy in appearance or style; pretentious; ostentatious. **4** Delicate of perception; refined; sensitive; nice. **5** Refined, as sirup. **6** Having a high or specified degree of purity, as gold or silver. **7** Distinguished or noteworthy. **8** Enjoyable; pleasant. **9** Trained to the highest point of efficiency: said of an athlete, a horse, etc. **10** Cloudless; rainless. — *adv.* **1** *Colloq.* Very much; finely; well; excellently. **2** In billiards, in a manner producing a fine carom, etc. — *v.t.* & *v.i.* **fined, fin·ing** To make or become purified, thin, or slender. [<OF *fin* perfected <LL *finus,* a back formation <L *finire* complete <*finis* end] — **fine′ly** *adv.*
Synonyms (adj.): beautiful, clarified, clear, comminuted, dainty, delicate, elegant, excellent, exquisite, gauzy, handsome, keen, minute, nice, polished, pure, refined, sensitive, sharp, slender, slight, small, smooth, splendid, subtile, subtle, tenuous, thin. *Fine* denotes that which has been brought to a full end, finished, consummated. From this root-sense many derived meanings branch out, causing words quite remote from each other to be synonyms of *fine.* That which is truly finished is *excellent* of its kind, and *beautiful,* if a thing that admits of beauty; as a *fine* house, *fine* trees, a *fine* woman, a *fine* morning. If it is a thing that admits of the removal of impurities, it is not finished till these are removed, and hence *fine* signifies *clarified, clear, pure, refined*; as, *fine* gold. That which is finished is apt to be *polished, smooth* to the touch, minutely exact in outline; hence *fine* comes to be a synonym for all words like *dainty, delicate, exquisite*; as, *fine* manners, a *fine* touch, *fine* perceptions. As that which is *delicate* is apt to be small, by an easy extension of meaning *fine* becomes a synonym for *slender, slight, minute, comminuted*; as, a *fine* thread, *fine* sand; or for *filmy, tenuous, thin*; as, a *fine* lace, *fine* wire; and as a *thin* edge is *keen* and *sharp, fine* becomes also a synonym for these words; as, a *fine* point, a *fine* edge. Compare BEAUTIFUL, EXCELLENT, MINUTE, TASTEFUL. *Antonyms*: big, blunt, clumsy, coarse, great, heavy, huge, immense, large, rude, stout, thick.
fine[2] (fīn) *n.* **1** A pecuniary penalty; the money so required, or anything forfeited as a penalty. **2** In English law, an amicable adjustment of a suit either actual or fictitious; a final agreement as for the possession of lands. **3** *Obs.* End; conclusion; death. — **in fine** Finally. — *v.t.* **fined, fin·ing** To punish by fine; exact a fine from. [<OF *fin* settlement <L *finis* end]
fine[3] (fēn) *n. French* A drink of brandy, especially one served with meals.
fi·ne[4] (fē′nā) *n. Music* A mark denoting the end; finis. [<Ital.]
fine·a·ble (fī′nə·bəl) See FINABLE.
fine arts See under ART[1].
Fi·ne·as (fē′nā·äs′) Spanish form of PHINEAS. Also *Ital.* **Fi·ne·o** (fē·nā′ō).
fine-cut (fīn′kut′) *n.* A kind of smoking or chewing tobacco, finely shredded.
fine-draw (fīn′drô′) *v.t.* **·drew, ·drawn, ·draw·ing** **1** To sew or close up, as a tear, so that the joining is imperceptible. **2** To draw out, as wire, to an extreme degree of fineness.
fine-drawn (fīn′drôn′) *adj.* Drawn out finely; hence, developed very subtly or too subtly.
fine-frame (fīn′frām′) *n.* A special frame used in making high-grade yarns of Sea Island cotton.
fine-grained (fīn′grānd′) *adj.* Having a close, fine grain, as in texture or surface: said of some leathers and woods.
fine·ness (fīn′nis) *n.* **1** The state or quality of being fine. **2** The degree of subdivision of the particles of a powder or other granular substance. **3** The purity of an alloy, especially one containing gold or silver, expressed in parts per thousand.
fin·er·y (fī′nər·ē) *n. pl.* **·er·ies** Showy or fine clothes or decoration.
fines herbes (fēn ârb) *French* A mixture of herbs used to season soups, stews, etc.
fine-spun (fīn′spun′) *adj.* **1** Drawn or spun out to an extreme degree of tenuity. **2** Subtle.
fi·nesse (fi·nes′) *n.* **1** Subtle contrivance; artifice; stratagem. **2** Dexterity; artfulness; skill. **3** In card-playing, an attempt on the part of a player to take a trick with a lower card when he holds a higher (as a queen when he holds the ace), in the hope that the opposing hand yet to play will not hold a taking card (as the king). See synonyms under ARTIFICE, DECEPTION. — *v.* **fi·nessed, fi·ness·ing** *v.t.* **1** To change or bring about by finesse. **2** In card games, to play as a finesse. — *v.i.* **3** To use finesse. **4** In card games, to make a finesse. [<F <*fin* FINE[1]]
fine-toothed comb (fīn′tōōtht′) A comb with fine teeth very close together. — **to go over with a fine-toothed comb** To search carefully; leave no part unsearched or unexamined.
fine·top (fīn′top′) *n.* Redtop.
fin·fish (fin′fish′) *n.* True fish: not shellfish.
fin-foot·ed (fin′fŏŏt′id) *adj.* **1** Having webbed feet. **2** Having lobate toes.
Fin·gal (fing′gəl) Hero of the spurious Ossianic poems, *Fingal* and *Temora,* by James Macpherson. See FIONN MACCUMAL.
Fingal's Cave A basaltic cavern on Staffa island, Inner Hebrides, Scotland; 227 feet long, 66 feet high.
fin·gan (fin·gän′) See FINJAN.
fin·gent (fin′jənt) *adj.* Forming; making; molding. [<L *fingens, -entis,* ppr. of *fingere* form]
fin·ger (fing′gər) *n.* **1** One of the digits of the hand, usually excluding the thumb. **2** Any small projecting piece or part, like a finger, as a lever. **3** A measure of length; the length of the middle finger. **4** A measure of depth, equal to the width of the finger. **5** That part of a glove which covers a finger. — **to burn one's fingers** To suffer the consequences of meddling or interfering. — **to have a finger in the pie** To take part in some matter. — **to have at one's finger tips** To have ready and available knowledge of. — **to put one's finger on** To identify or indicate correctly. — **to put the finger on** *U.S. Slang* **1** To betray to the police. **2** To indicate (the victim) of a planned crime. — **to twist around one's (little) finger** To be able to influence or manage with

ease. — *v.t.* 1 To touch or handle with the fingers; toy with. 2 To steal; purloin. 3 *Music* **a** To play (an instrument) with the fingers. **b** To mark the notes of (music) showing which fingers are to be used. 4 *U.S. Slang* **a** To betray. **b** To point out (the victim) of a planned crime. — *v.i.* 5 To touch or feel anything with the fingers. 6 *Music* **a** To use the fingers on a musical instrument in a certain manner. **b** To be arranged for playing by the fingers: said of instruments. [OE]

fin·ger·board (fing′gər·bôrd′, -bōrd′) *n.* 1 A guideboard bearing a pointing finger. 2 In stringed instruments, the strip of wood upon which the strings are pressed by the fingers of the player. 3 In instruments of the piano or organ class, a keyboard.

fin·ger·bowl (fing′gər·bōl′) *n.* A bowl containing water for cleansing the fingers at the table after eating.

fin·ger·breadth (fing′gər·bredth′) *n.* The breadth of a finger, from 3/4 inch to one inch.

fin·gered (fing′gərd) *adj.* 1 Having fingers; digitate. 2 Having figures to mark the fingering, as in music.

fin·ger·er (fing′gər·ər) *n.* One who fingers; a pilferer.

finger hole 1 A hole in any object into which a finger may be fitted, as in a bowling ball. 2 One of a series of holes in various wind instruments, as a flute, oboe, etc., over which the finger is manipulated in order to change the tones. 3 One of a series of small holes in a dial telephone.

fin·ger·ing[1] (fing′gər·ing) *n.* 1 The act of touching or feeling with the fingers. 2 *Music* **a** The act or order of using the fingers in playing an instrument, as the flute or piano. **b** The notation indicating what fingers are to be used.

fin·ger·ing[2] (fing′gər·ing) *n.* A finely twisted woolen yarn of medium weight, used for knitting and crocheting. Also **fingering yarn.**

Finger Lakes A group of long, narrow glacial lakes in west central New York.

fin·ger·ling (fing′gər·ling) *n.* 1 A young fish, especially a salmon or trout, no bigger than a man's finger. 2 A being of very small size. Compare THUMBLING. 3 *Obs.* A glove finger; a finger covering; a thimble.

finger mark A mark or stain left by a finger.

fin·ger–marked (fing′gər·märkt′) *adj.* Smudged with finger marks.

fin·ger·nail (fing′gər·nāl′) *n.* The horny growth on the end and along the upper surface of a finger.

finger painting A technique of applying paint to wet paper with the fingers and palms to form a design or picture.

fin·ger·post (fing′gər·pōst′) *n.* A guidepost in the shape of a pointing finger.

fin·ger·print (fing′gər·print′) *n.* An impression of the skin pattern on the inner surface of a finger tip: especially used in the identification of criminals, in the military, naval, and police services, and in various commercial transactions. — *v.t.* To take the fingerprints of. See synonyms under MARK[1]. — **fin′ger·print′ing** *n.*

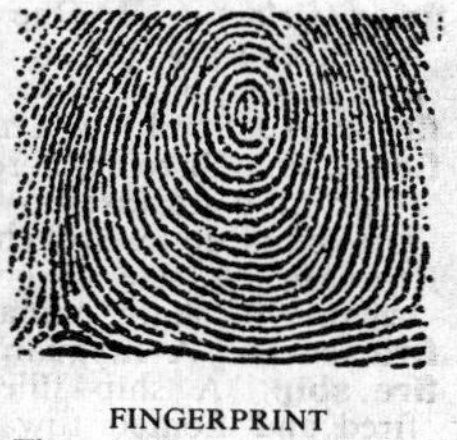

FINGERPRINT
The whorl type of print.

finger stall A cover to protect a finger.

finger wave A wave in the hair, shaped and set with the fingers, without the use of instruments.

fin·i·al (fin′ē·əl) *n.* 1 *Archit.* An ornament at the apex of a spire, pinnacle, or the like. 2 Any terminal part pointing upward. [<L *finis* end + -IAL]

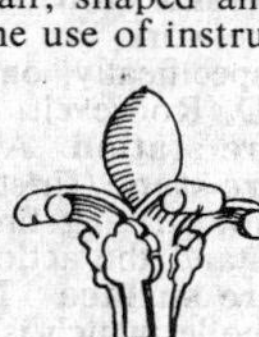

FINIAL

fin·i·cal (fin′i·kəl) *adj.* Over-nice or fastidious in dress, manners, and the like. Also **fin′ick·ing, fin′ick·y, fin′i·kin.** See synonyms under SQUEAMISH. [<FINE[1]] — **fin′i·cal·ly** *adv.* — **fin′·i·cal·ness** *n.*

fin·i·cal·i·ty (fin′ə·kal′ə·tē) *n.* 1 The characteristic of being finical. 2 That which is finical.

fin·ing (fī′ning) *n.* 1 The process of making fine. 2 The removal of gas bubbles from fused glass. 3 The purification and clarifying of wines. 4 Any substance used in clarifying liquids.

fi·nis (fī′nis, fin′is) *n.* *pl.* **fi·nis·es** *Latin* The end.

fin·ish (fin′ish) *v.t.* 1 To complete or bring to an end; come to the end of. 2 To perfect finally or in detail, as a portrait. 3 To use up; dispose of. 4 *Colloq.* To kill or destroy. 5 *Colloq.* To defeat; make powerless. — *v.i.* 6 To reach or come to an end; stop. 7 *Obs.* To die. — *n.* 1 The conclusion or last stage of anything. 2 The process or effect of perfecting or beautifying anything: the *finish* of a statue; cloth of a fine *finish.* 3 Perfection in speech or manner; social poise. 4 The joinery and cabinetwork necessary to complete the interior of a building. 5 That which finishes or completes. 6 A material, as oil, used in finishing. See synonyms under END. [<OF *feniss-*, stem of *fenir* end <L *finire* <*finis* an end]

Synonyms (verb): accomplish, achieve, close, complete, conclude, elaborate, end, perfect, polish, terminate. In addition to its meaning of *completing* by which it is synonymous with *close, conclude, end, terminate,* etc., *finish* has come to denote the bringing to perfection of every minutest detail, especially of superficial elegance, refinement, or beauty, and is thus a close synonym of *elaborate, perfect, polish,* etc., as in the expression, to add the *finishing* touches. Compare END *v. Antonyms*: begin, commence, found, inaugurate, initiate, institute, open, originate, start, undertake. Compare synonyms for BEGIN.

fin·ished (fin′isht) *adj.* 1 Carried to a high degree of perfection; polished. 2 Ended; concluded. 3 Completed; done. See synonyms under PERFECT, RIPE.

fin·ish·er (fin′ish·ər) *n.* One who or that which finishes, completes, ends, or perfects anything.

fin·ish·ing (fin′ish·ing) *n.* The final operation or set of operations in any manufacturing process: the *finishing* of furs, etc.

finishing school See under SCHOOL.

Fin·is·terre (fin′is·târ′, *Sp.* fē′nēs·ter′rä), **Cape** A headland in Galicia, the most westerly point of Spain.

fi·nite (fī′nīt) *adj.* 1 Having bounds, ends, or limits, as opposed to that which is infinite. 2 That may be determined, counted, or measured. 3 Subject to creature limitations, especially those that affect human life. 4 *Gram.* Limited by number and person: said of verb forms that can serve as predicates in sentences: distinguished from infinitives, participles, and gerunds that have no such limitations. 5 *Math.* **a** That may be equaled or exceeded by counting: said of numbers. **b** Limited and determinate, in theory or by observation; not infinite or infinitesimal: said of a magnitude. — *n.* Finite things collectively, or that which is finite: usually with *the.* [<L *finitus* limited; orig. pp. of *finire* end] — **fi′·nite·ly** *adv.* — **fi′nite·ness** *n.*

fin·i·tes·i·mal (fin′ə·tes′ə·məl) *adj. Math.* Denoted by the ordinal of a finite number. [<FINITE + *-esimal*, as in *centesimal* <L *-esimus*, suffix of ordinal numbers]

fin·i·tude (fin′ə·tōōd, -tyōōd, fī′nə-) *n.* The mode or fact of being finite; limitation. [<L *finitus* limited]

fin·jan (fin′jən) *n.* A small handleless coffee cup of Asia Minor: also spelled *fingan.* [< Arabic]

fink (fingk) *n. U.S. Slang* A non-working strikebreaker. [? <FINGER, *v.* (def. 4)]

fin keel See under KEEL.

Fin·land (fin′lənd) A republic of northern Europe, NE of the Baltic Sea; 130,091 square miles; capital, Helsinki: Finnish *Suomi.*

Finland, Gulf of An eastern arm of the Baltic Sea, between Finland and the U.S.S.R.

Fin·land·er (fin′lən·dər) *n.* A native or naturalized inhabitant of Finland.

Fin·lay (fin′lē, *Sp.* fin·lī′), **Carlos Juan,** 1833–1915, Cuban physician and biologist.

Finlay River (fin′lē) The chief tributary of the Peace River, flowing 210 miles SE through northern British Columbia.

Finn (fin) See FIONN MACCUMAL.

Finn (fin) *n.* 1 A native or inhabitant of Finland. 2 A member of a people speaking a Finnic language. [OE *Finnas* Finns]

fin·nan had·die (fin′ən had′ē) Smoked haddock. Also **fin′nan had·dock** (had′ək). [<*Findhorn haddock*, from *Findhorn*, a Scottish town where originally prepared]

finned (find) *adj.* Having fins or finlike extensions.

Finn·ic (fin′ik) *n.* A branch of the Finno-Ugric subfamily of Uralic languages, including Finnish, Estonian, and Lapp. — *adj.* Finnish.

fin·nick·ing (fin′i·king), **fin·nick·y** (fin′i·kē) See FINICAL.

Finn·ish (fin′ish) *adj.* Of or pertaining to Finland, the Finns, or their language. — *n.* The Uralic language of the Finns.

Fin·no–U·gric (fin′ō·ōō′grik, -yōō′grik) *n.* A subfamily of the Uralic languages, embracing the Finnic (Finnish, Estonian, Lapp, etc.) and Ugric (Magyar, Ostyak, Vogul) branches. — *adj.* Pertaining to the Finns and the Ugrians, or to their languages. Also **Fin′no–U′gri·an.**

fin·ny (fin′ē) *adj.* 1 Having fins; fishlike. 2 Abounding in fish.

fi·no·chi·o (fi·nō′kē·ō) *n.* A variety of fennel (*Foeniculum vulgare dulce*) whose young sweet shoots are esteemed as a food and salad. [<Ital. *finocchio* <L *faeniculum* FENNEL]

fin ray One of the cartilaginous or bony rods supporting the membrane of a fish's fin: also called *ray.*

Fin·sen light (fin′sən) A strong actinic light obtained either from an electric lamp or by passing sunlight through an ammoniacal solution of copper sulfate: used in treating certain skin diseases. [after N. R. *Finsen*, 1860–1904, Danish physician, its originator]

Fin·ster·aar·horn (fin′stər·är′hôrn) The highest peak of the Bernese Alps, Switzerland; 14,026 feet high.

Fio·na Mc·Leod (fē′nə mə·kloud′) Pseudonym of William Sharp.

Fionn Mac·Cumal (fin mə·kōōl′) The hero of the Fenian cycle of Old Irish legend, a chieftain of third century Ireland; father of the poet Ossian. Also spelled *Finn.*

fiord (fyôrd, fyōrd) *n.* A long and narrow arm of the sea, with high rocky banks: also spelled *fjord.* [<Norw. *fjord*]

fip·pence (fip′əns) *n. Brit.* Fivepence.

fip·pen·ny (fip′ə·nē, fip′nē) Short for FIVEPENNY.

fippenny bit *U.S.* A Spanish or Mexican silver piece current before the Civil War at about 6 cents.

fip·ple (fip′əl) *n.* A plug with a lip, as in certain wind instruments, such as the *fipple* flute. [? <ON *flipi* lip of a horse]

fi·que (fē′kā) *n.* A succulent plant of the amaryllis family (*Furcraea macrophylla*) native in tropical America, yielding a fiber similar to jute. [<Sp.]

fir (fûr) *n.* 1 An evergreen tree of the pine family (genus *Abies*), cone-bearing and resinous, especially the balsam fir (*A. balsamea*). 2 Its wood. ◆ Homophone: *fur.* [OE *fyrh*]

Fir·bolg (fir′bul·əg) Literally, men of the leather boats: one of a legendary pre-Celtic people of Ireland, defeated and run out by the Fomorians. [<Irish *fir* men + *bolg* leather coracle]

Fir·dau·si (fir·dou′sē) Pseudonym of Abul Kasim Mansur, 939?–1020, Persian epic poet. Also **Fir·du·si** (fir·dōō′sē).

fire (fīr) *n.* 1 The evolution of heat and light by combustion. 2 The combustion thus manifested, especially the flame, or the fuel as burning. 3 A destructive burning, as of a building. 4 The discharge of firearms. 5 A spark or sparks; a light, luster, or flash. 6 Intensity of feeling or action; ardor; passion; vivacity. 7 Any raging evil; affliction; trial. 8 Fever. 9 A combustible device or substance for producing fire or for display; fireworks. 10 Lightning. 11 *Poetic* A luminous object in the sky, as a star or meteor. 12 Torture or death by or as by burning;

add,āce,câre,pälm; end,ēven; it,īce; odd,ōpen,ôrder; tŏŏk,pōōl; up,bûrn; ə = a in *above,* e in *sicken,* i in *clarity,* o in *melon,* u in *focus;* yōō = u in *fuse;* oi,oil; ou,pout; ch,check; g,go; ng,ring; th,thin; th,this; zh,vision. Foreign sounds à,œ,ü,kh,ṅ; and ◆: see page xx. < from; + plus; ? possibly.

also, any severe trial. **13** *Obs.* A North American Indian term for a family or a nation; hence, by transference, one of the United States, especially one of the first thirteen. — **colored fire** A mixture of combustibles, as sulfur with a mineral salt that yields a colored light when burning: used for signals, fireworks, etc. — **Greek fire** An incendiary composition, used by the Byzantine Greeks to fire enemy ships: said to ignite on contact with water. — **on fire** Burning; ablaze; hence, ardent; zealous. — **under fire** Exposed to gunshot or artillery fire; hence, under attack of any kind. — *v.* **fired, fir·ing** *v.t.* **1** To set on fire; cause to burn. **2** To tend the fire of; put fuel in: to *fire* a furnace. **3** To bake, as pottery, in a kiln. **4** To cure, as tobacco, by exposure to heat. **5** To cauterize. **6** To inflame the emotions or passions of; excite. **7** To discharge, as a gun or bullet. **8** *Colloq.* To impel or hurl, as with force: to *fire* questions. **9** To cause to glow or shine. **10** *U.S. Colloq.* To discharge peremptorily from employment. — *v.i.* **11** To take fire; become ignited. **12** To discharge firearms. **13** To discharge a missile. **14** To become inflamed or excited. **15** To tend a fire. **16** To become blotched or yellow: said of flax and grain. See synonyms under INCENSE[1]. — **to fire away** To begin; start. — **to fire up** **1** To start a fire, as in a furnace. **2** To become enraged. [OE *fȳr*]
Synonyms (noun): blaze, burning, combustion, conflagration, flame. *Combustion* is the essential fact which is at the basis of that assemblage of visible phenomena which we call *fire*, *combustion* being the continuous chemical combination of a substance with some element, as oxygen, evolving heat, and extending from slow processes, such as those by which the heat of the human body is maintained, to the processes producing the most intense light also, as in a blast furnace, or on the surface of the sun. *Fire* is always attended with light, as well as heat; *blaze*, *flame*, etc., designate the mingled light and heat of a *fire*. *Combustion* is the scientific, *fire* the popular term. A *conflagration* is an extensive *fire*. Compare LIGHT[1].
fire-ac·tion (fīr′ak′shən) *n.* The fire of small arms or artillery estimated as a force in attack or defense.
fire alarm **1** An alarm calling attention to a fire or its whereabouts. **2** An apparatus for giving an alarm of fire, especially a telegraphic alarm.
fire–and–brim·stone (fīr′ən·brim′stōn′) *adj.* Impassioned; also, threatening hell: a *fire–and–brimstone* sermon.
fire ant A destructive, mound–building red ant (*Solenopsis geminata*) common in the SE United States: its sting is very painful and often fatal to animals.
fire·arm (fīr′ärm′) *n.* Any weapon from which a missile, as a bullet, is hurled by an explosive: usually restricted to small arms.
fire at will **1** The command given to riflemen or to gun crews to fire independently of each other and of their commanding officer. **2** The act of so firing.
fire·back (fīr′bak′) *n.* **1** The rear wall of a furnace or fireplace. **2** One of various Asian pheasants, having the plumage of the back a bright metallic red.
fire·ball (fīr′bôl′) *n.* **1** A sack of canvas filled with combustibles. **2** A meteor brighter than the planet Venus. **3** Ball-shaped lightning. **4** *Physics* The dense, mushroom-shaped or globular mass of radioactive debris and fall-out material produced by the explosion of an atomic or thermonuclear bomb.

FIREBALL *(def. 4)*

fire balloon **1** A balloon inflated with hot air supplied by fire from underneath, particularly a paper toy balloon carrying a lighted ball or sponge. **2** A balloon carrying inflammable explosives or fireworks, to ignite at a certain height.

fire beetle Any of various elaterid beetles (genus *Pyrophorus*) of the West Indies, especially the cucubano (*P. luminosus*), which emits a greenish light from two spots near the head and a red light from the abdomen.
fire·bird (fīr′bûrd′) *n.* Any of various, small, brilliantly colored birds, as the Baltimore oriole, the vermilion flycatcher, and the scarlet tanager.
fire·blight (fīr′blīt′) *n.* A serious bacterial disease of various pome fruits, caused by *Erwina amylovora* and attacking blossoms, leaves, twigs, and fruit.
fire·board (fīr′bôrd′, -bōrd′) *n.* A board to close a fireplace not in use; chimney board.
fire boat A steamboat provided with fire-extinguishing apparatus: used to protect shipping and wharves.
fire·box (fīr′boks′) *n.* The chamber in which the fuel of a locomotive, furnace, etc., is burnt.
fire·brand (fīr′brand′) *n.* **1** A burning or glowing piece of wood or other substance. **2** An incendiary; a mischief-maker.
fire·brat (fīr′brat′) *n.* A small, wingless, scaly insect (*Thermobia domestica*) which inhabits warm houses and is destructive of wallpaper, clothing, and starchy materials: related to the silverfish. For illustration see under INSECT (injurious).
fire·break (fīr′brāk′) *n.* A strip of plowed or cleared land made to prevent the spread of fire in woods or on a prairie.
fire·brick (fīr′brik′) *n.* A brick made of fire-clay, used for lining furnaces.
fire brigade A company of firemen.
fire·bug (fīr′bug′) *n.* *U.S. Colloq.* An incendiary; a pyromaniac.
fire bug The harlequin bug.
fire·clay (fīr′klā′) *n.* A refractory material, usually finely powdered aluminum silicate, mixed with iron oxide, lime, and other constituents to improve its fire-resistant qualities.
fire company **1** A company of men employed to extinguish fires. **2** A fire-insurance company.
fire control *Mil.* The control of artillery fire by automatic instruments and technical supervision.
fire·crack·er (fīr′krak′ər) *n.* A firework made of a small paper cylinder charged with gunpowder.
fire–cure (fīr′kyŏŏr′) *v.t.* **-cured, -cur·ing** To season with the heat and smoke of an open fire, as tobacco; to smoke.
fire·damp (fīr′damp′) *n.* **1** A combustible gas (chiefly methane) which enters mines from coal seams. **2** The explosive mixture formed by this gas and air.
fire department That part of the public service, including buildings, fire-extinguishing apparatus, and men, devoted to the prevention or extinguishment of fires.
fire·dog (fīr′dôg′, -dog′) *n.* An andiron.
fire·drake (fīr′drāk′) *n.* A fire-breathing dragon of Germanic mythology; specifically, the dragon that killed Beowulf. Also **fire′drag′on** (-drag′ən). [OE *fȳrdraca* < *fȳr* fire + *draca* a dragon]
fire drill **1** The drilling of a fire company. **2** Drilling, as of pupils in a school, to accustom them to proper action in case of fire.
fire–eat·er (fīr′ē′tər) *n.* **1** A juggler who pretends to eat fire. **2** A hot-headed person eager to fight or quarrel.
fire engine A heavy motor truck equipped with fire-fighting apparatus, especially power-driven pumps for throwing water and chemicals under high pressure.
fire escape A ladder or other device attached to the outside of a building and furnishing a means of escape from a burning building.
fire extinguisher A portable fire-fighting apparatus containing certain chemicals that are ejected by pressure through a short hose.
fire·fang (fīr′fang′) *v.i.* To deteriorate by oxidation, as cheese. [< FIRE + FANG, *v.*]
fire·find·er (fīr′fīn′dər) *n.* An instrument consisting of a map with an azimuth circle, an alidade, spirit level, and other accessories: used by forest rangers to locate the position of a fire.
fire·flaught (fīr′flôt′, -fläkht′) *n. Scot.* **1** A flash of lightning. **2** The aurora borealis.
fire·fly (fīr′flī′) *n. pl.* **·flies** Any of various phosphorescent, night-flying beetles (family

Lampyridae); specifically, the North American genera *Photinus* and *Photuris*, whose females and phosphorescent larvae are called *glowworms*.
fire–foam (fīr′fōm′) *n.* A thick foamlike substance, formed by the chemical union of aluminum sulfate and sodium bicarbonate with other materials, which smothers a fire: a trade name.
fire–guard (fīr′gärd′) *n.* **1** A space in fields, grasslands, woods, and forests, cleared of all combustible matter and serving as a protection against the spread of fire. **2** A metal screen placed before an open fire as a guard against sparks.
fire–house (fīr′hous′) *n.* A building for the housing of fire-fighting equipment and personnel.
fire insurance Insurance covering loss resulting from fire.
fire–i·rons (fīr′ī′ərnz) *n.* Poker, shovel, and tongs.
fire·less (fīr′lis) *adj.* Having no fire.
fireless cooker An insulated container in which hot foods may be placed to finish cooking or to be kept warm.
fire·light (fīr′līt′) *n.* The light from a fire, as a campfire.
fire line **1** A firebreak. **2** A barrier made by police against approach to a burning building.
fire·lock (fīr′lok′) *n.* An old form of musket discharged by any device for producing sparks; a flintlock.
fire·man (fīr′mən) *n. pl.* **·men** (-mən) **1** One who aids in extinguishing fires; a member of a professional fire-fighting company or crew. **2** One who tends the firing on a locomotive; a stoker.
fire–new (fīr′nōō′, -nyōō′) *adj. Archaic* Fresh from the fire; brand-new.
Fi·ren·ze (fē·ren′tzā) The Italian name for FLORENCE.
fire opal See under OPAL.
fire–pan (fīr′pan′) *n.* **1** A brazier; a grate. **2** The priming receptacle of a flintlock gun.
fire–pink (fīr′pingk′) *n.* A catchfly (*Silene virginica*) of the eastern United States, with crimson or scarlet flowers.
fire·place (fīr′plās′) *n.* A recess or structure in or on which a fire is built; especially that part of a chimney that opens into a room.
fire·plug (fīr′plug′) *n.* A hydrant for use in case of fire.
fire point A flash point.
fire·pow·er (fīr′pou′ər) *n. Mil.* **1** Capacity for delivering fire, as from the guns of a ship, battery, etc. **2** The total amount of fire delivered by a given weapon or unit.
fire·proof (fīr′prōōf′) *adj.* **1** Made resistant against fire; incombustible. **2** Of a nature to protect from fire. — *v.t.* To make resistant to fire.
fir·er (fīr′ər) *n.* **1** One who kindles fires. **2** An incendiary. **3** A stoker. **4** One who fires a weapon.
fire–reel (fīr′rēl) *n. Canadian* A fire engine.
fire–room (fīr′rōōm′, -rŏŏm′) *n.* The boiler-room on a steamship, where the firing of the furnace is done; stokehole.
fire sale A sale of goods reduced in price because of slight damage by fire.
fire screen A fireguard (def. 2).
fire ship A ship filled with combustibles, fired and floated toward an enemy for the purpose of destroying ships, bridges, etc.
fire–side (fīr′sīd′) *n.* The hearth or space about the fireplace; hence, the place of family cheer. See synonyms under HOME.
fireside chat An informal talk, over a radio network, on subjects of national interest; specifically, one given by President Franklin D. Roosevelt.
fire station A firehouse.
fire·stone (fīr′stōn′) *n.* **1** Flint or pyrites used for striking fire. **2** A stone that will withstand the action of fire.
fire surface That part of the surface of a boiler which is exposed to the fire; the heating surface.
fire·thorn (fīr′thôrn′) *n.* An evergreen, typically thorny shrub (genus *Pyracantha*) of the rose family, bearing white flowers and a scarlet or orange fruit, and cultivated as an ornamental hedge plant.
fire·tow·er (fīr′tou′ər) *n.* A watchtower, usually in a wooded area, from which a fire can be seen and reported.

fire·trap (fīr'trap') *n.* A building notoriously inflammable, or one not provided with an escape for use in case of fire.

fire·wall (fīr'wôl') *n.* **1** A fireproof wall designed to block the progress of a fire. **2** *Aeron.* A bulkhead of fire-resistant material placed between the engine compartment of an aircraft and the rest of the structure to limit the spread of fire from the engines.

fire·war·den (fīr'wôr'dən) *n.* An officer who has charge of the prevention and extinguishing of fires.

fire·wa·ter (fīr'wô'tər, -wot'ər) *n.* Whisky: a term first used by the North American Indians.

fire·weed (fīr'wēd') *n.* **1** The willow herb. **2** The jimsonweed.

fire·wood[1] (fīr'wŏŏd') *n.* Wood used, or fit to use, as fuel.

fire·wood[2] (fīr'wŏŏd') *n.* An ironwood (*Cyrilla racemiflora*) of Central America and the SE United States.

fire·works (fīr'wûrks') *n.* **1** A case or cases containing combustibles and explosives, producing brilliant or colored light or scintillations in burning. **2** A pyrotechnic display.

fire·worm (fīr'wûrm') *n.* **1** A glowworm. **2** The larva of a tortricid moth (*Rhopobota naevana*), which devours the leaves of the cranberry, leaving the plant apparently burned.

fire·wor·ship (fīr'wûr'ship) *n.* The worship of fire as a deity.

fir·ing (fīr'ing) *n.* **1** The act or process of applying fire or intense heat to anything, as in stoking, burning, baking, or vitrifying, as bricks or pottery in a kiln; also, in cauterizing. **2** The discharge of firearms. **3** Fuel, as wood or coal.

firing line 1 The line of active engagement in battle. **2** The main body of troops in action within effective rifle range of the enemy. **3** The foremost position in any activity.

firing pin That part of a firearm or a fuze which, on being actuated, strikes the primer or detonator. See illustration under BOMB (aerial).

firing squad A military or naval detachment selected to show honor to a deceased person by firing over his grave, or to execute a sentence of death by shooting.

firing tread A banquette tread; banquette.

fir·kin (fûr'kən) *n.* **1** A wooden vessel for lard, etc. **2** An English measure equal to one fourth of a barrel, or 40.9 liters: in the United States, 34.068 liters. [ME *ferdekyn* <MDu. *vierde* fourth + -KIN]

fir·lot (fûr'lot) *n.* An old Scottish dry measure, used also on the Isle of Man: from 1 to 1 1/2 bushels.

firm[1] (fûrm) *adj.* **1** Solidly compacted; unyielding; solid. **2** Fixedly settled; difficult to move; stable. **3** Strong, steadfast, or determined in character; vigorous; resolute; enduring. **4** Solid; not liquid or gaseous. **5** Not fluctuating widely, as prices. — *v.t.* & *v.i.* **1** To make or become firm, solid, or compact. **2** *Obs.* To confirm; establish. — *adv.* Solidly; resolutely; fixedly: to stand *firm* against the foe. [<L *firmus*] — **firm'ly** *adv.* — **firm'ness** *n.* *Synonyms (adj.):* close, compact, decided, determined, established, fast, fixed, hard, immovable, immutable, resolute, robust, rugged, secure, solid, steadfast, steady, strong, sturdy, unchanging, unfailing, unfaltering, unshaken. See FAITHFUL, HARD, IMPLICIT, OBSTINATE.

firm[2] (fûrm) *n.* **1** A union of two or more persons for the purpose of conducting business; a commercial, industrial, or financial partnership; a business house. **2** The style or title under which such a house carries on business; firm name. [<Ital. *firma* a signature <L *firmare* confirm <*firmus* firm]

fir·ma·ment (fûr'mə·mənt) *n.* The expanse of the heavens; sky. [<L *firmamentum* a support <*firmare* make firm] — **fir'ma·men'tal** *adj.*

fir·man (fûr'mən, fər-män') *n. pl.* **·mans** A special decree or edict of an Oriental sovereign; a grant or license. Also **fir'maun**. [<Persian *fermān* a command]

firm·er (fûr'mər) *adj.* Designating a cutting tool with a thin, narrow blade, for manual use in shaping wood. — *n.* A firmer chisel

or gouge. For illustration see under GOUGE.

firm power Electric power from a generating station available for use under all conditions.

firn (fîrn) *n. Meteorol.* Snow, partly consolidated into ice, found in Alpine regions; névé. [<G <*firn*, adj., of last year]

fir·ry (fûr'ē) *adj.* Pertaining to the fir; made of fir; wooded with firs.

first (fûrst) *adj.* **1** Preceding all others in the order of numbering: the ordinal of *one.* **2** Prior to all others in time; earliest. **3** Nearest or foremost in place from a given point. **4** Highest or foremost in character, rank, etc.; leading; chief; best. — **at (the) first blush** On first presentation; at first thought, without mature consideration. — **at first hand** Directly from the original source; without intervening assistance. — *n.* **1** That which comes or is first; the beginning. **2** *Music* The leading or upper part, voice, or instrument; also, a unison. **3** In English universities, the highest rank in examinations for honors; also, one taking the highest rank. **4** A winning position in a contest. **5** The first day of a month; the first year in a period or reign. **6** *pl.* The best grade of certain commercial products, as butter, sugar, etc. — **at first** (or **from the first**) At the beginning or origin. — *adv.* **1** Before all others in order, as in counting, time, place, or rank; also, in formal discourse, **first'ly.** **2** Before, or in preference to, some proposed act or anticipated event; sooner: He will never confess: he would die *first.* **3** For the first time. [OE *fyrst,* superlative of *fore* before] *Synonyms (adj.):* chief, earliest, foremost, front, highest, leading, original, primary, primeval, primitive, primordial, principal, pristine, supreme. *Antonyms:* hindmost, inferior, insignificant, last, least, lowest, secondary, subordinate, subsequent, subservient, subsidiary, trifling, trivial, unimportant.

first aid Treatment given in any emergency while awaiting qualified medical or surgical attention. — **first-aid** (fûrst'ād') *adj.*

first base In baseball, the base first reached by the runner, at the right-hand angle of the infield. Compare illustration under BASEBALL. — **to get to first base** *U.S. Slang* To succeed in the first phase of an enterprise.

first-born (fûrst'bôrn') *adj.* First brought forth; eldest; first, best, or highest; preeminent. — *n.* The child first born; an heir; also, a first product or result.

First Cause 1 God as uncaused, the original source and creator of all things. **2** In Aristotelian philosophy, prime mover.

first-class (fûrst'klas', -kläs') *adj.* **1** Belonging to the first class; of the highest rank or the best quality. **2** Consisting of sealed letters or other sealed matter transmitted by the post: *first-class* mail. **3** Pertaining to, for, or using, the most luxurious accommodations on a steamer, train, plane, etc.

First Day Sunday: name used by the Society of Friends.

first floor 1 *U.S.* The ground floor. **2** The floor just above the ground floor: a designation used generally in Great Britain, on the Continent, and occasionally in the United States.

first-fruit (fûrst'frŏŏt') *n., usually pl.* **1** The first gatherings of a season's produce. *Ex.* xxiii 19. **2** The first outcome, effects, results, or rewards of anything.

first-hand (fûrst'hand') *adj.* Obtained direct from the origin or producer; without intermediary. — *adv.* Direct from the original source.

First Lady The wife of the President of the United States or if he has no wife, the lady chosen by him to be the hostess of the White House.

first·ling (fûrst'ling) *n.* The first of anything; especially, the first-born of a flock. — *adj.* First produced.

first·ly (fûrst'lē) See under FIRST.

first mortgage A mortgage having priority over all other liens.

first night The first public performance of a play or opera; also, the night of this performance. — **first-night** (fûrst'nīt') *adj.*

first-night·er (fûrst'nī'tər) *n.* One who habitually attends opening performances; anyone present at an opening performance.

first officer In the merchant marine, a first mate.

first papers Papers declaring intent to become a citizen of the United States: first step in the naturalization of a foreigner.

first-rate (fûrst'rāt') *adj.* Of the first or finest class, quality, or character. — *adv.* In a high degree; well; excellently. — **first'-rat'er** *n.*

first water 1 The finest quality and purest luster: said of gems, especially of diamonds and pearls. **2** The utmost excellence of anything.

First World War See WORLD WAR I in table under WAR.

firth (fûrth) *n. Scot.* An arm of the sea: also spelled **frith.**

Firth of Forth See FORTH, FIRTH OF.

Firth of Tay See TAY RIVER.

fisc (fisk) *n.* The treasury of a state; any treasury. [<F <L *fiscus* a purse]

fis·cal (fis'kəl) *adj.* **1** Of or pertaining to the treasury or finances of a government. **2** Financial. — *n.* In Spain, Portugal, and some other countries in Europe, a public prosecutor.

fiscal agent A person or company representing another financially.

fiscal year See under YEAR.

Fisch·er (fish'ər), **Emil,** 1852–1919, German chemist. — **Hans** 1881–1945, German chemist.

fish (fish) *n. pl.* **fish** or (with reference to different species) **fish·es** **1** A vertebrate, cold-blooded craniate animal with permanent gills, belonging to the superclass *Pisces* in the phylum *Chordata*; adapted solely for aquatic life, it has a typically elongate, tapering body, usually covered with scales and provided with

FISH

(Anatomical features of a trout)
a Eye socket. *b* Brain case. *c* Dorsal fin. *d* Fin ray. *e* Adipose fin. *f* Caudal fin. *g* Anal fin. *h* Anus. *i* Ventral fin (also called abdominal, thoracic, or jugular, according to its deviation from normal position). *j* Ribs. *k* Pectoral fin.

fins for locomotion. ◆ Collateral adjective: *piscine.* **2** Loosely, any animal habitually living in the water. **3** The flesh of a fish used as food. **4** *Naut.* **a** A strip used to strengthen or mend a spar, rail joint, etc., or to join parts. **b** An apparatus for weighing anchor; anchor tackle: also called **fish tackle. 5** A person with fishlike characteristics, such as cold-bloodedness, stupidity, etc. — **to have other fish to fry** To have other business to do. — *adj.* Pertaining to, like, consisting of, or made from, fish: *fish* market, *fish* beam, *fish* glue; also, for fish: *fish* bowl, *fish* sauce. — *v.t.* **1** To catch or try to catch fish in (a body of water). **2** To catch or try to catch (fish, eels, etc.). **3** To search for by dragging, diving, etc. **4** To grope for and bring out: usually with *up* or *out.* **5** *Naut.* **a** To repair or strengthen by strips fastened lengthwise: to *fish* a spar. **b** To bring the flukes of (an anchor) to the gunwale or rail. — *v.i.* **6** To catch or try to catch fish. **7** To try to get something in an artful or indirect manner: usually with *for*: to *fish* for compliments. — **to fish or cut bait** To make a choice, as of joining or being left out of an enterprise. — **to fish out** To exhaust of fish. [OE *fisc*] — **fish'a·ble** *adj.*

Fish Either of two star groups regarded as together composing the constellation Pisces. See CONSTELLATION.

Fish (fish), **Hamilton,** 1808–93, governor of New York; secretary of state under President Grant 1869–77.

fish and chips *Brit.* Fish fillets and potatoes sliced and French-fried.

fish ball A fried ball or cake made of chopped

fish (often salt codfish) mixed with mashed potatoes. Also **fish cake.**

fish beam A beam cut with a downward bulge, like the belly of a fish.

fish·ber·ry (fish′ber′ē) *n. pl.* **·ber·ries** The berry of an East Indian vine *(Anamirta cocculus),* yielding picrotoxin. Also called *cocculus indicus.*

fish·bolt (fish′bōlt′) *n.* A bolt for securing fishplates at a fish joint.

fish·bone (fish′bōn′) *n.* **1** A bone of a fish. **2** *Mil.* A network of subterranean passages constructed by military engineers for purposes of defense, attack, and as listening posts close to enemy positions.

fish bowl (fish′bōl′) *n.* A bowl, usually glass, serving as a small aquarium for fish.

fish crow A crow *(Corvus ossifragus)* of the Atlantic coast of the United States that feeds mainly on fish.

fish–cul·ture (fish′kul′chər) *n.* The artificial breeding of fishes; pisciculture. **— fish′–cul′·tur·ist** *n.*

fish–di·vert·er (fish′di·vûr′tər) *n.* An electrical device for generating currents in selected areas of water, as power dams, irrigation ditches, etc., for the purpose of diverting fish from entering them.

fish·er (fish′ər) *n.* **1** One who fishes; a fisherman. **2** A weasel–like carnivore *(Martes pennanti)* of eastern North America, related to the martens. **3** The dark–brown fur of this animal. ◆ Homophone: *fissure.*

Fisher (fish′ər), **Dorothy Canfield** See CANFIELD. **— Herbert Albert Laurens,** 1865–1940, English historian. **— Irving,** 1867–1947, U.S. economist. **— Sir John Arbuthnot,** 1841–1920, Baron of Kilverstone, English admiral, first sea lord 1904–10, 1914–15.

fish·er·man (fish′ər·mən) *n. pl.* **·men** (-mən) **1** One who catches fish; a fisher; an angler. **2** A fishing boat.

fish·er·y (fish′ər·ē) *n. pl.* **·er·ies** **1** The operation or business of catching fish; fishing industry. **2** A place for fishing. **3** *Law* The right to fish in a given place at a given time. **4** A fish–hatchery.

fish·gig (fish′gig′) *n.* A staff with prongs for spearing fish. [<FISH + GIG[2]]

fish·grass (fish′gras′, -gräs′) *n.* Fanwort.

fish–hatch·er·y (fish′hach′ər·ē) *n. pl.* **·er·ies** A place designed for the artificial propagation, hatching, and nurture of fish.

fish hawk The osprey.

fish hook A hook, usually barbed, for catching fish.

fish·ing (fish′ing) *n.* **1** The operation or the sport of catching or trying to catch fish. **2** A right of, a place for, fishing; a fishery. ◆ Collateral adjective: *piscatorial.*

fish·ing–frog (fish′ing·frog′, -frôg′) *n.* The angler (def. 1).

fishing line A line or cord used in catching fish with a hook. Also **fish line.**

fishing tackle Rod, reel, line, leader, hooks, and harness, used in fishing.

fish joint A splice made by fastening two rails together by fishplates bolted across the meeting ends.

fish knife **1** A broad knife, often with a serrated edge, for serving fish. **2** A heavy knife for scaling and dressing fish.

fish ladder A chute or series of steps in a dam, covered with flowing water, to facilitate the upstream migrations of fish: also called *fishway.*

fish·meal (fish′mēl′) *n.* **1** Ground dried fish: used in soups. **2** Ground fish waste: used as fertilizer.

fish·mon·ger (fish′mung′gər, -mong′-) *n.* A dealer in fish.

fish·net (fish′net′) *n.* **1** A net for catching fish. **2** A similar net for holding camouflage materials in place.

fish owl A large Asian or African owl (genera *Ketupa* and *Scotopelia*), feeding mostly on fish.

fish·plate (fish′plāt′) *n.* One of the iron plates used in forming a fish joint.

fish·pole (fish′pōl′) *n.* A long, flexible rod to which a line and hook are attached for catching fish.

fish·pot (fish′pot′) *n.* A basketlike trap for catching fish, eels, or lobsters.

fish·pound (fish′pound′) *n.* A weir.

fish·skin (fish′skin′) *n.* The skin of a fish or marine animal, as of a dogfish or shark (used for abrading), of a porpoise (tanned for leather), or the like.

fishskin disease Ichthyosis.

fish·spear (fish′spir′) *n.* **1** A spear for catching or killing fish; a fishgig. **2** A lance for bleeding captured whales.

fish story *Colloq.* An extravagant or incredible narrative.

fish tackle A tackle used to raise an anchor to the gunwale of a ship by means of an iron hook.

fish·tail (fish′tāl′) *adj.* Like the tail of a fish in shape or in action. **—** *v.i. Aeron.* To swing the tail of an aircraft from side to side as a retarding action: also called *yaw.*

fishtail kick In swimming, a kick in which both legs are drawn up and then thrust simultaneously backward while held together.

fish–tracks (fish′traks′) *n. pl. Physics* Visible trails made by the particles activated in a cloud chamber.

fish warden A local officer to enforce laws relating to the protection of fish or fisheries.

fish·way (fish′wā′) *n.* A fish ladder.

fish–well (fish′wel′) *n.* A compartment, as in the hold of a fishing smack, open to the water beneath, used for storing live fish.

fish·wife (fish′wīf′) *n. pl.* **·wives** (-wīvz′) **1** A woman who sells fish. **2** An abusive virago.

fish·y (fish′ē) *adj.* **fish·i·er, fish·i·est** **1** Suggestive of, pertaining to, or like fish. **2** Abounding in fish. **3** *Colloq.* Of the nature of a fish story; incredible. **4** Vacant of expression; dull, as the eyes; lacking luster. **— fish′·i·ly** *adv.* **— fish′i·ness** *n.*

Fiske (fisk), **Bradley Allen,** 1854–1942, U.S. admiral and inventor. **— John,** 1842–1901, U.S. philosopher and historian. **— Minnie Maddern,** 1865–1932, *née* Davey, U.S. actress.

fis·sate (fis′āt) *adj.* Deeply cleft; fissured.

fissi– *combining form* Split; cleft: *fissiparous.* Also, before vowels, **fiss–.** [<L *fissus,* pp. of *findere* split]

fis·sile (fis′əl) *adj.* **1** Capable of being split or separated into layers. **2** Tending to split. [<L *fissilis* <*findere* split] **— fis·sil·i·ty** (fi·sil′ə·tē) *n.*

fis·sion (fish′ən) *n.* **1** The act of splitting or breaking apart. **2** *Biol.* Spontaneous division of a cell or organism into new cells or organisms, especially as a mode of reproduction; cell division. **3** *Physics* The disintegration of the nucleus of a radioactive atom initiated by bombardment with nucleons or gamma rays, leading to the formation of nuclei of more stable atoms and the release of energy. **4** In astrophysics, the breaking up of a large gaseous body into separate masses subject to mutual attraction: regarded as the possible origin of binary and double stars. [<L *fissio, -onis* <*fissus,* pp. of *findere* split] **— fis′sion·a·ble** *adj.*

fission fungus A bacterium; any member of the group *Schizomycetes* of the *Thallophyta* division of plants.

fis·si·pal·mate (fis′i·pal′māt) *adj.* Partially web–footed. **— fis′si·pal·ma′tion** *n.*

fis·sip·a·rous (fi·sip′ər·əs) *adj. Biol.* **1** Reproducing by fission. **2** Separating by fission. **— fis·sip′a·rous·ly** *adv.*

fis·si·ped (fis′i·ped) *adj.* Having the toes separated: also **fis·sip·e·dal** (fi·sip′ə·dəl, fis′i·ped′l), **fis′si·pe′di·al** (-pē′dē·əl). **—** *n. Zool.* Any of a suborder *(Fissipedia)* of terrestrial carnivores with separate toes, as cats, bears, etc. [<LL *fissipes, -pedis*]

fis·si·ros·tral (fis′i·ros′trəl) *adj. Ornithol.* Having a wide beak deeply cleft, as swifts, nighthawks, etc.

fis·sle (fis′əl) *Scot. v.i.* **·sled, ·sling** To rustle; bustle about; also, to fidget. **—** *n.* Fuss; bustle.

fis·sure (fish′ər) *n.* **1** A narrow opening, cleft, crevice, or furrow. **2** Cleavage. **3** *Anat.* **a** Any cleft or furrow of the body, as between the lobes of the liver or the bones of the skull. **b** One of the furrows on the surface of the brain. See synonyms under BREACH. **—** *v.t.* & *v.i.* **fis·sured, fis·sur·ing** To crack; split; cleave. ◆ Homophone: *fisher.* [<L *fissura* <*findere* split]

fissure of Sylvius The Sylvian fissure.

fist[1] (fist) *n.* **1** The hand closed tightly, as for striking; the clenched hand; also, grip, clutch. **2** *Colloq.* The hand. **3** *Colloq.* Handwriting. **4** *Printing* An index mark (☞). **—** *v.t.* **1** To strike with the fist. **2** *Naut.* To grasp with the fist. [OE *fȳst*] **— fist′ful** *n.*

fist[2] (fist) See FICE.

fist·ic (fis′tik) *adj.* Pertaining to the fist; pugilistic.

fist·i·cuff (fis′ti·kuf) *v.t.* & *v.i.* To beat or fight with the fist. **—** *n.* **1** A cuff with the fist. **2** *pl.* A pugilistic encounter.

fist·i·cuff·er (fis′ti·kuf′ər) *n.* A pugilist; boxer.

fis·tu·la (fis′chŏŏ·lə) *n. pl.* **·las** or **·lae** (-lē) **1** *Pathol.* Any abnormal opening or duct leading into a natural canal, hollow organ, or other part of the body. **2** A deep-seated suppurative inflammation, as in the withers of horses, ordinarily resulting from a bruise. **3** *Obs.* A reed or pipe. **— gastric fistula** An opening into the stomach through the abdominal wall, usually of traumatic origin. [<L, a pipe] **— fis′tu·lar** *adj.*

fis·tu·lous (fis′chŏŏ·ləs) *adj.* **1** Cylindrical and hollow like a reed. **2** Of or pertaining to a fistula. Also **fis′tu·late** (-lit, -lāt), **fis′tu·lat′ed.**

fist·wise (fist′wīz′) *adj.* & *adv.* Like a fist.

fit[1] (fit) *adj.* **fit·ter, fit·test** **1** Adapted to an end, aim, or design; adequate; competent; qualified. **2** Conformed to a standard, suitable; appropriate. **3** In a state of preparation; ready. **4** In good physical condition and training: originally a sporting use. **5** Suitable to the person or occasion; convenient; becoming; proper. See synonyms under ADEQUATE, APPROPRIATE, BECOMING, COMPETENT, CONVENIENT, GOOD, RIPE. **—** *v.* **fit·ted** or **fit, fit·ting** *v.t.* **1** To be suitable for: Dark days *fit* dark deeds. **2** To be of the right size and shape for. **3** To make or alter to the proper size or purpose: to *fit* a suit. **4** To provide with what is suitable or necessary: to *fit* a ship for sea. **5** To prepare or make qualified or ready: His experience *fits* him for the position. **6** To put in place carefully or exactly: to *fit* an arrow to a bow. **—** *v.i.* **7** To be suitable or proper. **8** To be of the proper size, shape, etc.: This shoe *fits.* See synonyms under ADAPT, ACCOMMODATE, TEMPER. **—** *n.* **1** An adjustment or agreement in size, form, or the like; suitability; adaptation. **2** A making ready; preparation. **3** *Mech.* **a** A part upon which something fits snugly; specifically, that part of a car axle upon which the wheel is forced. **b** The closeness or completeness of contact in machine parts, usually classified as loose, free, medium, snug, and wringing. **4** That which fits, as a piece of clothing. [ME *fyt*; origin uncertain] **— fit′ly** *adv.* **— fit′ness** *n.* **— fit′·ter** *n.*

fit[2] (fit) *n.* **1** A sudden onset of an organic or functional disorder, often attended by convulsions, as in epilepsy; spasm. **2** A sudden overmastering emotion or feeling; a mood: a *fit* of rage. **3** Impulsive and irregular exertion or action: a *fit* of industry. **— by fits** (or **by fits and starts**) Spasmodically; irregularly. [OE *fitt* struggle]

fit[3] (fit) *n.* **1** A song, story, or ballad. **2** A division of a ballad or song. [OE *fitt*]

fit[4] (fit) *n. Scot.* A foot; step.

fitch[1] (fich) *n.* A fitchew or its fur. [<MDu. *vitsche* a polecat]

fitch[2] (fich) *n. Archaic.* A vetch: commonly in the plural. The plural form in the Bible represents two different Hebrew words, meaning in *Isa.* xxviii 25, 27, black cumin, and in *Ezek.* iv 9, spelt. [Var. of VETCH]

Fitch (fich), **John,** 1743–98, U.S. inventor; pioneer in steam navigation. **— (William) Clyde,** 1865–1909, U.S. playwright.

fitch·ew (fich′ōō) *n.* **1** The polecat of Europe. **2** The fur of this animal: also called *fitch.* Also **fitch′et** (-it), **fitch′ole** (-ōl). [<OF *fissel, fissau.* Cf. MDu. *fisse, vitsche.*]

fit·ful (fit′fəl) *adj.* Occurring in fits; marked by fits; spasmodic; capricious; unstable. See synonyms under FICKLE, IRREGULAR, IRRESOLUTE. **— fit′ful·ly** *adv.* **— fit′ful·ness** *n.*

fit·tie–lan′ (fit′i·län′, -lôn′) *n. Scot.* The near horse of the hind pair in a plow team; the horse that walks on the unplowed part of the land.

fit·ting (fit′ing) *adj.* Fit or suitable for any purpose; proper; appropriate. **—** *n.* **1** The act of adjusting or connecting properly. **2** A fixture or a piece of apparatus. **3** Anything designed as an accessory to any system of working parts in a machine: usually in the plural. See synonyms under ADEQUATE, BE-

LONGING, JUST. — **fit′ting·ly** *adv.* — **fit′ting·ness** *n.*

fit to kill *Colloq.* Excessively: He laughed *fit to kill.*

Fitz– *prefix* Son of: an element in surnames, as in *Fitzgerald*: formerly used in forming the surnames of illegitimate children of royalty. [<AF, var. of OF *fiz, filz* <L *filius* son]

Fitz·Ger·ald (fits′jer′əld), **Edward,** 1809–83, English poet; translator of the *Rubáiyát* of Omar Khayyám.

Fitz·ger·ald (fits′jer′əld), **F(rancis) Scott,** 1896–1940, U.S. novelist.

Fiu·me (fyōō′mā) The Italian name for RIJEKA.

Fiu·mi·ci·no (fyōō′mē·chē′nō) Modern name for the Rubicon.

five (fīv) *n.* **1** The cardinal number following four and preceding six, or any of the symbols (5, v, V) used to represent it. **2** Anything made up of five units or members, as a basketball team, or representing five, as a playing card having five spots, or a five–dollar bill. ◆ Collateral adjective: *quinary.* — *adj.* Being five. [OE *fīf*]

five– and ten–cent store (fīv′ən·ten′sent′) A store selling miscellaneous articles priced at five and ten cents: extended to include stores selling articles priced from five cents to one dollar or more. Also called *dime store.* Also **five′–and–ten′, five–and–dime** (fīv′ən·dīm′).

Five Civilized Nations or **Tribes** The Cherokee, Chickasaw, Choctaw, Creek, and Seminole tribes of Oklahoma.

five–fin·gers (fīv′fing′gərz) *n.* **1** Any of several plants, as cinquefoil, bird's–foot trefoil, oxlip, Virginia creeper. **2** A starfish with five arms.

five·fold (fīv′fōld′) *adj.* Made up of five; five times as much or as great; quintuplicate. — *adv.* In a fivefold manner or degree.

Five Forks A locality in SE Virginia; scene of a Federal victory in the Civil War, April 1, 1865.

five hundred A card game developed from euchre, with the joker as high card and 500 points for game.

Five Nations Five confederated tribes of Iroquois Indians within the borders of the State of New York; namely, Mohawks, Oneidas, Onondagas, Cayugas, and Senecas. These five tribes, together with a sixth, the Tuscaroras, which returned from self–exile in 1712, formed the famous *Six Nations* of American history.

five·pence (fīv′pəns, *Brit. Colloq.* fip′əns) *n.* **1** Five English pennies. **2** Formerly, an American half–dime.

five·pen·ny (fīv′pə·nē, *Brit. Colloq.* fip′ən·ē) *adj.* **1** Worth five pence. **2** Having a length of 1 3/4 inches: a *fivepenny* nail.

fiv·er (fī′vər) *n. Colloq.* **1** A five–dollar bill or a five–pound note. **2** Anything counting five, as a hit in cricket permitting five runs, etc.

fives[1] (fīvz) *n. pl. Brit.* A game similar to handball.

fives[2] (fīvz) See VIVES.

five–spot (fīv′spot′) *n.* A small delicate annual herb (*Nemophila maculata*) of the waterleaf family, with white purple–spotted flowers: common in California.

Five–Year Plan (fīv′yir′) A plan for national economic development: a term originating with the first of such plans adopted by the U.S.S.R. in 1928.

fix (fiks) *v.t.* **1** To make firm or secure; attach securely; fasten. **2** To set or direct (attention, gaze, etc.) steadily: He *fixed* his eyes on the door. **3** To look at steadily or piercingly: He *fixed* her with his eyes. **4** To attract and hold; get, as attention or regard. **5** To decide definitely; settle: The decision *fixed* his fate. **6** To decide or agree on; determine: We *fixed* a date for the next meeting. **7** To place firmly in the mind. **8** To lay, as blame or responsibility, on. **9** *U.S.* To repair. **10** To arrange or put in order; adjust, as clothing or the hair. **11** *U.S.* To make ready and cook (food or a meal). **12** *U.S. Colloq.* To arrange or influence the outcome, decision, etc., of (a race, game, jury, etc.) by bribery or collusion: to *fix* a race. **13** To prepare (specimens) for microscopic study. **14** *Chem.* To cause to form a non–volatile or solid compound. **15** *Phot.* To bathe (a film or plate) in chemicals which remove substances still sensitive to light, thus preventing fading. **16** To regulate or stabilize (wages, prices, etc.). — *v.i.* **17** To become firm or fixed. **18** *Colloq.* To intend or prepare: I'm *fixing* to go. — **to fix on** To decide upon; choose. — **to fix up** *Colloq.* **1** To repair. **2** To arrange or put in order. **3** To supply the needs of. — *n.* **1** *Colloq.* A position of embarrassment; dilemma. **2** *Naut.* A ship's position as decided by reference to certain fixed points on shore or to astronomical observations; location. **3** On a chart or map, the point of intersection of two or more bearings, which serve to establish the position of an aircraft on its course. [<Med. L *fixare* fasten <L *fixus,* pp. of *figere* fasten] — **fix′·a·ble** *adj.*

Synonyms (verb): See BIND, CONFIRM, SET, SETTLE. The best usage avoids such expressions as "*Fix* the furniture in the room," "*Fix* the books on the shelves," when the meaning is *set* or *arrange* them. We *fix* a statue on its pedestal, a stone in the wall. *Fix* in the sense of *repair* is a convenient American and British colloquialism, rooted in popular use. In the United States, to *fix* a thing is to do to or with it whatever is needed to make it answer its purpose; to *fix* a furnace is to put it in working order by whatever process.

fix·ate (fik′sāt) *v.t* & *v.i.* **·at·ed, ·at·ing** **1** To render fixed; become fixed. **2** To fix or concentrate, as the eyes or attention, upon something. **3** To render constant or unchanged. **4** *Psychoanal.* To concentrate the libido on a particular object, blocking further development or new attachment. [<Med. L *fixatus,* pp. of *fixare.* See FIX.]

fix·a·tion (fik·sā′shən) *n.* **1** The act of fixing, or the state of being fixed; stability. **2** *Chem.* **a** A state of non–volatility in a chemical compound, or the entering into such a state. **b** The making permanent of a dye or color. **c** The conversion of free nitrogen from the air into useful compounds; any similar process applied to an oil or a gas. **3** *Psychoanal.* An excessive concentration of the libido on a particular object, as the exaggerated attachment of a child for one of its parents, manifested in periods of adult emotional stress in some types of psychosis or psychoneurosis. **4** A sustained focusing of the eyes upon a definite object. **5** *Bacteriol.* The prevention of hemolysis by the action of the complement.

fix·a·tive (fik′sə·tiv) *adj.* Serving to render permanent. — *n.* **1** That which serves to render permanent, as a mordant or varnish. **2** In art, a solution applied to pastel and crayon pictures to reduce fragility.

fixed (fikst) *adj.* **1** Of an established, unchanging, or permanent character; settled; lasting; stable. **2** Keeping nearly the same relative position. **3** Without days of grace: said of bills, notes, etc. **4** Attached; not locomotory: said of plants and certain organisms. **5** Equipped: all *fixed* for camp. **6** Settled; located: *fixed* in a new home. **7** *U.S. Colloq.* Bribed: a *fixed* jury. **8** *U.S. Colloq.* Provided with money, possessions, etc.: He's well *fixed.* — **fix·ed·ly** (fik′sid·lē) *adv.* — **fix′ed·ness** *n.*

fixed bridge Any bridge constructed on permanent supports: distinguished from a *pontoon bridge.*

fixed charge A charge that cannot be changed or escaped; specifically, such a charge payable at fixed intervals.

fixed idea *Psychiatry* An obsessional idea, often delusional, which tends to influence a person's whole attitude or mental life: also *idée fixe.*

fixed oil *Chem.* An oil, as olein, which leaves a permanent greasy stain, and cannot be volatilized without decomposition.

fixed star *Astron.* A self–luminous celestial body far beyond the bounds of our solar system: so called because such bodies preserve the same relative positions as observed from the earth.

fix·er (fik′sər) *n. U.S. Colloq.* An adjuster; specifically, a person who bribes or influences a jury, an election board, etc.

fix·ing (fik′sing) *n.* **1** The act of fastening, securing, repairing, solidifying, deciding, etc. See FIX. **2** *Phot.* The process of treating a developed picture so that it will not be changed by the further action of light. **3** *pl. U.S. Colloq.* Furnishings, ornaments, or trappings of any kind. **4** *pl. U.S. Colloq.* Foods prepared as accompaniments to a main dish.

fix·i·ty (fik′sə·tē) The state of being fixed; permanent character or condition; fixedness; stability.

fix·ture (fiks′chər) *n.* **1** Anything fixed firmly in its place; gas *fixtures.* **2** One who or that which is regarded as permanently fixed. **3** *Law* **a** Personal articles or chattels affixed to a freehold which may be removed by the tenant only without injury to the realty: also **movable fixtures. b** Anything affixed to a freehold of such a permanent nature as to be a legal part thereof: also **immovable fixtures.** [<FIXURE; infl. in form by *mixture*]

fix·ure (fik′shər) *n. Obs.* Fixed condition; firmness. [<LL *fixura* a fastening <L *figere* fasten]

Fi·zeau (fē·zō′), **Armand Hippolyte Louis,** 1819–96, French physicist.

fiz·gig (fiz′gig′) *n.* **1** A silly flirt; a giddy girl. **2** A firework that makes a fizzing noise when ignited. [? <FIZZ + GIG[1]]

fizz (fiz) *v.i.* To make a hissing noise. — *n.* **1** A hissing noise. **2** An effervescing beverage. **3** *Brit.* Champagne. Also **fiz.** [Imit.] — **fizz′y** *adj.*

fiz·zle (fiz′əl) *v.i.* **fiz·zled, fiz·zling** **1** To make a hissing noise, as wet wood or gunpowder when burning. **2** *Colloq.* To fail, especially after a good start. — **to fizzle out** To become a failure. — *n.* **1** A spluttering; fizzing. **2** A person, an attempt, or an undertaking that fails or comes to nothing; an ignominious failure, as in a recitation. [Freq. of obs. *fise* break wind]

fjeld (fyeld) *n.* In Scandinavian countries, a high, barren plateau or tableland: also spelled *field.*

fjord (fyôrd) See FIORD.

flab (flab) *n.* Flabby body tissue. [Back formation <FLABBY]

flab·ber·gast (flab′ər·gast) *v.t. Colloq.* To astound; confound, as by extraordinary news. [? Blend of FLABBY and AGHAST] — **flab′ber·gas·ta′tion** *n.*

flab·by (flab′ē) *adj.* **·bi·er, ·bi·est** **1** Lacking muscle or healthy fiber; flaccid. **2** Lacking in moral or intellectual vigor; languid; feeble. [Var. of *flappy* <FLAP + -Y[1]] — **flab′bi·ly** *adv.* — **flab′bi·ness** *n.*

fla·bel·late (flə·bel′it, -āt) *adj. Zool.* Fan–shaped: *flabellate* antennae.

flabelli– *combining form* Fan–shaped: *flabelliform.* [<L *flabellum* a fan, orig. dim. of *flabrum* a breeze <*flare* blow]

fla·bel·li·form (flə·bel′ə·fôrm) *adj.* Fan–shaped; flabellate.

fla·bel·lum (flə·bel′əm) *n. pl.* **·la** (-ə) **1** A fan, especially one used ceremonially in the Greek and Roman Catholic churches. **2** Any fan–shaped structure. **3** *Anat.* A group of fibers radiating from the corpus striatum of the brain. [<L, fan]

flac·cid (flak′sid) *adj.* Lacking firmness or elasticity; having no resistance; flabby. [<F *flaccide* <L *flaccidus* <*flaccus* limp] — **flac′·cid·ly** *adv.* — **flac·cid′i·ty, flac′cid·ness** *n.*

flack (flak) *n. Slang* A press agent.

fla·con (flà·kôn′) *n. French* A stoppered bottle or flask.

flaf·fin (flăf′in) *n. Scot.* Fluttering; flapping.

flag[1] (flag) *n.* **1** A piece of cloth commonly bearing a device and attached to a staff or halyard: used as a standard, symbol, or signal. See COLOR, ENSIGN, GUIDON, PENNANT, STANDARD. **2** The bushy part of the tail of a dog, as that of a setter. **3** *pl. Ornithol.* The long feathers on the leg of a hawk or other bird of prey; also, those on the second joint of a bird's wing. **4** The tail of a deer. — **black flag** A flag with a black field surmounted by white skull and crossbones, traditionally flown by pirate ships; the Jolly Roger.— **Christian flag** A flag with a white field (peace) and a blue canton (sincerity), emblazoned with a red cross: adopted by most Protestant churches. — **papal flag** A yellow–and–white banner, in which the crossed keys of Saint Peter surmounted by the papal triple crown occupy the center of the white half. — **service flag** A flag with red border and white center on which one or more blue or gold stars are

sewn, each representing a man or woman in or formerly in the armed forces. — *v.t.* **flagged, flag·ging 1** To mark out or adorn with flags. **2** To signal with a flag. **3** To send (information) by signals. **4** To decoy, as deer, by or as by waving a flag. — **to flag down** To cause to stop, as a train, by signaling with a flag or with a waving motion. [? <FLAG^{2}] — **flag′ger** *n.* — **flag′gy** *adj.*

flag^{2} (flag) *n.* **1** One of various monocotyledonous plants of the genus *Iris,* having sword–shaped leaves and growing in moist places; especially, the **yellow flag** of Europe *(I. pseudacorus)* and the common **blue flag** *(I. versicolor)* of the United States, the State flower of Tennessee. **2** The leaf of a flag. — *v.t.* **flagged, flag·ging** To calk the seams of (a cask) with flags or rushes. [Cf. Du. *vlag* iris]

flag^{3} (flag) *v.i.* **flagged, flag·ging 1** To grow spiritless or languid; become tired or weak. **2** To hang down; become limp. [? <obs. *flack* flutter; infl. by OF *flaquir* droop <*flac* droopy <L *flaccus*]

flag^{4} (flag) *n.* Split stone for paving; a flagstone. — *v.t.* **flagged, flag·ging** To pave with flagstones. [<ON *flaga* slab of stone. Akin to FLAKE.] — **flag′ger** *n.*

Flag Day A holiday commemorating the day, June 14, 1777, on which Congress proclaimed the Stars and Stripes the national standard of the United States.

flag·el·lant (flaj′ə·lənt, flə·jel′ənt) *n.* A zealot given to whipping or scourging himself, to secure pardon from sin: also **flag′el·la′tor.** — *adj.* Using a scourge; scourging; practicing flagellation. [<L *flagellans, -antis,* ppr. of *flagellare* scourge <*flagellum* a whip]

flag·el·late (flaj′ə·lāt) *v.t.* **·lat·ed, ·lat·ing** To whip; scourge. — *adj. Biol.* **1** Having or producing flagella or whiplike processes, or runnerlike branches. **2** Shaped like a flagellum. Also **flag′el·lat′ed** *adj.* [<L *flagellatus,* pp. of *flagellare.* See FLAGELLANT.]

flag·el·la·tion (flaj′ə·lā′shən) *n.* **1** A scourging, specifically as an incitement of abnormal sexual desire. **2** A massaging by strokes or blows. **3** Self–scourging as a means of religious discipline. **4** *Biol.* The development of flagella by certain protozoan organisms.

fla·gel·li·form (flə·jel′ə·fôrm) *adj.* Long, slender, and flexible, like a whiplash. [<L *flagellum* a whip + -FORM]

fla·gel·lum (flə·jel′əm) *n. pl.* **·la** (-ə) **1** *Biol.* A lashlike appendage, as the terminal part of an antenna in insects, or the mobile process of a protozoan. **2** A scourge. [<L, whip]

flag·eo·let (flaj′ə·let′) *n.* **1** A musical instrument resembling the flute, but blown at the end instead of at the side. It usually has six finger holes and a mouthpiece with a fipple.

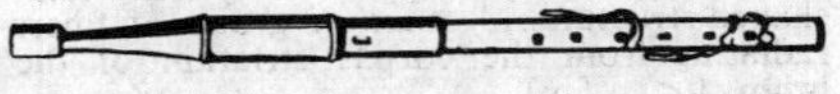

FLAGEOLET

2 An organ stop. [<F, dim. of OF *flageol*; ult. origin uncertain]

Flagg (flag), **James Montgomery,** 1877–1960, U.S. artist and illustrator.

flag·ging^{1} (flag′ing) *adj.* Growing weak; becoming languid or exhausted; failing; drooping.

flag·ging^{2} (flag′ing) *n.* **1** A pavement of flagstones; flagstones collectively. **2** The act of paving with flagstones.

flag·gy^{1} (flag′ē) *adj.* **·gi·er, ·gi·est** Lax; languid; limp. — **flag′gi·ness** *n.*

flag·gy^{2} (flag′ē) *adj.* **·gi·er, ·gi·est** Resembling or consisting of flagstones; laminate.

flag·gy^{3} (flag′ē) *adj.* **·gi·er, ·gi·est** Covered with irises.

fla·gi·tious (flə·jish′əs) *adj.* **1** Flagrantly wicked; atrocious; heinous. **2** Guilty of extraordinary vice; extremely criminal. See synonyms under CRIMINAL, FLAGRANT. [<L *flagitiosus* <*flagitium* disgraceful act] — **fla·gi′tious·ly** *adv.* — **fla·gi′tious·ness** *n.*

flag–lil·y (flag′lil′ē) *n. pl.* **–lil·ies** The American blue iris; blue flag.

flag·man (flag′mən) *n. pl.* **·men** (-mən) One who carries a flag, as for signaling trains on a railway.

flag officer Formerly, the captain of a flagship; now, the commander of a fleet or squadron, entitled to fly the flag of his command, as a fleet admiral, admiral, vice admiral, or rear admiral.

flag of truce A white flag displayed to the enemy to denote that a conference is desired; also, the bearer of the flag, or a vessel bearing such a flag.

flag·on (flag′ən) *n.* **1** A vessel with a handle and a spout, and often having a hinged lid, used to serve liquors at table. **2** A large wine bottle. [<OF *flacon, flascon* <Med. L *flasco, -onis* <Gmc.]

flag·pole (flag′pōl′) *n.* A pole of some length on which a flag is displayed.

fla·gran·cy (flā′grən·sē) *n. pl.* **·cies** Notoriousness; heinousness. Also **fla′grance.**

fla·grant (flā′grənt) *adj.* **1** Openly scandalous; notorious; heinous. **2** *Obs.* Burning; blazing; also, raging. [<L *flagrans, -antis,* ppr. of *flagrare* blaze, burn] — **fla′grant·ly** *adv.*

Synonyms: atrocious, disgraceful, enormous, flagitious, heinous, monstrous, nefarious, outrageous, scandalous, shameful, shocking. *Antonyms*: see synonyms for EXCELLENT.

fla·gran·te de·lic·to (flə·gran′tē di·lik′tō) *Latin* In the act of committing a crime; literally, while the crime was blazing.

flag·ship (flag′ship′) *n.* The ship in a naval formation that carries a flag officer and displays his flag. See FLAG OFFICER.

flag–smut (flag′smut′) *n.* A disease of wheat, caused by the smut fungus *Ustilago tritici* affecting the leaves and culms.

Flag·stad (flag′stad, *Norw.* fläg′stä), **Kirsten,** 1895–1963, Norwegian soprano active in the United States.

flag·staff (flag′staf′, -stäf′) *n.* A staff on which a flag is hung or displayed.

Flag·staff (flag′staf, -stäf) A city in north central Arizona.

flag station A station on a railway at which a train stops only on signal. Also **flag stop.**

flag·stone (flag′stōn′) *n.* **1** A broad, flat stone suitable for pavements. **2** Any fine–grained rock from which such slabs may be split. [<FLAG^{4} + STONE]

flail (flāl) *n.* **1** An implement consisting of a wooden bar (the swingle) hinged or tied to a handle, for separating grain by beating. **2** A medieval weapon with spiked iron swingle. — *v.t.* & *v.i.* To beat with or as with a flail; use a flail; thresh. [OE *flygel,* prob. <L *flagellum* a whip]

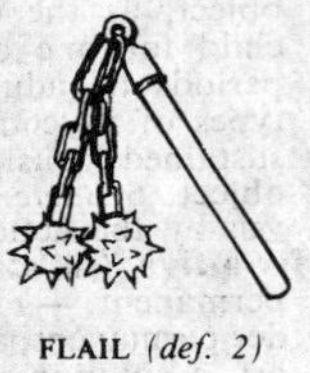

FLAIL *(def. 2)*

flail joint *Pathol.* A disorder characterized by excessive mobility of a limb, usually after resection of a joint.

flair (flâr) *n.* **1** Discernment; talent; aptitude. **2** Inclination; fondness; strong liking. **3** *Colloq.* A showy or dashing style: to wear clothes with *flair.* [<OF <*flairer* smell, ult. <L *fragrare*]

flak (flak) *n.* **1** Anti–aircraft fire. **2** *U.S. Colloq.* Criticism: political *flak.* [<G *fl(ieger)* aircraft + *a(bwehr)* defense + *k(anonen)* guns]

flake^{1} (flāk) *n.* **1** A small flat fragment or loosely cohering mass; a thin piece or chip of anything; scale; fleck. **2** A carnation having stripes of any single color on a white ground. **3** A gleam of light; flash. **4** *Naut.* The flat coil of a stowed cable; a fake. — *adj. Anthropol.* Denoting that form of Paleolithic stone implement shaped from the thin flakes chipped off the core of a large lump. — *v.t.* & *v.i.* **flaked, flak·ing 1** To peel off in flakes. **2** To form into flakes. **3** To spot or become spotted with flakes. [ME <Scand. Akin to FLAG^{4}.]

flake^{2} (flāk) *n.* **1** A light staging or platform for drying fish. **2** A flap on a saddle to keep the rider's knee from the horse. [<ON *flaki* hurdle]

flake^{3} (flāk) *v.* **flaked, flak·ing** *Slang v.i.* **1** To retire or go to sleep, as from exhaustion: usually with *out.* — *v.t.* **2** To fatigue; exhaust: usually with *out.*

flake–white (flāk′hwīt′) *n.* Pure white lead in scales used by artists as a pigment.

flak·ing (flā′king) *n.* **1** The operation of making flint flakes by chipping, as for gunlocks. **2** The breaking away of small bits of paint or plaster from covered surfaces.

flak·y (flā′kē) *adj.* **flak·i·er, flak·i·est** Resembling or consisting of flakes; easily separable into flakes. — **flak′i·ly** *adv.* — **flak′i·ness** *n.*

flam (flam) *n. Colloq.* **1** A false pretense; sham; falsehood. **2** A freak or whim. **3** An appoggiatura on the drum. — *v.t.* **flammed, flam·ming** *U.S. Colloq.* To deceive by imposture; to flim–flam. [Short for FLIM–FLAM]

flam·beau (flam′bō) *n. pl.* **·beaux** (-bōz) **1** A burning torch, as one made of a bundle of wicks covered with wax; any torch. **2** A large decorated candlestick. **3** A large sugar–boiling kettle. [<F <*flambe* <OF *flamme* FLAME]

Flam·bor·ough Head (flam′bûr′ə) A chalk peninsula and lighthouse in eastern Yorkshire, England.

flam·boy·ant (flam·boi′ənt) *adj.* **1** Characterized by extravagance; showy; bombastic. **2** Bursting into flame; blazing. **3** Having a wavy edge, as of flame. [<F, ppr. of *flamboyer* <OF *flambeiier* <*flambe* FLAME] — **flam·boy′·ance, flam·boy′an·cy** *n.* — **flam·boy′ant·ly** *adv.*

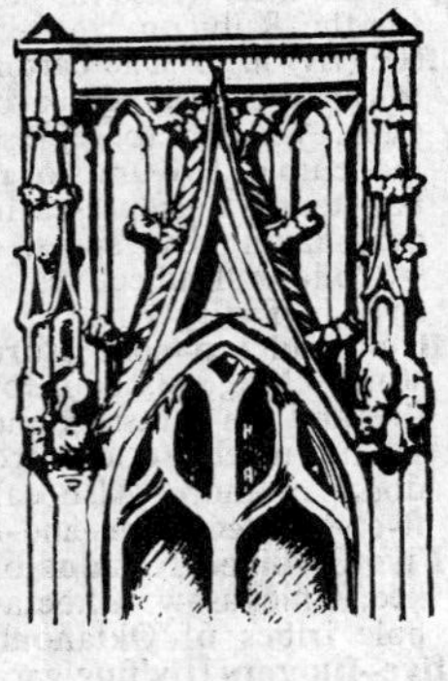

FLAMBOYANT ARCHITECTURE

flamboyant architecture A highly florid style of French Gothic architecture.

flame (flām) *n.* **1** A stream of vapor or gas made luminous by heat; gas or vapor in combustion. **2** An appearance or color like that of a blaze; glow; brilliancy; a red–yellow color, called **flame–scarlet.** **3** Excitement, as from rage, strife, or passionate desire. **4** An ardent affection; passionate love. **5** *Slang* A sweetheart. See synonyms under FIRE, LIGHT^{1}. — *v.* **flamed, flam·ing** *v.i.* **1** To give out flame; blaze; burn. **2** To light up or burn as if on fire; flash: His face *flamed* with rage. **3** To become enraged or excited (with anger, indignation, etc.): He *flamed* with indignation. — *v.t.* **4** To subject to heat or fire. **5** *Obs.* To inflame; excite. See synonyms under BURN. [<OF *flamme, flambe* <L *flamma* a flame] — **flam′ing** *adj.* — **flam′ing·ly** *adv.*

flame arc An electric arc produced and maintained between two carbons impregnated with mineral salts.

fla·men (flā′men) *n. pl.* **fla·mens** or **flam·in·es** (flam′ə·nēz) In ancient Rome, a priest devoted to the service of a particular god. [<L]

fla·men·co (flə·meng′kō, -men′-, flä-) *n.* A style of singing and dancing practiced by the Gipsies of Andalusia; also, a song or dance in this style. [<Sp., Flemish, because the Gipsies were thought to be from Flanders]

flame·out (flām′out′) *n.* The sudden extinguishing of the flame in a jet engine caused by an excess of fuel.

flame test *Chem.* The determination of the presence of an element or certain of its compounds, by holding the substance in the flame of a Bunsen burner and noting the resulting color.

flame–throw·er (flām′thrō′ər) *n. Mil.* A weapon that throws a stream of burning napalm or other gasoline mixture.

fla·min·go (flə·ming′gō) *n. pl.* **·gos** or **·goes** A long–necked, small–bodied wading bird (genus *Phoenicopterus*) of a pink or red color, having very long legs, webbed feet, and a bent bill. [<Pg. *flamingo* or Sp. *flamenco,* ult. <L *flamma* flame + Gmc. *-enc* -ING^{3}]

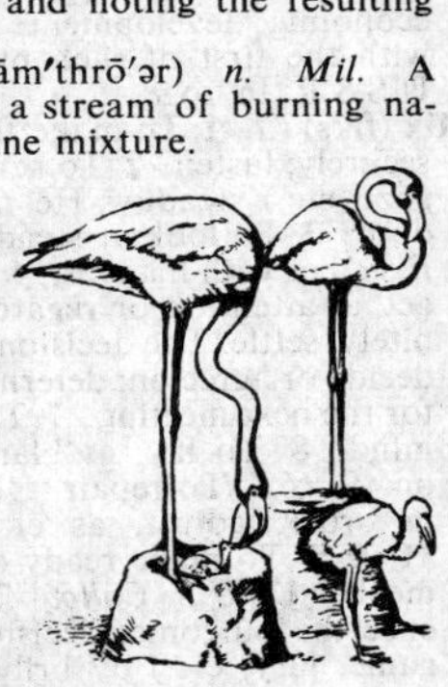

FLAMINGO
(From 4 to 4 1/2 feet standing height over–all)

Fla·min·i·an Way (flə·min′ē·ən) One of the chief ancient Roman roads from Rome to Cisalpine Gaul, built in 220 B.C. by Gaius Flaminius: Latin *Via Flaminia.*

Flam·i·ni·nus (flam′ə·nī′nəs), **Titus Quinctius,** 230?–174 B.C., Roman general.

Fla·min·i·us (flə·min′ē·əs), **Gaius,** died 217 B.C., Roman statesman.

flam·ma·ble (flam′ə·bəl) *adj.* Combustible; inflammable.

Flam·ma·rion (flà·mà·ryôṅ′), **Nicolas Camille,** 1842–1925, French astronomer and writer.

flam·y (flā′mē) *adj.* **flam·i·er, flam·i·est** Relating to, composed of, or resembling flame.

flan (flan, *Fr.* flàṅ) *n.* **1** A piece of metal ready to be made into a coin by receiving the stamp or the die; a blank. **2** A tart filled with cheese, cream, or fruit; also a custard or soufflé. [<F]

flanch (flanch, flänch) *n. Her.* A subordinary on the right or left side of the fess point of an escutcheon. Also **flanque** (flank). See illustration under ESCUTCHEON. [<OF *flanche,* var. of *flanc* flank]

flan·dan (flan′dan) *n. Archaic* A woman's cap or headdress with long hanging flaps. [Origin unknown]

Flan·ders (flan′dərz) A former county in the Low Countries, divided into: **1** Belgian Flanders, *Flemish* **Vlaan·de·ren** (vlàn′də·rən), comprising the provinces of **East Flanders,** *Flemish* **Oost–Vlaan·de·ren** (ōst′vlàn′də·rən); 1,147 square miles, capital, Ghent; and **West Flanders,** *Flemish* **West–Vlaan·de·ren** (vest′·vlàn′də·rən); 1,249 square miles; capital, Bruges; and **2** French Flanders, *French* **Flan·dre** (flàṅ′dr′), a region and former province of northern France.

flâ·ne·rie (flän·rē′) *n. French* Lounging; idling.

flâ·neur (flä·nœr′) *n. French* A dawdler; idler.

flange (flanj) *n.* **1** A spreading or flaring part. **2** A projecting rim or edge, as on a car wheel, a section of pipe, length of shafting, etc. **3** A tool used to shape flanges. **— *v.* flanged, flang·ing** *v.t.* To supply with a flange. **—** *v.i.* To have or take the form of a flange. [Prob. <OF *flangir* bend]

flank (flangk) *n.* **1** The hinder part of an animal's side, between the ribs and the hip. See illustration under HORSE. **2** *Entomol.* The side of an insect's thorax; the pleura. **3** The side, or the lateral portion or anything, especially of a military or naval force, or of a marching column. **4** That part of a bastion between the curtain and the face, or any part of a fortification that defends another work by a fire along its face; also, the lateral part of a fortification. See illustration under BASTION. **— by the right** or **left flank** A drill command preparatory to the marching maneuver in which every marcher makes a 90–degree turn to the right or left. **—** *v.t.* **1** To stand or be on one or both sides of. **2** *Mil.* **a** To get around and in back of (an enemy position or unit); turn the flank of. **b** To attack or threaten the flank of. **c** To guard the flank of (a friendly position or unit). **—** *adj.* **1** Pertaining to the flank or side. **2** Cut from the side, or situated at the side: a *flank* steak. **3** Coming from or toward the side: a *flank* attack. [<F *flanc* <Gmc.]

flank·er (flang′kər) *n.* **1** One of a body of troops thrown out to protect the flank or side of a marching column. **2** An addition to a fortification built at an angle to protect the main fortification, or to command the flank of an attacking enemy.

flan·nel (flan′əl) *n.* **1** A loosely–woven fabric of cotton, or of cotton and wool, with soft, naplike surface. **2** Plain cloth in the first stage of manufacture. **3** *pl.* Clothing made of flannel. **—** *v.t.* **·neled** or **·nelled, ·nel·ing** or **·nel·ling** To wrap in or rub with flannel. [Prob. <Welsh *gwlanen* flannel < *gwlan* wool] **— flan′nel·ly** *adj.*

flannel cake A pancake.

flan·nel·et (flan′əl·et′) *n.* A cotton fabric similar to flannel: plain, figured, or striped: used for underwear, etc. Also **flan′nel·ette′.**

flap (flap) *n.* **1** A broad, limber, and loosely hanging part or attachment. **2** The act of flapping. **3** An implement for brushing away flies. **4** *Surg.* A piece of skin or flesh cut away except at its base. **5** The flapping tongue of a valve. **6** *pl.* A disease of the lips of horses. **7** *Aeron.* A movable hinged section along the rear or trailing edge of a wing of an airplane, used to increase drag. **8** *Slang* An agitated or tempestuous reaction. [< *v.*] **— *v.* flapped, flap·ping** *v.t.* **1** To move by beating: to *flap* the wings. **2** To move with a flapping sound. **3** To strike with something flat and flexible. **—** *v.i.* **4** To beat the wings or move by beating the wings. **5** To move to and fro, as if blown by the wind. **6** *Slang* To lose one's composure. [Imit.]

flap·doo·dle (flap′do͞od′l) *n. Slang.* Boastful talk; twaddle; nonsense. [Arbitrary coinage]

flap·drag·on (flap′drag′ən) *n.* **1** A game in which raisins or other edibles are snatched by the players out of burning spirits and swallowed. **2** One of the articles thus used.

flap·jack (flap′jak′) *n.* A griddle cake.

flap·per (flap′ər) *n.* **1** One who or that which flaps or slaps, or calls attention. **2** A young bird unable to fly. **3** A flipper. **4** *Colloq.* A young girl, especially, in the 1920's, given to exaggerated styles and to sophisticated conduct.

flare (flâr) *v.* **flared, flar·ing** *v.i.* **1** To blaze or burn with a brilliant, wavering light, as a candle in the wind. **2** To break out in sudden or violent emotion: often with *up* or *out.* **3** To open or spread outward: A ship's bows *flare.* **—** *v.t.* **4** To cause to flare. **5** To signal (information) with flares. **—** *n.* **1** A large, bright, but unsteady and flickering light; unsteady glare. **2** A widening or spreading outward, as of the sides of a funnel. Compare illustrations under FUNNEL. **3** *Phot.* Unwanted light falling on the image plane in a camera projector or printer due to reflection of light between the lens surface or the interior of the lens barrel. **4** A brilliant brief burst of flame or light used as a signal or guide or as illumination. **5** Any sudden display, as of temper. See synonyms under LIGHT. [? Blend of FLY[1] and BARE[1]]

flare·back (flâr′bak′) *n.* Flame caused by ignition of gases released by opening the breech of a gun after firing.

flare–up (flâr′up′) *n.* **1** A sudden outburst of flame or light. **2** A sudden outbreak of anger.

flash (flash) *v.i.* **1** To break forth with light or fire suddenly and briefly: Lightning *flashed* across the sky. **2** To gleam; glisten: Their helmets *flashed* in the sun. **3** To be in view fleetingly; move very quickly: A train *flashed* by. **4** To come suddenly; be known or perceived in an instant: The memory *flashed* into my mind. **5** *Colloq.* To make a display. **—** *v.t.* **6** To send forth (fire, light, etc.) in brief flashes; cause to flash: His sword *flashed* fire in the sun. **7** To send or communicate with great speed: to *flash* news. **8** *Colloq.* To show or display briefly or ostentatiously: to *flash* a badge. **9** In glassmaking: **a** To cover with a thin coating of colored glass. **b** To apply (colored glass) as a coating. See synonyms under BURN[1]. **—** *n.* **1** A sudden and transient blaze; gleam. **2** A sudden outburst, as of wit, anger, etc. **3** A moment; instant. **4** Display; pomp; specifically, a vulgar display. **5** The coating of glass which is flashed upon other glass. **6** A mixture of capsicum, caramel, etc.: used in adulterating liquors. **7** A reservoir and sluiceway in a stream for storing water to float boats over a shoal. **8** A brief news dispatch sent right after the event, usually as a preliminary to fuller coverage. **9** *Archaic* Thieves' jargon. See synonyms under LIGHT[1]. **— a flash in the pan** **1** An explosion of the powder in the pan of a flintlock that does not discharge the weapon. **2** Hence, any abortive attempt, or weak outburst. **—** *adj.* **1** Obtained by flashlight, as a photograph. **2** Flashy; smart; sporty. **3** *Archaic* Of, pertaining to, or used by thieves: *flash* slang. [ME *flaschen;* prob. imit.]

flash·back (flash′bak′) *n.* **1** In fiction, drama, motion pictures, etc., a break in continuity made by the presentation of a scene, episode, or event occurring earlier. **2** The scene, episode, or event so presented.

flash·board (flash′bôrd′, -bōrd′) *n.* A board at the top of a dam to increase the height of water: also called *flushboard.*

flash bulb A photoflash bulb.

flash·cube (flash′kyo͞ob′) *n.* A small, rotatable cube containing four flash bulbs for use with a camera.

flash·er (flash′ər) *n.* **1** One who or that which flashes. **2** A device for intermittently opening and closing an electric circuit connected with incandescent lamps: used in advertising signs, etc.

flash flood A sudden, rushing flood of short duration.

flash house A house frequented by thieves, etc., where stolen goods are received.

flash·ing (flash′ing) *n.* **1** The act of one who flashes, in any sense. **2** A reheating of imperfectly formed glassware. **3** The twirling of a hollow globe of heated glass to spread it into a flat disk. **4** The fusing of a thin coating of colored glass on plain glass. **5** A lap joint, or a turned–up flange, usually of metal, to keep a roof watertight at an angle or where it joins a chimney, etc. **6** The act of flushing, as a stream or sewer. **7** The operation of perfecting the vacuum in a lamp bulb or vacuum tube by suddenly increasing the voltage passing through the filaments or cathode. **—** *adj.* Emitting flashes. **— flash′·ing·ly** *adv.*

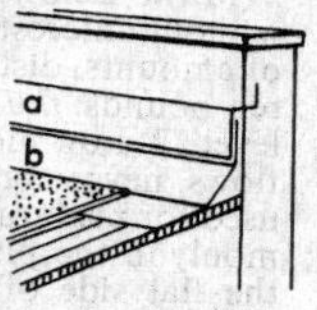

FLASHING
a, b. Parts of a lap joint.

flash lamp A lamp for taking flashlight photographs.

flash·light (flash′līt′) *n.* **1** *U.S.* A light, as in a lighthouse, shown only at regular intervals. **2** A brief and brilliant light for taking photographs. **3** A small portable electric light. Also **flash light.**

flash·o·ver (flash′ō′vər) *n. Electr.* A disruptive leakage of current through or around an insulator.

flash point The lowest temperature at which the vapors of petroleum or other combustible liquids will give a flash or slight explosion on exposure to a flame.

flash spectrum *Astron.* In a total eclipse of the sun, the instantaneous emission of bright lines in the spectrum of the chromosphere at the moment of totality.

flash·y (flash′ē) *adj.* **flash·i·er, flash·i·est** **1** Flashing; bright for a moment. **2** Pretentious and cheap; showy; tawdry. **— flash′i·ly** *adv.* **— flash′i·ness** *n.*

flask[1] (flask, fläsk) *n.* **1** A small bottle or similar vessel. **2** A small container, often of metal, for carrying liquids or liquor on the person. **3** A metal or horn vessel used by hunters to carry gunpowder. **4** A thin long–necked glass bottle covered with straw, as for oil. **5** A frame for holding a founding mold. **6** Any of variously shaped receptacles of glass or other material, used in laboratory work. **7** The commercial unit for the measurement and sale of mercury, equal to 76 pounds. **8** The iron container in which mercury is sold. [<F *flasque* <Med. L *flasca,* var. of *flasco.* See FLAGON.]

flask[2] (flask, fläsk) *n. Mil.* **1** The side plates forming the trail of a gun carriage. **2** *Obs.* The bed of a gun carriage. [<F *flasque* cheek of a gun carriage]

flas·ket (flas′kit, fläs′-) *n.* **1** A shallow basket, as for laundry. **2** A small flask.

flat[1] (flat) *adj.* **flat·ter, flat·test** **1** Having a surface that is a horizontal plane, or nearly so; level; without unevenness or inclination. **2** Without prominences or depressions; not curved or round or uneven: a *flat* country. **3** Lying prone upon the ground; prostrate; hence, overthrown; ruined. **4** Not qualified or softened in any way; positive; absolute: a *flat* refusal. **5** Deficient in distinctness, form, or interesting qualities; monotonous; stupid; tasteless; dull; insipid: a *flat* sermon, a *flat* market, *flat* wine. **6** *Music* Below pitch; minor or diminished: a *flat* third; having flats in the signature: a *flat* key. **7** *Phonet.* **a** Designating the vowel sound in *man,* as opposed to the sound in *calm.* **b** Of consonants, voiced: opposed to *sharp.* **8** Without gloss, as a painted surface. **9** Uniform in tint. **10** Lacking in contrast; without distinguishing light and shadow: an effect often aimed at in mural–painting. **11** Of a golf club, having the head set at a very obtuse angle to the shaft. **12** *Gram.* Having no inflectional or distinguishing ending or mark, as an adverb not ending in *-ly,* or a noun used as an adjective without the addition of

a characterizing suffix, as in such expressions as to breathe *deep,* the *sister* arts, etc. **13** Not varying with changing conditions; uniform: a *flat* rate. **14** Wanting in tonal quality: said of a sound or accent. — *adv.* **1** In a level state or position; so as to be flat; flatly. **2** *Music* Below the true pitch. **3** In finance, without interest. **4** Exactly; precisely: used of amounts, distances, and the like: It weighed ten pounds *flat.* — *n.* **1** A plane surface; a level. **2** Low meadowland over which the tide flows, never completely submerged by water: used for pasturage or planting. **3** Shoal: commonly in the plural. **4** Anything that is flat; the flat side of a thing. **5** *Music* A tone a half step lower than a tone from which it is named, represented by the character ♭. **6** A strip of high, level land. **7** An oblong wooden frame covered with canvas; a unit of a box–set of stage scenery. **8** A platform car. **9** A flat–bottomed boat, used for transporting heavy cargoes; a flatboat. **10** A deflated automobile tire. **11** A shallow, earth–filled tray for earlier seed germination to advance the flowering period. — *v.* **flat·ted, flat·ting** *v.t.* **1** To make flat. **2** *Music* To lower (a tone) in playing or composing, especially by a semitone. — *v.i.* **3** To become flat. **4** *Music* To sing or play below pitch. [ON *flatr*] — **flat′ly** *adv.* — **flat′ness** *n.*

Synonyms (adj.): absolute, characterless, downright, dull, empty, even, horizontal, insipid, level, lifeless, mawkish, pointless, spiritless, stupid, tame, vapid. As a dead level is monotonous and uninteresting, we have a *flat* joke, a *flat* remark, for one that is *dull, insipid, pointless.* As what is perfectly *level* is without variation or relief, we have a *flat* refusal, in the sense of what is *absolute.* See HORIZONTAL, LEVEL, SMOOTH.

◆ *Flat* is the first element in many self–explaining compound adjectives: *flat*–billed, *flat*–bottomed, *flat*–breasted, etc.

flat[2] (flat) *n.* **1** A set of rooms on one floor, for the occupancy of a family; apartment. **2** A house containing such flats. [Var. of obs. *flet,* a floor OE *flet*; infl. by FLAT[1]]

flat·boat (flat′bōt′) *n.* A large boat with a flat bottom much in use on rivers for freighting merchandise: also *flat.* Also **flat′bot′tom** (-bot′·əm).

flat–bot·tomed (flat′bot′əmd) *adj.* Having the bottom flat: usually said of boats.

flat car A railroad freight car, usually without sides or covering; a platform car. Also *flat.*

flat·fish (flat′fish′) *n. pl.* **·fish** or **·fish·es** Any of an order *(Heterosomata)* of fishes having a compressed body with unsymmetrical sides and with both eyes on one side, as the flounder, halibut, sole, etc.

flat·foot (flat′fo͝ot′) *n.* **1** *Pathol.* The deformed condition of a foot caused by a falling of the arch. **2** *pl.* **flat·feet** *Slang* A policeman.

flat foot A foot having a flat sole.

flat–foot·ed (flat′fo͝ot′id) *adj.* **1** Having flat feet. **2** Uncompromising; resolute; positive. — **flat′–foot′ed·ly** *adv.*

Flat·head (flat′hed′) *n.* **1** One of the Salishan tribe of North American Indians. **2** One of the Chinook Indians.

flat·i·ron (flat′ī′ərn) *n.* An iron with a smooth, polished surface for smoothing cloth by the action of heat and pressure.

flat knot A reef knot.

flat·ling (flat′ling) *adj. Obs.* Given with the flat side of a weapon; hence, oppressive, crushing. — *adv.* **1** *Brit. Dial.* Positively; peremptorily. **2** *Scot.* Flatlong. Also **flat′lings.**

flat·long (flat′lông) *adv. Obs.* With the flat side, as of a sword.

flat–nose (flat′nōz′) *adj.* Designating a type of pliers whose gripping surfaces meet along a common edge. See illustration under PLIERS.

flat silver Silver spoons, knives, forks, etc., collectively, as distinguished from silver bowls, pitchers, goblets, etc.

flat·ten (flat′n) *v.t.* & *v.i.* **1** To make or become flat or flatter. **2** To make or become prostrate. — **to flatten out** **1** To make or become flat or flatter. **2** *Aeron.* To change or become changed in angle of flight so as to fly horizontally, as after diving or climbing. — **flat′ten·er** *n.*

flat·ter[1] (flat′ər) *v.t.* **1** To praise unduly or insincerely. **2** To try to win over or gain the favor of by flattery. **3** To play upon the hopes or vanity of; beguile. **4** To please or gratify: She *flattered* me by saying "Yes." **5** To represent too favorably: The picture *flatters* her. — *v.i.* **6** To use flattery. See synonyms under CARESS, PRAISE, PUFF. — **to flatter oneself** To believe: I *flatter* myself that my gifts are acceptable. [<OF *flater* fawn, caress. Akin to FLAT[1].] — **flat′ter·er** *n.* — **flat′ter·ing** *adj.* — **flat′ter·ing·ly** *adv.*

flat·ter[2] (flat′ər) *n.* **1** One who or that which flattens. **2** A flat–holed drawplate through which watch springs, skirt wire, etc., are drawn. **3** A flat–faced hammer used by blacksmiths.

flat·ter·y (flat′er·ē) *n. pl.* **·ter·ies** **1** The act or practice of the flatterer. **2** Undue or insincere compliment; adulation. See synonyms under PRAISE. [<OF *flaterie* <*flater* fawn, caress]

Flat·ter·y (flat′ər·ē), **Cape** A high promontory and lighthouse at the entrance to Juan de Fuca Strait, NW Washington.

flat·ting (flat′ing) *n.* **1** The act, process, or operation of making or becoming flat or smooth. **2** A method of applying paint so that it will dry without gloss.

flat·tish (flat′ish) *adj.* Rather flat.

flat–top (flat′top′) *n.* A U.S. naval aircraft–carrier.

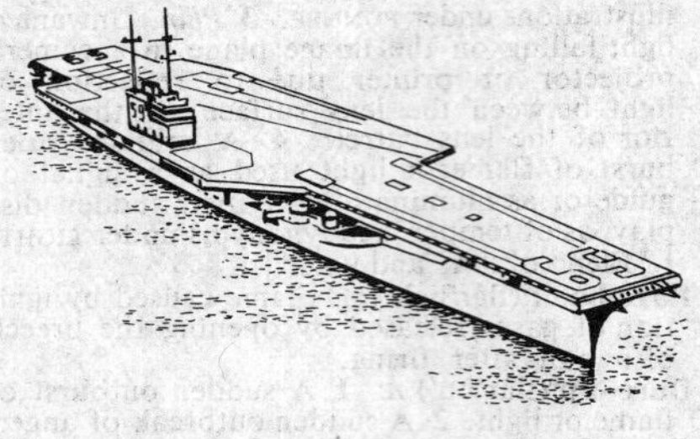

FLAT–TOP — AN AIRCRAFT–CARRIER

flat·u·lence (flach′ə·ləns, -yo͞o-) *n.* **1** The accumulation of gas in the stomach and bowels. **2** Windiness; vanity. Also **flat′u·len·cy.** [<F, ult. <L *flatus* a blowing <*flare* blow] — **flat′u·lent, flat′u·ous** *adj.* — **flat′u·lent·ly** *adv.*

fla·tus (flā′təs) *n. pl.* **·tus·es** **1** A breath; puff of wind. **2** Windiness; wind or gas in the stomach or bowels. **3** The condition of being puffed out with wind; inflation. [<L <*flare* blow]

flat·ware (flat′wâr′) *n.* **1** Dishes that are more or less flat, as plates and saucers, taken collectively: distinguished from *hollowware.* **2** Table utensils, as knives, forks, and spoons.

flat·wise (flat′wīz′) *adv.* With the flat side downward or next to another object. Also **flat′ways′** (-wāz′).

flat·work (flat′wûrk′) *n.* Household linen which can be ironed out on a mangle, as sheets, tablecloths, napkins, towels, etc.

flat·worm (flat′wûrm′) *n.* Any flat–bodied worm, as a tapeworm, fluke, planarian, etc.

Flau·bert (flō·bâr′), **Gustave,** 1821–80, French novelist.

flaunt (flônt) *v.i.* **1** To make an ostentatious or gaudy display; parade impudently: to *flaunt* through the streets. **2** To wave or flutter freely. — *v.t.* **3** To show or display in an ostentatious or impudent manner. — *n.* **1** The act of flaunting. **2** A boast; vaunt. [ME *flant* <Scand. Cf. Norw. *flanta* gad about.] — **flaunt′er** *n.*

Synonyms (verb): boast, display, exhibit, flourish, flutter, parade, vaunt, wave.

flaunt·ing (flôn′ting) *adj.* Making a parade or ostentatious display; jaunty and gay. Also **flaunt′y.** — **flaunt′ing·ly** *adv.*

flau·tist (flô′tist) *n.* One who plays the flute; a flutist.

fla·ves·cent (flə·ves′ənt) *adj.* Turning yellow; yellowish. [<L *flavescens, -entis,* ppr. of *flavescere* become yellow <*flavus* yellow]

Fla·vi·an (flā′vē·ən) *adj.* Of or pertaining to the emperor Titus Flavius Vespasianus (Vespasian) or to his sons and successors Titus and Domitian.

fla·vin (flā′vən) *n.* **1** *Biochem.* One of a group of yellow pigments widely distributed in plant and animal tissues and constituting an important element of the vitamin B_2 complex, as ribo*flavin.* **2** Quercetin. [<L *flavus* yellow + -IN]

fla·vism (flā′viz·əm) *n.* The condition or state of being yellow.

fla·vone (flā′vōn, flə·vōn′, flav′ōn) *n.* A colorless, crystalline, vegetable pigment, $C_{15}H_{10}O_2$, the parent substance of certain yellow dyes, as quercetin, etc. [<L *flavus* yellow + -ONE]

fla·vo·pro·te·in (flā′vō·prō′tē·in, -tēn) *n. Biochem.* An enzyme chemically linked with a protein and serving to oxidize nutrients in animal cells. [<FLAVIN + PROTEIN]

fla·vo·pur·pu·rin (flā′vō·pûr′pyə·rin) *n. Chem.* A crystalline coal–tar dye, $C_{14}H_8O_5$, isomeric with purpurin and similar to alizarin except that it produces colors with a yellowish tinge. [<L *flavus* yellow + PURPURIN]

fla·vor (flā′vər) *n.* **1** The quality of a thing as affecting the sense of taste or the senses of taste and smell; odor; scent. **2** The characteristic taste of a thing, especially if pleasant. **3** Distinctive quality or characteristic: the *flavor* of speech. **4** Flavoring. — *v.t.* To give flavor or any distinguishing quality to. Also, *Brit.,* **fla′vour.** [<OF *flaor, fleur,* prob. ult. <L *flare* blow; *v* added on analogy with *savor*] — **fla′vor·y** *adj.*

fla·vor·ing (flā′vər·ing) *n.* A substance, as an essence or extract, for giving a flavor to anything.

fla·vor·ous (flā′vər·əs) *adj.* Pleasantly flavored; savory. See synonyms under RACY.

fla·vous (flā′vəs) *adj.* Nearly pure yellow.

flaw[1] (flô) *n.* **1** An inherent defect, as in construction or constitution; especially, a defect that destroys or impairs strength, force, or legal validity; weak spot. **2** A crack; fissure: a *flaw* in a casting. See synonyms under BLEMISH, BREACH. — *v.t.* & *v.i.* To make flaws in; become cracked or defective. [? <ON *flaga* slab of stone] — **flaw′less** *adj.* — **flaw′less·ness** *n.* — **flaw′less·ly** *adv.*

flaw[2] (flô) *n.* **1** A sudden squall of wind; a transient but violent windstorm. **2** *Obs.* A tumult. [Prob. <ON *flaga* gust]

flaw·y (flô′ē) *adj.* Having flaws; defective.

flax (flaks) *n.* **1** An annual plant (genus *Linum*) with stems about two feet high and blue flowers, having a mucilaginous seed, called *flaxseed* or *linseed,* and an inner bark which yields the flax of commerce. **2** The soft fiber obtained from the bark of the flax plant, used in the manufacture of linen. **3** Any plant resembling flax. — *v.t.* & *v.i.* To beat or thrash. — **to flax around** *U.S. Colloq.* To stir about busily. — **to flax out** *U.S. Colloq.* **1** To knock out; beat, as in a fight. **2** To become fatigued or exhausted. [OE *fleax*]

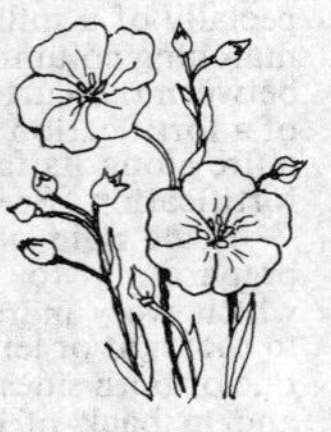

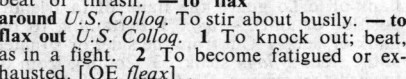

FLAX

flax·en (flak′sən) *adj.* **1** Of, pertaining to, or made of flax. **2** Like flax. **3** Of a light golden color.

Flax·man (flaks′mən), **John,** 1755–1826, English sculptor and draughtsman.

flax·seed (flaks′sēd′, flak′-) *n.* **1** The mucilaginous seed borne by the common flax; linseed: used medicinally for soothing and softening. **2** A low European herb of the flax family, having similar seed vessels.

flax·wort (flaks′wûrt′) *n.* Any plant of the flax family *(Linaceae).*

flax·y (flak′sē) *adj.* Like flax; fair; flaxen.

flay (flā) *v.t.* **1** To strip off the skin from, as by flogging. **2** To pillage; rob. **3** To attack with scathing criticism. [OE *flēan*] — **flay′er** *n.*

F–layer (ef′lā′ər) See APPLETON LAYER.

flea (flē) *n.* **1** A wingless insect (order *Siphonaptera*), parasitic upon a mammal or a bird, and having a compressed body, limbs adapted for leaping, and a head armed with piercing mandibles and a suctorial proboscis. For illustration see under INSECT (injurious). ◆ Collateral adjective: *pulicene.* **2** One of several small beetles or crustaceans that jump like fleas, as a beach flea or sand hopper. ◆ Homophone: *flee.* [OE *flēa.* Akin to FLEE.] — **a flea in one's** (or **the**) **ear** A warning; caution; sometimes, an irritating reply or rebuff.

flea·bane (flē′bān′) *n.* One of various plants of the composite family, especially *Erigeron philadelphicus* of the U.S., supposed to repel fleas.

flea·bite (flē'bīt') *n.* 1 The bite of a flea. 2 Any trifling wound or discomfort. 3 A minute quantity.

flea-bit·ten (flē'bit'n) *adj.* 1 Bitten by a flea. 2 White, flecked with bay or sorrel spots: said of the color of a horse.

fleam (flēm) *n.* 1 A surgeon's lancet. 2 The angle made by the cutting edge of a saw tooth with the plane of the blade. [< OF *flieme*, ult. < LL *flebotomum* < Gk. *phlebotomon*. See PHLEBOTOMY.]

flea market A market, often outdoors, for the sale of a wide assortment of old or second-hand articles, antiques, etc.

flea·wort (flē'wûrt') *n.* 1 A European plant (genus *Inula*) of the composite family: a reputed repellent of fleas. 2 A plant (*Plantago psyllium*) of the plantain family, whose seeds are used medicinally.

flèche (flesh) *n. Archit.* Any spire; more particularly, one over the intersection of the nave and transepts. [< F, lit., arrow]

fleck (flek) *n.* A dot or speck; a spot; dapple. —*v.t.* To mark with spots or flecks. [Cf. ON *flekkr* spot] —**fleck'less** *adj.* —**fleck'y** *adj.*

Fleck·er (flek'ər), **Herman James Elroy,** 1884–1915, English poet.

flec·tion (flek'shən) *n.* 1 The act of bending or turning. 2 A curved or bent part. 3 A turning as of the eye; glance; cast. 4 *Anat.* Flexion. 5 *Gram.* Inflection. Also, for defs. 1–3, *Brit.* flexion. [< L *flexio, -onis* < *flectere* bend]

flec·tion·al (flek'shən·əl) *adj.* Pertaining to flection or inflection, especially that of words by declension, etc. ◆ In anatomy and physiology the form *flexional* is preferred.

fled (fled) Past tense and past participle of FLEE[1].

fledge (flej) *v.* **fledged, fledg·ing** *v.t.* 1 To furnish with feathers, as an arrow. 2 To bring up (a young bird) until ready for flight. —*v.i.* 3 To grow enough feathers for flight. [< obs. *fledge* ready to fly, ME *flegge*, OE *-flycge* in *unflycge* not ready to fly]

fledg·ling (flej'ling) *n.* 1 A young bird just fledged. 2 A tyro; an inexperienced person. Also **fledge'ling.**

fledg·y (flej'ē) *adj.* **fledg·i·er, fledg·i·est** Feathery; downy; feathered.

flee[1] (flē) *v.* **fled, flee·ing** *v.i.* 1 To run away, as from danger, harm, or enemies. 2 To move away quickly; disappear. 3 To move swiftly; leave abruptly. —*v.t.* 4 To run away from; avoid or try to avoid. 5 To leave or go away from abruptly: to *flee* the country. See synonyms under ESCAPE, FLY[1]. ◆ Homophone: *flea.* [OE *flēon.* Akin to FLEA.]

flee[2] (flē, flā) *Scot. v.t. & v.i.* To fly; let fly. —*n.* A fly: also spelled *flie.*

fleece (flēs) *n.* 1 The coat of wool covering a sheep. 2 The entire coat of wool sheared from a sheep. 3 Anything resembling a fleece in quality or appearance. 4 A textile fabric with a soft silky pile, used for linings, etc.; also, the nap. 5 Meat from the ribs of buffalo. 6 Bear fat, used as food. —*v.t.* **fleeced, fleec·ing** 1 To shear the fleece from. 2 To swindle; defraud. 3 To cover or fleck as with fleece. [OE *flēos*] —**fleece'a·ble** *adj.*

fleec·er (flē'sər) *n.* One who fleeces; especially, one who takes by fraud.

fleech (flēch) *v.t. Scot.* To cajole; coax. —*n.* Flattery.

fleec·y (flē'sē) *adj.* **fleec·i·er, fleec·i·est** Pertaining to, like, or covered with a fleece. —**fleec'i·ly** *adv.*

fleer (flir) *v.t.* To jeer at; deride. —*v.i.* To laugh or grin coarsely or scornfully; sneer. —*n.* A derision or scorn. 2 A leer. [Prob. < Scand. Cf. Norw. *flira* laugh, grin.] —**fleer'ing** *adj.* —**fleer'ing·ly** *adv.*

fleet[1] (flēt) *v.i.* 1 To move swiftly. 2 *Naut.* To change place; shift. 3 *Archaic* To fade. 4 *Obs.* To float. —*v.t.* 5 *Rare* To cause to pass quickly; while away. 6 *Naut.* To change the position of, as a cable. —*adj.* 1 Moving, or capable of moving, swiftly; rapid; swift; nimble. 2 Passing; evanescent. 3 *Brit. Dial.* Thin; shallow. [OE *flēotan* float] —**fleet'ly** *adv.* —**fleet'ness** *n.*

fleet[2] (flēt) *n.* 1 A number of vessels in company or under one command; especially ships of war. 2 The entire number of vessels belonging to one government; a navy. 3 The number of vessels in one command: the Pacific *fleet.* 4 A number of vessels, aircraft, or vehicles, collectively, engaged in the same activity, or operated as a unit: a fishing *fleet,* a *fleet* of trucks. [OE *flēot* ship]

fleet[3] (flēt) *n. Dial.* An inlet, creek, or sewer: now chiefly an element in place names: *Fleet* Street. [OE *flēot* estuary]

Fleet Admiral See ADMIRAL OF THE FLEET.

fleet·ing (flē'ting) *adj.* Passing quickly; transitory. See synonyms under TRANSIENT.

Fleet Prison A former debtors' prison in London. Also **the Fleet.**

Fleet Street An old street in London, center of the newspaper and printing business; hence, London journalism.

fleg (fleg) *Scot. v.t.* To frighten. —*v.i.* To flee. —*n.* A stroke.

Flem·ing (flem'ing) *n.* A native of Flanders; one of Flemish blood and speech, of Dutch descent. [< MDu. *Vlaming*]

Flem·ing (flem'ing), **Sir Alexander,** 1881–1955, British bacteriologist; discovered penicillin. —**Sir John Ambrose,** 1849–1945, English electrical engineer.

Flem·ish (flem'ish) *adj.* Of or pertaining to Flanders, its people, literature, or language. —*n.* 1 Flemings collectively: with the definite article. 2 The language of Flanders, belonging to the Low German branch of the Germanic languages. [< MDu. *Vlaemisch*]

Flens·burg (flens'bŏŏrk) A port in NW Germany near the Danish border.

flense (flens) *v.t.* **flensed, flens·ing** To strip the blubber or the skin from, as a whale or a seal. Also **flench** (flench). [< Dan. *flense*] —**flens'er** *n.*

flesh (flesh) *n.* 1 The portion of an animal body that consists of the softer tissues; especially, the muscular part of the body, but the fats being often included: distinguished from the fluids, bones, and integuments. 2 Animal food or meat as distinguished from vegetable; in a restricted sense, the meat of mammals and birds as distinguished from fish. 3 The material part of man as distinguished from the spiritual; the body as opposed to the soul. 4 Mankind in general; the human race. 5 In Scriptural and theological use, human nature; specifically, the carnal nature of man as affected with evil inclinations. 6 Desire for the gratification of sensual passions. 7 *Poetic* Kind-heartedness; gentleness of nature. 8 The outer appearance or color of a person's body: a man of dark *flesh.* 9 Animal life as a whole. 10 The soft, pulpy parts of fruits and vegetables, as distinguished from skin, etc. 11 The color of the skin of a white person; flesh-colored. 12 Kin; family stock. —**in the flesh** 1 In person. 2 Alive. —**own flesh and blood** One's own family, relations, or descendants. —*v.t.* 1 To plunge, as a sword, into the flesh, especially for the first time. 2 To inure or initiate, as troops, by giving a first experience of warfare. 3 To incite, as hawks for hunting, with a first experience of killing. 4 To scrape the flesh from, as a hide. 5 To invest or pad out with flesh. 6 To make fat or fleshy. —*v.i.* 7 To become fat or fleshy. —**flesh out** To give substance or the appearance of reality to; develop fully: to *flesh out* an idea. [OE *flǣsc*]

flesh-col·ored (flesh'kul'ərd) *adj.* Having the color of the skin of a white person; pinkish.

flesh·er (flesh'ər) *n.* 1 One who strips the flesh from hides; also, an instrument used for this. 2 *Scot.* A butcher.

flesh fly A carnivorous dipterous insect (genus *Sarcophaga*) that deposits its eggs or larvae in animal matter.

flesh·i·ness (flesh'ē·nis) *n.* Plumpness; corpulence.

flesh·ing (flesh'ing) *n.* The process of cleaning the inner side of hides and skins of adhering flesh and fat.

flesh·ings (flesh'ingz) *n. pl.* Flesh-colored tights.

flesh·li·ly (flesh'li·lē) *adj. Rare* Sensually.

flesh·li·ness (flesh'lē·nis) *n.* 1 Sensuality. 2 Fleshiness.

flesh·ly (flesh'lē) *adj.* **·li·er, ·li·est** 1 Pertaining to the body; corporeal. 2 Sensual; carnal. 3 Fleshy; fat; plump. —*adv.* In a fleshly manner.

flesh·mon·ger (flesh'mung'gər, -mong'-) *n.* 1 A dealer in meat; butcher. 2 A procurer.

flesh·pot (flesh'pot') *n.* 1 A pot to cook flesh in. 2 *pl.* Any form of indulgence; luxury; soft living.

flesh wound A superficial wound not injuring the bones or vital organs.

flesh·y (flesh'ē) *adj.* **flesh·i·er, flesh·i·est** 1 Having much flesh; plump; corpulent; fat. 2 Pertaining to flesh or carnal nature; composed of flesh. 3 Consisting of firm pulp; succulent, as a peach or an apple.

fletch (flech) *v.t.* To provide with feathers, as arrows; fledge. [Alter. of FLEDGE; infl. by *fletcher*]

fletch·er (flech'ər) *n. Archaic* One who fletches arrows; an arrowmaker. [< OF *flechier, flecher* < *fleche* arrow]

Fletch·er (flech'ər), **John,** 1579–1625, English dramatist; collaborated with Beaumont. —**John Gould,** 1886–1950, U.S. poet.

Fletch·er·ism (flech'ə·riz'əm) *n.* 1 The doctrine that perfect health requires complete mastication of food. 2 The practice of this doctrine. [after Horace *Fletcher,* 1849–1919, U.S. dietician]

Fletch·er·ize (flech'ə·rīz) *v.t.* **·ized, ·iz·ing** To masticate until converted into pulp.

Fletsch·horn (flech'hôrn) A peak in southern Switzerland; 13,121 feet.

fleur-de-lis (flœr'də·lē', -lēs') *n. pl.* **fleurs-de-lis** (-də·lēz') 1 The iris. 2 A heraldic device, the bearing of the former royal family of France. Also **fleur'-de-lys'.** [< F, flower of lily]

fleured (flœrd) *adj.* Decorated with fleurs-de-lis.

Fleu·rus (flœ·rüs') A town in south central Belgium; scene of Spanish defeat in 1622, French victories in 1690, 1794.

fleu·ry (flŏŏ'rē) *adj. Her.* Terminating in the three leaves of, or strewed with, the fleur-de-lis; specifically, tipped with a fleur-de-lis: said of the arms of a cross. For illustration see under CROSS.

flew[1] (flŏŏ) See FLUE[1].

flew[2] (flŏŏ) Past tense of FLY[1].

flew·it (flŏŏ'it) *n. Scot.* A box on the ears; a slap.

flews (flŏŏz) *n. pl.* The large chops or hanging parts of the upper lip of certain dogs: term used especially of hounds. See illustration under DOG. [Origin unknown] —**flewed** *adj.*

flex (fleks) *v.t. & v.i.* 1 To bend. 2 To contract, as a muscle. —*n.* 1 A bend; flexure. 2 *Brit.* A length of pliant, usually insulated, copper wire, as for an electric plug-in connection. [< L *flexus,* pp. of *flectere* bend]

flex·i·ble (flek'sə·bəl) *adj.* 1 Capable of being bent, turned, or twisted, without breaking. 2 Pliant; plastic. 3 Tractable; yielding; compliant. Also **flex·ile** (flek'sil). —**flex'i·bil'i·ty, flex'i·ble·ness** *n.* —**flex'i·bly** *adv.*

flex·ion (flek'shən) *n.* 1 *Anat.* The bending or turning of a part, as a limb, muscle, etc.: opposed to *extension.* 2 *Brit.* Flection (defs. 1–3).

Flex·ner (fleks'nər), **Abraham,** 1866–1959, U.S. educator. —**Simon,** 1863–1946, bacteriologist; brother of the preceding.

flex·or (flek'sər) *n. Anat.* A muscle that operates to bend a joint.

flex·time (fleks'tīm') *n.* The system of allowing workers to arrange working hours according to their own convenience.

flex·u·ose (flek'shŏŏ·ōs) *adj.* 1 *Bot.* Bending gently to and fro in opposite directions, as certain plants; zigzag. 2 Flexuous. [< L *flexuosus* < *flexus* bent. See FLEX.]

flex·u·ous (flek'shŏŏ·əs) *adj.* 1 Winding or turning about; having bends or turns. 2 Unsteady; wavering. 3 Flexuose. [< L *flexuosus* < *flexus;* see FLEX] —**flex·u·os'i·ty** (flek'shŏŏ·os'ə·tē), **flex'u·ous·ness** *n.* —**flex'u·ous·ly** *adv.*

flex·u·ral (flek'shər·əl) *adj.* Of or pertaining to bending or curving.

flex·ure (flek'shər) *n.* 1 A bending; the state of being bent or flexed. 2 A bent part; turn; curve; fold.

FLEUR-DE-LIS

fley (flā) *Scot. v.t.* To frighten; affright. —*n.* A fright.

fli·aum (flī'ôm) *n.* The orange rockfish (*Sebastodes pinniger*) of the American Pacific coast. [Origin uncertain]

flib·ber·ti·gib·bet (flib'ər·tē·jib'it) *n.* An impulsive, flighty, or gossipy person. Also **flib'ber·di·gib'bit, flib'ber·ty·gib'bet.** [Imit.]

flich·ter (flikh'tər) *Scot. v.i.* To flutter; flicker. —*n.* A flicker.

flick[1] (flik) *v.t.* 1 To strike with a quick, light stroke, as with a whip or finger. 2 To throw or remove with such a motion: to *flick* dust. 3 To cause to move, as a whip, in a quick, darting manner. —*v.i.* 4 To move in a quick, darting manner: His fist *flicked* out. 5 To flutter. [< *n.*] —*n.* 1 A quick, light stroke, as with a whip. 2 The sound of such a stroke. 3 A streak or splash. [Imit.]

flick[2] (flik) *n. Slang* A movie. [Short for FLICKER[1]]

flick·er[1] (flik'ər) *v.i.* 1 To burn or shine with an unsteady or wavering light. 2 To move quickly or jerkily, as lightning. 3 To flutter the wings. —*v.t.* 4 To cause to flicker. —*n.* 1 A waving or fluctuating light. 2 A flickering or fluttering motion. See synonyms under LIGHT[1]. 3 In motion pictures, the effect of discontinuity due to faulty projection. [OE *flicorian* move the wings] —**flick'er·ing** *adj.* —**flick'er·ing·ly** *adv.* —**flick'er·y** *adj.*

flick·er[2] (flik'ər) *n.* A woodpecker, especially the golden–winged woodpecker (*Colaptes auratus*) of eastern North America. [Imit.]

flick·er·tail (flik'ər·tāl') *n.* A medium–sized ground squirrel (*Citellus richardsonii*) with a buff–to–grayish coat and a bushy tail, black above and brown beneath: common in Montana and North Dakota.

Flickertail State Nickname of NORTH DAKOTA.

flicks (fliks) *n. pl. Brit. Slang* Motion pictures.

flied (flīd) Past tense and past participle of FLY[1] (def. 7).

fli·er (flī'ər) *n.* 1 That which flies; a flying bird, airplane, or the like; a fugitive. 2 An aviator or airman. 3 A rapidly moving piece in a machine. 4 *U.S.* A printed handbill. 5 A single step in a straight flight of stairs: in the plural, a straight flight. 6 A bus or express train with a fast schedule. 7 *Colloq.* A venture, as in the stock market. Also spelled *flyer.*

flight (flīt) *n.* 1 The act, process, or power of flying; swift movement of any kind. ◆ Collateral adjective: *volar.* 2 The distance traveled, as by a projectile. 3 A group or flock flying through the air together. 4 The art of traveling through the air in aircraft. 5 A single trip of an airplane. 6 In the U.S. Air Force, a tactical unit of two or more aircraft. 7 A soaring and sustained effort or utterance. 8 An ascent or continuous series (of stairs or steps). 9 A light, slender arrow for shooting at long distances: also **flight arrow.** 10 In angling, a device for whirling the bait rapidly. 11 The act of fleeing or escaping. See synonyms under CAREER. —**to put to flight** To cause to flee or run; defeat decisively; rout. —*v.i. Obs.* To migrate or move in flights, as birds. [OE *flyht*] —**flight'less** *adj.*

flight attendant An employee of an airline who attends passengers on board an aircraft, as a steward or stewardess.

flight deck The top deck of an aircraft–carrier, on which aircraft land and takeoff.

flight engineer *Aeron.* The crew member of an airplane in charge of mechanical performance during flight.

flight feather *Ornithol.* One of the strong, stiff feathers that are essential to the flight of a bird.

flight formation *Aeron.* A maneuver in which two or more aircraft fly in a definite pattern with reference to the complete unit.

flight line *Aeron.* The part of an airfield adjacent to the hangars, where aircraft are serviced, parked, etc.

flight officer *U.S.* In World War II, a specially created rank in the Air Force, corresponding to a warrant officer in grade.

flight path *Aeron.* The path traced out by the center of gravity of an aircraft with reference to the earth.

flight plan *Aeron.* The essential details of a proposed aircraft flight, including type of airplane, points of departure and arrival, cruising altitude, course, speed, etc.

flight·re·cord·er (flīt'ri·kôr'dər) *n. Aeron.* An automatic electronic device for recording temperature and pressure changes in an aircraft in flight: used primarily on test flights.

flight station *Aeron.* The compartment of a large airplane containing equipment for controlling mechanical performance during flight, and manned by crew members other than the pilot.

flight strip *Aeron.* An auxiliary landing field for aircraft.

flight·y (flī'tē) *adj.* **flight·i·er, flight·i·est** 1 Given to light–headed fancies or caprices; volatile. 2 Slightly delirious. 3 Fleeting; passing swiftly. —**flight'i·ly** *adv.* —**flight'i·ness** *n.*

flim–flam (flim'flam') *Colloq. v.t.* —**flammed, –flam·ming** To deceive; swindle; trick. —*adj.* Shifty; deceptive; tricky. —*n.* 1 Nonsense. 2 A deception; sham; pretense; specifically, a process of cheating a person when making change. [Cf. Norw. *flim* a lampoon, *flimta* mock] —**flim'–flam'mer** *n.* —**flim'–flam'mer·y** *n.*

flim·sy (flim'zē) *adj.* **·si·er, ·si·est** Lacking substantial texture or structure; thin and weak; ineffective. —*n. pl.* **flim·sies** 1 A thin paper used for carbon copies. 2 A dispatch or article received on thin paper. [< FILM, by metathesis; infl. in form by *clumsy, tipsy,* etc.] —**flim'si·ly** *adv.* —**flim'si·ness** *n.*

flinch (flinch) *v.i.* 1 To shrink back, as from pain or danger; waver; wince. 2 In croquet, to allow the foot to slip from one's ball during the action of driving an opponent's ball from the field of play. —*n.* Any act of shrinking back, wavering, or wincing. [< OF *flenchir,* var. of *flechier* bend; ult. origin uncertain] —**flinch'er** *n.* —**flinch'ing·ly** *adv.*

flin·der (flin'dər) *n.* A small fragment; splinter; shred: usually in the plural. [Cf. Norw. *flindra* splinter]

Flin·ders Island (flin'dərz) Largest of the Furneaux group; 802 square miles.

Flinders Ranges A mountain range in eastern South Australia; highest peak, 3,900 feet.

Flinders River A river in northern Queensland, Australia, flowing 520 miles NW to the Gulf of Carpentaria.

F lines Fraunhofer's lines.

fling (fling) *v.* **flung, fling·ing** *v.t.* 1 To cast or throw with violence; hurl. 2 To cast off; discard. 3 To put abruptly or violently, as if by throwing: They *flung* him into prison. 4 To put (oneself) into something completely or with energy: He *flung* himself into the battle. 5 To throw to the ground, as in wrestling; overthrow. 6 To send forth; emit, as a fragrance. —*v.i.* 7 To move, rush, or flounce, as with anger or contempt. 8 To make abusive remarks; speak bitterly or critically. 9 To kick and plunge: said of horses. —*n.* 1 The act of casting out, down, or away; a throw. 2 A sneering insinuation; aspersion. 3 A kick, flounce, leap, or the like. 4 Free range for action or indulgence; dash; swagger. 5 A lively Scotch dance. [ME *flingen* < Scand. Cf. ON *flegja* beat.] —**fling'er** *n.*

fling·ing–tree (fling'ing·trē) *n. Scot.* 1 A flail. 2 A timber hung between horses in a stall.

flint (flint) *n.* 1 A dull–colored variety of quartz resembling chalcedony but more opaque; it is very hard, and produces a spark when struck with steel. 2 A piece of such stone, shaped for some purpose, as for striking fire. 3 Anything very hard, obdurate, or cruel. —*v.t.* To provide with a flint. [OE]

Flint (flint) 1 A city in central Michigan. 2 A county in NE Wales; 256 square miles; county town, Mold: also **Flint'shire** (-shir).

Flint (flint), **Austin,** 1812–86, U.S. physician. —**Austin,** 1836–1915, U.S. physiologist and physician; son of the preceding.

flint corn A kind of Indian corn (*Zea mays indurata*), having especially hard smooth kernels which do not shrivel.

flint glass See under GLASS.

flint·lock (flint'lok') *n.* 1 A gunlock in which a flint was used to ignite the powder in the pan. 2 A firearm equipped with such a gunlock.

flint paper A paper covered with powdered flint, resembling sandpaper.

Flint River (flint) A river in western Georgia, flowing 330 miles south to the Chattahoochee to form the Apalachicola.

flint·y (flin'tē) *adj.* **flint·i·er, flint·i·est** 1 Made of, containing, or resembling flint. 2 Hard; cruel; obdurate. See synonyms under HARD. —**flint'i·ly** *adv.* —**flint'i·ness** *n.*

flip (flip) *v.* **flipped, flip·ping** *v.t.* 1 To throw or put in motion with a jerk; flick. 2 To toss, as a coin or cigarette, by or as by a fillip. —*v.i.* 3 To move abruptly or with a jerk. 4 To make a fillip; strike lightly and quickly. —*n.* 1 A quick movement of the hand or finger; sudden toss; snap; fillip; flick. 2 A drink made with some liquor, as sherry, mixed with egg, sugar, and spices. —*adj. Colloq.* Pert; saucy; impertinent. [Imit.]

flip–flop (flip'flop') *n.* 1 A somersault or handspring. 2 In advertising presentations, an easel device permitting display cards to be flipped over the top. [Varied reduplication of FLIP]

flip·pant (flip'ənt) *adj.* 1 Light, pert, and trifling; shallow and impertinent. 2 *Obs.* Fluent; free of speech. [< FLIP, *v.* + -ANT] —**flip'pan·cy, flip'pant·ness** *n.* —**flip'pant·ly** *adv.*

flip·per (flip'ər) *n.* 1 A limb used to swim with, as by seals, turtles, etc. 2 *Usually pl.* One of a pair of rubber shoes having a long, flat, paddlelike piece projecting beyond the toes, used by skin divers and other swimmers: also called *fin.* 3 *Slang* The hand.

flip side The back or second side of a phonograph record, esp. the side with the recording of lesser importance.

flirt (flûrt) *v.i.* 1 To play at courtship; try to attract attention or admiration; coquet. 2 To trifle; toy: to *flirt* with danger. 3 To move with sudden jerky motions. —*v.t.* 4 To toss or throw with a jerk. 5 To move briskly or back and forth. —*n.* 1 A person, especially a woman, who coquets; a trifler. 2 The act of flirting; a flirting motion; fling. [Imit.] —**flirt'er** *n.* —**flirt'y** *adj.*

flir·ta·tion (flər·tā'shən) *n.* Insincere lovemaking. Also **flirt'ing.** —**flir·ta'tious** *adj.* —**flir·ta'tious·ly** *adv.* —**flir·ta'tious·ness** *n.*

flirt·gill (flûrt'gil') *n. Obs.* A forward or frivolous girl.

flit (flit) *v.* **flit·ted, flit·ting** *v.i.* 1 To move or fly rapidly and lightly; dart; skim. 2 To pass away, as time. 3 *Dial.* To leave; depart. 4 *Scot. & Brit. Dial.* To move from one dwelling to another. —*v.t.* 5 *Scot.* To transfer; move. See synonyms under FLY[1]. —*n.* A flitting motion or action; flutter. [< ON *flytja* remove, move] —**flit'ter** *n.* —**flit'ting** *n.*

flitch (flich) *n.* 1 A side (of a hog) salted and cured; side of bacon. 2 A strip or steak cut from the side of certain fishes, smoked or adapted for smoking. 3 In carpentry, one of the parts of a compound beam. 4 A length of stripped log from whose circumference thin sheets of veneer are cut; also, the sheet so cut. —*v.t.* To cut into flitches. [OE *flicce*]

flite (flīt) *Scot. v.t. & v.i.* **flit·ed, flit·ing** 1 To scold; quarrel. 2 To wrangle with (a person). —*n.* A quarreling; railing; scolding. Also spelled *flyte.* —**flit'ing** *n.*

flit·ter[1] (flit'ər) *n.* A thin bit or bits of tin, brass, or the like, used in decorative work. [Alter. of obs. *fitters* pieces, fragments]

flit·ter[2] (flit'ər) *v.t. & v.i.* To flutter; flit. [Freq. of FLIT]

flit·ter·mouse (flit'ər·mous') *n. pl.* **·mice** (-mīs') A bat. [Cf. G *fledermaus*]

fliv·ver (fliv'ər) *Slang v.i.* To fail. —*n.* 1 A cheap motorcar. 2 Hence, anything small of its kind or of low price. [Origin unknown]

float (flōt) *v.i.* 1 To rest on the surface of a liquid. 2 To drift on or as on the surface of a liquid; move gently. 3 To move or drift without purpose or destination. 4 To hover; stay vaguely: The image *floated* in his mind. —*v.t.* 5 To cause to rest on the surface of a liquid. 6 To put in circulation; place on sale: to *float* a loan. 7 To find support for, as a business venture. 8 To irrigate; flood. 9 To smooth the surface of (soft plaster). —*n.* 1 An object, as a ball, that floats on a liquid or buoys up something, as a cork on a bait line or a hollow ball in a cistern. 2 One of various devices or appliances, as a plasterer's spreading trowel, a shoemaker's rasp, etc. 3 A truck or wheeled platform, decorated for display in

a pageant. **4** *Naut.* A dock or basin in which a ship is floated. For illustration see DRYDOCK. **5** *Geol.* Rock or rocky debris detached from the original formation. **6** *Aeron.* That portion of the landing gear of a seaplane which provides buoyancy when it is resting on the surface of the water. **7** In banking, time drafts and out-of-town checks in transit for collection. See TRANSIT. **8** A mechanical device for elevating performers above the stage in spectacular plays; also, the footlights. **9** The passage of a filling thread under or over several warp threads without engaging them. **10** *Electr.* A voltage equalizer; storage battery. **11** *Biol.* A hollow or inflated organ that supports an animal in water. **12** A milk shake with a ball of ice-cream floating in it. [OE *flotian* float] **—float′a·ble, float′y** *adj.*

Synonym (verb): swim. An object *floats* which is upborne in a fluid without action; a living being *swims* when borne up, or borne onward, in a liquid by action; one wearied with *swimming* may rest himself by *floating*; a cork *floats* on water; the hawk seems to *float* in the upper air. *Antonyms*: drown, sink.

float·age (flō′tij), **float·a·tion** (flō·tā′shən) See FLOTAGE, etc.

float·board (flōt′bôrd′, -bōrd′) *n.* One of the paddles of a water wheel or of a paddle wheel.

float·er (flō′tər) *n.* **1** One who or that which floats; a float. **2** *U.S.* An unattached voter, especially one whose vote may be bought; also, one who votes fraudulently elsewhere than in his own district.

float-feed (flōt′fēd′) *adj. Mech.* Furnished with a feed controlled by a float, as the carburetor of an internal-combustion engine.

float·ing (flō′ting) *adj.* **1** Buoyed up or carried along by a liquid or gas; borne on the surface of a liquid. **2** Unattached to moorings or anchorage; afloat. **3** Moving about; not settled; fluctuating. **4** Not funded; due at various times and in various sums: said of an indebtedness. **5** Not invested permanently; in circulation; available: said of funds or capital.—*n.* **1** The act, operation, or process of floating, in any sense of the verb. **2** A second coat of plastering.

floating axle *Mech.* In an automobile, a live axle which floats in a housing: it supports none of the weight, its sole function being to transmit propelling power to the wheels.

floating debt The general unfunded indebtedness of a state or a corporation.

floating dock A double caisson having a floored open space between air chambers: used for lifting a vessel out of water by pumping the water out of the air chambers. Also **floating drydock.**

float·ing-heart (flō′ting·härt′) *n.* An aquatic herb (genus *Nymphoides*), with floating heart-shaped leaves.

float·ing-island (flō′ting·ī′lənd) *n.* A dessert consisting of boiled custard with the beaten whites of eggs or whipped cream floating on the surface.

floating kidney *Pathol.* An abnormal condition, usually congenital, in which the kidneys are movable or unstable in position: also called *movable kidney, wandering kidney.*

floating ribs See RIB.

floc (flok) *n.* A tiny flaky mass, as in smoke; a chemical precipitate: also spelled *flock.* [Short for FLOCCULE]

floc·cil·la·tion (flok′si·lā′shən) *n. Pathol.* A delirious picking at the bedclothes by a patient. [<NL *floccillus,* dim. of *floccus* lock of wool + ATION]

floc·cose (flok′ōs, flo·kōs′) *adj.* **1** Woolly. **2** *Bot.* Having tufts of soft hairs or wool. [<LL *floccosus* <*floccus* lock of wool]

floc·cu·late (flok′yə·lāt) *v.t. & v.i.* **·lat·ed, ·lat·ing 1** To gather or be joined together in small lumps, as some soils. **2** To collect in flaky masses, as the particles of a finely divided precipitate. **3** To form large masses, as clouds. *—adj.* (-lit) Having a tuft of stiff hairs or a flocculus. **—floc′cu·la′tion** *n.*

floc·cule (flok′yōōl) *n.* **1** A loose tuft, like wool. **2** *Chem.* One of the flakes in a flocculent precipitate. **3** A small flocculent mass. Also **floc·cus** (flok′əs). [<NL *flocculus,* dim. of *floccus* lock of wool]

floc·cu·lent (flok′yə·lənt) *adj.* **1** Resembling wool; woolly. **2** Of, pertaining to, or like the down of a young bird. **3** Covered with a soft waxy secretion, as certain insects. **4** Coalescing in flakes, as the clumping together of microscopic particles in a liquid. **—floc′cu·lence, floc′cu·len·cy** *n.* **—floc′cu·lent·ly** *adv.*

floc·cu·lus (flok′yə·ləs) *n. pl.* **·li** (-lī) **1** A little flake; floccule. **2** A small tuft of wool or wool-like hairs. **3** *Astron.* One of the gaseous cloudlike masses in the chromosphere of the sun. **4** *Anat.* One of a pair of small lateral lobes in the cerebellum of the higher vertebrates. [<NL. See FLOCCULE.]

flock[1] (flok) *n.* **1** A company or collection of animals, as sheep, goats, or birds. **2** The persons belonging to a congregation, church, parish, or diocese. **3** An unorganized company of persons; a crowd. *—v.i.* To assemble or go in flocks, crowds, etc.; congregate. [OE *flocc*]

Synonyms (noun): bevy, brood, company, covey, drove, gam, group, hatch, herd, litter, lot, pack, set, swarm. *Group* is the general word for any gathering of a small number of objects, whether of persons, animals, or inanimate things. The individuals in a *brood* or *litter* are related to each other; those in the other *groups* may not be. *Brood* is used chiefly of fowls and birds, *litter* of certain quadrupeds which bring forth many young at a birth; we speak of a *brood* of chickens, a *litter* of puppies. *Bevy* is used of birds, and figuratively of any bright and lively *group* of women or children, but rarely of men. *Flock* is applied to birds and to some of the smaller animals; *herd* is confined to the larger animals; we speak of a *bevy* of quail, a *covey* of partridges, a *flock* of blackbirds, or a *flock* of sheep, a *gam* of whales, a *herd* of cattle, horses, buffaloes, or elephants, a *pack* of wolves, a *pack* of hounds, a *swarm* of bees. A collection of animals driven or gathered for driving is called a *drove.*

flock[2] (flok) *n.* **1** Finely ground wool, felt or vegetable fiber; wool dust. **2** A tuft of wool, or the like. **3** Short refuse wool, used as stuffing and in upholstery. **4** A tufted or flakelike mass, especially if produced by precipitation: also spelled *floc.* *—v.t.* To cover or fill with flock, as a cushion. [Prob. <OF *floc* <L *floccus* lock of wool]

flock paper Wallpaper sized and covered or figured with flock; velvet paper.

flock·y (flok′ē) *adj.* **flock·i·er, flock·i·est** Resembling flock; floccose.

Flod·den (flod′n) A small hill in north Cumberland, England, surrounded by **Flodden Field,** scene of the defeat of James IV of Scotland by English forces, 1513.

floe (flō) *n.* A tabular mass, or a collection of such masses, of floating ice. ◆ Homophone: *flow.* [<ON *flo* a layer]

flog (flog, flôg) *v.t.* **flogged, flog·ging** To beat with a whip, rod, etc.; to whip. See synonyms under BEAT. *—n.* A sound resembling the impact of a blow; also, the act of flogging. [? <L *flagellare*] **—flog′ger** *n.* **—flog′ging** *n.*

flong (flong) *n.* A sheet of specially prepared paper used for making a stereotype mold or matrix. [Var. of FLAN]

flood (flud) *n.* **1** An unusually large flow of water; freshet; inundation; deluge. ◆ Collateral adjective: *diluvial.* **2** The coming in of the tide; the tide at its height; high tide: also called *flood tide.* **3** A copious flow or stream, as of sunlight, lava, etc.; abundant or excessive supply. **4** Any great body of water; the sea; a river. **5** A stage light that throws a broad beam. **—the Flood** or **Noah's flood** See under DELUGE. *—v.t.* **1** To cover or inundate with a flood; deluge. **2** To fill or overwhelm as with a flood: They *flooded* him with advice. **3** To supply with too much: He *flooded* the engine with gasoline. *—v.i.* **4** To rise to a flood; overflow. **5** To flow in a flood; gush. [OE *flōd*] **—flood′er** *n.*

flood control The use of dikes, dams, tunnels, artificial channels, and other engineering techniques as a means of regulating and controlling flood waters.

flood·gate (flud′gāt′) *n.* **1** *Engin.* A gate for regulating the flow of water, as a raceway. **2** Any free vent for an outpouring, as of wrath or tears.

flood·light (flud′līt′) *n.* Artificial illumination of great brilliancy and broad beam; specifically, a lighting unit equipped with a highpowered projector, enveloping the desired object in a broad flood of light.

flood plain An area of flat country bordering a stream and subject to flooding in periods of high water.

flood tide See FLOOD *n.* (def. 2).

floor (flôr, flōr) *n.* **1** The surface in a room or building upon which one walks. **2** The space between two adjacent levels of a building; a story. **3** Any natural area made smooth or level, corresponding in character or use to a floor; also, the surface of something built, as a bridge. **4** In any parliamentary body, the part of the hall occupied by its members; hence, the right or privilege to address the house during a given time and to the exclusion of other speakers. **5** The main business hall of an exchange. **6** *Naut.* The vertical plates between the inner and outer bottoms of a ship extending from one side (bilge) to the other. **7** The bottom limit of anything; specifically, the lowest price charged for a given thing. *—v.t.* **1** To cover or provide with a floor. **2** To throw or knock down; overthrow. **3** *Colloq.* To silence; defeat. **4** *Colloq.* To baffle; confound. [OE *flōr*] **—floor′er** *n.*

floor·age (flôr′ij, flō′rij) *n.* The area of a floor; floor space.

floor·board (flôr′bôrd′, flōr′bōrd′) *n.* A board in a floor; flooring.

floor·cloth (flôr′klôth′, -kloth′, flōr′-) *n.* **1** Any fabric used to cover floors, as oilcloth. **2** A cloth used to clean a floor.

floor·ing (flôr′ing, flō′ring) *n.* **1** Material for the making of a floor. **2** Floors collectively. **3** A floor.

floor leader A party leader in either house of the U.S. Congress, in charge of party organization and many of the privileges of the floor.

floor plan An architectural plan of the rooms and other spaces on one floor of a building.

floor show Entertainment consisting of dancing, singing, etc., presented on the dance floor of a night club or cabaret.

floor·walk·er (flôr′wô′kər, flōr′-) *n.* In a retail store, one who oversees the employees on a floor, directs customers, etc.

flooz·y (flōō′zē) *n. pl.* **flooz·ies** *Slang* A dissolute young woman; a tart. [Cf. FLOSSY]

flop (flop) *v.* **flopped, flop·ping** *v.i.* **1** To move or beat about with or as with thuds. **2** To fall loosely and heavily: to *flop* to the ground. **3** *Colloq.* To fail. *—v.t.* **4** To cause to strike, slap, or drop with or as with a thud. *—n.* **1** The sound or act of flopping. **2** *Colloq.* An utter failure, or a person who has failed. [Var. of FLAP] **—flop′per** *n.* **— flop′py** *adj.* **—flop′pi·ly** *adv.* **—flop′pi·ness** *n.*

flop·house (flop′hous′) *n.* A cheap lodging house or hotel.

floppy disc A small, flexible recording disc on which data may be stored in the memory of a digital computer.

flo·ra (flôr′ə, flō′rə) *n. pl.* **·ras** or **·rae** (-ē) **1** The aggregate of plants indigenous to a country or district: distinguished from *fauna.* **2** A work systematically describing such plants. [<NL, after L *Flora,* goddess of flowers]

Flo·ra (flôr′ə, flō′rə) A feminine personal name. Also *Fr.* **Flore** (flôr). [<L, flower]

—Flora In Roman mythology, the goddess of flowers and spring.

flo·ral (flôr′əl, flō′rəl) *adj.* Of, like, or pertaining to flowers.

Flo·ral (flôr′əl, flō′rəl) *adj.* Of, belonging, or relating to Flora.

floral envelope *Bot.* The corolla and calyx of a flower.

Flo·ré·al (flôr′ē·əl, *Fr.* flô·rā·àl′) See CALENDAR (Republican).

Flor·ence (flôr′əns, flor′-) A city on the Arno in central Italy: Italian *Firenze.* Ancient **Flo·ren·ti·a** (flō·ren′shē·ə).

Flor·ence (flôr′əns, flor′-; *Fr.* flô·räns′) A feminine personal name. Also *Dan., Ger., Sw.*

add,āce,câre,pälm; end,ēven; it,īce; odd,ōpen,ôrder; tŏŏk,pōōl; up,bûrn; ə = a in *above,* e in *sicken,* i in *clarity,* o in *melon,* u in *focus* ; yōō = u in *fuse,* oi,oil; ou,pout; ch,check; g,go; ng,ring; th,thin; th,this; zh,vision. Foreign sounds à,œ,ü,kh,ṅ; and ◆: see page xx. <from; + plus; ? possibly.

Flo·renz (flô·rents′), *Du.* **Flo·ren·ti·a** (flô·ren′tsē·ä), *Sp.* **Flo·ren·cia** (flō·ren′thyä). [< L, blooming]

Florence flask **1** A round or pear-shaped bottle of thin glass in which liquids are heated. **2** A straw-covered glass flask in which olive oil or wine is imported from Italy.

flor·en·tine (flôr′ən·tēn, -tīn, flor′-) *n.* A stout and durable kind of silk dress goods.

Flor·en·tine (flôr′ən·tēn, -tīn, flor′-) *adj.* Of or pertaining to the city of Florence, Italy. —*n.* An inhabitant or native of Florence.

Flo·res (flō′res) **1** One of the Lesser Sunda Islands, east of Sumbawa; 6,000 square miles. **2** (flō′rish) An island in the western Azores; 57 square miles.

flo·res·cence (flô·res′əns, flō-) *n. Bot.* **1** The state of being in blossom. **2** Inflorescence. For illustrations see INFLORESCENCE. [< NL *florescentia* < L *florescere,* inceptive of *florere* bloom]—**flo·res′cent** *adj.*

Flo·res Sea (flō′res) A part of the Indian Ocean between Sulawesi and the Lesser Sunda Islands.

flo·ret (flôr′it, flō′rit) *n.* **1** A little flower. **2** *Bot.* One of the small individual flowers that make up a cluster or head, as in sunflowers, dandelions, etc., of the composite family. **3** A silk yarn or floss. [< OF *florete,* dim. of *flor* a flower < L *flos, floris*]

Flo·rey (flôr′ē, flō′rē), **Sir Howard Walter,** 1898–1968, British pathologist born in Australia.

Florey unit The Oxford unit.

Flo·ri·an·ó·po·lis (flôr′ē·ən·op′ə·lis, flō′rē-) A port in southern Brazil, capital of Santa Catarina state. Formerly **Des·têr·ro** (dish·tār′·rōō).

flo·ri·at·ed (flôr′ē·ā′tid, flō′rē-) *adj.* Decorated with flower designs.

flo·ri·cul·ture (flôr′ə·kul′chər, flō′rə-) *n.* The cultivation of flowers or ornamental plants. See synonyms under AGRICULTURE. [< L *flos, floris* a flower + CULTURE]—**flo′ri·cul′tur·al** *adj.* —**flo′ri·cul′tur·al·ly** *adv.* —**flo′ri·cul′tur·ist** *n.*

flor·id (flôr′id, flor′-) *adj.* **1** Having a bright color; of a lively reddish hue. **2** Excessively ornate. **3** Blooming; flowery. **4** Full of ornamental musical phrases. [< L *floridus* flowery < *flos, floris* a flower]—**flo·rid·i·ty** (flə·rid′ə·te), **flor′id·ness** *n.* —**flor′id·ly** *adv.*

Flor·i·da (flôr′ə·də, flor′-) The southernmost Atlantic State of the United States; 58,560 square miles; capital, Tallahassee; entered the Union March 3, 1845: nickname, *Everglade State.* Abbr. FL —**Flo·rid·i·an** (flô·rid′ē·ən, flō-, flo-), **Flor·i·dan** (flôr′-, flor′-) *adj. & n.*

Florida Keys A chain of islands curving 150 miles SW around the tip of the Florida peninsula from Virginia Key to Key West.

Florida moss Spanish moss.

Florida, Straits of A passage separating the southern tip of Florida from the Bahamas and Cuba.

flo·rif·er·ous (flô·rif′ər·əs, flō-) *adj.* Bearing flowers. [< L *florifer* bearing flowers + -OUS]

flor·in (flôr′in, flor′in) *n.* **1** The unit of value of the Netherlands: also called *guilder.* **2** A British silver coin, equal to one tenth of a pound, or two shillings. **3** A gold coin first issued in England in 1343. **4** A coin first issued by Florence, made of gold, and weighing about 54 grains: also **flor′ence.** **5** Any of several ancient coins of England, Tuscany, Germany, etc. [< OF < Ital. *fiorino* < *fiore* a flower; so called from the figure of a lily stamped on it]

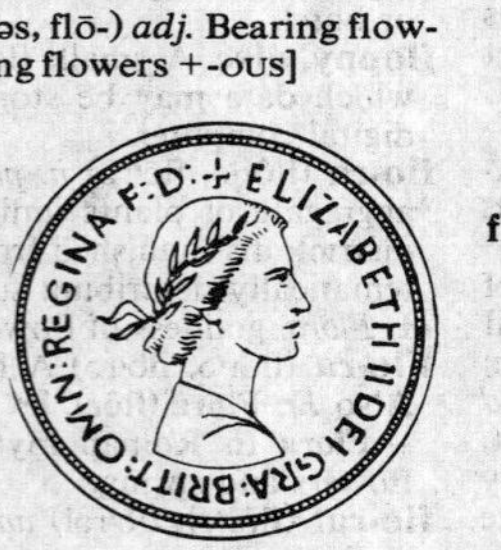

FLORIN
(Obverse)

Flo·ri·o (flôr′ē·ō, flō′rē·ō), **John,** 1553?–1625, English writer; translator of Montaigne's *Essays.*

flo·rist (flôr′ist, flō′rist, flor′ist) *n.* A grower of or dealer in flowers.

-florous *combining form Bot.* Having (a specified number, kind, etc., of) flowers: *uniflorous.* [< L *-florus* < *flos, floris* a flower]

flo·ru·it (flôr′yōō·it, flō′rōō·it) *Latin* He (or she) flourished.

flos fer·ri (flos′ fer′ī) A variety of aragonite, suggesting coral. [< L, flower of iron]

floss¹ (flôs, flos) *n.* **1** Floss silk. **2** The silk of some plants, as Indian corn. **3** The stray silk on the outside of cocoons of silkworms and of spiders. **4** A flossy surface; fluff. [< OF *flosche*]

floss² (flôs, flos) *n. Metall.* A slag that floats on molten metal. [< G *flosz*]

Flos·sie (flôs′ē, flos′ē) Diminutive of FLORENCE.

floss silk A soft, downy silk fiber suitable for embroidery.

floss·y (flôs′ē, flos′ē) *adj.* **floss·i·er, floss·i·est** **1** Of, pertaining to, or like floss; light; downy. **2** *Colloq.* Elegant; fine; beautiful.

flo·tage (flō′tij) *n.* **1** Things that float, collectively. **2** The capacity of anything to buoy up or to float. Also spelled *floatage.*

flo·ta·tion (flō·tā′shən) *n.* **1** The act or state of floating. **2** The science of bodies that float. **3** The act of floating or financing, as of an issue of bonds, etc., by bankers. **4** *Metall.* A method of separating pulverized ores by placing them in a froth of oils and chemicals in water, and applying a current of air so that the valuable ore particles float on or adhere to the surface. Also spelled *floatation.*

flotation gear *Aeron.* A buoyant apparatus attached to an aircraft to enable it to float when forced to alight on water.

flo·til·la (flō·til′ə) *n.* **1** A fleet of small vessels; a small fleet. **2** In the U.S. Navy, an organized group of destroyers, composed of two or more squadrons. **3** In the U.S. Army, a seagoing unit for laying mines. [< Sp., dim. of *flota* a fleet]

Flo·tow (flō′tō), **Friedrich von,** 1812–83, German opera composer.

flot·sam (flot′səm) *n.* **1** *Law* Goods cast or swept from a vessel into the sea and found floating. Compare JETSAM, LAGAN. **2** Any objects floating on the sea. **3** Hence, vagrants or unattached persons: the *flotsam* of society. Also spelled **flot′san** (-sən), **flot′son.** [< AF *floteson* < *floter* float < OE *flotian*]

flounce¹ (flouns) *n.* A gathered or plaited strip on a skirt. —*v.t.* **flounced, flounc·ing** To furnish with flounces. [Var. of FROUNCE]

flounce² (flouns) *v.i.* **flounced, flounc·ing** **1** To move or go with exaggerated tosses of the body, as in anger or petulance. **2** To plunge; founder: said of animals. —*n.* The act of flouncing; a fling. [< Scand. Cf. dial. Sw. *flunsa* plunge.]

flounc·ing (floun′sing) *n.* Material for flounces; also, flounces collectively.

floun·der¹ (floun′dər) *v.i.* **1** To struggle clumsily; move awkwardly as if mired or injured. **2** To proceed, as in speech or action, in a clumsy or confused manner; muddle. —*n.* A stumbling or struggling motion. [? Blend of FLOUNCE² and FOUNDER²]—**floun′der·ing·ly** *adv.*

floun·der² (floun′dər) *n.* **1** One of certain species of flatfish, valued as a food fish; especially, the winter flounder *(Pseudopleuronectes americanus)* of the North Atlantic coast, and the California flounder *(Platichthys stellatus).* **2** Any of several flat fish other than sole. [< AF *floundre,* prob. < Scand. Cf. Sw. *flundra.*]

flour (flour) *n.* **1** The ground and bolted substance of wheat. **2** The finely ground particles of any specified cereal: rye *flour.* **3** Any finely powdered substance. **4** Loose, finely crystallized saltpeter, used in making gunpowder. —*v.t.* **1** To make into flour; pulverize, as wheat. **2** *Metall.* To break up into minute particles: to *flour* mercury in the amalgamating process. **3** To sprinkle or cover with flour. [Var. of FLOWER]—**flour′y** *adj.*

flour·ish (flûr′ish) *v.i.* **1** To grow or fare well or prosperously; thrive. **2** To be at the peak of success or development; be at the height or in the prime: Alchemy *flourished* in the Middle Ages. **3** To move with sweeping motions; be displayed or waved about: Swords *flourished* in the air. **4** To write with sweeping or ornamental strokes. **5** *Music* **a** To play a showy passage. **b** To sound a fanfare. **6** *Obs.* To blossom. —*v.t.* **7** To wave about or brandish; flaunt, as a weapon or flag. **8** To embellish, as with ornamental lines or figures. —*n.* **1** An ornamental mark or design, especially a sweeping stroke, as in writing or embroidery; anything done for display alone. **2** The act of brandishing or waving. **3** A musical passage for display; fanfare. See synonyms under OSTENTATION. [< OF *floriss-,* stem of *florir* < L *florere* bloom]—**flour′ish·er** *n.* —**flour′ish·ing** *adj.* —**flour′ish·ing·ly** *adv.*

Synonyms (verb): advance, blossom, flower, gain, grow, increase, prosper, thrive. See FLAUNT, GAIN¹, SUCCEED. *Antonyms:* see synonyms for FALL.

flout (flout) *v.t.* To show or express scorn or contempt for; scoff at. —*v.i.* To express one's contempt; mock; jeer. See synonyms under MOCK. —*n.* A gibe; scoff; mockery. [Prob. ME *flouten* play the flute, deride]—**flout′er** *n.* —**flout′ing·ly** *adv.*

flow (flō) *v.i.* **1** To move along in a stream, as water or other fluid. **2** To move along, as with the qualities of a liquid: The crowd *flowed* through the gates. **3** To stream forth; proceed from a source. **4** To move with continuity and pleasing rhythm, as verse or music. **5** To fall or lie in waves, as garments or hair. **6** To be full or too full; abound; overflow: The creeks are *flowing* with gold. **7** To come in or rise, as the tide: opposed to ebb. —*v.t.* **8** To flood; inundate. **9** *Obs.* To cause to flow. —*n.* **1** The act of flowing, or that which flows; also, a continuous stream or current. **2** The incoming of the tide. **3** The quantity, as of water, that passes through an orifice or by a given point in a given time. **4** A copious outpouring. **5** Any easy, gentle movement, as of speech. ◆Homophone: *floe.* [OE *flowan*]—**flow′ing** *adj. & n.* —**flow′ing·ly** *adv.* —**flow′ing·ness** *n.*

flow·age (flō′ij) *n.* **1** The act of flowing or overflowing, or the state of being overflowed. **2** Liquid which flows or overflows. **3** *Physics* Deformation of a solid body by intermolecular movement like that of a viscous fluid: distinguished from or opposed to *fracture.*

flow·chart (flō′chärt′) *n.* A diagram showing all the steps in a logical sequence, as in a computer program.

flow·er (flou′ər, flour) *n.* **1** *Bot.* **a** The organ, or the combination of organs of reproduction in a plant; blossom; bloom. **b** In mosses, the reproductive organs with their enveloped or associated leaves. **2** A blooming plant. **3** The brightest, finest, choicest part, period, or specimen of anything. **4** Any flower-like ornament. **5** A flowery figure of speech. **6** *pl.* A very light powder obtained by sublimation and usually a metallic oxide: *flowers* of antimony; flour (def. 3). —*v.i.* **1** To put forth blossoms; bloom. **2** To come to full development; be at the full: The Renaissance *flowered* in Italy. —*v.t.* **3** To decorate with flowers or a floral pattern. [< OF *flour, flor* < L *flos, floris* a flower]—**flow′er·er** *n.* —**flow′er·less** *adj.* —**flow′er·y** *adj.* —**flow′er·i·ly** *adv.* —**flow′er·i·ness** *n.*

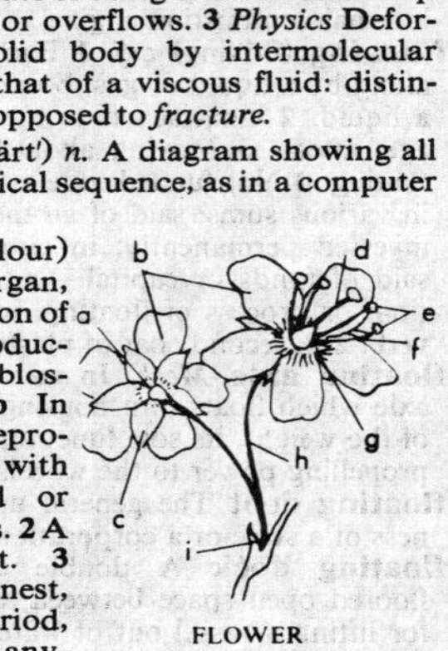

FLOWER
a. Calyx. *e.* Pollen.
b. Petal. *f.* Stamen.
c. Sepal. *g.* Corolla.
d. Pistil. *h.* Pedicel.
i. Bract.

flow·er·age (flou′ər·ij, flou′rij) *n.* **1** The act or state of flowering. **2** An ornamentation of flowers, or flowers collectively.

flower bed A plot of ground in which flowers are planted.

flow·er-de-luce (flou′ər·də·lōōs′, flour′-) *n. pl.* **flow·ers-de-luce** A flower of the iris variety. FLEUR-DE-LIS.

flow·er·et (flou′ər·it, flou′rit) *n.* A small flower, or a floret.

flower girl **1** A girl who sells flowers. **2** A small girl who carries flowers before the bride in a wedding procession.

flower head *Bot.* A dense headlike cluster of sessile florets.

flowering maple A plant *(Abutilon striatum)* with maplelike leaves and orange flowers veined in dark crimson: also called *redvein maple.*

flow·er-of-an-hour (flou′ər·uv·ən·our′, flour′-) *n.* The bladder ketmia.

flower pot A pot for holding growing plants.

flowers of benzoin See BENZOIN¹.

flow·me·ter (flō′mē′tər) *n.* An apparatus designed to measure the rate of flow of a liquid or a gas through any part of a transmitting system.
flown[1] (flōn) Past participle of FLY[1].
flown[2] (flōn) *adj.* **1** Coated, as a glaze, with color freely blended or flowed. **2** Eased off; slack, as a sheet. [< obs. pp. of FLOW]
flow relay *Electr.* A relay circuit adjusted to operate under specified conditions of flow in a gas or liquid.
flow-sheet (flō′shēt′) *n.* A diagram, chart, or expository outline showing the successive operations through which material progresses in a manufacturing process.
Floyd (floid) A masculine personal name. [< Welsh, gray]
flu (flōō) *n. Colloq.* Influenza: a contraction.
flub (flub) *U.S. Colloq. v.t. & v.i.* **flubbed, flub·bing** To do or manage (something) badly; botch or bungle: to *flub* one's chance. —*n.* A blunder; failure. [Origin unknown]
flub·dub (flub′dub) *n.* **1** Drivel; twaddle; flapdoodle. **2** *Printing* An insignificant stock ornament. [Imit.] **—flub·dub′ber·y** *n.*
fluc·tu·ant (fluk′chōō·ənt) *adj.* **1** Showing fluctuation. **2** Moving or shaped like a wave.
fluc·tu·ate (fluk′chōō·āt) *v.* **·at·ed, ·at·ing** *v.i.* **1** To change or vary often and in an irregular manner; waver; be unsteady. **2** To move with successive rise and fall; undulate. —*v.t.* **3** To cause to fluctuate. [< L *fluctuatus,* pp. of *fluctuare* wave < *fluctus* a wave < *fluere* flow] **—fluc′tu·a·bil′i·ty** *n.* **—fluc′tu·a·ble** *adj.*
Synonyms: hesitate, oscillate, swerve, undulate, vacillate, vary, veer, waver. To *fluctuate* is to move like a wave with alternate rise and fall. A pendulum *oscillates;* waves *fluctuate* or *undulate;* a light or a flame *wavers;* a frightened steed *swerves* from his course; a tool or weapon *swerves* from the mark or line; the temperature *varies;* the wind *veers* when it suddenly changes its direction. That which *veers* may steadily hold the new direction; that which *oscillates, fluctuates, undulates,* or *wavers* returns upon its way. As regards mental states, he who *hesitates* sticks (L *haerere*) on the verge of decision; he who *wavers* does not stick to a decision; he who *vacillates* decides now one way, and now another; one *vacillates* between contrasted decisions or actions; he may *waver* between decision and indecision, or between action and inaction. Persons *hesitate, vacillate, waver;* feelings *fluctuate* or *vary.* Compare SHAKE. *Antonyms*: abide, adhere, persist.
fluc·tu·a·tion (fluk′chōō·ā′shən) *n.* **1** Frequent irregular change; varying movement or action. **2** A rising and falling, as of prices. **3** *Biol.* A variation in an organism which is not inherited.
flue[1] (flōō) *n.* **1** A channel or passage for smoke, air, or gases of combustion; a chimney. **2** An organ pipe of flute or diapason quality. **3** Any of several types of fishing nets. Also spelled *flew.* [Origin uncertain]
flue[2] (flōō) *n.* Any fine, flocklike refuse of wool or the like; lint; down. [< Flemish *vluwe* down]
flue[3] (flōō) *n.* A fluke; barb, as of a harpoon, feather, or anchor. [Cf. Sw. *fly*]
flue gas The by-product of combustion in a heating system, consisting mostly of nitrogen, with varying proportions of carbon dioxide, oxygen, and, under improper conditions, carbon monoxide.
flu·ent (flōō′ənt) *adj.* **1** Ready in speaking or writing; voluble; copious. **2** Marked by fluency; flowing; smooth. **3** Flowing freely; mobile; changeable. [< L *fluens, -entis,* ppr. of *fluere* flow] **—flu′en·cy** (-sē), **flu′ent·ness** *n.* **—flu′ent·ly** *adv.*
flue pipe *Music* An organ pipe in which the tone is produced by a current of air striking an aperture or flue.
flue stop *Music* A stop controlling the flue pipes of an organ.
flue·y (flōō′ē) *adj.* Containing or like flue or lint; downy; fluffy.
fluff[1] (fluf) *n.* **1** Nap or down. **2** Anything downy or fluffy. **3** *Colloq.* An error made in reading or speaking (lines): said of actors, etc. —*v.t.* **1** To shake or pound so as to cause to puff out and become fluffy. **2** *Colloq.* To make an error in reading or speaking (lines). —*v.i.* **3** To become fluffy. **4** *Colloq.* To make a fluff (def. 3). [? Blend of FLUE[2] + PUFF]
fluff[2] (fluf) *n.* A flash, as of loose powder; puff. [Imit.]
fluff·y (fluf′ē) *adj.* **fluff·i·er, fluff·i·est** Downy; feathery. **—fluff′i·ly** *adv.* **—fluff′i·ness** *n.*
fluffy glider A flying phalanger *(Petaurus australis)* of Australia: also called *yellow-bellied glider.*
Flü·gel·horn (flōō′gəl·hôrn′, *Ger.* flü′gəl·hôrn′) *n.* A brass wind instrument similar in pitch and design to a cornet yet mellower in tone. [< G *flügel* wing + *horn* a horn; so called from its shape]
flu·id (flōō′id) *adj.* Capable of flowing; liquid or gaseous. —*n.* A substance that yields to any force tending to change its form; a liquid or gas. [< F *fluide* < L *fluidus* < *fluere* flow] **—flu·id′ic** *adj.* **—flu·id′i·ty, flu′id·ness** *n.* **—flu′id·ly** *adv.*
Synonyms (noun): gas, liquid. In comparison with the substance, *fluid,* a *liquid* is a body in a state in which the particles move freely among themselves, but remain in one mass, keeping the same volume, but taking always the form of the containing vessel; a *liquid* is an inelastic *fluid;* a gas is an elastic *fluid* that tends to expand to the utmost limits of the containing space. All *liquids* are *fluids,* but not all *fluids* are *liquids;* air and all the *gases* are *fluids,* but they are not *liquids* under ordinary circumstances, even if capable of being reduced to a *liquid* form by special means, as by cold and pressure. Water at the ordinary temperature is at once a *fluid* and a *liquid. Antonym*: solid.
fluid dram or **drachm** See under DRAM.
fluid drive An automobile transmission in which a driving rotor, turning in oil, transmits driving force to a driven rotor by forcing it to rotate in response to the action of the oil: usually automatically operated. Also called *hydraulic transmission.*
flu·id·ex·tract (flōō′id·eks′trakt) *n.* A solution in alcohol of the active principle of a vegetable drug so prepared that 1 cubic centimeter has the strength of 1 gram of the dry drug.
fluid ounce See under OUNCE (def. 1).
fluid pressure See under PRESSURE.
flu·i·dram (flōō′i·dram′) See FLUID DRAM under DRAM. Also **flu′i·drachm′.**
fluid wax Any liquid wax obtained from the oils of marine animals.
fluke[1] (flŏŏk) *n.* **1** *Naut.* The part of an anchor that holds to the ground. **2** One of the lobes of the tail of a whale. **3** A barb on a harpoon, arrow, etc. [? < FLUKE[2]]

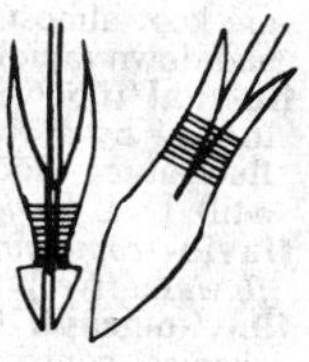
FLUKE[1] *(def. 3)*

fluke[2] (flŏŏk) *n.* **1** A leaflike, parasitic, trematode worm infesting sheep, and also man and other animals: also called **fluke worm. 2** A flatfish or flounder. [OE *flōc*]
fluke[3] (flŏŏk) *n.* **1** A lucky stroke or accident, as in billiards, etc. **2** *Colloq.* An accidental failure or disappointment, as from a capricious wind in sailing. [Origin unknown]
fluk·y (flōō′kē) *adj.* **fluk·i·er, fluk·i·est 1** Occurring by lucky chance. **2** Variable; capricious, as wind. Also **fluk′ey.**
flume (flōōm) *n.* **1** A conduit, as for a millwheel. **2** A narrow passage through which a torrent passes. **3** A chute. —*v.t.* **flumed, flum·ing 1** To drain away or divert by means of a water chute or conduit, as in mining. **2** To move or transport, as logs, by means of a flume. See synonyms under STREAM. [< OF *flum* < L *flumen* river < *fluere* flow]
flu·mi·nous (flōō′mə·nəs) *adj.* Of or pertaining to rivers; watered by streams. [< L *flumen, -inis* a river]
flum·mer·y (flum′er·ē) *n. pl.* **·mer·ies 1** A light dish made of flour or cornstarch; blanc-mange. **2** A glutinous refuse product of the manufacture of wheat starch. **3** Originally, a dish of oatmeal steeped in water and turned sour; pap. **4** Hence, anything vapid or insipid; empty compliment; flimsy show; humbug. [< Welsh *llymru*]
flum·mox (flum′əks) *v.t. Slang* To confuse; confound; perplex. [Cf. dial. E *flummocks* maul, mangle]
flump (flump) *v.t. & v.i. Colloq.* To drop heavily and clumsily; flop. —*n.* The act of flumping or the sound so produced. [Imit.]
flung (flung) Past tense and past participle of FLING.
flunk (flungk) *U.S. Colloq. v.t.* **1** To fail in, as an examination. **2** To give a failing grade to. —*v.i.* **3** To fail, as in an examination. **4** To back out; give up. **—to flunk out** To leave or cause to leave a class, school, or college because of failure in studies. —*n.* A complete failure; a giving up. [? Blend of FLINCH and FUNK]
flunk·y (flung′kē) *n. pl.* **flunk·ies 1** An obsequious fellow; servile imitator; toady. **2** A servant in livery. Also **flunk′ey.** [? Alter. of *flanker* < FLANK, *v.*] **—flunk′y·ism** *n.*
fluo- See FLUORO-.
flu·o·bo·rate (flōō′ō·bôr′āt, -bō′rāt) *n. Chem.* **1** The negative ion BO_2Fe_2. **2** Any compound containing this ion.
flu·o·phos·phate (flōō′ō·fos′fāt) *n. Chem.* A double salt of hydrofluoric and phosphoric acids.
flu·or (flōō′ər, -ôr) *n.* Fluorite. [< NL < L, a flowing < *fluere* flow; a trans. of G *flusse*]
fluor- Var. of FLUORO-.
flu·or·an (flōō′ə·ran) *n. Chem.* A crystalline anhydride, $C_{20}H_{12}O_3$, fluorescing in solution, formed as a by-product in making phenolphthalein. Also **flu′or·ane** (-ə·rān).
flu·or·ap·a·tite (flōō′ə·rap′ə·tīt) *n.* Apatite in which fluorine but little or no chlorine is present.
flu·o·rate (flōō′ə·rāt, -rit) *n. Chem.* **1** The negative ion FO_3. **2** Any compound containing this ion.
flu·o·resce (flōō′ə·res′) *v.i.* **·resced, ·resc·ing** To become fluorescent; exhibit fluorescence. [Back formation < FLUORESCENCE]
flu·o·res·ce·in (flōō′ə·res′ē·in) *n. Chem.* A darkred crystalline compound, $C_{20}H_{12}O_5$, obtained by heating phthalic anhydride, and subsequent separation: used in medicine and in the making of dyestuffs. Also **flu′o·res′ce·ine** (-ēn).
flu·o·res·cence (flōō′ə·res′əns) *n. Physics* **1** The property of certain substances to absorb radiation of a particular wavelength and to re-emit it as light of a different, usually greater, wavelength; the emitted radiation persists only as long as the stimulus is active: distinguished from *phosphorescence.* **2** The light so produced. [< FLUOR(SPAR); coined on analogy with OPALESCENCE]
flu·o·res·cent (flōō′ə·res′ənt) *adj.* Having or exhibiting fluorescence.
fluorescent lamp An electric-discharge lamp, usually tubular in shape, containing a metallic vapor which becomes luminous on the passing of the current and energizes a layer of fluorescent material coating the tube.
fluorescent screen A surface of glass coated with a fluorescent material, as platinocyanide; it fluoresces on exposure to electron bombardment and is used in cathode-ray vacuum tubes.
flu·or·ic (flōō·ôr′ik, -or′-) *adj.* Pertaining to, derived from, or containing fluorine or fluorite.
fluor·i·date (flŏŏr′ə·dāt, flōō′ə·ri·dāt) *v.t.* **·dat·ed, ·dat·ing** To add sodium fluoride to (drinking water), especially as a means of preventing tooth decay. **—fluor′i·da′tion** *n.*
flu·o·ride (flōō′ə·rīd, -rid) *n. Chem.* A binary compound of fluorine and another element. Also **flu′o·rid** (-rid).
fluor·i·dize (flŏŏr′ə·dīz, flōō′ə·ri·dīz) *v.t.* **·dized, ·diz·ing** To treat (teeth) with a fluoride, especially as a preventive of tooth decay. **—fluor′i·di·za′tion** *n.*
flu·o·rim·e·ter (flōō′ə·rim′ə·tər) *n. Physics* An absorbing screen used to measure the intensity of fluorescence from different sources, as X-rays, radium, etc.
flu·o·ri·na·tion (flōō′ər·i·nā′shən, flŏŏr′ə–) *n.* The act or process of introducing fluorine into an organic compound.
flu·o·rine (flōō′ə·rēn, -rin) *n.* A pale yellow, toxic, corrosive gaseous element (symbol F, atomic number 9), the most electronegative and reactive of all elements. See PERIODIC TABLE.

flu·o·rite (flo͞o'ə·rīt) *n.* A cleavable, isometric, variously colored calcium fluoride, CaF_2: used as a flux in making steel and glass: also called *fluor, fluorspar.*

fluoro- *combining form* **1** *Chem.* Indicating the presence of fluorine in a compound. **2** Fluorescence: *fluoroscope*: also, before vowels, *fluor-*, as in *fluoride.*

flu·o·ro·car·bon (flo͞o'ə·rō·kär'bən) *n. Chem.* Any of a group of very stable compounds in which hydrogen has been replaced by fluorine: used as solvents, lubricants, and insulators.

flu·o·ro·chem·i·cal (flo͞o'ə·rō·kem'ə·kəl) *n.* Any of various chemicals containing fluorine, as the fluorocarbons.

flu·o·rom·e·try (flo͞o'ə·rom'ə·trē) *n.* The measurement of the color and intensity of fluorescence.

fluor·o·scope (flo͝or'ə·skōp, flo͞o'ər·ə-) *n.* A device for observing, by means of some fluorescent substance, the shadows of objects enclosed in media opaque to ordinary light, but transparent to X-rays. **—fluor'o·scop'ic** (-skop'ik) *adj.*

fluor·os·co·py (flo͝or·os'kə·pē, flo͞o'ə·ros'-) *n.* Examination conducted by means of a fluoroscope.

flu·or·o·sis (flo͞o'ə·rō'sis, flo͞o·rō'-) *n. Pathol.* Chronic poisoning with fluorine.

flu·or·spar (flo͞o'ôr·spär', flo͞o'ər-) *n.* Fluorite.

flu·o·sil·i·cate (flo͞o'ə·sil'ə·kāt, -kit) *n. Chem.* A salt of silicic acid.

flu·o·si·lic·ic (flo͞o'ə·sə·lis'ik) *adj.* **1** Of, pertaining to, or containing fluorine and silicon. **2** Designating a colorless suffocating gaseous compound, **fluosilicic acid,** H_2SiF_6, formed by the action of hydrofluoric acid on silica.

flur·ry (flûr'ē) *v.* **·ried, ·ry·ing** *v.t.* To bewilder or confuse; agitate; fluster. *—v.i.* To move in a flurry. [< *n.*] *—n. pl.* **flur·ries 1** A sudden commotion; nervous agitation. **2** Flutter; hurry. **3** A light gust of wind. **4** A light snowfall or rain. **5** The spasmodic contortions of a dying whale. See synonyms under TUMULT. [Blend of FLUTTER and HURRY]

flush[1] (flush) *v.i.* **1** To become red in the face or overspread with color; redden; blush. **2** To flow and spread suddenly; rush: The blood *flushes* in his veins. **3** To be washed out or cleansed by a sudden flow of water. *—v.t.* **4** To cause to color, as with a rush of blood; make red or florid. **5** To encourage; excite: *flushed* with victory. **6** To wash out by a flow of water, as a sewer or an obstacle. *—n.* **1** A heightened color; warm glow; blush. **2** Sudden elation or excitement. **3** A sudden blossoming out; growth; bloom. **4** A sudden gush or flow of water. *—adj.* **1** Full of life; vigorous. **2** Powerful and direct, as a blow. *—adv.* In a direct manner; squarely; straight. [? <FLUSH[4]; infl. in meaning by *flash, flow, bluish,* etc.] **—flush'er** *n.*

flush[2] (flush) *adj.* **1** Having the surfaces in the same plane; level. **2** *Printing* Set even with the left edge of the type page; having no indention. **3** *Naut.* Of or pertaining to a ship with an upper deck extending in one level from stern to stern. **4** Full; copious. **5** Well supplied with money; spending freely. *—v.t.* To make level or straight. *—n.* **1** A level or unbroken surface. **2** Abundance. *—adv.* **1** With level, unbroken surface or form. **2** *Printing* Without indention; straight. [? <FLUSH[1]]

flush[3] (flush) *n.* In some card games, a hand of cards all of one color; specifically, in poker, of one suit. **—royal flush** A hand of cards containing the ace, king, queen, jack, and ten of one suit. **—straight flush** A poker hand having all the cards of the same suit and in sequence. [Cf. F *flux, flus* <L *fluxus* A flow]

flush[4] (flush) *v.t. & v.i.* To drive or to be startled from cover; start up, as birds. *—n.* The act of startling a bird; also a bird or birds startled from cover. [ME *flusschen;* origin uncertain]

flush·board (flush'bôrd', -bōrd') *n.* A flashboard.

Flush·ing (flush'ing) **1** A port in SW Netherlands, on the English Channel: Dutch *Vlissingen.* **2** A section of the Borough of Queens, New York City, including **Flushing Meadow,** site of the 1939–40 World's Fair and headquarters of the United Nations, 1946–51.

flus·ter (flus'tər) *v.t. & v.i.* To make or become confused, agitated, or befuddled. *—n.* Confusion of mind; flurry; intoxication. [Cf. Icel. *flaustr* hurry]

flus·trate (flus'trāt) *v.t.* **·trat·ed, ·trat·ing** To fluster; befuddle. Also **flus'ter·ate.** [<FLUSTER + -ATE[1]] **—flus'ter·a'tion, flus·tra'tion** *n.*

flute (flo͞ot) *n.* **1** A tubular wind instrument of small diameter with holes along the side. **2** A flute stop in an organ; flue. **3** *Archit.* A groove, usually of semicircular section, as in a column. **4** A corrugation; crimping. **5** A tall, slender wineglass. *—v.* **flut·ed, flut·ing.** *—v.i.* **1** To play on a flute. **2** To produce a flutelike sound. *—v.t.* **3** To sing or utter with flutelike tones. **4** To make flutes in, as a column. [<OF *flaüte*] **—flut'y** *adj.*

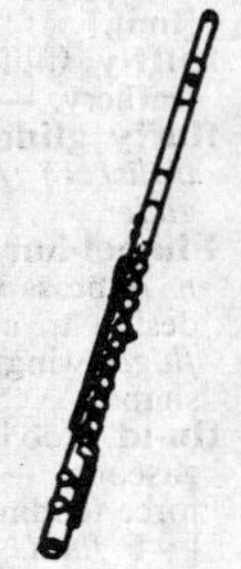

FLUTE

flut·ed (flo͞o'tid) *adj.* **1** Having parallel grooves or flutes. **2** Having the tone of a flute.

flut·er (flo͞o'tər) *n.* **1** A flutist. **2** One who or that which makes fluted work.

flut·ing (flo͞o'ting) *n.* **1** A flute or groove. **2** Flutes or grooves collectively. **3** The act of making a flute, as by carving a column: the reverse of *reeding.* **4** A crimp, as in the ruffle of a woman's dress.

flut·ist (flo͞o'tist) *n.* A flute-player: also called *flautist.*

flut·ter (flut'ər) *v.i.* **1** To wave or flap rapidly and irregularly, as in the wind. **2** To flap the wings rapidly, in or as in erratic flight. **3** To move or proceed with irregular motion: to *flutter* to the ground. **4** To move about lightly and quickly; flit. **5** To be excited or nervous, as with hope, fear, or expectation. *—v.t.* **6** To cause to flutter. **7** To excite; fluster. See synonyms under SHAKE. *—n.* **1** The act of vibrating or quivering. **2** Agitation; confused or tumultous emotion. **3** An up-and-down motion of the feet used in various swimming strokes, especially the crawl. **4** *Aeron.* A periodic oscillation set up in any part of an airplane by mechanical disturbances and maintained by inertia, structural characteristics, etc. **5** Tremololike pulsations in the sound track of a motion picture, due to rapid fluctuations in motor speed. **6** *Pathol.* An abnormally rapid but rhythmical contraction of the atria of the heart; also **auricular flutter.** [OE *flotorian*] **—flut'ter·er** *n.* **—flut'ter·y** *adj.*

flutter kick In swimming, a kick, usually performed with the crawl stroke, in which the legs are kept almost straight while being moved up and down rapidly.

flu·vi·al (flo͞o'vē·əl) *adj.* **1** Of, pertaining to or formed by a river. **2** Existing in a river. Also **flu·vi·at·ic** (flo͞o'vē·at'ik), **flu·vi·a·tile** (flo͞o'vē·ə·til). [<L *fluvialis* <*fluvius* river]

fluvio- *combining form* River: *fluviograph.* [<L *fluvius* a river]

flu·vi·o·graph (flo͞o'vē·ə·graf', -gräf') *n.* A mechanical contrivance for measuring the rise and fall of a river.

flu·vi·o·ma·rine (flo͞o'vē·ō'mə·rēn') *adj.* Formed by or pertaining to the joint action of the sea and flowing streams, as delta deposits.

flux (fluks) *n.* **1** A continuous flowing or discharge: a thermal or electrical *flux.* **2** The act or process of melting. **3** *Pathol.* A morbid discharge of fluid matter from the body. **4** *Metall.* A substance that promotes the fusing of minerals or metals, as borax. **5** Any readily fusible glass or enamel used as a base or ground in ceramic work. **6** *Physics* The rate of flow or transfer of water, heat, electricity, etc. **7** A state of constant movement: the *flux* of the tide. See synonyms under STREAM. **—bloody flux** Dysentery. *—v.t.* **1** To make fluid; melt; fuse. **2** To treat, as metal, with a flux. **3** *Obs.* To purge. *—v.i.* **4** *Obs.* To flow; move. [<F <L *fluxus* <*fluere* flow] **—flux·a'tion** *n.*

flux density *Physics* The induction of lines of electrical or magnetic force per unit section.

flux·ion (fluk'shən) *n.* **1** The act of flowing or melting; that which flows or melts; continuous change. **2** *Math. Obs.* The rate of variation of a changing quantity; also, a differential. **3** *Pathol.* An abnormal or excessive flow of body fluids.

flux·ion·al (fluk'shən·əl) *adj.* **1** *Obs.* Of or pertaining to mathematical fluxions. **2** *Obs.* Of a nature to flow. Also **flux'ion·ar'y.** **—flux'·ion·al·ly** *adv.*

fly[1] (flī) *v.* **flew** or **flied** (def. 7), **flown, fly·ing** *v.i.* **1** To move through the air by using wings, as a bird. **2** To move through the air in an aircraft; travel by aircraft. **3** To move through the air with speed, as an arrow or bullet. **4** To wave or move in the air, as a flag. **5** To pass swiftly: The years *flew* by. **6** To move swiftly or with violence: The door *flew* open. **7** In baseball, to bat a fly. **8** To take flight; flee. **9** In hawking, to hunt with or as with a hawk. *—v.t.* **10** To cause to wave or float in the air. **11** To operate (an aircraft). **12** To pass over in an aircraft: to *fly* the Atlantic. **13** To transport by aircraft. **14** To flee from. **15** In hawking, to hunt with a hawk. **—to fly at** To attack. **—to fly in the face of** To defy openly. **—to fly out** In baseball, to be retired by batting a ball which is caught by an opposing player before it touches the ground. *—n. pl.* **flies. 1** An object or device that moves or swings rapidly through the air, or has some relation to such motion. **2** A speed-regulating device, as of vanes upon a rotating shaft, used in music boxes, in the striking part of clocks. **3** *Printing* A long-fingered frame oscillating quickly upon a horizontal axis, taking the sheets from the tapes or cylinder of a printing press and delivering them flat upon a pile. **4** A knitting-machine latch. **5** The length of a flag measured from the staff to its farthest edge, as distinguished from the *hoist.* **6** That part of a flag farthest from the staff, or beyond the canton. **7** The revolving part of a vane that shows the direction of the wind. **8** *Mech.* **a** A flywheel, a weighted arm, or other mechanical device involving the flywheel principle. **b** The heavily weighted lever which enables a fly press to acquire momentum. **c** A fly press. **9** A strip or lap on a garment, to cover the buttons or other fasteners; hence, something used to cover or connect; a flap, as of a bootee. **10** An upper covering to a ridge-pole tent; also, the flap at the entrance of a tent. **11** The condition or movement of a ball when sent flying through the air as in baseball; also, the ball thus flying. **12** Waste cotton. **13** The act or state of flying; flight. **14** A public carriage; also, a delivery wagon. **15** In a theater, the space above the stage and behind the proscenium containing the borders, the mechanism for handling and setting the scenery, the overhead lights, etc. **—on the fly** While flying; while in the air; in haste. [OE *flēogan*]

Synonyms (verb): flee, flit, haste, hasten, run, soar, speed. See ESCAPE.

fly[2] (flī) *n. pl.* **flies 1** One of various small dipterous insects (family *Muscidae*), especially the common housefly *(Musca domestica).* **2** Any of various other flying insects not of the family *Muscidae*: the Spanish *fly,* or the *mayfly.* **3** A fish hook concealed by feathers, etc., to imitate some insect. **4** *pl.* **flys** A light carriage. [OE *flȳge*]

fly[3] (flī) *adj. Slang* Sharp; wide-awake.

fly·a·gar·ic (flī'ə·gar'ik, -ag'ə·rik) *n.* A common species of poisonous mushroom *(Amanita muscaria)* with a brightly colored pileus. Also **fly-am·a·ni·ta** (-am'ə·nī'tə).

fly·a·way (flī'ə·wā') *adj.* Disposed to flightiness; fluttering; restless; giddy. *—n.* A person or thing that is flighty, swift, or elusive.

fly·blow (flī'blō') *n.* The egg or young larva of a blowfly. *—v.t. & v.t.* **·blew, ·blown, ·blow·ing 1** To taint (food) with flyblows. **2** To spoil.

fly·blown (flī'blōn') *adj.* Tainted with flyblows.

fly·boat (flī'bōt') *n.* **1** A large flat-bottomed Dutch coasting boat. **2** A narrow English canal boat. **3** Any very swift vessel.

fly book A booklike case for holding artificial flies.

fly-by (flī'bī') *n. pl.* **-bys** The passage of a spacecraft relatively near a heavenly body, as for obtaining photographs of its surface.

fly-by-night (flī'bī·nīt') *adj.* Financially precarious or irresponsible. *—n.* One who is financially insecure or untrustworthy; one who cheats a creditor by decamping at night.

fly·catch·er (flī'kach'ər) *n.* Any of a large order of perching birds *(Passeriformes)* that feed upon insects; especially, the American tyrant flycatcher (family *Tyrannidae*) and the Old World flycatcher (family *Muscicapidae*)–**least flycatcher** A small American flycatcher; the chebec *(Empidonax minimus).*

fly·er (flī'ər) See FLIER.

fly-fish (flī′fish′) *v.i.* To fish with artificial flies as bait. —**fly′-fish′ing** *n.*

fly·flap·per (flī′flap′ər) *n.* A device for whisking flies.

fly-frame (flī′frām′) *n.* Any of several machines used to draw and twist textile fibers preparatory to spinning, as a roving frame.

fly-front (flī′frunt′) *adj.* Having a fly that covers buttons or a zipper.

fly·ing (flī′ing) *adj.* **1** Intended or adapted for swift or easy motion, or motion through the air; moving with or as with wings. **2** Moving rapidly or continuously; hurried: a *flying* bird or trip. **3** Floating or suspended so as to float in the air: a *flying* banner. **4** Extending or being beyond the ordinary; extra: a *flying* jib. —*n.* **1** The act of flight; flight, as of a bird or an aircraft. **2** *pl.* Loose material, as fibers, floating in the air. —**instrument flying** Navigation of an aircraft by means of instruments alone: also called **blind flying.**

flying boat A large seaplane, supported on water by its own hull rather than by floats.

flying bomb See under BOMB.

flying buttress *Archit.* A rampant arch extending from a wall or pier to a supporting abutment, usually receiving the thrust of another arch on the other side of the wall.

flying cadet An aviation cadet.

flying circus 1 In World War I, a squadron of fighter planes. **2** Aerial acrobatics performed by several planes. **3** The group giving such a performance.

flying colors Outward signs of victory or success: an allusion to passing through combat without striking the colors.

flying column *Mil.* A body of troops equipped to move swiftly and operate independently of the main force.

flying doctor *Austral.* A physician serving with the Royal Flying Doctor Service, which since 1928 has been providing medical care in remote inland places.

Flying Dutchman 1 A spectral Dutch ship supposed to be seen near the Cape of Good Hope in stormy weather: an omen of bad luck. **2** The captain of this ship, doomed to sail the seas forever for his sins: subject of an opera (1843) by Richard Wagner.

flying fatigue Aeroneurosis.

flying field *Aeron.* A field with a graded portion for taking off and landing and an unimproved area for flying operations.

flying fish A fish (family *Exocoetidae*) of warm and temperate seas, with large pectoral fins that enable it to glide through the air for short distances.

fly·ing-fox (flī′ing-foks′) *n.* A large fruit-eating bat, especially a genus (*Pteropus*) of the warmer parts of the Old World, with foxlike snout.

flying frog A ranoid tree frog (*Rhacophorus pardalis*) of Borneo, having elongated, webbed toes which serve as supports during leaps.

flying gurnard A marine fish (family *Dactylopteridae*) having very long horizontal pectoral fins divided into a smaller upper and a longer lower or posterior portion and able to flutter for short distances in the air.

flying jib, flying-jib boom See under JIB[1].

flying lemur An insect-eating mammal (genus *Cynocephalus*) having the fore and hind limbs connected by a fold of skin, by the aid of which it makes flying leaps: native of East Indies: also called *colugo.*

flying lizard A dragon (def. 6).

flying machine 1 An aircraft which is sustained by aerodynamic forces; an airplane. **2** An airship.

fly·ing-mare (flī′ing-mâr′) *n.* In wrestling, a throw accomplished by seizing an opponent's wrist, turning around and jerking the opponent over one's shoulder.

flying officer An officer who belongs to the crew of an aircraft, as a pilot, navigator, bombardier, or the like.

flying phalanger Any of several arboreal marsupials (genera *Acrobates, Petaurus, Schoinobates*) of Australia and New Guinea, having folds of skin along the sides that enable them to make long, gliding leaps. Also called *glider, gliding possum, possum glider.*

flying saucer Any of various oddly shaped objects alleged to have been seen flying at high altitudes; an unidentified flying object (UFO).

flying squirrel A squirrel (genus *Glaucomys*) having on each side a fold of skin forming a parachute, by the help of which the animal can make long sailing leaps.

flying start 1 In racing, the passing of the starting post at full speed. **2** Any rapid beginning.

flying trip A quick, hurried trip.

flying wing 1 An airplane without a fuselage. **2** *Canadian* In football, a player whose position varies behind the line of scrimmage.

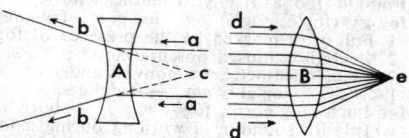

FLYING SQUIRREL
(Head and body about 5 inches long; tail, 4 inches)

fly·leaf (flī′lēf′) *n. pl.* **·leaves** A blank leaf at the beginning or end of a book, pamphlet, or similar printed matter.

fly·net (flī′net′) *n.* **1** A net worn by horses to keep off flies. **2** Any netting, as in a window, for excluding insects.

fly-o·ver (flī′ō′vər) *n.* A public display of military aircraft as a demonstration of strength, variety of types, and maneuverability; a military air show. Also **fly′-past** (-past′).

fly·pa·per (flī′pā′pər) *n.* An adhesive paper, or one impregnated with poison, for catching or killing flies.

fly press A press for stamping and punching metal blanks, equipped with a hand screw and a heavily weighted cross arm.

fly·speck (flī′spek′) *n.* **1** The dot made by the excrement of a fly. **2** Any slight speck. —*v.t.* To mark with flyspecks.

fly·stone (flī′stōn′) *n.* Cobalt, used as a poison for flies, worms, etc., when ground and mixed with sugar and water.

fly·trap (flī′trap′) *n.* **1** A trap for catching flies. **2** An insectivorous plant, as the pitcher plant and the Venus flytrap.

fly·weight (flī′wāt′) *n.* A boxer weighing 112 lbs. or less: the lightest weight class.

fly·wheel (flī′hwēl′) *n.* A heavy wheel whose weight resists sudden changes of speed, thus securing uniform motion in the working parts of an engine or machine.

Fm *Chem.* Fermium (symbol Fm).

F N 300 A gas-operated, clip-fed rifle designed in Belgium and manufactured in England, having a bore of 7.62 mm, and capable of full automatic fire at 650 to 700 rounds per minute. It supersedes the Lee Enfield as the standard British service weapon. [from *F(abrique) N(ationale) d'Armes de Guerre)*, where it was designed]

F-num·ber (ef′num′bər) *n. Phot.* A number obtained by dividing the focal length of a lens by its effective diameter: the smaller the F-number, the wider the aperture and the shorter the exposure required: also called *F-stop.* Also **F, F/, F:, f, f/, f.**

Fo (fō) Buddha: the Chinese name.

foal (fōl) *n.* The young of an equine animal; a colt. —*v.t. & v.i.* To give birth to (a foal). [OE *fola*]

foam (fōm) *n.* **1** A collection of minute bubbles forming a frothy mass. **2** *Chem.* A colloid system of gas dispersed in liquid. **3** Frothy saliva or sweat. **4** The white crest of a breaking wave; hence, the sea. **5** Figuratively, rage or fury. —*v.i.* To gather, produce, or form foam; froth. —*v.t.* To cause to foam. [OE *fam*] —**foam′less** *adj.*

foam-flow·er (fōm′flou′ər) *n.* A hardy herbaceous perennial (*Tiarella cordifolia*) of the saxifrage family, with purple or red flowers and decorative foliage.

Foam·ite (fō′mīt) *n.* A fire-extinguishing substance composed of licorice in a solution of bicarbonate of soda; in contact with flame it yields a heavy foam which smothers the fire: a trade name.

foam rubber Natural or synthetic rubber which has been treated with various chemicals and expanded into a cellular structure adapted for a wide range of uses as an insulating and buoyancy material and in upholstery.

foam·y (fō′mē) *adj.* **foam·i·er, foam·i·est** Covered with or full of foam; foamlike. —**foam′i·ly** *adv.* —**foam′i·ness** *n.*

fob[1] (fob) *n.* **1** A watch pocket in the waistband of trousers. **2** A chain or ribbon hanging from it; also, an ornament on a watch chain or ribbon. [Cf. dial. G *fuppe* a pocket]

fob[2] (fob) *v.t.* **fobbed, fob·bing** *Archaic* To cheat; trick: also spelled *fub.* —**to fob off 1** To dispose of or palm off by craft or deceit. **2** To put off; attempt to placate, as with promises. [? < FOB[1]]

fo·cal (fō′kəl) *adj.* Pertaining to, at, or limited to a certain point or focus.

focal epilepsy Jacksonian epilepsy.

focal infection *Pathol.* An infection originating in and often spreading from a circumscribed region of the body.

fo·cal·ize (fō′kəl·īz) *v.t. & v.i.* **·ized, ·iz·ing 1** To adjust or come to a focus; focus. **2** *Med.* To confine or be confined to a small area, as an infection. —**fo′cal·i·za′tion** *n.*

focal length *Optics* The distance from the second principal plane of a lens or mirror to the point where rays from a distant object converge. Also **focal distance.**

Foch (fôsh), **Ferdinand,** 1851–1929, marshal of France; commander in chief (1918) of the Allied Armies on the western front in World War I.

fo′c's′le (fōk′səl) *n. Naut.* Forecastle.

fo·cus (fō′kəs) *n. pl.* **·cus·es** or **·ci** (-sī) **1** *Optics* **a** The point to which a system of light rays converges after passage through a lens or other optical arrangement, or after reflection from

FOCI

A. Concavo-concave lens—showing light rays *a, a,* refracting as at *b, b,* and forming the virtual focus at *c.*

B. Convexo-convex lens—showing light rays *d, d,* converging to the principal focus at *e.*

a mirror. **b** The point from which such rays appear to diverge. **c** The place where a visual image is clearly formed, as in the eye or a camera. The point of convergence of the rays is called the **real focus;** the point where diverging rays would meet if their directions were reversed is called the **virtual focus. 2** *Physics* The meeting point of any system of rays, beams, or waves: an acoustic *focus.* **3** *Geom.* **a** One of two points, the sum or difference of whose distances to a conic section is a constant. **b** A point in some other curve, having similar properties. **4** Any central point: the *focus* of an earthquake. —*v.t. & v.i.* **fo·cused** or **fo·cussed, fo·cus·ing** or **fo·cussing 1** To adjust the focus of (the eye or an optical instrument). **2** To bring or come to a focus or point, as rays. [< L, hearth] —**fo′cal** *adj.*

fod·der (fod′ər) *n.* Coarse feed, for horses, cattle, etc., as the stalks and leaves of field corn. See synonyms under FOOD. —*v.t.* To supply with fodder. [OE *fódor*]

fodg·el (foj′əl) *adj. Scot.* Fat; corpulent; squat.

foe (fō) *n.* **1** One actively hostile. **2** A hostile force; an enemy; adversary. **3** One who or that which opposes or injures; anything injurious or detrimental. See synonyms under ENEMY. [Fusion of OE *fah* hostile and *gefa* an enemy]

foehn (fœn) *n. Meteorol.* A warm and dry southerly wind of Alpine valleys: also spelled *föhn, fön.* [< dial. G *föhn* < L *Favonius,* the west wind]

foe·man (fō′mən) *n. pl.* **·men** (-mən) An active or open enemy.

foe·tal (fē′təl), **foe·ta·tion** (fē·tā′shən), **foe·tus** (fē′təs), etc. See FETAL, etc.

fog[1] (fog, fôg) *n. Agric.* **1** Dead or decaying grass. **2** Aftermath (def. 2). Also *foggage.*

[ME *fogge*, prob. <Scand. Cf. Norw. *fogg* long grass on wet ground.] **— fog'gy** *adj.*

fog[2] (fog, fôg) *n.* **1** Condensed watery vapor suspended in the atmosphere at or near the earth's surface. **2** *Chem.* A colloid system of the liquid-in-gas type (see COLLOID SYSTEM). **3** *Meteorol.* Any hazy condition of the atmosphere, or the material causing it: a dust *fog.* **4** Bewilderment; obscurity. **5** *Phot.* A coating obscuring a developed photographic plate. — *v.* **fogged, fog·ging** *v.t.* **1** To surround with or as with fog. **2** To confuse; bewilder. **3** *Phot.* To cloud (a plate) with a fog. — *v.i.* **4** To become foggy. [Prob. back formation < *foggy,* in the sense "marshy" <FOG[1]; infl. in meaning by Dan. *fog* spray]

Fo·gaz·za·ro (fō'gät·tsä'rō), **Antonio,** 1842–1911, Italian novelist and poet.

fog bank A mass of fog seen at a distance, especially at sea.

fog·bound (fog'bound', fôg'-) *adj.* Detained by fog; prevented because of fog from traveling, sailing, flying, etc.

fog·bow (fog'bō', fôg'-) *n. Meteorol.* A white or very faintly colored arc of light seen opposite the sun in fog.

fog chamber A cloud chamber. See under CHAMBER.

fog dog A clearing spot in a fog bank, indicating the lifting of the fog: also called *sea dog.*

fog·fruit (fog'frōōt', fôg'-) *n.* An American creeping plant (genus *Lippia*) of the vervain family bearing closely bracted heads of bluish-white flowers, especially *L. lanceolata.*

fog·gage (fog'ij, fôg'-) *n.* **1** Long grass, left standing over winter, for feeding cattle in the spring. **2** The privilege of pasturing cattle on fog; also, such pasturing.

Fog·gia (fôd'jä) A city in southern Italy.

fog·gy (fog'ē, fôg'ē) *adj.* **fog·gi·er, fog·gi·est** **1** Full of or marked by the presence of fog. **2** Mentally confused; obscure; cloudy. **3** *Phot.* Fogged; indistinct. See synonyms under THICK. [<FOG[1]] **— fog'gi·ly** *adv.* **— fog'gi·ness** *n.*

fog·horn (fog'hôrn', fôg'-) *n.* **1** A horn or whistle for sounding a warning during a fog on the water: also **fog'-sig'nal, fog'-whis'tle.** **2** Hence, a powerful, harsh voice.

fo·gy (fō'gē) *n. pl.* **fo·gies** A person of old-fashioned notions. — *adj.* Old-fashioned; out-of-date; fusty. Also **fo'gey, fo'gie.** [? <FOGGY] **— fo'gy·ish** *adj.* **— fo'gy·ism** *n.*

fogy pay *U.S. Mil. Slang* Longevity pay. Also **fo'gey pay.**

foh (fô) *interj.* An exclamation of contempt, dislike, or disgust. [Var. of FAUGH]

föhn (fœn) See FOEHN.

foi·ble (foi'bəl) *n.* **1** A personal weakness; slight fault of character. **2** The portion of a sword blade or foil blade from the middle to the point: distinguished from *forte.* [<F, obs. var. of *faible* FEEBLE]

Synonyms: defect, error, failing, frailty, imperfection, infirmity, peccadillo, weakness.

foil[1] (foil) *v.t.* **1** To prevent the success of; balk; frustrate; baffle. **2** In hunting, to cross and recross (a scent or trail) so as to confuse pursuers. See synonyms under BAFFLE, HINDER[1]. — *n.* **1** *Archaic* A thwarting; frustration. **2** In wrestling, an incomplete fall. **3** An animal's trail. [<OF *fouler, fuler* crush, trample down <LL *fullare* full cloth < *fullo* a fuller]

foil[2] (foil) *n.* **1** Metal in very thin pliable sheets or leaves. **2** A leaf of bright metal placed by jewelers beneath an inferior gem to heighten the color or luster. **3** Anything serving to adorn or set off by contrast something different or superior. **4** The reflecting amalgam on the back of a mirror. **5** *Archit.* A leaflike division in ornamentation; a lobe, as in tracery. A group of three foils is called *trefoil*; of four, *quatrefoil*; of five, *cinquefoil*; etc. **6** *Obs.* A leaf. — *v.t.* **1** To apply foil to; cover with foil. **2** To intensify or set off by contrast. **3** *Archit.* To adorn, as windows, with foils. [<OF <L *folium* leaf]

FOILS (*def. 5*)
Foliated tracery in Gothic window, Grace Church Chantry, New York.

foil[3] (foil) *n.* **1** A blunted rapierlike implement, sometimes having a button on its end, used in fencing. **2** The art of fencing. [Origin uncertain]

foiled (foild) *adj.* Having foils, as a window.

foils·man (foilz'mən) *n. pl.* **·men** (-mən) A fencer; one skilled in fencing.

foin (foin) *Obs. v.i.* To lunge or thrust, with or as with a weapon. — *n.* A thrust or pass with a weapon. [<OF *foine* a fishspear <L *fuscina*]

Fo·ism (fō'iz·əm) *n.* Chinese Buddhism. [<Fo] **— Fo'ist** *n.*

foi·son (foi'zən) *n. Archaic* **1** Power, strength. **2** *pl.* Resources. **3** Abundance. [<OF, a pouring out <L *fusio, -onis* < *fundere* pour]

foist (foist) *v.t.* **1** To put in or introduce slyly or improperly: to *foist* a candidate on a party. **2** To pass off (something spurious) as genuine. [Prob. < dial. Du. *vuisten* hold in the hand, palm]

Fo·kine (fō·kēn', *Russ.* fô'kin), **Michel,** 1880–1942, U.S. choreographer born in Russia.

Fok·ker (fok'ər), **Anthony H. G.,** 1890–1939, Dutch airplane designer active in Germany and the United States.

fold[1] (fōld) *v.t.* **1** To turn back (something) upon itself one or more times. **2** To bring down upon itself; close; collapse: to *fold* an umbrella; to *fold* wings. **3** To place together and interlock: to *fold* one's hands. **4** To wrap up; enclose. **5** To mix, as beaten egg whites or whipped cream, into other ingredients, by gently turning one part over the other with a spoon: with *in.* **6** To embrace; enfold: She *folded* him in her arms. — *v.i.* **7** To come together in folds. **8** *U.S. Slang* To fail; close: often with *up.* — *n.* **1** One part doubled over another; a plait; ply; a lap; also, the space between two folded-over parts. **2** The crease made by folding. **3** *Geol.* A smooth bend or flexure in a layer of rock; an anticline or syncline. **4** That which envelops; an embrace. [OE *fealdan*]

fold[2] (fōld) *n.* **1** A pen, as for sheep. **2** A flock of sheep. **3** Any group needing care, as the congregation of a church. **4** *Brit. Dial.* A farmstead. — *v.t.* To shut up in a fold, as sheep. [OE *fald*]

-fold *suffix* **1** Having (a specified number of) parts: a *threefold* blessing. **2** (A specified number of) times as great, or as much: to reward *tenfold.* [OE *-feald* < *fealdan* fold]

fold·boat (fōld'bōt') *n.* A faltboat.

fold·er (fōl'dər) *n.* **1** One who or that which folds. **2** A timetable or other printed paper that may be readily folded or readily spread out. **3** A large envelope or binder for loose papers.

fol·de·rol (fol'də·rol) See FALDERAL.

fold·ing (fōl'ding) *n.* The gathering or keeping of sheep in a fold.

fo·li·a (fō'lē·ə) Plural of FOLIUM.

fo·li·a·ceous (fō'lē·ā'shəs) *adj.* **1** Of the nature or form of a leaf. **2** Leaflike. **3** Having leaves; foliate. [<L *foliaceus* < *folium* a leaf]

fo·li·age (fō'lē·ij) *n.* **1** Any growth of leaves; leaves collectively. **2** A representation of leaves, flowers, and branches, used in architectural ornamentation. [Earlier *foillage* <F *feuillage* < *feuille* a leaf <L *folium*; refashioned after the Latin form]

fo·li·aged (fō'lē·ijd) *adj.* Having, or ornamented with, foliage.

foliage green Any of several shades of dark, dull green; a color like that of the leaves of trees in the summer.

fo·li·ar (fō'lē·ər) *adj.* Of, pertaining to, consisting of, or resembling leaves.

fo·li·ate (fō'lē·āt, -it) *adj.* **1** Having leaves; leafy; leaf-shaped. **2** Decorated with leaf-shaped ornaments; beaten into leaf. — *v.* **·at·ed, ·at·ing** *v.t.* **1** To beat or form into a leaf or thin plate, as gold. **2** To coat or back with metal foil. **3** To number the leaves of (a book). **4** *Archit.* To adorn or ornament with foils or foliage. — *v.i.* **5** To split into leaves or laminae. **6** To put forth leaves. [<L *foliatus* leafy < *folium* a leaf] **— fo'li·at'ed** *adj.*

fo·li·a·tion (fō'lē·ā'shən) *n.* **1** *Bot.* **a** The leafing-out of plants. **b** The disposition of leaves in a bud. **2** The act or process of making into thin sheet metal or foil, or of covering or backing with foil, as a mirror. **3** *Archit.* Decoration or enrichment with cusps, lobes, or foliated tracery; also, one of such ornaments. **4** The state of being foliaceous or foliated. **5** *Geol.* A crystalline segregation of certain minerals in a rock, in dominant planes. **6** The numbering of the leaves of a book, etc., instead of its pages. Also **fo·li·a·ture** (fō'lē·ə·chŏŏr').

fo·lic acid (fō'lik) *Biochem.* A nitrogen-containing acid having vitaminlike properties and often included in the vitamin-B complex. It is found abundantly in green leaves, and in mushrooms, yeast, and some animal tissues.

fo·li·o (fō'lē·ō, fōl'yō) *n. pl.* **·li·os** **1** A sheet of paper folded once or of a size adapted to folding once. **2** A book, or the like, composed of sheets folded but once; hence, a book of the largest size. **3** The size of a book so made up. **4** A page of a book; sometimes, in bookkeeping, two opposite pages numbered alike. **5** *Printing* The number of a page. **6** *Law* A certain number of words (72–100), recognized as a unit for estimating the length of a document. **7** A leaf of manuscript or of a book. **8** A holder made of heavy paper for protecting sheets of manuscript, music, etc. — *adj.* Consisting of or resulting from a sheet or sheets folded once; having two leaves, hence, four pages. — *v.t.* To number the pages or locate the folios of (a book or manuscript) consecutively. [<L, ablative sing. of *folium* a leaf]

fo·li·o·late (fō'lē·ə·lāt') *adj. Bot.* Of, pertaining to, or composed of leaflets: used in composition: *bifoliolate,* composed of two leaflets. [<L *foliolum,* dim. of *folium* a leaf + -ATE[1]]

fo·li·ose (fō'lē·ōs) *adj.* Bearing leaves or leaflike appendages. [<L *foliosus* < *folium* a leaf]

-folious *suffix* Leaflike or leafy: used in the formation of adjectives. [<L *foliosus* < *folium* leaf]

fo·li·um (fō'lē·əm) *n. pl.* **·li·ums** or **·li·a** (-lē·ə) **1** *Usually pl.* A thin layer or stratum, especially of rocks. **2** *Geom.* A segment of a curve closed by its node; a loop. [<L, a leaf]

folium of Descartes *Geom.* A plane cubic curve with one loop, a node, and two branches asymptotic to the same line.

folk (fōk) *n. pl.* **folk** or **folks** **1** A people; nation; race. **2** *Usually pl.* People of a particular group or class: old *folks*; poor *folks*; town *folk.* **3** *pl. Colloq.* People in general: *Folks* say; *folks* disagree. **4** *pl. Colloq.* One's family or relatives. — *adj.* Originating among or characteristic of the common people of a district or country. [OE *folc*]

Folk, in the adjectival use, may appear as the first element in two-word phrases; as in:

folk air	**folk faith**	**folk song**
folk art	**folk life**	**folk speech**
folk belief	**folk literature**	**folk story**
folk custom	**folk music**	**folk tale**
folk dance	**folk name**	**folk tune**

Folke·stone (fōk'stən) A port and resort in Kent, England.

Fol·ke·ting (fōl'kə·ting) *n.* The lower branch of the Danish Rigsdag or legislature. Also **Fol'ke·thing.**

folk etymology **1** Modification of an unfamiliar word resulting from an incorrect analysis of the elements, causing it to assume the shape or pronunciation of better known forms, as *agnail* (in Middle English, a painful nail) became *hangnail.* **2** Nonscientific word derivation. Also called *popular etymology.*

folk·free (fōk'frē') *adj.* Having the lawful rights of a freeman.

folk·land (fōk'land') *n.* In old English law, land of the folk or people, of the community, or of the nation, held by folkright: distinguished from *bookland,* requiring written title. [OE *folcland*]

folk laws The laws of the common people; specifically, the laws of the Salian Franks.

folk·lore (fōk'lôr', -lōr') *n.* **1** The traditions, beliefs, customs, sayings, stories, etc., preserved among the common people. **2** The study of folk cultures. **— folk'lor'ist** *n.*

folk·mote (fōk'mōt') *n.* In early English history, a general assembly of the people of a town, county, etc. Also **folk'moot'** (-mōōt'). [OE *folcmōt* < *folc* folk + *mōt* meeting]

folk·right (fōk'rīt') *n.* The common law of the people; the public right.

folk·sy (fōk'sē) *adj.* **·si·er, ·si·est** *Colloq.* Friendly; sociable; unpretentious.

folk·ways (fōk′wāz′) *n. pl.* The traditional habits, customs, and behavior of a given group, tribe, or nation. [Coined by W. G. Sumner]

fol·li·cle (fol′i·kəl) *n.* **1** *Anat.* A small cavity or saclike structure in certain parts of the animal body, having a protective or secretory function: a hair *follicle.* See illustration under HAIR. **2** *Bot.* **a** A dry seed vessel of one carpel. **b** A small bladder on the leaves of some mosses. [<L *folliculus,* dim. of *follis* bag]

fol·lic·u·lar (fə·lik′yə·lər) *adj.* **1** Of, pertaining to, or like a follicle. **2** Affecting the follicles, as of the pharynx.

fol·lic·u·lat·ed (fə·lik′yə·lā′tid) *adj.* Having a follicle or a cocoon; follicular. Also **fol·lic′u·late** (-lit).

fol·lies (fol′ēz) *n. pl. of* **folly** A theatrical performance having no plot sequence, consisting of many elaborate scenes of music and dance; revue.

fol·low (fol′ō) *v.t.* **1** To go or come after and in the same direction. **2** To succeed in time or order. **3** To seek to overtake or capture; pursue. **4** To accompany; attend. **5** To hold to the course of: to *follow* a road. **6** To conform to; act in accordance with. **7** To move or act in the cause of; be under the leadership or authority of: He *follows* Plato. **8** To work at as a profession or livelihood; employ oneself in: men who *follow* the sea. **9** To come after as a consequence or result: The effect *follows* the cause. **10** To use or take as a model; imitate: to *follow* an example. **11** To watch or observe closely; be attentive to: to *follow* sports. **12** To understand the course, sequence, or meaning of, as an explanation. **13** To strive after; try to attain or obtain: to *follow* one's star. —*v.i.* **14** To move or come after or in the direction of something preceding in time, sequence, or motion. **15** To attend; understand: Do you *follow*? **16** To come as a result or consequence. —**to follow out 1** To follow to the end, as an argument. **2** To comply with, as orders or instructions. —**to follow suit 1** In card games, to play a card of the suit led. **2** To follow another's example. —**to follow through 1** To swing to the full extent of the stroke after having struck the ball, as in tennis or golf. **2** To perform fully; complete. —**to follow up 1** To pursue closely. **2** To achieve more by acting upon what has already been achieved, as an advantage. —*n.* The act of following; specifically, a stroke in billiards that causes the cue ball, after impact, to follow the object ball. [OE *folgian*]

Synonyms (verb): accompany, attend, chase, copy, ensue, heed, imitate, obey, observe, practice, pursue, result, succeed. A servant *follows* or *attends* his master, a victorious general may *follow* the retiring enemy merely to watch and hold him in check; he *chases* or *pursues* with intent to overtake and attack; the chase is closer and hotter than the pursuit. (Compare synonyms for HUNT.) One event may *follow* another either with or without special connection; if it *ensues,* there is some orderly connection; if it *results* from another, there is some relation of effect, consequence, or inference. A clerk *observes* his employer's directions. A child *obeys* his parent's commands, *follows* or *copies* his example, *imitates* his speech and manners. The compositor *follows* copy; the incoming official *succeeds* the outgoing official. See IMITATE. *Antonyms*: anticipate, direct, flee, guide, lead, pass, precede, surpass.

fol·low·er (fol′ō·ər) *n.* **1** One who or that which follows; an adherent, imitator, or attendant. **2** *Mech.* A part of a machine put into action by another part, as a driven pulley. **3** *Brit. Colloq.* An admirer; a beau.

fol·low·ing (fol′ō·ing) *adj.* **1** Next in order; succeeding or ensuing. **2** That is about to follow, be recounted, be mentioned, or the like. —*n.* A body of adherents, attendants, or disciples.

fol·low–through (fol′ō·thrōō′) *n.* **1** In some sports, the continuing and completion of a motion, as the swing of the racket, club, or bat after contact with the ball. **2** Any continuing or completion.

fol·low–up (fol′ō·up′) *adj.* Pertaining to steady or repeated action or to a second or immediately following action or thing; reinforcing; supplementary. —*n.* A supplementary letter or visit to a business prospect, urging favorable action on a previous proposal.

fol·ly (fol′ē) *n. pl.* **·lies 1** The condition or state of being foolish, or deficient in understanding; foolish conduct, idea, or act. **2** The result of a ruinous undertaking or enterprise, as a costly and useless structure left unfinished; also, any extravagant structure or undertaking, considered as showing the bad judgment of the originator. **3** An object of foolish or vicious attention or pursuit. **4** Immoral conduct; sin. See synonyms under IDIOCY. [<F *folie* <*fol* fool]

Fol·som culture (fol′səm) *Anthropol.* A supposed prehistoric North American culture represented by typically Neolithic artifacts discovered near Folsom, northeastern New Mexico.

Folsom point *Anthropol.* One of various chipped points, first found near Folsom, New Mexico, in 1925.

Fo·mal·haut (fō′məl·hôt) The bright star Alpha in the constellation of Piscis Austrinus; magnitude, 1.3.

fo·ment (fō·ment′) *v.t.* **1** To stir up or instigate; incite, as rebellion or discord. **2** To treat with warm water or medicated lotions; apply a poultice to. See synonyms under PROMOTE. [<F *fomenter* <LL *fomentare* <*fomentum* a poultice <*fovere* warm, keep warm] —**fo·ment′er** *n.*

fo·men·ta·tion (fō′mən·tā′shən) *n.* **1** The act of fomenting, warming, or cherishing. **2** The use of any warm, moist application, as a poultice; also, the lotion applied. **3** Instigation or incitement, as to mutiny.

fo·mes (fō′mēz) *n. pl.* **fom·i·tes** (fom′i·tēz, fō′·mi-) *Med.* An object or substance other than food capable of transmitting an infection, as bedding, clothes, etc. [<L, tinder]

Fo·mor·i·an (fə·môr′ē·ən, -mō′rē-) *n.* In Old Irish mythology, one of a people who dwelt under the sea and ravaged Ireland: generally associated with the powers of evil. [<Irish *fomhor* pirate]

Fön (fœn) See FOEHN.

fond[1] (fond) *adj.* **1** Disposed to love or to regard with pleasure, tenderness, or desire; enamored: followed by *of,* formerly by *on.* **2** Loving or affectionate; devotedly attached: sometimes with an implication of unwise tenderness or weak indulgence. **3** Cherished or regarded with affection; doted on. **4** *Archaic.* Foolish or simple; silly. See synonyms under FRIENDLY. [Earlier *fonned,* pp. of obs. *fon* be foolish]

fond[2] (fond, *Fr.* fôṅ) *n.* A groundwork or background, especially of lace. [<F <L *fundus* bottom]

fon·dant (fon′dənt, *Fr.* fôṅ·däṅ′) *n.* A soft, molded confection. [<F, orig. ppr. of *fondre* melt]

fon·dle (fon′dəl) *v.* **·dled, ·dling** *v.t.* **1** To handle lovingly; caress. **2** *Obs.* To pamper; coddle. —*v.i.* **3** To display fondness, as by caressing. See synonyms under CARESS. [Freq. of obs. *fond* caress] —**fon′dler** *n.*

fon·dling (fond′ling) *n.* One who or that which is fondled.

fond·ly (fond′lē) *adv.* **1** In a fond manner; tenderly; dotingly. **2** Credulously. **3** *Obs.* Foolishly.

fond·ness (fond′nis) *n.* **1** Extravagant or foolish affection. **2** Strong preferment, liking or relish. **3** *Obs.* Foolishness.

fon·du (fôṅ·dü′) *adj. French* Melting into or blending gradually with one another, as colors.

fon·due (fon·dōō′, *Fr.* fôṅ·dü′) *n.* A dish made of grated cheese, melted with eggs, butter, etc. [<F]

Fon·se·ca (fōn·sā′kä), **Gulf of** An inlet of the Pacific in Salvador, Honduras, and Nicaragua.

font[1] (font) *n.* **1** A receptacle for the water used in baptizing. **2** A receptacle for holy water. **3** A fountain; hence, origin; source. [OE <LL *fons, fontis* a fountain]

font[2] (font) *n.* A full assortment of printing type of a particular face and size: also *Brit.* *fount.* [<F *fonte* <*fondre* melt]

Fon·taine·bleau (fôṅ·ten·blō′) A town in central France in the **Forest of Fontainebleau;** site of the **Palace of Fontainebleau,** a former residence of French kings, now a museum.

font·al (fon′təl) *adj.* Pertaining to a font or fountain, and hence to an origin or source.

fon·ta·nel (fon′tə·nel′) *n.* **1** *Anat.* A soft, pulsating, unossified area in the fetal and infantile skull. **2** *Surg.* An artificial opening for the discharge of body fluids; a seton. Also **fon′ta·nelle′.** [<F *fontanelle,* dim. of *fontaine.* See FOUNTAIN.]

Fon·tanne (fon·tan′), **Lynn,** born 1887?, U.S. actress born in England; wife of Alfred Lunt.

Fon·te·noy (fon′tə·noi, *Fr.* fôṅ·tə·nwä′) **1** A village in western Belgium; scene of a French victory over British forces, 1745. **2** A village of north central France; scene of a victory of Charles II of France, 841: also **Fon·te·nailles** (fôṅ·tə·nä′y′), **Fon·ta·net** (fôṅ·tà·ne′).

Foo·chow (fōō′chou′, *Chinese* fōō′jō′) A port in SE China; capital of Fukien province: formerly *Minhow.* Also **Fu′chow′.**

food (fōōd) *n.* **1** That which is eaten or drunk or absorbed for the growth and repair of organisms and the maintenance of life; nourishment; nutriment; aliment. **2** Nourishment taken in solid as opposed to liquid form: *food* and drink. **3** That which increases, keeps active, or sustains. [OE *fōda*]

Synonyms: aliment, diet, fare, feed, fodder, forage, nourishment, nutriment, nutrition, pabulum, provender, regimen, sustenance, viands, victuals. *Food* is, in the popular sense, whatever one eats in contradistinction to what one drinks. Thus we speak of *food* and drink, of wholesome, unwholesome, or indigestible *food*; in a more scientific sense whatever, when taken into an organism, serves to build up structure or supply waste may be termed *food*; thus we speak of liquid *food,* plant *food,* etc.; in this wider sense *food* is closely synonymous with *nutriment, nourishment,* and *sustenance. Victuals* is a plain, homely word for whatever may be eaten; we speak of choice *viands,* cold *victuals. Diet* refers to the quantity and quality of *food* habitually taken, with reference to preservation of health. *Regimen* considers *food* as taken by strict rule, in which use it is closely synonymous with *diet,* but applies more widely to the whole ordering of life. *Fare* is a general word for all table supplies, good or bad; as, sumptuous *fare*; wretched *fare. Feed, fodder,* and *provender* are used only of the food of the lower animals, *feed* denoting anything consumed, but more commonly grain, *fodder* denoting hay, corn stalks, or the like, sometimes called long *feed*; *provender* is dry *feed,* whether grain or hay, straw, etc. *Forage* denotes any kind of *food* suitable for horses and cattle, primarily as obtained by a military force in scouring the country, especially an enemy's country. Compare NUTRIMENT.

Food and Drug Administration A division of the U.S. Department of Health, Education, and Welfare, which enforces laws relating to the purity, standards, branding, and labeling of foods, drugs, and cosmetics.

food chain *Ecol.* The relationship of organisms considered as food sources or consumers or both, as the relationship of a flowering plant to a bee to a bird.

Foo dog (fōō) A lion dog (def. 1): a western commercial term. [<Chinese *Foo,* var. of *Fo* Buddha + dog]

food·stuff (fōōd′stuf′) *n.* Anything used as nourishment, or entering into the composition of food: often in the plural.

foo·fa·raw (fōō′fə·rô) *n. Colloq.* **1** Gaudy trimmings; tinsel. **2** Nonsense. [Origin unknown]

fool[1] (fōōl) *n.* **1** A person lacking in understanding, judgment, or common sense; a simpleton. **2** A person, fantastically dressed and equipped, formerly kept at court and in great households to make sport; a professional jester. **3** One who is fooled or made a fool of; butt; victim. **4** *Obs.* An idiot; imbecile. **5** *Obs.* One without spiritual wisdom; wicked person. —*v.i.* To act like a fool; be foolish or playful. —*v.t.* To make a fool of; impose upon; deceive. —**to fool around** *U.S. Colloq.* **1** To waste time on trifles. **2** To

hang about idly. — **to fool away** *Colloq*. To spend foolishly; squander, as money. — **to fool with** 1 To meddle with. 2 To joke with. 3 To play with. — *adj. Colloq.* 1 Stupid: that *fool* cook. 2 Foolish: a *fool* story. [<F *fou* <L *follis* a bellows; later, a windbag, a simpleton]

fool² (fōol) *n.* Crushed stewed fruit with whipped cream. [Prob. <FOOL¹]

fool·er·y (fōo′lə·rē) *n. pl.* **·er·ies** Foolish conduct; anything foolish.

fool·har·dy (fōol′här′dē) *adj.* Bold without judgment; reckless; rash. See synonyms under IMPRUDENT. — **fool′har′di·ly** *adv.* — **fool′har′di·ness** *n.*

fool·ing (fōol′ing) *n.* 1 Playing the fool; jesting. 2 Loitering.

fool·ish (fōol′ish) *adj.* 1 Showing folly; wanting in judgment. 2 Resulting from folly or stupidity. 3 *Archaic* Insignificant; small; humble. See synonyms under ABSURD, CHILDISH. — **fool′ish·ly** *adv.* — **fool′ish·ness** *n.*

fool·proof (fōol′prōof′) *adj.* So simple as to be understood or operated by a fool; so constructed as to operate smoothly and safely no matter how ignorant the operator.

fools·cap (fōolz′kap′) *n.* 1 A size of writing paper about 13 by 16 inches, making when folded a page 13 by 8 inches. 2 *Brit.* A size of printing paper 13 1/2 by 17 inches: so called from the watermark of a fool's cap and bells used by old papermakers. 3 A fool's cap.

fool's cap 1 A pointed, belled cap, formerly worn by jesters. 2 A dunce's cap of this shape: formerly used as a punishment for school children.

fool's errand A profitless undertaking.

fool's gold Pyrite, a gold-colored mineral.

fool's paradise A state of deceptive happiness based on vain hopes or delusions.

fool's–parsley (fōolz′pärs′lē) *n.* A fetid, poisonous herb (*Aethusa cynapium*) naturalized in NE United States and eastern Canada: so called because it resembles parsley: also **fool's–cic′e·ly** (fōolz′sis′ə·lē).

foot (fōot) *n. pl.* **feet** 1 The terminal segment of the limb of a vertebrate animal upon which it rests in standing or moving. ◆ Collateral adjective: *pedal.* 2 Any part serving as or likened to a foot. 3 Anything corresponding in form, use, or position to the foot. 4 The part of a boot or stocking which receives the wearer's foot. 5 A part in a sewing machine, to hold the fabric down: also called **presser foot.** 6 *Naut.* The lower edge of a four–sided sail. 7 The lowest part; bottom; base; foundation; also, the last row, line, or series; the inferior part or end. 8 A measure of length, equivalent to 12 inches, or 30.48 centimeters. 9 Soldiers, collectively, who march and fight on foot: distinguished from *horse* (cavalry). 10 A primary measure of poetic rhythm, corresponding to a *bar* in music. — **on foot** 1 Walking; not riding. 2 Happening; going on; proceeding. — **to put one's foot down** To be decisive or determined. — **to put one's foot in it** To get into a difficulty or scrape. — **under foot** 1 Under the feet; hence, in the way. 2 On the ground: wet *under foot.* — *v.i.* 1 To go afoot; walk. 2 To move the foot to music; dance. 3 *Naut.* To move or sail faster. — *v.t.* 4 To move on or through by walking or dancing; set foot on. 5 To furnish with a foot, as a stocking. 6 To add, as a column of figures, and place the sum at the bottom. 7 *Colloq.* To pay, as a bill. — **to foot it** To walk, run, or dance. — **to foot up** To amount to when counted or added. [OE *fōt*]

foot·age (fōot′ij) *n.* 1 Length in running feet, as of lumber, of tunneling or mining, or of film in a motion picture. 2 Payment at a rate of so much a foot for work done.

foot–and–mouth disease (fōot′ən·mouth′) A contagious, febrile disease of domestic animals, in which ulcers are formed about the mouth and hoofs. It is caused by a filtrable virus.

foot·ball (fōot′bôl′) *n.* 1 *U.S.* A game played between two teams, properly of eleven men

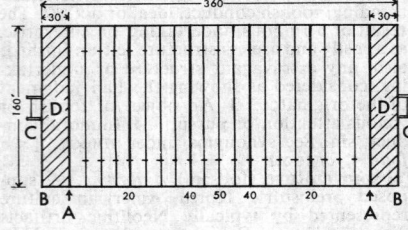

FOOTBALL PLAYING FIELD
A. Goal lines.　　*C.* Goal posts.
B. End lines.　　*D.* End zones.
The field of play is marked off in guidelines spaced 5 yards apart and so identified, as 20-yard line, etc.

each, on a field with goals at each end, points being scored by running or passing an ellipsoidal leather ball across the opponent's goal line, or kicking it between the goal posts placed on or behind the goal line. 2 The ball itself. 3 *Brit.* **a** Soccer. **b** Rugby football. 4 Any person, idea, etc., bandied or shunted back and forth.

foot·board (fōot′bôrd′, -bōrd′) *n.* 1 Something to rest the feet upon. 2 An upright piece at the foot of a bedstead.

foot·boy (fōot′boi′) *n.* A page.

foot brake A brake operated by pressure of the foot.

foot·breadth (fōot′bredth′) *n.* The breadth of a foot, as a measure.

foot·bridge (fōot′brij′) *n.* A bridge for persons on foot.

foot·can·dle (fōot′kan′dəl) *n.* The illumination on one square foot of surface, all points of which are at a distance of one foot from one international candle. — **apparent foot·candle** See FOOT–LAMBERT.

foot·cloth (fōot′klôth′, -kloth′) *n.* 1 A carpet to walk upon on occasions of ceremony. 2 *Obs.* A caparison for a horse.

foot·ed (fōot′id) *adj.* Having a foot or feet: four–*footed*; also, shaped like a foot.

foot·er (fōot′ər) *n.* 1 A person who goes on foot. 2 A person or thing having a certain number of feet in height or length: a six–*footer.*

foot·fall (fōot′fôl′) *n.* The sound of a footstep; a footstep.

foot·gear (fōot′gir′) *n.* Footwear.

foot·guard (fōot′gärd′) *n.* A horse's boot.

foot·hill (fōot′hil′) *n.* A low hill at the base of a mountain.

foot·hold (fōot′hōld′) *n.* 1 A firm support for the foot. 2 Secure footing. 3 Established position.

foot·ing (fōot′ing) *n.* 1 A place to stand or walk on; hence, position or condition; especially, secure position. 2 An established mode of mutual consideration and treatment. 3 The adding of a column or columns of figures, or the sum thus obtained. 4 A footstep; tread; especially, measured tread; dancing. 5 The act of adding a foot to anything; that which is added as a foot. 6 A strong foundation of greater lateral dimensions than the wall, embankment, or structural member which it supports.

foot ladder A ladder with flat steps to place the feet upon.

foot–lam·bert (fōot′lam′bərt) *n.* A unit of brightness, equal to the brightness of a uniformly diffusing surface which emits or reflects one lumen per square foot: also called **apparent foot-candle.**

foot·le (fōot′l) *Colloq. v.t. & v.i.* **foot·led, foot·ling** To talk or act in a silly or foolish manner. — *adj.* Nonsensical: also **foot′ling.** — *n.* Foolish talk; nonsense. [Origin uncertain]

foot·less (fōot′lis) *adj.* 1 Having no feet. 2 Having no footing or basis. 3 *Colloq.* Awkward; inept.

foot·lights (fōot′līts′) *n. pl.* 1 Lights in a row near the front of the stage, as in a theater. 2 The stage.

foot·ling (fōot′ling) *adj. & adv.* 1 Foolish;

trifling. 2 Having or with the feet foremost: said of a position of the fetus at birth.

foot·lock·er (fōot′lok′ər) *n.* A small trunk, usually used by soldiers for personal belongings and clothing.

foot·log (fōot′lôg′, -log′) *n.* A log across a stream from bank to bank, on which a person may cross.

foot·loose (fōot′lōos′) *adj.* Free to travel or rove around; not bound to any person or duty; unattached.

foot·man (fōot′mən) *n. pl.* **·men** (-mən) 1 A male servant in livery who attends a carriage, answers the door, waits at table, etc. 2 *Obs.* A pedestrian.

foot·mark (fōot′märk′) *n.* A footprint. See synonyms under TRACE.

foot·note (fōot′nōt′) *n.* A note at the foot of a page or column.

foot·pace (fōot′pās′) *n.* 1 A slow pace. 2 A staircase landing. 3 A dais.

foot·pad (fōot′pad′) *n.* A highwayman or robber on foot.

foot·path (fōot′path′, -päth′) *n.* A path for persons on foot.

foot–pound (fōot′pound′) *n.* The work done in moving a pound's weight one foot against gravity: a unit of mechanical work.

foot–pound·al (fōot′poun′dəl) *n.* A measure of the work done in moving through one foot against a force of one poundal.

foot·print (fōot′print′) *n.* An impression left by a foot. See synonyms under MARK, TRACE.

foot·rest (fōot′rest′) *n.* A stool, chair extension, etc., for supporting the feet.

foot–rope (fōot′rōp′) *n. Naut.* 1 A rope stretched under a yard for sailors to stand on while reefing or furling. 2 A boltrope sewed to the lower edge of a sail.

foot–rot (fōot′rot′) *n.* An infectious disease of sheep, characterized by inflammation of the foot, progressive degeneration of the tissues, ill-smelling discharges, and lameness: caused by any of several micro-organisms, bacterial or of fungous origin.

foots (fōots) *n. pl.* Settlings or sediment, as of molasses or oil.

foot soldier An infantryman.

foot·sore (fōot′sôr′, -sōr′) *adj.* Having sore feet, as from walking.

foot·stalk (fōot′stôk′) *n. Bot.* 1 The petiole of a leaf, or the peduncle of a flower. 2 A stem or part supporting the body or an organ; a pedicel.

foot·stall (fōot′stôl′) *n.* 1 *Archit.* The base or pedestal of a column or pillar. 2 The stirrup of a side–saddle.

foot·step (fōot′step′) *n.* 1 The impression or mark of a foot; footprint; track. 2 The action of a foot in stepping. 3 The sound of a step; tread; footfall. See synonyms under TRACE.

foot·stock (fōot′stok′) *n. Mech.* In turning or boring machinery, a tailstock or loose headstock.

foot·stone (fōot′stōn′) *n.* The stone at the foot of a grave.

foot·stool (fōot′stōol′) *n.* A low stool for the feet.

foot·stove (fōot′stōv′) *n.* A metal container for live coals, enclosed in a box having a perforated top: used for warming the feet.

foot–ton (fōot′tun′) *n.* The work done in raising a long ton a distance of one foot against the force of gravity.

foot·wall (fōot′wôl′) *n.* 1 *Mining* The layer of rock lying just beneath a vein of ore. 2 *Geol.* That side of an inclined fault that lies below the hanging wall.

foot–wash·ing (fōot′wosh′ing, -wôsh′-) *n.* The washing of one another's feet as an act of humility: a religious ceremony performed by certain sects in remembrance of the washing of the disciples' feet by Jesus.

foot·way (fōot′wā′) *n.* A path or passage for pedestrians; footpath.

foot·wear (fōot′wâr′) *n.* Clothing for the feet; boots, shoes, socks, stockings.

foot·work (fōot′wûrk′) *n.* Use or control of the feet, as in boxing or tennis.

foot–worn (fōot′wôrn′, -wōrn′) *adj.* 1 Weary with walking. 2 Worn by the feet, as a path.

foot·y (fōot′ē) *adj.* **foot·i·er, foot·i·est** *Colloq.* Foolish; insignificant; worthless. [<F *foutu*, pp. of *foutre* damn]

foo·zle (fōo′zəl) *v.t. & v.i.* **·zled, ·zling** To do

Center column image caption (human foot):

LONGITUDINAL SECTION
OF HUMAN FOOT
a. Tibia.
b. Astragal.
c. Calcaneum.
d. Navicular.
e. Internal cuneiform bone.
f. First metatarsal.
g, h. Phalanges of great toe.
i. Inferior ligament.
j. Plantar fasciae, supporting the plantar arch.
k. Achilles' tendon.

awkwardly; fumble. —*n.* A misstroke or misplay, especially in golf. [Cf. dial. G *fuseln* work badly]—**foo'zler** *n.*

fop (fop) *n.* A man affectedly fastidious in dress or deportment; a dandy. [Cf. Du. *foppen* cheat]

fop·ling (fop'ling) *n.* A petty fop.

fop·per·y (fop'ər·ē) *n. pl.* **·per·ies** The conduct or practices of a fop. Also **fop'pish·ness.**

fop·pish (fop'ish) *adj.* Characteristic of a fop; dandified. —**fop'pish·ly** *adv.*

for (fôr, *unstressed* fər) *prep.* **1** To the extent of: The ground is flat *for miles.* **2** Through the duration or period of: The coupon is good *for* a week. **3** To the number or amount of: a check *for* six dollars. **4** At the price or payment of: He bought the hat *for* ten dollars. **5** On account of; as a result of: He is respected *for* his ability. **6** In honor of; by the name of: He is called Walter *for* his grandfather. **7** Appropriate to: a time *for* work. **8** In place or instead of: using a book *for* a desk. **9** In favor, support, or approval of: a vote *for* peace. **10** In the interest or behalf of: My lawyers will speak *for* me. **11** Tending toward, as with longing or desire: a passion *for* jewelry; an eye *for* bargains. **12** As affecting (in a particular way): good *for* your health. **13** Belonging, given, attributed, or assigned to: a package *for* you; the reason *for* going. **14** In proportion to: big *for* his age. **15** As the equivalent to or requital of: blow *for* blow. **16** In spite of: I believe in it *for* all your sophistry! **17** In order to reach or go toward: He left *for* his office. **18** In order to become, find, keep, or obtain: suing *for* damages; looking *for* a hat. **19** At (a particular time or occasion): We agreed to meet *for* Easter. **20** In the character of; as being, seeming, or supposed to be: We took him *for* an honest man. —**for . . . to . . .** To have: The child pulled at her skirt *for* her *to* notice him. —**O (Now, etc.) for . . .** ! Would that I had!: O *for* a horse! —*conj.* **1** In view of the reason that; seeing that: It is no easy matter to decide, *for* its elements are complex. **2** Owing to the fact that; because: He could not leave, *for* he was expecting a visitor. See synonyms under BECAUSE. [OE]

for- *prefix* **1** Away; off (in a privative sense); past: *forget, forgo.* **2** Very; extremely: *forlorn.* [OE *for-, fær-*]

for- See also words beginning FORE-.

for·age (fôr'ij, for'-) *n.* **1** Any food suitable for horses or cattle. **2** The act of foraging or seeking food. —*v.* **for·aged, for·ag·ing** *v.t.* **1** To strip of provisions; search through for supplies; ravage. **2** To provide with forage. **3** To obtain or provide by or as by foraging. —*v.i.* **4** To search for food or supplies. **5** To search: usually with *out* or *for.* **6** To make a foray. See synonyms under FOOD. [<F *fourrage* <OF *feurre* <Gmc.]—**for'ag·er** *n.*

forage cap *Brit.* A small, undress military cap.

foraging ant Any of various tropical ants (family *Formicidae*) that make forays for food in large bodies; especially, the driver ant and army ant of Africa, and the tropical American legionary ant (genus *Eciton*).

Fo·rain (fô·raṅ', **Jean Louis,** 1852–1931, French painter.

For·a·ker, Mount (fôr'ə·kər, for'-) A peak in south central Alaska; 17,280 feet.

fo·ra·men (fô·rā'mən) *n. pl.* **·ram·i·na** (-ram'ə·nə) *Anat.* **1** An orifice or short passage, as in a bone. **2** An opening; aperture. [<L <*forare* bore]

foramen magnum *Anat.* The large orifice by which the spinal cord passes into the skull and becomes continuous with the medulla oblongata.

for·a·min·i·fer (fôr'ə·min'ə·fər, for'-) *n.* One of a large order *(Foraminifera)* of rhizopods usually having a typically calcareous or chitinous shell perforated by many minute apertures. They are chiefly marine and virtually microscopic. [<L *foramen, -inis* a hole +*-fer* having <*ferre* bear]—**fo·ram·i·nif·er·al** (fə·ram'ə·nif'ər·əl), **fo·ram'i·nif'er·ous** *adj.*

for·as·much as (fôr'əz·much') **1** Seeing or considering that; since; because. **2** *Obs.* So far as. Also **for as much as.**

for·ay (fôr'ā, for'ā) *v.t.* & *v.i.* To ravage; pillage; raid. —*n.* A marauding expedition; raid. See synonyms under INVASION. [Prob. back formation <*forayer* a raider <OF *forrier* <*forre,* var. of *feurre* FORAGE]

forb (fôrb) *n.* A weed, in the range stockman's usage; a non-grasslike herb. [Appar. <Gk. *phorbē* fodder]

for·bade, for·bad (fər·bad', fôr-) Past tense of FORBID.

for·bear[1] (fôr·bâr', fər-) *v.* **·bore, ·borne, ·bear·ing** *v.t.* **1** To refrain or abstain from; avoid (an action) voluntarily. **2** *Archaic* To put up with; endure. —*v.i.* **3** To abstain or refrain. **4** To be patient or act patiently. See synonyms under REFRAIN. [OE]—**for·bear'er** *n.*

for·bear[2] (fôr'bâr') See FOREBEAR.

for·bear·ance (fôr·bâr'əns, fər-) *n.* **1** The act of forbearing; patient endurance of offenses. **2** *Law* A refraining from claiming or enforcing a right. **3** A refraining from retaliation or retribution. See synonyms under MERCY, PATIENCE, RESPITE.

for·bear·ing (fôr·bâr'ing, fər-) *adj.* Disposed to forbear; patient.

Forbes–Rob·ert·son (fôrbz'rob'ərt·sən), **Sir Johnston,** 1853–1937, English actor.

for·bid (fər·bid', fôr-) *v.t.* **for·bade** or **for·bad, for·bid·den** or **for·bid, for·bid·ding 1** To command (a person) not to do, use, enter, etc. **2** To prohibit the use or doing of; interdict. **3** To make impossible. See synonyms under PROHIBIT. [OE *forbēodan*]—**for·bid'dance** *n.* —**for·bid'der** *n.*

for·bid·den (fər·bid'n, fôr-) *adj.* Not allowed; prohibited.

Forbidden City 1 Lhasa, Tibet. **2** A walled section of Peking, China, containing the royal palaces of the former Chinese Empire.

forbidden fruit 1 In the Bible, the fruit of the tree of knowledge of good and evil, forbidden to Adam and Eve. **2** Prohibited pleasure.

for·bid·ding (fər·bid'ing, fôr-) *adj.* **1** Such as to repel; unfriendly and repellent in manner. **2** Repulsive, or causing aversion: a *forbidding* countenance. —**for·bid'ding·ly** *adv.* —**for·bid'·ding·ness** *n.*

for·bore (fôr·bôr', -bōr') Past tense of FORBEAR[1].

for·borne (fôr·bôrn', -bōrn') Past participle of FORBEAR[1].

for·by (fôr·bī') *adv.* & *prep. Scot.* **1** Besides; over and above. **2** Near; hard by. **3** Past, in time. Also **for·bye'.**

force (fôrs, fōrs) *n.* **1** *Physics* Anything that changes or tends to change the state of rest or motion in a body: the fundamental cgs unit of force is the dyne. **2** The action of one body upon another; any operating energy. **3** Any moral, social, or political cause, or aggregate of causes. **4** Power or energy as lodged in an individual agent. **5** Power or energy considered as exerting constraint or compulsion; coercion. **6** The capacity to convince or move; weight; import. **7** Binding effect; efficacy. **8** An organized or aggregated body of individuals; especially, a military aggregate; an army; troop or naval unit. **9** Rhetorical vigor; energy; animation; strength. **10** A group of workers. See synonyms under ARMY, IMPULSE, OPERATION, POWER. —**coercive** or **coercitive force** *Physics* The power of resisting magnetization or demagnetization. —**the force** The police of a certain district. —*v.t.* **forced, forc·ing 1** To compel to do something by or as by force; coerce; constrain. **2** To get or obtain by or as by force: to *force* an answer. **3** To bring forth or about by or as by effort: to *force* a smile. **4** To drive or move despite resistance; press: to *force* the enemy back. **5** To assault and capture, as a fortification. **6** To break open, as a door or lock. **7** To make, as a passage or way, by force. **8** To press or impose upon someone as by force: to *force* one's opinion on someone. **9** To exert to or beyond the utmost; strain, as the voice. **10** To stimulate the growth of artificially, as plants in a hothouse. **11** To rape. **12** *Obs.* To put in force, as a law. **13** In baseball: **a** To put out (a base runner) who has been compelled by another baserunner to leave one base for the next. **b** To allow (the base runner on third base) to score by walking the batter when the bases are full. **c** To allow (a run) in such a manner. **14** In card games: **a** To compel (a player) to trump a trick by leading a suit of which he has none. **b** To play so as to compel (a player) to reveal the strength of his hand. **c** To compel a player to play (a particular card). [<F <L *fortis* brave, strong]—**force'a·ble** *adj.* —**forc'er** *n.*

forced (fôrst, fōrst) *adj.* **1** Compulsory. **2** Strained; affected: *forced* gaiety. **3** Speeded up, with few or no pauses: a *forced* march.

forced draft A current of air artificially supplied as to a furnace.

forced feeding Compulsory feeding of a person.

forced landing *Aeron.* The landing of an aircraft because of adverse weather conditions, mechanical failure, or the like.

forced oscillations *Electr.* Oscillations imposed upon an electrical system by outside forces which determine the amplitude and frequency of the oscillation. Compare FREE OSCILLATION.

force-feed (fōrs'fēd', fôrs'-) *n.* The supply of lubricating oil under pressure to an internal-combustion engine.

force·ful (fôrs'fəl, fōrs'-) *adj.* Acting with force; strong; effective. —**force'ful·ly** *adv.* —**force'ful·ness** *n.*

force ma·jeure (ma̤·zhœr') *French* **1** Superior and irresistible force. **2** *Law* The virtual equivalent of *act of God* or *inevitable accident.*

force·meat (fôrs'mēt', fōrs'-) *n.* Finely chopped, seasoned meat served separately or used as stuffing. [<*force,* alter. of FARCE, *v.* +MEAT]

force-out (fôrs'out', fōrs'-) *n.* In baseball, an out made when a runner, forced from his base, fails to reach the next base before it is tagged by a fielder holding the ball.

for·ceps (fôr'səps) *n.* **1** A pair of pincers for grasping and manipulating small or delicate objects: used by watchmakers, surgeons, dentists, etc. **2** *Anat.* A bundle of fibers uniting the corpus callosum with the cerebral hemispheres of the brain. **3** A pincerslike structure. [<L <*formus* warm +*capere* take]

force pump A pump that delivers fluid at a pressure greater than that at which it is received: distinguished from *lift pump.*

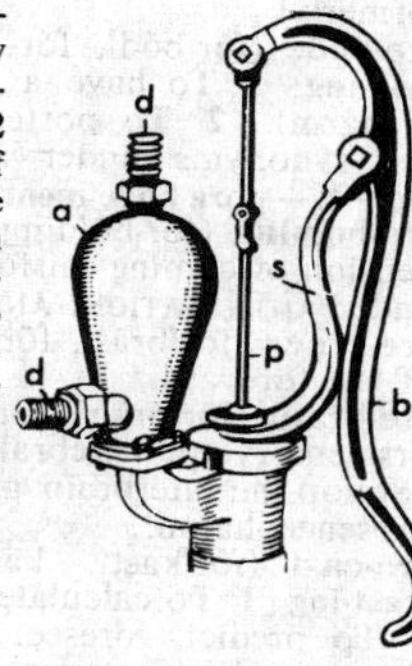

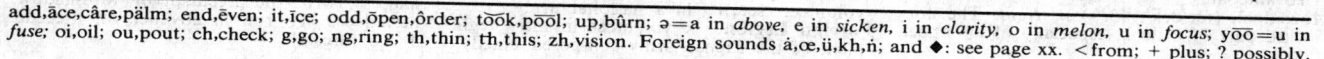

SIDE–SUCTION FORCE PUMP
a. Air chamber. *b.* Brake. *d, d.* Discharge pipes. *p.* Piston rod. *s.* Stand.

for·ci·ble (fôr'sə·bəl) *adj.* **1** Accomplished by force. **2** Energetic; cogent. See synonyms under POWERFUL, RACY. —**for'ci·ble·ness** *n.* —**for'ci·bly** *adv.*

ford (fôrd, fōrd) *n.* A place in a stream that can be crossed in a vehicle or by wading. —*v.t.* **1** To go on foot or in a vehicle across (a stream, river, etc.). **2** To drive across a river or stream at a ford, as cattle, etc. [OE *ford*]—**ford'a·ble** *adj.* —**ford'less** *adj.*

Ford (fôrd, fōrd), **Ford Madox,** 1873–1939, English writer: original surname Hueffer. —**Gerald Rudolph,** born 1913, 38th president of the United States 1974-1977. —**Henry,** 1863–1947, U.S. automobile manufacturer. —**John,** 1586?–1639?, English dramatist.

for·do (fôr·do͞o') *v.t.* **·did, ·done, ·do·ing** *Archaic* **1** To kill; destroy. **2** To ruin; undo. Also spelled *foredo.* [OE *fordōn*]

for·done (fôr·dun') *adj. Archaic* Worn out with fatigue; exhausted.

fore (fôr, fōr) *adj.* **1** Preceding in place or time; forward; antecedent; prior. **2** Situated at or toward the front in relation to something else. —*n.* **1** The foremost part; the leading place. **2** *Naut.* The foremast. —**to the fore 1** To or at the front; into promi-

nence or conspicuous view. 2 At hand; available. 3 Alive; still active. —*prep.* & *conj.* *Archaic* or *Dial.* Before. —*adv.* 1 *Naut.* At or toward the bow of a ship. 2 Before; forward; in front. —*interj.* In golf, a warning to any person who stands in the way of a stroke or of the ball. [OE]

fore–[1] See also words beginning FOR–.

fore–[2] *prefix* 1 Prior in time, place, or rank; as in:

fore–acquaint	**fore–assign**	**foreman**
fore–adapt	**forebeing**	**forenotice**
fore–age	**forebless**	**foreparent**
fore–announce	**forecited**	**fore–quoted**
fore–answer	**foreconclude**	**foresignify**

2 Front; in or at the front; as in:

forebay	**foreboom**	**fore–edge**
forebody	**forecabin**	**fore–end**

[OE *fore-*, *for-* before]

fore–and–aft (fôr′ən·aft′, fōr′-) *adj.* & *adv.* *Naut.* Lying or going in the direction of the ship's length; also, toward both bow and stern; in or at the bow and stern.

fore–and–aft rigged *Naut.* Fitted with sails whose forward edge (luff) is set on travelers attached to the mast: distinguished from *square–rigged.* See SCHOONER (def. 1).

fore–and–after (fôr′ən·af′ter, fōr′-) *n. Naut.* 1 Anything set along the length of a ship, as a hatch beam. 2 A vessel having only fore–and–aft sails.

fore·arm[1] (fôr·ärm′, fōr-) *v.t.* To arm beforehand.

fore·arm[2] (fôr′ärm′, fōr′-) *n.* 1 The part of the arm between the elbow and the wrist. ◆ Collateral adjective: *cubital.* 2 A wooden grip on the barrel of a gun to guard the firer's hand against being burned.

fore·bear (fôr′bâr′, fōr′-) *n.* An ancestor. [<Earlier *fore–be–er*, one who has existed formerly]

fore·bode (fôr·bōd′, fōr-) *v.t.* & *v.i.* **·bod·ed, ·bod·ing** 1 To have a premonition of (evil or harm). 2 To portend; presage; foretell. See synonyms under AUGUR. [<FORE- + BODE[2]] —**fore·bode′ment** *n.* —**fore·bod′er** *n.*

fore·bod·ing (fôr·bō′ding, fōr-) *n.* The apprehension of coming misfortune. See synonyms under ANTICIPATION, ANXIETY.

fore·brace (fôr′brās′, fōr′-) *n. Naut.* A brace of the foreyard.

fore·brain (fôr′brān′, fōr′-) *n. Anat.* 1 The first embryonic cerebral vesicle, from which develop the interbrain and endbrain. 2 The prosencephalon.

fore·cast (fôr′kast′, -käst′, fōr′-) *v.t.* **·cast, ·cast·ing** 1 To calculate or plan beforehand. 2 To predict; foresee. 3 To foreshadow. See synonyms under ANTICIPATE, AUGUR. —*n.* 1 *Meteorol.* An antecedent calculation or determination, especially in regard to weather conditions over a short period of time on the basis of charted data. 2 Previous contrivance; also, plan. 3 Forethought; foresight. 4 A prophecy. See synonyms under ANTICIPATION, PRUDENCE.

fore·cast·er (fôr′kas′tər, -käs′-, fōr′-) *n.* One who forecasts, as the weather.

fore·cas·tle (fôr′kas′əl, -käs′-, fōr′-, fōk′səl) *n. Naut.* 1 The forward part of a ship. 2 In a merchant vessel, the forward part or compartment with living quarters for common sailors. Also spelled *fo'c's'le.*

fore·close (fôr·klōz′, fōr-) *v.* **·closed, ·clos·ing** *v.t.* 1 *Law* **a** To deprive (a mortgager in default) of the right to redeem mortgaged property. **b** To take away the power to redeem (a mortgage or pledge). 2 To shut out; exclude. —*v.i.* 3 To foreclose a mortgage. [<OF *forclos*, pp. of *forclore* exclude <*for-* outside (<L *fors*) + *clore* <L *claudere* close] —**fore·clos′a·ble** *adj.* —**fore·clo′sure** (-klō′zhər) *n.*

fore·con·scious (fôr·kon′shəs, fōr-) *n.* The preconscious.

fore·course (fôr′kôrs′, fōr′kōrs′) *n. Naut.* In a square–rigged vessel, the foresail.

fore·court (fôr′kôrt′, fōr′kōrt′) *n.* In tennis, handball, etc., the zone nearest the net or wall.

fore·date (fôr·dāt′, fōr-) *v.t.* **·dat·ed, ·dat·ing** To antedate.

fore·deck (fôr′dek′, fōr′-) *n. Naut.* The forward part of a deck, especially of an upper deck.

fore·do (fôr·do͞o′, fōr-) See FORDO.

fore·doom (fôr·do͞om′, fōr-) *v.t.* To doom in advance; condemn beforehand. —*n.* (fôr′·do͞om′, fōr′-) Doom in advance.

fore·fa·ther (fôr′fä′thər, fōr′-) *n.* An ancestor, especially a remote ancestor.

Forefathers' Day The anniversary of the landing of the Pilgrims at Plymouth, Mass. (Dec. 21, 1620), usually celebrated on Dec. 22, through an error in changing from the Old Style calendar to the New Style.

fore·feel (fôr·fēl′, fōr-) *v.t.* **·felt, ·feel·ing** To have a premonition of; feel before.

fore·foot (fôr′fo͝ot′, fōr′-) *n. pl.* **·feet** 1 A front foot. 2 *Naut.* The bow or cutwater of a vessel.

fore·front (fôr′frunt′, fōr′-) *n.* The foremost part or position.

fore·gath·er (fôr·gath′ər, fōr-) See FORGATHER.

fore·glimpse (fôr′glimps′, fōr′-) *n.* A glimpse of the future, or a glance ahead at the outset.

fore·go[1] (fôr·gō′, fōr-) See FORGO.

fore·go[2] (fôr·gō′, fōr-) *v.t.* & *v.i.* **fore·went, fore·gone, fore·go·ing** To go before or precede in time, place, etc. [OE *foregān*]

fore·go·er (fôr·gō′ər, fōr-) *n.* One who or that which precedes; especially, the leader of a dog team.

fore·go·ing (fôr·gō′ing, fōr-) *adj.* Occurring previously; antecedent. See synonyms under ANTECEDENT.

fore·gone (fôr′gôn′, -gon′, fōr′-) *adj.* Determined already; previous. —**fore′gone′ness** *n.*

foregone conclusion 1 A conclusion determined in advance of the evidence. 2 An obvious, foreseen, or foreseeable result.

fore·ground (fôr′ground′, fōr′-) *n.* That part of a landscape or picture nearest the spectator.

fore·gut (fôr′gut′, fōr′-) *n. Zool.* In vertebrates, the anterior part of the embryonic alimentary canal.

fore·hand (fôr′hand′, fōr′-) *adj.* 1 Done prior to. 2 Front. 3 Of or pertaining to a tennis stroke made to the right of the body (when the player is right–handed): distinguished from *backhand.* —*n.* 1 The part of a horse in front of the rider. 2 Superiority; advantage. 3 A forehand tennis stroke; also, the position in playing such a stroke.

fore·hand·ed (fôr′han′did, fōr′-) *adj.* 1 Done in good time; early. 2 Having money saved; thrifty. 3 In tennis, forehand. 4 Referring to the forehand or foreparts of a horse. —**fore′hand′ed·ness** *n.*

fore·head (fôr′id, -hed, for′-) *n.* 1 The upper part of the face, between the eyes and the natural line of the hair. ◆ Collateral adjective: *frontal.* 2 The front part of a thing.

for·eign (fôr′in, for′-) *adj.* 1 Belonging to, situated in, or derived from another country; not native; alien. 2 Connected with other countries; bearing a relation to other countries. 3 Of, pertaining to, or resulting from some person or thing aside from that under discussion. 4 *Biol.* Occurring in that place or body in which it is not normally or organically found. 5 Having only remote relation or no relation; not pertinent; irrelevant. 6 *Law* Not subject to the laws or jurisdiction of a country; extraterritorial. 7 *Obs.* Outside one's family circle. See synonyms under ALIEN. [<F *forain*, ult. <L *foras* out of doors]

foreign affairs International affairs in relation to the home government.

foreign bill A bill of exchange drawn in one country or state and made payable in another: also called **foreign draft.**

for·eign–born (fôr′in·bôrn′, for′-) *adj.* Born in another country; not native.

for·eign·er (fôr′in·ər, for′-) *n.* A native or citizen of a foreign country. See synonyms under ALIEN.

foreign exchange 1 The transaction of monetary affairs, payment of debts, etc., between residents of different countries. 2 The value of the money of one country in terms of the money of another; also, the difference between this and par.

for·eign·ism (fôr′ən·iz′əm, for′-) *n.* 1 The state of being foreign. 2 A foreign peculiarity, idiom, or custom.

foreign legion A military unit of foreign volunteers serving in a national army.

Foreign Legion A volunteer infantry regiment of the French army composed chiefly, in its enlisted ranks, of non–French troops and originally serving in North Africa. Also **French Foreign Legion.**

foreign mission 1 A group of people organized and sent to spread religious teaching, medical knowledge, etc., in a foreign country. 2 A group of government representatives sent to a foreign country on diplomatic or other business.

for·eign·ness (fôr′in·nis, for′-) *n.* 1 The state or quality of being foreign. 2 Absence of connection or relation; extraneousness.

foreign office A department or bureau of a government in charge of foreign affairs; also, the building in which it is housed. Also **Foreign Office.**

fore·judge[1] (fôr·juj′, fōr-) See FORJUDGE.

fore·judge[2] (fôr·juj′, fōr-) *v.t.* **·judged, ·judg·ing** To prejudge; pass judgment on before hearing the evidence.

fore·know (fôr·nō′, fōr-) *v.t.* **·knew, ·known, ·know·ing** To know beforehand. —**fore·know′a·ble** *adj.*

fore·knowl·edge (fôr′nol′ij, fōr′-) *n.* Knowledge of a thing before it manifests itself or of an event before it takes place; prescience.

fore·la·dy (fôr′lā′dē, fōr′-) *n. pl.* **·la·dies** A forewoman.

fore·land (fôr′land, fōr′-) *n.* 1 A projecting point of land; a cape. 2 Territory situated in front: opposed to *hinterland.*

fore·lay (fôr·lā′, fōr-) *v.t.* **·laid, ·lay·ing** *Dial.* To plan or lay down beforehand.

fore·leg (fôr′leg′, fōr′-) *n.* A front leg of a quadruped. Also **fore leg.**

fore·lock[1] (fôr′lok′, fōr′-) *n.* A lock of hair growing over the forehead.

fore·lock[2] (fôr′lok′, fōr′-) *n. Mech.* An iron pin or wedge passed through the end of a bolt or the like, to prevent its withdrawal; linchpin; key.

fore·look (fôr′lo͝ok′, fōr′-) *n. U.S.* A look into the future.

fore·man (fôr′mən, fōr′-) *n. pl.* **·men** (-mən) 1 The overseer of a body of workmen. 2 The head man; chief man; especially, the spokesman of a jury. See synonyms under MASTER. —**fore′man·ship** *n.*

fore·mast (fôr′mast′, -mäst′, -məst, fōr′-) *n. Naut.* The foremost mast of a vessel.

fore·mast·man (fôr′mast′mən, -mäst′-, fōr′-) *n. pl.* **·men** (-mən) An ordinary sailor.

fore·most (fôr′mōst, -məst, fōr′-) *adj.* First in place, time, rank, or order; chief. See synonyms under FIRST, PARAMOUNT. —*adv.* In the first place; soonest; first. [OE *formest*]

fore·name (fôr·nām′, fōr-) *v.t.* **·named, ·nam·ing** To name before; mention previously. —*n.* (fôr′nām′, fōr′-) A name placed before the family name or surname; a prenomen. —**fore′named′** *adj.*

fore·noon (fôr′no͞on′, fōr′-, fôr·no͞on′, fōr-) *n.* The period of daylight preceding midday; the morning.

fo·ren·sic (fə·ren′sik) *adj.* 1 Pertaining to courts of justice or to public disputation; argumentative; rhetorical. 2 Relating to or used in legal proceedings: *forensic* medicine. Also **fo·ren′si·cal.** [<L *forensis* <*forum* market place, forum] —**fo·ren′si·cal·ly** *adv.*

fore·or·dain (fôr′ôr·dān′, fōr′-) *v.t.* To ordain beforehand; predestinate.

fore·or·dain·ment (fôr′ôr·dān′mənt, fōr′-) *n.* Foreordination.

fore·or·di·na·tion (fôr·ôr′də·nā′shən, fōr-) *n.* Predestination; predetermination. See PREDESTINATION.

fore·part (fôr′pärt′, fōr′-) *n.* The first part in time, place, or sequence.

fore·past (fôr′past′, -päst′, fōr′-) *adj. Rare* Past; bygone. Also **fore′passed′.**

fore·peak (fôr′pēk′, fōr′-) *n. Naut.* The extreme forward part of a ship's hold within the angle of the bow under the lowest deck.

fore·quar·ter (fôr′kwôr′tər, fōr′-) *n.* The front portion of a side of beef, etc., including the leg and adjacent parts.

fore·rank (fôr′rangk′, fōr′-) *n.* The front or first rank.

fore·reach (fôr·rēch′, fōr-) *v.t. Naut.* 1 To gain upon or pass, as a ship. —*v.i.* 2 To move forward suddenly and unexpectedly. 3 To gain.

fore·run (fôr·run′, fōr-) *v.t.* **·ran, ·run, ·run·ning** 1 To be the precursor of; foreshadow; herald. 2 To run in advance of; precede. 3 To forestall.

fore·run·ner (fôr·run′ər, fōr-, fôr′run′ər, fōr′-) *n.*. 1 A precursor; predecessor; ancestor. 2 One who or that which runs before; a herald; a harbinger. 3 A portent or prognostic. — **the Forerunner** John the Baptist. See synonyms under HERALD.

fore·said (fôr′sed′, fōr′-) *adj.* Aforesaid.

fore·sail (fôr′sāl′, -səl, fōr′-, fō′səl) *n. Naut.* 1 A square sail, bent to the foreyard; the lowest sail on the foremast of a square-rigged vessel. 2 The fore-and-aft sail on a schooner's foremast, set on a boom and gaff. 3 The forestaysail of a cutter or sloop.

fore·see (fôr·sē′, fōr-) *v.t.* **fore·saw, fore·seen, fore·see·ing** To see beforehand; anticipate. — **fore·see′a·ble** *adj.* — **fore·seer′** *n.*

fore·shad·ow (fôr·shad′ō, fōr-) *v.t.* To suggest or indicate beforehand; prefigure. — *n.* The indistinct representation or indication of something to come. — **fore·shad′ow·er** *n.*

fore·sheet (fôr′shēt′, fōr′-) *n. Naut.* 1 A rope holding one of the clews of a foresail. 2 *pl.* The forward space in a boat.

fore·shore (fôr′shôr′, fōr′shōr′) *n.* That part of a shore uncovered at low tide.

fore·short·en (fôr·shôr′tən, fōr-) *v.t.* In drawing, to reduce the lines or parts of (a drawing, etc.) so as to create the illusion of depth and distance while retaining the proper proportions of size and extent. — **fore·short′·en·ing** *n.*

fore·show (fôr·shō′, fōr-) *v.t.* **·showed, ·shown, ·show·ing** To show or indicate beforehand; prophesy. Also *Archaic* **fore·shew′** (-shō).

fore·side (fôr′sīd′, fōr′-) *n.* 1 The front. 2 Land along the shore.

fore·sight (fôr′sīt′, fōr′-) *n.* 1 The act or capacity of foreseeing; a looking forward. 2 Thoughtful care for the future. See synonyms under ANTICIPATION, PRUDENCE, WISDOM. — **fore′sight′ed** *adj.* — **fore′sight′ed·ness** *n.*

fore·skin (fôr′skin′, fōr′-) *n.* The prepuce.

fore·spur·rer (fôr·spûr′ər, fōr-) *n. Obs.* One who rides in advance as a herald.

for·est (fôr′ist, for′-) *n.* 1 A large tract of land covered with a natural growth of trees and underbrush. ◆ Collateral adjective: *sylvan.* 2 In English law, wild land generally belonging to the crown and kept for the protection of game. — *adj.* Of, pertaining to, or inhabiting woods or forest. — *v.t.* To overspread or plant with trees; make a forest of. [<OF <Med. L *(silva) foresta* an unenclosed (wood) < *foris* outside]

for·est·age (fôr′is·tij, for′-) *n. Brit.* 1 *Law* Tribute payable to a forester. 2 A forester's service to the king.

fore·stall (fôr·stôl′, fōr-) *v.t.* 1 To hinder, prevent, or guard against by taking preventive measures. 2 To deal with, think of, or realize beforehand; anticipate. 3 To affect (the market) in one's favor by buying up or diverting goods. 4 *Obs.* To intercept. See synonyms under PREVENT. [OE *foresteall* an ambush] — **fore·stall′er** *n.* — **fore·stall′ing** *n.*

for·est·a·tion (fôr′is·tā′shən, for′-) *n.* 1 Forest extension; the planting of, or conversion of land into, forests. 2 Practical forestry.

fore·stay (fôr′stā′, fōr′-) *n. Naut.* A guy from the head of the foremast to the stem.

fore·stay·sail (fôr′stā′sāl′, -səl, fōr′-) *n. Naut.* A triangular sail in front of the foremast, hoisted on the forestay: in some rigs called *foresail.*

forest cover The sum total of vegetation in a forest; more especially, herbs, shrubs, and the litter of leaves, branches, fallen trees, and decayed vegetable matter composing the **forest floor.**

for·est·ed (fôr′is·tid, for′-) *adj.* Covered with trees or woods.

for·est·er (fôr′is·tər, for′-) *n.* 1 One skilled in the science of forestry; one in charge of a forest, its timber, or its game. 2 Any forest dweller. 3 A spotted moth (family *Agaristidae*) of the United States; especially, the velvety-black eight-spotted forester *(Alypia octomaculata).* 4 The great gray kangaroo of Australia *(Macropus giganteus).*

For·es·ter (fôr′is·tər, for′-), **C(ecil) S(cott),** 1899–1966, English novelist.

forest fly A small, dipterous insect *(Hippobosca equina)* widely distributed in the Old World, infesting horses, mules, camels, and related quadrupeds: also called *horse tick.*

Forest Hills A section of New York City on Long Island, site of the national lawn tennis tournaments.

forest reserve A tract of forest land set aside by government order for protection and cultivation.

for·est·ry (fôr′is·trē, for′-) *n.* The science of planting, developing, and managing forests.

Forest Service A branch of the Department of Agriculture which administers the National Forests, directs forest research, and promotes the conservation of forest resources.

fore·taste (fôr·tāst′, fōr-) *v.t.* **·tast·ed, ·tast·ing** To have some experience or taste of beforehand. See synonyms under ANTICIPATE. — *n.* (fôr′tāst′, fōr′-) A taste or brief experience beforehand. See synonyms under ANTICIPATION.

fore·tell (fôr·tel′, fōr-) *v.t.* & *v.i.* **·told, ·tell·ing** To tell or declare in advance; predict; prophesy. See synonyms under AUGUR, PROPHESY. — **fore·tell′er** *n.*

fore·think (fôr·thingk′, fōr-) *v.t. Rare* To think over or out in advance; anticipate.

fore·thought (fôr′thôt′, fōr′-) *adj.* Devised or thought of in advance; planned. — *n.* 1 Consideration beforehand; deliberate planning. 2 Prudent care for the future. See synonyms under ANTICIPATION, CARE, PRUDENCE. — **fore·thought′ful** *adj.* — **fore·thought′·ful·ly** *adv.* — **fore·thought′ful·ness** *n.*

fore·time (fôr′tīm′, fōr′-) *n.* Time gone by; the past.

fore·to·ken (fôr·tō′kən, fōr-) *v.t.* To foreshow or presage; foreshadow. — *n.* (fôr′tō′kən, fōr′-) A token in advance.

fore·tooth (fôr′tōōth′, fōr′-) *n. pl.* **·teeth** An incisor.

fore·top (fôr′top′, fōr′-; *for def. 3, also* fôr′təp, fōr′-) *n.* 1 The forelock; especially of a horse. 2 The front part of a wig. 3 *Naut.* A platform at the head of the lower section of a foremast.

fore·top·gal·lant (fôr′top·gal′ənt, -tə-, fōr′-) *adj. Naut.* Of, pertaining to, or designating the mast, sail, yard, etc., immediately above the foretopmast.

fore·top·gal·lant·mast (fôr′top·gal′ənt·mast′, -mäst′, -məst, -tə-, fōr′-) *n. Naut.* The mast or section of a mast above the foretopmast.

fore·top·man (fôr′top′mən, fōr′-) *n. pl.* **·men** (-mən) *Naut.* A sailor assigned to duty on the upper parts of a foremast.

fore·top·mast (fôr·top′mast′, -mäst′, -məst, fōr-) *n. Naut.* The section of a mast above the foretop.

fore·top·sail (fôr·top′sāl′, -səl, fōr-) *n.* The sail set on the foretopmast.

for·ev·er (fôr·ev′ər, fər-) *adv.* 1 Throughout eternity; to the end of time; everlastingly. 2 Incessantly. Also *Brit.* **for ever.**

forever and a day To all eternity: emphatic form.

for·ev·er·more (fôr·ev′ər·môr, -mōr, fər-) *adv.* For all time and eternity; forever: emphatic form.

fore·warn (fôr·wôrn′, fōr-) *v.t.* To caution beforehand; inform or instruct in advance. — **fore·warn′ing** *n.*

fore·wom·an (fôr′wōōm′ən, fōr′-) *n. pl.* **·women** (-wim′in) A woman who oversees other employees.

fore·word (fôr′wûrd′, fōr′-) *n.* An introduction; preface.

fore·yard[1] (fôr′yärd′, fōr′-) *n. Naut.* The lowest yard on the foremast of a square-rigged vessel.

fore·yard[2] (fôr′yärd′, fōr′-) *n.* A front yard of a house, temple, etc.

for·fairn (fôr·fârn′, fōr-) *adj. Scot.* Tired out; forlorn.

For·far (fôr′fər, -fär) 1 A former name for ANGUS county, Scotland: also **For′far·shire** (-shir). 2 The county town of Angus county, Scotland.

for·feit (fôr′fit) *v.t.* To incur the loss of through some fault, omission, error, or offense. [< *n.*] — *adj.* Forfeited. — *n.* 1 A thing lost by way of penalty for some default. 2 *pl.* Any game in which some piece of personal property is taken as a fine for a breach of the rules, and is redeemable by some playful penalty; also, the articles so taken. 3 Forfeiture. [<OF *forfait* a misdeed <Med. L *foris factum* < *foris* outside + *factum.* See FACT.] — **for′feit·a·ble** *adj.* — **for′·feit·er** *n.*

for·fei·ture (fôr′fi·chər) *n.* 1 The act of forfeiting. 2 That which is forfeited.

for·fend (fôr·fend′) *v.t. Archaic* 1 To ward off, prevent. 2 To forbid. Also spelled *forefend.*

for·fi·cate (fôr′fi·kit) *adj.* Deeply furcate, or forked, as the tail of a frigate bird. [<L *forfex, forficis* scissors + -ATE[1]]

for·gat (fôr·gat′, fər-) *Archaic* Past tense of FORGET.

for·gath·er (fôr·gath′ər) *v.i.* 1 To meet or gather together; assemble. 2 To meet or encounter, especially by chance. 3 To associate; converse socially. Also spelled *foregather.*

for·gave (fôr·gāv′, fər-) Past tense of FORGIVE.

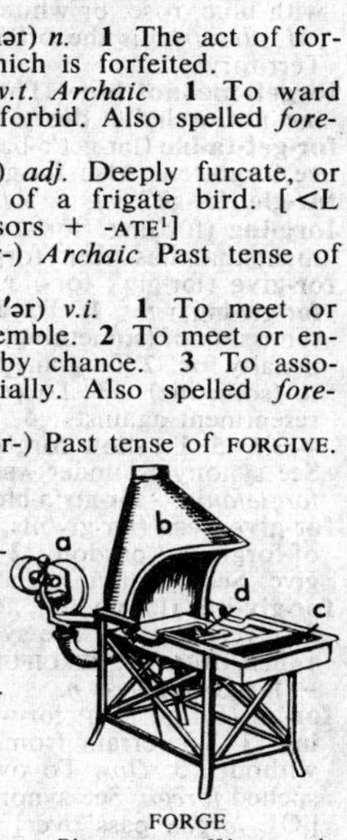

FORGE
a. Blower. *b.* Hood. *c.* Water tank. *d.* Coal bed.
The blower keeps fuel burning steadily by forced draft under the fire bed.

forge[1] (fôrj, fōrj) *n.* 1 An open fireplace or hearth with forced draft, for heating metal ready for hammering or shaping. 2 A smithy. 3 A place where metal is refined. — *v.* **forged, forg·ing** *v.t.* 1 To shape by heating and hammering, as a horseshoe; beat or stamp into shape. 2 To fashion or form in any way; invent. 3 To make, alter, or imitate with intent to defraud. — *v.i.* 4 To commit forgery. 5 To work as a smith. [<OF, ult. <L *fabrica.* Doublet of FABRIC.] — **forged** *adj.*

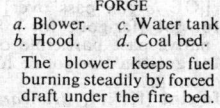

forge[2] (fôrj, fōrj) *v.t.* & *v.i.* **forged, forg·ing** To move, go, or impel slowly forward. [? Alter. of FORCE]

forg·er (fôr′jər, fōr′-) *n.* 1 One who counterfeits or commits forgery. 2 A smith. 3 A fabricator.

for·ger·y (fôr′jər·ē, fōr′-) *n. pl.* **·ger·ies** 1 The act of falsely making or materially altering, with intent to defraud, any writing which, if genuine, might be of legal efficacy or the foundation of a legal liability. 2 The act of counterfeiting coin. 3 A spurious article bearing a false signature, as a painting, sculpture, or book. 4 *Obs.* The exercise of invention.

Synonym: counterfeiting. Imitating or altering a coin or note which passes as currency or money is *counterfeiting*; the making of a fraudulent writing, or the material alteration of a genuine writing with intent to defraud, is *forgery*; the changing of the figures in a genuine note or check, the unauthorized appending of another's signature, the transferring of a genuine signature to a document for which it was not intended, are all instances of *forgery*; the making of spurious coins, the raising of government notes, bonds, etc., to higher values, are instances of *counterfeiting.*

for·get (fər·get′, fôr-) *v.* **for·got** (*Archaic* **for·gat**), **for·got·ten** or **for·got, for·get·ting** *v.t.* 1 To be unable to recall (something previously known) to the mind; fail or cease to remember. 2 To fail (to do something) unintentionally; neglect. 3 To fail to take through forgetfulness; leave behind accidentally. 4 To lose interest in or regard for; overlook purposely; disregard or slight: I will never *forget* you. 5 To leave unmentioned; fail to think of. — *v.i.* 6 To lose remembrance of something. — **to forget oneself** 1 To be unselfish. 2 To lose self-control and act in an unbecoming manner. 3 To lose consciousness. 4 To be lost in thought. [OE *forgietan*] — **for·get′ter** *n.*

for·get·ful (fər·get′fəl, fôr-) *adj.* 1 Having little power to retain or recall. 2 Neglectful; inattentive; careless. 3 *Obs.* Producing forgetfulness or oblivion. — **for·get′ful·ly** *adv.* — **for·get′ful·ness** *n.*

for·ge·tive (fôr′jə·tiv, fōr-) *adj. Archaic* Creative; inventive. [? < *forge*¹, *v.*]
for·get–me–not (fər·get′mē·not′) *n.* A small herb (genus *Myosotis*) of the borage family, with blue, rose, or white flowers. One species (*M. alpestris*) is the official flower of Alaska Territory.
forget–me–not blue The color of the forget–me–not, a light, dusty blue.
for·get·ta·ble (fər·get′ə·bəl, fôr-) *adj.* That may be forgotten. Also **for·get′a·ble.**
for·gie (fər·gē′) *v.t.* & *v.i. Scot.* To forgive.
forg·ing (fôr′jing, fōr′-) *n.* A tool or implement that has been forged.
for·give (fər·giv′, fôr-) *v.* **for·gave, for·giv·en, for·giv·ing** *v.t.* **1** To grant pardon for or remission of (something); cease to demand the penalty for. **2** To grant freedom from penalty to (someone). **3** To cease to blame or feel resentment against. **4** To remit, as a debt. — *v.i.* **5** To show forgiveness; grant pardon. See synonyms under ABSOLVE, PARDON. [OE *forgiefan*] — **for·giv′a·ble** *adj.* — **for·giv′er** *n.*
for·give·ness (fər·giv′nis, fôr-) *n.* **1** The act of forgiving; pardon. **2** A disposition to forgive. See synonyms under MERCY.
for·giv·ing (fər·giv′ing, fôr-) *adj.* Disposed to forgive; merciful. See synonyms under CHARITABLE, HUMANE, MERCIFUL. — **for·giv′ing·ly** *adv.* — **for·giv′ing·ness** *n.*
for·go (fôr·gō′) *v.t.* **for·went, for·gone, for·go·ing** **1** To refrain from. **2** To give up; go without. **3** *Obs.* To overlook; neglect. Also spelled *forego.* See synonyms under ABANDON. [OE *forgān* pass over] — **for·go′er** *n.*
for·got (fər·got′, fôr-) Past tense and alternative past participle of FORGET.
for·got·ten (fər·got′n, fôr-) Past participle of FORGET.
fo·rint (fôr′int, *Hungarian* fô·rēnt′) *n.* The basic monetary unit of Hungary since 1946, subdivided into 100 fillér.
for·jes·kit (fər·jes′kit) *adj. Scot.* Exhausted by labor.
for·judge (fôr·juj′) *v.t.* **·judged, ·judg·ing** *Law* **1** To deprive, as of a right, by judgment of court. **2** To expel (an attorney or officer) from court for some offense. Sometimes spelled *forejudge.* [<OF *forjugier* < *fors-* outside (<L *foris*) + *jugier* <L *judicare* judge]
fork (fôrk) *n.* **1** A utensil consisting of a handle and two or more tines or prongs, used for handling food at the table or in cooking. **2** A pronged agricultural or mechanical implement for tossing, turning, carrying, digging, lifting, etc.: a *pitchfork.* **3** Anything of like use or shape. **4** An offshoot: diverging branch. **5** The angular opening or place of division. **6** The point at which two roads or streams unite. **7** Each of the roads or streams: the west *fork*; also, the ground in the angle made by the junction of two streams. **8** A dilemma. **9** The barb of an arrow. — *v.t.* **1** To make fork–shaped. **2** To pierce, pitch, or dig with or as with a fork. **3** In chess, to attack (two pieces) simultaneously. — *v.i.* **4** To branch; bifurcate: The trail *forked.* — **to fork out** (or **over** or **up**) *Slang* To pay or hand over. [OE *forca* <L *furca*]

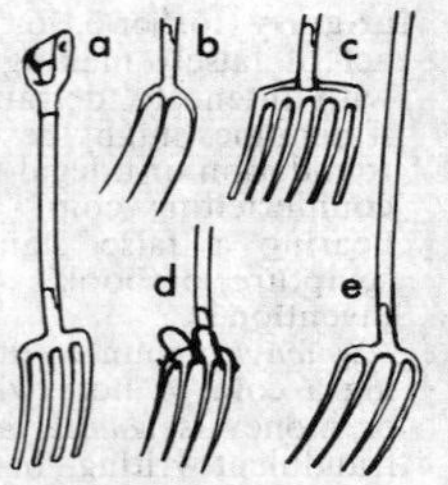

FARM FORKS
a. Spading fork.
b. Hay fork.
c. Ensilage fork.
d. Barley fork.
e. Manure fork.

forked (fôrkt, fôr′kid) *adj.* **1** Having a fork, or shaped like a fork. **2** Diverging into two branches: *forked* lightning. — **fork′ed·ly** *adv.* — **fork′ed·ness** *n.*
forked tongue A lying or treacherous tongue.
fork·y (fôr′kē) *adj.* Like a fork; forked; bifurcate.
For·lì (fôr·lē′) A city in north central Italy on the Montone. Ancient **Fo·rum Liv·i·i** (fôr′əm liv′ē·ī, fō′rəm).
for·lorn (fər·lôrn, fôr-) *adj.* **1** Left in distress without help or hope; deserted. **2** Miserable; pitiable. **3** Lonely; dreary. [Orig. pp. of obs. *forlese* lose, abandon, OE *forleosan*] — **for·lorn′ly** *adv.* — **for·lorn′ness** *n.*
forlorn hope **1** A desperate enterprise. **2** Those who undertake a hopeless task, as the members of a storming party. [<Du. *verloren hoop* lost troop]
form (fôrm) *n.* **1** The outward or visible shape of a body as distinguished from its substance or color. **2** *Philos.* The intelligible structure of a thing, which determines its substance or species, as distinguished from its matter. **3** A body, especially of a living being. **4** A mold or frame for shaping. **5** A specific structure, condition, or appearance: carbon in the *form* of diamonds; disease in all its *forms.* **6** A specific type or species of a larger group: democracy as a *form* of government. **7** In art, music, and literature, style and manner, as opposed to content. **8** System; order; formal procedure: to convene as a matter of *form.* **9** Behavior or conduct according to custom, ceremony, or decorum; formality; manners. **10** Manner or fashion of doing something: He swam in good *form.* **11** Fitness in respect to health, spirits, training, etc.: The horse was in good *form* for the race. **12** A formula or draft; a specimen document used as a guide in drawing up others. **13** A document with spaces left for the insertion of information: an application *form.* **14** The lair of an animal, especially of a hare. **15** A cotton bud. **16** A long bench without a back. **17** *Brit.* A grade or class in a school. **18** *Printing* The body of type and cuts secured in a chase. Also *Brit.* **forme.** **19** *Gram.* Any of the various shapes assumed by a word in a particular context, as *talk, talks, talked, talking.* **20** *Ling.* A linguistic form. See BOUND FORM, FREE FORM. — *v.t.* **1** To give shape to; mold; fashion. **2** To construct in the mind; devise: to *form* a plan. **3** To combine into; organize into: The men *formed* a club. **4** To develop; acquire, as a habit or liking. **5** To give a specific or exemplified shape or character to: He *formed* his ideals on those of Wilson. **6** To go to make up; be an element of: Guesswork *forms* the larger part of his theory. **7** To shape by discipline or training; mold: Education *forms* the mind. **8** *Gram.* To construct (a word) by adding or combining elements: to *form* an adverb by adding *-ly* to an adjective. — *v.i.* **9** To take shape; assume a specific form or arrangement. **10** To begin to exist. See synonyms under CONSTRUCT. [<OF *fourme* <L *forma*]
Synonyms (noun): appearance, aspect, ceremonial, ceremony, configuration, conformation, contour, fashion, figure, formality, method, mode, mold, observance, outline, rite, ritual, shape. See BODY, FIGURE, FRAME.
-form *combining form* Like; in the shape of: *ensiform.* [<L *-formis* -like < *forma* form]
for·mal¹ (fôr′məl) *adj.* **1** Made, framed, or done in accordance with regular and established forms and methods, or with proper dignity and impressiveness; orderly. **2** Of or pertaining to established forms or methods. **3** Of or pertaining to the external appearance or form as opposed to real substance: *formal* religion; perfunctory. **4** Having outward show, but lacking reality; outward; mechanical. **5** Having regard to or done in accordance with a scrupulous observance of social forms, customs, and etiquette; punctilious; ceremonious; conventional. **6** Of or pertaining to the form as opposed to the content of logical reasoning. **7** *Philos.* Of or pertaining to the characteristic composition of anything; essential instead of material.
for·mal² (fôr·mal′) *n.* Methylal.
for·mal·de·hyde (fôr·mal′də·hīd) *n. Chem.* A colorless pungent gas, CH_2O, obtained variously by the partial oxidation of methyl alcohol: used as an antiseptic, reagent, preservative, and disinfectant, for which it is prepared by solution in water or absorption into porous materials. It is also the basis of many important plastic materials, such as Bakelite, Formica, etc. Also **for·mal′de·hyd** (-hīd). [<FORM(IC) + ALDEHYDE]
for·mal·ism (fôr′məl·iz′əm) *n.* **1** Scrupulous observance of prescribed forms, especially in religious worship, social life, art, etc. **2** An instance of such observance. **3** Gestalt or configuration psychology. — **for′mal·ist** *n.* — **for′mal·is′tic** *adj.*
for·mal·i·ty (fôr·mal′ə·tē) *n. pl.* **·ties** **1** The state or character of being formal, precise, stiff, or elaborately ceremonious. **2** Adherence to standards and rules; ceremony; conventionality. **3** A proper order of procedure. **4** Form without substance or meaning. See synonyms under FORM.
for·mal·ize (fôr·məl·īz) *v.* **·ized, ·iz·ing** *v.t.* **1** To make formal. **2** To give form to; reduce to form. — *v.i.* **3** To be formal; act formally. — **for′mal·i·za′tion** *n.* — **for′mal·iz′er** *n.*
formal logic The branch of logic which deals only with the formal structure of propositions and with the operations by which conclusions are deduced from them; the art of deductive reasoning.
for·mal·ly (fôr′mə·lē) *adv.* **1** In accordance with forms; in a formal manner; stiffly. **2** In an authorized manner.
for·mat (fôr′mat) *n.* The form, size, type face, margins, and general style of a book or other publication, when printed and bound; especially, its shape and size as determined by the number of times the original sheet forming the leaves has been folded. [<F <L (*liber*) *formatus* a (book) made up < *formare* form]
for·mate (fôr′māt) *n. Chem.* A salt or ester of formic acid.
for·ma·tion (fôr·mā′shən) *n.* **1** The act or process of forming or of making by the combination of materials; also, the taking on of specific form; development. **2** Manner in which anything is shaped or composed. **3** The disposition of military troops as in column, line, or square. **4** Anything that is formed. **5** *Geol.* **a** Earthy or mineral deposits, or rock masses, named with reference to mode of origin. **b** A series of associated rocks, having similar conditions of origin. **6** *Ecol.* A fully developed plant association in a given area.
form·a·tive (fôr′mə·tiv) *adj.* **1** Competent, serving, or aiding to form; capable of being formed or influenced; plastic. **2** Pertaining to formation. **3** *Gram.* Serving to form words. — *n. Gram.* **1** An element, as an affix, added to the root of a word to give it a new and special grammatical form. **2** A word formed by the addition of a new element to, or a modification of, the root.
form class A group of linguistic forms having certain syntactical characteristics in common, as all words functioning as the subjects of sentences in English.
form drag *Physics* That component of fluid resistance which is due to the form of the object moving through it and which may be reduced or neutralized by streamlining.
For·men·te·ra (fôr·men·tā′rä) Smallest of the major islands of the Balearic group; 37 square miles.
form·er¹ (fôr′mər) *n.* One who or that which forms or molds; a maker; pattern.
for·mer² (fôr′mər) *adj.* Going before in time; previously mentioned; preceding; ancient. — **the former** The first of two mentioned persons or things: opposed to *the latter.* See synonyms under ANTECEDENT, ANTERIOR, CAUSE. [ME *formere,* a back formation < *foremost*]
for·mer·ly (fôr′mər·lē) *adv.* **1** Some time or a long time ago; heretofore. **2** *Obs.* At a time immediately preceding the present; just now.
for·mic (fôr′mik) *adj.* **1** Pertaining to or derived from ants. **2** Derived from formic acid. [<L *formica* ant]
For·mi·ca (fôr·mī′kə, fôr′mə·kə) *n.* A thermosetting phenolic resin used in transparent or colored sheets as wallboard, table tops, paneling, etc.; a trade name.
formic acid *Chem.* A colorless corrosive liquid compound, HCOOH, with a penetrating odor, found in the bodies of ants and spiders, in the hairs and other parts of certain caterpillars, and in stinging nettles, and made commercially by the reaction of carbon monoxide with sodium hydroxide.
for·mi·cant (fôr′mə·kənt) *adj.* **1** Antlike. **2** *Med.* Pertaining to the feeble, creeping motion of the pulse noted in certain conditions.
for·mi·car·y (fôr′mə·ker′ē) *n. pl.* **·car·ies** A nest of ants, consisting of galleries and chambers excavated in the earth and covered by a mound of debris.
for·mi·cate (fôr′mə·kāt) *v.i.* **·cat·ed, ·cat·ing** To swarm; collect in swarms, as ants. [<L *formicatus,* pp. of *formicare* crawl < *formica* an ant]
for·mi·ca·tion (fôr′mə·kā′shən) *n. Med.* An

itching sensation like the creeping of ants.
for·mi·ci·a·sis (fôr′mə·sī′ə·sis) *n. Pathol.* The itching, swollen condition following ant bite.

for·mi·da·ble (fôr′mi·də·bəl) *adj.* **1** Exciting fear; felt as dangerous to encounter. **2** Difficult to accomplish. [<MF <L *formidabilis* <*formidare* fear] — **for′mi·da·ble·ness** *n.* — **for′mi·da·bly** *adv.*

Synonyms: dangerous, redoubtable, redoubted, terrible, tremendous. That which is *formidable* is worthy of fear if encountered or opposed; as, a *formidable* array of troops, or of evidence. *Formidable* is a word of more dignity than *dangerous*, and suggests more calm and collected power than *terrible; formidable* is less overwhelming than *tremendous*. A loaded gun is *dangerous*; a battery of artillery is *formidable*. A *dangerous* man is likely to do mischief, and needs watching; a *formidable* man may not be *dangerous* if not attacked; an enraged maniac is *terrible*; the force of ocean waves in a storm, the silent pressure in the ocean depths, are *tremendous*. *Antonyms:* contemptible, despicable, feeble, harmless, helpless, powerless, weak.

form·less (fôrm′lis) *adj.* Without form; shapeless. — **form′less·ly** *adv.* — **form′less·ness** *n.*

For·mo·sa (fôr·mō′sə) **1** A former name for TAIWAN. **2** A province of northern Argentina; 28,778 square miles; capital, Formosa.

For·mo·san (fôr·mō′sən) *n.* **1** A native or inhabitant of the island of Formosa (Taiwan). **2** The Indonesian language of the Malay aborigines of Formosa. — *adj.* Of or pertaining to Formosa, its people, or their Indonesian language.

Formosa Strait The channel between China and Taiwan. *Chinese* **Tai·wan Hai·hsia** (tī′wän′ hī′shyä′)

for·mu·la (fôr′myə·lə) *n. pl.* **·las** or **·lae** (-lē) **1** An exact method or form of words prescribed as a guide for thought, action, expression, or statement; fixed rule or set form. **2** A medical prescription. **3** *Math.* A rule or combination expressed in algebraic or symbolic form. **4** *Chem.* A symbolic representation of the nature, composition, and structure of a chemical compound. The principal types are: the **empirical formula**, giving the quantitative values of the constituents, as H_2SO_4, sulfuric acid; the **structural formula**, showing the linkages of each atom, as CH_3CH_3, ethane; and the **graphic formula**, showing the spatial relations of the constituents, as

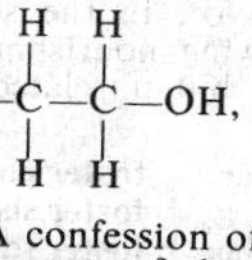

$$H-\overset{\overset{\displaystyle H}{|}}{C}-\overset{\overset{\displaystyle H}{|}}{C}-OH,\ \text{ethyl alcohol } C_2H_6O, \text{ or } CH_3CH_2OH.$$

5 A confession of religious faith, or a formal statement of doctrine. See synonyms under LAW, RULE. [<L, dim. of *forma* form]

for·mu·lar·ize (fôr′myə·lə·rīz) *v.t.* **·ized**, **·iz·ing** To formulate.

for·mu·lar·y (fôr′myə·ler′ē) *adj.* Stated in or as in a formula; formal. — *n. pl.* **·lar·ies 1** A collection of forms, formulas, etc.: a *formulary* of drugs. **2** Specifically, a church ritual. **3** A prescribed form; formula.

for·mu·late (fôr′myə·lāt) *v.t.* **·lat·ed**, **·lat·ing 1** To express in a formula, or as a formula. **2** To put or state in exact, concise, and systematic form. — **for′mu·la′tion** *n.* — **for′mu·la′tor** *n.*

for·mu·lism (fôr′myə·liz′əm) *n.* Observance or use of, or adherence to, formulas. — **for′mu·lis′tic** *adj.*

for·mu·lize (fôr′myə·līz) *v.t. & v.i.* **·lized**, **·liz·ing** To formulate. — **for′mu·li·za′tion** *n.* — **for′mu·li′zer** *n.*

for·myl (fôr′mil) *n. Chem.* The univalent radical CHO, constituting the base of formic acid. [<FORM(IC) + -YL]

For·nax (fôr′naks) A southern constellation near Eridanus. See CONSTELLATION.

for·ni·cate[1] (fôr′nə·kit) *adj. Archit.* Arched; vaulted. [<L *fornicatus* <*fornix, -icis* an arch]

for·ni·cate[2] (fôr′nə·kāt) *v.i.* **·cat·ed**, **·cat·ing** To commit fornication. [<L *fornicatus*, pp. of *fornicare* <*fornix, -icis* a vault, brothel] — **for′ni·ca′tor** *n.*

for·ni·ca·tion (fôr′nə·kā′shən) *n.* **1** Illicit sexual intercourse of unmarried persons. **2** In Scriptural use: **a** Adultery or harlotry, or incest. **b** Idolatry.

for·nix (fôr′niks) *n. pl.* **for·ni·ces** (-nə·sēz) **1** *Anat.* **a** A vaulted or reflected surface. **b** The bands of white fibers beneath the corpus callosum of the brain, connecting the two hemispheres of the cerebellum. **2** *Archit.* A vault or arch, commonly one within a building. [<L, vault]

For·rest (fôr′ist, for′-), **Edwin**, 1806–72, U.S. tragic actor. — **Nathan Bedford,** 1821–77, American Confederate general.

For·res·tal (fôr′is·tôl, for′-), **James Vincent,** 1892–1949, U.S. banker; first U.S. secretary of defense 1947–49.

for·rit (fôr′it, for′-) *adv. Scot.* Forward.

for·sake (fər·sāk′, fôr-) *v.t.* **for·sook, for·sak·en, for·sak·ing 1** To leave or withdraw from; renounce. **2** To abandon; desert. **3** *Obs.* To reject. See synonyms under ABANDON. [OE *forsacan*]

For·se·ti (fôr′se·tē) In Norse mythology, the god of justice; son of Balder. Also **For′se·te.**

for·sooth (fôr·sōōth′, fôr-) *adv.* In truth; certainly: chiefly ironical. [OE *forsōth*]

for·speak (fôr·spēk′) *v.t. Scot. & Brit. Dial.* **1** To bewitch. **2** *Obs.* To forbid.

for·spent (fôr·spent′) *adj.* Tired out; exhausted: also spelled *forespent.* [Orig. pp. of *forspend* exhaust, OE *forspendan*]

For·ster (fôr′stər), **E(dward) M(organ),** 1879–1970, English novelist.

for·swear (fôr·swâr′) *v.* **·swore, ·sworn, ·swear·ing** *v.t.* **1** To renounce upon oath; repudiate; abjure. **2** To deny upon oath. — *v.i.* **3** To swear falsely; commit perjury. — **to forswear oneself** To swear falsely. See synonyms under ABANDON, RENOUNCE. [OE *forswerian* swear falsely]

for·sworn (fôr·swôrn′, -swōrn′) *adj.* Perjured.

For·syth (fôr·sīth′), **Alexander John,** 1769–1843, Scottish clergyman and inventor.

for·syth·i·a (fôr·sith′ē·ə, -sī′thē·ə, fər-) *n.* One of a genus (*Forsythia*) of slender shrubs of the olive family native to China and Japan. Two species, *F. viridissima* and *F. suspensa,* are widely cultivated as ornamental plants. [after Wm. *Forsyth,* 1737–1804, British botanist, who brought the shrub from China]

fort (fôrt, fōrt) *n.* A single enclosed military work capable of independent defense; any fortification held by a garrison; a fortification: fortress. [<F, orig. an adj. <L *fortis* strong]

For·ta·le·za (fôr′tə·lā′zə) A port in eastern Brazil, capital of Ceará state.

fort·a·lice (fôr′tə·lis) *n.* An outwork of a fortification; a small fort. [<Med. L *fortalitia* <*fortis* strong]

Fort Dear·born (dir′bôrn) A military post established in 1803 on the present site of Chicago, Illinois.

Fort–de–France (fôr·də·fräns′) A port, the capital of Martinique.

Fort Don·el·son National Military Park (don′əl·sən) A locality in NW Tennessee on the Cumberland River; site of a Confederate defeat, 1862. See FORT HENRY.

Fort Du·quesne (dōō·kān′, dyōō-) An 18th century French trading post on the later site of Pittsburgh, Pennsylvania. See FORT PITT.

forte[1] (fôrt) *n.* **1** That which one does most readily or excellently. **2** The strongest part of a sword blade: distinguished from *foible.* [<F *fort.* See FORT.]

for·te[2] (fôr′tā, -tē) *Music n.* A musical chord or passage to be performed loudly. — *adj. & adv.* Loud: often as a direction to the player. [<Ital., strong <L *fortis*]

Fort Fish·er (fish′ər) An earthwork near the mouth of the Cape Fear River in North Carolina; besieged and captured by Union forces in the Civil War, 1865.

Fort Fred·e·ri·ca National Monument (fred′ə·rē′kə) A locality on St. Simons Island, SE Georgia; site of the ruins of an English fort built in 1736 by James Oglethorpe.

forth (fôrth, fōrth) *adv.* **1** Forward in place, time, or order. **2** Outward, as from seclusion. **3** Away; out, as from a place of origin; abroad. — *prep. Archaic* Forth from; out of. [OE, forwards]

Forth (fôrth, fōrth), **Firth of** The estuary, extending 51 miles to the North Sea, of the **Forth,** a river that flows 65 miles east in SE Scotland. The estuary is spanned by **Forth Bridge;** 3,770 feet, 8,295 feet with approaches.

forth·com·ing (fôrth′kum′ing, fōrth′-) *adj.* Ready or about to appear. — *n.* A coming forth.

Fort Hen·ry (hen′rē) A fort in NW Tennessee on the Tennessee River, 12 miles from Fort Donelson; captured by Northern forces, 1862.

forth·right (fôrth′rīt′, fōrth′-) *adj.* Straightforward; direct. — *n. Archaic* A direct path or course. — *adv.* **1** Straightforwardly; with directness or frankness. **2** At once; straightway.

forth·with (fôrth′with′, -with′, fōrth′-) *adv.* Without delay; immediately.

for·ti·eth (fôr′tē·ith) *adj.* **1** Tenth in order after the thirtieth: the ordinal of *forty.* **2** Being one of forty equal parts. — *n.* One of forty equal parts of anything; the quotient of a unit divided by forty.

for·ti·fi·ca·tion (fôr′tə·fə·kā′shən) *n.* **1** The act, art, or science of fortifying. **2** A military defensive work; a fort. **3** A strengthening of any kind.

Synonyms: castle, citadel, fastness, fort, fortress, stronghold. *Fortification* is the general word for any artificial defensive work; a *fortress* is a *fortification* of especial size and strength, regarded as permanent, and ordinarily an independent work; a *fort* or *fortification* may be temporary; a *fortification* may be but part of a defensive system; we speak of the *fortifications* of a city. A *citadel* is a *fortification* within a city, or the fortified inner part of a city, or a *fortress* within which a garrison may be placed to overawe the citizens, or to which the defenders may retire if the outer works are captured; the medieval *castle* was the fortified residence of a king or baron. *Fort* is the common military term for a detached fortified building or enclosure of moderate size occupied or designed to be occupied by troops. The *fortifications* of a modern city usually consist of a chain of *forts.* Any defensible place, whether made so by nature or by art, is a *fastness* or *stronghold.* See RAMPART.

for·ti·fied (fôr′tə·fīd) *adj.* **1** Strengthened; said especially of wines whose alcoholic content has been increased by the addition of brandy. **2** Enriched, as bread.

for·ti·fy (fôr′tə·fī) *v.* **·fied**, **·fy·ing** *v.t.* **1** To provide with defensive works; strengthen against attack. **2** To give physical or moral strength to; invigorate or encourage. **3** To confirm; corroborate. **4** To strengthen the structure of; reenforce. **5** To strengthen, as wine, by adding alcohol. **6** To enrich (food) by adding minerals, vitamins, etc. — *v.i.* **7** To raise defensive works. [<F *fortifier* <L *fortificare* <*fortis* strong + *facere* make] — **for′ti·fi′a·ble** *adj.* — **for′ti·fi′er** *n.*

for·tis (fôr′tis) *Phonet. adj.* Strongly articulated: opposed to *lenis.* — *n.* A consonant, usually a stop, pronounced with tension of the speech organs or with strong plosion. [<L, strong]

for·tis·si·mo (fôr·tis′ə·mō, *Ital.* fôr·tēs′sē·mō) *adj. & adv. Music* Very loud. [<Ital., superl. of *forte* strong]

for·ti·tude (fôr′tə·tōōd, -tyōōd) *n.* **1** Strength of mind to meet or endure unfalteringly pain, adversity, or peril; patient and constant courage. **2** *Obs.* Physical strength or force. [<F <L *fortitudo* <*fortis* strong]

Synonyms: courage, endurance, heroism, resolution. *Fortitude* (L. *fortis,* strong) is the strength or firmness of mind or soul to endure pain or adversity patiently and determinedly. *Fortitude* has been defined as "passive *courage,*" which is a good definition, but not complete. *Fortitude* might be termed "still *courage,*" or "enduring *courage*"; it is that quality which is able not merely to endure pain or trial, but steadily to confront dangers that cannot be actively opposed, or against which one has no adequate defense; it takes *courage* to charge a trench, *fortitude* to withstand an enemy's fire. *Resolution* is of the mind; *endurance* is

partly physical; it requires *resolution* to resist temptation, *endurance* to resist hunger and cold. Compare COURAGE, PATIENCE.

for·ti·tu·di·nous (fôr′tə·to͞o′də·nəs, -tyo͞o′-) *adj.* Having or showing courage and endurance.

Fort Knox (noks) A military reservation in north central Kentucky; site (since 1936) of Federal gold bullion depository.

Fort–La·my (fôr·là·mē′) The capital of Chad in north central Africa.

Fort Mc·Hen·ry National Monument (mək·hen′rē) A fort in the harbor of Baltimore, Maryland. Its bombardment by the British, Sept. 13, 1814, was the occasion of Francis Scott Key's writing *The Star Spangled Banner.*

Fort Meigs (megz) A former fort on the Maumee River, NW Ohio; unsuccessfully besieged by British and Indian forces, 1813.

Fort Mims (mimz) A stockade near Mobile, Alabama, site of an Indian massacre, Aug. 30, 1813.

Fort Mon·roe (mən·rō′) A military post in SE Virginia at the entrance to Hampton Roads. Also **Fortress Monroe.**

Fort Moul·trie (mōl′trē, mo͞ol′-, mo͞o′-) A fort in Charleston harbor, South Carolina; scene of battles in the Revolutionary War and in the Civil War. See MOULTRIE, WILLIAM.

Fort Ni·ag·a·ra (nī·ag′ər·ə, -ag′rə) A fort at the mouth of the Niagara River in New York; scene of battles in 1759, 1812, and 1813.

fort·night (fôrt′nīt′, -nit′) *n.* A period of two weeks; fourteen days. [OE *fēowertēne* fourteen + *niht* nights]

fort·night·ly (fôrt′nīt′lē) *adj.* Occurring, coming, or issued every fortnight. — *adv.* Once a fortnight.

Fort Peck Dam (pek) One of the world's largest earth–fill dams, in the Missouri River, NE Montana; 250 feet high, 4 miles long; on **Fort Peck Reservoir,** the second largest in the United States; 383 square miles.

Fort Pick·ens (pik′ənz) A fort at the entrance to Pensacola harbor, NW Florida.

Fort Pitt (pit) The British name for FORT DUQUESNE after they captured it from the French in 1758: on the present site of Pittsburgh.

Fort Pulaski National Monument (po͞o·las′kē) A fort in the mouth of the Savannah River, built in 1829.

for·tress (fôr′tris) *n.* A large permanent fort; a stronghold; castle. See synonyms under DEFENSE, FORTIFICATION. — *v.t.* To furnish or strengthen with a fortress; fortify. [<OF *forteresse* <L *fortis* strong]

Fort Smith (smith) A city on the Arkansas River in western Arkansas.

Fort Sum·ter National Monument (sum′tər) A fort in Charleston harbor, South Carolina; object of a Confederate attack, Apr. 12, 1861, that began the Civil War.

for·tu·i·tism (fôr·to͞o′ə·tiz′əm, -tyo͞o′-) *n.* The doctrine that phenomena or events come to pass by chance rather than in accordance with intelligent design or natural law. — **for·tu′i·tist** *n.* & *adj.*

for·tu·i·tous (fôr·to͞o′ə·təs, -tyo͞o′-) *adj.* **1** Occurring by chance; casual; accidental. **2** Fortunate; lucky. See synonyms under INCIDENTAL. [<L *fortuitus* <*fors* chance] — **for·tu′i·tous·ly** *adv.* — **for·tu′i·tous·ness** *n.*

for·tu·i·ty (fôr·to͞o′ə·tē, -tyo͞o′-) *n.* *pl.* **·ties** Chance occurrence; also, chance. See synonyms under ACCIDENT, HAZARD.

For·tu·na (fôr·to͞o′nə, -tyo͞o′-) In Roman mythology, the goddess of chance: identified with the Greek *Tyche.*

for·tu·nate (fôr′chə·nit) *adj.* **1** Happening by a favorable chance; lucky. **2** Favored with good fortune. — **for′tu·nate·ly** *adv.* — **for′tu·nate·ness** *n.*

Synonyms: favored, happy, lucky, prospered, prosperous, successful. A man is *successful* in any case if he achieves or gains what he seeks; he is known as a *successful* man if he has achieved or gained worthy objects of endeavor; he is *fortunate* or *lucky* if advantages have come to him without or beyond his direct planning or achieving. *Lucky* is the more common and colloquial, *fortunate* the more elegant word; *fortunate* is more naturally applied to the graver matters, as we speak of the *fortunate,* rather than the *lucky,* issue of a great battle; *lucky* more strongly emphasizes the element of chance, as when we speak of a *lucky* hit, a *lucky* guess, or of one as "born under a *lucky* star." *Favored* is used in a religious sense, implying that one is the object of divine favor. *Happy,* in this connection, signifies possessed of the means of happiness. One is said to be *happy* or *prosperous* whether his prosperity be the result of fortune or of achievement; *prospered* rather denotes the action of a superintending Providence. See AUSPICIOUS, HAPPY. *Antonyms*: broken, crushed, fallen, ill–starred, miserable, unfortunate, unhappy, unlucky, woeful, wretched.

for·tune (fôr′chən) *n.* **1** Chance or luck as the cause of changes in human affairs: often personified. **2** That which befalls one as his lot; good or bad luck. **3** Future destiny; fate: to tell *fortunes.* **4** Good luck; success; prosperity. **5** An amount of wealth; usually great wealth. See synonyms under EVENT. — *v.* **·tuned, ·tun·ing** *v.t.* *Rare* To bestow wealth upon. — *v.i.* To happen; occur by chance. [<OF <L *fortuna* <*fors* chance] — **for′tune·less** *adj.*

for·tune–hunt·er (fôr′chən·hun′tər) *n.* One who seeks to obtain wealth by marriage. — **for′tune–hunt′ing** *n.*

for·tune–tell·er (fôr′chən·tel′ər) *n.* One who claims to foretell events in a person's future. — **for′tune–tell′ing** *n.* & *adj.*

Fort Wayne (wān) A city in NE Indiana.

Fort Worth (wûrth) A city in northern Texas.

for·ty (fôr′tē) *adj.* Consisting of ten more than thirty, or of four times ten. — *n.* *pl.* **·ties** **1** The sum of ten and thirty; four times ten: a cardinal number. **2** Any of the symbols (40, xl, XL) representing this number. **3** *U.S.* Forty acres, or one-sixteenth of a section of land. [OE *fēowertig*]

for·ty–nin·er (fôr′tē·nī′nər) *n.* *U.S.* An adventurer or pioneer who went to California in 1849, the year of the gold rush.

Forty Thieves See ALI BABA.

forty winks *Colloq.* A short nap.

fo·rum (fôr′əm, fō′rəm) *n.* *pl.* **·rums** or **·ra** (-rə) **1** The public market place of an ancient Roman city, where popular assemblies met, and most legal and political business was transacted. **2** A tribunal; a court. **3** An assembly for free discussion of public affairs. [<L]

for·ward (fôr′wərd) *adj.* **1** At, or belonging to, the fore part, as of a ship. **2** Directed toward a position in front; onward: a *forward* course. **3** For deferred delivery: a *forward* purchase. **4** Advanced toward maturity or completion; specifically, precocious. **5** Bold; presumptuous. **6** Advanced; extreme; said of opinions or actions. — *adv.* **1** Toward the future. **2** Toward the front; ahead; onward. **3** At or in the fore part, as of a ship. **4** To a prominent position; forth; into view: to come *forward*; to bring *forward* an idea. Also *forwards.* — **forward of** In advance of. — *n.* **1** In American football, one of the players in the front line who attack in advance of the backfield and try to thwart the opponents. **2** In basketball, soccer, hockey, etc., one of those players who lead the attack and specialize in making goals. — *v.t.* **1** To help onward or ahead; promote. **2** To send; transmit; especially, to send (mail) on to a new address. **3** To prepare (a book) for finishing by covering, etc. See synonyms under ENCOURAGE, PROMOTE. [OE *foreweard*]

forward delivery Delivery at a future time.

for·ward·er (fôr′wər·dər) *n.* **1** A person, firm, or corporation whose business it is to receive goods for transportation and send them to their destination; a forwarding merchant or agent. **2** One who carries or promotes anything, as a reform.

for·ward·ly (fôr′wərd·lē) *adv.* **1** In a forward or front position. **2** In a forward manner; eagerly; boldly.

for·ward·ness (fôr′wərd·nis) *n.* **1** Presumption; overeagerness to put oneself forward; boldness; brazenness. **2** Willing readiness; eagerness. **3** State of being forward or in advance; precocity.

forward pass See under PASS.

forward quotation A price set for goods to be delivered at a future time.

for·wards (fôr′wərdz) See FORWARD *adv.*

for·why (fôr′hwī′) *Obs.* *adv.* Why; wherefore. — *conj.* Because.

for·worn (fôr·wôrn′) *adj.* *Archaic* Worn out: also spelled *foreworn.* [Orig. pp. of obs. *forwear* exhaust]

for·zan·do (fôr·tsän′dō) See SFORZANDO.

Fos·ca·ri (fôs·kä′rē), **Francesco,** 1372?–1457, doge of Venice; waged three wars with Milan.

Fos·dick (foz′dik), **Harry Emerson,** 1878–1969, U.S. clergyman and writer.

foss (fôs, fos) *n.* An artificial ditch or moat, as in a fortification. Also **fosse.** [<F *fosse* <L *fossa* <*fodire* dig]

fos·sa (fôs′ə, fos′ə) *n.* *pl.* **fos·sae** (-ē) *Anat.* A shallow depression or cavity in the body. [<L. See FOSS.]

fos·sette (fô·set′, fo-) *n.* *French* **1** A dimple. **2** *Anat.* A small depression, as in the crown of a tooth. [<F, dim. of *fosse.* See FOSS.]

fos·sick (fôs′ik, fos′-) *v.i.* *Austral.* **1** *Mining* To search for gold in abandoned mines, waste heaps, etc.; also, to search for surface gold. **2** To rummage about for something: used with *about* or *around.* [Cf. dial. E *fussock* bustle] — **fos′sick·er** *n.*

fos·sil (fos′əl, fôs′-) *n.* *Paleontol.* **1** The actual remains of plants or animals, preserved in the rocks of the earth's crust; also, material evidences of early organisms, as in petrified forms, coprolites, casts, impressions, imprints, etc. **2** *Geol.* One of certain inorganic objects or substances which in extinct or mineralized forms preserve in themselves records of the natural activities or phenomena of ancient geological ages, as solidified ripple marks. **3** Buried records of human activities, even within historic times. **4** *Colloq.* A person or thing that is behind the times, antiquated, or out of date. — *adj.* **1** Dug out of the earth; petrified. **2** Of or like a fossil; outworn; antiquated. [<F *fossile* <L *fossilis* dug up <*fossa.* See FOSS.]

fos·sil·if·er·ous (fos′əl·if′ər·əs) *adj.* Containing fossils.

fos·sil·ize (fos′əl·īz) *v.* **·ized, ·iz·ing** *v.t.* **1** To change into a fossil; petrify. **2** To make antiquated or out of date. — *v.i.* **3** To become a fossil. **4** To search for or gather fossil specimens. — **fos′sil·i·za′tion** *n.*

fos·so·ri·al (fo·sôr′ē·əl, -sō′rē-) *adj.* **1** Digging; burrowing: a *fossorial* animal. **2** Adapted for or used in digging in the earth, as the legs and other organs of the moles, armadillos, etc. [<LL *fossorius* <L *fodire* dig]

fos·ter (fôs′tər, fos′-) *v.t.* **1** To rear; bring up, as a child. **2** To promote the growth of; forward; help: to *foster* genius. **3** To keep as if affectionately; cherish; nurse: to *foster* a grudge. **4** *Obs.* To provide with food. See synonyms under AID, CHERISH, HELP, PROMOTE. — *adj.* Having the relation of, in the sense of giving, sharing, or receiving nourishment, shelter, affection, and care, but unrelated by blood; as in

foster brother	**foster father**	**foster parent**
foster child	**foster land**	**foster sister**
foster daughter	**foster mother**	**foster son**

[OE *fostrian* nourish] — **fos′ter·age** *n.* — **fos′ter·er** *n.* — **fos′tress** *n.* *fem.*

Fos·ter (fôs′tər, fos′-), **Sir Michael,** 1836–1907, English physiologist. — **Stephen Collins,** 1826–64, U. S. song writer. — **William Zebulon,** 1881–1961, U. S. labor leader and former Communist party chairman.

fos·ter·ling (fôs′tər·ling, fos′-) *n.* A foster child.

Foth·er·in·ghay Castle (foth′ər·ing·gā′) A castle in Northamptonshire, England; scene of imprisonment and execution of Mary Queen of Scots.

Fou·cault (fo͞o·kō′), **Jean Bernard Léon,** 1819–68, French physicist.

Foucault current See under CURRENT.

Fouc·quet (fo͞o·ke′) See FOUQUET.

fou·droy·ant (fo͞o·droi′ənt, *Fr.* fo͞o·drwà·yäN′) *adj.* **1** Sudden and overwhelming, as lightning. **2** *Pathol.* Beginning in an aggravated form, as a disease. [<F, ppr. of *foudroyer* strike with lightning <*foudre* lightning]

fought (fôt) Past tense and past participle of FIGHT.

fought·en (fôt′n) *Archaic* Past participle of FIGHT.

foul (foul) *adj.* **1** Offensive or loathsome to the physical, moral, or esthetic sense; filthy. **2** Obstructing, entangling or injuring by anything that clogs or is harmful; contrary; disagreeable. **3** Impeded or encumbered by something detrimental; clogged; entangled; encumbered; a *foul* chimney, a *foul* anchor. **4** Not according to justice or rule; unfair.

5 *Printing* **a** Full of errors; inaccurate; dirty. **b** Having the characters badly mixed; said of a type case. 6 Unfavorable; unlucky: a *foul* wind. 7 *Obs.* Ugly; homely. 8 In baseball, of or pertaining to a foul ball or foul line. — *n.* 1 An act of fouling, colliding, or becoming entangled. 2 A breach of rule in various sports and games. 3 In baseball, a foul ball. — *adv.* In a foul manner. — *v.t.* 1 To make foul or dirty; befoul. 2 To clog or choke, as a drain. 3 To entangle; snarl, as a rope in a pulley. 4 *Naut.* To cover or encumber (a ship's bottom) with barnacles, seaweed, etc. 5 To collide with. 6 To dishonor; disgrace. 7 In sports, to commit a foul against. 8 In baseball, to bat (the ball) outside of the foul lines. — *v.i.* 9 To become foul or dirty. 10 To become clogged or encumbered. 11 To become entangled. 12 To collide. 13 In sports, to violate a rule. 14 In baseball: **a** To bat a foul ball. **b** To be retired by batting a foul ball which is caught before it strikes the ground: usually with *out.* — **to foul up** *Slang* To bungle; make a mess (of). ◆ Homophone: *fowl.* [OE *ful*]

Synonyms (adj.): defiled, dirty, filthy, gross, impure, indelicate, muddy, nasty, obscene, odious, offensive, soiled, stained, sullied, unclean, vile. See BAD, NOISOME. *Antonyms*: see synonyms for PURE.

fou·lard (fōō·lärd′) *n.* 1 A lightweight, washable silk fabric, usually printed, used for dresses, ties, etc. 2 A highly mercerized cotton or rayon fabric in imitation of this. [<F <Swiss F *foulat* <OF *fouler.* See FOIL[1].]

foul ball In baseball, a ball batted so that it falls outside the foul lines.

foul line 1 In baseball, a line drawn from home plate through first or third base to the limits of the field. 2 In basketball, the line from which foul shots are made. 3 In bowling, tennis, etc., any line limiting the area of play or action.

foul·ly (foul′lē) *adv.* 1 In a foul manner. 2 Undeservedly: *foully* maligned.

foul–mouthed (foul′mouthd′, -moutht′) *adj.* Using abusive, profane, or obscene language.

foul·ness (foul′nis) *n.* 1 The state or quality of being foul. 2 Foul matter.

foul play 1 Unfairness; in games and sports, a violation of rule. 2 Any unfair or treacherous conduct, often with the implication of murder.

foul shot In basketball, a free throw awarded a player who has been fouled by an opposing player, and if successful scored as one point.

foul tip In baseball, a pitched ball swung at by the batter and glancing off the bat into the catcher's hands: the batter is retired if there are two strikes against him.

fou·mart (fōō′märt) *n.* The European polecat; the fitchew. Also **fou·li·mart** (fōō′lē·märt). [ME *fulmard,* OE *fūl* foul + *mearth* marten]

found[1] (found) *v.t.* 1 To lay the foundation of; establish on a foundation or basis: to *found* a theory. 2 To give origin to; establish; set up: to *found* a college or a family. — **to found on** 1 To form and base one's opinion. 2 To rest as on a foundation. [<OF *fonder* <L *fundare* <*fundus* base, bottom] — **found′er** *n.*

found[2] (found) *v.t.* 1 To cast, as iron, by melting and pouring into a mold. 2 To make by casting molten metal. [<F *fondre* <L *fundere* pour]

found[3] (found) Past tense and past participle of FIND. — *adj.* Provided with food, lodging, equipment, etc. — **and found** Plus board and lodging, as part payment.

foun·da·tion (foun·dā′shən) *n.* 1 The act of founding or establishing. 2 That on which anything is founded and by which it is supported or sustained. 3 A fund for the permanent maintenance of an institution; an endowment. 4 An endowed institution. 5 A structure upon which a building or a machine is erected, usually wholly or principally of masonry; that part of a building below the surface of the ground, or the portion that constitutes a base; sometimes, a platform, on which the upper portions rest. 6 An inner, fitted lining of a garment. 7 Theatrical grease-paint applied to the face, hands, etc., before adding the final make-up details. — **foun·da′·tion·al** *adj.*

foundation garment A girdle or corset, often combined with a brassière.

foundation sire In horse breeding, the named stallion from which the genealogy of all horses of a given breed is traced.

found·er[1] (foun′dər) *n.* One who makes metal castings.

foun·der[2] (foun′dər) *v.i.* 1 *Naut.* To fill with water and sink. 2 To collapse; cave in; fail. 3 To stumble; go lame, as a horse. 4 To have founder. — *v.t.* 5 *Naut.* To cause to sink. 6 To cause to go lame. — *n.* 1 Inflammation of the tissue in the foot of a horse, commonly due to overfeeding: also called *laminitis.* 2 Act of foundering. [<OF *fondrer* sink <*fond* bottom <L *fundus*]

foun·der·ous (foun′dər·əs) *adj.* Causing to founder; miry; swampy.

founders' shares Shares of stock, often privileged to extra dividends, issued to the promoters or founders of a company as payment for organizing expenses and reward for initiative.

found·ing (foun′ding) *n.* The business of making articles of cast iron, brass, etc.

found·ling (found′ling) *n.* A deserted infant of unknown parentage. [ME *fundeling* <*funde,* pp. of *find* + -LING[1]]

foun·dry (foun′drē) *n. pl.* **·dries** 1 An establishment in which articles are cast from metal. 2 The act or operation of founding. Also **foun′der·y.**

foundry proof *Printing* A final proof of composed type before stereotyping or electrotyping.

fount[1] (fount) *n.* A fountain; hence, any source. [<F *font* <L *fons, fontis* fountain]

fount[2] (fount) See FONT[2].

foun·tain (foun′tən) *n.* 1 A spring or jet of water issuing from the earth; especially, the source of a stream. ◆ Collateral adjective: *fontal.* 2 The origin or source of anything. 3 A jet or spray of water forced upward artificially, to provide water for drinking, cooling the air, or display. 4 A structure designed for such a jet to rise and fall in. 5 A reservoir or supply chamber for holding oil, ink, etc., as in a lamp, printing press, or inkstand. 6 A soda fountain. See synonyms under BEGINNING, CAUSE. [<OF *fontaine* <LL *fontana,* orig. fem. singular of *fontanus* of a spring <*fons, fontis* fountain]

foun·tain·head (foun′tən·hed′) *n.* 1 The source of a stream. 2 Any primal source or originating cause.

Fountain of Youth A legendary fountain said to have the power of rejuvenation: sought by Ponce de León and others in Florida and the West Indies.

fountain pen A pen having a reservoir for ink within the holder.

Fou·qué (fōō·kā′), **Friedrich H. K.,** 1777–1843, Baron de la Motte, German poet and dramatist.

Fou·quet (fōō·ke′), **Jean,** 1416?–80?, French painter. — **Nicolas,** 1615–80, Marquis de Belle Isle, French statesman. Also spelled *Foucquet.*

Fou·qui·e·ri·a (fōō′kē·ir′ē·ə) *n.* A genus of thorny shrubs, native to Mexico and the southern United States.

four (fôr, fōr) *adj.* Consisting of one more than three; twice two; quaternary. — *n.* 1 The cardinal number following three and preceding five, or any of the symbols (4, iv, IV) used to represent it. 2 Anything made up of four units or members; especially, a crew of four oarsmen, a team of four horses, a playing card with four pips, etc. [OE *feower*]

four bits *U.S. Slang* Fifty cents.

four·chette (fōōr·shet′) *n.* 1 A forked piece between glove fingers, uniting the front and back parts. 2 *Ornithol.* The furculum or wishbone of a bird. 3 The frog of a horse. 4 *Anat.* A fold of mucous membrane forming the posterior commissure of the vulva. [<F, dim. of *fourche* a fork <L *furca*]

four–cy·cle (fôr′sī′kəl, fōr′-) A cycle of operation in an engine in which fuel is taken into the cylinder, compressed, burned, and exhausted in four successive strokes.

four–di·men·sion·al (fôr′di·men′shən·əl, fōr′-) *adj.* 1 Having, or pertaining to, four dimensions. 2 *Math.* Relating to a system or a set of magnitudes whose elements can be completely defined only by four coordinates.

Four·drin·i·er (fōōr·drin′ē·ər) *adj.* Of, pertaining to, or designating a papermaking machine, the first to make a continuous web: invented by Louis Robert of France and patented by him there, but improved in England by Henry and Sealy Fourdrinier early in the 19th century. — *n.* A Fourdrinier machine.

four–eyed fish (fôr′īd′, fōr′-) The anableps.

four–flush (fôr′flush′, fōr′-) *n.* A valueless poker hand containing four cards of one suit and one of another. — *v.i.* 1 To bet on a hand containing four cards of one suit but lacking the fifth. 2 *Slang* To bluff.

four–flush·er (fôr′flush′ər, fōr′-) *n. Slang* A bluffer; one whose abilities and performance are less than his pretensions or promises.

four·fold (fôr′fōld′, fōr′-) *adj.* Made up of four; quadruplicate. — *n.* That which is four times as many or as much. — *adv.* In quadrupled measure.

four–foot·ed (fôr′fōōt′id, fōr′-) *adj.* Having four feet; quadruped.

Four Forest Cantons, Lake of the See LAKE OF LUCERNE.

Four Freedoms Freedom of speech and religion and freedom from want and fear: the world–wide goals of U.S. foreign policy stated by President F. D. Roosevelt in a message to Congress, January 6, 1941.

four·gon (fōōr·gôṅ′) *n. French* A covered wagon or van for carrying baggage, military supplies, etc.

four–hand·ed (fôr′han′did, fōr′-) *adj.* 1 Having four hands; quadrumanous, as monkeys. 2 Needing four hands, as certain games, a piano duet, etc.

Four–H Club (fôr′āch′, fōr′-) A youth organization, sponsored by the Department of Agriculture, offering education in home economics and agriculture: so called because it aims to improve the head, heart, hands, and health of its members. Also **4–H Club.**

four hundred The most exclusive social group of a place: a term originally applied to the wealthiest set in New York by Ward McAllister.

Fou·rier (fōō·ryā′), **François Marie Charles,** 1772–1837, French socialist. — **Jean Baptiste Joseph,** 1768–1830, French mathematician and physicist.

Fou·ri·er·ism (fōōr′ē·ə·riz′əm) *n.* The social reform system advocated by F. M. C. Fourier about 1815, proposing small, voluntary cooperative groups for economic production and maintenance, the achievement of social justice, and the fulfilment of individual desires. — **Fou′ri·er·ist, Fou′ri·er·ite′** *n.*

four–in–hand (fôr′in·hand′, fōr′-) *adj.* 1 Consisting of a four–horse team driven by one person. 2 Designating a necktie tied in a slipknot with the ends hanging vertically. — *n.* 1 A four–horse team driven by one person; also, a vehicle drawn by four horses. 2 A four–in–hand necktie.

four–leafed rose (fôr′lēft′, fōr′-) *Geom.* The polar curve of equation $r = a \sin 2\theta$: a curve of four symmetrical loops with the node at the origin.

four–let·ter word (fôr′let′ər, fōr′-) Any of several short words considered profane or obscene.

four–mast·ed (fôr′mas′tid, -mäs′-, fōr′-) *adj. Naut.* Having four masts. — **four′–mast′er** *n.*

Four·nier d'Albe (fōōr′nyā dalb′), **Edmund Edward,** 1868–1933, English physicist.

four–o'clock (fôr′ə·klok′, fōr′-) *n.* 1 An ornamental herb from Peru (*Mirabilis jalapa*) with flowers of a great variety of color that bloom from late afternoon till the next morning. 2 The Australian friarbird.

four·pence (fôr′pəns, fōr′-) *n.* 1 The sum of four English pennies; also, a silver piece of that value. 2 A silver coin used before the Civil War, worth 6 1/4 cents; the Spanish half–real: called *fourpence halfpenny* in New England, *fippenny bit* in Pennsylvania and elsewhere.

four–post·er (fôr′pōs′tər, fōr′-) *n.* A bedstead with four tall posts at the corners.

four·ra·gère (fōō·rà·zhâr′) *n.* A braided, metal–tipped cord awarded to individual soldiers or to a unit of troops for distinguished service;

and worn around the left shoulder. [<F]

four·score (fôr′skôr′, fōr′skôr′) *adj.* & *n.* Four times twenty; eighty.

four·some (fôr′səm, fōr′-) *adj.* Consisting of four: said of anything in which four are needed to take part together. —*n.* 1 A game, especially of golf, in which four players take part, two on each side; also the players. 2 Any group of four.

four·square (fôr′skwâr′, fōr′-) *adj.* 1 Having four equal sides and angles; square. 2 Hence, firm; solid; also, sincere; without guile. —*n.* An object having four equal sides; a square.

four·teen (fôr′tēn′, fōr′-) *adj.* Consisting of four more than ten, or of twice seven. —*n.* 1 The sum of ten and four; twice seven. 2 Any symbol (14, xiv, XIV) representing this number. [OE *fēowertēne*]

Fourteen Points The peace aims set forth by President Woodrow Wilson in an address, January 8, 1918, ten months before the end of World War I. Also **Fourteen Peace Points.**

four·teenth (fôr′tēnth′, fōr′-) *adj.* 1 Fourth in order after the tenth. 2 Being one of fourteen equal parts. —*n.* 1 One of fourteen equal parts of anything; the quotient of a unit divided by fourteen. 2 A fourteenth person, thing, or group.

fourth (fôrth, fōrth) *adj.* 1 Next in order after the third. 2 Being one of four equal parts. —*n.* 1 One of four equal parts of anything; the quotient of a unit divided by four; a quarter. 2 A fourth person, thing, or group. 3 *Music* a The interval between any note and the fourth note above it in a diatonic scale, counting the starting point as one. b A note at this interval above or below any other, considered in relation to that other; specifically, the fourth above the keynote; the subdominant. c Two notes at this interval written or sounded together; the consonance thus produced. See INTERVAL. —**the Fourth** July 4th; Independence Day. —*adv.* In the fourth order, rank, or place: also, in formal discourse, *fourthly.* ◆ Homophone: *forth.*

fourth-class (fôrth′klas′, -kläs′, fōrth′-) *adj.* Designating mail matter consisting of merchandise, and carried at the lowest rate.

fourth dimension 1 *Math.* A hypothetical, usually spatial dimension in addition to height, width, and thickness. 2 In the theory of relativity, the temporal coordinate of space time. —**fourth′-di·men′sion·al** *adj.*

fourth estate 1 The newspapers; journalism in general. 2 *Brit.* The reporters' gallery in the House of Commons.

fourth·ly (fôrth′lē, fōrth′-) *adv.* In the fourth place. See under FOURTH.

Fourth of July *U.S.* Independence Day.

Fourth Republic The republic formed in France in 1945.

four-wheel (fôr′hwēl, fōr′-) *adj.* 1 Having four wheels. 2 Affecting or controlling all four wheels: *four-wheel* drive.

Fou·ta Djal·lon (fōō′tä jä·lôn′) See FUTA JALLON.

fo·ve·a (fō′vē·ə) *n. pl.* **·ve·ae** (-vi·ē) *Anat.* A shallow rounded depression: the central *fovea* of the retina directly in the axis of vision; a fossa. [<L, a small pit] —**fo′ve·al** *adj.*

fo·ve·ate (fō′vē·āt, -it) *adj.* Having foveae; covered with little pits.

fo·ve·o·la (fə·vē′ə·lə) *n. pl.* **·lae** (-lē) A small fovea or pit. Also **fo·ve·ole** (fō′vē·ōl), **fo′ve·o·let** (-let). [<L, dim. of *fovea* a small pit]

fo·ve·o·late (fō′vē·ə·lāt) *adj.* Having foveolae or little pits. Also **fo′ve·o·lat′ed.**

fowl (foul) *n. pl.* **fowl** or **fowls** 1 The common domestic cock, hen, or chicken. 2 The flesh of fowls, especially of the full-grown domestic hen. 3 Poultry in general. 4 Birds collectively: wild *fowl.* 5 *Obs.* Any bird. —*v.i.* To catch or hunt wild fowl. ◆ Homophone: *foul.* [OE *fugol*] —**fowl′er** *n.*

fowl cholera An infectious intestinal disease, chronic or acute, of domestic fowl caused by a pathogenic bacterium, *Pasteurella avicida.*

Fowl·er (fou′lər), **Henry Watson**, 1858–1933, English lexicographer.

harles James Fowler's solution An aqueous solution of potassium arsenite containing arsenious acid: very poisonous: used in medicine as an alterative and tonic. [after Thomas *Fowler*, 1736–1801, English physician]

Fow·liang (fō′lyäng′, fōō′-) A city in NE Kiangsi province, SE China: formerly *Kingtehchen.*

fowl·ing (fou′ling) *n.* The hunting of birds for sport or food.

fowling net A net for catching birds.

fowl·ing-piece (fou′ling-pēs′) *n.* A light gun for bird-shooting.

fowl pox A disease affecting many species of domestic fowl and wild birds, characterized by skin lesions, tissue injuries, and sometimes diphtheria symptoms of the mucous membrane: caused by certain strains of filtrable viruses.

fowl tick A hardy, bloodsucking tick *(Argas persicus)* parasitic on fowls, especially prevalent in the SW United States.

fowl typhoid A sporadic disease of domestic fowl caused by the bacterium *Shigella gallinarum.*

fox (foks) *n.* 1 A burrowing canine mammal (family *Canidae,* genus *Vulpes*) having a long, pointed muzzle and long bushy tail, commonly reddish-brown in color, noted for its cunning. The common **European red fox** *(V. vulpes)* is reddish-brown above and white beneath, with a white-tipped tail. It inhabits a burrow, and preys on poultry, rabbits, etc. The **North American red fox** *(V. fulva)* is a similar species of which the **cross fox** (having a dark cross mark on its back) and **black** or **silver fox** are color varieties. The **gray fox** *(Urocyon cinereoargenteus)* is found from Pennsylvania southward, and differs in habits from the red. ◆ Collateral adjective: *vulpine.* 2 The fur of the fox. 3 A sly, crafty person. 4 A small rope made by hand of two or more rope yarns. 5 *Obs.* A sword. —*v.t.* 1 To trick; outwit. 2 To make drunk; intoxicate. 3 To stain, as paper or timber, with a reddish color. 4 To make sour, as beer, in fermenting. 5 To repair or mend, as shoes, with new uppers. —*v.i.* 6 To become drunk. 7 To become sour. 8 To become reddish in color. [OE]

NORTH AMERICAN
RED FOX
(Average length 2 feet; tail,
13 inches; height, 13 inches)

Fox (foks) *n.* One of an Algonquian tribe of North American Indians, formerly inhabiting the neighborhood of Green Bay, Wisconsin: combined with the Sacs, 1760.

Fox (foks), **Charles James**, 1749–1806, English statesman; opposed American policy of George III. —**George**, 1624–91, English preacher; founded the Society of Friends. —**Henry**, 1705–74, first Baron Holland, British statesman. —**John Williams**, 1863–1919, U.S. novelist.

fox·bane (foks′bān′) *n.* A European herb *(Aconitum lycoctonum)* of the crowfoot family; wolf's-bane.

FOWL
Nomenclature for anatomical parts.

fox·ber·ry (foks′ber′ē) *n. pl.* **·ries** The cowberry.

fox brush The tail of a fox.

fox-chase (foks′chās′) *n.* A fox hunt.

Foxe (foks), **John**, 1516–87, English divine and historian. —**Richard**, 1448?–1528, English prelate and statesman; also **Fox.**

Foxe Basin An arm of the Atlantic between Melville Peninsula and Baffin Island.

fox earth The burrow of a fox.

foxed (fokst) *adj.* 1 Discolored by decay: applied to timber. 2 Having light-brown stains or spots, as the paper of books, prints, etc. 3 Repaired or ornamented with a foxing, as the upper leather of a shoe.

fox-fire (foks′fīr′) *n.* The phosphorescent light emitted by foxed or rotten wood.

fox-fish (foks′fish′) *n. pl.* **-fish** or **-fish·es** 1 The dragonet. 2 The fox shark.

fox-glove (foks′gluv′) *n.* Any plant of a genus *(Digitalis)* of the figwort family, especially the English variety *(D. purpurea),* having flowers in long one-sided racemes; the leaves are a source of digitalis.

ENGLISH
FOXGLOVE
(From 2 1/2 to
5 feet tall)

fox grape Either of two species of American grapes, called the **northern fox grape** *(Vitio labrusca)* and the **southern fox grape** *(V. rotundifolia).*

fox-hole (foks′hōl′) *n.* A shallow pit dug by a combatant as cover against enemy fire: so called from the earth burrow of a fox.

fox-hound (foks′hound′) *n.* One of a breed of large, strong, very swift dogs trained for foxhunting.

fox-hunt (foks′hunt′) *n.* The hunting of foxes with hounds. Also **fox hunt.**

fox-hunt·ing (foks′hun′ting) *n.* The sport of hunting foxes with hounds. —**fox′hunt′er** *n.*

fox-ing (fok′sing) *n.* A piece of leather put on the upper leather of a shoe along the edge next to the sole.

Fox Islands (foks) The easternmost group of the Aleutian Islands.

fox shark The thresher shark *(Alopias vulpes),* having a powerful tail as long as its body: also called *foxfish.*

fox-skin (foks′skin′) *n.* 1 The dressed skin of a fox. 2 A fur cap made of such skin.

fox squirrel Any of several large North American arboreal squirrels; especially *Sciurus niger.*

fox-tail (foks′tāl′) *n.* 1 The tail of a fox. 2 Any of various species of grass bearing a dense spike of flowers like a fox's tail; especially the meadows foxtail *(Alopecurus pratensis).*

fox terrier See under TERRIER.

fox-trot (foks′trot′) *n.* 1 A pace between a trot and a walk: used of horses. 2 A modern dance step of syncopated two-four time.

fox-wood (foks′wood′) *n.* Decayed or foxed wood.

fox·y (fok′sē) *adj.* **fox·i·er, fox·i·est** 1 Of or like a fox; crafty. 2 Reddish-brown in color. 3 Discolored; foxed. 4 Soured; improperly fermented, as wine. 5 Defective, as in quality. 6 Denoting a wild flavor found in wine made from some American grapes. —**fox′i·ness** *n.*

foy (foi) *n. Dial.* A feast given before one goes on a journey. [<MDu. *foie,* prob. <OF *voie* <L *via* a road, way]

foy·er (foi′ər, -ā; *Fr.* fwä·yā′) *n.* 1 A public room or lobby, as in a theater or hotel. 2 An entrance room in a house. [<F <LL *focarium* hearth <*focus*]

Foynes (foinz) A town in County Limerick, Ireland; site of a transoceanic airport superseded by Shannon after World War II. *Irish Gaelic* **Faeng.**

Fr *Chem.* Francium (symbol Fr).

Fra (frä) *n.* Brother: a friar's title. [<Ital., short for *frate* <L *frater* brother]

Fra Angelico See ANGELICO, FRA.

fra·cas (frä′kəs) *n.* A noisy fight; brawl. See synonyms under ALTERCATION, QUARREL. [<Ital. *fracasso* an uproar <*fracassare* shatter]

Fra·ca·sto·ro (frä′käs·tō′rō), **Girolamo**, 1483–1553, Italian physician and poet.

frac·tion (frak′shən) *n.* 1 A disconnected part; fragment; hence, a tiny bit. 2 *Math.* A quantity less than a unit, or one expressed as the sum of a number of aliquot parts of a unit. See list of principal kinds of fractions below. 3 *Obs.* The act of breaking. 4 A piece of land smaller than the standard unit of measurement. 5 *Chem.* One of the components separated from a substance by fractional distillation: Naphtha is a *fraction* of petroleum. —*v.t.* To set or separate into fractions. See synonyms under PART. [<OF <LL *fractio, -onis* <*fractus,* pp. of *frangere* break]

—**common fraction** A fraction expressed by two numbers, a denominator, indicating the number of equal parts into which the unit is to be divided, and a numerator, indicating

the number of those parts to be taken. Also called **vulgar fraction.**
—complex fraction A fraction in which either the numerator or the denominator is a fraction. Also called **compound fraction.**
—continued fraction A fraction whose denominator is another integer plus another fraction, and so on.
—decimal fraction A fraction whose denominator is any power of 10 and which may be expressed in decimal form, as 7/10 (0.7), 3/100 (0.03), etc.
—improper fraction A fraction in which the numerator exceeds the denominator.
—partial fraction One of a set of fractions whose algebraic sum is a given fraction.
—proper fraction A fraction in which the numerator is less than the denominator.
—similar fraction Any of a group of fractions having a common denominator or the same number of decimal places.
—simple fraction A fraction in which both numerator and denominator are integers.
—unit fraction A fraction whose numerator is unity.

frac·tion·al (frak′shən·əl) *adj.* **1** Pertaining to or constituting a fraction. **2** Broken; small. **3** *Chem.* Designating a process or method of separating a complex of substances into component parts on the basis of specific differences in selected properties, as solubility, boiling point, crystallization, etc.

fractional currency Money or coins of any denomination less than the standard monetary unit: in the United States, less than a dollar.

fractional distillation *Chem.* The separation of the various components of a mixture, as petroleum, by distillation into fractions having more or less fixed properties but not necessarily being definite compounds: also **frac′tion·a′tion.**

frac·tion·al·ism (frak′shə·nə·liz·əm) *n.* A tendency to fractionalize.

frac·tion·al·ize (frak′shə·nə·līz) *v.t.* **·ized, ·iz·ing** To divide into parts or fractions.

fractional section A piece of land of less than 640 acres, having topographical irregularities.

fractional township A tract of land of more or less than 36 sections, having various topographical irregularities.

frac·tion·ate (frak′shən·āt) *v.t.* **·at·ed, ·at·ing** To subject to fractional distillation.

fractionating column *Chem.* A long vertical tube divided into segments and attached to a still for the fractional distillation of liquid mixtures: also called *dephlegmator.*

frac·tion·ize (frak′shən·īz) *v.t.* & *v.i.* **·ized, ·iz·ing** To divide into fractions. **—frac′tion·i·za′tion** *n.*

frac·tious (frak′shəs) *adj.* Disposed to rebel; restive; unruly; peevish. See synonyms under FRETFUL, PERVERSE, RESTIVE. **—frac′tious·ly** *adv.* **—frac′tious·ness** *n.*

frac·tog·ra·phy (frak·tog′rə·fē) *n.* The microscopic study of the fractures and other structural defects occurring in metals. [<L *fractus* broken + -GRAPHY] **—frac·to·graph·ic** (frak′tə·Jean graf′·ik) *adj.*

frac·tur (fräk·tŏŏr′) See FRAKTUR.

frac·ture (frak′chər) *n.* **1** The act, mode, or result of breaking, or the state of being broken. **2** A break. **3** The breaking of a bone; a break in a bone. **—comminuted fracture** A fracture in which the bone is splintered or crushed. **—compound fracture** One leading to an open wound, often exposing the bone. **—impacted fracture** One in which the broken parts are driven into each other. **—simple fracture** One without any break in the skin: also **closed fracture. 4** A rupture; crack. **5** The characteristic appearance of the freshly broken surface of a mineral, as a conchoidal *fracture.* —*v.t.* & *v.i.* **·tured, ·tur·ing** To break or be broken; crack. See synonyms under BREAK, RUPTURE. **—frac′tur·a·ble** *adj.* **—frac′·tur·al** *adj.*

frae (frā) *prep. Scot.* From.

frae·num (frē′nəm) See FRENUM.

frag·ile (fraj′əl) *adj.* Easily broken; frail; delicate. [<L *fragilis* <*frangere* break. Doublet of FRAIL.] **—frag′ile·ly** *adv.* **—fra·gil·i·ty** (frə·jil′·ə·tē), **frag′ile·ness** *n.*
Synonyms: breakable, brittle, delicate, frail, frangible, infirm, slight, tender, weak.

frag·ment (frag′mənt) *n.* A part broken off; a small detached portion. See synonyms under PART. [<F <L *fragmentum* fragment, remnant]

frag·men·tar·y (frag′mən·ter′ē) *adj.* Composed of fragments; broken; incomplete. Also **frag·men′tal. —frag′men·tar′i·ly** *adv.* **—frag′men·tar′i·ness** *n.*

frag·men·ta·tion (frag′mən·tā′shən) *n.* **1** The breaking up into fragments. **2** The scattering in all directions of the fragments of an exploding grenade, shell, or bomb. **3** *Biol.* In cell division, the breaking up of one or more chromosomes into pieces smaller than the normal.

fragmentation bomb See under BOMB.

frag·ment·ed (frag′mən·tid) *adj.* Broken into pieces or fragments.

frag·ment·ize (frag′mən·tīz) *v.t.* **·ized, ·iz·ing** To break into small pieces.

Fra·go·nard (frȧ·gō·när′), **Jean Honoré,** 1732–1806, French painter.

fra·grance (frā′grəns) *n.* The state or quality of being fragrant; a sweet odor. Also **fra′gran·cy.**

fra·grant (frā′grənt) *adj.* Having an agreeable or sweet smell. [<L *fragrans, -antis,* ppr. of *fragrare* smell sweet] **—fra′grant·ly** *adv.*

frail[1] (frāl) *n.* **1** A basket made of rushes: used for containing dried fruits, and as a measure. **2** The weight measure of raisins in such a basket, about 50 pounds avoirdupois. [<OF *fraiel* basket]

frail[2] (frāl) *adj.* **1** Delicately constituted; easily broken or destroyed. **2** Easily tempted; liable to be led astray. See synonyms under FRAGILE. [<OF *fraile* <L *fragilis.* Doublet of FRAGILE.] **—frail′ly** *adv.*

frail·ty (frāl′tē) *n. pl.* **·ties 1** The state of being frail. **2** A fault or moral weakness. Also **frail′ness.** See synonyms under FOIBLE.

fraim (frām) See FREM.

fraise (frāz) *n.* **1** A defense of pointed stakes planted in a rampart horizontally or in an inclined position. **2** A ruff of the kind worn in Europe in the 16th century. [<F <*fraiser* curl, ult. <Gmc.]

frai·ter (frā′tər) *n. Obs.* A monastery or convent dining-room: also spelled *frater.* Also **frai′tor.** [<OF *fraitur,* short for *refreitor* <Med. L *refectorium* a dining-hall]

frak·tur (fräk·tŏŏr′) *n.* A form of Latin letter formerly widely used in German printing, characterized by thin shape, pointed ends, and bristling serifs: also spelled *fractur.* See ALPHABET. [<G <L *fractura* a breaking]

fram·be·si·a (fram·bē′zhē·ə, -zē·ə, -zhə) *n.* Yaws. Also **fram·boe′si·a.** [<NL <F *framboise* a raspberry]

frame (frām) *v.* **framed, fram·ing** *v.t.* **1** To surround with or put in a frame. **2** *Colloq.* To incriminate falsely. **3** To put together; build, as a house. **4** To put in words; utter: to *frame* a reply. **5** To draw up; put in proper form: to *frame* a law. **6** To think out; arrange; conceive, as a plan or theory. **7** To shape or adapt to a purpose; dispose: to *frame* oneself to obedience. —*v.i.* **8** *Obs.* To move; go. See synonyms under CONSTRUCT, MAKE. —*n.* **1** Something composed or constructed of parts, whether physical or mental, united and adjusted to one another in a system; a construction. **2** The general arrangement or constitution of a thing. **3** Structure or build, as of a person. **4** The supporting and formative parts of a structure, put together so as to sustain and give shape to the whole. **5** A machine characterized by a wooden framework or structure: a silk *frame.* **6** A case or border made to enclose or surround a thing. **7** A mental state or condition; mood. **8** In tenpins and bowling, a division of the game during which a player bowls at one setting of the pins. **9** The triangular frame in which the balls in a pool game are bunched ready for the break. **10** One of the complete exposures in a roll of motion-picture film. **11** In television, a single complete scanning of the field of view by the electronic or other scanning device. **12** Form; proportion. **13** The act of contriving or inventing. **14** *Colloq.* A frame-up. [OE *framian* benefit]
Synonyms (noun): fabric, form, framework, order, structure, system. See BODY, FORM, TEMPER.

frame frequency In television, the number of frames per second completed by the scanning spot.

frame house A house built on a wooden framework covered on the outside by shingles, boards, stucco, etc.

fram·er (frā′mər) *n.* One who or that which frames; a maker.

frame-up (frām′up′) *n. Colloq.* **1** Anything prearranged. **2** A conspiracy to convict a person on a false charge.

frame·work (frām′wûrk′) *n.* A skeleton structure for supporting or enclosing something.

fram·ing (frā′ming) *n.* **1** A framework. **2** The act of erecting or making a frame; the act of composing or drawing up. **3** *Colloq.* The act of conspiring against.

fram·mit (fram′it) *adj. Scot.* Foreign; strange.

franc (frangk) *n.* **1** A French coin, originally silver and once valued at about 19 1/2 cents: equivalent to 100 centimes: the monetary unit of France. **2** The corresponding monetary unit of Belgium, Switzerland, etc. **3** A French gold piece, first coined in 1360; also, a silver piece, first coined in 1575. [<OF *Franc(orum rex)* king of the Franks, the motto on the first of these coins]

France (frans, fräns), **Anatole** Pseudonym of Jacques Anatole Thibault, 1844–1924, French novelist and critic.

France (frans, fräns) A republic in western Europe; 212,659 square miles; capital, Paris. Abbr. *Fr.*

Fran·ces (fran′sis, frän′-) A feminine personal name. Compare FRANCIS. Also **Fran·cis·ca** (*Dan., Du., Pg.* frän·sēs′kä; *Ger.* frän·tsēs′kä; *Sp.* frän·thēs′kä), *Ital.* **Fran·ces·ca** (frän·ches′·kä), *Sw.* **Fran·cis·ka** (frän·sis′kä), *Fr.* **Fran·çoise** (fräṅ·swȧz′) or **Fran·cisque** (fräṅ·sēsk′).

Fran·ces·ca (frän·ches′kä), **Piero della** See under PIERO.

Fran·ces·ca da Ri·mi·ni (frän·ches′kä dä rē′mē·nē), died 1205?, Italian lady; killed, together with her lover, Paolo, by her husband, Giovanni the Lame: immortalized by Dante.

Franche-Com·té (fräṅsh·kôṅ·tā′) A region and former province of eastern France. Also **Free County of Burgundy.**

fran·chise (fran′chīz) *n.* **1** A political or constitutional right reserved to or vested in the people, as the right of suffrage. **2** *Law* A special privilege emanating from the government by legislative or royal grant and vested in an individual person or in a body politic and corporate; a right to do something, as run a railroad, a bus line, etc. **3** The territory or boundary of a special privilege or immunity. **4** Authorization granted by a manufacturer to distributor or retailer to sell his products. See synonyms under RIGHT. —*v.t. Obs.* To enfranchise. [<OF <*franc, franche* free]

Fran·cis (fran′sis, frän′-) A masculine personal name. Also **Fran·cis·cus** (*Dan., Du.* frän·sēs′kəs; *Ger.* frän·tsēs′kəs), *Fr.* **Fran·çois** (fräṅ·swȧ′), *Ital.* **Fran·ces·co** (frän·ches′kō), *Pg., Sp.* **Fran·cis·co** (*Pg.* frän·sēs′kōō, *Sp.* frän·thēs′kō). Compare FRANCES. [<Gmc., free]
—Francis I, 1494–1547, king of France 1515–1547.
—Francis II, 1768–1835, Holy Roman Emperor 1792–1806, emperor of Austria 1804–35.
—Francis Ferdinand, 1863–1914, archduke of Austria; assassinated.
—Francis Joseph, 1830–1916, emperor of Austria 1848–1916. Also *Ger.* **Franz Josef.**
—Francis of Assisi, Saint, 1182–1226, Italian mendicant; founder of the Franciscan order.
—Francis of Sales, Saint, 1567–1622, French prelate; founded the Order of Visitation, 1610. See SALESIAN.
—Francis Xavier, Saint See XAVIER.

Fran·cis·can (fran·sis′kən) *n.* A member of the mendicant order *(Gray Friars* or *Minorites)* founded in 1209 by St. Francis of Assisi. The three branches of the order are *Capuchins, Conventuals,* and *Observantines.* See also POOR CLARE. —*adj.* **1** Of or pertaining to St. Francis. **2** Belonging to a religious order or institution following the rule of St. Francis.

fran·ci·um (fran′sē·əm) *n.* A short-lived radioactive metallic element (symbol Fr, atomic number 87) occurring as a decay product of actinium and having a half-life of 22 minutes. See PERIODIC TABLE. [after FRANCE]

Franck (frängk), **César Auguste,** 1822–90, French composer born in Belgium. **—James,** 1882–1964, German physicist.

Fran·co (fräng′kō) Italian and Spanish form of FRANCIS.

Fran·co (frang′kō, *Sp.* fräng′kō), **Francisco,** 1892–1975; chief of state 1939–75.

Franco- *combining form* French: *Franco-Prussian.* [< L *Francus* a Frank]

Fran·co-Ger·man War (frang′kō·jûr′mən) See FRANCO-PRUSSIAN WAR in table under WAR.

fran·co·lin (frang′kə·lin) *n.* An Old World, now chiefly Asian, partridge (genus *Francolinus*), having richly colored plumage and a rather long tail and bill. [< F < Ital. *francolino*]

Fran·co·ni·a (frang·kō′nē·ə) A medieval duchy in south Germany, divided into the present administrative districts of Lower, Middle, and Upper Franconia. *German* **Fran·ken** (fräng′·kən) **—Fran·co′ni·an** *adj.* & *n.*

Fran·co·phile (frang′kə·fil) *n.* A non-French admirer of France or of French customs, etc. *—adj.* Kindly disposed toward France. — **Fran′co·phil′i·a** (-fil′ē·ə) *n.*

Fran·co·phobe (frang′kə·fōb) *n.* A person who fears or dislikes France or French things. *—adj.* Fearful of France. **—Fran′co·pho′bi·a** *n.*

Fran·co-Prus·sian War (frang′kō·prush′ən) See table under WAR.

franc-ti·reur (frän·tē·rœr′) *n. pl.* **francs-ti·reurs** (frän·tē·rœr′) A French soldier, one of the sharpshooters of a light infantry force. [< F < *franc* free + *tireur* shooter < *tirer* shoot]

fran·gi·ble (fran′jə·bəl) *adj.* Easily broken; brittle; fragile. [< OF < L *frangere* break] — **fran′gi·bil′i·ty, fran′gi·ble·ness** *n.*

fran·gi·pan·i (fran′ji·pan′ē, -pä′nē) *n.* **1** A perfume derived from or resembling that of the West Indian red jasmine *(Plumera rubra).* **2** The plant. Also **fran′gi·pane** (-pān). [after Marquis *Frangipani,* who created the perfume]

Fran·glais (frang·glā′) *n.* The French language as used by speakers who utilize many English borrowings. [< F *français* French + *anglais* English]

frank (frangk) *adj.* **1** Candid and open; ingenuous. **2** *Obs.* Giving freely; generous. **3** *Law* Free, in the sense of privileged, exempt, or unhindered in action. See synonyms under BLUFF, CANDID, HONEST. *—v.t.* **1** To mark, as a letter or package, so as to be sent free of charge. **2** To send, as a letter, free of charge. **3** To convey free of charge. **4** *Chiefly Brit.* To mark or stamp (mail) by machine (a **franking machine**) to indicate that postage has been paid. *—n.* **1** The right to send mail matter free. **2** The package so sent. **3** The signature that authenticates it: extended commercially to telegrams, etc. [< OF *franc* frank, free] — **frank′ly** *adv.* **—frank′ness** *n.* **—frank′er** *n.*

Frank (frangk) A masculine personal name; also shortened form of FRANCIS, FRANKLIN.

Frank (frangk) *n.* **1** A member of one of the Germanic tribes settled on the Rhine early in the Christian era. **2** In the Near East, any European. [< L *Francus* a Frank < Gmc., a spear (cf. OE *franca* lance); named from their weapon]

Frank (frangk), **Glenn,** 1877–1940, U.S. educator. **—Waldo David,** 1889–1967, U.S. writer.

Frank·en·stein (frangk′ən·stīn) *n.* **1** The hero of Mary Wollstonecraft Shelley's *Frankenstein,* a medical student who fashions a man monster which commits numerous atrocities and finally slays its maker. **2** Any person destroyed by his own handiwork. **3** Loosely, Frankenstein's monster. **4** Any work or created thing that gets beyond the control of the inventor and causes his destruction.

Frank·fort (frangk′fərt) The capital of Kentucky.

Frankfort on the Main (mān) A city in Hesse, West Germany; birthplace of Goethe. *German* **Frank·furt** or **Frank·furt-am-Main** (frängk′fo͝ort·äm·mīn′).

Frankfort on the O·der (ō′dər) A city in Brandenburg, East Germany. *German* **Frank·furt** or **Frank·furt-an-der-O·der** (frängk′fo͝ort·än·dər·ō′dər).

frank·furt·er (frangk′fər·tər) *n.* A highly seasoned sausage of mixed meats. Compare WIENERWURST. Also **frank′fort·er, frankfurt** (or **frankfort**) **sausage.** [after *Frankfurt,* Germany]

Frank·furt·er (frangk′fər·tər), **Felix,** 1882–1965, U.S. jurist born in Austria; associate justice of the Supreme Court, 1939–1962.

frank·in·cense (frangk′in·sens) *n.* An aromatic gum or resin from various trees of East Africa, especially *Boswellia carteri*: used as an incense and in medicine as a stimulant and expectorant: also called *olibanum.* [< OF *franc* pure + *encens* incense]

Frank·ish (frang′kish) *adj.* Of or pertaining to the Franks, or, in the Near East, to Europeans in general. *—n.* The language spoken by the Franks, belonging to the western branch of the Germanic languages.

frank·lin (frangk′lin) *n.* In late medieval England, a freeholder; a non-noble landholder ranking below the gentry. [ME *frankeleyn* < Med. L *francus* free]

Frank·lin (frangk′lin), **Benjamin,** 1706–90, American patriot, writer, scientist, and diplomat; signer of the Declaration of Independence. **—Sir John,** 1786–1847, English Arctic explorer.

Frank·lin (frangk′lin) **1** A temporary state, 1784–88, comprising lands of western North Carolina ceded to Congress in 1784; now part of eastern Tennessee. **2** The northernmost district of Northwest Territories, Canada; 541,753 square miles.

frank·lin·ite (frangk′lin·īt) *n.* A metallic, iron-black, slightly magnetic oxide of zinc, iron, and manganese, crystallizing in the isometric system: a valuable ore of zinc. [after *Franklin,* N. J., where it is found]

Franklin stove An open-faced cast-iron stove resembling a fireplace: invented by Benjamin Franklin.

FRANKLIN STOVE

frank·ly (frangk′lē) *adv.* Candidly; openly.

frank·pledge (frangk′plej′) *n.* **1** In old English law, a system of mutual suretyship that required all men to combine in groups of ten to stand as sureties for one another's good behavior. **2** A member of such a group. **3** One such group; a tithing.

Frans (fräns) Swedish and Dutch form of FRANCIS.

fran·tic (fran′tik) *adj.* Manifesting, or caused by, excessive excitement; frenzied. See synonyms under INSANE. [< OF *frenetique* < LL *phreneticus* < Gk. *phrenitikos* delirious < *phrenitis* delirium < *phrēn* mind] **—fran′ti·cal·ly, fran′tic·ly** *adv.* — **fran′tic·ness** *n.*

Frants (fränts) Danish form of FRANCIS.

Franz (fränts) German form of FRANCIS.

Franz Jo·sef Land (fränts jō′zəf, *Ger.* fränts yō′zəf) An archipelago in the Arctic Ocean, the most northerly land of the eastern hemisphere; annexed by the U.S.S.R. in 1926: also *Fridtjof Nansen land. Russian* **Zem·lya Fran·tsa Io·si·fa** (zyim·lyä′ frän′tsä ō′zyi·fä).

frap (frap) *v.t.* **frapped, frap·ping** *Naut.* To draw or bind firmly. [< OF *fraper* strike]

frap·pé (fra·pā′) *U.S. adj.* **frap·pée** *fem.* Iced; chilled. *—n.* **1** A fruit juice frozen to a mush. **2** A liqueur or other beverage poured over shaved ice. [< F, pp. of *frapper* chill]

Fra·ser River (frā′zər) The chief river of British Columbia, flowing 850 miles SW to the Gulf of Georgia.

frat (frat) *n. U.S. Colloq.* A college fraternity.

fratch (frach) *v.i.* & *n. Brit. Dial.* Quarrel.

fra·ter[1] (frā′tər) *n.* A brother; a comrade. [< L]

fra·ter[2] (frā′tər) *n. Obs.* a fraiter.

fra·ter·nal (frə·tûr′nəl) *adj.* **1** Pertaining to or befitting a brother; brotherly. **2** Of or pertaining to a fraternal order or association. [< L *fraternus* < *frater* brother] **—fra·ter′nal·ism** *n.* — **fra·ter′nal·ly** *adv.*

fraternal society An organization for the attainment of some mutual benefit. Also **fraternal association** or **order.**

fraternal twins *Genetics* Twins that develop from separately fertilized ova and thus are as distinct in hereditary characteristics as though born at different times. They may be of the same or opposite sex: distinguished from *identical* twins.

fra·ter·ni·ty (frə·tûr′nə·tē) *n. pl.* **·ties 1** The condition or relation of brotherhood; brotherly affection. **2** An organization, for social or other purposes, of men students of American colleges, usually having Greek letter names and secret rites, and represented by chapters in many institutions. **3** A similar organization outside of colleges. **4** A group of men of the same profession, sporting interests, etc.: the medical *fraternity.*

frat·er·ni·za·tion (frat′ər·nə·zā′shən) *n.* The act of fraternizing; specifically, intercourse between occupying military forces and civilians, often in contravention of regulations.

frat·er·nize (frat′ər·nīz) *v.* **·nized, ·niz·ing** *v.i.* **1** To be friendly or fraternal. **2** To be friendly with the enemy or with the people of an occupied or conquered territory; especially, to have sexual relations with women of such a territory. *—v.t.* **3** To bring into fraternal association. — **frat′er·niz′er** *n.*

Fra·tres Ar·va·les (frā′trēz är·vā′lēz) The Arval Brethren.

Fratres Mi·no·res (mī·nôr′ēz, -nō′rēz) See MINORITE.

Fratres Prae·di·ca·tor·es (prē′dik·ə·tôr′ēz, -tō′rēz) See DOMINICAN.

frat·ri·ci·dal (frat′rə·sī′dəl) *adj.* Of, pertaining to, or guilty of fratricide.

frat·ri·cide (frat′rə·sīd) *n.* **1** One who kills his brother. **2** The killing of a brother. [Def. 1 < F < L *fratricida* < *frater* brother + *caedere* kill; def. 2 < F < L *fratricidium*]

Frau (frou) *n. pl.* **Frau·en** (-ən) *German* A married woman; a wife; a lady: as a title, the German equivalent of *Mistress, Mrs.*

fraud (frôd) *n.* **1** Deception in order to gain by another's loss; craft; trickery; guile. **2** One who acts fraudulently; a cheat. **3** A deceptive or spurious thing. **4** *Law* Any artifice or deception practiced to cheat, deceive, or circumvent another to his injury. [< OF *fraude* < L *fraus, fraudis* deceit] **—fraud′ful** *adj.* **—fraud′ful·ly** *adv.* **—fraud′less** *adj.* **fraud′·less·ly** *adv.* — **fraud′less·ness** *n.*

Synonyms: artifice, cheat, cheating, deceit, deception, dishonesty, duplicity, imposition, imposture, swindle, swindling, treachery, treason, trick. A *fraud* is an act of deliberate *deception* with the design of securing something by taking unfair advantage of another. *A deceit* or *deception* may be designed merely to gain some end of one's own, with no intent of harming another; an *imposition* is intended to take some small advantage of another, or simply to make another ridiculous. An *imposture* is designed to obtain money, credit, or position to which one is not entitled, and may be practiced by a street beggar or by the pretender to a throne. All action that is not honest is *dishonesty,* but the term *dishonesty* is generally applied in business, politics, etc., to deceitful practices which are not distinctly criminal. *Fraud* includes *deceit,* but *deceit* may not reach the gravity of *fraud;* a *cheat* is of the nature of *fraud,* but of a petty sort; a *swindle* is more serious than a *cheat,* involving larger values and more flagrant *dishonesty. Fraud* is commonly actionable at law; *cheating* and *swindling* are for the most part out of the reach of legal proceedings. Compare ARTIFICE, DECEPTION, TREACHERY. *Antonyms*: fairness, honesty, integrity, truth, uprightness.

fraud·u·lence (frô′jə·ləns) *n.* The quality to being fraudulent; unfairness. Also **fraud′u·len·cy.**

fraud·u·lent (frô′jə·lənt) *adj.* Proceeding from, characterized by, or practicing fraud. See synonyms under BAD, COUNTERFEIT. **—fraud′·u·lent·ly** *adv.*

fraught (frôt) *adj.* **1** Involving; full of. **2** *Archaic* Freighted; laden. *—n. Obs.* Freight; cargo. [Orig. pp. of obs. *fraught* load, ult. < MDu. *vrachten*]

Frau Hol·le (frou hôl′ə) See HOLDA.

Fräu·lein (froi′līn) *n. German* An unmarried woman; a young woman: as a title, the German equivalent of *Miss.*

Fraun·ho·fer (froun′hō′fər), **Joseph von,** 1787–1826, German optician and physicist; mapped dark lines of the spectrum.

Fraunhofer's lines A series of groups of dark lines in the spectrum of the sun and other stars, each group appearing to the eye as a single transverse line: also called *F lines.*

frax·i·nel·la (frak′sə·nel′ə) *n.* A Eurasian herb *(Dictamnus albus)* of the rue family with white flowers and a powerful odor: also called *dittany* and *gas plant.* [< NL, dim. of L *fraxinus* ash tree]

fray[1] (frā) *n.* A fight; an affray. *—v.t. Obs.* To frighten. *—v.i. Obs.* To fight. [Aphetic var. of AFFRAY]

fray[2] (frā) *v.t.* & *v.i.* To wear, rub, or become

worn, as by friction; ravel. — *n.* A fretted spot in a cloth, etc. [<F *frayer* <L *fricare* rub]
Fra·zer (frā′zər), **Sir James George,** 1854–1941, Scottish anthropologist.
fra·zil (frə·zil′, fraz′əl, frā′zəl) *n.* Ice of a granular, spicular, or platelike shape formed in agitated or flowing water. Also **frazil ice.** [Cf. F *fraisil* cinders]
fraz·zle (fraz′əl) *Colloq. v.t. & v.i.* **·zled, ·zling** 1 To fray or become frayed; fret, or tatter. 2 To tire out; weary. — *n.* Frayed ends; state of being frayed. — **beat to a frazzle** Beat into shreds and tatters; hence, overcome completely. — **worn to a frazzle** Worn to shreds; hence, tired out; utterly exhausted. [? Blend of FRAY[2] + obs. *fasel* ravel]
freak (frēk) *n.* 1 A sudden causeless change of mind; a whim. 2 A malformation; monstrosity. 3 *Slang* One given to the use of drugs, especially illegal drugs. 4 *Slang* One who is very unconventional. 5 *Slang* One who is very enthusiastic about something: an opera *freak.* — *adj.* Strange; abnormal. — **to freak out** *Slang* 1 To experience, often unpleasantly, the effects of drugs, especially psychedelic drugs. 2 To behave as though one were under the influence of a psychedelic drug. [Origin unknown] — **freak′y** *adj.*
freak·ish (frē′kish) *adj.* Inclined to freaks; eccentric; also, like a freak, capricious; prankish. — **freak′ish·ly** *adv.* — **freak′ish·ness** *n.*
freath (frēth, frēth) *n. & v. Scot.* Lather; froth.
Fré·chette (frā·shet′), **Louis Honoré,** 1839–1908, Canadian journalist and poet.
freck·le (frek′əl) *n.* A small, brownish, or dark-colored spot on the skin. — *v.* **freck·led, freck·ling** *v.t.* To mark or cover with freckles. — *v.i.* To become marked with freckles. [ME *fracel,* var. of *frekne* <ON *freknur* freckles]
freck·led (frek′əld) *adj.* Marked with freckles. Also **freck′ly.**
Fred (fred) Shortened form of FREDERICK, ALFRED, WILFRED.
Fred·er·i·ca (fred′ə·rē′kə) A feminine personal name. Compare FREDERICK. Also *Pg., Sp.* **Fre·de·ri·ca** (frā′dā·rē′kä), *Fr.* **Fré·dé·rique** (frā·dā·rēk′).
Fred·er·ick (fred′ər·ik, -rik) 1 A masculine personal name. 2 Name of many European monarchs. Also **Fred′er·ic,** *Fr.* **Fré·dé·ric** (frā·dā·rēk′), *Dan.* **Fre·der·ik** (freth′ə·rēk), *Du.* **Fre·de·rik** (frā′dā·rēk). See also FEDERICO, FRIEDRICH. [<Gmc., peaceful ruler]
— **Frederick I,** 1121–90, Holy Roman Emperor 1152–90: known as *Barbarossa* (Redbeard).
— **Frederick I,** 1657–1713, elector of Brandenburg 1688–1701; first king of Prussia 1701–13.
— **Frederick II,** 1194–1250, Holy Roman Emperor 1215–50.
— **Frederick II,** 1712–86, king of Prussia 1740–86: known as **Frederick the Great.**
— **Frederick III,** 1415–93, Holy Roman Emperor 1440–93; king of Germany as Frederick IV.
— **Frederick William,** 1620–88, elector of Brandenburg 1640–88; secured Prussian independence: called "the Great Elector."
— **Frederick William I,** 1688–1740, king of Prussia 1713–40; succeeded Frederick I.
— **Frederick William II,** 1744–97, king of Prussia 1786–97; succeeded Frederick II.
— **Frederick William III,** 1770–1840, king of Prussia 1797–1840.
— **Frederick William IV,** 1795–1861, king of Prussia 1840–61.
Fred·er·icks·burg (fred′riks·bûrg, fred′ər·iks-) A city in NE Virginia; scene of Confederate victory in the Civil War, 1862.
Fred·er·ic·ton (fred′ər·ik·tən, fred′rik-) The capital of New Brunswick province, Canada.
Fre·der·iks·berg (fred′ər·iks·bûrg, fred′riks-; *Dan.* freth′ə·rēks·berkh′) The chief suburb of Copenhagen, Denmark, comprising a separate commune.
free (frē) *adj.* **fre·er, fre·est** 1 Not bound by restrictions, physical, governmental, or moral; exempt from arbitrary domination or distinction; independent. 2 Not enslaved or in bondage. 3 Not believing in or permitting slavery. 4 Self-determining, whether as implying the absence of control through external causes in the form of physical forces, legal commands, or moral influences, or as asserting the mysterious and inexplicable spontaneity of the self as possessed of so-called *free* will. 5 Having, conferring, or characterized by political liberty; not subject to despotic or arbitrary rule; living under a government based on the consent of the people: a *free* nation. 6 Liberated, by reason of age, from the authority of parents or guardians: At 21 years a man is *free.* 7 Invested with certain franchises; enjoying certain immunities; given or allowed all privileges of: *free* of the city. 8 Exempt from or not subject to; not dominated by; clear of: followed by *from,* or rarely by *of.* 9 Characterized by disregard of conventionality, ceremony, or formality; accessible; frank; ingenuous. 10 Characterized by disregard of duty or propriety; forward; impertinent, indelicate or immodest; careless; immoderate; reckless. 11 Without impediment or restraint; moving or ranging at will; not repressed, checked, or hampered; unobstructed; unrestricted; unconstrained. 12 Without restriction; especially, without charge or cost; open; gratuitous: *free* seats. 13 Employing or giving unrestrainedly or without parsimony; liberal; profuse; generous; also, not obtained by solicitation. 14 Expending energy without stint; ready and prompt in action or movement without urging; ready; spirited. 15 Not closely bound to an original or pattern, nor limited by strict technical rules; exercising some liberty or discretion: a *free* choice, a *free* translation. 16 Not attached, bound, or fixed; capable of moving; loose: the *free* end of a rope. 17 Uncombined chemically: *free* hydrogen. 18 Available: *free* energy. 19 *Naut.* Favorable: applied to winds more than six points from being dead ahead. 20 Of or pertaining to a freeman: opposed to *base.* — *adv.* 1 Gratuitously. 2 Freely; willingly. 3 With the wind more than six points from being dead ahead. — *v.t.* **freed, free·ing** 1 To make free; release from bondage, obligation, worry, etc. 2 To clear or rid of obstruction or hindrance; disentangle; disengage. See synonyms under ABSOLVE, DELIVER, RELEASE. [OE *frēo*] — **free′ly** *adv.*
Synonyms (adj.): clear, emancipated, exempt, independent, unchecked, unconfined, unfettered, unhindered, unimpeded, unobstructed, unrestrained, untrammeled. See GENEROUS. *Antonyms*: bound, clogged, dependent, enslaved, fettered, hindered, impeded, restrained, restricted, shackled, subdued, subjected, subjugated.
-free *combining form* Free of; devoid of: *carefree, duty-free.*
free agency The power or capacity of a personality to act freely without constraint of his will. See WILL.
free agent A person regarded as self-determining and thus capable of responsible choice, and whose actions are determined by his own unconstrained will.
free alongside ship or **vessel** Delivered without charge to the pier where a ship is docked: abbreviated *f.a.s.*
free-and-eas·y (frē′ənd·ē′zē) *adj.* Unconventional; unrestrained.
free association 1 *Psychol.* An association of ideas unrestricted by definite control or limiting factors. 2 *Psychoanal.* A method of revealing unconscious processes by encouraging a spontaneous and unselective association of ideas.
free balloon A balloon floating freely in the atmosphere, its height controlled only by ballast and regulation of gas content.
free·bie (frē′bē) *n. Slang* Anything, as a ticket to a sports event, that is given free.
free·board (frē′bôrd′, -bōrd′) *n.* 1 *Naut.* The side of a vessel between the water line and the main deck. 2 The distance between the underframe of an automobile and the ground.
free·boot (frē′bo͞ot′) *v.i.* To act as a freebooter.
free·boot·er (frē′bo͞o′tər) *n.* One who plunders; especially a pirate or buccaneer. [<MDu. *vrijbuiter* < *vrij* free + *buit* booty]
free·boot·y (frē′bo͞o′tē) *n. Obs.* 1 Spoil; loot. 2 Pillaging.
free-born (frē′bôrn′) *adj.* Not born in servitude.
free city A city having an independent government, as certain German cities, that at one time were virtually small republics.
free coinage The mintage of certain specified bullion that may be offered at the mint by any person, with or without a fixed charge.
free companion See FREE LANCE (def. 1).
free company A company of medieval mercenaries.
freed·man (frēd′mən) *n. pl.* **·men** (-mən) An emancipated slave, especially an emancipated American Negro after the Civil War. — **freed′wom′an** *n. fem.*
free·dom (frē′dəm) *n.* 1 Exemption or liberation from slavery or imprisonment. 2 Exemption from political restraint or autocratic control; independence. 3 Liberty of choice or action. 4 *Philos.* The state of the will as the first cause of human actions; self-determination in rational beings. 5 Exemption; immunity: *freedom* from want; *freedom* from arrest. 6 Exemption or release from obligations, ties, etc. 7 Ease; facility. 8 Frankness or familiarity in speech or manner. 9 The right to enjoy the privileges of membership or citizenship: *freedom* of the city. 10 Unrestricted use: He had *freedom* of the library. 11 Ease of motion. See synonyms under LIBERTY. — **free′dom·less** *adj.* [OE *frēodōm*]
freedom of the press The right freely to publish without censorship or other government interference, usually restricted in practice by laws barring obscenity, sedition, and libel.
freedom of the seas Exemption from seizure at sea in war, by armed vessels of belligerents, of all private property of neutrals except contraband of war.
free electron See under ELECTRON.
free energy *Physics* That portion of the energy of a physicochemical system that is available to perform work.
free enterprise See PRIVATE ENTERPRISE.
free fight A general fight; a free-for-all.
free-for-all (frē′fər·ôl′) *n.* A fight, game, or competition, open to all comers.
free form *Ling.* A morpheme which can occur meaningfully in isolation: opposed to *bound form.*
free gold 1 Gold held by the U. S. Treasury over and above that in the gold reserve. 2 Pure gold found loose, as in placer mining.
free·hand (frē′hand′) *adj.* Executed with the hand without aid of measurements or drawing instruments: *freehand* drawing.
free hand Authority to act on one's own.
free-hand·ed (frē′han′did) *adj.* 1 Having the hands free or unrestricted. 2 Open-handed; generous. — **free′-hand′ed·ness** *n.*
free-heart·ed (frē′här′tid) *adj.* Generous; frank; open-hearted.
free·hold (frē′hōld′) *n.* 1 An estate in lands. 2 Land held without limitations or conditions; absolute ownership of an estate. — **free′hold′er** *n.*
free lance 1 A medieval soldier who sold his services to any state or cause. 2 One who writes, performs, or offers services without being regularly employed. 3 One who supports a cause or causes independently and without personal allegiance.
free-lance (frē′lans′, -läns′) *v.i.* **-lanced, -lanc·ing** To serve or work as a free lance. — *adj.* Working or acting as a free lance.
free list 1 A list of goods not subject to tariff charges. 2 A list of persons admitted free.
free-liv·er (frē′liv′ər) *n.* One addicted to personal indulgence, as in eating and drinking.
free-liv·ing (frē′liv′ing) *adj.* 1 Given to easy-going or self-indulgent habits of life. 2 *Zool.* Having or characterized by freedom of movement; motile.
free·load (frē′lōd′) *v.i. Slang* To act as a freeloader.
free·load·er (frē′lō′dər) *n. Slang* One who attends social gatherings for free food and drink.
free love The doctrine or custom of free choice in sexual relations, without the constraint of legal marriage or any permanent obligations.
free·man (frē′mən) *n. pl.* **·men** (-mən) 1 A man who is free; one not a slave or serf. 2 An inhabitant of a city. 3 In English law, a person admitted to the freedom of a corporate town or borough or of any other corporate

body and hence having full rights and privileges. **4** In feudal law, an allodial proprietor, as distinct from a vassal. **5** In old English law, a freeholder, as distinct from a villein. **6** In colonial America, a freeholder and hence, in most colonies, an enfranchised citizen.

Free·man (frē′mən), **Douglas Southall,** 1886–1953, U.S. editor and historian. — **Edward Augustus,** 1823–92, English historian. — **Mary Eleanor,** 1852–1930, *née* Wilkins, U.S. writer.

free·mar·tin (frē′mär′tən) *n.* A female calf twinned with a male calf and generally barren. [Origin uncertain]

free·ma·son (frē′mā′sən) *n.* In the Middle Ages, a stonemason belonging to a craft guild that had secret signs and passwords, and that admitted as honorary members persons not connected with their craft, who were designated *accepted masons.*

Free·ma·son (frē′mā′sən) *n.* A member of an extensive secret order or fraternity, dating from the Middle Ages, the members denoting themselves *Free and Accepted Masons.* — **Free·ma·son·ic** (frē′mə·son′ik) *adj.* — **Free′ma′·son·ry** *n.*

free·ma·son·ry (frē′mā′sən·rē) *n.* Instinctive sympathy or community of interests.

free·ness (frē′nis) *n.* The state of being free.

free on board Put on board a train, ship, or other freight or baggage carrier, without charge: abbreviated *f.o.b.*

free oscillations *Electr.* Oscillations within a circuit of a frequency determined by the inductance and capacity of the circuit uninfluenced by impressed voltages. Compare FORCED OSCILLATIONS.

free path *Physics* The distance traveled by a particle, as an ion, electron, or molecule, before colliding with another.

free port **1** A port open to all trading vessels on equal terms. **2** The whole or part of a port area where no customs duties are levied on goods intended for transshipment rather than for import.

free press An uncensored press; newspapers, magazines, etc., not accountable to a government for the news or opinions they print.

free ship **1** A ship belonging to a neutral power, and hence free from liability to seizure in time of war. **2** A ship that, while foreign-built, may receive U.S. registry when owned by a citizen or citizens of the United States.

free·si·a (frē′zhē·ə, -sē·ə, -zhə) *n.* A South African plant (genus *Freesia*) of the iris family, having bell-shaped, various colored, fragrant flowers. [<NL, after E. M. *Fries,* 1794–1878, Swedish botanist]

free silver The free and unlimited coinage of silver, particularly at a fixed ratio to gold, as 16 to 1 (advocated by a section of the Democratic party in 1896). — **free′-sil′ver** *adj.*

Free-soil (frē′soil′) *adj. U.S.* Of or pertaining to the Free-soil party, organized in 1848 to oppose the extension of slavery. — **Free′-soil′er** *n.*

free-spo·ken (frē′spō′kən) *adj.* Unreserved or frank in speech. — **free′spo′ken·ly** *adv.* — **free′·spo′ken·ness** *n.*

Free State **1** Before the Civil War, any State where slavery did not exist or was forbidden. **2** The Irish Free State.

free·stone (frē′stōn′) *adj.* Having a pit from which the pulp easily separates, as a plum or peach. — *n.* **1** Any stone, as sandstone or limestone, easily wrought for building purposes. **2** A peach easily freed from its pit.

free-style (frē′stīl′) *adj.* In competitive swimming, using or marked by the freedom to use whichever stroke the swimmer chooses. — *n.* Free-style swimming.

free-swim·mer (frē′swim′ər) *n.* A fish that swims habitually near the surface.

free-swim·ming (frē′swim′ing) *adj. Zool.* Swimming freely, as an aquatic animal: said especially of certain organisms that are attached or immovable during other stages of their development.

free·think·er (frē′thing′kər) *n.* An independent thinker; especially, one who forms his own religious beliefs without regard to church authority. — **free′think′ing** *adj.* & *n.*

free thought Thought or belief, especially in religious matters, based on reason alone and uninfluenced by authority or dogma.

Free·town (frē′toun) A port, capital of Sierra Leone.

free trade **1** Commerce between different countries free from restrictions or burdens, as tariff or customs; specifically, commerce not subjected to restrictions, discriminations, or favors of any kind designed to influence its normal course. **2** The practice, policy, or system of unrestricted trade. **3** The trade system of a country whose duties are levied only for revenue and without regard to their effect on home industries. Compare PROTECTION, PROTECTIVE TARIFF. **4** *Archaic* or *Obs.* Smuggling.

free-trad·er (frē′trā′dər) *n.* An advocate of or believer in free trade.

free verse Verse depending for its poetic effect upon irregular rhythmical pattern, either absence or irregularity of rime, and the use of cadenced speech rhythms rather than conventional verse forms; vers libre.

free·war·ren (frē′wôr′ən, -wor′-) *n.* In English law, the exclusive right of killing game within warren.

free water Soil water in excess of that absorbed by the soil: also called *gravity water.*

free·way (frē′wā′) *n.* A multiple-lane road designed for rapid transportation.

free wheel *Mech.* **1** A form of automotive transmission including a clutch which allows the driving shaft to run freely when its speed exceeds that of the engine shaft. **2** A brake device attached to the rear wheel of a bicycle which permits wheel motion without pedal action. — **free′-wheel′ing** *n.* & *adj.*

free will **1** The power of self-determination regarded as a special faculty. **2** *Philos.* The doctrine that man is entirely unrestricted in his ability to choose between good and evil: opposed to *determinism.*

free-will (frē′wil′) *adj.* Made, done, or given of one's own free choice; voluntary.

freeze (frēz) *v.* **froze, fro·zen, freez·ing** *v.i.* **1** To become converted from a fluid to a solid state by loss of heat; become ice. **2** To become stiff or hard with cold, as wet clothes. **3** To be very cold: It's *freezing* in here! **4** To become covered or obstructed with ice. **5** To adhere by freezing: It *froze* to the ground. **6** To be damaged or killed by freezing or frost. **7** To become motionless, as if frozen. **8** To be chilled or made motionless, as if by fear or other emotion. **9** To become formal or unyielding in manner. — *v.t.* **10** To change into ice; cause to become frozen. **11** To make stiff or hard by freezing the moisture of. **12** To cover or obstruct with ice. **13** To damage or kill by freezing or frost. **14** To make or hold motionless or in position. **15** To chill or make motionless, as if by fear, awe, or other emotion; frighten; discourage. **16** To fix or stabilize (prices, stocks, wages, etc.) so as to prevent change, as by government order. **17** *Med.* To anesthetize: to *freeze* a tooth. — **to freeze to** (or **onto**) **1** To keep close or cling to (a person). **2** To hold on to. — **to freeze out** *U.S. Colloq.* To exclude or drive away, as by unfriendliness or severe competition. — *n.* **1** The act of freezing or the state of being frozen. **2** A spell of freezing weather. **3** The stabilizing or fixing of prices, labor, etc., in order to prevent profiteering, migration of workers, etc. ◆ Homophone: *frieze.* [OE *frēosan*]

freeze-out (frēz′out′) *n.* **1** A kind of poker game in which each player drops out as soon as all his money is lost, the last player winning all. **2** An exclusion, as by unfriendliness, outwitting, or trickery.

freez·er (frē′zər) *n.* **1** That which freezes. **2** A refrigerator within which a low temperature is maintained for the purpose of preserving or freezing foods, etc. **3** An apparatus containing ice or brine, for freezing ice-cream.

freeze-up (frēz′up′) *n.* The freezing over of lakes, rivers, streams, etc., in severe winter weather; also, such weather.

freezing mixture Any mixture, as of salt and ice, that can lower the temperature of surrounding bodies or substances to various levels below the freezing point.

freezing point *Physics* The temperature at which a liquid passes into the solid state under given pressure; for fresh water at sea-level pressure this temperature is 32 degrees above zero Fahrenheit, or zero degrees Celsius. Compare MELTING POINT.

free zone A section of a port or city for the receipt and storage of goods, duty-free.

Frei·berg (frī′bûrg, *Ger.* frī′berkh) A city in the former state of Saxony, SE East Germany.

Frei·burg (frī′bûrg, *Ger.* frī′bŏŏrkh) **1** A city in SW Germany: also **Freiburg-im-Breis·gau** (im brīs′gou). **2** The German name for FRIBOURG.

freight (frāt) *n.* **1** *U.S. & Can.* **a** The service of transporting commodities by land, air, or water; specifically, ordinary transportation as opposed to *express.* **b** The commodities so transported. **2** *Brit.* **a** The service of transporting commodities by air or water. **b** The commodities so transported. In Great Britain, commodities transported by land are known as *goods.* **3** The price paid for the transportation of commodities. **4** *U.S. & Can.* A freight train: in Great Britain, called a *goods* train. — **dead freight** Money paid for cargo space, as on shipboard, that was not used. — *v.t.* **1** To load with commodities for transportation. **2** To load; burden. **3** To send or transport as or by freight. [<MDu. *vrecht,* var. of *vracht.* See FRAUGHT.]

freight·age (frā′tij) *n.* **1** A cargo; lading. **2** The price charged or paid for carrying goods. **3** The transportation of merchandise.

freight car A railway car for carrying freight.

freight·er (frā′tər) *n.* **1** One who has freight transported. **2** One who contracts to transport freight for others; especially, the charterer of a ship for carrying merchandise. **3** One engaged in transporting merchandise by fleets or trains of vehicles. **4** A freight-carrying vessel or aircraft.

freight train *U.S.* A railroad train comprised of freight cars.

Fré·jus (frā·zhüs′), **Pointe de** An Alpine peak on the Franco-Italian border; 9,659 feet; crossed by the **Fréjus Pass** at 8,370 feet.

frem (frem) *Scot. adj.* Alien; strange. — *n.* A stranger. Also **fremd** (fremd), **frem·it** (frem′·it), **fremt** (fremt): sometimes spelled *fraim.*

Fre·man·tle (frē′man·təl) A port in SW Western Australia.

fre·mes·cent (frə·mes′ənt) *adj. Obs.* Growing increasingly noisy; tumultuous. [<L *fremere* roar + -ESCENT]

frem·i·tus (frem′i·təs) *n. pl.* **·tus** *Pathol.* A palpable vibration, as of the wall of the chest; resonant thrill. [<L, a roar]

Fré·mont (frē′mont), **John Charles,** 1813–90, U.S. explorer, general, and politician.

Frem·stad (frem′städ), **Olive,** 1872–1951, U.S. soprano born in Sweden.

fre·na·tor (frē′nā·tər) *n. Anat.* Anything which checks or restrains body motion. [<L, a tamer <*frenare* curb, restrain]

french (french) *v.t.* To prepare (chops or rib roasts) by trimming the meat from the ends of the bones.

French (french), **Daniel Chester,** 1850–1931, U. S. sculptor. — **Sir John Denton Pinkstone,** 1852–1925, first Earl of Ypres, British field marshal in World War I.

French (french) *adj.* Pertaining to, from, or characteristic of France, its people, or their language. — *n.* **1** The people of France collectively: with *the.* **2** The Romance language of France, belonging to the Italic subfamily of Indo-European languages. — **Old French** The French language from about 850 to 1400, directly descended from Vulgar Latin as it developed in Gaul. Old French had two especially important dialects, the *langue d'oïl,* spoken north of the Loire, and the *langue d'oc* (Provençal), spoken south of it. Modern French is derived from the former, with the central French dialect of Paris as the standard. Abbr. *OF* — **Middle French** The French language as spoken from about 1400 to 1600. Abbr. *MF* — **Modern French** The language of France after 1600. Abbr. *F* [OE *Frencisc* <*Franca* a Frank]

French Academy An association of forty scholars, writers, and intellectuals, known as "the Immortals," established in 1685 by Cardinal Richelieu to exercise control over the French language and literature. *French* **A·ca·dé·mie Fran·çaise** (à·kà·dā·mē′ fräṅ·sez′).

French and Indian War That part of the war between France and England, 1754–60, waged in America, in which the French received support from Indian allies.

French blue Ultramarine.

French Broad River A river in western North Carolina and eastern Tennessee, flowing 204 miles north to the Tennessee River.

French bulldog A breed of small, compact, bat-eared bulldog, generally of a dark or brindle color, developed in France.

French Canada 1 The province of Quebec. 2 French-Canadians collectively.

French-Ca·na·di·an (french'kə-nā'dē-ən) *n.* A French settler in Canada or a descendant of French settlers in Canada.

French casement A casement for a French window.

French chop A rib chop of lamb with the top of the bone scraped bare.

French Community A political association that includes France, Central African Republic, Chad, Congo Republic, Dahomey, Gabon Republic, Ivory Coast Republic, Malagasy Republic, Mauritania, Republic of Niger, Senegal, and Republic of the Upper Volta, together with the French overseas departments and territories.

French cuff A cuff of a sleeve turned back and secured to itself with a link.

French curve An instrument used by draftsmen and architects for drawing curves.

French disease Syphilis.

French doors A pair of adjoining doors, often set with glass panes, attached to opposite door jambs and opening in the middle.

French dressing A salad dressing consisting of olive oil, spices, vinegar, salt, etc.

French Equatorial Africa A former group of French overseas territories in west central Africa. Formerly **French Congo.** See CENTRAL AFRICAN REPUBLIC, CHAD, CONGO REPUBLIC, GABON REPUBLIC.

French-fried (french'frīd') *adj.* Cooked by frying crisp in deep fat.

French gray A light, clear, somewhat greenish gray.

French Gui·an·a (gē·an'ə) An overseas department of France on the NE coast of South America, including the inland Territory of Inini; 34,740 square miles; capital, Cayenne. *French* **Guy·ane Fran·çaise** (gē·än' frän·sez').

French heel A high, forward-slanting heel, used on women's dress shoes.

French horn A keyed, brass wind instrument with long twisted tube whose diameter increases gradually from the mouthpiece to a widely flaring bell shape: developed from the hunting horn.

French·i·fy (fren'chə·fī) *v.t.* **·fied**, **·fy·ing** To make French in form or characteristics.

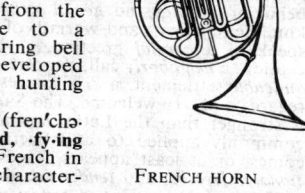

FRENCH HORN

French India Formerly, the overseas territories of France in India, consisting of the settlements of Chandernagore, Karikal, Mahé, Pondicherry, and Yanam, with adjoining territory; total, 193 square miles; capital, Pondicherry. *French* **É·ta·blisse·ments fran·çais dans l'Inde** (ā·tá·blēs·män' frän·sā' dän laňd').

French Indochina A former name for INDO-CHINA (def. 2).

French leave An informal, unauthorized, or hurried departure.

French·man (french'mən) *n.* *pl.* **·men** (-mən) A native or citizen of France; one of the French people. — **French'wom'an** *n. fem.*

French Morocco A former French protectorate and associated state in the French Union, in NW Africa: since 1956 a part of the sultanate of Morocco.

French North Africa A former name for Algeria, French Morocco, and Tunisia.

French Polynesia A French overseas territory spread over a wide area of the South Pacific, comprising Gambier, Tubuai, Marquesas, and Society Islands, and Tuamotu Archipelago; 1,575 square miles; capital, Papeete, on Tahiti; *French* **Po·ly·né·sie Fran·çaise** (pô·lē·nä·zē' frän·sez'). Formerly called **French Oceania,** *French* **Établissements français de l'Océanie.**

French pancake A very thin, rolled pancake,

usually covered with preserved fruit, sugar, and cinnamon.

French pastry A rich fancy pastry often having a filling of whipped cream, custard, or preserved fruits.

French Revolution See under REVOLUTION.

French roof A modified mansard roof.

French seam A seam sewed on both sides so that no raw edges are exposed.

French Shore The parts of the Newfoundland coast included in various British treaties granting rights to French fishermen from 1713 to 1904.

French Somaliland See SOMALILAND, FRENCH.

French Sudan See MALI.

French telephone A handset telephone, with the receiver and the transmitter mounted on one handle.

French toast Bread dipped in a batter of beaten eggs and milk, and fried in shallow fat.

French Togoland See TOGO.

French Union A former political association of France, its overseas departments and territories, and other associated states and territories. See also FRENCH COMMUNITY.

French West Africa A former group of French overseas territories comprised in the western bulge of Africa. See DAHOMEY, GUINEA, IVORY COAST REPUBLIC, MALI, MAURITANIA, REPUBLIC OF NIGER, REPUBLIC OF SENEGAL, REPUBLIC OF THE UPPER VOLTA.

French West Indies Islands in the Caribbean, comprising two overseas departments of France: Martinique and Guadeloupe.

French windows A casement window with adjoining sashes attached to opposite jambs and opening in the middle.

French·y (fren'chē) *Colloq. adj.* **·i·er**, **·i·est** Having or assuming French characteristics. — *n. pl.* **French·ies** A Frenchman.

Fre·neau (fre·nō'), **Philip,** 1752–1832, American poet.

fre·net·ic (frə·net'ik) *adj.* Frenzied, frantic; also, pertaining to mental disorder: also **fre·net'i·cal.** — *n.* A frantic or mentally disordered person; a phrenetic. [Var. of PHRENETIC] — **fre·net'i·cal·ly** *adv.*

fre·num (frē'nəm) *n.* *pl.* **·na** (-nə) *Anat.* A restraining band or fold; the *frenum* of the tongue: also spelled **fraenum.** [<L, bridle]

fren·zied (fren'zēd) *adj.* Affected with frenzy or madness; frantic.

fren·zy (fren'zē) *n. pl.* **·zies** Violent agitation; fury; madness; delirium. — *v.t.* **·zied**, **·zy·ing** To throw into frenzy; make frantic. [<OF *frenesie* <LL *phrenesis* <LGk. *phrenēsis,* var. of *phrenitis* delirium < *phrēn* mind]

Synonyms (noun): fanaticism, fury, insanity, madness, mania, raving. See ENTHUSIASM, INSANITY. *Antonyms:* composure, coolness, equanimity, equipoise, sanity, sobriety.

Fre·on (frē'on) *n. Chem.* Any of a group of stable, colorless, non-toxic, non-flammable organic compounds of chlorine and fluorine used as solvents, refrigerants, and propellants for aerosol insecticides: a trade name.

fre·quence (frē'kwəns) *n.* Frequency.

fre·quen·cy (frē'kwən·sē) *n. pl.* **·cies** 1 The property or state of being frequent. 2 *Physics* The number of occurrences of a periodic quantity, as waves, vibrations, oscillations, in a unit of time; usually expressed as cycles per second. 3 *Stat.* A ratio expressing the number of times a given case, value, or score occurs in a total of relevant classified data: the *frequency* of marriage in a specified population. 4 *Ecol.* The relative number of plant and animal species in a given region.

frequency band *Telecom.* A channel included between certain specified wavelengths for the efficient transmission of radio, television, and other forms of electromagnetic signals.

frequency bridge *Electr.* A device similar to

the Wheatstone bridge, used in the measurement of alternating-current frequencies.

frequency condition *Physics* The state of an atom or molecule in which it may emit radiation of a given frequency.

frequency curve *Stat.* A graphic representation of the frequencies of the values of specified variables as presented in a **frequency distribution** table and arranged by order of magnitude: also called *distribution curve.* See HISTOGRAM.

frequency level *Physics* A logarithmic expression of the tone interval between a given sound frequency and a reference keynote; one octave has a frequency level of unity.

frequency meter An instrument, calibrated in cycles, kilocycles, or megacycles, for measuring the wavelength or frequency of radio signals.

frequency modulation *Telecom.* A system of radio transmission in which the carrier wave is varied by the modulation signal in frequency rather than in amplitude. This system can utilize narrower channels than does the amplitude modulation system and is exceptionally free of static and other atmospheric disturbances.

fre·quent (frē'kwənt) *adj.* 1 Occurring or appearing often. 2 Repeating or inclined to repeat often; reiterating; persistent. 3 *Obs.* Crowded; full; thronged. — *v.t.* (fri·kwent') 1 To visit often. 2 To be in or at often or habitually. [<L *frequens, -entis* crowded] — **fre·quent'er** *n.*

Synonyms (adj.): common, constant, general, numerous, recurrent, recurring, repeated, returning, usual. See COMMON, GENERAL, MANY, USUAL. *Antonyms:* few, occasional, rare, scanty, solitary, uncommon, unusual.

fre·quen·ta·tion (frē'kwən·tā'shən) *n.* The practice of frequenting or resorting; frequent visiting.

fre·quen·ta·tive (fri·kwen'tə·tiv) *Gram. adj.* Denoting repeated or habitual action: a *frequentative* verb. — *n.* An iterative or frequentative verb.

fre·quent·ly (frē'kwənt·lē) *adv.* Often; repeatedly; at short intervals.

frère (frâr) *n.* *pl.* **frères** (frâr) *French* 1 Brother. 2 Friar; monk.

fres·co (fres'kō) *n. pl.* **·coes** or **·cos** 1 The art of painting on a surface of plaster, especially while the plaster is still fresh. 2 A picture so painted. — *v.t.* **fres·coed, fres·co·ing** To paint in fresco. [<Ital., fresh] — **fres'co·er, fres'co·ist** *n.*

fresh¹ (fresh) *adj.* 1 Newly made, obtained, received, etc.: *fresh* coffee; *fresh* footprints. 2 New; recent: *fresh* news. 3 Additional; further: *fresh* supplies. 4 Not salted, pickled, smoked, etc. 5 Not spoiled, stale, musty, etc. 6 Not faded, worn, etc.: *fresh* colors; *fresh* memories. 7 Not salt: *fresh* water. 8 Pure; refreshing: *fresh* air. 9 Appearing healthy or youthful. 10 Not fatigued; active. 11 Inexperienced; unsophisticated. 12 *Meteorol.* Moderately rapid and strong; specifically designating a breeze (No. 5) or a gale (No. 8) of the Beaufort scale. 13 Having a renewed supply of milk: said of a cow that has recently calved. — *n.* 1 A freshet. 2 A pool or stream of fresh water. 3 A fresh-water stream running into tidewater; also the adjoining lands. [OE *fersc,* infl. by OF *freis,* both ult. <Gmc.] — **fresh'ly** *adv.* — **fresh'ness** *n.*

Synonyms (adj.): blooming, bright, cool, green, new, novel, recent, renewed, ruddy, undimmed, unfaded, unimpaired, unskilled, untarnished, untried, unworn, verdant, vigorous, young, youthful. See MODERN, NEW. *Antonyms:* blasé, decayed, dim, dull, exhausted, faded, jaded, moldy, musty.

fresh² (fresh) *adj. Slang* Forward; presumptuous. [<G *frech* impudent]

fresh-air (fresh'âr') *adj.* Fond of, providing, or organized to provide fresh or uncontaminated air.

fresh·en (fresh'ən) *v.t.* 1 To make fresh, vigorous, or less salty. 2 *Naut.* To relieve (a hawser or rope) by changing the position of the part exposed to chafing. — *v.i.* 3 To become fresh. 4 To have a calf: said of cows. 5 To come into milk. — **fresh'en·er** *n.*

fresh·et (fresh'it) *n.* 1 A sudden flood in a

stream; an inundation. **2** A fresh-water stream flowing into the sea.

fresh·man (fresh′mən) *n. pl.* **·men** (-mən) A student in the first year of the course in a college, high school, etc.

fresh-wa·ter (fresh′wô′tər, -wot′ər) *adj.* **1** Pertaining to or living in fresh water. **2** Experienced in sailing on fresh water only; hence, untrained; of no experience. **3** Inland; not situated on the coast. **4** *U.S.* Not well known; somewhat provincial: a *fresh-water* college. **5** Untrained; unskilled.

fres·nel (frā·nel′) *n. Physics* A unit of wave frequency, equal to 10^{12} cycles per second. [after A. J. *Fresnel*]

Fres·nel (frā·nel′), **Augustin Jean,** 1788–1827, French physicist.

fres·no (frez′nō) *n. pl.* **·noes** or **·nos** A wide, shallow, scooplike, metal scraper for moving earth. Also **fresno scraper.** [after *Fresno,* Cal., where first made]

Fres·no (frez′nō) A city in central California.

fret[1] (fret) *v.* **fret·ted, fret·ting** *v.t.* **1** To irritate; worry; annoy. **2** To wear or eat away, as by chafing or gnawing; corrode; fray. **3** To form or make by wearing away. **4** To make rough; agitate: to *fret* the surface of a pond. — *v.i.* **5** To be angry, troubled, or irritated; chafe. **6** To be worn or eaten away. **7** To become rough or agitated. See synonyms under PIQUE. — *n.* **1** The act of fretting. **2** An abrasion, corrosion, or wearing away. **3** An abraded, worn, or eroded spot. **4** A state of irritation, ill temper, or vexation. [OE *fretan* devour]

fret[2] (fret) *n.* A ridge on a musical instrument, as a guitar, against which the strings may be stopped. — *v.t.* **fret·ted, fret·ting** To provide with frets, as of a stringed instrument. [Cf. OF *frete* ring]

fret[3] (fret) *n.* **1** Ornamental work in relief,

TYPES OF FRET

done by carving, cutting, or embossing; in a broad sense, perforated or interlaced ornamental work in wood or stone or in painting. **2** An ornament characterized by angular interlocked or interlacing lines. **3** A headdress of wire of precious metal, often ornamented with gems: worn by women in medieval times. — *v.t.* **fret·ted, fret·ting** To ornament with fretwork; embroider with gold or silver thread. [Prob. <OF *frette* a lattice, trellis]

fret·ful (fret′fəl) *adj.* Inclined to fret; peevish; worrying; agitated. — **fret′ful·ly** *adv.* — **fret′ful·ness** *n.* — **fret·some** *adj.*

Synonyms (adj.): complaining, cross, fractious, fretting, impatient, irritable, peevish, pettish, petulant, snappish, snarling, testy, touchy, vexed, waspish, worried, worrying. See RESTIVE. *Antonyms*: forbearing, genial, gentle, kind, lovely, loving, meek, mild, patient, sweet, uncomplaining.

fret saw A saw with a long, narrow blade and fine teeth: used for fretwork, scrollwork, etc.

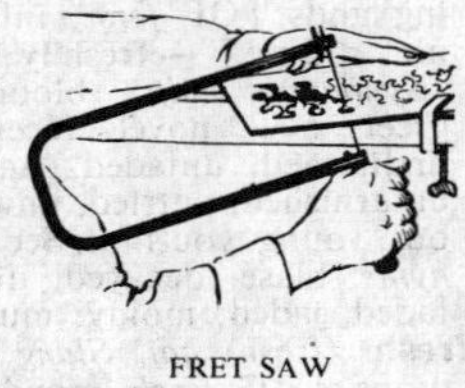

FRET SAW

fret·ty (fret′ē) *adj.* **·ti·er, ·ti·est 1** Fretful; peevish. **2** *Colloq.* Rubbed; inflamed, as a sore.

fret·work (fret′wûrk′) *n.* **1** Interlaced ornamental work composed of frets. **2** Perforated architectural work. **3** Variable movement, as of light and shade.

Freud (froid, *Ger.* froit), **Sigmund,** 1856–1939, Austrian neurologist; founder of modern theory of psychoanalysis.

Freu·di·an (froi′dē·ən) *adj.* Of, pertaining to, or conforming to the teachings of Sigmund Freud, especially regarding the cause and cure of neurotic and psychotic disorders, and the significance of dreams. — *n.* One who upholds the theories of Freud. — **Freu′di·an·ism** *n.*

Frey (frā) In Norse mythology, the god of rain and sunshine, and specifically of fruitfulness and prosperity. Also **Freyr** (frār).

Frey·a (frā′ə) In Norse mythology, the goddess of love; daughter of Njord and sister of Frey. Compare FRIGG. Also **Frey′ja.**

Frey·tag (frī′täkh), **Gustav,** 1816–95, German novelist and historian.

fri·a·ble (frī′ə·bəl) *adj.* Easily crumbled or pulverized. [<F <L *friabilis* <*friare* crumble] — **fri′a·bil′i·ty, fri′a·ble·ness** *n.*

fri·ar (frī′ər) *n.* **1** A brother or member of one of the mendicant religious orders, as the Augustinians, Carmelites *(White Friars),* Dominicans *(Black Friars),* or Franciscans *(Gray Friars).* **2** *Printing* An area on a printed sheet or page containing too little ink: opposed to *monk.* [<OF *frere* <L *frater* brother]

fri·ar·bird (frī′ər·bûrd′) *n.* An Australian honey-eating bird (genus *Philemon*) having a bare head: also called *four-o'clock.*

friar's balsam A soothing balsam, composed of benzoin, myrrh, aloe, balsam of Tolu, and other ingredients dissolved in alcohol.

fri·ar's-lan·tern (frī′ərz·lan′tərn) *n.* The will-o'-the-wisp.

Friar Tuck In medieval English legend, a jovial priest; associate of Robin Hood.

fri·ar·y (frī′ər·ē) *n. pl.* **·ar·ies 1** A monastery of a mendicant order. **2** The institution of friars. See synonyms under CLOISTER. — *adj.* Pertaining to friars or to a monastery.

frib·ble (frib′əl) *v.* **frib·bled, frib·bling** *v.t.* To waste; fritter away. — *v.i.* To act in a frivolous way; trifle. — *adj.* Of little importance; frivolous. — *n.* **1** Trifling action. **2** A trifler. [Cf. FRIVOLOUS] — **frib′bler** *n.* — **frib′bling** *adj.*

Fri·bourg (frī′bûrg, *Fr.* frē·bōōr′) A city in west central Switzerland: German *Freiburg.*

fric·an·deau (frik′ən·dō′) *n. pl.* **·deaux** (-dōz) A cutlet of veal or other meat, roasted or braised and served with sauce. Also **fric′an·do′.** [<F]

fric·as·see (frik′ə·sē′) *n.* A dish of meat cut small, stewed, and served with gravy. — *v.t.* **·seed, ·see·ing** To make into a fricassee. [<F *fricassé,* orig. pp. of *fricasser* sauté]

fric·a·tive (frik′ə·tiv) *Phonet. adj.* Describing those consonants that are produced by the forced escape and friction of the breath through a narrow aperture, as (f), (v), (th). — *n.* A consonant so produced. Also called *spirant.* [<NL *fricativus* <L *fricare* rub]

Frick (frik), **Henry Clay,** 1849–1919, U.S. industrialist and philanthropist.

fric·tion (frik′shən) *n.* **1** The rubbing together of two bodies. **2** Resistance to motion due to the contact of two surfaces moving relatively to each other. **3** Lack of harmony; conflict of opinions; disagreement. [<F <L *frictio, -onis* <*fricare* rub] — **fric′tion·al** *adj.* — **fric′tion·al·ly** *adv.*

Synonyms: abrasion, attrition, chafing, fretting, grating, grinding, interference, rubbing, wearing.

friction clutch *Mech.* Any of various arrangements for transferring the motion of one system of parts to another by regulating the frictional contact between designated elements. Also **friction coupling.**

friction drive *Mech.* A drive in which motion is obtained by the frictional contact of surfaces, one being connected with the power system, the other with the transmission system.

friction fabric Fabric impregnated with rubber: used in the making of automobile tires. Also **friction stock.**

friction gear *Mech.* Any machine element that transmits power by frictional contact between surfaces, as of rotating wheels, disks, etc.

friction layer *Meteorol.* That portion of the atmosphere, from 1,500 to 3,000 feet altitude, in which air flow is strongly affected by the rotational friction of the earth.

friction loss Loss of power through friction, as in the contact surfaces of a machine, the surface tension of flowing water in pipes, etc.

friction match A match tipped with a chemical mixture that ignites by friction.

friction tape Cotton tape impregnated with an adhesive, moisture-resisting compound: used in electrical and mechanical work.

friction test A test for determining the amount of power absorbed by a specified lubricant.

Fri·day (frī′dē, -dā) The sixth day of the week. — **Good Friday** The Friday before Easter. [OE *Frigedæg* Frigg's day; trans. of LL *Veneris dies* day of Venus]

Fri·day (frī′dē, -dā) In Defoe's *Robinson Crusoe,* Crusoe's native servant, whom he saves from death on a Friday.

Fridt·jof Nan·sen Land (frit′yôf nän′sən) An unofficial name for FRANZ JOSEF LAND.

fried (frīd) Past tense and past participle of FRY.

fried cake A cruller or doughnut fried in deep fat.

Fried·e·ri·ke (frē′də·rē′kə) German form of FREDERICA.

Fried·land (frēd′land, *Ger.* frēt′länt) The former German name for PRAVDINSK.

Fried·rich (frēd′rikh) German form of FREDERICK.

friend (frend) *n.* **1** One who cherishes kind regard for another person; an intimate and trustworthy companion. **2** One who regards a thing with favor; a promoter. **3** An adherent; ally; one of the same nation or party. See synonyms under ASSOCIATE. — *v.t. Obs.* To befriend. [OE *frēond*]

Friend (frend) *n.* A member of the Society of Friends; a Quaker. — **Friend′ly** *adj.*

friend·ed (fren′did) *adj.* Having friends; with friends.

friend·less (frend′lis) *adj.* Having no friends; forlorn. — **friend′less·ness** *n.*

friend·ly (frend′lē) *adj.* **·li·er, ·li·est 1** Pertaining to or like a friend; befitting friendship; amicable. **2** Propitious; favorable. — **friend′li·ly, friend′ly** *adv.* — **friend′li·ness** *n.*

Synonyms: accessible, affable, affectionate, amicable, brotherly, companionable, complaisant, cordial, favorable, fond, genial, hearty, kind, kindly, loving, neighborly, sociable, social, tender, well-disposed. *Friendly,* as said of persons, signifies having the disposition of a friend; as said of acts, it signifies befitting or worthy of a friend. The adjective *friendly* does not reach the full significance of the nouns "friend" and "friendship"; one may be *friendly* to those who are not his friends, and to be in *friendly* relations often signifies little more than not to be hostile. *Affable* and *accessible* are distinctively used of public and eminent persons, who might, if disposed, hold themselves at a distance from others. *Companionable* and *sociable* refer to manner and behavior, *cordial* and *genial* express genuine kindliness of heart and warmth of feeling. We speak of a *cordial* greeting, a *favorable* reception, a *neighborly* call, a *sociable* visitor, an *amicable* settlement, a *kind* interest, a *friendly* regard, a *hearty* welcome. The Saxon *friendly* is stronger than the Latin *amicable. Fond* is commonly applied to an affection that becomes, or at least appears, excessive. *Affectionate, devoted,* and *tender* are almost always used in a high and good sense; as, an *affectionate* son; a *devoted* friend; "the *tender* mercy of our God," *Luke* i 78. See AMICABLE, GOOD, PROPITIOUS. Compare FRIENDSHIP. *Antonyms*: adverse, alienated, antagonistic, bellicose, belligerent, cold, contentious, disaffected, distant, estranged, frigid, hostile, ill-disposed, indifferent, inimical, unfriendly, unkind, warlike.

Friendly Islands See TONGA ISLANDS.

friend·ship (frend′ship) *n.* **1** Mutual regard cherished by kindred minds. **2** The state or fact of being friends.

Synonyms: affection, amity, attachment, comity, consideration, devotion, esteem, favor, friendliness, love, regard. *Friendship* is a deep, quiet, enduring *affection,* founded upon mutual respect and *esteem. Friendship* is always mutual; one may have friendly feelings toward an enemy, but while there is hostility or coldness on one side there cannot be *friendship* between the two. *Friendliness* is a quality of friendly feeling, without the deep and settled *attachment* implied in the state of *friendship. Comity* is mutual, kindly courtesy, with care of each other's right, and *amity* a friendly feeling and relation not necessarily implying special *friendliness*; as, the *comity* of nations, or *amity* between neighboring countries. *Affection* may be purely natural; *friendship* is a growth. *Friendship* is more intellectual and less emotional than *love*; it is easier to give reasons for *friendship* than for *love*; *friendship* is more calm and quiet, *love* more fervent, often rising to intensest passion.

Compare ACQUAINTANCE, ASSOCIATION, ATTACHMENT, LOVE. *Antonyms*: see synonyms for BATTLE, ENMITY, FEUD, HATRED.

fri·er (frī′ər) See FRYER.

Frie·sian (frē′zhən) See FRISIAN.

Fries·land (frēz′lənd, -land) The most northerly province of the Netherlands; 1,249 square miles; capital, Leeuwarden. Ancient **Fri·sia** (frizh′ə).

frieze[1] (frēz) *n. Archit.* **1** The middle division of an entablature. It may be flat and plain, as in the Roman Tuscan order; conventionally ornamented, as in the Greek Doric; or highly enriched with sculpture. For illustration see ENTABLATURE. **2** Any ornamented horizontal band or strip in a wall. ◆ Homophone: *freeze.* [<F *frise* <Med. L *frisium,* ? ult. <L *Phrygium (opus)* Phrygian (work, ornament)]

frieze[2] (frēz) *n.* A coarse woolen cloth with shaggy nap, now made almost exclusively in Ireland. — *v.t.* **friezed, friez·ing** *Obs.* To produce a nap on. ◆ Homophone: *freeze.* [<MF *frise* <*friser* curl]

FRIGATE

frig·ate (frig′it) *n.* **1** A sailing war vessel, in use from 1650 to 1840, smaller than a ship of the line but larger than a corvette. **2** A modern anti-submarine warship, somewhat larger than the 600-ton corvette; used to escort merchant convoys. **3** Originally, a light and swift vessel of the Mediterranean, propelled by both oars and sails. [<F *frégate* <Ital. *fregata*]

frigate bird Either of two species of large raptorial birds (genus *Fregata*) with great powers of flight, having the upper mandible hooked and extraordinarily long wings and tail feathers: also called *man-of-war bird.*

Frigg (frig) In Norse mythology, the wife of Odin and goddess of marriage: often confused with *Freya.* Also **Frig′ga.**

fright (frīt) *n.* **1** Sudden and violent alarm or fear. **2** *Colloq.* Anything ugly, ridiculous, or shocking in appearance, producing aversion or alarm. — *v.t. Poetic* To frighten. [OE *fryhto*]

Synonyms (noun): affright, dismay, dread, fear, horror, panic, terror. *Affright, fright,* and *terror* are always sudden, and in actual presence of that which is terrible; *fear* may be controlled by force of will; *fright* and *terror* overwhelm the will; *terror* paralyzes; *fright* may cause wild or desperate action. *Fright* is largely a matter of the nerves; *fear* of the intellect and the imagination; *terror* of all the faculties, bodily and mental. *Panic* is a sudden *fear* or *fright,* affecting numbers at once; vast armies or crowded audiences are liable to *panic* upon slight occasion. In a like sense we speak of a financial *panic.* Compare ALARM, FEAR.

fright disease A nervous disorder of dogs, characterized by sporadic attacks of running and barking, with manifestations of great fear: also called *running fits, canine hysteria.*

fright·en (frīt′n) *v.t.* **1** To throw into a state of fear or fright; terrify; scare. **2** To drive by scaring: with *away* or *off.* — **fright′en·er** *n.* — **fright′en·ing** *adj.* — **fright′en·ing·ly** *adv.*

Synonyms: affright, alarm, appal, browbeat, cow, daunt, dismay, intimidate, scare, terrify. The sudden rush of an armed madman may *frighten*; the quiet leveling of a highwayman's pistol *intimidates.* A savage beast is *intimidated* by the keeper's whip. Employers may *intimidate* their employees from voting contrary to their will by threat of discharge. To *browbeat* or *cow* is to bring into a state of submissive fear; to *daunt* is to give pause or check to a violent, threatening, or even a brave spirit. To *scare* is to cause sudden, unnerving fear; to *terrify* is to awaken fear that is overwhelming. To *appal* (literally to make *pale*) is to overcome momentarily by some staggering or chilling fear or shocked repugnance; to *dismay* (literally to deprive of power) is to cause a sinking fear, make faint with dread or terror. Compare ALARM, FRIGHT.

fright·ened (frīt′nd) *adj.* Terrified; alarmed.

fright·ful (frīt′fəl) *adj.* Apt to induce terror; shocking. — **fright′ful·ly** *adv.* — **fright′ful·ness** *n.*

Synonyms: alarming, appalling, awful, direful, dreadful, fearful, hideous, horrible, horrid, portentous, shocking, terrible, terrific, terrifying. See AWFUL.

frig·id (frij′id) *adj.* **1** Of low temperature; cold. **2** Lacking in warmth of feeling; stiff, formal, and forbidding. **3** Lacking in sexual feeling or response: said of women. Compare IMPOTENT. [<L *frigidus* <*frigere* be cold] — **frig′id·ly** *adv.* — **frig′id·ness** *n.*

Frig·id·aire (frij′i·dâr′) *n.* An electric refrigerator: a trade name.

fri·gid·i·ty (fri·jid′ə·tē) *n.* **1** Coldness; formality. **2** Sexual unresponsiveness. Compare IMPOTENCE.

frigid zone See under ZONE.

frig·o·rif·ic (frig′ə·rif′ik) *adj.* Producing cold; chilling. Also **frig′o·rif′i·cal.** [<F *frigorifique* <L *frigorificus* <*frigor* cold + *facere* make]

fri·jole (frē′hōl, *Sp.* frē·hō′lā) *n. pl.* **·joles** (-hōlz, *Sp.* -hō′lās) A bean or beanlike seed (genus *Phaseolus*) used as food by Latin-American peoples. Also **fri′jol.** [<Sp.]

frill (fril) *n.* **1** An ornamental band of textile fabric, especially of lace or fine lawn, gathered in folds on one edge, the other edge being left loose; a flounce; ruffle. **2** *pl.* Affected airs and manners; fripperies, as of dress. **3** *Zool.* A ruff or frill-like part, appendage, or fold, as of elongated feathers on the neck of some birds, of long hairs on the neck of some dogs, and of membrane on the frilled lizard. **4** *Bot.* A thin membrane surrounding the stem of certain fungi near the pileus or hood, as in *Agaricus*: also called *armilla.* **5** *Phot.* A loosening and bulging of a plate or film around the edges, caused by uneven action of the emulsion; frilling. — *v.t.* **1** To make into a frill. **2** To put frills on. — *v.i.* **3** *Phot.* To wrinkle at the edges, as a gelatin film. [Origin uncertain] — **frill′er** *n.* — **frill′y** *adj.*

frilled lizard A large arboreal lizard (*Chlamydosaurus kingii*) of Australia, about three feet long, and having on each side of the neck a broad erectile membrane.

frill·ing (fril′ing) *n.* Gathered trimming in general; ruffles; frills.

Fri·maire (frē·mâr′) See under CALENDAR (Republican).

Friml (frim′əl), **Rudolf,** 1881–1972, Czech composer, active in the United States.

fringe (frinj) *n.* **1** An ornamental border or trimming of pendent cords, loose threads, or tassels. **2** Any fringelike border, edging, or margin. **3** Any outer or bounding portion: a *fringe* of shrubs in a garden, a *fringe* of land seen in the distance. **4** *Optics* One of the alternate light and dark bands produced by the interference of light, as in diffraction. — *v.t.* **fringed, fring·ing** **1** To ornament with or as with a fringe. **2** To serve as a fringe or border for. [<OF *frenge* <L *fimbria* a fringe]

fringe bell A Japanese stemless evergreen herb (*Schizocodon soldanelloides*) with toothed leaves and deep-rose flowers blue or white near the edges.

fringe benefit Any of various benefits received from an employer apart from salary, as insurance, pension, vacation, etc.

fringed gentian See under GENTIAN.

fringed orchis An orchid of the hardy terrestrial group (genus *Habenaria*) with tuberous roots and flowers having a fringed lip.

fringe lily A perennial herb of the lily family (genus *Thysanotus*) having clusters of purple flowers with fringed edges, native in Western Australia, but now found in California. Also **fringed violet.**

fringe tree A small tree (*Chionanthus virginicus*) of the olive family of the eastern United States with dark-blue drupes and white flowers; the dried root bark has medicinal properties.

frin·gil·line (frin·jil′īn, -in) *adj.* **1** Finchlike. **2** Of or pertaining to a family (*Fringillidae*) of small birds of which the finches and sparrows are characteristic. [<L *fringilla,* a small bird + -INE[1]]

fring·y (frin′jē) *adj.* **fring·i·er, fring·i·est** Resembling fringe; having a fringe.

frip·per·y (frip′ər·ē) *n. pl.* **·per·ies** **1** Mean or worthless things; trumpery; tawdry finery; gew-gaws. **2** *Obs.* Cast-off or old clothes. **3** *Obs.* Traffic in old clothes, or a place where they are sold. [<F *friperie* <OF *freperie* <*frepe* a rag]

Fris·bee (friz′bē) *n.* A light plastic disk used in play by being tossed with a spin from person to person: a trade name. Also **fris′·bee.**

Frisch·es Haff (frish′əs häf′) The German name for VISTULA LAGOON.

Fris·co (fris′kō) *Colloq.* San Francisco, California.

fri·sé (fri·zā′) *n.* An upholstery or rug fabric faced with a thick pile of uncut loops or of cut and uncut loops in design. [<F, orig. pp. of *friser* curl]

fri·sette (fri·zet′) See FRIZETTE.

fri·seur (frē·zœr′) *n. French* A hairdresser.

Fris·ian (frizh′ən, -ē·ən) *adj.* **1** Of or pertaining to the Dutch province of Friesland, its people, or their language. **2** Of or pertaining to the Frisii, an ancient Germanic tribe of the Netherlands. — *n.* **1** A native or inhabitant of modern Friesland. **2** A member of the tribe of the ancient Frisii. **3** The Low German, West Germanic language of the Frisians, closely related to English. Also *Friesian.*

Frisian Islands An island chain of the North Sea, divided into three major groups, the **West, North,** and **East Frisian Islands.**

frisk (frisk) *v.t.* **1** To move briskly or playfully. **2** *U.S. Slang* To search (someone) for concealed weapons, smuggled goods, etc., by running the hand rapidly over his clothing. **3** *U.S. Slang* To steal from in this way. — *v.i.* **4** To leap about playfully; gambol; frolic. — *n.* **1** A playful skipping about. **2** *U.S. Slang* A frisking or searching. [<obs. *frisk* lively <F *frisque*; ult. origin unknown] — **frisk′er** *n.*

Synonyms (verb): caper, dance, frolic, gambol, play, sport. See LEAP. *Antonyms*: droop, mope, muse, repose, rest.

fris·ket (fris′kit) *n. Printing* **1** A light frame to hold the printing surface between the tympan and the form of a platen press. **2** A similar frame attached to a hand press of the Washington type. [<F *frisquette*]

frisk·y (fris′kē) *adj.* **frisk·i·er, frisk·i·est** Lively or playful. See synonyms under RESTIVE. — **frisk′i·ly** *adv.* — **frisk′i·ness** *n.*

frit (frit) *v.t.* **frit·ted, frit·ting** To decompose and partly melt: to *frit* glassmaking materials before final fusion. — *n.* **1** An imperfectly vitrified mass, formed in making glass. **2** The material from which soft fictile wares are made. **3** A partially fused composition used as a basis for glazes. Also **fritt.** [<F *fritte* <Ital. *fritta,* pp. of *friggere* fry]

frit fly A small fly (*Oscinosoma frit*), very destructive of cereal grains.

frith (frith) *n. Scot.* A firth.

frit·il·lar·y (frit′ə·ler′ē) *n. pl.* **·lar·ies** **1** One of a genus (*Fritillaria*) of arctic or north-temperate bulbous plants of the lily family in which the flowers are checkered with pale and dark purple. **2** One of various butterflies (*Argynnis, Dione,* and related genera) having wings checkered with black and light brown, whose caterpillars feed on the violet and related plants. [<NL *Fritillaria* <L *fritillus* a dice box; from its checkered markings]

frit·ter[1] (frit′ər) *v.t.* **1** To waste or disperse little by little: usually with *away.* **2** To break or tear into small pieces. [<*n.*] — *n.* A small piece or fragment: a shred. [Cf. OF *fraiture* <L *fractura* <*frangere* break]

frit·ter[2] (frit′ər) *n.* A small fried cake, often

containing fruit or pieces of meat. [<F *friture* <L *frigere* fry]

Fritz (frits) Shortened form of FRIEDRICH.

Fri·u·li (frē·ōō′lē) A historical region of northern Italy on the Adriatic, now partly in Yugoslavia.

Fri·u·li·an (frē·ōō′lē·ən) *n.* 1 One of a people of Celtic origin inhabiting the region of Friuli. 2 The Rhaeto–Romanic dialect of these people.

friv·ol (friv′əl) *v.* **friv·oled** or **friv·olled**, **friv·ol·ing** or **friv·ol·ling** *Colloq.* *v.i.* To behave frivolously; trifle. — *v.t.* To fritter: with *away*. [Back formation <FRIVOLOUS] — **friv′ol·er**, **friv′ol·ler** *n.*

fri·vol·i·ty (fri·vol′ə·tē) *n.* *pl.* **·ties** 1 The quality or condition of being frivolous. 2 A frivolous act, thing, or practice. See synonyms under LEVITY.

friv·o·lous (friv′ə·ləs) *adj.* 1 Void of significance or reason; petty; trivial; unimportant. 2 Characterized by lack of seriousness, sense, or reverence; trifling; silly. [<L *frivolus* silly] — **friv′o·lous·ly** *adv.* — **friv′o·lous·ness** *n.*

fri·zette (fri·zet′) *n.* A frizz of hair, worn as a bang.

frizz[1] (friz) *v.t.* & *v.i.* **frizzed**, **frizz·ing** 1 To form into tight, crisp curls, as the hair. 2 To make or form into small, tight tufts or knots, as the nap of cloth. — *n.* 1 That which is frizzed, as hair. 2 The condition of being frizzed. Also **friz.** [Var. of FRIEZE[2], *v.*] — **friz′zer**, **friz′er** *n.* — **frizz′i·ness** *n.*

frizz[2] (friz) *v.t.* & *v.i.* **frizzed**, **friz·zing** To fry with a sizzling noise. [<FRY + imit. suffix]

friz·zle[1] (friz′əl) *v.t.* & *v.i.* **friz·zled**, **friz·zling** 1 To fry or cook with a sizzling noise. 2 To make or become curled or crisp, as by frying. [Blend of FRY and SIZZLE; ? infl. by FRIZZLE[2]]

friz·zle[2] (friz′əl) *v.t.* & *v.i.* **friz·zled**, **friz·zling** To form into tight, crisp curls, as the hair. [? Freq. of FRIEZE[2], *v.*]

fro (frō) *adv.* Away from; back: used in the phrase *to-and-fro.* — *prep.* *Scot.* From. [<ON *fra* from]

Fro·bish·er (frō′bish·ər), **Sir Martin**, 1535?–1594, English navigator and explorer.

Frobisher Bay An inlet of the Atlantic in SE Baffin Island.

frock (frok) *n.* 1 The principal outer garment of women and girls; a dress. 2 A monk's robe, long and very loose. 3 A coarse loose outer garment worn by laborers, brewers, butchers, etc. 4 A woolen jersey worn by sailors. 5 In English military service, an undress regimental coat. 6 A frock coat. — *v.t.* 1 To furnish with or clothe in a frock. 2 To invest with ecclesiastic office. [<OF *froc*; ult. origin uncertain]

frock coat A coat for men's wear, usually double-breasted, having knee-length skirts.

froe (frō) *n.* A cleaving knife with the blade at right angles to the handle, used for riving staves, shingles, etc. Also spelled *frow.* [Appar. <FROWARD, in sense "turned away," with ref. to the blade]

Froe·bel (frā′bəl, *Ger.* frœ′bəl), **Friedrich Wilhelm August**, 1782–1852, German educator; founder of the kindergarten system.

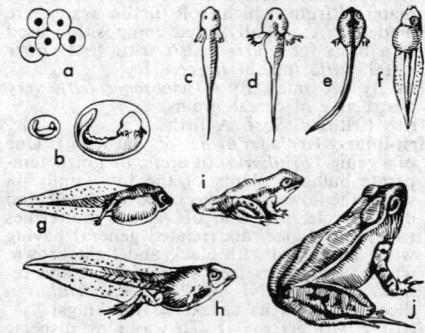

STAGES IN THE DEVELOPMENT OF THE FROG
a. Eggs. *b.* Embryo. *c–h.* Development of the tadpole. *i.* Young frog. *j.* Adult frog.

frog (frog, frôg) *n.* 1 One of a genus (*Rana*) of small, tailless, amphibious, web-footed ani-

mals; especially, the North American bullfrog (*R. catesbiana*), the leopard frog (*R. pipiens*), and the green edible European frog (*R. esculenta*). Frogs are distinguished from the toads in having smooth skin, webbed feet, and greater leaping and swimming powers. 2 Any of several arboreal frogs (family *Ranidae*), as the tree frog, flying frog. 3 The triangular prominence in the sole of a horse's foot. 4 A section of a railway track where one rail crosses or diverges from another. 5 A metal device used to stop the action in a power loom when the warp becomes entangled with the shuttle. 6 A small bundle of certain types of Cuban, Puerto Rican, or other imported tobaccos, having a V-shaped notch at the ends where the heaviest part of the stems has been removed. 7 An ornamental fastening on a cloak or a coat. 8 The loop of a scabbard. 9 *Slang* A Frenchman: a derogatory term. — **a frog in one's throat** A slight laryngeal hoarseness. — *v.i.* **frogged**, **frog·ging** To hunt frogs. [OE *frogga*] — **frog′like′** *adj.*

frog·bit (frog′bit′, frôg′-) *n.* 1 A little aquatic European plant (*Hydrocharis morsusranae*) which floats on water and bears white flowers. 2 An American plant (*Limnobium spongia*) of the same family (*Hydrocharitaceae*), found in stagnant water. Also **frog's′-bit′**.

frog-eye (frog′ī′, frôg′ī′) *n.* 1 A fungus disease affecting the leaves of apple trees and caused by various species of a fungus (*Physalospora*). 2 Any similar leaf blight of fungus origin characterized by concentric whitish spots. — **frog′-eyed′** *adj.*

frog fish The angler: so called from its wide mouth.

frog·ger·y (frog′ər·ē, frôg′-) *n.* *pl.* **·ger·ies** 1 A place frequented by frogs, or one where frogs are raised. 2 A collection of frogs.

frog·gy (frog′ē, frôg′ē) *adj.* **·gi·er**, **·gi·est** Of, pertaining to, or abounding in frogs. — **frog′gi·ness** *n.*

frog·hop·per (frog′hop′ər, frôg′-) *n.* A broad, squat leafhopping insect (family *Cercopidae*); the nymphs of many species are enclosed in a frothy mass; a spittle insect. See FROG SPIT.

frog kick In swimming, a kick in which both legs are drawn up with the heels together and the knees apart, then simultaneously thrust backward.

frog lily The yellow waterlily (*Nuphar advena*).

frog·man (frog′mən, -man′, frôg′-) *n.* *pl.* **·men** (-mən, -men′) One who is dressed in a waterproof suit and equipped with a portable diving unit and various implements for underwater military or naval reconnaissance.

frog·mouth (frog′mouth′, frôg′-) *n.* 1 An East Indian nocturnal bird (genus *Podargus*) with very broad, deeply cleft bill: found also in Australia and locally named *mopoke.* 2 The snapdragon.

frog spit 1 *Entomol.* The frothy exudation from the nymphs of a froghopper; cuckoo spit; toad spittle. 2 *Bot.* A green fresh-water alga whose filaments clump in foamlike floating masses.

Froh·man (frō′mən), **Charles**, 1860–1915, U.S. theatrical manager.

Frois·sart (froi′särt, *Fr.* frwȧ·sàr′), **Jean**, 1337?–1410?, French chronicler.

frol·ic (frol′ik) *n.* 1 A scene of gaiety. 2 A gay or sportive outburst or act; a prank. 3 A gathering for social merriment; a party. 4 A gathering of neighbors to do or finish some kind of work; a bee: a harvesting *frolic.* [<*adj.*] — *v.i.* **frol·icked**, **frol·ick·ing** To play merrily; gambol. — *adj.* Full of or characterized by mirth or playfulness; sportive; merry. [<Du. *vrolijk* merry <MDu. *vro* glad] — **frol′ick·er** *n.* — **frol′ick·y** *adj.*

Synonyms (*noun*): amusement, caper, carousal, entertainment, festivity, fun, gambol, game, gaiety, lark, merrymaking, prank, spree, sport. See AMUSEMENT, ENTERTAINMENT, SPORT.

frol·ic·some (frol′ik·səm) *adj.* Full of frolic; playful. Also **frol′ick·y.** See synonyms under AIRY, MERRY. — **frol′ic·some·ly** *adv.* — **frol′ic·some·ness** *n.*

from (frum, from; *unstressed* frəm) *prep.* 1 Starting at (a particular place or time): the plane *from* Chicago; busy *from* six until nine. 2 Out of (something serving as a holder or container): She drew a pistol *from* her purse. 3 Not near to or in contact with: far *from* the madding crowd. 4 Out of the control

or authority of: released *from* custody. 5 Out of the totality of: six cigarettes *from* the pack. 6 As being other or another than: He couldn't tell me *from* my brother. 7 As being in adverse relation to: *from* grave to gay. 8 Because of: having as the foundation, origin, or cause: Skill comes *from* practice. 9 With (some person, place, or thing) as the instrument, maker, or source: a note *from* your mother; silks *from* Rome. [OE *fram, from*]

fro·men·ty (frō′mən·tē) See FRUMENTY.

frond (frond) *n.* *Bot.* 1 A leaflike expansion in which the functions of stem and leaf are not fully differentiated, as the so-called leaf of ferns and seaweeds. See illustration under FERN. 2 The leaf of a palm. [<L *frons, frondis* leaf]

Fronde (frônd) *n.* A political party established in France during the minority of Louis XIV, opposing the court and Cardinal Mazarin, and precipitating the civil wars of 1648, 1650, and 1651. [<F, a sling]

frond·ed (fron′did) *adj.* Provided with fronds; leafy.

fron·des·cence (fron·des′əns) *n.* *Bot.* 1 The period or act of leafing. 2 Leaves collectively. — **fron·des′cent** *adj.*

fron·dif·er·ous (fron·dif′ər·əs) *adj.* Frond-bearing.

front (frunt) *n.* 1 The fore part or side of anything: opposed to *back.* 2 The position directly before a person or thing: the steps in *front* of the church. 3 A face of a building; usually the face on the entrance side. 4 The foremost ground occupied by an army; battle zone. 5 Land facing a road, body of water, etc.; frontage. 6 *Brit.* A promenade facing a beach. 7 In the theater, the audience part of the auditorium. 8 *Archaic* The forehead; by extension, the face. 9 Bearing or attitude in facing a problem, etc.: a bold *front.* 10 Bold assurance; effrontery. 11 *Colloq.* An outward semblance of wealth or position. 12 A person chosen for his prestige to serve as an official, usually titular, of an organization; a figurehead. 13 A person, group, or business serving as a cover for underhanded activities. 14 A coalition of diverse forces working for a common political or ideological aim: a labor *front.* 15 A dickey (def. 1); also, a large cravat. 16 In hotels, the bellhop first in line: generally used as a call to the desk. 17 *Meteorol.* The boundary, diffuse or sharp, which separates masses of cold air and warm air. 18 *Phonet.* The part of the tongue immediately behind the blade and directly below the hard palate. — *adj.* 1 Of or pertaining to the front; situated in front. 2 Considered from the front: a *front* view. 3 *Phonet.* Describing those vowels produced with the front of the tongue raised toward the hard palate, as (ē) in *feed.* See synonyms under ANTERIOR, FIRST. — *v.t.* 1 To have the front opposite to or in the direction of; face. 2 To confront; meet face to face; defy. 3 To furnish with a front. 4 To serve as a front for. — *v.i.* 5 To have the front or face turned in a specific direction. [<OF <L *frons, frontis* forehead]

front·age (frunt′ij) *n.* 1 Linear extent of front: the *frontage* of a lot. 2 The fact or action of facing in a certain direction; outlook; exposure.

fron·tal[1] (frun′təl) *adj.* Pertaining to the front or to the forehead. — *n.* *Anat.* A bone of the anterior part of the skull, forming the skeleton of the forehead. [<NL *frontalis* <L *frons, frontis* forehead] — **fron′tal·ly** *adv.*

fron·tal[2] (frun′təl) *n.* 1 A front part. 2 Something to cover the front or forehead. 3 *Eccl.* A movable hanging to cover the front of an altar. 4 *Archit.* A small pediment or other front piece above a minor door or window. [<OF *frontel* <LL *frontale* <*frons, frontis* forehead, front]

front bench *Brit.* In the House of Commons, the seats closest to the Speaker, reserved for the party leaders.

front·ed (frun′tid) *adj.* 1 Having a front. 2 Formed in line.

Fron·te·nac (fron′tə·nak, *Fr.* frônt·nàk′), **Comte Louis de Buade de**, 1620–98, French governor of Canada.

fron·tier (frun·tir′) *n.* 1 The part of a nation's territory that abuts upon another country; the border; confines. 2 That portion of a country bordering on the wilderness, newly

or thinly settled by pioneer settlers. **3** Any region of thought or knowledge not yet explored: a *frontier* of science. **4** *Obs.* A fort. See synonyms under BOUNDARY. — *adj.* Of, from, inhabiting, situated on, or characteristic of a frontier. [<OF *frontiere* <*front* FRONT]

fron·tiers·man (fruntirz′mən) *n.* pl. **·men** (-mən) One who lives on the frontier or on or beyond the borders of civilization. Also **fron·tier′man.**

fron·tis·piece (frun′tis·pēs′, fron′-) *n.* **1** An illustration in the front of a book. **2** An ornamental front; a façade. [Earlier *frontispice* <F <Med. L′ *frontispicium* face <L *frons, frontis* forehead + *specere* look at; infl. in form by *piece*]

front·less (frunt′lis) *adj.* Without a front.

front·let (frunt′lit) *n.* **1** A band worn on the forehead. **2** The forehead of a bird or animal when distinguished by color or the like. **3** A frontstall. [<OF *frontelet*, dim. of *frontel.* See FRONTAL.]

front line The foremost line of battle.

fronto– *combining form* **1** *Anat.* Pertaining to the frontal bone or frontal region of the skull. **2** *Meteorol.* Pertaining to a front. [<L *frons, frontis* forehead, front]

front office The main office, or office of the highest ranking executive, in an organization.

fron·to·gen·e·sis (frun′tō·jen′ə·sis) *n. Meteorol.* The development of a boundary between cold air and warm air masses, or the intensification of an already existing boundary.

fron·tol·y·sis (frun·tol′ə·sis) *n. Meteorol.* The disappearance or subsidence of a front: opposed to *frontogenesis.*

fron·to·ma·lar (frun′tō·mā′lər) *adj. Anat.* Pertaining to the frontal and cheek bones.

fron·tón (frən·tōn′) *n.* The court in which jai alai is played. [<Sp.]

front–page (frunt′pāj′) *′adj.* Of great significance or importance; meriting placement on the front page of a publication.

Front Range The easternmost range of the Rocky Mountains, in Colorado and Wyoming; highest peak, 14,225 feet.

front·stall (frunt′stôl′) *n. Obs.* A perforated headplate for a horse.

frore (frôr, frōr) *adj. Archaic* Frosty; frozen. [Early pp. of FREEZE]

frosh (frosh) *n.* pl. **frosh** *U.S. Slang* A college freshman.

frost (frôst, frost) *n.* **1** Minute crystals of ice

FROST PATTERNS
a. Spongiform. *b.* Filicoid. *c.* Stellate.

formed directly from atmospheric water vapor; frozen dew; hoarfrost. **2** Freezing weather; the **degree of frost** is the number of degrees below the freezing point. **3** The formation of ice; frozen moisture within a porous substance. **4** Coldness and austerity of manner. **5** *Slang* A failure. — *v.t.* **1** To cover with frost. **2** To damage or kill by frost. **3** To apply frosting to. [OE] — **frost′less** *adj.*

Frost (frôst, frost), **Robert Lee**, 1875–1963, U.S. poet and essayist.

frost·bite (frôst′bīt′, frost′-) *n.* The gangrenous condition of having some part of the body, as the ears or fingers, partially frozen. — *v.t.* **·bit, ·bit·ten, ·bit·ing** To injure, as a part of the body, by partial freezing. — **frost′bit′ten** *adj.*

frost·ed (frôs′tid, fros′-) *adj.* **1** Covered with frost or frosting. **2** Presenting a surface resembling frost, as an iced cake or matted electric bulb. **3** Frostbitten.

frost–fish (frôst′fish′, frost′-) *n.* pl. **·fish** or **·fish·es** The tomcod.

frost–flow·er (frôst′flou′ər, frost′-) *n.* A small bulbous plant of the lily family (*Milla biflora*) with scape 6–18 inches high, bearing starlike, fragrant, white, waxy flowers; native in southwestern U. S.

frost fog A pogonip.

frost·ing (frôs′ting, fros′-) *n.* **1** A mixture of sugar, egg white or fat, and flavoring of various kinds, used to coat or cover a cake; also called *icing.* **2** The rough surface produced on metal, glass, etc., in imitation of frost. **3** Coarsely powdered glass, etc., used for decorative work.

frost itch A complaint affecting certain persons only in winter and usually in dry climates; a form of pruritis: also called *winter itch.*

frost line The depth to which frost penetrates the ground, expressed in terms of a single season, a seasonal average, or the maximum attained.

frost·weed (frôst′wēd′, frost′-) *n.* A cistaceous plant, the rockrose (*Crocanthemum canadense*). Also **frost′wort′** (-wûrt′).

frost·work (frôst′wûrk′, frost′-) *n.* **1** Hoarfrost deposited upon exposed objects in delicate tracery. **2** Any surface ornamentation in imitation of such effect.

frost·y (frôs′tē, fros′-) *adj.* **frost·i·er, frost·i·est 1** Attended with frost; freezing: *frosty* weather. **2** Affected or covered by or like frost. **3** Lacking in warmth of manner; chilling; distant. **4** Having white hair; hoary. — **frost′i·ly** *adv.* — **frost′i·ness** *n.*

froth (frôth, froth) *n.* **1** A mass of bubbles resulting from fermentation or agitation; a colloid system of gas dispersed in a liquid. **2** Any foamy excretion or exudation; foam. **3** Any light, unsubstantial matter; vain or senseless display of wit; idle pleasure; vanity. — *v.t.* **1** To cause to foam. **2** To cover with froth. **3** To give forth in the form of foam. — *v.i.* **1** To form or give off froth; foam. [<ON *frodha*]

froth·er (frô′thər, froth′ər) *n.* **1** One who or that which froths. **2** A substance or chemical agent used to develop the foam in the flotation process of separating minerals from their ores.

froth·ing–a·gent (frô′thing·ā′jənt, froth′ing-) *n. Chem.* Any substance, as saponin or oleic acid, which will produce froth in an agitated liquid.

froth·y (frô′thē, froth′ē) *adj.* **froth·i·er, froth·i·est 1** Consisting of, covered with, or full of froth. **2** As unsubstantial as froth; empty; pretentious; trivial. — **froth′i·ly** *adv.* — **froth′i·ness** *n.*

Froude (frōōd), **James Anthony**, 1818–94, English historian.

frou–frou (frōō′frōō′) *n.* **1** A rustling, as of silk; the swish of a woman's dress. **2** *Colloq.* Affected elegance; fanciness. [<F]

frounce (frouns) *v.t. & v.i.* **frounced, frounc·ing 1** To curl. **2** *Archaic* To wrinkle; pleat. — *n. Archaic* Affectation; empty pretence. [<OF *froncier* <*fronce* a fold, ? <Gmc.]

frou·zy (frou′zē) See FROWZY.

frow[1] (frou) *n.* **1** A Dutch or German woman. **2** A wife; a married woman. [<MDu. *frouwe* woman, lady]

frow[2] (frō) See FROE.

fro·ward (frō′ərd, -wərd) *adj.* Disobedient; intractable; perverse. [<FRO + WARD] — **fro′ward·ly** *adv.* — **fro′ward·ness** *n.*

frown (froun) *v.i.* **1** To contract the brow, as in displeasure or concentration; scowl. **2** To look one's displeasure or disapproval: with *on* or *upon.* — *v.t.* **1** To make known (one's displeasure, disgust, etc.) by contracting one's brow. **2** To silence, rebuke, etc., by or as by a frown. — *n.* **1** A wrinkling of the brow, as in dislike, anger or abstraction; a scowl. **2** Hence, any manifestation of displeasure or lack of favor. [<OF *froignier*, prob. <Gmc.] — **frown′er** *n.* — **frown′ing** *adj.* — **frown′ing·ly** *adv.*

frow·sy (frous′tē) *adj. Brit. Colloq.* Musty; stuffy. [Cf. OF *frouste* decayed]

frow·zled (frou′zəld) *adj.* Unkempt; disheveled.

frow·zy (frou′zē) *adj.* **·zi·er, ·zi·est** Slovenly in appearance; unkempt; untidy. Also **frou′zy, frow′sy.** [? Akin to FROWSTY]

froze (frōz) Past tense of FREEZE.

fro·zen (frō′zən) *adj.* **1** Congealed, benumbed, or killed by cold; having become, or overspread with, ice. **2** Subject to extreme cold, as a climate or region. **3** Quick-frozen, as *frozen* food. **4** *Econ.* Arbitrarily maintained at a given level: said of prices, wages, employment status, etc.

frozen assets Property still valuable but not readily available for conversion into cash.

frozen sleep *Med.* A form of therapy that consists in putting the patient to sleep and lowering the body temperature to from 70° to 90° F.: also called *cryotherapy.*

Fruc·ti·dor (fruk′ti·dôr, *Fr.* frük·tē·dôr′) See under CALENDAR (Republican).

fruc·tif·er·ous (fruk·tif′ər·əs) *adj.* Fruit-bearing.

fruc·ti·fy (fruk′tə·fī) *v.* **·fied, ·fy·ing** *v.t.* To make fruitful; fertilize. — *v.i.* To bear fruit. [<F *fructifier* <L *fructificare* <*fructus* fruit + *facere* do, make] — **fruc′ti·fi·ca′tion** *n.*

fruc·tose (fruk′tōs) *n.* A very sweet, levorotatory monosaccharide, $C_6H_{12}O_6$, occurring in sugar cane and fruits: also called *fruit sugar, levulose.*

fruc·tu·ous (fruk′chōō·əs) *adj.* Productive; fertile; fruitful. [<OF <L *fructuosus* <*fructus* fruit]

fru·gal (frōō′gəl) *adj.* **1** Exercising economy; saving; sparing. **2** Marked by economy; meager; stinted. [<L *frugalis* <*frugi* temperate, orig. dative singular of *frux* food] — **fru′gal·ly** *adv.*

fru·gal·i·ty (frōō·gal′ə·tē) *n.* pl. **·ties 1** Strict economy; thrift. **2** Wise and sparing use: *frugality* of praise. Also **fru′gal·ness.**

— **Synonyms:** economy, miserliness, parsimoniousness, parsimony, providence, prudence, saving, scrimping, sparing, thrift. *Economy* is a wise and careful administration of the means at one's disposal; *frugality* is a withholding of expenditure, or *sparing* of supplies or provision, to a noticeable and often to a painful degree; *parsimony* is excessive and unreasonable *saving* for the sake of *saving. Frugality* exalted into a virtue to be practiced for its own sake, instead of as a means to an end, becomes the vice of *parsimony. Miserliness* is the denying oneself and others the ordinary comforts or even necessaries of life, for the sake of hoarding. *Prudence* and *providence* look far ahead, and sacrifice the present to the future, saving as much as may be necessary for that end. (See PRUDENCE.) *Thrift* seeks not merely to save, but to earn. *Economy* manages, *frugality* saves, *providence* plans, *thrift* at once earns and saves, with a view to wholesome and profitable expenditure at a fitting time. See ABSTINENCE. *Antonyms:* abundance, bounty, extravagance, liberality, luxury, opulence, riches, waste, wealth.

fru·giv·o·rous (frōō·jiv′ər·əs) *adj.* Fruit-eating. [<L *frux, frugis* fruit + -VOROUS]

fruit (frōōt) *n.* **1** *Bot.* **a** The edible, pulpy mass covering the seeds of various plants and

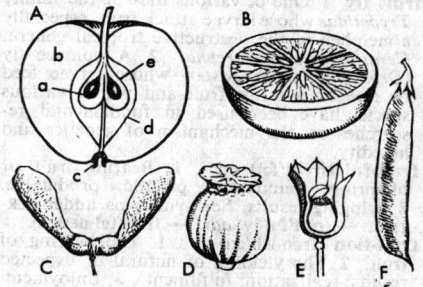

FRUIT
A. Cross-section of an apple:
  a. Seeds. *b.* Pulp. *c.* Limb of calyx. *d.* Core. *e.* Carpels.
B. Cross-section of an orange.
C. Schizocarpous fruit of the maple.
D. Ripe capsule of a poppy.
E. Pyxis of henbane with outer carpel removed.
F. Legume of pea.

trees. They are classified as *fleshy*, as gourds, melons, oranges, apples, pears, berries, etc.; *drupaceous*, as cherries, peaches, plums, apricots, and others containing stones; *dry*, as nuts, capsules, achenia, follicles, legumes, etc. **b** In flowering plants, the mature seed vessel and its contents, together with such accessory or external parts of the inflorescence as seem to be integral with them. **c** In cryptogams, the spores with their enveloping or accessory organs. **2** Any vegetable product used as

food, or otherwise serviceable to man, as grain, cotton, or flax; also, such products collectively: the *fruits* of the earth. **3** That which is produced, as the young of man or animals. **4** The consequence or result of any action; any outcome, effect, or result: the *fruit* of evil, the *fruits* of industry. — *v.t.* & *v.i.* To bear or make bear fruit. [<OF <L *fructus* <*frui* enjoy]

Synonym (noun): vegetable. In the botanical sense not only apples, pears, peaches, tomatoes, figs, etc., but all berries, nuts, grains, beans, peas, pumpkins, squashes, cucumbers, and melons, as well as pine cones, the samaras or winged seeds of the maple, ash, or elm, and many other products, are *fruits*. Popular usage, however, is narrower. The *grains* have been dropped, and the tendency is to drop *nuts* also, so that a *fruit* is now generally understood to be the fleshy and juicy product of some plant, usually tree or shrub (and nearly always containing the seed), which, when ripe, is edible without cooking, and adapted for use as a dessert as well as a salad. The quince, however, while usually cooked before eating, is classed among *fruits*, and we sometimes speak of poisonous *fruits* as the *berries* of the nightshade. A *vegetable*, in the popular sense, is any part of a herbaceous plant commonly used for culinary purposes, and may consist of the *root*, as in the beet and turnip; the *stem*, as in the asparagus, celery, and rhubarb; a *tuber*, or underground stem, as in the potato; the *foliage*, as in cabbage and spinach, or of that which is botanically the *fruit*, as in the tomato, bean, pea, and eggplant. See synonyms under HARVEST, PRODUCT.

fruit·age (frōō′tij) *n.* **1** Fruit collectively. **2** The state, process, or time of producing fruit. **3** Any result or effect of action; consequence.

frui·tar·i·an (frōō·târ′ē·ən) *n.* One whose food consists mainly of fruits, with or without milk and nuts. — **frui·tar′i·an·ism** *n.*

fruit cake A cake containing fruit, generally raisins, currants, and citron.

fruit–cup (frōōt′kup′) *n.* A mixture of cut fruits, fresh or preserved, served in a cup or glass.

fruit dot Sorus.

fruit·ed (frōō′tid) *adj.* Bearing or containing fruit.

fruit·er (frōō′tər) *n.* **1** A vessel that carries fruit. **2** A fruit–bearing tree.

fruit·er·er (frōō′tər·ər) *n. Brit.* A dealer in fruits.

fruit fly **1** One of various flies of the family *Trypetidae* whose larvae attack fruit, especially a member of the destructive tropical genera, *Ceratitis* and *Anastrepha.* **2** A pomace fly (*Drosophila melanogaster*) whose larvae feed on ripe or overripe fruit and whose various species have been used in fundamental researches on the mechanism of genetics and heredity.

fruit·ful (frōōt′fəl) *adj.* **1** Bearing fruit or offspring abundantly; prolific; productive. **2** Bringing results. See synonyms under FERTILE. — **fruit′ful·ly** *adv.* — **fruit′ful·ness** *n.*

fru·i·tion (frōō·ish′ən) *n.* **1** The bearing of fruit. **2** The yielding of natural or expected results; realization; fulfilment. **3** Enjoyment. [<OF <LL *fruitio, -onis* enjoyment <*frui* enjoy]

fruit·less (frōōt′lis) *adj.* **1** Yielding no fruit; barren. **2** Yielding no good results; useless; idle. See synonyms under USELESS, VAIN. — **fruit′less·ly** *adv.* — **fruit′less·ness** *n.*

fruit rot Leaf rot.

fruit sugar Fructose.

fruit tree A tree, particularly a cultivated tree, producing an edible, succulent fruit.

fruit·y (frōō′tē) *adj.* **fruit·i·er, fruit·i·est** Like fruit in taste, flavor, etc. — **fruit′i·ness** *n.*

fru·men·ta·ceous (frōō′mən·tā′shəs) *adj.* **1** Belonging to the cereals. **2** Resembling or made of cereal grain. [<LL *frumentaceus* <*frumentum* grain]

fru·men·ty (frōō′mən·tē) *n.* A seasoned dish of hulled wheat boiled in milk: also spelled *fromenty, furmenty.* [<OF *frumentée* <L *frumentum* grain]

frump (frump) *n.* A dowdily dressed, sometimes ill–tempered, woman. [? <MDu. *frompelen*, var. of *verrompelen* wrinkle]

frump·ish (frum′pish) *adj.* **1** Dowdy; old-fashioned in dress. **2** Ill–tempered; morose. Also **frump′y.**

Frun·ze (frōōn′ze) The capital of Kirghiz S.S.R. in Soviet Central Asia. Formerly **Pish·pek** (pish′pek).

frus·trate (frus′trāt) *v.t.* **·trat·ed, ·trat·ing** **1** To keep (someone) from doing or achieving something; baffle the efforts or hopes of. **2** To keep, as plans or schemes, from being fulfilled; thwart; bring to naught. See synonyms under BAFFLE, HINDER. — *adj.* **1** Without effect; vain; null; void. **2** Frustrated; baffled. [<L *frustratus*, pp. of *frustrari* disappoint <*frustra* in vain] — **frus′trat·er** *n.* — **frus′tra·tive** *adj.*

frus·tra·tion (frus·trā′shən) *n.* State of being frustrated or thwarted; bafflement.

frus·tule (frus′chōōl) *n.* The siliceous shell of a diatom. [<F <LL *frustulum*, dim. of *frustum* a bit, small piece]

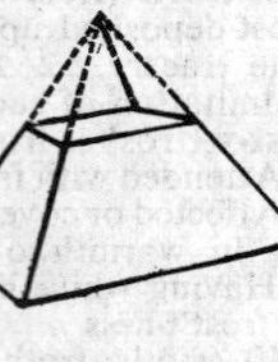

FRUSTUM OF A PYRAMID

frus·tum (frus′təm) *n. pl.* **·tums** or **·ta** (-tə) **1** *Geom.* **a** That which is left of a solid after cutting off the upper part: said of a cone or a pyramid. **b** That part of a solid included between any two planes, or, in the case of a sphere, that part between two parallel planes. **2** *Archit.* A fragment; a broken shaft of a column. [<L, fragment]

fru·tes·cent (frōō·tes′ənt) *adj.* **1** Somewhat shrubby. **2** Becoming a shrub. [<L *frutex* a shrub + -ESCENT] — **fru·tes′cence** *n.*

fru·ti·cose (frōō′ti·kōs) *adj.* Of, pertaining to, or having the characteristics of a true shrub. [<L *fruticosus* <*frutex, fruticis* a shrub]

fry[1] (frī) *v.t.* & *v.i.* **fried, fry·ing** **1** To cook or be cooked in hot fat, usually over direct heat. **2** *Obs.* To vex; worry; be agitated. — *n. pl.* **fries** **1** A dish of anything fried. **2** A social occasion, usually a picnic, at which foods are fried and eaten: a fish *fry.* **3** The viscera or testes of an animal fried and served for the table: calf's *fry* (pluck), pig's *fry* (liver), lamb's *fries* (testes). [<F *frier* <L *frigere*]

fry[2] (frī) *n. pl.* **fry** **1** Very young fish. **2** The young of other animals, especially when spawned or littered in large numbers. **3** Small adult fish. **4** A multitude or quantity of persons or objects of little importance. [<ON *friō* seed]

Fry (frī), **Christopher,** born 1907, English dramatist.

fry·er (frī′ər) *n.* **1** One who or that which fries. **2** A young chicken, suitable for frying. **3** A high–power electric lamp for use in color photography. Also spelled *frier.*

frying pan A shallow metal pan, with a long handle, for frying food.

F–stop (ef′stop′) *n.* F–number.

fu′ (fōō) *adj. Scot.* Full; intoxicated.

Fu·ad I (fōō·äd′), 1868–1936, sultan 1917–22, and king 1922–36, of Egypt: original name *Ahmed Fuad.*

fub (fub) See FOB[2].

fub·sy (fub′zē) *adj.* **·si·er, ·si·est** Plump.

fuch·sia (fyōō′shə, -shē·ə) *n.* **1** A plant (genus *Fuchsia*) of the evening–primrose family, with red, pink, white, or purple drooping, four-petaled flowers. **2** A perennial herb, the California fuchsia (*Zauschneria californica*), with scarlet flowers. **3** A bright bluish–red, the typical color of the fuchsia. [after Leonhard *Fuchs*, 1501–66, German botanist]

fuch·sin (fōōk′sin) *n. Chem.* A crystalline coal-tar product, superficially green in the solid state, but deep red in solution. Obtained by treating rosaniline with hydrochloric acid, it is used as a dye and in printing. Also called *magenta.* Also **fuch′sine** (-sin, -sēn). [<FUCHSIA + -IN]

fu·coid (fyōō′koid) *adj.* **1** Resembling or belonging to seaweeds; of the family *Fucaceae* which includes the rockweeds. **2** Containing fucoids or impressions of them. Also **fu·coi′dal, fu′cous.** — *n.* **1** A large, coarse, olive-brown seaweed. **2** A plant, either living or fossil, that resembles a seaweed.

fu·co·xan·thin (fyōō′kō·zan′thin) *n. Biochem.* The reddish–brown pigment found in red algae: also called *phycophaein.*

fu·cus (fyōō′kəs) *n. pl.* **·ci** (-sī) or **·cus·es** **1** Any of a genus (*Fucus*) of algae, typified by certain large olive–brown seaweeds, known as *rockweed* or *bladderwrack.* **2** *Obs.* A paint or dye. [<L]

fud·dle (fud′l) *v.* **·dled, ·dling** *v.t.* To confuse or make stupid with drink. — *v.i.* To tipple. [Cf. dial. G *fuddeln* swindle]

fud·dy–dud·dy (fud′ē·dud′ē) *n. Colloq.* **1** An old–fashioned person. **2** A faultfinding, fussy person. [Origin uncertain]

fudge (fuj) *n.* **1** A soft confection made of butter, sugar, chocolate, etc. **2** Humbug; nonsense: commonly used as a contemptuous interjection. **3** An attachment to a rotary newspaper press, for printing late news, usually in a different color from the remainder of the publication. **4** The news so printed. — *v.t.* **fudged, fudg·ing** To make, adjust, or fit together in a clumsy or dishonest manner. [Origin uncertain]

Fu·e·gi·an (fyōō·ē′jē·ən, fwā′jē·ən) *adj.* Of or pertaining to Tierra del Fuego or to its native people. — *n.* An Indian of Tierra del Fuego.

Fuehr·er (fyōōr′ər, *Ger.* fü′rər) *German* Leader: a title of distinction applied to Adolf Hitler by his adherents. Also **Führ′er.**

fu·el (fyōō′əl) *n.* **1** Combustible matter, as wood or coal, used to feed a fire. **2** Whatever feeds or sustains any expenditure, outlay, passion, or excitement. — *v.t.* & *v.i.* **fu·eled** or **fu·elled, fu·el·ing** or **fu·el·ling** To supply with or take in fuel. [<OF *fouaille* <LL *focalia* <*focus* hearth] — **fu′el·er, fu′el·ler** *n.*

fuel cell Any of various devices for the generation of electrical energy from the chemical energy of continuously supplied fuels, chiefly hydrogen and oxygen, in contact with a suitable electrolyte.

fuel injection The providing of fuel to an engine by direct injection into the cylinders for the purpose of obtaining precise distribution of the fuel.

fuel tank A tank for holding fuel.

Fuer·te·ven·tu·ra (fwer′tā·ven·tōō′rä) The second largest of the Canary Islands; 666 square miles.

fuff (fuf) *v.t.* & *v.i. Scot.* To puff.

fu·ga·cious (fyōō·gā′shəs) *adj.* **1** Having a fugitive tendency; transitory; volatile. **2** *Bot.* Falling very early, as the petals of a poppy. [<L *fugax, fugacis* <*fugere* flee] — **fu·ga′cious·ly** *adv.* — **fu·ga′cious·ness** *n.*

fu·gac·i·ty (fyōō·gas′ə·tē) *n.* **1** The quality of being transitory; fugaciousness. **2** In thermodynamics, the tendency of a substance in a heterogeneous mixture to escape from a given phase in order to reestablish chemical equilibrium. **3** The amount of this tendency.

Fug·ger (fōōg′ər) The name of a wealthy family of merchants and financiers who flourished in Germany in the 16th century.

fu·gi·o (fyōō′jē·ō) *n.* A copper coin, issued 1787, bearing the word *fugio* beside a meridian sun; the Franklin cent: the first U.S. coinage authorized by Congress. [<L, I flee]

FUGIO

fu·gi·tive (fyōō′jə·tiv) *adj.* **1** Fleeing or having fled, as from pursuit, danger, arrest, etc.; escaping or escaped; runaway. **2** Not fixed or lasting; transient; fading or liable to fade; evanescent. **3** Treating of subjects of passing interest; occasional. See synonyms under TRANSIENT. — *n.* **1** One who or that which flees, as from pursuit, danger, bondage, restraint, or duty; a runaway or deserter. **2** An exile or refugee. [<F *fugitif* <L *fugitivus* <*fugere* flee] — **fu′gi·tive·ly** *adv.* — **fu′gi·tive·ness** *n.*

fu·gle (fyōō′gəl) *v.i.* **·gled, ·gling** *Rare* **1** To act as fugleman. **2** To make signals.

fu·gle·man (fyōō′gəl·mən) *n. pl.* **·men** (-mən) **1** A soldier who stands in front of a line or body of men and leads them in military exercises; a file–leader. **2** One who leads or sets an example in anything. [<G *flügelmann* <*flügel* wing + *mann* man]

fugue (fyōōg) *n. Music* **1** A form, or sometimes a complete composition in strict poly-

phonic style in which a theme is introduced by one part, harmonized by contrapuntal rule, and reintroduced throughout. 2 *Psychiatry* An interval of flight from reality, during which an individual will assume a personality and perform actions in themselves rational but entirely forgotten upon the return of normal consciousness: a form of amnesia. [<F <Ital. *fuga* <L, a flight] — **fug′al** *adj.*

Fu·ji (fo͞o·jē) The highest peak of Japan, an extinct volcano on Honshu island: 12,300 feet. Also **Fu·ji-no-ya·ma** (fo͞o·jē·nō·yä·mä), **Fu·ji·san** (fo͞o·jē·sän), **Fu·ji·ya·ma** (fo͞o·jē·yä·mä).

Fu·kien (fo͞o′kyen′) A province of SE China; 45,000 square miles; capital, Foochow. Also **Fu′-chien′.**

Fu·ku·o·ka (fo͞o·ko͞o·ō·kä) A city on northern Kyushu island, Japan.

-ful *suffix* 1 Full of; characterized by: *joyful.* 2 Able to; tending to: *fearful.* 3 Having the character of: *manful.* 4 The quantity or number that will fill: *cupful.* [OE *-full, -ful* <*full* full] ◆ Nouns ending in **-ful** form the plural by adding *-s,* as in *cupfuls, spoonfuls.*

Fu·la (fo͞o′lä) *n.* 1 One of a Moslem people of the Egyptian Sudan, basically of Hamitic stock but mixed with Negro, having straight or curly hair, aquiline features, and light reddish-brown complexion. 2 The Sudanic language of these people. Also **Fu′lah.**

Ful·bright Act (fo͝ol′brīt) A Congressional act of 1946 that provides for a large part of the proceeds from the sale of United States war surplus property in foreign countries to be used for financing the mutual exchange of students, teachers, and other cultural workers: named for James William Fulbright, born 1905, U. S. senator.

ful·crum (fo͝ol′krəm) *n. pl.* **·crums** or **·cra** (-krə) 1 The support on or against which a lever rests. 2 Any prop or support. 3 *Zool.* In many ganoid fishes one of the rows of spinelike scales arranged along the forward edge of the median and paired fins: usually in the plural. [<L, bed post <*fulcire* prop up]

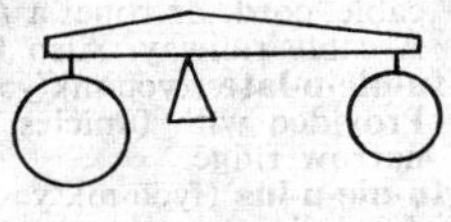

FULCRUM

Ful·da (fo͝ol′dä), **Ludwig,** 1862–1939, German writer.

ful·fil (fo͝ol·fil′) *v.t.* **ful·filled, ful·fil·ling** 1 To perform, as a duty or command. 2 To bring into effect or to consummation. 3 To finish; come to the end of. 4 To fill the requirements of; satisfy, as the conditions of a contract. Also **ful·fill′.** See synonyms under EFFECT, KEEP. [OE *fullfyllan*] — **ful·fil′ler** *n.* — **ful·fil′·ment, ful·fill′ment** *n.*

ful·gent (ful′jənt) *adj.* Beaming or shining brightly; radiant; gleaming; effulgent; resplendent. [<L *fulgens, -entis,* ppr. of *fulgere* gleam] — **ful′gen·cy** *n.* — **ful′gent·ly** *adv.*

ful·gid (ful′jid) *adj.* 1 Fulgent. 2 Fiery red. [<L *fulgidus* <*fulgere* gleam]

ful·gor (ful′gər) *n. Archaic* Dazzling brightness. Also **ful′gour.** [<L <*fulgere* gleam]

ful·gu·rant (ful′gyər·ənt) *adj.* Flashing; lightninglike.

ful·gu·rate (ful′gyə·rāt) *v.i.* **·rat·ed, ·rat·ing** To flash or throw out flashes, as of lightning. [<L *fulguratus,* pp. of *fulgurare* lighten <*fulgur* lightning]

ful·gu·rat·ing (ful′gyə·rā′ting) *adj.* Flashing; emitting flashes; darting; lancinating: *fulgurating* pains.

ful·gu·ra·tion (ful′gyə·rā′shən) *n.* 1 The act of flashing or lightening. 2 The sensation of stabbing pain. 3 Lightning stroke. 4 Destruction of animal tissue by electric sparks.

ful·gu·rite (ful′gyə·rīt) *n.* 1 A vertical tube with fused walls, formed in sand or rock by the passage of lightning. 2 An explosive: a type of dynamite.

ful·gu·rous (ful′gyər·əs) *adj.* Flashing, moving, or acting like lightning.

ful·ham (fo͝ol′əm) *n. Archaic* 1 A fraudulent or loaded die. 2 *Usually pl.* Any sham or fraud. Also **ful′lam.** [? from *Fulham,* a section of London once frequented by gamblers]

fu·lig·i·nous (fyo͞o·lij′ə·nəs) *adj.* 1 Like soot or smoke; also, sooty-brown. 2 Dark, as if shrouded in smoke. [<L *fuliginosus* <*fuligo, -inis* soot] — **fu·lig′i·nous·ly** *adv.*

full[1] (fo͝ol) *adj.* 1 Containing or having all that can or should be admitted; having no empty or vacant space; filled. 2 Abounding in something; also, engrossed or excited as with some thought: with *of.* 3 Perfectly sufficient or complete. 4 Ample in extent or volume; well-filled or rounded out; plump. 5 Having the disk wholly illuminated, as the moon. 6 Filled or satisfied with food or drink; hence, intoxicated. 7 Filled with emotion or with knowledge. 8 High, as the tide. 9 Possessing depth or volume: said of sounds. 10 Unblended; pure: said of color. 11 Having plenty of body: said of wines, etc. 12 Distended by wind, as a sail. 13 Having folds or plaits: a *full* skirt. See synonyms under AMPLE, IMPLICIT. — *n.* 1 The highest state, point, or degree. 2 The phase (of the moon) when the whole disk is illuminated. — *adv.* 1 Without abatement, diminution, qualification, etc.; fully; completely; to the utmost extent. 2 Very: to run *full* fast. — *v.t.* To make full; gather, as a sleeve. — *v.i.* To become full. [OE *ful*] — **full′ness, ful′ness** *n.* — **ful′ly** *adv.*

The adjective is the first element of many compound adjectives, as:

full-armed	**full-fed**	**full-opening**
full-bearded	**full-flowering**	**full-resounding**
full-built	**full-leaved**	**full-shouldered**
full-chested	**full-mouthed**	**full-strength**

full[2] (fo͝ol) *v.t.* & *v.i.* To make or become thicker and more compact, by shrinking: said of cloth. [Back formation <FULLER, *n.*]

full and by *Naut.* Close to the wind but with the sails full.

full·back (fo͝ol′bak′) *n.* In American football, one of the backfield, originally the player farthest from the line of scrimmage.

full-blood (fo͝ol′blud′) *n.* A person or animal of unmixed breed.

full blood 1 The condition of being thoroughbred: an Indian of *full blood.* 2 The relationship between kindred of any degree who possess to the full the degree of kinship named. — **full′-blood′** *adj.*

full-blood·ed (fo͝ol′blud′id) *adj.* 1 Having a large supply of blood; plethoric. 2 Of pure or unmixed blood; thoroughbred.

full-blown (fo͝ol′blōn′) *adj.* 1 Fully expanded or blossomed out. 2 Fully matured, perfected, or attired. 3 Filled with wind.

full-dress (fo͝ol′dres′) *adj.* 1 Characterized by or requiring full dress: a *full-dress* dinner. 2 Formal and thoroughgoing: a *full-dress* debate.

full dress Costume worn at court receptions or at formal social gatherings.

full·er[1] (fo͝ol′ər) *n.* One who fulls and cleanses cloth. [OE *fullere* <L *fullo*]

full·er[2] (fo͝ol′ər) *n.* 1 A blacksmith's tool with a round edge, used in grooving or spreading hot iron; a form of swage. 2 A groove made by a fuller. — *v.t.* To groove or crease by the use of a fuller: to *fuller* a bayonet blade. [? <FULL[1], *v.*]

Full·er (fo͝ol′ər), **George,** 1822–84, U. S. painter. — **Melville Weston,** 1833–1910, jurist, chief justice of the U. S. Supreme Court 1888–1910. — **(Sarah) Margaret,** 1810–50, Marchioness Ossoli, U. S. writer. — **Thomas,** 1608–61, English divine and author.

Full·er·board (fo͝ol′ər·bôrd′, -bōrd′) *n.* A cardboard used as insulating material and for other protective purposes in the electrical industry: a trade name. Also called *electrical pressboard, presspahn.*

fuller's earth A soft earthy material occurring in nature as an impure hydrous aluminum silicate: it is used as a filter and in removing grease from cloth and wool, and also in medicine, as a dusting powder and, with glycerin, in poultices.

ful·ler's-tea·sel (fo͝ol′ərz·tē′zəl) *n.* A stout coarse herb *(Dipsacus fullonum)* resembling a thistle, with opposite connate leaves, and oblong heads of flowers.

full·er·y (fo͝ol′ər·ē) *n. pl.* **·er·ies** A place where cloth is fulled; a fulling mill.

full-fashioned (fo͝ol′fash′ənd) *adj.* Knitted to conform to the shape of the lower leg, the human figure, etc.: said of hosiery and sweaters.

full-fledged (fo͝ol′flejd′) *adj.* 1 Full-feathered. 2 Fully developed; having gone into full operation. 3 Of full rank.

full house In poker, three of a kind and a pair, a hand next in value below four of a kind. Also **full hand.**

fulling mill 1 A machine for fulling woolen cloth. 2 A mill where cloth is fulled.

full moon 1 The moon when it shows its whole disk illuminated. 2 The time when this occurs.

full-rigged (fo͝ol′rigd′) *adj. Naut.* Completely equipped, with three or more masts, each fully supplied with square sails.

full-scale (fo͝ol′skāl′) *adj.* 1 Unreduced; scaled to actual size: a *full-scale* drawing. 2 All-out: a *full-scale* attack.

full stop A period.

full swing Unrestrained liberty or license; free course. — **in full swing** Going on vigorously and unrestrainedly.

full-time (fo͝ol′tīm′) *adj.* Requiring all one's working hours.

full-track (fo͝ol′trak′) *adj.* Designating a vehicle, as a tank, which rides entirely on and is steered by an endless belt on each side. Compare HALF-TRACK.

ful·mar (fo͝ol′mər) *n.* A large sea bird *(Fulmarus glacialis)* of the Arctic; also, the **giant fulmar** *(Macronectes giganteus)* of southern seas. [<ON *full mar* stinking mew]

ful·mi·nant (ful′mə·nənt) *adj.* 1 Fulminating. 2 Beginning suddenly, as a fever.

ful·mi·nate (ful′mə·nāt) *v.* **·nat·ed, ·nat·ing** *v.i.* 1 To explode or detonate violently. 2 To shout accusations, threats, etc.; denounce. 3 *Rare* To thunder and lighten. — *v.t.* 4 To cause to explode violently. 5 To shout (accusations, threats, etc.). — *n. Chem.* 1 A salt of fulminic acid, that explodes under percussion. 2 A mixture containing such a salt. [<L *fulminatus,* pp. of *fulminare* lighten <*fulmen, fulminis* lightning] — **ful′mi·na′tion** *n.* — **ful′mi·na′tor** *n.* — **ful′mi·na·to′ry** (-tôr′ē, -tō′rē) *adj.*

fulminating compound A fulminate. Also **fulminating powder.**

ful·mine (ful′min) *v.t.* & *v.i.* **·mined, ·min·ing** To fulminate. [<F *fulminer* <L *fulminare.* See FULMINATE.]

ful·min·ic (ful·min′ik) *adj.* Relating to or producing a detonation.

fulminic acid *Chem.* An isomer of cyanic acid, CNOH, that unites with bases to form explosive salts, called fulminates.

ful·mi·nous (ful′mə·nəs) *adj.* Of, pertaining to, or like thunder and lightning.

ful·some (fo͝ol′səm, ful′-) *adj.* 1 Offensive and distasteful because excessive: *fulsome* praise. 2 Coarse; indelicate. [<FULL, *adj.* + -SOME; infl. by FOUL] — **ful′some·ly** *adv.* — **ful′some·ness** *n.*

Ful·ton (fo͝ol′tən), **John Farquhar,** 1899–1960, U. S. physiologist. — **Robert,** 1765–1815, U. S. inventor; launched first steamboat 1803.

ful·vous (ful′vəs) *adj.* Reddish-yellow; tawny. [<L *fulvus*]

fu·mar·ic (fyo͞o·mar′ik) *adj. Chem.* Of, pertaining to, or occurring in fumitory plants: *fumaric* acid, $C_4H_4O_4$.

fu·ma·role (fyo͞o′mə·rōl) *n.* A small hole from which volcanic vapors issue. [<F *fumerolle* <LL *fumariolum,* dim. of *fumarium* chimney <*fumus* smoke]

fu·ma·to·ri·um (fyo͞o′mə·tôr′ē·əm, -tō′rē-) *n. pl.* **·ri·ums** or **·ri·a** An airtight chamber or apparatus for an arboretum, etc., to contain gases or the like, with which to destroy insects, fungous scales, etc. [<NL <L *fumare* smoke <*fumus* smoke]

fu·ma·to·ry (fyo͞o′mə·tôr′ē, -tō′rē) *adj.* Of or pertaining to smoking. — *n.* A fumatorium.

fum·ble (fum′bəl) *v.* **fum·bled, fum·bling** *v.i.* 1 To feel about blindly or clumsily; grope: with *for, at, with,* or *after.* 2 In sports, to fail to catch or hold the ball. — *v.t.* 3 To handle clumsily or awkwardly. 4 In sports, to fumble (the ball). — *n.* The act of fumbling. [Prob. <Scand. Cf. Sw. *fumla* grope] — **fum′bler** *n.*

fume (fyo͞om) *n.* 1 Reek; smoke. 2 Vapor, visible or invisible, especially as having

narcotic or choking qualities. **3** Any odorous smoke or vapor. **4** Furious anger. **5** Incense; aromatic smoke. — *v.* **fumed, fum·ing** *v.i.* **1** To give off smoke, vapor, etc. **2** To pass off in a mist or vapor. **3** To express or show anger, irritation, etc. — *v.t.* **4** To expose to or treat or fill with fumes, smoke, etc. [<OF *fum* <L *fumus* smoke] — **fum'er** *n.* — **fum'·ing** *adj.*

fumed (fyo͞omd) *adj.* Treated with fumes: said especially of wood coated with filler and then exposed to chemical fumes: *fumed* oak.

fume fading The fading of synthetic dyes in textiles exposed to certain chemical fumes. Also called *gas fading.*

fu·met (fyo͞o'met) *n. Obs.* **1** The odor of long-kept game. **2** The savory odor of meats while cooking. Also **fu·mette'.** [<F <L *fumus* smoke]

fu·mi·gant (fyo͞o'mə·gənt) *n.* Any substance, as hydrogen cyanide, whose vapors are capable of destroying vermin, rats, insects, etc., in an enclosed space; a gaseous disinfectant or insecticide.

fu·mi·gate (fyo͞o'mə·gāt) *v.t.* **·gat·ed, ·gat·ing** **1** To subject to smoke or fumes, as for disinfection. **2** *Archaic* To perfume. [<L *fumigatus,* pp. of *fumigare* smoke <*fumus* smoke + *agere* drive] — **fu'mi·ga'tion** *n.* — **fu'·mi·ga'tor** *n.*

fu·mi·to·ry (fyo͞o'mə·tôr'ē, -tō'rē) *n. pl.* **·ries** Any of a genus *(Fumaria)* of climbing herbs; especially, a low herb *(F. officinalis)* with terminal racemes of rose-colored flowers, used medicinally as an alterative and tonic. [<F *fumeterre* <Med. L *fumus terrae* smoke of the earth]

fu·mu·lus (fyo͞o'myə·ləs) *n. Meteorol.* A delicate, almost invisible veil of cloud that may form at all heights from cirrus to stratus: most observable in low latitudes and on hot days. [<NL, dim. of *fumus* smoke]

fum·y (fyo͞o'mē) *adj.* **fum·i·er, fum·i·est** Yielding or containing fumes; smoky; vaporous. — **fum'i·ly** *adv.* — **fum'i·ness** *n.*

fun (fun) *n.* **1** That which excites merriment; frolic; sport; amusement. **2** Drollery; jocularity; a joke. **3** Frolicsome doings; also, the mirth and enjoyment derived therefrom. See synonyms under ENTERTAINMENT, LAUGHTER, SPORT, WIT. — **to make fun of** To ridicule. — **for** or **in fun** Not seriously; sportively, jokingly. — *v.i.* **funned, fun·ning** *Colloq.* To indulge in fun; make sport; jest. [<obs. *fonnen* befool]

Fu·na·fu·ti (fo͞o'nə·fo͞o'tē) The island headquarters of the Gilbert Islands district of the Gilbert and Ellice Islands colony; one square mile.

fu·nam·bu·list (fyo͞o·nam'byə·list) *n.* A performer on a tight or slack rope. [<L *funambulus* <*funis* rope + *ambulare* walk] — **fu·nam'bu·la·to'ry** (-tôr'ē, -tō'rē) *adj.* — **fu·nam'·bu·lism** *n.*

Fun·chal (fo͞oṅ·shäl') **1** A port, capital of Madeira. **2** An administrative district of Portugal comprising Madeira.

func·tion (fungk'shən) *n.* **1** The specific, natural, or proper action that belongs to an agent. **2** One's appropriate or assigned business, duty, part, or office. **3** The proper employment of faculties or powers. **4** The normal action of any organ or set of organs: the respiratory *function.* **5** A public or official ceremony or formal entertainment. **6** *Math.* A quantity whose value is dependent on the value of some other quantity. **7** *Ling.* The part played by a linguistic element in a form or construction. See synonyms under DUTY. — *v.i.* **1** To perform as expected or required; operate properly. **2** To perform the rôle of something else. **3** *Ling.* To perform a specific function. [<OF <L *functio, -onis* <*fungi* perform]

func·tion·al (fungk'shən·əl) *adj.* **1** Of or belonging to the proper office or work of an agent or agency. **2** Designed for or suited to a particular operation or use: *functional* architecture. **3** *Med.* Affecting only the functions of an organ or part; not structural or organic: a *functional* disease. — **func'tion·al·ly** *adv.*

func·tion·al·ism (fungk'shən·əl·iz'əm) *n.* In art, architecture, etc., a doctrine that holds function to be of prime importance, modifying such factors as form and structure so that they may contribute the utmost to the effective functioning of the finished product. — **func'·tion·al·ist** *n.*

functional shift *Ling.* The assuming of a new syntactic function by a word, without a change in form, as when an adjective serves as a noun in English.

func·tion·ar·y (funk'shən·er'ē) *n. pl.* **·ar·ies** A public official.

function word *Ling.* A word which is used to indicate the function of, or the relationship between, other words in a phrase or sentence, as a preposition or conjunction.

fund (fund) *n.* **1** A sum of money or stock of convertible wealth employed in, set aside for, or available for a business enterprise or other purpose; specifically, the quick capital or available assets of a business firm or corporation. **2** *pl.* Money lent to government; a funded debt. **3** A reserve store; an ample stock: a *fund* of humor. **4** *pl.* Money in general: out of *funds.* **5** *Obs.* Bottom. See synonyms under STOCK, MONEY. — *v.t.* **1** To convert into a more or less permanent debt bearing a fixed rate of interest: to *fund* a public debt. **2** To furnish a fund for the payment of the principal or interest of (a debt). **3** To make a fund of; amass. [<L *fundus* bottom] — **fund'a·ble** *adj.*

fun·da·ment (fun'də·mənt) *n.* **1** A fundamental principle or element. **2** The part on which the body rests in sitting; the buttocks; also, the anus. **3** *Geog.* The natural features of a region considered in the aggregate and as unmodified by human action. **4** *Obs.* Foundation. [<L *fundamentum* <*fundus* bottom]

fun·da·men·tal (fun'də·men'təl) *adj.* **1** Relating to or constituting a foundation; indispensable; basal. **2** *Geol.* Located at the bottom; constituting the lowest stratum or formation: *fundamental* rock. **3** *Music* Radical: applied to the lowest note of a chord, considered as being its foundation or root. **4** *Physics* Designating that component of a wave form or other periodic oscillation on which all harmonic frequencies are based. See synonyms under RADICAL. — *n.* **1** Anything that serves as the foundation or basis of a system of belief, as a truth, law, or principle; a primary and necessary truth; an essential. **2** *Music* The note on which a chord is formed. **3** *Physics* That frequency on which a harmonic or group of harmonics is based. — **fun'·da·men'tal·ly** *adv.*

fun·da·men·tal·ism (fun'də·men'təl·iz'əm) *n.* **1** The belief that all statements made in the Bible are literally true. **2** In the United States, a movement among Protestants holding that such belief is essential to Christian faith: opposed to *modernism.* — **fun'da·men'tal·ist** *n.*

fun·dus (fun'dəs) *n. Anat.* The rounded base, bottom, or farther end or part of any hollow organ: the *fundus* of the eye. [<L]

Fun·dy (fun'dē), **Bay of** An inlet of the Atlantic between Nova Scotia and New Brunswick and NE Maine; its tides are among the highest in the world, rising to 70 feet.

Fü·nen (fü'nən) German name for FYN.

fu·ner·al (fyo͞o'nər·əl) *n.* **1** The rites and ceremonies preceding and accompanying burial; obsequies. **2** A gathering or procession of persons on the occasion of a burial. — *adj.* Pertaining to, suitable for, or used at a funeral. [<OF *funeraille* <Med. L *funeralia,* neut. pl. of *funeralis* <*funus, funeris* a burial rite]

fu·ne·re·al (fyo͞o·nir'ē·əl) *adj.* Pertaining to or suitable for a funeral; mournful; lugubrious. [<L *funereus* <*funus* FUNERAL] — **fu·ne'·re·al·ly** *adv.*

fu·nest (fyo͞o·nest') *adj. Rare* Portending or causing death or evil; fatal; doleful. [<F *funeste* <L *funestus* <*funus* FUNERAL]

Fünf·kir·chen (fünf'·kėr'khən) The German name for PÉCS.

fun·gal (fung'gəl) *adj.* Fungous. — *n.* A fungus.

Fun·gi (fun'jī) *n. pl.* One of the subdivisions of the *Thallophyta:* non-flowering plants of wide distribution and great variety, devoid of chlorophyll, reproducing chiefly by asexual means and obtaining nourishment either as *parasites* on living organisms or as *saprophytes* on dead organic matter. They include the molds, mildews, rusts, and mushrooms, and are subdivided into bacteria or fission fungi *(Schizomycetes),* slime fungi *(Myxomycetes),* algal fungi *(Phycomycetes),* ascus fungi *(Ascomycetes),* basidium fungi *(Basidiomycetes),* and the Fungi Imperfecti, not yet classified. [See FUNGUS]

fungi- *combining form* Fungus: *fungicide.* Also, before vowels, **fung-.** [<L *fungus* a mushroom]

fun·gi·ble (fun'jə·bəl) *adj.* **1** Capable of being replaced in kind, as movables. **2** That may be measured, counted, or weighed. — *n.* **1** Anything fungible. **2** *Law* A thing of which one portion may be taken or used in the place of another portion to fulfil an obligation. [<Med. L *fungibilis* <*fungi* perform] — **fun'·gi·bil'i·ty** *n.*

fun·gi·cide (fun'jə·sīd) *n.* Anything that kills fungi or destroys their spores; especially, any chemical compound used for this purpose. — **fun'gi·ci'dal** *adj.*

fun·gi·form (fun'jə·fôrm) *adj.* Having a form or a head like that of a mushroom or fungus.

fun·goid (fung'goid) *adj.* Resembling a mushroom or fungus. — *n.* A fungus.

fun·gous (fung'gəs) *adj.* **1** Pertaining to or of the nature of a fungus; spongy. **2** Springing up suddenly. **3** Bearing or containing fungi.

fun·gus (fung'gəs) *n. pl.* **fun·gus·es** or **fun·gi** (fun'jī) **1** Any of the *Fungi* group of thallophytic plants, comprising the mushrooms, puffballs, molds, smuts, etc. **2** A soft, spongy growth on an animal body. [<L, a mushroom. Akin to SPONGE.]

fu·ni·cle (fyo͞o'ni·kəl) *n. Anat.* **1** A small cord, ligature, or fiber. **2** A funiculus. [<L *funiculus,* dim. of *funis* a rope]

fu·nic·u·lar (fyo͞o·nik'yə·lər) *adj.* **1** Pertaining to, consisting of, or like a funicle. **2** Pertaining to a cord or funiculus. **3** Operated by a cable, cord, or rope: a *funicular* railway. — *n.* A cable railway. Also **funicular railway.**

fu·nic·u·late (fyo͞o·nik'yə·lit, -lāt) *adj.* **1** *Bot.* Provided with funicles. **2** *Zool.* Forming a narrow ridge.

fu·nic·u·lus (fyo͞o·nik'yə·ləs) *n. pl.* **·li** (-lī) **1** A small cord, rope, or the like. **2** *Anat.* The umbilical cord. **3** *Bot.* The cord or stalk that connects the ovule or seed with the peridium of a plant. [<L]

funk (fungk) *n. Colloq.* Cowardly fright; panic. — *v.t.* **1** To shrink from; be afraid of. **2** To frighten; scare. — *v.i.* **3** To shrink through fear or aversion; try to back out. [Cf. Flemish *fonck* fear]

Funk (fungk), **Casimir,** 1884–1967, Polish biochemist. — **Charles Earle,** 1881–1957, U.S. lexicographer. — **Isaac Kauffman,** 1838–1912, U.S. publisher and lexicographer; founder of *The Literary Digest;* editor in chief of the *Standard Dictionary* and *New Standard Dictionary of the English Language.*

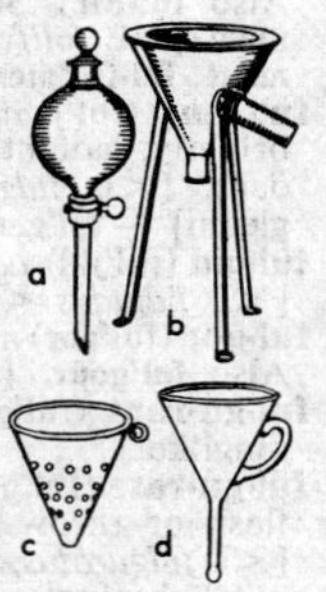

fun·nel (fun'əl) *n.* **1** A wide-mouthed conical vessel, terminating in a tube, for filling close-necked vessels with liquids: also called *tunnel.* **2** A smoke pipe, chimney, or flue. **3** A smokestack on a steamship. **4** Any funnel-like part or process: the *funnel* cell in a leaf. — *v.t.* & *v.i.* **·neled** or **·nelled, ·nel·ing** or **·nel·ling** To pass or move through or as through a funnel; focus. [Earlier *fonel,* ult. <L *infundibulum* <*infundere* pour <*in-* into + *fundere* pour]

FUNNELS
a. Separatory funnel.
b. Hot filtration funnel.
c. Filter funnel.
d. Glass funnel, with olivary tip.

fun·nies (fun'ēz) *n. pl. U.S. Colloq.* Comic strips.

fun·ny (fun'ē) *adj.* **·ni·er, ·ni·est** **1** Affording fun; comical; ludicrous; laughable. **2** *Colloq.* Puzzling; strange; unusual. — **fun'ni·ly** *adv.* — **fun'ni·ness** *n.*

Synonyms: amusing, comical, diverting, droll, facetious, farcical, grotesque, humorous, jocose, jocular, jolly, jovial, laughable, ludicrous, merry, mirthful, odd, queer, ridiculous, whimsical, witty. Compare AMUSE. *Antonyms:* see synonyms for SAD.

funny bone The part of the humerus where the ulnar nerve is exposed at the elbow; crazy bone.

funny paper *U.S. Colloq.* A newspaper supplement containing comic strips.

Fun·ston (fun′stən), **Frederick,** 1865–1917, U. S. general.

Fun·za (fōōn′sä) See BOGOTÁ (def. 2).

fur (fûr) *n.* **1** The soft, fine, hairy coat covering the skin of many mammals. **2** *pl.* or *collective sing.* Skins of fur-bearing animals, as ermine, sable, beaver, etc.; also, apparel made of them. **3** Any fuzzy covering, as coating on the tongue. **4** A piece of wood nailed under a bent rafter to straighten it. [< *v.*] **— to make the fur fly** To attack a person or thing vigorously; fight. *— v.t.* **furred, fur·ring 1** To cover, line, or trim with fur. **2** To clothe with fur. **3** To cover with a coating, as of scum. **4** To apply furring to, as for lathing. ◆ Homophone: *fir.* [<OF *forrer* line with fur <Gmc.]

fu·ran (fyōōr′·an, fyōō·ran′) *n. Chem.* A colorless liquid heterocyclic hydrocarbon, C_4H_4O, obtained from pine tar and an important source of furfural: also *furfuran.* Also **fu·rane** (fyōōr′ān). [Short for *furfurane* <L *furfur* bran + -AN(E)²]

fur·be·low (fûr′bə·lō) *n.* **1** A plaited flounce, ruffle, or similar ornament. **2** Hence, any ornament in feminine dress. *— v.t.* To decorate elaborately or fussily. [Alter. of FALBALA]

fur·bish (fûr′bish) *v.t.* **1** To make bright by rubbing; burnish. **2** To restore to brightness or beauty; renovate: often with *up.* See synonyms under GARNISH. [<OF *forbiss-*, stem of *forbir* <OHG *furban* clean] **— fur′bish·er** *n.*

fur·cal (fûr′kəl) *adj.* Forked; branched; furcate.

fur·cate (fûr′kāt) *v.i.* **·cat·ed, ·cat·ing** To separate into diverging parts; fork. *— adj.* Forked: also **fur′cat·ed.** [<Med. L *furcatus* cloven < *furca* fork] **— fur′cate·ly** *adv.* **— fur·ca′tion** *n.*

fur·crae·a (fər·krē′ə) *n.* One of a genus *(Furcraea)* of tropical American plants of the amaryllis family; especially *F. macrophylla,* which yields a valuable fiber. See FIQUE. [<NL, after A. F. *Fourcroy,* 1755–1809, French chemist]

fur·cu·lum (fûr′kyə·ləm) *n. pl.* **·la** (-lə) The united clavicles of a bird; the wishbone. [< NL, incorrectly formed as dim. of *furca* fork]

fur·fur (fûr′fər) *n. pl.* **·fur·es** (-fə·rēz) Dandruff, or branlike scales of skin; scurf. [<L, bran] **— fur′fur·a′ceous** *adj.*

fur·fur·al (fûr′fə·ral) *n. Chem.* A colorless liquid heterocyclic aldehyde, $C_5H_4O_2$, obtained by distillation of the pentose sugars occurring in corncobs, oat hulls, and other agricultural waste products: widely used as a solvent and reagent in the dyestuffs, plastics, and other industries. Also **fur′fur·ol** (-ôl, -ol). [<L *furfur* bran + AL(DEHYDE)]

fur·fu·ran (fûr′fə·ran) *n.* Furan.

fu·ri·bund (fyōōr′i·bund′) *adj. Rare* Filled with rage or fury; raging. [<L *furibundus* < *furere* rage]

Fu·ries (fyōōr′ēz) *n. pl.* In Greek and Roman mythology, the three goddesses who take vengeance on unpunished criminals—Alecto, Megaera, and Tisiphone: also called *Erinyes, Eumenides.*

fu·ri·o·so (fyōō′rē·ō′sō) *adj. Music* With fury or vehemence. [<Ital.]

fu·ri·ous (fyōōr′ē·əs) *adj.* **1** Full of fury; raging; frantic. **2** Wildly rushing; violent; tempestuous; as waves, a storm, etc. See synonyms under FIERCE. [<L *furiosus* < *furere* rage] **— fu′ri·ous·ly** *adv.* **— fu′ri·ous·ness** *n.*

furl (fûrl) *v.t.* To roll up and make secure, as a sail to a spar. *— v.i.* To become furled. *— n.* **1** The act of furling. **2** Something furled. [<F *ferler* <OF *fermlier* < *ferm* close (<L *firmus*) + *lier* bind <L *ligare*]

fur·long (fûr′lông, -long) *n.* A measure of length, one eighth of a mile, 220 yards, or 201.168 meters. [OE *furlang* < *furh* furrow + *lang* long]

fur·lough (fûr′lō) *n.* An authorized leave of absence of more than three days granted to an enlisted man in the army or navy. Compare LEAVE, PASS. *— v.t.* To grant a furlough to. [<Du. *verlof*]

furm (fûrm) *n. Scot.* A form; bench.

fur·men·ty (fûr′mən·tē), **fur·me·ty** (fûr′mə·tē), **fur·mi·ty** See FRUMENTY.

fur·nace (fûr′nis) *n.* **1** A structure or apparatus containing a chamber for heating, fusing, hardening, etc., by means of a fire beneath, as for melting metal, baking pottery, evaporating water, etc. **2** A large stove in the basement or cellar of a house, equipped with conduits for heating the upper rooms. See ELECTRIC FURNACE. [<OF *fornais* <L *fornax, fornacis* < *furnus* oven]

Fur·neaux Islands (fûr′nō) An Australian island group between Australia and Tasmania; 1,031 square miles.

Fur·ness (fûr′nis), **Horace Howard,** 1833–1912, U. S. scholar.

fur·nish (fûr′nish) *v.t.* **1** To equip, or fit out, as with fittings or furniture. **2** To supply; provide. See synonyms under ACCOMMODATE, GIVE, PRODUCE, PROVIDE. [<OF *furniss-*, stem of *furnir* <OHG *frumjan* provide] **— fur′nish·er** *n.*

fur·nish·ing (fûr′nish·ing) *n.* **1** *pl.* Fixtures or fittings, as hardware for cabinetwork, etc. **2** The act of supplying with furniture.

fur·ni·ture (fûr′nə·chər) *n.* **1** That with which anything is furnished or supplied; equipment or outfit; specifically, movable household articles, such as chairs, tables, bureaus. **2** Ornamental appendages or external adjuncts that serve to complete anything. **3** *Printing* The strips and blocks of wood or metal, made in multiples of picas, which are locked between the page forms and the chase. **4** *Obs.* The action of providing for, equipping, or furnishing. [<F *fourniture* < *fournir* FURNISH]

Fur·ni·vall (fûr′nə·vəl), **Frederick James,** 1825–1910, English philologist.

fu·ror (fyōōr′ôr) *n.* **1** Fury. **2** Great excitement or enthusiasm. **3** An object of enthusiasm; a fad; a craze. **4** Religious frenzy. Also **fu·rore** (fyōōr′ôr, fyōō·rôr′ē, -rō′rē). [<L *furor* < *furere* rage]

fu·ror lo·quen·di (fyōōr′ōr lō·kwen′dī) *Latin* Enthusiasm for speaking.

furor po·et·i·cus (pō·et′i·kəs) *Latin* Poetic frenzy.

furor scri·ben·di (skri·ben′dī) *Latin* Enthusiasm for writing.

fur·phy (fûr′fē) *Austral.* A rumor; canard. [after *Furphy,* a foundry owner]

furred (fûrd) *adj.* **1** Bearing fur; also, trimmed with fur. **2** Provided with furring.

fur·ri·er (fûr′ē·ər, -yər) *n.* A dealer in furs or fur goods; a dresser of furs for garments.

fur·ri·er·y (fûr′ē·ər·ē) *n. pl.* **·er·ies 1** Furs in general. **2** The business of a furrier.

fur·ring (fûr′ing) *n.* **1** Fur, or fur trimmings. **2** A coating or scale, as on the inner surface of boiler pipes; also, the process of removing it. **3** Pieces of wood attached to a surface, as for lathing. **4** The act of applying or adjusting, as pieces of wood or metal for lathing.

fur·row (fûr′ō) *n.* **1** A trench made in the earth by a plow. **2** One of the grooves in the face of a millstone. **3** Any groove or wrinkle. **4** *Obs.* A plowed field. *— v.t.* **1** To make furrows in; plow. **2** To make wrinkles in, as the brow. *— v.i.* **3** To become wrinkled. [OE *furh*] **— fur′row·er** *n.*

fur·ry (fûr′ē) *adj.* **1** Of or like fur. **2** Covered with or clad in fur. **— fur′ri·ness** *n.*

fur seal An eared seal that yields a fur of great commercial value, especially *Callorhinus alascanus,* the Alaska fur seal of the Pribilof Islands. See SEAL².

Fürth (fürt) A city in Bavaria, Germany.

fur·ther (fûr′thər) Comparative of FAR. *— adj.* **1** More distant or advanced in time or degree. **2** Wider or fuller; additional. **3** More distant in space; farther. See note under FARTHER. *— adv.* **1** More remotely; farther. **2** In addition; besides; also. See synonyms under YET. *— v.t.* To help forward; promote. See synonyms under PROMOTE. [OE *furthra*] **— fur′ther·er** *n.*

fur·ther·ance (fûr′thər·əns) *n.* **1** The act of furthering; advancement. **2** That which furthers.

fur·ther·more (fûr′thər·môr′, -mōr′) *adv.* In addition; moreover.

fur·ther·most (fûr′thər·mōst′) *adj.* Furthest or most remote.

fur·ther·some (fûr′thər·səm) *adj.* Tending to further or advance; promotive; helpful.

fur·thest (fûr′thist) Superlative of FAR. *— adj.* **1** Most distant, remote, or advanced in time or degree. **2** Most distant in space. *— adv.* **1** At or to the greatest distance in time or degree. **2** Farthest.

fur·tive (fûr′tiv) *adj.* Stealthy or sly; stolen; secret; elusive. See synonyms under SECRET. [<F *furtif* <L *furtivus* stolen < *fur* a thief] **— fur′tive·ly** *adv.* **— fur′tive·ness** *n.*

fu·run·cle (fyōōr′ung·kəl) *n.* A boil or inflammatory sore caused by bacterial infection of the subcutaneous tissue. [<L *furunculus,* dim. of *fur* thief] **— fu·run·cu·lar** (fyōō·rung′kyə·lər) *adj.* **— fu·run′cu·lous** *adj.*

fu·ry (fyōōr′ē) *n. pl.* **·ries 1** A state of violent anger; ungovernable rage. **2** A storm of anger; a fit of raving passion. **3** Violent action or agitation; impetuosity; fierceness; frenzy. **4** Intense passion of any kind; inspiration; enthusiasm. **5** A person of violent temper, especially a turbulent woman; termagant. See synonyms under ANGER, FRENZY, VIOLENCE. [<L *furia* < *furere* rave]

furze (fûrz) *n.* A spiny evergreen shrub *(Ulex europaeus)* of the bean family, having many branches and yellow flowers: also called *gorse, whin.* [OE *fyrs*] **— furz′y** *adj.*

fu·sain (fyōō·zān′, *Fr.* fü·zaṅ′) *n.* **1** A crayon of fine charcoal, or a drawing made with it. **2** One of the constituents of bituminous coal, consisting of patches and wedges of fibrous strands; mineral charcoal. [<F, spindle tree <L *fusus* spindle]

Fu·san (fōō·sän) Japanese name for PUSAN.

fus·cous (fus′kəs) *adj.* Grayish-brown or tawny; dusky. [<L *fuscus* dusky]

fuse¹ (fyōōz) *n.* **1** *Electr.* A protective device of fusible metal set in a circuit so as to be directly heated and destroyed by the passage of an excess current through it. **2** A textile cord, ribbon, or the like impregnated with combustible material for communicating fire to explosives, as in mining, blasting, and pyrotechnics; black match: distinguished from *fuze.* [<Ital. *fuso* <L *fusus* a spindle]

fuse² (fyōōz) *v.t.* & *v.i.* **fused, fus·ing 1** To liquefy by heat; melt. **2** To join or cause to join as if by melting together. See synonyms under MELT, MIX, UNITE. [<L *fusus,* pp. of *fundere* pour]

fu·see (fyōō·zē′) *n.* **1** A wooden match having a bulb of inflammable material at its end and not extinguishable by wind. **2** A flare used as a railroad signal. **3** *Mech.* A spirally grooved cone, as in a watch or a spring clock, about which is wrapped a chain or cord, which is also wound about a cylindrical barrel containing or driven by a spiral spring. Its use is to give the spring increasing leverage as its power lessens by unwinding. Also spelled *fuzee.* [<F *fusée* <Med. L *fusata* <L *fusus* spindle]

fu·se·lage (fyōō′sə·lij, -läzh, -zə-) *n. Aeron.* The main structural framework of an airplane which supports the power plant, cockpit, fuel container, wings, cargo, crew and passenger space, etc. See illustration under AIRPLANE. [<F, ult. <L *fusus* a spindle]

fu·sel oil (fyōō′zəl, -səl) A volatile, poisonous, oily liquid, consisting largely of amyl alcohol, and having a disagreeable odor and taste, obtained when corn, potato, or grape spirits are rectified: used as a solvent in various chemical processes. Also **fu′sel.** [<G *fusel* inferior spirits]

Fu·shih (fōō′shir′) See YENAN.

Fu·shun (fōō′shōōn′) A city in south central Manchuria, near Mukden.

fu·si·bil·i·ty (fyōō′zə·bil′ə·tē) *n.* Quality of being fusible, or the degree of this quality.

fu·si·ble (fyōō′zə·bəl) *adj.* Capable of being fused or melted by heat. **— fu′si·ble·ness** *n.* **— fu′si·bly** *adv.*

fusible metal Any alloy, as one containing bismuth, which melts at a comparatively low temperature. Also **fusible alloy.**

fu·si·form (fyōō′zə·fôrm) *adj.* Tapering from the middle toward each end; spindle-shaped. [<L *fusus* spindle + -FORM]

fu·sil (fyōō′zəl) *n.* A flintlock musket: also spelled *fuzil.* [<F <OF *foisil* a steel for striking sparks, ult. <L *focus* a hearth]

fu·sile (fyōō′zəl, -səl, -sīl) *adj.* **1** Made by melting or casting. **2** *Obs.* Capable of being fused. [<L *fusilis* < *fundere* pour]

fu·si·liers (fyōō′zə·lirz′) *n. pl.* A title borne by certain British infantry regiments: from soldiers who formerly carried fusils. Also **fu′si·leers′.**

fu·sil·lade (fyōō′zə·lād′) *n.* A simultaneous discharge of firearms. —*v.t.* **·lad·ed, ·lad·ing** To attack or kill by a fusillade. Also **fu′si·lade′.** [<F <*fusiller* shoot <*fusil* a musket]

fu·sion (fyōō′zhən) *n.* **1** The act of blending, or the state of being blended throughout. **2** The act of coalescing of two political parties, or the state of coalescence: also used attributively: a *fusion* ticket. **3** The act or process of changing, or the state of being in the course of change, from a solid into a liquid by the agency of heat; melting. **4** A state of fluidity due to the action of heat. **5** *Physics* A thermonuclear reaction in which the nuclei of a light element undergo transformation into those of a heavier element, with the release of great energy: the reverse of *fission.* **6** *Ling.* A coalescing of two originally distinct words because of a similarity in form and meaning, as in the development of the verb *bid* from the Old English verbs *biddan* "ask" and *bēodan* "command." See synonyms under ALLIANCE. [<L *fusio, -onis* <*fundere* pour]

fu·sion·ism (fyōō′zhən·iz′əm) *n.* The doctrine, advocacy, or practice of fusion in politics. —**fu′sion·ist** *n.*

fusion welding A process of joining metal parts by applying high temperatures to the contact surfaces, thus bonding them together without the use of rivets or other mechanical means.

fuss (fus) *n.* **1** Disturbance about trivial matters; trouble; ado. **2** One who worries about trifles: also **fuss′er.** See synonyms under QUARREL. —*v.i.* To make a fuss or bustle over trifles. —*v.t.* To bother or perplex with trifles. [Origin unknown]

fuss·budg·et (fus′buj′it) *n. Colloq.* A nervous, fussy person.

fuss·y (fus′ē) *adj.* **fuss·i·er, fuss·i·est** **1** Inclined to fuss; fidgety; fretful. **2** Troublesome to do or make. —**fuss′i·ly** *adv.* —**fuss′i·ness** *n.*

fust (fust) *n. Obs.* A musty, rank smell. —*v.i.* To become musty or moldy in taste or smell. [<OF *fust* cask]

fus·ta·nel·la (fus′tə·nel′ə) *n.* A short white skirt worn by men in modern Greece. Also **fus′ta·nelle′** (-nel′). [<Ital.]

fus·tian (fus′chən) *n.* **1** Formerly, a kind of stout cloth made of cotton and flax; now, a coarse, twilled cotton fabric, such as corduroy or velveteen. **2** Pretentious verbiage; bombast. —*adj.* **1** Made of fustian. **2** Pompous, bombastic. [<OF *fustaine* <Med. L (*pannus*) *fustaneus* (<L *fustis* a cudgel), trans. of Gk. *xylinon* wooden <*xylon* wood]

fus·tic (fus′tik) *n.* **1** The wood of a tropical tree (*Chlorophora tinctoria*) used as a yellow dyestuff; yellow wood. **2** Any of several other

woods used for dyeing. [<F *fustoc* <Sp. < Arabic *fustuq,* prob. <Gk. *pistakē* pistachio]

fus·ti·gate (fus′tə·gāt) *v.t.* **·gat·ed, ·gat·ing** To beat with a stick; cudgel: now in humorous use. [<L *fustigatus,* pp. of *fustigare* <*fustis* club + *agere* do, drive] —**fus′ti·ga′tion** *n.*

fus·tin (fus′tin) *n.* **1** The coloring matter of fustic and sumac. **2** *Chem.* A glucoside, $C_{36}H_{26}O_{14}$, from the wood of the smoke tree. [<FUST(IC) + -IN]

fust·y (fus′tē) *adj.* **fust·i·er, fust·i·est** **1** Musty; moldy; rank. **2** Old-fashioned; fogeyish. —**fust′i·ly** *adv.* —**fust′i·ness** *n.*

fu·thark (fōō′thärk) *n.* The runic alphabet. Also **fu′tharc, fu′thorc** (-thôrk), **fu′thork.** [from the first six letters, *f, u, þ (th), a (or o), r, c*]

fu·tile (fyōō′təl, -til; *Brit.* -tīl) *adj.* **1** Of no avail; done in vain; useless. **2** Frivolous; trivial: *futile* chatter. See synonyms under USELESS, VAIN. [<F <L *futilis* pouring out easily, useless] —**fu′tile·ly** *adv.* —**fu′tile·ness** *n.*

fu·til·i·tar·i·an (fyoo·til′ə·târ′ē·ən) *adj.* Convinced of the futility of human enterprise. —*n.* One so convinced.

fu·til·i·ty (fyōō·til′ə·tē) *n. pl.* **·ties** **1** The quality of being ineffective or useless. **2** Unimportance; triviality. **3** A futile act, event, thing, etc.

fut·tock (fut′ək) *n. Naut.* One of the curved or crooked timbers in the built-up rib or frame of a wooden ship. [? Alter, of FOOT HOOK]

futtock shrouds *Naut.* Shrouds extending from the outer extremities of the crosstrees to a band in the mast below.

Fu·tu·na (fōō·tōō′nə) See WALLIS AND FUTUNA ISLANDS.

fu·tur·al (fyōō′chər·əl) *adj.* Of or pertaining to the future or futures.

fu·ture (fyōō′chər) *n.* **1** The time yet to come. **2** Prospects or outlook. **3** Any security sold or bought upon agreement for future delivery: usually plural: to deal in *futures.* **4** *Gram.* **a** A verb tense denoting action that will take place at some time to come. **b** A verb in this tense. —*adj.* **1** Such as will or may be hereafter. **2** Pertaining to or expressing time to come. **3** Pertaining to the state of the soul after death: the *future* life. [<OF *futur* <L *futurus,* future participle of *esse* be]

fu·ture·less (fyōō′chər·lis) *adj.* Having or knowing no future; lacking foresight or forethought.

future life Spiritual existence after death.

future perfect *Gram.* The verb tense expressing an action completed before a specified future time. Example: He *will have finished* by tomorrow.

future shock A state of stress and disorientation brought on by a quick succession of changes, esp. in new standards of behavior and values.

fu·tur·ism (fyōō′chə·riz′əm) *n.* A movement in art, music, and literature originating in Italy in 1910, and aiming at originality, intensity, and force unhampered by tradition. —**fu′·tur·ist** *n.*

fu·tu·ri·ty (fyōō·tōōr′ə·tē, -tyōōr′-) *n. pl.* **·ties** **1** Time to come; the future. **2** The state of being future. **3** The people of the future. **4** A future possibility. **5** A futurity race.

futurity race *U.S.* A horse race for which entry nominations long precede the running.

futurity stakes *U.S.* Stakes to be raced for, long after the entries or nominations are made.

fuze (fyōōz) *n.* A mechanical or electrical device that initiates the explosive charge of a shell, bomb, grenade, etc.: distinguished from *fuse* (def. 2). —**all-ways fuze** A fuze, used especially on mortar shells, which detonates the explosive charge on contact, regardless of the position of the projectile. —**non-delay fuze** A fuze which detonates on impact. [Var. of FUSE[1]]

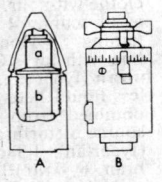

FUZES
A. Artillery VT (proximity) fuze:
a. Radio unit.
b. Battery.
B. Aerial bomb time fuze.

fu·zee (fyōō·zē′) See FUSEE.

fu·zil (fyōō′zəl) See FUSIL.

fuzz (fuz) *n.* **1** Loose, light, or fluffy matter. **2** A mass or coating of such matter. **3** *Slang* A policeman or the police. —*v.t.* & *v.i.* To cover or become covered with fuzz. [Origin unknown]

fuzz·y (fuz′ē) *adj.* **fuzz·i·er, fuzz·i·est** **1** Covered with fuzz. **2** Lacking sharpness: said of motion-picture sound track on visual inspection. **3** Having distorted sound: said of recorded music, especially of high frequencies. —**fuzz′i·ly** *adv.* —**fuzz′i·ness** *n.*

-fy *suffix of verbs* **1** Make; form into: *deify.* **2** Cause to be; become: *liquefy.* [<OF *-fier* <L *-ficare* <*facere* do, make]

fyke[1] (fīk) *Scot.* *n.* **1** Uneasiness; fidgetiness; fidget. **2** Fussy, unnecessary, or annoying exactness, or any crotchety peculiarity. —*v.t.* & *v.i.* To fidget. Also spelled *fike.*

fyke[2] (fīk) *n.* A fish trap consisting of several successive conical nets with wide-stretched mouths; a bag net; bow net. Also **fyke net.** [<Du. *fuik* bow net]

fyl·fot (fil′fot) *n.* The swastika. [<FILL, *v.* + FOOT; so called because used to fill in the foot or base of stained glass windows]

Fyn (fün) *n.* A Danish island in the Baltic Sea; 1,149 square miles: German *Fünen.* Also **Fyen.**

fyrd (fûrd, fird) *n.* An army or military force in England before the Norman conquest. [OE]

Fy·za·bad (fī′zä·bäd) A former spelling of FAIZABAD.

G

g, G (jē) *n. pl.* **g's, G's** or **gs, Gs, gees** (jēz) **1** The seventh letter of the English alphabet: from Phoenician *gimel,* through Greek *gamma,* Roman G. **2** A sound of the letter *g.* See ALPHABET. —*symbol* **1** *Music* **a** The fifth, or dominant, tone in the scale of C major. **b** The pitch of this tone. **c** A printed or written note representing it. **d** A scale built upon G. **e** The treble clef. **2** *Physics* The acceleration of a body due to gravity, about 32 feet per second per second: written in lower case.

G–1, G–2, G–3 See under GENERAL STAFF.

gab[1] (gab) *n. Colloq.* Idle talk; loquacity. —*v.i.* **gabbed, gab·bing** To talk much or idly; chatter. [Prob. <ON *gabba* mock]

gab[2] (gab) *n. Mech.* A hook, as on a rod conveying the motion of an eccentric. For illustration see ECCENTRIC. [Cf. Flemish *gabbe* a notch]

gab[3] (gab, gäb) *n. Scot.* The mouth.

gab·ar·dine (gab′ər·dēn, gab′ər·dēn′) *n.* **1** A firm, twilled, worsted fabric, having a diagonal raised weave, used for coats, suits, etc. **2** A similar, softer fabric of mercerized cotton. **3** A gaberdine. [Var. of GABERDINE]

gab·bart (gab′ərt) *n. Scot.* A vessel used for inland trade; a lighter. Also **gab′bard** (-ərd).

gab·ble (gab′əl) *v.* **·bled, ·bling** *v.i.* **1** To talk rapidly and incoherently; babble. **2** To utter rapid, cackling sounds, as geese. —*v.t.* **3** To utter rapidly and incoherently. —*n.* **1** Noisy and incoherent or foolish talk. **2** Cackling, as of geese. See synonyms under BABBLE. [Freq. of GAB[1]] —**gab′bler** *n.*

gab·bro (gab′rō) *n. pl.* **·bros** *Geol.* Any of a class of igneous rocks of granular texture, consisting essentially of pyroxene, usually augite or diallage, and plagioclase. [<Ital.] —**gab′broid** *adj.*

gab·by (gab′ē) *adj.* *Colloq.* **·bi·er, ·bi·est** Given to talk; loquacious.

ga·belle (gə·bel′) *n.* In old English and French law, a tax, excise, impost, or duty; specifically, in French history, a tax on salt, abolished in 1790. Also **ga·bel′.** [<F <Med. L *gabella* < *gablum* tax <Gmc.] —**ga·belled′** *adj.*

gab·er·dine (gab′ər·dēn, gab′ər·dēn′) *n.* **1** A loose, coarse coat or frock. **2** A long, loose, coarse cloak worn by Jews in medieval times. **3** Gabardine. [<Sp. *garbardina* <MHG *wallevart* a pilgrimage]

gab·er·lun·yie (gab′ər·lün′yē,-lōōn′-) *n. Scot.* A beggar who carries a bag or pouch; a mendicant. Also **gab′er·lun′zie** (-lun′zē).

Ga·bès (gä′bes) A port on the **Gulf of Gabès** (ancient *Syrtis Minor*), an inlet of the Mediterranean on the SE coast of Tunisia.

gab·fest (gab′fest) *n. Slang* A "feast" of talking; prolonged empty talk; also, an occasion marked by prolonged talking. [<GAB[1] + G *fest* feast]

ga·bi·on (gā′bē·ən) *n.* A bottomless wicker

basket or cylinder, to be stuffed with sand or earth to form a fortification, foundation, etc. [< F < Ital. *gabbione*, aug. of *gabbia* a cage < L *cavea* cage]

ga·bi·on·ade (gā'bē·on·ād') *n.* A defensive work formed principally of gabions. Also **ga'bi·on·nade'**.

ga·ble (gā'bəl) *n. Archit.* 1 The upper part of an end wall, above the level of the eaves, beneath the end of a ridge roof that is not hipped or returned on itself: commonly triangular. 2 The entire end wall of a building; a gable end. —*v.t. & v.i.* **ga·bled, ga·bling** To build or be built with gables; form or end in gables. [< OF, prob. < ON *gafl* gable] —**ga'bled** *adj.*

GABLES

gable end *Archit.* The triangular wall between the eaves and the apex of the roof on the end of a building having a gable.

gable roof A ridge roof terminating in a gable at each end.

gable window A window in a gable, or one having a gable top.

Ga·bon (gä·bôń) An estuary tributary to the Gulf of Guinea in western Gabon; 40 miles long.

Gabon Republic An independent republic of the French Community on the west coast of equatorial Africa; 102,290 square miles; capital, Libreville; formerly a French overseas territory. Also **Ga·boon** (gə·bōōn'), **Ga·bun'**. —**Ga'bon·ese'** (-nēz, -nēs) *adj. & n.*

Ga·bo·riau (gà·bô·ryō'), **Emile**, 1835–73, French novelist.

Ga·bri·el (gā'brē·əl, *Fr.* gà·brē·el'; *Ger., Sw.* gä'brē·äl; *Pg., Sp.* gä'brē·äl') A masculine personal name. Also *Ital.* **Ga·bri·el·lo** (gä'brē·el'lō). [< Hebrew, hero of God] —**Gabriel** In the Bible, an archangel, appearing as the messenger of God. *Dan.* viii 16, *Luke* i 26.

ga·bri·elle (gā'brē·el') *n.* A flowing house dress of flimsy material. [from a proper name]

Ga·bri·lo·witsch (gä'vri·lō'vich), **Ossip**, 1878–1936, Russian pianist and conductor.

gad[1] (gad) *v.i.* **gad·ded, gad·ding** To roam abroad idly; ramble; stray. —*n.* The act of gadding. [? Back formation from obs. *gadling* vagabond] —**gad'der** *n.*

gad[2] (gad) *n.* 1 A punch or metal-pointed tool for breaking up ore or rock; also, a percussion drill. 2 A goad for driving cattle; any small rod or switch. 3 A large nail, spike, or wedge. —*v.t.* **gad·ded, gad·ding** 1 To break up with a gad. 2 To use a gad or rod upon. [< ON *gaddr* goad, spike]

Gad (gad) *interj. & n. Archaic* God: a variant form used euphemistically in oaths.

Gad (gad) In the Bible, Jacob's seventh son; also, the tribe descended from him, or its territory east of Jordan. *Gen.* xxx 11.

gad·a·bout (gad'ə·bout') *n.* One who gads habitually. —*adj.* Fond of gadding.

Gad·a·ra (gad'ə·rə) An ancient city of Palestine SE of the Sea of Galilee. —**Gad·a·rene** (gad'-ə·rēn, gad'ə·rēn') *adj. & n.*

gad·bee (gad'bē') *n.* A gadfly.

Ga·del·ic (gə·del'ik, -dē'lik) See GOIDELIC.

gad·fly (gad'flī') *n. pl.* **·flies** 1 A large fly (family *Tabanidae*) that torments cattle and horses. 2 A botfly or warblefly. 3 A restless, annoying busybody. [< GAD[2] + FLY]

gadg·et (gaj'it) *n.* 1 Any small mechanical device or contrivance, especially one of which the name cannot be recalled. 2 In glassmaking, a tool for grasping a piece of ware in the course of treatment. [Origin uncertain]

gadg·e·teer (gaj'ə·tir') *n.* A habitual user or contriver of gadgets.

gadg·et·ry (gaj'ət·rē) *n.* 1 The devising of gadgets. 2 Gadgets collectively.

Gadhel (gā'dəl) See GAEL.

ga·doid (gā'doid) *adj.* Of or pertaining to a large family (*Gadidae*) of chiefly marine fishes with soft fins, somewhat elongated bodies, large mouths, and wide gill openings. The family includes the codfish, hake, and haddock. —*n.* One

of the *Gadidae*. Also **ga'did**. [< NL *gadus* codfish < Gk. *gados*, a kind of fish + -OID]

gad·o·lin·ite (gad'ə·lin·īt') *n.* A black, vitreous silicate ore which yields gadolinium and other rare-earth elements.

gad·o·lin·i·um (gad'ə·lin'ē·əm) *n.* A metallic element (symbol Gd, atomic number 64) of the lanthanide series, having six naturally occurring stable isotopes and one weakly radioactive isotope. See PERIODIC TABLE. [after John *Gadolin*, 1760–1852, Finnish chemist]

ga·droon (gə·drōōn') See GODROON.

Gads·den (gadz'dən), **James**, 1788–1858, U.S. soldier and diplomat; by treaty with Mexico, 1853, secured for the United States a tract (45,535 square miles) known as the **Gadsden Purchase**, now part of Arizona and New Mexico.

gad·wall (gad'wôl) *n. pl.* **·walls** or **·wall** A large fresh-water duck (*Chaulelasmus streperus*) of the northern hemisphere, with black and white markings and numerous fine lamellae on the bill: highly esteemed as game. [Origin unknown]

gae[1] (gā) *v.i. Scot.* **gaed, gaen, gae·ing** To go: also spelled *gay.*

gae[2] (gā) Past tense of GIVE.

Gae·a (jē'ə) In Greek mythology, the goddess of earth, mother and wife of Uranus, and mother of the Titans, etc.: identified with the Roman *Tellus*: also called *Gaia*, *Ge*. Also **Gæ'a**. [< Gk. *Gaia* Earth]

Gae·dhel·ic (gə·del'ik, -dē'lik) See GOIDELIC.

Gaek·war (gīk'wär, jēk'-) *n.* Title of the native ruler of Baroda, India: also spelled *Gaikwar, Guicowar.* [< Marathi *Gāekvād*, a family name; lit., cowherd]

Gael (gāl) *n.* One of the Celtic people of Ireland, the Scottish Highlands, and the Isle of Man: also spelled *Gadhel.* [< Scottish Gaelic *Gaidheal*]

Gael·ic (gā'lik) *adj.* Belonging or relating to the Celtic Gaels, or to their languages. —*n.* 1 The languages of the Gaels; namely, Irish (*Irish Gaelic*), Manx, and, specifically, the speech of the Scottish Highlanders (*Scottish Gaelic*). 2 The Goidelic branch of the Celtic languages.

gaet (gāt) *n. Scot.* Manner; way; gait: also spelled *gait.*

gaff[1] (gaf) *n.* 1 A sharp iron hook at the end of a pole, for landing a large fish. 2 *Naut.* A spar for extending the upper edge of a fore-and-aft sail. 3 A gamecock's steel spur. —*v.t.* 1 To strike or land with a gaff: to *gaff* a sailfish. 2 *Brit. Slang* To trick; cheat. —**to stand the gaff** *U.S. Colloq.* To endure hardship, ridicule, or pain without complaining or quitting; be game. [< OF *gaffe*, prob. < Celtic]

gaff[2] (gaf) *n.* 1 Loud, rude talk; raillery. 2 An outburst of laughter; a guffaw. [Cf. OE *gafspræc* ribald talk]

gaff[3] (gaf) *n. Brit. Slang* A cheap theater or low-priced place of amusement. [Origin unknown]

gaffe (gaf) *n. French Colloq.* A clumsy mistake; a blunder; faux pas.

gaf·fer (gaf'ər) *n.* 1 An old man: correlative of *gammer*; an aged rustic: now contemptuous. 2 *Brit.* A foreman of laborers. 3 *U.S. Slang* The chief electrician in a motion-picture studio. [Alter. of GODFATHER]

gaff-headed (gaf'hed'id) *adj. Naut.* Having a gaff rig.

gaff rig *Naut.* A type of rig consisting of a fore-and-aft sail with the head supported by a gaff. —**gaff'-rigged'** *adj.*

gaff-top·sail (gaf'top'səl, -sāl) *n. Naut.* A light sail set above a gaff and having its foot extended thereby.

Gaf·sa (gaf'sə) A town in south central Tunisia; site of prehistoric discoveries; scene of first engagement (February, 1943) between American and German forces in the Tunisian campaign of World War II: ancient *Capsa.*

gag (gag) *n.* 1 Any appliance for completely obstructing the vocal organs or restraining speech; hence, any restraint upon free speech or discussion. 2 Something nauseating. 3 An instrument for holding open the jaws during an operation. 4 An interpolation by an actor in a play; a joke, humorous remark, story, etc.; also, a practical joke. [< v.] —**to pull a gag** *U.S. Slang* To perpetrate a hoax; tell an untrue story in a playful spirit. —*v.* **gagged, gag·ging** 1 To keep from

speaking or crying out by means of a gag. 2 To keep from speaking or discussing freely, as by force or authority: to *gag* the press. 3 To cause nausea in; cause to retch. 4 *Surg.* To hold open (the mouth) with a gag. 5 *Slang* To make fun of; hoax. 6 *Slang* To introduce one's own words or speeches into (a theatrical role): often with *up.* —*v.i.* 7 To heave with nausea; retch. 8 *Slang* To make jokes or speeches of an improvised nature. [ME *gaggen*; prob. imit.]

ga·ga (gä'gä) *adj. Slang* Foolish; crazy. [< F (slang), a foolish old man]

Ga·ga·rin (gä·gä'rēn), **Yuri Alekseyevitch**, 1934–1968, U.S.S.R. air force officer; first astronaut to make a successful space flight and first man to orbit the earth, April 12, 1961.

gage[1] (gāj) *v.t.* **gaged, gag·ing** 1 To determine the dimensions, amount, force, etc., of by means of a gage. 2 To determine the contents or capacity of, as a cask. 3 To estimate; appraise or judge. 4 To cut or rub (stones or bricks) to uniform size. 5 To mix (plaster) in the right proportions so as to dry in a desired time. —*n.* 1 An instrument for measuring, indicating, or regulating the capacity, quantity, dimensions, power, amount, proportions, etc., of anything. 2 A standard of comparison: the *gage* of the boiler; and, figuratively: the *gage* of his genius. 3 A standard measurement, dimension, quantity, or amount. 4 The distance between rails or between wheel treads, as in a railway. See the adjectives BROAD-GAGE, NARROW-GAGE, and STANDARD-GAGE. 5 The exposed length of a tile, slate, or shingle. 6 The amount of gypsum added to lime plaster to hasten its setting. 7 The composition of plaster of Paris and other substances used in making moldings, decorations, etc. 8 The diameter of the bore of a gun. 9 *Printing* A strip of metal or other material by which the exact space occupied by type of a certain kind, or the length of a page, or the width of a margin, is determined. 10 *Naut.* a The position of a vessel with regard to the wind and to another vessel. When to windward of another vessel, a ship is said to have the *weather gage;* when to leeward, the *lee gage.* b The draft of a vessel. 11 A measurement standard indicating relative fineness of hose, as determined by the number of needles used per inch. Also spelled *gauge.* [< OF *gauger* measure]

gage[2] (gāj) *v.t.* **gaged, gag·ing** *Archaic* 1 To bind or pledge as a guaranty or forfeit. 2 To wager; stake. —*n.* Something given or thrown down as security for some act, as a gauntlet in token of readiness for combat; a pledge. See synonyms under SECURITY. [< OF *gager* < *gage* a pledge < Gmc. Doublet of WAGE.]

gage[3] (gāj) *n.* One of several varieties of plum, as the *greengage.* [after Sir William *Gage*, 1777–1864, who introduced it into England]

Gage (gāj), **Thomas**, 1721–87, British general and administrator; commanded the British army at Bunker Hill in the Revolutionary War.

gage d'a·mour (gäzh dä·mōōr') *French* Pledge of love.

gag·er (gā'jər) *n.* 1 One who gages. 2 An officer of the revenue service who measures the contents of casks, etc. Also spelled *gauger.*

gag·ger (gag'ər) *n.* 1 One who gags. 2 A piece of iron used to keep a core in its place in a mold.

gag·gle (gag'əl) *v.i.* **gag·gled, gag·gling** To utter the cackle of the goose; gabble. —*n.* 1 A flock of geese. 2 A group, as of talkative women. 3 A cackle. [Imit.]

gag·man (gag'man') *n. pl.* **·men** (-men') A professional humorist; one employed to write humorous lines and sketches for stage, screen, radio, etc.

gag rule A rule of parliamentary procedure limiting speech or discussion; especially, a rule adopted by the U.S. Congress in 1836 tabling all matters relating to slavery.

gahn·ite (gän'īt) *n.* A zinc aluminate, sub-

translucent to opaque and varying in color from green to black and brown, crystallizing in the isometric system. [after J. G. *Gahn,* 1745–1818, Swedish chemist]

Gai·a (gā′ə, gī′ə) See GAEA.

gai·e·ty (gā′ə·tē) *n. pl.* **·ties 1** The state of being gay; merriment; fun: often used in the plural. **2** Gay appearance; finery; show: *gaiety* of attire. Also spelled *gayety.* See synonyms under FROLIC, HAPPINESS, SPORT. [< F *gaieté* < *gai.* See GAY.]

Gaik·war (gīk′wär) See GAEKWAR.

Gail·lard Cut (gā′lärd, gil·yärd′) A passage about 10 miles from the city of Panama, made in constructing the Panama Canal; 8 miles long, 300 feet wide at the bottom, 45 feet deep: formerly *Culebra Cut.* [after David DuB. *Gaillard,* 1859–1913, American army engineer]

gail·lar·di·a (gā·lär′dē·ə) *n.* Any plant of a genus *(Gaillardia)* of western American herbs of the composite family with alternate resinous dotted leaves and large shiny terminal heads of fragrant yellow or reddish-purple flowers. [after *Gaillard* de Charentonneau, French botanist]

gai·ly (gā′lē) *adv.* In a gay manner; joyously; merrily; showily: also spelled *gayly.*

gain[1] (gān) *v.t.* **1** To obtain by or as by effort; earn. **2** To get in competition; win. **3** To reach; arrive at. **4** To get or undergo as an increase, profit, addition, etc.: to *gain* interest or weight. **5** To get the friendship or support of; win over. —*v.i.* **6** To make progress; increase; improve. **7** To draw nearer or farther away: He *gained* on me steadily. —*n.* **1** That which is obtained as an advantage; a desired acquisition; commercial profit. **2** Amount of increase; accession. **3** The pursuit or the acquisition of riches. **4** *Electronics* The ratio of output to input in a sound-transmitting circuit. See synonyms under PROFIT. [< F *gagner* < OF *gaaignier* < Gmc.]

Synonyms (verb): achieve, acquire, attain, conquer, earn, flourish, get, learn, master, obtain, procure, realize, reap, win. See ACHIEVE, FLOURISH, GET, OBTAIN, REACH. *Antonyms*: forfeit, lose, miss, surrender.

gain[2] (gān) *n.* **1** A groove across a board or plank; a cut to receive a timber, as a girder. **2** A beveled shoulder in a binding joist. —*v.t.* To fasten with notches or gains, or cut gains in, as floor timbers. [Origin uncertain]

gain·er (gā′nər) *n.* **1** One who gains profit or advantage for himself. **2** A fancy dive, consisting of a back somersault from a front-diving take-off.

gain·ful (gān′fəl) *adj.* Yielding profit; lucrative. **—gain′ful·ly** *adv.* **—gain′ful·ness** *n.*

gain·giv·ing (gān′giv′ing) *n. Obs.* Uncertainty of mind; misgiving.

gain·less (gān′lis) *adj.* Profitless. **—gain′·less·ness** *n.*

gain·ly (gān′lē) *adj. Obs.* **1** Well built; comely; graceful. **2** Convenient. [< obs. *gain* fit, favorable (< ON *gegn*) + -LY] **—gain′li·ness** *n.*

gain·say (gān′sā′) *v.t.* **gain·said, gain·say·ing 1** To deny. **2** To contradict; controvert. **3** To speak or act against; oppose. —*n. Rare* A contradiction. [OE *gegn-* against + SAY[2]] **—gain′say′er** *n.*

Gains·bor·ough (gānz′bûr·ō), **Thomas,** 1727–1788, English painter.

'gainst (genst) *prep.* Against: an abbreviated form.

gair (gâr) *n. Scot.* A gore, as in a field. See GORE[2] (def. 1).

gair·ish (gâr′ish), **gair·ish·ly,** etc. See GARISH, etc.

gaist (gāst) *n. Scot.* A ghost.

gait (gāt) *n.* **1** The manner of walking or stepping; carriage of the body in going; walk. **2** The movement of a horse's feet in going, as the canter, pace, trot, run, single-foot, etc. —*v.t.* **1** To train to or cause to take a particular gait: to *gait* a horse. **2** To put in working order; set up: to *gait* a loom. ◆ Homophone: *gate.* [< ON *gata* way]

gait·ed (gā′tid) *adj.* Having a (particular) gait.

gai·ter (gā′tər) *n.* **1** A covering for the lower leg or ankle, fastened at the side and usually strapped under the foot. **2** A shoe covering the ankle and having no opening in front and usually elastic sides. **3** An overshoe with a cloth top. [< F *guêtre*]

gaiting pole A device for keeping a horse straight in the shafts of a racing sulky; a pole on which a roller is mounted which rubs against the horse when he swerves.

Ga·ius (gā′əs, gī′-) A Roman praenomen: also *Caius.*

—Gaius Roman jurist of the second century A.D.

gal (gal) *n. U.S. Colloq.* A girl.

ga·la (gā′lə, gal′ə, gä′lə) *n.* A festivity; show. —*adj.* Festive; appropriate for a festive occasion. [< F < Ital., holiday dress]

ga·lac·ta·gog (gə·lak′tə·gôg, -gog) *adj.* Promotive of the flow of milk. —*n.* Any medicine promoting the secretion of milk. Also **ga·lac′·ta·gogue, ga·lac′to·gogue.** [< GALACT(O)- + Gk. *agōgos* producing]

ga·lac·tan (gə·lak′tən) *n. Biochem.* A polymeric anhydride of galactose, found in gums, algae, lichens, agar, and in fruit pectins. [< GALACT(O)- + AN(HYDRIDE)]

ga·lac·tic (gə·lak′tik) *adj. Astron.* Pertaining to the Galaxy or Milky Way.

galactic circle *Astron.* The great circle passing centrally along the Milky Way.

galactic latitude *Astron.* The angular distance of a celestial body from the galactic plane.

galactic plane The plane of the galactic circle.

galactic poles The poles of the galactic circle.

galacto- *combining form* Milk; milky: *galactopoietic.* Also, before vowels, **galact-.** [< Gk. *gala, galaktos* milk]

ga·lac·to·cele (gə·lak′tə·sēl) *n. Pathol.* A tumor of the female breast caused by blockage of a milk duct.

ga·lac·to·lip·in (gə·lak′tō·lip′in) See CEREBROSIDE.

gal·ac·tom·e·ter (gal′ək·tom′ə·tər) *n.* A lactometer.

ga·lac·to·poi·et·ic (gə·lak′tō·poi·et′ik) *adj.* Promoting the secretion of milk. [< GALACTO- + Gk. *poiētikos* capable of making]

ga·lac·to·scope (gə·lak′tə·skōp) *n.* An instrument for testing milk for butterfat content.

ga·lac·tose (gə·lak′tōs) *n. Chem.* A sweet crystalline glucose, $C_6H_{12}O_6$, the dextrorotatory form of which is obtained when milk sugar is treated with dilute acids.

ga·lac·to·se·mi·a (gə·lak′tə·sē′mē·ə) *n. Pathol.* A metabolic disease in which the body is unable to tolerate milk in any form because of the lack of an enzyme which converts galactose into glucose: often fatal in newborn children. [< GALACTOSE + -EMIA]

ga·lac·to·ther·a·py (gə·lak′tō·ther′ə·pē) *n.* Treatment of disease by means of milk.

gala day A holiday; festival.

gala dress Gay costume for gala days.

ga·la·go (gə·lā′gō) *n. pl.* **-gos** Bush baby.

Gal·a·had (gal′ə·had), **Sir** In Arthurian romance, the purest and noblest knight of the Round Table, son of Lancelot and Elaine.

gal·a·lith (gal′ə·lith) *n.* A hard, thermoplastic casein plastic, available in colors, used to make buttons, clips, etc., and for trimming apparel and accessories. Also called *milkstone.* [< Gk. *gala* milk + *lithos* stone]

ga·lan·gal (gə·lang′gəl) *n.* The aromatic rootstocks of various East Indian herbs (genus *Alpinia)* of the ginger family: also spelled *galingale.* [< OF *galingal* < Arabic *khalanjān* < Chinese *Ko-liang-kiang* mild ginger from the province Ko]

gal·an·tine (gal′ən·tēn) *n.* A cold preparation of boned, stuffed, and seasoned chicken, veal, etc., served in its own jelly. [< F]

ga·lan·ty show (gə·lan′tē) A shadow pantomime in miniature, the shadows being cast by figures cut from paper. [Prob. < Ital. *galante* gallant]

Ga·lá·pa·gos Islands (gä·lä′pä·gōs) An Ecuadorian island group 600 miles west of Ecuador; 3,028 square miles: officially *Colón Archipelago.*

Gal·a·ta (gä′lä·tä) A commercial section of Istanbul on the north side of the Golden Horn; originally a Genoese settlement.

gal·a·te·a (gal′ə·tē′ə) *n.* A strong twill cotton fabric, white or striped, used in making women's and children's garments. [after the *Galatea,* a British warship]

Gal·a·te·a (gal′ə·tē′ə) In Greek mythology, an ivory statue of a maiden brought to life by Aphrodite after its sculptor Pygmalion had fallen in love with it.

Ga·la·ti (gä·läts′, -lä′tsē) A city in eastern Rumania on the Danube. Also **Ga·latz′.**

Ga·la·tia (gə·lā′shə, -shē·ə) An ancient country of central Asia Minor, so called from the Gauls who invaded and conquered the region in the third century B.C. *Greek* **Ga·la′tei·a.**

Ga·la·tian (gə·lā′shən) *adj.* Belonging or relating to the ancient Galatia: also **Ga·lat·ic** (gə·lat′ik) —*n.* A native of ancient Galatia. *Gal.* iii 1. **—Epistle to the Galatians** A letter written by the apostle Paul, about A.D. 56, to the Christians of Galatia, and included in the New Testament.

gal·a·vant (gal′ə·vant) See GALLIVANT.

ga·lax (gā′laks) *n.* A stemless evergreen herb *(Galax aphylla)* bearing a raceme of white flowers; its leaves are much used for funeral decoration. [< NL < Gk. *gala* milk]

gal·ax·y (gal′ək·sē) *n. pl.* **·ax·ies 1** *Astron.* Any of the very large systems of stars, nebulae, and other celestial bodies, comparable with but assumed to be independent of our own; an island universe. **2** Any brilliant group, as of persons. [< F *galaxie* < L *galaxias* the Milky Way < Gk. < *gala* milk]

Gal·ax·y (gal′ək·sē) *n. Astron.* The aggregate of all celestial bodies in the universe to which the sun belongs, including the luminous band of stars known as the Milky Way.

Gal·ba (gal′bə, gôl′-), **Servius Sulpicius,** 3 B.C.–A.D. 69, Roman emperor 68–69; killed by his soldiers.

gal·ba·num (gal′bə·nəm) *n.* A bitter and odorous gum resin obtained from certain umbelliferous herbs, especially the giant fennel: used as a stimulant, expectorant, and anti-spasmodic. [< L *galbanum* < Gk. *chalbanē* < Hebrew *helbenah*]

gale[1] (gāl) *n.* **1** A strong wind less violent than a hurricane, but stronger than a stiff breeze (7–10 on the Beaufort scale). **2** In poetic usage, a breeze; zephyr. **3** Figuratively, a noisy outburst: *gales* of merriment. [Origin uncertain]

gale[2] (gāl) *n.* A branching, sweet-smelling marsh shrub (*Myrica gala*) of the eastern United States. See SWEETGALE. [OE *gagel*]

gale[3] (gāl) *n. Brit.* A payment, at certain stated intervals, such as rent, interest, etc. [Var. of GAVEL[3]]

Gale (gāl), **Zona,** 1874–1938, U.S. novelist and playwright.

ga·le·a (gā′lē·ə) *n. pl.* **·le·ae** (-li·ē) **1** *Entomol.* A helmetlike membrane attached to the maxillae of certain insects. **2** *Bot.* The upper sepal of the flower of monkshood. **3** *Anat.* A structure connecting the separate parts of one of the muscles of the scalp. **4** *Med.* A type of bandage for the head. [< L, helmet]

ga·le·ate (gā′lē·āt) *adj.* Covered with, wearing, or having a galea. Also **ga′le·at′ed.**

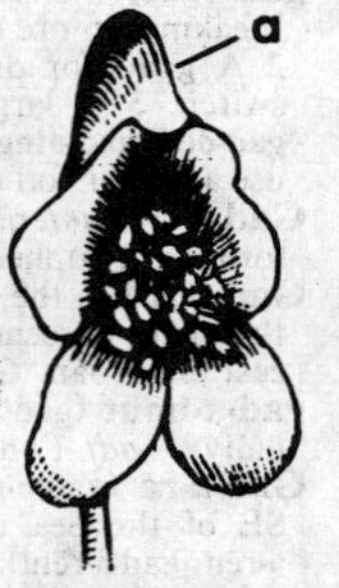

GALEATE SEPAL
A monkshood flower showing galeate upper sepal *(a).*

ga·le·i·form (gā′lē·ə·fôrm) *adj.* Helmet-shaped; resembling a casque or helm. [< L *galea* helmet + *-i-* + -FORM]

Ga·len (gā′lən), **Claudius,** 130?–200?, Greek physician and writer on medicine. **—Ga·len·ic** (ga·len′ik, -lē′·nik) or **·i·cal** *adj.*

ga·le·na (gə·lē′nə) *n.* A metallic, lead-gray, cleavable, isometric lead sulfide, PbS: an important ore of lead; lead glance. Also **ga·le·nite** (gə·lē′nīt). [< L, lead ore]

ga·len·i·cal (gə·len′i·kəl, -lē′·ni-) *n.* **1** A medicine or drug prepared in accordance with the principles of Galen. **2** A drug containing a standard proportion of naturally occurring organic substances as distinguished from chemical ingredients.

Ga·len·ism (gā′lən·iz′əm) *n.* The theory or practice of medicine followed by Galen. **—Ga′len·ist** *n.*

ga·le·o·pi·the·cus (gā′lē·ō·pi·thē′kəs) *n.* Any member of a genus *(Galeopithecus,* family *Galeopithecidae)* of insectivorous mammals, as the flying lemur. [< Gk. *galeē* weasel + *pithēkos* ape]

Ga·ler·as Volcano (gä·ler′äs) See PASTO VOLCANO.

gal·er·o·pi·a (gal′ə·rō′pē·ə) *n.* Abnormally clear vision and perception of objects. Also **gal′er·op′si·a** (-op′sē·ə) [< Gk. *galeros* cheerful + *ōps* eye]

Ga·li·bi (gä·lē'bē) *n.* A Carib Indian, especially of the tribes in the Guianas.

Ga·li·cia (gə·lish'ə) **1** (*Polish* gä·lē'tsē·ä) A region in SE Poland and NW Ukrainian S.S.R., formerly an Austrian crownland. **2** (*Sp.* gä·lē'thyä) A region and former kingdom in NW Spain.

Ga·li·cian (gə·lish'ən) *adj.* **1** Of or pertaining to Spanish Galicia, its people, or their language. **2** Of or pertaining to Polish Galicia or its native people. — *n.* **1** A native or inhabitant of Spanish Galicia. **2** The Portuguese dialect spoken in Spanish Galicia. **3** A native of Polish Galicia.

Gal·i·le·an (gal'ə·lē'ən) *adj.* Belonging or relating to Galilee. — *n.* **1** A native or inhabitant of Galilee. **2** A Christian: so called opprobriously in ancient times by the Jews. — **The Galilean** Jesus Christ. Also **Gal'i·lae'an.**

Gal·i·le·an (gal'ə·lē'ən) *adj.* Of or pertaining to Galileo.

Gal·i·lee (gal'ə·lē) A region in northern Palestine.

Galilee, Sea of A fresh-water lake in northern Palestine on the Israel-Jordan border, through which the river Jordan flows: Old Testament *Sea of Chinnereth*; New Testament *Sea of Gennesaret*: also *Lake Tiberias*.

Galilee porch A porch or chapel at the west end of some abbey churches. Also **Gal'i·lee.**

Gal·i·le·o (gal'ə·lē'ō), 1564–1642, Italian astronomer and founder of the science of mechanics; condemned by the Roman Inquisition: full name **Galileo Galilei.**

gal·i·ma·ti·as (gal'ə·mā'shē·əs, -mat'ē·əs) *n.* Confused or meaningless talk; gibberish. [<F]

gal·in·gale (gal'in·gāl) *n.* **1** A tall, perennial, and rare sedge (*Cyperus longus*) of southern England, with aromatic tuberous roots. **2** Galangal. [See GALANGAL]

gal·i·ot (gal'ē·ət) *n.* **1** A small galley propelled by sails and oars. **2** A one- or two-masted Dutch or Flemish merchant vessel. Also spelled *galliot.* [<OF, dim. of *galie* <Med.L *galea* a galley]

gal·i·pe·a (gal'ə·pē'ə) *n.* A tropical American shrub (*Galipea officinalis*) of the rutaceous family which yields angostura bark. [<NL]

gal·i·pot (gal'i·pot) *n.* The white turpentine resin formed on the bark of a pine (*Pinus pinaster*) of southern Europe: when refined it is called *white, yellow,* or *Burgundy pitch*: also spelled *gallipot.* [<F]

gall¹ (gôl) *n.* **1** *Physiol.* The bitter fluid secreted by the liver; bile. **2** Bitter feeling; malignity. **3** Any bitter and trying experience. **4** *Anat.* The sac containing the bile: also *gall bladder.* **5** *U.S. Slang* Cool impudence; effrontery. [OE *gealla*]

gall² (gôl) *n.* **1** An abrasion or excoriation, as by the friction of harness on a horse. **2** *Brit.* A blemish. **3** A locality made barren by exhaustion of the soil. **4** *U.S. Dial.* Low-lying wet land. **5** A person or thing that irritates or galls. — *v.t.* **1** To make sore or injure (the skin) by friction; chafe. **2** To vex or irritate. — *v.i.* **3** To be or become chafed or irritated. See synonyms under INCENSE. [Prob. <GALL¹]

gall³ (gôl) *n.* **1** An excrescence on plants, caused by insects, bacteria, or a parasitic fungus. The galls of commerce are produced by a gallfly which lays its eggs in the soft twigs of an oak (*Quercus lusitanica*) of western Asia and southern Europe. Galls contain tannin, and are used in inkmaking, dyeing, etc. **2** A similar excrescence on animals. [<F *galle* <L *galla* the gallnut]

Gal·la (gal'ə) *n.* **1** A member of a tribe of Hamitic origin inhabiting Ethiopia. **2** The language of this tribe.

gal·lant (gal'ənt) *adj.* **1** Possessing an intrepid spirit; brave; chivalrous. **2** Stately; imposing; noble. **3** Marked by showiness; gay: said chiefly of attire. **4** (gə·lant', gal'ənt) Polite and attentive to women; courteous. See synonyms under BRAVE. — *n.* (gal'ənt, gə·lant') **1** A man of gay and dashing manners; an intrepid youth. **2** A man who pays court to women; also, a man of fashion. — *v.t.* (gə·lant') **1** To accompany (a woman); escort. **2** To court or dally with (a woman). — *v.i.*

3 To play the gallant. [<OF *galant,* ppr. of *galer* rejoice]

gal·lant·ly (gal'ənt·lē) *adv.* Bravely; politely.

gal·lant·ry (gal'ən·trē) *n. pl.* **·ries** **1** Courage; heroism; chivalrousness. **2** Polite or excessive attention to women. **3** A gallant act or polite speech. **4** The calling or manner of a gallant. **5** Gallants collectively. See synonyms under COURAGE, PROWESS.

gall-ap·ple (gôl'ap'əl) *n.* A gallnut.

Gal·la·tin (gal'ə·tin), **Albert,** 1761–1849, U.S. statesman and financier born in Switzerland.

Gal·la·tin Range (gal'ə·tin) A range of the Rockies in NW Wyoming and SW Montana; highest peak, 11,155 feet.

Gal·lau·det (gal'ə·det'), **Thomas Hopkins,** 1787–1851, U.S. teacher of the deaf and dumb.

gall-ber·ry (gôl'ber'ē) *n. pl.* **·ries** The inkberry.

gall bladder *Anat.* A small, pear-shaped muscular pouch situated beneath the liver in man and serving as a reservoir for bile conducted through the **gall duct.**

Galle (gäl) A port of SW Ceylon: formerly *Point de Galle.*

Gal·le (gäl'ə), **Johann Gottfried,** 1812–1910, German astronomer; discoverer of Neptune, 1846.

gal·le·ass (gal'ē·as, -əs) *n.* A large galley of the 15th to 17th centuries, carrying three masts and heavily armed: used chiefly in the Mediterranean as a war vessel. [<F *galeace* <Ital. *galeazza,* aug. of *galea* <Med.L. See GALLEY.]

GALLEASS

Gal·le·gos Frei·re (gä·yā'gōs frā'rā), **Rómulo,** born 1884, Venezuelan novelist; president of Venezuela 1948.

gal·le·on (gal'ē·ən) *n.* A sailing vessel of the 15th to 17th centuries, usually armed and

GALLEON

having three or four decks; especially, the vessel used by Spain in trade with her Central American possessions. [<Sp. *galeón,* aug. of *galea* <Med.L. See GALLEY.]

gal·ler·y (gal'ər·ē) *n. pl.* **·ler·ies** **1** A long, narrow balcony or other passage having balustrades or rails and projecting from the inner or outer wall of a building. **2** *U.S.* In the South, a veranda. **3** A platform with seats which projects from the rear or side walls of a theater, legislative chamber, church, etc., out over the main floor; specifically, in a theater, the highest of such platforms, containing the cheapest seats. **4** The audience occupying the gallery seats; hence, the general public. **5** *Naut.* A balcony projecting from the after part of a ship's hull. **6** A long, narrow room or corridor. **7** A room or building used for the display of works of art. **8** A collection of works of art. **9** A room suggestive of a gallery, used for business purposes: a shooting *gallery*; a photographer's *gallery.* **10** *Mil. & Mining* A horizontal underground passage; a driftway. **11** An underground passage made by an animal. — *v.* **gal·ler·ied,** **gal·ler·y·ing** *v.t.* To furnish or adorn with a gallery or galleries. — *v.i. Mil.* To make an

underground passage. [<F *galerie* <Med.L *galeria,* ? alter. of *galilaea* a Galilee porch]

gal·let (gal'it) *n.* A small piece of stone; a chip. — *v.t.* To fill the joints of (a wall) with bits of stone. [<F *galet* a pebble]

gal·ley (gal'ē) *n. pl.* **·leys** **1** A long, low vessel used in ancient and medieval times, propelled by oars and sails or by oars alone. **2** A large rowboat. **3** The kitchen of a ship; also, the cookstove. **4** *Printing* **a** A long tray, for holding composed type. **b** A proof (**galley proof**) printed from such type. [< OF *galee* <Med.L *galea* <LGk. *galaia*]

galley slave **1** A slave who rowed in a galley. **2** Formerly, a convict sentenced to labor at the oar of a galley. **3** Hence, a drudge; hack.

galley west *adv. U.S. Colloq.* All askew: to knock *galley west.*

gall-fly (gôl'flī') *n. pl.* **·flies** **1** Any of various small hymenopterous insects (family *Cynipidae*), resembling wasps in appearance, whose larvae promote the growth of galls on plants. Also called *gall wasp.* **2** A gall midge.

Gal·li·a (gal'ē·ə) The Latin name for GAUL.

gal·liard (gal'yərd) *adj. Archaic* Full of gaiety; dashing; jaunty; spirited. — *n.* **1** A dance of brisk movement, popular in the 16th and 17th centuries. **2** The music for such a dance. [<OF *gaillard*]

gal·lic (gal'ik) *adj. Chem.* **1** Of, pertaining to, or derived from the element gallium. **2** Relating to or derived from gallnuts; specifically, designating a white, odorless, crystalline organic compound, **gallic acid,** $C_7H_6O_5 \cdot H_2O$, widely distributed in the vegetable kingdom and used in the making of inks, dyestuffs, paper, etc.

Gal·lic (gal'ik) *adj.* Of or pertaining to ancient Gaul or modern France. [<L *Gallicus* <*Gallus* inhabitant of Gaul]

Gal·li·can (gal'ə·kən) *adj.* Of or pertaining to Gaul or France, or especially to a former party in the Roman Catholic Church there. — *n.* A member of the Gallican party.

Gal·li·can·ism (gal'ə·kən·iz'əm) *n.* The doctrine of the national party in the Roman Catholic Church of France, adopted March 19, 1682, limiting the papal power and extending that of the national church: opposed to *Ultramontanism.*

Gal·li·cism (gal'ə·siz'əm) *n.* A French idiom, as used in any other language.

Gal·li·cize (gal'ə·sīz) *v.t. & v.i.* **·cized,** **·ciz·ing** To make or become French in character, language, etc.; Frenchify.

Gal·li-Cur·ci (gäl'lē·koor'chē), **Amelita,** 1889–1963, Italian coloratura soprano active in the United States.

Gal·lié·ni (gà·lyā·nē'), **Joseph,** 1849–1916, French general in World War I.

gal·li·fi·ca·tion (gal'ə·fi·kā'shən) *n.* The production of galls.

gal·li·gas·kins (gal'i·gas'kinz) *n. pl.* **1** Long loose hose, worn in the 16th century. **2** Loose breeches. **3** A sportsman's leather leggings. [Alter. of MF *garguesque,* var. of *greguesque* <Ital. *grechesca,* fem. of *grechesco* Greek]

gal·li·mau·fry (gal'i·mô'frē) *n. pl.* **·fries** **1** A hash or hodgepodge. **2** A confused jumble or medley of any kind. [<F *gallimafrée*; ult. origin unknown]

gal·li·na·cean (gal'ə·nā'shən) *n.* A gallinaceous bird.

gal·li·na·ceous (gal'ə·nā'shəs) *adj.* Of or pertaining to an order of birds (*Galliformes*), including the common hen, turkeys, partridges, etc. [<L *gallinaceus* <*gallina* a hen]

Gal·li·nas Point (gä·yē'näs) A cape in northern Colombia; the northernmost point of South America. Spanish **Punta Gallinas.**

gal·li·na·zo (gal'i·nä'zō) *n. pl.* **·zos** or **·zoes** **1** A turkey buzzard. **2** A tropical carrion crow. [<Sp. *gallinaza* vulture, aug. of *gallina* a hen]

gall·ing (gô'ling) *adj.* Chafing and rendering sore; hence, irritating; harrowing: *galling* bondage. — **gall'ing·ly** *adv.*

gal·li·nip·per (gal'ə·nip'ər) *n.* A large mosquito; a cranefly. [Origin uncertain]

gal·li·nule (gal'ə·nyōōl, -nōōl) *n.* Any of several cootlike birds allied to the rails; especially, the **Florida gallinule** (*Gallinula chloropus*). [<NL *gallinula,* dim. of *gallina* a hen]

Gal·li·o (gal'ē·ō) A Roman proconsul in

Achaia in the first century. *Acts* xviii 17. —**care-less Gallio** An indifferent or careless person.

gal·li·ot (gal'ē·ət) See GALIOT.

Gal·lip·o·li (gə·lip'ə·lē) A port on **Gallipoli Peninsula** in European Turkey, between the Gulf of Saros and the Dardanelles. Turkish *Gelibolu*.

gal·li·pot[1] (gal'i·pot) *n.* A small earthen jar as for ointments, jam, etc., especially as used by apothecaries. [< GALLEY + POT, because orig. imported on galleys]

gal·li·pot[2] (gal'i·pot) See GALIPOT.

gal·li·um (gal'ē·əm) *n.* A rare metallic element (symbol Ga, atomic number 31) having a low melting point. See PERIODIC TABLE. [< NL < L *gallus* a cock, trans. of *Lecoq* de Boisbaudran, 1838–1912, its discoverer]

gal·li·vant (gal'ə·vant, gal'ə·vant') *v.i.* To go about, especially with members of the opposite sex, in search of fun and pleasure; gad: also spelled *galavant, galivant*. [? Alter. of GALLANT]

gal·li·vat (gal'ə·vat) *n.* A large boat propelled by oars and a large, triangular sail: formerly used by Malay pirates. [Ult. < Pg. *galeota* a galley]

gal·li·wasp (gal'i·wosp', -wôsp') *n.* **1** A lizard (genus *Diploglossus*) of Jamaica, greatly feared, but harmless. **2** A lizard fish. Also spelled *gallywasp*. [Appar. < GALLEY + WASP; orig. an insect which infested West Indian ships]

gall midge Any of various small, slender, hairy gnats (family *Cecidomyiidae*) whose larvae produce galls on plants, especially on those of the composite and willow families. Also **gall'fly', gall gnat.** For illustration see INSECT (injurious).

gall·nut (gôl'nut') *n.* The gall of any gall-bearing oak: a source of tannic acid. Also **gall'-ap'ple.**

Gallo- *combining form* French; pertaining to the French or to France: *Gallomania.* [< L *Gallus* a Gaul]

gal·lo·bro·mal (gal'ō·brō'məl) *n. Chem.* An organic compound, $C_7H_4O_3Br_3$, obtained by treating bromine with gallic acid: used in medicine as a sedative and hypnotic.

Gal·lo·ma·ni·a (gal'ə·mā'nē·ə, -mān'yə) *n.* A craze for imitating French manners, fashions, etc. —**Gal'lo·ma'ni·ac** (-ak) *n.*

gal·lon (gal'ən) *n.* **1** An English and American liquid measure of various capacities: the **Winchester** or **wine gallon,** containing 231 cubic inches or four quarts, or 3.78 liters, which is the common standard of the United States; the **imperial gallon** of Great Britain of 277.42 cubic inches, or 4.5459 liters. **2** *Brit.* A dry measure; one eighth of a bushel. [< OF *galon*, ? < Celtic]

gal·lon·age (gal'ən·ij) *n.* Quantity or capacity reckoned in gallons.

gal·loon (gə·lōōn') *n.* A narrow braid, tape, or trimming of worsted, silk, or rayon, sometimes of gold or silver thread. [< OF *galon* < *galonner* adorn with ribbons] —**gal·looned', ga·looned'** *adj.*

gal·loot (gə·lōōt') See GALOOT.

gal·lop (gal'əp) *n.* **1** A gait of a quadruped characterized by a regular succession of leaps, in which the foot sequence is left hind, right hind, left fore, right fore, in repeating sequence. **2** The act of riding, or a ride at a gallop. **3** Speedy and careless action. —*v.i.* **1** To ride at a gallop. **2** To go, run, or move very fast or at a gallop. —*v.t.* **3** To cause to run at a gallop. [< OF *galop* < *galoper* < Gmc. Doublet of WALLOP.] —**gal'lop·er** *n.*

gal·lo·pade (gal'ə·pād') *n.* **1** A sidewise gallop, or curveting motion. **2** A brisk dance, or the music for it.

gal·lous (gal'əs) *adj. Chem.* Designating a compound containing bivalent gallium: *gallous* bromide.

Gal·lo·way (gal'ə·wā) A district of SW Scotland comprising the counties of Wigtownshire and Kirkcudbrightshire.

Gal·lo·way (gal'ə·wā) *n.* **1** A small horse, originally from Galloway, Scotland, now nearly or quite extinct. **2** A breed of dark cattle from Galloway, Scotland.

gall·low·glass (gal'ō·glas', -gläs') *n.* In ancient Ireland, an armed retainer of a chief. Also **gall'lo·glass'.** [< Irish *galloglach* < *gall* stranger + *ōglach* soldier]

---

gal·lows (gal'ōz) *n. pl.* **·lows·es** or **·lows 1** A framework consisting of two or more uprights supporting a crossbeam, used for hanging criminals. **2** *Naut.* A similar structure used to support spars on a vessel, or for other purposes: also called *gallows bitts.* [OE *galga*]

gal·lows-bird (gal'-ōz·bûrd') *n.* One who either has been hanged or deserves hanging.

gal·lows-tree (gal'-ōz·trē') *n.* A gallows.

gall·stone (gôl'stōn') *n. Pathol.* A solid substance found in the gall bladder, liver, etc.; biliary calculus.

Gal·lup poll (gal'əp) A sampling or cross-section of public opinion on given subjects, as conducted by George Horace *Gallup*, born 1901, U.S. statistician.

gal·lus·es (gal'əs·əs) *n. pl. U.S. Dial.* Suspenders for trousers. [< GALLOWS]

gall wasp A gallfly.

gal·ly·gas·kins (gal'i·gas'kinz) See GALLIGASKINS.

ga·loot (gə·lōōt') *n. U.S. Slang* An awkward or uncouth fellow: often used as a term of good-natured depreciation: also spelled *galloot.* [Cf. Du. *gelubt* castrated]

gal·op (gal'əp) *n.* **1** A lively dance in double measure. **2** The music for it. Also **gal·o·pade** (gal'ə·pād'). [< F, gallop]

ga·lore (gə·lôr', -lōr') *adj.* Very many; abundant: used after its noun. —*n. Obs.* Abundance. —*adv.* In abundance. [< Irish *go leór*, enough]

ga·losh (gə·losh') *n.* **1** *Usually pl.* An overshoe reaching above the ankle and worn in stormy weather. **2** *Obs.* A heavy wooden shoe; a clog or patten; hence, any boot or shoe. Also spelled *golosh.* Also **ga·loshe'.** [< F *galoche*, ult. < Gk. *kalopous* wooden shoe]

Gals·wor·thy (gôlz'wûr·thē), **John,** 1867–1933, English novelist and playwright.

Gal·ton (gôl'tən), **Sir Francis,** 1822–1911, English scientist and anthropologist; introduced fingerprint identification in England and established the science of biometrics for the study of heredity. —**Gal·to·ni·an** (gôl·tō'nē·ən) *adj.*

ga·lu·chat (gà·lü·shä') *n.* **1** Ornamental sharkskin leather, tanned without removal of pebbly surface. **2** A type of sharkskin fabric. [< F]

Gal·va·ni (gäl·vä'nē), **Luigi,** 1737–98, Italian physiologist.

gal·van·ic (gal·van'ik) *adj.* **1** Pertaining to galvanism. **2** Resembling the movement of a limb of a dead animal subjected to an electric current; spasmodic. Also **gal·van'i·cal.** —**gal·van'i·cal·ly** *adv.*

galvanic battery A battery of primary cells.

galvanic pile A voltaic pile.

gal·va·nism (gal'və·niz'əm) *n.* **1** A flow of electricity as produced by chemical action. **2** *Med.* The therapeutic application of a continuous electric current from voltaic cells. [after Luigi *Galvani* + -ISM] —**gal·va·nist** *n.*

gal·va·nize (gal'və·nīz) *v.t.* **·nized, ·niz·ing 1** To stimulate to muscular action by electricity. **2** To rouse to action; startle; excite. **3** To coat with metal by galvanic process; also, to coat iron with zinc. Also *Brit.* **gal'va·nise.** —**gal·va·ni·za'tion** *n.* —**gal'va·niz'er** *n.*

galvanized iron Iron coated with zinc, primarily by the electrolytic process.

galvano- *combining form* Galvanic; galvanism; produced by a galvanic current: *galvanometer.*

gal·va·no·cau·ter·y (gal'və·nō·kô'tər·ē) *n. pl.* **·ter·ies** *Med.* The operation or result of cauterizing by electricity.

gal·va·nom·e·ter (gal'və·nom'ə·tər) *n. Electr.* An apparatus for measuring current strength or potential difference. —**gal·va·no·met·ric** (gal'və·nō·met'rik, gal·van'ō-) or **·ri·cal** *adj.*

gal·va·nom·e·try (gal'və·nom'ə·trē) *n.* The science, art, or process of measuring electric currents.

---

gal·va·no·plas·ty (gal'və·nō·plas'tē, gal·van'ō-) *n.* The reproduction of the forms of objects by electrodeposition; electrotypy. Also **gal'va·no·plas'tics.** —**gal·va·no·plas'tic** *adj.*

gal·va·no·scope (gal'və·nō·skōp', gal·van'ə-) *n.* An instrument for detecting an electric current and showing its direction, differing from a galvanometer in being only qualitative. —**gal·va·no·scop·ic** (gal'və·nō·skop'ik, gal·van'ō-) *adj.*

gal·va·nos·co·py (gal'və·nos'kə·pē) *n.* **1** Use of the galvanoscope. **2** *Med.* Diagnosis by galvanism.

gal·va·no·sur·ger·y (gal'və·nō·sûr'jər·ē) *n.* Use of galvanic electricity in surgery.

gal·va·no·tax·is (gal'və·nō·tak'sis) *n.* Electrotaxis. Also **gal·va·not·ro·pism** (gal'və·not'rə·piz'əm).

gal·va·no·ther·my (gal'və·nō·thûr'mē) *n.* Production of heat by galvanism.

Gal·ves·ton (gal'vəs·tən) A port on the NE end of **Galveston Island** in **Galveston Bay,** an inlet of the Gulf of Mexico in SE Texas.

Galveston plan The commission plan of municipal government.

Gal·way (gôl'wā) A maritime county in western Ireland; 2,293 square miles; capital, Galway.

Galway Bay An inlet of the Atlantic Ocean between County Galway and County Clare, Ireland.

Gal·we·gian (gal·wē'jən) *adj.* Of or pertaining to the people or the district of Galloway, Scotland. —*n.* A native or inhabitant of this region.

gal·yak (gal'yak) *n.* A flat fur from the skin of a prematurely born kid or lamb. [< Russian *golyak* bare]

gam[1] (gam) *n.* **1** A herd or school of whales. **2** *U.S. Dial.* An exchange of visits between whaling vessels and crews. —*v.* **gammed, gam·ming** *v.i.* **1** *U.S. Dial.* To visit back and forth while at sea. **2** To come together in a gam: said of whales. —*v.t.* **3** *U.S. Dial.* To make a visit or visits to. [? Var. of GAME[1]]

gam[2] (gam) *n. Slang* A leg or calf, especially of a woman. [Var. of GAMB]

Ga·ma (gam'ə, *Pg.* gä'mə), **Vasco da,** 1469?–1524, Portuguese navigator; first to sail around Africa and to reach India (1498) by sea.

Ga·ma·li·el (gə·mā'lē·əl, -māl'yəl) A masculine personal name. [< Hebrew, reward of God] —**Gamaliel** A Pharisee; preceptor of the apostle Paul. *Acts* v 34; xxii 3.

ga·mash·es (gə·mash'əz, -mäsh'-) *n. pl. Brit. Dial.* Leggings, or high boots worn by horseback riders. [< F *gamache*]

gamb (gamb) *n.* **1** A leg; shank. **2** *Her.* The entire foreleg of a beast, especially of a lion. [< OF *gambe,* var. of *jambe.* See JAMB.]

gam·ba·do (gam·bā'dō) *n. pl.* **·dos** or **·does 1** A legging; gaiter. **2** *pl.* Bootlike leathers attached to a saddle, protecting the feet and serving as stirrups. **3** A curveting, prank, or flourish; antic. Also **gam·bade'** (-bād'). [< Ital. *gamba* leg]

gam·be·son (gam'bə·sən) *n.* A coat of medieval times, made of leather or of cloth stuffed and quilted, worn as armor. [< OF *gambison* < Gmc.]

Gam·bet·ta (gam·bet'ə, *Fr.* gän·be·tà'), **Léon Michel,** 1838–82, French statesman.

GAMBESON

Gam·bi·a (gam'bē·ə) An independent state in the Commonwealth of Nations, in western Africa; 4,000 square miles; capital, Bathurst; comprising an enclave along 300 miles of the lower course of the **Gambia River,** a river flowing 700 miles west from French Guinea to the Atlantic: *French* **Gam·bie** (gän·bē').

Gam·bier Islands (gam'bir) A part of French Oceania at the southern end of the Tuamotu group; 12 square miles; capital, Rikitea on Mangareva: also *Mangareva.*

gam·bir (gam'bir) *n.* Pale catechu, the dried

A TYPE OF GALLOWS

extract from the leaves and twigs of an Asian woody vine (*Uncaria gambir*): used as an astringent and tonic, and in tanning, dyeing, etc. Also **gam′bi·a** (-bē·ə), **gam′bier**. [<Malay]

gam·bit (gam′bit) *n.* One of various openings in chess, in which a pawn or piece is risked to obtain an attack. [<F <OF *gambet*, a tripping up, ult. <LL *gamba* a leg]

gam·ble (gam′bəl) *v.* **gam·bled**, **gam·bling** *v.i.* **1** To risk or bet something of value on the outcome of an event, a game of chance, etc. **2** To take a risk to obtain a desired result: He *gambled* on finding the window open. — *v.t.* **3** To wager or bet (something of value). **4** To lose or squander by gaming: usually with *away*. — *n.* *Colloq.* **1** Any risky or uncertain venture. **2** A gambling venture or transaction. ◆ Homophone: *gambol*. [Cf. ME *gamenen*, OE *gamenian* sport, play] — **gam′bling** *n.*

gam·bler (gam′blər) *n.* One who gambles.

gam·boge (gam·bōj′, -bōozh′) *n.* A brownish Oriental gum resin obtained from a tropical tree (*Garcinia hanburyi*), used as a pigment and cathartic. [<NL *gambogium*, from *Cambodia*, where found]

gam·bol (gam′bəl) *v.i.* **·boled** or **·bolled**, **·bol·ing** or **·bol·ling** To skip or leap about in play; frolic. See synonyms under FRISK, LEAP. — *n.* A skipping about in sport. See synonyms under FROLIC, SPORT. ◆ Homophone: *gamble*. [Earlier *gambald* <F *gambader* <*gambade* a spring, leap <Ital. *gambata* <*gamba* leg]

gam·brel (gam′brəl) *n.* **1** The hock of an animal. **2** A stick used for hanging meat. **3** *Archit.* A roof having its slope broken by an obtuse angle: also called **gambrel roof.** [<OF *gamberel*, dim. of *gambe* leg <LL *gamba* leg]

Gam·bri·nus (gam·brī′nəs), 1251-94, duke of Brabant, reputed to be the inventor of lager beer.

GAMBREL (*def. 3*)

game¹ (gām) *n.* **1** Any contest undertaken for recreation or prizes, played according to rules, and depending on strength, skill, or luck to win. **2** *pl.* Organized athletic contests. **3** Amusement: diversion; play. **4** Fun; sport. **5** A strategy; scheme; plan. **6** A proceeding conducted like a game: the *game* of diplomacy. **7** A set of equipment used in playing certain games, as backgammon or darts. **8** Success in a match: The *game* is ours. **9** The number of points required to win: *Game* is 100 points. **10** A definite portion of a match terminated by a victory or draw, as a *game* in bridge or tennis. **11** Manner or art of playing: He plays a poor *game*. **12** That which is hunted in a chase; prey. **13** Wild animals or birds, collectively, pursued or caught for sport or profit; also their flesh. **14** Any object of pursuit or attack: They were fair *game* for ridicule. **15** Pluck; spirit; intrepidity. **16** *Slang* A business; vocation; especially one involving risk: the advertising *game*. See synonyms under FROLIC. — *v.* **gamed**, **gam·ing** *v.i.* To gamble at cards, dice, etc., for money or other stakes. — *v.t.* To lose or squander by gambling: with *away*. — *adj.* **1** Of or pertaining to hunted wild animals or their flesh. **2** Plucky; spirited; intrepid. **3** Ready; willing. [OE *gamen*]

game² (gām) *adj. Colloq.* Lame or crooked: a *game* leg. [Origin uncertain]

game bird Any bird commonly hunted as game, as pheasant, wild duck, or partridge.

game·cock (gām′kok′) *n.* A rooster bred and trained for fighting. Also **game cock.**

game fowl 1 One of several breeds of fowl used in cockfighting. **2** Any bird hunted as game.

game·keep·er (gām′kē′pər) *n.* A person having the care of game, as in a preserve or park.

game laws Laws passed by Federal or State legislatures to protect wild game (animals, birds, fish) by setting the season and manner of capture and sale.

game·ly (gām′lē) *adv.* In a game manner; pluckily. Also **gam′i·ly.**

game·ness (gām′nis) *n.* Pluck; bravery; endurance.

game preserve A large tract of land set apart by law as a refuge and natural breeding ground for wild game.

games·man·ship (gāmz′mən·ship) *n.* The art of winning by the use of any and all means available while seeming to honor the recognized dictates of sportsmanship. [Coined by Stephen Potter, born 1900, English writer]

game·some (gām′səm) *adj.* Playful; sportive; gay; merry. — **game′some·ly** *adv.* — **game′some·ness** *n.*

game·ster (gām′stər) *n.* **1** A gambler. **2** *Obs.* A lewd, lecherous man or woman.

gam·e·tan·gi·um (gam′ə·tan′jē·əm) *n.* *pl.* **·gi·a** (-jē·ə) *Bot.* The plant cell or organ in which gametes are produced. [<GAMETE + Gk. *angeion* vessel]

gam·ete (gam′ēt, gə·mēt′) *n. Biol.* Either of two mature reproductive cells, an ovum or sperm, which in uniting produce a zygote. [<NL *gameta* <Gk. *gametē* wife, or *gametēs* husband] — **ga·met·ic** (gə·met′ik) *adj.* — **ga·met′i·cal·ly** *adv.*

gameto– *combining form* Gamete: *gametophore.* [<Gk. *gametēs* husband <*gamos* marriage]

gam·e·to·cyte (gə·mē′tə·sīt) *n. Biol.* A cell which produces gametes.

gam·e·tog·e·ny (gam′ə·toj′ə·nē) *n. Biol.* The formation of gametes. Also **gam·e·to·gen·e·sis** (gam′ə·tō·jen′ə·sis). — **gam·e·to·gen′ic** *adj.*

ga·me·to·phore (gə·mē′tə·fôr, -fōr) *n. Bot.* A modified branch or filament which bears reproductive organs or gametes, as in certain liverworts.

ga·me·to·phyte (gə·mē′tə·fīt) *n. Bot.* That phase or generation of a plant which produces the sexual organs: distinguished from the non-sexual form. — **gam·e·to·phyt·ic** (gam′ə·tō·fit′ik) *adj.*

gam·ic (gam′ik) *adj.* **1** Pertaining to or produced by the congress of the sexes; sexual. **2** *Biol.* Capable of development only after fecundation: *gamic* ova. [<Gk. *gamikos* <*gamos* marriage]

gam·in (gam′in, *Fr.* gà·man′) *n.* A neglected boy or girl of city streets; a street Arab. [<F]

gam·ing (gā′ming) *n.* The act or practice of gambling.

gaming table A table furnished with apparatus for gaming; especially, one in a **gaming house.**

gam·ma (gam′ə) *n.* **1** The third letter in the Greek alphabet (Γ, γ): corresponding to *g* (as in *go*). As a numeral it denotes 3. **2** *Physics* A unit of magnetic field intensity, equal to 10⁻⁵ gauss. **3** A unit of weight, equal to one thousandth of a milligram. **4** *Phot.* A number expressing the degree to which a negative has been developed as compared with the range of light values in the subject photographed. [<Gk.]

gam·ma·cism (gam′ə·siz′əm) *n.* Inability to utter such letters as *g, k*; baby talk.

gam·ma·di·on (gə·mā′dē·ən) *n.* **1** A cross made of four capital gammas; a swastika; a fylfot. **2** A Greek cross formed of four capital gammas all facing outward so that the ends of the arms of the cross are open. Also **gam·ma′tion** (-shən). [<LGk. <*gamma*, the letter G]

gamma globulin A globulin present in blood plasma which contains antibodies effective against certain pathogenic micro-organisms.

gamma rays *Physics* A type of emission from radioactive substances, consisting of electromagnetic radiation of great penetrating power and of wavelengths lying beyond the region of the shortest X-rays.

gamma test *Phot.* A test using a strip of film to determine the degree of density in a photographic image in comparison with the degree of illumination of the object photographed.

gam·mer (gam′ər) *n. Brit. Dial.* An old woman; grandmother: correlative of *gaffer.* [Alter. of GODMOTHER]

gam·mon¹ (gam′ən) *n.* In backgammon, a defeat in which the winner throws all his men before the loser throws off any. — *v.t.* To obtain a gammon over. [? ME *gamen* a game]

gam·mon² (gam′ən) *n. Brit. Colloq.* Deceitful nonsense or trickery. — *v.t.* To hoodwink by deceitful talk. — *v.i.* To talk deceitful nonsense. [Origin uncertain] — **gam′mon·er** *n.*

gam·mon³ (gam′ən) *n.* **1** A cured ham. **2** The bottom part of a flitch of bacon. — *v.t.* To cure by salting and smoking. [<OF *gambon* <*gambe* a leg <LL *gamba*]

gam·mon⁴ (gam′ən) *Naut. n.* Gammoning. — *v.t.* To make fast (the bowsprit) to the stem by means of gammoning. [Origin unknown]

gam·mon·ing (gam′ən·ing) *n. Naut.* The rope, chain, or iron lashing that fastens the bowsprit down to the stem of a vessel.

gamo– *combining form* **1** Sexually joined: *gamogenesis.* **2** Fused; united: *gamophyllous.* [<Gk. *gamos* marriage]

gam·o·gen·e·sis (gam′ə·jen′ə·sis) *n. Biol.* Sexual generation.

gam·o·ge·net·ic (gam′ə·jə·net′ik) *adj.* Of, pertaining to, or resulting from gamogenesis. — **gam′o·ge·net′i·cal·ly** *adv.*

gam·o·ma·ni·a (gam′ə·mā′nē·ə, -mān′yə) *n.* An excessive desire to marry.

gam·o·pet·al·ous (gam′ə·pet′əl·əs) *adj. Bot.* Pertaining to a division of dicotyledonous plants in which the flowers possess both calyx and corolla.

gam·o·phyl·lous (gam′ə·fil′əs) *adj. Bot.* Having cohering perianth leaves. [<GAMO– + Gk. *phyllon* leaf]

gam·o·sep·al·ous (gam′ə·sep′ə·ləs) *adj. Bot.* Having the sepals more or less united; monosepalous.

–gamous *combining form* Pertaining to marriage or union for reproduction: used in adjectives corresponding to nouns in *–gamy: polygamous.* [<Gk. *gamos* marriage + -OUS]

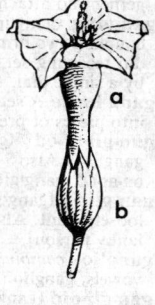

GAMOPETALOUS
Gamopetalous corolla (*a*) and gamosepalous calyx (*b*) of the flower of the tobacco plant.

gamp¹ (gamp) *n. Brit.* A large heavy umbrella: a humorous usage. [With ref. to one carried by Mrs. *Gamp*, a character in Dickens' *Martin Chuzzlewit*]

gamp² (gamp) *n.* A long piece of metal with a raised center, fitted to a sewing machine to produce a rounded tuck on fabric. [<F *guimpe.* See GUIMPE]

gam·ut (gam′ət) *n.* **1** *Music* The diatonic scale of musical notes. **2** The whole range of anything: the *gamut* of emotions. [<Med. L *gamma ut* <*gamma*, the first note of the early musical scale + *ut* (later, *do*); the names of the notes of the scale were taken from a medieval Latin hymn: *Ut* queant laxis *Resonare fibris, Mira* gestorum *Famuli* tuorum, *Solve* polluti *Labii* reatum, *Sancte Iohannes*]

gam·y (gā′mē) *adj.* **gam·i·er**, **gam·i·est 1** Having the flavor of game, especially game that has been kept raw until somewhat tainted, as preferred by gourmets. **2** Full of pluck; disposed to fight.

–gamy *combining form* Marriage or union for reproduction: used in anthropology, biology, and sociology: *polygamy.* [<Gk. *gamos* marriage]

gan (gan) *Archaic & Poetic* Began.

Gand (gän) The French name for GHENT.

Gan·dak (gun′duk) A river in Nepal and NW Bihar, India, flowing south 420 miles to the Ganges. Also **Great Gandak.**

gan·der (gan′dər) *n.* **1** A male goose. **2** A dunce. [OE *gandra*]

Gan·der (gan′dər) A town in eastern Newfoundland; site of transatlantic airport, a North American transit point for air services to Europe.

Gan·dhi (gän′dē, gan′-), **Mohandas Karamchand,** 1869-1948, Hindu nationalist leader: known as *Mahatma Gandhi.*

Gan·do (gän′dō) A former emirate including parts of Nigeria and French West Africa. Also **Gan′du** (-dō).

gan·dou·rah (gän·dōō′rä) *n.* A sleeveless garment resembling a shirt, worn by Arabs in the Near East. Also **gan·dou′ra.** [<Arabic *ghandūrah*]

gan·dy dancer (gan′dē) *U.S.* A railroad laborer. Also **gandy.**

Gan·dzha (gän′jä) A former name for KIROVABAD.

gane (gān) *Scot.* Gone.

ga·nef (gä′nəf) *n. Yiddish* A thief: also spelled *gonof, gonoph.* Also **ga′nof.**

gang[1] (gang) *n.* **1** A number of persons acting or operating together; a group; squad. **2** A group cooperating for evil purposes. **3** A set of tools or other objects of one kind operated together. **4** Gangue. See synonyms under CABAL. —*v.t.* **1** To unite into or as into a gang. **2** *Colloq.* To attack as a group. —*v.i.* **3** To come together as a gang; form a gang. **—to gang up on** *U.S. Slang* To attack or act against together: They *ganged up on* me. [OE *gang* a going < *gangan* go]

gang[2] (gang) *v.i. Scot.* To go.

gang·er (gang′ər) *n. Brit.* The foreman of a gang.

Gan·ges (gan′jēz) A river sacred to the Hindus in northern India and eastern Pakistan, flowing 1,560 miles from the Himalayas to the Bay of Bengal. *Sanskrit* and *Hindi* **Gan·ga** (gung′gä).

gang hook Two or three fish hooks, joined together and attached to one line.

gang·ing (gang′ing) *n. Electronics* A system of coupling two or more coils or condensers of a radio receiving set so that they may be controlled by a single dial.

gang knife A set of knives used to slice fish, etc., into pieces of predetermined length.

gan·gli·at·ed (gang′glē·ā′tid) *adj.* Possessing ganglia. Also **gan′gli·ate** (-it, -āt), **gan·gli·on·at·ed** (gang′glē·ən·ā′tid).

gan·gling (gang′gling) *adj.* Awkwardly tall and loosely built. Also **gan′gly.** [Cf. dial. E *gangrel* a lanky person]

ganglio- *combining form* Ganglion. Also, before vowels, **ganglion-,** as in *ganglionitis.*

gan·gli·oid (gang′glē·oid) *adj.* Resembling a ganglion.

gan·gli·on (gang′glē·ən) *n. pl.* **·gli·ons** or **·gli·a** (glē·ə) *Physiol.* **1** A collection of nerve cells, acting as a center of nervous influence. **2** Any center of energy, activity, or strength. **3** *Pathol.* A hard globular tumor proceeding from a tendon. [< LL < Gk. *ganglion* tumor] **—gan·gli·on·ic** (gang′glē·on′ik) *adj.*

gan·gli·on·ec·to·my (gang′glē·ən·ek′tə·mē) *n. Surg.* Removal of a ganglion.

gan·gli·on·i·tis (gang′glē·ən·ī′tis) *n. Pathol.* Inflammation of a ganglion.

gang·plank (gang′plangk′) *n.* A temporary bridge for passengers between a vessel and a wharf.

gang plow A set of plowshares arranged to work simultaneously.

gan·grel (gang′grəl, -rəl) *n. Scot.* **1** An awkward fellow. **2** A wanderer; vagrant. Also **gan′grell.**

gan·grene (gang′grēn, gang·grēn′) *n. Pathol.* Mortification or death of a part of the body, caused by failure or lack of an adequate blood supply; massive necrosis of the tissue. —*v.t.* & *v.i.* **gan·grened, gan·gren·ing** To cause gangrene in or become affected by gangrene. [< L *gangraena* < Gk. *gangraina*] **—gan′gre·nous** (-grə·nəs) *adj.*

gang saw An arrangement of circular saws geared to one shaft and used to perform several cutting operations simultaneously.

gang·ster (gang′stər) *n.* A member of a gang of toughs, gunmen, or the like. **—gang′ster·dom** *n.*

Gang·tok (gung′tok) The capital of Sikkim protectorate.

gangue (gang) *n. Mining* The non-metalliferous or worthless minerals found in a vein of ore. [< F < G *gang* vein of ore]

gang·way (gang′wā′) *n.* **1** A passageway through, into, or out of any enclosure; especially, a temporary passageway made of planks. **2** *Brit.* An aisle between rows of seats in the British House of Commons, separating members of the government or ex-ministers who are in opposition from the rank and file of their parties. **3** *Naut.* **a** Either side of the upper deck of a ship, from the mainmast to the quarter-deck. **b** An opening in a vessel's bulwarks to afford entrance for passengers or freight; also, a gangplank. **4** *Mining* The main level in a coal mine. **5** The gradient up which logs are conveyed into a sawmill: also called *logway.* —*interj.* Get out of the way! Stand aside! [OE *gangweg*]

gan·is·ter (gan′is·tər) *n.* **1** A very siliceous claystone of the lower coal measures of England, used chiefly for flagging and refractory furnace linings. **2** A mixture of ground quartz and fire clay used in lining Bessemer converters. Also **gan′nis·ter.** [< dial. G *ganster* < MHG, a spark]

gan·net (gan′it) *n.* **1** Any of several large sea birds (family *Sulidae*) related to the pelicans. The common gannet *(Moris bassana)* of the North Atlantic coasts is of a prevailing white color with blackish feet. **2** The wood ibis of Florida. [OE *ganot*]

gan·oid (gan′oid) *adj.* **1** Pertaining to a subclass *(Ganoidei)* of teleost fishes having scales consisting of laminated bone covered with a shiny enamel surface, as sturgeons, bowfins, etc. —*n.* A ganoid fish. [< Gk. *ganos* brightness + -OID]

gant·let[1] (gônt′lit, gant′-) *n.* **1** A punishment wherein the victim runs between two rows of men who strike him with clubs or switches as he passes. **2** A series of risks or unpleasant events. **3** A narrowing of two lines of railway track almost into the space of one, as on a bridge or in a tunnel, without breaking the continuity of either track. **—to run the gantlet** To be exposed to a series of hostile attacks or unpleasant incidents. —*v.t.* To form a gantlet by running together (railway tracks). Also spelled *gauntlet.* [Earlier *gantlope,* alter. of Sw. *gatlopp* a running down a lane]

gant·let[2] (gônt′lit, gant′-) See GAUNTLET[1].

gant·line (gant′līn′) *n. Naut.* A rope rove through a block at the masthead of a vessel for temporary use. [Alter. of *girtline.* See GIRT, LINE]

gan·try (gan′trē) *n. pl.* **·tries** **1** The frame of a traveling crane, or the crane and frame together. **2** A framework for supporting railway signals usually bridging the tracks. **3** A frame to hold a barrel horizontally. Also spelled *gauntry, gauntree.* [Alter. of OF *gantier, chantier* < L *canterius* beast of burden, framework < Gk. *kanthēlios* pack ass]

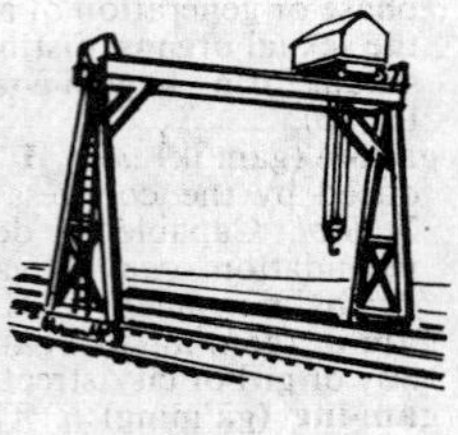

GANTRY *(def. 1)*

Gan·y·mede (gan′ə·mēd) **1** In Greek mythology, a beautiful shepherd boy of Troy whom Zeus, in the form of an eagle, carried up to Olympus to succeed Hebe as cupbearer to the gods; hence, any boy who serves drinks; a cupbearer. **2** *Astron.* The fourth (commonly called third) and largest satellite of Jupiter. [< Gk. *Ganymēdēs*]

Ga·o (gä′ō) A town in eastern Mali.

gaol (jāl) *n. Brit.* Jail. [Var. of JAIL] **—gaol′er** *n.*

gap (gap) *n.* **1** An opening or parting in anything; aperture; breach; chasm. **2** *Geog.* A deep notch or ravine in a mountain ridge. **3** A break in continuity; an interruption; a period in chronology or a range of phenomena about which nothing is known. **4** *Aeron.* The vertical distance between two supporting planes of an airplane. See synonyms under BREACH, HOLE. —*v.t.* **gapped, gap·ping** To make a breach or opening in. [< ON *gap* gap, abyss < *gapa* gape] **—gap′less** *adj.*

gape (gāp, gap) *v.i.* **gaped, gap·ing** **1** To stare with or as with open mouth, as in awe or surprise. **2** To open the mouth wide, as in yawning. **3** To be or become open wide; present a wide opening. —*n.* **1** The act of gaping. **2** *Zool.* The expanse of the open mouth, as in birds; also, the opening between the shells of a bivalve the edges of which do not naturally shut tight together, as in soft clams. **3** A gap. **—the gapes** **1** A fit of gaping or yawning. **2** A disease of young fowls, caused by the presence of gapeworms obstructing the breathing and causing much gaping. [< ON *gapa*] **—gap′er** *n.*

gape·seed (gāp′sēd′, gap′-, gäp′-) *n.* **1** *Brit.* Anything that causes wonder or astonishment to the ignorant or simple. **2** One who stares in a gaping manner.

gape·worm (gāp′wûrm′, gap′-) *n.* A nematode worm *(Syngamus trachealis)* that causes the gapes.

gap·py (gap′ē) *adj.* Having gaps; disconnected.

gap·y (gā′pē, gap′ē) *adj.* Affected with the gapes.

gar[1] (gär) *n. pl.* **gars** or **gar** Any of several fishes having a spearlike snout and elongate body, including the North American species *(Tylosurus marinus)*; the common European species *(Belone vulgaris),* esteemed as a food fish; and the teleost marine varieties also called *billfishes, needlefishes.* [Short for GARFISH]

gar[2] (gär) *v.t. Scot.* To make; cause.

ga·rage (gə·räzh′, -räj′, *Brit.* gar′ij) *n.* A building in which motor vehicles are stored and cared for. —*v.t.* **ga·raged, ga·rag·ing** To put or keep in a garage. [< F < *garer* protect, ult. < Gmc.]

Gar·a·mond (gar′ə·mond, *Fr.* gå·rå·môn′), **Claude,** died 1561, French printer and type founder.

Gar·and rifle (gar′ənd, gə·rand′) A semi-automatic, gas-operated, .30-caliber rifle adopted by the U.S. Army in World War II. [after J. C. *Garand,* born 1888, U.S. inventor]

garb (gärb) *n.* **1** Style of apparel, especially as characteristic of some office, rank, etc. **2** Clothes. **3** *Obs.* External seeming; appearance; demeanor; manner. **4** *Obs.* Custom; style. See synonyms under DRESS. —*v.t.* To clothe; dress. [< MF *garbe* gracefulness, ult. < Gmc.]

gar·bage (gär′bij) *n.* **1** Animal or household refuse. **2** Low or vile things collectively. [Prob. < AF. Cf. OF *garbe* a sheaf of grain, animal fodder]

gar·ban·zo bean (gär·bän′sō) The Mexican chickpea.

gar·ble (gär′bəl) *v.t.* **gar·bled, gar·bling** **1** To mix up or confuse; make incomprehensible: to *garble* a message. **2** To change or alter the meaning or emphasis of (a document, report, etc.) with intent to mislead or misrepresent. **3** *Obs.* To take the best part of. **4** *Obs.* To cull or sift. See synonyms under PERVERT. —*n.* **1** The act of garbling; a perversion, as of a text. **2** *pl.* Impurities separated from drugs, spices, etc.; refuse; trash. [< Ital. *garbellare* < Arabic *gharbala* sift < *ghirbal* a sieve, ult. < L *cribellum,* dim. of *cribrum* a sieve]

gar·board (gär′bôrd′, -bōrd′) *n. Naut.* One of the planks on a ship's bottom next to the keel. Also **garboard plank** or **strake.** [< Du. *gaarboord*]

gar·boil (gär′boil) *n. Obs.* An uproar; commotion. [< MF *garbouil* < Ital. *garbuglio,* appar. < L *bullire* boil]

Gar·cí·a Lor·ca (gär·thē′ä lôr′kä), **Federico,** 1899–1936, Spanish poet, dramatist, and essayist.

gar·çon (gȧr·sôn′) *n. pl.* **·çons** (-sôn′) *French* **1** A boy. **2** A waiter. **3** A male servant.

Gar·da (gär′dä), **Lake** The largest lake in Italy, on the Lombardy-Veneto border; 143 square miles: also *Lago di Garda.* Also **La·go di Be·na·co** (lä′gō dē be·nä′kō).

gar·dant (gär′dənt) *adj. Her.* Looking directly toward the observer, as an animal on a shield: also spelled *guardant.* [< F, orig. ppr. of *garder* watch]

gar·den (gär′dən) *n.* **1** A place for the cultivation of flowers, vegetables, or small plants. **2** Hence, any fertile or highly cultivated territory. **3** A piece of ground, commonly with ornamental plants or trees, used as a place of public resort: a botanical *garden.* —*adj.* **1** Grown, or capable of being grown in a garden; hence, hardy. **2** Ordinary; common. **3** Like a garden; ornamental: *garden* spot of the world. —*v.t.* To cultivate as a garden. —*v.i.* To till or work in a garden. [< AF *gardin* < Gmc.]

Gar·den (gär′dən), **Mary,** 1877–1967, U.S. operatic soprano.

garden balsam An ornamental plant *(Impatiens balsamina),* cultivated in many varieties.

gar·den·er (gärd′nər, gär′dən·ər) *n.* One who tends gardens, or is skilled in gardening.

garden heliotrope A species of valerian *(Valeriana officinalis)* having clusters of small pink or white flowers and roots with a penetrating aroma, reputed to have curative properties. Also called *allheal, valerian.*

gar·de·ni·a (gär·dē′nē·ə, -dēn′yə) *n.* Any of a considerable genus *(Gardenia)* of mainly tropical shrubs or trees of the madder family, with large and fragrant yellow or white axillary flowers. The Cape jasmine *(G. jasminoides)* is the best known in cultivation. [< NL, after

Alexander *Garden,* 1730–91, U.S. botanist]

gar·den·ing (gärd′ning, gär′dən·ing) *n.* The art of making and caring for a garden; also, the work involved. See synonyms under AGRICULTURE.

Garden of the Gods An area of curiously eroded sandstone formations in central Colorado.

garden sorrel The common sorrel, or sour dock.

Garden State Nickname of NEW JERSEY.

garde·robe (gärd′rōb) *n.* 1 *Archaic* A locked-up storeroom or wardrobe; also, its contents. 2 A private room, as a bedchamber. [< F *garder* keep + *robe* a robe]

gar·dez bien (gàr·dā′ byan′) *French* Take good care (of yourself).

gar·dez la foi (gàr·dā′ là fwä′) *French* Keep faith.

Gar·di·ner (gärd′nər, gär′də·nər), **Samuel Rawson**, 1829–1902, English historian. —**Stephen**, 1483–1555, English prelate and statesman.

gar·dy·loo (gär′dē·lōō′) *n. Scot.* Beware of the water: formerly said in Edinburgh, to warn passers-by to avoid slops thrown from a window.

Gar·eth (gar′ith) The "kitchen-scullion" knight of the Round Table, brother of Gawain.

Gar·field (gär′fēld), **James Abram**, 1831–81, 20th president of the United States, March 4 to September 19, 1881; assassinated.

gar·fish (gär′fish′) *n. pl.* **·fish** or **·fish·es** A fish with a spearlike snout, as a garpike. See GAR[1]. [OE *gar* spear + FISH]

gar·ga·ney (gär′gə·nē) *n.* A teal (*Anas querquedula*) of Europe and Asia, having a broad white line on each side of the head and neck. [< Ital. *garganello*]

Gar·gan·tu·a (gär·gan′chōō·ə) The peace-loving giant prince of Rabelais' satirical romance *Gargantua* (1534); mouthpiece for educational reform; possessor of an enormous appetite.

Gar·gan·tu·an (gär·gan′chōō·ən) *adj.* Huge; gigantic; prodigious.

gar·get (gär′git) *n.* 1 An infectious bacterial disease of cattle, sheep, and swine, characterized by inflammation of the udder, deficient or contaminated milk, distemper, and other symptoms: also called *mastitis.* 2 The pokeweed. [< OF *gargate* throat < L *gurges* a whirlpool]

gar·gle (gär′gəl) *v.* **gar·gled, gar·gling** *v.t.* 1 To rinse (the throat) with a liquid agitated by air from the windpipe. —*v.i.* 2 To use a gargle. 3 To make a sound as if gargling. —*n.* A liquid for gargling. [< OF *gargouiller* gargle < *gargouille* throat]

GARGOYLES

a. On cathedral of Amiens, 13th cent.
b. On cathedral of St. Eustache, Paris, 16th cent.
c. On church of Montmartre, 19th cent.
d. On Chrysler Building, New York, 20th cent.

gar·goyle (gär′goil) *n.* A waterspout, usually carved in a grotesque human or animal figure, projecting from the gutter of a building. Also spelled *gurgoyle.* [< OF *gargouille* throat] —**gar′goyled** *adj.*

gar·i·bal·di (gar′ə·bôl′dē) *n.* A loose blouse resembling those worn by the soldiers of Garibaldi.

Gar·i·bal·di (gar′ə·bôl′dē, *Ital.* gä′rē·bäl′dē), **Giuseppe**, 1807–82, Italian patriot and general; secured unity of Italy.

Gar·i·bal·di·an (gar′ə·bôl′dē·ən) *adj.* Of or pertaining to Giuseppe Garibaldi or his troops. —*n.* One of the soldiers of Giuseppe Garibaldi

Ga·ri·glia·no (gä′rē·lyä′nō) The lower reaches of the Liri.

gar·ish (gâr′ish) *adj.* 1 Marked by a dazzling glare. 2 Displaying a gaudy effect. 3 Extravagantly conceited. Also formerly spelled *gairish.* [Cf. obs. *gaure* stare] —**gar′ish·ly** *adv.* —**gar′ish·ness** *n.*

gar·land (gär′lənd) *n.* 1 A wreath of leaves, flowers, etc., as a token of victory, joy, or honor. 2 A collection of literary gems. 3 A wire framework covered with cloth or burlap strips and used in camouflage. 4 Something resembling a garland or wreath. 5 A strop used to hoist spars. —*v.t.* To deck with or as with a garland. [< OF *garlande*]

Gar·land (gär′lənd), **(Hannibal) Hamlin**, 1860–1940, U.S. writer.

gar·lic (gär′lik) *n.* 1 A hardy bulbous perennial (*Allium sativum*) of the same genus as the onion. 2 Its pungent bulb, used in cooking. [OE *gárlēac* < *gār* spear + *lēac* leek] —**gar′lick·y** *adj.*

gar·ment (gär′mənt) *n.* An article of clothing. See synonyms under DRESS. —*v.t.* To clothe: usually in the past participle. [< OF *garnement* < *garnir* garnish]

Gar·misch-Par·ten·kir·chen (gär′mish·pär′tən·kir′khən) A resort town in Upper Bavaria, Germany.

Gar·mo Peak (gär′mō) A former name for STALIN PEAK, U.S.S.R.

gar·ner (gär′nər) *v.t.* To gather or store as in a garner; collect. —*n.* 1 A place for the storing of grain; a granary. 2 Any storage place. [< OF *gernier, grenier* < L *granarium* a granary < *granum* grain]

Gar·ner (gär′nər), **John Nance**, 1868–1967, U.S. politician; vice president of the United States 1933–41.

gar·net[1] (gär′nit) *n.* 1 Any of a group of mineral double salts (silicates) of isometric crystalline form and varied composition, used as gemstones and abrasives. 2 A variable deep red color characteristic of certain varieties of garnet, as pyrope and almandine. [< OF *grenat* < Med. L *granatum* < L, a pomegranate; so called from its color]

gar·net[2] (gär′nit) *n. Naut.* A form of tackle or purchase. [Origin uncertain]

Gar·nett (gär′nit), **Constance**, 1862–1946, *née* Black; English translator of Russian literature. — **David**, born 1892, English writer; son of the preceding.

gar·net·ting (gär·net′ing) *n.* A process of reducing wool or cotton shoddy and rags to fibers that can be re-used. [from *Garnett* machine, named after the inventor]

gar·ni·er·ite (gär′nē·ə·rīt′) *n.* An amorphous, apple-green, hydrous silicate of nickel and magnesium, forming an important ore of nickel. [after Jules *Garnier,* French geologist]

gar·nish (gär′nish) *v.t.* 1 To decorate, as with ornaments; embellish. 2 In cookery, to decorate (a dish) with flavorsome or colorful trimmings for the table. 3 *Law* To give warning to (someone) to answer to an action; garnishee. —*n.* 1 Something placed around a dish for ornamentation or a relish. 2 Anything added as an ornament; embellishment. 3 *Obs.* In English jails, a fee collected from a new prisoner by the jailer. [< OF *garniss-,* stem of *garnir* prepare. Akin to WARN.]

Synonyms (verb): adorn, beautify, deck, decorate, dress, embellish, furbish, ornament. See ADORN. *Antonyms:* blemish, deface, denude, disfigure, dismantle, spoil, strip.

gar·nish·ee (gär′nish·ē′) *v.t.* **·eed, ·ee·ing** *Law* 1 To secure by garnishment (any debt or property, in the hands of a third person, which is due or belonging to the defendant in attachment). 2 To warn (a person) by garnishment. —*n. Law* A person warned not to pay or deliver money or effects to a defendant, pending a judgment of a court.

gar·nish·er (gär′nish·ər) One who garnishes or garnishees.

gar·nish·ment (gär′nish·mənt) *n.* 1 The act of garnishing. 2 That which garnishes; embellishment; ornament. 3 *Law* A warning or summons; specifically, a notice not to pay or deliver money or effects to a defendant, but to appear and answer the plaintiff's suit.

gar·ni·ture (gär′ni·chər) *n.* Anything used to garnish; embellishment. [< F < *garnir.* See GARNISH.]

Ga·ronne (gà·rôn′) A river in SW France, flowing NW 402 miles to the Gironde.

gar·pike (gär′pīk′) *n. pl.* **·pike** or **·pikes** 1 A large ganoid fish of the fresh waters of eastern North America (family *Lepirosteidae*), having an elongated spearlike snout. 2 A garfish. [< GAR[1] + PIKE]

gar·ret (gar′it) *n.* A story or room directly under a sloping roof. [< OF *garite* a watchtower < *garir* watch, defend < Gmc.]

gar·ret·eer (gar′it·ir′) *n.* One who lives in a garret.

Gar·rick (gar′ik), **David**, 1717–79, English actor and author.

gar·ri·son (gar′ə·sən) *n.* 1 The military force defending a fort, town, etc. 2 The place where such a force is stationed. ◆ Collateral adjective: *presidial.* —*v.t.* 1 To place troops in, as a fort or town, for its defense. 2 To station (troops) in a fort, town, etc. 3 To be the garrison of. [< OF *garison* < *garir* defend < Gmc.]

Gar·ri·son (gar′ə·sən), **Fielding Hudson**, 1870–1935, U.S. medical historian. —**William Lloyd**, 1805–79, U.S. abolitionist.

garrison cap A military cap having a round cloth top and a stiff, shiny visor, worn with the dress uniform.

gar·rote (gə·rot′, -rōt′) *n.* 1 A Spanish instrument for strangling, formerly used as a means of capital punishment. 2 The mode of punishment inflicted by the garrote. 3 Any similar method of strangulation, especially in order to rob. —*v.t.* **gar·rot·ed, gar·rot·ing** 1 To execute with a garrote. 2 To throttle in order to rob. Also **ga·rote′, ga·rotte′, gar·rotte′.** [< Sp. *garotte,* orig. a stick, cudgel < Celtic]

gar·rot·er (gə·rot′ər, -rōt′ər) *n.* A strangler; especially, a highwayman who throttles his victim. Also **gar·rot′ter.**

gar·ru·line (gar′ōō·lin, -lin, -yōō-) *adj.* Of or pertaining to a subfamily of corvine birds (*Garrulinae*), which includes the jays. —*n.* Any bird of this subfamily. [< NL < L *garrulus* talkative]

gar·ru·li·ty (gə·rōō′lə·tē) *n.* Idle and empty talkativeness.

gar·ru·lous (gar′ə·ləs, -yə-) *adj.* Given to continual and tedious talking; habitually loquacious. [< L *garrulus* talkative] —**gar′ru·lous·ly** *adv.* —**gar′ru·lous·ness** *n.*

Synonyms: chattering, loquacious, talkative, verbose. *Garrulous* signifies given to constant trivial talking. *Chattering* signifies uttering rapid, noisy, and unintelligible, or scarcely intelligible, sounds, whether articulate words or such as resemble them. The *talkative* person has a strong disposition to talk, with or without an abundance of words, or many ideas; the *loquacious* person has an abundant flow of language and much to say on any subject suggested; either may be lively and for a time entertaining; the *garrulous* person is tedious, repetitious, petty, and self-absorbed. *Verbose* is applied to utterances more formal than conversation, as to writings, or public addresses. Compare CIRCUMLOCUTION. *Antonyms:* laconic, reserved, reticent, silent, speechless, taciturn.

gar·ter (gär′tər) *n.* A band worn around the leg to hold a stocking in place; loosely, any stocking supporter. —*v.t.* To support or fasten with a garter. [< AF *gartier* < OF *garet* bend of the knee < Celtic]

Gar·ter (gär′tər) *n.* 1 The distinctive badge of the **Order of the Garter,** the highest order of knighthood in Great Britain. 2 The order itself, or membership therein.

garter snake Any of various small, harmless, viviparous, brightly striped snakes (genus *Thamnophis*): most common of American snakes.

garth (gärth) *n.* 1 The open space or courtyard enclosed by a cloister. 2 *Archaic* A yard; garden. [< ON *gardhr* a yard]

Gar·y (gâr′ē) A city in NW Indiana, on Lake Michigan.

Gar·y (gâr′ē), **Elbert Henry**, 1846–1927, U.S. lawyer and financier.

gas (gas) *n.* 1 *Physics* That fluid form of matter which is compressible within limits, and which, owing to the relatively free movement of its molecules, diffuses readily and is capable of indefinite expansion in all directions. 2 Any gaseous or vaporous mixture other than air: illuminating *gas,* fuel *gas,* etc. 3 A single jet of flame supplied by illuminating gas. **4**

Laughing gas. **5** *Mining* An explosive mixture of atmospheric air with firedamp. **6** *Slang* Empty boasting; chatter. **7** *U.S. Colloq.* Gasoline. **8** Chlorine or some other highly poisonous or asphyxiating substance used in warfare: also **poison gas. 9** Flatulence. See synonyms under FLUID. —*v.* **gassed, gas·sing** *v.t.* **1** To overcome, affect, or kill by gas or gas fumes. **2** To treat or saturate with gas. **3** To supply with gas or gasoline. **4** To singe so as to free of loose fibers: to *gas* lace. **5** *U.S. Slang* To talk boastfully or nonsensically to. —*v.i.* **6** To give off gas. **7** *U.S. Slang* To talk in an idle or empty manner; boast. [Coined by J. B. van Helmont, 1577–1644, Belgian chemist]

gas alarm 1 A warning of a gas attack. **2** The device by which the warning is given.

gas·a·lier (gas′ə·lir′) See GASOLIER.

gas analysis The qualitative and quantitative determination of gases, especially in regard to their physiological and thermodynamic properties.

gas attack A military attack using asphyxiating or poisonous gases to overcome the enemy, as by bombardment with gas shells.

gas bacillus The micro-organism producing gas gangrene in gunshot wounds, specifically *Bacillus welchii.*

gas·bag (gas′bag′) *n.* **1** An expansible container for holding gas. **2** *Slang* A tiresome, garrulous person.

gas balance An instrument for determining the specific gravity of gases.

gas black Carbon black, produced by carbonizing natural gas: used as a substitute for animal and vegetable carbon.

gas bleaching Bleaching by means of a gas, as by chlorine.

gas bomb A bomb or shell filled with poison gas which is released when the shell explodes. Also **gas shell.**

gas bracket A bracket bearing one or more gas burners.

gas burner A tube or tip, usually attached to a gas fixture, for regulating the flame of the gas consumed.

gas carbon A compact, amorphous carbon deposited in the retorts of gasworks, which is a good conductor of heat and electricity, and is used for battery plates and in the electric arc light. Also **gas coke.**

gas cell 1 *Aeron.* One of the individual compartments containing the gas in an airship: also **gas container. 2** An electrolytic cell composed of two gas electrodes: also **gas battery.**

gas chamber A chamber in which executions are performed by means of poisonous gas.

gas coal A bituminous coal from which illuminating gas may be made.

Gas·coigne (gas′koin), **George,** 1525?–77, English poet.

gas·con (gas′kən) *n.* A boaster. —*adj.* Boastful; blustering. [<F, a native of Gascony]

Gas·con (gas′kən) *adj.* Of, native of, or pertaining to Gascony. —*n.* A native of Gascony.

gas·con·ade (gas′kə·nād′) *v.i.* **·ad·ed, ·ad·ing** To brag; bluster. —*n.* Boastful or blustering talk, boasting; braggadocio; bluster. [<F *gasconnade* <*gascon* GASCON] **—gas′con·ad′er** *n.*

Gas·co·ny (gas′kə·nē) A region and former province of SW France. *French* **Gas·cogne** (gȧs·kôn′y′).

gas electrode An electrode capable of dissolving a gas or holding it on its surface; it is usually made of finely divided metal and in the solution behaves as a reversible electrode.

gas·e·lier (gas′ə·lir′) See GASOLIER.

gas engine An internal-combustion engine, especially one using illuminating or natural gas.

gas·e·ous (gas′ē·əs, -yəs) *adj.* **1** Having the nature or form of gas; aeriform. **2** Unsubstantial.

gas fading Fume fading.

gas filter A filter for removing solid or liquid particles from a gas.

gas fitter One who fits and puts up gas fixtures.

gas fittings The appliances connected with the introduction and use of gas in a building.

gas fixture A tube, with burners and stopcocks, connected with a gas pipe.

gas focusing *Physics* A method of focusing a stream of electrons through the action of an ionized gas.

gas furnace A furnace in which gas is used for fuel, or one for making gas.

gas gangrene *Pathol.* Gangrene with gas formation in the tissues of gunshot wounds; caused chiefly by anaerobic bacteria, as *Bacillus welchii.*

gas groove *Chem.* A groove formed by a stream of hydrogen or other gas rising continuously along the surface of an electrochemical metallic deposit while it is forming.

gash[1] (gash) *v.t.* To make a long, deep cut in. See synonyms under CUT. —*n.* A long, deep incision; a flesh wound. [Earlier *garse* <OF *garser* scratch]

gash[2] (gäsh) *adj. Scot.* **1** Fluent; intelligent **2** Neat; trim.

gas helmet A gas mask.

gas-hold·er (gas′hōl′dər) See GASOMETER.

gas·house (gas′hous′) *n.* A gasworks: often used figuratively to designate the rowdy district around a gashouse.

gas·i·form (gas′ə·fôrm) *adj.* Gaseous.

gas·i·fy (gas′ə·fī) *v.t. & v.i.* **·fied, ·fy·ing** To make into or become gas. **—gas′i·fi′a·ble** *adj.* **—gas′i·fi·ca′tion** *n.* **—gas′i·fi′er** *n.*

gas jet 1 A burner on a gas fixture. **2** The jet of flame on a gas burner.

Gas·kell (gas′kəl), **Elizabeth Cleghorn,** 1810–1865, *née* Stevenson, English novelist.

gas·ket (gas′kit) *n.* **1** *Mech.* A ring, disk, or plate of packing to make a joint watertight. **2** *Naut.* A rope or cord used to confine furled sails to the yard or boom. Also **gas′kin** (-kin), **gas′king** (-king). [Cf. Ital. *gaschetta* end of rope]

gas·kin (gas′kin) *n.* **1** The hinder part of a horse's leg, between the stifle and the hock. See illustration under HORSE. **2** *pl.* Galligaskins. See GASKET (def. 2). [? <GALLIGASKINS]

gas·light (gas′līt′) *n.* **1** Light produced by gas: also **gas light. 2** A gas jet or burner. **—gas′light′ing** *n.*

gas liquor A by-product obtained by subjecting soft coal to destructive distillation: the chief source of ammonia.

gas log An imitation log concealing a gas burner, used in a fireplace.

gas main A trunk gas pipe for conveying gas to the service pipes.

gas·man (gas′man′) *n. pl.* **·men** (-men′) **1** One who manufactures or supplies gas for lighting. **2** A gas fitter. **3** *Mining* One who superintends ventilation and guards against firedamp. **4** A man employed by a gas-supplying company to examine and read gas meters, note the amount used, etc.

gas mantle A mantle surrounding the flame of a gas jet, which radiates light when heated.

gas mask A protective headpiece worn to prevent poisoning by noxious fumes or gases.

gas meter An apparatus for measuring the quantity of gas that passes through it.

gas·o·gene (gas′ə·jēn) *n.* **1** A fuel gas made from charcoal. **2** A portable contrivance for producing gas for aerating water. [<F *gazogène*]

gas·o·hol (gas′ə·hôl, -hol) *n.* A mixture of 90 percent gasoline and usu. 10 percent alcohol, used in internal-combustion engines as a petroleum-saving fuel.

gas·o·lier (gas′ə·lir′) *n.* A pendent fixture having branches ending in gas burners: also spelled *gasalier, gaselier.* [<*gaso-* (<GAS) + (CHANDE)LIER]

gas·o·line (gas′ə·lēn, gas′ə·lēn′) *n.* A colorless, volatile, inflammable hydrocarbon product of the distillation of crude petroleum, having a specific gravity of .629 to .667 and boiling at from 75° to 90° C. It is used as fuel, for carbonizing water gases, to propel machinery, and as a solvent for fats. Also **gas′o·lene.** [<GAS + -OL[2] + -INE[2]]

gasoline bomb See FRANGIBLE GRENADE under GRENADE.

gas·om·e·ter (gas·om′ə·tər) *n.* **1** An apparatus for measuring gases, used in chemical manipulations. **2** An apparatus adapted to collecting, holding, or mixing gases; a gas-holder.

gas·om·e·try (gas·om′ə·trē) *n.* The measurement of gases. **—gas·o·met·ric** (gas′ə·met′rik) *adj.*

gas·op·er·at·ed (gas′op′ə·rā′tid) *adj.* Operated by the action of expanding gases: said especially of certain automatic and semi-automatic weapons. See GARAND RIFLE.

gas oven An oven heated by gas.

gasp (gasp, gäsp) *v.i.* **1** To take in the breath suddenly and sharply; breathe convulsively, as from fear or exhaustion. **2** To have great longing or desire: with *for* or *after.* —*v.t.* **3** To say or utter with gasps. —*n.* An act of convulsive and interrupted breathing. [<ON *geispa* yawn]

Gas·par (gäs·pär′) Portuguese and Spanish form of JASPER. Also *Fr.* **Gas·pard** (gȧs·pär′), *Ital.* **Gas·pa·ro** (gäs′pä·rō).

—Gaspar Traditional name of one of the three kings, the Magi, who honored the infant Jesus. Also called *Kasper.*

Gas·pé Peninsula (gȧs·pā′) A peninsula of the Province of Quebec, Canada, in the Gulf of St. Lawrence.

gasp·er (gas′pər, gäs′-) *n.* **1** One who or that which gasps. **2** *Brit. Slang* A cigarette.

gas pipe A pipe for carrying gas, especially illuminating gas.

gas plant The herb fraxinella.

gas pot A receptacle containing lacrimatory or other poison gases and used principally in training for chemical warfare.

gas sand Any sandstone that contains or yields natural gas.

gas shaft A corridor to permit the escape of gas released or discharged from the gas cells of an airship.

gas·sing (gas′ing) *n.* **1** Subjection to the action of a gas, as lime to chlorine. **2** The act of poisoning by gas warfare. **3** *Slang* Conversation; especially, idle or boastful talk.

gas station A filling station.

gas·sy (gas′ē) *adj.* **gas·si·er, gas·si·est 1** Characteristic of or impregnated with gas. **2** *Slang* Addicted to idle chatter or boastful talk.

gast (gast) *v.t. Obs.* To terrify. Compare AGHAST. [OE *gǣstan*]

gas tank 1 A gasometer. **2** A tank for holding gas or gasoline, as the fuel tank of an airplane or motor vehicle.

gastero- *combining form* Gastro-.

gas·ter·o·my·ce·tous (gas′tər·ō·mī·sē′təs) *adj.* Of or pertaining to a subgroup *(Gasteromycetes)* of fleshy fungi having spores enclosed in cavities within the fruit body, as puffballs and earthstars. [<GASTERO- + Gk. *mykēs, mykētos* fungus + -OUS]

Gas·ter·oph·i·lus (gas′tə·rof′ə·ləs) See GASTROPHILUS.

gas thermometer A thermometer which indicates temperature changes by variations in the pressure or volume of a contained gas, usually hydrogen.

gas·tight (gas′tīt′) *adj.* Not permitting the escape of gas.

gas·tral·gi·a (gas·tral′jē·ə) *n.* **1** *Pathol.* Neuralgia in the stomach. **2** Gastric pain.

gas·trec·to·my (gas·trek′tə·mē) *n. Surg.* An operation to remove a portion of the stomach.

gas·tric (gas′trik) *adj.* Of, pertaining to, or near the stomach. Compare illustration under ABDOMINAL.

gastric fever *Pathol.* **1** A bilious remittent fever; harvest fever. **2** Acute dyspepsia.

gastric juice *Biochem.* A thin acid fluid secreted by the glands of the stomach and containing several enzymes; the chief digestive fluid, acting mainly on proteins.

gas·trin (gas′trin) *n. Biochem.* A hormone secreted by the stomach membrane and promoting digestion by activating gastric juices.

gas·tri·tis (gas·trī′tis) *n. Pathol.* Inflammation of the stomach. **—gas·trit·ic** (gas·trit′ik) *adj.*

gastro- *combining form* **1** Stomach: *gastrolith.* **2** Stomach and: *gastroenterology.* Also **gastero-.** [<Gk. *gastēr* stomach]

gas·tro·coel (gas′trə·sēl) *n. Anat.* The archenteron. [<GASTRO- + Gk. *koilia* cavity]

gas·tro·col·ic (gas′trə·kol′ik) *adj. Anat.* Of, pertaining to, or attached to the stomach and the transverse colon.

gas·tro·di·aph·a·ny (gas′trō·dī·af′ə·nē) *n. Med.* Examination of the stomach by means of a small electric light inserted through the esophagus. Also **gas·tro·di·aph·a·nos·co·py** (gas′trō·dī·af′ə·nos′kə·pē). [<GASTRO- + Gk. *diaphanēs* transparent <*dia-* through + *phainein* appear]

gas·tro·en·ter·i·tis (gas′trō·en′tə·rī′tis) *n. Pathol.* Inflammation of the lining membrane of the stomach and bowels. **—gas′tro·en′te·rit′ic** (-tə·rit′ik) *adj.*

gas·tro·en·ter·ol·o·gy (gas′trō·en′tə·rol′ə·jē) *n.* The study of the anatomy, physiology, and

pathology of the stomach and intestines. —
gas·tro·en·ter·ol·o·gist n.

gas·tro·en·ter·os·to·my (gas'trō-en'tə-ros'tə-mē) n. Surg. An operation by which a passage is formed between the stomach and the intestine.

gas·tro·ga·vage (gas'trō-gə-väzh') n. Med. Artificial feeding through an opening in the abdominal wall to the stomach. Also **gas·tros·to·ga·vage** (gas·tros'tō-gə-väzh'). [< GASTRO- + F gavage cramming < gaver gorge]

gas·tro·he·pat·ic (gas'trō-hi-pat'ik) adj. Anat. Of or pertaining to the stomach and the liver.

gas·tro·in·tes·ti·nal (gas'trō-in·tes'tə·nəl) adj. Anat. Of or pertaining to the stomach and the intestines.

gas·tro·lith (gas'trō-lith) n. Pathol. A calculus or stony formation in the gastric region.

gas·trol·o·gy (gas·trol'ə-jē) n. The study of the anatomy, physiology, and pathology of the stomach.

gas·tron·o·mer (gas·tron'ə-mər) n. An epicure. Also **gas·tro·nome** (gas'trə-nōm), **gas·tron'o·mist.**

gas·tro·nom·ic (gas'trə-nom'ik) adj. Of or pertaining to gastronomy. Also **gas·tro·nom'i·cal.** — **gas·tro·nom'i·cal·ly** adv.

gas·tron·o·my (gas·tron'ə-mē) n. The art of good eating; epicurism. [< F gastronomie < Gk. gastronomia < gastēr stomach + nomos law]

Gas·troph·i·lus (gas-trof'ə-ləs) n. A genus of dipterous insects whose larvae are parasitic on horses, especially G. intestinalis, a botfly: also called Gasterophilus. [< NL < Gk. gastēr stomach + philos loving]

gas·tro·pod (gas'trə-pod) n. Any of a large and diverse class (Gastropoda) of mollusks usually having a spiral shell and moving by means of a ventral muscular organ, including snails, slugs, limpets, and conches. —adj. Of or pertaining to the class of gastropods. [< NL < Gk. gastēr stomach + pous, podos foot] —**gas·trop·o·dan** (gas·trop'ə-dən), **gas·trop'o·dous** adj.

gas·trop·to·sis (gas'trop·tō'sis) n. Pathol Prolapse of the stomach. [< GASTRO- + Gk. ptosis a falling]

gas·tro·scope (gas'trə-skōp) n. Med. An electrical apparatus for illuminating and inspecting the human stomach. —**gas·tro·scop'ic** (-skop'ik) adj.

gas·tros·co·py (gas·tros'kə-pē) n. Med. An examination of the abdomen to discover disease.

gas·tro·stege (gas'trə-stēj) n. Zool. One of the abdominal scales of a reptile. [< GASTRO- + Gk. stegē a covering]

gas·trot·o·my (gas·trot'ə-mē) n. Surg. An opening of or cutting into the stomach or abdomen, as to remove a foreign substance.

gas·trot·ri·chan (gas·trot'rə-kən) n. Any of a class (Gastrotricha) of minute fresh-water animals, possibly related to the rotifers, having spindle-shaped bodies partly or entirely covered with spines, bristles, or scales. [< GASTRO- + Gk. thrix, trichos hair]

gas·tro·vas·cu·lar (gas'trō-vas'kyə-lər) adj. Physiol. 1 Serving both a circulating and a digestive function. 2 Of or pertaining to organs having such a dual function.

gas·tru·la (gas'trōō-lə) n. pl. **·lae** (-lē) Biol. That embryonic form of metazoic animals which consists of a two-layered sac enclosing a central cavity or archenteron and having an opening at one end. [< NL, dim. of Gk. gastēr stomach] —**gas'tru·lar** adj.

gas·tru·la·tion (gas'trōō-lā'shən) n. The formation of a gastrula.

gas tube Physics A vacuum tube in which the pressure of the contained gas or vapor is such as to affect the electrical characteristics of the tube appreciably.

gas turbine A turbine engine in which liquid or gaseous fuel is burned under pressure and the expansion gases sent through a rotor unit connected with a generator.

gas warfare Warfare in which noxious or poisonous gases are dispersed by gas bombs or other means among enemy forces.

gas weld A fusion of metals by use of high-temperature gas flames, mixtures of hydrogen and acetylene with oxygen.

gas well A well from which natural gas flows.

gas·works (gas'wûrks') n. A factory where illuminating gas or heating gas is made.

gat¹ (gat) Archaic Past tense of GET.

gat² (gat) n. A ship channel in an otherwise shallow place. [< ON, an opening]

gat³ (gat) n. Slang A pistol. [Short for GATLING GUN]

gate¹ (gāt) n. 1 A movable barrier, commonly swinging on hinges: often distinguished from a door by having openwork. 2 An opening or passageway, as in a barrier, fence, wall, or enclosure, often with its surrounding masonry or woodwork; a portal. 3 Geog. A mountain gap or natural passageway. 4 That which gives or affords access: the gates of hell. 5 A frame in which a saw (or set of saws) is stretched. 6 Mech. A valve controlling the water supply of a water wheel or the like. 7 Metall. a A pouring hole in a mold. b A sprue or waste piece on a casting formed in a pouring hole. 8 A hinge. See illustration under HINGE. 9 The total paid admissions at a sports event; the total attendance. See synonyms under ENTRANCE. —v.t. **gat·ed**, **gat·ing** Brit. To keep (a college student) within the gates as a punishment. ◆ Homophone: gait. [OE gatu, plural of geat opening]

gate² (gāt) n. Scot. 1 Method of doing; manner; way. 2 A course or path. ◆ Homophone: gait. [< ON gata way]

gate·age (gā'tij) n. 1 Use of gates as in controlling the flow of water; also, the gates used. 2 Area of gate opening, as of a turbine gate.

gate·crash·er (gāt'krash'ər) n. Slang A person who gains admittance to a function without paying or without an invitation.

gate hinge Mech. A type of hinge formed of two detachable sections, one of which pivots on a cylindrical core projecting from the other. See illustration under HINGE.

gate·house (gāt'hous') n. A house beside, over, or at a gate, as a power station, a porter's lodge, or a medieval defensive structure.

gate·keep·er (gāt'kē'pər) n. One in charge of a gate. Also **gate'man.**

gate-leg table (gāt'leg') A table with swinging legs which support drop leaves and fold against the frame when the leaves are let down.

gate money Money paid for admission to a sports event, theatrical performance, etc.

gate-post (gāt'pōst') n. Either of two posts between which a gate swings.

Gates (gāts), **Horatio**, 1728–1806, American general in the Revolution. —**Reginald Ruggles**, 1882–1962, Canadian botanist and geneticist.

Gates·head (gāts'hed) A port on the Tyne in NE Durham, England.

gate·way (gāt'wā') n. 1 An entrance that is or may be closed with a gate. 2 That which is regarded as a means of ingress or egress. 3 The guides of a saw frame. See synonyms under ENTRANCE.

Gath (gath) In the Bible, one of the five cities of the Philistines; the home of Goliath: I Samuel v 17.

gath·er (gath'ər) v.t. 1 To bring together in one place or group. 2 To bring together from various places, sources, etc. 3 To pick, harvest, or collect. 4 To collect or summon up, as one's energies, for an effort, trial, etc. 5 To acquire or gain in increasing amount or degree: The storm gathered force. 6 To come to understand, believe, or infer. 7 To clasp or enfold: to gather someone into one's arms. 8 To draw into folds or plaits, as by shirring. 9 To wrinkle (the brow). —v.i. 10 To come together. 11 To increase by accumulation. 12 To wrinkle up, as the brow. 13 To come to a head; contract, as a boil. See synonyms under AMASS, CONVOKE. —**to gather up** To pick up and collect together in one place. —n. A plait or fold in cloth, held by a thread passing through the folds; a drawing together. [OE gadrian] —**gath'er·a·ble** adj.

gath·er·er (gath'ər-ər) n. 1 One who or that which gathers. 2 A sewing-machine attachment for gathering cloth. 3 One who collects taxes, fees, etc.

gath·er·ing (gath'ər-ing) n. 1 The action of that which gathers. 2 An assemblage of people. 3 An accumulation or collection of anything. 4 The contraction of a passage, as in a chimney or drain. 5 A series of gathers. 6 An abscess or

boil. 7 In bookbinding, a collection of printed sheets in proper order. See synonyms under ASSEMBLY, COMPANY.

gat·ing (gā'ting) n. 1 A form of punishment. See GATE¹ v. 2 Mech. A gate in a lock tumbler for the passage of the stub.

Gat·ling gun (gat'ling) An early machine-gun having numerous barrels rotating about a central axis, each being loaded and discharged as it was brought to firing position by the turning of a crank. [after R. J. Gatling, 1818–1903, U.S. inventor]

Ga·tun (gä-tōōn') A town in northern Panama Canal Zone. Spanish **Ga·tún'.**

Gatun Dam A dam of the Panama Canal at Gatun; 7,700 feet long, 115 feet high; impounding **Gatun Lake**, 163 square miles; 85 feet above sea level.

gauche (gōsh) adj. Awkward; clumsy; boorish. [< F, left-handed]

gauche·rie (gōsh-rē') n. 1 An awkward or tactless action. 2 Clumsiness; tactlessness. [< F]

Gau·cho (gou'chō) n. pl. **·chos** A native of the South American pampas of mixed Indian and Spanish ancestry; a cowboy. [< Sp.]

gaud (gôd) n. An article of vulgar finery. [< OF gaudir be merry < L gaudere rejoice]
   Synonyms: bauble, finery, gew-gaw, gimcrack, kickshaw, toy, trinket, trumpery.

gau·de·a·mus ig·i·tur (gô'dē·ä'məs ij'ə·tər, gou'dā·ä'mōōs ē'gi·tōōr') Latin Therefore let us be merry: the first words of a famous medieval student song.

gaud·er·y (gô'dər-ē) n. Showy ornament; finery.

Gau·dier-Br·zes·ka (gō-dyä'bər-zes-kà'), **Henri**, 1891–1915, French sculptor.

gaud·y¹ (gô'dē) adj. **gaud·i·er**, **gaud·i·est** Obtrusively brilliant in color: garish; flashy. — **gaud'i·ly** adv. —**gaud'i·ness** n.

gaud·y² (gô'dē) n. Brit. A feast or festival; an entertainment; especially, an annual dinner given by a college in one of the English universities. [< L gaudium joy]

gauf·fer (gôfər) See GOFFER.

gauge (gāj) See GAGE¹.

Gau·guin (gō-gan'), **Paul**, 1848–1903, French painter.

Gaul (gôl) An ancient name for the territory south and west of the Rhine, west of the Alps, and north of the Pyrenees; roughly the area of modern France: Latin Gallia. See also CISALPINE GAUL, TRANSALPINE GAUL, TRANSPADANE GAUL.

Gaul (gôl) n. 1 A native of ancient Gaul. 2 A Frenchman. [< F Gaule < L Gallus]

Gau·leit·er (gou'lī-tər) n. German A district leader of the Nazi party.

Gaul·ish (gôl'ish) adj. Of ancient Gaul, its people, or their Celtic language. —n. The extinct continental Celtic language of Gaul.

Gaull·ism (gôl'iz'əm) n. The policies or philosophy of Charles de Gaulle and his followers. — **Gaull'ist** adj. & n.

gaul·the·ri·a (gôl-thir'ē-ə) n. 1 Any of a large genus (Gaultheria) of aromatic shrubs or undershrubs with thick, shining, evergreen leaves and axillary white or rose-colored nodding flowers. The wintergreen is a well-known North American species. 2 Oil of wintergreen: also called **oil of gaultheria.** [< NL, after Dr. Jean-François Gaultier, 1708?–56, Canadian physician and botanist]

gaum (gôm) v.t. Dial. To smear, as with something sticky. [Var. of GUM]

gaunt (gônt) adj. 1 Emaciated, as from lack of food; lank; lean; meager; thin. 2 Grim; desolate. [? < OF gent elegant, infl. in meaning by ON gand a tall, thin person] —**gaunt'ly** adv. —**gaunt'ness** n.
   Synonyms: emaciated, famished, hungry, lank, lean, meager, pinched, thin, wan, wasted. See MEAGER.

gaunt·let¹ (gônt'lit, gänt'-) n. 1 In medieval armor, a leather glove covered with metal plates. 2 A modern glove with long wrist-extension; also, the part of the glove covering the wrist.

GAUNTLET (def. 1)

—to throw (or **fling**) **down the gauntlet** To challenge to combat or contest. Also spelled *gantlet.* [<OF *gantelet,* dim. of *gant* mitten] —**gaunt′let·ed** *adj.*

gaunt·let[2] (gônt′lit, gänt′-) See GANTLET[1].

gaun·try (gôn′trē), **gaun·tree** See GANTRY.

gaur (gour) *n.* A large wild ox *(Bos gaurus)* of southeastern Asia, having a hump on the dorsal ridge and horns curving backward. [<Hind.]

gauss (gous) *n. pl.* **gauss** *Physics* The cgs unit of magnetic induction, equal to a field exerting a force of one dyne on unit magnetic pole, or 0.7958 ampere-turn per centimeter. [after K. F. *Gauss*]

Gauss (gous), **Karl Friedrich,** 1777–1855, German mathematician.

Gau·ta·ma (gôt′ə·mə, gou′-) See BUDDHA. Also spelled *Gotama.*

Gau·tier (gō·yā′), **Théophile,** 1811–72, French writer.

gauze (gôz) *n.* **1** A light perforated fabric in which the warp threads are crossed or twisted around the filling. **2** Any thin open-woven material: wire *gauze.* **3** A mist; light fog. *—adj.* Resembling or made of gauze. [<MF *gaze,* appar. from *Gaza,* where originally made]

gauz·y (gô′zē) *adj.* **gauz·i·er, gauz·i·est** Thin and diaphanous, like gauze. See synonyms under FINE[1]. —**gauz′i·ly** *adv.* —**gauz′i·ness** *n.*

ga·vage (gə·väzh′, *Fr.* gȧ·väzh′) *n.* **1** A method of fattening poultry by forcing them to swallow a prepared food. **2** *Med.* A method of forcing patients to eat, as through a stomach tube. [<F <*gaver* gorge]

gave (gāv) Past tense of GIVE.

gav·el[1] (gav′əl) *n.* A mallet used by a presiding officer to call for order or attention. [Prob. var. of KEVEL]

gav·el[2] (gav′əl) *n. Brit. Dial.* An unbound bundle of grain. [<AF *gavelle* sheaf]

gav·el[3] (gav′əl) *n.* In old English law, customs duties or tribute; also, rent. [OE *gafol* tribute]

gav·el·kind (gav′əl·kīnd′) *n. Brit.* **1** A tenure of land whereby the lands of a deceased person are divided equally among his sons or nearest heirs; can be alienated by an heir after reaching the age of fifteen; and cannot escheat for felony: a custom once wide-spread in England, but now limited to Kent. **2** Any custom of dividing property equally among male heirs. [<GAVEL[3] + KIND]

gav·e·lock (gav′ə·lok) *n. Brit. Dial.* An iron crowbar. [OE *gafeluc* spear]

ga·vi·al (gā′vē·əl) *n.* The great Indian crocodile *(Gavialis gangeticus)*, having long, slender jaws, the upper one knobbed at the end. [<F <Hind. *ghariyal*]

ga·votte (gə·vot′) *n.* **1** A vivacious French dance, resembling the minuet. **2** Music appropriate to such a dance. Also **ga·vot′.** [<F <Provençal *gavoto* Alpine dance <*gavot* an inhabitant of the Alps]

Ga·wain (gä′win, gô′-) The "perfect knight" of Arthurian legend, nephew of King Arthur, appearing in the earliest sources, and in Malory. Also **Ga′waine.**

gawd (gôd), etc. See GAUD, etc.

gawk (gôk) *v.i. Colloq.* To stare or behave awkwardly and stupidly. *—n.* An awkward, stupid fellow. [Cf. dial. E *gawk* left-handed]

gawk·y (gô′kē) *adj.* **gawk·i·er, gawk·i·est** Awkward and dull; clownish; clumsy. See synonyms under AWKWARD. *—n. pl.* **gawk·ies** A gawk. —**gawk′i·ly** *adv.* —**gawk′i·ness** *n.*

gay (gā) *adj.* **1** Filled with or inspiring mirth; merry; sportive. **2** Brilliant; showy. **3** Loving pleasure; wanton. **3** *Slang* Homosexual; also, intended for homosexuals: a *gay* bar. See synonyms under AIRY, CHEERFUL, HAPPY, MERRY, VIVACIOUS, WANTON. *—n. Slang* A homosexual person. *—adv. Scot.* Fairly; considerably: sometimes spelled *gey;* also **gay′lie.** [<OF <Gmc.] —**gay′ness** *n.* —**gay′some** *adj.*

Gay (gā), **John,** 1685–1732, English poet and playwright.

Gay·a (gī′ə) A city and pilgrimage center in central Bihar, India.

gay·al (gā′əl, gə·yäl′) *n.* A semi-domesticated bovine (*Bos frontalis*) of southeastern Asia, very similar to the closely related wild and slightly larger gaur. [<Hind.]

gay·e·ty (gā′ə·tē), **gay·ly** (gā′lē), etc. See GAIETY, GAILY, etc.

Gay-Lus·sac (gā·lü·sȧk′), **Joseph Louis,** 1778–1850, French chemist and physicist.

Gay-Lussac's law See CHARLES'S LAW.

Gay Nine·ties (nīn′tēz) The decade from 1890 to 1900.

Gay-Pay-Oo (gā′pā′o͞o′) See OGPU.

Ga·za (gä′zə) A city in SW Palestine; since 1948 administered with the surrounding coastal district **(Gaza strip)** by Egypt, since 1957, by United Nations. *Arabic* **Ghaz·ze** (gaz′zē).

ga·za·bo (gə·zā′bō) *n. U.S. Slang* An awkward or eccentric man or boy; a queer fellow. [Cf. Sp. *gazapo* a shrewd fellow]

gaze (gāz) *v.i.* **gazed, gaz·ing** To look earnestly and steadily, as in scrutiny, admiration, or concern. *—n.* **1** A continued or intense look. **2** Something gazed at. See synonyms under LOOK. **—at gaze** *Brit.* In a gazing attitude; in the act of looking around with fear or apprehension, as a stag on hearing hounds. [ME *gasen* <Scand. Cf. dial Sw. *gasa* stare.] —**gaz′er** *n.*

ga·ze·bo (gə·zē′bō, -zā′-) *n. pl.* **·bos** or **·boes** A structure commanding a wide view, such as a summerhouse, or projecting window or balcony; a belvedere. [? <GAZE, imitating a Latin form]

gaze·hound (gāz′hound′) *n.* A hound that hunts by sight.

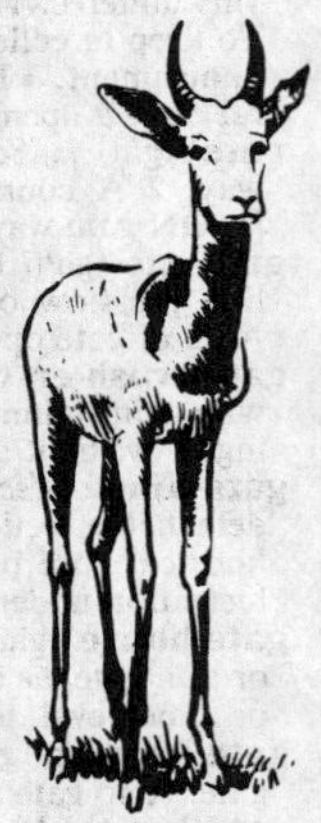

GAZELLE (Species vary from 2 to 3 feet in height)

ga·zelle (gə·zel′) *n.* A small, delicately formed antelope of northern Africa and Arabia (genus *Gazella*), with recurved horns and large, gentle eyes. [<OF <Arabic *ghazāl* gazelle]

ga·zette (gə·zet′) *n.* **1** A newspaper, or printed account of current events. **2** *Brit.* Any official government journal announcing appointments, promotions, etc. *—v.t. Brit.* **ga·zet·ted, ga·zet·ting** To publish or announce in a gazette. [<F <Ital. *gazzetta* <dial. Ital. (Venetian) *gazeta* a coin, orig. the price of the paper]

gaz·et·teer (gaz′ə·tir′) *n.* **1** A dictionary of geographical names. **2** A writer or contributor of news for a gazette.

Ga·zi·an·tep (gä′zē·än·tep′) A city in southern Turkey in Asia: formerly *Aintab.*

gaz·pa·cho (gäz·pä′chō) *n. pl.* **·chos** A cold Spanish soup made with fresh tomatoes, peppers, olive oil, vinegar, garlic, and spices, to which cucumber and bread are added. [<Sp.]

Gd *Chem.* Gadolinium (symbol Gd).

Gdańsk (gə·dänsk′, *Polish* gdän′y′sk) The Polish name for DANZIG.

Gdy·nia (gə·din′yə, *Polish* gdē′nyä) A port in NW Poland.

Ge (jē, gē) See GAEA.

Ge (zhā) *n.* A large and important South American Indian linguistic stock of eastern and central Brazil: also called *Tapuyan.*

Ge *Chem.* Germanium (symbol Ge).

ge·an·ti·cline (jē·an′tə·klīn) *n. Geol.* A vast upward flexure of the earth's crust: opposed to *geosyncline.* [<Gk. *gē* earth + ANTICLINE] —**ge·an′ti·cli′nal** *adj.* & *n.*

gear (gir) *n.* **1** *Mech.* **a** The moving parts or appliances that constitute a whole or set, serving to transmit motion or change its rate or direction: valve *gear,* reversing *gear.* **b** A cogwheel. **c** The engagement of toothed wheels or other parts in a mechanical assembly. **2** *Naut.* The ropes, blocks, etc., used in working a spar or sail; all the rigging of a ship. **3** Fitness for harmonious and effective action; working relationship: out of *gear.* **4** Any equipment, as dress, vestments, warlike accouterments, harness, tools, or household necessaries. **5** *Archaic* Property; possessions; goods. **6** *Archaic* Arms; armor. *—v.t.* **1** *Mech.* **a** To put into gear. **b** To equip with gears. **c** To connect by means of gears. **2** To regulate so as to match or suit something else: to *gear* production to demand. **3** To put gear on; harness; dress. *—v.i.* **4** To come into or be in gear; mesh. [<ON *gervi* equipment]

gear·box (gir′boks′) *n.* The gears and gearcase comprising the variable transmission of an automobile.

gear·case (gir′kās′) *n. Mech.* A metal housing for the gears of machinery.

gear·ing (gir′ing) *n. Mech.* **1** Power-transmitting gear in general. **2** Working parts collectively. **3** Ropes and tackle.

gear·shift (gir′shift′) *n. Mech.* A device for engaging or disengaging the gears in a power-transmission system.

gear·wheel (gir′hwēl′) *n. Mech.* A cogwheel.

geck (gek) *v.t.* & *v.i. Scot.* & *Brit. Dial.* **1** To show contempt; toss (the head); jeer. **2** *Obs.* To fool; cheat. *—n. Scot.* **1** Scorn or derision; jeer; taunt. **2** An object of contempt or derision; dupe.

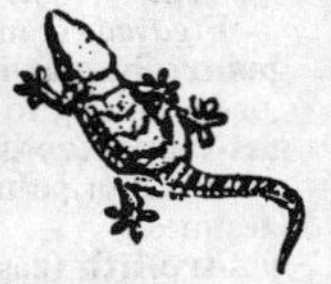

GECKO (Varies from 4 to over 12 inches in length)

geck·o (gek′ō) *n. pl.* **geck·os** or **geck·oes** Any of a family (*Geckonidae*) of small lizards having toes with adhesive disks; wall lizard. [<Malay *gēkoq,* imit. of its cry]

ged (ged) *n. Scot.* A fish, the pike. Also **gedd.**

Ged·des (ged′ēz), **Norman Bel,** 1893–1958, U.S. industrial and stage designer. **—Sir Patrick,** 1854–1932, Scottish biologist.

Gé·dé·on (zhā·dā·ôn′) French form of GIDEON. Also *Ital.* **Ge·de·o·ne** (gā′dā·ō′nā).

Ge·diz (gə·dēz′) A river in western Turkey, flowing 215 miles SW to the Gulf of Smyrna: formerly *Sarabat.*

gee[1] (jē) *n.* The letter G, g, or its sound.

gee[2] (jē) *v.t.* & *v.i.* **1** To turn to the right. **2** To evade; swerve. *—interj.* Turn to the right! a call in driving animals without reins: opposed to *haw*[4]. Also spelled *jee.* [Origin uncertain]

Gee (jē) *interj.* A minced oath: a euphemism for Jesus.

geek (gēk) *n.* A carnival performer who publicly eats or swallows live animals as a sensational spectacle. [Prob. var. of GECK]

Gee·long (jē·lông′) A port in southern Victoria, Australia.

Geel·vink Bay (khāl′vingk) An inlet of the Pacific in NW New Guinea.

gee·pound (jē′pound′) See SLUG (def. 5).

Geer·trui·da (hâr·troi′dä) Dutch form of GERTRUDE.

geese (gēs) Plural of GOOSE[1].

geest (gēst) *n. Geol.* **1** Material derived from rock decay in its natural place. **2** Gravel; especially, alluvium. [<Du., barren, dry soil]

Ge·ez (gē·ez′, gēz) *n.* Ethiopic.

gee·zer (gē′zər) *n. Slang* A queer old person. [Var. of *guiser* mummer <GUISE, *v.* (def. 3)]

Gef·le (yev′lə) See GAVLE.

ge·gen·schein (gā′gən·shīn) *n. Astron.* A patch of faint, hazy light sometimes observable at night on the point of the ecliptic opposite the sun: associated with the zodiacal light. Also called *counterglow.* [<G]

Ge·hen·na (gi·hen′ə) *n.* **1** In the Bible, the valley of Hinnom near Jerusalem, where offal was thrown and fires kept burning to purify the air. **2** A place of torment. **3** In the New Testament, hell; hellfire. [<LL <Gk. *geenna* <Hebrew *gehinnom* valley of *Hinnom*]

Gei·ger (gī′gər), **Hans,** 1882–1945, German physicist.

Gei·ger counter (gī′gər) *Physics* A sensitive instrument for counting ionizing particles in the air, as alpha particles or cosmic rays and also for detecting the amount of radioactivity in a given area. Also called *counting tube.* [after Hans *Geiger*]

Gei·kie (gī′kē), **Sir Archibald,** 1835–1924, English geologist and writer.

gei·sha (gā′shə) *n. pl.* **·sha** or **·shas** A Japanese girl trained to furnish entertainment by singing, dancing, etc. [<Japanese]

Geiss·ler tube (gīs′lər) *Physics* A sealed and partly evacuated glass tube containing electrodes: used for the study of electric discharges through gases. [after Heinrich *Geissler,* 1814–79, German physicist]

gel (jel) *n. Chem.* A colloidal dispersion of a solid in a liquid which may range from the nearly liquid to the solid state, but is typically a semisolid and of a jellylike consistency, as gelatin, mucilage, uncooked egg white, etc. *—v.i.* **gelled, gel·ling** To change into a gel; jellify. [Short for GELATIN]

ge·län·de·sprung (gə·len′də·shpro͝ong) *n.* In skiing, a jump, using both poles, made from a crouching position. [<G <*gelände* level ground + *sprung* jump]

gel·a·tin (jel′ə·tin) *n.* A hard, transparent, tasteless, colloidal protein produced from

bones, white connective tissue, and skin of animals. It is soluble in hot water, cooling to a jelly, but insoluble in alcohol or chloroform. Edible gelatin, used for foods, drugs, etc., is a highly refined product of yellowish tint; technical gelatin is used in photography, lithography, in the manufacture of sizing, plastics, etc. Also **gel′a·tine** (-tin, -tēn). [<F *gélatine,* orig. a soup made from fish <Ital. *gelatina* <*gelata* jelly <L. See JELLY.]

ge·lat·i·nate (ji·lat′ə·nāt) *v.t.* & *v.i.* **·nat·ed, ·nat·ing** To change into gelatin or a jellylike substance. **—ge·lat′i·na′tion** *n.*

ge·lat·i·nize (ji·lat′ə·nīz) *v.* **·nized, ·niz·ing** *v.t.* **1** To gelatinate. **2** To treat or coat with gelatin. —*v.i.* **3** To be changed into gelatin or jelly. **—ge·lat′i·ni·za′tion** *n.*

ge·lat·i·noid (ji·lat′ə·noid) *adj.* Like jelly or gelatin. —*n.* A gelatinlike substance.

ge·lat·i·nous (ji·lat′ə·nəs) *adj.* **1** Of the nature of gelatin; like jelly. **2** Of or pertaining to or consisting of gelatin. **—ge·lat′i·nous·ly** *adv.* **—ge·lat′i·nous·ness** *n.*

ge·la·tion (ji·lā′shən) *n.* Solidification, especially by cooling.

geld[1] (geld) *n.* In early English history, a tax or tribute. [OE]

geld[2] (geld) *v.t.* **geld·ed** or **gelt, geld·ing 1** To castrate; emasculate; also, to spay. **2** To deprive of an essential part; weaken. [<ON *gelda* castrate]

Gel·der·land (gel′dər·land, *Du.* hel′dər·länt) A province of eastern and central Netherlands; 1,921 square miles; capital, Arnhem: also *Guelderland, Guelders.*

geld·ing (gel′ding) *n.* A castrated animal, especially a horse.

Ge·lée (zhə·lā′), **Claude** See LORRAIN, CLAUDE.

Ge·li·bo·lu (ge′lē·bō·lōō′) The Turkish name for GALLIPOLI.

gel·id (jel′id) *adj.* Very cold; icy; frozen. [<L *gelidus*] **—ge·lid′i·ty** *n.* **—gel′id·ly** *adv.*

gel·se·mine (jel′sə·mīn, -min) *n. Chem.* A white, crystalline, very poisonous alkaloid, $C_{22}H_{26}O_2N_2$, obtained from gelsemium: used as a depressant and mydriatic.

gel·se·mi·um (jel·se′mē·əm) *n.* **1** The poisonous root of the yellow jasmine *(Gelsemium sempervirens).* **2** A medical preparation made from it. [<NL <Ital. *gelsomino* jasmine]

Gel·sen·kir·chen (gel′zən·kir′khən) A city in the Ruhr valley, North Rhine-Westphalia, Germany.

gelt (gelt) *n. Slang* Money. [<G *geld* money]

gem (jem) *n.* **1** A precious stone, especially when set as an ornament. **2** Anything rare, delicate, and perfect, as a work of literature or art. **3** A carved or engraved semiprecious stone; any jewel. **4** *Printing* A size of type between brilliant and diamond. **5** A light cake somewhat like a muffin. —*v.t.* **gemmed, gem·ming** To adorn with or as with gems. [OE *gim* <L *gemma* jewel]

Ge·ma·ra (gə·mä′rə, -môr′ə) *n.* The second part of the Jewish Talmud, an exposition of the first part (Mishna). [<Aramaic, completion]

gem·el (jem′əl) *adj.* Paired; coupled: a *gemel* window. [<OF <L *gemellus* doubled]

gem·i·nate (jem′ə·nāt) *v.t.* & *v.i.* **·nat·ed, ·nat·ing 1** To make or become double; pair. **2** *Ling.* To double a phoneme, particularly a consonant. —*adj.* (-nit) *Bot.* Occurring in pairs or couples, as leaves. [<L *geminatus,* pp. of *geminare* <*geminus* a twin] **—gem′i·na′tion** *n.*

Gem·i·ni (jem′ə·nī) **1** A constellation, the Twins. See CONSTELLATION. **2** The third sign of the zodiac.

gem·ma (jem′ə) *n. pl.* **·mae** (-ē) *Bot.* **1** A bud. **2** The budlike product of gemmation. [<L]

gem·mate (jem′āt) *adj. Bot.* Bearing buds; reproducing by buds. [<L *gemmatus,* pp. of *gemmare* bud]

gem·ma·tion (jem·ā′shən) *n. Bot.* **1** Reproduction by budlike outgrowth that becomes an independent individual. **2** The period of the expansion of buds.

gem·me·ous (jem′ē·əs) *adj.* Relating to, having the nature of, or resembling gems.

gem·mip·a·rous (jem·ip′ər·əs) *adj. Bot.* Reproducing by, or producing, buds. [<L *gemma* bud + -PAROUS] **—gem·mip′a·rous·ly** *adv.*

gem·mu·la·tion (jem′yōō·lā′shən) *n. Biol.* Reproduction by, or formation of, gemmules.

gem·mule (jem′yōōl) *n.* **1** *Bot.* A small bud or gemma. **2** *Biol.* One of the minute hypothetical granules that, according to the doctrine of pangenesis, reproduce the cells or organic units from which they are thrown off. **3** *Zool.* A small internal reproductive bud in certain fresh-water sponges. [<LL *gemmula,* dim. of *gemma* bud]

gem·my (jem′ē) *adj.* **1** Full of, set with, or containing gems. **2** Like a gem; bright; sparkling.

gem·ol·o·gy (jem·ol′ə·jē) *n.* The scientific study and investigation of gems. **—gem·o·log·i·cal** (jem′ə·loj′i·kəl) *adj.* **—gem·ol′o·gist** *n.*

ge·mot (gə·mōt′) *n.* In early English history, a public meeting or assembly: the folk *gemot*; a local court. Also **ge·mote′.** [OE *gemōt*]

gems·bok (gemz′bok) *n. pl.* **·bok** or **·boks** A South African antelope (*Oryx gazella*) having long, sharp, nearly straight horns and a tufted tail. [<Afrikaans <G *gemse* chamois + *bock* a buck]

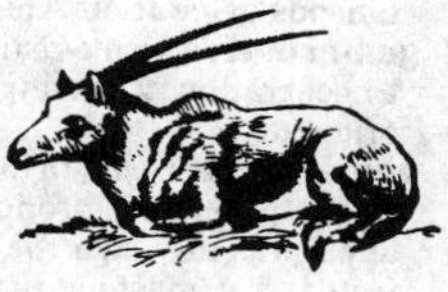

GEMSBOK
(About 3 feet high at the shoulder; horns to 3 feet)

Gem State Nickname of IDAHO.

gem·stone (jem′stōn′) *n.* A mineral or petrified organic material of a quality suitable for cutting, polishing, and using in jewelry.

ge·müt·lich (gə·müt′likh) *adj. German* Full of good feeling; genial; comfortable.

Ge·müt·lich·keit (gə·müt′likh·kīt) *n. German* Good feeling; a feeling of comfort.

-gen *suffix of nouns* **1** *Chem.* That which produces: *oxygen.* **2** *Biol.* That which is produced: *antigen.* [<F *-gène* <Gk. *-genēs,* <*gen-,* stem of *gignesthai* be born, become]

gen·darme (zhän′därm, *Fr.* zhäṅ·dȧrm′) *n. pl.* **·darmes** (-därmz, *Fr.* -dȧrm′) One of a corps of armed police, especially in France. [<F <*gens d'armes* men-at-arms]

gen·darm·e·rie (zhän′där·mə·rē, zhän·därm′·ə·rē; *Fr.* zhäṅ·dȧrm·rē′) *n.* Gendarmes collectively. Also **gen·darm′e·ry.**

gen·der (jen′dər) *n.* **1** *Gram.* In many languages, as in the Indo-European and Semitic families, a grammatical category of nouns governing the form assumed by the words which modify or refer to them. **Natural gender** corresponds to sex or lack of sex; animate beings are either masculine or feminine, inanimate objects are neuter. This is true of English, which indicates natural gender by pronoun reference (*he, she, it,* etc.), by suffixes and prefixes (*aviator, aviatrix, emperor, empress, he-bear, she-bear,* etc.), or by completely different forms (*cow, bull,* etc.). **Grammatical gender** may have a partial correspondence to sex for animate beings, but sexless objects can be of any gender. Latin and German have three grammatical genders (masculine, feminine, and neuter) often without reference to sex, as seen in Latin *nauta* sailor, which is in a feminine declension. French and Hebrew have two genders, the names of inanimate objects being either masculine or feminine. In some languages, as in the Algonquian family, gender classification is made on another basis entirely—that of animate and inanimate categories. **2** *Colloq.* Sex. **3** *Obs.* A kind; genus. —*v.t.* & *v.i. Obs.* To engender. [<OF *gendre* <L *genus, -eris.* Doublet of GENUS, GENRE.]

gene (jēn) *n. Biol.* The chemically complex unit which is assumed to be the carrier of specific physical characters from parents to offspring, being transmitted through the chromosomes of the gametes and subject to many influences, as mutation, translocation, crossing over, radiation. X-rays, etc.: also called *factor.* [<Gk. *genea* breed, kind]

Gene (jēn) Diminutive of EUGENE.

ge·ne·al·o·gist (jē′nē·al′ə·jist, jen′ē-) *n.* One versed in genealogies.

ge·ne·al·o·gy (jē′nē·al′ə·jē, jen′ē-) *n. pl.* **·gies 1** A record of descent from some ancestor; a list of ancestors and their descendants. **2** Descent in a direct line; pedigree. **3** The science that treats of pedigrees. [<Gk. *genea* race + -LOGY] **—ge·ne·a·log·i·cal** (jē′nē·ə·loj′i·kəl, jen′ē-) *adj.* **—ge′ne·a·log′i·cal·ly** *adv.*

gen·e·ra (jen′ər·ə) Plural of GENUS. [<L]

gen·er·a·ble (jen′ə·ər·bəl) *adj.* Capable of being generated. [<L *generabilis* <*generare* generate]

gen·er·al (jen′ər·əl) *adj.* **1** Pertaining to, including, or affecting all of the whole; not local or particular: a *general* election; a *general* anesthetic. **2** Common to or current among the majority; prevalent: the *general* opinion. **3** Extended in scope, meaning, or content; not restricted in application: a *general* principle. **4** Not limited to a special class; miscellaneous: a *general* cargo. **5** Not detailed or precise: a *general* idea. **6** Usual or customary: one's *general* habit. **7** Dealing with all branches of a business or pursuit; not specialized: a *general* store; a *general* practitioner. **8** Superior in rank: attorney *general.* —*n.* **1** *Mil.* **a** In the U.S. Army, Air Force, or Marine Corps, an officer ranking next above a lieutenant general, equivalent in rank to an admiral in the Navy. **b** Any general officer, as a brigadier general, lieutenant general, etc.: a shortened form. **c** In

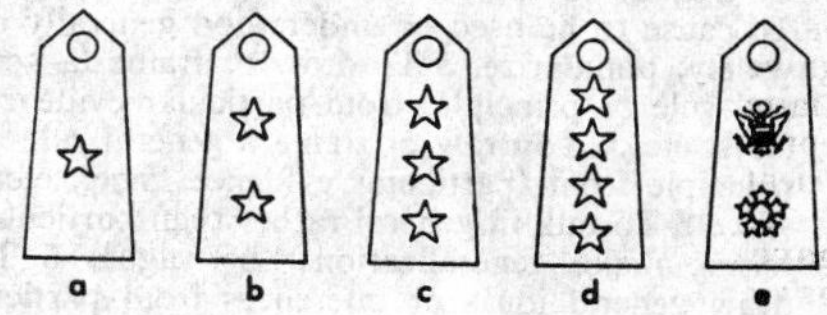

INSIGNIA OF GENERALS—UNITED STATES ARMY
a. Brigadier general. *c.* Lieutenant general.
b. Major general. *d.* General.
e. General of the Army.

many foreign armies, an officer of superior grade, usually ranking just below a marshal or field marshal. **2** *Eccl.* The chief of a religious order. **3** A general statement, fact, or principle. **4** *Archaic* The people or the public. **—brigadier general** An officer in the U.S. Army, Air Force, or Marine Corps ranking next above a colonel and next below a major general. **—in general** For the most part; in the main. **—lieutenant general** An officer in the U.S. Army, Air Force, or Marine Corps ranking next above a major general and next below a general. **—major general** An officer in the U.S. Army, Air Force, or Marine Corps ranking next above a brigadier general and next below a lieutenant general. [<OF <L *generalis* of a race or kind <*genus, generis* kind]

Synonyms (adj.): common, commonplace, customary, everyday, familiar, frequent, habitual, normal, ordinary, popular, prevalent, public, universal, usual. *Common* signifies frequently occurring, not out of the regular course, not exceptional; hence, not above the average, not excellent or distinguished; inferior, or even low; it also signifies pertaining to or participated in by two or more persons or things; as, Sorrow is *common* to the race. *General* may signify pertaining equally to all of a class, race, etc., but often signifies pertaining to the greater number, but not necessarily to all. *Universal* applies to all without exception; *general* applies to all with possible or comparatively few exceptions; *common* applies to very many without deciding whether or not they are all. A *common* remark is one we often hear; a *general* experience is one that comes to the majority of people; a *universal* experience is one from which no human being is exempt. Compare COMMON, FREQUENT, HABITUAL, NORMAL, USUAL. *Antonyms*: exceptional, infrequent, odd, peculiar, queer, rare, singular, strange, uncommon, unfamiliar, unknown, unparalleled, unprecedented, unusual.

general agent *Law* One appointed by a principal to act for him solely or particularly.

General Assembly 1 The deliberative body of the United Nations, meeting in annual or special sessions, in which every member nation is represented. **2** *U.S.* The legislature in some States. **3** The highest ecclesiastical governing body of certain denominations.

General Court The legislature in Massachusetts and New Hampshire.

gen·er·al·cy (jen′ər·əl·sē) *n.* Rank, authority, or tenure of office of a general.

general delivery 1 A post-office department that delivers mail to an addressee when called for. 2 Mail so addressed.

general election An election on a set date in which every constituency chooses a representative.

gen·er·al·is·si·mo (jen′ər·əl·is′i·mō) *n. pl.* **·mos** A supreme military or military and naval commander. [< Ital.]

gen·er·al·i·ty (jen′ə·ral′ə·tē) *n. pl.* **·ties** 1 The main part; chief portion; majority: the *generality* of voters. 2 Anything general or not specific; especially, a vague general statement: to deal in *generalities.* 3 The state of being general or generalized. Also **gen·er·al·ty** (jen′ər·əl·tē).

gen·er·al·i·za·tion (jen′ər·əl·ə·zā′shən, -ī·zā′-) *n.* 1 Act of generalizing. 2 A statement or proposition expressed in general terms, applying to a class or numerous members of a class, rather than covering only an individual case; opposite of *particularization.*

gen·er·al·ize (jen′ər·əl·īz′) *v.* **·ized, ·iz·ing** *v.t.* 1 To treat as having general or wide application. 2 To cause to be used or understood generally or widely; popularize. 3 To draw or frame (a general rule or principle) from particular evidence, facts, etc. 4 To draw or frame a general rule or principle from (particular evidence, facts, etc.). —*v.i.* 5 To talk in general rather than particular terms; make generalizations; be vague. 6 To draw general ideas or inferences from particulars.

General Land Office A U.S. government bureau in charge of surveying, selling, and disposing of claims to public land.

gen·er·al·ly (jen′ər·əl·ē) *adv.* 1 For the most part; ordinarily; in most but not all cases. 2 Without going into particulars. 3 So as to include or apply to all; collectively or universally.

general officer Any army officer holding a rank higher than colonel.

General of the Air Force The highest ranking officer of the U.S. Air Force.

General of the Armies A special title and rank conferred upon John J. Pershing in 1919.

General of the Army An officer of the highest rank in the U.S. Army: equivalent to marshal or field marshal in other armies. For insignia see illustration under GENERAL.

general paralysis See under PARESIS.

gen·er·al-pur·pose (jen′ər·əl·pûr′pəs) *adj.* Good for many purposes: A good *general-purpose* horse may be used as a draft horse or for pleasure driving.

general semantics A discipline for human living, formulated by Alfred Korzybski, involving a critical analysis of verbal and non-verbal symbols as these enter into behavioral responses, and a denial of the universality of Aristotelian logic: in practice using a methodology based on modern science, distinguishing carefully between levels of abstraction, between statements and the events they represent, generalizations and the particular, etc., avoiding polarized (either-or) orientations, and emphasizing unity and relationships within wholes.

gen·er·al·ship (jen′ər·əl·ship) *n.* 1 A general's office or rank. 2 A general's military skill or management. 3 Management or leadership of any sort.

general staff 1 A body of officers who direct the military policy and strategy of a national state. 2 A group of officers charged with directing a division or higher unit and operating from a headquarters under a commander in chief.

General Staff In the U.S. Army, the supreme military staff for policy and strategy, consisting of the Chief of Staff, several deputy and assistant Chiefs of Staff, including those heading sections of personnel administration (G-1), military intelligence (G-2), and operations and training (G-3), the Comptroller of the Army, the Director of the Women's Army Corps, and other officers.

gen·er·ate (jen′ə·rāt) *v.t.* **·at·ed, ·at·ing** 1 To produce or cause to be; bring into being. 2 To beget as a parent; procreate. 3 *Geom.* To trace out by motion: A moving point *generates* a line, or a line a surface. See synonyms under PRODUCE, PROPAGATE. [< L *generatus,* pp. of *generare* generate]

gen·er·a·tion (jen′ə·rā′shən) *n.* 1 The process, act, or function of begetting or procreating; reproduction. 2 Production or origination by any process; creation: the *generation* of electricity. 3 A step or degree in natural descent. 4 The period between successive steps in natural descent, usually taken at 30 years in humans. 5 All persons removed in the same degree from an ancestor. 6 A body of persons existing at the same time or period. 7 A body of persons overlapping other existing bodies, but typified by difference in mental, moral, or ethical outlook: the jazz *generation.* 8 The average lifetime of the persons in a community. 9 *Geom.* The formation of a magnitude by the motion of a point, line, or surface. 10 Race or family. 11 Progeny; offspring. —**spontaneous generation** Abiogenesis.

gen·er·a·tive (jen′ə·rā′tiv) *adj.* 1 Of or pertaining to generation. 2 Having the power to produce or originate.

gen·er·a·tor (jen′ə·rā′tər) *n.* 1 One who or that which generates, produces, or originates. 2 An apparatus in which the generation of a gas is effected. 3 A machine that transforms heat or mechanical work directly into electric energy; a dynamo.

gen·er·a·trix (jen′ə·rā′triks) *n. pl.* **gen·er·a·tri·ces** (jen′ər·ə·trī′sēz) 1 *Geom.* A line, point, or figure that generates another figure by its motion. 2 A female that generates or produces.

ge·ner·ic (ji·ner′ik) *adj.* 1 Pertaining to a genus or a class of related things: contrasted with *specific* or *varietal.* 2 Having a general application; abstract; not concrete. Also **ge·ner′i·cal.** [< L *genus, -eris* race, kind + -IC] —**ge·ner′i·cal·ly** *adv.*

gen·er·os·i·ty (jen′ə·ros′ə·tē) *n. pl.* **·ties** 1 The quality of being generous; liberality. 2 A generous act. See synonyms under BENEVOLENCE.

gen·er·ous (jen′ər·əs) *adj.* 1 Giving or bestowing heartily and munificently; munificent: a *generous* contributor. 2 Having noble qualities; honorable; high-minded: a *generous* nature. 3 Abundant; bountiful: a *generous* fare. 4 *Obs.* Of good descent: said either of men or of animals. 5 Having stimulating qualities; strong: *generous* wine. [< F *généreux* < L *generosus* of noble birth < *genus.* See GENUS.] —**gen′er·ous·ly** *adv.* —**gen′er·ous·ness** *n.*

Synonyms: bountiful, chivalrous, disinterested, free, free-handed, free-hearted, liberal, magnanimous, munificent, noble, open-handed, openhearted. *Generous* primarily signifies having the qualities worthy of noble or honorable birth; hence, free and abundant in giving, giving freely, heartily, and unselfishly. As regards giving, *generous* refers rather to the heartiness of the giver; *liberal* to the amount of the gift; a child may show himself *generous* in the gift of an apple, a millionaire makes a *liberal* donation; a *generous* gift, however, is commonly thought of as both ample and hearty. A *munificent* gift is vast in amount, whatever the motive of its bestowal. One may be *free* with another's money; he can be *generous* only with his own. *Disinterested* means without self-interest or selfish motive. One is *magnanimous* by a greatness of soul that rises above all that is poor, mean, or weak, and above resentment of injury or insult. *Antonyms*: avaricious, close, covetous, greedy, ignoble, illiberal, mean, miserly, niggardly, parsimonious, penurious, petty, rapacious, stingy.

Gen·e·see River (jen′ə·sē′) A river in Pennsylvania and western New York, rising in the Alleghenies, which flows 158 miles north to Lake Ontario.

ge·ne·si·al (ji·nē′zē·əl) *adj.* Of or pertaining to reproduction or generation. Also **ge·ne·sic** (ji·nē′zik).

ge·ne·si·ol·o·gy (ji·nē′zē·ol′ə·jē) *n.* The study of the reproduction of organisms. [< GENESIS + -(O)LOGY]

gen·e·sis (jen′ə·sis) *n. pl.* **·ses** (-sēz) 1 The act or mode of originating; creation. 2 Origin; beginning. [< L < Gk. *genesis* creation, origin]

Gen·e·sis (jen′ə·sis) The first book of the Pentateuch in the Old Testament.

-genesis *combining form* Development; genesis; evolution: *biogenesis.* [< Gk. *genesis* origin]

gen·et[1] (jen′it, jə·net′) *n.* 1 Any of certain small carnivores (genus *Genetta*) related to the civets but having only rudimentary scent glands. 2 The fur of the genet. Also **ge·nette′.** [< F *genette* < Sp. *gineta* < Arabic *jarnait* genet]

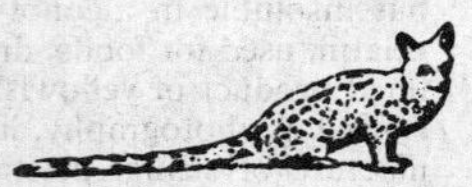
GENET
(Body 1 foot, 10 inches; tail, 1 foot, 6 inches)

gen·et[2] (jen′it) *n.* A jennet.

Ge·nêt (zhə·ne′), **Edmond Charles,** 1763–1834, French diplomat in the United States: also known as *Citizen Genêt.*

ge·neth·li·ac (jə·neth′lē·ak) *adj.* Relating to nativities or their calculation; showing the position of the stars at birth. Also **gen·eth·li·a·cal** (jen′əth·lī′ə·kəl). [< F *généthliaque* < LL *genethliacus* < Gk. *genethliakos* of one's birth] —**gen′eth·li′a·cal·ly** *adv.*

ge·net·ic (jə·net′ik) *adj.* 1 Of, pertaining to, dealing with, or based on genesis. 2 Of or relating to genetics. 3 *Biol.* Designating those characteristics of an organism due to inheritance or to the action of genes. Also **ge·net′i·cal.** [< GENESIS; formed on analogy with *synthetic, antithetic,* etc.] —**ge·net′i·cal·ly** *adv.*

genetic engineering The application of techniques of genetic recombination to produce desired alterations in genetic material.

ge·net·ics (jə·net′iks) *n.* 1 That branch of biology which deals with the interaction of the genes in producing the similarities and differences between individuals related by descent. 2 The science of plant- and animal-breeding. 3 The inherited characteristics of an organism or group of organisms. —**ge·net′i·cist** *n.*

ge·net·o·troph·ic (jə·net′ə·trof′ik, -trō′fik) *adj.* *Biol.* Pertaining to, exhibiting, or characterized by inherited defects in body chemistry resulting in an inability to assimilate enough of the essential elements in nutrition. [< GENETIC + TROPHIC]

ge·ne·va (jə·nē′və) *n.* Gin, especially Holland gin. [< MDu. *genever* < OF *genevre* gin < L *juniperus* juniper]

Ge·ne·va (jə·nē′və) 1 A canton of SW Switzerland; 107 square miles. 2 A city on the Lake of Geneva; capital of Geneva canton. *French* **Ge·nève** (zhə·nev′); *German* **Genf** (genf).

Geneva, Lake of The largest lake in Switzerland; 224 square miles: also *Lake Leman.*

Geneva bands A pair of linen strips, hanging from the front of the neck: worn with clerical or academic garments.

Geneva Convention A convention for the amelioration of the condition of the wounded and of prisoners in time of war, signed at Geneva, Switzerland, in 1864: also called *Red Cross Convention.*

Geneva cross See under CROSS.

Geneva gown A loose academic gown with large sleeves: used as an ecclesiastical vestment.

Geneva movement *Mech.* The movement effected by a mechanism having its driving wheel so geared as to give intermittent motion to another wheel which is toothed: used in watches, motion-picture projectors, etc.

Ge·ne·van (jə·nē′vən) *adj.* 1 Of or pertaining to Geneva, Switzerland. 2 Of or pertaining to the theology taught there by Calvin; Calvinistic. —*n.* 1 A native or inhabitant of Geneva. 2 A Calvinist.

Gen·e·vese (jen′ə·vēz′, -vēs′) *adj. & n.* Genevan.

Gen·ghis Khan (jen′giz kän′, jeng′gis), 1162–1227, Mongol conqueror of northern China, Iran, etc. Also spelled *Jenghiz.*

gen·ial[1] (jēn′yəl, jē′nē·əl) *adj.* 1 Kindly in disposition; cordial and pleasant in manner. 2 Imparting warmth, comfort, or life; supporting life or growth. 3 *Rare* Exhibiting or relating to genius. See synonyms under BLAND, CHEERFUL, COMFORTABLE, FRIENDLY, GOOD. [< L *genialis* of one's tutelary deity < *genius.* See GENIUS.] —**ge′nial·ly** *adv.*

ge·ni·al[2] (jə·nī′əl) *adj. Anat.* Of, pertaining to, or near the chin. [< Gk. *geneion* chin]

ge·ni·al·i·ty (jē′nē·al′ə·tē) *n.* Kindness of disposition; warmth; friendly cheerfulness.

gen·ic (jen′ik) *adj.* Of, pertaining to, or like a gene or genes; genetic.

-genic *combining form* Related to generation or production: *biogenic.* [<-GEN+-IC]

ge·nic·u·late (jə·nik'yə·lāt, -lit) *adj. Biol.* 1 Having kneelike joints or protuberances. 2 Bent abruptly, like a knee. [< L *geniculatus* < *geniculum,* dim. of *genu* knee]

ge·nie (jē'nē) *n.* A jinni.

Ge·nie (jē'nē) Diminutive of EUGENIA.

ge·ni·i (jē'nē·ī) 1 Plural of GENIUS (defs. 6 and 9). 2 Jinn.

ge·ni·o·plas·ty (jə·nī'ə·plas'tē) *n.* Plastic surgery of the chin and lower cheek.

gen·i·pap (jen'ə·pap) *n.* 1 A tropical American tree (*Genipa americana*) of the madder family. 2 Its edible fruit, about the size of an orange. [< Pg. *genipapo* < native name]

gen·i·tal (jen'ə·təl) *adj.* 1 Of or pertaining to the reproductive organs, or to the process of generation. 2 *Psychoanal.* Of or relating to a stage of psychosexual development in which the genitals are the dominant source of libidinal gratification in the context of mature personal relations with others: compare ANAL, ORAL. [< L *genitalis* of generation < *genitus,* pp. of *gignere* beget]

gen·i·ta·li·a (jen'ə·tā'lē·ə, -tāl'yə) *n. pl.* The genitals. [< L, neut. plural of *genitalis.* See GENITAL.]

gen·i·tals (jen'ə·təlz) *n. pl.* The external organs of generation; sexual organs.

gen·i·ti·val (jen'ə·tī'vəl) *adj.* Pertaining to the genitive case; having a genitive form. —**gen'·i·ti'val·ly** *adv.*

gen·i·tive (jen'ə·tiv) *adj.* 1 Indicating source, origin, possession, or the like. 2 *Gram.* Pertaining to a case in Latin, Greek, etc., corresponding in part to the English possessive. —*n. Gram.* 1 The genitive case. 2 A word in this case. [< L *genitivus* < *gignere* beget]

genito- *combining form* Of or related to the genitals. [< L *genitus,* pp. of *gignere* beget]

gen·i·tor (jen'ə·tər, -tôr) *n. Obs.* A progenitor; a begetter. [< L]

gen·i·to·u·ri·nar·y (jen'ə·tō·yŏŏr'ə·ner'ē) *adj. Anat.* Of or pertaining to the genital and the urinary organs.

gen·i·us (jēn'yəs) *n. pl.* **gen·ius·es** *for defs.* 2–5, 7, 8; **ge·ni·i** *for defs.* 6 *and* 9. 1 Extraordinary intellectual gifts, evidenced in original creation, expression, or achievement. 2 Remarkable aptitude for some special pursuit; a distinguishing natural capacity or tendency: a *genius* for oratory. 3 A person of phenomenal and original powers for productivity in art, science, statesmanship, etc.: such a *genius* as Mozart, Shakespeare, Napoleon, Einstein, etc. 4 The dominant influence or essential animating principle of anything; the prevalent feeling or thought (of a nation or era). 5 A representative type; impersonation; embodiment. 6 In Roman antiquity, a beneficent spirit or demon supposed to accompany one through life, or either of two attendant spirits, one good, the other bad; a guardian or tutelary spirit of a person, place, or thing. 7 Hence, a person having an extraordinary influence over another. 8 The traditions, history, associations, influences, etc., of a locality or place. 9 In Mohammedan folklore, a jinni. [< L, tutelary spirit < *gen-,* stem of *gignere* beget]
Synonyms: talent, talents. *Genius* is exalted intellectual power capable of operating independently of tuition and training, and marked by extraordinary faculty for original creation, invention, discovery, expression, etc. *Talent* is marked mental ability, and in a special sense, a particular and uncommon aptitude for some special mental work or attainment. *Genius* is higher than *talent,* more spontaneous, less dependent upon instruction, less amenable to training; *talent* is largely the capacity to learn, acquire, appropriate, adapt oneself to demand. Compare CHARACTER, INGENUITY, MIND, POWER. *Antonyms:* dulness, folly, imbecility, obtuseness, senselessness, stupidity.

ge·ni·us lo·ci (jē'nē·əs lō'sī, -kē) *Latin* 1 The spirit or guardian deity of the place. 2 The unique quality of a place as felt by an observer.

Gen·nes·a·ret (gə·nes'ə·ret), Sea of *or* Lake The New Testament name for the SEA OF GALILEE. Also **Gen·nes'a·reth.**

Gen·o·a (jen'ō·ə) A port in NW Italy on the Gulf of Genoa, the northern portion of the Ligurian Sea. *Italian* **Ge·no·va** (je'nō·vä).

gen·o·cide (jen'ə·sīd) *n.* The systematic extermination of racial and national groups: term first used in indictment of German war criminals after World War II. [< Gk. *genos* race, tribe +-CIDE; coined by Raphael Lemkin, 1944.]

Gen·o·ese (jen'ō·ēz', -ēs') *adj.* Of or pertaining to Genoa. —*n.* A native or legally constituted citizen of Genoa: used as singular, plural, or collective.

gen·om (jen'om) *n. Biol.* A full set of chromosomes with their associated genes. Also **gen'ome** (-ōm). [< GENE+-OM(E)]

gen·o·type (jen'ə·tīp) *n. Biol.* 1 The genetic constitution of an organism, expressed and latent: contrasted with *phenotype.* 2 A type representative of a group of organisms; the most typical species of a genus. [< Gk. *genos* race, kind +-TYPE] —**gen·o·typ·ic** (jen'ə·tip'·ik) *or* **·i·cal** *adj.*

-genous *suffix of adjectives* 1 Generating; yielding: *sporogenous.* 2 Produced or generated by: *parthenogenous.* [< -GEN+-OUS]

gen·re (zhän'rə) *n.* 1 A genus, sort, or style; especially, a category of art or literature characterized by a certain form, style, subject matter, or atmosphere. 2 A class of painting or other art portraying everyday life; distinguished from the historical, romantic, etc., style. [< F < L *genus,* *-eris* race, kind. Doublet of GENDER, GENUS.]

gen·ro (gen·rō') *n. pl.* **gen·ros** One of the Japanese elder statesmen. [< Japanese *genrō* first (of the) elders]

gens (jenz) *n. pl.* **gen·tes** (jen'tēz) 1 *Anthropol.* In primitive society, a body of blood kindred having a common gentile name, and distinguished by a totem or crest. 2 In Roman antiquity, a clan or house composed of several families having a common ancestor; a subdivision of a tribe. [< L]

Gen·san (gen·sän') The Japanese name for WONSAN, Korea.

Gen·ser·ic (gen'sər·ik, gen'-), 406?–77, king of the Vandals; conquered north Africa; sacked Rome, 455.

gent¹ (jent) *adj. Obs.* 1 Of gentle birth; genteel; noble. 2 Neat; pretty. [< OF < L *genitus,* orig. pp. of *gignere* beget]

gent² (jent) *n. Slang.* A gentleman.

Gent (gent) The Flemish name for GHENT.

gen·teel (jen·tēl') *adj.* 1 Well-bred or refined; elegant; polite. 2 Suitable for or pertaining to the station or needs of well-bred persons. 3 Stylish or fashionable. ◆This word is now used chiefly in a somewhat derogatory or humorous sense: *genteel* poverty. See synonyms under POLITE. [< MF *gentil.* Doublet of GENTLE.] —**gen·teel'ly** *adv.* —**gen·teel'ness** *n.*

gen·teel·ism (jen·tēl'iz·əm) *n.* An expression that is pretentious, affected, or overly elegant for what it describes or designates.

gen·tian (jen'shən) *n.* 1 Any of a large genus (*Gentiana*) of European and American flowering herbs, as the **yellow gentian** of Europe (*G. lutea*), the **fringed gentian** of America (*G. crinita*), with blue, conspicuously fringed solitary flowers, and the **closed** or **bottle gentian** (*G. andrewsi*), with purple-blue, non-opening flowers. 2 The root of the yellow gentian, having tonic properties. [< L *gentiana,* appar. after *Gentius,* an Illyrian king]

GENTIAN
a. Bottle or closed.
b. Fringed.

gen·tian·a·ceous (jen'shən·ā'shəs) *adj. Bot.* Belonging to a family (*Gentianaceae*) of annual or perennial herbs, with showy, perfect, regular flowers.

gen·tian·el·la (jen'shən·el'ə) *n.* 1 A European alpine dwarf gentian (*Gentiana acaulis*) having attractive blue flowers. 2 A shade of blue. [< NL, dim. of L *gentiana* GENTIAN]

gentian violet *Chem.* A purple dye of the rosaniline group, used medicinally as an antiseptic and bactericide: also called *methylrosaniline.*

gen·tile (jen'tīl) *adj.* 1 Of or pertaining to a nation, gens, or clan. 2 *Gram.* Denoting racial, national, or local extraction: said of a noun or adjective. 3 Heathen; pagan. —*n.* 1 *Gram.* A noun or adjective denoting race, country, etc. 2 In Roman law, a member of a gens or clan. [< F *gentil* < LL *gentilis* foreign. Doublet of GENTILE.]

Gen·tile (jen'tīl) *n.* 1 Among the Jews, one of a non-Jewish people; one not a Jew. 2 Among Christians: a One who is not a Jew; a pagan. b A Christian, especially one formerly a pagan. 3 Among Mormons, a non-Mormon. —*adj.* 1 Pertaining to or characteristic of a non-Jewish people. 2 Belonging to or like Christians, as distinguished from Jews. 3 Of or pertaining to non-Mormons.

gen·ti·lesse (jen'tə·les) *n. Archaic* Gentle birth or manners. [< OF < *gentil.* See GENTLE.]

gen·til·ism (jen'təl·iz'əm) *n.* 1 The character of being Gentile in birth and spirit; formerly, heathenism. 2 Clannishness; attachment to one's gens or tribe.

gen·til·i·ty (jen·til'ə·tē) *n. pl.* **·ties** 1 The quality of being genteel or well-bred; refinement: now often used ironically. 2 Gentle birth; good extraction. 3 Well-born or well-bred persons collectively; gentry. [< OF *gentilite* < L *gentilitas,* *-tatis* < *gentilis.* See GENTLE.]

gen·tle (jen'təl) *adj.* 1 Belonging to a family distinguished by blood, birth, or station. 2 Befitting one of high birth or station. 3 *Archaic* Noble; chivalrous: a *gentle* knight. 4 Considerate; generously inclined: a *gentle* reader. 5 Mild in disposition; refined in manners. 6 Tame; docile: a *gentle* horse. 7 Soft; moderate; not harsh: a *gentle* touch. 8 Not steep, sharp, or abrupt: a *gentle* slope. 9 *Meteorol.* Designating a moderate breeze, No. 3 on the Beaufort scale. —*v.t.* **gen·tled, gen·tling** 1 To make easy to control; tame, as a horse. 2 To make gentle. 3 *Obs.* To raise to the rank of gentility. [< OF *gentil* < L *gentilis* of good birth < *gens, gentis* race, clan. Doublet of GENTEEL, GENTILE.] —**gen'tly** *adv.* —**gen'tle·ness** *n.*

gentle craft 1 Shoemaking. 2 Angling.

gen·tle·folk (jen'təl·fōk') *n. pl.* Persons of good family and good breeding. Also **gen'tle·folks'.**

gen·tle·man (jen'təl·mən) *n. pl.* **·men** (-mən) 1 A well-bred man with good manners. 2 Any man: in the plural the usual form of address in public assemblies: Ladies and *gentlemen.* 3 *Brit.* A man above a yeoman in social rank. —**fine gentleman** A fashionable gentleman; also a dandy; fop.

gen·tle·man-at-arms (jen'təl·mən·at·ärmz') *n. pl.* **·men·(·mən·)** *Brit.* One of forty-six gentlemen who attend the sovereign on various state and solemn occasions.

gentleman farmer One who owns a farm, but hires others to work it.

gen·tle·man·ly (jen'təl·mən·lē) *adj.* Pertaining to or befitting a gentleman; courteous; gracious. Also **gen'tle·man·like'.**

gentleman of fortune Formerly, a gentleman who sought his fortune in dangerous pursuits; now, an adventurer living by his wits.

gentleman of the road 1 A highwayman. 2 *U.S.* A hobo.

gentleman's agreement An agreement, usually diplomatic or political, and less formal than a treaty or contract, guaranteed only by the honor of the parties involved.

gentleman's gentleman A valet serving a man of social position.

gentle sex Women collectively.

gen·tle·wom·an (jen'təl·wŏŏm'ən) *n. pl.* **·wom·en** (-wim'in) 1 A woman of good birth and social position: a lady. 2 A considerate, gracious, well-mannered woman. 3 Formerly, a woman in attendance on a lady of rank.

Gen·too (jen·tōō') *n. pl.* **·toos** (-tōōz') 1 In India, a Hindu, especially a Telugu, as distinguished from a Moslem. 2 The language of the Gentoos. [< Pg. *gentio* gentile < L *gentilis*]

gen·tri·fi·ca·tion (jen'trə·fə·kā'shən) *n.* The rebuilding or restoration of deteriorating city residential properties for purchase or use by middle- or upper-class buyers.

gen·try (jen′trē) *n.* **1** People of good position or birth; in England, the upper class exclusive of the nobility. **2** Any specified class of people: commonly an ironical term. **3** *Obs.* Gentle birth or condition. **4** *Obs.* Urbanity; politeness. [Appar. a back formation from GENTRICE, incorrectly taken as a plural]

gen·ty (jen′tē) *adj. Scot.* Shapely; trim; jaunty.

ge·nu (jē′nōō, -nyōō) *n. pl.* **gen·u·a** (jen′yōō·ə) *Anat.* **1** The knee. **2** A kneelike structure, as a bend of the corpus callosum. [<L]

gen·u·flect (jen′yə·flekt) *v.i.* To bend the knee, as in worship. [<Med. L *genuflectere* < *genu* knee + *flectere* bend]

gen·u·flec·tion (jen′yə·flek′shən) *n.* A bending of the knee, as in worship. Also *Brit.* **gen′·u·flex′ion.**

gen·u·ine (jen′yōō·in) *adj.* **1** Of the original or true stock. **2** Authentic; of the authorship claimed. **3** Not spurious, adulterated, or counterfeit. **4** Not affected or hypocritical; frank; sincere; true. See synonyms under AUTHENTIC, HONEST, PURE. [<L *genuinus* innate] — **gen′u·ine·ly** *adv.* — **gen′u·ine·ness** *n.*

ge·nus (jē′nəs) *n. pl.* **gen·e·ra** (jen′ər·ə) **1** *Biol.* A class or category of plants and animals ranking next above the species and next below the family or subfamily. The genus and species names together constitute the scientific name of an organism, the genus name (capitalized) standing first; as *Homo sapiens* for the human species. **2** *Logic* A class of things divisible into two or more subordinate classes, or species. **3** A kind; class. [<L, race, kind]

-geny *combining form* Mode of production of; generation or development of: *anthropogeny, cosmogeny.* [<F *-génie* <L *-genia* <Gk. *-geneia* < *gen-*, stem of *gignesthai* become]

geo- *combining form* Earth; ground; soil: *geocentric, geology.*

ge·o·ben·thos (jē′ə·ben′thəs) *n. Ecol.* That portion of the bottom of a river, stream, or lake which is destitute of vegetation. Compare PHYTOBENTHON. [<GEO- + Gk. *benthos* depth]

ge·o·bi·on (jē′ə·bī′on) *n. Ecol.* A plant community adapted to the land, as distinguished from aquatic communities. [<GEO- + Gk. *bios* life]

ge·o·bot·a·ny (jē′ō·bot′ə·nē) *n.* Phytogeography.

ge·o·cen·tric (jē′ō·sen′trik) *adj.* **1** Relating to the earth as a center. **2** Measured from the earth or the earth's center. — **ge′o·cen′tri·cal** *adj.* — **ge′o·cen′tri·cal·ly** *adv.*

ge·o·cen·tri·cism (jē′ō·sen′trə·siz′əm) *n.* The ancient theory that the earth is the center of the planetary system, or the central object of divine providential care.

ge·o·chem·i·cal (jē′ō·kem′i·kəl) *adj.* Showing the results of both geological and chemical action.

ge·o·chem·is·try (jē′ō·kem′is·trē) *n.* The chemistry of geological processes and of the substances taking part in them; chemical geology.

ge·o·chro·nol·o·gy (jē′ō·krə·nol′ə·jē) *n.* The age of the earth, as determined by the observation and study of geologic, geographic, climatic, and biological processes. — **ge·o·chron·o·log·ic** (jē′ō·kron′ə·loj′ik) or **·i·cal** *adj.*

ge·ode (jē′ōd) *n. Geol.* **1** A stone having a cavity lined with crystals. **2** The cavity in such a stone. [<F *géode* <L *geodes*, a precious stone <Gk. *geōdēs* earthy] — **ge·od·ic** (jē·od′ik) *adj.*

ge·o·des·ic (jē′ə·des′ik) *adj.* Of or pertaining to geodesy. — *n.* A geodesic line.

geodesic line *Math.* The shortest line connecting two points on a given surface.

ge·od·e·sy (jē·od′ə·sē) *n. Math.* The study and measurement of extensive areas of the earth's surface, especially with reference to the determination of the magnitude and figure of the earth: distinguished from *surveying* (of limited areas). [<F *géodésie* <NL *geodaesia* <Gk. *geodaisia* < *gē* earth + *daiein* divide] — **ge·od′e·sist** *n.*

ge·o·det·ic (jē′ə·det′ik) *adj.* **1** Of, pertaining to, determined, or effected by geodesy: a *geodetic* survey. **2** *Aeron.* Denoting a type of aircraft construction in which all parts of the fuselage, wings, and other exposed surfaces are built along the contours where the aerodynamic strain and load stress are greatest. **3** Geodesic. Also **ge′o·det′i·cal.** — **ge′o·det′i·cal·ly** *adv.*

ge·o·dy·nam·ics (jē′ō·dī·nam′iks) *n.* The study of the forces that affect the structure and

modifications of the earth. — **ge′o·dy·nam′ic, ge′o·dy·nam′i·cal** *adj.*

Geof·frey (jef′rē) A masculine personal name. See GODFREY. Also *Fr.* **Geof·froi** (zhō·frwä′). — **Geoffrey of Anjou,** 1113–50, father of Henry II of England: also known as *Geoffrey Plantagenet.* — **Geoffrey of Monmouth,** 1100?–54?, English chronicler.

Geof·froy Saint–Hi·laire (zhō·frwä′ saṅ·tē·lâr′), Étienne, 1772–1844, French zoologist.

ge·og·no·sy (jē·og′nə·sē) *n.* The study of the istics, especially in terms of large areas and the complex of interrelationships obtaining among them. **2** The natural aspect, features, etc., of a place or area: the *geography* of the Arctic. [<L *geographia* <Gk. < *gē* earth + *graphein* write, describe] — **ge·og′ra·pher** *n.* — **ge′o·graph′ic** or **·i·cal** *adj.* — **ge′o·graph′i·cal·ly** *adv.*

ge·oid (jē′oid) *n.* The earth considered as an ellipsoidal solid whose surface coincides with the mean level of the ocean. [<Gk. *geoidēs* earthlike < *gē* earth + *eidos* form]

GEOLOGICAL TIME SCALE

Read from bottom to top.

ERAS	TIME PERIODS ROCK SYSTEMS		TIME EPOCHS ROCK SERIES	APPROX. DURATION MILLION YEARS	APPROX. PERCENT TOTAL AGE	LIFE FORMS
CENOZOIC	QUATERNARY		RECENT PLEISTOCENE	1		Rise and dominance of Man.
CENOZOIC	UPPER TERTIARY		PLIOCENE MIOCENE	65	2	Modern animals and plants.
CENOZOIC	LOWER TERTIARY		OLIGOCENE EOCENE PALEOCENE			Rapid development of modern mammals, insects, and plants.
MESOZOIC	UPPER CRETACEOUS			75	5	Primitive mammals; last dinosaurs; last ammonites.
MESOZOIC	LOWER CRETACEOUS					Rise of flowering plants.
MESOZOIC	JURASSIC			45		First birds, first mammals. Diversification of reptiles; climax of ammonites; coniferous trees.
MESOZOIC	TRIASSIC			45		Rise of dinosaurs; cycadlike plants; bony fishes.
PALEOZOIC	PERMIAN			45	9	Rise of reptiles. Modern insects. Last of many plant and animal groups.
PALEOZOIC	PENNSYLVANIAN	CARBONIFEROUS		75		First reptiles. Amphibians; primitive insects; seed ferns; primitive conifers.
PALEOZOIC	MISSISSIPPIAN	CARBONIFEROUS				Climax of shell–crushing sharks. Primitive ammonites.
PALEOZOIC	DEVONIAN			50		First amphibians, first land snails. Primitive land plants. Climax of brachiopods.
PALEOZOIC	SILURIAN			20		First traces of land life. Scorpions. First lungfishes. Widespread coral reefs.
PALEOZOIC	ORDOVICIAN			70		First fish. Climax of trilobites. First appearance of many marine invertebrates.
PALEOZOIC	CAMBRIAN			50		First marine invertebrates, including trilobites.
PROTEROZOIC	PROTEROZOIC	PRE-CAMBRIAN		About 3,000	84	First signs of life. Algae.
ARCHEOZOIC	ARCHEOZOIC	PRE-CAMBRIAN				

Age of oldest dated rocks: about 3,500,000,000 years.

materials of the earth, their structure, characteristics, and interrelationships; structural geology. [<GEO- + Gk. *gnōsis* knowledge]

ge·o·graph·ic determinism (jē′ə·graf′ik) *Sociol.* The theory that attributes the forms and characteristics of a given society, community, or nation to the molding influence of geographic factors.

geographic mile See under MILE.

ge·og·ra·phy (jē·og′rə·fē) *n. pl.* **·phies 1** The science that describes the surface of the earth and its associated physical, biological, economic, political, and demographic character-

ge·ol·o·gist (jē·ol′ə·jist) *n.* One versed in geology. Also **ge·ol′o·ger.**

ge·ol·o·gize (jē·ol′ə·jīz) *v.i.* **·gized, ·giz·ing 1** To study, or discourse on, geology. **2** To make geological investigations, especially in the field.

ge·ol·o·gy (jē·ol′ə·jē) *n. pl.* **·gies 1** The science that treats of the origin, history, constitution, and structure of the earth, including the operation of the physical forces affecting its development and appearance and the history of living or extinct forms as recorded in the rocks. See Time Scale above. **2** A treatise

on this subject. See HISTORICAL GEOLOGY. — **ge·o·log·ic** (jē′ə·loj′ik) or **·i·cal** *adj.* —**ge′o·log′i·cal·ly** *adv.*

ge·o·man·cy (jē′ə·man′sē) *n.* Divination by means of some aspect of the earth, particularly by the observation of points and lines on the earth. —**ge′o·man′cer** *n.* —**ge′o·man′tic** *adj.*

ge·o·med·i·cine (jē′ō·med′ə·sin) *n.* The branch of medicine that treats the geographic factors of disease.

ge·om·e·ter (jē·om′ə·tər) *n.* One skilled in geometry. Also **ge·om·e·tri·cian** (jē·om′ə·trish′ən, jē′ə·mə-). [< L *geometres* < Gk. *geōmetrēs* one who measures land]

ge·o·met·ric (jē′ə·met′rik) *adj.* **1** Pertaining to or according to the rules and principles of geometry. **2** Forming, consisting of, or characterized by regular lines, curves, and angles, as the markings on certain insects, or on the primitive pottery of the Mycenaean era, which is recognized by its rectilinear decorations. Also **ge′o·met′ri·cal** — **ge′o·met′ri·cal·ly** *adv.*

geometric progression *Math.* A sequence of terms of which each member except the first is greater than its predecessor by a constant ratio, as 2, 4, 8, 16, 32, 64: distinguished from *arithmetic progression.*

ge·om·e·trid (jē·om′ə·trid) *n.* Any of a family (*Geometridae*) of moths whose larvae are called measuring worms, because they walk by moving their abdominal and anal prolegs, thus forming the body into a loop, giving the impression that they are measuring the space below. [< NL *Geometridae* < L *geometres*. See GEOMETER.]

ge·om·e·trize (jē·om′ə·trīz) *v.i.* **·trized, ·triz·ing 1** To study geometry. **2** To apply geometric methods or principles.

ge·om·e·try (jē·om′ə·trē) *n. pl.* **·tries** The branch of mathematics that treats of space and its relations, especially as shown in the properties and measurement of points, lines, angles, surfaces, and solids. [< OF *geometrie* < L *geometria* < Gk. *geōmetria* < *gē* earth + *metrein* measure]

ge·o·mor·phic (jē′ə·môr′fik) *adj.* **1** Resembling the earth, as in contour. **2** Of or pertaining to the earth's form or the configuration of its surface features.

ge·o·mor·phol·o·gy (jē′ō·môr·fol′ə·jē) *n.* The study of the development, configuration, and distribution of the surface features of the earth; physiographical geology. Also **ge′o·mor·phog′e·ny** (-foj′ə·nē). —**ge′o·mor·pho·log′i·cal** (-fə·loj′i·kəl) *adj.*

ge·on·o·my (jē·on′ə·mē) *n.* The study of the earth in all its geological, physical, chemical, and mechanical aspects; earth science. —**ge·o·nom·ic** (jē′ə·nom′ik) *adj.*

ge·oph·a·gy (jē·of′ə·jē) *n.* Dirt-eating; morbid appetite for dirt, clay, etc. —**ge·oph′a·gism** (-jiz′əm) *n.* —**ge·oph′a·gist** *n.*

ge·o·phys·ics (jē′ə·fiz′iks) *n.* The science that treats of the physical forces and phenomena associated with the earth, and studies the nature of deep-lying areas by means of seismographs, the torsion balance, and various electromagnetic instruments. —**ge′o·phys′i·cal** *adj.* —**ge′o·phys′i·cist** *n.*

ge·o·phyte (jē′ə·fīt) *n. Bot.* An earth-growing plant; especially, one whose buds, mycelia, etc., are deeply buried in the substratum.

ge·o·pol·i·tics (jē′ō·pol′ə·tiks) *n.* **1** The study of geography, geology, climate, and the natural resources of the earth in relation to the development of peoples, cultures, and states. **2** A method of studying geography and power politics in terms of national security in international relations, embracing geography, natural resources, industrial development, and political strength. **3** The former German doctrine of living space as the primary element in, and strongest guaranty of, state power and world domination. See LEBENSRAUM.

ge·o·pon·ic (jē′ə·pon′ik) *adj.* Pertaining to agriculture; hence, rustic. [< Gk. *geōponikos* < *geōponos* a farmer < *gē* earth + *ponos* labor]

ge·o·pon·ics (jē′ə·pon′iks) *n. pl.* The art or science of agriculture.

ge·o·po·ten·tial (jē′ə·pə·ten′shəl) *n. Meteorol.* The potential energy of unit mass, equal to the work required to lift it from the zero potential of sea level to its actual position: applied especially in air-mass analysis.

geor·die (jôr′dē) *n. Scot.* A guinea.

George (jôrj) A masculine personal name. Also *Dan., Ger., Sw.* **Ge·org** (gā′ôrg), *Fr.* **Georges** (zhôrzh) or **Geor·get** (zhôr·zhe′), *Latin* **Geor·gi·us** (jôr′jē·əs). [< Gk., husbandman]
—**George I,** 1660–1727, elector of Hanover; king of England 1714–27.
—**George I,** 1845–1913, king of Greece 1863–1913.
—**George II,** 1683–1760, king of England 1727–60.
—**George II,** 1890–1947, king of Greece 1922–23, 1935–47.
—**George III,** 1738–1820, king of England 1760–1820.
—**George IV,** 1762–1830, king of England 1820–30.
—**George V,** 1865–1936, king of England 1910–36.
—**George VI,** 1895–1952, king of England 1936–52.
—**George, Saint,** martyred 303?, patron saint of England.

George (jôrj) *n.* **1** A jewel carved with the figure of St. George slaying the dragon: one of the insignia of the Knights of the Garter. **2** An old coin minted in England during the reign of Henry VIII, and bearing the figure of St. George.

George (jôrj), **David Lloyd** See LLOYD GEORGE, DAVID. —**Henry,** 1839–97, U.S. economist.

Ge·or·ge (gā·ôr′gä), **Stefan,** 1868–1933, German lyric poet.

George (jôrj), **Lake** A lake in eastern New York, 33 miles long: called *Lake Horicon* in the novels of J. F. Cooper.

George V Coast A region of the coast of Antarctica south of Australia.

George Town A port on Penang Island, capital of Penang State, Malaya.

George·town (jôrj′toun) The capital of Guyana.

geor·gette crepe (jôr·jet′) A sheer, dull fabric with a crepelike surface, originally made of silk: used for blouses, gowns, millinery, etc.: a trade name. [after Mme. *Georgette* de la Plante, French modiste]

Geor·gia (jôr′jə) **1** A southern Atlantic State of the United States; 58,876 square miles; capital, Atlanta; entered the Union Jan. 2, 1788, one of the original thirteen States: nickname, *Cracker State*: abbr. GA **2** A constituent republic of the U.S.S.R. in the southern Caucasus on the Black Sea; 29,400 square miles; capital, Tiflis: Russian *Gruziya;* Georgian *Sakartvelo*: also **Georgian Soviet Socialist Republic.**

Geor·gia (jôr′jə), **Strait of** A channel between the mainland of British Columbia and Vancouver Island; 150 miles long, 20 to 40 miles wide.

Geor·gian (jôr′jən) *adj.* **1** Of or pertaining to the reigns or period of the four Georges in England, 1714–1830, or of George V, 1910–36. **2** Of or pertaining to the State of Georgia. **3** Of or pertaining to Georgia in the U.S.S.R., to the Georgians, or to their language. —*n.* **1** A native or inhabitant of the State of Georgia. **2** One of an ancient mountain people native to the Caucasus; also, one of their modern descendants, a native of the Georgian Republic. **3** The agglutinative South Caucasian language of the Georgians of the Soviet Union. **4** A person belonging to either of the Georgian periods in England, or having Georgian taste.

Geor·gi·an·a (jôr′jē·an′ə) A feminine personal name. Also **Geor·gi·na** (jôr·jē′nə, *Ger.* gā′ôr·gē′nä), *Fr.* **Geor·gine** (zhôr·zhēn) or **Georgette** (zhôr·zhet′). [See GEORGE]

Georgian Bay An inlet in the NE part of Lake Huron, Ontario, Canada; 110 by 50 miles.

Georgia pine 1 The long-leaved southern yellow pine (*Pinus palustris*). **2** The wood of this tree.

geor·gic (jôr′jik) *adj.* Pertaining to husbandry or rural affairs: also **geor′gi·cal.** —*n.* A poem on husbandry. [< L *georgicus* < Gk. *geōrgikos* < *geōrgia* husbandry]

ge·o·stat·ic (jē′ə·stat′ik) *adj.* Of or pertaining to the pressure of the earth.

ge·o·stat·ics (jē′ə·stat′iks) *n.* The statics of rigid bodies in relation to balanced forces on or beneath the earth's surface.

ge·o·strat·e·gist (jē′ō·strat′ə·jist) *n.* A specialist in the problems, objectives, and doctrines of geostrategy.

ge·o·strat·e·gy (jē′ō·strat′ə·jē) *n.* Military strategy as related to and determined by geopolitical factors. [< GEO(POLITICS) + STRATEGY] — **ge′o·stra·te′gic** (-strə·tē′jik) *adj.*

ge·o·stroph·ic (jē′ə·strof′ik) *adj. Meteorol.* Designating a regional drift of air masses caused by the rotation of the earth. Compare CYCLOSTROPHIC. [< GEO- + Gk. *strephein* turn]

ge·o·syn·cline (jē′ə·sin′klīn) *n. Geol.* A massive downward flexure of the earth's crust: opposed to *geanticline.* —**ge′o·syn·cli′nal** *adj. & n.*

ge·o·tax·is (jē′ə·tak′sis) *n. Biol.* The arrangement of an organism or any of its parts with respect to the force of gravitation. See GEOTROPISM.

ge·o·tech·nol·o·gy (jē′ō·tek·nol′ə·jē) *n.* The application of the mineral arts and sciences to the improvement of old and development of new methods, techniques, processes, and products, as in ceramics, glassmaking, metallurgy, etc. — **ge′o·tech′no·log′i·cal** (-nə·loj′i·kəl) *adj.* — **ge′o·tech·nol′o·gist** *n.*

ge·o·tec·ton·ic (jē′ō·tek·ton′ik) *adj. Geol.* Relating to the structure of the rock masses of the earth's crust and to their shape, composition, and distribution.

ge·o·ther·mal (jē′ə·thûr′məl) *adj.* Pertaining to or of the earth's internal heat. Also **ge′o·ther′mic.**

ge·ot·ro·pism (jē·ot′rə·piz′əm) *n. Biol.* A tendency exhibited by organisms, especially the roots of growing plants, to turn toward the center of the earth: distinguished from *apogeotropism.* Compare GEOTAXIS. —**ge·o·trop·ic** (jē′ə·trop′ik) *adj.* —**ge′o·trop′i·cal·ly** *adv.*

Ge·ra (gā′rä) A city in Thuringia, S East Germany.

ge·rah (gē′rə) *n.* An ancient Hebrew unit of weight, one twentieth of a shekel. *Ezek.* xlv 12.

Ge·raint (jə·rānt′) In Arthurian legend, one of the knights of the Round Table; husband of Enid. Tennyson used his story in *Idylls of the King.*

Ger·ald (jer′əld) A masculine personal name. [< Gmc., spear ruler]

Ger·al·dine (jer′əl·dēn) A feminine personal name. Also *Fr.* **Gé·ral·dine** (zhā·rál·dēn′). [See GERALD]

ge·ra·ni·a·ceous (ji·rā′nē·ā′shəs) *adj. Bot.* Belonging or pertaining to a family (*Geraniaceae*) of polypetalous herbs, shrubs, and trees, the geranium family, widely scattered in temperate and subtropical regions. [< NL *Geraniaceae* < L *geranium* GERANIUM]

ge·ra·ni·al (ji·rā′nē·əl) *n.* Citral.

ge·ra·ni·ol (ji·rā′nē·ôl, -ōl) *n. Chem.* An oily colorless alcohol of the terpene group, $C_{10}H_{18}O$, a constituent of oil of roses, geranium, citronella, and other plants: used in perfumery and cosmetics.

ge·ra·ni·um (ji·rā′nē·əm) *n.* **1** Any of a widespread genus (*Geranium*) of plants typical of the family Geraniaceae. Also called *cranesbill.* **2** Pelargonium. **3** A very deep pink to vivid red color. [< L < Gk. *geranion* < *geranos* crane]

Ge·rard (ji·rärd′, *Du.* hā′rärt) A masculine personal name: same as GERALD. Also *Fr.* **Gé·rard** (zhā·rár′), *Ital.* **Ge·rar·do** (jā·rär′dō), *Lat.* **Ge·rar·dus** (jə·rär′dəs) [< Gmc., hard spear]

Ge·rard (ji·rärd′), **Ralph Waldo,** born 1900, U.S. physiologist. —**John,** 1545–1612, English surgeon and botanist.

Gé·raud (zhā·rō′) French form of GERALD.

ger·bil (jûr′bil) *n.* Any of a subfamily (*Gerbillinae*) of rodents found in Asia, Africa, and SE Europe, with long hind legs, hairy tail, and narrow incisors. Also **ger·bille′.** [< F *gerbille* < NL *gerbillus,* dim. of *gerbo* a jerboa]

Ger·da (gûr′dä) In Norse mythology, a giantess who was loved by Frey and became his wife: also spelled *Gerd, Gerdh, Gerthr.*

Ge·re·mi·a (jä′rā·mē′ä) Italian form of JEREMIAH.

ge·rent (jir′ənt) *n.* A governing power; ruler;

manager. [<L *gerens, -entis,* ppr. of *gerere* carry on, do]

ge·re·nuk (ge′rə·no͝ok) *n.* An East African antelope *(Lithocranius walleri)* with extremely long legs and a massive head. [<native name]

ger·e·ol·ogy (jer·ē·ol′ə·jē) *n.* Gerontology. Also **ger′a·tol′o·gy** (-ə·tol′ə·jē). [<Gk. *gēras* old age + -LOGY]

ger·fal·con (jûr′fôl′kən, -fô′-) *n.* A large falcon *(Falco rusticolus)* of the Arctic regions, with feathered shanks: also spelled *gyrfalcon.* [<OF *gerfaucon* <OHG *gir* vulture + OF *faucon* a falcon]

Ger·hard (*Dan.* ger′härth, *Du.* kher′ärt, *Sw.* yer′härd) See GERALD. Also *Ger.* **Ger·hart** (ger′härt).

Ger·har·di·ne (ger′här·dē′nə) German form of GERALDINE.

ger·i·at·ric (jer′ē·at′rik) *adj.* Of or pertaining to geriatrics or to old people.

ger·i·a·tri·cian (jer′ē·ə·trish′ən) *n.* A specialist in the diseases of old age. Also **ger·i·at·rist** (jer′ē·at′rist).

ger·i·at·rics (jer′ē·at′riks) *n.* **1** The branch of medicine which deals with the structural changes, physiology, diseases, and hygiene of old age. **2** Gerontology. [<Gk. *gēras* old age + -IATRICS]

Gé·ri·cault (zhā·rē·kō′), **Jean Louis André Théodore,** 1791–1824, French painter.

ger·i·o·psy·cho·sis (jer′ē·ō·sī·kō′sis) *n.* Mental disorder associated with old age; a psychosis of the senile. [<Gk. *gēras* old age + PSYCHOSIS]

ger·kin (gûr′kin) See GHERKIN.

Ger·la·chov·ka (ger·lä·khôf′kä) The former name of STALIN PEAK. Czechoslovakia. *German* **Gerls·dor·fer Spit·ze** (gerls′dôr·fər shpit′sə). Also **Ger·lach** (ger′läkh).

germ (jûrm) *n.* **1** Any rudimentary vital element. **2** *Biol.* **a** The formative protoplasm of an egg or ovum, or of an ovule; a gamete; germ cell. **b** The earliest stage of an organism. **3** *Bot.* A growing point, as a young bud. **4** The primary source of anything; that from which a thing may be developed as from a seed. **5** A micro-organism; especially, one likely to cause disease; a microbe. **6** An embryo. —*adj.* **1** Germinative. **2** Pertaining to or arising from disease germs. [<F *germe* <L *germen* sprig]

ger·man[1] (jûr′mən) *n.* The cotillion, or a dance at which it is the chief feature. [Short for *German* cotillion]

ger·man[2] (jûr′mən) *adj.* Having the same parents or grandparents: used after the noun: cousins *german,* brothers *german.* [<OF *germain* <L *germanus* closely related]

Ger·man (jûr′mən) *n.* **1** A native or citizen of Germany. **2** The West Germanic language of the Germans. —**High German** The standard literary and spoken language used throughout most of Germany and in parts of Switzerland, Austria, and Alsace: also called **New High German.** Abbr. *HG* —**Low German 1** The collective languages of the Low Countries, including Dutch, Flemish, and Frisian, and of the northern lowlands of Germany (Plattdeutsch). **2** The division of West Germanic which includes Dutch, Flemish, Frisian, English, etc. Abbr. *LG* —**Old High German** The language of southern Germany from about 800 to 1100. Abbr. *OHG* —**Middle High German** The High German language from 1100 to 1450, as exemplified in the *Nibelungenlied.* Abbr. *MHG* —**Middle Low German** The low German language from 1100 to 1450. Abbr. *MLG*

German Baptist Brethren The Dunkers: official name.

German cockroach The Croton bug.

German Democratic Republic See under GERMANY.

ger·man·der (jər·man′dər) *n.* **1** A labiate herb (genus *Teucrium*) of the mint family, with pale purple flowers; especially the American germander *(T. canadense).* **2** The germander speedwell. See under SPEEDWELL. [<OF *germandree* <Med. L. *germandra,* alter. of LGk. *chamandrya* <Gk. *chamaidrys* <*chamai* on the ground + *drys* an oak]

ger·mane (jər·mān′) *adj.* **1** In close relationship; relevant; appropriate; pertinent. **2** Akin; german. [See GERMAN[2]]

German East Africa A former German protectorate occupying Tanganyika, 1885–1916.

German Empire See under GERMANY.

ger·man·ic (jər·man′ik) *adj. Chem.* Containing germanium in its higher valence.

Ger·man·ic (gər·man′ik) *adj.* **1** Of or pertaining to a group of early Indo-European tribes living in the region between the Rhine, Danube, and Vistula rivers: later extended to include the Germans, English, Dutch, Flemings, Danes, Scandinavians, and German-Swiss. **2** Relating to the language or customs of any of these people. —*n.* **1** A subfamily of the Indo-European family of languages, divided into the branches **East Germanic,** including Gothic (extinct); **North Germanic** or Scandinavian, including Norwegian, Swedish, Danish, Icelandic, and Faroese; and **West Germanic,** including all the High and Low German languages and dialects, among which are German, Dutch, Flemish, Frisian, English, Yiddish, Plattdeutsch, etc. **2** The prehistoric parent of these languages: called **Primitive Germanic.** Also called *Teutonic.*

Ger·man·i·cus Cae·sar (jər·man′i·kəs sē′zər), 15 B.C.–A.D. 19, Roman general. See also DRUSUS.

Ger·man·ism (jûr′mən·iz′əm) *n.* **1** A German idiom, word, or phrase, or an imitation of German idiom. **2** The characteristic German spirit; admiration of things German; anything copied after German customs, ideas, etc.

ger·ma·ni·um (jər·mā′nē·əm) *n.* A brittle, grayish white crystalline element (symbol Ge, atomic number 32) with a metallic luster, important as a semiconductor in the manufacture of electronic instruments. See PERIODIC TABLE. [<NL <L *Germania* Germany]

Ger·man·ize (jûr′mən·īz) *v.* **·ized, ·z·ing** *v.t.* **1** To cause to conform to German speech, customs, etc. **2** To translate into German. —*v.t.* **3** To adopt German opinions, customs, etc. —**Ger′man·i·za′tion** *n.* —**Ger′man·iz′er** *n.*

German measles Rubella.

Germano- *combining form* German: *Germanophile.*

German Ocean A former name for the NORTH SEA.

Ger·man·o·phile (jər·man′ə·fīl) *n.* One who has love for Germany or what is German.

Ger·man·o·phobe (jər·man′ə·fōb) *n.* One who dislikes Germany or what is German.

ger·man·ous (jûr′mən·əs) *adj. Chem.* Of or pertaining to germanium in its lower valence.

German shepherd A breed of dog having a large, muscular body, a thick, smooth coat, and unusual adaptability to work with policemen, blind persons, etc. Also called *police dog, Alsatian.*

German silver A white alloy of copper, nickel, and zinc, used in cutlery and as a base for plated ware; nickel silver.

German Southwest Africa A former name for South-West Africa. Now NAMIBIA.

German tinder Amadou.

Ger·man·town (jûr′mən·toun) A northern suburb of Philadelphia; scene of Washington's defeat during the Revolutionary War, Oct. 4, 1777.

Ger·ma·ny (jûr′mə·nē) A country of central Europe, known as the *German Empire* 1871–1918, divided in 1949 into: **a** The *Federal Republic of Germany (West Germany)*; 84,634 square miles; capital, Bonn; **b** The *German Democratic Republic (East Germany)*; 41,700 square miles; capital, Berlin: German *Deutschland,* French *Allemagne.*

ger·mar·i·um (jər·mâr′ē·əm) *n. Zool.* The formative part of the ovary of certain invertebrates, as the flatworm, containing the primary cell elements. [<NL <L *germen* a sprig]

germ cell *Biol.* A cell specialized for reproduction: distinguished from *somatic cell.*

ger·mi·cide (jûr′mə·sīd) *n.* That which is capable of killing germs; any agent used to destroy disease germs or other micro-organisms, as chlorine. [<GERM + -(I)CIDE] —**ger′mi·ci′dal** *adj.*

ger·mi·cul·ture (jûr′mə·kul′chər) *n.* The artificial cultivation of bacteria or disease germs for scientific research. —**ger′mi·cul′tur·ist** *n.*

ger·mi·nal (jûr′mə·nəl) *adj.* Pertaining to or constituting a germ; germinative [<NL *germinalis* <L *germen, -inis* a sprig]

Ger·mi·nal (jûr′mə·nəl, *Fr.* zhâr·mē·nál′) See under CALENDAR (Republican).

germinal disk *Biol.* **1** A disklike area of the blastoderm of eggs of amniotic vertebrates, in which the embryo proper first appears. **2** In meroblastic eggs with much yolk, the disklike protoplasmic part, which undergoes segmentation. Also called *blastodisk.* Compare illustration under EMBRYOLOGY.

germinal vesicle 1 *Biol.* The nucleus of the animal ovum. **2** *Bot.* The oospore within the embryo sac of the ovule of plants.

ger·mi·nate (jûr′mə·nāt) *v.* **·nat·ed, ·nat·ing** *v.i.* To begin to grow or develop; sprout. —*v.t.* To cause to sprout. [<L *germinatus,* pp. of *germinare* sprout] —**ger′mi·na·ble** (-nə·bəl) *adj.* —**ger′mi·nant** *adj.* —**ger′mi·na′tion** *n.* —**ger′mi·na′tor** *n.*

ger·mi·na·tive (jûr′mə·nā′tiv) *adj.* **1** Pertaining to or tending to produce germination; capable of germinating. **2** Capable of growing.

Ger·mis·ton (jûr′məs·tən) A city in Gauteng province, Republic of South Africa.

germ layer *Biol.* One of the three principal layers of cells from which the embryo develops, as the ectoderm, mesoderm, or endoderm.

germ plasm *Biol.* The part of the cell protoplasm which is the material basis of heredity, transferred from one generation to another. Also **germ plasma.**

germ theory 1 *Pathol.* The theory that infectious diseases, as typhoid fever, are caused by bacteria or other micro-organisms. **2** The doctrine of biogenesis.

ger·o·don·tia (jer′ə·don′shə) *n.* The branch of dentistry which specializes in the dental condition of elderly people. [<NL <Gk. *gēras* old age + *odous, odontos* tooth]

Gé·rold (zhā·rō′) French form of GERALD. Also *Ger.* **Ge′rold, Ge·rolt** (gā′rōlt).

Gé·rome (zhā·rōm′), **Jean Léon,** 1824–1904, French painter.

ger·o·mor·phism (jer′ə·môr′fiz·əm) *n. Pathol.* Premature senility and old age. [<Gk. *gēras* old age + *morphē* form + -ISM] —**ger′o·mor′phic** *adj.*

Ge·ro·ni·mo (jä·rô′nē·mō) Italian form of JEROME. —**Ge·ron·i·mo** (jə·ron′ə·mō) An Apache chief, 1829–1909, who led an insurrection against U.S. forces, 1884–86.

ge·ron·tic (ji·ron′tik) *adj.* Senile; of or pertaining to an old person or to old age. [<Gk. *gerontikos* <*gerōn, gerontos* old man]

geronto- *combining form* Old age; pertaining to old people: *gerontology.* Also, before vowels, **geront-.** [<Gk. *gerōn, gerontos* old man]

ger·on·toc·ra·cy (jer′on·tok′rəsē) *n.* Government by the old; specifically, in certain primitive African cultures, the control of social life by members of the oldest age group. —**ge·ron·to·crat·ic** (ji·ron′tō·krat′ik) *adj.*

ge·ron·to·ge·ic (ji·ron′tō·jē′ik) *adj.* Of or pertaining to the Old World: opposed to *neogeic.* [<GERONTO- + Gk. *gē* earth]

ger·on·tol·o·gy (jer′on·tol′ə·jē) *n.* **1** The scientific study of the processes and phenomena of aging. **2** Geriatrics. —**ger′on·tol′o·gist** *n.*

ger·on·to·pi·a (jer′on·tō′pē·ə) *n.* Senopia.

ge·ron·to·ther·a·py (ji·ron′tō·ther′ə·pē) *n.* The therapeutic management of the disorders and processes associated with aging: distinguished from *geriatrics.*

-gerous *suffix* Bearing or producing: crystalligerous. [<L *gerere* bear + -OUS]

Ger·ry (ger′ē), **Elbridge,** 1744–1814, American statesman; signer of the Declaration of Independence.

ger·ry·man·der (jer′i·man′dər, ger′-) *n.t.* To alter unfairly or abnormally, as the political map of a state, etc. —*n.* An unnatural and arbitrary redistricting of a state or county. [<GERRY + (SALA)MANDER: from the salamander shape of one of the districts formed in Massachusetts while Elbridge Gerry was governor]

Gersh·win (gûrsh′win), **George,** 1898–1937, U.S. composer. —**Ira,** 1896–1983 U.S. lyricist; brother of George.

Ger·tie (gûr′tē) Diminutive of GERTRUDE.

Ger·trude (gûr′tro͞od, *Fr.* zher·trüd′; *Ital.* jer·tro͞o′dā) A feminine personal name. Also *Ger.* **Ger·traud** (ger′trout), *Ger., Sw.* **Ger·trud** (ger′tro͞ot), *Pg.* **Ger·tru·des** (zher·tro͞o′desh), *Sp.* **Ger·trú·dis** (her·tro͞o′dēs). [<Gmc., spear maid]

ger·und (jer′ənd) *n. Gram.* **1** In Latin, a verbal noun used only in the oblique cases of the singular, as furor *scribendi,* a rage for *writing.*

2 In English, a verbal noun ending in *-ing,* functioning as a noun, but capable of taking objects and adverbial modifiers. Example: *Writing* poetry well is an art. [< LL *gerundium* < *gerere* carry on, do] —**ge·rundi·al** (jə·run′dē·əl) *adj.*

ge·run·dive (jə·run′div) *Gram. adj.* Like, pertaining to, or having the nature of the gerund. —*n.* In Latin, a verbal adjective having the gerund stem and used as future passive participle, expressing obligation, fitness, or necessity, as *regendus,* that must or should be ruled, or *amandus,* to be loved, that should be loved, etc. [< LL *gerundivus* < *gerundium* GERUND]

Ge·ry·on (jē′rē·ən, ger′ē-) In Greek mythology, a three-headed monster of Erytheia, killed by Hercules for his herd of red cattle.

Ge·sell (gə·zel′), **Arnold Lucius,** 1880–1961, U.S. psychologist.

ges·so (jes′ō) *n.* **1** A ground of plaster, as gypsum or plaster of Paris, prepared to be painted on. **2** Gypsum or plaster of Paris prepared for use in sculpture. [< Ital. < L *gypsum* GYPSUM]

gest[1] (jest) *n.* **1** *Archaic* A deed; exploit. **2** A tale of adventure; a romance, especially a metrical romance. Also **geste.** ◆ Homophone: *jest.* [< OF < L *gesta* deeds, orig. neut. plural of *gestus,* pp. of *gerere* do]

gest[2] (jest) *n. Archaic* A gesture; carriage; bearing. Also **geste.** ◆ Homophone: *jest.* [< OF *geste* < L *gestus* bearing < *gerere* carry on, do]

gest[3] (jest) *n. Obs.* **1** A halting place. **2** An itinerary, especially of a royal progress. ◆ Homophone: *jest.* [Var. of GIST]

Ge·stalt (gə·shtält′) *n. pl.* **·stalt·en** (-shtält′ən) *Psychol.* An arrangement of separate elements of experience, emotion, etc., in a form, pattern, or configuration so integrated as to appear and function as a unit that is more than a simple summation of its parts. [< G, form]

Gestalt psychology A school of psychology which interprets biological and psychic processes in terms of the action and interplay of closely integrated patterns or *Gestalten*; the observed effect of a Gestalt, as well as the mechanism of its action, cannot be adequately explained through a simple analysis of its constituent parts.

Ge·sta·po (gə·stä′pō) *n.* The secret police of Nazi Germany. [< G *Ge(heime) Sta(ats)-po(lizei)* Secret State Police]

Ges·ta Ro·ma·no·rum (jes′tə rō′mə·nôr′əm, -nō′rəm) A collection of tales compiled in Latin in Europe in the 14th century, used as a source book by Chaucer, Shakespeare, and others. [< L, deeds of the Romans]

ges·tate (jes′tāt) *v.t.* **·tat·ed, ·tat·ing** To carry in the womb during gestation. [< L *gestatus,* pp. of *gestare* carry young]

ges·ta·tion (jes·tā′shən) *n.* Pregnancy; especially, the period of carrying a fetus in the womb from conception until birth. —**ges′ta·to′ry** (-tôr′ē, -tō′rē) *adj.*

ges·tic (jes′tik) *adj.* Of or pertaining to bodily motion, especially dancing. Also **ges′ti·cal.**

ges·tic·u·late (jes·tik′yə·lāt) *v.* **·lat·ed, ·lat·ing** *v.i.* To make motions with the hands or arms, as in speaking. —*v.t.* To express by gestures. [< L *gesticulatus,* pp. of *gesticulari* < *gesticulus,* dim. of *gestus* bearing, gesture] —**ges·tic′u·la′tive** *adj.* —**ges·tic′u·la′tor** *n.*

ges·tic·u·la·tion (jes·tik′yə·lā′shən) *n.* **1** A motion of the body or limbs, designed to illustrate speech; a gesture. **2** The act or art of making gestures. See synonyms under GESTURE. —**ges·tic′u·la·to′ry** (-tôr′ē, -tō′rē) *adj.*

ges·tion (jes′chən) *n. Obs.* Management; operation.

ges·ture (jes′chər) *n.* **1** An expressive motion or action, as of the hand or hands in speaking, used for emphasis or to express some idea or emotion. **2** Such motions collectively, or the art of making them. **3** Something said or done as a mere concession to manners, courtesy, etc. **4** *Obs.* Deportment; posture. —*v.* **·tured, ·tur·ing** *v.i.* To make gestures; gesticulate. —*v.t.* To express by gestures. [< Med. L *gestura* < *gerere* carry on, do] —**ges′tur·er** *n.*

Synonym (noun): gesticulation. *Gesticulation* often conveys the idea of jerky, sudden, or undignified motions; a *gesture* is any expressive movement of the limbs or body.

Ge·sund·heit (gə·zŏŏnt′hīt) *German* (Your) health: a salutation or a toast, or an expression of good will after a sneeze.

get (get) *v.* **got** or *Archaic* **gat, got** or *U.S.* **got·ten, get·ting** *v.t.* **1** To come into possession of; obtain. **2** To go and bring back or obtain: to *get* one's hat. **3** To cause to come, go, move, etc.: to *get* baggage through customs. **4** To take; carry away: *Get* your things out of this house. **5** To prepare; make ready: to *get* breakfast. **6** To cause to be; bring to a state or condition: to *get* the work done. **7** To find out; ascertain by calculation, experiment, etc.: To *get* the range of a gun. **8** To obtain as a result: Divide two into six and you will *get* three. **9** To receive as a reward, punishment, evaluation, etc.: to *get* ten years in jail for robbery. **10** To obtain, receive, or earn (something desired or needed): to *get* permission. **11** To receive as a salary, gift, etc.: What did you *get* for Christmas? **12** To learn by memorizing: to *get* a lesson by heart. **13** To become sick with; contract: to *get* malaria. **14** To board; catch, as a train. **15** To beget: said chiefly of animals. **16** *U.S. Colloq.* To come to an understanding of; comprehend: I *get* the idea. **17** *Colloq.* To possess, or to have as a characteristic: with *have* or *has*: He has *got* quite a temper. See note under GOT. **18** To square accounts with: I'll *get* you yet. **19** *Colloq.* To be obliged or forced to do: with *have* or *has*: I have *got* to go home. See note under GOT. **20** *Colloq.* To strike; hit: That shot *got* him in the arm. **21** *Slang* To puzzle; baffle; also, to cause irritation or pleasure to: His impudence *gets* me. **22** *Archaic* Betake: *Get* thee behind me. —*v.i.* **23** To arrive: When does the train *get* there? **24** To come or go: *Get* in here! **25** To board; enter: to *get* on a train or into a car. **26** To become: arrive at a condition or state: to *get* drunk; to *get* stuck in the mud. **27** To acquire profits or property. **28** *Colloq.* To find time, means, or opportunity: to *get* to go. —**to get about 1** To become known. **2** To move about. —**to get across 1** To make or be convincing or clear, as to an audience. **2** To be successful, as in projecting one's personality, entertaining, etc. —**to get ahead** To succeed; prosper. —**to get along 1** To leave; go. **2** To be successful or fairly successful, as in business. **3** To be friendly; harmonize. **4** To proceed. **5** To grow old or older. —**to get around 1** To become known. **2** To move about. **3** To avoid; circumvent. **4** To flatter, cajole, etc., so as to obtain the favor of. —**to get at 1** To reach; arrive at: to *get at* the truth. **2** To intend; mean: I don't see what you're *getting at.* **3** To apply oneself to: to *get at* a problem. **4** *Colloq.* To bribe; corrupt. —**to get away 1** To escape. **2** To leave; go. **3** To start. —**to get away with** *Slang* To do (something) without discovery, criticism, or punishment. —**to get back at** *Slang* To revenge oneself on. —**to get by 1** To pass: This *got by* the censor. **2** *Colloq.* To manage to survive. —**to get in 1** To arrive. **2** To interject effectively, as a remark or the last word. —**to get off 1** To descend from; dismount. **2** To leave; depart. **3** To be relieved, as of duty. **4** To be released without punishment; escape penalty. **5** To utter: to *get off* a joke. —**to get on 1** To mount, as a horse. **2** To get along. —**to get out 1** To depart. **2** To escape. **3** To become known, as a secret. **4** To publish; issue. —**to get over 1** To recover from, as illness or surprise. **2** To get across. —**to get together 1** To collect, as facts or goods. **2** To meet; assemble. **3** *Colloq.* To come to an agreement. —**to get up 1** To rise, as from sleep. **2** To prepare and arrange; devise. **3** *Colloq.* To dress up; bedeck, as with finery. **4** To acquire or work up knowledge of: to *get up* German for an examination. **5** To climb; ascend. —*n.* **1** The act of begetting, or that which is begotten; breed; progeny: the *get* of the stallion. **2** In tennis, handball, etc., the retrieval of a shot apparently beyond reach. [< ON *geta*] —**get′ta·ble** *adj.*

Synonyms (verb): achieve, acquire, attain, earn, gain, obtain, procure, receive, secure, win. *Get* is a most comprehensive word. A person *gets* whatever he comes to possess or experience, with or without endeavor, expectation, or desire; he *gets* a bargain, a blow, a fall, a fever; he *gains* what he comes to by effort or striving; the swimmer *gains* the shore; a man *acquires* by continuous and ordinarily by slow process; as, One *acquires* a foreign language. A person is sometimes said to *gain* and often to *acquire* what has not been an object of direct endeavor; in the pursuits of trade, he incidentally *gains* some knowledge of foreign countries; he *acquires* by association with others a correct or incorrect accent; he *acquires* a bronzed complexion by exposure to a tropical sun; in such use, what he *gains* is viewed as desirable, what he *acquires* as slowly and gradually resulting. A person *earns* what he gives an equivalent of labor for, but he may not *get* it. On the other hand, he may *get* what he has not *earned*; the temptation to all dishonesty is the desire to *get* a living or a fortune without *earning* it. Compare ATTAIN, GAIN[1], LEARN, MAKE, OBTAIN, PURCHASE, REACH. *Antonyms*: see synonyms for ABANDON.

get-at-a·ble (get′at′ə·bəl) *adj. Colloq.* That one may get at or reach; obtainable; accessible. —**get′-at′-a·bil′i·ty** *n.*

get-a·way (get′ə·wā′) *n.* **1** An escape, as of a criminal or of a fox from covert. **2** The start, as of a horse in a race. Also **get′a·way′.**

geth·sem·a·ne (geth·sem′ə·nē) *n.* A place or time of agony.

Geth·sem·a·ne (geth·sem′ə·nē) A garden outside Jerusalem at the foot of the Mount of Olives; the scene of the agony, betrayal, and arrest of Jesus. *Matt.* xxvi 36. [< Gk. *Gethsēmanē* < Aramaic *gath shemānīm* oil press]

get-rich-quick (get′rich′kwik′) *adj.* Aiming at quick and lucrative gains.

get·ter (get′ər) *n.* **1** One who gets. **2** *Electronics* A substance, as magnesium, placed inside a vacuum tube during manufacture and acting by incandescence to remove any gases left by the vacuum pump. **3** *Electr.* A coating of metal on the filament of a tungsten lamp, designed to prolong its life.

get-to·geth·er (get′tə·geth′ər) *n.* An informal gathering or meeting.

Get·tys·burg (get′iz·bûrg) A town in southern Pennsylvania; scene of a Confederate defeat in the Civil War, July 1–3, 1863.

get-up (get′up′) *n. Colloq.* **1** The manner in which a thing is put together; general appearance; make-up. **2** Style of dress.

Gev *abbr. Physics* Giga (10^9) electron volts.

gew-gaw (gyōō′gô) *adj.* Showy; gaudy. —*n.* A flashy, useless ornament; bauble. See synonyms under GAUD. [ME *giue-goue;* origin uncertain]

gey (gā) *adj. Scot.* Moderate; considerable. —*adv.* Very.

gey·ser (gī′zər) *n.* **1** A natural hot spring from which intermittent jets of steam, hot water, or mud are ejected in a fountainlike column. **2** *Brit.* A gas hot-water heater. [< Icel. *geysir* gusher, name of a hot spring < *geysa* gush]

gey·ser·ite (gī′zər·īt) *n.* A concretionary opaline quartz deposited in various forms around the orifices of geysers and hot springs, sometimes forming terraces.

Ge·zi·ra (je·zē′rə) An irrigated region in east central Sudan between the Blue Nile and the White Nile.

ghaist (gāst) *n. Scot.* A ghost.

Gha·na (gä′nä) An independent state (1957) in the Commonwealth of Nations, comprising the former Gold Coast Colony and the protectorates of Ashanti, Northern Territories, and British Togoland in western Africa; 91,690 square miles; capital, Accra: formerly *Gold Coast.*

ghar·ry (gar′ē) *n. pl.* **·ries** *Anglo-Indian* A wheeled vehicle; a cart or carriage for hire. Also **ghar′ri.** [< Hind. *gārī* cart]

ghast·ly (gast′lē, gäst′-) *adj.* **·li·er, ·li·est 1** Having a haggard, deathlike appearance. **2** Terrifying or shocking. —*adv.* Like a specter; fearfully. [ME *gastlich,* OE *gæstan* terrify + *-lich* LY[1]] —**ghast′li·ness** *n.*

Synonyms (adj.): cadaverous, deathlike, deathly, hideous, pale, pallid, spectral, wan. See PALE². *Antonyms:* blooming, bright, buxom, comely, fresh, ruddy.

ghat (gôt) *n.* Anglo-Indian **1** A stairway on a river bank leading to a temple, or to a landing place or wharf. **2** A mountain pass or a descent from a mountain range. Also **ghaut.** [< Hind. *ghāt*]

Ghats (gôts, gäts), **Eastern** and **Western** The two principal mountain ranges of southern India, parallel to its coasts; average height of the Western Ghats, 3,000 to 5,000 feet; average height of the Eastern Ghats, 1,500 to 2,000 feet.

gha·zi (gä′zē) *n.* **1** In Moslem countries, a hero or champion, especially one who has fought against infidels. **2** In Turkey, an honorary title bestowed on eminent national leaders. [< Arabic, orig. ppr. of *ghazā* fight] —**gha′zism** *n.*

Ghaz·ni (gäz′nē) A city in eastern Afghanistan; former capital of the first Moslem dynasty in Afghanistan.

Ghe·ber (gā′bər, gē′-) *n.* A fire-worshiper or Parsee; a Zoroastrian: so called by Mohammedans: often spelled *Gueber, Guebre.* Also **Ghe′bre.** See GIAOUR. [< F. *guèbre* < Persian *gabr*]

ghee (gē) *n.* Anglo-Indian **1** Clarified butter. **2** A solid white oil obtained from a tree of northern India *(Madhuca butyracea),* used in soaps and ointments. Also **ghi.** [< Hind. *ghī* < Skt. *ghṛta*]

Gheel (khāl) A city in northern Belgium, known since the 14th century for its community treatment of the insane. Also **Geel.**

Ghent (gent) A city in NW Belgium: Flemish *Gent,* French *Gand.*

gher·kin (gûr′kin) *n.* **1** A small prickly cucumber *(Cucumis anguria),* used for pickles. **2** Any small, immature cucumber used for pickling: also spelled *gerkin.* [< Du. *agurk* cucumber < G < Slavic, ult. < LGk. *angourion*]

GHERKIN — VINE, FLOWER AND FRUIT

ghet·to (get′ō) *n. pl.* **·tos** or **·ti** (-tē) **1** A part of a city or town, especially in Italy, in which Jews were formerly required to live. **2** A section of a city, often rundown or overcrowded, inhabited chiefly by a minority group that is effectively barred from living in other communities, as because of racial prejudice or for economic or social reasons. [< Ital.]

Ghib·el·line (gib′əl·in, -ēn) *n.* A supporter in Italy of the German emperor (11th–14th centuries); one of the imperial party opposed to the papal party. See GUELF. —*adj.* Of or pertaining to this party. [< Ital. *Ghibellino,* alter. of G *Waiblingen,* an imperial estate] —**Ghib′el·lin·ism** *n.*

Ghi·ber·ti (gē·ber′tē), **Lorenzo,** 1378–1455, Florentine sculptor, painter, and goldsmith.

ghost (gōst) *n.* **1** A disembodied spirit. **2** The soul or spirit. **3** A shadow or semblance; slight trace. **4** A spirit of any kind. **5** *Optics* **a** A false or secondary image, or a spot of light, as from a defect in a lens or instrument. **b** In television, a secondary image, appearing as a doubling of the image to the right, caused by reception of a reflected signal a fraction of a second later than the primary image. **6** *Obs.* The Holy Ghost. **7** *U.S. Slang* An addict to opium-smoking. **8** *Metall.* A narrow band of metal on steel ingots or forgings, harder than the adjoining parts; it becomes more evident on machining: also **ghost line.** See synonyms under SPECTER. —**to give up the ghost,** To die. —*v.t.* & *v.i.* **1** To haunt as a ghost. **2** *Colloq.* To write as a ghost writer. [OE *gāst* spirit] —**ghost′like′** *adj.*

ghost dance A dance performed by certain North American Indian tribes, in which both sexes take part, believed to bring the dancer into communion with the souls of dead friends.

ghost·ly (gōst′lē) *adj.* **·li·er, ·li·est 1** Pertaining to the soul or religion; spiritual. **2** Pertaining to apparitions; spectral. —**ghost′li·ness** *n.*

ghost town A deserted town; especially, a former boom town now empty and decayed.

ghost-write (gōst′rīt′) *v.i.* & *v.t.* **-wrote, -written, -writ·ing** To do literary work credited to another. —**ghost writer.**

ghoul (gool) *n.* **1** In Oriental legend, an evil spirit supposed to prey on corpses. **2** A person who robs dead bodies; a grave-robber; body-snatcher. **3** One who delights in morbid and revolting things. [< Arabic *ghūl*] —**ghoul′ish** *adj.* —**ghoul′ish·ly** *adv.* —**ghoul′ish·ness** *n.*

ghur·ry (gûr′ē) *n. pl.* **·ries 1** In India, a clepsydra or water clock; hence, any timepiece. **2** In Hindu custom, the sixtieth part of a day. Also **ghur′rie.** [< Hind. *gharī* < Skt. *ghaṭī*]

ghyll (gil) See GILL³.

GI (jē′ī′) *n. Colloq.* A soldier, especially an enlisted man, in the U.S. Army —*adj.* Of, pertaining to, or issued by the U.S. Army. See GOVERNMENT ISSUE. Also **G.I.** [< G(overnment) I(ssue)]

Gia·cob·be (jä·kôb′bā) Italian form of JACOB.

Gia·co·mo (jä′kō·mō) Italian form of JAMES.

gi·ant (jī′ənt) *n.* **1** In mythology, a being of human form, but of enormous size. **2** Any person or thing of great size, either physically, mentally, or figuratively. **3** Any imaginary person of gigantic size. —*adj.* Gigantic. [< OF *géant* < L *gigas, -antis* < Gk. *gigas, -antos*] —**gi′ant·ess** *n. fem.* —**gi′ant·ship** *n.*

giant cactus A large desert cactus of SW United States *(Cereus giganteus),* with an erect columnar trunk, sometimes branching, many ribs, strong spines, and flowering tops: also called *saguaro, sahuaro.*

giant fennel See under FENNEL.

giant hyssop See under HYSSOP.

gi·ant·ism (jī′ənt·iz′əm) *n.* **1** The quality or condition of being a giant. **2** Gigantism.

giant kelp A very large, tough and massive seaweed *(Macrocystis pyrifera)* belonging to the brown algae, found mainly in the Pacific.

giant panda See under PANDA.

giant powder A variety of dynamite.

Giant's Causeway A headland on the northern coast of County Antrim, Northern Ireland, consisting of thousands of small basaltic columns of volcanic origin.

giant star See under STAR.

giaour (jour) *n.* An unbeliever; a term of opprobrium applied by Moslems. See GHEBER. [< Turkish *giaur* < Persian *gaur,* var. of *gabr*]

gi·ar·di·a·sis (jē′är·dī′ə·sis) *n. Pathol.* An intestinal disorder attributed to the presence of a parasitic flagellate protozoan, *Giardia lamblia;* flagellate diarrhea. [< NL *Giardia,* a genus name + -IASIS]

gib (gib) *n. Mech.* **1** A wedge-shaped or other piece of metal that holds another in place or adjusts a bearing, etc. **2** A bearing surface, usually of brass, let into the cross-head of a steam engine to reduce friction. —*v.t.* **gibbed, gib·bing** To fasten with a gib or gibs; supply with a gib. [? < GIBBET]

gib·ber¹ (jib′ər, gib′-) *v.i.* To talk rapidly and incoherently; jabber. —*n.* Gibberish. [Imit.]

gib·ber² (jib′ər) *n. Austral.* A boulder; stone. [< native Australian]

gibber country *Austral.* An inland area covered with stones. Also *gibber plain.*

gib·ber·el·lic acid (jib′ə·rel′ik) *Chem.* A fermentation product of gibberellin, $C_{19}H_{22}O_6$, used as a plant-growth regulator.

gib·ber·el·lin (jib′ə·rel′in) *n. Chem.* Any of a group of closely related plant hormones that regulate certain processes in all higher plants, as flowering, germination of seeds, stem elongation, etc. [after *Gibberella fujikuroi,* a pathogenic fungus from which they were first isolated]

gib·ber·ish (jib′ər·ish, gib′-) *n.* Incoherent or unintelligible gabble. See synonyms under LANGUAGE.

gib·bet (jib′it) *n.* An upright timber with a crosspiece projecting at right angles from its upper end, upon which criminals were formerly hanged; hence, any gallows. —*v.t.* **·bet·ed** or **·bet·ted, ·bet·ing** or **·bet·ting 1** To execute by hanging. **2** To hang and expose on a gibbet. **3** To hold up to public contempt. [< OF *gibet,* dim. of *gibe* a staff]

gib·bon (gib′ən) *n.* A slender, long-armed arboreal anthropoid ape of southern Asia (genus *Hylobates).* [< F; ult. origin uncertain]

BLACK-CAPPED GIBBON
(Standing erect, usually about 2 1/2 feet)

Gib·bon (gib′ən), **Edward,** 1737–94, English historian.

Gib·bons (gib′ənz), **James,** 1834–1921, U.S. cardinal. —**Orlando,** 1583–1625, English composer.

gib·bos·i·ty (gi·bos′ə·tē) *n. pl.* **·ties 1** The state of being gibbous, or convex. **2** A rounded protuberance; hump.

gib·bous (gib′əs) *adj.* **1** Irregularly rounded; convex, as the moon when less than full and yet more than half full. **2** Humpbacked. **3** *Bot.* Swollen on one side, as the calyx of a lupine. Also **gib·bose** (gib′ōs, gi·bōs′). [< L *gibbosus* < *gibbus* a hump] —**gib′bous·ly** *adv.* —**gib′bous·ness** *n.*

Gibbs (gibz), **Josiah Willard,** 1839–1903, U.S. mathematician and physicist. —**Sir Philip,** 1877–1962, English author and journalist. —**William Francis,** 1886–1967, U.S. naval architect.

gibe¹ (jīb) *v.t.* & *v.i.* **gibed, gib·ing** To mock; sneer; scoff. See synonyms under MOCK, SCOFF. —*n.* An expression of sarcasm and ridicule. See synonyms under SNEER. Also spelled *jibe.* [Cf. OF *giber* treat roughly in play] —**gib′er** *n.* —**gib′ing·ly** *adv.*

gibe² (jīb) See JIBE¹.

Gib·e·on (gib′ē·ən) A city NW of Jerusalem in ancient Palestine.

Gib·e·on·ite (gib′ē·ən·īt) *n.* **1** One of the inhabitants of Gibeon, condemned by Joshua to be "hewers of wood and drawers of water" for the Israelites. *Josh.* ix 27. **2** *Obs.* A drudge; a slave's slave.

gib·let (jib′lit) *n.* One of the edible visceral parts of a fowl, as the gizzard, heart, or liver. [< OF *gibelet* a stew made from game]

Gi·bral·tar (ji·brôl′tər) A British crown colony, fortress, and naval base on the southern coast of Spain: called *Key of the Mediterranean* and identified with one of the *Pillars of Hercules;* 2 1/4 square miles, including the **Rock of Gibraltar** (ancient *Calpe:* also *the Rock*) 1,396 feet high, and dominating the **Strait of Gibraltar,** the passage between Spain and Africa at the western end of the Mediterranean.

Gib·son (gib′sən), **Charles Dana,** 1867–1944, U.S. illustrator.

Gibson Desert (gib′sən) The central belt of the Western Australian desert, between the Great Sandy Desert and Victoria Desert.

Gibson girl An idealization of the American girl of the 1890's as portrayed by Charles Dana Gibson; also, the style of dress fashionable in that period. —**Gib′son-girl′** *adj.*

gid (gid) *n.* A parasitic disease chiefly affecting sheep and goats, caused by the presence in the brain or spinal cord of the cysticercus of a tapeworm *(Coenurus cerebralis).* [< GIDDY]

gid·dy (gid′ē) *adj.* **·di·er, ·di·est 1** Having a whirling or swimming sensation in the head; dizzy. **2** Tending to cause such a sensation: a *giddy* precipice. **3** Marked by foolish levity or impudence; heedless; fickle. —*v.t.* & *v.i.* **gid·died, gid·dy·ing** To make or become dizzy or unsteady. [OE *gydig* insane] —**gid′di·ly** *adv.* —**gid′di·ness** *n.*

Gide (zhēd), **André,** 1869–1951, French author. —**Charles,** 1847–1932, French economist.

Gid·e·on (gid′ē·ən) A masculine personal name. [< Hebrew, hewer] —**Gideon** An Israelite judge. *Judges* vi 11.

Gid·e·ons (gid′ē·ənz), **The International** A society of American businessmen founded in 1899 to advance the distribution of Bibles in hotels, hospitals, prisons, and public schools.

gie (gē) *v.t. Scot.* To give.

gier-ea·gle (jir′ē′gəl) *n.* A bird of prey, probably the Egyptian vulture *(Neophron percnopterus). Lev.* xi 18. [<Du. *gier* vulture + EAGLE]
Gi·e·ron·y·mus (jē′ə·ron′i·məs) A Latin form of JEROME.
Gies·sen (gē′sən) A city in central Hesse, West Germany.
gif (gif) *conj. Scot. & Brit. Dial.* If. Also **giff.**
gift (gift) *n.* **1** That which is given; a donation; present. **2** The act, right, or power of giving. **3** A natural endowment; aptitude; talent. **4** *Obs.* A bribe; also, an offering. —*v.t.* **1** To bestow or confer upon. **2** To endow with a talent or faculty. [OE <*gifan* give]
Synonyms (noun): benefaction, bequest, boon, bounty, bribe, donation, grant, gratuity, largess, present, tip. A *gift* is that which is voluntarily bestowed without expectation of return or compensation. *Gift* is almost always used in the good sense, *bribe* is the evil sense to signify payment for a dishonorable service under the semblance of a *gift*. A *benefaction* is a charitable *gift*, generally of large amount, and viewed as of enduring value, as an endowment for a college. A *donation* is something, perhaps of great, seldom of trivial value, given to a cause or to a person representing a cause; as, a *donation* to a charity. A *gratuity* is usually of moderate value and is always given as of favor, not of right; as, a *gratuity* to a waiter; commonly called a *tip. Largess* is archaic for a bountiful *gratuity*, usually to be distributed among many, as among the heralds at ancient tournaments. A *present* is a *gift* of friendship, or conciliation, and given as to an equal or a superior. A *boon* is something that has been desired or craved or perhaps asked, or something freely given that meets some great desire. A *grant* is commonly considerable in amount and given by public authority; as, a *grant* of public lands for a college. See FAVOR, SUBSIDY. *Antonyms*: compensation, earnings, guerdon, penalty, remuneration, wages.
gift·ed (gif′tid) *adj.* Endowed with mental power or talent. See synonyms under CLEVER. —**gift′ed·ness** *n.*
gift·ie (gif′tē) *n. Scot.* Faculty; power; gift.
gift of gab *Colloq.* Fluency in speaking.
gift of tongues In the Bible, a miraculous power of speaking in unknown tongues.
Gi·fu (gē·fōō) A city on central Honshu island, Japan.
gig[1] (gig) *n.* **1** A light, two-wheeled, one-seated vehicle drawn by one horse. **2** A machine for raising a nap on a cloth by passing it over cylinders fitted with teasels. **3** *Naut.* A ship's boat in which the oarsmen are seated on alternate thwarts; also, a speedy, light rowboat. —*v.* **gigged, gig·ging** *v.i.* To ride in a gig. —*v.t.* To raise the nap on (cloth). [Origin uncertain]
gig[2] (gig) *n.* **1** A pronged fishspear. **2** An arrangement of four barbless fish hooks fastened back to back and drawn through a school of fish to catch them in the bodies. —*v.t. & v.i.* **gigged, gig·ging** To spear or catch (fish) with a gig. [<FISHGIG]
gig[3] (gig) *Slang n.* A demerit, as in the army, school, etc. —*v.t.* **gigged, gig·ging** **1** To give a demerit to. **2** To punish with a gig. [Origin unknown]
giga- *combining form* In systems of measurement, one billion (10^9) times (the specified unit): *gigavolt.*
gi·gan·tesque (jī′gan·tesk′) *adj.* Like or suited to giants.
gi·gan·tic (jī·gan′tik) *adj.* **1** Like a giant; colossal; huge. **2** Tremendous; extraordinary. Also **gi·gan·te·an** (jī′gan·tē′ən). See synonyms under IMMENSE, LARGE. [<L *gigas, -antis* GIANT + -IC]
gi·gan·tism (jī·gan′tiz·əm) *n.* **1** Abnormal size. **2** *Pathol.* Excessive growth of the body due to disturbances in the function and growth of the anterior lobe of the pituitary gland: also called *giantism.* Also **gi′gan·to·so′ma** (-tə·sō′mə).
giganto- *combining form* Gigantic; very large: *gigantocyte.* Also, before vowels, **gigant-.** [<Gk. *gigas, -antos* giant]
gi·gan·to·cyte (jī·gan′tə·sīt) *n. Physiol.* An excessively large erythrocyte.
gi·gan·tom·a·chy (jī′gan·tom′ə·kē) *n.* In classical mythology, the battle of the giants; the war of the giants against Zeus and the Olympian gods. Also **gi·gan·to·ma·chi·a** (jī·gan′tō·mā′kē·ə). [<Gk. *gigantomachia* <*gigas, -antos* giant + *machē* battle]
Gi·gan·to·pith·e·cus (jī·gan′tō·pith′ə·kəs) *n. Paleontol.* A giant hominoid primate of the early Pleistocene, represented only by several very large fossilized molar teeth discovered in Hong Kong apothecary shops between 1935 and 1939. Also **Gi·gant·an·thro·pus** (jī′gan·tan′thrə·pəs). [<NL <Gk. *gigas, -antos* giant + *pithēkos* ape]
gig·gle (gig′əl) *v.i.* **gig·gled, gig·gling** To laugh in a high-pitched, nervous manner; titter. —*n.* A convulsive laugh; titter. [Imit.] —**gig′gler** *n.* —**gig′gle·some** *adj.* —**gig′gling** *adj. & n.* —**gig′gly** *adj.*
gig·let (gig′lit) *n. Brit.* A giddy girl; romp; minx. Also **gig′lot.** [Origin uncertain]
gig·o·lo (jig′ə·lō, *Fr.* zhē·gô·lō′) *n. pl.* **·los** (-lōz, *Fr.* -lō′) **1** A professional male dancer in dance halls, cabarets, or the like, who attends women patrons or visitors. **2** A woman's paid escort. **3** A man who is supported by a woman; a kept man. [<F, prob. <*gigolette* a prostitute]
gig·ot (jig′ət) *n.* **1** A leg of mutton. **2** A sleeve having the shape of a leg of mutton. [<F]
gigue (zhēg) *n. Music* A lively composition often forming the final movement of a suite. [<F. See JIG.]
Gi·hulng·an (hi·hōōlng′än) A municipality on the NE coast of Negros island, Philippines.
Gi·jón (hi·hôn′) A port in Asturias, NW Spain.
Gi·la monster (hē′·lə) A large, poisonous lizard *(Heloderma suspectum)* with a stout orange-and-black body, ranging from southern Utah and Nevada through Arizona and New Mexico into northern Mexico. The beaded lizard *(H. horridum)*, an allied form found in Mexico, is also poisonous.

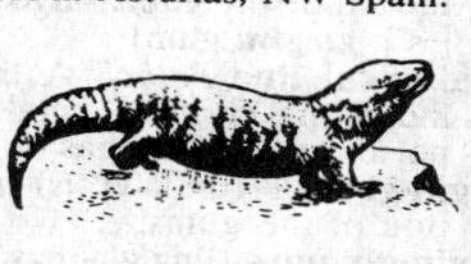
GILA MONSTER
(Up to 20 inches over all in length)

Gi·la River (hē′lə) A river in New Mexico and Arizona, flowing 650 miles SW to the Colorado River.
Gila woodpecker A woodpecker *(Centurus uropygialis)* of the SW United States, habitually nesting in the stem of the giant cactus.
gil·bert (gil′bərt) *n. Electr.* The cgs unit of magnetomotive force; equal to 0.7958 ampere-turn. [after William *Gilbert*, 1540–1603, English physicist]
Gil·bert (gil′bərt; *Dan.* gil′bert; *Du.* hil′bərt; *Fr.* zhel·bâr′; *Ger.* gel′bert) A masculine personal name. Also *Ital.* **Gil·ber·to** (jēl·ber′tō, *Sp.* hel·ber′tō), *Lat.* **Gil·ber·tus** (gil·bûr′tus, *Sw.* yil·ber′tōōs). [<Gmc., bright wish]
Gil·bert (gil′bərt), **Cass,** 1859–1934, U.S. architect. —**Sir Humphrey,** 1539?–83, English navigator. —**William,** 1540–1603, English physicist and physician. —**Sir William Schwenck,** 1836–1911, English humorous poet and librettist; collaborator with Sir Arthur Sullivan.
Gilbert and Ellice Islands A British colony in the west central and SW Pacific, comprising Ocean Island, the Gilbert Islands, the Ellice Islands, and several of the Phoenix and Line islands; total, about 375 square miles; headquarters on Tarawa, in the Gilbert Islands.
Gil·ber·ti·an (gil·bûr′tē·ən) *adj.* Pertaining to or resembling the style or humor of Sir W. S. Gilbert.
Gilbert Islands A group of atolls SE of the Marshall Islands, comprising a district of the Gilbert and Ellice Islands colony; 144 square miles; headquarters of the district and the colony, Tarawa.
Gil Blas (zhēl bläs′) The hero and title of a satiric picaresque romance by A. R. Le Sage.
Gil·bo·a (gil·bō′ə) A hilly district at the SE end of the Plain of Jezreel, scene of Saul's defeat and death. I *Sam.* xxxi 2–4.
gild[1] (gild) *v.t.* **gild·ed** or **gilt, gild·ing** **1** To coat with or as with gold or gold leaf. **2** To give a pleasing or attractive appearance to; gloss over. **3** *Obs.* To redden or smear (with blood). See synonyms under ADORN. ◆ Homophone: *guild.* [OE *gyldan*] —**gild′er** *n.*
gild[2] (gild), **gild·hall** (gild′hôl′), **gild·ry** (gild′rē), etc. See GUILD, etc.
gild·ed (gil′did) *adj.* **1** Thinly overlaid with or as with gold. **2** Fashionable; wealthy.
Gilded Age, the A post-Civil War period (1870–98) of waxing plutocratic accumulation and display in the United States: from *The Gilded Age* (1871), a novel by Mark Twain and Charles Dudley Warner depicting the newly emergent plutocracy with its conspicuous consumption and waste.
gild·er (gil′dər) See GUILDER.
gild·ing (gil′ding) *n.* **1** The art of overlaying a surface thinly with gold. **2** A mixture of finely divided gold, brass, or other substance to simulate gold, and a drying liquid: used as a decorative paint. **3** A specious or superficial appearance. Also **gilt, gild.**
Gil·e·ad (gil′ē·əd) A mountainous region of ancient Palestine east of the Jordan. *Josh.* xii 2.
Gil·e·ad·ite (gil′ē·əd·īt′) *n.* An inhabitant of Gilead. *Judges* xii 4.
Giles (jīlz) A masculine personal name. [<OF <L, having the aegis]
—**Giles** A seventh century hermit and saint; patron of cripples.
Gil·ga·mesh (gil′gə·mesh) A mythical Babylonian king, later identified with the sun-god: hero of the **Gilgamesh epic,** a literary epic written on cuneiform tablets found in the library of Ashurbanipal.
gill[1] (gil) *n.* **1** An organ for breathing the air dissolved in water, consisting, in aquatic vertebrates, as fishes and amphibians, of leaflike or threadlike vascular processes of mucous membrane on either side of the neck. Fishes take in water for the gills through the mouth and force it out mostly through the gill slits. **2** A gill-like part, as the wattle of a fowl. **3** *Bot.* One of the thin radial plates on the under side of the cap of a mushroom. —*v.t.* **1** To catch by the gills, as fish in a gill net. **2** To gut (fish). [ME *gile*, prob. <Scand. Cf. Sw. *gäl* gill.]
gill[2] (jil) *n.* A liquid measure, one fourth of a pint or 0.118 liter: also spelled *jill.* [<OF *gelle* measure for wine]
gill[3] (gil) *n.* **1** A ravine; a deep narrow gully. **2** A brook; narrow mountain stream. Also *ghyll.* [<ON *gil* gorge]
gill[4] (jil) *n.* **1** A girl or woman, especially a wanton one; sweetheart. **2** The ground ivy. [Short for GILLIAN]
gill arch *Zool.* One of the arches in gill-bearing vertebrates that carry the gills. In the higher vertebrates, the gill arches are transformed to perform other functions.
gill cleft Gill slit.
Gil·lette (ji·let′), **King Camp,** 1855–1932, U.S. inventor of safety razor. —**William,** 1855–1937, U.S. actor.
gill filament *Zool.* A threadlike vascular process of the mucous membrane of the gill.
gill fungus Any fungus of the genus *Agaricus*; an agaric.
Gil·li·an (jil′ē·ən) British form of JULIANA.
gil·lie (gil′ē) *n. Scot.* A manservant; attendant; especially one attending a sportsman in the field. Also **gil′ly.**
gil·li·flow·er (jil′ē·flou′ər) *n.* **1** One of various plants of the mustard family, as the common stock, the wallflower, or the rocket. **2** A plant of the pink family, as the clove pink: the Middle English and Elizabethan sense. **3** The feathered gilliflower *(Dianthus plumarius)* and ragged robin. **4** A variety of apple. Also **gil′ly·flow′er.** [Alter. of ME *gilofre* <OF, var. of *girofle* a clove <L *caryophyllum* <Gk. *karyophyllon* a clove tree]
gill net A net, set upright in the water by means of weighted stakes, in the meshes of which fish become entangled by their gills.
gill raker *Zool.* One of a row of processes projecting from the gill arches of fishes and screening the gills from injurious substances.
gill slit Any of a bilateral series of narrow external openings in the pharynx of embryonic chordates which persists throughout life in some aquatic forms, as sharks. Also called *gill cleft, branchial cleft.*

Gil·man (gil′mən), **Daniel Coit,** 1831–1908, U. S. educator.

gil·py (gil′pē) *n. pl.* **·pies** or **·peys** *Scot.* A lively, frolicsome young person of either sex. Also **gil′pey.**

gil·rav·age (gil·rav′ij) *Scot. v.i.* To feast or make merry in riotous fashion. — *n.* Noisy, riotous merriment.

gil·son·ite (gil′sən·īt) See UINTAHITE.

gilt[1] (gilt) Alternative past tense and past participle of GILD. — *adj.* Gilded; yellow like gold. — *n.* **1** The material used in gilding. **2** Superficial or meretricious show. ◆ Homophone: *guilt.*

gilt[2] (gilt) *n.* A young female pig. ◆ Homophone: *guilt.* [<ON *gyltr*]

gilt–edge (gilt′ej′) *adj.* **1** Having the edges gilded: said of leaves of paper either for writing or as bound in a book. **2** Of the best quality or highest price; first-class: *gilt-edge securities.* Also **gilt′–edged′.**

gilt–head (gilt′hed′) *n.* **1** One of various European fishes, as the sea bream (*Pagrus auratus*) of the Mediterranean. **2** A cunner.

gim·bals (jim′bəlz, gim′-) *n. Naut.* A contrivance for allowing a suspended object, as a ship's compass, to tip freely in all directions, thus remaining level, however the ship moves: also spelled *gymbals.* [Alter. of OF *gemelle* twin <L *gemellus,* dim. of *geminus* twin, double]

GIMBALS

gim·crack (jim′krak) *n.* A gew-gaw; bauble. See synonyms under GAUD. — *adj.* Cheap and showy. [Origin uncertain]

gim·crack·er·y (jim′krak·ər·ē) *n.* Worthless ornament or show.

gim·el (gim′əl) *n.* The third Hebrew letter. See ALPHABET.

gim·let (gim′lit) *n.* A small boring tool with a cross-head and a cutter-pointed screw tip. See illustration under AUGER. — *v.t.* To make a hole in with a gimlet. [<OF *guimbelet.* Akin to WIMBLE.]

gim·mick (gim′ik) *n. Slang* **1** A secret device for controlling the movements of a prize wheel. **2** Any tricky device or means. **3** Any contrivance, the name of which is not known or cannot be recalled. [Origin uncertain]

gimp[1] (gimp) *n.* **1** A narrow, flat, ornamental trimming, used for dresses, furniture, etc.: also **gimp′ing. 2** A coarse thread for forming edges and outlines in pillow lace. — *v.t.* To border with gimp. [Cf. OF *guimpre,* var. of *guipure,* a kind of trimming]

gimp[2] (gimp) *U.S. Slang n.* **1** Lameness; a limp. **2** One who limps; a cripple. — *v.i.* To limp. [Origin unknown]

gin[1] (jin) *n.* An aromatic alcoholic liquor, distilled from various grains and flavored with juniper berries; also, such a liquor with other flavoring. [Short for GENEVA]

gin[2] (gin) *v.t. & v.i.* **gan, gin·ning** *Archaic & Poetic* To begin.

gin[3] (jin) *n.* **1** A machine for separating cotton fibers from the seeds. **2** A portable hoisting machine. **3** A pump worked by a windmill. **4** A pile driver. **5** A snare or trap. **6** *Obs.* Artifice of any sort. — *v.t.* **ginned, gin·ning 1** To catch in or as in a gin or trap. **2** To remove the seeds from (cotton) in a gin. [Aphetic var. of OF *engin* ingenuity. See ENGINE.]

gin[4] (gin) *prep. Scot.* By; against (a certain) time. — *conj.* If; whether.

gin[5] (jin) *n. Austral.* An adult aboriginal female. [<native Australian]

gin·gal (jin′gôl) **gin·gall** See JINGAL.

gin·ge·ley (jin′ji·lē) *n.* The sesame. Also **gin′·ge·li, gin′gel·ly, gin·ge·ly.** [<Hind. *jingalī*]

gin·ger (jin′jər) *n.* **1** The pungent, spicy rootstock of a tropical plant (*Zingiber officinale*), either whole or pulverized: used in medicine and cookery. With the outer covering scraped off, the rootstock is called **white ginger,** and is regarded as superior to the East Indian or **black ginger,** in which the covering is not removed. **2** The plant itself. **3** A tawny, sandy, or reddish-brown color. **4** *Colloq.* Something of pungent quality; liveliness; spunk. — *v.t.* **1** To treat or spice with ginger. **2** *Colloq.* To make lively or piquant; enliven: often with *up.* [OE *gingifer* <LL *gingiber* <Gk. *zingiberis,* ult. <Skt.]

ginger ale An effervescent soft drink flavored with ginger.

ginger beer An effervescent drink made with yeast and flavored with ginger, popular in England, Canada, etc.

gin·ger·bread (jin′jər·bred′) *n.* **1** A light sweet cake flavored with ginger. **2** A ginger-flavored cooky cut into odd shapes and ornamented with colored icings. **3** Gaudy or unnecessary ornament. [Alter. of OF *gingembras* preserved ginger <LL *gingiber* GINGER]

gingerbread tree 1 The doom palm. **2** A tree of the rose family of West Africa (*Parinarium macrophylla*), bearing a farinaceous stone fruit called the gingerbread plum.

gingerbread work Cheap and tawdry ornamental work.

gin·ger·ly (jin′jər·lē) *adj.* Cautious, or fastidious, as an act or movement. — *adv.* **1** In a cautious, scrupulous, or fastidious manner. **2** *Obs.* Daintily. [Cf. OF *gensor, gentchur,* compar. of *gent* delicate]

gin·ger·snap (jin′jər·snap′) *n.* A small, flat, brittle cooky or biscuit flavored with ginger and molasses.

gin·ger·y (jin′jər·ē) *adj.* **1** Resembling ginger; spicy; hot-flavored. **2** Having a reddish or sandy color.

ging·ham (ging′əm) *n.* A plain-weave cotton fabric, usually in checks or stripes. [<F *guingan,* ult. <Malay *ginggang* striped]

gin·gi·val (jin·jī′vəl, jin′jə-) *adj.* **1** Of or pertaining to the gums. **2** *Phonet.* Produced with the aid of the gums; alveolar: *gingival* sounds. [<L *gingiva* gum]

gingival line *Pathol.* A line across the gums indicating chronic metal poisoning: in lead poisoning the line has a bluish tinge.

gin·gi·vi·tis (jin′jə·vī′tis) *n. Pathol.* Inflammation of the gums.

gin·gly·mus (jing′glə·məs, ging′-) *n. pl.* **·mi** (-mī) *Anat.* A joint that permits flexion and extension in a single plane, as at the elbow and knee; a hinge joint. [<NL <Gk. *ginglymos* a hinge]

gink (gingk) *n. Slang* An odd or peculiar person; guy. [Cf. dial. E *gink* trick]

gink·go (ging′kō, jing′kō) *n. pl.* **·goes** A deciduous resinous tree (*Ginkgo biloba*), native in China but cultivated in the United States for its fanlike foliage; the maidenhair tree: also spelled *jinkgo.* Also **ging′ko.** [<Japanese]

GINKGO
Branch showing leaf and nut. Regarded as the only surviving member of a family that had flourished millions of years ago, during the time of the dinosaurs.

gin·mill (jin′mil′) *n. Slang* A saloon.

gin·ner (jin′ər) *n.* One who operates a gin.

gin rummy A variety of rummy, in which a player may meld his hand whenever his unmatched cards are worth 10 points or less.

gin·seng (jin′seng) *n.* **1** An herb (genus *Panax*) native in North America and China, having a root of aromatic and stimulant properties, in great esteem in China. **2** The root, or a preparation made from it. [<Chinese *jen shen*]

Giob·be (jôb′bā) Italian form of JOB.

Gio·con·da (jō·kôn′dä), **La** Mona Lisa.

Gior·gia (jôr′jä) Italian form of GEORGIANA.

Gior·gio (jôr′jō) Italian form of GEORGE.

Gior·gio·ne (jôr·jō′nä), 1478?–1511, Venetian painter. Also **Gior·gio′ne da Cas·tel·fran·co** (käs′tel·frän′kō). Original name *Giorgio Barbarelli.*

Gio·si·a·de (jō·zē′ä·dä) Italian form of JOSIAH.

Giot·to (jôt′tō) Italian form of GODFREY.

Giot·to di Bon·do·ne (jôt′tō dē bôn·dō′nä), 1266–1337, Italian painter, architect, and sculptor.

Gio·van·na (jō·vän′nä) Italian form of JOAN.

Gio·van·ni (jō·vän′nē) Italian form of JOHN.

gip[1] (jip) *v.t. Brit.* To gut (fish). [Origin unknown]

gip[2] (jip) See GYP[1].

gi·pon (ji·pon′, jip′on) See JUPON.

gip·si·fy (jip′sə·fī) *v.t.* **·fied, ·fy·ing** To cause to be or to look like a gipsy.

gip·sy (jip′sē) *n. pl.* **·sies** One of any wandering group of people living the gipsy life; an itinerant tinker, farrier, etc. — *v.i.* **·sied, ·sy·ing** To live or wander like a gipsy. — *adj.* Of, pertaining to, or like a gipsy or the Gipsies; unconventional; wandering; Bohemian. Also spelled *gypsy.*

Gip·sy (jip′sē) *n. pl.* **·sies 1** A member of a wandering, dark-haired, dark-skinned people originating in India and appearing in Europe in the 15th century, now known in every part of the world as itinerant metalworkers, musicians, fortune-tellers, and, formerly, horse dealers. **2** Romany, their language. Also spelled *Gypsy.* [<Earlier *gipcyan,* aphetic var. of *Egypcyan* Egyptian]

gip·sy·ish (jip′sē·ish) *adj.* Like a gipsy; roving; hoydenish. — **gip′sy·ism** *n.*

gipsy moth A European moth (*Porthetria* or *Lymantria dispar*) naturalized in eastern New England about 1869, having larvae highly destructive to foliage: the male is light-brown, the larger female nearly white. For illustration see under INSECT (injurious).

gi·raffe (jə·raf′, -räf′) *n. pl.* **·raffes** or **·raffe 1** A large spotted African ruminant (*Giraffa camelopardalis*), having a very long neck and limbs; the tallest of the quadrupeds, sometimes attaining a height of 18 feet. **2** A cagelike mine car especially adapted for inclines. [<F, ult. <Arabic *zarāfah*]

GIRAFFE

Gi·raffe (jə·raf′, -räf′) The constellation Camelopard. See CONSTELLATION.

Gi·ral·da (jē·räl′dä) Italian form of GERALDINE.

Gi·ral·da (hē·räl′dä), **La** The square bell tower of the cathedral of Seville, Spain, surmounted by a bronze figure of Faith. [<Sp. *giralda* weathercock in the form of a person]

gir·an·dole (jir′ən·dōl) *n.* **1** A branching chandelier or bracket light. **2** A rotating firework. **3** A rotating water jet. **4** In fortification, a connection of several mines. **5** A pendent piece of jewelry. [<F <Ital. *girandola* <*girare* rotate <L *gyrare.* See GYRATE.]

Gi·rard (ji·rärd′), **Stephen,** 1750–1831, U. S. banker and philanthropist.

gir·a·sol (jir′ə·sōl, -sol) *n.* **1** A bluish-white translucent opal with reddish reflections: also called *fire opal.* **2** Any plant of the sunflower family; especially, the Jerusalem artichoke. Also **gir′a·sole.** [<Ital. *girasole* sunflower <*girare* turn + *sole* sun]

Gi·raud (zhē·rō′) French form of GERALD. Also **Gi·rauld′.**

Gi·raud (zhē·rō′), **Henri Honoré,** 1879–1949, French general in World War II.

Gi·rau·doux (zhē·rō·dōō′), **Jean,** 1882–1944, French novelist and playwright.

gird[1] (gûrd) *v.t.* **gird·ed** or **girt, gird·ing 1** To surround with a belt or girdle. **2** To encircle; hem in. **3** To prepare (oneself) for action. **4** To clothe; equip; endue, etc. [OE *gyrdan*]

gird[2] (gûrd) *n.* **1** A sarcastic thrust; taunt; gibe; sneer. **2** *Obs.* A cutting stroke; hence, a pang. **3** *Obs.* A spurt. — *v.t. & v.i.* To attack with sarcasm; gibe; jeer. [ME *girden;* origin unknown] — **gird′er** *n.*

gird·er (gûr′dər) *n.* **1** A principal horizontal beam, or a compound structure acting as a beam, receiving a vertical load and bearing vertically upon its supports. **2** One who or that which girds or encompasses.

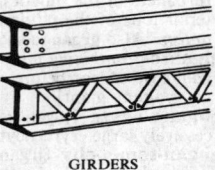

GIRDERS

gird·er·age (gûr′dər·ij) *n.* Girders collectively.

gir·dle[1] (gûr′dəl) *n.* **1** A belt used for girding

a loose garment about the waist; specifically, in ecclesiastical language, the narrow belt adorned with tassels, used to secure the alb; called also *cincture.* 2 Anything which encircles like a belt; especially, a woman's undergarment, more flexible and lighter than a corset, not coming above the waistline. 3 *Obs.* A small band or fillet encompassing a column. 4 *Mining* A thin sandstone stratum in a vein of coal. 5 *Anat.* The ringlike arrangement of bones, by which the limbs of a vertebrate animal are attached to the trunk. 6 The peripheral line of a cut gem, at which it is held in the setting. 7 An encircling cut through the bark of a branch or tree. — *v.t.* **gir·dled, gir·dling** 1 To fasten a girdle or belt around. 2 To encircle; encompass. 3 To make an encircling cut through the bark of (a branch or tree). [OE *gyrdel*]

gir·dle² (gûr′dəl) *n. Scot.* A griddle.

gir·dle-cake (gûr′dəl·kāk′) *n. Scot.* A griddle-cake.

gir·dler (gûrd′lər) *n.* 1 One who makes girdles. 2 One who or that which girdles or encircles. 3 *Entomol.* Any insect which cuts through the bark of twigs or branches; especially, the American twig girdler *(Oncideres cingulata),* which severs the twigs of hickory, poplar, and many other trees.

Gir·gen·ti (jir·jen′tē) The former name of AGRIGENTO.

girl (gûrl) *n.* 1 A female infant or child, or a young unmarried woman. 2 A maid servant. 3 A sweetheart. [ME *gurle*; origin uncertain]

girl Friday A female office worker who performs various tasks. [<GIRL + (MAN) FRIDAY]

girl friend *Colloq.* 1 A boy or man's sweetheart, favorite female companion, etc. 2 A female friend.

girl guide A member of an English organization, the **Girl Guides,** resembling the Girl Scouts.

girl·hood (gûrl′hŏŏd) *n.* The state or time of being a girl.

girl·ie (gûr′lē) *adj. Colloq.* Featuring nude or nearly nude women or pictures of them: a *girlie* magazine or show. Also **girl′y.**

girl·ish (gûr′lish) *adj.* Like or pertaining to a girl. See synonyms under YOUTHFUL. — **girl′·ish·ly** *adv.* — **girl′ish·ness** *n.*

girl scout A member of an organization, **Girl Scouts of America,** formed in the United States in 1912 by Juliette Low to develop health, character, etc.

girn (gûrn, girn) *v.i. Scot.* To snarl; growl.

Gi·ronde (jə·rond′, *Fr.* zhē·rôṅd′) An estuary in SW France formed by the Garonne and Dordogne rivers, extending 45 miles to the Bay of Biscay.

Gi·ronde (jə·rond′) The moderate republican party at the time of the first French assembly (1791–93). [from *Gironde,* because its leaders came from this area] — **Gi·ron′dist** (jə·ron′·dist), *Fr.* **Gi·ron·din** (zhē·rôṅ·daṅ′) *n.* & *adj.*

gir·o·sol (jir′ə·sôl, -sol) See GIRASOL.

girt¹ (gûrt) *v.t.* 1 To gird. 2 To measure the girth of. 3 To fasten with a girth, strap, etc. — *v.i.* 4 To measure in girth. — *n.* Girth. [<GIRD¹; also partly <*n.*]

girt² (gûrt) Past tense and past participle of GIRD¹. — *adj.* 1 Encircled; bound or fastened with a girth or girdle. 2 *Naut.* Moored with taut cables, so as to prevent swinging by wind or tide, as a vessel. 3 *Entomol.* Braced, as a chrysalis.

girth¹ (gûrth) *n.* 1 A band or strap for fastening a pack or saddle to a horse's back. 2 Anything that girds or binds; a girdle. 3 The circumference of a circular or cylindrical object; especially, the measure around the waist. 4 A circular bandage. — *v.t.* 1 To bind with a girth. 2 To encircle; girdle. 3 To find the girth of. [<ON *gjordh*]

girth² (gûrth) See GRITH.

Gis·borne (giz′bərn) A port in eastern North Island, New Zealand.

Gis·sing (gis′ing), **George Robert,** 1857–1903, English novelist.

gist (jist) *n.* 1 The substance or fundamental fact of a matter in law, the essential cause of legal action. 2 The substance or pith of any matter; the point or main idea. [<OF *giste* place of rest <*gesir* lie <L *jacere*]

git·a·lin (jit′ə·lin, jə·tā′lin, -tal′in) *n. Chem.* A glucoside, $C_{35}H_{56}O_{12}$, in crystalline or powdered form, from the leaves of digitalis, similar in action to digitalis. [<(DI)GITAL(IS) + -IN]

gi·ta·no (ji·tä′nō, *Sp.* hē·tä′nō) *n. pl.* **·nos** A Spanish gipsy. [<Sp.]

git·tern (git′ərn) *n.* A medieval musical instrument, like a cithern, but having gut instead of metal strings: predecessor of the guitar. [<OF *guiterne*]

Giu·ba (jōō′bä) The Italian name for JUBA.

Giu·dit·ta (jōō·dēt′tä) Italian form of JUDITH.

Giu·lia·na (jōō·lyä′nä) Italian form of JULIANA.

Giu·lia·no (jōō·lyä′nä) Italian form of JULIAN.

Giu·lio (jōōl′yō) Italian form of JULIUS.

Giu·lio Ro·ma·no (jōōl′yō rō·mä′nō), 1492–1546, Italian painter.

Giu·sep·pe (jōō·sep′pā) Italian form of JOSEPH.

Giu·sep·pi·na (jōō′sep·pē′nä) Italian form of JOSEPHINE. Also **Giu·sep·pa** (jōō·sep′pä).

Gius·ti·na (jōōs·tē′nä) Italian form of JUSTINA.

Gius·to (jōōs′tō) Italian form of JUSTUS.

give (giv) *v.* **gave, giv·en, giv·ing** *v.t.* 1 To transfer the possession or title of to another without compensation of any kind. 2 To transfer to the possession or control of another for a price or equal value. 3 To hand over to another for safekeeping, delivery, etc.: to *give* a letter to a postman. 4 To offer as entertainment: to *give* a play, party, etc. 5 To yield as a product or result: Two plus two *gives* four. 6 To be the cause or source of: The sun *gives* light. 7 To provide or furnish; impart: to *give* evidence; to *give* form to an idea. 8 To express in words; declare: to *give* a ruling or reply. 9 To impose or grant, as a punishment or reward: They *gave* him the death penalty. 10 To emit or show, as a movement, shout, etc. 11 To administer, as medicine. 12 To deal; inflict, as a blow or pain. 13 To concede; yield or grant: to *give* ground; to *give* permission. 14 To devote or sacrifice, as to a cause: to *give* one's time or one's life. — *v.i.* 15 To make gifts. 16 To yield, as from pressure, melting, or thawing; collapse. 17 To be springy or resilient; bend. — **to give away** 1 To bestow as a gift. 2 To bestow (the bride) upon the bridegroom in a marriage ceremony. 3 *Colloq.* To reveal or disclose; betray. — **to give birth (to)** 1 To bear (offspring). 2 To result in. — **to give in** 1 To yield, as in a fight or argument. 2 To collapse, as under stress. — **to give off** To send forth; emit, as odors. — **to give out** 1 To send forth; emit. 2 To serve out or distribute. 3 To make known; publish. 4 To fail; become worn out or exhausted. — **to give over** 1 To hand over, as to another's care. 2 To cease; desist. — **to give rise to** To cause or result in. — **to give tongue** To bark or bay: said of hunting dogs in pursuit. — **to give up** 1 To surrender; cede; hand over. 2 To stop; cease. 3 To desist from as hopeless. 4 To lose all hope for, as a sick person. 5 To devote wholly: to *give* oneself *up* to art. — *n.* The quality of being yielding; elasticity; the process or act of giving way. [Fusion of OE *giefan* and ON *gefa*] — **giv′er** *n.*

Synonyms (verb): bestow, cede, communicate, confer, deliver, furnish, grant, impart, supply. To *give* is primarily to transfer to another's possession or ownership without compensation; in its secondary sense in popular use, it is to put into another's possession by any means and on any terms whatever; a buyer may say "*Give* me the goods, and I will *give* you the money"; we speak of *giving* answers, information, etc., and often of *giving* what is not agreeable to the recipient, as blows, medicine, reproof. To *grant* is to put into one's possession in some formal way, or by authoritative act; as, Congress *grants* lands to a railroad corporation. *Confer* has a similar sense; as, to *confer* a degree or an honor; we *grant* a request or petition, but do not *confer* it. To *impart* is to *give* of that which one still, to a greater or less degree, retains; the teacher *imparts* instruction. To *bestow* is to *give* that of which the receiver stands in especial need; we *bestow* charity.

give-and-take (giv′ən·tāk′) *n.* 1 Fair exchange; equal compromise. 2 Repartee; a flow or exchange of ideas or wit: He is adept at such *give-and-take.*

give-a·way (giv′ə·wā′) *n.* 1 A betrayal to ridicule or detection, often unintentional. 2 That which betrays a secret or a person. — *adj.* Featuring awards of money or prizes: said of a radio or television show.

giv·en (giv′ən) *adj.* 1 Habitually inclined: with *to.* 2 Specified; stated; also, in law, dated. 3 Donated; presented. 4 Admitted as a fact or a premise. — *n.* A datum; premise.

given name The name given at birth or baptism.

give-up (giv′up′) *n.* The practice of splitting a stockbroker's commission with another broker at the direction of the customer.

Gi·za (gē′zə) A city in Upper Egypt on the Nile; site of the pyramids: also *El Gizeh.*

giz·mo (giz′mō) *n. pl.* **·mos** *U.S. Slang* Any gadget. [Origin unknown]

giz·zard (giz′ərd) *n.* 1 The second stomach of birds, in which the food is ground. 2 *Entomol.* The first stomach of insects, provided with horny plates for macerating or sifting food. 3 *Slang* The stomach. [<OF *gezier* <L *gigeria* cooked entrails of poultry]

gla·bel·la (glə·bel′ə) *n. pl.* **·lae** (-ē) *Anat.* The smooth prominence on the forehead just above the nose and between the eyebrows. See illustration under FACIAL ANGLE. [<NL <L, dim. of *glaber* smooth]

gla·brate (glā′brāt) *adj.* 1 Glabrous. 2 Becoming glabrous.

gla·bres·cent (glə·bres′ənt) *adj.* Shedding hair; becoming glabrous.

gla·bri·ros·tral (glā′brē·ros′trəl) *adj. Ornithol.* Having the mouth free from bristles, as some birds. [<L *glaber* smooth + ROSTRAL]

gla·brous (glā′brəs) *adj. Biol.* 1 Without hair or down. 2 Having a smooth surface. [<L *glaber* smooth]

gla·cé (gla·sā′, *Fr.* glȧ·sā′) *adj.* 1 Iced; frozen or cooled. 2 Having a glossy surface resembling ice. 3 Smooth and glossy, as certain leathers. — *v.t.* **·céed, ·cé·ing** 1 To cover with icing. 2 To render smooth and glossy. [<F, pp. of *glacer* freeze <*glace* ice]

gla·cial (glā′shəl) *adj.* 1 Pertaining to or caused by ice masses. 2 Icy, or icily cold. 3 Of or pertaining to the glacial epoch. 4 *Chem.* Crystallizing or assuming an ice-like appearance at ordinary temperature: *glacial* acetic acid. [<F <L *glacialis* <*glacies* ice] — **gla′cial·ly** *adv.*

glacial deposits *Geol.* Unstratified earth materials and debris transported by glaciers and left at the place of melting.

glacial epoch *Geol.* 1 Any portion of geological time characterized by the formation of ice sheets over large portions of the earth's surface. 2 One of four such epochs identified as succeeding one another during the Pleistocene: beginning with the oldest, they are the Günz, the Mindel, the Riss, and the Würm.

gla·cial·ist (glā′shəl·ist) *n.* One who studies geological processes as they are affected by the action of ice.

glacial period The period of time covering the glacial epochs.

gla·ci·ate (glā′shē·āt) *v.t.* **·at·ed, ·at·ing** 1 To cover with glacial ice. 2 To affect or change by glacial action. 3 To convert into ice. [<L *glaciatus,* pp. of *glaciare* freeze <*glacies* ice] — **gla′ci·a′tion** *n.*

gla·cier (glā′shər) *n.* A field of ice, formed in regions of perennial frost from compacted snow, which moves slowly downward over slopes or through valleys until it either melts, as in the lowlands, or breaks off in the form of icebergs on the borders of the sea. [<F <L *glacies* ice] — **gla′ciered** *adj.*

Glacier Bay National Monument A region of SE Alaska on the border of British Columbia; 3,590 square miles; established 1925.

glacier meal See ROCK FLOUR.

glacier milk The milky water of a stream issuing from a glacier and containing suspended silt or finely divided rock particles.

Glacier National Park A mountainous area in NW Montana; 1,560 square miles; established 1910.

glacier theory *Geol.* The theory that large elevated portions of the temperate and frigid zones were covered during the earlier geologic

epochs by slowly moving glaciers that transported vast masses of drift to lower latitudes.

gla·ci·ol·o·gy (glā'sē·ol'ə·jē) *n.* That branch of geology which studies the forms, movements, causes, and effects of glaciers. —**gla·ci·o·log·ic** (glā'sē·ə·loj'ik) or **·i·cal** *adj.* —**gla'ci·ol'o·gist** *n.*

gla·cis (glā'sis, glas'is) *n.* A defensive slope in front of a fortification. See illustration under BASTION. [< F, orig. a slippery place < OF *glacier* slip]

Glack·ens (glak'ənz), **William James,** 1870–1938, U.S. painter.

glad (glad) *adj.* **glad·der, glad·dest** 1 Having a feeling of joy, pleasure, or contentment; joyful; gratified: often with *of* or *at.* 1 Having an appearance of joy or brightness; gladsome; joyous. 3 Suggestive of or exciting joy: *glad* tidings. See synonyms under HAPPY, MERRY. —*v.t. & v.i.* **glad·ded, glad·ding** *Obs.* To gladden. [OE *glæd* shining, glad]—**glad'ly** *adv.* —**glad'ness** *n.*

Glad·beck (glät'bek) A city in North Rhine – Westphalia, Germany.

glad·den (glad'n) *v.t. & v.i.* To make or become glad. See synonyms under REJOICE. —**glad'den·er** *n.*

glade (glād) *n.* 1 A clearing or open space in a wood. 2 A smooth tract of uncovered ice, or an unfrozen open space in the ice of a river or lake. 3 An everglade. [Prob. akin to *glad* in obs. sense "bright," "sunny"]

glad eye *Slang* A provocative or flirtatious glance.

glad hand *Slang* A hearty welcome.

glad·i·ate (glad'ē·āt) *adj.* Sword-shaped. [< L *gladius* sword + -ATE[1]]

glad·i·a·tor (glad'ē·ā'tər) *n.* 1 A man who fought with deadly weapons, as in the ancient Roman amphitheater, for popular amusement. 2 Hence, one who engages in any kind of spirited contest. [< L < *gladius* sword]

ROMAN GLADIATORS
a. Retiarius.   *c.* Andabata.
b. Mirmillon.   *d.* Thracian.

glad·i·a·to·ri·al (glad'ē·ə·tôr'ē·əl, -tō'rē-) *adj.* Of or pertaining to gladiators or combats.

glad·i·o·lus (glad'ē·ō'ləs, glə·dī'ə·ləs) *n. pl.* **·lus·es** or **·li** (-lī) 1 Any of a large Old World genus (*Gladiolus*) of plants of the iris family with fleshy bulbs, sword-shaped leaves, and spikes of colored flowers. 2 Its corm or flower. Also **glad·i·o·la** (glad'ē·ō'lə, glə·dī'ə·lə), **glad'i·ole** (-ōl). [< L, dim. of *gladius* sword]

glad·some (glad'səm) *adj.* 1 Causing, feeling, or expressive of joy; joyous; pleasing. 2 Having a feeling of joy or pleasure: cheerful. See synonyms under MERRY. —**glad'some·ly** *adv.* —**glad'some·ness** *n.*

Glad·stone (glad'stōn, -stən) *n.* 1 A suitcase, generally of leather, hinged in the middle lengthwise so that it may open into halves: also called **Gladstone bag.** 2 A four-wheeled pleasure carriage having a driver's seat and two inside seats. [after W. E. *Gladstone*]

Glad·stone (glad'stōn, -stən), **William Ewart,** 1809–98, English statesman and Liberal leader; premier 1868–74; 1880–85; 1886; 1892–1894. —**Glad·sto·ni·an** (glad·stō'nē·ən), **Glad'ston·ite** *adj. & n.*

Glag·ol (glag'əl) *n.* An ancient Slavic alphabet: still used in many Roman Catholic dioceses in Dalmatia and Croatia, where Church Slavonic is the liturgical language. [< Russian *glagoly'* a word]—**Glag·o·lit·ic** (glag'ə·lit'ik) *adj.*

glaik (glāk) *n. Scot.* 1 A fraud or trick. 2 A gleam; glance. 3 Mockery; deception.

glaik·it (glā'kit) *adj. Scot.* Unsteady; giddy; silly; stupid. Also **glaik'et.**

glair (glâr) *n.* 1 The white of eggs mixed with vinegar: used as a size in gilding, etc. 2 Any similar viscous matter; anything slimy or slippery. —*v.t.* To treat with glair, as a book cover before gilding. Also **glaire.** ◆Homophone: *glare.* [< F *glaire* < L *clarus* clear]

glair·e·ous (glâr'ē·əs) *adj.* Of the nature of glair; glairy.

glair·y (glâr'ē) *adj.* 1 Like glair. 2 Exhibiting glair. —**glair'i·ness** *n.*

glaive (glāv) *n. Archaic* 1 A weapon consisting of a long blade fastened to a pole and resembling a halberd. 2 A broadsword. [< OF, lance]

glai·zie (glā'zē) *adj. Scot.* Glossy; sleek.

Gla·mor·gan (glə·môr'gən) A county in SE Wales; 813 square miles; county town, Cardiff. Also **Gla·mor'gan·shire** (-shir).

glam·or·ous (glam'ər·əs) *adj.* Radiating glamour; gorgeous. —**glam'or·ous·ly** *adv.*

glam·our (glam'ər) *n.* 1 A delusion wrought by magic spells; charm; enchantment. 2 Any artificial interest or association by which an object is made to appear delusively magnified or glorified; illusion; fascination; witchery. Also **glam'or.** [Scottish alter. of GRAMARY. Related to GRAMMAR.]

glance[1] (glans, gläns) *v.* **glanced, glanc·ing** *v.i.* 1 To strike something at an angle and bounce off. 2 To look quickly or hurriedly. 3 To glint; flash. 4 To make passing reference; allude. —*v.t.* 5 To cause to strike something at an angle and bounce off. See synonyms under LOOK. —*n.* 1 A quick or passing look; sudden or transient thought. 2 A momentary gleam. 3 An oblique movement or rebound. 4 In cricket, a stroke with the bat held slanting and thus sending the ball to one side of the wicket. [< OF *glacier* slip, ? infl. by ME *glenten* shine]

glance[2] (glans, gläns) *n.* A mineral, usually a sulfide, having a vitreous sheen: lead *glance.* [Short for *glance ore* < Du. *glanserts* luster ore]

gland (gland) *n.* 1 *Anat.* Any of various organs, composed of specialized epithelial tissue, intended for the secretion of materials essential to the bodily system or for the elimination of waste products: the salivary *glands,* endocrine *glands.* 2 A glandlike structure; a lymph *gland.* 3 *Aeron.* A tube so fitted to the envelope or gas bag of an airship as to allow the passing of a line through it without leakage of air or gas. 4 *Bot.* A special secreting organ in plants. 5 *Mech.* One of various parts of a mechanism that hold something in place; especially, a device for compressing the packing in a stuffing box in order to prevent leakage of a fluid under pressure. [< F *glande* < OF *glandre* < L *glandula,* dim. of *glans, glandis* acorn]

glan·ders (glan'dərz) *n.* A serious contagious disease of horses, mules, and other equines, caused by a bacillus (*Malleomyces mallei*) and characterized by nasal discharges and ulcerative lesions of the lungs and other organs: occasionally found in other animals and in man. When affecting the skin it is called *farcy.* [< OF *glandres,* pl. of *glandre* a gland]—**glan'dered, glan'der·ous** *adj.*

glan·dif·er·ous (glan·dif'ər·əs) *adj.* Acorn-bearing. [< L *glans, glandis* an acorn + -(I)FEROUS]

glan·di·form (glan'də·fôrm) *adj.* Acorn-shaped.

glan·du·lar (glan'jə·lər) *adj.* 1 Pertaining to, bearing, or of the nature of glands. 2 Affecting glands: a *glandular* infection. Also **glan'·du·lous.**

glandular fever Infectious mononucleosis.

glan·dule (glan'jool) *n.* A small gland.

glans (glanz) *n. pl.* **glan·des** (-dēz) 1 An acorn, or an acornlike part or instrument. 2 *Anat.* The rounded extremity of the penis or clitoris. [< L, an acorn]

glare[1] (glâr) *v.* **glared, glar·ing** *v.i.* 1 To shine with great and dazzling intensity. 2 To gaze or stare fiercely. 3 To be conspicuous or ostentatious. —*v.t.* 4 To express or send forth with a glare. —*n.* 1 A dazzling light. 2 An intense and piercing look or gaze, usually hostile. 3 Gaudiness; vulgar splendor. See synonyms under LIGHT[1]. ◆Homophone: *glair.* [ME *glaren* < LG]

glare[2] (glâr) *n.* A glassy, smooth surface. —*adj.* Having a glassy, smooth surface. ◆Homophone: *glair.* [? < GLARE[1], *n.*]

glar·ing (glâr'ing) *adj.* 1 Looking or staring fixedly or hostilely. 2 Emitting an excessively brilliant light. 3 Plainly or unpleasantly conspicuous: a *glaring* mistake. —**glar'ing·ly** *adv.*

Gla·rus (glä'roos) A city in eastern Switzerland.

glar·y[1] (glâr'ē) *adj.* Dazzling; glaring.

glar·y[2] (glâr'ē) *adj. U.S.* Slippery, as ice.

Glas·gow (glas'gō, -kō, gläs'-) A port on the Clyde river, SW Scotland: a native of Glasgow is known as a *Glaswegian.*

Glas·gow (glas'gō), **Ellen,** 1874–1945, U.S. novelist.

glas·nost (glas'nost) *n.* Openness, in present-day Soviet Union, in describing the actual conditions of society. [< Russian]

Glas·pell (glas'pel), **Susan,** 1882–1948, U.S. novelist and dramatist.

glass (glas, gläs) *n.* 1 A hard, amorphous, brittle, usually transparent substance made by fusing one or more of the oxides of silicon, boron, or phosphorus with certain basic oxides, followed by rapid cooling to prevent crystallization. ◆ Collateral adjectives: *hyaline, vitreous.* Principal types are:
—**borosilicate glass** A tough optical and thermal glass; Pyrex glass.
—**bottle glass** A soda-lime-silica glass with a greenish color caused by iron impurities.
—**crown glass** Hard optical sodium-silicate glass of low refraction.
—**cut glass** Glass ornamented by cutting or grinding on a wheel of stone, iron, or wood into grooves, leaving prismatic or crystal-like elevations between them.
—**flint glass** Soft optical lead-oxide glass of high refraction.
—**ground glass** Glass having a smooth, semiopaque surface that diffuses light.
—**lime glass** Plate, window, and container glass; made of lime and soda.
—**milk glass** Opaque milky glass containing cryolite.
—**optical glass** High-quality glass specialized in refractive and dispersive powers for lenses.
—**plate glass** Sheets of glass poured, rolled, and polished: used for mirrors and display windows.
—**safety glass** Glass in two sheets enclosing a film of transparent adhesive plastic tightly pressed between them; laminated glass: often called *shatterproof glass.*
—**stained glass** Glass colored by the addition of pigments in the form of metallic oxides: used decoratively, as for church windows.
—**window glass** Ordinary blown glass, flattened from cylinder shapes.
—**wire glass** Glass sheets reinforced with wire netting. 2 Any fused substance resembling glass. 3 Any article made of glass, as a window pane, a goblet or tumbler, a mirror, spectacles, etc. 4 A telescope; also, a barometer. 5 A glass devised for measuring time by the passage of sand or the like through an orifice. See HOURGLASS. 6 The contents of a glass or drinking vessel: He drank a *glass* of wine. 7 Glassware collectively. —*v.t.* 1 To enclose with glass. 2 To reflect; mirror. 3 To give a glazed surface to. —*adj.* Made of, relating to, or like glass. [OE *glæs*]
Glass may appear as a combining form in hyphemes and solidemes, or as the first element in two-word phrases; as in:

glass-bottomed	glass-lined
glass-clear	glassmaking
glass-colered	glass-painter
glass-covered	glass-paneled
glass-cutter	glass-sided
glass-cutting	glass-staining
glass-engraving	glass-topped
glass-green	glass wall
glass-hard	glass window

Glass (glas, gläs), **Carter,** 1858–1946, U.S. statesman.

glass bead Any small, solid or hollow sphere of glass.

glass-blow·ing (glas'blō'ing, gläs'-) *n.* The process of blowing viscid molten glass into any desired form. —**glass'-blow'er** *n.*

glass eye An artificial eye made of glass.
glass·ful (glas'fŏŏl, gläs'-) *n. pl.* **·fuls** As much as can be contained in a drinking glass.
glass furnace A furnace for fusing the materials of which glass is made, or one for remelting glass frit and making it ready for working.
glass gall A porous scum of impurities formed on the surface of molten glass.
glass·house (glas'hous', gläs'-) *n.* **1** A factory where glass is made. **2** *Brit.* A hothouse or greenhouse.
glass·ine (gla·sēn') *n.* A tough, thin, glazed, almost transparent paper made from thoroughly beaten pulp.
glass·mak·er (glas'mā'kər, gläs'-) *n.* One who makes glass.
glass·man (glas'mən, gläs'-) *n. pl.* **·men** (-mən) **1** One who sells glass or glassware. **2** A glassmaker. **3** A glazier.
glass paper Paper coated with glue and sprinkled with powdered glass: used as an abrasive.
glass snake **1** A slender legless lizard of the southern United States (*Ophisaurus ventralis*) having a very brittle tail. **2** A similar Old World snakelike lizard (*O. apus*).
glass·ware (glas'wâr', gläs'-) *n.* Articles made of glass.

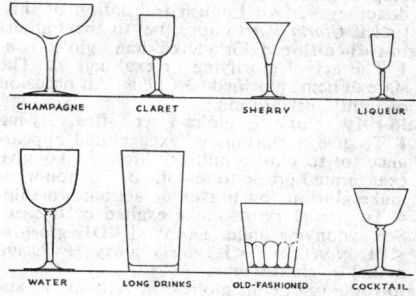

CHAMPAGNE   CLARET   SHERRY   LIQUEUR

WATER   LONG DRINKS   OLD-FASHIONED   COCKTAIL

GLASSWARE FOR MODERN TABLE USE

glass·wool (glas'wŏŏl', gläs'-) *n.* Fibers of spun glass of wool-like appearance: used in fireproofing fabrics, as insulator material, as a filter, and in draining wounds.
glass·work (glas'wûrk', gläs'-) *n.* **1** The manufacture of glass articles, etc. **2** Articles made of glass. — **glass'work'er** *n.*
glass·works (glas'wûrks', gläs'-) *n. sing. & pl.* A glass factory.
glass·worm (glas'wûrm', gläs'-) *n.* The arrowworm.
glass·wort (glas'wûrt', gläs'-) *n.* Any of several low saline seaside herbs (genus *Salicornia*) whose ashes were formerly used in glassmaking.
glass·y (glas'ē, gläs'ē) *adj.* **glass·i·er, glass·i·est** **1** Composed of or like glass; having a hard, fixed appearance. **2** Fixed, blank, and uncomprehending: a *glassy* stare. — **glass'i·ly** *adv.* — **glass'i·ness** *n.*
Glas·ton·bur·y (glas'tən·ber'ē) A municipal borough in central Somersetshire, England; the ruins of its abbey, originally built in the eighth century, are traditionally regarded as on the site of the first Christian church in England.
Glas·we·gi·an (glas·wē'jən, -jē·ən, gläs-) *adj.* Of or pertaining to Glasgow. — *n.* A native or inhabitant of Glasgow.
Glau·ber (glou'bər), **Johann Rudolf,** 1604–1668, German physician and alchemist who discovered muriatic acid and Glauber's salts.
Glauber's salts A white crystalline sodium sulfate, used medicinally as a cathartic. Also **Glauber salt.**
glau·cine (glô'sēn, -sin) *n. Biochem.* A yellowish, bitter, crystalline alkaloid, $C_{21}H_{25}O_4N$, from the sap of the yellow-horned poppy (*Glaucium flavum*): it suspends heart action and inhibits muscular sensibility.
glauco- *combining form* Bluish-gray: *glauconite.* Also, before vowels, **glauc-.** [<Gk. *glaukos* bluish-gray]
glau·co·ma (glô·kō'mə) *n. Pathol.* An affection of the eye characterized by opacity of the vitreous humor and impaired vision that may, if not given early therapeutic treatment,

lead to blindness. [<L <Gk. *glaukōma* < *glaukos* bluish-gray] — **glau·com·a·tous** (glô·kom'ə·təs) *adj.*
glau·co·nite (glô'kə·nīt) *n.* An amorphous, olive-green, loosely granular, massive hydrous silicate, chiefly of iron and potassium, found in greensand. [<Gk. *glaukon,* neut. of *glaukos* bluish-gray + -ITE¹]
glau·cous (glô·kəs) *adj.* **1** Having a yellowish-green color; also, sea green. **2** *Bot.* Covered with a bluish-white bloom, as grapes, blueberries, etc. [<L *glaucus* <Gk. *glaukos* bluish-gray]
glaucous gull See BURGOMASTER (def. 2).
glaucous willow The pussy willow.
glaum (gläm, glôm) *v.i. Scot.* To clutch; grasp.
glaze (glāz) *v.* **glazed, glaz·ing** *v.t.* **1** To fit, as a window, with glass panes. **2** To provide (a building, etc.) with windows. **3** To coat, as pottery, with a glasslike surface applied by fusing. **4** To cover with a glaze, as meat or biscuits. **5** To make glossy, as by polishing. **6** In painting, to cover with a thin, transparent color so as to modify the tone. — *v.i.* **7** To become glassy; take on a glaze. — *n.* **1** A smooth, shining, transparent surface; a glossy coating, or a substance used to produce it, as on pottery or tiles: distinguished from *enamel.* **2** A sheet of ice; an icy surface. **3** Stock or icing cooked to a thin paste and applied to the surface of meat, fish, vegetables, fruits, or nuts. [ME *glasen* < *glas* glass] — **glaz'er** *n.* — **glaz'i·ness** *n.* — **glaz'y** *adj.*
gla·zier (glā'zhər) *n.* **1** One who fits panes of glass. **2** One who applies glaze to pottery. — **gla'zier·y** *n.*
glaz·ing (glā'zing) *n.* **1** A glaze; material used to produce a glaze. **2** The act or art of applying glaze. **3** Window panes collectively; glasswork. **4** The act or art of setting glass.
Gla·zu·nov (glä'zŏŏ-nôf), **Alexander,** 1865–1936, Russian composer.
gleam (glēm) *n.* **1** A moderate light; a passing or intermittent glimmer; flash. **2** Something likened to a flash of light: a *gleam* of wit. See synonyms under LIGHT. — *v.i.* **1** To shine or glitter with a gleam or gleams. **2** To appear clearly and briefly, as a signal fire. — *v.t.* **3** To show with a gleam or gleams: His eyes *gleamed* hatred. See synonyms under SHINE. [OE *glæm.* Akin to GLIM, GLIMMER.]
gleam·y (glē'mē) *adj.* **gleam·i·er, gleam·i·est** **1** Sending forth gleams. **2** Characterized by fitful gleams of sunlight; uncertain: said of the weather.
glean (glēn) *v.t. & v.i.* **1** To collect (information, facts, etc.) by patient effort. **2** To gather (the leavings) from a field after the crop has been reaped. **3** To gather the leavings from (a field, etc.). [<OF *glener* <LL *glenare* <Celtic] — **glean'er** *n.*
glean·ing (glē'ning) *n.* **1** *pl.* That which is collected by a gleaner; a remaining portion. **2** The act of gleaning.
gle·ba (glē'bə) *n. pl.* **·bae** (-bē) *Bot.* The chambered spore-bearing tissue within the closed sac or peridium of a puffball fungus. [<NL <L, a clod]
glebe (glēb) *n.* **1** *Brit.* A portion of land attached to an ecclesiastical benefice as part of its endowment. **2** *Poetic* Any field; cultivated land. [<OF <L *gleba* clod]
glede (glēd) *n.* **1** The European kite (genus *Milvus*). **2** Any of several similar birds. Also **gled** (gled). [OE *glida*]
glee¹ (glē) *n.* **1** Mirth; gaiety; merriment. **2** A musical composition for three or more voices, without accompaniment. See synonyms under LAUGHTER. [OE *glēo*] — **glee'some** (-səm) *adj.*
glee² (glē) *Scot. v.i.* To squint. — *n.* A squint. Also **gley** (glē, glī).
glee club A musical club or group organized, formerly, to sing glees, now, any songs.
gleed (glēd) *n. Obs.* A coal of fire; flame; cinder. [OE *glēd*]
glee·ful (glē'fəl) *adj.* Feeling or exhibiting glee; mirthful. — **glee'ful·ly** *adv.* — **glee'ful·ness** *n.*
glee·man (glē'mən) *n. pl.* **·men** (-mən) *Archaic* A wandering singer or minstrel.
gleet (glēt) *Pathol. n.* **1 a** A slimy mucous discharge succeeding inflammation of the urethra. **b** A chronic discharge from any mucous membrane. **2** A chronic discharge from the nasal cavities, as in horses. — *v.i.* To emit

a thin, watery liquid; ooze. [<OF *glette* mucus, pus] — **gleet'y** *adj.*
gleg (gleg) *adj. Scot.* Quick; nimble; happy. — **gleg'ly** *adv.*
Glei·witz (glī'vits) A city in southern Poland; formerly in Germany. *Polish* **Gli·wi·ce** (glē·vē'tse).
glei·za·tion (glī·zā'shən) *n. Geol.* The process by which moisture acts upon rock materials to produce a greenish or bluish waterlogged soil, often with formation of peat bogs.
glen (glen) *n.* A small, secluded valley. [<Scottish Gaelic *glenn*]
Glen·coe (glen·kō') A valley in Argyllshire, Scotland; scene of massacre of the MacDonalds by the Campbells and the English, 1692.
Glen·dow·er (glen'dŏŏr, -dou·ər), **Owen,** 1359?–1416?, Welsh chieftain; rebelled against Henry IV.
Glen·gar·ry (glen·gar'ē) *n.* A woolen Scottish cap, high in front and sloping backward: also called **Glengarry bonnet.** [from *Glengarry,* a valley in Scotland]
Glen More (glen môr', mōr') See GREAT GLEN OF SCOTLAND.
Glenn (glen) **John H., Jr.,** born 1921, U.S. Marine Corps officer; first U.S. astronaut to orbit the earth, Feb. 20, 1962.
gle·noid (glē'noid) *adj.* **1** *Anat.* Hollowed like a shallow pit, as the articular cavities or fossae of the scapula and the temporal bone. **2** Having a shallow cavity. [<Gk. *glēnoeidēs* like a socket <*glēnē* a socket]
gli·a·din (glī'ə·din) *n. Biochem.* Any of a group of simple proteins derived from the gluten of wheat, rye, or other grains. [<F *gliadine* <Gk. *glia* glue]
glib (glib) *adj.* **glib·ber, glib·best** **1** Speaking with smooth fluency without much thought: a *glib* talker. **2** More facile than sincere: a *glib* compliment. **3** Characterized by easiness or quickness, as of manner. [Cf. obs. *glibbery* <MLG *glibberich* slippery] — **glib'ly** *adv.* — **glib'ness** *n.*
glid·der (glid'ər) *Brit. Dial. adj.* Slippery: also **glid'der·y.** — *v.t.* To make icy or smooth. — *v.i.* To slip. [OE]
glide (glīd) *v.* **glid·ed, glid·ing** *v.i.* **1** To move, slip, or flow smoothly or easily. **2** To pass unnoticed or imperceptibly, as time: often with *by.* **3** *Aeron.* To descend gradually and without the use of motor power: also, to operate or fly in a glider. **4** *Music & Phonet.* To produce a glide. — *v.t.* **5** To cause to glide. — *n.* **1** The act of gliding; a gliding motion. **2** *Music* An unbroken passage from tone to tone; a slur. **3** *Phonet.* **a** A transitional sound made in passing from the position of one speech sound to that of another, as the (w) heard between (ŏŏ) and (a) in *bivouac.* **b** A semivowel. **4** A gliding step in waltzing; also, a waltz in which this movement is used. **5** The movement of a glider. [OE *glīdan*]
glid·er (glī'dər) *n.* **1** One who or that which glides. **2** *Aeron.* An aircraft similar in general structure to an airplane but without an engine, supported by rising currents of air. **3** A couch hung in a metal frame and arranged so as to glide back and forth. **4** *Austral.* A flying phalanger: also **gliding possum.**

GLIDER—TWO-SEATED TRAINER

glid·ing (glī'ding) *n.* The act of one who or that which glides. — *adj.* Having the action or motion of a glide.
gliding angle See under ANGLE.
gliding plane *Mineral.* A plane parallel to which a differential movement of the parts of a crystal can take place without rupture.
gliding range *Aeron.* The greatest distance that can be traveled by an aircraft from a given height under normal gliding conditions. Also **gliding distance.**
gliff (glif) *n. Scot.* **1** A glimpse; a moment. **2** Fright. **3** A look; expression.
glim (glim) *n.* **1** *Slang* A light; a candle. **2** *Scot.* A momentary glance. **3** *Slang* An eye. [Akin to GLEAM]
glim·mer (glim'ər) *v.i.* **1** To shine with a faint,

unsteady light; flicker. 2 To appear fitfully or faintly. — *n.* 1 A faint, unsteady light; a flickering gleam. 2 A momentary apprehension; glimpse; a vague idea: a *glimmer* of the truth. See synonyms under LIGHT[1]. [ME *glimeren* shine. Akin to GLEAM.]
glimpse (glimps) *n.* 1 A momentary view or look. 2 A swift, passing appearance. 3 An inkling. 4 A sudden, passing gleam. — *v.* **glimpsed, glimps·ing** *v.t.* 1 To see for an instant; catch a glimpse of. — *v.i.* 2 To look for an instant; glance. [ME *glimsen* shine faintly. Akin to GLEAM.]
Glin·ka (glēn′kə), **Mikhail Ivanovich,** 1803–1857, Russian composer.
glint (glint) *v.i.* 1 To gleam; glitter. 2 To move quickly; glance aside. — *v.t.* 3 To reflect; shine. — *n.* 1 A gleam; flash. 2 *Scot.* A glimpse. [ME *glinten,* var. of *glenten* shine <Scand. Cf. dial. Sw. *glänta* shine.]
gli·o·ma (glī·ō′mə) *n. pl.* **·ma·ta** *Pathol.* A tumor containing elements similar to neuroglia cells, occurring in connective tissue. [<NL <Gk. *glia* glue + *-ōma* -OMA] — **gli·o·ma·tous** (glī·ō′mə·təs, -om′ə-) *adj.*
gli·o·sa (glī·ō′sə) *n. Anat.* The gray matter which surrounds the central canal of the spinal cord. [<NL <Gk. *glia* glue]
glis·sade (gli·säd′, -sād′) *v.i.* **·sad·ed, ·sad·ing** To slide or glide. — *n.* 1 The act of gliding down a slope, as of ice or snow. 2 A sliding step in dancing; glide. [<F <*glisser* slip]
glis·san·do (gli·sän′dō) *n. pl.* **·di** (-dē) A gliding effect, as in the playing of a run on the piano by sliding a finger rapidly over the keys. [<F *glissant,* ppr. of *glisser* slip + Ital. *-ando,* ppr. suffix]
glis·ten (glis′ən) *v.i.* To sparkle, especially with reflected light; shine; gleam. See synonyms under SHINE. — *n.* A shining, as by reflection from a wet surface. See synonyms under LIGHT[1]. [OE *glisnian* shine] — **glis′ten·ing** *adj.*
glis·ter (glis′tər) *v.i. Archaic* To glitter; glisten. — *n.* Glitter; glistening. [<MDu. *glisteren*]
glitch (glich) *n. Slang* 1 A malfunction or mishap. 2 A sudden shift from normal function, as in electric power. 3 A false or spurious electronic signal. [Prob. <G *glitschen* to slide, slip]
glit·ter (glit′ər) *v.i.* 1 To shine with a gleaming light; sparkle. 2 To be bright or colorful. — *n.* Sparkle; brilliancy. See synonyms under LIGHT[1]. [<ON *glitra*]
glit·ter·y (glit′ər·ē) *adj.* Having, or shining with, a glitter.
gloam (glōm) *v.t.* & *v.i. Scot.* To darken; make or become dusk. — *n. Rare* Twilight.
gloam·ing (glō′ming) *n.* The twilight; dusk. Also *gloam.* [OE *glōmung*]
gloat (glōt) *v.i.* To look with cruel or triumphant satisfaction; think about something with exultation or avarice: usually with *over.* [Cf. ON *glotta* grin]
glob·al (glō′bəl) *adj.* 1 Spherical. 2 Pertaining to or involving the world in its entirety: *global* war. 3 *Pathol.* Entire; all-inclusive: *global* aphasia.
glo·bate (glō′bāt) *adj.* Globe-shaped; spherical; hence, rounded; complete. Also **glo′bat·ed.**
globe (glōb) *n.* 1 A perfectly round body; ball; sphere. 2 The earth: with the definite article. 3 A sphere on which is a map of the earth or of the heavens: also **terrestrial** or **celestial globe.** 4 A hollow globular vessel or the like. 5 Any planetary or celestial body. 6 A ball, usually of gold, borne as an emblem of authority. — *v.t.* & *v.i.* **globed, glob·ing** To form into a globe. [<F <L *globus* ball]
globe daisy See under GLOBULARIN.
globe·fish (glōb′fish′) *n. pl.* **·fish** or **·fish·es** 1 A teleost fish (*Diodon hystrix*) of tropical seas, covered with long, horny spines and able, when disturbed, to inflate its body into a globular form: also called *porcupine fish.* 2 A puffer.

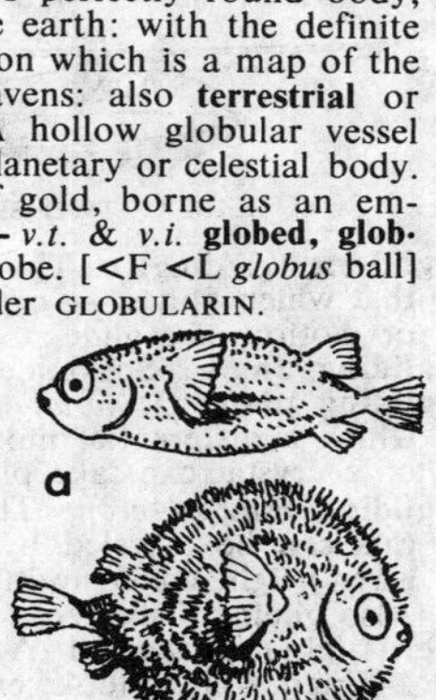

GLOBEFISH
a. Normal. *b.* Inflated.
(About 7 inches long)

globe·flow·er (glōb′flou′ər) *n.* Any of a genus (*Trollius*) of ranunculaceous plants having globular, yellow flowers.
globe-trot·ter (glōb′trot′ər) *n.* A habitual traveler; especially, one who travels all over the world. — **globe′-trot′ting** *n.* & *adj.*
Glo·big·er·i·na (glō·bij′ə·rī′nə) *n.* A genus of small marine foraminifers whose calcareous shells accumulate in vast quantities on the sea bottoms, forming the deposits known as **globigerina ooze.** [<NL <L *globus* a ball + *gerere* bear]
glo·bin (glō′bin) *n. Biochem.* A protein constituent of red blood corpuscles. [<L *globus* a ball + -IN]
glo·boid (glō′boid) *adj.* Having a spherical or globular shape; globate. — *n.* Any globate body or mass.
glo·bose (glō′bōs) *adj.* Spherical. Also **glo′bous** (-bəs). [<L *globosus* <*globus* a ball] — **glo·bose′ness** *n.* — **glo·bos·i·ty** (glō·bos′ə·tē) *n.*
glob·u·lar (glob′yə·lər) *adj.* 1 Spherical. 2 Formed of globules. 3 World-wide.
glob·u·lar·in (glob′yə·lər·in) *n.* A white, bitter powder, $C_{15}H_{20}O_8$, obtained from the leaves of the globe daisy (*Globularia alypum*): a glucoside similar to caffeine in action.
glob·ule (glob′yōōl) *n.* 1 A small globe or spherical particle. 2 A small pill. 3 *Med.* A corpuscle (def. 3). [<F <L *globulus,* dim. of *globus* a ball]
glob·u·li·cide (glob′yə·lə·sīd′) *n.* An agent destructive of red blood corpuscles. — **glob′u·li·ci′dal** *adj.*
glob·u·lif·er·ous (glob′yə·lif′ər·əs) *adj.* 1 Having or containing globules. 2 Containing red blood corpuscles.
glob·u·lim·e·ter (glob′yə·lim′ə·tər) *n.* An instrument for determining the number of red blood corpuscles in a given amount of blood.
glob·u·lin (glob′yə·lin) *n. Biochem.* Any one of a class of simple plant and animal proteins, insoluble in water but soluble in dilute saline solutions. [<GLOBULE]
glob·u·lous (glob′yə·ləs) *adj.* Of the shape of a small globe; globular; spherical. Also **glob′u·lose** (-lōs).
glo·chid·i·ate (glō·kid′ē·āt) *adj. Biol.* Barbed, as hairs and bristles.
glo·chid·i·um (glō·kid′ē·əm) *n. pl.* **·chid·i·a** (-kid′ē·ə) *Zool.* A larva of a mussel with a bivalve embryonic shell provided with hooked processes by which it may attach itself to a fish and there pass a brief phase of its life. [<NL, dim. of Gk. *glōchis* point of an arrow]
glock·en·spiel (glok′ən·spēl) *n.* 1 A portable musical instrument consisting of a series of metal bars tuned in chromatic range and played by striking with two wooden or composition hammers. 2 A set of bells; a carillon. [<G *glocken* bells + *spiel* play]

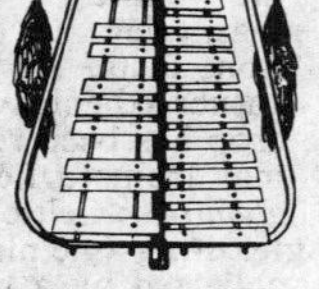

GLOCKENSPIEL

glom·er·ate (glom′ər·āt, -it) *v.t.* & *v.i. Obs.* **·at·ed, ·at·ing** To gather or wind into a ball or spherical mass. — *adj.* Clustered compactly. [<L *glomeratus,* pp. of *glomerare* collect <*glomus, -eris* a mass]
glom·er·a·tion (glom′ə·rā′shən) *n.* 1 A conglomerated mass. 2 Agglomeration. 3 A ball, or anything made into a ball or rounded mass.
glom·er·ule (glom′ər·ōōl) *n. Bot.* A cymose flower cluster which is condensed into a head-like form. [<F <NL *glomerulus,* dim. of *glomus, -eris* a mass]
glo·mer·u·lus (glə·mer′yə·ləs) *n. pl.* **·li** (-lī) 1 A glomerule. 2 *Anat.* A coil of blood vessels forming a small tuft at the expanded end of each uriniferous tubule. [<NL. See GLOMERULE.]
Glom·ma (glôm′ä) A river in SE Norway, flowing 185 miles south to the Skagerrak. Also **Gla′ma.**
glon·o·in (glon′ō·in) *n.* Nitroglycerin, especially as used in medicine. Also **glon′o·ine** (-in, -ēn). [<GL(YCERIN) + *O,* oxygen, and NO_3, nitric anhydride + -IN]
gloom (glōōm) *n.* 1 Partial or total darkness; heavy shadow. 2 Darkness or depression of the mind or spirits. 3 A dark or gloomy place. 4 *Scot.* A sulky look; frown. [<*v.*] — *v.i.* 1 To look sullen, displeased, or dejected. 2 To be or become dark or threatening. — *v.t.* 3 To make dark, sad, or sullen. ◆ Homophone: *glume.* [ME *glom(b)en* look sad]
gloom·ing (glōō′ming) *n.* 1 Gloaming. 2 A frown; sulky fit.
gloom·y (glōō′mē) *adj.* **gloom·i·er, gloom·i·est** 1 Dark; dismal; obscure. 2 Affected with gloom or melancholy; morose. 3 Productive of gloom or melancholy. See synonyms under DARK, MOROSE, SAD. — **gloom′i·ly** *adv.* — **gloom′i·ness** *n.*
glo·ri·a (glôr′ē·ə, glō′rē·ə) *n.* 1 *Eccl.* A hymn or ascription of praise to God; a doxology. 2 *Eccl. Usually cap.* **a** A movement of the mass, following the Kyrie, during which the *Gloria in excelsis* is sung. **b** In the Anglican and some other churches, a similar section in the Eucharist. 3 A musical setting for a gloria, especially the *Gloria in excelsis.* 4 A gloriole; glory. 5 An ornament for the head in imitation of a gloriole. 6 A mixture of wool and silk or similar material, used as a substitute for silk in covering umbrellas and in dressmaking. [<L, glory]
Gloria in ex·cel·sis (ek·sel′sis) 1 A Latin doxology beginning *Gloria in excelsis*; the greater doxology. 2 An English translation of this. [<LL *Gloria in excelsis (Deo)* Glory (to God) in the highest. See *Luke* ii 14.]
Gloria Pa·tri (pat′rē) 1 A short Latin doxology which begins *Gloria Patri*: the lesser doxology. 2 An English translation of this. [<LL *Gloria Patri* Glory (be) to the Father]
glo·ri·fi·ca·tion (glôr′ə·fə·kā′shən, glō′rə-) *n.* 1 The act of glorifying or exalting. 2 The state of being glorified. 3 *Colloq.* An occasion of jollity; celebration.
glo·ri·fy (glôr′ə·fī, glō′rə-) *v.t.* **·fied, ·fy·ing** 1 To give a glorious or exaggerated appearance to: to *glorify* military life. 2 To give exaggerated praise to; extol. 3 To honor or make glorious by prayer or action; worship. 4 To give glory to; make exalted or blessed. See synonyms under PRAISE. [<OF *glorifier* <LL *glorificare* <L *gloria* glory + *facere* make] — **glo′ri·fi′er** *n.*
glo·ri·ole (glôr′ē·ōl, glō′rē-) *n.* A halo or aureole. [<F <L *gloriola,* dim. of *gloria* glory]
glo·ri·ous (glôr′ē·əs, glō′rē-) *adj.* 1 Full of glory; of exalted honor, dignity, or majesty. 2 Extremely delightful; splendid: a *glorious* time. 3 *Obs.* Resplendent. 4 Eager for glory or distinction; vainglorious. See synonyms under BRIGHT, ILLUSTRIOUS. [<L *gloriosus* <*gloria* glory] — **glo′ri·ous·ly** *adv.* — **glo′ri·ous·ness** *n.*
glo·ry (glôr′ē, glō′rē) *n. pl.* **·ries** 1 Distinguished honor or praise; exalted reputation. 2 Something which occasions praise or renown; an object of praise. 3 Adoration; worshipful praise: give *glory* to God. 4 Splendor; magnificence: the *glory* of Rome. 5 The bliss of heaven: to go to *glory.* 6 A state of exaltation or extreme well-being: He was in his *glory.* 7 Radiance; brilliancy. 8 The emanation of light surrounding the head or the entire figure of a divine being; a nimbus; halo. See synonyms under FAME. — *v.i.* **glo·ried, glo·ry·ing** To rejoice proudly or triumphantly; exult; take pride: with *in.* [<OF *glorie* <L *gloria*]
glo·ry·flow·er (glôr′ē·flou′ər, glō′rē-) *n.* A climbing shrub of the bignonia family, native in Chile and Peru (*Eccremocarpus scaber*), with pinnate leaves and orange, yellow, or scarlet tubular flowers. Also called **glo′ry·vine′** (-vīn′).
glo·ry-lil·y (glôr′ē·lil′ē, glō′rē-) *n.* A climbing plant (genus *Gloriosa*) of the lily family, with solitary red and yellow flowers; especially *G. superba,* whose root yields superbine.
gloss[1] (glôs, glos) *n.* 1 The brightness or sheen of a polished surface. 2 A deceptive or superficial show. — *v.t.* 1 To make smooth or lustrous, as by polishing or buffing. 2 To hide or attempt to hide (errors, defects, etc.) by falsehood or equivocation: with *over.* — *v.i.* 3 To become shiny. [<Scand. Cf. ON *glossi* blaze, spark.] — **gloss′er** *n.*
gloss[2] (glôs, glos) *n.* 1 An explanatory note; especially, a marginal or interlinear note. 2 A glossary. 3 A plausible explanation to cover fault or defect. — *v.t.* 1 To write marginal explanations for (a text, word, etc.); annotate. 2 To excuse or change by false explanations: to *gloss* the truth of a matter. — *v.i.* 3 To make glosses. [<OF *glose* a note <L *glossa* a difficult word (in a text) <Gk. *glōssa* a foreign word; orig., tongue] — **gloss′er** *n.*

Glos·sa (glôs′ə, glos′ə), **Cape** A promontory in SW Albania; ancient *Acroceraunia*: Italian *Capo Linguetta.*

glos·sal (glôs′əl, glos′-) *adj.* Of or pertaining to the tongue; having a tongue; lingual.

glos·sa·rist (glos′ə·rist, glôs′-) *n.* One who writes glosses; also, one who compiles a glossary. Also **glos·sa·tor** (glo·sā′tər, glô-).

glos·sa·ry (glos′ə·rē, glôs′-) *n. pl.* **·ries 1** A lexicon of the obsolete, obscure, or foreign words of a work. **2** Any explanatory vocabulary, as of a science. [<L *glossarium* <*glossa* GLOSS²] —**glos·sar·i·al** (glo·sâr′ē·əl, glô-) *adj.*

glos·sec·to·my (glo·sek′tə·mē, glô-) *n. Surg.* Total or partial removal of the tongue or of a glossal lesion.

Glos·si·na (glo·sī′nə, glô-) *n.* An Ethiopian genus of biting flies which includes the tsetse fly, carrier of the infective agent of African sleeping sickness. For illustration see under INSECT (injurious). [<NL <Gk. *glōssa* tongue]

glos·si·tis (glo·sī′tis, glô-) *n. Pathol.* Inflammation of the tongue. —**glos·sit·ic** (-sit′ik) *adj.*

glosso- *combining form* The tongue; pertaining to the tongue: *glossography.* Also, before vowels, **gloss-.** [<Gk. *glōssa* tongue]

glos·sog·ra·phy (glo·sog′rə·fē, glô-) *n.* **1** A description of the tongue. **2** The making of glosses or of glossaries. —**glos·sog′ra·pher** *n.*

glos·so·la·li·a (glôs′ə·lā′lē·ə, glos-) *n.* **1** The gift of tongues. **2** (In some Pentecostal churches) a speaking in sounds that do not correspond linguistically to those of any known language.

glos·sol·o·gy (glo·sol′ə·jē, glô-) *n. Obs.* The science of language; comparative philology: also called *glottology.*

gloss·y (glôs′ē, glos′ē) *adj.* **gloss·i·er, gloss·i·est 1** Having a lustrous surface; polished. **2** Outwardly or speciously fair. See synonyms under SMOOTH. —**gloss′i·ly** *adv.* —**gloss′i·ness** *n.*

glost (glôst, glost) *n.* Lead glaze used in making pottery; also, glazed pottery. [Variant of GLOSS¹]

-glot *combining form* Able to speak, or written in, a number of languages: *polyglot.* [<Gk. *glōtta,* var. of *glōssa* tongue, language]

glot·tal (glot′l) *adj.* Of, pertaining to, or articulated in the glottis.

glottal stop *Phonet.* A sound produced in the larynx by an instantaneous closure of the glottis, as at the beginning of a cough, or in one pronunciation of *bottle*: not a phoneme in English.

glot·tic (glot′ik) *adj.* **1** Of or pertaining to the tongue. **2** Of, pertaining to, or produced by the glottis; glottal. **3** *Obs.* Linguistic.

glot·tis (glot′is) *n. pl.* **·ti·des** (-ə·dēz) *Anat.* The cleft or opening between the vocal folds at the upper orifice of the larynx, the mouth of the windpipe. [<NL <Gk. *glōttis* <*glōtta* tongue]

glot·tol·o·gy (glo·tol′ə·jē) See GLOSSOLOGY.

Glouces·ter (glos′tər, glôs′-), **Duke of** See under HUMPHREY. —**Richard,** 1452–85, Duke of Gloucester, became king of England 1483, as Richard III.

Glouces·ter (glos′tər, glôs′-) **1** A county in west central England; 1,257 square miles; county town, Gloucester. Also **Glouces′ter·shire** (-shir). **2** A port and resort in NE Massachusetts.

glove (gluv) *n.* A covering for the hand, having a separate sheath for each finger. —**the gloves** Boxing gloves. —*v.t.* **gloved, glov·ing 1** To put gloves on. **2** To cover with or as with a glove. **3** To serve as a glove for. [OE *glōf*]

glov·er (gluv′ər) *n.* A maker of or a dealer in gloves.

Glov·ers·ville (gluv′ərz·vil) A city in central New York; center of leather glove and mitten manufacture.

glow (glō) *v.i.* **1** To give off light and heat, especially without flame; be incandescent. **2** To shine as if greatly heated. **3** To show a strong, bright color; be bright or red, as with heat or animation; blush. **4** To be animated with strong emotion. **5** To be excessively hot; burn. —*n.* **1** The incandescence of a heated substance. **2** Bright color; redness; flush; ruddiness. **3** Fervid heat; strong emotion or ardor. **4** Bodily warmth, as caused by exercise, etc. See synonyms under LIGHT¹, WARMTH. [OE *glōwan*]

glow-dis·charge (glō′dis·chärj′) *n.* The initial luminous electrical discharge in a gas, as observed in neon lamps, etc.

glow·er (glou′ər) *v.i.* **1** To stare with an angry frown; scowl sullenly. **2** *Scot.* To stare. —*n.* The act of glowering; a fierce or threatening stare. Also *Scot.* **glour, glowr.** [? Freq. of obs. *glow* stare] —**glow′er·ing** *adj.* —**glow′er·ing·ly** *adv.*

glow·fly (glō′flī′) *n.* A firefly.

glow·ing (glō′ing) *adj.* Having a glow; ardent; bright; also, enthusiastic. —**glow′ing·ly** *adv.*

glow lamp An incandescent lamp, usually electrical.

glow potential The voltage marking the beginning of a glow-discharge.

glow·worm (glō′wûrm′) *n.* **1** A European beetle (genus *Lampyris*), the larva and wingless female of which display phosphorescent light. **2** The luminous larva of American fireflies.

glox·in·i·a (glok·sin′ē·ə) *n.* Any plant of a genus *(Sinningia),* with opposite leaves and large bell-shaped spotted flowers. [after B. P. *Gloxin,* 18th century German physician]

gloze¹ (glōz) *v.* **glozed, gloz·ing** *v.t.* **1** To explain away; palliate: usually with *over.* **2** *Obs.* To flatter. **3** *Obs.* To explain by notes or glosses. —*v.i.* **4** *Obs.* To make notes or glosses. —*n. Obs.* **1** Specious show; gloss. **2** A note, gloss, or comment. **3** Flattery. [<OF *gloser* explain <*glose* a note <L *glossa.* See GLOSS².]

gloze² (glōz) *v.t.* & *v.i.* **glozed, gloz·ing** *Rare* To shine; light up; gleam. [Cf. GLOSS¹]

gloz·ing (glō′zing) *n.* **1** Specious flattery. **2** Annotation.

glu·ca·gon (glōō′kə·gon) *n.* A hormone secreted by the pancreas that increases the level of sugar in the blood by stimulating the breakdown of glycogen to glucose.

glu·ci·num (glōō·sī′nəm) *n.* The former name for beryllium. [<NL <Gk. *glykys* sweet; because some of its salts are sweet to taste]

Gluck (glŏŏk), **Alma,** 1884–1938, U.S. soprano, born in Rumania. —**Christoph Willibald,** 1714–87, German composer.

glu·co·pro·te·in (glōō′kō·prō′tē·in, -tēn) See GLYCOPROTEIN.

glu·cose (glōō′kōs) *n. Chem.* **1** Dextrose or grape sugar; a monosaccharide carbohydrate having the formula $C_6H_{12}O_6$. It is widely distributed in plants and animals and is obtained by the hydrolysis of starch and other carbohydrates. It is fermentable but less sweet than cane sugar. **2** A thick yellowish sirup containing dextrose, maltose, and dextrin, obtained by incomplete hydrolysis of starch and used in confectionery, baking, etc. [<Gk. *glykys* sweet + -OSE²] —**glu·cos′ic** (-kos′ik) *adj.*

glu·co·side (glōō′kə·sīd) See GLYCOSIDE.

glu·co·su·ri·a (glōō′kō·sŏŏr′ē·ə) See GLYCOSURIA.

glue (glōō) *n.* **1** A viscid cement or adhesive preparation, usually a form of impure gelatin derived from boiling certain animal substances, as skin, bones, and cartilage, in water. It is a typical colloid. **2** Any of a number of sticky substances. —*v.t.* **glued, glu·ing** To stick or fasten with or as with glue. [<OF *glu* birdlime <LL *glus, glutis*] —**glue′y** *adj.*

glum (glum) *adj.* **glum·mer, glum·mest** Moody and silent; sullen. [Akin to GLOOM] —**glum′ly** *adv.* —**glum′ness** *n.*

glu·ma·ceous (glōō·mā′shəs) *adj.* Bearing, or pertaining to, glumes.

glume (glōōm) *n. Bot.* A chafflike scale on the lowest bracts of a grass spikelet. ◆ Homophone: *gloom.* [<L *gluma* husk]

glump·y (glum′pē) *adj.* Sullen; sulky; grumpy. [? Blend of GLUM and GRUMPY]

glunch (glōōnsh, glunsh) *Scot. v.i.* To frown; look sullen. —*adj.* Sullen and sour. —*n.* A look expressive of displeasure.

glut¹ (glut) *v.* **glut·ted, glut·ting** *v.t.* **1** To fill or supply to excess; satiate; gorge. **2** To supply (the market) with an excessive quantity of an article and bring on a lowering of prices. —*v.i.* **3** To eat gluttonously; gormandize. See synonyms under PAMPER, SATISFY. —*n.* **1** An excessive supply; plethora. **2** A full supply. **3** The condition of being glutted; act of glutting. [<obs. *glut* a glutton <OF *gloutir* swallow <L *glutire*]

glut² (glut) *n.* A wooden wedge used in splitting logs. [Cf. dial. *clut* a cleat]

glu·tam·ic acid (glōō·tam′ik) *Chem.* An amino acid, $C_5H_9O_4N$, present in many animal and vegetable proteins.

glu·ta·mine (glōō′tə·mēn, -min) *n. Biochem.* An amino acid, $C_5H_{10}O_3N_2$, commonly present in animal and vegetable proteins. [<GLUT(EN) + -AMINE]

glu·ta·thi·one (glōō′tə·thī′ōn) *n. Biochem.* A peptide of glutamic acid, cystine, and glycine, $C_{10}H_{17}O_6N_3S$, obtained from yeast; found also in muscle tissue, blood, and plants. [<GLUTA(MIC) + THI- + -ONE]

glu·te·al (glōō·tē′əl, glōō′tē·əl) *adj. Anat.* Of or pertaining to the muscles of the buttocks. [<GLUTEUS]

glu·te·lin (glōō′tə·lin) *n. Biochem.* Any of a class of simple proteins found in certain plants, as wheat. [<GLUTEN + *-lin,* an arbitrary ending]

glu·ten (glōōt′n) *n.* A mixture of plant proteins found in cereal grains; a tough, sticky substance obtained by washing out the starch from wheat flour: used as an adhesive and thickener. [<L, glue] —**glu′te·nous** *adj.*

gluten bread Bread made from flour rich in gluten and containing little starch.

glu·te·us (glōō·tē′əs) *n. pl.* **·te·i** (-tē′ī) *Anat.* Any of three muscles in the region of the buttocks. [<NL <Gk. *gloutos* rump]

glu·ti·nous (glōō′tə·nəs) *adj.* **1** Resembling glue; sticky. **2** Pervaded with sticky matter. See synonyms under ADHESIVE. —**glu′ti·nous·ly** *adv.* —**glu′ti·nous·ness** *n.*

glut·ton¹ (glut′n) *n.* **1** One who gluts himself; an excessive eater. **2** One who has an excessive appetite for anything. [<OF *glouton* <L *gluto, -onis* a glutton]

glut·ton² (glut′n) *n.* A musteline carnivore, the wolverine *(Gulo luscus),* especially the Old World form. [Trans. of G *vielfrass* great eater]

glut·ton·ize (glut′ən·īz) *v.t.* & *v.i.* **·ized, ·iz·ing** To eat (food) gluttonously.

glut·ton·ous (glut′ən·əs) *adj.* Voracious. —**glut′ton·ous·ly** *adv.*

glut·ton·y (glut′ən·ē) *n. pl.* **·ton·ies** The act or habit of eating to excess.

gly·cer·ic (gli·ser′ik, glis′ər-) *adj.* Of or derived from glycerol.

glyceric acid *Chem.* A colorless, sirupy compound, $C_3H_6O_4$, formed during alcoholic fermentation and by oxidizing glycerol with nitric acid.

glyc·er·ide (glis′ər·īd, -id) *n. Chem.* An ether or ester of glycerol with a fatty acid.

glyc·er·in (glis′ər·in) See GLYCEROL. Also **glyc′er·ine** (-in, -ēn).

glyc·er·ol (glis′ər·ōl, -ol) *n. Chem.* A sweet, oily, nearly colorless trihydric alcohol, $C_3H_8O_3$, formed by decomposition of natural fats with alkalis or superheated steam; also obtained from petroleum products. Also called *glycerin.* [<Gk. *glykeros* sweet + -OL²]

glyc·er·yl (glis′ər·il) *n. Chem.* The trivalent glycerol radical C_3H_5. [<GLYCER(IN) + -YL]

gly·cine (glī′sēn, glī·sēn′) *n. Chem.* A sweet, colorless amino acid, $C_2H_5O_2N$, obtained from various proteins. [<Gk. *glykys* sweet + -INE²]

gly·co·gen (glī′kə·jən) *n. Biochem.* A white, mealy, amorphous polysaccharide, $(C_6H_{10}O_5)_x$, contained in animal tissues, principally the liver: also called *animal starch.* [<Gk. *glykys* sweet + -GEN]

gly·co·gen·ase (glī′kə·jə·nās′) *n. Biochem.* An enzyme present in the liver which converts glycogen to a saccharide. [<GLYCOGEN + -ASE]

gly·co·gen·ic (glī′kə·jen′ik) *adj.* **1** Relating to the formation of glycogen. **2** Caused by glycogen.

gly·col (glī′kōl, -kol) *n. Chem.* **1** A colorless, sweetish compound, $C_2H_6O_2$, formed by decomposing certain ethylene compounds: used as a solvent, as a freezing mixture, and in the manufacture of explosives, intermediates, etc. **2** Any dihydroxyl alcohol of the glycol group having the general formula $C_nH_{2n}(OH)_2$. [<GLYC(ERIN) + -OL¹]

gly·col·ic acid (glī·kol′ik) *Chem.* An acid, $C_2H_4O_3$, found in the juice of cane sugar and unripe grapes: also made synthetically.

gly·co·pro·te·in (glī′kə·prō′tē·in, -tēn) *n. Biochem.* Any of a group of proteins containing a carbohydrate group other than nucleic acid, as mucin: also spelled *glucoprotein.* [<Gk. *glykys* sweet + PROTEIN]

gly·co·side (glī′kə·sīd) *n. Chem.* Any of a group of compounds which, when decomposed by dilute acids, alkalis, or certain ferments, yield glucose or some other sugar and a principle, as digitalin, quercetin, salicin, etc.: also spelled *glucoside.* [<GLUCOSE + -IDE]

gly·co·su·ri·a (glī′kə·sŏŏr′ē·ə) *n. Pathol.* A condition, as diabetes mellitus, in which the urine contains glucose: also spelled *glucosuria.* [<NL <F *glycose* glucose + Gk. *ouron* urine] **— gly′co·su′ric** *adj.*

Glyc·yr·rhi·za (glis′i·rī′zə) *n.* A genus of leguminous plants native in southern Europe and central Asia, the roots of which yield the common licorice of commerce. [<Gk. <*glykys* sweet + *rhiza* root]

Glyn (glin), **Elinor,** 1864–1943, *née* Sutherland, English novelist born in Canada.

gly·ox·a·line (glī·ok′sə·lin) *n.* Imidazole. [< GLY(COL) + OXAL(IC) + -INE[2]]

glyph (glif) *n.* **1** *Archit.* A vertical groove or channel, as in a Doric frieze. Compare TRIGLYPH. **2** A picture or carving representing an idea; hieroglyph. [<Gk. *glyphē* a carving <*glyphein* carve] **— glyph′ic** *adj.*

glyph·og·ra·phy (glif·og′rə·fē) *n.* A process for making relief plates for printing by engraving the design on a copperplate covered with a wax film. [<Gk. *glyphē* a carving + -GRAPHY]

Glyp·tal (glip′təl) *n.* A synthetic resin made from phthalic anhydride and glycerol: used as a bonding material, in paints and lacquers, etc.: a trade name.

glyp·tic (glip′tik) *adj.* **1** Pertaining to carving or engraving. **2** Exhibiting figures, as in a mineral. [<Gk. *glyptikos* <*glyphē* a carving]

glyp·tics (glip′tiks) *n. pl.* The art of cutting designs on precious stones, shells, etc.

glyp·to·dont (glip′tə·dont) *n.* Any of a genus *(Glyptodon)* of extinct American armadillos. [<NL *Glyptodon* <Gk. *glyptos* carved + *odous, odontos* a tooth]

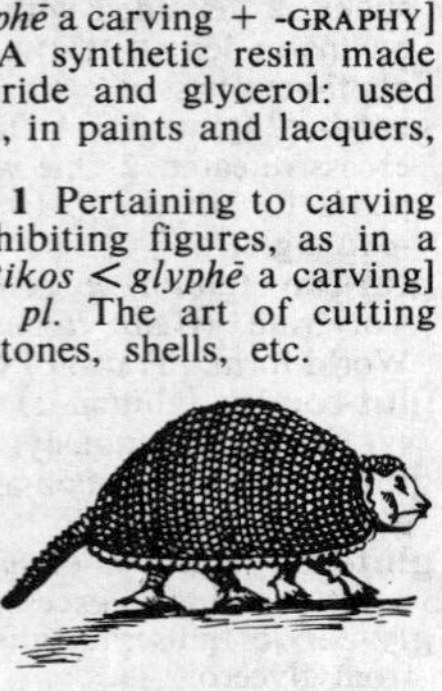

GLYPTODONT
(From 12 to 14 feet long)

glyp·to·graph (glip′tə·graf, -gräf) *n.* A design cut on a gem. **— glyp·tog·ra·pher** (glip·tog′rə·fər) *n.* **— glyp′·to·graph′ic** *adj.*

glyp·tog·ra·phy (glip·tog′rə·fē) *n.* **1** The art or operation of engraving on gems. **2** The study of engraved gems. [<Gk. *glyptos* carved + -GRAPHY]

G–man (jē′man′) *n. pl.* **–men** (-men′) An operative of the Federal Bureau of Investigation. [<G(OVERNMENT) MAN]

gnar (när) *v.i.* **gnarred, gnar·ring** To snarl or growl. Also **gnarr.** [Imit.]

gnarl[1] (närl) *v.i.* To snarl; growl. [Freq. of GNAR]

gnarl[2] (närl) *n.* A protuberance on a tree; a tough knot. [Back formation from GNARLED]

gnarled (närld) *adj.* Exhibiting gnarls; knotty; cross–grained; distorted. Also **gnarl′y.** [Var. of KNURLED]

gnash (nash) *v.t.* **1** To grind or snap (the teeth) together, as in rage or pain. **2** To bite or chew with grinding teeth. *—v.i.* **3** To grind the teeth together. *—n.* A snap or bite of the teeth. [Var. of obs. *gnast* <Scand. Cf. ON *gnista* gnash.]

gnat (nat) *n.* **1** Any of various small dipterous flies with long, many–jointed antennae, as the buffalo gnats, punkies, and midges. **2** A mosquito. [OE *gnæt*]

gnat·catch·er (nat′kach′ər) *n.* A small American bird (genus *Polioptila*) having a black, white–bordered tail and short wings.

gnath·ic (nath′ik) *adj.* Of or pertaining to the jaw. [<Gk. *gnathos* jaw]

gnathic index A measure of the prominence of the jaw, expressed as the ratio of the distance from nasion to basion taken as 100, to the distance from the basion to the alveolar point. Compare illustration under FACIAL ANGLE.

gna·thi·on (nā′thē·on, nath′ē·on) *n. Anat.* The lower end of the symphysis of the jaw. [<NL, dim. of Gk. *gnathos* the jaw]

gnatho– *combining form* Jaw: *gnathostome.* [<Gk. *gnathos* jaw]

gna·thon·ic (na·thon′ik) *adj.* Fawning; flattering. [after *Gnatho,* a sycophant in Terence's *Eunuchus*]

gnath·o·stome (nath′ə·stōm) *n.* Any of a division *(Gnathostomata)* of vertebrates having mouths provided with jaws.

–gnathous *combining form* Jaw: *prognathous.* [<Gk. *gnathos* jaw + -OUS]

gnaw (nô) *v.t.* **gnawed, gnawed** or **gnawn, gnaw·ing 1** To bite or eat away little by little with or as with the teeth. **2** To make by gnawing: to *gnaw* a hole. **3** To bite on repeatedly: He *gnawed* his lip in rage. **4** To torment or oppress with fear, pain, etc. *—v.i.* **5** To bite, chew, or corrode persistently or continually. **6** To cause constant worry, pain, etc. [OE *gnagan*] **— gnaw′er** *n.*

gnaw·ing (nô′ing) *n.* A constant biting, fretting pain.

gneiss (nīs) *n.* **1** A metamorphic rock consisting essentially of the same components as granite but in which there is a more or less distinctly foliated arrangement of the components, and especially of the mica. **2** Any of a number of highly metamorphic rocks containing feldspar. ◆ Homophone: *nice.* [<G] **— gneiss′ic** *adj.*

gneiss·oid (nīs′oid) *adj.* Resembling gneiss.

gnome[1] (nōm) *n.* **1** In folklore, one of a race of dwarfs believed to live underground as guardians of treasure, mines, etc. **2** The pigmy owl of North America. [<F <NL *gnomus*] **— gnom′ish** *adj.*

gnome[2] (nōm) *n.* A pithy proverbial saying; maxim. [<Gk. *gnōmē* thought, maxim]

gno·mic (nō′mik, nom′ik) *adj.* **1** Dealing in maxims. **2** Expressing a maxim or a universal truth. Also **gno′mi·cal.**

gno·mol·o·gy (nə·mol′ə·jē) *n.* A compilation of or a treatise on gnomic sayings.

gno·mon (nō′mon) *n.* **1** The triangular piece whose shadow points out the time of day on a sundial, or anything, as a pillar, used for a similar purpose. **2** The index of the hour circle of a globe. **3** *Geom.* The figure that remains after a parallelogram has been removed from the corner of a similar but larger parallelogram, as *BCIGDE* or *FCAGHE.* The diagonally opposite parallelograms *ADEB, EHIF,* or *GHED, EFCB,* are called *complements* of each other or of the whole parallelogram. **4** *Math.* One of the terms of an arithmetical series by which polygonal numbers are found: also **gnomonic number.** [<Gk. *gnōmōn* an indicator <*gnō–,* stem of *gignōskein* know]

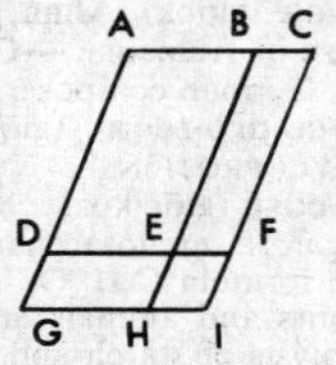

GNOMON

gno·mon·ic (nō·mon′ik) *adj.* **1** Of the nature of a gnomon. **2** Pertaining to the measurement of time by sundials. Also **gno·mon′i·cal.**

gno·mon·ics (nō·mon′iks) *n. pl.* The science of constructing sundials.

–gnomy *combining form* Knowledge or art of judging: *physiognomy.* [<Gk. *gnōmē* judgment]

gno·si·ol·o·gy (nō′sē·ol′ə·jē, nō′zē-) *n.* The branch of philosophy that treats of the sources, limits, and validity of knowledge; the systematic and critical treatment of philosophic principles underlying the activities of the cognitive faculties. [<GNOSIS + -(O)LOGY]

gno·sis (nō′sis) *n.* Cognition; especially, the knowledge of spiritual mysteries; Gnosticism. [<NL <Gk. *gnōsis* knowledge <*gignōskein* know]

–gnosis *combining form Med.* Knowledge; recognition: *prognosis.* [<Gk. *gnōsis* knowledge]

gnos·tic (nos′tik) *adj.* Of, pertaining to, or possessing knowledge; claiming esoteric insight or wisdom. Also **gnos′ti·cal.** [<Gk. *gnōstikos* knowing <*gnōsis.* See GNOSIS.] **— gnos′ti·cal·ly** *adv.*

Gnos·tic (nos′tik) *adj.* Of or pertaining to the Gnostics or Gnosticism. *—n.* An adherent or advocate of Gnosticism.

Gnos·ti·cism (nos′tə·siz′əm) *n.* A philosophical and religious system (first to sixth century) teaching that knowledge rather than faith was the key to salvation.

gnu (nōō, nyōō) *n. pl.* **gnus** or **gnu** A South African antelope (genus *Connochaetes*) having an oxlike head with curved horns, a mane, and a long tail; a wildebeest. Also **gnoo.** ◆ Homophone: *new.* [<Kaffir *nqu*]

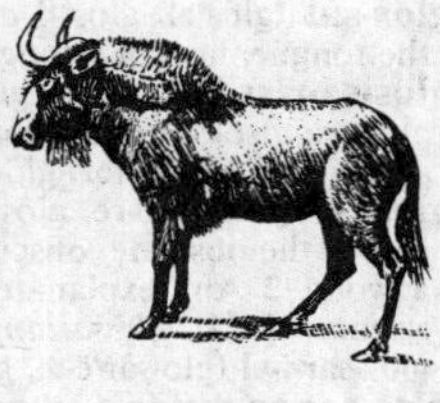

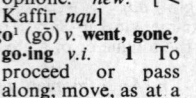

GNU
(From 4 to 4 1/2 feet high at the shoulder)

go[1] (gō) *v.* **went, gone, go·ing** *v.i.* **1** To proceed or pass along; move, as at a given speed. **2** To move from a place; leave; depart. **3** To move from one place to another for or as for a purpose: She *went* to dress for dinner. **4** To pass away; disappear; end: The opportunity has *gone.* **5** To be free or freed: They let him *go.* **6** To be in motion or operation; work properly: The watch is *going* now. **7** To extend or reach: The pipe *goes* into the next room. **8** To be, continue, or appear in a specified state or condition: Should these crimes *go* unpunished? **9** To pass into a state or condition; become: to *go* insane. **10** To proceed or end in a specified manner: The election *went* badly for him. **11** To be suitable; have its usual place; fit; belong: The music *goes* with these words. **12** To be considered or ranked: a good lunch, as lunches *go.* **13** To be phrased or expressed; have proper form or order: The song *goes* like this. **14** To emit or produce a specified sound or signal: The chain *goes* clank. **15** To attend; engage oneself in an occupation: to *go* to sea; to *go* fishing. **16** To pass: said of time. **17** To be guided or regulated; conform: to *go* with the times. **18** To be awarded, given, or applied: This *goes* toward canceling the debt. **19** To have recourse; make appeal; resort: to *go* to court. **20** To be known: What name does she *go* by? **21** To be sold or bid for: These shoes will *go* at a high price. **22** To help; tend: This *goes* to prove my argument. **23** To serve as a part; contribute: the graces that *go* to make a lady. **24** To be abolished or surrendered: The poll tax must *go.* **25** To collapse; fail: The walls *went* last in the fire. **26** To subject or put oneself: He *went* to great pains to do it. **27** To die. **28** To be about to do or act: used only in the progressive form and followed by the present infinitive: They were *going* to protest. *—v.t.* **29** To furnish; put up: to *go* bail. **30** To contribute; share: to *go* halves. **31** *Colloq.* To risk or bet; wager. **32** *Colloq.* To put up with; tolerate: I cannot *go* that music. **— to go about 1** To be occupied or busy with. **2** To set about to do (something). **3** *Naut.* To change to the other tack. **— to go around 1** To move about or circulate. **2** To be enough to furnish even shares. **— to go at 1** To attack. **2** To work at. **— to go back on 1** To forsake; be untrue to. **2** To fail to fulfil or abide by. **— to go by 1** To pass. **2** To conform to or be guided by: to *go by* the rules. **— to go for 1** To reach for; try to get: He *went for* his gun. **2** To attack. **3** *Colloq.* To be strongly attracted by. **— to go in for** *Colloq.* **1** To strive for or advocate: to *go in for* social reform. **2** To prefer; have a liking for: to *go in for* classical music. **— to go into 1** To investigate. **2** To take up, as an occupation: He *went into* business for himself. **3** To be contained in: Four *goes into* twelve three times. **— to go in with 1** To join. **2** To share expenses or risks with. **— to go off 1** To explode or be discharged, as a gun. **2** *Colloq.* To succeed; result: How did the party *go off*? **— to go on 1** To act; behave. **2** To happen: What's *going on* here? **3** *Colloq.* To talk aimlessly; chatter. **4** In the theater, to appear on stage. **— to go one better (than)** To surpass by a single degree or quality. **— to go out 1** To cease or be extinguished, as a light. **2** To advance or be drawn forth in sympathy: My heart *goes out* to him. **3** To strike: The union *went out* for higher wages. **4** To become obsolete. **5** To go to social affairs, the theater, etc. **— to go over 1** To turn on its side: The car *went over.* **2** To rehearse; repeat. **3** To examine closely or carefully. **4** *Colloq.* To succeed. **— to go**

through 1 To search thoroughly. 2 To experience; undergo. 3 To practice, as a role or part. 4 To be passed, as legislation. 5 To spend completely; use up: to *go through* a fortune. **— to go through with** To complete; undertake to finish. **— to go together** 1 To be suitable; harmonize. 2 *Colloq.* To keep company, as sweethearts. **— to go under** 1 To be overwhelmed or conquered. 2 To fail, as a business. **— to go up** To increase, as prices or values. **— to go with** 1 To be suitable to; harmonize with. 2 *Colloq.* To keep company with. **— to go without** To do or be without. **— to let go of** 1 To release one's hold of. 2 To abandon one's interest or share in. **—** *n.* 1 The act of going: the come and *go* of the seasons. 2 *Colloq.* The capacity for energetic action; vigor: He has plenty of *go.* 3 *Colloq.* A try; attempt: to have a *go* at something. 4 *Colloq.* A success: He made a *go* of it. 5 *Colloq.* A bargain. 6 *Colloq.* The fashion; mode: with *the.* 7 *Colloq.* A proceeding; turn of affairs. **— no go** *Colloq.* Useless; hopeless. **— on the go** *Colloq.* Busy; in constant motion. — *adj. Aerospace* Operating or proceeding as planned. [OE *gān*] **— go'er** *n.*

go² (gō) *n.* A Japanese game played with counters or stones on the intersections of lines on a board. [<Japanese]

go·a (gō'ə) *n.* A black-tailed gazelle (*Procapra picticaudata*) of the mountains of Tibet. [< Tibetan *dgoba*]

Go·a (gō'ə) A district of the former Portuguese India, on the west coast of India; annexed by India in 1961; 1,394 square miles; capital, New Goa.

goad (gōd) *n.* 1 A point set in the end of a stick for urging oxen or other beasts. 2 Something that spurs or incites. — *v.t.* To prick or drive with or as with a goad; incite. See synonyms under INCENSE¹, PIQUE¹, SPUR. [OE *gād*]

Goad (gōd) See GUDE.

goads·man (gōdz'mən) *n. pl.* **·men** (-mən) A driver of oxen, cattle, etc.

go-a·head (gō'ə·hed') *adj. Colloq.* Disposed to make rapid progress; energetic.

goal (gōl) *n.* 1 A point toward which effort or movement is directed; the objective point or terminus that one is striving to reach; the end aimed at: the *goal* of one's ambition. 2 In any game, race, contest, or competition, a mark, line, post, pole, or the like, made or set up to indicate the limit, winning point, or safety place of the game; in football, a pair of upright posts, **goal posts,** with a crosspiece over which the players strive to kick the ball. 3 In football and similar games, the act of propelling the ball over or past the goal, so as to win a point; also, the point so won. See synonyms under AIM, END. [ME *gol*; origin uncertain]

goal·ie (gō'lē) *n. Colloq.* A goalkeeper.

goal·keep·er (gōl'kē'pər) *n.* In certain games, as hockey, soccer, etc., a player stationed to protect the goal. Also **goal'tend'er.**

go·an·na (gō·an'ə) *n.* Any of several large, predatory, Australian lizards (family *Varanidae*) resembling the iguana, especially the black-and-yellow tree goanna (*Varanus varius*). [Alter. of IGUANA]

Goa powder A bitter yellow powder found in cavities of the Brazilian araroba tree (*Andira araroba*): used in medicine.

goat (gōt) *n.* 1 A hollow-horned ruminant (genus *Capra*) of rocky and mountainous regions, related to the sheep and including wild and domesticated forms. ◆ Collateral adjective: *hircine.* 2 A lecherous man. 3 *Slang* A scapegoat; the butt of a joke. **— to get one's goat** *Slang* To get a strong reaction (from someone) by teasing, tormenting, etc. [OE *gāt*] **— goat'like'** *adj.*

Goat (gōt) See CAPRICORN under CONSTELLATION.

goat antelope Any of certain ruminant mammals related to the goats and antelopes, as the chamois, Rocky Mountain goat, etc.

goat·beard (gōt'bird') *n.* 1 A European plant, the salsify (*Tragopogon pratensis*) with long, feathery pappus, naturalized in the United States. 2 A perennial herb of the rose family (*Aruncus sylvester*) with long compound panicles of whitish flowers. Also **goats'beard'.**

goat·ee (gō·tē') *n.* A man's beard so trimmed as to resemble the pointed beard of a goat.

goat·fish (gōt'fish') *n. pl.* **·fish** or **·fish·es** 1 A tropical marine fish of the mullet family, having a beardlike appendage below the mouth, especially the European red mullet, esteemed as a food fish. 2 The European filefish.

goat-god (gōt'god') *n.* Pan.

goat·herd (gōt'hûrd') *n.* One who tends goats.

goat·ish (gō'tish) *adj.* Resembling a goat; lustful. **— goat'ish·ly** *adv.* **— goat'ish·ness** *n.*

Goat Island An island in the Niagara River, dividing Niagara Falls into American Falls and Horseshoe (Canadian) Falls.

goat·skin (gōt'skin') *n.* 1 The hide of a goat. 2 Leather made from it.

goats·rue (gōts'rōō') *n.* 1 A hardy perennial herb (*Galega officinalis*) of the Old World. 2 An American herb of the pea family (*Tephrosia virginiana*).

goat·suck·er (gōt'suk'ər) *n.* 1 Any of numerous nocturnal, insectivorous birds (family *Caprimulgidae*) with flattened heads and wide mouths, as the whippoorwill or nighthawk. 2 The frogmouth.

goave (gōv) *v.i. Scot.* To stare stupidly.

goav·ing (gō'ving) *adj. Scot.* Staring stupidly; dreaming.

gob¹ (gob) *n.* A small piece, mass, or chunk; a lump. [<OF *gobe* mouthful, lump, ? <Celtic]

gob² (gob) *n. Brit.* 1 An abandoned mine-works filled with refuse. 2 Rubbish. [Cf. dial. E *goaf, goave* an empty space from which coal has been mined]

gob³ (gob) *n. Slang* A sailor of the U. S. Navy. [Origin uncertain]

go·bang (gō·bäng') *n.* A Japanese game played on a checkerboard, usually of 256 squares, the object being to first to arrange 5 counters in a row on intersecting lines. Also **go·ban'.** [<Japanese *goban* chessboard]

gobbe (gob) *n.* A creeping annual (*Voandzeia subterranea*), resembling the common peanut: much cultivated in Africa and South America. [< native Cariban name]

gob·bet (gob'it) *n.* 1 A piece or fragment, especially a morsel of cooked meat, highly seasoned. 2 A chunk; lump. 3 *Archaic* A mouthful. [<F *gobet,* dim. of *gobe* GOB¹]

gob·ble¹ (gob'əl) *v.* **gob·bled, gob·bling** *v.t.* 1 To swallow (food) greedily and in gulps. 2 *U.S. Slang* To seize or acquire in a grasping manner. — *v.i.* 3 To eat greedily and quickly. [<F *gover* bolt, devour] **— gob'bler** *n.*

gob·ble² (gob'əl) *n.* The sound made by the turkey cock. — *v.i.* **gob·bled, gob·bling** To utter a gobble, as turkeys. [Var. of GABBLE]

gob·ble·dy·gook (gob'əl·dē·gŏŏk') *n. Colloq.* Involved, pedantic, repetitious, and pompous jargon, relying heavily upon Latinized expressions and meaningless clichés: applied especially to the language of bureaucrats and professional politicians. [Coined by M. Maverick, U. S. Congressman, about 1940]

gob·bler (gob'lər) *n.* A turkey cock.

Gob·e·lin tapestry (gob'ə·lin, gō'bə-; *Fr.* gō·blaṅ') Any tapestry woven at the Parisian factory of the Gobelins, a family by whom the industry was begun in the 15th century.

go-be·tween (gō'bə·twēn') *n.* One who acts as an agent, assistant, or mediator between other persons in relation to business, intrigue, or other matters; an intermediary.

Go·bi (gō'bē) A desert in central Asia; 500,000 square miles: Chinese *Shamo.* Also **Gobi Desert.**

gob·let (gob'lit) *n.* 1 A drinking vessel with a stem and no handle. 2 A large, shallow bowl or drinking vessel for ceremonious or festive occasions. [<OF *gobelet,* dim. of *gobel* a drinking cup <Celtic]

gob·lin (gob'lin) *n.* A supernatural, grotesque creature regarded as malicious or mischievous. [<OF *gobelin* <Med. L *gobelinus,* ? <Gk. *kobalos* a rogue]

go·bo (gō'bō) *n. pl.* **·bos** 1 A portable sound-absorbing panel used to control sound effects in motion-picture production. 2 A device for shielding the lens of a television camera from the direct rays of light. [Origin uncertain]

gob·stick (gob'stik') *n.* An implement for removing a hook from a fish's mouth. [< dial. E *gob* the mouth + STICK]

go·by (gō'bē) *n. pl.* **·by** or **·bies** Any of a widely distributed family (*Gobiidae*) of spiny-rayed, chiefly marine fishes having ventral fins united into a funnel-shaped suction disk, as the rock goby (*Gobius paganellus*) and the California blind goby (genus *Typhlogobius*). [<L *gobius* <Gk. *kōbios,* a small fish]

go-by (gō'bī') *n. Colloq.* An intended slight.

go-cart (gō'kärt') *n.* 1 A light framework on rollers designed to support a baby learning to walk. 2 A small, light, baby carriage having the front wheels smaller than the rear. 3 A light carriage.

god (god) *n.* 1 A being regarded as possessing superhuman or supernatural qualities or powers, and made an object of worship or propitiation; a higher intelligence supposed to control the forces of good and of evil; a personification of any of the forces of nature or of some human attribute, interest, or relation; a divinity; deity. 2 Any person or thing exalted as the chief good, or made an object of supreme devotion. 3 Anything that absorbs one's attentions or aspirations: Money is his *god.* 4 The embodiment of some aspect of reality or of some being regarded as the ultimate principle of the universe: the *god* of justice. 5 An image or symbol of a deity; idol. — *v.t. Rare* **god·ded, god·ding** To deify; idolize. [OE]

God (god) The one Supreme Being, self-existent and eternal; the infinite creator, sustainer, and ruler of the universe: conceived of as omniscient, good, and almighty.

Go·da·va·ri (gō·dä'və·rē) A river in central India, flowing about 900 miles to the Bay of Bengal.

god·child (god'chīld') *n.* A child for whom a person becomes sponsor at baptism.

god·daugh·ter (god'dô'tər) *n.* A female god-child.

god·den (god·den') *Brit. Dial.* Good evening: a salutation. [Contraction of *good even*]

god·dess (god'is) 1 A female divinity. 2 Figuratively, a woman surpassingly beloved, good, or beautiful. **— god'dess·hood** *n.*

Go·des·berg (gō'des·berkh) A resort town on the Rhine in North Rhine-Westphalia. Also **Bad Godesberg** (bäd).

go-dev·il (gō'dev'əl) *n.* 1 A dray sled for hauling rocks, logs, etc. 2 A pointed iron weight dropped into the bore of an oil well to explode the charge of dynamite. 3 A railroad handcar used by work gangs. 4 A jointed, flexible device for cleaning a pipeline of obstructions.

god·fa·ther (god'fä'thər) *n.* A man who becomes sponsor for a child at its baptism or confirmation. — *v.t.* To act as a godfather to.

God·frey (god'frē) A masculine personal name. Also *Du.* **God·fried** (gōt'frēt), *Fr.* **Gode·froi** (gôd·frwä'), *Ital.* **Go·de·fre·do** (gō'dā·frā'dō), *Sp.* **Go·do·fre·do** (gō'thō·frā'thō). [<Gmc., peace of God]

— Godfrey of Bouillon, 1061–1100, duke of lower Lorraine; leader of the first crusade, 1096–1100.

God·havn (gôth'houn) A Danish settlement on the southern tip of Disko Island.

god·head (god'hed') *n.* Godhood; divinity.

God·head (god'hed') *n.* The essential nature of God; the Deity.

god·hood (god'hŏŏd) *n.* The state or quality of being divine.

Go·di·va (gə·dī'və) The wife of Leofric, 11th century Earl of Mercia, who according to English legend rode naked through Coventry as the condition of the removal of oppressive taxes.

god·less (god'lis) *adj.* Ungodly; atheistical; wicked. See synonyms under PROFANE. **— god'less·ness** *n.*

god·like (god'līk') *adj.* Similar to God or to a god; divine; of supreme excellence or beauty. **— god'like'ness** *n.*

god·ling (god'ling) *n.* A minor divinity.

god·ly (god'lē) *adj.* **·li·er, ·li·est** Filled with reverence and love for God; pious. **— god'li·ly** *adv.* **— god'li·ness** *n.*

god·moth·er (god'muth'ər) *n.* A female sponsor at baptism. — *v.t.* To act as godmother to.

Go·dol·phin (gō·dol'fin), **Sidney,** 1645–1712, first Earl of Godolphin, English statesman.

go·down (gō·doun') *n.* In China and the East Indies, a warehouse. [<Malay *godong* warehouse]

Go·doy (gō·thoi′), **Manuel de,** 1767–1851, Spanish statesman.

god·par·ent (god′pâr′ənt) *n.* A godfather or godmother.

go·droon (gə·drōōn′) *n.* **1** *Archit.* An ornament of notched or carved rounded form. **2** Fluted or oval decoration used in silverwork. Also spelled *gadroon.* [<F *godron* plait] **—go·drooned′** *adj.*

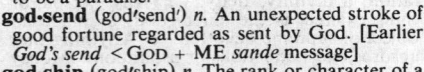

GODROON

God's acre A burying ground.

God's country *U.S.* A region considered to be a paradise.

god·send (god′send′) *n.* An unexpected stroke of good fortune regarded as sent by God. [Earlier *God's send* <GOD + ME *sande* message]

god·ship (god′ship) *n.* The rank or character of a god; deity.

god·son (god′sun′) *n.* A male godchild.

God·speed (god′spēd′) *n.* God speed you: a wish for a safe journey or for success.

Godt·haab (gôt′hôp) A port in SW Greenland.

Go·du·nov (gô·dōō·nôf′), **Boris,** 1552?–1605, czar of Russia 1598–1605.

God·ward (god′wərd) *adv.* Toward or in connection with God. Also **God′wards.**

God·win (god′win) A masculine personal name. Also **God′wine,** *Du.* **Go·de·wijn** (gō′də·vīn), *Lat.* **God·wi·nus** (god·wī′nəs). [<Gmc., friend of God]
—**Godwin,** died 1053, earl of the West Saxons, English statesman; chief minister to Edward the Confessor.

Godwin (god′win), **William,** 1756–1836, English philosopher and author.

God·win Aus·ten (god′win ôs′tin) See K2.

god·wit (god′wit) *n.* A curlewlike shore bird (genus *Limosa)* with long legs and a long, tilted bill, as the American marbled godwit *(L. fedoa).* [Origin uncertain]

Goeb·bels (gœb′əls), **Joseph Paul,** 1897–1945, German politician; Nazi minister of propaganda 1933–45.

Goe·ring (gœ′ring) See GORING.

Goe·thals (gō′thəlz), **George Washington,** 1858–1928, U.S. engineer; builder of Panama Canal.

Goe·the (gœ′tə), **Johann Wolfgang von,** 1749–1832, German poet, dramatist, novelist, and statesman.

goe·thite (gō′thīt, gœ′tīt) *n.* An imperfect, adamantine, reddish or blackish-brown ferric hydroxide, crystallizing in the orthorhombic system: also spelled *göthite.* [after *Goethe*]

gof·fer (gof′ər, gôf′-) *n.* **1** A fluting or crimp. **2** A tool used in crimping lace, paper, etc. —*v.t.* **1** To form plaits or flutes in; crimp, as lace or paper. **2** To raise in relief. Also spelled *gauffer.* [<F *gaufrer* crimp cloth <*gaufre* a honeycomb]

Gof·fre·do (gôf·frā′dō) Italian form of GODFREY. Also *Sp.* **Go·fre·do** (gō·frā′thō).

Gog (gog) **and Ma·gog** (mā′gog) In the Bible, the nations, led by Satan, which will war against the kingdom of God. *Rev.* xx 8.

go-get·ter (gō′get′ər) *n. U.S. Colloq.* A hustling, energetic, aggressive person.

gog·gle (gog′əl) *n.* **1** A rolling of the eyes. **2** *pl.* Spectacles, often with colored lenses, and attachments to fit close to the face as protection against strong light, wind, and dust. [<v.] —*adj.* Prominent; staring. —*v.* **gog·gled, gog·gling** *v.i.* **1** To roll the eyes about or stare with bulging eyes. **2** To roll sidewise or stare protrusively: said of the eyes. —*v.t.* **3** To roll (the eyes). [ME *gogelen* look aside, prob. <Celtic]

gog·gle-eye (gog′əl·ī′) *n.* A staring eye. —**gog′gle-eyed′** *adj.*

Gogh (gō, gôk; *Du.* khôkh), **Vincent van** See VAN GOGH.

gog·let (gog′lit) *n.* In the East Indies, a jar or vase of porous pottery for keeping water cool by evaporation: also called *gurglet.* [<Pg. *gorgoleta*]

go-go (gō′gō′) *adj. Slang* **1** Of or describing discothèques, the usually unrestrained, erotic dances performed there, or the dancers, typically young women, who entertain with such dances. **2** Lively, modern, glamorous, etc. **3** In finance, characterized by rapid speculative trading to realize profit quickly. **4** Aggressively enterprising or ambitious [<F *à gogo* joyfully]

Go·gol (gō′gəl, *Russian* gô′gôl), **Nikolai Vasilievich,** 1809–52, Russian novelist.

Gog·ra (gog′rə) A river in Tibet, Nepal, and India, flowing 640 miles, generally south, to the Ganges.

Goi·â·ni·a (goi·a′nē·ə) Capital of Goiás, Brazil.

Goi·ás (goi·äs′) A state of central Brazil; 240,444 square miles: formerly *Goyaz.*

Goi·del·ic (goi·del′ik) *n.* A branch of the Celtic languages including Irish, the Gaelic of the Scottish Highlands, and Manx; Gaelic. —*adj.* Of or pertaining to the Gaels or their languages. Also spelled *Gadelic, Gaedhelic.* Also **Goi·dhel′ic.** [<OIrish *Gōidel* a Gael]

go·ing (gō′ing) *n.* **1** The act of departing or moving; leaving. **2** The condition of the ground, paths, or roads. **3** Style of walking; gait. **4** *Obs.* The manner of conducting oneself; deportment. **—goings on** *Colloq.* Behavior; conduct; actions: used to express disapproval. —*adj.* **1** Continuing to function: a *going* concern. **2** Arising from continued operation: the *going* value of a business. **3** In existence: available: the best bargain *going.* **4** Departing; leaving. **—going on** *Colloq.* Approaching (a particular age or time).

goi·ter (goi′tər) *n. Pathol.* **1** A morbid enlargement of the thyroid gland, variously caused, visible as a swelling on the front part of the neck. **2** The condition itself; bronchocele. See also EXOPHTHALMIC GOITER. Also **goi′tre.** [<F, back formation from *goitreux,* ult. <L *guttur* throat] **—goi′trous** *adj.*

goi·tro·gen (goi′trə·jən) *n.* Any substance capable of initiating or promoting a goiter.

Gol·con·da (gol·kon′də) A city in Hyderabad, India, famous in the 16th century for diamond marketing.

Gol·con·da (gol·kon′də) *n.* A mine or other source of wealth. Also **gol·con′da.**

gold (gōld) *n.* **1** A soft, heavy, malleable and ductile metallic element (symbol Au, atomic number 79) found uncombined in nature, resistant to oxidation and to most chemical reagents. See PERIODIC TABLE. **2** The metal in the form of a coin. **3** Wealth; riches. **4** Gilding, or a golden-yellow color. See synonyms under MONEY. —*adj.* Pertaining to, like, made of, containing, or producing gold, or used in mining gold. [OE]

gold-band lily (gōld′band′) See under LILY.

gold basis The basis of values calculated on a gold standard.

gold·beat·er (gōld′bē′tər) *n.* One who makes gold leaf.

gold·beat·er's-skin (gōld′bē′tərz·skin′) *n.* The outer coat of the cecum of the ox, prepared for the use of the goldbeater.

gold·beat·ing (gōld′bē′ting) *n.* The act or operation of making gold leaf by hammering.

gold beetle **1** A leaf beetle *(Coptocycla bicolor)*: so called from its metallic luster. **2** A brilliant beetle (family *Chrysomelidae)* found on the sweet potato.

Gold·berg (gōld′bûrg), **Arthur Joseph,** born 1908, U.S. labor lawyer; secretary of labor 1961–62; associate justice of the Supreme Court 1962–65; U.S. ambassador to the UN, 1965–68.

gold·brick (gōld′brik′) *n.* **1** *Colloq.* A brick or bar of base metal gilded, used by swindlers, or a brick or bar of gold for which something else is substituted in delivery to the purchaser; hence, any swindle: also **gold brick. 2** *Slang* A soldier or sailor who shirks or tries to shirk work: also **gold′brick′er.** —*v.t. & v.i. Slang* **1** To shirk (work or duty). **2** To cheat.

gold·bug (gōld′bug′) *n.* **1** A gold beetle. **2** *U.S. Colloq.* An advocate of the gold standard.

gold certificate A U.S. Treasury note redeemable in gold at its face value, not now issued.

Gold Coast **1** A former name for GHANA. **2** A section of the African shore line on the Gulf of Guinea between the Ivory Coast and the Slave Coast. **3** *U.S.* Any residential or resort district frequented by rich people.

Gold Coast Colony A former British colony on the coast of western Africa. See GHANA.

gold-dig·ger (gōld′dig′ər) *n.* **1** One who or that which digs for gold. **2** *Colloq.* A woman who uses her personal relations with men to get money and gifts from them.

gold dust Gold in fine particles.

gold·en (gōl′dən) *adj.* **1** Made of or consisting of gold. **2** Having the color or luster of gold; bright-yellow; resplendent. **3** Resembling gold in worth or scarcity; unusually valuable or excellent; rare. **4** Characterized by a condition of great happiness and prosperity: the *golden* age. **—gold′en·ly** *adv.* **—gold′en·ness** *n.*

golden age **1** In Greek and Roman legend, a mythical period when perfect innocence, peace, and happiness reigned. **2** The most flourishing period of a nation's history. **3** In Roman literature, the period (27 B.C. to A.D. 14) of the finest classical writers; hence, in any country, the periods of literature most nearly corresponding to this: also called *Augustan age.*

golden anniversary See under ANNIVERSARY.

golden aster A North American perennial (genus *Chrysopsis)* of the composite family, with yellow-rayed flowers.

Golden Chersonese The Malay Peninsula.

golden eagle A rare eagle *(Aquila chrysaetos)* ranging throughout the Northern Hemisphere, having dark brown feathers tipped with golden brown at the nape.

gold·en·eye (gōl′dən·ī′) *n.* A large sea duck *(Glaucionetta clangula)* having the upper parts black and the lower parts white.

Golden Fleece In Greek legend, a fleece of gold that hung in a sacred grove in Colchis, guarded by a dragon: stolen by Jason with the aid of Medea. See PHRIXUS.

Golden Gate A strait leading from the Pacific Ocean to San Francisco Bay.

gold·en·glow (gōl′dən·glō′) *n.* A summer-flowering, erect herb *(Rudbeckia laciniata)* of the composite family, with showy terminal heads of yellow-rayed flowers.

golden goose In Greek legend, a goose that laid golden eggs, killed by its owner who thought to obtain all of them at once.

Golden Horde See under HORDE.

Golden Horn The crescent-shaped inlet of the Bosporus in Turkey in Europe, forming the harbor of Istanbul.

Golden Legend The name given by Caxton to his translation, published in 1483, of a medieval collection of the lives of the saints, composed in Latin by Jacobus de Voragine, 1230–98, archbishop of Genoa: also called *Legenda Aurea.*

golden mean A wise moderation; the avoidance of extremes.

golden number *Eccl.* A number indicating the place of a year in a Metonic cycle of 19 years, used in calculating the movable feasts.

golden pheasant A vividly colored pheasant *(Chrysolophus pictus)* of China and Tibet.

golden robin The Baltimore oriole.

gold·en·rod (gōl′dən·rod′) *n.* A widely distributed North American biennial or perennial herb (genus *Solidago)* of the composite family, with erect stalks carrying small heads of flowers, usually yellow and sometimes in clusters, blooming in summer and autumn. State flower of Alabama, Kentucky, and Nebraska.

golden rule The rule of life given in *Matt.* vii 12: "Whatsoever ye would that men should do to you, do ye even so to them."

gold·en·seal (gōl′dən·sēl′) *n.* **1** An herb *(Hydrastis canadensis)* of the United States, with a yellow rootstock, a single radical leaf, a hairy stem, and a single greenish-white flower. **2** This plant's rootstock.

golden section **1** In Euclidean geometry, the division of a line segment in extreme and mean ratio. **2** In esthetics, the division of a line or of a figure in which the smaller length or area is to the larger as the larger is to the whole; also, that proportion of a plane figure in which the smaller dimension is to the larger as the larger is to the sum of the dimensions; broadly a ratio of 3:5, thought to be especially pleasing esthetically. In sculpture, this is applied to the proportion of the frontal plane of the figure. In the Petrarchan sonnet, the relationship between the octave and the sestet is very like that of

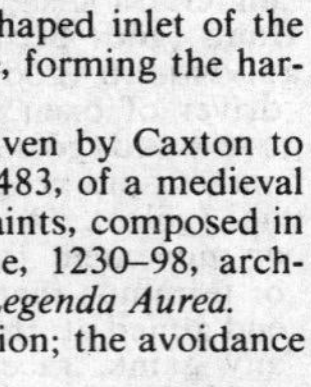

GOLDEN SECTION On line *AB,* square *ABIG* is constructed; *AG* is bisected at *C,* whereby *CD* = *CB,* and square *DEFA* is constructed. Ratio: *DA* : *AG* : : *AG* : *DG.*

the golden section, with the 14 lines divided in a ratio of 8:6. (The true section of 14 is 8.65:5.35.) In bookbinding, the proportion of an octavo binding also approximates this ratio.

Golden State Nickname of CALIFORNIA.

golden wattle A plant of the genus *Acacia* (especially *A. pycnantha*) related to the mimosa and having yellow flowers: widely distributed in Australasia.

golden wedding Fiftieth wedding anniversary.

gold·en–winged warbler (gōl′dən·wingd′) A North American warbler with yellow wings (*Vermivora chrysoptera*).

gold–ex·change standard (gōld′iks·chānj′) A monetary system based on currency at par in another country that maintains a gold standard.

gold·eye (gōld′ī′) *n.* A small fresh-water fish (*Amphiodon alosoides*) of northern and western North America: also called *Winnipeg goldeye.*

gold–filled (gōld′fild′) *adj.* Denoting an extra heavy or thick plate of gold on a base metal foundation, as in watchmaking.

gold·finch (gōld′finch′) *n.* 1 A European finch (genus *Carduelis*) having a black hood and a yellow patch on the wings. 2 An American finch (*Spinus tristis*) of which the male, in the summer, has a yellow body with black tail.

gold·fin·ny (gōld′fin′ē) *n. pl.* **·nies** A bright-colored European wrasse (genus *Ctenolabrus*).

gold·fish (gōld′fish′) *n. pl.* **·fish** or **·fish·es** A small carp of golden color (genus *Carassius*), originally of China, now cultivated in many varieties as an ornamental aquarium fish.

gold foil Thin sheets of gold, thicker than gold leaf. — **gold–foil** (gōld′foil′) *adj.*

gold·i·locks (gōld′ē·loks′) *n.* 1 A European herb (*Linosyris vulgaris*) with yellow flower heads. 2 The European buttercup. 3 A girl with golden hair.

gold lace A lace wrought with gold or gilt thread.

gold leaf A very fine leaf made from beaten gold. — **gold–leaf** (gōld′lēf′) *adj.*

Gold·mark (gōld′märk), **Karl**, 1830–1915, Hungarian composer.

gold note A banknote to be paid in gold.

gold number *Chem.* A number expressing the weight in milligrams of a lyophilic colloid (gelatin) just insufficient to prevent a change from red to violet in 10 cc. of colloidal gold to which has been added 1 cc. of a 10 percent solution of sodium chloride.

gold–of–pleas·ure (gōld′əv·plezh′ər) *n.* An erect annual herb (*Camelina sativa*) with long, lanceolate leaves, small, numerous flowers, and obovoid or pear-shaped pods: naturalized from Europe; false flax.

Gol·do·ni (gōl·dō′nē), **Carlo**, 1707–93, Italian dramatist.

gold point 1 That point in the rate of foreign exchange at which bullion can be shipped in payment of accounts without entailing a loss. 2 *Physics* The melting point of gold, 1063° C., used as a reference temperature.

gold reserve 1 Gold held in reserve by the U.S. Treasury to protect and formerly to redeem U.S. promissory notes; established by Congress, 1882. 2 The quantity of gold bullion or coin owned by the central bank of a country.

gold rush A mass movement of people to an area where gold has been discovered.

gold shell A copper-zinc alloy thinly plated with gold and used for making cheap jewelry: also called *Talmi gold.*

gold·smith (gōld′smith′) *n.* A worker in gold. — **gold·smith′er·y** *n.* — **gold·smith′ing** *n.*

Gold·smith (gōld′smith), **Oliver**, 1728–74, English poet, novelist, and dramatist.

goldsmith beetle A large European scarabaeid beetle (*Cetonia aurata*) of a brilliant golden color: also called *rose beetle.*

gold standard A monetary system based on gold of a specified weight and fineness as the unit of value.

gold–star mother (gōld′stär′) A mother of a member of the U.S. armed forces killed in action during wartime.

gold stick 1 An official of the British royal household who attends the sovereign on state occasions. 2 The gilt rod he carries as an emblem of office.

gold·stone (gōld′stōn′) *n.* Aventurine glass having numerous gold specks which give it a jeweled appearance.

gold–thread (gōld′thred′) *n.* 1 A North American evergreen herb (*Coptis groenlandica*) of the crowfoot family, with long, bright-yellow, fibrous roots. 2 The roots of this plant.

golf (gôlf, golf) *n.* An outdoor game played on a large course with a small resilient ball and a set of clubs, the object being to direct the ball into a series of variously distributed holes (usually nine or eighteen) in as few strokes as possible. — *v.i.* To play golf. [Cf. dial. E (Scottish) *gowf* strike] — **golf′er** *n.*

golf club 1 One of several clubs used in playing golf. 2 An organization of golfers; also, the building and grounds used by them.

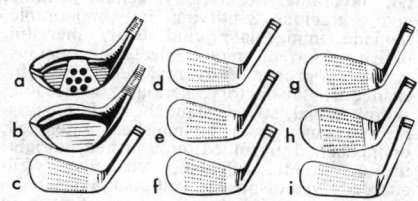

TYPES OF GOLF CLUBS

a. Driver.	d. No. 5 iron	g. No. 8 iron
b. Brassie.	or mashie.	h. No. 9 iron
c. No. 2 iron	e. No. 6 iron.	or niblick.
or midiron.	f. No 7 iron.	i. Putter.

golf links The course over which a game of golf is played. Also **golf course.**

Gol·gi (gôl′jē), **Camillo**, 1844–1926, Italian anatomist.

Golgi apparatus *Biol.* A netlike structure of rod-shaped elements found in the cytoplasm of animal cells. Also **Golgi body.** See illustration under CELL.

gol·go·tha (gol′gə·thə) *n.* 1 A burial place; graveyard; charnel house. 2 Any place of torment or sacrifice. [from *Golgotha*]

Gol·go·tha (gol′gə·thə) A place near Jerusalem where Jesus was crucified. *Matt.* xxvii 33. [<LL <Gk. <Aramaic *gogoltha* skull <Hebrew *gulgōleth*]

gol·iard (gōl′yərd) *n.* One of a class of wandering student jesters of the 12th and 13th centuries who wrote and sang Latin satirical verses. [<OF, a glutton <*gole* gluttony <L *gula*] — **gol·iar·der·y** (gōl·yär′dər·ē) *n.* — **gol·iar′dic** *adj.*

Go·li·ath (gə·lī′əth) A Philistine giant, slain by David. I *Sam.* xvii 4.

gol·li·wog (gol′ē·wog) *n.* 1 A grotesque, black doll. 2 A grotesque person. Also **gol′li·wogg.** [after illustrations drawn (1895) by Florence Upton for a series of children's books]

go·losh (gə·losh′) See GALOSH.

Goltz (gôlts), **Baron Kolmar von der**, 1843–1916, German field marshal of World War I.

gom·broon (gom·broon′) *n.* A Persian pottery of a semitransparent white. Also **gom·broon′-ware.** [from a town on the Persian Gulf]

Go·mel (gô′mel) A city in SE Belorussian S.S.R.

Go·me·ra (gō·mā′rä) One of the Canary Islands; 146 square miles.

Gó·mez (gō′mes), **Juan Vicente**, 1857?–1935, Venezuelan general; dictator 1908–35.

Go·mor·rah (gə·môr′ə, -mor′ə) A city on the shore of the Dead Sea, destroyed with Sodom because of the wickedness of its people. *Gen.* xiii 10. Also **Go·mor′rha.**

Gom·pers (gom′pərz), **Samuel**, 1850–1924, U.S. labor leader; president, American Federation of Labor 1886–95, 1896–1924.

gom·pho·sis (gom·fō′sis) *n. Anat.* An articulation or union by the firm implantation of one part in a socket situated in another, as the setting of teeth in the jaw or the styloid process in the temporal bone. [<NL <Gk. *gomphos* a bolt]

go·mu·ti (gō·moo′tē) *n.* 1 The Malayan feather palm (*Arenga pinnata*): a source of palm sugar. 2 A durable, black, hairlike fiber obtained from this palm: valuable for cordage, etc., because it does not rot in water. [<Malay *gumuti*]

gon– Var. of GONO-.

–gon *combining form* Having (a certain number of) angles: *pentagon.* [<Gk. *gonia* an angle]

gon·ad (gon′ad, gō′nad) *n. Anat.* A male or female sex gland, in which the gametes develop; an ovary or testis. [<GON- + -AD¹] — **gon′a·dal, go·na·di·al** (gō·nā′dē·əl), **go·nad·ic** (gō·nad′ik) *adj.*

gon·ad·o·ther·a·py (gon′ə·dō·ther′ə·pē, gə·nad′-ə-) *n.* Treatment of the gonads by the use of sex hormones.

gon·a·do·trop·ic (gon′ə·dō·trop′ik, -trō′pik, gə·nad′ə-) *adj.* Stimulating or nourishing the gonads. Also **gon′a·do·troph′ic** (-trof′ik, -trō′-fik).

gon·ad·ot·ro·pism (gon′ad·ot′rə·piz′əm) *n.* A physical constitution marked by a strong dominance of the gonads.

Go·na·ïves (gə·nä·ēv′), **Gulf of** A wide bay on the west coast of Haiti.

gon·a·poph·y·ses (gon′ə·pof′ə·sēz) *n. pl. Entomol.* The genital organs of insects collectively. [<GON- + APOPHYSIS]

Gon·court (gôn·koor′), **Edmond Louis Antoine Huot de**, 1822–96, French novelist; collaborator with his brother, **Jules Alfred Huot de**, 1830–70.

Gond (gond) *n.* A Dravidian of the hilly country of central India.

Gon·dar (gon′dər) A city in NW Ethiopia.

Gon·di (gon′dē) *n.* The Dravidian language of the Gonds, closely related to Khond.

gon·do·la (gon′də·lə) *n.* 1 A long, narrow, flat-bottomed Venetian boat, high-peaked at the ends, and rowed with one oar by a gondolier who stands near the stern. 2 A large flat-bottomed river boat of light build. 3 A long, shallow, open freight car. 4 *Aeron.* The car hanging below or attached to a dirigible balloon for the accommodation of engines, crew, or the like. [<Ital. <*gondolar* rock]

TRADITIONAL VENETIAN GONDOLA

gon·do·lier (gon′də·lir′) *n.* The rower of a gondola.

Gond·wa·na (gond·wä′nə) 1 A historical region comprising most of Madhya Pradesh, India. 2 A hypothetical Paleozoic continent believed to have existed in the southern Indian Ocean.

gone (gôn, gon) Past participle of GO. —*adj.* 1 Passed beyond help or hope; ruined; lost: a *gone* case. 2 Marked by faintness or weakness: a *gone* sensation. 3 Ended; past; dead. 4 Depressed and hopeless. — **gone on** *Colloq.* In love with.

gone·ness (gôn′nis, gon′-) *n.* A state of weakness or exhaustion.

gon·er (gôn′ər, gon′-) *n. Colloq.* A person or thing that is ruined or beyond saving; one who is as good as dead.

Gon·er·il (gon′ər·il) In Shakespeare's *King Lear*, Lear's eldest daughter, a symbol of filial ingratitude.

gon·fa·lon (gon′fə·lon) *n.* An ensign fixed to a revolving frame or a crossyard, generally with two or three streamers; a banderole. Also **gon·fa·non** (gon′fə·nən). [<Ital. *gonfalone* <OHG *gundfano* war banner]

gon·fa·lon·ier (gon′fə·lə·nir′) *n.* 1 A gonfalon-bearer; a chief standard-bearer, as of the Church of Rome. 2 The title of the chief magistrate of Florence, after 1293, and of other Italian medieval republics.

gong (gông, gong) *n.* 1 A metal musical instrument shaped like a shallow dish, sounded by beating. 2 A fixed signal bell of flattened curvature. [<Malay]

Gon·gor·ism (gong′gə·riz′əm) *n.* An ornate and

euphuistic literary style of the type cultivated by the Spanish poet **Luis de Gongora y Argote,**1561– 1627.

go·nid·i·um (gō·nid′ē· əm) *n. pl.* **·nid·i·a** (-ə) *Bot.* **1** In algae, a naked or membranous-coated propagative cell produced asexually. **2** In mosses, a cell filled with green granules. **3** In lichens, one of the green algal cells of a thallus. [<NL, dim. of Gk. *gonos* seed] **—go·nid′i·al** *adj.*

gonio- *combining form* Angle; corner: *goniometry* [<Gk. *gōnia* a corner]

go·ni·om·e·ter (gō′nē· om′ə·tər) *n.* **1** An instrument for measuring angles, as in crystallography, surveying, etc., either by direct contact as in the **contact goniometer,** or more accurately, by utilizing beams of light, as in the **reflecting goniometer. 2** An electrical direction-finder for aircraft. **—go·ni·o·met·ric** (gō′nē·ə·met′rik) or **·ri·cal** *adj.*

go·ni·om·e·try (gō′nē·om′ə·trē) *n.* **1** The art of measuring angles. **2** The branch of trigonometry that treats of angles.

go·ni·on (gō′nē·on) *n.* pl. **·ni·a** (-ə) *Anat.* The tip of the angle of the lower jaw. [<NL <Gk. *gonia* an angle]

go·ni·um (gō′nē·əm) *n. pl.* **·ni·a**(-ə) *Biol.* One of the primitive germ cells which aggregate from male or female sex cells. [<NL] **—gonium** *combining form* Seed; reproductive cell: *sporogonium.* [<Gk. *gonos* seed]

gono- *combining form* Procreative; sexual: *gonophore.* Also, before vowels, *gon-.* [< Gk. *gonos* seed]

gon·o·coc·cus (gon′ə·kok′əs) *n. pl.* **·coc·ci** (-kok′sī) The Gram-negative, strictly parasitic bacterium *(Neisseria gonorrheae)* which causes gonorrhea. [<NL. See GONO-, COCCUS.]

gon·of (gon′əf) *n. Slang* A pickpocket; a thief: also spelled *ganef.* Also **gon′iff, gon′oph.** [<Hebrew *gannābh* thief]

gon·o·phore (gon′ə·fôr, -fōr) *n.* **1** *Bot.* A stalk bearing male and female organs; an elongation of the axis of a flower lifting the stamens and pistil high above the floral envelopes. **2** *Biol.* An accessory generative organ that conveys the generative products, as an oviduct or spermiduct.

gon·o·poi·et·ic (gon′ə·poi·et′ik) *adj. Biol.* Yielding or producing reproductive elements, as ova or spermatozoa.

gon·or·rhe·a (gon′ə·rē′ə) *n. Pathol.* A specific contagious inflammation of the mucous membrane of the genital organs, caused by the gonococcus and accompanied by a discharge of morbid matter. Also **gon′or·rhoe′a.** [<LL <Gk. *gonorrhoia* <*gonos* seed + *rheein* flow]

gon·or·rhe·al (gon′ə·rē′əl) *adj.* Relating to, proceeding from, or affected with, gonorrhea. Also **gon′or·rhoe′al.**

gon·sil (gon′sil) See GUNSEL.

go·ny (gō′nē) See GOONEY.

-gony *combining form* Generation or production of: *cosmogony.* [<L *-gonia* < Gk. <*gonos* seed, reproduction; cf. -GENY]

Gon·za·ga (gôn·tsä′gä) Name of a princely Italian family, rulers of Mantua from the 14th to the 17th century; especially, **Federigo II,** died 1540, duke of Mantua 1519–40; **Luigi,** 1568–91, Jesuit philosopher, canonized as *Saint Aloysius.*

Gon·zá·lez·Vi·de·la (gōn·sä′lās·bē·thä′lä), **Gabriel,** born 1898, Chilean lawyer; president of Chile 1946–52.

goo (go͞o) *n. U.S. Slang* Any sticky fluid or semifluid. [? <BURGOO]

goo·ber (go͞o′bər) *n. U.S.* A peanut. Also **goober pea.** [<Bantu *nguba*]

good (go͝od) *adj.* **bet·ter, best 1** Satisfactory in quality or kind: *good* food; *good* soil. **2** Striking in appearance: a *good* figure. **3** Morally excellent; virtuous. **4** Worthy: in *good* standing; a *good* name; a *good* family. **5** Kind; benevolent. **6** Well-behaved: a *good* child. **7** Proper; desirable: *good* manners. **8** Pleasing; agreeable: *good* company; *good* news. **9** Beneficial; salutary: *good* for business; *good* advice. **10** Favorable; approving a *good* opinion. **11** Skilful; proficient: *good* at arithmetic; a *good* swimmer. **12** Orthodox; conforming: a *good* Democrat. **13** Reliable; safe: a *good* investment. **14** Considerable; rather great in degree, measure, or extent: a *good* supply; a *good* while; a *good* beating. **15** Full: a *good* two miles off. **—as good as** Practically; virtually: It is *as good as* done. **—to make good 1** To compensate for; replace. **2** To carry out; accomplish. **3** To prove; substantiate. **4** To be successful. —*n.* **1** That which is desirable, fit, serviceable, etc.: opposed to the *bad* or *evil.* **2** Benefit; profit; advantage: for the *good* of mankind; to get some *good* out of it. **3** That which is morally or ethically desirable: to do *good.* See synonyms under PROFIT, SERVICE —for good (and all) Finally; for the last time. **—to the good** In excess of assets over liabilities: fifty dollars *to the good.* —*interj.* An exclamation of satisfaction or assent. —*adv. Illit. Dial.* Well. [OE *gōd*] **—good′ ness** *n.*

Synonyms (adj.) : able, adequate, admirable, advantageous, agreeable, beneficial, benevolent, capital, cheerful, cheering, companionable, competent, complete, considerable, convenient, dexterous, dutiful, excellent, expert, fair, favorable, fit, friendly, genial, genuine, godly, gracious, gratifying, holy, honorable, humane, immaculate, kind, lively, merciful, obliging, perfect, pious, pleasant, precious, profitable, proper, ready, real, religious, right, righteous, satisfactory, serious, serviceable, skilful, social, sound, staunch, sterling, suitable, thorough, true, unblemished, unfeigned, unimpeached, unsullied, untarnished, upright, useful, valid, valuable, virtuous, well-adapted, well-disposed, well-qualified, wholesome, worthy. *Good* may at some time be a synonym of almost any adjective in the language implying advantage, benefit, utility, worth, etc. *Good* almost always carries a silent connotation of the connection or purpose with reference to which it is affirmed. A horse that is sound, kind, and serviceable, whether swift, as a racer, or strong and heavy, as a dray horse, is a *good* horse; a ship that is *staunch* and seaworthy is a *good* ship; a use of money that brings in sure and ample returns is a *good* investment; a man of high and true moral character is a *good* man; one of very different character, if brave and skilful in war, is a *good* soldier. Compare AMIABLE, BENEFICIAL, CHOICE, EXCELLENT, HONEST, MORAL, RIGHT, USEFUL, VIRTUOUS, WELL[2]. *Antonyms:* see synonyms for BAD.

good and *Colloq.* **1** Very: He's *good and* hungry. **2** Completely: when I'm *good and* ready.

good book, the The Bible. Also **the Good Book.**

good-by (go͝od′bī′) *adj., n. interj. pl.* **-bys** (-bīz′) Farewell; adieu. Also **good-bye.** See synonyms under FAREWELL. [Contraction of GOD BE WITH YOU]

Good Conduct Medal A decoration awarded for efficiency, honor, and fidelity in the U.S. Army: a bronze medal on which is an eagle standing on a closed book.

good fellow A boon companion; any sociable person.

good-fel·low·ship (go͝od′fel′ō·ship) *n.* Merry society; companionableness. Also **good′-fel′low·hood** (-ho͝od).

good for 1 Able or likely to produce: That patch is *good for* ten bushels. **2** Entitling (one) to, or acceptable for: a ticket *good for* ten trips, or *good for* a year. **3** Admitting to: The pass is *good for* any performance.

good-for-nothing (go͝od′fər·nuth′ing) *n.* A worthless person. —*adj.* Having no use or value.

Good Friday The Friday before Easter.

good-heart·ed (go͝od′här′tid) *adj.* Kind. **—good′heart′ed·ly** *adv.* **—good′heart′ed·ness** *n.*

Good Hope, Cape of A promontory in Western Cape Province, Republic of South Africa.

good humor A cheery, kindly mood or temper.

good-hu·mored (go͝od′hyo͞o′mərd, -yo͞o′-) *adj.* **1** Having or marked by a cheerful, kindly temper; pleasant. **2** Done or said in a pleasant, kindly way. **—good′hu′mored·ly** *adv.*

good·ish (go͝od′ish) *adj.* **1** Somewhat good; not bad; rather good. **2** Of appreciable extent; considerable.

good-look·ing (go͝od′lo͝ok′ing) *adj.* Attractive; handsome.

good·ly (go͝od′lē) *adj.* **·li·er, ·li·est 1** Having a pleasing appearance or superior qualities; comely; attractive. **2** Large; sizable. **—good′·li·ness** *n.*

good·man (go͝od′mən) *n. pl.* **·men** (-mən) *Archaic* **1** Master; Mr.: a familiar appellation of civility for a man below the rank of gentleman. **2** A husband; head of a family.

good-na·tured (go͝od′nā′chərd) *adj.* Having a pleasant disposition; not easily provoked. See synonyms under AMIABLE, PLEASANT. **—good′na′tured·ly** *adv.* **—good′na′tured·ness** *n.*

Good Neighbor Policy A policy of the U.S. government for promoting political and economic amity with the Central and South American countries: first enunciated in 1933 by President Franklin D. Roosevelt.

goods (go͝odz) *n. pl.* **1** Merchandise: dry *goods,* green *goods;* also, property, especially personal property. **2** A fabric: linen *goods,* dress *goods.* **3** *Colloq.* Qualifications; resources; abilities. **4** *Brit.* Freight: a *goods* train. **—to deliver the goods** To produce what was specified, promised, or expected.

Good Samaritan See under SAMARITAN.

Good Shepherd A designation of Jesus. *John* x 11, 12.

good speed Good luck: a wish for a safe journey or for success.

good-tem·pered (go͝od′tem′pərd) *adj.* Of a good disposition. **—good′tem′pered·ly** *adv.*

good usuage Standard use: said of diction, phraseology, and idioms acceptable to cultivated speakers and writers of a language. Also **good use.**

good·wife (go͝od′wīf′) *n. pl.* **·wives** (-wīvz′) *Archaic* **1** The mistress of the house. **2** A title of respect for a woman: the correlative of *goodman.*

good-will (go͝od′wil′) *n.* The prestige and friendly relations with customers built up by a business or member of a profession.

good will 1 A desire for the well-being of others. **2** Benevolence; charity; kindly intent. See synonyms under BENEVOLENCE, FAVOR, FRIENDSHIP.

Good·win Sands (go͝od′win) An area of shoals, 10 miles long, in the Straits of Dover, enclosing the Downs.

good·y[1] (go͝od′ē) *n.* A term of civility to women of humble station, formerly used in New England. [<GOODWIFE]

good·y[2] (go͝od′ē) *Colloq. adj.* Mawkishly good; weakly pious: also **good′y-good′y.** —*n. pl.* **good·ies 1** A weakly good person. **2** A sweetmeat.

Good·year (go͝od′yir), **Charles,** 1800–60, U.S. inventor.

goo·ey (go͞o′ē) *adj.* **goo·i·er, goo·i·est** *Slang* Like goo; sticky.

goof (go͞of) *n. Slang* A blockhead; simpleton; stupid, foolish person. —*v.i. v.t.* To blunder; botch. [Cf. obs. *goff* a stupid person <F *goffe*] **—goof′y** *adj.* **—goof′i·ly** *adv.* **—goof′i·ness** *n.*

goo·gly (go͞o′glē) *n.* In cricket, a ball bowled at a slow pace which breaks one way and then swerves in the other. [Cf. dial. E *goggle* roll, sway]

goo·gol (go͞o′gol) *n.* **1** *Math.* The number 10 raised to the hundredth power (10^{100}) or 1 followed by 100 zeros. **2** Any enormous number. [Adopted by E. Kasner, 1878–1955, U.S. mathematician, from a child's word]

goo·gol·plex (go͞o′gol·pleks′) *n. Math.* The number 10 raised to the googol power: this is equivalent to the number 1 followed by a googol of zeros.

gook (go͞ok *for def. 1,* go͝ok *for def. 2*) *n.* **1** *Mil. Slang* A Filipino: later applied to Chinese, Koreans, Polynesians, etc.: a contemptuous use. **2** *U.S. Slang* Excessive or gaudy ornamentation. [? <GOO]

goon (go͞on) *n.* U.S. Slang **1** A roughneck; thug; especially, one employed during labor disputes: most commonly used in the phrase **goon squad. 2** A dolt; stupid person. [after a character created by E. C. Segar, 1894–1938, U.S. cartoonist]

goo·ney (go͞o′nē) *n.* The black-footed albatross *(Diomedea nigripes)* of Pacific waters, having a sooty-brown plumage, whitish face, and saberlike wings with a spread up to 7 feet: also called *gony.* Also **gooney bird.** [Cf. dial. E *gawney* a fool]

goop (go͞op) *n. U.S. Slang* A rude, clownish, boorish person. [after a nonsensical creature created by Gelett Burgess]

goo·ral (go͞o′rəl) See GORAL.

goos·an·der (go͞os·an′dər) *n.* A merganser. [Origin uncertain]

goose[1] (go͞os) *n. pl.* **geese** (gēs) **1** One of a subfamily *(Anserinae)* of wild or domesticated web-footed birds larger than ducks and smaller than swans. See GRAYLAG. ◆Col-

lateral adjective: *anserine.* **2** The female of the goose: distinguished from *gander.* **3** *pl.* **goos·es** A tailor's heavy smoothing iron, having a curved handle. **4** A silly creature; ninny. **5** *Obs.* An old game of chance, played with dice and counters. —**Canada goose** The common North American wild goose *(Branta canadensis),* brownish-gray with black neck and head. —**to cook one's goose** *Colloq.* To spoil one's chances; ruin a person. —**the goose hangs** (or **honks**) **high** The prospect is good; everything is favorable. [OE *gōs*]

goose² (goos) *Slang v.t.* **goosed, goos·ing** **1** To prod or poke unexpectedly from behind. **2** To accelerate an engine in irregular spurts. —*n. pl.* **goos·es** A sudden or unexpected prod or poke in the backside. [? Special use of GOOSE¹]

goose·ber·ry (goos′ber′ē, -bər·ē, gōoz′-) *n. pl.* **·ries** **1** The tart fruit of a spiny shrub (genus *Grossularia* or *Ribes*). **2** This shrub. **3** A casklike portable frame around which barbed wire is wound in forming entanglements.

goose-egg (goos′eg′) *n. Slang* A cipher; naught; zero, as in the score of a game.

goose-flesh (goos′flesh′) *n.* A roughened condition of the skin produced by cold, fear, etc. Also **goose′-pim′ples** (-pim′pəlz), **goose′-skin** (-skin′).

goose·foot (goos′foot′) *n. pl.* **·foots 1** Any plant of a widely distributed genus *(Chenopodium)* of mealy-leaved shrubs and herbs with small green flowers; the pigweed. **2** A plant of the family *(Chenopodiaceae)* of which the goosefoot is typical.

goose·grass (goos′gras′, -gräs′) *n.* Any of various herbs and grasses, especially the cleavers, the silverweed, and a weed common in the West Indies and warmer parts of the United States *(Eleusine indica).*

goose·herd (goos′hûrd′) *n.* A tender of geese.

goose·neck (goos′nek′) *n.* **1** A mechanical contrivance curved like a goose's neck. **2** *Naut.* A swivel forming the fastening between a boom and a mast. **3** A curved shaft for a seat on a bicycle. **4** A bent pipe or tube having a swivel joint so that its outer end may be revolved.

goose-step (goos′step′) *n.* **1** The act of marking time with the feet. **2** A gymnastic exercise, or setting-up drill for the legs, which are alternately lifted and held straight out. **3** In some European armies, a stiff manner of marching on parade, which suggests this exercise. —*v.i.* To move or march in this manner.

goos·y (goo′sē) *adj.* **goos·i·er, goos·i·est 1** Like a goose. **2** Appearing like goose-flesh. **3** *Slang* Extremely nervous or ticklish: said of a person. Also **goos′ey.** —**goos′i·ness** *n.*

go·pher (gō′fər) *n.* **1** A burrowing American rodent (family *Geomyidae*), especially one with large cheek pouches, as the **pocket gopher** (genera *Thomomys* and *Geomys*). **2** One of various western North American ground squirrels, especially *Citellus columbianus* and related forms. **3** A large, nocturnal, burrowing land tortoise *(Gopherus polyphemus)* of the southern United States. [< F *gaufre* a honeycomb]

gopher snake **1** A nonpoisonous burrowing snake *(Drymarchon corais couperi)* of the southern United States: also called *indigo snake.* **2** Any of several nonpoisonous snakes (genus *Pituophis*) of the United States that feed on gophers and other rodents: also called *bull snake.*

Gopher State Nickname of MINNESOTA.

go·pher·wood (gō′fər·wood′) *n.* **1** Yellowwood. **2** The wood of which Noah's ark was made. *Gen.* vi 14. [< Hebrew *gōfer, gopher*]

go·ral (gō′rəl) *n. pl.* **·rals** or **·ral** A Himalayan goat antelope (genus *Nemorhedus*) having a short grayish coat speckled with black, short horns, and a white throat: also spelled *gooral.* [< native name]

Gor·ba·chev (gôr′bə·chof), **Mikhail Ser·geyevich,** 1931-, first secretary of the Communist party 1985-

gor·cock (gôr′kok′) *n.* The moorcock. [Origin uncertain]

Gor·di·an (gôr′dē·ən) *adj.* Pertaining to Gordius, or to the knot tied by him.

Gordian knot 1 The knot tied by Gordius. **2** A difficulty that can be overcome only by the application of unusual or bold measures.

Gor·di·us (gôr′dē·əs) An ancient king of Phrygia who tied a knot which, according to an oracle,

was to be undone only by the man who should rule Asia: Alexander the Great, unable to untie the knot, cut it in two with his sword.

Gor·don (gôr′dən), **Charles George,** 1833–85, English general; killed at Khartoum: called "Chinese Gordon." —**Lord George,** 1751–93, English political agitator; instigated "No Popery" riots in 1780.

gore¹ (gôr, gōr) *v.t.* **gored, gor·ing** To pierce, as with a tusk or a horn; wound. [ME *goren;* prob. akin to OE *gār* a spear]

gore² (gôr, gōr) *n.* **1** A wedge-shaped or triangular piece, as a tapering or triangular piece of land; also, in Maine and Vermont, a minor civil division. **2** A triangular piece of cloth let into a garment, sail, etc.; also, one of the separate fabric sections of a balloon, airship, or parachute. **3** *Naut.* A triangular piece of plank used in fitting a vessel. —*v.t.* **gored, gor·ing** To cut into triangular or tapering form, as a garment, or the deck of a vessel. [OE *gāra* triangular piece of land]

gore³ (gôr, gōr) *n.* Blood after effusion, especially clotted blood. [OE *gor* dirt, filth]

Go·rée (gô·rā′) An island off the SE tip of Cape Verde, French West Africa; first French stronghold in French West Africa.

Gor·gas (gôr′gəs), **William Crawford,** 1854–1920, U.S. sanitation expert and surgeon general of U.S. Army.

gorge (gôrj) *n.* **1** The throat; gullet. **2** A narrow passage between hills; ravine. **3** The act of gorging, or that which is gorged. **4** The part of a garment about the throat. **5** A jam: an ice *gorge.* **6** An entrance into a bastion or similar part of a fortification; hence, the rear of a redan or other work. For illustration see BASTION. **7** Bait used on a gorge hook. **8** *Colloq.* A full meal. **9** In falconry, the crop of a hawk. See synonyms under VALLEY. —*v.* **gorged, gorg·ing** *v.t.* **1** To stuff with food; glut. **2** To swallow gluttonously; gulp down. —*v.i.* **3** To stuff oneself with food. [< OF < L *gurges* a whirlpool]

gorge hook A pair of small fishhooks joined in a heavily leaded shank.

gor·geous (gôr′jəs) *adj.* Conspicuous by splendor of colors; very beautiful; magnificent; resplendent. [< OF *gorgias* elegant; ult. origin uncertain] —**gor′geous·ly** *adv.* —**gor′geous·ness** *n.*

gorg·er (gôr′jər) *n.* **1** One who eats to excess. **2** A heavy haul of fish.

gor·get (gôr′jit) *n.* **1** A piece of armor protecting the junction of the helmet and cuirass. **2** An ornament, often crescent-shaped, worn on the neck or breast. **3** A ruff formerly worn by women. **4** *Zool.* A throat patch distinguished by color or texture. [< OF *gorgete,* dim. of *gorge* throat]

Gor·gi·as (gôr′jē·əs) 485?–380? B.C., Greek orator and sophist.

gor·gon (gôr′gən) *n.* Any hideous object, especially a repulsive-looking woman. [< GORGON]

Gor·gon (gôr′gən) In Greek mythology, one of three sisters (Stheno, Euryale, and Medusa) with serpents for hair, so hideous that they turned the beholder to stone. [< L *Gorgo, -onis* < Gk. *Gorgō* < *gorgos* terrible]

gor·go·ne·an (gôr·gō′nē·ən) *adj.* Of or relating to the Gorgons; Gorgonlike. Also **gor·go′ni·an.**

gor·go·nei·on (gôr′gə·nē′ən) *n. pl.* **·nei·a** (-nē′ə) In classical mythology, a mask or head of Medusa; an emblem or attribute of Athena, borne as the centerpiece of the aegis and on her shield. Also **gor·go·ne′um** (-nē′əm). [< Gk., neut. of *gorgoneios* of a Gorgon]

GORGONEION
The Gorgon Medusa

gor·gon·ize (gôr′gə·nīz) *v.t.* **·ized, ·iz·ing** To paralyze as if by the Gorgon's spell; petrify or transfix.

Gor·gon·zo·la (gôr′gən·zō′lə) *n.* A white Italian cheese of pressed milk somewhat like Roquefort. [from *Gorgonzola,* a town in Italy]

gor·hen (gôr′hen′) *n.* The moorhen; the female red grouse. [See GORCOCK]

go·ril·la (gə·ril′ə) *n.* **1** Any of a dwindling species *(Gorilla gorilla)* of herbivorous great apes native to equatorial Africa, living in a close family groups and having an unearned reputation for aggressiveness due in part to their ritual threat displays, large size, and great strength. **2** *Slang* A tough; a brutal person; especially, a gangster. [< NL < Gk., appar. < native name]

GORILLA
(Weight up to 600 pounds; female about 1/5 less in stature and weight)

Gö·ring (gœ′ring), **Hermann,** 1893–1946, German field marshal and Nazi politician. Also spelled *Goering.*

Go·ri·zia (gō·rē′tsyä) A city in NE Italy on the Yugoslav border. Slovenian **Go·ri·ca** (gô·rē′tsä).

Gor·ki (gôr′kē), **Maxim** Pseudonym of Alexei Maximovich Pyeshkov, 1868–1936, Russian author.

Gor·ki (gôr′kē) A city on the Volga in west central Russian S.F.S.R.: formerly *Nizhni Novgorod.* Also **Gor′ky.**

Gör·litz (gœr′lits) A manufacturing city on the Neisse river in Saxony, Germany.

Gor·lov·ka (gôr·lôf′kə) A city in eastern Ukrainian S.S.R.

gor·mand (gôr′mənd), etc. See GOURMAND, etc.

gor·mand·ize (gôr′mən·dīz) *v.t.* & *v.i.* **·ized, ·iz·ing** To eat voraciously or gluttonously. —**gor′mand·iz′er** *n.*

Gor·no-Al·tai Autonomous Region (gôr′nō·äl·tī′) An administrative division of SE Altai Territory; 35,800 square miles. Formerly **Oi·rot Autonomous Region** (oi′rət).

Gor·no-Ba·dakh·shan Autonomous Region (gôr′nō·bä·däkh·shän′) An administrative district of SE Tadzhik S.S.R.; 23,600 square miles.

gorse (gôrs) *n. Brit.* Furze. [OE *gors(t)*] —**gors′y** *adj.*

go·ry (gôr′ē, gō′rē) *adj.* **·ri·er, ·ri·est 1** Covered with or stained with gore. **2** Resembling gore. See synonyms under BLOODY. [< GORE³] —**go′ri·ness** *n.*

gosh (gosh) *interj.* A minced oath. [Alter. of GOD]

gos·hawk (gos′hôk′, gôs′-) *n.* **1** A powerfully built, short-winged hawk (genus *Accipiter*), formerly used in falconry. **2** The eastern goshawk of North America *(Astur atricapillus).* [OE *gōshafoc* < *gōs* a goose + *hafoc* a hawk]

Go·shen (gō′shən) **1** The district in Egypt occupied by the Israelites. *Gen.* xiv 10. **2** A land of plenty.

gos·ling (goz′ling) *n.* **1** A young goose. **2** The pasqueflower. **3** A catkin or ament. **4** A silly person.

gos·ling-green (goz′ling·grēn′) *n.* A yellowish-green color.

gos·pel (gos′pəl) *n.* **1** Good news or tidings, especially the message of salvation preached by Jesus Christ and the apostles; the teaching of the Christian church. **2** *Usually cap.* A portion of the Gospels read during the eucharistic services of some churches. **3** Any doctrine concerning human welfare which is considered of great importance. **4** Anything which is regarded as absolutely true. —*v.t.* **·peled** or **·pelled, ·pel·ing** or **·pel·ling** *Obs.* To preach the gospel to. —*adj.* Relating to or agreeing with the gospel; evangelical; veritable. [OE *godspell* good news, trans. of Gk. *euangelion.* See EVANGEL.]

Gos·pel (gos′pəl) *n.* A narrative of Christ's life and teaching as given in one of the first four books of the New Testament.

gos·pel·er (gos′pəl·ər) *n.* **1** An ardent adherent of the Reformation, as distinguished from a Roman Catholic. **2** The cleric who

reads the Gospel at a church service. **3** An evangelist; missionary. Also **gos'pel·ler.**

Gos·plan (gôs′plän′) *n.* An economic planning commission of the Soviet Union, established in 1921, one of its functions now being the direction of the Five-Year Plans. [<Russian *gos(udar)* national + *plan* a plan]

gos·po·din (gôs′pô-dēn′) *n. Russian* Mister: since 1917, a courtesy title for non-Russians.

Gos·port (gos′pôrt, -pōrt) A port and municipal borough in SE Hampshire, England: yacht-building center and site of a naval base.

gos·sa·mer (gos′ə-mər) *n.* **1** An exceedingly fine thread or web of spider's silk that may float in the air. **2** A fine fabric like gauze. **3** A thin waterproof outer garment. —*adj.* Thin and light as gauze; flimsy: also **gos'sa·mer·y.** [<ME *gossamer* Indian summer, lit. goose summer; appar. so called because often seen in autumn when geese are in season]

gos·san (gos′ən, goz′-) *n. Mining* Decomposed material, usually reddish or ferruginous, forming the upper part of mineral veins and ore deposits. [<Cornish]

gos·san·if·er·ous (gos′ən-if′ər-əs) *adj.* Yielding or producing gossan.

Gosse (gôs, gos), **Sir Edmund William,** 1849–1928, English poet and critic.

gos·sip (gos′əp) *n.* **1** Familiar or idle talk; groundless rumor; mischievous tattle. **2** One who tattles or talks idly: also **gos'sip·er. 3** *Archaic* A boon companion. —*v.i.* To talk idly, usually about the affairs of others; be a gossip. —*v.t.* To repeat as gossip. See synonyms under BABBLE. [OE *godsibb* a baptismal sponsor < *god* God + *sib* a relative]

gos·sip·ing (gos′əp-ing) *n.* **1** Gossipy talk; a prating. **2** *Brit.Dial.* A christening.

gos·sip·mong·er (gos′əp-mung′gər, -mong′-) *n.* A zealous spreader of gossip.

gos·sip·y (gos′əp-ē) *adj.* Devoted to gossip; chatty.

gos·soon (go-soon′) *n. Irish* A lad; a serving boy. [Alter. of F *garçon* a boy]

got (got) Past tense and past participle of GET. ◆ **have got** In the sense of must, *have got* is in wide colloquial use to add emphasis: I *have* (or *I've*) *got* to leave. In the sense of possess, *have got* is still more common in informal speech: We *have got* (or *We've got*) plenty and intend to keep it. This usage has long been challenged on the grounds (1) that *have got* properly means "have acquired," and (2) that *got* is superfluous, since *have* alone would convey the same meaning. The usage is now defended as acceptable colloquial idiom on the grounds that *have* is so much used as an auxiliary that it has lost much of its primary sense of possess, and *got* therefore serves to restore and emphasize this meaning. When *have* is dropped, and *got* stands alone in the sense of must or of possess, it is illiterate, or at best dialectal, as in "I *got* rhythm" or "All God's chillun *got* wings."

Go·ta·ma (gō′tə·mə) See GAUTAMA.

Gö·te·borg (yœ′tə-bôr′y) A port in SW Sweden. Also **Goth·en·burg** (got′ən-bûrg, goth′-).

Goth (goth, gôth) *n.* **1** A member of an ancient East Germanic people, originating in the basin of the Vistula, that overran the Roman Empire in the third and fourth centuries: divided into the Ostrogoths, or **East Goths,** and Visigoths, or **West Goths. 2** A barbarian; rude or uncivilized person. [<LL *Gothi* the Goths < Gk. *Gothoi* <Gothic]

Go·tha (gō′tä) A city in the former state of Thuringia, SW East Germany.

Goth·am (goth′əm, gō′thəm) **1** A village near Nottingham, England, noted in stories for the foolishness of its inhabitants. **2** New York City. — **Goth'am·ite** (-īt) *n.*

Goth·ic (goth′ik) *adj.* **1** Of or pertaining to the Goths or to their language. **2** Rude, barbaric. **3** Of or pertaining to Gothic architecture. **4** *Obs.* Germanic or Teutonic. **5** Romantic; medieval: distinguished from *classic.* —*n.* **1** The East Germanic language of the Goths, known chiefly from fragments of a translation of the Bible made by Bishop Ulfilas in the fourth century: extinct by the ninth century. **2** The pointed style in architecture. — **Goth'i·cal·ly** *adv.*

Gothic arch See POINTED ARCH.

Gothic architecture The pointed type of medieval architecture prevalent in Europe from the full evolution of the Romanesque style

until the Renaissance, or roughly from 1200 to 1500.

GOTHIC ARCHITECTURE
Westminster Abbey, London, 13th–15th centuries A.D.

Goth·i·cism (goth′ə-siz′əm) *n.* **1** A Gothic idiom. **2** Imitation of or inclination for Gothic architecture. **3** Rudeness of manners; barbarousness.

Goth·i·cize (goth′ə-sīz) *v.t.* **·cized, ·ciz·ing** To make Gothic.

Gothic novel A type of romance developed in the late 18th and early 19th centuries, characterized by the supernatural and grotesque in a medieval setting: first used by Horace Walpole in "*The Castle of Otranto: A Gothic Story,*" 1764.

gothic type 1 *U.S.* A type face having all the strokes of uniform width and without serifs. **2** *Brit.* Black letter.

go·thite (gō′thīt) See GOETHITE.

Got·land (got′lənd, *Sw.* gôt′länd) A Swedish island in the Baltic Sea; 1,224 square miles; chief town, Visby. Formerly **Gott'land, Goth'land.**

got·ten (got′n) Past participle of GET. ◆ *Gotten,* obsolete in British, is current in American English in the sense of "obtained"; We have *gotten* the necessary funds. *Gotten* is also used in the sense of "become": He has *gotten* fat.

Göt·ter·däm·mer·ung (gœt′ər-dem′ər-ŏŏng) *German* Twilight of the gods. See RING OF THE NIBELUNG.

Gott·fried (gôt′frēt) German form of GODFREY.

Göt·ting·en (gœt′ing-ən) A city in Lower Saxony, West Germany.

Gott·lieb (gôt′lēp) Danish and German equivalent of THEOPHILUS. [<G, love of God]

Götz von Berlichingen (gœts fôn ber′likh·ing·ən) See BERLICHINGEN, GÖTZ VON.

gouache (gwäsh) *n.* **1** A method of watercolor painting with opaque colors mixed with water and gum. **2** A painting executed by this method, or the pigment used for it. [<F <Ital. *guazzo* a spray <L *aquatio* a watering < *aqua* water]

Gou·da cheese (gou′də, gōō′-) A mild cheese similar to Edam cheese.

Gou·dy (gou′dē), **Frederic William,** 1865–1947, U. S. type designer.

gouge (gouj) *n.* **1** A chisel having a curved cutting edge. **2** A groove made, or as made,

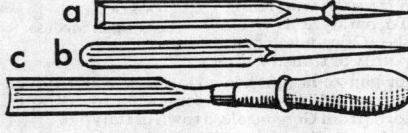

TYPES OF GOUGES
a. Paring. *b.* Turning. *c.* Firmer.

by it. **3** A layer of soft clay or decomposed rock along the wall of a vein; selvage. **4** A

tool for stamping metal. **5** *U.S. Colloq.* Stealing or cheating; also, one who cheats or defrauds. —*v.t.* **gouged, goug·ing 1** To cut or scoop out with or as with a gouge. **2** To scoop, force, or tear out as with a gouge: to *gouge* out an eye. **3** *U.S. Colloq.* To cheat in a bargain; swindle. [<F <LL *gulbia,* prob. <Celtic] — **goug'er** *n.*

Gou·jon (gōō-zhôn′), **Jean,** 1515?–72?, French sculptor.

gou·lash (gōō′läsh, -lash) *n.* A stew made with beef or veal and seasoned with paprika: generally known as **Hungarian goulash.** Also spelled *gulash.* [<Magyar *gulyas (hus)* shepherd's (meat)]

Gould (gōōld), **Jay,** 1836–92, U.S. financier.

Gou·nod (gōō-nō′), **Charles François,** 1818–1893, French composer.

gou·ra·mi (gōōr′ə·mē) *n. pl.* **·mis 1** A large, air-breathing, fresh-water Asian fish (*Osphromenus olfax*) which builds nests and is highly esteemed as food. **2** Any of several related fishes cultivated in home aquaria, as the banded gourami (*Colisa fasciata*), the three-spot gourami (*Trichogaster trichopterus*), and the dwarf gourami (*C. lalia*). [< Malay *gurami*]

gourd (gôrd, gōrd, gŏŏrd) *n.* **1** The melonlike fruit of certain plants of the cucurbit family, having a hard rind, as the pumpkin, squash, etc. **2** The fruit of any of various bottle gourds of the genus *Lagenaria.* **3** The plant that bears this fruit, or a vessel, as a dipper, made of its shell. **4** A hollow dried gourd used by gamblers for cheating. [<F *gourde* <L *cucurbita* gourd]

gourde (gŏŏrd) *n.* The monetary unit of Haiti.

gour·mand (gŏŏr′mənd, *Fr.* gŏŏr-män′) *n.* **1** A glutton. **2** Loosely, an epicure. Also spelled *gormand.* [<F, a glutton]

gour·met (gŏŏr-mā′, *Fr.* gŏŏr-me′) *n.* An epicure. [<F <OF, a winetaster]

Gour·mont (gŏŏr-môn′), **Remy de,** 1858–1915, French novelist and critic.

gout (gout) *n.* **1** *Pathol.* A disease of metabolism characterized by inflammation of a joint, as of the great toe, paroxysmal recurrent pain, and an excess of uric acid in the blood. Also called *podagra.* **2** A drop; clot. [<F *goutte* a drop <L *gutta*]

goût (gōō) *n. French* Taste; relish.

goutte (gōōt) *n. Her.* A subordinate ordinary representing a drop or tear. [<F. See GOUT.]

gout·y (gou′tē) *adj.* **gout·i·er, gout·i·est 1** Affected with gout. **2** Of or pertaining to the gout. **3** Swollen; protuberant. — **gout'i·ly** *adv.* — **gout'i·ness** *n.*

gou·ver·nante (gōō-ver-nänt′) *n. French* **1** A chaperon. **2** A governess; housekeeper.

Gov·an (guv′ən) A suburb of Glasgow, Scotland.

gov·ern (guv′ərn) *v.t.* **1** To rule or control by right or authority: to *govern* a kingdom. **2** To control or influence morally or physically; direct: His ideals *govern* his life. **3** To serve as a rule or regulation for; determine: This decision *governed* the case. **4** To hold back; curb, as one's temper. **5** *Gram.* **a** To regulate (a word) as to form: In *Take me home,* the verb *governs* the pronoun. **b** To require (a particular case, mood, or form): In English, a transitive verb *governs* the objective case of a pronoun. —*v.i.* **6** To exercise authority. [<OF *governer* <L *gubernare* steer <Gk. *kubernaein*] — **gov'ern·a·ble** *adj.*

Synonyms: command, control, curb, direct, influence, manage, reign, restrain, rule, sway. A person *commands* another when he has, or claims, the right to make that other do his will, with power of inflicting penalty if not obeyed; he *controls* another whom he can prevent from doing anything contrary to his will; he *governs* one whom he actually does cause to obey his will. A wise mother, by gentle means, *sways* the feelings and *molds* the lives of her children; to be able to *manage* servants is an important element of good housekeeping. The word *reign,* once so absolute, now simply denotes that one holds the official station of sovereign with or without effective power. See COMMAND, REGULATE. *Antonyms:* comply, obey, submit, yield.

gov·ern·ance (guv′ər-nəns) *n.* **1** Exercise of authority; direction; control. **2** Manner or system of government or regulation.

gov·ern·ess (guv′ər-nis) *n.* A woman employed in a private home to train and in-

struct children. —*v.i.* To act or serve as a governess.

gov·ern·ment (guv′ərn·mənt, -ər-) *n.* **1** The authoritative direction of the affairs of men in a community; rule and administration. **2** The governing body of a community, considered either as a continuous entity or as the group of administrators currently in power. **3** The form by which a community is managed: democratic *government*; ecclesiastical *government.* **4** A governed territory. **5** Management; control: the *government* of one's behavior. **6** *Gram.* A syntactical relation which requires a word to assume a certain case or mood when related to another word.

gov·ern·men·tal (guv′ərn·men′təl, -ər-) *adj.* Relating or pertaining to government; made by or proceeding from the government. —**gov′ern·men′tal·ly** *adv.*

Government House In British colonies, the official residence of a governor.

Government Issue Something which is furnished by a governmental agency, as uniforms to Army personnel. Abbr. *G.I.*

Government land Land owned by the U.S. government, available to the public at low cost and under specific conditions.

gov·er·nor (guv′ər·nər) *n.* **1** One who governs; especially, the chief executive of a state or colony. **2** *Mech.* A device for regulating the speed of an engine, motor, compressor, etc., usually by the centrifugal force of two or more balls or weights, which so control the motive fluid as to reduce speed: also called *ball–governor.* **3** *Brit. Colloq.* One's father. **4** *Brit. Colloq.* An employer. See synonyms under MASTER.

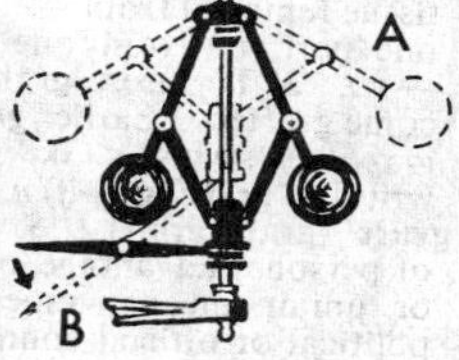

BALL–GOVERNOR
The balls, revolving, raise levers to position *A*, thus reducing excess speed of engine by closing valve at *B*.

governor general A governor who has deputy or lieutenant governors under him: the *governor general* of Canada. Also *Brit.* **gov′er·nor–gen′er·al.** —**gov′er·nor–gen′er·al·ship** *n.*

gov·er·nor·ship (guv′ər·nər·ship) *n.* The office of a governor; his term of office; or the territory under his jurisdiction.

Governors Island A small island at the mouth of the East River, New York Harbor; site of a United States military reservation and historic Fort Jay.

gow·an (gou′ən) *n. Scot.* **1** The English or garden daisy. **2** A yellow flower of any one of several species. Also **gow′un.** —**gow′an·y** *adj.*

gowd (goud) *n. Scot.* Gold. —**gow·den** (gou′dən), **gow′dun** *adj.*

Gow·er (gou′ər, gōr), **John,** 1325?–1408, English poet.

gowf (gouf) *Scot. n.* Golf. —*v.t.* To strike as in playing golf; beat; strike.

gowk (gouk) *n. Scot.* **1** The cuckoo. **2** A fool; simpleton.

gowk·it (gouk′it) *adj. Scot.* Foolish.

gown (goun) *n.* **1** A woman's dress or outer garment, especially when elaborate or costly. **2** A long and loose outer robe worn as a distinctive or official habit, as by clergymen, judges, barristers, professors, or university students, especially in England. See GENEVA GOWN. **3** Any loose outer garment or wrapper, especially when long: a dressing *gown.* **4** *Obs.* Dress; garb: the *gown* of humility. **5** *Obs.* A toga.—*v.t.* & *v.i.* To dress in a gown. [<OF *goune* < Med. L *gunna* a loose robe]

gowns·man (gounz′mən) *n. pl.* **·men** (-mən) **1** One who wears a gown professionally, as a clergyman, a graduate or student in a university, or a barrister. **2** *Brit.* A collegian as distinguished from a townsman: also **gown′man.**

goy (goi) *n. pl.* **goy·im** (goi′im) *Yiddish* A non–Jew; a Gentile.

Go·ya (gô′yə), **Francisco José de,** 1746–1828, Spanish painter and etcher: full surname *Goya y Lucientes.*

Go·yaz (goi·äs′) A former name for GOIÁS.

Graaf·i·an follicle (grä′fē·ən) *Anat.* The small sac in which the ova are developed in the ovary. Also **Graafian vesicle.** [after Regnier de *Graaf,* 1641–73, Dutch physician and anatomist]

graal (grāl) See GRAIL.

grab[1] (grab) *v.* **grabbed, grab·bing** *v.t.* **1** To grasp or seize forcibly or suddenly. **2** To take possession of violently or dishonestly. —*v.i.* **3** To make a sudden grasp. See synonyms under GRASP. —*n.* **1** The act of grabbing, or that which is grabbed. **2** A dishonest or unlawful taking possession or acquisition. **3** An apparatus for grappling. [Cf. MDu. *grabben* grip] —**grab′ber** *n.*

grab[2] (grab) *n.* A coasting vessel of the East Indies, with two or three masts. [<Arabic *ghurāb*]

grab–bag (grab′bag′) *n.* A bag or box filled with miscellaneous articles, from which one draws something unseen on payment of a price for each grab or draw.

grab·ble (grab′əl) *v.i.* **grab·bled, grab·bling** **1** To feel about with the hands; grope. **2** To flounder; sprawl. [Cf. Du. *grabbelen,* freq. of *grabben* grab]

gra·ben (grä′bən) *n. Geol.* A valleylike depression of the land caused by the subsidence of a series of blocks of the earth's crust. [<G, ditch]

grab rope *Naut.* A rope which runs along the side of a vessel for the use of boats coming alongside.

Grac·chi (grak′ī) Two Roman political reformers, **Gaius Sempronius Grac·chus** (grak′əs), 153–121 B.C., and his brother **Tiberius Sempronius Gracchus,** 163–133 B.C.

grace (grās) *n.* **1** Beauty or harmony of form, attitude, etc.; ease and elegance of speech. **2** Any excellence or attractive characteristic, quality, or endowment. **3** Unmerited favor or good will; clemency; hence, any kindness, favor, or service freely rendered. **4** *Theol.* The unmerited love and favor of God in Christ; hence, free gift; the divine influence acting within the heart, to regenerate, sanctify, and keep it; a state of reconciliation to God through Christ; the power or disposition to exercise saving faith and to live the Christian life; any spiritual gift or attainment. See CHARISMA. **5** A short prayer before or after a meal. **6** Something granted in the exercise of favor or discretion and not as of right. **7** A courteous or gracious demeanor; graciousness; demeanor in general. **8** *Music* An ornament or embellishment, as a trill, turn, or the like. **9** *Obs.* Physical virtue or efficiency. See synonyms under FAVOR, MERCY. —**good graces** Favorable regard; friendship. —*v.t.* **graced, grac·ing** **1** To add grace and beauty to; adorn. **2** To dignify; honor. **3** *Music* To ornament with grace notes or other embellishments. [<OF <L *gratia* favor]

Grace (grās) *n.* Goodness; clemency: a title applied in Great Britain and Ireland to a duke, duchess, or archbishop, formerly to the sovereign, and used with a possessive adjective: His *Grace.*

Grace (grās) A feminine personal name. [<L, favor]

grâce à Dieu (gräs à dyœ′) *French* Thanks to God.

grace cup A cup passed at the end of a meal for the drinking of the concluding health.

grace·ful (grās′fəl) *adj.* Characterized by grace; elegant; easy; becoming. —**grace′ful·ly** *adv.* —**grace′ful·ness** *n.*

Synonym: beautiful. That which is *graceful* is marked by elegance and harmony, with ease of action, attitude, or posture, or delicacy of form. *Graceful* commonly suggests motion or the possibility of motion; *beautiful* may apply to absolute fixity; a landscape or a blue sky is *beautiful,* but neither is *graceful. Graceful* commonly applies to beauty as addressed to the eye, but we often speak of a *graceful* poem or a *graceful* compliment. *Graceful* applies to the perfection of motion, especially of the lighter motions, which convey no suggestion of stress or strain, and are in harmonious curves. Apart from the thought of motion, *graceful* denotes a pleasing harmony of outline, proportion, etc., with a certain degree of delicacy; a Hercules is massive, an Apollo is *graceful.* We speak of a *graceful* attitude, *graceful* drapery. Compare BEAUTIFUL, BECOMING. *Antonyms*: see synonyms for AWKWARD.

graceful tree frog A tiny frog (*Hyla gracilenta*) of Australia, often kept as a pet.

grace·less (grās′lis) *adj.* Lacking grace, charm, or tact. —**grace′less·ly** *adv.* —**grace′less·ness** *n.*

grace note *Music* An ornamental note introduced as an embellishment, but not actually essential to the harmony or melody; an appoggiatura.

Grac·es (grā′siz) In Greek mythology, three sister goddesses: Aglaia (splendor), Euphrosyne (joy), and Thalia (abundance). Also **the three Graces.**

gra·ci·as (grä′thē·äs, -sē·əs) *interj. Spanish* Thanks.

grac·ile (gras′il) *adj.* Gracefully slender or slight. [<L *gracilis* slender] —**grac′ile·ness, gra·cil·i·ty** (grə·sil′ə·tē) *n.*

Gra·cio·sa (grə·syô′zə) An island in the central Azores; 27 square miles.

gra·ci·os·i·ty (grā′shē·os′ə·tē) *n. Rare* The quality or state of being gracious.

gra·ci·o·so (grā′shē·ō′sō, *Sp.* grä·thyō′sō) *n. pl.* **·sos** **1** A clown in Spanish comedy. **2** A low comic character. **3** *Obs.* A favorite. [<Sp., graceful]

gra·cious (grā′shəs) *adj.* **1** Disposed to show grace or favor; full of kindness or love. **2** Courteous and condescending; kind; affable. **3** Possessing or exhibiting divine grace. **4** *Obs.* Happy; fortunate. See synonyms under BLAND, HUMANE, MERCIFUL, POLITE, PROPITIOUS. [<OF <L *gratiosus* < *gratia* favor] —**gra′cious·ly** *adv.* —**gra′cious·ness** *n.*

grack·le (grak′əl) *n.* **1** One of various Old World starlinglike birds (family *Sturnidae*), usually black or black and white, as the myna. **2** An American blackbird; especially, the **purple grackle** (*Quiscalus quiscula*), with vivid iridescent plumage. [<NL *Gracula,* name of a genus < *graculus* a jackdaw]

gra·date (grā′dāt) *v.t.* & *v.i.* **·dat·ed, ·dat·ing** To pass or cause to pass imperceptibly from one shade or degree of intensity to another. —*adj.* Graduated according to size.

gra·da·tion (grā·dā′shən) *n.* **1** Orderly or continuous succession, progression, or arrangement, as according to size, quality, state, rank, or proficiency; regular advance upward or downward, as by steps or degrees. **2** A step, degree, rank, or relative position in an order or series; grade. **3** In art and architecture, a relative subordination or arrangement of parts so as to produce a desired effect; such a blending and variation of color and light as will produce effects of depth, relief, etc. **4** *Ling.* Ablaut. [<F <L *gradatio, -onis* a going by steps < *gradus* a step] —**gra·da′tion·al** *adj.* —**gra·da′tion·al·ly** *adv.*

grad·a·to·ry (grad′ə·tôr′ē, -tō′rē, grā′də-) *adj.* **1** Proceeding by gradations; gradual. **2** Adapted for stepping.

grade (grād) *n.* **1** A degree or step in any scale, as of quality, ability, dignity, etc. **2** A group of persons of the same rank or station: all *grades* of society. **3** Rate or rank in the U.S. armed forces. See page 548. **4** A class of things of the same quality or value: a high *grade* of wool. **5** *U.S.* **a** One of the divisions of an elementary or secondary school covering a year of work. **b** The pupils in such a division. **6** *pl. U.S.* A grade school. **7** A scholastic rating or mark on an examination or in a course. **8** A part of a road, track, or surface inclined to the horizontal. **9** The degree of inclination of a road or the like as compared with the horizontal. **10** *Agric.* An animal (as a cow or sheep) or a class of animals produced by crossing a common or other breed with a pure or better breed. —**at grade** At the same point of grade or inclination: a road crossing another *at grade.* —*v.* **grad·ed, grad·ing** *v.t.* **1** To arrange or classify by grades or degrees, according to size or quality. **2** To assign a grade to. **3** To gradate. **4** To make level or properly inclined: to *grade* a road. **5** To improve by crossbreeding with better stock: often with *up*: to *grade* up a herd of cattle. —*v.i.* **6** To take rank; be of a grade. [<F <L *gradus* step] —**grad′er** *n.*

-grade *combining form Zool.* Manner of walking: *plantigrade.* [<L *gradi* walk]

grade crossing A place where a road crosses a railroad on the same level.

grad·ed (grā′did) *adj.* **1** Leveled, as a road or railroad. **2** Improved by crossbreeding.

grade school An elementary school.

gra·di·ent (grā′dē·ənt) *adj.* **1** Running on legs; adapted for walking or running: a *gradient* animal or automaton, *gradient* feet. **2** Rising or descending gently or by degrees: a *gradient* road. — *n.* **1** A grade: a *gradient* of 1 to 50. **2** An incline; also, a ramp. **3** *Meteorol.* A rate of change in certain elements affecting weather conditions, as pressure, temperature, etc.: usually with reference to horizontal distance. [<L *gradiens, -entis,* ppr. of *gradi* walk]

gra·din (grā′din, *Fr.* grȧ·dań′) *n.* **1** One of a series of rising seats or steps, as in an amphitheater. **2** A raised step back of an altar; superaltar. Also **gra′dine** (-dēn). [<F <Ital. *gradino,* dim. of *grado* <L *gradus* a step]

gra·di·om·e·ter (grā′dē·om′ə·tər) *n.* **1** A surveyor's instrument for determining grades: also **gra·dom·e·ter** (grā·dom′ə·tər). **2** An instrument for measuring the gradient of the field of gravity in a given locality.

grad·u·al (graj′ōō·əl) *adj.* **1** Proceeding by steps or degrees; moving or changing slowly and regularly; slow. **2** Divided into degrees; graduated. — *n. Eccl.* **1** An antiphon sung at the Eucharist after the epistle. **2** A book containing the music for the sung parts of the Eucharist. *Ital.* **gra·du·a·le** (grä·dwä′lä) *n.* [< Med. L *gradualis* <L *gradus* a step] — **grad′·u·al·ly** *adv.* — **grad′u·al·ness** *n.*

  Synonyms (adj.): continuous, moderate, progressive, regular, slow. See SLOW. *Antonyms:* instant, instantaneous, momentary, prompt, quick, sudden.

grad·u·and (graj′ōō·ənd) *n. Canadian* A student who is about to graduate.

grad·u·ate (graj′ōō·āt) *v.* **·at·ed, ·at·ing** *v.t.* **1** To grant a diploma or degree to upon completion of a course of study, as at a college. **2** To mark in units or degrees, as a thermometer scale; calibrate. **3** To arrange into grades or divisions, as according to size or quality. — *v.i.* **4** To receive a diploma or degree upon completion of a course of study. **5** To change by degrees. — *n.* (graj′ōō·it) **1** One who has been graduated by an institution of learning, or who has completed any prescribed academic or professional course. **2** A graduated vessel used in measuring liquids, etc. — *adj.* (graj′ōō·it) **1** Holding a bachelor's degree: a *graduate* student. **2** Designed for or pertaining to graduate students: a *graduate* school. [<Med. L *graduatus,* pp. of *graduare* <L *gradus* step, degree] — **grad′u·a′tor** *n.*

graduate nurse A nurse who has graduated from a recognized school of nursing.

graduate student A student working toward an advanced degree at a graduate school, as in a university or college.

grad·u·a·tion (graj′ōō·ā′shən) *n.* **1** The act of graduating, as a scale, or state of being graduated, as a series of colors. **2** An equal division or dividing line in a graduated scale. **3** In education, commencement.

gra·dus (grā′dəs) *n.* **1** A dictionary of quantities in prosody. **2** *Music* A collection of graded exercises. [<L *Gradus (ad Parnassum)* step (to Parnassus), title of a Latin dictionary, 1702]

Grae·ae (grē′ē) In Greek mythology, the three daughters of Phorcus who guarded the habitation of the Gorgons and had but one eye and one tooth among them: also spelled *Graiae.* Also **Græ′æ.**

Grae·cia Mag·na (grē′shə mag′nə) In classical geography, the Greek colonies in southern Italy: also *Magna Graecia.* Also **Græ′cia Mag′na.**

Grae·cize (grē′sīz) See GRECIZE.

Graeco- See GRECO-.

Graf (gräf) *n.* **Graf·en** (gräf′ən) A count: title of a German or Swedish nobleman equivalent in rank to an English earl or a French count.

graff (gräf) *n. Scot.* A grave.

graf·fi·to (grə·fē′tō) *n. pl.* **·ti** (-tē) **1** Any design or scribbled motto, etc., drawn on a wall or other exposed surface. **2** *Archeol.* A pictograph scratched on an escarpment, wall, or any other surface. [<Ital. <*graffio* a scratch, ult. <Gk. *graphein* write]

graft[1] (graft, gräft) *n.* **1** *Bot.* **a** A shoot inserted into a tree or plant, so as to become a living part of it. **b** The place where the cion is inserted in a stock. **2** Something amalgamated with a foreign stock: The family was a Spanish *graft* upon an American tree. **3** *Surg.* **a** A juncture between a piece of animal tissue cut from a living person or animal and the tissue of another subject. **b** The piece so implanted. — *v.t.* **1** *Bot.* **a** To insert (a cion or bud) into a tree or plant. **b** To insert a shoot or shoots upon: to *graft* a tree with a new variety. **c** To obtain by such process. **2** *Surg.* To transplant tissue removed from one part, or from one animal, to another. — *v.i.* **3** To insert grafts. **4** To be or become grafted. [Earlier *graff* <OF *grafe* <LL *graphium* stylus <Gk. *grapheion* < *graphein* write] — **graft′age** (-ij) *n.* — **graft′er** *n.*

graft[2] (graft, gräft) *U.S. n.* **1** The attainment of personal advantage or profit by dishonest or unfair means, especially through one's political or official connections. **2** Anything thus gained. **3** *Austral. Slang* Work. — *v.t.* **1** To obtain by graft. — *v.i.* **2** To practice graft. **3** *Austral. Slang* To work. [Cf. dial. E *graft* work, livelihood] — **graft′er** *n.*

grafting wax A composition of beeswax, tallow, etc., used in grafting to exclude air.

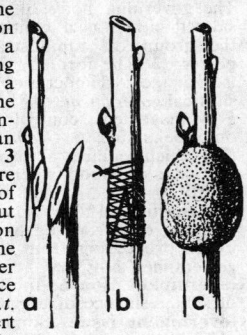

GRAFTING
a. Method of cutting for ligule–grafting, showing shape of ligule.
b. Graft and stock bound together.
c. Protection of the union by a ball of clay.

TABLE OF COMPARATIVE GRADES (UNITED STATES ARMED SERVICES)

Army	Air Force	Marine Corps	Navy	Coast Guard
General of the Army	General of the Air Force	(no equivalent)	Admiral of the Fleet	(no equivalent)
General	General	General	Admiral	Admiral
Lieutenant General	Lieutenant General	Lieutenant General	Vice Admiral	Vice Admiral
Major General	Major General	Major General	Rear Admiral (upper half)	Rear Admiral (upper half)
Brigadier General	Brigadier General	Brigadier General	Rear Admiral (lower half)	Rear Admiral (lower half)
Colonel	Colonel	Colonel	Captain	Captain
Lieutenant Colonel	Lieutenant Colonel	Lieutenant Colonel	Commander	Commander
Major	Major	Major	Lieutenant Commander	Lieutenant Commander
Captain	Captain	Captain	Lieutenant	Lieutenant
1st Lieutenant	1st Lieutenant	1st Lieutenant	Lieutenant (Junior Grade)	Lieutenant (Junior Grade)
2nd Lieutenant	2nd Lieutenant	2nd Lieutenant	Ensign	Ensign
Chief Warrant Officer W-4 Chief Warrant Officer W-3 Chief Warrant Officer W-2 Warrant Officer W-1	SAME	SAME	SAME	SAME
Sergeant Major of the Army Sergeant Major or Specialist 9	Chief Master Sergeant	Master Gunnery Sergeant Sergeant Major	Master Chief Petty Officer	Master Chief Petty Officer
Master Sergeant First Sergeant or Specialist 8	Senior Master Sergeant	Master Sergeant First Sergeant	Senior Chief Petty Officer	Senior Chief Petty Officer
Sergeant First Class Platoon Sergeant or Specialist 7	Master Sergeant	Gunnery Sergeant	Chief Petty Officer	Chief Petty Officer
Staff Sergeant or Specialist 6	Technical Sergeant	Staff Sergeant	Petty Officer First Class	Petty Officer First Class
Sergeant or Specialist 5	Staff Sergeant	Sergeant	Petty Officer Second Class	Petty Officer Second Class
Corporal or Specialist 4	Airman First Class	Corporal	Petty Officer Third Class	Petty Officer Third Class
Private First Class	Airman Second Class	Lance Corporal	Seaman	Seaman
Private E-2	Airman Third Class	Private First Class	Seaman Apprentice	Seaman Apprentice
Private E-1	Airman Basic	Private	Seaman Recruit	Seaman Recruit

Gra·ham (grā′əm), **John,** 1650?–89, Viscount Dundee, Scottish soldier: called "Graham of Claverhouse." **—Thomas,** 1805–69, Scottish chemist. **—William Franklin,** born 1918, U.S. evangelist: called **Billy Graham.**

Gra·hame (grā′əm), **Kenneth,** 1859–1932, English author.

graham flour Unbolted wheat flour. [after Sylvester *Graham,* 1794–1851, U.S. clergyman and vegetarian]

Graham Land A British name for PALMER PENINSULA. Also **Graham Coast.**

Grai·ae (grā′ē, grī′ē) See GRAEAE.

Gra·ian Alps (grā′ən, grī′-) A section of the Alps on the French-Italian border; highest peak, 13,324 feet.

grail (grāl) *n.* A broad bowl or chalice; specifically, in medieval legend, the **Holy Grail,** or *Sangreal,* the cup used by Jesus at the Last Supper, preserved by Joseph of Arimathea, who received some of Christ's blood into it at the Crucifixion, and brought it to Britain, after which it disappeared because of the impurity of its guardians. Also spelled *graal.* [< OF *graal* < Med. L *gradalis;* ult. origin uncertain]

grain (grān) *n.* **1** Any very small, hard mass: a *grain* of sand; especially, a seed resembling this; a kernel. **2** Any of the common cereals; specifically, the seed or fruit of any cereal, collectively, as wheat, oats, rye, barley, etc. **3** A minute particle. **4** A unit of weight, equal to 1/20 of a scruple apothecary: 1 oz. apothecary or troy contains 480 grains; 1 oz. avoirdupois contains 437.5 grains. **5** A unit of weight for pearls, equal to 1/4 of a metric carat or 50 milligrams. **6** The arrangement of the particles of a body of granular texture; hence, degree of coarseness, roughness, fineness of surface, direction or set of fibers, etc.: the *grain* of wood or leather. **7** The innate quality or character of a thing. **8** The cochineal insect, originally mistaken for a seed; hence, a red or purple dye, or any fast color. **9** *pl.* Refuse grain or malt after brewing. **10** Natural disposition; temper. See synonyms under PARTICLE, TEMPER. **—in grain** or **in the grain** **1** Set; fixed: said of dye. **2** Figuratively, innate; deeply rooted; ineradicable. —*v.t.* **1** To form into grains; granulate. **2** To paint or stain in imitation of the grain of wood, marble, etc. **3** In leather-making: **a** To scrape off hair from with a grainer. **b** To soften or raise the grain or pattern of. —*v.i.* **4** To form grains. [Fusion of OF *grain* a seed and *graine* seed, grain, both < L *granum* a seed]

grain alcohol Alcohol (def. 1), especially if produced by the fermentation of a cereal grain.

Grain Coast The coastal region of Liberia and some of Sierra Leone: so called for its former trade in grains of paradise.

graine (grān) *n.* The eggs of the silkworm. [< F, grain]

grain elevator **1** A warehouse or series of storage tanks for the storage, lifting, and distribution of grain. **2** A system of belt conveyors to carry grain to and from storage bins.

grain·er (grā′nər) *n.* **1** One who imitates the grain of wood with paint. **2** A knife used by tanners for removing hair. **3** A tool or machine used to simulate or raise the grain of wood, leather, etc.

Grain·ger (grān′jər), **Percy Aldridge,** 1882–1961, U.S. composer and pianist born in Australia.

grains (grānz) *n. pl. (often construed as singular)* A strong, iron fish spear with a line attached, having several points half-barbed inwardly. [< ON *grein* division]

grains of paradise The seeds of a West African plant *(Aframomum melegueta)* of the ginger family, used in medicine as an aromatic stimulant: also called *guinea grains.*

grain·y (grā′nē) *adj.* **grain·i·er, grain·i·est** **1** Full of grains or kernels. **2** Of the appearance of wood. **3** Granular. **—grain′i·ness** *n.*

graith (grāth) *Scot. n.* Equipment for any work or undertaking; tackle or tools. —*v.t.* To prepare (equipment for use).

gral·la·to·ri·al (gral′ə·tôr′ē·əl, -tō′rē-) *adj.* Of or pertaining to a former order *(Grallatores)* of long-legged wading birds, including the herons and snipes. [< L *grallator* a stilt-walker < *grallae* stilts]

gram[1] (gram) *n.* The basic unit of mass (or weight) in the metric system, equal to 15.432 grains: originally defined as the mass of 1 cubic centimeter of water at 4° C., but now as one thousandth of the mass of the kilogram at Sèvres, France. See METRIC SYSTEM. Also **gramme.** [< F *gramme* < LL *gramma* < Gk. *gramma* a small weight]

gram[2] (gram) *n.* **1** The chickpea of the East Indies: used as food for men, horses, and cattle. **2** One of various kinds of pulse, as **black gram** *(Phaseolus mungo).* [< Pg. *grão* < L *granum* a seed]

-gram[1] *combining form* Something written or drawn: *telegram.* [< Gk. *gramma* a letter, writing < *graphein* write.]

-gram[2] *combining form* A gram: used in the metric system: *kilogram.* [< GRAM[1]]

Gram (gram, *Dan.* gräm), **Hans Christian Joachim,** 1855–1938, Danish physician.

gra·ma (grä′mə) *n.* Any of various species of low pasture grasses of the western and SW United States, especially **blue grama** *(Bouteloua gracilis).* Also **gram′ma, grama grass, gramma grass.** [< Sp. < L *gramen* grass]

gram·a·ry (gram′ər·ē) *n.* **1** *Archaic* Occult lore; magic. **2** *Obs.* Grammar; erudition. Also **gram′a·rye, gram′ma·rye.** [< OF *gramaire.* See GRAMMAR.]

gram-at·om (gram′at′əm) *n. Chem.* That quantity of an element of which the weight in grams is the same as the atomic weight of the element. Also **gram′-a·tom′ic weight** (-ə·tom′ik).**—gram′-a·tom′ic** *adj.*

gram-e·quiv·a·lent (gram′i·kwiv′ə·lənt) *n.* The weight in grams of a substance which displaces or otherwise reacts with 1.008 gram of hydrogen or combines with 8 grams of oxygen. **—gram-equivalent** *adj.*

gra·mer·cy (grə·mûr′sē) *interj. Archaic* Many thanks; great thanks. [< OF *grand merci* great thanks]

gram·i·cid·in (gram′ə·sīd′n, grə·mis′ə·din) *n. Biochem.* A crystalline bacteriostatic and bactericidal substance isolated from an aerobic spore-forming soil bacterium *(Bacillus brevis).* It is a constituent of tyrothricin and has a powerful selective effect against Gram-positive micro-organisms. [< GRAM(-POSITIVE) + -(I)CIDE + -IN]

Gra·min·e·ae (grə·min′i·ē), **Gram·i·na·ce·ae** (gram′i·nā′si·ē) Former name of POACEAE. See POACEOUS. [< L *gramen, -inis* grass]

gra·min·e·ous (grə·min′ē·əs) *adj.* Of, pertaining to, or like grasses; poaceous.

gram·i·niv·or·ous (gram′i·niv′ər·əs) *adj.* Grass-eating.

gram·mar (gram′ər) *n.* **1** The systematic analysis of the classes and structure of words (morphology) and of their arrangements and interrelationships in larger constructions (syntax). **2** Formerly, the study of all aspects of language, as phonology, orthography, syntax, etymology, semantics, and prosody. **3** A system of morphological and syntactical rules and principles assumed for a given language. **4** A treatise or book dealing with such rules. **5** Speech or writing considered with regard to current standard of correctness: He employs poor *grammar.* **6** The elements of any science or art, or a book or treatise dealing with them. [< OF *gramaire* < L *grammatica* < Gk. *grammatikē (technē)* literary (art) < *grammata* literature, orig. plural of *gramma* letter < *graphein* write. Related to GLAMOUR.]

gram·mar·i·an (grə·mâr′ē·ən) *n.* **1** One skilled in grammar. **2** A writer or compiler of grammars. **3** Formerly, a learned humanist. **4** A writer on the principles of an art or science.

gram·mat·i·cal (grə·mat′i·kəl) *adj.* **1** Conforming to the principles of grammar. **2** Of or pertaining to grammar. Also **gram·mat′ic.— gram·mat′i·cal·ly** *adv.* **—gram·mat′i·cal·ness** *n.*

grammatical gender See under GENDER.

gramme (gram) See GRAM[1].

Gramme (gråm), **Zénobe Théophile,** 1826–1901, Belgian electrical scientist.

gram-mol·e·cule (gram′mol′ə·kyōōl) *n. Chem.* That quantity of a substance containing a weight in grams numerically equal to its molecular weight: also called *mol, mole.* Also **gram-mo·lec·u·lar weight** (gram′mə·lek′yə·lər).**— gram′-mo·lec′u·lar** *adj.*

Gram-neg·a·tive (gram′neg′ə·tiv) *adj.* See GRAM'S METHOD.

Gra·mont (grå·môṅ′), **Philibert,** 1621–1707, Comte de Gramont, French courtier, adventurer, and soldier.

Gram·o·phone (gram′ə·fōn) *n.* A type of phonograph; a trade name.

Gram·pi·ans (gram′pē·ənz) A mountain chain in Scotland dividing the Highlands from the Lowlands; highest peak, Ben Nevis, 4,406 feet. Also **Grampian Hills, Grampian Mountains.**

Gram-pos·i·tive (gram′poz′ə·tiv) *adj.* See GRAM'S METHOD.

gram·pus (gram′pəs) *n. pl.* **·pus·es** **1** A large dolphinlike cetacean (genus *Grampus*) found in North Atlantic and North Pacific waters. **2** The killer whale (genus *Orcinus*). [Alter. of obs. *grapeys* < OF *grapois, graspeis* < Med. L *crassus piscis* fat fish]

GRAMPUS
(Killer whale: from 20 to 30 feet in length)

Gram's method A method for the differentiation and classification of bacteria which depends upon the reaction to treatment, first with aniline gentian violet, then with an iodine solution, followed by immersion in alcohol. Those bacteria which are decolorized by the alcohol are *Gram-negative,* and those which retain the purple dye are *Gram-positive.* [after Hans C. J. *Gram*]

gran (gran) *adj. Scot.* Grand.

Gra·na·da (grə·nä′də, *Sp.* grä·nä′thä) **1** A province of southern Spain; 4,438 square miles. **2** Its capital; site of the Alhambra and former capital of a Moorish kingdom.

gran·a·dil·la (gran′ə·dil′ə) *n.* **1** The edible fruit of various species of passionflower *(Passiflora)* of tropical America, especially the giant granadilla *(P. quadrangularis),* oblong, with a soft pulp of a sweet acid flavor. **2** Any plant yielding this fruit. [< Sp., dim. of *granada* a pomegranate]

gran·a·dil·lo (gran′ə·dil′ō) *n.* **1** Any of a large number of tropical American trees, especially a West Indian tree *(Brya ebenus)* yielding a hard, durable wood used in making flutes, clarinets, recorders, etc. **2** The fine-grained rosewood or cocobolo *(Dalbergia retusa),* valued for furniture and cabinetwork. **3** The wood of such trees, especially that used in making musical instruments. Also called *grenadilla, grenadillo.* [< Sp.]

gran·a·ry (grā′nər·ē, gran′ər-) *n. pl.* **·ries** **1** A storehouse for grain. **2** A country or region where grain grows in abundance. [< L *granarium* < *granum* grain]

Gran Ca·na·ria (gräng kä·nä′ryä) One of the Canary Islands; 592 square miles; capital, Las Palmas. Also **Grand Ca·nar·y** (grand′ kə·nâr′ē).

Gran Cha·co (grän chä′kō) An extensive lowland plain of central South America, divided among Paraguay, Bolivia, and Argentina: also **El Chaco.**

grand (grand) *adj.* **1** Of imposing character or aspect; magnificent in proportion, extent, or belongings: *grand* scenery. **2** Characterized by striking excellence or impressive dignity; inspiring: a *grand* oration. **3** Preeminent by reason of great ability or high character; noble; worthy of exalted respect: the *grand* old man. **4** Preeminent in rank or order; also, of prime importance; principal: a *grand* climax. **5** Covering the whole field, or including all details; comprehensive; complete: the *grand* total. **6** *Music* Containing all the parts or movements that belong to a given style of composition. **7** Being one degree of relationship more distant than that ordinarily indicated by the word qualified: used in composition: *grandfather, granduncle, granddaughter, grandniece.* **8** Main; leading: the *grand* hall. —*n. U.S. Slang* One thousand dollars. [< OF < L *grandis*] **—grand′ly** *adv.* **—grand′ness** *n.*

Synonyms (adj.): august, dignified, elevated, exalted, great, illustrious, imposing, impressive, lofty, magnificent, majestic, stately, sublime. Aside from material dimensions,

great is said of that which is more than ordinarily powerful and influential, *grand* of that which is worthily so; a *great* victory may be simply an overwhelming triumph of might over right. We can speak of a *great* bad man, but not of a *grand* bad man; of a *great*, but not of a *grand*, tyrant. Compare AWFUL, IMPERIAL, LARGE, SUBLIME.

gran·dam (gran′dam, -dəm) *n. Archaic* A grandmother; an old woman. Also **gran′dame** (-dām, -dəm). [< AF *graund dame*]

Grand Army of the Republic An organization of Union army and navy veterans of the Civil War in the United States, organized (1866) in memory of the dead and to aid widows and dependents of the dead.

grand·aunt (grand′ant′, -änt′) *n.* The aunt of one's parent; sister of one's grandparent; a great-aunt.

Grand Banks A submarine shoal in the North Atlantic east and south of Newfoundland; 420 by 350 miles; a major fishing ground.

Grand Canal 1 A large canal in Venice, Italy, comprising the city's main thoroughfare. **2** The longest canal of China, comprising the main north-south waterway of north China; 1,000 miles long.

Grand Canyon A gorge formed by the Colorado River in NW Arizona; about 250 miles long; width, from 4 to 18 miles; depth, about one mile; partly in **Grand Canyon National Park;** 1,008 square miles; established 1919.

grand·child (grand′chīld′) *n. pl.* **·chil·dren** The child of one's son or daughter.

grand climacteric See under CLIMACTERIC.

Grand Cou·lee (kōō′lē) A dry canyon cut by the Columbia River in eastern Washington during the glacial epoch: site of **Grand Coulee Dam,** 550 feet high, 4,300 feet long, forming Franklin D. Roosevelt Lake.

grand·dad (gran′dad′) *n. Colloq.* Grandfather: a childish or familiar term. Also **grand′dad′dy.**

grand·daugh·ter (gran′dô′tər, grand′-) *n.* The daughter of one's child.

grand duchess 1 The wife or widow of a grand duke. **2** A woman holding sovereign rights over a grand duchy. **3** Formerly, in Russia, a daughter of a czar, or a daughter of any of his descendants in the male line.

grand duchy The domain of a grand duke or grand duchess.

grand duke 1 A sovereign who ranks just below a king. **2** In Russia, formerly, a ruler of a principality; later, any brother, son, uncle, or nephew of a czar.

gran·dee (gran·dē′) *n.* A Spanish or Portuguese nobleman of the highest rank. [< Sp. *grande* great]

grande pas·sion (gränd′ pä·syôn′) *French* Supreme love; great passion.

Grande-Terre (grän·târ′) See GUADELOUPE.

grande toi·lette (gränd′ twȧ·let′) *French* Full dress.

gran·deur (gran′jər, -jōōr) *n.* The quality of being grand; magnificence; sublimity. [< F < *grand* great]

Grand Falls A waterfall on the upper Hamilton River in Labrador; 245 feet high; 200 feet wide.

grand·fa·ther (grand′fä′thər) *n.* The father of one's father or mother. Also **grand′pa′** (-pä′), **grand′pa·pa′** (-pə·pä′). **—grand′fa′ther·ly** *adj.*

Grand Forks A city on the Red River in North Dakota.

gran·dil·o·quence (gran·dil′ə·kwəns) *n.* **1** The quality of being grandiloquent. **2** Lofty or bombastic speech.

gran·dil·o·quent (gran·dil′ə·kwənt) *adj.* Speaking in or characterized by a pompous or bombastic style. Also **gran·dil′o·quous** (-kwəs). [< L *grandiloquus* < *grandis* great + *loqui* speak; infl. in form by ELOQUENT] **—gran·dil′o·quent·ly** *adv.*

gran·di·ose (gran′dē·ōs) *adj.* **1** Having an imposing style; impressive; grand. **2** Affecting grandeur; pompous; bombastic. [< F < Ital. *grandioso* < L *grandis* great] **—gran′di·ose·ly** *adv.* **—gran·di·os·i·ty** (gran′dē·os′ə·tē) *n.*

gran·di·o·so (gran′dē·ō′sō) *adj. & adv. Music* In a grand or imposing manner. [< Ital.]

grand jury See under JURY.

Grand Lac (grän läk) The French name for TONLE SAP.

Grand Lama The Dalai Lama.

grand larceny See under LARCENY.

grand mal (grän mäl′) *Pathol.* An epileptic seizure characterized by severe convulsions followed by coma, often preceded by warning symptoms: distinguished from *petit mal.* [< F, lit. great sickness]

Grand Ma·nan (mə·nan′) An island in Bay of Fundy, SW New Brunswick, Canada; 57 square miles.

grand mer·ci (grän mer·sē′) *French* Many thanks.

grand monde (grän mônd′) *French* Fashionable society: literally, the great world.

grand·moth·er (grand′muth′ər) *n.* The mother of one's father or mother. Also **grand′ma′** (-mä′), **grand′ma·ma′** (-mə·mä′). **—grand′moth′er·ly** *adj.*

grand·neph·ew (grand′nef′yōō, -nev′-, gran′-) *n.* A son of one's nephew or niece; grandson of one's brother or sister.

grand·niece (grand′nēs′, gran′-) *n.* A daughter of one's nephew or niece; granddaughter of one's brother or sister.

Grand Old Party In U.S. politics, the Republican party.

grand opera See under OPERA.

grand·par·ent (grand′pâr′ənt, gran′-) *n.* The parent of one's parent.

grand piano See under PIANO.

grand prix (grän prē′) *French* Grand prize.

Grand Rapids A city in western Michigan.

gran·drelle (gran·drel′) *n.* **1** Two-ply yarn of contrasting colors. **2** A varicolored fabric made of such yarn.

Grand River 1 The former name of a source stream of the Colorado River. **2** A river in southern Iowa and NW Missouri, flowing 215 miles SE to the Missouri. **3** A river in SW Michigan, flowing NW 260 miles to Lake Michigan. **4** A river in NW South Dakota, flowing SE 209 miles to the Missouri. **5** A river in southern Ontario, flowing south 165 miles to Lake Erie.

grand·sire (grand′sīr′) *n.* **1** A grandfather; any male ancestor preceding a father. **2** Any venerable man. Also **grand′sir** (-sûr, gran′-).

grand·son (grand′sun′, gran′-) *n.* The son of one's son or daughter.

grand·stand (grand′stand′, gran′-) *n.* The principal stand on a racecourse; hence, a similar erection for spectators at any public spectacle. —*v.i. U.S. Colloq.* To show off in an attempt to win applause.

grandstand play Anything done to show off, or to win applause.

Grand Teton National Park A glaciated mountainous region of NW Wyoming including part of the Teton Range; 465 square miles; established 1929.

grand tour See under TOUR.

grand·un·cle (grand′ung′kəl) *n.* The uncle of one's father or mother; brother of one's grandparent.

grange (grānj) *n.* **1** *Brit.* A farm, with its dwelling house and appurtenances; specifically, the residence of a gentleman farmer. **2** *Obs.* A granary. **3** Formerly, a farm establishment belonging to a feudal manor or a monastery: the grain paid in as rent or tithes was stored in its granaries. [< AF *graunge,* OF *grange* < Med. L *granea* < L *granum* grain]

Grange (grānj) *n.* **1** The order of Patrons of Husbandry, a nation-wide association of U.S. farmers, founded in 1867 for the furtherance of agricultural interests. **2** One of the subordinate lodges of the Patrons of Husbandry.

grang·er (grān′jər) *n.* **1** A member of a Grange. **2** A countryman. **—grang′er·ism** *n.*

grang·er·ize (grān′jər·īz) *v.t.* **·ized, ·iz·ing 1** To illustrate (a book) with prints, engravings, etc., taken from other books. **2** To mutilate (a book) by cutting out the illustrations. [after Rev. James *Granger,* 1723–76, whose *Biographical History of England* (1769) was so illustrated] **—grang′er·ism** *n.* **—grang′er·i·za′tion** *n.* **—grang′er·iz′er** *n.*

grani- *combining form* Grain: *graniform.* [< L *granum* grain]

Gra·ni·cus (grə·nī′kəs) A river in NW Turkey, flowing 45 miles NE to the Sea of Marmara; scene of Alexander the Great's victory over the Persians in 334 B.C. *Turkish* **Ko·ca·baş** (kô·jä·bäsh′).

gra·nif·er·ous (grə·nif′ər·əs) *adj.* Bearing grain.

gran·i·form (gran′ə·fôrm) *adj.* Formed like a grain or a granule.

gran·ite (gran′it) *n.* **1** A hard, coarse-grained, igneous rock composed principally of quartz, feldspar, and mica, of great strength and taking a high polish. **2** Great hardness or rigidity. [< Ital. *granito,* orig. pp. of *granire* make seeds < *grano* a seed < L *granum*] **—gra·nit·ic** (grə·nit′ik) or **·i·cal** *adj.*

granite paper A wove paper containing very short silk threads of different colors.

Granite State Nickname of NEW HAMPSHIRE.

gran·ite·ware (gran′it·wâr′) *n.* **1** A variety of ironware coated with hard, granite-colored enamel. **2** A fine, hard pottery resembling ironstone china.

gran·it·ite (gran′it·īt) *n.* A variety of granite containing biotite.

gran·it·oid (gran′it·oid) *adj.* Designating any igneous rock of granitelike texture.

gra·niv·o·rous (grə·niv′ər·əs) *adj.* Living on grain or seeds. **—gran·i·vore** (gran′ə·vôr, -vōr) *n.*

gran·ny (gran′ē) *n. pl.* **·nies** *Colloq.* **1** A grandmother. **2** An old woman. **3** *U.S.* In the South, a nurse. **4** A finical, fussy person. **5** A granny knot. Also **gran′nie.**

granny knot *Naut.* An imperfect sailor's knot, differing from a reef knot in having the second tie crosswise. See illustration under KNOT. Also **granny's knot, granny's bend.**

grano- *combining form* Granitic: *granolith.* [< L *granum* a grain]

gra·no·la (grə·nō′lə) *n.* A mixture of dry cereals, nuts, and raisins, chopped fine and marketed as a health food.

gran·o·lith (gran′ə·lith) *n.* Pulverized granite cement used as artificial stone for paving. **—gran·o·lith·ic** (gran′ə·lith′ik) *adj.*

gran·o·phyre (gran′ə·fīr) *n.* A granite porphyry. [< GRANO- + (POR)PHYRY] **—gran·o·phy·ric** (gran′ə·fī′rik) *adj.*

grant (grant, gränt) *v.t.* **1** To give or accord, as permission, a request, etc. **2** To confer or bestow, as a privilege, charter, favor, etc. **3** To admit as true, especially something not proved, as for the sake of argument; concede. **4** To transfer (property), especially by deed. See synonyms under ACKNOWLEDGE, ALLOT, ALLOW, APPORTION, CONFESS, GIVE. —*n.* **1** The act of granting; a bestowing or conferring. **2** The thing granted; specifically, a piece of land granted to a person, state, etc., by the government. **3** An admission, concession. **4** One of certain tracts of land in New Hampshire, Maine, and Vermont, once belonging to Indian tribes, but allocated to settlers during the 18th century, and the subject of territorial controversy in colonial days. **5** A transfer of real property by deed. See synonyms under GIFT, SUBSIDY. [< AF *graunter, granter,* ult. < L *credens, -entis,* ppr. of *credere* believe] **—grant′a·ble** *adj.* **—grant′er** *n.*

Grant (grant), **Ulysses Simpson,** 1822-85, U.S. general in the Civil War; 18th president of the United States 1869-77.

Gran·ta (gran′tə) See CAM.

grant·ee (gran·tē′, grän-) *n. Law* The person to whom property is transferred by deed, or to whom rights are granted by patent or charter.

grant-in-aid (grant′in·ād′, gränt′-) *n.* A grant made by a central to a local government to assist in some public undertaking.

gran·tor (gran′tər, gran·tôr′, grän-) *n. Law* The person by whom a grant is made; maker of a deed.

gran·u·lar (gran′yə·lər) *adj.* Composed of, like, or containing grains or granules. Also **gran′u·lose** (-lōs), **gran′u·lous** (-ləs).

gran·u·lar·i·ty (gran′yə·lar′ə·tē) *n.* **1** The state or condition of being granular. **2** A coarseness in the silver graining of a motion-picture film.

gran·u·late (gran′yə·lāt) *v.t. & v.i.* **·lat·ed, ·lat·ing 1** To make or become granular; form into grains. **2** To become or cause to become rough on the surface by the formation of granules. **—gran′u·lat′ed** *adj.* **—gran′u·la′tor, gran′u·lat′er** *n.*

gran·u·la·tion (gran′yə·lā′shən) *n.* **1** The forming into grains or granules. **2** A granulated surface, or one of the elevations in such surface. **3** *Physiol.* **a** The process of forming new tissue in the healing of wounds. **b** The minute, flesh-colored, breadlike projections so formed. **4** *Astron.* An evanescent mottled appearance observed in the photosphere of the sun, attributed to gaseous convection currents in the outer layers. **—gran′u·la′tive** *adj.*

gran·ule (gran′yōōl) *n.* **1** A small grain; particle; corpuscle. **2** *Biol.* One of the small protoplasmic bodies suspended in the cytoplasm of the cell. [< LL *granulum,* dim. of L *granum* grain]

gran·u·lite (gran′yə·līt) *n.* A finely granulated, crystalline, foliated rock composed mainly of quartz and feldspar, but generally carrying garnet. —**gran·u·lit·ic** (gran′yə·lit′ik) *adj.*

gran·u·lo·cyte (gran′yə·lə·sīt) *n.* Any of several types of leukocyte in which the cytoplasm contains granules. —**gran·u·lo·cytic** (gran′yə·lə·sit′ik) *adj.*

gran·u·lo·ma (gran′yə·lō′mə) *n. Pathol.* A tumor composed of granulation tissue.

gran·u·lose (gran′yə·lōs) *n.* That portion of starch granules capable of being changed into sugar by certain ferments: distinguished from *cellulose.*

grape (grāp) *n.* **1** The smooth-skinned, edible, juicy, berrylike fruit of various species of the grapevine, from which most wines are made. **2** Any grapevine yielding this fruit. **3** Figuratively, wine. **4** Grapeshot. **5** A dark-blue color with a slight reddish tint. **6** *pl.* A cluster of nodular excrescences on a horse's fetlock, caused by a parasitic fungus. [< OF, bunch of grapes < *graper* gather grapes < *grape* a hook < Gmc.]

grape-eat·er (grāp′ē′tər) *n.* An Australian fruit-eating bird (*Zosterops lateralis*).

grape·fruit (grāp′frōōt′) *n.* A large, round, pale-yellow citrus fruit of tropical regions (*Citrus paradisi* and varieties), cultivated also in the United States.

grape hyacinth A plant (genus *Muscari*) of the lily family, differing from the common hyacinth in having its small blue flowers ovoid or globular and minutely six-toothed.

grape juice The unfermented juice of the grape: used as a beverage.

grape rot A wide-spread and malignant disease of grapes, caused by a parasitic fungus (*Plasmopara viticola*) and characterized by the formation of a milky coating on the leaves, sometimes having the appearance of oil spots: also called *downy mildew.* Also **grape blight.**

grap·er·y (grā′pər·ē) *n. pl.* **·er·ies** A building for the growing of grapes.

grape·shot (grāp′shot′) *n.* A cluster of cast-iron shot, to be discharged from a cannon.

grape·stone (grāp′stōn′) *n.* A seed of the grape.

grape sugar Dextrose: occurring in ripe grapes.

grape·vine (grāp′vīn′) *n.* **1** Any of a genus (*Vitis*) of woody, climbing vines characterized by profuse clusters of berrylike fruit, especially the American species *V. labrusca* and the Old World *V. vinifera.* **2** *U.S. Colloq.* **a** Grapevine telegraph. **b** An unverified report or rumor. **3** *U.S.* Grapevine twist.

grapevine telegraph *U.S.* Any hidden means by which information, rumor, etc., not available through regular channels becomes rapidly widespread.

grapevine twist *U.S.* A complicated figure in dancing used by Negroes of the South: also *grapevine.*

graph (graf, gräf) *n.* **1** A diagram indicating any sort of relationship between two or more things by means of a system of dots, curves, bars, or lines. **2** *Math.* The locus of a point moving in relation to coordinates so that all of its values satisfy a function of an equation. —*v.t.* To trace or represent in the form of a graph. [Short for *graphic formula*]

-graph *combining form* **1** One who or that which writes or records: *phonograph.* **2** A writing or record: *monograph.* [< F *-graphe* < L *-graphus* < Gk. *-graphos* < *graphein* write]

Graph·al·loy (graf′ə·loi′) *n.* A composition consisting of graphite into which bronze or Babbitt metal has been forced by hydraulic pressure: a trade name.

-grapher *combining form* A writer or one engaged in a graphic or kindred art: *bibliographer, photographer.*

graph·ic (graf′ik) *adj.* **1** Of or pertaining to the art of writing, or of indicating by letters or written signs. **2** Describing with pictorial effect; portraying with vividness. **3** Written, engraved, or recorded by means of letters or inscriptions. **4** Having the appearance of written or printed signs: *graphic granite.* **5** *Stat.* Indicating or calculating by lines, areas, diagrams, etc. **6** *Math.*

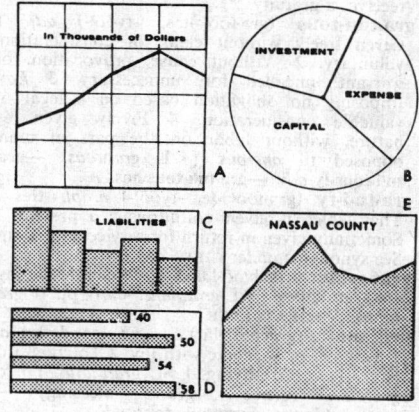

TYPES OF GRAPHS
A. Line graph. *B.* Pie or sector graph.
C. D. Bar graphs. *E.* Area graph.

Of or pertaining to the use of plotted curves to represent or solve an equation **7** *Geol.* Denoting a rock texture produced by a blending of crystalline constituents in such a way as to give a graphic appearance to a freshly cut section. Also **graph′i·cal.** [< L *graphicus* < Gk. *graphikos* of writing < *graphē* writing] —**graph′i·cal·ly, graph′ic·ly** *adv.*

Synonyms: descriptive, forcible, illustrative, pictorial, picturesque, vivid. See VIVID. *Antonyms:* dreary, dull, flat, monotonous, prosy, stupid, uninteresting.

graphic accent A written or printed sign of emphasis, as in many Spanish words.

graphic arts **1** Those arts involving the use of lines or strokes on a flat surface, as painting, drawing, engraving, etc. **2** Those arts which involve impressions printed on flat surfaces, as printing, lithography, etching, wood-engraving, etc.

graphic gold, graphic tellurium See SYLVANITE.

graph·ics (graf′iks) *n. pl.* The science or art of drawing, particularly of mechanical drawing, or of drawing to mathematical rules as in engineering.

graph·ite (graf′īt) *n.* A soft, black, chemically inert, hexagonal variety of carbon with a metallic luster and oily feel: used as a lubricant and in the making of lead pencils, electrodes, crucibles, etc.: also called *plumbago, black-lead.* [< G *graphit* < Gk. *graphein* write + *-it* -ITE[1]] —**gra·phit·ic** (grə·fit′ik) *adj.*

graph·i·tize (graf′ə·tīz) *v.t.* **·tized, ·tiz·ing** **1** To coat with graphite. **2** To make into graphite by a heating process. —**graph′i·ti·za′tion** (-tə·zā′shən, -tī·zā′-) *n.*

grapho- *combining form* Of or pertaining to writing: *graphology.* Also, before vowels, **graph-.** [< Gk. *graphē* writing < *graphein* write]

graph·ol·o·gy (graf·ol′ə·jē) *n.* **1** The scientific study and analysis of handwriting, especially with reference to forgeries and questioned documents. **2** The art of interpreting character and personality from the diagnostic peculiarities of handwriting. **3** The study of handwriting as an aid in the diagnosis of diseases of the brain and nervous system. —**graph·o·log·i·cal** (graf′ə·loj′i·kəl) *adj.* —**graph·ol′o·gist** *n.*

graph·o·ma·ni·a (graf′ə·mā′nē·ə, -mān′yə) *n.* A compulsive desire to write.

graph·o·mo·tor (graf′ə·mō′tər) *adj. Med.* Pertaining to or having influence upon the movements required in writing.

Graph·o·phone (graf′ə·fōn) *n.* A type of phonograph: a trade name.

graph·o·spasm (graf′ə·spaz′əm) *n.* Writer's cramp.

graph·o·type (graf′ə·tīp) *n.* **1** A process for producing engravings quickly by drawing with siliceous ink upon a plate faced with chalk afterward brushed away. **2** A plate so made.

graph paper Paper variously ruled to facilitate the drawing of a graph: usually quadrille paper, divided into equal squares.

-graphy *combining form* A written description of: *geography, biography.* [< Gk. *-graphia* < *graphein* write]

grap·lin (grap′lin) *n.* A grapnel. Also **grap′line** (-lin). [Alter. of GRAPNEL]

grap·nel (grap′nəl) *n.* **1** A device for grappling, consisting of several hooks or clamps on one stem, designed to catch hold of any object across which it is thrown or drawn; a grapple. Also *grappling iron.* **2** *Naut.* A boat's anchor with many flukes. See illustration under ANCHOR. [ME *grapenel,* dim. of OF *grapin* a hook]

grap·ple (grap′əl) *v.* **grap·pled, grap·pling** *v.t.* **1** To take hold of; grasp firmly. —*v.i.* **2** To use a grapnel. **3** To seize or come to grips with another, as in wrestling. **4** To deal or contend: with *with:* to *grapple* with a problem. See synonyms under CONTEND, GRASP. [< *n.*] —*n.* **1** A close hold, as in wrestling. **2** A grapnel. [< OF *grappil* grapnel] —**grap′pler** *n.*

grap·pling (grap′ling) *n.* **1** The act of seizing or grasping, or that by which anything is seized and held. **2** A grapnel.

grappling iron A grapnel. Also **grappling hook.**

grap·y (grā′pē) *adj.* Pertaining to, composed of, or resembling grapes.

Gras·mere (gras′mir, gräs′-) A small lake in Westmorland, England.

grasp (grasp, gräsp) *v.t.* **1** To lay hold of with or as with the hand; grip. **2** To seize greedily or eagerly; snatch. **3** To take hold of with the mind; understand. —*v.i.* **4** To make grasping motions. —**to grasp at 1** To try to seize. **2** To clutch at eagerly or desperately: to *grasp at* straws. —*n.* **1** The act of seizing or attempting to lay hold of something, as with the hand. **2** The ability to seize and hold; possession taken and kept by force. **3** Power of comprehension, or the exercise of this power. [ME *graspen,* metathetic var. of *grapsen* < LG] —**grasp′er** *n.*

Synonyms (verb): catch, clasp, clutch, comprehend, grab, grapple, grip, gripe, hold, seize, snatch, understand. See CATCH, EMBRACE[1]. *Antonyms:* abandon, fail, loose, lose, miss, release, relinquish.

grasp·ing (gras′ping, gräs′-) *adj.* Avaricious. See synonyms under GREEDY. —**grasp′ing·ly** *adv.* —**grasp′ing·ness** *n.*

grass (gras, gräs) *n.* **1** The green plants on which cattle feed. **2** Any of a large natural family of plants (*Poaceae*) with mostly rounded and hollow jointed stems, sheathing leaves, flowers borne on spikelets, and the fruit a seedlike grain, including all the common cereals, canes, bamboos, and a great variety of pasture plants. **3** *pl.* Spires or sprays of grass. **4** Grassland used for pasture; also, ground covered with grass; lawn. **5** Any of numerous plants with foliage suggesting or resembling the true grasses, as the sedges, the rushes, etc. **6** *Slang* Marihuana. —*v.t.* **1** To cover with grass or turf. **2** To feed with grass; pasture. **3** To spread on grass for bleaching by the sun. —*v.i.* **4** To graze on grass. **5** To produce grass; become covered with grass. [OE *græs.* Akin to GREEN, GROW.]

Grasse (gräs), **François Joseph Paul,** 1722–1788, Comte de Grasse, French admiral.

grass finch 1 The vesper sparrow. **2** An Australian weaverbird.

grass·hop·per (gras′hop′ər, gräs′-) *n.* Any of several orthopterous insects, including the locust and katydid (families *Locustidae* and *Tettigonidae*), having powerful hind legs adapted for leaping. The males of most species make a chirping sound with their wings or by friction of the hind legs against parts of the wings or wing covers. For illustration, see under INSECT (injurious).

grass·land (gras′land′, gräs′-) *n.* **1** Land reserved for pasturage or mowing. **2** Land in which grasses predominate, as the American prairies.

grass-of-Par·nas·sus (gräs′əv·pär·nas′əs, gräs′) *n.* Any of a genus (*Parnassia*) of smooth perennial herbs of the saxifrage family, bearing handsome white flowers.

grass-plot (gras′plot′, gräs′-) *n.* A plot of

ground covered with grass, sometimes with groups of shrubs, flowers, etc. Also *Obs.* **grass′plat′** (-plat).

grass·quit (gras′kwit, gräs′-) *n.* A small fringilline bird *(Tiaris bicolor* and *T. canora)* of Cuba and the Bahamas.

grass·roots (gras′rōōts′, -rōōts′, gräs′-) *n.* The rural sections of the country; the hinterland. —*adj.* Of or pertaining to such sections: a *grass-roots* region.

grass snipe The pectoral sandpiper.

grass tree 1 Any of various Australian plants of the lily family (genus *Xanthorrhoea)* having a thick, woody trunk crowned with long grasslike leaves and yielding a fragrant resin. **2** Any of several Australasian plants with grasslike foliage, as the ti.

grass widow A woman separated from her husband by causes other than death.

grass·y (gras′ē, gräs′ē) *adj.* **grass·i·er, grass·i·est** Abounding in, covered with, consisting of, or resembling grass. **—grass′i·ly** *adv.* **—grass′i·ness** *n.*

grat (grat) *Scot.* Past participle of GREET[2].

grate[1] (grāt) *v.* **grat·ed, grat·ing,** *v.t.* **1** To reduce to small particles by rubbing with a rough surface or through a grate. **2** To rub or grind so as to produce a harsh, scraping sound. **3** To annoy; irritate: to *grate* the nerves. **4** *Archaic* To wear or scrape away. —*v.i.* **5** To sound harshly, from or as from scraping or grinding; creak. **6** To have an irritating effect: with *on* or *upon.* —*n.* A harsh, grinding noise. ◆ Homophone: *great.* [< OF *grater* < Gmc.]

grate[2] (grāt) *n.* **1** A framework of bars, as to close an opening, or to hold fuel in burning. **2** A perforated metallic plate through which the ores pass after being crushed under stamps. **3** A fireplace. **4** *Obs.* A cage furnished with grates; a place of confinement. —*v.t.* **grat·ed, grat·ing** To fit with a grate or grates. ◆ Homophone: *great.* [< Med. L *grata* < Ital. < L *cratis* a lattice]

grate·ful (grāt′fəl) *adj.* **1** Having a due sense of benefits received; thankful. **2** Affording gratification; pleasurable; agreeable. **3** Expressing or denoting thankfulness; indicative of gratitude. [< obs. *grate* pleasing (< L *gratus*) + -FUL] **—grate′ful·ly** *adv.* **—grate′ful·ness** *n.*

Synonyms: obliged, thankful. See AGREEABLE, DELIGHTFUL.

grat·er (grā′tər) *n.* **1** Someone or something that grates. **2** A kitchen utensil used to grate vegetables, cheese, etc.

Gra·ti·an (grā′shē·ən, -shən), 359–83, Roman emperor 375–83: real name *Flavius Gratianus.*

grat·i·fi·ca·tion (grat′ə·fə·kā′shən) *n.* **1** The act of gratifying; a satisfying or pleasing. **2** The state of being gratified; specifically, the satisfaction of sexual craving. **3** *Obs.* That which gratifies; a reward; recompense; gratuity. See synonyms under HAPPINESS, SATISFACTION.

grat·i·fy (grat′ə·fī) *v.t.* **·fied, ·fy·ing 1** To give pleasure or satisfaction to. **2** To satisfy or indulge, as a desire or need. **3** *Obs.* To reward. See synonyms under ENTERTAIN, INDULGE, REJOICE. [< MF *gratifier* < L *gratificari* < *gratus* pleasing + *facere* make] **—grat′i·fi′er** *n.* **—grat′i·fy′ing·ly** *adv.*

gra·tin (grät′n, grat′n; *Fr.* grȧ·tan′) See AU GRATIN.

grat·i·nate (grat′ə·nāt) *v.t.* **·nat·ed, ·nat·ing** To prepare with a crust, as of grated bread, and cook until browned and crisp. [< F *gratiner* form a crust]

grat·ing[1] (grā′ting) *n.* **1** A grate. **2** *Physics* An optical device for the dispersion of light waves and the production of spectra, usually consisting of a series of very fine parallel grooves cut in the surface of polished metal or glass, sometimes of a suitably mounted crystal: also called **diffraction grating.**

grat·ing[2] (grā′ting) *adj.* Harsh in sound; rasping; irritating. —*n.* The act or sound of rasping. **—grat′ing·ly** *adv.*

gra·tis (grā′tis, grat′is) *adv.* Without recompense; freely. —*adj.* Given free of charge. [< L, var. of *gratiis* out of kindness, orig. ablative of *gratia* favor]

grat·i·tude (grat′ə·tōōd, -tyōōd) *n.* The state of being grateful; thankfulness. [< F < LL *gratitudo* < *gratus* pleasing]

Grat·tan (grat′ən), **Henry,** 1746–1820, Irish statesman and orator.

gra·tu·i·tant (grə·tōō′ə·tənt, -tyōō′-) *n.* One who receives a gratuity.

gra·tu·i·tous (grə·tōō′ə·təs, -tyōō′-) *adj.* **1** Given freely without claim or consideration; voluntary. **2** Without cause, provocation, or warrant; uncalled for; unnecessary. **3** *Law* Imposing no obligation based on a legal or valuable consideration. **4** Freely given by nature, without labor on the part of man: opposed to *onerous.* [< L *gratuitus*] **—gra·tu′i·tous·ly** *adv.* **—gra·tu′i·tous·ness** *n.*

gra·tu·i·ty (grə·tōō′ə·tē, -tyōō′-) *n. pl.* **·ties 1** That which is given gratuitously; a present. **2** Something given in return for service, etc.; a tip. See synonyms under GIFT.

grat·u·lant (grach′ōō·lənt) *adj.* Wishing one joy; congratulatory. [< L *gratulans, -antis,* pp. of *gratulari.* See GRATULATE.]

grat·u·late (grach′ōō·lāt) *Obs. v.t.* **·lat·ed, ·lat·ing 1** To greet or welcome with joy. **2** To congratulate. —*adj.* Gratifying. [< L *gratulatus,* pp. of *gratulari* rejoice < *gratus* pleasing] **—grat′u·la′tion** *n.* **—grat′u·la·to′ry** *adj.*

Grau·denz (grou′dents) The German name for GRUDZIADZ.

graul (grôl) See GRILSE.

grau·pel (grou′pəl) *n.* Small, compact pellets of snow: often called *soft hail.* [< G, hailstone]

gra·va·men (grə·vā′men) *n. pl.* **·vam·i·na** (-vam′ə·nə) The essence of a charge or grievance; the burden of a complaint. [< Med. L, grievance < L *gravare* burden < *gravis* heavy]

grave[1] (grāv) *adj.* **1** Of momentous import; solemn; important. **2** Serious, as in mind, manner, or speech; dignified; sedate. **3** Sober in color or fashion. **4** *Phonet.* **a** Having the tonal quality of the grave accent, or marked with it, as the vowel *è.* **b** Unaccented, as a syllable. See synonyms under IMPORTANT, SAD, SEDATE, SERIOUS. —*n.* **1** A mark (`) used in French to indicate the open quality of *e* or a distinction in meaning, as in *ou, où;* in English elocution to indicate a falling inflection or the pronunciation of a final *ed,* as in *preparèd;* in Greek to indicate a lowering of the tone from a higher pitch: also **grave accent.** See ACCENT. **2** *Music* A passage or movement in the slowest tempo. [< F < L *gravis* heavy] **—grave′ly** *adv.* **—grave′ness** *n.*

grave[2] (grāv) *n.* **1** An excavation in the earth for the burial of a dead body; a tomb. **2** Hence, death or ruin. **3** The abode of the dead. [OE *græf.* Related to GRAVE[3].] **—grave′less** *adj.*

grave[3] (grāv) *v.t.* **graved, grav·en, grav·ing 1** To engrave; carve with a chisel. **2** To sculpture. **3** To impress deeply, as on the memory. **4** *Brit. Dial.* To dig. **5** *Archaic* To bury. [OE *grafan* dig. Related to GRAVE[2].]

grave[4] (grāv) *v.t.* **graved, grav·ing** *Naut.* To clean, as a ship's bottom, by scraping or burning off seaweed, etc., and coating with pitch. [< OF, beach]

gra·ve[5] (grä′vā) *adv. Music* Slowly and solemnly. [< Ital.]

grave·clothes (grāv′klōz′, -klōthz′) *n. pl.* The clothes or wrappings in which a dead person is interred.

grave·dig·ger (grāv′dig′ər) *n.* One who digs graves.

grav·el (grav′əl) *n.* **1** A mixture of sand and small, usually rounded, pebbles or stones. **2** *Pathol.* A disease characterized by formation in the kidneys of granular concretions. **3** *Obs.* Sand. —*v.t.* **grav·eled** or **grav·elled, grav·el·ing** or **grav·el·ling 1** To cover or fill with gravel. **2** To bring up short, as in embarrassment or confusion. **3** *U.S. Colloq.* To irritate; annoy. **4** *Obs.* To run (a vessel) aground. [< OF *gravele,* dim. of *grave* beach] **—grav′el·ly, grav′el·y** *adj.*

grav·el-blind (grav′əl·blīnd′) *adj.* Almost blind: intermediate between *sandblind* and *stone-blind.*

gravel pit An excavation from which gravel is taken.

gravel road A road surfaced with gravel.

grav·en (grā′vən) *adj.* Carved or cut.

graven image A carved or graven idol.

Grav·en·stein (grav′ən·stēn, -stīn, grä′vən-) *n.* A large yellowish-red apple. [from *Gravenstein,* resort in southern Denmark]

grav·er (grā′vər) *n.* **1** An engraver's burin; also, a sculptor's chisel. **2** An engraver or a stonecarver.

graves (grāvz) See GREAVES.

Graves (grāvz, *Fr.* gräv) *n.* Wine produced in a district of SW France.

Graves (grāvz), **Robert,** born 1895, English poet, critic, and novelist.

Graves' disease *Pathol.* Exophthalmic goiter. [after Robert J. *Graves,* 1797–1853, Irish physician]

Graves·end (grāvz′end′) A port on the Thames river in NW Kent, England.

grave·stone (grāv′stōn′) *n.* A memorial stone, placed at a grave.

Gra·vet·ti·an (grə·vet′ē·ən) *adj. Anthropol.* Denoting a later extension of the Aurignacian culture period, merging with the Solutrean. Also called *Upper Perigordian.*

grave·yard (grāv′yärd′) *n.* A burial place; a cemetery.

graveyard shift A work shift during the late night, generally from midnight to eight in the morning.

grav·id (grav′id) *adj.* Pregnant. [< L *gravidus* < *gravis* heavy] **—grav′id·ly** *adv.* **—grav′id·ness, gra·vid·i·ty** (grə·vid′ə·tē) *n.*

gra·vim·e·ter (grə·vim′ə·tər) *n.* An instrument for determining specific gravity; a type of hydrometer. [< L *gravis* heavy + -METER]

grav·i·met·ric (grav′ə·met′rik) *adj.* **1** Determined by weight, or of a kind usually so determined. **2** Pertaining to measurement by weight. **—grav′i·met′ri·cal·ly** *adv.*

gra·vim·e·try (grə·vim′ə·trē) *n.* The measurement of weight or specific gravity with the gravimeter.

grav·ing (grā′ving) *n.* **1** The act or operation of incising or engraving. **2** *Naut.* The act of cleaning a ship's bottom by burning, scraping, and coating with pitch.

graving dock A drydock for examining, cleaning, and repairing a ship's bottom.

grav·i·pause (grav′ə·pôz) *n.* The region in space where the gravitational field of one celestial body ends, or is neutralized by that of another. [< GRAVI(TY) + PAUSE]

grav·i·sphere (grav′ə·sfir) *n.* The spherical area within which the gravitational field of a body is dominant. [< GRAVI(TY) + SPHERE]

grav·i·tate (grav′ə·tāt) *v.i.* **·tat·ed, ·tat·ing 1** To tend by or as by force of gravity. **2** To move as though drawn by a powerful force. **3** To sink or fall to the lowest level. [< NL *gravitatus,* pp. of *gravitare* press down < *gravis* heavy] **—grav′i·tat′er** *n.* **—grav′i·ta′tive** *adj.*

grav·i·ta·tion (grav′ə·tā′shən) *n.* **1** *Physics* The force whereby any two bodies attract each other in proportion to the product of their masses and inversely as the square of the distance between them. **2** The act of gravitating or its effect. **—grav′i·ta′tion·al** *adj.* **—grav′i·ta′tion·al·ly** *adv.*

grav·i·ty (grav′ə·tē) *n. pl.* **·ties 1** The accelerating tendency of bodies toward the center of the earth. **2** A similar tendency toward the center of any heavenly body. **3** Weight. **4** Gravitation. **5** The quality of being charged with or involving great interests; importance. **6** Dignified reserve; sedateness. **7** Lowness of pitch. **8** Something of grave import; a serious subject. See synonyms under WEIGHT. —*adj.* Employing gravity; worked by gravity: the *gravity* feed of an oil burner. [< F *gravité* < L *gravitas, -tatis* heaviness < *gravis* heavy]

gravity cell *Electr.* A primary cell in which the two electrolytes are kept separate by differences in specific gravity.

gravity fault *Geol.* A downward-sloping fault in which the upper portion or hanging wall appears to have moved under gravity to a level lower than that of the lower portion or footwall.

gra·vure (grə·vyōōr′) *n.* **1** An engraved copperplate or wooden block used in photogravure. **2** The print made from it. [< F < *graver* engrave]

gra·vy (grā′vē) *n. pl.* **·vies 1** The juice that drips from roasting or baking meat, or a sauce made from it. **2** *U.S. Slang* Any added, easily acquired, or extra payment or income; also, graft; illegally acquired money. **—gravy train** *U.S. Slang* A line of endeavor that is easy and lucrative. [ME *gravey*]

gravy boat A boat-shaped dish in which gravy is served.

gray (grā) *adj.* **1** Of the color of white and black mixed and without brilliancy. **2** Having gray hair; hoary. **3** Hence, old; aged. **4** Wearing a gray habit: a *Gray* Friar. See synonyms under ANCIENT. —*n.* **1** A gray color;

any dull, whitish tint; specifically, an achromatic color; one which may have brilliance but no hue. See COLOR 2 Something gray; specifically, a gray animal. —*v.t. & v.i.* To make or become gray. Also *esp. Brit.* grey. [OE *grǣg*] —**gray′ly** *adv.* —**gray′ness** *n.*

Gray (grā) *n.* A soldier of the Confederate Army in the American Civil War; also, collectively, the Confederate Army itself: the Blue and the *Gray.* Compare BLUE.

Gray (grā), **Asa,** 1810–88, U.S. botanist. —**Elisha,** 1835–1901, U.S. electrician and inventor. —**Thomas,** 1716–71, English poet.

gray·back (grā′bak′) *n.* 1 One of various animals, as the gray whale, the hooded crow (*Corvus cornix*), the American sandpiper, etc. 2 *Colloq.* A member of the Confederate Army during the Civil War. 3 *Colloq.* The body louse. Also spelled *greyback.*

gray·beard (grā′bird′) *n.* An old man, or one with a gray beard.

gray eagle The American bald eagle. See under EAGLE.

gray·fish (grā′fish′) *n. pl.* **·fish** or **·fish·es** The dogfish: also spelled *greyfish.*

gray goods Greige.

gray·ish (grā′ish) *adj.* Somewhat gray: also spelled *greyish.*

gray·lag (grā′lag′) *n. pl.* **·lag** or **·lags** the common wild gray goose (*Anser anser*) of Europe: so called because it migrates late. See GOOSE. Also spelled *greylag.*

gray·ling (grā′ling) *n. pl.* **·ling** or **·lings** 1 A small troutlike fish (genus *Thymallus*), with a richly colored, long, high dorsal fin. 2 A North American butterfly (*Minois alope*), with gray and brown markings (subfamily *Satyrinae*). Also spelled *greyling.*

gray market A trade operation involving the selling of scarce goods at exorbitant prices, a practice considered unethical but not necessarily illegal.

gray matter 1 *Anat.* The grayish substance of the brain, composed largely of ganglionic cell bodies and few fibers. 2 *Colloq.* Brains; intelligence.

gray·out grā′out′ *n.* A temporary loss or blurring of vision caused by oxygen deficiency: noted especially in aviators subjected to high acceleration.

gray plover A large plover of nearly cosmopolitan range (*Squatarola squatarola*), having a plumage which is gray in winter and black during the breeding season.

Grays Peak The highest peak of the Front Range in Colorado; 14,274 feet.

Gray·son (grā′sən), **David** Pseudonym of RAY STANNARD BAKER.

gray squirrel See under SQUIRREL.

gray·wacke (grā′wak, -wak·ə) *n. Geol.* A sedimentary rock composed of rounded or subangular grains of quartz, feldspar, etc., or rock fragments in a siliceous, argillaceous, or calcareous cement: also spelled *greywacke.* [<G *grauwacke* gray wacke]

gray whale A whalebone whale (*Rhachianectes glaucus*) of the northern Pacific coast.

gray wolf A large wolf of northern North America; the timber wolf.

Graz (gräts) The second largest city in Austria, capital of Styria.

graze¹ (grāz) *v.* **grazed, graz·ing** *v.i.* 1 To feed upon growing herbage. —*v.t.* 2 To put (cattle, etc.) to feed on growing herbage. 3 To put cattle, etc., to feed on, as a pasture, grass, etc. 4 To tend (cattle, etc.) at pasture. —*n.* The act of cropping or feeding upon growing grass or the like. [OE *grasian* <*græs* grass] —**graz′er** *n.*

graze² (grāz) *v.* **grazed, graz·ing** *v.t.* 1 To touch or rub against lightly in passing. 2 To scrape or cut slightly in passing: The bullet *grazed* his arm. —*v.i.* 3 To touch lightly in passing. 4 To scrape slightly. —*n.* 1 A light or passing touch; a scrape or abrasion. 2 *Mil.* The explosion of a bomb or shell immediately upon impact with the gound. [? <GRAZE¹] —**graz′er** *n.* —**graz′ing·ly** *adv.*

gra·zier (grā′zhər) *n.* 1 One who is engaged in grazing or pasturing cattle, or in raising them for the market. 2 *Austral.* One who occupies grazing land for sheep farming under a lease or license.

gra·zing (grā′zing) *n.* A pasture.

gra·zio·so (grä·tsyō′sō) *adv. & adj. Music* With grace. [<Ital.]

grease (grēs) *n.* 1 Animal fat, especially when soft. 2 A thick, oily or unctuous substance resembling animal fat, derived from the distillation of petroleum. 3 Wool, after shearing and before cleansing: also **grease wool.** 4 The condition of wool or furs before being cleansed: wool in the *grease.* 5 A scabrous inflammation of a horse's pastern and fetlock, characterized by an odorous, oily secretion, and, in the later stages, formation of fungoid masses: also called *grease-heel.* 6 Fat or fatness in an animal, as a deer: a hunting term. 7 *Slang* A bribe; money used for bribery. —*v.t.* (grēs, grēz) **greased, greas·ing** 1 To lubricate or smear with grease; put grease in or on. 2 *Slang* To influence by gifts or bribes: to *grease* the hand or palm. [<OF *graisse,* ult. <L *crassus* fat]

grease cup A receptacle for lubricating oil or grease. Also **grease box, grease cock.**

grease-heel (grēs′hēl′) See under GREASE.

grease-paint (grēs′pānt′) *n.* A paste, with a grease base, used in theatrical make-up.

greas·er (grē′sər, -zər) *n.* 1 One who or that which greases. 2 *Slang* A Mexican or Spanish-American: a contemptuous term.

grease·wood (grēs′wŏŏd′) *n.* Any one of various stunted and prickly shrubs of the goosefoot family (genus *Sarcobatus*) found on the alkaline plains of the western United States. Also **grease′bush′** (-bŏŏsh′).

greas·y (grē′sē, -zē) *adj.* **greas·i·er, greas·i·est** 1 Smeared or spotted with grease. 2 Containing much grease or fat; unctuous; oily. 3 Resembling grease; smooth. 4 Affected with scabby sores, as a horse's heels. —**greas′i·ly** *adv.* —**greas′i·ness** *n.*

great (grāt) *adj.* 1 Very large; big; immense; vast. 2 Being much more numerous than the average: a *great* army. 3 Extending through a long time; prolonged. 4 Of very considerable degree; extreme: *great* foolishness. 5 Of large or the largest importance; mighty; foremost. 6 Having large mental, moral, or other endowments; eminent; excellent. 7 *Colloq.* Adept; skilled: He's *great* at carpentry. 8 Important; weighty; momentous. 9 Characterized by or showing elevation, as of feeling, act, or aspect; high-minded; magnanimous. 10 *Archaic* Large in or as in pregnancy; teeming; gravid. 11 More remote by a single generation than the relationship indicated by the word qualified: used in combination with a hyphen: *great-uncle, great-grandson.* 12 *Colloq.* Excellent: We had a *great* time. 13 Intimately acquainted: *great* friends. See synonyms under GRAND, LARGE, SERIOUS. —*n.* 1 One who is or those who are powerful, noble, influential, or rich: usually with *the.* 2 *pl.* Great go. 3 The mass, lump, or lot; the whole: to do work by the *great.* ◆Homophone: *grate.* [OE *grēat*] —**great′ness** *n.*

great ape Any of the large anthropoid apes; a chimpanzee, gorilla, or orangutan.

Great Appalachian Valley A longitudinal chain of lowlands of the Appalachian Mountains extending from Canada to Alabama: also *Great Valley.*

Great Artesian Basin An area of about 680,000 square miles in eastern Australia, chiefly in Queensland, providing artesian wells. Also **Great Australian Basin.**

great auk See under AUK.

great-aunt (grāt′ant′, -änt′) *n.* A grandaunt.

Great Australian Bight A bay of the Indian Ocean in the coast of southern Australia.

Great Barrier Reef The world's largest chain of coral reefs, off the eastern coast of Queensland, Australia, extending about 1,260 miles: also *Barrier Reef.*

Great Basin An inland drainage region in the western United States, between the Wasatch and the Sierra Nevada mountains; 200,000 square miles.

Great Bear Ursa Major. See CONSTELLATION.

Great Bear Lake A lake in western Northwest Territories, Canada; 12,000 square miles; drained by the **Great Bear River,** flowing 100 miles west to the Mackenzie River.

Great Britain The principal island of the United Kingdom, comprising England, Scot-

land, and Wales; 88,745 square miles; capital, London.

great calorie See under CALORIE.

Great Channel A passage from the Indian Ocean to the Andaman Sea between Sumatra and the Nicobar Islands.

great circle *Geom.* A circle formed on the surface of a sphere by a plane which passes through the center of the sphere, dividing it into two equal parts.

great-cir·cle course (grāt′sûr′kəl) A course, as of a ship or aircraft, plotted along a great circle of the earth.

great·coat (grāt′kōt′) *n.* A heavy overcoat.

Great Commoner Nickname applied to William Pitt, Henry Clay, Thaddeus Stevens, and William Jennings Bryan.

Great Dane One of a breed of close-haired dogs of large size and great strength.

Great Divide See CONTINENTAL DIVIDE.

Great Dividing Range The mountains and plateaus of Australia forming the watershed of rivers flowing to the Coral and Tasman seas and those flowing to the Gulf of Carpentaria and the Indian Ocean.

great·en (grāt′n) *v.t. & v.i. Archaic* To make or become great or greater.

Greater Antilles See under ANTILLES.

greater glider A flying phalanger (*Schoinobates volans*) of Australia: also called *dusky glider.*

Greater New York See NEW YORK (def. 2).

Greater Sunda Islands See SUNDA ISLANDS.

Greater Walachia See MUNTENIA.

Great Falls A city in west central Montana.

Great Glen of Scotland A depression extending 60 miles across Scotland, dividing the central from the NW Highlands: also *Glen More.*

great go In British universities, the final examination for a degree.

great-grand·child (grāt′grand′chīld′) *n.* A child of a grandchild.

great-grand·daugh·ter (grāt′gran′dô′tər) *n.* A daughter of a grandchild.

great-grand·fa·ther (grāt′grand′fä′thər) *n.* The father of a grandparent.

great-grand·moth·er (grāt′grand′muth′ər) *n.* The mother of a grandparent.

great gray owl See under OWL.

great gross Twelve gross, as a unit.

great-heart·ed (grāt′här′tid) *adj.* high-spirited; courageous; also, magnanimous.

great horned owl A large American owl (*Bubo virginianus*) with tufted ears that resemble horns: also called *cat owl.*

Great Kar·roo (kə·rōō′) A plateau region of S Northern Cape Province, Republic of South Africa: also *Central Karroo.*

Great Khing·an Mountains (king′än′, shing′) See KHINGHAN MOUNTAINS.

Great Lakes A chain of five lakes, the largest group of fresh-water lakes in the world, in central North America on the Canada-United States border: Lakes Superior, Michigan, Huron, Erie, and Ontario; total 94,710 square miles; drained by the Saint Lawrence River.

great laurel The rosebay rhododendron.

great·ly (grāt′lē) *adv.* 1 In a great manner. 2 In or to a great degree.

Great Miami River See MIAMI RIVER.

Great Mogul See under MOGUL.

Great Mother Cybele.

great northern diver See under LOON.

Great Plains A sloping plateau, generally 400 miles wide, in western North America bordering the eastern base of the Rocky Mountains from Canada to New Mexico and Texas.

great power One of the countries exercising

a predominant influence in world affairs.
great primer *Printing* A size of type (18-point).
great Pyr·e·nees (pir'ə·nēz) One of a breed of large dog with a heavy, bearlike head, broad straight back, and long thick coat.
Great Rebellion See CIVIL WAR (ENGLISH) in table under WAR.
Great Rift Valley A great depression of the Near East and eastern Africa, extending from Syria to Mozambique, and traceable by the lakes and seas filling its elongated pockets: also *Rift Valley.*
Great Russian See under RUSSIAN.
Great Sandy Desert The northern belt of the Western Australian desert, north of the Gibson Desert.
Great Salt Lake A salt lake in NW Utah having no outlet and fluctuating in size from 1,000 to 2,000 square miles: also *Salt Lake.*
Great Schism The division in the Roman Catholic Church, 1378–1417, when rival popes ruled at Rome and Avignon.
Great Seal 1 The chief seal of a government, used to authenticate important documents and commissions in the name of the sovereign or highest executive of the government. **2** The Lord Chancellor of England, custodian of the British Great Seal, or his office. See SEAL[1].
Great Slave Lake A lake in southern Northwest Territories, Canada; 11,170 square miles.
Great Slave River See SLAVE RIVER.
Great Smoky Mountains A mountain range in North Carolina and Tennessee; highest point, 6,642 feet; site of **Great Smoky Mountains National Park,** 789 square miles, established 1930. Also **Great Smokies.**
Great St. Bernard Pass See under ST. BERNARD.
great–un·cle (grāt'ung'kəl) *n.* A granduncle.
Great Valley See CENTRAL VALLEY, GREAT APPALACHIAN VALLEY.
Great Victoria Desert See VICTORIA DESERT.
Great Wall of China A monumental wall in northern China, extending 1,500 miles between China proper and Mongolia; 20 feet wide at the base, 12 feet wide at the top; from 15 to 50 feet high; constructed 246–209 B.C.: also *Chinese Wall.*
Great War See WORLD WAR I in table under WAR.
Great Week In the Greek Orthodox Church, the week before Easter.
Great White Father A name used by American Indians for the president of the United States.
great white heron 1 A large white heron *(Ardea occidentalis)* of southern North America. **2** An egret *(Casmerodius albus)* of America and the Old World.
Great White Way The brightly lighted theater district of New York City; specifically, the section near Broadway and Times Square.
Great Yarmouth A port and county borough in SE Norfolk, England, on the North Sea: also *Yarmouth.*
great year See PRECESSION OF THE EQUINOXES.
greave (grēv) *n.* Armor to protect the leg from knee to ankle. [<OF *greve;* ult. origin unknown]
greaves (grēvz) *n. pl.* Pieces of boiled tallow scrap; cracklings; also, dregs of melted tallow: also spelled *graves.* [Akin to LG *greve* refuse of tallow]
grebe (grēb) *n.* Any of a family *(Colymbidae)* of four–toed swimming and diving birds, smaller than loons and of fresh–water habitat, as the **horned grebe** *(Colymbus auritus)* and the **pied–billed grebe,** or dabchick of America. [<F *grebe;* ult. origin uncertain]
Gre·cian (grē'shən) *adj.* Greek. —*n.* **1** A Greek. **2** A scholar of Greek.
Grecian bend 1 An affected posture, fashionable among women in the nineteenth century, in which the body inclined forward from the hips. **2** A type of bustle emphasizing this posture.
Gre·cism (grē'siz·əm) *n.* **1** A Greek idiom. **2** The style or spirit of Greek art, culture, etc. Also spelled *Graecism.*
Gre·cize (grē'sīz) *v.* **·cized, ·ciz·ing** *v.t.* **1** To make Greek in form, character, etc.; Hellenize. **2** To translate into Greek. —*v.i.* **3** To adopt or imitate Greek customs, speech, etc. [<F *gréciser* <L *graecizare* <*Graecus* a Greek]
Greco– *combining form* Greek: *Greco–Roman.* Also spelled *Graeco–.* [<L *Graecus* a Greek]
Gre·co (grā'kō, grek'ō), **El,** 1541–1614, Spanish painter, born in Crete: real name *Domenico Theotocopuli.* [<Sp., the Greek]
Gre·co–Per·sian Wars (grē'kō·pûr'zhən) See table under WAR.
Gre·co–Ro·man (grē'kō·rō'mən) *adj.* Of or pertaining to Greece and Rome together: *Greco–Roman* art, *Greco–Roman* style of wrestling.
gree[1] (grē) *v.t. & v.i. Scot. & Brit. Dial.* To bring or come to agreement.
gree[2] (grē) *n. Obs.* **1** Satisfaction; legal redress. **2** Good will; favor. [<OF *gré,* ult. < L *gratus* pleasing]
gree[3] (grē) *n. Scot. & Archaic* **1** Superiority; victory. **2** The prize of victory.
Greece (grēs) A kingdom of SE Europe; 51,182 square miles; capital, Athens: Greek *Hellas.*
greed (grēd) *n.* Eager and selfish desire; greediness; avarice. [Back formation <GREEDY]
greed·y (grē'dē) *adj.* **greed·i·er, greed·i·est 1** Eager to obtain; avaricious; grasping. **2** Having excessive appetite for food or drink. [OE *grǣdig*] —**greed'i·ly** *adv.* —**greed'i·ness** *n.*
Synonyms: gluttonous, grasping, insatiable, insatiate, ravenous, selfish, voracious. See AVARICIOUS.
gree·gree (grē'grē') See GRIGRI.
Greek (grēk) *adj.* Pertaining to Greece, its inhabitants, their language, or culture; Grecian; resembling the people of Greece. —*n.* **1** One of the people of ancient Greece; specifically, a member of one of the four major tribes: Achaean, Aeolian, Dorian, and Ionian. **2** One of the people of modern Greece, descended, with admixture, from the ancient Greeks. **3** The Indo–European, Hellenic language of ancient or modern Greece. Ancient, or classical, Greek, from Homer to about A.D. 200, is divided into four literary dialects: Aeolic, Attic, Doric, and Ionic. Abbr. *Gk.* —**Late Greek,** the language from about A.D. 200 to 600, including the patristic writings. See KOINE. Abbr. *LGk.* —**Medieval Greek,** the language of the Byzantine period, from 600 to 1500. Abbr. *Med. Gk.* —**Modern Greek,** the language of Greece since 1500, in its literary form retaining many classical features: also called *Romaic,* especially in its spoken form. **4** Language or things not understood: It's all *Greek* to me. **5** A member of the Greek Church. **6** *Colloq.* A tricky fellow; sharper; rogue. **7** *Archaic* A gay fellow; roisterer: a merry *Greek.* **8** *U.S. Slang* A member of a student fraternity designated by a combination of Greek letters. [<L *Graecus* <Gk. *Graikos* Greek] —**Greek'ish** *adj.*
Greek calends See CALENDS.
Greek Catholic A member of the Greek Church.
Greek Church 1 The Eastern or Oriental Church (officially, the Holy Oriental Orthodox Catholic Apostolic Church), which finally separated from the Roman or Western Church in the 15th century, on doctrinal and liturgical grounds: also **Greek Orthodox Church. 2** The Oriental Church in communion with Rome.
Greek cross See under CROSS.
Greek fire See under FIRE.
Greek Revival A style of architecture developed in the 18th and early 19th centuries, depending for its effect on the use of modified Greek motifs and structural elements.
Gree·ley (grē'lē), **Horace,** 1811–72, U.S. editor and politician.
Gree·ly (grē'lē), **Adolphus Washington,** 1844–1935, U.S. general and Arctic explorer.
green (grēn) *adj.* **1** Having the spectrum color between blue and yellow. **2** In leaf; grass-covered; verdant: *green* hills. **3** Not arrived at perfect or mature form or condition; unripe. **4** Of or due to immature or unskilled judgment or lack of knowledge; inexperienced; also, gullible. **5** Not seasoned or made ready for use; new; fresh; unrefined; raw. **6** Pale-greenish; pale; sickly; wan. **7** Characterized by strength or youthful vigor; flourishing. See synonyms under FRESH. —*n.* **1** The color of spring foliage; the color in the solar spectrum between the blue and the yellow. **2** A grassy level or piece of ground covered with herbage; a common; specifically, a golf putting green, or a whole golf course. **3** A green pigment or substance. **4** *pl.* The leaves and stems of young plants, as dandelion and spinach, used as food: usually boiled. **5** *pl.* Leaves or branches of trees; wreaths. **6** Something green used as an emblem. —*v.t. & v.i.* To become or cause to become green. [OE *grēne.* Akin to GRASS, GROW.] —**green'·ly** *adv.* —**green'ness** *n.*
Green (grēn), **Anna Katharine,** 1846–1935, U.S. writer. —**Hetty Howland,** 1835–1916, *née* Robinson, U.S. financier. —**John Richard,** 1837–83, English historian. —**Julian,** born 1900, French novelist born in America. —**William,** 1873–1952, U.S. labor leader, president of the American Federation of Labor 1924–52.
green algae A class *(Chlorophyceae)* of algae in which the chlorophyll–bearing cells are dominant; especially, *Protococcus viridis,* found as a coating on rocks, trees, fence posts, etc.
Green·a·way (grē'nə·wā), **Kate,** 1846–1901, English painter and illustrator of children's books, whose drawings popularized a style of children's clothes known by her name.
green·back (grēn'bak') *n.* **1** One of a class of legal–tender notes of the United States: so called because the back is printed in green. **2** The golden plover.
Greenback party A U.S. political party, 1874–84, that advocated the restriction of the currency to Treasury notes. —**Green'back'er** *n.*
Green Bay A city in eastern Wisconsin on the Fox River at the head of **Green Bay,** an inlet of Lake Michigan in Michigan and Wisconsin.
green·belt (grēn'belt') *n.* A strip of recreational or unoccupied land, encircling a community as a protection against objectionable property uses.
Green Berets The nickname of an elite unit of the U.S. Army, officially called Special Forces.
green·bri·er (grēn'brī'ər) *n.* Any of a genus *(Smilax)* of plants, especially a thorny vine *(S. rotundifolia)* of the United States and Canada, having small greenish flowers.
green comma A butterfly of North America *(Polygonia faunus),* so called from the greenish color and comma–shaped markings on the under side of its hind wings.
green corn Indian corn in the unripe, milky stage: boiled or roasted on the cob for eating.
green crop Green manure.
green dragon An American herb *(Arisaema dracontium)* related to the jack–in–the–pulpit: also called *dragonroot.*
Greene (grēn), **Graham,** born 1904, English novelist. —**Nathanael,** 1742–86, American general in the Revolutionary War. —**Robert,** 1558?–92, English dramatist and pamphleteer.
green earth Native clay containing small amounts of manganese and iron: used as a pigment in dyeing and as a base for some green lakes.
green·er·y (grē'nər·ē) *n. pl.* **·er·ies 1** A place where plants are grown. **2** A verdant mass of plants; verdure.
green–eyed (grēn'īd') *adj.* **1** Having green eyes. **2** Influenced by jealousy.
green felt A cluster of green algae (genus *Vaucheria*).
green·finch (grēn'finch') *n.* **1** An Old World finch *(Chloris chloris),* the male of which has green–and–gold plumage. **2** The Texas sparrow *(Arremonops rufivirgatus).*
green fingers Green thumb. —**green'–fin'·gered** *adj.*
green flash A vivid green hue sometimes seen on the upper edge of the sun's disk during sunrise or sunset.
green·fly (grēn'flī') *n. pl.* **·flies** A green plant louse; an aphid.
green·gage (grēn'gāj') *n.* A small, green-fleshed plum, originally developed in France. [<GREEN + GAGE[3]]
green gland *Zool.* One of two excretory organs near the head in decapod crustaceans.
green glass The viscid melted glass used for making bottles: also called *bottle glass.*
green gold An alloy of gold, silver, and copper in varying proportions, ranging from 14 to 18 karats in fineness, the deepest shade of green being of 18 karats: used in jewelry.
green·gro·cer (grēn'grō'sər) *n. Brit.* A retailer of fresh vegetables, fruit, etc. —**green'gro'·cer·y** *n.*
green·head (grēn'hed') *n. pl.* **·heads** or **·head 1** The striped bass. **2** Any of various American horseflies with green eyes *(Tabanus line-*

ola or *T. costalis).* **3** The male mallard duck **4** The scaup duck. **5** The golden plover. **6** The black-bellied plover.

green-heart (grēn'härt') *n.* A large hardwood tree *(Ocotea rodiaei)* of Guyana and the Pacific coast of the United States, with a tough, durable wood ranging in color from yellowish-green to black: used in shipbuilding: also called *bebeeru.*

green heron A small, wide-ranging American heron *(Butorides virescens)* with a greenish-black head and a white throat.

green-horn (grēn'hôrn') *n. Colloq.* An inexperienced person. [< GREEN *(adj.* def. 3) + HORN; with ref. to an immature animal]

green-house (grēn'hous') *n.* A building having glass walls and roof, for the protection or propagation of plants.

greenhouse effect A postulated warming of the earth due to an increase in atmospheric carbon dioxide, which is relatively transparent to incident solar radiation but opaque to reflected radiation at thermal wavelengths.

green-ing (grē'ning) *n.* One of several varieties of apples having a green skin when ripe.

green-ish (grē'nish) *adj.* Somewhat green.

Green-land (grēn'lənd) The largest island in the world, off NE North America, comprising a Danish colony; 840,000 square miles. *Danish* **Grön-land** (grœn'län').

Greenland Sea The southern Arctic Ocean off NE Greenland and north of Iceland.

green-let (grēn'lit) *n.* A vireo.

green light 1 A green signal used in the control of traffic and indicating that traffic may proceed. **2** *Colloq.* Approval or authorization of an intended action, program, etc.

green-ling (grēn'ling) *n.* Any of a genus *(Hexagrammos)* of large, carnivorous food fishes, found in North Pacific waters.

green lizard 1 A small, harmless, insectivorous lizard *(Anolis carolinensis)* of the southern United States. **2** A slender, long-tailed bright-green lizard *(Lacerta viridis)* of Europe and Asia Minor.

green manure 1 A crop, as of beans, clover, etc., plowed under before ripening to improve the fertility of the soil: also **green crop, green dressing. 2** Unaged stable manure.

green mold See BLUE MOLD.

green monkey A monkey *(Cercopithecus sabaeus)* of West Africa having an olive-greenish coat and a white ruff.

Green Mountain Boys Vermont soldiers of the American Revolution, led by Ethan Allen.

Green Mountains A Vermont range of the Appalachians; highest peak, 4,393 feet.

Green Mountain State Nickname of VERMONT.

green pepper The unripe fruit of the red pepper (genus *Capsicum):* eaten as a vegetable.

green revolution The large-scale development of inexpensive varieties of wheat, rice, and other grains, esp. to improve the economy of underdeveloped countries.

Green River 1 A headstream of the Colorado River, flowing 730 miles south through Wyo-

ming, Colorado, and Utah. **2** A river in central Kentucky, flowing 370 miles NW to the Ohio River.

green-room (grēn'room', -room') *n.* The common waiting room for performers in a theater when they are off stage.

green-sand (grēn'sand') *n. Geol.* Either of two sandstone strata of the Cretaceous system: so called from the color imparted to it by the glauconite with which it is mingled: often used as a fertilizer and water softener. See MARL[2].

Greens-bor-o (grēnz'bûr-ō) A city in north central North Carolina.

green-shank (grēn'shangk') *n.* A European sandpiper *(Tringa nebularia)* with greenish-gray legs and feet.

green-sick-ness (grēn'sik'nis) *n.* Chlorosis.

green soap A soft soap made from linseed oil and the hydroxides of potassium and sodium: used in the treatment of skin diseases.

green-stone (grēn'stōn') *n.* One of various kinds of compact, igneous rocks to which a green color has been imparted by chlorite, such as diabase and diorite.

green-sward (grēn'swôrd') *n.* Turf green with grass.

green tea Tea leaves withered and rolled but not allowed to undergo fermentation.

greenth (grēnth) *n. Rare* Verdure.

green thumb Success or skill in making plants grow easily.

Green-ville (grēn'vil) A city in NW South Carolina.

green vitriol Copperas.

Green-wich (grēn'ich, -ij, grin-) A metropolitan borough of SE London on the Thames, England; former site of the Royal Observatory; location of the prime meridian.

Greenwich time See under TIME.

Green-wich Village (grēn'ich, -ij) A section of New York City on the lower west side of the borough of Manhattan, formerly a village: traditionally frequented by artists, students, and writers.

green-wood (grēn'wood') *n.* A forest in leaf.

green woodpecker A European woodpecker *(Picus viridis)* with greenish upper plumage, a scarlet crown, and a fringed band on the cheek. Also called *hickwall, yaffle.*

greet[1] (grēt) *v.t.* **1** To address words of friendliness, courtesy, respect, etc., to, as in speaking or writing. **2** To receive or meet in a specified manner: He was *greeted* with a chorus of boos. **3** To come into the sight or awareness of; appear to: The sea *greeted* their eyes. See synonyms under ADDRESS. [OE *grētan*] —**greet'er** *n.*

greet[2] (grēt) *Scot. v.i.* **grat, greet-ing** To weep. —*n.* A crying; weeping. —**greet'ing** *n.*

greet-ing (grē'ting) *n.* Salutation on meeting, or by letter or message; welcome.

greg-a-rine (greg'ə-rēn, -rin) One of an order *(Gregarinina)* of sporozoans, parasitic in arthropods, insects, crustaceans, etc. [< NL < L *gregarius* gregarious]

gre-gar-i-ous (gri-gâr'ē-əs) *adj.* **1** Having the habit of associating in flocks, herds, or companies; not habitually solitary or living alone. **2** Of or pertaining to a flock; characteristic of a crowd or aggregation. **3** *Bot.* Growing in association, but not matted together, as certain mosses; clustered. [< L *gregarius* < *grex, gregis* a flock] —**gre-gar'i-ous-ly** *adv.* —**gre-gar'i-ous-ness** *n.*

gre-go (grē'gō, grā'-) *n.* A short, hooded cloak of coarse cloth, worn in the Levant. [< Ital. *greco* Greek < L *Graecus*]

Gre-go-ri-an (gri-gôr'ē-ən, -gō'rē-) *adj.* Pertaining to one named Gregory; especially to one of the two popes, Gregory I and Gregory XIII.

Gregorian calendar See under CALENDAR.

Gregorian chant 1 The system of church music ascribed to Gregory I, used as ritual music in the Roman Catholic and some other churches. **2** Any of the traditional melodies of this music.

Greg-o-ry (greg'ər-ē) A masculine personal name: the name of sixteen popes. Also **Greg-or** (greg'ər), *Dan., Ger.* **Gre-gor** (grā'gôr), *Du., Ger.* **Gre-go-ri-us** (grā-gō'rē-ōōs), *Fr.* **Gré-goire** (grā-gwär'), *Ital., Pg., Sp.* **Gre-go-ri-o** (grā-gō'-rē-ō). [< Gk., *watchman*]

—**Gregory I,** 540?-604, pope 590-604; reformed

the church service: known as **Gregory the Great.**

—**Gregory VII,** 1015-85, pope 1073-85; deposed by Emperor Henry IV, who appointed an anti-pope 1080: original name *Hildebrand.*

—**Gregory XIII,** 1502-85, pope 1572-85; reformed the Julian calendar.

—**Gregory Naz-i-an-zus** (naz'ē-an'zəs), 328?-389?, bishop of Constantinople: called "The Theologian."

—**Gregory of Ne-o-cae-sar-e-a** (nē'ō-si-zâr'ē-ə), Saint, 213?-270?, bishop of Neocaesarea, a city of Pontus, Asia Minor: called "Thaumaturgus."

—**Gregory of Nys-sa** (nis'ə), Saint, 332?-398?, Greek ecclesiastic; bishop of Nyssa.

—**Gregory of Tours,** 544?-594, Frankish historian and ecclesiastic; bishop of Tours.

Greg-o-ry (greg'ər-ē), **Lady Augusta,** 1852-1932, *née* Persse, Irish playwright. —**James,** 1638-75, Scottish mathematician and inventor.

Greifs-wald (grīfs'vält) A university city in Mecklenburg, northern East Germany.

greige (grā, grāzh) *n.* Cotton, linen, silk, rayon, or wool fabric before dyeing, sizing, or other processing: named for its gray unfinished appearance: also called *gray goods.* [< F *grège* raw, finished; infl. in form by *beige*]

grei-sen (grī'zən) *n.* A crystalline mixture of quartz and mica. [< G]

gre-mi-al (grē'mē-əl) *n.* A silken apron laid on the lap of a bishop when celebrating the Eucharist or anointing. [< L *gremium* lap]

grem-lin (grem'lin) *n.* A mischievous, invisible imp said to ride airplanes and cause mechanical trouble: a coinage of British aviators in World War II. [Origin uncertain]

Gre-na-da (gri-nā'də) An island republic in the West Indies, a member of the Commonwealth of Nations; the southernmost of the Windward Islands, with its dependencies in the Grenadines, 133 sq. mi.; capital, St. George's.

gre-nade (gri-nād') *n.* **1** A small bomb designed to be thrown by hand (**hand grenade**) or fired from a rifle or launching device, exploding on impact or by the action of a time fuze. **2** A glass bottle containing chemicals for extinguishing a fire. —**frangible grenade** A glass bottle filled with inflammable fluid, as gasoline, which is ignited on striking any object, as an armored vehicle or tank: popularly called *Molotov cocktail* or *gasoline bomb.* [< F, a pomegranate < Sp. *granada* < L *granatus* having seeds < *granum* a eed]

gre-nade-launch-er (gri-nād'lôn'chər) *n.* An attachment to the muzzle of a rifle or other weapon by which grenades are fired.

gren-a-dier (gren'ə-dir') *n.* **1** Formerly, a soldier assigned to throw grenades. **2** A member of a specially constituted corps or regiment, as the British Grenadier Guards. **3** Any of a family *(Macrouridae)* of deep-sea, soft-finned fishes related to the cod. [< F < *grenade.* See GRENADE.]

gren-a-dil-la (gren'ə-dil'ə), **gren-a-dil-lo** (-dil'ō) See GRANADILLO.

gren-a-dine[1] (gren'ə-dēn', gren'ə-dēn) *n.* **1** A silk or woolen, loosely woven fabric, usually mixed with cotton: used for curtains. **2** Silk cord made of several twisted strands braided together. [< F, ? after Grenada]

gren-a-dine[2] (gren'ə-dēn', gren'ə-dēn) *n.* A beverage sirup made from currants or pomegranates. [< F < *grenade* a pomegranate]

Gren-a-dines (gren'ə-dēnz) An island group of the Windward Islands, comprising dependencies of Grenada and St. Vincent; 30 square miles.

Gren-fell (gren'fel), **Sir Wilfred Thomason,** 1865-1940, English physician and author; missionary to Labrador.

Gre-no-ble (grə-nō'bəl, *Fr.* grə-nô'bl') A city in SE France.

Gren-ville (gren'vil), **George,** 1712-70, English statesman; premier 1763-65. —**Sir Richard,** 1541?-91, English vice admiral: also **Greyn'-ville.**

Gresh-am (gresh'əm), **Sir Thomas,** 1519?-79, English merchant and financier.

Gresh-am's law (gresh'əmz) In political economy, the law that of two forms of currency the inferior or more depreciated tends to drive the other from circulation, owing to the

hoarding and exportation of the better form: as commonly stated, "bad money drives out good." Also **Gresham's theorem.** [after Sir Thomas *Gresham*]

gres·so·ri·al (gre·sôr′ē·əl, -sō′rē-) *adj. Zool.* Having legs or feet adapted for walking; ambulatory: a *gressorial* bird or insect. Also **gres·so′ri·ous** (-sôr′ē-, -sō′rē). [< L *gressus,* pp. of *gradi* walk]

Gre·ta (grā′tə, gret′ə; *Ger.* grā′tä) Diminutive of MARGARET.

Gretch·en (grech′ən) See under MARGARET.

Gret·na Green (gret′nə) A village in Dumfriesshire, Scotland, near the English border: former scene of run-away marriages.

Greuze (grœz), **Jean Baptiste,** 1725–1805, French painter.

Grev·ille (grev′il), **Sir Fulke** See BROOKE.

grew (grōō) Past tense of GROW.

Grew (grōō), **Joseph Clark,** 1880–1965, U.S. diplomat.

grew·some (grōō′səm) See GRUESOME.

grey (grā) *adj. Brit.* Gray.

Grey (grā), **Charles,** 1764–1845, Earl Grey, English statesman. **—Sir Edward,** 1862–1933, Viscount Grey of Fallodon, English statesman; foreign secretary 1905–16. **—Lady Jane,** 1537–54, great-granddaughter of Henry VII; made heir to English throne by Edward VI; proclaimed queen 1553; deposed; beheaded.

grey·hound (grā′hound′) *n.* **1** One of a breed of tall, slender dogs with a long narrow head and smooth short coat: used for hunting and racing. **2** A fast ocean vessel. [OE *grighund*]

GREYHOUND
(About 26 to 28 inches high at the shoulder)

Grey·lock (grā′lok), **Mount** The highest point in Massachusetts, in the Berkshires; 3,505 eet.

grib·ble (grib′əl) *n.* A small isopod, as *Limnoria terebrans* or *L. lignorum,* that bores into and destroys submerged timber. [? Akin to GRUB]

grice (grīs) *n. Scot.* A pig; especially, a suckling pig.

grid (grid) *n.* **1** A grating of parallel bars. **2** A gridiron. **3** *Electr.* A metallic framework employed in a storage cell or battery for conducting the electric current and supporting the active material. **4** *Electronics* An electrode mounted between the cathode and anode of a vacuum tube for the control of electrons: usually in the form of a screen. **5** A system of coordinate lines superimposed upon a map and used as a basis for reference from a designated point. **6** A network of catwalks suspended from the ceiling of a motion-picture studio or other enclosure. **7** *Brit.* A network of high-tension lines for distributing electric power throughout a large area. [Short for GRIDIRON]

grid bias *Electronics* The direct-current potential applied to the grid of a vacuum tube to make it negative with respect to the filament or the cathode: also called *C-bias.*

grid circuit *Electronics* The part of a circuit between the cathode and grid of a vacuum tube.

grid condenser *Electronics* A small condenser connected in series with the grid or control circuit of a vacuum tube.

grid current *Electronics* The current flowing between the grid of a vacuum tube and the cathode.

grid·dle (grid′l) *n.* **1** A shallow pan for baking or frying thin cakes. **2** A cover for a hole in a cookstove. **—***v.t.* **grid·dled, grid·dling** To cook on a griddle. [< AF *grédil,* var. of OF *greil* < LL *craticulum,* dim. of *cratis* wickerwork]

grid·dle·cake (grid′l·kāk′) *n.* A thin, flat cake baked on a griddle, especially one of thin batter; a pancake.

gride (grīd) *v.t. & v.i.* **grid·ed, grid·ing 1** To grind or scrape harshly; grate. **2** To cut; pierce. **—***n.* A harsh cutting, grinding, or hacking. [Metathetic var. of GIRD[2]]

grid emission *Electronics* The emission of electrons from the overheated grid electrode of a vacuum tube.

grid·i·ron (grid′ī′ərn) *n.* **1** A grated utensil for broiling. **2** Any object resembling or likened to a gridiron, as a football field prepared for the game, or a network of pipe lines, railroad tracks, or the like. **3** The framework above a theater stage supporting the pulleys that raise and lower scenery; a storage space for scenery. [ME *gredire,* var. of *gredile* < AF *grédil* GRIDDLE; infl. by IRON]

grid leak *Electronics* A high-resistance unit connected directly or indirectly between the grid and cathode of a vacuum tube to allow escape of excess negative charges from the grid.

grid line One of the reference lines forming part of the grid on a map or chart.

grid·lock (grid′lok′) *n.* A clogged traffic situation which prevents vehicles from moving in any direction.

grid meridian A grid line extending in a north–south direction on the grid: the prime grid meridian usually coincides with the zero meridian of Greenwich.

grid north That direction on a grid map or chart which corresponds with the direction of the North Pole along the meridian of Greenwich.

grid return *Electronics* The connection which allows electrons to flow from the grid to the cathode of a vacuum tube.

grid road *Canadian* A road following a grid line of the original survey.

grid variation The angle between the magnetic and grid meridian at any place, expressed in degrees east or west to show the variation of the magnetic compass-card axis from grid north. Also called *grivation.*

grief (grēf) *n.* **1** Sorrow or mental suffering resulting from loss, affliction, regret, etc. **2** A cause of sorrow; an affliction; grievance. **3** An accident, as in hunting or racing; a mishap. **4** *Obs.* Physical pain; distress; also, a cause of pain. **—to come to grief** To have misfortune; fail. [< OF < *grever* GRIEVE] **—grief′less** *adj.* **—grief′less·ness** *n.*

Synonyms: affliction, agony, distress, melancholy, mourning, regret, sadness, sorrow, tribulation, trouble, woe. *Grief* is acute mental pain resulting from loss, misfortune, or deep disappointment. *Grief* is more acute and less enduring than *sorrow. Sorrow* and *grief* are for definite cause; *sadness* and *melancholy* may arise from a vague sense of want or loss, from a low state of health, or other ill-defined cause; *sadness* may be momentary; *melancholy* is more enduring, and may become chronic. *Affliction* is a deep *sorrow* and is applied also to the misfortune producing such *sorrow; mourning* most frequently denotes *sorrow* publicly expressed. *Antonyms:* see synonyms for HAPPINESS.

grief-strick·en (grēf′strik′ən) *adj.* Overwhelmed or bowed down by sorrow.

Grieg (grēg), **Edvard Hagerup,** 1843–1907, Norwegian composer.

griev·ance (grē′vəns) *n.* **1** That which oppresses, injures, or causes grief and a sense of wrong; a cause of annoyance. **2** A complaint, or a cause for complaint, because of a wrong suffered. **3** *Obs.* Mental or physical pain; also, anger; grief. See synonyms under INJUSTICE.

grieve (grēv) *v.* **grieved, griev·ing** *v.t.* **1** To cause great sorrow or grief to; make sad. **2** *Obs.* To injure or offend. **—***v.i.* **3** To feel sorrow or grief; mourn; lament. See synonyms under HURT, MOURN. [< OF *grever* < L *gravare* oppress < *gravis* heavy] **—griev′er** *n.* **—griev′·ing** *adj.* **—griev′ing·ly** *adv.*

griev·ous (grē′vəs) *adj.* **1** Causing grief or sorrow; hard to be borne; oppressive. **2** Causing mischief or destruction; hurtful; injurious. **3** Expressive of or connected with grief or distress: a *grievous* complaint. **4** Severe: a *grievous* pain or illness. **5** Atrocious; heinous: *grievous* sin. See synonyms under HARD, HEAVY. **—griev′ous·ly** *adv.* **—griev′ous·ness** *n.*

griff (grif) *n.* **1** A series of horizontal blades in a reciprocating frame, to raise and lower the shedding mechanism of a Jacquard loom in forming the pattern. **2** Griffe[1]. **3** A claw. [< F *griffe* a claw. See GRIFFE[1].]

griffe[1] (grif) *n. Archit.* An ornament in the form of a claw at an angle of the base of a column: also spelled *griff:* also called *spur.* [< F, claw < *griffer* grasp]

griffe[2] (grif) *n. U.S. Dial.* **1** A person having one Negro and one mulatto parent; also, a mulatto. **2** A person of mixed Negro and American Indian descent. Also **griff, grif′fin** (-in). [< F < Sp. *grifo,* orig. a griffin]

grif·fin[1] (grif′in) *n.* In Greek mythology, a creature with the head and wings of an eagle and the body of a lion: also spelled *griffon.* [< OF *grifoun* < L *gryphus* < Gk. *gryps* griffin] **—grif′fin·esque′** (-esk′) *adj.*

STYLIZED HERALDIC GRIFFIN

grif·fin[2] (grif′in) *n. Anglo-Indian* A newcomer to India from England; greenhorn. [Origin uncertain]

Grif·fith (grif′ith), **D(avid Lewelyn) W(ark),** 1875–1948, U.S. motion-picture producer.

grif·fon (grif′ən) *n.* **1** A griffin. **2** A breed of large sporting dog of European origin, having a gray, wiry coat and long head: also *wire-haired griffon.* Compare BRUSSELS GRIFFON, BELGIAN GRIFFON, BRABANÇON GRIFFON. [< F]

grift·er (grif′tər) *n. U.S. Colloq.* A person given a concession with a circus or carnival to run a freak show or refreshment stand, or operate games of chance, etc. [? < GRAFTER]

grig (grig) *n.* **1** A cricket or grasshopper. **2** A sand eel. **3** A very lively person. [Origin uncertain]

Gri·gnard (grē·nyár′), **Victor,** 1871–1934, French chemist.

gri·gri (grē′grē′) *n.* An African Negro talisman or charm; fetish: also spelled *greegree.* [< native name]

grigri man An African Negro witch doctor or magician.

grill (gril) *v.t.* **1** To cook on a gridiron; broil. **2** To torment with heat. **3** *U.S. Colloq.* To cross-examine persistently and searchingly. **—***v.i.* To be cooked on a gridiron. **—***n.* **1** A gridiron. **2** That which is broiled on a gridiron. **3** A grillroom. **4** The action of grilling. **5** A grille or grating of any kind. [< F *griler* < *gril* < OF *greil.* See GRIDDLE.] **—grill′er** *n.*

gril·lage (gril′ij) *n.* A heavy framework of crossed timbers or steel beams to sustain a foundation, especially on yielding soil. [< F < *grille,* var. of *gril* a grill]

grille (gril) *n.* **1** A grating or screen; especially one of wrought metal, as in a grate for shielding an open door or window. **2** In court tennis, a square opening at the rear of the hazard court. Also **grill.** [< F, var. of *gril.* See GRILL.]

grilled (grild) *adj.* **1** Having a grille. **2** Broiled.

Grill·par·zer (gril′pär·tsər), **Franz,** 1791–1872, Austrian dramatist and poet.

grill·room (gril′rōōm′, -rōōm′) *n.* A restaurant or eating place where grilling is done or grilled food is served.

grill·work (gril′wûrk′) *n.* **1** A grille (def. 1). **2** The design or structure of a grille.

grilse (grils) *n. pl.* **grilse** or **grils·es** A young salmon after its first return to fresh water: also called *graul.* [Origin unknown]

grim (grim) *adj.* **1** Stern and forbidding in aspect or nature; fierce; ferocious. **2** Harsh; severe; dreadful. **3** Unyielding; formidable. [OE] **—grim′ly** *adv.* **—grim′ness** *n.*

Synonyms: ferocious, fierce, hideous, savage, stern, sullen, terrible. *Grim* expresses or suggests a silent but most determined ferocity; as, the *grim* aspect of the executioner. Compare FIERCE. *Antonyms:* benign, genial, gentle, kind, mild, placid, sweet, tender.

gri·mace (gri·mās′) *n.* A distortion of the features, either habitual or occasioned by annoyance, disgust, contempt, etc.; a wry face. **—***v.i.* **·maced, ·mac·ing** To make grimaces. [< MF < Sp. *grimazo,* prob. < Gmc.] **—gri·mac′er** *n.*

Gri·mal·di (grē·mäl′dē), **Joseph,** 1779–1837, English clown.

Grimaldi man *Anthropol.* A type of early man represented by skeletons found in the caves of Grimaldi near Menton, on the French–Italian border: variously interpreted as ancestral to the Caucasoid or Negroid type.

gri·mal·kin (gri·mal′kin, -môl-) *n.* **1** A cat,

particularly an old female cat. 2 A malevolent old woman. [<GRAY + MALKIN]

grime (grīm) *n.* That which soils; soot; dirt ground into a surface. —*v.t.* **grimed, grim·ing** To make dirty; begrime. [<Flemish *grijm*]

Grimes Golden A variety of golden-yellow eating apple. [after T. P. *Grimes,* c. 1790, who first grew it in W. Virginia]

Grimm (grim), **Jacob Ludwig Karl,** 1785–1862, and his brother **Wilhelm Karl,** 1786–1859, German philologists, noted for their collection of fairy tales.

Grimm's Law A statement by J. L. K. Grimm (earlier enunciated by Rasmus Rask) of the development of the consonants from Indo-European into Germanic. Among the commonest consonantal changes are: Indo-European voiceless plosives *(p, t, k),* represented by Sanskrit *pitár,* Greek *treis,* Latin *centum,* becoming voiceless fricatives *(f, th, h),* as seen in English *father, three, hundred;* Indo-European aspirated voiced plosives *(bh, dh, gh),* represented by Sanskrit *bhrātar,* Sanskrit *dhā,* Latin *hostis* (IE *ghostis*), to unaspirated voiced plosives *(b, d, g),* as in English *brother, do, guest;* Indo-European voiced plosives *(b, d, g),* represented by Latin *cannabis,* Greek *damaein,* Latin *ager,* to voiceless plosives *(p, t, k),* as in English *hemp, tame, acre.* A further development in High German accounts for the difference between English *pound,* German *pfund;* English *ten,* German *zehn,* English *make,* German *machen;* English *that,* German *das.* See VERNER'S LAW.

Grims·by (grimz′bē) The largest British fishing port, in northern Lincolnshire, England.

grim·y (grī′mē) *adj.* **grim·i·er, grim·i·est** Full of or covered with grime; dirty. **—grim′i·ly** *adv.* **—grim′i·ness** *n.*

grin[1] (grin) *v.* **grinned, grin·ning** *v.i.* **1** To smile broadly. **2** To draw back the lips so as to show the teeth, as in pain, rage, or foolish laughter. —*v.t.* **3** To express by grinning. —*n.* The act of grinning; a broad smile. [OE *grennian*] **—grin′ner** *n.* **—grin′ning·ly** *adv.*

grin[2] (grin) *n. Archaic* A snare; trap. [OE]

grind (grīnd) *v.* **ground, grind·ing** *v.t.* **1** To sharpen, polish, or shape by friction. **2** To reduce to fine particles, as by crushing or friction; triturate. **3** To rub or press gratingly or harshly: to *grind* one's teeth. **4** To oppress; harass cruelly. **5** To operate by turning a crank, as a coffee mill. **6** To produce by or as by grinding. **7** *Colloq.* To teach laboriously. —*v.i.* **8** To perform the operation of grinding. **9** To undergo grinding; become ground. **10** To rub; grate. **11** *Colloq.* To study or work steadily; drudge. —*n.* **1** The act of grinding, or the sound made by grinding. **2** *Colloq.* Work or study that is tediously and laboriously performed. **3** *Colloq.* A laborious student. [OE *grindan*] **—grind′ing** *adj. n.* **—grind′ing·ly** *adv.*

grin·de·li·a (grin·dē′lē ·ə) *n.* **1** Any plant of an American genus *(Grindelia)* of coarse herbaceous or shrubby plants with sessile, rigid leaves and large heads of yellow flowers. **2** The dried leaves and flowering tops of certain species of this plant *(G. camporum* or *G. humilis), yielding a balsam used in the treatment of asthma, bronchitis, and ivy poisoning. Also called gum plant.* [<NL, after D. H. *Grindel,* Russian botanist]

grind·er (grīn′dər) *n.* **1** One who or that which grinds, as a knife sharpener, coffee mill, etc. **2** A molar tooth.

grind·er·y (grīn′dər·ē) *n. pl.* **·er·ies** **1** A place where edged tools or other instruments are ground. **2** *Brit.* Materials and tools used by leatherworkers.

grind·stone (grīnd′stōn′) *n.* **1** A flat circular stone so hung that it can be rotated upon an axis: used for sharpening tools, abrading, etc. **2** A millstone.

grin·go (grin′gō) *n. pl.* **·gos** In Latin America, a foreigner, particularly an American or Englishman: a contemptuous term. [<Am. Sp., gibberish]

Grin·nel (gri·nel′), **Henry,** 1799–1874, U.S. merchant; fitted out Arctic expeditions.

Grin·nell Land (gri·nel′) Formerly, a central section of Ellesmere Island in NE Franklin district, Northwest Territories, Canada.

grip[1] (grip) See GRIPPE.

grip[2] (grip) *n.* **1** The act of grasping firmly; a holding fast; clutch; a firm grasp. **2** A particular mode of grasping hands, as among members of a secret society, for mutual recognition. **3** *U.S.* A valise; gripsack. **4** That part of a thing by which it is grasped. **5** One of various mechanical grasping devices. **6** Ability to seize and hold physically or mentally; intellectual grasping power. **7** *Slang* A stagehand; a scene-shifter. **8** A twinge of pain. —*v.* **gripped** or **gript, grip·ping** *v.t.* **1** To take firm hold of with or as with the hand; hold onto tightly. **2** To join or attach securely with a grip (def. 5). **3** To seize or capture, as the mind; attract and hold the attention or imagination of. —*v.i.* **4** To take firm hold. **5** To take hold of the attention, imagination, etc. See synonyms under CATCH, GRASP. [Fusion of OE *gripe* a grasp and *gripa* handful, both <*gripan* seize. Akin to GROPE.] **—grip′per** *n.* **—grip′ping** *adj.* **—grip′ping·ly** *adv.*

gripe (grīp) *v.* **griped, grip·ing** *v.t.* **1** To seize and hold firmly; grasp; grip. **2** To cause pain in the bowels of, as if by sudden constriction. **3** To cause mental pain to; oppress; grieve. —*v.i.* **4** *U.S. Colloq.* To grumble; complain. **5** To suffer pains in the bowels. **6** *Obs.* To reach for or clutch something firmly. **7** *Naut.* To tend to come up into the wind. See synonyms under CATCH, GRASP. —*n.* **1** A fast or firm hold; grip; control. **2** *pl.* Intermittent pains in the bowels. [OE *gripan*] **—grip′er** *n.* **—grip′y** *adj.*

grippe (grip) *n. Influenza.* Also *grip.* [<F <*gripper* seize] **—grip′py** *adj.*

grip·ple (grip′əl) *adj. Scot.* Tenacious; greedy; covetous.

grip·sack (grip′sak′) *n.* U.S. A traveling bag, valise, or portmanteau.

Gri·qua (grē′kwə, grik′wə) *n.* A half-breed of South Africa of European (usually Dutch) and Hottentot or Bushman parents. [<Afrikaans]

Gri·qua·land East (grē′kwə· land, grik′wə-) Previous Transkeian province in Northern-Cape Province, Republic of South Africa; 6,602 square miles.

Griqualand West Previous Transkeian province in Northern Cape Province, Republic of South Africa; 15,007 square miles; chief city, Kimberley.

Gris (grēs), **Juan,** 1887–1927, Spanish painter.

gri·saille (gri·zāl, *Fr.* grē ·zä′y′) *n.* **1** A style of painting in grayish monochrome, in imitation of bas-relief: especially adapted for decoration. **2** Any object, especially glass, thus painted. [<F <*gris* gray]

Gri·sel·da (gri·zel′də, *Ital.* grē·sel′dä) A feminine personal name. Also **Gris·sel** (gris′əl). [<Gmc., stone heroine] *Griselda* In Boccaccio's *Decameron,* a lady of proverbial virtue and patience: called "Patient Griselda."

gris·e·ous (gris′ē·əs, griz′-) *adj.* Bluish-gray; having a mottled or grizzled grayish color. [<Med. L *griseus*]

gri·sette (gri·zet′) *n.* **1** A Parisian working-girl, especially one of easy, gay manners. **2** A gray woolen dress fabric worn by French working-women. [<F, orig. a gray woolen fabric < *gris* gray]

gris·kin (gris′kin) *n.* Brit. A loin of pork. [<obs. *grice* a pig + -KIN]

gris·ly[1] (griz′lē) *adj.* **·li·er, ·li·est** Savage-looking; fear-inspiring; horrifying. ◆Homophone: *grizzly.* [OE *grislic*] **—gris′li·ness** *n.*

gris·ly[2] (griz′lē) See GRIZZLY.

Gris-Nez (grē-nā′), **Cape** A headland and lighthouse of northern France on the narrowest part of the Strait of Dover.

gri·son (grī′sən, griz′·ən) *n.* A South American carnivore *(Grison vittata)* resembling a weasel. [<F *grison* <*gris* gray]

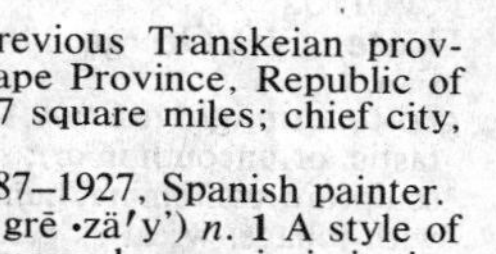

GRISON
(About 12 to 14 inches in body length)

Gri·sons (grē·zôn′) The largest canton in Switzerland; 2,746 square miles; capital, Chur. *German* **Grau·bün·den** (grou·bün′·dən), *Italian* **Gri·gi·o·ni** (grē·jyō′nē).

grist (grist) *n.* **1** A portion of grain brought to a mill to be ground; hence, that which is ground. **2** A supply; provision. **3** *U.S. Colloq.* A number or quantity of anything: a *grist* of flies. [OE <*grindan* grind]

gris·tle (gris′əl) *n.* Cartilage, especially in meat. [OE] **—gris′tled, gris′tly, gris′ly** *adj.* **—gris′tli·ness, gris′li·ness** *n.*

grist·mill (grist′mil′) *n.* A mill for grinding grain.

grit[1] (grit) *n.* **1** Rough, hard particles; sand or fine gravel. **2** A coarse compact sandstone adapted for grindstones. **3** *U.S.* Firmness of character, especially in pain or danger; pluck; courage. **4** Degree of hardness with openness of texture or composition: applied to burrstone, etc. — *v.* **grit·ted, grit·ting** *v.t.* To grind or press (the teeth) together, as in anger or determination. — *v.i.* To give forth a grating sound. [OE *grēot*]

grit[2] (grit) *n.* **1** Coarse meal. **2** *pl. U.S.* Coarsely ground hominy. [OE *grytte*]

grit[3] (grit) *adj. Scot.* Great; influential.

Grit (grit) *Canadian n.* A member of the Liberal Party. —*adj.* Of or pertaining to the Liberal Party.

grith (grith) *n.* Obs. **1** Security; specifically, in Old English law, **church grith,** the sanctuary or refuge afforded by a church. **2** A place of safety; sanctuary; refuge. Also spelled *girth.* [OE <ON *gridh* home; in pl., asylum]

grit·ty (grit′ē) *adj.* **·ti· er, ·ti·est** **1** Like, containing, or consisting of grit. **2** *U.S.* Full of pluck. **—grit′ti·ly** *adv.* **—grit′ti·ness** *n.*

gri·va·tion (gri·vā′shən) *n.* Grid variation.

griv·et (griv′it) *n.* A small monkey *(Cercopithecus aethiops)* of Abyssinia, greenish above, whitish below. [Origin unknown]

Griz·el (griz′əl) See GRISELDA. Also *Scot.* **Griz′zle.**

griz·zle[1] (griz′əl) *v.t. & v.i.* **griz·zled, griz·zling** To become or cause to become gray. [<*adj.*] —*n.* **1** A mixture of white and black; gray. **2** A gray wig. **3** *Obs.* A gray-haired person. —*adj.* Gray. [<OF *grisel* <*gris* gray] **—griz′zled** *adj.*

griz·zle[2] (griz′əl) *v.i.* **griz·zled, griz·zling** *Brit. Colloq.* To grumble or fret continuously. [Freq. of dial. E *grize* grind the teeth]

griz·zly (griz′lē) *adj.* **·zli·er, zli·est** Grayish; somewhat gray: also spelled *grisly.* ◆ Homophone: *grisly*[1]. — *n. pl.* **·zlies** A grizzly bear.

grizzly bear A large, powerful, yellowish or brownish bear *(Ursus horribilis)* of western North America.

groan (grōn) *v.i.* **1** To utter a low, prolonged sound of or as of pain, sorrow, etc.; moan. **2** To be oppressed or overburdened: The people *groaned* under the heavy taxes. —*v.t.* **3** To utter or express with groans. —*n.* A low moaning sound uttered in anguish, distress, or derision. [OE *grānian*] **—groan′er** *n.* **—groan′ ing** *adj. n.* **—groan′ing·ly** *adv.*

groat (grōt) *n.* **1** A former English silver coin of the 14th–17th centuries; fourpence. **2** A trifle. [<MDu. *groot,* orig. great, large]

groats (grōts) *n. pl.* Hulled and crushed oats or wheat; fragments of wheat larger than grits. [OE *grotan*]

gro·cer (grō′sər) *n.* One who deals in supplies for the table, as sugar, tea, coffee, spices, country produce, etc., and in other household articles. [<OF *grossier,* lit., one who trades in grosses, a wholesaler <Med. L *grossarius* < *grossus* gross, great]

gro·cer·y (grō′sər·ē) *n. pl.* **·cer·ies** **1** *U.S.* A grocer's store or shop. **2** *pl.* Supplies sold by a grocer.

Grod·no (grôd′nô) A city on the Nieman in western Belorussia; formerly in Poland.

grog (grog) *n.* A mixture of spirits and water; especially, rum and water; hence, any intoxicating drink. [after Old *Grog,* nickname (with ref. to his grogram cloak) of Admiral E. Vernon, 1684–1757, who first rationed it to English sailors]

grog·ger·y (grog′ər·ē) *n. pl.* **·ger·ies** *U.S. Slang* A low drinking place; a grogshop.

grog·gy (grog′ē) *adj.* **·gi·er, ·gi·est** **1** Unsteady on the feet or not fully conscious; dazed, as from weakness or exhaustion. **2** Drunk. **—grog′gi·ly** *adv.* **—grog′gi·ness** *n.*

grog·ram (grog′rəm) *n.* Grosgrain. [<F *gros grain.* See GROSGRAIN.]

grog·shop (grog′shop′) *n. Brit.* A low barroom.

groin (groin) *n.* 1 *Anat.* The fleshy hollow where the thigh joins the abdomen. ◆ Collateral adjective: *inguinal.* 2 *Archit.* The line of intersection of two vaults. —*v.t.* To build with or form into groins. [? OE *grynde* abyss, hollow]

groin-rib (groin′·rib′) *n. Archit.* A rib supporting or masking a groin; an ogive.

GROIN–RIBS
In a cathedral vault.

Gro·lier de Ser·vières (grō·lyā′ də ser·vyâr′), **Jean,** 1479–1565, French collector of books and designer of bindings.

Gro·lier design (grō′lē·ər, *Fr.* grō·lyā′) In bookbinding, an ornamental design characterized by geometrical or arabesque figures and leaf sprays in gold lines. Also **Grolier scroll.** [after Jean *Grolier* de Servières]

grom·met (grom′it) *n.* 1 *Naut.* A ring of rope, as on the peak of a sail. 2 A metallic eyelet, as for a mailbag. Also spelled *grummet.* [<F *gromette* <*gourmer* curb]

grom·well (grom′wəl) *n.* 1 A rough grayish herb *(Lithospermum officinale)* of the borage family. 2 Any plant of this genus. [<OF *gromil* <L *gruinum milium* <*gruinum* a crane + *milium* millet]

Gro·my·ko (grō·mē′kō), **Andrei A.,** born 1909, U.S.S.R. Communist leader and diplomat.

Gro·ning·en (grō′ning·ən, *Du.* khrō′ning·ən) A city in northern Netherlands.

groom (grōōm, grŏŏm) *n.* 1 A person who cares for horses in the stable; hostler. 2 A bridegroom. 3 *Archaic* A menial; page; servitor. 4 A dignitary in an English royal household under the chamberlain, having nominal offices to perform. —*v.t.* 1 To take care of; especially, to clean, curry, and brush (a horse). 2 To make neat, clean, and smart. 3 *U.S.* To prepare by training and developing, as for political office: to *groom* a candidate. [ME *grom.* Cf. OF *gromet* a servant.]

groomed (grōōmd, grŏŏmd) *adj.* Brushed and cleaned; cared for: often in combination: ill-*groomed,* well-*groomed.*

grooms·man (grōōmz′mən, grŏŏms′-) *n. pl.* **·men** (-mən) The best man at a wedding.

Groot (grōt), **Gerhard,** 1340–84, Dutch reformer and preacher: known as *Gerardus Magnus.* Also **Groete, Groote.**

groove (grōōv) *n.* 1 A furrow, channel, or long hollow, especially one cut by a tool for something to fit into or work in. 2 A fixed routine in the affairs of life. 3 *U.S. Slang* A satisfying or delightful experience. **—in the groove** *Slang* Acting or performing deftly and smoothly. —*v.* **grooved, groov·ing** *v.t.* 1 To form a groove in. 2 To fix in a groove. 3 *U.S. Slang* To take satisfaction or delight in; dig. —*v.i.* 4 *U.S. Slang* To find satisfaction or delight. [<Du. *groeve.* Akin to GRAVE[2], GRAVE[3].] **—groov′er** *n.*

groov·y (grōō′vē) *adj.* **groov·i·er, groov·i·est** *U.S. Slang* Satisfying; delightful; great; super: a *groovy* feeling; *groovy* people.

grope (grōp) *v.* **groped, grop·ing** *v.i.* To feel about with or as with the hands, as in the dark; feel one's way. —*v.t.* To seek out or find by or as by groping. [OE *grāpian.* Akin to GRIP.] **—grop′er** *n.* **—grop′ing** *adj.*

Gro·pi·us (grō′pē·əs), **Walter,** 1883–1969, German architect active in the United States.

Gros (grō), **Baron Antoine Jean,** 1771–1835, French painter.

gros·beak (grōs′bēk′) *n.* Any of certain species of finches or of other small birds allied to the finches and having a large stout beak, including the **rose-breasted grosbeak** *(Hedymeles ludovicianus)* and the **pine grosbeak** *(Pinicola enucleator)* of North America. [<F *grosbec* large beak]

gro·schen (grō′shən) *n. pl.* **·schen** A former silver coin of Germany and Austria, of small value; also a current Austrian coin, a hundredth part of a schilling.

gros de Lon·dres (grō də lôn′dr′) A heavy silk material having alternating horizontal ribs of varied fineness of yarns or of different colors. [<F, heavy (silk) of London]

gro·ser (grō′zər) *n. Scot.* A gooseberry.

gros·grain (grō′grān) *n.* A closely woven corded silk or rayon fabric, often having a cotton filling, and of dull luster: used for ribbons, collar facings, etc.: also called *grogram.* [<F, large grain]

gross (grōs) *adj.* 1 Conspicuous by reason of size or openness; glaring; flagrant: said of errors, wrongs, faults, untruths, etc. 2 Undiminished by deduction; entire: opposed to *net*: *gross* earnings, *gross* weight. 3 Coarse in meaning or sense; indelicate; obscene: *gross* epithets. 4 Of excessive or repulsive size combined with coarseness; big; fat; bulky: a *gross* woman. 5 Wanting in fineness; coarse in composition or structure: *gross* material. 6 Closely compacted, so as to be thick or dense: *gross* vapors. 7 Wanting in delicacy of perception or sensibility; dull of apprehension or feeling; stupid. 8 Not specific or detailed; general. 9 *Obs.* Palpable; obvious. See synonyms under CORPULENT, FOUL, IMMODEST, THICK, VULGAR. —*n. pl.* **gross** 1 Twelve dozen, as a unit. 2 The greater part; mass; entire amount. **—in gross** or **in the gross** In bulk; all together. —*v.t.* & *v.i.* To make or earn (total profit) before deduction of expenses, taxes, etc. [<OF *gros* <LL *grossus* thick] **—gross′ly** *adv.* **—gross′ness** *n.*

gross national product The total market value of a nation's goods and services, before any deductions or allowances are made.

gros·su·lar·ite (gros′yə·lə·rīt′) *n.* A variety of garnet composed of calcium aluminum silicate and varying from colorless when pure to pale green, gray, pink, or brown, depending on trace impurities. [<NL *grossularia* a gooseberry + -ITE[1]]

Gross·war·dein (grōs′vär·dīn′) The German name for ORADEA.

grosz (grôsh) *n. pl.* **grosz·y** (grôsh′ē) A hundredth part of a zloty. [<Polish]

Grosz (grōs), **George,** 1893–1959, German painter active in the United States.

grot (grot) *n. Poetic* A grotto. [<F *grotte.* See GROTTO.]

Grote (grōt), **George,** 1794–1871, English historian.

gro·tesque (grō·tesk′) *n.* 1 The incongruous, fantastic, or uncouth in art; specifically, painting or sculpture combining human and animal forms with foliage, wreaths, etc. 2 Any disproportionate or ludicrous person, figure, or design. —*adj.* 1 Incongruously composed or ill-proportioned; fantastic; ludicrously or whimsically odd or extravagant. 2 Containing or comprised of incongruous or fantastic details; pertaining to grotesques. See synonyms under FANCIFUL, ODD, RIDICULOUS. [<F <Ital. *grottesco* <*grotta* a grotto, excavation; with ref. to works of art found in excavations of ancient houses] **—gro·tesque′ness** *n.*

gro·tes·que·ry (grō·tes′kə·rē) *n. pl.* **·ries** 1 The quality of being grotesque; grotesqueness. 2 A grotesque object, action, event, etc. 3 A grotesque ornamental style or detail, as in architecture. Also **gro·tes′que·rie.**

Gro·ti·us (grō′shē·əs), **Hugo,** 1583–1645, Dutch jurist and statesman: called the "Father of International Law": originally, *Huig van Groot.*

grot·to (grot′ō) *n. pl.* **·toes** or **·tos** A small cave; an artificial cavernlike retreat. [<Ital. *grotta* <L *crypta.* Doublet of CRYPT.]

grouch (grouch) *U.S. Colloq. v.i.* To grumble; be surly or discontented. —*n.* 1 A discontented, grumbling person. 2 A grumbling, sulky mood. [<OF *groucher* murmur] **—grouch′er** *n.* **—grouch′i·ly** *adv.* **—grouch′i·ness** *n.* **—grouch′y** *adj.*

ground[1] (ground) *n.* 1 The firm, solid portion of the earth at and near its surface. 2 Hence, soil; earth; dirt. 3 Any region or tract of land, especially a portion put to special use: a parade *ground,* hunting *ground,* etc. 4 *Often pl.* A starting point; good reason; basis; sufficient cause: On what *ground* is the argument based?; also, pretext. 5 Position or distance: to gain, hold, or lose *ground.* 6 *pl.* The particles that settle at the bottom of a liquid preparation; dregs. 7 In various arts, some preparative work or part, as a surface to be worked on; in painting, a first coat or color or a surface prepared therewith. 8 *Music* The plain song or air as a basis for development and variation. 9 *Electr.* a A connection of a circuit with the earth. b An object or place to which a ground wire is attached. 10 *Often pl.* Private land; landed estate; especially in the plural, the enclosed spaces immediately appertaining to a mansion. 11 *Often pl.* The base or foundation, as of belief or knowledge. 12 The bottom, as of a lake or the ocean; lowest depth. See synonyms under LAND, REASON. **—to gain ground** 1 To conquer land. 2 To make progress; win favor, position, influence, etc. **—to stand one's ground** To maintain an argument or a purpose. —*adj.* 1 Being on the ground or on a level with it. 2 Fundamental: the *ground* form of a word. 3 Terrestrial: said of birds: the *ground* sparrow, *ground* warbler. 4 Burrowing: the *ground* squirrel, *ground* snake. 5 Growing on the ground; trailing or dwarfed: *ground* ivy, *ground* hemlock. —*v.t.* 1 To put, place, or set on the ground. 2 To fix firmly on a basis; found; establish. 3 To train (someone) in first principles or elements, as of Latin or science. 4 *Aeron.* To cause to stay on the ground. 5 *Naut.* To cause to run aground, as a ship. 6 To furnish (a surface) with a ground or background for painting, etc. 7 *Electr.* To place in connection with the earth, as a circuit. —*v.i.* 8 To come or fall to the ground. 9 In baseball, to be retired on a grounder batted to an opposing player: usually with *out.* 10 *Naut.* To run aground. 11 To sink to the bottom: The bait *grounds.* [OE *grund*]

ground[2] (ground) Past tense and past participle of GRIND.

ground·age (groun′dij) *n. Brit.* A charge for space occupied by a vessel while in port.

ground bait Bait dropped to the bottom to attract fish.

ground bass *Music* A short bass part or phrase repeated continually against varied melody and harmony in the upper parts.

ground beetle Any of various insectivorous beetles of the family *Carabidae,* often found under logs, stones, etc. For illustration see under INSECT (beneficial).

ground bird A field sparrow or vesper sparrow.

ground cherry Any of several plants of the nightshade family (genus *Physalis*), as the Cape gooseberry *(P. peruviana),* having yellow, edible berries, or the common strawberry tomato *(P. pruinosa).*

ground connection *Electr.* A wire or other conductor for grounding a current.

ground cover Low-growing plants, shrubs, and other vegetation.

ground crew *Aeron.* The crew required for the landing, servicing, repairing, and maintenance of aircraft, including the landing crew, mechanics, etc.

ground·er (groun′dər) *n.* 1 One who or that which grounds. 2 In baseball, a batted ball that rolls or bounces along the ground.

ground floor The floor of a building level or almost level with the ground. —*U.S. Colloq.* **to get in on the ground floor** To enter a company or join a business undertaking at its inception and hence receive equal profits with the promoters.

ground fog *Meteorol.* A narrow layer of fog formed over a cool land surface, and not exceeding the height of a man.

ground frost A ground temperature low enough to cause injury to growing plants: usually reckoned at 30° F.

ground gear *Aeron.* The apparatus and equipment needed for the landing of aircraft and their handling while on the ground.

ground glass See under GLASS.

ground hemlock A low, evergreen shrub *(Taxus canadensis)* of the northern United States with long, straggling branches and a red fruit; the American yew: also called *moosegrass.*

ground hog 1 The woodchuck. 2 The aardvark. 3 A sandhog.

ground-hog day (ground′hôg′, -hog′) February 2, Candlemas: according to rural tradition, if the ground hog, emerging after hibernation, sees his shadow on this day, he retreats to his hole, thus indicating six weeks more of winter; if he does not see his shadow it is a sign of an early spring.

ground ivy A creeping herb *(Nepeta hederacea)* with roundish, kidney-shaped, scalloped leaves and bluish-purple flowers.

ground laurel The trailing arbutus.

ground·less (ground′lis) *adj.* Without foundation, reason, or cause. —**ground′less·ly** *adv.* —**ground′less·ness** *n.*

ground·ling (ground′ling) *n.* 1 An animal of terrestrial habits. 2 A plant which creeps on the ground. 3 A fish that keeps to the bottom. 4 Formerly, one of the audience in the pit of a theater; hence, a person of unrefined tastes.

ground loop *Aeron.* An acute, ungovernable turning of an aircraft during a landing or a take-off.

ground·mass (ground′mas′) *n. Geol.* A compact and fine-grained or glassy portion of porphyritic igneous rock, in which the phenocrysts, or larger, distinct crystals, are embedded.

ground·nut (ground′nut′) *n.* 1 The peanut. 2 Any of several plants having edible tubers attached to the roots, as the **ground pea,** a North American wild bean (*Apios americana*), and the dwarf ginseng (*Panax trifolium*). 3 St. Anthony's nut.

ground owl A small, long-legged, terrestrial owl (*Speotyto cunicularia*) common in the western United States, where it digs extensive nesting burrows in open prairie country: also called *burrowing owl.*

ground pine 1 An evergreen, generally creeping plant (*Lycopodium obscurum*); clubmoss. 2 An evergreen European herb (*Ajuga chamaepitys*): so called from its resinous odor.

ground pink The moss pink.

ground plan 1 The plan of the ground floor of a building. 2 Any preliminary plan or outline.

ground plate 1 A groundsill. 2 A bedplate, as for railroad ties. 3 *Electr.* A metal plate in the ground forming the earth connection of a circuit.

ground plum 1 A plant (*Astragalus crassicarpus*) of the bean family, found in the western Mississippi valley from Minnesota to Texas. 2 Its thick, fleshy, plum-shaped pod. Also called *milkvetch.*

ground rattlesnake The massasauga.

ground rent Compensation paid each year, or for a term of years, for grounds leased for building or other improvement.

ground-re·turn circuit (ground′ri·tûrn′) See EARTH RETURN.

ground robin The towhee.

ground·sel (ground′səl) *n.* 1 A common herb of the composite family (genus *Senecio*), having yellow tubular flowers. 2 Groundsill. [OE *gundæswelgiæ,* lit., that swallows pus (with ref. to its use in poultices); infl. in form by OE *grund* ground]

groundsel tree A small tree of the North American Atlantic coast (*Baccharis halimifolia*), with showy white or yellow flowers.

ground·sill (ground′sil′) *n.* The lowest horizontal timber in a frame building: also *groundsel.*

ground sparrow Any of various small sparrows that nest on the ground, as the vesper sparrow or the song sparrow.

ground speed *Aeron.* The speed of an airplane with relation to the earth. See AIR SPEED.

ground squirrel 1 A chipmunk. 2 A gopher.

ground state *Physics* That condition of an atom which corresponds to its lowest level of energy and, hence, to its maximum stability.

ground swell A broad, deep swell or heaving of the sea caused by prolonged storm, continuing into calm weather, and frequently reaching open stretches of coast remote from the area of the storm.

ground water Free subsurface water, the top of which is the water table; all water in and saturating the soil.

ground wave A radio wave which travels along the surface of the ground.

ground·ways (ground′wāz′) *n. pl. Naut.* Timbers fixed to the ground and extending fore and aft under the hull of a ship and on each side of the keel, to form the surface track on which a ship is launched.

ground wire The wire connecting an electrical apparatus with the ground or with a grounded object.

ground·work (ground′wûrk′) *n.* A fundamental part; basis.

ground zero The point on the ground vertically beneath or above the point of detonation of an atomic or thermonuclear bomb.

group (groop) *n.* 1 A number of persons, animals, or things existing or brought together; an assemblage; cluster. 2 In painting or sculpture, an assemblage of figures or objects affording a harmonious unit or design. 3 A number of plants or animals classed together because of certain common characteristics. 4 In the U.S. Air Force, a tactical, maintenance, medical, or administrative subdivision of a wing. 5 In the U.S. Army or Marine Corps, a tactical unit consisting of two or more battalions. 6 *Chem.* **a** A number of connected atoms constituting a part of a molecule: the hydroxyl *group* (OH). **b** A set of elements having similar properties, as in the periodic table. 7 *Geol.* A rock system of highest rank, corresponding with an era in the time scale. 8 An ethnological or linguistic division ranking below a branch. —*v.t. & v.i.* To gather or form into a group or groups. [<F *groupe* <Ital. *groppo* knot, lump <Gmc.]

group·er (groo′pər) *n.* Any of certain serranoid food fishes of warm seas, of *Mycteroperca, Epinephalus,* and related genera. [<Pg. *garupa,* appar. <S. Am. Ind.]

group·ie (groo′pē) *n. Slang* A fan or supporter, especially a young woman who follows a performer in a rock-and-roll group on tour.

group·ment (groop′mənt) *n.* A grouping; specifically, a grouping of battalions or larger units.

grouse[1] (grous) *n. pl.* **grouse** Any of a family (*Tetraonidae*) of game birds of the northern hemisphere, related to the pheasants, smaller than the domestic hen, and having mottled plumage; especially, the **red grouse** (*Lagopus scoticus*) of the British Isles, the **ruffed grouse** or partridge (*Bonasa umbellus*) of the

RUFFED GROUSE
(From 12 to 17 inches tall)

United States, the **pinnated grouse** or prairie chicken (*Tympanuchus cupido*), the **sage grouse** or cock of the plains, the **spruce grouse** or spruce partridge (*Canachites canadensis*), and the capercaillie. [Origin uncertain]

grouse[2] (grous) *Slang v.i.* **groused, grous·ing** To grumble; grouch. [<OF *grousser* murmur] —**grous′er** *n.* —**grous′ing** *n.*

grout (grout) *n.* 1 A light, semi-liquid cement mortar used to fill joints between stones, bricks or tiles. 2 A finishing coat for surfaces. 3 Coarse meal. 4 *pl.* Groats. 5 *pl.* Dregs; lees; grounds. 6 A wall coating of rough plaster studded with small stones. —*v.t.* To fill, surround, or finish with grout. [OE *grūt* coarse meal] —**grout′er** *n.*

grout·y (grou′tē) *adj.* 1 Turbid, as liquor. 2 *Slang* Cross or surly; sulky.

grove (grōv) *n.* A group of trees, smaller than a forest; a small wood, especially when cleared of underbrush. ♦ Collateral adjective: *nemoral.* [OE *grāf*]

grov·el (gruv′əl, grov′-) *v.i.* **grov·eled** or **grov·elled, grov·el·ing** or **grov·el·ling** 1 To creep or crawl face downward; lie abjectly prostrate. 2 To act with abject humility; abase oneself, as from fear or servility. 3 To take pleasure in what is base or sensual. [Back formation <GROVELING] —**grov′el·er** or **grov′el·ler** *n.*

grov·el·ing (gruv′əl·ing, grov′-) *adj.* Lying prostrate; abject; low; mean; sordid. Also **grov·el·ling.** See synonyms under BASE[2]. [ME *grovelynge, adv.* <on gruff face down (<ON *á grufu*) + -LING[2]] —**grov′el·ing·ly** *adv.*

groves of Ac·a·deme (ak′ə·dēm′) See under ACADEME.

grow (grō) *v.* **grew, grown, grow·ing** *v.i.* 1 To increase in size by the assimilation of nutriment; progress toward maturity. 2 To sprout and develop to maturity, as from a seed or spore. 3 To flourish; thrive: Moss *grows* in damp places. 4 To become more in size, quantity, or degree: The storm was *growing.* 5 To become; come to be gradually: She was *growing* angry. 6 To become fixed or attached by or as by growth: The vine *grew* to the wall. 7 To cause to grow; raise by cultivation. 8 To develop: This crab will *grow* a new shell. 9 To cover with a growth: used in the passive: The hull was *grown* with weeds. —**grow on** To become gradually more pleasing or important to. —**grow up** To reach adult maturity. See synonyms under FLOURISH. [OE *grōwan*] —**grow′er** *n.*

grow·ing-pains (grō′ing·pānz′) *n. pl.* 1 Pains of a rheumatic or neuralgic character sometimes experienced during the period of growth in children. 2 Problems encountered in the early phases of an enterprise.

growl (groul) *n.* 1 The guttural threatening sound made by an angry animal. 2 Angry fault-finding; grumbling. —*v.i.* 1 To utter a growl, as an angry dog. 2 To grumble or find fault in a surly manner. 3 To rumble, as distant thunder. —*v.t.* 4 To express by growling. See synonyms under COMPLAIN. [? <OF *grouler* mumble <Gmc.]

growl·er (grou′lər) *n.* 1 One who or that which growls. 2 *U.S. Slang* A vessel in which beer is carried home from the place of sale. 3 *Brit. Slang* A four-wheeled cab. 4 *Electr.* A device which indicates the presence of a short circuit by a growling sound produced by two field poles arranged as in a motor. 5 An irregular fragment of an iceberg or mass of floe ice large enough to be dangerous to ships.

grown (grōn) *adj.* Mature; fully developed.

grown-up (grōn′up′) *n.* A mature person. —*adj.* (grōn′up′) Adult or like adults.

growth (grōth) *n.* 1 The process of growing; gradual increase of a living organism by natural process; development to maturity or full size. 2 Any gradual increase or development; augmentation; progress. 3 Anything grown or produced, or in the process of growing; product; effect. 4 *Pathol.* A morbid formation: a cancerous *growth.* See synonyms under HARVEST, INCREASE, PROGRESS.

growth industry An industry with a rate of growth or development greater than the rate of growth of the economy as a whole.

growth ring An annual ring.

Groz·ny (grôz′nē) A city east of the Caspian Sea, Russian S.F.S.R. Also **Groz′nyy.**

grub (grub) *v.* **grubbed, grub·bing** *v.i.* 1 To dig in the ground. 2 To do menial labor; toil: to *grub* for a living. 3 To make careful or plodding search; rummage. 4 *Slang* To eat. —*v.t.* 5 To dig from the ground; root out: often with *up* or *out.* 6 To clear (ground) of roots, stumps, etc. 7 *Slang* To provide with food. —*n.* 1 The wormlike larva of certain insects, as of the June beetle and most of the *Hymenoptera.* See illustration under INSECT. 2 One who grubs; a grind or drudge. 3 *Slang* Food. [ME *grubben.* Akin to GRAVE[1], GRAVE[2].]

grub·ber (grub′ər) *n.* 1 One who or that which grubs. 2 A grub hoe. 3 A machine or tool for pulling up stumps.

grub·by (grub′ē) *adj.* **·bi·er, ·bi·est** 1 Dirty; unclean. 2 Full of grubs: specifically used in the western United States of cattle or sheep attacked by the larvae of botflies or warbleflies. —**grub′bi·ly** *adv.* —**grub′bi·ness** *n.*

grub hoe A heavy hoe for digging or for grubbing out stumps; a mattock. See illustration under HOE.

grub·stake (grub′stāk′) *U.S. n.* Money, supplies, or equipment provided a prospector on condition of a share of his finds. —*v.t.* **·staked, ·stak·ing** To supply with a grubstake.

grub·street (grub′strēt′) *adj.* Characteristic of literary hacks or their work; second-rate. —*n.* Inferior authors and literary hacks as a class, or their work.

Grub Street The former name of Milton Street, London, once frequented by needy authors and literary hacks.

grudge (gruj) *v.* **grudged, grudg·ing** *v.t.* 1 To envy the possessions or good fortunes of (another). 2 To give or allow unwillingly and resentfully; begrudge. —*v.i.* 3 *Obs.* To be envious or discontented; grumble. —*n.* 1 Ill will cherished for some remembered wrong. 2 Reluctance; unwillingness. See synonyms under HATRED, PIQUE[1]. [<OF *groucher.* Cf. GROUCH.] —**grudg′er** *n.* —**grudg′ing·ly** *adv.*

Gru·dziadz (groo′jônts) A city on the Vistula in northern Poland: German *Graudenz.*

grue (gro͞o) *v.i. Scot.* & *Brit. Dial.* To feel dread or horror; shudder. [Akin to Du. *gruwen* shudder]

gru·el (gro͞o′əl) *n.* A semi-liquid food made by boiling meal in water or milk. — **to take one's gruel** To take one's punishment. — *v.t.* **gru·eled** or **gru·elled, gru·el·ing** or **gru·el·ling** To wear out, disable, or exhaust by hard work, punishment, etc. [<OF, meal, ult. <Med. L *grutum* coarse meal <Gmc.] — **gru′el·er** or **gru′el·ler** *n.* — **gru′el·ly** *adj.*

gru·el·ing (gro͞o′əl·ing) *adj.* Severe; exhausting; punishing. — *n.* Punishment; exhausting labor; prolonged and relentless questioning, etc. Also **gru′el·ling.**

grue·some (gro͞o′səm) *adj.* Frightening; grisly: also spelled *grewsome.* [<GRUE + -SOME] — **grue′some·ly** *adv.* — **grue′some·ness** *n.*

gruff (gruf) *adj.* Having a rough or brusque manner, voice, or countenance; harsh; surly. See synonyms under MOROSE. [<Du. *grof* rough] — **gruff′ish, gruff′y** *adj.* — **gruff′ly, gruff′i·ly** *adv.* — **gruff′ness, gruff′i·ness** *n.*

gru–gru (gro͞o′gro͞o′) *n.* **1** Either of two West Indian palms *(Acrocomia aculeata* or *A. sclerocarpa)* the nuts of which yield a butter-like oil used for scenting toilet soap: also **gru–gru palm. 2** The larva of a South American palm weevil *(Rhynchophorus palmarum),* destructive to the gru–gru and other palms and sugarcane, and eaten as a delicacy: also **gru–gru worm.** [<Sp. *grugrú* <Cariban]

grum (grum) *adj.* **grum·mer, grum·mest** *Rare* **1** Morose, sullen, or sour; surly. **2** Guttural; gruff. [Prob. blend of GRIM and GLUM]

grum·ble (grum′bəl) *v.* **grum·bled, grum·bling** *v.i.* **1** To complain in a surly manner; mutter. **2** To make growling sounds in the throat. **3** To rumble, as thunder. — *v.t.* **4** To say with a grumble. See synonyms under COMPLAIN. — *n.* **1** A surly, discontented sound or complaint; murmur. **2** *pl.* An ill-tempered, complaining mood. **3** A rumble. [Cf. Du. *grommelen* < *grommen* growl] — **grum′bler** *n.* — **grum′bling·ly** *adv.* — **grum′bly** *adj.*

Grum·ble·to·ni·an (grum′bəl·tō′nē·ən) *n.* A political nickname for one who opposed the policies of William III of England.

grume (gro͞om) *n.* **1** A viscid, semifluid mass. **2** A clot, as of blood. [<F <L *grumus* little pile]

grum·met (grum′it) See GROMMET.

gru·mose (gro͞o′mōs) *adj. Bot.* Consisting of clustered grains.

gru·mous (gro͞o′məs) *adj.* **1** Like grume; clotted. **2** Grumose.

grumph (grumf) *Scot. v.t.* & *v.i.* To grunt. — *n.* A grunt.

grumph·ie (grum′fē) *n. Scot.* A pig; especially, a sow. Also **grumph′y.**

grump·y (grum′pē) *adj.* **grump·i·er, grump·i·est** Exhibiting surliness or gruffness; cranky. Also **grump′ish.** [Blend of GRUNT and DUMP] — **grump′i·ly** *adv.* — **grump′i·ness** *n.*

grund (gro͝ond) *Scot. v.* & *n.* Ground. Also **grun.**

Grun·dy (grun′dē), **Mrs.** A character in Morton's comedy, *Speed the Plough* (1798): now symbolizing society in general as a censor of morals and manners. — **Grun′dy·ism** *n.*

grun·ion (gro͞on·yōn′) *n.* A silversides *(Leuresthes tenuis),* common on the coast of California. [Prob. <Sp. *gruñón* grunter]

grun·stane (gro͞on′stən) *n. Scot.* A grindstone. Also **grun′stun.**

grunt (grunt) *v.i.* **1** To make the deep, guttural sound of a hog. **2** To make a similar sound, as in annoyance, assent, effort, etc. — *v.t.* **3** To express, as dissent or disapproval, by grunting. See synonyms under COMPLAIN. — *n.* **1** A short, guttural sound, as of a hog. **2** A food fish of warm American seas related to the snappers (*Haemulon* and related genera): so called from the noise it makes when caught. [OE *grunnettan*] — **grunt′er** *n.*

grun·tle (grun′təl) *Brit. Dial. v.i.* To grunt; sulk. — *n.* A grunt; a snout. [Freq. of GRUNT]

grun·yie (gro͞on′yē) *n. Scot.* A snout. Also **grun′zie.**

Grus (grus) A constellation, the Crane. See under CONSTELLATION.

grush·ie (grush′ē, gro͞osh′ē) *adj. Scot.* Growing luxuriantly; thick.

grutch (gruch, gro͞och) *v.t.* & *v.i. Scot.* & *Brit. Dial.* Grudge.

Gru·yère (grē·yâr′, gro͞o-; *Fr.* grü·yâr′) *n.* A light-yellow, whole-milk Swiss cheese, usually without holes. [from *Gruyère,* a town in Switzerland]

Gru·zi·ya (gro͞o′zyē·yə) The Russian name for GEORGIA, U.S.S.R.

gryl·lid (gril′id) *n.* One of a family *(Gryllidae)* of orthopterous insects having the hind legs specialized for jumping, long, slender antennae, and wings frequently reduced or absent; a cricket. — *adj.* Of or pertaining to the *Gryllidae.* [<NL <L *gryllus* a grasshopper <Gk. *gryllos*]

G–string (jē′string′) *n.* **1** A strip of cloth passed between the legs and supported at the waist by a band or cord; a loincloth. **2** A thin strip of cloth, often ornamented with tassels and spangles, worn about the groin and hip by strip-teasers.

gua·cha·ro (gwä′chä·rō) *n.* The oilbird *(Steatornis caripensis)* of South America and Trinidad, of frugivorous and nocturnal habits, from whose young an oil is extracted and used by the natives as butter and for illumination. [<Sp. *guácharo*]

gua·co (gwä′kō) *n.* Any of certain tropical American climbing plants used as antidotes to snake bites; especially, the birthworts (genus *Aristolochia*), closely allied to the Virginia snakeroot, and a climbing Brazilian plant (genus *Mikania*), of the composite family. [<Sp. < native name]

Gua·da·la·ja·ra (gwä′thä·lä·hä′rä) A city of west central Mexico, capital of Jalisco state.

Gua·dal·ca·nal (gwä′dəl·kə·nal′) The largest island in the British Solomon Islands protectorate; 2,500 square miles; scene of first Allied invasion northward in the Pacific in World War II, August, 1943.

Gua·dal·qui·vir (gwä′thäl·kē·vir′) A river in southern Spain, flowing over 360 miles SW to the Gulf of Cadiz.

Gua·da·lupe Hi·dal·go (gwä′də·lo͞op′ hi·dal′gō, *Sp.* gwä′thä·lo͞o′pä ē·thäl′gō) A former town, part of Gustavo A. Madero federal district in south central Mexico; site of the shrine of Our Lady of Guadalupe and of the signing of the treaty ending the Mexican War, 1848.

Gua·da·lupe Mountains (gô′də·lo͞op′, gwä′·də·lo͞op′) A range in SW Texas and southern New Mexico between the Pecos and Rio Grande rivers; highest point, **Guadalupe Peak,** is highest point in Texas, 8,751 feet.

Gua·da·lupe River (gô′də·lo͞op′, gwä′də·lo͞op′) A river in Texas, flowing 458 miles SE to San Antonio Bay.

Gua·de·loupe (gô′də·lo͞op′, *Fr.* gwȧ·də·lo͞op′) An overseas department of France in the Lesser Antilles, comprising the twin islands of Basse-Terre (also called *Guadeloupe*) and Grande-Terre; together 583 square miles; with island dependencies, 639 square miles; capital, Basse-Terre.

Gua·di·a·na (gwä′dē·ä′nə, *Pg.* gwə·thya′nə; *Sp.* gwä·thyä′nä) A river in SW Spain and SE Portugal, flowing west 510 miles to the Gulf of Cádiz.

guai·ac (gwī′ak) *n.* **1** A brown or greenish-brown resin extracted from guaiacum: used in medicine, in making paints and varnishes, etc.: also **guai′a·cum** (-ə·kəm). **2** The Tonka bean.

guai·a·col (gwī′ə·kōl, -kol) *n. Chem.* A colorless fluid or white crystalline compound, $C_7H_8O_2$, obtained by distilling guaiacum, found in hardwood tar, and also made synthetically: its compounds are widely used in medicine. [<GUAIAC(UM) + -OL[2]]

guai·a·cum (gwī′ə·kəm) *n.* **1** Any of a genus *(Guajacum)* of tropical American trees or shrubs of the caltrop family, especially *G. officinale* and *G. sanctum.* **2** The hard, durable, resinous wood of this tree or shrub; lignumvitae. **3** Guaiac. [<NL <Sp. *guayacán* <Taino]

Guai·ra (gwī′rə), **La** See LA GUAIRA.

Gual·te·ri·o (gwäl·tā′rē·ō) Spanish form of WALTER. *Ital.* **Gual·tie·ro** (gwäl·tyâ′rō).

Guam (gwäm) The largest island of the Marianas group, comprising an unincorporated territory of the United States; ceded by Spain in 1898; 217 square miles; capital, Agaña. — **Gua·ma·ni·an** (gwə·mā′nē·ən) *adj.* & *n.*

guan (gwän) *n.* A Central and South American gallinaceous bird (subfamily *Penelopinae*), related to the curassows, having a long tail. [<Sp. <Cariban]

Gua·na·ba·ra Bay (gwu·nə·vä′rə) An inlet of the Atlantic in SE Brazil; Rio de Janeiro is on the SW shore. Also **Río de Janeiro Bay.**

gua·na·co (gwä·nä′kō) *n. pl.* **·cos** or **·co** A South American ruminant of the llama family *(Lama huanacus),* of light-brown color, passing into white below: also spelled *huanaco.* [<Sp. < Quechua]

GUANACO
(From 4 to 4 1/2 feet high at the shoulder)

Gua·na·jua·to (gwä′·nä·hwä′tō) A state in central Mexico; 11,804 square miles; capital Guanajuato.

gua·nase (gwä′nās) *n. Biochem.* An autolytic enzyme capable of changing guanine into xanthine.

gua·ni·dine (gwä′nə·dēn, -din, gwan′ə-) *n. Chem.* A strongly basic crystalline compound, CH_5N_3, formed by the oxidation of guanine: many of its derivatives are used in the making of plastics, resins, explosives, etc. Also **gua′·ni·din** (-din).

gua·nine (gwä′nēn) *n. Biochem.* A white amorphous compound, $C_5H_5N_5O$, contained in guano, fish scales, muscle tissue, the pancreas: it is also a decomposition product of nucleoproteins. Also **gua′nin** (-nin). [<GUANO + -INE[2]]

gua·no (gwä′nō) *n. pl.* **·nos 1** The accumulated excrement of sea birds found in the dry climate of the Peruvian coast and elsewhere: used as a fertilizer. **2** A manufactured nitrogenous fertilizer; also, decomposing animal remains used as a fertilizer. [<Sp. <Quechua *huanu* dung]

Guan·tá·na·mo (gwän·tä′nä·mō) A city near **Guantánamo Bay,** a sheltered Caribbean inlet, site of a U. S. naval station in SE Cuba.

Guap (wäp) A former spelling of YAP.

Gua·po·ré (gwä·pô·rā′) **1** A river of central South America, forming part of the boundary between Brazil and NE Bolivia and flowing 750 miles NW to the Mamore: also *Iténez.* **2** The former name of RONDÔNIA.

gua·ra·ni (gwä′rä·nē′) *n.* The basic monetary unit of Paraguay, equal to 100 centavos.

Gua·ra·ni (gwä′rä·nē′) *n. pl.* **·nis** or **·ni 1** A member of any of a group of South American Indian tribes, comprising the southern branch of the Tupian stock, and formerly occupying the valleys of the Paraná and the Uruguay. **2** The Tupian language of these tribes. [< Tupian, a warrior]

guar·an·tee (gar′ən·tē′) *n.* **1** A pledge or formal assurance that something will meet stated specifications or that a specified act will be performed. **2** Something given as security. **3** A guarantor. **4** Something which assures a certain outcome: Diligence is a *guarantee* of success. — *v.t.* **·teed, ·tee·ing 1** To certify or vouch for the performance of (something); warrant. **2** To make (oneself) responsible for the obligation of another. **3** To secure against loss or damage. **4** To affirm with certainty; promise; swear: He *guarantees* to be there. [Var. of GUARANTY]

guar·an·tor (gar′ən·tər, -tôr′) *n.* One who or that which guarantees or warrants; one who makes a guaranty or makes himself responsible for the obligation of another.

guar·an·ty (gar′ən·tē) *n. pl.* **·ties 1** A pledge, made in separate contract, to be responsible for the contract, debt, or duty of another person in case of his default or miscarriage. **2** A deposit or security made in place of such a pledge. **3** The assumption of such responsibility by pledge or security. **4** A guarantor. — *v.t.* **·tied, ·ty·ing** To guarantee. [<OF *guarantie* < *guarantir* warrant < *guarant* a warrant <Gmc. Doublet of WARRANTY.]

guard (gärd) *v.t.* **1** To stand guard over (a door, pass, etc.). **2** To watch over so as to keep from harm, loss, etc.; protect. **3** To watch over so as to keep from escaping. **4** To keep a check on; restrain: *Guard* your tongue. **5** *Archaic* To escort. — *v.i.* **6** To take precautions; be on guard. See synonyms under KEEP, PRESERVE, SHELTER. — *n.* **1** One who or that which protects, defends, or secures from loss, injury, or attack; hence, defense; protection; watch. **2** Specifically, a man or a

body of men occupied in preserving a person or place from attack, or in controlling prisoners or preventing their escape. **3** Precaution against surprise or attack; care; attention. **4** A posture, attitude, or condition of defense. **5** Any of various protective or defensive devices for wearing, or for attaching to an object, as a machine or implement. **6** *Brit.* A railway official in charge of a train; a conductor. **7** *U.S.* An official employed on elevated and subway trains at points of entrance and egress. **8** In football, one of two line players (the **right guard** and **left guard**) who support the center; also, one of two players in basketball with similar positions and titles. See synonyms under DEFENSE, RAMPART. **—on guard 1** Ready for defense or protection; on the watch, as a military guard. **2** The first position in fencing or in bayonet exercises. Also, *French, en garde.* [<OF *guarder, garder* <Gmc. Akin to WARD.] — **guard′er** *n.*

Guar·da·fui (gwär′dä·fwē′), **Cape** A cape of eastern Africa, at the eastern tip of the Gulf of Aden.

guar·dant (gär′dənt) *Obs. adj.* **1** Exercising guardianship; guarding. **2** Gardant. —*n.* A guardian. [<OF *gardant,* pp. of *garder* guard]

guard cell *Bot.* A specialized epidermal cell in plants, controlling the pores by which gases enter and pass out from the leaves and young stems.

guard·ed (gär′did) *adj.* Exhibiting caution; circumspect; also, protected. —**guard′ed·ly** *adv.* —**guard′ed·ness** *n.*

guard·house (gärd′hous′) *n.* **1** A quarters and headquarters for military guards. **2** A building for confinement of military personnel convicted of minor offenses or awaiting court martial.

guard·i·an (gär′dē·ən) *n.* **1** *Law* A person who legally has the care of the person or property, or both, of one who is incompetent to act for himself, especially of an infant or minor. **2** One to whom anything is committed for safekeeping or preservation. **3** One who guards; a warden. ◆ Collateral adjective: *custodial.* —*adj.* Keeping guard; watching; protecting; tutelary. [<OF *guarden* <*guarder* guard. Doublet of WARDEN.] —**guard′i·an·ship** *n.*

guard·rail (gärd′rāl′) *n.* **1** *Naut.* A timber bolted to a ship's side to serve as a fender. **2** On railroads, a beam or rail parallel to a main rail in a track to prevent the wheels from jumping the track: used on curves and other dangerous places. **3** A protective railing around any dangerous place.

guard·room (gärd′ro͞om′, -ro͝om′) *n.* **1** The room occupied by a military guard while on duty. **2** A room where prisoners are kept under guard.

guards·man (gärdz′mən) *n. pl.* **·men** (-mən) **1** A man who serves as a guard. **2** *U.S.* A member of the National Guard.

guard–wire (gärd′wīr′) *n. Electr.* A grounded wire erected near a low–voltage circuit or public crossing as a safeguard against accidental contact with a high–voltage overhead conductor.

Guá·ri·co (gwä′rē·kō) A state in central Venezuela; 25,640 square miles; capital, San Juan de los Morros.

Guar·ne·ri (gwär·nā′rē) Name of a family of Italian violin–makers, notably **Giuseppe Antonio,** 1687?–1745. Also **Guar·nie′ri** (-nyâ′rē).

Guar·ne·ri·us (gwär·nā′rē·əs) *n.* A violin made by a member of the Guarneri family.

Gua·te·ma·la (gwä′tə·mä′lä) A Central American republic south and east of Mexico; 42,042 square miles; capital, Guatemala City. — **Gua′te·ma′lan** *adj.* & *n.*

gua·va (gwä′və) *n.* **1** A small tropical American tree or shrub of the myrtle family (genus *Psidium*). **2** Its fruit, about the size of a crab apple, chiefly used in making guava jelly. [<Sp. *guayaba,* appar. <S. Am. Ind.]

Gua·via·re (gwä·vyä′rā) A river in eastern and central Colombia, flowing 650 miles east to the Orinoco.

Guay·a·quil (gwī′ä·kēl′) A port of western Ecuador on the **Gulf of Guayaquil,** a Pacific bay in SW Ecuador.

gua·yu·le (gwä·yo͞o′lā) *n.* **1** A perennial herb (*Parthenium argentatum*) of the composite family, grown in Mexico, Texas, and California. **2** The resinous latex of this tree, yielding a natural rubber: also **guayule rubber.** [<Sp. <Nahuatl]

gu·ber·na·to·ri·al (go͞o′bər·nə·tôr′ē·əl, -tō′rē-, gyo͞o′-) *adj.* Of or pertaining to a governor or the office of governor. [<L *gubernator* a governor <*gubernare* govern]

gu·ber·ni·ya (go͞o·ber′nē·yä) *n.* **1** In the U.S.S.R., an administrative subdivision under a rural soviet. **2** In Russia before 1917, an administrative division corresponding to a province. [<Russian, ult. <L *gubernare* govern]

guck (guk) *n. U.S. & Canadian Slang* Goo; muck.

gude (güd) *adj. Scot.* Good: also spelled *guid.*

Gude (güd) *n. Scot.* God: also spelled *Goad.*

gude·fa·ther (güd′fä′thər) *n. Scot.* Father–in–law: also spelled *guidfather.*

gude·man (güd′män) *n. Scot.* Husband; the head of a house; goodman: also spelled *guidman.*

gude·wife (güd′wīf′) *n. Scot.* **1** The mistress of a house; goodwife. **2** A landlady.

gudg·eon[1] (guj′ən) *n.* **1** An Old World, carplike, fresh–water fish (genus *Gobio*), very easily caught. **2** A minnow. **3** A simpleton. **4** Anything swallowed credulously; bait. —*v.t.* To impose upon; cheat; dupe. [<OF *goujon* <L *gobio,* var. of *gobios.* See GOBY.]

gudg·eon[2] (guj′ən) *n.* **1** *Mech.* The bearing of a shaft, especially when made of a separate piece. **2** A metallic journal piece let into the end of a wooden shaft. [<OF *gougeon* pin of a pulley]

Gud·run (go͝od′ro͞on) **1** In the *Gudrun Lied,* a 13th century German national epic, a princess, daughter of Hettal, king of Denmark. **2** In the *Volsunga Saga,* the daughter of the king of the Nibelungs and wife of Sigurd, later married to Atli. Also spelled *Guthrun.*

Gue·ber (gā′bər), **Gue·bre** See GHEBER.

Guel·der·land (gel′dər·land) See GELDERLAND.

guel·der–rose (gel′dər·rōz′) *n.* The snowball tree, a cultivated variety of cranberry with white flowers. [from *Guelder(land) rose*]

Guel·ders (gel′dərz) See GELDERLAND.

Guelf (gwelf) *n.* **1** A member of a medieval political faction in Italy that supported the papacy in its struggle against the influence of the German emperors: opposed to the *Ghibellines.* **2** A member of a German princely family, founded in the time of Charlemagne by Welf I in Swabia, from which the Hanoverian line of English kings descended. Also **Guelph.** [<Ital. *Guelfo,* ult. after OHG *Welf,* a family name] —**Guelf′i·an, Guelf′ic** *adj.* —**Guelf′ism** *n.*

gue·non (gə·nōn′, *Fr.* gə·nôṅ′) *n.* A long–tailed monkey (genus *Cercopithecus*) found in Mozambique, Africa: its banded hairs give it a mottled appearance. [<F; ult. origin unknown]

guer·don (gûr′dən) *n.* An honorable reward; requital. [<OF <Med. L *widerdonum* <OHG *widarlōn* <*widar* in turn + *lōn* reward] — **guer′don·er** *n.*

Gue·rick·e (gā′rik·ə), **Otto von,** 1602–86, German physicist.

Guer·ni·ca (ger·nē′kä) A town in northern Spain; bombed by German planes in 1937.

guern·sey (gûrn′zē) *n.* A knitted shirt; jersey.

Guern·sey (gûrn′zē) *n.* One of a breed of dairy cattle from the island of Guernsey, Channel Islands.

Guern·sey (gûrn′zē) One of the Channel Islands; 25 square miles.

guerre à mort (gâr à môr′) *French* War to the death.

Guer·re·ro (ger·rā′rō) A state in SW Mexico; 24,885 square miles; capital, Chilpancingo.

guer·ril·la (gə·ril′ə) *n.* One of an irregular, independent band of partisan soldiers. Also **gue·ril′la.** [<Sp. *guerrilla,* dim. of *guerra* a war]

Guesde (ged), **Jules Basile,** 1845–1922, French socialist. —**Guesd′ism** *n.* —**Guesd′ist** *adj.* & *n.*

guess (ges) *v.t.* **1** To form a judgment or opinion of (something) on uncertain or incomplete knowledge; surmise; conjecture. **2** To conjecture correctly: to *guess* the answer. **3** To believe; think: I *guess* we'll be late. —*v.i.* **4** To form a judgment or opinion on uncertain or incomplete knowledge. **5** To conjecture correctly: How did you *guess*? —*n.* **1** A tentative opinion or conclusion; a supposition; surmise; conjecture. **2** The act of guessing. [ME *gessen,* prob. <Scand. Cf. Sw. *gissa,* Dan. *gisse* guess.] —**guess′er** *n.*

Synonyms (verb): conjecture, divine, fancy, imagine, suppose, surmise, suspect. See SOLVE, SUPPOSE. *Antonyms*: demonstrate, establish, prove.

Synonyms (noun): conjecture, hypothesis, supposition, surmise. A *guess* is a conclusion from data directly at hand, and held as probable or tentative, while one confessedly lacks material for certainty. A *conjecture* is preliminary and tentative, but more methodical than a *guess*; a *supposition* is more nearly final; a *surmise* is an imagination or a suspicion. *Antonyms*: assurance, certainty, confidence, conviction, demonstration, proof.

guess·ti·mate (ges′tə·mit) *n. U.S. Colloq.* A prediction or extrapolation based, in part, on guesswork.

guess·work (ges′wûrk′) *n.* The process of guessing, or the result obtained thereby; a guess, or guesses collectively.

guest (gest) *n.* **1** A person received and entertained at the house of another; a visitor. **2** A lodger or boarder. **3** A parasitic animal; especially, any of various inquilines or insects living or breeding in the nests of other species: *guest* ants, *guest* wasps, etc. **4** *Obs.* A foreigner; stranger. —*v.t.* To entertain as a guest. —*v.i.* To be a guest. [OE *giest*; infl. in form by ON *gastr* stranger. Akin to HOST[1], HOST[2].]

Guest (gest), **Edgar Albert,** 1881–1959, U.S. humorist and poet.

guest room A room, as in a private home or inn, which is used for the lodging of guests.

guest rope *Naut.* **1** A hawser carried and paid out by a boat so as to connect a vessel with an object towards which it is to be warped. **2** A rope used to assist the towline of a boat in towing; also, a line by which a boat is fastened to a vessel or eased into a gangway. Also **guess rope, guess warp, ges·warp** (ges′wôrp′).

Gueux (gœ) *n. pl.* The Dutch nobles and burghers who from 1566 resisted the Inquisition and Philip II in the Netherlands. [<F, beggars]

guff (guf) *n.* **1** A sudden or slight gust of air; puff. **2** *Slang* Nonsense; buncombe. [Imit.]

guf·faw (gə·fô′) *n.* A shout of boisterous laughter; horselaugh. —*v.i.* To utter such laughter. [Imit.]

Gug·gen·heim (go͝og′ən·hīm), **Daniel,** 1856–1930, U.S. industrialist and philanthropist.

Gu·gliel·ma (go͞o·lyel′mä) Italian form of WILHELMINA.

Gu·gliel·mo (go͞o·lyel′mō) Italian form of WILLIAM.

gu·ha (go͞o′hä, go͞o′ä) *n. Pathol.* A type of bronchial asthma endemic on the island of Guam. Also **gu′ja.**

Gui·an·a (gē·an′ə, -ä′nə) A region of NE South America, comprising British and French Guiana, Surinam, and sometimes including northern Brazil and eastern Venezuela. —**the Guianas**: British Guiana, French Guiana, Surinam.

guid (güd) See GUDE.

gui·dance (gīd′ns) *n.* **1** The act, process, or result of guiding. **2** A leading; direction. **3** *Mil.* The principles and techniques of assembling, interpreting, and transmitting intelligence necessary to the maneuvering of guided missiles along their flight paths to the designated targets.

guide (gīd) *v.* **guid·ed, guid·ing** *v.t.* **1** To show the way to; lead or accompany as a guide. **2** To direct the motion or action of, as a vehicle, tool, etc. **3** To lead or direct the affairs, standards, opinions, etc., of: Let these principles *guide* your life. —*v.i.* **4** To act as a guide. See synonyms under LEAD[1], REGULATE. —*n.* **1** One who leads or directs another in any path or direction; one who shows the way by accompanying or going in advance; specifically, one who conducts sightseers, or an expert woodsman who conducts hunters, fishermen, etc. **2** Something serving to guide; a guidebook or guidepost. **3** *Mech.*

Any device acting as an indicator or serving to keep a part or object in position or to regulate its operation. **4** *Mil.* A soldier on the flank of a line to mark a pivot or regulate an alinement. See synonyms under RULE. [< OF *guider*] —**guid'a·ble** *adj.* —**guid'er** *n.*

guide·board (gīd'bôrd', -bōrd') *n.* A board bearing directions for travelers, usually at the junction of highways: also called *fingerpost.*

guide·book (gīd'bŏok') *n.* A handbook for travelers or tourists, containing descriptions of places, routes, etc.

guided missile *Mil.* An unmanned aerial missile whose course can be altered during flight by mechanisms within it and sometimes under the control of radio signals transmitted from ground stations or from aircraft.

guide·line (gīd'līn') *n.* **1** A line, as a rope, for guiding. **2** A word, phrase, etc., often printed as a guide along the upper margin of printed copy. **3** Any indication of the limits or scope of an undertaking.

guide·post (gīd'pōst') *n.* **1** A post with an attached sign giving directions to travelers, as at a roadside. **2** Anything that guides, directs, or limits; guideline.

guide·rope (gīd'rōp') *n.* **1** *Aeron.* **a** A long rope suspended from a balloon or dirigible and trailed along the ground as a brake and to maintain altitude. **b** Any similar rope for hauling down and mooring an airship; a grab line: also called *trail rope.* **2** A line attached to a rope to hold it in position.

Gui·do d'A·rez·zo (gwē'dō dä·ret'tsō), 990?–1050?, Italian Benedictine monk; musician.

gui·don (gīd'n) *n.* **1** A forked flag carried by mounted troops. **2** The man who carries it. **3** A small flag carried by a unit of the U.S. Army as a company emblem. [< F < Ital. *guidone*]

Gui·do Re·ni (gwē'dō rā'nē) See RENI, GUIDO.

Gui·enne (gwē·yen', gē-) A former province of SW France; formerly the kingdom of Aquitaine: also *Guyenne.*

Guil·bert (gēl·bâr') French form of GILBERT.

guild (gild) *n.* **1** A corporation or association of persons engaged in kindred pursuits for mutual protection, aid, etc., known in England from the seventh century. **2** A church or religious association organized for benevolent and other parish work. **3** *Ecol.* **a** One of four groups of plants having characteristic modes of life, namely, the lianas, epiphytes, saprophytes, and parasites. **b** A group of plants which, under certain ecological conditions, adapt themselves in mass to a new locality. Also spelled *gild.* ◆ Homophone: *gild.* [Fusion of OE *gild* payment, *gegyld* association, and ON *gildi* payment] —**guild'ship** *n.* —**guilds'man** *n.*

guil·der (gil'dər) *n.* Gulden: also spelled *gilder.* also called *florin.* [Earlier *guldren,* alter. of Du. *gulden* golden]

Guild·ford (gil'fəd) The county town of Surrey, England.

guild·hall (gild'hôl') *n. Brit.* **1** The hall where a guild meets. **2** A town hall.

Guild·hall (gild'hôl') The hall of the Corporation of the City of London, England.

guild socialism See under SOCIALISM.

guile (gīl) *n.* **1** The act of deceiving, or the disposition to deceive; craft; duplicity; treachery. **2** *Obs.* A stratagem. See synonyms under ARTIFICE, DECEPTION. [< OF < Gmc. ? Akin to WILE.] —**guile'ful** *adj.*

guile·less (gīl'lis) *adj.* Free from guile; artless; frank. See synonyms under CANDID, INNOCENT, PURE. —**guile'less·ly** *adv.* —**guile'less·ness** *n.*

Guil·ford Courthouse (gil'fərd) A national military park in north central North Carolina, scene of a Revolutionary War battle, 1781.

Guil·laume (gē·yōm') French form of WILLIAM. Also *Sp.* **Guil·ler·mo** (gē·lyer'mō), *Pg.* **Guil·her·me** (gē·lyer'mā).

Guil·laume (gē·yōm'), **Charles Édouard,** 1861–1938, French physicist.

Guil·lel·mine (gē·yel·mēn') French form of WILHELMINA. Also **Guil·lel·mette** (-met'), *Sp.* **Guil·lel·mi·na** (gē·lyel·mē'nä).

guil·le·mot (gil'ə·mot) *n.* Any of several narrowbilled auks (genera *Uria* and *Cepphus*), found in northern latitudes; specifically, the **black guillemot** (*C. grylle*) or cuttie, and the murres, including the **foolish guillemot** (*Uria aalge*). [< F, dim. of *Guillaume* William]

guil·loche (gi·lōsh') *n.* An ornament formed by two or more intertwining bands or intersecting lines; an ornamental braid. [< F *guillochis;* ult. origin unknown]

guil·lo·tine (gil'ə·tēn') *n.* **1** The instrument of capital punishment in France, consisting of a weighted knife which falls and beheads the victim: invented by Antoine Louis, 1723–92, French physician. **2** A form of papercutting machine. **3** *Surg.* An instrument for cutting the tonsils. —*v.t.* **·tined, ·tin·ing** To behead with the guillotine. [< F, after Dr. J. I. *Guillotin,* 1738–1814, who advocated its use]

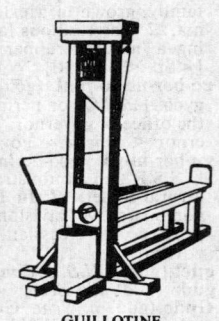
GUILLOTINE
Showing the basket for the body and receptacle for the head.

guilt (gilt) *n.* **1** The state of one who, by violation of law, has made himself liable to or deserving of punishment; culpability. **2** Wrongdoing; wickedness. See synonyms under SIN. ◆ Homophone: *gilt.* [OE *gylt*]

guilt·less (gilt'lis) *adj.* **1** Free from guilt; innocent. **2** Ignorant: with *of.* **3** Devoid: with *of.* See synonyms under INNOCENT, PURE. —**guilt'less·ly** *adv.* —**guilt'less·ness** *n.*

guilt·y (gil'tē) *adj.* **guilt·i·er, guilt·i·est 1** Having violated a law or rule of duty; liable to penalty. **2** Involving, expressing, feeling, or characterized by guilt. See synonyms under CRIMINAL. —**guilt'i·ly** *adv.* —**guilt'i·ness** *n.*

guin·ea (gin'ē) *n.* **1** A former English gold coin, so called because first coined (1663) from Guinea gold: last issued in 1813; now, money of account: equal to 21 shillings. **2** The guinea fowl.

Guin·ea (gin'ē) **1** A term formerly used to describe a coastal region in western Africa, divided by the Niger delta into **Upper Guinea** and **Lower Guinea.** It was broadly considered to consist of the littoral portions of the British, French, and Portuguese equatorial possessions from Senegal to Angola. **2** The littoral portion of the territory extending from the Niger delta to southern Senegal. See PORTUGUESE GUINEA, SPANISH GUINEA. **3** A republic in west Africa, coextensive with former French Guinea; 95,350 square miles; Capital, Conakry.

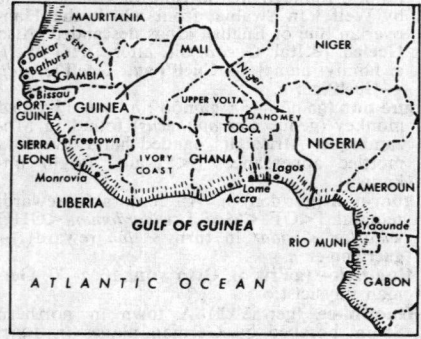

Guinea, Gulf of An inlet of the Atlantic in the western coast of Africa, south of the great bulge of the continent.

Guinea corn Durra.

guinea fowl A gallinaceous bird (*Numida meleagris*) of African origin, having dark-gray plumage speckled with white spots: long domesticated in Europe and America: also *guinea, guinea hen.*

guinea grains Grains of paradise.

guinea grass A hardy, perennial, erect grass (*Panicum maximum*) native to Africa: grown in the southern United States for forage.

guinea green A crystalline substance, $C_{37}H_{35}N_2O_6S_2Na$, dark-green in powder form.

GUINEA FOWL
(About 15 inches tall)

guinea hen 1 A female guinea fowl. **2** A guinea fowl.

Guinea pepper Cayenne pepper.

guinea pig 1 A small, domesticated rodent, usually white, variegated with red and black, having short ears and lacking a visible tail, widely used as an experimental animal in biological and medical research. **2** Any object or victim of experimentation.

Guinea worm A slender, threadlike nematode worm (*Dracunculus medinensis*), common in tropical Africa and Asia. The larva parasitically enters the stomach of man or animal, usually in drinking water, and makes its way to the subcutaneous connective tissue, especially, in man, of the legs and feet.

Guin·e·vere (gwin'ə·vir) In Arthurian legend, Arthur's unfaithful queen; the paramour of Lancelot. Also **Guin'e·ver** (-vər).

gui·pure (gi·pyŏor', *Fr.* gē·pür') *n.* A lace having no ground mesh, but having the pattern held in place by connecting threads. [< F < *guiper* cover with silk < Gmc.]

guise (gīz) *n.* **1** The external appearance as produced by garb or costume; outward seeming; mien; aspect; habit; dress. **2** The manner; behavior; also, customary manner; fashion; way. **3** A mask or pretense; cover. —*v.* **guised, guis·ing** *v.t.* **1** *Archaic* To dress; costume. **2** *Brit. Dial.* To disguise. —*v.i.* **3** *Brit. Dial.* To go about in disguise or costume. [< OF < Gmc. Akin to WISE².]

Guise (gēz, gwēz; *Fr.* gēz, gü·ēz') A French ducal family; specifically, either **François de Lorraine,** 1519–63, second Duc de Guise, French commander; or **Henri de Lorraine,** 1550–88, third Duc de Guise, French commander who instigated the massacre of St. Bartholomew.

Guise (gēz) A town in northern France.

gui·tar (gi·tär') *n.* A musical instrument having a fretted fingerboard and usually six strings, played with the fingers. [< Sp. *guitarra* < Gk. *kithara.* Doublet of CITHARA, ZITHER.]

gui·tar·fish (gi·tär'fish') *n. pl.* **·fish** or **·fish·es** Any of a family (Rhinobatidae) of viviparous, sharklike rays having a long tail and wide body.

guit·guit (gwit'gwit') *n.* Any of several tropical American birds, the honey creepers. [Imit.]

Gui·try (gē·trē'), **Sacha** 1885–1957, French playwright and actor.

Gui·zot (gē·zō'), **François Pierre Guillaume,** 1787–1874, French statesman and historian.

Gu·ja·rat (gŏoj'ə·rät') A fertile plain in northern Bombay State, India. Also **Gu'ze·rat** (gŏoz'-).

Gu·ja·ra·ti (gŏoj'ə·rä'tē) *n.* The language of the natives of Gujarat, Baroda, and the adjoining states, belonging to the Indic branch of Indo-Iranian languages.

Gujarat States A group of former princely states included since 1949 in various districts of Bombay State, India; 7,493 square miles.

gu·la (gyŏo'lə) *n. pl.* **·lae** (-lē) **1** *Anat.* The esophagus or gullet. **2** *Ornithol.* The upper part of the throat next the chin, as in a bird. **3** *Entomol.* The ventral part of the neck in insects; also, the submentum in a beetle. [< L, throat] —**gu'lar** *adj.*

gu·lash (gŏo'läsh) See GOULASH.

gulch (gulch) *n. U.S.* A ravine; hollow; gully. [? < dial. *gulch* swallow greedily]

gul·den (gŏol'dən) *n.* **1** The monetary unit of value in the Netherlands. **2** The Austro-Hungarian florin: a former monetary unit. **3** One of various coins formerly current in Germany and the Netherlands. Also *guilder, gilder.* [< Du. and G, lit., golden]

GUITAR

Gü·lek Bo·ghaz (gü·lek' bō·gäz') A pass over the Taurus mountains in southern Turkey: ancient Cilician Gates.

gules (gyŏolz) *n. Her.* The tincture red: in a blazon without color, indicated by parallel vertical lines. [< OF *gueules* red-dyed ermine fur, ? < L *gula* throat]

gulf (gulf) *n.* **1** The tract of water within an

indentation or curve of the coastline, in size between a bay and a sea. **2** An abyss; chasm. **3** That which engulfs irretrievably; a whirlpool. **4** A wide or impassable space; a separation not easily bridged. —*v.t.* To swallow up as in a gulf; engulf. [< OF *golfe* < Ital. *golfo* < LGk. *kolphos* < Gk. *kolpos* a bay]

Gulf of Lyons See LION, GULF OF THE

Gulf States The States of the United States bordering on the Gulf of Mexico: Florida, Alabama, Mississippi, Louisiana, and Texas.

Gulf Stream The largest of the warm ocean current systems, flowing from the Gulf of Mexico along the coast of the United States to Nantucket, and thence eastward as far as Norway.

gulf·weed (gulf′wēd′) *n.* Any of a genus (*Sargassum*) of brown algae that grow in warm seas and are found drifting in the Gulf Stream and the Sargasso Sea. Also called *sargasso.*

gull¹ (gul) *n.* **1** A long-winged, usually white, web-footed swimming bird (family *Laridae*) having the upper mandible hooked. **2** One of various sea birds related to the gull, as a tern or gannet. [ME < Celtic. Cf. Welsh *gwylan* a gull.]

gull² (gul) *n.* **1** A simple, credulous person; dupe. **2** A deceit; fraud; trick. —*v.t.* To deceive; outwit; cheat. [? < obs. *gull* swallow; infl. by ME *goll* a gosling]

Gul·lah (gul′ə) *n.* **1** One of a group of Negroes dwelling on a narrow, coastal strip and outlying islands of South Carolina, Georgia, and NE Florida. **2** The creolized language spoken by these people.

gul·let (gul′it) *n.* **1** *Anat.* The passage from the mouth to the stomach; the esophagus. **2** The throat or neck. **3** A channel for water; ravine; gully. [< OF *goulet,* dim. of *goule* throat < L *gula*]

gul·li·ble (gul′ə-bəl) *adj.* Capable of being easily gulled, duped, or deceived; simple; credulous. Also **gul′la·ble.** —**gul′li·bil′i·ty, gul′la·bil′i·ty** *n.*

Gul·li·ver (gul′ə-vər), **Lemuel** Hero of Jonathan Swift's *Gulliver's Travels* (1726), a political and social satire in four books.

gul·ly¹ (gul′ē) *n. pl.* **·lies 1** A channel or ravine cut in the earth by running water; narrow ravine. **2** A watercourse. —*v.t.* **gul·lied, gul·ly·ing** To cut or wear a gully in. [Var. of GULLET]

gul·ly² (gul′ē) *n. Scot.* A knife.

gulp (gulp) *v.t.* **1** To swallow eagerly and in large amounts: usually with *down.* **2** To keep back as if by swallowing: to *gulp* down a retort. —*v.i.* **3** To gasp or choke as if taking a large drink of liquid. —*n.* The act of gulping, or something gulped down; a swallow; also, the amount swallowed: a *gulp* of milk. [< Du. *gulpen;* of imit. origin] —**gulp′er** *n.* —**gulp′ing·ly** *adv.*

gum¹ (gum) *n.* **1** An amorphous, brittle, colloidal mass resulting from the drying of the exuded sap of trees or shrubs. True gums are complex hydrocarbons; they are usually soluble in water, but not in alcohol, ether, and the oils; but the name is popularly applied also to true resins and to gum resins, especially when used as mucilage, etc. **2** The gum tree. **3** Rubber. **4** *pl. U.S. Dial.* Rubber overshoes; also, automobile tires. **5** A preparation of some natural gum (as cherry gum or balsam of Tolu), or some other tenacious substance, flavored and sweetened for use as a masticatory: also **chewing gum. 6** *U.S. Dial.* A section of a gum tree made into a well-curb, a watering trough, a bin, etc.; also, a beehive made of a similar hollow log. **7** Any sticky, viscous substance. **8** The adhesive wash on the reverse side of postage stamps. —*v.* **gummed, gum·ming** *v.t.* **1** To smear gum. **2** To stiffen or unite with gum. —*v.i.* **3** To exude or form gum. **4** To become stiff and sticky. —**to gum up** *U.S. Slang* To bungle or ruin. [< OF *gomme* < L *gummi* < Gk. *kommi*] —**gum′mer** *n.*

gum² (gum) *n. Anat.* The fleshy tissue that covers the alveolar arches of the jaws and invests the necks of the teeth. ◆ Collateral adjective: *gingival.* —*v.t.* **gummed, gum·ming** To chew with the gums: He *gums* his food. [OE *goma* inside of mouth]

gum ammoniac See AMMONIAC².

gum arabic The dried, yellowish-white or amber gum from various species of *Acacia,* especially *A. senegal* and *A. arabica,* composed chiefly of the salts of arabic acid: widely used in medicine and the arts.

Gum·bin·nen (gŏom·bin′ən) The former German name for GUSEV.

gum·bo (gum′bō) *n.* **1** Okra. **2** The stratified portion of the lower till of the Mississippi Valley; especially, those soils which form a sticky or soapy mud when wet. **3** Clay encountered in drilling for oil or sulfur. —*adj.* Resembling or pertaining to gumbo soil (see *n.* def. 3). [< Bantu language of Angola]

gum·boil (gum′boil′) *n.* A small boil or abscess formed on the gum.

gum·bo·til (gum′bō·til) *n. Geol.* A gray or brown plastic clay resulting from the prolonged weathering of glacial deposits; the varying thicknesses of its layers sometimes give indications of the length of interglacial periods. [< GUMBO + TILL⁴]

gum·drop (gum′drop′) *n.* A molded sweetmeat, often soft inside, made usually of gum arabic, but sometimes also of gelatin, glucose, etc.

gum elastic Rubber.

gum·lie (gum′lē) *adj. Scot.* Muddy; gloomy. Also **gum′ly.**

gum·ma (gum′ə) *n. pl.* **gum·ma·ta** (gum′ə·tə) or **gum·mas** *Pathol.* A soft tumor occurring in tertiary syphilis. [< NL < L *gummi* gum] —**gum′ma·tous** *adj.*

gum·mif·er·ous (gu·mif′ər·əs) *adj.* Yielding or producing gum.

gum·mite (gum′īt) *n.* A greasy, viscid material of red or yellow color, formed as an alteration product of pitchblende.

gum·mo·sis (gu·mō′sis) *n. Bot.* The extensive change of tissue into gum, as in cherry gum.

gum·my (gum′ē) *adj.* **·mi·er, ·mi·est** Like or covered with gum; sticky; viscous. Also **gum′mous.** See synonyms under ADHESIVE. —**gum′mi·ness** *n.*

gum plant Any of several plants of the western United States (genus *Grindelia*), covered with a glutinous varnish when young. Also **gum weed.**

gump·tion (gump′shən) *n. Colloq.* **1** Ready perception; quick-wittedness; initiative. **2** Shrewd common sense. [< dial. E (Scottish). Cf. ME *gome* care, heed.]

gum resin Any of a kind of combined gum and resin which oozes as a milky juice from incisions in the stems, roots, or branches of certain plants and gradually solidifies in the air.

gum·shoe (gum′shoō′) *n.* **1** *U.S. Slang* A detective. **2** *Pl.* Sneakers. **3** A rubber shoe or overshoe. —*adj. U.S. Slang* **1** Done secretly; undercover. **2** Pertaining to detectives. —*v.i.* **·shoed, ·shoe·ing** *U.S. Slang* To go stealthily and noiselessly; sneak.

Gum·ti (gŏom′tē) A river in central Uttar Pradesh, India, flowing SE 500 miles to the Ganges.

gum·tree (gum′trē′) *n.* Any of various species of Australian eucalyptus trees.

gum tree An American gum-producing and hardwood lumber tree, as the sour or black gum and the tupelo.

gum·wood (gum′wŏod′) *n.* The wood of several Australasian trees (genus *Eucalyptus*), especially the blue gum (*E. globulus*) and the salmon gum (*E. salmonophloia*), now grown in the United States: used for construction and furniture.

gun (gun) *n.* **1** A metal tube for firing projectiles by the force of an explosive, by compressed air, or a spring, together with its stock and other attachments. **2** A piece of ordnance with a flat trajectory. **3** Any portable firearm except a pistol or revolver, as a rifle, musket, carbine, etc. **4** *U.S. Colloq.* A pistol or revolver. **5** The discharge of a cannon, as in firing salutes or signaling. **6** The throttle controlling the action of an internal-combustion engine, as in an automobile or airplane. **7** Any device resembling a gun in shape or operation: a grease *gun.* —*v.* **gunned, gun·ning** *v.i.* **1** To go hunting with a gun. **2** To shoot with a gun. **3** To seek with intent to harm or kill: with *for.* **4** To seek eagerly: with *for:* to *gun* for votes. **5** *U.S. Colloq.* To go or drive at great speed. —*v.t.* **6** *U.S. Colloq.* To shoot (someone). **7** *U.S. Colloq.* To open the throttle of, as an engine, so as to increase the speed of operation. [ME *gonne, gunne* < ON *gunna,* orig. a nickname for *Gunnhildr,* fem. personal name]

gun barrel Barrel (def. 7).

gun·boat (gun′bōt′) *n.* A lightly armed, unarmored naval vessel, used for patrolling rivers and coastal waters.

gun carriage A carriage upon which a cannon is mounted.

gun·cot·ton (gun′kot′n) *n.* A highly explosive compound prepared by treating cotton with nitric and sulfuric acids: also called *nitrocotton.*

gun deck A covered deck carrying the principal battery of a warship.

gun dog A hunting dog; a dog bred and trained to accompany and assist a hunter, as a setter, pointer, etc.

gun·fight (gun′fīt′) *n. U.S.* In the old West, a fight with revolvers or pistols. —**gun′fight′er** *n.* —**gun′fight′ing** *n.*

gun·fire (gun′fīr′) *n.* **1** The firing or discharge of a gun or guns. **2** *Mil.* **a** An artillery action in which guns fire independently of each other, with or without ordered interval. **b** The use of artillery or small arms in warfare, as distinguished from bayonets, or from charge tactics.

gun·flint (gun′flint′) *n.* A piece of flint fitted to the hammer of a flintlock musket.

gung ho (gung′ hō′) *Chinese* Work together: a motto adopted by a body of U.S. Marine raiders in World War II.

gun·lock (gun′lok′) *n.* The mechanism of a gun by which the hammer or needle is driven and the charge exploded. See RIFLE.

gun·man (gun′mən) *n. pl.* **·men** (-mən) **1** *U.S.* A man armed with a gun, especially a criminal or killer. **2** A gunsmith.

gun metal 1 A bronze alloy, composed of nine parts copper to one part tin, formerly much used for smaller cannon, and still used for other purposes. **2** Any other material used in making guns, as gun iron, steel, certain kinds of brass, etc. **3** Any of various alloys treated with sulfur and the like to imitate the color of gun metal: used for metal novelties. **4** A neutral gray color with a bluish tinge: also **gun-met·al gray** (gun′met′l).

gun moll *U.S. Slang* A woman who associates with criminals.

Gun·nar (gŏon′är) In the *Volsunga Saga,* a hero who wins Brynhild as his wife; brother to Gudrun. Compare GUNTHER.

gun·nel¹ (gun′əl) See GUNWALE.

gun·nel² (gun′əl) *n. pl.* **·nels** or **·nel** A blenny (fish) of the North Atlantic (*Pholis gunnellus*). [Origin unknown]

gun·ner (gun′ər) *n.* **1** A soldier or sailor who operates a gun or cannon. **2** A member of an aircraft crew who operates a gun mounted on a swivel base. **3** One who hunts game with a gun.

gun·ner·y (gun′ər·ē) *n.* **1** The science and art of operating cannon. **2** The use of artillery. **3** Guns collectively.

gun·ning (gun′ing) *n.* The sport of hunting game with a gun.

Gun·ni·son River (gun′ə·sən) A river of west central Colorado, flowing 180 miles NW to the Colorado River.

gun·ny (gun′ē) *n. pl.* **·nies 1** Coarse sacking of jute or hemp. **2** A bag or sack made of it: also **gunny bag** or **gunny sack.** [< Hind. *gonī* gunny sack]

gun·pa·per (gun′pā′pər) *n.* A cellulose compound used as an absorbent foundation for the preparation of a form of guncotton.

gun·pow·der (gun′pou′dər) *n.* An explosive mixture of potassium nitrate, charcoal, and sulfur, black or brown in color, used especially in gunnery.

Gunpowder Plot See under GUY FAWKES DAY.

gunpowder tea A fine green tea, each leaf of which is rolled into a tiny round pellet.

gun·room (gun′rŏom′, -rŏom′) *n.* **1** A room in which guns are kept. **2** In the British navy, a room for the accommodation of junior officers.

gun·run·ner (gun′run′ər) *n.* One who smuggles

or carries on illegal traffic in firearms and ammunition. — **gun′run′ning** *n.*

gun·sel (gun′səl) *n. Slang* **1** A young armed robber or killer. **2** A young sexual pervert. **3** A callow, unsophisticated youth. Also **gon·sil** (gon′səl). [Origin uncertain]

gun·shot (gun′shot′) *n.* **1** The range or reach of a gun. **2** The act of discharging a firearm. — *adj.* Made by the shot of a gun: a *gunshot* wound.

gun–shy (gun′shī′) *adj.* Afraid of the sound of a gun, as a dog.

gun·sight (gun′sīt′) *n.* A device on a gun which assists in aiming; a sight.

gun·sling·er (gun′sling′ər) *n. U.S. Slang* A gunfighter.

gun·smith (gun′smith′) *n.* One who makes or repairs firearms.

gun·stock (gun′stok′) *n.* The wooden part of a firearm, as a rifle, etc., holding the lock and the barrel.

Gun·ter (gun′tər), **Edmund,** 1581–1626, English mathematician.

Gunter's chain See under CHAIN.

Gun·ther (gŏŏn′tər) In the *Nibelungenlied,* the brother of Kriemhild and husband of Brünhilde: identified with *Gunnar.*

gun·wale (gun′əl) *n. Naut.* **1** The upper wale of a war vessel with apertures for guns. **2** The strake which tops a ship's side or bounds the top plank of the side of a vessel: also spelled *gunnel.* [< GUN + WALE (plank)]

Günz (gŭnts) See GLACIAL EPOCH.

gup·py (gup′ē) *n. pl.* **·pies** A small, tropical, fresh–water fish (genus *Lebistes*), valued as an aquarium fish for the brilliant coloring of the males, and for mosquito control. [after R. J. L. *Guppy,* British scientist]

Gup·ta (gŏŏp′tə) A dynasty, 320?–544?, of North India, founded by Chandragupta II.

gur·gle (gûr′gəl) *v.* **gur·gled, gur·gling** *v.i.* **1** To flow with a bubbling, liquid sound. **2** To make such a sound. — *v.t.* **3** To utter with a gurgling sound. — *n.* A gurgling flow or sound: also **gur′gling.** [Var. of GARGLE]

gur·glet (gûr′glit) See GOGLET.

Gur·kha (gŏŏr′kə) *n.* One of a warlike Rajput people of Hindu religion in Nepal.

gur·nard (gûr′nərd) *n. pl.* **·nards** or **·nard** One of various spiny–finned marine fishes (family *Triglidae*) with mailed cheeks: some species are called *sea robins.* [< F *grognard* grumbler < *grogner* grunt < L *grunnire*]

gur·ney (gûr′nē) *n. pl.* **·neys** A stretcher mounted on wheels. [Origin uncertain]

gu·ru (gōō′rōō) *n. pl.* **·rus** **1** One who provides instruction or spiritual leadership in Hindu mysticism. **2** A teacher or leader regarded as having special knowledge, powers, etc. [< Hind.]

Gus (gus) Diminutive of AUGUSTUS.

Gu·sev (gōō′syəf) A city in Russian S.F.S.R., formerly in East Prussia: former German *Gumbinnen.*

gush (gush) *v.i.* **1** To flow out suddenly and in volume, as tears or blood. **2** To produce a sudden flood, as of blood, tears, etc.: Her eyes *gushed* with tears. **3** *Colloq.* To express oneself with extravagant and affected emotion; be overly enthusiastic. — *v.t.* **4** To pour forth (blood, tears, etc.). — *n.* **1** A sudden outpouring of fluid or of something likened to it, as of sound, or the thing thus emitted. **2** *Colloq.* An extravagant display of sentiment. [ME *guschen,* prob. < Scand. Cf. ON *gusa* gush.] — **gush′i·ness** *n.* — **gush′y** *adj.*

gush·er (gush′ər) *n.* **1** One who or that which gushes. **2** A free–flowing oil well.

gush·ing (gush′ing) *adj.* Flowing freely; sentimental. — **gush′ing·ly** *adv.* — **gush′ing·ness** *n.*

gus·set (gus′it) *n.* **1** A small triangular piece of cloth fitted into a garment to give added strength or more room. **2** In metalworking, an angle–iron or bracket for stiffening an angle in construction. **3** A chain–mail connection between two armor plates. — *v.t.* To furnish with a gusset. [< OF *gousset,* dim. of *gousse* a pod, shell]

gust[1] (gust) *n.* **1** A violent blast of wind; rapid fluctuations in the force of a wind near the earth's surface. **2** A sudden outburst of feeling. [< ON *gustr*] — **gust′i·ly** *adv.* — **gust′i·ness** *n.* — **gust′y** *adj.*

gust[2] (gust) *n.* **1** Taste; relish; gratification; gusto. **2** Flavor, as of food. [< L *gustus* taste] — **gust′a·ble** *adj.*

gus·ta·tion (gus·tā′shən) *n.* The act or power of tasting. — **gus·ta·tive** (gus′tə·tiv) *adj.* — **gus′ta·tive·ness** *n.* — **gus′ta·to′ry** (-tôr′ē, -tō′rē) *adj.*

Gus·ta·vo A. Ma·de·ro (gōōs·tä′vō ä mä·thā′·rō) The Federal district of central Mexico including Guadalupe Hidalgo.

Gus·ta·vus (gus·tā′vəs, -tä′-) A masculine personal name. Also *Du.* **Gus·taaf** (khōōs′täf), *Fr.* **Gus·tave** (güs·tȧv′), *Ger.* **Gus·tav** (gōōs′·täf), *Ital., Sp.* **Gus·ta·vo** (gōōs·tä′vō), *Sw.* **Gus·taf** (gōōs′täf). [< Gmc., divine staff]

— **Gustavus I,** 1496–1560, king of Sweden who defeated the Danes (king, 1523–60): known as *Gustavus Vasa.*

— **Gustavus II,** 1594–1632, prominent in the Thirty Years' War: known as *Gustavus Adolphus.*

— **Gustavus V,** 1858–1950, king of Sweden 1907–50: known as *Gustaf.*

— **Gustavus VI,** 1882–1973, king of Sweden 1950–1973: known as *Gustaf Adolf.*

gus·to (gus′tō) *n.* **1** Keen enjoyment; relish; zest. **2** Individual taste. See synonyms under RELISH. [< Ital. < L *gustus* taste]

gut (gut) *n.* **1** *pl.* The alimentary canal; an intestine: regarded as indelicate usage. **2** The dried entrails of an animal, used for strings for musical instruments, etc.; catgut. **3** A contracted strait connecting two bodies of water. **4** A strong cord made from fiber drawn out of a silkworm when ready to spin its cocoon, used like catgut for snells, etc. **5** *pl. Slang* Stamina; courage; grit. — *v.t.* **gut·ted, gut·ting** **1** To take out the intestines of; eviscerate. **2** To plunder. **3** To remove or destroy the contents of: The fire *gutted* the interior of the building. — *adj. Slang* **1** Central; basic; fundamental: *gut* issues. **2** Deeply felt, as though physically experienced: a *gut* conviction. [OE *guttas* viscera] — **gut′·ter** *n.*

Gu·ten·berg (gōō′tən·bûrg, *Ger.* gōō′tən·berkh), **Johann,** 1397?–1468, German printer; reputed inventor of movable type. Compare COSTER.

Gutenberg Bible A Vulgate edition printed in Mainz sometime before 1456, generally ascribed to J. Gutenberg and regarded as the first large work printed from movable type.

Guth·run (gōōth′rōōn) See GUDRUN.

Gu·tru·ne (gōō·trōō′nə) In Wagner's *Ring des Nibelungen,* the wife of Siegfried and the sister of Gunther.

gut·sy (gut′sē) *adj.* **gut·si·er, gut·si·est** *Slang* Courageous; dauntless; gritty.

gut·ta (gut′ə) *n. pl.* **·tae** (-ē) **1** In pharmacy, a drop. **2** *Archit.* One of the small droplike ornaments, usually in the form of truncated cones, enriching the under part of mutules and regulae of the Doric entablature. [< L]

gut·ta–per·cha (gut′ə·pûr′chə) *n.* The purified and coagulated exudate, grayish–white to red in color, from various sapotaceous Malayan trees (genera *Palaquium* and *Payena*): used as an electrical insulator, a dental plastic, etc. [< Malay *getah* gum + *percha* gum tree]

gut·tate (gut′āt) *adj.* **1** Spotted, as if by colored drops. **2** Containing drops or little round masses likened to drops. Also **gut′tat·ed.** [< L *guttatus* speckled < *gutta* a drop]

gut·té (gōō·tā′) *adj. Her.* Covered with drops. Also **gut·tée′, gut′ty.** [< AF *gutté* < L *guttatus.* See GUTTATE.]

gut·ter (gut′ər) *n.* **1** A channel along the eaves of a house to carry off rain water. **2** A waterway for carrying off surface water, constructed generally at the side of a road or street. **3** Slum areas of a community: language of the *gutter.* **4** Any slight channel, trench, or trough. — *v.t.* **1** To form channels or grooves

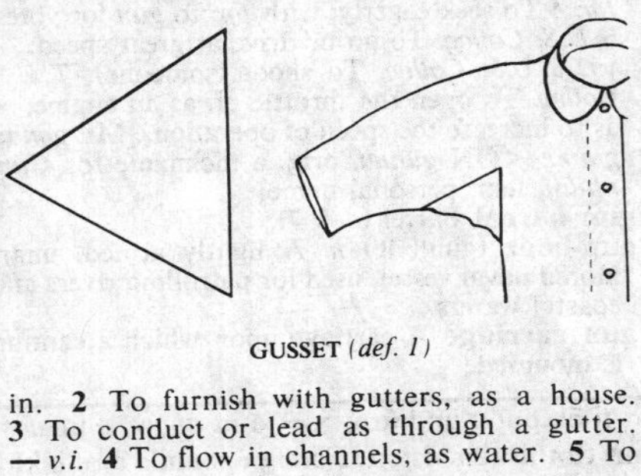

GUSSET *(def. 1)*

in. **2** To furnish with gutters, as a house. **3** To conduct or lead as through a gutter. — *v.i.* **4** To flow in channels, as water. **5** To melt rapidly into streams of wax: said of candles. [< OF *goutiere* < *goute* a drop < L *gutta*] — **gut′ter·y** *adj.*

gut·ter·bird (gut′ər·bûrd′) *n.* **1** A sparrow. **2** A mean or contemptible person.

gut·ter·snipe (gut′ər·snīp′) *n.* A neglected child who runs loose on the streets; a slum child; a street Arab.

gut·tur·al (gut′ər·əl) *adj.* **1** Pertaining to the throat. **2** Produced or formed in the throat; hence, harsh; grating: a *guttural* sound. **3** *Phonet.* Velar. — *n. Phonet.* A velar sound. [< NL *gutturalis* < *guttur* throat] — **gut·tur·al·i·ty** (gut′ə·ral′ə·tē), **gut′tur·al·ness** *n.* — **gut′·tur·al·ly** *adv.*

gut·tur·al·ize (gut′ər·əl·īz′) *v.t.* & *v.i.* **·ized, ·iz·ing** **1** To speak or utter gutturally. **2** *Phonet.* To velarize. — **gut′tur·al·i·za′tion** *n.*

gut·ty (gut′ē) *adj.* **gut·ti·er, gut·ti·est** *Slang* Courageous; strong; plucky.

guy[1] (gī) *n. Naut.* A rope, cord, or the like, as for steadying a mast. — *v.t.* To secure, steady, or guide with a guy. [< OF *guie* < *guier,* var. of *guider* guide]

guy[2] (gī) *n.* **1** *Slang* A person; fellow; man. **2** *Brit.* A person of grotesque appearance. **3** An effigy of Guy Fawkes. See GUY FAWKES DAY. — *v.t.* **guyed, guy·ing** *Slang* To ridicule; make fun of. [after *Guy* Fawkes] — **guy′er** *n.*

Guy (gī, *Fr.* gē) A masculine personal name. Also *Du., Ger., Sp.* **Gui·do** (gē′dō, *Dan., Ital., Sw.* gwē′dō). [< Celtic, sense]

— **Guy de Lusignan** (lü·sē·nyäṅ′), died 1194, French Crusader; king of Jerusalem 1186–92, and of Cyprus.

Guy (gī), **Thomas,** 1644–1724, English philanthropist; founded Guy's Hospital, London, England.

Guy·enne (gwē·yen′, gē-) See GUIENNE.

Guy Fawkes Day (gī′ fôks′) An English celebration, November 5, commemorating the Gunpowder Plot, an abortive conspiracy (1605) led by **Guy Fawkes** (1570–1606) to blow up the Parliament buildings while King James I and Parliament were in assembly.

guy·ot (gē′ō) *n.* A seamount having a flat top: also called *tablemount.* [after A. H. *Guyot,* 1807–84, Swiss-born U.S. geographer]

guz·zle (guz′əl) *v.t.* & *v.i.* **guz·zled, guz·zling** To drink immoderately or frequently. [? < OF *gosiller* < *gosier* throat] — **guz′zler** *n.*

Gwa·li·or (gwä′lē·ôr) A former princely state in central India; 26,008 square miles.

Gwin·nett (gwi·net′), **Button,** 1735?–77, American patriot; signer of Declaration of Independence.

Gwyn (gwin), **Nell,** 1650–87, English actress, mistress of Charles II.

Gyang·tse (gyäng′tse′) A town in southern Tibet.

gybe (jīb) See JIBE[1].

Gy·ges (gī′jēz, jī′-) **1** One of the Hecatoncheires. **2** A king of Lydia, 716–678 B.C., said by Plato to possess a magic ring that could make the wearer invisible.

gym (jim) *n. U.S. Colloq.* **1** A gymnasium. **2** A course in physical training. [Short for GYMNASIUM]

gym·bals (jim′bəlz, gim′-) See GIMBALS.

gym·kha·na (jim·kä′nə) *n. Brit.* An athletic meet, especially for racing; the meeting place. [< Hind. *gend–khana* a racket court; infl. by *gymnastics*]

gym·na·si·arch (jim·nā′zē·ärk) *n.* An official in ancient Greece entrusted with the management of the gymnasia. [< L *gymnasiarchus* < Gk. *gymnasiarchos* < *gymnasion* a gymnasium + *archein* rule]

gym·na·si·um (jim·nā′zē·əm) *n. pl.* **·si·ums** or **·si·a** (-zē·ə) **1** A building or room used for physical education activities and sports, and usually having gymnastic equipment. **2** In ancient Greece, a place where youths met for physical exercise and discussion. [< L < Gk. *gymnasion* < *gymnazein* exercise, train naked < *gymnos* naked]

Gym·na·si·um (gim·nä′zē·ōōm) *n.* In continental Europe, especially Germany, a classical school preparatory to the universities.

gym·nast (jim′nast) *n.* One expert in gymnastics. [< Gk. *gymnastēs* a trainer < *gymnazein.* See GYMNASIUM.]

gym·nas·tic (jim·nas′tik) *adj.* Relating to gymnastics. — **gym·nas′ti·cal·ly** *adv.*

gym·nas·tics (jim·nas′tiks) *n.* **1** Gymnastic exercises for the development of bodily strength and agility. **2** Exercises in a gymnasium, as

distinguished from outdoor athletics. **3** Feats of bodily skill.

gymno- *combining form* Naked: *gymnosperm.* Also, before vowels, *gymn-.* [< Gk. *gymnos* naked]

gym·no·bac·te·ri·um (jim′nō-bak-tir′ē-əm) *n. pl.* **·ri·a** (-ē-ə) A type of bacterium without flagella: distinguished from *trichobacterium.*

gym·no·car·pous (jim′nə-kär′pəs) *adj. Bot.* Provided with naked fruits in flowering plants: said of a fruit without pubescence. Also **gym′no·car′pic.**

gym·nos·o·phist (jim-nos′ə-fist) *n.* **1** One of an ancient Hindu sect of ascetic philosophers who wore little or no clothing. **2** A nudist. [< L *gymnosophistae,* pl. < Gk. *gymnosophistai* < *gymnos* naked + *sophistēs* a sophist] **—gym·nos′o·phy** *n.*

gym·no·sperm (jim′nə-spûrm′) *n.* One of a class of plants (the *Gymnospermae*) having their ovules and seeds naked, as certain evergreens: distinguished from *angiosperm.* **—gym′no·sper′mous, gym′no·sper′mic** *adj.*

gyn- Var. of GYNO.

gy·nae·ce·um (jī′nə-sē′əm, jin′ə-) See GYNECEUM.

gynaeco- See GYNECO.

gy·nan·der (jī-nan′dər, ji-, gī-) *n.* **1** *Biol.* An organism exhibiting bisexual characteristics, usually localized on one or the other side of the midline of the body, as certain insects: also **gy·nan·dro·morph** (jī-nan′drō-môrf, ji-, gī-). **2** A masculine woman. [< Gk. *gynandros* of doubtful sex < *gynē* woman + *anēr, andros* man]

gy·nan·droid (jī-nan′droid, ji-, gī-) *n.* A hermaphrodite with predominantly female characteristics.

gy·nan·dro·mor·phism (jī-nan′drō-môr′fiz-əm, ji-, gī-) *n. Biol.* The occurrence of male and female characteristics in the same individual. **—gy·nan·dro·mor′phic, gy·nan·dro·mor′phous** *adj.*

gy·nan·drous (jī-nan′drəs, ji-, gī-) *adj.* **1** *Bot.* Having the stamens united with or seemingly borne upon the pistil. **2** Exhibiting gynandry.

gy·nan·dry (jī-nan′drē, ji-, gī-) *n.* Hermaphroditism. Also **gy·nan′drism.**

gy·nar·chy (jī′när·kē, jin′är-) *n. pl.* **·chies** Female authority or domination; the supremacy of women; government by a woman or by women. **—gy·nar′chic** *adj.*

gyne (jīn) *n.* The female or queen ant. [< NL < Gk. *gynē* a woman]

gy·ne·ce·um (jī′nə-sē′əm, jin′ə-) *n. pl.* **·ce·a** (-sē′ə) **1** The part of a Greek house reserved for the women, usually the rear. **2** The gynoecium. Also **gynaeceum.** [< L *gynaecium* < Gk. *gynaikeion* < *gynē, gynaikos* a woman]

gyneco- *combining form* Female; pertaining to women: *gynecomorphous:* also spelled *gynaeco-.* Also, before vowels, *gynec-.* [< Gk. *gynē, gynaikos* a woman]

gy·ne·coc·ra·cy (jī′nə-kok′rə-sē, jin′ə-) *n. pl.* **·cies** Rule by a woman or by women; female supremacy. [< Gk. *gynaikokratia* < *gynē, gynaikos* a woman + *krateein* rule] **—gy·ne·co·crat** (jī′nə-kō·krat, ji-) *n.* **—gy·ne·co·crat·ic** (jī′nə-kō·krat′ik, jin′ə-) *adj.*

gy·ne·coid (jī′nə·koid, jin′ə-) *n.* A worker ant capable of laying eggs.

gy·ne·col·o·gy (gī′nə-kol′ə-jē, jī′nə-, jin′ə-) *n.* The study of the female reproductive system and the disorders peculiar to it. **—gy·ne·co·log′i·cal** *adj.* **—gy′ne·col′o·gist** *n.*

gy·ne·co·mor·phous (jī-nē·kō·môr′fəs, jin′-kō-, gī-) *adj.* Having the characteristics, shape, or appearance of a female.

gy·ni·at·rics (jī′nē·at′riks, jin′ē-) *n.* The diagnosis and treatment of women's diseases. Also **gy·ni·at·ry** (jī′nē·at′rē, jin′ē-, ji·nī′ə·trē).

gyno- *combining form* **1** Woman; female: *gynophobia.* **2** *Bot. & Med.* Female reproductive organ; ovary; pistil: *gynophore.* Also, before vowels, *gyn-.* [< Gk. *gynē* a woman]

gy·no·base (jī′nə-bās, jin′ə-) *n. Bot.* The conical or flat enlargement of the receptacle of a flower, bearing the gynaecium. **—gy′no·ba′sic, gy′no·ba′seous** (-bā′shəs) *adj.*

gy·noe·ci·um (jī·nē′sē·əm, ji-) *n. Bot.* The female parts of a flower; the pistil or pistils taken as a unit. Compare ANDROECIUM. [< NL < L *gynaeceum.* See GYNECEUM.]

gy·no·gen·e·sis (jī′nō·jen′ə·sis, jin′ō-) *n. Biol.* The development of an egg after fertilization by a sperm whose nucleus is either absent or inactive, as in certain nematodes. **—gy′no·gen′ic** *adj.*

gy·nop·a·thy (jī·nop′ə·thē, ji-) *n.* Any disease of women. **—gy·no·path·ic** (jī′nə·path′ik, jin′-) *adj.*

gy·no·phore (jī′nə·fôr, -fōr, jin′ə-) *n. Bot.* A stalk supporting the ovary of certain plants, as in the cleome and some crucifers.

-gynous *combining form* **1** Female; of women: *philogynous.* **2** *Bot.* Denoting location, number, etc., of the pistils: *acrogynous.* [< Gk. *gynē* a woman]

gyp¹ (jip) *U.S. Slang n.* **1** A swindler. **2** A swindling transaction. **—v.t. & v.i. gypped, gyp·ping** To cheat or swindle. Also spelled *gip.* [? < GYPSY]

gyp² (jip) *n. Brit. Colloq.* A male servant at a university. [< obs. *gippo* a scullion < F *jupeau* tunic]

gyp·soph·i·la (jip·sof′ə·lə) *n.* Any of a large genus (*Gypsophila*) of hardy annual and perennial herbs with sparse foliage and small rosy or white flowers; babysbreath. [< NL < Gk. *gypsos* chalk + *philein* love]

gyp·sum (jip′səm) *n.* Hydrous sulfate of lime, $CaSO_4 \cdot 2H_2O$, occurring in massive, fibrous, foliated, or granular form. The crystalline and usually transparent form is called *selenite;* the massive fine-grained, white or delicately colored variety is called *alabaster;* when calcined, it is called *plaster of Paris.* [< L < Gk. *gypsos* chalk] **—gyp′se·ous** *adj.* **—gyp·sif·er·ous** (jip·sif′ər·əs) *adj.*

Gyp·sy (jip′sē) See GIPSY.

gypsy moth A European moth with mottled light brown or near-white wings (*Porthetria dispar*), which has become established as a destructive pest in the Eastern United States and Canada, its hairy caterpillar devouring the leaves of deciduous trees.

gy·ral (jī′rəl) *adj.* **1** Having a circular, revolving, or whirling motion. **2** Of or pertaining to the convolutions of the brain. **—gy′ral·ly** *adv.*

gy·rate (jī′rāt) *v.i.* **gy·rat·ed, gy·rat·ing 1** To rotate or revolve. **2** To move in a spiral path; whirl, as a cyclone. **—adj. Zool.** Having spiral or convoluted parts. [< L *gyratus,* pp. of *gyrare* gyrate < *gyrus* a circle < Gk. *gyrus*]

gy·ra·tion (jī·rā′shən) *n.* **1** A rotating whirling or spiral motion; a revolution. **2** A single whorl of a spiral shell.

gy·ra·to·ry (jī′rə·tôr′ē, -tō′rē) *adj.* Gyrating.

gyre¹ (jīr) *n.* **1** A circular or swirling motion. **2** A ring; vortex; a spiral or round form. **3** In ocean-

ography, a ringlike movement of ocean currents set up by variable wind systems acting upon large ocean areas of different chemical and biological properties. [< L *gyrus* a circle]

gyre² (jīr) *n. Scot.* An evil spirit; ogre.

gyr·fal·con (jûr′fôl′kən, -fô′-) See GERFALCON.

gy·ro (jī′rō) *n.* A gyroscope or gyrocompass.

gyro- *combining form* Circle, ring, or spiral: *gyroscope.* Also, before vowels, *gyr-.*

gy·ro·com·pass (jī′rō·kum′pəs, -kom′-) *n.* A compass operating on the principle of a gyroscope; an instrument of navigation indicating a change in the direction of a ship or aircraft by the resistance of a gyroscope to such change.

gyro control 1 *Aeron.* The gyroscope element of an automatic pilot. **2** A gyro stabilizer.

gy·ro·dy·nam·ics (jī′rō·dī·nam′iks, -di-) *n.* The dynamics of rotating bodies.

gy·ro·ho·ri·zon (jī′rō·hə·rī′zən) *n. Aeron.* A gyroscopic instrument designed to simulate the natural horizons and thus indicate the exact lateral and longitudinal position of an aircraft.

gy·ro·mag·net·ic (jī′rō·mag·net′ik) *adj.* Of or pertaining to the magnetic properties of electric charges in rotation, specifically of electron movements in atoms.

gy·ron (jī′ron) *n. Her.* A charge formed by two straight lines meeting in an acute angle at the center of a shield, its fess point. [< F *giron* < OHG *gēro* gusset, triangular piece]

gyro pilot An automatic pilot.

gy·ro·plane (jī′rə·plān′) *n.* An airplane whose chief support is obtained from the rapid rotation of airfoils about a vertical or nearly vertical axis.

gy·ro·scope (jī′rə·skōp) *n.* A heavy rotating wheel, the axis of which is free to turn in any direction, and which can be set to rotate in any plane, independently of forces tending to change the position of the axis. [< F] **—gy·ro·scop·ic** (-skop′ik) *adj.*

gyro stabilizer A gyroscopic device which operates to maintain a structural unit in a steady position, as a gun, despite the rolling of a ship or the motion of the vehicle upon which it is mounted.

GYROSCOPE
Showing possible directional movements.

gy·ro·stat (jī′rə·stat) *n.* A modification of the gyroscope, used to illustrate the dynamics of rotating rigid bodies. [< GYRO(SCOPE) + -STAT]

gy·ro·stat·ic (jī′rə·stat′ik) *adj.* Pertaining to the gyrostat or to the law that a rapidly rotating body tends to keep in the same plane. **—gy′ro·stat′i·cal·ly** *adv.*

gy·ro·stat·ics (jī′rə·stat′iks) *n. pl.* The laws governing the rotation of solid bodies.

gy·rus (jī′rəs) *n. pl.* **·ri** (-rī) *Anat.* A rounded, serpentine ridge between two fissures or sulci; especially, one of the convolutions of the cortex of the brain. [< NL < L *gyrus* a circle]

gyve (jīv) *n. Usually pl.* A fetter for the limbs of prisoners. See synonyms under FETTER. **—v.t. gyved, gyv·ing** To bind with fetters; shackle. [ME *give, gyves;* origin uncertain]

H

h, H (āch) *n. pl.* **h's, H's** or **hs, Hs, aitch·es** (ā′chiz) **1** The eighth letter of the English alphabet, from Phoenician *cheth,* which eventually developed into Greek *eta,* Roman *H.* **2** The sound of the letter *h,* a voiceless, glottal fricative. In a few English words of French origin, as

heir, honor, hour, etc., initial *h* is still written but not pronounced; usage varies in certain other words, as herb, homage, etc., in which some persons pronounce the *h* and some do not. See ALPHABET. **—symbol Chem.** Hydrogen (symbol H).

ha (hä) *n. & interj.* **1** An exclamation or sound made by a quick expulsion of breath expressing surprise, joy, grief, laughter, etc. **2** A sound indicating hesitation, indecision, etc. Also spelled *hah.*

ha' (hô) *n. Scot.* A hall; principal room.

Ha·a·bai (hä·ä·bī′) An island group of the central Tonga Islands. Also **Ha·a·pai′.**

haaf (häf) *n.* A deep-sea fishing ground off the coast of the Shetland or Orkney Islands. [<ON *haf* sea]

haak (häk) See HAKE.

Haa·kon (hô′ko͝on) The name of several kings of Norway. — **Haakon VII,** 1872–1957, king of Norway 1905–57.

haar (här) *n. Scot.* Mist; especially, a chilly fog.

Haar·lem (här′ləm) A city of western Netherlands; capital of North Holland province: also *Harlem.*

Ha·bak·kuk (hə·bak′ək, hab′ə·kuk) A minor Hebrew prophet of about the seventh century B.C.; also, the book of the Old Testament written by him. Also **Ha·bac′uc.**

Ha·ba·na (ä·vä′nä), **La** The Spanish name for HAVANA.

ha·ba·ne·ra (ä′bä·nā′rä) *n.* **1** A dance of African origin common in Cuba. **2** The slow rhythmic music for this dance. [<Sp., of Havana]

Ha·ba·ne·ro (ä′vä·nā′rō) *n.* A native or inhabitant of Havana, Cuba.

Hab·ba·ni·ya (häb·bä′nē·yə), **Lake** A salt lake of central Iraq; 54 square miles.

ha·be·as cor·pus (hā′bē·əs kôr′pəs) *Law* A writ commanding a person having another in custody to produce the detained person before a court. [<L, (you) have the body]

ha·ben·dum (hə·ben′dəm) *n. pl.* **·da** (-də) *Law* The clause in a deed beginning "to have and to hold" (in Latin, *habendum et tenendum*), which determines what interest or estate is granted by the deed. [<L, gerundive of *habere* have]

Ha·ber (hä′bər), **Fritz,** 1868–1934, German electrochemist; developed the **Haber process** for the fixation of atmospheric nitrogen.

hab·er·dash·er (hab′ər·dash′ər) *n.* **1** A dealer in men's furnishings. **2** *Brit.* A dealer in or peddler of ribbons, trimmings, thread, needles, and other small wares. [Prob. <AF *hapertas* kind of fabric]

hab·er·dash·er·y (hab′ər·dash′ər·ē) *n. pl.* **·er·ies** **1** The goods sold by haberdashers. **2** A haberdasher's shop.

hab·er·geon (hab′ər·jən) *n.* A coat of mail for the breast and neck, shorter than a hauberk. [<OF *haubergeon,* dim. of *hauberc.* See HAUBERK.]

hab·ile (hab′il) *adj.* Skilful; able. [Var. of ABLE; infl. in form by F *habile* able or L *habilis* apt]

ha·bil·i·ment (hə·bil′ə·mənt) *n.* **1** An article of clothing. **2** *pl.* Clothes; garb. See synonyms under DRESS. [<OF *habillement* <*habiller* dress, make fit <L *habilis* fit, apt]

ha·bil·i·tate (hə·bil′ə·tāt) *v.t.* **·tat·ed, ·tat·ing** **1** *U.S.* In the West, to furnish with suitable means of equipment, to work (a mine). **2** *Rare* To dress: clothe. [<Med. L *habilitatus,* pp. of *habilitare* enable <*habilis* fit] — **ha·bil′·i·ta′tion** *n.*

hab·it (hab′it) *n.* **1** A tendency toward an action or condition, which by repetition has become spontaneous. **2** An action so induced; habitual course of action or conduct. **3** Habitual condition, appearance, or temperament; physical or mental make-up. **4** *Biol.* A characteristic mode of growth or aspect of a plant or animal. **5** An outer garment or garments; costume; especially, a woman's dress or costume for horseback riding. **6** The distinctive garment of a religious order. **7** *Psychol.* An acquired response or set of responses; a cultivated tendency. Compare INSTINCT. **8** *Obs.* Intimate acquaintance; familiarity. — *v.t.* **1** To furnish with a habit; clothe; dress. **2** *Obs.* To inhabit. [<OF <L *habitus* condition, dress <*habere* have]

Synonyms (noun): custom, fashion, habitude, practice, routine, rule, system, usage, use, wont. *Habit* is a tendency or inclination toward an action or condition, which by repetition has become easy, spontaneous, or even unconscious, or an action or regular series of actions, or a condition so induced. *Habitude* is habitual relation or association. *Custom* is the uniform doing of the same act in the same circumstance, usually, at least in the origin of the *custom,* for a definite reason; *routine* is the doing of customary acts in a regular and uniform sequence and is more mechanical than *custom.* It is the *custom* of shopkeepers to open at a uniform hour, and to follow a regular *routine* of business until closing time. *Custom* is chiefly used of the action of many; *habit* of the action of one; we speak of the *customs* of society, the *habits* of an individual. *Fashion* is the generally recognized *custom* in the smaller matters, especially in dress. A *rule* is prescribed either by some external authority or by one's own will; as, It is the *rule* of the house; or, my invariable *rule. Practice* is the active doing of something in a systematic way; we do not speak of the *practice,* but of the *habit* of going to sleep. *Wont* is established *usage* or *custom* and now chiefly poetical. Compare CUSTOM, DRESS, MANNER, PRACTICE, USE.

hab·it·able (hab′it·ə·bəl) *adj.* Fit to be inhabited. [<L *habitabilis* <*habitare* inhabit] — **hab·it·a·bil·i·ty** (hab′it·ə·bil′ə·tē), **hab′it·a·ble·ness** *n.* — **hab′it·a·bly** *adv.*

hab·i·tan·cy (hab′ə·tən·sē) *n. pl.* **·cies** *Rare* **1** Inhabitance; residence. **2** Inhabitants collectively.

hab·i·tant (hab′ə·tənt) *n.* **1** An inhabitant. **2** (*Fr.* à·bē·tän′) A small rural proprietor, or resident, of French descent, in Canada or Louisiana: also **ha·bi·tan′.** [<F <L *habitans, -antis,* ppr. of *habitare* dwell]

hab·i·tat (hab′ə·tat) *n.* **1** The region where a race, species, or individual naturally or usually lives or is found. **2** Natural environment. [<NL, it dwells]

hab·i·ta·tion (hab′ə·tā′shən) *n.* **1** A place of abode. **2** The act or state of inhabiting. See synonyms under HOME, HOUSE.

hab·it·ed (hab′ə·tid) *adj.* **1** Clothed; arrayed; wearing a habit. **2** *Obs* Habituated.

ha·bit·u·al (hə·bich′o͞o·əl) *adj.* **1** Of, pertaining to, or constituting a habit. **2** Acquired by or resulting from habit, repeated use, or continued causes. **3** Characterized by repeated or constant practice or indulgence; inveterate: a *habitual* liar. [<Med. L *habitualis* <*habitus.* See HABIT.] — **ha·bit′u·al·ly** *adv.* — **ha·bit′u·al·ness** *n.*

Synonyms: accustomed, common, customary, familiar, general, ordinary, regular, stated, usual, wonted. See COMMON, GENERAL, USUAL. Compare synonyms for HABIT. *Antonyms*: exceptional, extraordinary, infrequent, irregular, occasional, rare, unusual, unwonted.

ha·bit·u·ate (hə·bich′o͞o·āt) *v.t.* **·at·ed, ·at·ing** **1** To make familiar by repetition or use; accustom. **2** *U.S. Colloq.* To frequent. [<L *habituatus,* pp. of *habituare* condition] — **ha·bit′u·at′ed** *adj.* — **ha·bit′u·a′tion** *n.*

hab·i·tude (hab′ə·to͞od, -tyo͞od) *n.* **1** Habitual method, state, character, constitution, or tendency; habit. **2** Customary relation or association. **3** Habitual practice. See synonyms under HABIT. [<MF <L *habitudo* condition]

ha·bit·u·é (hə·bich′o͞o·ā, *Fr.* à·bē·twā′) *n.* A habitual visitor or frequenter of a place. [<F, pp. of *habituer* accustom]

Habs·burg (häps′bo͝orkh) See HAPSBURG.

ha·bu (hä·bo͞o) *n.* A very poisonous crotaline snake (genus *Trimeresurus*) of Okinawa and the Ryukyu archipelago, patterned in green and yellow: related to the American rattlesnake and copperhead. [<Japanese]

ha·chure (ha·sho͝or′, hash′o͝or) *n.* **1** In art, a hatching. **2** In mapmaking, the shading or lines used to indicate hills or elevations. — *v.t.* (ha·sho͝or′) **·chured, ·chur·ing** To mark or indicate with hatchings. [<F *hacher* HATCH[3]]

ha·ci·en·da (hä′sē·en′də, *Sp.* ä·syen′dä) *n.* In Spanish America: **1** A landed estate; a country house. **2** A farming, mining, or manufacturing establishment in the country. [<Am. Sp. <L *facienda* things to be done <*facere* do, make]

hack[1] (hak) *v.t.* **1** To cut or chop crudely or irregularly, as with an ax or sword. **2** To break up, as clods of earth. **3** In basketball, to strike (an opposing player) on the arm. **4** In Rugby football, to kick (an opposing player) in the shins. — *v.i.* **5** To make cuts or notches with heavy, crude blows. **6** To emit short, dry coughs. See synonyms under CUT. — **to hack it** *Slang* To cope with it; do it. — *n.* **1** A gash, cut, or nick made by or as by a sharp instrument. **2** An ax or other tool for hacking. **3** A kick on the shins, as in Rugby football. **4** A short, dry cough. [OE *haccian* cut] — **hack′er** *n.*

hack[2] (hak) *n.* **1** A horse for hire. **2** A horse used for general work or for ordinary riding, as distinguished from one bred or trained for special use. **3** An old, worn-out horse. **4** A hackney coach. **5** A taxicab. **6** A writer who hires himself out for any kind of writing jobs; a literary drudge. — *v.t.* **1** To let out for hire, as a horse. **2** To make stale or trite by constant use; hackney. — *v.i.* **3** *Colloq.* To drive a taxicab. **4** *Brit.* To ride on or move at the pace of a hack (*n.* def. 2). — *adj.* **1** Of or designated for a hack: a *hack* stand. **2** For hire or drudging work: a *hack* horse; a *hack* writer. **3** Done by a hack; requiring drudgery: a *hack* job. **4** Trite; hackneyed. [<HACKNEY]

hack[3] (hak) *n.* **1** A frame or rack on which to dry cheese, fish, bricks, etc. **2** A row of bricks laid out to dry. **3** A pile of green brick. [Var. of HATCH[1]]

hack·a·more (hak′ə·môr, -mōr) *n. U.S.* A special headstall of a halter of rawhide or horsehair used to break colts to respond to a bridle. [Alter. of Sp. *jaquima* halter]

hack·ber·ry (hak′ber′ē, -bər·ē) *n. pl.* **·ries** **1** An American tree (genus *Celtis*) resembling the elm and having small, sweet, edible fruit. **2** The fruit or wood of this tree. Also called *hagberry.* [Var. of *hagberry* <ON *heggr* hedge + BERRY]

hack·but (hak′but) *n.* A harquebus. Also spelled *hagbut.* [<MF *hacquebut* <Du. *hakebus* <*hake* hook + *bus* gun]

hack·ee (hak′ē) *n.* The chipmunk: sometimes spelled *hacky.* [Imit.]

Hack·en·sack (hak′ən·sak) A city in eastern New Jersey, on the **Hackensack River,** which flows 45 miles south to Newark Bay.

hack·er·y (hak′ər·ē) *n. pl.* **·er·ies** *Anglo-Indian* A bullock cart with rude and primitive wooden wheels. [<Hind. *chhakṛā*]

hack·ham·mer (hak′ham′ər) *n.* An implement for dressing grindstones.

hack·le[1] (hak′əl) *n.* **1** One of the long narrow feathers on the neck of a cock, used by anglers in making artificial flies; also, a similar feather on other birds. **2** An artificial feather fly for angling: also **hackle fly.** **3** *pl.* The erectile hairs on the neck and back of a dog: also spelled *heckle.* **4** A hatchel. **5** Unspun fiber, as raw silk. — *v.t.* **hack·led, hack·ling** **1** To furnish (a fly) with a hackle. **2** To hatchel. [See HATCHEL] — **hack′ler** *n.*

hack·le[2] (hak′əl) *v.t.* & *v.i.* **hack·led, hack·ling** To cut or chop roughly or crudely; mangle; hack. [Freq. of HACK[1]]

hack·ly (hak′lē) *adj.* Jagged; rough.

hack·man (hak′mən) *n. pl.* **·men** (-mən) The driver of a hack or public carriage.

hack·ma·tack (hak′mə·tak) *n.* The American larch; tamarack. [<N. Am. Ind.]

hack·ney (hak′nē) *n. pl.* **·neys** **1** One of a breed of driving and saddle horses. **2** A horse kept for hire. **3** A hackney coach. **4** A drudge. — *v.t.* **1** To make trite by constant use. **2** To let out or use as a hackney. — *adj.* Let out for hire; common. [<OF *haquenée* a horse; ult. origin unknown] — **hack′ney·ism** *n.*

hackney coach A coach kept for hire.

hack·neyed (hak′nēd) *adj.* Worn out; made commonplace by frequent use; trite. See synonyms under TRITE.

hack·saw (hak′sô′) *n.* A narrow-bladed, close-toothed saw for cutting metal.

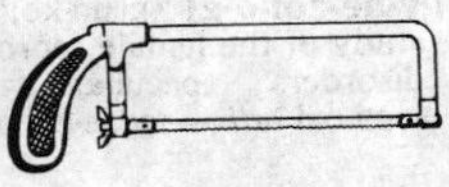

HACKSAW

hack work The work of a literary hack.

had[1] (had) Past tense and past participle of HAVE.

had[2] (had) *v.t. Scot.* To hold.

had better, had liefer, had rather See usage note under HAVE.

had·die (had′ē) *n. Scot.* A haddock.

had·din (had′ən) *n. Scot.* A dwelling; holding.

Had·ding·ton (had′ing·tən) The county seat of East Lothian, Scotland.

had·dock (had′ək) *n. pl.* **·dock** or **·docks** A food fish (*Melanogrammus aeglefinus*) of the North Atlantic, allied to the cod and with a black lateral line and blackish shoulder spot. [ME; origin unknown]

hade (hād) *n. Geol.* The inclination of a fault plane or vein from the vertical; an underlay: also **had′ing.** See FAULT (def. 3). — *v.i.* **had·ed, had·ing** To incline from a vertical position, as a fault plane. [Cf. dial. E *hade* slope]

Ha·des (hā′dēz) **1** In Greek mythology,

brother of Zeus, god of the underworld and lord of the dead: identified with the Greek and Roman *Pluto* and the Roman *Dis*. **2** The kingdom over which Pluto rules, the abode of the dead. See TARTARUS, ORCUS. **3** *Colloq.* A euphemism for HELL. [< Gk. *Haidēs* < *a*- not + *idein* see]

Had·field (had′fēld), **Sir Robert Abbott,** 1858–1940. English metallurgist.

Ha·dhra·maut (hä′drä·mout′, -môt′) A region on the southern coast of Arabia. Also **Ha′dra·maut′**.

hadj (haj)′ *n.* The pilgrimage to Mecca required of every free Mohammedan at least once in his life. Also spelled *haj, hajj.* See HEGIRA. [< Turkish < Arabic *hajj* pilgrimage. Akin to HEGIRA.]

hadj·i (haj′ē) *n.* **1** A Mohammedan who has made the pilgrimage to Mecca: used also before a name as a title. **2** An Armenian or a Greek who has made a pilgrimage to the holy sepulcher at Jerusalem. Also **hadj′ee.** [< Arabic *hajj* pilgrim]

Had·ley (had′lē), **Henry Kimball,** 1871–1937, U.S. composer.

had·n't (had′nt) Contraction of HAD NOT.

Ha·dri·an (hā′drē·ən), 76–138, Roman emperor 117–138: full name *Publius Aelius Hadrianus:* sometimes called "Adrian."

Ha·dri·an·op·o·lis (hā′drē·ən·op′ə·lis) The ancient name for ADRIANOPLE.

Hadrian's Wall A wall extending from Solway Firth to the Tyne, built by Hadrian, 122–128, to protect Roman Britain from the Picts and Scots.

Had·ru·me·tum (had′rə·mē′təm) The ancient name for SOUSSE.

hae (hā, ha) *v.t. Scot.* To have.

Haeck·el (hek′əl), **Ernst Heinrich,** 1834–1919, German biologist.

Hae·ju (hī·jōō) A port of central Korea on the Yellow Sea. *Japanese* **Kai·shu** (kī·shōō).

haem-, haemo- See HEMO-.

haema- See HEMA-.

haemat-, haemato- See HEMATO-.

hae·ma·to·cry·al (hē′mə·tō·krī′əl) See HEMATOCRYAL.

hae·ma·to·therm·al (hē′mə·tō·thûr′məl) See HEMATOTHERMAL.

hae·ma·tox·y·lon (hē′mə·tok′sə·lon, hem′ə-) *n.* **1** Any of a genus (*Haematoxylon*) of tropical American trees, especially the logwood or bloodwood tree (*H. campechianum*), whose heartwood supplies a purple-red coloring matter. **2** The wood of this tree. [< NL < Gk. *haima, -atos* blood + *xylon* wood]

haem·or·rhoid (hem′ə·roid), **haem·or·rhoi·dal** See HEMORRHOID, etc.

haen (hän) *Scot.* Past participle of HAE; had.

hae·res (hē′rēz) See HERES.

haf·fet (haf′it) *n. Scot.* Side of the head; temple.

ha·fiz (hä′fiz) *n.* One who has memorized the Koran: a Moslem title of respect. [< Arabic *hāfiz* one who remembers]

Ha·fiz (hä′fiz) Pseudonym of Shams ud-din Mohammed, Persian poet and philosopher of the 14th century.

haf·ni·um (haf′nē·əm) *n.* A metallic element (symbol Hf, atomic number 72) found combined in zirconium ores and used to control fission in nuclear reactors. See PERIODIC TABLE. [< NL, from L *Hafnia* Copenhagen]

haft (haft, häft) *n.* A handle; specifically, the handle of a cutting weapon. —*v.t.* To supply with or set in a haft or handle. Also spelled *heft*. [OE *hæft* handle < *habban* hold, have]

hag[1] (hag) *n.* **1** A forbidding or malicious old woman; an ugly crone. **2** A witch; sorceress; she-devil; a woman in league with the devil. **3** A hagfish. [OE *hægtes* witch] —**hag′gish** *adj.*

hag[2] (hag) *Scot. & Brit. Dial. v.t. & v.i.* **1** To hack or hew. **2** To harass; torment. —*n.* **1** A stroke with a chopping tool; hack. **2** A notch; cut. **3** One man's section of wood for felling. **4** Broken or mossy ground in a bog. **5** Cut branches. Also **hagg.** [< ON *höggva* hew]

Ha·gar (hā′gər) Abraham's concubine, mother of Ishmael. *Gen.* xvi 1.

hag·ber·ry (hag′ber′ē, -bər·ē) *n. pl.* **·ries** The hackberry. [See HACKBERRY]

hag·bush (hag′bŏŏsh′) *n.* The azedarach. [? OE *haga* hedge + BUSH]

hag·but (hag′but) *n.* A hackbut.

hag·don (hag′dən) *n.* The shearwater: also calle *haglet, haglin.* Also **hag′del** (-dəl), **hag′den** (-dən). [? < HAG[2] *v.*]

Ha·gen (hä′gən) **1** In the *Nibelungenlied,* Siegfried's murderer. **2** In Wagner's *Götterdämmerung,* the half-brother of Gunther and Gutrune.

Ha·gen (hä′gən) A city in North Rhine-Westphalia, Germany. Also **Ha·gen-in-West·fal·en** (in vest·fäl′ən).

hag·fish (hag′fish′) *n. pl.* **·fish** or **·fish·es** A primitive eel-like marine cyclostome (order or subclass *Myxinoidea*), allied to the lamprey, which bores its way into the bodies of living fishes by means of a rasping suctorial mouth. [< HAG[2], *v.* + FISH]

Hag·ga·dah (hə·gä′də, *Hebrew* hä·gô′dô) *n. pl.* **·doth** (-dōth) **1** A free interpretation or application: specifically, an illustrative anecdote or parable of the Midrash: distinguished from *halacha.* **2** The ritual, including the exposition of the story of the Exodus, read during the Seder on the first two nights of Passover. Also **Ha·ga′dah, Hag·ga′da.** [< Hebrew < *higgid* tell]

hag·gad·ic (hə·gad′ik, -gäd′-) *adj.* Of or pertaining to the Haggadah. Also **ha·gad′ic, haggad′i·cal.**

hag·ga·dist (hə·gä′dist) *n.* A haggadic writer or scholar. Also **ha·ga′dist.** —**hag·ga·dis·tic** (hag′ə·dis′tik), **hag′a·dis′tic** *adj.*

Hag·ga·i (hag′ē·ī, hag′ī) A minor Hebrew prophet of about 520 B.C.; also, the Old Testament book written by him.

hag·gard[1] (hag′ərd) *adj.* **1** Worn and gaunt in appearance. **2** Wild or intractable, as a hawk. —*n.* **1** In falconry, a wild hawk caught in its adult plumage. **2** Hence, an untamed fierce creature. [< OF *hagard* wild < MHG *hag* hedge] —**hag′gard·ly** *adv.* —**hag′gard·ness** *n.*

hag·gard[2] (hag′ərd) *n. Obs.* A wanton woman. [< HAG[1]]

Hag·gard (hag′ərd), **Sir Henry Rider,** 1856–1925, English novelist.

hag·gis (hag′is) *n.* A Scottish dish commonly made of a sheep's heart and liver with onions and suet, mixed with oatmeal and boiled in a sheep's stomach. [ME *hagas* < *haggen* chop + *es* food]

hag·gish (hag′ish) *adj.* Resembling or characteristic of a hag.

hag·gle (hag′əl) *v.* **hag·gled, hag·gling** *v.t.* **1** To cut unskilfully; mangle. **2** To tire or confuse, as by wrangling. —*v.i.* **3** To argue about price or terms. —*n.* The act of haggling or higgling. [Freq. of HAG[2]] —**hag′gler** *n.*

hag·i·ar·chy (hag′ē·är′kē, hā′jē-) *n. pl.* **·chies** A government, or the principle of government, by priests; sacerdotal government. Also **hag·i·oc·ra·cy** (hag′ē·ok′rə·sē, hā′jē-).

hagio- *combining form* Sacred: *hagiography.* Also, before vowels, **hagi-.** [< Gk. *hagios* sacred]

Hag·i·og·ra·pha (hag′ē·og′rə·fə, hā′jē-) *n. pl.* The third of the three ancient divisions of the Old Testament, comprising all books not reckoned in the Law or the Prophets. [< Gk. < *hagios* sacred + *graphein* writing]

hag·i·og·ra·phy (hag′ē·og′rə·fē, hā′jē-) *n. pl.* **·phies** **1** The writing or study of saints' lives. **2** A collection of biographies of saints. —**hag·i·og′ra·phal** *adj.* —**hag′i·og′ra·pher** *n.* —**hag·i·o·graph·ic** (hag′ē·ō·graf′ik, hā′jē-) or **·i·cal** *adj.*

hag·i·ol·a·try (hag′ē·ol′ə·trē, hā′jē-) *n.* The veneration or invocation of saints. —**hag·i·ol′a·ter** *n.* —**hag′i·ol′a·trous** *adj.*

hag·i·ol·o·gy (hag′ē·ol′ə·jē, hā′jē-) *n. pl.* **·gies** **1** A list of saints. **2** A treatise on saints' lives; sacred writings. —**hag·i·o·log·ic** (hag′ē·ō·loj′ik, hā′jē-) *adj.* —**hag′i·ol′o·gist** *n.*

hag·i·o·scope (hag′ē·ō·skōp′, hā′jē-) *n.* An oblique opening in the screen or chancel wall of a medieval church, to permit those in a side chapel or aisle to see the main altar. —**hag′i·o·scop′ic** (-skop′ik) *adj.*

hag·let, hag·lin (hag′lin) See HAGDON.

hag·rid·den (hag′rid′n) *adj.* **1** Ridden by a hag or witch. **2** Tormented or distressed by or as by nightmares or hallucinations. **3** By extension, tormented by a woman.

Hague (åg), **Cap de la** A cape of NW France on the English Channel.

Hague (hāg), **The** The de facto capital of the Netherlands: Dutch *'s Gravenhage.*

—**Hague Conferences** The first international peace conferences, held at The Hague in 1899 (26 states) and 1907 (44 states). The **Hague Conventions,** relating to the conduct of war and to the arbitration of international disputes, were adopted by the conferences, and the **Hague Tribunal** was created by the first. See PERMANENT COURT OF ARBITRATION under COURT.

hah (hä) See HA.

ha-ha (hä′hä) *n.* A hedge or wall set in a ditch, so as not to obstruct the view: also spelled *hawhaw.* [< F *haha*]

Hahn (hän), **Otto,** 1879–1968, German physical chemist.

Hah·ne·mann (hä′nə·män), **(Christian Friedrich) Samuel,** 1755–1843, German physician; founder of homeopathy. —**Hah·ne·man·i·an** (hä′nə·man′ē·ən, -män′ē-), **Hah′ne·man′ni·an** *adj.*

Hah·ne·mann·ism (hä′nə·män·iz′əm) *n.* The original homeopathy.

Hai·da (hī′də) *n.* **1** A member of any of the tribes of North American Indians inhabiting the Queen Charlotte Islands, British Columbia, and Prince of Wales Island, Alaska. **2** The family of languages spoken by these tribes.

Hai·dar·a·bad (hī′dər·ə·bad′) See HYDERABAD.

Hai·dar A·li (hī′dər ä′lē) See HYDER ALI.

Hai·duk (hī′dŏŏk) *n.* **1** One of a body of Hungarian mercenaries of the 16th century, or Magyar race, who served the Protestant cause. **2** One of the bandit mountaineers of the Balkans who took part in the struggle for independence against Turkey. Also spelled *Heyduck.* Also **Hai′duck.** [< Hungarian *hajduk* drover]

Hai·fa (hī′fə) A port of NW Israel on the Bay of Acre.

Haig (hāg), **Douglas,** 1861–1928, first Earl Haig, British field marshal.

haik (hīk, häk) *n.* An Oriental outside garment made of an oblong woolen cloth. Also **haick.** [< Arabic *hayk* < *hāk* to weave]

HAIK

hai·ku (hī·kōō) *n.* A poem in imitation of a Japanese verse form, consisting of three lines of five, seven, five syllables respectively. Also *hokku.* [< Japanese *haikai*]

hai·kwan (hī′kwän′) *n.* The maritime custom duties of China. [< Chinese < *hai* sea + *kuan* gate]

hail[1] (hāl) *n.* **1** Frozen rain or congealed vapor, often falling in pellets during thunderstorms. **2** Figuratively, anything falling thickly and with violence: a *hail* of blows. **3** A hailstorm. —*v.i.* To pour down hail: used impersonally. —*v.t.* To hurl or pour down like hail: to *hail* curses on someone. ◆ Homophone: *hale.* [OE *hægel*] —**hail′y** *adj.*

hail[2] (hāl) *v.t.* **1** To call loudly to in greeting; salute. **2** To call to so as to attract attention: to *hail* a cab. **3** To name as; designate: They *hailed* him captain. —*v.i.* **4** To call out so as to attract attention or give greeting. —**to hail from** To come from; have as one's original home or residence. See synonyms under ADDRESS. —*n.* **1** A call to attract attention; greeting. **2** The distance a shout can be heard: within *hail.* —*interj.* An exclamation of greeting. ◆ Homophone: *hale.* [ME *hailen, heilen* < ON *heilla* < *heill* whole, hale. Akin to HALE[2].] —**hail′er** *n.*

hail[3] (hāl) *adj. Scot.* Healthy; hale; whole.

hail Columbia *U.S. Slang* **1** A severe punishment or reprimand. **2** A beating or drubbing: to give the enemy *hail Columbia.* **3** A rumpus: to raise *hail Columbia.* [Euphemism for HELL]

Hai·le Se·las·sie (hī′lē sə·las′ē, -lä′sē), 1891–1975, emperor of Ethiopia 1930–74; in exile 1936–41.

hail-fel·low (hāl′fel′ō) *adj.* On very familiar or cordial terms. —*n.* A close companion. Also **hail′-fel′low-well′-met′.**

Hail Mary See AVE MARIA.

hail·stone (hāl′stōn′) *n.* A pellet of hail.

hail·storm (hāl′stôrm′) *n.* A storm in which hail falls: also **hail storm.**

hain (hain) *v.t. Scot.* To save; spare; preserve.

Hai·nan (hī′nän′) An island of SE China; 13,000 square miles; separated from the mainland by **Hainan Strait,** an arm of the South China Sea.

Hai·naut (e·nō′) A province of SW Belgium; 1,437 square miles; capital, Mons. *Flemish* **He·ne·gou·wen** (hā′nə·gou′wən).

hain't (hānt) *Illit. & Dial.* Contraction of *have not* or *has not.*

Hai·phong (hī′fong′) A port of North Vietnam.

hair (hâr) *n.* **1** One of the filaments of modified epidermal tissue growing from the skin or outer covering of a mammal. ◆ Collateral adjectives: *capillary, pilar.* **2** Any mass of such filaments, especially that which grows upon the head. **3** Any filamentous process. **4** *Bot.* An outgrowth of the epidermis in plants. **5** Haircloth; specifically, mats woven from horsehair, used in expressing oils, etc.

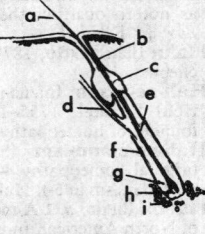

HAIR

Section through the skin:
a. Shaft.
b. Root.
c. Sebaceous gland.
d. Erector pili muscle.
e. Root sheath.
f. Follicle.
g. Bulb.
h. Papilla.
i. Fat-cells.

6 Figuratively, an exceedingly minute, slight, or delicate thing, space, etc. — *adj.* Like, or made of, hair. — **to a hair line** With the utmost exactness. — **to split hairs** To quibble; make petty or excessive distinctions. — **to let down one's hair** To disclose the actual state of one's affairs. — **not to turn a hair** To show or reveal no sign of exhaustion nor a lack of composure. ◆ Homophone: *hare.* [OE *hær*] — **hair′less** *adj.*

Hair may appear as a combining form in hyphemes or solidemes, or as the first element in two–word phrases; as in:

hairband	hairmonger
hair bleacher	hairmongering
hair braid	hair net
haircap	hair oil
hair carder	hair powder
hair clipper	hair remover
hair–collecting	hair restorer
hair–collector	hair ribbon
hair crimper	hair sorter
hair curler	hair straightener
hair drawer	hair tonic
hair dye	hair wash
hair dyer	hair washer
hair dyeing	hair waver
hairlock	hair–waving
hair mattress	hairwork

hair·bird (hâr′bûrd′) *n.* The chipping sparrow: so called because it lines its nest with hair.

hair·breadth (hâr′bredth′) *n.* A hair's breadth; an extremely small space or distance. — *adj.* Having only the breadth of a hair; very narrow. Also **hairs′–breadth′, hair′s′–breadth′.**

hair·brush (hâr′brush′) *n.* A brush used for the hair.

hair cell *Anat.* One of the delicate filamentous cells situated in the organ of Corti in the cochlea, and responsible for the transmission of sound vibrations.

hair·cloth (hâr′klôth′, -kloth′) *n.* A fabric having a warp of either cotton or linen yarn with a horsehair filling.

hair·cut (hâr′kut′) *n.* The act of cutting the hair or the style in which it is cut. — **hair′cut′ter** *n.* — **hair′cut′ting** *adj. & n.*

hair–do (hâr′dōō′) *n.* A style of dressing the hair; coiffure.

hair·dress·er (hâr′dres′ər) *n.* One who arranges the hair, especially women's hair. — **hair′dress′ing** *n.*

hair·line (hâr′līn′) *n.* **1** *Printing* **a** A very thin line on a type face; also, the type itself. **b** A thin rule. **2** A narrow stripe in textile fabrics. **3** The outline of hair on the head.

hair·pin (hâr′pin′) *n.* A U–shaped pin made of wire, bone, celluloid, or the like, for supporting the hair or headdress.

hair–rais·ing (hâr′rā′zing) *adj.* Causing fright or shock. — **hair′–rais′er** *n.*

hair seal The eared seal or sea lion, not valued for its fur.

hair shirt A rough cloth garment of goats' hair worn as a shirt or as a girdle for penance or mortification.

hair space *Printing* The thinnest of the metal spaces for separating letters and words.

hair–split·ting (hâr′split′ing) *n.* Insistence upon minute or trivial distinctions. See synonyms under SOPHISTRY. — *adj.* Drawing excessively nice distinctions. — **hair′–split′ter** *n.*

hair·spring (hâr′spring′) *n.* The fine spring of the balance wheel of a watch.

hairst (hârst) *n. Scot.* Harvest.

hair·streak (hâr′strēk′) *n.* A small butterfly (family *Lycaenidae*) with narrow stripes on the underside of the wings.

hair·stroke (hâr′strōk′) *n.* **1** A very fine stroke in writing. **2** A serif.

hair–trig·ger (hâr′trig′ər) *n.* **1** A trigger so delicately adjusted that a very slight pressure discharges the firearm. **2** A pistol or revolver having such a trigger. — *adj.* Stimulated or set in operation by the slightest provocation.

hair·worm (hâr′wûrm′) *n.* Any of various nematode worms (families *Gordiidae* and *Mermithidae*) which inhabit running water and whose larvae are parasitic in insects: sometimes called *horsehair–snake.*

hair·y (hâr′ē) *adj.* **hair·i·er, hair·i·est** **1** Covered with, made of, or like hair. **2** *Slang* **a** Troublesome; difficult. **b** Dangerous; harrowing. — **hair′i·ness** *n.*

Hai·ti (hā′tē) **1** A republic comprising the western portion of Hispaniola; 10,714 square miles; capital, Port-au-Prince. **2** Former name of HISPANIOLA. *French* **Ha·ï·ti** (à.ē.tē′).

Hai·ti·an (hā′tē·ən, -shən) *adj.* Of or pertaining to Haiti, its people, or their culture. — *n.* **1** A native or inhabitant of Haiti. **2** A French patois spoken by the Haitians: also **Haitian Creole. 3** Taino.

haj (haj), **hajj** See HADJ.

ha·je (hä′jē) *n.* The African cobra or asp (*Naja haje*). See also illustration under URAEUS. [<Arabic *ḥayyah* snake]

haj·i (haj′ē), **haj·ji** See HADJI.

hake (hāk) *n. pl.* **hake** or **hakes** **1** A fish (genus *Merluccius*) having a short first dorsal fin, and long, sinuated second dorsal and anal fins; especially, the European hake (*M. smiridus*) and the American silver hake or whiting (*M. bilinearis*). **2** A North American food fish (genus *Phycis*), the codling. Also spelled **haak.** [OE *hacod* pike < *haca* hook]

Ha·ken·kreuz (hä′kən-kroits) *n.* A swastika: especially as the symbol of Nazism. [<G, lit., hooked cross]

ha·kim (hä·kēm′) *n.* In Moslem countries, a governor; also, a sage or physician. Also **hakeem′, ha·kem′.** [<Arabic, wise, learned]

Hak·luyt (hak′lōōt), **Richard,** 1553?–1616, English historian and geographer.

Ha·ko·da·te (hä·kō·dä·tā) A port on SW Hokkaido island, Japan.

hal– Var. of HALO–.

ha·la·cha (hä′lä·khä′, *Hebrew* hä·lô′khô) *n. pl.* **·choth** (-khōth) In the Talmud, Jewish traditional law embracing minute precepts not found in the written law; the legal part of the Midrash. Compare HAGGADAH. Also **ha′la·kah′.** [<Hebrew *halakāh* a rule to go by < *hālak* walk, go] — **ha·lach·ic** (hə·lak′ik) *adj.*

ha·la·chist (hä′lə·kist, hə·lä′kist) *n.* One who frames from the Biblical laws precepts of the halacha. Also **ha′la·kist.**

ha·la·tion (hā·lā′shən, ha-) *n. Phot.* An appearance somewhat like a halo: caused by the radiation of light from a window or other object in the scene of a photograph, or by reflection of light from the plate; ghost. [< HALO]

hal·berd (hal′bərd) *n.* A weapon in the form of a battle–ax and pike at the end of a long staff. Also **hal′bard, hal′bert** (-bərt). [<OF *hallebarde* <MHG *helmbarte* < *helm* handle + *barte* broad-ax]

HAJE
The royal serpent of ancient Egypt; widely represented as a religious symbol and in the royal headdress (*a*) as sign of the royal power. (From 3 to 4 feet long, with neck skin dilatable)

hal·ber·dier (hal′bər·dir′) *n.* A soldier armed with a halberd.

hal·cy·on (hal′sē·ən) *n.* **1** A mythical bird, identified with the kingfisher, said to have nested on the sea at the time of the winter solstice, when the sea was supposed to become calm. **2** Any kingfisher of the genus *Halcyon* of Australasia. — *adj.* **1** Of or pertaining to the halcyon. **2** Calm; peaceful. [<L *halcyon,* var. of *alcyon* <Gk. *alkyōn* kingfisher]

halcyon days **1** The seven days before and the seven days after the winter solstice, when the halcyon bred and brought calm, peaceful weather. **2** Any period of peace and tranquillity.

Hal·cy·o·ne (hal·sī′ə·nē) See ALCYONE.

Hal·dane (hôl′dān), **J(ohn) B(urdon) S(anderson),** 1892–1964, English biologist. — **John Scott,** 1860–1936, English physiologist, father of the preceding. — **Richard Burdon,** 1856–1928, Viscount Haldane of Cloan, English philosopher and statesman, brother of John Scott.

hale¹ (hāl) *v.t.* **haled, hal·ing** **1** To drag by force; haul; pull. **2** To compel to go: to *hale* someone into court. ◆ Homophone: *hail.* [Var. of HAUL] — **hal′er** *n.*

hale² (hāl) *adj.* **1** Of sound and vigorous health; robust. **2** *Scot.* Free from defect or injury. See synonyms under HEALTHY. ◆ Homophone: *hail.* [OE *hāl.* Related to WHOLE.] — **hale′ly** *adv.* — **hale′ness** *n.*

Hale (hāl), **Edward Everett,** 1822–1909, U.S. clergyman and author. — **George Ellery,** 1868–1938, U.S. astronomer. — **Sir Matthew,** 1609–76, English judge and historian. — **Nathan,** 1755–75, American Revolutionary officer; hanged as a spy by the British.

Ha·le·a·ka·la (hä′lā·ä·kä·lä′) The largest extinct volcanic crater in the world, on eastern Maui island, Hawaii; 10,032 feet high; 19 square miles; 2,000 feet deep.

Ha·le·mau·mau (hä′lā·mou′mou) The fiery pit in the Kilauea crater of Mauna Loa, Hawaii.

Ha·le·vi (hä·lē′vī), **Judah,** 1085?–1140?, Spanish Hebrew poet and Arabic philosopher: also **ha–Le′vi.**

Ha·lé·vy (à·lā·vē′), **Jacques François Fromental Élie,** 1799–1862, French composer. — **Ludovic,** 1834–1908, French playwright and novelist.

half (haf, häf) *n. pl.* **halves** (havz, hävz) One of two equal parts into which a thing is or may be divided, or a quantity equal to such a part. — **to, for, at,** or **on halves** For half the crop or profits: for rent *at halves,* to farm *on halves.* — *adj.* **1** Being one of two equal parts of a thing. **2** Partial; approximately one half of, in amount or value. — *adv.* To the degree or extent of a half; partially. — **not half bad** *Brit.* Actually quite good, don't you know! [OE *hælf*]

Half frequently appears as the first element in hyphenated compounds, with the following meanings:

1 Exactly half; as in:

half–acre	half–foot	half–pounder
half–barrel	half–full	half–price
half–century	half–inch	half–rod
half–circle	half–liter	half–round
half–day	half–mile	half–thick
half–dozen	half–mystic	half–timer
half–fill	half–pound	half–weight

2 Partial or partially; approximately half; as in:

half–admitted	half–deserted	half–mad
half–afraid	half–digested	half–make
half–alive	half–done	half–murder
half–altered	half–dressed	half–open
half–angry	half–drunk	half–opened
half–ashamed	half–earnest	half–raw
half–awake	half–eaten	half–ripe
half–belief	half–ebb	half–ruined
half–believe	half–educated	half–safe
half–bent	half–finished	half–serious
half–blind	half–frozen	half–shut
half–buried	half–gloom	half–sleep
half–civilized	half–grown	half–spoiled
half–cleaned	half–hidden	half–strength
half–clear	half–human	half–submerge
half–conscious	half–humorous	half–true
half–crazy	half–joking	half–whisper
half–dead	half–knowledge	half–wild

half–and–half (haf′ənd·haf′, häf′ənd·häf′) *adj.* Half of one thing and half of another. — *n.* A mixture of two liquors; specifically, beer

and ale. — *adv.* Equally; in two equal divisions.

Hal·fa·ya Pass (häl·fä′yä) A pass through the coastal hills of NW Egypt; scene of heavy fighting in World War II, 1941–42.

half·back (haf′bak′, häf′-) *n.* In American football, either of two players in the backfield, originally stationed half-way between the line and the fullback.

half–baked (haf′bākt′, häf′-) *adj.* **1** Baked on one side or not baked through; doughy. **2** Imperfectly planned or conceived. **3** Raw; immature; unseasoned.

halfbeak (haf′bēk′, häf′-) *n.* A fish (genus *Hemiramphus*), related to the saury, having the lower jaw prolonged into a flat, narrow extension.

half–bind·ing (haf′bīn′ding, häf′-) *n.* A style of bookbinding in which only the back and corners of the volume are covered with leather. — **half′–bound′** (-bound′) *adj.*

half blood 1 *Law* The relationship between persons who have one parent only in common. **2** The condition of being of mixed stock: an Indian of *half blood.*

half–blood (haf′blud′) *n.* **1** A person having only one parent of a specified stock; one whose parents are of different stocks; a half-breed. **2** An animal, as a cow, sheep, etc., of crossed inferior and superior stock. **3** A person of Indian and white, or Negro and white parentage. — *adj.* Being a half-blood or half-breed; in a loose sense, of mixed blood or breed: also **half′–blood′ed.**

half–boot (haf′bōōt′, häf′-) *n.* A boot extending slightly above the ankle.

half–breed (haf′brēd′, häf′-) *n.* **1** One having parents of different blood or ethnic stock: a Canadian *half–breed.* **2** One having a white father and an American Indian mother. **3** An adherent of President Garfield in the factional struggles of 1881 within the Republican party. See STALWART. — *adj.* Half of one breed and half of another; coming of mixed ethnic or racial stock: also **half′–bred′** (-bred′).

half–breed buffalo A catalo.

half–broth·er (haf′bruth′ər, häf′-) *n.* A brother related through only one parent.

half–case (haf′kās′, häf′-) *n. Printing* A type case about half the width of the standard upper case.

half–caste (haf′kast′, häf′käst′) *n.* One born of mixed European and Asian blood; also, any half-breed. — *adj.* Of mixed European and other blood.

half–cock (haf′kok′, häf′-) *n.* The position of the hammer of a firearm when partly raised, but not releasable by the trigger. — **to go off at half–cock 1** To be discharged prematurely. **2** Hence, to act or speak without deliberation. Also **to go off half–cocked.** — *v.t.* To raise the hammer of (a gun) to the position of half-cock.

half–cracked (haf′krakt′, häf′-) *adj.* Half-witted.

half–crown (haf′kroun′, häf′-) *n.* **1** An English silver coin of the value of 2s. 6d. **2** *Naut.* A method of passing a rope around a spar.

half–dime (haf′dīm′, häf′-) *n.* A U.S. silver coin worth five cents: first minted, 1792; discontinued, 1873. Also **half′–disme′.**

half–dol·lar (haf′dol′ər, häf′-) *n.* A U.S. silver coin worth fifty cents: first minted, 1794.

half–ea·gle (haf′ē′gəl, häf′-) *n.* A gold coin of the United States having a value of five dollars.

half gainer A backward somersault from the standing position of a front dive.

half hatchet A hatchet, the blade of which is trimmed flush with the wedge of the shaft. See illustration under HATCHET.

half–heart·ed (haf′här′tid, häf′-) *adj.* Showing little interest or enthusiasm. See synonyms under FAINT, IRRESOLUTE. — **half′–heart′ed·ly** *adv.* — **half′–heart′ed·ness** *n.*

half–hitch (haf′hich′, häf′-) *n.* A hitch formed by an overhand knot. See illustration under HITCH.

half–hose (haf′hōz′, häf′-) *n.* Socks or stockings extending halfway to the knee.

half–hour (haf′our′, häf′-) *n.* **1** A period of thirty minutes. **2** The point midway between the hours. — **half′–hour′ly** *adv.*

half leather A style of bookbinding in which

the volume has a leather back and muslin sides.

half–length (haf′length′, häf′-) *adj.* Of half the full length, as of a portrait. — *n.* A portrait showing only the upper half of the body.

half–life (haf′līf′, häf′-) *n. Physics* The period of time during which half the atoms of a radioactive element or isotope will disintegrate. The half-life of radium is about 1,620 years, at the end of which period the amount remaining will require another 1,620 years to decline by half. Also called *half–value period.* Also **half period.**

half–lift (haf′lift′, häf′-) *n.* A layer of heel leather split to half the standard thickness, and used for close adjustment in built-up heels.

half–light (haf′līt′, häf′-) *n.* A dim, grayish light, as at evening.

half–loop (haf′lōōp′, häf′-) *n. Aeron.* A flight maneuver in which an airplane makes one half of a complete loop.

half–mast (haf′mast′, häf′mäst′) *n.* The position of a flag when half-way up the staff, as a tribute of respect to the dead or as a signal of distress. — *v.t.* To put, as a flag, at half-mast. Also called *half–staff.*

half–meas·ure (haf′mezh′ər, häf′-) *n.* An imperfect or inadequate measure or plan.

half–mitt (haf′mit′, häf′-) *n.* A type of mitten extending only to the knuckles. Also **half′–mit′ten.**

half–moon (haf′mōōn′, häf′-) *n.* **1** The moon when half its disk is illuminated. **2** Something similar in shape to a half-moon.

half–nel·son (haf′nel′sən, häf′-) *n.* A wrestling hold in which one arm is passed below the opponent's armpit and the hand is pressed against the back of his neck.

half note *Music* A note held half the measure of a whole note; a minim.

half–pace (haf′pās′, häf′-) *n. Brit.* **1** A floor raised above the adjoining level, in a bay window or the like; the raised place at the head of steps on which an altar stands; a dais. **2** A resting place at the end of a flight of stairs; a footpace.

half–pay (haf′pā′, häf′-) *n.* Literally, half of full pay; most commonly, the reduced pay of an officer not in regular service or on the retired list, generally more than half.

half–pen·ny (hā′pən-ē, häf′pen-ē) *n. pl.* **half·pence** (hā′pəns) or **half–pen·nies** (hā′pən-ēz, hāp′nēz) A British copper coin equivalent to one half of a penny.

half–pike (haf′pīk′, häf′-) *n.* A spearing weapon having a staff about half as long as that of the pike.

half pint 1 A measure of capacity equal to one half of a pint. **2** *Slang* A small person.

half relief Mezzo–relievo.

half rime Near rime.

half–roll (haf′rōl′, häf′-) *n. Aeron.* The turning of an airplane through an angle of 180° about its long axis.

half–sec·tion (haf′sek′shən, häf′-) *n.* Half a square mile, or 320 acres of land.

half–shot (haf′shot′, häf′-) *adj. Slang* **1** Very tired. **2** Half drunk.

half–sis·ter (haf′sis′tər, häf′-) *n.* A sister related through only one parent.

half–sole (haf′sōl′, häf′-) *n.* A tap sole on a shoe, extending only to the shank. — *v.t.* **·soled, ·sol·ing** To repair by attaching a half-sole.

half–sov·er·eign (haf′sov′rin, -suv′rən, häf′-) *n.* A British gold coin of the value of ten shillings: no longer in active circulation.

half–staff (haf′staf′, häf′stäf′) See HALF-MAST.

half–step (haf′step′, häf′-) *n.* **1** *Music.* A semitone. **2** *Mil.* A step of fifteen inches at quick time; in double time, one of eighteen inches.

half–stuff (haf′stuf′, häf′-) *n.* Crude paper pulp before it goes into the papermaking machine.

half–sword (haf′sôrd′, -sōrd′, häf′-) *n.* Half the length of a sword.

half tide The interval midway between high and low tide.

half–tim·bered (haf′tim′bərd, häf′-) *adj.* Built of heavy timbers, with the spaces between filled with masonry or plaster: said of the framework of a house.

half time The middle break in a field or court game played in definite time intervals.

half–time (haf′tīm′, häf′-) *adj.* Requiring half a person's usual working hours.

half–tint (haf′tint′, häf′-) *n.* A tint or tone of color intermediate between two strong tones of different values.

half–ti·tle (haf′tīt′l, häf′-) *n.* **1** The title of a book, usually abridged, printed on the leaf preceding the title page. **2** The title of any part or section of a book printed on the leaf preceding the text proper: often called *mock title.*

halftone (haf′tōn′, häf′-) *n.* **1** An illustration made from a relief plate obtained by photographing an original through a finely ruled glass screen, the lights and shadows appearing when printed as minutely lined or dotted surfaces. **2** A half-tint. **3** *Music* A semitone. — *adj.* Made by the process of printing halftones.

half–track (haf′trak′, häf′-) *adj.* Designating a type of military vehicle propelled by endless tracks, but steered by a pair of wheels in front. — *n.* A half-track vehicle. Compare FULL–TRACK.

half–truth (haf′trōōth′, häf′-) *n.* An assertion that is true as far as it goes, but that omits or conceals part of the truth.

half–val·ue period (haf′val′yōō, häf′-) See HALF–LIFE.

half–vol·ley (haf′vol′ē, häf′-) *n.* In tennis, cricket, etc., a ball, or the return, struck close to the ground, the instant after it bounces.

half–way (haf′wā′, häf′-) *adv.* At or to half the distance. — *adj.* **1** Midway between two points. **2** Partial; inadequate: *half-way measures.*

half–wit (haf′wit′, häf′-) *n.* A feeble-minded person; idiot. — **half′–wit′ted** *adj.*

half–year (haf′yir′, häf′-) *n.* **1** Half of a calendar year, or six months. **2** Half the time regularly used in a year, as of a school year. — **half′–year′ly** *adj. & adv.*

hal·i·but (hal′ə-bət, hol′-) *n. pl.* **·but** or **·buts** A large flatfish (*Hippoglossus hippoglossus*) of northern seas, much esteemed as food, sometimes attaining a weight of 400 pounds: also spelled *holibut.* [ME *halybutte*, OE *halig* holy + BUT²]

hal·ic (hal′ik, hā′lik) *adj. Ecol.* Of or pertaining to plant communities associated with saline soils.

Hal·i·car·nas·sus (hal′ə-kär-nas′əs) An ancient Greek city in SW Asia Minor; site of the Mausoleum, one of the Seven Wonders of the Ancient World; modern *Bodrum.*

hal·ide (hal′īd, -id, hā′līd, -lid) *n. Chem.* Any compound of a halogen with an element or radical, as a bromide, chloride, etc. — *adj.* Resembling sea salt; haloid. Also **hal·id** (hal′id, hā′lid).

hal·i·dom (hal′ə-dom) *n. Archaic* **1** Holiness. **2** A holy relic. **3** A holy place; sanctuary. [OE *haligdom* < *halig* holy + -DOM]

Hal·i·fax (hal′ə-faks), **Earl of,** 1881–1959, Edward Frederick Lindley Wood, English statesman.

Hal·i·fax (hal′ə-faks) **1** The capital of Nova Scotia province, Canada; the principal Atlantic port in Canada. **2** A county borough in SW Yorkshire, England. — **Hal·i·go·ni·an** (hal′i-gō′nē-ən) *adj. & n.*

hal·i·plank·ton (hal′ə-plangk′tən) *n.* Marine plankton, as opposed to lacustrine plankton.

hal·ite (hal′īt, hā′līt) *n.* A massive or granular, white or variously colored sodium chloride, NaCl; rock salt.

hal·i·to·sis (hal′ə-tō′sis) *n.* A malodorous condition of the breath. [< L *halitus* breath + -OSIS]

hal·i·tus (hal′ə-təs) *n.* **1** The breath. **2** The vapor from a living body or from blood newly drawn. [< L]

hall (hôl) *n.* **1** A passage or corridor in a building. **2** A small room or enclosure at the entry of a house; a vestibule; lobby. **3** A large building or room devoted to public or semipublic business or entertainments. **4** In a university or college, a large building used as a dormitory, classroom building, laboratory, etc. **5** A meeting place for a fraternity or society; also the society itself: Tammany

Hall. 6 *Brit.* A college dining-room; also, the dinner served there. 7 In medieval times, the large main room of a castle or other great house, used for dining, entertaining, and, often, sleeping. 8 The country residence of a baron, squire, etc. See synonyms under HOUSE.◆ Homophone: haul. [OE *heall*]

Hall (hôl), **Charles Francis,** 1821–71, U.S. Arctic explorer. —**G(ranville) Stanley,** 1846–1924, U.S. psychologist and editor.

Hal·lam (hal′əm), **Henry,** 1777–1859, English historian.

hal·lan (hal′ən, häl′-) *n. Scot.* A wall or partition in cottages, to screen the occupants from the cold air when the door is opened.

hall bedroom A small bedroom opening into a hall, especially one at the head of a stairway.

Hal·le (häl′ə) A city in SW East Germany, capital of former Saxony-Anhalt state. Also **Hal·le-an-der-Saa·le** (häl′ə-än-dər-zä′lə).

Hal·leck (hal′ək), **Fitz-Greene,** 1790–1867, U.S. poet.

hal·lel (hal′el, hə-lāl′) *n.* In Jewish religious observances, the Psalms from cxiii to cxviii inclusive, chanted at the Passover, Pentecost, and Sukkoth. [< Hebrew *hallēl* praise]

hal·le·lu·jah (hal′ə-lōō′yə) *interj.* Praise ye the Lord! —*n.* 1 A musical composition whose principal theme is found in the word *hallelujah.* 2 A flower of the wood sorrel family (*Oxalidaceae*). Also **hal′le·lu′iah.** [< Gk. < Hebrew *hallēlū* praise + *yāh* Jehovah]

Hal·ley (hal′ē), **Edmund,** 1656–1742, English astronomer royal. See under COMET.

hal·liard (hal′yərd) See HALYARD.

hal·lion (hal′yən) *n. Scot.* A rascal, hellion.

hall·mark (hôl′märk′) *n.* 1 An official mark stamped on gold and silver articles in England to guarantee their purity. 2 Any mark or proof of genuineness or excellence. —*v.t.* To stamp with a hallmark. [< Goldsmiths' *Hall,* London, where the assaying and stamping were formerly exclusively done + MARK]

hal·loo (hə-lōō′) *interj.* 1 An exclamation to attract attention, express surprise, etc. 2 A shout to incite hounds to the chase. —*n.* A cry of "halloo." —*v.i.* To shout "halloo"; cry out. —*v.t.* 1 To incite or encourage with shouts. 2 To shout to; hail. 3 To shout (something). Also **hal·lo, hal·loa** (hə-lō′): also spelled *holla, hollo, holloa, hillo, hilloa, hullo.* [< OF *halloer* pursue noisily]

hal·low (hal′ō) *v.t.* 1 To make holy; consecrate. 2 To look upon as holy; reverence. [OE *halgian* < *halig* holy] —**hal·lowed** (hal′ōd, in liturgical use hal′ō·id) *adj.*

Hal·low·e'en (hal′ō-ēn′) *n.* The evening of Oct. 31, vigil of All Saints' Day. [< (ALL-) HALLOW(S) E(V)EN]

Hal·low·mass (hal′ō·məs) *n. Archaic* The feast of All-hallows or All Saints' Day. Also **Hal′low·mas.** [< (ALL-)HALLOW-MASS]

Hall process A process for the electrolytic reduction of aluminum from its ores. [after C. M. *Hall,* 1863–1914, U.S. inventor]

Hall·statt (häl′shtät) A village of Upper Austria on the SW shore of the Lake of Hallstatt, where prehistoric implements were found.

Hall·statt (häl′shtät) *adj.* Pertaining to or denoting the earlier of two principal divisions of the prehistoric Iron Age of Europe, extending from about the ninth to the fifth century B.C. — **Hall·statt′i·an** (-ē-ən) *adj.*

hall tree A clothestree.

hal·lu·ci·nate (hə-lōō′sə-nāt) *v.t.* **·nat·ed, ·nat·ing** To affect or afflict with hallucinations. [< L *hallucinatus,* pp. of *hallucinari, alucinari* wander mentally]

hal·lu·ci·na·tion (hə-lōō′sə-nā′shən) *n.* 1 An apparent perception without any corresponding external object. 2 *Psychiatry* Any of numerous sensations, auditory, visual, or tactile, experienced without external stimulus, and caused by mental derangement, intoxication, or fever. See ILLUSION. 3 A mistaken notion. See synonyms under DELUSION, DREAM, ERROR. —**hal·lu·ci·na·to·ry** (hə-lōō′sə-nə-tôr′ē, -tō′rē) *adj.*

hal·lu·ci·no·gen (hə-lōō′sin-ə-jən) *n.* Any drug or chemical, as peyote, capable of inducing hallucinations.

hal·lu·ci·no·gen·ic (hə-lōō′sə-nə-jen′ik) *adj.* 1 Causing or having to do with hallucinations or with a distortion of perception or consciousness: *hallucinogenic* drugs. 2 Of or pertaining to hallucinogens.

hal·lu·ci·no·sis (hə-lōō′sə-nō′sis) *n. Psychiatry* A mental or nervous disorder characterized by persistent hallucinations.

hal·lux (hal′əks) *n. pl.* **hal·lu·ces** (hal′yōō-sēz) *Biol.* 1 The first or innermost digit of the foot; the great toe. 2 In a bird, the hind toe. [< NL < L *hallex;* infl. by *hallus* thumb]

hall·way (hôl′wā′) *n.* A passage giving entrance to a building or communicating with its various apartments.

halm (hôm) See HAULM.

hal·ma (hal′mə) *n.* In the exercise of the pentathlon, the long jump with weights in the hands. [< Gk. < *halesthai* leap]

Hal·ma·he·ra (häl′mä-hā′rä) An Indonesian island NE of Celebes; 6,870 square miles: also *Djailolo, Jailolo, Jilolo.*

ha·lo (hā′lō) *n. pl.* **·los** or **·loes** 1 *Meteorol.* A luminous circle around the sun or the moon, caused by the refraction of light passing through ice crystals floating in the air. 2 A nimbus; a radiance encircling the head in portrayals of a sacred personage. 3 The ideal brightness with which imagination surrounds an object of affection or sentiment. —*v.t.* To enclose in a halo. —*v.i.* To form a halo. [< L < Gk. *halos* a circular threshing floor]

halo- *combining form* 1 The sea; of or related to the sea: *halophyte.* 2 Related to a halogen. Also, before vowels, *hal-,* as in *haloid.* [< Gk. *hals, halos* salt, the sea]

hal·o·bi·os (hal′ə-bī′əs) *n.* Life in the oceans; marine life collectively. [< HALO- + Gk. *bios* life] —**hal′o·bi·ot′ic** (-bī-ot′ik) *adj.*

hal·o·gen (hal′ə-jən) *n. Chem.* One of certain non-metallic elements belonging to the seventh group in the periodic table, as iodine, fluorine, chlorine, and bromine, which combine directly with metals to form halides. [< Gk. *hals* sea, salt + -GEN] —**ha·log·e·nous** (hə-loj′ə-nəs) *adj.*

hal·o·ge·na·tion (hal′ə-jə-nā′shən) *n. Chem.* The introduction of a halogen into an organic molecule, by substitution or addition.

hal·oid (hal′oid, hā′loid) *adj.* 1 Resembling sea salt. 2 Pertaining to or derived from a halogen. —*n.* A haloid salt.

hal·o·man·cy (hal′ə-man′sē) *n.* Divination by means of salt thrown into a flame: also spelled *alomancy.*

hal·o·per·i·dol (hal′ō-per′ə-dōl, -dôl) *n.* An ataractic drug, $C_{21}H_{23}ClFNO_2$.

ha·loph·i·lous (hə-lof′ə-ləs) *adj. Bot.* Adapted to salt; said of plants growing in saline soil. Also **hal·o·phil** (hal′ə-fil), **hal′o·phile** (-fil, -fil).

hal·o·phyte (hal′ə-fīt) *n. Bot.* A plant of saline soil, such as those of the genera *Salsola* and *Salicornia,* growing in salt marshes and yielding salt. —**hal′o·phyt′ic** (-fit′ik) *adj.*

Hals (häls), **Frans,** 1580?–1666, Dutch painter.

halse (hôls) *n. Brit. Dial.* The neck. [OE *hals*]

Hal·sey (hôl′zē), **William Frederick,** 1882–1959, U.S. admiral in World War II.

Häl·sing·borg (hel′sing·bôr′y) A port in SW Sweden.

halt[1] (hôlt) *n.* A complete stop, or cessation of progress in any movement, as of marching troops. —**to call a halt** To put a stop to, or demand that something be stopped. —*v.t. & v.i.* To stop; bring or come to a halt. See synonyms under REST[1], STAND. [< F *halte* < G *halt,* orig. imperative of *halten* stop]

halt[2] (hôlt) *v.i.* 1 To be imperfect; proceed lamely, as verse or logic. 2 To be in doubt; waver. 3 *Archaic* To walk with a limp; hobble. —*adj. Archaic* Crippled; limping in gait; lame. —*n. Archaic* The act of limping; lameness. [OE *healt* lame] —**halt′ing** *adj.* —**halt′ing·ly** *adv.* — **halt′ing·ness** *n.*

hal·ter[1] (hôl′tər) *n.* 1 A strap or rope, especially one with a headstall at one end, by which to hold a horse or other animal. 2 A hangman's rope; hence, death by the rope. 3 A woman's waist designed for exposing the back and arms to the sun, fastened around the neck and waist. —*v.t.* 1 To put a halter on; secure with a halter. 2 To hang (someone). [OE *hælftre*]

hal·ter[2] (hal′tər) *n. pl.* **hal·te·res** (hal-tir′ēz) *Entomol.* One of a pair of small, knobbed, filamentous appendages on each side of the thorax in dipterous insects, replacing the hind wings; a balancer. [< NL < Gk. *haltēres* jumping weights (as used in the halma)]

ha·lutz (khä-lōōts′) *n. pl.* **ha·lu·tzim** (khä-lōō-tsēm′) A pioneer agriculturist in Israel: also spelled *chalutz.* [< Hebrew *chalutz* a warrior]

halve (hav, häv) *v.t.* **halved, halv·ing** 1 To divide into two equal parts; share equally. 2 To lessen by half; take away half of. 3 In golf, to play (a match or hole) in the same number of strokes as one's opponent. [< HALF]

halves (havz, hävz) Plural of HALF.

ha·ly (hā′lē) *adj. Scot.* Holy.

hal·yard (hal′yərd) *n. Naut.* A rope for hoisting or lowering a sail, a yard, or a flag: also spelled *halliard, haulyard.* [< HALE[1] + YARD[1]]

Ha·lys (hā′lis) Ancient name for KIZIL-IRMAK.

ham (ham) *n.* 1 The thigh of an animal, as a hog, prepared for food. 2 *pl.* The buttocks. 3 The space or region behind the knee joint; the hock of quadrupeds. 4 *Slang* A third-rate actor; one who overdramatizes scenes, or portrays a character in amateur fashion. 5 An amateur radio operator. [OE *hamm*] —**ham′my** *adj.*

Ham (ham) The youngest son of Noah. *Gen.* v 32, ix 24.

Ha·ma (hä′mä) A town in western Syria on the Orontes: *Old Testament* **Ha·math** (hä′māth). Also **Ha′mah.**

Ha·ma·dan (hä′mä-dän′) A city in western Iran; ancient *Ecbatana.*

ham·a·dry·ad (ham′ə-drī′əd, -ad) *n. pl.* **·ads** or **·a·des** (-ə-dēz) 1 In Greek mythology, a wood nymph whose life was connected with that of the tree she inhabited. 2 The king cobra. [< Gk. *hamadryas, -ados* < *hama* together with + *drys* oak tree]

ha·mal (hə-mäl′, -môl′) *n.* 1 In Oriental countries, one who bears burdens; a porter; a carrier. 2 In India, a man servant: also spelled *hammal.* Also **ha·maul′.** [< Arabic *hammāl* < *hamala* carry]

Ha·ma·mat·su (hä-mä-mät-sōō′) A city on south central Honshu island, Japan.

Ham·a·me·lis (ham′ə-mē′lis) *n.* A genus of shrubs of the witch hazel family (*Hamamelidaceae*) having alternate simple leaves and heads or spikes of monoecious or polygamous flowers. *H. virginiana* is the common witch hazel. [< NL < Gk. *hamamēlis* tree with pearlike fruit] —**ham·a·me·li·da·ceous** (ham′ə-mē′lə-dā′shəs) *adj.*

Ha·man (hā′mən) The chief minister of Ahasuerus, whose plot against the Jews recoiled upon himself (*Esth.* iii–vii), and who was hanged on a gallows fifty cubits high; hence, the phrase **hanged as high as Haman.**

Ham·ble·to·ni·an (ham′bəl-tō′nē·ən) *n.* 1 One of a famous breed of American trotting horses. 2 The chief harness race for three-year-old trotters, held annually, formerly at Goshen, New York. —*adj.* Of or pertaining to a horse of the Hambletonian breed. [after *Hambletonian,* famous American stud, from Black *Hambleton,* a racecourse in Yorkshire, England]

Ham·born (häm′bôrn) See DUISBURG-HAMBORN.

Ham·bro (häm′brō), **Carl Joachim,** 1885–1964, Norwegian statesman.

ham·burg (ham′bûrg) *n.* Hamburger (defs. 1 and 2). Also **hamburg steak.**

Ham·burg (ham′bûrg) *n.* 1 A European variety of the domestic fowl, having lead-gray legs and a rose-colored comb. 2 A black, sweet and juicy grape, indigenous to the Tyrol and widely cultivated in hothouses throughout the northern latitudes. Also **Ham′burgh.**

Ham·burg (ham′bûrg, *Ger.* häm′bŏŏrkh) A state comprising the chief port and second largest city in Germany, at the head of the Elbe estuary in NW Germany; 288 square miles.

ham·burg·er (ham′bûr′gər) *n.* 1 Finely ground beef. 2 Such meat fried or broiled in the form of a patty. Also **hamburger steak:** also called *Salisbury steak.* 3 A sandwich consisting of such meat placed between the halves of a round roll. [from *Hamburg,* Germany]

hame[1] (hām) *n.* One of two curved bars fitted to the collar, that hold the traces of a draft harness. [OE *hama* dress, covering]

hame[2] (hām) *n. Scot.* Home. —**hame′ly** *adj.*

Ha·meln (hä′meln) A town on the Weser in Lower Saxony, West Germany. Also **Ham·e·lin** (ham′ə·lin).

Ham·hung (häm·hŏŏng′) A city in North Korea. *Japanese* **Kan·ko.**

Ha·mil·car Bar·ca (hə·mil′kär bär′kə, ham′əl·kär), died in battle 229? B.C., Carthaginian general; father of Hannibal.

Ham·il·ton (ham′əl·tən), **Alexander,** 1757–1804, American statesman; joint author of *The Federalist.* — **Lady Emma,** 1761?–1815, mistress of Lord Nelson. — **Sir William,** 1788–1856, Scottish philosopher. — **Sir William Rowan,** 1805–65, Irish mathematician and astronomer.

Ham·il·ton (ham′əl·tən) **1** A port in southern Ontario, Canada, on Lake Ontario. **2** The chief port and capital of Bermuda, on Bermuda Island. **3** A burgh of Lanarkshire, Scotland.

Ham·il·ton (ham′əl·tən), **Mount** A peak of the Coast Ranges in western California; 4,372 feet; site of the Lick Observatory.

Hamilton River A river in southern Labrador, flowing 600 miles to **Hamilton Inlet,** a bay of the Atlantic.

Ham·ite (ham′īt) *n.* **1** A descendant of Ham, youngest son of Noah. **2** A member of the Caucasoid ethnic stock which from earliest days inhabited NE Africa and the Canary Islands.

Ha·mit·ic (ha·mit′ik) *adj.* Of or pertaining to Ham, or the Hamites, or their languages. — *n.* A North African subfamily of the Hamito-Semitic family of languages, divided into three branches — ancient Egyptian, Libyco-Berber (extinct Libyan and the modern Berber dialects), and the Cushitic languages of Ethiopia and Somaliland.

Ham·i·to–Se·mit·ic (ham′ə·tō·sə·mit′ik) *n.* A large family of languages spoken in northern Africa and part of SW Asia, consisting of the subfamilies *Hamitic* (ancient Egyptian, Libyan, the modern Berber dialects, and the Cushitic languages) and *Semitic* (Akkadian, Phoenician, Aramaic, Syriac, Arabic, Hebrew, Amharic, etc.). The family is characterized grammatically by triliteral or biliteral word bases.

ham·let (ham′lit) *n.* **1** A little village; a cluster of houses in the country. **2** *Brit.* A village without a church of its own. [<OF *hamelet,* dim. of *hamel* <LL *hamellum* village <Gmc.]

Ham·let (ham′lit) In Shakespeare's play of this name, the hero, prince of Denmark, who seeks to avenge the murder of his father at the bidding of his father's ghost.

ham·mal (hə·mäl′, -môl′) See HAMAL.

Hamm (häm) A city in North Rhine–Westphalia, West Germany. Also **Hamm–in–West·fal·en** (häm·in·vest′fäl·ən).

Ham·mar·skjold (häm′är·shüld), **Dag,** 1905–1961, Swedish statesman; secretary general of the United Nations 1953–61.

ham·mer (ham′ər) *n.* **1** A hand implement with a head at right angles to the handle, used for driving nails, pounding, swaging, etc. See under CLAW HAMMER, TACK HAMMER. **2** A machine, as a steam hammer or trip hammer, performing functions similar to those of a heavy hand hammer. **3** A part or piece of a machine or apparatus performing functions similar to those of a hammer: especially, the piece by which a gong or the like is struck. **4** That part of a gunlock which strikes the cap or cartridge. **5** A padded piece that strikes the string of a pianoforte. **6** An auctioneer's mallet. **7** A lever in an internal combustion engine which controls the exhaust. **8** *Anat.* The malleus of the middle ear. **9** A metal ball weighing 16 pounds with a long wire or wooden handle: used for throwing in track meets. — **under the hammer** For sale at auction. — *v.t.* **1** To strike or beat with or as with a hammer; drive, as a nail. **2** To shape or fasten with a hammer. **3** To form or force as if with hammer blows: to *hammer* an idea into his head. — *v.i.* **4** To strike blows with or as with a hammer. [OE *hamer*] — **ham′mer·er** *n.*

hammer and sickle The Communist party emblem, in which a crossed sickle and hammer symbolize the peasant and the worker.

hammer and tongs Forcefully; with vehemence: to go at it *hammer and tongs.*

ham·mer·cloth (ham′ər·klôth′, -kloth′) *n.* The cloth covering a coachman's box. [? Alter. of *hamper cloth*]

hammered work Work in thin metal having

the design hammered or beaten by hand, as in repoussé work.

Ham·mer·fest (häm′ər·fest) A city in northern Norway.

ham·mer·har·den (ham′ər·här′dən) *v.t.* To harden (metals) by beating with a hammer.

ham·mer·head (ham′ər·hed′) *n.* **1** The head of a hammer. **2** A heronlike wading bird (order *Ciconiiformes*) native to Africa and Madagascar, with a blunt–pointed beak, clove-brown plumage, and a large crest. **3** A voracious shark (family *Sphynidae*) of warm seas, having a transversely elongated head with the eyes at each end. **4** The hogsucker. **5** An African fruit bat (family *Pteropidae*) with an elongated snout, related to the flying fox.

ham·mer·less (ham′ər·lis) *adj.* Having no hammer visible: said of firearms.

hammer lock A wrestling grip in which the arm is twisted behind the back and upwards.

ham·mer·smith (ham′ər·smith′) *n.* One who works metal with a hammer.

Ham·mer·stein (ham′ər·stīn), **Oscar,** 1847–1919, U.S. theatrical manager born in Germany. — **Oscar,** 1895–1960, U.S. songwriter and librettist; grandson of the preceding.

ham·mer·toe (ham′ər·tō′) *n. Pathol.* A deformity of the toe, usually the second, in which the joint nearest the foot is bent downward.

ham·mock[1] (ham′ək) *n.* A couch of canvas or netting, swung by the ends. [<Sp. *hamaca* <native name]

ham·mock[2] (ham′ək) *n. U.S.* In the South, a thickly wooded tract of fertile land, often elevated: also called *hummock.* [Var. of HUMMOCK]

Ham·mu·ra·bi (hä′mŏŏ·rä′bē, ham′ə-) Founder of the first Babylonian dynasty at the beginning of the second millenium B.C.; famous lawgiver who promulgated the **Code of Hammurabi.**

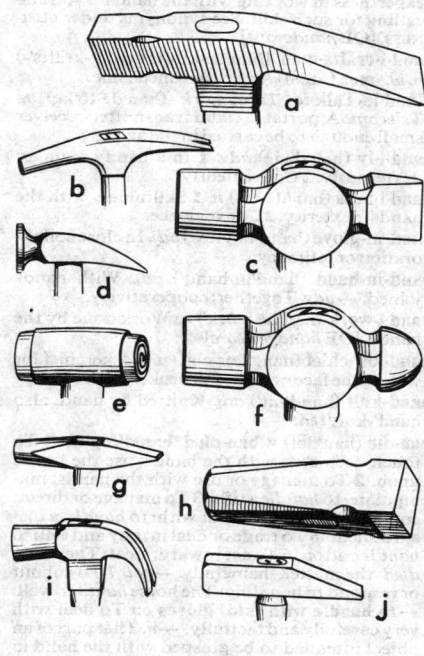

HAMMERS
a. Bricklayer's hammer.
b. Upholsterer's or tack hammer.
c. Machinist's straight–peen.
d. Shoemaker's hammer.
e. Rawhide–faced hammer.
f. Machinist's ball–peen.
g. Riveting hammer.
h. Blacksmith's set–hammer.
i. Claw hammer.
j. Tinner's hammer.

Hamp·den (ham′dən), **John,** 1594–1643, English patriot; refused to pay ship money exacted by Charles I. — **Walter,** stage name of W. H. Dougherty, 1879–1955, U.S. actor.

ham·per[1] (ham′pər) *v.t.* To hinder the movements of; encumber; restrain. — *n.* **1** *Naut.* Necessary but encumbering equipment of a ship, as the rigging. **2** A fetter. See synonyms under EMBARRASS, HINDER. [ME *hampren*; origin uncertain]

ham·per[2] (ham′pər) *n.* A large packing basket, as for food. — *v.t.* To put into hampers. [<OF *hanapier* case to hold a cup or goblet <*hanap* cup <LG. Doublet of HANAPER.]

Hamp·shire (hamp′shir) A county in southern England; 1,650 square miles; capital, Winchester; including the administrative counties of Southampton and the Isle of Wight: shortened form *Hants.*

Hamp·stead (hamp′sted, -stid) A metropolitan borough of London north of the Thames, including **Hampstead Heath,** a public common, once the resort of highwaymen.

Hamp·ton (hamp′tən), **Wade,** 1752?–1835, American Revolutionary officer. — **Wade,** 1818–1902, Confederate general and politician; grandson of the preceding.

Hampton Roads A channel in SE Virginia through which the James, Nansemond, and Elizabeth Rivers flow to Chesapeake Bay; scene of the Civil War engagement of the armored warships "Monitor" and "Merrimac," Mar. 9, 1862.

ham·shack·le (ham′shak′əl) *v.t.* **·led, ·ling** **1** To hobble, as a horse, by connecting the head and forelegs with a short rope or strap, so as to impede movement. **2** To restrain or impede. Also spelled *hapshackle.* [<HAM[1] + SHACKLE]

ham·ster (ham′stər) *n.* A sturdy burrowing rodent. The common hamster (*Cricetus cricetus*) of Europe and Asia has very large cheek pouches and a short tail; it stores up grain in subterranean galleries. [<G]

ham·string (ham′string′) *n.* **1** A tendon of the thigh, back of the knee. **2** The large sinew at the back of the hock of the hind leg of a quadruped. — *v.t.* **·strung, ·string·ing** **1** To cut the hamstring of; cripple; disable. **2** To cripple (a whale) by cutting the fluke-tendons.

Ham·sun (häm′sŏŏn, ham′sən), **Knut,** 1859–1952, Norwegian novelist.

Ham·tramck (ham·tram′ik) A city of SE Michigan, entirely surrounded by Detroit.

ham·u·late (ham′yə·lāt, -lit) *adj.* **1** Having little hooks, as certain plants. **2** Curved.

ham·u·lus (ham′yə·ləs) *n. pl.* **·li** (-lī) **1** A little hook. **2** A hooklike process of a bone. **3** A hooked barbicel of a feather. [<L]

ham·za (ham′zə) *n.* In Arabic orthography, the sign of the glottal stop, transliterated with an apostrophe.

han (han) *n. Scot.* Hand.

Han (hän) The fifth Chinese dynasty, 207 B.C.–A.D. 220.

Han (hän) **1** A river in east central China, flowing 750 miles SE to the Yangtze. **2** A river in southern China, flowing 210 miles south to the China Sea.

han·a·per (han′ə·pər) *n.* A wicker receptacle for documents or valuables. [<OF *hanapier.* Doublet of HAMPER[2].]

hance (hans) *n.* **1** *Archit.* **a** The haunch of an arch; the lower part of a many–centered arch, above the springing. **b** A small arch joining a straight lintel to its jamb. **2** A break or sudden departure from a natural form; an irregularity, as in a fife rail. [ME, aphetic var. of ENHANCE.]

Han Cities (hän) See WUHAN.

Han·cock (han′kok), **John,** 1737–93, American statesman; signer of the Declaration of Independence. — **Winfield Scott,** 1824–86, U.S. general.

hand (hand) *n.* **1** The part of the forelimb in man and other primates that is attached to the lower extremity of the forearm, and is adapted for grasping; it consists of the carpus, metacarpus, and fingers. **2** The end or distal segment of a limb when serving as a prehensile organ, as in bats. **3** Side or direction: At his right *hand* sat the president. **4** A side or viewpoint of a subject or question: on the one *hand* this and on the other *hand* that. **5** A part or role in doing something: They all had a *hand* in it. **6** *pl.* Possession; control; supervision: The work is in my *hands.* **7** Aid;

assistance: to lend a *hand.* **8** A pledge of betrothal, or a giving in marriage. **9** A manual laborer: a farm *hand.* **10** A person, as the performer of some action or task: a book written by various *hands.* **11** A person, considered with reference to his skill or ability: He was quite a *hand* with the violin. **12** Skill; ability; touch: The painting showed the *hand* of a master. **13** The members of a group or company: All *hands* joined in the sport. **14** A (specified) remove from a source of supply or information: a story heard at second-*hand.* **15** The cards held by a player at one deal; also, the player. **16** The playing of the cards at one deal. **17** Clapping of hands; a round of applause. **18** Handwriting; style of writing: a legible *hand.* **19** A person's signature. **20** Something resembling a hand in appearance or function. **21** The figure ☞ used as an index; fist. **22** The pointer of a clock. **23** A bunch of tobacco leaves on the stem, tied together. **24** A small cluster of bananas. **25** The approximate width of the palm; specifically, four inches: a horse 16 *hands* high. **26** The part of a gunstock grasped by the hand. **27** *Law* A manus. **—a great hand at** or **for** A person specially fond of or clever at. **—at first hand** At the source. **—at hand** Within reach; nearby; convenient. **—at the hand of** From the hand of; by the operation of. **—by hand** With the hands; not aided by machinery. **—to have one's hands full** To have all or more than one can do. **—in hand 1** Delivered in advance; paid in the hand. **2** In process of execution or under consideration: I have the matter *in hand.* **3** Entirely under control **—laying on of hands** The act or ceremony of laying the hands on the head of another for the purpose of consecrating to a special office, or of blessing or healing. **—to lend a hand** To help. **—off one's hands** Out of one's care or control. **—on hand 1** In present or rightful possession: We have too many goods *on hand.* **2** In place; present: He was promptly *on hand.* **—on one's hands** In one's care or possession; entailing responsibility on one. **—out of hand 1** Unruly; lawless: The rioters got *out of hand.* **2** Immediately; without delay; offhand. **—to hand** At hand; close by; readily accessible. **—to wash one's hands of** To take no further responsibility in; dismiss from consideration. *—v.t.* **1** To give, pass, or deliver with or as with the hand; transmit; transfer. **2** To lead or help with the hand. **3** *Naut.* To furl, as sail. **—to hand down 1** To transmit, as to one's heirs or successors. **2** To deliver, as the decision of a court. **—to hand it to** *U.S. Slang* To acknowledge the abilities, success, etc., of. **—to hand on** To pass on; transmit. **—to hand out** To mete out; distribute. **—to hand over** To give up possession of; surrender. [OE *hand*]

Hand (hand), **Learned,** 1872–1961, U.S. jurist.

hand·bag (hand′bag′) *n.* A small, portable bag, as a small satchel or a woman's purse.

hand·ball (hand′bôl′) *n.* **1** A game in which a small ball is struck with the hand and kept bounding against a wall or walls by, usually, two or four players. **2** The rubber ball used in this game.

hand·bar·row (hand′bar′ō) *n.* **1** A litter or stretcher. **2** A wheelbarrow.

hand·bill (hand′bil′) *n.* A small advertising sheet or public notice, usually distributed by hand.

hand·book (hand′bo͝ok′) *n.* A small guidebook or manual.

hand·breadth (hand′bredth′) *n.* The breadth of the hand; a palm. Also *hand's breadth.*

hand car A small open railroad car, propelled by a hand pump or motor, used by section men and other railroad workers.

hand cart A cart pushed by hand.

hand·clasp (hand′klasp′, -kläsp′) *n.* A clasping of a person's hand in greeting, agreement, farewell, etc.

hand·cuff (hand′·kuf′) *n.* One of two manacles connected by a chain, and designed to be locked around the wrists. See synonyms under FETTER. *—v.t.* To put handcuffs on; manacle.

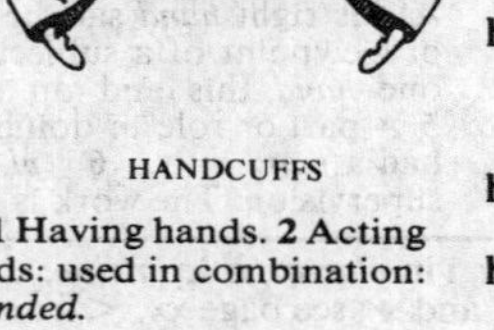

HANDCUFFS

hand·ed (han′did) *adj.* **1** Having hands. **2** Acting or provided with hands: used in combination: right-*handed,* four-*handed.*

hand·ed·ness (han′did·nis) *n.* The tendency of an individual to prefer the use of either the right or the left hand.

Han·del (han′dəl), **George Frederick,** 1685–1759, German composer active in England. Also *Ger.* **Georg Friedrich Hän·del** (he·n′dəl).

hand·fast (hand′fast′, -fäst′) *n. Obs.* A contract signified and sealed by clasping hands; hence, a betrothal or marriage contract. *—v.t. Archaic* **1** To grasp with the hand. **2** To betroth. **—hand′fast′ing** *n.*

hand·ful (hand′fo͝ol) *n. pl.* **hand·fuls 1** As much or as many as a hand can hold at once. See -FUL. **2** A comparatively small number or quantity. **3** *Colloq.* Something or someone difficult to control.

hand·gal·lop (hand′gal′əp) *n.* A moderate gallop.

hand glass 1 A mirror intended to be held in the hand. **2** A reading glass. **3** A time glass to measure a ship's log.

hand grenade See under GRENADE.

hand·grip (hand′grip′) *n.* **1** A grip of the hand. **2** *Usually pl.* Close conflict; struggle.

hand·gun (hand′gun′) *n.* A firearm held and fired in one hand, as a pistol.

hand·i·cap (han′dē·kap′) *n.* **1** A condition imposed to equalize the chances of competitors in a race or athletic contest, as the carrying of extra weight, or the requirement of a greater distance or a later start than is assigned to an inferior competitor; also, the weight, etc., so required. **2** A race or contest in which such conditions are imposed. **3** Any disadvantage or hindrance making success in an undertaking more difficult. *—v.t.* **·capped, ·cap·ping 1** To impose a handicap on, as a contestant in a race. **2** To be a handicap to: His leg *handicaps* his movements. [< *hand in cap,* a lottery game in which winners were penalized] **—hand′i·cap′per** *n.*

hand·i·craft (han′dē·kraft′, -kräft′) *n.* **1** Skill and expertness in working with the hands. **2** A trade calling for such skill. See synonyms under BUSINESS. [OE *handcræft*]

hand·i·crafts·man (han′dē·krafts′mən, -kräfts′-) *n. pl.* **·men** (-mən) An artisan; mechanic.

Hand·ie-Talk·ie *Trademark* (han′dē·tô′kē) *n. Telecom.* A portable radio transmitter-receiver small enough to be carried in the hand.

hand·i·ly (han′də·lē) *adv.* **1** In a handy manner; dexterously. **2** Conveniently.

hand·i·ness (han′dē·nis) *n.* **1** Skilfulness with the hands; dexterity. **2** Convenience.

hand-in-glove (hand′in·gluv′) *adj.* In close collaboration or intimacy.

hand-in-hand (hand′in·hand′) *adj.* With hands joined. *—adv.* Together; cooperatively.

hand·i·work (han′dē·wûrk′) *n.* Work done by the hands. [OE *handgeweorc*]

hand·ker·chief (hang′kər·chif) *n.* **1** A kerchief for wiping the face or nose. **2** A neckerchief.

hand-knit (hand′nit′) *adj.* Knitted by hand: also **hand′-knit′ted.**

han·dle (han′dəl) *v.* **han·dled, han·dling** *v.t.* **1** To touch, feel, etc., with the hands; use the hands upon. **2** To manage or use with the hands; manipulate: to *handle* a rifle. **3** To manage or direct; control. **4** To deal or treat with: to *handle* a disagreement. **5** To trade or deal in; buy and sell: to *handle* cotton. **6** To act toward; treat: They *handled* the matter shamefully. *—v.i.* **7** To submit or respond to handling: The horse *handles* well. **—to handle with (kid) gloves on** To deal with very carefully and tactfully. *—n.* That part of an object intended to be grasped with the hand in lifting or using, as a haft, helve, hilt, crank, bail, or knob. **—to fly off the handle** To be suddenly and unreasonably angry; make an emotional scene. [OE *handlian* < *hand* hand]

han·dle·bar (han′dəl·bär′) *n.* **1** A handle or handles in the form of a bar; specifically, the steering bar of a bicycle, motorcycle, or similar vehicle. **2** *pl. U.S. Colloq.* A long mustache curved like a handlebar.

han·dler (hand′lər) *n.* **1** One who or that which handles; specifically, one who trains, breaks in, or manages certain animals, as dogs, colts, fighting cocks, etc. **2** The trainer of a pugilist.

hand·less (hand′lis) *adj.* **1** Without hands. **2** Awkward; clumsy.

hand level A telescopic hand instrument used in surveying to find approximate elevations.

han·dling (hand′ling) *n.* **1** The act of touching or turning with the hands. **2** Manner of treatment, as in writing, drawing, arguing, etc.

hand-made (hand′mād′) *adj.* Made by hand or by hand tools.

hand·maid (hand′mād′) *n.* A female servant or attendant. Also **hand′maid′en.**

hand-me-down (hand′mē·doun′) *n. U.S. Colloq.* **1** A garment which has been outgrown and is passed to a smaller person. **2** A shabby or second-hand garment. **3** A cheap, ready-made garment. **—hand′-me-down′** *adj.*

hand organ A musical instrument consisting of a boxed revolving cylinder turned by a hand crank; a portable barrel organ.

hand-out (hand′out′) *n. U.S. Colloq.* **1** Anything given to a beggar, especially food. **2** A printed or mimeographed press release usually distributed at a press conference.

hand-pick (hand′pik′) *v.t.* **1** To pick by hand. **2** To select with care. **3** To choose for an ulterior purpose: to *hand-pick* a candidate.

hand pump Any pump worked by hand; especially, an auxiliary fuel pump used to start an engine or for emergency: also called *wobble pump.*

hand rail A rail that can be grasped by the hand, as at the edge of a gallery or along the outer edge of a stairway.

hand saw A saw made to be used with one hand.

hand's breadth See HANDBREADTH.

hand·sel (hand′səl, han′-) *n.* **1** A gift as a token of good will or to secure good luck. **2** Earnest money on a contract. **3** A bridegroom's gift to a bride. **4** Money given as a gift at New Year's. *—v.t.* **·seled** or **·selled, ·sel·ing** or **·sel·ling 1** To give handsel to. **2** To do or use for the first time. **3** To inaugurate, as with a ceremony. Also spelled *hansel.* [OE *handselen* < *hand* hand + *selen* gift]

hand·set (hand′set′) *n.* An apparatus, device, or instrument, especially a telephone, designed to be held in or operated by one hand.

hand·shake (hand′shāk′) *n.* A clasping and shaking of a person's hand, as in greeting, agreement, parting, etc.

hand·some (han′səm) *adj.* **1** Agreeable to the eye or to good taste; of pleasing aspect. **2** Of liberal dimensions or proportions. **3** Marked by magnanimity, generosity, or liberality. **4** Marked by propriety. **5** *Obs.* Handy; convenient; dexterous. See synonyms under BEAUTIFUL, FINE. ◆ Homophone: *hansom.* [< HAND + -SOME, orig. with sense "easy to handle"] **—hand′some·ness** *n.*

hand·some·ly (han′səm·lē) *adv.* **1** Becomingly; liberally; generously. **2** Cleverly; neatly.

hands-on (handz′on′; -ôn′) *adj.* Designating an action that requires active participation; *hands-on techniques.*

hand·spike (hand′spīk′) *n.* A bar used as a lever.

hand·spring (hand′spring′) *n.* A somersault in which only the hands, when the feet are in the air, touch the ground.

hand-to-hand (hand′tə·hand′) *adj.* At close quarters: a *hand-to-hand* fight.

hand-to-mouth (hand′tə·mouth′) *adj.* Spending as fast as one earns; improvident.

hand·work (hand′wûrk′) *n.* Work done by hand, not by machine.

hand·writ·ing (hand′rī′ting) *n.* **1** The form of writing peculiar to a given person. **2** Penmanship. **3** Written matter.

hand·y (han′dē) *adj.* **hand·i·er, hand·i·est 1** Ready at hand or convenient for use; nearby. **2** Skilful with the hands. **3** Easy to handle: said of a ship or a tool. See synonyms under CONVENIENT, SKILFUL.

handy man One good at odd jobs; a jack-of-all-trades.

Ha·ne·da (hä·nē·dä) The airport of Tokyo, on central Honshu island, Japan.

hang (hang) *v.* **hung** or (*esp. for v. defs.* **3** *and* **9**) **hanged, hang·ing** *v.t.* **1** To fasten or attach to something above; suspend. **2** To attach, as upon hinges, so as to allow some motion. **3** To put (someone) to death by suspending from a gallows, cross, etc.; execute on a gallows. **4** To ornament, cover, or furnish by or as by something suspended: to *hang* walls with tapestry. **5** To fasten in position or at the correct angle: to *hang* a scythe.

6 *U.S.* To cause, as a jury, to come to or remain in deadlock, as one juror by refusing to vote with the rest. —*v.i.* **7** To be suspended; swing; dangle. **8** To be suspended without visible support; float, as in the air. **9** To be put to death on the gallows. **10** To project out; overhang. **11** To droop; incline downward. **12** To be imminent or impending: War *hangs* over the world. **13** To be dependent or contingent, as on a decision. **14** To be uncertain or in doubt. **15** To watch or attend closely: to *hang* on someone's words. **16** *U.S.* To be or remain in deadlock, as a jury. —**to hang around** (or **about**) **1** To linger or loiter. **2** To group around. —**to hang back** To be reluctant or unwilling. —**to hang fire 1** To fail to fire promptly, as a firearm. **2** To be delayed, as an event. **3** To be undecided, as a business agreement. —**to hang in** *Slang* To stay; persevere; hold on. —**to hang out 1** To lean out. **2** To suspend out in the open: to *hang out* the wash. **3** *Slang* To reside or spend one's time: usually with *at* or *in*. —**to hang together 1** To stay together. **2** To be coherent or consistent, as an explanation. —**to hang up 1** To place on hooks or hangers. **2** To place a telephone receiver on the hook and thus break off communication. —**to let it all hang out** *Slang* **1** To make no effort to conceal one's motives, fears, desires, etc. **2** To be altogether free of restraint or inhibition. —*n.* **1** The way a thing hangs: the *hang* of a drape. **2** *U.S. Colloq.* Familiar knowledge or wont; knack. **3** A bit: I don't give a *hang*: euphemism for *damn*. **4** Rake, as of a mast. —**to get the hang of** *U.S. Colloq.* To come to understand or be able to do. [Fusion of ME *hangen* (OE *hangian* hang down), OE *hon* suspend, and ME *henge* cause or condemn to hang (< ON *hengjan*)]

han·gar (hang′ər, -gär) *n.* A shelter or shed, especially one for the maintenance and storage of aircraft. [< F]

Hang·chow (hang′chou′, *Chinese* häng′jō′) A port in eastern China, capital of Chekiang province, at the head of **Hangchow Bay**, an inlet of the East China Sea.

hang·dog (hang′dôg′, -dog′) *adj.* Of mean, sneaking, or abject character or appearance. —*n.* A skulking person; sneak.

hang·er (hang′ər) *n.* **1** One who hangs, as a hangman. **2** A device on which something is hung. **3** A shaped frame on which a garment is suspended or draped.

hang·er-on (hang′ər·on′) *n. pl.* **hang·ers-on** A self-attached dependent; parasite.

hang glider A kitelike metal and cloth frame to which a person is harnessed while soaring through the air.

hang·ing (hang′ing) *adj.* **1** Suspended from something; dangling. **2** Involving or suggesting death on the gallows. **3** Lying on a steep slope: a *hanging* garden. **4** Drooping and dejected: said of the countenance. **5** Held in abeyance. —*n.* **1** The act of suspending. **2** Execution on the gallows. **3** *pl.* Drapery for a room, as tapestry.

hanging wall *Geol.* The layer of an inclined fault plane which overlies the footwall.

hang·man (hang′mən) *n. pl.* **·men** (-mən) A public executioner.

hang·nail (hang′nāl′) *n.* Skin partially torn loose at the side or root of a fingernail. [Alter. of AGNAIL; infl. by HANG]

hang·nest (hang′nest′) *n.* A hangbird's nest.

Hang·ö (häng′œ) A port on the Baltic in SW Finland. *Finnish* **Han·ko** (häng′kô).

hang·out (hang′out′) *n. Slang* A habitual meeting place or resort.

hang·o·ver (hang′ō′vər) *n. U.S. Colloq.* **1** A person or thing remaining from something that is past; a survival, as of a tradition. **2** The aftereffects of alcoholic dissipation, as headache and nausea.

hang·up (hang′up′) *n. Slang* **1** A psychological difficulty; especially, a neurotic preoccupation or obsession. **2** Anything blocking a natural or normal process.

hank (hangk) *n.* **1** A bundle of two or more skeins of yarn tied together; also, a single skein. **2** A measure of yarn varying for different materials: a hank of No. 1 cotton is 840 yards long and weighs 1 pound; a hank of woolen yarn is 560 yards long. **3** *Naut.* **a** A rope, string, coil, or tie. **b** Any fastening; specifically, a ring of rope

or iron on the edge of a jib or staysail, used for fastening it. [ME < Scand. Cf. Icel. *hankar*, genitive of *hönk* a skein, coil.]

Han·ka, Lake See KHANKA, LAKE.

han·ker (hang′kər) *v.i.* To yearn; have desire: with *after*, *for*, or an infinitive. [Cf. Flemish *hankeren* long for] —**han′ker·er** *n.* —**han′ker·ing** *n.*

Han·kow (hang′kou′, *Chinese* häng′jō′) A city in east central China on the Yangtze.

han·ky-pan·ky (hang′kē·pang′kē) *n. Slang* **1** Trickery. **2** Jugglery; sleight-of-hand. [An arbitrary formation, ? < HAND]

Han·na (hän′ə) Dutch form of JOAN.

Han·na (han′ə), **Marcus Alonzo**, 1837–1904, U.S. financier and politician: known as *Mark Hanna.*

Han·nah (han′ə) A feminine personal name. [< Hebrew, grace]
—**Hannah** A Jewish prophetess; mother of the prophet Samuel. 1 *Sam.* i 2.

Han·ni·bal (han′ə·bəl) A masculine personal name. [< Phoenician, grace of Baal]
— **Hannibal**, 247–183 B.C., Carthaginian general who invaded Italy by crossing the Alps; son of Hamilcar Barca.

Han·no (han′ō), third century B.C. Carthaginian leader.

Ha·noi (hä·noi′) A city in North Vietnam, capital of the Democratic Republic of Vietnam (Vietminh).

Ha·no·taux (à·nô·tō′), **Albert Auguste Gabriel**, 1853–1944, French statesman and author.

Han·o·ver (han′ō·vər) A former Prussian province included since 1945 in the state of Lower Saxony, Germany. *German* **Han·no·ver** (hä·nō′vər). —**Han·o·ve·ri·an** (han′ō·vir′ē·ən) *adj.* & *n.*

Hanoverian dynasty A reigning family of Great Britain, founded by George I, who was elector of Hanover, and ending with Victoria: also called **House of Hanover.**

Hans (häns) Dutch, German, and Swedish diminutive form of JOHANNES.

Han·sard (han′sərd) *n.* The printed record of the proceedings of the British Parliament. [after Luke *Hansard*, 1752–1828, its first publisher]

hanse (hans) *n.* **1** A guild of medieval merchants. **2** An entrance fee; especially, one paid by merchants not members of a guild. [< OF < OHG *hansa* band]

Hanse (hans) *n.* The Hanseatic League.

Han·se·at·ic (han′sē·at′ik) *adj.* Pertaining to the Hanse towns of Germany.

Hanseatic League A league of about 85 towns and cities in northern Germany and neighboring countries, called **Hanse towns,** which banded together in the Middle Ages (about 1241–1669) for mutual protection and trade advantages. Hamburg, Lübeck, and Bremen are still called Hanse towns.

han·sel (han′səl) See HANDSEL.

Han·sen's disease (han′sənz) Leprosy.

han·som (han′səm) *n.* A low, two-wheeled, one-horse cab, with the driver mounted back of the top: also **hansom cab.** ◆ Homophone: *handsome.* [after J. A. *Hansom*, 1803–82, English inventor]

HANSOM

Hants (hants) Hampshire: a shortened form of *Hantesshire*, the Middle English spelling.

Ha·nuk·kah (khä′nŏŏ·kə) A Jewish festival lasting eight days from Kislew 25th (early December), in memory of the rededication of the temple at Jerusalem under the Maccabees in 164 B.C. It is also known, usually by Christians, as the *Feast of Dedication.* Also **Ha′nu·kah:** also spelled *Chanuca.* [< Hebrew *hanukkah* dedication]

han·u·man (hän′ŏŏ·mən) *n.* The entellus monkey. [< Hind., lit., the one with a jaw]

Han·u·man (hän′ŏŏ·mən) In Hindu mythology, a monkey god.

Han·yang (hän′yäng′) A city on the Yangtse in east central China.

hap (hap) *Archaic n.* **1** A casual occurrence; happening; chance. **2** Luck; good fortune. See synonyms under ACCIDENT. —*v.i.* **happed, hap·ping** To happen; chance. [< ON *happ*]

ha·pax le·go·me·non (hā′paks lə·gom′ə·non) *Greek* Occurring but once: said in reference to rare or nonce words or phrases.

hap·haz·ard (hap′haz′ərd) *adj.* Accidental; happening by chance. —*n.* Mere chance; hazard. —*adv.* By chance; at random. [< HAP + HAZARD] —**hap′haz′ard·ly** *adv.*

haph·e·pho·bi·a (haf′ə·fō′bē·ə) See HAPTEPHOBIA.

haph·ta·rah (häf′tä·rä′, -tô′rô) *n. pl.* **·roth** (-rōth′, -rōth) The selection from the prophets read in the synagog service after each lesson from the law. See PARASHAH. [< Hebrew *haphtārāh* conclusion]

hap·less (hap′lis) *adj.* Having no luck; unfortunate; unlucky. —**hap′less·ly** *adv.* —**hap′less·ness** *n.*

hap·lite (hap′līt) *n.* A fine-grained, acid granite, composed mostly of quartz and feldspar and occurring in dikes. Its micaceous constituent, when present, is usually muscovite. Also called *aplite.* [< HAPL(O)- + -ITE¹] —**hap·lit·ic** (hap·lit′ik) *adj.*

haplo- *combining form* Simple; single. Also, before vowels, **hapl-.** [< Gk. *haploos* simple]

hap·loid (hap′loid) *adj. Biol.* Having the character of gametes with a reduced number of chromosomes, in contradistinction to the diploid with the doubled number found in somatic cells. Also **hap·loid′ic.**

hap·lo·sis (hap·lō′sis) *n. Biol.* The halving of the chromosome number during meiosis.

hap·ly (hap′lē) *adv.* By chance.

hap·pen (hap′ən) *v.i.* **1** To take place or occur; come to pass. **2** To come about or occur by chance or without expectation or design. **3** To chance; have the fortune: We *happened* to be there. **4** To come by chance: to *happen* upon the answer. **5** To come or go by chance: with *in*, *along*, *by*, etc. —**to happen to 1** To befall. **2** To become of: What *happened to* your old friend? [< HAP]

Synonyms: bechance, betide, chance, fall, occur, supervene. A thing is said to *happen* when no design is manifest or thought of; it is said to *chance* when it appears to be the result of accident (compare synonyms for ACCIDENT). An incident *happens* or *occurs;* something external or actual *happens* to one; a thought or fancy *occurs* to him. *Befall* and *betide* are transitive; *happen* is intransitive; something *befalls* or *betides* a person or *happens* to him. *Betide* is especially used for anticipated evil, thought of as waiting and coming at its appointed time; as, Woe *betide* him. One event *supervenes* upon another event, one disease upon another, etc.

hap·pen·ing (hap′ən·ing) *n.* **1** Something that happens; an event. See synonyms under ACCIDENT. **2** A staged but usually partly improvised event, often bizarre or spectacular, intended to engage the attention or elicit a response through shock or novelty.

hap·pen·stance (hap′ən·stans, -stəns) *n. U.S. Colloq.* A chance occurrence. [< HAPPEN + (CIR·CUM)STANCE]

hap·per (hap′ər) *n. Scot.* The hopper of a mill.

hap·pi·ly (hap′ə·lē) *adv.* **1** In a happy manner; cheerfully. **2** Fortunately; luckily. **3** Felicitously. **4** *Obs.* Haply; by chance.

hap·pi·ness (hap′ē·nis) *n.* **1** The state or quality of being happy; the pleasurable experience that springs from possession of good or the gratification of desires; enjoyment; blessedness. **2** Good fortune; luck; prosperity. **3** Unstudied grace; aptness or felicitousness, as of a remark or turn of phrase.

Synonyms: blessedness, bliss, cheer, comfort, contentment, delight, ecstasy, enjoyment, felicity, gaiety, gladness, gratification,

joy, merriment, mirth, pleasure, rapture, rejoicing, satisfaction, triumph. *Comfort* may be almost wholly negative, being found in security or relief from that which pains or annoys. *Enjoyment* is more positive and *pleasure* still more vivid; *satisfaction* is more tranquil than *pleasure;* when a worthy *pleasure* is past, a worthy *satisfaction* remains. *Happiness* is more complete than *comfort, enjoyment,* or *satisfaction,* more serene and rational than *pleasure. Felicity* is a colder and more formal term than *happiness. Gladness* is *happiness* that overflows. *Joy* is more intense than *happiness,* deeper than *gladness,* to which it is akin, nobler and more enduring than *pleasure. Bliss* is ecstatic, perfected *happiness.* See RAPTURE.

hap·py (hap′ē) *adj.* **·pi·er, ·pi·est 1** Enjoying, giving or indicating pleasure; joyous; blessed. **2** Dexterously or fortunately effective; opportune; felicitous. **3** Yielding or marked by happiness: *happy* moments. [< HAP]

Synonyms: blessed, blissful, blithe, blithesome, bright, buoyant, cheerful, cheering, cheery, delighted, delightful, dexterous, felicitous, fortunate, gay, glad, jocund, jolly, joyful, joyous, lucky, merry, mirthful, pleased, prosperous, rapturous, rejoiced, rejoicing, smiling, sprightly, successful, sunny. *Happy* primarily refers to something that comes "by good hap," a chance that brings prosperity, benefit, or success. In its most frequent present use, *happy* is applied to the state of one enjoying happiness, or to that by which happiness is expressed; as, a *happy* heart, *happy* laughter. (Compare synonyms for HAPPINESS.) *Cheerful* applies to the possession or expression of a moderate and tranquil happiness. A *cheery* word spontaneously gives cheer to others; a *cheering* word is more distinctly planned to cheer and encourage. *Gay* applies to an effusive and superficial happiness perhaps resulting largely from abundant animal spirits. A *buoyant* spirit is, as it were, borne up by joy and hope. A *sunny* disposition has a tranquil brightness that irradiates all who come within its influence. See AUSPICIOUS, CHEERFUL, CLEVER, FORTUNATE, SKILFUL, WELL. *Antonyms*: despondent, gloomy, melancholy, miserable, mournful, regretful, sad, sorrowful, woeful, wretched.

hap·py-go-luck·y (hap′ē·gō·luk′ē) *adj.* Trusting easily to luck; improvident; haphazard. *—adv.* As one pleases; anyhow; at will.

Haps·burg (haps′bûrg, *Ger.* häps′bŏŏrkh) An ancient German family from which were descended rulers of Austria, Hungary and Bohemia, the Holy Roman Empire, and Spain; the male line ended 1740: also called **House of Hapsburg.** Also spelled *Habsburg.*

Haps·burg-Lor·raine (haps′bûrg·lə·rān′, *Ger.* häps′bŏŏrkh·lō·rān′) The royal house of Austria, 1740–1918.

hap·shack·le (hap′shak′əl) See HAMSHACKLE.

hap·tene (hap′tēn) *n. Biochem.* A partial antigen: a substance which, when combined with certain proteins, has the power of conferring on them specific antigenic properties. Also **hap′ten** (-ten). [< Gk. *haptein* touch + -ENE]

hap·te·pho·bi·a (hap′tə·fō′bē·ə) *n.* A morbid fear of being touched: also called *haphephobia.* [< Gk. *haptein* touch + -PHOBIA] **—hap′te·pho′bic** *adj.*

hap·ter·on (hap′tər·on) *n. pl.* **·ter·a** (-tər·ə) *Bot.* A special organ of attachment developed by many aquatic plants, or marine algae, by which they anchor themselves to rocks. Also **hap′tere** (-tir). [< NL < Gk. *haptein* touch]

hap·to·phore (hap′tə·fôr, -fōr) *n. Biochem.* The thermostable portion of a toxin molecule which combines with an antitoxin cell to neutralize the toxic thermolabile portion. [< Gk. *haptein* touch + -PHORE]

hap·tot·ro·pism (hap·tot′rə·piz′əm) *n. Bot.* A one-sided growth in plants, induced by pressure or other stimuli. [< Gk. *haptein* + -TROPISM] **—hap′to·trop′ic** (-trop′ik, -trō′pik) *adj.*

ha·ra-ki·ri (hä′rä·kē′rē) *n.* Suicide by disembowelment: traditional form of suicide practiced by the Japanese samurai when disgraced or in lieu of execution: also *hari-kari.* Also **ha′ra-ka′ri** (-kä′rē). [< Japanese *hara* belly + *kiri* cut]

ha·rangue (hə·rang′) *n.* An oration; especially, a loud and vehement speech. *—v.* **·rangued, ·rangu·ing** *v.t.* To address in a harangue. *—v.i.* To deliver a harangue. See synonyms under SPEECH. [< F < Med. L *harenga* < OHG *hari* host + *hringa* ring] **—ha·rangu′er** *n.*

Ha·rar (hä′rər) A town in east central Ethiopia: formerly *Harrar.*

har·ass (har′əs, hə·ras′) *v.t.* **1** To trouble or worry persistently with cares, annoyances, etc.; torment. **2** *Mil.* To worry (an enemy) by raids and small attacks. **3** *Obs.* To ravage; raid. See synonyms under PERSECUTE, PERPLEX, TIRE[1]. [< OF *harasser* < *harer* set dogs on, prob. < OHG *haren* cry out] **—har′ass·er** *n.* **—har′ass·ment** *n.*

Har·bin (här′bin) A port on the Sungari, capital of Sungkiang province, NE Manchuria.

har·bin·ger (här′bin·jər) *n.* **1** One who or that which foreruns and announces the coming of something. **2** Formerly, a courier who rode in advance of a party to arrange for their lodging and entertainment. See synonyms under HERALD. *—v.t.* To act as a harbinger to; presage. [< OF *herbergeor* provider of shelter < *herberge* shelter < Gmc.]

har·bor (här′bər) *n.* **1** A port or haven so protected, naturally or artificially, as to provide shelter for ships. **2** Any place of refuge or rest. See synonyms under REFUGE, SHELTER. *—v.t.* **1** To give refuge to; shelter; protect. **2** To entertain in the mind; cherish, as a grudge. *—v.i.* **3** To take shelter in or as in a harbor. See synonyms under CHERISH, SHELTER. Also, *Brit.,* **har′bour.** [ME *herberwe* < OE *here* army + *beorg* refuge] **—har′bor·er** *n.*

har·bor·age (här′bər·ij) *n.* **1** A port or place of shelter for ships. **2** Shelter; entertainment.

har·bor·mas·ter (här′bər·mas′tər, -mäs′-) *n.* **1** An officer who inspects vessels in harbor to see that they are properly berthed and moored. **2** The chief of the harbor police.

hard (härd) *adj.* **1** Solid and firm in substance and consistency; not easily receiving indentation or impression: opposed to *soft.* **2** Capable of endurance; hardy. **3** Difficult of accomplishment, management, or solution; troublesome: opposed to *easy.* **4** Obdurate or callous in character or demeanor; hard-hearted. **5** Harsh or cruel: He was too *hard* on her; *hard* words. **6** Shrewd and obstinate. **7** Oppressive; difficult to endure: a *hard* life; *hard* times. **8** Strict or exacting in terms: a *hard* bargain. **9** Vigorous; persistent; energetic: *hard* study; a *hard* worker. **10** Sound; trustworthy. **11** Esthetically harsh or unpleasant: a *hard* face. **12** Stormy; inclement; rigorous: a *hard* winter. **13** Indisputable; definite: *hard* facts. **14** Strictly factual: *hard* news. **15** In specie; metallic: said of money. **16** Containing certain mineral salts in solution which interfere with the cleansing action of soap: said of water. **17** Containing much alcohol; strong: said of liquor. **18** Addictive: said of drugs. **19** *Agric.* High in gluten content: said of wheat. **20** Denoting *c* or *g* when articulated as a stop, as in *cod* and *god,* rather than as a fricative or an affricate. *—adv.* **1** With great energy or force; vigorously: to work *hard*; to rain *hard.* **2** Intently; earnestly: to look *hard* for something. **3** Harshly or severely. **4** With effort or difficulty. **5** Securely; tightly: to hold on *hard.* **6** So as to become hard: It was frozen *hard.* **7** In close proximity; near: often with *after, by,* or *upon.* [OE *heard*]

Synonyms (adj.): arduous, austere, bad, callous, compact, cruel, dense, difficult, distressing, exacting, firm, flinty, grievous, hardened, harsh, impenetrable, obdurate, oppressive, rigid, severe, solid, stern, stubborn, unfeeling, unforgiving, unrelenting, unyielding. See ARDUOUS, AUSTERE, BAD, COMPACT, DIFFICULT, FIRM, IMPENETRABLE, TROUBLESOME. *Antonyms*: easy, facile, fluid, genial, gentle, intelligible, kind, lenient, meek, mild, penetrable, soft, submissive, tender, yielding.

hard-and-fast (härd′ən·fast′, -fäst′) *adj.* Absolutely binding; fixed and unalterable.

hard·back (härd′bak′) *adj.* Hard-cover. *—n.* A hard-cover book.

hard·ball (härd′bôl′) *n.* **1** A baseball. *—adj. U.S. Colloq.* Tough; intense: a *hardball* confrontation.

hard-bit·ten (härd′bit′n) *adj.* Tough; unyielding.

hard·board (härd′bôrd′, -bōrd′) *n.* A material composed of fibers from wood chips pressed into sheets.

hard-boiled (härd′boild′) *adj.* **1** Boiled until cooked through; said of an egg. **2** *Colloq.* Hardened or unyielding in character; tough.

hard·bound (härd′bound′) *adj.* Hard-cover.

hard by *Archaic* or *Dial.* Close by.

hard cash Actual money as distinguished from debts or claims to be collected or settled.

hard coal Anthracite.

hard-core (härd′kôr′) *adj.* **1** Thoroughly dedicated, determined, loyal, etc., to a cause or movement: *hard-core* radicals. **2** Extremely explicit: *hard-core* pornography. **3** Of or pertaining to the hard core.

hard core 1 The basic, central, or most important part; nucleus. **2** Unemployed or underemployed people not trained for any job.

hard-cov·er (härd′kuv′ər) *adj.* Designating a book having rigid sides, as of cardboard bound in cloth or another material: contrasted to *softcover.*

hard-earned (härd′ûrnd′) *adj.* Earned or gained with difficulty; obtained by hard work.

Har·de·ca·nute (här′də·kə·nōōt′, -nyōōt′), 1019?–42, king of England and Denmark 1040–42; son of Canute.

hard·en (här′dən) *v.t.* **1** To make hard or harder; make solid. **2** To make unyielding, pitiless, or indifferent. **3** To strengthen or make firm in any element of character, disposition, etc. **4** To make tough, strong, or hardy; inure. *—v.i.* **5** To become hard. **6** In commerce: **a** To become higher, as prices. **b** To become stable. [< ON *harthna*]

hard·en·ing (här′dən·ing) *n.* Any substance or material that hardens another; specifically, any metal added to iron to make steel.

hard-fea·tured (härd′fē′chərd) *adj.* Stern or forbidding in countenance or aspect.

hard-fist·ed (härd′fis′tid) *adj.* **1** Of an avaricious or miserly disposition. **2** Having hard, horny, or strong hands. **—hard′-fist′ed·ness** *n.*

hard·hack (härd′hak′) *n.* The steeplebush.

hard-hand·ed (härd′han′did) *adj.* **1** Having hard or horny hands. **2** Governing with severity or cruelty; despotic; tyrannical.

hard-hat (härd′hat′) *n. U.S. Colloq.* A construction worker.

hard hat 1 Any of various helmets worn for protection, as by construction workers, motorcyclists, etc. **2** *Brit.* Any hat having a hard crown, as a derby or bowler.

hard·head (härd′hed′) *n. pl.* **·heads** *for defs.* **1, 2; ·head** or **·heads** *for defs.* **3, 4. 1** A shrewd, tough-minded person. **2** An obstinate or stupid person. **3** The menhaden. **4** The alewife.

hard-head·ed (härd′hed′id) *adj.* **1** Possessing shrewdness and a practical turn. **2** Inclined to obstinacy; stubborn. **—hard′-head′ed·ness** *n.*

hard-heart·ed (härd′här′tid) *adj.* Lacking pity or sympathy; unfeeling; obdurate. **—hard′-heart′ed·ly** *adv.* **—hard′-heart′ed·ness** *n.*

har·di·hood (här′dē·hood) *n.* **1** Sturdy courage. **2** Rash or foolish daring; presumptuous boldness; audacity; effrontery. **3** The quality of being hardy; physical endurance. See synonyms under COURAGE, EFFRONTERY, TEMERITY.

har·di·ly (här′də·lē) *adv.* With hardihood; boldly.

har·di·ness (här′dē·nis) *n.* **1** The state of being hardy or physically strong. **2** Stout-heartedness; intrepidity.

Har·ding (här′ding), **Warren Gamaliel,** 1865–1923, president of the United States 1921–23.

hard labor Heavy labor, such as stone-breaking, etc., imposed as a form of punishment upon imprisoned convicts.

hard line An unyielding position, as in negotiation. **—hard′-line′** *adj.* **—hard′-lin′er** *n.*

hard-look·ing (härd′lŏŏk′ing) *adj.* Appearing hard; tough-looking.

hard·ly (härd′lē) *adv.* **1** Scarcely; not quite: She was *hardly* aware of what she was doing. **2** With difficulty or great pains. **3** Improbably. **4** Rigorously; harshly; severly.

hard maple Sugar maple.

hard-mouthed (härd′mouthd′, -moutht′) *adj.* Having a hard mouth, as a horse; hence, not easily guided or controlled.

hard·ness (härd′nis) *n.* **1** The state of being hard. **2** Unyieldingness of spirit; insensitivity; callousness. **3** A property of water that contains mineral salts. **4** *Med.* Tension: said of the pulse. **5** In art, harsh effect or treatment. **6** That quality of a mineral that resists scratching: see MOHS SCALE. **7** The toughness of a metal or alloy: see BRINELL HARDNESS. **8** *Physics* A high-penetrating

power of X-rays or other forms of radiant energy.

hard-nosed (härd′nōzd′) *adj. Slang* Hard-bitten, unyielding, or firmly businesslike: a *hard-nosed* approach to government spending. Also **hard-nose** (härd′nōz′).

hard of hearing Deaf or partially deaf.

hard-pan (härd′pan′) *n.* 1 A layer of firm detritus under soft soil. 2 A firm foundation; solid basis.

hard rubber Vulcanite.

hard sauce Butter, sugar, and flavorings creamed together and used as a sauce with puddings, etc.

hard sell *U.S. Colloq.* The use of aggressive methods of salesmanship.

hard-set (härd′set′) *adj.* 1 In a difficult situation; beset. 2 Firmly resolved; obstinate.

hard-shell (härd′shel′) *adj.* 1 Having a hard shell, as a lobster or crab, previous to shedding the carapace. 2 Stubbornly devoted to one's principles; uncompromising; inflexible.

Hardshell Baptist A Primitive or Old School Baptist.

hard-shell clam (härd′shel′) The quahaug.

hard-shell crab A crab, particularly the blue crab (*Callinectes sapidus*) of North America, before it has molted: after it has molted it is known as a *soft-shell crab.*

hard-ship (härd′ship) *n.* 1 Something hard to endure, as injustice. 2 *Obs.* Rigor; severity. See synonyms under MISFORTUNE.

hard-spun (härd′spun′) *adj.* Spun with a fine twist.

hard-stand (härd′stand′) *n. Aeron.* A paved, hard-surfaced area adjacent to a runway, for the parking of aircraft and ground vehicles.

hard-tack (härd′tak′) *n.* Large, unsalted, crackerlike, hard-baked biscuit for army and navy use: also called *ship biscuit.*

hard-top (härd′top′) *adj.* Describing an automobile with the body design of a convertible, but with a rigid top. —*n.* Such a car.

hard up 1 In need or want, as of money. 2 Having a meager choice.

hard-ware (härd′wâr′) *n.* 1 Manufactured articles of metal, as utensils or tools. 2 Weapons: military *hardware.* 3 Mechanical, electronic, or other devices or materials, as distinguished from people, planning, operational procedures, etc. 4 Any of the machinery that makes up a computer installation: distinguished from *software.*

hard-wood (härd′wood′) *n.* 1 Wood from broadleaved deciduous trees as distinguished from the wood of coniferous or needle-leaved trees. 2 Any such tree.

har-dy[1] (här′dē) *adj.* **-di-er, -di-est** 1 Inured to hardship; robust. 2 Showing hardihood; bold; audacious; strenuous. 3 Able to survive the winter in the open air; perennial: said of plants. 4 Rigid; strong; durable. See synonyms under STRONG. [< OF *hardi*, pp. of *hardir* embolden < OHG *hartjan* make hard]

har-dy[2] (här′dē) *n. pl.* **-dies** A square-shanked chisel or fuller for insertion in a hardy-hole. [< HARD + -Y[1]]

Har-dy (här′dē), **Thomas,** 1840–1928, English novelist and poet.

har-dy-hole (här′dē-hōl′) *n.* A hole in a blacksmith's anvil in which a hardy or other tool may be placed.

hare (hâr) *n. pl.* **hares** or **hare** 1 A rodent (genus *Lepus*) with cleft upper lip, long ears, and long hind legs: proverbial for its timidity and swiftness. 2 The common American rabbit. ◆ Collateral adjective: *leporine.* ◆ Homophone: *hair.* [OE *hara*]

hare-and-hounds (hâr′ən-houndz′) *n.* An outdoor sport in which some players (*hounds*) pursue others (*hares*) who have scattered scraps of paper as "scent" behind them.

hare-bell (hâr′bel′) *n.* 1 A perennial Scottish herb (*Campanula rotundifolia*) with blue, bell-shaped flowers. 2 Any of several related plants, as the western harebell of the U.S. (*C. petiolata*). Also called *bluebell.*

hare-brained (hâr′brānd′) *adj.* Foolish; flighty; giddy.

Ha-re Krish-na (hä′rē krish′nə) The name of a U.S. cult, adopted from the title of a Buddhist love chant dedicated to the Hindu god Krishna.

hare-lip (hâr′lip′) *n.* A congenital fissure of the upper lip a short distance from the median line.

har-em (hâr′əm, har′-) *n.* 1 The apartments of a Moslem household reserved for females. 2 The wives, concubines, etc., occupying the harem. 3 A Moslem holy place forbidden to all but the faithful. Also **ha-reem** (hä-rēm′). [< Arabic *harim* (something) forbidden, sacred < *harama* forbid]

hare's-eye (hârz′ī′) *n.* Lagophthalmos.

Har-fleur (är-flœr′) A port on the Seine near Le Havre, northern France.

Har-gei-sa (här-gā′sə) A city in NW Somalia, capital of the former British Somaliland.

Har-greaves (här′grēvz), **James,** died 1778, English weaver; inventor of the spinning jenny.

har-i-cot (har′ə-kō) *n.* 1 A stew of meat, especially mutton, and vegetables. 2 The ripe seeds or green pods of the kidney bean and other string beans; also, the kidney bean. [< F < Nahuatl *ayecotl*]

ha-ri-ka-ri (hä′rē-kä′rē) See HARA-KIRI.

Har-ing-ton (har′ing-tən), **Sir John,** 1561–1622, English writer and translator: also *Harrington.*

hark (härk) *v.i.* To listen; harken: usually in the imperative. —*v.t. Archaic* To hear; listen to. —**to hark back** 1 In hunting, to retrace the trail so as to find again a lost scent: said of hounds. 2 To return to some previous point, as after a digression. —*n.* The cry "hark" as used to urge on or guide hounds in the chase. [ME *herkien*]

hark-en (här′kən) *v.t. Archaic* To hear; listen to; heed. —*v.i. Poetic* To listen; give heed. Also spelled *hearken.* See synonyms under LISTEN. [OE *heorcnian*]

hark-er (här′kər) *n. Scot.* A listener.

harl[1] (härl) *v.t. & v.i. Scot. & Brit. Dial.* To drag or be dragged; scrape. Also **harle.**

harl[2] (härl) *n.* 1 Filaments of flax or hemp drawn out or hackled; hence, any fibrous substance. 2 A barb of a large feather, as from a peacock: used for making artificial flies in angling. [Prob. < MLG *herle*]

Har-lan (här′lən), **John Marshall,** 1899–1971, U.S. jurist; associate justice of the Supreme Court 1954–1971.

Har-le-ian (här-lē′ən) *adj.* Belonging to or connected with **Robert Har-ley** (här′lē), 1661–1724, and his son **Edward,** 1689–1741, earls of Oxford and Mortimer and founders of the Harleian collection of books and manuscripts in the British Museum.

Har-lem (här′ləm) 1 A former village of NE Manhattan Island; now a section of New York City with a large Negro population. 2 Haarlem.

Harlem River A navigable tidal stream forming the northern boundary of Manhattan Island, connected with the Hudson River by a ship canal.

har-le-quin (här′lə-kwin, -kin) *n.* A buffoon. —*adj.* 1 Comic; buffoonlike. 2 Parti-colored, like the dress of a Harlequin. —*v.i. Rare* To play the harlequin. —**har-le-quin-esque′** (-esk′) *adj.*

Har-le-quin (här′lə-kwin, -kin) A traditional pantomime character, originally from old Italian comedy, the lover of Columbine, traditionally dressed in parti-colored tights, with shaved head, masked face, and bearing a light wooden sword.

har-le-quin-ade (här′lə-kwin-ād′, -kin-) *n.* 1 That part of a pantomime in which the harlequin and clown play the principal parts; hence, pantomime. 2 Fantastic antics or show; buffoonery.

harlequin brant The laughing goose.

harlequin bug A shiny, black or blue bug with red or red and yellow spots (*Murgantia histrionica*) which feeds on cabbage and related plants: also called *cabbage bug, fire bug.*

harlequin duck A northern sea duck (*Histrionicus histrionicus*) the male of which is brilliantly and variously colored.

harlequin snake One of the coral snakes.

Har-ley Street (här′lē) A street in the West End of London, occupied chiefly by specialists in medicine and surgery.

har-lot (här′lət) *n.* 1 A lewd woman; prostitute. 2 *Obs.* A knave or vagabond. [< OF *herlot* fellow, rogue]

har-lot-ry (här′lət-rē) *n.* The trade of a harlot; habitual lewdness.

harm (härm) *n.* 1 That which inflicts injury or loss. 2 The injury inflicted; hurt. 3 Offense against right or morality; wrong. See synonyms under INJURY, MISFORTUNE. —*v.t.* To do harm to; damage; hurt. See synonyms under ABUSE, HURT. [OE *hearm* insult]

har-mat-tan (här′mə-tan′) *n.* A dry, sandy wind of the west coast of Africa, blowing from the interior during December, January, and February. [< Sp. *harmatán* < native name]

H-ar-ma-ture (āch′är′mə-chər, -chōōr) *n. Electr.* An early form of armature having a section shaped like an H: also called *shuttle armature.*

harm-ful (härm′fəl) *adj.* Having power to injure; noxious. See synonyms under INIMICAL, NOISOME, PERNICIOUS. —**harm′ful-ly** *adv.* —**harm′ful-ness** *n.*

har-mine (här′mēn, -min) *n.* Banisterine. Also **har′min** (-min). [< Gk. *harmala* wild rue + -INE[2]]

harm-less (härm′lis) *adj.* 1 Not harmful; innoxious. 2 Without hurt, loss, or liability. See synonyms under INNOCENT. —**harm′less-ly** *adv.* —**harm′less-ness** *n.*

har-mon-ic (här-mon′ik) *adj.* 1 Producing, characterized by, or pertaining to harmony; consonant; harmonious. 2 *Music* **a** Pertaining to harmony, as distinguished from melody or rhythm. **b** Pertaining to a tone whose rate of vibration is an exact multiple of a given primary tone. 3 *Math.* Derived from or originally suggested by the numerical relations between the vibrations of the musical harmonics or overtones of the same fundamental tone: *harmonic* functions. —*n.* 1 An attendant or secondary tone, produced by the vibration in aliquot parts of the same body or string which gives, by its complete simultaneous vibration, the primary or fundamental tone; overtone. 2 *Music* A note on a stringed instrument produced by stopping a string at a specific point. 3 *Physics* Any component of a periodic quantity which is an integral multiple of the fundamental frequency. Also **har-mon′i-cal.** [< L *harmonicus* < Gk. *harmonikos* < *harmonia* harmony] —**har-mon′i-cal-ly** *adv.*

har-mon-i-ca (här-mon′i-kə) *n.* 1 A musical instrument consisting of small metal reeds fixed within a series of slots in a narrow case, and played by blowing through the slots. 2 An instrument composed of a series of glass tubes, goblets, or the like, graduated to a musical scale and played by rubbing the rims. 3 An instrument composed of glass or metal strips struck by hammers. [< L, fem. of *harmonicus* harmonic]

harmonic analyzer *Physics* An instrument which separates the components of a complex sound wave into the corresponding sine waves.

harmonic distortion *Physics* A wave form distortion which contains both fundamental and harmonic frequencies.

har-mon-i-con (här-mon′i-kən) *n.* 1 An orchestrion. 2 A mouth organ; harmonica. [< Gk. *harmonikon*, neuter of *harmonikos* harmonic]

har-mon-ics (här-mon′iks) *n. pl.* 1 That branch of acoustics dealing with musical sounds: construed as singular. 2 The overtones or partials of a fundamental: construed as plural.

har-mo-ni-ous (här-mō′nē-əs) *adj.* 1 Characterized by harmony or agreement; free from discord. 2 Having the parts related in pleasing combination; symmetrical; congruous. 3 Melodious; pleasing to the ear.

har-mo-nist (här′mə-nist) *n.* 1 A master of the principles of musical harmony. 2 A student or expounder of the harmony of different writings, as of the Christian Gospels. 3 A musician. 4 A harmonizer.

har-mo-nis-tic (här′mə-nis′tik) *adj.* Pertaining or relating to harmony, specifically to the work of literary harmonists.

har-mo-ni-um (här-mō′nē-əm) *n.* A reed organ. [< F < L *harmonia*]

har-mo-nize (här′mə-nīz) *v.t. & v.i.* **-nized, -niz-ing** 1 To make or become harmonious or suitable. 2 To arrange or sing in musical

harmony. Also, *Brit.,* **har′mo·nise.** See synonyms under ACCOMMODATE, ADAPT, AGREE. — **har′mo·ni·za′tion** *n.* — **har′mo·niz′er** *n.*

har·mo·ny (här′mə·nē) *n. pl.* **·nies** 1 Accord or agreement in feeling, manner, or action: the *harmony* of a loving family. 2 A state of order, agreement, or completeness in the relations of things or of parts of a whole to each other. 3 Pleasing sounds; music. 4 *Music* **a** Any agreeable combination of simultaneous tones. **b** The science or study of the relations of combinations of tones or chords, their progressions, resolutions, modulations, etc., as distinguished from melody and rhythm. 5 A literary work to display the agreement of different books: a *harmony* of the Gospels. [<OF *armonie* <L *harmonia* <Gk. <*harmos* joint <*harmozein* join]

Synonyms: accord, accordance, agreement, amity, concord, concurrence, conformity, congruity, consent, consistency, consonance, symmetry, unanimity, uniformity, union, unison, unity. When tones, thoughts, or feelings, individually different, combine to form a consistent and pleasing whole, there is *harmony. Harmony* is deeper and more essential than *agreement. Concord* implies more volition than *accord. Conformity* is submission to authority or necessity. *Congruity* involves the element of suitableness; *consent* and *concurrence* refer to decision or action, but *consent* is more passive than *concurrence.* See MELODY, TUNE, SYMMETRY. *Antonyms:* antagonism, conflict, controversy, disagreement, discord, disproportion, dissension, disunion, hostility, incongruity, inconsistency, opposition, schism, variance.

har·mo·tome (här′mə·tōm) *n.* A vitreous hydrous silicate of potassium, barium, and aluminum, crystallizing in the monoclinic system, and forming characteristic cross-shaped crystals. [<Gk. *harmos* joint + -TOME]

harn (härn) *n. Scot.* A very coarse linen.

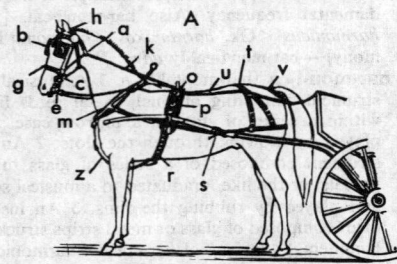

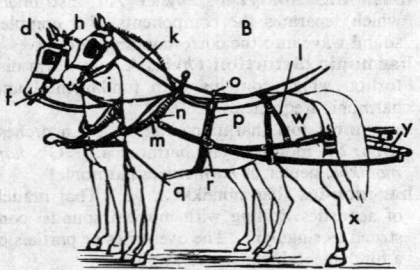

NOMENCLATURE OF HARNESS
A. Single harness. *B.* Double harness.

a. Runner.	*o.* Terrets.
b. Blinder.	*p.* Saddle.
c. Throatlatch.	*q.* Pole chain.
d. Browband or front piece.	*r.* Bellyband strap.
e. Bit.	*s.* Breeching strap.
f. Curb bit.	*t.* Hipstrap.
g. Nose piece.	*u.* Backstrap.
h. Crownpiece.	*v.* Crupper.
i. Curb chain.	*w.* Breeching.
k. Checkrein.	*x.* Traces.
l. Breech stay.	*y.* Whiffletree or swingletree.
m. Hame.	*z.* Martingale.
n. Collar showing afterwale.	

har·ness (här′nis) *n.* 1 The combination of traces, straps, and other pieces forming the gear of a draft animal and used to attach it for work to a wheeled vehicle or plow. 2 *Archaic* The defensive armor of a soldier or of his horse. 3 Any arrangement of straps, cords, etc., as for lifting or performing some mechanical operation. 4 A device on a loom comprising the heddles which shift the sets of warp threads alternately. 5 The routine or obligations of work or business. — *v.t.* 1 To put harness on, as a horse. 2 To make use of the power or potential of: to *harness* a waterfall. 3 *Archaic* To dress in or equip with armor. [<OF *harneis*; ult. origin unknown] — **har′ness·er** *n.*

harnessed antelope Any of several African antelopes with harnesslike markings, especially the bushbuck.

harness race A race for pacers or trotters harnessed to sulkies.

Har·ney Peak (här′nē) A mountain in the Black Hills, the highest point in South Dakota; 7,242 feet.

Har·old (har′əld, *Fr.* à·rôld′) A masculine personal name; also, the name of several kings of England, Norway, and Denmark. Also *Lat.* **Ha·rol·dus** (hä·rōl′dəs), *Dan.* **Ha·rald** (hä′räld). [<Gmc., chief of the army] — **Harold I,** died 1040, king of England 1035–1040: called "Harold Harefoot." — **Harold II,** 1022?–66, king of England Jan.–Oct. 1066; killed at battle of Hastings. — **Harold III,** 1015–66, king of Norway; killed at battle of Stamford Bridge, where he was defeated by Harold II of England: known as *Harald Haardraade.*

harp (härp) *n.* 1 A stringed musical instrument, nearly triangular in modern form, played with the fingers. 2 One of several old Irish coins of various values. 3 A harplike part in a mechanism. — *v.i.* 1 To play on a harp. 2 To speak or write persistently; dwell tediously: with *on* or *upon.* — *v.t.* 3 *Archaic* To give utterance to; express. 4 *Poetic* To affect in some way by playing the harp: to *harp* one to sleep. [OE *hearpe*]

Harp (härp) The constellation Lyra.

harp·er (här′pər) *n.* One who plays the harp; a harpist.

Harpers Ferry A town in NE West Virginia; scene of John Brown's raid and capture.

harp·ings (här′pingz) *n. pl. Naut.* 1 The foreparts of the wales surrounding the bow of a ship. 2 Extensions of the ribbands. Also **harp′ins.** [Prob. <F *harper* grip]

harp·ist (här′pist) *n.* One who plays the harp; a minstrel.

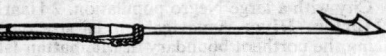

TOGGLED HAND HARPOON

har·poon (här·pōon′) *n.* A barbed missile weapon, carrying a long cord, for striking whales or large fish. — *v.t.* To strike, take, or kill with a harpoon. [<F *harpon* grappling iron <*harper* grip <*harpe* claw] — **har·poon′er, har·poon·eer** (-ir′) *n.*

harpoon gun A small cannon which fires a harpoon: used in whaling.

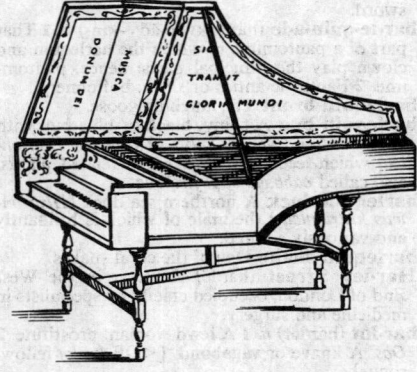

HARPSICHORD

harp·si·chord (härp′sə·kôrd) *n.* A keyboard instrument in wide-spread use from the 16th to the 18th century, and revived in the 20th, precursor of the piano, but having the strings plucked by quills instead of struck. [<MF *harpechorde* <Ital. *arpicordo* <LL *harpa* harp + L *chorda* string <Gk. ·*chordē*]

har·py (här′pē) *n. pl.* **·pies** 1 Any rapacious person; a plunderer; extortioner. 2 A very large, crested, voracious tropical American eagle, the **harpy eagle** (*Thrasaetus harpyia*): also called *winged wolf.* [<HARPY]

Har·py (här′pē) *n.* In Greek mythology, a filthy, winged monster with the head of a woman and the tail, legs, and talons of a bird; usually three (the Harpies), Aello, Celaeno, and Ocypete, who fouled or seized the food of their victims, carried off the souls of the dead, etc. [<F *Harpie* <L *Harpyia* <Gk. <*harpazein* seize]

har·que·bus (här′kwə·bəs) *n.* 1 An ancient hand firearm, the predecessor of the musket. 2 A number of soldiers armed with harquebuses. Also spelled *arquebus.* Also **har′que·buse, har′que·buss.** [<F *harquebuse* <MLG *hakebusse* hook-gun]

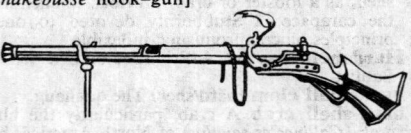

HARQUEBUS

har·que·bus·ier (här′kwə·bəs·ir′) *n.* One armed with a harquebus.

Har·rar (har′rər) A former spelling of HARAR.

har·ri·dan (har′ə·dən) *n.* A vixenish old woman; a hag. [<OF *haridelle* jade]

har·ri·er[1] (har′ē·ər) *n.* 1 One who or that which harries. 2 The marsh hawk.

har·ri·er[2] (har′ē·ər) *n.* 1 A small hound used for hunting hares. 2 *Brit.* A member of a hare-and-hounds team. [<HARE + -IER]

Har·ri·et (har′ē·ət) A feminine personal name. Also **Har′ri·ot, Har′ri·ott.** [<Gmc., home-ruler]

Har·ring·ton (har′ing·tən), **Sir John** See HARINGTON.

Har·ris (har′is), **Joel Chandler,** 1848–1908, U.S. writer. — **Roy,** born 1898, U.S. composer.

Har·ris·burg (har′is·bûrg) The capital of Pennsylvania, on the Susquehanna River.

Har·ri·son (har′ə·sən) Name of a prominent American political family including: **Benjamin,** 1726?–91, signer of the Declaration of Independence; his son **William Henry,** 1773–1841, U.S. general, president of the United States March 4–April 4, 1841; **Benjamin,** 1833–1901, president of the United States 1889–93, grandson of William Henry Harrison.

Har·ro·gate (har′ə·git, -gāt) A municipal borough in central Yorkshire, England.

Har·ro·vi·an (ha·rō′vē·ən, hə-) *adj.* Of or pertaining to the school at Harrow-on-the-Hill, England. — *n.* A student at or alumnus of Harrow.

har·row (har′ō) *n.* A farm implement, commonly a frame set with spikes or teeth, or disks, for leveling plowed ground, breaking clods, etc. — *v.t.* 1 To draw a harrow over (a field, etc.). 2 To disturb the mind or feelings of painfully; distress. — *v.i.* 3 To undergo harrowing. [ME *harwe,* prob. <Scand. Cf. ON *herfi.*] — **har′row·er** *n.*

har·row·ing (har′ō·ing) *adj.* Lacerating or tormenting to the feelings. — **har′row·ing·ly** *adv.*

Harrowing of Hell The descent of Christ into hell between his crucifixion and resurrection, when he is supposed to have brought salvation to the souls of the dead; a frequent subject in literature and art.

Har·row-on-the-Hill (har′ō·on·thə·hil′) An urban district in Middlesex NW of London; seat of Harrow, a public school founded 1571. Also **Har′row.**

har·ry (har′ē) *v.* **har·ried, har·ry·ing** *v.t.* 1 To lay waste, as in war or invasion; pillage; sack. 2 To harass in any way. 3 *Scot.* To carry off in a raid; seize. — *v.i.* 4 To make raids for plunder. Also *Obs.* **har′row.** See synonyms under PERSECUTE. [OE *hergian* ravage]

Har·ry (har′ē) Diminutive of HAROLD or HENRY.

har·ry-soph (har′i·sof′) *n. Brit.* At Cambridge University, a student with a B.A. degree who is a candidate for a medical or law degree. [<*Harry,* a nickname for Henry VIII + SOPHISTER]

harsh (härsh) *adj.* 1 Grating or rough to any of the senses; violently disagreeable; dis-

cordant; rasping; irritating. **2** Irritating to the mind; offensive. **3** Rigorous; severe; also, unfeeling: a *harsh* judge, a *harsh* sentence. See synonyms under ARBITRARY, AUSTERE, BITTER, HARD, ROUGH. [ME *harsk*, prob. < Scand. Cf. Sw. *härsk*, Dan. *harsk* rancid.] — **harsh'ly** *adv.* —**harsh'ness** *n.*

harsh·en (här'shən) *v.t.* To make harsh, rough, or severe.

hars·let (härs'lit) See HASLET.

hart (härt) *n.* The male of the red deer, especially after it has passed its fifth year. ◆ Homophone: *heart.* [OE *heort*]

Hart (härt), **Moss,** 1904–1961, U.S. playwright and librettist.

har·tal (här·täl') *n.* In India, a suspension or stopping of business, as a form of mourning or passive protest against a political measure or situation. [<Hind. *hartāl* <*hat* shop + *tāla* lock]

Harte (härt), **(Francis) Bret,** 1836–1902, U.S. novelist and story writer.

harte·beest (härt'bēst, här'tə-) *n.* **1** A large antelope of Africa (genera *Bubalis* and *Alcelaphus*), grayish-brown above and white below. **2** The bontebok. Also **hart'beest.** [< Afrikaans <Du. *hert* hart + *beest* beast]

Hart·ford (härt'fərd) The capital of Connecticut, on the Connecticut River.

harts·horn (härts'hôrn') *n.* **1** A volatile preparation of ammonia, used as smelling salts, formerly distilled from deer horns. **2** Sal volatile. **3** The antler of a hart.

hart's–tongue (härts'tung') *n.* A fern *(Phyllitis scolopendrium)* having bright green fronds, found throughout the temperate zone.

har·um–scar·um (hâr'əm·skâr'əm) *adj.* Reckless; irresponsible. —*n.* A wild, reckless, or thoughtless person. [<obs. *hare* frighten + SCARE]

Ha·run al–Ra·shid (hä·rōōn' äl'rə·shēd') 766?–809, caliph of Bagdad; hero of the *Arabian Nights.*

ha·rus·pex (hə·rus'peks, har'əs·peks) *n. pl.* **ha·rus·pi·ces** (hə·rus'pə·sēz) A soothsayer or diviner of ancient Rome who interpreted the will of the gods from inspection of the entrails of sacrificed animals: also spelled *aruspex.* [< L] —**ha·rus'pi·cal** (-kəl) *adj.* —**ha·rus·pi·ca·tion** (hə·rus'pə·kā'shən) *n.* —**ha·rus·pi·cy** (hə·rus'pə·sē) *n.*

Har·vard (här'vərd), **John,** 1607–1638, English nonconformist clergyman, who emigrated to America; endowed Harvard College, 1636.

har·vest (här'vist) *n.* **1** A crop, as of grain, gathered or ready for gathering. **2** The time of gathering. **3** The product of any toil or effort. —*v.t.* & *v.i.* **1** To gather (a crop). **2** To gather the crop of (a field, etc.). [OE *hærfest* autumn, harvest]

Synonyms (noun): crop, fruit, growth, harvesting, harvest time, increase, ingathering, proceeds, produce, product, reaping, result, return, yield. *Harvest* is the generic word; *crop* is the common and commercial expression; we say a man sells his *crop,* but we should not speak of his selling his *harvest;* we speak of an ample or abundant *harvest,* a good *crop. Harvest* is applied almost wholly to grain; *crop* applies to almost anything that is gathered in; we speak of the potato *crop,* not the potato *harvest;* we may say either the wheat *crop* or the wheat *harvest.* We speak of *produce* collectively, but of a *product* or various *products;* vegetables, fruits, eggs, butter, etc., may be termed farm *produce,* or the *products* of the farm. *Product* is a word of wider application than *produce;* we speak of the *products* of manufacturing, the *product* obtained by multiplying one number by another, etc. The word *proceeds* is chiefly used of the *return* from an investment; we speak of the *produce* of a farm, but of the *proceeds* of the money invested in farming. The *yield* is what the land gives up to the farmer's demand, as the *yield* of corn or oats. *Harvest* has also a figurative use; as, The result of lax enforcement of law is a *harvest* of crime. See INCREASE, PRODUCT.

harvest bug 1 The harvest tick. **2** A harvest fly.

har·vest·er (här'vis·tər) *n.* **1** One who harvests **2** A reaping machine.

harvest feast A feast after the harvest has been gathered or the season in which it occurs: also called **harvest festival.**

harvest fly A large cicada *(Tibicen linnei)* of North America, noted for its shrill, noisy cry.

harvest home 1 An Old English festival held at the bringing home of the harvest. **2** The song sung at such festivals. **3** The season for garnering the harvest.

har·vest·man (här'vist·mən) *n. pl.* **·men** (-mən) **1** One who labors in the harvest. **2** An arachnid of the order *Phalangida;* a daddy-long-legs.

harvest moon The full moon that occurs near the autumnal equinox.

harvest tick An acaridan mite (genus *Trombicula*), mostly red, that attaches itself to the skin, being especially abundant about harvest time; a chigger.

Har·vey (här'vē) A masculine personal name. [<Gmc., army battle]

Har·vey (här'vē), **William,** 1578–1657, English physician; discovered the circulation of the blood.

Har·wich (har'ij, -ich) A port in NE Essex, England.

Harz Mountains (härts) A mountain range between the Elbe and Weser rivers, central Germany; highest peak, 3,747 feet. Also **Hartz.**

has (haz) Present indicative, third person singular, of HAVE.

Ha·sa (hä'sə, has'ə), A province and eastern dependency of Nejd, Saudi Arabia, on the Persian Gulf; capital, Hofuf: also *Al Ahsa.*

has–been (haz'bin') *n. Colloq.* A person or thing no longer popular or effective.

Has·dru·bal (haz'drōō·bəl, haz·drōō'bəl) Name of several Carthaginian generals, especially Hannibal's brother; killed 207 B.C.

ha·sen·pfef·fer (hä'zən·fef'ər) *n.* A stew made with marinated rabbit meat. [G]

hash (hash) *n.* **1** A dish of chopped and cooked meat and vegetables, usually sautéed. **2** A mess; a jumble. **3** A rehash; any old thing brought forth in new form. **4** *Scot.* A wasteful or slovenly person; blockhead; dunce. —**to make a hash of** *Colloq.* To bungle; spoil. —**to settle (one's) hash** *Colloq.* To silence, finish off, or put down (a person). —*v.t.* **1** To cut or chop into small pieces; mince. **2** *U.S. Colloq.* To make a mess of; bungle. —**to hash over** *U.S. Colloq.* To talk or think about carefully; mull. [<OF *hacher* chop. See HATCH[3].]

Hash·e·mite Kingdom of the Jordan (hash'ə·mīt) See JORDAN, HASHEMITE KINGDOM OF THE.

hash house *U.S. Slang* A cheap restaurant.

hash·ish (häsh'ēsh, -ish) *n.* **1** The tops and sprouts of Indian hemp, used as a narcotic and intoxicant. **2** An intoxicating preparation of this plant. Also **hash'eesh.** [<Arabic *hashish* hemp]

hash mark *Mil. Slang* A service stripe worn on the uniform sleeve.

hash–sling·er (hash'sling'ər) *n. U.S. Slang* A waiter or waitress in a cheap restaurant.

Has·i·dim (has'i·dim, *Hebrew* khä·sē'dim) See CHASSIDIM.

has·let (häs'lit, haz'-) *n.* The heart, liver, etc., especially of a hog, used as food: also spelled *harslet.* [<OF *hastelet* broiled meat <*haste* spit <L *hasta* spear]

has·lock (has'lok') *n.* The fine short wool on the throat of a sheep. [<HALSE + LOCK[3]]

Has·mo·ne·an (haz'mə·nē'ən) *n.* One of the Jewish family to which the Maccabees belonged, noted for its leadership and patriotism.—*adj.* Of or pertaining to the Hasmoneans. Also **Has'mo·nae'an.**

has·n't (haz'ənt) Contraction of HAS NOT.

hasp (hasp, häsp) *n.* A fastening passing over a staple and secured as by a padlock. See synonyms under LOCK. —*v.t.* To shut or fasten with or as with a hasp. [OE *hæpse*]

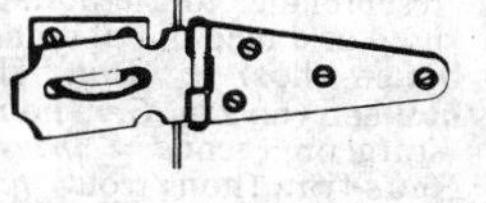
HASP

Has·sam (has'əm), **Childe,** 1859–1935, U.S. painter and etcher.

Has·selt (häs'əlt) The capital of Limburg province, Belgium.

has·sle (has'əl) *Slang n.* An argument; squabble. —*v.i.* **·sled, ·sling** To argue. Also **has'sel.** [? <HAGGLE + TUSSLE]

has·sock (has'ək) *n.* **1** An upholstered footstool. **2** A rank tuft of coarse or boggy grass. **3** *Scot.* A shock of hair. [OE *hassuc* coarse grass <Celtic]

hast (hast) Have: archaic or poetic second person singular, present tense,of HAVE: used with *thou.*

has·tate (has'tāt) *adj. Bot.* Triangular or halberd-shaped, with the base diverging on each side into an acute lobe: said of plant leaves. Also **has'tat·ed.** [<L *hasta* spear]

haste (hāst) *n.* **1** Celerity of movement or action; speed; dispatch. **2** Necessity for speed; urgency. **3** Hurry; precipitancy; unpremeditated or impulsive action. —*v.t.* & *v.i.* **hast·ed, hast·ing** *Poetic* To hasten. [<OF <Gmc.]

hast·en (hā'sən) *v.t.* To cause to hurry or move quickly; expedite. —*v.i.* To move with speed or haste; be quick; hurry. See synonyms under FLY, PUSH, QUICKEN. —**hast'en·er** *n.*

Has·tings (häs'tingz) A county borough on the coast of SE Sussex, England; scene of **Battle of Hastings,** 1066, fought at Senlac Hill, where William of Normandy defeated Harold II of England.

Has·tings (häs'tingz), **Warren,** 1732–1818, first British governor general of India.

hast·y (hās'tē) *adj.* **hast·i·er, hast·i·est 1** Acting with, or done with haste. **2** Acting or done without due consideration; rash. **3** Quick-tempered; impetuous; irascible. **4** *Obs.* Eager; in a hurry. See synonyms under IMPETUOUS, SWIFT. —**hast'i·ly** *adv.* —**hast'i·ness** *n.*

hasty pudding 1 Pudding made of meal, seasoning, and boiling water or milk. **2** *U.S.* Cornmeal mush.

hat (hat) *n.* **1** A covering for the head, generally with a crown and brim; also, any piece of millinery worn for a hat. **2** A cardinal's red hat; hence, the rank or dignity of a cardinal. —**to pass the hat** To take up a collection. —**to talk through one's hat** *Colloq.* To talk nonsense; also, to bluff. —**under one's hat** *Colloq.* Secret; private: Keep it *under your hat.* [OE *hæt.* Akin to HOOD.]

Hat may appear as a combining form in hyphemes or solidemes, or as the first element in two-word phrases; as in:

hat brim	**hatmaking**	**hat–shaped**
hat brush	**hat peg**	**hat shop**
hatful	**hatpin**	**hat–sizing**
hatless	**hatrack**	**hat–tipping**
hatmaker	**hatrail**	**hat–wearing**

hat·band (hat'band') *n.* A narrow ribbon or other band of silk or cloth surrounding a hat just above the brim.

hat·box (hat'boks') *n.* A case, often of leather, for a hat; also, a small compartment in a trunk for a hat.

hatch[1] (hach) *n.* **1** *Naut.* **a** An opening in the deck of a vessel affording passage to the hold, as for cargo, etc.: also called *hatchway.* **b** The cover over a hatch. **2** Any similar opening in the floor or roof of a warehouse or other building, or the cover or grating for such an opening. **3** A door or gate with an opening above; a divided door; wicket. **4** A sluice gate. [OE *hæcc* grating]

hatch[2] (hach) *v.t.* **1** To bring forth (young) from the egg by incubation. **2** To bring forth young from (the egg). **3** To devise, as a plan; contrive secretly, as a plot. —*v.i.* **4** To emerge from the egg. **5** To produce young. —*n.* **1** The act of hatching. **2** The brood hatched at one time. **3** The result or outcome of any plan. [ME *hacchen;* origin uncertain]

hatch[3] (hach) *v.t.* To mark with hatchings. —*n.* A shade line in drawing or engraving. [< OF *hacher* chop <*hache* an ax <Gmc.]

hatch·back (hach'bak') *n.* An automobile having a hatch or door at the back of the sloping roof.

hatch·el (hach'əl) *n.* An implement for cleaning flax or hemp, consisting of a set of teeth fastened in a board: also *hackle.* —*v.t.* **hatch·eled** or **·elled, hatch·el·ing** or **·el·ling 1** To comb or clean with a hatchel, as flax or hemp: also *hackle.* **2** *Rare* To irritate; heckle. [ME *hechele*] —**hatch'el·er, hatch'el·ler** *n.*

add,āce,câre,pälm; end,ēven; it,īce; odd,ōpen,ôrder; tŏŏk,pōōl; up,bûrn; ə = a in *above,* e in *sicken,* i in *clarity,* o in *melon,* u in *focus;* yōō = u in *fuse;* oi,oil; ou,pout; ch,check; g,go; ng,ring; th,thin; th,this; zh,vision. Foreign sounds à,œ,ü,kh,ṅ; and ◆ : see page xx. <from; + plus; ? possibly.

hatch·er (hach′ər) *n.* **1** A bird that incubates; also, an incubator. **2** One who hatches or contrives.

hatch·er·y (hach′ər·ē) *n. pl.* **·er·ies** A place where eggs are hatched; especially, a place for producing poultry on a large scale, or a place for hatching fish to restock streams.

hatch·et (hach′it) *n.* A small short-handled ax, for use with one hand. **— to bury the hatchet** To cease from hostilities; forget injuries; make peace. [<F *hachette,* dim. of *hache* an ax <Gmc.]

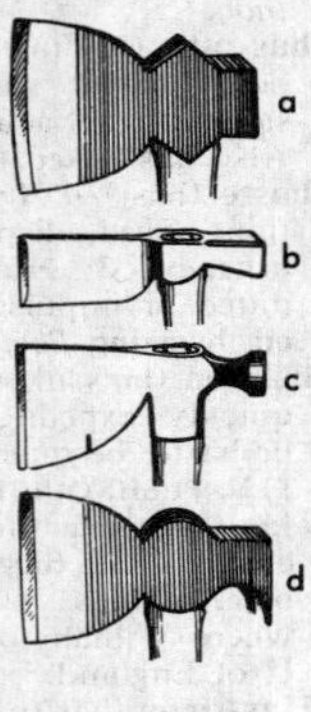

HATCHETS
a. Broad.
b. Lathing.
c. Half.
d. Claw.

hatch·et·face (hach′it·fās′) *n.* A thin sharp-featured face. **— hatch′et-faced′** *adj.*

hatch·ing (hach′ing) *n.* In drawing or engraving, the marking with fine parallel lines for shading; also, the result of such lines or shading.

hatch·ment (hach′mənt) *n. Her.* The armorial bearings of a deceased person, so blazoned as to indicate the rank, sex, etc.: usually in a lozenge-shaped panel, as over a tomb. [Alter. of ACHIEVEMENT]

hatch·way (hach′wā′) See HATCH[1].

hate (hāt) *v.* **hat·ed, hat·ing** *v.t.* **1** To regard with extreme aversion; have great dislike for; detest. **2** To be unwilling; dislike: with a clause or an infinitive as object: I *hate* doing that. **—** *v.i.* **3** To feel hatred. See synonyms under ABHOR. **—** *n.* **1** Intense aversion; animosity; malignity. **2** A person or thing detested. See synonyms under HATRED. [OE *hatian*] **— hat′a·ble** *adj.* **— hat′er** *n.*

hate·ful (hāt′fəl) *adj.* **1** Exciting strong aversion; odious. **2** Feeling or manifesting hatred. **— hate′ful·ly** *adv.* **— hate′ful·ness** *n.*

hath (hath) Has: archaic or poetic third person singular, present tense, of HAVE.

Hath·a·way (hath′ə·wā), **Anne,** 1557?–1623, wife of Shakespeare.

Ha·thor (hä′thôr) The Egyptian goddess of love and joy: identified with the Greek *Aphrodite*: represented as having a cow's head.

Ha·thor·ic (hə·thôr′ik, -thor′-) *adj. Archit.* Denoting columns with sculptures on the capitals representing the head of Hathor.

ha·tred (hā′trid) *n.* Bitter dislike or aversion; antipathy; animosity; enmity.

Synonyms: abhorrence, anger, animosity, antipathy, aversion, detestation, dislike, enmity, grudge, hate, hostility, malevolence, malice, malignity, odium, rancor, repugnance, resentment, revenge, spite. *Repugnance* applies to that which one feels when summoned or impelled to do or to endure something from which he instinctively draws back. *Aversion* is the turning away of the mind or feelings from some person or thing, or from some course of action, etc. *Hate,* or *hatred,* as applied to persons, is intense and continued *aversion,* usually with disposition to injure; *anger* is sudden and brief, *hatred* is lingering and enduring. As applied to things, *hatred* is intense *aversion,* with desire to destroy or remove; *hatred* of evil is a righteous passion, akin to *abhorrence,* but more vehement. *Malice* involves the active intent to injure; *malignity* is deep, lingering, and venomous, while often impotent to act; *rancor* (akin to *rancid*) is cherished *malignity* that has soured and festered and is virulent and implacable. *Spite* is petty *malice* that delights to inflict stinging pain; *grudge* is deeper than *spite*; it is sinister and bitter; *resentment* always holds itself to be justifiable, but looks less certainly to action than *grudge* or *revenge.* Compare ABOMINATION, ANGER, ANTIPATHY, ENMITY, REVENGE. *Antonyms*: see synonyms for FRIENDSHIP, LOVE.

Ha·tshep·sut (ha·chep′so͞ot) Queen of Egypt 1501?–1481? B.C.

hat·ter (hat′ər) *n.* **1** One who makes or deals in hats. **2** *Austral.* A person who lives alone, especially in a remote area.

Hat·ter·as (hat′ər·əs), **Cape** A promontory on SE **Hatteras Island,** a narrow barrier beach between the Atlantic and Pamlico Sound off North Carolina.

hat·te·ri·a (ha·tir′ē·ə) *n.* The sphenodon. [Origin uncertain]

hat-tree (hat′trē′) *n.* A frame with hooks or pegs on which to hang hats.

hau·berk (hô′bûrk) *n.* A coat of chain mail. [<OF *hauberc* <OHG *halsberc* neck-protector]

haugh·ty (hô′tē) *adj.* **·ti·er, ·ti·est** **1** Proud and disdainful; arrogant. **2** *Obs.* Lofty; bold. [<OF *haut* high] **— haugh′ti·ly** *adv.* **— haugh′·ti·ness** *n.*

Synonyms: austere, churlish, cold, contemptuous, disdainful, distant, high, insolent, proud, reserved, stately, supercilious, surly, unapproachable, uncivil, unsociable. Compare ABSOLUTE, ARROGANT, IMPERIOUS, PROUD.

haul (hôl) *v.t.* **1** To pull or draw with force; drag. **2** To transport as if by pulling, as in a truck or cart. **3** *Naut.* To shift the course of (a ship), especially so as to sail nearer the wind. **—** *v.i.* **4** To drag or pull. **5** To shift in direction: said of the wind. **6** To change one's views or course of action. **7** *Naut.* To change course, especially so as to sail nearer the wind. See synonyms under DRAW. **— to haul off** **1** To draw back the arm so as to deliver a blow. **2** *Naut.* To change course so as to move further away from an object. **— to haul up** **1** To come to a stop. **2** *Naut.* To sail nearer the wind. **—** *n.* **1** A pulling with force. **2** That which is obtained by hauling. **3** The drawing of a fish net. **4** The amount of fish caught in a single drawing of a net. **5** The distance over which anything is hauled. ◆ Homophone: *hall.* [<OF *haler* <Gmc.]

haul·age (hô′lij) *n.* **1** The act, process, or operation of hauling. **2** A charge for hauling. **3** The charge made by a railroad company for the use of a line or track.

haul·er (hô′lər) *n.* **1** One who or that which hauls; specifically a carter: also *Brit.* **haul·ier** (hôl′yər). **2** A fish-hauling apparatus.

haulm (hôm) *n.* **1** The stalks or stems of any of the grains, or of hops, beans, etc. **2** Any plant stem. Also spelled *halm.* [OE *healm*] **— haulm′y** *adj.*

haul·yard (hôl′yərd) See HALYARD.

haun (hôn) *n. Scot.* A hand.

haunch (hônch, hänch) *n.* **1** The fleshy part of the hip and buttock; the hip or a hindquarter: a *haunch* of venison. **2** *Archit.* The part of an arch on either side of its crown: also spelled *hanch.* [<OF *hanche* <Gmc.] **— haunched** *adj.*

haunch bone The innominate bone.

haunt (hônt, hänt) *v.t.* **1** To visit frequently or customarily in disembodied form; appear to as a ghost or other spirit. **2** To recur persistently to the mind or memory of: The face *haunts* me. **3** To visit often; frequent, as a saloon. **—** *v.i.* **4** To make ghostly appearances. **5** *Rare* To be present often. **—** *n.* **1** A place often visited; specifically, a place where wild animals come habitually to feed. **2** *Dial.* A ghost. [<OF *hanter*]

haunt·ed (hôn′tid, hän′-) *adj.* Frequently visited or resorted to, especially by ghosts or apparitions.

haunt·ing (hôn′ting, hän′-) *adj.* Difficult to forget; frequently occurring to memory: a *haunting* melody. **— haunt′ing·ly** *adv.*

Haupt·mann (houpt′män), **Gerhart,** 1862–1946, German poet and dramatist.

Hau·ra·ki Gulf (hou·rä′kē, -rak′ē) An inlet of the South Pacific in northern North Island, New Zealand.

Hau·sa (hou′sə) *n.* **1** A Negroid people occupying a tract of central Sudan north of the confluence of the Niger and Benue rivers. **2** The language of these people, bearing some resemblance to the Sudanic family, and much used as a medium of commerce. Also **Haus′sa.**

hause (hôs) *n. Scot.* The throat; halse.

hau·sen (hô′zən, *Ger.* hou′zən) *n.* The Russian sturgeon (genus *Acipenser*). [<G]

Haus·frau (hous′frou′) *n. German* Housewife.

Haus·ho·fer (hous′hō·fər), **Karl,** 1869–1946, German general and exponent of geopolitics.

haus·mann·ite (hous′mən·īt) *n.* A submetallic brownish-black manganese oxide, Mn_3O_4, crystallizing in the tetragonal system. [after J. F. L. *Hausmann,* 1782–1859, German metallurgist]

Hauss·mann (ōs·män′), **Baron Georges,** 1809–1891, French administrator; redesigned Paris streets and public buildings.

haus·tel·lum (hôs·tel′əm) *n. pl.* **·tel·la** (-tel′ə) *Zool.* The proboscis or sucking organ of certain insects and crustaceans. [<NL, dim of L *haustrum* water-drawing machine < *haurire* draw]

haus·to·ri·um (hôs·tôr′ē·əm, -tō′rē-) *n. pl.* **·to·ri·a** (-tôr′ē·ə, -tō′rē·ə) *Bot.* A root or sucker found in certain fungi and parasitic plants by which they absorb nutriment without damage to the host. [<NL <L *haustor* drainer < *haurire* draw]

haut·boy (hō′boi, ō′-) *n.* A woodwind instrument; oboe. [<F *hautbois* < *haut* high (in tone) + *bois* wood]

haute cou·ture (ōt ko͞o·tür′) *French* High fashion, represented especially by the leading designers of stylish apparel.

haute cui·sine (ōt kwē·zēn′) *French* An elaborate or elegant cuisine.

Haute-Ga·ronne (ōt·gȧ·rôn′) A department in SW France; 2,457 square miles; capital, Toulouse.

Haute-Marne (ōt·mȧrn′) A department in NE France; 2,416 square miles; capital, Charmont.

Haute-Saône (ōt·sōn′) A department in E France; 2,074 square miles; capital, Vesoul.

Haute-Sa·voie (ōt·sȧ·vwȧ′) A department in E France; 1,774 square miles; capital, Annecy.

hau·teur (hō·tûr′, *Fr.* ō·tœr′) *n.* Haughty manner or spirit; haughtiness. [<F]

Haute-Vol·ta (ōt·vôl·tȧ′) The French name for UPPER VOLTA.

haut monde (ō môṅd′) *French* The upper class; high society.

Haut-Rhin (ō·raṅ′) A department of eastern France; 1,354 square miles; capital, Colmar.

Ha·van·a (hə·van′ə) **1** A province of western Cuba; 3,174 square miles. **2** Its capital, the largest port of the West Indies and capital of Cuba: Spanish *La Habana.* **— Hav·a·nese** (hav′ə·nēz′, -nēs′) *adj.* & *n.*

Ha·vas (ȧ·vȧ′) A French news agency.

have (hav) *v.t.* Present indicative: I, you, we, they **have** (*Archaic* **thou hast**), he, she, it **has** (*Archaic* **hath**); past indicative **had** (*Archaic* **thou hadst**); present subjunctive **have**; past subjunctive **had**; *pp.* **had**; *ppr.* **hav·ing** **1** To hold as a possession; own. **2** To possess as a characteristic, attribute, etc.: He *has* only one leg; The very walls *have* ears. **3** To receive; get: I *had* a letter this morning. **4** To hold in the mind; entertain, as an opinion or a doubt. **5** To manifest or exercise: *Have* patience! **6** To experience; undergo: to *have* an operation. **7** To be affected with: to *have* a cold. **8** To carry on; engage in: to *have* a party. **9** To cause to be: to *have* someone shot; *Have* him leave. **10** To allow or permit; tolerate: I will *have* no interference. **11** To possess a certain relation to: to *have* the wind at one's back. **12** To be in relationship to or association with: to *have* three children. **13** To bring forth or beget (young): to *have* a baby. **14** To maintain or declare: so rumor *has* it. **15** *Colloq.* To gain or possess an advantage over; baffle: He *had* me there. **16** *Colloq.* To trick; cheat: I've been *had!* **17** To engage in sexual intercourse with. **—** *auxiliary* As an auxiliary *have* is used: **a** With past participles to form perfect tenses expressing completed action: often with the addition of other auxiliary verbs: I *have* gone; I *have* been given; I shall *have* gone. **b** With the infinitive to express obligation or compulsion: I *have* to go. **— to have at** To attack. **— to have done** To stop; desist. **— to have it in for** *Colloq.* To hold a grudge against. **— to have it out** To continue a fight or discussion to a final settlement. **— to have on** To be wearing; be clothed in. ◆ *Have* is used in the form *had* (early *hadde,* past subjunctive) in certain phrases of preference: you *had better* hurry = You would be wiser to hurry; I *had rather* (or *liefer*) die = I would prefer to die. **—** *n.* A person or country possessing relatively much wealth. [OE *habban*]

Synonyms: hold, occupy, own, possess. *Have* is applied to whatever belongs to or is connected with one; a man may be said to *have* what is his own, what he has borrowed, what has been entrusted to him, or what he has stolen. To *possess* a thing is to *have* the ownership with control and enjoyment of it. To *hold* is to *have* in one's hand, or securely in one's control; a man *holds* his friend's coat for a moment, or he *holds* a struggling horse; he *holds* a promissory note, or *holds* an office.

To *own* is to *have* the right of property in; to *possess* is to *have* that right in actual exercise; to *occupy* is to *have* possession and use with or without ownership. A man *occupies* his own house or a room in a hotel; he may *own* a farm of which he is not in possession because a tenant *occupies* it and is determined to *hold* it. To be in possession differs from *possess* in that to *possess* denotes both right and fact, while to be in possession denotes simply the fact with no affirmation as to the right. To *have* reason is to be endowed with the faculty; to be in possession of one's reason denotes that the faculty is in actual present exercise.

Ha·vel (hä′fəl) A river in NE East Germany, flowing 215 miles south to the Elbe.

have·lock (hav′lok) *n.* A cover for a military cap, made with a long rear flap, as a protection from the sun. [after Sir Henry *Havelock*, 1795–1857, British general]

ha·ven (hā′vən) *n.* **1** A place of anchorage for ships; a harbor; port. **2** A refuge; shelter. See synonyms under SHELTER. —*v.t.* To shelter (a vessel, etc.) in or as in a haven. [OE *hæfen*]

have–not (hav′not′) *n.* A person or country relatively lacking in wealth: the haves and *have–nots*.

have·n't (hav′ənt) Contraction of HAVE NOT.

hav·er[1] (hav′ər, häv′-, av′-, äv′-) *n. Scot.* Oats.

ha·ver[2] (hā′vər) *v.i. Scot.* To babble.

hav·er·el (hä′vər·əl, ā′-) *adj.* Half–witted; silly. Also **hav′·rel** (hav′rəl).

hav·er·meal (hav′ər·mēl′, häv′-, av′-, äv′) *n. Scot.* Oatmeal.

ha·vers (hā′vərz) *n. Scot.* Foolish talk.

hav·er·sack (hav′ər·sak) *n.* A bag, slung from the shoulder, for a soldier's rations. [<F *havresac* <G *habersack* oat sack]

Ha·ver·sian canals (hə·vûr′shən) *Anat.* The numerous channels for capillary blood vessels in bone substance. [after Clopton *Havers*, 1650–1702, English anatomist]

hav·er·sine (hav′ər·sin) *n. Trig.* Half of a versed sine.

haves and have–nots The rich and the poor; of nations, those possessing and those lacking the raw materials for autarchy.

hav·ing (hav′ing) *n. Scot.* Good behavior or breeding; good manners.

hav·iour (hāv′yər) *n. Obs.* Behavior. Also **hav′·ior**.

hav·oc (hav′ək) *n.* **1** General carnage or destruction; ruin. **2** Tumultuous disorder, confusion, or uproar. See synonyms under MASSACRE —**to cry havoc** To give a signal for pillage and destruction. —*v.t.* **hav·ocked**, **hav·ock·ing** *Rare* To lay waste; destroy. [<OF *havot* plunder <Gmc.]

Ha·vre (hä′vər, -vrə; *Fr.* äv′r′), **Le** A port of NW France on the English Channel. Founded as **Ha–vre–le–Grâce** (äv′r′·də·gräs′).

haw[1] (hô) *interj.* A meaningless utterance occurring in hesitating or drawling speech. —*v.i.* To hesitate in speaking.

haw[2] (hô) *n.* The fruit of the hawthorn. [OE *haga*]

haw[3] (hô) *n.* **1** The nictitating membrane or third eyelid of certain animals. **2** *pl.* A disease of this membrane. [Origin uncertain]

haw[4] (hô) *n. & interj.* An order to turn to the left or near side in driving, usually to a yoked team without reins: opposed to *gee.* —*v.t. & v.i.* To turn to the left. [Origin uncertain]

Ha·wai·i (hə·wä′ē, hə·wī′yə) **1** A State of the United States comprising the Hawaiian Islands; 6,435 square miles; capital, Honolulu; entered the Union Aug. 21, 1959; nickname, *Aloha State*: Abbr. HI **2** The largest of the Hawaiian Islands; 4,030 square miles; chief town, Hilo.

Ha·wai·ian (hə·wī′yən) *adj.* Of or pertaining to Hawaii or its inhabitants. —*n.* **1** A native or naturalized inhabitant of Hawaii. **2** The Polynesian language of the aboriginal inhabitants of Hawaii.

Hawaiian Islands A group of islands in the North Pacific constituting the State of Hawaii: formerly *Sandwich Islands*.

Hawaii National Park Two volcanic areas containing the active volcanoes Mauna Loa and Kilauea on the island of Hawaii and the extinct crater of Haleakala on Maui Island; 276 square miles; established 1916.

Ha·wash (hä′wäsh) A former name for AWASH.

haw·finch (hô′finch′) *n.* The European grosbeak (genus *Coccothraustes*), having a very large beak.

haw–haw[1] (hô′hô′) *n.* A loud coarse laugh.

haw–haw[2] (hô′hô′) See HA–HA.

Haw–Haw, (hô′hô′), **Lord** Sobriquet of William Joyce, 1906–46, born in the United States, propagandist for Germany in World War II, executed as a British traitor.

hawk[1] (hôk) *n.* **1** A diurnal bird of prey (family *Accipitridae*) with relatively short rounded wings, a hooked beak, and strong claws; including the North American species, Cooper's hawk (*Accipiter cooperi*) and the sharp–shinned hawk (*A. velox*). **2** The goshawk (genus *Astur*) and the red–tailed hawk (genus *Buteo*). **3** Any falconine bird except a vulture or an eagle, as a falcon, buzzard, or kite. **4** One who seeks to resolve a war primarily by means of military force: opposed to *dove[1]* (def. 4). —*v.i.* **1** To hunt game with hawks; practice falconry. **2** To fly in search of prey; soar, as a hawk. [OE *hafoc, hafuc*]

AMERICAN ROUGH–LEGGED HAWK (About 20 to 23 inches)

hawk[2] (hôk) *v.t. & v.i.* To cry (goods) for sale in the streets or in public places; peddle. [Back formation <HAWKER[2]]

hawk[3] (hôk) *v.t.* To cough up (phlegm). —*v.i.* To clear the throat with a coughing sound. —*n.* A forcible effort to raise phlegm from the throat; also, the sound of this. [Imit.]

hawk[4] (hôk) *n.* A small square board with a handle underneath, used to hold plaster or mortar. [Origin uncertain]

hawk·bill (hôk′bil′) *n.* A small tropical marine turtle (*Eretmochelys imbricata*) which furnishes the best grade of tortoise shell used in commerce: also **hawk's–bill**.

hawk·er[1] (hô′kər) *n.* One who hunts with hawks; a falconer.

hawk·er[2] (hô′kər) *n.* A street peddler; one who cries goods for sale in the streets. [< MLG *hoker* a peddler, huckster]

Hawk·eye (hôk′ī′) *n.* A native or inhabitant of Iowa.

Hawk·eye (hôk′ī′) In Cooper's *Last of the Mohicans*, a sobriquet of Leatherstocking or Natty Bumppo.

hawk·eyed (hôk′īd′) *adj.* Having keen, piercing eyes; keen–sighted.

Hawkeye State Nickname of IOWA.

hawk·ing (hô′king) *n.* The sport of hunting small game with hawks or falcons; falconry.

Haw·kins (hô′kinz), **Sir John,** 1532–1595, English admiral; aided defeat of Spanish Armada. Also **Haw′kyns.** —**Sir Anthony Hope,** 1863–1933, English novelist; wrote under the name *Anthony Hope*.

hawk·ish (hôk′ish) *adj.* Disposed to rely on military force to resolve a war: opposed to *dovish*.

hawk moth A large stout–bodied moth (family *Sphingidae*) which flies by twilight and sucks the nectar from flowers: also called *hummingbird moth*.

hawk's–beard (hôks′bird′) *n.* Any species of a genus (*Crepis*) of European herbs: so called from the long bristly pappus.

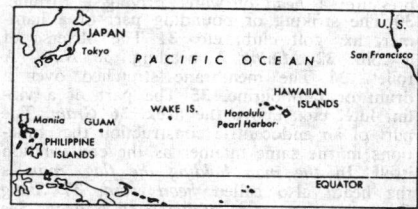

hawks·beak (hôks′bēk) *n. Archit.* A compound molding, often ornamented with a Doric leaf pattern.

hawk's–bill turtle (hôks′bil′) See HAWKBILL.

hawk's–eye (hôks′ī′) *n.* **1** The American golden plover (*Pluvialis dominica*). **2** The tiger–eye.

hawk·shaw (hôk′shô) *n. Colloq.* A detective: a humorous term. [after a character in *The Ticket of Leave Man* by Tom Taylor, 1817–1880, English novelist]

hawk·weed (hôk′wēd′) *n.* Any species of a genus (*Hieracium*) of weedy perennial herbs of the composite family having small yellow or orange flowers.

Ha·worth (hā′wûrth), **Sir Walter Norman,** 1883–1950, English chemist.

hawse (hôz) *n. Naut.* **1** The part of a vessel's bow having openings, usually steel–lined, for the passage of cables. **2** A hawsehole. **3** The situation of the cables that lead from a moored vessel to her anchors. **4** The horizontal distance between the vessel and her anchors. [<ON *hals* neck, bow of a ship]

hawse·hole (hôz′hōl′) *n. Naut.* A hole in the bow of a vessel for the passage of a cable or hawser.

haw·ser (hô′zər) *n. Naut.* A large rope or cable used in mooring, towing, etc. [<OF *haucier* lift]

haw·ser–laid (hô′zər·lād′) *adj.* Made of three small ropes laid up into one; cable–laid.

haw·thorn (hô′thôrn) *n.* A thorny, spring–flowering, ornamental shrub or small tree of the rose family (genus *Crataegus*) with white or pink flowers and small pome fruits called *haws*. The American **downy hawthorn** is the State flower of Missouri. [OE *haguthorn*]

Haw·thorne (hô′thôrn), **Nathaniel,** 1804–1864, U.S. novelist.

hay[1] (hā) *n.* Grass, clover, or the like, cut and dried for fodder. —**to hit the hay** *U.S. Slang* To go to bed. —**to make hay while the sun shines** To take full advantage of an opportunity. —*v.t.* **1** To make, as clover, into hay. **2** To feed with hay. **3** To plant (land) with hay. —*v.i.* **4** To make hay. [OE *hēg*]

hay[2] (hā) *n. Obs.* A net or snare, especially a net enclosing the burrow, hole, or haunt of an animal. [<AF *haie*; ult. origin uncertain]

hay[3] (hā) *n. Obs.* A hedge, palisade, or fence; also, a place enclosed by such. [OE *hege*]

hay[4] (hā) *n.* A country dance with a winding in–and–out movement. [<MF *haye*]

Hay (hā), **John,** 1838–1905, U.S. statesman, diplomat, author, and poet.

hay·cock (hā′kok′) *n.* A dome–shaped pile of hay in the field

Hay·dn (hīd′n), **Franz Joseph,** 1732–1809, Austrian composer.

Hayes (hāz), **Helen,** born 1900, U.S. actress: married name Mrs. Charles MacArthur. —**Roland,** born 1887, U.S. Negro tenor. —**Rutherford Birchard,** 1822–93, president of the United States 1877–81.

hay fever *Pathol.* An annually recurring catarrhal affection of the mucous membranes of the eyes and air passages, caused chiefly by the pollen of certain plants.

hay foot One of the alternate marching steps in military drill, as in the phrase *hayfoot, straw foot*: from the alleged use of hay and straw to help country recruits tell the difference between right and left.

hay·fork (hā′fôrk′) *n.* **1** A long–handled fork for turning or pitching hay by hand. **2** A large power–driven fork for moving hay.

hay·ing (hā′ing) *n.* The act or process of cutting, curing, and storing hay.

hay·loft (hā′lôft′, -loft′) *n.* A loft in a barn or stable for storing hay.

hay·mak·er (hā′mā′kər) *n.* **1** One who makes hay, especially, one who spreads it to dry. **2** A haytedder. **3** A rustic dance. **4** *Colloq.* A wide, swinging blow of the fist; in boxing, a knockout punch.

Hay·mar·ket (hā′mär′kit) **1** A street in London between Piccadilly Circus and Pall Mall; site of many theaters. **2** A square in Chicago; site of a riot for better labor conditions, 1886.

hay·mow (hā′mou′) *n.* **1** A mass of hay; especially, one stored in a loft or bay. **2** A hayloft.

Haynes (hānz), **Elwood,** 1857–1925, U.S. inventor; pioneer automobile designer.

hay·rack (hā′rak′) *n.* **1** A broad, long, open frame or rack mounted on wheels or placed on a wagon body, in which hay, straw, etc.,

are hauled. 2 A framework for holding hay to feed cattle, horses, etc.

hay ride A pleasure ride in a wagon or hayrack half full of hay or straw.

Hays (hāz), **Will H.,** 1879–1954, U.S. politician; first president of the Motion Picture Producers and Distributors of America.

hay seed Grass seed; also, the mingled seeds, chaff, etc., that fall from hay, as on a barn floor.

hay·seed (hā′sēd′) *n. U.S. Slang* A country person; a rustic.

hay·stack (hā′stak′) *n.* A conical pile of hay, stacked in the open air, and sometimes covered. Also **hay′rick′.**

hay·ted·der (hā′ted′ər) *n.* One who or that which teds hay; especially, a wheeled farm implement for stirring and spreading newly cut hay.

Hay·ti·an (hā′tē·ən, -shən) See HAITIAN.

hay·ward (hā′wôrd′, -wərd) *n. Obs.* An officer of a parish, township, or manor charged with inspecting fences and enclosures for cattle or impounding strays. [< HAY³ + WARD]

hay·wire (hā′wīr′) *n.* Wire for baling hay. —*adj. U.S. Slang* **1** Confused; mixed up; scrambled. **2** Crazy: to go *haywire.* [Slang sense < *haywire outfit,* loggers' term for a camp with poor or broken equipment which had to be mended with haywire]

Ha·za (hä′zä), **El** See HASA, EL.

haz·ard (haz′ərd) *n.* **1** Exposure to the chance of loss or injury; risk; peril. **2** A chance or fortuitous event or consequence, as the result of dice; a chance. **3** That which is hazarded, risked, or staked; the stake in gambling. **4** A gambling game played with a dice box and two dice by any number of players. **5** An obstacle on a golf course, such as a bunker, water (except casual water), sand trap, path, etc. **6** In English billiards, the pocketing of a ball, or the stroke that puts a ball into a pocket. When the object ball is forced into a pocket the stroke is called a **winning hazard;** when the striker's ball falls into a pocket after contact with the object ball it is a **losing hazard. 7** In court tennis, a stroke in which the server drives the ball, either direct from the racket or on the first bound, into the grille or the winning gallery. **—moral hazard** The element of personal character of a property-owner as it affects the willingness of an insurance company to insure his property. —*v.t.* **1** To put to hazard; imperil. **2** To venture; to take the risk involved in; risk. [< OF *hasard* < Arabic *alzahr* the die]

Synonyms (noun): accident, casualty, chance, contingency, danger, fortuity, jeopardy, peril, risk, venture. *Hazard* is the incurring of the possibility of loss or harm for the possibility of gain; *danger* may have no compensating alternative. In *hazard* the possibilities of gain or loss are nearly balanced; in *risk* the possibility of loss is the chief thought; in *chance* and *venture* the hope of good predominates; we speak of a merchant's *venture,* but of an insurance company's *risk;* one may be driven by circumstances to run a *risk;* he freely seeks a *venture;* we speak of the *chance* of winning, the *hazard* or *risk* of losing. A *contingency* is simply an indeterminable future event, which may or may not be attended with *danger* or *risk.* See ACCIDENT, DANGER. *Antonyms*: assurance, certainty, necessity, plan, protection, safeguard, safety, security, surety.

haz·ard·ous (haz′ər·dəs) *adj.* **1** Exposed to, exposing to, or involving danger of risk or loss. **2** Dependent on chance; fortuitous. See synonyms under PRECARIOUS. **—haz′ard·ous·ly** *adv.* **—haz′ard·ous·ness** *n.*

haze¹ (hāz) *n.* **1** Very fine suspended particles in the air, often with little or no moisture. **2** Dimness, as of perception or knowledge. [? Back formation < HAZY]

haze² (hāz) *v.t.* **hazed, haz·ing 1** *U.S.* To subject (new students) to pranks and humiliating horseplay. **2** *Naut.* To punish or harass by the imposition of heavy or disagreeable tasks. [< OF *haser* irritate] **—haz′er** *n.*

ha·zel (hā′zəl) *n.* **1** A bushy shrub or small tree of the birch family (genus *Corylus*) yielding a hard-shelled edible nut enclosed in a leafy involucre. **2** The wood or nut of the hazel. **3** The color of the hazelnut shell, a medium yellowish-brown. —*adj.* **1** Made of hazel wood. **2** Of the color of hazel. [OE *hæsel*] **—ha′zel·ly** *adj.*

Ha·zel (hā′zəl) A feminine personal name. [< Hebrew, God sees]

ha·zel·nut (hā′zəl·nut′) *n.* **1** The nut of the hazel: also called *filbert.* **2** The hazel shrub or tree.

haz·ing (hā′zing) *n.* **1** Imposition of heavy or disagreeable tasks. **2** *U.S.* The subjection (of new students or initiates) to pranks and humiliating ordeals. **3** A thorough beating.

Haz·litt (haz′lit), **William,** 1778–1830, English essayist.

ha·zy (hā′zē) *adj.* **haz·i·er, haz·i·est 1** Obscured with haze. **2** Figuratively, lacking clearness; dim; obscure. See synonyms under THICK. [Cf. OE *hasu* gray] **—haz′i·ly** *adv.* **—haz′i·ness** *n.*

haz·zan (khä·zän′, khä′zən) *n.* A cantor of a synagog: also spelled *chazan, khazen.* [< Hebrew *hazzan* prefect]

H-beam (āch′bēm′) *n.* A structural member having a cross-section resembling an H: also called *H-girder.*

H-bomb (āch′bom′) *n.* The hydrogen bomb.

he¹ (hē) *pron.* **1** The male person or being previously mentioned or understood, in the nominative case. **2** Anyone; any man: *He* who hesitates is lost. —*n.* A male, as a man, boy, bull, etc. [OE]

he² (hā) *n.* The fifth Hebrew letter. See ALPHABET.

He *Chem.* Helium (symbol He).

he- *combining form* Male; masculine: in hyphenated compounds: *he-goat.* [< HE]

head (hed) *n.* **1** The part of the body of an animal that contains the brain and the organs of special sense, the ears, eyes, mouth, and nose. ◆ Collateral adjective: *cephalic.* **2** Something having the shape or position of a head, or being in some way analogous to a head, as a barrel top. **3** The length of the head: taller by a *head.* **4** Mind; intelligence: He used his *head.* **5** Mental aptitude: a good *head* for mathematics. **6** Mental poise; self-possession: He kept his *head.* **7** A person: crowned *heads;* learned *heads.* **8** An individual or single entity, considered as a unit of counting: a price of two dollars a *head.* In this sense *head* may appear as a plural: six *head* of cattle. **9** The end regarded as the uppermost or higher part of something: the *head* of a valley, bed, table, etc. **10** The source, as of a river. **11** The fore or forward part of anything: the *head* of a column of troops. **12** The bow of a ship. **13** A headland; cape: chiefly in place names: Beachy *Head.* **14** A leader; chief; director. **15** The position or rank of a leader: the *head* of one's profession. **16** The top or summit of something: the *head* of the stairs; the *head* of a page. **17** The heading of a book, composition, chapter, etc. **18** The headlines of a single newspaper item. **19** A division of a subject, discourse, composition, or the like: He had little to say on that *head.* **20** Culmination: climax: to come to a *head.* **21** The maturated part of a boil or abscess before breaking. **22** Advance in the face of opposition: to make *head* against the storm. **23** A compact cluster of leaves or leaf stalks, as a *head* of cabbage, lettuce, or celery. **24** A rounded, compact bud, as a *head* of cauliflower. **25** A capitulum. **26** A cluster of cereal grain at the top of a stem. **27** The foam that rises to the surface of a fermenting liquid, as of beer or ale. **28** The measure of stored-up force or capacity, as of steam. **29** The height of a column or body of fluid above a certain point, considered as causing pressure: a *head* of water driving a turbine. **30** The striking or pounding part of a hammer, ax, golf club, etc. **31** The obverse of a coin. **32** *Mining* A heading. **33** *Naut.* A toilet. **34** The membrane stretched over a drum or tambourine. **35** The part of a violin, lute, etc., above the neck. **36** *Gram.* The part of an endocentric construction that functions in the same manner as the construction itself. In *the man holding the flag, man* is the head: also called *head word.* **37** *Slang* One who uses or is addicted to a drug. See synonyms under CHIEF, MASTER. —*v.t.* **1** To be first or most prominent on: to *head* the list. **2** To be chief or leader of; command. **3** To furnish with a head. **4** To cut off the head or top of, as a person or tree. **5** To turn or direct the course of: to *head* a vessel toward shore. **6** To pass around the head of: to *head* a stream. **7** To excel; beat, as in sports. **8** In soccer, to bunt (the ball) with the head. —*v.i.* **9** To move in a specified direction or toward a specified point. **10** To come to or form a head. **11** To originate; rise: said of rivers and streams. **—to head off** To intercept the course of: We'll *head* him *off* at the pass. **—to head up** *Colloq.* To be the leader or manager of; command. See synonyms under LEAD, PRECEDE. —*adj.* **1** Principal; chief. **2** Situated at the top or front. **3** Bearing against the front: a *head* wind. [OE *hēafod*]

-head *suffix* Condition, state, totality: *godhead.* [ME *-hede*]

head·ache (hed′āk′) *n.* **1** A pain in the head. **2** *Colloq.* A source of vexation or trouble. **—head′a′chy** (-ā′kē) *adj.*

head·band (hed′band′) *n.* **1** A band worn on the head. **2** A decorative terminal cord or roll forming the end of the inner back of a book. **3** A decorative band at the head of a page or chapter in a printed book.

head·board (hed′bôrd′, -bōrd′) *n.* A board placed at or forming the head, as of a bed.

head·cheese (hed′chēz′) *n.* A pressed and jellied cheeselike mass made of small pieces of the head and feet of a hog or calf.

head·dress (hed′dres′) *n.* **1** A covering or ornament for the head. **2** The style in which the hair is arranged; coiffure.

head·ed (hed′id) *adj.* **1** Furnished with a head. **2** Formed or grown into a head, as cabbage. **3** Furnished with a heading.

-headed *combining form* Having a (specified number or kind of) head: clear-*headed.*

head·er (hed′ər) *n.* **1** A person who makes or puts on heads, as in barrelmaking. **2** *Colloq.* A plunge or fall headforemost, as diving. **3** One of various machines or tools for making, attaching, or removing heads; especially, a kind of harvesting machine that cuts the ripe heads off grain in the field. **4** A brick or stone placed with its end toward the face of a wall. **5** In building, a timber resting in trimmers and carrying the ends or heads of the tail beams. **6** A pipe, duct, channel, or conduit which serves as a central distributing point of a fluid flow to auxiliary branches.

head·first (hed′fûrst′) *adv.* With the head first; precipitately. Also **head′fore′most′** (-fôr′mōst′, -məst, -fōr′-).

head gate The upstream gate of a canal lock; a watergate or floodgate of any race or sluice.

head·gear (hed′gir′) *n.* **1** A headdress or the like. **2** That part of the hoisting apparatus at the top of a mine shaft. **3** The parts of the harness that belong about the horse's head. **4** *Naut.* The running rigging of headsails.

head-hunt·ing (hed′hun′ting) *n.* Among certain savage tribes, the custom of decapitating slain enemies and preserving the heads as trophies. **—head′-hunt′er** *n.*

head·ing (hed′ing) *n.* **1** Something located at the head, as a title. **2** *Mining* A driftway in the line of a tunnel; also, any place where work is done in driving a horizontal passage. **3** The action of providing with a head. **4** Boards or other material from which the heads of casks, barrels, etc., are made. **5** A strip along the edge of a piece of lace; also, the part of a ruffle above the gathering line.

head·ker·chief (hed′kûr′chif) *n.* A kerchief for the head.

head·land (hed′lənd *for def. 1;* hed′land′ *for def. 2*) *n.* **1** A cliff projecting into the sea. **2** A strip of unplowed land at the ends of furrows or near a fence.

head·less (hed′lis) *adj.* **1** Without a head; decapitated. **2** Without a leader. **3** Stupid; erratic; brainless.

head·light (hed′līt′) *n.* A powerful light, as at the front of a locomotive, motor vehicle, or street car.

head·line (hed′līn′) *n.* **1** A word or words set in bold type at the head of a newspaper column or news story, indicating or summarizing the content, especially the heading of the main front-page story. **2** A line at the head of a page, containing title, page number, etc. **3** A line inside a hat where the brim joins the crown. **4** A rope attached to an animal's head. **5** *Naut.* A rope used to fasten the bow of a vessel to a pier or shore.

head·lin·er (hed′lī′nər) *n.* The main attraction at a theatrical performance; the actor or per-

former whose name appears in large letters.

head·lock (hed′lok′) *n.* A wrestling grip in which the head is held between the opponent's arm and body.

head·long (hed′lông′, -long′) *adv.* 1 Headfirst. 2 Without deliberation; rashly; recklessly. 3 With unbridled speed or force. —*adj.* Precipitate; impetuous; rash.

head man 1 A leader or person of authority in a community. 2 A North American Indian chief. 3 A workman in charge of other workers.

head·mas·ter (hed′mas′tər, -mäs′-) *n.* The principal of a school. —**head′mas′ter·ly** *adj.* — **head′mas′ter·ship** *n.*

head·mis·tress (hed′mis′tris) *n. fem.* The female principal of a school. —**head′mis′tress·ship** *n.*

head money 1 Prize money per head for prisoners captured in war, or for the apprehension of outlaws. 2 A per capita tax; a poll tax.

head·most (hed′mōst′) *adj.* Most advanced; foremost.

head-on (hed′on′, -ôn′) *adj. & adv.* Front end to front end; a *head-on* collision.

head over heels 1 Somersaulting or tumbling heels over head. 2 Completely: *head over heels* in love. 3 Rashly; impetuously.

head·phone (hed′fōn′) *n.* A device for telephone or radio reception, single or paired, usually attached by a band passing over the head.

head·piece (hed′pēs′) *n.* 1 A piece of armor to protect the head. 2 A decorative design at the top of a printed page. 3 The head; hence, the wits.

head·pin (hed′pin′) *n.* In tenpins, a kingpin.

head·quar·ters (hed′kwôr′tərz) *n. sing. & pl.* 1 The quarters or operating base of an officer in command, as of an army unit, police force, etc. 2 Any center of operations.

head·race (hed′rās′) *n.* The channel by which water is led to a water wheel, or to any machinery. [< HEAD + RACE²]

head resistance *Aeron.* Parasite drag.

head·rest (hed′rest′) *n.* Any device to support the head.

head·right (hed′rīt′) *n.* 1 The right of ownership to a piece of public land granted by a government to a head of a family settling on it; also, the land so granted. 2 In the State of Texas, a similar grant; also, the land so granted, usually 640 acres. 3 The right of a North American Indian to a share of the tribal property.

head·sail (hed′sāl′, -səl) *n. Naut.* A sail set forward of the foremast, as a jib; also, one set on the foremast.

head·set (hed′set′) *n.* A radio or telephone headphone.

head·ship (hed′ship) *n.* The office of a chief; chief authority.

heads·man (hedz′mən) *n. pl.* **-men** (-mən) A public executioner.

head·spin (hed′spin′) *n.* A wrestling movement used to break away from a half-nelson.

head·spring (hed′spring′) *n.* 1 The fountainhead; source. 2 A gymnastic feat in which the performer springs, without using his hands and using his head as lever, from a supine position to his feet.

head·stall (hed′stôl′) *n.* The part of a bridle that fits over the horse's head.

head·stand (hed′stand′) *n.* The act of holding one's body upside-down in a vertical position, with one's weight resting on one's head and, usually, on one's hands or arms.

head start An advance start; an advantage in time or distance, as in a handicap race.

head·stock (hed′stok′) *n. Mech.* One of various devices supporting the end or head of a part or member, as the live spindle of a lathe.

head·stone (hed′stōn′) *n.* 1 The stone at the head of a grave. 2 The cornerstone or keystone of a structure: also **head stone.**

head·strong (hed′strông′, -strong′) *adj.* 1 Stubbornly bent on having one's own way; obstinate; determined. 2 Involving or proceeding from wilfulness or obstinacy. —**head′strong·ly** *adv.* — **head′strong·ness** *n.*

head waiter An employee, as of a restaurant, who supervises the seating of guests, the serving of food and drink, etc.

head·wa·ters (hed′wô′tərz, -wot′ərz) *n. pl.* The waters at or near the source of any stream, river, or the like: sometimes in the singular.

head·way (hed′wā′) *n.* 1 Forward motion; momentum; progress. 2 The interval of time between consecutive trains, etc. 3 The clear distance under a girder arch, etc.

head wind A wind from ahead, blowing directly opposite to the course of a ship, airplane, etc.

head word 1 A word or expression that introduces or begins, as a chapter. 2 *Gram.* A head (def. 36).

head·work (hed′wûrk′) *n.* Mental labor. — **head′work·er** *n.* —**head′work′ing** *n.*

head·y (hed′ē) *adj.* **head·i·er, head·i·est** 1 Headstrong. 2 Tending to affect the head, as liquor. —**head′i·ly** *adv.* —**head′i·ness** *n.*

heal (hēl) *v.t.* 1 To restore to health or soundness; make healthy again; cure. 2 To bring about the remedy or cure of, as a wound or disease. 3 To remedy, repair, or counteract, as a quarrel, breach, etc. 4 To free from sin, grief, worry, etc.; purify: to *heal* the spirit. —*v.i.* 5 To become well or sound. 6 To perform a cure or cures. See synonyms under RECOVER. ♦ Homophone: *heel.* [OE *halan*] —**heal′a·ble** *adj.* —**heal′ing** *adj. & n.* —**heal′ing·ly** *adv.*

heal-all (hēl′ôl′) *n.* 1 A catholicon; remedy for all diseases. 2 The allheal.

heald (held) *n.* In weaving, a device for holding and guiding the heddles in a loom. [OE *hefeld*]

heal·er (hē′lər) *n.* 1 Someone or something that heals. 2 One who undertakes to heal through prayer and faith.

heal·some (hēl′səm) *adj. Scot.* Wholesome. — **heal′some·ness** *n.*

health (helth) *n.* 1 Soundness of any living organism. 2 General condition of body or mind, as to vigor and soundness. 3 A toast wishing health. —*adj.* 1 Pertaining to, connected with, or engaged in public-health work: *health* education, *health* inspector. 2 Conducive to good health: a *health* food. [OE *hoelth* < *hāl* whole]

Health, Education, and Welfare, Department of An executive department of the U.S. government (established in 1953), headed by the Secretary of Health, Education, and Welfare, which administers Federal services relating to health, education, and social security.

health food Any food believed to have special health-giving benefits.

health·ful (helth′fəl) *adj.* 1 Promoting health; salubrious. 2 Being in health: properly *healthy.* See synonyms under HEALTHY. —**health′ful·ly** *adv.* —**health′ful·ness** *n.*

health officer A quarantine officer; an officer of a health board.

health·y (hel′thē) *adj.* **health·i·er, health·i·est** 1 Having good health; sound; well. 2 Conducive to health; salutary: *healthy* recreation. 3 Indicative or characteristic of sound health: a *healthy* complexion. —**health′i·ly** *adv.* —**health′i·ness** *n.*

Synonyms: hale, healthful, hearty, hygienic, salubrious, salutary, sanitary, sound, strong, vigorous, well, wholesome. *Healthy* is correctly used to signify possessing or enjoying health or its results; as, a *healthy* person, a *healthy* condition. *Healthful* signifies promotive of health, tending or adapted to confer, preserve, or promote health; as, a *healthful* climate, a *healthful* diet. *Salubrious* is always used in the physical sense, and is chiefly applied to air or climate. *Salutary* is now chiefly used in the moral sense; as, a *salutary* lesson. See SANE. *Antonyms:* delicate, diseased, emaciated, exhausted, failing, fainting, fragile, frail, ill, sick, unhealthy, unsound, wasted, weak, worn.

heap (hēp) *n.* 1 A collection of things piled up; a pile; mass. 2 A large number; lot. 3 A crowd. 4 *Slang* An old, broken-down automobile. —*v.t.* 1 To pile into a heap; make a mound or mass of. 2 To fill or pile (a container) full or more than full. 3 To strew with heaps: to *heap* a field with bodies. 4 To give or bestow in great quantities: to *heap* insults on someone. 5 To give or bestow great quantities upon: to *heap* someone with riches. —*v.i.* 6 To form or rise in a heap or pile. —*adv.* Very; very much: North American Indian term. [OE *hēap* a crowd]

Synonyms (noun): accumulation, agglomeration, aggregate, aggregation, collection, drift, hoard, mass, pile, store. See COLLECTION, MASS.

heaped measure A measure in which the contents more than fill the container, rising in a mound above its rim. See STRUCK MEASURE.

heap·ing (hē′ping) *adj.* Having the contents raised above the top; heaped.

hear (hir) *v.* **heard** (hûrd), **hear·ing** *v.t.* 1 To perceive by means of the ear. 2 To listen to; give audience to: *Hear* what I say! 3 To attend as part of the audience: to *hear* a concert. 4 To learn or be informed of: I *hear* you are leaving town. 5 To listen to officially, judicially, or by way of examination: to *hear* a case in court; to *hear* a lesson. 6 To respond or accede to; grant: to *hear* a prayer. —*v.i.* 7 To perceive or be capable of perceiving sound by means of the ear. 8 To be informed or made aware; receive information: with *of, about,* or *from.* See synonyms under LISTEN. —**hear! hear!** *Brit.* Listen! An expression of approval accorded a public speaker. —**to hear of** To approve of: usually in the negative: He will not *hear of* it. [OE *hēran*] —**hear′er** *n.*

hear·ing (hir′ing) *n.* 1 The capacity to hear. 2 The special sense by which sounds are perceived. 3 An opportunity to be heard; audience. 4 The distance or space within which sound may be heard. 5 The examination of a person charged with an offense, and of the witnesses; a judicial trial, especially without a jury, as in an equity suit.

hearing aid Any of various portable instruments for the improvement of hearing, especially those which amplify sound waves by the use of microphones connected with transistors or vacuum tubes operated by small batteries.

hear·ing-loss (hir′ing-lôs′) *n.* A measure of defective hearing, expressed as a percentage of the tones normally audible under standard conditions: determined by audiograms.

heark·en (här′kən) See HARKEN.

Hearn (hûrn), **Lafcadio,** 1850–1904, U.S. writer born in Europe, who became a Japanese citizen under the name of Yakumo Koizumi.

hear·say (hir′sā′) *n.* Information received indirectly; common talk; report; rumor; also, hearsay evidence.

hearsay evidence Evidence, oral or written, derived from something the witness has heard others say; any evidence depending upon the credibility and competency of some person other than the witness: generally excluded but admissible in some litigations.

hearse (hûrs) *n.* 1 A vehicle for carrying the dead to the grave. 2 A symbolical triangular frame set with spikes, resembling teeth of a harrow, on which lighted candles are placed during the singing of Tenebrae in Holy Week. —*v.t.* **hearsed, hears·ing** 1 To put in or on a hearse. 2 To bury. [< F *herse* a harrow < L *hirpex, -icis;* so called because the frame for candles about a coffin resembled a harrow]

Hearst (hûrst), **William Randolph,** 1863–1951, U.S. publisher.

heart (härt) *n.* 1 The central organ of the

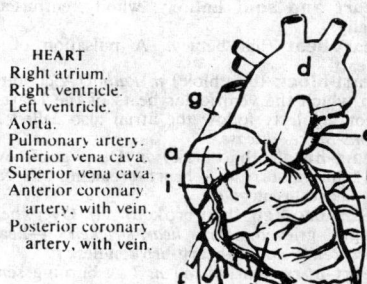

HEART
a. Right atrium.
b. Right ventricle.
c. Left ventricle.
d. Aorta.
e. Pulmonary artery.
f. Inferior vena cava.
g. Superior vena cava.
h. Anterior coronary artery, with vein.
i. Posterior coronary artery, with vein.

vascular system of animals; a hollow muscular structure which maintains the circulation of

the blood by alternate contraction (systole) and dilatation (diastole). ◆ Collateral adjective: *cardiac.* **2** The breast regarded as the seat of the heart. **3** The seat of the affections and emotions, as distinguished from the head as the center of intellect and will. **4** One's inmost thoughts or feelings: to pour out one's *heart.* **5** Affection; love: to win one's *heart.* **6** Tenderness; capacity for sympathy: to have no *heart.* **7** Courage; resolution; firmness of will: The men lost *heart.* **8** Ardor; enthusiasm; energy: He put his whole *heart* into the task. **9** Mood; spirit: a heavy *heart.* **10** A person, especially a dear or courageous one: a brave *heart.* **11** The central part of anything; the core: the *heart* of the city. **12** The inner part or core of a tree, plant, vegetable, etc. **13** The vital or essential part; the essence: the *heart* of the matter. **14** Anything represented as or shaped like a heart; especially the conventional roundish figure with a point opposite two lobes. **15** A playing card bearing red, heart-shaped spots or pips. **16** *pl.* The suit of such playing cards. **17** *pl.* A game of cards played with a full pack, in which the object is to take no hearts. —**after one's own heart** Suiting one perfectly; conforming to one's ideas; to one's taste: a man *after one's own heart.* —**at heart** At the center or bottom; essentially; substantially; in fact. —**athletic heart** Enlargement of the heart induced by excessive participation in athletic sports. —**by heart** By rote, so as to be memorized perfectly: said of recitations. —**from one's heart** With all sincerity. —**to have at heart** To cherish; be concerned for earnestly. —**to have one's heart in one's mouth** To be excessively excited or frightened. —**to have the heart** To be callous or cruel enough. —**to take to heart** To consider seriously. —**to wear one's heart on one's sleeve** To show one's feelings plainly. —**with all one's heart** Intensely; thoroughly; completely; wholly. —*v.t. Rare* **1** To hearten. **2** To place in the heart. —*v.i.* **3** To form a heart. ◆ Homophone: *hart.* [OE *heorte*]

Heart may appear as a combining form (in hyphemes or solidemes) or as the first element in two-word phrases; as in:

heart action	**heart murmur**
heart-affecting	**heart-purifying**
heart-angry	**heart-ravishing**
heart-bred	**heart-robbing**
heart-burdened	**heart-shaking**
heart-cheering	**heartsickening**
heart-chilling	**heartsickness**
heart complaint	**heart-sorrowing**
heart-corroding	**heart-stimulant**
heart-dulling	**heart strain**
heart-fashioned	**heart-swelling**
heart-freezing	**heart-swollen**
heart-fretting	**heart-tearing**
heart-gnawing	**heart-thrilling**
heart-gripping	**heart-throb**
heart-happy	**heart-throbbing**
heart-hardened	**heart-tickling**
heart-hardening	**heart-warm**
heartheaviness	**heart-warming**
heartheavy	**heart-weariness**
heart-ill	**heart-weary**
heart-melting	**heart-wounded**
heart-moving	**heart-wringing**

heart·ache (härt′āk′) *n.* Mental anguish; grief; sorrow.

heart and soul Entirely; wholly; enthusiastically.

heart·beat (härt′bēt′) *n.* A pulsation of the heart.

heart·block (härt′blok′) *n. Pathol.* A condition in which the ventricular beats of the heart do not regularly follow the atrial also called *Adams-Stokes disease.*

heart·break (härt′brāk′) *n.* Deep grief; overwhelming sorrow. —**heart′-break′ing** *adj.* & *n.* —**heart′-break′er** *n.*

heart·bro·ken (härt′brō′kən) *adj.* Overwhelmingly grieved: also *heart-stricken.* —**heart′-bro′ken·ly** *adv.* —**heart′-bro′ken·ness** *n.*

heart·burn (härt′bûrn′) *n.* **1** A burning sensation in the esophagus, due to acidity of the stomach. **2** Discontent; jealousy.

heart·burn·ing (härt′bûr′ning) *n.* Gnawing discontent or rancor, as from envy or jealousy. —*adj.* Deeply felt; distressful.

heart cherry A variety of cherry having heart-shaped fruit.

heart disease Any morbid condition of the heart, whether organic or functional.

heart·ed (här′tid) *adj.* **1** Having a heart of a specified kind: used in combination: kind-*hearted.* **2** Heart-shaped: a *hearted* shield.

heart·en (här′tən) *v.t.* To give heart or courage to; strengthen. See synonyms under ENCOURAGE.

heart failure **1** Inability of the heart to pump enough blood to maintain normal circulation. **2** Sudden and fatal stoppage of the action of the heart.

heart·felt (härt′felt′) *adj.* Deeply felt; most sincere.

heart·free (härt′frē′) *adj.* Having the affections disengaged.

hearth (härth) *n.* **1** The floor of a fireplace, furnace, or the like. **2** The fireside; home. **3** *Metall.* That part of a reverberatory furnace upon which the ore is laid to be subjected to the action of fire; in a blast furnace, the lowest part, through which the melted metal flows. **4** A bloomery. See synonyms under HOME. [OE *heorth*]

hearth money **1** Peter's pence (def. 2). **2** In English law (1662–1689), a tax of two shillings laid on hearths in houses paying church and poor rates: also called *chimney money.*

hearth·stone (härth′stōn′) *n.* **1** A stone forming a hearth. **2** Figuratively, a fireside. **3** A soft stone used for scouring floors, doorsteps, etc. See synonyms under HOME.

heart·i·ly (här′tə·lē) *adv.* **1** With sincerity or cordiality. **2** Earnestly; enthusiastically. **3** Abundantly and with good appetite: to eat *heartily.* **4** Completely; thoroughly: to be *heartily* beaten.

heart·i·ness (här′tē·nis) *n.* The state or quality of being hearty.

heart·land (härt′land′) *n.* **1** That portion of a country essential to the maintenance of its defensive and offensive strength in wartime. **2** The interior of a country as distinguished from its more exposed peripheral areas. **3** Any large geographic area supposed to give the nation controlling it decisive strategic advantage in any struggle for world domination: compare GEOPOLITICS.

heart·less (härt′lis) *adj.* **1** Without sympathy or affection; hard-hearted; pitiless. **2** Without courage; cowardly; craven. —**heart′less·ly** *adv.* —**heart′less·ness** *n.*

heart-rend·ing (härt′ren′ding) *adj.* Extremely distressing; causing anguish.

hearts·ease (härts′ēz′) *n.* **1** The pansy or violet. **2** Freedom from sorrow or care. Also **heart's′-ease′.**

heart·seed (härt′sēd′) *n.* Balloonvine, an ornamental climbing vine.

heart-shaped (härt′shāpt′) *adj.* Shaped like a heart; oval, with one end obtusely pointed and the other notched.

heart·sick (härt′sik′) *adj.* Deeply disappointed or despondent. Also **heart′sore′** (-sôr′, -sōr′).

heart·some (härt′səm) *adj.* Cheerful or animated; lively; merry; gay. —**heart′some·ly** *adv.*

heart-strick·en (härt′strik′ən) *adj.* Overwhelmed with grief or fear.

heart·strings (härt′stringz′) *n. pl.* The strongest feelings or affections.

heart-struck (härt′struk′) *adj.* **1** Heart-stricken. **2** Ineradicable.

heart-to-heart (härt′tə·härt′) *adj.* Marked by frankness, intimacy, and sincerity.

heart·wa·ter (härt′wô′tər, -wot′ər) *n.* A disease of cattle, sheep, and goats due to the destruction of blood corpuscles by a filtrable virus.

heart·whole (härt′hōl′) *adj.* **1** Having the affections free; not in love. **2** Undaunted; sincere. —**heart′whole′ness** *n.*

heart·wood (härt′wŏŏd′) *n.* The older, nonfunctioning xylem in the central part of a woody stem, usually denser and darker than the surrounding sapwood. Also called *duramen.*

heart·worm (härt′wûrm′) *n.* A nematode worm (genus *Filaria*) parasitic in the heart and blood stream of dogs, occasionally of cats and other animals.

heart-worn (härt′wôrn′) *adj.* Worn with care and trouble.

heart·y (här′tē) *adj.* **heart·i·er, heart·i·est** **1** Full of affection or cordiality; genial. **2** Strongly felt; vigorous: a *hearty* dislike. **3** Healthy and strong. **4** Supplying abundant nourishment: a *hearty* meal. **5** Enjoying or requiring abundant nourishment: a *hearty* appetite. **6** Fertile: said of land. —*n. pl.* **heart·ies** A hearty fellow or sailor.

heat (hēt) *n.* **1** That which raises the temperature of a body or substance or any material system; also the rise itself, however produced. **2** *Physics* A form of energy directly associated with and proportional to the random molecular motions of a substance or body; it may be variously generated (as by combustion, friction, chemical action, radiation, etc.), converted by suitable processes into other forms of energy, and its total absence corresponds with that complete cessation of all translational molecular motion known as absolute zero. ◆ Collateral adjective: *thermal.* **3** The sensation produced by a rise in temperature. **4** The state of being hot; a temperature high as compared with a mean, standard, or normal temperature: summer *heat.* **5** Color, appearance, or condition indicating high temperature; high color; redness; flush. **6** *Metall.* A single heating, melting, or smelting operation, as in working iron or steel; also, the material heated, melted, etc., at one time: The foundry runs three *heats* a day. **7** A single effort or action, or one of an interrupted series of such efforts; especially, a single course or division of a race: to run several *heats.* **8** Greatest vehemence or fury; excitement or agitation; unusual animation; ardor; fervency: the *heat* of battle. **9** Sexual excitement in animals, especially in females; estrus. **10** *Physiol.* The sensation of warmth experienced when certain receptors in the skin are stimulated. **11** A fundamental quality of elements, humors, and bodies in general: opposed to *cold.* See synonyms under WARMTH. —*v.t.* & *v.i.* **1** To make or become hot or warm. **2** To excite or become excited; arouse. See synonyms under INCENSE. [OE *hætu*] —**heat′ed** *adj.* —**heat′ed·ly** *adv.*

heat-bal·ance (hēt′bal′əns) *n. Physics* A method of accounting for all the heat units supplied, transferred, and consumed in a given process, as in a diesel engine, steam turbine, furnace, refrigerating system, etc.

heat capacity The amount of heat required to raise the temperature of a given mass of a substance or material by one degree.

heat content Enthalpy.

heat death *Physics* The state of complete thermodynamic equilibrium in a material system; maximum entropy.

heat engine Any engine for the conversion of heat into mechanical energy, as a steam or diesel engine.

heat·er (hē′tər) *n.* **1** Any device, apparatus, or contrivance designed to generate, impart, transmit, or conserve heat, as a stove, radiator, etc. **2** One who attends to the heating of something: often in combination: a rivet *heater.* **3** *Electronics* An element which supplies current for heating the cathode of a vacuum tube. **4** *Colloq.* A pistol or revolver.

heath (hēth) *n.* **1** A low, hardy, evergreen shrub of a large genus *(Erica)* with narrow, usually whorled leaves and small tubular or globose, rose, white, or yellow flowers. Two of the most durable species are the fine-leaved heath *(E. cinerea)* and the cross-leaved heath *(E. tetralix).* **2** The common heather. **3** *Brit.* An area of open land overgrown with heath or with coarse herbage. **4** In Coverdale's and later versions of the Old Testament, a desert plant; identified both as tamarisk and savin. *Jer.* xvii 6; xlviii 6. [OE *hǣth*]

heath aster A common aster of the eastern United States *(Aster ericoides),* having thick clusters of small white or pink flowers.

heath·ber·ry (hēth′ber′ē, -bər·ē) *n. pl.* **·ries** The crowberry.

heath bird The heath grouse. Also **heath cock.**

hea·then (hē′thən) *n. pl.* **·thens** or **·then** **1** One who is not a believer in the God of the Bible; one who is neither Christian, Jew, nor Mohammedan; a pagan; Gentile; idolater. **2** Any irreligious, rude, or uncultured person. —*adj.* **1** Unbelieving; Gentile; pagan. **2** Irreligious; uncultured. **3** Of or pertaining to the heathen or their customs. [OE *hæthen.* Akin to HEATH.]

hea·then·dom (hē′thən·dəm) *n.* **1** Heathenism. **2** The regions of the world, collectively, inhabited by heathen peoples. **3** Heathen peoples collectively.

hea·then·ish (hē′thən·ish) *adj.* Pertaining to, characteristic of, or resembling heathen; hence, irreligious; rude; barbarous; cruel. — **hea′then·ish·ly** *adv.* — **hea′then·ish·ness** *n.*
hea·then·ism (hē′thən·iz′əm) *n.* **1** Paganism; idolatry. **2** The condition, manners, or morals of heathen ignorance; barbarism. Also **hea′then·ry** (-rē).
hea·then·ize (hē′thən·īz) *v.t.* & *v.i.* **·ized, ·iz·ing** To make or become heathenish or heathen.
hea·then·ness (hē′thən·is) *n.* **1** The state of being heathen. **2** The regions inhabited by the heathen.
heath·er (heth′ər) *n.* **1** A hardy evergreen shrub related to the heath; especially, the true heather of Scotland *(Calluna vulgaris)*, with minute leaves and close, one-sided, spikelike racemes of pinkish-lavender flowers. **2** The heath. **3** A dull, grayish-red color. [ME *hadder*; origin unknown; infl. in form by HEATH]
heath·er-bleat (heth′ər·blēt′) *n.* The snipe. Also **heath′er-bleat′er, heath′er-bluit′er** (-blo͞ot′·ər, -blüt′ər), **heath′er-blut′ter.**
heather mixture A combination of colored fibers giving a flecked appearance suggesting heather fields: used chiefly in tweeds or other woolen fabrics.
heath·er·y (heth′ər·ē) *adj.* **1** Resembling heather. **2** Abounding in heather.
heath grass A perennial grass *(Sieglingia decumbens)* found growing on heaths and moors in Europe. Also **heather grass.**
heath grouse A European grouse *(Tetrao tetrix)* found in the heath country of Great Britain, the male of which is mostly black, with a lyre-shaped tail: also called *heath bird.*
heath hen An American grouse *(Tympanuchus cupido cupido)* related to the prairie chicken of western North America: now extinct.
heath·y (hē′thē) *adj.* **heath·i·er, heath·i·est** **1** Of, pertaining to, or resembling heath. **2** Covered by or abounding in heath.
heat index An index expressing the heating value of an oil, determined by the rise in temperature from mixing 50 cc. of a specified oil with 10 cc. of concentrated sulfuric acid. Also **heat number.**
heat lightning A fitful play of lightning unattended by thunder, usually seen near the horizon at the close of a hot day, due to the reflection from distant clouds of far-off flashes, causing a diffused glow.
heat of formation The quantity of heat absorbed or evolved in the formation of a gram-molecule of a compound from its constituents at constant volume. Also **heat of combination.**
heat of fusion The quantity of heat required to convert into the liquid state a given mass of a solid which has already been brought to the melting point.
heat of vaporization The latent heat required to vaporize one gram of a liquid.
hea·tron·ic (hē·tron′ik) *adj.* Of or pertaining to the subjection of a material to a required uniform temperature through the application of high-frequency radio waves: applied in the rapid and accurate molding of plastics. [<HEAT + (ELECT)RONIC]
heat stroke The state of exhaustion and collapse caused by prolonged exposure to heat, as in furnace rooms, foundries, or from the sun's rays. Also **heat prostration.**
heat treatment *Metall.* The application of heat to metals and alloys under such conditions of temperature, time, range of variation, etc., as will give the desired properties, as hardness, to the product.
heaume (hōm) *n.* In medieval armor, a large supplemental helmet fitting over an inner helmet and resting on the shoulders; a casque. [<F <OF *helme.* Related to HELM².]
heave (hēv) *v.* **heaved** or **hove, heav·ing** *v.t.* **1** To raise with effort; lift; hoist. **2** To lift and throw, especially with effort; hurl. **3** To cause to swell, rise, or bulge out, as the chest in breathing. **4** To cause to rise and fall repeatedly: The waves *heaved* the ship up and down. **5** To emit or bring forth (a sigh, groan, etc.) as with effort or pain. **6** *Naut.* **a** To raise or haul up (the anchor); pull on (a cable, etc.). **b** To cause (a ship) to move in a specified direction by or as by hauling on cables or ropes. **7** *Geol.* To fracture and displace (a vein or stratum). — *v.i.* **8** To rise or swell up; bulge. **9** To rise and fall repeatedly. **10** To breathe with effort; gasp; pant. **11** To vomit or make an effort to vomit; retch. **12** *Naut.* **a** To move or proceed: said of ships. **b** To haul or pull, as on a rope; push, as on a capstan. — **heave, ho!** *Naut.* Pull (or push) hard together! — **to heave in** (or **into**) **sight** To come into view, as a ship at sea. — **to heave to** *Naut.* **1** To bring (a ship) to a standstill by heading into the wind with one or more sails aback. **2** To cause a ship to lie to, as in a storm. — *n.* **1** An upward and onward throw; an effort to lift or raise. **2** A rising or an upward movement. **3** A swell or an expansion, as of sea waves, or the earth in an earthquake. **4** *Geol.* The amount of actual displacement of the parts of a fractured mineral vein or stratum, vertically or horizontally or in both directions combined. [OE *hebban* lift]
heav·en (hev′ən) *n.* **1** *Theol.* The abode of God and of blest spirits; the dwelling place or state of existence of righteous souls after their life on earth. **2** *Usually pl.* The region or regions surrounding the earth; especially, the domelike expanse over the earth; the sky; firmament. **3** Any place or condition of supreme happiness; a state of bliss. **4** In Christian Science, harmony; the atmosphere of Soul. **5** Climate, especially as regards the sky of a particular place. [OE *heofon*] — **heav′en·li·ness** *n.* — **heav′en·ward** *adj.* & *adv.* — **heav′en·wards** *adv.*
Heav·en (hev′ən) God, or the Supreme Being; Providence: *Heaven* keep thee.
heav·en·ly (hev′ən·lē) *adj.* **1** Of or belonging to the heaven of God. **2** Of or pertaining to the natural sky: chiefly in the phrase, *heavenly* bodies. **3** Having excellence or beauty or giving pleasure that belongs to heaven: often, in colloquial usage, a general expression of approval.
heave offering An offering of the Jewish service: so called because heaved or lifted up.
heav·er (hē′vər) *n.* **1** One who heaves or lifts. **2** A short bar or stick used as a lever for twisting rope; handspike.
heaves (hēvz) *n. pl.* An asthmatic disease of horses; quick, labored breathing; broken wind. [Plural of HEAVE]
heav·i·er-than-air (hev′ē·ər·thən·âr′) *adj.* Describing any aircraft whose weight is greater than that of the air it displaces. See AERODYNE.
heav·i·ly (hev′ə·lē) *adv.* **1** With great weight or burden; oppressively; also, densely. **2** With depressing affliction or misfortune; grievously; tediously.
heav·i·ness (hev′ē·nis) *n.* **1** The quality of being heavy; ponderousness. **2** Despondency; grief. See synonyms under WEIGHT.
Heav·i·side (hev′ē·sīd), **Oliver,** 1850–1925, English physicist.
Heaviside layer A layer of the ionosphere which begins at about 65 miles above the earth and acts as a reflector of radio waves: also called *E-layer, Kennelly-Heaviside layer.*
heav·y (hev′ē) *adj.* **heav·i·er, heav·i·est** **1** Hard to lift or carry; weighty: opposed to *light.* **2** Having great specific gravity; hence, of dense or concentrated weight: *heavy* as lead. **3** Over the usual weight: *heavy* luggage; *heavy* woolens. **4** Of great quantity or amount; abundant: a *heavy* crop; a *heavy* vote. **5** Dealing in large amounts: *heavy* trade; a *heavy* investor. **6** Laden or weighted: an atmosphere *heavy* with moisture. **7** Permeating; diffuse: a *heavy* odor. **8** Forceful; powerful: *heavy* gunfire; a *heavy* blow. **9** Tempestuous; violent: a *heavy* sea, storm, etc. **10** *Mil.* **a** Of large size: said of weapons. **b** Heavily armed: *heavy* infantry. **11** Clayey; cloggy: said of soils, roads, etc. **12** Doughy; dense and compact: said of bread, pastries, etc. **13** Not easily digested: *heavy* food. **14** Thick; massive; coarse: *heavy* lines, features, etc. **15** Slow and cumbrous: a *heavy* step. **16** Loud and intense: *heavy* applause. **17** Hard to do or accomplish; laborious: *heavy* work. **18** Hard to bear or suffer; oppressive: *heavy* taxes; *heavy* sorrow. **19** Weary; sleepy. **20** Tedious; dull: a *heavy* style. **21** Profound; intense: a *heavy* silence. **22** Gloomy; overcast: a *heavy* sky. **23** Feeling or expressing sorrow or grief; sad; despondent: a *heavy* heart. **24** Serious; grave: a *heavy* role; a *heavy* offense. **25** Pregnant. **26** Steep: a *heavy* grade. — *adv.* Heavily. — *n. pl.* **heav·ies** **1** A serious role in a play, representing dignity or self-importance in middle life or vigorous age; often the villain. **2** An actor who interprets such a role. [OE *hefig*]

Synonyms (adj.): burdensome, crushing, cumbrous, dull, grievous, inert, oppressive, ponderous, slow, sluggish, stolid, stupid, weighty. See DROWSY, SAD. *Antonyms*: airy, buoyant, ethereal, light, lively, subtile, trifling, trivial, volatile.
heav·y-dut·y (hev′ē·do͞o′tē, -dyo͞o′-) *adj.* Stoutly constructed so as to bear up under severe or long strain, usage, etc.
heavy earth Baryta.
heav·y-foot·ed (hev′ē·fo͝ot′id) *adj.* Clumsy or plodding in gait. — **heav′y-foot′ed·ly** *adv.* — **heav′y-foot′ed·ness** *n.*
heav·y-hand·ed (hev′ē·han′did) *adj.* **1** Lacking lightness of touch; clumsy. **2** Oppressive; overbearing; dogmatic. — **heav′y-hand′ed·ly** *adv.* — **heav′y-hand′ed·ness** *n.*
heav·y-heart·ed (hev′ē·här′tid) *adj.* Sad; melancholy. — **heav′y-heart′ed·ly** *adv.* — **heav′y-heart′ed·ness** *n.*
heavy hydrogen Deuterium.
heav·y-lad·en (hev′ē·lād′n) *adj.* **1** Bearing a heavy burden. **2** Troubled; oppressed.
heavy metal Any metal with a specific gravity greater than 4.
heavy spar Barite.
heavy timber **1** Dense, unbroken forest; thick woods. **2** Big trees. **3** Big logs.
heavy water Deuterium oxide, D_2O, the compound of oxygen and the heavy isotope of hydrogen.
heav·y·weight (hev′ē·wāt′) *n.* A person of more than average weight; specifically, a boxer or wrestler over 175 pounds in weight. — *adj.* Of more than average weight or thickness.
Heb·bel (heb′əl), **Friedrich,** 1813–63, German dramatist.
heb·do·mad (heb′də·mad) *n.* The number seven; any seven things; especially, a period of seven days; a week. [<L *hebdomas, -adis* <Gk. *hebdomas* < *hepta* seven]
heb·dom·a·dal (heb·dom′ə·dəl) *adj.* **1** Composed of seven days. **2** Occurring weekly. — **heb·dom′a·dal·ly** *adv.*
heb·dom·a·dar·y (heb·dom′ə·der′ē) *n. pl.* **·dar·ies** *Eccl.* A member of a chapter or monastic choir who presides over the recitation of the breviary for the week.
He·be (hē′bē) In Greek mythology, the daughter of Zeus and Hera, goddess of youth and, before she was replaced by Ganymede, the cupbearer of the gods.
he·be·phre·ni·a (hē′bə·frē′nē·ə) *n. Psychiatry* A type of dementia precox occurring at puberty. [<NL <Gk. *hēbē* youth + *phrēn* mind] — **he′be·phre′nic** (-frē′nik, -fren′ik) *adj.*
He·ber (hē′bər), **Reginald,** 1783–1826, English bishop and hymn writer.
He·ber·to (ā·ber′tō) Spanish form of HERBERT.
heb·e·tate (heb′ə·tāt) *v.i.* & *v.t.* **·tat·ed, ·tat·ing** To make or become blunt or dull. — *adj.* **1** *Bot.* Having a blunt, soft point, as certain plants. **2** Stupid; dull. [<L *hebetatus,* pp. of *hebetare* be dull < *hebes* dull] — **heb′e·ta′tion** *n.* — **heb′e·ta′tive** *adj.*
he·bet·ic (hə·bet′ik) *adj.* Of or pertaining to the period of puberty.
heb·e·tude (heb′ə·to͞od, -tyo͞od) *n.* Stupidity and dulness of the senses, especially as noted in grave fevers. [<LL *hebetudo* <*hebes, -etis* dull]
He·bra·ic (hi·brā′ik) *adj.* Relating to or characteristic of the Hebrews. Also **He·bra′i·cal.** [<LL *Hebraicus* <Gk. *Hebraikos* < *Hebraios* a Hebrew] — **He·bra′i·cal·ly** *adv.*
He·bra·ism (hē′brā·iz′əm, -brə-) *n.* **1** A distinctive characteristic of the Hebrews. **2** A Hebrew idiom. **3** The religion of the Hebrews; Judaism.
He·bra·ist (hē′brā·ist, -brə-) *n.* **1** One proficient in or a student of Hebrew. **2** One who conforms to Hebraic thought and traditions. **3** Among the early Jews, one who upheld

the Hebrew language and traditions in opposition to the Hellenists. Also **He′brew·ist.**

He·bra·is·tic (hē′brā·is′tik, -brə-) *adj.* Belonging to or resembling the Hebrew language, thought, or manners. Also **He′bra·is′ti·cal.**

He·bra·ize (hē′brā·īz, -brə-) *v.* **·ized, ·iz·ing** *v.t.* To make Hebrew. — *v.i.* To adopt Hebrew customs, language, etc.

He·brew (hē′brōō) *n.* **1** A member of one of a group of Semitic tribes; especially, an Israelite. **2** The Semitic language of the ancient Hebrews, used in the Old Testament: retained as a scholarly and religious language after its decline as a vernacular about the fourth century B.C. **3** The modern descendant of ancient Hebrew, the official language of the republic of Israel. — **Epistle to the Hebrews** A New Testament book of uncertain authorship, addressed to Hebrew Christians: also **Hebrews.** — *adj.* Relating or belonging to the Hebrews; Hebraic. [<OF *Hebreu* <L *Hebraeus* <Gk. *Hebraios* <Hebrew *'ibhri*, lit., one from beyond (Jordan)]

Hebrew calendar See under CALENDAR.

Heb·ri·des (heb′rə·dēz) The islands off the western coast of Scotland, divided into two groups, the *Inner Hebrides* and the *Outer Hebrides*; total, 2,900 square miles: also *Western Islands.* — **Heb′ri·de′an** (-dē′ən) or **He·brid·i·an** (hə·brid′ē·ən) *adj.* & *n.*

He·bron (hē′brən) A town in Palestine SW of Jerusalem: ancient *Kirjath-Arba*: Arabic *El Khalil.*

Hec·a·te (hek′ə·tē) In Greek mythology, a goddess of earth, moon, and underworld: later associated with sorcery: also *Hekate.*

Hec·a·te Strait (hek′ə·tē) A channel separating Queen Charlotte Islands from western British Columbia.

hec·a·tomb (hek′ə·tōm, -tōōm) *n.* A great sacrifice, originally of a hundred oxen. [<L *hecatombe* <Gk. *hecatombē* < *hekaton* a hundred + *bous* an ox]

Hec·a·ton·chei·res (hek′ə·tən·kī′rēz) In Greek mythology, the three hundred-handed, fifty-headed giants, sons of Uranus and Gaea: Briareus, Cottus, and Gyes: identified with the Roman *Centimanus.* [<Gk. < *hekaton* a hundred + *cheir* hand]

hec·is·to·ther·mic (hek′is·tə·thûr′mik) See HEKISTOTHERMIC.

heck (hek) *interj. Slang* An exclamation: euphemism for hell.

heck·le (hek′əl) *v.t.* **heck·led, heck·ling 1** To try to confuse or annoy (a speaker) with taunts, questions, etc. **2** To hackle (flax, etc.). — *n.* A hackle or hatchel. [ME *hechelen* < *hechele* a hatchel] — **heck′ler** *n.*

Hec·la (hek′lə) See HEKLA.

hec·tare (hek′târ) *n.* A unit of area in the metric system; 100 ares; equal to 10,000 square meters, or 2.471 acres: also spelled *hektare.* See METRIC SYSTEM. [<F <Gk. *hekaton* a hundred + F *are* ARE[2]]

hec·tic (hek′tik) *adj.* **1** Characterized by intense excitement or wild feeling. **2** Characterized by or denoting a wasting habit or condition of body. **3** Pertaining to or affected with hectic fever; consumptive. Also **hec′ti·cal.** [<F *hectique* <LL *hecticus* <Gk. *hektikos* consumptive < *hexis* state of the body < *echein* have] — **hec′ti·cal·ly** *adv.*

hectic fever *Pathol.* A fever connected with some organic disease, as pulmonary tuberculosis.

hectic flush A flush on the cheek in hectic fever.

hecto- *combining form* A hundred: *hectogram.* Also, before vowels, **hect-.** For words beginning thus see below or under METRIC SYSTEM. [<F <Gk. *hekaton* a hundred]

hec·to·cot·y·lus (hek′tə·kot′ə·ləs) *n. pl.* **·li** (-lī) *Zool.* One of the arms in male cephalopods that is modified to serve a reproductive function. [<HECTO- + Gk. *kotylē* cup]

hec·to·gram (hek′tə·gram) *n.* A measure of weight equal to 100 grams or 3.527 ounces avoirdupois: also spelled *hektogram.* See METRIC SYSTEM. Also **hec′to·gramme.**

hec·to·graph (hek′tə·graf, -gräf) *n.* A gelatin pad for making multiple copies of a writing or drawing. — *v.t.* To copy by hectograph. — **hec′to·graph′ic** *adj.*

hec·to·li·ter (hek′tə·lē′tər) *n.* A measure of capacity equal to 100 liters or 2.838 U.S. bushels. See METRIC SYSTEM. Also **hec′to·li′tre.**

hec·to·me·ter (hek′tə·mē′tər, hek·tom′ə·tər) *n.* A measure of length equal to 100 meters or 328.08 feet. See METRIC SYSTEM. Also **hec′to·me′tre.**

hec·tor (hek′tər) *v.t.* & *v.i.* **1** To bully; bluster. **2** To tease; torment. [< *n.*] — *n.* A quarrelsome, domineering fellow; bully. [after HECTOR]

Hec·tor (hek′tər) In the *Iliad,* a Trojan hero, son of Priam and Hecuba: killed by Achilles to avenge the death of Patroclus.

hec·to·stere (hek′tə·stir) *n.* A measure of volume equal to 100 steres.

Hec·u·ba (hek′yōō·bə) In the *Iliad,* the wife of Priam and mother of Hector, Troilus, Paris, and Cassandra.

he'd (hēd) **1** He had. **2** He would.

hed·dle (hed′l) *n.* In weaving, the parallel vertical cords or wires of a loom through which the warp is threaded: used to separate, raise, or lower the warp. See illustration under LOOM. [OE *hefeld* thread for weaving]

hedge (hej) *n.* **1** A fence or barrier formed by bushes set close together. **2** Any barrier or boundary. **3** The act of hedging. — *v.* **hedged, hedg·ing** *v.t.* **1** To surround or border with a hedge; separate with a hedge. **2** To surround, guard, or hem in with or as with obstructions or barriers: usually with *in.* **3** To try to compensate for possible loss from (a bet, investment, etc.) by making offsetting bets or investments. — *v.i.* **4** To hide, as in or behind a hedge; skulk. **5** To make offsetting bets, investments, etc. **6** To avoid definite statement or involvement; refuse to commit oneself. [OE *hegg*] — **hedg′er** *n.* — **hedg′y** *adj.*

hedge apple The Osage orange.

hedge bill A tool used in pruning hedges; billhook. Also **hedging bill.**

hedge garlic A tall hedge weed *(Sisymbrium alliaria)* of the mustard family, with heart-shaped leaves, white flowers, erect pods, and a garlicky odor.

EUROPEAN HEDGEHOG
(Average length: 10 inches)

hedge·hog (hej′hôg′, -hog′) *n.* **1** A small, nocturnal, insectivorous mammal of the Old World (family *Erinaceidae*), having the back and sides covered with stout spines; also **hedge′pig′. 2** The porcupine. **3** *Mil.* **a** One of a chain of strongly fortified villages. **b** A wooden rack or frame, on which barbed wire is strung: used in trench warfare.

hedge·hop (hej′hop′) *v.i.* **·hopped, ·hop·ping** To fly close to the ground in an airplane, rising over houses, trees, etc., as in spraying insecticide or strafing enemy positions. — **hedge′hop′per** *n.* — **hedge′hop′ping** *n.* & *adj.*

hedge hyssop 1 A European perennial herb *(Gratiola officinalis)* of the figwort family, once used medicinally as an emetic and purgative. **2** The skullcap (genus *Scutellaria*).

hedge marriage *Brit.* A marriage performed by a hedge parson; a clandestine marriage.

hedge parson *Brit.* Formerly, one of a class of vagabond and illiterate clergy. Also **hedge priest.**

hedge·row (hej′rō′) *n.* A row of shrubs, planted as a hedge.

hedge school *Brit.* Formerly, a school kept in the open air; a makeshift school.

hedge sparrow A small brownish European warbler *(Prunella modularis)* that frequents hedges.

He·din (he·dēn′), **Sven Anders,** 1865–1952, Swedish explorer.

He·djaz (hē·jaz′, he-) See HEJAZ.

he·don·ic (hē·don′ik) *adj.* **1** Pertaining to or of the nature of pleasure. **2** Of or pertaining to hedonism or hedonics. [<Gk. *hēdonikos* < *hēdonē* pleasure < *hēdys* sweet]

he·don·ics (hē·don′iks) *n. pl. (construed as singular)* **1** The science of pleasure or positive enjoyment: as a branch of ethics it treats of pleasure in its relation to duty. **2** That branch of psychology which considers pleasurable sensations in their bearing on life.

he·don·ism (hē′dən·iz′əm) *n.* **1** The doctrine of certain Greek philosophers (Aristippus and the Cyrenaics) that pleasure, of whatever kind, is the only good. **2** In ethics, gross self-interest; self-indulgence. **3** A tendency to exaggerate and dwell upon pleasurable sensations. — **he′don·ist** *n.* — **he′don·is′tic** *adj.* — **he′don·is′ti·cal·ly** *adv.*

-hedral *combining form* Having a (given) form or number of sides: *octahedral*: used in adjectives corresponding to nouns in *-hedron.* [<-HEDR(ON) + -AL]

-hedron *combining form Geom.* & *Mineral.* A figure or crystal having a (given) form or a (specific) number of surfaces: *octahedron.* [<Gk. *hedra* side, surface]

hee·bie-jee·bies (hē′bē·jē′bēz) *n. pl. U.S. Slang* A fit of nervousness. [Coined by Billy de Beck, U.S. comic cartoonist, died 1942]

heed (hēd) *v.t.* To take notice of; pay attention to. — *v.i.* To pay attention. See synonyms under CARE, FOLLOW, LISTEN. — *n.* Careful attention or consideration. [OE *hēdan*] — **heed′er** *n.*

heed·ful (hēd′fəl) *adj.* Attentive. See synonyms under THOUGHTFUL. — **heed′ful·ly** *adv.* — **heed′ful·ness** *n.*

heed·less (hēd′lis) *adj.* Careless, thoughtless. See synonyms under IMPRUDENT, INATTENTIVE. — **heed′less·ly** *adv.* — **heed′less·ness** *n.*

hee-haw (hē′hô′) *n.* **1** The braying sound of an ass. **2** Loud, rude laughter. — *v.i.* **1** To bray, as an ass. **2** To laugh in a loud, rude manner. [Imit.]

heel[1] (hēl) *n.* **1** In man, the rounded posterior part of the foot; the calcaneum with its associated structures. **2** The corresponding part of the foot or tarsus in any other animal. **3** The part of a shoe, or other foot covering, that surrounds or lies just beneath or around this part of the foot; in a boot or shoe, the built-up portion on which the rear of the foot rests; in hosiery, the separately knitted rear part of the foot. **4** The whole foot, as seen from the rear; sometimes, *pl.,* the hind feet of an animal. **5** Something resembling a heel or located like a heel, as cyma reversa, a form of molding; the lower end of a stud or rafter. **6** *Naut.* **a** The hindmost part of a vessel's keel. **b** The lower end of a mast. **7** That part of the head of a golf club that is nearest to the neck; also, that part of a tool that is nearest to the handle. **8** The last part or remainder: the *heel* of tobacco in a pipe. **9** *Colloq.* A cad. — **down at the heel** Presenting a seedy or slovenly appearance. — **to be at, on,** or **upon the heels of** To follow closely. — **to heel** To a position close behind a master: said of dogs. — *v.t.* **1** To supply with a heel. **2** To follow at the heels of; pursue closely. **3** To touch or strike with the heel. **4** To arm (a fighting cock) with steel spurs. **5** In golf, to strike (the ball) with the heel of the club. **6** *Slang* To supply with money, etc. — *v.i.* **7** To follow at the heels of someone. **8** To touch the ground with or move the heels, as in dancing. ◆ Homophone: *heal.* [OE *hela*] — **heel′less** *adj.*

heel[2] (hēl) *v.t.* & *v.i. Naut.* To lean or cause to lean to one side; cant, as a ship. — *n.* The act of heeling or inclining laterally from an upright position; a cant; list: also **heel′ing.** ◆ Homophone: *heal.* [Earlier *heeld,* OE *hieldan*]

heel-and-toe (hēl′ən·tō′) *adj.* Designating a manner of walking in which the heel of one foot touches the ground before the toes of the other foot leave it.

heel bone The calcaneum.

heeled (hēld) *adj.* **1** Having heels; fitted with heels. **2** *Slang* **a** Supplied with money. **b** Armed, as with a gun.

heel·er (hē′lər) *n.* **1** *U.S. Slang* A disreputable political retainer: often called **ward heeler. 2** One who heels shoes.

heel·piece (hēl′pēs′) *n.* **1** That part of a stocking which encloses the heel. **2** One thickness of leather in making the heel of a shoe. **3** The bar of iron which connects the soft iron cores in an electromagnet.

heel·post (hēl′pōst′) *n.* The post in a doorframe to which the door is hinged.

heel·tap (hēl′tap′) *n.* **1** A thickness of leather on the heel of a shoe. **2** A small quantity of liquor left in a glass.

Heep (hēp), **Uriah** In Dickens' *David Copperfield,* an obsequious, dishonest, and hypocritical clerk.

Heer·len (hâr′lən) A city of SE Netherlands.

heeze (hēz) *v.t. Scot.* To hoist.

Hef·ner lamp (hef′nər) See STANDARD LAMP.

heft[1] (heft) *v.t. Colloq.* **1** To test the weight of by lifting. **2** To lift up; heave. — *v.i.*

3 *Colloq.* To weigh. —*n. U.S. Colloq.* **1** The bulk or gist of a thing; major part. **2** Weight. [Related to HEAVE]

heft² (heft) See HAFT.

heft·y (hef'tē) *adj.* **heft·i·er, heft·i·est** *Colloq.* **1** Heavy; weighty. **2** Big and powerful; muscular.

He·gel (hā'gəl), **Georg Wilhelm Friedrich,** 1770–1831, German philosopher.

He·ge·li·an (hā·gā'lē·ən, hə·jēl'yən) *adj.* According with or pertaining to the philosophical system of Hegel. —*n.* An adherent of this system.

He·ge·li·an·ism (hā·gā'lē·ən·iz'əm, hə·jēl'yən-) *n.* The philosophical system of Hegel. Its controlling assumption was the so-called Hegelian *dialectic,* or principle which enables reflective thinking to arrange all the categories, or necessary conceptions of reason, in an order of development that corresponds to the actual order, in development, of all reality. The system is customarily characterized as *absolute idealism.* Also **He·gel·ism** (hā'gəl·iz'əm).

he·gem·o·ny (hə·jem'ə·nē, hej'ə·mō'nē, hē'jə-) *n. pl.* **·nies 1** Predominant influence of one state over others as in a league or alliance. **2** Leadership, or supreme command. [< Gk. *hēgemonia* < *hēgeesthai* lead] —**heg·e·mon·ic** (hej'ə·mon'ik) *adj.*

he·gi·ra (hə·jī'rə, hej'ə·rə) *n.* Any precipitate flight or departure: also spelled *hejira.* [< Med. L < Arabic *hijrah* departure < *hajara* go away]

He·gi·ra (hi·jī'rə, hej'ə·rə) *n.* **1** The flight of Mohammed from Mecca to Medina in 622; now taken as the beginning of the Mohammedan era. **2** The Mohammedan era. Also spelled *Hejira.*

he·gu·men (hə·gyōō'men) *n.* In the Eastern Church, the head of a body of monks: an office of dignity rather than jurisdiction. See ARCHIMANDRITE. Also **he·gu·me·nos** (-nos), **he·gou'me·nos.** [< Med. L *hegumenus* < Gk. *hēgoumenos,* var. of *hēgeomenos,* ppr. of *hēgeesthai* lead]

he·gu·me·ne (hə·gyōō'mə·nē) *n.* In the Eastern Church, the head of a nunnery: similar to an abbess in the Western Church. [< Gk. *hēgoumenē,* fem. var. of *hēgeomenos.* See HEGUMEN.]

he·gu·me·ny (hə·gyōō'mə·nē) *n. pl.* **·nies** The office or position of a hegumen.

Hei·del·berg (hī'dəl·bûrg, *Ger.* hī'dəl·berkh) A city in Baden-Württemberg, Germany.

Heidelberg man A primitive human type *(Homo heidelbergensis)* reconstructed from a massive lower jaw with teeth which was discovered in 1907 in a sandpit near Heidelberg: considered by some authorities to form a single genus with Sinanthropus and Pithecanthropus.

heif·er (hef'ər) *n.* A young cow. [OE *heahfore*]

Hei·fetz (hī'fits), **Ja·scha** (yä'shə), born 1901, U.S. violinist born in Lithuania.

heigh (hā, hī) *interj.* An exclamation to attract attention, or to encourage, as a race horse.

heigh-ho (hī'hō', hā'-) *interj.* An exclamation of varying significance, as of weariness, disappointment, surprise, etc.

height (hīt) *n.* **1** Distance above a base; altitude; highness. **2** An eminence. **3** The acme; culmination. [OE *hiehtho*]
Synonyms: acclivity, altitude, elevation, eminence, exaltation, loftiness. See SUMMIT. Compare HIGH. *Antonyms:* depression, depth, descent, lowliness, lowness.

height·en (hīt'n) *v.t. & v.i.* **1** To make or become high or higher; raise or lift. **2** To make or become more in degree, amount, size, etc.; intensify. —**height'en·er** *n.*
Synonyms: elevate, enhance, exalt, lift, raise, uplift. See AGGRAVATE, INCREASE. *Antonyms:* abase, debase, depress, deteriorate, diminish, lower, reduce.

height-find·er (hīt'fīn'dər) *n. Aeron.* An optical instrument used to determine the height of aircraft.

height-to-pa·per (hīt'tə·pā'pər) *n. Printing* The standard height of type: in the United States, 0.9186 inch; in England, 0.9175 inch. Compare TYPE-HIGH.

heil (hīl) *German interj.* Hail! —*v.t.* To salute with "heil."

Heil·bronn (hīl'brôn) A city in Baden-Württemberg, Germany.

Hei·lung·kiang (hā'lōōng·jyäng') A province of north central Manchuria; 130,000 square miles; capital, Tsitsihar. Also **Hei·lung·chiang.**

Heim·dall (hām'däl) In Norse mythology, the guardian of Bifröst, the rainbow bridge that leads to Asgard. Also **Heim'dal, Heim'dallr** (-däl·r').

Heim·lich maneuver (hīm'lik) A life-saving method of preventing a person's choking on food lodged in the windpipe by firmly grasping the victim around the midsection from behind, and pressing a fist hard against the diaphragm to produce a burst of air up through the throat.

Hei·ne (hī'nə), **Heinrich,** 1797–1856, German poet.

hei·nie (hī'nē) *n. Slang* A German soldier: a term of contempt. [< G *Heine,* dim. of *Heinrich*]

hei·nous (hā'nəs) *adj.* Extremely wicked; atrocious; odiously sinful. See synonyms under FLAGRANT, INFAMOUS. [< OF *haïnos* < *haine* hatred < *haïr* hate] —**hei'nous·ly** *adv.* —**hei'nous·ness** *n.*

heir (âr) *n.* **1** *Law* One who on the death of another becomes entitled by operation of law to succeed to the deceased person's estate, as an estate of inheritance: also **heir at law. 2** In states and countries which have adopted the civil law, all persons called to the succession. **3** Anyone inheriting from a deceased person. **4** One who or that which succeeds to any qualities of another by reason of community of origin, or inherits anything by transmission. **5** *Obs.* Offspring. ◆ Homophone: *air.* [< OF < L *heres*] —**heir'ess** *n. fem.* —**heir'less** *adj.*

heir apparent One who must by course of law become the heir if he survives his ancestor.

heir·loom (âr'lōōm) *n.* **1** Any movable chattel that descends to an heir; especially, something that has been handed down for generations. **2** Any personal quality, endowment, or family characteristic inherited from ancestors. [< HEIR + LOOM, in obs. sense "tool"]

heir presumptive One who is at present heir to another but whose claims may become void by birth of a nearer relative.

heir·ship (âr'ship) *n.* **1** The state or condition of an heir. **2** Succession by inheritance. Also **heir'dom** (-dəm).

Hei·sen·berg (hī'zən·berkh), **Werner,** 1901–76, German physicist.

heist (hīst) *v.t. Slang* To steal. [Var. of HOIST]

He·jaz (hē·jaz', he-) A viceroyalty of Saudi Arabia extending along the Red Sea; 150,000 square miles; capital, Mecca: also *Hedjaz.*

he·ji·ra (hə·jī'rə, hej'ə·rə) See HEGIRA.

Hek·a·te (hek'ə·tē) See HECATE.

hek·is·to·ther·mic (hek'is·tə·thûr'mik) *adj. Ecol.* Of or designating plants adapted for living beyond the limits of tree growth and in the prolonged absence of light and warmth. Also spelled *hecistothermic.* [< Gk. *hēkistos* least + *thermē* heat]

Hek·la (hek'lə) An active volcano in SW Iceland; 4,747 feet: also *Hecla.*

hek·tare (hek'târ), **hek·to·gram** (hek'tə·gram), etc. See HECTARE, etc.

Hel (hel) In Norse mythology: **1** The daughter of Loki, goddess of those who died of old age or disease. **2** The kingdom of the dead not killed in battle: see VALHALLA.

hel·co·sis (hel·kō'sis) *n. Pathol.* The development of an ulcer. [< Gk. *helkos* an ulcer + -OSIS] —**hel·cot'ic** (-kot'ik) *adj.*

held (held) Past tense of HOLD.

Hel·der (hel'dər) A port of NW Netherlands. Also **Den Helder** (den).

Hel·en (hel'ən) A feminine personal name. Also **Hel·e·na** (hel'ə·nə), *Dan., Du.* **He·le·na** (hā·lā'nä), *Fr.* **Hé·lène** (ā·len'), **He·lene** (*Ger.* hā·lā'nə, *Greek* hā·lā'nä). [< Gk., a torch]

—**Helen of Troy** In Greek mythology, the most beautiful woman in the world, daughter of Zeus and Leda and wife of Menelaus; awarded as a prize to Paris by Aphrodite, she eloped with him to Troy, thus causing the Trojan War.

Hel·e·na (hel'ə·nə) The capital of Montana.

Hel·e·na (hel'ə·nə), **Saint,** 247?–327?, mother of Constantine the Great.

Hel·e·nus (hel'ə·nəs) In Greek legend, a son of Priam and Hecuba, endowed like his twin sister Cassandra with the gift of prophecy: captured by the Greeks, he was forced to reveal how Troy could be taken. *Greek* **Hel'e·nos.**

Hel·go·land (hel'gō·länt) A small island in the North Sea off NW Germany; formerly a resort and German naval base: English *Heligoland.*

he·li·a·cal (hi·lī'ə·kəl) *adj. Astron.* **1** Pertaining to the sun. **2** Designating those risings and settings of the stars that take place as near the sun as they can be observed. Also **he·li·ac** (hē'lē·ak). [< LL *heliacus* < Gk. *hēliakos* < *hēlios* the sun] —**he·li'a·cal·ly** *adv.*

He·li·an·thus (hē'lē·an'thəs) *n.* A large genus of mainly North American annual or perennial plants of the composite family, the sunflowers, with usually opposite leaves and large heads of yellow flowers. [< NL < Gk. *hēlios* sun + *anthos* a flower]

he·li·ast (hē'lē·ast) *n.* A dicast. [< Gk. *heliastēs* < *heliazesthai* sit in court]

hel·i·cal (hel'i·kəl) *adj.* Pertaining to or shaped like a helix. —**hel'i·cal·ly** *adv.*

helical gear *Mech.* A gear wheel whose teeth are cut across the face at an angle with the axis.

hel·i·cline (hel'ə·klīn) *n.* A ramp with a curving or spiral passageway. [< HELI(X) + (IN-)CLINE]

helico- *combining form* Spiral; helical: *helicodromic.* Also, before vowels, **helic-.** [< Gk. *helix* spiral]

hel·i·co·dro·mic (hel'i·kō·drō'mik, -drom'ik) *adj.* Having a flight path curving like a corkscrew or a bent skew spiral: said of guided missiles. [< HELICO- + -DROM(OUS) + -IC]

hel·i·coid (hel'ə·koid) *adj.* Coiled spirally, as certain univalve shells: also **hel'i·coi'dal.** —*n.* A geometrical surface resembling that of a screw. —**hel·i·coi'dal·ly** *adv.*

hel·i·con (hel'i·kon, -kən) *n.* A horn-shaped bass or contrabass tuba. [< L < Gk. *Helikōn,* the mountain of the Muses; infl. by HELIX]

Hel·i·con (hel'i·kon, -kən) A mountain range in Boeotia, east central Greece; highest point, 5,736 feet; legendary home of the Muses; site of the fountains of Aganippe and Hippocrene. —**Hel·i·co·ni·an** (hel'i·kō'nē·ən) *adj.*

hel·i·cop·ter (hel'ə·kop'tər, hē'lə-) *n. Aeron.* A type of aircraft whose aerodynamic support is obtained from propellers rotating on a vertical axis and which is capable of rising and descending vertically. [< F *hélicoptère* < Gk. *helix, -ikos* a spiral + *pteron* a wing]

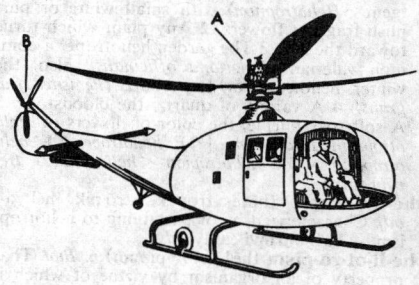

FOUR-PASSENGER HELICOPTER
A. Pitch control mechanism. *B.* Torque control rotor.

hel·i·co·tre·ma (hel'ə·kō·trē'mə) *n. Anat.* The opening in the inner ear which connects the inner and outer spiral canals at the apex of the cochlea. [< NL < Gk. *helix, -ikos* a spiral + *trēma* hole]

Hel·i·go·land (hel'ə·gō·land') See HELGOLAND.

Heligoland Bight An arm of the North Sea between Helgoland and the German mainland; scene of a British naval victory in World War I, August 28, 1914. *German* **Hel·go·län·der Bucht** (hel'gō·len'dər bōōkht').

he·li·o (hē'lē·ō) *n. pl.* **·os** *Colloq.* A heliograph.

helio- *combining form* Sun; of the sun: *heliotropic.* [< Gk. *hēlios* the sun]

he·li·o·cen·tric (hē′lē·ə·sen′trik) *adj.* Having reference to the sun as a center: a *heliocentric* system. Also **he′li·o·cen′tri·cal.**

he·li·o·chrome (hē′lē·ə·krōm′) *n.* A photograph in natural colors. —**he′li·o·chro′mic** *adj.*

He·li·o·gab·a·lus (hē′lē·ə·gab′ə·ləs), 204–222, emperor of Rome 218–222, under name of Marcus Aurelius Antoninus: also spelled *Elagabalus.*

he·li·o·gram (hē′lē·ə·gram′) *n.* A message sent by means of a heliograph.

he·li·o·graph (hē′lē·ə·graf′, -gräf′) *n.* **1** An instrument for taking photographs of the sun. **2** A photograph taken by sunlight. **3** A mirror for signaling by flashes of light. —*v.t.* & *v.i.* To signal with a heliograph. —**he·li·og·ra·pher** (hē′lē·og′rə·fər) *n.* —**he′li·o·graph′ic** *adj.* —**he′li·og′ra·phy** *n.*

he·li·o·gra·vure (hē′lē·ō·grə·vyŏŏr′) *n.* Photo engraving, or a print or plate produced by it. See PHOTOGRAVURE.

he·li·ol·a·try (hē′lē·ol′ə·trē) *n.* Worship of the sun. —**he′li·ol′a·ter** *n.* —**he′li·ol′a·trous** *adj.*

he·li·o·lith·ic (hē′lē·ə·lith′ik) *adj.* Denoting a culture characterized by sun-worship and megaliths. [< HELIO- + (MEGA)LITHIC]

he·li·ol·o·gy (hē′lē·ol′ə·jē) *n. Obs.* The science of the sun's energy and action. —**he′li·ol′o·gist** *n.*

he·li·om·e·ter (hē′lē·om′ə·tər) *n. Astron.* An instrument for the accurate measurement of small angles in the heavens. —**he·li·o·met·ric** (hē′lē·ə·met′rik) or **·ri·cal** *adj.* —**he′li·om′e·try** *n.*

he·li·oph·i·lous (hē′lē·of′ə·ləs) *adj. Bot.* Fond of or turning toward the sun, as the sunflower. [< HELIO- + Gk. *philos* loving]

he·li·o·pho·bi·a (hē′lē·ə·fō′bē·ə) *n.* Morbid aversion to sunlight.

he·li·o·phyte (hē′lē·ə·fīt′) *n. Bot.* A plant growing in the light.

He·li·op·o·lis (hē′lē·op′ə·lis) **1** An ancient city at the apex of the Nile delta in lower Egypt: Egyptian *On.* **2** The Greek name for BAALBEK.

He·li·os (hē′lē·os) In Greek mythology, the sun god, son of Hyperion: also called *Hyperion.*

he·li·o·scope (hē′lē·ə·skōp′) *n. Astron.* A telescope in which the eyes are protected during observations of the sun.

he·li·o·stat (hē′lē·ə·stat′) *n. Astron.* An instrument consisting of a mirror moved by clockwork so that the rays of the sun shall be reflected from it in a fixed direction.

he·li·o·tax·is (hē′lē·ə·tak′sis) *n.* Phototaxis resulting from the effect of the sun's rays. [< HELIO- + (PHOTO)TAXIS] —**he′li·o·tac′tic** (-tak′tik) *adj.*

he·li·o·ther·a·py (hē′lē·ō·ther′ə·pē) *n. Med.* Exposure to the sun for remedial purposes.

he·li·o·trope (hē′lē·ə·trōp′, hēl′yə-) *n.* **1** An herb (genus *Heliotropium*) with small white or purplish fragrant flowers. **2** Any plant which turns toward the sun. **3** The garden heliotrope or common valerian *(Valeriana officinalis)*; also, the winter heliotrope or butterburr *(Petasites fragrans).* **4** A variety of quartz, the bloodstone. **5** A soft rosy-purple, the color of flowers of *Heliotropium arborescens.* [<F *héliotrope* <L *heliotropium* <Gk. *hēliotropion* <*hēlios* sun + *trepein* turn]

he·li·o·tro·pic (hē′lē·ə·trop′ik, -trō′pik, hēl′yə-) *adj.* Characterized by or pertaining to heliotropism. —**he′li·o·trop′i·cal·ly** *adv.*

he·li·ot·ro·pism (hē′lē·ot′rə·piz′əm) *n. Biol.* That property of an organism by virtue of which it tends, when not symmetrically illuminated on all sides, to move either toward or away from the source of light. Also **he′li·ot′ro·py.**

he·li·o·type (hē′lē·ə·tīp′) *n.* A photoengraving from which impressions can be taken by a printing press; an impression so taken. —*adj.* Of or pertaining to such photoengravings, or to the process of making them. Also **he′li·o·typ′ic** (-tip′ik). —**he′li·o·ty′py** (-tī′pē) *n.*

He·li·o·zo·a (hē′lē·ə·zō′ə) *n. pl.* An order of protozoan aquatic organisms with filamentous pseudopodia radiating from a spherical body. [<NL <Gk. *hēlios* sun + *zōon* animal]

hel·i·port (hel′ə·pôrt′, -pōrt′, hē′lə-) *n.* An airport for helicopters. [<HELI(COPTER) + PORT[1] a harbor]

hel·i·spher·ic (hel′ə·sfer′ik) *adj.* Turning spirally on a sphere. See HELIX, SPHERIC. Also **hel′i·spher′i·cal.** [<Gk. *helix* a spiral + SPHERE]

he·li·um (hē′lē·əm) *n.* A chemically inert, odorless, colorless, gaseous element (symbol He, atomic number 2) having a boiling point near absolute zero, found in natural gas deposits and comprising only about 5 parts per million of the atmosphere but the second most abundant element, after hydrogen, in the universe. See PERIODIC TABLE. [<NL <Gk. *hēlios* sun]

he·lix (hē′liks) *n. pl.* **he·lix·es** or **hel·i·ces** (hel′·ə·sēz) **1** *Geom.* A line, thread, wire, or the like, curved into a shape such as it would assume if wound in a single layer round a cylinder; a form like a screw thread. **2** Any spiral. **3** *Anat.* The recurved border of the external ear. **4** *Archit.* A small volute. [<L, a spiral <Gk.]

hell (hel) *n.* **1** The abode of evil spirits; infernal regions; place of eternal punishment, of extreme torment, etc. See GEHENNA, INFERNO, TARTARUS. **2** Any condition of extreme physical or mental suffering. **3** In ancient times, the place of departed spirits; called by the Greeks *Hades,* by the Hebrews *Sheol,* and by the Scandinavians *Hel.* **4** A place of evil, as a gambling house; also, a place for rejected things or refuse. **5** In Christian Science, mortal belief; error; lust; remorse; hatred; revenge; sin. **6** Hellbox. [OE *hel*]

he'll (hēl) Contraction of HE WILL.

Hel·lad·ic (he·lad′ik) *adj.* Of or pertaining to the pre-Greek civilization of the Aegean.

Hel·las (hel′əs) **1** Originally, a small district and town in Thessaly; later, by extension, all lands inhabited by Greek-speaking peoples. **2** The Greek name as well as a poetic and literary usage for GREECE.

hell·bend·er (hel′ben′dər) *n.* **1** A large and voracious amphibian *(Cryptobranchus alleghenien-sis)* common in the valley of the Ohio River, and very tenacious of life. **2** *U.S. Slang* A drunken debauch; also, a debauchee.

hell-bent (hel′bent′) *adj. U.S. Slang* Determined; recklessly eager: *hell-bent* for election.

hell·box (hel′boks′) *n. Printing* A receptacle for broken and battered type.

hell·broth (hel′brôth′, -broth′) *n.* A magical mixture prepared for malignant purposes.

hell·cat (hel′kat′) *n.* **1** A furious or spiteful woman. **2** A witch; hag.

hell·div·er (hel′dī′vər) *n.* The dabchick.

Hel·le (hel′ē) In Greek legend, the daughter of Nephele and Athamas who, fleeing with her brother Phrixus on a ram with golden fleece, fell off and was drowned in the strait thenceforth called *Hellespont,* or "sea of Helle."

hel·le·bo·ras·ter (hel′ə·bə·ras′tər) *n.* An English species of hellebore *(Helleborus foetidus)* with numerous globular flowers, often cultivated for ornament: also called *bear's-foot, stinking* or *fetid hellebore.*

hel·le·bore (hel′ə·bôr, -bōr) *n.* **1** A perennial herb (genus *Helleborus*) of the crowfoot family having serrated leaves and large flowers. Cultivated species are, in the United States, the green hellebore *(H. viridis),* and in Europe, the black hellebore or *Christmas rose (H. niger),* the black roots of which are a powerful cathartic. **2** Any of certain herbs (genus *Veratrum*) of the lily family whose dried rootstocks yield poisonous alkaloids of use in medicine and as insecticides; especially the American or green hellebore *(V. viride)* and the European white hellebore *(V. album)*; also called *false hellebore.* **3** The powdered root of the American hellebore, used to destroy plant vermin. [<L *helleborus* <Gk. *helleboros*]

hel·le·bo·re·in (hel′ə·bôr′ē·in, -bō′rē-) *n. Chem.* A toxic glucoside, $C_{37}H_{56}O_{18}$, from the rhizome of *Helleborus niger* and *H. viridis*: a powerful cardiac stimulant.

hel·leb·o·rin (hə·leb′ə·rin, hel′ə·bôr′in, -bō′rin) *n. Chem.* A colorless crystalline glucoside, $C_{28}H_{36}O_6$, from the same sources as helleborein: a powerful cathartic and emmenagog.

Hel·len (hel′ən) In Greek legend, son of Deucalion and Pyrrha and progenitor, through his sons Aeolus, Dorus, and Xuthus, of the Greek race.

Hel·lene (hel′ēn) *n.* A Greek. Also **Hel·le′ni·an.** [<Gk. *Hellēn*]

Hel·len·ic (he·len′ik, -lē′nik) *adj.* Greek; Grecian. —*n.* A subfamily of the Indo-European languages, consisting of the Greek language and its dialects, ancient and modern. See GREEK.

Hel·le·nism (hel′ə·niz′əm) *n.* **1** Ancient Greek character, ideals, or civilization. **2** A Greek idiom or phrase. **3** Assimilation of Greek speech, manners, and culture, as by the Romans or the Jews of the Diaspora.

Hel·le·nist (hel′ə·nist) *n.* **1** An adopter of Greek customs, language, and usages; especially, a Grecizing Jew in the time of the Apostles or in the Alexandrian church: called in the English versions of the New Testament *Grecian Jew* or *Grecian.* **2** A Greek scholar; a specialist in Greek. **3** One of the Byzantine Greeks who contributed to the revival of classical learning in Europe in the 15th century.

Hel·le·nis·tic (hel′ə·nis′tik) *adj.* **1** Of or pertaining to Hellenists. **2** Resembling, representing, or akin to the Greek in thought or style; especially, Greek with an admixture of foreign elements. **3** Of or pertaining to the Hellenistic Age. Also **Hel′le·nis′ti·cal.**

Hellenistic Age The period which began with the conquests of Alexander the Great and ended about 300 years later: characterized by the spread of Greek language and culture throughout the Near East.

Hellenistic Greek See KOINÉ.

Hel·le·nize (hel′ə·nīz) *v.t.* & *v.i.* **·nized, ·niz·ing** To make or become Greek or Hellenic; adopt or imbue with Greek language or customs; Grecize. —**Hel·le·ni·za·tion** (hel′ə·nə·zā′shən, -nī·zā′-) *n.* —**Hel′le·niz′er** *n.*

hel·ler (hel′ər) *n.* Any one of several small silver or copper coins formerly current in Germany, Switzerland, and Austria. [<G, from *Hall,* a Swabian town where first minted]

Hel·les (hel′əs), **Cape** The southern extremity of Gallipoli Peninsula, European Turkey.

Hel·les·pont (hel′əs·pont) The ancient Greek name for the DARDANELLES. See HELLE.

hell·fire (hel′fīr′) *n.* One of the torments of the damned; the flames of hell.

Hell Gate A narrow channel of the East River in New York City.

hell·gram·mite (hel′grə·mīt) *n.* The large aquatic larva of a megalopterous insect, the four-winged dobson fly, much used as a bait for black bass and other fish: also called *dobson.* See DOBSON FLY. [Origin unknown]

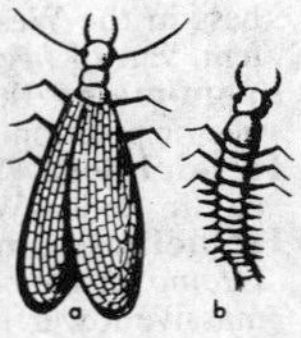

HELLGRAMMITE
Dobson fly *(a)* and larva *(b).*

hell·hound (hel′hound′) *n.* A hound of hell; a fierce and cruel pursuer.

hel·lion (hel′yən) *n. Colloq.* A mischievous person; one given to wild and unpredictable actions. Also called *hallion.* [<HELL]

hell·ish (hel′ish) *adj.* Of or like hell; diabolical; also, wicked; malignant; horrible. See synonyms under INFERNAL. —**hell′ish·ly** *adv.* —**hell′ish·ness** *n.*

hell·kite (hel′kīt′) *n.* **1** A fierce bird of prey. **2** A wantonly malignant or cruel person.

hel·lo (hə·lō′) *interj.* **1** An exclamation used in calling the attention and in greeting, especially over the telephone. **2** An exclamation of surpise. —*n. pl.* **hel·loes** The call "hello." —*v.t.* & *v.i.* **·loed, ·lo·ing** To call "hello" to.

Hells Canyon A canyon of the Snake River on the Idaho-Oregon border; maximum depth, 7,900 feet.

helm[1] (helm) *n.* **1** *Naut.* The steering apparatus of a vessel, especially the tiller. **2** Metaphorically, any place of control or responsibility; administration. —*v.t.* To manage the helm of; steer; direct. [OE *helma* rudder]

helm[2] (helm) *n. Archaic* & *Poetic* A helmet; covering. —*v.t.* To cover or supply with a helmet. [OE *helm* covering]

Hel·mand (hel′mənd) A river in Afghanistan, flowing 700 miles SW to the Seistan depression. Also **Hil·mand** (hil′mənd).

hel·met (hel′mit) *n.* **1** A covering of defensive or protective armor for the head, made of metal, as worn by soldiers of all times, or of leather, as worn by football players. **2** Something resembling head armor in shape, position, or function: as, protective headgear, etc.; the metal head covering of a diving suit,

or the wire-mesh headguard worn by fencers. [<OF, dim. of *helme* a helmet <Gmc.] — **hel′met·ed** *adj.*

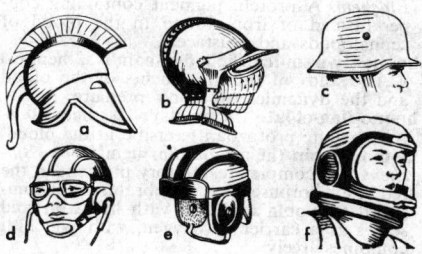

TYPES OF HELMETS

a. Helmet of Grecian warrior.
b. Casque, 16th century knight.
c. German, World War II.
d. Aviator's with head-phone.
e. Football player.
f. Space pilot.

Helm·holtz (helm′hōlts), **Baron von,** 1821–1894, Hermann Ludwig Ferdinand, German physiologist and physicist.

hel·minth (hel′minth) *n.* A worm; specifically, a parasitic intestinal worm. [<Gk. *helmins, -inthos* a worm]

hel·min·thi·a·sis (hel′min·thī′ə·sis) *n. Pathol.* Any disorder caused by infestation with worms. [<Gk. *helmins, -inthos* a worm + -IASIS]

hel·min·thic (hel·min′thik) *adj.* 1 Worm-expelling. 2 Pertaining to helminths. — *n.* A vermifuge; an anthelmintic.

hel·min·thol·o·gy (hel′min·thol′ə·jē) *n.* 1 The study of intestinal worms and their effects. 2 The branch of zoology that treats of worms, especially of parasitic worms. [<Gk. *helmins, -inthos* a worm + -LOGY]

helms·man (helmz′mən) *n. pl.* **·men** (-mən) A steersman; one who guides a ship.

helm roof *Archit.* A pointed roof with four inclined faces, gabled at the apex.

Helm·stedt (helm′shtet) A city in Lower Saxony, Germany. Formerly **Helm′städt** (-shtet).

He·lo·der·ma (hē′lə·dûr′mə) *n.* A genus of American lizards, including the Gila monster. [<NL *hēlos* a nail + *derma* skin] — **he′lo·der′ma·toid** (-toid) *adj. & n.* — **he′lo·der′mid** (-mid) *n.* — **he′lo·der′moid** (-moid) *adj. & n.*

Hé·lo·ïse (ā·lō·ēz′) French form of LOUISE. — Héloïse, 1101–64, French abbess; pupil and mistress of Abélard and, later, his wife.

he·lo·phyte (hē′lə·fīt) *n. Bot.* A plant growing in marshes and adapted to an amphibious life. [<Gk. *helos* marsh + -PHYTE]

hel·o·plank·ton (hel′ə·plangk′tən) See HELEO-PLANKTON.

hel·ot (hel′ət, hē′lət) *n.* 1 One of a class of serfs of ancient Sparta, bound to the soil, and in most cases descended from prisoners of war. 2 Any slave. [<L *helotes* <Gk. *heilōs, heilōtos;* appar. from *Helos,* a Laconian town enslaved by Sparta]

hel·ot·ism (hel′ət·iz′əm, hē′lət-) *n.* 1 Serfdom, as that of ancient Sparta. 2 *Bot.* A type of symbiosis, especially the relation between algae and fungi in forming lichens.

hel·ot·ry (hel′ət·rē, hē′lət-) *n.* 1 Serfdom. 2 Helots as a class.

help (help) *v.t.* 1 To give or provide assistance to; aid. 2 To assist in some action, motion, etc.: with *on, into, out of, up, down,* etc. 3 To rescue, as from death or danger. 4 To give relief to; ease; comfort: to *help* a cold. 5 To be responsible for: He can't *help* it if he's lame. 6 To avoid; refrain from: I couldn't *help* seeing her. 7 To serve; wait on as a waiter, clerk, etc. — *v.i.* 8 To give assistance; be of service. — *n.* 1 Assistance afforded toward the promotion of an object or the attainment of an end. 2 Remedy or relief. 3 Rescue or succor. 4 One who or that which aids; a helper. 5 *U.S.* A hired servant; domestic: often used collectively: The *help* are on strike. 6 *Dial.* A portion of food. [OE *helpan*] — **help′er** *n.*

Synonyms (verb): abet, aid, assist, befriend, cooperate, encourage, foster, relieve, second,

succor, support, sustain, uphold. *Help* expresses greater dependence and deeper need than *aid.* In extremity we say "God *help* me" rather than "God *aid* me." In time of danger we cry *"Help! Help!"* rather than *"Aid! Aid!"* To *aid* is to *second* another's own exertions. We speak of *helping* the helpless, rather than of *aiding* them. *Help* includes *aid,* but *aid* may fall short of the meaning of *help.* In law to *aid* or *abet* makes one a principal. (Compare synonyms for ACCESSORY.) To *cooperate* is to *aid* as an equal; to *assist* implies a subordinate and secondary relation. One *assists* a fallen friend to rise; he *cooperates* with him in helping others. *Encourage,* and usually *uphold,* refer to mental *aid; succor* and *support,* oftenest to material assistance. We *encourage* the timid or despondent, *succor* the endangered, *support* the weak, *uphold* those who else might be shaken or cast down. Compare ABET, AID, PROMOTE, SERVE. *Antonyms:* see synonyms for HINDER.

help·ful (help′fəl) *adj.* Affording aid; beneficial. — **help′ful·ly** *adv.* — **help′ful·ness** *n.*

help·ing (hel′ping) *n.* 1 A giving of aid. 2 A portion of food.

helping verb An auxiliary verb. See *auxiliary* (*n.,* def. 2a).

help·less (help′lis) *adj.* 1 Unable to help oneself; feeble. 2 Incompetent; incapable. 3 Destitute of help.

help·mate (help′māt) *n.* 1 A helper; partner. 2 A wife. See synonyms under ASSOCIATE.

help·meet (help′mēt) *n.* A helpmate.

Hel·sing·ør (hel′sing·œr′) The Danish name for ELSINORE.

Hel·sin·ki (hel′sing·kē) The capital of Finland, on the Gulf of Finland. *Swedish* **Hel·sing·fors** (hel′sing·fôrz)

hel·ter-skel·ter (hel′tər·skel′tər) *adv.* In a hurried and confused manner. — *adj.* Hurried and confused. — *n.* Disorderly hurry; confused and hasty action. [Imit.]

helve (helv) *n.* The handle, as of an ax or hatchet. [OE *helfe*]

Hel·ve·tia (hel·vē′shə) The Latin name for SWITZERLAND. — **Hel·ve′tian** *adj. & n.*

Hel·vet·ic (hel·vet′ik) *adj.* Pertaining to the people of Helvetia (Switzerland); Swiss. — *n.* An adherent of Zwingli and the other Swiss reformers; a Swiss Protestant.

Hel·ve·ti·i (hel·vē′shē·ī) *n. pl.* The members of an ancient Germano-Celtic tribe, originally living in the region bounded by the Black Forest, the Main, and the Rhine; also, in the time of Julius Caesar, in western Switzerland.

Hel·vé·tius (hel·vē′shəs, *Fr.* el·vā·syüs′), **Claude,** 1715–71, French philosopher.

hem[1] (hem) *n.* A finished edge made on a fabric by turning over the raw edge (usually twice) and sewing down the first fold: done to prevent raveling or as an ornament. — *v.t.* **hemmed, hem·ming** 1 To make a hem on; border; edge. 2 To shut in; enclose; restrict: usually with *in, about,* etc. [OE] — **hem′mer** *n.*

hem[2] (hem) *n. & interj.* A sound made as in clearing the throat; ahem. — *v.i.* **hemmed, hem·ming** 1 To make the sound "hem." 2 To hesitate in speaking. [Imit.]

hem- See also words beginning HAEM-.

hem- Var. of HEMO-.

hema- *combining form* Blood: *hemapoiesis.* Also spelled *haema-.* [<Gk. *haima* blood]

he·ma·ba·rom·e·ter (hē′mə·bə·rom′ə·tər, hem′ə-) *n. Med.* An instrument for determining the specific gravity of blood.

he·ma·chrome (hē′mə·krōm, hem′ə-) *n. Biochem.* The red coloring matter of the blood.

he·ma·cy·tom·e·ter (hē′mə·sī·tom′ə·tər, hem′ə-) *n.* An instrument used in counting blood cells and micro-organisms. — **he′ma·cy·tom′e·try** *n.*

he·ma·gog (hē′mə·gôg, -gog, hem′ə-) *n. Med.* An agent which promotes or favors the discharge of blood. Also **he′ma·gogue.** [<HEM- + -AGOG] — **he′ma·gog′ic** (-goj′ik) *adj.*

he·mal (hē′məl) *adj.* 1 Pertaining to blood or the vascular system; of the nature of blood. 2 Pertaining to or situated on the side of the body that contains the heart. Also spelled *haemal.* [<Gk. *haima* blood + -AL]

he-man (hē′man′) *n. pl.* **-men** (-men′) *Slang* A virile, muscular man.

Hem·ans (hem′ənz, hē′mənz), **Felicia Dorothea,** 1793–1835, *née* Browne, English poet.

he·ma·pho·bi·a (hē′mə·fō′bē·ə, hem′ə-) See HEMOPHOBIA.

he·ma·poi·e·sis (hē′mə·poi·ē′sis, hem′ə-) *n.* The promotion or production of blood. Also called *hematopoiesis.* [<HEMA- + Gk. *poiēsis* a making <*poieein* make] — **he′ma·poi·et′ic** (-poi·et′ik) *adj.*

hemat- Var. of HEMATO-.

he·ma·tal (hē′mə·təl, hem′ə-) *adj.* Of, relating to, or associated with the blood or blood vessels.

he·ma·tal·los·co·py (hē′mə·təl·os′kə·pē, hem′ə-) *n.* The scientific analysis of blood to determine the blood type to which it belongs. [HEMAT- + ALLO- (def. 3) + -SCOPY]

he·ma·te·in (hē′mə·tē′in, hem′ə-) *n. Chem.* A reddish-brown, crystalline substance, $C_{16}H_{12}O_6$, extracted from logwood, and used as an indicator and stain. [<HEMAT- + -EIN]

he·ma·tem·e·sis (hē′mə·tem′ə·sis, hem′ə-) *n. Pathol.* Vomiting of blood; gastric hemorrhage.

he·ma·ther·mal (hē′mə·thûr′məl, hem′ə-) See HEMATOTHERMAL.

he·mat·ic (hi·mat′ik) *adj.* 1 Of, pertaining to, or contained in blood. 2 Effecting a change in the blood. — *n.* A medicine that produces a change in the blood.

hem·a·tin (hem′ə·tin, hē′mə-) *n.* A brownish-black, iron-containing powder formed from hemoglobin by treatment with acid.

hem·a·tin·ic (hem′ə·tin′ik, hē′mə-) *n. Med.* Any agent which increases the number of red corpuscles in the blood. — *adj.* Of or pertaining to hematin.

hem·a·tite (hem′ə·tīt, hē′mə-) *n.* Red ferric oxide, Fe_2O_3, one of the important ores of iron, occurring in columnar, granular, or other forms, and crystallizing in the hexagonal system. Also spelled *haematite.* [<L *haematites* <Gk. *haimatitēs* bloodlike < *haima* blood] — **hem·a·tit·ic** (hem′ə·tit′ik, hē′mə-) *adj.*

hemato- *combining form* Blood: *hematoblast:* also, before vowels, *hemat-.* Also spelled *haemato-.* [<Gk. *haima, haimatos* blood]

hem·a·to·blast (hem′ə·tō·blast′, hē′mə-) *n. Biol.* A cell in the bone marrow or liver which produces the red corpuscles of the blood; a blood platelet.

hem·a·to·cele (hem′ə·tō·sēl′, hē′mə-) *n. Pathol.* A tumor containing blood.

hem·a·to·crit (hem′ə·tō·krit′, hē′mə-) *n.* An instrument which, by centrifugal action, separates the corpuscles and the serum in blood in order to determine the relative amounts. Also spelled *haematokrit.* [<HEMATO- + Gk. *kritēs* a judge < *krinein* judge]

hem·a·toc·ry·al (hem′ə·tok′rē·əl, hē′mə-) *adj. Zool.* Cold-blooded, as fishes and reptiles: also spelled *haematocryal.* [<HEMATO- + Gk. *kryos* cold]

hem·a·to·gen·e·sis (hem′ə·tō·jen′ə·sis, hē′mə-) *n.* Formation of blood. — **hem′a·to·gen′ic** or **hem′a·to·ge·net′ic** (-jə·net′ik) *adj.*

hem·a·toid (hē′mə·toid, hem′ə-) *adj.* Bloody, or resembling blood.

he·ma·tol·o·gy (hē′mə·tol′ə·jē, hem′ə-) *n.* The branch of medical science that treats of the blood, its formation, functions, and diseases: also spelled *haematology.* Also **he′ma·to·lo′gi·a** (-tə·lō′jē·ə).

he·ma·tol·y·sis (hē′mə·tol′ə·sis, hem′ə-), **he·ma·to·lyt·ic** (hē′mə·tō·lit′ik, hem′ə-) See HEMOLYSIS, etc.

he·ma·to·ma (hē′mə·tō′mə, hem′ə-) *n. pl.* **·to·ma·ta** (-tō′mə·tə) *Pathol.* A blood tumor. [<HEMAT- + -OMA]

he·ma·tom·e·ter (hē′mə·tom′ə·tər, hem′ə-) *n.* An instrument for determining the number of corpuscles in a given quantity of blood. — **he′ma·tom′e·try** *n.*

he·ma·to·pho·bi·a (hē′mə·tō·fō′bē·ə, hem′ə-) See HEMOPHOBIA.

he·ma·to·poi·e·sis (hē′mə·tō·poi′ē·sis, hem′ə-), **he·ma·to·poi·et·ic** (hē′mə·tō′poi·et′ik, hem′ə-) See HEMAPOIESIS, etc.

he·ma·tose (hē′mə·tōs, hem′ə-) *adj.* Fully or abnormally charged with blood.

he·ma·to·sis (hē′mə·tō′sis, hem′ə-) *n. Physiol.* The formation of blood; conversion of chyle or venous blood into arterial blood. [<NL

<Gk. *haimatōsis* < *haimatoein* make into blood]

he·ma·to·ther·a·py (hē′mə·tō·ther′ə·pē, hem′ə-) See HEMOTHERAPY.

he·ma·to·ther·mal (hē′mə·tō·thûr′məl, hem′ə-) *adj. Zool.* Warm-blooded, as mammals and birds: also spelled *haematothermal.*

hem·a·tox·y·lin (hem′ə·tok′sə·lin, hē′mə-) *n. Chem.* A colorless crystalline compound, $C_{16}H_{14}O_6 \cdot 3H_2O$, containing the coloring matter of logwood: used as a dye and indicator. [<HEMATO- + XYL- + -IN]

hem·a·to·zo·on (hem′ə·tō·zō′on, hē′mə-) *n. pl.* **·zo·a** (-zō′ə) An animal parasite living in the blood. [<HEMATO- + Gk. *zōon* animal]

hem·a·tu·ri·a (hem′ə·tŏŏr′ē·ə, -tyŏŏr′-, hē′mə-) *n. Pathol.* Bloody urine. [<HEMAT- + -URIA]

hem·el·y·tron (hem·el′ə·tron) *n. pl.* **·tra** (-trə) *Entomol.* One of the partially thickened and hardened forewings of certain insects: also called *hemielytron.* Also **hem·el′y·trum** (-trəm). [<HEMI- + ELYTRON] **— hem·el′y·tral** *adj.*

hem·er·a·lo·pi·a (hem′ər·ə·lō′pē·ə) *n. Pathol.* Day blindness, in which sight is less distinct by daylight than by night or by artificial light. See NYCTALOPIA. [<NL <Gk. *hēmera* day + *alaos* blind + *ōps* eye] **— hem′er·a·lo′·pic** *adj.*

Hem·er·o·bap·tist (hem′ər·ə·bap′tist) *n.* **1** A member of an ancient Jewish sect practicing daily ceremonial ablution. **2** One of an early Christian sect holding to daily baptism. [<Med. L *Hemerobaptista* <Gk. *Hēmerobaptistēs* < *hēmera* day + *baptistēs* baptizer]

hem·er·o·phyte (hem′ər·ə·fīt′) *n. Bot.* A plant introduced through the agency of man. [<Gk. *hēmeros* cultivated + -PHYTE]

hemi- *prefix* Half: *hemisphere.* [<Gk., half]

-hemia See -EMIA.

hem·i·al·gi·a (hem′ē·al′jē·ə) *n. Pathol.* Pain, especially in the head, confined to one side; unilateral pain. [<HEMI- on one side + -ALGIA]

hem·i·a·nop·si·a (hem′ē·ə·nop′sē·ə) *n. Pathol.* A paralysis, partial or total, of some of the fibers of the optic nerve, with the result that part of the field of vision is obscured or obliterated in one or both eyes. Also **hem′i·a·no′pi·a** (-nō′pē·ə). [<NL <Gk. *hēmi-* half + *an-* without + *ōps* eye] **— hem′i·a·nop′tic** (-nop′tik) *adj.*

hem·i·at·ro·phy (hem′ē·at′rə·fē) *n. Pathol.* The wasting away of one side, as of the face.

he·mic (hē′mik, hem′ik) *adj.* Pertaining or relating to blood: *hemic* diseases. Also spelled *haemic.*

hem·i·cel·lu·lose (hem′i·sel′yə·lōs) *n. Biochem.* Any of a class of polysaccharide carbohydrates more readily hydrolyzed than cellulose; they occur widely in plants.

hem·i·chor·date (hem′i·kôr′dāt) *adj.* Of, pertaining to or belonging to a division of chordates *(Hemichordata)* characterized by paired gill slits and a primitive notochord including many small marine forms. **—** *n.* A member of this division; a tongue worm. [<NL <Gk. *hēmi-* half + *chordata* chordate]

hem·i·cra·ny (hem′i·krā′nē) *n. Pathol.* Migraine, or nervous headache. Also **hem′i·cra′·ni·a** (-nē·ə). [<F *hemicraine* <LL *hemicrania* <Gk. *hemikrania* < *hēmi-* half + *kranion* skull]

hem·i·cy·cle (hem′i·sī′kəl) *n.* **1** A semicircular arena, as in a theater. **2** A semicircle, or objects arranged in a semicircle. **— hem′i·cy′·clic** (-sī′klik, -sik′lik) *adj.*

hem·i·dem·i·sem·i·qua·ver (hem′ē·dem′ē·sem′·ē·kwā′vər) *n. Music* A sixty-fourth note.

hem·i·dome (hem′i·dōm) *n. Mineral.* That form in a crystal composed of two parallel domed planes in the triclinic, or of two parallel orthodomic planes in the monoclinic system of crystallization.

hem·i·el·y·tron (hem′ē·el′ə·tron) See HEMELYTRON, etc.

he·mig·na·thous (hə·mig′nə·thəs) *adj.* Having one jaw shorter than the other, as in certain birds. [<HEMI- + Gk. *gnathos* jaw]

hem·i·he·dral (hem′i·hē′drəl) *adj. Mineral.* Pertaining to crystal forms that possess only one half as many planes as are required for complete symmetry in the class to which they belong. [<HEMI- + Gk. *hedra* seat, surface] **— hem′i·he′dral·ly** *adv.*

hem·i·he·dron (hem′i·hē′drən) *n. pl.* **·dra** (-drə) A hemihedral crystal form.

hem·i·met·a·bol·ic (hem′i·met′ə·bol′ik) *adj. Entomol.* Designating those insects whose larvae have an incomplete metamorphosis, developing gradually into the adult stage: opposed to *holometabolic.* Also **hem·i·me·tab·o·lous** (hem′i·mə·tab′ə·ləs). **— hem′i·me·tab′o·lism** (-tab′ə·liz′əm) *n.*

hem·i·mor·phic (hem′i·môr′fik) *adj. Mineral.* **1** Pertaining to crystals that are unsymmetric with reference to the opposite ends of a symmetry axis. **2** Pertaining to a class in the monoclinic system. **— hem′i·mor′phism** (-fiz·əm) *n.*

hem·i·mor·phite (hem′i·môr′fīt) *n.* A white to yellowish or brown orthorhombic hydrous zinc silicate, $Zn_2SiO_4 \cdot H_2O$, pyroelectric and sometimes called *electric calamine*: an important ore of zinc.

he·min (hē′min) *n. Biochem.* A brownish-red, crystalline compound, $C_{34}H_{32}O_4N_4FeCl$, formed by the action of glacial acetic or hydrochloric acid on hemoglobin; hematin hydrochloride: also spelled *haemin.* [<Gk. *haima* blood]

Hem·ing·way (hem′ing·wā), **Ernest,** 1899–1961, U.S. novelist.

hem·i·par·a·site (hem′i·par′ə·sīt) *n. Bot.* A plant partly parasitic, as the mistletoe. **— hem′i·par′a·sit′ic** (-par′ə·sit′ik) *adj.*

hem·i·ple·gi·a (hem′i·plē′jē·ə) *n. Pathol.* Paralysis of one side of the body. Also **hem′i·ple′gy. — hem′i·ple′gic** (-plē′jik, -plej′ik) *adj.*

He·mip·ter·a (hi·mip′tər·ə) *n. pl.* An order of insects generally with suctorial mouth parts, and usually with four wings thick at the base and membranous at the free end, including the true bugs, cicadas, crickets, plant lice, etc. [<NL <Gk. *hēmi-* half + *pteron* wing] **— he·mip′ter** *n.* **— he·mip′ter·al** or **he·mip′·ter·ous** *adj.* **— he·mip′ter·an** *adj.* & *n.*

hem·i·sphere (hem′ə·sfir) *n.* **1** A half-sphere, formed by a plane passing through the center of the sphere. **2** A half of the terrestrial or of the celestial globe, or a map or projection of the half of either on a plane surface. The world is usually considered as divided either at the equator into the *northern* and *southern* hemispheres, or at some meridian between Europe and America into the *eastern* and *western,* usually at the twentieth meridian west of Greenwich. **3** *Anat.* One of two large convoluted, semiovoid masses forming the bulk of the cerebrum. [<F *hémisphère* <L *hemisphaerium* <Gk. *hēmisphairion* < *hēmi-* half + *sphaira* a sphere] **— hem·i·spher·ic** (hem′ə·sfer′ik) or **·i·cal** *adj.*

hem·i·sphe·roid (hem′ə·sfir′oid) *n.* A half of a spheroid. **— hem′i·sphe·roi′dal** (-sfi·roid′l) *adj.*

hem·i·stich (hem′i·stik) *n.* A half of a poetic line; an incomplete poetic line. [<LL *hemistichium* <Gk. *hēmistichion* < *hēmi-* half + *stichos* a row, line of poetry]

hem·i·sys·to·le (hem′i·sis′tə·lē) *n. Med.* Contraction of only one of the heart ventricles, producing only one pulse beat for every two heartbeats.

hem·i·ter·pene (hem′i·tûr′pēn) *n. Chem.* Any of a group of isomeric hydrocarbons related to the terpenes, and having the general formula C_5H_8.

hem·i·trope (hem′i·trōp) *n.* A twin crystal. **—** *adj.* **1** Having one part in reverse position with reference to the other: said of a crystal form. **2** Half inverted. Also **hem′i·trop′ic** (-trop′ik, -trō′pik) *adj.* [<F *hémitrope* <Gk. *hēmi-* half + *tropē* a turning < *trepein* turn]

he·mit·ro·pous (hə·mit′rə·pəs) *adj.* **1** *Bot.* Half anatropous: said of a half-inverted ovule. **2** *Entomol.* Adapted for pollinating certain kinds of flowers: said of bees, etc.

hem·line (hem′līn′) *n.* The line formed by the lower edge of a garment, as a dress.

hem·lock (hem′lok) *n.* **1** An evergreen tree (genus *Tsuga*) of North America and Asia. **2** The wood of this tree. **3** The hemlock spruce. **4** The spotted hemlock *(Conium maculatum),* a large biennial herb of the parsley or carrot family, yielding coniine: also **poison hemlock. 5** A poison made from the unripe dried fruit of this herb: Socrates drank the *hemlock.* **6** Any of several related herbs, as the water hemlock *(Cicuta maculata).* [OE *hymlice*]

hemlock spruce A North American coniferous tree of the pine family *(Tsuga canadense),* having a coarse non-resinous wood used for paper pulp and packing boxes, and a bark which yields an important tanning material.

hemo- *combining form* Blood: *hemoglobin*: also, before vowels, *hem-.* Also spelled *haemo-.* [<Gk. *haima* blood]

he·mo·cy·a·nin (hē′mə·sī′ə·nin, hem′ə-) *n. Biochem.* A protein pigment containing copper instead of iron, found in the blood of cephalopods and crustacea.

he·mo·dy·nam·ics (hē′mō·dī·nam′iks, hem′ō-) *n.* The study of the movements of the blood and the dynamics of blood pressure.

he·mo·flag·el·late (hē′mə·flaj′ə·lāt, hem′ə-) *n.* A flagellate protozoan parasitic in the blood.

he·mo·glo·bin (hē′mə·glō′bin, hem′ə-) *n. Biochem.* The complex respiratory pigment in the red blood corpuscles of vertebrates. It is composed of globin in union with hematin, and serves as a carrier of oxygen, with which it combines freely.

he·mo·hy·per·ox·i·a (hē′mō·hī′pər·ok′sē·ə, hem′ō-) *n. Med.* Hyperoxia of the blood.

he·mo·hy·pox·i·a (hē′mō·hī·pok′sē·ə, hem′ō-) *n. Med.* Hypoxia of the blood.

he·moid (hē′moid) *adj.* Resembling blood; hematoid: also spelled *haemoid.*

he·mo·leu·ko·cyte (hē′mə·lōō′kə·sīt, hem′ə-) *n.* A white blood corpuscle. Also **he′mo·leu′·co·cyte.**

he·mo·ly·sin (hē′mə·lī′sin, hem′ə-, hi·mol′ə·sin) *n. Biochem.* A substance contained or formed in the blood and having the power to liberate hemoglobin from the red blood corpuscles.

he·mol·y·sis (hi·mol′ə·sis) *n.* Dissolution or breakdown of red blood corpuscles with liberation of their contained hemoglobin: also called *hematolysis.* **— he·mo·lyt·ic** (hē′·mə·lit′ik, hem′ə-) *adj.*

Hé·mon (ā·môn′), **Louis,** 1880–1913, French novelist.

he·mo·phil·i·a (hē′mə·fil′ē·ə, -fil′yə, hem′ə-) *n. Pathol.* A disorder characterized by profuse and excessive bleeding even from slight injuries: typically affecting only males, who inherit it as a sex-linked genetic factor transmitted through the mother; the bleeder's disease. Also spelled *haemophilia.* [<NL <Gk. *haima* blood + *philia* fondness]

he·mo·phil·i·ac (hē′mə·fil′ē·ak, hem′ə-) *n.* One afflicted with hemophilia; a bleeder. Also **he′mo·phile** (-fīl).

he·mo·phil·ic (hē′mə·fil′ik, hem′ə-) *adj.* **1** Pertaining to hemophilia. **2** Thriving in blood, as certain bacteria.

he·mo·pho·bi·a (hē′mə·fō′bē·ə, hem′ə-) *n.* A morbid fear of blood: also *hemaphobia, hematophobia.* **— he′mo·pho′bic** *adj.*

he·mo·ple·o·nex·i·a (hē′mə·plē′ə·nek′sē·ə, hem′ə-) *n.* Pleonexia.

hem·op·ty·sis (hem·op′tə·sis) *n. Pathol.* Bleeding from the lungs or bronchial tubes. [<HEMO- + *ptysis* spitting <Gk. *ptyein* spit]

hem·or·rhage (hem′ər·ij, hem′rij) *n.* Discharge of blood from a ruptured blood vessel. **—** *v.i.* **hem·or·rhaged, hem·or·rhag·ing** To bleed copiously. Also spelled *haemorrhage.* [<L *haemorrhagia* <Gk. *haimorrhagia* < *haima* blood + *-rhagia* < *rhēgnynai* burst] **— hem·or·rhag·ic** (hem′ə·raj′ik) *adj.*

hem·or·rhoid (hem′ə·roid) *n. Often pl.* A swollen mass of varicose veins in the rectal mucous membrane: also called (in the plural) *piles.* Also spelled *haemorrhoid.* [<F <L <Gk. *haimorrhoides (phlebes)* bleeding (veins) < *haima* blood + *rheein* flow] **— hem·or·rhoi·dal** (hem′ə·roid′l) *adj.*

he·mo·spa·sia (hē′mə·spā′zhə, -zhē·ə, hem′ə-) *n.* The drawing of blood to a given part of the body by means of a suction cup. [<HEMO- + Gk. *spasis* suction < *spaein* draw]

he·mo·sta·sia (hē′mə·stā′zhə, -zhē·ə, hem′ə-) *n.* **1** Congestion of blood in a part. **2** The checking of hemorrhage. Also **he·mos·ta·sis** (hi·mos′tə·sis). [<NL <Gk. *haima* blood + *stasis* a standing]

he·mo·stat (hē′mə·stat, hem′ə-) *n. Med.* A device or drug for checking the flow of blood.

he·mo·stat·ic (hē′mə·stat′ik, hem′ə-) *adj. Med.* **1** Stopping the flow of blood. **2** Preventive of bleeding. **—** *n.* A hemostat.

he·mo·ther·a·py (hē′mə·ther′ə·pē, hem′ə-) *n. Med.* The treatment of disease by the administration of blood or blood preparations: also called *hematotherapy.*

he·mo·tho·rax (hē′mə·thôr′aks, -thō′raks, hem′ə-) *n.* Effusion of blood into the chest.

he·mo·thy·mi·a (hē′mə·thī′mē·ə, hem′ə-) *n. Psychiatry* A morbid craving for blood; im-

pulse to murder. [< NL < Gk. *haima* blood + *thymos* passion < *thyein* rage] **—he'mo·thy'mic** *adj.*

hemp (hemp) *n.* **1** A tall, annual Asian herb *(Cannabis sativa)* of the mulberry family, with small green flowers and a tough bark; Indian hemp. **2** The tough and strong fiber obtained from this plant, used for cloth and cordage. **3** A narcotic prepared from the plant, as bhang or hashish. **4** *Colloq.* The hangman's rope. **—Bengal, Bombay, Madras,** or **sunn hemp** See SUNN. [OE *henep*]

hemp agrimony A coarse European herb *(Eupatorium cannabinum)* resembling the boneset of the United States.

hemp dogbane See INDIAN HEMP (def. 2).

hemp·en (hem'pən) *adj.* **1** Made of hemp. **2** Of or pertaining to hemp.

hemp nettle A common weed *(Galeopsis tetrahit)* of the mint family, having stems covered with prickly deflexed bristles and leaves hairy on both sides.

hemp·seed (hemp'sēd') *n.* The seed of hemp.

hemp·y (hem'pē) *adj.* **hemp·i·er, hemp·i·est 1** Hempen. **2** *Scot. & Brit. Dial.* Worthy of hanging: used humorously. Also **hemp'ie.**

hem·stitch (hem'stich') *n.* The ornamental finishing of the inner edge of a hem, made by pulling out several threads adjoining it and drawing the cross-threads together in groups by successive stitches. *—v.t.* To embroider with a hemstitch. **—hem'stitch'er** *n.*

hen (hen) *n.* **1** The mature female of the common domestic fowl. **2** Any female bird. **3** The female of the lobster and certain fishes. [OE *henn*]

hen-and-chickens (hen'ən·chik'ənz) *n.* A plant which propagates by means of offshoots, runners, and other ground parts, as the ground ivy and the European houseleek.

hen·bane (hen'bān') *n.* A poisonous, Old World herb *(Hyoscyamus niger)* of the nightshade family, with sticky, malodorous foliage and reddish-brown flowers: the source of hyoscyamine.

hen·bit (hen'bit') *n.* **1** A low herb *(Lamium amplexicaule)* of the mint family; deadnettle. **2** The ivy-leaved speedwell *(Veronica hederaefolia)*. [Trans. of MLG *hoenderbeet*]

hence (hens) *adv.* **1** Away from this place. **2** In the future. **3** From this cause or source; consequently; therefore. See synonyms under THEREFORE. *—interj.* Depart! [ME *hennes* < *henne* (OE *heonan* from here) + *-s*, adverbial suffix]

hence·forth (hens'fôrth', -fōrth', hens'fôrth', -fōrth') *adv.* From this time on. Also **hence'for'ward** (-fôr'wərd).

hench·man (hench'mən) *n. pl.* **·men** (-mən) **1** A servile assistant. **2** A faithful follower. **3** A male servant. See synonyms under ACCESSORY. [ME *henxstman* < OE *hengst* horse + *man* a groom]

hen·coop (hen'kōōp', -kōōp') *n.* A cage or crib for confining poultry.

hen·dec·a·gon (hen·dek'ə·gon) *n.* A plane figure, with eleven sides and eleven angles: also spelled *endecagon.* [< Gk. *hendeka* eleven + *-GON*] **—hen·de·cag·o·nal** (hen'də·kag'ə·nəl) *adj.*

hen·dec·a·syl·lab·ic (hen'dek·ə·si·lab'ik) *adj.* Containing eleven syllables. *—n.* A metrical line containing eleven syllables: also **hen'dec·a·syl'la·ble.** [< L *hendecasyllabus* < Gk. *hendekasyllabos* + *-IC*]

hen·di·a·dys (hen·dī'ə·dis) *n.* In rhetoric, the use of two words connected by a conjunction to express the same idea as a single word with a qualifier; as, with *might and main* instead of by *main strength.* [< LL < Gk. *hen dia dyoin* one through two]

Hen·don (hen'dən) A municipal borough of Middlesex, England; site of Royal Air Force airfield and scene of annual air show.

hen·e·quen (hen'ə·kin) *n.* **1** A tough fiber obtained from the leaves of the Mexican plant *Agave fourcroydes,* or from the related *A. sisalana;* Mexican sisal. **2** The plant from which this fiber is obtained. Also **hen'e·quin.** [< Sp. < Taino]

Hen·gist (heng'gist, hen'jist), died 488, and his brother **Hor·sa** (hôr'sə), died 455, leaders of the Jutish invaders of Kent, England.

Heng·yang (hung'yäng') A city of SE central China. Formerly **Heng·chow** (hung'jō').

Hen·ley (hen'lē) A municipal borough of Oxfordshire, England; site of an annual rowing regatta since 1839. Also **Hen'ley-on-Thames'** (-temz').

Hen·ley (hen'lē), **William Ernest,** 1849–1903, English journalist, poet, and author.

Hen·lo·pen (hen·lō'pən), **Cape** A cape in Delaware opposite Cape May, New Jersey, at the entrance to Delaware Bay.

hen·na (hen'ə) *n.* **1** An Oriental shrub or small tree *(Lawsonia inermis)* with lance-shaped, entire leaves. **2** A cosmetic preparation from the leaves of this plant: used for dyeing the fingernails, hair, etc. **3** The color of this dye, varying from reddish-orange to coppery-brown. [< Arabic *henna*]

Hen·ne·pin (hen'ə·pin, *Fr.* en·pan'), **Louis,** 1640–1708?, Flemish Franciscan missionary to Canada.

hen·ner·y (hen'ər·ē) *n. pl.* **·ner·ies** A place where hens are kept.

hen·o·the·ism (hen'ō·thē·iz'əm) *n.* The doctrine that ascribes supreme power to some one of several gods in turn; also, the belief in a special supreme god for each region, race, or nation. [< Gk. *hen* one + THEISM] **—hen'o·the·ist** *n.* **—hen'o·the·is'tic** *adj.*

hen·peck (hen'pek') *v.t.* To harass or domineer over (the husband): said of wives.

Hen·ri (hen'rī), **Robert,** 1865–1929, U.S. painter.

Hen·ri·et·ta (hen'rē·et'ə, Du., Sw. hen'rē·et'ä) A feminine personal name. Also **Hen·ri·et·te** (Dan. hen'rē·et'ä; Ger. hen'rē·et'ə), Fr. **Hen·ri·ette** (än·rē·et'), Pg. **Hen·ri·que·ta** (en·rē·kā'tä). [< Gmc., ruler of the home]

hen·roost (hen'rōōst') *n.* A place where poultry roost.

hen·ry (hen'rē) *n. Electr.* The practical unit of inductance; the inductance of a circuit in which the variation of the current at the rate of one ampere per second induces an electromotive force of one volt. [after Joseph Henry]

Hen·ry (hen'rē) A masculine personal name; also, the name of many European monarchs. Also *Du., Dan.* **Hen·drik** (hen'drik), *Fr.* **Hen·ri** (än·rē'), *Latin* **Hen·ri·cus** (hen·rē'kəs), *Sw.* **Hen·rik** (hen'rik), *Pg.* **Hen·ri·que** (en·rē'kä). [< Gmc., ruler of the home]

—Henry I, 1068–1135, king of England 1100–1135; son of William the Conqueror, conquered Normandy: called "Beauclerc."

—Henry II, 1133–89, king of England 1154–1189, first Plantagenet king.

—Henry III, 1207–72, king of England 1216–1272; barons rebelled against his rule under leadership of Simon de Montfort.

—Henry III, 1551–89, king of France 1574–1589; with his mother, Catherine de' Medici, plotted the Massacre of St. Bartholomew's, 1572.

—Henry IV, 1050–1106, Holy Roman Emperor 1056–1106; excommunicated by Pope Gregory VII.

—Henry IV, 1367–1413, king of England 1399–1413; first Lancastrian king: called "Bolingbroke."

—Henry IV, 1553–1610, king of France 1589–1610; first Bourbon king: also known as **Henry of Navarre.**

—Henry V, 1387–1422, king of England 1413–22; conquered France.

—Henry VI, 1421–71, king of England 1422–1461 and 1470–71.

—Henry VII, 1457–1509, king of England 1485–1509; first Tudor king.

—Henry VIII, 1491–1547, king of England 1509–47; threw off papal authority.

—Henry the Navigator, 1394–1460, prince of Portugal; patron of voyagers and explorers.

Henry, Cape A cape in southern Virginia at the southern entrance of Chesapeake Bay.

Hen·ry (hen'rē), **Joseph,** 1797–1878, U.S. physicist. **—O.** See O. HENRY. **—Patrick,** 1736–99, U.S. statesman and orator.

Hens·lowe (henz'lō), **Philip,** died 1616, English theatrical manager.

hent (hent) *v.t. Archaic* To seize; catch. *—n. Obs.* A catch or grasp. [OE *hentan*]

hep (hep) *adj. U.S. Slang* Aware; informed; cognizant: often with *to.* [? Alter. of STEP, as pronounced in counting time for marching]

he·par (hē'pär) *n. Med.* A liver-brown alkaline sulfide formed by fusing an alkaline carbonate, as potash, with sulfur: used as an antacid and alterative: also called *liver of sulfur.* [< Med. L < Gk. *hēpar* the liver]

hep·a·rin (hep'ə·rin) *n. Biochem.* A polysaccharide found in liver and other animal tissues and having the power to prevent the coagulation of blood: used in medicine and surgery. [< Gk. *hēpar* liver + *-IN*]

he·pat·ic (hi·pat'ik) *adj.* **1** Of, pertaining to, or resembling the liver. **2** Occurring in, affecting, or acting upon the liver. **3** *Bot.* Pertaining to or resembling a class of plants, the liverworts. **4** Liver-colored. *—n.* **1** A drug acting on the liver. **2** A liverwort. Also **he·pat'i·cal.** [< L *hepaticus* < Gk. *hēpatikos* < *hēpar* the liver]

he·pat·i·ca (hi·pat'ə·kə) *n. pl.* **·cas** or **·cae** (-sē) Any of a genus *(Hepatica)* of small perennial herbs of the crowfoot family, with three-lobed leaves and delicate, variously colored flowers; the liverleaf. [< NL < L *hepaticus* of the liver]

hepatic cells The functional cells of the liver.

hep·a·ti·tis (hep'ə·tī'tis) *n. Pathol.* Inflammation of the liver.

hep·a·ti·za·tion (hep'ə·tə·zā'shən, -tī·zā'-) *n.* The conversion of any tissue into a substance resembling liver. Also *Brit.* **hep'a·ti·sa'tion.**

hepato- *combining form* Pertaining to the liver: *hepatogenic.* Also, before vowels, **hepat-.** [< Gk. *hēpar, hēpatos* the liver]

hep·a·to·gen·ic (hep'ə·tō·jen'ik) *adj.* Produced by or proceeding from the liver. Also **hep·a·tog·e·nous** (hep'ə·toj'ə·nəs).

hep·a·to·pan·cre·as (hep'ə·tō·pan'krē·əs) *n. Zool.* A glandular organ of many invertebrates, supposed to have the function of the liver and the pancreas.

hep·a·tos·co·py (hep'ə·tos'kə·pē) *n.* **1** Divination by inspecting the livers of animals. **2** Inspection of the liver.

hep·cat (hep'kat') *n. Slang* A jazz expert or enthusiast. [< HEP + CAT (def. 11)]

He·phaes·tus (hi·fes'təs) In Greek mythology, the ugly, lame god of fire and of metallurgy; son of Zeus and Hera, and, in the *Odyssey,* the husband of Aphrodite: identified with the Roman *Vulcan:* also called the *Lemnian smith.* Greek **He·phais'tos.** Also **He·phæs'tus.**

Hep·ple·white (hep'əl·hwīt) *adj.* Denoting an English style of furniture characterized by graceful curves and light, slender woodwork: developed in the reign of George III. [after G. *Hepplewhite,* died 1786, the designer]

hepta- *combining form* Seven: *heptachord.* Also, before vowels, **hept-.** [< Gk. *hepta* seven]

HEPPLEWHITE CHAIR

hep·ta·chlor (hep'tə·klôr, -klōr) *n.* A chlorinated hydrocarbon, $C_{10}H_7Cl_7$, toxic to humans and used as an insecticide.

hep·ta·chord (hep'tə·kôrd) *n. Music* **1** A diatonic octave considered without the upper note. **2** An instrument with seven strings. **3** The interval of the major seventh. [< Gk.

heptachordos < *hepta-* seven + *chordē* a string]

hep·tad (hep′tad) *adj.* Having a combining power of seven; of or belonging to a heptad. — *n.* 1 A collection of seven things. 2 *Chem.* An atom, radical, or element that has a valence of seven. [<Gk. *heptas, -ados* a group of seven]

hep·ta·glot (hep′tə·glot) *adj.* Written in seven languages. — *n.* A book in seven languages.

hep·ta·gon (hep′tə·gon) *n.* A plane figure having seven sides and seven angles. — **hep·tag·o·nal** (hep·tag′ə·nəl) *adj.*

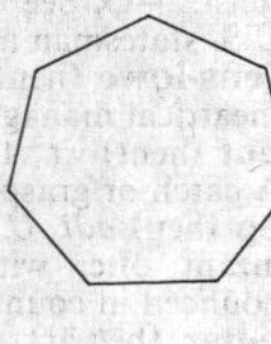

HEPTAGON

hep·ta·he·dron (hep′tə·hē′·drən) *n.* A solid bounded by seven plane faces. — **hep′ta·he′dral** (-drəl) *adj.*

hep·tam·er·ous (hep·tam′ər·əs) *adj.* 1 Having seven parts. 2 *Bot.* Having seven members in each whorl: said of flowers. [<HEPTA- + -MEROUS]

hep·tam·e·ter (hep·tam′ə·tər) *n.* A verse of seven feet or measures.

hep·tane (hep′tān) *n.* A colorless, inflammable, liquid hydrocarbon of the methane series, C_7H_{16}: used as a solvent and in the determination of the octane number of motor fuels. [<HEPT(A)- + -ANE[2]]

hep·tan·gu·lar (hep·tang′gyə·lər) *adj.* Having seven angles.

hep·tar·chy (hep′tär·kē) *n. pl.* **·chies** 1 A group of seven kingdoms or governments; specifically, the seven Saxon kingdoms in England (fifth to ninth century). 2 Government by seven persons.

hep·ta·stich (hep′tə·stik) *n.* A heptameter.

Hep·ta·teuch (hep′tə·tōōk, -tyōōk) *n.* The first seven books of the Old Testament. [<HEPTA- + Gk. *teuchos* book]

hep·tode (hep′tōd) *n. Electronics* A seven-electrode vacuum tube containing an anode, cathode, control electrode, and four additional electrodes ordinarily acting as grids. [<HEPT(A)- + -ODE[1]]

her (hûr) *pron.* The objective case of *she.* — *pronominal adj.* Belonging or pertaining to a female person, animal, etc.: the form of the possessive case of the pronoun *she* when used attributively: *her* garden. [OE *hire*]

He·ra (hir′ə) In Greek mythology, the queen of the gods and goddess of women and marriage, sister and wife of Zeus: identified with the Roman *Juno.* Also spelled *Here.*

Her·a·cle·a (her′ə·klē′ə) An ancient city of southern Italy; scene of a Roman defeat by Pyrrhus of Epirus, 280 B.C.

Her·a·cles (her′ə·klēz) Hercules. Also **Her′a·kles.** — **Her·a·cle·an** (her′ə·klē′ən) *adj.*

Her·a·clid (her′ə·klid) *n. pl.* **Her·a·cli·dae** (her′ə·klī′dē) A descendant of Hercules; one of the ancient Spartan royalty, who claimed such descent. [<Gk. *Herakleidēs*] — **Her·a·cli·dan** (her′ə·klī′dən) *adj.*

Her·a·cli·tus (her′ə·klī′təs), 535?–475? B.C., Greek philosopher.

He·rak·lei·on (hə·rak′lē·ən, her′ə·klī′ən) The Greek name for CANDIA. Also **I·rá·kli·on** (i·räk′lē·ôn).

her·ald (her′əld) *n.* 1 Formerly, an officer whose business it was to bear messages, challenges, etc., from a sovereign or from the commander of an army. 2 *Brit.* An official whose duty and profession it is to grant or record arms, trace and record genealogies, record the creation of peers, etc. 3 An official bearer of important tidings; hence, any bearer of news. 4 A precursor; harbinger. — *v.t.* To announce publicly; usher in; proclaim. See synonyms under ANNOUNCE, PRECEDE. [<OF *heralt,* ? <OHG *heren* call] — **he·ral·dic** (hi·ral′dik) *adj.*

Synonyms (noun): ambassador, courier, forerunner, harbinger, pioneer, precursor.

her·ald·ry (her′əl·drē) *n.* 1 The science that treats of blazoning or describing armorial bearings, etc. 2 An emblazonment. 3 The symbolism of heraldic bearings. 4 The ceremony attendant upon heraldry.

Heralds' College In England, a corporate body of officials, instituted in 1484 to determine all questions concerning heraldry, the use of heraldic devices, the rights of those privileged to use them, etc.

her·ald·ship (her′əld·ship) *n.* The office or rank of a herald.

Her·at (he·rät′) A province of NW Afghanistan; 50,000 square miles; capital, Herat.

herb (ûrb, hûrb) *n.* 1 A seed plant devoid of woody tissue which dies completely, or down to the ground, after flowering. 2 A herbaceous plant valued for its medicinal qualities or for its smell or taste. 3 *Rare* Herbage. [<L *herba* grass, herbage]

her·ba·ceous (hûr·bā′shəs) *adj.* 1 Pertaining to, having the character of, or similar to herbs. 2 Having the semblance, color, or structure of an ordinary leaf.

herb·age (ûr′bij, hûr′-) *n.* 1 Herbs collectively. 2 Pasturage. 3 The leaves, stems, and other succulent parts of herbaceous plants.

herb·al (hûr′bəl, ûr′-) *adj.* Of or pertaining to herbs. — *n.* 1 A book containing classifications and descriptions of herbs or plants. 2 A herbarium.

herb·al·ist (hûr′bəl·ist, ûr′-) *n.* 1 A dealer in herbs, especially medicinal herbs. 2 Formerly, one skilled in the study of herbs or plants. Also **herb′ist.**

her·bar·i·um (hûr·bâr′ē·əm) *n. pl.* **·bar·i·ums** or **·bar·i·a** (-bâr′ē·ə) 1 A collection of dried plants scientifically arranged. 2 A room or building containing such a collection. [<LL <L *herba* grass]

Her·bart (hûr′bärt, *Ger.* her′bärt), **Johann Friedrich,** 1776–1841, German philosopher. — **Her·bar·ti·an** (hûr·bär′tē·ən) *adj.* — **Her·bar′ti·an·ism** *n.*

herb·a·ry (hûr′bə·rē) *n. pl.* **·ries** A garden containing only herbs or vegetables.

herb–ben·net (ûrb′ben′it, hûrb′-) *n.* A European herb of the rose family (*Geum urbanum*); avens. [<OF *herbe beneite* <Med. L *herba benedicta,* lit., blessed herb]

Her·bert (hûr′bərt, *Ger., Sw.* her′bərt; *Fr.* er·bâr′) A masculine personal name. Also *Lat.* **Her·ber·tus** (hər·bûr′təs), *Pg.* **Her·ber·to** (er·ber′tōō). [<Gmc., bright warrior]

Herbert (hûr′bərt), **George,** 1593–1633, English clergyman and poet. — **Victor,** 1859–1924, U. S. composer born in Ireland.

her·bes·cent (hûr·bes′ənt) *adj.* 1 Herblike. 2 Tending to become herbaceous.

her·bi·cide (hûr′bə·sīd) *n.* A weed–killer.

her·bif·er·ous (hûr·bif′ər·əs) *adj.* Producing herbs or vegetation. [<L *herbifer* < *herba* grass + *ferre* bear]

her·bi·vore (hûr′bə·vôr, -vōr) *n.* A herbivorous animal.

her·biv·o·rous (hûr·biv′ər·əs) *adj.* 1 Feeding on vegetable matter. 2 Belonging to a group or division (*Herbivora*) of mammals (now generally called *Ungulata*) that feed mainly on herbage, as cows, horses, camels, etc. [<L *herba* grass + -VOROUS]

herb–Par·is (ûrb′par′is, hûrb′-) *n.* A European herb of the lily family (*Paris quadrifolia*) closely allied to the wakerobin: also called *paris.*

herb–rob·ert (ûrb′rob′ərt, hûrb′-) *n.* A species of cranebill or geranium (*Geranium robertianum*).

herb·y (ûr′bē, hûr′-) *adj.* 1 Of the nature of herbs. 2 Relating to or abounding with herbs.

Her·ce·go·vi·na (hûr′tsə·gô·vē′nə, *Serbian* her′·tsə·gō′vi·nä) The Serbo–Croatian spelling of HERZEGOVINA.

Her·cu·la·ne·um (hûr′kyə·lā′nē·əm) A Roman city near Naples, buried by an eruption of Vesuvius in A.D. 79.

her·cu·le·an (hûr·kyōō′lē·ən, hûr′kyə·lē′ən) *adj.* Possessing or requiring great strength; laborious; mighty.

Her·cu·le·an (hûr·kyōō′lē·ən, hûr′kyə·lē′ən) *adj.* Like or pertaining to Hercules (Heracles), the ancient hero.

Her·cu·les (hûr′kyə·lēz) 1 In Greek mythology, the son of Alcmene and Zeus, renowned for his strength and endurance: also spelled *Heracles.* 2 Any man of great size and strength. 3 A large northern constellation. See CONSTELLATION. — **labors of Hercules** A series of twelve great tasks imposed by Eurystheus upon Hercules, because of the hostility of Hera: the killing of the Nemean lion; the killing of the Hydra of Lerna; the capture of the Erymanthian boar; the capture of the stag of Ceryneia; the killing of the man-eating birds of Stymphalus; the cleansing of the stables of Augeas; the capture of the Cretan bull; the capture of the horses of Diomedes; the theft of the girdle of Hippolyta; the capture of the cattle of Geryon; the theft of the apples of the Hesperides; and the capture of Cerberus from Hades.

Her·cu·les–club (hûr′kyə·lēz·klub′) *n.* 1 One of several small trees or shrubs, as the prickly ash, the spikenard, etc.: also called *angelica–tree.* 2 A large variety of the common gourd.

her·cy·nite (hûr′sə·nīt) *n.* A vitreous, black iron spinel, $FeAl_2O_4$, crystallizing in the isometric system. [<L *Hercynia (silva)* the Bohemian (forest) + -ITE[1]]

herd[1] (hûrd) *n.* 1 A number of animals feeding or traveling together. 2 A large crowd; especially, the common people; rabble. — *v.t.* & *v.i.* To bring or group together in or as in a herd. [OE *heord*]

herd[2] (hûrd) *n. Scot.* & *Brit. Dial.* A herdsman; shepherd. — *v.t.* To care for or drive (sheep, cattle, etc.).

-herd *combining form* Herdsman: *swineherd, cowherd,* etc. [OE *hirde* herdsman]

herd·book (hûrd′bŏŏk′) *n.* A record of the pedigrees of cattle in important herds.

Her·der (hûr′dər, *Ger.* her′dər), **Johann Gottfried von,** 1744–1803, German poet, theologian, and philosopher.

herd·er (hûr′dər) *n.* 1 A herdsman. 2 *U.S.* One who looks after a herd of cattle or a flock of sheep.

her·dic (hûr′dik) *n.* A carriage, usually two–wheeled, with low–hung body, back entrance, and side seats. [after Peter *Herdic,* 1824–88, its inventor]

herd's–grass (hûrdz′gras′, -gräs′) *n.* 1 Redtop. 2 Timothy. Also **herd′–grass′.** [after John *Herd,* early New Hampshire farmer]

herds·man (hûrdz′mən) *n. pl.* **·men** (-mən) *Brit.* One who owns or tends a herd. Also **herd′man.**

here (hir) *adv.* 1 In or at this place. 2 To this place; hither. 3 At this point of time or stage of proceedings; now. 4 At a place indicated. 5 In the present life. ◆ Homophone: *hear.* [OE *hēr*]

He·re (hir′ē) See HERA.

here·a·bout (hir′ə·bout′) *adv.* About this place; in this vicinity. Also **here′a·bouts′.**

here·af·ter (hir·af′tər, -äf′-) *adj.* 1 At some future time. 2 From this time forth. 3 In the state of life after death; after the present life. — *n.* A future state or existence. [OE *hēræfter*]

here and there In one place and another; so as to be irregularly scattered. — **neither here nor there** Foreign to the subject under discussion; unimportant; irrelevant.

here·at (hir·at′) *adv.* 1 At this time. 2 By reason of this; because of this.

here·by (hir·bī′) *adv.* 1 By means or by virtue of this. 2 Near this.

He·re·dia (ā·rā′thyä), **José Maria de,** 1842–1905, French poet born in Cuba.

he·red·i·ta·bil·i·ty (hə·red′i·tə·bil′ə·tē), **he·red·i·ta·ble** (hə·red′i·tə·bəl), etc. See HERITABILITY, etc.

her·e·dit·a·ment (her′ə·dit′ə·mənt) *n. Law* That capable of being inherited. — **corporeal hereditament** Property of such a nature as to be cognizable by the senses and in any way connected with land. — **incorporeal hereditament** An inheritable right issuing out of and annexed to some corporeal inheritance, as the right of way over another's land, or the right to the use of running water. [<Med. L *hereditamentum* <L *heres, -edis* an heir]

he·red·i·tar·y (hə·red′ə·ter′ē) *adj.* 1 *Law* Passing, capable of passing, or that must necessarily pass by inheritance, or from an ancestor, to an heir; deriving by inheritance. 2 Passing naturally from parent to child. 3 *Biol.* Transmitted or transmissible directly from a plant or animal to its offspring: distinguished from *congenital.* 4 Endowed with certain qualities derived from an ancestor. 5 Of or pertaining to heredity or inheritance. [<L *hereditarius* < *hereditas.* See HEREDITY.] — **he·red′i·tar′i·ly** *adv.* — **he·red′i·tar′i·ness** *n.*

he·red·i·tist (hə·red′ə·tist) *n.* An adherent of the theory that individuality is determined by heredity.

he·red·i·ty (hə·red′ə·tē) *n. pl.* **·ties** 1 Transmission of physical characteristics, mental traits, tendency to disease, etc., from parents to offspring. 2 *Biol.* The tendency manifested by an organism to develop in the likeness of a progenitor, because of the transmission of genetic factors in the reproductive process. 3 The sum total of an individual's inherited

characteristics. [<F *hérédité* <L *hereditas, -tatis* an inheritance < *heres, -edis* an heir]

Her·e·ford (her′ə·fərd) *n.* One of a breed of cattle, commonly red with a white face and markings. [from HEREFORD]

Her·e·ford (her′ə·fərd) A county in western England; 842 square miles; county seat, Hereford. Also **Her′e·ford·shire** (-shir′, -shər).

her·e·geld (her′ə·geld) *n.* In Old Scots law, a due analogous to the English heriot. Also **her′e·gild** (-gild). [OE *heregield* < *here* army + *gield* tribute]

here·in (hir·in′) *adv.* In this; in this place, circumstance, etc. [OE *hērinne*]

here·in·af·ter (hir′in·af′tər, -äf′-) *adv.* In a subsequent part of this (document).

here·in·be·fore (hir′in·bi·fôr′, -fōr′) *adv.* In a preceding part of this (document).

here·in·to (hir′in·tōō′) *adv.* Into this.

here·of (hir·uv′) *adv.* 1 Of this; about this. 2 From this; because of this.

here·on (hir·on′, -ôn′) *adv.* On this; hereupon.

he·res (hir′ēz) *n. pl.* **he·re·des** (hi·rē′dēz) *Law* An heir. Also spelled *haeres.* [<L]

he·re·si·arch (hi·rē′sē·ärk, her′ə·sē·ärk′) *n.* The chief exponent of a heresy. See synonyms under HERETIC. [<LL *haeresiarcha* <Gk. *hairesiarchēs* < *hairesis* a sect + *archēs* leader < *archein* rule]

her·e·sy (her′ə·sē) *n. pl.* **·sies** 1 A doctrinal view or belief at variance with the recognized tenets of a system, church, school, or party. 2 The maintenance of such a doctrinal view or tenet. 3 *Obs.* Any course of conduct or instruction tending to produce dissension and schism in the church. [<OF *heresie,* ult. <Gk. *hairesis* a sect, lit., a choosing < *haire-esthai* choose]

her·e·tic (her′ə·tik) *n.* 1 One who holds a heresy. 2 An actual or former member of a church, or one whose allegiance is claimed by it, who holds religious opinions contrary to the fundamental doctrines and tenets of that church. [<MF *hérétique* <LL *haereticus* <Gk. *hairetikos* able to choose < *haireesthai* choose] — **he·ret·i·cal** (hə·ret′i·kəl) *adj.* — **he·ret′i·cal·ly** *adv.*

Synonyms: dissenter, heresiarch, nonconformist, schismatic. Etymologically, a *heretic* is one who takes or chooses his own belief, instead of the belief of his church; a *schismatic* is primarily one who produces a split or rent in the church. A *heretic* differs in doctrine from the religious body with which he is connected; a *schismatic* differs in doctrine or practice, or in both. A *heretic* may be reticent, or even silent; a *schismatic* introduces divisions. A *heresiarch* is the author of a heresy or the leader of a heretical party, and is thus at once a *heretic* and a *schismatic.* With advancing ideas of religious liberty, the odious sense once attached to these words is largely modified, and *heretic* is often used playfully. *Dissenter* and *nonconformist* are terms specifically applied to English subjects who hold themselves aloof from the Church of England.

here·to (hir·tōō′) *adv.* To this time, place, or end.

here·to·fore (hir′tə·fôr′, -fōr′) *adv.* Previously; hitherto.

here·un·to (hir′un·tōō′) *adv.* To this; hereto; up to this point, or to this end or result.

here·up·on (hir′ə·pon′, -pôn′) *adv.* Upon this; following immediately after this.

here·with (hir·with′, -with′) *adv.* Along with this.

Her·ges·hei·mer (hûr′gəs·hī′mər), **Joseph,** 1880–1954, U.S. novelist.

Her·ing window (her′ing) *Optics* An apparatus for demonstrating color contrast by means of a shutter whose two openings contain samples of the desired colors. [after Ewald *Hering,* 1834–1918, German psychologist]

her·i·ot (her′ē·ət) *n.* In feudal law, a tribute or contribution to the lord of the manor from the heir of a tenant upon succeeding his father. [OE *heregeatwa* < *here* army + *geatwa* equipment]

her·i·ta·ble (her′ə·tə·bəl) *adj.* 1 That can be inherited. 2 Capable of inheriting. [<OF < *heriter* inherit] — **her′i·ta·bil′i·ty** *n.* — **her′i·ta·bly** *adv.*

her·i·tage (her′ə·tij) *n.* 1 Property that is or can be inherited. 2 Any condition or culture

which is allotted or handed down to one, as by ancestors. 3 The chosen people of God, as the Israelites or the Christian elect. [<OF < *heriter* inherit <L *hereditare* < *heres, -edis* an heir]

her·i·tor (her′ə·tər) *n.* An inheritor. [<AF *heritor,* OF *heritier* <L *hereditarius.* See HEREDITARY.] — **her′i·trix** (-triks) *n. fem.*

Her·ki·mer (hûr′kə·mər), **Nicholas,** 1728–77, American general in the Revolutionary War.

herl (hûrl) *n.* 1 A barb of a feather, used in making artificial flies for angling. 2 A fly so made. [Cf. MLG *herle* a fiber]

her·ma (hûr′mə) *n. pl.* **·mae** (-mē) or **·mai** (-mī) In ancient Greece, a rough square stone, broader at the base than above, with a sculptured head of Hermes or some other deity on the top, placed in front of houses and to mark boundaries of estates, streets, etc.; also, such a stone with the head of a mortal. [<L <Gk. *Hermēs* Hermes]

Her·ma·ic (hûr·mā′ik) *adj.* Pertaining to or characteristic of the Greek god Hermes (Mercury), or the Egyptian Thoth (Hermes Trismegistus).

Her·man (hûr′mən, *Du., Sw.* her′män) A masculine personal name. Also *Ger.* **Her·mann** (her′män), *Fr.* **Ar·mand** (är·män′), *Ital.* **Er·man·no** (er·män′nō), *Lat.* **Ar·min·i·us** (är·min′ē·əs). [<Gmc., man of the army]

Her·mann·stadt (her′män·shtät) The German name for SIBIU.

her·maph·ro·dite (hûr·maf′rə·dīt) *adj.* 1 Having the characteristics of both sexes; bisexual. 2 *Naut.* Denoting a type of ship which is square-rigged forward and schooner-rigged aft. 3 *Bot.* Monoclinous. — *n.* 1 *Biol.* A plant or animal organism that combines the characteristics of both sexes. 2 *Naut.* A hermaphrodite brig. [<L *hermaphroditus* <Gk. *hermaphroditos,* after *Hermaphroditos* HERMAPHRODITUS] — **her·maph′ro·dit′ic** (-dit′ik) or **·i·cal** *adj.* — **her·maph′ro·dit′i·cal·ly** *adv.* — **her·maph′ro·dit·ism, her·maph′ro·dism** *n.*

hermaphrodite brig A brigantine.

Her·maph·ro·di·tus (hûr·maf′rə·dī′təs) In Greek mythology, the son of Hermes and Aphrodite, who, after loving the nymph Salmacis, became united with her in a single body combining both sexes.

her·me·neu·tics (hûr′mə·nōō′tiks, -nyōō′-) *n.* The science or art of interpretation, especially of the Scriptures. [<Gk. *hermēneutikē* (*technē*) interpretive (art) < *hermēneutēs* an interpreter] — **her′me·neu′tic** or **·ti·cal** *adj.* — **her′me·neu′ti·cal·ly** *adv.*

Her·mes (hûr′mēz) In Greek mythology, the son of Zeus and Maia, messenger and herald of the gods, god of science, eloquence, and cunning, patron of thieves, travelers, and commerce, protector of boundaries, and guide of souls on their way to Hades: identified with the Roman *Mercury.*

Hermes Tris·me·gis·tus (tris′mə·jis′təs) The Greek name for the Egyptian god Thoth, regarded as the founder of alchemy and other occult sciences: partially identified with *Hermes.*

her·met·ic (hûr·met′ik) *adj.* Made airtight; impervious to air and liquids, as by fusion. Also **her·met′i·cal.** [<Med. L *hermeticus* < *Hermes* (*Trismegistus*); with ref. to alchemy]

Her·met·ic (hûr·met′ik) *adj.* Belonging or relating to Hermes, or to Hermes Trismegistus. — **Her·met′i·cal·ly** *adv.*

her·met·i·cal·ly (hûr·met′ik·lē) *adv.* So as to be airtight or impervious.

hermetic art Alchemy.

Her·mi·o·ne (hûr·mī′ə·nē) In Greek legend, the daughter of Menelaus and Helen, wife of Neoptolemus and later of Orestes.

her·mit (hûr′mit) *n.* 1 A person who abandons society and lives alone, especially for religious contemplation; an anchorite. 2 A molasses cooky containing spice and sometimes raisins. 3 *Obs.* A beadsman. Also *Obs.* **ermyte.** [<OF *hermite* <L *eremita* <Gk. *erēmitēs* < *erēmia* a desert < *erēmos* solitary] — **her·mit′ic** or **·i·cal** *adj.* — **her·mit′i·cal·ly** *adv.* — **her′mit·like′** *adj.*

her·mit·age (hûr′mə·tij) *n.* The retreat or cell of a hermit. See synonyms under CLOISTER.

hermit crab A decapod crustacean (genus *Pagurus*) usually having a soft abdomen which

for protection is thrust into the empty shell of a univalve mollusk.

hermit thrush A thrush (*Hylocichla guttata*) of eastern North America, having a spotted breast and reddish tail.

hermit warbler A brilliantly colored songbird (*Dendroica occidentalis*) of the Sierra Nevadas.

Her·mod (hûr′məd) In Norse mythology, the son of Odin, and messenger of the gods, who went to Hel to bring back Balder. Also **Her′modr.**

Her·mon (hûr′mən), **Mount** A mountain on the Syria-Lebanon border; the highest peak in ancient Palestine; 9,232 feet.

hern (hûrn) *n. Archaic* The heron. [OE *hyrne*]

Her·nan·do (er·nän′dō) Spanish form of FERDINAND.

Her·ne (her′nə) A city in North Rhine-Westphalia, Germany.

her·ni·a (hûr′nē·ə) *n. Pathol.* Protrusion, as of an intestine or other organ from its normal position; rupture. [<L] — **her′ni·al** *adj.*

hernio- *combining form* Hernia: *hernioplasty.* [<L *hernia*]

her·ni·o·plas·ty (hûr′nē·ə·plas′tē) *n. Surg.* An operation for the radical cure of hernia. — **her′ni·o·plas′tic** *adj.*

her·ni·ot·o·my (hûr′nē·ot′ə·mē) *n. pl.* **·mies** *Surg.* The operation of cutting down to and severing the constricting part in strangulated hernia.

hern·shaw (hûrn′shô) *n.* 1 A heron. 2 Her. The representation of a heron or similar bird. [Var. of HERONSEW]

he·ro (hir′ō) *n. pl.* **·roes** 1 A person distinguished for valor, fortitude, or bold enterprise; anyone regarded as having displayed great courage or exceptionally noble qualities. 2 In classical mythology, the son of a god or goddess and a mortal: the eponymous founder of a city or family, as Cadmus, was sometimes locally worshiped as a hero. 3 The central male figure of a poem, play, romance, or the like; in modern fiction, the male character in whom the principal interest centers. [<L *heros* <Gk. *hērōs*]

He·ro (hir′ō) In Greek legend, a priestess of Aphrodite at Sestos, for whom Leander, her lover, swam the Hellespont from Abydos every night: when he drowned one night, Hero cast herself into the sea.

Her·od (her′əd), 73?–4 B.C., king of Judea 37–4 B.C.: known as **Herod the Great.**
— **Herod Agrippa I,** 10? B.C.–A.D. 44, king of Judea 41–44.
— **Herod Antipas,** 4 B.C.–A.D. 39, tetrarch of Galilee; son of Herod the Great. — **He·ro·di·an** (hi·rō′dē·ən) *adj. & n.*

He·ro·di·as (hi·rō′dē·əs) Second wife of Herod Antipas. *Mark* vi 17–28.

He·rod·o·tus (hi·rod′ə·təs), 484?–424? B.C., Greek historian: called the "Father of History."

he·ro·ic (hi·rō′ik) *adj.* 1 Characteristic of a hero; brave; noble: *heroic* courage; a *heroic* death. 2 Of or involving the heroes of antiquity: a *heroic* age. 3 Describing heroes and their deeds: a *heroic* poem. 4 Like heroic poetry in style; magniloquent; high-flown: *heroic* language. 5 Bold; daring; extreme: a *heroic* attempt. 6 In art and sculpture, larger than life and smaller than colossal. Also **he·ro′i·cal.** — *n.* 1 *pl.* Heroic verse. 2 *pl.* High-flown or extravagant language, sentiments, or actions: Cut out the *heroics.* — **he·ro′i·cal·ly** *adv.*

heroic age The mythical age when heroes and demigods lived on earth.

heroic couplet An English verse form consisting of two riming lines of iambic pentameter, often epigrammatic in character.

heroic poetry Epic poetry, especially as dealing with heroes and demigods.

heroic verse A verse form adapted to heroic or lofty themes, and used especially in epic and dramatic poetry, as the hexameter in Greek and Latin, the hendecasyllabic ottava rima in Italian, the Alexandrine in French drama, and the heroic couplet and blank verse, with various other combinations of iambic verse, in English.

her·o·in (her′ō·in) *n.* Diacetylmorphine, $C_{21}H_{23}O_5N$, a white, odorless, crystalline

derivative of morphine with a bitter taste: a powerful, habit-forming narcotic of which the manufacture is prohibited in the United States. [<G]

her·o·ine (her′ō·in) *n. fem.* **1** A woman of heroic character. **2** The chief female character in a story, play, or the like. [<L *heroina* <Gk. *hērōinē*, fem. of *hērōs* a hero]

her·o·ism (her′ō·iz′əm) *n.* **1** Heroic character or qualities. **2** A heroic act. See synonyms under FORTITUDE, PROWESS.

He·rold (he′rōlt) Dutch form of HAROLD.

her·on (her′ən) *n.* A long-necked and long-legged wading bird; specifically, one of a family *(Ardeidae)* of birds with 12 stiff tail feathers and the outer toe as long as or longer than the inner. See EGRET. **— great blue heron** A large, bluish-gray American heron *(Ardea herodias)*. [<OF *hairon*, ult. <Gmc.]

GREAT BLUE HERON (About 4 feet tall)

her·on·bill (her′ən·bil′) *n.* Any of a genus *(Erodium)* of annual or perennial herbs with toothed leaves, widely distributed in temperate regions. Also **her′on's-bill′**, **her′ons·bill′**.

her·on·ry (her′ən·rē) *n. pl.* **·ries** A place where herons congregate and breed.

he·ro-wor·ship (hir′ō·wûr′ship) *n.* Enthusiastic or extravagant admiration for heroes or other distinguished personages.

her·pes (hûr′pēz) *n. Pathol.* An inflammatory eruption on the skin, forming groups of small blisters which tend to spread. [<L <Gk. *herpēs* <*herpein* creep]

herpes sim·plex (sim′pleks) Cold sore.

herpes zos·ter (zos′tər) Shingles.

her·pet·ic (hûr·pet′ik) *adj.* Relating to or like herpes. Also **her·pet′i·cal.** **—her·pe·tism** (hûr′pə·tiz′əm) *n.*

her·pe·tol·o·gy (hûr′pə·tol′ə·jē) *n.* The branch of zoology that treats of reptiles and amphibians. [<Gk. *herpeton* a reptile <*herpein* creep + -LOGY] **— her·pe·to·log·i·cal** (hûr′pə·tə·loj′i·kəl) *adj.* **— her′pe·tol′o·gist** *n.*

Herr (her) *n. pl.* **Her·ren** (her′ən) *German* A title of respectful address, equivalent to the English *mister.*

Herr·en·volk (her′ən·fôlk′) *n. German* The master race.

Her·re·ra (er·rā′rä), **Francisco de,** 1576–1656, Spanish painter.

Her·rick (her′ik), **Robert,** 1591–1674, English poet.

her·ring (her′ing) *n. pl.* **·rings** or **·ring** **1** A small food fish *(Clupea harengus)* frequenting moderate depths of the North Atlantic in great numbers. The young are canned as sardines and the adults are smoked or salted. **2** A fish allied to the herring (family *Clupeidae)*, especially *Clupea cacruteus* of Pacific waters and the pilchard or sardine. [OE *hǣring*]

her·ring·bone (her′ing·bōn′) *adj.* Similar to the spinal structure of a herring; especially, laid out, arranged, woven, or stitched in rows of parallel lines with the lines of adjoining rows slanting in opposite directions: said of masonry, textiles, etc. **—** *n.* Anything made or arranged in such a pattern. **—** *v.t.* & *v.i.* **·boned, ·bon·ing** **1** To ornament with or arrange in herringbone stitches, patterns, etc. **2** To walk on skis (up an incline) with the toes pointed out: so called from the herringbone tracks made by the skis.

her·ring·bone-work (her′ing·bōn′wûrk′) *n.* **1** Masonry in which the stones are laid slanting in opposite directions alternately. **2** A cross-stitch made of rows of diagonal stitches.

herring gull A small American gull *(Larus argentatus smithsonianus)* of the Atlantic coast that feeds on herring.

Her·riot (e·ryō′), **Édouard,** 1872–1957, French statesman; premier 1924–25, 1932.

her·ry (her′ē) *v.t. Scot.* To harry. **— her′ri·ment** (-mənt) or **her′ry·ment** *n.*

hers (hûrz) *pron.* **1** Belonging or pertaining to her: the form of the possessive case of *she* when used in predicative position, without a following noun, or after *of*: That book is *hers*; those eyes of *hers.* **2** The things or persons belonging to or relating to her: John's story is funnier than *hers*; She provides for herself and *hers.* [OE *hire* + *-s* (after *his*)]

Her·schel (hûr′shəl), **Sir John Frederick William,** 1792–1871, English astronomer. **— Sir William,** 1738–1822, English astronomer of German birth: original name *Friedrich Wilhelm Herschel*; father of the preceding.

her·self (hər·self′) *pron.* **1** Reflexive form of *her.* **2** Emphatic or intensive form of *she.*

Herst·mon·ceux (hûrst′mən·sōō, hûrs′-) A village of SE Sussex, England: the British meteorological station and time clocks were moved here from Greenwich in 1946: also *Hurstmonceux.*

Hert·ford (här′fərd, härt′-) A county in SE England; 633 square miles; county seat, Hertford. Also **Hert′ford·shire** (-shir, -shər). Shortened form **Herts** (härts, hûrts).

Her·to·gen·bosch, 's (ser′tō·khən·bôs′) See 's HERTOGENBOSCH.

hertz (hûrts) *n. Physics* A unit of electromagnetic wave frequency, equal to one cycle per second. [after Heinrich *Hertz*]

Hertz (herts), **Gustav,** born 1887, German physicist. **—Heinrich,** 1857–94, German physicist. **— Hertz′i·an** *adj.*

Hertzian wave One of the electromagnetic waves; a radio wave: also **Hertzian radiation.** [after Heinrich *Hertz*]

Hertz·sprung-Rus·sell diagram (hert′sprung′rus′əl) *Astron.* A classification of stars plotted on a chart in which the luminosity increases on a vertical scale from bottom to top and the color or spectral type changes from blue or white to red on a horizontal scale from left to right: also called *Russell diagram.* See MAIN SEQUENCE. [after Ejnar *Hertzsprung*, born 1873, Dutch astronomer, and Henry Norris *Russell*, 1877–1957, U.S. astronomer]

Her·ze·go·vi·na (hûr′tsə·gō·vē′nə) See BOSNIA AND HERZEGOVINA: Serbo-Croatian *Hercegovina.* **— Her′ze·go·vin′i·an** (-vin′ē·ən) *adj.* & *n.*

Her·zl (her′tsəl), **Theodor,** 1860–1904, Hungarian journalist; founder of the Zionist movement. See ZIONISM.

he's (hēz) **1** He is. **2** He has.

He·se·kiel (hā·zā′kē·el) German form of EZEKIEL.

Hesh·wan (hesh′van, *Hebrew* khesh′vän) A Hebrew month: also called *Marchesvan* or *Bul.* Also spelled *Hesvan.* Also **Hesh′van.** See CALENDAR (Hebrew).

He·si·od (hē′sē·əd, hes′ē·əd) Greek poet of the eighth century B.C. **— He·si·od·ic** (hē′sē·od′ik, hes′ē-) *adj.*

He·si·o·ne (hi·sī′ə·nē) In Greek legend, the daughter of Laomedon, who was rescued from a monster by Hercules.

hes·i·tan·cy (hez′ə·tən·sē) *n. pl.* **·cies** **1** The act or manner of one who falters or is uncertain; hesitation; vacillation. **2** A faltering in speech. Also **hes′i·tance.** See synonyms under DOUBT.

hes·i·tant (hez′ə·tənt) *adj.* Hesitating; uncertain. [<L *haesitans, -antis*, ppr. of *haestare.* See HESITATE.] **— hes′i·tant·ly** *adv.*

hes·i·tate (hez′ə·tāt) *v.i.* **·tat·ed, ·tat·ing** **1** To be uncertain as to decision or action; waver. **2** To pause. **3** To be slow or faltering in speech. [<L *haesitatus*, pp. of *haesitare*, freq. of *haerere* stick] **— hes′i·ta′tive** *adj.* **— hes′i·ta′tive·ly** *adv.*

hes·i·ta·tion (hez′ə·tā′shən) *n.* **1** The act of hesitating; a delay caused by indecision or uncertainty. **2** A state of uncertainty; doubt. **3** A pause or faltering in speech.

hesp (hesp) *n. Scot.* & *Brit. Dial.* **1** A hasp. **2** The length of two linen-thread hanks.

Hes·per·es·thu·sa (hes′pər·əs·thōō′zə) One of the Hesperides.

Hes·pe·ri·a (hes·pir′ē·ə) Land of the West: the ancient Greek name for Italy and the Latin name for the Iberian Peninsula.

Hes·pe·ri·an (hes·pir′ē·ən) *adj.* **1** *Poetic* In or of the west; western. **2** Of or pertaining to the Hesperides. [<L *hesperius* <Gk. *hesperios* western]

Hes·per·id (hes′pər·id) Any of the Hesperides.

Hes·per·i·des (hes·per′ə·dēz) In Greek mythology, the daughters of Atlas (Aegle, Erytheia, and Hesperesthusa), who with the dragon, Ladon, guarded the golden apples given to Hera by Gaea and later stolen by Hercules: also called *Atlantides.* [<Gk. *hesperis* western] **— Hes·per·id·i·an** (hes′pə·rid′ē·ən) or **·e·an** *adj.*

hes·per·i·din (hes·per′ə·din) *n.* A glycoside, $C_{28}H_{34}O_{15}$, obtained from citrus fruits as a white, tasteless, odorless, crystalline powder. [<HESPERIDIUM + -IN]

hes·per·id·i·um (hes′pə·rid′ē·əm) *n. pl.* **·i·a** (-ē·ə) *Bot.* An indehiscent, many-celled, fleshy fruit with a spongy or leathery rind; a berry with a hard rind, as the lemon. [<NL <Gk. *Hesperides* the Hesperides; with ref. to the golden apples]

Hes·per·or·nis (hes′pər·ôr′nis) *n.* One of a genus *(Hesperornis)* of extinct swimming birds from the Cretaceous of Kansas with pointed teeth and serpentlike jaws. The type species was six feet long. [<NL <Gk. *hesperos* western + *ornis* a bird]

Hes·pe·rus (hes′pər·əs) The evening star, especially Venus. Also **Hes′per.** [<L <Gk. *Hesperos*]

Hess (hess), **Myra,** born 1890, English pianist. **— Rudolf,** born 1894, German Nazi leader; sentenced to life imprisonment in 1946.

Hes·se (hes′ə), **Hermann,** 1877–1962, German novelist.

Hesse (hes) A state of western Germany; 8,153 square miles; capital, Wiesbaden. *German* **Hes·sen** (hes′ən).

Hesse-Cas·sel (hes′kas′əl) A former landgravate of Germany; incorporated into Prussia, 1866: also **Electoral Hesse, Hesse′-Kas′sel.** *German* **Hes·sen-Kas·sel** (hes′ən·käs′əl).

Hesse-Darm·stadt (hes′därm′shtät) A former grand duchy of Germany. *German* **Hes′sen-Darm′stadt.**

Hesse-Nas·sau (hes′nas′ô) A former province of Prussia in western Germany. *German* **Hes·sen-Nas·sau** (hes′ən·näs′ou).

hes·sian (hesh′ən) *n.* A strong coarse hempen cloth. [from *Hesse*]

Hes·sian (hesh′ən) *n.* **1** A native or citizen of Hesse. **2** A soldier from Hesse hired by the British to fight in the American Revolution. **3** *pl.* Hessian boots. **—** *adj.* Of or pertaining to Hesse or its inhabitants.

Hessian boots High boots, reaching to the knees, worn early in the 19th century.

Hessian fly A small blackish fly or midge *(Mayetiola* or *Phytophaga destructor)* with red lines on the upper surface, very destructive to wheat, barley, and rye: supposedly introduced into America by the Hessian troops during the Revolutionary War.

hess·ite (hes′īt) *n.* A metallic, lead-gray, silver telluride, Ag_2Te, crystallizing in the isometric system. [after G. H. *Hess*, 1802–50, Swiss chemist]

hes·son·ite (hes′ən·īt) See ESSONITE.

hest (hest) *n. Archaic* Behest.

Hes·ter (hes′tər) See ESTHER. Also **Hes′ther.**

Hes·ti·a (hes′tē·ə) In Greek mythology, the eldest daughter of Kronos and Rhea, and goddess of the hearth: identified with the Roman *Vesta.*

Hes·van (hes′van) See HESHWAN.

Hes·y·chast (hes′i·kast) *n.* A quietist; especially, one of a mystic and quietistic sect that originated in the Greek Church among the monks of Mt. Athos in the 14th century. See ILLUMINATI. [<Med. L *hesychasta* <Gk. *hēsychastēs* <*hēsychazein* be still <*hēsychos* quiet] **— hes′y·chas′tic** *adj.*

het (het) Dialectal past tense and past participle of HEAT. **— to get het up** *Dial.* To become angry, disturbed, or excited.

he·tae·ra (hi·tir′ə) *n. pl.* **·tae·rae** (-tir′ē) In ancient Greece, one of a class of professional entertainers or courtesans: composed of slaves, freedwomen, and foreigners. Also **he·tai·ra** (hi·tī′rə). [<Gk. *hetaira*, fem. of *hetairos* a companion]

he·tae·rism (hi·tir′iz·əm) *n.* **1** Promiscuous concubinage. **2** The theory that this condition characterized all primitive society. Also **he·tai·rism** (hi·tī′riz·əm).

hetero- *combining form* Other; different: *heterogeneous*: opposed to *homo-*. Also, before vowels, **heter-**. [<Gk. *hetero-* <*heteros* other]

het·er·o·cer·cy (het′ər·ə·sûr′sē) *n. Zool.* Inequality of the caudal fin of a fish produced by the extension of the vertebral column upward and consequent enlargement of one of the lobes, as in sharks, sturgeons, etc. [<HETERO- + Gk. *kerkos* tail] **— het′er·o·cer′cal** (-sûr′kəl) *adj.*

het·er·o·chro·mat·ic (het′ər·ə·krō·mat′ik) *adj.* Of, pertaining to, characterized by, or desig-

nating an array or pattern of different colors. Also **het′er·o·chrome′** (-krōm′), **het′er·o·chro′·mous** (-krō′məs).

het·er·o·chro·ma·tin (het′ər·ə·krō′mə·tin) *n. Biol.* An inert fraction of chromatin, unchanged during mitosis.

het·er·o·chro·mo·some (het′ər·ə·krō′mə·sōm) *n.* **1** Sex chromosome. **2** Any aberrant chromosome.

het·er·o·chron·ic (het′ər·ə·kron′ik) *adj. Med.* Occurring at irregular or abnormal times: said of an illness. Also **het·er·och·ro·nous** (het′ər·ok′·rə·nəs).

het·er·och·tho·nous (het′ər·ok′thə·nəs) *adj.* Foreign; not indigenous or native. [< HETERO- + Gk. *chthōn* land, country]

het·er·o·clite (het′ər·ə·klīt′) *n.* **1** *Gram.* A word that varies or is irregular in inflection; particularly, a noun inflected from more than one stem, as Latin *domus.* **2** A person or thing deviating from the ordinary or correct form. —*adj.* **1** Anomalous. **2** *Gram.* With an irregular inflection: also **het′er·o·clit′ic** (-klit′ik) or **·i·cal.** [< F *hétéroclite* < L *heteroclitus* < Gk. *heteroklitos* irregular < *hetero-* other + *klinein* bend]

het·er·o·cy·clic (het′ər·ə·sī′klik, -sik′lik) *adj. Chem.* Pertaining to or designating an organic ring compound containing one or more types of atoms other than carbon: opposed to *homocyclic.*

het·er·o·cyst (het′ər·ə·sist′) *n. Bot.* A cell of doubtful function, larger than its neighbors, developed in some blue-green algae.

het·er·o·dox (het′ər·ə·doks′) *adj.* **1** At variance with a commonly accepted doctrine in religion. **2** In general, at variance with any commonly accepted doctrine or opinion: opposed to *orthodox.* [< Gk. *heterodoxos* < *hetero-* other + *doxa* opinion]

het·er·o·dox·y (het′ər·ə·dok′sē) *n. pl.* **·dox·ies** **1** The character of being heterodox. **2** A heterodox doctrine or opinion. See synonyms under SECT.

het·er·o·dyne (het′ər·ə·dīn′) *adj. Telecom.* Describing the manner by which oscillations of a frequency almost equal to that of the transmitted waves are developed in a separate tube of a radio receiving set, the two oscillations forming beats. —*v.t.* **·dyned, ·dyn·ing** To effect such oscillations.

het·er·oe·cism (het′ə·rē′siz·əm) *n. Bot.* A type of parasitism associated with certain fungi and characterized by the development of different stages of the parasite on different hosts: also called *metoxeny.* [< HETER(O)- + Gk. *oikos* house] —**het′er·oe′cious** (-shəs) *adj.*

het·er·o·gam·ete (het′ər·ə·gam′ēt, -gə·mēt′) *n. Biol.* A gamete sexually or otherwise differentiated: also called *anisogamete.*

het·er·og·a·mous (het′ər·og′ə·məs) *adj.* **1** *Bot.* Bearing flowers that are sexually of two kinds: opposed to *homogamous.* **2** *Biol.* Having unlike gametes: opposed to *isogamous.*

het·er·og·a·my (het′ər·og′ə·mē) *n.* The character or condition of being heterogamous. —**het·er·o·gam·ic** (het′ər·ə·gam′ik) *adj.*

het·er·o·ge·ne·ous (het′ər·ə·jē′nē·əs) *adj.* Consisting of dissimilar elements or ingredients. [< Med. L *heterogeneus* < Gk. *heterogenēs* < *hetero-* other + *genos* kind] —**het·er·o·ge·ne·i·ty** (het′ər·ə·jə·nē′ə·tē) *n.* —**het′er·o·ge′ne·ous·ly** *adv.*

Synonyms: confused, conglomerate, discordant, dissimilar, mingled, miscellaneous, mixed, nonhomogeneous, unhomogeneous, unlike, variant, various. Substances quite *unlike* are *heterogeneous* as regards each other. A *heterogeneous* mixture is one whose constituents are not only *unlike* in kind, but unevenly distributed; cement is composed of substances such as lime, sand, and clay, which are *heterogeneous* as regards each other, but the cement is said to be homogeneous if the different constituents are evenly *mixed* throughout, so that any one portion of the mixture is exactly like any other. A substance may fail of being homogeneous and yet not be *heterogeneous,* in which case it is said to be *nonhomogeneous* or *unhomogeneous;* a bar of iron that contains flaws, air bubbles, etc., or for any reason is not of uniform structure and density throughout, even if no foreign substance be *mixed* with the iron, is said to be *non-homogeneous.* A *miscellaneous* mixture may or may not be *heterogeneous;* if the objects are alike in kind, but different in size, form, quality, use, etc., and without special order or relation, the collection is *miscellaneous;* if the objects differ in kind, such a mixture is also, and more strictly, *heterogeneous.* See COMPLEX. *Antonyms*: alike, homogeneous, identical, like, pure, same, similar, uniform.

het·er·o·gen·e·sis (het′ər·ə·jen′ə·sis) *n. Biol.* **1** Asexual generation. **2** Metagenesis. —**het·er·o·ge·net·ic** (het′ər·ə·jə·net′ik) *adj.*

het·er·og·o·ny (het′ər·og′ə·nē) *n.* **1** *Bot.* The state of having flowers differing in kind, length of stamens and styles: opposed to *homogony.* **2** Metagenesis. —**het′er·og′o·nous** *adj.* —**het′·er·og′o·nous·ly** *adv.*

het·er·o·grade (het′ər·ə·grād′) *adj. Stat.* Having or denoting a variable magnitude, grade, or intensity. Compare HOMOGRADE.

het·er·og·ra·phy (het′ə·rog′rə·fē) *n.* **1** Orthography in which the same letter represents different sounds in different words or syllables, as *c* in *camp* and *cent.* **2** Spelling varying from the standard everyday usage. —**het·er·o·graph·ic** (het′ər·ə·graf′ik) or **·i·cal** *adj.*

het·er·og·y·nous (het′ə·roj′ə·nəs) *adj. Biol.* Having the females differentiated into sexual and neuter forms, as a bee or an ant.

het·er·o·ki·ne·sis (het′ər·ə·ki·nē′sis, -kī-) *n. Biol.* A differential distribution of the sex chromosomes in meiosis. —**het′er·o·ki·net′ic** (-net′ik) *adj.*

het·er·ol·o·gy (het′ə·rol′ə·jē) *n. Biol.* **1** Difference of structure as compared with a type; lack of homology; abnormality. **2** Analogy between unrelated organisms: contrasted with *homology* between related organisms. —**het′er·ol′ogous** (-gəs) *adj.*

het·er·ol·y·sis (het′ə·rol′ə·sis) *n. Biochem.* Dissolution effected by an outside agent; specifically, the destruction of a cell by external enzymes or lysins: opposed to *autolysis.* —**het·er·o·lyt·ic** (het′ər·ə·lit′ik) *adj.*

het·er·om·er·ous (het′ə·rom′ər·əs) *adj. Bot.* Possessing parts that differ in number, form, or composition, as the whorls of a flower: opposed to *isomerous.*

het·er·o·mor·phic (het′ər·ə·môr′fik) *adj. Biol.* **1** Deviating from the normal form or standard type. **2** Undergoing complete metamorphosis, as certain insects. Also **het′er·o·mor′phous** (-fəs). —**het′er·o·mor′phism** (-fiz·əm) *n.*

het·er·on·o·mous (het′ə·ron′ə·məs) *adj.* **1** *Biol.* Divergent or differing from the common type: said of one of a series of related things, as the somites of an arthropod. **2** Subject to the law or rule of another. [< HETERO- + Gk. *nomos* law, rule] —**het·er·on′o·my** *n.*

het·er·o·nym (het′ər·ə·nim′) *n.* **1** A word spelled like another, but having a different sound and meaning, as *bass* (a male voice) and *bass* (a fish). **2** Another name for the same thing; especially, one of two precisely equivalent terms in different languages: "Water" is a *heteronym* of the French word "eau." Compare HOMONYM. [< HETER(O)- + Gk. *onyma,* var. of *onoma* name; on analogy with *synonym*]

het·er·on·y·mous het′ə·ron′ə·məs) *adj.* **1** Relating to, having the nature of, or containing a heteronym. **2** *Optics* Appearing on the side opposite to that of the eye that produced it: said of double images of an object when the image seen by the right eye is on the left side and vice versa.

Het·er·o·ou·si·an (het′ər·ō·ōō′sē·ən, -ou′sē-), etc. See HETEROUSIAN, etc.

het·er·o·pha·sia (het′ər·ə·fā′zhə, -zhē·ə) *n. Psychiatry* A form of aphasia in which the patient says or writes one thing when he means another. [< NL < Gk. *hetero-* other + *-phasia* < *phanai* speak]

het·er·o·phyl·lous (het′ər·ə·fil′əs) *adj. Bot.* Having leaves that differ, as in size, form, or function, on the same plant. —**het′er·o·phyl′ly** (-fil′ē) *n.*

het·er·o·pla·sia (het′ər·ə·plā′zhə, -zhē·ə) *n. Pathol.* The development of abnormal tissue by diseased action where the cells of the abnormal tissues differ from the normal ones. [< NL]

het·er·o·plas·ty (het′ər·ə·plas′tē) *n. Surg.* A plastic operation in which the portion grafted is taken from an organism or person other than the patient.

het·er·o·po·lar (het′ər·ə·pō′lər) *adj. Electr.* Designating an unequal distribution of an electric charge: opposed to *homopolar.*

Het·er·op·ter·a (het′ə·rop′tər·ə) *n. pl.* A suborder of the *Hemiptera* that includes many of the true bugs. [< NL < Gk. *hetero-* other + *pteron* wing] —**het′er·op′ter·ous** *adj.*

het·er·o·sex·u·al (het′ər·ə·sek′shōō·əl) *adj.* **1** Pertaining to or characterized by sexual attraction toward a person of the opposite sex. **2** *Biol.* Pertaining to different sexes. —*n.* A heterosexual person. Compare BISEXUAL, HOMOSEXUAL. —**het′er·o·sex′u·al′i·ty** (-sek′shōō·al′ə·tē) *n.*

het·er·o·sis (het′ə·rō′sis) *n. Biol.* Exceptional vigor of plant and animal organisms through crossbreeding between two different types; hybrid vigor. [< NL < Gk. *heterōsis* alteration < *heteros* other]

het·er·os·po·rous (het′ə·ros′pər·əs, het′ər·ə·spôr′əs, -spō′rəs) *adj. Bot.* **1** Producing both large and small spores. **2** Producing spores of more than one sex. Also **het·er·o·spor·ic** (het′ər·ə·spôr′ik, -spor′ik).

het·er·o·stat·ic (het′ər·ə·stat′ik) *adj. Electr.* Measuring by the aid of a charge other than the one to be measured: applied to an electrometer, thus distinguishing it from an *idiostatic* one.

het·er·o·sty·ly (het′ər·ə·stī′lē) *n. Bot.* A difference in the length of the styles in flowers of the same species, whereby certain plants insure cross-pollination. Also **het′er·o·sty′lism** (-stī′·liz·əm). [< HETERO- + STYLE[2]]

het·er·o·tax·is (het′ər·ə·tak′sis) *n.* **1** *Pathol.* A malformation caused by displacement or lateral transposition of organs. **2** Any irregular or abnormal arrangement of parts, as of rock strata, geographic features, etc.: opposed to *homotaxis.* Also **het′er·o·tax′i·a** (-tak′sē·ə), **het′er·o·tax′y** (-tak′sē). [< NL < Gk. *hetero-* other + *taxis* arrangement] —**het′er·o·tac′tic** (-tak′tik), **het′er·o·tax′ic** (-tak′sik) *adj.*

het·er·o·thal·lism (het′ər·ə·thal′iz·əm) *n. Bot.* A form of sexual differentiation in certain fungi, as the bread mold (*Rhizopus nigricans*), characterized by the possession of two types of mycelia whose hyphae conjugate to produce zygotes. [< HETERO- + Gk. *thallos* sprout] —**het′er·o·thal′lic** *adj.*

het·er·o·to·pi·a (het′ər·ə·tō′pē·ə) *n. Pathol.* A misplacement of an organ, or a growth abnormally situated in the body. Also **het′er·ot′o·py** (-ot′ə·pē). [< NL < Gk. *hetero-* other + *topos* place] —**het′er·o·top′ic** (-top′ik), **het′er·ot′o·pous** (-ot′ə·pəs) *adj.*

het·er·ot·ri·chous (het′ə·rot′rə·kəs) *adj.* **1** Having unlike cilia. **2** Of or pertaining to an order (*Heterotrichida*) of ciliate infusorians. [< HETERO- + Gk. *trichos* hair]

het·er·ot·ro·phy (het′ə·rot′rə·fē) *n.* **1** Any disorder of nutrition. **2** *Bot.* An abnormal manner of obtaining nourishment: applied to certain plants having no true root hairs, and obtaining all nourishment by a fungus, the hyphae of which closely invest the roots and take the place of root hairs. [< HETERO- + Gk. *trophē* nurture < *trephein* feed] —**het′er·o·troph′ic** (-ə·trof′ik, -trō′fik) *adj.*

het·er·o·tro·pi·a (het′ər·ə·trō′pē·ə) *n. Pathol.* A deviation of the eyes in which the two visual lines so diverge that binocular vision is impaired; a form of strabismus. [< HETERO- + -TROP(E) + -IA]

het·er·o·typ·ic (het′ər·ə·tip′ik) *adj. Biol.* Denoting a form of meiosis in which the chromosomes split at an early period, the halves remaining united at the ends and opening out into rings, each of which represents two chromosomes: contrasted with *homeotypic.* Also **het′er·o·typ′i·cal.**

het·er·ou·si·a (het′ə·rōō′sē·ə, -rou′sē-) *n.* Difference in substance or essence: a theological term. [< LGk. *heterousia* < *heterousios* of different essence < *heteros* other + *ousia* being] —**het′er·ou′si·ous, het′er·ou′si·an** *adj.*

Het·er·ou·si·an (het′ə·rōō′sē·ən, -rou′sē-) *n.* One of a party in the early Christian church that affirmed that the substance of the Son is essentially different from that of the Father; an Arian: distinguished from *Homoousian:*

Also **Het′er·ou′si·ast** (-ast). —*adj.* Pertaining to the Heterousians or their belief.

het·er·o·zy·go·sis (het′ər·ə·zi·gō′sis, -zi-) *n. Biol.* The descent of an organism from two different races, species, or varieties; hybridism. [< NL]

het·er·o·zy·gote (het′ər·ə·zī′gōt, -zig′ōt) *n. Biol.* A hybrid resulting from the fusion of two gametes that bear different allelomorphs of the same character and which in consequence does not breed true; a heterozygous individual: contrasted with *homozygote.*

het·er·o·zy·gous (het′ər·ə·zī′gəs) *adj. Biol.* Designating that condition of an individual in which any given genetic factor has been derived from only one of the two generating gametes.

heth (kheth) *n.* The eighth Hebrew letter: also spelled *cheth.* See ALPHABET.

het·man (het′mən) *n. pl.* **·mans** (-mənz) The chieftain of the Cossacks. See ATAMAN. [< Polish < G. *hauptmann* head man, captain]

heugh (hyōōkh) *n. Scot.* **1** A precipice; a crag. **2** A ravine with steep sides. **3** A coalpit. Also **heuch.**

heu·land·ite (hyōō′lən·dīt) *n.* A pearly, variously colored, transparent, hydrous silicate of aluminum and calcium, belonging to the group of zeolites. [after H. *Heuland,* 19th c. English mineralogist]

heu·ris·tic (hyōō·ris′tik) *adj.* **1** Aiding or guiding in discovery. **2** Inciting to find out. [< Gk. *heuriskein* find out]

hew (hyōō) *v.* **hewed, hewn** or **hewed, hew·ing** *v.t.* **1** To make or shape with or as with blows of an ax: often with *out.* **2** To cut with blows of an ax, sword, etc.; chop; hack. **3** To bring down or fell with or as with blows of an ax: usually with *down.* —*v.i.* **4** To make cutting and repeated blows, as with an ax or sword. ◆ Homophone: *hue.* [OE *hēawan*] **—hew′er** *n.*

Hew·lett (hyōō′lit), **Maurice Henry,** 1861–1923, English novelist and essayist.

hex (heks) *U.S. Colloq. v.t.* To bewitch; enchant. —*n.* **1** A witch; sorceress; specifically, a witch doctor. **2** A bewitchment; enchantment: to put a *hex* on one. [< G *hexe* witch]

hexa- *combining form* Six: *hexagon.* Also, before vowels, **hex-.** [< Gk. *hexa-* < *hex* six]

hex·a·ba·sic (hek′sə·bā′sik) *adj. Chem.* **1** Denoting an acid in which six hydrogen atoms can be replaced by a basic radical. **2** Any compound containing six atoms of a univalent metal or their equivalent.

hex·a·chlo·ro·eth·ane (hek′sə·klôr′ō·eth′ān, -klō′rō-) *n. Chem.* A white crystalline trichloride of carbon, C_2Cl_6, used in the manufacture of explosives, dyestuffs, disinfectants, and smoke screens.

hex·a·chlo·ro·phene (hek′sə·klôr′ə·fēn) *n.* An antibacterial agent used in some soaps.

hex·a·chord (hek′sə·kôrd) *n. Music* A series of six tones with a half-step between the third and fourth tones, and whole steps between the others.

hex·ad (hek′sad) *n.* **1** The number six. **2** A group or series of six. [< LL *hexas, hexadis* the number six < Gk. *hexas, hexados*]

hex·ad·ic (hek·sad′ik) *adj.* **1** Of the nature of a hexad. **2** Arranged in groups of six. **3** Based on the number six.

hex·a·em·er·on (hek′sə·em′ər·on) *n.* **1** A period of six days, usually applied specifically to those of the creation. **2** An account of the creation. Also **hex′a·hem′er·on** (-hem′-). [< LL < Gk. *hexaēmeros* the six days' work, lit., of six days < *hex* six + *hēmera* day] **—hex′a·em′er·ic, hex′a·hem′er·ic** *adj.*

hex·a·gon (hek′sə·gon) *n.* A figure with six sides and six angles. [< L *hexagonum* < Gk. *hexagonos* six-cornered < *hex* six + *gōnia* angle]

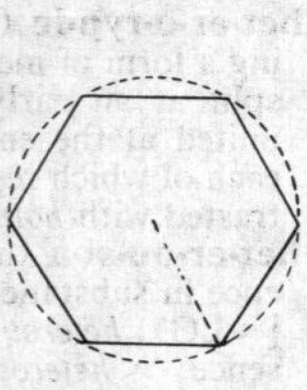

HEXAGON

hex·ag·o·nal (hek·sag′ə·nəl) *adj.* **1** Having the form of a hexagon. **2** Having its section a hexagon; six-sided. —**hex·ag′o·nal·ly** *adv.*

hexagonal system A crystal system having three equal axes intersecting in one plane at 60°, and one of different length intersecting the others at right angles. See CRYSTAL.

hex·a·gram (hek′sə·gram) *n.* One of various figures formed by six intersecting lines, especially one made by completing the equilateral triangles based on the sides of a regular hexagon.

hex·a·he·dron (hek′sə·hē′drən) *n. pl.* **·drons** or **·dra** (-drə) A solid bounded by six plane faces. [< NL] **—hex′a·he′dral** *adj.*

hex·a·hy·drate (hek′sə·hī′drāt) *n. Chem.* A hydrate with six molecules of water.

hex·a·hy·dric (hek′sə·hī′drik) *adj. Chem.* Composed of six hydroxyl groups.

hex·am·er·ous (hek·sam′ər·əs) *adj.* **1** *Bot.* Having a six-parted floral whorl: generally written 6-*merous.* **2** *Zool.* Having six parts or divisions; arranged in sixes or multiples of sixes, as in corals. Also **hex·am′er·al.** [< HEXA- + -MEROUS]

hex·am·e·ter (hek·sam′ə·tər) *n.* A verse of six feet or measures, especially the dactylic verse of the Greek and Latin epics. —*adj.* Having six metrical feet in a verse. [< L < Gk. *hexametros*] **—hex·a·met·ric** (hek′sə·met′rik), **hex·am′e·tral** (-ə·trəl), **hex′a·met′ri·cal** *adj.*

hex·a·meth·yl·ene·tet·ra·mine (hek′sə·meth′ə·lēn·tet′rə·mēn) See METHENAMINE.

hex·ane (hek′sān) *n. Chem.* One of five isomers, C_6H_{14}, of the methane series of saturated hydrocarbon compounds; especially, a volatile colorless oil contained in petroleum. [< HEX(A)- + -ANE]

hex·an·gu·lar (hek·sang′gyə·lər) *adj.* Having six angles.

Hex·a·pla (hek′sə·plə) *n. pl.* An edition of the Holy Scriptures containing six versions in parallel columns; especially, a collection of Hebrew and Greek versions of the Old Testament thus arranged, published by Origen in the third century: construed as singular. [< Gk., pl. of *hexaploos* < *hex* six + *-ploos* -fold] **—hex′a·plar** *adj.*

hex·a·pod (hek′sə·pod) *adj.* Having six feet. —*n.* One of the true or six-legged insects *(Hexapoda).* [< Gk. *hexapous, hexapodos* six-footed] — **hex·ap·o·dous** (hek·sap′ə·dəs) *adj.*

hex·ap·o·dy (hek·sap′ə·dē) *n. pl.* **·dies** Six metrical feet taken together, or a verse or line consisting of six feet.

hex·arch·y (hek′sär·kē) *n. pl.* **·arch·ies** **1** A group of six states. **2** Government by six persons.

hex·a·stich (hek′sə·stik) *n.* In Greek or Latin prosody, a section or stanza of six lines. Also **hex·as·ti·chon** (heks·as′tə·kon). [< L *hexastichus* < Gk. *hexastichos* < *hex* six + *stichos* line] — **hex′a·stich′ic** *adj.*

hex·a·style (hek′sə·stīl) *adj. Archit.* Having a front with six columns, as a temple. [< L *hexastylus* < Gk. *hexastylos* having six columns in front < *hex* six + *stylos* column] **—hex′a·sty′los** (-stī′ləs) *n.*

Hex·a·teuch (hek′sə·tōōk, -tyōōk) *n.* The first six books of the Bible considered as constituting one series. [< HEXA- + Gk. *teuchos* tool, book] **—Hex′a·teu′chal** *adj.*

hex·en·be·sen (hek′sən·bā′zən) *n.* A compact broomlike growth of various trees; witches'-broom. [< G, witches'-broom]

hex·oc·ta·he·dron (heks·ok′tə·hē′drən) *n.* A form of the isometric crystal system consisting of 48 similar triangular planes. [< HEX- + OCTA- + -HEDRON] **—hex·oc′ta·he′dral** (-drəl) *adj.*

hex·one (hek′sōn) *n. Chem.* A colorless liquid ketone compound, $C_6H_{12}O$, used as a solvent for gums and resins.

hex·o·san (hek′sə·san) *n. Biochem.* Any of a group of polysaccharides which hydrolyze to a hexose. [< HEXOSE + -AN]

hex·ose (hek′sōs) *n. Biochem.* Any simple sugar containing six oxygen atoms to the molecule.

hex·tet·ra·he·dron (heks·tet′rə·hē′drən) *n.* A variety of crystal in the isometric system consisting of 24 similar triangular faces. — **hex·tet′ra·he′dral** (-drəl) *adj.*

hex·yl (hek′səl) *n. Chem.* The univalent hydrocarbon radical, C_6H_{13}, of hexane and its derivatives.

hex·yl·re·sor·ci·nol (hek′səl·rə·zôr′sə·nōl) *n.* A yellowish-white compound, $C_{12}H_{18}O_2$, with a pungent odor and astringent taste, used as a germicide and antiseptic.

hey (hā) *interj.* An exclamation of surprise, pleasure, inquiry, incitement, etc., or calling for attention. [Imit.]

hey·day[1] (hā′dā′) *n.* **1** The time of greatest vitality and vigor. **2** Exuberant spirits; wildness. [Prob. < HIGH DAY]

hey·day[2] (hā′dā′) *interj.* An exclamation of surprise, joy, etc. [< Du. *heida!* hey there!]

Hey·drich (hī′drikh), **Reinhard,** 1904–42, German Nazi politician; assassinated.

Hey·duck (hī′dōōk) See HAIDUK.

Hey·mans (hī′mäns), **Corneille,** born 1892, Belgian physiologist.

Hey·se (hī′zə), **Paul von,** 1830–1914, German dramatist and novelist.

Hey·ward (hā′wərd), **Du·Bose** (də·bōz′), 1885–1940, U.S. novelist and playwright.

Hey·wood (hā′wōōd), **John,** 1497?–1580?, English writer of interludes. **—Thomas,** 1575?–1641?, English playwright and actor.

Hez·e·ki·ah (hez′ə·kī′ə) A masculine personal name. [< Hebrew, Jehovah is strength]
—Hezekiah Twelfth king of Judah; son of Ahaz; reigned 726–715 B.C. II *Kings* xviii 1. Also *Ezechias.*

Hg *Chem.* Mercury (symbol Hg). [L *hydrargyrum*]

H-hinge (āch′hinj′) *n.* A hinge with long, narrow leaves, which, when open, resembles the letter H. See illustration under HINGE.

H-hour (āch′our′) *n.* The hour appointed for a military operation to begin: also called *zero hour.*

hi (hī) *interj. Colloq.* Hello: an exclamation of greeting. [Contraction of *how are you?*]

Hi·a·le·ah (hī′ə·lē′ə) A city in SE Florida, just NW of Miami; noted for its race track.

hi·a·tus (hī·ā′təs) *n. pl.* **·tus·es** or **·tus** **1** A gap or opening; break, with a part missing; lacuna; interruption. **2** A pause or break due to the concurrence of two separate vowels without an intervening consonant.

Hi·a·wath·a (hī′ə·woth′ə, -wôth′ə, hē′ə-) Mohawk chief and venerated counselor of the League of the Iroquois, shortly before the advent of the Europeans: name used by Longfellow for the hero of his poem *Hiawatha.*

hi·ba·chi (hi·bä′chē) *n. pl.* **·chis** A charcoal-burning brazier, used for cooking food, etc. [< Jap. *hi* fire + *bachi* bowl]

hi·ber·nac·le (hī′bər·nak′əl) *n.* Hibernaculum (def. 3). [< L *hibernaculum* < *hibernare* pass the winter + -CULUM, dim. suffix]

hi·ber·nac·u·lum (hī′bər·nak′yə·ləm) *n. pl.* **·la** (-lə) *Biol.* **1** An encysted winter polyzoon bud capable of germinating in the spring. **2** A hibernating case constructed of foreign materials by certain insects. A den or shelter occupied by a hibernating animal. [< NL]

hi·ber·nal (hī·bûr′nəl) *adj.* Pertaining to winter; wintry. [< L *hibernalis* < *hibernus* wintry]

hi·ber·nate (hī′bər·nāt) *v.i.* **·nat·ed, ·nat·ing** **1** To pass the winter, especially in a torpid state, as certain animals. **2** To pass the time in seclusion. [< L *hibernatus,* pp. of *hibernare* < *hiems* winter] **—hi′ber·na′tion** *n.*

Hi·ber·ni·a (hī·bûr′nē·ə) The Latin and poetic name for Ireland. [< L, alter. of *Iverna* < Celtic. Related to ERIN.]

Hi·ber·ni·an (hī·bûr′nē·ən) *adj.* Pertaining to Hibernia or Ireland, or its people; Irish. —*n.* A native or naturalized inhabitant of Ireland.

Hi·ber·ni·an·ism (hī·bûr′nē·ən·iz′əm) *n.* An Irish idiom or peculiarity of speech. Also **Hi·ber′ni·cism** (-nə·siz′əm).

Hi·ber·ni·cize (hī·bûr′nə·sīz) *v.t.* **·cized, ·ciz·ing** To make Irish. **—Hi·ber′ni·ci·za′tion** *n.*

hi·bis·cus (hī·bis′kəs, hi-) *n.* Any of various malvaceous herbs, shrubs and trees of the genus *Hibiscus,* having large, showy flowers of various colors. [< L < Gk. *hibiskos* mallow]

Hi·bok·hi·bok (hē′bôk·hē′bôk) A volcano on Camiguin island, Philippines; erupted 1948; 4,370 feet: also *Mount Camiguin.*

hic·cup (hik′əp) *n.* A short, catching sound, caused by spasmodic contraction of the diaphragm and windpipe. —*v.i.* **1** To have the hiccups; make a hiccup. —*v.t.* **2** To utter with hiccups. Also **hic·cough** (hik′əp): also spelled *hickup.* [Imit.]

hic et u·bi·que (hik et yōō·bī′kwē) *Latin* Here and everywhere.

hic ja·cet (hik jā′set) *Latin* Here lies: often inscribed on tombstones.

hick (hik) *n. Slang* One characterized by countrified manners, speech, or dress. [Alter. of RICHARD]

hick·ey (hik′ē) *n. pl.* **·eys** **1** *Mech.* A T-shaped device of iron pipe used for bending a conduit. **2** *Electr.* A small fitting employed to secure an electric fixture to an outlet box. [Origin unknown]

Hick·ok (hik′ok), **James Butler,** 1837–76, U.S. frontier scout: called "Wild Bill Hickok."

hick·o·ry (hik′ər·ē) *n. pl.* **·ries** **1** An Amer-

ican tree of the walnut family (genus *Carya*), yielding an edible nut and having hard, tough, heavy wood: also called *shellbark*. **2** Something made of this wood, as a walking stick or a switch. **3** A strong cotton fabric, usually twilled: used for men's trousers and shirts. **— Old Hickory** Andrew Jackson: so nicknamed for his tough unyielding character. *— adj.* **1** Having a growth of hickory trees. **2** Made of hickory. **3** Tough, like hickory wood. **4** Pertaining to a hickory switch, used in punishment: *hickory* discipline. [<Algonquian *pawcohiccora*]

hick·up (hik′əp) See HICCUP.

hick·wall (hik′wôl′) *n.* The green woodpecker. [ME *hyghwhele*; prob. imit.]

Hic·po·chee (hik′pə·chē), **Lake** A lake of central Florida, comprising a link of the Cross–Florida Waterway.

hic se·pul·tus (hik sə·pul′təs) *Latin* Here (is) buried.

hid (hid) Past tense and alternative past participle of HIDE. *— adj.* Hidden.

hi·dal·go (hi·dal′gō, *Sp.* ē·thäl′gō) *n. pl.* **·gos** (-gōz, *Sp.* -gōs) A Spanish nobleman of the lower rank. [<Sp. < *hijo de algo* son of something] **— hi·dal′ga** (-gä) *n. fem.*

Hi·dal·go (hi·dal′gō, *Sp.* ē·thäl′gō) A state in central Mexico; 8,057 square miles; capital, Pachuca.

Hid·de·kel (hid′i·kəl) The Biblical name for the TIGRIS.

hid·den (hid′n) Past participle of HIDE. *— adj.* Put out of sight; secreted; not known; unseen: also *hid.* See synonyms under SECRET.

hid·den·ite (hid′ən·īt) *n.* A transparent, yellow to green variety of spodumene found in Alexander County, N.C.: used as a gemstone. [after W. E. *Hidden*, 1853–1918, U.S. mineralogist]

hide[1] (hīd) *v.* **hid, hid·den** or **hid, hid·ing** *v.t.* **1** To put or keep out of sight; conceal. **2** To keep secret; withhold from knowledge: to *hide* one's fears. **3** To block or obstruct the sight of; keep from view: The smoke *hid* the buildings. **4** To turn away, as from shame or so as to ignore: *Hide* not thy face from me. *— v.i.* **5** To keep oneself out of sight; remain concealed. **— to hide out** To go into hiding. [OE *hȳdan*] **— hid′er** *n.*

Synonyms: bury, cloak, conceal, cover, disguise, dissemble, entomb, inter, mask, overwhelm, screen, secrete, suppress, veil. *Hide* is the general term, including all the rest, signifying to put out of sight or beyond ready observation or approach; a thing may be *hidden* by intention, by accident, or by the imperfection of the faculties of the one from whom it is *hidden.* As an act of persons, to *conceal* is always intentional; one may *hide* his face in anger, grief, or abstraction; he *conceals* his face when he fears recognition. A house is *hidden* by foliage; the bird's nest is artfully *concealed.* A thing is *covered* by putting something over or around it, by accident or design; it is *screened* by putting something before it, always for protection from observation, inconvenience, attack, censure, etc. In the figurative use, a person may *hide* honorable feelings; he *conceals* an evil or hostile intent. Compare BURY, MASK, PALLIATE. *Antonyms*: admit, advertise, avow, betray, confess, disclose, discover, disinter, divulge, exhibit, exhume, expose, manifest, promulgate, publish, raise, reveal, show, tell, uncover, unmask, unveil.

hide[2] (hīd) *n.* **1** The skin of a large animal, as an ox, especially as material for leather. **2** The human skin: humorously or with contempt. *— v.t.* **hid·ed, hid·ing 1** To whip; flog severely. **2** To remove the hide from. [OE *hȳd* skin]

hide[3] (hīd) *n.* In Old English law, a measure of land, originally about 120 acres, considered enough to support a family. [OE *hīd, hīgid*]

hide–and–seek (hīd′ən·sēk′) *n.* A children's game in which those who hide are sought by one who is "it." Also **hide′–and–go–seek′.**

hide·bound (hīd′bound′) *adj.* **1** Obstinately fixed in opinion; narrow–minded; bigoted. **2** Having the bark so closely adherent that it impedes growth: said of trees.

hid·e·ous (hid′ē·əs) *adj.* Shocking or dreadful, especially in looks; ghastly; revolting. See synonyms under FRIGHTFUL, GHASTLY, GRIM. [<AF *hidous*, OF *hideus* < *hisde, hide* fright; ult. origin unknown] **— hid′e·ous·ly** *adv.* **— hid′e·ous·ness** *n.*

hide–out (hīd′out′) *n.* A place of concealment and safety; hiding place.

hid·ing[1] (hī′ding) *n.* The act of secreting, or the state of being secreted; concealment.

hid·ing[2] (hī′ding) *n. Colloq.* A flogging.

hiding power 1 The opacity of a paint. **2** The ability of a paint to reduce the contrast of a black–and–white surface.

hi·dro·sis (hi·drō′sis) *n.* **1** *Med.* The formation and excretion of sweat. **2** *Pathol.* **a** Any skin disease characterized by sweating. **b** Profuse sweating. [<NL <Gk. *hidroein* sweat < *hidrōs* sweat]

hi·drot·ic (hi·drot′ik) *n.* A drug or other substance to promote sweating; a sudorific. [<Med. L *hidroticus* <Gk. *hidrōtikos*]

hie (hī) *v.t.* & *v.i.* **hied, hie·ing** or **hy·ing** To hasten; hurry: often reflexive. [OE *hīgian*]

hie·la·man (hē′lə·mən) *n.* A shield of wood or bark about 3 feet long and 4 inches wide, used by Australian aborigines. [<native word]

hi·e·mal (hī′ə·məl) *adj.* Hibernal. [<L *hiemalis* < *hiems* winter]

hi·er·a·co·sphinx (hī′ər·ā′kō·sfingks) *n.* In ancient Egyptian art, a hawk–headed sphinx. See SPHINX. [<Gk. *hierax* hawk + SPHINX]

hi·er·arch (hī′ər·ärk) *n.* **1** An ecclesiastical chief ruler. **2** An official of ancient Greece who had charge of the votive offerings in a temple. [<Med. L *hierarcha* < *hierarchēs* < *hieros* sacred + *archos* ruler < *archein* rule]

hi·er·ar·chism (hī′ər·är′kiz·əm) *n.* The principles, character, and rule of a hierarchy. **— hi′er·ar′chist** *n.*

hi·er·ar·chy (hī′ər·är′kē) *n. pl.* **·chies 1** A body of persons, especially ecclesiastics, ranked according to successive orders or classes. **2** Government or rule by a body of ecclesiastics organized in ranks or orders. **3** *Theol.* **a** Any of three ranks of angels. See ANGEL. **b** The body of angels collectively. **4** In science and logic, a series of systematic groups, as kingdoms, classes, orders, families, genera, and species. [<LL *hierarchia* <Gk. *hierarchia* rule of a *hierarch*] **— hi′er·ar′chic, hi′er·ar′chi·cal, hi′er·ar′chal** *adj.*

hi·er·at·ic (hī′ə·rat′ik) *adj.* **1** Of or pertaining to priests; devoted to sacred uses; sacerdotal; consecrated. **2** Of or pertaining to a cursive form of ancient Egyptian hieroglyphs, more complex than the demotic or popular cursive: employed for state papers, rituals, etc. Also **hi′er·at′i·cal.** [<L *hieraticus* <Gk. *hieratikos* of a priest's office < *hieros* sacred]

hi·er·at·i·ca (hī′ə·rat′i·kə) *n.* A fine grade of papyrus.

hiero– *combining form* Sacred; divine. [<Gk. *hieros* sacred]

Hi·er·o I (hī′ər·ō), died 467 B.C., tyrant of Syracuse 478–467 B.C.; patron of literature. Also **Hi′er·on** (-on).

hi·er·oc·ra·cy (hī′ə·rok′rə·sē) *n. pl.* **·cies** Ecclesiastical rule or supremacy. [<HIERO- + -CRACY] **— hi·er·o·crat·ic** (hī′ər·ə·krat′ik) or **·i·cal** *adj.*

hi·er·o·dule (hī′ər·ə·dyōōl) *n.* In ancient Greece, a temple slave, or one set apart as the property of some deity. [<Gk. *hierodoulos* < *hieron* temple + *doulos* slave]

hi·er·o·glyph (hī′ər·ə·glif′, hī′rə·glif) *n.* **1** Picture writing, especially of the ancient Egyptians: usually in the plural. **2** A character or word supposed to convey a hidden meaning. **3** *pl.* Humorously, illegible handwriting; unintelligible scribbling. Also **hi′·er·o·glyph′ic.** [<LL *hieroglyphicus* <Gk. *hieroglyphikos* hieroglyphic < *hieros* sacred + *glyphein* carve] **— hi′er·o·glyph′ic** or **·i·cal** *adj.* **— hi′er·o·glyph′i·cal·ly** *adv.*

HIEROGLYPHS (*n. def. 1*)

hi·er·og·ly·phist (hī′ər·og′lə·fist, hī·rog′-) *n.* One skilled in the art of reading hieroglyphs.

hi·er·o·gram (hī′ər·ə·gram′, hī′·rə-) *n.* **1** A sacred writing. **2** A character or symbol of sacred significance.

hi·er·ol·o·gy (hī′ə·rol′ə·jē, hī·rol′-) *n.* **1** The science of or a treatise on ancient Egyptian writings and inscriptions. **2** The scientific study and comparison of religions. [<HIERO- + -LOGY] **— hi·er·o·log·ic** (hī′ər·ə·loj′ik, hī′rə-) or **·i·cal** *adj.* **— hi′er·ol′o·gist** *n.*

hi·er·o·man·cy (hī′ər·ə·man′sē, hī′rə-) *n.* The act of divining by observing things offered in sacrifice.

Hi·er·on·y·mite (hī′ə·ron′ə·mīt) *n.* A follower of St. Jerome (Hieronymus); also, a member of one of the several monastic orders named after him. [<Med. L *Hieronymita* <LL *Hieronymus* Jerome. See HIERONYMUS.]

Hi·er·on·y·mus (hī′ə·ron′ə·məs, *Du., Ger., Sw.* ē·ā·rō′ni·mōōs) Latin form of JEROME. Also *Pg.* **Hi·e·ro·ni·mo** (ē·ā·rō′ni·mō). [<L <Gk. *hieronymos* having a sacred name < *hieros* sacred + *onyma, onoma* name]

hi·er·o·phant (hī′ər·ə·fant′, hī·er′-) *n.* **1** In ancient Greece, an official expounder of religious mysteries or rites. **2** One who expounds any esoteric cult or doctrine. [<LL *hierophanta* <Gk. *hierophantēs* < *hieros* sacred + *phainein* show] **— hi′er·o·phan′tic** *adj.*

hi·er·o·pho·bi·a (hī′ər·ə·fō′bē·ə) *n.* Morbid fear of sacred and religious things.

Hier·ro (yer′rō) The westernmost of the Canary Islands; 106 square miles: formerly *Ferro.*

Hi·er·o·sol·y·ma (hī′ər·ə·sol′i·mə) The ancient name for JERUSALEM.

hi·er·o·ther·a·py (hī′ər·ə·ther′ə·pē) *n.* Treatment of disease by religious symbolism and exercises. **— hi′er·o·ther′a·pist** *n.*

hi–fi (hī′fī′) *adj.* High–fidelity. *— n.* A radio receiver or phonograph capable of reproducing high–fidelity sound.

hig·gle (hig′əl) *v.i.* **hig·gled, hig·gling** To dispute about terms; haggle; chaffer. [Var. of HAGGLE] **— hig′gler** *n.*

hig·gle·dy–pig·gle·dy (hig′əl·dē·pig′əl·dē) *adj.* In a disordered state; jumbled; muddled. *— n.* Great confusion; a jumble. *— adv.* In a confused manner. [<obs. *higle–pigle*, a varied reduplication, ? < *pig*]

high (hī) *adj.* **1** Greatly elevated; lofty. **2** Having a (specified) elevation: an inch *high.* **3** Of or pertaining to an elevated, or inland, district: *High* German. **4** Extending to or performed from a height: *high* jump; *high* dive. **5** *Geog.* Far from the equator: said of latitudes. **6** Remote; old: *high* antiquity. **7** Of exalted rank or estimation: *high* heaven. **8** Of superior character or kind: *high* art. **9** Important; serious: *high* crimes. **10** Expensive; costly: Rent is *high.* **11** Intensified; of great degree, measure, force, etc.: *high* wind; *high* explosives. **12** Fully advanced or culminated: *high* noon. **13** Haughty; arrogant: *high* words. **14** Strict, as in opinion or doctrine: *high* Tory. **15** Elated; merry: *high* spirits. **16** Complex: usually in the comparative degree: *higher* mathematics, *higher* mammals. **17** Slightly tainted: said of meat. **18** *Music* Acute in pitch; shrill. **19** *Phonet.* Produced with the tongue raised close to the roof of the mouth; close: said of vowel sounds, as the (ē) in *bead*: opposed to *low.* **20** *Mech.* Designating a step–up gear mechanism operating at its greatest speed transmission. **21** *Colloq.* Feeling the effects of liquor, drugs, etc.; intoxicated. *— adv.* **1** To or at a high level, position, degree, etc. **2** In a high manner. **3** At a high pitch. *— n.* **1** A high level, position, etc. **2** *Meteorol.* An anti-cyclone. **3** *Mech.* An arrangement of gears for the greatest speed transmission. **— on high 1** High above. **2** In heaven. [OE *hēah*] **— high′ly** *adv.* **— high′ness** *n.*

Synonyms (adj.): elevated, eminent, exalted, lofty, noble, proud, steep, tall, towering, uplifted. *Deep*, while an antonym of *high* in usage, may apply to the very same distance simply measured in an opposite direction, *high* applying to vertical distance measured from below upward, and *deep* to vertical distance measured from above downward; as, a *deep* valley nestling between *high* mountains. *High* is a relative term signifying greatly raised above any object, base, or surface, in comparison with what is usual, or with some standard; a table is *high* if it exceeds thirty inches; a hill is not *high* at a hundred feet. That is

tall whose height is greatly in excess of its breadth or diameter, and whose actual height is great for an object of its kind; as, a *tall* tree; a *tall* man; *tall* grass. That is *lofty* which is imposing or majestic in height; we term a spire *tall* with reference to its altitude, or *lofty* with reference to its majestic appearance. That is *elevated* which is raised somewhat above its surroundings; that is *eminent* which is far above them; as, an *elevated* platform; an *eminent* promontory. In the figurative sense, *elevated* is less than *eminent*, and this less than *exalted;* we speak of *high, lofty,* or *elevated* thoughts, aims, etc., in the good sense, but sometimes of *high* feelings, looks, words, etc., in the invidious sense of haughty or arrogant. A *high* ambition may be merely selfish; a *lofty* ambition is worthy and *noble.* Compare HAUGHTY, STEEP¹. *Antonyms*: base, deep, degraded, depressed, dwarfed, inferior, low, mean, short, stunted.

high and dry 1 On shore above the reach of water. **2** Stranded; helpless.

high and low Everywhere.

high and mighty Haughty; imperious.

high-ball¹ (hī′bôl′) *n.* An alcoholic drink, consisting of whisky to which is added soda water, mineral water, or ginger ale, served with ice in a tall glass. [Prob. < HIGH + *ball* whisky glass (in bartender's slang)]

high-ball² (hī′bôl′) *n.* A railroad signal meaning to "go ahead." —*v.i. U.S. Slang* To go at great speed. [From a large ball that could be raised or lowered, once used as a semaphore]

high-bind-er (hī′bīn′dər) *n. U.S. Slang* **1** A member of a Chinese secret society of blackmailers. **2** A ruffian; a tough. [? < HELLBENDER]

high-born (hī′bôrn′) *adj.* Of noble birth or extraction.

high-boy (hī′boi′) *n.* A tall chest of drawers usually in two sections, the lower a tablelike structure: called *tallboy* in England. See LOWBOY. [Origin unknown]

high-bred (hī′bred′) *adj.* **1** Of a fine pedigree. **2** Characterized by fine manners or good breeding.

high-brow (hī′brou′) *Colloq. n.* A person of cultivated or intellectual tastes: sometimes a term of derision. —*adj.* Of or suitable for such a person: also **high′browed′.** —**high′brow′ism** *n.*

HIGHBOY

high-chair (hī′châr′) *n.* A baby's chair provided with an eating tray and standing on tall legs.

High Church The group in the Anglican Church that exalts the authority of the church and emphasizes the value of ritual. See LOW CHURCH. —**High′-Church′man** *n.*

high-class (hī′klas′, -kläs′) *adj. Colloq.* Superior; of high quality.

high comedy Comedy presenting the world of polite society and relying chiefly on witty dialog.

high day A holiday; feast day.

higher criticism The scientific and historical study of literature, especially the Bible. Compare LOWER CRITICISM.

higher education 1 College education. **2** Any education beyond secondary schooling, giving advanced opportunities in general or special fields of learning.

Higher Thought New Thought.

high-er-up (hī′ər-up′) *n. Colloq.* A person of superior rank or position.

high explosive 1 A bursting charge that explodes by detonation and with extreme rapidity. **2** A shell charged with high explosive.

high-fa-lu-tin (hī′fə-lōōt′n) *Colloq. adj.* Highflown in manner or speech. —*n.* High-sounding language or writing; pompous speech. Also **high′fa·lu′ting.** [? < HIGH-FLOWN]

high-fi-del-i-ty (hī′fi-del′ə-tē) *adj. Electronics* Capable of reproducing sound with a minimum of distortion: said of certain radio and phonographic equipment: also *hi-fi.*

high-fli-er (hī′flī′ər) *n.* **1** One who or that which flies high. **2** One who goes to extremes or lives extravagantly. Also **high′-fly′er.**

high-flown (hī′flōn′) *adj.* **1** Pretentious. **2** Extravagant in style.

high-fly-ing (hī′flī′ing) *adj.* **1** That flies high, as a bird or airplane. **2** Having pretentious ideas and aims; extravagant in claims or opinions.

high-fre-quen-cy (hī′frē′kwən-sē) *adj. Physics* Of or pertaining to a band of wave frequencies, usually from 3 to 30 megacycles.

High German See under GERMAN.

high-grade (hī′grād′) *adj.* Of superior quality.

high-hand-ed (hī′han′did) *adj.* Carried on in an overbearing manner.

high-hat (hī′hat′) *Colloq. n.* One who wears a top hat; hence, an aristocrat; snob. —*adj.* Aristocratic; snobbish. —*v.t.* To snub; treat snobbishly.

high-hole (hī′hōl′) *n.* A bird, the flicker. Also **high′hold′er.**

high-jinks (hī′jingks′) *n.* **1** An old Scottish game of forfeits, in which one was chosen by lot to perform a task. **2** *Colloq.* Rough sports or jollification. [Origin uncertain]

high jump An athletic event in which the contestants jump for height over a horizontal bar.

high-keyed (hī′kēd′) *adj.* **1** With high musical pitch. **2** Sensitive; spirited.

high-land (hī′lənd) *n.* An elevation of land.

high-land-er (hī′lən-dər) *n.* A mountaineer. Also **high′land·man** (-mən).

High-land-er (hī′lən-dər) *n.* A native of the Scottish Highlands; a Gael.

Highland fling A lively Scotch dance.

High-lands (hī′ləndz) *n. pl.* The mountainous part of northern and western Scotland in and north of the Grampians.

Highlands of the Hudson A mountainous region in SE New York; intersected by the Hudson River.

high life The life of fashionable society.

high-light (hī′līt′) *n.* **1** *pl.* The white or bright spots in a photograph or picture; conversely, the dark spots on the negative of a photograph. **2** A part or detail of special importance or vividness: That touchdown was the *highlight* of the game. —*v.t.* To give special emphasis to; feature.

high living A luxurious manner of life, as in diet.

high mass In the Roman Catholic Church, a mass that is sung and accompanied by full ceremonial.

high-mind-ed (hī′mīn′did) *adj.* **1** Showing an elevated mind; with lofty ethics or feelings. **2** Haughty; arrogant. —**high′-mind′ed·ly** *adv.* —**high′-mind′ed·ness** *n.*

high-muck-a-muck (hī′muk′ə-muk) *n. U.S. Colloq.* A person of importance, real or pretended. [< HIGH + reduplication of MUCKLE]

High-ness (hī′nis) *n.* A title of honor belonging to persons of royal rank: with *His, Her,* or *Your.*

high-oc-tane (hī′ok′tān) *adj.* Having a high octane number, indicating superior antiknock properties.

high-pitched (hī′picht′) *adj.* **1** Shrill. **2** Having a steep slope: said of roofs.

high place Among Semitic peoples, an altar or place of worship, generally on a bare, lofty hill or mountain. —**high′-placed′** *adj.*

high-pres-sure (hī′presh′ər) *adj.* **1** Having or using a high steam pressure: said of steam engines. **2** Exerting vigorous tactics, pressing; urgent: *high-pressure* salesmanship. —*v.t.* **-sured, -sur-ing** To persuade or influence by such methods.

high priest A chief priest.

high-proof (hī′prōōf′) *adj.* Containing a high percentage of alcohol: *high-proof* whisky.

high relief Alto-relievo.

high-rise (hī′rīz′) *adj.* Describing a relatively tall building or structure. —*n.* A tall building, as a many-storied apartment house: also **high rise.**

high-road (hī′rōd′) *n.* **1** A main road. **2** A common or easy method or course. See synonyms under WAY.

high school See under SCHOOL. —**high′-school′** *adj.*

high seas The unenclosed waters of the ocean or sea, especially those beyond the territorial jurisdiction of any one country or nation.

high-sea-soned (hī′sē′zənd) *adj.* **1** Made rich in flavor, as by the addition of spices. **2** Racy; sparkling; lively.

High Sierras The highest portion of the Sierra Nevada, south of Lake Tahoe.

high-sign (hī′sīn′) *n. Colloq.* An informing or warning gesture or grimace.

high-sound-ing (hī′soun′ding) *adj.* Ostentatious or imposing in sound or import.

high-spir-it-ed (hī′spir′ə-tid) *adj.* Full of spirit; not brooking restraint.

high-strung (hī′strung′) *adj.* Strung to a high pitch; strained; highly sensitive.

hight¹ (hīt) *adj. Archaic* Called or named. [OE *heht,* pt. of *hātan* call]

hight² (hīt) See HEIGHT. Also *Obs.* **highth** (hītth, hīth).

high-tail (hī′tāl′) *v.i. U.S. Slang* To depart hastily, especially in fright.

high tea A substantial afternoon or early evening meal at which meat is served.

high-ten-sion (hī′ten′shən) *adj. Electr.* Pertaining to, characterized by, or operating under very high voltage, usually in excess of 1,000 volts.

high-test (hī′test′) *adj.* **1** Designating a material or substance which has passed severe tests of fitness. **2** Denoting a grade of gasoline with a low boiling-point range.

high tide 1 The maximum tidal elevation of the water at any point; also, the time of its occurrence. **2** Any culminating point in a series of events. Also **high water.**

high time 1 About time; past the proper time. **2** *Slang* An occasion of revelry and excitement.

high-toned (hī′tōnd′) *adj.* **1** Of high principles; honorable. **2** Having a high pitch. **3** *U.S. Colloq.* Aristocratic; fashionable.

high treason Treason against the sovereign or state.

high-ty-tigh-ty (hī′tē-tī′tē) *adj. & interj.* Hoity-toity.

high-up (hī′up′) *adj.* In a high or superior position.

High Veld (velt) See NORTHERN KARROO.

high-water (hī′wô′tər, -wot′ər) *adj.* Pertaining to high tide or to its time or highest elevation.

high-way (hī′wā′) *n.* **1** A public thoroughfare; specified line of travel. **2** A common or open way or course. See synonyms under ROAD, WAY.

high-way-man (hī′wā′mən) *n. pl.* **-men** (-mən) One who practices robbery on the highway. See synonyms under ROBBER.

high wine Grain spirits distilled to a high percentage of alcohol; usually in the plural.

high-wrought (hī′rôt′) *adj.* **1** Skilfully or finely wrought. **2** Highly agitated; impassioned.

Hii-u-maa (hē′ōō-mä) See KHIUMA.

hi-jack (hī′jak′) *v.t. U.S. Colloq.* **1** To steal a shipment of (goods, bootleg liquor, etc.) by force. **2** To rob or steal (a truck, etc., carrying such goods). **3** To seize control of (an aircraft) while in flight by the threat or use of force and redirect it to a different destination; skyjack. **4** To rob, swindle, etc., by force or coercion. [Origin unknown] —**hi′jack′er** *n.*

hike (hīk) *v.* **hiked, hik-ing** *v.i.* To go on foot, as for pleasure or on a military march; tramp. —*v.t.* To raise or lift: usually with *up* —*n.* **1** A weary journey on foot; a long walk. **2** *Colloq.* An increase: a price *hike.* [? Var. of HITCH]

hi-lar-i-ous (hi-lâr′ē-əs, hī-) *adj.* Boisterously merry; romping. See synonyms under MERRY. —**hi-lar′i-ous-ly** *adv.*

hi-lar-i-ty (hi-lar′ə-tē, hī-) *n.* Boisterous mirth. See synonyms under LAUGHTER. [< OF *hilarité* < L *hilaritas, -tatis* < *hilaris* < Gk. *hilaros* cheerful]

Hil-a-ry (hil′ər-ē) A masculine personal name. Also **Hi-la-ri-us** (*Dan., Du., Ger., Sw.* hē-lä′rē-ōōs; *Lat.* hi-lä′rē-əs), *Fr.* **Hi-laire** (ē-lâr′), *Sp.* **Hi-la-ri-o** (ē-lä′rē-ō). [< L, joyful] —**Hilary, Saint,** 300?-367?, anti-Arian bishop of Poitiers.

Hilary term or **sitting** One of the four terms recognized in English courts of law, lasting from Jan. 11 to March 23: so called from the festival of St. Hilary (Jan. 13).

Hil-da (hil′də) A feminine personal name. [< Gmc., war]

Hil-de-brand (hil′də-brand) Personal name of

Gregory VII. —**Hil·de·bran·dine** (-din, -dīn) *adj.*

Hil·des·heim (hil′dəs-hīm) A city in SW Lower Saxony, north central West Germany.

hill (hil) *n.* 1 A conspicuous natural elevation rising above the earth's surface and smaller than a mountain. 2 A heap or pile: a *mole-hill.* 3 A small mound of earth placed over or around certain plants and tubers. 4 The plants and tubers so surrounded. — **the Hill** Capitol Hill. — *v.t.* 1 To surround or cover with hills, as potatoes. 2 To form a hill or heap of. — *adj.* Living in, or coming from, a hilly country: *hill* folk, *hill* songs; also, having many hills: *hill* country. [OE *hyll*]

Hill (hil), **Ambrose Powell,** 1825–65, American Confederate general. — **Archibald Vivian,** born 1886, English physiologist. — **James Jerome,** 1838–1916, U.S. railroad promoter; financier.

Hil·la (hil′ə) A town in central Iraq on the Euphrates, near the ruins of Babylon. Also **Hil′lah.**

hill–and–dale (hil′ən-dāl′) *adj.* Designating a method of phonograph recording by making the cuts perpendicular to the surface of the disk, the varying depth corresponding with the sound values. Compare LATERAL-CUT.

Hil·lar·y (hil′ər-ē), **Sir Edmond,** born 1919, New Zealand apiarist; scaled Mt. Everest 1953 with Tensing Norkay of Nepal.

hill·bil·ly (hil′bil′ē) *n. pl.* **·lies** *Colloq.* A person inhabiting or from the mountains or a backwoods area, especially of the southern United States: originally a derogatory term. — *adj. Colloq.* Of or characteristic of hillbillies: *hillbilly* music. [<HILL + BILLY²]

hill·er (hil′ər) *n.* 1 One who makes hills about seeding plants. 2 A mechanical appliance for this purpose.

hill·man (hil′mən) *n. pl.* **·men** (-men′) 1 A dweller in a hilly country; highlander; especially, a member of any hill tribe of India. 2 A climber of hills. 3 A Cameronian. 4 A fairy; troll.

Hill·man (hil′mən), **Sidney,** 1887–1946, U.S. labor leader.

hill mi·na (mī′nə) An East Indian starling-like bird (*Eulabes religiosa*) that can be taught to speak. Also **hill my′na.**

hil·lo (hil′ō, hi-lō′), **hil·loa** See HALLOO.

hill·ock (hil′ək) *n.* A small hill; a mound. — **hill′ock·y** *adj.*

Hill·quit (hil′kwit), **Morris,** 1869–1933, U.S. lawyer and socialist born in Latvia.

hill·side (hil′sīd′) *n.* The side of a hill; a slope or rise of ground.

hill·top (hil′top′) *n.* The summit of a hill.

hill·y (hil′ē) *adj.* **hill·i·er, hill·i·est** 1 Full of hills; swelling; rounded. 2 Like a hill; steep. — **hill′i·ness** *n.*

Hi·lo (hē′lō) A port, the chief city on the island of Hawaii.

hilt (hilt) *n.* The handle and guard of a sword or dagger. — **to the hilt** Thoroughly; completely. — *v.t.* To provide with a hilt. [OE]

hi·lum (hī′ləm) *n. pl.* **·la** (-lə) 1 *Bot.* The scar on a seed indicating its point of attachment; also, the nucleus of a starch grain or the eye of a bean. 2 *Anat.* The fissurelike interval where ducts, vessels, and nerves enter and leave an organ. Also **hi′lus** (-ləs). [<L, a trifle]

Hil·ver·sum (hil′vər-sum) A city in west central Netherlands.

him (him) *pron.* The objective case of *he.* [OE]

Hi·ma·chal Pra·desh (hi·mä′chəl prə-dāsh′) A Union Territory of NE central India, bordering on Tibet; it contains twenty–two former princely states, of which nineteen, before 1936, were grouped in the Punjab Hill States agency, and the rest, 1921–36, in the Punjab States agency; 10,904 square miles; capital, Simla.

Hi·ma·la·yas (hi·mäl′yəz, -mä′lə·yəz, him′ə-lā′əz) A mountain chain between Tibet and India and in Nepal; highest point, 29,002 feet, world's highest point. Also **the Hi·ma′· la·ya.** — **Hi·ma·la·yan** *adj.*

hi·mat·i·on (hi·mat′ē·on) *n. pl.* **·i·a** (-ē·ə) A large square or oblong piece of cloth worn as a mantle by ancient Greeks. [<Gk.]

Hi·me·ji (hē·me·jē) A city on southern Honshu island, Japan.

Himm·ler (him′lər), **Heinrich,** 1900–45, Ger-

man Nazi official; head of the Gestapo, 1936–45.

him·self (him·self′) *pron.* 1 A reflexive and usually intensive or emphatic form of the third–person pronoun, masculine gender. 2 One's normal physical or mental condition; one's consciousness; one's individuality: He stumbled, but soon recovered *himself.* 3 *Dial.* He: used as nominative alone without noun or pronoun: The dagger which *himself* gave Edith was lost; *himself* has said so.

Him·yar·ite (him′yə-rīt) *n.* 1 One of an ancient tribe of SW Arabia and the opposite African mainland. 2 An Arab of a group of ancient kindred tribes, or of their descendants, inhabiting southern Arabia. [after Arabic *Himyar* a legendary king of Yemen + -ITE¹] — **Him·yar·it·ic** (him′yə-rit′ik) *adj.*

hind¹ (hīnd) *adj.* **hind·er, hind·most** or **hind·er·most** Belonging to the rear. [OE *hindan* behind]

hind² (hīnd) *n.* The female of the red deer or stag. [OE]

hind³ (hīnd) *n. Archaic* A farm laborer; also, a peasant. [OE *hīna, hīgna,* genitive pl. of *hīgan* domestics]

hind·brain (hīnd′brān′) *n. Anat.* That part of the brain which develops from the posterior or third embryonic vesicle, including the cerebellum and pons, the medulla oblongata and its membranous roof, or the epencephalon, metencephalon, etc.

Hin·de·mith (hin′də-mit), **Paul,** 1895–1963, German composer active in the United States.

Hin·den·burg (hin′dən-bûrg, *Ger.* hin′dən-bŏŏrkh) The German name for ZABRZE.

Hin·den·burg (hin′dən-bûrg, *Ger.* hin′dən-bŏŏrkh), **Paul von Beneckendorff und von,** 1847–1934, German general and statesman; president of the German Republic 1925–34.

Hindenburg line A strongly fortified line of defense in World War I, established by the Germans in 1916, and running through Saint Laurent, Cambrai, Canal du Nord, Saint Quentin, and La Fère; abandoned in October, 1918. [after Paul von *Hindenburg*]

hin·der¹ (hin′dər) *v.t.* 1 To keep back or delay; check. 2 To prevent; obstruct. — *v.i.* 3 To be an obstruction or obstacle. [OE *hindrian* <*hinder* behind] — **hin′der·er** *n.*
Synonyms: baffle, balk, bar, block, check, clog, counteract, delay, embarrass, encumber, foil, frustrate, hamper, impede, obstruct, prevent, resist, retard, stay, stop, thwart. A railroad train may be *hindered* by a snowstorm from arriving on time; it may by special order be *prevented* from starting. To *retard* is simply to make slow by any means whatever. To *obstruct* is to *hinder,* or possibly to *prevent* advance or passage by putting something in the way; to *oppose* or *resist* is to *hinder,* or possibly to *prevent,* by directly contrary or hostile action, *resist* being the stronger term and having more suggestion of physical force; *obstructed* roads *hinder* the march of an enemy, though there may be no force strong enough to *oppose* it. Compare EMBARRASS, IMPEDE, LIMIT, PROHIBIT, RESTRAIN, SUSPEND. *Antonyms:* see synonyms for HELP, QUICKEN.

hind·er² (hīn′dər) *adj.* Pertaining to or constituting the rear. [OE]

hind·gut (hīnd′gut′) *n. Anat.* The embryonic structure from which the colon develops.

Hin·di (hin′dē) *n.* The principal language of northern India, belonging to the Indic branch of the Indo–Iranian languages. It includes **Western Hindi,** of which Hindustani is the major dialect, and **Eastern Hindi.** [<Hind. *hindī* <*Hind* India <Persian <OPersian *Hindu* land on the Indus <Skt. *sindhu* river, the Indus]

hind·most (hīnd′mōst′) *adj.* Situated in the extreme rear. Also **hind′er·most′** (hīn′dər-).

Hin·doo (hin′dōō), **Hin·doo·ism** (-iz′əm), etc. See HINDU, etc.

hind·quar·ter (hīnd′kwôr′tər) *n.* One of the two back parts into which the sagittal half of a carcass of a quadruped is usually divided, including a hind leg.

hin·drance (hin′drəns) *n.* 1 The act of hindering. 2 An obstacle or check. See synonyms under IMPEDIMENT.

hind·sight (hīnd′sīt′, hīn′sīt′) *n.* 1 Insight into

the nature and difficulties of a situation after the event or after the difficulties have been resolved. 2 The rear sight of a gun or rifle.

Hin·du (hin′dōō) *n.* 1 A member of the native Aryan race of India. 2 Any native of India who professes Hinduism. — *adj.* Of or pertaining to the people or religion of India. Also *Hindoo.* [<Persian *Hindū* < *Hind.* See HINDI.]

Hin·du·ism (hin′dōō-iz′əm) *n.* The popular religion of India, consisting of the ancient religion of the Brahmans, with an admixture of Buddhism and other philosophies: its supreme deities are the triad of Brahma, Vishnu, and Siva, while numberless inferior divinities and natural objects, as trees, serpents, etc., are objects of worship. Also *Hindooism.*

Hin·du·ize (hin′dōō-īz) *v.t.* **·ized, ·iz·ing** To make Hindu in customs, speech, etc.

Hindu Kush (kŏŏsh) A mountain range in central Asia, on the Afghanistan–Pakistan border; highest point, 25,263 feet; ancient *Caucasus Indicus.*

Hin·du·stan (hin′dōō-stan′, -stän′) 1 The Persian name for the land east of the Indus. 2 The region of the Ganges plain where Hindi is largely spoken. 3 The Republic of India as opposed to Pakistan. Also **Hin′do·stan′** (-dō-).

Hin·du·sta·ni (hin′dōō-stä′nē, -stän′ē) *n.* The principal dialect of Western Hindi: the official language and general medium of communication in India. See URDU. — *adj.* Of or pertaining to Hindustan, its people, or to Hindustani. Abbr. *Hind.*

hing (hing) *v.t.* & *v.i. Scot.* To hang.

hinge (hinj) *n.* 1 A device allowing one part to turn upon another: the hook or joint on which a door or shutter swings or turns.

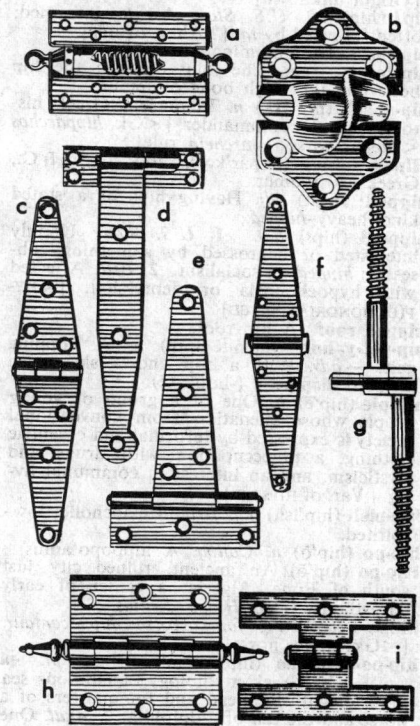

HINGES

a. Spring hinge. *d.* Plate hinge. *g.* Gate hinge.
b. Blind hinge. *e.* T-hinge. *h.* Butt hinge.
c. Strap hinge. *f.* Link hinge. *i.* H-hinge.

2 A device consisting of two metal plates joined by a rod, used as to connect a lid to a box. 3 A natural articulation; a joint, as in the shell of an oyster. 4 A pivotal point on which anything depends for its effect or course. — *v.* **hinged, hing·ing** 1 To have one's course determined by an action or eventuality; be dependent: with *on* or *upon*: The

deal *hinged* on his acceptance of the offer.
— *v.t.* **2** To attach by or equip with a hinge or hinges. [ME *hengen*, prob. <ON *hengja* hang. Related to HANG.]

hinge joint *Anat.* A joint in which angular motion occurs in but one plane, as the elbow joint.

hin·ny[1] (hin′ē) *n. pl.* **·nies** The offspring of a stallion and a she-ass. [<L *hinnus* <Gk. *ginnos*]

hin·ny[2] (hin′ē) *v.i.* **·nied, ·ny·ing** To whinny; neigh. [Var. of WHINNY]

hint (hint) *n.* **1** An indirect suggestion or implication in avoidance of or allusion to a direct statement. **2** A small amount or part: *a hint* of rain. **3** *Obs.* An opportunity; occasion. See synonyms under SUGGESTION. — *v.t.* To suggest indirectly; imply. — *v.i.* To make hints: often with *at*. See synonyms under ALLUDE. [OE *hentan* seize, grasp]

hin·ter·land (hin′tər·land′) *n.* **1** The region lying behind the district along a seacoast or riverside. **2** The region remote from urban areas; the back country. [<G]

Hi·ob (hē′ôp) German form of JOB.

hip[1] (hip) *n.* **1** The lateral part of the body between the brim of the pelvis and the free part of the thigh. ♦ Collateral adjective: *coxal.* **2** The hip joint. **3** The coxa in insects. **4** *Archit.* The external angle in which adjacent roof slopes meet each other. — **on** (or **upon**) **the hip** In a position prejudicial to success: in allusion to a wrestler's trick. — *v.t.* **hipped, hip·ping 1** To fracture or sprain the hip of (an animal). **2** *Archit.* To build with a hip or hips, as a roof. [OE *hype*]

hip[2] (hip) *n.* The fruit of a rose, especially of the dogrose. [OE *hēope*]

hip[3] (hip) *interj.* An exclamation used to introduce a hurrah, or to give the signal for it. [Origin unknown]

hip[4] (hip) *adj. U.S. Slang* Aware; informed: often followed by *to*. [? Alter. of HEP]

hip bone The innominate bone.

hip joint *Anat.* The joint between the hip bone and the thigh bone or femur.

hip·parch (hip′ärk) *n.* In ancient Greek history, a cavalry commander. [<Gk. *hipparchos* <*hippos* horse + *archein* rule]

Hip·par·chus (hi·pär′kəs), 160?–125? B.C., Greek astronomer.

hipped[1] (hipt) *adj.* Having hips of a stated kind: heavy-*hipped.*

hipped[2] (hipt) *adj.* **1** *U.S. Slang* Unduly interested or engrossed by something; obsessed: *hipped* on socialism. **2** *Brit.* Affected with hypochondria or depression. [<HYPO(CHONDRIA) + -ED]

hipped roof A hip roof.

hip·pet·y-hop (hip′ə·tē·hop′) *n.* A hopping gait. — *adv.* With a hop and a skip: also **hip′pet·y-hop·pet·y** (-hop′ə·tē).

hip·pie (hip′ē) *n.* One of a group of young people whose alienation from conventional society is expressed by informal and eccentric clothing, a preoccupation with drugs and mysticism, and an interest in communal living. [Var. of HIPSTER]

hip·pish (hip′ish) *adj. Brit.* Melancholic; low-spirited.

hip·po (hip′ō) *n. Colloq.* A hippopotamus.

Hip·po (hip′ō) An ancient, ruined city just south of Bône, Algeria: a center of early Christianity: also **Hippo Regius.**

hippo- *combining form* Horse: *hippocentaur.* [<Gk. *hippos* horse]

hip·po·cam·pus (hip′ə·kam′pəs) *n. pl.* **·pi** (-pī) **1** In Greek mythology, a fabulous sea monster with the head and forequarters of a horse and the tail of a dolphin. **2** *Anat.* One of two eminences found on the floor of the lateral ventricles of the brain. The larger, **hippocampus major,** is in the descending or temporal cornu of the ventricle; the smaller, **hippocampus minor,** is in the occipital cornu. **3** The sea horse. [<L <Gk. *hippos* horse + *kampos* sea monster] — **hip′po·cam′pal** *adj.*

hip·po·cen·taur (hip′ə·sen′tôr) *n.* A centaur.

hip·po·cras (hip′ə·kras) *n.* A cordial made of spiced wine, lemon, etc.: used for medicinal purposes: popular in the Middle Ages. [<OF *ypocras,* after *Hippocrates*]

Hip·poc·ra·tes (hi·pok′rə·tēz), 460?–377 B.C., Greek physician: called the "Father of Medicine."

Hip·po·crat·ic (hip′ə·krat′ik) *adj.* Of or pertaining to Hippocrates.

Hippocratic oath An oath administered to those entering the practice of medicine in early days and credited to Hippocrates, and still administered to graduates about to receive a medical degree.

Hip·po·crene (hip′ə·krēn, hip′ə·krē′nē) A fountain on Mount Helicon, Greece, traditionally sacred to the Muses. [<L <Gk. *hippokrēnē* <*hippos* horse + *krēnē* fountain]

Hip·po·da·mi·a (hip′ō·dā′mē·ə) In Greek legend, the wife of Pirithous, abused at a banquet by centaurs: the subject of the Parthenon metopes.

hip·po·drome (hip′ə·drōm) *n.* **1** An arena, stadium, or large structure for equestrian exhibitions, circuses, etc. **2** In ancient Greece and Rome, a course or track for horse races and chariot races. [<F <L *hippodromos* <Gk. <*hippos* horse + *dromos* running, course <*dramein* run]

hip·po·griff (hip′ə·grif) *n.* A mythological beast with the wings, head, and claws of a griffin, and the hoofs and tail of a horse. Also **hip′po·gryph.** [<F *hippogriffe* <Ital. *ippogrifo* <Gk. *hippos* horse + LL *gryphus* GRIFFIN]

HIPPOGRIFF

Hip·pol·y·ta (hi·pol′ə·tə) In Greek mythology, a queen of the Amazons: according to one tradition Hercules killed her to obtain her girdle, but she is also said to have been the wife of Theseus and by him the mother of Hippolytus: also called *Antiope.* Also **Hip·pol′y·te** (-tē).

Hip·pol·y·tus (hi·pol′ə·təs) In Greek mythology, the son of Theseus and Hippolyta, who spurned the love of his stepmother Phaedra and was killed by Poseidon at his father's request after Phaedra had turned Theseus against him.

Hip·pom·e·don (hi·pom′ə·don) See SEVEN AGAINST THEBES.

Hip·pom·e·nes (hi·pom′ə·nēz) In Greek mythology, the man who won Atalanta by beating her in a race.

hip·poph·a·gist (hi·pof′ə·jist) *n.* An eater of horseflesh. Also **hip·poph′a·gus** (-ə·gəs). [<HIPPO- + Gk. *phagein* eat] — **hip·poph′a·gous** (-gəs) *adj.*

hip·poph·a·gy (hi·pof′ə·jē) *n.* The act or habit of eating horseflesh. [<HIPPO- + -PHAGY]

hip·po·pot·a·mus (hip′ə·pot′ə·məs) *n. pl.* **·mus·es** or **·mi** (-mī) A large, amphibious, short-legged, thick-skinned African pachyderm related to the pigs (*Hippopotamus amphibius*), having a massive body and very broad obtuse muzzle; river horse. Among living quadrupeds it ranks next to the elephant in size. [<L <Gk. *hippopotamos* <*hippos* horse + *potamos* river]

HIPPOPOTAMUS
(From 4 1/2 to 5 feet at shoulder; length about 12 feet)

Hip·po Re·gi·us (hip′ō rē′jē·əs) See HIPPO.

Hippo Za·ry·tus (zə·rī′təs) An ancient name for BIZERTE.

hip·pus (hip′əs) *n. Pathol.* A disorder of the eyes characterized by rapid, spasmodic changes in size of the pupil when exposed to light. [<NL <Gk. *hippos* horse; from the movement of the eye]

-hippus *combining form Paleontol.* Horse: *Eohippus.* [<Gk. *hippos* horse]

hip roof *Archit.* **1** A roof rising directly from the wall plate on all sides, and thus having no gable. **2** A short portion of a roof over a truncated gable. Also called **hipped roof.**

hip-shot (hip′shot′) *adj.* **1** Having the hip joint dislocated. **2** Lame; awkward.

hip·ster (hip′stər) *n. U.S. Slang* One who is hip, as one versed in jazz. [<HIP[4] + -STER]

Hi·ram (hī′rəm) A masculine personal name. [<Hebrew, nobly born]
— **Hiram,** 980?–936 B.C., king of Tyre who helped to build Solomon's temple. I *Kings* v.

hi·ran (hī′ran) *n. Telecom.* A form of radar designed for operations requiring extreme precision and accuracy in the location of positions. [<HI(GH PRECISION SHO)RAN]

hir·cine (hûr′sin, -sīn) *adj.* Like a goat; especially, having a goatlike smell. [<L *hircinus* <*hircus* goat]

hire (hīr) *v.t.* **hired, hir·ing 1** To obtain the services of (a person) or the use of (a thing) for a compensation; employ; rent. **2** To grant the use of (a thing) or the services of (a person) for a compensation; let: often with *out.* See synonyms under EMPLOY, RETAIN. — **to hire out** To give one's services for a compensation. — *n.* **1** Compensation for labor, services, etc. **2** The act of hiring. See synonyms under SALARY. — **for hire** Offered for use or rent for a compensation. [OE *hȳr*] — **hir′a·ble, hire′a·ble** *adj.* — **hir′er** *n.*

hired girl A woman hired to do household or farm chores.

hired hand A person employed on a farm.

hired man A man hired to do odd jobs, especially about a farm.

hire·ling (hīr′ling) *adj.* Serving for hire; venal. See synonyms under VENAL. — *n.* One who serves for or only for hire.

Hi·ro·hi·to (hir·ō·hē·tō), born 1901, emperor of Japan 1926–.

Hi·ro·shi·ge (hir·ō·shē′ge), **Ando,** 1797–1858, Japanese painter and printmaker.

Hi·ro·shi·ma (hir′ō·shē′mä, hi·rō′shē·mä) A port in SW Honshu island, Japan; devastated by first atomic bomb used in warfare, August 6, 1945.

hir·sel[1] (hûr′səl) *Scot. v.t.* To arrange in flocks, as sheep. — *n.* A flock of sheep. Also *hissel.*

hir·sel[2] (hûr′səl) *v.i. Scot. & Brit. Dial.* To move along with friction or with a rustling effect. Also **hir′sle.**

hir·sute (hûr′sōōt, hûr·sōōt′) *adj.* **1** Having a hairy covering; set with bristles; shaggy. **2** Covered with coarse hairs or hairlike processes. **3** Covered with fine hairlike feathers, as the feet of certain birds. [<L *hirsutus* rough] — **hir′sute·ness** *n.*

Hir·u·din·e·a (hir′ə·din′ē·ə) *n. pl.* A class of annelids which includes the leeches. [<NL <L *hirudo, -inis* leech]

hi·ru·di·noid (hi·rōō′də·noid) *adj.* Pertaining to or resembling a leech.

hi·run·dine (hi·run′din, -dīn) *adj.* Of, pertaining to, or resembling the swallow; swallow-like. [<L *hirundo, -dinis* a swallow]

his (hiz) *pron.* **1** Belonging or pertaining to him: the possessive case of *he* used predicatively or after *of:* This room is *his;* that laugh of *his.* **2** The things, persons, etc., belonging or pertaining to him: Her book is better than *his;* He protects himself and *his.* — *pronominal adj.* Belonging or relating to him: the possessive case of *he* used attributively: *his* book. [OE]

His·ki·a (his·kē′ä) Dutch form of HEZEKIAH.

his′n (hiz′ən) *pron. Archaic* or *Dial.* His. Also **hisn.**

His·pan·ic (his·pan′ik) *adj.* Of or pertaining to the countries or people of Spain, Portugal, and Latin America, or to their languages, customs, or culture. — *n. U.S.* A native or inhabitant of Spanish America; Spanish American.

Hispanic America See SPANISH AMERICA.

His·pan·i·cism (his·pan′ə·siz′əm) *n.* A turn of phrase peculiar to the Spanish.

His·pa·nio·la (his′pə·nyō′lə) An island of the West Indies; 30,000 square miles; formerly *Haiti;* divided into Haiti and the Dominican Republic. *Spanish* **Es·pa·ño·la** (es′pä·nyō′lä).

His·pa·no-Mo·resque (his·pä′nō·mô·resk′) *adj.* Pertaining to or naming the art of Spain having Moorish characteristics.

his·pid (his′pid) *adj. Biol.* Rough with stiff hairs or bristles; bristly. [<L *hispidus* hairy] — **his·pid·i·ty** (his·pid′ə·tē) *n.*

hiss (his) *n.* **1** The prolonged sound of *s,* as that made by escaping air. **2** Such a sound made to express disapproval, hatred, etc. — *v.i.* **1** To make or emit a hiss or hisses. **2** To express disapproval or hatred by hissing. — *v.t.* **3** To express disapproval or hatred of by hissing. **4** To express by means of a hiss or hisses. **5** To pursue, drive off, silence, etc., by hissing: usually with *off, down,* etc. [OE *hyscan* jeer at]

His·sar·lik (his·sär·lik′) The site of ancient Troy in NW Turkey in Asia.

his·sel (his′əl) *Scot.* See HIRSEL[1].

hiss·ing (his′ing) *n.* **1** The act of uttering a

hiss. 2 *Archaic* An object of scorn or contempt.

hist (hist) *interj.* Be silent! hush! hark! —*v.t. Poetic* To urge on or signal by making a hissing sound. [Imit.]

his·tam·i·nase (his·tam′ə·nās) *n. Biochem.* An enzyme capable of inactivating histamine: used in the treatment of allergic conditions. [< HISTAMINE + -ASE]

his·ta·mine (his′tə·mēn, -min) *n. Biochem.* A white crystalline substance, $C_5H_9N_3$, found in plant and animal tissues and as a decomposition product of histidine. It stimulates gastric secretion, reduces blood pressure, and has a contracting action on the uterus. [< HIST(IDINE) + AMINE]

his·ti·dine (his′tə·dēn, -din) *n.* A basic amino acid, $C_6H_9N_3O_3$, obtained upon hydrolysis of most proteins. [< Gk. *histion* tissue + -IDE(E) + INE[2]]

his·ti·o·cyte (his′tē·ə·sīt) *n.* A macrophage that functions in connective tissue. Also **his·to·cyte.** —**his·ti·o·cyt·ic** (his′tē·ə·sit′ik) *adj.*

his·ti·oid (his′tē·oid) *adj.* Appearing like a normal tissue. Also **his·toid** (his′toid). [< Gk. *histos* web + -OID]

histo- *combining form* Tissue: histology. Also, before vowels, **hist-.** [< Gk. *histos* a web]

his·to·blast (his′tə·blast) *n.* A tissue-forming cell

his·to·chem·is·try (his′tə·kem′is·trē) *n.* The chemistry of tissue structures in organisms.

his·to·gen·e·sis (his′tə·jen′ə·sis) *n.* The formation and development of tissues. Also **his·tog·e·ny** (his·toj′ə·nē). —**his′to·gen′ic** *adj.*

his·to·gram (his′tə·gram) *n. Stat.* A graph of frequency distribution in the form of a series of rectangles whose width and area correspond to the range of the class interval and the quantities represented. See HISTORIGRAM.

his·tol·o·gy (his·tol′ə·jē) *n.* 1 The branch of biology treating of the structure of the tissues of organized bodies; microscopic anatomy. 2 The tissue structure of a plant or animal organism. [< HISTO- + -LOGY] —**his·to·log·i·cal** (his′tə·loj′i·kəl) *adj.* —**his·tol′o·gist** *n.*

his·tol·y·sis (his·tol′ə·sis) *n.* 1 *Biol.* The degeneration and dissolution of the organic tissue. 2 *Entomol.* The process by which the larval organs of many insects dissolve into a creamy consistency during the pupa stage, save for certain cell groups which develop into the organs of the future imago. [< HISTO- + -LYSIS]

his·tone (his′tōn) *n. Biochem.* One of a group of simple proteins which yield amino acids on hydrolysis: occurs frequently with nucleic acid and hematin. Also **his′ton** (-ton). [< HIST(O)- + -ONE]

his·to·plas·mo·sis (his′tə·plaz·mō′sis) *n. Pathol.* A serious fungous disease that may infect the lymph nodes and the lungs.

his·to·ri·an (his·tôr′ē·ən, -tō′rē-) *n.* 1 One who writes a history; a chronicler. 2 One versed in history.

his·to·ri·at·ed (his·tôr′ē·ā′tid, -tō′rē-) *adj.* Adorned with figures or designs, especially human or animal figures, as the illuminated manuscripts and capitals of columns of the Middle Ages. [< LL *historiatus,* pp. of *historiare* relate a history < *historia* a history]

his·tor·ic (his·tôr′ik, -tor′-) *adj.* 1 Mentioned or celebrated in history; notable. 2 Historical.

his·tor·i·cal (his·tôr′i·kəl, -tor′-) *adj.* 1 Belonging or relating to history or historians; containing the record or representation of facts. 2 Relating to the past. 3 Pertaining to things as known by testimony, or purely as matters of fact: Memory is the *historical* faculty. 4 Phylogenetic. 5 Historic. —**his·tor′i·cal·ly** *adv.* —**his·tor′i·cal·ness** *n.*

historical geology That branch of geology which treats of the chronological succession of earth events, including past forms of plant and animal life as revealed in fossils, etc.

historical linguistics See under LINGUISTICS.

historical method The method which would found conclusions on a detailed and critical study of the history of the development of the object under consideration.

historical present *Gram.* The present tense used to narrate a past event as if it were happening contemporaneously with the narrative.

historical school Followers of and believers in the historical method.

his·tor·i·cism (his·tôr′ə·siz′əm, -tor′ə-) *n.* The conception that the history of anything sufficiently accounts for its nature or values. —**his·tor′i·cist** *n.*

his·to·ric·i·ty (his′tə·ris′ə·tē) *n.* Historical authenticity.

his·to·ried (his′tə·rēd) *adj. Rare* Rich in historic deeds or events; storied.

his·tor·i·fy (his·tôr′ə·fī, -tor′-) **·fied, ·fy·ing** To write the history of; chronicle.

his·tor·i·gram (his·tôr′ə·gram, -tor′-) *n. Stat.* A graph illustrating the changes of a given variable as a function of time: distinguished from *histogram.* [< HISTORY + -GRAM]

his·to·ri·og·ra·pher (his·tôr′ē·og′rə·fər, -tō′rē-) *n.* One who writes history, especially in an official capacity.

his·to·ri·og·ra·phy (his·tôr′ē·og′rə·fē, -tō′rē-) *n.* 1 The writing of history. 2 History that is written. —**his·to·ri·o·graph·ic** (his·tôr′ē·ə·graf′ik, -tō′rē-) or **·i·cal** *adj.* —**his·to′ri·o·graph′i·cal·ly** *adv.*

his·to·ry (his′tə·rē, his′trē) *n. pl.* **·ries** 1 A recorded narrative of past events, especially those concerning a particular period, nation, individual, etc. 2 The branch of knowledge dealing with the records of the past, especially those involving human affairs. 3 The aggregate of events concerning a given subject, recorded or unrecorded. 4 Past events in general: in the course of *history.* 5 A past worthy of notice; an eventful career. 6 Something in the past: This is all *history* now. 7 *Med.* The facts received from a patient concerning his health, past and present, together with current symptoms: in full, **medical history.** 8 A historical drama. [< L *historia* < Gk., knowledge, narrative < *histōr* knowing. Doublet of STORY.]

Synonyms: account, annals, archives, autobiography, biography, chronicle, memoir, memorial, muniment, narration, narrative, recital, record, register, story. *History* is a systematic *record* of past events. *Annals* and *chronicles* relate events with little regard to their relative importance, and with complete subserviency to their succession in time. *Annals* (L *annus,* year) are yearly records; *chronicles* (Gk. *chronos,* time) follow the order of time. Both necessarily lack emphasis, selection, and perspective. *Archives* are public *records,* which may be *annals,* or *chronicles,* or deeds of property, etc. *Memoirs* generally record the lives of individuals or facts pertaining to individual lives. A *biography* is distinctively a written *account* of one person's life and actions; an *autobiography* is a *biography* written by the person whose life it records. *Annals, archives, chronicles, biographies,* and *memoirs* and other *records* furnish the materials of *history. History* recounts events with careful attention to their importance, their mutual relations, their causes and consequences, selecting and grouping events on the ground of interest or importance. *History* is usually applied to such an *account* of events affecting communities and nations, yet sometimes we speak of the *history* of a single eminent life. Compare RECORD. *Antonyms:* see synonyms for FICTION.

his·tri·on·ic (his′trē·on′ik) *adj.* 1 Pertaining to the stage; theatrical. 2 Having a theatrical manner; artificial; affected. Also **his′tri·on′i·cal.** [< L *histrionicus* < *histrio* actor] —**his′tri·on′i·cal·ly** *adv.*

his·tri·on·ics (his′trē·on′iks) *n. pl.* 1 The art of dramatic representation. 2 Theatrical affectation.

his·tri·on·i·cism (his′trē·on′ə·siz′əm) *n.* A use of histrionic art; stage effect.

hit (hit) *v.* **hit, hit·ting** *v.t.* 1 To come against or in contact with, usually with impact or force. 2 To inflict (a blow, etc.). 3 To strike with a blow: She *hit* him too hard. 4 To strike with or as with a missile: He *hit* the robber in the leg. 5 To move or propel by striking: He *hit* the ball over the fence. 6 To arrive at or achieve, as after effort or search: often with *upon:* to *hit* upon the right answer. 7 To suit; be in accordance with: The idea *hit* her fancy. 8 To affect the emotion, well-being, etc., of: His father's

death *hit* him hard. 9 *Colloq.* To go at vigorously or to excess: to *hit* the bottle. 10 In baseball, to make a (specified base) hit: to *hit* a triple. —*v.i.* 11 To deliver a blow or blows: often with *out.* 12 To strike with force; bump: often with *against.* 13 To fire the cylinder charges of an internal-combustion engine: The car was *hitting* on all eight cylinders. See synonyms under REACH. —**to hit it off** *Colloq.* To take pleasure in one another's company; be congenial. —**to hit off** 1 To imitate. 2 To express or describe exactly. —*n.* 1 A striking against something; a stroke; blow. 2 A stroke of wit or sarcasm; repartee. 3 A stroke of luck; success. 4 Anything enjoying quick public acclaim: The play was a *hit.* 5 In baseball, a base hit. 6 In backgammon, a move that throws one of the opponent's men back to the entering point, or a game won after one or more men are thrown off by the opponent. See synonyms under BLOW. —**clean hit** In baseball, a hit which drives the ball so that it cannot be fielded in time to prevent the earning of a base. [OE *hittan* < ON *hitta* come upon]

hit-and-run (hit′ən·run′) *adj.* 1 Designating an automobile operator who hits a pedestrian and drives away without stopping. 2 Describing the tactics of a military force which makes small harassing attacks on a larger force without venturing a major engagement. 3 In baseball, describing a maneuver in which the batter and the base runners work together by a prearranged plan.

hitch (hich) *n.* 1 A stop or sudden halt; obstruction; hence, an obstacle to an enterprise. 2 The act of catching or fastening, as by a rope, hook, etc.; also a connection so made. 3 *Naut.* Any of various knots made with

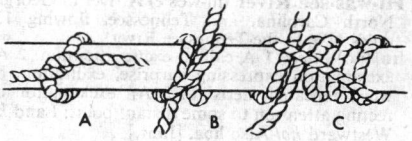

HITCHES
A. Half hitch. B. Clove hitch. C. Rolling hitch.

rope, rigging, etc. 4 A quick or sudden push or pull; a jerk. 5 A limp; halt; hobble. 6 *U.S. Colloq.* A period of enlistment in military service, especially in the U.S. Navy. —*v.t.* 1 To fasten or tie, especially temporarily, with a knot, rope, strap, etc. 2 To harness to a vehicle: often with *up:* to *hitch* a horse to a buggy. 3 To move or shift with a jerk or jerks: He *hitched* himself around in his chair. 4 To marry: often with *up.* 5 *U.S. Slang* To obtain (a ride) by hitchhiking. —*v.i.* 6 To move with jerks: to *hitch* forward. 7 To become caught or entangled. 8 To strike the feet together, as in trotting: said of horses. 9 *U.S. Colloq.* To get on together; agree: He and I don't *hitch.* 10 *U.S. Slang* To travel by hitchhiking. [ME *hicchen;* origin uncertain]

Hitch·cock (hich′kok), **Alfred,** 1900-1980, English motion-picture director active in the United States. —**Edward,** 1793-1864, U.S. geologist.

hitch·hike (hich′hīk′) *v.i. U.S. Colloq.* To travel on foot and by asking rides from passing vehicles. —**hitch′hik′er** *n.*

hitching post A post having iron loops or rings to which a horse, team, etc., may be hitched.

hith·er (hith′ər) *adj.* Near to or toward the person speaking: opposed to *farther.* —*adv.* In this direction; toward this place. [OE *hider*]

hith·er·most (hith′ər·mōst′) *adj.* Nearest.

hith·er·to (hith′ər·tōō′, hith′ər·tōō′) *adv.* 1 Till now. 2 *Archaic* Thus far. See synonyms under YET.

hith·er·ward (hith′ər·wərd) *adv.* Hither. Also **hith′er·wards.**

Hit·ler (hit′lər), **Adolf,** 1889-1945, head of the Nazi party and dictator, officially chancellor of Germany 1933-45; born in Austria: called

"der Führer." **—Hit'ler·ism** (hit·lir'ē·ən) *adj.* — **Hit'ler·ism** *n.*

hit-or-miss (hit'ər·mis') *adj.* **1** Heedless; haphazard: to live a *hit-or-miss* life. **2** Varicolored. —*adv.* Haphazardly.

hit·ter (hit'ər) *n.* One who strikes or hits.

Hit·tite (hit'īt) *n.* **1** One of an ancient people who established a powerful empire in Asia Minor and Northern Syria about 2000–1200 B.C. **2** The language of the Hittites, known from cuneiform inscriptions discovered in Asia Minor which date from about 1400 B.C. **(Cuneiform Hittite).** Hieroglyphic inscriptions from about 1000 B.C., found in Asia Minor and Northern Syria, have also been attributed to the Hittites **(Hieroglyphic Hittite).** Although Hittite has been established as having a definite connection with Indo-European, it exhibits characteristics which distinguish it so markedly from the rest of the Indo-European family that the exact nature of the relationship remains uncertain. See INDO-HITTITE. —*adj.* Of or relating to the Hittites or their language. [<Hebrew *hittīm*]

Hit·torf (hit'ôrf), **Johann Wilhelm,** 1824–1914, German physicist.

Hittorf tube Physics **1** A glass tube having metallic electrodes almost touching, so as to show the insulating effects of a vacuum. **2** A Crookes tube. [after J. W. *Hittorf*]

Hi·va O·a (hē'və ō'ə) The second largest of the Marquesas Islands; capital, Atuona.

hive (hīv) *n.* **1** A structure in which bees may dwell. **2** A colony of bees. **3** A place full of activity. —*v.* **hived, hiv·ing** *v.t.* **1** To cause (bees) to enter a hive; gather into a hive. **2** To store (honey) in a hive. **3** To store (anything) for future use. —*v.i.* **4** To enter or dwell in or as in a hive. [OE *hȳf*]

hives (hīvz) *n.* Any of various skin diseases, especially urticaria. [Origin unknown]

Hi·was·see River (hī·wos'ē) A river in Georgia, North Carolina, and Tennessee, flowing 132 miles NW to the Tennessee River.

ho (hō) *interj.* **1** A call to excite attention. **2** An exclamation expressing surprise, exultation, or, when repeated, derision. **3** An exclamation directing attention to some distant point: Land *ho!* Westward *ho!* Also **hoa.** [Imit.]

Ho *Chem.* Holmium (symbol Ho).

ho·ac·tzin (hō·ak'tsin) See HOATZIN.

Hoang Ho (hwäng' hō') See HWANG HO.

hoar (hôr, hōr) *adj.* **1** White or gray with age; hoary. **2** White or grayish-white in color. **3** Ancient. **4** *Obs.* Musty; moldy. —*n.* **1** Hoarfrost. **2** The condition of being white with age or frost; hoariness. ◆ Homophone: *whore.* [OE *hār* gray-haired]

hoard (hôrd, hōrd) *n.* An accumulation stored away for safeguarding or for future use. See synonyms under HEAP, STOCK. —*v.t.* To gather and store away or hide for future use. —*v.i.* To gather and store away food, jewels, etc. ◆ Homophone: *horde.* [OE *hord* treasure] **—hoard'er** *n.*

hoard·ing[1] (hôr'ding, hōr'-) *n.* **1** The act of accumulating a hoard. **2** *pl.* Treasure laid by; savings.

hoard·ing[2] (hôr'ding, hōr'-) *n. Brit.* **1** A fence, as about a place where building is in progress. **2** A billboard. [<OF *hourd* palisade <Gmc.]

hoar·frost (hôr'frôst', -frost', hōr'-) *n.* Frost having the form of silvery ice needles. [ME *horfrost*]

hoar·hound (hôr'hound', hōr'-) *n.* Horehound.

hoarse (hôrs, hōrs) *adj.* **1** Harsh and rough in sound. **2** Having the voice harsh and rough. [OE *hā(r)s*] **—hoarse'ly** *adv.* **—hoarse'ness** *n.*

hoars·en (hôr'sən, hōr'-) *v.t.* & *v.i.* To make or become hoarse or harsh.

hoar·y (hôr'ē, hō'rē) *adj.* **hoar·i·er, hoar·i·est** **1** White, as from age. **2** Ancient. **3** Covered with short and dense grayish-white hairs, as certain animals. See synonyms under ANCIENT. —**hoar'i·ness** *n.*

hoast (hōst) *Scot.* & *Brit. Dial. v.i.* To cough. —*n.* A cough; hoarseness.

ho·at·zin (hō·at'sin) *n.* A South American bird (genus *Opisthocomus*) resembling the curassow in appearance, prevailingly olive, with a yellowish crest and a pair of hooked claws on each wing: also called *hoactzin.* Also **ho·az'in.** [<Sp. Am. <Nahuatl *uatzin*]

hoax (hōks) *v.t.* To deceive by a trick. —*n.* **1** A deception practiced for sport. **2** A practical joke or fraud. [<HOCUS(-POCUS)] **—hoax'er** *n.*

hob[1] (hob) *n.* **1** A projection on the side of a fireplace; also, its top, serving as a shelf. **2** The nave of a wheel. **3** A hardened fluted steel mandrel for cutting screw threads. **4** A steel punch with a design in relief. **5** A game in which quoits or other objects are tossed at a stake; also, the stake. [? Var. of HUB]

hob[2] (hob) *n.* A fairy; hobgoblin; elf. **—to play hob with** To throw into confusion; upset; ruin. [Orig., a nickname for ROBERT, ROBIN]

Ho·bart (hō'bərt, -bärt) The capital of Tasmania, on the Derwent river.

Hob·be·ma (hob'ə·mä), **Meindert,** 1638–1709, Dutch painter.

Hobbes (hobz), **Thomas,** 1588–1679, English philosopher.

Hobb·ism (hob'iz·əm) *n.* The philosophy of Thomas Hobbes; especially his theory that an absolute monarch is necessary to control the antagonisms of individual interests. Also **Hob·bi·an·ism** (hob'ē·ən·iz'əm). **—Hobbes·i·an** (hobz'ē·ən), **Hob·bi·an** (hob'ē·ən) *adj.* **—Hob·bist** (hob'ist) *n.*

hob·bit (hob'it) *n.* One of a fictitious race of amiable, elflike creatures with furry feet, created by the British author John Ronald Reuel Tolkien (1882–1973).

hob·ble (hob'əl) *v.* **hob·bled, hob·bling** *v.i.* **1** walk with or as with a limp; go lamely or on crutches. **2** To move or proceed in an irregular or clumsy manner. —*v.t.* **3** To hamper the free movement of (a horse, etc.), as by tying the legs together. **4** To cause to move lamely or awkwardly. —*n.* **1** A limping gait. **2** A fetter for the legs; specifically, a rope, strap, or pair of linked rings used to fetter the forelegs of an animal. **3** An embarrassment; difficulty. [? Freq. of HOP. Cf. G *hoppeln* hobble.] **—hob'bler** *n.*

hob·ble-bush (hob'əl·bŏŏsh') *n.* A straggling shrub *(Viburnum alnifolium)* of the honeysuckle family, having flowers resembling those of hydrangea, and the fruit coral-red drupes.

hob·ble·de·hoy (hob'əl·dē·hoi') *n.* **1** An awkward youth. **2** An adolescent boy. Also **hob'be·de·hoy'** (hob'ə·dē-). [Origin uncertain]

hob·ble·show (hob'əl·shō) See HUBBLESHOW.

hobble skirt A narrow skirt, formerly worn by women, so made below the knee as to permit the wearer to take only short steps.

hob·by (hob'ē) *n. pl.* **·bies** **1** A subject or pursuit in which one takes absorbing interest. **2** A hobbyhorse. **3** An ambling nag. **4** A small falcon *(Falco subbuteo)* with long wings. [from *Robin,* a personal name]

hob·by·horse (hob'ē·hôrs') *n.* **1** A rocking-horse; also, a toy consisting of a stick with a wooden horse's head attached. **2** The figure of a horse attached to a person's waist so that he appears to be riding it: used in morris dances, pantomimes, etc.

hob·gob·lin (hob'gob'lin) *n.* **1** A mischievous imp. **2** Anything that causes superstitious terror, particularly anything imagined. See synonyms under SCARECROW. [<HOB[2] + GOBLIN]

hob·nail (hob'nāl') *n.* A nail for studding the soles of heavy shoes.

hob·nailed (hob'nāld') *adj.* **1** Provided or armed with hobnails. **2** Wearing hobnailed boots or shoes; clownish. **3** Ornamented with knobs, as glassware.

hobnail liver The liver in an advanced stage of cirrhosis, characterized by warty surface projections resembling hobnails.

hob·nob (hob'nob) *v.i.* **·nobbed, ·nob·bing** **1** To drink together familiarly and convivially. **2** To be on familiar terms; chat socially. —*n.* A friendly talk. Also **hob-or-nob** (hob'ər·nob'). [OE *habban* have + *nabban* have not]

ho·bo (hō'bō) *n. pl.* **·boes** or **·bos** *U.S.* **1** A migratory, unskilled workman. **2** A professional idler; a tramp. —*v.i.* To live or wander as a hobo. [<*Hey, Bo,* a vagrant's greeting] **—ho'bo·ism** *n.*

Ho·bo·ken (hō'bō·kən) A port of entry in NE New Jersey on the Hudson River.

Hob·son-Job·son (hob'sən·job'sən) *n.* Anglo-Indian (*n.* def. 3).

Hob·son's choice (hob'sənz) This or nothing; a choice with no alternative: in allusion to the practice of Thomas Hobson, 1544–1631, English liveryman, who required each customer to take the horse nearest the door.

Hoc·cleve (hok'lēv), **Thomas,** 1370–1450, English poet.

Ho Chi Minh (hō' chē' min'), 1890?–1969, leader of the Viet Minh; president of North Vietnam 1945–1969.

Ho Chi Minh City A city in S Vietnam; formerly called *Saigon* and formerly capital of South Vietnam.

hock[1] (hok) *n.* **1** The joint of the hind leg in digitigrade mammals, as the horse and ox, corresponding to the ankle in man. **2** The knee joint of a fowl. **3** In man, the back part of the knee joint. —*v.t.* To disable by cutting the tendons of the hock; hamstring. [OE *hōh* heel]

hock[2] (hok) *n.* Any white Rhine wine; originally, that known as *Hochheimer.* [Contraction of *hockamore* <G *Hochheimer* <*Hochheim,* a German town where it was first produced]

hock[3] (hok) *v.t.* & *n.* *U.S. Slang* Pawn. **—in hock** *Slang* **1** In pawn. **2** In prison. [Du. *hok* prison, debt]

hock·ey (hok'ē) *n.* **1** A game played either on a field or on ice, in which opposing players, equipped with curved or hooked sticks, try to drive a small block (puck) or ball into or past the opposite goals. **2** A hockey stick. [<*hock* bent stick, var. of HOOK]

hockey stick The curved stick used to hit the ball or puck in hockey.

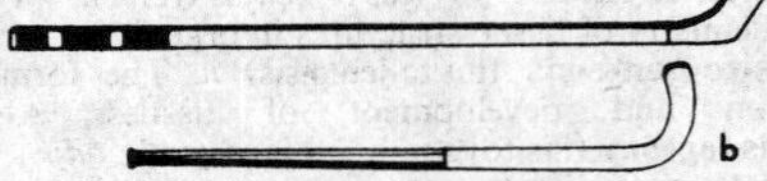

HOCKEY STICKS
a. Ice hockey. *b.* Field hockey.

hock·shop (hok'shop') *n.* *U.S. Slang* A pawnshop.

ho·cus (hō'kəs) *v.t.* **·cused** or **·cussed, ·cus·ing** or **·cus·sing** **1** To deceive by a trick; impose upon. **2** To drug. **3** To add drugs to, as a drink. [Abbreviation of HOCUS-POCUS]

ho·cus-po·cus (hō'kəs·pō'kəs) *n.* **1** A verbal formula used in conjuring or juggling. **2** A conjurer's trick, or deception wrought as if by the conjurer's art. —*v.t.* & *v.i.* To cheat; trick. [A sham Latin phrase, ? alter. of *hoc est corpus* this is my body, a eucharistic formula]

hod (hod) *n.* **1** A long-handled receptacle for holding bricks and mortar, carried on the shoulder. **2** A coal scuttle or a box for coals. [<obs. *hot* <OF *hotte* pannier <Gmc. Cf. MDu. *hodde.*]

hod·car·ri·er (hod'kar'ē·ər) *n.* A man who carries a hod. Also **hod'man** (-mən).

hod·den gray (hod'n) A coarse cloth having the natural color of the wool: formerly worn in northern England and Scotland.

Ho·dei·da (hō·dā'də, -dī'-) A port on the Red Sea in western Yemen. Also *Hudaida.*

Hö·der (hœ'thər) In Norse mythology, a blind son of Odin, slayer of Balder: also spelled *Hoth, Höthr.* Also **Ho'dur.**

Hodge (hoj) *Brit.* A nickname for an agricultural laborer. [from ROGER, a personal name]

Hodg·en·ville (hoj'ən·vil) A town in central Kentucky. See ABRAHAM LINCOLN NATIONAL PARK.

hodge-podge (hoj'poj') *n.* **1** A stew of mixed meats and vegetables. **2** A jumbled mixture; conglomeration. Also *hotch-potch.* [Var. of HOTCHPOTCH]

Hodg·kin's disease (hoj'kinz) *Pathol.* A progressive and fatal enlargement of the lymph nodes, lymphoid tissue, and spleen; a form of granuloma. [after Dr. Thomas *Hodgkin,* 1798–1866, English physician, who first described it]

ho·di·er·nal (hō'dī·ûr'nəl) *adj.* Of or pertaining to the present day. [<L *hodiernus* <*hoc die* (on) this day]

Hód·me·zö·vá·sár·hely (hōd'me·zœ·vä'shär·hey') A city in southern Hungary.

ho·do·graph (hō'də·graf, -gräf) *n.* *Math.* The curve traced by the terminal point of a vector drawn from a fixed origin and representing the acceleration of a particle moving at a

known velocity along any given path. [<Gk. *hodos* way + GRAPH]

ho·dom·e·ter (hō-dom′ə-tər) *n.* An odometer.

ho·do·scope (hō′də-skōp) *n. Physics* A device for indicating the path of cosmic rays, consisting of a series of Geiger counters connected with a neon lamp to record the passage of the separate particles. [<Gk. *hodos* way + -SCOPE]

hoe (hō) *n.* A flat-bladed implement for digging, scraping, and tilling, having in the simplest form a flat and thin blade set nearly at

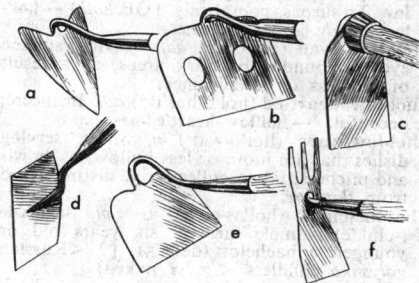

TYPES OF HOES
a. Warren hoe. *c.* Grub hoe. *e.* Garden hoe.
b. Mortar hoe. *d.* Scuffle hoe. *f.* Weeding hoe.

a right angle to a long handle. —*v.t. & v.i.* **hoed, hoe·ing** To dig, scrape, or till with a hoe. [<OF *houe* <OHG *houwa* < *houwan* cut] —**ho′er** *n.*

Hoe (hō) Name of a family identified with the manufacture and improvement of the printing press in America: especially, **Robert,** 1784–1833; his son, **Richard March,** 1812–86, and grandson, **Robert,** 1839–1909.

hoe·cake (hō′kāk′) *n. U.S.* A thin cake of Indian meal: originally baked on a hoe.

hoe-down (hō′doun′) *n. U.S.* **1** A lively, shuffling dance: originally Southern. **2** The music for such a dance. [Origin uncertain]

Hoek van Hol·land (hœk van hôl′änt) The Dutch name for HOOK OF HOLLAND.

Hœ·nir (hœ′nir) In Norse mythology, one of the creators of Ask, the first man, and Embla, the first woman.

Hof (hôf) A city in Franconia, West Germany.

Ho·fer (hō′fər), **Andreas,** 1767–1810, Tirolese patriot.

Hoff·man (hof′mən), **Malvina,** 1887–1966, U. S. sculptor.

Hoff·mann (hôf′män), **Ernst Theodor Amadeus,** 1776–1822, German writer and composer.

Hof·mann (hôf′män), **August Wilhelm von,** 1818–92, German chemist. —**Josef,** 1876–1957, Polish pianist and composer.

Hof·mans·thal (hôf′mäns·täl), **Hugo von,** 1874–1929, Austrian poet and dramatist.

Ho·fuf (hoō-foōf′) The capital of El Hasa, Saudi Arabia. Also *Hufuf.*

hog (hôg, hog) *n.* **1** An omnivorous ungulate having a long mobile snout with flat, expanded end containing the nostrils; especially, any domestic variety of the wild boar (family *Suidae*) bred and raised for its meat, called *pork.* **2** Some animal like the foregoing, as the peccary, warthog, etc. **3** *Colloq.* A filthy, gluttonous person. **4** A stirrer in a paper-pulp vat. —*v.* **hogged, hog·ging** *v.t.* **1** *U.S. Slang* To take more than one's share of; grab selfishly. **2** To arch (the back) upward like a hog's. **3** To cut short, as a horse's mane. —*v.i.* **4** To sag at both ends: said of ships. [OE *hogg*]

ho·gan (hō′gən) *n.* The rude hut of the Navaho and other roving tribes of the SW United States. [<Navaho *qoghan* house]

Ho·garth (hō′gärth), **William,** 1697–1764, English painter and engraver.

Hogarth line A serpentine curve drawn by William Hogarth and later explained, in his *Analysis of Beauty* (1753), as the most perfect figure that man can devise.

hog·back (hôg′bak′, hog′-) *n.* **1** A back humped like that of certain hogs. **2** A sandy or rocky ridge caused by unequal erosion or the outcropping edge of tilted strata. Also called *hog's-back.*

hog-backed (hôg′bakt′, hog′-) *adj.* Elevated toward the middle, like the back of a hog.

Hog·ben (hog′bən), **Lancelot,** born 1895, English biologist and writer.

hog-chain (hôg′chān′, hog′-) *n. Naut.* A tension chain passing from bow to stern of a vessel and fastened to posts amidships: used to prevent the ends from sagging.

hog cholera A highly infectious and contagious disease of swine caused by a filtrable virus, characterized by loss of appetite, fever, exhaustion, and high mortality.

hog·fish (hôg′fish′, hog′-) *n. pl.* **·fish** or **·fish·es** **1** A labroid fish (*Lachnolaemus maximus*) of Florida and the West Indies, with the first three dorsal spines filamentous. **2** A grunt or pigfish; especially, the sailor's-choice.

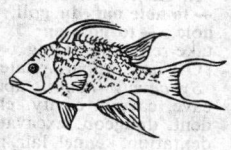

HOGFISH
(About 14 inches long)

Hogg (hog), **James,** 1770–1835, Scottish poet: called "the Ettrick Shepherd."

hog·gish (hôg′ish, hog′-) *adj.* Like a hog. —**hog′gish·ly** *adv.* —**hog′gish·ness** *n.*

hog·ma·nay (hog′mə·nā′) *n. Scot. & Brit. Dial.* The day before New Year's, when gifts or refreshments are sought and bestowed. Also **hog′me·nay′.**

hog·nose (hôg′nōz′, hog′-) *n.* Any North American non-venomous colubrine snake (genus *Heterodon*) with a flattened head and prominent snout, known for its formidable appearance and contorted movements when disturbed. Also **hog′-nosed′ snake.**

hog-nosed skunk (hôg′nōzd′, hog′-) See under CONEPATE.

hog·nut (hôg′nut′, hog′-) *n.* **1** The nut of the pignut hickory. **2** *Brit.* The earth chestnut.

hog peanut A slender vine (*Amphicarpa bracteata*) of the bean family bearing usually a one-seeded pod: also called *earth pea.*

hog pen A pigsty.

hog's-back (hôgz′bak′, hogz′-) *n.* A hogback.

hog-score (hôg′skôr′, -skōr′, hog′-) *n.* A line drawn across the rink in curling, one sixth of the way from each tee to the other.

hogs·head (hôgz′hed′, hogz′-) *n.* **1** A large cask. **2** A liquid measure of varying capacity: in the United States and Great Britain ordinarily 63 gallons, or 0.238 cubic meter, or 52 1/2 imperial gallons.

hog-shou·ther (hôg′shōōth′ər, hog′-) *v.i. Scot.* To jostle with the shoulder.

hog's-pud·ding (hôgz′pŏŏd′ing, hogz′-) *n. Brit. Dial.* A pudding of flour, with currants, etc., stuffed into a hog's entrail like a sausage.

hog-suck·er (hôg′suk′ər, hog′-) *n.* A freshwater fish (*Catostomus nigricans*) of central United States.

hog-tie (hôg′tī′, hog′-) *v.t.* **·tied, ·ty·ing** or **·tie·ing** **1** To tie all four feet or the hands and feet of. **2** *Colloq.* To bind fast; keep from taking action.

hog-tight (hôg′tīt′, hog′-) *adj.* Strong enough to keep swine in or out: said of a fence.

Hog·town (hôg′toun′, hog′-) *Canadian Slang* Toronto. —**Hog′town′er**

Hogue (ôg), **La** A roadstead off the coast of NW France; scene of French naval defeat, 1692.

hog-wal·low (hôg′wol′ō, hog′-) *n.* **1** A damp, muddy place in which hogs wallow. **2** A depression in a prairie that remains damp and grassy.

hog·wash (hôg′wosh′, -wôsh′, hog′-) *n.* **1** Kitchen refuse, swill, etc., fed to hogs. **2** Any worthless rubbish; nonsense; foolishness.

hog·weed (hôg′wēd′, hog′-) *n.* Any of numerous coarse weeds of persistent growth, including the ragweeds, knotweed, dogfennel, etc.

hog wild *U. S. Slang* Wildly excited.

Ho·hen·lin·den (hō′ən·lin′dən) A village east of Munich; scene of French victory over the Austrians, 1800.

Ho·hen·lo·he (hō′ən·lō′ə) A family of German princes.

Ho·hen·stau·fen (hō′ən·shtou′fən) A German princely family, prominent especially in the 12th and 13th centuries.

Ho·hen·zol·lern (hō′ən·tsôl′ərn) A family of

Prussian kings of the 18th and 19th centuries and German emperors, 1871–1918.

Ho·hen·zol·lern (hō′ən·tsôl′ərn) A former Prussian province in southern Germany.

hoick (hoik) *Aeron. v.t.* To throw (an aircraft) into sharp, sudden changes of direction, as in making a steep climb. —*v.i.* To engage in this kind of maneuver or operation: usually with *about* or *around.* [Origin unknown]

hoicks (hoiks) *interj.* A cry used to stir up the hounds in hunting. Also *yoicks.*

hoi·den (hoid′n) *n.* See HOYDEN.

hoigh (hoi) See HOY[2].

hoi pol·loi (hoi′ pə·loi′) The common people; the masses; the herd: usually used contemptuously, and preceded by a redundant *the.* [<Gk., the many]

hoist (hoist) *v.t.* To raise to a higher position; lift or heave up, especially by some mechanical means. —*n.* **1** A hoisting machine; lift. **2** The act of hoisting; a boost. **3** The vertical dimension of a flag or the like, measured along the pole or halyard: distinguished from the *fly.* **4** *Naut.* **a** The length of a sail between the boom and the peak or the jaws of the gaff. **b** The midship depth of a square sail set by hoisting the yard. [? <Du. *hijschen*] —**hoist′er** *n.*

hoi·ty-toi·ty (hoi′tē·toi′tē) *interj.* Think of that! what now! —*adj.* **1** Self-important; putting on airs. **2** Flighty; giddy. **3** Petulant; huffy. Also spelled *highty-tighty.* [Reduplication of obs. *hoit* romp; infl. in meaning by HIGH]

ho·key-po·key (hō′kē·pō′kē) *n.* **1** Ice-cream sold by street peddlers in small quantities: also **ho′ky-po′ky.** **2** Hocus-pocus.

Hok·kai·do (hôk·kī′dō) A northern island of Japan; 29,600 square miles: formerly *Yezo.* Also **Ho·ku·shu** (hō·koō·shōō).

hok·ku (hôk·koō) See HAIKU.

ho·kum (hō′kəm) *n. Slang* **1** A phrase or device deliberately used by an actor, writer, or speaker to win a laugh or catch attention. **2** Contrived sentimental or pathetic effects in a play or story. **3** Nonsense; bunk. [Alter. of HOCUS]

Ho·ku·sai (hō·koō·sī), **Katsuhika,** 1760–1849, Japanese painter and engraver.

hol- Var. of HOLO-.

Hol·arc·tic (hol·ärk′tik, -är′tik, hōl-) *adj.* Pertaining to or designating a zoogeographical region of the world, including the Nearctic and Palearctic realms. See ZOOGEOGRAPHIC REALM.

ho·lard (hō′lärd) *n.* The total quantity of water found in the soil. See CHRESARD, ECHARD. [<HOL- + Gk. *ardeia* irrigation]

Hol·bein (hōl′bīn, *Ger.* hôl′bīn), **Hans,** 1465?–1524, German painter: called "the Elder." —**Hans,** 1497?–1543, German painter, son of the preceding: called "the Younger."

hol·co·dont (hol′kə·dont) *adj. Zool.* Having teeth set in a continuous groove. [<Gk. *holkos* furrow + *odous, odontos* tooth]

hold[1] (hōld) *v.* **held, held** or *in legal use* **hold·en, hold·ing** *v.t.* **1** To take and keep in the hand; retain. **2** To prevent the movement or escape of: He *held* her so that she could not move. **3** To restrain from acting or speaking: *Hold* your tongue! **4** To keep in a specified state: to *hold* one a prisoner. **5** To regard in a specified manner; consider: to *hold* someone dear. **6** To require to fulfil, as the conditions of a contract; obligate. **7** To support or keep in position: Ropes *held* the tower in position. **8** To be capable of enclosing or containing: The barrel *holds* ten gallons. **9** To maintain in the mind; believe: to *hold* an opinion or a grudge. **10** To conduct or engage in; carry on: to *hold* court or services. **11** To have and retain ownership or control of; keep as one's own; occupy: to *hold* the chair. **12** To retain possession or control of, as against an enemy: They *held* the town against the enemy. —*v.i.* **13** To maintain a grip or grasp. **14** To remain firm or unbroken: if the rope *holds*; He *held* to his purpose. **15** To remain or continue unchanged: The breeze *held* all day. **16** To be relevant; remain true, correct, etc.: This decision *holds* for all such cases. **17** To check or restrain oneself; forbear: usually used in the imperative. See synonyms under AR-

REST, EMBRACE, ESTEEM, GRASP, HAVE, INTEREST, KEEP, OCCUPY, RESTRAIN, RETAIN. **— to hold back** 1 To prevent from acting or doing. 2 To refrain. 3 To keep apart or aside; retain, as for an undisclosed purpose. **— to hold down** 1 To suppress; keep under control. 2 *Colloq.* To occupy (a job, etc.) successfully. **— to hold forth** To harangue; preach or speak at length. **— to hold in** To keep in check; restrain. **— to hold off** 1 To keep at a distance. 2 To refrain. **— to hold on** 1 To maintain a grip or hold. 2 To persist; continue. 3 *Colloq.* To stop or wait: used in the imperative. **— to hold one's own** To maintain one's position, as in a contest; lose no ground. **— to hold out** 1 To stretch forth; offer. 2 To last to the end: Our supplies *held out.* 3 To continue resistance; endure; persist. 4 *U.S. Slang* To keep back part or all of (something). **— to hold out for** *Colloq.* To insist upon as a condition of an agreement: He *held out for* a higher salary. **— to hold over** 1 To put off to a later date; delay. 2 To remain beyond the expected time or limit; extend. **— to hold up** 1 To support; prop. 2 To exhibit to view. 3 *Colloq.* To last; endure. 4 To delay; stop. 5 *Colloq.* To stop and rob; also, to rob. **—** *n.* 1 The act of holding, as with the hands; a seizure; figuratively, a controlling force or influence; restraint. 2 A place to grasp. 3 A place of security; a fortified place; stronghold; refuge. 4 The state of being held; possession. 5 *Law* A holding or tenure: in composition: *copyhold, freehold.* 6 *Music* A character (𝄐) indicating the sustention of a tone. 7 A cell in jail. 8 Something to hold articles; a receptacle. 9 A lock or latch. [OE *haldan*]

hold² (hōld) *n. Naut.* The space below the decks of a vessel where cargo is stowed. [<HOLE or <MDu. *hol*]

Hol·da (hôl'dä) In German folklore, the feminine spirit who leads the souls of the dead in their aerial flight. She was associated as well with fruitfulness and the hearth, and was also called "Frau Holle."

hold–all (hōld'ôl') *n.* A general receptacle; especially, a sort of bag used by travelers.

hold·back (hōld'bak') *n.* 1 That which keeps back; a check. 2 A strap passing from the shafts of a horse–drawn vehicle and through the breeching harness, permitting the horse to hold back the vehicle or to push it back.

hold·en (hōl'd'n) Alternative past participle of HOLD, obsolete except in legal use.

hold·er (hōl'dər) *n.* 1 One who or that which holds. 2 An owner; possessor: chiefly in compounds: *householder.* 3 *Law* One who has legal possession of a bill of exchange, check, or promissory note for which he is entitled to receive payment.

hold·fast (hōld'fast', -fäst') *n.* 1 That by which something is held securely in place. 2 Something to cling to; a support. 3 A firm grasp. 4 *Bot.* A specialized organ of attachment at the base of certain algae: also **holdfast cell.**

hold·ing (hōl'ding) *n.* 1 The action of someone or something that holds. 2 A tenure or right of possession. 3 *Often pl.* Property held by legal right, especially stocks or bonds. 4 In football, basketball, etc., the act of obstructing an opponent, as with the arms or hands, contrary to the rules of the game.

holding company A company that holds stock in one or more companies for investment or operating purposes, or both.

hold·o·ver (hōld'ō'vər) *n.* 1 Something remaining from a previous time or situation. 2 A place of detention for prisoners awaiting trial. 3 One who continues in office after his term has expired, or after a change of administration. 4 One who is kept on from one engagement to another.

hold–up (hōld'up') *n.* 1 Stoppage, delay, or obstruction of some activity. 2 A forcible stoppage to commit robbery, especially of a traveler, a train, etc. 3 An overcharge, extortion.

hole (hōl) *n.* 1 A cavity extending into any solid body; a pit; hollow; cave. 2 An opening running or made through a body; aperture or orifice; perforation. 3 An animal's burrow or den. 4 Hence, a vile place; also, a place of hiding. 5 In golf, a cavity in a putting green into which the ball must be played; the distance within bounds between the teeing ground and the flag marking the hole toward which the play is moving; also, one of the points in the game of golf scored by the player who holes out, hole by hole, in the fewest strokes. 6 In various other games, a cavity into which a ball is played, or a point thus scored. 7 *Colloq.* A dilemma. 8 A fault; defect: to expose the *holes* in an argument. **— in the hole** *Colloq.* In debt. **—** *v.* **holed, hol·ing** *v.t.* 1 To make a hole or holes in; perforate. 2 To drive or put into a hole, as in billiards or golf. 3 To dig (a shaft, tunnel, etc.). **—** *v.i.* 4 To make a hole or holes. **— to hole out** In golf, to hit the ball into a hole. **— to hole up** 1 To hibernate. 2 To take refuge in hiding. ◆ Homophone: *whole.* [OE *hol.* Appar. related to HOLLOW.]

Synonyms (noun): aperture, bore, breach, cave, cavern, cavity, chasm, concavity, den, dent, dungeon, excavation, gap, hollow, indentation, kennel, lair, notch, opening, orifice, perforation, rent. A *hole* is an *opening* in a solid body; it may extend entirely through it, forming a passageway or vent, or only partly through it, forming a *cavity,* and may be of any shape, provided the axes are not greatly unequal. An *opening* very long in proportion to its width is more commonly called a crack, fissure, slit, etc., or on the surface of the earth such an opening is designated as a *chasm,* gorge, or ravine; a *rent* in a garment is made by tearing, a slit by cutting. An *orifice* is the mouth of a *hole* or tube. *Aperture* is a very general word; the crack of a partly opened door is an *aperture,* but not a *hole.* The noun *hollow* denotes a shallow *concavity* on the outer surface of a solid, usually round or oval. A *dent* is a depression on the surface of a solid, usually sharp or angular, as if beaten in. A *breach* is roughly broken, generally from the top or edge down through a wall or other object; a *gap* may be between portions that never were joined. See BREACH, BREAK.

hole in one In golf, the act of sinking the ball into a hole in one drive.

hole·y (hō'lē) *adj.* Having holes.

hol·i·but (hol'ə·bət) See HALIBUT.

hol·i·day (hol'ə·dā) *n.* 1 A day appointed by law or custom for the suspension of general business, usually in commemoration of some person or event. 2 Any day of rest or exemption from work. ◆ Collateral adjective: *ferial.* 3 A period of festivity or leisure; a vacation. 4 *Archaic* A day for special religious observance: now usually spelled *holy day.* **—** *adj.* Suitable for a holiday; festive. **—** *v.i.* To vacation. [OE *hālig dæg* holy day]

ho·li·er–than–thou (hō'lē·ər·thən·thou') *adj.* Affecting an attitude of superior goodness or virtue; sanctimonious.

ho·li·ly (hō'lə·lē) *adv.* In a holy manner; piously; sacredly.

ho·li·ness (hō'lē·nis) *n.* 1 The state of being holy; piety. 2 *Theol.* Completeness of moral and spiritual purity. 3 The state of anything hallowed or consecrated to God. See synonyms under SANCTITY. **— His (or Your) Holiness** A title of the pope.

Hol·ins·hed (hol'inz·hed, -in·shed), **Raphael,** died 1580?, English chronicler. Also **Hol·lings·head** (hol'ingz·hed).

ho·lism (hō'liz·əm, hol'iz-) *n. Philos.* The theory that nature tends to synthesize units into organized wholes. [<HOL- + -ISM] **— ho·lis·tic** (hō·lis'tik) *adj.* **— ho·lis'ti·cal·ly** *adv.*

holk (hōk) See HOWK.

hol·la (hol'ə, hə·lä'), **hol·lo** (hol'ō, hə·lō'), **hol·loa** (hol'ō, hə·lō') See HALLOO.

hol·land (hol'ənd) *n.* 1 Unbleached linen, glazed or unglazed: used sometimes in the plural, but construed as a singular. 2 In dressmaking, a form–fitting foundation used as a guide to size. 3 *pl.* Spirit flavored with juniper alone, especially that made in the Netherlands; gin: also **Holland gin** or **Hol·lands.** [from HOLLAND, where first made]

Hol·land (hol'ənd) See NETHERLANDS.

hol·lan·daise sauce (hol'ən·dāz') A creamy sauce made of butter, yolks of eggs, lemon juice or vinegar, and seasoning. [<F, fem. of *hollandais* of Holland]

Hol·land·er (hol'ən·dər) *n.* A native of the Netherlands; a Dutchman.

Hol·lan·di·a (hô·län'dē·ä) The former name of KOTABARU.

hol·ler (hol'ər) *v.t.* & *v.i.* To call out loudly; shout; yell. **—** *n.* A loud shout; yell. [Imit.]

hol·low (hol'ō) *adj.* 1 Having a cavity or depression scooped out; not solid: a *hollow* tree. 2 Sunken; fallen: *hollow* cheeks. 3 Empty; vacant; hence, worthless; fruitless; insincere. 4 Sounding like the reverberation from an empty vessel or cavity; deep; murmuring. **—** *n.* 1 Any depression in a body; a cavity. 2 A valley. 3 A concave tool for making grooves and moldings. See synonyms under HOLE. **—** *v.t.* & *v.i.* To make or become hollow: usually with *out.* **—** *adv. Colloq.* Completely; thoroughly. **— to beat all hollow** To surpass completely. [OE *holh*] **— hol'·low·ly** *adv.* **— hol'low·ness** *n.*

hol·low–eyed (hol'ō·īd') *adj.* Having sunken eyes surrounded by dark areas, as a result of sickness or sleeplessness.

hol·low–heart·ed (hol'ō·här'tid) *adj.* Insincere; deceitful. **— hol'low–heart'ed·ness** *n.*

hol·low·ware (hol'ō·wâr') *n.* Silver serving dishes that are more or less hollow, as bowls and pitchers, taken collectively: distinguished from *flatware.*

hol·lus·chick (hol'əs·chik) *n. pl.* **·chick·ie** (-chik'ē) A male fur seal six years old or younger; a bachelor (def. 5). [? <Russian *golyshka* childless <*golyī* naked]

hol·ly (hol'ē) *n. pl.* **·lies** 1 A tree or shrub (genus *Ilex*) with alternate leaves, white flowers, and the fruit a red berry. 2 The holm oak: also **holly oak.** [OE *holen*]

hol·ly·hock (hol'ē·hok) *n.* A tall biennial herb (*Althaea rosea*) of the mallow family, with large flowers of numerous shades. It was originally a native of China. [ME *holihoc* <*holi* holy + *hoc* mallow]

HOLLYHOCK
a. Single.
b. Double.

Hol·ly·wood (hol'ē·wŏŏd) *n.* The American motion–picture industry, its character, life, etc. **—** *adj.* Of, pertaining to, or characteristic of Hollywood.

Hol·ly·wood (hol'ē·wŏŏd) A NW section of Los Angeles, California, considered the center of the motion–picture industry.

holm¹ (hōm) *n.* 1 An island in a river. 2 *Brit.* Low–lying land by a stream. [OE; infl. in meaning by ON *holmr* land by water, island]

holm² (hōm) *n.* A European evergreen oak (*Quercus ilex*). Also **holly oak, holm oak.** [OE *holen* holly. Doublet of HOLLY.]

Hol·man–Hunt (hōl'mən·hunt'), **William,** 1827–1910, English painter.

Holmes (hōmz), **Oliver Wendell,** 1809–94, U. S. physician, poet, and humorist. **— Oliver Wendell,** 1841–1935, U. S. jurist, associate justice of the Supreme Court 1902–32; son of preceding. **— Sherlock** See SHERLOCK HOLMES.

hol·mi·a (hōl'mē·ə) *n. Chem.* The oxide of holmium. [<NL <HOLMIUM] **— hol'mic** *adj.*

hol·mi·um (hōl'mē·əm) *n.* A metallic element (symbol Ho) of the lanthanide series found in gadolinite. See ELEMENT. [from *Holmia,* Latinized name of Stockholm, Sweden]

holo– *combining form* Whole; wholly: *holograph.* Also, before vowels, *hol–.* [<Gk. *holos* whole]

hol·o·ax·i·al (hol'ō·ak'sē·əl) *adj.* Designating a crystal having all the possible axes of symmetry but without symmetrical planes.

hol·o·blas·tic (hol'ə·blas'tik) *adj. Biol.* 1 Undergoing segmentation throughout the entire mass; wholly germinal, as the ova of all mammals except the monotremes. 2 Of or pertaining to such ova: opposed to *meroblastic.*

Hol·o·caine (hol'ə·kān) *n.* Proprietary name for a brand of phenacaine.

hol·o·caust (hol'ə·kôst) *n.* 1 A sacrifice wholly consumed by fire. 2 Wholesale destruction or loss of life by fire, war, etc. [<F *holocauste* <LL *holocaustum* <Gk. *holokauston,* neut. of *holokaustos* <*holos* whole + *kaustos* burnt] **— hol'o·caus'tal, hol'·o·caus'tic** *adj.*

Hol·o·cene (hol'ə·sēn) *Geol. n.* The epoch following the Pleistocene and extending to the present time. **—** *adj.* Pertaining to the epoch

following the Pleistocene. [<HOLO- + Gk. *kainos* recent]

Hol·o·fer·nes (hol′ə-fûr′nēz) In the book of Judith in the Apocrypha, an Assyrian general slain by Judith.

hol·o·gram (hol′ə-gram) *n.* Photosensitive film containing a three-dimensional image produced by holography. [<HOLO- + -GRAM¹]

hol·o·graph (hol′ə-graf, -gräf) *adj.* Denoting a document wholly in the handwriting of the person whose signature it bears. — *n.* A document so written. [<F *holographe* <Gk. *holographos* < *holos* entire + *graphein* write]

hol·o·graph·ic (hol′ə-graf′ik, -gräf′-) *adj.* 1 Holograph. 2 Of or pertaining to holography. Also **hol′o·graph′i·cal**.

ho·log·ra·phy (hə-log′rə-fē) *n.* A photographic process utilizing a split beam of laser light to produce on a photographic plate, without the use of a lens, the interference pattern of light waves, thus recording a three-dimensional image that can be reconstructed and viewed. [<HOLO- + -GRAPHY]

hol·o·he·dron (hol′ə-hē′drən) *n.* A crystal form having the full number of symmetrically arranged planes crystallographically possible. — **hol′o·he′dral** (-drəl) *adj.*

hol·o·me·tab·o·lism (hol′ə-mə-tab′ə-liz′əm) *n.* *Entomol.* The condition of having a complete metamorphosis, with a larval and pupal stage preceding the adult: opposed to *hemimetabolism.* — **hol′o·met′a·bol′ic** (-met′ə-bol′ik), **hol′o·me·tab′o·lous** *adj.*

hol·o·mor·phic (hol′ə-môr′fik) *adj.* Denoting likeness of form at the ends, as of crystals.

hol·o·phote (hol′ə-fōt) *n.* A lamp for a lighthouse, etc., so arranged that all light is utilized and thrown in the desired direction by reflectors, refracting lenses, or both. [<HOLO- + Gk. *phos, phōtos* light] — **hol′o·pho′tal** *adj.*

ho·loph·ra·sis (hə-lof′rə-sis) *n.* Expression of a sentence or a complex idea in the form of a single word, as in some American Indian languages. [<HOLO- + Gk. *phrasis* phrase] — **hol·o·phras·tic** (hol′ə-fras′tik) *adj.*

hol·o·phyte (hol′ə-fīt) *n.* *Bot.* A plant possessing chlorophyll, and therefore capable of manufacturing its own food. — **hol·o·phyt·ic** (hol′ə-fit′ik) *adj.*

hol·o·sym·met·ric (hol′ə-si-met′rik) *adj.* Wholly symmetrical. — **hol′o·sym′me·try** (-sim′ə-trē) *n.*

hol·o·thu·ri·an (hol′ə-thŏŏr′ē-ən) *n.* Any of a class (*Holothurioidea*) of echinoderms with generally wormlike shape, skinlike integument, and tentacles about the mouth: including trepangs, sea cucumbers, sea slugs, etc. [<L *holothurium,* a kind of zoophyte <Gk. *holothurion*]

Hol·o·trich·i·da (hol′ə-trik′ə-də) *n.* An order of ciliate infusorians with cilia nearly uniformly disposed over the surface of the body. [<NL <HOLO- + Gk. *trix, trichos* hair] — **ho·lot·ri·chal** (hə-lot′ri-kəl), **ho·lot′ri·chous** *adj.*

hol·o·type (hol′ə-tīp) *n.* In taxonomy, the single specimen of a plant or animal which is taken as representative of a new species.

hol·o·zo·ic (hol′ə-zō′ik) *adj.* Wholly like an animal; distinguished from *holophytic.*

holp (hōlp), **holp·en** (hōl′pən) Obsolete forms of past tense and past participle of HELP.

Hol·stein (hōl′stīn, -stēn) *n.* One of a breed of cattle originally developed in the Netherlands province of Friesland and adjoining German provinces: valued for both beef and milk: also **Hol′stein–Frie′sian** (-frē′zhən).

Hol·stein (hōl′stīn, *Ger.* hōl′shtīn) A former Danish duchy, now part of Schleswig–Holstein, northern West Germany.

hol·ster (hōl′stər) *n.* A pistol case. [<Du.]

Hol·ston River (hōl′stən) A river in NE Tennessee, flowing 110 miles SW to the Tennessee River.

holt (hōlt) *n. Archaic* 1 A wooded hill. 2 A wood. [OE]

ho·lus-bo·lus (hō′ləs-bō′ləs) *n.* The whole lot or quantity. — *adv.* All together; at a gulp. [Dog Latin <WHOLE + BOLUS]

ho·ly (hō′lē) *adj.* **·li·er, ·li·est** 1 Devoted to religious or sacred use; consecrated; hallowed. 2 Of highest spiritual purity; saintly: a *holy* martyr. 3 Befitting a saintly character; devout: *holy* fear. 4 Of divine nature or origin. 5 Worthy of veneration because

associated with something divine. — *n. pl.* **ho·lies** A holy thing or quality. [OE *hālig*]

Synonyms (adj.): blessed, consecrated, devoted, devout, divine, hallowed, sacred, saintly. *Sacred* is applied to that which is to be regarded as inviolable on any account, and so is not restricted to divine things; therefore in its lower applications it is less than *holy.* That which is *sacred* may be made so by institution, decree, or association; that which is *holy* is so by its own nature, possessing intrinsic moral purity, and, in the highest sense, absolute moral perfection. God is *holy*; his commands are *sacred. Holy* may be applied also to that which is *hallowed*; as, "the place whereon thou standest is *holy* ground," *Ex.* iii 5. In such use *holy* is more than *sacred*, as if the very qualities of a spiritual or divine presence were imparted to the place or object. *Divine* has been used with great looseness, denoting goodness or power in eloquence, music, etc., but the tendency is to restrict its use to attributes of the Divine Being. See PERFECT, PURE. *Antonyms:* abominable, common, cursed, impure, polluted, secular, unconsecrated, unhallowed, unholy, unsanctified, wicked, worldly.

Holy Alliance A treaty concluded by Russia, Austria, and Prussia at Paris, France, in 1815, binding the sovereign rulers in brotherhood and proclaiming Christianity the foundation of government.

Holy City A city considered sacred by the believers in a religion, as Jerusalem or Mecca.

Holy Communion The Eucharist or Lord's Supper.

Holy Cross, Mount of the A peak of the Sawatch Range in Colorado; 13,986 feet.

holy day A sacred day, as the Sabbath, or one set apart for religious uses.

Holy Father A title of the pope.

Holy Ghost See HOLY SPIRIT.

Holy Grail See GRAIL.

Hol·y·head (hol′i·hed) An island and its chief port in NW Wales. *Welsh* Caer Gy·bi (kīr gē′bē).

Holy Land Palestine.

Holy Mother The Virgin Mary.

Holy Office See CONGREGATION OF THE HOLY OFFICE.

holy of holies The innermost and most sacred shrine of the Jewish tabernacle.

Hol·yoke (hōl′yōk) A city in west central Massachusetts.

holy orders The state of being ordained to the ministry of a church: a term used chiefly in the Anglican, Eastern, and Roman Catholic churches. See also under ORDER.

Holy Roller One belonging to a Protestant sect whose members express religious emotion by violent bodily movements and shouting: a humorous or derogatory term.

Holy Roman Empire An empire in central and western Europe, established in 962 and lasting until 1806: regarded as an extension

of the Western Roman Empire and as the temporal form of the dominion of which the pope was spiritual head: sometimes considered as established with the crowning of Charlemagne. See map below: extent in 11th cent.

holy rood The cross over the entrance to the chancel of many churches and cathedrals.

Holy Rood The cross on which Jesus was crucified.

Holy Saturday The Saturday before Easter.

Holy See See under SEE².

Holy Sepulcher See under SEPULCHER.

Holy Spirit The third person of the Trinity: also called *Holy Ghost.*

ho·ly·stone (hō′lē·stōn) *n.* A flat piece of soft sandstone used for cleaning the wood decks of a vessel. — *v.t.* **·stoned, ·ston·ing** To scrub with a holystone. [Said to be so called because used to clean decks for Sunday]

Holy Synod The supreme governing body in any of the Greek Catholic churches.

Holy Thursday 1 In the Roman Catholic Church, the Thursday of Holy Week, or Maundy Thursday. 2 *Rare* In the Anglican Church, Ascension Day.

ho·ly·tide (hō′lē·tīd′) *n.* A holy season.

holy water Water regarded as sacred; especially, in the Eastern and Roman Catholic churches, water blessed by a priest.

Holy Week In the Christian church, the week before Easter.

Holy Writ The Scriptures.

hom·age (hom′ij, om′-) *n.* 1 Reverential regard or worship; deference. 2 In feudal law, formal acknowledgment of tenure by a tenant to his lord. 3 An act evincing deference or vassalage. See synonyms under ALLEGIANCE, REVERENCE. — *v.t. Obs.* **·aged, ·ag·ing** To pay respect or allegiance to. [<OF <LL *hominaticum* < *homo, -inis* vassal, client, man]

hom·ag·er (hom′ə·jər, om′-) *n.* One who does homage or holds land under tenure of homage.

hom·bre (ôm′brä, om′brē) *n. U.S. Slang* A man. [<Sp.]

Hom·burg (hom′bûrg) *n.* 1 A man's hat of soft felt with slightly rolled-up brim and crown dented lengthwise: so called because originally worn by men in Homburg, Germany. 2 A woman's hat styled after this.

home (hōm) *n.* 1 One's fixed place of abode; the family residence. 2 A family circle; household: a happy *home.* 3 The place of abode of one's affections, peace, or rest: He found a *home* in the church. 4 One's native place or country. 5 The seat or habitat of something; the place of origin: New Orleans is the *home* of jazz. 6 An establishment for the shelter and care of the needy or infirm. 7 In some games, the goal that must be reached in order to win or score. — **at home** 1 In one's own house, place, or country. 2 At ease, as if in familiar surroundings. 3 Prepared to receive callers. — *adj.* 1 Of or pertaining to one's home or country. 2 At the place regarded as the base of operations: the *home* office; a *home* game. 3 Going to the point; effective: a *home* thrust. — *adv.* 1 To or at home. 2 To the place or point intended: to thrust the dagger *home.* 3 Deeply and intimately; to the heart: Her words struck *home.* — *v.* **homed, hom·ing** *v.t.* 1 To carry or send to a home. 2 To furnish with a home. — *v.i.* 3 To go to a home; fly home, as homing pigeons. 4 To have residence. — **to home on** (or **in on**) 1 *Mil.* To direct toward, seek, or find the target, as a guided missile. 2 *Aeron.* To direct (an aircraft) to or toward a given spot by radio or other signals. [OE *hām*]

Synonyms (noun): abode, domicile, dwelling, fireside, habitation, hearth, hearthstone, house, ingleside, residence. See HOUSE.

Home may appear as a combining form in hyphemes or solidemes, or as the first element in two-word phrases, with the following meanings:

1 Of or pertaining to one's home or country:

home address	homekeeper	homemaking
home base	homekeeping	home–owner
home–builder	home lot	home–owning
home–defense	home–lover	home–seeker
home–folks	home–loving	home site
home island	homemaker	home worship

2 At or in the home:

home-abiding	**homelife**
home-baked	**home-raised**
home-built	**home-reared**
home-cooked	**home-sheltered**
home-fed	**home-staying**
home-grown	**home-woven**

3 To or toward the home:

home-bound	**home letter**
homecomer	**home-longing**
home correspondent	**home-wind**

4 Relating to, produced or carried on in, one's home or country; domestic; hence, also, belonging to headquarters:

home affairs	**home market**
home farm	**home office**
home manufacture	**home trade**

Home (hyo͞om), **Earl of** See DOUGLAS-HOME.
home•bod•y (hōm′bod′ē) *n. pl.* **•bod•ies** A person who habitually stays at home.
home-born (hōm′bôrn′) *adj.* Native to the home; derived through the home.
home-bred (hōm′bred′) *adj.* **1** Bred at home; native; domestic. **2**Uncultivated.
home-brew (hōm′bro͞o′) *n.* Spirituous or malt liquor distilled or brewed at home. **—home′-brewed′** *adj.*
home•com•ing (hōm′kum′ing) *n.* **1** A return home. **2** *U.S.* In colleges, an annual celebration for visiting alumni.
home economics The science that treats of the economic and social interests and activities of the home: food, clothing, hygiene, heating and ventilation, thrifty management, etc.
home guard Local volunteers organized to defend the home region or country when the standing army is afield.
home•land (hōm′land′) *n.* The country of one's birth or allegiance.
home•less (hōm′lis) *adj.* Having no home. **—home′less•ness** *n.*
home•like (hōm′līk′) *adj.* Like home; reminding of home. **—home′like′ness** *n.*
home•ly (hōm′lē) *adj.* **•li•er, •li•est 1** Having a familiar everyday character; unpretentious. **2** *U.S.* Having plain features; not good-looking. **3** Domestic. **—home′li•ness** *n.*
home-made (hōm′mād′) *adj.* **1** Of household or domestic manufacture, as distinguished from factory or foreign make. **2** Simple; homely.
homeo- *combining form* Like; similar: *homeothermal: also spelled homoeo-.* Also, before vowels, **home-.** [<**Gk.** *homoios* similar]
Home Office In the British government, the department handling domestic affairs, particularly supervision of the police, elections, and naturalization.
ho•me•o•mor•phism (hō′mē•ə•môr′fiz•əm, hom′ē-) *n.* A close similarity in the crystalline forms of unlike chemical compounds. **—ho′me•o•mor′phous** *adj.*
ho•me•o•path•ic (hō′mē•ə•path′ik, hom′ē-) *adj.* **1** Relating to homeopathy. **2** Diluted in nature. Also spelled *homeopathic*.
ho•me•op•a•thist (hō′mē•op′ə•thist, hom′ē-) *n.* One who advocates or practices homeopathy. Also **ho•me•o• path** (hō′mē•ə•path′, hom′ē-).
ho•me•op•a•thy (hō′mē•op′ə•thē, hom′ē-) *n.* A system of medicine formulated by Dr. Samuel Hahnemann, 1755–1843. It is founded on the principle that "like cures like," and prescribes minute doses of such medicines as would produce in a healty person the symptoms of the disease treated. Also spelled *homoeopathy.* [< HOMEO- + -PATHY]
ho•me•o•pla•sia (hō′mē• ə•plā′zhə, -zhē•ə, hom′•ē-) *n. Med.* The formation of tissue similar in appearance to the adjacent tissue. **—ho′me•o•plas′tic** (-plas′tik) *adj.*
ho•me•o•sta•sis (hō′mē•ə•stā′sis, hom′ē-) *n.* The tendency of an organism to maintain a uniform and beneficial physiological stability within and between its parts; organic equilibrium. **—ho′me•o•stat′ic** (-stat′ik) *adj.*
ho•me•o•typ•ic (hō′mē•ə•tip′ik, hom′ē-) *adj. Biol.* Of or pertaining to the second meiotic division in cells, more nearly resembling typical mitosis: contrasted with *heterotypic.* Also **ho′me•o•typ′i•cal.**
home plate In baseball, the base at which the batter stands when batting: a run is scored when the batter touches first, second, and third base, and home plate consecutively without being retired. See illustration under BASEBALL.
hom•er[1] (hē′mər) *n. U.S. Colloq.* A home run.
ho•mer[2] (hō′mər) *n.* **1** In Jewish antiquity, a liquid measure of 10 baths. See BATH[2]. **2** A dry measure of 10 ephahs. [<Hebrew *hōmer* <*hāmar* swell up]
Ho•mer (hō′mər) A masculine personal name. Also *Du., Ger.* **Ho•me•rus** (hô•mā′ro͞os), *Fr.* **Ho•mère** (ō•mâr′), *Gk.* **Ho•me•ros** (hō•me′•rōs). [<Gk. (Cumaean), blind] **—Homer** A Greek epic poet of about the ninth century B.C.; traditional author of the *Iliad* and *Odyssey.*
Ho•mer (hō′mər), **Winslow,** 1836–1910, U.S. painter.
Ho•mer•ic (hō•mer′ik) *adj.* Of or pertaining to Homer or his age or writings. Also **Ho•me•ri•an** (hō•mir′ē•ən), **Ho•mer′i•cal.**
Homeric laughter Loud and irrepressible laughter.
home•room (hōm′ro͝om′, -ro͞om′) *n.* The schoolroom in which a class meets daily for attendance check, hearing of bulletins, guidance, etc.
home rule 1 Self-government in local affairs within the framework of state or national laws. **2** A political movement, begun about 1870, to gain autonomy for Ireland.
home•rul•er (hōm′ro͞o′lər) *n.* One who favors home rule.
home run In baseball, a base hit in which the ball is driven beyond reach of the opposing fielders, thus allowing the batter to touch all bases and score a run.
home•sick (hōm′sik′) *adj.* Suffering because of absence from home; ill in mind or body through longing for home; nostalgic. **—home′•sick′ness** *n.*
home•spun (hōm′spun′) *adj.* **1** Of domestic manufacture. **2**Plain and homely in character. *—n.* **1** Fabric woven at home. **2** A loose, rough fabric having the appearance of tweed.
home•stake (hōm′stāk′) *n.* Enough money to get back home.
home•stead (hōm′sted) *n.* **1** The place of a home; the house, subsidiary buildings, and adjacent land occupied as a home. **2** *U.S.* A tract of land occupied by a settler under the Homestead Act (1862) or its revisions. *—v.i. U.S.* To become a settler on a homestead under the Homestead Act. *—v.t. U.S.* To settle on land under the Homestead Act.
Homestead Act A Congressional enactment of 1862, later revised and extended, which enables a settler to acquire 160 acres of free public land providing he reside on, cultivate, and improve his land for five years (in 1912, reduced to three years), after which time he may obtain full title and unrestricted ownership. In less fertile areas, 320 or even 640 acres were later allowed.
home•stead•er (hōm′sted′ər) *n.* **1** One who has a homestead. **2** One who holds lands acquired under the Homestead Act of Congress.
homestead law *U.S.* A law in many States exempting a homestead from seizure or sale to satisfy general debts of a certain amount. Also **homestead exemption law.**
home•stretch (hōm′strech′) *n.* **1** The last part of a racecourse before the winning post is reached; the last part of a horse race. **2** The last part of any journey or endeavor.
home•ward (hōm′wərd) *adj.* Directed toward home. *—adv.* Toward home. Also **home′•wards.**
home•work (hōm′wûrk′) *n.* Work performed or assigned for performance at home; work done at home by wage-earners, or lessons assigned to students for home study.
home•y (hō′mē) *adj.* **•hom•i•er, hom•i•est** *Colloq.* Reminding of home; homelike: also spelled *homy.* **—home′y•ness, hom′i•ness** *n.*
hom•i•cide (hom′ə•sīd, hō ′mə-) *n.* **1** The killing of one human being by another. **2** A person who has killed another. [<F <L *homicidium* <*homicida* murderer <*homo* man + *-cidere* <*caedere* cut, kill] **—hom′i•ci′dal** *adj.* **—hom′i•ci′dal•ly** *adv.*
hom•i•let•ics (hom′ə•let′ iks) *n.* The branch of rhetoric that treats of the composition and delivery of sermons. [<Gk. *homilētikos* sociable <*homileein* be in company with <*homilos* assembly]
hom•i•list (hom′ə•list) *n.* **1** A writer of homilies. **2** One who delivers homilies or preaches to a congregation.
hom•i•ly (hom′ə•lē) *n. pl.* **•lies 1** A didactic sermon on some text or topic from the Bible. **2** A serious admonition, especially upon morals or conduct. **3** A tedious, moralizing discourse. [<OF *omelie* <LL *homilia* <Gk. *homilia* <*homilos* assembly < *homos* the same + *ilē* crowd] **—hom′i•let′ic** or **•i•cal** *adj.*
hom•i•nal (hom′ə•nəl) *adj.* Pertaining to man. [<L *homo, hominis* man]
hom•ing (hō′ming) *adj.* **1** Readily finding the way home, returning home. **2** Pertaining to any of various methods and devices for directing an aircraft or guided missile to a specified spot: a *homing* beacon. *—n.* The act of heading for or reaching home.
homing pigeon A pigeon with remarkable capability of making its way home from great distances: used for conveying messages. Also called *carrier pigeon.*
hom•i•nid (hom′ə•nid, hō′mə-) *n. Zool.* A member of the family *Hominidae* of the primate order, now represented by only one living species, *Homo sapiens.* *—adj.* Of or pertaining to any member of this group. [<NL <L *homo, hominis* man]
hom•i•noid (hom′ə•noid, hō′mə-) *adj.* **1** Manlike. **2** *Zool.* Pertaining to or describing any member of the superfamily or group *Hominoidea* of the primate order, including the large tailless apes, as the gibbons, orangutans, gorillas, and chimpanzees, and the genus *Homo* as its most advanced form. *—n.* **1** An animal resembling man. **2** Any primate of the superfamily *Hominoidea.* [<NL <L *homo, hominis* man]
hom•i•ny (hom′ə•nē) *n.* Hulled corn (maize), broken up or coarsely ground, boiled in water or milk for food. Also (**hominy grits.** [< Algonquian *rockahominie* parched corn]
Ho•mo (hō′mō) *n.* **1** Man. **2** *Zool.* Generic name of various species of erect, large-brained anthropoids belonging to the family *Hominidae* of the primate order of vertebrates, now represented only by *Homo sapiens.* [<L]
homo- *combining form* Same; similar; equal: *homogeneous* : opposed to *hetero-.* [<Gk. *homo-* <*homos* same]
ho•mo•cen•tric (hō′mə•sen′trik, hom′ə-) *adj.* Having a common center. Also **ho′mo•cen′•tri•cal.**
ho•mo•cer•cal (hō′mə•sûr′kəl, hom′ə-) *adj.* Zool. Characterized by a similarity of the upper and lower halves of the caudal fin in fishes, due to the straight, central position of the caudal verdtebrae. [<HOMO- + Gk. *kerkos* tail] **—ho′mo•cer′cy** (-sûr′sē) *n.*
ho•mo•chro•mat•ic (hō′mə•krō•mat′ik, hom′ə-) *adj.* Pertaining to or consisting of one color; monochromatic. Also **ho•mo•chrome** (hō′mə•krōm, hom′ə-). **—ho•mo•chro•ma•tism** (hō′mə•krō′mə•tiz′əm, hom′ə-) *n.*
ho•mo•chro•mous (hō′mə•krō′məs, hom′ə-) *adj. Bot.* Of one color, as a flower head with similar florets. [< HOMO- + Gk. *chrōma* color]
ho•mo•cy•clic (hō′mə•sī′klik, -sik′lik, hom′ə-) *adj. Chem.* Pertaining to or designating an organic compound of the closed-chain or ring type, as benzene: opposed to *heterocyclic.*
ho•mo•dyne (hō′mə•dīn, hom′ə-) *adj.* Electronics Pertaining to or designating a system of radio reception by the aid of a locally generated voltage of carrier frequency; zero-beat in reception. Compare HETERODYNE. [<HOMO- + Gk. *dynamos* power]
homoeo- See HOMEO-.
ho•mo•er•o•tism (hō′mō•er′ə•tiz′əm) *n.* Sexual attraction to members of the same sex, normally well sublimated. Also **ho•mo•e•rot•i•cism** (hō′mō•i•rot′ə•siz′əm). **—ho′mo•e•rot′ic** *adj.*
ho•mog•a•mous (hō•mog′ə•məs) *adj. Bot.* **1** Having but one kind of flowers; opposed to *heterogamous.* **2** Having pistils and stamens which ripen at the same time: opposed to *dichogamous.* Also **ho•mo•gam•ic** (hō′mə•gam′•ik). [<HOMO- + -GAMOUS]
ho•mog•a•my (hō•mog′ə•mē) *n.* **1** *Bot.* **a** The simultaneous maturity of stamens and pistils in a flower: distinguished from *dichogamy.* **b** The condition of having all flowers alike: distinguished from *heterogamy.* **2** *Biol.* Interbreeding among an isolated group of individuals having similar characters, or characters different from those from which they are isolated. [<HOMO- + -GAMY]
ho•mo•ge•ne•i•ty (hō′mə•jə•nē′ə•tē, hom′ə-) *n.*

Identity or similarity of kind or structure.

ho·mo·ge·ne·ous (hō′mə·jē′nē·əs, hom′ə-) *adj.* **1** Of the same composition or character throughout. **2** Of the same kind, nature, etc. (with another); like; similar: opposed to *heterogeneous.* **3** *Math.* Having all its terms of the same degree, as an algebraic equation. Also **ho·mo·gene** (ho′mə·jēn), **ho′mo·ge′ne·al.** See synonyms under ALIKE. [< Med. L *homogeneus* < Gk. *homogenēs* of the same race < *homos* the same + *genos* race] —**ho′mo·ge′ne·ous·ly** *adv.* —**ho′mo·ge′ne·ous·ness** *n.*

ho·mo·gen·e·sis (hō′mə·jen′ə·sis, hom′ə-) *n. Biol.* **1** A mode of reproduction in which the offspring are like the parent and have the same cycle of existence: opposed to *heterogenesis.* **2** Homogeny.

ho·mog·en·ize (hə·moj′ə·nīz, hō′mə·jə·nīz′) *v.t.* **·ized, ·iz·ing 1** To make or render homogeneous. **2** To process, as milk, by subjecting to high temperature and pressure so as to break up fat globules and disperse them uniformly throughout; emulsify. —**ho·mog′en·ized** *adj.* —**ho·mog′en·i·za′tion** *n.* —**ho·mog′en·iz′er** *n.*

ho·mog·e·nous (hə·moj′ə·nəs) *adj. Biol.* Having a similarity in structure due to descent from a common ancestor or development from a common stock.

ho·mog·e·ny (hə·moj′ə·nē) *n. Biol.* Homology of structures genetically related through a common ancestor: opposed to *homoplasy.* [< Gk. *homogeneia* community of birth < *homos* the same + *genos* race]

ho·mog·o·ny (hə·mog′ə·nē) *n. Bot.* The condition of having stamens and pistils of uniform respective length in all flowers of the same species; opposed to *heterogony.* [< HOMO- + -GONY] —**ho·mog′o·nous** *adj.* —**ho·mog′o·nous·ly** *adv.*

ho·mo·grade (hō′mə·grād) *adj. Stat.* Expressed in one or the other of two contrasting categories, as male or female. Compare HETEROGRADE.

hom·o·graph (hom′ə·graf, -gräf, hō′mə-) *n.* A word identical with another in spelling, but differing from it in origin and meaning, and sometimes in pronunciation, as *bass,* a fish, and *bass,* a male voice: also called *homonym.* ◆ See note under HOMONYM. [< Gk. *homographos* having the same letters < *homos* same + *graphein* to write] —**hom′o·graph′ic** *adj.*

homoio- *combining form* Homeo-. [< Gk. *homoios* similar]

ho·moi·o·ther·mal (hə·moi′ə·thûr′məl) *adj.* Preserving a uniform temperature, as warm-blooded animals: opposed to *poikilothermal.* Also **homothermal.**

ho·moi·ou·sian (hō′moi·o͞o′sē·ən, -ou′sē-) *adj.* Alike in nature or characteristics. Also **ho′moi·ou′si·ous.**

Ho·moi·ou·si·an (hō′moi·o͞o′sē·ən, -ou′sē-) *n.* One of the Arian sectaries of the fourth century who held that Christ was of a similar nature but not of the same nature with the Father: opposed to *Homoousian.* —*adj.* Of or pertaining to the Homoiousians or their beliefs: also **Ho′moi·ou′si·ous.** [< Gk. *homoios* like + *ousia* being] —**Ho′moi·ou′si·an·ism** *n.*

hom·o·log (hom′ə·lôg, -log) *n.* **1** Something that answers in position, proportion, or type to, or has structural affinity with, something else; a member or form of a homologous series: Ethane is a *homolog* of methane. **2** *Biol.* A structure or part of an organism showing homology: The wing of a bat is the *homolog* of the arm of a man: distinguished from *analog.* Also **hom′o·logue.**

ho·mol·o·gate (hō·mol′ə·gāt) *v.* **·gat·ed, ·gat·ing** *v.t.* **1** To acknowledge; express approval of. **2** In Scots law, to make valid; ratify. —*v.i.* **3** To agree; to express assent. [< Med. L *homologatus,* pp. of *homologare* < Gk. *homologein* agree]

ho·mo·log·ic (hō′mə·loj′ik, hom′ə-) *adj.* **1** *Geom.* Designating two figures so related that either may be the projection of the other upon a plane. **2** Relating to or governed by homology; corresponding in structure; homologous. Also **ho′mo·log′i·cal.** —**ho·mo·log′i·cal·ly** *adv.*

ho·mol·o·gize (hō·mol′ə·jīz) *v.* **·gized, ·giz·ing** *v.t.* **1** To make homologous. **2** To demonstrate the homologies of. —*v.i.* **3** To be homologous; correspond in structure or value.

ho·mol·o·gous (hō·mol′ə·gəs) *adj.* **1** Having a similar structure, proportion, value, or position. **2** Proportional to each other. **3** Identical in nature, relation, or the like. **4** *Biol.* Denoting either of a pair of sexually differentiated chromosomes which unite at meiosis. **5** *Med.* Pertaining to or designating a serum protecting against the same bacterium from which it was prepared. [< Gk. *homologos* agreeing < *homos* the same + *logos* speech < *legein* speak]

hom·o·lo·graph·ic (hom′ə·lə·graf′ik) *adj.* Pertaining to homolography.

homolographic projection A method of map drawing by which the relative areas of different countries are accurately indicated.

homo·log·ra·phy (hom′ə·log′rə·fē) *n.* The study or presentation of proportions, anatomical or geodetic. [< Gk. *homalos* even + *graphein* write]

ho·mol·o·gy (hō·mol′ə·jē) *n.* **1** The state or quality of being homologous; correspondence in structure and properties. **2** *Biol.* The correspondence of a part or organ of one animal with a similar part or organ of another, determined by agreement in derivation and development from a like primitive origin, as the foreleg of a quadruped, the wing of a bird, and the pectoral fin of a fish: distinguished from *analogy* and contrasted with *heterology.* **3** *Chem.* A similarity in compounds having the same fundamental structure but differing in constituents by a regular succession of changes, as the alcohols. **4** *Bacteriol.* A relationship between a bacterium and the serum obtained from it. [< HOMO- + -LOGY]

ho·mol·o·sine (hə·mol′ə·sin, -sīn) *adj.* Designating a world map combining two homolographic projections so as to portray continents with the least distortion possible. [< Gk. *homalas* even + L *sinus* curve]

ho·mo·mor·phism (hō′mə·môr′fiz·əm, hom′ə-) *n.* **1** *Biol.* Resemblance in form, as among the members of a zoophytic colony. **2** *Entomol.* The exhibition of imperfect metamorphosis in insects; resemblance of larva to adult. **3** *Bot.* The possession of perfect flowers of only one form or kind. Compare HETEROMORPHISM. —**ho′mo·mor′phic, ho′mo·mor′phous** *adj.*

ho·mo·mor·phy (hō′mə·môr′fē, hom′ə-) *n. Biol.* Imitative resemblance between unrelated organisms; adaptive mimicry without structural similarity.

hom·o·nym (hom′ə·nim, hō′mə-) *n.* **1** A word identical with another in pronunciation, but differing from it in spelling and meaning, as *fair* and *fare, read* and *reed* : also called *homophone.* **2** A homograph. **3** A word identical with another in spelling and pronunciation, but differing from it in origin and meaning, as *butter,* the food, and *butter,* one who butts. **4** One who has the same name as another; namesake. **5** *Biol.* A generic or specific name rejected because of previous application to another animal or plant. [< Gk. *homos* same + *onyma* name] —**hom·o·nym·ic** (hom′ə·nim′ik, hō′mə-) or **·i·cal** *adj.*

◆*Homonym* is used with a variety of meanings, the most common sense being that of definition 1 above. Although *homophone* is etymologically more precise and is unambiguous in meaning, *homonym* is nevertheless the more commonly used form in this sense. *Homonym* is also, but less commonly, used interchangeably with *homograph.*

ho·mon·y·mous (hō·mon′ə·məs) *adj.* **1** Of the nature of a homonym; ambiguous. **2** Indicated by the same name because occupying the same relation.

ho·mon·y·my (hō·mon′ə·mē) *n.* Identity of sound or name with diversity of sense; ambiguity.

ho·mo·ou·si·an (hō′mō·o͞o′sē·ən, -ou′sē-, hom′·ō-) *adj.* Identical in nature. Also **ho′mo·ou′·si·ous.**

Ho·mo·ou·si·an (hō′mō·o͞o′sē·ən, -ou′sē-, hom′ō-) *n.* One of the Christians, who, in the great controversy of the fourth century about the nature of Christ, maintained that it was identical with that of the Father, instead of similar, or different, as maintained by the less strict and more rigid Arians respectively: distinguished from *Homoiousian* and *Heterousian.* —*adj.* Of or pertaining to the Homoousians or their beliefs: also **Ho′·mo·ou′si·ous.** [< Gk. *homos* the same + *ousia* being] —**Ho′mo·ou′si·an·ism** *n.*

ho·mo·phile (hō′mō·fīl) *n.* A homosexual.

ho·mo·pho·bi·a (hō′mō·fō′bē·ə) *n.* Extreme hatred or fear of either homosexuals or of homosexuality.

hom·o·phone (hom′ə·fōn, hō′mə-) *n.* A homonym (def. 1). ◆See note under HOMONYM. [< Gk. *homophōnos* of the same sound < *homos* same + *phōnē* sound]

hom·o·phon·ic (hom′ə·fon′ik, hō′mə-) *adj.* **1** *Music* **a** Consisting of sounds having the same pitch; in unison: said of ancient music. **b** Having one predominant part carrying the melody, with the other parts used for harmonic rather than for contrapuntal effect: opposed to *polyphonic.* **2** Of or pertaining to homophones; having the same sound. Also **ho·moph·o·nous** (hō·mof′ə·nəs).

ho·moph·o·ny (hō·mof′ə·nē) *n.* **1** Identity of sound, with difference of meaning. **2** *Music* The condition or quality of being homophonic.

ho·mo·plas·tic (hō′mə·plas′tik, hom′ə-) *adj. Biol.* Pertaining to a resemblance (in forms or organs) not traceable to homogeny: opposed to *homogenous.*

ho·mo·po·lar (hō′mə·pō′lər) *adj. Chem.* Having uniform distribution of an electric charge, as in compounds linked by a covalent bond: opposed to *heteropolar.*

Ho·mop·ter·a (hō·mop′tər·ə) *n. pl.* A suborder of hemipterous insects with sucking mouth parts and usually two pairs of wings, including the cicadas, aphids, etc. [< NL < Gk. *homos* same + *pteron* wing] —**ho·mop′ter·an** *adj. & n.*

ho·mop·ter·ous (hō·mop′tər·əs) *adj.* Of, pertaining to, or belonging to the suborder *Homoptera.*

ho·mor·gan·ic (hō′môr·gan′ik) *adj. Phonet.* Describing speech sounds which are produced in a similar position in the mouth, as (p) and (b).

Homo sa·pi·ens (sā′pē·enz) See HOMO.

ho·mo·sex·u·al (hō′mə·sek′sho͞o·əl, hom′ə-) *adj.* Pertaining to or characterized by homosexuality. —*n.* A homosexual person. Compare BISEXUAL, HETEROSEXUAL.

ho·mo·sex·u·al·i·ty (hō′mə·sek′sho͞o·al′ə·tē, hom′ə-) *n.* **1** Sexual attraction toward a person of the same sex. **2** Sexual relations between persons of the same sex.

ho·mos·po·rous (hō·mos′pər·əs, hō′mə·spôr′·əs, -spō′rəs) *adj. Bot.* Having or producing asexual spores of one kind only. —**ho·mos′·po·ry** (hō·mos′pər·ē, hō′mə·spôr′ē, -spō′rē) *n.*

ho·mo·tax·is (hō′mə·tak′sis, hom′ə-) *n.* **1** Classification in the same category. **2** *Geol.* The assignment to the same period in the life history of the earth of those groups of strata exhibiting the same general faunal characteristics, however widely separated from one another geographically; similarity of fossil formations. —**ho′mo·tax′i·al, ho·mo·tax′ic** *adj.* —**ho′mo·tax′i·al·ly** *adv.*

ho·mo·thal·lic (hō′mə·thal′ik, hom′ə-) *adj. Bot.* Designating that condition of the mold fungi in which the sexual gametes which conjugate arise from the same mycelium: opposed to *heterothallic.* [< Gk. *homos* same + *thallos* branch]

ho·mo·ther·mal (hō′mə·thûr′məl, hom′ə-) *adj.* Homoiothermal.

ho·mo·type (hō′mə·tīp) *n. Biol.* A part or organ similar to a preceeding, succeeding, or opposite one in the same animal, as one of the legs or arms. —**ho′mo·typ′ic** (-tip′ik) or **·i·cal** *adj.*

ho·mo·ty·py (hō′mə·tī′pē) *n. Biol.* The correspondence of a part or organ of one region with that of another in the same animal.

homo vul·ga·is (vul·gā′ris) *n. Latin* The average or common man.

ho·mo·zy·go·sis (hō′mə·zī·gō′sis, -zi-, hom′ə-) *n. Biol.* The formation of a homozygote by the union of gametes.

ho·mo·zy·gote (hō′mə·zī′gōt, -zig′ōt, hom′ə-) *n. Biol.* A zygote formed by the conjugation of two gametes having the same genetic factors; a homozygous individual. See HETEROZYGOTE.

ho·mo·zy·gous (hō'mə·zī'gəs, hom'ə-) *adj.* *Biol.* Designating that condition of an individual in which any given genetic factor is doubly present, due usually to conjugating gametes which were alike in respect to this factor. [<HOMO- + Gk. *zygōsis* joining < *zygon* a yoke]

Homs (hôms) A city on the Orontes in western Syria: ancient *Emesa*.

ho·mun·cu·lus (hō·mung'kyə·ləs) *n.* *pl.* **·li** (-lī) **1** According to Paracelsus, a tiny man produced artificially and endowed with magic power. **2** An undersized man; dwarf; manikin. **3** The human fetus. [<L, dim. of *homo* man] — **ho·mun'cu·lar** *adj.*

ho·my (hō'mē) See HOMEY.

Ho·nan (hō'nän') *n.* A fine Chinese silk, sometimes distinguished by blue edges.

Ho·nan (hō'nän') A province of north central China; 55,000 square miles; capital, Kaifeng.

Hon·do (hon·dō) See HONSHU.

Hon·du·ran (hon·dŏor'ən, -dyŏor'-) *adj.* Of or relating to Honduras. — *n.* A native or inhabitant of Honduras.

Hon·du·ras (hon·dŏor'əs, -dyŏor'-) A republic of NE Central America; 43,278 square miles; capital, Tegucigalpa.

Honduras, British See BRITISH HONDURAS.

Honduras, Gulf of An inlet of the Caribbean Sea in Honduras, British Honduras, and Guatemala. Also **Bay of Honduras.**

hone[1] (hōn) *n.* A block of fine compact stone for sharpening edged tools, razors, etc. — *v.t.* **honed, hon·ing** To sharpen, as a razor, on a hone. [OE *hān* stone]

hone[2] (hōn) *v.i.* **honed, hon·ing** *Dial.* **1** To pine; long for. **2** To moan; grumble. [<F *hogner* mutter]

Ho·neg·ger (hō'neg·ər, *Fr.* ô·ne·gâr'), **Arthur,** 1892–1955, French composer.

hon·est (on'ist) *adj.* **1** Fair and candid in dealing with others; true; just; upright; trustworthy. **2** Chaste; virtuous. **3** Free from fraud; equitable; fair. **4** Of respectable quality or appearance; creditable; unimpeached. **5** Characterized by openness or sincerity; frank. [<OF *honeste* <L *honestus* < *honos* honor] — **hon'est·ly** *adv.*
Synonyms: candid, equitable, fair, faithful, frank, genuine, good, honorable, ingenuous, just, sincere, straightforward, true, trustworthy, trusty, upright. One who is *honest* in the ordinary sense is disposed to act with regard for the rights of others, especially in matters of business or property; one who is *honorable* scrupulously observes the dictates of a personal honor that is higher than any demands of mercantile law or public opinion. Compare CANDID, JUST, MORAL, RIGHT, VIRTUOUS. *Antonyms:* deceitful, dishonest, disingenuous, faithless, false, fraudulent, hypocritical, lying, mendacious, perfidious, traitorous, treacherous, unfaithful, unscrupulous, untrue.

hone·stone (hōn'stōn') *n.* **1** Any fine-grained stone from which hones are made, as novaculite. **2** A hone.

hon·es·ty (on'is·tē) *n.* **1** The character or quality of being honest; uprightness of conduct in general; justice; fairness. **2** Chastity; virtue. **3** An ornamental garden plant (*Lundria annua*) of the mustard family.

hone·wort (hōn'wûrt') *n.* Any of a number of plants formerly believed to have medicinal properties, as the stone parsley, goldenrod, etc.

hon·ey (hun'ē) *n.* **1** A sweet, sirupy secretion, deposited by bees and derived chiefly from the nectaries of flowers. **2** Sweetness or lusciousness in general. **3** Sweet one: a pet name. — *v.* **hon·eyed** or **hon·ied, hon·ey·ing** — *v.t.* **1** To talk in an endearing or flattering manner to. **2** To sweeten. — *v.i.* **3** To talk fondly or in a coaxing manner. — *adj.* Honeylike; sweet. [OE *hunig*]

honey ant A small ant of the SW United States (genus *Myrmecocystus*), having one form of worker which receives and stores in its abdomen the honey gathered by the other workers.

honey bag The receptacle or dilatation of the esophagus in which the bee carries honey. Also **honey sac.**

hon·ey·balls (hun'ē·bôlz') *n.* *pl.* *U.S. Dial.* The spherical, white flower heads of the buttonbush.

honey bee A bee that collects honey; spe-

cifically, the common hive bee (*Apis mellifera*).

hon·ey·comb (hun'ē·kōm') *n.* **1** A structure of hexagonal waxen cells, made by bees to contain honey, eggs, etc. **2** Anything full of small holes or cells. — *v.t.* **1** To fill with small holes or passages. **2** To pervade; corrupt. — *v.i.* **3** To become full of holes or passages. [OE *hunig·camb*] — **hon'ey·combed'** *adj.*

HONEYCOMB

honeycomb moth A moth (*Galleria melonella*) that infests beehives; bee moth. Also called *waxworm.*

honey creeper A small, brightly colored bird (family *Coeribidae*) of the warmer parts of America; the guitguit.

hon·ey·dew (hun'ē·dōo', -dyōo') *n.* **1** A sweet secretion of plants or insects, as of aphids. **2** A honeydew melon. **3** A light pinkish orange. — **hon'ey·dewed'** *adj.*

honeydew melon A variety of muskmelon with a smooth white skin and sweet pulp.

hon·ey–eat·er (hun'ē·ē'tər) *n.* One of several Australian oscine birds (family *Meliphagidae*) which extract honey from flowers.

hon·eyed (hun'ēd) *adj.* **1** Covered with or full of honey. **2** Sweet; hence, soothing; agreeable; sweetly flattering. Also spelled *honied.* — **hon'eyed·ly** *adv.* — **hon'eyed·ness** *n.*

honey guide A small plain-colored bird of Africa, Asia, and the East Indies (genera *Indicator* and *Prodotiscus*) said to lead persons to the nests of wild bees.

honey locust A large, thorny North American tree (*Gleditsia triacanthos*) of the bean family, bearing long pods with a sweet pulp between the seeds.

honey lotus See under MELILOT.

honey mesquite See under MESQUITE.

hon·ey·moon (hun'ē·mōōn) *n.* **1** A wedding trip. **2** The first month or so after marriage.

honey mouse A small marsupial of southern Australia (family *Phalangeridae*) with a long, pointed nose and extensible tongue. It feeds on nectar and small insects.

hon·ey·pot (hun'ē·pot') *n.* A receptacle, of wax or other substance, made by many species of wild bees to store their honey.

honey shucks The beans of the honey locust.

hon·ey·stone (hun'ē·stōn') *n.* A soft, yellowish or reddish aluminum mineral having a resinous appearance and crystallizing in the octahedral system: also called *mellite.*

hon·ey·suck·er (hun'ē·suk'ər) See HONEY-EATER.

hon·ey·suck·le (hun'ē·suk'əl) *n.* **1** Any of a genus (*Lonicera*) of ornamental erect or climbing shrubs having tubular white, buff, or crimson flowers. **2** Any one of a number of other plants, as the bush honeysuckle. [OE *hunisuce*]

honeysuckle pattern The anthemion.

honey tree 1 A honey locust. **2** A hollow tree in which wild bees have stored honey.

honey yellow A soft yellow, as of honey.

Hon·fleur (ôn·flœr') A port of the Seine estuary opposite Le Havre, NW France.

hong (hong, hông) *n.* **1** A mercantile warehouse in China, comprising a number of connecting rooms; also, a connected row of warehouses. **2** A foreign trading establishment in China. [<Chinese *hang* row of houses, mercantile association]

Hong Kong (hong' kong', hông' kông') A British crown colony in SE China; 391 square miles, comprising **Hong Kong Island** (32 square miles), Kowloon peninsula, and the New Territories; capital, Victoria on Hong Kong Island; under Japanese occupation, 1941–45.

Ho·ni·a·ra (hō'nē·ä'rä) A coast town of NW

Guadalcanal, capital of the British Solomon Islands protectorate.

hon·ied (hun'ēd) See HONEYED.

ho·ni soit qui mal y pense (ô·nē swà' kē màl ē päns') *French* Evil be to him who evil thinks: motto of the Order of the Garter.

honk (hôngk, hongk) *n.* The cry of a wild goose or a sound imitating it, as that of an automobile horn. — *v.i.* To utter or make a honk or honks. — *v.t.* To cause to emit a honk or honks, as an automobile horn. [Imit.]

honk·er (hông'kər, hong'-) *n.* **1** A wild goose. **2** One who honks.

hon·ky (hôngk'ē, hungk'ē) *n.* *pl.* **·kies** *U.S. Slang* A white man: an offensive term. Also **hon'kie.** [? <HUNKY. See BOHUNK.]

hon·ky-tonk (hông'kē·tôngk', hong'kē·tongk') *n.* *Slang* A noisy, low-class barroom or night club. [Prob. imit.]

Hon·o·lu·lu (hon'ə·lōō'lōō) A port on SE Oahu; capital of Hawaii.

hon·or (on'ər) *n.* **1** Consideration due or paid, as to worth; respectful regard. **2** Any outward token of such feeling, such as college distinctions. **3** A nice sense of what is right. **4** That to which respect is due; a cause of esteem. **5** A title used in addressing judges, mayors, etc.: used with a possessive pronoun: *his honor*, the mayor. **6** In whist, one of the four highest trump cards; in bridge, one of the five highest cards of the trump suit, or one of the four aces when there are no trumps. **7** In golf, the privilege of playing first from the tee. See synonyms under FAME, JUSTICE, REVERENCE, VIRTUE. — **to do the honors** To act as host. — *v.t.* **1** To regard with honor or respect; treat with courtesy or respect. **2** To worship. **3** To do honor to; dignify; ennoble. **4** To accept or pay, as a check or draft. See synonyms under ADMIRE, VENERATE, WORSHIP. — *adj.* Having received recognition for outstanding academic work: an *honor* student. Also, *Brit.*, **honour.** [<OF <L] — **hon'or·er** *n.*

Ho·no·ra (ə·nôr'ə, ə·nō'rə) A feminine personal name. Also **Ho·no·ri·a** (ə·nôr'ē·ə, ə·nō'rē·ə).

hon·or·a·ble (on'ər·ə·bəl) *adj.* **1** Worthy of honor, in any degree from simple respectability to eminence; creditable; estimable; illustrious. **2** Conferring honor. **3** Consistent with or acting in accordance with principles of honor; conforming to a code of honor. **4** Betokening honor; accompanied by marks or testimonials of honor: *honorable* burial. **5** Entitled to honor: formal epithet of respect prefixed to the names of persons holding important offices. See synonyms under GOOD, HONEST, ILLUSTRIOUS, JUST, MORAL. Also *Brit.* **hon'our·a·ble.** — **hon'or·a·ble·ness** *n.* — **hon'or·a·bly** *adv.*

hon·o·rar·i·um (on'ə·râr'ē·əm) *n.* *pl.* **·i·ums** or **·i·a** A gratuity given, as to a professional man, for services rendered when law, custom, or propriety forbids a set fee. See synonyms under SALARY. [<L *honorarium* (*donum*) honorary (gift), neut. of *honorarius* honorary]

hon·or·ar·y (on'ə·rer'ē) *adj.* **1** Done, conferred, or held merely as an honor. **2** Designating an office or title bestowed as a sign of honor, without emoluments or without powers or duties. **3** Depending solely on one's honor: said of a debt or other obligation not legally binding. [<L *honorarius*]

Ho·no·ré (ô·nô·rā') A French masculine personal name. [<F, honored]

hon·or·if·ic (on'ə·rif'ik) *adj.* **1** Conferring or implying honor or respect. **2** Denoting certain phrases, words, or word elements, as in Oriental languages, used in respectful address. — *n.* Any honorific title, word, phrase, etc. [<L *honorificus* <*honor* + *facere* make] — **hon'or·if'i·cal·ly** *adv.*

Ho·no·ri·us (hə·nôr'ē·əs, -nō'rē-), **Flavius Augustus,** 384–423, emperor of the Western (Roman) Empire 395–423.

honor point *Her.* The point just above the fess point. See illustration under ESCUTCHEON.

honors of war Marks of respect or honorable terms granted to a capitulating force.

honors system In some colleges and universities, a plan of advanced study for selected students, in which the student is excused from classroom routine to undertake individual, specialized work.

honor system A system of administering examinations and schoolwork without supervision

and relying upon the honor of the students not to cheat.

Hon·shu (hon·shōō) The largest island of Japan; 88,745 square miles, including outlying islands; capital, Tokyo: also *Hondo.*

hooch (hōōch) *n. U.S. Slang* Intoxicating liquor. Also spelled *hootch.* [< *hoochinoo,* alter. of *Hutanuwu,* name of Alaskan Indian tribe that made liquor]

Hooch (hōkh), **Pieter de,** 1629–77?, Dutch painter.

hood¹ (hōod) *n.* **1** A soft or flexible covering for the head and the back of the neck. **2** Anything of similar form or character. **3** A monk's cowl. **4** An ornamental fold attached to the back of an academic gown. **5** In falconry, a cover for the entire head of a hawk. **6** A projecting cover to a hearth, forge, or ventilator. **7** The movable cover of a machine, as of the engine of an automobile. **8** *Biol.* A concave expansion of any organ, resembling a hood; a crest. — *v.t.* To cover or furnish with or as with a hood. [OE *hōd*]

hood² (hōod) *n. U.S. Slang* A hoodlum. [< HOODLUM]

-hood *suffix of nouns* **1** Condition of; state of being: *babyhood, falsehood.* **2** Class or totality of those having a certain character: *priesthood.* [OE *had* state, condition]

Hood (hōod), **John Bell,** 1831–79, American Confederate general. — **Samuel,** 1724–1816, first Viscount Hood, English admiral. — **Thomas,** 1799–1845, English poet and humorist. — **Robin** See ROBIN HOOD.

Hood (hōod), **Mount** A volcanic peak in the Cascade Range, NW Oregon; 11,245 feet.

hood·ed (hōod′id) *adj.* **1** Wearing or having a hood. **2** Shaped like a hood. **3** Having a hoodlike part. **4** *Ornithol.* A conspicuous patch of feathers on the head of a bird. **5** *Zool.* The folds of skin near the head of certain animals and capable of voluntary expansion, as in the cobra and certain other snakes.

hooded seal One of the more abundant seals of the North Atlantic (*Cystophora cristata*). The males have an inflatable bag on the top of the head.

hood·er (hōod′ər) *n. Brit.* The top sheaf of a shock of grain; hence, a finishing touch.

hood·ie (hōod′ē) *n. Scot.* The hooded crow of Europe (*Corvus cornix*).

hood·lum (hōod′ləm) *n. U.S.* One of a class of street rowdies; any ruffian or rowdy. [? < dial. G *hodalum* a rowdy] — **hood′lum·ism** *n.*

hood·man (hōod′mən) *n. pl.* **·men** (-mən) The person blindfolded in the game of **hoodman-blind,** an old form of blindman's-buff.

hoo·doo (hōo′dōo) *n.* **1** Voodoo. **2** *Colloq.* A person or thing that brings bad luck; a jinx. — *v.t. Colloq.* To bring bad luck to; bewitch. [Var. of VOODOO]

Hood River A city on the Columbia River in northern Oregon.

hood·wink (hōod′wingk′) *v.t.* **1** To deceive as if by blinding; impose upon; delude. **2** To blindfold. **3** *Obs.* To cover; conceal. [< HOOD + WINK] — **hood′wink′er** *n.*

hoo·ey (hōo′ē) *n. & interj. U.S. Slang* Nonsense.

hoof (hōof, hōof) *n. pl.* **hoofs** (*Rare* **hooves**) **1** The horny sheath incasing the ends of the digits or foot in various mammals. ◆ Collateral adjective: *ungular.* **2** An animal with hoofs. — **cloven hoof** The sign of Satan. — **on the hoof** Alive; not butchered: said of cattle. — *v.t. & v.i.* **1** To trample with the hoofs. **2** *Colloq.* To walk or dance: usually with *it.* [OE *hōf*] — **hoofed** (hōoft, hōoft) *adj.*

hoof-and-mouth disease (hōof′ən·mouth′) See FOOT-AND-MOUTH DISEASE.

hoof-bound (hōof′bound′, hōof′-) *adj.* Having a contraction of the hoof, causing pain and lameness.

hoof·er (hōof′ər, hōof′-) *n. U.S. Slang* A professional dancer, especially a tap dancer.

hoof·print (hōof′print′, hōof′-) *n.* The print left by a hoof on the ground; a track.

hook (hōok) *n.* **1** A curved or bent piece serving to catch or hold another object. **2** A tool in hooked form; especially, a sickle. **3** *Music* The flag-shaped projection from the stem of an eighth note, or one of still shorter duration. **4** A hook-shaped part, as of a written character. **5** The act of hooking. **6** Something that catches or snares; a trap. **7** In golf, a shot in which the ball deviates to the side on which the player stands. **8** In baseball, a sharp-breaking curve. **9** In boxing, a short blow delivered in a swinging manner crosswise and with the elbow bent and rigid. **10** A bend in a river; a point of land; a cape: *Sandy Hook.* See synonyms under LOCK. — **by hook or by crook** By one way or another. — **on one's own hook 1** By oneself. **2** On one's own authority. — *v.t.* **1** To fasten, attach, or take hold of with or as with a hook. **2** To catch on or with a hook, as fish. **3** To trick; take in: I've been *hooked.* **4** To make or bend in the shape of a hook; crook. **5** To catch on or toss with the horns: said of bulls; etc. **6** To make, as a rug, by looping thread, yarn, etc., through burlap with a hook. **7** *Slang* To steal; pilfer. **8** In baseball, to throw (a ball) with a hook. **9** In boxing, to strike with a hook. **10** In golf, to drive (the ball) in a hook. — *v.i.* **11** To curve like a hook; bend. **12** To be fastened with a hook. — **to hook up 1** To fasten or attach with hooks. **2** To put together, as the parts of a machine. — **to hook up to** To connect (apparatus) to a source of power: The trailer was *hooked up to* the car. — **to hook up with** *Colloq.* To join; become a companion or adherent of. [OE *hōc*]

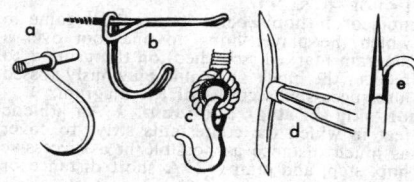

HOOKS
a. Box hook.   *c.* Eyehook.   *e.* Boat hook.
b. Coat hook.   *d.* Ice hook.

hook·ah (hōok′ə) *n.* In India and Iran, a form of tobacco pipe by which the smoke is drawn through water; a narghile. Also **hook′a.** [< Arabic *ḥuqqah*]

hook-and-lad·der (hōok′ən·lad′ər) *n.* A vehicle, equipped with ladders for effecting rescues, and hooks, axes, etc., for tearing down walls, used by fire departments. Also **hook-and-ladder truck.**

Hooke (hōok), **Robert,** 1635–1703, English physicist.

hooked (hōokt) *adj.* **1** Curved like a hook. **2** Supplied with a hook. **3** Made with a hook. — **hook·ed·ness** (hōok′id·nis) *n.*

hook·er¹ (hōok′ər) *n.* **1** A two-masted Dutch vessel. **2** A fishing boat used on the English and Irish coasts. **3** An old or clumsy craft. [< Du. *hoeker* < *hoek* hook]

hook·er² (hōok′ər) *n. Slang* A drink, especially an alcoholic one. [< HOOK, prob. with ref. to the bend of the arm in drinking]

hook·er³ (hōok′ər) *n. Slang* A prostitute. [from Corlears *Hook,* formerly a notorious waterfront district in Manhattan]

Hook·er (hōok′ər), **Joseph,** 1814–79, Union general in the American Civil War. — **Sir Joseph Dalton,** 1817–1911, English botanist. — **Richard,** 1554?–1600, English theologian. — **Thomas,** 1586?–1647, English clergyman, one of the founders of Connecticut. — **Sir William Jackson,** 1785–1865, English botanist; father of Sir J. D. Hooker.

Hooker's green A green pigment composed of Prussian blue and gamboge.

Hooke's law (hōoks) *Physics* The law that the elastic distortion of a body under stress is proportional to the stress producing the distortion. [after Robert *Hooke*]

hook, line, and sinker Completely; without question or reservation.

hook-nose (hōok′nōz′) *n.* An aquiline nose, or a person having such a nose. — **hook′nosed′** *adj.*

Hook of Holland A headland and harbor of SW Netherlands: Dutch *Hoek van Holland.*

hook-up (hōok′up′) *n.* **1** *Telecom.* **a** The assembled apparatus for a radio broadcast or other electrical transmission. **b** The diagram giving the connections for such transmission. **2** A mechanical connection, as of

gas or water lines. **3** *Colloq.* An alliance or pact between governments, organizations, etc.

hook·worm (hōok′wûrm′) *n.* Any of various nematode worms of the genera *Ancylostoma, Necator,* etc., infesting man and several animals, such as sheep, dogs, cattle, etc.

hookworm disease Ancylostomiasis.

hook·y¹ (hōok′ē) *adj.* Full of hooks, pertaining to hooks, or like a hook.

hook·y² (hōok′ē) *n. U.S. Colloq.* The condition of being illegitimately absent, truant, etc.: used only in the phrase **to play hooky,** to be a truant. [< HOOK, in dial. sense of "make off"]

hoo·li·gan (hōo′lə·gən) *n.* A hoodlum; a gangster. [after *Hooligan,* name of an Irish family in London] — **hoo′li·gan·ism** *n.*

hoop¹ (hōop, hōop) *n.* **1** A circular band of stiff material, especially one used to confine the staves of a barrel, cask, etc. **2** A child's toy in the shape of a large circular ring of metal or wood that is trundled along the ground. **3** A large ring of flexible material used for expanding a woman's skirt. **4** The band of a finger ring. **5** An arched wicket in croquet. **6** Anything shaped like a ring or band. — *v.t.* **1** To surround or fasten with hoops, as a cask. **2** To encircle. [OE *hōp*]

hoop² (hōop) *n.* **1** A whoop; shout. **2** The sound made in whooping cough. — *v.t. & v.i.* To whoop. [Var. of WHOOP]

hoop·er (hōop′ər, hōop′ər) *n.* One who hoops casks or tubs; a cooper.

Hoop·er·at·ing (hōo′pə·rā′ting) *n.* A rating of the popularity of television or radio programs or performers by means of telephone interviews with a sample poll of listeners taken during the performance: given in terms of millions of estimated listeners. Also **Hoop·er rating** (hōo′pər). [after Claude E. *Hooper,* 1898–1954, U.S. statistician]

hoop·ing (hōo′ping, hōop′ing) *n.* **1** Material from which to make hoops; also, hoops in general. **2** A system of hoops, as on some breechloading guns.

hoop·la (hōop′lä) *n. U.S. Slang* Excitement; fervor. [Orig., a coach driver's exclamation]

hoop·le (hōo′pəl) *n.* A child's hoop.

hoo·poe (hōo′pōo) *n.* An Old World bird (family *Upupidae*), having a long, pointed, curved bill and an erectile crest. Also **hoo′poo.** [< F *huppe* < L *upupa*]

HOOPOE
(About 12 inches long; bill: 2 1/2 inches)

hoop skirt A framework of hoops or crinoline for expanding a skirt; also, the skirt itself.

hoop snake A harmless snake of the southern United States (*Abastor erythrogrammus*): formerly believed to take its tail in its mouth and roll like a hoop.

hoo·ray (hōo·rā′, hə-, hōo-) See HURRAH.

hoord (hōord) *v.t. & v.i. Scot.* To hoard. — **hoord′et** (-it) *adj.*

Hoo·sac Range (hōo′sək) A spur of the Green Mountains in western Massachusetts; highest point, 3,000 feet; pierced by the **Hoosac Tunnel,** a railway tunnel 25,000 feet long.

hoose (hōos) *n. Scot.* A house.

hoose·gow (hōos′gou) *n. U.S. Slang* Jail or prison. Also **hoos′gow.** [< Sp. *juzgado* tribunal]

Hoo·sier (hōo′zhər) *n. U.S.* A native or citizen of the **Hoosier State,** a nickname for Indiana. [Prob. < dial. *hoosier* mountaineer, in ref. to Kentucky settlers in southern part of the State]

hoot (hōot) *v.i.* **1** To jeer or call out, as in contempt or disapproval. **2** To utter the low, hollow cry of an owl. — *v.t.* **3** To jeer at or mock with hooting cries. **4** To drive off with shouts of contempt, disapproval, etc. **5** To express by hooting. — *n.* **1** A cry uttered in derision. **2** The cry of an owl. **3** *Slang* A whit: not worth a *hoot.* [< Scand. Cf. Sw. *huta.*]

hootch (hōoch) See HOOCH.

hoot·chy-koot·chy (ho͞o′chē·ko͞o′chē) *n. U.S. Slang* A suggestive dance involving much hip and abdominal movement. [Origin unknown]
hoot·en·an·ny (ho͞ot′n·an′ē) *n. Slang* A gathering of folk singers. [Origin unknown]
hoot owl An owl that hoots, especially the American northern barred owl (*Strix varia*).
Hoo·ver (ho͞o′vər), **Herbert Clark,** 1874–1964, president of the United States 1929–33. — **J(ohn) Edgar,** 1895–1972, U.S. criminologist: director of the Federal Bureau of Investigation 1924–1972.
Hoover Dam A dam in the Colorado River on the Arizona–Nevada border, forming Lake Mead; 727 feet high; 1,282 feet long: formerly *Boulder Dam.*
Hoo·ver·ville (ho͞o′vər·vil) *n.* Any group of ramshackle huts, usually on the outskirts of a town, in which the jobless camped during the depression of the early 1930's. [after Herbert *Hoover* + *-ville* city, town]
hooves (ho͝ovz, ho͞ovz) Alternative plural of HOOF.
hooy (hoi) See HOY².
hop¹ (hop) *v.* **hopped, hop·ping** *v.i.* **1** To move in short leaps with the feet off the ground. **2** To jump about on one foot. —*v.t.* **3** To jump over, as a fence. **4** To board or catch; get on: to *hop* a train. See synonyms under LEAP. —*n.* **1** The act or result of hopping. **2** *Colloq.* A dance or dancing party. **3** *Colloq.* An ascent, flight, or trip in an airplane. [OE *hoppian*]
hop² (hop) *n.* **1** A perennial climbing herb (*Humulus lupulus*) with opposite lobed leaves and scaly fruit. **2** *pl.* The ripe and carefully dried multiple fruit of this plant: used in the brewing of beer and in medicine as an aromatic bitter stomachic. [<MDu. *hoppe*]
hop·cal·ite (hop′kəl·īt) *n.* A granular mixture of the oxides of copper, cobalt, manganese, and silver: effective as a catalyzing material to protect against carbon monoxide. [< (*Johns*) *Hop*(*kins University*) + (*University of*) *Cal*(*ifornia*) + -ITE¹]
hop clover Yellow clover (*Trifolium procumbens*) whose dried flowers resemble hops.
hope (hōp) *v.* **hoped, hop·ing** *v.t.* **1** To desire with expectation of fulfilment: I *hope* to be able to join you. **2** To wish; want: I *hope* that you will be happy. —*v.i.* **3** To have desire or expectation: usually with *for*: to *hope* for the best. See synonyms under ANTICIPATE, TRUST. —*n.* **1** Desire accompanied by expectation. **2** The cause of hopeful expectation. **3** The thing confidently desired or hoped for. —**in hopes** Having hope. See synonyms under TRUST. [OE *hopa*]
Hope (hōp), **Anthony** See HAWKINS, ANTHONY HOPE.
hope chest A box or chest used by young women to hold linen, clothing, etc., in anticipation of marriage.
hope·ful (hōp′fəl) *adj.* **1** Full of hope; promising. **2** Having qualities that excite hope. See synonyms under AUSPICIOUS, SANGUINE. —*n.* A young person who seems likely to succeed in life: a humorous or ironic use. —**hope′ful·ness** *n.*
hope·ful·ly (hōp′fə·lē) *adv.* **1** In a hopeful manner. **2** It is hoped; one hopes: *Hopefully,* a strike can be averted.
Ho·peh (hō′pā′) A province in NE China; 50,000 square miles; capital, Paoting: formerly *Chihli.* Also **Ho′pei′.**
hope·less (hōp′lis) *adj.* **1** Without hope; despairing. **2** Affording no ground of hope. —**hope′less·ly** *adv.* —**hope′less·ness** *n.*
hope·sick (hōp′sik′) *adj.* Sick at heart with unfulfilled hope or ungratified longing.
Ho·pi (hō′pē) *n.* **1** One of a group of North American Pueblo Indians of Shoshonean linguistic stock: now on a reservation in NE Arizona: also called *Moqui* or *Moki.* **2** Their Shoshonean language. [<Hopi *hópitu,* lit., peaceful ones]
Hop·kins (hop′kinz), **Sir Frederick Gowland,** 1861–1947, English biochemist. —**Gerard Manley,** 1844–89, English poet. —**Harry Lloyd,** 1890–1946, U.S. statesman; advisor to President F. D. Roosevelt. —**Johns,** 1795–1873, U.S. financier and philanthropist. —**Mark,** 1802–87, U.S. educator.
Hop·kin·son (hop′kin·sən), **Francis,** 1737–91, American writer; signed the Declaration of Independence.
hop·lite (hop′līt) *n.* In ancient Greece, a heavily armed foot soldier. [<Gk. *hoplitēs* <*hoplon* a shield]
hop-o'-my-thumb (hop′ə·mī·thum′) *n.* A very small person. [after *Hop-o'-my-thumb,* tiny hero of a fairy tale by Perrault]
hopped-up (hopt′up′) *adj. U.S. Slang* **1** Stimulated by a narcotic drug. **2** Excited; exhilarated. **3** Supercharged for high speed: said of an automobile. [? <HOP²]
hop·per (hop′ər) *n.* **1** One who or that which hops. **2** A saltatorial insect or larva, as a grasshopper or the larva of a fly that infests cheese. **3** A shaking or conveying receiver, funnel, or trough in which something is placed to be passed or fed, as to a mill. **4** A funnel-shaped spout or tank with a movable bottom or no bottom, as for conveying grain to cars. **5** A tilting, dumping, or discharging bottom or receptacle, as in a car or boat. **6** A tank or boxlike receptacle for holding water, grain, sugar, etc., which may be emptied by opening its bottom.
hopper car A car for coal, gravel, etc., with an opening to discharge the contents.
hop·ple (hop′əl) *v.t.* **·pled, ·pling** To hamper; hobble. —*n.* A fetter for the legs of a horse, etc. [Var. of HOBBLE]
hop·sack·ing (hop′sak′ing) *n.* A coarse fabric with rough surface: used for dresses, etc. [<HOP² + SACK]
hop·scotch (hop′skoch′) *n.* A child's game in which the player hops on one foot over a diagram marked (scotched) on the ground to recover the block or pebble previously tossed into successive sections of the diagram.
hop, skip (or **step**), **and jump** **1** An athletic feat in which the contestants strive to cover as much distance as possible in a successive hop, step, and jump. **2** A short distance or interval.
hop trefoil **1** Hop clover. **2** Black medic.
Hor (hôr), **Mount** A mountain in SW Jordan; 4,430 feet.
Hor·ace (hôr′is, hor′-) A masculine personal name: see HORATIO. Also *Fr.* **Ho·race** (ô·räs′), **Ho·ra·ci·o** (*Pg.* ô·rä′sē·o͞o, *Sp.* ō·rä′thē·ō). [<L, light of the sun, keeper of the hours] —**Horace** Anglicized name of *Quintus Horatius Flaccus,* 65–8 B.C., Roman poet. —**Ho·ra·tian** (hə·rā′shən) *adj.*
Ho·rae (hō′rē) In Greek mythology, the three goddesses of natural order and the seasons.
ho·ral (hō′rəl) *adj.* Pertaining to an hour; hourly. [<L *hora* hour]
ho·rar·i·ous (hō·râr′ē·əs) *adj. Bot.* Lasting but one or two hours: said of flowers. [<L *hor*(*a*) hour + -ARIOUS]
ho·ra·ry (hō′rə·rē) *adj.* **1** Pertaining to an hour; designating the hours. **2** Continuing only an hour; occurring hourly. **3** In astrology, referring to propitious or specific times. [<L *hora* hour]
Ho·ra·ti·i (hə·rā′shē·ī) In Roman legend, three Roman brothers who fought and killed the Curiatii, three brothers from Alba Longa.
Ho·ra·ti·o (hə·rā′shē·ō, -shō) A masculine personal name. Also **Ho·ra·ti·us** (*Du.* hô·rä′sē·o͞os, *Ger.* hô·rä′tsē·o͞os, *Lat.* hô·rā′shē·əs), *Dan.* **Ho·rats** (hô·räts′). [See HORACE]
—**Horatio** In Shakespeare's *Hamlet,* the close friend of Hamlet.
Ho·ra·tius Co·cles (hə·rā′shəs kō′klēz) In Roman legend, a hero who with two comrades held the bridge over the Tiber against the Etruscan army.
horde (hôrd, hōrd) *n.* **1** A clan or tribe of Mongolian, especially Tatar, nomads; hence, any nomadic group. **2** A multitude; a pack or swarm, as of men, animals, or insects. —**Golden Horde** A fierce and powerful Mongol horde, named from the golden tent of Batu Khan, under whose lead they laid waste eastern Europe in the 13th century; the Kipchaks. —*v.i.* **hord·ed, hord·ing** To gather in a horde. ◆ Homophone: *hoard.* [<F <G <Polish *horda* <Turkish *ordū* camp. Related to URDU.]
hor·de·in (hôr′dē·in, hōr′-) *n. Biochem.* An alcohol-soluble protein from barley: of the prolamine group of simple proteins. [<L *hordeum* barley]
hor·de·nine (hôr′də·nēn, -nin, hōr′-) *n.* A white, crystalline, almost tasteless alkaloid, $C_{10}H_{15}ON$, obtained from malt sprouts: its sulfate is used in the treatment of diarrhea and as a heart stimulant. [<L *hordeum* barley + -INE²]
Hor·de·um (hôr′dē·əm, hōr′-) *n.* A genus of true grasses, one species of which is the cultivated barley. [<L]
hore (hôr, hōr) *Obs.* See HOAR.
Ho·reb (hō′reb) The mountain where the law was given to Moses; generally identified with Mount Sinai. *Ex.* iii 1.
hore·hound (hôr′hound′, hōr′-) *n.* **1** A whitish, bitter, perennial herb of the mint family (genus *Marrubium*): used as a remedy for colds. **2** A candy flavored with an extract of this herb. **3** One of various allied plants. Also spelled *hoarhound.* [OE *harhune*]
Hor·i·con (hôr′i·kon, hor′-), **Lake** Lake George in the novels of J. Fenimore Cooper.
ho·ri·zon (hə·rī′zən) *n.* **1** The line of the apparent meeting of earth or sea and sky: called the **local** or **visible horizon.** **2** The bounds of observation or experience. **3** *Astron.* **a** The plane passing through a position on the earth's surface at right angles to the line of gravity: called the **sensible horizon.** **b** The great circle in which the sensible horizon cuts the celestial sphere: called the **celestial, geometric, rational,** or **true horizon.** **4** *Geol.* **a** A definite position in the stratigraphic column, or in the scheme of classification of strata according to age. **b** A bed or limited number of beds characterized by one or more distinctive fossils; a zone. **5** One of the layers in a cross-section of soil. **6** The imaginary line, taking the place of the natural horizon, in a picture of a landscape, on which is projected the point of sight of the viewer. See PERSPECTIVE. [<OF *orizonte* <L *horizon* <Gk. *horizōn* (*kyklos*) bounding (circle), ppr. of *horizein* bound <*horos* limit, bound]
horizon blue A soft gray-blue.
hor·i·zon·tal (hôr′ə·zon′təl, hor′-) *adj.* **1** Parallel to the horizon; on a level. **2** Included or measured in a plane of the horizon. **3** Of, pertaining to, on, or close to the horizon. **4** Equal and uniform: a *horizontal* tariff. **5** Made up of similar units: a *horizontal* trust. —*n.* A line or plane assumed, for the purpose of measurement or description, to be parallel with the horizon. —**hor′i·zon′tal·ly** *adv.*
Synonyms (*adj.*): flat, level, plain, plane. For practical purposes *level* and *horizontal* are identical, but *level* is more loosely used of that which has no especially noticeable elevations or inequalities; as, a *level* road. *Flat* applies to a surface only, and, in the first, most usual sense, to a surface that is *horizontal* or *level* in all directions; *flat* is also applied to any *plane* surface without irregularities or elevations, as a picture may be painted on the *flat* surface of a perpendicular wall. *Plane* applies only to a surface, and is used with more mathematical exactness than *flat. Plain,* originally the same word as *plane,* is now rarely used except in senses pertaining to *level* ground. We speak of a *horizontal* line, a *flat* morass, a *level* road, a *plain* country, a *plane* surface (especially in the scientific sense). See FLAT, LEVEL. *Antonyms*: broken, hilly, inclined, irregular, rolling, rough, rugged, slanting, sloping, uneven.
hor·i·zon·tal·ism (hôr′ə·zon′təl·iz′əm, hor′-) *n.* The character of being horizontal; horizontal extension. —**hor′i·zon·tal′i·ty** (-zon·tal′ə·tē) *n.*
hor·mone (hôr′mōn) *n. Physiol.* An internal secretion, produced in and by one of the endocrine glands; specifically, one of a group of complex chemical compounds evolved in one part of an organism and carried thence by the blood stream or body fluids to other parts, on which it exercises a specific physiological action. Many important hormones are now made synthetically. Compare COLYONE. See ENDOCRINE. [<Gk. *hormōn,* ppr. of *hormaein* excite] —**hor·mo·nal** (hôr·mō′nəl), **hor·mon·ic** (hôr·mon′ik) *adj.*
Hor·muz (hôr′muz) A small island of SE Iran in the **Strait of Hormuz,** a channel connecting the Persian Gulf and the Gulf of Oman: also *Ormuz.*
horn (hôrn) *n.* **1** A hard bonelike growth projecting from the head of various hoofed mammals, as oxen, sheep, cattle, etc.; also, the antler of a deer, shed annually. **2** Any hardened and thickened outgrowth of epidermal tissue, as a feeler, antenna, tentacle, etc. **3** A feather tuft, as on the head of some birds. **4** The appendage like an animal's horn attributed to demons, deities, etc. **5** An imag-

inary projection from the forehead of a cuck-old. **6** The substance of which animal horn consists, as keratin, calcium phosphate, etc. **7** A vessel or implement formed from or shaped like a horn: a powder *horn*. **8** A wind instru-ment, made formerly of animal horn, now of brass, in the shape of a long tube constricted at one end and widening out to a large bell at the other. **9** *Slang* A trumpet. **10** Any pointed or tapering projection. **11** One of the extremities of a crescent moon. **12** One of the branches forming the delta of a stream. **13** A cape or peninsula. **14** The pommel of a sad-dle. **15** The point of an anvil. **16** *Aeron.* The lever which operates the wire connecting with the rudder, aileron, or elevator of an aircraft. **17** A hollow conical device with a bell-shaped aperture, for collecting sound waves, as in a sound locator. **18** A device for sounding warning signals: an automobile *horn*. — **on the horns of a dilemma** Forced to choose be-tween two painful alternatives. — **to haul (or pull or draw) in one's horns** To check one's anger, zeal, pretensions, etc. — *adj.* Of horn or horns. — *v.t.* **1** To provide with horns. **2** To shape like a horn. **3** To attack with the horns; gore. **4** *Obs.* To cuckold. — **to horn in** To enter without invitation. [OE. Akin to CORN².] — **horn′less** *adj.* — **horn′like′** *adj.*

Horn, Cape The southern extremity of South America, on the last island of the Fuegian archipelago. Also **the Horn.**

horn angle *Geom.* The angle formed by two curved lines tangent to each other at one point.

horn·beam (hôrn′bēm′) *n.* A small tree of the birch family (genus *Carpinus*), resembling the beech, with white, hard wood.

horn·bill (hôrn′bil′) *n.* A large bird of tropical Asia and Africa, related to the kingfishers (family *Bucerotidae*) and having a large bill surmounted by a hornlike extension.

horn·blende (hôrn′blend) *n.* A common miner-al, greenish-black or black, containing iron and silicate of magnesium, calcium, and alu-minum. — **horn′blend′ic** *adj.*

hornblende schist A schistose rock consisting essentially of hornblende in parallel layers.

horn·book (hôrn′book′) *n.* **1** A leaf or page con-taining a printed alphabet, etc., covered with transparent horn and framed: formerly used in teaching reading to children. **2** A primer or book of rudimentary knowledge.

horn bug The stag beetle.

Horn·church (hôrn′chûrch) An urban district of SW Essex, England.

horned (hôrnd, *Poetic* hôr′nid) *adj.* Having a horn or horns.

horned horse The gnu.

horned owl Any of various American owls with conspicuous ear tufts; especially, the great horned owl or the screech owl.

horned pout A fresh-water catfish of North America (*Ameiurus nebulosus*); one of the bullheads. Also **horn pout.**

horned toad A harmless, flat-bod-ied, spiny lizard (*Phrynosoma cornu-tum*) with a very short tail and toad-like appearance: common in semi-arid regions of the western part of the United States: also *horn toad.*

horned viper A ven-omous African or Indian viper (*Cer-astes cornutus*) with a horn over each eye.

HORNED TOAD
(From 3 to 7 inches long)

hor·net (hôr′nit) *n.* Any of various strong-bodied social wasps (family *Vespidae*) capable of inflicting a severe sting; especially, the American bald-faced hornet (*Dolichovespula maculata*) and the European giant hornet (*Vespa crabo*). [OE *hyrnet*]

hornets′ nest A nest of hornets; hence, a troubled, angry, and dangerous situation. — **to stir up a hornets′ nest** To bring about

an angry and dangerous situation, often in-advertently.

horn·fels (hôrn′fels′) *n.* A speckled, fine-grained rock produced by the intrusion of granite into slate. [<G, horn rock]

horn fly A small black fly (*Siphona irritans*) that attacks cattle, clustering about their horns, and seriously affects vitality and milk production.

Horn·ie (hôr′nē) See HORNY.

horn·ing (hôr′ning) *n.* **1** *U.S. Dial.* A cha-rivari. **2** The act of one who or that which horns.

hor·ni·to (hôr·nē′tō, *Sp.* ôr·nē′tō) *n.* *pl.* **·tos** (-tōz, *Sp.* -tōs) A low, oven-shaped fumarole, common in South American volcanic regions. Also **hor′nite** (-nīt). [<Sp., lit., little oven]

horn-mad (hôrn′mad′) *adj.* **1** Mad enough to gore: said of a bull. **2** Crazy; insane; wild. — **horn′-mad′ness** *n.*

horn of plenty 1 In Greek mythology, the horn of Amalthea. **2** A symbol of abundance in general, represented in art as a curved horn filled with fruit, etc.: also called *cornucopia*.

horn·pipe (hôrn′pīp′) *n.* **1** A lively English country dance. **2** The music of such a dance, or similar music. **3** A musical instrument resembling the clarinet formerly used in Eng-land and Wales.

horn-rimmed (hôrn′rimd′) *adj.* Having frames of horn or of dark-colored plastic, often rel-atively thick and heavy: said of spectacles or eyeglasses.

horn silver 1 Fused silver chloride. **2** Cerar-gyrite.

horn spoon A scoop made of cow horn: used by miners for testing washings.

horn·stone (hôrn′stōn′) *n.* Chert.

horn-swog·gle (hôrn′swog′əl) *v.t.* **·gled, ·gling** *Slang* To deceive; bamboozle; cheat.

horn·tail (hôrn′tāl′) *n.* A large type of saw-fly (family *Siricidae*) with a horn at the end of the abdomen. The larva is a wood borer. For illustration see under INSECT (in-jurious).

horn toad The horned toad.

horn·work (hôrn′wûrk′) *n.* **1** The art of work-ing horn. **2** Objects collectively that are made of horn. **3** *Mil.* A fortification outwork made up of two half bastions connected by a curtain.

horn·worm (hôrn′wûrm′) *n.* A caterpillar with a hornlike hind appendage: the larva of a hawk moth.

horn·wort (hôrn′wûrt′) *n.* An aquatic herb (*Ceratophyllum demersum*) widely distributed in lakes, ponds, and slow streams.

horn·y (hôr′nē) *adj.* **horn·i·er, horn·i·est 1** Re-sembling horn; callous. **2** Made of horn. **3** Having horns. **4** *Slang* Lustful; lecherous.

Horn·y (hôr′nē) *n. Scot. & Brit. Dial.* The devil: also spelled *Hornie*.

horn·y-hand·ed (hôr′nē·han′did) *adj.* Having hard or calloused hands.

hor·o·loge (hôr′ə·lōj, hor′-) *n.* **1** A timepiece. **2** A clock tower. [<OF *horloge* <L *horolo-gium* <Gk. *hōrologion* <*hōra* time + *legein* tell]

ho·rol·o·ger (hô·rol′ə·jər, hō-) *n.* One skilled in horology; also, one who makes or sells time-pieces. Also **ho·rol′o·gist.**

hor·o·log·ic (hôr′ə·loj′ik, hor′-) *adj.* **1** Per-taining to horology or to a horologe. **2** *Bot.* Opening and closing at certain hours, as some flowers. Also **hor′o·log′i·cal.**

Hor·o·lo·gi·um (hôr′ə·lō′jē·əm, hor′-) A south-ern constellation, the Clock. See CONSTELLA-TION.

ho·rol·o·gy (hô·rol′ə·jē, hō-) *n.* The science of time-measurement or of the construction of timepieces.

hor·o·scope (hôr′ə·skōp, hor′-) *n.* **1** In astrol-ogy, the aspect of the heavens, with special reference to the positions of the planets at any instant. **2** A figure or statement showing such aspect, from which astrologers profess to foretell the future of an individual. **3** The diagram of the twelve divisions or houses of the heavens, used by astrologers in predicting the future. [<L *horoscopus* <Gk. *hōroskopos* observer of hour of nativity <*hōra* hour + *skopos* watcher <*skopeein* watch]

ho·ros·co·py (hô·ros′kə·pē, hō-) *n.* **1** The art of casting horoscopes or of determining the future from the positions of the heavenly

bodies. **2** In astrology, the situation of the heavenly bodies at the time of a person's birth; a horoscope.

Ho·ro·witz (hôr′ə·wits, hor′-; *Russian* hôr′ə·vits), **Vladimir,** born 1904, U.S. pianist born in Russia.

hor·ren·dous (hô·ren′dəs, ho-) *adj.* Frightful; fearful. [<L *horrendus*, gerundive of *horrere* bristle] — **hor·ren′dous·ly** *adv.*

hor·rent (hôr′ənt, hor′-) *adj.* **1** Standing erect like bristles; bristling. **2** Causing terror and abhorrence. **3** Feeling or expressing horror. [<L *horrens, -entis*, ppr. of *horrere* bristle]

hor·ri·bi·le dic·tu (hô·rē′bə·lā dik′tōō) *Latin* Horrible to be told.

hor·ri·ble (hôr′ə·bəl, hor′-) *adj.* Exciting abhor-rence; terrible. See synonyms under AWFUL, FRIGHTFUL. [<F <L *horribilis* <*horrere* bristle] — **hor′ri·ble·ness** *n.* — **hor′ri·bly** *adj.*

hor·rid (hôr′id, hor′-) *adj.* **1** Fitted to inspire horror; dreadful. **2** *Colloq.* Highly obnox-ious; outrageous. See synonyms under FRIGHT-FUL. [<L *horridus* bristling <*horrere* bristle] — **hor′rid·ly** *adv.* — **hor′rid·ness** *n.*

hor·rif·ic (hô·rif′ik, ho-) *adj.* Causing horror.

hor·ri·fy (hôr′ə·fī, hor′-) *v.t.* **·fied, ·fy·ing** To affect or fill with horror. — **hor′ri·fi·ca′tion** *n.*

hor·rip·i·la·tion (hô·rip′ə·lā′shən, ho-) *n.* A chilliness accompanied by the appearance of goose-pimples and bristling of the hair over the body, preceding fever; goose-flesh. [<L *horripilatio, -onis* <*horripilare* <*horrere* bristle + *pilus* hair]

hor·ror (hôr′ər, hor′-) *n.* **1** The painful emo-tion of extreme fear or abhorrence; dread. **2** Extreme repugnance. **3** That which excites fear or dread; especially, some great accident or calamity. **4** *Obs.* The shivering fit that precedes a fever. See synonyms under ABOMI-NATION, FEAR, FRIGHT. — **the horrors** *Colloq.* **1** The blues. **2** Delirium tremens. [<L]

Hor·sa (hôr′sə) See HENGIST.

hors de com·bat (ôr də kôn′bà′) *French* Out of the fight.

hors de sai·son (ôr də se·zôn′) *French* Out of season.

hors d′oeuvre (ôr dûrv′, *Fr.* ôr dœ′vr′) An appetizer served before a meal. ◆ This form is both singular and plural in French. An English plural, **hors d′oeuvres,** is also seen. [<F]

horse (hôrs) *n. pl.* **hors·es** or **horse 1** A large, solid-hoofed quadruped (*Equus caballus*) with coarse mane and tail: commonly, in the domestic state, employed as a beast of draught and burden and especially for riding upon.

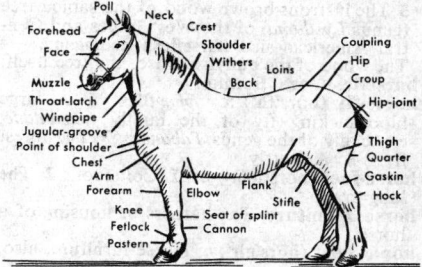

HORSE
Nomenclature for anatomical parts.

◆ Collateral adjective: *equine.* **2** Any of various extinct mammals related to or sup-posed to be of the ancestral line of the horse, as the eohippus. **3** A male horse, especially when castrated; a gelding. **4** Cavalry: a regi-ment of *horse.* **5** A device used to support anything or suggesting the uses of a horse: usually used in combination: a *clotheshorse.* **6** *Mining* A mass of rock, similar to the wall rock, found in a vein of ore. **7** *U.S. Slang* A translation or other similar aid used by pupils in working out lessons; pony; crib. **8** A man: a friendly, joking, or opprobrious term. **9** *U.S. Slang* Horseplay; foolery. **10** *Colloq.* In chess, a knight. **11** In gymnastics, a wooden block on four legs used for vaulting and other exercises. — **a horse of another (or different) color** A completely different matter. — **to hold one's horses** To be patient; curb

one's impetuosity; wait; take things easy. **— to horse** 1 The bugle call summoning mounted troops to saddle and stand equipped at their horses' heads. 2 A signal to mount. *— v.* **horsed, hors·ing** *v.t.* 1 To furnish with horses; mount. 2 To put on another's back or on a sawhorse for flogging. 3 To flog. 4 *Aeron.* To jerk violently at (the controls of an aircraft). 5 *U.S. Slang* To subject to pranks or horseplay. *— v.i.* 6 To mount or ride on a horse. 7 *U.S. Slang* To engage in horseplay: usually with *around.* *— adj.* Coarse; large for its kind: *horse* chestnut, *horselaugh.* [OE *hors*]

horse·back (hôrs′bak′) *n.* 1 A horse's back. 2 An object shaped like a horse's back. *— adv.* On a horse's back.

horse balm Richweed.

horse·block (hôrs′blok′) *n.* 1 A block or platform used in mounting a horse. 2 A frame of boards used as a support.

horse·boat (hôrs′bōt′) *n.* 1 A boat moved by horsepower. 2 A boat for carrying horses.

horse·boot (hôrs′bōōt′) *n.* A leather covering to protect a horse's pastern against injury.

horse·bot (hôrs′bot′) *n.* A botfly or its larva that infests the stomach and intestines of the horse.

horse·boy (hôrs′boi′) *n.* A stableboy.

horse·break·er (hôrs′brā′kər) *n.* One who trains horses to work in harness or under the saddle.

horse·brush (hôrs′brush′) *n.* Any of a genus (*Tetradymia*) of low, tough, hoary, sometimes spiny shrubs of the western United States, especially the little-leaf horsebrush (*T. glabrata*), considered poisonous to sheep.

horse car 1 A car drawn by horses; tramcar. 2 A car for transporting horses by rail.

horse chestnut 1 A tree (*Aesculus hippocastanum*) of Asian origin, having digitate leaves, clusters of flowers, and large chestnutlike fruits: in the United States some species are known as *buckeyes.* 2 The fruit of this tree.

horse·cloth (hôrs′klôth′, -kloth′) *n.* A cloth to cover a horse.

horse collar A stuffed collar for a horse's neck, used to support the hames of a draft harness and to ease the pressure on the shoulders in drawing.

horse·drench (hôrs′drench′) *n.* A medicinal dose for a horse, or the instrument with which it is administered.

horse·fish (hôrs′fish′) *n.* *pl.* **·fish** or **·fish·es** The moonfish.

horse·flesh (hôrs′flesh′) *n.* 1 The flesh of a horse. 2 Horses, considered collectively. 3 The lustrous brown wood of the sabicu tree (genus *Lysiloma*) of the West Indies and Central America: also **horseflesh mahogany.** 4 The wood of the bullytree; also, the tree itself.

horseflesh ore Bornite.

horse·fly (hôrs′flī′) *n.* *pl.* **·flies** 1 A large bloodsucking fly of the family *Tabanidae,* especially of the genus *Tabanus.* 2 The forest fly. 3 A botfly.

horse·foot (hôrs′fŏŏt′) *n.* 1 Coltsfoot. 2 The king crab.

horse furniture The harness or housing of a horse.

horse-gear (hôrs′gir′) *n.* Horse furniture; also, horsepower.

horse gentian A perennial weedy herb (genus *Triosteum*) of the honeysuckle family, especially the feverwort.

Horse Guards 1 In the British Army, a body of cavalry serving as guards, especially the **Royal Horse Guards** (2nd Regiment) forming the personal escort of the sovereign. 2 A building in Whitehall, London, the headquarters of the Horse Guards and offices for some departments of the War Office. 3 The chief military officials of the British Army, as distinguished from civilian officials.

horse·hair (hôrs′hâr′) *n.* 1 The hair of horses, especially of their manes and tails. 2 Haircloth.

horse·hair-snake (hôrs′hâr′snāk′) *n.* A hairworm.

horse·head (hôrs′hed′) *n.* A tropical American moonfish (*Selene vomer*).

horse·hide (hôrs′hīd′) *n.* 1 The hide of a horse. 2 Leather made from a horse's hide.

horse latitudes *Naut.* A belt of high pressure at about 35° north or south latitude, characterized by calms and light variable winds, with diminishing to prevailing westerlies toward the poles and trade winds toward the equator.

horse·laugh (hôrs′laf′, -läf′) *n.* A loud, boisterous laugh.

horse·leech (hôrs′lēch′) *n.* 1 A large leech (genus *Haemopis*), said to enter the nostrils of cattle, horses, etc., when they are drinking. 2 One who is perpetually begging or teasing: *Prov.* xxx 15: also **horse′leach′.**

horse·less (hôrs′lis) *adj.* Not possessing, using, or requiring a horse: usually in such phrases as *horseless* carriage.

horse mackerel 1 A carangoid fish of Pacific waters (*Trachurus symmetricus*). 2 The tunny.

horse·man (hôrs′mən) *n.* *pl.* **·men** (-mən) 1 One who rides a horse. 2 A cavalryman. 3 A man who is skilled in riding or managing horses.

horse·man·ship (hôrs′mən·ship) *n.* Equestrian skill.

horse marine 1 A member of an imaginary corps of mounted marines. 2 One who is as awkward and out of place as a mounted marine would be aboard ship. 3 A mounted marine or sailor on duty ashore.

horse·mint (hôrs′mint′) *n.* 1 An erect American herb (*Monarda punctata*) of the mint family; wild bergamot. 2 Either of two European woodland mints (*Mentha longifolia* and *M. aquatica*), both naturalized in the United States.

horse·net·tle (hôrs′net′l) *n.* A rough roadside weed (*Solanum carolinense*) with straw-colored prickles, white flowers, and yellow berries, found in the central and southern United States.

horse opera *U.S. Slang* A motion picture dealing with ranch life in the western United States.

horse pistol A large pistol formerly carried in a holster by horsemen.

horse·play (hôrs′plā′) *n.* Rough, boisterous play.

horse·pond (hôrs′pond′) *n.* A pond for watering horses.

horse-post (hôrs′pōst′) *n.* A system of sending mail by a carrier on horseback; also, the carrier. See PONY EXPRESS.

horse post A hitching post.

horse·pow·er (hôrs′pou′ər) *n.* 1 The force exerted by, or rate of work maintained by, an average dray horse. 2 *Mech.* The standard theoretical unit of the rate of work, equal to 33,000 pounds lifted one foot in one minute, or 550 foot-pounds per second. 3 A mechanical arrangement for utilizing a horse's power.

horse·pow·er-hour (hôrs′pou′ər·our′) *n.* A measure of work performed at the rate of one horsepower in one hour. Expressed in foot-pounds it is equal to 33,000 × 60, or 1,980,000 foot-pounds.

horse race A race by horses. **— horse′-rac′er** *n.* **— horse′-rac′ing** *n.*

horse rack A long pole supported by posts to which horses are hitched.

horse·rad·ish (hôrs′rad′ish) *n.* 1 A coarse, tall, common garden herb (*Armoracia lapathifolia*) of the mustard family. 2 Its pungent root, used as a condiment.

horse·rake (hôrs′rāk′) *n.* A large mechanical rake worked by horsepower.

horse sense *Colloq.* Innate practical intelligence; common sense; shrewdness.

horse·shoe (hôr′shōō′, hôrs′-) *n.* 1 A metal shoe for a horse, U-shaped like the edge of a horse's hoof, to which it is nailed. 2 Something roughly U-shaped, especially if the opening is narrower than the sweep of the curve. 3 The horseshoe crab. *— v.t.* **·shoed, ·shoe·ing** To furnish with horseshoes.

horseshoe crab A king crab.

horse·shoes (hôr′shōōz′, hôrs′-) *n.* A game, similar to quoits, originally played with discarded horseshoes, now often with new or imitation horseshoes.

horse sugar The sweetleaf, a shrub (*Symplocos tinctoria*) of the southern United States: eaten by cattle and horses.

horse·tail (hôrs′tāl′) *n.* 1 The tail of a horse, especially when severed from the body and used as a distinction of rank or as a standard. In Turkey the two ranks of pashas were distinguished by two and three horsetails. 2 A perennial, hollow-stemmed, pteridophytic plant (genus *Equisetum*); the scouring rush.

horse-tam·er (hôrs′tā′mər) *n.* A horsebreaker.

horse tick The forest fly.

horse·weed (hôrs′wēd′) *n.* 1 A common weed (*Erigeron canadensis*) of the composite family, found in most parts of North America. 2 The wild lettuce. 3 The great ragweed.

horse·whip (hôrs′hwip′) *n.* A whip for driving or managing horses. *— v.t.* **·whipped, ·whip·ping** To chastise with a horsewhip.

horse·wom·an (hôrs′wŏŏm′ən) *n.* *pl.* **·wom·en** (-wim′in) 1 A woman who rides on horseback. 2 A woman who is skilled in riding or managing horses.

horst (hôrst) *n.* *Geol.* A portion of the earth's crust slightly elevated from the surrounding tracts by faults. Also **horste.** [<G]

hors·y (hôr′sē) *adj.* **hors·i·er, hors·i·est** 1 Pertaining to or suggestive of horses. 2 Devoted to horses or horse-racing. 3 *Slang* Coarse or gross in appearance. Also **hors′ey.** **— hors′i·ly** *adv.* **— hors′i·ness** *n.*

Hor·ta (hôr′tə, *Pg.* ôr′tə) Westernmost of the three districts of the Azores, comprising Pico, Fayal, Flores, and Corvo islands; total, 294 square miles; capital, Horta, on Fayal.

hor·ta·tive (hôr′tə·tiv) *adj.* Hortatory. [<L *hortativus* <*hortari* urge] **— hor′ta·tive·ly** *adv.*

hor·ta·to·ry (hôr′tə·tôr′ē, -tō′rē) *adj.* 1 Giving exhortation. 2 *Ling.* Pertaining to a mood used in some languages to express exhortation, encouragement, etc., or to the imperative or subjunctive moods when used in this manner. [<L *hortatorius*]

Hor·tense (hôr′tens, *Fr.* ôr·täṅs′) A feminine personal name. Also **Hor·ten·si·a** (*Ger.* hôr·ten′sē·ä, *Lat.* hôr·ten′shē·ə). [<F <L, gardener]

Hor·thy (hôr′tē), **Nicholas von,** 1868–1957, Hungarian admiral and statesman; regent of Hungary 1920–44: also known as *Miklos von Horthy.*

hor·ti·cul·ture (hôr′tə·kul′chər) *n.* 1 The cultivation of a garden, or the mode of cultivation employed in a garden. 2 That department of the science of agriculture which relates to the cultivation of gardens or orchards, including the growing of vegetables, fruits, flowers, and ornamental shrubs and trees. See synonyms under AGRICULTURE. [<L *hortus* garden + *cultura* cultivation] **— hor′ti·cul′tor** (-kul′tər) *n.* **— hor′ti·cul′tur·al** *adj.* **— hor′ti·cul′tur·ist, hor′ti·cul′tist, hor′ti·cul′tur·al·ist** *n.*

hor·tus sic·cus (hôr′təs sik′əs) *Latin* Literally, a dry garden; a herbarium.

Ho·rus (hō′rəs) In Egyptian mythology, the hawk-headed god of the sun.

HORUS
In legend, the son of Isis and Osiris.

ho·san·na (hō·zan′ə) *interj.* An exclamation of praise to God. *— n.* A cry of hosanna; hence, any exultant acclamation in praise of the Almighty. [<LL <Gk. *hōsanna* <Hebrew *hōshī'āhnnā* save, I pray]

hose (hōz) *n.* *pl.* **hose** (*Archaic* **hos·en**) 1 *Usually pl.* Formerly, a garment worn by men, covering the legs and the lower part of the body, like very tight trousers. 2 *pl.* Stockings; socks. 3 *pl.* **hos·es** A flexible tube or pipe, of leather, rubber, cotton, etc., for conveying water and other fluids. *— v.t.* **hosed, hos·ing** To drench or douse with a hose. [OE *hosa*]

Ho·se·a (hō·zē′ə, -zā′ə) A masculine personal name. [<Hebrew *Hōshēa',* lit., salvation <*yasha* save]

— Hosea One of the Hebrew minor prophets, eighth century B.C.; also, the Old Testament book bearing his name.

hose company A group of men who convey and man the hose for extinguishing fires.

ho·sier (hō′zhər) *n.* A dealer in hose, etc.

ho·sier·y (hō′zhər·ē) *n.* Hosiers' wares; stockings; hose; the hosier's business.

Hos·kins (hos′kinz), **Roy Graham,** 1880–1964, U. S. physiologist.

hos·pice (hos′pis) *n.* A place of entertainment or shelter, as a monastery in an Alpine pass. [<F <L *hospitium* inn, hospitality <*hospes* host, guest]

hos·pi·ta·ble (hos'pi·tə·bəl, hos·pit'ə·bəl) *adj.* 1 Disposed to behave in a warm manner or to entertain with generous kindness. 2 Characterized by hospitality. 3 Figuratively, very receptive. [<OF <L *hospitare* entertain] — **hos'pi·ta·ble·ness** *n.* — **hos'pi·ta·bly** *adv.*

hos·pi·tal (hos'pi·təl) *n.* 1 An institution for the reception, care, and medical treatment of the sick or wounded; also, the building used for that purpose. 2 *Obs.* An inn or hospice. 3 Formerly, a place of hospitality for those in need of shelter and maintenance: foundling *hospital*, Greenwich *Hospital* (a home for retired seamen in London). [<OF <L *hospitalis* of a guest <*hospes* guest. Doublet of HOTEL, HOSTEL.]

hos·pi·tal·er (hos'pi·təl·ər) *n.* 1 One cared for or supported in a hospital. 2 The title of the chief resident official in certain London hospitals which were originally religious foundations. See HOSTELER (def. 2). Also **hos'pi·tal·ler.**

Hos·pi·tal·er (hos'pi·təl·ər) *n.* A member of one of various charitable brotherhoods or military orders of the Middle Ages, of which the best known is the **Knights Hospitalers of St. John of Jerusalem**, which originated during the crusades in a hospital built at Jerusalem by merchants of Amalfi and dedicated to St. John the Baptist. When the order had to move its seat elsewhere, it was known as *Knights of Malta* and *Knights of Rhodes.*

hos·pi·tal·i·ty (hos'pə·tal'ə·tē) *n. pl.* **·ties** The spirit, practice, or act of being hospitable. ◆ Collateral adjective: *xenial.*

hos·pi·tal·ize (hos'pi·təl·īz') *v.t.* **·ized, ·iz·ing** To put in a hospital for treatment. — **hos'pi·tal·i·za'tion** *n.*

hos·pi·ti·um (hos·pish'ē·əm) *n. pl.* **·ti·a** (-ē·ə) *Archaic* 1 A monastic inn. 2 An inn; hostel. [<L <*hospes* guest]

hos·po·dar (hos'pə·där) *n.* A title of dignity formerly borne by the princes of Lithuania and the kings of Poland, later by the princes or governors of Moldavia and Wallachia and the emperor of Russia. [<Rumanian, ult. <Slavic]

host[1] (hōst) *n.* 1 One who entertains guests in private life. 2 The landlord of a hotel. 3 *Biol.* Any living plant or animal that harbors another as a parasite. — *v.i. Colloq.* To conduct or entertain in the role of a host. [<OF *hoste* <L *hospes* guest, host. Akin to GUEST, HOST[2].]

host[2] (hōst) *n.* 1 An army. 2 A large body of men; a multitude. See synonyms under ARMY, ASSEMBLY, COMPANY, THRONG. [<OF <L *hostis* enemy. Akin to GUEST, HOST[1].]

host[3] (hōst) *n.* 1 *Usually cap.* In the Roman Catholic, Greek, Lutheran, and some other churches, the eucharistic bread or wafer before or after consecration. 2 *Obs.* An offering; sacrifice. [<OF *hoiste* <L *hostia* sacrificial victim]

hos·tage (hos'tij) *n.* 1 A person held as a pledge, as in war, for the performance of some stipulation. 2 Hence, anything given as a pledge. [<OF]

hos·tel (hos'təl) *n.* An inn; a lodging house; especially, a **youth hostel**, a supervised shelter for the use of young people on walking trips. Also **hos'tel·ry** (-rē). — **hos·tler·y** (hos'lər·ē). [<OF <LL *hospitale* inn <*hospes* guest. Doublet of HOTEL, HOSPITAL.]

hos·tel·er (hos'təl·ər) *n.* 1 A student living in a hostel. 2 The monk who acted as host in a monastery. 3 *Archaic* An innkeeper. Also **hos'tel·ler.**

host·ess (hōs'tis) *n.* A female host.

hos·tile (hos'təl, *esp. Brit.* hos'tīl) *adj.* 1 Having a spirit of enmity. 2 Pertaining to an enemy. See synonyms under ALIEN, MALICIOUS. — *n.* An enemy; antagonist. [<F <L *hostilis*] — **hos'tile·ly** *adv.*

hos·til·i·ty (hos·til'ə·tē) *n. pl.* **·ties** 1 The state of being hostile. 2 *Obs.* Hostile action. 3 *pl.* Warlike measures. See synonyms under ANTIPATHY, ENMITY, FEUD, HATRED.

host·ing (hōs'ting) *n. Obs.* 1 The gathering of an armed host; a muster. 2 An encounter.

hos·tler (hos'lər, os'-) *n.* 1 A stableman; groom: also spelled *ostler.* 2 A man who prepares locomotives for their succeeding trips. [<OF *hostelier* innkeeper]

hot (hot) *adj.* **hot·ter, hot·test** 1 Having or giving heat; of high temperature: opposed to *cold* and exceeding *warm* in degree. 2 Producing a burning or biting sensation to the taste or touch: *hot* pepper; *hot* acid. 3 Marked by passion or zeal; fiery; fervent: *hot* words. 4 *Slang* Excited with sexual desire. 5 Violent; intense; raging: a *hot* battle. 6 *Slang* So new as not to have lost its freshness, currency, excitement, etc. 7 *Slang* Recently stolen or smuggled: *hot* goods. 8 *Music Slang* **a** In jazz, characterized by fervent and exciting rhythm and spirit, a lively tempo, and improvised variations on the original score. **b** Performing such music. 9 Following very closely: in *hot* pursuit. 10 In games, near to the subject or solution sought. 11 In hunting, distinct; strong: said of a scent. 12 Having an electrical charge, especially of high voltage: a *hot* wire. 13 Dangerously radioactive, as the fall-out of an atomic bomb. — **to make it hot for** *Slang* To make the situation extremely uncomfortable for. — *adv.* In a hot manner. [OE *hāt*] — **hot'ly** *adv.* — **hot'ness** *n.*

Synonyms: burning, choleric, fervent, fervid, fiery, glowing, heated, irascible, passionate, peppery, pungent, stinging, vehement, violent. See ARDENT, EAGER[1]. *Antonyms:* arctic, bleak, boreal, chill, chilly, cold, cool, freezing, frigid, frosty, frozen, gelid, icy, polar, wintry.

hot–air (hot'âr') *adj.* 1 Heating by means of hot air: a *hot–air* furnace. 2 Inflated with hot air: a *hot–air* balloon.

hot air 1 Heated air. 2 *Slang* Empty or pretentious talk; humbug.

hot·bed (hot'bed') *n.* 1 A bed of rich earth, protected by glass, and warmed for promoting the growth of plants. 2 A place or condition favoring rapid growth or heated activity.

hot blast A blast of hot air blown into a smelting furnace. — **hot'–blast'** *adj.*

hot–blood·ed (hot'blud'id) *adj.* Being of hot blood; passionate; amorous.

hot·box (hot'boks') *n.* The overheated journal box of a railroad car or other fast-moving wheeled vehicle: caused by friction.

hot cake A pancake or fritter.

hotch (hoch) *v.t. & v.i. Scot. & Brit. Dial.* To shake; jiggle or fidget.

hotch·pot (hoch'pot') *n. Law* A commixture of property made in order to secure an equable division. [<OF *hochepot* <MDu. *hutspot*]

hotch–potch (hoch'poch') *n.* 1 A hodgepodge. 2 *Law* A hotchpot. [Var. of HOTCHPOT]

hot cross bun A circular cake or bun marked with a cross of frosting, eaten especially during Lent.

hot dog *Colloq.* A cooked frankfurter, usually grilled and served in a split roll.

ho·tel (hō·tel') *n.* 1 An establishment or building providing lodging, food, etc., for travelers and others; an inn. 2 In French usage: **a** An official residence or private dwelling in a city or town. **b** A building for the transaction of public business in a city or town. [<F *hôtel* <OF *hostel* inn. Doublet of HOSTEL, HOSPITAL.]

Hô·tel des In·va·lides (ô·tel' dā·zań·vȧ·lēd') An institution in Paris, originally founded in 1607 for disabled veterans, now a military museum containing the tomb of Napoleon.

hô·tel de ville (ô·tel' də vēl') *French* A town hall.

hô·tel Dieu (ô·tel' dyœ') *French* A hospital.

ho·te·lier (hō'təl·ir') *n.* A hotel-keeper; hotelman. [<F]

hot·foot (hot'fŏŏt') *v.i. Colloq.* To hurry; go hastily. — *adv. Colloq.* In all haste; hastily. — *n. Slang* The prank of furtively wedging a match between the upper and sole of a victim's shoe, lighting it, and letting it burn down.

Hoth (hoth) *Höder.* Also **Höthr** (hœ'thər).

hot·head (hot'hed') *n.* A hasty, impetuous, or quick-tempered person. — **hot'–head'ed** *adj.* — **hot'–head'ed·ly** *adv.* — **hot'–head'ed·ness** *n.*

hot·house (hot'hous') *n.* 1 A structure kept warm artificially, as for the forced growth of flowers, etc. 2 *Obs.* A brothel.

Ho·tien (hō'tyen') The Chinese name for KHOTAN.

hot line A direct means of communication; specifically, a telephone line for emergency use by heads of state of nuclear powers, or for immediate communication between an official and his chief subordinates.

hot plate 1 A heated metal plate for maintaining at a uniform temperature anything set upon it. 2 A small portable gas or electric stove.

hot·pot (hot'pot') *n.* A dish of meat stewed with potatoes in a covered pot.

hot·press (hot'pres') *v.t.* To subject to heat and mechanical pressure, as for calendering or to extract oil. — *n.* A machine for hot-pressing. — **hot'pressed'** *adj.* — **hot'press'er** *n.* — **hot'press'ing** *n.*

hot rod *Slang* An automobile, popularly a jalopy, with a motor modified for speed.

hot seat *U.S. Slang* The electric chair.

hot spring A natural spring, the waters of which issue forth at 98° F. or above.

Hot Springs A resort in western Virginia.

Hot Springs National Park A resort area in central Arkansas containing mineral-bearing thermal springs; established 1921.

hot·spur (hot'spûr') *n.* A person who pushes on, heedless of advice or warning; a hot-headed person. — *adj.* Impetuous; reckless: also **hot'spurred'.**

Hot·ten·tot (hot'ən·tot) *n.* 1 One of a yellowish-brown South African people believed to be related to both the Bantus and Bushmen. 2 The agglutinative language of these people, forming a subfamily of the Khoisan family of African languages: related to and having some of the clicks of Bushman.

Hottentot bread A plant, the elephant foot. Also **Hottentot's bread.**

hou·dah (hou'də) See HOWDAH.

Hou·dan (hŏŏ'dan) *n.* A breed of domestic fowls having black-and-white coloring, flesh-colored and blue legs, and V-shaped comb. [from *Houdan*, a town in France]

Hou·di·ni (hŏŏ·dē'nē), **Harry**, 1874–1926, U.S. magician and author: real name *Erich Weiss.*

Hou·don (ŏŏ·dôń'), **Jean Antoine**, 1741?–1828, French sculptor.

Hou·ma·youn (hŏŏ·mä'yŏŏn) See HUMAYUN.

hound (hound) *n.* 1 A hunting dog which hunts by scent; specifically, in Great Britain, a foxhound. 2 A dastardly fellow. 3 In the game of hare-and-hounds, one who acts the part of a hound. 4 *pl. Naut.* Projections at the head of a mast which support the top trestletrees and the lower rigging. 5 *Mech.* A brace to strengthen the running gear of a vehicle: if between the reach and hinder axle, called **hind hound;** if between the tongue and forward axle, **fore hound.** — *v.t.* 1 To hunt with or as with hounds; nag persistently. 2 To incite to pursue; set on the chase. [OE *hund* dog]

hound's–tongue (houndz'tung') *n.* 1 A coarse hairy weed (*Cynoglossum officinale*) found in pastures and waste grounds, with tongue-shaped leaves, dull-red flowers, and prickly nutlets. 2 The vanilla plant.

hound's–tooth check (houndz'tŏŏth') A design of small broken checks in cloth.

hour (our) *n.* 1 A space of time equal to one twenty-fourth of a day; sixty minutes; before the general use of timepieces, one twelfth of the interval from sunrise to sunset (called *hour of the day*), or one twelfth that from sunset to sunrise (called *hour of the night*). 2 A measure of time as indicated by the sun in relation to the horizon: the sun was two *hours* high. 3 The point of time indicated by a chronometer, watch, or clock; the time of day. 4 A set, appointed, or definite time; specifically, the time of death. 5 *pl.* Prayers to be repeated at stated times of the day; also, the time for these devotions, or the book containing them. 6 An hour's journey: commonly a league or three miles. 7 A sidereal hour. See SIDEREAL (def. 2). 8 *Astron.* An angular measure of right ascension or longitude, being 15 degrees or the 24th part of a great circle of the sphere. — **after hours** After the prescribed hours for school, business, etc. — **the small hours** The early morning hours. ◆ Collateral

adjective: *horal.* [<L *hora* <Gk. *hōra* time, period]

hour angle *Astron.* The angle subtended by a place on the celestial sphere between the meridian and the hour circle passing through the object: used in determining time.

hour circle *Astron.* A great circle which passes through the celestial pole: used in the determination of the hour angle.

hour·glass (our′glas′, -gläs′) *n.* A glass vessel having two globular parts connected by a narrow neck: used for measuring time by the running of sand from the upper into the lower compartment, the passage taking a full hour.

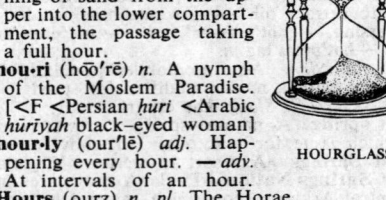

HOURGLASS

hou·ri (ho͞o′rē) *n.* A nymph of the Moslem Paradise. [<F <Persian *ḥūri* <Arabic *ḥūrīyah* black-eyed woman]

hour·ly (our′lē) *adj.* Happening every hour. — *adv.* At intervals of an hour.

Hours (ourz) *n. pl.* The Horae.

house (hous) *n.* **1** A building intended for human habitation, especially one used as the residence of a family or single tenant. **2** A household; family. **3** A building used for any purpose: a coffee *house;* a *house* of worship. **4** The abode of a fraternity, order, etc.: a sorority *house.* **5** A dormitory or residence hall in a college or university; also, its resident students, collectively. **6** *Brit.* A college in a university; also, its member students, collectively. **7** A legislative body; also, the chamber it occupies. **8** *Eccl.* The deliberative body of a congregation or convocation. **9** A place of business. **10** A business firm: the *house* of Morgan. **11** A theater. **12** An audience at a public entertainment or service: to speak to a full *house.* **13** A line of ancestors and descendants regarded as forming a single family: the *House* of Tudor. **14** In astrology, one of the twelve divisions of the heavens, made by projecting great circles through the north and south points of the horizon. Each division, having special significance, is used in casting horoscopes. See ZODIAC. **15** A sign of the zodiac considered as the seat of greatest influence of a particular planet. **— on the house** At the expense of the proprietor; gratis. **— to bring down the house** To receive loud and enthusiastic applause. **— to clean house** *Colloq.* To get rid of undesirable conditions or persons in an organization. **— to keep house** To manage the affairs or work of a home. — *v.* (houz) **housed, hous·ing** *v.t.* **1** To take or put into a house; furnish with a house; lodge. **2** To store in a house or building. **3** To fit into a mortise, joint, etc. **4** *Naut.* To place in a secure or safe position, as in time of storms. — *v.i.* **5** To take shelter or lodgings; dwell. [OE *hūs*] **— house′ful** *n.*

Synonyms (noun): abode, building, cabin, cot, cottage, domicile, dwelling, dwelling place, edifice, habitation, hall, home, hovel, hut, manor, mansion, palace, residence, shanty, villa. See EDIFICE, HOME.

House (hous), **Edward Mandell,** 1858–1938, U.S. diplomat; adviser to President Wilson: known as *Colonel House.*

house arrest Detention in one's own house by authority of law.

house·boat (hous′bōt′) *n.* A boat or barge fitted out as a dwelling.

house·boy (hous′boi′) *n.* A houseman.

house·break·er (hous′brā′kər) *n.* One who breaks into a house to rob. **— house′break′·ing** *n.*

house·bro·ken (hous′brō′kən) *adj.* Trained to live cleanly in a house: said of animals.

house·carl (hous′kärl) *n.* A member of the bodyguard or household troops of a Danish or early English king or noble.

house coat A long, loose-skirted garment designed for informal indoor wear.

house·fly (hous′flī′) *n. pl.* **·flies** The common fly *(Musca domestica),* found in nearly all parts of the world: an agent in transmitting certain diseases. For illustration see under INSECTS (injurious).

house guest A guest invited to stay one or more nights.

house·hold (hous′hōld) *n.* A number of persons dwelling under the same roof. — *adj.* Domestic. [<HOUSE + HOLD, *n.*]

household arts See under ART.

house·hold·er (hous′hōl′dər) *n.* The head of a family; specifically, in England, one who inhabits a dwelling or tenement of such a nature as to qualify him for the exercise of the franchise.

household goods The furniture, utensils, and supplies necessary for keeping house.

household linen See FLATWORK.

household troops A special body of soldiers detailed for the protection of a sovereign, his family, and residence.

house·keep·er (hous′kē′pər) *n.* One who directs the affairs or work of a household either as mistress or as an upper servant. **— house′keep′ing** *n.*

hou·sel (hou′zəl) *n. Obs.* The Eucharist. [OE *hūsel*]

house·leek (hous′lēk′) *n.* An Old World garden plant *(Sempervivum tectorum)* of the orpine family, with pink flowers and thick fleshy leaves that grow on walls and roofs.

house·line (hous′līn′) *n. Naut.* A small three-stranded line of fine-dressed hemp, used for seizings, etc.: sometimes called *housing.* Also spelled *houslin.*

house·maid (hous′mād′) *n.* A girl employed to do housework.

housemaid's knee *Pathol.* A chronic inflammation of the bursa in front of the knee, afflicting housemaids and others who kneel in working.

house·man (hous′mən) *n.* A handy man employed to do heavy work about a house, hotel, etc.: also called *houseboy.*

house·mas·ter (hous′mas′tər, -mäs′-) *n.* The master having charge of a school residence, specifically in a British school.

House of Burgesses In colonial times, the lower house of the legislature of Virginia.

house of cards Any weak, unstable organization, plan, etc.

House of Commons The lower house of the British Parliament.

house of correction An institution for minor criminals; reform school.

House of Delegates The lower house of the legislature in Maryland, Virginia, and West Virginia.

House of Keys The lower house of the legislature of the Isle of Man. See KEYS.

House of Lords The upper house of the British Parliament.

House of Peers The upper chamber of the Japanese Diet.

House of Representatives **1** The lower, larger branch of the United States Congress, and of many State legislatures, composed of members elected popularly on the basis of population. **2** A similar legislative body, as in Australia, Japan, or Mexico.

House of Saxe-Coburg-Gotha See under WINDSOR.

house organ A publication issued by a commercial enterprise to promote the interest of customers in its products, or to maintain efficiency among its employees.

house party An entertainment of guests for several days, usually in a country house or a college fraternity; also, the guests.

house physician A physician resident by appointment in a hospital or other institution.

house·room (hous′ro͞om;, -ro͝om′) *n.* Room or lodging in a house or hotel; accommodation.

house snake A harmless snake *(Lampropeltis triangulum)* of the northern United States that frequents houses and preys on rats and mice: also called *milk snake* and *spotted adder.*

house sparrow See under SPARROW (def. 1).

house·top (hous′top′) *n.* **1** The top or roof of a house. **2** Figuratively, an exposed or public place: to cry it from the *housetops.*

house·ware (hous′wâr′) *n.* Kitchen equipment and other wares used in a home.

house·warm·ing (hous′wôr′ming) *n.* A festivity on entering a new home.

house·wife (hous′wīf′) *n. pl.* **·wives** (-wīvz′) **1** A married woman who manages the affairs of her own household as a full-time occupation. **2** (hous′wīf′, *esp. Brit.* huz′if) A receptable for small articles required in sewing. **— house′wife′ly** *adj. & adv.* **— house′·wife′li·ness** *n.*

house·wife·ry (hous′wīf′rē) *n.* The part of household management under a woman's direction; housekeeping processes. Also **house′·wife′ship** (-ship).

house·work (hous′wûrk′) *n.* Work in keeping house, especially the more menial tasks.

house wren See under WREN.

hous·ie (ho͞o′sē) *n. Scot.* A small house.

hous·ing[1] (hou′zing) *n.* **1** The act of providing with a house or shelter. **2** The act of bringing into a house, or putting under cover. **3** Shelter from the weather. **4** *Mech.* **a** A hollow made in one member of an engine or machine to receive a portion of another member. **b** That part of a frame of a machine which sustains a journal box; a jaw. **c** The casing containing either the differential gear or a set of ball bearings in the transmission of an automobile. **5** A niche for a statue. **6** *Naut.* **a** A houseline. **b** A hoarding to protect a ship's deck when in repair dock. **c** That part of a mast or bowsprit below the deck or abaft the knightheads. **7** A mortise in a timber, for receiving the end of another timber.

hous·ing[2] (hou′zing) *n.* The ornamental trappings of a horse, especially the saddlecloth: usually in the plural. See synonyms under CAPARISON. [<OF *houce;* of uncertain origin]

hous·lin (hous′lin) See HOUSELINE.

Hous·man (hous′mən), **Alfred Edward,** 1859–1936, English poet and classical scholar.

Hous·say (ou′sī), **Bernardo Alberto,** born 1887, Argentine physiologist.

Hous·ton (hyo͞os′tən), **Sam,** 1793–1863, U.S. statesman and general; president of the Republic of Texas 1836–38, 1841–44.

Hous·ton (hyo͞os′tən) A city in SE Texas.

Hous·to·ni·a (ho͞os·tō′nē·ə) *n.* A genus of low, slender North American plants of the madder family, including the bluet. [after Dr. William *Houston,* 1695–1733, English naturalist]

Hou·yhn·hnm (ho͞o·in′əm, hwin′əm) In Swift's *Gulliver's Travels,* one of a race of horses having reason and all the noble qualities of ideal man: contrasted with the apelike *Yahoo,* having all the vices of man. [Imit. of the whinny of a horse]

hove[1] (hōv) *v.t. & v.i. Obs.* **1** To raise or move upward. **2** To inflate. [<HEAVE]

hove[2] (hōv) Past tense of HEAVE.

hov·el (huv′əl, hov′-) *n.* **1** A wretched dwelling; hut. **2** An open shed for sheltering cattle, tools, or produce. See synonyms under HOUSE, HUT. — *v.t.* **hov·eled** or **hov·elled, hov·el·ing** or **hov·el·ling** **1** To shelter in a hovel. **2** To build like a hovel. [? Dim. of OE *hof* building]

hov·er (huv′ər, hov′-) *v.i.* **1** To remain suspended in or near one place in the air, as by fluttering the wings. **2** To linger; be nearby, as if waiting or watching: with *around, near,* etc. **3** To remain in an uncertain or irresolute state: with *between.* — *n.* **1** A shelter or retreat. **2** The act of hovering. [< obs. *hove* float] **— hov′er·er** *n.*

Hov·er·craft (huv′ər·kraft′, hov′-, -kräft′) *n.* A vehicle traveling on a thin cushion of air produced by fans directed downward: a trade name. Also **hov′er·craft′.**

how[1] (hou) *adv.* **1** In what way or manner: I knew *how* it was done. **2** To what degree, extent, or amount; in what proportion: showing *how* great was the concentration of ions. **3** In what state or condition: Let me see *how* the account stands. **4** For what reason or purpose: I can't see *how* he came to do it. **5** For what price; at what sum: I inquired *how* the stock sold. **6** By what name or designation: We know *how* he is called among his own people. **7** To what effect; with what meaning: *How* do you intend that remark to be taken? **8** *Colloq.* What? — *n.* Way of doing or becoming; means: Teach me the *how* of it. [OE *hū*]

how[2] (hou) *adj. Scot.* Hollow or deep; also, hollow in sound. — *n.* A valley; glen. Also spelled *howe.*

how[3] (hou) *interj.* An expression of greeting attributed to and used humorously in imitation of American Indians.

How·ard (hou′ərd) A masculine personal name. [<Gmc., hedge guard]

How·ard (hou′ərd), **Catherine,** 1522?–42, fifth wife of Henry VIII of England; executed.

how·be·it (hou·bē′it) *adv.* Nevertheless. — *conj. Obs.* Although; be that as it may. See synonyms under NOTWITHSTANDING.

how·dah (hou′də) *n.* A railed or canopied seat on the back of an elephant: also spelled *houdah.* [<Hind. *haudah*]

how·die (hou′dē, ou′-, hō′, ō′-) *n. Scot.* A midwife.

how-do-you-do (hou′də-yə-ədōō′) *n. Colloq.* An awkward situation or occasion: usually preceded by an intensive *fine, pretty, nice,* etc. Also **how-d′ye-do** (hou′dyə-dōō′).

How do you do? What is the state of your health?: a phrase often used as a greeting when being introduced to or meeting a person.

how·dy (hou′dē) *interj. Colloq.* An expression of greeting. [Contraction of HOW DO YOU (DO)?]

howe (hō) See HOW².

Howe (hou), **Elias,** 1819-67, U.S. inventor of the sewing machine. — **Julia Ward,** 1819-1910, U.S. author. — **Richard,** 1725-99, Earl Howe, English admiral in the American Revolution. — **William,** 1729-1814, fifth Viscount Howe, English general; commander in chief during American Revolution; brother of the preceding.

how·el (hou′əl) *n.* A cooper's plane for smoothing the inside of casks. — *v.t.* To make smooth with a howel. [<MLG *hövel*]

How·ells (hou′əlz), **William Dean,** 1837-1920, U.S. novelist and editor.

how·ev·er (hou-ev′ər) *adv.* **1** In whatever manner; by whatever means. **2** To whatever degree or extent: Spend *however* much it costs. **3** How; in what manner: *However* did it happen? — *conj.* Notwithstanding; still; yet. See synonyms under BUT, NOTWITHSTANDING. Also **how·e′er′** (-âr′).

how·it·zer (hou′it-sər) *n.* A piece of artillery having a barrel longer than a mortar's, and firing at angles up to 65° with medium muzzle velocity. [Appar. <Du. *houwitzer,* ult. <Czech *houfnice* catapult]

HOWITZER—BRITISH ARMY, 1914

howk (hōk) *v.t. & v.i. Brit. Dial.* To dig; burrow: also spelled *holk.* — **howk′it** (-it) *adj.*

howl (houl) *v.i.* **1** To utter the loud, mournful wail of a wolf or dog. **2** To utter such a cry in rage, grief, etc. **3** To make such a sound: The storm *howled.* — *v.i.* **4** To utter or express with a howl or howls. **5** To drive or effect with a howl or howls. — *n.* **1** The cry of a wolf or dog. **2** Any resonant cry expressive of grief or rage. **3** An undesirable sound distortion in radio reception, due to acoustic or electrical feedback. [Imit.]

How·land Island (hou′lənd) A United States possession in the mid-Pacific near the equator.

howl·er (hou′lər) *n.* **1** One who or that which howls. **2** A siren for signaling, or, when attached to a military airplane, for creating confusion or panic among the enemy. **3** A tropical American monkey having a long, prehensile tail and great vocal power: the ursine *howler* (*Alouatta ursinus*): also **howling monkey.** **4** *Colloq.* Gross exaggeration; also, an absurd mistake or blunder.

how·let (hou′lit) *n. Obs.* An owl; owlet. [<F *hulotte*]

howl·ing (hou′ling) *adj.* **1** Filled with or abounding in howls; dismal: the *howling* wilderness. **2** *Slang* Prodigious; tremendous; enormous: a *howling* success, a *howling* lie.

How·rah (hou′rä) A city on the Hooghly opposite Calcutta, NE India.

how·so·ev·er (hou′sō-ev′ər) *adv.* In whatever manner; to whatever extent.

hoy[1] (hoi) *n.* **1** A barge used to convey bulky cargo to ships in port. **2** A single-masted,

heavy, coastwise vessel or tender of obsolete type. [<MDu. *hoei*]

hoy[2] (hoi) *interj.* Ho; hallo: a cry to attract attention. Compare AHOY. Also spelled *hoigh, hooy.* [Imit. Cf. Du. *hui!*]

hoy·den (hoid′n) *n.* A romping or bold girl; tomboy. — *adj.* Inelegant or unseemly; bold. — *v.i.* To romp rudely or indecently. Also spelled *hoiden.* [? <obs. *hoit* romp] — **hoy′den·ish** *adj.*

Hoyle (hoil) *n.* A book or rules and instructions for indoor games, especially for card games: so called from the original author, **Edmund Hoyle,** 1672-1769, English writer on card games. — **according to Hoyle** Following the rules laid down in Hoyle; hence, sportsmanlike; acting fairly in a game or sport, or in any matter.

hoyte (hoit) *v.i. Scot.* To walk or run awkwardly; limp.

Hra·dec Krá·lo·vé (hrä′dets krä′lô-ve) A city in NE Bohemia, Czechoslovakia: German *Königgrätz.*

Hr·dlič·ka (hûrd′lich-kə), **A·leš** (ä′lesh), 1869-1943, U.S. anthropologist born in Czechoslovakia.

hsien (shyen) *n.* A subprefecture of Chinese provincial administration.

Hsin·chu (shin′chōō′) A city in NW Taiwan.

Hsin-king (shin′jing′) A former name for CHANGCHUN. Also **Hsin′ching′.**

Hual·la·ga (wä-yä′gä) A river in central and northern Peru, flowing 700 miles NE to the Amazon basin.

Huam·bo (wäm′bō) The former name of NOVA LISBOA.

hua·na·co (wä-nä′kō) See GUANACO.

hua·ra·che (wä-rä′chä) *n.* A Mexican sandal woven of strips of leather and having leather heel straps. Also **hua·ra′cho** (-chō). [<Am. Sp. <Quechua *huaraca* leather thong]

Huás·car (wäs′kär) An Inca ruler of Peru, 1495-1532, who was put to death by his brother Atahualpa.

Huas·ca·rán (wäs′kä-rän′) An extinct Andean volcano; the highest point in Peru; 22,205 feet.

hub (hub) *n.* **1** The central part of a wheel. **2** Anything central; a center of traffic. — **the Hub** Boston, Massachusetts. [Prob. var. of HOB]

hub·ba hub·ba (hub′ə hub′ə) *Colloq.* An exclamation expressing emphatic approval. [Imit.]

Hub·bard (hub′ərd), **Elbert Green,** 1856-1915, U.S. writer and publisher.

hub·ble (hub′əl) *n.* A small protuberance or lump, as in a road; roughness. [Dim. of HUB] — **hub′bly** (-lē) *adj.*

hub·ble-bub·ble (hub′əl-bub′əl) *n.* **1** A continuous bubbling or gurgling sound. **2** A hookah or water pipe. [Reduplication of BUBBLE]

hub·ble·show (hub′əl-shō′) *n. Brit. Dial.* Uproar; confusion.

hub·bub (hub′ub) *n.* A confused noise; uproar. See synonyms under NOISE, TUMULT. [Said to be an Irish cry]

Hu·ber·tus·burg (hōō′ber·təs·bōōrkh) A town in former Saxony, East Germany, east of Leipzig: scene of the signing of the treaty ending the Seven Years War, 1763.

hu·bris (hyōō′bris) *n.* Wanton arrogance. [<Gk.]

huck·a·back (huk′ə-bak) *n.* A coarse, durable linen or cotton cloth used for towels. Also **huck, huck′a·buck** (-buk). [Origin uncertain]

huck·le (huk′əl) *n.* The hip; also, a hump or projection resembling the hip. [Dim. of obs. *huck* hip; ult. origin unknown]

huck·le·ber·ry (huk′əl·ber′ē) *n. pl.* **·ries** **1** The edible black or dark-blue berry of a species of heath (genus *Gaylussacia*), often confused with the blueberry. **2** The European whortleberry. **3** The shrub producing either of these berries. Also called *hurtleberry, whortleberry.* [Prob. alter. of HURTLEBERRY]

Huck·le·ber·ry Finn (huk′əl·ber′ē fin′) The title character of Mark Twain's novel *The Adventures of Huckleberry Finn.*

huckle bone The innominate bone; hip bone.

huck·ster (huk′stər) *n.* **1** One who retails small wares, provisions, or the like; a peddler; hawker; especially, one who raises and sells

garden products. **2** A mean, venal fellow; a petty jobber or trickster. **3** *U.S. Slang* An advertising man. — *v.t.* **1** To put up for sale; peddle. **2** To haggle over. — *v.i.* **3** To haggle. [<MDu. *hoekster* <*heuken* retail] — **huck′ster·ism** *n.*

Hu·dai·da (hō-dā′də, -dī′-) See HODEIDA.

Hud·ders·field (hud′ərz·fēld) A county borough of SW Yorkshire, England.

hud·dle (hud′l) *v.* **hud·dled, hud·dling** *v.i.* **1** To crowd closely together, as from fear or for warmth. **2** To draw or hunch oneself together, as from cold. **3** In football, to gather in a huddle. — *v.t.* **4** To bring together in a group or mass. **5** To draw or hunch (oneself) together. **6** To make or do hurriedly or carelessly. **7** To push or put hastily or confusedly. — *n.* **1** A confused crowd or collection. **2** In football, the grouping of a team before each play, in which signals and instructions are given. **3** Any small, intimate conference. [Origin uncertain]

Hu·di·bras (hyōō′di·bras) Hero of Samuel Butler's *Hudibras,* a mock-heroic poem caricaturing the Puritans.

Hu·di·bras·tic (hyōō′di·bras′tik) *adj.* Pertaining to or in the style or meter of *Hudibras*; in tetrameter couplets, with elaborate, often comical, rimes.

Hud·son (hud′sən), **Henry,** died 1611?, English navigator in the service of Dutch merchants; explored the Hudson River, 1609; discovered Hudson Bay, 1611. — **William Henry,** 1841-1922, English author and naturalist.

Hudson Bay An inland sea in northern Canada; 850 miles long; 600 miles wide.

Hudson River A river in eastern New York State, flowing 306 miles south to New York Bay.

Hudson's Bay Company **1** A British joint-stock association chartered in 1670 to conduct the fur trade in lands beyond the Hudson Strait. **2** A large private corporation in Canada.

Hudson seal Muskrat fur dyed and trimmed to resemble Alaskan sealskin.

Hudson Strait The strait connecting Hudson Bay with the Atlantic Ocean; 450 miles long.

hue[1] (hyōō) *n.* **1** The particular shade of a color; that in which one color or shade differs from another; color; tint. **2** That attribute of a chromatic color, as red, green, blue, which determines the character of its difference from the nearest achromatic color. Compare BRIGHTNESS, LIGHTNESS, SATURATION. See COLOR. **3** A compound color, especially one in which one or more of the primary colors is predominant. **4** *Obs.* Appearance; form. ◆ Homophone: hew. [OE *heow* appearance]

hue[2] (hyōō) *n.* A vociferous cry; shouting. ◆ Homophone: hew. [<OF *hu* cry <*huer*]

Hué (hwä, hyōō·ä′) A port, capital of Central Vietnam.

hue and cry **1** A great stir and clamor about any matter. **2** Formerly, the common-law process of pursuing felons by shouts and cries until taken.

hued (hyōōd) *adj.* Having a hue or color: usually in combination: dark-*hued.*

Huel·va (wel′vä) A province of SW Spain; 3,894 square miles; capital, Huelva.

Hues·ca (wes′kä) **1** A province of NE Spain; 6,054 square miles. **2** Its capital, the former residence of the kings of Aragon.

huff (huf) *v.t.* **1** To offend; make angry. **2** To treat insolently or arrogantly; bully; hector. **3** *Obs.* To cause to swell; blow up. **4** In checkers, to remove (an opponent's piece) from the board as a forfeit for neglecting to capture an opposing piece. — *v.i.* **5** To be offended. **6** To puff; blow. **7** *Obs.* To puff or swell with anger or pride; bluster. — *n.* **1** Offense suddenly taken. **2** In checkers, the act of huffing. [Imit.]

huff·ish (huf′ish) *adj.* Petulant; irascible. — **huff′ish·ly** *adv.* — **huff′ish·ness** *n.*

huff·y (huf′ē) *adj.* **huff·i·er, huff·i·est** **1** Easily offended. **2** Puffed up. — **huff′i·ly** *adv.* — **huff′i·ness** *n.*

Hu·fuf (hōō-fōōf′) See HOFUF.

hug (hug) *v.* **hugged, hug·ging** *v.t.* **1** To clasp tightly within the arms, as from affection. **2** To keep fondly in the mind; cherish, as a belief or opinion. **3** To keep close to, as a

shore. — *v.i.* 4 To lie close; nestle. See synonyms under EMBRACE. — *n.* A close embrace. [Prob. <ON *hugga* console]

huge (hyōōj) *adj.* Having great bulk; vast. See synonyms under IMMENSE, LARGE. Also *Colloq.* **huge′ous.** [<OF *ahuge* high] — **huge′ly** *adv.* — **huge′ness** *n.*

hug·ger-mug·ger (hug′ər·mug′ər) *n.* 1 Secrecy; privacy. 2 Confusion and disorder. — *adj.* 1 Secret; sly. 2 Slovenly. [< obs. *hoker-moker*, prob. reduplication of ME *mokern* conceal]

Hug·gins (hug′inz), **Sir William,** 1824–1910, English astronomer.

Hugh (hyōō) A masculine personal name. Also **Hu·go** (hyōō′gō; *Dan., Du., Ger., Sw.* hōō′gō; *Pg., Sp.* ōō′gō), *Fr.* **Hugues** (üg). [<Gmc., intelligent]
— **Hugh Ca·pet** (kā′pit, kap′it; *Fr.* kȧ·pe′), 940?–996, king of France 987–996, founder of the Capetian dynasty.

Hughes (hyōōz), **Charles Evans,** 1862–1948, U.S. jurist and statesman; chief justice, U.S. Supreme Court 1930–41. — **(James) Langston,** 1902–1967, U.S. poet and author. — **Thomas,** 1822–96, English author.

hug-me-tight (hug′mē·tīt′) *n.* A short, close-fitting jacket, usually knitted.

Hu·go (hyōō′gō, *Fr.* ü·gō′), **Victor (Marie),** 1802–85, French poet, novelist, and dramatist.

Hu·gue·not (hyōō′gə·not) *n.* A French Protestant of the 16th and 17th centuries: persecuted during the religious wars of the time. [<F <G *Eidgenoss* confederate] — **Hu′gue·not′ic** *adj.*

Hu·gue·not·ism (hyōō′gə·not′iz·əm) *n.* The doctrines of the Huguenots; French Protestantism.

huh (hu) *interj.* An exclamation of inquiry, surprise, contempt, etc. [Imit.]

Hui·la (wē′lä), **Ne·va·do del** (nā·vä′thō thel) A volcanic peak in south central Colombia; 18,865 feet.

hu·la (hōō′lə) *n.* A native Hawaiian dance performed by women, with intricate arm movements that tell a story in pantomime. Also **hu′la-hu′la.** [<Hawaiian]

Hu·la (hōō′lä), **Lake** An expansion of the Jordan headwaters in NE Israel near the Syrian border: also *Waters of Merom.* Also **Hu′le** (-le).

hulk (hulk) *n.* 1 The body of a ship or decked vessel, especially of an old, unseaworthy vessel, or of one wrecked. 2 An old ship used for a prison or for purposes other than seagoing. 3 Any bulky or unwieldy object or person. 4 A heavy, clumsy ship. — *v.i.* 1 To rise or loom bulkily: usually with *up.* 2 *Brit. Dial.* To lounge or slouch in a lazy, clumsy manner. [OE *hulc* ship, prob. < Med. L *hulcus* <Gk. *holkas* towed vessel < *hélkein* drag]

hulk·ing (hul′king) *adj.* Bulky; unwieldy. Also **hulk′y.**

hull (hul) *n.* 1 The outer covering, as of a kernel of grain or of a nut; husk; pod; also, any outer covering; specifically, in the plural, garments, clothes. 2 *Naut.* The body of a ship, exclusive of the masts, sails, yards, and rigging. 3 *Aeron.* The main covered structure of a rigid airship; also, that part of a flying boat which rests upon the water. — *v.t.* 1 To shell; free from the hull. 2 To strike or pierce the hull of (a vessel). [OE *hulu* a covering] — **hull′er** *n.*

Hull (hul), **Cordell,** 1871–1955, U.S. secretary of state 1933–44. — **Isaac,** 1773–1843, American commodore.

Hull (hul) A port in SE Yorkshire, England: officially *Kingston-upon-Hull.*

hul·la·ba·loo (hul′ə·bə·lōō′) *n.* A loud and confused noise; uproar; tumult. Also **hul′la·bal·loo′.** [Imit. reduplication of HULLO]

hull down *Naut.* So far away as to have the hull hidden by the curvature of the earth.

hul·lo (hə·lō′) See HALLOO.

hum[1] (hum) *v.* **hummed, hum·ming** *v.i.* 1 To make a low, continuous, buzzing sound, as a bee. 2 To sing with the lips closed, not articulating the words. 3 To give forth a confused, indistinct sound, as of mingled voices. 4 To pause in speaking, as from confusion; hem. 5 *Colloq.* To be busily active: The office *hummed.* — *v.t.* 6 To sing, as a tune, with the lips closed. 7 To put into a specified state or condition by humming: to *hum* someone to sleep. See synonyms under SING. — *n.* A low, monotonous, or inarticulate sound (as of *h′m*). — *interj.* A sound as of *h′m* or *hem.* [Imit.] — **hum′mer** *n.*

hu·man (hyōō′mən) *adj.* 1 Pertaining to or characterizing man or mankind. See synonyms under HUMANE. 2 Possessed by or suitable for man. — *n. Colloq.* One of the human race; a human being. [<OF *humain* <L *humanus*] — **hu′man·ness** *n.*

hu·mane (hyōō·mān′) *adj.* 1 Having or showing kindness and tenderness; compassionate. 2 Tending to refine; polite; elegant. [Var. of HUMAN] — **hu·mane′ly** *adv.* — **hu·mane′ness** *n.*
Synonyms: benevolent, benignant, charitable, clement, compassionate, forgiving, gentle, gracious, human, kind, kind-hearted, merciful, pitying, sympathetic, tender, tender-hearted. *Human* denotes what pertains to mankind, with no suggestion as to its being good or evil. *Humane* denotes what may rightly be expected of mankind at its best in the treatment of sentient beings; a *humane* enterprise or endeavor is one that is intended to prevent or relieve suffering. The *humane* man will not needlessly inflict pain upon the meanest thing that lives; a *merciful* man is disposed to withhold or mitigate the suffering even of the guilty. The *compassionate* man sympathizes with and desires to relieve actual suffering, while one who is *humane* would forestall and prevent the suffering which he sees to be possible. Compare GOOD, PITIFUL. *Antonyms*: barbarous, brutal, cruel, fierce, ferocious, inhuman, merciless, pitiless, ruthless, savage, selfish, unmerciful, unpitying.

hu·man·ism (hyōō′mən·iz′əm) *n.* 1 Culture derived from classical training; polite learning. 2 A system of thinking in which man, his interests and development are made central and dominant, tending to exalt the cultural and practical rather than the scientific and speculative. 3 Humanity.

Hu·man·ism (hyōō′mən·iz′əm) *n.* The intellectual, scientific, and literary movement of the 14th to 16th centuries which exalted Greek and Roman culture and learning: opposed to *Scholasticism.*

hu·man·ist (hyōō′mən·ist) *n.* 1 One versed in the study of humanities; a classical scholar. 2 One who is versed in human nature. — **hu′man·is′tic** *adj.* — **hu′man·is′ti·cal·ly** *adv.*

hu·man·i·tar·i·an (hyōō·man′ə·târ′ē·ən) *n.* 1 One who is broadly philanthropic and humane: a philanthropist. 2 One who seeks to forward the welfare of humanity by ameliorating pain and suffering in any of their manifestations. 3 One who believes that Christ was a mere man; an anti-Trinitarian. 4 One who holds that the perfectibility of the human race is attainable without superhuman aid. — *adj.* Of or pertaining to humanitarianism or the humanitarians.

hu·man·i·tar·i·an·ism (hyōō·man′ə·târ′ē·ən·iz′·əm) *n.* 1 The doctrines, principles, or practices of humanitarians, in any sense. 2 In Comtism, the theory that humanity is the ultimate reality.

hu·man·i·ty (hyōō·man′ə·tē) *n. pl.* **·ties** 1 Mankind collectively. 2 Human nature. 3 The state or quality of being human. 4 The state or quality of being humane; also, a humane act. 5 *pl.* The branches of learning including literature, language, and philosophy, especially as distinguished from the natural and social sciences. [<OF *humanité* <L *humanitas, -tatis* < *humanus* human]
Synonyms: civilization, culture, refinement; (*pl.* the humanities) belles-lettres. See BENEVOLENCE, MANKIND. *Antonyms*: barbarism, boorishness, coarseness, rudeness.

hu·man·ize (hyōō′mən·īz) *v.t.* & *v.i.* **·ized, ·iz·ing** To make or become humane or human. Also *Brit.* **hu′man·ise.** — **hu′man·i·za′tion** (-ə·zā′shən, -ī·zā′-) *n.*

hu·man·kind (hyōō′mən·kīnd′) *n.* The human race. See synonyms under MANKIND.

hu·man·ly (hyōō′mən·lē) *adv.* 1 In accordance with man's nature. 2 Within human power or experience. 3 In a humane or kindly manner.

hu·ma·noid (hyōō′mə·noid) *adj.* 1 Resembling a human being in structure, function, and general appearance. 2 Imperfectly or deceptively human. — *n.* An imaginary creature having some resemblance to a human being.

hu·ma·num est er·ra·re (hyōō·mā′nəm est e·rā′rē) *Latin* To err is human.

Hu·ma·yun (hōō·mä′yōōn), 1508–56, Mogul emperor of India: also *Houmayoun.*

Hum·ber (hum′bər) An estuary of the Ouse and Trent rivers, flowing into the North Sea from the NE English coast.

Hum·bert (hum′bərt) A masculine personal name. [<Gmc., bright giant]
— **Humbert I,** 1844–1900, king of Italy 1878–1900; assassinated. — **Humbert II,** born 1904, Prince of Piedmont, king of Italy May to June 1946; abdicated.

hum·ble (hum′bəl) *adj.* **·bler, ·blest** 1 Having or expressing a sense of inferiority, dependence, or unworthiness; meek. 2 Lowly in condition; unpretending; obscure. 3 Lowly in feeling or manner; submissive; deferential. — *v.t.* **hum·bled, hum·bling** 1 To reduce the pride of; make meek; humiliate. 2 To lower in rank or dignity; abase. [<F <L *humilis* low < *humus* ground] — **hum′ble·ness** *n.* — **hum′bler** *n.* — **hum′bling** *adj.* — **hum′bling·ly** *adv.* — **hum′bly** *adv.*
Synonyms (adj.): low, lowly, meek, modest, obscure, poor, submissive, unassuming, unobtrusive, unpretending, unpretentious. See MODEST. *Antonyms*: arrogant, boastful, exalted, haughty, high, lofty, presuming, pretentious, proud.

hum·ble-bee (hum′bəl·bē′) *n.* A bumblebee. [ME *humbylbee* < *humbler,* freq. of HUM + BEE]

humble pie A pie made of the humbles of a deer, formerly served to the huntsmen and servants at hunting feasts. — **to eat humble pie** To make humble apologies; be humiliated: also **to eat umble pie.**

hum·bles (hum′bəlz) *n. pl.* The entrails, etc., of a deer. [<OF *numbles* <L *lumbulus,* dim. of *lumbus* loin]

Hum·boldt (hum′bōlt, *Ger.* hōōm′bōlt), **Baron (Friedrich Heinrich) Alexander von,** 1769–1859, German naturalist and explorer. — **Baron (Karl) Wilhelm von,** 1767–1835, German philologist, statesman, and poet.

Hum·boldt Bay (hum′bōlt) A Pacific inlet on the coast of NW California.

Humboldt River A river in northern Nevada, flowing 300 miles SW to the **Humboldt Sink,** a lake in west central Nevada.

hum·bug (hum′bug) *n.* 1 Anything intended or calculated to deceive; a sham. 2 An impostor. 3 The spirit or practice of deception; sham. See synonyms under QUACK[2]. — *v.* **·bugged, ·bug·ging** *v.t.* To impose upon; deceive. — *v.i.* To practice deceit. [Origin unknown] — **hum′bug·ger** *n.* — **hum′bug·ger·y** *n.*

hum·ding·er (hum·ding′ər) *n. Slang* One who or that which excels.

hum·drum (hum′drum′) *adj.* Without interest; tedious. — *n.* 1 Monotonous existence; tedious talk; anything tiresome. 2 A dull or tedious fellow; bore. [<HUM + DRUM]

Hume (hyōōm), **David,** 1711–76, Scottish historian and philosopher.

hu·mec·tant (hyōō·mek′tənt) *adj.* Moistening. — *n.* A moistening preparation or drug; a diluent. [<L *humectans, -antis,* ppr. of *humectare* moisten]

hu·mer·al (hyōō′mər·əl) *adj.* 1 Of or pertaining to the humerus. 2 Of or pertaining to the shoulder. [<L *humerus* shoulder]

humeral veil *Eccl.* A veil or scarf worn round the shoulders by the subdeacon at high mass from the offertory to the paternoster, and also by the officiating priest in processions and benediction of the sacrament.

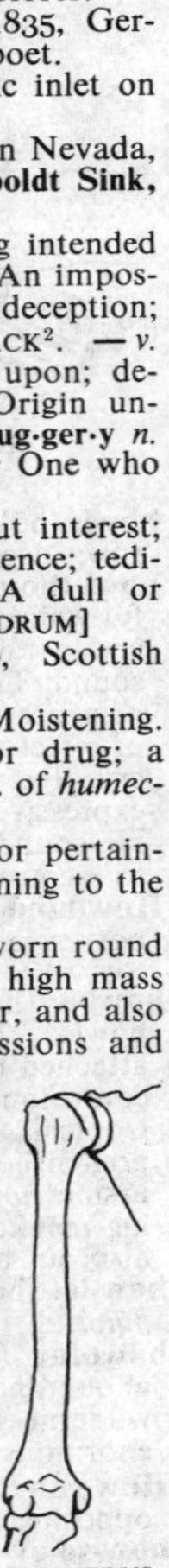
HUMERUS

hu·mer·us (hyōō′mər·əs) *n. pl.* **·mer·i** (-mər·ī) 1 *Anat.* The bone of the upper part of the arm or forelimb; also, the upper arm or brachium. 2 *Entomol.* **a** The front upper corner or angle of the thorax of a wing cover or elytron. **b** The subcostal nervure in the forewings of certain *Hymenoptera,* or femur of a foreleg in *Orthoptera.* ◆ Homophone: *humorous.* [<L, shoulder]

Hum·fried (hōōm′frēt) Dutch and German form of HUMPHREY. Also *Sw.* **Hum′frid.**

hu·mic (hyōō′mik) *adj.* Of, pertaining to, or derived from humus. [<L *humus* ground, soil]

hu·mic·o·lous (hyōō·mik′ə·ləs) *adj. Bot.* Of or pertaining to plants growing on medium-dry soil. [<L *humus* soil + *colere* dwell]

hu·mid (hyōō′mid) *adj.* Containing sensible moisture; damp. [<L *humidus* <*humere, umere* be moist] —**hu′mid·ly** *adv.*

hu·mid·i·fy (hyōō·mid′ə·fī) *v.t.* **·fied, ·fy·ing** To make moist or humid, as the atmosphere of a room. —**hu·mid′i·fi·ca′tion** *n.*

hu·mid·i·stat (hyōō·mid′ə·stat) *n.* A device for measuring the relative humidity of air.

hu·mid·i·ty (hyōō·mid′ə·tē) *n.* **1** Moisture; dampness. **2** *Meteorol.* The percentage of water vapor in the air to the total amount possible at the same temperature (**relative humidity**). The actual amount of water vapor per unit of volume is known as **absolute humidity.** Also **hu′mid·ness.** [<OF *humidité* <L *humiditas* <*humidus* humid]

hu·mi·dor (hyōō′mə·dôr) *n.* **1** A place for storing cigars or tobacco where the percentage of moisture is regulated; also, a small box fitted for the same purpose. **2** *Printing* A cabinet in which mats are stored to keep them sufficiently moist for proper impression by type.

hu·mil·i·ate (hyōō·mil′ē·āt) *v.t.* **·at·ed, ·at·ing** To lower or offend the pride or self–respect of. See synonyms under ABASE, ABASH. [<L *humiliatus,* pp. of *humiliare* <*humilis* lowly] —**hu·mil′i·at′ing, hu·mil′i·a·to′ry** (-tôr′ē, -tō′rē) *adj.*

hu·mil·i·a·tion (hyōō·mil′ē·ā′shən) *n.* The act of humiliating, or the state of being humiliated; abasement; mortification; also, that which humiliates. See synonyms under CHAGRIN.

hu·mil·i·ty (hyōō·mil′ə·tē) *n. pl.* **·ties 1** The quality of being humble. **2** Deference; courtesy; kindness. **3** An act of submission or of humbleness. [<L *humilitas, -tatis* lowness]

hu·mit (hyōō′mit) *n.* One degree in the measurement of humiture.

hu·mi·ture (hyōō′mə·chər) *n.* The combined effect of humidity and temperature; expressed quantitatively by adding the values of the relative humidity and the temperature and dividing by 2. [<HUMI(DITY) + (TEMPERA)TURE; coined (1937) by O. F. Hevener, U.S. banker]

hum·mel (hum′əl) *Scot. n.* **1** A cow or other animal with its horns broken off. **2** Grain with the awns broken off. —*adj.* **1** Without horns. **2** Without awns. —*v.t.* **·meled** or **·melled, ·mel·ing** or **·mel·ling** To remove the horns or awns of.

hum·ming (hum′ing) *adj.* **1** Making a low murmuring or buzzing. **2** Lively; frothing; hence, strong or stimulating. **3** *Colloq.* Speedy; spirited. —**hum′ming·ly** *adv.*

hum·ming·bird (hum′ing·bûrd′) *n.* A small, brilliantly colored bird of the New World (family *Trochilidae*), mostly tropical, related to the swifts. They feed chiefly upon insects and the sweets of flowers, and are named from the humming sound produced by the rapid motion of their wings as they hover over the flowers. The common hummingbird of the eastern United States is known as the *rubythroat.*

hummingbird moth The hawk moth.

hum·mock (hum′ək) *n.* **1** A small elevation; hillock. See HAMMOCK². **2** A pile or ridge of ice on an ice field. [Origin unknown] —**hum′mock·y** *adj.*

hu·mor (hyōō′mər, yōō′-) *n.* **1** Disposition of mind or feeling; caprice; freak; whim. **2** A facetious turn of thought; playful fancy; jocularity; drollery. **3** The capacity to perceive, appreciate, or express what is funny, amusing, incongruous, ludicrous, etc.; also, the capacity to make something seem funny, amusing, ludicrous, etc.; specifically in literature, the expression of this in speech or action. **4** Moisture; specifically, an animal fluid: the serous *humor.* In medieval times, the humors, consisting of blood, phlegm, yellow bile, and black bile, were supposed to give rise to the sanguine, phlegmatic, choleric, and melancholic temperaments, respectively. **5** *Pathol.* Any chronic cutaneous eruption supposed to be due to disorder of the blood. See synonyms under FANCY, TEMPER, WHIM, WIT. —**out of humor** Irritated; annoyed. —*v.t.* **1** To comply with the moods or caprices of. **2** To accommodate or adapt oneself to. See synonyms under INDULGE. Also *Brit.* **hu′mour.** [<OF <L *umor* <*umere* be moist]

hu·mor·al (hyōō′mər·əl, yōō′-) *adj.* Relating to or arising from the humors of the body.

hu·mor·esque (hyōō′mə·resk′) *n. Music* A lively or fanciful instrumental composition. [<G *humoreske*]

hu·mor·ism (hyōō′mər·iz′əm, yōō′-) *n.* **1** The theory that disease proceeds from vitiated humors in the body. **2** The spirit of a humorist. Also **hu·mor·al·ism** (hyōō′mər·əl·iz′əm)

hu·mor·ist (hyōō′mər·ist, yōō′-) *n.* **1** One who displays or exercises humor; a wag. **2** A professional writer or entertainer whose work is humorous. —**hu′mor·is′tic** *adj.*

hu·mor·ous (hyōō′mər·əs, yōō′-) *adj.* **1** Adapted to excite merriment; amusing. **2** Moved by caprice; whimsical; also, irritable; peevish. **3** *Obs.* Humid; watery; moist. ◆ Homophone: *humerus.* —**hu′mor·ous·ly** *adv.* —**hu′mor·ous·ness** *n.*

Synonyms: amusing, comic, comical, droll, facetious, funny, jocose, jocular, ludicrous, sportive, witty. See JOCOSE. *Antonyms:* dreary, dull, grave, melancholy, mournful, sad, serious, sober, solemn.

hu·mor·some (hyōō′mər·səm, yōō′-) *adj.* **1** Full of humor or whims. **2** Characterized by humor; droll. —**hu′mor·some·ly** *adv.* —**hu′· mor·some·ness** *n.*

hu·mous (hyōō′məs) *adj.* Relating to or derived from the ground or humus. [<HUMUS]

hump (hump) *n.* **1** A protuberance, especially that formed by a curved spine or a fleshy growth on the back: the *hump* of a camel or bison. **2** A mound in a railroad switchyard up one side of which cars are taken by an engine and then allowed to coast down the other; hence, any obstacle. **3** *Brit. Slang* An attack of ill temper; blues. **4** *Colloq.* A long tramp or hike, especially with a load on the back. —**over the hump** Beyond the point where force or effort is needed; at the point where all is easy going. —**The Hump** The Himalayas: name applied by aviators in World War II. —*v.t.* **1** To bend or round (the back) in a hump; hunch. **2** *U.S. Slang* To put forth great effort: used reflexively: *Hump* yourself. **3** *Austral. Slang* To carry on the shoulders or back; also, to carry. [Origin uncertain]

hump·back (hump′bak′) *n.* **1** A crooked back. **2** A hunchback. **3** A whalebone whale (genus *Megaptera*) with a low humplike dorsal fin. —**hump′backed′** *adj.*

Hum·per·dinck (hŏŏm′pər·dingk), **Engelbert,** 1854–1921, German composer.

humph (humf) *interj.* An exclamation of doubt or dissatisfaction. [<HUM¹]

Hum·phrey (hum′frē) A masculine personal name. Also *Lat.* **Hum·phre·dus** (hum·frē′dəs). [<Gmc., peaceful giant]
— **Humphrey,** 1391–1447, Duke of Gloucester, son of Henry IV of England; Protector during minority of Henry VI: called "the Good Duke."
— **Humphrey, Hubert Horatio,** 1911–1978, American politician, vice president of the United States, 1965–69.

Hum·phrey Island (hum′frē) See MANIHIKI.

Hump·ty Dump·ty (hump′tē dump′tē) A personified egg in English and European nursery rhyme; an important character in Lewis Carroll's *Through the Looking–Glass.*

hump·y¹ (hum′pē) *adj.* **hump·i·er, hump·i·est** Marked by or covered with humps.

hump·y² (hum′pē) *n. Austral.* Any small hut or shack. [<native Australian]

hu·mus (hyōō′məs) *n.* The organic matter of the soil, usually leaf mold and other materials, in which decomposition is well advanced. [<L, ground]

Hun (hun) *n.* **1** One of a barbarous nomadic Asian people which invaded Europe in the fourth and fifth centuries. See ATTILA. **2** Any barbarous or destructive warrior; a vandal. [OE *Hune* <LL *Hunnus*]—**Hun′nish** *adj.* —**Hun′nish·ness** *n.*

Hu·nan (hōō′nän′) A province in south central China; 80,000 square miles; capital, Changsha.

hunch (hunch) *n.* **1** A hump. **2** A lump or hunk. **3** A sudden shove. **4** *U.S. Colloq.* A premonition: from the belief that good luck attends the touching of a hunchback's hunch. —*v.t.* **1** To bend, as the back, so as to form

a hump; arch. **2** *Obs.* To push or jostle. —*v.i.* **3** To move or thrust oneself forward. [Origin uncertain]

hunch·back (hunch′bak′) *n.* A person having a crooked or deformed back. —**hunch′backed′** *adj.*

hun·der (hun′dər) *adj. & n. Scot.* Hundred.

hun·dred (hun′drid) *adj.* Being one more than ninety–nine; ten times ten. —*n.* **1** The product of ten multiplied by ten; the number following ninety–nine; also, the symbols (100, c, C) representing it. ◆ Collateral adjective: *cental.* **2** An ancient subdivision of a county, common in England and Ireland and still used in the State of Delaware. [OE]

Hundred Days, the The period from March 20 to June 28, 1815, between Napoleon's arrival in Paris after his escape from Elba and the restoration of Louis XVIII after Waterloo.

hun·dred·fold (hun′drid·fōld′) *n.* An amount or number a hundred times as great as a given unit. —*adj.* Indicating a hundred times as much or as many; centuplicate. —*adv.* By a hundred: now always used with *a* (in British usage, with *an*).

hun·dred–per·cent·er (hun′drid·pər·sen′tər) *n. Colloq.* An overpatriotic person; a Jingo.

hun·dredth (hun′dridth) *n.* **1** The last in a series of a hundred. **2** One of a hundred equal parts of anything; the quotient of a unit divided by one hundred. —*adj.* **1** Being the tenth group of ten in order after the ninetieth: the ordinal of *one hundred.* **2** Being one of a hundred equal parts.

hun·dred·weight (hun′drid·wāt′) *n.* A weight commonly reckoned in the United States at 100 pounds avoirdupois, in England at 112 pounds. Abbreviated *cwt.*

Hundred Years' War See table under WAR.

Hun·e·ker (hun′ə·kər), **James Gibbons,** 1860–1921, U.S. author and critic.

hung (hung) Past tense and past participle of HANG.

Hun·gar·i·an (hung·gâr′ē·ən) *adj.* Of or pertaining to Hungary, its people, or their language. —*n.* **1** A native or citizen of Hungary; one of a people formerly Magyar, Ruthenian, Slovak, Serbo–Croatian, German, etc., existing side by side: now dominantly Magyar; hence, a Magyar. **2** The Finno–Ugric language of the Hungarians: also called *Magyar.* [<Med. L *Hungarus*]

Hun·ga·ry (hung′gə·rē) A state in central Europe; 35,902 square miles; capital, Budapest. Hungarian *Magyarország.* Officially **Hungarian People's Republic.**

hun·ger (hung′gər) *n.* **1** Craving for food; also, the weakness caused by the lack of it. **2** Any strong desire. —*v.i.* **1** To feel hunger; be hungry. **2** To have a craving or desire: with *for* or *after.* —*v.t.* **3** To starve; famish. [OE]

hun·ger–strike (hung′gər·strīk′) *n.* Persistent abstention from food in order to obtain concessions from authority: sometimes practiced by prisoners with the object of securing release or a melioration of punishment.

Hung·nam (hŏŏng·näm′) A city of North Korea. Japanese **Ko·nan** (kō·nän).

hun·gry (hung′grē) *adj.* **·gri·er, ·gri·est 1** Having a keen appetite; suffering from want of food. **2** Eagerly desiring; craving. **3** Indicating hunger. **4** Poor or barren. See synonyms under GAUNT. [OE *hungrig* <*hunger*] —**hun′gri·ly** *adv.* —**hun′gri·ness** *n.*

Hung–shui (hŏŏng′shwā′) A river in southern China, flowing 900 miles to the West River.

hung up *Slang* **1** Psychologically disturbed; especially, preoccupied or obsessed. **2** Sidetracked or impeded, as from a natural or normal process: *hung up* on legal technicalities.

hunk (hungk) *n. Colloq.* A large piece; lump. [Prob. <Flemish *hunke*]

hun·ker (hung′kər) *v.i.* To squat or stoop so that the body rests on the calves of the legs. —*n. pl.* The buttocks resting on the calves of the legs. —**on one's hunkers** In a stooping or squatting position.

Hun·ker (hung′kər) *n.* **1** A member of one of the conservative factions of the Democratic party in New York State in 1842: opposed to the *Barnburners.* **2** Hence, one opposed to political progress; old fogy. [? <Du. *honk* home, goal]

hun·ker·ish (hung′kər·ish) *adj.* Extremely conservative. —**hun′ker·ism** *n.*
hunks (hungks) *n. sing.* & *pl.* A niggardly fellow; miser. [Origin unknown]
hunk·y (hung′kē) See BOHUNK.
hun·ky–do·ry (hung′kē·dôr′ē, -dō′rē) *adj. U.S. Slang* Done satisfactorily or in a satisfactory condition; all right. Also **hunk′y.** [Fanciful extension of slang *hunky* safe, satisfactory]
hunt (hunt) *v.t.* **1** To pursue (game or other wild animals) for the purpose of killing or catching. **2 a** To search (a region) for game. **b** To search (a place): to *hunt* a room. **3** To search for diligently; look for. **4** To manage or use in hunting: to *hunt* a pack of hounds. **5** To chase or drive away; pursue. **6** To persecute; harass. —*v.i.* **7** To pursue game or other wild animals; follow the chase. **8** To make a search; seek. **9** *Aeron.* To make weaving motions about its normal flight path, as an aircraft or guided missile. **10** *Mech.* To run alternately fast and slow owing to unsteady action in the governor: said of stationary engines, etc. —**to hunt down 1** To pursue until caught or killed. **2** To search for until found. —**to hunt up 1** To search for until found. **2** To go in search of. —*n.* **1** The act of hunting game; chase. **2** A search. **3** An association of huntsmen; the participants in a hunt. **4** A district hunted over. —**still hunt 1** A hunting for game in quiet manner. **2** Any quiet and cautious hunt for something. [OE *huntian*]
Synonyms (noun): chase, hunting, inquisition, pursuit, search. A *hunt* may be either the act of pursuing or the act of seeking, or a combination of the two. A *chase* or *pursuit* is after that which is fleeing or departing; a *search* is for that which is hidden; a *hunt* may be for that which is either hidden or fleeing; a *search* is a minute and careful seeking, and is especially applied to a locality; we make a *search* of or through a house, for an object, in which connection it would be colloquial to say a *hunt. Hunt* never quite loses its association with field sports, where it includes both *search* and *chase*; the *search* till the game is hunted out, and the *chase* till it is hunted down. Figuratively, we speak of literary *pursuits*, or of the *pursuit* of knowledge; a *search* for reasons; the *chase* of fame or honor; *hunt*, in figurative use, inclines to the unfavorable sense of *inquisition*, but with aggressiveness; as, a *hunt* for heresy.
Hunt (hunt), **(James Henry) Leigh,** 1784–1859, English poet and essayist. —**William Holman** See HOLMAN-HUNT.
hunt·er (hun′tər) *n.* **1** A person who hunts in any way; especially, one who hunts game. **2** A horse or dog used in hunting. **3** A hunting watch.
Hunt·er (hun′tər), **John,** 1728–93, Scottish surgeon and anatomist.
Hun·ter River (hun′tər) A river in eastern New South Wales, Australia, flowing 287 miles SW to the Pacific.
hunt·er's–green (hun′tərz·grēn′) *n.* A dark, dull-green color formerly used for hunting costume. Also **hunt′er–green′.**
hunt·ing (hun′ting) *n.* The act of pursuing, as game.
hunting bit Snafflebit.
hunting case The case of a hunting watch, designed with a hinged cover for the crystal.
Hunt·ing·don (hun′ting·dən) A county in east central England; 366 square miles; county seat, Huntingdon. Also **Hunt′ing·don·shire** (-shir). Shortened form **Hunts.**
hunting knife A long, sharp, single- or double-edged knife used by hunters and campers.
Hunt·ing·ton (hun′ting·tən), **Collis Potter,** 1821–1900, U.S. railroad builder. —**Ellsworth,** 1876–1947, U.S. geographer and explorer. —**Samuel,** 1731–96, Connecticut patriot; signer of the Declaration of Independence.
Hunt·ing·ton (hun′ting·tən) A city on the Ohio River in western West Virginia.
hunting watch A watch having the dial side as well as the reverse protected by a metal cap or lid.
hunt·ress (hun′tris) *n.* A woman who hunts.
hunts·man (hunts′mən) *n. pl.* **·men** (-mən) **1** One who practices hunting. **2** The attendant who has charge of the pack of hounds in a hunt.
hunts·man's–cup (hunts′mənz·kup′) *n.* The common American pitcherplant.
hunt's–up (hunts′up′) *n.* A tune played on a horn to awaken huntsmen in the morning; hence, anything that awakens.
Hun·ya·dy (hōōn′yô·dē), **Já·nos** (yä′nôsh), 1385?–1456, Hungarian general and national hero; checked the Moslem advance in SE Europe. Also **Hun′ya·di.**
Hu·on de Bor·deaux (ü·ôn′ də bôr·dō′) The hero of a 13th century French *chanson de geste* belonging to the Charlemagne cycle.
Hu·on pine (hyōō′on) A large evergreen tree (*Dacrydium franklini*) growing in Tasmania. [from *Huon* River, Tasmania]
Hu·peh (hōō′pe′) A province in east central China; 70,000 square miles; capital, Wuchang. Also **Hu′pei′.**
hur·cheon (hûr′chən) *n. Brit. Dial.* **1** An urchin. **2** A hedgehog.
hur·dle (hûr′dəl) *n.* **1** A movable framework wattled together and used for making fences, etc. **2** A framework to be leaped over in racing. **3** Formerly, a sledge for conveying criminals to execution. **4** *pl.* A race over hurdles. —*v.* **·dled, ·dling** *v.t.* **1** To leap over, as an obstacle in a race. **2** To make, cover, or enclose with hurdles. **3** To surmount (a difficulty, etc.). —*v.i.* **4** To leap over hurdles, obstacles, etc. [OE *hyrdel*] —**hur′dler** *n.*

HURDLE (*def. 2*)

hur·dles (hûr′dəlz) *n. pl. Scot.* The loins; buttocks.
hurds (hûrdz) See HARDS.
hur·dy–gur·dy (hûr′dē·gûr′dē) *n. pl.* **·dies** One of various musical instruments played by turning a crank; specifically, a hand organ played by street musicians. [Appar. imit. of the instrument]
hurl (hûrl) *v.t.* **1** To throw with violence; fling. **2** To throw down; overthrow. **3** To utter with vehemence. —*v.i.* **4** *Rare* To throw a missile. **5** In baseball, to pitch. See synonyms under SEND. —*n.* The act of throwing with violence; a cast. [ME *hurlen*, ? <Scand. Cf. Dan. *hurle* whirr, Norw. *hurla* buzz.]
hurl·bar·row (hûrl′bar′ō) *n. Scot.* A wheelbarrow.
hur·ley (hûr′lē) *n. Irish* The game of hurling.
hur·ley–hack·et (hûr′lē·hak′it) *n.* A small trough or sledge for sliding down a steep hill or an inclined plane. [Origin uncertain]
hurl·ing (hûr′ling) *n.* **1** A former game similar to football. **2** In Ireland, the game of hockey. [<HURL]
hur·ly (hûr′lē) *n. pl.* **·lies** Confusion; noise; uproar.
hur·ly–bur·ly (hûr′lē·bûr′lē) *n. pl.* **·lies** Tumult; uproar. See synonyms under TUMULT. [Origin uncertain]
Hu·ron (hyŏŏr′on) *n.* A member of any one of four confederated tribes of North American Indians of Iroquoian stock, originally occupying the territory between Lakes Huron and Ontario: destroyed or dispersed by Iroquois tribes to the south of them, 1648–50. [<F, ruffian]
Hu·ron (hyŏŏr′ən), **Lake** The second largest of the Great Lakes of North America, between Michigan and Ontario; 23,200 square miles.
hur·rah (hōō·rô′, hə·rä′) *interj.* An exclamation expressing triumph or joy. —*n.* A shout of triumph. —*v.t.* To cheer, as a speaker, with hurrahs. —*v.i.* To shout a hurrah or hurrahs: sometimes spelled *hooray.* Also **hur·ra′.** [Imit. Cf. Sw., Dan. *hurra!* and Du. *hoera!*]
hur·rah's–nest (hōō·rôz′nest′, hə·räz′-) *n.* A disorderly, untidy mess; wild confusion. [Origin unknown]
hur·ri·cane (hûr′ə·kān) *n. Meteorol.* **1** A tropical cyclone, especially one originating in the West Indies. **2** In the Beaufort scale, a wind force of the 12th or highest degree, moving at more than 75 miles an hour. Also *Obs.* **hur′ri·ca′no** (-kā′nō). See synonyms under CYCLONE. [<Sp. *huracán* <Cariban]
hurricane deck *Naut.* The upper deck of a passenger steamer, as those on the larger rivers of the United States.
hur·ry (hûr′ē) *v.* **hur·ried, hur·ry·ing** *v.i.* **1** To act or move rapidly or in haste; hasten. —*v.t.* **2** To cause or urge to act or move more rapidly: often with *up.* **3** To cause to act or move too hastily: I was *hurried* into it. **4** To hasten the progress, completion, etc., of, often unduly: to *hurry* a decision. See synonyms under HUSTLE, QUICKEN. —*n. pl.* **hur·ries** **1** Haste; precipitation. **2** The act of hurrying. [Origin uncertain] —**hur′ried** *adj.* —**hur′ried·ly** *adv.* —**hur′ried·ness** *n.*
hur·ry–scur·ry (hûr′ē·skûr′ē) *v.i.* To rush in haste and confusion; act hurriedly. —*adj.* Hurried; confused. —*n.* Hasty, confused, or disorderly movement; bustling haste. —*adv.* With disorderly haste; pell-mell; confusedly.
Hurst·mon·ceux (hûrst′mən·sōō′, hûrs′-) See HERSTMONCEUX.
hurt (hûrt) *v.* **hurt, hurt·ing** *v.t.* **1** To cause physical harm or suffering to; injure. **2** To cause material damage to; mark; score. **3** To have a bad effect on; do harm to: Another drink won't *hurt* you. **4** To cause mental suffering to; grieve; worry. —*v.i.* **5** To cause suffering: My feet *hurt.* **6** To cause damage, hurt, etc. —*n.* **1** An injury, especially one causing pain, as a bruise. **2** Damage; detriment. **3** An injury to the feelings; a slight. [<OF *hurter* hit] —**hurt′er** *n.*
Synonyms (verb): afflict, damage, grieve, harm, impair, injure, mar, pain, wound. See VIOLATE. *Antonyms*: benefit, comfort, console, delight, heal, help, please, profit, rejoice, relieve, repair, soothe.
hur·ter (hûr′tər) *n.* **1** The shoulder of the axle of a vehicle, or a reenforcing piece thereon. **2** A buffer, to check the motion of a gun carriage. [<F *heurtoir* knocker]
hurt·ful (hûrt′fəl) *adj.* Causing hurt. See synonyms under BAD, INIMICAL, NOISOME, PERNICIOUS. —**hurt′ful·ly** *adv.* —**hurt′ful·ness** *n.*
Hürt·gen (hürt′gən) A village in North Rhine-Westphalia, Germany, near **Hürtgen Forest,** scene of heavy fighting (November, 1944) in World War II.
hur·tle (hûr′təl) *v.* **hur·tled, hur·tling** *v.i.* **1** To come with violence or noise; crash: with *against* or *together.* **2** To make a crashing, rushing sound; move with noisy speed: The shell *hurtled* through the air. **3** To move or rush headlong or impetuously: He *hurtled* from the room. —*v.t.* **4** To drive, shoot, or throw violently. **5** *Archaic* To strike against; collide with. [Freq. of ME *hurten* hit, hurt]
hur·tle·ber·ry (hûr′təl·ber′ē) *n. pl.* **·ries** The huckleberry. [Appar. <dial. *hurt,* OE *hórta* a hurtleberry + BERRY]
hurt·less (hûrt′lis) *adj.* **1** Harmless. **2** Unharmed.
Hus (hus, *Czech* hōōs), **Jan** See HUSS, JOHN.
hus·band (huz′bənd) *n.* **1** A married man; man with a wife. **2** *Obs.* A thrifty manager. **3** *Obs.* A husbandman. —*v.t.* **1** To use or spend wisely; economize on; conserve. **2** To be a husband to; marry. **3** *Archaic* To provide with a husband. **4** *Archaic* To till; cultivate. [OE *hūsbonda* <*hūs* house + *bonda* freeholder] —**hus′band·less** *adj.* —**hus′band·like′** *adj.* —**hus′band·ly** *adj.*
hus·band·man (huz′bənd·mən) *n. pl.* **·men** (-mən) A farmer.
hus·band·ry (huz′bən·drē) *n.* **1** Agriculture. **2** Economical management; also, any management, good or bad. See synonyms under AGRICULTURE. —**Patrons of Husbandry** See GRANGE.
Hu·sein ibn–A·li (hōō·sīn′ ib′n·ä′lē), 1856–1931, first king of Hejaz 1916–24.
hush (hush) *v.t.* **1** To make silent; repress the noise of. **2** To suppress mention of; keep from being public. **3** To soothe; allay, as fears. —*v.i.* **4** To be or become silent or still. [<*adj.*] —*n.* Deep silence; stillness; quiet. —*adj. Obs.* Quiet; still; silent. —*interj.* Be still; calm yourself. [ME *husht* quiet]
hush·a·by (hush′ə·bī) *interj.* Hush: an expression used to lull a child to sleep.
hush–hush (hush′hush′) *adj. Colloq.* Secret.
Hu Shih (hōō′ shir′), 1891–1962, Chinese philosopher and author; invented modern simplified Chinese.
hush·ion (hush′ən) *n. Scot.* A footless stocking.
hush money A bribe to secure silence or secrecy.

hush·pup·py (hush'pup'ē) *n.* *pl.* **·pies** *U.S.* In the South, a fried ball of cornmeal dough.

husk (husk) *n.* **1** The outer covering of certain fruits or seeds; rind; hull; especially, that of an ear of maize or Indian corn. **2** The carob pod. *Luke* xv 16. **3** Any covering, especially when comparatively worthless. — *v.t.* To remove the husk of. [ME *huske*, ? OE *hosu* husk] — **husk'er** *n.*

husk·ing (hus'king) *n.* **1** The act of stripping off husks, as from maize. **2** A gathering of friends to aid in husking corn: also **husking bee.**

husk·y¹ (hus'kē) *adj.* **husk·i·er, husk·i·est** **1** Abounding in husks; like husks. **2** Dry as a husk; hoarse: said of the voice. [<HUSK] — **husk'i·ly** *adv.* — **husk'i·ness** *n.*

husk·y² (hus'kē) *U.S. Colloq.* *adj.* **husk·i·er, husk·i·est** Strong; burly. — *n.* A strong or powerfully built person. [Special use of HUSKY¹, with ref. to toughness of husks]

Husk·y (hus'kē) *n.* *pl.* **Husk·ies** A heavy-furred Eskimo dog. See SIBERIAN HUSKY. Also **husk'y.** [? Alter. of ESKIMO]

Huss (hus), **John,** 1369–1415, Bohemian religious reformer; burned as a heretic: also *Jan Hus.*

hus·sar (hŏŏ·zär') *n.* Originally, a light-armed horse trooper of the Hungarian army; later, a member of any light-armed cavalry regiment in other European armies, usually with brilliant dress uniforms. [<Hungarian *huszár* <Serbian *gusar* <Ital. *corsaro* <Med. L *corsarius.* Doublet of CORSAIR.]

Hus·serl (hŏŏs'ərl), **Edmund,** 1859–1938, German philosopher.

Huss·ite (hus'īt) *n.* A follower of John Huss. — **Huss·it·ism** (hus'it·iz'əm) *n.*

hus·sy (huz'ē, hus'ē) *n.* *pl.* **·sies** **1** A pert or forward girl; jade: in reproach or playfully. Also **huzzy.** **2** A case or bag. See HOUSEWIFE (def. 2). [Alter. of HOUSEWIFE]

hust·ing (hus'ting) *n.* **1** A British court formerly held in the larger cities (and still in existence in London): now more commonly in the plural. **2** *pl.* The temporary platform on which the nomination of parliamentary candidates was made prior to the Ballot Act of 1872; hence, the proceedings at an election; now, any platform or place where political speeches are made; hence, a political campaign. [OE *hūsting* council <ON *hūsthing* <*hūs* house + *thing* assembly]

hus·tle (hus'əl) *v.* **hus·tled, hus·tling** *v.t.* **1** To push or knock about roughly or rudely; jostle. **2** To force or impel roughly and hurriedly: to *hustle* a man from a room. **3** *U.S. Colloq.* To hurry; cause to proceed rapidly. **4** *U.S. Slang* **a** To sell aggressively, as for quick profit. **b** To obtain by aggressive action. **c** To dupe; victimize. — *v.i.* **5** To push one's way; elbow; elbow. **6** *U.S. Colloq.* To act or work with energy and speed. **7** *U.S. Slang* To be a prostitute. **8** *U.S. Slang* To live by one's wits, as by gambling, petty thievery, etc. **9** In sports, to put forth extra effort. — *n.* **1** The act of hustling. **2** *Colloq.* Energetic activity; push. **3** *U.S. Slang* A way of getting money illegitimately, as by fraud or thievery; a racket. [<Du *hutselen* shake, toss]

Synonyms (verb): crowd, elbow, hasten, hurry, jam, jostle, push, rush, shove. *Antonyms*: dally, dawdle, delay, hold back, loaf.

hus·tler (hus'lər, hus'əl·ər) *n.* **1** *U.S. Colloq.* An aggressive, energetic person; go-getter. **2** *U.S. Slang* A prostitute. **3** *U.S. Slang* One who lives by his wits, as a gambler, confidence man, petty thief, etc.

hus·wife (huz'if) *n. Obs.* **1** A housewife. **2** A hussy. [Var. of HOUSEWIFE]

hut (hut) *n.* A small rude dwelling. — *v.t.* & *v.i.* **hut·ted, hut·ting** To shelter or live in a hut. [<OF *hutte* <OHG *hutta*]

Synonyms (noun): cabin, cot, cottage, hovel, shanty, shed. See HOUSE. *Antonyms*: castle, hall, mansion, palace.

hutch (huch) *n.* **1** A place for storing anything. **2** A small or dark room. **3** A coop or pen for rabbits, etc. **4** A chest or locker. **5** A measure; also, a basket. — *v.t.* To store up or hoard. [<F *huche* <LL *hutica*]

Hutch·ins (huch'inz), **Robert Maynard,** born 1899, U.S. educator; president of the University of Chicago 1929–45; chancellor 1945–51.

Hutchinson's teeth *Pathol.* The notched permanent incisor teeth sometimes associated with congenital syphilis. [after Sir Jonathan Hutchinson, 1828–1913, English physician]

hut·ment (hut'mənt) *n.* **1** A group of huts, as in an encampment. **2** The housing of people in huts.

Hux·ley (huks'lē) Name of an English family distinguished in science and literature: especially **Thomas Henry,** 1825–95, biologist and author; upheld Darwin's views on evolution; **Sir Julian Sorell,** 1887–1975, biologist; grandson of Thomas Henry; **Aldous Leonard,** 1894–1963, novelist; brother of the preceding.

Huy·gens (hi'gənz), **Christian,** 1629–95, Dutch mathematician, physicist, and astronomer. Also **Huy'ghens.**

Huys·mans (wēs·mäns'), **Joris Karl,** 1848–1907, French novelist.

huz·za (hə·zä') *n.* & *interj.* Hurrah: a shout of joy. Also **huz·zah', huz·zay'** (-zā'). [Imit.]

huz·zy (huz'ē) See HUSSY.

Hwai (hwī) A river in east central China, flowing 600 miles NE.

Hwai·ning (hwī'ning') A former name of AN-KING.

Hwang Hai (hwäng' hī') The Chinese name for the YELLOW SEA.

Hwang Ho (hwäng' hō') The second-longest river of China, flowing 2,900 miles east from the Tibetan highlands across northern China to the Gulf of Chihli: also *Yellow River, Hoang Ho.*

Hwang·poo (hwäng'pŏŏ') A river in eastern China, flowing 100 miles north to the Yangtse: also *Whangpoo.*

hy·a·cinth (hi'ə·sinth) *n.* **1** A bulbous plant of the lily family (genus *Hyacinthus*) cultivated for its spikelike cluster of flowers. **2** The bulb or flower of this plant. **3** A gem, anciently bluish-violet, probably the sapphire, now a brownish, reddish, or orange zircon. **4** A plant frequently alluded to by the Greek poets, fabled to have sprung from the blood of Hyacinthus, beloved of Apollo, and to have borne on its petals the words of grief, *Ai, Ai*: sometimes identified as the iris, larkspur, or gladiolus. [Var. of older *jacynth* <OF *jacincte* <L *hyacinthus* <Gk. *hyakinthos.* Doublet of JACINTH.]

HYACINTH (def. 1)

hyacinth blue A medium purplish-blue, the color of certain hyacinths.

hy·a·cin·thine (hi'ə·sin'thin, -thīn) *adj.* Pertaining to or like the hyacinth.

Hy·a·cin·thus (hi'ə·sin'thəs) In Greek mythology, a youth loved and accidentally killed by Apollo who caused a flower to spring from his blood.

Hy·a·des (hi'ə·dēz) **1** In Greek mythology, five daughters of Atlas whom Zeus set among the stars. **2** *Astron.* A cluster of five stars in Taurus, including Aldebaran, shaped like the letter V: when they rose with the sun they were considered to be a sign of rain by ancient astronomers. [<L <Gk., ? <*hyein* rain] Also **Hy·ads** (hi'adz).

hy·ae·na (hi·ē'nə) See HYENA.

hy·a·line (hi'ə·lin, -līn) *n.* **1** A glassy surface, as of the sea; something transparent. **2** *Biochem.* A nitrogenous compound, related to chitin, the chief constituent of hydatid cysts, which on decomposition yields a reducing sugar. **3** *Anat.* The hyaloid membrane. Also **hy'a·lin** (-lin). — *adj.* Consisting of or resembling glass; transparent: the *hyaline* substance of a cell. [<L *hyalinus* <Gk. *hyalos* glass]

hyaline cartilage *Anat.* That form of cartilage in which the cells are embedded in a homogeneous translucent matrix.

hy·a·lite (hi'ə·līt) *n.* A pellucid glassy variety of opal.

hyalo– *combining form* Glass; of or resembling glass: *hyaloplasm.* Also, before vowels, **hyal–.** [<Gk. *hyalos* glass]

hy·al·o·gen (hi·al'ə·jən) *n. Biochem.* Any of various insoluble substances found in animal tissues and related to mucin; it yields hyaline on hydrolysis.

hy·a·loid (hi'ə·loid) *adj.* Like glass; pellucid: the *hyaloid* membrane. [<Gk. *hyaloeidēs* glassy]

hyaloid membrane *Anat.* A delicate membrane enveloping the vitreous humor of the eye.

hy·a·lo·plasm (hi'ə·lō·plaz'əm) *n. Biol.* The clear, fluid or semifluid ground substance of protoplasm, as distinguished from the granular substance. Also **hy'a·lo·plas'ma** (-plaz'mə). — **hy'a·lo·plas'mic** *adj.*

Hy·bla (hi'blə) An ancient town in Sicily on the site of modern Paternó. Also **Hybla Major.**

Hy·blae·an (hi·blē'ən) *adj.* Of or relating to Hybla or the famous honey produced there in ancient times; hence, smoothly flowing. Also **Hy·blæ'an, Hy·ble'an.**

hy·brid (hi'brid) *adj.* **1** Produced by interbreeding or cross-fertilization. **2** Derived from incongruous sources; mixed. — *n.* **1** An animal or plant of mixed parentage; a mongrel. **2** Anything of heterogeneous origin or incongruous parts. **3** *Ling.* A word composed of elements from more than one language, as *genocide.* [<L *hybrida* offspring of tame sow and wild boar]

hy·brid·ism (hi'brid·iz'əm) *n.* **1** The state of being hybrid: also **hy·brid·i·ty** (hi·brid'ə·tē). **2** The act of interbreeding, or of inducing hybridization. **3** *Ling.* The mingling in one word of elements from more than one language.

hy·brid·ize (hi'brid·iz) *v.t.* & *v.i.* **·ized, ·iz·ing** To produce or cause to produce hybrids; crossbreed. Also *Brit.* **hy'brid·ise.** — **hy·brid·i·za·tion** (hi'brid·ə·zā'shən, -i·zā'-) *n.* — **hy'brid·iz'er** *n.* — **hy'brid·ous** *adj.*

hybrid vigor Heterosis.

hy·dan·to·in (hi·dan'tō·in) *n.* A white crystalline derivative of allantoin, $C_3H_4ON.$ [<Gk. *hydōr, hydatos* water + (ALL)ANTOIN]

Hy·das·pes (hi·das'pēz) The ancient name for the JHELUM.

hy·da·thode (hi'də·thōd) *n. Bot.* An epidermal cellular structure, as a gland, that exudes water: found in plants. [<Gk. *hydōr, hydatos* water + *hodos* way]

hy·da·tid (hi'də·tid) *n.* **1** An encysted vesicle containing an aqueous fluid. **2** An encysted larval stage of a tapeworm. — *adj.* Of or pertaining to a water-containing cyst. [<Gk. *hydatis* drop of water]

hy·da·to·gen·e·sis (hi'də·tō·jen'ə·sis) *n.* Formation of water, as in the tissues and cavities of the body. [<Gk. *hydōr, hydatos* water + GENESIS]

Hyde (hid), **Douglas,** 1860–1949, Irish Gaelic scholar; president of Ireland 1938–45. — **Edward,** 1609–74, first Earl of Clarendon, English historian and statesman.

Hyde (hid), **Mr.** See JEKYLL.

Hyde Park 1 A public park in the West End of London, England; noted as a meeting place of soapbox orators. **2** A village on the Hudson in southern New York; site of the estate and burial place of Franklin Roosevelt.

Hy·der·a·bad (hi'dər·ə·bad', -bäd') **1** A former State of south central India on the Deccan Plateau, merged, November 1, 1956, into the States of Andhra Pradesh, Bombay, and Mysore; 82,698 square miles; former capital, Hyderabad: formerly *Nizam's Dominions*: also *Haidarabad.* **2** A Commissioners' Division of SE West Pakistan, formerly a district of the former province of Sind; 35,998 square miles. **3** A city on the Indus, SE West Pakistan, formerly capital of the former province of Sind. **4** A city on the Deccan Plateau, south central India, capital of Andhra Pradesh State; formerly capital of the former State of Hyderabad.

Hy·der A·li (hi'dər ä'lē), 1728–82, regent of Mysore who fought against the British; father of Tipu Sahib.

hyd·no·car·pate (hid'nə·kär'pāt) *n. Chem.* A salt or ester of hydnocarpic acid, especially the sodium salt or ethyl ester, used in the treatment of leprosy.

hyd·no·car·pic (hid'nə·kär'pik) *adj. Chem.* Denoting an acid, $C_{16}H_{28}O_2,$ extracted from the seeds and oil of the chaulmoogra tree, and used in the treatment of leprosy. [<Gk. *hydnon* truffle + *karpos* fruit]

hydr– Var. of HYDRO–.

hy·dra (hī′drə) n. pl. **·dras** or **·drae** (-drē) 1 Any evil having many forms. 2 A freshwater polyp (genus *Hydra*). [<Gk. *hydra* water serpent]

Hy·dra (hī′drə) 1 In Greek mythology, the nine-headed serpent of Lerna, which grew two heads for each one that was cut off: slain by Hercules with a firebrand. 2 *Astron.* A southern constellation. See CONSTELLATION.

hy·drac·id (hī-dras′id) n. *Chem.* An acid that contains no oxygen, as hydrochloric acid: contrasted with *oxyacid*.

hy·dra·gog (hī′drə-gŏg, -gog) n. Any medicine that causes abundant watery evacuations. Also **hy′dra·gogue.** [<F <L *hydragogus* <Gk. *hydragōgos* <*hydōr* water + *agein* lead]

hy·dra·head·ed (hī′drə-hed′id) adj. Having many heads; hard to destroy.

hy·dran·ge·a (hī-drān′jē-ə, -jə) n. A plant of a genus (*Hydrangea*) of trees and shrubs of the saxifrage family, with opposite, usually serrate, leaves and cymose clusters of large, showy flowers. [<NL <Gk. *hydōr* water + *angeion* vessel]

hy·drant (hī′drənt) n. A valved discharge pipe connected with a water main; a plug. [<Gk. *hydōr* water]

hy·dranth (hī′drănth) n. *Zool.* A nutritive zooid in a hydroid colony, or the part with the mouth and digestive cavity. [<HYDRA + Gk. *anthos* flower]

Hy·dra·o·tes (hī′drā-ō′tēz) The ancient name for the RAVI.

hy·drar·gyr·ic (hī′drär-jir′ik) adj. Of, pertaining to, or containing mercury.

hy·drar·gy·rism (hī-drär′jə-riz′əm) n. Mercury poisoning; mercurialism.

hy·drar·gy·rum (hī-drär′jə-rəm) n. Mercury: especially so called in pharmacy. [<NL <L *hydrargyrus* <Gk. *hydrargyros* <*hydōr* water + *argyros* silver]

hy·dras·tine (hī-dras′tēn, -tin) n. *Chem.* A bitter, crystalline alkaloid, $C_{21}H_{21}NO_6$, contained in the roots of goldenseal, having tonic and febrifuge properties. [<NL *Hydrastis* botanical genus name <Gk. *hydōr* water]

hy·drate (hī′drāt) n. *Chem.* Any of a class of compounds formed by the union of molecules of water with other molecules or atoms. — v.t. **·drat·ed, ·drat·ing** To combine with water or its elements to form a hydrate. [<HYDR– + -ATE³] — **hy′drat·ed** adj. — **hy·dra·tion** (hī-drā′shən) n.

hy·drau·lic (hī-drô′lik) adj. 1 Pertaining to hydraulics, involving the moving of water, or force exerted by water: *hydraulic* engineering, mining, etc. 2 Denoting any of various machines and structures operating by means of water or other liquid under pressure: a *hydraulic* elevator, crane, ram, press, etc. 3 Hardening under water: *hydraulic* cement. Also **hy·drau′li·cal.** [<L *hydraulicus* <Gk. *hydraulikos* of a water organ <*hydraulos* water organ <*hydōr* water + *aulos* pipe] — **hy·drau′li·cal·ly** adv.

hydraulic brake A brake actuated by fluids under pressure in cylinders and tubular connecting lines.

hydraulic press A machine which operates by means of fluid under pressure to exert a large force over an extended area: used in forming steel dies, in baling, etc.

hydraulic ram An automatic device by which the fall of a comparatively large quantity of water furnishes the power to raise a smaller quantity to a height above that of the source.

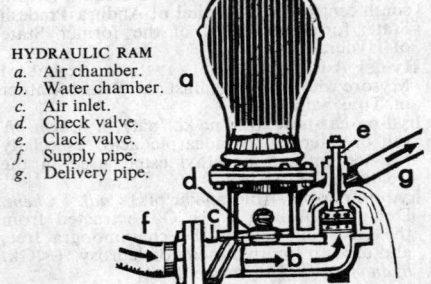

HYDRAULIC RAM
a. Air chamber.
b. Water chamber.
c. Air inlet.
d. Check valve.
e. Clack valve.
f. Supply pipe.
g. Delivery pipe.

hy·drau·lics (hī-drô′liks) n. pl. (construed as singular) The science of the laws of motion

of water and other liquids and of their practical applications.

hydraulic transmission See FLUID DRIVE.

hy·dra·zine (hī′drə-zēn, -zin) n. *Chem.* 1 A colorless fuming liquid, N_2H_4, derived from diazoacetic acid: used as a reducing agent in organic synthesis and as a fuel in jet engines. 2 One of a group of compounds derived from the foregoing by replacement of one or more hydrogen atoms by another radical: phenyl *hydrazine*. [<HYDR– + AZ(O) + -INE²]

hy·dra·zo·ic (hī′drə-zō′ik) adj. *Chem.* Of or pertaining to a colorless, very toxic acid, HN_3, obtained from hydrazine by various methods; its salts, **hy·dra·zo·ates** (hī′drə-zō′āts), explode with great violence when heated.

hy·dric (hī′drik) adj. Of or pertaining to hydrogen in combination.

hy·dride (hī′drīd, -drid) n. *Chem.* 1 A compound of hydrogen with another element or a radical acting as an element. 2 A hydroxide. Also **hy′drid** (-drid).

hy·dri·od·ic (hī′drē-od′ik) adj. *Chem.* Pertaining to or designating a dense, colorless, suffocating acid, HI, soluble in water, formed by the union of hydrogen and iodine.

hydro– *combining form* 1 Water; of, related to, or resembling water: *hydrophone.* 2 *Chem.* Denoting a compound of hydrogen: *hydrochloric.* Also, before vowels, **hydr–.** [<Gk. *hydro–* <*hydōr* water]

hy·dro·air·plane (hī′drō-âr′plān′) See HYDROPLANE (def. 1).

hy·dro·bro·mic (hī′drə-brō′mik) adj. *Chem.* Designating a colorless, pungent acid, HBr, formed by the union of hydrogen and bromine.

hy·dro·car·bon (hī′drə-kär′bən) n. *Chem.* One of a large and important group of compounds that contain hydrogen and carbon only. There are many types and classes, including the aliphatic, aromatic, saturated, and unsaturated hydrocarbons.

hy·dro·cele (hī′drə-sēl) n. *Pathol.* A localized accumulation of fluid surrounding the testicles or along the spermatic cord. [<L <Gk. *hydrokēle* <*hydōr* water + *kēlē* tumor]

hy·dro·ceph·a·lus (hī′drə-sef′ə-ləs) n. *Pathol.* An accumulation of watery fluid within the ventricles or between the membranes of the brain. [<HYDRO– + Gk. *kephalē* head] — **hy′·dro·ceph′a·loid** (-loid), **hy′dro·ceph′a·lous** adj.

hy·dro·chlo·ric (hī′drə-klôr′ik, -klō′rik) adj. *Chem.* Pertaining to or designating a colorless, corrosive, fuming acid, HCl, exceedingly soluble in water, in which form it is largely used in manufactures and sometimes called *muriatic acid.*

hy·dro·chlo·ride (hī′drə-klôr′īd, -klō′rīd) n. *Chem.* A compound produced by the union of hydrochloric acid with an element or radical.

hy·dro·cy·an·ic (hī′drō-sī-an′ik) adj. *Chem.* Of, pertaining to, or designating an unstable, volatile, colorless, and extremely poisonous acid, HCN, formed by decomposing metallic cyanides with hydrochloric acid. It is only slightly dissociated in water, and has a characteristic odor resembling that of bitter almonds: also called *prussic acid.*

hy·dro·dy·nam·ic (hī′drō-dī-nam′ik) adj. Of or pertaining to the force or pressure of water or other fluids. Also **hy′dro·dy·nam′i·cal.**

hy·dro·dy·nam·ics (hī′drō-dī-nam′iks) n. pl. (construed as singular) The branch of mechanics that treats of the dynamics of fluids, chiefly water and other liquids.

hy·dro·e·lec·tric (hī′drō-i-lek′trik) adj. Of or pertaining to electricity developed by water power, or by the escape of steam under high pressure, etc. — **hy·dro·e·lec·tric·i·ty** (hī′drō·i·lek·tris′ə·tē) n.

hy·dro·flu·or·ic (hī′drō-flŏŏ-ôr′ik, -or′-) adj. *Chem.* Pertaining to or designating a volatile, colorless, hygroscopic, corrosive acid, HF, formed by decomposing metallic fluorides. It readily attacks silica, hence is used for etching on glass.

hy·dro·foil (hī′drə-foil) n. A streamlined surface designed to provide support in or obtain a reaction from the water through which it moves, as an attachment to a boat, submarine, or hydroplane.

hy·dro·gel (hī′drə-jel) n. *Chem.* A colloid which has assumed a jellylike form in the presence of water.

hy·dro·gen (hī′drə-jən) n. The lightest of the elements (symbol H) occurring chiefly in combination with oxygen as water, and in hydro-

carbons and other organic compounds. When isolated it is usually a colorless, odorless, tasteless, inflammable gas, lighter than air and liquefying under great pressure and low temperature. — **heavy hydrogen** See DEUTERIUM. [<F *hydrogène* <Gk. *hydōr* water + *gen–*, stem of *gignesthai* be born; so called with ref. to the water formed by its combustion] — **hy·drog·e·nous** (hī-droj′ə-nəs) adj.

hy·dro·gen·ate (hī′drə-jə-nāt′) v.t. **·at·ed, ·at·ing** *Chem.* 1 To cause to combine with hydrogen. 2 To expose to hydrogen, or to effect chemical action of by the use of or by exposure to hydrogen: to *hydrogenate* fats and oils. Also **hy′dro·gen·ize′** (-īz′).

hy·dro·gen·a·tion (hī′drə-jə-nā′shən) n. *Chem.* The act or process of subjecting to the action of hydrogen, usually in the presence of a catalyst: the *hydrogenation* of coal to form liquid hydrocarbons.

hydrogen bomb A bomb of great destructive power, releasing enormous quantities of energy by the fusion, under extremely high temperatures, of deuterium or tritium atoms, with the formation of helium.

hydrogen cyanide Hydrocyanic acid.

hydrogen ion *Chem.* The positively charged hydrogen ion (H⁺) present in all acids. The number of hydrogen ions per unit volume of an aqueous solution is known as the **hydrogen ion concentration**, or *pH* value.

hydrogen peroxide *Chem.* A sirupy liquid, H_2O_2, whose aqueous solutions are important as antiseptics and bleaching agents, the usual solution being a slightly acid one containing about 3 percent by weight of pure hydrogen peroxide. Also called *peroxide.*

hydrogen sulfide *Chem.* A colorless, gaseous compound, H_2S, having a characteristic odor of rotten eggs, made by decomposing certain metallic sulfides, chiefly iron, by means of acids. It is poisonous and is a valuable laboratory reagent.

hy·dro·glid·er (hī′drə-glī′dər) n. A glider with floats attached to permit it to land on or take off from water.

Hy·dro·graph·ic Office (hī′drə-graf′ik) A bureau of the U. S. Navy Department in charge of the charting of navigable waters and the studying of oceanography.

hy·drog·ra·phy (hī-drog′rə-fē) n. The science of determining and making known the conditions of navigable waters, charting rivers, coasts, etc. — **hy·drog′ra·pher** n. — **hy′dro·graph′ic** or **·i·cal** adj.

hy·droid (hī′droid) adj. 1 Of or pertaining to a class (*Hydrozoa*) of mostly marine coelenterates resembling the hydra; like a polyp. 2 Designating a reproductive phase in the development of certain hydrozoans characterized by the formation of colonies. — n. A hydrozoan.

hy·dro·ki·net·ic (hī′drō-ki-net′ik) adj. Relating to the motion and kinetic energy of fluids. Also **hy′dro·ki·net′i·cal.**

hy·dro·ki·net·ics (hī′drō-ki-net′iks) n. pl. (construed as singular) The branch of hydrodynamics that treats of fluids in motion.

hy·drol·o·gy (hī-drol′ə-jē) n. The branch of physical geography that treats of the waters of the earth, their distribution, characteristics, and effects. [<HYDRO– + -LOGY] — **hy·dro·log·ic** (hī′drə-loj′ik) or **·i·cal** adj. — **hy′dro·log′i·cal·ly** adv. — **hy·drol′o·gist** n.

hy·drol·y·sis (hī-drol′ə-sis) n. *Chem.* Any decomposition involving the addition of water; specifically, a double decomposition reaction between water and some other compound, as phosphorus trichloride. [<HYDRO– + -LYSIS] — **hy·dro·lyt·ic** (hī′drə-lit′ik) adj.

hy·dro·lyte (hī′drə-līt) n. Any substance affected by hydrolysis.

hy·dro·lyze (hī′drə-līz) v.t. & v.i. **·lyzed, ·lyz·ing** To undergo or cause to undergo the process of hydrolysis. — **hy′dro·lyz′a·ble** adj. — **hy·dro·ly·za·tion** (hī′drə-lə-zā′shən, -lī-zā′-) n.

hy·dro·man·cy (hī′drə-man′sē) n. Divination by means of water. — **hy′dro·manc′er** n. — **hy′dro·man′tic** (-tik) adj.

hy·dro·me·chan·ics (hī′drō-mə-kan′iks) n. The mechanics of fluids, including hydrostatics, hydrodynamics, hydrokinetics, and pneumatics. — **hy′dro·me·chan′i·cal** adj.

hy·dro·me·du·sa (hī′drō-mə-dōō′sə, -dyōō′-) n. pl. **·sae** (-sē) A type of coelenterate produced by budding from an individual, as the jellyfish and medusa.

hy·dro·mel (hī′drə·mel) *n.* A liquor, usually unfermented, consisting of honey diluted with water; when fermented, it is called *mead.* [<L <Gk. *hydromeli* <*hydōr* water + *meli* honey]

hy·dro·met·al·lur·gy (hī′drō·met′əl·ûr′jē) *n.* The process of assaying or reducing ore by means of liquid reagents. — **hy′dro·met′al·lur′gi·cal** *adj.*

hy·dro·me·te·or (hī′drō·mē′tē·ər) *n. Meteorol.* A watery or aqueous meteor; any of the conditions or effects produced by water, as rain, snow, hail, etc.

hy·dro·me·te·or·ol·o·gy (hī′drō·mē′tē·ə·rol′ə·jē) *n.* The branch of meteorology that treats of hydrometeors or of water in the atmosphere.

hy·drom·e·ter (hī·drom′ə·tər) *n.* **1** A calibrated sealed tube weighted at one end for determining the density or specific gravity, especially of liquids and solutions: also called *densimeter.* **2** A current gage. — **hy·dro·met·ric** (hī′drə·met′rik) or **·ri·cal** *adj.* — **hy·drom′e·try** *n.*

hy·drop·a·thy (hī·drop′ə·thē) *n.* The treatment of diseases by the use of water; water cure. — **hy·dro·path·ic** (hī′drə·path′ik) or **·i·cal** *adj.* — **hy·drop′a·thist, hy′dro·path** *n.*

hy·dro·phane (hī′drə·fān) *n.* A whitish or light-colored opal, opaque when dry, but translucent when wet. — **hy·droph·a·nous** (hī·drof′ə·nəs) *adj.*

hy·droph·i·lous (hī·drof′ə·ləs) *adj. Bot.* Having the flowers pollinated by the agency of water: said of certain higher plants. [< HYDRO- + Gk. *philos* loving]

hy·dro·pho·bi·a (hī′drə·fō′bē·ə) *n.* **1** Rabies. **2** Any morbid dread of water. [<L <Gk., <*hydōr* water + *phobos* fear] — **hy′dro·pho′bic** *adj.*

hy·dro·phone (hī′drə·fōn) *n.* **1** An electrical instrument for detecting underwater sounds, especially of enemy submarines. **2** A device used for the purpose of detecting leaks in water pipes.

hy·dro·phyte (hī′drə·fīt) *n. Bot.* A plant living in water or in wet ground. — **hy·dro·phyt·ic** (hī′drə·fit′ik) *adj.*

hy·drop·ic (hī·drop′ik) *adj.* Dropsical; affected with dropsy. Also **hy·drop′i·cal.** [<OF *idropique* <L *hydropicus* <Gk. *hydrōpikos* <*hydrōps* dropsy <*hydōr* water] — **hy·drop′i·cal·ly** *adv.*

hy·dro·plane (hī′drə·plān) *n.* **1** An airplane constructed for alighting upon or rising from the water: also called *hydroairplane.* **2** A motorboat of extremely light construction driven either by submerged screws or by aerial propellers. **3** A hydrofoil. — *v.i.* **·planed, ·plan·ing 1** To move on water at a speed sufficient to give support through hydrodynamic and aerodynamic forces alone. **2** To drive or ride in a hydroplane.

hy·dro·pon·ics (hī′drə·pon′iks) *n. pl.* (*construed as singular*) Soilless agriculture; the raising of plants in nutrient mineral solutions without earth around the roots: also called *water culture, tank farming.* [<HYDRO- + Gk. *ponos* labor] — **hy′dro·pon′ic** *adj.*

hy·drop·sy (hī′drop′sē) *n.* Dropsy. Also **hy′drops, hy·drop′si·a.**

hy·dro·qui·none (hī′drō·kwi·nōn′) *n. Chem.* A white crystalline compound, $C_6H_4(OH)_2$, derived from quinone: used in medicine as an antiseptic and antipyretic, and in photography as a developing agent. Also **hy′dro·quin′ol** (-kwin′ōl, -ol).

hy·dro·scope (hī′drə·skōp) *n.* **1** An instrument for detecting moisture, especially in the air. **2** An instrument for seeing through considerable depths of water. — **hy′dro·scop′ic** (-skop′ik) or **·i·cal** *adj.*

hy·dro·sere (hī′drə·sir) *n. Ecol.* In plant succession, the series of changes in vegetation which take place in the water. [<HYDRO- + SERE[2]]

hy·dro·sol (hī′drə·sol, -sōl) *n. Chem.* A water solution of a colloid. [<HYDRO- + SOL(UTION)]

hy·dro·some (hī′drə·sōm) *n. Zool.* A hydroid colony as a whole. Also **hy′dro·so′ma** (-sō′mə). [<HYDRO- + -SOME[2]]

hy·dro·sphere (hī′drə·sfir) *n.* **1** The total water surrounding the earth. **2** The atmospheric moisture enveloping the globe, in distinction from the atmosphere itself.

hy·dro·stat (hī′drə·stat) *n.* **1** A contrivance for preventing the explosion of steam boilers. **2** An electrical device for making known the presence of water, as a protection against leakage, overflow, etc.

hy·dro·stat·ic (hī′drə·stat′ik) *adj.* Pertaining to hydrostatics. Also **hy′dro·stat′i·cal.**

hy·dro·stat·ics (hī′drə·stat′iks) *n. pl.* (*construed as singular*) The science of the pressure and equilibrium of fluids, as water.

hy·dro·sul·fate (hī′drə·sul′fāt) *n. Chem.* A compound of sulfuric acid and an alkaloid or other organic base.

hy·dro·sul·fide (hī′drə·sul′fīd) *n. Chem.* A compound derived from hydrogen sulfide, by replacing one of the hydrogen atoms with a basic radical or a base.

hy·dro·sul·fite (hī′drə·sul′fīt) *n.* Sodium hydrosulfite.

hy·dro·sul·fu·rous (hī′drō·sul·fyŏŏr′əs, hī′drə·sul′fər·əs) See HYPOSULFUROUS.

hy·dro·tax·is (hī′drə·tak′sis) *n. Biol.* **1** The irritable response or turning of organisms under the influence of humidity or water. **2** The action of moisture in determining the direction of motion, as in protoplasm. — **hy′dro·tac′tic** (-tak′tik) *adj.*

hy·dro·the·ca (hī′drə·thē′kə) *n.* A calicle. [< NL <Gk. *hydōr* water + *thēkē* case]

hy·dro·ther·a·peu·tics (hī′drō·ther′ə·pyōō′tiks) *n.* Hydropathy. Also **hy′dro·ther′a·py** (-ther′ə·pē). — **hy′dro·ther′a·peu′tic** *adj.*

hy·dro·ther·mal (hī′drə·thûr′məl) *adj. Geol.* Of, pertaining to, or produced by action of heated or superheated water, especially the action of such water in dissolving, transporting, and redepositing mineral matter.

hy·dro·tho·rax (hī′drə·thôr′aks, -thō′raks) *n. Pathol.* An accumulation of fluid in the pleural cavity; dropsy of the chest. — **hy·dro·tho·rac·ic** (hī′drō·thə·ras′ik) *adj.*

hy·drot·ro·pism (hī·drot′rə·piz′əm) *n. Bot.* The phenomena of curvature induced in a growing plant organ by the stimulation of moisture. — **hy·dro·trop·ic** (hī′drə·trop′ik) *adj.*

hy·drous (hī′drəs) *adj. Chem.* **1** Watery; containing water of crystallization or hydration. **2** Containing hydrogen.

Hy·dro·vize (hī′drə·vīz) *v.t.* **·vized, ·viz·ing** To make (a textile fabric) rainproof and resistant to stains, winds, and perspiration by the application to its surface of a water repellent: a trade name.

hy·drox·ide (hī·drok′sīd) *n. Chem.* A compound containing hydroxyl.

hy·drox·y (hī·drok′sē) *adj. Chem.* Any of a class of compounds containing the hydroxyl radical: a *hydroxy* acid.

hy·drox·yl (hī·drok′sil) *n. Chem.* The univalent radical OH, consisting of one atom of oxygen and one of hydrogen. It occurs in alcohols, most acids, and many organic compounds. [<HYDR- + OX(YGEN) + -YL]

hy·drox·yl·a·mine (hī·drok′sil·ə·mēn′, -am′in) *n. Chem.* A colorless crystalline organic base, NH_2OH, formed by the partial reduction of nitric acid, but usually obtained as an unstable solution in water. In chemical behavior it is similar to ammonia.

Hy·dro·zo·a (hī′drə·zō′ə) *n. pl.* A class of coelenterates, mostly marine, including jellyfishes, polyps, etc. — **hy′dro·zo′an** *adj.* & *n.*

Hy·drus (hī′drəs) A southern constellation. [<Gk. *hydros* water snake]

hy·e·na (hī·ē′nə) *n.* A catlike carnivorous mammal of Africa and Asia (family *Hyaenidae*) with very strong, large teeth, striped or spotted body, and skulking habits, as the African laughing hyena (*Hyaena brunnea*) and the spotted hyena (*Crocuta crocuta*): also spelled *hyaena.* [<L *hyaena* <Gk. *hyaina* <*hys* pig]

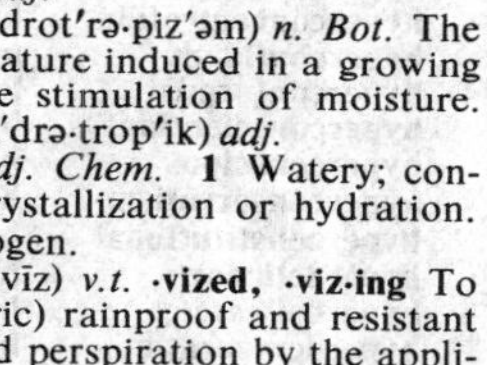

HYENA
(About 2 feet high at the shoulder)

Hyères (yâr′) A port and resort in SE France.

hy·e·tal (hī′ə·təl) *adj. Meteorol.* **1** Of or pertaining to rain or the amount of the rainfall at different places and seasons. **2** Rainy.

hyeto– *combining form* Rain: *hyetograph.* Also, before vowels, **hyet–.** [<Gk. *hyetos* rain < *hyein* rain]

hy·e·to·graph (hī′i·tə·graf′, -gräf′) *n. Meteorol.* A chart showing the distribution of rainfall over the earth, or over any part of it.

hy·e·to·graph·ic (hī′i·tə·graf′ik) *adj. Meteorol.* Relating to or showing the amount of rainfall: a *hyetographic* map. Also **hy′e·to·graph′i·cal.**

hy·e·tog·ra·phy (hī′i·tog′rə·fē) *n.* The branch of meteorology that treats of the distribution of rainfall, and of the exhibition of it graphically in charts, maps, etc.

hy·e·tol·o·gy (hī′i·tol′ə·jē) *n.* That branch of meteorology which treats of precipitation. [<HYETO- + -LOGY] — **hy·e·to·log·i·cal** (hī′i·tə·loj′i·kəl) *adj.*

Hy·ge·ia (hī·jē′ə) In Greek mythology, the goddess of health; daughter of Aesculapius, the god of medicine: identified with the Roman *Salus.* Also **Hy·ge′a, Hy·gi′a** (-jī′ə). [<Gk. *hygeia* health] — **Hy·ge′ian** *adj.*

hy·giene (hī′jēn, -ji·ēn) *n.* The branch of medical science that relates to the preservation of health; sanitary science. [<F *hygiène* <Gk. *hygienios* healthful]

hy·gi·en·ic (hī′jē·en′ik, hī·jē′nik) *adj.* Pertaining to hygiene; sanitary. See synonyms under HEALTHY. — **hy′gi·en′i·cal·ly** *adv.*

hy·gi·en·ics (hī′jē·en′iks, hī·jē′niks) *n.* The science of preserving and promoting health.

hy·gi·en·ist (hī′jē·ən·ist) *n.* One who studies or is versed in the principles of hygiene. Also **hy′ge·ist** (-jē·ist), **hy′gie·ist.**

hygro– *combining form* Wet; denoting relation to moisture. [<Gk. *hygros* wet]

hy·gro·graph (hī′grə·graf, -gräf) *n.* A recording hygrometer.

hy·grom·e·ter (hī·grom′ə·tər) *n.* An instrument for ascertaining the humidity or degree of moisture in the atmosphere. [<HYGRO- + -METER]

hy·gro·met·ric (hī′grə·met′rik) *adj.* **1** Pertaining to hygrometry or the state of the atmosphere as to moisture. **2** Readily absorbing and retaining moisture. Also **hy′gro·met′ri·cal.**

hy·grom·e·try (hī·grom′ə·trē) *n.* The branch of physics that treats of the measurement of degrees of moisture, especially the moisture of the air.

hy·gro·scope (hī′grə·skōp) *n.* A device for approximating the humidity of the air.

hy·gro·scop·ic (hī′grə·skop′ik) *adj.* **1** Pertaining to the hygroscope, or capable of being detected only by it. **2** Able to absorb or condense moisture from the atmosphere, as glycerol. **3** Expanding or shrinking according to the amount of moisture: said of plants.

Hyk·sos (hik′sōs, -sos) A dynasty of kings of Egypt, probably of Syro-Semitic origin, who ruled at Memphis 1685–1580 B.C.: often called *Shepherd Kings.*

hy·la (hī′lə) *n.* The tree frog (genus *Hyla*). [<NL <Gk. *hyle* wood]

Hy·las (hī′ləs) In Greek mythology, a beautiful youth, loved by Hercules, whose companion he was on the cruise of the Argonauts; he was stolen by Naiads while bathing in a spring at Mysia.

hy·lic (hī′lik) *adj.* Relating to or of the nature of matter; material. — **hy′li·cism** (-lə·siz′əm) *n.*

hy·li·cist (hī′lə·sist) *n.* A believer or teacher of materialism; specifically, one of the early Ionic philosophers.

hy·lism (hī′liz·əm) *n.* **1** Materialism. **2** The theory that matter is the principle or source of evil.

hylo– *combining form* Related to matter; material: *hylotropic.* Also, before vowels, **hyl–.** [<Gk. *hylē* wood]

hy·lo·the·ism (hī′lə·thē′iz·əm) *n.* The doctrine of belief that the material universe is God; pantheism.

hy·lo·trop·ic (hī′lə·trop′ik, -trō′pik) *adj.* Having the capacity to change in form without a change in composition; as ice, water, and steam.

hy·lo·zo·ism (hī′lə·zō′iz·əm) *n.* The doctrine that life and matter are inseparable. [<HYLO- + Gk. *zōē* life] — **hy′lo·zo′ic** *adj.* — **hy′lo·zo′ist** *n.* — **hy′lo·zo·is′tic** *adj.*

hy·men (hī′mən) *n.* **1** *Anat.* A thin mucous membrane partially covering the entrance of

the vagina; the virginal membrane or maiden-head. **2** The wedded state; marriage. [<Gk. *hymēn* membrane]

Hy·men (hī′mən) In Greek mythology, the god of marriage and of the wedding feast. Also **Hy′me·nae′us** (-nē′əs).

hy·me·ne·al (hī′mə·nē′əl) *adj.* Pertaining to marriage: also **hy′me·ne′an.** See synonyms under MATRIMONIAL. — *n.* A wedding song.

hy·me·ni·um (hī·mē′nē·əm) *n. pl.* **·ni·a** (-nē·ə) or **·ni·ums** *Bot.* The fruit-bearing surface or stratum in the higher fungi of the *Ascomycetes* or *Basidiomycetes,* as the two vertical faces on the gills of the common mushroom. It consists of a collection of basidia, sometimes interspersed with sterile cells in a layer or stratum. [<NL <Gk. *hymenion,* dim. of *hymen* membrane]

hymeno– *combining form* Membrane: *hymenophore.* Also, before vowels, **hymen–.** [<Gk. *hymēn* skin, membrane]

Hy·men·o·my·ce·tes (hī′mən·ō·mī·sē′tēz) *n. pl.* A subgroup of fleshy, leathery, or woody fungi, having an exposed hymenium, including the common edible mushroom, *Agaricus campestris.* — **hy′men·o·my·ce′tal** or **·tous** *adj.*

hy·men·o·phore (hī′mən·ə·fôr′, -fōr′) *n. Bot.* The stem and pileus of a hymenomycetous fungus; more specifically, that part of the sporophore which bears the hymenium. Also **hy·men·i·o·phore** (hī·men′ē·ə·fôr′, -fōr′), **hy′men·o·pho′rum** (-fôr′əm, -fō′rəm).

Hy·men·op·ter·a (hī′mən·op′tər·ə) *n. pl.* An extensive and highly developed order of insects typically having four membranous wings, of which the front pair are larger, and mostly a wormlike larva and inactive pupa, including bees, wasps, sawflies, ants, etc. [<NL <Gk. *hymen* membrane + *ptera,* pl. of *pteron* a wing] — **hy′men·op′ter** *n.* — **hy′men·op′ter·an** *adj.* & *n.* — **hy′men·op′ter·ous** *adj.*

Hy·met·tus (hī·met′əs) A mountain range in east central Greece; highest point, 3,367 feet. *Greek* **Hy·met′tos.**

hymn (him) *n.* A song expressive of praise, adoration, or elevated emotion; specifically, a metrical composition, divided into stanzas or verses, intended to be sung in religious worship; also, a religious or patriotic ode, song, lyric, or other poem. — *v.* **hymned, hymn·ing** *v.t.* **1** To praise or worship in hymns. **2** To express by singing: to *hymn* praises. — *v.i.* **3** To sing hymns or praises. See synonyms under SONG. [Fusion of OE *hymen* and OF *ymne,* both <LL *ymnus, hymnus* <Gk. *hymnos* a song, ode] — **hym′nic** (-nik) *adj.*

hym·nal (him′nəl) *n.* A book of hymns: also **hymn book.** — *adj.* Of or concerning a hymn or hymns.

hymnal stanza Common measure.

hym·nist (him′nist) *n.* A writer of hymns. Also **hym′no·dist** (-nə·dist).

hym·no·dy (him′nə·dē) *n. pl.* **·dies 1** Hymns collectively; hymnology. **2** The practice of singing hymns. [<LL *hymnodia* <Gk. *hymnōidia* <*hymnos* hymn + *ōidē* singing]

hym·nog·ra·phy (him·nog′rə·fē) *n.* The art of composing hymns.

hym·nol·o·gy (him·nol′ə·jē) *n.* **1** The study or science of hymns, including their history, use, and classification. **2** A treatise on hymns, or hymns collectively. [<HYMN + -(O)LOGY] — **hym·no·log·ic** (him′nə·loj′ik) or **·i·cal** *adj.* — **hym·nol′o·gist** *n.*

hy·oid (hī′oid) *n. Anat.* A U-shaped bone at the base of the tongue, for the attachment of the muscles of deglutition: also **hyoid bone.** — *adj.* **1** Pertaining to the hyoid bone. **2** Having the form of the Greek letter upsilon (Υ, υ). [<F *hyoïde* <Gk. *hyoeidēs* <Υ upsilon + *eidos* form]

hy·os·cine (hī′ə·sēn) *n.* Scopolamine. [<HYOS-C(YAMUS) + -INE]

hy·os·cy·a·mine (hī′ə·sī′ə·mēn, -min) *n. Chem.* A white, crystalline, poisonous alkaloid, $C_{17}H_{23}NO_3$, contained in henbane, thorn apple, deadly nightshade, and other plants; used medicinally. Also **hy·os·cy′a·min** (-min).

hy·os·cy·a·mus (hī′ə·sī′ə·məs) *n.* The henbane, containing alkaloids used for their anodyne and antispasmodic properties. [<Gk. *hyoskyamos* henbane <*hys* hog + *kyamos* bean]

hyp– Var. of HYPO–.

hyp·a·bys·sal (hip′ə·bis′əl) *adj. Geol.* Pertaining to or designating igneous rocks which form minor intrusions, such as dikes and

sills; also, the intrusions themselves. [<HYP-+ ABYSSAL]

hyp·aes·the·si·a (hip′əs·thē′zhē·ə, -zhə), **hy·pae·thral** (hi·pē′thrəl), etc. See HYPESTHESIA, etc.

Hy·pa·tia (hī·pā′shə, -shē·ə) A Greek philosopher celebrated for her beauty, killed by a mob A.D. 415.

hype (hīp) *Slang v.t.* **hyped, hyp·ing 1** To deceive; fool. **2** To stimulate with or as with drugs: with *up.* — *n.* **1** A deception; fraud. **2** A promotional talk or message. [<HYPO-DERMIC, with ref. to the injection of drugs]

hyper– *prefix* **1** Over; above; excessive: *hypertension:* opposed to *hypo–.* **2** *Chem.* Denoting the highest in a series of compounds: now generally replaced by *per–.* [<Gk. *hyper–* <*hyper* above]

In the following self-explanatory compounds, *hyper–* appears in sense 1:

hyperabsorption	hypermoral
hyperaccurate	hypermotile
hyperacoustics	hypermotility
hyperaction	hypermystical
hyperactive	hypernatural
hyperacuity	hyperneurotic
hyperacute	hypernormal
hyperacuteness	hypernote
hyperaltruism	hypernutrition
hyperanarchy	hyperobtrusive
hyperangelical	hyperorganic
hyperbarbarous	hyperorthodox
hyperbrutal	hyperorthodoxy
hypercarnal	hyperpanegyric
hypercatharsis	hyperparoxysm
hypercathartic	hyperpathetic
hypercivilization	hyperpatriotic
hypercivilized	hyperpersonal
hyperclassical	hyperpigmentation
hyperclimax	hyperplagiarism
hyperconcentration	hyperpolysyllabic
hyperconfident	hyperproduction
hyperconformist	hyperprophetical
hyperconscientious	hyperpure
hyperconscious	hyperpurist
hyperconservatism	hyperrational
hyperconstitutional	hyperreactive
hyperdelicacy	hyperrealize
hyperdelicate	hyperresonance
hyperdemocratic	hyperresonant
hyperdiabolical	hyperreverential
hyperdistention	hyperridiculous
hyper–Dorian	hyperritualism
hyperelegant	hyper–Romantic
hyperemphasize	hypersaintly
hyperenthusiasm	hyperscholastic
hyperethical	hyperscrupulosity
hyperexaltation	hypersecretion
hyperexcitability	hypersensitization
hyperexcitable	hypersensual
hyperexcitement	hypersensualism
hyperfastidious	hypersensuous
hypergenesis	hypersentimental
hypergrammatical	hyperskeptical
hyperhilarious	hypersophisticated
hyperhypocrisy	hyperspeculative
hyperidealistic	hyperspiritualizing
hyperimmune	hyperstoic
hyperimmunity	hypersubtlety
hyperingenuity	hypersuggestibility
hyperintellectual	hypersuperlative
hyperintelligence	hypertechnical
hyperlogical	hypertense
hyperlustrous	hypertorrid
hypermagical	hypertoxic
hypermedication	hypertragical
hypermetaphorical	hypertragically
hypermetaphysical	hypertropical
hypermiraculous	hypervigilant
hypermodest	hypervitalize

hyp·er·ac·id (hī′pər·as′id) *adj.* Excessively acid. — **hy′per·a·cid′i·ty** (-ə·sid′ə·tē) *n.*

hy·per·a·cu·si·a (hī′pər·ə·kyoo′zhē·ə) *n. Pathol.* Morbid acuteness of hearing. Also **hy′per·a·cu′sis** (-sis). [<HYPER- + Gk. *akousis* hearing]

hy·per·a·dre·ni·a (hī′pər·ə·drē′nē·ə) *n. Pathol.* A disorder caused by excessive secretory activity of the adrenal glands, and characterized by sudden increases in blood pressure. Also **hy·per·ad·re·nal·ism** (hī′pər·ə·drē′nəl·iz′-əm).

hy·per·ae·mi·a (hī′pər·ē′mē·ə), **hy·per·aes·the·si·a** (hī′pər·es·thē′zhē·ə, -zhə) See HYPEREMIA, etc.

hy·per·al·ge·si·a (hī′pər·al·jē′zē·ə, -sē·ə) *n. Pathol.* Excessive sensitiveness to pain. Also

hy′per·al·ge′sis. [<HYPER- + Gk. *algēsis* sense of pain <*algos* pain] — **hy′per·al·ge′sic** (-zik, -sik) *adj.*

hy·per·bar·ic (hī′pər·bar′ik) *adj. Med.* **1** Of, pertaining to, or affected by hyperbarism. **2** Designating a spinal anesthetic solution having a density greater than that of the spinal fluid.

hy·per·bar·ism (hī·per′bə·riz′əm) *n. Med.* A disturbed condition caused by an atmospheric pressure which is greater than the pressure within the tissues, fluids, or cavities of the body: occurs in a sudden descent from a high to a low altitude. Opposed to *hypobarism.* [<HYPER- + Gk. *baros* weight]

hy·per·bo·la (hī·pûr′bə·lə) *n. Math.* A curve traced by a point moving so that the difference between its distances from two fixed points, or foci, remains constant; the curves traced by the edges where a plane intersects the nappes of a right circular cone. [<NL <Gk. *hyperbolē* a throwing beyond, excess. See HYPERBOLE.]

hy·per·bo·le (hī·pûr′bə·lē) *n.* Poetic or rhetorical overstatement; exaggeration. [<L <Gk. *hyperbolē* a throwing beyond, excess <*hyper–* over + *ballein* throw]

hy·per·bol·ic (hī′pər·bol′ik) *adj.* **1** Relating to or containing hyperbole; exaggerating. **2** Of, pertaining to, or having the shape of a hyperbola. Also **hy′per·bol′i·cal.** — **hy′per·bol′i·cal·ly** *adv.*

hyperbolic paraboloid *Math.* A quadric surface generated in such a way that, parallel to one plane, its sections are hyperbolas, and, parallel to the other planes, all sections are parabolas.

hyperbolic sine curve *Math.* A sine curve with hyperbolic convolutions.

hyperbolic spiral *Math.* A polar curve traced by a point moving so that its distance from the pole varies inversely as its polar angle: it is asymptotic to a line parallel to the polar axis.

hy·per·bo·lize (hī·pûr′bə·līz) *v.t.* & *v.i.* **·lized, ·liz·ing** To express in or use hyperbole; exaggerate. Also *Brit.* **hy·per′bo·lise.** — **hy·per′bo·lism** (-liz′əm) *n.*

hy·per·bo·loid (hī·pûr′bə·loid) *n. Math.* A quadratic surface generated by a hyperbola revolving about a fixed line: also called a **hyperboloid of one sheet.** A **hyperboloid of two sheets** is a quadratic surface generated by an ellipse moving so as to remain parallel to a common transverse axis, and varying so that the ends of its axes coincide with given hyperbolas having the same transverse axis.

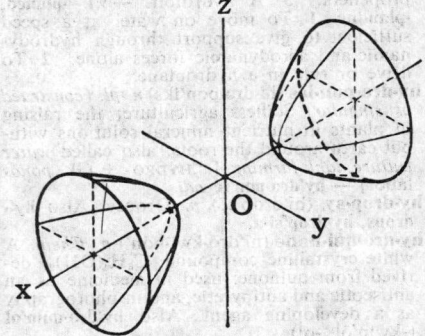

HYPERBOLOID OF TWO SHEETS
O. Origin. *x.* Transverse axis. *y, z.* Coordinate axes.

hy·per·bo·re·an (hī′pər·bôr′ē·ən, -bō′rē-) *adj.* Of the far north; frigid.

Hy·per·bo·re·an (hī′pər·bôr′ē·ən, -bō′rē-) *n.* One of a people supposed by the ancient Greeks to dwell in a blessed land lying beyond the north wind and inaccessible by land or sea. — *adj.* Pertaining to the Hyperboreans. [<L *hyperboreus* <Gk. *hyperboreos* <*hyper–* beyond + *Boreas* north wind]

hy·per·cat·a·lec·tic (hī′pər·kat′ə·lek′tik) *adj.* Having one or two syllables beyond the final regular measure: said of a line of poetry; hypermetric. [<L *hypercatalecticus* <Gk. *hyperkatalēktikos* <*hyper–* beyond + *katalēktikos* CATALECTIC] — **hy′per·cat′a·lex′is** (-lek′sis) *n.*

hy·per·crit·ic (hī′pər·krit′ik) *n.* A very severe critic.

hy·per·crit·i·cal (hī′pər·krit′i·kəl) *adj.* **1**

Given to strained or captious criticism. 2 Excessively exact or precise. See synonyms under CAPTIOUS. — **hy′per·crit′i·cal·ly** *adv.* — **hy′per·crit′i·cism** (-siz′əm) *n.*

hy·per·cube (hī′pər·kyōōb) *n.* A tesseract.

hy·per·du·li·a (hī′pər·dōō′lē·ə, -dyōō′-) *n. Eccl.* Worship given to the Virgin Mary as the most sacred of mortal creatures: superior to *dulia.* Compare LATRIA. [<Med. L < *hyper-* beyond + *dulia* service]

hy·per·e·mi·a (hī′pər·ē′mē·ə) *n. Pathol.* Abnormal accumulation of the blood in any part of the body: also spelled *hyperaemia.* — **hy′per·e′mic** *adj.*

hy·per·es·the·si·a (hī′pər·es·thē′zhē·ə, -zhə) *n.* Exaggerated sensitiveness to touch, heat, pain, etc.: also spelled *hyperaesthesia.*

hy·per·es·thet·ic (hī′pər·es·thet′ik) *adj.* 1 Morbidly sensitive. 2 Immoderately esthetic. Also spelled *hyperaesthetic.*

hy·per·eu·tec·tic (hī′pər·yōō·tek′tik) *adj.* Having the minor component in a proportion greater than that of the corresponding eutectic mixture: said of a mineral, alloy, or solution.

hy·per·ex·ten·sion (hī′pər·ik·sten′shən) *n. Physiol.* The maximum extension of an arm or leg beyond the plane of the body.

hy·per·fine (hī′pər·fīn′) *adj. Physics* Of, pertaining to, or characterized by very closely spaced lines, as in the spectra of certain elements and isotopes.

hy·per·fo·cal (hī′pər·fō′kəl) *adj. Phot.* Designating that distance in front of a given camera lens under specified conditions, at and beyond which all objects are in substantially clear focus.

hy·per·gol·ic (hī′pər·gol′ik) *adj.* Pertaining to or describing a type of rocket propellant that ignites spontaneously on contact with an oxidizer. [HYPER- + G *gola* a code word used in German rocketry]

hy·per·hi·dro·sis (hī′pər·hi·drō′sis) *n.* Abnormal sweating. Also **hy′per·i·dro′sis** (-ī·drō′sis).

Hy·pe·ri·on (hī·pir′ē·ən) 1 In Greek mythology, a Titan, the son of Uranus and Gaea and father of Helios, Selene, and Eos. 2 Helios.

hy·per·ki·ne·si·a (hī′pər·ki·nē′zhē·ə, -zhə) *n. Pathol.* Exaggerated muscular action; spasm. Also **hy′per·ki·ne′sis** (-nē′sis). — **hy′per·ki·net′ic** (-net′ik) *adj.*

hy·per·me·ter (hī·pûr′mə·tər) *n.* A hypercatalectic line; also, a period containing a redundant syllable. — **hy·per·met·ric** (hī′pər·met′rik) or **·ri·cal** *adj.*

hy·per·me·tro·pi·a (hī′pər·mə·trō′pē·ə) *n. Pathol.* An abnormal condition of the eye in which objects at a distance are seen more plainly than those near at hand; far-sightedness. Also **hy′per·met′ro·py** (-met′rə·pē), **hy′per·o′pi·a** (-ō′pē·ə). [<NL <Gk. *hypermetros* excessive + *ōps* eye] — **hy′per·me·trop′ic** (-mə·trop′ik, -trō′pik) *adj.*

hy·perm·ne·si·a (hī′pərm·nē′zhē·ə, -zhə) *n.* A condition marked by an abnormal retentivity and acuteness of memory; total recall: distinguished from *amnesia.* Also **hy′perm·ne′sis** (-nē′sis). [<HYPER- + Gk. *mnesis* remembrance]

Hy·perm·nes·tra (hī′pərm·nes′trə) In Greek mythology, the only one of the Danaides who did not kill her husband on her wedding night.

hy·per·on (hī′pər·on) *n. Physics* Any of a class of atomic particles having a mass intermediate between that of a neutron and a deuteron. Symbol, Λ (lambda), followed by an identifying superscript. Also called *V-particle.* [<NL <Gk. *hyper-* above, more]

hy·per·o·pi·a (hī′pər·ō′pē·ə) *n.* Hypermetropia.

hy·per·os·mi·a (hī′pər·oz′mē·ə) *n.* Morbid sensitiveness to odors. [<HYPER- + Gk. *osmē* smell]

hy·per·os·to·sis (hī′pər·os·tō′sis) *n. pl.* **·ses** (-sēz) *Pathol.* An abnormal increase in or thickening of bony tissue.

hy·per·ox·i·a (hī′pər·ok′sē·ə) *n. Med.* An excess of oxygen in the atmosphere or in an animal body. [<NL <HYPER- + OX(Y)- + -IA]

hy·per·par·a·site (hī′pər·par′ə·sīt) *n.* An organism parasitic on another parasite. — **hy′per·par′a·sit′ic** (-sit′ik) *adj.* — **hy′per·par′a·sit·ism** (-ə·sit·iz′əm) *n.*

hy·per·phe·nom·e·nal (hī′pər·fə·nom′ə·nəl) *adj.* Transcending phenomena; real.

hy·per·phys·i·cal (hī′pər·fiz′i·kəl) *adj.* 1 Independent of the physical. 2 Supernatural. — **hy′per·phys′i·cal·ly** *adv.*

hy·per·pi·e·si·a (hī′pər·pī·ē′zhē·ə, -zhə) *n. Pathol.* Abnormally high blood pressure. Also **hy′per·pi·e′sis** (-sis). [<NL <Gk. *hyper-* beyond + *piesis* pressure < *piezein* press]

hy·per·pi·tu·i·ta·rism (hī′pər·pi·tōō′i·tə·riz′əm, -tyōō′-) *n. Pathol.* Abnormal functioning of the pituitary gland; also, the disorders resulting from it.

hy·per·pla·si·a (hī′pər·plā′zhē·ə, -zhə) *n. Pathol.* Excessive production of cells in a part; enlargement from quantitative increase produced by cell division: distinguished from *hypertrophy.* — **hy′per·plas′ic** (-plas′ik), **hy′per·plas′tic** (-plas′tik) *adj.*

hy·per·ploid (hī′pər·ploid) *adj. Biol.* Pertaining to or designating a chromosome number greater than the normal number but not an exact multiple of it. — **hy′per·ploid′y** *n.*

hy·perp·ne·a (hī′pərp·nē′ə) *n. Pathol.* Violent or labored breathing caused by a deficiency of oxygen in the blood. Also **hy′perp·noe′a.** [<NL <Gk. *hyper-* above + *pnoē* breathing < *pneein* breathe]

hy·per·pro·sex·i·a (hī′pər·prō·sek′sē·ə) *n. Psychiatry* An inordinate and exaggerated attention to certain things, as the symptoms of an illness or mental disorder. [<HYPER- + Gk. *prosexis* attention]

hy·per·py·rex·i·a (hī′pər·pī·rek′sē·ə) *n. Pathol.* Very high fever. — **hy′per·py·ret′ic** (-ret′ik), **hy′per·py·rex′i·al** *adj.*

hy·per·sen·si·tive (hī′pər·sen′sə·tiv) *adj.* 1 Excessively sensitive. 2 Allergic. — **hy′per·sen′si·tive·ness, hy′per·sen′si·tiv′i·ty** (-sen′sə·tiv′ə·tē) *n.*

hy·per·sen·si·tize (hī′pər·sen′sə·tīz) *v.t.* **·tized, ·tiz·ing** *Phot.* To increase the sensitiveness or speed of, as a plate or film, usually by immersion in a suitable solution or by exposure to mercury vapor. — **hy′per·sen′si·ti·za′tion** ... — **hy′per·sen′si·tiz′ing** *n.*

hy·per·son·ic (hī′pər·son′ik) *adj.* Of, pertaining to, or characterized by supersonic speeds of mach 5 or greater.

hy·per·son·ics (hī′pər·son′iks) *n. pl. (construed as singular)* That branch of dynamics which studies the design, characteristics, and performance of objects moving at supersonic speeds of mach 5 or greater: applied especially to jet planes, guided missiles, rockets, and the like.

hy·per·space (hī′pər·spās′) *n.* Space regarded as having more than three dimensions.

hy·per·sthene (hī′pər·sthēn) *n.* A pearly, dark-colored, ferrous magnesium-pyroxene mineral found in igneous rocks. [<HYPER- + Gk. *sthenos* strength]

hy·per·sthe·ni·a (hī′pər·sthē′nē·ə) *n.* Excessive physical vigor and tone. [<HYPER- + Gk. *sthenos* strength] — **hy′per·sthen′ic** (-sthen′ik) *adj.*

hy·per·ten·sion (hī′pər·ten′shən) *n. Pathol.* 1 Excessively high blood pressure. 2 A disease of the arteries caused by or associated with such pressure.

Hy·per·therm (hī′pər·thûrm) *n.* An apparatus for producing hyperthermia: a trade name.

hy·per·ther·mi·a (hī′pər·thûr′mē·ə) *n. Med.* 1 An abnormally high temperature. 2 Therapeutic treatment by means of artificially induced fever. Also **hy′per·ther′my.** [<HYPER- + Gk. *thermē* heat] — **hy′per·ther′mal** *adj.*

hy·per·thy·mic (hī′pər·thī′mik) *adj.* 1 *Psychiatry* Denoting a state of morbidly exaggerated activity of mind or body. 2 Designating a constitutional type associated with persistent overdevelopment of the thymus gland. [<HYPER- + Gk. *thymos* spirit, passion]

hy·per·thy·roid (hī′pər·thī′roid) *adj.* Marked by hyperthyroidism. — *n.* One affected by hyperthyroidism.

hy·per·thy·roid·ism (hī′pər·thī′roid·iz′əm) *n. Pathol.* 1 Abnormal activity of the thyroid gland. 2 Any disorder caused by such activity: opposed to *hypothyroidism.*

hy·per·ton·ic (hī′pər·ton′ik) *adj. Pathol.* Pertaining to or designating a higher osmotic pressure than the normal, as of blood: opposed to *isotonic.* — **hy′per·to·nic′i·ty** (-tō·nis′ə·tē) *n.*

hy·per·tro·phy (hī·pûr′trə·fē) *n. Pathol.* 1 The excessive development of an organ or part. 2 The morbid enlargement of a part from increased nutrition without increase of waste: opposed to *atrophy.* — *v.i.* **·phied, ·phy·ing** To grow excessively; develop abnormally. — **hy·per·troph·ic** (hī′pər·trof′ik, -trō′fik) or **·i·cal** *adj.*

hy·per·ven·ti·la·tion (hī′pər·ven′tə·lā′shən) *n.* 1 An excess supply of air to the lungs, as when airplane pilots resort to deep and rapid breathing to ensure adequate oxygen: often resulting in lowering carbon dioxide content of the blood. 2 Physical therapy by exposure of the body to drafts of air.

hy·per·vi·ta·mi·no·sis (hī′pər·vī′tə·mi·nō′sis) *n. Pathol.* A condition due to an excess of vitamins, either in the diet or in prepared form: opposed to *avitaminosis.*

hyp·es·the·si·a (hip′əs·thē′zhē·ə, -zhə) *n. Pathol.* Diminished sensitiveness; partial loss of capacity for sensation: also spelled *hypaesthesia.* — **hyp′es·the′sic** (-sik) or **·thet′ic** (-thet′ik) *adj.*

hy·pe·thral (hi·pē′thrəl, hī-) *adj.* Roofless, as a building open to the sky: said of a building whose roof has been destroyed or never completed, or of a sanctuary, etc., never intended to be roofed. Also spelled *hypaethral.* [<L *hypaethrus* <Gk. *hypaithros* < *hypo-* under + *aithēr* ether, clear sky]

hy·pha (hī′fə) *n. pl.* **·phae** (-fē) *Bot.* A long, threadlike, usually branching body in the thallus of a fungus: the vegetative hyphae, as opposed to the reproductive ones, constitute the mycelium of fungi. [<NL <Gk. *hyphē* web] — **hy′phal** *adj.*

hy·pheme (hī′fēm) *n.* A hyphened compound word. Compare SOLIDEME. [<HYPH(EN) + (PHON)EME]

hy·phe·mi·a (hī·fē′mē·ə) *n. Pathol.* 1 Deficiency of blood, or a lack of supply of the red corpuscles in the blood. 2 Extravasation of the blood into a surrounding tissue, especially in the eye. Also **hy·phae′mi·a.** [<HYPO- + -HEMIA]

hy·phen (hī′fən) *n.* A mark (- or - or ₌) indicating connection: used to connect the elements of certain compound words, to show division of a word at the end of a line, and to indicate a unit modifier: a *hit-and-run* driver. — *v.t.* To hyphenate. [<LL <Gk. *hyph′ hen* under one, together < *hypo-* under + *hen* one]

hy·phen·ate (hī′fən·āt) *v.t.* **·at·ed, ·at·ing** 1 To connect by a hyphen. 2 To print or write with a hyphen. Also **hy′phen·ize.** — **hy′phen·a′tion, hy′phen·i·za′tion** (-ə·zā′shən, -ī·zā′-) *n.*

hy·phen·at·ed (hī′fən·ā′tid) *adj.* Implying or relating to a naturalized person of foreign birth, especially to one whose sympathies are with the land of his birth.

hyp·na·gog·ic (hip′nə·goj′ik) *adj.* 1 Inducing or promoting sleep, as by a drug or by hypnosis. 2 Of or pertaining to the mental condition occurring just before sleep; dreamlike; visionary. [<HYPN(O)- + -AGOG]

hyp·na·pa·gog·ic (hip′nə·pə·goj′ik) *adj.* Preventing or inhibiting sleep. [<HYPN(O)- + AP(O)- + -AGOG]

hyp·nic (hip′nik) *adj.* Calculated to induce sleep; pertaining to sleep. — *n.* A soporific.

hypno- *combining form* Sleep; of or related to sleep: *hypnology.* Also, before vowels, **hypn-.** [<Gk. *hypnos* sleep]

hyp·no·a·nal·y·sis (hip′nō·ə·nal′ə·sis) *n.* A psychoanalytic technique which utilizes data obtained by or under the conditions resulting from hypnosis. — **hyp′no·an′a·lyt′ic** (-an′ə·lit′ik) *adj.*

hyp·no·gen·e·sis (hip′nō·jen′ə·sis) *n.* The production of hypnotic sleep. — **hyp′no·ge·net′ic** (-jə·net′ik), **hyp′no·ge·net′i·cal, hyp·nog·e·nous** (hip·noj′ə·nəs) *adj.*

hyp·noid·al (hip·noid′l) *adj. Psychiatry* Characterizing a condition of the nervous organization resembling slight hypnosis, with heightened suggestibility, partial anesthesia, etc.

hyp·nol·o·gy (hip·nol′ə·jē) *n.* The science of the phenomena of sleep. — **hyp·no·log·ic** (hip′nə·loj′ik) or **·i·cal** *adj.* — **hyp·nol′o·gist** *n.*

hyp·no·pae·di·a (hip′nə·pē′dē·ə) *n.* Training and instruction during sleep: a word used by Aldous Huxley in his novel *Brave New World* (1932), now applied to a technique

in actual use. [<HYPNO- + Gk. *paideia* education] **—hyp′no·pae′dic** (-pē′dik) *adj.*

hyp·no·pho·bi·a (hip′nə·fō′bē·ə) *n.* A morbid fear of sleep or of falling asleep. **—hyp′no·pho′bic** *adj.*

hyp·no·pom·pic (hip′nə·pom′pik) *adj. Psychol.* Persisting after or emerging from sleep: describing the semiconscious state between sleep and waking often marked by visions and fantasies. [<HYPNO- + Gk. *pompaios* accompanying]

Hyp·nos (hip′nos) In Greek mythology, the god of sleep: identified with the Roman *Somnus.* Also **Hyp′nus** (-nəs).

hyp·no·sis (hip·nō′sis) *n. pl.* **·ses** (-sēz) *Psychol.* **1** A trancelike condition that may be psychically induced by another person, characterized by loss of consciousness and a greater or lesser degree of responsiveness to the suggestions of the hypnotist. **2** The causing of such a condition.

hyp·no·ther·a·py (hip′nə·ther′ə·pē) *n. Med.* The use of hypnotism in treating disease.

hyp·not·ic (hip·not′ik) *adj.* **1** Pertaining to hypnotism or tending to produce hypnosis. **2** Tending to produce sleep. *—n.* **1** An agent efficacious in producing sleep. **2** A hypnotized person. [<Gk. *hypnōtikos* <*hypnos* sleep] **—hyp·not′i·cal·ly** *adv.*

hyp·no·tism (hip′nə·tiz′əm) *n.* The theory and practice of hypnosis. **—hyp′no·tist, hyp′no·tiz′er** *n.*

hyp·no·tize (hip′nə·tīz) *v.t.* **·tized, ·tiz·ing** **1** To produce hypnosis in. **2** *Colloq.* To fascinate; entrance. Also *Brit.* **hyp′no·tise.** **—hyp′·no·tiz′a·ble** *adj.* **—hyp′no·ti·za′tion** (-tə·zā′·shən, -tī·zā′-) *n.*

hy·po (hī′pō) *n.* **1** *Chem.* Sodium thiosulfate. **2** *Slang* Hypochondria; also, a hypochondriac. **3** *Colloq.* A hypodermic injection or needle.

hypo– *prefix* **1** Under; beneath; less than: *hypodermic*: opposed to *hyper–*. **2** *Chem.* Indicating the lowest member in a series of compounds, that is, the lowest degree of oxidation: *hypophosphate.* **3** *Med.* Denoting a lack of or deficiency in: *hypofunction.* Also, before vowels, **hyp–**. [<Gk. *hypo-* <*hypo* under]

hy·po·a·cid·i·ty (hī′pō·ə·sid′ə·tē) *n. Med.* Deficient or subnormal acidity, as of the gastric juices.

hy·po·bar·ic (hī′pə·bar′ik) *adj. Med.* **1** Pertaining to or affected by hypobarism. **2** Denoting a spinal anesthetic solution whose density is less than that of the spinal fluid. Opposed to *hyperbaric.*

hy·po·bar·ism (hī′pə·bär′iz·əm) *n. Med.* A condition brought about when the pressure of the gases within the body is in excess of the atmospheric pressure: opposed to *hyperbarism.* Compare *aeroembolism.* [<HYPO- + Gk. *baros* weight]

hy·po·blast (hī′pə·blast) *n. Biol.* The innermost of the blastodermic membranes, from which is derived the epithelium of the digestive tract and its annexes. **—hy′po·blas′·tic** *adj.*

hy·po·bran·chi·al (hī′pə·brang′kē·əl) *adj. Zool.* Of or pertaining to the lower segment of the branchial arch in animals.

hy·po·cap·ni·a (hī′pə·kap′nē·ə) *n. Med.* A deficiency of carbon dioxide in the blood, often due to hyperventilation. [<HYPO- + Gk. *kapnos* smoke] **—hy′po·cap′nic** *adj.*

hy·po·caust (hī′pə·kôst) *n.* In ancient Roman houses, a hollow space for the accumulation of heat under the floor. [<L *hypocaustum* <Gk. *hypokauston* <*hypo* beneath + *kaiein* burn]

hy·po·cen·ter (hī′pə·sen′tər) *n.* That point on the earth's surface directly beneath or above the burst of an atomic or thermonuclear bomb; ground zero.

hy·po·chlo·rite (hī′pə·klôr′īt, -klō′rīt) *n. Chem.* A salt of hypochlorous acid.

hy·po·chlo·rous (hī′pə·klôr′əs, -klō′rəs) *adj. Chem.* Denoting an acid, HClO, obtained by the action of chlorine on mercurous oxide and water, and in other ways. It acts as an oxidizing and bleaching agent.

hy·po·chon·dri·a (hī′pə·kon′drē·ə, hip′ə-) *n. Psychiatry* **1** A morbid melancholy and depression of mind or spirits. **2** A morbidly extreme anxiety about one's health, usually associated with one or another part of the body, and accompanied by imagined symptoms of illness. Also **hy·po·chon·dri·a·sis** (hī′·pō·kən·drī′ə·sis). [<L, abdomen (once taken to be the seat of this condition) <Gk. *hypochondria,* neut. pl. from *hypochondrios* under the cartilage <*hypo-* under + *chondros* cartilage]

hy·po·chon·dri·ac (hī′pə·kon′drē·ak, hip′ə-) *adj.* **1** Pertaining to or affected by hypochondria. **2** Of, pertaining to, or situated in the hypochondrium. Also **hy·po·chon·dri·a·cal** (hī′pō·kən·drī′ə·kəl). *—n.* A person subject to or afflicted by hypochondria. **—hy′po·chon·dri′a·cal·ly** *adv.*

hy·po·chon·dri·um (hī′pə·kon′drē·əm, hip′ə-) *n. pl.* **·dri·a** (-drē·ə) *Anat.* That region of the abdomen situated on either side under the costal cartilages and short ribs. [<NL <Gk. *hypochondrion.* See HYPOCHONDRIA.]

hy·po·co·ris·tic (hī′pō·kə·ris′tik) *adj.* Of or pertaining to an endearing diminutive or pet name. [<Gk. *hypokoristikos* <*hypo-* under + *korizesthai* caress <*koros* child]

hy·po·cot·yl (hī′pə·kot′l) *n. Bot.* That part of the seedling axis of a plant below the seed leaves or cotyledons. [<HYPO- + COTYL(EDON)] **—hy′po·cot′y·lous** *adj.*

hy·poc·ri·sy (hi·pok′rə·sē) *n. pl.* **·sies** The feigning to be what one is not; extreme insincerity; dissimulation. [<OF *ypocrisie* <L *hypocrisis* <Gk. *hypokrisis* acting a part, feigning <*hypo-* under + *krinein* decide]

Synonyms: affectation, cant, dissimulation, formalism, pharisaism, pietism, pretense, sanctimoniousness, sanctimony, sham. *Pretense* (L. *praetendo*) primarily signifies the holding something forward as having certain rights or claims, whether truly or falsely; in the good sense, it is now rarely used except with a negative; as, There can be no *pretense* that this is due; a false *pretense* implies the possibility of a true *pretense*; but, alone and unlimited, *pretense* commonly signifies the offering of something for what it is not. *Hypocrisy* is the false *pretense* of moral excellence, either as a cover for actual wrong, or for the sake of the credit and advantage attaching to virtue. *Cant* (L. *cantus,* a song), primarily the singsong iteration of the language of any party, school, or sect, denotes the mechanical and pretentious use of religious phraseology, without corresponding feeling or character; *sanctimoniousness* is the assumption of a saintly manner without a saintly character. *Affectation* is in matters of intellect, taste, etc., much what *hypocrisy* is in morals and religion: *affectation* might be termed petty *hypocrisy.* Compare DECEPTION. *Antonyms:* candor, frankness, genuineness, honesty, ingenuousness, openness, sincerity, transparency, truth, truthfulness.

hyp·o·crite (hip′ə·krit) *n.* One who acts a false part or makes false professions. [<Gk. *hypokritēs* an actor. See HYPOCRISY.] **—hyp′o·crit′i·cal** *adj.* **—hyp′o·crit′i·cal·ly** *adv.*

Synonyms: cheat, deceiver, dissembler, impostor, pretender. A *hypocrite* is one who acts a false part, or assumes a character other than the real. The *deceiver* seeks to give false impressions of any matter where he has an end to gain; the *dissembler* or *hypocrite* seeks to give false impressions in regard to himself. The *dissembler* is content if he can keep some base conduct or evil purpose from being discovered; the *hypocrite* seeks not merely to cover his vices, but to gain credit for virtue. The *cheat* and *impostor* endeavor to make something out of those whom they may deceive. The *cheat* is the inferior and more mercenary, as the thimblerig gambler; the *impostor* may aspire to a fortune or a throne. Compare HYPOCRISY.

hy·po·cy·cloid (hī′pə·sī′kloid, hip′ə-) *n. Math.* A curve generated by a point on the circumference of a circle which rolls, without slipping, on the inside of another circle.

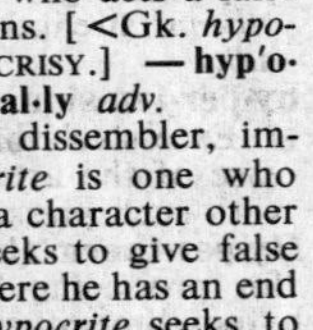

HYPOCYCLOID
B. Center of circle.
AC. Arc on which circle rolls.

hy·po·derm (hī′pə·dûrm) *n. Zool.* The cellular layer between the cuticle and the basal membrane of an arthropod. Also **hy′po·der′·mis.**

hy·po·der·ma (hī′pə·dûr′mə) *n.* **1** *Bot.* The distinct sheath of strengthening tissue beneath the epidermis of stems in plants. **2** The hypoderm. **3** Any of a genus (*Hypoderma*) of dipterous insects, the botflies. [<NL <Gk. *hypo-* under + *derma* skin]

hy·po·der·mal (hī′pə·dûr′məl) *adj.* **1** Pertaining to the hypoderma; situated below the epidermis. **2** Hypodermic.

hy·po·der·mic (hī′pə·dûr′mik) *adj.* **1** Of or pertaining to the area under the skin. **2** Of or pertaining to the hypoderma. *—n.* A hypodermic injection or syringe.

hypodermic injection An injection under the skin.

hypodermic medication Medical treatment by subcutaneous means, as by hypodermic injection.

hypodermic needle The needle of a hypodermic syringe.

hypodermic syringe A syringe having a sharp, hollow needle for injection of substances beneath the skin.

hy·po·der·mis (hī′pə·dûr′məs) *n.* The hypoderm. [<NL]

hy·po·eu·tec·tic (hī′pō·yōō·tek′tik, hip′ō-) *adj.* Having the minor component in a proportion less than that in the corresponding eutectic mixture: said of a mineral, alloy, or solution.

hy·po·gas·tri·um (hī′pə·gas′trē·əm) *n. pl.* **·tri·a** (-trē·ə) *Anat.* The region at the lower part of the abdomen on the middle line. [<NL <Gk. *hypogastrion* <*hypo-* below + *gastēr* belly] **—hy′po·gas′tric** *adj.*

hy·po·ge·al (hī′pə·jē′əl, hip′ə-) *adj.* **1** *Geol.* Situated beneath the surface of the earth, or underlying the superficial outcropping strata. **2** Hypogeous. [<HYPO- + Gk. *gē* earth]

hyp·o·gene (hip′ə·jēn) *adj. Geol.* **1** Formed beneath the earth's surface, as granite. **2** Pertaining to or caused by subterranean agencies; plutonic: contrasted with *epigene* and *volcanic.*

hy·pog·e·nous (hī·poj′ə·nəs, hi-) *adj. Bot.* Growing beneath, as fungi on the under surface of a leaf. Compare EPIGENOUS. [<HYPO- + -GENOUS]

hyp·o·ge·ous (hip′ə·jē′əs, hī′pə-) *adj.* **1** Underground. **2** *Bot.* Growing or fruiting underground, as truffles and other fungi. [<L *hypogeus* <Gk. *hypogeios* <*hypo-* under + *gē* earth]

hyp·o·ge·um (hip′ə·jē′əm, hī′pə-) *n. pl.* **·ge·a** (-jē′ə) **1** *Archit.* The part of a building below the ground. **2** Any underground structure; an artificial cave. [<L <Gk. *hypogeios* subterranean]

hy·po·glos·sal (hī′pə·glos′əl, hip′ə-) *adj. Biol.* Of or pertaining to a nerve situated under the tongue in birds, reptiles, and mammals; underneath the tongue. *—n.* A hypoglossal nerve. [<HYPO- + Gk. *glōssa* tongue]

hy·pog·y·nous (hī·poj′ə·nəs, hi-) *adj. Bot.* Situated on or growing from the receptacle of the flower beneath the ovary or pistil. [<HYPO- + GYNOUS] **—hy·pog′y·ny** *n.*

hy·po·ma·ni·a (hī′pə·mā′nē·ə, -mān′yə, hip′ə-) *n.* A mild form of mania; a condition of moderate elation and overactivity.

hy·po·nas·ty (hip′ə·nas′tē, hī′pə-) *n. Bot.* A state of curvature induced in an extending plant organ by the excessively active growth of its lower side, causing it to bend downward. Compare EPINASTY. [<HYPO- + Gk. *nastos* compact] **—hyp′o·nas′tic** *adj.* **—hyp′o·nas′ti·cal·ly** *adv.*

hy·po·ni·trous (hī′pə·nī′trəs) *adj. Chem.* Designating an unstable white crystalline nitrogenous acid, $(HNO)_2$, formed by the union of hydroxylamine and nitrous acid, and in other ways. Its salts are known as **hy′po·ni′trites** (-trīts).

hy·po·phos·phate (hī′pə·fos′fāt) *n. Chem.* A salt of hypophosphoric acid.

hy·po·phos·phite (hī′pə·fos′fīt) *n. Chem.* A salt of hypophosphorous acid.

hy·po·phos·phor·ic (hī′pō·fos·fôr′ik, -for′ik) *adj. Chem.* Denoting a crystalline tetrabasic acid, $H_4P_2O_6$, formed from moist phosphorus by oxidation.

hy·po·phos·pho·rous (hī′pə·fos′fər·əs) *adj. Chem.* Denoting a monobasic acid derived from phosphorus, H_3PO_2, a powerful reducing agent.

hy·poph·y·ge (hī·pof′ə·jē, hi-) *n. Archit.* A horizontal rounded groove under a structural member, as in the case of archaic Doric capitals. [<Gk. *hypophygē* refuge, recess <*hypo-* under + *pheugein* flee]

hy·poph·y·sis (hī·pof′ə·sis, hi-) *n. pl.* **·ses** (-sēz) *Anat.* A process or outgrowth. [<NL <Gk.,

an undergrowth <*hypo-* under + *physis* nature <*phyein* grow]

hypophysis cer·e·bri (ser′ə·brī) *Anat.* The pituitary gland. [<NL, outgrowth of the brain]

hy·po·pi·tu·i·ta·rism (hī′pō·pi·to͞o′i·tə·riz′əm, -tyo͞o′-) *n. Pathol.* **1** Diminished activity of the pituitary gland. **2** Any condition produced by this, marked by excessive fat and by adolescent traits.

hy·po·pla·si·a (hī′pə·plā′zhē·ə, -zhə, hip′ə-) *n. Pathol.* The condition of arrested development. —**hy′po·plas′tic** (-plas′tik) *adj.*

hy·po·ploid (hī′pə·ploid, hip′ə-) *adj. Biol.* Denoting a chromosome number less than the basic number. —**hy′po·ploid′y** *n.*

hy·po·pne·a (hī′pə·nē′ə, hip′ə-) *n. Med.* Abnormal rapidity and shallowness of breathing, as from hypoventilation. Also **hy′po·pnoe′a.** [<NL <Gk. *hypo-* under + *pnoē* breathing <*pneein* breathe]

hy·po·po·di·um (hī′pə·pō′dē·əm, hip′ə-) *n. pl.* **·di·a** (-dē·ə) *Bot.* The basal portion of a leaf, including the stalk; a supporting structure in plants. [<NL <Gk. *hypo-* under + *podion,* dim. of *pous, podos* a foot]

hy·po·py·on (hī·pō′pē·on, hi-) *n. Pathol.* An accumulation of pus in the cavity of the eye which contains the aqueous humor. [<NL <Gk., a kind of ulcer <*hypo-* under + *pyon* pus]

hy·po·scope (hī′pə·skōp) *n.* A form of altiscope for military use, as a sighting attachment to a rifle, etc.

hy·pos·ta·sis (hī·pos′tə·sis, hi-) *n.* **1** That which forms, either in fact or hypothesis, a groundwork or support for anything; a basis. **2** *Philos.* A distinct individual subsistence; also, a logical substance. **3** *Theol.* Any one of the persons of the Trinity; also, the separate personal subsistence of each of the three persons of the Trinity in one divine substance. **4** *Med.* A settling down of a fluid of the body. **5** *Pathol.* A morbid deposition of sedimentary matter within the body. [<L <Gk. *hypostasis* substance, subsistence < *hypo-* under + *histhastai* stand, middle voice of *histanai* cause to stand]

hy·po·stat·ic (hī′pə·stat′ik, hip′ə-) *adj.* **1** Of, pertaining to, or constituting a distinct personality or substance; distinctly personal. **2** Of, relating to, or proceeding from hypostasis; elemental. **3** *Med.* Resulting from downward pressure or deposition of sediment in the body: *hypostatic* congestion. **4** *Genetics* Denoting a factor hidden or masked by another which is not an allelomorph. Also **hy′po·stat′i·cal.** [<Gk. *hypostatikos*] —**hy′po·stat′i·cal·ly** *adv.*

hypostatic union *Theol.* The union of two natures in the one person or hypostasis of Christ.

hy·pos·ta·tize (hī·pos′tə·tīz, hi-) *v.t.* **·tized, ·tiz·ing** To treat as real; ascribe substantial or distinct existence to. —**hy·pos′ta·ti·za′tion** (-tə·ti·zā′shən, -tə·tī·zā′-) *n.*

hy·po·sthe·ni·a (hī′pə·sthē′nē·ə) *n. Pathol.* Deficient vitality. Compare HYPERSTHENIA. [<HYPO- + Gk. *sthenos* strength] —**hy′po·sthen′ic** (-sthen′ik) *adj.*

hy·pos·to·ma (hī·pos′tə·mə, hi-) *n. pl.* **hy·po·sto·ma·ta** (hī′pə·stō′mə·tə) *Zool.* A part or organ lying below the mouth, as in certain crustaceans and coelenterates. Also **hyp·o·stome** (hip′ə·stōm). [<NL <Gk. *hypo-* under + *stoma* mouth] —**hy′po·sto′mi·al** *adj.*

hyp·o·style (hip′ə·stīl, hī′pə-) *n. Archit.* **1** Any structure having a ceiling resting upon columns; a pillared hall. **2** One of the halls with huge pillars characteristic of Egyptian architecture. —*adj.* Of, similar to, or pertaining to such a structure. [<HYPO- + Gk. *stylos* pillar]

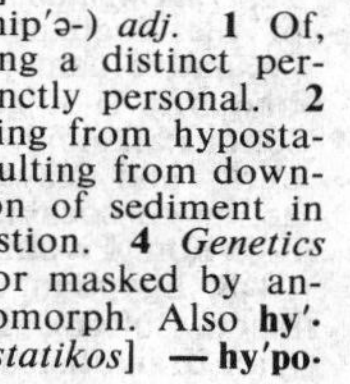
HYPOSTYLE

hy·po·sul·fite (hī′po·sul′fīt) *n. Chem.* **1** Sodium thiosulfate. **2** A salt of hyposulfurous acid.

hy·po·sul·fur·ic (hī′pō·sul·fyo͝or′ik, hī′pə·sul′fər·ik) *adj. Chem.* Of or pertaining to an unstable, colorless acid, $H_2S_2O_6$, having no odor and forming soluble salts with certain bases: also *dithionic.*

hy·po·sul·fu·rous (hī′pō·sul·fyo͝or′əs, hī′pə·sul′fər·əs) *adj. Chem.* Pertaining to or designating an unstable acid, $H_2S_2O_4$, of strong reducing and bleaching properties: also *hydrosulfurous.*

hy·po·tax·is (hī′pə·tak′sis, hip′ə-) *n. Gram.* Subordinate or dependent arrangement of clauses, phrases, etc.: opposed to *parataxis.* —**hy′po·tac′tic** (-tak′tik) or **·ti·cal** *adj.* —**hy′po·tac′ti·cal·ly** *adv.*

hy·pot·e·nuse (hī·pot′ə·no͞os, -nyo͞os, hi-) *n. Geom.* The side of a right-angled triangle opposite the right angle. Also **hy·poth′e·nuse** (-poth′-). [<L *hypotenusa* <Gk. *hypoteinousa (grammē)* a subtending (line) <*hypo-* under + *teinein* stretch]

hy·po·thal·a·mus (hī′pə·thal′ə·məs, hip′ə-) *n. Anat.* The region below the thalamus, controlling visceral activities. —**hy·po·tha·lam·ic** (hī′pə·thə·lam′ik) *adj.*

hy·po·thal·lus (hī′pə·thal′əs, hip′ə-) *n. pl.* **·li** (-ī) *Bot.* **1** The delicate hyphal filaments upon which a lichen thallus is first developed; a mycelial or hyphal outgrowth from the margin of the thallus of a crustaceous lichen. **2** In fungi, an under thallus on which spore cases are produced. [<HYPO- + Gk. *thallos* young shoot] —**hy′po·thal′line** (-ēn, -in) *adj.*

hy·poth·ec (hī·poth′ik, hi-) *n.* A pledge or mortgage of either lands or goods as security for debt where the property pledged remains in possession of the debtor. [<F *hypothèque* <LL *hypotheca* <Gk. *hypothēkē* pledge < *hypotithenai* deposit as a pledge <*hypo-* under + *tithenai* put] —**hy·poth′e·car′y** (-ə·ker′ē) *adj.*

hy·poth·e·cate (hī·poth′ə·kāt, hi-) *v.t.* **·cat·ed, ·cat·ing** To give (personal property) in pledge as security for debt. [<Med. L *hypothecatus,* pp. of *hypothecare* <LL *hypotheca* pledge] —**hy·poth′e·ca′tion** *n.* —**hy·poth′e·ca′tor** *n.*

hy·poth·e·nar (hī·poth′ə·nər, hi-) *n. Biol.* The ridge on the palm at the base of the little finger, or at a corresponding part in the forefoot of a quadruped. [<HYPO- + Gk. *thenar* palm]

hy·po·ther·mal (hī′pō·thûr′məl, hip′ō-) *adj.* Tepid; moderately warm.

hy·po·ther·mi·a (hī′pō·thûr′mē·ə, hip′ō-) *n. Med.* **1** An abnormally low temperature. **2** Therapeutic anesthesia produced by gradually reducing body temperature to as low as 75° F.; frozen sleep. Also **hy′po·ther′my.** [<HYPO- + Gk. *thermē* heat] —**hy′po·ther′mal** *adj.*

hy·poth·e·sis (hī·poth′ə·sis, hi-) *n. pl.* **·ses** (-sēz) **1** A set of assumptions provisionally accepted as a basis of reasoning, experiment, or investigation. **2** An unsupported or ill-supported theory. [<NL <Gk., foundation, supposition <*hypotithenai* put under <*hypo-* under + *tithenai* put]

Synonyms: conjecture, guess, scheme, speculation, supposition, surmise, system, theory. A *hypothesis* is a statement of what is deemed possibly true, assumed and reasoned upon as if certainly true, with a view of reaching truth not yet surely known; especially, in the sciences, a *hypothesis* is a comprehensive tentative explanation of certain phenomena, which is meant to include all other facts of the same class, and which is assumed as true till there has been opportunity to bring all related facts into comparison; if the *hypothesis* explains all the facts, it is regarded as verified; till then it is regarded as a working *hypothesis,* that is, one that may answer for present practical purposes. A *hypothesis* may be termed a comprehensive *guess.* Compare GUESS, SYSTEM, THEORY. *Antonyms:* certainty, demonstration, discovery, evidence, fact, proof.

hy·poth·e·size (hī·poth′ə·sīz, hi-) *v.* **·sized, ·siz·ing** *v.t.* To make a hypothesis of. —*v.i.* To conceive or suggest hypotheses.

hy·po·thet·ic (hī′pə·thet′ik) *adj.* **1** Having the nature of or based on hypothesis; assumed conditionally or tentatively as a basis for argument or investigation; also, involving a formal hypothesis. **2** Given to using hypotheses. Also **hy′po·thet′i·cal.** See synonyms under IMAGINARY. [<L *hypotheticus* <Gk. *hypothetikos*] —**hy′po·thet′i·cal·ly** *adv.*

hy·po·thy·roid (hī′pō·thī′roid) *adj.* Manifesting hypothyroidism. —*n.* One affected by hypothyroidism.

hy·po·thy·roid·ism (hī′pō·thī′roid·iz′əm) *n. Pathol.* **1** Deficient functioning of the thyroid gland. **2** The resulting psychosomatic disorders: sometimes called *cretinism,* and opposed to *hyperthyroidism.*

hy·po·ton·ic (hī′po·ton′ik) *adj.* **1** Deficient in body tone. **2** Below the osmotic pressure of an isotonic fluid. —**hy′po·to·nic′i·ty** (-tō·nis′ə·tē) *n.*

hy·po·tro·choid (hī′pə·trō′koid) *n. Math.* The curve traced by a point inside a circle, or on its extended radius, as the circle rolls, without slipping, on the inside of another given, fixed circle.

hy·po·tro·phy (hī′pə·trō′fē) *n. Med.* Abiotrophy.

hy·po·ven·ti·la·tion (hī′pō·ven′tə·lā′shən) *n.* Deficient or inadequate ventilation.

hy·po·xan·thine (hī′pə·zan′thēn, -thin) *n. Biochem.* A crystalline alkaloid, $C_5H_4N_4O$, found in various organs, and especially in the muscular tissue of animals, also in certain seeds. Also **hy′po·xan′thin** (-thin). [<Gk. *hypoxanthos* yellowish-brown <*hypo-* under + *xanthos* yellow] —**hy′po·xan′thic** *adj.*

hy·po·xe·mi·a (hī′pok·sē′mē·ə) *n. Med.* Deficient oxygenation of the blood, as from hypoxia. [<HYP- + OX(Y)- + -EMIA]

hy·pox·i·a (hī·pok′sē·ə) *n. Med.* Low oxygen intake by the body, especially as resulting from decreased pressure at high altitudes. [<HYP- + OX(Y)- + -IA]

hypped (hipt), **hyp·pish** (hip′ish) See HIPPED[2], etc.

hypso– *combining form* Height: *hypsometer.* Also, before vowels, **hyps–.** [<Gk. *hypsos* height]

hyp·sog·ra·phy (hip·sog′rə·fē) *n.* **1** The science of observing or describing the topographical features of the earth's surface above sea level. **2** Topographic relief. [<HYPSO- + -GRAPHY] —**hyp·so·graph·ic** (hip′sə·graf′ik) or **·i·cal** *adj.*

hyp·som·e·ter (hip·som′ə·tər) *n.* An instrument for the measurement of heights above sea level by determining the atmospheric pressure through observation of the boiling point of water. [<HYPSO- + -METER]

hyp·som·e·try (hip·som′ə·trē) *n.* The art of measuring, by any method, the heights of points upon the earth's surface above sea level. —**hyp·so·met·ric** (hip′sə·met′rik) or **·ri·cal** *adj.* —**hyp′so·met′ri·cal·ly** *adv.* —**hyp·som′e·trist** *n.*

hyp·so·phyl·lum (hip′sə·fil′əm) *n. Bot.* A bract, or the like, in plant inflorescence. Also **hyp′so·phyl, hyp′so·phyll.** [<HYPSO- + Gk. *phyllon* leaf]

hy·ra·coid (hī′rə·koid) *n.* A hyrax. —*adj.* Of or pertaining to a hyrax. Also **hy′ra·coi′de·an.** [<NL *Hyracoidea,* genus name]

hy·rax (hī′raks) *n. pl.* **·rax·es** or **·ra·ces** (-rə·sēz) A small, harelike ungulate mammal (order *Hyracoidea*) of Africa and SW Asia; the cony of the Bible; the rock hyrax (genus *Procavia*) shelters in crevices and the tree hyrax (genus *Dendrohyrax*) is arboreal. [<Gk., shrewmouse]

Hyr·ca·ni·a (hûr·kā′nē·ə) A province of the ancient Persian Empire, on the SE shore of the Caspian Sea. —**Hyr·ca′ni·an** *adj.* & *n.*

hy·son (hī′sən) *n.* A grade of green tea from China. The early crop is known as **young hyson.** [<Chinese *hsi-ch'un,* lit., blooming spring]

hys·sop (his′əp) *n.* **1** A bushy, medicinal herb *(Hyssopus officinalis)* of the mint family, about 2 feet high, with small clusters of blue flowers. **2** An unidentified plant furnishing the twigs used in the Mosaic purificatory and sacrificial rites, etc. **3** One of various other plants, as the **giant hyssop** (genus *Agastache*). [OE *ysope* <OF <L *hyssopus* <Gk. *hyssōpos* <Hebrew *ēzōb*]

hys·ter·ec·to·my (his′tə·rek′tə·mē) *n. Surg.* Complete removal of the uterus by excision.

hys·ter·e·sis (his′tə·rē′sis) *n.* **1** *Physics* **a** The tendency of a magnetic substance to persist in any state of magnetization; that property of a medium by virtue of which work is done in changing the direction or intensity of magnetic force among its parts. **b** Some

analogous phenomenon, as in dielectrics. When there has been a decrease in magnetization it is called *hysteretic loss,* and the hysteretic loss in ergs per cubic centimeter per cycle is called the *hysteretic constant.* **2** *Biochem.* The influence of the past history of a colloid upon its present condition and behavior. **3** Any state of a material or substance which can be adequately described only in terms of its previous history. [<Gk. *hysterēsis* deficiency <*hystereein* lag] —**hys·ter·et·ic** (his′tə·ret′ik) *adj.*

hys·te·ri·a (his·tir′ē·ə, -ter′-) *n.* **1** *Psychiatry* A psychoneurotic condition characterized by violent emotional paroxysms, anxiety, and morbid effects, as of the sensory and motor functions. **2** Abnormal excitement; morbid emotionalism, as in wild outbursts of alternate laughing and crying. Also **hys·ter·ics** (his·ter′iks). [<NL <Gk. *hystera* the womb; because the condition was thought to affect

women more than men] —**hys·ter·i·cal** (his·ter′i·kəl), **hys·ter′ic** *adj.* —**hys·ter′i·cal·ly** *adv.*
hys·ter·i·tis (his′tə·rī′tis) *n. Pathol.* Inflammation of the womb.
hystero– *combining form* **1** The womb; uterine: *hysteropexy.* **2** Hysteria; hysteric: *hysterogenic.* Also, before vowels, **hyster–.** [< Gk. *hystera* the womb]
hys·ter·o·gen·ic (his′tər·ə·jen′ik) *adj.* Producing or concerned in the production of hysteria.
hys·ter·oid (his′tər·oid) *adj.* Resembling hysteria.
hys·ter·on prot·er·on (his′tər·on prot′ər·on) **1** A figure of speech that reverses the natural order of words or clauses. Example: "Is your father well? is he yet alive?" **2** That form of fallacy in which one asserts a consequent and then infers the antecedent. [<LL <Gk., the latter (put) first]
hys·ter·o·pex·y (his′tər·ə·pek′sē) *n. Surg.* The

operation of fixing the uterus to the abdominal wall to relieve prolapsus. [<HYSTERO- + Gk. *pēxis* fixing]
hys·ter·o·phyte (his′tər·ə·fīt′) *n.* A plant included in an obsolete group (*Hysterophyta*) embracing fungi. —**hys·ter·o·phyt′ic** (-fit′ik) *adj.*
hys·ter·ot·o·my (his′tə·rot′ə·mē) *n. Surg.* **1** The operation of cutting into the womb. **2** Caesarean section. [<HYSTERO- + -TOMY]
hys·tri·co mor·phic (his′tri·kō·môr′fik) *adj.* Of or pertaining to a division (*Hystricomorpha*) of rodents, including porcupines, cavies, etc. [<Gk. *hystrix* porcupine + -MORPHIC]
hyte (hīt) *adj. Scot.* Crazy; mad.
hy·ther (hī′thər) *n. Biol.* The combined effect of moisture and heat on an organism. [<Gk. *hy(dōr)* water + *ther(mē)* heat]
hy·zone (hī′zōn) *n.* Tritium. [<HY(DROGEN) + Gk. *ozein* smell; with ref. to its strong odor]

I

i, I (ī) *n. pl.* **i's, I's** or **Is, eyes** (īz) **1** The ninth letter of the English alphabet: from Phoenician *yod,* Greek *iota,* Roman *I.* **2** Any sound of the letter *i.* See ALPHABET. — *symbol* **1** The Roman numeral one: written I or i. See under NUMERAL. **2** *Chem.* Iodine (symbol I).
I¹ (ī) *pron.* The person speaking or writing, as he denotes himself in the nominative case. — *n.* **1** The self; the pronoun *I* employed as a noun. **2** *Philos.* The ego. [OE *ic*]
I² (ī) *adj.* Shaped like the letter I: an *I-*beam, *I-*rail.
I³ (ī) *interj. Obs.* See AYE or AY.
i′ (i) *prep. Scot.* This.
i–¹ Reduced var. of IN-¹.
i–² See Y-.
–ia¹ *suffix of nouns* Used in: **1** *Geog.* Names of countries: *Australia.* **2** *Pathol.* Names of diseases and related terms: *hysteria.* **3** *Bot.* Names of genera: *Lobelia.* **4** *Chem.* Names of alkaloids: *morphia.* **5** Words borrowed directly from Greek and Latin: *militia.* [<L and Gk. *-ia,* suffix of fem. nouns]
–ia² *suffix of nouns* Used in: **1** *Biol.* Names of classes: *Mammalia.* **2** Names of classical festivals: *Bacchanalia.* **3** Words, usually collectives, borrowed from Latin or Greek: *regalia.* [< L and Gk. *-ia,* plural suffix of neut. nouns]
I·a·go (ē·ä′gō) The perfidious adviser of Othello.
Ia·ko·bos (yä′kə·bôs) Greek form of JAMES.
–ial *suffix of adjectives* Of, pertaining to, or like the first element of the word: *nuptial, filial.* [Var. of -AL¹, with connective *-i*]
i·am·bic (ī·am′bik) *adj.* **1** Pertaining to or employing the iambus: *iambic* poetry. **2** Having characteristics of iambics. — *n.* **1** An iambus. **2** A verse, line, or stanza composed of iambic feet. **3** A satire or invective poem in iambic verse. [<L *iambicus* <Gk. *iambikos*]
i·am·bus (ī·am′bəs) *n. pl.* ·**bi** (-bī) A foot of two syllables, a short or unaccented followed by a long or accented one. Also **i·amb** (ī′amb). [<L <Gk. *iambos* <*iambein* assail verbally; because orig. utilized by satiric poets]
–ian *suffix* Of, pertaining to, from, or like the proper name appearing in the stem: *Baconian, Bostonian,* etc. [Var. of -AN, with connective *-i*]
–iana See -ANA.
–iasis *suffix Med.* Denoting a process and its results, especially in diseased conditions: *psoriasis.* [Var. of -OSIS]
Ia·sy (yä′shē, yäsh) See JASSY.
i·at·ric (ī·at′rik) *adj.* Relating to physicians and the healing art; medical. Also **i·at′ri·cal.** [<Gk. *iatrikos* healing <*iatros* physician <*iasthai* heal]
–iatrics *combining form* Denoting treatment of disease: *pediatrics.* [<Gk. *iatrikos* pertaining to the art of healing]

iatro– *combining form* Signifying a connection with or relation to medicine: *iatrochemistry, iatrophysics,* etc. [<Gk. *iatros* physician]
i·at·ro·gen·ic (ī·at′rə·jen′ik) *adj. Med.* Generated or induced by the physician; said especially of disorders resulting from autosuggestion based on the physician's manner of handling or discussing a case.
–iatry *combining form* Medical or curative treatment: *psychiatry.* [<Gk. *iatreia* healing]
I·ba·dan (ē·bä′dän) A city in SW Nigeria.
I·ba·ñez (ē·vä′nyeth) See BLASCO Y IBAÑEZ.
I–beam (ī′bēm′) *n.* A beam or joist having a cross-section in the shape of an I.
I·be·ri·a (ī·bir′ē·ə) **1** The part of SW Europe comprising Spain and Portugal: also **Iberian Peninsula.** **2** An ancient country between the Caucasus and Armenia, corresponding to modern Georgia.
I·be·ri·an (ī·bir′ē·ən) *adj.* **1** Of or pertaining to ancient Iberia in Asia, now Transcaucasian Georgia. **2** Of or pertaining to the Iberian Peninsula, including Spain and Portugal, or relating to the people of this region. — *n.* **1** One of the inhabitants of ancient Iberia in Asia, conquered by the Arabs in the seventh century. **2** A member of the oldest ethnological group of Europe, which existed on the Iberian Peninsula as early as the Neolithic era. **3** The unclassified language of the ancient inhabitants of the Iberian Peninsula, of which Basque may be a modern survivor: known only through some proper names and about 150 inscriptions. [<L *Iberus* <Gk. *Iberes* Spaniards]
I·ber·ville (dē′bər·vil, *Fr.* dē·ber·vēl′), **Sieur d',** 1661–1706, Pierre Lemoyne (or Le Moyne), French-Canadian explorer; colonized Louisiana.
i·bex (ī′beks) *n. pl.* **i·bex·es** or **i·bi·ces** (ī′bə·sēz, ib′ə-) One of various wild goats of Europe and Asia, with long, recurved horns, especially the Alpine ibex (*Capra ibex*) and the Cretan ibex (*C. hircus*). [<L]
I·bi·cuí (ē·bē·kwē′) A river in southern Brazil, flowing 300 miles west to the Uruguay.
i·bi·dem (i·bī′dem) *adv. Latin* In the same place. Abbr. *ibid.*
i·bis (ī′bis) *n. pl.* **i·bis·es** or **i·bis 1** A wading bird related to the heron (family *Threskiornithidae*), with cylindrical

IBEX
(Species vary from 2 1/2 to 3 1/2 feet tall)

bill bent downward; especially the sacred ibis (*Threskiornis aethiopica*), venerated among the ancient Egyptians. **2** The wood ibis. [<L <Gk. <Egyptian *hab*]
–ible See -ABLE.
Ib·lees (ib′lēs) See EBLIS.
Ibn Sa·ud (ib′n sä·ōōd′), **Abdul Aziz,** 1880–1953, king of Saudi Arabia 1932–53. See SAUD.
I·bo (ē′bō) *n. pl.* **I·bo 1** A member of a group of Negro tribes of western Africa. **2** The Sudanic language of these tribes. [< the native name]
i·bo·ga (i·bō′gə) *n.* A cultivated shrub (genus *Tabernaemontana,* formerly *Tabernanthe iboga*) of the dogbane family, of central Africa. [< native name]
i·bo·gaine (i·bō′gän, -gə·ēn) *n. Chem.* A poisonous alkaloid, $C_{52}H_{66}O_2N_6$, from the root, bark, and leaves of the iboga: similar in action to cocaine.
Ib·ra·him Pa·sha (ib·rä·hēm′ pä′shə), 1789–1848, Egyptian commander and viceroy.
Ib·sen (ib′sən), **Henrik,** 1828–1906, Norwegian dramatist and poet.
Ib·sen·ism (ib′sən·iz′əm) *n.* A theory or doctrine concerning Ibsen's plays, which were conceived by his imitators and critics, though not by Ibsen himself, as problem plays in which social conventions and attitudes were criticized.
–ic *suffix* Of adjectives: **1** Of or pertaining to: *volcanic.* **2** Like; resembling; characteristic of: *angelic.* **3** Consisting of; containing: *alcoholic.* **4** Produced or caused by: *Homeric.* **5** Related to; connected with: *domestic.* **6** *Chem.* Having a higher valence than that indicated by *-ous:* said of elements in compounds: *cupric* oxide, *sulfuric* acid. — Of nouns: **1** By the conversion of adjectives in any of the above senses: *Stoic, public.* **2** The art or knowledge of: *rhetoric, music.* [<F *-ique* <L *-icus* <Gk. *-ikos*]
   ◆ –ic, –icly A few adjectives in *-ic* form adverbs in *-icly,* as, *publicly,* but the adverb is usually formed by adding *-ally: musically, rhythmically, volcanically.* See also note under *-ICAL, -ICS.*
I·çá (ē·sä′) The Putumayo in its lower courses in Brazil.
–ical *suffix* **1** Like; pertaining to: *ethical:* used in adjectives derived from nouns in *-ic, -ics.* **2** With the same general meaning as *-ic: comical;* sometimes with extended or special meaning: *economical.* [<LL *-icalis* < *-icus* -IC + *-alis* -AL]
   ◆ –ic, –ical In cases where both forms exist and do not differ greatly in meaning, there is no set rule governing usage. Euphony and past usage alone generally determine the choice of one form over the other.
I·car·i·a (i·kâr′ē·ə, ī-) A Greek Aegean island SW of Samos; 99 square miles; formerly *Nicaria:* also *Ikaria.*

I·car·i·an (ī-kâr′ē-ən, ĭ-) *adj.* Of or pertaining to Icarus, son of Daedalus; hence, high-flying; rash or adventurous; presumptuous. [<L *Icarus* <Gk. *Ikarios*]

Icarian Sea The Aegean Sea off the coast of Asia Minor, where Icarus was supposed to have fallen after his flight.

Ic·a·rus (ĭk′ə-rəs, ī′kə-) In Greek mythology, the son of Daedalus, who, escaping with his father from Crete, flew too near the sun so that the wax that fastened his artificial wings melted and he fell into the sea and drowned.

ICBM The intercontinental ballistic missile, having a range of at least 5,000 miles. Compare *IRBM*.

ice (īs) *n.* 1 Congealed or frozen water; the solid condition assumed by water at or below 32° F. or 0° C. ◆ Collateral adjective: *glacial.* 2 A frozen dessert made without cream, as a sherbet, water ice, or frappé. 3 Something resembling ice in appearance: camphor *ice.* 4 Frosting or icing for cake. 5 Chilly reserve; a very formal or dignified attitude. 6 *Slang* A diamond; also, diamonds collectively. — **to break the ice** To break through reserve or formality. — **to cut no ice** *U.S. Slang* To have no importance. — **on ice** *U.S. Slang* 1 Set aside or reserved for future action. 2 In prison. 3 Sure; already determined. — *v.* **iced, ic·ing** *v.t.* 1 To cause to freeze; congeal into ice. 2 To cover with ice. 3 To chill with or as with ice. 4 To frost, as cake, with icing. — *v.i.* 5 To freeze; congeal into ice. — *adj.* Made of ice; to be used on ice: *ice skates.* [OE *īs*]

-ice *suffix of nouns* Condition, quality, or state of: *justice.* [<OF *-ice* <L *-itius, -itia, -itium*]

ice age The glacial epoch.

ice anchor See ICE HOOK (def. 2).

ice ax An ax used by mountaineers for cutting steps in the ice: usually equipped with a spiked butt.

ice·berg (īs′bûrg) *n.* 1 A thick mass of ice found floating in the sea at high latitudes; a portion of a glacier discharged into the sea: distinguished from *field ice.* 2 A cold, unemotional person. [<Du. *ijsberg*]

ice-blink (īs′blingk) *n.* A shining whiteness on the horizon produced by the reflection of distant masses of ice. [Cf. Du. *ijsblin,* Dan. *iisblink*]

ice-boat (īs′bōt′) *n.* 1 A framework with skatelike runners and sails for sailing over ice. 2 An icebreaker (def. 2).

ice·bone (īs′bōn′) *n.* The aitchbone. [Prob. <L *ischium* ischium + BONE. Cf. MDu. *yschbeen.*]

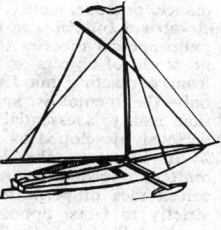

ICEBOAT

ice boulder A boulder transported and deposited through glacial action.

ice·bound (īs′bound′) *adj.* Surrounded, beset, or obstructed by ice; frozen in: an *icebound* ship, an *icebound* harbor.

ice·box (īs′boks′) *n.* A refrigerator. Also **ice′-chest′** (-chest′).

ice·break·er (īs′brā′kər) *n.* 1 A structure for deflecting ice from a bridge pier or the like: also **ice′-a′pron** (-ā′prən). 2 A specially constructed ship having a strong prow and powerful engines, used to break up ice in navigable channels of icebound waters and harbors.

ice cap An extensive covering of ice and snow permanently overlying a tract of land and moving in all directions from a center. See ICE SHEET.

ice-cream (īs′krēm′) *n.* A mixture of cream or butterfat, flavoring, sweetening, and often eggs, beaten to a uniform consistency and frozen. Also **ice cream.** [Orig., *iced cream*]

iced (īst) *adj.* 1 Coated or covered with ice or sleet. 2 Made cold with ice. 3 Covered with icing, as cake.

ice·fall (īs′fôl′) *n.* The steepest part or the precipice of a glacier, resembling a frozen waterfall.

ice field A large field of floating ice. Also **ice float, ice floe.**

ice fishing Fishing through holes cut in the ice.

ice-foot (īs′fŏot′) *n.* A wall of ice formed by sea water and snow frozen along the shore in polar regions. [Trans. of Dan. *isfod*]

ice hook 1 A hook attached to a pole: used in handling large blocks of ice. See illustration under HOOK. 2 An S-shaped iron bar sharpened at one point: used with a hawser to secure a vessel to ice: also *ice anchor.*

ice-house (īs′hous′) *n.* A building for storing ice.

I·cel (ē-chel′) A city in southern Turkey: also *Mersin.* Turkish *I·çel′.*

Ice·land (īs′lənd) The westernmost state of Europe, comprising an independent island republic in the North Atlantic; 39,709 square miles; capital, Reykjavík; a Danish possession until 1944. Icelandic **Ís·land** (ēs′länt).

Ice·land·er (īs′lan′dər) *n.* A native or naturalized inhabitant of Iceland.

Ice·land·ic (īs-lan′dik) *adj.* Of or pertaining to Iceland. — *n.* The North Germanic language of Iceland; strictly, this language since the 16th century. — **Old Icelandic** The language of Iceland before the 16th century, exemplified in the Eddas: the best literary representative of Old Norse, and sometimes used synonymously for it.

Iceland moss An edible and medicinal lichen (*Cetraria islandica*) of the arctic regions.

Iceland poppy See under POPPY.

ice·man (īs′man′, -mən) *n. pl.* **·men** (-men′, -mən) 1 One who gathers and stores or deals in ice; also, one who carts and delivers ice to consumers. 2 One skilled in traveling upon ice or navigating among masses of ice.

ice needle *Meteorol.* A thin crystal of ice, so light that it floats suspended in the air.

I·ce·ni (ī-sē′nī) *n. pl.* An ancient British tribe, led by its queen, Boadicea, against the Romans; defeated by Suetonius Paulinus, A.D. 61. [<L]

ice pack 1 A large tract of floating ice cakes closely compacted and held together. 2 A container for cracked ice, used for medical applications.

ice pick An awl-like tool for breaking ice into small pieces.

ice plant A fig marigold of southern Africa, the Mediterranean region, and southern California (*Mesembryanthemum crystallinum*) having leaves covered with glistening frostlike protuberances.

ice point *Physics* The melting point of ice at standard atmospheric pressure, 0.0° C: one of the fixed points of the international temperature scale.

ice·quake (īs′kwāk′) *n.* The disturbance attending the rupture of masses of ice.

ice rain 1 A rain that congeals quickly in a deposit of glaze. 2 Falling pellets of clear ice; sleet.

ice sheet A large ice cap; a continental glacier.

ice-skate (īs′skāt′) *v.i.* **-skat·ed, -skat·ing** To skate on the ice.

ice skate A skate with a metal runner for skating on ice.

ice-up (īs′up′) *n. Aeron.* The formation of ice on the leading edges or other exposed surfaces of airplanes when passing through moist air at low temperatures. Also **ic′ing.**

ice water 1 Water chilled by ice. 2 Melted ice.

Ich·a·bod (ik′ə-bod) A grandson of Eli. 1 *Sam.* iv 21. [<Hebrew, ? inglorious]

Ich·a·bod Crane (ik′ə-bod krān′) A Yankee schoolteacher in Irving's *Legend of Sleepy Hollow.*

I·chang (ē′chäng′) A port on the Yangtze, south central China.

ich dien (ikh dēn) *German* I serve: motto of the Prince of Wales.

ich·neu·mon (ik-nōō′mən, -nyōō′-) *n.* 1 An Old World civetlike carnivore of somewhat weasel-like aspect (genus *Herpestes*), as the mongoose, feeding on mice, eggs, snakes, etc. 2 An ichneumon fly. [<L *ichneumon,* lit., tracker <*ichneuein* track down <*ichnos* footstep, trace; because it was believed to track down and eat crocodiles' eggs]

ichneumon fly A hymenopterous insect (family *Ichneumonidae*) that deposits its eggs upon or in other insects which its larvae will feed upon. For illustration see under INSECT (beneficial).

ich·nite (ik′nīt) *n. Paleontol.* A fossil footprint. Also **ich′no·lite** (-nə-līt). [<Gk. *ichnos* footprint]

ich·no·graph (ik′nə-graf, -gräf) *n.* A ground plan.

ich·nog·ra·phy (ik-nog′rə-fē) *n.* 1 The art of drawing by means of compass and rule, or of tracing plans, etc. 2 The plan drawn. [<LL *ichnografia* <Gk. <*ichnos* trace + *graphein* write] — **ich·no·graph·ic** (ik′nə-graf′ik) or **-i·cal** *adj.*

i·chor (ī′kôr, ī′kər) *n.* 1 In classical mythology, the ethereal fluid supposed to flow in the veins of the gods. 2 A watery acrid humor discharged from sores. [<Gk. *ichōr*]

i·chor·ous (ī′kər-əs) *adj.* Full of, mingled with, or like ichor.

ich·thy·ic (ik′thē-ik) *adj.* Fishlike.

ichthyo- *combining form* Fish: *ichthyology.* Also, before vowels, **ichthy-.** [<Gk. *ichthys* fish]

ich·thy·o·cen·taur (ik′thē-ə-sen′tôr) *n.* A fabulous monster, combining the form of man and fish.

ich·thy·oid (ik′thē-oid) *adj.* Of or like a fish: also **ich′thy·oi′dal.** — *n.* A fishlike vertebrate.

ich·thy·ol (ik′thē-ōl, -ol) *n.* Proprietary name for a compound of sulfonated hydrocarbons obtained by the distillation of certain shales: used mainly in skin diseases.

ich·thy·o·lite (ik′thē-ə-līt′) *n. Paleontol.* A fossil fish.

ich·thy·ol·o·gy (ik′thē-ol′ə-jē) *n.* The branch of zoology that treats of fishes. [<ICHTHYO- + -LOGY] — **ich·thy·o·log·ic** (ik′thē-ə-loj′ik) *adj.* — **ich′thy·o·log′i·cal** *adj.*

ich·thy·oph·a·gist (ik′thē-of′ə-jist) *n.* One who feeds on fish.

ich·thy·oph·a·gous (ik′thē-of′ə-gəs) *adj.* Fish-eating.

ich·thy·oph·a·gy (ik′thē-of′ə-jē) *n.* The practice of feeding on fish.

ich·thy·or·nis (ik′thē-ôr′nis) *n. Paleontol.* One of a genus (*Ichthyornis*) of extinct toothed birds of the Cretaceous having fishlike vertebrae. [<ICHTHY- + Gk. *ornis* bird]

ich·thy·o·sau·rus (ik′thē-ə-sôr′əs) *n. pl.* **·sau·ri** (-sôr′ī) *Paleontol.* Any of an order (*Ichthyosauria*) of extinct marine reptiles of the Mesozoic era, having a porpoise-like form with four paddlelike limbs, a large, elongated head, long tail, and

ICHTHYOSAURUS
(The largest are thought to have been about 30 feet long)

broad vertebrae resembling those of fishes. Also **ich′thy·o·saur′.** [<ICHTHYO- + Gk. *sauros* lizard]

ich·thy·o·sis (ik′thē-ō′sis) *n. Pathol.* A congenital skin disease characterized by dry, scaly or horny formations. — **ich′thy·ot′ic** (-ot′ik) *adj.*

-ician *suffix of nouns* One skilled in, or engaged in, the field of: *logician, mathematician:* originally used with names of arts and sciences ending in *-ic* or *-ics,* but now, by analogy, with any stem, as in *beautician, mortician.* [<F *-icien*]

i·ci·cle (ī′si-kəl) *n.* A pendent, tapering mass or rod of ice formed by the freezing of drops of dripping water. [OE *īsgicel* <*īs* ice + *gicel* piece of ice, icicle] — **i′ci·cled** *adj.*

i·ci·ly (ī′sə-lē) *adv.* In an icy manner; frigidly; frostily.

ic·ing (ī′sing) *n.* A glazing or coating of sugar, usually mixed with white of egg or cream, for a cake; frosting.

i·ci on parle fran·çais (ē-sē′ ôṅ pàrl′ frän-se′) *French* French is spoken here.

ick·er (ik′ər) *n. Scot.* A head of grain; an ear of corn.

Ick·es (ik′əs, -ēz), **Harold,** 1874–1952, U.S. public administrator and writer.

Ic·olm·kill (ik′əlm-kil) See IONA.

i·con (ī′kon) *n. pl.* **·cons** or **i·co·nes** (ī′kə-nēz) 1 An image or likeness. 2 In the Greek Church, a holy picture, mosaic, etc.: also

spelled *ikon.* 3 Formerly, any book illustration. Also called *eikon.* See synonyms under IMAGE. [<Gk. *eikōn* image]

i·con·ic (ī·kon′ik) *adj.* 1 Relating to or of the nature of an icon. 2 Relating to portraiture. 3 Customary or conventional, in art: applied originally to the portraits or statues of athletes who had been victorious in the contests, and later to memorial busts, etc., made after conventional types. Also **i·con′i·cal.**

I·co·ni·um (ī·kō′nē·əm) The ancient name for KONYA.

icono– *combining form* Image; of or related to images: *iconography.* Also, before vowels, **icon–.** [<Gk. *eikōn* image]

i·con·o·clast (ī·kon′ə·klast) *n.* 1 An image breaker. 2 One of certain religious parties devoted to the destruction of images that were venerated or worshiped. 3 One who assails traditional beliefs. [<LL *iconoclastes* <Gk. *eikonoklastēs* <*eikōn* image + *-klastēs* breaker <*klaein* break, destroy] **—i·con′o·clas′tic** *adj.*

i·con·o·ge·net·ic (ī·kon′ə·jə·net′ik) *adj.* 1 Image–forming. 2 *Biol.* Capable of gathering visual information about external objects, as the eyes of animals.

i·co·nog·ra·phy (ī′kə·nog′rə·fē) *n. pl.* **·phies** 1 The science of the description and study of paintings, sculptures, portraits, busts, statues, emblems, and symbolism: Christian *iconography.* 2 The art of illustration by figures; pictorial representation. 3 *Obs.* A picture or other representation, or a collection of representations. [<Med. L *iconografia* <Gk. *eikonografia* <*eikōn* icon + *graphein* write] **—i·con·o·graph·ic** (ī·kon′ə·graf′ik) or **·i·cal** *adj.*

i·co·nol·a·ter (ī′kə·nol′ə·tər) *n.* A worshiper of images; an idolater. [<ICONO-+ -LATRY] **—i′co·nol′a·try** *n.*

i·co·nol·o·gy (ī′kə·nol′ə·jē) *n. pl.* **·gies** 1 The science of pictorial or emblematic representation. 2 A study or description of works of art, emblematic figures, and particularly the attributes of religious, mythological and historical personages. [<ICONO- + -LOGY] **—i·con·o·log·i·cal** (ī·kon′ə·loj′i·kəl) *adj.*

i·con·o·ma·ni·a (ī·kon′ə·mā′nē·ə, -mān′yə) *n.* A morbid interest in, or obsession with, images, fancied or real.

i·con·o·scope (ī·kon′ə·skōp) *n. Telecom.* A scanning device used in television, consisting of an evacuated glass bulb containing a photosensitive screen from whose surface the image is picked up by a narrow, intense, swiftly moving beam of electrons.

i·co·nos·ta·sis (ī′kə·nos′tə·sis) *n. pl.* **·ses** (-sēz) In the Eastern Church, the screen separating the sacristy, bema, and chapel of prothesis from the rest of the church. Also **i·con·o·stas** (ī·kon′ə·stas). [<NL <NGk. *eikonostasis* < *eikōn* icon + *stasis* standing]

i·co·sa·he·dron (ī′kō·sə·hē′drən) *n. pl.* **·dra** (-drə) *Geom.* A solid bounded by 20 plane faces. [<Gk. *eikosaedron*] **—i′co·sa·he′dral** (-drəl) *adj.*

icosi– *combining form* Twenty. Also, before vowels, **icos–.** [<Gk. *eikosi* twenty]

–ics *suffix of nouns* 1 Art, science, or field of study of: *mathematics.* 2 Methods, practices, or activities of: *athletics.* [See -IC]

◆ **–ic, –ics** Adjectives in Greek, ending in *–ikē* (feminine singular) and *–ika* (neuter plural) were often used as nouns to indicate the names of arts or the various departments of life and knowledge. These words were borrowed, through Latin *–ica,* as singular nouns in the Romance languages and later into English. After the 16th century, it became customary to use the plural form in *–ics,* on analogy with Greek *–ika*: *optics, logistics, acoustics.* Nouns ending in *–ics* are construed as singular when they strictly denote an art, science, or system (as, mathematics is difficult; politics offers an uncertain future); they are construed as plural if they denote personal attributes (as, his mathematics are poor; his politics are suspect), if they denote inherent qualities (as, the acoustics are bad) or specific activities (as, athletics are compulsory; hysterics are unseemly; our tactics are superior to the enemy's).

ic·ter·ic (ik·ter′ik) *adj. Pathol.* Affected with jaundice. Also **ic·ter′i·cal.** [<Gk. *ikterikos*]

ic·ter·us (ik′tər·əs) *n.* 1 *Pathol.* Jaundice. 2 *Bot.* Yellowness in the leaves of plants, caused by protracted wet or cold weather. [<LL <Gk. *ikteros* jaundice]

Ic·ti·nus (ik·tī′nəs) Fifth century B.C. Greek architect; designed the Parthenon.

ic·tus (ik′təs) *n. pl.* **·tus·es** or **·tus** 1 *Pathol.* a A stroke or blow. b A sudden attack or fit. 2 The sting of an insect. 3 A metrical stress or a syllable. [<L, pp. of *icere* strike]

i·cy (ī′sē) *adj.* **i·ci·er, i·ci·est** 1 Pertaining to ice; frigid; as cold as ice; full of or like ice. 2 Marked by coldness of manner, aspect, etc.; chilling. [OE *isig*] **—i′ci·ness, i′cy·ness** *n.*

id (id) *n.* 1 *Biol.* In Weismann's theory of heredity, a unit of germ plasm representing the characteristics of an ancestral member of the species: supposedly composed of determinants, which are made up of biophores. 2 *Psychoanal.* The concealed, inaccessible part of the psyche, seated in the unconscious, independent of a sense of reality, logic, and morality, but actuated by fundamental impulses towards fulfilling instinctual needs; the reservoir of psychic energy or libido. [Def. 1, short for IDIOPLASM; def. 2, <NL <L *id* it, trans. of G *es*]

I'd (īd) 1 I would. 2 I had.

–id[1] *suffix* 1 *Zool.* a A member of a family: *leporid.* b A member of a class: *arachnid.* 2 *Astron.* A meteor from: used to denote meteors which seem to radiate from certain constellations: *Perseid.* 3 An epic about: *Aeneid.* 4 Son or daughter of: often used in personal names from classical myth or legend: *Danaid.* [<L *-is, -idis* <Gk.*-is, -idos,* suffix of patronymics]

–id[2] *suffix of adjectives* Having a particular quality, or in a specified state: *fluid, vivid.* [< F *-ide* <L *-idus;* or directly <L]

I·da (ī′də, *Du., Ger., Ital.* ē′dä; *Fr.* ē·dȧ′) A feminine personal name. [<Gmc., happy]

I·da (ī′də) 1 A mountain range in NW Asia Minor near the site of ancient Troy; highest peak, 5,797 feet: *Turkish* **Kaz Da·gi** (käz′dä·ē′). 2 The highest mountain in Crete; 8,058 feet: also *Psiloriti*: *Greek* **I·dhi** (ē′thi).

–idae *suffix Zool.* Used to form the names of families of animals when added to the stem of the name of the type genus: *Canidae.* [<NL *-idae* <L <Gk. *-idai,* plural patronymic suffix]

I·dae·an (ī·dē′ən) *adj.* Of or pertaining to Mount Ida.

I·da·ho (ī′də·hō) A NW State of the United States; 83,557 square miles; capital, Boise; entered the Union July 3, 1890; nickname, *Gem State*: abbr. ID **—I′da·ho′an** *adj. & n.*

–ide *suffix Chem.* Used in the names of compounds, usually binary, and attached to the electronegative or non–metallic element or radical: sodium *chloride.* Also **–id.** [<F *-ide.* See -ID[2].]

i·de·a (ī·dē′ə) *n.* 1 Any notion or thought: the *idea* of a horse or of happiness. 2 The result of thinking; a definitely formulated thought; an opinion: a clear *idea* of social justice. 3 A plan or project: to have an *idea* of going into business. 4 A concept; a mental representation of something perceived through the senses. 5 A vague thought or fancy; supposition: I had no *idea* you'd come. 6 *Colloq.* Meaning; aim: What's the *idea*? 7 In Platonic philosophy, the archetype or external pattern of which all existing things are imperfect representations. 8 *Obs.* The embodiment of a conception, belief, or view. [<L <Gk. < *idein* see]

Synonyms: apprehension, archetype, belief, conceit, concept, conception, design, fancy, fantasy, ideal, image, imagination, impression, judgment, model, notion, opinion, pattern, plan, purpose, sentiment, supposition, theory, thought. *Idea* is in Greek a *form* or an *image.* The sense implied by early Platonic philosophy has nearly disappeared and has been largely appropriated by *ideal,* but something of the original meaning still appears when in theological or philosophical language we speak of the *ideas* of God. The present popular use of *idea* makes it signify any product of mental *apprehension* or activity, considered as an object of knowledge or thought; this coincides with the primitive sense at but a single point—that an *idea* is mental as opposed to anything substantial or physical; thus, almost any mental product, as a *belief, conception, design, opinion,* etc., may now be called an *idea.* Compare FANCY, IDEAL, IMAGE, THOUGHT[1]. *Antonyms*: actuality, fact, reality, substance.

i·de·al (ī·dē′əl, ī·dēl′) *adj.* 1 Pertaining to or existing in ideas; conceptional. 2 Of or pertaining to an ideal or perfection. 3 Conceived as perfect, supremely excellent, or very desirable. 4 Existing only in imagination or notion; of such perfection as to be practically unattainable. 5 In philosophy, existing as an archetypal idea or pattern. **—***n.* 1 That which is taken as a standard of excellence or beauty; an ultimate object of attainment; model; type. 2 That which exists only in imagination. [<L *idealis*]

Synonyms (adj.): fancied, fanciful, imaginary, unreal, visionary. Compare IMAGINARY, ROMANTIC. See also PERFECT. *Antonyms*: actual, material, palpable, physical, real, substantial, tangible, visible.

Synonyms (noun): archetype, idea, model, original, pattern, prototype, standard. An *ideal* is that which is conceived or taken as the highest type of excellence or ultimate object of attainment. The *archetype* is the primal form, actual or imaginary, according to which any existing thing is constructed; the *prototype* has or has had actual existence; in the derived sense, as in metrology, a *prototype* may not be the original form, but one having equal authority with that as a standard. An *ideal* may be primal, or may be slowly developed even from failures and by negations; an *ideal* is meant to be perfect, the best conceivable thing that could by possibility be attained. The artist's *ideal* is his own mental image, of which his finished work is but an imperfect expression. The *original* is the first specimen, good or bad; the *original* of a master is superior to all copies. The *standard* may be below the *ideal.* The *ideal* is ordinarily unattainable; the *standard* is concrete, and ordinarily attainable, being a measure to which all else of its kind must conform; as, the *standard* of weights and measures, of corn, or of cotton. The *idea* of virtue is the mental concept or image of virtue in general: the *ideal* of virtue is the mental concept or image of virtue in its highest conceivable perfection. Compare EXAMPLE, IDEA. *Antonyms*: accomplishment, achievement, act, action, attainment, development, doing, embodiment, execution, fact, incarnation, performance, practice, reality, realization.

i·de·al·ism (ī·dē′əl·iz′əm) *n.* 1 Any of several philosophical theories that there is no reality, no world of objects or "thing–in–itself" apart from a reacting mind or consciousness; that only the mental is knowable, and therefore that reality is essentially spiritual or mental: variously developed by Berkeley, Kant, Hegel. 2 In literature, the development of subject matter following an imaginative or preconceived idea of perfection instead of adhering strictly to facts: opposed to *realism.* 3 The quest of the ideal; the habit of forming ideals and of striving after their realization; by extension, that which is so realized; the attainment of an ideal. 4 In art, the endeavor to attain perfection by improving and uniting in one form all the best qualities to be found in different individual forms. *Idealism* creates in conformity with a preconceived ideal; *realism* restricts the imaginative faculty.

i·de·al·ist (ī·dē′əl·ist) *n.* 1 One who idealizes, or seeks an ideal or ideal conditions; a visionary; a romantic. 2 An exponent of idealism in art or literature. 3 One who holds the doctrines of any philosophic idealism. **—i·de′al·is′tic** or **·ti·cal** *adj.***—i·de′al·is′ti·cal·ly** *adv.*

i·de·al·i·ty (ī′dē·al′ə·tē) *n. pl.* **·ties** 1 The condition or character of being ideal; existence only in the mind 2 The power or tendency to form ideals; imagination.

i·de·al·ize (ī·dē′əl·īz) *v.* **·ized, ·iz·ing** *v.t.* To represent or think of as conforming to some standard of perfection or beauty; make ideal; exalt. **—***v.i.* To form an ideal or ideals. **—i·de·al·i·za·tion** (ī·dē′əl·ə·zā′shən, -ī·zā′-) *n.* **—i·de′al·iz′er** *n.*

i·de·al·ly (ī·dē′əl·ē) *adv.* 1 Conforming to an ideal. 2 In idea or imagination; mentally; intellectually.

i·de·ate (ī·dē′āt) *v.* **·at·ed, ·at·ing** *v.t.* To form an idea of; frame in the mind; conceive. **—***v.i.* To form ideas; think. **—***n. Philos.* The object corresponding to an idea: so distinguished by

those who regard the object not simply as perceived, but as the product of perception: also **i·de·a·tum** (ī′dē·ā′təm).

i·de·a·tion (ī′dē·ā′shən) *n.* **1** The mental power to form ideas. **2** The mental process of forming and using ideas. — **i′de·a′tion·al** *adj.*

i·dée fixe (ē·dā′ fēks′) *French pl.* **idées fixes** (ē·dā′ fēks′) A fixed idea; obsession.

i·dem (ī′dem) *n.* & *adj. Latin* The same: often as referring to what was previously mentioned.

i·den·tic (ī·den′tik) *adj.* **1** Identical. **2** In diplomatic correspondence, identical in form: said of notes sent by two governments dealing with a third.

i·den·ti·cal (ī·den′ti·kəl) *adj.* **1** Absolutely the same; the very same. **2** Uniform with something else in quality, condition, execution, appearance, etc. [<Med. L *identicus* < *idem* the same] — **i·den′ti·cal·ly** *adv.* — **i·den′ti·cal·ness** *n.*

Synonyms: alike, equivalent, interchangeable, same, selfsame. Strictly, no two persons or things can be *identical* or the *same*. In looser usage, two volumes may be said to be *identical* or the *same* in contents; a carbon copy is *identical* in substance with the original, but it is not the *same* document. Two synonyms, as "begin" and "commence," may be in most cases *equivalent* and *interchangeable*, but one is not the *same* as the other, and at some point they will be found to draw apart, either in meaning or use. A check may be *equivalent* to the money specified, but it is not the *same* as cash. When a person or thing is surely recognized as the very one referred to, and no other, we say, "This is the *identical* man, the *identical* document," or "the *same* man, document." See SYNONYMOUS. *Antonyms*: contrary, different, dissimilar, distinct, unlike.

identical twin *Genetics* One of a pair of human offspring which develop from a division of a single fertilized egg cell. They are invariably of the same sex and exhibit similarities due to participation in the same genetic factors: distinguished from *fraternal twin*.

i·den·ti·fi·ca·tion (ī·den′tə·fə·kā′shən) *n.* **1** The act or process of showing to be the same. **2** The state of being shown or proved to be identical. **3** Anything by which identity can be established. **4** *Psychoanal.* A process by which an individual, usually subconsciously, behaves or imagines himself behaving as if he were a person with whom he has formed an emotional tie. **5** The act or state of feeling sympathy for a fictitious or dramatic character, sometimes extending to projection of the image of the self into the character. See EMPATHY.

identification tag **1** *Mil.* Either of two metal disks worn by a soldier, and bearing his name, serial number, and other personal data: popularly called *dog tag*. **2** Any tag affixed, as to a suitcase or trunk, for purpose of identification.

i·den·ti·fy (ī·den′tə·fī) *v.t.* **·fied, ·fy·ing** **1** To determine or establish as a particular person or thing; ascertain the nature or supposed identity of. **2** To consider or treat as the same; make the same or identical: He *identifies* money with happiness. **3** To serve as a means of recognition or identification of: The teeth *identified* the skull. **4** To join or associate in interest, action, etc.: usually with *with*: He *identified* his name with a well-known charity. **5** *Biol.* To determine the proper genus, order, etc., of. **6** *Psychoanal.* To make identification of (oneself) with someone else. [<LL *identificare*] — **i·den′ti·fi′a·ble** *adj.* — **i·den′ti·fi′er** *n.*

i·den·ti·ty (ī·den′tə·tē) *n.* *pl.* **·ties** **1** The state of being identical or absolutely the same; selfsameness. **2** Sameness of character or quality. Identity may be of two sorts: *absolute*, which involves exact equality with itself, or selfsameness, as the equation $a = a$; and *relative*, a less rigid sense, which implies a close material resemblance or similarity, as that of the green of two leaves. **3** The distinctive character belonging to an individual; personality; individuality. **4** The state of being what is asserted or described. [<LL *identitas, -tatis* < *idem* the same]

ideo– *combining form* Idea; of or pertaining to ideas: *ideograph*. [<Gk. *idea* a form, idea]

i·de·o·graph (ī′dē·ə·graf′, -gräf′, id′ē-) *n.* **1** A picture symbol or sign of an object, or the graphic representation of a thought, as distinguished from a representation of the sound of a word in the given language. **2** A symbol, as +, =, ¶, $, etc. Also **i′de·o·gram′** (-gram′). — **i′de·o·graph′ic** or **·i·cal** *adj.* — **i′de·o·graph′i·cal·ly** *adv.*

i·de·og·ra·phy (ī′dē·og′rə·fē, id′ē-) *n.* The graphic representation of ideas by symbolic characters: use of ideographs. [<IDEO- + -GRAPHY]

i·de·ol·o·gist (ī′dē·ol′ə·jist, id′ē-) *n.* **1** One who formulates or is expert in an ideology. **2** A visionary.

i·de·ol·o·gize (ī′dē·ol′ə·jīz, id′ē-) *v.t.* To imbue, as a person, group, or nation, with a certain ideology; to indoctrinate.

i·de·o·logue (ī′dē·ə·lôg, -log, id′ē-) *n.* One who is committed to an ideology. [<F]

i·de·ol·o·gy (ī′dē·ol′ə·jē, id′ē-) *n.* **1** The ideas or kind of thinking characteristic of an individual or group; specifically, the ideas and objectives that influence a whole group or national culture, shaping especially their political and social procedure: German *ideology*. **2** The science that treats of the evolution of human ideas. [<IDEO- + -LOGY] — **i·de·o·log·ic** (ī′dē·ə·loj′ik, id′ē-) or **·i·cal** *adj.*

i·de·o·mo·tor (ī′dē·ə·mō′tər, id′ē-) *adj. Psychol.* Of or pertaining to involuntary muscular or other movements induced by a dominant idea. Compare SENSORIMOTOR. — **i′de·o·mo′·tion** (-mō′shən) *n.*

i·de·o·phone (ī′dē·ə·fōn′, id′ē-) *n.* A sound or combination of sounds representing a thought or an idea; an uttered word or phrase.

ides (īdz) *n. pl.* In the ancient Roman calendar, the 15th of March, May, July, and October, and the 13th of the other months. [<L *idus*]

id est (id est) *Latin* That is. Abbr. *i.e.*

Id·fu (id′fōō) See EDFU.

idio– *combining form* One's own, individual, peculiar: *idiosyncratic*. [<Gk. *idios* own, private, peculiar]

id·i·o·blast (id′ē·ə·blast′) *n. Biol.* One of the hypothetical structural units that are thought to make up animal and vegetable cells.

id·i·o·chro·mat·ic (id′ē·ō·krō·mat′ik) *adj. Mineral.* Pertaining to or designating a crystal whose color and optical properties are due to the material of the pure crystal itself and not to any foreign substance.

id·i·oc·ra·sy (id′ē·ok′rə·sē) *n.* *pl.* **·sies** Idiosyncrasy. [<Gk. *idiokrasia* < *idios* one's own + *krasis* mixture]

id·i·o·cy (id′ē·ə·sē) *n.* *pl.* **·cies** **1** The condition of being an idiot; mental deficiency amounting almost to total absence of understanding, caused by non-development or abnormality of the brain tissue. **2** *Psychiatry* The lowest grade of mental capacity and intelligence, often accompanied by physical abnormalities. **3** An idiotic utterance or act. [<IDIOT]

Synonyms: fatuity, folly, foolishness, imbecility, incapacity, senselessness, stupidity. *Idiocy* is a state of mental deficiency amounting almost or quite to total absence of understanding. *Imbecility* is a condition of mental weakness, which incapacitates for the serious duties of life. *Incapacity*, or lack of legal qualification for certain acts, necessarily results from *imbecility*, but may also result from other causes, as from insanity or from age, sex, etc.; as, the *incapacity* of a minor to make a contract. *Idiocy* or *imbecility* is deficiency of mind, while insanity is disorder or abnormal action of the brain. *Folly* and *foolishness* denote a want of mental and often of moral balance. *Fatuity* is sometimes used as equivalent to *idiocy*, but more frequently signifies conceited and excessive *folly*. *Stupidity* is dulness and slowness of mental action which may range all the way from lack of normal readiness to absolute *imbecility*. Compare INSANITY.

id·i·o·e·lec·tric (id′ē·ō·i·lek′trik) *adj.* Electric by virtue of inherent properties: formerly said of bodies readily electrified by friction: distinguished from *anelectric*. Also **id′i·o·e·lec′·tri·cal**.

id·i·o·glos·si·a (id′ē·ō·glos′ē·ə, -glôs′-) *n. Psychiatry* Defective speech, characterized by a succession of meaningless sounds. [<IDIO- + Gk. *glōssa* tongue]

id·i·o·graph (id′ē·ə·graf′, -gräf′) *n.* One's private mark or signature; a trademark. — **id′i·o·graph′ic** or **·i·cal** *adj.*

id·i·om (id′ē·əm) *n.* **1** An expression peculiar to a language, not readily analyzable from its grammatical construction or from the meaning of its component parts, as *to put up with* (tolerate, endure). **2** A speech pattern, dialect, or language characteristic of a certain group, class, trade, region, etc.: legal *idiom*. **3** The peculiar genius or spirit of a language. **4** Specific character, peculiarity, or style, as in art or literature. See synonyms under LANGUAGE. [<L *idioma* <Gk. *idiōma* peculiarity, property < *idioein* appropriate < *idios* one's own]

id·i·o·mat·ic (id′ē·ə·mat′ik) *adj.* **1** Full of idiom; vernacular. **2** Peculiar to or characteristic of a certain language or dialect. Also **id′i·o·mat′i·cal.** [<Gk. *idiōmatikos* characteristic < *idiōma*. See IDIOM.] — **id′i·o·mat′·i·cal·ly** *adv.*

id·i·o·mor·phic (id′ē·ō·môr′fik) *adj.* **1** *Mineral.* Possessing its characteristic crystallographic faces: said of one of the constituent minerals of a rock. **2** Having its own peculiar form. — **id′i·o·mor′phi·cal·ly** *adv.*

id·i·op·a·thy (id′ē·op′ə·thē) *n.* *pl.* **·thies** *Pathol.* **1** A disease of unknown or indeterminate origin. **2** A disease generated by an allergy or by some forms of eczema and gastro-intestinal disorder. [<IDIO- + -PATHY] — **id·i·o·path·ic** (id′ē·ō·path′ik) or **·i·cal** *adj.*

id·i·o·plasm (id′ē·ō·plaz′əm) *n. Biol.* The portion of a cell derived from the parent organism, in distinction from that which is the product of the growth of the individual; germ plasm. — **id′i·o·plas·mat′ic** (-plaz·mat′ik) *adj.*

id·i·o·stat·ic (id′ē·ō·stat′ik) *adj. Electr.* Effecting measurement by repulsion of charges instead of by attraction: said of electrometry: distinguished from *heterostatic*.

id·i·o·syn·cra·sy (id′ē·ō·sing′krə·sē) *n.* *pl.* **·sies** **1** A constitutional peculiarity, as of susceptibility or aversion. **2** Any quality, characteristic, tendency, or mode of expression peculiar to an individual; quirk. [<Gk. *idiosynkrasia* < *idios* peculiar + *synkrasis* a mixing together < *syn* together + *krasis* mixing] — **id′i·o·syn·crat′ic** (-sin·krat′ik) *adj.* — **id′i·o·syn·crat′i·cal·ly** *adv.*

id·i·ot (id′ē·ət) *n.* **1** A human being conspicuously deficient in mental powers and in the capacity for self-protection. **2** *Psychiatry* A person exhibiting the lowest grade of mental development. **3** A foolish fellow; a simpleton. [<OF *idiot* <L *idiota* <Gk. *idiōtēs* private person < *idios* one's own]

id·i·ot·ic (id′ē·ot′ik) *adj.* Like or pertaining to an idiot; senseless; stupid. Also **id′i·ot′i·cal.** — **id′i·ot′i·cal·ly** *adv.*

id·i·ot·ism (id′ē·ət·iz′əm) *n.* **1** Excessive stupidity; a senseless course of action. **2** Idiocy. **3** *Obs.* An idiom. [<F *idiotisme*]

i·dle (īd′l) *adj.* **1** Not occupied; doing nothing. **2** Averse to labor; lazy. **3** Affording leisure. **4** Without effect; useless; unavailing: *idle* talk, *idle* rage. — *v.* **i·dled, i·dling** *v.i.* **1** To spend time in idleness. **2** To saunter or move idly; loaf. **3** *Mech.* To operate without transmitting power, usually at reduced speed: said of motors and machines. — *v.t.* **4** To pass in idleness; waste, as a day. **5** To cause to be idle, as a person or an industry. ◆ Homophones: *idol, idyl*. [OE *īdel* empty, useless]

Synonyms (adj.): inactive, indolent, inert, lazy, slothful, sluggish, trifling, unemployed, unoccupied, vacant. *Idle* etymologically denotes not the absence of action, but vain, useless action—the absence of useful, effective action; the *idle* schoolboy may be very actively whittling his desk or tormenting his neighbors. Doing nothing whatever is the secondary meaning of *idle*. A *lazy* person may chance to be employed in useful work, but he acts without energy or impetus. We speak figuratively of a *lazy* stream. *Slothful* belongs in the moral realm, denoting a self-indulgent aversion to exertion. *Indolent* is a milder term for the same quality. See INSIGNIFICANT. *Antonyms*: active, busy, diligent, employed, industrious, occupied, working.

i·dle·ness (īd′l·nis) *n.* The state of being idle in any sense; slothfulness; inactivity. [OE *īdelnes*]

idle pulley *Mech.* A pulley to guide a driving belt, increase its tension, or increase its arc of contact on one of the working pulleys.

i·dler (īd′lər) *n.* **1** One who idles; a lazy person; a loafer. **2** An idle wheel. **3** One of a ship's crew who stands no night watches, having special day duties.

i·dlesse (īd′les) *n. Archaic* Idleness. [A pseudo-antique formation]

idle wheel *Mech.* **1** A gear wheel to convey motion from one wheel to another, all three being upon different axes. **2** An idle pulley. Also *idler.*

IDLE WHEEL

I·dle·wild (īd′l·wīld) A locality in Queens borough, New York City: site of New York International Airport.

i·dly (īd′lē) *adv.* **1** In an idle manner. **2** Uselessly; vainly; without effect.

I·do (ē′dō) *n.* An artificial language, a simplification of the principles of Esperanto: developed in 1907. [<Esperanto, offspring]

id·o·crase (id′ō·krās, ī′dō-) *n.* Vesuvianite. [<IDIO- + Gk. *krasis* mixture]

i·dol (īd′l) *n.* **1** An image of a god or saint, or an object to which or through which worship is offered. **2** The image of a heathen god. **3** That on which the affections are passionately set. **4** A source of error; a fallacy. **5** An unsubstantial apparition; a phantom due to reflection, as in a mirror. **6** *Obs.* An impostor; counterfeit. See synonyms under IMAGE. ◆ Homophones: *idle, idyl.* [<OF *idele* <L *idolum* <Gk. *eidōlon* image, phantom < *eidos* form, shape]

i·dol·a·ter (ī·dol′ə·tər) *n.* **1** An adorer of images. **2** One who is inordinately fond of some person or thing. [<OF *idolatre* <LL *idololatres* <Gk. *eidōlolatrēs* < *eidōlon* an idol + *latreuein* worship] — **i·dol′a·tress** *n. fem.*

i·dol·a·trize (ī·dol′ə·trīz) *v.* **·trized, ·triz·ing** *v.t.* To make an idol of; idolize. — *v.i.* To practice idolatry.

i·dol·a·trous (ī·dol′ə·trəs) *adj.* **1** Pertaining to idolatry. **2** Extravagant in admiration. — **i·dol′a·trous·ly** *adv.* — **i·dol′a·trous·ness** *n.*

i·dol·a·try (ī·dol′ə·trē) *n. pl.* **·tries** **1** The worship of idols. **2** Idolatrous admiration. [<OF *idolatrie* <LL *idololatria* <Gk. *eidōlolatreia* < *eidolon* an idol + *latreuein* worship]

i·dol·ism (ī′dəl·iz′əm) *n.* **1** A fanciful or false notion. **2** Idol-worship.

i·dol·ize (ī′dəl·īz) *v.* **·ized, ·iz·ing** *v.t.* **1** To have inordinate love for; adore. **2** To worship as an idol. — *v.i.* **3** To worship idols. Also *Brit.* **i′dol·ise.** See synonyms under WORSHIP. — **i·dol·i·za·tion** (ī′dəl·ə·zā′shən, -ī·zā′-) *n.* — **i′dol·iz′er** *n.*

i·dol·o·clast (ī·dol′ə·klast) *n.* A breaker of images. [<IDOL + (ICON)OCLAST]

i·dol·o·clas·tic (ī·dol′ə·klas′tik) *adj.* Of or pertaining to the breaking of images.

I·dom·e·neus (ī·dom′ə·nōōs, -nyōōs) In Greek legend, a king of Crete who fought on the Greek side in the Trojan War.

i·do·ne·ous (ī·dō′nē·əs) *adj.* Proper; suitable; proportionate. [<L *idoneus* fitting]

I·du·mae·a (ī′dyōō·mē′ə, id′yōō-) An ancient country SE of Palestine: also *Edom.* Also **I′du·me′a, I′du·mæ′a.** — **I′du·mae′an** *adj.*

i·dyl (īd′l) *n.* **1** A short poem or prose piece depicting simple scenes of pastoral, domestic, or country life; also, a more extended descriptive or narrative poem. **2** Any event, scene, or circumstance of a kind suitable for such a work. **3** *Music* A composition of simple or pastoral character. Also **i′dyll.** ◆ Homophones: *idle, idol.* [<L *idyllium* <Gk. *eidyllion,* dim. of *eidos* form] — **i′dyl·ist, i′dyl·list** *n.*

i·dyl·lic (ī·dil′ik) *adj.* Of or pertaining to the idyl; having the essential qualities of an idyl or pastoral poem. Also **i·dyl′li·cal.** — **i·dyl′·li·cal·ly** *adv.*

-ie *suffix* Little; dear: *birdie*: often used in nicknames or affectionately, as in *Annie.* [Var. of -Y³]

-ier *suffix of nouns* One who is concerned with or works with: *cashier.* Also, after vowels and *w,* *-yer,* as in *lawyer.* [<F. See -EER]

If (ēf) An islet SW of Marseilles, France: site of the **Château d'If,** formerly a state prison.

if (if) *conj.* **1** On the supposition or condition that: We'll go by plane *if* the weather permits. **2** Allowing that; although: *If* he was there, I didn't see him. **3** Whether: I am not sure *if* he is at home. ◆ *If* is also used in exclamatory clauses to introduce (a) a wish or determination: *If* I had only thought of that!; and (b) surprise or irritation: Well, *if* he hasn't run away again! — *n.* **1** The word *if* itself. **2** A condition; supposition. [OE *gif*]

if·fy (if′ē) *adj. Colloq.* Conditional; hypothetical. [<IF]

If·ni (ēf′nē) A Spanish territory comprising an enclave on the west coast of Morocco; 741 square miles; capital, Sidi Ifni.

Ig·dra·sil (ig′drə·sil) See YGDRASIL.

ig·loo (ig′lōō) *n. pl.* **·loos** **1** An Eskimo house, dome-shaped and usually built of blocks of packed snow. **2** A conical mound, for protecting munitions, made of earth and concrete. Also **ig′lu.** [<Eskimo *igdlu*]

ig·na·ti·a (ig·nā′shē·ə, -shə) *n.* The dried seed of a small tree (*Strychnos ignatia*) native to the Philippines: used like nux vomica. [<NL (*faba*) *ignatia* (bean) of Ignatius]

Ig·na·ti·us (ig·nā′shē·əs, -shəs; *Du.* ig·nä′sē·ōōs; *Ger.* ig·nä′tsē·ōōs) A masculine personal name. Also *Fr.* **I·gnace** (ē·nyàs′), *Ger.* **Ig·naz** (ig·näts′), *Ital.* **I·gna·zi·o** (ē·nyä′tsē·ō) or **I·gna·ci·o** (ē·nyä′chē·ō, *Pg.* ig·nä′sē·ōō, *Sp.* ig·nä′thē·ō), *Polish* **Ig·na·cy** (ēg·nä′tsē). [<L, fiery]
— **Ignatius, Saint,** 67?–107?, bishop of Antioch: called "Theophorus."
— **Ignatius, Saint,** 798?–878, patriarch of Constantinople.
— **Ignatius of Loyola** See LOYOLA.

ig·ne·ous (ig′nē·əs) *adj.* **1** Pertaining to or resembling fire. **2** *Geol.* Formed by the action of a fusing heat within the earth: said especially of rocks consolidated from a molten state: distinguished from *sedimentary.* [<L *igneus* < *ignis* fire]

ig·nes·cent (ig·nes′ənt) *adj.* **1** Emitting sparks of fire when struck with steel or iron. **2** Coruscating. [<L *ignescere* burn < *ignis* fire]

igni- *combining form* Fire: *ignify.* [<L *ignis* fire]

ig·ni·fy (ig′nə·fī) *v.t.* **·fied, ·fy·ing** *Rare* **1** To set on fire; burn. **2** To fuse or melt. [Cf. LL *ignifacere* set on fire]

ig·nis fat·u·us (ig′nis fach′ōō·əs) *pl.* **ig·nes fat·u·i** (ig′nēz fach′ōō·ī) **1** A phosphorescent light seen in the air over marshy places; jack-o'-lantern; will-o'-the-wisp. **2** Figuratively, a delusion; deceptive attraction. [< Med. L, foolish fire]

ig·nite (ig·nīt′) *v.* **ig·nit·ed, ig·nit·ing** *v.t.* **1** To set on fire; cause to burn. **2** To cause to glow with intense heat; make incandescent. **3** *Chem.* To bring to the point of combustion. — *v.i.* **4** To take fire; start burning. See synonyms under BURN. [<L *ignitus,* pp. of *ignire* set on fire] — **ig·nit′i·ble, ig·nit′a·ble** *adj.* — **ig·nit′i·bil′i·ty, ig·nit′a·bil′i·ty** *n.*

ig·nit·er (ig·nī′tər) *n.* **1** One who or that which ignites. **2** A device for exploding a shell or torpedo, for setting off a blasting charge, etc. **3** An ignitor.

ig·ni·tion (ig·nish′ən) *n.* **1** The act of, or system employed in, igniting. **2** The act of exploding the charge of gases in the cylinder of an internal-combustion engine. **3** The electrical apparatus that fires these gases. [<Med. L *ignitio, -onis* burning < *ignire* burn]

ig·ni·tor (ig·nī′tər) *n. Electronics* A silicon carbide electrode used to initiate the action of an Ignitron. Also spelled *igniter.*

Ig·ni·tron (ig·nī′trən, ig′nə·tron) *n. Electronics* A gas-discharge rectifier tube with a mercury electrode and an ignitor: used to control the starting of a unidirectional current flow: a trade name.

ig·no·ble (ig·nō′bəl) *adj.* **1** Unworthy or degraded in character. **2** *Rare* Low-born. **3** Of inferior kind; specifically, in falconry, said of the short-winged hawks, which chase their prey, as distinguished from the *noble* falcons which attack by a single swoop. See synonyms under BASE, VULGAR. [<F <L *ignobilis* < *in-* not + *gnobilis* noble, known] — **ig·no·bil·i·ty** (ig′nə·bil′ə·tē), **ig·no′ble·ness** *n.* — **ig·no′bly** *adv.*

ig·no·min·i·ous (ig′nə·min′ē·əs) *adj.* **1** Entailing or implying dishonor or disgrace. **2** Deserving ignominy; despicable. **3** Abasing; humiliating. See synonyms under INFAMOUS. [<L *ignominiosus* < *ignominia* IGNOMINY] — **ig′no·min′i·ous·ly** *adv.* — **ig′no·min′i·ous·ness** *n.*

ig·no·min·y (ig′nə·min′ē) *n. pl.* **·min·ies** **1** Disgrace or dishonor. **2** That which causes disgrace; disgraceful action or conduct. [<L *ignominia* < *in-* not + *nomen* name, reputation]

ig·no·ra·mus (ig′nə·rā′məs, -ram′əs) *n.* An ignorant pretender to knowledge. [<L, we do not know]

ig·no·rance (ig′nər·əns) *n.* **1** The state of being ignorant; the condition of not being informed; lack of knowledge. **2** An act, offense, or sin due to ignorance. [<F <L *ignorantia*]

ig·no·rant (ig′nər·ənt) *adj.* **1** Destitute of education or knowledge. **2** Unacquainted; unaware. **3** Manifesting or characterized by ignorance. [<OF <L *ignorans, -antis,* ppr. of *ignorare* not to know. See IGNORE.] — **ig′no·rant·ly** *adv.*

Synonyms (adj.): ill-informed, illiterate, uneducated, unenlightened, uninformed, uninstructed, unlearned, unlettered, unskilled, untaught, untutored. *Ignorant* signifies destitute of education or knowledge, or lacking knowledge or information; it is thus a relative term. The most learned man is still *ignorant* of many things; persons are spoken of as *ignorant* who have not the knowledge that has become generally diffused in the world; the *ignorant* savage may be well-instructed in matters of the field and the chase, and is thus more properly *untutored* than *ignorant. Illiterate* is without letters and the knowledge that comes through reading. *Unlettered* is similar in meaning to *illiterate,* but less absolute; the *unlettered* man may have acquired the art of reading and writing and some elementary knowledge; the *uneducated* man has never taken any systematic course of mental training. *Ignorance* is relative; *illiteracy* is absolute; we have statistics of *illiteracy*; no statistics of *ignorance* are possible. See BRUTISH. *Antonyms*: educated, instructed, learned, sage, skilled, trained, well-informed, wise.

ig·nore (ig·nôr′, -nōr′) *v.t.* **·nored, ·nor·ing** **1** To refuse to notice or recognize; disregard intentionally. **2** *Law* To reject (a bill of indictment) for insufficient evidence. [<F *ignorer* <L *ignorare* < *in-* not + *gno-,* stem of *gnoscere* know] — **ig·nor′er** *n.*

I·go·rot (ē′gə·rōt′, ig′ə-) *n. pl.* **·rot** or **·rots** **1** One belonging to a group of Malay tribes of northern Luzon, Philippines, some of whom are head-hunters. **2** The Indonesian language of these tribes. Also **I·gor·ro·te** (ē′gôr·rō′tā). [<Sp. *Igorrote,* prob. <Tagalog]

I·graine (i·grān′) In Arthurian legend, the mother of King Arthur: also *Ygerne.*

i·gua·na (i·gwä′nə) *n.* **1** An edible, tropical American lizard (family *Iguanidae*); especially *Iguana iguana,* which sometimes attains a length of 6 feet: it is partly arboreal, partly herbivorous, and, unless attacked, is harmless. **2** Any one of several lizards related to the iguana. [<Sp. <Cariban]

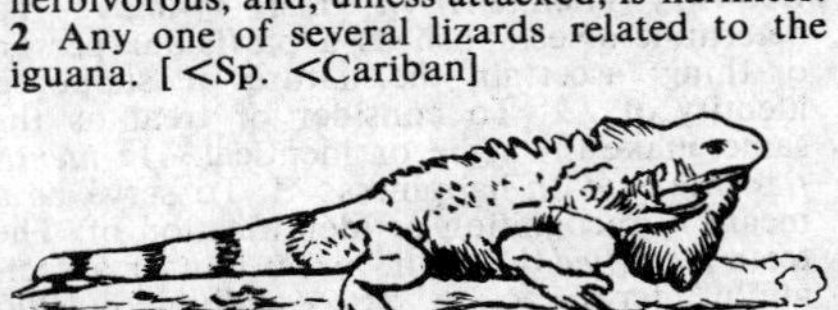

COMMON IGUANA
Grass-green in color with black and white markings; the dewlap and spiny crest are characteristic of the true iguana.

i·guan·o·don (i·gwan′ə·don) *n.* A large, powerfully built, herbivorous, bipedal dinosaur (order *Ornithischia*), associated with the Lower Cretaceous period in Belgium. [<NL < IGUANA + Gk. *odōn* tooth]

I·guas·sú (ē′gwä·sōō′) A river in SE Brazil, flowing about 820 miles west to the Paraná; 14 miles above its mouth are the **Iguassú Falls,** 210 feet high and almost a mile wide. Also **I′gua·çu′.** *Spanish* **I′gua·zú′.**

ih·ram (ē·räm′) *n.* **1** A two-piece, white cotton dress worn by the Moslem pilgrims to Mecca, of which one piece is girded round the waist and the other is worn over the left shoulder. **2** A pilgrim who has assumed this garb. **3** The regulations that he must observe. [<Arabic *iḥram* interdiction < *ḥarama* forbid]

IHS, ihs A monogram of the name Jesus, derived from the Greek IH(ΣΟΥ)Σ, Jesus.

Ijs·sel (ī′səl) A branch of the lower Rhine in the Netherlands, flowing 72 miles north to Lake Ijssel: also *Yssel. Dutch* **IJs′sel.**

Ijs·sel (ī′səl), **Lake** A fresh-water lake enclosed by a dam from the Zuyder Zee, central Netherlands. *Dutch* **IJs′sel·meer′**(-mär′).

I·ka·ri·a (ē′kä·rē′ə) See ICARIA.

Ikh·na·ton (ik·nä′tən) Egyptian king 1375–1358 B.C.; monotheist religious reformer: also known as *Amenhotep IV.* Also spelled *Akhnaton.*

i·kon (ī′kon) See ICON (def. 2).

i·lang–i·lang (ē′läng·ē′lang) See YLANG–YLANG.

I·la·ri·o (ē·lä′rē·ō) Italian form of HILARY.

Il·de·fon·so (ēl′dā·fōn′sō) Spanish form of ALPHONSO.

-ile *suffix* Of, like, pertaining to; capable of; suited to: *docile, mobile.* Also, sometimes, **-il,** as in *civil, fossil.* [<F *-il, -ile* <L *-ilis,* suffix of adjectives; or directly <L]

il·e·ac (il′ē·ak) *adj.* Of or pertaining to the ileum. Also **il′e·al.** [A refashioning of ILIAC]

Île de France (ēl də fräns′) A region and former province of north central France at the center of the Paris Basin.

Île du Dia·ble (ēl dü dyà′bl′) The French name for DEVIL'S ISLAND.

il·e·i·tis (il′ē·ī′tis) *n. Pathol.* Inflammation of the ileum.

ileo– *combining form* Of or pertaining to the ileum: *ileostomy.* Also, before vowels, **ile–.** [< L *ileum* the ileum]

il·e·os·to·my (il′ē·os′tə·mē) *n. Surg.* The operation of forming an artificial opening into the ileum. [<ILEO- + -STOMY]

I·ler·da (i·lûr′də) The ancient name for LÉRIDA.

il·e·um (il′ē·əm) *n. Anat.* The lower three fifths of the small intestine from the jejunum to the cecum, excluding the duodenum. [<L <Gk. *eilein* roll, twist]

il·e·us (il′ē·əs) *n. Pathol.* An obstruction of the intestines, variously caused and resulting in severe colic. [<L <Gk. *eileos* colic <*eilein* twist]

i·lex (ī′leks) *n.* **1** A tree or shrub (genus *Ilex*) of the holly family. **2** The holm oak. **3** The holly. [<L, holm oak]

Il·ford (il′fərd) A municipal borough in SW Essex, England.

I·li (ē′lē) A river flowing 590 miles west from Sinkiang province, China, to Lake Balkash in the S.R.

il·i·ac (il′ē·ak) *adj.* Pertaining to or near the ilium. [<LL *iliacus* suffering from colic <*ileus* colic]

Il·i·ac (il′ē·ak) *adj.* Pertaining to ancient Ilium or Troy; also, pertaining to the Trojan War. Also **Il′i·an.**

Il·i·ad (il′ē·əd) **1** An ancient Greek epic poem in 24 books on the siege of Ilium (Troy), traditionally ascribed to Homer. **2** Any similar long narrative poem. **3** A tale of many sorrows or miseries. [<L *Ilias, -adis* <Gk. *Ilias, -ados* <*Ilios, Ilion* Ilium (Troy)]

il·i·um (il′ē·əm) *n. pl.* **·i·a** (-ē·ə) *Anat.* The large upper portion of the innominate bone. [<L, flank]

Il·i·um (il′ē·əm) See TROY (def. 1). Also **Il′i·on** (-ən).

ilk[1] (ilk) *adj. & n. Obs.* Same. **—of that ilk 1** Of that same: a phrase denoting that a person's surname and the name of his estate are the same: Kent *of that ilk*—that is, Kent of Kent. **2** Of that race, class, or kind. [OE *ilka* the same]

ilk[2] (ilk) *adj. Scot. & Dial.* **1** Each; every. **2** Ordinary; common. Also **il′ka** (-kə). [Var. of EACH]

ill (il) *adj.* **1** Disordered in physical condition; diseased; unwell; sick. **2** Evil in effect or tendency; baneful; harmful; unjust; unkind. **3** Of inferior quality; wretched. **4** Lacking skill; ineffective. **5** Evil; malevolent; wrong: *ill* wind, *ill* repute. **6** *Scot.* Difficult; also, grieved; afflicted with sorrow. See synonyms under BAD[1], SICKLY.—*n.* Anything that prevents or impairs what is good or desirable, as sickness, misfortune, or bad luck. See synonyms under MISFORTUNE. —*adv.* **1** Not well. **2** With difficulty; hardly. **3** Badly; unfavorably. **—ill at ease** Uneasy; uncomfortable. [<ON *illr*]

Ill may appear as a combining form in hyphemes, as in:

ill–accoutered	**ill–disposed**	**ill–matched**
ill–accustomed	**ill–doing**	**ill–mated**
ill–advised	**ill–equipped**	**ill–minded**
ill–affected	**ill–fated**	**ill–omened**
ill–afford	**ill–health**	**ill–placed**
ill–assorted	**ill–housed**	**ill–pleased**
ill–breeding	**ill–informed**	**ill–seeming**
ill–concealed	**ill–judged**	**ill–timed**
ill–conceived	**ill–judging**	**ill–tongued**
ill–considered	**ill–kept**	**ill–trained**
ill–contrived	**ill–luck**	**ill–wisher**
ill–defined	**ill–mannered**	**ill–wishing**

I'll (īl) **1** I will. **2** I shall.

Il·lam·pu (ē·yäm′po͞o) A peak in western Bolivia; 21,490 feet: also *Sorata.*

il·la·tion (i·lā′shən) *n.* **1** The act of inferring. **2** That which is inferred; deduction. [<L *illatio, -onis* <*illatus,* pp. of *inferre* bring in, infer]

il·la·tive (il′ə·tiv) *adj.* Pertaining to, denoting, or derived by inference, especially legitimate inference. —*n.* A word denoting an inference, as *therefore.* **—il′la·tive·ly** *adv.*

il·laud·a·ble (i·lô′də·bəl) *adj.* Blameworthy.

ill–be·ing (il′bē′ing) *n.* The condition of being ill or evil: opposed to *well-being.*

ill–bod·ing (il′bō′ding) *adj.* Ill-omened; inauspicious.

ill–bred (il′bred′) *adj.* Badly taught, reared, or trained; rude.

il·le·gal (i·lē′gəl) *adj.* Contrary to the law; not legal. See synonyms under CRIMINAL. **—il·le′·gal·ly** *adv.*

il·le·gal·i·ty (il′ē·gal′ə·tē) *n. pl.* **·ties 1** The state of being illegal. **2** Something unlawful.

il·le·gal·ize (i·lē′gəl·īz) *v.t.* **·ized, ·iz·ing** To make illegal or unlawful.

il·leg·i·ble (i·lej′ə·bəl) *adj.* Not legible; undecipherable. **—il·leg′i·bil′i·ty, il·leg′i·ble·ness** *n.* **—il·leg′i·bly** *adv.*

il·le·git·i·ma·cy (il′i·jit′ə·mə·sē) *n. pl.* **·cies 1** The character or condition of being born out of lawful wedlock; bastardy. **2** Unsoundness, spuriousness, or irregularity, as of an argument; illogicality.

il·le·git·i·mate (il′i·jit′ə·mit) *adj.* **1** Not legitimate; contrary to law. **2** Born out of wedlock. **3** Illogical; unsound. **4** Contrary to good usage; irregular. [<L *illegitimus* < *in-* not + *legitimus.* See LEGITIMATE.] **—il′le·git′i·ma′tion** *n.* **—il′le·git′i·mate·ly** *adv.*

ill fame Bad repute.

ill–fa·vored (il′fā′vərd) *adj.* **1** Repulsive; ugly. **2** Objectionable. Also *Brit.* **ill′–fa′voured.**

ill–got·ten (il′got′n) *adj.* Obtained dishonestly.

ill–hu·mor (il′hyo͞o′mər) *n.* A morose, disagreeable, or choleric state of mind; sullenness. **—ill′–hu′mored** *adj.*

il·lib·er·al (i·lib′ər·əl) *adj.* **1** Not liberal; not generous in giving; parsimonious. **2** Narrow-minded. **3** Lacking breadth of culture; vulgar. **—il·lib′er·al·ism** (-iz′əm) *n.* **—il·lib′er·al′·i·ty** (-al′ə·tē) *n.* **—il·lib′er·al·ly** *adv.* **—il·lib′er·al·ness** *n.*

il·lic·it (i·lis′it) *adj.* **1** Not permitted; unlawful. **2** Having to do with unlawful things or actions. [<F *illicite* <L *illicitus* <*in-* not + *licitus.* See LICIT.] **—il·lic′it·ly** *adv.* **—il·lic′it·ness** *n.*

Il·li·ma·ni (ē′yē·mä′nē) A peak in western Bolivia; 21,185 feet.

il·lim·it·a·ble (i·lim′i·tə·bəl) *adj.* That can not be limited; boundless. See synonyms under INFINITE.**—il·lim′it·a·bil′i·ty, il·lim′it·a·ble·ness, il·lim′i·ta′tion** (-ə·tā′shən) *n.* **—il·lim′it·a·bly** *adv.*

il·lin·i·um (i·lin′ē·əm) *n.* A former name for PROMETHEUM. [<NL, from *Illinois*]

Il·li·nois (il′ə·noi′, -noiz′) *n. pl.* **·nois** A North American Indian belonging to any one of the Algonquian tribes of the Illinois Confederacy. [<F <N. Am. Ind.]

Il·li·nois (il′ə·noi′, -noiz′) A north central State of the United States; 56,400 square miles; capital, Springfield; entered the Union Dec. 3, 1818; nickname, *Prairie State:* abbr. IL **—Il′li·nois′an** (-noi′ən, -noi′zən) *adj. & n.*

Illinois Confederacy A confederacy of Algonquian tribes of North American Indians whose territory included Illinois and parts of Wisconsin and Iowa.

Illinois River A river in Illinois, flowing 273 miles west and SW to the Mississippi.

il·liq·uid (i·lik′wid) *adj. Law* Not clearly manifest or proved: said of a debt, right, or claim which has no legal standing. [<IL- + LIQUID]

il·lit·er·a·cy (i·lit′ər·ə·sē) *n. pl.* **·cies 1** The state of being illiterate or untaught; lack of culture; ignorance of letters; especially, as in census statistics, inability to read or to read and write. **2** A literary blunder or series of such blunders.

il·lit·er·ate (i·lit′ər·it) *adj.* **1** Unable to read or write. **2** Ignorant of letters; not literate; manifesting want of culture; uneducated. See synonyms under IGNORANT. —*n.* An illiterate person; especially, one who cannot read or write. [<L *illiteratus* <*in-* not + *literatus.* See LITERATE.] **—il·lit′er·ate·ly** *adv.* **—il·lit′·er·ate·ness** *n.*

ill–look·ing (il′look′ing) *adj.* Looking ill; homely; uncomely.

ill nature Peevishness; surliness; sullenness.

ill–na·tured (il′nā′chərd) *adj.* Surly; cross. See synonyms under MALICIOUS, MOROSE. **—ill′–na′tured·ly** *adv.* **—ill′–na′tured·ness** *n.*

ill·ness (il′nis) *n.* **1** The state of being out of health. **2** An ailment; sickness. **3** *Obs.* Badness; evil.

Synonyms: ailment, complaint, disease, disorder, distemper, indisposition, infirmity, sickness. See DISEASE. *Antonyms:* health, soundness, strength, vigor.

il·lo·cal (i·lō′kəl) *adj.* Having no location in space; without place. [<LL *illocalis* <*in-* not + *localis.* See LOCAL.] **—il·lo·cal·i·ty** (il′ō·kal′ə·tē) *n.*

il·log·ic (i·loj′ik) *n.* That which is not logical.

il·log·i·cal (i·loj′i·kəl) *adj.* Not logical; contrary to or neglectful of the rules of logic; not reasonable. **—il·log′i·cal′i·ty, il·log′i·cal·ness** *n.* **—il·log′i·cal·ly** *adv.*

ill–set (il′set′) *adj.* Incorrectly or improperly set.

ill–sort·ed (il′sôr′tid) *adj.* Not well sorted; unharmonious; unsuitably matched.

ill–starred (il′stärd′) *adj.* Unfortunate; as if under an evil star.

ill temper Irritability; moroseness.

ill–tem·pered (il′tem′pərd) *adj.* **1** Characterized by bad temper. **2** *Obs.* In an unhealthy condition.

ill–treat (il′trēt′) *v.t.* To treat badly; maltreat. See synonyms under ABUSE. **—ill′–treat′ment** *n.*

ill turn An act of unkindness or hostility.

il·lude (i·lo͞od′) *v.t. Obs.* To trick; cheat. [<L *illudere* make sport of <*in-* toward, against + *ludere* play]

il·lume (i·lo͞om′) *v.t.* **·lumed, ·lum·ing** *Poetic* To illumine; illuminate. [<ILLUMINE, prob. influenced in form by F *rallumer* light]

il·lu·min·ance (i·lo͞o′mə·nəns) *n. Physics* The luminous flux per unit area of a uniformly illuminated surface.

il·lu·mi·nant (i·lo͞o′mə·nənt) *adj.* Giving light; illuminating. —*n.* Any material used for illuminating. [<L *illuminans, -antis,* ppr. of *illuminare* give light]

il·lu·mi·nate (i·lo͞o′mə·nāt) *v.* **·nat·ed, ·nat·ing** *v.t.* **1** To give light to; light up. **2** To explain; make clear. **3** To enlighten, as the mind. **4** To make illustrious or resplendent. **5** To decorate with lights. **6** To decorate (a manuscript, letter, etc.) with ornamental borders, figures, etc., of gold or other colors. —*v.i.* **7** To light up. —*adj.* **1** Lighted up. **2** *Obs.* Enlightened. —*n.* One of the illuminati. [<L *illuminatus,* pp. of *illuminare* < *in-* thoroughly+ *luminare* light <*lumen* light]

il·lu·mi·na·ti (i·lo͞o′mə·nä′tī, -nä′tē) *n. pl. sing.* **·na·to** (-nä′tō, -nä′tō) **1** Those who have or profess to have remarkable discernment or spiritual enlightenment. **2** In early church usage, baptized persons, to whom in the ceremony a lighted taper was given as a symbol of spiritual enlightenment. [<L, pl. of *illuminatus,* pp of *illuminare* light up]

Il·lu·mi·na·ti (i·lo͞o′mə·nä′tī, -nä′tē) *n. pl.* **1** Any of various European religious sects which claimed to have received a special religious enlightenment. **2** A select, secret, deistic and republican society founded by Adam Weishaupt at Ingolstadt, Bavaria, in 1776, aiming at emancipation from despotism: also called *Perfectibilists.*

add,āce,câre,pälm; end,ēven; it,īce; odd,ōpen,ôrder; to͝ok,po͞ol; up,bûrn; ə = a in *above,* e in *sicken,* i in *clarity,* o in *melon,* u in *focus;* yo͞o = u in *fuse;* oi,oil; ou,pout; ch,check; g,go; ng,ring; th,thin; th,this; zh,vision. Foreign sounds à,œ,ü,kh,ṅ; and ◆: see page xx. <from; + plus; ? possibly.

il·lu·mi·nat·ing gas (i·lo͞o'mə·nā'ting) Gas consisting of hydrogen mixed with carbon monoxide, methane, ethylene, and other hydrocarbons (as well as impurities such as carbon dioxide, nitrogen, etc.): used for lighting purposes.

il·lu·mi·na·tion (i·lo͞o'mə·nā'shən) *n.* 1 The act of illuminating. 2 The fact or state of being illuminated. 3 A lighting up, especially for festal purposes. 4 Illuminance. 5 Mental enlightenment; imparted light; spiritual enlightenment. 6 *Often cap.* The specific doctrines held by the Illuminati. 7 Embellishment of manuscript, with colors and gold, or a particular figure or design in such ornamentation. See synonyms under LIGHT. [<L *illuminatio, -onis*]

il·lu·mi·na·tive (i·lo͞o'mə·nā'tiv) *adj.* 1 Having power or tending to illuminate; illustrative. 2 Relating to adornment or decoration of books or manuscripts.

il·lu·mi·na·tor (i·lo͞o'mə·nā'tər) *n.* 1 One who or that which gives light. 2 A lamp, lens, etc., for throwing light on particular objects or places. 3 One who executes illuminations on manuscripts. [<L *illuminator*]

il·lu·mine (i·lo͞o'min) *v.t.* & *v.i.* **·mined, ·min·ing** To illuminate or be illuminated. [<F *illuminer* <L *illuminare* illuminate. Related to LIMN.] — **il·lu'mi·na·ble** *adj.*

Il·lu·mi·nism (i·lo͞o'mə·niz'əm) *n.* The principles of the Illuminati.

il·lu·mi·nist (i·lo͞o'mə·nist) *n.* 1 One aspiring to or claiming high spiritual enlightenment. 2 One who professionally illuminates manuscripts, etc.; an illuminator.

Il·lu·mi·nist (i·lo͞o'mə·nist) *n.* One of the Illuminati.

ill–use (il'yo͞oz') *v.t.* **·used, ·us·ing** To treat roughly, cruelly, or unjustly; misuse; abuse. — *n.* (-yo͞os') Bad treatment; misuse. — **ill'–us'age** (-yo͞o'sij, -yo͞o'zij) *n.*

il·lu·sion (i·lo͞o'zhən) *n.* 1 An unreal image seemingly presented to the senses; any misleading appearance; a false show. 2 *Psychol.* A sensory impression which misrepresents the true character of the object perceived; false perception. See HALLUCINATION. 3 The act of deceiving or misleading by a false appearance. 4 The state of being deceived; delusion; false impression. 5 A thin material resembling tulle, usually of silk: used for veils and garments. 6 An artistic effect giving the appearance of reality to a painting. See synonyms under DELUSION, DREAM. [<OF <L *illusio, -onis* mocking, deceit < *illudere* make sport of. See ILLUDE.] — **il·lu'sion·al** *adj.*

il·lu·sion·ism (i·lo͞o'zhən·iz'əm) *n.* Any doctrine that treats the material world as an illusion of the senses.

il·lu·sion·ist (i·lo͞o'zhən·ist) *n.* 1 One given to illusions; a visionary; a dreamer. 2 One who creates illusions; a sleight–of–hand performer. 3 A believer in illusionism.

il·lu·sive (i·lo͞o'siv) *adj.* Misleading; deceptive; unreal. Also **il·lu'so·ry** (-sər·ē). See synonyms under DECEPTIVE, IMAGINARY. — **il·lu'sive·ly** *adv.* — **il·lu'sive·ness** *n.*

il·lus·trate (il'əs·trāt, i·lus'trāt) *v.t.* **·trat·ed, ·trat·ing** 1 To explain or make clear by means of figures, examples, etc.; exemplify. 2 To furnish with drawings, pictures, etc., for decoration or explanation, as a book or article. 3 *Obs.* To make luminous or bright. 4 *Obs.* To make illustrious. See synonyms under ADORN. [<L *illustratus*, pp. of *illustrare* light up < *in-* thoroughly + *lustrare* illuminate] — **il'lus·tra'tor** *n.*

il·lus·tra·tive (i·lus'trə·tiv, il'əs·trā'tiv) *adj.* Serving to illustrate or exemplify. — **il·lus'tra·tive·ly** *adv.*

il·lus·tra·tion (il'əs·trā'shən) *n.* 1 That which illustrates, as an example, comparison, anecdote, etc., by which a subject or statement is elucidated or explained. 2 A print, drawing, or picture of any kind inserted in written or printed text to elucidate or adorn it. 3 The act or art of illustrating. See synonyms under ALLEGORY, SAMPLE, SIMILE. [<L *illustratio, -onis*]

il·lus·tri·ous (i·lus'trē·əs) *adj.* 1 Greatly distinguished; renowned. 2 Conferring luster. 3 *Obs.* Luminous; bright. [<L *illustris* < *in-* in + *lustrum* light] — **il·lus'tri·ous·ly** *adv.* — **il·lus'tri·ous·ness** *n.*

Synonyms: celebrated, distinguished, eminent, famed, famous, glorious, honorable, honored, noble, noted, renowned. See GRAND. *Antonyms*: base, besmirched, degraded, despised, disgraced, dishonored, disreputable, ignominious, infamous, inglorious, notorious, stained, sullied, unhonored, unknown.

ill will Enmity; malevolence.

il·ly (il'lē) *adv.* In an ill or evil manner; not well; ill. ◆ While *illy* is regularly formed from the adjective *ill*, discriminating writers prefer to use *ill* as the adverb as well.

Il·lyr·i·a (i·lir'ē·ə) An ancient country north and east of the Adriatic.

Il·lyr·i·an (i·lir'ē·ən) *n.* 1 One of the inhabitants of ancient Illyria. 2 The Indo–European language of the Illyrians, of which few traces remain: regarded by some as the ancestor of modern Albanian. — *adj.* Of or pertaining to ancient Illyria, its inhabitants, or their language.

Il·lyr·i·cum (i·lir'i·kəm) One of the earliest of the ancient Roman colonies, established in Illyria.

Il·men (il'mən), **Lake** A lake south of Novgorod, Russian S.F.S.R.; 850 square miles.

il·men·ite (il'mən·īt) *n.* An iron–black, opaque titanium–iron oxide, $FeTiO_3$, crystallizing in the hexagonal system. [from Lake *Ilmen*]

I·lo·ca·no (ē'lō·kä'nō) *n.* 1 A member of one of the most highly developed peoples of the Philippines, inhabiting western and NW Luzon. 2 The Indonesian language of these peoples. Also **I'lo·ka'no.** [<Philippine Sp. *Ilocano*, lit., river man <Tagalog *ilog* river]

I·lo·i·lo (ē'lō·ē'lō) A port and chief city on Panay island, Philippines.

Il Pen·se·ro·so (il pen'sə·rō'sō) The pensive man: title of a poem by Milton. [<Ital.]

I·lus (ī'ləs) In Greek mythology, the father of Laomedon and grandfather of Priam; founder of Troy (Ilium). [<Gk. *Ilos*]

im–[1] See also words beginning with **em–**.

im–[2] Assimilated var. of IN–[1] and IN–[2].

I'm (īm) I am.

im·age (im'ij) *n.* 1 A visible representation of something; a statue, picture, idol, etc. 2 *Optics* The picture or counterpart of an object produced by reflection or refraction, or the passage of rays through a small aperture. If such an image can be actually thrown on a surface as in a camera, it is a **real image**; but if it is visible only as in a mirror, it is a **virtual image.** 3 A natural resemblance; also, that which resembles something; counterpart. 4 A representation in the mind of something not perceived at the moment through the senses; a product of the reproductive imagination or memory, of things seen, heard, touched, etc., including the accompanying emotion. 5 A mental picture or idea: a false *image* of oneself. 6 The way in which a person or thing is popularly perceived or regarded, especially through the agency of the mass media, as television, magazines, etc.; public impression: a politician striving to improve his *image*; a distorted *image* of the U.S. 7 A metaphor or a simile that reproduces or suggests in words the form, color, aspect, or semblance of an object. 6 A symbol of anything; embodiment; type. 7 *Telecom.* The optical replica of a scene produced by a television camera. 8 *Obs.* An apparition. — *v.t.* **·aged, ·ag·ing** 1 To form a mental picture of; imagine. 2 To make a visible representation of; portray; delineate. 3 To mirror; reflect. 4 To describe vividly in speech or writing, as with images, figures of speech, etc. 5 To symbolize. [<OF <L *imago* <the base of *imitari* imitate]

Synonyms (noun): conception, copy, effigy, emblem, figure, icon, idea, idol, likeness, picture, representation, semblance, similitude, shadow, statue. See FANCY, FIGURE, IDEA, MODEL, PICTURE, SIMILE.

image point The point whose depth below ground zero is equal to the height of an exploding atomic or hydrogen bomb: it is considered as a source of radiating reflected shock.

im·age·ry (im'ij·rē) *n. pl.* **·ries** 1 The act of forming images; images collectively. 2 Figurative description in speech or writing. See synonyms under SIMILE.

im·ag·i·na·ble (i·maj'ə·nə·bəl) *adj.* Conceivable. [<LL *imaginabilis*] — **im·ag'i·na·bly** *adv.*

im·ag·i·nal (i·maj'ə·nəl) *adj. Entomol.* Of or pertaining to the imago, or complete adult stage of an insect.

im·ag·i·nar·y (i·maj'ə·ner'ē) *adj.* Existing only in imagination; unreal. — *n. Math.* An algebraic quantity or value that involves the square root of a negative quantity. — **im·ag'i·nar'i·ly** *adv.* — **im·ag'i·nar'i·ness** *n.*

Synonyms (adj.): airy, chimerical, dreamy, fancied, fanciful, hypothetical, ideal, illusive, illusory, quixotic, shadowy, utopian, visionary. See IDEAL. *Antonyms*: actual, material, palpable, physical, real, realized, substantial, tangible, visible.

im·ag·i·na·tion (i·maj'ə·nā'shən) *n.* 1 The picturing power or act of the mind. 2 *Psychol.* The constructive or creative faculty, expressed in terms of images which either reproduce past experiences or recombine them in ideal or creative forms. 3 That which is imagined; a mental image; a fantasy. 4 An irrational notion or belief. 5 *Archaic* Planning, plotting, or scheming, as involving mental construction. [<L *imaginatio, -onis* < *imaginatus*, pp. of *imaginari* IMAGINE]

Synonyms: fancy, fantasy. *Fancy* and *imagination* both belong to the productive or, more properly, the constructive faculty. Both recombine and modify mental images; the one great distinction between them is that *fancy* is superficial, while *imagination* is deep, essential, spiritual. *Fantasy* in ordinary usage simply denotes capricious or erratic *fancy*, as appears in the adjective *fantastic*. Compare FANCY, IDEA, THOUGHT[1].

im·ag·i·na·tion·al (i·maj'ə·nā'shən·əl) *adj.* Pertaining to, resulting from, or affected by the imagination.

im·ag·i·na·tive (i·maj'ə·nə·tiv, -nā'tiv) *adj.* 1 Creative or constructive; having capacity for imagining. 2 Characterized by or proceeding from imagination. See synonyms under FANCIFUL, ROMANTIC. [<L *imaginatus*, pp. of *imaginari* IMAGINE] — **im·ag'i·na·tive·ly** *adv.* — **im·ag'i·na·tive·ness** *n.*

im·ag·ine (i·maj'in) *v.* **·ined, ·in·ing** *v.t.* 1 To form a mental image of; conceive or create in the mind. 2 To suppose or conjecture; think. — *v.i.* 3 To use the imagination. 4 To make conjectures; suppose. See synonyms under GUESS, SUPPOSE. [<L *imaginari* imagine < *imago* image]

im·a·gism (im'ə·jiz'əm) *n.* A movement in modern poetry, originating around 1910 and characterized by the use of precise, concrete images and freedom from convention in versification and form. [<F *Des Imagistes*, the title of the first anthology of imagist poetry] — **im'a·gist** (-jist) *n.* — **im'a·gis'tic** *adj.*

i·ma·go (i·mā'gō) *n. pl.* **i·ma·goes** or **i·mag·i·nes** (i·maj'ə·nēz) 1 *Entomol.* An adult, sexually matured insect. 2 *Psychoanal.* The infantile, subconscious idea of the parent or other loved one persisting in the adult. [<L]

i·mam (i·mäm') *n.* A Moslem priest, who recites prayers and leads devotions. Also **i·maum** (i·mäm', i·môm'). [<Arabic *imām* leader < *amma* lead]

I·mam (i·mäm') *n.* 1 A title of Mohammed and his four immediate successors: so called because they conducted the devotions of the faithful. 2 A title of a Moslem religious leader or chief. 3 The title of the leaders of the Shiahs, or heterodox Persian sect of Moslems; Ali and his ten successors: ascribed also to the Mahdi. Compare MAHDI. Also **I·maum** (i·mäm', i·môm').

i·mam·ate (i·mäm'āt) *n.* The office or jurisdiction of an imam.

i·ma·ret (i·mä'ret) *n.* In Turkey, an inn or hotel. [<Turkish *'imāret* <Arabic *'imārah* building]

im·bal·ance (im·bal'əns) *n.* 1 A lack of balance. 2 Inability to maintain an erect position. 3 Defective coordination of the eye muscles, endocrine glands, etc.

im·balm (im·bäm') See EMBALM.

im·be·cile (im'bə·sil) *adj.* 1 Having the mental faculties feeble or defective; feeble–minded. 2 Characterized by stupidity. — *n. Psychiatry* A person of feeble mind; one intermediate between an idiot and a moron. See IDIOT. [<F *imbécile* <L *imbecillus* weak]

im·be·cil·i·ty (im'bə·sil'ə·tē) *n. pl.* **·ties** 1 The condition or quality of being imbecile or impotent; feebleness, especially of the mind. 2 *Psychiatry* The next to the lowest grade of mental capacity and intelligence. See IDIOCY. 3 Any expression of character or opinion that indicates mental feebleness. 4 Incompetency;

inability. 5 Absurdity; folly; silliness. [<MF *imbécillité* <L *imbecillitas* feebleness]

im·bibe (im·bīb′) *v.* **·bibed, ·bib·ing** *v.t.* 1 To drink in; drink. 2 To take in as if drinking; absorb. 3 To receive into the mind or character: to *imbibe* good principles. 4 *Obs.* To saturate; imbue. —*v.i.* 5 To drink. See synonyms under ABSORB. [<F *imbiber* <L *imbibere* < *in-* in + *bibere* drink] —**im·bib′er** *n.*

im·bi·bi·tion (im′bi·bish′ən) *n.* 1 The act or process of imbibing, drinking in, or absorbing. 2 The absorption of moisture by any porous body.

im·bri·cate (im′brə·kāt) *v.* **·cat·ed, ·cat·ing** *v.t.* To lay or arrange regularly so as to overlap, as tiles on a roof. —*v.i.* To overlap. —*adj.* (-brə·kit) 1 Lying regularly over one another like shingles or slates, so as to break joints. 2 *Biol.* Overlapping with the extremities or margins, as the scales of fishes, the feathers of birds, or flower petals in the bud. 3 Decorated with overlapping scales, or so as to represent a surface of overlapping scales or tiles. Also **im′bri·cat′ed, im′bri·ca′tive.** [<L *imbricatus,* pp. of *imbricare* cover with gutter tiles < *imbrex* gutter tile < *imber* rain] —**im′bri·ca′tive·ly** *adv.*

im·bri·ca·tion (im′brə·kā′shən) *n.* 1 The condition of being imbricate: especially applied to shingles or tiles. 2 An imbricated organ, part, or structure.

im·bro·glio (im·brōl′yō) *n. pl.* **·glios** 1 A troublesome complication of affairs; a misunderstanding attended by ill feeling, perplexity, or strife; an entanglement. 2 An intricate plot, as of a tale or drama. [<Ital.]

Im·bros (im′brəs) The largest Turkish island in the Aegean, west of the mouth of the Dardanelles: Turkish *İmroz.*

im·brue (im·bro͞o′) *v.t.* **·brued, ·bru·ing** To stain or wet; moisten, especially with blood. [<OF *embreuver* <L *imbibere* drink]

im·brute (im·bro͞ot′) *v.t.* & *v.i.* **·brut·ed, ·brut·ing** To make or become brutal or brutish; brutalize.

im·bue (im·byo͞o′) *v.t.* **·bued, ·bu·ing** 1 To wet thoroughly; saturate. 2 To impregnate with color; dye; imbrue. 3 To impregnate or fill, as the mind, with emotions, principles, etc. [<OF *imbuer* <L *imbuere* wet, soak]

im·id·az·ole (im′id·az′ōl, -ə·zōl′) *n. Chem.* A white, crystalline, monacid base, $C_3H_4N_2$, isomeric with pyrazole; also called *glyoxaline.* [<IMID(O)- + AZOLE]

im·ide (im′īd, -id) *n. Chem.* A compound containing the bivalent radical NH united to a bivalent acid radical. Also **im′id** (-id). [< AMIDE]

imido– *combining form Chem.* 1 Used to indicate the presence of an imide in a compound. 2 Loosely, imino–. Also, before vowels, **imid–.** [<IMIDE]

i·mine (i·mēn′, im′in) *n. Chem.* An organic compound in which a non–acid radical is united with the NH radical. [<AMINE]

imino– *combining form Chem.* Used to indicate the presence of an imine in a compound. Also, before vowels, **imin–.** [<IMINE]

im·i·tate (im′ə·tāt) *v.t.* **·tat·ed, ·tat·ing** 1 To do or try to do after the manner of; try to be the same as. 2 To mimic; counterfeit, as a tone of voice. 3 To make a copy or reproduction of; duplicate. 4 To use as a pattern or model. 5 To assume the appearance of; look like: lead painted to *imitate* gold. See IMITATION. [<L *imitatus,* pp. of *imitari* imitate] —**im·i·ta·ble** (im′ə·tə·bəl) *adj.* —**im′·i·ta·bil′i·ty** *n.* —**im′i·ta′tor** *n.*

Synonyms: ape, copy, counterfeit, duplicate, follow, impersonate, mimic, mock, pattern, personate, portray, repeat, represent, resemble, simulate. See FOLLOW. *Antonyms*: alter, change, differentiate, distort, misrepresent, modify, pervert, remodel, transform, vary.

im·i·ta·tion (im′ə·tā′shən) *n.* 1 The act of imitating. 2 Something done or made in resemblance of something else; a likeness; also, a counterfeit: *imitation* of money. 3 *Music* The repetition of a phrase or subject in another voice or a different key. 4 *Biol.* Mimicry of environment or of another animal, plant, etc., for concealment or protection. See synonyms under CARICATURE, DUPLICATE, MODEL. —*adj.* Counterfeit; imitating something genuine or superior: *imitation* diamonds. [<L *imitatio, -onis*]

im·i·ta·tive (im′ə·tā′tiv) *adj.* 1 Inclined to imitate; given to or characterized by imitation. 2 Formed after a copy or model; resembling an original. 3 Fictitious; counterfeit. 4 *Ling.* Designating a word that approximates a natural sound, as *buzz, clink, swish.* Abbr. *imit.* —**im′i·ta′tive·ly** *adv.* —**im′i·ta′·tive·ness** *n.*

im·mac·u·late (i·mak′yə·lit) *adj.* 1 Without spot or blemish; pure; without taint of evil or sin. 2 Faultless; flawless. 3 Of one color; not spotted. See synonyms under GOOD, INNOCENT, PERFECT, PURE. [<L *immaculatus* < *in-* not + *maculatus* spotted] —**im·mac′u·late·ly** *adv.* —**im·mac′u·late·ness** *n.*

Immaculate Conception In the Roman Catholic Church, the doctrine that the Virgin Mary was conceived in her mother's womb without the stain of original sin: distinguished from *Virgin Birth.*

im·man·a·cle (i·man′ə·kəl) *v.t. Rare* To put manacles on; fetter.

im·mane (i·mān′) *adj. Archaic* Of vast size; gigantic; cruel. [<L *immanis*]

im·ma·nence (im′ə·nəns) *n.* 1 A permanent abiding within; an indwelling. 2 The doctrine that the ultimate principle of the universe is not to be distinguished from the universe itself, that God dwells in all things and permeates the spirit of man. Also **im′ma·nen·cy.**

im·ma·nent (im′ə·nənt) *adj.* 1 Remaining within; indwelling; inherent: opposed to *transeunt, transcendent.* 2 Pertaining to the philosophical or the theological doctrine of immanence. See synonyms under INHERENT. [<L *immanens, -entis,* ppr. of *immanere* remain in < *in-* in + *manere* stay] —**im′ma·nent·ly** *adv.*

Im·man·u·el (i·man′yo͞o·əl, *Ger.* i·mä′no͞o·el) A masculine personal name. See EMMANUEL. [<Hebrew, God with us]

—**Immanuel** A name of the Messiah. *Isa.* vii 14; *Matt.* i 23.

im·ma·te·ri·al (im′ə·tir′ē·əl) *adj.* 1 Not material; incorporeal: opposed to corporeal. 2 Unimportant. See synonyms under INSIGNIFICANT. [<Med. L *immaterialis*] —**im′ma·te′ri·al·ly** *adv.* —**im′ma·te′ri·al·ness** *n.*

im·ma·te·ri·al·ism (im′ə·tir′ē·əl·iz′əm) *n.* The doctrine that the objective world has no existence apart from perception by the consciousness; specifically, the idealism of Berkeley. —**im′ma·te′ri·al·ist** *n.*

im·ma·te·ri·al·i·ty (im′ə·tir′ē·al′ə·tē) *n. pl.* **·ties** 1 The state or quality of being immaterial. 2 That which has no material existence or essence.

im·ma·te·ri·al·ize (im′ə·tir′ē·əl·īz) *v.t.* **·ized, ·iz·ing** To make immaterial or incorporeal.

im·ma·ture (im′ə·cho͝or′, -tyo͝or′, -to͝or′) *adj.* 1 Not mature or ripe; not full–grown; undeveloped. 2 Not brought to a complete state; imperfect. 3 In physical geography, not in accordance with or thoroughly adapted to surrounding or local conditions, particularly of base level: *immature* topography. 4 *Obs.* Too early; premature. [<L *immaturus*] —**im′·ma·ture′ly** *adv.* —**im′ma·tur′i·ty, im′ma·ture′·ness** *n.*

im·meas·ur·a·ble (i·mezh′ər·ə·bəl) *adj.* Not capable of being measured; indefinitely extensive; boundless. See synonyms under INFINITE. —**im·meas′ur·a·ble·ness, im·meas′ur·a·bil′i·ty** *n.* —**im·meas′ur·a·bly** *adv.*

im·me·di·a·cy (i·mē′dē·ə·sē) *n.* 1 The state or quality of being immediate; freedom from the intervention of any intermediate person or thing. 2 In the feudal system, the condition of being next in rank to the suzerain. 3 *Philos.* **a** Independent or non–relative existence or being. **b** Consciousness or direct awareness, apart from memory or reasoning. **c** Intuitive knowledge as distinguished from that arrived at by proof or reasoning.

im·me·di·ate (i·mē′dē·it) *adj.* 1 Without delay; instant. 2 Separated by no appreciable space; nearly related; close. 3 Acting without the intervention of anything; direct: opposed to *mediate.* 4 Pertaining to a direct perception; intuitive. 5 Directly concerning; having a direct bearing. [<Med. L *immediatus*] —**im·me′di·ate·ness** *n.*

Synonyms: close, contiguous, direct, instant, intimate, next, present, proximate. *Antonyms*: distant, far, future, remote.

im·me·di·ate·ly (i·mē′dē·it·lē) *adv.* 1 In an immediate manner; without lapse of time; instantly; at once. 2 Without the intervention of anything; directly. —*conj.* As soon as.

Synonyms (adv.): directly, forthwith, instanter, instantly, now, presently, straightway. *Immediately* primarily signifies without the intervention of anything as a medium, hence without the intervention of any, even the briefest, interval or lapse of time. *Directly,* which once meant with no intervening time, now means after some little while; *presently* no longer means in this very present, but before very long. Even *immediately* is sliding from its instantaneousness, so that we are fain to substitute *at once, instantly,* etc., when we would make promptness emphatic.

im·med·i·ca·ble (i·med′i·kə·bəl) *adj.* Incurable. [<L *immedicabilis* < *in-* not + *medicabilis* curable]

Im·mel·mann turn (im′əl·män, -mən) *Aeron.* An airplane maneuver consisting of a partial loop followed by a half–roll on the longitudinal axis: used to gain altitude while simultaneously reversing the direction of flight. [after Max *Immelmann,* 1890–1916, German aviator]

im·me·mo·ri·al (im′ə·môr′ē·əl, -mō′rē-) *adj.* Reaching back beyond memory; having its origin in the indefinite past. See synonyms under PRIMEVAL. [<Med. L *immemorialis*] —**im′me·mo′ri·al·ly** *adv.*

im·mense (i·mens′) *adj.* 1 Very great in degree or size; vast; huge. 2 Infinite. —*n.* The limitless void; infinity. [<F <L *immensus* < *in-* not + *mensus,* pp. of *metiri* measure] —**im·mense′ly** *adj.*

Synonyms (adj.): colossal, enormous, gigantic, huge, prodigious, stupendous, vast. See LARGE.

im·men·si·ty (i·men′sə·tē) *n. pl.* **·ties** 1 The state or quality of being immense; vastness. 2 Boundless space. See synonyms under MAGNITUDE. Also **im·mense′ness.** [<MF *immensité* <L *immensitas* < *immensus* IMMENSE]

im·men·sur·a·ble (i·men′sho͝or·ə·bəl) *adj.* Immeasurable. [<MF <L *immensurabilis* < *in-* not + *mensurabilis* MENSURABLE] —**im·men′sur·a·bil′i·ty** *n.*

im·merge (i·mûrj′) *v.* **·merged, ·merg·ing** *v.t.* To immerse. —*v.i.* To plunge, as into a liquid; sink. [<L *immergere* < *in-* in + *mergere* dip] —**im·mer′gence** *n.*

im·merse (i·mûrs′) *v.t.* **·mersed, ·mers·ing** 1 To plunge or dip entirely in water or other fluid. 2 To involve deeply; engross: He *immersed* himself in study. 3 To baptize by immersion. [<L *immersus,* pp. of *immergere* dip]

Synonyms: bury, dip, douse, duck, immerge, plunge, sink, submerge. *Dip* is a native word, while *immerse* is a Latin borrowing; *dip* is accordingly the more popular and commonplace, *immerse* the more elegant and dignified expression in many cases. To speak of baptism by immersion as *dipping* now seems rude, but was entirely proper and usual in early English. Baptists now universally use the word *immerse.* To *dip* and to *immerse* alike signify to *bury* or *submerge* some object in a liquid; but *dip* implies that the object *dipped* is at once removed from the liquid. *Immerse* suggests more absolute completeness of the action; one may *dip* his sleeve or *dip* a sponge in a liquid, if he but touches the edge; if he *immerses* it, he completely *sinks* it under, and covers it with the liquid. *Submerge* implies that the object cannot readily be removed, if at all; as, a *submerged* wreck. To *plunge* is to *immerse* suddenly and violently, for which *douse* and *duck* are colloquial terms. *Dip* is used, also, unlike the other words, to denote the putting of a hollow vessel into a liquid in order to remove a portion of it; in this sense we say *dip up, dip out.* Compare synonyms for BURY[1].

im·mer·sion (i·mûr′zhən, -shən) *n.* 1 The act of immersing or the state of being immersed; specifically, baptism by submersion in water. 2 The state of being overwhelmed or deeply engaged; absorption: *immersion* in business. 3 *Astron.* The disappearance of a heavenly body, either by passing behind another or by entering into the light of the sun or the shadow of the earth. [<L *immersio, -onis*]

im·mer·sion·ism (i·mûr′zhən·iz′əm, -shən-) *n.* **1** The theological doctrine of immersion. **2** The custom of baptizing by immersion.

im·mesh (i·mesh′) See ENMESH.

im·mew (i·myōō′) *v.t. Obs.* To coop up; imprison. [See MEW¹.]

im·mi·grant (im′ə·grənt) *n.* **1** One who or that which immigrates. **2** A foreigner who enters a country to settle there. Compare EMIGRANT. —*adj.* Immigrating.

im·mi·grate (im′ə·grāt) *v.* **·grat·ed, ·grat·ing** *v.i.* To come into a new country or region for the purpose of settling there. —*v.t.* To bring in as an immigrant or settler. See synonyms under EMIGRATE. [<L *immigratus,* pp. of *immigrare* go into <*in-* in + *migrare* migrate] —**im′mi·gra·to′ry** (-tôr′ē, -tō′rē) *adj.*

im·mi·gra·tion (im′ə·grā′shən) *n.* **1** The act of immigrating; entrance of a settler or settlers from a foreign country. **2** The total number of aliens entering a country for permanent residence during a stated period. **3** Immigrants collectively.

im·mi·nence (im′ə·nəns) *n.* **1** The state or quality of being imminent. **2** Impending evil. Also **im′mi·nen·cy.** [<LL *imminentia*]

im·mi·nent (im′ə·nənt) *adj.* **1** About to happen; impending; said especially of danger or evil. **2** Overhanging as if about to fall. [<L *imminens, -entis* <*imminere* lean over, impend <*in-* on + *-minere* project] —**im′mi·nent·ly** *adv.*

Synonyms : impending, threatening. *Imminent,* from the Latin, with the sense of projecting over, signifies liable to happen at once, as some calamity, dangerous and close at hand. *Impending,* also from the Latin, with the sense of hanging over, is closely akin to *imminent,* but somewhat less emphatic. *Imminent* is more immediate, *impending* more remote, *threatening* more contingent. An *impending* evil is almost sure to happen at some uncertain time, near or remote; an *imminent* peril is one liable to befall very speedily; a *threatening* peril may be near or remote, but always with hope that it may be averted. *Antonyms* : chimerical, contingent, doubtful, improbable, problematical, unexpected, unlikely.

im·min·gle (i·ming′gəl) *v.t.* & *v.i.* **·gled, ·gling** To mix thoroughly; mingle.

im·mis·ci·ble (i·mis′ə·bəl) *adj.* Not capable of mixing, as oil and water. Also **im·mix′a·ble** (-mik′sə-). [? <L *immiscibilis* <*in-* not + *miscere* mix] —**im·mis′ci·bil′i·ty** *n.*

im·mit (i·mit′) *v.t. Obs.* To send in; inject. [<L *immittere* <*in-* in + *mittere* send] —**im·mis·sion** (i·mish′ən) *n.*

im·mit·i·ga·ble (i·mit′ə·gə·bəl) *adj.* That cannot be mitigated. [<L *immitigabilis*] —**im·mit′i·ga·bly** *adv.*

im·mix (i·miks′) *v.t.* To mingle; mix in. [<L *immixtus,* pp. of *immiscere* <*in-* in + *miscere* mix]

im·mix·ture (i·miks′chər) *n.* An intermingling; association with; commingling.

im·mo·bile (i·mō′bəl, -bēl) *adj.* **1** Unmovable; stable. **2** Not to be touched through the emotions. [<OF <L *immobilis*]

im·mo·bil·i·ty (im′ō·bil′ə·tē) *n.* The condition of being immovable or immobile; fixedness. See synonyms under APATHY.

im·mo·bi·lize (i·mō′bə·līz) *v.t.* **·lized, ·liz·ing** **1** To make immovable; fix in place, as a limb by splints or bandages. **2** To make unable to move or mobilize, as a fleet or body of troops. **3** To withdraw (specie) from circulation and hold as security for banknotes. [<F *immobiliser*] —**im·mo′bi·li·za′tion** (-lə·zā′shən, -lī·zā′-) *n.*

im·mod·er·ate (i·mod′ər·it) *adj.* Not moderate; exceeding reasonable bounds. [<L *immoderatus*] —**im·mod′er·ate·ly** *adv.* —**im·mod′er·ate·ness** *n.*

Synonyms : excessive, exorbitant, extravagant, inordinate, intemperate, unreasonable, violent. Compare IRREGULAR, VIOLENT. *Antonyms*: see synonyms for MODERATE.

im·mod·er·a·tion (i·mod′ə·rā′shən) *n.* Want of moderation; excess. Also **im·mod′er·a·cy** (-ə·sē). [<L *immoderatio, -onis*]

im·mod·est (i·mod′ist) *adj.* **1** Wanting in modesty; indelicate or indecent. **2** Impudent; bold. [<L *immodestus*] —**im·mod′est·ly** *adv.* —**im·mod′es·ty** *n.*

Synonyms : bold, brazen, coarse, forward, gross, impure, indecent, indecorous, indelicate, lewd, obscene, shameless, unchaste, wanton. Compare synonyms for IMPUDENT. *Antonyms* : see synonyms for PURE.

im·mo·late (im′ə·lāt) *v.t.* **·lat·ed, ·lat·ing** To sacrifice; especially, to kill as a sacrifice. [<L *immolatus,* pp. of *immolare* sprinkle with sacrificial meal <*in-* on + *mola* meal] **im′mo·la′tor** *n.*

im·mo·la·tion (im′ə·lā′shən) *n.* **1** The act of immolating. **2** The state of being immolated. **3** That which is immolated or sacrificed. [<L *immolatio, -onis*]

im·mor·al (i·môr′əl, i·mor′-) *adj.* **1** Violating the moral law; contrary to rectitude or public morality. **2** Habitually licentious. —**im·mor′al·ly** *adv.*

Synonyms : bad, corrupt, criminal, depraved, dishonest, dissolute, evil, loose, profligate, sinful, unprincipled, vicious, vile, wicked, wrong. See BAD¹, CRIMINAL, SINFUL. *Antonyms* : chaste, devout, dutiful, godly, good, just, moral, pious, pure, religious, righteous, upright, virtuous, worthy.

im·mo·ral·i·ty (im′ə·ral′ə·tē) *n. pl.* **·ties** **1** The quality or condition of being immoral; vice; wickedness; licentiousness. **2** An act of licentiousness. **3** An immoral act. See synonyms under SIN.

im·mor·tal (i·môr′təl) *adj.* Having unending existence; deathless; enduring. —*n.* **1** A person considered worthy of immortality. **2** In mythology, a god. —**the Immortals** **1** The members of the French Academy, forty in number: also called **the Forty Immortals.** **2** The royal guard of ancient Persia; hence, any band or group that has conducted itself with marked gallantry in the face of extraordinary perils (especially of war). [<L *immortalis*] —**im·mor′tal·ly** *adv.*

Synonyms (*adj.*): deathless, endless, eternal, everlasting, imperishable, incorruptible, indestructible, indissoluble, never-dying, neverfading, never-failing, sempiternal, undying, unfading, unfailing. See ETERNAL. *Antonyms* : dying, ephemeral, fading, failing, fleeting, mortal, perishable, perishing, transient, transitory.

im·mor·tal·i·ty (im′ôr·tal′ə·tē) *n.* **1** Exemption from death or oblivion; eternal life. **2** Eternal fame. [<OF *immortalité* <L *immortalitas*]

im·mor·tal·ize (i·môr′təl·īz) *v.t.* **·ized, ·iz·ing** To make immortal; give perpetual fame or life to.

im·mor·telle (im′ôr·tel′) *n.* **1** A flower (genus *Xeranthemum*) of the composite family that retains its form and color for a long time after being gathered. **2** The everlasting. [<F]

im·mo·tile (i·mō′til) *adj.* Not motile; stationary.

im·mov·a·ble (i·mōō′və·bəl) *adj.* **1** That cannot be moved or stirred from its place; fixed: an *immovable* foundation. **2** Steadfast; unchangeable: an *immovable* purpose. **3** Not having the feelings easily roused; impassive. **4** *Law* Not liable to be removed; permanent in place: *immovable* property. See synonyms under FIRM, INFLEXIBLE, OBSTINATE. —*n.* **1** That which cannot be moved. **2** *Law* Any piece of land, together with trees, buildings, etc., strictly appertaining to it, either naturally or otherwise, so as not to be movable: opposed to *movable.* —**im·mov′a·bil′i·ty, im·mov′a·ble·ness** *n.* —**im·mov′a·bly** *adv.*

im·mune (i·myōōn′) *adj.* **1** Exempt, as from taxation. **2** *Med.* Protected from disease by inoculation. —*n.* A person not susceptible to some particular disease. [<F <L *immunis*]

im·mu·ni·ty (i·myōō′nə·tē) *n. pl.* **·ties** **1** Freedom or exemption, as from a penalty, burden, duty, or evil, such as the exemption of ecclesiastical persons and places from duties and burdens thought unbecoming their sacred character: followed by *from.* **2** *Med.* Exemption from contagion or infection or from liability to suffer from epidemic or endemic disease. It may be *active* through the formation of specific antibodies in the organism, or *passive* through the effect of a serum injected from another organism. See synonyms under RIGHT. [<OF *immunité* <L *immunitas* <*immunis* exempt <*in-* not + *munis* serviceable <*munus* service, duty]

im·mu·nize (im′yə·nīz) *v.t.* **·nized, ·niz·ing** To make immune; protect, as from infection. —**im·mu·ni·za·tion** (im′yə·nə·zā′shən, -nī·zā′-) *n.*

immuno- *combining form* Immune; immunity: *immunology.* [<IMMUNE]

im·mu·no·gen·ic (i·myōō′nō·jen′ik) *adj. Med.* Producing or conferring immunity to a specified disease.

im·mu·no·ge·net·ics (i·myōō′nō·jə·net′iks) *n.* The study of immunity to disease as conditioned by and associated with the transmission of specific genetic factors.

im·mu·nol·o·gy (im′yə·nol′ə·jē) *n.* The science which treats of the phenomena and techniques of immunity from disease. [<IMMUNO- + -LOGY] —**im·mu·no·log·i·cal** (i·myōō′nə·loj′i·kəl) *adj.*

im·mu·no·re·ac·tion (i·myōō′nō·rē·ak′shən) *n. Med.* The reaction which takes place between an antigen and its antibody, as in the blood.

im·mu·no·sup·pres·sive (i·myōō′nō·sə·pres′iv) *adj.* Preventing the action of an antibody in order to permit an organism to accept foreign material, such as an organ transplant.

im·mure (i·myŏŏr′) *v.t.* **·mured, ·mur·ing** To shut up within or as within walls; imprison. [<Med. L *immurare* <*in-* in + LL *murare* wall <*murus* wall] —**im·mure′ment** *n.*

im·mu·si·cal (i·myōō′zi·kəl) *adj.* Unmusical.

im·mu·ta·bil·i·ty (i·myōō′tə·bil′ə·tē) *n.* The state or quality of being immutable or unchangeable. Also **im·mu′ta·ble·ness.** [<L *immutabilitas, -tatis*]

im·mu·ta·ble (i·myōō′tə·bəl) *adj.* Not mutable; unchangeable. See synonyms under FIRM, PERMANENT. [<L *immutabilis*] —**im·mu′ta·bly** *adv.*

Im·o·gen (im′ə·jən) In Shakespeare's *Cymbeline,* the heroine, a model of conjugal fidelity.

imp (imp) *n.* **1** An evil spirit; a little devil; a child of the devil. **2** A mischievous or malicious person: especially applied to a child. **3** *Obs.* Progeny; offspring. —*v.t.* **1** To mend or repair by something inserted or added. **2** To furnish with wings. **3** In falconry, to repair or improve powers of flight by grafting feathers to (a falcon, a falcon's wing, tail, etc.); to graft (a feather or feathers). **4** *Obs.* To graft; implant [OE *impa* a graft <*impian* ingraft <LL *impotus* a shoot <Gk. *emphytos* <*emphyein* implant <*en-* in + *phyein* produce]

im·pact (im·pakt′) *v.t.* To press or drive firmly together; pack; wedge. —*n.* (im′pakt) **1** The act of striking; collision. **2** The forcible momentary contact of a moving body with another either moving or at rest: the *impact* of a bullet against a target. **3** A continuing, powerful influence: the *impact* of science on culture. See synonyms under COLLISION. [<L *impactus,* pp. of *impingere.* See IMPINGE]

im·pact·ed (im·pak′tid) *adj.* **1** Packed firmly. **2** *Dent.* Denoting a tooth wedged between the jawbone and another tooth in such a way as to prevent its emergence through the gums.

im·pac·tion (im·pak′shən) *n.* **1** An overloading of an organ, as of the intestine. **2** A wedging of one part into another. **3** *Dent.* An impacted tooth. [<L *impactio, -onis* a striking]

im·pair (im·pâr′) *v.t.* To diminish in quality, strength, or value; injure. [<OF *empeirer* <LL *in-* thoroughly + *pejorare* make worse <L *pejor* worse]

Synonyms : debase, decrease, deteriorate, diminish, enervate, enfeeble, lessen, reduce, weaken. See HURT, WEAKEN, WEAR. *Antonyms* : see synonyms for AMEND, INCREASE.

im·pair·ment (im·pâr′mənt) *n.* **1** The act of impairing. **2** The state of being impaired. **3** Deterioration; injury. [<OF *empeirement*]

im·pa·la (im·pä′lə) *n.* A South African antelope (*Aepyceros melampus*), dark red fading into clear white below, with the spreading horns in the male: also called *pallah.* [<native name]

im·pale (im·pāl′) *v.t.* **·paled, ·pal·ing** **1** To fix upon a pale or sharp stake. **2** To torture or put to death by thrusting a sharp stake through the body. **3** To make helpless as if by fixing upon a stake; transfix: to *impale* someone with a glance. **4** *Her.* To place (two coats of arms) side by side on an escutcheon. Also spelled *empale.* [<OF *empaler* <LL *impalare* <*in-* in + *palus* a stake]

im·pale·ment (im·pāl′mənt) *n.* **1** The act of impaling. **2** That which impales, or the space impaled; an enclosure. **3** The displaying of two coats of arms side by side on one escutcheon. Also spelled *empalement.*

im·pal·pa·ble (im·pal′pə·bəl) *adj.* **1** Imperceptible to the touch; specifically, ground so fine that no grit can be felt. **2** Intangible unreal. **3** Immaterial: incorporeal. [<Med. L

impalpabilis] — **im·pal'pa·bil'i·ty** *n.* — **im·pal'·pa·bly** *adv.*

im·pal·u·dism (im·pal'yə·diz'əm) *n. Pathol.* Chronic malarial infection: often called *marsh poisoning.* [<L *in-* in + *palus, paludis* swamp]

im·pa·na·tion (im'pə·nā'shən) *n.* The doctrine that the body and blood of Christ are united into one substance with the consecrated bread and wine: distinguished from *transubstantiation.* [<Med. L *impanatus*, pp. of *impanare* embody in bread <*in-* in + *panis* bread] — **im·pa·nate** (im·pā'nit, -nāt), **im·pa·nat·ed** (im·pā'nā·tid) *adj.*

im·pan·el (im·pan'əl) *v.t.* **·eled** or **·elled, ·el·ing** or **·el·ling** 1 To enrol upon a panel or list, as for jury duty. 2 To draw from such a list, as a jury. Also spelled *empanel.* — **im·pan'el·ment** *n.*

im·par (im·pär') *adj.* Odd or unequal; without a corresponding part; not paired. [<L <*in-* not + *par* equal]

im·par·a·dise (im·par'ə·dīs) *v.t.* **·dised, ·dis·ing** To place in or as in paradise; make supremely happy.

im·par·i·pin·nate (im·par'ə·pin'āt) *adj. Bot.* Pinnate with an odd terminal leaflet; odd-pinnate. [<L *impar* unequal + PINNATE]

im·par·i·ty (im·par'ə·tē) *n. pl.* **·ties** Lack of correspondence; inequality; diversity. [<LL *imparitas, -tatis*]

im·park (im·pärk') *v.t.* 1 To enclose (land) as a park. 2 To place (animals) in or as in a park or enclosure. [<AF *enparker*, OF *emparquer*] — **im·par·ka·tion** (im'pär·kā'shən) *n.*

im·part (im·pärt') *v.t.* 1 To make known; tell; communicate. 2 To give a portion of; give. — *v.i.* 3 To give a part; share. See synonyms under GIVE, INFORM, PUBLISH. [<OF *empartir* <L *impartire* <*in-* on + *partire* share <*pars, partis* part, share] — **im·part'er** *n.*

im·par·ta·tion (im'pär·tā'shən) *n.* The act of imparting, as knowledge. Also **im·part'ment.**

im·par·tial (im·pär'shəl) *adj.* Not partial; unbiased; just. See synonyms under CANDID, JUST. — **im·par'tial·ly** *adv.*

im·par·ti·al·i·ty (im'pär·shē·al'ə·tē, im·pär'-) *n.* The quality or character of being impartial; fairness. Also **im·par'tial·ness.**

im·part·i·ble[1] (im·pär'tə·bəl) *adj.* Not subject to partition; not dividable. [<LL *impartibilis*] — **im·part'i·bil'i·ty** *n.* — **im·part'i·bly** *adv.*

im·part·i·ble[2] (im·pär'tə·bəl) *adj. Obs.* Capable of being imparted, shared, or made known.

im·pass·a·ble (im·pas'ə·bəl, -päs'-) *adj.* Not passable. See synonyms under IMPENETRABLE. — **im·pass'a·bil'i·ty, im·pass'a·ble·ness** *n.* — **im·pass'a·bly** *adv.*

im·passe (im'pas, im·pas'; *Fr.* aṅ·päs') *n.* 1 A blind alley, or passage open only at one end; cul–de–sac. 2 Any serious and insurmountable obstacle or problem. [<F]

im·pas·si·bil·i·ty (im·pas'ə·bil'ə·tē) *n.* 1 Essential incapacity for suffering. 2 The state of being unfeeling or apathetic. Also **im·pas'si·ble·ness.** [<OF *impassibilité* <L *impassibilitas* <*impassibilis* impassible]

im·pas·si·ble (im·pas'ə·bəl) *adj.* 1 Incapable of suffering or sympathizing. 2 Not affected by feeling; apathetic. [<OF *impassible* <Med. L *impassibilis* <*in-* not + *passibilis*. See PASSIBLE.] — **im·pas'si·bly** *adv.*

im·pas·sion (im·pash'ən) *v.t.* To affect with passion; inflame. [<Ital. *impassionare*]

im·pas·sion·ate (im·pash'ən·it) *adj.* Without passion; dispassionate.

im·pas·sioned (im·pash'ənd) *adj.* Fervent; stirring. See synonyms under ARDENT.

im·pas·sive (im·pas'iv) *adj.* 1 Insensible to or unaffected by suffering or pain; unimpressionable. 2 Unmoved by or not exhibiting feeling; apathetic. 3 Not susceptible of injury. 4 Lifeless; insensible; also, unconscious. — **im·pas'sive·ly** *adv.* — **im·pas'sive·ness, im·pas·siv·i·ty** (im'pa·siv'ə·tē) *n.*

im·paste (im·pāst') *v.t.* **·past·ed, ·past·ing** 1 To encrust with or as with paste. 2 To make into a paste or crust. 3 To apply paint thickly to; employ the technique of impasto on. [<Ital. *impastare*] — **im·pas·ta·tion** (im'pās·tā'shən) *n.*

im·pas·to (im·päs'tō) *n.* 1 A technique of painting in which thick pigment is applied to a surface to give relief or force. 2 The pigment so applied. [<Ital.]

im·pa·tience (im·pā'shəns) *n.* 1 Lack of patience; unwillingness to brook delay. 2 Intolerance of opposition or control. [<OF *impacience* <L *impatientia*]

Synonyms: fretfulness, irritation, peevishness, pettishness, petulance, vexation. These words express the slighter forms of anger. *Irritation, petulance,* and *vexation* are temporary and for immediate cause. *Fretfulness, pettishness,* and *peevishness* are chronic states finding in any petty matter an occasion for their exercise. Compare ACRIMONY, ANGER. *Antonyms:* amiability, benignity, forbearance, gentleness, leniency, lenity, long-suffering, mildness, patience, peace, peaceableness, peacefulness, self-control, self-restraint.

im·pa·ti·ens (im·pā'shē·enz) *n.* Any of a large genus (*Impatiens*) of herbs with stems enlarged at the joints, opposite leaves, and irregular flowers, as the *jewelweed, snapweed,* or *touch-me-not.* The ripe elastic seed vessels, when touched, burst open and scatter the seeds. [<L]

im·pa·tient (im·pā'shənt) *adj.* 1 Not possessed of or not exercising patience; intolerant; disturbed by or complaining about pain, delay, strain, etc. 2 Exhibiting or expressing impatience. See synonyms under EAGER, FRETFUL, RESTIVE. [<OF *impacient* <L *impatiens, -entis* <*in-* not + *patiens*. See PATIENT.] — **im·pa'tient·ly** *adv.*

im·pav·id (im·pav'id) *adj.* Without fear; intrepid; bold. [<L *impavidus* <*in-* not + *pavidus* timid] — **im·pa·vid·i·ty** (im'pə·vid'ə·tē) *n.* — **im·pav'id·ly** *adv.*

im·pawn (im·pôn') *v.t.* To pledge as security; pawn.

im·peach (im·pēch') *v.t.* 1 To bring discredit upon; challenge: to *impeach* one's honesty. 2 To charge with crime or misdemeanor in office; arraign (a public official) before a competent tribunal on such a charge. See synonyms under ARRAIGN. [<OF *empescher* hinder <LL *impedicare* entangle <*in-* in + *pedica* fetter <*pes, pedis* foot] — **im·peach'er** *n.*

im·peach·a·ble (im·pē'chə·bəl) *adj.* Liable to be impeached; censurable. — **im·peach'a·bil'i·ty** *n.*

im·peach·ment (im·pēch'mənt) *n.* 1 A discrediting. 2 The act of impeaching; especially the arraignment of a high civil officer. [<OF *empeschement* obstruction]

im·pearl (im·pûrl') *v.t.* 1 To form into pearl-like drops. 2 To make pearl-like. 3 To adorn with or as with pearls. [<F *emperler*]

im·pec·ca·ble (im·pek'ə·bəl) *adj.* 1 Not liable to commit sin or wrong. 2 Faultless. — *n.* An impeccable person. [<LL *impeccabilis* <*in-* not + *peccare* sin] — **im·pec'ca·bil'i·ty** *n.* — **im·pec'ca·bly** *adv.*

im·pec·cant (im·pek'ənt) *adj.* Free from sin or error; blameless. — **im·pec'cance, im·pec'·can·cy** *n.*

im·pe·cu·ni·ar·y (im'pə·kyōō'nē·er'ē) *adj.* Impecunious.

im·pe·cu·ni·ous (im'pə·kyōō'nē·əs) *adj.* Having no money; habitually poor. [<F *impécunieux*] — **im'pe·cu·ni·os'i·ty** (-kyōō'nē·os'ə·tē) *n.* — **im'pe·cu'ni·ous·ly** *adv.* — **im'pe·cu'ni·ous·ness** *n.*

im·pe·dance (im·pēd'ns) *n.* 1 *Electr.* a The resistance met by an alternating current on passing through a conductor. b The ratio of the effective electromotive force to the effective current of an alternating–current circuit. 2 *Physics* In a sound-transmitting medium, the ratio of the force per unit area to the volume velocity of a given surface.

im·pede (im·pēd') *v.t.* **·ped·ed, ·ped·ing** To retard or hinder in progress or action; obstruct. See synonyms under EMBARRASS, HINDER[1], LIMIT, OBSTRUCT. [<L *impedire*, lit., shackle the feet <*in-* in + *pes, pedis* foot] — **im·ped'er** *n.*

im·pe·di·ent (im·pē'dē·ənt) *adj.* That impedes. — *n.* That which impedes. [<L *impediens, -ientis*, ppr. of *impedire*. See IMPEDE.]

im·ped·i·ment (im·ped'ə·mənt) *n.* 1 That which hinders or impedes; an obstruction. 2 An organic hindrance to easy speech; a stammer. 3 *Law* Anything that prevents the contraction of a valid marriage. — **absolute impediment** *Law* A condition which makes it impossible for a person to contract a valid marriage. — **prohibitive impediment** *Law* A condition under which persons who have contracted marriage are subject to punishment for having done so. — **relative impediment** *Law* A state of facts which bars only people of a certain degree of consanguinity from contracting marriage with each other, as a brother with a sister. See also DIRIMENT IMPEDIMENT OF MARRIAGE. [<L *impedimentum*]

Synonyms: bar, barrier, clog, difficulty, encumbrance, hindrance, obstacle, obstruction. *Difficulty* makes an undertaking not easy. That which rests upon one as a burden is an *encumbrance.* A *hindrance* (kindred with *hind, behind*) is anything that makes one come behind or short of his purpose. An *impediment* (literally, that which checks the foot) may be either what one finds in his way or what he carries with him; *impedimenta* was the Latin name for the baggage of a soldier or of an army. The tendency is to view an *impediment* as something constant or, at least for a time, continuous; as, an *impediment* in one's speech. A *difficulty* or a *hindrance* may be either within one or without; a speaker may find *difficulty* in expressing himself, or *difficulty* in holding the attention of restless children. An *encumbrance* is always what one carries with him; an *obstacle* or an *obstruction* is always without. To an infantryman the steepness of a mountain path is a *difficulty*, loose stones are *impediments*, a fence is an *obstruction*, a cliff or a boulder across the way is an *obstacle*, a bed-roll is an *encumbrance. Antonyms:* advantage, aid, assistance, benefit, help, relief, succor.

im·ped·i·men·ta (im·ped'ə·men'tə) *n. pl.* 1 Baggage or other supplies of an army. 2 *Law* Impediments. 3 Any drawbacks or burdens. [<L]

im·ped·i·tive (im·ped'ə·tiv) *adj.* Causing hindrance; obstructive.

im·pel (im·pel') *v.t.* **·pelled, ·pel·ling** 1 To drive or push (something) forward or onward. 2 To urge or force (someone) to an action, course, etc.; incite; compel. See synonyms under ACTUATE, DRIVE, ENCOURAGE, INFLUENCE, PERSUADE, PUSH, SEND[1], SPUR. [<L *impellere* <*in-* on + *pellere* drive]

im·pel·lent (im·pel'ənt) *adj.* Tending to impel. — *n.* An impelling person, thing, or force. [<L *impellens, -entis*, ppr. of *impellere*. See IMPEL.]

im·pel·ler (im·pel'ər) *n.* 1 One who or that which impels. 2 *Mech.* The rotor of a pump or blower.

im·pend (im·pend') *v.i.* 1 To be imminent; threaten, as something evil or destructive. 2 To be suspended; hang: with *over.* [<L *impendere* overhang <*in-* on + *pendere* hang] — **im·pen'dence, im·pen'den·cy** *n.*

im·pen·dent (im·pen'dənt) *adj.* Imminent; threatening. [<L *impendens, -entis*, ppr. of *impendere*. See IMPEND.]

im·pend·ing (im·pen'ding) *adj.* Hanging over; threatening; about to happen. See synonyms under IMMINENT.

im·pen·e·tra·bil·i·ty (im·pen'ə·trə·bil'ə·tē) *n.* 1 The quality of being impenetrable. 2 *Physics* The property of matter which prevents two bodies from occupying the same space at the same time. Also **im·pen'e·tra·ble·ness.**

im·pen·e·tra·ble (im·pen'ə·trə·bəl) *adj.* 1 That cannot be penetrated or pierced: said of material things. 2 That cannot be penetrated by the eye or mind; abstruse; dense: an *impenetrable* darkness or mystery. 3 Not to be affected by moral considerations: an *impenetrable* conscience. 4 Possessing the property of impenetrability. [<OF *impenetrable* <L *impenetrabilis*] — **im·pen'e·tra·bly** *adv.*

Synonyms: close, dense, hard, impassable, impermeable, impervious, solid. See HARD. *Antonyms:* fluid, loose, open, penetrable, pervious, soft, yielding.

im·pen·i·tence (im·pen'ə·təns) *n.* Want of penitence or repentance; hardness of heart. Also **im·pen'i·ten·cy.** [<LL *impaenitentia*]

im·pen·i·tent (im·pen'ə·tənt) *adj.* Not penitent; hardened; obdurate. [<LL *impaenitens, -entis* <*in-* not + *paenitens*. See PENITENT.] — **im·pen'i·tent·ly** *adv.* — **im·pen'i·tent·ness** *n.*

im·pen·nate (im·pen'āt) *adj. Ornithol.* Having short wings with scalelike feathers, as a penguin.

im·per·a·tive (im·per′ə·tiv) *adj.* 1 Expressive of or containing positive, as distinguished from advisory or discretionary, command; authoritative; peremptory. 2 *Gram.* Designating that mood of the verb which expresses command, entreaty, or exhortation. 3 Not to be evaded or avoided; obligatory. — *n.* 1 That which is imperative. 2 *Gram.* The mood of the verb which expresses command; also, a verb in this mood. [<L *imperativus* <*imperare* command] — **im·per′a·tive·ly** *adv.* — **im·per′a·tive·ness** *n.*

im·pe·ra·tor (im′pə·rā′tər, -tôr) *n.* 1 The official designation of the Roman emperors; originally a commander in chief. 2 Any emperor or absolute ruler.

im·per·a·to·ri·al (im·per′ə·tôr′ē·əl, -tō′rē·əl) *adj.* Of or pertaining to the title or office of imperator. [<L *imperatorius*] — **im·per′a·to′ri·al·ly** *adv.*

im·pe·ra·trice (im′pə·rā′tris) *n. Obs.* An empress. Also **im′pe·ra′trix** (-triks). [<F *impératrice* <L *imperatrix, -icis*]

im·per·cep·ti·ble (im′pər·sep′tə·bəl) *adj.* That cannot be perceived, as by reason of smallness, extreme tenuity or delicacy, distance or gradual progress; inappreciable by the mind or sense; undiscernible: an *imperceptible* change. [<F <L *imperceptibilis*] — **im′per·cep′ti·ble·ness, im′per·cep′ti·bil′i·ty** *n.* — **im′·per·cep′ti·bly** *adv.*

im·per·cep·tive (im′pər·sep′tiv) *adj.* Not perceptive; deficient in perception. — **im·per·cep·tiv·i·ty** (im′pər·sep·tiv′ə·tē), **im′per·cep′tive·ness** *n.*

im·per·fect (im·pûr′fikt) *adj.* 1 Not perfect; incomplete; defective. 2 *Gram.* Pertaining to a tense of the verb that indicates past action as uncompleted, continuous, or synchronous with some other action. 3 *Law* Without binding force; not enforceable by law. 4 *Music* Diminished: an *imperfect* interval. 5 *Bot.* Lacking certain parts normally present; diclinous. See synonyms under BAD[1]. — *n. Gram.* The imperfect tense, or a verb or verbal form expressing this tense. [<OF *imparfait* <L *imperfectus*; refashioned after L] — **im·per′fect·ly** *adv.* — **im·per′fect·ness** *n.*

imperfect flower *Bot.* A flower which lacks some essential part or member.

im·per·fec·tion (im′pər·fek′shən) *n.* 1 Lack of perfection: also **im·per′fect·ness.** 2 A defect. See synonyms under BLEMISH, FOIBLE. [<OF *imperfection* <LL *imperfectio, -onis* <L *imperfectus* incomplete]

im·per·fec·tive (im′pər·fek′tiv) *Gram. adj.* Of or pertaining to an aspect of the verb which expresses continuing action or repetition; durative. — *n.* The imperfective aspect, or a verb in this aspect. — **im′per·fec′tive·ly** *adv.*

im·per·fo·ra·ble (im·pûr′fər·ə·bəl) *adj.* That cannot be perforated.

im·per·fo·rate (im·pûr′fər·it) *adj.* 1 Without perforations; not perforated. 2 Not separated by a line of perforations, as stamps. Also **im·per′fo·rat′ed** (-rā′tid). — *n.* An unperforated stamp.

im·per·fo·ra·tion (im·pûr′fər·ā′shən) *n.* The state of being imperforate.

im·pe·ri·al (im·pir′ē·əl) *adj.* 1 Of or pertaining to an empire, or to an emperor or an empress. 2 Designating the legal weights and measures of the United Kingdom. 3 Of or pertaining to a state as supreme over colonies or the like. 4 Possessing commanding power or dignity; predominant. 5 Superior in size or quality. — *n.* 1 A pointed tuft of hair on the chin: from the emperor Napoleon III, who wore such a beard. 2 Anything of more than usual size of the class to which it belongs, or of superior excellence. 3 A size of paper: in the United States, 23 in. × 31 in.; in Great Britain, 22 in. × 30 in. 4 A size of slate 24 inches wide and from 12 to 30 inches long. 5 A former Russian gold coin worth 15 rubles. 6 The top of a carriage, as of a diligence. [<OF <L *imperialis* <*imperium* rule] — **im·pe′ri·al·ly** *adv.*

Synonyms (adj.): exalted, grand, kingly, magnificent, majestic, noble, queenly, regal, royal, sovereign, supreme. *Antonyms*: base, beggarly, cowering, cringing, ignoble, inferior, mean, paltry, poor, servile, slavish.

Im·pe·ri·al (im·pir′ē·əl) *n.* An adherent or soldier of the Holy Roman Empire.

Imperial City 1 The capital city of an empire. 2 Specifically, Rome, Italy, in the ancient Roman or Holy Roman empires.

imperial eagle See under EAGLE.

imperial gallon See under GALLON.

im·pe·ri·al·ism (im·pir′ē·əl·iz′əm) *n.* 1 A policy that aims at creating, maintaining, or extending an empire or superstate, comprising many nations and areas, all controlled by a central government. 2 A governmental policy of developing foreign trade and exploiting the raw materials of backward countries through the use of political and military pressures, without necessarily assuming direct political control of the nations affected. 3 A system of imperial government. 4 Imperial character, authority, or spirit.

im·pe·ri·al·ist (im·pir′ē·əl·ist) *n.* 1 One who advocates or upholds imperialism. 2 A partisan or supporter of an emperor. — *adj.* Imperialistic.

im·pe·ri·al·is·tic (im·pir′ē·əl·is′tik) *adj.* 1 Of, pertaining to, or characteristic of imperialism. 2 Favoring imperialism or government by an emperor. — **im·pe′ri·al·is′ti·cal·ly** *adv.*

imperial jade A green-tinted aventurine quartz: used as a gem.

imperial moth A beautiful, large American moth (*Eacles* or *Basilona imperialis*) having yellow wings sprinkled and barred with lavender, with wing spread often of 5 inches.

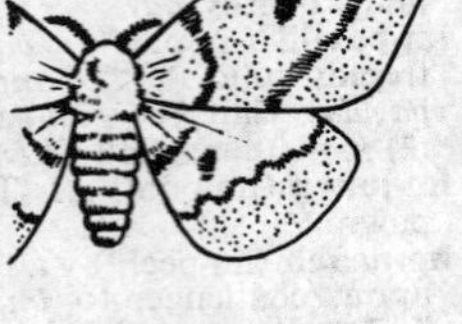

IMPERIAL MOTH
Showing the character of the markings.

imperial quart One fourth of an imperial gallon.

Imperial Valley A region of SE California, mostly below sea level, reclaimed from the Colorado Desert.

im·per·il (im·per′il) *v.t.* ·iled or ·illed, ·il·ing or ·il·ling To place in peril; endanger.

im·pe·ri·ous (im·pir′ē·əs) *adj.* 1 Assuming and determined to command; domineering; arrogant. 2 Urgent; imperative. 3 *Obs.* Imperial; lordly. [<L *imperiosus*] — **im·pe′ri·ous·ly** *adv.* — **im·pe′ri·ous·ness** *n.*

Synonyms: arbitrary, arrogant, authoritative, commanding, controlling, despotic, dictatorial, dogmatic, domineering, exacting, haughty, imperative, irresistible, lordly, overbearing. An *imperious* demand or requirement may have in it nothing offensive; it is simply one that resolutely insists upon compliance, and will not brook refusal; an *arrogant* demand is offensive by its tone of superiority, an *arbitrary* demand by its unreasonableness; an *imperious* disposition is liable to become *arbitrary* and *arrogant.* A person of an independent spirit is inclined to resent an *imperious* manner in anyone, especially in one whose superiority or authority is not clearly recognized. *Commanding* is always used in a good sense; as, a *commanding* appearance; a *commanding* eminence. See ARBITRARY, DOGMATIC. *Antonyms*: complaisant, compliant, docile, ductile, gentle, humble, lenient, lowly, meek, mild, submissive.

im·per·ish·a·ble (im·per′ish·ə·bəl) *adj.* Not perishable or subject to decay. See synonyms under ETERNAL, IMMORTAL. — **im·per′ish·a·bil′i·ty, im·per′ish·a·ble·ness** *n.* — **im·per′ish·a·bly** *adv.*

im·pe·ri·um (im·pir′ē·əm) *n. pl.* ·ri·a (-ē·ə) 1 Command not subject to definition or limitation of function; absolute command. 2 *Law* The right to command, which includes authority to use the force of the state to enforce its laws. [<L. See EMPIRE.]

im·per·ma·nence (im·pûr′mə·nəns) *n.* The state or quality of being impermanent; also, something impermanent. Also **im·per′ma·nen·cy.**

im·per·ma·nent (im·pûr′mə·nənt) *adj.* Not permanent.

im·per·me·a·ble (im·pûr′mē·ə·bəl) *adj.* 1 Not permeable. 2 Impervious to moisture. See synonyms under IMPENETRABLE. [<LL *impermeabilis*] — **im·per′me·a·bil′i·ty** *n.* — **im·per′me·a·bly** *adv.*

im·per·son·al (im·pûr′sən·əl) *adj.* 1 Not having personality: an *impersonal* deity. 2 Not relating to a particular person or thing: an *impersonal* statement. 3 *Gram.* Having or containing an indeterminate subject: an *impersonal* verb. In English the subject of an impersonal verb is usually the pronoun *it,* as *it thunders*: often in apposition with a following clause or phrase, as *it is fun to swim.* — *n.* That which lacks personality; especially, an impersonal verb. [<LL *impersonalis*] — **im·per′son·al′i·ty** (-al′ə·tē) *n.* — **im·per′son·al·ly** *adv.*

im·per·son·al·ize (im·pûr′sən·əl·īz′) *v.t.* ·ized, ·iz·ing To render impersonal.

im·per·son·ate (im·pûr′sən·āt) *v.t.* ·at·ed, ·at·ing 1 To adopt or mimic the appearance, mannerisms, etc., of. 2 To act or play the part of. 3 To represent in human form; personify: He *impersonates* the quality of virtue. See synonyms under IMITATE. — *adj.* (-it) Embodied in a person; having personality.

im·per·son·a·tion (im·pûr′sən·ā′shən) *n.* 1 The act of impersonating. 2 Personification.

im·per·son·a·tor (im·pûr′sən·ā′tər) *n.* One who impersonates or plays a character part.

im·per·ti·nence (im·pûr′tə·nəns) *n.* 1 The state, quality, or instance of being impertinent. 2 Improper intrusion: rudeness. 3 Irrelevancy; inappropriateness. Also **im·per′·ti·nen·cy.**

im·per·ti·nent (im·pûr′tə·nənt) *adj.* 1 Rude; impudent. 2 Irrelevant; not to the point. 3 Not suitable or fitting. See synonyms under IMPUDENT, MEDDLESOME. [<F <L *impertinens, -entis* <*in-* not + *pertinens.* See PERTINENT.] — **im·per′ti·nent·ly** *adv.*

im·per·turb·a·ble (im′pər·tûr′bə·bəl) *adj.* Incapable of being agitated. See synonyms under CALM. [<LL *imperturbabilis*] — **im′per·turb′a·bil′i·ty, im′per·turb′a·ble·ness** *n.* — **im′·per·turb′a·bly** *adv.*

im·per·tur·ba·tion (im·pûr′tər·bā′shən) *n.* Freedom from agitation; calmness.

im·per·turbed (im′pər·tûrbd′) *adj.* Not perturbed or agitated.

im·per·vi·a·ble (im·pûr′vē·ə·bəl) *adj.* Impervious.

im·per·vi·ous (im·pûr′vē·əs) *adj.* 1 Permitting no passage into or through; impenetrable; impermeable. 2 Not permeable by fluids, light rays, etc. 3 Not capable of being influenced by; deaf to: a mind *impervious* to reason. See synonyms under IMPENETRABLE. [<L *impervius* <*in-* not + *per-* through + *via* way, road] — **im·per′vi·ous·ly** *adv.* — **im·per′vi·ous·ness** *n.*

im·pe·ti·go (im′pə·tī′gō) *n. Pathol.* A contagious skin disease characterized by pustular eruptions. [<L <*impetere* attack. See IMPETUS.] — **im·pe·tig·i·nous** (im′pə·tij′ə·nəs) *adj.*

im·pe·trate (im′pə·trāt) *v.t.* ·trat·ed, ·trat·ing 1 To obtain by request or entreaty. 2 *Rare* To importune; beseech. [<L *impetratus,* pp. of *impetrare* obtain by request <*in-* to + *patrare* bring to pass] — **im′pe·tra′tion** *n.* — **im′pe·tra′tor** *n.*

im·pe·tra·tive (im′pə·trā′tiv) *adj.* Using prayer or entreaty, or tending to obtain by entreaty. [<L *impetrativus*]

im·pet·u·ous (im·pech′ōō·əs) *adj.* 1 Characterized by impetus, energy, or violent force: *impetuous* haste. 2 Characterized by spontaneous or vehement impulse of action or emotion: *impetuous* affection. [<MF *impétueux* <L *impetuosus*] — **im·pet′u·os′i·ty** (-os′·ə·tē) *n.* — **im·pet′u·ous·ly** *adv.* — **im·pet′u·ous·ness** *n.*

Synonyms: excitable, fiery, hasty, headlong, impulsive, passionate, precipitate, quick, rash, sudden, swift. See EAGER, FIERCE, VIOLENT. *Antonyms*: calm, careful, cautious, circumspect, considerate, deliberate, lazy, leisurely, slow, sluggish, steady.

im·pe·tus (im′pə·təs) *n.* 1 The energy with which anything moves or is driven. 2 Momentum. 3 Any impulse or incentive. See synonyms under IMPULSE. [<L <*impetere* rush upon <*in-* upon + *petere* seek]

Imp·hal (imp′hul) The capital of Manipur, India.

im·phee (im′fē) *n.* An African cereal grass (*Sorghum vulgare*) which yields a sirup: also used for fodder and grain. [<Zulu *imfe*]

im·pi (im′pē) *n. pl.* A body of armed Zulus or other native warriors. [<Zulu]

im·pi·e·ty (im·pī′ə·tē) *n. pl.* ·ties 1 Ungodliness; irreverence. 2 An impious act. 3 Want of natural dutifulness toward parents. [<OF *impieté* <L *impietas, -tatis*]

imp·ing (im′ping) *n.* The process of grafting;

a graft, as of feathers on a hawk's wing. [OE *impian* graft. See IMP.]

im·pinge (im·pinj′) *v.i.* **·pinged, ·ping·ing** **1** To come into contact; strike; collide, especially sharply: with *on, upon,* or *against.* **2** To encroach; infringe: with *on* or *upon.* [<L *impingere* <*in-* against + *pangere* strike] — **im·pinge′ment** *n.* — **im·ping′er** *n.*

im·pi·ous (im′pē·əs) *adj.* **1** Destitute of reverence for the divine character or will; ungodly; wicked. **2** Characterized by irreverence; blasphemous. **3** Unfilial; lacking reverence, especially to one's parents. See synonyms under PROFANE. [<L *impius* <*in-* not + *pius* reverent] — **im′pi·ous·ly** *adv.* — **im′pi·ous·ness** *n.*

imp·ish (im′pish) *adj.* Implike. — **imp′ish·ly** *adv.* — **imp·ish·ness** *n.*

im·pla·ca·ble (im·plā′kə·bəl, -plak′ə-) *adj.* That cannot be placated; inexorable. [<F <L *implacabilis* <*in-* not + *placere* please] — **im·pla′ca·bil′i·ty, im·pla′ca·ble·ness** *n.* — **im·pla′ca·bly** *adv.*

Synonyms: cruel, inexorable, irreconcilable, merciless, pitiless, relentless, severe, unappeasable, unforgiving, unrelenting. *Antonyms*: forgiving, gentle, mild, placable, tender, yielding.

im·pla·cen·tal (im′plə·sen′təl) *adj. Zool.* **1** Having no placenta. **2** Of or pertaining to a former division of mammals *(Implacentalia),* including the monotremes and marsupials, having no placenta. — *n.* An implacental mammal. Also **im′pla·cen′tate** (-tāt).

im·plant (im·plant′, -plänt′) *v.t.* **1** To insert or graft, as living tissue. **2** To inculcate or instil, as principles. **3** To plant, as seeds. — *n.* (im′plant′, -plänt′) *Med.* **1** A tissue implanted in the body. **2** A small tube containing radon or other radioactive material, embedded in tissue for therapeutic or remedial purposes. [<F *implanter*] — **im·plant′er** *n.*

im·plan·ta·tion (im′plan·tā′shən) *n.* **1** The act of implanting. **2** The introduction of a solid drug under the skin. **3** The subcutaneous injection of a drug: called **hypodermic implantation.** **4** Skin– or tissue–grafting. **5** The self–planting of body cells, especially tumor cells, in a new part of the body; spontaneous metastasis. **6** The setting of a new tooth in a jaw. [<F]

im·plau·si·ble (im·plô′zə·bəl) *adj.* Not plausible. — **im·plau′si·bly** *adv.*

im·plead (im·plēd′) *v.t. Law* **1** To sue in a court of justice. **2** To accuse; arraign. **3** To plead, as a cause. — *v.i.* **4** To bring a suit at law. [<AF *enpleder,* OF *empleidier*] — **im·plead′a·ble** *adj.*

im·plead·er (im·plē′dər) *n.* A complainant or prosecutor.

im·pledge (im·plej′) *v.t.* **·pledged, ·pledg·ing** To put in pledge; pawn.

im·ple·ment (im′plə·mənt) *n.* **1** A thing used in work, especially in manual work; a utensil; tool. **2** Originally, that which supplies a want; any means or agent for the accomplishment of a purpose. See synonyms under TOOL. — *v.t.* (-ment) **1** To carry into effect; fulfil; accomplish. **2** To provide what is needed for; supplement. **3** To furnish with implements. [<L *implementum* a filling up <*implere* fill up <*in-* in + *plere* fill] — **im′ple·men′tal** *adj.*

im·ple·men·ta·tion (im′plə·men·tā′shən) *n.* A putting into effect, fulfilment, or carrying through, as of ideas, a program, etc.

im·ple·tion (im·plē′shən) *n.* The act of filling, or the state of being full; also, that which fills. [<LL *impletio, -onis* <*implere.* See IMPLEMENT.]

im·pli·cate (im′plə·kāt) *v.t.* **·cat·ed, ·cat·ing** **1** To show to be involved or concerned, as in a plot or crime. **2** To imply. **3** To fold or twist together; entangle; intertwine. See synonyms under INVOLVE. [<L *implicatus,* pp. of *implicare* involve <*in-* in + *plicare* fold]

im·pli·ca·tion (im′plə·kā′shən) *n.* **1** The act of implying; something implied; especially, something that leads to a deduction. **2** An entanglement. — **im′pli·ca′tion·al** *adj.*

im·pli·ca·tive (im′plə·kā′tiv) *adj.* Tending to imply or to implicate. Also **im·pli·ca·to·ry** (im′pli·kə·tôr′ē, -tō′rē). — **im′pli·ca′tive·ly** *adv.*

im·plic·it (im·plis′it) *adj.* **1** Fairly to be understood, but not specifically stated; implied. **2** Arising from thorough confidence in another; unquestioning: *implicit* trust. **3** Virtually contained in; essential, though not apparent; potential: The man is *implicit* in the child. **4** *Obs.* Infolded; entangled. [<F *implicite* <L *implicitus,* later form of *implicatus,* pp. of *implicare* involve. See IMPLICATE.] — **im·plic′it·ly** *adv.* — **im·plic′it·ness** *n.*

Synonyms: absolute, blind, complete, firm, full, perfect, steadfast, submissive, undoubting, unhesitating, unquestioning, unreserved, unshaken. *Implicit* primarily signifies "implied." *Implicit* faith assumes all reasons for belief or action to be "implied" in the fact that a statement, for instance, comes from some trusted source, as the Scriptures or the church; *implicit* obedience assumes that all reasons for action are "implied" in the mere command given by adequate authority. As contrasted with *explicit, implicit* belief is given to an *explicit* statement, *implicit* obedience rendered to an *explicit* command. Compare EXPLICIT; see, also, TACIT.

im·plied (im·plīd′) *adj.* Contained or included, but not directly stated. See synonyms under TACIT. — **im·pli·ed·ly** (im·plī′id·lē) *adv.*

implied powers *U.S.* Powers not expressly granted by the Constitution to the Federal government but inferred because of their necessary relation to powers which are expressly granted.

im·plode (im·plōd′) *v.t.* & *v.i.* **·plod·ed, ·plod·ing** **1** To burst inward. **2** *Phonet.* To pronounce by implosion. [<IM- + (EX)PLODE]

im·plo·ra·tion (im′plə·rā′shən) *n.* The act of imploring; entreaty. [<F *imploratio, -onis*]

im·plore (im·plôr′, -plōr′) *v.* **·plored, ·plor·ing** *v.t.* **1** To call upon in supplication; beseech; entreat. **2** To beg for urgently; pray for. — *v.i.* **3** To make urgent supplication. See synonyms under ASK, PLEAD, PRAY. [<L *implorare* <*in-* thoroughly + *plorare* cry out]

im·plor·er (im·plôr′ər, -plō′rər) *n.* One who implores; a suppliant.

im·plor·ing (im·plôr′ing, -plō′ring) *adj.* That implores; beseeching. — **im·plor′ing·ly** *adv.* — **im·plor′ing·ness** *n.*

im·plo·sion (im·plō′zhən) *n.* **1** A bursting inward; sudden collapse: opposed to *explosion.* **2** *Phonet.* The initial, sudden blockage of the breath stream in the production of a stop consonant: opposed to *plosion.* [<IMPLODE, on analogy with *explosion*] — **im·plo′·sive** (-siv) *adj.*

im·plu·vi·um (im·plo͞o′vē·əm) *n. pl.* **·vi·a** (-vē·ə) A basin in the floor of the atrium of an ancient Roman house to receive the rain that fell through the compluvium. [<L *impluere* rain into <*in-* in + *pluere* rain]

im·ply (im·plī′) *v.t.* **·plied, ·ply·ing** **1** To involve necessarily as a circumstance, condition, effect, etc.: An action *implies* an agent. **2** To indicate (a meaning not expressed); hint at; intimate. **3** *Obs.* To entangle; infold. See synonyms under ALLUDE, IMPORT, INVOLVE. [<OF *emplier* <L *implicare* involve <*in-* in + *plicare* fold. Doublet of EMPLOY.]

im·pol·i·cy (im·pol′ə·sē) *n.* Unsuitableness to the end proposed; inexpediency. [<IMPOLITIC, on analogy with *policy*]

im·po·lite (im′pə·līt′) *adj.* Lacking in politeness; rude. See synonyms under BLUFF. [<L *impolitus* <*in-* not + *politus.* See POLITE.] — **im′po·lite′ly** *adv.* — **im′po·lite′ness** *n.*

im·pol·i·tic (im·pol′ə·tik) *adj.* **1** Pursuing unwise measures. **2** Adapted to injure the interests involved; inexpedient; injudicious. See synonyms under IMPRUDENT. Also **im·po·lit·i·cal** (im′pə·lit′i·kəl). — **im·pol′i·tic·ly, im′po·lit′i·cal·ly** *adv.*

im·pon·der·a·ble (im·pon′dər·ə·bəl) *adj.* **1** Without weight. **2** Impossible of reckoning. — *n.* A factor in a situation which cannot be definitely foreseen. — **im·pon′der·a·bil′i·ty, im·pon′der·a·ble·ness** *n.* — **im·pon′der·a·bly** *adv.*

impone (im·pōn′) *v.t. Obs.* To wager; stake. [<L *imponere* place upon <*in-* on + *ponere* place]

im·po·rous (im·pôr′əs, -pō′rəs) *adj.* Very close or compact in texture; without pores; solid. — **im·po·ros·i·ty** (im′pə·ros′ə·tē) *n.*

im·port (im·pôrt′, -pōrt′, im′pôrt, -pōrt) *v.t.* **1** To bring (goods) into one country from a foreign country in commerce: opposed to *export.* **2** To bring in; introduce: to *import* acrimony into a debate. **3** To mean; signify: His expression *imports* no good for me. **4** To be of importance or significance to; concern. — *v.i.* **5** To be of importance or significance; matter: The argument does not *import.* — *n.* (im′pôrt, -pōrt) **1** That which is implied; meaning; significance. **2** That which is brought from one country into another. **3** Importance. See synonyms under WEIGHT. [<F *importer* <L *importare* bring in <*in-* in + *portare* carry; prob. infl. in meaning by L *oportet* it is necessary] — **im·port′a·ble** *adj.*

Synonyms (verb): betoken, denote, imply, mean, purport, signify, suggest. See INTEREST.

im·por·tance (im·pôr′təns) *n.* **1** The quality of being important or momentous. **2** Weight or consequence, as in public estimation or in self–esteem. **3** Consequential manner; pretentiousness. **4** *Obs.* Significance; meaning; also, urgency. Also *Obs.* **im·por′tan·cy.** [<F <Med. L *importantia*]

im·por·tant (im·pôr′tənt) *adj.* **1** Of great import, consequence, prominence, or value. **2** Mattering greatly: with *to*: evidence *important* to the case. **3** Pompous; pretentious. **4** *Obs.* Importunate; urgent. [<F <L *importans, -antis,* ppr. of *importare.* See IMPORT.] — **im·por′tant·ly** *adv.*

Synonyms: grave, influential, material, momentous, prominent, serious, significant, valuable, weighty. See SERIOUS. *Antonyms*: empty, idle, inconsiderable, irrelevant, mean, petty, slight, trifling, trivial, unimportant, useless, worthless.

im·por·ta·tion (im′pôr·tā′shən, -pōr-) *n.* **1** The act of importing, or bringing from one country into another merchandise for sale, processing, etc. **2** That which is imported.

im·port·er (im·pôr′tər, -pōr′-) *n.* One who imports or brings in goods from a foreign country.

im·por·tu·nate (im·pôr′chə·nit) *adj.* **1** Urgent in character, request, or demand; insistent; pertinacious. **2** *Obs.* Vexatious. See synonyms under EAGER[1], TROUBLESOME, URGENT. [<Med. L *importunatus,* pp. of *importunari.* See IMPORTUNE.] — **im·por′tu·nate·ly** *adv.* — **im·por′tu·nate·ness** *n.*

im·por·tune (im′pôr·to͞on′, -tyo͞on′, im·pôr′·chən) *v.* **·tuned, ·tun·ing** *v.t.* **1** To beset with persistent requests or demands. **2** To ask for persistently or urgently. **3** *Obs.* To annoy. **4** *Obs.* To impel; urge. — *v.i.* **5** To make persistent requests or demands. — *adj.* Persistent; importunate. [<F *importuner* <Med. L *importunari* be troublesome <L *importunus* having no access, vexatious <*in-* without + *portus* a port] — **im′por·tune′ly** *adv.* — **im′por·tun′er** *n.*

im·por·tu·ni·ty (im′pôr·to͞o′nə·tē, -tyo͞o′-) *n. pl.* **·ties** **1** The act of importuning. **2** The state of being importunate. **3** *pl.* Importunate demands. Also **im·por·tu·na·cy** (im·pôr′chə·nə·sē). [<L *importunitas, -tatis*]

im·pose (im·pōz′) *v.t.* **·posed, ·pos·ing** **1** To place or lay by authority, as something to be borne, endured, or obeyed: to *impose* a tax or penalty. **2** To place by or as by force: to *impose* opinions on another. **3** To obtrude or force (oneself, one's presence, etc.) upon others. **4** To palm off (something) as true or genuine; foist. **5** *Printing* To arrange in a form, as pages of type. **6** *Eccl.* To lay on (hands), as in confirmation or ordination. **7** *Obs.* To lay down; deposit. — **to impose on** (or **upon**) **1** To take advantage of; presume. **2** To cheat or deceive by trickery or false representation. **3** To make an impression; influence. — *n. Obs.* An injunction; command. [<F *imposer* <*im-* on + *poser.* See POSE[1].] — **im·pos′a·ble** *adj.* — **im·pos′er** *n.*

im·pos·ing (im·pō′zing) *adj.* Adapted to make an impression; grand; elegant.

imposing stone A flat, level slab, on which printers impose forms of type. Also **imposing table.**

im·po·si·tion (im′pə·zish′ən) *n.* **1** The act of imposing, in any sense of the word. **2** An unjust requirement. **3** A trick of deception; imposture. **4** *Printing* The arrangement of pages of type or plates, in the right order for printing. **5** The act of laying on hands,

as in confirmation or ordination. 6 A tax, toll, or duty. See synonyms under DECEPTION, FRAUD. [<L *impositio, -onis* <*impositus.* See IMPOST.]

im·pos·si·bil·i·ty (im·pos'ə·bil'ə·tē) *n. pl.* **·ties** 1 The fact or state of being impossible. 2 That which is impossible; something that cannot exist or be done. [<L *impossibilitas, -tatis*]

im·pos·si·ble (im·pos'ə·bəl) *adj.* 1 Not possible. 2 *Law* Impracticable in the nature of the case. 3 Unimaginable; hopelessly objectionable; intolerable; absurd. See synonyms under IMPRACTICABLE. [<F] —**im·pos'·si·bly** *adv.*

im·post (im'pōst) *n.* 1 That which is imposed; specifically, a customs duty. 2 *Archit.* A projecting band or block placed at the top of a column or pier, and from which an arch springs. See illustration under ARCH. 3 A weight carried by a horse in a handicap race. See synonyms under TAX. —*v.t.* To classify so as to fix the customs duty: said of imported goods. [<OF <Med. L *impostum* <L *impositus,* pp. of *imponere* lay on <*in-* on + *ponere* lay, place]

im·pos·tor (im·pos'tər) *n.* One who deceives by false pretenses, especially under an assumed name or character. See synonyms under HYPOCRITE, QUACK². [<F *imposteur* <LL *impostor* <*impositus,* pp. of *imponere* lay on, impose]

im·pos·tu·mate (im·pos'chə·māt) *v.t.* & *v.i.* *Obs.* To affect with an abscess; become abscessed or ulcerous. Also **im·pos'thu·mate.** [<IMPOSTUME] —**im·pos'tu·ma'tion** *n.*

im·pos·tume (im·pos'chōōm, -tyōōm) *n. Rare* An abscess. Also **im·pos'thume.** [Alter. of APOSTEME]

im·pos·ture (im·pos'chər) *n.* Deception by means of false pretenses. See synonyms under ARTIFICE, FRAUD. [<F <LL *impostura*]

im·po·tence (im'pə·təns) *n.* 1 The state or quality of being impotent; feebleness. 2 Loss or lack of capacity for sexual intercourse: said of men. Compare FRIGIDITY. Also **im'·po·ten·cy.** [<OF <L *impotentia*]

im·po·tent (im'pə·tənt) *adj.* 1 Destitute of or lacking in power, physical, moral, or intellectual; not potent; weak; feeble. 2 Destitute of sexual power: said usually of the male; also, occasionally, barren; sterile. 3 Lacking in self-control. [<OF <L *impotens, -entis* <*in-* not + *potens.* See POTENT.] —**im'po·tent·ly** *adv.*

im·pound (im·pound') *v.t.* 1 To shut up in a pound, as a stray dog. 2 To place in custody of a court of law. 3 To collect (water) in a pond, reservoir, etc., as for irrigation. —**im·pound'age** (-poun'dij) *n.* —**im·pound'er** *n.*

im·pov·er·ish (im·pov'ər·ish) *v.t.* 1 To reduce to poverty. 2 To exhaust the fertility or quality of, as soil; deteriorate. Also spelled EMPOVERISH. [<OF *empovrir* <*em-* thoroughly + L *pauperare* impoverish <*pauper* poor]

im·pov·er·ish·ment (im·pov'ər·ish·mənt) *n.* The act of impoverishing, or the state of being impoverished.

im·prac·ti·ca·ble (im·prak'ti·kə·bəl) *adj.* 1 Impossible or unreasonably difficult of performance. 2 Unserviceable. 3 Hard to get on with; unreasonable; intractable: said of persons. —**im·prac'ti·ca·bil'i·ty, im·prac'ti·ca·ble·ness** *n.* —**im·prac'ti·ca·bly** *adv.*

Synonyms: impossible, impractical, intractable. That which is *impossible* cannot be done at all; that which is *impracticable* is theoretically possible, but cannot be done under existing conditions. *Impractical,* which strictly means not practical, is coming into frequent popular use as the equivalent of *impracticable,* but the difference should be maintained; an *impractical* man lacks practical judgment or efficiency; an *impracticable* man is difficult to deal with (compare OBSTINATE, PERVERSE); an *impractical* scheme lacks practical fitness, is theoretic or visionary; an *impracticable* scheme has some inherent difficulties that would insure its failure in action. *Antonyms*: easy, feasible, possible, practicable.

im·prac·ti·cal (im·prak'ti·kəl) *adj.* Not practical; unpractical. See synonyms under IMPRACTICABLE. —**im·prac'ti·cal'i·ty** (-kal'ə·tē) *n.*

im·pre·cate (im'prə·kāt) *v.t.* **·cat·ed, ·cat·ing** To invoke or call down, as a judgment, calamity, or curse. [<L *imprecatus,* pp. of *imprecare* pray to <*in-* to + *precari* pray <*prex, precis* prayer] —**im'pre·ca'tor** *n.* —**im'pre·ca·to'ry** (-kə·tôr'ē, -tō'rē) *adj.*

im·pre·ca·tion (im'prə·kā'shən) *n.* A malediction; curse. [<L *imprecatio, -onis*]

Synonyms: anathema, curse, execration, malediction. See OATH. *Antonyms*: benediction, benison, blessing, praise.

im·pre·ci·sion (im'pri·sizh'ən) *n.* Want of precision.

im·preg (im'preg) *n.* A tough, durable, weather-resistant plywood whose layers are impregnated with an aqueous solution of resin-forming chemicals, then dried, cured, and bonded with resin glue. [Short for IMPREGNATED]

im·pregn (im·prēn') *v.t. Obs.* To impregnate. [<LL *impraegnare* make pregnant]

im·preg·na·ble (im·preg'nə·bəl) *adj.* 1 Proof against attack; that cannot be taken. 2 Not to be overcome by temptation. See synonyms under INCONTESTABLE, SECURE. [<OF *imprenable* <*im-* not (<L *in-*) + *prenable* pregnable <*prendre* take <L *prehendere*] —**im·preg'na·bil'i·ty** *n.* —**im·preg'na·bly** *adv.*

im·preg·nate (im·preg'nāt) *v.t.* **·nat·ed, ·nat·ing** 1 To make pregnant; get with child. 2 To fertilize. 3 To saturate or permeate with another substance. 4 To fill or imbue with emotion, ideas, principles, etc.: to *impregnate* a book with religious feeling. —*adj.* Made pregnant. [<LL *impraegnatus,* pp. of *impraegnare* impregnate <*in-* in + *praegnans* pregnant] —**im·preg'na·ble** (-nə·bəl) *adj.* —**im·preg'na·tor** *n.*

im·preg·na·tion (im'preg·nā'shən) *n.* 1 The act of impregnating. 2 The state of being impregnated. 3 That with which anything is impregnated.

im·pre·sa·ri·o (im'prə·sä'rē·ō) *n. pl.* **·sa·ri·os** One who organizes, manages, or is responsible for an opera company or public musical performance. [<Ital. <*impresa* undertaking <*imprendere* undertake <L *in-* on + *prehendere* take]

im·pre·scrip·ti·ble (im'pri·skrip'tə·bəl) *adj.* 1 Incapable of being either lost or acquired by usage or prescription. 2 Inalienable. [<F] —**im'pre·scrip'ti·bil'i·ty** *n.* —**im'pre·scrip'·ti·bly** *adv.*

im·prese (im·prēz') *n. Obs.* A heraldic device or emblematic design. Also **im·pre·sa** (im·prä'zä). [<F <Ital. *impresa* undertaking]

im·press¹ (im·pres') *v.t.* 1 To produce a marked effect upon, as the mind; influence: His proposal *impressed* me. 2 To fix firmly in the mind, as ideas, beliefs, etc.: to *impress* a fact on the memory. 3 To form or make (an imprint or mark) by pressure; stamp: to *impress* a design on metal. 4 To form or make an imprint or mark upon. 5 To apply with pressure; press: to *impress* one's hand into the mud. 6 *Electr.* To create or establish (a difference of potential) in a conductor by means of a dynamo, battery, or other source of electrical energy. —*n.* (im'pres) 1 A mark or indentation produced by pressure. 2 The effect of a force. 3 The act or process of making an impression. 4 Peculiar character or form; stamp. [<L *impressus,* pp. of *imprimere* impress <*in-* on + *premere* press]

Synonyms (verb): imprint, inculcate, press, print, stamp. *Antonyms*: see synonyms for CANCEL.

im·press² (im·pres') *v.t.* 1 To compel to enter public service: to *impress* seamen. 2 To seize (property) for public use. —*n.* Impressment. [<IM- in + PRESS¹] —**im·press'er** *n.*

im·press·i·ble (im·pres'ə·bəl) *adj.* Capable of being impressed or of receiving an impression; sensitive; susceptible. —**im·press'i·bil'i·ty, im·press'i·ble·ness** *n.* —**im·press'i·bly** *adv.*

im·pres·sion (im·presh'ən) *n.* 1 The act of impressing or imprinting; the imparting of a distinguishing mark, form, or character. 2 The result of exterior influence, as impressment; a stamp, mark, or figure made by pressure. 3 An effect produced on the senses, the mind, the feelings, or the conscience. 4 A slight or indistinct remembrance; a notion or belief held by the mind without adequate grounds. 5 An effect left upon the mind, which resembles in any way, or bears the marks of, some past experience; specifically, any mental effect regarded as the resultant of a previous experience. 6 *Printing* **a** The imprint of types, illustrations, etc., on a page or sheet. **b** All the copies of a book printed at one time: especially, an unaltered reprint from standing type or from plates, as distinguished from *edition.* **c** One copy of a book, engraving, etching, etc. See synonyms under FEELING, IDEA, MARK¹. [<OF <L *impressio, -onis*] —**im·pres'sion·al** *adj.*

im·pres·sion·a·ble (im·presh'ən·ə·bəl) *adj.* Subject to or susceptible of impression; easily molded; plastic. [<F] —**im·pres'sion·a·bil'·i·ty, im·pres'sion·a·ble·ness** *n.*

im·pres·sion·ism (im·presh'ən·iz'əm) *n.* 1 In painting, a theory and school of art, developed in the third quarter of the 19th century, which attempted to produce, with the vividness and immediacy of nature and particularly of light itself, the impressions made by the subject on the artist. See IMPRESSIONIST SCHOOL. 2 In literature, a theory and practice of presenting the most immediate and arresting aspects of character, emotion, scene, or situation with relatively little study of explicit realistic detail. 3 *Music* A theory and school of composition, developed in the late 19th and early 20th centuries, as by Debussy and Ravel, striving to create impressions, moods, and atmospheric qualities by new tonal effects and other characteristic devices. —**im·pres'·sion·ist** *adj.* & *n.* —**im·pres'sion·is'tic** *adj.*

Impressionist School A group of French painters of the later 19th century who developed the doctrines and style of impressionism, including Manet, Monet, Pissarro, Sisley, Renoir, Degas, and others.

im·pres·sive (im·pres'iv) *adj.* Producing or tending to produce an impression; holding the attention; exciting emotion or admiration. See synonyms under GRAND. [<IMPRESS¹] —**im·pres'sive·ly** *adv.* —**im·pres'sive·ness** *n.*

im·press·ment (im·pres'mənt) *n.* 1 The act of impressing into the public service, or of seizing property for public use. 2 The seizure of civilians for service in the navy or the seizure of members of a ship's crew by a foreign vessel.

im·pres·sure (im·presh'ər) *n.* An impression.

im·prest (im·prest') *adj. Obs.* Given as a loan in advance: said of money given, as to soldiers, sailors, or government employees. —*n.* A prepayment of money, especially to carry on some public service. [<*in prest* on loan, after Ital. *impresto* loan. See PREST.]

im·pri·ma·tur (im'pri·mā'tər, -prī-) *n.* 1 Literally, let it be printed: an official formula of license to print or publish, affixed by a censor or board of censors to a book or pamphlet. 2 License or approval in general; sanction. [<L, let it be printed <*imprimere* impress]

im·pri·mis (im·prī'mis) *adv.* In the first place; first in order. [<L]

im·print (im·print') *v.t.* 1 To produce or reproduce (a figure, mark, etc.) by pressure: to *imprint* a design on wax. 2 To mark (something), as with a stamp or seal. 3 To fix firmly in the heart, mind, etc. See synonyms under IMPRESS¹, INSCRIBE. —*n.* (im'print) 1 A mark or character made by printing, stamping, or pressing. 2 The effect left by impression. 3 A publisher's or printer's name, place of publication, date, etc., printed in a book or other publication. 4 An impression, as of a medal, etc. [<OF *empreinte,* pp. of *empreinter* <L *imprimere* <*in-* in + *premere* press]

im·pris·on (im·priz'ən) *v.t.* 1 To put into or keep in a prison. 2 To confine or restrain in any way. See synonyms under SHUT. [<OF *emprisoner* <*en-* in + *prison.* See PRISON.]

im·pris·on·ment (im·priz'ən·mənt) *n.* 1 The act of imprisoning. 2 Confinement in, or as in a prison.

im·prob·a·ble (im·prob'ə·bəl) *adj.* Not likely to be true; not reasonably to be expected. [<L *improbabilis*] —**im·prob·a·bil·i·ty** (im'·prob·ə·bil'ə·tē, im·prob'-), **im·prob'a·ble·ness** *n.* —**im·prob'a·bly** *adv.*

im·pro·bi·ty (im·prō'bə·tē) *n. pl.* **·ties** Want of probity; dishonesty. [<L *improbitas, -tatis* <*improbus* wicked <*in-* not + *probus* honest]

im·promp·tu (im·promp'tōō, -tyōō) *adj.* Made, done, or uttered on the spur of the moment; extempore; offhand. See synonyms under EXTEMPORANEOUS. —*n.* Anything done on the impulse of the moment. —*adv.* Without preparation. [<F <L *in promptu* in readiness]

im·prop·er (im·prop'ər) *adj.* 1 Not proper;

not strictly belonging or appropriate; inapplicable. **2** Not in accord with the proprieties of speech, manners, or conduct; indecorous. **3** Unsuitable; inappropriate. **4** Irregular or abnormal. [<OF *impropre* <L *improprius*] — **im·prop′er·ly** *adv.*

improper fraction See under FRACTION.

im·pro·pri·ate (im·prō′prē·āt) *v.t.* **·at·ed, ·at·ing** To transfer (ecclesiastical property or revenues) to laymen. — *adj.* (-prē·it) Vested or placed in the hands of a layman; impropriated. [<Med. L *impropriatus,* pp. of *impropriare* take as one's own <L *in-* on + *proprius* one's own] — **im·pro′pri·a′tion** *n.* — **im·pro′·pri·a′tor** *n.*

im·pro·pri·e·ty (im′prə·prī′ə·tē) *n. pl.* **·ties** **1** The state or quality of being improper. **2** Anything that is improper, as an act. **3** A violation of good usage in speech or writing. See synonyms under INDECENCY. [<L *improprietas, -tatis*]

im·prove (im·pro͞ov′) *v.* **·proved, ·prov·ing** *v.t.* **1** To make better the quality, condition, etc., of. **2** To use to good advantage; utilize: to *improve* one's opportunities. **3** *U.S.* To increase the value or profit of, as land by cultivation or lots by construction of buildings. — *v.i.* **4** To become better. **5** To make improvements: with *on* or *upon.* See synonyms under AMEND. [<AF *emprower* <OF *en-* into + *prou* profit] — **im·prov′a·bil′i·ty, im·prov′a·ble·ness** *n.* — **im·prov′a·ble** *adj.* — **im·prov′a·bly** *adv.* — **im·prov′er** *n.*

im·prove·ment (im·pro͞ov′mənt) *n.* **1** The act or process of improving; betterment; amelioration. **2** Something that is better than (something previous): Diesel power is an *improvement* over steam. **3** A beneficial change or addition; an advance. **4** *U.S.* A tract of land developed by cultivation, buildings, enclosures, etc. **5** *pl. U.S.* The enclosures, buildings, clearings, etc., produced on a piece of land. See synonyms under INCREASE, PROFIT, PROGRESS.

im·prov·i·dent (im·prov′ə·dənt) *adj.* **1** Lacking foresight; incautious. **2** Taking no thought for future needs. — **im·prov′i·dence** *n.* — **im·prov′i·dent·ly** *adv.*

Synonyms: careless, imprudent, prodigal, reckless, shiftless, thoughtless, thriftless, unthrifty. See IMPRUDENT. *Antonyms*: careful, economical, provident, prudent, saving, thoughtful, thrifty.

im·pro·vise (im′prə·vīz) *v.t.* & *v.i.* **·vised, ·vis·ing** **1** To compose, recite, sing, etc., without previous preparation; extemporize. **2** To make or devise on the spur of the moment, especially from what is at hand: to *improvise* a raft from driftwood. Also **im·prov′i·sate** (im·prov′ə·zāt). [<F *improviser* <Ital. *improvvisare* <*improvviso* unforeseen <L *improvisus* <*in-* not + *provisus* foreseen] — **im·prov·i·sa·tion** (im·prov′ə·zā′shən, im′prə·vī·zā′shən) *n.* — **im′pro·vis′er, im·prov′i·sa′tor** *n.* — **im·prov·i·sa·to·ri·al** (im·prov′ə·zə·tôr′ē·əl, -tō′rē·əl), **im·prov′i·sa·to′ry** (-tôr′ē, -tō′rē) *adj.*

im·prov·vi·sa·to·re (ēm′prôv·vē·zä·tō′rā) *n. pl.* **·ri** (-rē) *Italian* An improviser, especially of poems and songs.

im·pru·dent (im·pro͞o′dənt) *adj.* Not prudent; lacking discretion. [<L *imprudens, -entis* < *in-* not + *prudens* PRUDENT] — **im·pru′dent·ly** *adv.* — **im·pru′dence** *n.*

Synonyms: careless, foolhardy, heedless, ill-advised, ill-judged, impolitic, improvident, incautious, inconsiderate, indiscreet, injudicious, rash, reckless, short-sighted, thoughtless, thriftless, unthinking, unthrifty, venturesome, venturous. *Improvident* is chiefly used of lack of provision for future need, supply, support, etc.; *imprudent,* of a lack of provision against future danger, loss, or harm. Each word has also acquired a positive meaning: *improvident* referring to *careless* or *reckless* waste of present resources without thought of future need; *imprudent,* to *thoughtless* or *reckless* disregard of possible or probable future dangers. See IMPROVIDENT. *Antonyms*: see synonyms for ASTUTE.

im·pu·dence (im′pyə·dəns) *n.* **1** Effrontery; insolence. **2** Insolent language or behavior. **3** *Obs.* Shamelessness; immodesty. Also **im′·pu·den·cy.** [<OF <L *impudentia*]

Synonyms: assurance, boldness, effrontery, forwardness, impertinence, incivility, insolence, intrusiveness, officiousness, pertness, presumption, rudeness, sauciness. *Impertinence* primarily denotes what does not pertain or belong to the occasion or the person, and hence comes to signify interference by word or act not consistent with the age, position, or relation of the person interfered with or of the one who interferes; especially, forward, presumptuous, or meddlesome speech. *Impudence* is shameless *impertinence.* What would be arrogance in a superior becomes *impertinence* or *impudence* in an inferior. *Impertinence* has less of intent and determination than *impudence.* We speak of thoughtless *impertinence,* shameless *impudence. Insolence* is literally that which is against custom, that is, the violation of customary respect and courtesy. *Officiousness* is thrusting upon others unasked and undesired service, and is often as well-meant as it is annoying. *Rudeness* is the behavior that might be expected from a thoroughly uncultured person, and may be either deliberate and insulting or unintentional and even unconscious. Compare ARROGANCE, ASSURANCE, EFFRONTERY. *Antonyms*: bashfulness, coyness, diffidence, humility, lowliness, meekness, modesty, submissiveness.

im·pu·dent (im′pyə·dənt) *adj.* **1** Offensively bold; insolently assured. **2** *Obs.* Immodest; shameless. [<OF <L *impudens* < *in-* not + *pudens* modest, orig. ppr. of *pudere* feel shame] — **im′pu·dent·ly** *adv.*

Synonyms: bold, bold-faced, brazen, brazen-faced, forward, immodest, impertinent, insolent, pert, rude, saucy, shameless. Compare synonyms for IMPUDENCE. *Antonyms*: bashful, deferential, diffident, modest, obsequious, retiring, shrinking, shy, timid.

im·pu·dic·i·ty (im′pyə·dis′ə·tē) *n.* Immodesty; shamelessness. [<F *impudicité* <L *impudicitia* < *impudicus* shameless < *in-* not + *pudicus* modest < *pudor* shame]

im·pugn (im·pyo͞on′) *v.t.* To assail by words or arguments; attack as false or untrustworthy; challenge. [<OF *impugner* <L *impugnare* < *in-* against + *pugnare* fight < *pugna* battle < *pugnus* fist] — **im·pugn′a·ble** *adj.* — **im·pug·na·tion** (im′pəg·nā′shən) *n.* — **im·pugn′er** *n.* — **im·pugn′ment** *n.*

im·pu·is·sance (im·pyo͞o′ə·səns) *n.* Want of power or ability; impotence. [<F] — **im·pu′·is·sant** *adj.*

im·pulse (im′puls) *n.* **1** An impelling force, especially one that acts suddenly and produces motion; impulsion. **2** The motion produced by a sudden impelling force; impetus. **3** A sudden or transient mental urge resulting in undeliberated action, caused by the feelings or by some objective stimulus. **4** Any natural, unreasoned motive or tendency to act: a kind *impulse.* **5** An instinctive or reactive craving for action; a desire to act resulting from instantaneous judgments as to how to meet an emergency. **6** *Physiol.* A stimulus. **7** *Mech.* A great force acting for a very short time; also, the momentum due to a force. **8** *Electr.* A surge of current flowing in one direction. [<L *impulsus,* pp. of *impellere.* See IMPEL.]

Synonyms: feeling, force, impetus, incentive, incitement, influence, instigation, motive. See INFLUENCE.

impulse excitation See SHOCK EXCITATION.

im·pul·sion (im·pul′shən) *n.* **1** The act of impelling. **2** The state of being impelled. **3** An impulse or motion suddenly communicated; impetus. **4** That which impels, whether a force or motive. **5** Mental impetus. **6** Incitement; instigation. [<OF <L *impulsio, -onis*]

im·pul·sive (im·pul′siv) *adj.* **1** Actuated by impulse. **2** Having the power of impelling. **3** Acting by instantaneous or intermittent force or impulse. See synonyms under IMPETUOUS. [<OF *impulsif* <Med. L *impulsivus*] — **im·pul′sive·ly** *adv.* — **im·pul′sive·ness** *n.*

im·pu·ni·ty (im·pyo͞o′nə·tē) *n. pl.* **·ties** Freedom from punishment or from injurious consequences. [<L *impunitas, -tatis* < *impunis* unpunished < *in-* not + *poena* punishment]

im·pure (im·pyo͝or′) *adj.* **1** Not pure; containing some foreign substance; adulterated. **2** Unchaste. **3** Containing foreign idioms or grammatical blemishes. **4** Unfit for religious use; unhallowed. **5** Mixed with or having a tendency toward extraneous, corporeal, or foreign matter. See synonyms under FOUL, IMMODEST. [<L *impurus*] — **im·pure′ly** *adv.* — **im·pure′ness** *n.*

im·pu·ri·ty (im·pyo͝or′ə·tē) *n. pl.* **·ties** **1** The state of being impure. **2** Adulteration. **3** Moral pollution. **4** That which is impure or polluting. See synonyms under INDECENCY. [<OF *impurité* <L *impuritas, -tatis* < *in-* not + *purus* pure]

im·pur·ple (im·pûr′pəl) See EMPURPLE.

im·pu·ta·tion (im′pyo͞o·tā′shən) *n.* **1** The act of imputing. **2** Whatever is ascribed or charged; especially, censure or reproach. [<LL *imputatio, -onis*]

im·pu·ta·tive (im·pyo͞o′tə·tiv) *adj.* **1** Transferred or transmitted by imputation; imputed. **2** Addicted to making imputations. [<LL *imputativus*] — **im·pu′ta·tive·ly** *adv.*

im·pute (im·pyo͞ot′) *v.t.* **·put·ed, ·put·ing** **1** To attribute, as a fault or crime, to a person; ascribe. **2** *Theol.* To attribute, as righteousness or guilt, vicariously. See synonyms under ATTRIBUTE. [<OF *emputer* <L *imputare* enter into the account < *in-* in + *putare* reckon, think] — **im·put′a·bil′i·ty, im·put′a·ble·ness** *n.* — **im·put′a·ble** *adj.* — **im·put′er** *n.*

im·pu·tres·ci·ble (im′pyo͞o·tres′ə·bəl) *adj.* Not subject to corruption.

Im·roz (ēm·rôs′) The Turkish name for IMBROS.

in (in) *prep.* **1** Within the bounds of; contained or included within: six rooms *in* the house. **2** Amidst; surrounded by: *in* the rain; buried *in* sand. **3** Within the class or group of; being a worker at, investor *in,* etc.: a man *in* a thousand; He is *in* munitions. **4** Occupied or concerned with: *in* search of truth. **5** Wearing, decorated with, etc.: that girl *in* blue; a room *in* green. **6** Made out of: I can show you this watch *in* gold. **7** So as to form or constitute: ornaments arranged *in* a spiral. **8** So as to enter into or remain within: sinking *in* the mud; putting his hands *in* his pockets. **9** As a part or function of; belonging to: We knew you had it *in* you. **10** According to or within the scope or range of: *In* my opinion you're mistaken; to come *in* hearing. **11** During; throughout the course of: a concert given *in* the evening. **12** At or before the end or expiration of: the note due *in* three days; I'll be there *in* no time. **13** With regard or respect to: Students vary *in* talent. **14** Affected by; under the influence of: *in* doubt as to the outcome. **15** By means of; with the use of: speaking *in* whispers; painted *in* water colors. **16** For the purpose of: to run *in* pursuit. **17** By reason or as a result of: to run *in* fear. — *adv.* **1** To or toward the interior or inside from the exterior or outside: Please come *in.* **2** So as to be part of, contained by, or included with: to join *in*; to stir *in* flour. — **all in** *Colloq.* Exhausted; worn out. — **in that** Because; since: *In that* you're here already, you might as well stay. — **in with** In association or friendship with. — **to be in for** *Colloq.* To have the certain expectation of receiving (usually something unpleasant). — **to have it in for** *Colloq.* To resent; bear ill will toward. — *adj.* **1** That is successful; having control or authority. **2** On the inside; inner. **3** Leading or going in: the *in* train. **4** *Colloq.* **a** Privileged in status. **b** Much publicized and often admired. **5** *Colloq.* Understandable only to a select few: *in* jokes. — *n.* **1** A member of a party in office or power, a team at bat, etc. **2** *Colloq.* A door or other means of entrance or access. **3** *Colloq.* Favored position or influence: an *in* with the boss. **4** A nook or corner. — **ins and outs** **1** All the twists and turns, nooks and corners, etc. **2** The full complexities, details, etc.: the *ins and outs* of a question. — *v.t.* **inned, in·ning** **1** To gather, as hay. **2** *Dial.* To enclose, as land. [OE]

in-[1] *prefix* Not; without; un-; non-. Also: *i-* before *gn,* as in *ignore*; *il-* before *l,* as in *illiterate*; *im-* before *b, m, p,* as in *imbalance, immiscible, impecunious*; *ir-* before *r,* as in *irrefragable.* [<L]

There follows a list of self-defining words with this prefix, most of them being variants

of words beginning with *un–*. *In–* as here used has the meaning of "want or lack of," "not" (as *incivility*, lack of civility; *indevout*, not devout). See the foot of this page, etc.

in–[2] *prefix* In; into; on; within; toward: *include, incur, invade*: also used intensively, as in *inflame*, or without perceptible force. Also *il–* before *l*, as in *illuminate*; *im–* before *b, m, p*, as in *imbibe, immigrate, impress*; ir– before *r*, as in *irradiate*. The form generally remains unassimilated in words formed in English, as in *inbreed*. [Fusion of IN, *prep. & adv.* + L *in–*]

in–[3] *prefix* In, into; within: *inlet*. [OE]

–in *suffix Chem.* Used generally to denote neutral compounds, as fats, proteins, and glycerides: *stearin*: sometimes spelled *–ine*. Also *–ein*. [Var. of -INE[2]]

in·a·bil·i·ty (in′ə·bil′ə·tē) *n.* The state of being unable; lack of necessary power.

in ab·sen·ti·a (in ab·sen′shē·ə, -shə) *Latin* In absence (of the person concerned).

in ab·strac·to (ab·strak′tō) *Latin* In the abstract.

in·ac·ces·si·ble (in′ak·ses′ə·bəl) *adj.* Not accessible; incapable of being reached. **— in′ac·ces′si·bil′i·ty** *n.*

in·ac·cu·ra·cy (in·ak′yər·ə·sē) *n. pl.* **·cies** 1 The state or condition of being inaccurate. 2 Something which is inaccurate.

in·ac·cu·rate (in·ak′yər·it) *adj.* Wanting in accuracy. **— in·ac′cu·rate·ly** *adv.* **— in·ac′cu·rate·ness** *n.*

In·a·chus (in′ə·kəs) In Greek mythology, a river god and the first king of Argos; son of Oceanus and Tethys and father of Io.

in·ac·tion (in·ak′shən) *n.* A state of inactivity; forbearance from action; idleness.

in·ac·ti·vate (in·ak′tə·vāt) *v.t.* **·vat·ed, ·vat·ing** 1 To render inactive. 2 *Med.* To stop the activity of (a serum or its complement) by heat or other means. **— in·ac′ti·va′tion** *n.*

in·ac·tive (in·ak′tiv) *adj.* 1 Characterized by inaction; not making special exertion or effort. 2 Marked by absence of effort or desire for action; indolent. 3 Without power to act. 4 *Physics* Having no effect or action upon polarized light. See synonyms under IDLE, PASSIVE, SLOW. **— in·ac′tive·ly** *adv.* **— in·ac·tiv·i·ty** (in′ak·tiv′ə·tē), **in·ac′tive·ness** *n.*

in ac·tu (ak′to͞o) *Latin* In reality.

in·ad·e·quate (in·ad′ə·kwit) *adj.* Not equal to that which is required; inapt; insufficient; imperfect. **— in·ad′e·qua·cy, in·ad′e·quate·ness** *n.* **— in·ad′e·quate·ly** *adv.*

in·ad·ver·tence (in′əd·vûr′təns) *n.* 1 The quality of being inadvertent; want of care or circumspection. 2 An effect of inattention; oversight: This error was a mere *inadvertence*. Also **in′ad·ver′ten·cy.** [<Med. L *inadvertentia*]

in·ad·ver·tent (in′əd·vûr′tənt) *adj.* 1 Done without consideration. 2 Habitually heedless. 3 Unintentional. **— in′ad·ver′tent·ly** *adv.*

in·ad·vis·a·ble (in′əd·vī′zə·bəl) *adj.* Not advisable. **— in′ad·vis′a·bil′i·ty** *n.*

–inae *suffix Zool.* Used in the names of subfamilies: *Cervinae* (see CERVINE). [<NL <L, fem. pl. of *-inus* -INE[1]]

in ae·ter·num (ē·tûr′nəm) *Latin* Forever.

in·af·fa·ble (in·af′ə·bəl) *adj.* Not affable; austere; disagreeable.

in·al·ien·a·ble (in·āl′yən·ə·bəl) *adj.* Not transferable; that cannot be rightfully taken away. **— in·al′ien·a·bil′i·ty, in·al′ien·a·ble·ness** *n.* **— in·al′ien·a·bly** *adv.*

in·al·ter·a·ble (in·ôl′tər·ə·bəl) *adj.* That cannot be altered; unalterable. **— in·al′ter·a·bil′i·ty, in·al′ter·a·ble·ness** *n.* **— in·al′ter·a·bly** *adv.*

in·am·o·ra·ta (in·am′ə·rä′tə, in′am-) *n.* A woman with whom one is enamored; sweetheart. [<Ital. *innamorata*, fem. pp. of *innamorare* enamor] **— in·am′o·ra′to** (-tō) *n. masc.*

in–and–in (in′ənd·in′) *adj. & adv.* 1 From animals of the same or closely related parentage: breeding *in–and–in*. 2 Figuratively, with continuous reciprocal action.

in·ane (in·ān′) *adj.* 1 Wanting in understanding; silly. 2 Having no substance or contents; vacant. **—** *n.* That which is void; any vacuity; infinite space. [<L *inanis* empty]

in·an·i·mate (in·an′ə·mit) *adj.* Wanting in life and animation; not animate: opposed to *sentient*. [<LL *inanimatus*] **— in·an′i·mate·ly** *adv.* **— in·an′i·mate·ness** *n.*

in·a·ni·tion (in′ə·nish′ən) *n.* 1 The state of being void or empty. 2 Exhaustion from lack of nourishment. [<F <LL *inanitio, -onis* < *inanitus*, pp. of *inanire* empty < *inanis* empty]

in·an·i·ty (in·an′ə·tē) *n. pl.* **·ties** 1 The condition of being inane or empty; inanition; lack of sense. 2 A frivolous or silly thing. 3 A stupid or trite remark. [<OF *inanité* <L *inanitas* < *inanis* empty]

in·ap·peas·a·ble (in′ə·pē′zə·bəl) *adj.* That cannot be appeased; not to be appeased.

in·ap·pe·tence (in·ap′ə·təns) *n.* A lack of appetite or desire. Also **in·ap′pe·ten·cy. — in·ap′pe·tent** *adj.*

in·ap·pro·pri·ate (in′ə·prō′prē·it) *adj.* Not appropriate; unsuitable; unfitting.

in·arch (in·ärch′) *v.t. Bot.* To graft by attaching (a branch) without severing it from the parent stock until it has become united with the new stock; graft by approach. [<IN-[2] + ARCH]

in·arm (in·ärm′) *v.t.* To encircle with or as with the arms; embrace.

In·ar·tic·u·la·ta (in′är·tik′yə·lā′tə) See ECARDINES.

in·ar·tic·u·late (in′är·tik′yə·lit) *adj.* 1 Indistinctly or unintelligibly uttered by the speech organs. 2 Incapable of speech; dumb. 3 Unable to speak coherently or to express oneself fully. 4 Unspoken; unexpressed. 5 *Anat.* Not jointed or segmented, as certain worms; also, not hinged. **— in′ar·tic′u·late·ly** *adv.* **— in′ar·tic′u·late·ness** *n.*

in ar·tic·u·lo mor·tis (in är·tik′yə·lō môr′tis) *Latin* At the moment of death.

in·as·much as (in′əz·much′ az′) 1 Since; because; seeing that. 2 *Archaic* In the measure that; to the degree that.

in·at·ten·tion (in′ə·ten′shən) *n.* Lack of or failure to give attention; heedlessness; negligence; disregard.

in·at·ten·tive (in′ə·ten′tiv) *adj.* Neglecting or failing to pay attention; careless. **— in′at·ten′tive·ly** *adv.* **— in′at·ten′tive·ness** *n.*

Synonyms: absent, absent–minded, careless, heedless, inconsiderate, listless, neglectful, negligent, regardless, remiss, restless, unmindful, unobservant. See ABSTRACTED. *Antonyms*: attentive, careful, considerate, heedful, listening, noticing, noting, observing, regardful, studious, thoughtful, watchful.

in·au·di·ble (in·ô′də·bəl) *adj.* That cannot be heard; beyond the range of hearing. **— in·au′di·bil′i·ty** *n.* **— in·au′di·bly** *adv.*

in·au·gu·rate (in·ô′gyə·rāt) *v.t.* **·rat·ed, ·rat·ing** 1 To induct into office with formal ceremony; invest. 2 To begin or commence upon formally; initiate: to *inaugurate* a reform. 3 To celebrate the public opening or first use of: to *inaugurate* a bridge. See synonyms under INSTALL. [<L *inauguratus*, pp. of *inaugurare* take omens, consecrate, install. See AUGUR.] **— in·au′gu·ral** (-rəl) *adj.* **— in·au′gu·ra′tor** *n.* **— in·au′gu·ra·to′ry** (-tôr′ē, -tō′rē) *adj.*

in·au·gu·ra·tion (in·ô′gyə·rā′shən) *n.* The act or ceremony of inaugurating. See synonyms under ACCESSION, BEGINNING. [<L *inauguratio, -onis*]

Inauguration Day The day for the inauguration of a president of the United States following his election: January 20. Prior to the inauguration of 1937 the date was March 4.

in·be·ing (in′bē′ing) *n.* 1 Inherent existence. 2 Essential nature; what a thing is in itself.

in·board (in′bôrd′, -bōrd′) *adj.* 1 *Naut.* Inside the hull or bulwarks of a ship: used also adverbially. 2 *Mech.* Toward the inside.

inboard brakes In automobiles, brake assemblies mounted within the chassis rather than on the wheels, the object being to reduce unsprung weight.

in·born (in′bôrn′) *adj.* Implanted by nature; innate. See synonyms under INHERENT.

in·bound (in′bound′) *adj.* Bound inward: an *inbound* ship.

in·breathe (in·brēth′) *v.t.* **·breathed, ·breath·ing** 1 To draw in, as breath; inhale. 2 To inspire.

in·bred (in′bred′) *adj.* 1 Bred within; innate. 2 Bred from closely related parents. See synonyms under INHERENT.

in·breed (in′brēd′, in′brēd′) *v.t.* **·bred, ·breed·ing** 1 To develop or produce within. 2 To breed by continual mating of closely related stock.

in·burst (in′bûrst′) *n.* 1 A bursting from without inward. 2 That which bursts in: an *inburst* of water.

in·by (in′bī′) *Scot. adv.* Inward; toward the interior or center. **—** *adj.* Located nearby.

In·ca (ing′kə) *n.* 1 An emperor or chief of Peru or one of its divisions, at the time of the Spanish conquest. 2 One of the native Quechuan Indians formerly dominant in Peru. [<Sp. <Quechua *Ynca* royal prince]

in·cage (in·kāj′) *v.t.* To encage.

in·cal·cu·la·ble (in·kal′kyə·lə·bəl) *adj.* 1 That cannot be counted or calculated. 2 Uncertain. 3 Not foreseeable. **— in·cal′cu·la·bil′i·ty** *n.* **— in·cal′cu·la·bly** *adv.*

in·ca·les·cent (in′kə·les′ənt) *adj.* Growing warm; increasing in heat. [<L *incalescens, -entis*, ppr. of *incalescere* grow hot < *in–* thoroughly + *calescens*. See CALESCENT.] **— in′ca·les′cence** *n.*

in cam·er·a (in kam′ər·ə) 1 In secret; privately. 2 *Law* In chambers. [<L, in a room]

In·can (ing′kən) *n.* 1 A member of the Inca empire. 2 Quechua. **—** *adj.* Of or pertaining to the Inca empire, its culture, or to its people.

in·can·desce (in′kən·des′) *v.t. & v.i.* **·desced, ·desc·ing** To be or become, or cause to become luminous with heat. [<L *incandescere*] **— in′can·des′cence, in′can·des′cen·cy** *n.*

in·can·des·cent (in′kən·des′ənt) *adj.* 1 Made luminous by heat; white or glowing with heat. 2 Of or pertaining to a lamp the light of which is derived from incandescing material, such as the filament in an electric lamp or the mantle in a Welsbach burner. [<L *incandescens, -entis*, ppr. of *incandescere* grow hot < *in–* in + *candescere*, inceptive of *candere* glow white] **— in′can·des′cent·ly** *adv.*

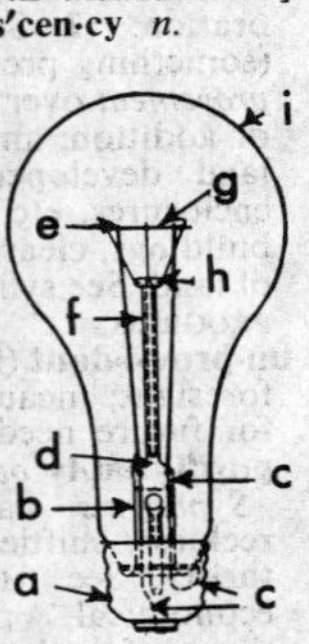

INCANDESCENT LIGHT BULB
a. Base.
b. Stem.
c. Leading–in wires.
d. Stem seal.
e, h. Anchors.
f. Hub.
g. Filament.
i. Bulb.

in·can·ta·tion (in′kan·tā′shən) 1 The utterance of magical words for enchantment or exorcism. 2 The formula so used. 3 Any magic or sorcery. See synonyms under SORCERY. [<F <L *incantatio, -onis* < *incantare* make an incantation. See ENCHANT.] **— in′can·ta′tor** *n.* **— in·can·ta·to·ry** (in·kan′tə·tôr′ē, -tō′rē) *adj.*

in·ca·pa·ble (in·kā′pə·bəl) *adj.* 1 Not capable; lacking power, capacity or ability: with *of*; incompetent. 2 Without legal qualifications or eligibility. **—** *n.* A totally incompetent person. **— in·ca′pa·bil′i·ty, in·ca′pa·ble·ness** *n.* **— in·ca′pa·bly** *adv.*

in·ca·pac·i·tate (in′kə·pas′ə·tāt) *v.t.* **·tat·ed, ·tat·ing** 1 To make incapable or unfit; deprive of capacity; disable. 2 *Law* To deprive of legal or political capacity; disqualify. **— in′ca·pac′i·ta′tion** *n.*

in·ca·pac·i·ty (in′kə·pas′ə·tē) *n. pl.* **·ties** 1 Lack of capacity; incapability. 2 *Law* Want of competency. See synonyms under IDIOCY.

in·cap·su·late (in·kap′sə·lāt, -syo͞o-) *v.t.* **·lat·ed, ·lat·ing** To enclose as in a capsule. [<IN- + CAPSUL(E) + -ATE[1]]

in·car·cer·ate (in·kär′sər·āt) *v.t.* **·at·ed, ·at·ing** 1 To imprison; put in jail. 2 To confine; enclose. **—** *adj.* Imprisoned. [<Med. L *incarceratus*, pp. of *incarcerare* imprison < *in–* in + *carcer* jail] **— in·car′cer·a′tion** *n.* **— in·car′cer·a′tor** *n.*

in·car·di·nate (in·kär′də·nāt) *v.t.* **·nat·ed, ·nat·ing** In the Roman Catholic Church: 1 To establish in a particular church, diocese, or place as principal priest, deacon, etc. 2 To

inacceptable	inadept	inappealable	inappreciable	inapproachability	inarable	inassimilate
inaccordance	inadmissibility	inapplicability	inappreciative	inapproachable	inartificial	inauspicious
inaccordancy	inadmissible	inapplicable	inapprehensible	inapt	inartistic	inauthentic
inacquaintance	inaffability	inapplication	inapprehension	inaptitude	inartistical	incapacious
inacquiescent	inaidable	inapposite	inapprehensive	inaqueous	inassignable	incaution

make a cardinal. [<Med. L *incardinatus,* pp. of *incardinare* install a priest < *in-* in + *cardinalis* a chief priest] — **in·car′di·na′tion** *n.*

in·car·na·dine (in·kär′nə·dīn, -din) *v.t.* **·dined, ·din·ing** To dye or stain red or flesh-color. — *adj.* Of pale-red. pink, flesh- or blood-color. [<F *incarnadin* <Ital. *incarnatino,* dim. of *incarnato* flesh-colored, pp. of *incarnare* INCARNATE]

in·car·nant (in·kär′nənt) *adj. Med.* Promoting the granulation of wounds. — *n.* An agent that promotes the healing of wounds. Also **in·car′na·tive.** [< earlier *incarn* cover with flesh, heal over <LL *incarnare* INCARNATE]

in·car·nate (in·kär′nāt) *v.t.* **·nat·ed, ·nat·ing** 1 To embody in flesh; give bodily form to. 2 To give concrete shape or form to; actualize: a doctrine *incarnated* in institutions. 3 To be the embodiment of; typify: The warrior *incarnates* the spirit of battle. — *adj.* (-nit) 1 Invested with flesh. 2 Embodied in human form: a fiend *incarnate.* 3 Personified or epitomized: savagery *incarnate.* 4 Flesh-colored; roseate. [<LL *incarnatus,* pp. of *incarnare* embody in flesh < *in-* in + *caro, carnis* flesh]

in·car·na·tion (in′kär·nā′shən) *n.* 1 The act of becoming incarnate. 2 *Often cap.* The assumption of the human nature by Jesus Christ as the second person of the Trinity. 3 That which is personified by, or embodied in or as in human form; personification; embodiment of a quality, idea, principle, etc.; specifically, an avatar. [<AF *incarnaciun* < LL *incarnatio, -onis*]

in·case (in·kās′) *v.t.* **·cased, ·cas·ing** To place or enclose in or as in a case or cases: often spelled *encase.*

in·case·ment (in·kās′mənt) *n.* 1 The act of incasing, or the state of being incased. 2 That which incases. — **theory of incasement** *Biol.* An old theory of reproduction that assumes each ovum to contain a fully formed organism in miniature; preformation.

in·ca·va·tion (in′kə·vā′shən) *n.* 1 The act of making hollow. 2 The hollow itself. [<L *incavatus,* pp. of *incavare* < *in-* in + *cavare* make hollow < *cavus* hollow]

in·cen·di·ar·y (in·sen′dē·er′ē) *adj.* 1 Pertaining to malicious setting on fire. 2 Tending to inflame passion. 3 Capable of generating intense heat, as any of various substances such as magnesium, thermit, or white phosphorus. 4 Pertaining to or containing such a substance: an *incendiary* bomb. — *n. pl.* **·ries** 1 One who maliciously sets a building on fire; one who commits arson. 2 One who excites to sedition, inflames evil passions, or the like. 3 An incendiary bomb or shell. [<L *incendiarius* < *incendium* a fire < *incendere* set on fire] — **in·cen′di·a·rism** (-ə·riz′əm) *n.*

incendiary bomb See under BOMB.

in·cense[1] (in·sens′) *v.t.* **·censed, ·cens·ing** To excite or arouse the wrath of; inflame to anger; enrage. [<OF *incenser* <L *incendere* set on fire < *in-* in + *candere* glow] — **in·cense′ment** *n.* — **in·cen′sor** *n.*

Synonyms: anger, chafe, enrage, exasperate, fire, gall, goad, heat, inflame, irritate, provoke, sting. *Antonyms*: allay, appease, conciliate, mollify, pacify, placate, soothe.

in·cense[2] (in′sens) *n.* 1 An aromatic substance that exhales perfume during combustion, as certain gums and spices. 2 The odor or fumes of spices, etc., burnt as an act of worship. 3 Any agreeable perfume. 4 Figuratively, pleasing attention; praise. — *v.* **·censed, ·cens·ing** *v.t.* 1 To perfume with incense. 2 To burn incense to. — *v.i.* 3 To burn incense. [<OF *encens* <L *incensus,* pp. of *incendere* set on fire]

in·cen·tive (in·sen′tiv) *adj.* Encouraging or impelling. — *n.* That which incites, or tends to incite, to action. See synonyms under IMPULSE, MOTIVE. [<L *incentivus* < *incentus,* pp. of *incinere* set the tune < *in-* in + *canere* sing] — **in·cen′tive·ly** *adv.*

in·cept (in·sept′) *v.t.* 1 *Biol.* To take in, as a cell or organism. 2 *Obs.* To begin; undertake. [<L *inceptus,* pp. of *incipere* begin < *in-* on + *capere* take]

in·cep·tion (in·sep′shən) *n.* 1 The act of beginning. 2 The state of being begun. 3 The initial period, as of an undertaking. See synonyms under BEGINNING. [<L *inceptio, -onis* < *inceptus,* pp. of *incipere.* See INCEPT.]

in·cep·tive (in·sep′tiv) *adj.* 1 Noting the beginning or commencement of an action or occurrence; initial. 2 *Gram.* Referring to a class of verbs or to the aspect of a verb denoting the commencement of an action; inchoative; ingressive. In Latin, for example, such verbs are formed by the addition of *-scere* to the present stem, as *cale(scere),* to grow warm, from *cale(re),* to be hot. — *n.* 1 That which tends to commence, as an inceptive word or construction. 2 *Gram.* An inceptive word or construction. [<OF *inceptif* <L *inceptus,* pp. of *incipere.* See INCEPT.] — **in·cep′tive·ly** *adv.*

in·cer·ti·tude (in·sûr′tə·tōōd, -tyōōd) *n.* 1 The state of being uncertain; uncertainty; doubtfulness. 2 Insecurity. [<F <Med. L *incertitudo* <L *incertus* uncertain]

in·ces·sant (in·ses′ənt) *adj.* Continued or repeated without cessation. See synonyms under CONTINUAL, PERPETUAL. [<F <LL *incessans, -antis* < *in-* not + *cessare* cease] — **in·ces′san·cy** (-ən·sē) *n.* — **in·ces′sant·ly** *adv.*

in·cest (in′sest) *n.* 1 Sexual intercourse between persons too closely related for legal marriage. 2 *Theol.* Spiritual incest. [<L *incestum* < *incestus* unchaste < *in-* not + *castus* chaste]

in·ces·tu·ous (in·ses′chōō·əs) *adj.* 1 Guilty of incest. 2 Of the nature of incest. [<L *incestuosus*] — **in·ces′tu·ous·ly** *adv.*

inch[1] (inch) *n.* 1 A linear measure: the twelfth part of a foot or 2.54 centimeters. 2 *Meteorol.* The amount of snow or rain which would cover a surface to the depth of an inch. 3 *Physics* The unit of pressure equivalent to the weight of a fluid column, as of mercury, having a height of one inch. 4 An exceedingly small distance, amount of time, or quantity of material. — **by inches** Gradually; very slowly. — *v.t.* & *v.i.* To move by inches or small degrees. [OE *ynce* <L *uncia* the twelfth part, inch, ounce. Doublet of OUNCE.]

inch[2] (inch) *n. Scot.* An island: often used in combination in Scottish local names.

inch·meal (inch′mēl′) *adv.* Inch by inch; piecemeal. — *n.* A fragment an inch long; a little piece. [<INCH + -MEAL]

in·cho·ate (in·kō′it, in′kō·āt) *adj.* Existing in its elements only; begun or entered upon, but not in full existence or operation; incipient. — *v.t.* & *v.i.* (in′kō·āt) **·at·ed, ·at·ing** *Rare* To begin. [<L *inchoatus, incohatus,* pp. of *incohare* begin] — **in·cho′ate·ly** *adv.* — **in′cho·a′tion, in·cho′ate·ness** *n.*

in·cho·a·tive (in·kō′ə·tiv) *adj.* 1 *Gram.* Inceptive. 2 *Rare* Inchoate; incipient. — *n.* That which begins or expresses beginning; an inceptive; especially, an inceptive verb.

In·chon (in·chon) A port on the Yellow Sea in central Korea: also *Chemulpo. Japanese* **Jin·sen** (jin·sen).

inch·worm (inch′wûrm′) *n.* A measuring worm. See under GEOMETRID.

in·ci·dence (in′sə·dəns) *n.* 1 A falling, or the direction or manner of falling. 2 *Physics* The angle which the path of a body or of any form of radiant energy makes with the perpendicular of a surface at the point of impact. 3 The fact or the manner of being incident. 4 The degree of occurrence or effect of something: a high *incidence* of typhus. 5 *Geom.* Partial coincidence in the position of two figures, as a line and a point on it.

in·ci·dent (in′sə·dənt) *n.* 1 Anything that takes place as part of an action or in connection with an event; a subordinate or concomitant event or act. 2 A happening in general, especially one of little importance; any event; an occurrence. 3 Something characteristically, naturally, or legally depending upon, connected with, or contained in another thing as its principal. See synonyms under ACCIDENT, CIRCUMSTANCE, EVENT, SCENE, STORY. — *adj.* 1 Falling or striking upon; impinging from without: *incident* rays. 2 Likely to befall; naturally or usually appertaining or attending: danger *incident* to travel. 3 Of the nature of an incident or concomitant; belonging subsidiarily; appurtenant: The right of alienation is *incident* to a title in fee simple. 4 *Obs.* Incidental. [<F <L *incidens, -entis,* ppr. of *incidere* fall upon < *in-* on + *cadere* fall]

in·ci·den·tal (in′sə·den′təl) *adj.* 1 Occurring in the course of something else; contingent. 2 Happening without regularity or design; casual. — *n.* 1 Something that is incidental, contingent, or fortuitous; a subordinate or minor occurrence, circumstance, or result. 2 *Music* In the tonic sol-fa system, a tone foreign to a chord. 3 *Usually pl.* Minor or casual expenses or items. — **in′ci·den′tal·ly** *adv.*

Synonyms (adj.): accessory, accidental, casual, chance, collateral, concomitant, concurrent, contingent, fortuitous, occasional. That is *incidental* which comes in the regular course of things, but is not viewed as primary or important; as, an *incidental* allusion, reference, or mention. That which is *incidental* is subordinate to the main design; that which is *accidental* occurs without design. Compare ACCIDENT. *Antonyms*: essential, fundamental, independent, inherent, invariable, regular, systematic, underlying.

in·cin·er·ate (in·sin′ər·āt) *v.t.* **·at·ed, ·at·ing** To consume with fire; reduce to ashes; cremate. See synonyms under BURN. [<Med. L *incineratus,* pp. of *incinerare* < *in-* in + *cinis, cineris* ashes]

in·cin·er·a·tion (in·sin′ə·rā′shən) *n.* The act or state of cremation. [<F]

in·cin·er·a·tor (in·sin′ə·rā′tər) *n.* 1 One who or that which incinerates. 2 A furnace or apparatus for reducing any substance to ashes, as for consuming refuse or for cremating.

in·cip·i·ence (in·sip′ē·əns) *n.* Inception; the state of being incipient. Also **in·cip′i·en·cy.** ◆ Homophone: *insipience.*

in·cip·i·ent (in·sip′ē·ənt) *adj.* Belonging to the first stages. [<L *incipiens, -entis,* ppr. of *incipere.* See INCEPT.] — **in·cip′i·ent·ly** *adv.*

in·ci·pit (in′si·pit) *Latin* Here begins: a term often found at the beginning of medieval manuscripts.

in·cise (in·sīz′) *v.t.* **·cised, ·cis·ing** 1 To cut into with a sharp instrument; gash. 2 To make (designs, marks, etc.) by cutting; engrave; carve. [<MF *inciser* <L *incidere* cut into < *in-* in + *caedere* cut]

in·cised (in·sīzd′) *adj.* 1 Cut in; engraved. 2 Notched irregularly but sharply, as a leaf or an insect's wing.

in·ci·sion (in·sizh′ən) *n.* 1 The act of incising. 2 An opening made with a cutting instrument: a cut; gash. 3 *Surg.* A division of soft parts with a cutting instrument, as in an operation. 4 Sharpness; incisiveness; trenchancy. 5 A slit or notch, having the appearance of a cut, as in the margin of a leaf, a butterfly's wing, etc. [<OF <L *incisio, -onis*]

in·ci·sive (in·sī′siv) *adj.* 1 Having the power of incising. 2 Cutting; trenchant; acute: *incisive* wit. 3 Pertaining to an incisor. Also **in·ci′so·ry** (-sər·ē). [<Med. L *incisivus*] — **in·ci′sive·ly** *adv.* — **in·ci′sive·ness** *n.*

in·ci·sor (in·sī′zər) *adj.* Adapted for cutting. — *n.* A front or cutting tooth; in man, one of eight such teeth, four in each jaw. [<NL]

in·ci·sure (in·sizh′ər) *n.* An incision; cut. [<L *incisura*]

in·ci·tant (in·sī′tənt) *adj.* Inciting; instigating. — *n.* One who or that which incites. [<L *incitans, -antis,* ppr. of *incitare.* See INCITE.]

in·ci·ta·tion (in′sī·tā′shən) *n.* 1 Incitement. 2 An incentive. [<OF <L *incitatio, -onis*]

in·cite (in·sīt′) *v.t.* **·cit·ed, ·cit·ing** To urge to a particular action; instigate; stir up. See synonyms under ABET, ACTUATE, INFLUENCE, PERSUADE, SPUR, STIR. [<OF *inciter* <L *incitare*

incautious	**incognoscible**	**incompact**	**incompressibility**	**incondensability**	**inconsiderable**	**incontrollable**
incelebrity	**incoherentness**	**incompassionate**	**incompressible**	**incondensable**	**inconsolable**	**incontrovertibility**
incertain	**incohesive**	**incompliance**	**incomputable**	**inconducive**	**inconsonance**	**incontrovertible**
incircumspect	**incommutability**	**incompliant**	**inconcealable**	**inconformity**	**inconsonant**	**inconversant**
incogent	**incommutable**	**incomposite**	**inconcrete**	**inconsecutive**	**inconsumable**	**inconversion**

< *in-* thoroughly + *citare* rouse, freq. of *ciere* set in motion] — **in·ci′ta·tive** (-tə·tiv) *adj.* — **in·cit′er** *n.*

in·cite·ment (in·sīt′mənt) *n.* **1** The act of inciting. **2** That which incites; incentive; motive. See synonyms under IMPULSE.

in·ci·vil·i·ty (in′sə·vil′ə·tē) *n. pl.* **·ties** **1** The state of being uncivil; discourteous manner. **2** An uncivil or rude act.

in·clasp (in·klasp′, -kläsp′) *v.t.* To enclasp.

in·clem·ent (in·klem′ənt) *adj.* Not clement; harsh; severe; rigorous, as weather; unpropitious or untoward. [<L *inclemens, -entis*] — **in·clem′en·cy** *n.*

in·cli·na·tion (in′klə·nā′shən) *n.* **1** Deviation from a given direction, especially from the vertical or horizontal. **2** The act of inclining or state of being inclined. **3** A slope or declivity. **4** A mental bent or tendency; predilection. **5** *Geom.* The angle between two lines, planes, etc. **6** *Astron.* The angle formed between the orbital plane of a planet and the ecliptic. [<F <L *inclinatio, -onis*] — **in·cli·na·to·ry** (in·klī′nə·tôr′ē, -tō′rē) *adj.*

Synonyms: appetite, attraction, bent, bias, desire, direction, disposition, drift, fancy, predilection, prepossession, proclivity, proneness, propensity, tendency. See AIM, APPETITE, ATTACHMENT, DESIRE, DIRECTION, FANCY, RELISH, WILL. *Antonyms*: aversion, disinclination, dislike, opposition, repulsion, resistance.

in·cline (in·klīn′) *v.* **·clined, ·clin·ing** *v.i.* **1** To deviate from the horizontal or vertical; slant; slope. **2** To have a tendency or disposition of the mind; be disposed or biased. **3** To tend in some quality or degree: purple *inclining* toward blue. **4** To bow or bend the head or body, as in courtesy. — *v.t.* **5** To cause to bend, lean, or slope. **6** To give a tendency or leaning to; influence. **7** To bow, as the head. See synonyms under ACTUATE, DRAW, INFLUENCE, LEAN[1], PERSUADE, TIP. — **to incline one's ear** To hear with favor; heed. — *n.* (in′klīn, in·klīn′) That which inclines from the horizontal; a gradient; slope. [<OF *encliner* <L *inclinare* < *in-* on + *clinare* lean] — **in·clin′a·ble** *adj.* — **in·clin′er** *n.*

in·clined (in·klīnd′) *adj.* **1** Bent out of line, or making an angle with some standard. **2** Having a tendency in some (specified) direction. **3** *Bot.* Bent out of the perpendicular, or with convex side up. **4** Toward the horizontal.

inclined plane A plane forming any but a right angle with a horizontal plane.

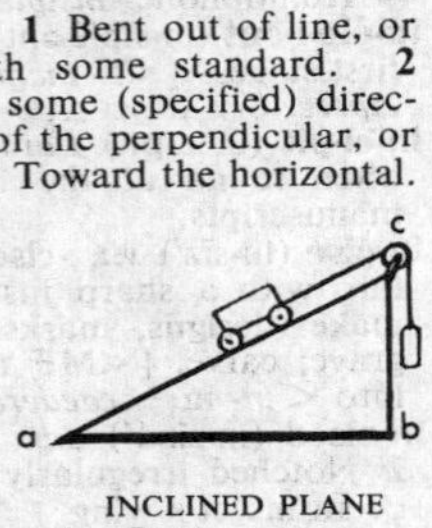

INCLINED PLANE
ab. Base.
bc. Height.
ac. Inclined plane.
bac. Angle formed by plane.

in·cli·nom·e·ter (in′klə·nom′ə·tər) *n.* **1** *Aeron.* An instrument for measuring inclination or slope of an aircraft with relation to the horizontal. **2** A magnetic needle pivoted to swing vertically in order to indicate the inclination of the earth's magnetic field; a dip needle. [<IN-CLIN(E) + -(O)METER]

in·close (in·klōz′), **in·clo·sure** (in·klō′zhər) See ENCLOSE, etc.

in·clude (in·klōōd′) *v.t.* **·clud·ed, clud·ing** **1** To have as a component part; contain. **2** To have or involve as a subordinate part, quality, element, etc.; imply: Religion *includes* morality. **3** To place in a general category, aggregate, etc. **4** To enclose within; confine. [<L *includere* < *in-* in + *claudere* shut] — **in·clud′a·ble, in·clud′i·ble** *adj.*

in·clud·ed (in·klōō′did) *adj. Bot.* Designating stamens or style not projecting above the corolla.

in·clu·sion (in·klōō′zhən) *n.* **1** The act of including. **2** That which is included. **3** *Mineral.* A substance either gaseous (as air), liquid (as water), or solid (as crystal), enclosed in a mineral, usually in a crystal. **4** *Biol.* Any inactive particle lodged in a living cell. [<L *inclusio, -onis* < *includere*. See INCLUDE.]

in·clu·sive (in·klōō′siv) *adj.* **1** Including the things, times, places, limits, or extremes mentioned: from A to Z *inclusive*. **2** Including within; surrounding: often with *of*: The list is *inclusive of* all the items. [<Med. L *inclusivus*] — **in·clu′sive·ly** *adv.* — **in·clu′sive·ness** *n.*

in·co·er·ci·ble (in′kō·ûr′sə·bəl) *adj.* **1** That cannot be coerced. **2** *Physics* Resistant to forces tending to change the form or properties of a substance or material.

in·cog·i·ta·ble (in·koj′ə·tə·bəl) *adj.* Not capable of being thought of; inconceivable. [<LL *incogitabilis*] — **in·cog′i·ta·bil′i·ty** *n.*

in·cog·i·tant (in·koj′ə·tənt) *adj.* Unthinking; thoughtless. [<L *incogitans, -antis*]

in·cog·ni·to (in·kog′nə·tō, in′kəg·nē′tō) *adj.* & *adv.* Unknown; under an assumed name, so as to avoid notice or ceremony. — *n. pl.* **·tos** (-tōz) **1** The state of being incognito. **2** One who passes under an assumed name. **3** The assumed name. [<Ital. <L *incognitus* unknown < *in-* not + *cognitus*, pp. of *cognoscere* know] — **in·cog′ni·ta** (-tə) *n.* & *adj. fem.*

in·co·her·ence (in′kō·hir′əns) *n.* **1** Want of coherence. **2** Looseness or separateness of material particles. **3** That which is incoherent. Also **in′co·her′en·cy.**

in·co·her·ent (in′kō·hir′ənt) *adj.* **1** Having little or no coherence; incongruous; unconnected. **2** Manifesting incoherence in thought, speech, or action. **3** Without physical coherence of parts. — **in′co·her′ent·ly** *adv.*

in·com·bus·ti·ble (in·kəm·bus′tə·bəl) *adj.* Incapable of burning or of being burned. — *n.* That which does not burn; an incombustible substance or material. — **in′com·bus′ti·bil′i·ty, in′com·bus′ti·ble·ness** *n.* — **in′com·bus′ti·bly** *adv.*

in·come (in′kum) *n.* **1** Money, or other benefit, periodically received; the amount so received. **2** The gain derived from capital, or labor, or both, inclusive of profit gained through the sale or conversion of capital assets. **3** *Obs.* The act of coming in; an incoming; specifically, the influx of divine grace into the soul. — **earned income** Income from labor, professional work, or business. — **unearned income** Income from capital investments, etc.

in·com·er (in′kum′ər) *n.* **1** One who or that which comes in. **2** One who follows or succeeds another.

income tax See under TAX.

in·com·ing (in′kum′ing) *adj.* Coming in or about to come in: an *incoming* tenant, *incoming* profits. — *n.* The act of coming in; entrance or arrival.

in·com·men·su·ra·ble (in′kə·men′shər·ə·bəl, -sər·ə-) *adj.* **1** Lacking a common measure or standard of comparison. **2** *Math.* Not expressible in terms of a common measure or unit: *incommensurable* numbers. **3** Conspicuously disproportionate. — *n.* That which is incommensurable. — **in′com·men′su·ra·bil′i·ty, in′com·men′su·ra·ble·ness** *n.* — **in′com·men′su·ra·bly** *adv.*

in·com·men·su·rate (in′kə·men′shər·it) *adj.* **1** Incommensurable. **2** Inadequate; disproportionate. — **in′com·men′su·rate·ly** *adv.* — **in′com·men′su·rate·ness** *n.*

in·com·mode (in′kə·mōd′) *v.t.* **·mod·ed, ·mod·ing** To cause inconvenience to; disturb. [<F *incommoder* <L *incommodare* < *incommodus* inconvenient < *in-* not + *commodus* proper measure]

in·com·mo·di·ous (in′kə·mō′dē·əs) *adj.* Not commodious; not affording sufficient accommodation; inconvenient. — **in′com·mo′di·ous·ly** *adv.* — **in′com·mo′di·ous·ness** *n.* — **in′com·mod′i·ty** (-mod′ə·tē) *n.*

in·com·mu·ni·ca·ble (in′kə·myōō′nə·kə·bəl) *adj.* **1** Not capable of being communicated or imparted. **2** Incommunicative. — **in′com·mu′ni·ca·bil′i·ty** *n.*

in·com·mu·ni·ca·do (in′kə·myōō′nə·kä′dō) *adj.* & *adv.* Confined without the opportunity to communicate, as a prisoner. [<Sp.]

in·com·mu·ni·ca·tive (in′kə·myōō′nə·kā′tiv, -kə·tiv) *adj.* Reserved; guarded in speech and manner. — **in′com·mu′ni·ca′tive·ly** *adv.* — **in′com·mu′ni·ca′tive·ness** *n.*

in·com·pa·ra·ble (in·kom′pər·ə·bəl) *adj.* **1** Not admitting of comparison, as being unapproachable; peerless. **2** Unsuitable for comparison. See synonyms under RARE[1]. [<F] — **in·com′pa·ra·bil′i·ty, in·com′pa·ra·ble·ness** *n.* — **in·com′pa·ra·bly** *adv.*

in·com·pat·i·ble (in′kəm·pat′ə·bəl) *adj.* **1** Not compatible; incapable of existing together in agreement or harmony; discordant. **2** Incapable of coexisting. **3** *Med.* **a** Incapable of use in combination, as certain drugs. **b** Mutually antagonistic, as different blood types. **4** *Logic* Incapable of being true simultaneously: said of two or more propositions. — *n. Usually pl.* Incompatible persons or things. See synonyms under CONTRARY, INCONGRUOUS. — **in′com·pat′i·bly** *adv.*

in·com·pat·i·bil·i·ty (in′kəm·pat′ə·bil′ə·tē) *n. pl.* **·ties** **1** The quality of being incompatible: also **in′com·pat′i·ble·ness.** **2** That which is incompatible. [<F *incompatibilité*]

in·com·pe·tent (in·kom′pə·tənt) *adj.* **1** Not competent; unable to do what is required. **2** Not legally qualified. See synonyms under BAD. — *n.* An incompetent person. [<F *incompétent*] — **in·com′pe·tence, in·com′pe·ten·cy** *n.* — **in·com′pe·tent·ly** *adv.*

in·com·plete (in′kəm·plēt′) *adj.* **1** Not complete; imperfect. **2** Lacking in certain parts, as some flowers. — **in′com·plete′ly** *adv.* — **in′com·plete′ness** *n.* — **in′com·ple′tion** *n.*

in·com·pre·hen·si·ble (in′kom·pri·hen′sə·bəl, in·kom′-) *adj.* **1** Not comprehensible; not understandable; inconceivable. **2** *Archaic* That cannot be included or confined within limits. See synonyms under MYSTERIOUS. [<L *incomprehensibilis*] — **in·com′pre·hen·si·bil′i·ty, in·com′pre·hen′si·ble·ness** *n.* — **in·com′pre·hen′si·bly** *adv.*

in·com·pre·hen·sion (in′kom·pri·hen′shən, in·kom′-) *n.* Lack of understanding.

in·com·pre·hen·sive (in′kom·pri·hen′siv, in·kom′-) *adj.* Not comprehensive; limited.

in·com·put·a·bil·i·ty (in′kəm·pyōō′tə·bil′ə·tē) *n.* That which is not computable.

in·con·ceiv·a·ble (in′kən·sē′və·bəl) *adj.* **1** That cannot be conceived; incomprehensible. **2** Incredible; impossible. **3** *Philos.* Involving a contradiction in terms; inherently contradictory. — **in′con·ceiv′a·ble·ness, in′con·ceiv′a·bil′i·ty** *n.* — **in′con·ceiv′a·bly** *adv.*

in·con·clu·sive (in′kən·klōō′siv) *adj.* **1** Not leading to an ultimate conclusion; indecisive. **2** Not achieving a definite result; ineffective: *inconclusive* efforts.

in·con·dite (in·kon′dit) *adj.* Badly constructed; irregular. [<L *inconditus* < *in-* not + *conditus*, pp. of *condere* put together]

in·con·gru·ent (in·kong′grōō·ənt) *adj.* Incongruous. — **in·con′gru·ence** *n.* — **in·con′gru·ent·ly** *adv.*

in·con·gru·i·ty (in′kən·grōō′ə·tē) *n. pl.* **·ties** **1** The state of being incongruous; lack of harmony or suitableness. **2** That which is incongruous. [<Med. L *incongruitas, -tatis*]

in·con·gru·ous (in·kong′grōō·əs) *adj.* **1** Not congruous. **2** Composed of inharmonious elements. — **in·con′gru·ous·ly** *adv.* — **in·con′gru·ous·ness** *n.*

Synonyms: absurd, conflicting, contradictory, contrary, discordant, discrepant, ill-matched, inapposite, inappropriate, incommensurable, incompatible, inconsistent, inharmonious, irreconcilable, mismatched, mismated, repugnant, unsuitable. Two or more things that do not fit well together, or are not adapted to each other, are said to be *incongruous*; a thing is said to be *incongruous* that is not adapted to the time, place, or occasion; the term is also applied to a thing made up of ill-assorted parts or *inharmonious* elements. *Discordant* is applied to all things that jar like musical notes that are not in accord; *inharmonious* has the same original sense, but is a milder term. Things are *incompatible* which cannot exist together in harmonious relations, and whose action when associated tends to ultimate extinction of one by the other. *Inconsistent* applies to things that cannot be made to agree in thought with each other, or with some standard of truth or right; slavery and freedom are *inconsistent* with each other in theory, and *incompatible* in fact. *Incongruous*

inconvincibility
inconvincible
incoordinate
incorresponding
incorrodible
increate
incurability
incurable
incuriosity
incurious
indecipherability
indecipherable
indeclinable
indecorous
indecorum
indefensibility
indeficiency
indefinitive
indemonstrability
indemonstrable
indescribable
indestructibility
indestructible
indestructibleness
indetectable
indevotion
indevout
indiscernible
indiscoverable
indiscussible
indisposable
indistinguishable
indivertible
individable
indivinity

applies to relations, *unsuitable* to purpose or use; two colors are *incongruous* which cannot be agreeably associated: either may be *unsuitable* for a person, a room, or an occasion. *Incommensurable* is a mathematical term, applying to two or more quantities that have no common measure or aliquot part. See CONTRARY. *Antonyms*: accordant, agreeing, compatible, consistent, harmonious, suitable.

in·con·se·quent (in·kon′sə·kwənt) *adj.* **1** Contrary to reasonable inference. **2** Not according to sequence; hence, irrelevant. **3** Illogical in thought or action; eccentric. **—in·con′se·quence** *n.* **—in·con′se·quent·ly** *adv.*

inconsequent drainage In physical geography, drainage established prior to the deformation of the drained section, and continuing after such a change in the earth's surface.

in·con·se·quen·tial (in′kon·sə·kwen′shəl, in·kon′-) *adj.* **1** Of little consequence; trivial. **2** Irrelevant. **—in·con′se·quen′ti·al′i·ty** (-kwen′·shē·al′ə·tē) *n.* **—in·con′se·quen′tial·ly** *adv.*

in·con·sid·er·ate (in′kən·sid′ər·it) *adj.* **1** Not considerate; thoughtless. **2** Showing want of consideration. See synonyms under BLUFF, IMPRUDENT, INATTENTIVE. **—in′con·sid′er·ate·ly** *adv.* **—in′con·sid′er·ate·ness** *n.* **—in′con·sid′·er·a′tion** *n.*

in·con·sis·ten·cy (in′kən·sis′tən·sē) *n. pl.* **·cies** **1** The state or quality of being inconsistent; logical incompatibility; lack of uniformity or coherence in thought or conduct. **2** That which is inconsistent. Also **in′con·sis′tence.**

in·con·sis·tent (in′kən·sis′tənt) *adj.* **1** Logically incompatible. **2** Self-contradictory. **3** Not consistent; capricious. See synonyms under CONTRARY, INCONGRUOUS. **—in′con·sis′tent·ly** *adv.*

in·con·spic·u·ous (in′kən·spik′yōō·əs) *adj.* **1** Not conspicuous; not prominent. **2** Not attracting attention to oneself.

in·con·stant (in·kon′stənt) *adj.* Not constant; fickle; variable. See synonyms under FICKLE, VAIN. [<F <L *inconstans, -antis*] **—in·con′·stan·cy** *n.* **—in·con′stant·ly** *adv.*

in·con·test·a·ble (in′kən·tes′tə·bəl) *adj.* Not admitting of controversy. [<F]

Synonyms: certain, impregnable, incontrovertible, indisputable, indubitable, irrefragable, unassailable, undeniable, undoubted, unquestionable. *Antonyms*: apocryphal, doubtful, dubious, fictitious, hypothetical, problematical, questionable, uncertain, unsustained, unverified.

in·con·ti·nent (in·kon′tə·nənt) *adj.* **1** Not continent; exercising no control over the appetites, especially sexual passion; unchaste. **2** Unrestrained: an *incontinent* passion. **3** *Pathol.* Unable to hold back bodily discharges or evacuations. **4** *Obs.* Immediate. **—** *adv.* *Archaic* Immediately. [<OF <L *incontinens, -entis.* See IN-[1], CONTINENT.] **—in·con′ti·nence, in·con′ti·nen·cy** *n.* **—in·con′ti·nent·ly** *adv.*

in·con·ven·ience (in′kən·vēn′yəns) *n.* **1** The state of being inconvenient. **2** A disadvantage; embarrassment. Also **in′con·ven′ien·cy.** **—** *v.t.* **·ienced, ·ienc·ing** To cause inconvenience to; incommode; trouble. [<OF]

in·con·ven·ient (in′kən·vēn′yənt) *adj.* **1** Not convenient; incommodious; embarrassing. **2** Not expedient; unsuitable. [<OF *inconvenient* <L *inconveniens, -entis.* See IN-[1], CONVENIENT.] **—in′con·ven′ient·ly** *adv.*

in·con·vert·i·ble (in′kən·vûr′tə·bəl) *adj.* Not interchangeable, as paper money into specie. **—in′con·vert′i·bil′i·ty** *n.*

in·co·or·di·na·tion (in′kō·ôr′də·nā′shən) *n.* **1** Lack of coordination. **2** *Physiol.* **a** Lack of balance or harmony between moving parts. **b** Inability to effect voluntary muscular actions in proper order and at adequate speed.

in·cor·po·rate[1] (in·kôr′pə·rāt) *v.* **·rat·ed, ·rat·ing** *v.t.* **1** To take into or include as part of a mass or whole: His philosophy *incorporates* the ideas of Hegel. **2** To form into a legal corporation. **3** To combine or unite into one body or whole; blend; mix. **4** *Rare* To give material form to; embody. **—** *v.i.* **5** To become combined or united as one body or whole. **6** To form a legal corporation. See synonyms under ENROL, MIX, UNITE. **—** *adj.* (-pər·it) **1** Joined, or intimately associated. **2** Incorporated. [<LL *incorporatus*, pp. of *incorporare* embody <*in-* in + *corporare.* See CORPORATE.] **—in·cor′po·ra′tive** *adj.*

in·cor·po·rate[2] (in·kôr′pər·it) *adj.* **1** Not consisting of matter; incorporeal. **2** Not formed into a corporation. [<L *incorporatus*]

in·cor·po·rat·ed (in·kôr′pə·rā′tid) *adj.* **1** Constituting a legal corporation. **2** Combined.

in·cor·po·ra·tion (in·kôr′pə·rā′shən) *n.* **1** The act of incorporating. **2** A corporation. **3** The combining of elements.

in·cor·po·ra·tor (in·kôr′pə·rā′tər) *n.* **1** One who forms a corporation. **2** One of the members of a corporation named in the incorporating charter.

in·cor·po·re·al (in′kôr·pôr′ē·əl, -pō′rē-) *adj.* **1** Not consisting of matter; immaterial. **2** Pertaining to the immaterial world. **3** Not appreciable by the senses. **4** *Law* Having no material existence, but regarded as existing by the law; intangible: *incorporeal* rights. Also *Obs.* **in·cor′po·ral** (in·kôr′pər·əl). [<L *incorporeus*] **—in′cor·po′re·al·ism** *n.* **—in′cor·po′re·al·ly** *adv.*

in·cor·po·re·i·ty (in′kôr·pə·rē′ə·tē) *n. pl.* **·ties** **1** The quality of being not material. **2** An incorporeal entity.

in·corpse (in·kôrps′) *v.t. Obs.* To incorporate.

in·cor·rect (in′kə·rekt′) *adj.* **1** Inaccurate or untrue. **2** Not proper; unsuitable. **3** Erroneous; faulty. **—in′cor·rect′ly** *adv.*

in·cor·ri·gi·ble (in·kôr′ə·jə·bəl, -kor′-) *adj.* **1** That cannot be corrected. **2** Depraved beyond reform. **—** *n.* One who is beyond correction. [<MF <*in-* not + *corrigible.* See CORRIGIBLE.] **—in·cor′ri·gi·ble·ness, in·cor′ri·gi·bil′i·ty** *n.* **—in·cor′ri·gi·bly** *adv.*

in·cor·rupt (in′kə·rupt′) *adj.* **1** Not depraved nor defiled morally; above the power of bribes; pure. **2** Not marred in physical substance; not acted upon by decay. **3** Not tainted by other idioms: free from error, as a language. **4** Unchanged; unaltered, as a text. Also **in′cor·rupt′ed.** [<L *incorruptus* <*in-* not + *corruptus.* See CORRUPT.] **—in′cor·rupt′ly** *adv.* **—in′cor·rupt′ness** *n.* **—in′cor·rup′tion** (-rup′shən) *n.* **—in′cor·rup′tive** *adj.*

in·cor·rupt·i·ble (in′kə·rup′tə·bəl) *adj.* Incapable of corruption; especially, not accessible to bribery. See synonyms under FAITHFUL, IMMORTAL, JUST, MORAL. **—in′cor·rupt′i·bil′i·ty, in′cor·rupt′i·ble·ness** *n.* **—in′cor·rupt′i·bly** *adv.*

in·cras·sate (in·kras′āt) *v.t.* & *v.i.* **·sat·ed, ·sat·ing** **1** To make or become thick or thicker. **2** To thicken (a fluid), as by mixing or evaporation. **—** *adj. Biol.* Thickened, as the antennae or femora of certain insects: also **in·cras′sat·ed.** [<L *incrassatus*, pp. of *incrassare* <*in-* very + *crassus* thick]

in·cras·sa·tion (in′kra·sā′shən) *n.* **1** The act or process of thickening. **2** A thickening or swelling. **—in·cras·sa·tive** (in·kras′ə·tiv) *adj.*

in·crease (in·krēs′) *v.* **·creased, ·creas·ing** *v.i.* **1** To become greater, as in amount, size, degree, etc.; grow. **2** To grow in numbers, especially by reproduction: May your tribe *increase.* **—** *v.t.* **3** To make greater, as in amount, size, degree, etc.; augment; enlarge. **—** *n.* (in′krēs) **1** The act or process of growing larger, as in quantity, size, degree, etc.; augmentation; enlargement; extension. **2** An added or increased amount; increment: an *increase* in pay. **3** A production of offspring; propagation: blessed with a large *increase.* **4** Offspring; progeny. **5** *Archaic.* Crops of the earth. [<OF *encreistre* <L *increscere* <*in-* in + *crescere* grow <*creare* create] **—in·creas′a·ble** *adj.* **—in·creas′ing·ly** *adv.*

Synonyms (verb): advance, aggravate, augment, enhance, enlarge, exaggerate, extend, heighten, intensify, magnify, prolong, raise. See ADD, AGGRAVATE, AMPLIFY, FLOURISH, PROPAGATE, SWELL. *Antonyms*: abbreviate, abridge, contract, curtail, decrease, diminish.

Synonyms (noun): access, accession, accretion, addendum, addition, aggravation, amplification, appendage, augmentation, complement, enhancement, enlargement, expansion, extension, growth, harvest, improvement, increment, product, reenforcement, return. See ACCESSION, HARVEST, PROGRESS. *Antonyms*: abbreviation, contraction, deduction, diminution, expenditure, loss, subtraction, waste.

in·creas·er (in·krē′sər) *n.* **1** One who or that which increases. **2** A breeder; grower. **3** A pipefitting for joining the female end of a small pipe to the male end of a large one. **4** *Obs.* One who advances or promotes.

in·cred·i·bil·i·ty (in·kred′ə·bil′ə·tē) *n. pl.* **·ties** **1** The state or quality of being unbelievable or hard to believe. **2** An unbelievable thing.

in·cred·i·ble (in·kred′ə·bəl) *adj.* **1** Seeming too far-fetched or extraordinary to be possible. **2** Beyond or difficult of belief. **—in·cred′i·ble·ness** *n.* **—in·cred′i·bly** *adv.*

in·cre·du·li·ty (in′krə·dōō′lə·tē, -dyōō′-) *n.* Indisposition or refusal to believe. See synonyms under DOUBT. Also **in·cred·u·lous·ness** (in·krej′ə·ləs·nis). [<OF *incredulité*]

in·cred·u·lous (in·krej′ə·ləs) *adj.* **1** Refusing belief; skeptical. **2** Characterized by, caused by, or manifesting doubt. **3** *Obs.* Incredible. [<L *incredulus* <*in-* not + *credulus.* See CREDULOUS.] **—in·cred′u·lous·ly** *adv.*

in·cre·mate (in′krə·māt) *v.t. Obs.* **·mat·ed, ·mat·ing** To cremate.

in·cre·ment (in′krə·mənt) *n.* **1** The act of increasing; enlargement. **2** That which is added; increase: opposed to *decrement.* **3** *Math.* The amount by which a varying quantity increases between two of its stages. **4** *Mil.* The quantity of powder added to, or subtracted from, the propelling charge of separate loaded artillery ammunition to compensate for differences in range. See synonyms under INCREASE. **—unearned increment** Any increase of value produced by forces independent of the person who receives it; specifically, increase of value in land that springs from the increase of population or other cause independent of the land itself and of its owner. [<L *incrementum* <*increscere* INCREASE] **—in′cre·men′tal** (-men′·təl) *adj.*

in·cres·cent (in·kres′ənt) *adj.* Characterized by increase; growing: said especially of the moon. [<L *increscens, -entis,* ppr. *of increscere* INCREASE]

in·cre·tion (in·krē′shən) *n.* Internal secretion or its product; a hormone. [<IN-[2] + (SE)CRETION]

in·crim·i·nate (in·krim′ə·nāt) *v.t.* **·nat·ed, ·nat·ing** **1** To charge with a crime or fault; accuse. **2** To show or appear to show the guilt or error of. [<Med. L *incriminatus,* pp. of *incriminare* <*in-* in + *criminare* accuse one of a crime] **—in·crim′i·na′tion** *n.* **—in·crim′i·na·to′ry** (-nə·tôr′ē, -tō′rē) *adj.*

in·croy·a·ble (aṅ·krwä·yà′bl′) *n. French* A member of the Royalist party in France who affected extravagance and foppery in dress and language during the French Directorate (1795–99). [<F, lit., incredible]

in·crust (in·krust′) *v.t.* **1** To cover with a crust or hard coat. **2** To decorate, as with jewels. Also spelled *encrust.* [<OF *encrouster* <L *incrustare* <*in-* on + *crustare* form a crust]

in·crus·ta·tion (in′krus·tā′shən) *n.* **1** The act of incrusting, or the state of being incrusted. **2** A crust, coating, or scale on the surface of a body.

in·cu·bate (in′kyə·bāt, ing′-) *v.* **·bat·ed, ·bat·ing** *v.t.* **1** To sit upon (eggs) in order to hatch; brood. **2** To hatch (eggs) in this manner or by artificial heat. **3** To maintain under conditions favoring optimum growth or development, as bacterial cultures. **—** *v.i.* **4** To sit on eggs; brood. **5** To undergo incubation. [<L *incubatus*, pp. of *incubare* <*in-* on + *cubare* lie] **—in′cu·ba′tive** *adj.*

in·cu·ba·tion (in′kyə·bā′shən, ing′-) *n.* **1** The act of hatching. **2** State of being hatched.

indivision	**inductile**	**ineffaceable**	**inelegance**	**inenergetic**	**inerrability**	**inevident**
indocibility	**inductility**	**inefficacious**	**inelegancy**	**inequable**	**inerrable**	**inexcitable**
indocible	**indurable**	**inefficacy**	**ineloquence**	**inequitable**	**inerratic**	**inexcusability**
indocile	**ineconomic**	**ineffulgent**	**ineloquent**	**ineradicable**	**inerroneous**	**inexecution**
indocility	**ineffaceability**	**inelaborate**	**ineludible**	**inerasable**	**inerudite**	**inexertion**

add,āce,câre,pälm; end,ēven; it,īce; odd,ōpen,ôrder; tŏŏk,pōōl; up,bûrn; ə = a in *above,* e in *sicken,* i in *clarity,* o in *melon,* u in *focus;* yōō = u in *fuse;* oi,oil; ou,pout; ch,check; g,go; ng,ring; th,thin; th,this; zh,vision. Foreign sounds à,œ,ü,kh,ṅ; and ◆: see page xx. < from; + plus; ? possibly.

3 A planning or producing. 4 Figuratively, a brooding upon, especially that of the Spirit of God over chaos at the Creation (*Gen.* i 2). 5 *Med.* The period between the time of exposure to an infectious disease and its development. [<L *incubatio, -onis*]

in·cu·ba·tor (in′kyə·bā′tər, ing′-) *n.* 1 An apparatus kept at a uniform warmth, as by a lamp, for artificial hatching of eggs. 2 *Bacteriol.* An apparatus for artificial development of micro-organisms, as bacteria, especially one in which the temperature may be regulated. 3 An appliance for keeping warm a prematurely born child. 4 One who or that which incubates. [<L, a hatcher]

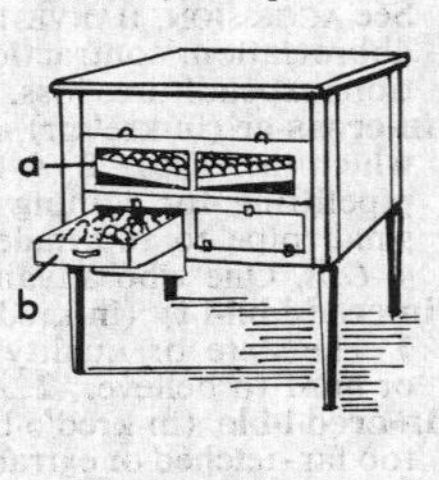

INCUBATOR
a. Egg tray.
b. Nursery drawer.
Incubators are variously heated by attached gas- or oil-fired heating units or by electrical units.

in·cu·bus (in′kyə·bəs, ing′-) *n.* *pl.* **·bus·es** or **·bi** (-bī) 1 Anything that tends to weigh down or discourage. 2 A nightmare. 3 A demon supposed to descend upon sleeping persons with whom it sought to have sexual intercourse. Compare SUCCUBUS. See synonyms under LOAD. [<Med. L, a demon that causes nightmare <LL, nightmare <L *incubare* lie on]

in·cu·des (in·kyōō′dēz) Plural of INCUS.

in·cul·cate (in·kul′kāt, in′kul-) *v.t.* **·cat·ed, ·cat·ing** To impress upon the mind by frequent and emphatic repetition; instil. See synonyms under IMPRESS. [<L *inculcatus*, pp. of *inculcare* tread on < *in-* on + *calcare* tread < *calx, calcis* heel] — **in·cul·ca·tion** (in′kul·kā′shən) *n.* — **in′cul·ca′tor** *n.*

in·cul·pa·ble (in·kul′pə·bəl) *adj.* Not culpable.

in·cul·pate (in·kul′pāt, in′kul-) *v.t.* **·pat·ed, ·pat·ing** 1 To charge with fault; blame. 2 To involve in guilt; implicate. [<Med. L *inculpatus*, pp. of *inculpare* blame < *in-* in + *culpa* fault] — **in′cul·pa′tion** *n.* — **in·cul′pa·to′ry** (-pə·tôr′ē, -tō′rē) *adj.*

in·cult (in·kult′) *adj.* *Obs.* 1 Uncultivated; unpolished. 2 Wanting in refinement. [<L < *in-* not + *cultus*, pp. of *colere* cultivate]

in·cum·ben·cy (in·kum′bən·sē) *n.* *pl.* **·cies** 1 The state of holding an office or discharging its duties or functions. 2 The period during which an office is held. 3 The state of being incumbent, or that which is incumbent, as a mental or physical burden. 4 *Rare* An obligation.

in·cum·bent (in·kum′bənt) *adj.* 1 Resting upon one as a moral obligation, or as necessary under the circumstances; obligatory. 2 Resting, leaning, or weighing wholly or partly upon something. — *n.* One who holds an office or performs official duties. [<L *incumbens, -entis*, ppr. of *incumbere* recline < *in-* on + *cubare* lie down]

in·cum·ber (in·kum′bər), **in·cum·brance** (in·kum′brəns), etc. See ENCUMBER, etc.

in·cu·nab·u·la (in′kyōō·nab′yə·lə) *n.* *pl.* *of* **in·cu·nab·u·lum** (-ləm) The beginnings or the earliest monuments of an art, race, or development; cradle; birthplace; specifically, specimens of printing and block engraving that appeared before A.D. 1500. [<L < *in-* in + *cunabula*, dim. of *cunae* a cradle] — **in′cu·nab′u·lar** *adj.*

in·cur (in·kûr′) *v.t.* **·curred, ·cur·ring** To meet with or become subject to, as unpleasant consequences, especially through one's own action; bring upon oneself. [<L *incurrere* run into < *in-* in + *currere* run]

in cu·ri·a (in kyŏŏr′ē·ə) *Latin* In court.

in·cur·rent (in·kûr′ənt) *adj.* Having or characterized by an inward-flowing current. [<L *incurrens, -entis*, ppr. of *incurrere* INCUR]

in·cur·sion (in·kûr′zhən, -shən) *n.* A hostile entrance into a territory; a temporary invasion; raid. See synonyms under AGGRESSION, ATTACK, INVASION. [<L *incursio, -onis* < *incurrere* INCUR] — **in·cur′sive** *adj.*

in·cur·vate (in·kûr′vāt) *v.t.* & *v.i.* **·vat·ed, ·vat·ing** To curve; bend, especially inwards. — *adj.* Curved. [<L *incurvatus*, pp. of *incurvare* curve inward < *in-* in + *curvare* curve]

in·cur·va·tion (in′kər·vā′shən) *n.* 1 The state of being curved or bent. 2 The act of bending. 3 The growing inward of the nails. 4 An ingrowing nail.

in·curve (in·kûrv′) *v.t.* & *v.i.* To curve inward. — *n.* (in′kûrv′) In baseball, a pitched ball that curves inward toward the batter.

in·cus (ing′kəs) *n.* *pl.* **in·cu·des** (in·kyōō′dēz) 1 *Anat.* The central one of three small bones in the tympanum or middle ear; so called from its fancied resemblance to an anvil. See illustration under EAR. 2 *Meteorol.* The anvil-shaped upper part of a cumulonimbus cloud; an anviltop. [<L, anvil] — **in′cu·dal** *adj.*

in·cuse (in·kyōōz′) *adj.* Formed by hammering or stamping. — *n.* An impression made by striking a coin with or against a die. [<L *incusus*, pp. of *incudere* forge with a hammer < *in-* on + *cudere* beat]

Ind (ind) 1 *Poetic* India. 2 *Obs.* The Indies.

In·da (in′də) See INDRA.

in·da·ba (in·dä′bä) *n.* A great meeting of South African natives; parliament; council. [<Zulu *in–daba* subject, matter]

in·da·gate (in′də·gāt) *v.t.* *Obs.* **·gat·ed, ·gat·ing** To investigate. [<L *indagatus*, pp. of *indagare* investigate] — **in′da·ga′tion** *n.* — **in′da·ga′tor** *n.*

in·da·mine (in′də·mēn, -min) *Chem.* Any of a class of weak, unstable, organic bases derived from anilines which form bluish and greenish salts: also called *phenylene blue*. Also **in′da·min** (-min). [<IND(IGO) + AMINE]

in·debt·ed (in·det′id) *adj.* 1 Having contracted a debt. 2 Owing gratitude; beholden. [<OF *endetté*, pp. of *endetter* < *en-* on + *dette* debt. See DEBT.]

in·debt·ed·ness (in·det′id·nis) *n.* 1 The state of being indebted. 2 The amount of one's debts.

in·de·cen·cy (in·dē′sən·sē) *n.* *pl.* **·cies** 1 The condition of being indecent; especially, vulgarity or immorality in actions, spoken or printed words, pictures, etc. 2 An indecent act. 3 Obscenity.

Synonyms: coarseness, filthiness, foulness, grossness, immodesty, impropriety, impurity, indecorum, indelicacy, obscenity, offensiveness, uncleanness, unseemliness, vileness. See OUTRAGE. *Antonyms*: delicacy, modesty, nicety, propriety, purity, refinement.

in·de·cent (in·dē′sənt) *adj.* 1 Offensive to decency or propriety; immodest; gross. 2 Contrary to what is fit and proper. See synonyms under IMMODEST. — **in·de′cent·ly** *adv.*

in·de·cid·u·ate (in′də·sij′ōō·it) *adj.* Without a decidua.

in·de·cid·u·ous (in′də·sij′ōō·əs) *adj.* *Bot.* Not dropping off at maturity; evergreen.

in·de·ci·sive (in′də·sī′siv) *adj.* 1 Not decisive. 2 Hesitant; irresolute. — **in′de·ci′sive·ly** *adv.* — **in′de·ci′sion** *n.*

in·deed (in·dēd′) *adv.* In fact; in truth: used to emphasize an affirmation, to mark a qualifying word or clause, to denote a concession, or interrogatively for the purpose of drawing forth confirmation of a fact stated. — *interj.* An exclamation of surprise, irony, incredulity, etc. [<IN + DEED]

in·de·fat·i·ga·ble (in′də·fat′ə·gə·bəl) *adj.* Not yielding readily to fatigue; tireless; unflagging. [<MF *indéfatigable* <L *indefatigabilis* < *in-* not + *defatigare* tire out] — **in′de·fat′i·ga·bil′i·ty, in′de·fat′i·ga·ble·ness** *n.* — **in′de·fat′i·ga·bly** *adv.*

Synonyms: assiduous, indomitable, industrious, never-failing, never-tiring, persevering, persistent, tireless, unfailing, unfaltering, unflagging, untiring, unwearied. *Antonyms*: defeated, despondent, discouraged, fainting, faltering, flagging, indolent, negligent, remiss, wearied.

in·de·fea·si·ble (in′də·fē′zə·bəl) *adj.* Not defeasible; incapable of being annulled, set aside, or made void. — **in′de·fea′si·bil′i·ty** *n.* — **in′de·fea′si·bly** *adv.*

in·de·fen·si·ble (in′di·fen′sə·bəl) *adj.* 1 Incapable of being justified, excused, etc. 2 Incapable of being defended.

in·de·fin·a·ble (in′di·fī′nə·bəl) *adj.* That cannot be defined or described; vague; subtle. — **in′de·fin′a·ble·ness** *n.* — **in′de·fin′a·bly** *adv.*

in·def·i·nite (in·def′ə·nit) *adj.* 1 Not definite or precise. 2 Indeterminate; without fixed boundaries; incapable of measurement. 3 So large as to have no definite or particular limit; also, infinite. 4 *Bot.* Uncertain: said of stamens when too many to be counted easily, and of inflorescence when not terminated absolutely by a flower. 5 *Gram.* Not defining or determining; tending to generalize, as the *indefinite* articles *a* and *an*. See synonyms under EQUIVOCAL, VAGUE. — **in·def′i·nite·ly** *adv.* — **in·def′i·nite·ness** *n.*

indefinite pronoun See under PRONOUN.

in·de·his·cent (in′də·his′ənt) *adj.* *Bot.* Not opening spontaneously or naturally when ripe: said of certain grains and fruits. — **in′de·his′cence** *n.*

in·del·i·ble (in·del′ə·bəl) *adj.* That cannot be blotted out; ineffaceable. [<L *indelibilis* < *in-* not + *delibilis* perishable < *delere* destroy] — **in·del′i·bil′i·ty, in·del′i·ble·ness** *n.* — **in·del′i·bly** *adv.*

in·del·i·ca·cy (in·del′ə·kə·sē) *n.* *pl.* **·cies** 1 The quality of being indelicate; coarseness. 2 An act offensive to propriety or refined feeling.

in·del·i·cate (in·del′ə·kit) *adj.* Not delicate; offensive to propriety; immodest. See synonyms under IMMODEST. — **in·del′i·cate·ly** *adv.*

in·dem·ni·fy (in·dem′nə·fī) *v.t.* **·fied, ·fy·ing** 1 To compensate for loss or damage sustained. 2 To make good (a loss). 3 To give security against future loss or punishment to. See synonyms under PAY. [<L *indemnis* unhurt (< *in-* not + *damnum* harm) + -FY] — **in·dem′ni·fi·ca′tion** *n.* — **in·dem′ni·tor** (-nə·tər) *n.*

in·dem·ni·ty (in·dem′nə·tē) *n.* *pl.* **·ties** 1 That which is given as compensation for a loss or for damage. 2 An undertaking to remunerate another for loss or to protect him against liability. 3 Exemption from penalties or liabilities incurred. See synonyms under RECOMPENSE, RESTITUTION, SUBSIDY. [<F *indemnité* <L *indemnitas* < *indemnis*. See INDEMNIFY.]

indemnity bond See under BOND.

in·dene (in′dēn) *n.* *Chem.* A colorless, oily hydrocarbon, C_9H_8, obtained from coal tar by fractional distillation. [<IND(OLE) + -ENE]

in·dent (in·dent′) *v.t.* 1 To set, as the first line of a paragraph, in from the margin. 2 To cut or mark the edge of with toothlike hollows or notches; serrate. 3 To make an order for goods upon. 4 To make an order for (goods). 5 To cut or tear (a document drawn in duplicate) along an irregular line in order to identify the halves when fitted together. 6 To cut or tear the edge or top of (a document) in an irregular line. 7 To indenture, as an apprentice. — *v.i.* 8 To be notched or cut; form a recess. 9 To set a line, etc., in from the margin. 10 To make out an order in duplicate; make a requisition. 11 *Archaic* To enter into a bargain or covenant. — *n.* (in′dent, in·dent′) 1 A cut or notch in the edge of anything; an opening like a notch; an indentation or impression. 2 An indented contract; indenture. 3 An indented certificate issued by the United States government at the close of the American Revolution, for principal or interest due on the public debt. 4 An official order for supplies. 5 In commerce, a foreign order for goods, with or without specified particulars as to quality, price, mode of shipment, etc. 6 An indention. [<OF *endenter* <Med. L *indentare* < *in-* in + *dens, dentis* tooth]

in·den·ta·tion (in′den·tā′shən) *n.* 1 The act of denting. 2 A cut or notch in an edge or border. 3 An indention. See synonyms under HOLE.

in·dent·ed (in·den′tid) *adj.* 1 *Archit.* **a** Notched or serrated. **b** Formed into several angles: said of a parapet. 2 *Her.* Toothed like a saw. 3 In printing or typewriting, set in from the margin. 4 Indentured.

in·den·tion (in·den′shən) *n.* 1 A dent. 2 *Printing* **a** The setting in of a line or body of type at the left side. **b** The space thus left blank.

inexhausted	**inexpectant**	**inexpert**	**inexplosive**	**inextinguishable**	**infeminine**	**inirritability**
inexhaustibility	**inexpedience**	**inexpiable**	**inexpressive**	**infeasible**	**infrequence**	**inobservable**
inexistence	**inexpediency**	**inexplainable**	**inextensibility**	**infecund**	**infrugal**	**inobtrusive**
inexistency	**inexpedient**	**inexplicability**	**inextensible**	**infecundity**	**inhomogeneity**	**inoppressive**
inexistent	**inexperience**	**inexplicit**	**inextension**	**infelonious**	**inhomogeneous**	**inoppugnable**

—hanging indention *Printing* Equal indention of all lines of a paragraph except the first, which is not indented.

in·den·ture (in·den′chər) *n.* 1 *Law* An instrument of contract under seal; an instrument in duplicate between parties, each party keeping a counterpart. 2 *Often pl.* A legal instrument for binding an apprentice or a servant to his master. 3 The act of indenting, or the state of being indented. —*v.t.* **·tured, ·tur·ing** 1 To bind by indenture, as an apprentice. 2 To indent; furrow. [<OF *endenture* <Med. L *indentare*. See INDENT.]

in·de·pen·dence (in′di·pen′dəns) *n.* 1 Freedom from dependence upon others, as for government or financial support. 2 A competency. 3 A spirit of self–reliance. See synonyms under LIBERTY, WEALTH. See DECLARATION OF INDEPENDENCE.

Independence Day The Fourth of July: so called in the United States in commemoration of the Declaration of Independence, adopted July 4, 1776.

in·de·pen·den·cy (in′di·pen′dən·sē) *n. pl.* **·cies** 1 Independence. 2 An independent state or territory.

In·de·pen·den·cy (in′di·pen′dən·sē) *n. Eccl.* The doctrine that each congregation of the Christian church is an entity independent of central ecclesiastical control.

in·de·pen·dent (in′di·pen′dənt) *adj.* 1 Not subordinate or subject to nor dependent for support upon another government, person, or thing. 2 Affording means of independence or freedom of action. 3 Indicating self–reliance; resentful of, or uninfluenced by, advice or assistance. 4 Separate or disconnected. 5 Pertaining to the Independents or Congregationalists. 6 Not identified with any political party. 7 Possessing sufficient means to live without labor. 8 *Math.* a Capable of taking any value without regard to the variation of other quantities. b Denoting two or more quantities such that the value of none of them depends upon that of the others. —*n.* 1 One who exercises his own will or judgment without the guidance or control of others. 2 *Often cap.* One who is not an adherent of any political party. —**in′de·pen′dent·ly** *adv.*

In·de·pen·dent (in′di·pen′dənt) *n.* 1 A believer in Independency. 2 In England, a Congregationalist.

independent clause *Gram.* A clause capable of constituting a sentence.

in–depth (in′depth′) *adj.* Extensive and thorough; not superficial; penetrating or profound: an *in–depth* study of world–wide intelligence operations.

in·de·ter·mi·na·ble (in′di·tûr′mi·nə·bəl) *adj.* 1 Not capable of exact determination or measurement. 2 Not decided or clearly established. —**in′de·ter′mi·na·bly** *adv.*

in·de·ter·mi·na·cy (in′di·tûr′mə·nə·sē) *n.* The state of being indefinite or undetermined; lack of certainty.

indeterminacy principle The uncertainty principle.

in·de·ter·mi·nate (in′di·tûr′mə·nit) *adj.* 1 Not definite in extent, amount, or nature. 2 Not clear or precise; vague. 3 Not decided; unsettled. 4 *Bot.* Not definitely terminated, as a raceme. 5 *Math.* Designating any of a class of undefined expressions, as infinity minus infinity, zero divided by infinity, zero to the zero power, etc. —**in′de·ter′mi·nate·ly** *adv.* —**in′de·ter′mi·nate·ness** *n.*

in·de·ter·mi·na·tion (in′di·tûr′mə·nā′shən) *n.* 1 Lack of determination. 2 The state of being indeterminate.

in·de·ter·min·ism (in′di·tûr′mə·niz′əm) *n.* The doctrine that the will, while influenced, is not absolutely determined by motives or environment. —**in′de·ter′min·ist** *n.*

in·dex (in′deks) *n. pl.* **·dex·es** or **·di·ces** (-də·sēz) 1 Anything used to indicate, point out, or guide, as the index finger, or forefinger, the hand of a clock, a pointer, etc. 2 Anything that manifests or denotes: an *index* of character. 3 An alphabetic list of matters or references, as in a book. 4 *Math.* An exponent. 5 A mark [☞] employed to direct attention. 6 A numerical expression of the ratio between one dimension or magnitude and another with which it is regarded as comparable: the cephalic *index*. 7 *Obs.* A prolog; prelude. —*v.t.* 1 To provide with an index. 2 To enter in an index. 3 To indicate; mark. [<L. See INDICATE.] —**in′dex·er** *n.* —**in·dex′i·cal** *adj.*

In·dex (in′deks) *n.* A list of interdicted books prepared by the Holy Office of the Roman Catholic Church. The *Index Expurgatorius*, no longer officially prepared, indicated those books which, with certain expurgations, might be read; the *Index Librorum Prohibitorum*, those which are forbidden.

index finger The forefinger: so called from its universal use as a pointer or indicator.

index number *Stat.* Any of a series of numbers indicating the quantitative time changes in a given statistical aggregate, as prices, costs, etc., with reference to an arbitrary base (usually 100) which represents the status of the aggregate at a specified previous time or period.

index of refraction *Optics* The ratio of the sine of the angle of incidence to that of the angle of refraction when light enters a transparent substance.

In·di·a (in′dē·ə) The central peninsula of southern Asia, south of the Himalayas; 1,581,000 square miles: ancient *Bharat*; divided into: (1) the **Republic of India**, a self–governing member of the Commonwealth of Nations; 1,138,814 square miles; capital, New Delhi; (2) Pakistan; (3) several smaller states unaffiliated with the Commonwealth.

India ink 1 A black pigment composed of a mixture of lampblack or burnt cork with gelatin and water, originally made in India, China, and Japan and molded in sticks or cakes. 2 A liquid ink made from this pigment. 3 Any of various heavy drawing inks in different colors, especially one containing sepia. Also called *Chinese ink.*

In·di·a·man (in′dē·ə·mən) *n. pl.* **·men** (-mən) A large merchant ship in the India trade, especially one in the service of the East India Company.

In·di·an (in′dē·ən) *adj.* 1 Pertaining to India or the East Indies or to Indians. 2 Pertaining to the American aboriginal race or to the West Indies. 3 Made from maize. —*n.* 1 A native of India or of the East Indies. 2 A member of the aboriginal race of America (American Indian) or of the West Indies. 3 Loosely, any of the languages of the American Indians. [<L *India* <Gk. <*Indos* the Indus river <OPersian *Hindu* India <Skt. *sindhu* river. Cf. HINDI.]

In·di·an·a (in′dē·an′ə) A north central State of the United States; 36,291 square miles; capital, Indianapolis; entered the Union Dec. 11, 1816; nickname, *Hoosier State*: abbr. IN —**In′·di·an′i·an** *adj. & n.*

Indian agent *U.S. & Canadian* A federal representative in Indian affairs, often on a reservation.

In·di·an·ap·o·lis (in′dē·ə·nap′ə·lis) The capital of Indiana.

Indian bean The catalpa tree (*Catalpa bignonioides*) of China, the West Indies, and the United States: it yields a fine, durable wood adapted for cabinetwork.

Indian bread Tuckahoe.

Indian clubs See under CLUB[1].

Indian corn Maize.

Indian Desert See THAR DESERT.

Indian field *U.S.* A clearing in a forest, known or believed to have once been cultivated by Indians.

Indian file Single file: the usual order of the American Indians when walking a trail.

Indian giver *U.S. Colloq.* One who gives a present and then wants it back.

Indian hemp 1 The common Asian hemp (*Cannabis sativa*). 2 A perennial American herb (*Apocynum cannabinum*) of the dogbane family, with a tough bark, greenish–white flowers, and a milky juice: its dried roots have medicinal properties: also called *Canada hemp, hemp dogbane, Indian physic.*

Indian licorice Jequirity.

Indian mallow A tall weed (*Abutilon incanum*) with large velvety leaves and small yellow flowers.

Indian meal Cornmeal.

Indian millet The tall grass (*Sorghum vulgare*) of which sorgo, broomcorn, and durra are varieties.

Indian mulberry The aal.

Indian Mutiny An uprising in India (1857–1858) occasioned by native resentment against British colonial policies: also called *Sepoy Mutiny.*

Indian Ocean The smallest of the three great oceans of the world, bounded by Africa, Asia, Australia, and Antarctica; 28,357,000 square miles.

Indian paintbrush A flower, the painted cup.

Indian physic 1 Either of two perennial herbs (genus *Gillenia*) common in the woods of the United States, and reputed to be emetic, cathartic, or tonic, according to the dose. 2 Indian hemp (def. 2).

Indian pipe A low, smooth, waxy–white, one-flowered, saprophytic, somewhat pipe–shaped herb (*Monotropa uniflora*) common in moist woodlands of Asia and North America.

Indian pudding A pudding made with cornmeal, milk, and molasses.

Indian red 1 A pure native iron oxide found in India and used as a pigment. 2 A red earth used by the American Indian and by early American painters.

Indian rice See WILD RICE.

Indian River A lagoon of eastern Florida, extending 120 miles between the mainland and a coastal strip.

Indian States Formerly, the 560 semi–independent states of British India ruled by native princes: also *Native States.*

Indian summer See under SUMMER.

Indian Territory Formerly, a Territory of the United States: now a part of Oklahoma.

Indian tobacco An erect, hairy, branched herb (*Lobelia inflata*) with ovate, obtusely toothed leaves and small, pale–blue flowers. Compare LOBELINE.

Indian turnip Jack–in–the–pulpit.

In·di·an–wres·tle (in′dē·ən·res′əl) *v.i.* **·tled, ·tling** To engage in any of various contests of strength and agility in which two people grasp hands, lock legs, etc., and attempt to force each other into an inferior position.

India paper 1 A thin, yellowish, absorbent printing paper, made in China and Japan from vegetable fiber, and used in taking the finest proofs from engraved plates. 2 A thin, tough, and opaque printing paper, originally from the Orient, used for Bibles, etc.

India print Lightweight cotton fabric, usually handblocked in Oriental patterns and rich colors.

India proof A proof taken on India paper.

India rubber A soft and elastic substance derived from the sap of various tropical plants and having many uses in industry and the arts; caoutchouc. See RUBBER.

In·dic (in′dik) *adj.* Pertaining to India, its peoples, languages, and culture; Indian. —*n.* A branch of the Indo–Iranian subfamily of Indo–European languages, including many of the ancient and modern languages of India, as Sanskrit, Gujarati, Hindi, Bengali, Romany, etc. [<L *Indicus* <Gk. *Indikos* <*India* INDIA]

in·di·can (in′də·kən) *n.* 1 *Chem.* A colorless, crystalline, toxic glycoside, $C_{14}H_{17}O_6N$, contained in several species of indigo plants. 2 *Biochem.* Potassium indoxyl sulfate, $C_8H_6NSO_4K$, contained in the urine and other body fluids of certain animals, including man:

inopulent	insapient	insonorous	intranquility	intranslatable	inurbanity	inverity
inostensible	insaturable	insubduable	intranscalent	intransmissible	inutilized	invirile
insagacity	insensuous	insubmergible	intransferable	intransmutable	inutterable	invirility
insalutary	inseverable	insubmissible	intransformable	intransparent	invalorous	inviscid
insalvable	insolidity	insubvertible	intransfusible	inurbane	inverisimilitude	invital

also called *uroxanthin.* [<L *indicum* INDIGO + -AN]

in·di·cant (in′də·kənt) *adj.* Indicating. —*n.* An indicator.

in·di·cate (in′də·kāt) *v.t.* **·cat·ed, ·cat·ing** **1** To be or give a sign of; betoken: Those clouds *indicate* rain. **2** To point out; direct attention to: to *indicate* the correct page. **3** To express or make known, especially briefly or indirectly: His smile *indicates* his approval. **4** *Med.* To show or suggest, as a disease or its remedy: said of symptoms, etc. [<L *indicatus,* pp. of *indicare* <*in-* in + *dicare* point out, proclaim] —**in′di·ca·to′ry** (-kə·tôr′ē, -tō′rē) *adj.*

in·di·ca·tion (in′də·kā′shən) *n.* **1** The act of indicating, in any sense; manifestation; prediction. **2** That which indicates or suggests; a token; sign; symptom. **3** *Med.* The manifestation afforded by the symptoms of a disease as to the course of treatment. See synonyms under CHARACTERISTIC, MARK[1], SIGN. [<F]

in·dic·a·tive (in·dik′ə·tiv) *adj.* **1** Suggestive; giving intimation. **2** *Gram.* Of or pertaining to a mood in which an act or condition is stated or questioned as an actual fact, rather than as a potentiality or an unrealized condition. —*n. Gram.* The indicative mood, or a verb in this mood. —**in·dic′a·tive·ly** *adv.*

in·di·ca·tor (in′də·kā′tər) *n.* **1** One who or that which indicates or points out. **2** Any contrivance or apparatus, automatic or otherwise, which makes a mark, record, or sign to indicate the condition or position of something: a water gage; a speed indicator; a dial showing the position of elevators, cages, etc.; a device for recording the arrival and departure of trains, the number of fares collected in street cars, etc. **3** An instrument attached to a steam engine which, by the action of the steam itself, draws an **indicator-diagram** from which may be ascertained the gross power, the correct adjustment of the distribution valves, the ratio of the pressure in the cylinder to the boiler pressure, etc. **4** *Chem.* A substance, as litmus, potassium permanganate, etc., which colors a solution and by its disappearance, reappearance, or change of color when a reagent is added, indicates alkalinity, acidity, etc. **5** *Ecol.* A type of vegetation or plant growth serving to indicate the general character of a habitat. [<LL]

in·di·ca·tor–reg·u·la·tor (in′də·kā′tər·reg′yə·lā′·tər) *n. Mil.* A device which supplies data on the various elements, as timing, elevation, etc., required for accurate firing of a gun.

in·di·ces (in′də·sēz) Plural of INDEX: used especially in mathematical or other abstract works.

in·di·cia (in·dish′ə) *n. pl. sing.,* **·di·cium** (-dish′·əm) Discriminating marks; indications; badges; tokens; symptoms. [<L, pl. of *indicium* sign]

in·dict (in·dīt′) *v.t.* **1** *Law* To prefer an indictment against: said of the action of grand juries. **2** To charge with a crime. See synonyms under ARRAIGN. ◆ Homophone: *indite.* [<AF *enditer* make known, inform; later infl. in form by Med. L *dictare* accuse. Related to INDITE.] —**in·dict′a·ble** *adj.* —**in·dict·ee** (in·dī·tē′) *n.* —**indict′er, in·dict′or** *n.*

in·dic·tion (in·dik′shən) *n.* **1** A cycle of fifteen years, introduced by Constantine as a fiscal term, and adopted by the popes as part of their chronological system. **2** The number of one of these cycles, or that of any particular year in its cycle. [<OF <L *indictio, -onis* <*indicere* announce <*in-* in + *dicere* say, tell]

in·dict·ment (in·dīt′mənt) *n.* **1** The act of indicting, or the state of being indicted; formal charge or accusation in general. **2** A formal written charge of crime, preferred at the suit of the government and presented by a grand jury on oath to the court in which it is impaneled, as the basis for trial of the accused; the legal document itself. [<AF *enditement*]

In·dies (in′dēz) **1** The East Indies. **2** The East Indies, India, and Indochina. **3** The West Indies.

in·dif·fer·ence (in·dif′ər·əns) *n.* **1** The state of being unconcerned or indifferent; lack of interest or feeling; apathy; freedom from prejudice or bias. **2** The quality of not arousing interest or approval; a low degree of excellence; immateriality; slight importance. See synonyms under APATHY, NEGLECT. Also **in·dif′fer·en·cy.**

in·dif·fer·ent (in·dif′ər·ənt) *adj.* **1** Having no inclination or interest; apathetic. **2** Only passably or tolerably good or large; mediocre; ordinary. **3** Awakening no concern or preference; unimportant. **4** Unprejudiced; with no predominating tendency; impartial. **5** *Biol.* **a** Undifferentiated; not specialized, as plant or animal tissue. **b** Denoting a species of plants or animals found in diversified habitats. **6** Not active; neutral: said of chemical compounds, parts of magnets, etc. —*n.* **1** An apathetic person. **2** An object of indifference. —*adv. Obs.* Tolerably. [<OF *indifferent* <L *indifferens.* See IN-[1], DIFFERENT.] —**in·dif′fer·ent·ly** *adv.*

in·dif·fer·ent·ism (in·dif′ər·ən·tiz′əm) *n.* **1** The doctrine that the differences in religious faiths are of no importance. **2** The doctrine that to be in thought and in reality are one and the same thing; the doctrine of absolute identity. **3** Habitual or systematic indifference. —**in·dif′fer·ent·ist** *n.*

in·di·gen (in′də·jən) *n.* A person, animal, or thing native to the soil; aboriginal; autochthon: distinguished from *cultigen.* Also **in′de·gene** (-jēn). [<F *indigène*]

in·dig·e·nous (in·dij′ə·nəs) *adj.* **1** Originating in a (specified) place or country; not exotic; native. **2** Innate; inherent. See synonyms under NATIVE, PRIMEVAL. Also **in·dig′e·nal.** [<LL *indigenus* <L *indigena* native <*indu-* within + *gen-,* root of *gignere* beget] —**in·dig′e·nous·ly** *adv.* —**in·dig′e·nous·ness** *n.*

in·di·gent (in′də·jənt) *adj.* Destitute of property; poor. [<F <L *indigens, -entis,* ppr. of *indigere* lack, want <*indu-* within + *egere* need] —**in′di·gence, in′di·gen·cy** *n.*

in·di·gest (in′də·jest′) *Obs. adj.* Undigested; confused. —*n.* A disordered mass. [<L *indigestus*] —**in′di·gest′ed** *adj.*

in·di·gest·i·ble (in′də·jes′tə·bəl) *adj.* Not digestible; difficult to digest. —**in′di·gest′i·bil′·i·ty, in′di·gest′i·ble·ness** *n.* —**in′di·gest′i·bly** *adv.*

in·di·ges·tion (in′də·jes′chən) *n.* Defective digestion; dyspepsia. [<F]

In·di·gir·ka (in′di·gir′kə) A river in NE Siberia, flowing 1,113 miles north to the Siberian Sea.

in·dign (in·dīn′) *adj. Obs.* Unworthy. [<MF *indigne* <L *indignus*]

in·dig·nant (in·dig′nənt) *adj.* **1** Having just anger and scorn. **2** Manifesting or provoked by such a feeling. [<L *indignans, -antis,* ppr. of *indignari* regard as unworthy <*indignus* unworthy] —**in·dig′nant·ly** *adv.*

in·dig·na·tion (in′dig·nā′shən) *n.* Just resentment. See synonyms under ANGER. [<OF <*indignatio, -onis* <*indignari* think unworthy]

in·dig·ni·ty (in·dig′nə·tē) *n. pl.* **·ties** **1** An act tending to degrade or mortify; an insult; affront. **2** *Obs.* Base character or conduct; also, anger aroused thereby. See synonyms under OFFENSE, OUTRAGE. [<L *indignitas, -tatis* <*indignus*]

in·di·go (in′də·gō) *n.* **1** A blue coloring substance, $C_{16}H_{10}N_2O_2$, obtained by the decomposition of indican, contained in the indigo plant and now synthetically produced from various aromatic hydrocarbons. Mixed with oil, it forms a paint of great body, but one easily decomposed by impure air. **2** A deep violet blue: often used adjectivally. **3** The indigo plant. [<Sp. <L *indicum* <Gk. *Indikon (pharmakon)* Indian (dye), neut. of *Indikos* Indian]

indigo blue **1** The blue coloring substance of crude indigo; indigotin. **2** Any similar dark-blue color.

indigo bunting A North American finch *(Passerina cyanea),* the male of brilliant indigo-blue color and the female brownish: often called *lazuli finch.* Also **indigo bird.**

in·di·goid (in′də·goid) *adj.* Pertaining to or designating a class of vat dyes resembling indigo.

indigo plant Any of several plants yielding indigo, especially the tropical shrub *Indigofera tinctoria,* and woad.

indigo snake The gopher snake.

in·dig·o·tin (in·dig′ə·tin, in′də·gō′tin) *n.* Pure indigo: it occurs as a dark-blue crystalline compound, $C_{16}H_{10}N_2O_2$, extracted from indican and made synthetically. Also **indigo blue.** [<INDIGO + *-t-* + -IN]

in·di·rect (in′də·rekt′) *adj.* **1** Deviating from a direct line in space. **2** Not in the direct line of derivation or succession: *indirect* descent. **3** Not in direct relation; not tending to a result by the shortest or plainest course; inferential. **4** Designating gunfire aimed at a target which cannot be seen by sighting at a known aiming point. **5** Not morally direct; tending to mislead or deceive: *indirect* conduct. **6** Not in the exact words of the speaker. —**in′di·rect′ly** *adv.* —**in′di·rect′ness** *n.*

indirect discourse See under DISCOURSE.

in·di·rec·tion (in′də·rek′shən) *n.* **1** Indirect course of practice. **2** Dishonest means; deceit.

indirect lighting Lighting that is reflected, as from a white ceiling, or diffused to give a minimum of glare and shadow.

indirect object See under OBJECT.

in·dis·creet (in′dis·krēt′) *adj.* Lacking discretion; imprudent. See synonyms under IMPRUDENT. —**in′dis·creet′ly** *adv.* —**in′dis·creet′·ness** *n.*

in·dis·cre·tion (in′dis·kresh′ən) *n.* **1** The state of being indiscreet. **2** An indiscreet act.

in·dis·crim·i·nate (in′dis·krim′ə·nit) *adj.* **1** Showing no discrimination. **2** Mingled in confusion. —**in′dis·crim′i·nate·ly** *adv.* —**in′·dis·crim′i·nate·ness** *n.* —**in′dis·crim′i·nat′ing** *adj.* —**in′dis·crim′i·na′tion** *n.*

in·dis·pen·sa·ble (in′dis·pen′sə·bəl) *adj.* Not to be dispensed with; necessary or requisite for a purpose. See synonyms under INHERENT, NECESSARY. —*n.* An indispensable person or thing. —**in′dis·pen′sa·bil′i·ty, in′dis·pen′sa·ble·ness** *n.* —**in′dis·pen′sa·bly** *adv.*

in·dis·pose (in′dis·pōz′) *v.t.* **·posed, ·pos·ing** **1** To render unwilling or averse; disincline. **2** To render unfit; disqualify. **3** To make ill or ailing.

in·dis·posed (in′dis·pōzd′) *adj.* **1** Ill; unwell. **2** Disinclined. See synonyms under RELUCTANT. —**in′dis·posed′ness** (-pōzd′-, -pō′zid-) *n.*

in·dis·po·si·tion (in′dis·pə·zish′ən) *n.* **1** Slight illness. **2** The state of being mentally disinclined. See synonyms under ILLNESS.

in·dis·put·a·ble (in′dis·pyōō′tə·bəl, in·dis′pyōō·tə·bəl) *adj.* Incapable of being disputed; unquestionable. See synonyms under INCONTESTABLE, SURE. [<LL *indisputabilis*] —**in′·dis·put′a·bil′i·ty, in′dis·put′a·ble·ness** *n.* —**in′·dis·put′a·bly** *adv.*

in·dis·sol·u·ble (in′di·sol′yə·bəl, in·dis′ə·lyə·bəl) *adj.* **1** That cannot be dissolved, liquefied, or melted. **2** Perpetually binding. Also **in·dis·solv·a·ble** (in′di·zol′və·bəl). See synonyms under IMMORTAL. [<L *indissolubilis*] —**in′dis·sol′u·bil′i·ty, in′dis·sol′u·ble·ness** *n.* —**in′dis·sol′u·bly** *adv.*

in·dis·tinct (in′dis·tingkt′) *adj.* **1** Not clearly distinguishable or separable by senses or intellect; not distinct; confused; dim; vague; obscure. **2** Not presenting clear and well-defined images or impressions; obscured. **3** Indiscriminate. See synonyms under EQUIVOCAL, OBSCURE. [<L *indistinctus*] —**in′dis·tinct′ly** *adv.*

in·dis·tinc·tion (in′dis·tingk′shən) *n.* **1** Want of distinction; indiscrimination; confusion. **2** Equality of rank or condition. **3** Indistinctness.

in·dis·tinc·tive (in′dis·tingk′tiv) *adj.* **1** Having no distinguishing quality. **2** Incapable of distinguishing. —**in′dis·tinc′tive·ly** *adv.* —**in′·dis·tinc′tive·ness** *n.*

in·dis·tinct·ness (in′dis·tingkt′nis) *n.* **1** Lack of distinctness; obscurity; faintness. **2** Lack of mental qualities necessary for the purpose of making a clear distinction; indistinguishableness.

in·dite (in·dīt′) *v.t.* **·dit·ed, ·dit·ing** **1** To put into words or writing; write; compose. **2** *Obs.* To dictate. ◆ Homophone: *indict.* [<AF *enditer* make known, inform <L *in-* in + *dictare* declare. Related to INDICT.] —**in·dite′·ment** *n.* —**in·dit′er** *n.*

in·di·um (in′dē·əm) *n.* A soft malleable silver-white metallic element (symbol In), found in very small quantities in sphalerite and many other ores. See ELEMENT. [<NL <*indicum* indigo + -IUM; with ref. to its spectrum color]

in·di·vid·u·al (in′də·vij′ōō·əl) *adj.* **1** Existing as an entity; single; particular. **2** Not divisible; not capable of actual division without loss of something essential to its existence. **3** Pertaining, belonging, or peculiar to one particular person or thing. **4** Differentiated from others by peculiar or distinctive characteristics: an *individual* style. See synonyms under PARTICULAR. —*n.* **1** A single person, animal, or thing; especially, a human being;

a person with distinctive or marked peculiarities. **2** Anything that cannot be divided or separated into parts without losing its identity. [<Med. L *individualis* <L *individuus* indivisible <*in*- not + *dividuus* divisible] — **in'di·vid'u·al·ly** *adv.*

in·di·vid·u·al·ism (in'də·vij'ōō·əl·iz'əm) *n.* **1** The quality of being separate. **2** Personal independence in action, character, or interest. **3** A personal peculiarity; idiosyncrasy. **4** A tendency or attitude, in religion, ethics, or politics, favoring the liberty of the individual: opposed to *socialism, totalitarianism,* etc. **5** Excessive self-interest; selfishness. **6** *Philos.* Egoism. — **in'di·vid'u·al·ist** *n.* — **in'di·vid'u·al·is'tic** *adj.*

in·di·vid·u·al·i·ty (in'də·vij'ōō·al'ə·tē) *n.* *pl.* **·ties 1** Something that distinguishes one person or thing from others. **2** Distinctive character or personality. **3** The quality or state of existing separately. **4** An individual; a personality. **5** *Archaic* State or quality of inseparability; indivisibility.

in·di·vid·u·al·ize (in'də·vij'ōō·əl·īz') *v.t.* **·ized, ·iz·ing 1** To make individual; give individual characteristics to; distinguish. **2** To treat, mention, or consider individually; particularize. — **in'di·vid'u·al·i·za'tion** (-ə·zā'shən, -ī·zā'-) *n.*

in·di·vid·u·ate (in'də·vij'ōō·āt) *v.t.* **·at·ed, ·at·ting 1** To distinguish from others; individualize. **2** To bring into existence as an individual. [<Med. L *individuatus,* pp. of *individuare* <*individuus* individual]

in·di·vid·u·a·tion (in'də·vij'ōō·ā'shən) *n.* **1** The action or process of rendering individual. **2** State of being individualized. **3** Personal identity; individuality. **4** *Zool.* The development of separate units in a colony of protozoans. **5** *Philos.* The differentiation of the individual from the species and from every other individual. [<Med. L *individuatio, -onis*]

in·di·vis·i·ble (in'də·viz'ə·bəl) *adj.* Not divisible; incapable of being divided. — **in'di·vis'i·bil'i·ty** *n.* — **in'di·vis'i·bly** *adv.*

Indo– *combining form* Indian: *Indonesia.* [< Gk. *Indos* Indian]

In·do–Af·ri·can (in'dō–af'ri·kən) *adj.* Of or pertaining to both India and Africa.

In·do–Ar·y·an (in'dō–âr'ē·ən) *adj.* Of the Indic branch of the Indo–Iranian subfamily. — *n.* An Aryan of India. See ARYAN.

In·do·chi·na (in'dō·chī'nə) **1** The SE peninsula of Asia, comprising the Union of Burma, Cambodia, Laos, the Federation of Malaya, Thailand, North Vietnam and South Vietnam: sometimes *Farther India.* **2** The states of Cambodia, Laos, North Vietnam and South Vietnam: formerly *French Indochina.* Also **Indo–China.**

In·do·chi·nese (in'dō·chī·nēz', -nēs') *adj.* Of or pertaining to Indochina or its inhabitants. — *n.* **1** A member of one of the native Mongoloid races inhabiting Indochina. **2** The Sino–Tibetan family of languages.

in·doc·tri·nate (in·dok'trə·nāt) *v.t.* **·nat·ed, ·nat·ing 1** To instruct in doctrines, principles, etc. **2** To instruct; teach. See synonyms under TEACH. [<Med. L *in*- into + *doctrinare* teach <*doctrina* teaching <*doctor* a teacher <*docere* teach] — **in·doc'tri·na'tion** *n.*

In·do–Eu·ro·pe·an (in'dō–yŏŏr'ə·pē'ən) *n.* **1** The largest family of languages in the world, assumed to have descended from an unrecorded common ancestor and comprising most of the languages of Europe and many languages of India and SW Asia. These languages are conventionally divided into two classifications, *centum* and *satem* (from the Latin and Avestan words for 'hundred'), primarily according to the representation of the proto-Indo-European palatalized velar (k) as velar stops in the *centum* (mainly western) division, and as sibilants in the *satem* (mainly eastern) division. The principal *centum* subfamilies are Hellenic, Italic, Celtic, and Germanic. The principal *satem* subfamilies are Indo-Iranian, Armenian, Albanian, and Balto-Slavic. Among the lesser-known, extinct languages which have been established as belonging to the Indo-European family are Hittite and Tocharian. Cuneiform Hittite is grouped with the *centum* languages, while Hieroglyphic Hittite is thought by some to

be a *satem* language. Tocharian is generally classed with the *centum* languages. See also THRACIAN, PHRYGIAN, LIGURIAN, SICEL, ILLYRIAN, MESSAPIAN, and VENETIC. **2** The assumed prehistoric parent language of this family of languages: now fairly well reconstructed by linguists. — *adj.* Of or pertaining to the Indo-European family of languages, or to the peoples speaking them. Also *Aryan, Indo–Germanic.*

In·do–French (in'dō–french') *adj.* Pertaining to both India and France.

In·do–Ger·man·ic (in'dō–jər·man'ik) *n., adj.* Indo–European: the German term.

In·do–Hit·tite (in'dō–hit'īt) *n.* A language hypothesized by some as the parent of both the Indo–European and Anatolian families. According to this theory, Hittite is a sister language to Indo–European, rather than an offspring of it.

In·do–I·ra·ni·an (in'dō·ī·rā'nē·ən) *n.* A subfamily of the Indo–European family of languages, consisting of Indic and Iranian branches. — *adj.* Of or pertaining to this subfamily. Also *Aryan.*

in·dole (in'dōl) *n. Chem.* A white, crystalline, malodorous compound, C_8H_7N, formed by the reduction of indigo, and also from putrefactive animal proteins and certain albuminous compounds by fermentation. Highly diluted, it is used in perfumery. Also **in'dol** (-dōl, -dol). [<IND(IGO) + -OLE]

in·do·lence (in'də·ləns) *n.* Habitual idleness; laziness. Also **in'do·len·cy.** [<L *indolentia* freedom from pain]

in·do·lent (in'də·lənt) *adj.* **1** Averse to exertion; habitually inactive or idle. **2** Without pain; sluggish. See synonyms under IDLE. [<LL *indolens, -entis* <*in*- not + *dolens,* ppr. of *dolere* feel pain] — **in'do·lent·ly** *adv.*

in·dom·i·ta·ble (in·dom'i·tə·bəl) *adj.* Not to be subdued. See synonyms under INDEFATIGABLE, OBSTINATE. [<LL *indomitabilis* <L *indomitus* untamed <*in*- not + *domitus* tamed, pp. of *domitare,* intens. of *domare* subdue] — **in·dom'i·ta·bly** *adv.*

In·do·ne·sia (in'dō·nē'zhə, -shə) Since 1950 a republic, the **Republic of Indonesia,** comprising Java, Sumatra, most of Borneo, half of Timor, Celebes, the Moluccas, and other islands of the Malay Archipelago: 575,893 square miles; capital, Jakarta: formerly *Netherlands East Indies.*

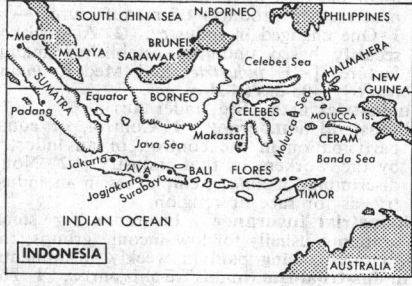

INDONESIA

In·do·ne·sian (in'dō·nē'zhən, -shən) *n.* **1** One of a small, light-brown-skinned people native throughout the Malay Peninsula and Archipelago, the Philippines, Sumatra, Java, etc.: believed to be an admixture of Polynesian and Mongoloid stocks. **2** A subfamily of the Austronesian family of languages spoken by these people, including Formosan, Igorot, Javanese, Malagasy, Malay, Tagalog, etc.: also called *Malayan.* — *adj.* Of or pertaining to Indonesia, its peoples, or their languages.

Indonesian Timor See TIMOR.

in·door (in'dôr', -dōr') *adj.* Being or done within doors; pertaining to the interior of a building.

in·doors (in'dôrz', -dōrz') *adv.* Inside or toward the inside of a building.

in·do·phe·nol (in'dō·fē'nōl, -nol) *n. Chem.* One of a series of synthetic quinonimine coloring compounds resembling indigo: used for dyeing cotton and wool blue. [<IND(IG)O + PHENOL]

In·dore (in·dôr', -dōr') **1** A former princely state in west central India; 9,934 square miles.

2 Its former capital, since 1948 the summer capital of Madhya Bharat.

in·dorse (in·dôrs'), **in·dorse·ment** (in·dôrs'mənt) See ENDORSE, ENDORSEMENT.

in·dor·see (in'dôr·sē', in·dôr'sē) See ENDORSEE.

in·dow (in·dou'), **in·dow·ment** (in·dou'mənt) See ENDOW, etc.

in·dox·yl (in·dok'sil) *n. Chem.* A crystalline compound, C_8H_7NO, formed from indole and used as an intermediate in the synthesis of indigo. [<IND(IGO) + (HYDR)OXYL]

In·dra (in'drə) In early Hindu mythology, the god of the firmament and of rain. In the Vedas he is a god of the first rank: in later mythology he falls to a second rank.

in·draft (in'draft', -dräft') *n.* The act of drawing in or that which is drawn in; an inward flow. Also **in'draught'.**

In·dra·pu·ra (in'drə·pŏŏr'ə) See KERINCHI.

in·drawn (in'drôn') *adj.* **1** Drawn in; uttered with suppressed breath. **2** Abstracted; preoccupied.

in·dri (in'drē) *n.* A lemur of Madagascar; especially, a species (*Indris brevicaudata*) about two feet long, with exserted ears, rudimentary tail, and usually prevailingly black in color. [<F <Malagasy *indry lo,* there he goes: mistaken for the name of the animal]

INDRA

Drawn from an early Indian sculpture of the Vedic period. Indra was the god of the east in Hindu legend.

in·du·bi·ta·ble (in·dōō'bə·tə·bəl, -dyōō'-) *adj.* Not open to doubt or question; unquestionable; certain. See synonyms under EVIDENT, INCONTESTABLE, MANIFEST. [<F] — **in·du'bi·ta·ble·ness** *n.* — **in·du'bi·ta·bly** *adv.*

in·duce (in·dōōs', -dyōōs') *v.t.* **·duced, ·duc·ing 1** To lead on to a specific action, belief, etc., by persuasion or influence; prevail on. **2** To bring on; produce; cause: a sickness *induced* by fatigue. **3** *Physics* To produce, as by exposure to electric, magnetic, or radioactive influences. **4** To reach as a conclusion by an inductive process of reasoning. **5** *Obs.* To lead in; introduce. [<L *inducere* introduce <*in*- in + *ducere* lead] — **in·duc'er** *n.* — **in·duc'i·ble** *adj.*

induced drag *Aeron.* That portion of the drag of an aircraft induced by the lift. Compare PARASITE DRAG, PROFILE DRAG.

in·duce·ment (in·dōōs'mənt, -dyōōs'-) *n.* **1** An incentive; motive. **2** The act of inducing. **3** *Law* In pleading, the preamble, or explanatory introduction to the particular charges and allegations.

in·duct (in·dukt') *v.t.* **1** To bring into or install in an office, benefice, etc., especially with formal ceremony. **2** To bring or lead in; introduce; initiate. **3** *U.S.* To bring (one who has been conscripted) into a military service. [<L *inductus,* pp. of *inducere.* See INDUCE.]

in·duc·tance (in·duk'təns) *n. Electr.* **1** The capacity of an electric circuit for responding to a magnetoelectrically induced current. **2** Self-induction in an electrical circuit or its equivalent, for purposes of measurement in terms of henries.

in·duc·tee (in'duk·tē') *n.* One inducted into military service.

in·duc·tion (in·duk'shən) *n.* **1** The process of causing an event or bringing about a conclusion by some particular path or course of reasoning. **2** *Logic* The process of inferring or aiming at the general from observation of the particular; specifically, the inference of a specific law of causational connection from the observation and analysis of some particular instance or instances. **3** Any conclusion reached by inductive reasoning. **4** In

English ecclesiastical law, the formal installation of a person into an office or church living. 5 An introduction; especially, a preamble, prolog, or prelude foreshadowing the argument or character of a literary work. 6 The bringing forward of separate facts as evidence in order to prove a general statement. 7 *Electr.* The production of magnetization or electrification in a body by the mere proximity of a magnetic field or electric charge, or of an electric current in a conductor by the variation of the magnetic field in its vicinity. 8 *Physiol.* The stimulating effect of one tissue upon the growth or alteration of another. 9 The act or process of inducting, as for military service; initiation; installation. 10 *Obs.* A beginning or introduction to anything; that which leads to or induces a thing. **— magnetic induction** The magnetization of iron, steel, etc., by its introduction into a magnetic field. [<OF <L *inductio, -onis*] **— in·duc'tion·al** *adj.*

Synonyms: deduction, inference. *Deduction* is reasoning from the general to the particular; *induction* is reasoning from the particular to the general. In *deduction*, if the general rule is true, and the special case falls under the rule, the conclusion is certain; *induction* can ordinarily give no more than a probable conclusion, because we can never be sure that we have collated all instances. An *induction* is of the nature of an *inference*, but while an *inference* may be partial and hasty, an *induction* is careful, and aims to be complete. Compare DEMONSTRATION, INFERENCE.

induction coil *Electr.* An apparatus for generating currents by electromagnetic induction, consisting usually of two concentric coils of insulated wire enclosing an iron core. One of the coils, called the *primary*, is usually short and of thick wire, and the *secondary* long and of thin wire. An alternating current of high tension is induced in the secondary coil by rapid automatic making and breaking of the circuit in the primary.

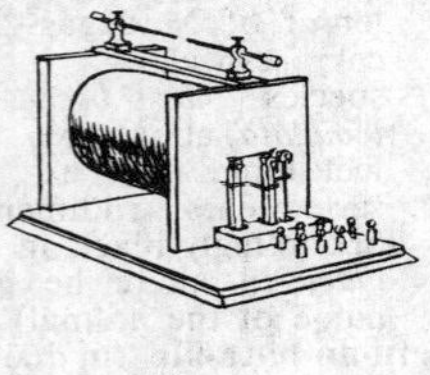

INDUCTION COIL

in·duc·tive (in·duk'tiv) *adj.* 1 Pertaining to or proceeding by induction. 2 Produced by induction. 3 Introductory. [<LL *inductivus*] **— in·duc'tive·ly** *adv.* **— in·duc'tive·ness** *n.*

in·duc·tiv·i·ty (in'duk·tiv'ə·tē) *n. Electr.* Specific capacity for induction.

in·duc·tor (in·duk'tər) *n.* 1 One who or that which inducts. 2 *Electr.* Any part of an electrical apparatus which acts inductively upon another. [<L]

in·due (in·do͞o', -dyo͞o') *v.t.* **·dued, ·du·ing** To endue. [See ENDUE]

in·dulge (in·dulj') *v.* **·dulged, ·dulg·ing** *v.t.* 1 To yield to or gratify, as desires or whims. 2 To yield to or gratify the desires, whims, etc., of. 3 *Eccl.* To grant a dispensation or indulgence to. 4 *Obs.* To grant as a privilege or favor. 5 In business: **a** To grant more time to (someone) to meet a bill. **b** To grant more time for (a bill) to be met. — *v.i.* 6 To yield to or gratify desires; indulge oneself; with *in.* [<L *indulgere* be kind to, concede] **— in·dulg'er** *n.*

Synonyms: content, favor, gratify, humor, pamper, please, satisfy, spoil. See PAMPER. *Antonyms*: check, contradict, control, deny, disappoint, discipline, displease, oppose, refuse, thwart.

in·dul·gence (in·dul'jəns) *n.* 1 The act of indulging; hence, excess; self-gratification. 2 That with which a person is indulged or indulges himself; an act of compliance, grace, or favor. 3 Permission to defer payment, as of a note. 4 In the Roman Catholic Church, remission, by those authorized, of the temporal punishment still due to sin after sacramental absolution, either in this world or in purgatory; also, a relaxation, in a person's favor, of a particular rule of ecclesiastical law: properly called *dispensation.* 5 The granting of special favors by the Declaration of Indulgence. Also **in·dul'gen·cy.** **— Declaration of Indulgence** In English history, a royal proclamation granting a larger measure of religious freedom to nonconformists: especially those of Charles II, 1671, and James II, 1687. [<OF <L *indulgentia*]

in·dul·gent (in·dul'jənt) *adj.* Prone to indulge; lenient. See synonyms under CHARITABLE. [<L *indulgens, -entis,* ppr. of *indulgere* concede] **— in·dul'gent·ly** *adv.*

in·dul·gen·tial (in'dul·jen'shəl) *adj.* Pertaining to ecclesiastical indulgences.

in·du·line (in'dyə·lēn, -lin) *n. Chem.* Any one of an extensive group of coal-tar dyestuffs yielding a violet to intense blue color. Also **in'du·lin** (-lin). [<IND(IGO) + -UL(E) + -INE[2]]

in·dult (in·dult') *n.* 1 An indulgence or privilege granted by the pope, to bishops and others, as exemption from some canonical or ecclesiastical duty. 2 In Spain, an import duty: also **in·dul'to** (-dul'tō). [<LL *indultum* <*indultus,* pp. of *indulgere* concede]

in·du·na (in·do͞o'nə) *n.* Among the Zulus, an officer serving under the king or chief. [<Zulu *in-duna*]

in·du·pli·cate (in·do͞o'plə·kit, -dyo͞o'-) *adj. Bot.* Having the edges turned or folded inward: said of calyx or corolla in estivation, or of leaves in vernation. Also **in·du'pli·ca'tive.** **— in·du'pli·ca'tion** *n.*

in·du·rate (in'do͞o·rāt, -dyo͞o-) *v.t. & v.i.* **·rat·ed, ·rat·ing** To make or become hard, hardy, or callous; harden; inure. — *adj.* (-rit) Hard or hardened: also **in'du·rat'ed.** [<L *induratus,* pp. of *indurare* make hard. See ENDURE.] **— in'du·ra'tive** *adj.*

in·du·ra·tion (in'do͞o·rā'shən, -dyo͞o-) *n.* 1 The act or process of indurating, or the state of being indurated. 2 Hardening of the heart; obduracy. 3 An indurated part. [<OF <Med. L *induratio, -onis*]

In·dus (in'dəs) A river in western Tibet and NW India, flowing over 1,900 miles NW to the Arabian Sea.

In·dus (in'dəs) A southern constellation, the Indian. See CONSTELLATION. [<L, an Indian]

in·du·si·um (in·do͞o'zē·əm, -zhē-, -dyo͞o'-) *n. pl.* **·si·a** (-zē·ə, -zhē·ə) 1 *Bot.* **a** An outgrowth of a fern leaf covering the immature sori or fruit clusters. **b** A hairy cup surrounding the stigma in a flower. 2 *Biol.* **a** The larval case of an insect. **b** Any similar membranous envelope, as the amnion. [<L, a tunic <*induere* put on; infl. in form by Gk. *endysis* dress, garment <*endyein* put on] **— in·du'si·al** *adj.*

in·dus·tri·al (in·dus'trē·əl) *adj.* 1 Pertaining to or engaged in industry. 2 Denoting the processes or products of manufacture. — *n.* 1 One engaged in industry. 2 A stock or security based upon an established manufacture. [<F *industriel* and Med. L *industrialis*] **— in·dus'tri·al·ly** *adv.*

industrial arts See under ART[1].

industrial democracy 1 Control, or equal participation in the control, of an industry by the workers in that industry. 2 Nondiscrimination among employees in an industry, as for race or religion.

industrial insurance Insurance for small amounts, usually for low-income groups, the premium being paid in weekly instalments.

in·dus·tri·al·ism (in·dus'trē·əl·iz'əm) *n.* 1 The modern industrial system, especially with reference to large-scale manufacturing industries; the organization of industries. 2 A condition of society in which the highest aim is success in peaceful industries. See CAPITALISM. **— in·dus'tri·al·ist** *adj.* & *n.*

in·dus·tri·al·ize (in·dus'trē·əl·īz') *v.t.* **·ized, ·iz·ing** To render industrial; affect with or devote to industrialism: to *industrialize* a village. **— in·dus'tri·al·i·za'tion** (-ə·zā'shən, -ī·zā'-) *n.*

industrial relations The relationships between employers and employees.

industrial revolution The period of economic transition from hand industry to the application of power-driven machinery which began in England in the second half of the 18th century.

industrial union A labor union in which membership is open to all workers in a particular industry. Compare CRAFT UNION.

Industrial Workers of the World A syndicalistic labor organization founded at Chicago in 1905 and flourishing through the early 1920's. *Abbr. IWW.* See WOBBLY.

in·dus·tri·ous (in·dus'trē·əs) *adj.* 1 Assiduously or habitually occupied in any work, business, or pursuit. 2 Indicating diligence. 3 Industrial. [<F *industrieux* <L *industriosus*] **— in·dus'tri·ous·ly** *adv.* **— in·dus'tri·ous·ness** *n.*

Synonyms: active, assiduous, busy, diligent, employed, engaged, occupied, sedulous. *Industrious* signifies zealously or habitually applying oneself to any work or business. *Busy* applies to an activity which may be temporary, *industrious* to a habit of life. We say a man is *busy* just now; that is, *occupied* at the moment with something that takes his full attention. It would be ridiculous or satirical to say, He is *industrious* just now. But *busy* can be used in the sense of *industrious,* as when we say he is a *busy* man. *Diligent* indicates also a disposition, which is ordinarily habitual, and suggests more of heartiness and volition than *industrious.* We say one is a *diligent,* rather than an *industrious,* reader of the Bible. Compare ACTIVE, BUSY, INDEFATIGABLE.

in·dus·try (in'dəs·trē) *n. pl.* **·tries** 1 Earnest or constant application to work or business. 2 Useful labor in general. 3 A special branch of productive work, or the capital or workers employed in it: the steel *industry,* the farming *industry.* 4 The mechanical and manufacturing branches of productive activity, as distinguished from agricultural. 5 *Obs.* Skill, dexterity; also, a clever device or contrivance. [<F *industrie* <L *industria* diligence <*industrius* diligent]

Synonyms: application, assiduity, attention, constancy, diligence, effort, exertion, intentness, labor, pains, patience, perseverance, persistence, sedulousness. *Industry* is the quality, action, or habit of earnest, steady, and continued attention or devotion to any useful or productive work or task, manual or mental. *Assiduity* (L *ad,* to, and *sedere,* sit), as the etymology suggests, sits down to a task until it is done. *Diligence* (L *diligere,* love, choose) invests more effort and exertion, with love of the work or deep interest in its accomplishment; *application* (L *ad,* to, and *plicare,* fold) bends to its work and concentrates all one's powers upon it with utmost intensity; hence, *application* can hardly be as unremitting as *assiduity. Constancy* is a steady devotion of heart and principle. *Patience* works on in spite of annoyances; *perseverance* overcomes hindrances and difficulties; *persistence* strives relentlessly against opposition; *persistence* has very frequently an unfavorable meaning, implying that one persists in spite of considerations that should induce him to desist. *Industry* is *diligence* applied to some vocation, business, or profession; hence, by derived use, the occupation itself. *Labor* and *pains* refer to the *exertions* of the worker and the tax upon him, while *assiduity, perseverance,* etc., refer to his continuance in the work. See BUSINESS. *Antonyms*: idleness, inattention, inconstancy, indolence, neglect, negligence, remissness, sloth.

in·dwell (in'dwel') *v.* **·dwelt, ·dwel·ling** *v.t.* To dwell in; inhabit. — *v.i.* To dwell; abide: with *in.* **— in'dwell'er** *n.* **— in'dwell'ing** *n.*

In·dy (daṅ·dē'), **Vincent d',** 1851–1931, French composer.

-ine[1] *suffix of adjectives* Like; pertaining to; of the nature of: *marine, canine.* [<F *-in, -ine* <L *-inus,* adj. suffix]

-ine[2] *suffix* 1 *Chem.* **a** Used in the names of halogens: *bromine, fluorine.* **b** Used to indicate an alkaloid or basic substance: *morphine, amine.* **c** Var. of -IN. 2 Used in names of commercial products: *gasoline, brilliantine.* [Special use of -INE[1]]

-ine[3] *suffix* Used to form feminine words, names, and titles: *heroine, Josephine.* [<F <L *-ina,* suffix of fem. nouns <Gk. *-inē*; or directly <L or <Gk.]

-ine[4] *suffix* Like; resembling: *crystalline.* [<L *-inus* <Gk. *-inos*]

in·earth (in·ûrth') *v.t. Poetic* To place in the earth; bury.

in·e·bri·ant (in·ē'brē·ənt) *adj.* Intoxicating. — *n.* Anything that intoxicates.

in·e·bri·ate (in·ē'brē·āt) *v.t.* **·at·ed, ·at·ing** 1 To make drunk; intoxicate. 2 To exhilarate; excite. — *n.* (-it, -āt) A habitual drunkard. — *adj.* (-it, -āt) Intoxicated: also **in·e'bri·at'ed.** [<L *inebriatus,* pp. of *inebriare* intoxicate <*in-* thoroughly + *ebriare* make drunk <*ebrius* drunk]

in·e·bri·a·tion (in·ē′brē·ā′shən) *n.* 1 Drunkenness; habitual intoxication. 2 Exhilaration. Also **in·e·bri·e·ty** (in′ē·brī′ə·tē).

in·ed·i·ble (in·ed′ə·bəl) *adj.* Not edible; not fit to eat. — **in·ed′i·bil′i·ty** *n.*

in·ef·fa·ble (in·ef′ə·bəl) *adj.* 1 That cannot be expressed in speech. 2 That must not be spoken; too lofty or sacred for expression. [<F <L *ineffabilis* < *in-* not + *effabilis* utterable < *effari* speak < *ex-* out + *fari* speak] — **in·ef′fa·bil′i·ty** *n.* — **in·ef′fa·bly** *adv.*

in·ef·fec·tive (in′i·fek′tiv) *adj.* 1 Not effective; not producing the effect expected. 2 Incompetent. — **in′ef·fec′tive·ly** *adv.* — **in′ef·fec′tive·ness** *n.*

in·ef·fec·tu·al (in′i·fek′chōō·əl) *adj.* 1 Not effectual; not able to produce an intended effect. 2 Unsuccessful; fruitless. — **in′ef·fec′tu·al·ly** *adv.*

in·ef·fi·cient (in′i·fish′ənt) *adj.* 1 Not efficient; uneconomical or wasteful. 2 Not capable; incompetent. — **in′ef·fi′cien·cy** *n.* — **in′ef·fi′cient·ly** *adv.*

in·e·las·tic (in′i·las′tik) *adj.* Not elastic; inflexible; unyielding; unadaptable. — **in·e·las·tic·i·ty** (in′i·las′tis′ə·tē) *n.*

in·el·e·gant (in·el′ə·gənt) *adj.* 1 Not elegant; lacking in beauty, polish, grace, refinement, good taste, or the like. 2 Coarse; crude.

in·el·i·gi·ble (in·el′ə·jə·bəl) *adj.* Not eligible; disqualified; unsuitable; inexpedient. — **in·el′i·gi·bil′i·ty** *n.* — **in·el′i·gi·bly** *adv.*

in·e·luc·ta·ble (in′i·luk′tə·bəl) *adj.* Not to be escaped; impossible to struggle against; irresistible. [<L *ineluctabilis* < *in-* not + *eluctabilis* surmountable < *eluctari* surmount] — **in′e·luc′ta·bil′i·ty** *n.* — **in′e·luc′ta·bly** *adv.*

in·ept (in·ept′) *adj.* 1 Not suitable or qualified; out of place. 2 Absurd; foolish. 3 Clumsy; awkward. [<L *ineptus* < *in-* not + *aptus* fit] — **in·ep′ti·tude** *n.* — **in·ept′ly** *adv.* — **in·ept′ness** *n.*

in·e·qual·i·ty (in′i·kwol′ə·tē) *n. pl.* **·ties** 1 The condition of being unequal; disparity. 2 Lack of evenness or proportion; variableness: *inequalities* of surface; *inequalities* of climate. 3 Inadequacy; incompetency. 4 *Math.* A statement that two quantities are not equal, made by placing the sign ≠ between them; or by the sign < or >, the angle being toward the symbol of smaller quantity. 5 The daily variation in rise of the tides due to varying lunar influences. See synonyms under DIFFERENCE.

in·eq·ui·ty (in·ek′wə·tē) *n. pl.* **·ties** 1 Want of equity; injustice. 2 An unfair act.

in·er·ran·cy (in·er′ən·sē, -ûr′-) *n.* 1 The state of being free from error. 2 As applied to Scripture, plenary inspiration.

in·ert (in·ûrt′) *adj.* 1 Destitute of inherent power to move; possessing inertia; inactive. 2 Sluggish. 3 *Chem.* Devoid of active properties; incapable of or resisting combination: the *inert* gases. See synonyms under HEAVY, IDLE, LIFELESS, PASSIVE, SLOW. [<L *iners, inertis* < *in-* not + *ars* art] — **in·ert′ly** *adv.* — **in·ert′ness** *n.* — **in·er′tion** (-ûr′shən) *n.*

in·er·tia (in·ûr′shə) *n.* 1 The state of being inert; sluggishness. 2 *Physics* **a** That property of matter by virtue of which any physical body persists in its state of rest or of uniform motion until acted upon by some external force; its quantitative expression is *mass.* **b** A similar property noted in certain forms of energy, as electricity and quanta. [<L, idleness] — **in·er′tial** *adj.*

inertial guidance *Aeron.* The control of the flight path of aircraft and guided missiles by built-in gyroscopic mechanisms which automatically compensate for the action of inertial forces tending to change the direction of a predetermined course.

in·es·cap·a·ble (in′ə·skā′pə·bəl) *adj.* Inevitable; unavoidable. — **in′es·cap′a·bly** *adv.*

in es·se (in es′ē) *Latin* In being; actually existing. Compare IN POSSE.

in·es·sen·tial (in′i·sen′shəl) *adj.* 1 Unessential; not essential. 2 Immaterial. — **in′es·sen′ti·al′i·ty** *n.*

in·es·ti·ma·ble (in·es′tə·mə·bəl) *adj.* Above price; very valuable. — **in·es′ti·ma·bly** *adv.*

in·ev·i·ta·ble (in·ev′ə·tə·bəl) *adj.* 1 That cannot be prevented; unavoidable. 2 Hence, customary; usual: a humorous usage. See synonyms under NECESSARY. [<L *inevitabilis* < *in-* not + *evitare* avoid < *ex-* completely + *vitare* avoid] — **in·ev′i·ta·ble·ness, in·ev′i·ta·bil′i·ty** *n.* — **in·ev′i·ta·bly** *adv.*

inevitable accident See FORCE MAJEURE.

in·ex·act (in′ig·zakt′) *adj.* Not exact, accurate, or true. — **in′ex·act′ly** *adv.* — **in′ex·act′ness, in′ex·act′i·tude** *n.*

in·ex·cus·a·ble (in′ik·skyōō′zə·bəl) *adj.* Not excusable; impossible to excuse or justify. — **in′·ex·cus′a·bly** *adv.*

in·ex·haust·i·ble (in′ig·zôs′tə·bəl) *adj.* 1 Incapable of being exhausted or used up. 2 Incapable of fatigue; tireless.

in·ex·o·ra·ble (in·ek′sər·ə·bəl) *adj.* Not to be moved by entreaty; unyielding. See synonyms under IMPLACABLE, INFLEXIBLE. [<L *inexorabilis.* See IN-², EXORABLE.] — **in·ex′o·ra·bil′i·ty, in·ex′o·ra·ble·ness** *n.* — **in·ex′o·ra·bly** *adv.*

in·ex·pen·sive (in′ik·spen′siv) *adj.* Not expensive; costing little.

in·ex·pe·ri·enced (in′ik·spir′ē·ənst) *adj.* Not experienced; lacking in the skill and knowledge derived from experience.

in·ex·plic·a·ble (in·eks′pli·kə·bəl, in′iks·plik′ə·bəl) *adj.* Not explicable; impossible to explain; inexplainable. — **in′ex·pli·ca·bil′i·ty, in′ex·plic′a·ble·ness** *n.* — **in·ex′pli·ca·bly** *adv.*

in·ex·press·i·ble (in′iks·pres′ə·bəl) *adj.* Incapable of being expressed; especially, that cannot be expressed in words; unutterable: often used loosely for *great.* — **in′ex·press′i·bil′i·ty, in′ex·press′i·ble·ness** *n.* — **in′ex·press′i·bly** *adv.*

in·ex·pug·na·ble (in′iks·pug′nə·bəl) *adj.* Impregnable; unconquerable. [<F <L *inexpugnabilis* < *in-* not + *ex-* out + *pugnare* fight] — **in′ex·pug′na·bil′i·ty, in′ex·pug′na·ble·ness** *n.* — **in′ex·pug′na·bly** *adv.*

in ex·ten·so (in ik·sten′sō) *Latin* At full length.

in ex·tre·mis (in iks·trē′mis) *Latin* At the point of death; at the last gasp.

in·ex·tri·ca·ble (in·eks′tri·kə·bəl) *adj.* So involved that extrication is impossible. [<L *inextricabilis* < *in-* not + *extricare.* See EXTRICATE.] — **in·ex′tri·ca·bil′i·ty, in·ex′tri·ca·ble·ness** *n.* — **in·ex′tri·ca·bly** *adv.*

I·nez (ī′nez′) Portuguese form of AGNES. Also *Sp.* **I·nés** (ē·nās′).

in·fal·li·ble (in·fal′ə·bəl) *adj.* 1 Exempt from fallacy or error of judgment. 2 Exempt from uncertainty or liability to error. 3 In Roman Catholic theology, insusceptible of error in matters relating to faith and morals: said of the pope speaking *ex cathedra.* — *n.* One who or that which is infallible. — **in·fal′li·bil′i·ty, in·fal′li·ble·ness** *n.* — **in·fal′li·bly** *adv.*

in·fa·mous (in′fə·məs) *adj.* 1 Having an odious reputation; notorious. 2 Involving infamy. 3 *Law* Convicted of infamy. [< Med. L *infamosus* <L *infamis* < *in-* not + *fama* fame < *fari* speak] — **in′fa·mous·ly** *adv.* — **in′fa·mous·ness** *n.*

Synonyms: atrocious, base, detestable, disgraceful, dishonorable, disreputable, heinous, ignominious, ill-famed, nefarious, odious, outrageous, scandalous, shameful, shameless, vile, villainous, wicked. See BASE.

in·fa·my (in′fə·mē) *n. pl.* **·mies** 1 Total lack of honor or reputation. 2 That which is odious; depravity; an infamous act. 3 *Law* The legal status of a person convicted of serious crimes which, in the United States, disqualify him as a witness or juror. [<F *infamie* <L *infamia* < *infamis.* See INFAMOUS.]

in·fan·cy (in′fən·sē) *n. pl.* **·cies** 1 The state of being an infant. 2 *Law* Minority. 3 The earliest period in the history of a thing.

in·fant (in′fənt) *n.* 1 A baby; a child under seven years of age. 2 *Law* A minor; in most States of the United States, a person under 21 years of age. — *adj.* 1 Babyish; infantile. 2 *Law* Minor; not yet of age. [<OF *enfant* <L *infans, -antis* not speaking < *in-* not + *fans, fantis,* ppr. of *fari* talk]

in·fan·ta (in·fan′tə) *n.* A daughter of a Spanish or Portuguese king. [<Sp., infant]

in·fan·te (in·fan′tā) *n.* A son, except the eldest, of a Spanish or Portuguese king. [<Sp., infant]

in·fan·ti·cide (in·fan′tə·sīd) *n.* 1 Child murder. 2 One who murders a child. [<F <LL *infanticidium* <L *infans, -antis* child + *caedere* kill; def. 2 <L *infanticida*]

in·fan·tile (in′fən·tīl, -til) *adj.* 1 Pertaining to or characteristic of infants or infancy. 2 *Geol.* In an early period of development succeeding an upheaval of the earth's crust or other change affecting basic level. See synonyms under CHILDISH. Also **in′an·tine** (-tīn, -tin).

infantile paralysis Poliomyelitis.

infantile scurvy *Pathol.* A disease of young children characterized by foul breath, diarrhea, anemia, hemorrhages, etc.: also called *Barlow's disease.*

in·fan·til·ism (in′fən·təl·iz′əm) *n.* 1 Abnormal prolonging of an infantile condition as to sex and body in adults. 2 Backwardness in physical and mental development.

in·fan·try (in′fən·trē) *n. pl.* **·tries** Soldiers or units of an army that fight on foot and are equipped with small arms. [<F *infanterie* < Ital. *infanteria* < *infante* boy, page, foot soldier <L *infans, infantis* child]

in·fan·try·man (in′fən·trē·mən) *n. pl.* **·men** (-mən) A foot soldier.

in·farct (in·färkt′) *n. Pathol.* A portion of tissue congested because of an embolus and undergoing necrosis. [<Med. L *infarctus* <L *infartus,* pp. of *infarcire* < *in-* in + *farcire* stuff] — **in·farc′tion** *n.*

in·fat·u·ate (in·fach′ōō·āt) *v.t.* **·at·ed, ·at·ing** 1 To make foolish or fatuous; deprive of sound judgment. 2 To inspire with foolish and unreasoning passion. [<L *infatuatus,* pp. of *infatuare* make a fool of < *in-* very + *fatuus* foolish] — **in·fat′u·at′ed** *adj.* — **in·fat′u·a′tion** *n.*

in·fect (in·fekt′) *v.t.* 1 To introduce pathogenic micro-organisms into, as a wound; communicate disease to, as a person, etc. 2 To contaminate, as a scalpel, with disease-bearing matter. 3 To affect or influence, as with emotion, beliefs, etc., especially harmfully; taint. 4 *Law* To taint with illegality; render subject to seizure or penalty. See synonyms under DEFILE, POLLUTE. [<L *infectus,* pp. of *inficere* dip into, stain < *in-* in + *facere* do, make] — **in·fect′er, in·fec′tor** *n.*

in·fec·tion (in·fek′shən) *n.* 1 The act of infecting, as with disease, attitude, mood, ideas, etc. 2 Communication of disease, as by entrance of pathogenic germs into an organism in any manner. 3 Any diseased condition so produced. 4 The instilation of a quality, usually evil, by influence or communication. 5 *Law* Taint of illegality. 6 That which infects; especially, infectious morbific matter. 7 *Rare* Liking; affection: in humorous use. See synonyms under CONTAGION. [<F] — **focal infection** A bacterial infection localized in certain body tissues, as the tonsils or a tooth, from which toxins are sent to other areas.

in·fec·tious (in·fek′shəs) *adj.* 1 That may be communicated by infection. 2 Able to communicate infection. 3 *Law* Tainting with illegality. 4 Having the quality of being transmitted from one to another: *infectious* laughter. 5 *Obs.* Infected. — **in·fec′tious·ly** *adv.* — **in·fec′tious·ness** *n.*

infectious disease Any disease due to the entrance into and growth in the body of micro-organisms.

infectious mononucleosis *Pathol.* An acute communicable disease marked by fever, sore throat, a swelling of the lymph nodes, especially in the cervical region, and an increase in abnormal mononuclear cells: also called *glandular fever.*

in·fec·tive (in·fek′tiv) *adj.* Infectious.

in·fe·lic·i·tous (in′fə·lis′ə·təs) *adj.* Not felicitous, happy, or suitable in application, condition, or result. — **in′fe·lic′i·tous·ly** *adv.* — **in′·fe·lic′i·tous·ness** *n.*

in·fe·lic·i·ty (in′fə·lis′ə·tē) *n. pl.* **·ties** 1 The state of being infelicitous; unhappiness. 2 That which is infelicitous; an inappropriate or inapt remark, act, etc. [<L *infelicitas, -tatis*]

in·felt (in′felt′) *adj.* Felt inwardly or deeply.

in·feoff (in·fēf′), **in·feoff·ment** (in·fēf′mənt) See ENFEOFF, etc.

in·fer (in·fûr′) *v.* **·ferred, ·fer·ring** *v.t.* 1 To derive by reasoning; conclude or accept from evidence or premises; deduce. Compare POSIT. 2 To involve or imply as a conclusion; give evidence of: said of facts, statements, etc.: His actions *infer* a motive. 3 Loosely, to imply; hint. 4 *Obs.* To bring in; advance; also, to cause. — *v.i.* 5 To draw inferences.

[<L *inferre* bring into <*in-* in + *ferre* bring, carry] — **in·fer′a·ble, in·fer′ri·ble** *adj.*

in·fer·ence (in′fər·əns) *n.* **1** The act of inferring. **2** That which is inferred; a deduction or conclusion. **3** Loosely, a conjecture. [< Med. L *inferentia* <L *inferens, -entis,* ppr. of *inferre.* See INFER.]

Synonyms: conclusion, consequence, deduction, demonstration, induction. A *conclusion* is the absolute and necessary result of the admission of certain premises; an *inference* is a probable *conclusion*, toward which known facts, statements, or admissions point, but which they do not absolutely establish; sound premises together with their necessary *conclusion* constitute a *demonstration.* See DEMONSTRATION, INDUCTION.

in·fer·en·tial (in′fə·ren′shəl) *adj.* Deducible by inference. — **in′fer·en′tial·ly** *adv.*

in·fe·ri·or (in·fir′ē·ər) *adj.* **1** Lower in quality, merit, importance, or rank. **2** *Biol.* Situated or placed lower, as certain parts of the body relative to others; in animals, situated on or pertaining to the lower or ventral side. **3** Later in point of time: the *inferior* limit of a year. **4** In music, having a lower pitch. **5** *Bot.* Below some other organ; in a blossom, anterior. **6** *Astron.* **a** Between the earth and the sun: an *inferior* planet. **b** Below the horizon; below the celestial pole. **7** *Printing* Set below the level of the line, as small characters without a shoulder below, used in chemical formulas. See synonyms under BAD[1]. — *n.* One who or that which is classed lower than others; a subordinate. [<L, lower, compar. of *inferus* low]

in·fe·ri·or·i·ty (in·fir′ē·ôr′ə·tē, -or′-) *n.* The state of being inferior; low condition.

inferiority complex *Psychol.* An emotional trend or state of mind characterized by a morbidly exaggerated sense of one's own limitations and incapacities, and sometimes compensated for by aggressive behavior.

in·fer·nal (in·fûr′nəl) *adj.* **1** Belonging to hell; diabolical: often used colloquially to express indignation or emphasis: an *infernal* rascal. **2** Pertaining to Tartarus. [<OF <L *infernalis* < *infernus* situated below < *inferus* below] — **in·fer′nal·ly** *adv.*

Synonyms: demoniac, demoniacal, devilish, diabolic, diabolical, fiendish, hellish, satanic.

infernal machine Any device for doing unusual damage by explosion.

in·fer·no (in·fûr′nō) *n.* *pl.* **·nos** **1** The infernal regions; hell. **2** Any place comparable to hell; especially, a hot or fiery place. [<Ital.]

In·fer·no (in·fûr′nō) The first of the three parts of the *Divina Commedia* of Dante, describing the poet's journey through Hell, under the guidance of Vergil.

infero– *combining form Anat. & Zool.* On the under side; below. [<L *inferus* low]

in·fer·o·lat·er·al (in′fər·ō·lat′ər·əl) *adj.* Below and on one side.

in·fer·tile (in·fûr′til) *adj.* Not fertile or productive; sterile; barren. — **in′fer·til′i·ty** *n.*

in·fest (in·fest′) *v.t.* To overrun or haunt in large numbers, especially so as to render unpleasant or unsafe: The barn is *infested* with rats. [<MF *infester* <L *infestare* assail < *infestus* hostile] — **in·fest′er** *n.*

in·fes·ta·tion (in′fes·tā′shən) *n.* **1** The act of infesting. **2** The state of being infested, as with parasites or vermin. [<LL *infestatio, -onis*]

in·feu·da·tion (in′fyōō·dā′shən) *n.* **1** In feudal law, the granting or the putting in possession of an estate in fee; also, the feudal relation. **2** The granting of tithes to laymen. [<Med. L *infeudatio, -onis* < *infeudare* enfeoff < *in-* in + *feudum* FEUD[2]]

in·fi·del (in′fi·dəl) *n.* **1** One who denies the existence of God. **2** An unbeliever, as viewed from the standpoint of a believer in any particular religion or belief. See synonyms under SKEPTIC. — *adj.* **1** Lacking the true faith; especially, rejecting the Christian religion. **2** Faithless; recreant. **3** Of, relating to, or characteristic of infidels or infidelity. [<OF *infidèle* <L *infidelis* unfaithful < *in-* not + *fidelis* faithful]

in·fi·del·i·ty (in′fi·del′ə·tē) *n.* *pl.* **·ties** **1** The state of being an infidel; lack of belief. **2** Lack of fidelity; specifically, violation of the marriage vow by adultery.

in·field (in′fēld′) *n.* **1** **a** The space thirty yards square enclosed within the base lines of a baseball field: distinguished from *outfield.* **b** The infielders collectively. See illustration under BASEBALL. **2** Land under tillage; distinguished from *outfield.*

in·field·er (in′fēl′dər) *n.* In baseball, a defensive player in the infield: the first, second, and third basemen, the shortstop, and, when fielding the ball, the pitcher and catcher: distinguished from *outfielder.*

in·fil·ter (in·fil′tər) *v.t.* & *v.i.* To enter by infiltration.

in·fil·trate (in·fil′trāt; *esp. for v. defs. 2, 3* in′fil·trāt) *v.* **·trat·ed, ·trat·ing** *v.t.* **1** To cause (a liquid or gas) to pass into or through pores or interstices. **2** To filter through or into; permeate. **3** *Mil.* To pass through, as enemy lines, singly or in small groups so as to attack from the rear or on the flanks. — *v.i.* **4** To pass into or through a substance, as in filtering. — *n.* **1** That which infiltrates or has infiltrated. **2** Any morbid substance that passes into the tissues of the body.

in·fil·tra·tion (in′fil·trā′shən) *n.* **1** The act or process of infiltrating. **2** That which infiltrates. — **in·fil·tra·tive** (in·fil′trə·tiv) *adj.*

in·fin·i·tate (in·fin′ə·tāt) *v.t.* **·tat·ed, ·tat·ing** *Logic* To make (a positive concept or proposition) infinite or indefinite by adding a negative prefix to one of its terms; also, to make (a negative concept or proposition) positive by the reverse of this method: "Tigers are not herbivorous" when *infinitated* becomes "Tigers are non–herbivorous." [<Med. L *infinitatus,* pp. of *infinitare* render infinite < *infinitus* infinite] — **in·fin′i·ta′tion** *n.*

in·fi·nite (in′fə·nit) *adj.* **1** So great as to be immeasurable and unbounded; limitless: *infinite* power or space. **2** All–embracing; perfect; absolute: the *infinite* God. **3** *Math.* **a** Of, pertaining to, or designating a quantity conceived as always increasing so as to exceed any other assignable quantity in value. **b** Consisting of as many elements as a proper part of a total assemblage. **4** In music, composed so that it can be repeated over and over, without finale. **5** Very numerous; very great: to take *infinite* pains. — *n.* That which is infinite; an infinite quantity or magnitude; infinity. — **the Infinite** God; Eternity; the Absolute. [<L *infinitus* unlimited < *in-* not + *finitus* finite < *finis* limit] — **in′fi·nite·ly** *adv.* — **in′fi·nite·ness** *n.*

Synonyms: absolute, boundless, countless, eternal, illimitable, immeasurable, innumerable, interminable, limitless, measureless, numberless, unbounded, unconditioned, unfathomable, unlimited, unmeasured. *Infinite* signifies without bounds or limits in any way, and may be applied to space, time, quantity, or number. *Countless, innumerable,* and *numberless,* which should be the same as *infinite*, are in common usage vaguely employed to denote what it is difficult or practically impossible to count or number, but still perhaps falling far short of *infinite*; as, *countless* leaves, the *countless* sands on the seashore, *numberless* battles, *innumerable* delays. So, too, *boundless, illimitable, limitless, measureless,* and *unlimited* are loosely used in reference to what has no apparent or readily determinable limits in space or time; as, we speak of the *boundless* ocean. *Infinite* space is without bounds, not only in fact, but in thought; *infinite* time is truly *eternal.* Compare ETERNAL, PERFECT. *Antonyms*: bounded, brief, circumscribed, evanescent, finite, limited, little, measurable, moderate, narrow, restricted, shallow, short, small, transient, transitory.

in·fin·i·tes·i·mal (in′fin·ə·tes′ə·məl) *adj.* **1** Infinitely small. **2** So small as to be incalculable and insignificant for all practical purposes. **3** *Math.* Denoting a quantity conceived as continually diminishing toward zero as a limit. — *n.* An infinitesimal quantity. [<NL *infinitesimus* < *infinitus* infinite + *-esimus* (after *centesimus* hundredth)] — **in′fin·i·tes′i·mal·ly** *adv.*

infinitesimal calculus **1** Differential and integral calculus taken together. See under CALCULUS. **2** A branch of calculus which deals with differentials and the sums of infinitesimals.

in·fin·i·ti·val (in·fin′ə·tī′vəl) *adj. Gram.* Of or pertaining to the infinitive mood of the verb. — **in·fin′i·ti′val·ly** *adv.*

in·fin·i·tive (in·fin′ə·tiv) *Gram. adj.* **1** Without limitation of person or number: opposed to *finite.* **2** Of, pertaining to, or using the infinitive mood. — *n.* In many languages, a mood of the verb expressing action or condition without the limitation of person or number, as *to run.* In English, its sign *to* is omitted after the auxiliaries *can, could, do, may, might, must, shall, should, will, would,* and after such phrases as *had better, had rather,* and is used optionally after *bid, dare, help, let, make, need, please, see,* etc. The infinitive may also function as a noun while retaining the ability of the verb to take objects and adverbial modifiers. Example: *To ride* horses was his favorite sport. Also **infinitive mood.** — **split infinitive** An expression in which the sign of the infinitive "to" is separated from its verb by an intervening word, usually an adverb, as in the phrase "to quickly return." Although the construction is often condemned, it is sometimes justified to escape ambiguity. [<LL *infinitivus*]

in·fin·i·tude (in·fin′ə·tōōd, -tyōōd) *n.* **1** The quality of being infinite or boundless. **2** An infinite or unlimited quantity.

in·fin·i·ty (in·fin′ə·tē) *n.* *pl.* **·ties** **1** The quality or state of being infinite; boundlessness; perfection. **2** Something, as space, regarded as boundless. **3** The portion of space that lies at an infinite distance. **4** *Math.* **a** An infinite number or quantity: denoted by ∞. **b** The point or series of points in space that by supposition lie at an infinite distance from the definite point in question. [<OF *infinité* <L *infinitas, -tatis* < *infinitus* INFINITE]

in·firm (in·fûrm′) *adj.* **1** Feeble or weak from age. **2** Lacking soundness, resolution, stability, or firmness. **3** Not legally secure; voidable. See synonyms under FRAGILE, SICKLY. [<OF *enferm* <L *infirmus*] — **in·firm′ly** *adv.* — **in·firm′ness** *n.*

in·fir·mar·i·an (in′fər·mâr′ē·ən) *n.* A person having charge of a hospital, especially in a monastery, or who is delegated to perform hospital service.

in·fir·ma·ry (in·fûr′mər·ē) *n.* *pl.* **·ries** **1** A place for the treatment of the sick; a dispensary. **2** A small hospital. [<Med. L *infirmaria* < *infirmus* infirm]

in·fir·mi·ty (in·fûr′mə·tē) *n.* *pl.* **·ties** **1** A physical, mental, or moral weakness or flaw. **2** Infirm condition. See synonyms under DISEASE, FOIBLE, ILLNESS.

in·fix (in·fiks′) *v.t.* **1** To fix or drive in, as by thrusting. **2** To implant firmly; instil; inculcate. **3** *Gram.* To insert (an infix) within a word. — *n.* (in′fiks) *Gram.* A modifying addition inserted in the body of a word. Compare PREFIX, SUFFIX. — **in·fix′ion** *n.*

in fla·gran·te de·lic·to (in flə·gran′tē di·lik′tō) *Latin* In the very act of committing a crime: literally, while the crime is blazing.

in·flame (in·flām′) *v.* **·flamed, ·flam·ing** *v.t.* **1** To set on fire; kindle. **2** To excite to violent emotion or activity; arouse the fury of. **3** To excite or make more intense, as anger or lust. **4** To make red or florid, as with rage. **5** To cause inflammation in; heat morbidly. — *v.i.* **6** To catch fire; burst into flame. **7** To become excited or aroused. **8** To become inflamed by infection, etc. See synonyms under INCENSE[1]. [<OF *enflammer* <L *inflammare* < *in-* in + *flammare* flame < *flamma* flame] — **in·flam′er** *n.*

in·flam·ma·ble (in·flam′ə·bəl) *adj.* **1** Readily set on fire; combustible: also *flammable.* **2** Easily excited or roused to passion. — *n.* A combustible substance or material. See synonyms under ARDENT. [<F] — **in·flam′ma·bil′i·ty, in·flam′ma·ble·ness** *n.* — **in·flam′ma·bly** *adv.*

in·flam·ma·tion (in′flə·mā′shən) *n.* **1** *Pathol.* A morbid process in some tissue, organ, or part of the body characterized by heat, redness, swelling, and pain. **2** The act of inflaming.

in·flam·ma·to·ry (in·flam′ə·tôr′ē, -tō′rē) *adj.* **1** Tending to produce heat or excitement. **2** Calculated to arouse evil passions, riot, etc.; seditious. **3** Characterized by or pertaining to inflammation. **4** Inducing or provoking inflammation.

in·flate (in·flāt′) *v.* **·flat·ed, ·flat·ing** *v.t.* **1** To fill with gas or air so as to distend or expand; blow up; dilate. **2** To increase the proportions of; puff up: to *inflate* one's pride. **3** To

increase unduly, especially so that the nominal value exceeds the real: to *inflate* currency or prices. — *v.i.* **4** To become distended or inflated. See synonyms under PUFF, SWELL. [<L *inflatus*, pp. of *inflare* blow into <*in-* in + *flare* blow] — **in·flat′a·ble** *adj.*

in·flat·ed (in·flā′tid) *adj.* **1** Puffed out; distended; swollen, as by air or gas. **2** Hollowed or puffed out, as a plant stem or capsule; bulbous; dilated. **3** Overloaded with figures of speech and high-sounding words; pompous; bombastic; magniloquent. **4** Enhanced

in·fla·tion·ist (in·flā′shən·ist) *n.* An advocate of or believer in the issuing of an abnormally large amount of currency.

in·flect (in·flekt′) *v.t.* **1** *Gram.* To give or recite the inflections of (a word); conjugate; decline. **2** To modulate, as the voice. **3** To turn inward or aside; deflect; curve. — *v.i.* **4** To take grammatical inflection. [<L *inflectere* <*in-* in + *flectere* bend]

in·flec·tion (in·flek′shən) *n.* **1** The act of inflecting, the state of being inflected, or that which is inflected; a bending or bend; curva-

adjectives and adverbs; *-ed* for the past and past participle of regular (or weak) verbs, and *-ing* for the present participle.

in·flec·tion·al (in·flek′shən·əl) *adj. Ling.* **1** Belonging to, relating to, or showing grammatical inflection. **2** Designating a language, such as Latin, that expresses grammatical relationships by means of inflections, rather than by auxiliary words; synthetic: opposed to *analytic.* Also *Brit.* **in·flex′ion·al.** — **in·flec′tion·al·ly** *adv.*

in·flexed (in·flekst′) *adj. Bot.* Abruptly turned or bent inward, as the petals of a flower.

in·flex·i·ble (in·flek′sə·bəl) *adj.* **1** Not to be turned from a purpose; unyielding; firm; inexorable: *inflexible* resolves, an *inflexible* will. **2** Incapable of being physically bent; unbending; rigid; not flexible. **3** That cannot be altered or varied: the *inflexible* laws of nature. [<L *inflexibilis*] — **in·flex′i·bil′i·ty, in·flex′i·ble·ness** *n.* — **in·flex′i·bly** *adv.*

Synonyms: immovable, inexorable, obstinate, persistent, pertinacious, resolute, rigid, steadfast, stiff, stubborn, unbending, unrelenting, unyielding. See OBSTINATE. *Antonyms:* ductile, elastic, flexible, indulgent, lithe, pliable, pliant, supple, yielding.

in·flict (in·flikt′) *v.t.* **1** To cause another to suffer or endure, as a blow or wound. **2** To impose, as punishment. **3** To impose as if by force or against opposition: to *inflict* one's views on the public. [<L *inflictus*, pp. of *infligere* strike on <*in-* on + *fligere* strike] — **in·flict′er, in·flic′tor** *n.* — **in·flic′tive** *adj.*

in·flic·tion (in·flik′shən) *n.* **1** The act or process of inflicting or imposing: the *infliction* of a penalty. **2** That which is inflicted, as pain or punishment.

in·flo·res·cence (in′flə·res′əns) *n. Bot.* **1** The act of flowering; the expanding of blossoms. **2** The mode of disposition of flowers: racemose and cymose *inflorescence.* **3** Flowers collectively: said of certain plants or of a tree or a group of trees: the *inflorescence* of the horse chestnut. **4** An axis along which all the buds are flower buds. [<NL *inflorescentia* <LL *inflorescens*, ppr. of *inflorescere* come into flower. See IN-², FLORESCENCE.] — **in′flo·res′cent** *adj.*

in·flow (in′flō′) *n.* The act of flowing in, or that which flows in.

in·flu·ence (in′floo·əns) *n.* **1** The power or process of producing an effect upon a person, by imperceptible or intangible means. **2** Power arising from social, financial, moral, or similar authority. **3** A person, group, or the like possessing such power. **4** *Electr.* Electrostatic induction. **5** In astrology, originally, an ethereal fluid flowing from the stars and affecting the character and actions of men; later, an occult force of the stars exercising a similar control. See synonyms under IMPULSE, OPERATION. — *v.t.* **·enced, ·enc·ing 1** To exert mental or moral influence upon or over; sway; persuade. **2** To act upon physically; affect the nature or condition of; modify: Fatigue often *influences* the eyesight. [<F <LL *influentia* <*influens, -entis*, ppr. of *influere* <*in-* in + *fluere* flow. Doublet of INFLUENZA.] — **in′flu·enc·er** *n.*

Synonyms (verb): activate, actuate, affect, command, compel, dispose, draw, drive, excite, impel, incite, incline, induce, instigate, lead, mold, move, persuade, prompt, stir, sway, urge. To *influence* is to affect, modify, or act upon by physical, mental, or moral power, especially in some gentle, subtle, and gradual way; as, Vegetation is *influenced* by light; Everyone is *influenced* to some extent by public opinion; *influence* is chiefly used of power acting from without, but it may be used of motives regarded as forces acting upon the will. *Activate* means to put or go into action, to make capable of acting. *Actuate* refers to that which initiates the action of a mechanism or apparatus, as well as to mental or moral power *impelling* one from within. One may *influence*, but cannot directly *actuate* another; but one may be *actuated* to cruelty by hatred. *Prompt* and *stir* are words of mere suggestion toward some course of action; *dispose, draw, incline, influence,* and *lead* refer to the use of mild means to awaken in another a purpose or disposition to act. To

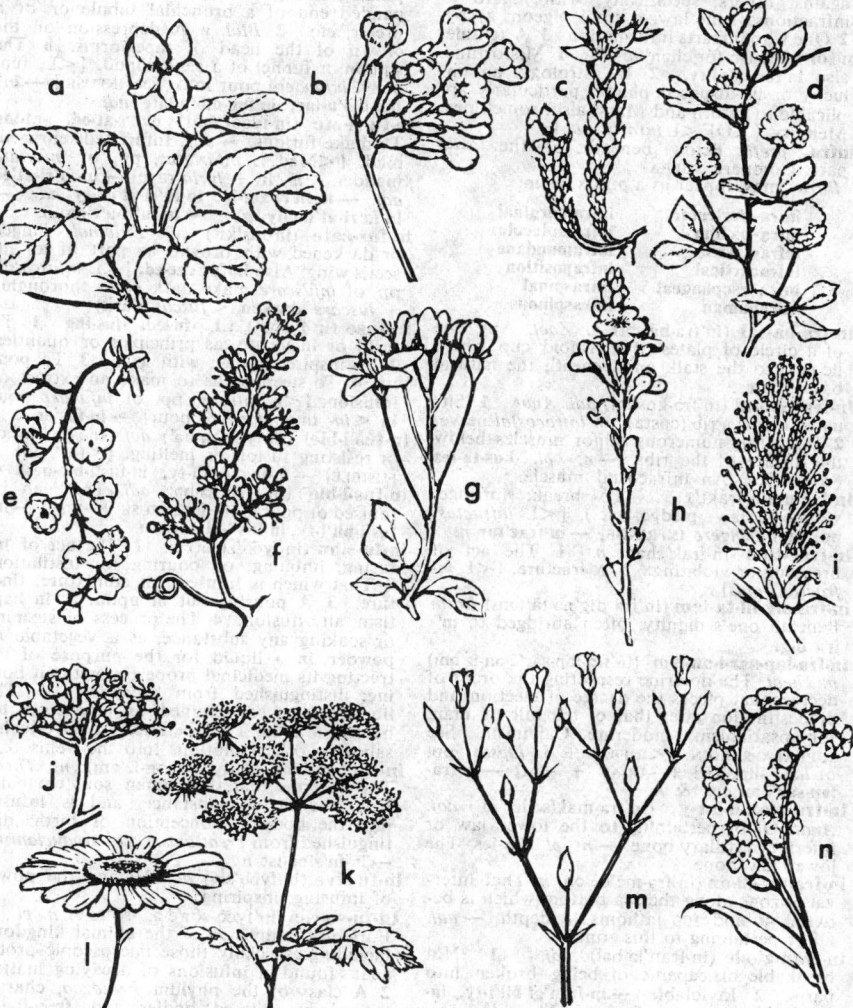

INFLORESCENCE

a. Uniflorous (violet).
b. Many-flowered (primrose).
c. Terminal (sedum).
d. Axillary (black medic).
e. Ordinary (grape currant).
f. Variegate (grapevine).
g. Clustered (cherry tree).
h. Corymb (verbena).
i. Catkin (willow).
j. Simple umbel (ivy).
k. Compound umbel (parsnips).
l. Capitulum (large marguerite).
m. Cyme: biparous or dichotomous (chickweed).
n. Cyme: uniparous or scorpion's-tail (forget-me-not).

or swollen abnormally or improperly; increased unjustifiably: *inflated* values. **5** Puffed up with conceit.

in·flat·er (in·flā′tər) *n.* One who or that which inflates; especially, any mechanical device, as an air pump, for inflating. Also **in·fla′tor.**

in·fla·tion (in·flā′shən) *n.* **1** The act of inflating, or the state of being inflated; distention: the *inflation* of a bubble or a balloon. **2** Bombast; conceit. **3** Expansion or extension beyond natural or proper limits or so as to exceed normal or just value; specifically, over-issue of currency, or the state resulting therefrom; also, increase in price levels arising from mounting effective demand without corresponding increase in commodity supply. **4** That which is inflated or puffed up. — **in·fla′tion·ar′y** *adj.*

ture; angle. **2** *Gram.* **a** A pattern of change undergone by words to express grammatical and syntactical relations, as of case, number, gender, person, tense, etc. The inflection of nouns, pronouns and adjectives is called *declension*; that of verbs, *conjugation.* **b** An element denoting the grammatical function of a word, as the use of *'s* to signify possession in *boy's.* **c** An inflected form. **3** Modulation or change of pitch in the voice. **4** *Geom.* A change in the nature of a curve, as from convex to concave. Also *Brit.* **in·flex′ion:** sometimes called *flection.*

◆ The few inflections surviving in English include: *s* for the regular plural of nouns, and for the third person singular present indicative of verbs; *'s* for the possessive; *-er* for the comparative, and *-est* for the superlative, of many

excite is to arouse one from lethargy or indifference to action. *Incite* and *instigate,* to spur or goad to action, differ in the fact that *incite* may be good, while *instigate* is usually to evil (compare ABET). To *urge* and *impel* signify to produce strong excitation toward some act. *Drive* and *compel* imply irresistible influence accomplishing its object. One may be *driven* either by his own passions or by external force or urgency; one is *compelled* only by some external power; as, The owner was *compelled* by his misfortunes to sell his estate. Compare ACTUATE, BEND, COMPEL, DRIVE, GOVERN, PERSUADE. *Antonyms*: deter, discourage, dissuade, hinder, impede, inhibit, prevent, restrain, retard.

influence fuze A proximity fuze.

in·flu·ent (in′flōō·ənt) *adj.* **1** Flowing in. **2** Relating to a channel through which either air or any fluid passes into a receptacle. — *n.* An inflow; a tributary stream or river; affluent. [<L *influens, -entis,* ppr. of *influere.* See INFLUENCE.]

in·flu·en·tial (in′flōō·en′shəl) *adj.* **1** Having or exercising influence. **2** Having or exercising a great influence or power; effective. — **in′flu·en′tial·ly** *adv.*

in·flu·en·za (in′flōō·en′zə) *n.* **1** *Pathol.* A contagious, infective, sometimes epidemic disease generally caused by a filtrable virus and commonly characterized by inflammation of the upper air passages, attended by fever and nervous and muscular prostration. **2** A contagious disease common among horses: characterized by its attack upon the mucous membranes of the throat and eyelids. [<Ital. <*influire* influence <L *influere* flow in. Doublet of INFLUENCE.] — **in′flu·en′zal** *adj.* — **in′flu·en′za·like′** *adj.*

in·flux (in′fluks′) *n.* **1** The act of flowing in; a continuous flowing in. **2** A pouring in or instilling. **3** The mouth of a river. **4** The place or point at which one stream flows into another. See synonyms under ACCESSION. [<F <LL *influxus,* pp. of *influere* flow in]

in·fold (in·fōld′) *v.t.* **1** To wrap in folds; enclose. **2** To embrace in or as in the arms; contain. **3** To turn or fold inward; make a fold in. Also *enfold.* — **in·fold′er** *n.*

in·form[1] (in·fôrm′) *v.t.* **1** To tell (someone) facts or information previously unknown; make something known to; notify: He *informed* me of the outcome. **2** To give character to; inspire; animate. **3** *Obs.* To give form or vitality to; shape. **4** *Rare* To teach; instruct. — *v.i.* **5** To give information, especially concerning infractions of the law: with *on* or *against.* [<OF *enformer* <L *informare* give form to, describe <*in-* in + *forma* form]

Synonyms: advertise, advise, apprise, communicate, disclose, divulge, impart, instruct, intimate, mention, notify, reveal, teach, tell. See LEARN, TEACH.

in·form[2] (in·fôrm′) *adj.* **1** Shapeless; unformed. **2** Deformed. [<F *informe* <L *informis* <*in-* not + *forma* form]

in·for·mal (in·fôr′məl) *adj.* **1** Not in the usual or prescribed form; unofficial: an *informal* truce. **2** Without ceremony or formality: an *informal* dinner. **3** Describing a manner of speech or writing characteristic of familiar conversation; colloquial. — **in·for′mal·ly** *adv.*

in·for·mal·i·ty (in′fôr·mal′ə·tē) *n. pl.* **·ties** **1** Absence of regular form; the state of being informal. **2** An informal act or proceeding.

in·form·ant (in·fôr′mənt) *n.* **1** One who imparts information. **2** *Ling.* A native speaker of a language whose speech is used by linguists in recording and studying linguistic forms, sounds, etc.

in for·ma pau·pe·ris (in fôr′mə pô′pər·is) *Latin* In the character or condition of a pauper; hence, in a lawsuit, free from costs.

in·for·ma·tion (in′fər·mā′shən) *n.* **1** Knowledge acquired or derived. **2** Timely or specific knowledge. **3** *Law* An accusation or complaint made without the intervention of a grand jury. **4** The act of informing. **5** Any distinct signal element forming part of a message or communication, especially one assembled and made available for use by automatic machines, as a digital computer: usually measured in bits. [<OF *enformacion*] — **in′for·ma′tion·al** *adj.* See synonyms under EDUCATION, KNOWLEDGE, TIDINGS, WISDOM.

information theory The scientific study of the characteristics, properties, and functions of any signal system designed to transmit information, with special emphasis on the number of bits that can be sent on a given power in a given time over a communication system operating under given conditions: also called *communication theory.*

in·form·a·tive (in·fôr′mə·tiv) *adj.* Instructive; affording information. Also **in·form′a·to′ry.** [<L *informatus,* pp. of *informare* describe]

in·formed (in·fôrmd′) *adj.* Having a high degree of knowledge, information, or education.

in·form·er (in·fôr′mər) *n.* **1** One who informs against others; specifically, with regard to infractions of the law; a stool pigeon; a spy. **2** One who imparts information. **3** A telltale.

in·for·tune (in·fôr′chən) *n. Obs.* **1** Misfortune: also **in′for·tu′ni·ty.** **2** In astrology, an unlucky or ill-disposed planet: particularly applicable to Saturn and Mars; also, sometimes, Mercury. [<OF <L *infortunium*]

infra– *prefix* Below; beneath; on the lower part. Compare SUPRA–.

Infra– may appear as a prefix, as in:

infra–auricular	**inframarginal**
infra–axillary	**inframolecular**
infraclavicle	**inframundane**
infracortical	**infraposition**
infra–esophageal	**infraspinal**
infrahuman	**infraspinous**

in·fra·ba·sal (in′frə·bā′səl) *n. Zool.* Any one of a circle of plates of a crinoid cup which lie next to the stalk and beneath the natural basal plates.

in·fra·cos·tal (in′frə·kos′təl) *adj. Anat.* **1** Situated below a rib (costa): an *infracostal* nerve. **2** Indicating numerous minor muscles below the surface of the ribs. — *n. pl.* **·kos·ta·les** (-kos·tā′lēz) An infracostal muscle.

in·fract (in·frakt′) *v.t.* To break; infringe; violate (a law, pledge, etc.). [<L *infractus,* pp. of *infringere* INFRINGE] — **in·frac′tor** *n.*

in·frac·tion (in·frak′shən) *n.* **1** The act of breaking or violating. **2** A fracture. [<L *infractio, -onis*]

in·fra dig·ni·ta·tem (in′frə dig′nə·tā′təm) *Latin* Beneath one's dignity: often abridged to **in′·fra dig.**

in·fra·lap·sar·i·an·ism (in′frə·lap·sâr′ē·ən·iz′əm) *n. Theol.* The doctrine respecting the order of decrees that places the decree of election and predestination after that of the fall of man; sublapsarianism; moderate Calvinism. See SUPRALAPSARIAN. [<INFRA- + L *lapsus,* pp. of *labi* slip, fall + -ARIAN + -ISM] — **in′fra·lap·sar′i·an** *adj.* & *n.*

in·fra·max·il·lar·y (in′frə·mak′sə·ler′ē) *adj. Anat.* Of or pertaining to the lower jaw or inferior maxillary bone. — *n. pl.* **·lar·ies** The lower jaw bone.

in·fra·me·di·an (in′frə·mē′dē·ən) *n.* That interval or zone along the sea bottom which is between 50 and 100 fathoms in depth. — *adj.* Of or pertaining to this zone.

in·fran·gi·ble (in·fran′jə·bəl) *adj.* **1** Not breakable or capable of being broken into parts. **2** Inviolable. — **in·fran′gi·bil′i·ty, in·fran′gi·ble·ness** *n.* — **in·fran′gi·bly** *adv.*

in·fra–o·ral (in′frə·ôr′əl, -ō′rəl) *adj. Anat.* Placed beneath the mouth.

in·fra–or·bit·al (in′frə·ôr′bit·əl) *adj. Anat.* Situated below the orbit of the eye.

in·fra·red (in′frə·red′) *adj. Physics* **1** Situated beyond the red end of the visible spectrum, as certain heat rays. **2** Designating radiations of wavelength in excess of about 7,600 angstroms but less than radio waves.

in·fra·son·ic (in′frə·son′ik) *adj.* Of, pertaining to, or characterized by a sound frequency below the range of audibility: also called *subsonic.* Compare ULTRASONIC.

in·fra·struc·ture (in′frə·struk′chər) *n.* The permanent foundation or essential elements of a structure, system, plan of operations, etc.; especially, the essential installations of a community, as schools, hospitals, transportation facilities, power plants, etc.

in·fre·quent (in·frē′kwənt) *adj.* Occurring at widely separate intervals; uncommon. — **in·fre′quent·ly** *adv.* — **in·fre′quen·cy** *n.*

in·fringe (in·frinj′) *v.t.* **·fringed, ·fring·ing** To break or disregard the terms or requirements of, as an oath or law; violate. — **to infringe on** (or **upon**) To transgress or trespass on rights or privileges; encroach: to *infringe on* a liberty or a patent. [<L *infringere* <*in-* in + *frangere* break] — **in·fring′er** *n.*

in·fringe·ment (in·frinj′mənt) *n.* **1** The act of infringing. **2** Any breaking in upon or violation of a right, privilege, regulation, law, contract, etc. **3** The wrongful use of trademarks or trade names.

in·fun·dib·u·li·form (in′fən·dib′yə·lə·fôrm′) *adj.* **1** Funnel-shaped. **2** *Bot.* Having a tube below and gradually enlarged above.

in·fun·dib·u·lum (in′fən·dib′yə·ləm) *n. pl.* **·la** (-lə) **1** *Anat.* **a** A structure or conduit shaped like a funnel, as that connecting the third ventricle of the brain with the pituitary body, passing through the hypothalamus. **b** An expanded end of a bronchial tubule or of a ureter, etc. **2** *Biol.* **a** A depression on the crown of the head of tapeworms. **b** The siphon or funnel of a cephalopod. [<L, funnel <*infundere* pour into. See INFUSE.] — **in′·fun·dib′u·lar, in′fun·dib′u·late** *adj.*

in·fu·ri·ate (in·fyŏŏr′ē·āt) *v.t.* **·at·ed, ·at·ing** To make furious. — *adj.* Infuriated; enraged; mad. [<Med. L *infuriatus,* pp. of *infuriare* madden <*in-* in + *furia* rage] — **in·fu′ri·at′ed** *adj.* — **in·fu′ri·ate·ly, in·fu′ri·at′ed·ly** *adv.* — **in·fu′ri·at′ing·ly** *adv.* — **in·fu′ri·a′tion** *n.*

in·fus·cate (in·fus′kit) *adj. Entomol.* Tinged or darkened with brown, as part of an insect's wing. Also **in·fus′cat·ed.** [<L *infuscatus,* pp. of *infuscare* make dark <*in-* thoroughly + *fuscare* darken <*fuscus* dark]

in·fuse (in·fyōōz′) *v.t.* **·fused, ·fus·ing** **1** To instil or inculcate, as principles or qualities. **2** To inspire; imbue: with *with.* **3** To pour in. **4** To steep, so as to make an extract or infusion. [<L *infusus,* pp. of *infunder* pour in <*in-* in + *fundere* pour] — **in·fus′er** *n.*

in·fus·i·ble[1] (in·fyōō′zə·bəl) *adj.* Incapable of or resisting fusion or melting. [<IN-[1] not + FUSIBLE] — **in·fus′i·bil′i·ty, in·fus′i·ble·ness** *n.*

in·fus·i·ble[2] (in·fyōō′zə·bəl) *adj.* That can be infused or poured in. [<INFUSE + -IBLE] — **in·fus′i·bil′i·ty, in·fus′i·ble·ness** *n.*

in·fu·sion (in·fyōō′zhən) *n.* **1** The act of infusing, imbuing, or pouring in; instilation. **2** That which is infused; an admixture; tincture. **3** A pouring out or upon, as in baptism; an affusion. **4** The process of steeping or soaking any substance, as a vegetable or powder, in a liquid for the purpose of extracting its medicinal properties without boiling: distinguished from *decoction.* **5** The liquid extract so obtained: an *infusion* of tobacco. **6** *Med.* The operation of introducing saline or other solutions into the veins.

in·fu·sion·ism (in·fyōō′zhən·iz′əm) *n. Theol.* The doctrine that the human soul emanates from the divine substance, and is infused into the body at conception or birth: distinguished from *creationism* and *traducianism.* — **in·fu′sion·ist** *n.*

in·fu·sive (in·fyōō′siv) *adj.* Having the power of infusing; inspiring.

In·fu·so·ri·a (in′fyōō·sôr′ē·ə, -sō′rē·ə) *n. pl.* **1** Formerly, a division of the animal kingdom, including especially those microscopic protozoans found in infusions of decaying matter. **2** A class of the phylum *Protozoa,* characterized by ciliated bodies and free-living aquatic habits, including *Paramecium* and *Stentor*: also called *Ciliata.* — **in′fu·so′ri·an** *adj.* & *n.* [<NL *infusus,* pp. of *infundere* pour into]

in·fu·so·ri·al (in′fyōō·sôr′ē·əl, -sō′rē-) *adj.* **1** Of or pertaining to infusorians. **2** Containing or composed of infusorians.

infusorial earth Kieselguhr.

in fu·tu·ro (in fyōō·tyōōr′ō) *Latin* In the future.

–ing[1] *suffix* **1** The act or art of doing the action expressed in the root verb: *hunting.* **2** The product or result of an action: a *painting,* a *building.* **3** Material for: *flooring.* **4** That which performs the action of the root verb: a *covering.* [OE *-ung, -ing*]

–ing[2] *suffix* Used in the present participle of verbs and in participial adjectives: He is *talking*; an *eating* apple. [ME *-inde* <OE *-ende*; infl. by ME *-inge* -ING[1]]

–ing[3] *suffix of nouns* **1** Related or belonging to; having the quality of: *farthing.* **2** Descendant of: *Browning.* **3** Small; little: *atheling.* [OE]

in·gath·er (in·gath′ər) *v.t.* & *v.i.* To gather in; harvest; assemble. — **in·gath′er·er** *n.*

in·gath·er·ing (in·gath′ər·ing) *n.* The act or occupation of gathering in, specifically, of a harvest. See synonyms under HARVEST.

Inge (ing), **William Ralph,** 1860–1954, English

churchman and author; dean of St. Paul's, London, 1911–34.

In·ge·low (in′jə·lō), **Jean,** 1820–97, English author.

in·gem·i·nate (in·jem′ə·nāt) *v.t.* **·nat·ed, ·nat·ing** To repeat or redouble; reiterate. —*adj.* (-it) Repeated; redoubled. [<L *ingeminatus,* pp. of *ingeminare* double. See IN-[1], GERMINATE.] —**in·gem′i·na′tion** *n.*

in·gen·er·ate[1] (in·jen′ər·āt) *v.t.* **·at·ed, ·at·ing** To generate or produce within. —*adj.* (-it) Inborn. [<L *ingeneratus,* pp. of *ingenerare* ENGENDER] —**in·gen′er·a′tion** *n.*

in·gen·er·ate[2] (in·jen′ər·it) *adj.* Not brought into being by generation. [<LL *ingeneratus* self-existent]

in·gen·ious (in·jēn′yəs) *adj.* **1** Possessed of or manifesting inventive faculty. **2** Characterized by ingenuity; well conceived; apt. **3** *Obs.* Of clever mind or genius, or displaying exceptional mental qualities. See synonyms under CLEVER. [<MF *ingénieux* <L *ingeniosus* talented < *ingenium* natural quality, ability < *in-* in + *gignere* beget] —**in·gen′ious·ly** *adv.* —**in·gen′ious·ness** *n.*

in·gen·i·tal (in·jen′ə·təl) *adj. Obs.* That is natural to one; inherent. [<L *ingenitus,* pp. of *ingignere* implant, beget]

in·gé·nue (an′zhə·nōō′, *Fr.* aṅ·zhā·nü′) *n. pl.* **·nues** (-nōōz′, *Fr.* ·nü′) **1** A young woman or girl who is artless, ingenuous, or innocent. **2** An actress who fills such a role; also, the role. [<F, fem. of *ingénu* <L *ingenuus* INGENUOUS]

in·ge·nu·i·ty (in′jə·nōō′ə·tē, -nyōō′-) *n.* **1** The quality of having inventive power; cleverness in contriving or originating. **2** Ingeniousness of execution or design. **3** *Obs.* Ingenuousness; candor.

Synonyms: acuteness, cleverness, cunning, dexterity, genius, ingeniousness, invention, inventiveness, readiness, skill. *Ingenuity* is inferior to *genius,* being rather mechanical than creative, and is shown in devising expedients, overcoming difficulties, inventing appliances, adapting means to ends. *Dexterity* is chiefly of the hand; *cleverness* may be either of the hand or of the mind, but chiefly of the latter. See ADDRESS. *Antonyms*: awkwardness, clumsiness, dulness, stupidity, unskilfulness.

in·gen·u·ous (in·jen′yōō·əs) *adj.* **1** Free from disguise or dissimulation; frank; artless. **2** High-minded; sincere. **3** Ingenious: an incorrect use. See synonyms under CANDID, HONEST. [<L *ingenuus* inborn, natural, frank < *in-gignere* beget, engender] —**in·gen′u·ous·ly** *adv.* —**in·gen′u·ous·ness** *n.*

In·ger·soll (ing′gər·səl, -sôl), **Robert Green,** 1833–99, U. S. lawyer, agnostic, and writer.

in·gest (in·jest′) *v.t.* To take in (food) for digestion. [<L *ingestus,* pp. of *ingere* carry in < *in-* in + *gerere* carry] —**in·ges′tion** *n.* —**in·ges′tive** *adj.*

in·ges·ta (in·jes′tə) *n. pl.* **1** Things introduced or taken into a living body, as food: opposed to *egesta.* **2** Anything incorporated. [<NL, neut. pl. of *ingestus,* pp. of *ingerere* carry in]

in·gine (in·jīn′) *n. Scot.* Natural ability; a gifted person.

in·gle (ing′gəl) *n. Scot.* A fire or fireplace.

in·gle·nook (ing′gəl·nŏŏk′) *n.* A corner by the fire.

in·gle·side (ing′gəl·sīd′) *n. Scot.* The fireside. Also **in′gle-cheek′** (-chēk).

in·glo·ri·ous (in·glôr′ē·əs, -glō′rē-) *adj.* **1** Characterized by failure or disgrace. **2** Without glory; obscure; humble. [<L *ingloriosus*] —**in·glo′ri·ous·ly** *adv.* —**in·glo′ri·ous·ness** *n.*

in·go·ing (in′gō′ing) *adj.* Entering; going in.

In·golds·by (ing′gəldz·bē), **Thomas** See BARHAM.

In·gol·stadt (ing′ôl·shtät) A city on the Danube in Upper Bavaria, West Germany.

in·got (ing′gət) *n.* **1** A mass of cast metal from the crucible, as a bar of gold. **2** *Obs.* A mold in which an ingot may be cast. [<IN-[2] + OE *goten,* pp. of *geoton* pour]

in·graft (in·graft′, -gräft′) See ENGRAFT.

in·grain (in·grān′) *v.t.* **1** To fix deeply; impress indelibly upon the mind or character. **2** To dye before weaving; dye with "grain" or scarlet. Also spelled *engrain.* —*n.* (in′grān′) A carpet made of ingrained worsted; also, the ingrained wool or other material of which it is made. —*adj.* (in′grān′) Dyed in the yarn before manufacture; hence, thoroughly inwrought. [Var. of ENGRAIN]

in·grained (in·grānd′) *adj.* **1** Dyed in the wool; deeply rooted or worked in. **2** Thorough; inveterate.

in·grate (in′grāt) *adj. Obs.* Ungrateful. Also **in·grate′ful.** —*n.* One who is ungrateful. [<OF *ingrat* <L *ingratus* unpleasant, ungrateful < *in-* not + *gratus* pleasing]

in·gra·ti·ate (in·grā′shē·āt) *v.t.* **·at·ed, ·at·ing** To bring (oneself) into the favor or confidence of others. —**in·gra′ti·at′ing·ly** *adv.* —**in·gra′ti·a′tion** *n.* —**in·gra′ti·a·to′ry** (-ə·tôr′ē, -tō′rē) *adj.* [<Ital. *ingraziare* <L *in gratiam* in favor]

in·grat·i·tude (in·grat′ə·tōōd, -tyōōd) *n.* Lack of gratitude; insensibility to kindness; thanklessness.

in·gra·ves·cent (in′grə·ves′ənt) *adj. Pathol.* Increasing in severity or gravity, as a disease. [<L *ingravescens, -entis,* ppr. of *ingravescere* grow heavier, worse < *in-* in + *gravis* heavy] —**in′gra·ves′cence** *n.*

in·gre·di·ent (in·grē′dē·ənt) *n.* **1** That which enters into the composition of a mixture: usually distinguished from the *constituent* of a chemical compound. **2** A component part of anything. See synonyms under PART. [<F *ingrédient* <L *ingrediens, -entis,* ppr. of *ingredi* entering into < *in-* in + *gradi* walk]

In·gres (aṅ′gr′), **Jean Auguste Dominique,** 1780–1867, French painter.

in·gress (in′gres) *n.* **1** Means or power of effecting entrance. **2** A place of entrance. **3** The act of entering. See synonyms under ENTRANCE[1]. [<L *ingressus,* pp. of *ingredi* enter]

in·gres·sion (in·gresh′ən) *n.* The act of entering, or an entrance into something.

in·gres·sive (in·gres′iv) *adj.* **1** Pertaining to entrance; entering. **2** *Gram.* Inceptive. —**in·gres′sive·ness** *n.*

in-group (in′grōōp′) *n. Sociol.* Any group considered by any of its members to have a certain exclusiveness: contrasted with *out-group.*

in·grown (in′grōn′) *adj.* **1** Grown into the flesh, as a toe nail. **2** Growing inward or within. —**in′grow′ing** *adj.*

in·growth (in′grōth′) *n.* An inward growth, or a thing that grows inward.

in·gui·nal (ing′gwə·nəl) *adj.* Of, pertaining to, or near the groin. See illustration under ABDOMINAL. [<L *inguinalis*]

inguino- *combining form* In, affecting, or related to the groin. Also, before vowels, **inguin-.** [<L *inguen, -inis* the groin]

in·gui·no-ab·dom·i·nal (ing′gwə·nō·ab·dom′ə·nəl) *adj.* Related to the groin and the abdomen.

in·gulf (in·gulf′) *v.t.* To engulf. —**in·gulf′·ment** *n.*

in·gur·gi·tate (in·gûr′jə·tāt) *v.t.* & *v.i.* **·tat·ed, ·tat·ing** To eat or drink greedily or to excess; gorge; swill. [<L *ingurgitatus,* pp. of *ingurgitare* pour in, gorge oneself < *in-* in + *gurges, -ites* whirlpool] —**in·gur′gi·ta′tion** *n.*

in·hab·it (in·hab′it) *v.t.* To live or dwell in; occupy as a home. —*v.i. Archaic* To dwell; abide. [<OF *enhabiter* <L *inhabitare* < *in-* in + *habitare* dwell, freq. of *habere* have] —**in·hab′it·a·bil′i·ty** *n.* —**in·hab′it·a·ble** *adj.* —**in·hab′it·er** *n.* —**in·hab′i·ta′tion** *n.*

in·hab·i·tance (in·hab′ə·təns) *n.* **1** The act of dwelling; state of being inhabited; residence, as distinguished from sojourn. **2** A habitation; abode. Also **in·hab′i·tan·cy.**

in·hab·i·tant (in·hab′ə·tənt) *n.* One making his home or dwelling permanently in a place, as distinguished from a lodger or visitor; a resident. [<AF <L *inhabitans -antis,* pp. of *inhabitare*]

in·hab·it·ed (in·hab′ə·tid) *adj.* **1** Having inhabitants; populated. **2** *Obs.* Lodged.

in·ha·lant (in·hā′lənt) *adj.* **1** That inhales or draws in. **2** Used for inhaling. —*n.* **1** An apparatus used for inhaling. **2** That which is to be inhaled. Also **in·ha′lent.**

in·ha·la·tion (in′hə·lā′shən) *n,* **1** The act of inhaling. **2** That which is inhaled; an inhalant.

in·hale (in·hāl′) *v.* **·haled, ·hal·ing** *v.t.* To draw into the lungs, as breath or tobacco smoke; breathe in. —*v.i.* To draw breath, tobacco smoke, etc., into the lungs. Opposed to *exhale.* [<L *inhalare* < *in-* in + *halare* breathe]

in·hal·er (in·hā′lər) *n.* **1** One who inhales. **2** Something from or through which one inhales; specifically an appliance or apparatus enabling one to inhale air, medicinal vapors, anesthetics, etc.

in·har·mo·ni·ous (in′här·mō′nē·əs) *adj.* Lacking in, or not in, harmony; discordant. Also **in′har·mon′ic** (-mon′ik), **in′har·mon′i·cal.** See synonyms under INCONGRUOUS. —**in′har·mo′·ni·ous·ly** *adv.* —**in′har·mo′ni·ous·ness** *n.*

in·haul (in′hôl′) *n. Naut.* A rope or rigging for bringing in a sail or spar, as the jib boom. Also **in′haul′er.**

in·here (in·hir′) *v.i.* **·hered, ·her·ing** To be a permanent or essential part: with *in.* [<L *inhaerere* < *in-* in + *haerere* stick] —**in·her′ence, in·her′en·cy** *n.*

in·her·ent (in·hir′ənt, -her′-) *adj.* **1** Permanently united; intrinsic; innate; essential. **2** Pertaining as a property or attribute. Also **in·he·ren·tial** (in′hi·ren′shəl). [<L *inhaerens, -entis,* ppr. of *inhaerere* INHERE] —**in·her′ent·ly** *adv.*

Synonyms: congenital, essential, immanent, inborn, inbred, indispensable, indwelling, infixed, ingrained, innate, inseparable, internal, intrinsic, inwrought, native, natural, subjective. *Immanent* is a philosophic word, to denote that which dwells in or pervades any substance or spirit without necessarily being a part of it. That which is *inherent* is an *inseparable* part of that in which it inheres, and is usually thought of with reference to some outworking or effect; as, an *inherent* difficulty. God is said to be *immanent* (not *inherent*) in the universe. Frequently *intrinsic* and *inherent* can be interchanged, but *inherent* applies to qualities, while *intrinsic* applies to essence, so that to speak of *intrinsic* excellence conveys higher praise than if we say *inherent* excellence. *Inherent* and *intrinsic* may be said of persons or things; *congenital, inborn, inbred, innate,* apply to living beings. *Congenital* is frequent in medical and legal use with special application to defects; as, *congenital* idiocy. *Innate* and *inborn* are almost identical, but *innate* is preferred in philosophic use, as when we speak of *innate* ideas; that which is *inborn, congenital,* or *innate* may be original with the individual, but that which is *inbred* is inherited. *Ingrained* signifies dyed in the grain, and denotes that which is deeply wrought into substance or character. See NATURAL. *Antonyms*: accidental, casual, external, extrinsic, fortuitous, incidental, outward, subsidiary, superadded, superficial, superfluous, superimposed, supplemental, transient, unconnected.

in·her·it (in·her′it) *v.t.* **1** To receive, as property or a title, by succession or will; fall heir to. **2** To receive (traits, qualities, etc.) as if by succession or will; have as hereditary traits. **3** *Obs.* To make heir; place (an heir) in possession: usually with *of.* —*v.i.* **4** To come into or possess an inheritance. **5** To receive traits, qualities, etc.: with *from.* [<OF *enheriter* <LL *inhereditare* inherit < *in-* in + *heres* heir]

in·her·it·a·ble (in·her′ə·tə·bəl) *adj.* **1** Transmissible by descent; descendible to an heir by mere operation of law. **2** Capacitated or qualified to take by inheritance: having *inheritable* blood. **3** That may be transmitted by ancestors; heritable. [<AF *enheritable*] —**in·her′it·a·bil′i·ty, in·her′it·a·ble·ness** *n.* —**in·her′it·a·bly** *adv.*

in·her·i·tance (in·her′ə·təns) *n.* **1** Anything acquired or possessed by descent or succession; something which is or can be inherited, as property or title acquired by an heir at the owner's death. **2** A heritage, especially in the sense of mental, cultural or spiritual legacies left by past generations to succeeding generations. **3** Physical or mental characteristics derived from ancestry. **4** Act or fact of inheriting.

inheritance tax A tax imposed on an inherited estate.

inherited character *Genetics* A modification of an organism considered as having been transmitted by inheritance: distinguished from *acquired character.*

in·her·i·tor (in·her′ə·tər) *n.* An heir. —**in·her′i·tress** (-tris), **in·her′i·trix** (-triks) *n. fem.*

in·he·sion (in·hē′zhən) *n.* The condition of inhering or being fixed in something; inherence. [<LL *inhaesio, -onis* < *inhaerere.* See INHERE.]

in·hib·it (in·hib′it) *v.t.* **1** To hold back; restrain, as an impulse. **2** To forbid (a cleric) to perform religious functions. **3** To check or block (one mental or nervous process) by another, nearly simultaneous, opposed process. See synonyms under PROHIBIT. [<L *inhibitus,* pp. of *inhibere* check < *in-* in + *habere* have, hold] — **in·hib′it·er, in·hib′i·tor** *n.* — **in·hib′it·a·ble** *adj.* — **in·hib′i·tive, in·hib′i·to′ry** (-tôr′ē, -tō′rē) *adj.*

in·hi·bi·tion (in′hi·bish′ən, in′i-) *n.* **1** The act of inhibiting or the state of being inhibited; restriction; repression; embargo; ban. **2** *Physiol.* **a** The checking of one stimulus or reflex by another acting in opposition. **b** A state of diminished activity at the synapses of the nerves. **3** *Psychol.* **a** The blocking of one mental impulse or process by another. **b** The restraint of will over the impulsive tendencies to habitual or strongly stimulated reactions. **c** Any mental or emotional block.

in·hib·i·tor (in·hib′ə·tər) *n.* **1** That which causes inhibitory action; especially, an inhibitory nerve. **2** A medicinal agent that tends or operates to check organic activity.

in hoc sig·no vin·ces (in hok sig′nō vin′sēz) *Latin* By this sign (i.e., of the cross) thou wilt conquer: motto of the emperor Constantine.

in·hos·pi·ta·ble (in·hos′pi·tə·bəl, in′hos·pit′ə·bəl) *adj.* **1** Not hospitable. **2** Barren; wild; cheerless; affording no shelter or subsistence. — **in·hos′pi·ta·ble·ness** *n.* — **in·hos′pi·ta·bly** *adv.* — **in·hos′pi·tal′i·ty** (-tal′ə·tē) *n.*

in·hu·man (in·hyōō′mən) *adj.* **1** Not possessed of human qualities; cruel; savage; barbarous. **2** Characterized by cruelty; manifesting lack of humanity. **3** Not of the ordinary human type. See synonyms under BARBAROUS, SANGUINARY. [<F *inhumain* <L *inhumanus*] — **in·hu′man·ly** *adv.* — **in·hu′man·ness** *n.*

in·hu·mane (in′hyōō·mān′) *adj.* Not humane; not kind; inhuman. — **in′hu·mane′ly** *adv.*

in·hu·man·i·ty (in′hyōō·man′ə·tē) *n. pl.* **·ties** The state of lacking human or humane qualities; cruelty; also, a cruel act, word, etc. [<F *inhumanité* <L *inhumanitas*]

in·hu·ma·tion (in′hyōō·mā′shən) *n.* Burial.

in·hume (in·hyōōm′) *v.t.* **·humed, ·hum·ing** To place in the earth, as a dead body; bury; inter. [<L *inhumare* < *in-* in + *humus* soil, earth] — **in·hum′er** *n.*

In·i·go (in′i·gō) A masculine personal name. [<Sp., fiery (lit., igneous)]

in·im·i·cal (in·im′i·kəl) *adj.* **1** Of a character regarded as hurtful in tendency or opposed in influence; antagonistic. **2** Unfriendly; hostile. [<LL *inimicalis* < *inimicus* unfriendly < *in-* not + *amicus* friend] — **in·im′i·cal′i·ty** (-kal′ə·tē) *n.* — **in·im′i·cal·ly** *adv.*

Synonyms: adverse, antagonistic, averse, contradictory, contrary, disaffected, harmful, hurtful, noxious, opposed, pernicious, repugnant, unfriendly, unwilling.

in·im·i·ta·ble (in·im′ə·tə·bəl) *adj.* That cannot be imitated; matchless; incomparable. [<L *inimitabilis*] — **in·im′i·ta·bil′i·ty, in·im′i·ta·ble·ness** *n.* — **in·im′i·ta·bly** *adv.*

I·ni·ni (ē·nē·nē′) A dependency of southern French Guiana bordering on Brazil; 30,300 square miles.

in·i·on (in′ē·ən) *n. pl.* **in·i·a** (in′ē·ə) *Anat.* The occipital protuberance on the exterior of the skull. [<NL <Gk., nape of the neck < *is, inos* muscle]

in·iq·ui·tous (in·ik′wə·təs) *adj.* Wicked; unjust. See synonyms under CRIMINAL, SINFUL. — **in·iq′ui·tous·ly** *adv.* — **in·iq′ui·tous·ness** *n.*

in·iq·ui·ty (in·ik′wə·tē) *n. pl.* **·ties** **1** Deviation from right; wickedness; gross injustice. **2** A wrongful act; unjust thing or deed. See synonyms under ABOMINATION, INJUSTICE, SIN. [<OF *iniquité* <L *iniquitas* < *iniquus* unequal < *in-* not + *aequus* equal]

in·i·tial (in·ish′əl) *adj.* **1** Standing at the beginning or head. **2** Pertaining to the first stage. — *n.* **1** The first letter of a word, name, etc. **2** In a book or manuscript, the first letter of a chapter, division of a chapter, or verse: often elaborately painted and gilded. — *v.t.* **·tialed** or **·tialled, ·tial·ing** or **·tial·ling** To mark or sign with initials. [<F <L *initialis* < *initium* beginning < *initus,* pp. of *inire* go into, enter upon < *in-* in + *ire* go] — **in·i′tial·ly** *adv.*

initial meridian axis *Math.* The vertical, fixed plane passing through the polar axis of a sphere in the spherical coordinate system.

Initial Teaching Alphabet An alphabet of 43 characters representing the sounds of English, used in teaching children to read: also called *Augmented Roman.* Abbr. *I.T.A.*

in·i·ti·ate (in·ish′ē·āt) *v.t.* **·at·ed, ·at·ing** **1** To begin; originate. **2** To introduce, as into a position or club, usually with rites or ceremony. **3** To instruct in fundamentals or principles. See synonyms under ENROL, INSTALL, TEACH. — *adj.* (-it, -āt) **1** Instructed in the rudiments or secrets; initiated; newly admitted, as into a secret society. **2** Initial; begun; commenced; new. **3** Characteristic of an inexperienced person or of one newly initiated. — *n.* (-it, -āt) One who has been initiated; also, a beginner. [<L *initiatus,* pp. of *initiare* enter upon < *initium* beginning. See INITIAL.] — **in·i′ti·a′tor** *n.*

in·i·ti·a·tion (in·ish′ē·ā′shən) *n.* **1** The act of initiating. **2** Ceremonial admission, as into a society; the rites or ceremonies which have to be undergone. See synonyms under BEGINNING.

in·i·ti·a·tive (in·ish′ē·ə·tiv) *n.* **1** A first move. **2** The power of initiating; ability for original conception and independent action. **3** The process by which the electorate initiates or enacts legislation. See REFERENDUM. — *adj.* Pertaining to initiation; serving to initiate; preliminary. — **in·i′ti·a·tive·ly** *adv.*

in·i·ti·a·to·ry (in·ish′ē·ə·tôr′ē, -tō′rē) *adj.* **1** Introductory. **2** Serving to initiate.

in·ject (in·jekt′) *v.t.* **1** To drive or force in: to *inject* gas into a carburetor. **2** To force a fluid into, as for anesthetizing, preserving, etc., especially by means of a syringe or hypodermic needle. **3** To introduce (something new or lacking): with *into*: to *inject* life into a play. **4** To throw in or interject, as a remark or comment, usually by way of interruption. [<L *injectus,* pp. of *inicere, injicere* throw, cast in < *in-* in + *jacere* throw]

in·jec·tion (in·jek′shən) *n.* **1** The act of injecting, the state of being injected, or that which is injected. **2** *Med.* The introduction by instruments of a fluid into some cavity or tissue of the body. **3** The similar introduction of a substance into a cadaver to facilitate dissection or anatomical demonstration. **4** Any liquid or substance so introduced. **5** An enema. **6** The state of being hyperemic.

in·jec·tor (in·jek′tər) *n.* **1** One who or that which injects. **2** An apparatus by which steam carries and delivers water to a boiler that is supplying steam.

in·ju·di·cious (in′jōō·dish′əs) *adj.* **1** Not judicious; indiscreet; ill-advised. **2** Wanting in judgment. See synonyms under IMPRUDENT. — **in′ju·di′cious·ly** *adv.* — **in′ju·di′cious·ness** *n.*

in·junc·tion (in·jungk′shən) *n.* **1** The act of enjoining. **2** An admonition or order given with authority. **3** *Law* A judicial order requiring the party enjoined to take or (usually) to refrain from some specified action. See synonyms under ORDER. [<LL *injunctio, -onis* < *injunctum,* pp. of *injungere* join to, enjoin. See IN-[2], JUNCTION.]

in·jure (in′jər) *v.t.* **·jured, ·jur·ing** **1** To do harm or hurt to; wound; damage; impair. **2** To do wrong to; treat with injustice. See synonyms under ABUSE, HURT, VIOLATE. [<F *injurier* <L *injurari* < *injuria* INJURY] — **in′jur·er** *n.*

in·ju·ri·ous (in·jŏŏr′ē·əs) *adj.* **1** Hurtful, deleterious, or detrimental in any way. **2** *Obs.* Disposed to inflict injury; inimical. **3** Slanderous; abusive. See synonyms under BAD, PERNICIOUS. Compare INJURY. [<F *injurieux* <L *injuriosus*] — **in·ju′ri·ous·ly** *adv.* — **in·ju′ri·ous·ness** *n.*

in·ju·ry (in′jər·ē) *n. pl.* **·ries** **1** Any wrong, damage, or mischief done or suffered. **2** A source of harm. **3** A wrong or damage done to another; the unlawful infringement or privation of rights. **4** *Obs.* Abuse; insult. [<AF *injurie* <L *injuria* < *injurius* injust < *in-* not + *jus, juris* right, law]

Synonyms: blemish, damage, detriment, disadvantage, evil, harm, hurt, impairment, injustice, loss, mischief, outrage, prejudice, wrong. *Injury* is the general term including all the rest. Whatever reduces the value, utility, beauty, or desirableness of anything is an *injury* to that thing; of persons, whatever is so done as to operate adversely to one in his person, rights, property, or reputation is an *injury. Damage* (L *damnum,* loss) is that which occasions *loss* to the possessor; hence, *damage* reduces value, utility, or beauty; *detriment* (L *deterere,* to rub or wear away) is similar in meaning, but far milder. As a rule, the slightest use of an article by a purchaser operates to its *detriment* if again offered for sale, even when the article may not have received the slightest *damage. Damage* is partial; *loss* is properly absolute as far as it is predicted at all; the *loss* of a ship implies that it is gone beyond recovery; the *loss* of the rudder is a *damage* to the ship; but since the *loss* of a part still leaves a part, we may speak of a partial or total *loss. Evil* commonly suggests suffering or sin, or both; as, the *evils* of poverty, the social *evil. Harm* is closely synonymous with *injury*; it may apply to body, mind, or estate, but always affects real worth, while *injury* may concern only estimated value. A *hurt* is an *injury* that causes pain, physical or mental; a slight *hurt* may be no real *harm. Mischief* is disarrangement, trouble, or *harm* usually caused by some voluntary agent, with or without injurious intent; a child's thoughtless sport may do great *mischief*; *wrong* is *harm* done with evil intent. An *outrage* combines insult and *injury.* Compare synonyms for BLEMISH, INJUSTICE, LOSS, OUTRAGE, VIOLENCE. *Antonyms*: advantage, amelioration, benefit, blessing, boon, help, improvement, remedy, service, utility.

in·jus·tice (in·jus′tis) *n.* **1** The violation or denial of justice. **2** An unjust act; a wrong. [<OF <L *injustitia*]

Synonyms: grievance, inequity, iniquity, injury, unfairness, unrighteousness, wrong. *Injustice* is a violation or denial of justice, an act or omission that is contrary to equity or justice; as, the *injustice* of unequal taxes. In legal usage a *wrong* involves *injury* to person, property, or reputation, as the result of evil intent; *injustice* applies to civil damage or loss, not necessarily involving *injury* to person or property, as by misrepresentation of goods which does not amount to a legal warranty. In popular usage, *injustice* may involve no direct *injury* to person, property, interest, or character, and no harmful intent, while *wrong* always involves both; one who attributes another's truly generous act to a selfish motive does him an *injustice.* Compare synonyms for INJURY, SIN. *Antonyms*: equity, fairness, faithfulness, honesty, honor, impartiality, integrity, justice, lawfulness, rectitude, right, righteousness, uprightness.

ink (ingk) *n.* **1** A colored liquid or viscous substance, used in writing, printing, etc. ◆ Collateral adjective: *atramental.* **2** The dark fluid secreted by a cuttlefish and ejected so as to color the water and thus assist in escaping an enemy. — *v.t.* To spread ink upon; mark or color with ink. [<OF *enque* <LL *encaustum* purple ink used by the Caesars <Gk. *enkauston,* neut. of *enkaustos* burned out. See ENCAUSTIC.] — **ink′er** *n.*

ink·ber·ry (ingk′ber′ē) *n. pl.* **·ries** **1** A small shrub (*Ilex glabra*) of the holly family, with oblong leaves and roundish, black, shining berries. **2** One of its berries. **3** Pokeweed.

Ink·er·man (ing′kər·mən, *Russian* in·ker·män′) An eastern suburb of Sevastopol: site of the Russian defeat in the Crimean War, 1854.

ink·horn (ingk′hôrn′) *n.* An inkholder: so called because formerly made of horn.

inkhorn term A bookish word. Also **ink′·horn′ism.**

in·kle (ing′kəl) *n.* **1** A broad linen tape; the thread or yarn from which it is made. **2** Formerly, a braid trimming.

ink·ling (ingk′ling) *n.* A slight intimation; a faint notion; hint. [ME *inkle* hint, ? <OE *inca* suspicion]

ink-sac (ingk′sak′) *n. Zool.* A pear-shaped glandular organ in the mantle cavity of cuttlefish from which a black substance is ejected as a protective screen.

ink·stand (ingk′stand′) *n.* A vessel to hold ink for writing: often combined with a rack for pens, etc. Also **ink′well′** (-wel′).

ink·wood (ingk′wŏŏd′) *n.* An evergreen pinnate-leaved tree (*Exothea paniculata*) found in southern Florida, the West Indies, and Guatemala, and yielding a reddish-brown, hard, heavy wood: also called *butterbough.*

ink·y (ing′kē) *adj.* **ink·i·er, ink·i·est** 1 Consisting of, stained with, like, or containing ink 2 Black. — **ink′i·ness** *n.*
ink·y-cap (ing′kē-kap′) *n.* A mushroom (genus *Coprinus*) whose gills dissolve into a black, inky liquid after the spores have matured.
in·lace (in·lās′) See ENLACE.
in·laid (in′lād′, in·lād′) *adj.* 1 Decorated by the insertion of wood, ivory, or other material. 2 Inserted to form such decoration. See INLAY.
in·land (in′lənd) *adj.* 1 Remote from the sea. 2 Located in or limited to the interior of a country. 3 Not foreign; domestic. — *n.* (in′lənd, -land′) The interior of a country. — *adv.* (in′lənd, -land′) Toward the interior of a land.
Inland Empire A region of the Columbia River basin in eastern Washington, northern Oregon, and northern Idaho.
in·land·er (in′lən·dər, -lan′dər) *n.* One living inland or from inland.
Inland Sea An arm of the Philippine Sea between Honshu and Shikoku and Kyushu islands, Japan. *Japanese* **Se·to-nai·kai** (se·tō·nī·kī).
in·law (in·lô′) *v.t.* In old English law, to free from outlawry; replace under protection of law; restore to civil rights. [OE *inlagian*]
in-law (in′lô′) *n. Colloq.* A member of the family of one's husband or wife, or the spouse of one's child.
in·law·ry (in′lô′rē) *n. pl.* **·ries** In old English law, annulment of outlawry; restoration to the protection of the law.
in·lay (in·lā′, in′lā′) *v.t.* **in·laid, in·lay·ing** 1 To set decorative patterns or designs of (ivory, gold, etc.) into the surface of an object. 2 To decorate, as a piece of furniture, by inserting such patterns or designs. 3 To attach (a page, illustration, etc.) in a place cut for it in a larger or heavier sheet, either for framing or enlarging the margin. — *n.* (in′lā) 1 That which is inlaid. 2 A pattern or design so produced. 3 *Dent.* A filling for a tooth, of gold, porcelain, etc., cemented into a cavity so as to be even with the surface. 4 An inlay graft. — **in′lay′er** *n.*
inlay graft *Bot.* A cion inserted at a place in the stock from which a closely matching piece of bark has been removed.
in·let (in·let′) *v.t.* **·let, ·let·ting** 1 To insert; inlay. 2 *Obs.* To admit. — *n.* (in′lit) 1 A small body of water leading into a larger, as a small bay or creek or a tributary of a lake. 2 An entrance, as to a culvert. 3 Something inserted. 4 *Obs.* The act of admitting. See synonyms under ENTRANCE[1].
in·li·er (in′lī′ər) *n. Geol.* An underlying uneroded formation of rock imbedded in a later deposit: opposed to *outlier.*
in lo·co (in lō′kō) *Latin* In the place; in the right or proper spot.
in lo·co pa·ren·tis (in lō′kō pə·ren′tis) *Latin* In the place of a parent.
in·ly (in′lē) *adv. Poetic* 1 In the inner parts; inwardly. 2 Intimately. — *adj. Obs.* Inward. [OE *inlīce*]
in·mate (in′māt′) *n.* 1 One who lives in a place with others; an associate or mate in occupancy. 2 One who is kept or confined in a prison, asylum, or similar institution. 3 *Obs.* An alien; a stranger; one not properly belonging to the place where he dwells. [? <INN + MATE]
in me·di·as res (in mē′dē·əs rēz′) *Latin* In the midst of things; into the heart of the matter.
in me·mo·ri·am (in mə·môr′ē·əm, -mō′rē-) *Latin* In memory (of); as a memorial (to).
in·mesh (in·mesh′) See ENMESH.
in-mi·grant (in′mī′grənt) *n.* A person who has moved from one locality to another in the same country. — **in′-mi·gra′tion** (-grā′·shən) *n.*
in·most (in′mōst′, -məst) *adj.* 1 Farthest from the exterior. 2 Figuratively, deepest, most secret, or most intimate. [OE *innemest,* a double superlative of *inne* in]
inn (in) *n.* 1 A public house for the entertainment of travelers; a place where meals and lodging are obtainable; hostelry; tavern. 2 *Brit.* A house of residence for students: now only in the names of such residences, as *Inns* of Court. 3 *Obs.* A dwelling place; abode. [OE < *inn* in]
Inn (in) A river of eastern Switzerland, western Austria, and southern Bavaria, flowing 320 miles NE to the Danube.
in·nards (in′ərdz) *n.pl. Dial.* or *Colloq.* Inner or interior parts or organs; the insides. [<INWARDS, *n.*]
in·nate (in′āt, i·nāt′) *adj.* 1 Native to or original with the individual; inborn; natural. 2 Immediately in or from the mind or intellect rather than acquired by experience; intuitive: *innate* truths. 3 *Bot.* Attached by its base to the apex of a filament: said of an anther. 4 Endogenous. Compare ADNATE. See synonyms under INHERENT, NATIVE, RADICAL. [<L *innatus,* pp. of *innasci* be born in < *in-* in + *nasci* be born] — **in′nate·ly** *adv.* — **in′nate·ness** *n.*
in·ner (in′ər) *adj.* 1 At a point farther in or inward; interior; nearer a center. 2 Pertaining to that which is within; specifically, denoting the spiritual or immaterial. 3 Not easily discerned or understood; esoteric; hidden. — *n.* 1 The inside of something. 2 The section of a target between the center and the outer. 3 A shot striking this section. [OE *innerra,* compar. of *inne* in]
inner city A central part of a large city, usually characterized by poverty and often populated by minority groups. — **in′ner-cit′y** *adj.*
Inner Hebrides See HEBRIDES.
Inner Light The presence of God in man, giving guidance and enlightenment: a doctrine of Quakerism. Also **Inner Word.**
Inner Mongolia See MONGOLIA.
in·ner·most (in′ər·mōst′) *adj.* Inmost; farthest within. — *n.* The inmost part, thing, or place.
in·ner·sole (in′ər·sōl′) *n.* A continuous piece of leather or other material cut to the contour of a shoe last and placed inside to give a smooth surface.
Inner Temple See INNS OF COURT.
inner tube A flexible, inflatable tube, usually of rubber, which together with an outer casing comprises a pneumatic tire.
in·ner·vate (i·nûr′vāt, in′ər·vāt) *v.t.* **·vat·ed, ·vat·ing** *Physiol.* 1 To supply with nerves or nervous filaments. 2 To give stimulus to (a nerve); innerve. [<INNERVE]
in·ner·va·tion (in′ər·vā′shən) *n.* 1 *Physiol.* The act of innervating. 2 *Anat.* The arrangement of nervous filaments in any part of the body.
in·nerve (i·nûrv′) *v.t.* **·nerved, ·nerv·ing** To impart nervous energy to; invigorate; animate; stimulate. [<IN-[2] + NERVE]
In·ness (in′is), **George,** 1825–94, U.S. painter.
in·ning (in′ing) *n.* 1 The period during which a party or person is in power, control, or action. 2 In baseball and other games, a turn at the bat; the period during which one side is at the bat, or the period when each side takes one turn at the bat. 3 *pl.* In cricket, the play of, or score made by, either side while batting or by any one batsman during his turn: construed in the singular. 4 Reclamation (of marsh or swamp land). 5 *pl.* Lands reclaimed from the sea. 6 An ingathering, as of grain into a barn; a harvest. [OE *innung,* gerund of *innian* get it, put in]
inn·keep·er (in′kē′pər) *n.* The proprietor or keeper of an inn. Also **inn′hold′er** (-hōl′dər).
in·no·cence (in′ə·səns) *n.* 1 The state of being innocent; the condition of being free from evil or guile, or from that which corrupts or vitiates; purity of heart; freedom from taint. 2 Freedom from guilt, as of some specific crime or charge; absence of legal guilt. 3 Freedom from harmful or noxious qualities; harmlessness; innocuousness. 4 Simplicity or ignorance through lack of intellect or imperfect development; hence, weak-mindedness. 5 Freedom from illegal taint, as violation of an embargo or blockade by conveying goods to a belligerent. 6 A bluet. 7 A slender-stemmed, erect herb *(Collinsia verna)* with a blue and white corolla; also a related California herb *(C. bicolor).* [<OF <L *innocentia*]
Synonyms: blamelessness, goodness, guilelessness, guiltlessness, harmlessness, innocuousness, inoffensiveness, purity, simplicity, sincerity, sinlessness, stainlessness, virtue. *Innocence,* which is *goodness* without temptation or trial, or perhaps without knowledge of evil, is less than *virtue* which is *goodness* that resists and overcomes temptation. Compare synonyms for INNOCENT. *Antonyms*: contamination, corruption, crime, criminality, evil, fault, guile, guilt, harm, harmfulness, hurt, hurtfulness, impurity, ruin, sin, sinfulness, stain, wrong.
in·no·cen·cy (in′ə·sən·sē) *n. pl.* **·cies** Innocence; also, an instance of innocence.
in·no·cent (in′ə·sənt) *adj.* 1 Not tainted with sin; pure; ignorant of evil; blameless: an *innocent* babe. 2 Free from the guilt of a particular evil action or crime. 3 Free from qualities that can harm or injure; innocuous; harmless. 4 Of artless or ingenuous disposition; naive. 5 Not maliciously intended: an *innocent* lie, an *innocent* remark. 6 Free from liability to forfeiture; not contraband; lawful; permitted. 7 Lacking in knowledge or sense; simple or ignorant; imbecile. 8 Lacking in worldly knowledge: an *innocent* girl. 9 Entirely lacking; devoid: with *of*: *innocent* of grammar. — *n.* 1 One unstained by sin. 2 A young child. 3 A simpleton. 4 The bluet. — **the Innocents** The children put to death by Herod: commemorated Dec. 28. Matt. *ii* 16. [<OF <L *innocens, -entis* < *in-* not + *nocens,* ppr. of *nocere* harm] — **in′no·cent·ly** *adv.*
Synonyms (adj.): blameless, clean, clear, faultless, guileless, guiltless, harmless, immaculate, innocuous, innoxious, inoffensive, pure, right, righteous, sinless, spotless, stainless, upright, virtuous. *Innocent,* in the full sense, signifies not tainted with sin; not having done wrong or violated legal or moral precept or duty; as, an *innocent* babe. *Innocent* is a negative word, expressing less than *righteous, upright,* or *virtuous,* which imply knowledge of good and evil, with free choice of the good. A little child or a lamb is *innocent*; a tried and faithful man is *righteous, upright, virtuous. Immaculate, pure,* and *sinless* may be used either of one who has never known the possibility of evil or of one who has perfectly and triumphantly resisted it. *Innocent,* in a specific case, signifies free from the guilt of a particular act, even when the total character may be very evil; as, The thief was found to be *innocent* of the murder. See CANDID, PURE. *Antonyms*: compare synonyms for CRIMINAL.
In·no·cent (in′ə·sənt, *Fr.* ē·nō·sän′) A masculine personal name; also, the appellation of 13 popes. Also *Lat.* **In·no·cen·tius** (in′ə·sen′·shəs, *Du.* in′ə·sen′sē·ŏŏs; *Ger.* in′ə·tsen′tsē·ŏŏs), *Ger.* **In·no·cenz** (in′ə·tsents), *Ital.* **In·no·cen·te** (ēn′nō·chen′tā) or **In·no·cen·zio** (ēn′nō·chen′·dzyō), *Sp.* **I·no·cen·ci·o** (ē′nō·then′thē·ō). [<L, blameless]
— **Innocent I,** died 417, pope 402–17, condemned Pelagianism: canonized *Saint Innocent.*
— **Innocent II,** died 1143, pope 1130–43, condemned Abelard: real name Gregorio Papareschi.
— **Innocent III,** 1161–1216, pope 1198–1216; raised the papal power to the highest point: real name Lotario de' Conti.
— **Innocent IV,** died 1254, pope 1243–54; proclaimed a crusade against Frederick II: real name Sinibaldo de' Freschi.
— **Innocent XI,** 1611–89, pope 1676–89; quarreled with Louis XIV on the limitation of papal powers in France (see GALLICANISM): real name Benedetto Odescalchi.
in·noc·u·ous (i·nok′yŏŏ·əs) *adj.* 1 Having no harmful qualities. 2 Non-poisonous: said of plants and animals, especially snakes. See synonyms under INNOCENT. [<L *innocuus* < *in-* not + *nocuus* harmful < *nocere* harm] — **in·noc′u·ous·ly** *adv.* — **in·noc′u·ous·ness** *n.*
in·nom·i·nate (i·nom′ə·nit) *adj.* 1 Without specific name. 2 Anonymous. [<LL *innominatus* < *in-* not + *nominatus,* pp. of *nominare* name. See NOMINATE.]
innominate artery *Anat.* A large but short trunk springing from the arch of the aorta near the heart.
innominate bone *Anat.* A large, irregular bone resulting from the consolidation of the ilium, ischium, and pubis to form one of the sides of the pelvis in adult mammals; the hip bone; haunch bone; huckle bone: also called *os innominatum.*
in no·mi·ne Do·mi·ni (in nom′ə·nē dom′ə·nī) *Latin* In the name of the Lord.
in·no·vate (in′ə·vāt) *v.* **·vat·ed, ·vat·ing** *v.i.* To

make changes or alterations in anything established; bring in new ideas, methods, etc.: often with *in, on,* or *upon.* — *v.t. Obs.* To bring in as an innovation. [<L *innovatus,* pp. of *innovare* renew < *in-* in + *novare* make new, alter < *novus* new] — **in′no·va′tor** *n.*

in·no·va·tion (in′ə·vā′shən) *n.* **1** The making of a change in something established. **2** A novelty. See synonyms under CHANGE. [<LL *innovatio, -onis*]

in·no·va·tive (in′ə·vā′tiv) *adj.* Characterized by or tending to introduce innovations.

in·no·va·to·ry (in′ə·vā′tər·ē) *adj.* Having the character of innovation.

in·nox·ious (i·nok′shəs) *adj.* Free from harmful qualities; not noxious. [<L *innoxius* < *in-* not + *noxius* NOXIOUS. Related to INNOCENT, INNOCUOUS.]

Inns·bruck (inz′brŏŏk, *Ger.* ins′brŏŏk) The capital of Tirol in Austria, on the Inn.

Inns of Chancery **1** Formerly, in London, residences in which students for the Chancery bar began their law studies; later occupied as offices by attorneys, solicitors, etc. **2** The law societies occupying these buildings.

Inns of Court The sets of buildings occupied by the four legal societies of London, the Inner Temple, Middle Temple, Lincoln's Inn, and Gray's Inn, that exercise the exclusive right of calling law students to the bar; hence, the societies themselves.

in·nu·en·do (in′yŏŏ·en′dō) *n. pl.* **·dos** or **·does** **1** A suggestion or hint about some person or thing; an indirect aspersion; insinuation: usually in derogation. **2** *Law* In pleading, an explanatory phrase employed to make a previous phrase more explicit, as in saying "the perjured villain, meaning the plaintiff," in which the phrase "meaning the plaintiff" is an innuendo. Also spelled *inuendo.* See synonyms under SUGGESTION. [<L, by nodding at, intimating, ablative gerund of *innuere* nod to, signify < *in-* to + *-nuere* nod]

In·nu·it (in′yŏŏ·it) *n. sing.* & *pl.* An Eskimo of Alaska: distinguished from the *Yuit,* or Asian Eskimos; also, Arctic Eskimos as distinct from the Aleuts. Compare YUIT. [<Eskimo]

in·nu·mer·a·ble (i·nōō′mər·ə·bəl, i·nyōō′-) *adj.* Too numerous to be counted; very numerous; countless. Also **in·nu′mer·ous.** See synonyms under INFINITE. [<L *innumerabilis*] — **in·nu′mer·a·bil′i·ty, in·nu′mer·a·ble·ness** *n.* — **in·nu′mer·a·bly** *adv.*

in·nu·tri·tion (in′nōō·trish′ən, -yōō-) *n.* Lack of nutrition; failure of nourishment. — **in′nu·tri′tious** *adj.*

in·ob·serv·ance (in′əb·zûr′vəns) *n.* Non–observance; inattention.

in·oc·u·la·ble (in·ok′yə·lə·bəl) *adj.* That can be inoculated or communicated by inoculation. — **in·oc′u·la·bil′i·ty** *n.* — **in·oc′u·la′tor** (-lā′tər) *n.*

in·oc·u·late (in·ok′yə·lāt) *v.t.* **·lat·ed, ·lat·ing** **1** To communicate a disease to (a person or animal) by inoculation. **2** To inject an immunizing serum into. **3** To implant ideas, opinions, etc., in the mind of. **4** *Bot.* To insert a bud in, as a tree, for propagation. [<L *inoculatus,* pp. of *inoculare* engraft an eye or bud < *in-* in + *oculus* bud, eye]

in·oc·u·la·tion (in·ok′yə·lā′shən) *n.* **1** *Med.* The introduction of specific disease organisms into the living tissues of animals and man, as a means of securing immunity through inducing a mild form of the disease. Inoculation may be *curative,* when an antitoxin is injected as a remedy, or *protective,* when the substance injected aims to secure immunity from disease. **2** *Bot.* The operation of inserting a bud in a tree for propagation. **3** Contamination; infection: the *inoculation* of vice. **4** The improvement of soils by introducing special micro–organisms: practiced especially in the cultivation of leguminous crops.

in·oc·u·lum (in·ok′yə·ləm) *n.* The prepared material, as bacteria, viruses, spores, etc., used in making an inoculation. [<NL <INOCULATE]

in·o·dor·ous (in·ō′dər·əs) *adj.* Having no odor; emitting no scent.

in·of·fen·sive (in′ə·fen′siv) *adj.* Giving no offense; unobjectionable; causing nothing displeasing, disturbing, or harmful. See synonyms under INNOCENT. — **in′of·fen′sive·ly** *adv.* — **in′of·fen′sive·ness** *n.*

in·of·fi·cious (in′ə·fish′əs) *adj.* **1** *Law* Without consideration of duty or natural obligation; regardless of office or duty: An *inofficious* will neglects to provide for those naturally dependent on the testator. **2** Without office; inoperative. **3** *Obs.* Not civil or attentive. [<L *inofficiosus*] — **in′of·fi′cious·ly** *adv.*

in om·ni·a pa·ra·tus (in om′nē·ə pə·rā′təs) *Latin* Prepared for anything.

I·nö·nü (e′nœ·nü), **Ismet,** 1884–1973, president of Turkey 1938–50.

in·op·er·a·ble (in·op′ər·ə·bəl) *adj.* **1** *Surg.* Not suitable for operative procedures without undue risk: an *inoperable* cancer. **2** Not practicable.

in·op·er·a·tive (in·op′ər·ə·tiv) *adj.* Not operative; having no effect or result; ineffectual. — **in·op′er·a·tive·ness** *n.*

in·op·por·tune (in·op′ər·tōōn′, -tyōōn′) *adj.* Unseasonable or inappropriate; unsuitable or inconvenient, especially as to time; not opportune. [<L *inopportunus*] — **in·op′por·tune′ly** *adv.* — **in·op′por·tune′ness** *n.*

in·or·di·nate (in·ôr′də·nit) *adj.* Not restrained by prescribed rules or bounds; immoderate; excessive. See synonyms under IMMODERATE, IRREGULAR. — **in·or′di·na·cy** (-nə·sē), **in·or′di·nate·ness** *n.* — **in·or′di·nate·ly** *adv.*

in·or·gan·ic (in′ôr·gan′ik) *adj.* **1** Devoid of organized vital structure; not organic; not being animal or vegetable; inanimate. **2** Not the result of living or organic processes. **3** Of, pertaining to, or designating the branch of chemistry that treats of substances lacking carbon, but including the carbonates and cyanides. **4** *Ling.* Not belonging to the normal development of a word; extraneous, as the final *t* in *against.* — **in′or·gan′i·cal·ly** *adv.*

in·os·cu·late (in·os′kyə·lāt) *v.t.* & *v.i.* **·lat·ed, ·lat·ing** **1** To unite by contact of openings, as two blood vessels. **2** To unite or join together, as in continuity.

in·os·cu·la·tion (in·os′kyə·lā′shən) *n.* **1** Union by tubelike passages; intercommunication. **2** A union that implies continuity.

in·o·si·tol (in·ō′sə·tōl, -tol) *n. Biochem.* An efflorescent, crystalline, water–soluble, polyhydric alcohol, $C_6H_6(OH)_6$, regarded as the anti–alopecia factor of the vitamin B complex. It is widely distributed in plant and animal tissue and also made synthetically. Also called *muscle sugar.* Also **in·o·site** (in′ə·sīt). [<Gk. *is, inos* muscle + -IT(E)[1] + -OL[1]]

in·ot·ro·pism (in·ot′rə·piz′əm, ī·not′-) *n. Med.* Any interference with the contractility of muscle. — **in·o·trop·ic** (in′ō·trop′ik, -trō′pik ī′nō-) *adj.* [<Gk. *is, inos* muscle + -TROPISM]

in·ox·i·dize (in·ok′sə·dīz) *v.t.* **·dized, ·diz·ing** To render incapable of oxidation.

in pa·ce (in pā′sē, pä′kā) *Latin* In peace.

in·pa·tient (in′pā′shənt) *n.* A patient who is lodged, fed, and receives treatment in a hospital or the like: distinguished from *outpatient.*

in per·pet·u·um (in pər·pech′ōō·əm) *Latin* Forever; perpetually.

in per·so·nam (in pər·sō′nəm) *Latin* Against the person, rather than against specific things: used in certain legal proceedings.

in pet·to (ēn pet′tō) *Italian* In the breast; secretly: said of Roman Catholic cardinals appointed in consistory as "reserves," but not officially announced.

in·phase (in′fāz′) *adj. Electr.* Being of the same phase: said of currents. See PHASE.

in pos·se (in pos′ē) *Latin* Having a possible but not an actual existence; potential. Compare IN ESSE.

in pro·pri·a per·so·na (in prō′prē·ə pər·sō′nə) *Latin* In one's own person.

in·put (in′pŏŏt′) *n.* **1** Something put into a system or device, as energy into a machine, food into the body, data into a computer, or a signal into an electronic device. **2** A place or point of introduction, as of data into a computer. **3** An effect or influence resulting from contributing opinions, information, suggestions, etc.: The staff had real *input* in the directive.

in·quest (in′kwest) *n.* **1** A judicial inquiry, aided by a jury, into a special matter, as a sudden death. **2** The body of men making such inquiry. **3** Inquiry; investigation. [<OF *enqueste* <L *inquisita (res)* (thing) inquired (into), fem. of *inquisitus, inquestus,* pp. of *inquirere* INQUIRE]

in·qui·e·tude (in·kwī′ə·tōōd, -tyōōd) *n.* **1** A state of restlessness; uneasiness. **2** *pl.* Anxieties; disquieting thoughts. [<F *inquiétude* <LL *inquietudo*] — **in·qui′et** *adj.* — **in·qui′et·ly** *adv.*

in·qui·line (in′kwə·līn, -lin) *adj. Zool.* Living in the abode of another, as an insect in a gall made by another: also **in·quil·i·nous** (in·kwil′ə·nəs). — *n.* An animal that lives in the abode of another; a commensal. [<L *inquilinus* lodger < *in-* in + *colere* dwell]

in·qui·nate (in′kwə·nāt) *v.t.* **·nat·ed, ·nat·ing** To pollute; corrupt. [<L *inquinatus,* pp. of *inquinare* pollute < *in-* in + *cunire* void excrement]

in·qui·na·tion (in′kwə·nā′shən) *n.* **1** The state of being defiled; corruption. **2** Pollution; infection. [<L *inquinatio, -onis*]

in·quire (in·kwīr′) *v.* **·quired, ·quir·ing** *v.t.* **1** To ask information about: They *inquired* the way. — *v.i.* **2** To seek information by asking questions: to *inquire* about one's health. **3** To make investigation, search, or inquiry: with *into.* Also spelled *enquire.* [<L *inquirere* inquire into < *in-* into + *quaerere* seek] — **in·quir′a·ble** *adj.* — **in·quir′er** *n.* — **in·quir′ing** *adj.* — **in·quir′ing·ly** *adv.*

Synonyms: ask, examine, interrogate, query, question. One may either *ask* or *inquire* one's way. In this sense *ask* and *inquire* are nearly interchangeable, chiefly differing in the fact that *ask* is the popular and *inquire* the more formal word, although *ask* has place in the best literary use. Also, *ask* has more reference to the presence of a second person; the solitary investigator *inquires* rather than *asks* the cause of some phenomenon: in this sense *ask* is often used reflexively; as, "I *asked* myself why this happened." *Inquire into* thus becomes a natural synonym for *examine, investigate,* etc. Compare ASK, EXAMINE, QUESTION.

in·quir·y (in·kwīr′ē, in′kwə·rē) *n. pl.* **·quir·ies** **1** The act of inquiring. **2** Investigation; research; search for knowledge. **3** A query. [ME *enquere*]

Synonyms: examination, interrogation, investigation, query, question, research, scrutiny, study. See QUESTION. *Antonyms:* see synonyms for ANSWER.

in·qui·si·tion (in′kwə·zish′ən) *n.* **1** The proceedings and findings of a jury of inquest. **2** The jury or other body making judicial inquiry into some particular matter. **3** Investigation. See synonyms under HUNT, QUESTION. [<OF <L *inquisitio, -onis* < *inquisitus.* See INQUIRE.]

In·qui·si·tion (in′kwə·zish′ən) *n.* **1** A court or tribunal of the Roman Catholic Church for the discovery, examination, and punishment of heretics; specifically, the ecclesiastical tribunal for the discovery and punishment of heretics, active in central and southern Europe in the 13th century; also, the **Spanish Inquisition** (1237–1834), the notoriously severe tribunal which continued its persecutions through the 16th century: put under state control 1480; abolished 1834: also called *Holy Office.* **2** The Congregation of the Holy Office. — **In′qui·si′tion·ist, In·quis·i·tor** (in·kwiz′ə·tər) *n.*

in·qui·si·tion·al (in′kwə·zish′ən·əl) *adj.* Of or pertaining to the Inquisition; characterized by searching investigation, or by severities like those of the Inquisition. — **in′qui·si′tion·al·ly** *adv.*

in·qui·si·tion·ist (in′kwə·zish′ən·ist) *n.* One who practices the methods of the Inquisition; an inquisitor.

in·quis·i·tive (in·kwiz′ə·tiv) *adj.* **1** Given to questioning, especially for the gratification of curiosity; prying: an *inquisitive* busybody. **2** Inclined to the pursuit of knowledge. [<L *inquisitus*] — **in·quis′i·tive·ly** *adv.* — **in·quis′i·tive·ness** *n.*

Synonyms: curious, inquiring, intrusive, meddlesome, meddling, peeping, prying, scrutinizing, searching. An *inquisitive* person is one who is bent on finding out all that can be found out by inquiry, especially of little and personal matters, and hence is generally *meddlesome* and *prying. Inquisitive* may be used in a good sense, but in such connection *inquiring* is to be preferred; as, an *inquiring* mind. As applied to a state of mind, *curious* denotes a keen and rather pleasurable desire to know fully something to which one's attention has been called, but without the active tendency that *inquisitive* implies; a well–bred person may be *curious* to know, but will not be *inquisitive* in trying to ascertain what is of interest in the affairs of another. *Antonyms:*

apathetic, careless, heedless, inattentive, indifferent, unconcerned, uninterested.

in·quis·i·tor (in·kwiz′ə·tər) *n.* **1** One who inquires or investigates; specifically, an official whose duty it is to investigate or examine. **2** A member of the Inquisition. [<OF *inquisiteur* <L *inquisitor*]

in·quis·i·to·ri·al (in·kwiz′ə·tôr′ē·əl, -tō′rē-, in′·kwiz-) *adj.* **1** After the manner of an inquisitor; disposed to ask cruel and offensive questions. **2** Pertaining to a court of inquisition or to an inquisitor or his duties. **3** *Law* Pertaining to a system of criminal procedure in which the proceedings are conducted secretly and the judge acts also as prosecutor. Compare ACCUSATORY, ACCUSATORIAL. **— in·quis′i·to′ri·al·ly** *adv.* **— in·quis′i·to′ri·al·ness** *n.*

in re (in rē′) *Law Latin* In the case or matter of; concerning: *in re* Smith vs. Jones.

in rem (in rem′) *Law Latin* Against the thing: designating a proceeding instituted for the disposition of property and not directed against any specific person.

in·ro (in′rō′) *n.* A set or nest of small lacquered boxes worn at the girdle by Japanese, designed to contain small articles of convenience, as medicines, a seal, and sealing wax. [<Japanese *in* seal + *ro* wax]

in·road (in′rōd′) *n.* **1** A hostile entrance into a country; raid; any forcible encroachment. **2** Any illegal, destructive, or wasteful encroachment: *inroads* upon one's health, time, savings, etc. See synonyms under INVASION. [<IN-[3] + obs. *road* riding]

in·rush (in′rush′) *n.* A sudden rushing in; invasion.

in·sal·i·vate (in·sal′ə·vāt) *v.t.* **·vat·ed, ·vat·ing** To mix with saliva, as food, in eating. **— in·sal′i·va′tion** *n.*

in·sa·lu·bri·ous (in′sə·lōō′brē·əs) *adj.* Not wholesome; not healthful. [<L *insalubris*] **— in′sa·lu′bri·ous·ly** *adv.* **— in′sa·lu′bri·ty** *n.*

ins and outs Minute details; particulars; ramifications.

in·sane (in·sān′) *adj.* **1** Not sane; mentally deranged or unsound; crazy; irrational. **2** Set apart for or used by the insane. **3** Characteristic of those who are mentally deranged; insensate. **4** Foolish, extravagant, or impractical: *insane* hopes. [<L *insanus* < *in-* not + *sanus* whole] **—in·sane′ly** *adv.* **—in·sane′ness** *n.*

Synonyms: absurd, cracked, crazed, crazy, delirious, demented, deranged, distracted, frantic, frenzied, irrational, lunatic, mad, maniac, maniacal, monomaniac, wandering, wild. *Antonyms*: clear, collected, level-headed, sage, sane, sensible, sober, sound, wise.

in·san·i·ty (in·san′ə·tē) *n.* **1** Any mental disorder characterized by temporary or permanent irrational or violent deviations from normal thinking, feeling, and behavior: not a technical term in medicine or psychiatry. **2** *Law* Any degree of mental unsoundness resulting in inability to distinguish between right and wrong, to control the will, foresee the consequences of an act, make a valid contract, or manage one's own affairs. **3** Lack of sound sense; extreme folly.

Synonyms: alienation, craziness, delirium, dementia, derangement, frenzy, lunacy, madness, mania, monomania. Of these terms *insanity* is the most comprehensive, including in a loose sense all morbid conditions of mind due to diseased action of the brain or nervous system. *Craziness* is a vague popular term for any sort of disordered mental action, or for conduct suggesting it. *Lunacy*, originally denoted intermittent *insanity*, supposed to be dependent on the changes of the moon (L *luna*). *Madness* is the old popular term, now suggesting excitement akin to *mania*. *Derangement* is a common euphemism for *insanity*. *Delirium* is always temporary, and is specifically the *insanity* of disease, as in acute fevers. *Dementia* is a general weakening of the mental powers: the word is specifically applied to the mental incapacities of senility. *Monomania* is mental *derangement* as to one subject or object. *Frenzy* and *mania* are forms of raving and furious *insanity*. Compare DELUSION, FRENZY, IDIOCY. *Antonyms*: clearness, lucidity, rationality, sanity.

in·sa·tia·ble (in·sā′shə·bəl, -shē·ə·bəl) *adj.* Not satiable; not to be sated or satisfied; unappeasable. Also **in·sa′ti·ate** (-it). See synonyms under GREEDY. [<OF *insaciable*] **— in·sa′ti·a·bil′i·ty, in·sa′tia·ble·ness** *n.* **— in·sa′tia·bly, in·sa′ti·ate·ly** *adv.* **— in·sa′ti·ate·ness** *n.*

in·sa·ti·e·ty (in′sə·tī′ə·tē) *n.* Lack of satiety or surfeit; unsatisfied wish or appetite. [<L *insatietas, -tatis*]

in·scribe (in·skrīb′) *v.t.* **·scribed, ·scrib·ing** **1** To write or engrave (signs, words, names, etc.). **2** To mark the surface of with engraved or written characters, especially in a durable or conspicuous way. **3** To dedicate, as a book, usually by an informal, written note. **4** To enter the name of on a list; enrol. **5** *Brit.* To register or record the names of holders of (stocks, securities, etc.). **6** *Geom.* To draw (one figure) in another so that the latter circumscribes the former. [<L *inscribere* < *in-* on, in + *scribere* write] **— in·scrib′er** *n.*

Synonyms: address, dedicate, engrave, impress, imprint, mark, stamp, write.

in·scrip·tion (in·skrip′shən) *n.* **1** The act or operation of inscribing, or that which is inscribed. **2** Incised or relief lettering; any legend or record marked in lasting characters on a solid and durable object. **3** Entry in a roll or the like. **4** *Brit.* A registry, as of securities. **5** The lettering on a print or similar work. **6** An address in a book; a dedication. See synonyms under RECORD, SUPERSCRIPTION. [<L *inscriptio, -onis* < *inscriptus*, pp. of *inscribere* INSCRIBE] **— in·scrip′tion·al, in·scrip′tive** *adj.*

in·scru·ta·ble (in·skrōō′tə·bəl) *adj.* That cannot be searched into; incomprehensible; unfathomable; impenetrable. See synonyms under MYSTERIOUS. [<LL *inscrutabilis* < *in-* not + *scrutare* look at] **— in·scru′ta·bil′i·ty, in·scru′ta·ble·ness** *n.* **— in·scru′ta·bly** *adv.*

in·sect (in′sekt) *n.* **1** A minute invertebrate animal; one of the class *Insecta*. The true insects or hexapods have the body divided into a head, a thorax of 3 segments, each of which bears a pair of legs, and an abdomen of 7 to 11 segments, and in development usually pass through a metamorphosis. There are usually 2 pairs of wings, sometimes one pair or none. **2** Loosely, any small, air-breathing invertebrate resembling or suggesting an insect, as spiders, centipedes, ticks, etc. See illustrations of INSECTS (injurious, beneficial) on pages 656 and 657. [<L *(animal) insectum* (animal) notched or cut into < *insectus*, pp. of *insecare* cut into, notch] **— in·sec′te·an** (-sek′tē·ən) *adj.* **— in′sect·like′** *adj.*

In·sec·ta (in·sek′tə) *n. pl.* A class of six-legged arthropods, including and restricted to the true insects or hexapods. [<NL]

in·sec·tar·i·um (in′sek·târ′ē·əm) *n. pl.* **·i·ums** or **·i·a** (-ē·ə) A place for keeping and breeding insects, as for the purpose of studying economic entomology. Also **in·sec·tar·y** (in′·sek·ter′ē). [<NL]

in·sec·ti·cide (in·sek′tə·sīd) *n.* A substance which kills insects, usually in powder, paste, or liquid form. [<INSECT + -CIDE]

in·sec·tion (in·sek′shən) *n.* A cutting into; incision. [<L *insectus*, pp. of *insecare* cut up]

in·sec·ti·val (in′sek·tī′vəl, in·sek′tə-) *adj.* Pertaining to, or like, insects.

in·sec·ti·vore (in·sek′tə·vôr, -vōr) *n.* **1** Any of an order *(Insectivora)* of insect-eating mammals, as shrews, moles, and hedgehogs. **2** An insectivorous animal or plant. [<F <L *insectum* insect + *-vorus* devouring < *vorare* devour]

in·sec·tiv·o·rous (in′sek·tiv′ər·əs) *adj.* **1** Feeding upon or subsisting upon insects. **2** Pertaining to the *Insectivora*.

in·sec·to·cu·tion (in·sek′tə·kyōō′shən) *n.* The destruction of insect pests by electric shock, with the use of electrified wire screens, grids, etc. [<INSECT (ELECTR)OCUTION] **— in·sec′·to·cu′tor** *n.*

insect wax Chinese wax.

in·se·cure (in′sə·kyŏŏr′) *adj.* **1** Not secure or safe; in danger of breaking or failing; infirm. **2** Not assured of safety; liable to suffer loss or harm. **— in′se·cure′ly** *adv.* **— in′·se·cure′ness** *n.*

in·se·cu·ri·ty (in′sə·kyŏŏr′ə·tē) *n.* The condition of being unsafe; liability to injury, loss or failure; uncertainty; instability.

in·sem·i·nate (in·sem′ə·nāt) *v.t.* **·nat·ed, ·nat·ing** **1** To impregnate; make pregnant. **2** To sow seed in, as soil. [<L *inseminatus*, pp. of *inseminare* sow < *in-* in + *seminare* sow < *semen* seed] **— in·sem′i·na′tion** *n.*

in·se·nes·cence (in′sə·nes′əns) *n.* The process of becoming old, especially in a normal manner and without undue loss of vigor. [<IN-[2] + SENESCENCE] **— in′se·nes′cent** *adj.*

in·sen·sate (in·sen′sāt, -sit) *adj.* **1** Manifesting or marked by a lack of sense or reason; brutish; mad. **2** Destitute of sensibility. **3** Inanimate. [<LL *insensatus*] **— in·sen′sate·ly** *adv.* **— in·sen′sate·ness** *n.*

in·sen·si·ble (in·sen′sə·bəl) *adj.* **1** That is not or cannot be felt or perceived by the sense; an *insensible* motion or change. **2** Blunted in feeling or perception: to be *insensible* to pity. **3** Deprived of sensation or perception; senseless. **4** Insensate; inanimate: *insensible* earth. **5** *Obs.* Without intelligent meaning; senseless. **6** Devoid of passion, emotion, or sensitiveness; apathetic; unaware. See synonyms under BRUTISH, NUMB. [<L *insensibilis*] **— in·sen′si·bil′i·ty, in·sen′si·ble·ness** *n.* **— in·sen′si·bly** *adv.*

in·sen·si·tive (in·sen′sə·tiv) *adj.* Not sensitive to impressions, whether physical, mental, or emotional. **— in·sen′si·tiv′i·ty, in·sen′si·tive·ness** *n.*

in·sen·ti·ent (in·sen′shē·ənt, -shənt) *adj.* Inanimate. **— in·sen′ti·ence, in·sen′ti·en·cy** *n.*

in·sep·a·ra·ble (in·sep′ər·ə·bəl) *adj.* Incapable of being separated or disjoined: *inseparable* friends. **— in·sep′a·ra·ble·ness** *n.* **— in·sep′a·ra·bly** *adv.*

in·sert (in·sûrt′) *v.t.* To put or place into something else; put between or among other things; introduce. **—** *n.* (in′sûrt) That which is inserted; an addition made by insertion; specifically, in bookbinding, an inset; also, a circular or the like placed within a newspaper or book for mailing. [<L *insertus*, pp. of *inserere* < *in-* in + *serere* place, join] **— in·sert′er** *n.*

in·sert·ed (in·sûr′tid) *adj.* **1** *Anat.* Attached to, as the tendon of a muscle to a bone. **2** *Bot.* Growing from a part, as stamens on the corolla of a flower.

in·ser·tion (in·sûr′shən) *n.* **1** The act of inserting, or the state of being inserted. **2** That which is inserted, as lace or embroidery placed between pieces of plain fabric. **3** *Bot.* Place or mode of attachment, as of a leaf to a branch. **4** *Anat.* The end of a muscle that is attached to the bone or part which it moves. **5** A word, paragraph, or written material inserted in a written or printed page; also, an advertisement in a newspaper. See INSERT.

in·ses·so·ri·al (in′sə·sôr′ē·əl, -sō′rē-) *adj.* **1** Of or pertaining to a former order or class *(Insessores)* of perching birds. **2** Perching or fitted for perching, as a bird's foot. [<L *insessor* a sitter < *insessum*, pp. of *insidere* sit on < *in-* on + *sedere* sit]

in·set (in·set′) *v.t.* To set in; implant; insert. **—** *n.* (in′set′) **1** A leaf or leaves inserted, as in a book or newspaper. **2** A small diagram, map, etc., inserted in the border of a larger one. **3** A piece of material let or set into a garment. **4** Influx, as of the tide.

in·sheathe (in·shēth′) *v.t.* **·sheathed, ·sheath·ing** To place or enclose in or as in a sheath.

in·shore (in′shôr′, -shōr′, in′shôr′, -shōr′) *adj.* **1** Being or occurring near the shore: *inshore* fishing. **2** Coming toward the shore: an *inshore* wind. **—** *adv.* Toward the shore.

in·shrine (in·shrīn′) *v.t.* To enshrine.

in·side (in′sīd′, -sīd′) *n.* **1** The side, surface, or part that is within; interior. **2** That which is contained; contents. **3** Inner thoughts or feelings: One cannot know the *inside* of a man's mind. **4** *pl. Colloq.* Inner organs; entrails. **5** *Printing* **a** *pl.* Sheets of paper that do not include any of the outer or soiled sheets of a ream or package. **b** The side of a sheet containing the second page. **6** An inside passenger or place for a passenger, as in a vehicle. **—** *adj.* **1** Situated or occurring on or in the inside; internal. **2** Suited for or pertaining to the inside. **3** For use indoors: *inside* paint. **4** Private; confidential: known only within a certain group or organization:

inside reports. — *adv.* (in'sīd') **1** In or into the interior; within. **2** Indoors. — **inside out** Reversed so that the inside is exposed. — *prep.* (in'sīd') In or into the interior of; within. — **inside of** *Colloq.* Within the time or distance of: a house *inside of* a mile away.

in·sid·er (in·sī'dər) *n.* One who is inside; hence, one who has special information or advantages.

inside track The inner and shorter way around a race track; hence, a position of advantage; the favored position.

in·sid·i·ous (in·sid'ē·əs) *adj.* **1** Designed to entrap; full of wiles. **2** Doing or contriving harm. **3** Awaiting a chance to harm. **4**

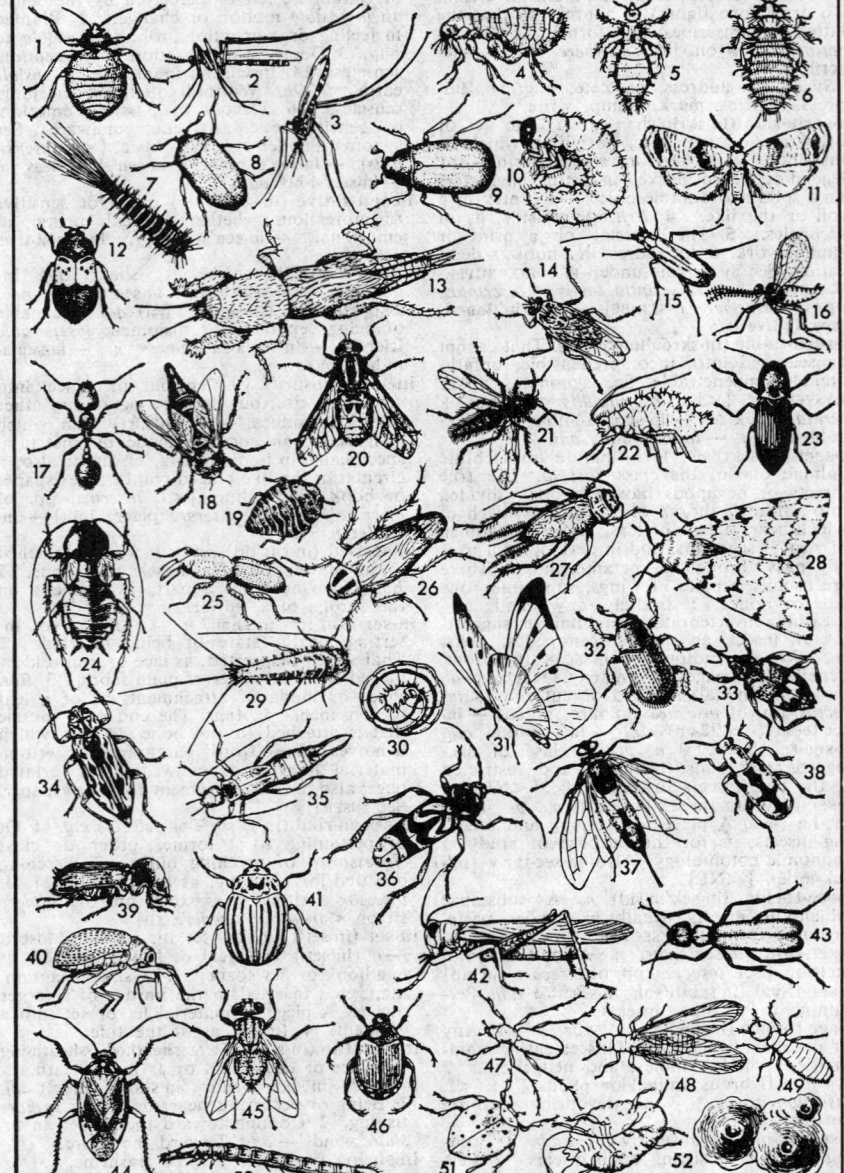

Causing harm by slow, stealthy, usually imperceptible means: an *insidious* disease. [< L *insidiosus* < *insidiae* ambush < *insidere* sit in, lie in wait] — **in·sid'i·ous·ly** *adv.* — **in·sid'i·ous·ness** *n.*

Synonyms: artful, crafty, cunning, deceitful, designing, guileful, intriguing, sly, subtle, treacherous, tricky, wily.

in·sight (in'sīt') *n.* **1** Intellectual discernment. **2** A perception of the inner nature of a thing; intuition. See synonyms under ACUMEN, WISDOM.

in·sig·ni·a (in·sig'nē·ə) *n.* *pl. of* **in·sig·ne** (in·sig'nē) **1** Badges, emblems, etc., used as marks of office or distinction. **2** Things significant or indicative of a calling. See illus-

tration under SHOULDER PATCH. [< L, neut pl. of *insignis* eminent < *in-* in + *signum* sign, emblem, badge]

in·sig·nif·i·cance (in'sig·nif'ə·kəns) *n.* The state of being insignificant; lack of import or of importance; triviality. Also **in'sig·nif'·i·can·cy.**

in·sig·nif·i·cant (in'sig·nif'ə·kənt) *adj.* **1** Not significant; without import, meaning, or bearing; without importance; trivial. **2** Small, little. — **in'sig·nif'i·cant·ly** *adv.*

Synonyms: idle, immaterial, irrelevant, little, mean, meaningless, paltry, petty, slight, small, trifling, trivial. See LITTLE. *Antonyms:* considerable, essential, grand, grave, great, im-

mense, influential, large, mighty, significant.

in·sin·cere (in'sin·sir') *adj.* Not sincere, honest, or genuine; hypocritical. — **in'sin·cere'ly** *adv.* — **in'sin·cer'i·ty** (-ser'ə·tē) *n.*

in·sin·u·ate (in·sin'yoo·āt) *v.t.* **·at·ed, ·at·ing** **1** To indicate slyly or deviously; imply; intimate. **2** To infuse or instil gradually or subtly into the mind: to *insinuate* distrust. **3** To introduce (someone) gradually or artfully into a position or relation: to *insinuate* oneself into another's confidence. See synonyms under ALLUDE. [< L *insinuatus*, pp. of *insinuare* curve < *in-* in + *sinus* bosom, curved surface]

in·sin·u·at·ing (in·sin'yoo·ā'ting) *adj.* Characterized by insinuation; winding, or creeping

in; insensibly or subtly winning favor and confidence; ingratiating.

in·sin·u·a·tion (in·sin'yoo·ā'shən) *n.* **1** The act of insinuating; indirect suggestion; implication; specifically, an injurious suggestion. **2** That which is insinuated; hint; a subtly ingratiating act, remark, etc. **3** Gradual or sly introduction. **4** Power or faculty of gaining affection, favor, or confidence. See synonyms under SUGGESTION.

in·sin·u·a·tive (in·sin'yoo·ā'tiv) *adj.* **1** Making use of insinuation, as to gain favor or confidence. **2** Tending to instil into the mind. **3** Characterized by or necessitating insinuation; suggestive.

in·sin·u·a·tor (in·sin'yoo·ā·tər) *n.* **1** One who worms his way into favor. **2** One who subtly hints or intimates (something usually malicious).

in·sip·id (in·sip'id) *adj.* **1** Without flavor; unsavory; tasteless. **2** Not qualified to interest; vapid; lacking in energy or ambition; dull. See synonyms under FLAT. [< F *insipide* < LL *insipidus* < *in-* not + *sapidus* savory < *sapere* savor, taste] — **in·si·pid·i·ty** (in'si·pid'ə·tē), **in·sip'id·ness** *n.* — **in·sip'id·ly** *adv.*

in·sip·i·ence (in·sip'ē·əns) *n.* Lack of wisdom; foolishness. ◆ Homophone: *incipience.* [< OF < L *insipientia* < *insipiens, -entis* unwise] **in·sip·i·ent** (in·sip'i·ənt) *adj.* Foolish; unwise.

INJURIOUS INSECTS

1. Bedbug, *Cimex lectularius.*
2. Mosquito, genus *Culex.*
3. Mosquito, genus *Anopheles.*
4. Flea, *Pulex irritans.*
5. Body louse, *Pediculus humanus.*
6. Chicken louse, genus *Mallophaga.*
7. Carpet beetle larva.
8. Carpet beetle, *Attagenus piceus.*
9. June beetle, genus *Scarabaeidae.*
10. June beetle grub.
11. Codling moth, *Carpocapsa pomonella.*
12. Larder beetle, *Dermestes lardarius.*
13. Mole cricket, genus *Gryllotalpa.*
14. Tsetse fly, genus *Glossina.*
15. Clothes moth, *Tineola bisselliella.*
16. Gall midge, family *Cecidomyidae.*
17. Ant, family *Formicidae.*
18. Botfly, genus *Gasterophilus.*
19. Phylloxera, *Dactylosphaera vitifoliae.*
20. Deer fly, *Chrysops discalis.*
21. Midge, genus *Culicoides.*
22. Plant louse or aphid, family *Aphididae.*
23. Click beetle, family *Elateridae.*
24. Oriental roach, *Blatta orientalis.*
25. Rice weevil, genus *Sitophilus.*
26. Cockroach, *Blatella germanica.*
27. Cricket, *Gryllus domesticus.*
28. Gipsy moth, *Lymantria dispar.*
29. Firebrat, genus *Thermobia.*
30. Cutworm larva, family *Noctuidae.*
31. Cabbage butterfly, *Pieris rapae.*
32. Bark beetle, family *Scolytidae.*
33. White pine weevil, genus *Pissodes.*
34. Metallic wood borer, family *Buprestidae.*
35. Earwig, *Forficula auricularia.*
36. Maple borer, family *Cerambycidae.*
37. Horntail, genus *Urocerus.*
38. Asparagus beetle, *Crioceris asparagi.*
39. Palm borer, family *Bostrichidae.*
40. Cotton boll weevil, *Anthonomus grandis.*
41. Potato beetle, *Leptinotarsus decemlineata.*
42. Grasshopper, family *Acrididae.*
43. Blister beetle, *Epicauta pennsylvanicus.*
44. Tarnished plant bug, *Lygus pratensis.*
45. House fly, *Musca domestica.*
46. Japanese beetle, *Popillia japonica.*
47. Rose chafer, *Macrodactylus subspinosus.*
48. Termite, genus *Kalotermes,* winged form.
49. Termite, wingless form.
50. Wireworm (larva of click beetle).
51. Mexican bean beetle, *Epilachna varivestris.*
52. San José scale, *Quadriaspidiotus perniciosus,* showing scales.

in·sist (in·sist') *v.i.* To make emphatic or repeated assertion, demand, or request: often with *on* or *upon:* He *insisted* on the correctness of his theory. — *v.t.* To state or demand emphatically: with a clause as object: He *insisted* that he was right. [< F *insister* < L *insistere* dwell upon, persist < *in-* on + *sistere* stand] — **in·sis'tence, in·sis'ten·cy** *n.*

Synonyms: persevere, persist. *Insist* implies some alleged authority or right; *persist* implies simply determination of will; we *insist* upon the action of others; we *persist* in our own. *Insist* is used of any urgency, good or bad, but largely in the good sense; *persist* is used chiefly in a bad sense, *persevere* being preferred for the better meaning. See PERSIST.

in·sis·tent (in·sis′tənt) *adj.* **1** Insisting; persistent; urgent. **2** Standing out prominently; conspicuous: *insistent* colors. **— in·sis′tent·ly** *adv.*

in si·tu (in sī′tyōō) *Latin* In its original site or position.

in·snare (in·snâr′) See ENSNARE.

in·so·bri·e·ty (in′sə·brī′ə·tē) *n.* Lack of moderation; intemperance; especially in drinking.

in·so·far as (in′sō·fär′ az′) To the extent that; in such measure as. Also **in so far as.**

in·so·late (in′sō·lāt) *v.t.* **·lat·ed, ·lat·ing** To expose to the rays of the sun, as for bleaching, drying, maturing, etc. [< L *insolatus,* pp. of *insolare* expose to the sun < *in-* in + *sol* sun]

in·so·la·tion (in′sō·lā′shən) *n.* **1** The act of insolating; exposure to the rays of the sun. **2** Sunstroke. **3** A method of treating disease by exposure to the rays of the sun. **4** A disease in plants caused by exposure to the sun. **5** *Meteorol.* **a** Solar radiation received by the earth and other planets. **b** The rate of delivery of such radiant energy per unit of horizontal surface.

in·sole (in′sōl′) *n.* **1** The fixed inner sole of a boot or shoe. **2** A removable inner sole placed within a shoe to improve its fit or as a protection against dampness.

in·so·lence (in′sə·ləns) *n.* **1** The quality of being insolent; pride or haughtiness exhibited in contemptuous and overbearing treatment of others; offensive impertinence. **2** An insult. See synonyms under ARROGANCE, IMPUDENCE. [< OF < L *insolentia* < *insolens, -entis* unwonted]

in·so·lent (in′sə·lənt) *adj.* **1** Presumptuously or defiantly offensive in language or manner; impudent. **2** Grossly disrespectful; characterized by insolence. See synonyms under HAUGHTY, IMPUDENT. [< L *insolens, -entis* unusual, haughty, insolent < *in-* not + *solens, -entis,* ppr. of *solere* be wont, accustomed] **— in′so·lent·ly** *adv.*

in·sol·u·ble (in·sol′yə·bəl) *adj.* **1** Not capable of being dissolved, as in a liquid; not soluble. **2** That cannot be explained or solved; insolv-

---

BENEFICIAL INSECTS
1. Tiger beetle, genus *Cicindella.*
2. Fiery hunter, *Calosoma calidus.*
3. Praying mantis nymph.
4. Ground beetle larva.
5. Syrphus or hover fly, genus *Syrphus.*
6. Tachina fly, genus *Winthemia.*
7. Praying mantis, *Paratenodera sinensis.*
8. Syrphus fly larva.
9. Ichneumon fly, genus *Ephialtes.*
10. Tachina fly, *Alophora diversa.*
11. Darning needle, *Anax junius.*
12. Dragon fly, *Libellula semifasciata.*
13. Scorpion fly, *Panorpa rufescens.*
14. Assassin fly, genus *Erax.*
15. Ichneumon fly, genus *Amblyteles.*
16. Big-headed fly, genus *Pipunculus.*
17. Bee fly, *Villa alternata.*
18. Spanish fly, *Lytta vesicatoria.*
19. Damsel fly, genus *Agrion.*
20. Dance fly, genus *Empis.*
21. Ladybird, *Adalia bipunctata.*
22. Digger wasp, genus *Ammophila.*
23. Ant lion, *Hesperoleon abdominalis.*
24. Ant lion larva and pit.
25. Lacewing, genus *Chrysopa,* with eggs.
26. Digger wasp, *Bembidula quadrifasciatus.*
27. Rove beetle, genus *Staphylinus.*
28. Assassin bug, *Sinea diadema.*
29. Mud dauber, genus *Scleripheron.*
30. Potter wasp, genus *Eumenes.*
31. Ground beetle, genus *Pterosticus.*
32. Caterpillar hunter, *Calosoma scrutator.*
33. Cicada killer, *Sphecius speciosus.*

---

who is not solvent; a bankrupt; specifically, a debtor whose property is taken to be divided among his creditors by a court under the operation of bankruptcy law.

in·som·ni·a (in·som′nē·ə) *n.* Chronic inability to sleep. [< L < *insomnis* sleepless]

in·som·ni·ac (in·som′nē·ak) *n.* One who suffers from sleeplessness.

in·som·ni·ous (in·som′nē·əs) *adj.* Affected with insomnia; sleepless.

in·som·no·lence (in·som′nə·ləns) *n.* Sleeplessness.

in·so·much (in′sō·much′) *adv.* **1** To such a degree or extent: with *that* or *as.* **2** Inasmuch: with *as.*

in·so·nate (in′sə·nāt) *v.t.* **·nat·ed, ·nat·ing** To expose or subject to the action of sound waves, especially those of very high frequency. [< IN-² + L *sonatus,* pp. of *sonare* sound] **— in′so·na′tion** *n.*

in·sou·ci·ance (in·sōō′sē·əns, *Fr.* aṅ·sōō·syäns′) *n.* Careless unconcern; indifference; heedlessness. [< F]

in·sou·ci·ant (in·sōō′sē·ənt, *Fr.* aṅ·sōō·syäṅ′) *adj.* Without concern or care; heedless; unmindful. [< F < *in-* not + *souciant,* ppr. of *soucier* care < OF *solcier* < L *sollicitare* disturb] **— in·sou·ci·ant·ly** (in·sōō′sē·ənt·lē) *adv.*

---

in·soul (in·sōl′) See ENSOUL.

in·span (in·span′) *v.t.* & *v.i.* **·spanned, ·span·ning** To harness or yoke (animals) to a vehicle. [< Afrikaans < Du. *inspannen*]

in·spect (in·spekt′) *v.t.* **1** To look at or examine carefully and critically. **2** To examine or review officially and with ceremony, as troops. See synonyms under EXAMINE, LOOK. [< L *inspectus,* pp. of *inspicere* look into < *in-* into + *specere* look]

in·spec·tion (in·spek′shən) *n.* Critical viewing or investigation; especially, an official examination. See synonyms under OVERSIGHT. [< OF < L *inspectio, -onis*] **— in·spec′tion·al** *adj.*

in·spec·tive (in·spek′tiv) *adj.* Of or pertaining

to inspection; tending to inspect, or that may be inspected.

in·spec·tor (in·spek′tər) *n.* **1** One who inspects. **2** An official designated to carry out inspection; a supervisor. **3** An officer of police usually ranking next below the superintendent. See synonyms under SUPERINTENDENT. [< L]

in·spec·tor·ate (in·spek′tər·it) *n.* The office or district of an inspector. Also **in·spec′tor·ship** (-ship).

Inspector General A military, air, or naval officer responsible for the conduct of inspec-

---

able. **3** Impossible to pay or discharge, as a debt or obligation. [< OF < L *insolubilis*] **— in·sol′u·bil′i·ty, in·sol′u·ble·ness** *n.* **— in·sol′u·bly** *adv.*

in·solv·a·ble (in·sol′və·bəl) *adj.* **1** Not admitting of explanation; insoluble. **2** *Obs.* That cannot be untied or loosened.

in·sol·ven·cy (in·sol′vən·sē) *n. pl.* **·cies** Bankruptcy.

in·sol·vent (in·sol′vənt) *adj.* **1** Unable to meet the claims of creditors; not solvent; bankrupt. **2** Inadequate for the payment of debts. **3** Pertaining to insolvency. **— n.** A debtor

tions and investigations of the economy, discipline, and efficiency of the branch of the armed forces in which he serves; also an officer of his department serving on the staff of a division or higher unit.

in·sphere (in·sfir′) *v.t.* To ensphere.

in·spir·a·ble (in·spīr′ə·bəl) *adj.* 1 That can be breathed; inhalable. 2 Capable of being inspired. — **in·spir′a·bil′i·ty** *n.*

in·spi·ra·tion (in′spə·rā′shən) *n.* 1 The infusion or imparting of an idea, an emotion, or a mental or spiritual influence. 2 That which is so infused or imparted. 3 An actuating or exalting influence; a stimulus to creativity in thought or action. 4 State of being inspired. 5 Divine or supernatural influence considered as exerted upon men so that their writings have divine authority; attributed by the Society of Friends to the direct teaching of the mind of man by the Holy Spirit. 6 A person or thing that inspires. 7 The act of drawing air into the lungs, inbreathing, or inspiring; inhalation: opposite of *expiration.* See synonyms under ENTHUSIASM. [<OF <LL *inspiratio, -onis*]

in·spi·ra·tion·al (in′spə·rā′shən·əl) *adj.* Of or pertaining to inspiration; bestowing or influenced by inspiration; inspiring. — **in′spi·ra′tion·al·ly** *adv.*

in·spi·ra·tion·al·ist (in′spə·rā′shən·əl·ist) *n.* One who inspires others, whether by speech, writing, or conduct.

in·spir·a·to·ry (in·spīr′ə·tôr′ē, -tō′rē) *adj.* Of or pertaining to inspiration or inhalation. [<L *inspiratus* + -ORY]

in·spire (in·spīr′) *v.* **·spired, ·spir·ing** *v.t.* 1 To stir or affect by some mental or spiritual influence; stimulate; animate: A brave leader *inspires* his followers. 2 To affect or imbue with a specified idea or feeling: to *inspire* survivors with hope. 3 To arouse or give rise to; generate: Fear *inspires* hatred. 4 To motivate or cause by supernatural influence or guidance. 5 To draw into the lungs; inhale. 6 To prompt the saying or writing of indirectly so as to avoid responsibility: This rumor was *inspired* by my enemies. 7 *Obs.* To blow or breathe into or upon. — *v.i.* 8 To draw in breath; inhale. 9 To give or provide inspiration. See synonyms under ENCOURAGE. [<OF *enspirer* <L *inspirare* breathe into <*in-* into + *spirare* breathe] — **in·spir′er** *n.*

in·spired (in·spīrd′) *adj.* 1 Communicated, imparted, or guided by inspiration: the *inspired* writings (Scriptures). 2 Prompted or kindled by ideas, emotions, etc.: an *inspired* speech. 3 Officially motivated or shaped: an *inspired* editorial. — **in·spir·ed·ly** (in·spīr′id·lē, -spīrd′lē) *adv.*

in·spir·it (in·spir′it) *v.t.* To fill with spirit or life; animate; exhilarate; enliven. See synonyms under ENCOURAGE. — **in·spir′it·ing·ly** *adv.*

in·spis·sate (in·spis′āt) *v.t.* & *v.i.* **·sat·ed, ·sat·ing** To thicken, as by evaporation. — *adj.* Thickened; inspissated. See synonyms under THICK. [<LL *inspissatus,* pp. of *inspissare* thicken <*in-* thoroughly + *spissare* thicken <*spissus* thick] — **in·spis·sa·tion** (in′spi·sā′shən) *n.* — **in′spis·sa·tor** *n.*

in·sta·bil·i·ty (in′stə·bil′ə·tē) *n.* *pl.* **·ties** 1 Lack of stability or firmness. 2 Mutability of opinion or conduct; inconstancy; changeableness. 3 Flimsiness of construction; liability to give way; insecurity: the *instability* of a bridge.

Synonyms: changeableness, fickleness, flightiness, inconstancy, mutability, unstableness, unsteadiness. *Antonyms*: certainty, constancy, firmness, persistence, stability, steadiness.

in·sta·ble (in·stā′bəl) *adj.* Unstable.

in·stall (in·stôl′) *v.t.* 1 To place in office, etc., with formal ceremony. 2 To establish in a place or position. 3 To place in position for service or use: to *install* a hot-water system. [<F *installer* <Med. L *installare* <*in-* in + *stallare* seat <OHG *stal* a seat] — **in·stall′er** *n.*

Synonyms: inaugurate, induct, initiate, ordain. *Antonyms*: break, cashier, depose, dismiss.

in·stal·la·tion (in′stə·lā′shən) *n.* 1 The act or ceremony of inducting into an office or place of honor. 2 An installing or being installed; especially, the introduction of apparatus or machines for use. 3 Such a machine or apparatus fixed for use: a ventilating *installation.* 4 Any large, fixed base of the armed service.

in·stal·ment (in·stôl′mənt) *n.* 1 A partial payment of a price due; a payment on account. 2 One of several parts of anything furnished at different times; especially a section of a novel or other writing running serially in a magazine, newspaper, etc. 3 The act of installing. Also **in·stall′ment.** [< obs. *estall* arrange payments <OF *estaler* stop <OHG *stal* seat, place]

instalment plan The purchase of goods or services by means of deferred payments at regular intervals.

in·stance (in′stəns) *n.* 1 Something offered or occurring as an exemplification. 2 A case. 3 Illustration, evidence, or proof: an *instance* of her forthrightness. 4 *Archaic* Urgency. 5 The act of asking, soliciting, suggesting or urging: They took action at the *instance* of aroused taxpayers. 6 *Obs.* An impelling motive. 7 A step in proceeding: in the first *instance.* 8 *Law* The institution of a process or suit. — **for instance** For example. — *v.t.* **·stanced, ·stanc·ing** 1 To refer to as illustration or example. 2 *Rare* To manifest or show. 3 *Rare* To cite an instance, or as an instance. [<OF <L *instantia* a standing near, urgent supplication <*instans, -antis* standing. See INSTANT.]

in·stan·cy (in′stən·sē) *n.* 1 Urgency; solicitation. 2 Immediateness.

in·stant (in′stənt) *adj.* 1 Immediately impending. 2 Now passing; current; present: the 10th *instant* (the 10th day of the month now passing). See PROXIMO, ULTIMO. 3 Direct; immediate. 4 Eager and active; urgent; importunate. See synonyms under IMMEDIATE. — *n.* 1 A particular point of time; the moment which in passing may be called now. 2 A very brief portion of time; moment. — *adv. Poetic* Instantaneously; instantly. [<OF <L *instans, -antis,* ppr. of *instare* stand near, urge <*in-* upon + *stare* stand]

in·stan·ta·ne·ous (in′stən·tā′nē·əs) *adj.* 1 Acting or done instantly. 2 Relating to a particular instant. [<INSTANT, on analogy with *simultaneous*] — **in′stan·ta′ne·ous·ly** *adv.* — **in′·stan·ta′ne·ous·ness** *n.*

in·stan·ter (in·stan′tər) *adj.* Without an instant of delay. See synonyms under IMMEDIATELY. [<L]

in·stant·ly (in′stənt·lē) *adv.* 1 On the instant; at once. 2 *Archaic* With urgency; insistently. — *conj.* As soon as. See synonyms under IMMEDIATELY.

in·star[1] (in·stär′) *v.t.* **·starred, ·star·ring** 1 To adorn or stud with or as with stars. 2 To set as a star; make a star of.

in·star[2] (in′stär′) *n. Entomol.* 1 Any stage in the metamorphosis of an insect or other arthropod between successive molts: the pupal *instar* of a butterfly. 2 The insect or arthropod while undergoing any of these stages. [<L, form, likeness]

in·state (in·stāt′) *v.t.* **·stat·ed, ·stat·ing** 1 To place or establish in a certain office or rank; induct. 2 *Obs.* To endow.

in sta·tu quo (in stā′tyōō kwō′, stach′ōō) *Latin* 1 In the present condition. 2 In the original state.

in·stau·rate (in·stôr′āt) *v.t.* **·rat·ed, ·rat·ing** *Rare* To renew; renovate; restore. [<L *instauratus,* pp. of *instaurare* renew] — **in·stau·ra·tion** (in′stô·rā′shən) *n.*

in·stead (in·sted′) *adv.* 1 In place or room; in lieu: with *of*: a friend *instead* of an enemy. 2 In one's (its, their, etc.) stead or place: They went prospecting for silver and found gold *instead.*

in·step (in′step′) *n.* 1 *Anat.* The arched upper part of the human foot, extending from the toes to the ankle. ◆ Collateral adjective: *tarsal.* 2 The front part of the hind leg of a horse, extending from the ham, or hock, to the pastern joint. 3 That part of a shoe or of a stocking that covers the instep.

in·sti·gate (in′stə·gāt) *v.t.* **·gat·ed, ·gat·ing** 1 To bring about by inciting; foment. 2 To urge or incite to an action or course: to *instigate* someone to treason. See synonyms under ABET, ENCOURAGE, INFLUENCE, SPUR, STIR. [<L *instigatus,* pp. of *instigare* <*in-* against + the root *-stig-* prick, goad] — **in′sti·ga′tive** *adj.* — **in′sti·ga′tor** *n.*

in·sti·ga·tion (in′stə·gā′shən) *n.* 1 The act of instigating, inciting, or urging, especially to evil. 2 That in which instigating is embodied; an incitement; stimulus.

in·stil (in·stil′) *v.t.* **·stilled, ·stil·ling** 1 To put into the mind gradually, as if drop by drop. 2 To pour in by drops. Also **in·still′.** [<L *instillare* drop, drip <*in-* in + *stillare* drop <*stilla* a drop] — **in·stil·a·tion** (in′stə·lā′shən) or **in′stil·la′tion, in·stil′ment** or **in·still′ment** *n.* — **in·still′er** *n.*

in·stinct (in′stingkt) *n.* 1 A natural impulse or innate propensity that incites animals (including man) to the actions that are essential to their existence, preservation, and development; animal intuition. 2 *Psychol.* **a** A strong, innate tendency to certain actions and forms of behavior, often accompanied by emotional excitement. **b** A complex, unlearned, adaptive response to some situation or experience. 3 A natural aptitude. — *adj.* (in·stingkt′) Animated from within; moved by or imbued with inward impulse; filled; alive: usually with *with.* [<L *instinctus,* pp. of *instinguere* impel]

in·stinc·tive (in·stingk′tiv) *adj.* Of the nature of, or prompted by, instinct; spontaneous; innate. Also **in·stinc′tu·al** (-chōō·əl). See synonyms under SPONTANEOUS. — **in·stinc′tive·ly, in·stinct′ly** *adv.*

in·sti·tute (in′stə·tōōt, -tyōōt) *v.t.* **·tut·ed, ·tut·ing** 1 To set up or establish; found. 2 To set in operation; initiate. 3 To appoint to an office, position, etc.; place in a benefice. 4 *Law* To nominate as heir or executor. — *n.* 1 An established organization or society pledged to some special purpose and work, or the building devoted to its use; an institution. 2 *pl.* Fundamental principles of law, or a digest of them, as for beginners. 3 An established principle, rule, or order. — **farmers' institute** An organization of farmers addressed by experts in agriculture for the purpose of disseminating knowledge in farming. — **naval institute** A society having as its object the development of naval knowledge. — **teachers' institute** A meeting of the schoolteachers of a state or county for the discussion of methods of teaching and problems which arise within a certain period. [<L *institutus,* pp. of *instituere* erect, establish <*in-* in, on + *statuere* set up, stand]

Synonyms (verb): appoint, begin, commence, erect, establish, found, ordain, organize, originate, start. *Antonyms*: see synonyms for ABOLISH.

Institute of France A national society established in 1795 to promote science, literature, and art, composed of a union of five academies: The French Academy; the Academy of Inscriptions and Belles-lettres; the Academy of Sciences; the Academy of Fine Arts; the Academy of Political and Moral Sciences. Also **the Institute.**

in·sti·tu·tion (in′stə·tōō′shən, -tyōō′-) *n.* 1 That which is instituted or established; an established order, principle, law, or usage as an element of organized society or of civilization: the *institution* of chivalry. 2 A corporate body or establishment instituted and organized for an educational, medical, charitable, or similar purpose, or the building occupied by such a corporate body: the Smithsonian *Institution.* 3 The act of instituting, establishing, or setting on foot: *institution* of an investigation. 4 *Eccl.* **a** The investment of a clergyman by a competent authority with the spiritualities of his office: contrasted with *induction,* which confers the temporalities. **b** The establishment of a sacrament, especially of the Eucharist. **c** That part of the ritual in baptism or the Eucharist at which the words used by Christ in establishing the sacrament are recited. 5 *Law* The formal designation by one person of another to be his heir. 6 *Colloq.* A well-established custom, object, or person: The postman was one of the *institutions* of the place. 7 *Obs.* Instruction, or a book of instruction. [<OF <L *institutio, -onis*]

in·sti·tu·tion·al (in′stə·tōō′shən·əl, -tyōō′-) *adj.* 1 Pertaining to or enjoined by institutions: *institutional* principles. 2 Relating to first principles or elements; rudimentary: *institutional* instruction. 3 Pertaining to investiture in office. 4 Designating a form of advertising intended to promote good will and prestige, as for an institution, rather than to get immediate sales. — **in′sti·tu′tion·al·ly** *adv.*

in·sti·tu·tion·al·ism (in′stə·to͞o′shən·əl·iz′əm, -tyo͞o′-) *n.* **1** The system of institutions. **2** Belief in and support of the usefulness and authority of institutions. **3** The spirit that exalts established institutions, especially in religion: opposed to *individualism.*

in·sti·tu·tion·al·ize (in′stə·to͞o′shen·əl·īz′, -tyo͞o′-) *v.t.* **·ized, ·iz·ing** **1** To make institutional. **2** To turn into or regard as an institution. **3** *U.S. Colloq.* To put (someone) in an institution (def. 2).

in·sti·tu·tion·ar·y (in′stə·to͞o′shən·er′ē, -tyo͞o′-) *adj.* Of or pertaining to legal or ecclesiastical institutions or to institutions of learning.

in·sti·tu·tive (in′stə·to͞o′tiv, -tyo͞o′-) *adj.* **1** Tending or intended to institute or establish; having power to ordain. **2** Established by authority; instituted. **— in′sti·tu′tive·ly** *adv.*

in·sti·tu·tor (in′stə·to͞o′tər, -tyo͞o′-) *n.* **1** One who establishes, organizes, or sets in operation; a founder. **2** *U.S.* In the Protestant Episcopal Church, one who institutes a clergyman into a church or parish. **3** *Obs.* An educator. Also **in′sti·tut′er.** [<L]

in·stroke (in′strōk′) *n.* **1** An inwardly directed stroke. **2** *Mech.* The thrust of an engine's piston away from the crankshaft. Compare OUTSTROKE.

in·struct (in·strukt′) *v.t.* **1** To impart knowledge or skill to, especially by systematic method; educate; teach. **2** To give specific orders or directions to; order: He *instructed* his men to break camp. **3** To give information or explanation to; inform. See synonyms under INFORM[1], LEARN, TEACH. [<L *instructus,* pp. of *instruere* <*in-* in + *struere* build]

in·struc·tion (in·struk′shən) *n.* **1** The act of instructing; teaching. **2** Imparted knowledge; precept. **3** The act of giving specific directions or commands. **4** The directions given. **5** *pl.* In English law, directions given to a solicitor or counsel. See synonyms under EDUCATION, LEARNING, NURTURE, ORDER. [<OF *enstruccion* <L *instructio, -onis*]

in·struc·tion·al (in·struk′shən·əl) *adj.* Pertaining or relating to instruction; educational; containing information.

in·struc·tive (in·struk′tiv) *adj.* Serving to instruct; conveying knowledge. **— in·struc′tive·ly** *adv.* **— in·struc′tive·ness** *n.*

in·struc·tor (in·struk′tər) *n.* **1** One who instructs; a teacher. **2** *U.S.* A college teacher of lower rank than the lowest professorial grade. Also **in·struct′er.** [<L]

in·struc·tor·ship (in·struk′tər·ship) *n.* The position or office of an instructor.

in·stru·ment (in′strə·mənt) *n.* **1** A means by which work is done; an implement or tool, especially a device or mechanism for scientific or professional purposes, as distinguished from an apparatus, tool, or machine for industrial use. **2** Any means of accomplishment: The hands are *instruments* of the will. **3** A mechanical or other contrivance for the production of musical sounds. **4** A person doing the will of another. **5** *Law* A formal document, as a contract, deed, etc. See synonyms under AGENT, RECORD, TOOL. **—** *v.t.* **1** *Law* To draw up an instrument. **2** *Music* To orchestrate. [<L *instrumentum* <*instruere* fit out, INSTRUCT]

in·stru·men·tal (in′strə·men′təl) *adj.* **1** Serving as a means or instrument; serviceable. **2** Fitted for or produced by musical instruments. **3** Traceable to a mechanical instrument, as errors in observation or measurement. **4** *Gram.* Pertaining to a case of the noun, as in Sanskrit, indicating the means or instrument by or with which something is done. **—** *n. Gram.* **1** The instrumental case. **2** A word in this case.

in·stru·men·tal·ism (in′strə·men′təl·iz′əm) *n.* *Philos.* The doctrine that experience (or use) determines the value of anything; hence, the doctrine that ideas are true or valid according to their usefulness; pragmatism.

in·stru·men·tal·ist (in′strə·men′təl·ist) *n.* **1** *Music* One who plays an instrument, as distinguished from a vocalist. **2** A believer in instrumentalism.

in·stru·men·tal·i·ty (in′strə·men·tal′ə·tē) *n. pl.* **·ties** **1** The condition of being instrumental; subordinate agency. **2** That which is instrumental; means.

in·stru·men·tal·ly (in′strə·men′təl·ē) *adv.* **1** By means of an instrument or agency; not directly. **2** With musical instruments.

in·stru·men·ta·tion (in′strə·men·tā′shən) *n.* **1** *Music* **a** The act or art of arranging compositions for performance by instruments; orchestration. **b** The use of an instrument, as for producing special or peculiar effects. **2** The art and technique of using instruments of precision. **3** Instrumentality; agency.

instrument board The panel containing the gages and other indicators of performance in an automobile, airplane, or other complex apparatus. Also **instrument panel.**

instrument flight *Aeron.* Control of the course of an aircraft by reference to instruments within the craft rather than by observation of landmarks: contrasted to *contact flight.*

in·sub·or·di·nate (in′sə·bôr′də·nit) *adj.* **1** Not subordinate or obedient; not submitting to authority; rebellious; mutinous. **2** Not lower or inferior in height: an *insubordinate* hill. **—** *n.* A disobedient or unsubmissive person. **— in′sub·or′di·nate·ly** *adv.*

in·sub·or·di·na·tion (in′sə·bôr′də·nā′shən) *n.* The state of being insubordinate; disobedience to constituted authorities; unruliness.

in·sub·stan·tial (in′səb·stan′shəl) *adj.* Unsubstantial; not material; illusive. **— in′sub·stan′ti·al′i·ty** (-shē·al′ə·tē) *n.*

in·suf·fer·a·ble (in·suf′ər·ə·bəl) *adj.* Not to be endured; intolerable. **— in·suf′fer·a·ble·ness** *n.* **— in·suf′fer·a·bly** *adv.*

in·suf·fi·cien·cy (in′sə·fish′ən·sē) *n. pl.* **·cies** **1** Lack of sufficiency; inadequacy in amount, value, power, fitness, etc.; deficiency; also, mental inability. **2** Anything that is not enough. [<F *insuffisance* <LL *insufficientia*]

in·suf·fi·cient (in′sə·fish′ənt) *adj.* **1** Inadequate for some need, purpose, or use. **2** Mentally or physically unfit. **— in′suf·fi′cient·ly** *adv.*

in·suf·flate (in·suf′lāt, in′sə·flāt) *v.t.* **·flat·ed, ·flat·ing** **1** To blow or breathe into or upon. **2** To blow a substance into: to *insufflate* a room with disinfectant. **3** *Med.* **a** To blow (air, medicinal gas, etc.) into an opening or upon some part of the body. **b** To treat by insufflation, as an asphyxiated person. **4** *Eccl.* To breathe upon, as at baptism. [<L *insufflatus,* pp. of *insufflare* <*in-* in + *sufflare* <blow from below <*sub-* under + *flare* blow] **— in·suf′fla·tor** *n.*

in·suf·fla·tion (in′sə·flā′shən) *n.* **1** The act or process of blowing or breathing upon or into. **2** *Eccl.* A breathing upon a person or thing as symbolic of the operation and entrance of the Holy Spirit, or the casting out of unclean spirits, as in some churches in the ordinance of baptism for the purification of catechumens. **3** *Med.* A forcible blowing, as of air into the lungs, or of a gas, vapor, or powder into some opening or cavity of the body. [<LL *insufflatio, -onis*]

in·su·la (in′sə·lə) *n. pl.* **·lae** (-lē) **1** *Anat.* Any detached or isolated area in an organ of the body, as the central lobe of the cerebral cortex. **2** In ancient Rome, a block of houses. [<L, island]

in·su·lar (in′sə·lər) *adj.* **1** Of or pertaining to, like, living on or characteristic of an island. **2** Standing alone; isolated. **3** *Biol.* Having an island as its habitat. **4** Of or pertaining to people inhabiting an island or otherwise isolated, or to their customs, opinions, etc. **5** Not broad, liberal, nor cosmopolitan; narrow: *insular* ideas or prejudices. **6** *Med.* **a** Breaking out or appearing sporadically in spots, as a rash on the body. **b** Characterized by spots appearing singly here and there. **7** *Anat.* Pertaining to an insula or to the islands of Langerhans in the pancreas. [<L *insularis* <*insula* island]

in·su·lar·i·ty (in′sə·lar′ə·tē) *n.* **1** The state or quality of being insular or belonging to an island. **2** Insular position, character, or condition. **3** Narrowness or illiberality. Compare PENINSULARITY. Also **in′su·lar·ism.**

in·su·late (in′sə·lāt) *v.t.* **·lat·ed, ·lat·ing** **1** To place in a detached state or situation; isolate. **2** To change into an island; surround by water. **3** *Physics* To separate from conducting bodies, as by a covering or support of a non-conducting substance, usually in order to prevent or lessen the leakage of an electric current, heat, sound, radiation, etc. [<L *insulatus* formed like an island <*insula* island]

in·su·la·tion (in′sə·lā′shən) *n.* **1** The act of insulating; isolation. **2** The act of surrounding a body with non-conductors. **3** Material used in insulating.

in·su·la·tor (in′sə·lā′tər) *n.* **1** One who or that which insulates. **2** *Electr.* A dielectric substance or material, as glass or porcelain, adapted to minimize leakage from a charged conductor which it supports.

in·su·lin (in′sə·lin) *n.* A protein hormone secreted by and obtained from the pancreas: used in the form of a standardized aqueous solution, it checks the accumulation of glucose in the blood and promotes the utilization of sugar in the treatment of diabetes. [<L *insula* island (of Langerhans) + -IN]

in·su·lize (in′sə·līz) *v.t.* **·lized, ·liz·ing** To inject insulin into; treat with insulin.

in·sult (in·sult′) *v.t.* **1** To treat with insolence or contempt; affront. **2** *Obs.* To attack suddenly; assault. **—** *v.i.* **3** *Obs.* To exult or behave insolently. See synonyms under AFFRONT, MOCK, OUTRAGE. **—** *n.* (in′sult) **1** Something offensive said or done; an indignity or affront. **2** Contumelious treatment; abuse; outrage. **3** *Obs.* A sudden attack or assault. See synonyms under OFFENSE. [<F *insulter* <L *insultare* leap at, insult, freq. of *insilire* leap upon <*in-* on + *salire* leap] **— in·sult′er** *n.*

in·sult·ing (in·sul′ting) *adj.* Conveying or intending to insult. **— in·sult′ing·ly** *adv.*

in·su·per·a·ble (in·so͞o′pər·ə·bəl) *adj.* Not to be surmounted or overcome; insurmountable. [<L *insuperabilis*] **— in·su′per·a·bil′i·ty, in·su′per·a·ble·ness** *n.* **— in·su′per·a·bly** *adv.*

in·sup·port·a·ble (in′sə·pôr′tə·bəl, -pōr′-) *adj.* **1** Intolerable; insufferable. **2** Without grounds; unjustifiable. **— in′sup·port′a·bly** *adv.*

in·sup·press·i·ble (in′sə·pres′ə·bəl) *adj.* Incapable of being suppressed or concealed; irrepressible. Also **in′sup·pres′sive** (-pres′iv).

in·sur·ance (in·sho͝or′əns) *n.* **1** An act, business, or system by which pecuniary indemnity is guaranteed by one party (as a company) to another party in certain contingencies, as of death, accident, damage, disaster, injury, loss, old age, risk, sickness, unemployment, etc., upon specified terms: in Great Britain, often *assurance.* **2** A contract made under such a system. **3** The consideration paid for insuring; premium. **4** The sum that the insurer has agreed to pay in case of the occurrence of the specified contingency. **5** The act of making safe or secure. **6** Something that provides protection or security.

— accident insurance A form of insurance covering loss due to accidental personal injury.

— casualty insurance Insurance of property against loss from accidental causes.

— endowment insurance A form of life insurance in which the whole amount agreed upon is paid to the insured if he survives beyond a specified date, or to some designated person or his heirs if he dies before that time.

— fire insurance Insurance covering loss or damage to property by fire or from the efforts to extinguish fire.

— life insurance Insurance on the life of oneself or another. The first life insurance company established in Great Britain was the "Amicable" in 1706, and the first in America was introduced from England in 1759 as the Presbyterian Ministers' Fund, and established in Philadelphia.

— marine insurance Insurance which covers loss on ships, cargo, and freight by shipwreck or disaster at sea.

— unemployment insurance A form of government insurance in which a worker is paid, during an extended period of involuntary unemployment, from a fund contributed to by employers and employees.

in·sur·ant (in·sho͝or′ənt) *n.* One to whom an insurance policy is issued; also, the beneficiary.

in·sure (in·sho͝or′) *v.* **·sured, ·sur·ing** *v.t.* **1** To contract to pay or be paid an indemnity in the event of harm to or the loss or death of; issue or take out a policy of insurance on. **2** To make safe; guard or protect: with *against* or *from*: Only vigilance *insures* freedom against tyranny. **3** To make sure or

certain; guarantee: His researches *insure* the accuracy of the report. — *v.i.* 4 To issue or take out a policy of insurance. Also spelled *ensure.* [<OF *enseurer* make sure <*en-* in + *seur* sure] — **in·sur'a·bil'i·ty** *n.* — **in·sur'·a·ble** *adj.*

in·sured (in·shŏŏrd') *n.* 1 The person or persons to whom insurance (as fire or marine) is to be paid after loss or damage. 2 The person or persons upon whose death or disability insurance (life or accident) becomes due.

in·sur·er (in·shŏŏr'ər) *n.* One who or that which insures; especially, a company or individual that undertakes, for compensation, to guarantee against loss; an underwriter.

in·sur·gence (in·sûr'jəns) *n.* The act of rising in insurrection; insurrection; uprising.

in·sur·gen·cy (in·sûr'jən·sē) *n.* 1 The state of being insurgent. 2 In international law, any uprising against a government of less gravity than a revolution.

in·sur·gent (in·sûr'jənt) *adj.* Rebellious; rising in rebellion against an existing government. See synonyms under TURBULENT. — *n.* One who takes part in active and forcible opposition or resistance to the constituted authorities; also, a rebel to whom belligerent rights have not been accorded. [<L *insurgens, -entis,* ppr. of *insurgere* rise up against <*in-* against + *surgere* rise]

in·sur·mount·a·ble (in'sər·moun'tə·bəl) *adj.* That cannot be surmounted, passed over, or overcome; insuperable. — **in'sur·mount'a·bly** *adv.*

in·sur·rec·tion (in'sə·rek'shən) *n.* An organized resistance to established government. See synonyms under REVOLUTION. [<F <LL *insurrectio, -onis* <*insurrectus,* pp. of *insurgere* rise up against. See INSURGENT.] — **in'sur·rec'tion·al** *adj.* — **in'sur·rec'tion·ar'y** *adj.* & *n.* — **in'sur·rec'tion·ism** *n.* — **in'sur·rec'tion·ist** *n.*

in·sus·cep·ti·ble (in'sə·sep'tə·bəl) *adj.* Not susceptible; incapable of being moved or impressed. — **in'sus·cep'ti·bil'i·ty** *n.*

in·swathe (in·swāth') See ENSWATHE.

in·swept (in'swept') *adj.* Narrowed or tapering in front, as an airplane wing.

in·tact (in·takt') *adj.* Left complete or unimpaired. [<L *intactus* untouched <*in-* not + *tactus,* pp. of *tangere* touch] — **in·tact'ness** *n.*

in·ta·glio (in·tal'yō, *Ital.* in·tä'lyō) *n.* *pl.* **·glios** or **·gli** (-lyē) 1 Incised carving; a sunken design: compare RILIEVO. 2 The art of making such designs. 3 A work, especially a gem, with incised carving: compare CAMEO. 4 A countersunk die for producing a relief design. — *v.t.* 1 To engrave with a sunken design. 2 To execute or represent in intaglio. [<Ital. <*intagliare* engrave <*in-* in + *tagliare* cut]

intaglio printing A method of printing from sunken or incised plates: also called *copperplate* or *steel-die printing.*

in·take (in'tāk') *n.* 1 That which is taken in; also, a taking in. 2 A point at which a knit or woven article is narrowed. 3 The area in which a water supply is formed. 4 The point at which a fluid is taken into a pipe or channel, as distinguished from the outlet. 5 The current flowing in such a pipe. 6 The amount so taken in. 7 The amount of energy or power taken into a machine or system.

in·tan·gi·ble (in·tan'jə·bəl) *adj.* 1 Not capable of being touched; not tangible; impalpable. 2 Not directly appreciable by the mind; unfathomable — *n.* Something intangible but often noteworthy or influential nevertheless. [<Med. L *intangibilis*] — **in·tan'gi·bil'i·ty, in·tan'gi·ble·ness** *n.* — **in·tan'gi·bly** *adv.*

in·tar·si·a (in·tär'sē·ə) *n.* Mosaic woodwork of tinted and natural woods. [<Ital. *intarsio* <*intarsiare* inlay, encrust <*in-* in + Arabic *tarsi* incrustation]

in·te·ger (in'tə·jər) *n.* 1 A whole. 2 A number that is not a fraction; a whole number. [<L <*in-* not + root *tag-,* of *tangere.* Doublet of ENTIRE.]

in·te·ger vi·tae (in'tə·jər vī'tē) *Latin* Innocent; pure: literally, blameless in life.

in·te·gra·ble (in'tə·grə·bəl) *adj.* Capable of being integrated.

in·te·gral (in'tə·grəl) *adj.* 1 Constituting a completed whole. 2 Constituting an essential part of a whole necessary for completeness; intrinsic. 3 *Math.* **a** Pertaining to an integer. **b** Produced by integration. — *n.* 1 An entire thing; a whole. 2 *Math.* The result of integration. [<LL *integralis*] — **in'te·gral'i·ty** (-gral'ə·tē) *n.* — **in'te·gral·ly** *adv.*

integral calculus See under CALCULUS.

in·te·grand (in'tə·grand) *n.* *Math.* An expression to be integrated, or whose integration is indicated. [<L *integrandus,* gerundive of *integrare* make whole]

in·te·grant (in'tə·grənt) *adj.* Contributing or essential to the making up of a whole; integral. — *n.* A component. [<L *integrans, -antis,* ppr. of *integrare* make whole]

in·te·grate (in'tə·grāt) *v.* **·grat·ed, ·grat·ing** *v.t.* 1 To make whole by the bringing together or addition of parts. 2 To give the sum total or mean value of. 3 *Math.* To find the integral of. 4 *U.S.* **a** To make (schools, housing, public facilities, etc.) available to people of all races and ethnic groups on an equal basis. **b** To remove any barriers imposing segregation upon (religious, racial, or other groups). — *v.i.* 5 To become integrated. [<L *integratus,* pp. of *integrare* make whole, renew <*integer* whole, intact] — **in'te·gra'tive** (-grā'·tiv) *adj.*

in·te·grat·ed (in'tə·grā'tid) *adj.* 1 Made whole by combining in systematic order or arrangement the component parts or factors: an *integrated* curriculum. 2 Well adjusted: an *integrated* personality. 3 *Econ.* Organized and equipped to produce all materials (usually excluding the raw materials) and components required by a manufacturing process without recourse to independent suppliers; a fully *integrated* plant. 4 *U.S.* Made up of individuals or groups of various cultural, economic, racial, etc., backgrounds functioning as a unit: an *integrated* school.

in·te·gra·tion (in'tə·grā'shən) *n.* 1 The act or operation of integrating; the bringing together of parts into a whole. 2 *Math.* The process of determining a function from its derivative; the inverse of *differentiation.* 3 *Physiol.* The combination of different nervous processes or reflexes so that they cooperate in a larger activity and thus unify the bodily functions. 4 *Psychol.* The orderly arrangement of the physical, emotional, and mental components of the personality into a more or less stable and harmonious pattern of behavior. 5 *U.S.* The act or process of integrating, especially racially, an institution, place, or group. — **in'te·gra'tion·ist** *(especially for def. 5) n.* [<L *integratio, -onis*]

in·te·gra·tor (in'tə·grā'tər) *n.* 1 One who or that which integrates. 2 Any mechanical device for obtaining the numerical value of an integral, especially the area of an irregular figure. 3 An integrating instrument, as a planimeter.

in·teg·ri·ty (in·teg'rə·tē) *n.* 1 Uprightness of character; probity; honesty. 2 Unimpaired state; soundness. 3 Undivided or unbroken state; completeness. See synonyms under FIDELITY, JUSTICE, VIRTUE, WORTH. [<L *integritas, -tatis* <*integer* whole]

in·teg·u·ment (in·teg'yə·mənt) *n.* 1 A covering; coating; investment. 2 *Biol.* Any natural outer covering or envelope, as the skin of an animal, coat of a seed, etc. [<L *integumentum* covering <*integere* cover <*in-* thoroughly + *tegere* cover] — **in·teg·u·men·ta·ry** (in·teg'·yə·men'tə·rē) *adj.*

in·tel·lect (in'tə·lekt) *n.* 1 The faculty or power of perception or thought; intelligence; mind; sometimes, the higher thinking powers, as distinguished from the senses and memory: *Intellect* distinguishes man from brutes. 2 Intelligent people collectively: The *intellect* of the age is enlisted in these inquiries. 3 The faculty or power of understanding, whether of the objects immediately presented in sense perception, or of those known by processes of reasoning. 4 Formerly, in the archaic threefold division of psychology, the faculty of knowing, as distinguished from sensibility and will. 5 The power to perceive things in a rational way, as involving a more than ordinary comprehension of their relations, laws, and profounder meanings; the scientific or philosophic mind: Aristotle was a man of mighty *intellect.* 6 The sum of the mental powers by which knowledge is acquired, retained, and extended, as distinguished from the senses; the understanding. [<L *intellectus* perception, understanding, sense <*intelligere* understand. See INTELLIGENT.]

Synonyms: intelligence, reason, reasoning, understanding. According to the long-established division of the mental powers into the *intellect,* the sensibilities, and the will, the *intellect* is that assemblage of faculties which is concerned with knowledge, as distinguished from emotion and volition. *Understanding* is the Saxon word of the same general import, but is chiefly used of the reasoning powers. See MIND, UNDERSTANDING. *Antonyms*: body, matter, passion, sensation, sense.

in·tel·lec·tion (in'tə·lek'shən) *n.* Exercise of the intellect; thought. [<Med. L *intellectio, -onis*]

in·tel·lec·tive (in'tə·lek'tiv) *adj.* Of or pertaining to the intellect; intelligent. [<OF *intellectif* <LL *intellectivus*] — **in'tel·lec'tive·ly** *adv.*

in·tel·lec·tu·al (in'tə·lek'chōō·əl) *adj.* 1 Pertaining to the intellect; bringing into action the intellect or higher capacities; mental. 2 Possessing intellect or intelligence; characterized by a high degree of intelligence. 3 Requiring intelligence or study: *intellectual* pursuits. See synonyms under CLEVER, WISE. — *n.* 1 An intellectual person. 2 *pl.* *Archaic* The mental faculties; intellect: often in the plural. [<L *intellectualis*] — **in'tel·lec'tu·al·ly** *adv.*

in·tel·lec·tu·al·ism (in'tə·lek'chōō·əl·iz'əm) *n.* 1 Intellectual quality or power; intellectuality. 2 Devotion to intellectual occupation. 3 Belief in the supremacy of the intellect among human faculties. 4 The doctrine that the ultimate principle of all reality is intellect or reason. — **in'tel·lec'tu·al·ist** *n.* — **in'tel·lec'tu·al·is'tic** *adj.*

in·tel·lec·tu·al·i·ty (in'tə·lek'chōō·al'ə·tē) *n.* The quality or state of being intellectual; possession of intellectual force or endowment.

in·tel·lec·tu·al·ize (in'tə·lek'chōō·əl·īz') *v.t.* & *v.i.* **·ized, ·iz·ing** To make or become intellectual.

in·tel·li·gence (in·tel'ə·jəns) *n.* 1 The quality, exercise, or product of active intellect; intellect; knowledge; ability to exercise the higher mental functions; readiness of comprehension. 2 The capacity to meet situations, especially if new or unforeseen, by a rapid and effective adjustment of behavior; also, the native ability to grasp the significant factors of a complex problem or situation. 3 Information acquired or communicated; notification; news; especially, secret information, political, military, etc. 4 Mutual understanding; interchange of information or thought: to exchange a look of *intelligence.* 5 An intelligent being; especially, a spirit not embodied: the Supreme *Intelligence.* See synonyms under INTELLECT, KNOWLEDGE, MIND, TIDINGS, UNDERSTANDING. [<OF <L *intelligentia* <*intelligens, -entis,* ppr. of *intelligere* understand]

intelligence department A department charged with getting information for a government, an army, or a navy, as by means of spies.

intelligence office 1 An office where information may be obtained. 2 *U.S.* Formerly, an employment bureau, especially for servants.

intelligence officer An officer in the service of an intelligence department.

intelligence quotient *Psychol.* A numerical quotient obtained by multiplying the mental age of a person by 100, and dividing the result by his chronological age. Abbr. *I.Q.* or *IQ.*

in·tel·li·genc·er (in·tel'ə·jən·sər) *n.* A sender or conveyor of intelligence or news; a messenger; spy.

intelligence test *Psychol.* Any test designed to show the relative mental capacity of a person.

in·tel·li·gent (in·tel'ə·jənt) *adj.* 1 Distinguished for intelligence; of active mind; discerning; acute: an *intelligent* reader. 2 Marked by intelligence: an *intelligent* reply. 3 Endowed with intellect; reasoning: Man is an *intelligent* animal. 4 *Archaic* Informed; cognizant: with *of.* 5 *Obs.* Communicating information. [<L *intelligens, -entis,* ppr. of *intelligere* understand, perceive <*inter-* between + *legere* choose, pick] — **in·tel'li·gent·ly** *adv.*

Synonyms: acute, astute, bright, clear-headed, clear-sighted, clever, discerning, educated, instructed, keen, keen-sighted, knowing, long-headed, quick-sighted, sensible, sharp-sighted, sharp-witted, shrewd, well-informed. *Antonyms*: see synonyms for IGNORANT.

in·tel·li·gen·tial (in·tel'ə·jen'shəl) *adj.* 1 Exercising or characterized by intelligence; rational. 2 Conveying intelligence.

in·tel·li·gent·si·a (in·tel'ə·jent'sē·ə, -gent'-) *n. pl.* Intellectual or learned people, collectively; especially those capable of thinking for themselves: sometimes used derisively: a term adopted during the Russian Revolution to differentiate the intellectual classes as such from the bourgeoisie and proletariat. Also **in·tel·li·gent'zi·a.** [<Russian *intelligentsiya* < Ital. *intelligenza* intelligence < L *intelligentia*]

in·tel·li·gi·bil·i·ty (in·tel'ə·jə·bil'ə·tē) *n. pl.* **·ties 1** Clearness; understandableness. **2** That which is intelligible.

in·tel·li·gi·ble (in·tel'ə·jə·bəl) *adj.* **1** Capable of being understood. **2** *Philos.* Capable of being apprehended only by the intellect, not by the senses. Compare SENSIBLE. See synonyms under CLEAR, PLAIN. [<L *intelligibilis*] — **in·tel'li·gi·bly** *adv.*

in·tem·er·ate (in·tem'ər·it) *adj.* Undefiled; pure. [<L *intemeratus* <*in-* not + *temeratus,* pp. of *temerare* violate < *temere* rashly, by chance]

in·tem·per·ance (in·tem'pər·əns) *n.* **1** Lack of moderation or due restraint. **2** Excess in speech or action, especially in the use of alcoholic drinks. **3** An intemperate act. See synonyms under EXCESS. [<OF <L *intemperantia*]

in·tem·per·ate (in·tem'pər·it) *adj.* **1** Characterized by lack of moderation, as in speech or action; unrestrained, as in indulgence or exertion. **2** Given to or characterized by excessive use of alcoholic drinks: *intemperate* habits. **3** Excessive in character or degree: inordinate; inclement: *intemperate* weather. — **in·tem'per·ate·ly** *adv.* — **in·tem'per·ate·ness** *n.*

in·tend (in·tend') *v.t.* **1** To have in mind to accomplish or do; purpose: He *intends* to go. **2** To make or destine for a purpose, use, etc.: Was that gift *intended* for me? **3** To have the purpose of meaning or expressing; mean: She *intended* nothing by the remark. **4** *Obs.* To direct, as one's course or thoughts. — *v.i.* **5** *Rare* To have intention; mean: to *intend* well. **6** *Obs.* To tend; incline. See synonyms under PURPOSE. [<OF *entendre* <L *intendere* stretch out (for) <*in-* in, at + *tendere* stretch] — **in·tend'er** *n.*

in·ten·dance (in·ten'dəns) *n.* **1** Business management or superintendence. **2** An intendancy. [<F]

in·ten·dan·cy (in·ten'dən·sē) *n. pl.* **·cies 1** The office or work of an intendant; intendants collectively. **2** An administrative district in Spanish America. Also **in·ten'den·cy.**

in·ten·dant (in·ten'dənt) *n.* **1** A superintendent; provincial administrator, as under the Bourbons in France. **2** A Spanish or Mexican district administrator or treasurer. Also **in·ten'dent,** *Spanish* **in·ten·den·te** (ēn'ten·den'tā). See synonyms under SUPERINTENDENT. [<F]

in·tend·ed (in·ten'did) *adj.* **1** Made the object of design or intent; designed. **2** Betrothed. — *n. Colloq.* One who is betrothed.

in·tend·ment (in·tend'mənt) *n.* **1** The true intent or meaning, or correct understanding, of the law, or of a legal instrument; also, a general presumption of law. **2** *Obs.* Intention; object, as of an action; purpose; design. [<OF *entendement*]

in·ten·er·ate (in·ten'ər·āt) *v.t.* **·at·ed, ·at·ing** *Rare* To make tender; soften. [<L *in-* very + *tener* tender + -ATE¹] — **in·ten'er·a'tion** *n.*

in·tense (in·tens') *adj.* **in·tens·er, in·tens·est 1** Strained or exerted to a high degree; ardent; unremitting; fervid: *intense* study. **2** Extreme in degree; very deep or strong; severe; violent; excessive: *intense* light or pain. **3** Putting forth strenuous effort; intent. **4** Susceptible to or exhibiting deep emotion, earnestness, or application: said of a person. **5** *Phot.* Having strength or marked contrast; dense: said of a negative. See synonyms under ARDENT, EAGER, VIOLENT, VIVID. [<OF <L *intensus,* pp. of *intendere* stretch out] — **in·tense'ly** *adv.* — **in·tense'ness** *n.*

in·ten·si·fi·ca·tion (in·ten'sə·fə·kā'shən) *n.* **1** The act or result of intensifying or of making intense. **2** *Phot.* The process of increasing the density of a negative.

in·ten·si·fi·er (in·ten'sə·fī'ər) *n.* **1** One who or that which intensifies. **2** *Phot.* A chemical solution used to effect intensification. **3** A

device by which fluid pressure is intensified.

in·ten·si·fy (in·ten'sə·fī) *v.* **·fied, ·fy·ing** *v.t.* **1** To make intense; increase in intensity. **2** *Phot.* To increase the density of (a film) so as to obtain stronger contrast between light and shadow. — *v.i.* **3** To become intense or more intense. See synonyms under AGGRAVATE, INCREASE.

in·ten·sion (in·ten'shən) *n.* **1** The act of straining or stretching, or state of being strained or made tense; tension. **2** Increase of energy or power; intensification. **3** *Logic* All the implications in a concept or term; connotation: distinguished from *extension.* **4** Intensity; degree. **5** Intense exertion of the mind or the will. [<L *intensio, -onis*]

in·ten·si·ty (in·ten'sə·tē) *n. pl.* **·ties 1** The state or quality of being intense; relative strength or degree of a quality or force; intenseness. **2** *Physics* The force, energy, or quantity of action of any physical agent, generally estimated by its ratio to the space within which it acts, or to the quantity of matter on which it acts: the *intensity* of pressure of a fluid, the *intensity* of gravity. **3** *Electr.* **a** The strength of an electric or magnetic field as measured by the number of force lines that pass through unit area of cross-section. **b** Current strength or density. **c** Potential or electromotive force. **4** *Phot.* Strong contrast between light and shade in a negative; density; also, opacity. See synonyms under ENTHUSIASM, VIOLENCE, WARMTH.

in·ten·sive (in·ten'siv) *adj.* **1** Serving or tending to intensify. **2** Admitting of increase of force or degree; capable of being intensified. **3** Thorough, as contrasted with extensive. **4** *Logic* Relating to intension or content. See CONTENT. **5** *Agric.* Of or pertaining to the tillage of land by the application of much labor and costly fertilization to a given area (usually small) which is thereby brought to a high degree of productiveness. **6** Of or relating to a way of making any industry more lucrative by perfecting methods and appliances without enlarging the scale of operations. **7** *Med.* **a** Characterizing a method of inoculation wherein the injections are successively increased in strength. **b** A method of administering increasingly strong remedies or doses. **8** *Gram.* Adding emphasis or force. **9** Intense; assiduous; concentrated: *intensive* research; *intensive* warfare. **10** Characterized by a relatively heavy investment in (something specified) as compared with other factors: used in combination: an *energy-intensive* method of heating; a *labor-intensive* industry. — *n.* **1** Whatever gives intensity or emphasis. **2** *Gram.* An intensive particle, word, or phrase. [<F *intensif*] — **in·ten'sive·ly** *adv.* — **in·ten'sive·ness** *n.*

intensive particle A particle or prefix expressing heightened meaning: as *be-* in *besmirch; for-* in *forlorn; de-* in *desiccate; per-* in *perjure.* Also **intensive prefix.**

in·tent (in·tent') *adj.* **1** Having the mind earnestly bent or fixed; attentive; earnest. **2** Firmly, constantly, or assiduously directed. See synonyms under EAGER. — *n.* **1** That which is designed; intention; meaning; connotation; aim; purpose. **2** *Law* The state of mind in which or the purpose with which one does an act; also, the character that the law imputes to an act. See synonyms under DESIGN, PURPOSE. [<OF *entent, entente* <L *intentus,* pp. of *intendere* stretch out, endeavor] — **in·tent'ly** *adv.* — **in·tent'ness** *n.*

in·ten·tion (in·ten'shən) *n.* **1** A settled direction of the mind toward the doing of a certain act. **2** That upon which the mind is set or which it wishes to express or achieve; meaning; purpose conceived. **3** *pl. Colloq.* Purpose with regard to marriage. **4** *Law* An intelligent purpose to do a criminal act; intent; purpose: an essential element in a criminal offense. **5** *Med.* Natural course, operation, or process, as in the healing of a wound. **6** *Logic* In scholasticism: **a** First intention, a general concept of an object, kind of object, or notion formed from something outside the mind, as *man, house, integrity, word, to run.* **b** Second intention, a general concept formed from or extended to abstractions of other concepts of objects and their relation-

ships, as *genus* and *species, property, ethics, language* and *meaning, physiological functions.* Compare CONSTRUCT *n.* (def. 2). **7** *Eccl.* **a** The inward intent or purpose on the part of the minister of a sacrament to do what the church requires to be done: considered essential to the validity of a sacrament. **b** The purpose for which a person offers up prayers or other devotions: often with *special* or *particular.* **8** Earnest attention; application. See synonyms under AIM, DESIGN, PURPOSE. [<OF *entencion* <L *intentio, -onis*]

in·ten·tion·al (in·ten'shən·əl) *adj.* Done with intention; designed. [<Med. L *intentionalis*] — **in·ten'tion·al·ly** *adv.*

in·ten·tioned (in·ten'shənd) *adj.* Having designs or intentions: used in composition with a qualifying adverb: well-*intentioned.*

in·ter (in·tûr') *v.t.* **·terred, ·ter·ring** To place in a grave or tomb; bury. See synonyms under BURY, HIDE. [<OF *enterrer* <LL *interrare* <*in-* in + *terra* earth]

inter- *prefix* **1** With each other; together: *interwind.* **2** Mutual; mutually: *intercommunion.* **3** Between (the units signified): *intercollegiate, intertribal.* **4** Occurring or situated between; intermediate: *intermural, interpolar.* [<L *inter-* < *inter* between, among]

A large number of words beginning with *inter-* are self-explaining or readily understood, as in the following list; those that require special definition will be found in their proper alphabetical place.

interagency	**interknot**
inter-American	**interlay**
interanimate	**interligamentous**
interblend	**interlocate**
interbrachial	**intermigration**
intercarotid	**intermolecular**
intercarpal	**intermundane**
interchain	**intermural**
intercirculate	**inter-oceanic**
interclasp	**inter-ocular**
intercolonial	**interplace**
intercommunion	**interplanetary**
intercomplexity	**interpolar**
intercontinental	**interracial**
interconversion	**interreceive**
interconvertible	**interregional**
intercross	**interrule**
interdenominational	**interscapular**
interdepartmental	**interscene**
interdependence	**interscholastic**
interdependency	**interseptal**
interdependent	**intersocial**
interdiffuse	**intersonant**
interdiffusion	**interspeech**
interdigital	**interstellar**
interfibrous	**interstratification**
interfold	**interstratify**
interfriction	**intertangle**
interfulgent	**interterritorial**
interfuse	**intertraffic**
interfusion	**intertribal**
interglandular	**intertropical**
interglobular	**intertubular**
intergovernmental	**intertwist**
intergrowth	**inter-union**
interisland	**inter-university**
interjoin	**interwind**
interjunction	**interwork**
interknit	**interwreathe**

in·ter·act (in'tər·akt') *v.i.* To act on each other. — **in'ter·ac'tive** *adj.*

in·ter·ac·tion (in'tər·ak'shən) *n.* Reciprocal action or influence: the *interaction* between the executive and legislative branches of government. — **in'ter·ac'tion·al** *adj.*

in·ter·ac·tion·ism (in'tər·ak'shən·iz'əm) *n. Psychol.* The theory that physical occurrences are the causes of mental modifications and that mental modifications give rise to physical changes.

in·ter a·li·a (in'tər ā'lē·ə) *Latin* Among other things.

in·ter a·li·os (in'tər ā'lē·ōs) *Latin* Among other persons.

in·ter·bed·ded (in'tər·bed'id) *adj. Geol.* Occurring between beds: said of rocks.

in·ter·bor·ough (in'tər·bûr'ō) *adj.* Pertaining to, situated in, or running in two or more boroughs: an *interborough* railroad.

in·ter·brain (in'tər·brān') *n. Anat.* The portion

of the brain that is derived from the second cerebral vesicle; the diencephalon.

in·ter·breed (in′tər·brēd′) *v.* **·bred, ·breed·ing** *v.t.* **1** To breed by crossing different stocks, varieties, etc.; crossbreed. **2** To cause (animals or plants) to breed by crossing. —*v.i.* **3** To breed with another: said of different varieties, stocks, etc.

in·ter·ca·lar·y (in·tûr′kə·ler′ē) *adj.* **1** Added to the calendar. **2** Containing an added day. **3** Interposed; inserted. [<L *intercalarius*]

in·ter·ca·late (in·tûr′kə·lāt) *v.t.* **·lat·ed, ·lat·ing 1** To insert or interpolate. **2** To insert, as an additional day or month, into the calendar. [<L *intercalatus,* pp. of *intercalare* insert <*inter-* between +*calare* proclaim, call]

in·ter·ca·la·tion (in·tûr′kə·lā′shən) *n.* **1** The insertion of one thing between other things, especially in an irregular manner. **2** An insertion of a day or days in the calendar. —**in·ter′ca·la′tive** *adj.*

in·ter·car·di·nal (in′tər·kär′də·nəl) *adj. Naut.* Between the cardinal points of the compass, as northeast, southwest, etc. —*n.* One of the intercardinal points of the compass.

in·ter·cede (in′tər·sēd′) *v.i.* **·ced·ed, ·ced·ing 1** To plead in behalf of another; make intercession. **2** To interpose a veto: said of the ancient Roman tribunes. See synonyms under INTERPOSE. [<L *intercedere* come between <*inter-* between +*cedere* pass, go]—**in′·ter·ced′er** *n.*

in·ter·cel·lu·lar (in′tər·sel′yə·lər) *adj. Biol.* Situated between or among cells: the *intercellular* substance or matrix of cartilage.

intercellular spaces *Bot.* The spaces or passages filled with air between or among the cells of plant tissues.

in·ter·cept (in′tər·sept′) *v.t.* **1** To seize or stop on the way to a destination; arrest in passage: to *intercept* a messenger. **2** To stop, interrupt, or prevent: to *intercept* the flow of water. **3** To cut off from connection, sight, etc. **4** *Math.* To contain or include between two points of a curve. See synonyms under INTERPOSE, SHUT. —*n.* (in′tər·sept) **1** That which is cut off or intercepted. **2** *Math.* The part of a curve contained between two points of intersection with other curves. [<L *interceptus,* pp. of *intercipere* <*inter-* between +*capere* seize]—**in′ter·cep′tion** *n.* —**in′ter·cep′tive** *adj.*

in·ter·cep·tor (in′tər·sep′tər) *n.* **1** One who or that which intercepts. **2** *Aeron.* **a** A lateral control device in an airplane. **b** An airplane adapted to the pursuit and interception of enemy aircraft. Also **in′ter·cept′er.** [<L]

in·ter·ces·sion (in′tər·sesh′ən) *n.* **1** The act of interceding between persons; entreaty in behalf of others. **2** A prayer, or series of prayers. [<L *intercessio, -onis* <*intercessus,* pp. of *intercedere* INTERCEDE]—**in′ter·ces′sion·al** *adj.*

in·ter·ces·sor (in′tər·ses′ər) *n.* One who intercedes; a mediator. [<L]—**in′ter·ces′so·ry** *adj.*

in·ter·change (in′tər·chānj′) *v.* **·changed, ·chang·ing** *v.t.* **1** To put each of (two things) in the place of the other. **2** To give and receive in return, as gifts; exchange. **3** To alternate: to *interchange* work and rest. —*v.i.* **4** To make an interchange. —*n.* (in′tər·chānj′) **1** Exchange. **2** Alternation. See synonyms under INTERCOURSE. [<OF *entrechangier* <*entre-* between (<L *inter-*) +*changier* <LL *cambiare* exchange]—**in′ter·chang′er** *n.*

in·ter·change·a·ble (in′tər·chān′jə·bəl) *adj.* Capable of being interchanged or substituted one for the other; permitting transposition. [<OF *entrechangeable*]—**in′ter·change′a·ble·ness, in′ter·change′a·bil′i·ty** *n.* —**in′ter·change′·a·bly** *adv.*

in·ter·cip·i·ent (in′tər·sip′ē·ənt) *adj.* Intercepting; stopping. —*n.* One who or that which intercepts. [<L *intercipiens, -entis,* ppr. of *intercipere.* See INTERCEPT.]

in·ter·clav·i·cle (in′tər·klav′i·kəl) *n. Anat.* The median ventral bone between the clavicles. —**in′ter·cla·vic′u·lar** (-klə·vik′yə·lər) *adj.*

in·ter·clude (in′tər·klo͞od′) *v.t.* **·clud·ed, ·clud·ing** *Obs.* To shut out; cut off; intercept. [<L *intercludere* <*inter-* between +*claudere* close]—**in′ter·clu′sion** (-zhən) *n.*

in·ter·col·le·giate (in′tər·kə·lē′jit, -jē·it) *adj.* Existing, representing, or conducted between, two or more colleges: an *intercollegiate* committee, *intercollegiate* rules, games, etc.

in·ter·co·lum·ni·a·tion (in′tər·kə·lum′nē·ā′shən) *n. Archit.* **1** The space or method of spacing between columns. **2** The space between two consecutive columns. [<L *intercolumnium* space between columns +-ATION]—**in′·ter·co·lum′nar** *adj.*

in·ter·com (in′tər·kom) *n. Colloq.* A system for intercommunication.

in·ter·com·mon (in′tər·kom′ən) *v.i. Brit. Law* To share the use of a common with a nearby town, village, etc. [<AF *entrecomuner* <*entre-* between (<L *inter-*) +*comuner* share <L *communis* common]

in·ter·com·mu·ni·cate (in′tər·kə·myo͞o′nə·kāt) *v.t.* **·cat·ed, ·cat·ing** To communicate mutually, as between individuals, rooms, different units of an organization, factory, etc. —**in′ter·com·mu′ni·ca′tion** *n.* —**in′ter·com·mu′ni·ca′tive** *adj.*

in·ter·com·mu·ni·ty (in′tər·kə·myo͞o′nə·tē) *n.* Mutual community or participation.

in·ter·con·nect (in′tər·kə·nekt′) *v.t.* & *v.i.* To connect with one another.

in·ter·con·nect·ed (in′tər·kə·nek′tid) *adj.* So joined as to move in unison; geared: said of mechanical parts. —**in′ter·con·nec′tion** *n.*

in·ter·con·ti·nen·tal (in′tər·kon′tə·nen′təl) *adj.* Being or operating between continents: an *intercontinental* ballistic missile.

in·ter·cos·tal (in′tər·kos′təl) *adj. Anat.* Being or occurring between the ribs. —*n.* An intercostal muscle. [<NL *intercostalis* <L *inter-* between +*costa* rib]—**in′ter·cos′tal·ly** *adv.*

in·ter·course (in′tər·kôrs, -kōrs) *n.* **1** Mutual exchange; commerce; communication. **2** The interchange of ideas. **3** Sexual connection; coitus. [<OF *entrecours* <L *intercursus,* pp. of *intercurrere* run between <*inter-* between +*currere* run]

Synonyms: association, commerce, communication, communion, connection, conversation, converse, correspondence, dealing, exchange, fellowship, interchange, intercommunication, intercommunion, reciprocation, reciprocity. See CONVERSATION. *Antonyms*: alienation, avoidance, boycotting, estrangement, ostracism, reserve, reticence, silence.

in·ter·crop (in′tər·krop′) *Agric. v.t.* & *v.i.* **·cropped, ·crop·ping 1** To raise (one crop) between the rows of another. **2** To raise (a quick-growing crop) between the harvesting and planting of the regular crops. —*n.* (in′·tər·krop′) **1** A crop cultivated between the rows of another crop. **2** A quickly maturing crop raised when ground is unoccupied by the crops grown in regular rotation.

in·ter·cur·rent (in′tər·kûr′ənt) *adj. Med.* Coming or taking place between: an *intercurrent* disease. [<L *intercurrens, -entis,* ppr. of *intercurrere* run between]

in·ter·den·tal (in′tər·den′təl) *adj.* **1** Situated between the teeth. **2** *Phonet.* Produced with the tip of the tongue between the teeth, as *th* in *thin*: also *dentilingual, linguadental.* —*n. Phonet.* An interdental consonant.

in·ter·dict (in′tər·dikt′) *v.t.* **1** To prohibit or restrain authoritatively. **2** *Eccl.* To exclude from religious privileges. —*n.* **1** A prohibitive order; ban. **2** A ban formerly declared by the pope, forbidding the clergy to perform religious services or administer the sacraments under certain circumstances. **3** In ancient Roman law, an interlocutory edict of the pretor, in matters affecting right of possession. **4** In Scots law, a judicial injunction. See synonyms under PROHIBIT. [<OF *entredit* <L *interdictum,* pp. of *interdicere* forbid <*inter-* between +*dicere* say; refashioned after L]—**in′ter·dic′tion** *n.* —**in′ter·dic′tive** *adj.* —**in′·ter·dic′tive·ly** *adv.* —**in′ter·dic′tor** *n.* —**in′ter·dic′to·ry** *adj.*

in·ter·est (in′tər·ist, -trist) *n.* **1** Attention with a sense of concern; lively sympathy or curiosity; also, the power to excite or hold such attention. **2** That which is of advantage or profit; benefit; also, selfish or private advantage. **3** Payment for the use of money, or money so paid; an agreed or statutory compensation accruing to a creditor during the time that a loan or debt remains unpaid, reckoned usually as a yearly percentage of the sum owed. **4** Something added in making a return; something more than is due. **5** Proprietary right or share; part ownership; participation in profit: sometimes used in the plural. **6** The persons interested in some department of work or business. **7** Power to procure favorable regard; influence. —*v.t.* (*also* in′tə·rest) **1** To excite or hold the curiosity or attention of. **2** To cause to have a share or interest in; induce to participate. **3** *Obs.* To relate to; affect; concern. [<OF <L *interest* it is of concern or advantage; 3rd person sing. of *interesse* lie between, be important <*inter-* between +*esse* be]

Synonyms (verb): amuse, attract, concern, engage, entertain, excite, hold, import, matter, occupy. *Interest* is used absolutely without a preposition, and with or without other qualification; *import* is now commonly used with a preposition and with some word or phrase indicating measure or estimate of value; as, It *imports* much *to* me. A matter may *interest* one financially or intellectually; in this sense the noun is commonly used; as, It is of *interest* to me. See AMUSE, CONCERN, ENTERTAIN. *Antonyms*: bore, disturb, fatigue, tire, weary, worry.

in·ter·est·ed (in′tər·is·tid, -tris-, -tə·res′-) *adj.* **1** Having the attention attracted or the feelings engaged. **2** Biased; not impartial. **3** Being a part owner. —**in′ter·est·ed·ly** *adv.* —**in′ter·est·ed·ness** *n.*

in·ter·est·ing (in′tər·is·ting, -tris-, -tə·res′-) *adj.* Possessing or exciting interest; attractive. —**in′ter·est·ing·ly** *adv.* —**in′ter·est·ing·ness** *n.*

in·ter·face (in′tər·fās) *n.* A surface, usually a plane surface, forming the boundary between adjacent solids, spaces, or immiscible liquids.

in·ter·fa·cial (in′tər·fā′shəl) *adj.* **1** Of or pertaining to an interface. **2** Denoting the surface tension between two adjacent bodies, as dissimilar fluids which do not mix.

in·ter·fas·cic·u·lar (in′tər·fə·sik′yə·lər) *adj.* **1** *Bot.* Situated between fascicles, as the cambium between the fibrovascular bundles in the stems of dicotyledons and gymnosperms. **2** *Anat.* Pertaining to or situated between fasciculi.

in·ter·fere (in′tər·fir′) *v.i.* **·fered, ·fer·ing 1** To come into mutual conflict or opposition; clash. **2** To get in the way; be an obstacle or obstruction; intervene: The noise *interferes* with concentration. **3** To enter into or take part unasked in the concerns of others; meddle. **4** To strike one foot against the opposite foot or fetlock in walking or running: said of horses. **5** *Physics* To counteract one another, as waves of light, sound, or electricity. **6** In sports, to obstruct the actions of an opponent in an illegal manner. **7** In patent law, to claim priority for an invention: distinguished from *infringe.* See synonyms under INTERPOSE. [<OF *(s')entreferir* strike each other <L *inter-* between +*ferire* strike]—**in′ter·fer′er** *n.* —**in′ter·fer′ing·ly** *adv.*

in·ter·fer·ence (in′tər·fir′əns) *n.* **1** The act of interfering; conflict; collision. **2** *Physics* The action of two or more wave trains, as of light, sound, electricity, radiation, etc., which on meeting tend to neutralize or to augment each other by a combination of dissimilar or like phases. With light rays, interference may produce alternate dark and bright bands; with sound, intervals of silence, or increased volume; in radio, a disturbance in reception due to conflict of signals, etc. **3** *Aeron.* The aerodynamic influence of two or more bodies on one another. **4** In patent law, the conflict created by an application for a patent, covering, wholly or partly, any pending application or unexpired patent. **5** In sports, obstruction of the actions of an opponent in an illegal manner. **6** In football: **a** The pro-

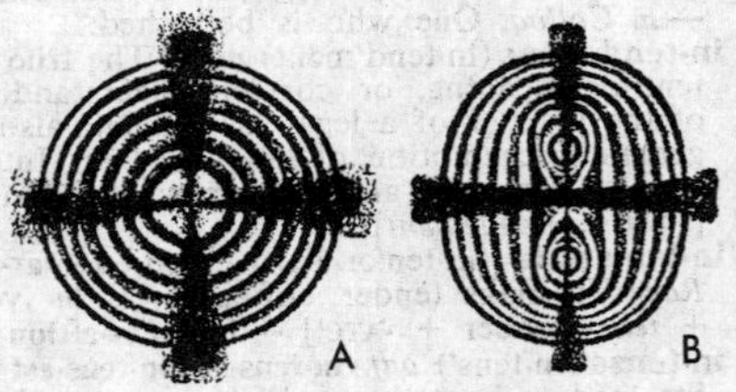

PATTERNS OF LIGHT INTERFERENCE

A. Interference pattern of a uniaxial crystal. *B.* Interference patterns of a biaxial crystal when the axes of the polarizer and analyzer are at right angles to each other.

tecting of the ball carrier from opposing tacklers. **b** The players providing this protection. See synonyms under FRICTION.

in·ter·fe·ren·tial (in′tər·fə·ren′shəl) *adj.* Of or pertaining to interference.

in·ter·fe·rom·e·ter (in′tər·fə·rom′ə·tər) *n. Physics* An instrument which utilizes the interference of light rays for the comparison of wavelengths and the measurement of very small distances: largely developed by A. A. Michelson, of Chicago. [<INTERFER(E) + -(O)METER] — **in′ter·fe·rom′e·try** *n.*

in·ter·fer·on (in′tər·fir′on) *n. Biochem.* A protein produced by virus-infected cells that halts the multiplication of the virus.

in·ter·fer·tile (in′tər·fûr′til) *adj. Biol.* Having the power to interbreed, as individuals of the same species.

in·ter·flu·ent (in·tûr′flo͞o·ənt) *adj.* **1** Flowing between. **2** Flowing together; blending. Also **in·ter′flu·ous** (-əs). [<L *interfluens, -entis,* ppr. of *interfluere* flow between] — **in·ter′flu·ence** *n.*

in·ter·fluve (in′tər·flo͞ov) *n. Geog.* The area between two neighboring rivers or river valleys. [<INTER- + L *fluvius* stream]

in·ter·ga·lac·tic (in′tər·gə·lak′tik) *adj. Astron.* Between or among the galaxies: *intergalactic* space.

in·ter·gla·cial (in′tər·glā′shəl) *adj. Geol.* Pertaining to, or occurring in, the interval between periods of continental glaciation.

In·ter·glos·sa (in′tər·glôs′ə, -glos′ə) *n.* An international language based chiefly on Greek and Latin roots and having few grammatical inflections. [<INTER- + Gk. *glōssa* tongue]

in·ter·gra·da·tion (in′tər·grā·dā′shən) *n. Biol.* A stage or grade between two types, varieties, genetic characters, or the like.

in·ter·grade (in′tər·grād′) *v.i.* **·grad·ed, ·grad·ing** To merge gradually with each other, as two varieties. —*n.* (in′tər·grād′) A form transitional or intermediate between others in a graded series. — **in′ter·gra′di·ent** (-grā′dē·ənt) *adj.*

in·ter·im (in′tər·im) *n.* **1** An intermediate season; time between periods or events. **2** An interval of time; the meantime. — *adj.* For or during an intervening period of time; temporary: an *interim* appointment. [<L, meanwhile]

in·te·ri·or (in·tir′ē·ər) *adj.* **1** Existing, pertaining to, or occurring within something or between limits; internal; inner: opposed to *exterior.* **2** Inland. **3** Of a private or confidential nature. **4** Of or pertaining to spiritual matters; not worldly. **5** *Astron.* Having an orbit within the earth's, as Mercury and Venus. — *n.* **1** The internal part; inside. **2** The inland or central region of a country. **3** A painted scene or drop representing the inside of a dwelling, etc. **4** The domestic affairs of a country; home ministry. **5** The spiritual nature or basic character. — **Department of the Interior** An executive department of the U.S. government (established in 1849), headed by the Secretary of the Interior, dealing with mines, government lands, parks and reservations, Indian affairs, wildlife, geological survey, etc. [<OF *interieur* <L *interior,* compar. of *inter* within] — **in·te′ri·or′i·ty** (-ôr′ə·tē, -or′-) *n.* — **in·te′ri·or·ly** *adv.*

interior angle See under ANGLE.

interior decorator One whose occupation is the furnishing and decorating of interiors of houses, offices, etc.

interior drainage Drainage whose waters are confined to and evaporate within a land area not connected with the ocean.

in·ter·ja·cent (in′tər·jā′sənt) *adj.* Situated between; intermediate. [<L *interjacens, -entis* lying between, pp. of *interjacere* <*inter-* between + *jacere* lie]

in·ter·ject (in′tər·jekt′) *v.t.* To throw between other things; introduce abruptly; insert; interpose. [<L *interjectus,* pp. of *interjicere* < *inter-* between + *jacere* throw]

in·ter·jec·tion (in′tər·jek′shən) *n.* **1** *Gram.* A word expressing emotion or simple exclamation, as *oh! alas! look!*: one of the eight traditional parts of speech. **2** The act of ejaculating. **3** A sudden interposition. [<OF <L *interjectio, -onis*] — **in′ter·jec′tion·al** *adj.* — **in′ter·jec′tion·al·ly** *adv.*

in·ter·jec·to·ry (in′tər·jek′tər·ē) *adj.* Full of interjections; also, interposed. — **in′ter·jec′to·ri·ly** *adv.*

in·ter·ki·ne·sis (in′tər·ki·nē′sis) *n. Biol.* The pause or interval of relative quiescence between two meiotic divisions of the cell: applied particularly to the vegetative stage of the nucleus. — **in′ter·ki·net′ic** (-net′ik) *adj.*

in·ter·lace (in′tər·lās′) *v.* **·laced, ·lac·ing** *v.t.* **1** To pass (branches, strips, etc.) over and under one another; interlock; lace; weave. **2** To blend; combine. **3** To mingle or cross; intersperse. — *v.i.* **4** To pass over and under one another. [<OF *entrelacier*] — **in′ter·lace′ment** *n.*

In·ter·la·ken (in′tər·lä′kən) A resort town in central Switzerland between the Lake of Brienz and the Lake of Thun.

in·ter·lam·i·nate (in′tər·lam′ə·nāt) *v.t.* **·nat·ed, ·nat·ing** To lay or insert between laminae; arrange in layers. — **in′ter·lam′i·na′tion** *n.* — **in′ter·lam′i·nar** (-nər) *adj.*

in·ter·lard (in′tər·lärd′) *v.t.* **1** To scatter throughout with something different from or irrelevant to the subject or material: to *interlard* a conversation with sarcasms. **2** To insert fat, bacon, etc., into (meat) for cooking. [<MF *entrelarder*]

in·ter·leaf (in′tər·lēf′) *n. pl.* **·leaves** (-lēvz′) A blank leaf inserted or bound between others; also, the printed or written matter on a leaf so inserted.

in·ter·leave (in′tər·lēv′) *v.t.* **·leaved, ·leav·ing** **1** To insert interleaves into (a book). **2** To insert an interleaf or interleaves between (printed leaves).

in·ter·line[1] (in′tər·līn′) *v.t.* **·lined, ·lin·ing** **1** To write or print between the lines of. **2** To insert between lines. [OF *entreligner* <Med. L *interlineare* <L *inter-* between + *linea* line] — **in′ter·lin′er** *n.*

in·ter·line[2] (in′tər·līn′) *v.t.* **·lined, ·lin·ing** To put a lining between the usual lining and the outer fabric of (a garment).

in·ter·lin·e·al (in′tər·lin′ē·əl) *adj.* **1** Interlinear. **2** Arranged in alternate lines. — **in′ter·lin′e·al·ly** *adv.*

in·ter·lin·e·ar (in′tər·lin′ē·ər) *adj.* **1** Situated or occurring between lines: *interlinear* annotations. **2** Having translations or glosses inserted between the lines of the text. [<Med. L *interlinearis*]

in·ter·lin·e·ate (in′tər·lin′ē·āt) *v.t.* **·at·ed, ·at·ing** To interline (a book, etc.). [<Med. L *interlineatus,* pp. of *interlineare.* See INTERLINE[1].]

in·ter·lin·e·a·tion (in′tər·lin′ē·ā′shən) *n.* **1** The act or process of interlining. **2** An interpolation between lines.

In·ter·lin·gua (in′tər·ling′gwə) *n.* An international auxiliary language, published in the United States in 1951, based primarily on English and the Romance languages. [<L *inter-* between + *lingua* tongue, language]

in·ter·lin·ing (in′tər·lī′ning) *n.* **1** Interlineation. **2** An intermediate lining in a garment; also, the material of which it is made.

in·ter·lock (in′tər·lok′) *v.t.* & *v.i.* **1** To join together; link with one another. **2** *Mech.* To connect or engage so that the operation of any part of a machine, apparatus, or system is interrelated with the operation of one or more other parts. — *n.* (in′tər·lok′) The action of interlocking, or the state of being interlocked.

interlocking directorates *Econ.* Boards of directors which, through shared membership, assume dominant control of and responsibility for the operation of many separately organized and legally distinct corporations, especially when in related fields of activity.

in·ter·lo·cu·tion (in′tər·lō·kyo͞o′shən) *n.* Interchange of speech; dialog. [<L *interlocutio, -onis* < *interlocutus,* pp. of *interloqui* speak between <*inter-* between + *loqui* speak]

in·ter·loc·u·tor (in′tər·lok′yə·tər) *n.* **1** One who takes part in a conversation; an interpreter; questioner. **2** The center man in a minstrel troupe. [<L *interlocutus,* pp. of *interloqui* speak between, converse] — **in′ter·loc′u·tress** (-tris) *n. fem.*

in·ter·loc·u·to·ry (in′tər·lok′yə·tôr′ē, -tō′rē) *adj.* **1** Consisting of or pertaining to dialog; conversational. **2** Interposed, as in a narrative. **3** *Law* Done during pendency of a lawsuit, but not final.

in·ter·lope (in′tər·lōp′) *v.i.* **·loped, ·lop·ing** **1** Originally, to engage in a commerce, trade, etc., legally belonging to others. **2** To intrude in the affairs of others. [<INTER- + *lope,* Du. *loopen* run]

in·ter·lop·er (in′tər·lō′pər) *n.* **1** One who thrusts himself into a place without right. **2** One who traffics in a trade legally belonging to others.

in·ter·lude (in′tər·lo͞od) *n.* **1** An action or event considered as coming between others of greater length or importance; a differing and intervening time or space. **2** A song of the chorus in Greek drama without dialog. **3** An independent performance, usually light or humorous, introduced between the acts of a play or the parts of a performance. **4** A short passage of music played to bridge a transition; an intermezzo; also, an instrumental passage between stanzas of a hymn, between portions of a formal church service, between the acts of a play or opera, or the like. **5** Anything introduced or inserted, breaking the regular order or aspect; any intervening time or act. [<Med. L *interludium* <L *inter-* between + *ludus* a game, play <*ludere* play]

in·ter·lu·nar (in′tər·lo͞o′nər) *adj. Astron.* Pertaining to the period, generally about four days, between old and new moon, during which the moon is invisible, owing to its proximity to the sun. Also **in′ter·lu′na·ry.** [<L *interlunium* period between old and new moon]

in·ter·mar·riage (in′tər·mar′ij) *n.* **1** Marriage between persons of different families, races, etc. **2** Marriage between blood kindred.

in·ter·mar·ry (in′tər·mar′ē) *v.i.* **·ried, ·ry·ing** **1** To become connected by marriage: said of different clans, families, etc. **2** To marry each other: said of members of the same clan, family, etc.

in·ter·max·il·lar·y (in′tər·mak′sə·ler′ē) *adj.* **1** *Anat.* **a** Situated between the two maxillae or bones of the upper jaw. **b** Of or pertaining to one of two or more bones at the anterior and median part of the upper jaw, carrying the incisor teeth. **2** *Zool.* Situated between the maxillary lobes, as in crustaceans.

in·ter·med·dle (in′tər·med′l) *v.i.* **·dled ·dling** To interfere unduly in the affairs of others; meddle. See synonyms under INTERPOSE. [<AF *entremedler*] — **in′ter·med′dler** *n.*

in·ter·me·di·a·cy (in′tər·mē′dē·ə·sē) *n.* The state or character of being intermediate; intermediate action or agency.

in·ter·me·di·ar·y (in′tər·mē′dē·er′ē) *adj.* **1** Situated, acting, or coming between; having an intermediate function. **2** Acting as a mediator; mediatory. — *n.* **1** An intermediate agent or medium. **2** A form, stage, or product intermediate between others. [<F *intermédiaire*]

in·ter·me·di·ate (in′tər·mē′dē·it) *adj.* **1** Being in a middle place or degree. **2** Situated or occurring between limits or extremes. — *n.* (-it) **1** An intermediator; adjuster. **2** Something intermediate. **3** A substance formed at a state between the raw material and the finished product. **4** *Chem.* An organic compound derived from coal tar or petroleum crude oil and used as a starting point in the manufacture of a wide range of drugs, cosmetics, plastics, and dyestuffs. — *v.i.* (-āt) **·at·ed, ·at·ing** To act as an intermediary; mediate. [<Med. L *intermediatus* <*intermedius*] — **in′ter·me′di·ate·ly** *adv.* — **in′ter·me′di·ate·ness** *n.*

in·ter·me·di·a·tion (in′tər·mē′dē·ā′shən) *n.* The act of intermediating; intervention.

in·ter·me·di·a·tor (in′tər·mē′dē·ā′tər) *n.* One who adjusts differences; a mediator; also, an intervening agent; intermediary. — **in′ter·me′di·a·to′ry** (-tôr′ē, -tō′rē) *adj.*

in·ter·ment (in·tûr′mənt) *n.* The act of interring; burial.

in·ter·mez·zo (in′tər·met′sō, -med′zō) *n. pl.* **·zos** or **·zi** (-sē, -zē) **1** A song, chorus, or short ballet given between the acts of a play or opera. **2** A short light movement connecting the main divisions of a large musical composition; also, a short piece of instrumental music composed in this style to be played independently. [<Ital. <L *intermedius* intermediate]

in·ter·mi·na·ble (in·tûr′mə·nə·bəl) *adj.* Having no limit or end; continuing for a very long time; endless. See synonyms under ETERNAL, INFINITE, PERPETUAL. [<OF] —**in·ter′mi·na·bly** *adv.*
in·ter·min·gle (in′tər·ming′gəl) *v.t.* & *v.i.* **·gled, ·gling** To mingle together; mix.
in·ter·mis·sion (in′tər·mish′ən) *n.* **1** Temporary cessation; interruption. **2** A recess; interval, as between acts in the theater; entr'acte. [<L *intermissio, -onis* < *intermissus*, pp. of *intermittere.* See INTERMIT.] —**in′ter·mis′sive** *adj.*
in·ter·mit (in′tər·mit′) *v.t.* & *v.i.* **·mit·ted, ·mit·ting** To stop temporarily or at intervals; cease or interrupt; pause. See synonyms under CEASE, SUSPEND. [<L *intermittere* < *inter-* between + *mittere* send, put] —**in′ter·mit′tence** *n.*
in·ter·mit·tent (in′tər·mit′ənt) *adj.* **1** Having periods of intermission. **2** Alternately ceasing and beginning: an *intermittent* fever. —**in′ter·mit′tent·ly** *adv.*
intermittent current *Electr.* An interrupted current flowing in one direction.
intermittent fever *Pathol.* A fever in which the paroxysms occur at regular intervals, as in malaria. See AGUE.
in·ter·mix (in′tər·miks′) *v.t.* & *v.i.* To mix together; intermingle.
in·ter·mix·ture (in′tər·miks′chər) *n.* **1** The act of mixing together, or the state of being so mixed. **2** A mass of mixed ingredients. **3** An additional ingredient; admixture.
in·ter·mod·u·late (in′tər·moj′o͞o·lāt) *v.t.* & *v.i.* **·lat·ed, ·lat·ing** *Electronics* To cause a reciprocal modulation of (the components of a complex wave), with the production of new waves having frequencies equal to the sums and differences of integral multiples of the original complex wave. —**in′ter·mod′u·la′tion** *n.*
in·ter·mon·tane (in′tər·mon′tān) *adj.* Situated between mountains: *intermontane* silt. Also **in′ter·moun′tain** (-moun′tən). [<INTER- + L *montanus* mountainous <*mons, montis* mountain]
in·tern (in·tûrn′) *v.t.* To confine or detain within the limits of a country or area, as enemy aliens, or, in neutral countries, soldiers, ships, etc., of warring countries. —*v.i.* To undergo resident training in medicine or surgery in a hospital; be an intern. —*adj. Archaic* Internal. —*n.* (in′tûrn) **1** An advanced medical student or graduate undergoing resident training in a hospital: opposed to *extern.* **2** A person confined and segregated in wartime as a prisoner of war or enemy alien. Also **in′terne.** [<F *interne* resident within <L *internus* internal] —**in′tern·ship** (-ship) *n.*
in·ter·nal (in·tûr′nəl) *adj.* **1** Situated in or applicable to the inside; interior: opposed to *external.* **2** Pertaining to or derived from the inside; based on the thing itself; inherent. **3** Pertaining to the inner self or the mind; subjective. **4** Pertaining to the domestic affairs of a country: opposed to *external* or *foreign.* **5** *Anat.* **a** Situated relatively nearer to the median plane of the body or farther from the surface. **b** Supplying the interior of an organ or region. See synonyms under INHERENT. —*n.* **1** A remedy to be taken internally. **2** *pl.* The internal bodily organs; entrails. **3** *pl.* The essential qualities of anything. [<LL *internalis* < *internus* < *in* in]
in·ter·nal-com·bus·tion (in·tûr′nəl·kəm·bus′chən) *adj.* Designating a type of engine in which the energy is produced by burning or exploding a mixture of compressed air and fuel, as gasoline, in one or more of its cylinders.
in·ter·nal·i·ty (in′tər·nal′ə·tē) *n.* The quality or state of lying within; inwardness; interiority.
in·ter·nal·ly (in·tûr′nəl·ē) *adv.* **1** As to the interior or inner part; interiorly: cold on the surface but hot *internally.* **2** Mentally or spiritually: *internally* content. **3** In respect to internal affairs.
internal medicine The branch of medicine which is concerned with diagnosis and treatment of internal diseases.
internal revenue See under REVENUE.
internal rime The riming of a word or group of syllables in a line of verse, as the word before the caesura, with a word or group of syllables at the end of the line or another line: also called *leonine rime.*
internal secretion *Physiol.* **1** A secretion of any one of the endocrine glands. **2** A hormone.
in·ter·na·sal (in′tər·nā′zəl) *n. Zool.* One of a pair of dermal scutes of some reptiles lying between the nasals.
in·ter·na·tion·al (in′tər·nash′ən·əl) *adj.* Pertaining to two or more nations; affecting nations generally. —*n.* A person who is a citizen of more than one nation. —**in′ter·na′tion·al·ly** *adv.*
In·ter·na·tion·al (in′tər·nash′ən·əl) *n.* **1** One of several international organizations of socialist workers. **2** A society formed in London in 1864 for the international political organization of workingmen, in the socialistic conflict with capital, of which Karl Marx was the dominant spirit; its full title was the **International Workingmen's Association:** last convention in Philadelphia, 1876. **3** See INTERNATIONALE. —**Second International** An organization, formed in 1889, to replace the First International, from which the Third International seceded: also called **Socialist International.** —**Third** or **Red International** A socialist workers' organization proclaimed in Russia March 5, 1919, representing twelve countries: dissolved in 1943: also called *Comintern.*
international candle A candela.
In·ter·na·tio·nale (in′tər·nash′ən·əl, *Fr.* an·ter·nȧ·syô·nȧl′) A French song written by Eugene Pottier in 1871 and adopted as a revolutionary hymn by French Socialists and those of other European countries: the national anthem of Soviet Russia until 1944, and still popular as a workers' song: usually written *L'Internationale.* [<F]
in·ter·na·tion·al·ism (in′tər·nash′ən·əl·iz′əm) *n.* **1** The character of being related to more nations than one or to nations generally. **2** The doctrine that common interest, mutual understanding, and friendly dependence among nations can be the foundation of world-wide equality, justice, and peace: opposed to *nationalism.* **3** The doctrine of a workers' international socialistic organization for the betterment of workers throughout the world. —**in′ter·na′tion·al·ist** *n.* —**in′ter·na′tion·al′i·ty** *n.*
in·ter·na·tion·al·ize (in′tər·nash′ən·əl·īz′) *v.t.* **·ized, ·iz·ing** To make international, as in character or administration. —**in′ter·na′tion·al·i·za′tion** *n.*
International Labor Organization A permanent administrative association of 77 nations including the United States, constituting a specialized agency of the United Nations, with tripartite representation of workers, employers, and governments, working for the improvement of labor conditions in member nations, and functioning through the **International Labor Conference** and the **International Labor Office.** Commonly known as the **ILO.**
International Morse code A variation, differing in eleven letters, of the telegraphic code devised by S. F. B. Morse: also called **continental Morse code.**
International News Service An organization for collecting news and distributing it to member newspapers. Abbr. *INS, I.N.S.*
International Phonetic Alphabet The alphabet of the International Phonetic Association (a society founded in 1886), in which the speech sounds of a language can be transcribed. Each of the symbols of this alphabet represents a specific sound, distinguished as to place and manner of articulation, regardless of the language being recorded. Abbr. *IPA.* See chart on page 665.
in·terne (in′tûrn) *n.* **1** Intern. **2** The inner nature: poetical usage. [<F]
in·ter·ne·cine (in′tər·nē′sin, -sīn) *adj.* Involving mutual slaughter; sanguinary. [<L *internecinus* < *internecare* kill, slaughter < *inter-* among + *necare* kill]
in·tern·ee (in′tûr·nē′) *n.* An interned person. [<INTERN + -EE]
in·ter·nist (in·tûr′nist) *n.* A specialist in internal medicine. [<INTERN(AL) + -IST]
in·tern·ment (in·tûrn′mənt) *n.* The act of interning; the state of being interned.
internment camp A military station for the detention of prisoners of war and enemy aliens.
in·ter·no·dal (in′tər·nōd′l) *adj.* **1** Of or pertaining to an internode. **2** Situated between two nodes or joints. —*n.* An internodal joint.
in·ter·node (in′tər·nōd′) *n.* **1** *Anat.* A part situated between two joints or nodes, as a phalanx or other segment of a limb. **2** *Bot.* The part of a plant stem between the nodes or places from which the leaves grow. **3** *Ornithol.* In a feather, the contracted part between the roots of the barbs. **4** The part of a vibrating string between two nodes. [<L *internodium* < *inter-* between + *nodus* node]
in·ter nos (in′tər nōs′) *Latin* Between ourselves.
in·ter·nun·ci·o (in′tər·nun′shē·ō) *n. pl.* **·ci·os** **1** A diplomatic representative of the pope in countries not represented by a papal nuncio. **2** A go-between; messenger between two parties. [<Ital. <L *inter-* between + *nuntius* messenger] —**in′ter·nun′cial** (-shəl) *adj.*
in·ter·o·cep·tor (in′tər·ə·sep′tər) *n. Physiol.* A peripheral sense organ excited by internal stimuli arising chiefly within the viscera: also spelled **enteroceptor**. Compare EXTEROCEPTOR. [< *intero-* <INTERNAL + (RE)CEPTOR] —**in′ter·o·cep′tive** *adj.*
in·ter·or·bi·tal (in′tər·ôr′bə·təl) *adj. Anat.* Situated between the orbits of the eyes.
in·ter·os·cu·late (in′tər·os′kyə·lāt) *v.i.* **1** To form a connecting link, as between objects, genera, etc.; osculate. **2** To inosculate with each other; interpenetrate. —**in′ter·os′cu·la′tion** *n.*
in·ter·os·se·ous (in′tər·os′ē·əs) *adj. Anat.* Pertaining to structures situated between bones: an *interosseous* membrane.
in·ter·pel·lant (in′tər·pel′ənt) *adj.* Causing interpellation. —*n.* One who interpellates: also **in·ter·pel·la·tor** (in′tər·pə·lā′tər, in·tûr′pə·lā′tər). [<L *interpellans, -antis,* ppr. of *interpellare.* See INTERPELLATE.]
in·ter·pel·late (in′tər·pel′āt, in·tûr′pə·lāt) *v.t.* **·lat·ed, ·lat·ing** To subject to an interpellation. [<L *interpellatus,* pp. of *interpellare* interrupt by speaking < *inter-* between + *pellere* drive]
in·ter·pel·la·tion (in′tər·pə·lā′shən, in·tûr′-) *n.* A formal demand upon a member of a government to explain an official action or policy. [<L *interpellatio, -onis*]
in·ter·pen·e·trate (in′tər·pen′ə·trāt) *v.* **·trat·ed, ·trat·ing** *v.t.* **1** To penetrate thoroughly; pervade; permeate. **2** To penetrate mutually. —*v.i.* **3** To penetrate each other. **4** To penetrate between or among parts or things. —**in′ter·pen′e·tra′tion** *n.*
in·ter·per·son·al (in′tər·pûr′sən·əl) *adj.* Existing between people: *interpersonal* relations.
in·ter·phone (in′tər·fōn′) *n.* A telephone for use exclusively within a building, office, ship, airplane, etc.
in·ter·plane (in′tər·plān′) *adj. Aeron.* Situated or placed between the wings of an airplane.
in·ter·plan·e·tary (in′tər·plan′ə·ter′ē) *adj.* Between or among planets: *interplanetary* travel.
in·ter·play (in′tər·plā′) *n.* Action or movement between parts of something, as parts of a machine; mutual or reciprocal action or influence. —*v.i.* (in′tər·plā′) To exert influence reciprocally.
in·ter·plead (in′tər·plēd′) *v.i. Law* To litigate adverse claims by bill of interpleader. [<AF *entrepleder*]
in·ter·plead·er (in′tər·plē′dər) *n. Law* A proceeding in which one who has money or goods claimed by two or more persons may ask that the claimants be required to litigate the title between themselves.
in·ter·po·late (in·tûr′pə·lāt) *v.* **·lat·ed, ·lat·ing** *v.t.* **1** To alter, as a manuscript, by the insertion of new or unauthorized matter; corrupt. **2** To insert (such matter). **3** To put (something different or irrelevant) between other things; intercalate; interpose. **4** *Math.* **a** To compute intermediate values of a quantity between a series of given values: distinguished from *extrapolate.* **b** To insert (an intermediate term or terms) in a series. —*v.i.* **5** To make interpolations. [<L *interpolatus,* pp. of *interpolare* polish, form anew < *interpolis* refurbished, vamped up < *inter-* between + root of *polire* polish] —**in·ter′po·la′tion** *n.* —**in·ter′po·la′tive** *adj.* —**in·ter′po·la′tor, in·ter′po·lat′er** *n.*
in·ter·pose (in′tər·pōz′) *v.* **·posed, ·pos·ing** *v.t.* **1** To place between other things; insert. **2** To put forward or introduce by way of intervention or interference: He *interposed* his authority. **3** To put in or inject, as a remark, into a conversation, argument, etc. —*v.i.* **4** To come between; intervene. **5** To put in a remark; interrupt. [<F *interposer* place between < *inter-* between (<L) + *poser.* See

POSE¹.] — **in·ter·po′sal** *n.* — **in′ter·pos′er** *n.* — **in′ter·pos′ing·ly** *adv.*

Synonyms: arbitrate, intercede, intercept, interfere, intermeddle, interrupt, meddle, mediate. To *interpose* is to place or come between other things or persons, usually as a means of obstruction or prevention of some effect or result that might otherwise occur. *Intercede* and *interpose* are used in a good sense; *intermeddle* always in a bad sense, and *interfere* frequently so. To *intercede* is to come between persons who are at variance, and plead with the stronger in behalf of the weaker. To *intermeddle* is to thrust oneself into the concerns of others with officiousness; *meddling* commonly arises from idle curiosity. To *interfere* is to intrude into others' affairs with more serious purpose, with or without acknowledged right or propriety. *Intercept* is applied to an object that may be seized or stopped while in transit; as, to *intercept* a letter or a messenger; *interrupt* is applied to an action which might or should be continuous, but is broken in upon (L *rumpere* to break) by some disturbing power. One who *arbitrates* or *mediates* must do so by the request or at least with the consent of the contending parties; the other words of the group imply that he steps in of his own accord. *Antonyms*: avoid, retire, withdraw.

in·ter·po·si·tion (in′tər·pə·zish′ən) *n.* **1** The act of interposing. **2** That which is interposed. **3** In U.S. political theory, the doctrine and practice of interposing the sovereign powers of a State between the people of that State and the enforcement of a Federal statute or judicial ruling that is deemed by the State government to infringe upon its sovereignty and the autonomy of its institutions. [<OF]

in·ter·pret (in·tûr′prit) *v.t.* **1** To give the meaning of; explain or make clear; elucidate: to *interpret* Scripture. **2** To derive a particular understanding of; give a certain explanation to; construe: We *interpreted* his silence as pride. **3** To bring out the meaning of by artistic representation or performance. **4** To translate. — *v.i.* **5** To act as interpreter. **6** To explain. [<F *interpréter* <L *interpretatus*, pp. of *interpretari* < *interpres* agent, interpreter] — **in·ter′pret·a·ble** *adj.* — **in·ter′pret·a·bil′i·ty, in·ter′pret·a·ble·ness** *n.*

Synonyms: construe, decipher, define, elucidate, explain, explicate, expound, render, translate, unfold, unravel. See synonyms for DEFINITION, SOLVE. *Antonyms*: confound, confuse, darken, distort, falsify, involve, jumble, mingle, misinterpret, misread, misrepresent, mistake, misunderstand, mix, perplex.

in·ter·pre·ta·tion (in·tûr′prə·tā′shən) *n.* **1** The act of interpreting. **2** The sense given by an interpreter or an expositor; meaning. **3** Histrionic or artistic representation. See synonyms under DEFINITION. — **authentic interpretation** *Law* An interpretation made by the author himself. — **close interpretation** *Law* One in which the words are taken in their narrowest meaning. — **extravagant interpretation** *Law* One which substitutes a broader meaning for the true one. — **free interpretation** *Law* One made in good faith but uncontrolled by any specific principle. — **judicial interpretation** *Law* Judge–made rulings construing the meaning and purport of a statute; the act of making such rulings. [<F] — **in·ter′pre·ta′tion·al** *adj.*

in·ter·pre·ta·tive (in·tûr′prə·tā′tiv) *adj.* **1** Designed or fitted to interpret; explanatory; defining. **2** Containing an interpretation; embodying ideas or facts; significative. **3** Admitting of interpretation; constructive. Also **in·ter′pre·tive.** — **in·ter′pre·ta′tive·ly** *adv.*

in·ter·pret·er (in·tûr′prit·ər) *n.* One who interprets or translates; specifically, one who serves as oral translator between people speaking different languages. [<OF *interpreteur* <LL *interpretor*]

in·ter·ra·di·al (in′tər·rā′dē·əl) *adj.* Between rays or radii.

in·ter·reg·num (in′tər·reg′nəm) *n.* **1** The time during which a throne is vacant. **2** A suspension of executive authority through a change of government. **3** Any period of abeyance or derangement.· **4** In Roman history, the interval filled by an interrex. [<L *interregnum* < *inter-* between + *regnum* reign]

in·ter·re·late (in′tər·ri·lāt′) *v.t. & v.i.* **·lat·ed ·lat·ing** To bring or come into reciprocal relation.

in·ter·re·lat·ed (in′tər·ri·lā′tid) *adj.* Reciprocally related.

in·ter·re·la·tion (in′tər·ri·lā′shən) *n.* Mutual or reciprocal relation. — **in′ter·re·la′tion·ship** *n.*

in·ter·rex (in′tər·reks) *n. pl.* **in·ter·re·ges** (in′tər·rē′jēz) One who governs during an interregnum; specifically, in Roman history, one of the magistrates appointed to govern during a vacancy on the throne or in the consulate. [<L *interrex* < *inter-* between + *rex* king]

in·ter·ro·gate (in·ter′ə·gāt) *v.* **·gat·ed, ·gat·ing** *v.t.* To put questions to; question. — *v.i.* To ask

THE INTERNATIONAL PHONETIC ALPHABET.
(Revised to 1951.)

		Bi-labial	Labio-dental	Dental and Alveolar	Retroflex	Palato-alveolar	Alveolo-palatal	Palatal	Velar	Uvular	Pharyngal	Glottal
CONSONANTS	Plosive . . .	p b		t d	ʈ ɖ			c ɟ	k g	q ɢ		ʔ
	Nasal . . .	m	ɱ	n	ɳ			ɲ	ŋ	N		
	Lateral Fricative .			ɬ ɮ								
	Lateral Non-fricative .			l	ɭ			ʎ				
	Rolled . . .			r						ʀ		
	Flapped . . .			ɾ	ɽ					ʀ		
	Fricative . .	ɸ β	f v	θ ð s z ɹ	ʂ ʐ	ʃ ʒ	ʑ ʑ	ç j	x ɣ	χ ʁ	ħ ʕ	h ɦ
	Frictionless Continuants and Semi-vowels	w ɥ	ʋ	ɹ				j (ɥ)	(w)	ʁ		
VOWELS	Close . . .	(y ʉ u)						Front Central Back i y ɨ ʉ ɯ u				
	Half-close . .	(ø o)						e ø ɤ o				
								ə				
	Half-open . .	(œ ɔ)						ɛ œ ɜ ɞ ʌ ɔ				
								æ ɐ				
	Open . .	(ɒ)						a ɑ ɒ				

(Secondary articulations are shown by symbols in brackets.)

OTHER SOUNDS.—Palatalized consonants: ƫ, ḓ, etc.; palatalized ʃ, ʒ: ɕ, ʑ. Velarized or pharyngalized consonants: ɫ, ɖ, ᵶ, etc. Ejective consonants (with simultaneous glottal stop): p', t', etc. Implosive voiced consonants: ɓ, ɗ, etc. ɼ fricative trill. σ, ϱ (labialized θ, ð, or s, z). ʅ, ʮ (labialized ʃ, ʒ). ɿ, ɿ, ɕ (clicks, Zulu c, q, x). ɺ (a sound between r and l). ɳ Japanese syllabic nasal. ʓ (combination of x and ʃ). ʍ (voiceless w). ɩ, ɣ, ɷ (lowered varieties of i, y, u). ɜ (a variety of ə). ɵ (a vowel between ø and o).

Affricates are normally represented by groups of two consonants (ts, tʃ, dʒ, etc.), but, when necessary, ligatures are used (ʦ, ʧ, ʤ, etc.), or the marks ‿ or ‿ (t͡s or t͜s, etc.). ‿ ‿ also denote synchronic articulation (m͡ŋ = simultaneous m and ŋ). c, ɟ may occasionally be used in place of tʃ, dʒ, and ꭤ, ꭦ for ts, dz. Aspirated plosives: ph, th, etc. r-coloured vowels: eɹ, aɹ, ɔɹ, etc., or eʵ aʵ, ɔʵ, etc., or ɚ, aᶭ, ᶗ, etc.; r-coloured ə: əɹ or əʵ or ɹ or ᶿ or ɚ.

LENGTH, STRESS, PITCH.— : (full length). · (half length). ˈ (stress, placed at beginning of the stressed syllable). ˌ (secondary stress). ˉ (high level pitch); ˍ (low level); ˊ (high rising); ˏ (low rising); ˋ (high falling); ˎ (low falling); ˆ (rise-fall); ˇ (fall-rise)

MODIFIERS.— ˜ nasality. ˏ breath (l̥ = breathed l). ˎ voice (ş = z). ʽ slight aspiration following p, t, etc. ˎ labialization (n̫ = labialized n). ˎ dental articulation (t̪ = dental t). ˙ palatalization (ž = ʑ). ˎ specially close vowel (ẹ = a very close e). ˏ specially open vowel (ẹ = a rather open e). ˔ tongue raised (e˔ or ẹ = ẹ). ˕ tongue lowered (e˕ or ẹ = ɛ). ˖ tongue advanced (u˖ or ṵ = an advanced u, t̟ = t̠). - or ˗ tongue retracted (i˗ or i = ɨ˕, t̠ = alveolar t). ˒ lips more rounded. ˓ lips more spread. Central vowels: ᵻ(= ɨ), ü(= ʉ), ë(= ɘ·), ö(= ɵ), ̈ɛ, ̈ɔ. ˌ (e.g. n̩) syllabic consonant. ˘ consonantal vowel. ʃ variety of ʃ resembling s, etc.

Courtesy, Association Phonétique Internationale

add,āce,câre,pälm; end,ēven; it,īce; odd,ōpen,ôrder; to͝ok,po͞ol; up,bûrn; ə = a in *above*, e in *sicken*, i in *clarity*, o in *melon*, u in *focus*; yo͞o = u in *fuse*; oi,oil; ou,pout; ch,check; g,go; ng,ring; th,thin; t͟h,this; zh,vision. Foreign sounds á,œ,ü,kh,ṅ; and ◆: see page xx. < from; + plus; ? possibly.

questions. See synonyms under EXAMINE, INQUIRE, QUESTION. [<L *interrogatus*, pp. of *interrogare* < *inter-* between + *rogare* ask]

in·ter·ro·ga·tion (in·ter′ə·gā′shən) *n.* **1** The act of interrogating. **2** A question; query. **3** An interrogation point. **4** *Telecom.* The transmission of a signal pulse or combination of such pulses by an interrogator. See synonyms under INQUIRY, QUESTION.

interrogation point A mark of punctuation (?) indicating that the foregoing sentence asks a direct question: sometimes called *question mark.* Also **interrogation mark.**

in·ter·rog·a·tive (in′tə·rog′ə·tiv) *adj.* **1** Denoting inquiry; questioning. **2** *Gram.* Of or pertaining to a word, phrase, or sentence which asks a question. — *n. Gram.* A word, phrase, or sentence used to ask a question, as *who, whose book, Who is there?* [<L *interrogativus*] — **in′ter·rog′a·tive·ly** *adv.*

interrogative pronoun See under PRONOUN.

in·ter·ro·ga·tor (in·ter′ə·gā′tər) *n.* **1** One who or that which interrogates. **2** *Telecom.* A device for transmitting pulses of challenge or inquiry to a transponder: usually connected with a responser for receiving and displaying the return pulses.

in·ter·rog·a·to·ry (in′tə·rog′ə·tôr′ē, -tō′rē) *adj.* Pertaining to, expressing, or implying a question; interrogative. — *n.* A question; interrogation. See synonyms under INQUIRY, QUESTION. — **in′ter·rog′a·to′ri·ly** (-tôr′ə·lē, -tō′rə-) *adv.*

in·ter·rupt (in′tə·rupt′) *v.t.* **1** To cause a delay or break in: to *interrupt* service; hinder the doing or completion of: to *interrupt* a speech. **2** To break the continuity, course, or sameness of: to *interrupt* work or a speech. **3** To break in on (someone) talking, working, etc. — *v.i.* **4** To break in upon an action or speech. See synonyms under HINDER[1], INTERPOSE, OBSTRUCT, SUSPEND. [<L *interruptus*, pp. of *interrumpere* < *inter-* between + *rumpere* break]

in·ter·rupt·ed (in′tə·rup′tid) *adj.* **1** Broken in upon; irregular; intermittent. **2** *Bot.* Suddenly or abruptly stopped. — **in′ter·rupt′ed·ly** *adv.*

interrupted screw *Mil.* A screw placed in the breech of certain guns, permitting the block to be engaged or released by turning through a small arc.

in·ter·rupt·er (in′tə·rup′tər) *n.* **1** One who or that which interrupts. **2** *Electr.* A device, usually automatic, for rapidly breaking and making an electric circuit, as in an induction coil. **3** *Mil.* An electrical device, in connection with a chronoscope, for causing a pencil to register the exact time of passage of a projectile through a wire screen. **4** *Mil.* An automatic device that interrupts the firing of a flexibly mounted gun, as in a turret, when structural parts of the craft or vehicle in which it is mounted come within the field of fire. Also **in′ter·rup′tor.**

in·ter·rup·tion (in′tə·rup′shən) *n.* **1** The act of interrupting. **2** The state of being interrupted; breach in continuity; an interval. **3** Obstruction caused by breaking in upon any course, progress, or motion; hindrance; stop; check. **4** In Scots law, the legal step necessary to terminate a period of prescription; exception or reply against prescription. **5** An intermission; a temporary cessation.

in·ter·rup·tive (in′tə·rup′tiv) *adj.* Tending to interrupt; interrupting. — **in′ter·rup′tive·ly** *adv.*

in·ter se (in′tər sē′) *Latin* Between (or among) themselves.

in·ter·sect (in′tər·sekt′) *v.t.* To pass across; cut through or into so as to divide. — *v.i.* To cross each other. [<L *intersectus*, pp. of *intersecare* < *inter-* between + *secare* cut]

in·ter·sec·tion (in′tər·sek′shən) *n.* **1** The act of intersecting. **2** A place of crossing. [<L *intersectio, -onis*]

in·ter·sex (in′tər·seks′) *n. Biol.* An individual, usually sterile, showing biological characteristics of both sexes. — **in′ter·sex′u·al** *adj.* — **in′ter·sex′u·al′i·ty** *n.*

in·ter·space (in′tər·spās′) *v.t.* **·spaced, ·spac·ing** **1** To make spaces between. **2** To occupy spaces between. — *n.* (in′tər·spās′) Intervening room; space between.

in·ter·sperse (in′tər·spûrs′) *v.t.* **·spersed, ·spers·ing** **1** To scatter among other things; set here and there. **2** To diversify or adorn with other things scattered here and there. [<L *interspersus*, pp. of *interspergere* < *inter-* among + *spargere* scatter] — **in′ter·spers′ed·ly** *adv.* — **in′ter·sper′sion** (-spûr′zhən) *n.*

in·ter·state (in′tər·stāt′) *adj.* Between different States, as of the United States, or their citizens: *interstate* commerce.

Interstate Commerce Act An act passed by Congress, and approved February 4, 1887, which established a commission of five (since increased to eleven) members to regulate commerce between States when carried by common carriers, as by railroad, vessel, motor vehicle, and pipeline (except water pipes). The **Interstate Commerce Commission** executes and enforces the act in the public interest, promotes safe service and conditions, prevents unjust rates and discriminatory practice, etc.

in·ter·stice (in·tûr′stis) *n.* **1** An opening in anything. **2** A narrow space between adjoining parts or things. **3** A crack; crevice; chink; cranny. **4** An interval of time; specifically, the interval that canon law requires between promotions from one order to another in the Roman Catholic Church. [<F <L *interstitium* < *interstitus*, pp. of *intersistere* stand between < *inter-* between + *sistere* cause to stand < *stare* stand]

in·ter·sti·tial (in′tər·stish′əl) *adj.* **1** Pertaining to, existing in, or forming an interstice. **2** *Biol.* Situated within the tissues of an organ or part; *interstitial* cells. [<L *interstitus*] — **in′ter·sti′tial·ly** *adv.*

in·ter·tex·ture (in′tər·teks′chər) *n.* **1** The act of interweaving. **2** The web or tissue interwoven.

in·ter·twine (in′tər·twīn′) *v.t.* & *v.i.* **·twined, ·twin·ing** To unite by twisting or interlacing.

in·ter·ur·ban (in′tər·ûr′bən) *adj.* Between cities.

in·ter·val (in′tər·vəl) *n.* **1** An open space between two objects; distance between points; intervening room. **2** The degree of difference between objects. **3** The time that intervenes between two events or periods or between a state or condition and its recurrence. **4** *U.S.* & *Can.* Intervale. **5** *Music* **a** The difference in pitch between two tones sounded in succession.

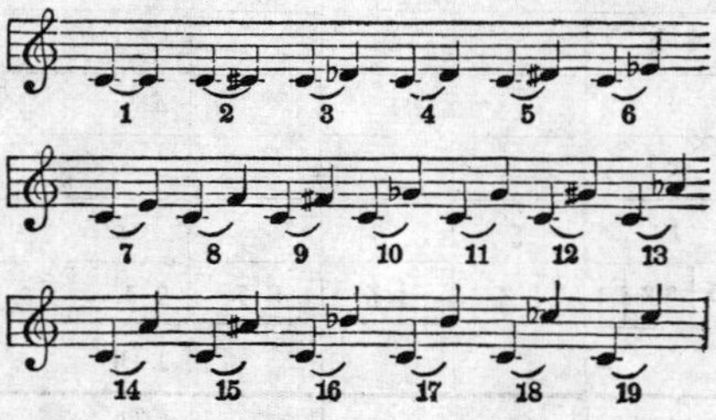

MUSICAL INTERVALS

1. Prime or unison. 2. Augmented prime. 3. Minor second. 4. Major second. 5. Augmented second. 6. Minor third. 7. Major third. 8. Perfect fourth. 9. Augmented fourth. 10. Diminished fifth. 11. Perfect fifth. 12. Augmented fifth. 13. Minor sixth. 14. Major sixth. 15. Augmented sixth. 16. Minor seventh. 17. Major seventh. 18. Diminished octave. 19. Octave. On a keyboard instrument where mechanical limitations make it necessary to make one tone serve for two slightly different ones, some of the intervals above appear identical, as 5 and 6.

b The difference in pitch of tones sounded at or near the same time. — **augmented interval** A musical interval longer than the indicated standard by a half-step or semitone. — **diminished interval** An interval that is a half-step shorter than the perfect or minor interval indicated. — **harmonic interval** An interval in which the tones are simultaneous. — **inverted interval** A simple interval in which the lower tone is transposed an octave upward, or the upper tone an octave downward. — **melodic interval** An interval in which the tones are successive. — **perfect interval.** An interval admitting of no change without destroying the consonance, as the prime, fourth, fifth, and octave. [<OF *entreval, intervalle* <L *intervallum* between the ramparts < *inter-* between + *vallum* rampart]

in·ter·vale (in′tər·vāl′) *n. U.S.* & *Can.* A low tract of land between hills, especially along a river; interval. [Fusion of INTERVAL + VALE[1]]

in·ter·va·ri·e·tal (in′tər·və·rī′ə·təl) *adj. Biol.* Pertaining to or designating a cross between two varieties, strains, or breeds of the same species.

in·ter·vein (in′tər·vān′) *v.t.* **1** To intersect with or as if with veins. **2** To set in alternate veins.

in·ter·vene (in′tər·vēn′) *v.i.* **·vened, ·ven·ing** **1** To come between by action or authority; interfere or mediate: The king *intervened* in the quarrel. **2** To occur, as something irrelevant or unexpected, so as to influence or modify an action, result, etc.: I will come if nothing *intervenes.* **3** To be located between; lie between. **4** To take place between other events or times; happen in the meantime: Many years *intervened.* **5** *Law* To interpose in a lawsuit so as to become a party to it. [<L *intervenire* < *inter-* between + *venire* come] — **in′ter·ven′er** *n.* — **in′ter·ven′ient** (-vēn′yənt) *adj.*

in·ter·ven·tion (in′tər·ven′shən) *n.* **1** The act of intervening or coming between. **2** Interference with the acts of others. **3** *Law* The becoming or applying to become a party to a suit in which the applicant has an interest. **4** In international law, interference in the affairs of one country by another by force or threat of force. **5** An intervening time, event, or thing. [<LL *interventio, -onis* < *interventus*, pp. of *intervenire* intervene] — **in′ter·ven′tion·al** *adj.*

in·ter·ven·tion·ist (in′tər·ven′shən·ist) *n.* One who advocates intervention, as in the affairs of another state.

in·ter·view (in′tər·vyōō) *n.* **1** A meeting of two persons, as by appointment. **2** Specifically, in journalism, a colloquy with one whose views are sought for publication. **3** The report of such a colloquy. — *v.t.* To have an interview with. [<MF *entrevu*, pp. of *entrevoir* glimpse, *s'entrevoir* see each other <L *inter-* between + *videre* see] — **in′ter·view′er** *n.*

in·ter·volve (in′tər·volv′) *v.t.* & *v.i.* **·volved, ·volv·ing** To wind or coil one within another; involve or be involved with each other. [<INTER- + L *volvere* roll]

in·ter·weave (in′tər·wēv′) *v.t.* & *v.i.* **·wove** or **·weaved, ·wo·ven** (*Obs.* **·wove**), **·weav·ing** To weave together; intermingle or connect closely; interlace; blend.

in·tes·ta·ble (in·tes′tə·bəl) *adj.* Legally disqualified from making a will, as a lunatic. [<LL *intestabilis.* See INTESTATE.]

in·tes·ta·cy (in·tes′tə·sē) The condition resulting from one's dying intestate: opposed to *testacy.*

in·tes·tate (in·tes′tāt) *adj.* **1** Not having made a valid will. **2** Not legally devised or disposed of by will. — *n.* A person who dies intestate. [<L *intestatus* < *in-* not + *testatus*, pp. of *testari* make a will < *testis* witness]

in·tes·ta·tion (in′tes·tā′shən) *n. Law* **1** Testamentary incapacity. **2** Withdrawal of the right to make a will.

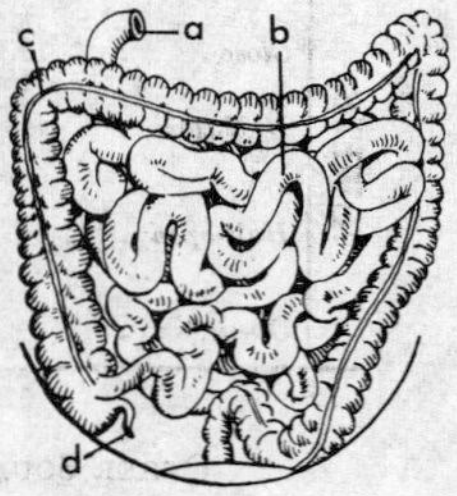

HUMAN INTESTINES
a. Duodenum. *b.* Small intestine. *c.* Colon. *d.* Vermiform appendix.

in·tes·tine (in·tes′tin) *n. Anat.* That part of the alimentary canal between the pylorus and the anus; bowel. In man the small intestine, divided into *duodenum, jejunum,* and *ileum,* is the upper part, and is much convoluted; the large intestine is of greater caliber, and is divided into *cecum, colon,* and *rectum.* ◆ Collateral adjective: *alvine.* — *adj.* **1** Internal with regard to state or community; domestic; civil. **2** Pertaining to the interior. [<L *intestinus* internal < *intus* within < *in* in] — **in·tes′ti·nal** *adj.*

in·thral (in·thrôl′), **in·throne** (in·thrōn′), etc. See ENTHRAL, etc.

in·ti·ma (in′tə·mə) *n. pl.* **·mae** (-mē) **1** *Anat.* The internal coat of a part or organ, as of a lymphatic, blood vessel, intestine, or artery. **2** *Entomol.* The lining membrane of the trachea of an insect. [<NL <L *intimus* innermost. See INTIMATE[1].] — **in′ti·mal** *adj.*

in·ti·ma·cy (in′tə·mə·sē) *n. pl.* **·cies** **1** Close or confidential friendship. **2** An intimate act;

especially, illicit sexual connection: a euphemistic use. See synonyms under ACQUAINTANCE.

in·ti·mate[1] (in′tə·mit) *adj.* **1** Closely connected by friendship or association; personal; confidential. **2** Pertaining to the inmost being; innermost; indwelling; *intimate* knowledge. **3** Adhering closely; close: *intimate* union. **4** Proceeding from within; inward; internal: an *intimate* impulse. **5** Having illicit sexual relations (with): a euphemism. — *n.* A close or confidential friend. [<F *intime* <L *intimus,* superl. of *intus* within] — **in′ti·mate·ly** *adv.*

in·ti·mate[2] (in′tə·māt) *v.t.* **·mat·ed, ·mat·ing** **1** To make known without direct statement; hint; imply. **2** *Rare* To make known formally; declare. [<L *intimatus,* pp. of *intimare* announce < *intimus,* superl. of *intus* within]

in·ti·ma·tion (in′tə·mā′shən) *n.* **1** Information communicated indirectly; a hint. **2** A declaration or notification. See synonyms under SUGGESTION. [<F]

in·tim·i·date (in·tim′ə·dāt) *v.t.* **·dat·ed, ·dat·ing** **1** To make timid; cause fear in; cow. **2** To force or restrain by threats or violence. See synonyms under FRIGHTEN. [<Med. L *intimidatus,* pp. of *intimidare* <L *in-* very + *timidus* afraid] — **in·tim′i·da′tor** *n.*

in·tim·i·da·tion (in·tim′ə·dā′shən) *n.* **1** The use of violence or threats to influence the conduct of another. **2** The state of being intimidated.

in·tinc·tion (in·tingk′shən) *n. Eccl.* A method of administering both elements of the Eucharist at once, by dipping the bread into the wine. [<LL *intinctio, -onis* < *intinctus,* pp. of *intingere* dip in < *in-* in + *tingere* tinge]

in·tine (in′tin, -tīn) *n. Bot.* The inner coating of the wall of a pollen grain. [<L *intus* within]

in·ti·tle (in·tīt′l) See ENTITLE.

in·tit·ule (in·tit′yōōl) *v.t.* **·uled, ·ul·ing** To give a title or designation to. [<F *intituler* <LL *intitulare* <L *in-* in, on + *titulus* title]

in·to (in′tōō) *prep.* **1** To or toward the inside of; penetrating or entering within: Come *into* the house. **2** Extending within (a period of time): talking well *into* the night. **3** So as to become: Boiling changes water *into* steam. **4** *Math.* Dividing: Two *into* six is three. **5** As an addition to: *into* the bargain. **6** In the direction of: *into* the northwest. **7** To the practice or study of: to go *into* medicine. **8** *Slang* Actively engaged or involved with, as an interest or enthusiasm: He's *into* oriental religion. [OE]

Synonyms: in, to. *Into* is the preposition of tendency, direction, destination, etc.; *in* is that of condition, state, position, or situation. *Into* should be used and not *in,* when entrance or insertion is intended; *into* indicates motion, change, entrance, in a more marked degree than *in.* "I throw the stone *into* the water, and it lies *in* the water." Used adverbially *in* follows verbs of motion, as *come, go, walk,* and such use has established certain phrases as idioms. One says, "Come *in* the house" but the preferred expression is "Come *into* the house." Where no object is expressed, we say "come *in,*" "go *in.*" *Antonyms:* beyond, by, from, out, past, through.

in·tol·er·a·ble (in·tol′ər·ə·bəl) *adj.* Not tolerable; that cannot be borne or endured; insufferable. — *adv. Obs.* Intolerably. — **in·tol′er·a·bil′i·ty, in·tol′er·a·ble·ness** *n.* — **in·tol′er·a·bly** *adv.*

in·tol·er·ance (in·tol′ər·əns) *n.* **1** Refusal to tolerate opposing beliefs; bigotry. **2** Incapacity or unwillingness to bear or endure. Also **in·tol′er·an·cy.** See synonyms under FANATICISM.

in·tol·er·ant (in·tol′ər·ənt) *adj.* **1** Not disposed to tolerate contrary beliefs or opinions; bigoted. **2** Unable or unwilling to bear or endure: with *of*: *intolerant* of opposition. — **in·tol′er·ant·ly** *adv.*

in·tomb (in·tōōm′), **in·tomb·ment** (in·tōōm′·mənt), etc. See ENTOMB, etc.

in·to·nate (in′tō·nāt) *v.t.* **·nat·ed, ·nat·ing** **1** To intone. **2** To sound the tones of the musical scale, as in sol-faing. [<Med. L *intonatus,* pp. of *intonare* intone, thunder < *in-* in + L *tonus* tone]

in·to·na·tion (in′tō·nā′shən) *n.* **1** The modulation of the voice in speaking: distinguished from *articulation*: Her *intonation* is soft and sweet. **2** The act of intoning, as of the church service by a priest. **3** *Music* Production of tones, as by the voice, especially in regard to precision of tone. **4** In plain song, the notes leading up to the reciting tone: commonly sung by a single voice.

in·tone (in·tōn′) *v.* **·toned, ·ton·ing** *v.t.* **1** To utter or recite in a musical monotone: chant. **2** To give particular tones or intonation to. — *v.i.* **3** To utter a musical monotone; chant. [<MF *entonner* < Med. L *intonare.* See INTONATE.] — **in·ton′er** *n.*

in to·to (in tō′tō) *Latin* In the whole; altogether; entirely.

in·tox·i·cate (in·tok′sə·kāt) *v.t.* **·cat·ed, ·cat·ing** **1** To make drunk; inebriate. **2** To elate or excite to a degree of frenzy. **3** To poison, as by bacterial toxins, serum injections, drugs, alcohol, etc. — *adj.* (-kit) Drunk; intoxicated. [<Med. L *intoxicatus,* pp. of *intoxicare* poison, drug <L *toxicum* poison] — **in·tox′i·cant** *adj.* & *n.* — **in·tox′i·ca′tion** *n.* — **in·tox′i·ca′·tive** *adj.*

intra– *prefix* Within; inside of. [<L *intra* < *intra* within]

Intra– may appear as a prefix in hyphemes or solidemes, with the meaning *situated* or *occurring within*; as in:

intra–abdominal	**intramedullary**
intra–abdominally	**intramembranous**
intra–acinous	**intrameningeal**
intra–alveolar	**intrametropolitan**
intra–appendicular	**intramontane**
intra–arachnoid	**intramundane**
intra–arterial	**intramuscularly**
intra–articular	**intramyocardial**
intra–aural	**intranarial**
intra–auricular	**intranasal**
intrabranchial	**intraneural**
intrabronchial	**intra–ocular**
intrabuccal	**intra–oral**
intracanalicular	**intra–orbital**
intracapsular	**intra–osseous**
intracardiac	**intra–osteal**
intracarpal	**intra–ovarian**
intracarpellary	**intra–ovular**
intracartilaginous	**intraparasitic**
intracellular	**intraparenchymatous**
intracephalic	**intraparochial**
intracerebellar	**intrapelvic**
intracerebral	**intrapericardiac**
intracervical	**intrapericardial**
intracloacal	**intraperineal**
intracolic	**intraperiosteal**
intracollegiate	**intraperitoneal**
intracontinental	**intraphilosophic**
intracorporeal	**intraplacental**
intracorpuscular	**intrapleural**
intracortical	**intrapolar**
intracostal	**intrapontine**
intracranial	**intraprostatic**
intracutaneous	**intrapulmonary**
intracystic	**intrarectal**
intradermal	**intrarenal**
intradermic	**intraretinal**
intradivisional	**intrascrotal**
intraduodenal	**intrasegmental**
intraecclesiastical	**intraseptal**
intraepiphyseal	**intraserous**
intraepithelial	**intraspinal**
intrafilamentary	**intraspinally**
intrafistular	**intrastation**
intragastric	**intrasynovial**
intraglandular	**intratarsal**
intraglobular	**intraterritorial**
intragyral	**intrathecal**
intrahepatic	**intrathoracic**
intrahyoid	**intratrabecular**
intra–imperial	**intratracheal**
intrajugular	**intratropical**
intralamellar	**intratubal**
intralaryngeal	**intratubular**
intraligamentary	**intratympanic**
intraligamentous	**intra–umbilical**
intralingual	**intra–urban**
intralobar	**intra–urethral**
intralobular	**intra–uterine**
intralocular	**intravalvular**
intralumbar	**intravascular**
intramammary	**intraventricular**
intramandibular	**intraverbal**
intramarginal	**intravertebral**
intramastoid	**intravesical**

in·tra–a·tom·ic (in′trə·ə·tom′ik) *adj. Physics* Within an atom or atoms; pertaining to atomic structure.

in·trac·ta·ble (in·trak′tə·bəl) *adj.* **1** Not tractable; refractory; unruly. **2** Lacking plastic quality; difficult to treat or work. See synonyms under IMPRACTICABLE, OBSTINATE, PERVERSE, REBELLIOUS, RESTIVE. — **in·trac′ta·bil′i·ty, in·trac′ta·ble·ness** *n.* — **in·trac′ta·bly** *adv.*

in·tra·dos (in·trā′dos) *n. Archit.* The interior or lower surface of an arch or vault. See illustration under ARCH. [<F *intrados* <L *intra-* within + F *dos* back <L *dorsum*]

in·tra·mo·lec·u·lar (in′trə·mə·lek′yə·lər) *adj. Chem.* Pertaining to or occurring in the interior of a molecule.

in·tra·mu·ral (in′trə·myŏŏr′əl) *adj.* **1** Situated within the walls of a city. **2** *Anat.* Situated within the walls of a hollow organ. **3** Taking place within the confines of an educational institution: *intramural* football: opposed to *extramural.*

in·tra mu·ros (in′trə myŏŏr′ōs) *Latin* Within the walls.

in·tra·mus·cu·lar (in′trə·mus′kyə·lər) *adj. Anat.* Within a muscle or muscular tissue, as an injection.

in·tra·na·tion·al (in′trə·nash′ən·əl) *adj.* Situated within or relating to matters within a nation: opposed to *international.*

in·tran·si·gent (in·tran′sə·jənt) *adj.* Refusing to agree or compromise; irreconcilable. — *n.* One who is intransigent; a radical or revolutionary: also **in·tran′si·gent·ist.** Also *French* **in·tran·si·geant** (aṅ·trän·sē·zhäṅ′). [<F *intransigeant* <Sp. *intransigente* <L *in-* not + *transigens, -entis,* ppr. of *transigere* agree. See TRANSACT.] — **in·tran′si·gence** *n.*

in·tran·si·tive (in·tran′sə·tiv) *Gram. adj.* **1** Not taking or requiring an object, as certain verbs. **2** Of or pertaining to such verbs. — *n.* An intransitive verb. — **in·tran′si·tive·ly** *adv.*

intransitive verb A verb whose action is not transferred to an object but terminates in the subject or doer. *Waits, sleeps, dreams, grows,* are intransitive in the following: the man waits, he sleeps, he dreams, the grass grows. Intransitive verbs become transitive only with a cognate object: I dreamed a dream; to sleep the sleep of the just; to die a soldier's death.

in tran·si·tu (in tran′sə·tyōō) *Latin* In transit; during transmission.

in·trant (in′trənt) *adj.* Entering. — *n.* An entrant; especially, one entering an association or institution. [<L *intrans, -antis,* ppr. of *intrare* enter. See ENTER.]

in·tra·nu·cle·ar (in′trə·nōō′klē·ər, -nyōō′-) *adj.* Within the nucleus, as of an atom or a cell.

in·tra·state (in′trə·stāt′) *adj.* Confined within or pertaining to a single state.

in·tra·tel·lu·ric (in′trə·tə·lŏŏr′ik) *adj. Geol.* **1** Formed or occurring within the earth. **2** Pertaining to the constituents of an effusive rock formed prior to their appearance on the surface, or to the period of their formation.

in·tra·ve·nous (in′trə·vē′nəs) *adj. Med.* Into or within a vein: an *intravenous* injection. — **in′tra·ve′nous·ly** *adv.*

in·tra·vi·tel·line (in′trə·vi·tel′in, -vī-) *adj. Biol.* Within the yolk of an egg.

in·trench (in·trench′), **in·trench·ment** (in·trench′mənt) See ENTRENCH, etc.

in·trench·ant (in·tren′chənt) *adj. Obs.* Indivisible.

in·trep·id (in·trep′id) *adj.* Unshaken in the presence of danger; dauntless. See synonyms under BRAVE. [<L *intrepidus* < *in-* not + *trepidus* agitated] — **in·tre·pid·i·ty** (in′trə·pid′ə·tē) *n.* — **in·trep′id·ly** *adv.*

in·tri·ca·cy (in′tri·kə·sē) *n. pl.* **·cies** **1** The quality of being complicated or entangled. **2** A complication; complexity.

in·tri·cate (in′tri·kit) *adj.* **1** Exceedingly or perplexingly entangled, complicated, or involved. **2** Difficult to follow or understand. See synonyms under COMPLEX. [<L *intricatus,* pp. of *intricare* entangle < *in-* in + *tricae* difficulties] — **in′tri·cate·ly** *adv.* — **in′tri·cate·ness** *n.*

in·tri·gant (in′trə·gənt, *Fr.* aṅ·trē·gäṅ′) *n. pl.* **·gants** (-gənts, *Fr.* -gäṅ′) One given to intrigue. [<F <Ital. *intrigante,* ppr. of *intrigare* intrigue <L *intricare* entangle. See INTRICATE.]

— **in·tri·gante** (in′trə·gant′, -gänt′; *Fr.* aṅ·trē·gäṅt′) *n. fem.*

in·trigue (in·trēg′, in′trēg) *n.* **1** The working for an end by secret or underhand means; a plot or scheme. **2** A clandestine and illicit love affair; liaison. **3** The plot of a play, poem, or story, or the complications in which the characters are involved. — *v.* **·trigued, ·tri·guing** *v.t.* **1** To arouse and hold the interest or curiosity of; beguile; allure. **2** To plot for; bring on or get by secret or underhand means. **3** *Rare* To puzzle; perplex. — *v.i.* **4** To use secret or underhand means; make plots. **5** To carry on a secret or illicit love affair. [<F *intriguer* <Ital. *intrigare* <L *intricare.* See INTRICATE.] — **in·tri′guer** *n.*

in·trinse (in·trins′) *adj. Obs.* Tightly drawn; intricate; entangled. [Short for obs. *intrinsecate* <Ital. *intrinsecato* familiar, confused in sense with *intricate* intricate]

in·trin·sic (in·trin′sik) *adj.* **1** Pertaining to the nature of a thing or person; inherent; real; true: opposed to *extrinsic.* **2** Contained or being within. **3** *Anat.* Contained within a certain portion of the body as nerves or muscles. Also **in·trin′si·cal.** See synonyms under INHERENT. [<OF *intrinseque* <Med. L <L *intrinsecus* internally] — **in·trin′si·cal·ly** *adv.*

intro– *prefix* In; into; within: *introvert.* [<L *intro-* < *intro* inwardly]

in·tro·cep·tion (in′trə·sep′shən) *n. Psychol.* The thorough acceptance by an individual of the fundamental moral standards and conventions of society; social conformity in motives and purpose. [<INTRO- + (RE)CEPTION]

in·tro·duce (in′trə·do͞os′, -dyo͞os′) *v.t.* **·duced, ·duc·ing** **1** To bring (someone) to acquaintance with another; cause to become acquainted: He *introduced* me to his cousin; He *introduced* the women to each other. **2** To present formally: to *introduce* one to society. **3** To bring (someone) to acquaintance with or knowledge of something: with *to*: to *introduce* someone to gambling. **4** To bring into notice, use, or practice: to *introduce* a new fashion. **5** To bring, lead, or put into; insert: to *introduce* a probe into a wound. **6** To bring forward for notice or consideration: to *introduce* a resolution. **7** To begin; start: to *introduce* a new line of questioning. See synonyms under ALLEGE. [<L *introducere* < *in-* within + *ducere* lead] — **in′tro·duc′er** *n.* — **in′·tro·duc′i·ble** *adj.*

in·tro·duc·tion (in′trə·duk′shən) *n.* **1** The act of introducing, as inserting, bringing into notice or use, or making acquainted. **2** The means of introducing one person to another, as by letter, card, etc. **3** Something that leads up to and tends to explain something else; specifically, a preliminary statement made by an author or speaker in explanation of the subject or design of his writing or discourse. **4** Hence, an elementary treatise in any branch of study: an *introduction* to chemistry. **5** *Music* A preparatory movement intended to foreshadow or lead up to the theme. See synonyms under ENTRANCE. [<OF] — **in′tro·duc′tor** *n.*

in·tro·duc·to·ry (in′trə·duk′tər·ē) *adj.* Serving as an introduction; prefatory; preliminary. Also **in′tro·duc′tive.** [<LL *introductorius*] — **in′tro·duc′to·ri·ly** *adv.*

in·tro·fac·tion (in′trə·fak′shən) *n. Chem.* A change in the wetting properties and fluidity of an impregnating substance when acted upon by an introfier. [<INTRO- + *-faction* doing <L *factus,* pp. of *facere* do]

in·tro·fi·er (in′trə·fī′ər) *n. Chem.* A substance which speeds up the impregnating capacity of fluids, as naphthalene or its derivatives when acting on molten sulfur. [<INTRO- + -FY]

in·tro·it (in·trō′it) *n.* **1** An antiphon said or chanted at the beginning of the Eucharist, as the priest enters the sanctuary. **2** In the Anglican Church, an anthem or hymn sung at the beginning of public worship. [<F <L *introitus* an entrance < *introire* < *intro-* in + *ire* go]

in·tro·ject (in′trə·jekt′) *v.t. Psychoanal.* To transform external realities, as persons and objects, into mental replicas or images with which one may enter into direct emotional relations. [<INTRO- + (PRO)JECT]

in·tro·jec·tion (in′trə·jek′shən) *n.* **1** *Psychoanal.* The incorporation into the ego of mental images of persons and objects to the extent of being emotionally affected by them: compare PROJECTION. **2** *Psychol.* The attribution of sentient qualities to inanimate objects; personification. [<intro- + (PRO)JECTION]

in·tro·mit (in′trə·mit′) *v.t.* **·mit·ted, ·mit·ting** **1** To send or place in; insert. **2** To permit to enter; admit. [<L *intromittere* < *intro-* within + *mittere* send] — **in′tro·mis′sion** (-mish′ən) *n.* — **in′tro·mis′sive** (-mis′iv), **in′tro·mit′tent** *adj.*

in·trorse (in·trôrs′) *adj. Bot.* Turned inward or toward the axis, as an anther that faces the axis of a flower. Compare EXTRORSE. [<L *introrsus* inward, contraction of *introversus* < *intro-* within + *versus* turned] — **in·trorse′ly** *adv.*

in·tro·spect (in′trə·spekt′) *v.t.* To look into; examine the interior of. — *v.i. Psychol.* To examine and analyze one's own thoughts and emotions; practice self-examination. [<L *introspectus,* pp. of *introspicere* < *intro-* within + *specere* look] — **in′tro·spec′tive** *adj.* — **in′·tro·spec′tive·ly** *adv.* — **in′tro·spec′tive·ness** *n.*

in·tro·spec·tion (in′trə·spek′shən) *n.* **1** The act of looking within. **2** *Psychol.* The contemplation of one's own mental processes and emotional states; self-examination.

in·tro·sus·cept (in′trə·sə·sept′) See INTUSSUSCEPT.

in·tro·ver·sion (in′trə·vûr′zhən, -shən) *n.* **1** The act or process of introverting. **2** *Psychol.* The direction or concentration of one's interest upon oneself. **3** *Psychoanal.* The concentration of the libido upon inwardly derived activities or satisfactions. Compare EXTROVERSION. [<NL *introversio, -onis* <L *intro-* within + *versio, -onis* a turning] — **in′tro·ver′sive** (-vûr′siv) *adj.*

in·tro·vert (in′trə·vûrt) *n.* **1** *Psychol.* An individual with strongly self-centered patterns of emotion, fantasy, and thought: opposed to *extrovert.* **2** *Biol.* An organ capable of being turned inward, as the eye tentacle of a land snail or the proboscis of a gastropod. — *v.t.* **1** To turn within; cause to take an inward direction, as the mind or one's thoughts. **2** *Biol.* To turn (an organ) inward upon itself. — *adj.* Characterized by or tending to introversion: *introvert* habits. [<INTRO- + L *vertere* turn]

in·trude (in·tro͞od′) *v.* **·trud·ed, ·trud·ing** *v.t.* **1** To thrust or force in without leave or excuse: to *intrude* one's views. **2** *Geol.* To cause to enter by intrusion. — *v.i.* **3** To come in without leave or invitation; thrust oneself in. [<L *intrudere* < *in-* in + *trudere* thrust] — **in·trud′er** *n.*

in·tru·sion (in·tro͞o′zhən) *n.* **1** The act of intruding; encroachment. **2** *Geol.* **a** The thrusting of molten rock within an earlier formation. **b** An intrusive rock.

in·tru·sive (in·tro͞o′siv) *adj* **1** Coming without warrant; intruding; obtrusive; prone to intrude. **2** *Geol.* Formed by solidification before reaching the surface of the earth, as certain igneous rocks; plutonic. **3** *Phonet.* Referring to speech sounds in a word which do not have etymological basis, but result from the adjustment of the vocal organs to the sounds preceding and following, as the *d* in *spindle* (Old English *spinel*). — **intrusive r** An *r* sound sometimes heard between a word ending in a vowel and a following word beginning with a vowel, as in law*r* office. [<L *intrusus,* pp. of *intrudere.* See INTRUDE.] — **in·tru′sive·ly** *adv.* — **in·tru′sive·ness** *n.*

in·trust (in·trust′) See ENTRUST.

in·tu·bate (in′tyo͞o·bāt, -to͞o-) *v.t.* **·bat·ed, ·bat·ing** *Med.* To treat by intubation. [<IN- + L *tuba* tube + -ATE[2]]

in·tu·ba·tion (in′tyo͞o·bā′shən, -to͞o-) *n. Med.* The insertion of a tube in an orifice, as in the larynx in cases of diphtheria.

in·tu·it (in′tyo͞o·it, in·to͞o′it) *v.t.* & *v.i.* To know by intuition. [<L *intuitus,* pp. of *intueri* look upon < *in-* on + *tueri* look]

in·tu·i·tion (in′to͞o·ish′ən, -tyo͞o-) *n.* **1** Quick perception of truth without conscious attention or reasoning. **2** Knowledge from within; instinctive knowledge or feeling. **3** *Philos.* **a** An immediate knowledge, or envisagement, of an object, truth, or principle, whether of a physical, rational, artistic, or ethical nature: a conception derived by analogy from the act and result of clear and concentrated vision. **b** That which is known intuitively; truth obtained by internal apprehension without the aid of perception or the reasoning powers. See synonyms under KNOWLEDGE. [<Med. L *intuitio, -onis* < *intuitus,* pp. of *intueri* look upon. See INTUIT.] — **in′tu·i′tion·al** *adj.* — **in′·tu·i′tion·al·ly** *adv.*

intuitional ethics The teaching of that school of ethics which holds that man has an intuitive apprehension and intrinsically valid judgment of moral values.

in·tu·i·tion·al·ism (in′to͞o·ish′ən·əl·iz′əm, -tyo͞o-) *n.* The doctrine that certain truths are immediately, and without discursive argument, cognized as fundamental and incontestable and are the foundation of all knowledge. Also **in′tu·i′tion·ism.** — **in′tu·i′tion·al·ist, in′tu·i′·tion·ist** *n.*

in·tu·i·tive (in·to͞o′ə·tiv, -tyo͞o′-) *adj.* **1** Perceived by the mind without the intervention of any process of thought: *intuitive* evidence. **2** Discovering truth or reaching a just conclusion without resort to the powers of reason: the *intuitive* faculty. — **in·tu′i·tive·ly** *adv.* — **in·tu′i·tive·ness** *n.*

in·tu·i·tiv·ism (in·to͞o′ə·tiv·iz′əm, -tyo͞o′-) *n.* **1** The doctrine that all ethical principles are intuitive. **2** Intuitive faculty; insight; instinct. — **in·tu′i·tiv·ist** *n.*

in·tu·mesce (in′to͞o·mes′, -tyo͞o-) *v.i.* **·mesced, ·mesc·ing** **1** To enlarge or expand, as from heat or congestion. **2** To swell or bubble up; become tumid. [<L *intumescere,* intens. of *tumescere,* inceptive of *tumere* swell]

in·tu·mes·cence (in′to͞o·mes′əns, -tyo͞o-) *n.* **1** A tumid state or process. **2** A tumid growth; a swelling. **3** The bubbling up of a molten mass. **4** Excited feeling or language. Also **in′tu·mes′cen·cy.** — **in′tu·mes′cent** *adj.*

in·turn (in′tûrn′) *n.* **1** The act of turning inward, or the state of being so turned, as of the toes. **2** A dancing step. Also **in′turn′ing.**

in·tus·sus·cept (in′təs·sə·sept′) *v.t.* To receive within itself or within something else; invaginate: also *introsuscept.* [<L *intus* within + *susceptus,* pp. of *suscipere* take up < *sub-* under + *capere* take] — **in′tus·sus·cep′tive** *adj.*

in·tus·sus·cep·tion (in′təs·sə·sep′shən) *n.* **1** A receiving within. **2** The state of being received within. **3** *Pathol.* The introversion of a portion of an intestine or other tube into the portion adjoining it. **4** *Physiol.* The reception into an organ of foreign matter, as food, and its conversion into living tissue; interstitial growth. **5** *Bot.* The interposition of new molecules between the molecules of the original material, as in the cell walls of plants or grains of starch.

in·twine (in·twīn′), **in·twist** (in·twist′), etc. See ENTWINE, etc.

in·u·en·do (in′yo͞o·en′dō) See INNUENDO.

in·u·lase (in′yə·lās) *n. Biochem.* An enzyme arising from the action of certain species of fungi on inulin, which it converts into levulose. [<INUL(IN) + -ASE]

in·u·lin (in′yə·lin) *n. Biochem.* A white, amorphous, soluble polysaccharide, $C_6H_{10}O_5$, isomeric with starch, and occurring in the underground parts of some composite plants such as the dahlia, the dandelion, and the elecampane: it yields a fructose on hydrolysis. [<L *inula* elecampane + -IN]

in·unc·tion (in·ungk′shən) *n.* **1** The act of anointing. **2** *Med.* The process of rubbing into the skin, as an ointment or liniment. [<L *inunctio, -onis* < *inunctus,* pp. of *inungere* anoint]

in·un·dant (in·un′dənt) *adj.* Inundating; overflowing.

in·un·date (in′un·dāt) *v.t.* **·dat·ed, ·dat·ing** To cover by overflowing; flood; fill to overflowing. [<L *inundatus,* pp. of *inundare* < *in-* in, on + *undare* overflow < *unda* wave] — **in′un·da′tor** *n.* — **in·un·da·to·ry** (in·un′də·tôr′ē, -tō′rē) *adj.*

Synonyms: deluge, flood, overflow, overwhelm, submerge. *Antonyms:* drain, dry, parch, scorch.

in·un·da·tion (in′un·dā′shən) *n.* **1** A flood. **2** A condition of superabundance.

in·ure (in·yo͝or′) *v.* **·ured, ·ur·ing** *v.t.* To harden or toughen by use or exercise; accustom; habituate. — *v.i.* To have or take effect; be applied. Also spelled *enure.* [<IN[2] + obs. *ure* work, use <OF *eure* <L *opera* work] — **in·ure′ment** *n.*

in·urn (in·ûrn′) *v.t.* To put into a cinerary urn; bury; entomb.

in·u·tile (in·yo͞o′til) *adj.* Useless. [<F <L *inutilis*] — **in·u′tile·ly** *adv.* — **in′u·til′i·ty** *n.*

in va·cu·o (in vak′yo͞o·ō) *Latin* In a vacuum.

in·vade (in·vād′) *v.* **·vad·ed, ·vad·ing** *v.t.* **1** To enter with or as with hostile intent, as for conquering or plundering. **2** To encroach upon; trespass on: to *invade* privacy. **3** To spread over or penetrate injuriously: Disease *invaded* the lungs. — *v.i.* **4** To make an invasion. [<L *invadere* < *in-* in + *vadere* go] — **in·vad′er** *n.*

in·vag·i·nate (in·vaj′ə·nāt) *v.* **·nat·ed, ·nat·ing** *v.t.* **1** To put or receive into a sheath. **2** To turn back within itself, as a tubular organ or part. — *v.i.* **3** To undergo invagination. [<L *in-* in + *vagina* sheath + -ATE[2]] — **in·vag′i·nat′ed** *adj.*

in·vag·i·na·tion (in·vaj′ə·nā′shən) *n.* **1** The act of invaginating, or the state of being invaginated; intussusception. **2** *Biol.* **a** The differentiation of the germinal layers by a pushing in of the wall of the blastula to form the gastrula, or by the growth of the epiblast cells as a thin layer over the hypoblast. **b** That which is invaginated; specifically, a pouch formed by an infolding of a membrane: the buccal *invagination.*

in·va·lid[1] (in′və·lid) *n.* A sickly person, or one disabled, as by wounds, disease, etc. — *adj.* **1** Enfeebled by ill health. **2** Pertaining to or for the use of sick persons. — *v.t.* **1** To cause to become an invalid; disable. **2** To classify, or release (a soldier, sailor, etc.) from active service as an invalid. — *v.i.* **3** To become an invalid. **4** To retire from active service because of ill health: said of soldiers, sailors, etc. [<F *invalide* <L *invalidus* not strong] — **in′va·lid·ism** *n.*

in·val·id[2] (in·val′id) *adj.* Having no force, weight, or cogency; null; void. [<L *invalidus*] — **in·va·lid·i·ty** (in′və·lid′ə·tē) *n.* — **in·val′id·ly** *adv.*

in·val·i·date (in·val′ə·dāt) *v.t.* **·dat·ed, ·dat·ing** To weaken or destroy the force or validity of; render invalid; annul. [<INVALID[2] + -ATE[1]] — **in·val′i·da′tion** *n.* — **in·val′i·da′tor** *n.*

in·val·u·a·ble (in·val′yōō·ə·bəl, -yŏŏ·bəl) *adj.* Of a value beyond estimation; very precious. — **in·val′u·a·bly** *adv.*

In·var (in·vär′) *n.* An alloy of nickel and steel, containing 36 percent of nickel, employed in the manufacture of instruments of precision and of standard measures, because it is practically free from expansion or contraction by heat or cold: a trade name. [<INVAR(IABLE)]

in·var·i·a·ble (in·vâr′ē·ə·bəl) *adj.* That does not or can not vary or be varied; always uniform. See synonyms under CONTINUAL, PERMANENT. — **in·var′i·a·bil′i·ty, in·var′i·a·ble·ness** *n.* — **in·var′i·a·bly** *adv.*

in·var·iance (in·vâr′ē·əns) *n.* The property or condition of being invariant.

in·var·i·ant (in·vâr′ē·ənt) *adj.* Constant; not subject to variation. — *n. Math.* A quantity which remains unchanged; a constant.

in·va·sion (in·vā′zhən) *n.* **1** The act of invading; a military inroad or incursion for conquest, reconquest, or plunder. **2** Hence, any attack with harmful intent or result: an *invasion* of disease. **3** Encroachment, as by an act of intrusion or trespass: the *invasion* of privacy. [<LL *invasio, -onis* < *invasum,* pp. of *invadere.* See INVADE.]

Synonyms: aggression, encroachment, foray, incursion, inroad, irruption, raid. See AGGRESSION, ATTACK.

in·va·sive (in·vā′siv) *adj.* Having the character or effect of an invasion; encroaching; aggressive.

in·vect·ed (in·vek′tid) *adj. Archit.* **1** Having a border line consisting of a series of convex arcs or scallops. **2** Consisting of such arcs, as a line, the edge of a molding, etc.: opposed to *engrailed.* [<L *invectus,* pp. of *invehere.* See INVEIGH.]

in·vec·tive (in·vek′tiv) *n.* Railing accusation; vituperation; abuse. — *adj.* Using or characterized by vituperation or abuse. [<OF *invectif* <LL *invectivus* <L *invectus,* pp. of *invehere.* See INVEIGH.] — **in·vec′tive·ly** *adv.* — **in·vec′tive·ness** *n.*

in·veigh (in·vā′) *v.i.* To utter vehement censure or invective: with *against.* [<L *invehere* carry into < *in-* into + *vehere* carry] — **in·veigh′er** *n.*

in·vei·gle (in·vē′gəl, -vā′-) *v.t.* **·gled, ·gling** **1** To lead on, as by trickery or flattery; draw; entice. **2** To win over or seduce; captivate. See synonyms under ALLURE. [<F *aveugler* blind, deceive < *aveugle* blind, ult. <L *ab-* without + *oculus* eye] — **in·vei′gle·ment** *n.* — **in·vei′gler** *n.*

in·veil (in·vāl′) *v.t. Obs.* To cover with a veil.

in·vent (in·vent′) *v.t.* **1** To create the idea, form, or existence of by original thought or effort; devise: to *invent* a better mousetrap. **2** To fabricate in the mind; make up, as something untrue or contrary to fact: He *invented* an excuse. **3** *Obs.* To come or chance upon; find. See synonyms under DISCOVER, PLAN. [<L *inventus,* pp. of *invenire* come upon, discover < *in-* on + *venire* come] — **in·vent′i·ble** *adj.*

in·ven·tion (in·ven′shən) *n.* **1** The act or process of inventing. **2** That which is invented: a useful *invention.* **3** Skill or ingenuity in contriving. **4** Mental fabrication or concoction. **5** In literature or art, creation by the exercise of imaginative powers: poetic *invention.* **6** In rhetoric, the finding out or selection of topics to be treated, or arguments to be used. **7** *Archaic* A finding; discovery. **8** *Law* **a** The process of devising and producing by independent investigation and experiment something not previously known or existing. **b** The article, device, or composition thus created. See synonyms under ARTIFICE, FICTION, INGENUITY, PROJECT. [<OF *invencion*]

in·ven·tive (in·ven′tiv) *adj.* Able to invent; quick at contrivance. — **in·ven′tive·ly** *adv.* — **in·ven′tive·ness** *n.*

in·ven·tor (in·ven′tər) *n.* One who invents; especially, one who has originated some method, process, or mechanical device, or who devotes his time to invention. Also **in·vent′er.** [<L]

in·ven·to·ry (in′vən·tôr′ē, -tō′rē) *n. pl.* **·ries** **1** An itemized list of articles, with the number and value of each. **2** The items so listed or to be listed, as the stock of goods of a business. **3** The process of listing articles, supplies, or materials with the description, quantity, and value of each. **4** The value of the goods or stock of a business. **5** A detailed account of the property of a deceased person. **6** A list of articles, with valuations, covered by an insurance policy. See synonyms under RECORD. — *v.t.* **·ried, ·ry·ing** **1** To make an inventory of; to list in detail. **2** To insert in an inventory. **3** To take stock of; appraise. [<Med. L *inventarium,* L *inventorium.* See INVENT.] — **in′ven·to′ri·al** (-tôr′ē·əl, -tō′rē-) *adj.* — **in′ven·to′ri·al·ly** *adv.*

in·ve·rac·i·ty (in′və·ras′ə·tē) *n. pl.* **·ties** **1** Lack of veracity; untruthfulness. **2** An untruth; lie.

In·ver·chap·el (in′vər·chap′əl) See KERR.

in·ver·ness (in′vər·nes′) *n.* A sleeveless, cloaklike garment. Also **Inverness cape.** [from *Inverness,* Scotland]

In·ver·ness (in′vər·nes′) A maritime county in NW Scotland; 4,211 square miles; county seat, Inverness. Also **In′ver·ness′shire** (-shir).

in·verse (in·vûrs′, in′vûrs) *adj.* Opposite in order or effect; inverted; reciprocal. — *n.* That which is inverted. — **in·verse′ly** *adv.*

in·ver·sion (in·vûr′zhən, -shən) *n.* **1** The act of inverting. **2** The state of being inverted; a reversal of the natural order of things. **3** In rhetoric: **a** A reversal of the natural order of words. **b** A form of discussion that makes use of a speaker's own argument against himself. **4** *Music* The alteration of a harmony or melody by inverting the relations of its intervals; also, the arrangement resulting from such change. **5** In marching, a reversal of the order of companies in line, so as to bring the left to the right, and vice versa. **6** *Chem.* A rearrangement of the molecular structure of compounds, with the forming of two new compounds whose effects on the plane of polarization are opposed to each other: Sucrose, by acid hydrolysis, is an *inversion* of glucose and fructose. **7** *Meteorol.* An increase of temperature with elevation often noted in anticyclones. **8** *Phonet.* A tongue position in which the tip is turned up and back. **9** Homosexuality. [<L *inversio, -onis* < *inversus,* pp. of *invertere.* See INVERT.] — **in·ver′sive** *adj.*

in·vert (in·vûrt′) *v.t.* **1** To turn upside down or inside out. **2** To reverse the position, order, or sequence of; turn in the opposite direction. **3** To change to the opposite: to *invert* a meaning. **4** *Music* To transpose, as an interval, phrase, or vocal part. **5** *Chem.* To alter, as a compound, by inversion. **6** *Phonet.* To articulate with inversion of the tongue. — *v.i.* **7** To undergo inversion. — *adj.* (in′vûrt) Inverted. — *n.* (in′vûrt) A homosexual. [<L *invertere* < *in-* in + *vertere* turn] — **in·vert′i·ble** *adj.* — **in·ver′tor** *n.*

in·ver·tase (in·vûr′tās) *n. Biochem.* An enzyme capable of splitting sucrose and related sugars into glucose and fructose, found in certain plants and the intestines of animals; specifically, a ferment which inverts cane sugar into fructose and glucose. Also **in·ver′tin** (-tin). [<INVERT + -ASE]

In·ver·te·bra·ta (in·vûr′tə·brā′tə) *n. pl.* A former name for a section of the animal kingdom including all animals without a spinal column: opposed to *Vertebrata.* [<NL]

in·ver·te·brate (in·vûr′tə·brit, -brāt) *adj.* **1** Destitute of a backbone; not vertebrate. **2** Of or pertaining to the *Invertebrata.* **3** Lacking force or firmness; irresolute: also **in·ver′te·bral.** — *n.* **1** An invertebrate animal; one of the *Invertebrata.* **2** One who lacks resolution.

in·vert·ed (in·vûr′tid) *adj.* **1** Turned in a contrary direction, or turned upside down; reversed in order or position. **2** Having a position the opposite of the usual or normal one: an *inverted* ovule in plants, *inverted* commas, etc. **3** *Phonet.* Cacuminal. — **in·vert′ed·ly** *adv.*

inverted arch *Archit.* An arch having its crown downward: used in foundations.

inverted commas *Brit.* Quotation marks.

inverted mordent See under MORDENT.

in·vert·er (in·vûr′tər) *n. Electr.* A device for converting direct current into alternating current; a converter.

invert soap A synthetic detergent with strong disinfectant qualities due to the presence of positive ions in its molecular structure causing its resistance to the action of acids and alkalis.

invert sugar A mixture of fructose and glucose occurring in some fruits and artificially produced by the hydrolysis of cane sugar.

in·vest (in·vest′) *v.t.* **1** To use (money or capital) for the purchase of property, stocks, securities, etc., with the expectation of future profit or income. **2** To place in office formally; install. **3** To give power, authority, or rank to. **4** To cover or surround as if with a garment: Mystery *invested* the whole affair. **5** To surround or hem in; lay siege to. **6** *Rare* To confer or settle (a right, power, etc.): with *in.* **7** *Obs.* To clothe; also, to don. — *v.i.* **8** To make an investment or investments. [<L *investire* clothe, enshroud < *in-* on + *vestire* clothe < *vestis* clothing; infl. in meaning by Ital. *investire* invest] — **in·ves′tor** *n.*

in·ves·ti·gate (in·ves′tə·gāt) *v.* **·gat·ed, ·gat·ing** To search or inquire into; examine in detail. — *v.i.* To make an investigation. See synonyms under EXAMINE, QUESTION. [<L *investigatus,* pp. of *investigare* < *in-* in + *vestigare* track, trace < *vestigium* track] — **in·ves′ti·ga·ble** (-tə·gə·bəl) *adj.* — **in·ves′ti·ga′tive** *adj.* — **in·ves′ti·ga′tor** *n.*

in·ves·ti·ga·tion (in·ves′tə·gā′shən) *n.* **1** The act of investigating; careful inquiry or research. **2** An inquiry by authority, as by a legislative committee, into certain facts. **3** A systematic examination of some scientific question, whether by experiment or mathematical treatment. [<F]

in·ves·ti·tive (in·ves′tə·tiv) *adj.* **1** Of or pertaining to investiture. **2** Having the function of investing; serving to invest. [<L *investitus,* pp. of *investire.* See INVEST.]

in·ves·ti·ture (in·ves′tə·chər) *n.* **1** The act or ceremony of investing with something, as robes of office. **2** That which invests or clothes. **3** In feudal law, the delivery of possession of lands in the presence of witnesses. **4** *Eccl.* The ceremony of inducting an abbot or bishop into his office by placing the symbols of the office in his hands and receiving his oath of fealty. **5** *Obs.* Clothing. [<Med. L *investitura.*]

in·vest·ment (in·vest′mənt) *n.* **1** The placing of money, capital, or other resources to gain

a profit, as in interest. 2 That which is invested. 3 That in which one invests. 4 Investiture. 5 *Biol.* An outer covering. 6 *Archaic* Clothing; a garment. 7 *Mil.* The surrounding of a fort or town by an enemy force to create a state of siege; a blockade.

investment trust A company that invests its capital in other companies.

in·vet·er·a·cy (in·vet′ər·ə·sē) *n. pl.* **·cies** 1 Persistence from habit; habitual nature or character. 2 Deep-rooted hostility.

in·vet·er·ate (in·vet′ər·it) *adj.* 1 Firmly established by long continuance; deep-rooted. 2 Confirmed in a particular character or habit. 3 *Obs.* Characteristic of long enmity; bitter; malignant; also, ancient. [<L *inveteratus*, pp. of *inveterare* make old < *in-* very + *vetus* old] — **in·vet′er·ate·ly** *adv.* — **in·vet′er·ate·ness** *n.*

in·vid·i·ous (in·vid′ē·əs) *adj.* 1 Expressing, prompted by, or provoking envy or ill will; unjustly discriminating; hence, displeasing. 2 *Obs.* Showing envy. See synonyms under MALICIOUS. [<L *invidiosus* < *invidia* envy. Doublet of ENVIOUS.] — **in·vid′i·ous·ly** *adv.* — **in·vid′i·ous·ness** *n.*

in·vig·i·late (in·vij′ə·lāt) *v.t.* **·lat·ed, ·lat·ing** 1 *Brit.* To keep watch over or proctor students at examination. 2 *Obs.* To watch carefully. [<L *invigilatus*, pp. of *invigilare* < *in-* thoroughly + *vigilare* watch < *vigilia* watch < *vigil* awake < *vigere* be vigorous] — **in·vig′i·la′tion** *n.* — **in·vig′i·la′tor** *n.*

in·vig·or·ate (in·vig′ər·āt) *v.t.* **·at·ed, ·at·ing** To give vigor and energy to; animate. [<L *in-* in + *vigor* vigor + -ATE^{2}] — **in·vig′or·at′ing·ly** *adv.* — **in·vig′or·a′tion** *n.*

in·vin·ci·ble (in·vin′sə·bəl) *adj.* Not to be overcome; unconquerable. [<F <L *invincibilis*. See IN^{1}-, VINCIBLE.] — **in·vin′ci·bil′i·ty, in·vin′ci·ble·ness** *n.* — **in·vin′ci·bly** *adv.*

in vi·no ver·i·tas (in vī′nō ver′i·tas) *Latin* In wine (there is) truth.

in·vi·o·la·ble (in·vī′ə·lə·bəl) *adj.* That must not or can not be violated. [<L *inviolabilis*] — **in·vi′o·la·bil′i·ty, in·vi′o·la·ble·ness** *n.* — **in·vi′o·la·bly** *adv.*

in·vi·o·la·cy (in·vī′ə·lə·sē) *n.* The state of being inviolate.

in·vi·o·late (in·vī′ə·lit) *adj.* 1 Not violated; unprofaned; pure; unbroken. 2 Inviolable; not to be violated. — **in·vi′o·late·ly** *adv.* — **in·vi′o·late·ness** *n.*

in·vis·i·ble (in·viz′ə·bəl) *adj.* 1 Not visible; not capable of being seen. 2 Not in sight; concealed. 3 *Econ.* Referring to resources or reserves that do not appear in regular processes or in financial statements: *invisible* products, *invisible* revenue, *invisible* assets. — *n.* 1 One who or that which is invisible. 2 *Often cap.* One of a sect of Protestants in the 16th century who denied the visibility of the church. 3 A Rosicrucian, as belonging to a secret fraternity. — **the Invisible** The Supreme Being; God. [<OF] — **in·vis′i·bil′i·ty, in·vis′i·ble·ness** *n.* — **in·vis′i·bly** *adv.*

invisible ink Sympathetic ink.

in·vi·ta·tion (in′və·tā′shən) *n.* 1 The act of inviting; courteous solicitation to come to some place or to do some act; especially, a requesting of another's company: a standing *invitation* to dinner. 2 The means of inviting; the words by which one is invited: a written *invitation*. 3 The act of alluring; incitement; attraction. 4 In the Anglican Church, the hortatory introduction preceding the confession in the communion office; the invitatory. [<L *invitatio, -onis*]

in·vi·ta·to·ry (in·vī′tə·tôr′ē, -tō′rē) *Eccl. adj.* Using or containing invitation: the *invitatory* psalm, "O come let us sing," *Ps.* xcv. — *n. pl.* **·ries** One of several forms of invitation to worship; especially, the antiphon to the Venite. [<Med. L *invitatorius*]

in·vite (in·vīt′) *v.* **·vit·ed, ·vit·ing** *v.t.* 1 To ask (someone) politely or graciously to be present in some place, to attend some event, or to perform some action. 2 To make formal or polite request for: to *invite* suggestions. 3 To present opportunity or inducement for; attract: The situation *invites* criticism. 4 To tempt; entice. — *v.i.* 5 To give invitation; entice. — *n.* (in′vīt) *Slang* An invitation. [<F *inviter* <L *invitare* entertain] — **in·vit′er** *n.*

in·vit·ing (in·vī′ting) *adj.* That invites or allures. — **in·vit′ing·ly** *adv.* —**in·vit′ing·ness** *n.*

in vi·tro (in vī′trō) *Latin* Within glass: said especially of experiments carried on in test tubes or outside of the living organisms.

in vi·vo (in vī′vō) *Latin* Within the living organism: opposed to *in vitro.*

in·vo·ca·tion (in′vō·kā′shən) *n.* 1 The act of invoking. 2 A judicial order. 3 *Eccl.* A form of prayer, as at the opening of a service. 4 An appeal invoking the Muses or some divine being, at the beginning of an epic or other work. 5 The act of conjuring an evil spirit. 6 The formula or incantation thus used. See synonyms under PRAYER. [<OF <L *invocatio, -onis* < *invocare*. See INVOKE.]

in·voc·a·to·ry (in·vok′ə·tôr′ē, -tō′rē) *adj.* Having the nature of, expressive of, or employed in invocation.

in·voice (in′vois) *n.* 1 A list sent to a purchaser, etc., containing the items and charges of merchandise. 2 The goods so listed. — *v.t.* **·voiced, ·voic·ing** To itemize; make an invoice of. [<F *envois*, pl. of *envoi* a thing sent < *envoyer* send. See ENVOY^{1}.]

in·voke (in·vōk′) *v.t.* **·voked, ·vok·ing** 1 To call on for aid, protection, etc.; address, as in prayer. 2 To call for, as in supplication: to *invoke* a blessing. 3 To summon or conjure by incantation, as evil spirits. 4 To appeal to for confirmation; quote as an authority. See synonyms under PRAY. [<F *invoquer* <L *invocare* call upon < *in-* on + *vocare* call] — **in·vok′er** *n.*

in·vol·u·cel (in·vol′yə·sel) *n. Bot.* 1 A secondary involucre. 2 A rosette of bracts beneath a calyx. Also **in·vol′u·cel′lum.** [<NL *involucellum*, dim. of L *involucrum* covering]

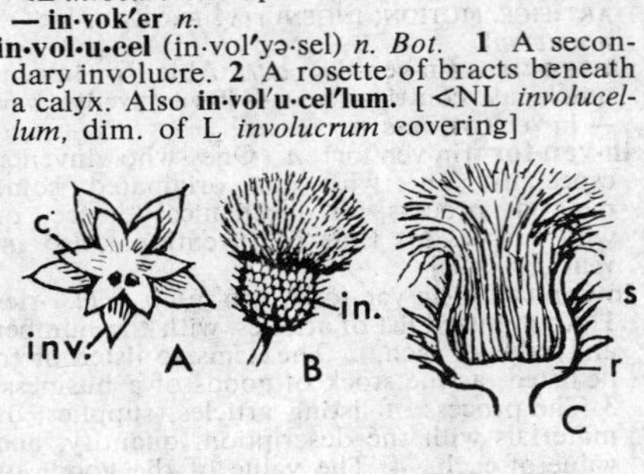

INVOLUCEL AND INVOLUCRE

A. Involucel of hollyhock; *c*, calyx; *inv.*, involucel.
B. Head of thistle; *in.*, involucre.
C. Section of thistle, showing arrangement of the scales (*s*) of the involucre, and the receptacle (*r*).

in·vo·lu·cral (in′və·lōō′krəl) *adj.* Pertaining to, resembling, or provided with an involucre.

in·vo·lu·crate (in′və·lōō′krit, -krāt) *adj.* Provided with or forming an involucre. Also **in′vo·lu′crat·ed.**

in·vo·lu·cre (in′və·lōō′kər) *n.* 1 An enveloping membrane or wrapper. 2 *Bot.* A ring or rosette of bracts surrounding the base of a flower cluster. In many flowers the subtending involucres resemble calyxes and all composites are involucrate. [<F <L *involucrum* covering < *involvere*. See INVOLVE.]

in·vo·lu·crum (in′və·lōō′krəm) *n. pl.* **·cra** (-krə) 1 An involucre. 2 *Zool.* The sheath at the base of a nematocyst. [<L]

in·vol·un·tar·y (in·vol′ən·ter′ē) *adj.* 1 Contrary to one's will or wish. 2 Not under the control of the will. 3 Unintentional. 4 *Physiol.* Describing those muscles, glands, and other bodily organs which act independently of conscious control. See synonyms under SPONTANEOUS. — **in·vol′un·tar′i·ly** *adv.* — **in·vol′un·tar′i·ness** *n.*

in·vo·lute (in′və·lōōt) *adj.* 1 Complicated by reason of the intertwinings or the interrelation of parts or elements. 2 *Bot.* Having the edges rolled inward, as a leaf. 3 *Zool.* Having the whorls nearly or quite concealing the axis, as a shell; also, coiled spirally, as certain antennae. Also **in′vo·lut′ed.** — *n. Geom.* The curve traced by a point on a line as the line unrolls from a fixed curve. [<L *involutus*, pp. of *involvere* involve]

in·vo·lu·tion (in′və·lōō′shən) *n.* 1 The act of involving, infolding, or rolling up, or the state of being involved or rolled up; complication; entanglement. 2 Something involved, rolled up, or entangled. 3 *Physiol.* **a** The return of an organ to its normal condition after a physiological increase in its size and structure: the *involution* of the womb after childbirth. **b** Retrograde development; the physiological decline preceding and accompanying old age. 4 *Math.* The multiplication of a quantity by itself any number of times; the raising of a quantity to any power. 5 In rhetoric, complicated or cumbrous arrangement of words, clauses, or phrases, caused by the insertion of qualifying or modifying phrases between words that belong together. 6 *Biol.* Degeneration; retrograde evolution.

in·volve (in·volv′) *v.t.* **·volved, ·volv·ing** 1 To have as a necessary circumstance, condition, or implication. 2 To have effect on; affect: The law will *involve* many people. 3 To draw within itself; swallow up; overwhelm: The whirlpool *involved* ten persons. 4 To draw into entanglement, trouble, etc.; implicate; entangle. 5 To make intricate or difficult; complicate. 6 To hold the attention of; engross: He was *involved* in his work. 7 To wrap up or infold; cover or conceal; envelop: to *involve* a place in darkness. 8 To wind in spirals or curves; coil, especially intricately. 9 *Math.* To raise (a number) to a given power. [<L *involvere* roll into or up < *in-* in + *volvere* roll] — **in·volve′ment** *n.*

Synonyms: complicate, embarrass, embroil, entangle, implicate, imply, include, overwhelm. To *involve* is to roll or wind up with or in, so as to combine inextricably or very nearly inseparably; as, The nation is *involved* in war; The bookkeeper's accounts, or the writer's sentences, are *involved. Involve* is a stronger word than *implicate*, denoting more complete entanglement. As applied to persons, *implicate* applies only to that which is wrong, while *involve* is more commonly used of that which is unfortunate; one is *implicated* in a crime, *involved* in embarrassments, misfortunes, or perplexities. One is *embroiled* in a serious conflict, *entangled* in a conspiracy, which, once the situation is *complicated* by treachery, may *overwhelm* the participants who are *involved*. As regards logical connection, that which is *included* is usually expressly stated; that which is *implied* is not stated, but is naturally to be inferred; that which is *involved* is necessarily to be inferred, as, a slate roof is *included* in the contract; that the roof shall be watertight is *implied*; the contrary supposition *involves* an absurdity. Compare COMPLEX, PERPLEX. *Antonyms*: disconnect, disentangle, distinguish, explicate, extricate, remove, separate.

in·volved (in·volvd′) *adj.* Intricate; complicated; not easily comprehended. — **in·volv·ed·ness** (in·vol′vid·nis) *n.*

in·vul·ner·a·ble (in·vul′nər·ə·bəl) *adj.* Not capable of being wounded; not to be overcome; having no weak point; unconquerable. — **in·vul′ner·a·bil′i·ty, in·vul′ner·a·ble·ness** *n.* — **in·vul′ner·a·bly** *adv.*

in·wall (in′wôl′) *n.* An inner wall or lining wall, particularly of a blast furnace. — *v.t.* (in·wôl′) To wall in; fortify with a wall.

in·ward (in′wərd) *adv.* 1 Toward the inside, center, or interior. 2 In or on the inside. 3 Into the spirit or mind. Also *inwards.* — *adj.* 1 Situated within, especially with reference to the body; inner: opposed to *outward.* 2 Pertaining to the mind or spirit: an *inward* light. 3 Muffled; low, as the voice. 4 Proceeding toward the inside. 5 Inland. 6 Inherent; intrinsic. — *n. Obs.* An intimate. [OE *inweard*]

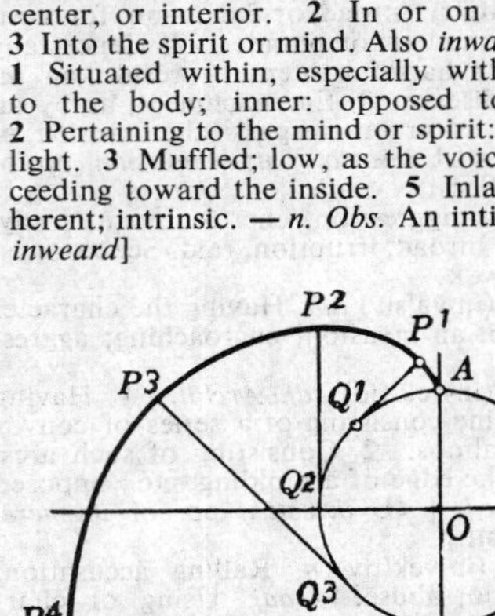

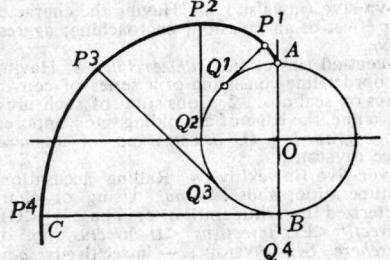

INVOLUTE

Involute *AC* is formed by the locus of point *P* (at P^1, P^2, P^3, P^4) as line *BC* unrolls from curve *BA*. Length of the tangent to the curve (P^1Q^1, P^2Q^2, etc.) from any point on the involute *AC* is equal to the length of the curve to the point of tangency ($AQ^1 = P^1Q^1$; $AQ^2 = P^2Q^2$; etc.).

in·ward·ly (in′wərd·lē) *adv.* 1 In an inward manner; especially, in one's thoughts and

feelings; with no outward manifestation; secretly. 2 *Rare* Toward the center or interior; inward: to turn *inwardly.* 3 Essentially; inherently; intrinsically. [OE *inweardlīce*]

in·ward·ness (in′wərd·nis) *n.* 1 The inner quality or meaning; true nature or import. 2 The state of being inward or internal, mentally or physically, actually or figuratively. 3 Collectively, the ideas and interests which belong to the life of the mind or spirit, and to its true development. 4 *Obs.* Intimacy.

in·wards (in′wərdz) *adv.* 1 Inward. 2 With respect to taxable imports: duties paid *inwards.* —*n. pl.* Inner or interior parts.

in·weave (in·wēv′) *v.t.* **·wove** or **·weaved, ·woven** (*Obs.* **·wove), ·weav·ing** To weave in or together; introduce into a fabric as a component part.

in·wind (in·wīnd′) *v.t.* **·wound, ·wind·ing** To wind in or around; entwine.

in·wo·ven (in·wō′vən) *adj.* Woven in; entwined.

in·wrap (in·rap′) See ENWRAP.

in·wreathe (in·rēth′) See ENWREATHE.

in·wrought (in·rôt′) *adj.* Worked into, as a fabric or metalwork, so as to form part of it. See synonyms under INHERENT.

i·o (ē′ō) *interj.* An exclamation expressive of gladness or exultation. [<L <Gk. *iō*]

I·o (ī′ō) In Greek mythology, the daughter of Inachus, who was loved by Zeus and changed by him into a heifer to escape the jealous wrath of Hera, who set hundred–eyed Argus to watch her; when Argus was killed by Hermes on Zeus's orders, Hera sent a gadfly which drove Io to Egypt where she regained her human form.

Io·an·ni·na (yô·ä′nē·nä) A city of NW Greece: also *Janina, Yanina.*

iod– Var. of IODO–.

i·o·date (ī′ə·dāt) *v.t.* **·dat·ed, ·dat·ing** To iodize. —*n. Chem.* A salt of iodic acid. [<IOD- + -ATE³] —**i′o·da′tion** *n.*

i·od·ic (ī·od′ik) *adj. Chem.* 1 Of, pertaining to, or containing iodine. 2 Designating a white crystalline acid, HIO_3, used as an oxidizing agent.

i·o·dide (ī′ə·dīd) *n. Chem.* 1 A binary compound of iodine. 2 A salt or compound in which iodine is the acid radical. 3 A salt of hydriodic acid: potassium *iodide.* Also **i′o·did** (-did). [<IOD- + -IDE]

i·o·dim·e·try (ī′ə·dim′ə·trē) *n.* Iodometry. [< *iodi-*, var. of IODO- + -METRY]

i·o·dine (ī′ə·dīn, -din, -dēn) *n.* A bluish–black crystalline element (symbol I) of the halogen group, having a metallic luster and yielding, when heated, corrosive fumes of a rich violet color. It is valuable for its powerful antiseptic properties, and is applied externally as a counterirritant. It is also extensively used in photography and organic synthesis. See ELEMENT. Also **i·o·din** (ī′ə·din). [<F *iode* <Gk. *iōdēs* violetlike (<*ion* a violet + *eidos* form) + -INE² (as in *chlorine*); from its violet–colored vapor]

iodine number *Biochem.* The number of milligrams of iodine absorbed from an iodine solution by 100 grams of fat.

i·o·dize (ī′ə·dīz) *v.t.* **·dized, ·diz·ing** 1 To treat with or bring under the influence of iodine. 2 To add iodine to: to *iodize* collodion. 3 To expose to the vapor of iodine. [<IOD- + -IZE] —**i′o·diz′er** *n.* —**i′o·di·za′tion** *n.*

iodo– *combining form* Denoting the presence of, or relation to, iodine: *iodoform.* Also, before vowels, *iod–.*

I·o·do·bis·mi·tol (ī′ə·dō·biz′mə·tol, ·tol) *n.* Proprietary name for a bismuth sodium iodide solution in ethylene glycol with acetic acid: used by intramuscular injection in the treatment of syphilis. [<IODO-+ BISMUTH (arbitrarily altered) + -OL]

i·o·do·form (ī·ō′də·fôrm) *n. Chem.* A light–yellow crystalline compound, CHI_3, formed by the action of iodine on alcohol in an alkaline solution: used in medicine as an antiseptic. [<IODO- + FORM(YL)]

i·o·dol (ī′ə·dōl, -dol) *n. Chem.* A yellowish–brown crystalline compound, C_4I_4NH: used as a substitute for iodoform. [<IOD- + -OL]

i·o·dom·e·try (ī′ə·dom′ə·trē) *n. Chem.* 1 The determination of iodine by volumetric methods. 2 The art of making quantitative determination by the use of standard solutions of iodine, or by the liberation of iodine from an iodide. Also *iodimetry.*[<IODO- + -METRY] —**i·o·do·met·ric** (ī′ə·dō·met′rik) or **·ri·cal** *adj.*

i·o·dous (ī′ə·dəs) *adj. Chem.* 1 Of, pertaining to, or like iodine. 2 Containing iodine in its lower valency. [<IOD- + -OUS]

I·ol·cus (ī·ol′kəs) In classical geography, a city at the foot of Mount Pelion in Thessaly, NE Greece, near modern Volos; traditionally the home of Jason.

i·o·lite (ī′ə·līt) *n.* Cordierite. [<Gk. *ion* violet + -LITE]

i·o moth (ī′ō) A large American moth *(Automeris io)* having conspicuous eyelike spots on the hind wings. The caterpillar has stinging spines. [See IO]

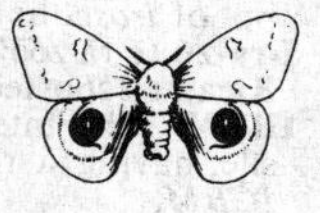

IO MOTH

i·on (ī′ən, ī′on) *n. Physics* 1 An electrically charged atom, radical, or molecule, formed by the dissolution of an electrolyte and becoming a *cation* with a positive (+) charge if electrons are lost, or an *anion* with a negative (−) charge if electrons are gained. Thus, a molecule of sodium chloride, NaCl, in aqueous solution, dissociates into the sodium cation Na^+, with a deficiency of one electron, and the chlorine anion Cl^-, with an excess of one electron. 2 In a gas, an electrified particle produced in various ways, as by the action of an electric current or of rays such as the ultraviolet and certain radium emanations. See HYDROGEN ION. [<Gk. *ion,* neut. of *iōn,* ppr. of *ienai* go]

–ion *suffix of nouns* 1 Action or process of: *communion.* 2 Condition or state of being: *union.* 3 Result of: *opinion.* Also *–ation, –tion.* [<F *ion* <L *-io, -ionis*]

I·o·na (ī·ō′nə) An island of the Inner Hebrides, Scotland; 1½ by 3½ miles; site of monastery established by St. Columba in 563: also *Icolmkill.*

ion engine A reaction engine producing a small but sustained thrust by emission of positive ions accelerated in an electrical field. Compare PLASMA ENGINE.

ion exchange *Chem.* 1 A process whereby ions may be reversibly interchanged at the boundary of a liquid and solid in contact, the composition of the solid not being altered: used especially in water softening with zeolites and in the purification of solutions. 2 A similar process occurring between immiscible electrolytes.

ion exchange resin *Chem.* Any of a class of substances which yield cations and anions in the ion–exchange process.

I·o·ni·a (ī·ō′nē·ə) The coastal region and adjacent islands of western Asia Minor, anciently colonized by Greeks.

I·o·ni·an (ī·ō′nē·ən) *adj.* Pertaining to Ionia, its people, or their culture. —*n.* A member of one of the four major tribes of ancient Greece. The Ionians settled eastern Greece and Ionia about 1100 B.C.

Ionian Islands An island group in the Ionian Sea off the western coast of Greece; 963 square miles.

Ionian Sea A part of the Mediterranean between Greece and Sicily and the foot of the Italian peninsula.

i·on·ic (ī·on′ik) *adj. Chem.* 1 Of, pertaining to, or containing ions. 2 Designating the theory of electrolytic dissociation, according to which the molecules of all acids, bases, and salts dissociate in varying degrees when they are dissolved in water and certain other solvents.

I·on·ic (ī·on′ik) *adj.* 1 Ionian. 2 *Archit.* Of or pertaining to an order of Greek architecture characterized by scroll–like ornaments of the capital. See illustration under CAPITAL. 3 In prosody, designating a metrical foot, consisting either of two long and two short syllables (– – ⏑ ⏑) and called **greater Ionic,** or *Ionic a majore,* or of two short and two long (⏑ ⏑ – –), when it is called **lesser Ionic** or *Ionic a minore.* —*n.* 1 In prosody, an Ionic foot; also, a verse composed of Ionic feet. 2 A dialect of ancient Greek spoken in Ionia and in most of the Aegean Islands, divided into **Old Ionic** or **Epic,** the language of the Homeric poems, and **New Ionic,** of the fifth century B.C., used by Herodotus and Hippocrates. 3 *Printing* A style of type with a large, heavy roman face. [<L *Ionicus* <Gk. *Iōnikos*]

ionic crystal *Physics* A crystal formed chiefly of ions held together by electrostatic attraction.

i·o·ni·um (ī·ō′nē·əm) *n. Physics* The immediate precursor of radium in the radioactive disintegration of uranium: it is an isotope of thorium, of mass 230 and a half–life of about 80,000 years.[<ION + (URAN)IUM; from its ionizing action]

i·on·i·za·tion (ī′ən·ə·zā′shən, -ī·zā′-) *n.* 1 *Chem.* The breaking apart of electrolytes into anions and cations, by solution or other process, mechanical or chemical; electrolytic dissociation. 2 *Physics* The generation of ions by radioactivity. —**degree of ionization** The fraction of the molecules of an electrolyte dissociated or ionized at a given temperature and concentration of solution, usually expressed as a percentage.

ionization chamber *Physics* An enclosed cylinder containing two oppositely charged electrodes and air or other gas: used to determine the intensity of an X–ray beam by its ionizing effect upon the gas.

ionization potential *Physics* The energy, expressed in electron volts, required to remove an electron from an atom by impact: 5.13 is the *ionization potential* for sodium.

i·on·ize (ī′ən·īz) *v.t.* **·ized, ·iz·ing** 1 To convert, totally or in part, into ions. 2 To divide into ions. —**i′on·iz′a·ble** *adj.* —**i′on·iz′er** *n.*

i·on·o·gen·ic (ī′ən·ə·jen′ik) *adj. Chem.* Forming or supplying ions, as an electrolyte.

i·o·none (ī′ə·nōn) *n. Chem.* Either of two isomeric compounds, $C_{13}H_{20}O$, related to the terpenes and containing the aromatic principle of violet and orrisroot. [<Gk. *ion* violet + -ONE]

i·on·o·pause (ī·on′ə·pôz) *n.* The zone of transition between the ionosphere and the exosphere, beginning at a height of about 400 miles beyond the earth's surface. [<IONO- (< ION)+ PAUSE]

i·on·o·sphere (ī·on′ə·sfir) *n.* An upper layer of the earth's atmosphere above the mesosphere consisting of several layers subject to ionization, with seasonal variations: it is a part of the Heaviside layer responsible for the reflection of radio waves [<IONO- (<ION) + SPHERE]

i·on·to·pho·re·sis (ī·on′to·fə·rē′sis) *n. Med.* Treatment by the introduction of ions into the body; therapeutic ionization of affected organs and tissues. Also **i·on·o·ther·a·py** (ī′ən·ō·ther′·ə·pē). [<*ionto-,* combining form of ION + PHORESIS]

i·o·pho·bi·a (ī′ə·fō′bē·ə) *n.* Toxicophobia. [< Gk. *ios* venom + -PHOBIA]

I·os (ē′os) An Aegean island in the Cyclades; 43 square miles: also *Nios.*

Iosh·kar–O·la (yosh·kär′o·lä′) The capital of Mari Autonomous S.S.R.

i·o·ta (ī·ō′tə) *n.* 1 The ninth letter and fourth vowel in the Greek alphabet (Ι, ι): corresponding to English I, i. As a numeral it denotes 10. 2 A small or insignificant mark or part. See synonyms under PARTICLE. [<L < Gk. *iōta.* Doublet of JOT.]

i·o·ta·cism (ī·ō′tə·siz′əm) *n.* Over–frequent use of the letter iota (I) or of its sound, also, the practice in modern Greek of giving the pronunciation of iota (ē) to certain diphthongs and long vowels. [<LL *iotacismus* <Gk. *iōtakismos*]

I O U 1 A paper having on it these letters (meaning *I owe you*) followed by a named sum and duly signed. 2 A symbol and acknowledgment of indebtedness. Also **I.O.U.**

I·o·wa (ī′ə·wə) *n. pl.* **·was** or **·wa** 1 One of a North American tribe of Siouan Indians, formerly living in Minnesota, and now on reservations in Oklahoma and Kansas. 2 The Siouan language of this tribe.

I·o·wa (ī′ə·wə, ī′ə·wä) A north central State of the United States; 56,280 square miles; capital, Des Moines; entered the Union Dec. 28, 1846; nickname *Hawkeye State*: abbr. IA —. **I′o·wan** *adj.* & *n.*

Iowa River A river in Iowa, flowing 329 miles SE to the Mississippi.

ip·e·cac (ip′ə·kak) *n.* 1 A South American creeping or shrubby plant *(Cephaelis ipecacuanha)* of the madder family, yielding the

medicinal alkaloids emetine and cephaeline.
2 An extract or tincture of the root of this plant, generally used as an emetic, but also having cathartic properties; also, the root itself. Also **ip·e·cac·u·an·ha** (ip'ə-kak'yōō-ä'nə). [<Pg. *ipecacuanha* <Tupian *ipi-kaa-guéne* < *ipe* little + *kaa* tree, herb + *guéne* causing sickness]

ipecacuanha wine Wine in which ipecac has been steeped: used medicinally.

Iph·i·cles (if'ə-klēz) In Greek legend, the son of Amphitryon and Alcmene; twin brother of Hercules.

Iph·i·ge·ni·a (if'ə-jə-nī'ə) In Greek legend, the daughter of Agamemnon and Clytemnestra, sacrificed by her father at Aulis to Artemis, who rescued her and made her a priestess in Tauris: here she later rescued her brother Orestes and fled with him to Greece.

I·pin (ē'pin') A city on the Yangtze in south central China: formerly *Suchow*.

I·poh (ē'pō) The capital of Perak State, Malaya.

ip·o·moe·a (ip'ə-mē'ə) *n.* Any of a large genus (*Ipomoea*) of mainly tropical herbs, or, rarely, shrubs or trees, of the convolvulus family, with trumpet-shaped flowers, including the morning-glory and sweet potato. Also **ip'o·me'a.** [<NL <Gk. *ips, ipos* sort of horn + *homoios* like]

IPOMOEA

Ip·po·li·tov-I·va·nov (ē-pô·lē'tôf-ē-vä'nôf), **Mik·hail,** 1859–1935, Russian composer.

Ip·sam·bul (ip·säm·bool') See ABU SIMBEL.

ip·se dix·it (ip'sē dik'sit) *Latin* Literally, he himself has said; hence, a dogmatic assertion; dictum. [<L]

ip·sis·si·ma ver·ba (ip·sis'ə-mə vûr'bə) *Latin* The very words; the exact language. In a different grammatical case, *ipsissimis verbis,* the phrase means "in the very words."

ip·so fac·to (ip'sō fak'tō) *Latin* By the fact itself, or in and by the very fact or act: *ipso facto* outlawed. [<L]

ip·so ju·re (ip'sō jŏŏr'ē) *Latin* By the law itself.

Ip·sus (ip'səs) An ancient town in southern Phrygia, Asia Minor; scene of a victory of Lysimachus, 301 B.C.

Ips·wich (ips'wich) The county town of Suffolk, SE England.

I·qui·que (ē-kē'kä) A port in northern Chile.

I·qui·tos (ē-kē'tōs) A port on the upper Amazon, NE Peru.

ir– Assimilated var. of IN-¹ and IN-².

i·ra·cund (ī'rə-kund) *adj.* Angry, or easily angered; choleric; passionate. [<L *iracundus* < *ira* anger] — **i'ra·cun'di·ty** *n.*

i·ra·de (i·rä'dē) *n.* A decree of the Sublime Porte or of any Moslem ruler. Also **i·ra'deh.** [<Turkish <Arabic *irādah* will, desire]

I·ran (i·ran', ē·rän') A kingdom of SW Asia; 630,000 square miles; capital, Teheran: officially called *Persia* until March, 1935.

I·ra·ni·an (i·rä'nē·ən) *adj.* Belonging or relating to Iran or Persia. —*n.* **1** A modern Persian. **2** A member of the ancient Persian or Iranian race. **3** A branch of the Indo-Iranian subfamily of Indo-European languages, embracing Afghan or Pushtu in the east and, in the west, Avestan, Old Persian, Middle Persian, Scythian, etc., modern Persian, Kurdish, and other ancient and modern tongues of Persia, Caucasia, etc. — **I·ran·ic** (i·ran'ik) *adj.*

Iranian Plateau The upland, mostly in Iran, extending from the Tigris to the Indus.

I·raq (i·rak', ē·räk') A kingdom approximately coextensive with ancient Mesopotamia in SW Asia; 168,040 square miles; capital, Baghdad; with Jordan, formed the Arab Federation, 1958. Also **I·rak'.**

I·ra·qi (ē·rä'kē) *adj.* Of or pertaining to Iraq, its inhabitants, or their language. —*n.* **1** A native or inhabitant of the kingdom of Iraq. **2** The dialect of Arabic spoken in Iraq.

i·ras·ci·ble (i·ras'ə·bəl, ī-) *adj.* **1** Prone to anger; choleric. **2** Caused by anger. See synonyms under HOT. [<F <LL *irascibilis* < *irasci* be angry < *ira* anger] — **i·ras'ci·bil'i·ty, i·ras'ci·ble·ness** *n.* — **i·ras'ci·bly** *adv.*

i·ra·ta·men·te (ē·rä'tä·men'tā) *adv. Music* Angrily; indignantly; passionately: a direction as to the style of playing a composition or passage. [<Ital.]

i·rate (ī'rāt, ī·rāt') *adj.* Moved to anger; wrathful. See synonyms under BITTER. [<L *iratus,* pp. of *irasci* be angry] — **i'rate·ly** *adv.*

I·ra·zú (ē·rä·zōō') A volcano in central Costa Rica; 11,260 feet.

IRBM The intermediate range ballistic missile, having a range of 1500 miles. Compare *ICBM.*

ire (īr) *n.* Strong resentment; wrath; anger. See synonyms under ANGER. [<OF <L *ira* anger]

ire·ful (īr'fəl) *adj.* Full of ire; wrathful; angry. — **ire'ful·ly** *adv.* — **ire'ful·ness** *n.*

Ire·land (īr'lənd) The westernmost and second largest of the British Isles; 31,838 square miles; divided into: **1 Northern Ireland,** a part of the United Kingdom comprising six counties and two boroughs of the former province of Ulster in the north; 5,237 square miles; capital, Belfast; and **2** the **Republic of Ireland,** independent (1949) of the Commonwealth of Nations and comprising 26 southern counties; 26,600 square miles; capital, Dublin: formerly *Irish Free State* (Irish *Saorstat Eireann*), 1922–37; *Eire,* 1937–49.

I·re·nae·us (ī'rə·nē'əs), **Saint** Greek church father of the second century; bishop of Lyons.

I·rene (ī·rēn'; *Ger.* ē·rā'nə, *Ital.* ē·rä'nä) A feminine personal name. Also *Fr.* **I·rène** (ē·ren'). [<Gk., peace]
— **Irene** In Greek mythology, the goddess of peace, daughter of Zeus and Themis: identified with the Roman *Pax.*
— **Irene,** 752–803, Byzantine empress, wife of Leo IV, East Roman emperor.

i·ren·ic (ī·ren'ik) *adj.* Tending to promote peace; conciliatory. Also **i·ren'i·cal.** [<Gk. *eirēnikos* < *eirēnē* peace]

i·ren·ics (ī·ren'iks) *n.* Irenical theology; theology concerned with promoting Christian unity.

Ire·ton (īr'tən), **Henry,** 1611–51, English parliamentary general.

i·ri·da·ceous (ī'rə·dā'shəs, ir'ə-) *adj.* Relating to a family (*Iridaceae*) of perennial herbs, the iris family. [<Gk. *iris, iridos* iris + -ACEOUS]

ir·i·dec·to·my (ir'ə·dek'tə·mē, ī'rə-) *n. Surg.* The operation of removing a part of the iris. [<IRID(O)- + -ECTOMY]

ir·i·des·cence (ir'ə·des'əns) *n. Optics* The many-colored appearance caused by the interference effect of light rays striking the outer and inner surface layers of various bodies, as clouds, mother-of-pearl, oil films, etc. [<IRIDESCENT <Gk. *iris, iridos* rainbow + -ESCENCE] — **ir'i·des'cent** (ir'ə-) *adj.* — **ir'i·des'cent·ly** *adv.*

i·rid·ic (i·rid'ik, ī-) *adj. Chem.* Of, pertaining to, or containing iridium in its higher valence: *iridic* bromide, IrBr₄. [<IRID(IUM) + -IC]

i·rid·i·um (i·rid'ē·əm, ī-) *n.* A brittle, silver-gray, metallic element (symbol Ir) of extreme hardness belonging to the platinum group: discovered by William Tennant in 1804. It is used in certain alloys, for penpoints, jewelry, etc. [<NL <L *iris, iridis* rainbow <Gk. *Iris* goddess of the rainbow + -IUM; from the iridescence of some of its salts]

irido– *combining form Med.* Iris of the eye: *iridotomy.* Also, before vowels, **irid-.** [<Gk. *iris, iridos* the iris]

i·rid·o·cyte (i·rid'ə·sīt, ī-) *n. Biol.* A cell having the power to produce color in an organism, especially a cell located in the integument of the cuttlefish. [<L *iris, iridos* rainbow <Gk. *iris* + -CYTE]

ir·i·do·ple·gi·a (ir'ə·dō·plē'jē·ə, ī'rə-) *n. Pathol.* Paralysis of the sphincter of the iris, resulting in an inability of the pupil to contract. — **ir'i·do·pleg'ic** (-plej'ik, -plē'jik) *adj.*

ir·i·dos·mi·um (ir'ə·doz'mē·əm, -dos'-, ī'rə-) *n.* Osmiridium. Also **ir·i·dos·mine** (ir'ə·doz'min, -dos'-, ī'rə-). [<IRID(IUM) + OSMIUM]

ir·i·dot·o·my (ir'ə·dot'ə·mē, ī'rə-) *n. pl.* **·mies** *Surg.* Any incision into the iris. [<IRIDO- + -TOMY]

I·ri·go·yen (ē·rē·gō'yen), **Hipólito,** 1852–1933,

president of Argentina 1916–22, and 1928–30.

i·ris (ī'ris) *n. pl.* **i·ris·es** or **ir·i·des** (ir'ə·dēz, ī'rə-) **1** *Anat.* The colored circular, contractile membrane between the cornea and the lens of the eye, whose central perforation is occupied by the pupil. See illustration under EYE. **2** *Bot.* Any one of a notable genus (*Iris*) of plants with sword-shaped leaves and large handsome flowers: the cultivated varieties are also known as *fleur-de-lis.* **3** The orris. **4** The rainbow; any similar iridescent appearance. **5** Rainbow quartz. [<L *iris* rainbow, iris <Gk. *iris*]

IRIS
a. Bearded iris.
b. Japanese iris.
c. Siberian iris.

I·ris (ī'ris) In Greek mythology the goddess of the rainbow, attendant of Zeus and Hera; in Homer's *Illiad,* the messenger of the gods.

I·ris (ī'ris) The ancient name for the YESIL IRMAK, Turkey.

i·ris·at·ed (ī'rə·sā'tid) *adj.* Iridescent. — **i'ris·a'tion** *n.*

iris diaphragm An adjustable diaphragm, like the iris of the eye, designed for regulating the size of an aperture, as in a camera lens.

i·rised (ī'rist) *adj.* Having colors like those of the rainbow.

I·rish (ī'rish) *adj.* Pertaining to Ireland, its people, or their language. — *n.* **1** The people of Ireland collectively: with *the.* **2** The ancient or modern language of Ireland, belonging to the Goidelic branch of the Celtic languages; Irish Gaelic: sometimes called *Erse.* Historically, the language is divided into **Old Irish,** from approximately 700 to 1100; **Middle Irish,** from 1100 to 1600; and **Modern Irish,** after 1600. **3** The dialect of English spoken in Ireland; Irish English. **4** *Colloq.* Temper: He got his *Irish* up. [ME *Irisc,* OE *Iras* <ON *Irar* the Irish <OIrish *Eriu* Ireland. Cf. EIRE.]

Irish bridge *Engin.* A surface of reinforced concrete laid on the bed of a river, over which flood waters may run without causing damage.

Irish English See IRISH (def. 3).

I·rish·er (ī'rish·ər) *n. U.S. Slang* An Irish settler in the United States.

Irish Free State A former name for the Republic of Ireland. See under IRELAND.

Irish Gaelic See IRISH (def 2).

I·rish·ism (ī'rish·iz'əm) *n.* **1** An expression or idiom characteristic of the Irish; Hibernianism. **2** Irish character or traits collectively.

I·rish·man (ī'rish·mən) *n. pl.* **·men** (-mən) A man of Irish birth or race.

Irish moss A seaweed (*Chondrus crispus*) found off the coasts of Ireland and North America: used as a food, especially in blancmange, and in medicine and industry; carrageen.

Irish potato The common or white potato (*Solanum tuberosum*), as distinguished from the sweet potato.

Irish Republican Army An anti-British secret organization originally organized in behalf of Irish independence and outlawed by the Irish government in 1936, but continuing terrorist activities to force annexation of Northern Ireland.

I·rish·ry (ī'rish·rē) *n. pl.* **·ries** **1** The Irish collectively, or a company of Irish. **2** Irishism.

Irish Sea The arm of the Atlantic separating Ireland from England, Scotland, and Wales; 130 miles long, 150 miles wide.

Irish setter See under SETTER.

Irish stew A stew made originally with mutton, potatoes, and onions; now with almost any meat and vegetables.

Irish terrier See under TERRIER.

Irish water spaniel See under SPANIEL.

Irish wolfhound A large, powerful dog of an ancient breed used in hunting wolf and elk; characterized by straight, heavy forelegs and a hard, rough coat, usually gray, brindle, black, fawn, or white in color.

IRISH WOLFHOUND
(From 30 to 38 inches high at the shoulder)

I·rish·wom·an (ī'rish·wŏŏm'ən) n. pl. **·wom·en** (-wim'in) A woman of Irish birth or race.

i·ri·tis (ī·rī'tis) n. Pathol. Inflammation of the iris. Also **i·ri·si·tis** (ī'rə·sī'tis). [<NL <L iris iris + -ITIS] — **i·rit·ic** (ī·rit'ik) adj.

irk (ûrk) v.t. To annoy or weary; irritate; disgust; vex. [ME irken; origin uncertain]

irk·some (ûrk'səm) adj. Troublesome or tiresome; tedious. See synonyms under TEDIOUS, TROUBLESOME, WEARISOME. — **irk'some·ly** adv. — **irk'some·ness** n.

Ir·kutsk 1 A region (oblast) in southern Siberia, Russia, near Lake Baikal in central Asia. 2 The chief city of this region, pop. 640,000.

i·ron (ī'ərn) n. 1 A tough, abundant, malleable, ductile, and strongly magnetic metallic element (symbol Fe). Easily oxidized in moist air and attacked by many reagents, iron is seldom obtained in its pure, silver-white form, but occurs widely in both ferrous and ferric compounds, and combines in varying proportions with carbon, phosphorus, silicon, sulfur, etc. Typical commercial varieties are: cast iron, pig iron, steel, and wrought iron. 2 An iron tool, weapon, utensil, or anything composed of iron. 3 pl. Fetters, especially shackles for the feet. 4 A metal-headed golf club with the face slightly laid back. 5 In the leather industry, a unit of thickness, equal to one forty-eighth of an inch. 6 A flatiron. — **in irons** 1 Fettered. 2 Naut. Unable to cast away on either side; in stays: said of a vessel coming about into the wind. — adj. 1 Made of iron. 2 Resembling iron; hard; rude; heavy; also, firm; unyielding: an iron will. 3 Of or pertaining to the Iron Age. — v.t. 1 To smooth or press with an iron implement, as cloth or clothing. 2 To fetter. 3 To furnish or arm with iron. — v.i. 4 To smooth or press cloth, clothing, etc., with an iron implement. — **to iron out** To smooth out; remove. [OE īren, īsen, isern] — **i'ron·er** n.

Iron Age Archeol. The last and most advanced of the three roughly classified prehistoric stages of human progress, preceded by the Stone Age and Bronze Age.

i·ron·bark (ī'ərn·bärk') n. Any one of a genus (Eucalyptus) of large, valuable Australian timber trees having a solid rather than a fibrous, stringy, or scaly bark.

iron black Finely divided antimony.

i·ron·bound (ī'ərn·bound') adj. 1 Bound with iron. 2 Faced or surrounded with rocks; rugged. 3 Hard to change; unyielding.

i·ron·clad (ī'ərn·klad') adj. 1 Protected by iron or steel armor, as warships. 2 Not to be evaded; rigorous. 3 Strong. — n. A warship sheathed with armor: a term not common since the Spanish-American War.

iron curtain An impenetrable barrier of secrecy and censorship: a term made current by Winston Churchill in a speech in Fulton, Missouri (1946), to describe the dividing line between Western Europe and the Soviet sphere of influence.

i·rone (ī·rōn') n. Chem. A colorless, volatile, aromatic oil, $C_{14}H_{22}O$, extracted from orrisroot and used in perfumery. [<IR(IS) + -ONE]

iron froth A spongy variety of hematite.

Iron Gate A narrow pass in the valley of the Danube, SW Rumania, on the Yugoslav border: German Eisernes Tor, Rumanian Por·ti·le de Fier (pôr'tsē'le de fyer'). Also **Iron Gates**.

iron glance A crystallized variety of hematite.

iron gray The color of freshly cut or broken iron. Also **iron grey**. — **i'ron·gray'** adj.

i·ron-hand·ed (ī'ərn·han'did) adj. Severe and rigorous; despotic.

iron hat See GOSSAN.

iron horse A railroad engine.

i·ron·ic (ī·ron'ik) adj. 1 Conveying a meaning that contradicts the literal sense of the words used: an ironic comment. 2 Being the reverse of what was expected: an ironic event. 3 Of the nature of or given to the use of irony. Also **i·ron'i·cal** (-i·kəl). — **i·ron'i·cal·ly** adv. — **i·ron'i·cal·ness** n.

i·ron·ing (ī'ər·ning) n. The process of pressing and smoothing with flatirons.

iron lung A cabinetlike enclosure used in the treatment of pulmonary disorders, fitted with automatically operated bellows, in order to promote the rhythmic action of the impaired lungs and thus maintain respiration in the patient who lies within it, his head only exposed: also called Drinker respirator.

i·ron·mas·ter (ī'ərn·mas'ter, -mäs'-) n. A manufacturer of iron.

i·ron·mon·ger (ī'ərn·mung'gər, -mong'-) n. A dealer in iron articles.

i·ron·mon·ger·y (ī'ərn·mung'gər·ē, -mong'-) n. pl. **·ger·ies** 1 Iron articles collectively; hardware. 2 Trade in such articles. 3 An ironmonger's place of business. 4 Humorously, firearms.

iron putty See under PUTTY.

iron pyrites 1 Ordinary pyrites; fool's-gold. 2 Marcasite. 3 Pyrrhotite.

i·ron·side (ī'ərn·sīd') n. A person or thing of tremendous strength or endurance.

I·ron·sides (ī'ərn·sīdz') n. pl. 1 Nickname of Edmund II of England. 2 Nickname of Oliver Cromwell. 3 One of Cromwell's soldiers. — **Old Ironsides** See CONSTITUTION.

i·ron·smith (ī'ərn·smith') n. A worker in iron; a blacksmith.

i·ron·stone (ī'ərn·stōn') n. Any mineral or rock containing iron; iron ore.

i·ron·ware (ī'ərn·wâr') n. Hardware; iron utensils.

i·ron·weed (ī'ərn·wēd') n. An herb or shrub (genus Vernonia) of the composite family, from three to six feet high, with alternate leaves, and heads of perfect, tubular, mostly purple or reddish flowers.

i·ron·wood (ī'ərn·wŏŏd') n. Any of various trees of unusually hard, heavy, or strong wood; especially, the Catalina ironwood (Lyonothamnus floribundus) of southern California and the hop hornbeam (Ostrya virginiana) of the eastern United States.

i·ron·work (ī'ərn·wûrk') n. Anything made of iron, as parts of a building. — **i'ron·work'er** n.

i·ron·works (ī'ərn·wûrks') n. sing. & pl. An establishment for the manufacture of iron or of heavy ironwork.

i·ron·wort (ī'ərn·wûrt') n. Any of various plants of the mint family, especially the red hemp nettle.

i·ro·ny¹ (ī'rə·nē) n. pl. **·nies** 1 The use of words to signify the opposite of what they usually express; ridicule disguised as praise or compliment; covert sarcasm or satire. 2 The feigning of ignorance, as in the Socratic method of questions and answers: hence **Socratic irony**. 3 A condition of affairs or events exactly the reverse of what was expected: the irony of fate. [<L ironia <Gk. eirōneia < eirōn dissembler < erein question, ask]

i·ron·y² (ī'ər·nē) adj. Of or like iron.

Ir·o·quoi·an (ir'ə·kwoi'ən) n. 1 A large North American Indian linguistic stock including the Cayuga, Cherokee, Conestoga, Erie, Mohawk, Oneida, Onondaga, Seneca, Tuscarora, Wyandot, and certain other tribes. 2 A member of any of the Iroquois tribes. — adj. Of or pertaining to the Iroquois Indians, or to any of their languages.

Ir·o·quois (ir'ə·kwoi, -kwoiz) n. pl. **·quois** 1 A member of any of the powerful North American Indian tribes comprising the confederacy known as the Five Nations. See FIVE NATIONS. 2 A member of any tribe belonging to the Iroquoian linguistic stock. [<F <Algonquian Irinakoiw, lit., real adders]

ir·ra·di·ant (i·rā'dē·ənt) adj. Sending out rays of light. [<L irradians, -antis, ppr. of irradiare shine] — **ir·ra'di·an·cy**, **ir·ra'di·ance** n.

ir·ra·di·ate (i·rā'dē·āt) v. **·at·ed**, **·at·ing** v.t.

1 To direct light upon; light up; illuminate. 2 To make clear or understandable; enlighten. 3 To send forth in or as in rays of light; diffuse; radiate. 4 To treat with or subject to X-rays, ultraviolet light, or other radiant energy. 5 To heat with radiant energy. — v.i. 6 To emit rays; shine. 7 To become radiant. [<L irradiatus, pp. of irradiare < in- thoroughly + radiare shine < radius ray] — **ir·ra'di·a·tive** adj. — **ir·ra'di·a·tor** n.

ir·ra·di·a·tion (i·rā'dē·ā'shən) n. 1 The act of irradiating. 2 The state of being irradiated. 3 Rays emitted: the irradiation of a candle. 4 Optics An apparent enlargement of a bright object, when seen against a dark background, due to the fact that the rays of light do not converge accurately to a focus upon the retina. 5 The application, to a person, substance, or object, of any form of radiant energy, for therapeutic, preservative, or other purposes. 6 The amount or intensity of radiation falling on a surface in a given time. 7 Physiol. A diffusion or branching out of afferent nerve impulses or of conditioned reflexes.

ir·ra·tion·al (i·rash'ən·əl) adj. 1 Not possessed of or not exercising reasoning powers. 2 Math. a Pertaining to an irrational number. b Denoting an algebraic expression containing variables that are irreducible, as $\sqrt{-1}$, $\sqrt[3]{x^2}$. Compare RATIONAL. 3 Contrary to reason; absurd. 4 In Greek and Latin prosody, not keeping the proper ratio between thesis and arsis, as a long syllable used in place of a short one. See synonyms under ABSURD, INSANE. [<L irrationalis] — **ir·ra'tion·al·ly** adv.

ir·ra·tion·al·ism (i·rash'ən·əl·iz'əm) n. A belief or philosophy that is not grounded in reason.

ir·ra·tion·al·i·ty (i·rash'ə·nal'ə·tē) n. pl. **·ties** 1 The state of lacking reason or understanding. 2 Something irrational or absurd. Also **ir·ra'tion·al·ness**.

irrational number See under NUMBER.

Ir·ra·wad·dy (ir'ə·wä'dē) A river rising in Tibet and flowing 1,000 miles south through Burma to the Bay of Bengal.

ir·re·cip·ro·cal (ir'i·sip'rə·kəl) adj. 1 Not reciprocal; wanting in mutual interaction, assistance, or exchange. 2 Designating a type of colony or group whose members do not contribute equally to the general welfare.

ir·re·claim·a·ble (ir'i·klā'mə·bəl) adj. That cannot be reclaimed or redeemed. — **ir're·claim'a·bil'i·ty**, **ir're·claim'a·ble·ness** n. — **ir're·claim'a·bly** adv.

ir·rec·on·cil·a·ble (i·rek'ən·sī'lə·bəl, i·rek'ən·sī'lə·bəl) adj. That cannot be reconciled: irreconcilable enemies. — n. One who will not agree or become reconciled: said especially of political factionists. — **ir·rec'on·cil'a·bil'i·ty**, **ir·rec'on·cil'a·ble·ness** n. — **ir·rec'on·cil'a·bly** adv.

ir·re·cov·er·a·ble (ir'i·kuv'er·ə·bəl) adj. That cannot be recovered or regained; irredeemable; lost beyond recall. — **ir're·cov'er·a·ble·ness** n. — **ir're·cov'er·a·bly** adv.

ir·re·cu·sa·ble (ir'i·kyōō'zə·bəl) adj. That cannot be rejected. [<F irrécusable <LL irrecusabilis < in- not + recusabilis that should be rejected < recusare reject] — **ir're·cu'sa·bly** adv.

ir·re·deem·a·ble (ir'i·dē'mə·bəl) adj. 1 Not to be redeemed or replaced by an equivalent. 2 That cannot be reclaimed; not to be atoned for or escaped from: an irredeemable scoundrel, crime, or slavery. 3 Not ended by payment of principal: an irredeemable annuity. — **ir're·deem'a·bly** adv.

ir·re·den·ta (ir'ā·den'tä) adj. Italian Unredeemed: said of a separated territory whose reunion with the mother country is sought.

Ir·re·den·tist (ir'i·den'tist) n. 1 One of a party formed in Italy about 1878 to secure the incorporation with that country of regions Italian in speech and race, but subject to other governments. 2 Any person or party that advocates the reunion with the "mother country" of a separate or separated national group or region. — adj. Of or pertaining to the Irredentists or their policies. [<Ital. irredentista <(Italia) irredenta unredeemed (Italy), fem. of irredento <L in- not + redemptus redeemed. See REDEEM.] — **Ir're·den'tism** n.

ir·re·duc·i·ble (ir′i·dōō′sə·bəl, -dyōō′-) *adj.* Not reducible.

ir·ref·ra·ga·ble (i·ref′rə·gə·bəl) *adj.* That cannot be refuted or disproved. [<LL *irrefragabilis* < *in-* not + *refragari* oppose] **— ir·ref′ra·ga·bil′i·ty, ir·ref′ra·ga·ble·ness** *n.* **— ir·ref′ra·ga·bly** *adv.*

ir·re·fran·gi·ble (ir′i·fran′jə·bəl) *adj.* **1** That cannot be broken or violated: an *irrefrangible* law. **2** Not susceptible of refraction: said of light rays. **— ir′re·fran′gi·bly** *adv.*

ir·ref·u·ta·ble (i·ref′yə·tə·bəl, ir′i·fyōō′tə·bəl) *adj.* Not refutable; that cannot be disproved; irrefragable, as an argument. **— ir·ref′u·ta·bil′i·ty** *n.* **— ir·ref′u·ta·bly** *adv.*

ir·re·gard·less (ir′i·gärd′lis) *adj.* & *adv.* *Illit.* Regardless: an incorrect or humorous usage.

ir·reg·u·lar (i·reg′yə·lər) *adj.* **1** Not regular; departing from or being out of the usual or proper form, order, course, method, proportion, etc. **2** Not conforming in action or character to rule, duty, discipline, etc.; lawless: *irregular* habits. **3** *Bot.* Exhibiting a want of symmetry in form and size: said of flowers in which the members of the various whorls differ from one another in size or shape. **4** Laboring under an ecclesiastical irregularity. See IRREGULARITY (def. 2). **5** Not belonging to a regular military force: *irregular* troops. **6** *Gram.* Not inflected or conjugated according to the most prevalent pattern: *irregular* verbs. See STRONG (def. 28). **7** *Law* Not according to rule; improper; not complying with legal formalities. **—** *n.* A person exercising a calling or profession without belonging to its regular organization or conforming to its regulations, as a soldier not in a regular military force. [<OF *irreguler* <Med. L *irregularis*] **— ir·reg′u·lar·ly** *adv.*

Synonyms (adj.): abnormal, anomalous, confused, crooked, desultory, devious, disorderly, dissolute, eccentric, erratic, exceptional, fitful, immoderate, inordinate, uneven, unnatural, unsettled, unsymmetrical, unsystematic, unusual, variable, vicious, wandering, wild. *Antonyms*: common, constant, established, fixed, formal, methodical, natural, normal, orderly, ordinary, periodical, punctual, regular, stated, steady, systematic, uniform, universal, unvarying, usual.

ir·reg·u·lar·i·ty (i·reg′yə·lar′ə·tē) *n.* *pl.* **·ties** **1** The condition of being irregular; an aberration, inconsistency, etc. **2** In the Roman Catholic and Anglican churches, an impediment to the taking or performing the functions of orders. See synonyms under DISORDER.

ir·rel·a·tive (i·rel′ə·tiv) *adj.* **1** Not relative; unconnected. **2** *Music* Having no common tone. **— ir·rel′a·tive·ly** *adv.* **— ir·rel′a·tive·ness** *n.*

ir·rel·e·vant (i·rel′ə·vənt) *adj.* Not relevant; not apposite; impertinent. See synonyms under ALIEN, INSIGNIFICANT. **— ir·rel′e·vance, ir·rel′e·van·cy** *n.* **— ir·rel′e·vant·ly** *adv.*

ir·re·liev·a·ble (ir′i·lē′və·bəl) *adj.* That cannot be relieved.

ir·re·lig·ion (ir′i·lij′ən) *n.* The state of being without or opposed to religion; unbelief; ungodliness. [<F *irréligion*] **— ir·re·lig′ion·ist** *n.*

ir·re·lig·ious (ir′i·lij′əs) *adj.* **1** Not religious; indifferent or hostile to religion. **2** Profane or sinful; ungodly. **— ir′re·lig′ious·ly** *adv.* **— ir′re·lig′ious·ness** *n.*

ir·rem·e·a·ble (i·rem′ē·ə·bəl, i·rē′mē-) *adj.* Admitting no return, irretraceable. [<L *irremeabilis* < *in-* not + *remeabilis* returning < *remeare* return < *re-* back + *meare* go] **— ir·rem′e·a·bly** *adv.*

ir·re·me·di·a·ble (ir′i·mē′dē·ə·bəl) *adj.* Not to be remedied; incurable; irreparable. [<L *irremediabilis*] **— ir′re·me′di·a·ble·ness** *n.* **— ir′re·me′di·a·bly** *adv.*

ir·re·mis·si·bil·i·ty (ir′i·mis′ə·bil′ə·tē) *n.* Impossibility of being forgiven; the state of being without remission. **— ir′re·mis′si·ble** *adj.* **— ir′re·mis′si·ble·ness** *n.* **— ir′re·mis′si·bly** *adv.*

ir·re·mov·a·bil·i·ty (ir′i·mōō′və·bil′ə·tē) *n.* **1** Perpetuity. **2** The quality of certain offices implying that the incumbent's appointment is for the term of his natural life.

ir·re·mov·a·ble (ir′i·mōō′və·bəl) *adj.* Not removable; permanent. **— ir′re·mov′a·bly** *adv.*

ir·rep·a·ra·ble (i·rep′ər·ə·bəl) *adj.* That cannot be repaired, rectified, or made amends for. **— ir·rep′a·ra·bil′i·ty, ir·rep′a·ra·ble·ness** *n.* **— ir·rep′a·ra·bly** *adv.*

ir·re·peal·a·ble (ir′i·pē′lə·bəl) *adj.* Not repealable.

ir·re·place·a·ble (ir′i·plā′sə·bəl) *adj.* Not capable of being replaced.

ir·re·plev·i·sa·ble (ir′i·plev′ə·sə·bəl) *adj.* *Law* That cannot be replevied. Also **ir′re·plev′i·a·ble** (-plev′ē·ə·bəl). [<IR- + AF *replevisable* repleviable <OF *replevir* replevy. See REPLEVIN.]

ir·re·pres·si·ble (ir′i·pres′ə·bəl) *adj.* Not repressible; that cannot be restrained. **— ir′re·pres′si·ble·ness, ir′re·pres′si·bil′i·ty** *n.* **— ir′re·pres′si·bly** *adv.*

ir·re·proach·a·ble (ir′i·prō′chə·bəl) *adj.* Not reproachable; blameless. [<F *irréprochable*] **— ir′re·proach′a·ble·ness** *n.* **— ir′re·proach′a·bly** *adv.*

ir·re·sis·ti·ble (ir′i·zis′tə·bəl) *adj.* Not resistible; that cannot be successfully withstood or opposed. **— ir′re·sis′ti·bil′i·ty, ir′re·sis′ti·ble·ness** *n.* **— ir′re·sis′ti·bly** *adv.*

ir·res·o·lu·ble (i·rez′ə·lōō·bəl) *adj.* **1** Not resoluble. **2** Not to be relieved; beyond help. **3** Not solvable; insoluble.

ir·res·o·lute (i·rez′ə·lōōt) *adj.* Not resolute or resolved; wavering; hesitating. **— ir·res′o·lute′·ly** *adv.* **— ir·res′o·lute′ness, ir·res′o·lu′tion** *n.*

Synonyms: capricious, doubtful, faint-hearted, faltering, fickle, fitful, half-hearted, hesitant, hesitating, indecisive, undecided, vacillating, wavering. Indecision denotes lack of intellectual conviction; irresolution denotes defect of volition, weakness of will. A thoughtful man may be *undecided* as to the course to take in perplexing circumstances; yet when decided he may act with promptness; an *irresolute* man lacks the nerve to act. Indecision commonly denotes a temporary state or condition, irresolution a trait of character. See FAINT, FICKLE. *Antonyms*: decided, determined, firm, persistent, resolute, resolved.

ir·re·solv·a·ble (ir′i·zol′və·bəl) *adj.* Not separable into parts; incapable of being resolved; not analyzable.

ir·re·spec·tive (ir′i·spek′tiv) *adj.* Lacking respect or relation; regardless: now used mostly with *of,* often adverbially. **— ir′re·spec′tive·ly** *adv.*

ir·re·spir·a·ble (ir′i·spīr′ə·bəl, ir·res′pi·rə·bəl) *adv.* Not respirable; not fit to be breathed. **— ir′re·spir′a·ble·ness** *n.*

ir·re·spon·si·ble (ir′i·spon′sə·bəl) *adj.* **1** Not accountable or amenable; not of sound mind. **2** Careless of responsibilities; unreliable. See synonyms under ARBITRARY. **—** *n.* A person who is irresponsible. **— ir′re·spon′si·bil′i·ty, ir′re·spon′si·ble·ness** *n.* **— ir′re·spon′si·bly** *adv.* **— ir′re·spon′sive** *adj.* **— ir′re·spon′sive·ness** *n.*

ir·re·ten·tion (ir′i·ten′shən) *n.* Lack of power of retaining. **— ir′re·ten′tive** *adj.* **— ir′re·ten′tive·ness** *n.*

ir·re·trace·a·ble (ir′i·trā′sə·bəl) *adj.* Not retraceable.

ir·re·triev·a·ble (ir′i·trē′və·bəl) *adj.* Not retrievable; irreparable. **— ir′re·triev′a·ble·ness, ir′re·triev′a·bil′i·ty** *n.* **— ir′re·triev′a·bly** *adv.*

ir·rev·er·ence (i·rev′ər·əns) *n.* **1** The quality or condition of being irreverent. **2** The condition of not being reverenced; lack of honor.

ir·rev·er·ent (i·rev′ər·ənt) *adj.* Lacking in proper reverence; without deep respect or veneration. **— ir·rev′er·ent·ly** *adv.*

ir·re·vers·i·ble (ir′i·vûr′sə·bəl) *adj.* **1** That cannot be reversed or inverted. **2** Of, pertaining to, or designating a chemical or biological process which can continue only in one direction, as the coagulation of the white of a raw egg by heat, a degenerative disease, or the path of a stimulus along the nerves. **— ir′re·vers′i·bil′i·ty, ir′re·vers′i·ble·ness** *n.* **— ir′re·vers′i·bly** *adv.*

ir·rev·o·ca·ble (i·rev′ə·kə·bəl) *adj.* Incapable of being revoked or repealed; unalterable. **— ir·rev′o·ca·bil′i·ty, ir·rev′o·ca·ble·ness** *n.* **— ir·rev′o·ca·bly** *adv.*

ir·ri·gate (ir′ə·gāt) *v.t.* **gat·ed, ·gat·ing** **1** To supply (land) with water by means of ditches or other artificial channels. **2** *Med.* To moisten, as a wound, with dropping water, or spray, jet, etc. **3** *Rare* To moisten; wet. [<L *irrigatus,* pp. of *irrigare* bring water to < *in-* to + *rigare* water] **— ir′ri·ga·ble** (ir′ə·gə·bəl) *adj.* **— ir′ri·ga′tor** *n.*

ir·ri·ga·tion (ir′ə·gā′shən) *n.* **1** The artificial watering of land. **2** The conditon of being irrigated. **3** *Med.* The steady maintenance of a flow of water over an affected part, for cleansing or therapeutic purposes. **— ir′ri·ga′·tion·al** *adj.*

ir·ri·ga·tion·ist (ir′ə·gā′shən·ist) *n.* One who conducts or is an authority on irrigation.

ir·ri·ga·tive (ir′ə·gā′tiv) *adj.* **1** Of or pertaining to irrigation. **2** Designed for irrigation.

ir·rig·u·ous (i·rig′yōō·əs) *adj.* **1** Watered or watery. **2** Supplying water. [<L *irriguus* < *in-* very + *riguus* watered < *rigare* wet, water]

ir·ri·ta·bil·i·ty (ir′ə·tə·bil′ə·tē) *n.* *pl.* **·ties** **1** The state of being irritable. **2** Susceptibility to anger or impatience. **3** *Biol.* **a** The responsiveness of living matter or protoplasm in general to changes in external conditions, manifested by motion, change of form, and in other ways; specifically, the response to stimuli characterizing certain tissues or organs of plants and animals. Compare STIMULUS. **b** A morbid condition of an organ, manifested by undue excitability under the action of a stimulant. Also **ir′ri·ta·ble·ness.**

ir·ri·ta·ble (ir′ə·tə·bəl) *adj.* **1** Showing impatience or ill temper on little provocation; irascible; petulant. **2** *Biol.* Responding easily to the action of external stimuli. **3** *Pathol.* Influenced to an abnormal degree by the action of stimulants or irritants. See synonyms under FRETFUL. [<L *irritabilis* < *irritare*] **— ir′ri·ta·bly** *adv.*

ir·ri·tant (ir′ə·tənt) *adj.* **1** Causing irritation. **2** *Med.* Irritating the eyes, nose, or digestive system: an *irritant* gas or smoke. **—** *n.* **1** *Pathol.* An agent of inflammation, pain, etc. **2** A provocation; spur. [<L *irritans, -antis,* ppr. of *irritare*] **— ir′ri·tan·cy** *n.*

ir·ri·tate (ir′ə·tāt) *v.t.* **·tat·ed, ·tat·ing** **1** To excite ill temper or impatience in; fret; exasperate. **2** To make sore or inflamed. **3** *Biol.* To excite, as organic tissue, to a characteristic function or action. See synonyms under AFFRONT, INCENSE[1], PIQUE[1]. [<L *irritatus,* pp. of *irritare* irritate]

ir·ri·ta·tion (ir′ə·tā′shən) *n.* **1** The act of irritating. **2** The state of being irritated. **3** *Pathol.* A condition of morbid irritability in an organ or part of the body.

ir·ri·ta·tive (ir′ə·tā′tiv) *adj.* **1** Serving to produce irritation. **2** Accompanied by irritation.

ir·ro·ta·tion·al (ir′rō·tā′shən·əl) *adj.* Without rotatory motion.

ir·rup·tion (i·rup′shən) *n.* **1** A breaking or rushing in. **2** A violent incursion. See synonyms under INVASION. [<L *irruptio, -onis* < *irruptus,* pp. of *irrumpere* burst in < *in-* in + *rumpere* break] **— ir·rup′tive** *adj.*

Ir·tish (ir·tish′) A river in western Siberian Russian S.F.S.R., flowing 1,844 miles west and NW to the Ob. Also **Ir·tysh′.**

Ir·ving (ûr′ving) A masculine personal name. [from a place name in Scotland]

Ir·ving (ûr′ving), **Sir Henry,** 1838–1905, English actor: original name *John Henry Brodribb.* **— Washington,** 1783–1859, U. S. author, historian, and humorist.

Ir·win (ûr′win) A masculine personal name. [Appar. var. of IRVING]

is (iz) Present tense, third person singular of BE. [OE]

is- Var. of ISO-.

I·saac (ī′zek, *Fr.* ē·zȧk′) A masculine personal name. Also *Ger.* **I·saak** (ē′zäk), *Latin* **I·sa·a·cus** (ī·sā′ə·kəs), *Ital.* **I·sac·co** (ē·zäk′kō), *Dan., Sw.* **I·sak** (ē′säk). [<Hebrew, laughter] **— Isaac** A Hebrew patriarch; son of Abraham and Sarah, and father of Esau and Jacob. *Gen.* xxi 3.

I·saacs (ī′zəks), **Rufus Daniel** See READING, MARQUIS OF.

Is·a·bel (iz′ə·bel, *Pg., Sp.* ē′sä·bel′) A feminine personal name. Also **Is·a·bel·la** (iz′ə·bel′ə, *Du.* iz′ä·bel′ä, *Ital.* ē′zä·bel′lä), **Is·a·belle** (iz′ə·bel, *Fr.* ē·zȧ·bel′, *Ger.* ē′zä·bel′ə), *Fr.* **I·sa·beau** (ē·zȧ·bō′). [<Hebrew, oath of Baal]

Is·a·bel (iz′ə·bel) See SANTA ISABEL (def. 2).

Is·a·bel·la I (iz′ə·bel′ə), 1451–1504, queen of Castile and León, wife of Ferdinand V of Aragon, with whom she unified Spain and subdued Granada; aided Columbus: known as Isabel la Católica.

i·sa·cous·tic (ī′sə·kōōs′tik, -kous′-) *adj.* *Physics* **1** Of or pertaining to equality in the clearness or intensity of sound. **2** Denoting a line, curve, or surface connecting all points within an enclosed space having the same acoustic characteristics. [<IS- + ACOUSTIC]

I·sae·us (ī·sē′əs), 420–348 B.C., Attic orator and rhetorician; reputed teacher of Demosthenes.

i·sa·go·ge (ī′sə·gō′jē) *n.* An introduction, as to a work of scholarship. [<L <Gk. *eisagōgē* < *eisagein* introduce < *eis-* into + *agein* lead] **— i′sa·gog′ic** (-goj′ik) *adj.*

i·sa·gog·ics (ī′sə·goj′iks) *n. pl.* (*construed as sing.*) That part of exegetical theology which has to do with the literary history of the books of the Bible, their inspiration, authorship, genuineness, and time and place of composition; Biblical introduction.

I·sa·iah (ī·zā′ə, ī·zī′ə) A masculine personal name. Also *Fr.* **I·sa·ie** (ē·zä·ē′), *Ital.* **I·sai·a** (ē·zī′ä), *Pg., Sp.* **I·sa·i·as** (ē′sä·ē′äs). [<Hebrew *yĕsha' yah* salvation]
— **Isaiah** A major Hebrew prophet of the eighth century B.C.; also, a book of the Old Testament attributed wholly or in part to him. See DEUTERO-ISAIAH. Also **I·sai′as** (-əs).

I·sa·ian (ī·zā′ən, ī·zī′-) *adj.* Pertaining or relating to Isaiah. Also **I·sa·ian·ic** (ī′zā·an′ik).

i·sal·lo·bar (ī·sal′ə·bär) *n. Meteorol.* A contour line on a chart connecting places which show equal changes in barometric pressure over a specified interval. [<ISO- + ALLO- + Gk. *baros* weight] **— i·sal′lo·bar′ic** *adj.*

i·san·drous (ī·san′drəs) *adj. Bot.* Having the stamens all similar and of the same number as the petals. [<ISO- + -ANDROUS]

i·sa·nom·al (ī′sə·nom′əl) *n. Meteorol.* A line on a map or chart, connecting all those places which exhibit the same types or degrees of meteorological anomaly, as of pressure, temperature, wind, etc. [<ISO- + ANOM(ALOUS)] **— i′sa·nom′a·lous** *adj.*

i·san·ther·ous (ī·san′thər·əs) *adj. Bot.* Having equal anthers. [<ISO- + Gk. *anthēros* flowery < *anthos* flower]

i·san·thous (ī·san′thəs) *adj. Bot.* Having regular flowers. [<ISO- + Gk. *anthos* flower]

I·sar (ē′zär) A river in the Tirol, Austria, and Bavaria, SW West Germany, flowing 163 miles NE to the Danube.

i·sa·tin (ī′sə·tin) *n. Chem.* A yellowish or brownish-red crystalline compound with a bitter taste, $C_8H_5NO_2$, obtained by oxidizing indigo: used as a reagent and in the manufacture of vat dyes. Also **i′sa·tine** (-tēn, -tin). [<L *isatis* woad <Gk. + -IN] **— i′sa·tin′ic** *adj.*

I·sau·ri·a (ī·sô′rē·ə) An ancient district of SE Asia Minor between Cilicia and Pisidia. **— I·sau′ri·an** *adj. & n.*

is·ba (ēs′bä) *n. Russian* A log cabin.

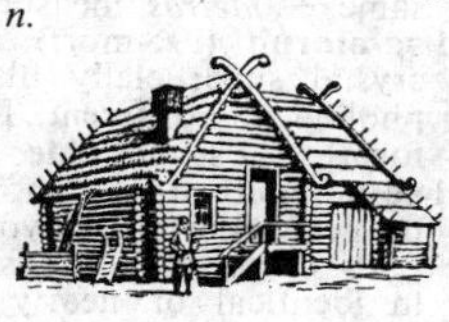

ISBA

Is·car·i·ot (is·kar′ē·ət) See JUDAS ISCARIOT.

is·che·mi·a (is·kē′mē·ə) *n. Pathol.* A localized deficiency of blood, as from a contracted blood vessel. Also **is·chae′mi·a.** [<NL <Gk. *ischein* hold, check + -EMIA] **— is·che′mic** *adj.*

Is·chia (ēs′kyä) An island in the Tyrrhenian Sea near Naples; 18 square miles.

is·chi·um (is′kē·əm) *n. pl.* **·chi·a** (-kē·ə) **1** *Anat.* The posterior part of the pelvic arch; in man, the part of the hip bone on which the body rests when sitting. **2** *Zool.* The third joint of any limb or lateral appendage in crustaceans. **3** *Entomol.* A side of the thorax in insects. Also **is·chi·on** (is′kē·ən). [<L <Gk. *ischion* hip, hip joint < *ischys* strong] **— is·chi·at·ic** (is′kē·at′ik) or **·ad·ic** (-ad′ik), **is′chi·ac** (-ak) or **is′ki·al** (-əl) *adj.*

I′se (īz) *Scot.* Contraction of *I shall.*

-ise Var. of -IZE.

I·se Bay (ē·se) An inlet of the Philippine Sea in central Honshu, Japan.

is·en·trop·ic (īs′en·trop′ik, -trō′pik) *adj. Physics* Without change in entropy.

I·ser (ē′zər) The German name for the JIZERA.

I·sère (ē·zâr′) A river in SE France, flowing 150 miles SW to the Rhone.

I·seult (i·sōōlt′) In medieval romance, either of two princesses: Iseult of the White Hand of Britanny, married to Tristan, or Iseult the Beautiful of Ireland, married to King Mark. See TRISTAN. Also spelled *Isolde, Isolt, Isoud, Yseult.*

Is·fa·han (is·fə·hän′) A city in west central Iran: formerly *Ispahan*: also *Esfahan.*

-ish[1] *suffix* **1** Of or belonging to (a national group): *Polish*; *Danish.* **2** Of the nature of; like: *boyish*; *clownish.* **3** Verging toward the character of: *feverish*; *bookish.* **4** Somewhat; rather: *bluish*; *tallish.* **5** *Colloq.* Approximately: *fortyish.* [OE *-isc,* adjectival suffix]

-ish[2] *suffix of verbs* Found in verbs of French origin: *brandish, demolish.* [<F *-iss-,* stem ending of *-ir* verbs <L *-isc-,* stem ending of inceptives]

I·shim (ē·shem′) A river in Russian S.F.S.R., flowing 1,123 miles NW to the Irtish.

Ish·ma·el (ish′mā·əl) **1** The son of Abraham and Hagar; exiled with the latter. **2** An outcast. [<Hebrew, God hears]

Ish·ma·el·ite (ish′mē·əl·īt′) *n.* **1** A traditional descendant of Ishmael; an Arab. *Gen.* xxi 9–21. **2** One having the character of Ishmael. *Gen.* xxi 9–21. **3** Any wanderer; outcast. **— Ish′ma·el·it′ic** (-īt′ik), **Ish·ma·el·it′ish** (-ī′·tish) *adj.* **— Ish′ma·el·it′ism** *n.*

Ish·tar (ish′tär) In Babylonian and Assyrian mythology, the wife of Tammuz and goddess of love and fertility.

I·si·ac (ī′sē·ak) *adj.* Belonging or relating to the goddess Isis: the *Isiac* tablet. [<L *Isiacus* <Gk. *Isiakos* <*Isis* Isis]

Is·i·dore (iz′ə·dôr, -dōr; *Fr.* ē·zē·dôr′) A masculine personal name. Also *Ital.* **I·si·do·ro** (ē′zē·dō′rō), *Latin* **Is·i·do·rus** (is′ə·dô′rəs). [<Gk., gift of Isis]
— Isidore, Saint, 560?–636, Spanish theologian and scholar; archbishop of Seville.

i·sin·glass (ē′zing·glas, -gläs, ī′zən-) *n.* **1** A preparation of nearly pure gelatin made from the swim bladders of certain fishes, as sturgeons, cod, and carp. **2** Mica, chiefly in the form of thin sheets. [<MDu. *huysenblas* sturgeon bladder < *huysen* sturgeon + *blase* bladder; infl. in form by GLASS]

I·sis (ī′sis) In Egyptian mythology, the goddess of fertility, sister and wife of Osiris.

Is·ken·de·run (ēs·ken′de·rōōn′) A port of southern Turkey at the NE Mediterranean: formerly *Alexandretta.* Also **Is·kan′de·run.**

Is·lam (is′ləm, iz′-, is·läm′) *n.* **1** The religion of the Muslims, which maintains that there is but one God, Allah, and that Mohammed is his prophet; Mohammedanism. **2** The body of Muslim believers, their culture, and the countries they inhabit. [<Arabic *islām* submission < *salama* to be resigned]

Is·lam·a·bad (iz·läm′ə·bäd) The capital of Pakistan.

Is·lam·ic (is·lam′ik, -läm′-, iz-) *adj.* Muslim.

Is·lam·ism (is′ləm·iz′əm, iz′-) *n.* Islam. **— Is′·lam·is′tic, Is′lam·it′ic** *adj.*

Is·lam·ite (is′ləm·īt, iz′-) *n.* A Muslim; Mussulman.

Is·lam·ize (is′ləm·īz, iz′-) *v.t. & v.i.* **·ized, ·iz·ing** To convert or conform to Islam.

is·land (ī′lənd) *n.* **1** A tract of land, usually of moderate extent, surrounded by water. **2** Anything isolated or like an island; anything set distinctly apart from its surroundings, as a piece of elevated woodland surrounded by prairie. **3** A patch of land differentiated from the surrounding area by a certain kind of vegetation: They walked to the oak *island.* **4** A cultivated or settled spot, especially a big farm in the woods or other unsettled area: often used as a place name. **5** *Anat.* Any of various isolated structures of the body; an insula. **—** *v.t.* **1** To make into an island or islands; insulate. **2** To isolate; set apart. **3** To intersperse with or as with islands. [OE *īgland,* lit., island land < *īg, ieg* isle + *land*; the *s* was added to the spelling in the 16th c. on a mistaken association from *isle*]

is·land·er (ī′lən·dər) *n.* An inhabitant of an island. Also **isles·man** (īlz′mən).

islands of Lang·er·hans (läng′ər·häns) *Anat.* Clusters of cells dispersed within the tissues of the pancreas and involved in the secretion of insulin. [after E. R. *Langerhans,* 1847–1888, German histologist]

Islands of the Blessed In Greek mythology, islands in the Western Ocean where the favorites of the gods lived after death.

island universe *Astron.* A galaxy.

isle (īl) *n.* **1** A small island. **2** *Poetic* An island. **—** *v.* **isled, isl·ing** *v.t.* To make into or place on an isle or island. **—** *v.i.* To live on an isle or island. ◆ Homophone: *aisle.* [<OF <L *insula* island]

Isle of Ely See ELY.

Isle of Man See MAN, ISLE OF.

Isle of Pines **1** A Cuban island SW of Havana; 1,182 square miles; chief town, Nueva Gerona. *Spanish* **Is·la de Pi·nos** (ēs′lä thā pē′·nōs). **2** A dependency of New Caledonia off its southern tip; 58 square miles: also *Kunie. French* **Ile des Pins** (ēl dā pań′).

Isle of Sheppey See SHEPPEY, ISLE OF.

Isle of Thanet See THANET, ISLE OF.

Isle of Wight See WIGHT, ISLE OF.

Isle Roy·ale (roi′əl, *Fr.* ēl rwȧ·yȧl′) An island in Lake Superior, within Michigan; 209 square miles: site of **Isle Royale National Park,** established 1940.

is·let (ī′lit) *n.* A little island. [<OF *islette,* dim. of *isle*]

Is·ling·ton (iz′ling·tən) A metropolitan borough of London north of the Thames.

ism (iz′əm) *n.* A doctrine or system: often applied satirically or with derogatory force. [<-ISM]

-ism *suffix of nouns* **1** The act, process, or result of: *ostracism.* **2** The condition of being: *skepticism.* **3** The characteristic action or behavior of: *heroism.* **4** The beliefs, teachings, or system of: *Calvinism.* **5** Devotion to; adherence to the teachings of: *nationalism.* **6** A characteristic or peculiarity of: said of language or idiom: *Americanism.* **7** *Med.* An abnormal condition resulting from an excess of: *alcoholism.* [<L *-ismus* <Gk. *-ismos*]

Is·ma·el·ite (is′mē·əl·īt′) *n.* **1** An Ishmaelite. **2** An Ismailian.

Is·ma·i·li·a (is′mä·ē′lē·ə) A town in NE Egypt at the mid-point of the Suez Canal. Also **Is′ma·i′li·ya.**

Is·ma·i·li·an (is′mä·ē′lē·ən) *n.* A member of a sect of the Shiah branch of Islam. Also **Is′ma·el′i·an.** [after *Ismail,* son of the sixth imam of the Moslems]

Is·ma·il Pa·sha (is′mä·ēl′ pä′shə), 1830–95, khedive of Egypt 1863–79.

Is·nik (ēz·nēk′) See IZNIK.

is·n't (iz′ənt) Is not: a contraction.

iso- *combining form* **1** Equal; the same; identical. **2** *Chem.* Isomeric with, or an isomer of (the compound named): *isoprene.* Also, before vowels, *is-*. [<Gk. *isos* equal]

i·so·ag·glu·ti·na·tion (ī′sō·ə·glōō′tə·nā′shən) *n. Med.* The agglutination of the red blood corpuscles of an animal by a serum taken from another individual of the same species.

i·so·ag·glu·tin·in (ī′sō·ə·glōō′tə·nin) *n. Physiol.* An agglutinin having the power to agglutinate the red blood corpuscles of another individual of the same species.

i·so·am·yl (ī′sō·am′il) *n. Chem.* The univalent radical C_5H_{11} which enters into many organic compounds: *isoamyl* acetate (pear oil), *isoamyl* alcohol (fusel oil), etc.

i·so·bar (ī′sə·bär) *n.* **1** *Meteorol.* A line on a chart or diagram connecting places on the earth's surface having the same barometric pressure for a specified time or period. **2** *Physics* Any of two or more atoms having the same atomic weights but different atomic numbers and chemical properties. [<ISO- + Gk. *baros* weight] **— i′so·bar′ic** (-bar′ik) *adj.* **— i′so·bar′o·met′ric** (-bar′ə·met′rik) *adj.*

i·so·bath (ī′sə·bath) *n.* A contour line connecting points of equal depth beneath the earth or along the ocean floor. [<ISO- + Gk. *bathys* deep]

i·so·bront (ī′sə·bront) *n. Meteorol.* A line joining points at which any specified phase of a thunderstorm occurs at the same time. [<ISO- + Gk. *brontē* thunder]

i·so·can·dle (ī′sə·kan′dəl) *adj. Physics* **1** Designating a curve drawn through those points about a source of light at which the candlepower is the same. **2** Denoting a diagram comprising several sets of such curves.

i·so·chasm (ī′sə·kaz′əm) *n.* An isogram indicating the same average frequency of auroral displays. [<ISO- + Gk. *chasma* gap]

i·so·cheim (ī′sə·kīm) *n. Meteorol.* A line joining points on the earth's surface which have the same mean winter temperature. Also **i′so·chime.** [<ISO- + Gk. *cheima* winter] **— i′so·chei′mal** *adj.*

i·so·chore (ī′sə·kôr) *n. Physics* An isogram for

which volume is the constant quantity. Also **i′so·chor.** [<ISO- + Gk. *chōra* space] —**i′so·chor′ic** *adj.*

i·so·chro·mat·ic (ī′sō·krō·mat′ik) *adj.* **1** *Optics* Having or denoting identity of color. **2** Orthochromatic.

i·so·chron (ī′sə·kron) *n. Biol.* In studies of growth, a mathematical function equal to one percent of the time required to attain maturity. Also **i′so·chrone** (-krōn). [<ISO- + Gk. *chronos* time]

i·soch·ro·nal (ī·sok′rə·nəl) *adj.* Relating to or characterized by equal intervals of time, as a pendulum that always vibrates in the same period. Also **i·so·chron·ic** (ī′sə·kron′ik), **i·soch′ro·nous.** —**i·soch′ro·nous·ly** *adv.*

i·soch·ro·nize (ī·sok′rə·nīz) *v.t.* **·nized, ·niz·ing** To make isochronal. —**i·soch′ro·nism** *n.*

i·soch·ro·ous (ī·sok′rō·əs) *adj.* Having the same color or tint throughout. [<ISO- + -CHROOUS]

i·so·cli·nal (ī′sə·klī′nəl) *adj.* **1** Dipping at the same angle and in the same direction. **2** Designating a line projected on the earth's surface connecting places that have the same inclination to the earth's magnetic field. **3** *Geol.* Pertaining to an isocline. —*n.* An isoclinal line.

i·so·cline (ī′sə·klīn) *n. Geol.* A rock fold in which the strata are so closely appressed that the sides are parallel. [<ISO- + Gk. *klinein* bend] —**i′so·clin′ic** (-klin′ik) *adj.*

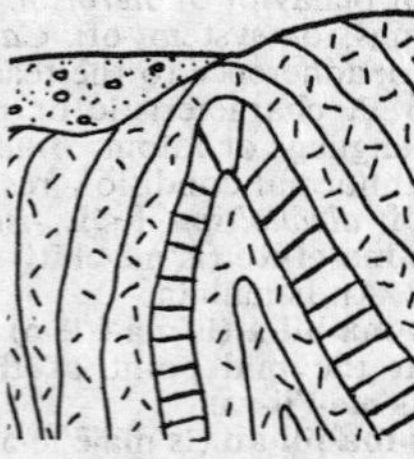

ISOCLINE
Vertical isoclinal folds.

i·so·cosm (ī′sə·koz′əm) *n. Physics* A line connecting points on the earth's surface showing an equal cosmic ray intensity. [<ISO- + Gk. *kosmos* world]

i·soc·ra·cy (ī·sok′rə·sē) *n. pl.* **·cies** Equality in government; government in which all have equal power. [<Gk. *isokratia* <*iso-* same + *-kratia* rule <*kratos* power] —**i·so·crat** (ī′sə·krat) *n.* —**i′so·crat′ic** *adj.*

I·soc·ra·tes (ī·sok′rə·tēz), 436–338 B.C., Athenian orator.

i·so·cy·a·nine (ī′sō·sī′ə·nēn, -nin) *n. Chem.* Any of a group of quinoline dyes used in sensitizing photographic plates. Also **i′so·cy′a·nin** (-nin).

i·so·cy·clic (ī′sō·sī′klik, -sik′lik) *adj.* **1** *Chem.* Pertaining to or designating any of two or more closed-chain hydrocarbon compounds containing the same number of atoms. **2** *Bot.* Denoting a flower whose whorls have an equal number of parts.

i·so·def (ī′sə·def) *n.* An isogram joining points that show an equal percentage deviation from the mean of some specified phenomenon or characteristic. [<ISO- + DEF(ICIENCY)]

i·so·des·mic (ī′sō·dez′mik) *adj. Physics* Pertaining to or denoting an ionic crystal structure in which all the bonds are of equal strength. [<ISO- + Gk. *desmos* chain]

i·so·di·a·met·ric (ī′sō·dī′ə·met′rik) *adj.* **1** Equal in the three dimensions. **2** Having only the lateral axes equal, as crystals of the tetragonal and hexagonal systems.

i·so·di·mor·phism (ī′sō·dī·môr′fiz·əm) *n.* The phenomenon in which two or more similar crystals are at the same time isomorphous and dimorphous. —**i′so·di·mor′phous** *adj.*

i·so·dose (ī′sə·dōs) *n.* The same or an equal dose, as of drugs, X-rays or other forms of radioactivity.

i·so·dy·nam·ic (ī′sō·dī·nam′ik) *adj.* **1** Relating to or characterized by equality of force. **2** Designating any line on the earth's surface at all points of which the intensity of terrestrial magnetism is the same. Also **i′so·dy·nam′i·cal.**

i·so·e·lec·tric (ī′sō·i·lek′trik) *adj.* **1** Exhibiting the same electric potential. **2** *Chem.* Designating the *p*H value at which a colloidal suspension is electrically neutral with respect to the surrounding medium. [<ISO- + ELECTRIC]

i·so·e·lec·tron·ic (ī′sō·i·lek·tron′ik) *adj. Physics* Pertaining to or denoting atoms having the same number of valence electrons and similar physical properties.

i·so·eu·ge·nol (ī′sō·yōō′jə·nōl, -nol) *n. Chem.* A colorless oily liquid, $C_{10}H_{12}O_2$, derived from ylang-ylang and used in the manufacture of vanillin. [<ISO- + EUGENOL]

i·so·gam·ete (ī′sō·gam′ēt, -gə·mēt′) *n. Biol.* One of a pair of uniting gametes similar in size, form, and structure: opposed to *heterogamete.*

i·sog·a·my (ī·sog′ə·mē) *n. Biol.* That form of sexual reproduction in which there is a union of two similarly formed sexual cells, or gametes. Compare OOGAMY. [<ISO- + -GAMY] —**i·sog′a·mous** *adj.*

i·sog·e·nous (ī·soj′ə·nəs) *adj.* **1** Having a similarity of origin. **2** *Biol.* Developed from the same cells or tissues. [<ISO- + -GENOUS] —**i·so·gen·e·sis** (ī′sō·jen′ə·sis), **i·sog′e·ny** *n.*

i·so·ge·o·therm (ī′sō·jē′ə·thərm) *n. Geol.* A line or surface along which the earth, below its surface, has the same temperature. [<ISO- + GEO- + Gk. *thermē* heat] —**i′so·ge′o·ther′mal, i′so·ge′o·ther′mic** *adj.*

i·so·gloss (ī′sə·glôs, -glos) *n. Ling.* A line on a map in a dialect atlas delimiting areas within which certain linguistic features, as pronunciation, vocabulary, etc., are exhibited in common.

i·so·gon (ī′sə·gon) *n.* A polygon whose angles are all equal. [<ISOGONIC]

i·so·gon·ic (ī′sə·gon′ik) *adj.* **1** Having equal angles. **2** Denoting an isogonic line. Also **i·sog·o·nal** (ī·sog′ə·nəl). —*n.* An isogonic line. [<Gk. *isogōnios*]

isogonic line A line connecting points on the earth's surface having equal magnetic declination.

i·so·gram (ī′sə·gram) *n.* A line connecting points on a chart, map, or diagram which have equal values in relation to specified geographic features, physical conditions, or meteorological phenomena.

i·so·griv (ī′sə·griv) *n. Nav.* A line connecting points of equal grid variation. [<ISO- + GRIV(ATION)]

i·so·hel (ī′sə·hel) *n. Meteorol.* An isogram showing places of equal sunshine. [<ISO- + Gk. *hēlios* sun]

i·so·hy·dric (ī′sə·hī′drik) *adj. Chem.* Pertaining to or designating a chemical neutralization in which the *p*H value remains constant.

i·so·hy·et (ī′sə·hī′ət) *n. Meteorol.* A curve joining places of equal rainfall. [<ISO- + Gk. *hyetos* rain]

i·so·late (ī′sə·lāt, is′ə-) *v.t.* **·lat·ed, ·lat·ing** **1** To place in a detached or separate situation; set apart. **2** *Electr.* To insulate. **3** *Chem.* To obtain in a free or uncombined state, as an element or compound. **4** *Med.* To set apart from others, as a person with a communicable disease. **5** *Bacteriol.* To obtain a pure bacterial culture of (a specified disease or bacterium). —*n.* **1** A definite constituent or factor of some natural phenomenon, or aspect of experience, set apart from the whole for purposes of study, experiment, and analysis. **2** *Chem.* A pure compound, as one derived from an essential oil. [Back formation of ISOLATED <Ital. *isolato,* pp. of *isolare* isolate <*isola* island <L *insula* island] —**i′so·la′tor** *n.*

i·so·lat·ing (ī′sə·lā′ting, is′ə-) *adj. Ling.* Describing a language, such as Chinese, in which there is no distinction in form between the parts of speech, with meaning being determined primarily by word order.

i·so·la·tion·ism (ī′sə·lā′shən·iz′əm) *n.* The advocacy of national self-sufficiency and freedom from foreign political and economic alliances. —**i′so·la′tion·ist** *n.*

I·solde (i·sōld′, *Ger.* i·zôl′də) See ISEULT. Also **I·solt′.**

i·so·lead (ī′sə·lēd) *n. Mil.* A curved line drawn on a chart which indicates instantly the required lead of a gun in relation to a moving target. Also **isolead curve.**

i·so·lec·i·thal (ī′sō·les′ə·thəl) *adj. Biol.* Having the yolk evenly distributed through the protoplasm of an egg. [<ISO- + Gk. *lekithos* yolk of an egg]

I·so·le E·o·lie (ē′zō·lā ē·ō′lyā) An Italian name for the LIPARI ISLANDS.

i·so·leu·cine (ī′sə·lōō′sēn) *n. Biochem.* An amino acid, $C_6H_{13}NO_2$, found in body tissues and believed to be essential in nutrition.

i·so·log (ī′sə·lôg, -log) *n. Chem.* An isologous compound. Also **i′so·logue.** [<ISOLOGOUS]

i·sol·o·gous (ī·sol′ə·gəs) *adj. Chem.* Having similar molecular structure but different atoms of the same valency: applied especially to those groups of hydrocarbon compounds that have a constant difference of two hydrogen atoms in their composition. [<ISO- + Gk. *logos* proportion]

i·so·lux (ī′sə·luks) *n. Optics* **1** A line plotted on an appropriate set of coordinates to connect points of equal illumination. **2** A diagram containing sets of such lines. [<ISO- + L *lux* light]

i·so·mag·net·ic (ī′sō·mag·net′ik) *adj.* Relating to or designating lines connecting points of equal magnetic force. —*n.* An isomagnetic line.

i·so·mer (ī′sə·mər) *n. Chem.* A compound having the same molecular weight and formula as another but with a different spatial arrangement of its atoms, resulting in different properties. [<Gk. *isomerēs* equally divided <*isos* equal + *meros* part] —**i·so·mer′ic** (-mer′ik) *adj.*

i·som·er·ism (ī·som′ər·iz′əm) *n. Chem.* The condition of having different chemical or physical properties, or both, but identical molecular composition.

i·som·er·ous (ī·som′ər·əs) *adj.* **1** *Bot.* Equal in number, as the members of the successive circles or whorls of a flower: opposed to *heteromerous.* **2** *Entomol.* Having an equal number of tarsal joints on all feet: said of certain coleopterous insects. **3** Isomeric.

i·so·met·ric (ī′sō·met′rik) *adj.* **1** Having equality in dimensions or measurements. **2** Pertaining to that system of crystallization in which the three axes are equal in length and at right angles to each other. **3** *Physics* Indicating or maintaining the same proportions, measure, dimensions, etc., as a constant volume in a gas. Also **i′so·met′ri·cal.** **4** Based upon the forceful contraction of muscles against immovable resistance without shortening muscle fibers, a means of strengthening muscles: *isometric* exercises. —*n.* An isometric line. [<Gk. *isometros* <*isos* equal + *metron* measure] —**i′so·met′ri·cal·ly** *adv.*

i·so·me·tro·pi·a (ī′sō·mə·trō′pē·ə) *n. Optics* Equality of the focal length of the two eyes. [<ISO- + Gk. *metron* measure + -OPIA]

i·som·e·try (ī·som′ə·trē) *n.* **1** Equality in measured parts or proportions. **2** *Geog.* Equality of elevation, as of mountain peaks. [<Gk. *isometria* equality of measure <*isos* same + *metros* measure]

i·so·morph (ī′sə·môrf) *n.* An organism or crystal superficially like another but morphologically different. [<ISO- + Gk. *morphē* form] —**i′so·mor′phic** *adj.*

i·so·mor·phism (ī′sə·môr′fiz·əm) *n.* **1** The property shown by two substances of analogous chemical composition that crystallize in identical or nearly identical forms. **2** *Biol.* The possession of like characters by organisms of different groups, resulting usually from like environmental influences. —**i′so·mor′phous** *adj.*

i·so·neph (ī′sə·nef) *n. Meteorol.* An isogram showing places of equal degrees of cloudiness. [<ISO- + Gk. *nephos* cloud]

i·son·o·my (ī·son′ə·mē) *n.* **1** Equality of civil rights. **2** Equality in rank, kind, or grade, in classification. [<Gk. *isonomia* <*isos* same + *nomos* law] —**i·so·nom·ic** (ī′sō·nom′ik) *adj.*

I·son·zo (ē·zôn′tsō) A river in NW Yugoslavia and NE Italy, flowing 84 miles south to the Gulf of Trieste.

i·so·oc·tane (ī′sō·ok′tān) *n. Chem.* Trimethylpentane.

i·sop·a·thy (ī·sop′ə·thē) *n. Med.* **1** The theory that a contagious disease contains in its own causative agent the means for its cure. **2** Treatment by the application or use of diseased matter. —**i·so·path·ic** (ī′sə·path′ik) *adj.*

i·so·phene (ī′sə·fēn) *n.* **1** *Ecol.* A contour line on a map indicating areas of equal frequency of a given plant or animal. **2** A line joining all places within a given area or region of the earth along which seasonal phenomena take place at the same time. [<ISO- + Gk. *phainein* reveal]

i·so·phot·ic (ī′sō·fot′ik) *adj. Bot.* Equally illuminated: said of leaves and other organs.

i·so·phyl·ly (ī′sō·fil′ē) *n. Bot.* The condition in which a plant bears only one kind of leaf. [<ISO- + Gk. *phyllon* leaf] —**i′so·phyl′lous** *adj.*

i·so·pi·es·tic (ī′sō·pī·es′tik) *adj.* Showing equal

pressure; isobaric. — *n.* An isobar. [<ISO-
+ Gk. *piezein* press]

i·so·pleth (ī′sə·pleth) *n.* 1 *Meteorol.* A graph
showing the variations of a specified climatic
element with respect to two coordinates, temporal and spatial, the latter generally being
an altitude factor. 2 An isogram. 3 A
nomograph. [<Gk. *isoplēthēs* equal in number or quantity < *iso-* equal + *plēthos* number, quantity]

i·so·pod (ī′sə·pod) *n.* Any of a large and varied
order (*Isopoda*) of terrestrial and aquatic
crustaceans, having sessile eyes, flattened
bodies lacking a carapace, and seven free
thoracic segments, of which each carries a
pair of closely similar legs. — *adj.* Of or pertaining to the *Isopoda*. [<NL <Gk. *isos* equal
+ *pous, podos* foot] — **i·sop·o·dan** (ī·sop′ə·dən)
adj.

i·so·pol·i·ty (ī′sō·pol′ə·tē) *n.* Reciprocity of
civil rights.

i·so·por (ī′sə·pôr, -pōr) *n.* An isogram indicating an equal rate of change in any element of the earth's magnetic field. [<ISO-
+ Gk. *poros* passage] — **i·so·por′ic** *adj.*

i·so·pract (ī′sə·prakt) *n.* A boundary enclosing areas of equal frequency or value of
specified physical conditions, as population,
snowfall, etc. [<ISO- + Gk. *praktikos* of
action]

i·so·prene (ī′sə·prēn) *n. Chem.* A volatile
liquid hydrocarbon of the terpene group,
C_5H_8, obtained when caoutchouc and gutta-
percha are subjected to dry distillation. [Ap-
par. an arbitrary coinage]

i·so·pro·pyl (ī′sə·prō′pil) *n. Chem.* The univalent radical $(CH_3)_2CH$, an important constituent of many organic compounds, as isopropyl alcohol, $(CH_3)_2CHOH$, used as a
solvent and in perfumery. Also called **i′so·
pro′pa·nol** (-pə·nōl, -nol).

i·sop·ter·ous (ī·sop′tər·əs) *adj.* Of or pertaining to an order (*Isoptera*) of small and
medium–sized social insects having soft bodies, strong mandibles, and well-developed
claws, the workers and soldiers being wingless and sterile. See WHITE ANT. [<ISO- +
-PTEROUS]

i·so·pyc·nic (ī′sə·pik′nik) *adj.* Of, pertaining
to, or having equal density, as sea water or
air masses. — *n.* A line connecting points of
equal density. [<ISO- + Gk. *pyknos* thick,
dense]

i·so·pyre (ī′sə·pīr) *n.* A variety of impure opal.

i·sos·ce·les (ī·sos′ə·lēz) *adj.*
Geom. Pertaining to or designating a triangle having
two sides of equal length.
[<LL <Gk. *isoskelēs* equal-
legged < *iso-* equal + *skelos*
leg]

i·so·seis·mal (ī′sə·sīz′məl,
-sīs′-) See COSEISMAL.

i·so·seis·mic (ī′sə·sīz′mik,
-sīs′-) *adj.* Pertaining to or
designating equal intensities
of earthquake shocks. — *n.*
A coseismal.

i·sos·mot·ic (ī′sos·mot′ik) Isotonic. [<ISO- +
(O)SMOTIC]

i·so·spo·ry (ī·sos′pər·ē) *n. Bot.* The condition
of having only one kind of spore, as in the
true ferns and club mosses. Also **i·so·spore**
(ī′sə·spôr, -spōr). [<ISO- + SPOR(E) + -Y¹]
— **i·sos′po·rous** *adj.*

i·sos·ta·sy (ī·sos′tə·sē) *n.* 1 *Geol.* The theoretical condition of equilibrium which the earth's
surface tends to assume under the action of
terrestrial gravitation, as affected by the
transference of material from regions of denudation to those of deposition, and by differences in density in various portions of the
earth's mass near the surface. 2 Equilibrium
resulting from equal pressure on all sides.
[<ISO- + Gk. *stasis* a standing still] — **i·so·
stat·ic** (ī′sə·stat′ik) *adj.*

i·so·stem·o·nous (ī′sə·stem′ə·nəs) *adj. Bot.*
Having the stamens in a single series and
of the same number as the petals and sepals.
[<ISO- + Gk. *stēmōn* thread + -OUS] — **i′so·
stem′o·ny** *n.*

i·so·stere (ī′sə·stir) *n.* 1 *Meteorol.* A line
connecting points of equal atmospheric density. 2 *Chem.* A compound or radical which

exhibits isosterism. [<ISO- + Gk. *stereos*
solid]

i·sos·ter·ism (ī·sos′tər·iz′əm) *n. Chem.* A similarity in the physical properties of certain
compounds, radicals, and elements, due to
their having the same number and arrangement of electrons. — **i·so·ster·ic** (ī′sə·ster′ik)
adj.

i·so·there (ī′sə·thir) *n. Meteorol.* An isogram
indicating places having the same mean summer temperature. [<ISO- + Gk. *theros* sum-
mer] — **i·soth·er·al** (ī·soth′ər·əl) *adj. & n.*

i·so·therm (ī′sə·thûrm) *n. Meteorol.* A line
passing through points on the earth's surface
which have the same temperature at a given
time or over the same period. [<ISO- + Gk.
thermē heat]

i·so·ther·mal (ī′sə·thûr′məl) *adj.* 1 Having
the same temperature. 2 Designating a
layer of the atmosphere lying above the region of convection: also called *stratospheric.*
3 Of or pertaining to an isotherm. — *n.*
An isotherm.

i·so·tone (ī′sə·tōn) *n. Physics* One of two or
more atomic nuclei having the same number of neutrons. [<ISOTONIC]

i·so·ton·ic (ī′sə·ton′ik) *adj.* 1 Having the
same tonicity. 2 *Physiol.* **a** Having the same
osmotic pressure on opposite sides of a
membrane: said of solutions, especially blood
or plasma: distinguished from *hypertonic*:
also *isosmotic.* **b** Denoting a muscle which
contracts against a small but uniform tension or the curve of such a contraction. 3
Music Pertaining to, characterized by, or
having equal tones. [<Gk. *isotonos* having
equal accent or tone < *iso-* equal + *tonos*
accent, tone] — **i·so·ton·ic·i·ty** (ī′sə·tō·nis′-
ə·tē) *n.*

i·so·tope (ī′sə·tōp) *n. Physics* Any of two or
more forms of an element having the same
atomic number and similar chemical properties but differing in atomic weight and
radioactive behavior. The accepted atomic
weight of an element is the average of the
nuclear masses of all the isotopes it may
contain. [<ISO- + Gk. *topos* place] — **i·so·
top·ic** (ī′sə·top′ik, -tō′pik) *adj.* — **i·sot·o·py**
(ī·sot′ə·pē) *n.*

i·so·tron (ī′sə·tron) *n.* An apparatus for the
electromagnetic separation of uranium isotopes, especially in the generation of atomic
energy. [<ISO(TOPE) + (ELEC)TRON]

i·so·trop·ic (ī′sə·trop′ik, -trō′pik) *adj.* 1 *Physics* Exhibiting the same physical properties
in every direction. 2 *Biol.* Having indifferent
structure, as various eggs. Also **i′so·trope,
i·sot·ro·pous** (ī·sot′rə·pəs).

i·sot·ro·pism (ī·sot′rə·piz′əm) *n.* 1 The quality of being isotropic. 2 *Biol.* An ability in
an unsegmented egg to develop an embryo
from any part. Also **i·sot·ro·py** (ī·sot′rə·pē).
[<ISO- + -TROPISM]

I·soud (i·sōōd′) See ISEULT.

Is·pa·han (is′pä·hän′) A former spelling of
ISFAHAN.

Is·ra·el (iz′rē·əl) A masculine personal name.
[<Hebrew, contender with God]
— **Israel** The patriarch Jacob. *Gen.* xxxii 28.

Is·ra·el (iz′rē·əl) *n.* 1 The Jewish people,
traditionally regarded as descended from
Israel (Jacob). 2 The kingdom in the northern part of ancient Palestine formed by the
ten tribes of Israel.

Is·ra·el (iz′rē·əl) A republic comprising parts
of Palestine, proclaimed as a Jewish national
state in May, 1948; 8,040 square miles; capital, Jerusalem. — **Is·rae·li** (iz·rā′lē) *adj. & n.*

Is·ra·el·ite (iz′rē·əl·īt′) *n.* 1 Any of the people
of Israel or their descendants; a Hebrew; a
Jew. 2 One of God's chosen people. — **Is′-
ra·el·it′ish** (-ī′tish), **Is′ra·el·it′ic** (-it′ik) *adj.*

Is·ra·fel (iz′rə·fel) In Moslem mythology, the
one of the four archangels who is to sound
the resurrection trumpet. Also **Is′ra·feel, Is′-
ra·fil** (-fēl).

Is·sa·char (is′ə·kär) The ninth son of Jacob.
Gen. xxx 18.

Is·sei (ēs·sā) *n. pl.* ·**seis** or ·**sei** A Japanese
who emigrated to the United States after
the Oriental exclusion proclamation of 1907,
and is not legally eligible to become an
American citizen. Compare NISEI, KIBEI.
[<Japanese *is* first + *sei* generation]

is·su·a·ble (ish′ōō·ə·bəl, -yōō-) *adj.* 1 That
can issue or be issued. 2 *Law* Tending to
an issue. — **is′su·a·bly** *adv.*

is·su·ance (ish′ōō·əns, -yōō-) *n.* The act of
putting, sending, or giving out; promulgation; distribution.

is·su·ant (ish′ōō·ənt, -yōō-) *adj.* 1 Issuing or
emerging. 2 *Her.* Denoting a beast of which
the upper half only is seen.

is·sue (ish′ōō, -yōō) *v.* ·**sued,** ·**su·ing** *v.t.* 1 To
give out or deliver in a public or official
manner; put into circulation; publish: to *issue*
a new stamp; to *issue* a magazine. 2 To deal
out or distribute: to *issue* ammunition. 3 To
send forth or emit; let out; discharge. — *v.i.*
4 To come forth or flow out; emerge: Water
issued from the pipe. 5 To come as a result
or consequence; proceed: His charity *issues*
from his good character. 6 To come to a
specified end: with *in*: The argument *issued*
in a duel. 7 To be given out or published;
appear. 8 To come as profit or revenue;
accrue: with *out of*. 9 *Rare* or *Law* To be
born or descended. — *n.* 1 The act of going
out; outflow. 2 A place or way of egress.
3 Result; outcome; upshot. 4 The action of
giving out or supplying officially or publicly.
5 An item or amount which is issued. 6 Offspring; progeny. 7 Profits; proceeds. 8 *Med.*
a A suppurating sore, produced and maintained by artificial means. **b** A discharge, as
of blood. 9 *Law* The point in question between parties to an action. 10 A subject of
discussion or interest. See synonyms under
CONSEQUENCE, END, EVENT, TOPIC. [<F *issue*
< *issir, eissir* <L *exire* < *ex-* out of + *ire*
go] — **at issue** Under dispute; in question.
— **to take issue** To disagree. — **is′su·er** *n.*

Is·sus (is′əs) An ancient port in Cilicia, NE
Asia Minor; scene of the victory of Alexander
the Great over Darius III, 333 B.C.

Is·syk Kul (ē′sik kōōl′) The second largest
mountain lake in the world, in eastern
Kirghiz S.S.R.; 2,395 square miles.

-ist *suffix of nouns* 1 One who or that
which does or has to do with: often used
with verbs in *-ize*: catechist. 2 One whose
profession is; one who practices: pharmacist.
3 A student or devotee of: genealogist. 4
One who advocates or adheres to: in extension from nouns ending in *-ism*: socialist.
[<L *-ista* <Gk. *-istēs*]

Is·tan·bul (is′tan·bōōl′, -tän-, *Turkish* is·täm′·
bōōl) The largest city of Turkey, a port on
both sides of the Bosporus at its entrance into
the Sea of Marmara: formerly *Byzantium* and,
as *Constantinople*, capital of Turkey until
1923: also *Stambul.* Also **Is′tan·boul′.**

isth·mi·an (is′mē·ən, *rarely* isth′-) *adj.* Of or
pertaining to an isthmus. — *n.* An inhabitant of an isthmus.

Isthmian Canal The Panama Canal.

Isthmian games The Pan-Hellenic festival,
celebrated every two years in ancient Greece
on the Isthmus of Corinth.

isth·mus (is′məs, *rarely* isth′-) *n. pl.* ·**mus·es**
or ·**mi** (-mī) 1 A narrow body of land connecting two larger bodies. 2 *Anat.* A contracted passage or portion of an organ between two larger cavities or parts: the portion
of the brain which joins the pons Varolii with
the interbrain and hemisphere. 3 *Bot.* The
constricted or contracted part of the cells of
desmids connecting the two hemicells. [<L
<Gk. *isthmos* narrow passage]

is·tle (ist′lē) *n.* 1 A fiber derived principally
from a tropical American agave plant (*Agave
fourcroydes* or *A. lophantha*): used for carpets, belting, cordage, etc.: also called *pita,
Tampico fiber.* 2 A similar fiber obtained
from certain plants of the pineapple family
(genus *Bromelia*). Also spelled *ixtle.* [<Am.
Sp. *ixtle* <Nahuatl *ichtli*]

Is·tri·a (is′trē·ə) A peninsula, mostly in Yugoslavia, in the north Adriatic Sea; 1,908 square
miles. *Serbo-Croation* **Is·tra** (ēs′trä). Also
Istrian Peninsula. — **Is′tri·an** *adj. & n.*

Ist·van (ēst·vän′) Hungarian form of STEPHEN.

it (it) *pron.* The neuter pronoun, nominative
(pl. *they*) and objective (pl. *them*), of the third
person singular, used: 1 As a substitute for
things or for infants and animals when the
sex is unspecified. 2 As the subject of an
impersonal verb: It rained. 3 As the subject

or object of a clause regarding a general condition or state of affairs: How was *it? It* was warm. **4** As the subject or predicate nominative of a verb whose logical subject is anticipated: Who was *it? It* was John. **5** As the indefinite subject of a verb introducing a clause or phrase: *It* seems that he knew. **6** *Colloq.* As the indefinite object after certain verbs in idiomatic expressions: to lord *it* over; to face *it*. — *n.* In certain children's games, the player required to perform some specified act. [OE *hit*]

I.T.A. Initial Teaching Alphabet.

I·ta·bi·ra (ē'tə·vir'ə) A town in SE Brazil.

i·tab·i·rite (i·tab'ə·rīt) *n.* A schist containing hematite in grains or scales. Also **i·tab'l·ryte.** [from *Itabira*, Brazil]

it·a·col·u·mite (it'ə·kol'yə·mīt) *n.* A laminated, granular, friable sandstone which is flexible in thin slabs. [from *Itacolumi*, mountain in eastern Brazil]

I·tal·ian (i·tal'yən) *adj.* Pertaining to Italy, its people, culture or language. — *n.* **1** A native or naturalized inhabitant of Italy. **2** The Romance language of modern Italy. [<L *Italianus* < *Italia* Italy]

I·tal·ian·ate (i·tal'yən·āt, -it) *adj.* Italian in nature or characteristics. — *v.t.* (-āt) **·at·ed, ·at·ing** To Italianize. [<earlier *Italianated* <Ital. *italianato* made Italian] — **I·tal'ian·a'·tion** *n.*

Italian East Africa A former Italian colony, comprising Eritrea, Italian Somaliland, and Ethiopia.

Italian hand The flowing script, developing from the 15th century, used in documents and forming the basis for modern English handwriting. Compare COURT HAND. — **fine Italian hand** Subtle cunning: The scheme showed her *fine Italian hand.*

I·tal·ian·ism (i·tal'yən·iz'əm) *n.* **1** An Italian idiom or expression; a custom or fashion peculiar to Italy. **2** The spirit, manner, or taste of the Italians. **3** A preference for or sympathy with Italy or things Italian.

I·tal·ian·ize (i·tal'yən·īz) *v.t.* & *v.i.* **·ized, ·iz·ing** To make or become Italian in manner, customs, language, etc. — **I·tal'ian·i·za'tion** *n.*

Italian millet See under MILLET.

Italian poplar The Lombardy poplar.

Italian Somaliland See SOMALILAND.

Italian squash Zucchini.

Italian sonnet See under SONNET.

i·tal·ic (i·tal'ik) *Printing n.* A style of type in which the letters slope, as *these*: also **i·tal'ics.** — *adj.* Designating, or printed in, italic. Compare ROMAN.

I·tal·ic (i·tal'ik) *adj.* Relating to any of the peoples of ancient Italy. — *n.* A subfamily of the Indo-European languages, comprising three branches—Falisco-Latinian (including Latin and the Romance languages), Osco-Umbrian, and Sabellian. [<L. *Italicus*]

i·tal·i·cize (i·tal'ə·sīz) *v.t.* & *v.i.* **·cized, ·ciz·ing** **1** To print in italics. **2** To underscore (written words or phrases) with a single line to indicate italics. Also *Brit.* **i·tal'i·cise.**

I·tal·i·ote (i·tal'ē·ōt) *n.* One of the Greek inhabitants of Italy. Also **I·tal'i·ot** (-ot). [<Gk. *Italiōtēs* <*Italia* Italy]

It·a·ly (it'ə·lē) A republic in southern Europe; 116,224 square miles; capital, Rome. *Italian* **I·ta·lia** (ē·tä'lyä).

I·tas·ca (ī·tas'kə), **Lake** A lake in northern Minnesota, considered to be the source of the Mississippi.

itch (ich) *v.i.* **1** To feel a peculiar irritation of the skin which inclines one to scratch the part affected. **2** To have a desire or longing; crave. — *n.* **1** Any of various usually contagious skin diseases accompanied by itching, as scabies. **2** An itching of the skin. **3** A restless desire or yearning. [OE *giccan*] — — **itch'i·ness** *n.* — **itch'ing** *n.* — **itch'y** *adj.*

itch mite A mite (*Sarcoptes scabiei*), the female of which burrows and lays eggs under the scarfskin, causing inflammation and intense itching.

-ite[1] *suffix of nouns* **1** A native of: *Brooklynite.* **2** An adherent of: *Darwinite.* **3** A descendant of: *Israelite.* **4** *Mineral.* A rock or mineral: *graphite.* **5** *Zool.* A part of the body or of an organ: *somite.* **6** *Paleontol.* A fossil: *ammonite.* **7** Like; resembling; related to: often used in the names of commercial products: *dynamite.* [<F *-ite* <L *-ita* <Gk. *-itēs*]

-ite[2] *suffix Chem.* A salt or ester of an acid whose name ends in *-ous: sulfite.* [<F *-ite*; arbitrarily coined (1787) from *-ate* -ATE[3]]

-ite[3] *suffix* Used in adjectives and verbs formed on the past participial stems of Latin verbs in the second, third, and fourth conjugations: *finite, unite.* [<L *-itus*]

i·tem (ī'təm) *n.* **1** A separate article or entry in an account, etc. **2** A newspaper paragraph. **3** *Obs.* An admonition; hint; especially, a maxim or saying, formerly introduced by the word *item.* See synonyms under CIRCUMSTANCE. — *v.t.* **1** To set down by items. **2** To make a note or memorandum of. — *adv.* Likewise. [<L, likewise]

i·tem·ize (ī'təm·īz) *v.t.* **·ized, ·iz·ing** To set down or specify by items. — **i'tem·iz'er** *n.* — **i'tem·i·za'tion** *n.*

item veto The power of a government executive to veto parts of a bill without vetoing the entire bill.

I·té·nez (ē·tā'nes) See GUAPORÉ.

it·er·ate (it'ə·rāt) *v.t.* **·at·ed, ·at·ing** **1** To utter or do again. **2** To utter or do repeatedly. [<L *iteratus*, pp. of *iterare* repeat < *iterum* again] — **it'er·a·ble** (it'ər·ə·bəl) *adj.* — **it'er·ant** *adj.* — **it'er·ance, it'er·a'tion** *n.*

it·er·a·tive (it'ə·rā'tiv, it'ər·ə·tiv) *adj.* **1** Characterized by repetition; repetitious. **2** *Gram.* Frequentative.

i·te·rum (it'ər·əm) *adv. Latin* Again; once more.

Ith·a·ca (ith'ə·kə) **1** A Greek island of the Ionian group; 36 square miles; legendary home of Odysseus. *Modern Greek* **I·thá·ki** (ē·thä'kē). **2** A city in south central New York. — **Ith'a·can** *adj.* & *n.*

ith·er (ith'ər) *adj.* & *pron. Scot.* Other.

I·thunn (ē'thōōn) In Norse mythology, keeper of the golden apples of youth; wife of Bragi. Also **I'thun.**

I·thu·ri·el (i·thyōōr'ē·əl) In Milton's *Paradise Lost*, an angel sent by Gabriel to search for Satan. [<Hebrew *Yithūrī'ēl* the superiority of God]

ith·y·phal·lic (ith'ə·fal'ik) *adj.* **1** Relating to the phallus used in the festivals of Bacchus; hence, obscene; lewd. **2** In classical prosody, describing a trochaic tripody: used in verse sung in the phallic processions. [<L *ithyphallicus* <Gk. *ithyphallikos* <*ithyphallos* <*ithys* erect, rigid + *phallos* a phallus]

i·tin·er·a·cy (ī·tin'ər·ə·sē, i·tin'-) *n.* A passing from place to place in circuit, as in the discharge of ministerial duties. Also **i·tin'er·an·cy.**

i·tin·er·ant (ī·tin'ər·ənt, i·tin'-) *adj.* Going from place to place. — *n.* One who travels from place to place, as a minister serving a circuit of churches. [<LL *itinerans, -antis*, ppr. of *itinerari* make a journey < *iter, itineris* journey] — **i·tin'er·ant·ly** *adv.*

i·tin·er·ar·y (ī·tin'ə·rer'ē, i·tin'-) *n. pl.* **·ar·ies** **1** A detailed account or diary of a journey. **2** A plan of a proposed tour. **3** An exploring tour, or its record. **4** A route pursued in traveling. **5** Originally, a book or chart giving the roads, places, and distances of a region or along a route. **6** A guidebook. **7** In the Roman Catholic Church, a form of prayer for clergy departing on a journey. — *adj.* **1** Pertaining to or done on a journey. **2** Itinerant. [<LL *itinerarium*, neut. of *itinerarius* pertaining to a journey < *iter, itineris* journey, route]

i·tin·er·ate (ī·tin'ər·āt, i·tin'-) *v.i.* **·at·ed, ·at·ing** To journey from place to place in or on circuit; to roam; wander. [<LL *itineratus*, pp. of *itinerari* make a journey. See ITINERANT.] — **i·tin'er·a'tion** *n.*

-itis *suffix* Inflammation of: *peritonitis, laryngitis.* [<Gk.]

it'll (it'l) **1** It will. **2** It shall.

its (its) *pronominal adj.* (possessive case of the pronoun *it*) Belonging or pertaining to it: *its* color. [<IT + *'s*, possessive case ending; written *it's* until the 19th century]

it's (its) **1** It is. **2** It has.

it·self (it·self') *pron.* It: an intensive or reflexive use. Also *Scot.* **it·sel'.**

it's me See note under ME.

I·tur·bi (ē·tōōr'bē), **José**, born 1895, U.S. pianist and conductor born in Spain.

-ity *suffix of nouns* The state or condition of being: *probity.* [<F *-ité* <L *-itas*]

I·tys (ī'tis) In Greek mythology, the son of Tereus, who was killed by his mother and aunt. See PHILOMELA.

I·u·lus (ī·yōō'ləs) See ASCANIUS.

I·van (ī'vən, *Russian* i·vän') Russian form of JOHN.

— **Ivan III,** 1440–1505, grand duke of Muscovy from 1462; founded the Russian Empire: known as *Ivan the Great.*

— **Ivan IV,** 1530–84, first czar of Russia 1547–1584: known as *Ivan the Terrible.*

I·van·hoe (ī'vən·hō) A historical romance by Sir Walter Scott based on the Norman-Saxon conflict in England at the time of Richard I.

I·va·no·vo (ē·vä'nô·vô) A city in Russian S.F.S.R. NE of Moscow. Formerly **Ivanovo-Voz·ne·sensk** (vôz·nye·syensk').

I've (īv) I have.

-ive *suffix of adjectives* **1** Having a tendency or predisposition to: *disruptive.* **2** Having the nature, character, or quality of: *massive.* Also *-ative.* [<F *-if* <L *-ivus*, suffix of adjectives]

Ives (īvz), **Charles,** 1874–1954, U.S. composer. — **Frederick Eugene,** 1856–1937, U.S. inventor, pioneer in photography. — **James Merritt** See CURRIER AND IVES.

i·vied (ī'vēd) *adj.* Covered or overgrown with ivy.

I·vi·za (ē·vē'thä) Third largest of the Balearic Islands; 230 square miles; capital, Iviza. *Spanish* **I·bi·za** (ē·vē'thä).

i·vo·ry (ī'vər·ē) *n. pl.* **·ries** **1** The hard, creamy-white, fine-grained, opaque dentine that constitutes the greater part of the tusks of certain animals, as the elephant, walrus, etc. ◆ Collateral adjective: *eburnean.* **2** Any form of dentine. **3** Some ivorylike substance. **4** *pl.* Things made of, consisting of, or similar to ivory; especially, in slang use, the teeth, billiard balls, dice, keys of a piano. **5** The ivory nut. **6** The color of ivory. — *adj.* Made of or resembling ivory. [<OF *ivurie* <L *eboreus* of ivory < *ebur* ivory]

i·vo·ry·bill (ī'vər·ē·bil') *n.* A large North American woodpecker (*Campephilus principalis*), now rare, having a white or ivory-like bill.

ivory black A deep-black pigment made by charring bones or ivory scraps; carbon black.

Ivory Coast The coastal region of western Africa along the Gulf of Guinea.

Ivory Coast Republic An independent republic of the French Community in western Africa; 127,520 miles; capital, Abidjan.

ivory gull The white arctic gull (*Pagophila alba*).

ivory nut The hard, ivorylike seed of the ivory palm, used for small carvings, buttons, etc.; vegetable ivory.

ivory palm The South American palm (*Phytelephas macrocarpa*) that bears ivory nuts.

ivory tower A place or condition of seclusion from the world and worldly attitudes, reality, action, etc.

i·vo·ry·type (ī'vər·ē·tīp') *n. Phot.* A picture made by fixing a translucent photograph over another.

I·vry-la-Ba·tail·le (ē·vrē'lá·bá·tä'y') A town in NW France; scene of a Huguenot victory under Henri of Navarre over the Catholic league, 1590.

i·vy (ī'vē) *n. pl.* **i·vies** **1** A European, evergreen, climbing or creeping shrub (*Hedera helix*) of the ginseng or ivy family, bearing glossy leaves, small yellowish flowers, and black berries: also called **English ivy.** **2** One of various other climbing plants, as the **Japanese** or **Boston ivy** (*Parthenocissus tricuspidata*) and the **ground ivy** (*Nepeta hederacea*). [OE *īfig*]

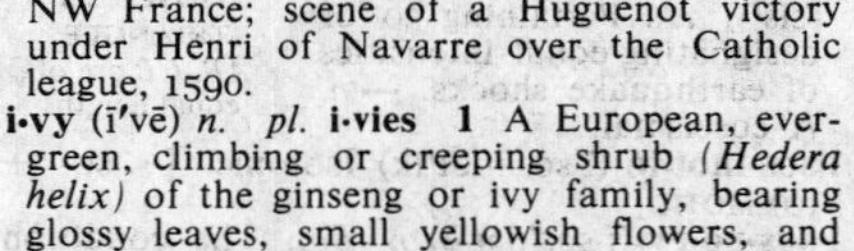

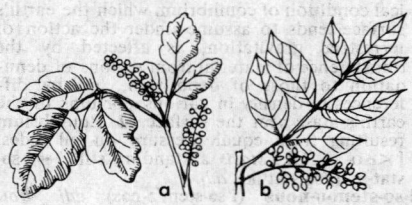

IVY
a. Poison ivy (*Rhus radicans*).
b. Poison sumac (*Rhus vernix*).

i·vy·ber·ry (ī'vē·ber'ē) *n. pl.* **·ries** Wintergreen.

Ivy League An association, primarily athletic, of colleges in the NE United States, comprising Brown, Columbia, Cornell, Dartmouth, Harvard, Princeton, the University of

Pennsylvania, and Yale: often used attributively to denote the fashions or manners characteristic of students in these colleges: *Ivy League* clothes.

ivy tod An ivy plant.

ivy vine **1** An American vitaceous plant (*Ampelopsis cordata*) with cordate leaves. **2** The Virginia creeper.

i·wis (i·wis′) *adv. Archaic* Certainly; surely; to wit: in later use written mistakenly *I wis*, through confusion with the verb *wit*. Also spelled *ywis*. [OE *gewis*]

I·wo Ji·ma (ē′wō jē′mä, ē′wə jē′mə) The largest of the Volcano Islands in the North Pacific; taken after severe fighting (1945) by American forces in World War II.

Ix·elles (ēk·sel′) A suburb SE of Brussels. *Flemish* **El·se·ne** (el′sə·nə).

ix·i·a (ik′sē·ə) *n.* Any of a genus (*Ixia*) of South African bulbous plants of the iris family, with narrow sword-shaped leaves, and spikes of large, showy, ornamental flowers. [<NL <Gk. *ixos* birdlime; from their viscid nature]

Ix·i·on (ik·sī′ən) In Greek mythology, a Thessalian king and father of the Centaurs, who was punished by Zeus for his love for Hera by being tied to a perpetually revolving wheel in Hades. [<Gk. *Ixíōn*]

ix·o·di·a·sis (ik′sə·dī′ə·sis) *n. Pathol.* Skin disease caused by ticks of the genus *Ixodes*; tick fever. [<NL *Ixodes,* genus of ticks + -IASIS]

Ix·ta·ci·hau·tl (ēs′tä·sē′wät·l) A dormant volcano in central Mexico; 17,342 feet; last eruption, 1868. Also **Iz·tac·ci·hua·tl** (ēs′täk·sē′wät·l).

ix·tle (iks′tlē, is′tlē) See ISTLE.

I·ye·ya·su (ē·yä·yä·sōō), 1543–1616, Japanese shogun, general, and statesman; founder of the Tokugawa shogunate.

Iy·yar (ē′yär) A Hebrew month. Also **I′yar.** See CALENDAR (Hebrew).

I·zaak (ē′zäk) Dutch and Polish form of ISAAC. Also *Hungarian* **I·zsák** (ē′zäk).

I·za·bal (ē·sä·bäl′), **Lake** A lake in eastern Guatemala.

iz·ar (iz′ər) *n. Arabic* A piece of white cotton fabric worn as the chief outer garment of Moslem women.

–ization *suffix* State or process of: used to form nouns from verbs in *-ize: oxidization.* [<-IZE + -ATION]

–ize *suffix of verbs* **1** To make; cause to become or resemble: *Christianize, concretize, Americanize.* **2** Subject to the action of; affect with: *oxidize.* **3** Change into; become: *mineralize.* **4** To act in the manner of; to practice: *sympathize.* Also *–ise.* [<F *-iser* <L *-izare* <Gk. *-izein*]

I·zhevsk (ē·zhefsk′) The capital of the Udmurt Autonomous S.S.R.

Iz·ma·il (ēz·mä·ēl′) A city on the Danube in Ukrainian S.S.R.

Iz·mir (ēz·mir′) The Turkish name for SMYRNA.

Iz·nik (ēz·nēk′) A village of NW Turkey on the site of ancient Nicaea. Also **Is·nik′.**

iz·zard (iz′ərd) *n. Colloq.* The letter Z. — **from A to izzard** From beginning to end. [Earlier *ezed,* var. of ZED]

J

j, J (jā) *n. pl.* **j's, J's** or **js, Js, jays** (jāz) **1** The tenth letter of the English alphabet: originally identical with Roman *I.* In the 17th century, the calligraphic practice of carrying initial *I* (which usually had consonant value) both above and below the line gradually developed into a graphic distinction between *i* the vowel and *i* or *j* the consonant. **2** A sound of the letter *j,* usually a voiced affricate, as in *judge* (juj); in borrowings from Modern French, often a voiced, alveolar fricative, as in *jabot.* See ALPHABET. — *symbol* **1** In Roman numerals, one: used as a variant of i at the end of a number, as *vij,* especially in medical prescriptions. **2** Anything shaped like a J, as a bolt or hook.

ja (yä) *interj. & adv. German* Yes.

jab (jab) *v.t. & v.i.* **jabbed, jab·bing 1** To poke or thrust sharply, as with the point of something. **2** To punch or strike with sharp blows. — *n.* A sharp thrust or poke: punch. [Var. of JOB²]

Jab·al·pur (jub′əl·pôr, -pōr) The Hindi name for JUBBULPORE.

jab·ber (jab′ər) *v.t. & v.i.* To speak rapidly or unintelligibly; chatter. See synonyms under BABBLE. — *n.* Rapid or unintelligible talk; chatter. [Prob. imit.] — **jab′ber·er** *n.*

Ja·bez (jā′biz) A masculine personal name. [<Hebrew, sorrow]

jab·i·ru (jab′ə·rōō) *n.* A large tropical American wading bird (*Jabiru mycteria*) of the stork family, with white plumage and a scarlet inflatable pouch. [<Tupian]

jab·o·ran·di (jab′ə·ran′dē) *n.* **1** Any of a genus (*Pilocarpus*) of numerous South American shrubs of the rue family, especially *P. jaborandi.* **2** The dried leaves of this and allied plants, which yield pilocarpine and other medicinal alkaloids. [<Tupian]

ja·bot (zha·bō′, jab′ō; *Fr.* zhà·bō′) *n. pl.* **·bots** (-bōz′, *Fr.* -bō′) A lace frill worn by women on the bodice; formerly, a ruffle on a man's shirt bosom. [<F, lit., a gizzard]

ja·bot·i·ca·ba (jə·bot′ə·kä′bə) *n.* A semitropical evergreen tree (*Myrciaria cauliflora*) of the myrtle family, with edible, grapelike fruit: cultivated in Florida and California. [< Tupian *jabuti* a tortoise + *caba* fat]

jab·o·ty (jab′ə·tē) *n.* **1** An oil-bearing seed from a tropical American tree (genus *Erisma*). **2** The oil from this seed, sometimes used as a substitute for cocoa butter. [<Tupian]

ja·cal (hä·käl′) *n. pl.* **·ca·les** (-kä′lās) A one-room Mexican hut built of upright poles laced together with wicker and plastered with mud or adobe. [<Sp. <Nahuatl]

jac·a·mar (jak′ə·mär) *n.* A tropical American insectivorous bird (family *Galbulidae*) of various genera, having golden–green or coppery plumage. [<F <Tupian *jacamaciri*]

ja·ça·na (zhä′sə·nä′) Any of a family (*Jacanidae*) of small tropical wading birds with long, straight claws by which they walk over the floating leaves of aquatic plants. [<Pg. <Tupian]

jac·a·ran·da (jak′ə·ran′də) *n.* **1** Any of a genus (*Jacaranda*) of tropical American trees and shrubs of the bignonia family, with a hard, fine-textured wood: some species, as *J. caroba,* are used in medicine. **2** Brazilian rosewood (*Dalbergia nigra*): used for making tool handles, radio cabinets, etc. [<Tupian]

Já·chy·mov (yä′khi·môv) A town in western Czechoslovakia, in the former province of Bohemia: German *Joachimsthal.*

ja·cinth (jä′sinth, jas′inth) *n.* **1** A reddish-orange variety of zircon: used as a gemstone. **2** *Obs.* A hyacinth. [<OF *iacinte* <L *hyacinthus.* Doublet of HYACINTH.]

jack¹ (jak) *n.* **1** *Mech.* **a** A device, appliance, or part of a machine: so called from its serving to supply the place of an assistant. **b** A portable device, operating by lever, screw, or other mechanical principle, for exerting considerable energy through a short distance: used in raising weights. **2** The male of the ass or of certain other animals. **3** A flag showing the canton or union of the national ensign without the fly, as of the United States or of Great Britain. See UNION JACK. **4** A playing card; in most games, the lowest of the face cards; a knave. **5** *U.S. Slang* Money. **6** *Electr.* A spring clip to which the wires of a circuit may be attached and which is arranged for the insertion of a plug. **7** A bootjack. **8** A jacklight. **9** A device to prevent back draft in a chimney or vent pipe. **10** *Naut.* An iron crosstree at the topgallant-masthead: also **jack crosstree. 11** An automatic figure of a man which strikes the time bell of a clock. **12** A small white ball used as the object played for in the game of bowls. **13** The hopper of a pianoforte; in a harpsichord, the piece of wood holding the quill which strikes the string. **14** One of various fishes, as a pike or pickerel. **15** *pl.* The game played with jackstones. — **hydraulic jack** A device for lifting heavy weights or exerting great force by fluid pressure from a hand pump connected with a large-bore cylinder and a piston: also **hydrostatic jack.** — *v.t.* **1** To raise or lift with or as with a jack. **2** *Colloq.* To advance, as a price or charge:

often with *up.* **3** *U.S.* To jack-light. [from *Jack,* a personal name]

jack² (jak) *n.* **1** A cultivated tree (*Artocarpus heterophyllus*) of SE Asia, resembling the breadfruit tree. **2** Its yellow wood, furnishing valuable lumber. **3** The large fruit, resembling the breadfruit, produced by this tree. [<Pg. *jaca* <Malayalam *chakka*]

jack³ (jak) *n.* A medieval coat of mail made of two thicknesses of leather or cloth and padded; a gambeson. [<OF *jacque* <Sp. *jaco,* ? <Arabic *shakk*]

Jack (jak) **1** A nickname for JOHN; earlier, for JAMES, as derived from JACOB. **2** Hence, from its frequency, a man; fellow; especially, a sailor; also, a handy man for odd jobs: in these senses usually **jack.** [<OF *Jacques* Jacob]

jack-a-dan·dy (jak′ə·dan′dē) *n. pl.* **·dies** A ridiculous fop.

jack·al (jak′ôl, -əl) *n.* **1** One of various dog-like carnivorous mammals (family *Canidae*), smaller than the wolf, with a long bushy tail, feeding on small animals and on carrion. **2** One who does base work to serve another's purpose: from the erroneous notion that the jackal finds prey for the lion. Also **jack′all.** — *v.i.* To do menial work. [<Turkish *chakal* <Persian *shaghal*]

Jack-a-Lent (jak′ə·lent′) See JACK-O'-LENT.

jack-a-napes (jak′ə·nāps) *n.* An impertinent fellow; an upstart. [<*Jack Napes,* nickname of William de la Pole, 15th c. Duke of Suffolk]

Jack and Jill In an old English nursery rime, a boy and girl who "went up a hill to fetch a pail of water." Hence, any man and his sweetheart or wife.

jack·ass (jak′as′) *n.* **1** The male ass. **2** A foolish person; blockhead.

jackass brig A brigantine.

jack bean A three-leaved climber of the bean family (*Canavalia ensiformis*) having purple flowers in auxiliary racemes and long pods: grown for stock feed in the southern United States: also called *overlook.*

jack·boots (jak′bōōts′) *n. pl.* Heavy topboots reaching above the knees.

jack box A unit for plugging a loudspeaker or individual headphone into a radio receiving system: used in airplanes, etc.

jack·daw (jak′dô′) *n.* **1** A small, glossy-black, crowlike bird (*Corvus monedual*) of Europe, often tamed as a pet. **2** Any of various American grackles, especially the boat-tailed grackle (*Cassidix mexicanus*).

jack·er (jak′ər) *n.* One who or that which jacks.

jack·e·roo (jak'ə·roo') n. Austral. Colloq. A station employee who is being trained for managerial status. Also **jack'a·roo'**. [<JACK¹ + (KANGA)ROO]

jack·et (jak'it) n. 1 A short coat, usually not extending below the hips. 2 Anything resembling a jacket. 3 A covering for a steam cylinder, to prevent radiation of heat. 4 A removable paper wrapper or cover for a bound book. 5 An open envelope or folder, used for filing letters, documents, papers, etc. 6 A covering of hard metal on a bullet or shell. 7 The skin of a potato. — v.t. To cover with a jacket. [<OF jaquette, dim. of jaque a coat] — **jack'et·ed** adj.

jack·ey (jak'ē), **jack·ie** See JACKY.

Jack Frost A personification of wintry or frosty weather.

jack·ham·mer (jak'ham'ər) A rock drill operated by compressed air.

jack-in-a-box (jak'in·ə·boks') n. 1 A toy consisting of a grotesque figure in a box, springing up when the lid is unfastened. 2 A tropical tree (Hernandia sonora) yielding a fruit that when shaken makes a rattling sound. 3 A rogue; swindler. Also **jack'-in-the-box'**.

jack-in-the-pul·pit (jak'in·thə·pool'pit) n. A common American herb (Arisaema triphyllum) of the arum family, growing from a turnip-shaped bulb, with an intensely acrid juice and a curious spike of flowers enclosed in a greenish-purple spathe: also called Indian turnip.

JACK-IN-THE-PULPIT
Fruit and flower.

Jack Ketch (kech) A public executioner or hangman. [after John Ketch, died 1686, executioner under James II]

jack·knife (jak'nīf') n. pl. **·knives** (-nīvz) 1 A large pocket knife with recessed handle into which the blade is folded. 2 A dive during which the body is doubled from the hips with the hands touching the ankles, and then straightened before entering the water.

jack·leg (jak'leg') n. One who professes more knowledge, skill, or standing than he has; especially, an unprincipled lawyer; a shyster. — adj. Untrained; incompetent; unprincipled.

jack·light (jak'līt') n. U.S. A torch or light used in hunting or fishing at night to attract and dazzle game or fish.

jack·light (jak'līt') v.t. & v.i. To seek (game or fish) with a jacklight.

jack·o (jak'ō) n. pl. **jack·os** An ape; jocko.

jack oak A black-barked oak of the eastern United States (Quercus marilandica).

jack-of-all-trades (jak'əv·ôl'trādz') n. One who is able to do many kinds of work.

jack-o'-lan·tern (jak'ə·lan'tərn) n. 1 A will-o'-the-wisp; ignis fatuus. 2 A lantern made of a pumpkin hollowed and carved into a grotesque face, or an imitation of this. Also **jack'-a-lan'tern**.

Jack-o'-Lent (jak'ə·lent') n. An effigy of Judas Iscariot, formerly carried in processions and pelted in Lent; hence, a target for criticism; butt. Also spelled Jack-a-lent.

jack pine The gray pine (Pinus banksiana), growing chiefly on barren tracts of North America.

jack·plane (jak'plān') n. A carpenter's roughing plane.

jack·pot (jak'pot') n. 1 In poker, a pot that must accumulate till one of the players gets a pair of jacks or cards of higher value on the deal; also, a game or part of it in which this rule is observed. 2 Hence, any pot or pool in which contributions accumulate. — **to hit the jackpot** U.S. Colloq. To win the biggest possible prize; to achieve a major success.

jack rabbit One of a genus (Lepus) of large American hares with long hind legs and long ears.

jack·screw (jak'skroo') n. A mechanical jack in which pressure is transmitted by the action of a screw.

jack·shaft (jak'shaft', -shäft') n. 1 A shaft sunk in a mine. 2 A bar or crosspiece for supporting a mechanical drill, held in place by jackscrews.

jack snipe 1 A small European snipe. 2 The pectoral sandpiper.

Jack·son (jak'sən) The capital of Mississippi.

Jack·son (jak'sən), **Andrew**, 1767–1845, president of the United States 1829–37: called "Old Hickory." — **Chevalier**, born 1865, U.S. laryngologist. — **Helen Hunt**, 1831–85, née Maria Fiske, U.S. novelist. — **Thomas Jonathan**, 1824–63, Confederate general: known as Stonewall Jackson from the firm stand of his command at the first battle of Bull Run, 1861.

Jackson Day An anniversary celebration of Andrew Jackson's victory at New Orleans on January 8, 1815: often commemorated by a Democratic party dinner.

Jack·so·ni·an (jak·sō'nē·ən) adj. Of, pertaining to, or brought into notice by a person named Jackson; specifically, relating to Andrew Jackson, seventh president of the United States. — n. An advocate of the political principles of Andrew Jackson.

Jacksonian epilepsy Pathol. A form of epilepsy characterized by local spasms which tend to spread gradually outward from the focal point, usually without loss of consciousness. Also called focal epilepsy. [after John Hughlings Jackson, 1834–1911, English physician]

Jack·son·ville (jak'sən·vil) A port near the mouth of the St. Johns River in northern Florida.

Jack Sprat A character in an English nursery rime.

jack·stay (jak'stā') n. Naut. 1 A rope or rod along the upper surface of a yard, to which to fasten a sail. 2 A rope or rod running up and down on the forward side of a mast, on which a yard travels; a traveler.

jack·stone (jak'stōn') n. 1 One of a set of stones or knobbed metal pieces used in a child's game: also jack. 2 pl. The game so played; jacks.

jack·straw (jak'strô') n. 1 A straw effigy; man of straw. 2 One of a set of straws or thin strips of wood, bone, etc., used in playing a child's game. 3 pl. The game played with them.

jack·tar (jak'tär') n. Colloq. A sailor. Also spelled jack'-tar', jack tar, Jack Tar.

jack towel A long coarse towel hanging on a roller.

jack·y (jak'ē) n. pl. **jack·ies** 1 A sailor. 2 Brit. Slang Gin. Also spelled jackey, jackie. [Dim. of JACK]

Ja·co (yä'kōō) An island dependency of Portuguese Timor; 5 square miles: also Yako.

Ja·cob (jā'kəb, Du., Ger. yä'kôp) A masculine personal name. Also Fr. **Ja·cob** (zhà·kôb'), Sp. **Ja·co·bo** (hä·kō'bō), Lat. **Ja·co·bus** (jə·kō'bəs), [<Hebrew Jacob, supplanter] — **Jacob** A Hebrew patriarch; second son of Isaac and father of the founders of the twelve tribes of Israel: also called Israel. Gen xxv 26.

Ja·cob (jā'kəb), **Arthur**, 1790–1874, Irish physician.

Ja·co·be·an (jak'ə·bē'ən) adj. 1 Of or pertaining to the time of James I of England and sometimes of James II; specifically, of or pertaining to an English architectural and furniture style of the early 17th century, representing the merging of English Tudor forms into those of the Renaissance, and sometimes, by extension, the architecture of the entire Stuart period and of the Commonwealth. 2 Of or pertaining to the apostle St. James the Less or the epistle ascribed to him. — n. A Jacobean writer or politician. Also **Jac'o·bae'an**. [<LL Jacobaeus <Jacobus James]

jac·o·bin (jak'ə·bin) n. A pigeon with neck feathers ruffed so as to form a hood.

Jac·o·bin (jak'ə·bin) n. 1 A member of a French revolutionary society that inaugurated the Reign of Terror, 1793; dissolved, 1799. 2 Hence, an extreme revolutionist. 3 pl. Dominican friars before the French Revolution. [<F Jacobin of St. James <Med. L Jacobinus <LL Jacobus James; with ref. to the church of St. James, in Paris, where they first met]

Jac·o·bin·i·cal (jak'ə·bin'i·kəl) adj. 1 Belonging to the French Jacobins. 2 Turbulently democratic; revolutionary; radical. Also **Jac'·o·bin'ic**. — **Jac'o·bin'i·cal·ly** adv.

Jac·o·bin·ism (jak'ə·bin·iz'əm) n. 1 Unreasonable or violent opposition to legitimate government; popular turbulence. 2 A Jacobinical characteristic or idea.

Jac·o·bin·ize (jak'ə·bin·īz') v.t. **·ized**, **·iz·ing** To affect with or convert to Jacobinism.

Jac·o·bite (jak'ə·bīt) n. 1 An adherent of James II of England after his abdication in 1688, or of his royal line. 2 An adherent of the Jacobite Church. — adj. Of or pertaining to the Jacobites: also **Jac·o·bit·ic** (jak'ə·bit'ik), **Jac'o·bit'i·cal**. [<L Jacobus James + -ITE¹]

Jacobite Church A Monophysitic sect of Syria, Mesopotamia, and Kurdistan, founded by Jacobus Baradaeus, died 578, a Greek monk of Constantinople: regarded as heretical by the Greek Church.

Jac·o·bit·ism (jak'ə·bīt'iz·əm) n. The tenets of the English Jacobites, or of the Syrian sect of Jacobites.

Jacob's ladder 1 A ladder from earth to heaven that Jacob saw in a dream. Gen. xxviii 12. 2 Naut. A rope ladder, often with wooden steps.

Ja·cob's-lad·der (jā'kəbz·lad'ər) n. 1 A common European ornamental herb (Polemonium caeruleum), having an arrangement of its leaves and leaflets suggestive of a ladder: often called makebate. 2 Any of several related species found in America.

ja·co·bus (jə·kō'bəs) n. An English gold coin of the reign of James I, varying in value from 20 to 22 shillings. [<L Jacobus James]

jac·o·net (jak'ə·net) n. 1 A soft, thin, white cotton cloth. 2 A cotton fabric with one side glazed. [from Jagganath (now Puri) in India, where first made]

Jac·quard (jə·kärd', Fr. zhà·kàr') adj. Invented by or pertaining to J. M. Jacquard, 1752–1834, a French weaver who invented the **Jacquard loom**, used in weaving figured materials.

Jacque·mi·not (jak'mi·nō, Fr. zhàk·mē·nō') n. A deep-red, hybrid perpetual rose. Also **General Jacqueminot**. [after J. F. Jacqueminot, 1787–1865, French general]

Jacque·rie (jə·krē') n. The peasant insurrection in France in 1358: so called from the scornful nickname Jacques Bonhomme given by the nobles to the peasantry; hence, any revolt of peasants.

Jacques (zhàk) The French form of JAMES.

jac·ta a·le·a est (jak'tə ā'lē·ə est) Latin The die has been cast.

jac·ta·tion (jak·tā'shən) n. 1 The act of throwing. 2 Jactitation (def. 2). 3 Exercise, as in riding. 4 Boasting. [<L jactatio, -onis <jactare, freq. of jacere throw]

jac·ti·ta·tion (jak'tə·tā'shən) n. 1 A public boasting; bragging. 2 Pathol. A morbid restlessness, as in acute disease. 3 Law A false assertion, as of marriage, repeated to the injury of another; an action to enjoin such false pretension. [<Med. L jactitatio, -onis <L jactitare say publicly, freq. of jactare hurl]

Ja·cuí (zhə·kwē') A river in central Río Grande do Sul state, Brazil, flowing 280 miles south and east to the Lagoa dos Patos.

jac·u·late (jak'yə·lāt) v.t. **·lat·ed**, **·lat·ing** Rare To hurl, as a dart. [<L jaculatus, pp. of jaculare throw] — **jac'u·la'tion** n.

jac·u·la·to·ry (jak'yə·lə·tôr'ē, -tō'rē) adj. Darting or thrown out suddenly.

jade¹ (jād) n. 1 A hard, tough, greenish or white silicate, used for making ornaments and including chiefly two species: jadeite and nephrite. 2 The greenish color of jade; jade green. [<F jade, var. of ejade <Sp. (piedra de) ijada (stone for) colic, lit., the side, ribs]

jade² (jād) n. 1 An old, worn-out horse. 2 A worthless person; specifically, a hussy. 3 A woman: ironical usage. — v.t. & v.i. **jad·ed**, **jad·ing** To weary or become weary by hard service; tire. See synonyms under TIRE¹. [Origin uncertain]

jad·ed (jā'did) adj. 1 Worn-out; exhausted. 2 Satiated; sated, as from overindulgence. — **jad'ed·ly** adv. — **jad'ed·ness** n.

jade green Any of several shades of green characteristic of jade.

jade·ite (jā'dīt) n. A translucent sodium-aluminum silicate of the pyroxene group. [<JADE¹ + -ITE¹]

jad·ish (jā'dish) adj. 1 Vicious: said of a horse. 2 Unchaste or wanton: said of a woman. Also **jad'y**. — **jad'ish·ly** adv. — **jad'ish·ness** n.

jae·ger (yā'gər) n. 1 (also jā'gər) Any of a genus (Stercorarius) of sea birds which pursue and harass gulls and terns until they drop or disgorge their prey. 2 A huntsman or hunting attendant. 3 Obs. A soldier of the Ger-

man or Austrian army especially trained in scouting, sharpshooting, and forestry: hired by England during the American Revolution. Also spelled *yager*. Also **jä'ger**. [<G, hunter <*jagen* hunt]

Ja·el (jā'əl) In the Bible, an Israelite heroine who killed Sisera. *Judges* iv 17.

Ja·én (hä·ān') A province of southern Spain; 5,205 square miles; capital Jaén.

Jaf·fa (jaf'ə, yaf'ə) A port in western Israel; included in Tel Aviv since 1950: Old Testament *Joppa*. *Hebrew* **Ya·fo** (yä·fō').

Jaff·na (jäf'nə) A port on **Jaffna Peninsula**, the northernmost part of Ceylon.

jag¹ (jag) *n.* **1** A projecting point; notch; tooth. **2** A bolt with barbed point. **3** *Brit. Dial.* A stab or jab, as of a dirk. — *v.t.* **jagged, jagging 1** To cut notches or jags in. **2** To cut unevenly or with slashing strokes, as a garment. Also **jagg.** [ME *jagge*; origin unknown]

jag² (jag) *n.* **1** A load for one horse; small load. **2** *Slang* Enough liquor to intoxicate; also, intoxication: to have a *jag* on. Also **jagg.** [Origin unknown]

Jag·a·nath (jug'ə·nät, -nôt), **Jag·a·na·tha** (jug'ə·nä'tə), **Jag·gur·nath** (jug'ər·nät) See JUGGERNAUT.

jag·ged (jag'id) *adj.* Having jags or notches. Also *jaggy*. See synonyms under ROUGH. — **jag'ged·ly** *adv.* — **jag'ged·ness** *n.*

jag·ger·y (jag'ər·ē) *n.* **1** A coarse sugar made in the East Indies from the sap of the date palm or from sugarcane. **2** A wine made from the coconut palm. Also **jag'gar·y, jag'gher·y, jag·ra** (jag'rə). [<Hind. *jāgrī* <Skt. *çarkara* sugar]

jag·gy (jag'ē) *adj.* **·gi·er, ·gi·est** Having notches; jagged.

ja·ghir (jä·gir') *n. Anglo-Indian* The government revenues of a tract of land assigned with the power to collect and administer. Also **ja·gheer', ja·ghire'.** [<Persian *jā* place + *gīr* holding]

jag·uar (jag'wär, jag'yōō·är) *n.* A large, tawny, spotted feline (*Panthera onca*) of tropical America. [<Tupian *jaguara*]

ja·gua·run·di (jä'gwä·run'dē) *n.* A carnivorous, weasel-like wildcat (genus *Felis*) of tropical America, having grayish-brown fur: also called *yaguarundi*. Also **ja'gua·ron'di.** [<Tupian]

JAGUAR
(Up to 9 feet in length; tail: about 2 1/2 feet)

Jah (jä, yä) *Hebrew* Jehovah. *Psalms* lxviii 4.

Jah·veh, Jah·we (yä've), **Jah·vism, Jah·wism** (yä'viz·əm), etc. See YAHWEH, etc.

jai a·lai (hī ə·lī') A Spanish game, popular in Latin America, played by two opposed couples in a court called a *frontón*: the ball is served against a wall, and each player wears a gauntlet from which projects a long, curved wicker racket, called the *cesta*, in which he alternately receives the ball and hurls it back against the wall. The first to miss loses the point. Compare *pelota*. [<Sp. <Basque, jolly festival]

Jai·hun (jī·hōōn') The Arabic name for the AMU DARYA.

jail (jāl) *n.* A building or place for the confinement of arrested persons or those guilty of minor offenses. — *v.t.* To put or hold in jail; imprison. Also, *Brit.,* gaol. [<OF *jaiole*, ult. <L *cavea* cave]

jail·bird (jāl'bûrd') *n. Colloq.* **1** One sentenced to or confined in prison. **2** A habitual lawbreaker; one often confined in jail. Also, *Brit.,* gaolbird.

jail-de·liv·er·y (jāl'di·liv'ər·ē) *n.* **1** *Law* The legal disposal, as by trial and condemnation or acquittal, of the cases of all prisoners awaiting trial. **2** The escape or forcible liberation of prisoners from jail.

jail·er (jā'lər) *n.* The officer in charge of a jail: also, *Brit.,* gaoler. Also **jail'or.**

Jai·lo·lo (jī·lō'lō) See HALMAHERA.

Jai·me (hī'mä) A Spanish form of JAMES.

Jain (jīn) *n.* An adherent of Jainism. — *adj.* Of or pertaining to Jainism. Also **Jai·na** (jī'nə). [<Hind. *Jaina* <*jina* victorious]

Jain·ism (jī'niz·əm) *n.* A Hindu religious system, founded about 500 B.C., which combines certain elements of Brahmanism and Buddhism, its principal distinctive features being the worship of sages or saints, known as *jinas*, and the great respect for the lives of animals.

Jai·pur (jī·pŏŏr') **1** A former princely state in the Rajputana States, India. **2** The capital of Rajasthan, formerly the capital of Jaipur.

Ja·kar·ta (jä·kär'tä) A port of NW Java, capital of the Republic of Indonesia: formerly *Batavia*: also *Djakarta*.

jake (jāk) *adj. Slang* All right; fine.

Jake (jāk) Diminutive of JACOB.

jakes (jāks) *n. Archaic* or *Dial.* A privy. [? from *Jake*, a personal name]

Ja·kob (yä'kôb) Danish, Polish, Swedish, and German form of JACOB.

jal·ap (jal'əp) *n.* **1** The dried root of any of several Mexican plants of the morning-glory family (especially *Exogonium purga*), used in medicine as a hydragog. **2** Any allied plant yielding a similar drug. Also *Obs.* **jal'op.** [<Sp. (*purga de*) *Jalapa* (medicine from) Jalapa] — **ja·lap·ic** (jə·lap'ik) *adj.*

Ja·la·pa (hä·lä'pä) The capital of Veracruz state, eastern Mexico. Officially **Ja·la'pa En·rí·quez** (en·rē'käs).

jal·a·pin (jal'ə·pin) *n.* A resinous glycoside contained in several convolvulaceous plants: used in medicine as a cathartic. [<JALAP + -IN]

Ja·lis·co (hä·lēs'kō) A state in west central Mexico, 31,152 square miles; capital, Guadalajara.

ja·lop·y (jə·lop'ē) *n. pl.* **·lop·ies** *U.S. Colloq.* A decrepit automobile. [Origin uncertain]

ja·lou·sie (jal'ōō·sē, zhal'ōō·zē') *n.* A Venetian blind. [<F, lit., jealousy]

Jal·u·it (jal'ōō·it) The largest atoll and administrative center of the Marshall Islands; 4 square miles.

jam¹ (jam) *v.* **jammed, jam·ming** *v.t.* **1** To press or force into a tight place or position; wedge or squeeze in. **2** To fill and block up by crowding: to *jam* a corridor. **3** To bruise or crush by violent pressure. **4** To cause (a machine, part, etc.) to become wedged or stuck fast so that it cannot work. **5** In radio, to interfere with (a broadcast, station, etc.) by transmitting on the same wavelength. — *v.i.* **6** To become wedged; stick fast. **7** To press or wedge; push: The crowd *jammed* into the room. **8** In jazz music, to improvise; also, to take part in a jam session. — *n.* **1** A number of people or objects closely crowded; a crush; the act of jamming. **2** A mass of logs, ice, etc., blocked in a stream. See synonyms under THRONG. — *adv.* Completely: *jam* full. ◆ Homophone: *jamb*. [Related to CHAMP¹]

Synonyms (verb): crowd, crush, force, pack, press, push, squeeze, throng. See HUSTLE. *Antonyms:* ease, free, liberate, loosen, release, relieve.

jam² (jam) *n.* A pulpy, sweet conserve of fruit boiled with sugar: distinguished from *jelly*. ◆ Homophone: *jamb*. [? <JAM¹, *v.*]

Ja·mai·ca (jə·mā'kə) *n.* Rum produced in Jamaica.

Ja·mai·ca (jə·mā'kə) An independent member of the Commonwealth of nations comprising the island of Jamaica, SE of Cuba; 4,411 square miles; capital, Kingston; and its dependencies, the Cayman Islands and Turks and Caicos Islands; total, 4,705 square miles. — **Ja·mai'can** *adj. & n.*

jamb (jam) *n.* **1** A side post or side of a doorway, window, etc. **2** A jambeau. ◆ Homophone: *jam*. [<OF *jambe* leg, support <LL *gamba* hoof, leg <Celtic]

jam·ba·la·ya (jam'bə·lä'yə, zham'-) *n.* A traditional Creole dish of rice cooked with seafood and fowl. [<Provençal *jambalaia*]

jam·beau (jam·bō') *n. pl.* **·beaux** (-bōz') A piece of armor for the leg. Also **jambe** (jam). [<OF *jambe* a leg]

Jam·bol (yäm'bôl) See YAMBOL.

jam·bo·ree (jam'bə·rē') *n.* **1** *Colloq.* A boisterous frolic or spree. **2** A large, especially international, assembly of Boy Scouts. **3** In euchre, a lone hand consisting of the five highest cards. [<JAM¹; on analogy with *corroboree, chivaree*]

James (jāmz) A masculine personal name. [<Sp. *Jaime*, var. of *Jacobo* JACOB]
— **James** One of the brothers of Jesus: identified by some with James the Less. *Mark* vi 3.
— **James I,** 1394-1437, king of Scotland 1406-1437: educated in England; author of *The Kingis Quair.*
— **James III,** 1451-88, king of Scotland 1460-1488, defeated at Bannockburn; murdered.
— **James IV,** 1473-1513, king of Scotland 1488-1513; defeated and killed at Flodden Field.
— **James I,** 1566-1625, first Stuart king of England 1603-25; as **James VI,** king of Scotland 1567-1625. See under BIBLE.
— **James II,** 1633-1701, king of England 1685-88; deposed.
— **James Edward** See STUART, JAMES EDWARD.
— **James the Greater** One of the Twelve Apostles; son of Zebedee, brother of John.
— **James the Less** One of the Twelve Apostles; son of Alphaeus.

James (jāmz), **Henry,** 1843-1916, U.S. novelist and critic active in England. — **Jesse (Woodson),** 1847-82, U.S. outlaw. — **William,** 1842-1910, U.S. psychologist; brother of Henry James.

James Bay The southern projection of Hudson Bay, Canada.

Jame·son (jām'sən), **Sir Leander Starr,** 1853-1917, administrator in South Africa; leader of the unsuccessful **Jameson's raid** into the Transvaal, Dec. 29, 1895.

James River 1 A river in Virginia, flowing 340 miles to Hampton Roads. **2** A river in North and South Dakota, flowing 710 miles SE to the Missouri: also *Dakota River.*

James·town (jāmz'toun) **1** A restored village in eastern Virginia: the first permanent English settlement within the limits of the United States, 1607. **2** A port and the capital of St. Helena.

Jamestown weed See JIMSONWEED.

jammed on the wind *Naut.* Sailing close-hauled.

Jam·mu (jum'ōō) **1** A province of Jammu and Kashmir; 12,378 square miles. **2** A city in SW Jammu and Kashmir, India, capital of Jammu province, and former winter capital of Jammu and Kashmir.

Jammu and Kashmir A constituent State of India, 1957; an independent republic, 1952-57; a princely state within the Dominion of India, 1947-52, and in British India, 1846-1947; an object of contention between India and Pakistan since 1947; 92,780 square miles in all, 85,861 square miles under Indian control, the rest under Pakistani occupation though claimed by both countries: capital, Srinagar. Formerly **Kashmir and Jammu.**

jam-packed (jam'pakt') *adj. Colloq.* Crowded to capacity; as tightly packed as possible.

jam session An informal gathering of jazz musicians performing improvisations on various themes, each exploring the possibilities of his instrument while following no set musical form other than a motif mutually evolved.

Jam·shed·pur (jäm'shed·pŏŏr') A city in SE Bihar, India.

Jam·shid (jam'shid) In Iranian mythology, an early king, said to have reigned 700 years. Also **Jam'shyd.**

Jan (yän) Dutch and Polish form of JOHN.

Ja·ná·ček (yä'nä·chek), **Leoš,** 1854-1928, Czech composer.

Jane (jān) A feminine personal name; variant form of JOAN.

Janes·ville (jānz'vil) A city in southern Wisconsin, near Beloit; pop. 35,164.

Jan·et (jan'it, jə·net') A feminine personal name. [See JOAN]

Ja·net (zhà·ne'), **Pierre Marie Félix,** 1859-1947, French psychologist and neurologist.

jan·gle (jang'gəl) *v.* **·gled, ·gling** *v.i.* **1** To make harsh, unmusical sounds. **2** To wrangle; bicker. — *v.t.* **3** To cause to sound discordantly. — *n.* Discordant sound; wrangling. See synonyms under NOISE, QUARREL. [<OF *jangler*] — **jan'gler** *n.* — **jan'gling** *n.*

Ja·nic·u·lum (jə·nik'yə·ləm) A hill in Rome on the Tiber, opposite the original seven.

Ja·ni·na (yä'nē·nä) See IOANNINA.

jan·i·tor (jan'i·tər) n. **1** One who has the care of a building, offices, etc. **2** A doorkeeper; porter. [<L <janua door]

jan·i·zar·y (jan'ə·zer'ē) n. pl. **·zar·ies** One of the former bodyguards of the Turkish sultans, originally composed of young prisoners trained to arms: suppressed in 1826; also, sometimes, any Turkish soldier. Also **jan'i·sar·y**, **jan'is·sar·y**. [<F janissaire <Turkish yenicheri new army]

Jan May·en (yän' mī'ən) A Norwegian island in the Arctic Ocean between Norway and Greenland; 144 square miles.

jan·nock (jan'ok) n. Scot. Oaten bread; a cake.

Já·nos (ya'nôsh) Hungarian form of JOHN.

Jan·sen (jan'sən, Du. yän'sən), **Cornelis**, 1585–1638, Roman Catholic theologian; bishop of Ypres in Flanders. Also **Jan·se·ni·us** (jan·sē'nē·əs).

Jan·sen·ism (jan'sən·iz'əm) n. Theol. The doctrines taught by Cornelis Jansen, emphasizing predestination and the irresistibility of God's grace, and denying free will. — **Jan'sen·ist** n. — **Jan'sen·is·tic** or **·ti·cal** adj.

jant·y (jan'tē) See JAUNTY.

Jan·u·ar·y (jan'yoō·er'ē) n. The first month of the year, containing 31 days. [<L Januarius < Janus Janus]

Ja·nus (jā'nəs) In Roman mythology, the god of portals and beginnings, having two faces, one on each side of his head.

Ja·nus–faced (jā'nəs–fāst') adj. Two-faced; looking both ways; deceitful.

Jap (jap) adj. & n. Slang Japanese: an opprobrious usage.

JANUS

jap·a·con·i·tine (jap'ə·kon'ə·tēn) n. Chem. A white, crystalline, extremely poisonous alkaloid, $C_{24}H_{47}O_{11}N$, from the root of the Japanese aconite (Aconitum japonicum). [<JAP(ANESE) + ACONIT(E) + -INE[2]]

ja·pan (jə·pan') n. **1** A varnish used as a medium in which to grind colors, and as a drier for pigments. **2** A hard jet-black lacquer for coating sheet metal; Brunswick-black. — adj. Pertaining to or lacquered with japan. — v.t. **·panned**, **·pan·ning** To lacquer with or as with japan. [from JAPAN] — **ja·pan'ner** n.

Ja·pan (jə·pan') A constitutional empire of eastern Asia, comprising the four main islands of Honshu, Hokkaido, Kyushu, and Shikoku with many adjacent smaller islands; 147,692 square miles; capital, Tokyo: also Nihon, Nippon, Dai Nippon.

Japan, Sea of The arm of the Pacific Ocean lying between the islands of Japan and the Asian mainland.

japan black See JAPAN (lacquer): also called black–japan.

Japan clover A perennial, cloverlike herb (Lespedeza striata) of the bean family, from eastern Asia, naturalized in the United States and used for feeding horses and cattle. Also **Japanese clover**.

Jap·a·nese (jap'ə·nēz', -nēs') adj. Belonging or relating to Japan, its language, or its people. — n. **1** A native of Japan. **2** The agglutinative language of Japan, showing a slight similarity to Korean, but generally considered to be unrelated to any language: see KANA.

Japanese barberry A dwarfed variety of barberry (Berberis thunbergi): used for hedges, etc.

Japanese beetle A small green and brown beetle (Popillia japonica) with a metallic luster introduced into this country from Japan and first noted in 1916. The adults eat the leaves and fruits of various plants; the larvae feed on grass roots. See illustration under INSECT (injurious).

Japanese ivy A climbing shrub (Parthenocissus tricuspidata) closely related to the Virginia creeper.

Japanese persimmon Kaki.

Japanese river fever Tsutsugamushi disease.

Japanese spaniel See under SPANIEL.

Japanese tissue A fine silky paper, originally made from the bark of the paper mulberry.

Japanese vellum A smooth, creamy, hand-made paper of exceptional strength, originally made from the paper mulberry.

Jap·a·nesque (jap'ə·nesk') adj. In the style of Japanese art or industry. — n. An article made in such style. — **Jap'a·nesque'ly** adv. — **Jap'a·nesque'ry** n.

Japan rose Any of several true roses native to Japan; specifically, Rosa multiflora and Rosa rugosa, both widely cultivated garden plants in the United States.

Japan Stream See under CURRENT.

Japan wax A vegetable fat containing palmitic acid and extracted from the berries of certain species of sumac (genus Rhus): used largely for adulterating beeswax: also called Japan tallow.

jape (jāp) v. **japed**, **jap·ing** v.i. Archaic To joke; make jests. — v.t. Obs. To mock; jibe at. — n. A jest; jibe. [ME jappen; origin uncertain] — **jap'er** n. — **jap'er·y** n.

Ja·pheth (jā'fith) A masculine proper name. Also **Ja'phet** (-fit). [<Hebrew, the extender] — **Japheth** Third son of Noah. Gen. v 32.

Ja·phet·ic (jə·fet'ik) adj. **1** Belonging to or descended from Japheth, Noah's son: distinguished from Hamitic and Semitic. **2** Obs. Indo-European.

Ja·pon·ic (jə·pon'ik) adj. Of, pertaining to, or from Japan. [<Japon, obs. var. of Japan + -IC]

ja·pon·i·ca (jə·pon'i·kə) n. **1** An eastern-Asian shrub (Chaenomeles lagenaria) with toothed leaves and bright scarlet flowers; the Japanese quince. **2** The camellia (Camellia japonica). [<NL, Japanese]

Jap·o·nism (jap'ə·niz'əm) n. A Japanese characteristic, as in art.

Ja·pu·rá (zhä'pōō·rä') A river rising in the Andes of SW Colombia and flowing 1,150 miles SE to the Amazon in NE Brazil: also Yapurá.

Ja·ques (jā'kwēz, -kwiz) In Shakespeare's As You Like It, a lord, melancholy and cynical, attending on the banished duke.

jar[1] (jär) n. **1** A deep, wide-mouthed vessel of earthenware or glass. **2** The quantity which a jar contains; jarful. [<F jarre < Arabic jarrah]

jar[2] (jär) v. **jarred**, **jar·ring** v.i. **1** To shake or rattle, as from a shock or blow. **2** To make a harsh, discordant sound. **3** To have an unpleasant or painful effect: Her manner jarred on my nerves. **4** To disagree or conflict; quarrel. — v.t. **5** To cause to shake or rattle, as by a shock or blow. **6** To affect unpleasantly or painfully, as one's nerves or feelings; shock. **7** To cause to make a harsh, discordant sound. See synonyms under SHAKE. — n. **1** A shaking, as from a sudden shock. **2** A discordant sound. **3** Discord; strife. See synonyms under QUARREL. [Imit.]

jar[3] (jär) n. A swinging, as of a door on its hinges: used only in the phrases **on a jar** and **on the jar**, meaning slightly opened. [OE cerr. See AJAR[1].]

ja·ra·be (hä·rä'bā) n. A Mexican dance. [<Sp., lit., sirup]

Ja·ra·bub (jä'rä·bōōb') An oasis in eastern Cyrenaica, Libya: Italian Giarabub.

jar·di·nière (jär'də·nir', Fr. zhàr·dē·nyàr') n. An ornamental pot or stand, as of porcelain, for flowers or plants. [<F, fem. of jardinier a gardener]

jar·fly (jär'flī') n. pl. **·flies** A cicada or harvest fly: so called because of the jarring noise it makes.

jar·gon[1] (jär'gən) n. **1** Confused, unintelligible speech; gibberish. **2** Any language thought to be meaningless or excessively confused. **3** The technical or specialized language characteristic of a particular sect, profession, or similarly restrictive group; cant; lingo: the jargon of the law courts. **4** A mixture of two or more dissimilar languages, often used as a lingua franca, as the Chinook jargon; pidgin. See synonyms under SLANG. — v.i. To talk in jargon; gabble. [<OF]

jar·gon[2] (jär'gon) n. A transparent, adamantine, colorless, yellowish, leaf-green, or smoky zircon found in Ceylon. Also **jar·goon'** (-gōōn'). [<F, ult. <Persian zargûn gold-colored]

jar·go·nelle (jär'gə·nel') n. An early variety of pear. Also **jar'go·nel'**, **jar'gon·nelle'**. [<F, dim. of jargon JARGON[2]]

jar·gon·ize (jär'gən·īz) v. **·ized**, **·iz·ing** v.t. To translate into jargon. — v.i. To speak in jargon.

ja·ri·na (jä·rē'nə) n. The ivory nut.

jarl (yärl) n. Formerly, a Scandinavian nobleman or chieftain; an earl. [<ON. Akin to EARL.]

jar·o·site (jar'ə·sīt, jə·rō'-) n. A hydrous sulfate of iron and potassium, occurring massive or in brown or yellow crystals. [from Barranco Jarosa, in Spain]

Jar·row (jar'ō) A port on the Tyne in NE Durham, England.

jar·vey (jär'vē) n. Brit. Colloq. The driver of a hackney coach; also, the driver of a jaunting car. [from Jarvis, a personal name]

Jar·vis Island (jär'vis) A United States possession (1936) in the central Pacific near the equator; 1 1/2 square miles.

jas·mine (jas'min, jaz'-) n. **1** An ornamental plant of the olive family (genus Jasminum) with fragrant, generally white, flowers. **2** Of various other plants, as the **Cape Jasmine** (Gardenia jasminoides), the **Carolina** or **yellow jasmine** (Gelsemium sempervirens), etc. **3** Frangipani. **4** Papaw. Also spelled jessamine. [<F jasmin <Persian yāsmin]

Ja·son (jā'sən) A masculine personal name. — **Jason** In Greek legend, a prince of Iolcus who led the Argonauts in search of the Golden Fleece which he obtained with the help of Medea. [<Gk., healer]

jas·pé (zhas·pā') adj. Veined or clouded on the surface in imitation of jasper; streaked. — n. A variety of plain-weave shaded cloth, usually printed or embroidered. [<F, like jasper]

jas·per (jas'pər) n. **1** An impure, opaque, usually red, brown, or yellow variety of quartz, admitting of a high polish and used for vases and other articles: also **jas'per·ite**. **2** A stone in the breastplate of the high priest. Exod. xxviii 20. [<MF jaspre, var. of jaspe <L jaspis <Gk. <Semitic. Cf. Hebrew yashpeh.]

Jas·per (jas'pər, Du. yäs'pər) A masculine personal name. Also **Dan. Jes·per** (yes'pər). [<Persian, bearer of treasure]

jas·per·ize (jas'pər·īz) v.t. **·ized**, **·iz·ing** To convert into jasper: the jasperized wood of Arizona.

Jasper National Park A park on the eastern slope of the Rockies, western Alberta, Canada; 4,200 square miles.

Jas·pers (yäs'pərz), **Karl**, 1883–1969, German philosopher.

jas·pid·e·an (jas·pid'ē·ən) adj. Consisting of or containing jasper; like jasper. Also **jas·pid'e·ous**. [<L jaspideus <jaspis, -idos jasper]

Jas·sy (yä'sē) A city in NE Rumania: also Iasi.

Jas·trow (jas'trō), **Joseph**, 1863–1944, U.S. psychologist born in Poland.

Jat (jät, jŏt) n. Hindi One of an important Indian race or caste in the Punjab, Rajputana, and the United Provinces, numbering over 8,000,000.

JA·TO (jā'tō) n. Aeron. A jet-propulsion unit attached to airplanes to facilitate quick takeoff. Also **jato**. [<J(ET) A(SSISTED) T(AKE)-O(FF)]

Jat·ro·pha (jat'rə·fə) n. A genus of tropical American herbs, shrubs, and trees of the spurge family, the seeds of which yield alkaloids having medicinal properties. [<NL < Gk. iatros physician + trophē food]

jaud (jäd, jôd) n. Scot. A jade.

jauk (jäk, jôk) v.i. Scot. To trifle; idle.

jaun·der (jän'dər, jôn'-) v.i. Scot. To talk idly. Also **jaun·er** (jä'nər, jô'-).

jaun·dice (jôn′dis, jän′-) n. 1 Pathol. A morbid condition due to excretion of bile pigments in the blood, characterized by yellowness of the skin, lassitude, and anorexia; icterus. 2 A mental condition, as in jealousy or prejudice, in which the judgment is warped. —v.t. ·diced, ·dic·ing 1 To affect with jaundice. 2 To affect with prejudice or envy. [<OF jaunisse <jaune yellow <L galbinus yellowish <galbus yellow]

jaun·diced (jôn′dist, jän′-) adj. 1 Affected with jaundice. 2 Yellow-colored. 3 Prejudiced because of envy or jealousy.

jaunt (jônt, jänt) n. 1 A short journey; pleasure trip; excursion. 2 A tiresome journey. 3 Obs. A jolting; jounce. —v.i. To make a short trip, especially for pleasure. [Cf. obs. jaunce prance]

jaunting car In Ireland, a horse-drawn, two-wheeled vehicle having seats placed lengthwise over the wheels, back to back or face to face: also called sidecar. Also **jaunty car.**

JAUNTING CAR

jaunt·y (jôn′tē, jän′-) adj. jaunt·i·er, jaunt·i·est 1 Affecting a careless ease or self-satisfaction; sprightly. 2 Obs. Genteel. Also spelled janty. [<F gentil GENTLE] —jaunt′i·ly adv. —jaunt′i·ness n.

Jau·rès (zhô·res′), Jean Léon, 1859–1914, French socialist; assassinated.

Ja·va (jä′və, jav′ə) n. 1 A type of coffee. 2 Coffee; a cup of Java. 3 A domestic fowl. [from Java, where first grown]

Ja·va (jä′və, jav′ə) An Indonesian island SE of Sumatra; with Madura and adjacent islands, 51,032 square miles; capital, Jakarta.

Java man Pithecanthropus.

Jav·a·nese (jav′ə·nēz′, -nēs′) adj. Of or pertaining to Java, its language, or its people. —n. pl. ·nese 1 A native or naturalized inhabitant of Java. 2 The Indonesian language of central Java, closely related to Malay, and containing some elements of Sanskrit.

Ja·va·ri (zhä′vä·rē′) A river forming about one-half the boundary of Brazil and Peru and flowing 600 miles NE to the Amazon: also Yavari. Also **Ja′va·ry′.**

Java Sea The part of the Pacific between Borneo and Java.

Java sparrow A seed-eating bird (Munia oryzivora) of Java: a common cage bird.

jave·lin (jav′lin, jav′ə·lin) n. 1 A short, light spear, used as a missile weapon for hunting or in war. 2 A long spear with wooden shaft, thrown for distance in an athletic contest. [<F, prob. <Celtic]

Ja·velle water (zhə·vel′) A solution of chlorinated potash or of sodium hypochlorite, used as an antiseptic and as a bleaching agent. Also **Ja·vel′ water.**

jaw (jô) n. 1 Anat. One of the two bony structures forming the framework of the mouth; a maxilla or a mandible. 2 The mouth. 3 Anything like or suggesting a jaw, as one of the gripping parts of a vise: often used figuratively: the jaws of death. 4 Slang Needless talk; scolding; abuse. —v.i. Slang 1 To talk; jabber. 2 To scold. —v.t. 3 Slang To scold. [Earlier jowe, chawe. ? Akin to chew, infl. by F joue cheek.]

HUMAN JAW

jaw·bone (jô′bōn′) n. One of the bones of the jaw; especially, the mandible. —v.t. ·boned, ·bon·ing U.S. Slang 1 To urge vigorously; especially, to urge to abide voluntarily by price or wage guidelines fixed by government. —v.i. 2 To argue vigorously. —adj. U.S. Slang Based on voluntary compliance.

jaw·break·er (jô′brā′kər) n. 1 Very hard candy. 2 A machine that crushes ore: also **jaw′crush′er.** 3 A word hard to pronounce.

Jax·ar·tes (jak·sär′tēz) The ancient name for the SYR DARYA.

Jay (jā), **John,** 1745–1829, American statesman; first chief justice of the United States, 1789–95.

jay (jā) n. 1 A small crowlike bird, usually of brilliant coloring, as the **European jay** (Garrulus glandarius), the **blue jay** (Cyanocitta cristata), the **Canada jay** (Perisoreus canadensis), etc. 2 Slang A poor actor; also, a country bumpkin; greenhorn. 3 An unscrupulous chatterbox. 4 Obs. A coarse or loud woman. [<OF; ult. origin unknown]

jay·hawk·er (jā′hô′kər) n. 1 A freebooting guerrilla; especially, one of the border ruffians who, in the Free-soil conflict in Kansas and during the Civil War, combined pillage with guerilla fighting in Missouri and the neighboring states. 2 Any freebooter or robber. 3 A native of Kansas. 4 A tarantula. [Origin uncertain]

jay·hawk·ing (jā′hô′king) n. Stealing; raiding.

Jay·me (zhā′me) Portuguese form of JAMES.

jay·walk (jā′wôk′) v.i. Colloq. To cross a street without observing the traffic regulations. [<JAY (def. 2) + WALK] —jay′walk′er n. —jay′walk′ing n.

jaz·er·ant (jaz′ər·ənt) n. Armor made of small overlapping metal plates quilted into a cloth or velvet jacket: also jesseraunte, jesseraunce. [<OF (hauberc) jazerant Algerian (mail) <Sp. jazarino <Arabic Al-jaza′ir Algiers]

jazz (jaz) n. 1 A kind of music, generally improvised but sometimes arranged, achieving its effects by syncopation, heavily accented rhythms, dissonance, melodic variation, and particular tonal qualities of the saxophone, trumpet, clarinet, and other instruments. It was originated by New Orleans Negro musicians. 2 Popular dance music. 3 Slang Nonsense; claptrap. —adj. Of or pertaining to jazz. —v.t. To play or arrange (music) as jazz. —v.i. To dance to or play jazz. —to jazz up Slang To make exciting or more exciting. [< Creole jass coition; from its origin in the brothels of New Orleans]

jazz age U. S. The 1920's regarded as a period of relaxed morality and gay, irresponsible behavior.

jazz·y (jaz′ē) adj. jazz·i·er, jazz·i·est 1 Resembling or characteristic of jazz. 2 Slang Showy or loud, as clothes; also, lively or swinging. —jazz′i·ly adv.

jeal·ous (jel′əs) adj. 1 Apprehensive of being displaced by a rival in affection or favor; revengeful on account of fickle treatment or the like. 2 Earnestly and anxiously suspicious; vigilant in guarding; watchful. 3 Demanding exclusive worship and love: applied to God. Ex. xx 5. 4 Obs. Zealous. 5 Obs. Fearful; doubtful. See synonyms under ENVIOUS. [<OF gelos <Med. L zelosus <LL zelus zeal <Gk. zēlos zeal. Doublet of ZEALOUS.] —jeal′ous·ly adv. —jeal′ous·ness n.

jeal·ous·y (jel′əs·ē) n. pl. ·ous·ies The state or quality of being jealous in any sense.

jean (jēn) n. 1 A sturdy, twilled cotton cloth, used especially in work clothes or for casual wear. 2 pl. Trousers made of jean, denim, or a similar fabric. 3 pl. U.S. Colloq. Trousers. [Orig. jene fustian <ME Jene, Gene Genoa, where it was made]

Jean (jēn) Scottish form of JOAN.

Jean (zhän) French form of JOHN.

Jeanne (jēn, Fr. zhän) See JOAN.

—**Jeanne d'Arc** (därk) See JOAN OF ARC.

Jean·nette (jə·net′) Diminutive of JANE.

Jean Paul (zhän pôl) Pseudonym of J. P. F. Richter.

Jeans (jēnz), **Sir James Hopwood,** 1877–1946, English astronomer and physicist.

Jebb (jeb), **Sir Richard Claverhouse,** 1841–1905, Scottish classical scholar.

jeb·el (jeb′əl) n. Arabic A mountain: used in geographical names of North Africa and Arabia: also French djebel.

Jeb·el Druze (jeb′əl drōōz′) A province of southern Syria; 2,584 square miles. Also **Jebel ed Druz** (ed drōōz′).

Jeb·el Mu·sa (jeb′əl mōō′sə) A mountain in northern Spanish Morocco on the Strait of Gibraltar: identified with one of the Pillars of Hercules; 2,790 feet.

Jed·burgh (jed′bûrg) The county town of Roxburghshire, Scotland.

Jed·da (jed′ə) See JIDDA.

Jed·dart (jed′ərt) adj. Scot. Of or pertaining to Jedburgh, Scotland. Also **Jed′wood** (-wood).

Jeddart justice Scot. Hanging a suspected criminal and holding the trial afterward. Also **Jedburgh (or Jedwood) justice.**

Jeddart staff Scot. A kind of battle-ax. Also **Jedburgh (or Jedwood) ax.**

jee (jē) See GEE[2].

Jeep (jēp) n. A military motor vehicle with four-wheel drive and a carrying capacity of one quarter of a ton, used for reconnaissance and for the transportation of passengers and light cargo: a trade name. [Alter. of G.P., for General Purpose Vehicle, its military designation]

jeep·a·ble (jē′pə·bəl) adj. Traversable by jeep.

jeer[1] (jir) v.i. To speak or shout in a derisive, mocking manner; scoff. —v.t. To treat with derision or mockery; scoff at. See synonyms under MOCK, SCOFF. —n. A derisive and flouting word or speech. See synonyms under SNEER. [? OE cēir clamor] —jeer′er n. —jeer′ing·ly adv.

jeer[2] (jir) n. Naut. A tackle for raising or lowering a lower yard of a sailing ship. [? <GEE[2] + -ER[1]]

je·fe (hā′fā) n. Spanish Chief; leader; head.

Jef·fers (jef′ərz), **(John) Robinson,** 1887–1961, U.S. poet.

Jef·fer·son (jef′ər·sən), **Joseph,** 1829–1905, U.S. actor. —**Thomas,** 1743–1826, American statesman: drafted the Declaration of Independence; president of the United States 1801–1809.

Jefferson (jef′ər·sən), **Mount** 1 A peak in the Cascade Range, NW central Oregon; 10,495 feet. 2 A peak in the White Mountains, New Hampshire, 5,725 feet.

Jefferson City The capital of Missouri, on the Missouri River.

Jefferson Day The anniversary of Thomas Jefferson's birthday, April 13th: often commemorated by a Democratic party dinner.

Jef·fer·so·ni·an (jef′ər·sō′nē·ən) adj. Of or relating to Thomas Jefferson or his political opinions; democratic. —**Jef′fer·so′ni·an·ism** n.

Jef·frey (jef′rē), **Francis,** 1773–1850, editor and Scottish jurist: as lord advocate known as Lord Jeffrey.

Jef·freys (jef′rēz), **George,** 1648–89, first Baron Jeffreys of Wem, English judge.

je·had (ji·häd′) See JIHAD.

Jeh·lam (jā′lum) See JHELUM.

Je·ho·ash (jə·hō′ash) Same as JOASH.

Je·hol (jə·hol′, hôl′; Chinese rə′hu′) A province of SW Manchuria; 40,000 square miles; capital Chengteh.

Je·hosh·a·phat (ji·hosh′ə·fat, -hos′-) King of Judah about 873–848 B.C. I Kings xxii 41.

Je·ho·vah (ji·hō′və) In the Old Testament, God; the Lord: the common transliteration of the Tetragrammaton. See YAHWEH. [<Hebrew JHVH Yahweh, with the substitution of vowels from 'adhonay my Lord] —**Je·ho′vi·an, Je·ho′vic** adj.

Jehovah's Witnesses A Christian sect, originally known as the International Bible Students' Association, strongly opposed to war and denying the authority of the government in matters of conscience.

Je·ho·vist (ji·hō′vist) n. 1 One who maintains that the vowel points of the word Jehovah as found in the Hebrew text of the Bible properly belong to it, and are not merely those of Adonai: opposed to Adonist. —**Je·ho′vism** n.

Je·ho·vis·tic (jē′hō·vis′tik) adj. Yahwistic.

je·hu (jē′hyōō) n. 1 A fast or furious driver. 2 A coachman or driver. [after JEHU]

Je·hu (jē′hyōō) The tenth king of Israel, reigned at the beginning of the ninth century B.C. II Kings ix 20. [<Hebrew, the Lord is He]

je·june (jə·jōōn′) adj. 1 Lifeless; dry; dull. 2 Wanting in substance; barren. 3 Not mature; puerile; childish. See synonyms under MEAGER. [<L jejunus hungry] —**je·june′ly** adv. —**je·june′ness** n.

je·ju·num (jə·jōō′nəm) n. pl. ·na (-nə) Anat. That portion of the small intestine that extends from the duodenum to the ileum. [<NL <L jejunus hungry, empty]

Je·kyll (jē′kəl, jek′əl), **Doctor** In Robert Louis Stevenson's Strange Case of Doctor Jekyll and Mr. Hyde, one half of the dual personality

consisting of a kindly physician (Jekyll) and a criminal ruffian (Hyde).

Jel·ga·va (yel′gä·vä) A city in west central Latvia: German *Mitau:* also *Yelgava.*

jel·ick (jel′ik) *n.* A long coat, open at the sides from the hip down, worn by Turkish women. [<Turkish *yelek*]

jell (jel) *v.i.* & *v.t.* **1** To jelly. **2** To assume or cause to assume definite form. [Back formation <JELLY]

Jel·li·coe (jel′i·kō), **John Rushworth,** 1859–1935, Earl Jellicoe, British admiral; governor general of New Zealand 1920–24.

jel·lied (jel′ēd) *adj.* Brought to a jelly.

jel·li·fy (jel′ə·fī) *v.t.* & *v.i.* **·fied, ·fy·ing** To make or turn into jelly. **— jel′li·fi·ca′tion** *n.*

jel·lo (jel′ō) *n.* A fruit-flavored gelatin dessert. [<*Jell-O,* a trade name]

jel·ly (jel′ē) *n. pl.* **·lies 1** Any semisolid gelatinous substance that will quiver when shaken, but will not flow, as fruit juice boiled with sugar or meat juice boiled down. **2** Any food preparation having the consistency of jelly. **3** A gelatin filter placed in front of electric lamps to change their color values; used with motion-picture cameras. **—** *v.t.* & *v.i.* **·lied, ·ly·ing** To bring or turn to jelly. [<OF *gelee* <L *gelata,* orig. pp. fem. of *gelare* freeze]

jel·ly·bean (jel′ē·bēn′) *n.* A bean-shaped candy consisting of a hard, often colored coating over a gelatinous center.

jel·ly·fish (jel′ē·fish′) *n. pl.* **·fish** or **·fish·es 1** Any of a number of marine coelenterates (classes *Hydrozoa* and *Scyphozoa*) of jellylike appearance, and usually umbrella-shaped bodies with trailing tentacles, as the medusa and the Portuguese man-of-war. **2** *Colloq.* A person without energy, determination, or stamina.

je·lu·tong (zhə·lo͞o·tong′) *n.* **1** The milky resinous exudate from a Malayan tree *(Dyera costulata),* resembling chicle and also used as a substitute for rubber. **2** The tree itself, or its soft, corklike timber. [<Malay]

Jem (jem), **Jem·my** (jem′ē) Diminutives of JAMES.

jem·a·dar (jem′ə·där′) *n. Anglo-Indian* **1** A native lieutenant in the army next in rank below a subahdar. **2** A head servant or employee in a household or other establishment; sometimes, a police or customs officer of the military caste. Also **jem′i·dar′.**

Je·mappes (zhə·måp′) A town in SW Belgium; scene of the first battle of the French Revolutionary War, in which the French defeated the Austrians, 1792.

Je·mi·ma (jə·mī′mə) A feminine personal name. Also **Je·mi′mah.** [<Hebrew, a dove]

jem·my (jem′ē) *n. pl.* **·mies** *Brit.* **1** A short crowbar; a jimmy. **2** A baked sheep's head. **3** *Obs.* A type of riding boot. **4** *Dial.* A greatcoat. [Var. of JIMMY]

Je·na (yā′nə) A city in the former state of Thuringia, East Germany; site of Napoleon's defeat of the Prussians, 1806.

je ne sais quoi (zhə nə se kwä′) *French* I know not what; an indefinable something.

Jen·ghiz Khan (jeng′giz kän′) See GENGHIS KHAN.

Jen·ner (jen′ər), **Edward,** 1749–1823, English physician; introduced vaccination. **— Sir William,** 1815–98, English physician and pathologist.

jen·net (jen′it) *n.* **1** A small Spanish horse, a cross of Arabian and native stock. **2** A female donkey: also spelled *genet.* [<OF *genet* <Sp. *jinete* a light horseman <Arabic *Zenāta,* a Barbary tribe]

jen·net·ing (jen′it·ing) *n. Brit.* A variety of early apple, ripening about St. John's Day (June 24). [<F *Jeannet,* dim. of *Jean* John]

Jen·nings (jen′ingz), **Herbert Spencer,** 1868–1947, U.S. naturalist and geneticist.

jen·ny (jen′ē) *n. pl.* **·nies 1** Short for spinning jenny. **2** A female: also used in combination or alone for a female bird or animal, as *jenny* wren, *jenny* ass. **3** A traveling crane. **4** A portable electric generator for use on a motion-picture set. **5** A man who interests himself or interferes in feminine matters: also called *betty.* **6** A jinny. Also spelled *jinny.* [from *Jenny,* a personal name]

Jen·ny (jen′ē) Diminutive of JANE. Also **Jen′nie.**

jeof·ail (jef′āl) *n. Law* An oversight; a mistake; the acknowledgement of an error in pleading. Also **jeof′aile.** [<AF *jeo fail* I am wrong]

jeop·ard·ize (jep′ər·dīz) *v.t.* **·ized, ·iz·ing** To put in jeopardy; expose to loss or injury; imperil. Also **jeop′ard.**

jeop·ard·y (jep′ər·dē) *n.* **1** Exposure to or danger of death, loss, or injury; danger; peril. **2** The peril in which a defendant is put when placed on trial for a crime. See synonyms under DANGER, HAZARD. [<OF *jeu parti* even chance]

Jeph·thah (jef′thə, jep′-) A judge in Israel; sacrificed his daughter. *Judges* xi 34–40.

je·quir·i·ty (ji·kwir′ə·tē) *n.* **1** A twining, tropical shrub *(Abrus praecatorius),* the Indian or wild licorice. **2** One of the handsome, poisonous seeds, **jequirity beans,** of this plant used in India as weights, ornaments, and in medicine: often called *jumble-beads.* Also **je·quer′·i·ty.** [<F *jéquirity* <Tupian]

Je·qui·ti·nho·nha (zhə·kē′ti·nyō′nyə) A river in eastern Brazil, flowing 500 miles NE to the Atlantic.

Je·rah·me·el (jə·rā′mē·əl) One of the seven archangels of Hebrew and Christian legend.

jer·bo·a (jər·bō′ə) *n.* An Old World, nocturnal, social rodent (family *Dipodidae*) with the hind legs much elongated for jumping, especially *Jaculus jaculus* of North Africa. [<NL <Arabic *yarbu*ʻ]

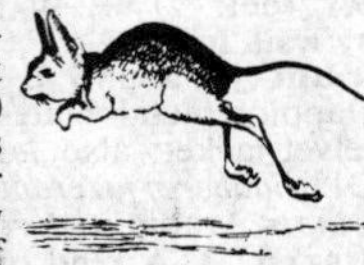

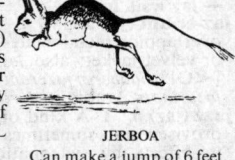

JERBOA
Can make a jump of 6 feet. (About 3 inches long; tail: 5 inches)

je·reed (je·rēd′) *n.* A javelin of Moslem countries; also, a game in which it is used: also spelled *jerreed, jerrid.* Also **je·rid′.** [<Arabic *jerīd*]

jer·e·mi·ad (jer′ə·mī′ad) *n.* A lament; tale of woe; a denunciation of existing conditions. [<F *jérémiade* <*Jérémie* Jeremiah]

Jer·e·mi·ah (jer′ə·mī′ə) A masculine personal name. Also **Jer·e·my** (jer′ə·mē), **Jer·e·ma·i** (jer′ə·mä′ē), *Dan., Du., Ger., Sw.* **Je·re·mi·as** (yā·rə·mē′äs), *Fr.* **Jé·ré·mie** (zhā·rā·mē′).

— Jeremiah A major Hebrew prophet who flourished in the seventh century B.C.; also, an Old Testament book containing his prophecies. Also **Jer′e·mi′as.** [<Hebrew, exalted of the Lord]

Je·rez (hā·rāth′, -rās′) A town in SW Spain: formerly *Xeres.* Also **Je·rez de la Fron·te·ra** (thə lä frōn·tā′rä).

Jer·i·cho (jer′i·kō) A village in western Jordan, north of the Dead Sea; site of an ancient city of the same name (*Num.* xxii 1).

Jericho rose See ROSE OF JERICHO.

Jer·it·za (yer′it·sä), **Maria,** born 1887, Austrian soprano active in the United States.

jerk[1] (jûrk) *v.t.* **1** To give a sharp, sudden pull, tug, or twist to. **2** To throw or move with a sharp, suddenly arrested motion. **3** To utter in broken or abrupt manner. **—** *v.i.* **4** To give a jerk or jerks. **5** To move with sharp, sudden motions; twitch. **—** *n.* **1** A short, sharp pull, twitch, or fling. **2** *Physiol.* An involuntary contraction of some muscle, due to the reflex action of nerves; specifically, an involuntary muscular spasm or twitching caused by religious excitement. **3** *Slang* A railroad local branch line. **4** *Slang* A stupid or unsophisticated person. [Prob. imit.] **— jerk′y** *adj.* **— jerk′i·ly** *adv.* **— jerk′i·ness** *n.*

jerk[2] (jûrk) *v.t.* To cure (meat) by cutting into strips and drying. **—** *n.* Jerky[2]. [Alter. of Sp. *charquear* < *charqui.* See CHARQUI.]

jer·kin (jûr′kin) *n.* A waistcoat; short coat; jacket; doublet: often made of leather. **— buff jerkin** A jerkin of buff leather or, later, of buff-colored cloth. [Origin unknown]

jerk·wa·ter (jûrk′wô′tər, -wot′ər) *adj. U.S. Colloq.* **1** Not on the main line: a *jerkwater* train or station. **2** Insignificant; small: a *jerkwater* college. **—** *n.* A train serving a branch line. [<JERK[1], *v.* + WATER]

jerk·y[1] (jûr′kē) *n.* A springless wagon or carriage: also spelled *jirky.* [<JERK[1], *n.* + -Y[1]]

jerk·y[2] (jûr′kē) *n.* Jerked meat: also called *charqui.* Also **jerked beef.** [Alter. of CHARQUI]

jer·o·bo·am (jer′ə·bō′əm) *n.* **1** An oversized champagne bottle holding about four quarts. **2** A drinking cup of great size. [after JEROBOAM]

Jer·o·bo·am (jer′ə·bō′əm) A Jewish leader who led the revolt of the ten tribes against Rehoboam and became first king of Israel, as distinguished from Judah; introduced idolatry. I *Kings* xi, xii.

— Jeroboam A king of Israel; son of Joash: reigned 790–749? B.C. II *Kings* xiv.

Je·rome (jə·rōm′, *Brit.* jer′əm) A masculine personal name. Also *Fr.* **Jé·rôme** (zhā·rōm′), *Dan.* **Je·ro·ny·mus** (ye·rō′ni·məs), *Pg., Sp.* **Je·ro·ni·mo** (*Pg.* zhe·rō′ni·mo͝o, *Sp.* hā·rō′nē·mō). [<Gk., holy name]

— Jerome, Saint, 340?–420, one of the four great Latin church fathers; prepared the Vulgate.

Je·rome (jə·rōm′, *Brit.* jer′əm), **Jerome K(lapka),** 1859–1927, English humorist.

jer·reed (je·rēd′), **jer·rid** See JEREED.

jer·ry[1] (jer′ē) *n. pl.* **·ries 1** One who erects buildings or does work in an unsubstantial and mean manner: also **jer′ry·build′er** (-bil′·dər). **2** Work that is inferior or fraudulent in material or construction. **—** *adj.* Cheaply and fraudulently constructed; flimsy. [Origin unknown]

jer·ry[2] (jer′ē) *n. pl.* **·ries** *Slang* A German; especially, a German soldier. [Alter. of GERMAN]

Jer·ry (jer′ē) Popular form of JEREMIAH, JEREMY, GERALD, etc.

jer·ry·build (jer′ē·bild′) *v.t.* **·built, ·build·ing** To build flimsily and of inferior materials. **— jer′ry·build′ing** *n.* **— jer′ry·built′** *adj.*

jer·sey (jûr′zē) *n.* **1** A plain-knitted, elastic, ribbed fabric of wool, cotton, rayon, etc. **2** A close-fitting knit shirt as worn by athletes; hence, any close-fitting upper garment of knitted material. **3** Fine woolen yarn, or fine-combed wool, as spun in the island of Jersey. [from *Jersey*]

Jer·sey (jûr′zē) *n.* One of a breed of cattle, usually fawn-colored, originating in the island of Jersey or the Channel Islands, noted for milk rich in butterfat content. **—** *adj.* Of or pertaining to the island of Jersey or to the State of New Jersey.

Jer·sey (jûr′zē) The largest of the Channel Islands; 45 square miles; capital, St. Hélier.

Jersey City A port on the Hudson River in NE New Jersey.

Je·ru·sa·lem (ji·ro͞o′sə·ləm, -lem) A holy city of Judaism and Christianity in central Palestine, partly in Israel (of which it is the capital) and partly in Jordan: identified with the Old Testament *Salem.* Ancient *Hierosolyma. Arabic* **El Quds esh She·rif** (al ko͞ots′ ash sha·rēf′).

Jerusalem artichoke A tall sunflower *(Helianthus tuberosus)* of the composite family of NE North America having an edible tuber. [Alter. of Ital. *girasole* sunflower + ARTICHOKE]

Jerusalem cherry A small, evergreen shrub *(Solanum pseudocapsicum)* of the nightshade family, from Mauritius. It has white flowers succeeded by scarlet or yellow, cherrylike berries.

Jerusalem cross See under CROSS.

Jerusalem oak See under OAK.

jer·vine (jûr′vēn) *n. Chem.* A white, crystalline, toxic alkaloid, $C_{26}H_{37}O_3N$, obtained from the rhizome of the white hellebore *(Veratrum album).* [<Sp. *yerva,* the root of the hellebore + -INE[2]]

Jer·vis Bay (jûr′vis, *Brit.* jär′vis) An inlet of the Pacific in eastern New South Wales, Australia.

Jes·per·sen (yes′pər·sən), **(Jens) Otto (Harry),** 1860–1943, Danish philologist.

jess (jes) *n.* **1** A short strap fastened to the leg of a hawk: used in falconry. **2** A ribbon hanging from a garland or crown. [<OF *ges* <L *jactus* a throw <*jacere* throw] **— jessed** *adj.*

jes·sa·mine (jes′ə·min) *n.* The jasmine: a popular name. [Var. of JASMINE]

jes·sant (jes′ənt) *adj. Her.* **1** Shooting forth as a plant. **2** Issuing, as an animal, from the middle of an ordinary. Compare ISSUANT. [<OF *issant,* ppr. of *isser* spring forth]

Jes·se (jes′ē) A masculine personal name. [<Hebrew, the Lord is]

— Jesse The father of David. I *Sam.* xvi 1.

Jes·sel·ton (jes′əl·tən) A port on the South China Sea, capital of Sabah.

jes·ser·aunte (jes′ər·ônt) See JAZERANT. Also **jes′ser·aunce.**

Jes·si·ca (jes′i·kə) A feminine personal name. [<Hebrew, the Lord's grace]

— Jessica In Shakespeare's *Merchant of Venice,* the daughter of Shylock, who elopes with Lorenzo.

Jes·sie (jes′ē) A feminine personal name.

jest (jest) *n.* **1** Something said or done in joke, plesantary, or raillery; a joke. **2** The object of laughter, sport, or raillery; a laughingstock. **3** *Obs.* An exploit, tale of exploits; a masquerade; pageant. See synonyms under WIT. —*v.i.* **1** To speak or act an a playful or trifling manner. **2** To scoff; jeer. —*v.t.* **3** To scoff at; ridicule. [<OF *geste, jeste* <L *gesta* deeds <*gerere* do]

jest·er (jest'ər) *n.* **1** One who jests; specifically. a medieval cort fool. **2** *Archaic* In the Middle Ages, a professional teller of romances.

jest·ing (jes'ting) *n.* The action of one who jokes; fun; raillery; —*adj.* Of the nature of a jest; prone to humor; mirthful; jocose. —**jest'ing·ly** *adv.*

Je·su (jē'zōō, -sōō) Jesus: used poetically, especially in the vocative.

Jes·u·ate (jezh'ōō·āt, jez'yōō-) *n. pl.* **Jes·u·ates** or **Jes·u·a·ti** (jezh'ōō·ā'tī, jez'yōō-) One of the order or congregation of *Jesuati,* founded by St. John Colombini of Siena in the 14th century, and suppressed by Pope Clement IX in 1688. Their chief occupation was care of the sick, especially the plague–stricken. Also **Jes'u·et.** [<Ital. *Gesuato* <*Gesú* Jesus]

Jes·u·it (jezh'ōō·at, jez'yōō-) *n.* **1** A member of the Society of Jesus, a Roman Catholic religious order founded in 1534 by Ignatious Loyola to combat the Reformation and propagate the faith among the heathen. Abbr. *S.J.* [<NL *Jesuita* <L *Jesus* Jesus]

Jes·u·it·ic (jezh'ōō·it'ik, jez'yōō-) *adj.* **1** Of, pertaining to, or like the Jesuits, or their principles, methods, or practices. **2** Using crafty or insidious arts or methods; designing; crafty; a derogatory use. Also **Jes'u·it'i·cal.** —**Jes'u·it'i·cal·ly** *adv.*

Jes·u·it·ism (jezh'ōō·it·iz'əm, jez'yōō-) *n.* **1** The doctrines, system, principles, and methods of the Jesuits. **2** Practices such as those attributed to the Jesuits. **3** Deceptive practices, subtle distinctions, or political duplicity: a derogatory use.

Jes·u·it·ize (jezh'ōō·it·īz', jez'yōō-) *v.t. & v.i.* **·ized, ·iz·ing** To be or make Jesuitic.

Jes·u·it·ry (jezh'ōō·t·trē, jer'yōō-) *n.* The methods or principles professed by or ascribed to the Jesuits.

Jesuits' bark **1** Peruvian bark, a species of cinchona, yielding quinine. **2** The marsh elder.

Je·sus (jē'zəs) A masculine personal name. [<Hebrew, the Lord is salvation]

—**Jesus** The source of Christianity; probably living from 6 B.C. to A.D. 29 or 30; son of Mary; regarded in all Christian faiths as Christ, the Messiah. Hence, also **Jesus Christ.** —**Jesus** The son of Sirach; lived about the third or fourth century B.C.; author of *Ecclesiasticus.*

jet[1] (jet) *n.* **1** A rich black variety of lignite, used for ornaments. **2** The color of jet; a deep, glossy black. **3** *Obs.* Black marble. —*adj.* Made of or having the appearance of jet. [<OF *jaiet* <L *gagates* <Gk. *gagatēs,* from *Gagai,* a Lycian town where it was mined]—**jet'–black'** (-blak') *adj. & n.*

jet[2] (jet) *n.* **1** That which spurts out from a narrow orifice; a gushing flow. **2** A spout or nozzle. **3** A projecting or overhanging course of bricks or the like; jut. **3** A jet plane. [<*v.*]—*v.t. & v.i.* **jet·ted, jet·ting** To spurt forth or emit in a stream; spout. [<F *jeter* throw, ult. <L *jactare,* freq. of *jacere* throw]

Jet. meaning operating by, of, or relating to jet propulsion, may appear as a combining form in hyphemes or solidemes or as the first element in two–word phrases; as in:

jet aircraft	**jet bomber**	**jet pilot**
jet airplane	**jet fighter**	**jet plane**
jet aviation	**jetliner**	**jet–propelled**

jet d'eau (zhe dō') *n. pl.* **jets d'eau** (zhe dō') *French* A jet of water; fountain. Also **jet·teau** (je·tō'), **jette d'eau** (jet dō'), **jet·to** (jet'ō).

jet deflection The directional control of the blast in a jet engine in order to change the speed or direction of a jet–propelled aircraft without loss of stability.

je·té (zhə·tā') *n.* In ballet, a wide leap with one leg forward and the other back. [<F, p.p. of *jeter,* to jump]

jet engine An engine that takes in outside air to oxidize fuel which is coverted into the energy of a powerful jet of heated gas expelled to the rear under high pressure: a special form of reaction engine.

Jeth·ro (jeth'rō) Moses' father–in–law. *Exod.* xviii.

jet lag A disruption of the body's accustomed rhythms of sleep, hunger, etc. owing to the change of time zones when traveling long distances by jet aircraft.

jet·lin·er (jet'lī'nər) *n.* A large, commercial jet aircraft.

jet·port (jet'pôrt', -pōrt') *n.* An airport designed to accomodate jet aircraft.

jet propulsion **1** Propulsion by meams of a jet of gas or other fluid. **2** *Aeron.* Aircraft propulsion by means of jet engines. —**jet'–pro·pul'sion** *adj.*

jet rotor The rotor unit of a helicopter powererd by jet engines mounted on the blades.

jet·sam (jet'səm) *n.* **1** Unbuoyed goods cast from a vessel in peril, and which sink: distinguished from *flotsam* and *lagan.* **2** Jettison [Earlier *jetson,* short for JETTISON]

jet set A group of wealthy, international celebrities who frequently travel long distances, as by jet aircraft, for social events, etc. —**jet–set·ter** (jet'set'ər) *n.*

jet stream **1** The strong flow of gas or other fluid expelled from a jet engine, rocket motor, and the like. **2** *Meteorol.* A high–velocity circumpolar wind circulating, usually from west to east, near the base of the stratosphere.

jet·ti·son (jet'ə·sən) *n.* **1** The throwing overboard of goods, or cargo, especially from a ship in danger of foundering. **2** Jetsam. —*v.t.* **1** To throw overboard, as goods or cargo. **2** Hence, to discard or abandon something that hampers. [<AF *getteson* <L *jactatio, -onis* a throwing <*jactare.* See JET[2].]

jet·ton (jet'ən) *n.* A counter or token. Also **jet'on.** [<MF *jeton* <*jeter* throw. See JET[2].]

jet·ty[1] (jet'ē) *n. pl.* **·ties** **1** A structure in a body of water serving to control or divert a current, protect a harbor or the like, or as a wharf or pier. **2** A part of a building projecting or overhanging. Also, *Obs. jutty.* [<OF *jetee,* jetee, orig. pp. of *jeter* throw. See JET[2].]

jet·ty[2] (jet'ē) *adj.* Like or made of jet; black as jet. —**jet'ti·ness** *n.*

jet vane A fixed or adjustable vane of heat–resistant material placed in a jet stream for purposes of stability and control.

jet wash *Aeron.* The backwash caused by a jet engine, rocket, guided missle, and the like.

jeu (zhœ) *n. pl.* **jeux** (zhœ) *French* Play; pastime; game.

jeu de mots (zhœ də mō') *French* Play on words; pun or quibble.

jeu d'es·prit (zhœ des·prē') A play of fancy; witticism. [<F]

jeune fille (zhœn fēy') *French* Young girl.

jeu·nesse do·rée (zhə·nes' do·rā') Any group of wealthy and fashionable young persons. [F, lit., gilded youth]

Jev·ons (jev'ənz), **William Stanley,** 1835–82, English logician and economist.

Jew (jōō) *n.* **1** A member of the ancient Near Eastern Hebrew people, the Israelites, or one tracing descent from them by genealogy or conversion. **2** Any person professing Judaism. **3** Originally, a member of the tribe or the kingdom of Judah. —**Wandering Jew** The shoemaker Ahasuerus, fabled to be condemned to wander perpetually for driving Christ from his door; hence, a restless wanderer. —*adj.* Jewish; relating to Jews. [OF *gui, jueu* <L *Judaeus* <Gk. *Ioudaios* <Hebrew *y'hudi* descendant of Judah.

Jew–bait·ing (jōō'bā'ting) *n. Slang (an offensive usage)* The act of harassing, harrying, or otherwise persecuting the Jews. —**Jew'–bait'er** *n.*

jew·el (jōō'əl) *n.* **1** A precious stone; gem, especially one set in precious metal. **2** Anything or rare excellence or special value. **3** A bit of precious stone, crystal, or glass used to form a durable bearing, as for a watch pivot. **4** One dearly beloved. —*v.t.* **·eled** or **·elled, ·el·ing** or **·el·ling** To adorn with jewels; set jewels in. [<OF *jouel,* ult. <L *jocus* a joke, sport]

jew·el·er (jōō'əl·ər) *n.* A dealer or maker of jewelry. Also **jew'el·ler.**

jew·el·ry (jōō'əl·rē) *n.* **1** Jewels collectively. **2** The art of mounting precious stones; trade of a jeweler. Also *Brit.* **jew'el·ler·y.**

jew·el·weed (jōō'əl·wēd') *n.* Either of two American plants of the genus *Impatiens,* the touch–me–nots (*I. biflora* or *I. pallida*).

Jew·ett (jōō'it), **Frank Baldwin,** 1879–1949. U.S. electrical engineer. —**Sarah Orne,** 1849–1909, U.S. novelist.

jew·fish (jōō'fish') *n. pl.* **·fish** or **·fishes** **1** One of various large groupers of American waters, especially *Stereolepis gigas* of the California coast. **2** The giant grouper *(Promicrops itaiara)* of the Florida coast. **3** The tarpon.

Jew·ish (jōō'ish) *Adj.* Belonging to, like, or characteristic of the Jews, their customs, religion, etc.; Hebrew. —**Jew'ish·ness** *n.*

Jewish Autonomous Oblast See BIRDOBIDZHAN.

Jewish calendar The Hebrew calendar. See under CALENDAR.

Jewish holidays See HANUKKAH, PESACH, ROSH HASHANA, SUKKOTH, and YOM KIPPUR for the principal holidays of Judaism.

Jew·ry (jōō'rē) *n.* **1** The country of the Jews; Judea. **2** The Jewish people or race.

jew's–harp (jōōz'härp') *n.* **1** A small musical instrument with a lyre–shaped metal frame and a bent metallic tounge. **2** *Naut.* The shackle that connects the chain cable with the anchor ring.

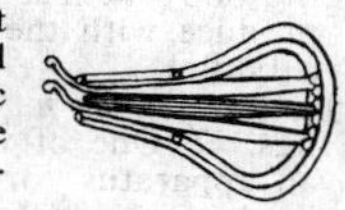

JEW'S–HARP
Held against the teeth and struck with the hand.

Jew's–pitch (jōōz'pich') *n.* Bitumen. Also **Jew's'–pitch'.**

Jew's–thorn (jōōz'thôrn') *n.* Christ's–thorn.

je·zail (jə·zīl') *n. Afghan* A long and heavy Afghan musket.

Je·za·jas (yā·zä'yäs) Dutch form of ISAIAH.

Jez·e·bel (jez'ə·bel) The wife of Ahab, notorious for her evil life (I *Kings* xvi 31); hence, a bold, vicious or cruel woman.

Jez·re·el (jer'rē·əl, jez·rēl'), **Plain of** A plain in northern Israel between the Jordan valley and Mount Carmel. *Judith* iii 9. Also *Esdraelon.*

Jhe·lum (jā'ləm) A river in Kashmir and West Pakistan, flowing 480 miles to the Chenab: ancient *Hydaspes:* also *Jehlem.*

jhong (jông) *n.* In India, a musical instrument resembling cymbals, used to accompany native folk music.

JHVH *Alt. of* YHWH.

jib[1] (jib) *n.* **1** *Naut.* A triangular sail, set on a stay and extending from the foretopmast head to the jib boom or the bowspirit. **2** The swinging boom of a crane or derrick. —**flying jib** A jib set out beyond the standing jib, or an extended boom, called the **flying–jib boom.** —**the cut of one's jib** One's appearance. —*v.t. & v.i.* **jibbed. jib·bing** *Naut.* To shift or swing; jibe. Also **jibb.** [? Short for GIBBET]

jib[2] (jib) *v.t.* **jibbed, jib·bing** **1** To move restively sidewise and backward; refuse to go forward, as a horse. **2** To refuse to do something; balk. —*n.* A horse that jibs; also **jib'ber** [Cf. OF *giber* kick]

jib·ba (jib'ə) *n. Arabic* A shirt, especially a patched shirt adopted as a uniform by followers of the Mahdi. Compare to JUBHA. Also **jib'bah, jib'beh.**

jib boom *Naut.* A spar forming a continuation of the bowsprit.

jib crane A crane having a swinging boom.

jibe[1] (jīb) *v.* **jibed, jib·ing** *v.t.* **1** *Naut.* To swing from one side of a vessel to the other; said of a fore–and–aft sail or its boom. **2** To change course so that the sails shift in this manner. —*v.t.* **3** To cause to swing from one side of a vessel to the other. Also spelled *gibe, gybe, jib.* [<Du. *gijben*]

jibe[2] (jīb) See GIBE[1].

jibe[3] (jīb) *v.i.* **jibed, jib·bing** *U.S. Colloq.* To agree; be in accordance. [Origin uncertain]

Ji·bu·ti (ji·bōō'tē) See DJIBOUTI.

ji·ca·ma (hē'kə·mə) *n.* A tropical plant with edible tuberous roots and with seeds that yield rotenone and oils [<Nahuatl *xicama*]

Jid·da (jid'ə) The port for Mecca, Saudi Arabia, on the Red Sea: also *Jedda.* Also **Jid'dah.**

jif·fy (jif′ē) *n. pl.* **·fies** *Colloq.* An instant; moment. Also **jiff.** [Origin unknown]

jig (jig) *n.* **1** A light, gay dance to a rapid tune, usually in triple time, or the music for it. **2** A practical joke. **3** *Mech.* A tool or fixture used to guide cutting tools. **4** A fish hook having a loaded shank. **5** *Mining* A wire sieve or system of sieves used in separating ore by vibration. **—the jig is up** *Colloq.* All is over and done. **—** *v.* **jigged, jig·ging** *v.i.* **1** To dance or play a jig. **2** To move with quick, jerky motions. **3** To fish with a jig. **4** *Mech.* To use a jig. **—** *v.t.* **5** To sing or play to the time of a jig. **6** To dance, as a jig. **7** To jerk up and down or to and fro. **8** To catch (fish) by hooking through the body with a jig. **9** *Mech.* To form or produce with the aid of jigs. [Cf. OF *gigue* a fiddle]

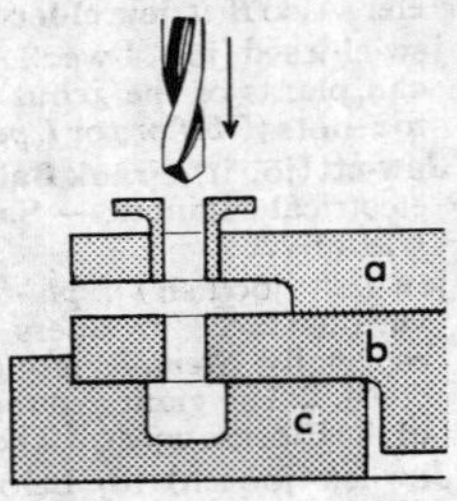

JIG
a. A drill jig.
b. Matter to be drilled.
c. Support block.

jig·ger[1] (jig′ər) *n.* **1** One who or that which jigs. **2** One of various jolting mechanisms: an apparatus for separating ores by jolting in sieves in water. **3** A potter's wheel. **4** *Naut.* A small spanker sail set on a short mast in the stern of a canoe; also, a small smacklike boat carrying such a sail. **5** Jiggermast. **6** A short, lofting, iron-headed golf club used for approaching. **7** A support for a billiard cue when about to strike a ball in an awkward position; a bridge. **8** A small glass or cup for measuring liquor, holding about one ounce; also, the amount of liquor so measured. **9** *Colloq.* Any small indefinite device.

jig·ger[2] (jig′ər) *n.* **1** A chigger or chigoe: also **jigger flea. 2** Some other insect of similar habits to the chigoe, as a harvest tick. [Alter. of CHIGGER]

jig·ger·mast (jig′ər·mast′, -mäst′) *n. Naut.* The aftermast in a yawl or a four-masted vessel.

jig·gle (jig′əl) *v.t. & v.i.* **·gled, ·gling** To move with slight, quick jerks. **—** *n.* An up-and-down unsteady movement. [Freq. of JIG, *v.*]

jig·saw (jig′sô′) *n.* A fine, narrow saw set vertically in a frame, so as to be moved rapidly up and down.

jigsaw puzzle A puzzle, the object of which is to reassemble into the original pattern a mounted picture which has been cut by a jigsaw into numerous irregularly shaped, and often interlocking pieces.

ji·had (ji·häd′) *n.* **1** A religious war of Moslems against the enemies of their faith. **2** Any war for a faith. Also spelled *jehad.* [<Arabic *jihād*]

jill[1] (jil) *n.* See GILL[2].

jill[2] (jil) *n.* **1** A young woman; sweetheart. **2** A female ferret. **3** A cup. [<from *Jill,* a personal name]

jil·let (jil′it) *n. Scot.* A sportive or wanton girl or woman; a flirt or jilt.

jill-flirt (jil′flûrt′) *n.* A wanton or depraved woman; gill-flirt.

Ji·lo·lo (ji·lō′lō) See HALMAHERA.

jilt (jilt) *v.t.* To cast off or discard (a previously favored lover or sweetheart); deceive in love. **—** *n.* One who capriciously discards a lover. [Cf. dial. E (Scottish) *jillet* a giddy girl] **— jilt′er** *n.*

Jim (jim), **Jim·my** (jim′ē) Diminutives of JAMES.

jim-crow (jim′krō′) *U.S. Colloq. adj.* Segregating Negroes: *jim-crow* buses; *jim-crow* laws. **—** *v.t.* To subject to Negro segregation. Also **Jim′-Crow′.**

Jim Crow *U.S. Colloq.* **1** A Negro: a term of contempt, from a Negro character in an old Negro song. **2** The segregation of Negroes. **— Jim-Crow·ism** (jim′krō′iz·əm) *n.*

Ji·mé·nez de Cis·ne·ros (hē·mā′nāth thā thēs·nā′rōs), **Francisco,** 1436–1517, Spanish cardinal and statesman.

jim-jams (jim′jamz′) *n. Slang* **1** Delirium tremens. **2** Extreme nervousness; the jitters.

jim·my (jim′ē) *n. pl.* **·mies** A burglar's crowbar: sometimes made in sections. **—** *v.t.* **·mied, ·my·ing** To break or pry open with a jimmy. Also, *Brit., jemmy.* [from *Jimmy,* dim. of *James,* a personal name]

Jim·my Wood·ser (jim′ē wood′zər) *Austral. Slang* **1** A solitary drinker. **2** A solitary drink.

jimp (jimp) *Scot. adj.* **1** Natty. **2** Scanty; scarce. Also **jimp′y. —** *adv.* **1** Neatly. **2** Barely; scarcely. Also **jimp′ly, jimp′y.**

jim·son·weed (jim′sən·wēd′) *n.* **1** A tall, coarse, evil-smelling, very poisonous annual weed of the nightshade family *(Datura stramonium)*: it yields several important alkaloids, as atropine and scopolamine. **2** Apple of Peru. Also **jimp·son weed** (jimp′sən). [Alter. of *Jamestown weed,* so called because first observed in Jamestown, Va.]

ji·na (ji′nə) See JAINISM.

jin·gal (jing′gôl) *n.* A heavy musket mounted on a swivel rest, formerly used in China and Burma: often spelled *gingal, gingall.* Also **jin′·gall.** [<Hind. *jangāl* large musket]

jing·ko (jing′kō) See GINKGO.

jin·gle (jing′gəl) *v.* **·gled, ·gling** *v.i.* **1** To make light, ringing sounds, as keys striking together. **2** To sound regularly or pleasingly on the ear, as verse, tunes, etc. **—** *v.t.* **3** To cause to jingle. **—** *n.* **1** A tinkling or clinking sound; also, that which produces it. **2** Any pleasing succession of rhythmical sounds in a verse; also, such a verse. **3** A one-horse, two-wheeled carriage or car, once used in Ireland and Australia. [Imit.] **—jin′gly** *adj.*

jin·glet (jing′glit) *n.* **1** A small, free, metallic ball used as the clapper of a globular sleigh bell. **2** Any small jingling appendage.

Jin·go (jing′gō) *n. pl.* **·goes 1** One who boasts of his patriotism and favors an aggressive foreign policy. **2** *Brit.* Originally, one of a party supporting Disraeli's Near Eastern policy. **— by Jingo!** A meaningless oath or ejaculation expressing strong conviction, surprise, etc. **—** *adj.* Of, pertaining to, or characteristic of the Jingoes. [Origin uncertain] **— Jin′go·ish** *adj.* **— Jin′go·ism** *n.* **— Jin′go·ist** *n.* **— Jin′go·is′tic** *adj.*

jink (jingk) *v.i. Scot.* To move quickly; dodge. **—** *n.* **1** *pl.* Frolics; pranks: high *jinks.* **2** *Scot.* A dodging turn; dodge. **— jink′er** *n.*

Jin·nah (jin′ə), **Mohammed Ali,** 1876–1948, Moslem leader; first governor general of Pakistan 1947–48.

jin·ni (ji·nē′) *n. pl.* **jinn** In Moslem mythology, an order of supernatural beings able to assume animal or human form, and often at the call and service of men through some magical controlling object: the plural form is often erroneously used as a singular: sometimes spelled *djinni, genie.* Also **jin·nee′.** [< Arabic *jinnī*]

jin·ny (jin′ē) *n. pl.* **·nies 1** An incline in a mine, upon which loaded cars descend by gravity: also **jinny road. 2** *Mech.* The traveler on the arm of a crane: also *jenny.* [Cf. JENNY]

Jin·ny (jin′ē) See JENNY.

jin·rik·sha (jin·rik′·shə, -shô) *n.* A small, two-wheeled passenger carriage drawn by one man. Also **jin·rick′sha, jin·rik′i·sha.** [<Japanese *jin* man + *riki* power + *sha* carriage]

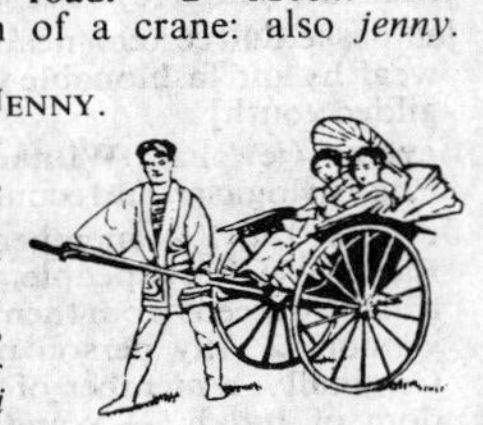

JINRIKSHA

Jin·sen (jin·sen) The Japanese name for INCHON.

jinx (jingks) *n.* A person or thing supposed to bring bad luck; a hoodoo. **—** *v.t.* To bring bad luck to. [<Earlier *jynx* <Gk. *iynx* the wryneck (a bird anciently used in witchcraft)]

ji·pi·ja·pa (hē′pē·hä′pä) *n.* A shrubby, stemless, palmlike plant *(Carludovica palmata),* native to South America; the fan-shaped leaves provide the fiber of which Panama hats are made. [from *Jipijapa,* town in Ecuador]

jirk·y (jûr′kē) See JERKY (def. 1).

jit·ney (jit′nē) *n. U.S. Colloq.* **1** A small coin; a nickel. **2** A motor vehicle that carries passengers for a small fare. [Cf. F *jeton* JETTON]

jit·ter (jit′ər) *v.i. Colloq.* To talk or act nervously. [Var. of CHITTER]

jit·ter·bug (jit′ər·bug′) *U.S. Slang n.* A person who responds to swing or jazz music by dancing in a fast, violent manner. **—** *v.i.* **·bugged, ·bug·ging** To dance to swing or jazz music in a fast, violent manner.

jit·ters (jit′ərz) *n. pl. Colloq.* Intense nervousness or a spell of nerves. **— jit′ter·y** *adj.*

jiu·jit·su (jōō·jit′sōō) *n.* A Japanese system of unarmed self-defense in which one's opponent is compelled to use his strength to his own disadvantage: also spelled *jujitsu, jujutsu.* Also **jiu·jut·su** (jōō·jit′sōō, -jōōt′sōō). Compare JUDO. [<Japanese *jiu, ju* gentle, pliant + *jitsu* art]

jive (jīv) *n. Slang* **1** The jargon of jazz music and musicians. **2** Jazz music. [Origin uncertain]

Jiz·er·a (yiz′ər·ä) A river in northern Bohemia, Czechoslovakia, flowing 100 miles SW to the Elbe: German *Iser.*

jo (jō) *n. Scot.* A sweetheart of either sex. Also **joe.**

Jo·ab (jō′ab) A masculine personal name. [<Hebrew, the Lord is father]
— Joab David's nephew, commander of the Hebrew army. II *Sam.* xviii 2.

Jo·a·chim (jō′ə·kim; *Du.* yō′ä·kim, *Fr.* zhō·ä·kaṅ′, *Ger.* yō′ä·khim) A masculine personal name. Also *Ital.* **Joa·chi·no** (jä·kē′nō) or **Joa·chi·mo** (jä·kē′mō), *Sp.* **Joa·quin** (hwä·kēn′) or **Joa·quim** (hwä·kēm′). [<Hebrew, the Lord will judge]

Jo·a·chim (yō′ə·kim), **Joseph,** 1831–1907, Hungarian violinist.

Jo·a·chims·thal (yō′ä·khims·täl′) A German name for JACHYMOV.

joad (jōd) *n.* A migratory worker. [after the *Joad* family in John Steinbeck's *Grapes of Wrath*]

Joan (jōn) A feminine personal name. Also **Jo·an·na** (jō·an′ə), **Jo·a·net·ta** (jō′ə·net′ə). [<Hebrew, the Lord's grace]
— Joan of Arc, 1412–31, a French heroine and martyr who compelled the English to raise the siege of Orléans; captured; burned as a sorceress and heretic: called the "Maid of Orleans"; beatified 1909; canonized 1920. Also French *Jeanne d'Arc.*
— Joan, Pope See POPE JOAN.

jo·an·nes (jō·an′əs) See JOHANNES.

Jo·an·nes (jō·an′ēz) Latin form of JOHN.

João (zhwouṅ) Portuguese form of JOHN.

João Pes·so·a (zhwouṅ pe·sō′ə) A city in NE Brazil, capital of Paraíba state: formerly *Parahiba.*

Jo·ash (jō′ash) Name of two Jewish kings: Joash, king of Judah 837–797 B.C., and Joash, king of Israel 800–785 B.C. Also called *Jehoash.*

job[1] (job) *n.* **1** A piece of work of a definite extent or character, especially one done in the course of one's profession or occupation. **2** A specific piece of work done for a certain fee. **3** Anything to be done. **4** *Colloq.* A situation or position of employment. **5** A material thing to be worked on. **6** A public service or transaction done ostensibly for the public good but actually for private or partisan gain. **7** *Colloq.* An affair; circumstance: to make the best of a bad *job.* **8** *Slang* A theft; robbery. **9** *Printing* The printing of small or miscellaneous circulars, cards, posters, etc. See synonyms under BUSINESS, TASK. **—** *v.* **jobbed, job·bing** *v.i.* **1** To work by the job or piece. **2** To be a jobber. **3** To turn a position of public trust improperly to private advantage. **—** *v.t.* **4** To buy in bulk from the importers or manufacturers and resell in lots to dealers. **5** To sublet (work) among separate contractors. **—** *adj.* That may be bought, sold, or used by the job: a *job* lot. [Origin unknown]

job[2] (job) *v.t. & v.i.* **jobbed, job·bing** To jab. **—** *n.* The act of thrusting, poking, or stabbing suddenly; a jab. [ME *jobben*]

Job (jōb; *Fr.* zhōb, *Sw.* yōb) A masculine personal name. Also *Lat.* **Jo·bus** (jō′bəs). [<Hebrew, persecuted]
— Job The chief personage of the Old Testament book of Job: often referred to as the symbol of patience on account of his many afflictions; also this book itself.

job·ber (job′ər) *n.* **1** One who buys goods in bulk from the manufacturer or importer and sells to the retailer. **2** *Brit.* A middleman, as among stockbrokers. **3** An intriguer, as in politics. **4** One who works by the job, or on small jobs.

job·ber·y (job′ər·ē) *n. pl.* **·ber·ies** Corrupt use

job·less (job′lis) adj. 1 Without a job. 2 Of or pertaining to those without a job. —**job′·less·ness** n.

job lot A collection of miscellaneous goods sold as a lot.

job printer One who does miscellaneous printing. —**job printing.**

Job's comforter One who, like the friends of Job, professes to console or comfort, but actually increases one's wretchedness.

Job's-tears (jōbz′tirz′) n. 1 A hardy, annual, tropical grass (Coix lacryma-jobi). 2 The white, pearly seeds of this plant, sometimes used as beads.

Jo·cas·ta (jō·kas′ta) In Greek legend, the wife of Laius, who unwittingly married her own son Oedipus and killed herself when she discovered it.

jock¹ (jok) n. 1 Colloq. A jockstrap. 2 Slang An athlete. [<JOCK(STRAP)]

jock² (jok) n. Colloq. 1 A jockey. 2 A disc jockey.

Jock (jok) n. Scot. 1 A nickname for the personal name JOHN. 2 A nickname for any Scotsman.

jock·ey (jok′ē) n. 1 One employed to ride horses, especially at races. 2 One who takes undue advantage in trade. 3 Obs. A strolling minstrel. 4 Obs. A lad; boy. 5 Obs. A horse dealer. —v. ·eyed, ·ey·ing v.i. 1 To maneuver for an advantage: to jockey for position. 2 To be tricky; cheat. 3 To ride as a jockey. —v.t. 4 To put or guide by skilful handling or control. 5 To trick; cheat. 6 To ride (a horse) in a race. [Dim. of JOCK]

jock·o (jok′ō) n. 1 A chimpanzee. 2 Any ape or monkey. Also called jacko.

jock·strap (jok′strap′) n. An elastic support for the genitals worn by male athletes. [< cant jock the male genitals + STRAP]

jo·cose (jō·kōs′) adj. Of the nature of a joke; jocular. [<L jocosus < jocus joke] —**jo·cose′ly** adv. —**jo·cose′ness** n.

Synonyms: droll, facetious, funny, humorous, jocular, merry, sportive, waggish. See HUMOROUS, MERRY, VIVACIOUS. Antonyms: care-worn, cheerless, doleful, dreary, dull, grave, lugubrious, melancholy, miserable, mordant, mournful, rueful, sad, serious, solemn, sorrowful, woeful.

jo·cos·i·ty (jō·kos′ə·tē) n. pl. ·ties 1 Jocularity; jocoseness; mirthfulness. 2 A joke.

joc·u·lar (jok′yə·lər) adj. 1 Being in a joking mood; making jokes. 2 Having the nature of, intended as, or appropriate to a joke or joking; comic; funny. Also joc′u·la·to·ry (-tôr′ē, -tō′rē). See synonyms under HUMOROUS, JOCOSE. [<L jocularis < joculus, dim. of jocus a joke] —**joc·u·lar·i·ty** (-lar′ə·tē) n. —**joc′u·lar·ly** adv.

joc·und (jok′ənd, jō′kənd) adj. Having a blithe or gay disposition or appearance; jovial; sportive. [<OF jocund <LL jocundus, alter. of L jucundus pleasant < juvare delight] —**joc′und·ly** adv. —**joc′und·ness** n.

jo·cun·di·ty (jō·kun′də·tē) n. pl. ·ties The state or quality of being jocund; sportiveness; mirth.

Jodh·pur (jōd·poor′, jōd′ poor) 1 A former princely state in the Rajputana States, India: also Marwar. 2 A city in central Rajasthan; formerly the capital of Jodhpur state.

jodh·pur boots (jod′pər) Riding shoes that end just above the ankle, buckled on the sides.

jodh·purs (jod′pərz) n. pl. Wide riding breeches, close-fitting from knee to ankle, designed to be worn with jodhpur boots. Also **jodhpur breeches.** [from Jodhpur, India]

Joe (jō) 1 Diminutive of JOSEPH. 2 U.S. Slang A person: a good Joe. —**G.I. Joe** U.S. Slang 1 An enlisted man in the U.S. Army. 2 An enlisted man in any of the U.S. armed services.

Jo·el (jō′əl) A masculine personal name. [<Hebrew, the Lord is God]
—**Joel** A prophet, son of Pethuel; also, the Old Testament book by this prophet. Joel i 1.

joe-pye weed (jō′pī′) Either of two tall American herbs, Eupatorium purpureum or E. maculatum, with pale-purple flowers.

jo·ey (jō′ē) n. Austral. The young of an animal, especially a young kangaroo.

Jof·fre (zhôf′r′), **Joseph Jacques Césaire**, 1852–1931. French marshal; commander in chief of French army in World War I.

jog (jog) v. **jogged, jog·ging** v.t. 1 To push or touch with a slight jar; shake. 2 To nudge; arouse the attention of. 3 To give a slight reminder to; stimulate: to jog the memory. —v.i. 4 To move with a slow, jolting pace or trot. 5 To proceed slowly or monotonously: with on or along. —n. 1 A slight push, as with the elbow; any slight incentive. 2 A slow, jolting motion or pace. 3 Any angle or break in a line or surface. 4 In the theater, a narrow flat used with other scenery to form a corner or projection in the stage set. [Prob. imit. Akin to SHOG.] —**jog′ger** n.

jog·ging (jog′ing) n. The exercise of running at a slow, regular pace, often alternately with walking.

jog·gle (jog′əl) v. ·gled, ·gling v.t. 1 To shake slightly; jog; jolt. 2 To fasten or join together by a joggle or joggles. —v.i. 3 To have an irregular or jolting motion; shake. See synonyms under SHAKE. —n. 1 An irregular shake; jog; jolt. 2 A joint by means of which a piece, as of stone, is fitted to another. 3 A dowel. 4 A shoulder to receive the thrust of a brace or strut. [Freq. of JOG, v.]

joggle post 1 A post having shoulders to receive the feet of struts; kingpost. 2 A post built of timbers joggled together.

Jog·ja·kar·ta (jog′yə·kär′tə) A town in southern Java; formerly capital of the Republic of Indonesia: also Djokjakarta, Jokjakarta.

jog trot 1 A slow, easy trot, as of a horse. 2 A slow, humdrum habit of living or doing the daily tasks.

Jo·hann (yō′hän) Dutch, German, and Swedish form of JOHN. Also **Jo·han·nes** (Ger. yō·hän′əs, Lat. jō·an′ēz).

Jo·han·na (jō·hän′ə, Ger. Sw. yō·hän′ə) German and Swedish form of JOAN. Also Dan. **Jo·han·ne** (yō·hän′ə).

jo·han·nes (jō·han′ēz) n. A former gold coin of Portugal: also joannes. [after Joannes V of Portugal]

Jo·han·nes·burg (jō·han′is·bûrg, yō·hän′is-) A city in Gauteng, Republic of South Africa.

Jo·hann·sen (yō·hän′sən), **Wilhelm Ludwig**, 1857–1927, Danish botanist and geneticist.

Jo·hans·son gage (yō·hän′sən) One of a series of metallically perfect, flat, steel blocks with parallel surfaces: used in precision measurements. [after C.E. Johansson, Swedish engineer]

john (jon) n. Slang 1 A toilet. 2 A man who patronizes a prostitute.

John (jon) A masculine personal name: often used, especially in phrases or compounds, to denote a man or boy in general. [<Hebrew, the grace of the Lord]
—**John** One of the twelve apostles, son of Zebedee and brother of James; also, the Gospel according to this apostle, or one of the three Epistles written by him: also called "Saint John the Evangelist."
—**John** Son of Zacharias; the forerunner of Jesus; beheaded by Herod Antipas; known as John the Baptist.
—**John,** 1166?–1216, king of England 1199–1216; signed Magna Carta, 1215: called "John Lackland."
—**John I,** 1357–1433, king of Portugal 1385–1433; made treaty alliance with England, 1386: called "John the Great."
—**John II,** 1319–64, king of France 1350–64; defeated at Poitiers, imprisoned in England: called "John the Good."
—**John III,** 1624–96, king of Poland 1674–96; fought against the Turks: real name John Sobieski.
—**John IV,** 1605–56, king of Portugal 1640–1656; founder of the Braganza dynasty: called "John the Fortunate."
—**John XXIII,** 1881–1963, real name Angelo Giuseppe Roncalli; pope 1958–63.
—**John Chrysostom, Saint,** 347?–407, one of the four Greek Christian fathers; patriarch of Constantinople.
—**John of Austria, Don,** 1547–78, natural son of Emperor Charles V; defeated Turks at Lepanto, 1571.
—**John of Damascus, Saint,** 700?–754?, Greek theologian: also called "John Damascene."
—**John of Gaunt,** 1340–99, duke of Lancaster, son of Edward III of England; patron of Chaucer and Wyclif.

—**John of Leiden,** 1500?–36, Dutch Anabaptist leader.
—**John of Salisbury,** died 1180, English churchman.
—**John of the Cross, Saint,** 1542–91, Spanish mystic: also Spanish San Juan de la Cruz.

John (jon), **Augustus Edwin,** 1878–1961, English portrait painter.

John apple Obs. See APPLEJOHN.

John Bull The Englishman personified: a nickname; hence, the English people. Also Johnny Bull. [after a character in a satire (1712) by John Arbuthnot] —**John-Bul·lism** (jon′bool′iz·əm) n.

John Doe (dō) A name commonly used to designate a fictitious or real personage: from the fictitious plaintiff in the action at common law for ejectment, the fictitious defendant being Richard Roe.

john do·ry (dôr′ē dō′rē) A small food fish (family Zeidae) of the Atlantic coast of Europe, the Mediterranean and Australian seas: of compressed form and a prevailing golden-yellow. Also **John Do′ry, John Do′ree:** also called dory.

John Hancock U.S. Colloq. A person's autograph. [after John Hancock, whose large signature is the first on the Declaration of Independence]

John·ny (jon′ē) n. pl. ·nies A Confederate soldier. Also **Johnny Reb.**

Johnny Appleseed See APPLESEED, J OHNNY.

john·ny·cake (jon′ē·kāk′) n. A flat cake of Indian meal, baked on a griddle; also, cornbread: often spelled johnnycake. [? < obs. jonikin, a type of bread (<N. Am. Ind.) + CAKE]

John·ny-come-late·ly (jon′ē·kum′lāt′lē) n. Colloq. A person who has recently arrived on the scene.

john·ny-jump-up (jon′ē·jump′up′) n. 1 A naturalized variety of the pansy (Viola kitaibeliana). 2 The bird's-foot violet. 3 The wild pansy. Also **john′ny-jump′er.**

Johnny on the spot Colloq. One who is always on hand and ready for anything. —**John·ny-on-the-spot** (jon′ē·on·thə·spot′) adj.

Johnny red Pathol. kwashiorkor.

John o' Groat's (ə grōts′) A locality of northern Scotland, often erroneously regarded as the northernmost point of Britain. Also **John o' Groat's House.**

John Paul Appellation of two popes.
— **John Paul I,** 1912–1978, real name Albino Luciani; pope 1978.
—**John Paul II,** born 1920, real name Karol Wojtyla, pope 1978.

John·son (jon′sən), **Andrew,** 1808–75, president of the United States 1865–69. — **James Weldon,** 1871–1938, U.S. lawyer and author. —**Lyndon Baines,** 1908–1973, 36th president of the United States 1963–1969. —**Samuel,** 1709–84, English author, critic, and lexicographer: known as Doctor Johnson. —**Sir William,** 1715–74, English official in the American colonies.

John·son·ese (jon′sən·ēz′, -ēs′) n. 1 Ponderous, oracular, and elaborate style attempting to imitate that of Dr. Samuel Johnson. 2 Johnsonian, in a derogatory sense.

Johnson grass A perennial pasture grass (Sorghum halepense) also valued for hay, but considered a weed in cultivated land: also called Arabian millet. [after Wm. Johnson, Alabama planter]

John·so·ni·an (jon·sō′nē ·ən) adj. Having the characteristics of the style of Dr. Samuel Johnson: precise, often sesquipedalian, carefully elaborated, judicious, and final. See JOHNSONESE. —n. One who follows or copies the style of Dr. Johnson. —**John·so′ni·an·ism, John′son·ism** n.

John·ston (jon′stən), **Albert Sidney,** 1803–62, American Confederate general; killed at Shiloh. —**Joseph Eggleston,** 1807–91, American Confederate general.

Johnston Island A small island in the central Pacific 700 miles SW of Honolulu, under jurisdiction of the United States Navy.

Jo·hore (jə·hôr′, -hōr′) The southernmost State of Malaya; 7,330 square miles: capital, Johore Bahru.

joie de vi·vre (zhwá də vēv′r′) French Joy of living.

join (join) *v.t.* **1** To set or bring together; connect; combine: to *join* girders. **2** To come to a junction with; become part of: The path *joins* the road here. **3** To become a member of, as a club. **4** To unite in act or purpose: to *join* forces. **5** To come to as a companion or participant; meet and accompany: When will you *join* us? **6** To unite in marriage. **7** To engage in (battle, etc.). **8** *Colloq.* To adjoin. **9** *Geom.* To draw a straight line or curve between. — *v.i.* **10** To come together; connect; unite: The roads *joined.* **11** To enter into association or agreement. **12** To take part: usually with *in.* — **to join up** To enlist in a military service. — *n.* A place of junction or contact; joint. [<OF *joign-*, stem of *joindre* <L *jungere*]

join·der (join′dər) *n.* **1** The act of joining. **2** *Law* A joining of causes of action or defense; a joining of parties in an action; also, the acceptance of an issue tendered. [<F *joindre* join]

join·er (joi′nər) **1** One who or that which joins. **2** An artisan who finishes woodwork in houses; also, loosely, any mechanic who puts together pieces of wood.

join·er·y (joi′nər·ē) *n.* **1** The art or work of a joiner. **2** The articles constructed by a joiner.

joint (joint) *n.* **1** The place, point, line, or surface where two or more things are joined together; a junction or mode of junction; hinge. **2** An articulation or place of natural or easy separation between two parts, as of a machine, animal, or plant; a node; also, an internode or portion between two nodes or joints. **3** *Anat.* A place of union of two bones or separate parts of the skeleton; an articulation. **4** *Geol.* One of a series of approximately parallel divisional planes occurring in many rocks. **5** One of the pieces into which a carcass is divided by the butcher. **6** *U.S. Slang* A marihuana cigarette. **7** *U.S. Slang* A place of low resort, as for gambling. **8** *U.S. Slang* Any place of dwelling or gathering. — **out of joint** **1** Not fitted at the joint; dislocated. **2** Disordered; disorganized. — *adj.* **1** Produced by combined action. **2** Sharing together. **3** Participated in or used by two or more; held or shared in common. **4** *Law* Joined together in unity of interest or of liability: opposed to *several.* **5** Of or relating to both branches of a legislature: a *joint* session. See synonyms under MUTUAL. — *v.t.* **1** To fasten by means of a joint or joints. **2** To form or shape with a joint or joints, as a board. **3** To separate into joints, as meat. [<OF <L *junctus*, pp. of *jungere* join] — **joint′less** *adj.*

joint account An account in the name of two or more persons.

joint committee A committee of representatives from both houses of a legislative body.

joint convention **1** A session of both houses of a legislature. **2** An assembly of delegates representing two or more political parties. Also **joint session.**

joint·ed (join′tid) *adj.* Having joints, knots, or nodes; articulated.

joint·er (join′tər) *n.* **1** One who or that which joints; especially, one of several instruments for constructing joints. **2** An edged part, triangular in shape, attached to the beam of a plow. **3** A trying plane.

joint evil *Pathol.* A form of leprosy which is anesthetic in its later stages, especially as known in the West Indies.

joint fir Any of a genus of shrubs *(Ephedra)* growing in dry or desert regions, with jointed green branches and red berries; especially, ma huang.

joint·grass (joint′gras′, -gräs′) *n.* A creeping grass *(Paspalum distichum)* of the southern United States, which roots at the joints: used as fodder.

joint·ly (joint′lē) *adv.* In a joint manner; unitedly.

joint·mouse (joint′mous′) *n.* A movable cartilage, calculus, or other foreign body in a joint.

joint·ress (join′tris) *n.* **1** A woman who has a jointure: also **join·tur·ess** (join′chər·is). **2** A woman who is a joint ruler or owner.

joint snake The glass snake.

joint stock Capital or stock that is held jointly.

joint-stock company (joint′stok′) A company or partnership whose capital is divided into shares (usually transferable), some of which are held by each of the members. Also **joint′-stock′ association.**

join·ture (join′chər) *n.* **1** *Law* A settlement, as of land, made to a woman in place of dower. **2** *Obs.* A joining together. — *v.t.* **join·tured, join·tur·ing** To settle a jointure on. [<F <L *junctura* <*jungere* join]

join·ture·less (join′chər·lis) *adj.* Having no jointure.

joint·weed (joint′wēd′) *n.* A slender, erect American annual herb *(Polygonella articulata)* with small, white flowers on jointed stems.

joint·worm (joint′wûrm′) *n.* The larva of a plant-feeding chalcidid hymenopterous fly (genus *Harmolita*), especially *H. tritici,* that does great damage to wheat, barley, etc., by causing a gall-like excrescence at the joints of the stalk.

Join·ville (zhwaṅ·vēl′), **Jean de,** 1224–1317, French crusader and chronicler.

joist (joist) *n.* A horizontal timber in a floor or ceiling. See synonyms under STICK. — *v.t.* To furnish with joists. [<OF *giste* <*gesir* lie <L *jacere*]

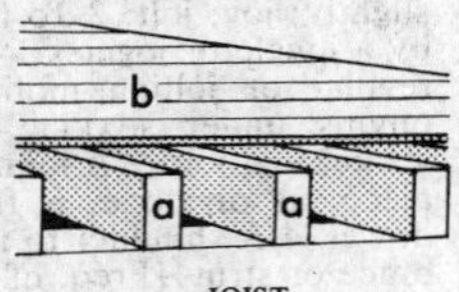

JOIST
a. Joists.
b. Floor boards.

Jó·kai (yō′koi), **Mau·rus,** 1825–1904, Hungarian novelist.

joke (jōk) *n.* **1** Something said or done for the purpose of creating amusement; a jest. **2** A subject of merriment. **3** Something not said or done in earnest; sport. See synonyms under WIT. — *v.* **joked, jok·ing** *v.t.* To make merry with. — *v.i.* To make jokes; jest. [<L *jocus*] — **jok′ing·ly** *adv.*

jok·er (jō′kər) *n.* **1** One who jokes. **2** In certain card games, as euchre, an extra card that counts as the highest trump, or, in poker, as any card the holder names. **3** *U.S.* An ambiguous or inconspicuous clause, inserted in a legislative bill to render it ineffectual or cause it to serve some purpose other than the original intention of the bill. **4** Any hidden device or ruse used for purposes of trickery or deception.

Jok·ja·kar·ta (jōk′yə·kär′tə) See JOGJAKARTA.

jole (jōl) See JOWL.

Jo·li·et (jō′lē·et, jō′lē·et′; *Fr.* zhô·lye′), **Louis,** 1645–1700, French-Canadian explorer. Also **Jol·liet** (jol′ē·et, *Fr.* zhô·lye′).

Jo·liot-Cu·rie (zhô·lyō′kü·rē′), **Frédéric,** 1900–1958, and his wife **Irène,** 1897–1956, daughter of Marie and Pierre Curie, French physicists.

jol·li·fi·ca·tion (jol′ə·fə·kā′shən) *n.* An act or occasion of festivity; a merrymaking.

jol·li·fy (jol′ə·fī) *v.t.* & *v.i.* **·fied, ·fy·ing** To be or cause to be merry or jolly.

jol·li·ness (jol′ē·nis) *n.* The state or quality of being jolly; gaiety. Also **jol·li·ty** (jol′ə·tē).

jol·ly (jol′ē) *adj.* **·li·er, ·li·est** **1** Full of life and mirth; jovial. **2** Expressing, inspiring, or characterized by mirth; exciting gaiety. **3** *Obs.* Exhilarated. See synonyms under HAPPY, MERRY. — *adv. Brit. Colloq.* Extremely; very: a *jolly* good time. — *n. pl.* **·lies** **1** Fun; banter; flattery. **2** *Brit. Slang* A British marine. **3** *Brit. Colloq.* A merry or festive gathering. — *v.t.* **·lied, ·ly·ing** *Colloq.* **1** To attempt to put or keep in good humor by agreeable or flattering attentions: often with *along* or *up.* **2** To make fun of; joke; rally. [<OF *joli*] — **jol′li·er** *n.* — **jol′li·ly** *adv.*

Jolly balance A spring balance used in the determination of specific gravities. [after Philip von *Jolly,* 1809–84, German physicist]

jol·ly·boat (jol′ē·bōt′) *n.* A small boat belonging to a ship. [<Dan. *jolle* yawl + BOAT]

Jolly Roger See BLACK FLAG under FLAG[1].

Jō·lo (hō′lō, hō·lō′) **1** The chief island in the Sulu archipelago, Philippines; 345 square miles. **2** Its chief city, capital of Sulu province.

jolt (jōlt) *v.t.* **1** To strike or knock against with a jarring shock. **2** To shake about with such shock. — *v.i.* **3** To move with jolts or bumps, as over a rough road. See synonyms under SHAKE. — *n.* A sudden, slight shock. [? Blend of ME *jot* bump and *joll* bump] — **jolt′er** *n.* — **jolt′y** *adj.*

Jo·ma·da (jō·mä′dä) The name of two Mohammedan months. See under CALENDAR (Mohammedan). Also spelled *Jumada.*

Jon (jon) An old form of JOHN.

Jo·nah (jō′nə) A masculine personal name. Also **Jo·nas** (jō′nəs; *Fr.* zhô·näs′, *Ger.* yō′näs). [<Hebrew, dove]
— **Jonah** **1** A Hebrew prophet of the eighth or ninth century B.C., who was cast overboard during a tempest sent because he had defied God: he was swallowed by a large fish, lived in its belly for three days, and was vomited up on shore alive. **2** The minor book of the Old Testament named for him and telling his story. **3** Any person or thing regarded as bringing bad luck: in allusion to the bad luck brought upon the sailors of the vessel the prophet traveled on. *Jonah* i 13–17. Also **Jo·nas** (jō′nəs).

Jon·a·than (jon′ə·thən) A masculine personal name. [<Hebrew, gift of the Lord]
— **Jonathan** Son of Saul and close friend of David. I *Sam.* xiv 1.
— **Jonathan** See BROTHER JONATHAN.

Jon·a·than (jon′ə·thən) *n.* A yellowish-red variety of late autumn apple.

Jones (jōnz), **Casey** See CASEY JONES. — **Daniel,** born 1881, English phonetician. — **Ernest,** 1879–1958, English psychologist and biographer of Sigmund Freud. — **Henry Arthur,** 1851–1929, English playwright. — **In·i·go** (in′i·gō), 1573–1652, English architect and stage designer. — **John Paul,** 1747–92, American naval commander born in Scotland. — **Rufus Matthew,** 1863–1948, U. S. Quaker leader, philosopher, and writer; co-founder of the American Friends Service Committee.

Jones Sound An arm of Baffin Bay between Ellesmere and Devon islands, Northwest Territories, Canada.

jon·gler·y (jong′glə·rē) *n. Archaic* Juggling; trickery. [<F *jonglerie* <*jongleur* a juggler]

jon·gleur (jong′glər, *Fr.* zhôṅ·glœr′) *n.* A medieval minstrel; also, later, a storyteller or buffoon. See JUGGLER. [<OF]

jon·ny·cake (jon′ē·kāk′) See JOHNNYCAKE.

jon·quil (jon′kwil, jong′-) *n.* **1** An ornamental bulbous plant *(Narcissus jonquilla)* related to the daffodil, having long, linear leaves and fragrant, white or yellow flowers. **2** The bulb or flower of this plant. **3** One of several other species of *Narcissus.* **4** A light-yellow color used in staining porcelains. Also **jon′quille.** [<F *jonquille,* ult. <L *juncus* a rush]

Jon·son (jon′sən), **Ben(jamin),** 1573–1637, English poet and dramatist.

Jop·pa (jop′ə) The Old Testament name for JAFFA. II *Chron.* ii 16.

Jor·daens (yôr′däns), **Jacob,** 1593–1678, Flemish painter.

jor·dan (jôr′dən) *n. Brit. Slang* A chamber pot.

Jor·dan (jôr′dən) The chief river of Palestine, flowing over 200 miles south to the Dead Sea.

Jor·dan (jôr′dən), **David Starr,** 1851–1931, U.S. zoologist and educator.

Jordan, Hashemite Kingdom of the A constitutional monarchy comprising the territories of Trans-Jordan and Arab Palestine; formed, with Iraq, The Arab Federation, 1958, but remains a sovereign state; 37,758 square miles: capital, Amman. *Arabic* **Al Ur·du·ni·yah** (al ŏŏr·dŏŏ·nē′yä). Also **Jordan.** — **Jor·da·ni·an** (jôr·dā′nē·ən) *adj.* & *n.*

Jordan almond A large Spanish almond, frequently sugar-coated as a confection.

Jor·ge (*Sp.* hôr′hā, *Pg.* zhôr′zhe) Spanish and Portuguese form of GEORGE.

jor·na·da (hôr·nä′thä) *n. SW U.S.* A stretch of desert land that can be crossed in a day's journey. [<Sp., ult. <L *diurnus* of a day]

jo·rum (jôr′əm, jō′rəm) *n.* A drinking bowl or its contents. Also **jo′ram.** [? after *Joram,* a Biblical character who brought vessels of silver and gold to David]

jo·seph (jō′zef) *n.* A long coat formerly worn by men; also, a similar garment formerly worn as a riding habit by women. [In allusion to the coat of *Joseph* (*Gen.* xxxvii 3)]

Jo·seph (jō′zəf, *Fr.* zhō·zef′; *Ger.* yō′zef) A masculine personal name. Also *Lat.* **Jo·se·phus** (jō·sē′fəs), *Pg., Sp.* **Jo·sé** (*Pg.* zhŏŏ·ze′, *Sp.* hō·sā′). [<Hebrew, addition]
— **Joseph** Hebrew patriarch; son of Jacob and Rachel: sold into slavery in Egypt by his brothers. *Gen.* xxx 24–5.
— **Joseph** Husband of Mary, the mother of Jesus. *Matt.* i 18.
— **Joseph II,** 1741–90; Holy Roman Emperor 1765–90.
— **Joseph of Arimathea** A wealthy Israelite who believed in Christ and provided a tomb for his burial. Compare GRAIL.

Joseph flower See GOATBEARD (def. 1). Also **Joseph's flower.**

Jo·se·phine (jō′zə·fēn, *Ger.* yō′zə·fē′nə) Feminine form of JOSEPH. Also *Fr.* **Jo·sé·phine**

(zhō·zä·fēn′) or **Jo·sèphe** (zhō·zef′) *Ger.* **Jo·seph·e** (yō·zef′ə), *Lat.* **Jo·se·pha** (jō·sē′fə), *Pg.* **Jo·se·phi·na** (zhō′zə·fē′nə), *Sp.* **Jo·se·fi·na** (hō′·sä·fē′nä).

—Josephine, 1763–1814, Marie Joséphine-Rose Tascher de la Pagerie, widow of Viscount Beauharnais; married Napoleon I 1796; divorced 1809.

Jo·seph·ite (jō′zəf·īt) *n.* A member of the Reorganized church of Jesus Christ of Latter-day Saints (the Mormon Church), established about 1860 by the followers of Joseph Smith.

Jo·se·phus (jō·sē′fəs), **Flavius,** A.D. 37–96?, Jewish historian.

josh (josh) *U.S. Slang v.t. & v.i.* To make good-humored fun of (someone); tease; banter. **—***n.* A hoax; a good-natured joke. [Blend of JOKE and BOSH] **—josh′er** *n.*

Josh Bil·lings (josh bil′ingz) Pseudonym of Henry Wheeler Shaw.

Josh·u·a (josh′ōō·ə) A masculine personal name. Also *Lat.* **Jos·u·a** (jos′ōō·ə; *Du., Sw.* yō′sōō·ä, *Ger.* yō′zōō·ə), *Fr.* **Jo·sué** (zhō·zwā′). [<Hebrew, the Lord is salvation]

—Joshua Son of Nun and successor of Moses as leader of the Israelites; also, the book of the Old Testament ascribed to him.

Joshua tree A tall, treelike desert plant (*Yucca brevifolia*) with forking branches that end in a cluster of leaves.

Jo·si·ah (jō·sī′ə) A masculine personal name. Also *Lat.* **Jo·si·as** (jō·sī′əs, *Dan.* yō·zī′äs; *Fr.* zhō·zē·äs′), *Du.* **Jo·zi·as** (yō·zē′äs). [<Hebrew, given to the Lord]

—Josiah A king of Judah in the seventh century B.C. II *Kings* xxii 1.

jos·kin (jos′kin) *n. Brit. Dial.* An awkward rustic; a boor.

Jos·quin des Prés (zhôs·kaṅ′ dā prā′), 1445?–1521, Flemish composer.

joss (jos) *n.* A Chinese god. [Pidgin English <Pg. *deos* God]

joss house A Chinese temple or place for idols.

joss paper Gold or silver paper burnt by the Chinese at funerals, etc.

joss stick A stick of perfumed paste burnt as incense.

jos·tle (jos′əl) *v.t. & v.i.* **·tled, ·tling** To push or crowd; elbow; hustle; bump. See synonyms under HUSTLE. **—***n.* A collision, bumping against, or slight shaking. Also spelled *justle.* [Freq. of JOUST] **—jos′tler** *n.*

jot (jot) *v.t.* **jot·ted, jot·ting** To make a hasty note of: usually with *down.* **—***n.* The least bit; an iota. See synonyms under PARTICLE. [<IOTA]

jo·ta (hō′tä) *n.* A lively Spanish dance in 3/4 time danced by a man and a woman with castanets.

Jo·tham (jō′thəm) A masculine personal name. [<Hebrew, the Lord is perfect]

— Jotham A son of Gideon, who survived the murder of his brothers. *Judges* ix 5–16.

jot·tings (jot′ingz) *n. pl.* Items of news, or memoranda.

Jö·tun (yœ′tōōn) In Norse mythology, one of the giants personifying the hostile powers of nature. Also **Jo·tun** (yô′tōōn, yō′-), **Jo′tunn.**

Jö·tunn·heim (yœ′tōōn·hām) See UTGARD. Also **Jo′tun·heim** (yô′-, yō′-).

Jou·bert (zhōō·bâr′), **Joseph,** 1754–1824, French moralist. **— Petrus Jacobus,** 1831–1900, Boer general.

jougs (jōōgz) *n. pl.* An old Scottish instrument of punishment, consisting of an iron yoke by which the culprit was fastened to a wall or post. [<OF *joug* yoke <L *jugum* yoke]

jouk (jōōk) *v.i. Scot.* To dodge; also, to bow.

joule (joul, jōōl) *n. Physics* The mks unit of work or energy: equivalent to the work done, or heat generated, in one second by an electric current of one ampere against a resistance of one ohm, or in raising the potential of one coulomb by one volt: equal to 10,000,000 ergs or .737324 foot-pounds. [after James Prescott *Joule*]

Joule (joul, jōōl), **James Prescott,** 1818–89, English physicist.

jounce (jouns) *v.t. & v.i.* **jounced, jounc·ing** To shake or move roughly up and down; bounce; jolt. **—***n.* A shake; a bump. [? Blend of GEE[2] and BOUNCE]

jour (zhōōr) *n. French* Day; daylight; dawn.

Jour·dan (zhōōr·däṅ′), **Comte Jean Baptiste,** 1762–1833, French marshal.

jour de fête (də fet′) *French* A feast day; festival.

jour·nal (jûr′nəl) *n.* **1** A record of daily occurrences of personal interest; a diary. **2** An official record of the daily proceedings of a legislature or other deliberative body. **3** A periodical recording news or other events of current interest. **4** A daily chronicle of a voyage. **5** *Naut.* A log or logbook. **6** In bookkeeping: **a** A daybook. **b** In double entry, a book in which transactions of the day are entered in systematic form, either as original entries or as transfers from the daybook, in order to facilitate later posting in the ledger. **7** *Mech.* That part of a shaft or axle which rotates in or against a bearing. [<OF <L *diurnalis.* Doublet of DIURNAL.]

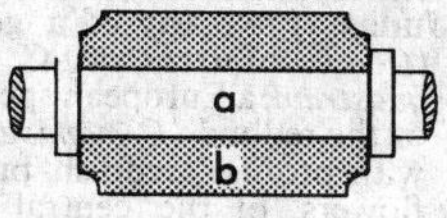

JOURNAL (*def. 7*)
a. Journal. *b.* Bearing.

journal box *Mech.* The box or bearing for a rotating axle or shaft.

jour·nal·ese (jûr′nəl·ēz′, -ēs′) *n.* A style of writing supposedly characteristic of newspapers; facile and sensational writing, hackneyed phrases and effects, etc.

jour·nal in·time (zhōōr·nȧl′ aṅ·tēm′) *French* Private diary.

jour·nal·ism (jûr′nəl·iz′əm) *n.* **1** The occupation of a journalist; the writing, editing, or publishing of newspapers or other periodicals. **2** Newspapers collectively.

jour·nal·ist (jûr′nəl·ist) *n.* One who manages, edits, or writes for a journal or newspaper.

jour·nal·is·tic (jûr′nəl·is′tik) *adj.* Pertaining to journalists or journalism. **—jour′nal·is′ti·cal·ly** *adv.*

jour·nal·ize (jûr′nəl·īz) *v.* **·ized, ·iz·ing** *v.t.* **1** To enter in a journal. **2** To write or describe in a journal. **—***v.i.* **3** To keep a journal or diary. Also *Brit.* **jour′nal·ise.**

jour·ney (jûr′nē) *n.* **1** Passage from one place to another, especially by land: sometimes applied figuratively to the passage through life. **2** The distance traversed, or traversable, in a specified time: a week's *journey* away. **3** In glassmaking, the round of work or the time taken in making raw material into glass. **—***v.i.* To travel; go on a journey. [<OF *journee* a day's travel <L *diurnum,* orig. neut. sing. of *diurnus* daily < *dies* a day] **—jour′ney·er** *n.*

Synonyms (noun): excursion, expedition, pilgrimage, tour, transit, travel, trip, voyage. A *journey* is a direct going from a starting point to a destination, ordinarily over a considerable distance; we speak of a day's *journey,* or the *journey* of life. *Travel* is a passing from place to place, not necessarily in a direct line or with a fixed destination. A *voyage,* which was formerly a *journey* of any kind, is now a going to a considerable distance by water, especially by sea. A *trip* is a short and direct *journey.* A *tour* is a *journey* that returns to the starting point, generally over a considerable distance; as, a bridal *tour,* or business *tour.* An *excursion* is a brief *tour* or *journey* taken for pleasure, often by many persons at once; as, an *excursion* to West Point. *Passage* is a general word for a *journey* by any conveyance, especially by water; as, rough *passage* across the Atlantic. *Transit,* literally the act of passing over or through, is used specifically of the conveyance of passengers or merchandise; rapid *transit* is demanded for surburban residents or perishable goods. *Pilgrimage,* once always of a sacred character, retains in derived uses something of that sense; as, a *pilgrimage* to Monticello.

jour·ney·man (jûr′nē·mən) *n. pl.* **·men** (-mən) A mechanic who has learned his trade and who works at it for another.

jour·ney·work (jûr′nē·wûrk′) *n.* Work done by a journeyman.

joust (just, joust, jōōst) *n.* A tilting match between mounted knights, usually with blunt lances and in single combat. **—***v.i.* To engage in a joust. Also spelled *just.* [<OF *jouste* <*jouster* <LL *juxtare* approach <*juxta* nearby] **—joust′er** *n.*

Jo·van·na (zhō·vä′nə) Portuguese form of JOAN.

Jove (jōv) Jupiter. **—by Jove!** A mild oath expressing surprise, emphasis, etc.

jo·vi·al (jō′vē·əl) *adj.* Possessing or expressive of good-natured mirth or gaiety; jolly. See synonyms under MERRY. [<F <LL *Jovialis* born under the influence of Jupiter] **—jo′·vi·al·ly** *adv.* **—jo′vi·al·ness** *n.*

Jo·vi·al (jō′vē·əl) *adj.* **1** In astrology, pertaining to the influence of the planet Jupiter; favorable; benignant. **2** *Obs.* Of or pertaining to the god Jupiter; Jovelike; majestic.

jo·vi·al·i·ty (jō′vē·al′ə·tē) *n.* **1** The quality of being jovial. **2** Merriment; conviviality; mirth. Also **jo·vi·al·ty** (jō′vē·əl·tē). See synonyms under SPORT.

jo·vi·al·ize (jō′vē·əl·īz′) *v.t.* **·ized, ·iz·ing** To make jovial.

Jo·vi·an (jō′vē·ən) *adj.* Of or pertaining to Jove or Jupiter.

Jo·vi·a·nus (jō′vē·ā′nəs), **Flavius Claudius,** 331?–364, Roman emperor 363–364. Also **Jo′·vi·an** (-ən).

jow (jou, jō) *Scot. v.t. & v.i.* To ring; toll. **—***n.* The stroke or sound of a bell.

Jow·ett (jou′it), **Benjamin,** 1817–93, English classical scholar.

jowl[1] (joul, jōl) *n.* **1** The fleshy part of the lower jaw, especially when fat and pendulous. **2** The wattle of fowls. **3** The dewlap of cattle. Also spelled *jole.* [ME *cholle,* ? OE *coelur* throat]

jowl[2] (joul, jōl) *n.* The cheek or jaw. Also spelled *jole.* [OE *ceafl*] **—jowled** *adj.*

jowl·er (jou′lər) *n.* A heavy-jawed hound.

joy (joi) *n.* **1** A lively emotion of happiness; gladness. **2** Anything which causes delight. **3** An expression or manifestation of this. **4** *Obs.* Festivity. See synonyms under HAPPINESS, RAPTURE. **—***v.i.* To be glad; rejoice. **—***v.t. Obs.* To gladden. See synonyms under REJOICE. [<OF *joie* <L *gaudium* <*gaudere* rejoice]

joy·ance (joi′əns) *n.* **1** *Poetic* Delight; enjoyment. **2** *Archaic* Gaiety; festivity.

Joyce (jois), **James,** 1882–1941, Irish novelist and poet. **— William** See HAW-HAW, LORD.

joy·ful (joi′fəl) *adj.* **1** Full of joy. **2** Manifesting or causing joy. See synonyms under HAPPY. **—joy′ful·ly** *adv.* **—joy′ful·ness** *n.*

joy·less (joi′lis) *adj.* Destitute of joy; having or causing no joy. **—joy′less·ly** *adv.* **—joy′·less·ness** *n.*

joy·ous (joi′əs) *adj.* Joyful. See synonyms under AIRY, CHEERFUL, HAPPY, MERRY. **—joy′·ous·ly** *adv.* **—joy′ous·ness** *n.*

joy-ride (joi′rīd′) *n. Colloq.* An automobile ride taken exclusively for pleasure: often with the idea of reckless driving in a stolen car. **—joy′-rid′er** *n.* **—joy′-rid′ing** *n.*

joy-stick (joi′stik′) *n. Slang* The control stick in an airplane.

Jo·zsef (*Hungarian* yō′sef, *Polish* yôsh′if) Hungarian and Polish form of JOSEPH.

Juan (hwän) Spanish form of JOHN. See also DON JUAN.

Jua·na (hwä′nä) Spanish form of JOAN.

Juan de Fu·ca Strait (hwän′ də fōō′kə) An arm of the Pacific Ocean between Vancouver Island and the Washington mainland.

Ju·an Fer·nan·dez (jōō′ən fər·nan′dēz, *Sp.* hwän fer·nän′dās) A group of Chilean islands lying 425 miles west of central Chile: total land area, 70 square miles. See SELKIRK, ALEXANDER.

Juá·rez (hwä′rās), **Benito Pablo,** 1806–72, Mexican patriot who opposed Maximilian; president of Mexico 1858–63, 1867–72.

Juárez, Ciudad See CIUDAD JUÁREZ.

ju·ba (jōō′bə) *n.* A lively Southern Negro dance. **—to pat juba** To keep time to the juba by patting with the hands and feet. [Of African origin]

Ju·ba (jōō′bä) A river in southern Italian Somaliland, flowing 548 miles south to the Indian Ocean: Italian *Giuba.*

Ju·bal (jōō′bəl) A descendant of Cain; a musician or inventor of musical instruments. *Gen.* iv 21.

ju·bate (jōō′bāt) *adj.* Having a manelike growth. [<L *jubatus* <*juba* a mane]

Jub·bul·pore (jub′əl·pôr′) A city in northern Madhya Pradesh, central India: also *Jabalpur.*

ju·be (jōō′bē) *n.* **1** *Archit.* A rood loft or screen and gallery at the entrance of the choir of a church. **2** *Obs.* An ambo. [<L *jube,* imperative of *jubere* bid; from the first word of a prayer anciently recited from this gallery]

jubh·a (jōōb′ə) *n.* A long, loose outer garment, worn in Moslem countries. Also **jub′·bah.** See JIBBA. [<Arabic *jubbah*]

ju·bi·lance (jōō′bə·ləns) *n.* Jubilation. Also **ju′bi·lan·cy.**

ju·bi·lant (jōō′bə·lənt) *adj.* **1** Manifesting great joy; exultingly glad. **2** Expressing triumph. [<L *jubilans, -antis,* ppr. of *jubilare* exult] **—ju′bi·lant·ly** *adv.*

ju·bi·late (jōō′bə·lāt) *v.t.* & *v.i.* **·lat·ed, ·lat·ing** To rejoice; exult. [<L *jubilatus,* pp. of *jubilare* exult]

Ju·bi·la·te (jōō′bə·lā′tē, -lä′-) *n.* **1** The 100th (in the Vulgate and Douai versions, the 99th) Psalm, or the music to which it may be set: from its opening word in the Latin version. **2** The third Sunday after Easter, whose introit begins *Jubilate.* [<L, imperative of *jubilare* exult, be joyful]

Ju·bi·la·te De·o (jōō′bə·lā′tē dē′ō, jōō′bə·lä′tē dā′ō) *Latin* Be joyful in the Lord.

ju·bi·la·tion (jōō′bə·lā′shən) *n.* Rejoicing; exultation.

ju·bi·lee (jōō′bə·lē) *n.* **1** In Jewish history, every fiftieth year, from the entrance of the Hebrews into Canaan. At its recurrence, all Hebrew slaves were emancipated and all alienated lands reverted to their former owners or their heirs. **2** In the Roman Catholic Church, a year of special indulgence, appointed by the Pope, during which compliance with certain conditions of confession, communion, good works, etc., will secure remission from the penal consequences of sin: also called *Annus Sanctus.* **3** The fiftieth or the twenty-fifth anniversary of an event; also, the celebration of this. **4** Any season of rejoicing or festivity. **5** *Obs.* A state or manifestation of exultation or delight. Also **ju′bi·le.** [<OF *jubile* <LL *jubilaeus* (infl. by *jubilum* a shout of joy) <Gk. *iōbēlaios* <Hebrew *yōbēl* ram's horn, trumpet]

jubilee singer One, especially a Negro, who sings jubilee songs.

jubilee song A Negro folk song or spiritual; originally, one of rejoicing over emancipation from slavery.

Ju·by (jōō′bē), **Cape** A headland of Spanish West Africa opposite the Canary Islands: also *Cape Yubi.*

Jú·car (hōō′kär) A river in eastern Spain, rising in NE Cuenca province and flowing 310 miles south and east to the Mediterranean.

ju chin (jōō′ chin′) **1** A creamy gold emulsion made by rubbing gold leaf under water with a circular motion of the fingers: used in Chinese and Japanese painting to outline rocks in landscapes, to impart bright highlights to birds and flowers, and to decorate the garments in Buddhistic portraits. **2** A brush technique for applying this emulsion. [<Chinese, lit., milk gold]

Ju·dae·a (jōō·dē′ə), **Ju·dae·an** (jōō·dē′ən) See JUDEA, etc.

Ju·dah (jōō′də) A masculine personal name. Also *Lat.* **Ju·das** (jōō′dəs, *Ger., Polish, Sw.* yōō′däs), **Jude** (jōōd, *Fr.* zhüd), *Fr.* **Ju·da** (zhü·dà′). [<Hebrew, praise]
—**Judah** The fourth son of Jacob and Leah, or the tribe descended from him; also, the kingdom, comprising the tribes of Judah and Benjamin, ruled over by the descendants of Solomon. I *Kings* xi–xii.

Ju·dah (jōō′də) An ancient kingdom of the Jews in southern Palestine.

Ju·da·ic (jōō·dā′ik) *adj.* Pertaining to the Jews. Also **Ju·da′i·cal.** [<L *Judaicus* <Gk. *Ioudaikos* <*Ioudaios.* See JEW.] **—Ju·da′i·cal·ly** *adv.*

Ju·da·ism (jōō′dē·iz′əm) *n.* **1** The religious beliefs or practices of the Jews. **2** The acceptance of Jewish rites or doctrines. **—Ju′da·ist** *n.* **—Ju′da·is′tic** *adj.*

Ju·da·ize (jōō′dē·īz) *v.t.* & *v.i.* **·ized, ·iz·ing** To bring over to or accept Judaism. Also *Brit.* **Ju′da·ise.**

Ju·da·iz·er (jōō′dē·ī′zər) *n.* **1** One who accepts or advocates Judaism. **2** In apostolic times, a Jew converted to Christianity who clung to the Mosaic ritual. Also *Brit.* **Ju′da·is′er.**

Ju·das (jōō′dəs) See JUDAH.
—**Judas** The disciple of Jesus who betrayed him with a kiss, thus identifying him to the Roman captors; hence, one who betrays another under the guise of friendship: also **Judas Iscariot.**
—**Judas** A brother of Jesus. *Matt.* xiii 55.
—**Judas Maccabeus** See under MACCABEUS.

Judas kiss A treacherous kiss or other gesture simulating friendliness.

Judas tree Any of a genus (*Cercis*) of trees, as *C. siliquastrum,* a European species, or the redbud (*C. canadensis*) with profuse, reddish-purple flowers, of the central and western United States. [From a tradition that Judas hanged himself upon a tree of this kind]

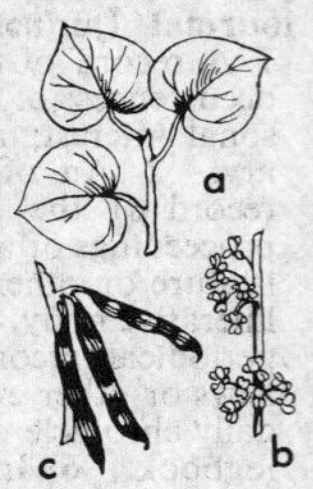

JUDAS TREE
a. Leaves.
b. Blossom.
c. Fruit.

Jude (jōōd) See JUDAH. —**Jude** One of the apostles, the brother of James, and possibly of Jesus: sometimes identified with Thaddeus (*Luke* vi 16); also, a New Testament epistle attributed to him.

Ju·de·a (jōō·dē′ə) The southern part of ancient Palestine under Persian, Greek, and Roman dominion: also *Judaea.*

Ju·de·an (jōō·dē′ən) *adj.* Of or pertaining to Judea. —*n.* A native of Judea. Also spelled *Judaean.*

judge (juj) *n.* **1** An officer invested with authority to administer justice. **2** One who decides upon the merits of things, as in contests. **3** One who is competent to decide upon the merits of persons, animals, things, etc.; a connoisseur. **4** In Jewish history, one of the Israelitish rulers from the death of Joshua to the anointing of Saul. —*v.* **judged, judg·ing** *v.t.* **1** To hear and decide in an official capacity the merits of (a case) or the guilt of (a person); examine and pass judgment on; try. **2** To form an opinion or judgment concerning; evaluate; estimate: to *judge* a painting. **3** To hold as judgment or opinion; consider; suppose: We *judged* it the proper time. **4** To govern: said of the ancient Hebrew judges. —*v.i.* **5** To act as a judge; sit in judgment. **6** To form a judgment or estimate. **7** To make a judgment or decision. [<OF *juge* <L *judex, -icis* <*ius* right + *dic-,* root of *dicere* speak] **—judg′er** *n.*
Synonyms (noun): arbiter, arbitrator, justice, referee, umpire. A *judge,* in the legal sense, is a judicial officer appointed or elected to preside in courts of law, and to decide legal questions duly brought before him; the name is sometimes given to other legally constituted officers; as, the *judges* of election; in other relations, any person duly appointed to pass upon the merits of contestants or of competing articles may be called a *judge.* In various sports the *judge* is called an *umpire* or in some cases the *referee,* as, the *umpire* of a ball game. In law, a *referee* is appointed by a court to decide disputed matters between litigants; an *arbitrator* is chosen by the contending parties to decide matters in dispute without action by a court. In certain cases, an *umpire* is appointed by a court to decide where *arbitrators* disagree. *Arbiter,* with its suggestion of final and absolute decision, has come to be used only in a high or sacred sense; as, war must now be the *arbiter*; the Supreme *Arbiter* of our destinies. The *judges* of certain courts, as the United States Supreme Court, are technically known as *justices.*

judge advocate *Mil.* **1** A commissioned officer of the U. S. Army belonging to the Judge Advocate General's Department. **2** The legal staff officer for a commander. **3** The prosecutor in a general or special court martial.

Judge Advocate General A major general in the U. S. Army serving as head of the Judge Advocate General's Department.

judge-made (juj′mād′) *adj.* Created or constituted by judges or judicial decision: frequently used in an opprobrious sense.

Judg·es (juj′iz) The seventh book of the Old Testament.

judge·ship (juj′ship) *n.* The office, or period in office, of a judge.

judg·mat·ic (juj·mat′ik) *adj. Colloq.* Evincing good judgment; skilful. Also **judg·mat′i·cal.** [<*judge*; on analogy with *dogmatic*] **—judg·mat′i·cal·ly** *adv.*

judg·ment (juj′mənt) *n.* **1** The act or faculty of affirming or denying a conclusion, whether as based upon a direct comparison of objects or ideas, or derived by a process of reasoning. **2** The result of judging; the decision or conclusion reached, as after consideration or deliberation. **3** *Law* The sentence or final order of a court in a civil or criminal proceeding; the sentence of the law; the final determination or adjudication of the rights of the parties to an action; decision; award; also, the obligation or debt created by the decision or verdict of a court, or the official certificate or record of such decision, which constitutes a lien on leviable property. **4** A disaster or affliction regarded as inflicted by God as a punishment for sin. **5** *Theol.* The final award or sentence of the human race; also, the time of this: also **Judgment** or **Last Judgment.** **6** *Psychol.* The mental act or attitude of decision with which the process of observation, comparison, or ratiocination is terminated; also, loosely, the rational faculty; thought. **7** *Logic* That form of thought in which two terms are compared and their fitness to be joined under a given relation is affirmed or denied; also, the result of judging, the verbal expression of which is called an assertion or proposition. **8** *Obs.* Uprightness; rectitude. Also *Brit.* **judge′ment.** See synonyms under IDEA, PRUDENCE, THOUGHT[1], UNDERSTANDING, WISDOM. **—general judgment** *Theol.* The final judgment of all men after the dissolution of the world. **—particular judgment** *Theol.* The judgment of the soul immediately after death.

Judgment Day *Theol.* The day or time of the Last Judgment.

judgment debtor *Law* A debtor against whom judgment of indebtedness has been recorded.

judgment of God Trial by single combat or by ordeal or the like, supposed to be under direct divine control.

judgment seat A judges' bench or a place where judgment is delivered.

ju·di·ca·ble (jōō′də·kə·bəl) *adj.* That can be tried or judged. Also **ju·di·ci·a·ble** (jōō·dish′ē·ə·bəl).

ju·di·ca·tive (jōō′də·kā′tiv, -kə-) *adj.* Competent to judge; judicial. [<L *judicatus,* pp. of *judicare* judge]

ju·di·ca·tor (jōō′də·kā′tər) *n.* One who performs the office of a judge.

ju·di·ca·to·ry (jōō′də·kə·tôr′ē, -tō′rē) *adj.* Pertaining to the administration of justice. —*n. pl.* **·ries** **1** A tribunal. **2** The judiciary. **3** *Obs.* Judicial power; justice.

ju·di·ca·ture (jōō′də·kə·chŏŏr) *n.* **1** The power of administering justice. **2** The jurisdiction of a court. **3** A court of justice; also, judges collectively. **4** *Obs.* Established right; legality; lawfulness.

ju·di·cial (jōō·dish′əl) *adj.* **1** Pertaining to the administration of justice. **2** Of, pertaining to, or connected with a court or judge. **3** Discriminating; impartial. **4** Serving to decide or determine; judging: *judicial* duels. **5** *Obs.* Established by formal enactment or positive law. [<L *judicialis* <*judex, -icis* a judge] **—ju·di′cial·ly** *adv.*

ju·di·ci·ar·y (jōō·dish′ē·er′ē, -dish′ə·rē) *adj.* Pertaining to courts of justice or to a judge. —*n. pl.* **·ar·ies** **1** That department of government which administers the law. **2** The judges of the courts considered collectively.

ju·di·cious (jōō·dish′əs) *adj.* **1** Having or acting on sound judgment; proceeding with discretion; manifesting forethought and sense; wise; prudent. **2** Done with sound judgment; well-calculated; planned or arranged with discretion. See synonyms under POLITIC, SAGACIOUS, WISE[1]. [<F *judicieux* <L *judicium* a judgment] **—ju·di′cious·ly** *adv.* **—ju·di′cious·ness** *n.*

Ju·dith (jōō′dith; *Fr.* zhü·dēt′, *Ger.* yōō′dēt) A feminine personal name. Also *Lat.* **Ju·di·tha** (jōō′di·tə). [<Hebrew, praise]
—**Judith** A Jewish woman, heroine of a book in the Apocrypha of the same name, who rescued her countrymen by slaying the Assyrian general, Holofernes.

ju·do (jōō′dō) *n.* A Japanese system of mental and physical conditioning based upon jiujitsu and often practiced as a sport. Compare JIUJITSU. [<Japanese *ju* gentle, pliant + *do* way of life]

Ju·dy (jōō′dē) **1** Diminutive of JUDITH. **2** The wife of Punch.

jug[1] (jug) *n.* **1** A narrow-necked, stout, bulging vessel with a cork, for keeping or carrying liquids. **2** A deep vessel for holding or serving liquids; a drinking vessel; pitcher. **3** A pint of ale or beer. **4** *Slang* A prison; jail. —*v.t.* **jugged, jug·ging** **1** To put into

a jug. **2** To cook in a jug. **3** *Slang* To imprison; jail. [from *Jug*, a nickname for *Joan*]

jug² (jug) *v.i.* **jugged, jug·ging** To utter a cry like that of the nightingale, as some birds. — *n.* The note of some birds, as the nightingale. [Imit.]

jug³ (jug) *v.i.* **jugged, jug·ging** To collect together and nestle in a flock or covey: said of partridges. [Cf. OF *jouquier* be at rest]

jug⁴ (jug) *n.* An act of worship by which Brahmans are said to acquire preternatural power. Also **jug′gul** (-gəl). [<Hind. *jag* <Skt. *jagata* the world]

ju·gal (jōō′gəl) *adj. Anat.* Of or pertaining to a bone of the zygomatic arch or malar bone. [<L *jugalis* <*jugum* a yoke]

ju·gate (jōō′git, -gāt) *adj.* **1** Occurring in pairs. **2** *Bot.* Having paired leaves, as certain plants. [<L *jugatus*, pp. of *jugare* bind together <*jugum* a yoke]

jug·ger·naut (jug′ər·nôt) *n.* **1** Anything to which one makes unquestioning sacrifices. **2** Any irresistible force. [after JUGGERNAUT]

Jug·ger·naut (jug′ər·nôt) The eighth avatar of Vishnu whose idol at Puri, India, was drawn on a heavy car under the wheels of which devotees were said to have thrown themselves to be crushed. Also spelled *Jaganath, Jaganatha, Jaggurnath.* [<Hind. *jagannāth* lord of the universe]

jug·gle (jug′əl) *v.* **·gled, ·gling** *v.t.* **1** To toss (a number of balls, plates, etc.) into the air, keeping them in continuous motion by successively catching and tossing them up again. **2** To perform tricks of sleight of hand with. **3** To manipulate for the purpose of deception or trickery: to *juggle* financial accounts. — *v.i.* **4** To perform as a juggler. **5** To practice deception or trickery. — *n.* **1** A feat of legerdemain. **2** A trick or deception. [<OF *jogler* <L *joculari* jest]

jug·gler (jug′lər) *n.* **1** One who juggles; a prestidigitator. **2** One who deceives by cheating; an impostor. [<OF *joglere* <L *joculator* jester]

jug·gler·y (jug′lər·ē) *n. pl.* **·gler·ies** **1** The art of a juggler; legerdemain. **2** Deception; trickery.

jug·gling (jug′ling) *adj.* Deceiving; cheating; relating to tricks of magic. — *n.* Jugglery.

jug–han·dled (jug′han′dəld) *adj.* One–sided; partial; hence, unjust.

jug·head (jug′hed′) *n. U. S. Slang* **1** A slow–witted horse. **2** A slow or stupid person.

ju·glan·da·ceous (jōō′glan·dā′shəs) *adj.* Designating a family *(Juglandaceae)* of trees with odd–pinnate leaves and monoecious flowers, including the walnut and hickory. [<NL *Juglandaceae*, the walnut family <L *juglans* a walnut]

ju·glone (jōō′glōn) *n.* A brownish–red crystalline compound, $C_{10}H_6O_3$, extracted from the bark or unripe fruit of the walnut tree *(Juglans cinerea)*. [<L *juglans* walnut + -ONE]

Ju·go·slav (yōō′gō·släv′, -slav′), **Ju·go·sla·vi·a** (yōō′gō·slä′vē·ə) See YUGOSLAV, YUGOSLAVIA.

jug·u·lar (jug′yə·lər, jōō′gyə-) *adj.* **1** *Anat.* Pertaining to the throat or to the jugular vein. **2** *Biol.* **a** Situated in front of the pectoral fins. **b** Having the ventral fins at the throat, as a fish. — *n.* One of the jugular veins. [<NL *jugularis* <L *jugulum* a collar bone]

jugular vein *Anat.* One of the large veins on either side of the neck that returns blood from the brain, face, and neck.

ju·gu·late (jōō′gyə·lāt) *v.t.* **·lat·ed, ·lat·ing** **1** *Med.* To arrest the course of (a disease) by drastic therapeutic measures. **2** *Obs.* To cut the throat of. [<L *jugulatus*, pp. of *jugulare* slay, cut the throat of <*jugulum* a collar bone] — **ju′gu·la′tion** *n.*

Ju·gur·tha (jōō·gûr′thə), died 104 B.C., Numidian king.

juice (jōōs) *n.* **1** The fluid part of vegetable or animal matter; especially, the expressible watery matter in fruits, containing usually the characteristic flavor. **2** *Usually pl.* The fluids of the body. **3** The essence of anything. **4** *Slang* Electric current, or other means of generating power, as oil, gasoline, etc. **5** The liquid extracted from anything. [<OF *jus* <L] — **juice′less** *adj.*

juiced rehearsal (jōōst) In television, a final or dress rehearsal, for which the mechanical equipment is used exactly as in the actual telecast.

juic·y (jōō′sē) *adj.* **juic·i·er, juic·i·est** **1** Abounding with juice; moist. **2** Full of interest; colorful; spicy. — **juic′i·ly** *adv.* — **juic′i·ness** *n.*

Juiz de Fo·ra (zhwēzh thə fô′rə) A city in southern Minas Gerais state, Brazil.

ju·jit·su (jōō·jit′sōō), **ju·jut·su** (jōō·jit′sōō, -jōōt′-) See JIUJITSU.

ju·ju (jōō′jōō) *n.* An African fetish or talisman; an object of religious veneration or awe; hence, anything inexplicable, mysterious, or magical; also, the charm said to be worked by a juju. [<native West African name, ? ult. <F *joujou* a toy] — **ju′ju·ism** *n.*

ju·jube (jōō′jōōb) *n.* **1** Any of a genus *(Zizyphus)* of several Old World trees or shrubs of the buckthorn family; especially, the common jujube *(Z. jujuba)*, the lotus tree. **2** Its edible fruit. **3** A lozenge. [<F <Med. L *jujuba*, alter. of L *zizyphum* <Gk. *zizyphon* <Persian *zizafūn*]

Ju·juy (hōō·hwē′) A province of NW Argentina; 22,952 square miles; capital, Jujuy.

juke box A large automatic phonograph, usually coin–operated and permitting selection of the records to be played.

juke joint *U.S. Slang* A roadhouse or barroom for drinking and dancing. [<Gullah *juke*, orig. a brothel (of West African origin) + JOINT (*n.* def. 6)]

Jukes, the A pseudonym used for the members of an actual New York family whose history, as investigated over several generations by 19th century sociologists, showed abnormal incidence of crime, disease, and pauperism. See KALLIKAK.

ju·lep (jōō′lip) *n.* **1** A drink composed usually of brandy or whisky, sugar, cracked ice, and some flavoring, commonly fresh green mint: also **mint julep.** **2** A subacid, mucilaginous, sweetened drink, often used as a vehicle for the administration of medicine. **3** A cool drink made with herbs. Also **ju′lap.** [<MF <Persian *gulāb* rose–water]

Jul·ia (jōōl′yə; *Du.* yōō′lē·ə, *Pg.* zhōō′lē·ə, *Sp.* hōō′lē·ä) A feminine personal name. Also **Ju·lie** (jōō′lē; *Fr.* zhü·lē′, *Ger.* yōō′lē·ä). [<L, fem. of *Julius* JULIUS]

Jul·ian (jōōl′yən; *Ger. Sw.* yōō′lē·än, *Sp.* hōō′lē·än′) A masculine personal name. Also *Lat.* **Ju·li·a·nus** (jōō′lē·ā′nəs, *Du.* yōō′lē·ä′nōōs), *Sp.* **Ju·li·a·no** (hōō′lē·ä′nō), *Fr.* **Ju·lien** (zhü·lyan′), *Pg.* **Ju·li·ão** (zhōō·lē·oun′). [<L, of Julius]

— **Julian the Apostate,** 331–363, Flavius Claudius Julianus, Roman emperor 361–63; renounced Christianity and revived paganism.

Jul·ian (jōōl′yən) *adj.* Of, pertaining to, or named after, Julius Caesar.

Ju·li·an·a (jōō′lē·an′ə; *Du., Sw.* yōō′lē·ä′nä, *Pg.* zhōō′lē·ä′nə, *Sp.* hōō′lē·ä′nä) A feminine personal name. Also *Ger.* **Ju·li·a·ne** (yōō′lē·ä′nə), *Fr.* **Ju·li·enne** (zhü·lē·en′). [<L, fem. of *Julianus* JULIAN]

— **Juliana Louise Emma Marie Wilhelmina,** born 1909, queen of the Netherlands 1948–.

Julian Alps A division of the eastern Alps in NW Yugoslavia and eastern Italy; highest peak, 9,394 feet.

Julian calendar. See under CALENDAR.

Ju·li·a·ne·haab (yōō′lē·ä′nə·hôp) A port in SW Greenland.

ju·li·enne (jōō′lē·en′) *n.* A clear meat soup containing vegetables chopped or cut into thin strips. — *adj.* Cut into thin strips: *julienne* potatoes. [<F, from *Julienne*, a personal name]

Ju·li·et (jōō′lē·et, jōōl′yit) A feminine personal name: diminutive of JULIA.

— **Juliet** The heroine of Shakespeare's *Romeo and Juliet.*

Jul·ius (jōōl′yəs; *Du., Ger.* yōō′lē·ōōs) A masculine personal name; also the name of three popes. *Fr.* **Jules** (zhül), *Pg., Sp.* **Ju·lio** (*Pg.* zhōō′lyō, *Sp.* hōō′lyō). [<L, downy beard]

— **Julius II,** 1443–1513, pope 1503–13; patron of the arts: real name Giuliano della Rovere.

— **Julius Caesar** See under CAESAR.

Jul·lun·der (jul′ən·dər) A city of central Punjab, India.

Ju·ly (jōō·lī′, jōō-) The seventh month of the calendar year, having 31 days. [<OF *Julie* <L *(mensis) Julius* (month) of Julius; because inserted in the calendar by Julius Caesar]

Ju·ma·da (jōō·mä′də) See JOMADA.

jum·ble (jum′bəl) *v.* **·bled, ·bling** *v.t.* **1** To mix in a confused mass; put or throw together without order. **2** To confuse in the mind. — *v.i.* **3** To meet or unite confusedly. See synonyms under DISPLACE. — *n.* **1** A confused mixture or collection: also **jum′ble·ment.** **2** A thin sweet cake. [Origin uncertain]

jum·ble–beads (jum′bəl·bēdz′) *n. pl.* The seeds of the jequirity.

jum·bo (jum′bō) *n. pl.* **·bos** A very large person, animal, or thing. — *adj.* Very large; especially, larger than usual. [after JUMBO]

Jum·bo (jum′bō) An elephant exhibited by P. T. Barnum: the largest ever captured; killed by accident, 1885.

jum·buck (jum′buk′) *n. Austral.* A sheep. [?<native Australian *jimbuc* small kangaroo]

Jum·na (jum′nə) A river in northern India, flowing 860 miles SW to the Ganges.

jump (jump) *v.i.* **1** To spring from the ground, floor, etc., by the action of the muscles of the feet and legs. **2** To move abruptly as by bounds or leaps. **3** To rise abruptly: The temperature *jumped.* **4** In checkers, to capture an opponent's piece by passing a man over it to a vacant square beyond. — *v.t.* **5** To leap over. **6** To cause to leap: to *jump* a horse over a barrier. **7** To cause to rise, as prices. **8** To pass over; leave out: to *jump* a stage in explaining a process. **9** To leave or move from abruptly: to *jump* the track. **10** To take possession of illegally: to *jump* a claim. **11** *U.S. Colloq.* To get on or off (a train, etc.) by or as by jumping. **12** *Colloq.* To assault; attack. **13** *Slang* To leave or quit abruptly or secretly: to *jump* town. **14** In checkers, to capture (an opponent's piece) by passing a man over it. **15** In bridge, to raise (the bid) in a partner's suit more than necessary, as in indicating a strong hand. **16** In hunting, to cause (game) to leave cover; start; flush. — **to jump at** **1** To accept quickly or eagerly. **2** To reach (a conclusion) hastily and illogically. — **to jump bail** *U.S. Slang* To forfeit by violating the terms of. — **to jump on** To scold; castigate. — **to jump ship** To desert a ship. — **to jump the gun** *Colloq.* **1** To begin before the starting signal is given. **2** To begin prematurely. — *n.* **1** The act of jumping; a leap; spring. **2** The length or height of a leap; also, that which is jumped over. **3** *Colloq.* A head start; advantage: He has the *jump* on me. **4** An involuntary twitch or movement, as when startled. **5** *pl.* Convulsive starts, as in delirium tremens. **6** *Mining* A fault or dislocation, as of a vein. **7** An abrupt break in a level course of masonry. **8** *Obs.* An effort; attempt. — **on the jump** *Colloq.* Hurrying from one thing to another; on the go; working hard and fast. [Origin uncertain]

jump area *Mil.* A locality, usually behind enemy lines, assigned for the landing of parachute troops: also called *landing area.*

jump ball In basketball, a ball tossed between two opposing players by the referee, as in beginning or resuming play.

jump bid In bridge, a bid higher than needed to beat or raise a previous declaration.

jump·er¹ (jum′pər) *n.* **1** One who or that which jumps. **2** The larva of a cheese fly. **3** A piece of mechanism or a tool having a jumping motion. **4** A rude sled. **5** *Electr.* A wire used to cut out part of a circuit, or to close a temporary gap in it.

jum·per² (jum′pər) *n.* **1** *Chiefly Brit.* A loose outer jacket, often of coarse cloth, worn over or instead of other clothes, as to protect them from getting soiled. **2** A hooded fur jacket used by Eskimos and Arctic explorers. **3** A one–piece, sleeveless dress, usually worn with a blouse or sweater by women and children: also **jumper dress.** [Prob. alter. of OF *juppe*

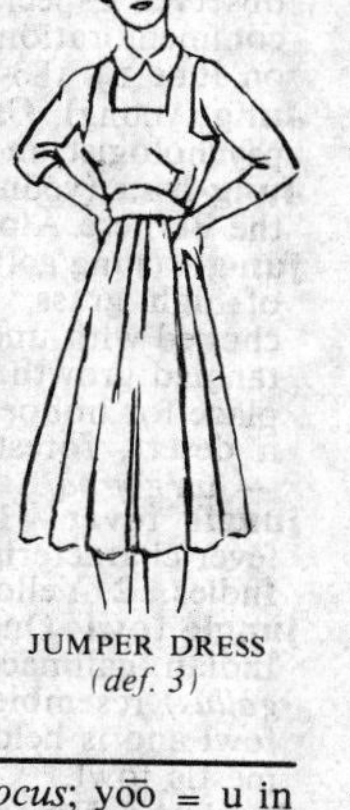

JUMPER DRESS
(def. 3)

a jacket, ult. <Arabic *jubbah* a short coat]

jumping bean The seed of certain tropical shrubs (genera *Sebastiania* and *Sapium*) of the spurge family, which jumps about owing to the movements of the larva of a small moth (*Carpocapsa saltitans*) inside.

jump·ing-jack (jum'ping-jak') *n.* A toy figure of a man, whose jointed limbs are moved by strings.

jumping mouse A small, hibernating mouse of North America (*Zapus hudsonius*) having long hind legs and tail: able to leap 9 to 15 feet.

jump·ing-off place (jum'ping-ôf', -of') 1 The end of a journey. 2 The utmost limit of settlement or civilization; a deserted, depressing place. 3 The edge of the world; the end of life. 4 The end or limit of one's resources.

jump-off (jump'ôf', -of') *n.* The commencement of a planned attack by ground forces.

jump seat An extra seat that folds up, as in the rear of a limousine or taxi.

jump shot In basketball, a shot attempted at the height of a leap.

jump spark A spark produced by electricity jumping across a fixed gap.

jump suit 1 A one-piece garment consisting of pants with a blouse or shirt attached. 2 A kind of coverall worn by parachutists, mechanics, etc.

jump weld A weld of metal effected by hammering together the butt ends of two pieces heated to the welding point.

jump·y (jum'pē) *adj.* **jump·i·er, jump·i·est** 1 Subject to sudden changes; fluctuating. 2 Characterized by nervous, spasmodic movements; apprehensive. — **jump'i·ness** *n.*

jun·ca·ceous (jung·kā'shəs) *adj. Bot.* Pertaining or belonging to a family (*Juncaceae*) of widely distributed grasslike plants, the rush family, mostly growing in moist places. [<NL *Juncaceae,* the rush family <L *juncus* bulrush]

jun·co (jung'kō) *n. pl.* **·cos** Any of a genus (*Junco*) of North American finches, mainly gray with white underparts: also called *snowbird.* [<Sp., a rush]

junc·tion (jungk'shən) *n.* 1 The act of joining, or condition of being joined. 2 A place of union or meeting, as of railroads. See synonyms under UNION. [<L *junctio, -onis* <*jungere* join] — **junc'tion·al** *adj.*

junc·ture (jungk'chər) *n.* 1 An act of joining; junction. 2 A point or line of junction, as of two bodies; an articulation, joint, or seam. 3 A coincidence of two chains of events; a crisis, exigency. See synonyms under UNION. [<L *junctura* <*jungere* join]

June (joon) The sixth month of the calendar year, having 30 days. [<OF *Juin* <L (*mensis*) *Junius* (month) of the Junii, a Roman gens]

Ju·neau (joo'nō) The capital of Alaska, a port on the SE coast.

June beetle 1 A large, brightly colored scarabaeid beetle (genus *Polyphylla*) that begins to fly early in June: often called *Maybug.* Also **June bug.** For illustrations see under INSECT (injurious). 2 The fig-eater of the southern United States.

June·ber·ry (joon'ber'ē) *n. pl.* **·ries** 1 A small tree (*Amelanchier canadensis*) bearing racemes of white flowers followed by purple edible berries. 2 One of the berries. Also called *shadbush, serviceberry, service tree.*

June·teenth (joon'tēnth') *n.* June 19, a holiday observed especially in Texas by Negroes in commemoration of the freeing of Texas slaves on June 19, 1865.

Jung (yoong), **Carl Gustav,** 1875–1961, Swiss psychologist and psychiatrist.

Jung·frau (yoong'frou') A mountain peak in the Bernese Alps, Switzerland; 13,653 feet.

jun·gle (jung'gəl) *n.* 1 A dense tropical thicket of high grass, reeds, vines, brush, or trees choked with undergrowth; hence, any similar tangled growth. 2 *U.S. Slang* A gathering place for hoboes and tramps. [<Hind. *jangal* a desert, forest <Skt. *jangala* dry, desert] — **jun'gly** *adj.*

jungle fever 1 A malarial or intermittent fever characteristic of the jungles of the East Indies. 2 Yellow fever.

jungle fowl One of a genus (*Gallus*) of East Indian gallinaceous birds: one species (*G. gallus*) resembles a black-breasted red game fowl and is held to be the original of the domestic fowl.

Ju·ni·at·a River (joo'nē·at'ə) A river in central Pennsylvania, flowing about 150 miles east to the Susquehanna.

Ju·nín (hoo·nēn') A city of central Peru; scene of Bolívar's defeat of the Spanish in 1824.

jun·ior (joon'yər) *adj.* 1 Younger in years or lower in rank. 2 Denoting the younger of two: opposed to *senior* and distinguishing a father from a son, usually abbreviated *Jr.* 3 Belonging to youth or earlier life. 4 Later in point of existence or occurrence: *junior* securities. 5 Pertaining to the third year of a high-school or collegiate course of four years. — *n.* 1 The younger of two; one later or lower in service or standing; a younger person. 2 A student in the third or junior year of a high-school, college, or university course. [<L *junior,* comp. of *juvenis* young]

junior college A college giving academic courses up to and including the sophomore year.

junior high school See under SCHOOL.

jun·ior·i·ty (joon·yôr'ə·tē, -yor'-) *n.* The state or rank of being a junior.

Junior League Any of the various local branches of the Association of the Junior Leagues of America, Inc., composed of young society women engaged in volunteer welfare work.

ju·ni·per (joo'nə·pər) *n.* 1 Any of a genus (*Juniperus*) of evergreen pinaceous shrubs; especially the common juniper (*J. communis*) of Europe and America. It has dark-blue berries of a pungent taste, which are used in making gin. 2 The dried berries of the juniper plant. 3 A leafless shrub (*Retama*) mentioned in the Old Testament. 4 Loosely, the American larch or tamarack. [<L *juniperus*]

Jun·ius (joon'yəs, joo'nē·əs) A masculine personal name. [<L, name of Roman gens] — **Junius** Pseudonym of an unknown English political writer from 1769?–72.

junk¹ (jungk) *n.* 1 A sea term for discarded cable or cordage. 2 Salt meat supplied to ships. 3 Cast-off materials of little or no value. 4 A chunk; small mass. 5 *Surg.* A type of cushion used in dressing wounds. — *v.t. Colloq.* To scrap; to demolish or cast aside. [<OF *jonc* <L *juncus* rush]

junk² (jungk) *n.* A large Chinese vessel with high poop, prominent stem, full stern and lug sails. [<Sp. and Pg. *junco* <Malay *djong* a ship]

CHINESE JUNK

Jun·ker (yoong'kər) *n.* 1 A younger member of a German noble family. 2 One of the reactionary aristocracy of Prussia seeking to maintain social and political supremacy. [<G <*jung* young + *herr* master] — **Jun'ker·dom** *n.* — **Jun'ker·ism** *n.*

Jun·kers (yoong'kərs), **Hugo,** 1859–1935, German airplane engineer and builder.

junk·et (jung'kit) *n.* 1 A feast, banquet, picnic, or pleasure trip. 2 A trip taken with all expenses paid, usually from public funds: also **jun'ket·ing.** 3 A delicacy made of curds or of sweetened milk and rennet. — *v.i.* 1 To have a feast; banquet. 2 To go on a pleasure trip, especially at public expense. — *v.t.* 3 To entertain by feasting; regale. [<AF *jonquette* rush basket <L *juncus* rush]

junk·ie (jung'kē) *n. Slang* One addicted to narcotic drugs, especially to heroin.

junk·man (jungk'man') *n. pl.* **·men** (-men') One who purchases, collects, and sells junk.

junk·yard (jungk'yärd') *n.* A place where junk is thrown or collected.

Ju·no (joo'nō) In Roman mythology, the wife of Jupiter, queen of the gods and goddess of marriage: identified with the Greek *Hera.*

Ju·no·esque (joo'nō·esk') *adj.* Resembling the stately beauty of Juno.

Ju·not (zhü·nō'), **Andoche,** 1771–1813, Duc d'Abrantès, French marshal.

jun·ta (jun'tə) *n.* 1 A Central or South American legislative council. 2 A junto. [<Sp. <L *juncta,* pp. fem. of *jungere* join]

jun·to (jun'tō) *n. pl.* **·tos** A faction; a cabal. See synonyms under CABAL. [<JUNTA]

jupe (joop) *n. Scot.* A jupon.

Ju·pi·ter (joo'pə·tər) 1 In Roman mythology, the god ruling over all the other gods and all men: identified with the Greek *Zeus*: also called *Jove.* 2 *Astron.* The fifth planet from the sun; its mean diameter is 87,000 miles, and it revolves around the sun in about 11 7/8 years at a mean distance of 483,000,-000 miles. See PLANET.

Ju·pi·ter-Am·mon (joo'pə·tər·am'ən) A Roman name for the Egyptian god AMMON. Also **Ju'pi·ter-A'men** or **Ju'pi·ter-A'mon** (ä'mən).

Ju·pi·ter Plu·vi·us (joo'pə·tər plōō'vē·əs) *Latin* Jupiter considered as the giver of rain.

ju·pon (joo'pon, joo·pon') 1 A petticoat. 2 A medieval doublet or tunic. [<OF <*juppe.* See JUMPER².]

ju·ra (joor'ə) Plural of JUS.

Ju·ra (joor'ə, *Fr.* zhü·rä') 1 A mountain range in eastern France and western Switzerland; highest peak, 5,652 feet. 2 One of the Inner Hebrides; 146 square miles.

ju·ral (joor'əl) *adj.* Relating to rights and obligations as subjects of jurisprudence. [<L *jus, juris* law]

Ju·ras·sic (joo·ras'ik) *adj. Geol.* Of or pertaining to a period of the Mesozoic era succeeding the Triassic and followed by the Cretaceous: it was characterized by the dominance of dinosaurian reptiles and the earliest bird forms. — *n.* The Jurassic period or corresponding rock system. [<F *jurassique,* from *Jura*]

ju·rat (joor'at) *n.* 1 One sworn to the faithful performance of a duty, as a magistrate or juror. 2 An officer with duties similar to those of an alderman, as in the English Cinque Ports. 3 A magistrate in the Channel Islands. 4 *Law* The clause in an official certificate testifying that the deposition has been duly sworn to at a stated time before a competent authority. [<L *juratus,* pp. of *jurare* swear]

ju·ra·to·ry (joor'ə·tôr'ē, -tō'rē) *adj. Law* Pertaining to an oath.

ju·re di·vi·no (joor'ē di·vī'nō) *Latin* By divine law.

ju·re hu·ma·no (joor'ē hyoo·man'ō) *Latin* By human law.

ju·rel (hoo·rel') *n. Spanish* One of various carangoid fishes (genus *Caranx*), especially *C. crysos* and *C. latus,* found along the southern Atlantic coast of the United States.

ju·rid·i·cal (joo·rid'i·kəl) *adj.* 1 Relating to law and judicial proceedings. 2 Pertaining to the judicial office, or to jurisprudence. Also **ju·rid'ic.** [<L *juridicus* <*jus, juris* law + *dicere* declare] — **ju·rid'i·cal·ly** *adv.*

ju·ris·con·sult (joor'is·kən·sult', -kon'sult) *n.* One learned in the law; a jurist. [<L *jurisconsultus* <*jus, juris* law + *consultus* skilled]

ju·ris·dic·tion (joor'is·dik'shən) *n.* 1 Lawful right to exercise official authority, whether executive, legislative, or judicial. 2 The territory within or the matter over which such authority may be lawfully exercised. 3 A judicature; a court, or series of courts, of justice. 4 Power of those in authority; control. [<OF *juridiction* <L *jurisdictio, -onis* <*jus, juris* law + *dicere* declare] — **ju'ris·dic'tion·al** *adj.* — **ju'ris·dic'tion·al·ly** *adv.*

ju·ris·pru·dence (joor'is·prood'ns) *n.* 1 The philosophy of positive law and its administration; the science of law. 2 A system of laws, as of a particular country. See synonyms under LEGISLATION. — **analytical jurisprudence** Jurisprudence formed by analysis and comparison of legal conceptions. — **comparative jurisprudence** The analytical comparison of systems of law prevailing in different countries and nations, ancient and modern. — **medical jurisprudence** The branch of jurisprudence that pertains to questions involving wounds, poisons, insanity, and presumption of survivorship. [<L *jurisprudentia* <*jus, juris* law + *prudentia* knowledge]

ju·ris·pru·dent (jŏŏr′is·prōōd′nt) *adj.* Skilled in jurisprudence. — *n.* A person learned in the law. — **ju′ris·pru·den′tial** (-prōō·den′shəl) *adj.*

ju·rist (jŏŏr′ist) *n.* One versed in the science of laws. [<F *juriste* <Med. L *jurista* <L *jus, juris* law]

ju·ris·tic (jōō·ris′tik) *adj.* Of or pertaining to a jurist or the profession of law. Also **ju·ris′ti·cal.** — **ju·ris′ti·cal·ly** *adv.*

juristic act A proceeding intended to have a legal result and having the necessary qualifications.

ju·ror (jŏŏr′ər) *n.* One who serves on a jury or is sworn in for jury duty. [<AF *jurour* <L *jurator* <*jurare* swear]

Ju·ruá (zhōō·rwä′) A river flowing 1,200 miles NW across Brazil to the Amazon from the mountains of Peru.

Ju·rue·na (zhōō·rwā′nə) A river in northern Mato Grosso, Brazil, flowing 500 miles north to the Tapajós.

ju·ry[1] (jŏŏr′ē) *n. pl.* **·ries 1** A body of persons (usually twelve) legally qualified and summoned to serve on a judicial tribunal, there sworn to try well and truly a cause and give a true verdict according to the evidence. **2** A committee of award in a competition. — **coroner's jury** A body of persons selected to attend a coroner's investigation and determine the causes of deaths not obviously due to natural causes. — **grand jury** A jury called to hear complaints of the commission of offenses and to ascertain whether there is prima-facie ground for a criminal accusation. — **petit jury** The jury that sits at a trial in civil and criminal cases: also **petty jury.** [<AF *juree* an oath <Med. L *jurata*, orig. pp. of L *jurare* swear <*jus, juris* law]

ju·ry[2] (jŏŏr′ē) *adj. Naut.* Rigged up temporarily, for relief, replacement, or emergency use: a *jury* mast. [Prob. <OF *ajurie* aid <L *adjutare* help]

ju·ry·man (jŏŏr′ē·mən) *n. pl.* **·men** (-mən) A juror.

jury mast 1 *Naut.* A temporary mast. **2** *Med.* An iron rod used for supporting the weight of the head in spinal disease or injury.

jus (jus) *n. pl.* **ju·ra** (jŏŏr′ə) **1** Law in its abstract sense distinguished from statute law; right; justice. **2** Any right that is enforceable by law. [<L, law]

jus ca·no·ni·cum (jus kə·non′i·kəm) *Latin* The canon law.

jus ci·vi·le (jus si·vī′lē) *Latin* Civil law.

jus di·vi·num (jus di·vī′nəm) *Latin* Divine law.

jus gen·ti·um (jus jen′shē·əm) *Latin* The law of nations.

jus na·tu·ra·le (jus nach′ə·rā′lē) *Latin* Natural law; the law of nature. Also **jus na·tu·rae** (nə·tyōō′rē).

Jus·se·rand (zhüs·räṅ′), **Jean Adrien Antoine Jules,** 1855–1932, French diplomat and author.

jus·sive (jus′iv) *adj. Gram.* In Semitic languages, denoting a mood expressing mild command. — *n.* A jussive mood, word, or construction. [<L *jussus*, pp. of *jubere* order]

jussive subjunctive *Gram.* The subjunctive used to express mild command, as in Latin *dicat*, let him speak: usually restricted to the second and third persons.

just[1] (just) *adj.* **1** Actuated by or doing justice; righteous; upright; honest: *just* to all concerned. **2** Based on or conforming to the principles of justice; impartial; legitimate. **3** Agreeing with a required standard; true. **4** Consistent with what is proper or reasonable: *just* in one's dealings. **5** Morally pure; perfect; righteous before God. **6** *Obs.* Faithful; true; exact. — *adv.* **1** To the exact point, instant, or degree; without lack, excess, or variation; exactly; precisely. **2** But now; this moment. **3** A moment ago; very lately: He has *just* left. **4** By very little; barely; only. **5** *Colloq.* Actually; positively: That gift is *just* wonderful. [<L *justus* <*jus* law] — **just′ly** *adv.*

Synonyms (adj.): equitable, even, exact, fair, fitting, honest, honorable, impartial, incorrupt, incorruptible, lawful, reasonable, right, righteous, rightful, square, straightforward, true, trusty, upright, virtuous. See HONEST, MORAL, RIGHT, VIRTUOUS. Compare synonyms for JUSTICE. *Antonyms*: corrupt, dishonest, dishonorable, faithless, false, inequitable, one-sided, partial, perfidious, treacherous, unfair, unfaithful, unjust, unreasonable, unrighteous, venal.

just[2] (just), **just·er** (jus′tər) See JOUST, etc.

juste mi·lieu (zhüst mē·lyœ′) *French* Golden mean.

jus·tice (jus′tis) *n.* **1** Conformity in conduct or practice to the principles of right or of positive law; regard for or fulfilment of obligations; rectitude; honesty. **2** The moral principle by which actions are determined as just or unjust. **3** Adherence to truth of fact; impartiality. **4** The rendering of what is due or merited; that which is due or merited; just requital or consideration. **5** The quality of being just or reasonable; rightness; equitableness. **6** A judge, as of the U.S. Supreme Court, etc. **7** Administration of law; the forms and processes by which it is made effective. **8** Right of authority; also, formerly, jurisdiction. **9** *Theol.* One of God's attributes, by virtue of which he wills equal laws and makes just awards. **10** *Obs.* Exactness or precision; justness. — **bed of justice** The seat occupied by the French king when attending the deliberations of the parliament; also, the session itself. — **Department of Justice** An executive department of the U. S. government (established in 1870) under the direction of the Attorney General: it supervises enforcement of Federal laws, directs the activities of U. S. judicial districts, and represents the government in legal matters generally. Also **Justice Department.** [<OF <L *justitia* < *justus* JUST]

Synonyms: equity, fairness, faithfulness, honor, impartiality, integrity, justness, law, lawfulness, legality, propriety, rectitude, right, righteousness, rightfulness, truth, uprightness, virtue. In its governmental relations, *justice* is the giving to every person exactly what he deserves, not necessarily involving any consideration of what any other may deserve; *equity* (the quality of being equal) is giving every one as much advantage, privilege, or consideration as is given to any other; it is that which is equally right or just to all concerned; *equity* is a close synonym for *fairness* and *impartiality*, but it has a legal precision that those words have not. In legal proceedings, the system of *equity*, devised to supply the insufficiencies of *law*, deals with cases to which the *law* by reason of its universality cannot apply. *Integrity, rectitude, right, righteousness*, and *virtue* denote conformity of personal conduct to the moral law, and thus necessarily include *justice*, which is giving others that which is their due. *Lawfulness* is an ambiguous word, meaning in its narrower sense mere *legality*, which may be far from *justice*, but in its higher sense signifying accordance with the supreme *law* or *right*, and thus including perfect *justice*. *Justness* refers rather to logical relations than to practical matters; as, we speak of the *justness* of a statement or of a criticism. See JUDGE, VIRTUE. *Antonyms*: dishonesty, inequity, injustice, partiality, unfairness, unlawfulness, unreasonableness, untruth, wrong.

justice of the peace An inferior magistrate elected or appointed to prevent breaches of the peace within a county or township, to punish violators of the law, and to discharge various other local magisterial duties.

jus·tic·er (jus′tis·ər) *n. Obs.* A magistrate; justice of the peace.

jus·tice·ship (jus′tis·ship) *n.* A justice's office or dignity.

jus·ti·ci·a·ble (jus·tish′ə·bəl) *adj.* Proper to be examined in a court of justice. — *n.* A person subject to the jurisdiction of another. [<AF <*justicier* try in court]

jus·ti·ci·ar (jus·tish′ē·ər) *n.* A justiciary (def. 2). Also **jus·ti′ci·er.**

jus·ti·ci·ar·y (jus·tish′ē·er′ē) *adj.* Pertaining to law or the administration of justice. — *n. pl.* **·ar·ies 1** A high judicial officer; a judge. **2** In medieval England, a high officer, or king's deputy, who, during the time of the Norman kings, exercised both administrative and judicial powers. [<Med. L *justiciarius* a judge <*justicia* JUSTICE]

jus·ti·fi·a·ble (jus′tə·fī′ə·bəl) *adj.* Capable of being justified. — **jus′ti·fi′a·bil′i·ty, jus′ti·fi·a·ble·ness** *n.* — **jus′ti·fi′a·bly** *adv.*

jus·ti·fi·ca·tion (jus′tə·fə·kā′shən) *n.* **1** The state of being justified. **2** The ground of justifying, or that which justifies. **3** *Theol.* The forensic, juridical, or gracious act of God by which the sinner is declared righteous, or justly free from obligation to penalty, and fully restored to divine favor. **4** *Printing* The even spacing of type within a fixed measure. **5** *Law* A plea in bar to a plaintiff's action alleging and showing the rightfulness or lawfulness of the act complained of and sued for: in slander, to plead the truth of the words spoken in *justification* of the speaking. See synonyms under APOLOGY, DEFENSE. [<LL *justificatio, -onis* <*justificare* JUSTIFY]

jus·ti·fi·ca·tive (jus′tə·fə·kā′tiv) *adj.* Tending to justify, or capable of justifying; vindicatory. Also, **jus·tif·i·ca·to·r·y** (jus·tif′ə·kə·tôr′ē, -tō′rē).

jus·ti·fi·er (jus′tə·fī′ər) *n.* One who justifies. Also **jus′ti·fi·ca′tor.**

jus·ti·fy (jus′tə·fī) *v.* **·fied, ·fy·ing** *v.t.* **1** To show to be just, right, or proper. **2** To declare or prove guiltless or blameless; exonerate; acquit. **3** *Law* To show sufficient reason for (something done). **4** *Printing* To adjust (lines) to the proper length by spacing. — *v.i.* **5** *Law* **a** To show sufficient reason for something done. **b** To qualify as a bondsman. **6** *Printing* To be properly spaced; fit. [<OF *justifier* <LL *justificare* pardon <*justus* just + *facere* make]

Synonyms: absolve, acquit, approve, authorize, clear, defend, endorse, exculpate, excuse, exonerate, maintain, sustain, uphold, vindicate, warrant. That may sometimes be *excused* which cannot be *justified*; that which can be *justified* does not need to be *excused*. See RATIFY. *Antonyms*: arraign, blame, censure, chide, condemn, convict, criminate, denounce, reprehend, reprobate, reprove.

Jus·tin (jus′tin; *Fr.* zhüs·taṅ′; *Ger.* yōōs′tēn) A masculine personal name. Also *Lat.* **Jus·ti·nus** (jus·tī′nəs), *Sp.* **Jus·ti·no** (hōōs·tē′nō). [<L, just]

— **Justin Martyr,** 100?–165?, a Greek father of the church; probably beheaded in Rome under Marcus Aurelius.

Jus·ti·na (jus·tī′nə, *Sp.* hōōs·tē′nä) A feminine personal name. Also *Fr., Ger.* **Jus·tine** (*Fr.* zhüs·tēn′, *Ger.* yōōs·tē′nä). [<L, fem. of *Justinus* JUSTIN]

Jus·tin·i·an (jus·tin′ē·ən) *adj.* Of or pertaining to Justinian. Also **Jus·tin′i·a′ni·an** (-ā′nē·ən).

Jus·tin·i·an (jus·tin′ē·ən), 483–565, Roman emperor of the East 527–565; codified the Roman laws.

Justinian Code The body of Roman law as codified by Justinian.

jus·ti·ti·a om·ni·bus (jus·tish′ē·ə om′nə·bəs) *Latin* Justice for all: motto of the District of Columbia.

jus·tle (jus′əl) See JOSTLE.

just·ness (just′nis) *n.* The quality of being just; justice. See synonyms under JUSTICE.

just now Scarcely a moment ago.

Jus·tus (jus′təs, *Ger.* yōōs′tōōs) A masculine personal name. Also *Fr.* **Juste** (zhüst), *Ger.* **Just** (yōōst), *Sp.* **Jus·to** (hōōs′tō). [<L, just]

jut (jut) *v.i.* **jut·ted, jut·ting** To extend beyond the main portion; project: often with *out*. — *n.* Anything that juts; a projection. [Var. of JET[2]]

jute (jōōt) *n.* **1** A tall annual Asian herb (*Corchorus capsularis* or *C. olitorius*) of the linden family. **2** The soft, lustrous fiber obtained from the inner bark of this plant, used for bags, cordage, etc. [<Bengali *jhuṭo* <Skt. *jūṭa* a braid of hair]

Jute (jōōt) *n.* A member of a Germanic tribe from Jutland that invaded Britain in the fifth century. [<LL *Jutae* the Jutes <OE *Iōtas*] — **Jut′ish** *adj.*

Jut·land (jut′lənd) A peninsula of northern Europe comprising continental Denmark and Germany north of the Eider; 11,411 square miles; Battle of Jutland, only major engagement of British and German fleets, was fought 70 miles to the west in 1916: also *Cimbrian Chersonese*: Danish *Jylland*.

jut·ty (jut′ē) See JETTY.

ju·ve·nal (jōō′və·nəl) *n.* **1** *Obs.* A youth;

young man. 2 *Ornithol.* The plumage acquired by a bird subsequent to leaving the nest. [<L *juvenalis* young]

Ju·ve·nal (jōo′və·nəl), 60?–140?, Roman poet: full name, Decimus Junius Juvenalis.

ju·ve·nes·cent (jōo′və·nəs′nt), *adj.* Becoming young; also, rejuvenating. [<L *juvenescens, -entis,* ppr. of *juvenescere* grow younger] —**ju′ve·nes′cence** *n.*

ju·ve·nile (jōo′və·nil, -nīl) *adj.* 1 Characteristic of youth; young. 2 Adapted to youth. —*n.* 1 A young person; a youth. 2 An actor who interprets youthful roles. 3 A book for children or youth. See synonyms under YOUTHFUL. [<L *juvenilis* <*juvenis* young]

juvenile court See under COURT.

ju·ve·nil·i·a (jōo′və·,-nil′yə) *n. pl.* Youthful writings. [<L, orig. neut. of *juvenalis* young]

ju·ve·nil·i·ty (jōo′və·nil′ə·tē) *n. pl.* **·ties** 1 A youthful act or character; juvenile character or manner. 2 Youthfulness; youth; the state of being juvenile. Also **ju′ve·nile·ness.**

K

k, K (kā) *n. pl.* **k's, K's** or **ks, Ks** or **kays** (kāz) 1 The eleventh letter of the English alphabet: from Phoenician *kaph,* Greek *kappa,* Roman *K.* 2 The sound of the letter *k,* a voiceless plosive which varies from velar to alveolar position according to the place of articulation of the accompanying vowel, as in *coop* and *keep.* It is normally not pronounced when initial before *n,* as in *knee, knight, know,* etc. See ALPHABET. —*symbol Chem.* Potassium (K for *kalium*).

K2 (kā′tōo′) The world's second highest mountain peak, in the Karakoram range, northern Kashmir, India; 28,250 feet: also *Dapsang, Godwin Austen.*

ka (kä) *n.* In Egyptian religion, the genius or spiritual self: believed to dwell in man and images and to survive in the tomb. [<Egyptian]

Ka·a·ba (kä′ə·bə, kä′bə) *n.* The Moslem shrine at Mecca enclosing a sacred black stone, supposedly given to Abraham by the angel Gabriel, toward which worshipers face when praying: also spelled *Caaba.*

kaas (käs) See KAS.²

kab (kab) See CAB.²

kab·a·la (kab′ə·lə, kə·bä′lə), **kab·ba·la,** etc. See CABALA, etc.

ka·bar (kä′bär) See CABER.

ka·ba·ra·go·ya (kä·bä′rä·gō′yä) See MONITOR (def. 5).

Ka·bar·din·i·an Autonomous Soviet Socialist Republic (kä′bər·din′ē·ən) An autonomous republic in southern European Russian S.F.S.R.; 4,550 square miles; capital, Nalchik. *Russian* **Kab·ar·din·ska·ya Av·to·no·mna·ya S.S.R.** (kab′är·dyēn′skä·yä äf·tô′no·mnä′yä).

ka·bob (kə·bob′) *n.* 1 A dish of small pieces of meat roasted or broiled on skewers and served with various condiments. 2 In India, any roast meat. Also **ka·bab′:** sometimes spelled *cabob.* [<Arabic *kabāb*]

ka·bu·ki (kä·bōo′kē) *n.* A kind of Japanese play on popular or comic themes, employing elaborate costume, stylized gesture, music, and dancing. Compare NO². [<Japanese]

Ka·bul (kÄU′/′bəl) 1 A river in eastern Afghanistan and western Pakistan, flowing 320 miles east to the Indus 2 A city on the Kabul river, capital of Afghanistan.

Ka·byle (kə·bīl′) *n.* 1 One of the Berbers living in Algeria or Tunisia. 2 The Berber dialect spoken by these people.

Ka·chin State (kə·chin′) A constituent unit of the Union of Burma in NW Upper Burma: 33,871 square miles; capital, Myitkyina.

kad·dish (kä′dish) *n. Often cap.* In Judaism, a daily prayer recited in the synagogue service, in one form used by mourners. [<Aramaic *qaddish* holy]

ka·di (kä′dē) See CADI.

Ka·di·ak (kä′dē·ak, *Russian* kə·dyäk′) See KODIAK ISLAND.

Kadiak bear A very large brown bear (*Ursus middendorffi*) found on Kodiak and adjacent islands off the Alaskan coast: also *Kodiak bear.*

kaf·fee·klatsch (kôf′ē·klach′, -kläch′, kof′-) *n.* A social gathering for conversation while coffee and refreshments are served. [<G, lit., coffee + gossip]

Kae·song (kā′sông′) A city in central Korea, NW of Seoul; an ancient capital of Korea. *Japanese* **Kai·jo** (kī·jō).

kaf·fir (kaf′ər) *n.* A variety of sorghum grown in dry regions as a grain and forage plant; East Indian millet. Also **kaf′ir:** erroneously **kaffir corn.** [after the *Kaffirs*]

Kaf·fir (kaf′ər) *n.* 1 A member of a group of southern African Bantu-speaking peoples. 2 An offensive and vulgar term of contempt for a black African, especially of the Republic of South Africa. A non-Moslem: term used contemptuously by Arab Moslems. Also **Kaf′ir:** sometimes spelled *Caffer, Caffre.* [<Arabic *kāfir* unbeliever]

kaf·fi·yeh (kə·fē′ye) *n. Arabic* A large, square kerchief worn by Arabs over the head and shoulders and held in place by an agal. Also **kef·fi′yeh.** [<Arabic *kafiyah,* ? <LL *cuphia, cofia.* See COIF.]

Kaf·fra·ri·a (Kə·frā′rē·ə) A region in Eastern Cape Province, Republic of South Africa.

Ka·fir (kä′fər, kaf′ər) *n.* One of the people of Kafiristan. Also **Kaf′fir.**

Ka·fi·ri (kä·fir′ē) *n.* The Indic language spoken by the Kafirs of Kafiristan.

Ka·fi·ri·stan (kä′fi·ri·stän′) A former name for NURISTAN.

Kaf·ka (käf′kä), **Franz,** 1883–1924, Austrian novelist and writer of short stories.

Kaf·ka·esque (käf′kə·esk′) *adj.* Characteristic of the novels of Franz Kafka; especially, bizarre or absurd, and often marked by the ineffectuality of the individual.

kaf·tan (kaf′tən, käf·tän′) See CAFTAN.

Ka·fu·e (kä·fōo′ā) A river in central Zambia, flowing 600 miles NE through **Kafue Gorge** to the Zambesi.

Ka·ga·wa (kä·gä·wä), **Toyohiko,** 1888–1960, Japanese Christian social reformer.

Ka·ge·ra (kä·gā′rä) A river in east central Africa, flowing 250 miles NE to Lake Victoria: also *Alexandra Nile.*

ka·go (kä′gō) *n.* A form of palanquin. [<Japanese *kango*]

Ka·go·shi·ma (kä·gō·shē·mÄU/) A port on southern Kyushu island, Japan. Also **Ka·go·si·ma.**

Ka·hoo·la·we (kä′hōō·lÄU/′we) An island in the south central Hawaiian Islands; 45 square miles. Also **Ka′hu·la′we.**

Kai Islands (kī) See KEI ISLANDS.

kai·ak (kī′ak) See KAYAK.

Ka·e·teur Falls (kī′ə·tr′) A waterfall in central British Guiana in the Potaro River; 741 feet.

Kai·feng (kī′fung′) A city in east central China, capital of Honan province.

kail (kāl), **kail·yard** (kāl′yärd′) See KALE, KALE-YARD.

kain (kān) *n.* Rental or tax paid in land produce, livestock, eggs, etc.: also spelled *cain, kane.* [<OIrish *cāin* law]

kai·nite (kī′nīt, kaā′ə·nīt) *n.* A colorless to dark flesh-red hydrous sulfate of potassium and magnesium and magnesium chloride, crystallizing in the monoclinic system: used as a fertilizer. [<G *kainit* <Gk. *kainos* recent]

Kair·ouan (kīr·wän′, *Fr.* ker·wän′) A city in NE Tunisia; holy city of the Moslems: also *Qairwan.* Also **Kair·wan′.**

kai·ser (kī′zər) *n.* Emperor: the German title applied to the emperors of the Holy Roman Empire, as successors to those of the old Roman Empire. [<G <L *Caesar* Caesar]

Kaiser Title of the German emperors, 1871–1918.

Kaiser (kī′zər), **Henry J.,** 1882–1967, U.S. industrialist.

juxta- *prefix* Near; next to: *juxtamarine,* bordering on the sea. [<L *juxta* near]

jux·ta·pose (juks′tə·pōz) *v.t* **posed, ·posing** To place close together; put side by side. [<F *juxtaposer* <L *juxta* near + *poser.* See POSE.²]

jux·ta·po·si·tion (juks′tə·pə·zish′ən) *n* A placing close together or side by side; contiguity.

Jyl·land (yūl′län) The Danish name for JUTLAND.

Kai·sers·lau·tern (kī′zərs·lou′tərn) A city in Rhineland-Palatinate. SW West Germany.

Kai·ser-Wil·helm's Land (kī′zər·vil′helms) A former German territory in NE New Guinea, part of the Territory of New Guinea.

kaj·e·put (kaj′ə·pət) See CAJUPUT.

ka·ka (kä′kə) *n.* A New Zealand parrot (genus *Nestor*), typically with olive-green body, gray crown, ad crimson-red on the rump and abdomen. [<Maori]

ka·ka·po (kä′kə·pō′) *n.* A nocturnal, flightless, greenish-brown New Zealand parrot (*Strigops habroptilus*). [<Maori *kaka* a parrot + *po* night]

ka·ke·mo·no (kä′ke·mō′nÅM/) *n.* A picture on paper or silk attached to a roller and used as a wall hanging. [<Japanese <*kake* hang + *mono* thing]

ka·ki (kä′kē) *n.* An Asian tree (*Diospyros kaki*) of the ebony family, with yellowish-white flowers and an edible orange or yellow fruit; cultivated in southern and western Untied States; also called *Japanese persimmon.* [<Japanese, persimmon]

ka·la-a·zar (kä′lä·zī′, -az′ər) *n. Pathol.* An infectious fever of India, China, and Egypt characterized by enlarged spleen, anemia, and emaciation: caused by a protozoan parasite (*Leishmania donovani*). [<Hind. *kālā-āzār* black disease]

Ka·la·ha·ri Desert (kä′lä·hä′rē) An arid plateau region in Namibia, Botswana, and the Republic of South Africa.

Ka·lakh (kä′läkh) An ancient city of Assyria, south of Nineveh on the site of modern, *Nimrud:* Biblical *Calah.*

Ka·la·ma·ta (kä′lä·mä′tä) A port of southern Greece; capital of Messenia. Also **Ka·la·mai** (kä·lä′me).

Kal·a·ma·zoo (kal′ə·mə·zōo′) A city in SW Michigan.

ka·lam·ka·ri (kä′läm·kä′rē) *n.* An East Indian cotton fabric having designs that are drawn and colored by hand [<Hind.]

Ka·lat (kə·lät′) A princely state of eastern Baluchistan. West Pakistan; 30,799 square miles; capital, Kalat: also *Khelat.*

Kalb (kalb, *Ger.* kälp), **Johann,** 1721–80, German general in the American Revolution; known as *Baron de Kalb.*

kale (kāl) *n.* 1 A variety of headless cabbage yielding curled leaves. 2 *Scot.* Cabbage of any kind; also, broth of kale; broth. 3 *U.S. Slang* Money. Also spelled **kail.** [Var. of COLE]

ka·lei·do·scope (kə·lī′də·skōp) *n.* An instrument which, by means of mirrors, presents bits of colored glass, viewed through it, in ever-changing symmetrical patterns, as the tube is rotated. [<Gk. *kalos* beautiful + *eidos* form + -SCOPE]

ka·lei·do·scop·ic (kə·lī′də·skop′ik) *adj.* Pertaining to a kaleidoscope; picturesquely diversified. Also **ka·lei′do·scop′i·cal.** —**ka·lei′do·scop′i·cal·ly** *adv.*

kal·ends (kal′əndz) See CALENDS.

kale runt *Scot.* A cabbage stem. Also **kale stock.**

Ka·le·va·la (kä′lə·vä′lä) The national epic of Finland: a collection of ancient poems embodying the myths and hero legends of Finland: compiled by Elias Lönnrott, 1849. [<Finnish, land of heroes]

kale·wife (kāl′wɪf) *n. pl.* **·wives** (-wɪvz′) *Scot.* A woman who sells vegetables.

kale·yard (kāl′yärd′) *n.* **1** *Scot.* A cabbage garden. **2** A kitchen garden. Also spelled *kailyard.*

kaleyard school A late 19th century school of fiction writers, including J. M. Barrie and Ian Maclaren, who described Scottish life with much use of dialect. Also *kailyard school.*

Kal·gan (käl′gän′) The capital of Chahar province, China.

kal·i (kal′e, ka′le) *n.* The common saltwort. [< Arabic *qalī.* See ALKALI.]

Ka·li (kä′le) In Hindu mythology, the goddess of destruction and wife of Siva: worshiped with bloody sacrifices.

kal·ian (käl·yän′) *n.* The hookah of Persia. [< Persian *kalīān*]

Ka·li·da·sa (kä′le·dä′sä) Indian poet and dramatist, who lived about the fifth century.

ka·lif (kā′lif, kal′if) See CALIPH.

Ka·li·nin (kä·le′nin) A city in western Russian S.F.S.R. on the Volga: formerly *Tver.*

Ka·li·nin (kä·le′nin), **Mikhail Ivanovich,** 1875–1946, president of the U.S.S.R. 1923–46.

Ka·li·nin·grad (kä·le′nin·grät′) A port on the Pregel River in Russian S.F.S.R.; formerly, as German *Königsberg,* the capital of East Prussia.

Ka·lisz (kä′lesh) A city in west central Poland: German **Ka·lisch** (kä′lish).

ka·li·um (kā′le·əm) *n.* Potassium: from this name, used by pharmacists and German chemists, its symbol K is derived. [< KALI]

Kal·li·kak (kal′ə·kak) A pseudonym used for the members of an actual New Jersey family whose history, as investigated by H. H. Goddard, in 1912, showed abnormal incidence of crime, disease, and pauperism. Compare JUKES. [< Gk. *kalli-* beautiful + *kakos* evil]

kal·li·type (kal′ə·tip) *n.* A photoprinting process by which ferric salts are reduced to ferrous salts, which in turn act upon soluble silver salts. [< Gk. *kalli-* beautiful + TYPE]

Kal·mar (käl′mär) A port in SE Sweden on **Kalmar Sound,** an arm of the Baltic between Sweden and Öland Island.

kal·mi·a (kal′me·ə) Any plant of a genus (*Kalmia*) of North American shrubs of the heath family, with evergreen leaves and umbellate clusters of rose, purple, or white flowers. [< NL, after Peter *Kalm,* 1716–79, Swedish botanist]

Kal·muck (kal′muk) *n.* **1** A member of one of the western Buddhistic Mongol tribes extending from western China to the valley of the Volga river. **2** The Mongolian language of these tribes. Also **Kal′muk.**

Kal·myk Autonomous Soviet Socialist Republic (kal′mik) A former administrative division of SE European Russian S.F.S.R. Also **Kal·muck Autonomous S.S.R.** (kal′muk).

ka·long (kä′lông) *n.* A fruit–eating bat (family *Pteropodidae*) of Africa, Asia, and Australia. [< Malay *kalong*]

kal·pac (kal′pak) See CALPAC.

kal·so·mine (kal′sə·min) See CALCIMINE.

Ka·lu·ga (kä·lōō′gä) A city in western Russian S.F.S.R. on the Oka river.

ka·lyp·tra (kə·lip′trə) *n.* A thin veil worn by women of ancient Greece over the face and as a headdress. [< Gk. < *kalyptein* hide]

Ka·ma (kä′mä) A river in eastern European Russian S.F.S.R., flowing 1,262 miles from the Urals to the Volga.

kam·a·cite (kam′ə·sit) *n.* A variety of meteoric iron containing nickel and showing, when polished, a fine network of bands. [< G *kamacit* < Gk. *kamax, -akos* a vine pole]

Ka·ma·ku·ra (kä·mä·kōōr·ä) A city on Honshu island, Japan; site of a 42–foot, 13th century bronze image of Buddha.

ka·ma·la (kə·ma′lə, kam′ə-) *n.* **1** An Indian tree (*Mallotus philippinensis*) of the spurge family. **2** The fine orange–red powder from its capsular fruit, used as a purgative and in dyeing. [< Skt.]

Kam·chat·ka (kam·chat′kə, *Russian* käm·chät′kä) A peninsula at the eastern end of U.S.S.R. extending 750 miles southward between the Bering and Okhotsk Seas; 104,200 square miles.

kame¹ (kam) *n. Scot.* Comb.

kame² (kam) *n. Geol.* A conical hill or short ridge of stratified sand and gravel formed by glacier deposition. [See COOMB]

Ka·me·ha·me·ha I (kä·mā′hä-mä′hä), 1753?–1819, first king of Hawaii; known as *Kamehameha the Great.*

Ka·me·rad (kä′mə-rät′) *n. pl.* **·rad·en** (-rä′dən) *German* Comrade: used by German soldiers to indicate readiness to surrender.

Kam·er·lingh On·nes (kä′mər·ling ôn′əs), **Heike,** 1853–1926, Dutch physicist.

Ka·me·run (kä′mə·rōōn) The German name for CAMEROONS.

kame·ster (käm′stər) *n. Scot.* A woolcomber.

Ka·met (kä′met) A mountain on the Tibetan border of Uttar Pradesh State, India; 25,447 feet.

ka·mi (kä′me) *n. Japanese* **1** The gods collectively of the first and second mythological dynasties of Japan; also, their descendants, the mikados. **2** The deified spirits of the heroes and famous men of Japan.

ka·mi·ka·ze (kä′mi·kä′ze) *n.* In World War II, a Japanese pilot pledged to die in crashing his bomb–laden plane against the target; also, the airplane itself on such a mission. [< Japanese, divine wind < *kami* a god + *kaze* the wind]

Kam·pa·la (käm·pä′lä) The capital of Uganda, in the southern part.

kam·pong (käm·pong′, käm′pong) *n.* An enclosed space; a compound. [< Malay]

kam·sin (kam′sin) See KHAMSIN.

Kan (gän) The chief river of Kiangsi province, China, flowing 540 miles north to Poyang Lake.

ka·na (kä′nə) *n.* Japanese syllabic writing: a system of 46 phonetic symbols normally used for foreign words, and used collaterally with Chinese ideographs to indicate Japanese grammatical inflections. [< Japanese]

Ka·nak·a (kə·nak′ə, kan′ə·kə) *n.* **1** A native of Hawaii. **2** Any South Sea Islander. [< Polynesian, man]

Ka·na·ra (kä′nə·rə, kə·nä′rə) **1** A region of the southern Deccan Plateau, India; 60,000 square miles: *Canarese* **Kar′na·tak. 2** A district of southern Bombay State, India, on the western edge of the Deccan Plateau; 3,961 square miles: also **North Kanara;** formerly *Canara.*

Ka·na·rese (kä′nə·rez′, -rēs′) *adj.* Of or pertaining to Kanara. —*n.* **1** A native or naturalized inhabitant of Kanara. **2** The Dravidian language of Kanara. Also spelled *Canarese.*

Ka·na·wha River (kə·nô′wə) A river in SW West Virginia, flowing 97 miles NW to the Ohio.

Ka·na·za·wa (kä·nä·zä·wä) A port of western Honshu island, Japan.

Kan·chen·jun·ga (kun′chən·jōōng′gə) The third highest mountain in the world, in the eastern Nepal Himalayas; 28,146 feet; formerly *Kinchi.*

Kan·da·har (kän′dä·här′) A city in southern Afghanistan; also *Qandahar.*

Kan·din·ski (kan·din′ske, *Russian* kän·dyēn′ski) **Vasili,** 1866–1946, Russian painter.

Kan·dy (kan′dē, kän′dē) A city in central Sri Lanka; formerly *Candy.*

kane (kān) See KAIN.

Kane (kān), **Elisha Kent,** 1820–57, U.S. arctic explorer.

Ka·nem (kä′nem) An administrative region of western Chad territory, French Equatorial Africa; formerly a state; 56,000 square miles.

Kan·gar (käng·gär′) Capital of Perlis state, Federation of Malaya.

kan·ga·roo (kang′gə-rōō′) *n.* Any of a large family (*Macropodidae*) of herbivorous marsupials of the Australian region, having weak forelimbs and strong hind limbs, with stout tail, moving by leaping bounds, and ranging in size from nine feet long to about the size of a rat. [Australian]

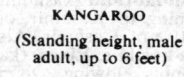

KANGAROO

(Standing height, male adult, up to 6 feet)

kangaroo court 1 An unofficial court in which the law is disregarded or wilfully misinterpreted. **2** A mock court or trial. **3** A frontier or backwoods court.

kangaroo rat 1 One of various pouched rodents (*Dipodomys agilis*) of the SW United States and Mexico, with elongated hind limbs and tail. **2** Any of several Australian rodents (genus *Notomys*) noted for their leaping habits.

K'ang–hsi (käng′she′), 1654–1722, also called Sheng–tsu. First Manchu emperor of China, 1662–1722; annexed Tibet and made the first Chinese treaty with a European power (Russia, 1689).

Kang Te (käng′ tä′) Emperor of Manchukuo, 1934–45. See PU–YI.

Kang–ting (käng′ting′) A city in SW China.

Kan·ka·kee (kang′kə·ke′) A river in Indiana and Illinois, flowing 135 miles to the Illinois River.

Ka·no (kä′nō) A city in northern Nigeria.

ka·noon (kä·nōōn′) A kind of dulcimer having fifty or sixty strings and played with the fingers. Also **ka·nun′.** [< Persian *qānūn*]

Kan·pur (kän′pōōr′) A city on the Ganges in Uttar Pradesh, India; formerly *Cawnpore.*

Kan·sas (kan′zəs) A north central State of the United States; 82,276 square miles; capital, Topeka; entered the Union Jan. 29, 1861; nickname, *Sunflower State.* Abbr. KS —**Kan′·san** (-zən) *adj. & n.*

Kansas City 1 A city on the Missouri River in NE Kansas. **2** A city on the Missouri River in western Missouri.

Kansas River A river in NE Kansas, flowing 200 miles east to the Missouri: also *Kaw.*

Kan·su (kän′sōō′, *Chinese* gän′sōō′) A province in NW China; 150,000 square miles; capital, Lanchow.

Kant (kant, *Ger.* känt), **Immanuel,** 1724–1804, German philosopher; author of *Critique of Pure Reason* (1781).

kan·tar (kän·tär′) See CANTAR.

Kant·i·an (kan′te·ən) *adj.* Of or pertaining to Kant or his philosophy. —*n.* A follower of Kantianism.

Kant·i·an·ism (kan′te·ən·iz′əm) *n.* The critical philosophy of Immanuel Kant that sets forth the doctrine of a priori knowledge: man experiences the material world through sense perception, but its form is determined by the mind alone. Also **Kant′ism.**

Kao·hsiung (gou′shyōōng′) A port in SW Taiwan.

Kao·lan (gou′län′) A former name for LANCHOW.

ka·o·li·ang (kä′ō·lē·ang′) *n. Chinese* Any of a variety of sorghums of eastern Asia, some introduced into the United States.

ka·o·lin (kä′ə·lin) *n.* A claylike, friable, hydrous aluminum silicate used in making porcelain. Also **ka′o·line.** [from Chinese *Kao Ling* High Ridge, a mountain range where first mined]

ka·o·lin·ite (kä′ə·lin·it′) *n.* A highly purified form of kaolin.

kap·a (kap′ə) *n. pl.* **kap·a–kap·a** A Tapa cloth. [< Hawaiian]

Ka·pell·meis·ter (kä·pel′mis′tər) *n.* The musical director of a choir, orchestra, etc.: also called *chapelmaster.* [< G, bandmaster]

Kap·e·naar (kap′ə·när′) *Afrikaans* A white person born in the Cape of Good Hope province.

kaph (käf) *n.* The eleventh Hebrew letter: also spelled *caph.* See ALPHABET.

Ka·pi·da·ği Peninsula (kä′pi·dä·gē′) An extension of NW Turkey into the Sea of Marmara: ancient *Cyzicus.* Also **Ka·pu Dagh** (kä′pōō däg).

ka·pok (kä′pok) *n.* A cottony or silky fiber covering the seeds of a tropical tree (*Ceiba pentandra*) of the silk–cotton family: used for mattresses, life–savers, insulation material, etc. [< Malay *kāpoq*]

kap·pa (kap′ə) *n. Greek* The tenth letter in the Greek alphabet (K, κ), equivalent to English *k.* See under ALPHABET.

kappa curve *Math.* A plane, kappa–shaped curve, symmetrical with respect to the coordinate axes and the origin, and having two cusps at the origin.

Ka·pu·as (kä′pōō·äs) A river in central Borneo, flowing 710 miles SW to the South China Sea. Also **Ka′poe·as.**

ka·put (kä·pōōt′) *adj. Slang* Ruined; done for; finished. [< G]

Ka·ra (kä′rə) A river in northern European

Russian S.F.S.R., flowing 130 miles north from the northern Urals.

kar·a·bi·ner (kar'ə·bē'nər) *n.* An article of mountaineering equipment: a steel loop or ring snapped into a piton, through which a rope may be passed, to hold climbers. [Short for G *karabinerhaken* carbine snap]

KARABINER
a. Closed.
b. Open.

Ka·ra·chi (kə·rä'chē) A port on the Arabian Sea NW of the Indus delta.

Ka·ra·fu·to (kä·rä·fōō·tō) The Japanese name for the southern part of SAKHALIN.

Ka·ra·gan·da (kä'rä·gän·dä') A city in central Kazakh S.S.R.

Kar·a·george (kar'ə·jôrj'), 1776–1817, Serbian leader and patriot: real name *George Petrovich.*

Ka·ra·Kal·pak Autonomous S.S.R. The former name of **Karakalpakstan**, the territory in NW Uzbekistan along the Amu Darya; 61,000 square miles; capital Nukus.

Kar·a·ko·ram (kar'ə·kôr'əm, -kō'rəm) A mountain range in NE Kashmir; highest peak, 28,250 feet: traversed by **Karakoram Pass** at 18,550 feet on the China-Kashmir trade route: also *Mustagh.* Also **Kar'a·ko'rum.**

kar·a·kul (kar'ə·kəl) *n.* **1** A breed of sheep of Bokhara. **2** Astrakhan of the best quality, obtained from the black, lustrous, tightly curled coat of young lambs of the karakul sheep. Also spelled *caracul.* [from *Kara Kul,* lake in central Siberia]

Ka·ra Kum (kä'rä kōōm') A desert in central Turkmen S.S.R., extending from the Caspian Sea to Amu Darya.

Ka·ra Sea (kä'rə) An arm of the Arctic Ocean between Novaya Zemlya and northern U.S.S.R.

kar·at (kar'ət) *n.* The twenty-fourth part by weight of gold in an article; thus, 18-karat gold means an article 18/24 or 3/4 gold by weight: distinguished from *carat.* [Var. of CARAT]

ka·ra·te (kä·rä'tä, -tē) *n.* An Oriental style of hand-to-hand fighting using sudden forceful blows, as with the side of the hand or with the fingertips. [<Japanese]

Kar·ba·la (kär'bə·lə) A city and Moslem pilgrimage center in central Iraq. Also **Kar'be·la.**

Ka·re·li·a (kə·rē'lē·ə, -rēl'yə) **1** A former autonomous republic of NW Russian S.F.S.R.; included since 1940 in Karelo-Finnish S.S.R. **2** Karelo-Finnish S.S.R.

Ka·re·li·an Isthmus (kə·rē'lē·ən, -rēl'yən) A glacial land bridge between the Gulf of Finland and Lake Ladoga in Russia.

Ka·re·lo-Fin·nish S.S.R. A former constituent republic of NW U.S.S.R., now a republic of Russia; 66,000 square miles; capital, Petrozavodsk; comprising territory ceded by Finland in March 1940, and joined with Karelia: also Karelia.

Ka·ren State A constituent unit of the Union of Myanmar; 11,700 square miles; capital, Pa-an.

Ka·ri·kal (kä'rē·käl') A free city and former French settlement in southern Madras, India; 52 square miles. Formerly **Ca'ri·cal'.**

Kar·kheh (kär'ke) A river in SW Iran, flowing 350 miles SE to the Tigris: ancient *Choaspes:* also *Kerkheh.*

Karl (kärl) The German and alternate Scandinavian form of CHARLES.

Kar·lov·ei A village on the Danube in Croatia: by a treaty signed here in 1699, Turkey ceded most of her European territories to Poland, Venice, and Austria.

Kar·lo·vy Va·ry (kär'lô·vē vä'rē) A town in NW Bohemia, Czech republic. *German* **Karlsbad:** also *Carlsbad.*

Karls·kro·na (kärls·krōō'nä) A city in southern Sweden, site of the chief Swedish naval base.

Karls·ruh·e A city in SW Germany, in the state of Baden-Wurttemberg: also Carlsruhe.

kar·ma (kär'mə, kûr'-) *n.* The effect of any act, religious or otherwise; the law of cause and effect regulating one's future life; inevitable retribution: a Brahmanic idea developed by the Buddhists. [<Sanskrit, action]

karn (kärn) *n. Brit.* A cairn.

Kar·nak (kär'nak) A village on the Nile in Upper Egypt, on the northern part of the site of ancient Thebes.

Kärn·ten (kern'tən) The German name for CARINTHIA.

Ká·rol·yi (kä'rō·yē), **Count Mihály,** 1875–1955, Hungarian politician.

ka·ross (kə·ros') *n. Afrikaans* **1** A native garment made of skins sewed together in the form of a square. **2** A rug made of skins.

Kar·pa·thos (kär'pə·thos) The third largest island of the Dodecanese group in the Aegean; 111 square miles: Italian *Scarpanto.*

kar·rer (kär'ər), **Paul,** 1889–1971, Swiss chemist.

kar·roo (kə·rōō', ka-) *n. pl.* **·roos** A dry plateau or tableland of South Africa. Also **ka·roo'.** See GREAT KARROO, SOUTHERN KARROO, NORTHERN KARROO. [<Hottentot]

Kar·roo (kə·rōō', ka-) *adj. Geol.* Belonging to or designating a period or rock system of the Paleozoic and Mesozoic eras, developed in South Africa. Also **Ka·roo'.**

Kars (kärs) A city in NE Turkey in Asia.

Karst (kärst) The German name for CARSO.

kart (kärt) *n.* A small, low, motorized vehicle for one person, used especially in racing. [Var. of CART] — **kart'ing** *n.*

Ka·run (kä·rōōn') A river in SW Iran, flowing SE, west and NW 500 miles from NE Khuzistan to the Shatt el Arab.

karyo- combining form *Biol.* Nucleus: *karyoplasm.* Also, before vowels, **kary–:** also spelled *caryo-.* [<Gk. *karyon* a nut]

kar·y·og·a·my (kar'ē·og'ə·mē) *n. Biol.* The merging or close union of the nuclei of two gametes to form the primary nucleus of the embryo. [<KARYO- + -GAMY]

kar·y·o·ki·ne·sis (kar'ē·ō·ki·nē'sis) *n. Biol.* **1** The series of changes which the nucleus goes through in indirect or mitotic cell division. **2** Such cell division; mitosis. Also spelled *caryokinesis.* [<KARYO- + Gk. *kinēsis* movement] — **kar'y·o·ki·net'ic** (-net'ik) *adj.*

kar·y·o·lymph (kar'ē·ə·limf') *n. Biol.* The clear protoplasmic fluid surrounding the structures of the cell nucleus.

kar·y·o·mere (kar'ē·ə·mir') *n. Biol.* One of the small vesicles formed in chromosomes in certain types of mitosis. Also **kar'y·om'er·ite** (-om'ər·īt).

kar·y·o·plasm (kar'ē·ə·plaz'əm) *n. Biol.* The protoplasm of the nucleus of a cell: also called *nucleoplasm.* — **kar'y·o·plas'mic** *adj.*

kar·y·o·some (kar'ē·ə·sōm') *n. Biol.* **1** A chromosome. **2** A mass of chromatin in the resting nucleus of the cell. **3** The cell nucleus itself. Also **kar'y·o·so'ma** (-sō'mə).

kar·y·o·tin (kar'ē·ō'tin) *n. Biol.* The stainable, usually reticulated substance of the cell nucleus; chromatin: also spelled *caryotin.* [<KARYO- + (CHROMA)TIN]

kar·y·o·type (kar'ē·ə·tīp') *n. Genetics* The particular chromosome number and gene arrangement in the gametes of any given species, type, or strain of organism.

Ka·sai (kä·sī') A river in southern central Africa, flowing 1,100 miles east and north to the Congo.

Kas·bah (käz'bä) See CASBAH.

Ka·schau (kä'shou) The German name for KOŠICE.

Ka·shan (kä·shän') A city in north central Iran.

ka·sher (kä'shər) *v.t.* To make or pronounce kosher. — *adj. & n.* See KOSHER.

Kash·gar (käsh·gär') A town in western Sinkiang province, China: Chinese *Shufu.*

Kash·mir (kash·mir', kash'mir) **1** See JAMMU AND KASHMIR. **2** A province of Jammu and Kashmir; 8,539 square miles; capital, Srinagar; containing the **Vale of Kashmir,** a valley in the Himalayas in western Kashmir province. Formerly *Cashmere.*

Kash·mi·ri (kash·mir'ē) *n.* The Indic language of the Kashmirians.

Kash·mi·ri·an (kash·mir'ē·ən) *adj.* Of or pertaining to Kashmir or its people. — *n.* A native of Kashmir. Also spelled *Cashmerian.*

Kas·kas·ki·a River (kas·kas'kē·ə) A river in Illinois, flowing 320 miles SW to the Mississippi.

Kas·par (käs'pär) German form of JASPAR and GASPAR. Also *Sw.* **Kas'per** (käs'pər).

Kas·sa (kôsh'shō) The Hungarian name for KOŠICE.

Kas·sa·la (kas'ə·lə) A city in NE Sudan.

Kas·sel (käs'əl) A city in Hesse, eastern West Germany: also *Cassel.*

Kas·tel·lo·ri·zo (käs·te·lô'ri·zô) The eastern-most island of the Dodecanese group in the Aegean: Italian *Castelrosso.*

Kas·tro (käs'trô) A former name of MYTILINE. Also **Kas'tron** (-trən).

kata- See CATA-.

ka·tab·a·sis (kə·tab'ə·sis) *n.* **1** The march back to the sea of the Greek mercenaries who followed Cyrus against Artaxerxes. See ANABASIS. **2** Any retreat. [<Gk., a going down]

kat·a·bat·ic (kat'ə·bat'ik) *adj. Meteorol.* Pertaining to or designating a down-flowing wind cooled by radiation, as one reaching a valley from high ground.

kat·a·bol·ic (kat'ə·bol'ik), **ka·tab·o·lism** (kə·tab'ə·liz'əm), etc. See CATABOLIC, etc.

Ka·tah·din (kə·tä'din), **Mount** A peak in central Maine; 5,268 feet.

ka·tal·y·sis (kə·tal'ə·sis), **kat·a·lyt·ic** (kat'ə·lit'ik), etc. See CATALYSIS, etc.

kat·a·mor·phism (kat'ə·môr'fiz·əm) *n.* Metamorphism.

Ka·tan·ga (kə·tang'gə) A SE province of the Republic of the Congo; 191,827 square miles; capital, Elisabethville.

Ka·ta·ri·na (kä·tä·rē'nä) Swedish form of CATHERINE.

Kate (kāt) Diminutive of CATHERINE.

Kath·e·rine (kath'ə·rin, kath'rin), **Kath·e·rine** See CATHERINE.

ka·thar·sis (kə·thär'sis), **ka·thar·tic** (kə·thär'tik) See CATHARSIS, etc.

Kath·er·i·na (kath'ə·rē'nə), **Ge·bel** (jeb'əl) A mountain in NE Egypt, highest peak in the Sinai Peninsula and in Egypt; 8,651 feet: also *Mount Catherine.*

Ka·thi·a·war (kä'tē·ə·wär') A peninsula of western India extending into the Arabian Sea between the Gulfs of Cambay and Cutch.

Kath·leen (kath'lēn, kath·lēn') See CATHERINE.

kath·ode (kath'ōd), etc. See CATHODE, etc.

kat·i·on (kat'ī'ən) See CATION.

Kat·mai National Monument (kat'mī) A region of the NE Alaska Peninsula, southern Alaska; 14,214 square miles; contains **Katmai Volcano;** 7,000 feet; last eruption, 1912; and the Valley of the Ten Thousand Smokes.

Kat·man·du (kät'män·dōō') The capital of Nepal. Also **Kath'man·du'.**

Ka·to·wi·ce (kä'tô·vē'tse) A city in southern Poland: German **Kat·to·witz** (kät'ō·vits).

Kat·rine (kat'rin), **Loch** A lake in SW Perthshire, Scotland.

Kat·te·gat (kat'ə·gat) An arm of the North Sea, between Sweden and Jutland: also *Cattegat.* Also **Kat·te·gott** (kät'ə·got).

ka·ty·did (kā'tē·did) *n.* An arboreal, green, long-horned insect allied to the grasshoppers and crickets (family *Tettigonidae*): named from the sound produced by the stridulating organs at the base of the wing covers in the male.

Kau·ai (kou'ī) The fourth largest of the Hawaiian Islands; 555 square miles.

Kauf·man (kôf'mən), **George S.,** 1889–1961, U.S. playwright.

Kau·nas (kou'näs) A city on the Nemen river in south central Lithuania: Russian *Kovno.*

kau·ri (kou'rē) *n.* **1** A large timber tree (*Agathis australis*) of New Zealand. **2** The wood of this tree. **3** Any other species of the genus *Agathis.* **4** Kauri gum. Also **kau'ry.** [<Maori]

kauri gum A colorless to amber or brown resinous exudation of the kauri tree, used in varnishes, for oilcloth, linoleum, etc. Also **kauri copal, kauri resin.**

ka·va (kä'və) *n.* **1** A shrub (*Piper methysticum*) of the pepper family. **2** An intoxicating and narcotic beverage made from the roots of this plant by the Polynesians: also **ka'va–ka'va.** [<Maori *kawa* bitter]

Ka·val·la (kä·vä'lä) A port of NE Greece.

ka·vass (kə·väs') *n.* A guard or military courier attending Turkish dignitaries; also, a Turkish police officer. [<Turkish. *qawwās* a maker of bows < *qaws* a bow]

Ka·ver·i (kō'vər·ē) A river in southern India, flowing 475 miles NE to the Bay of Bengal: also *Cauvery.*

Ka·vi (kä'vē) *n.* The extinct language of Java from which modern Javanese developed: preserved in ancient Buddhist writings.

Ka·vi·eng (kä'vē·eng) A port and the chief city of northern New Ireland, Bismarck Archipelago.

Ka·vir (kä·vir′) See DASHT-I-KAVIR.
Kaw (kô) *n.* A Kansas Indian.
Ka·wa·gu·chi (kä·wä·gōō·chē) A city of central Honshu island, Japan.
Ka·wa·sa·ki (kä·wä·sä·kē) A city of central Honshu island on Tokyo Bay.
Kaw River See KANSAS RIVER.
Ka·wu·la (kä·wōō′lä) See LOMBLEM. Also **Ka·woe′la.**
kay (kā) See KEY².
Kay (kā), **Sir** A braggart and spiteful knight of the Round Table; foster brother and seneschal of King Arthur. Also spelled *Kai* and, in French romances, *Queux.*
kay·ak (kī′ak) *n.* The hunting canoe of arctic America, made of sealskins stretched over a pointed frame, leaving a hole amidships where the navigator sits, excluding the water by fastening the deck covering around him. Also spelled *kaiak.* [<Eskimo]

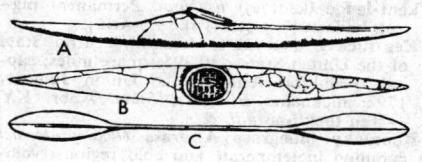

KAYAK
A. Side view. *B.* Top view. *C.* Paddle.

Kaye-Smith (kā′smith′), **Sheila,** 1889–1956, English novelist.
kayles (kālz) *n. pl. Brit. Dial.* 1 A game of ninepins or skittles. 2 The pins used in the game.
kay·o (kā′ō) *Slang v.t.* **kay·oed, kay·o·ing** In boxing, to knock out. — *n.* A knockout (def. 1). Also *KO.* [<k(nock) o(ut)]
Kay·se·ri (kī′sə·rē′) A city in central Turkey in Asia: ancient *Caesarea Mazaca.*
Ka·zakh *n.* 1 One of a Turkic people, formerly largely nomadic, dwelling in Kazakhstan. 2 A long-piled rug, usually in geometrical patterns, made by the Kazakhs.
Kazakhstan A republic in central Asia; pop. 17,000,000, 1,050,000 square miles; capital, Alma-Ata; formerly **Kazakh Soviet Socialist Republic** (1936–1991).
Ka·zan A city in west central Russia; capital of Tatarstan republic.
Ka·zan River (kə·zan′) A river in Northwest Territories, Canada, flowing 455 miles NE from SE Mackenzie to a lake in central Keewatin which drains into Hudson Bay.
ka·zoo (kə·zōō′) *n.* A toy musical instrument: a wooden or metal tube to which is attached a piece of stretched catgut or paper which vibrates when the tube is sung or hummed into. [Origin uncertain]
Kaz·vin (käz·vēn′) A city in NW Iran: also *Qazvin.*
ke·a (kā′ə, kē′ə) *n.* A large New Zealand parrot (*Nestor notabilis*), olive-brown variegated with blue and green, which feeds on carrion in addition to fruits, etc., and even attacks live sheep. [Maori]
Ke·a (kā′ä) See KEOS.
Kean (kēn), **Edmund,** 1787–1833, English actor.
Kear·ny (kär′nē), **Philip,** 1815?–62, U. S. general; served in Mexican and Civil wars.
keat (kēt) *n.* A young guinea fowl.
Keats (kēts), **John,** 1795–1821, English poet.
ke·bar (kē′bär) See CABER.
keb·bie (keb′ē) *n. Scot.* A cudgel, or rude walking stick.
keb·bock (keb′ək) *n. Scot.* A cheese. Also **keb′buck.**
Ke·ble (kē′bəl), **John,** 1792–1866, English divine and poet; one of the founders of the Oxford movement.
Kech·ua (kech′wä), **Kech·uan** (kech′wən) See QUECHUA, QUECHUAN.
keck¹ (kek) *v.i.* 1 To heave as in vomiting; retch. 2 To show or feel great disgust. — *n.* Nausea. [Prob. imit.]
keck² (kek) *n.* A hollow stalk of a plant. [Back formation <KEX, mistaken as a plural]
keck·le¹ (kek′əl) *v.t.* **keck·led, keck·ling** *Naut.* To wrap or serve, as a cable, with canvas, rope, etc., as a protection from chafing. [Origin unknown]
keck·le² (kek′əl) *Scot. v.i.* **keck·led, keck·ling** To cackle; chuckle. — *n.* A chuckle or giggle.
Kecs·ke·mét (kech′kə·māt) A city in central Hungary.
Ke·dah (kā′dä) One of the States of Malaya, in the NW part; 3,660 square miles; capital, Alor Star.
Ke·dar (kē′dər) A son of Ishmael; also, a tribe or confederacy of Arabian tent-dwellers descending from him. — **Ke′dar·ite** *adj.*
ked·dah (ked′ə) *n.* An enclosure or corral for the capture of wild elephants: also spelled *khedah.* [<Hind. *kheda*]
kedge (kej) *Naut. n.* A light anchor used in warping, freeing a vessel from shoals, etc.: also **kedge anchor.** — *v.i.* 1 To move a vessel by hauling up to a kedge anchor placed at a distance. 2 To be moved in this way. — *v.t.* 3 To move (a vessel) in this way. [<*kedge (anchor)* <CADGE]
Ke·dron (kē′drən) A valley east of Jerusalem. *John* xviii 1. Also *Kidron.*
ke·ef (kā·ef′) See KEF.
keek (kēk) *Scot.* To peep; pry. — *n.* A peep.
keek·ing-glass (kē′king·glas′, -gläs′) *n. Scot.* A looking-glass.
keel¹ (kēl) *n.* 1 *Naut.* The lowest lengthwise member of the framework of a vessel, serving to stiffen it and, when it projects below the planking or plating, as is usually the case, giving it stability. 2 Figuratively, a ship. 3 *Aeron.* **a** A vertical fin which extends longitudinally for a considerable length at the bottom of an airship. **b** The center bottom of an airplane fuselage. 4 Any keel-shaped part or object. 5 *Ornithol.* A median longitudinal ridge or process, as of the breast bone of a fowl. — **fin keel** An extension of a yacht's keel downward, suggesting the back fin of a fish: commonly of metal, and serving to ballast and prevent lateral drifting. — *v.t.* & *v.i.* To turn over with the keel uppermost; capsize. — **to keel over** 1 To turn bottom up; capsize. 2 To fall over or be felled, as from an injury. [<ON *kjölr* keel]
keel² (kēl) *n.* 1 A coal barge used on the Tyne in England. 2 The quantity of coal in a barge load. 3 A former British unit of weight for coal, equal to 21.54 metric tons. [<MDu. *kiel* ship]
keel³ (kēl) *v.t. Obs.* To cool. [OE *cēlan*]
keel⁴ (kēl) *n. Scot.* Red chalk or ocher; ruddle.
keel·age (kē′lij) *n. Naut.* The sum paid for anchoring a vessel in a harbor.
keel·boat (kēl′bōt′) *n.* A covered freight boat of shallow draft having a keel but no sails, usually propelled by poles or the current: used on rivers in the western United States.
keel·er (kē′lər) *n.* 1 A shallow tub. 2 A box used to hold salt in salting fish. [<KEEL³]
Kee·ley cure (kē′lē) A proprietary system for the treatment of drug addiction and alcoholism by the administration of gold chloride. [after Leslie J. *Keeley,* 1832–1900, American physician]
keel·haul (kēl′hôl′) *v.t.* 1 *Naut.* To haul (a man) through the water under a ship from one side to the other or from stem to stern: a former punishment. 2 To reprove severely; castigate. Also **keel-hale** (kēl′hāl′).
Kee·ling Islands (kē′ling) See COCOS ISLANDS.
keel·son (kēl′sən) *n.* 1 *Naut.* A beam running lengthwise above the keel of a ship. 2 A similar structural member running above the keel of a flying boat. Also spelled *kelson.* [Related to KEEL¹]
Kee·lung (kē′lŏŏng′) A port of northern Taiwan: also *Kilung, Chilung.*
keen¹ (kēn) *adj.* 1 Very sharp, as a knife. 2 Cutting; piercing, as wit. 3 Vivid; pungent. 4 Having or exhibiting sharpness or penetration; shrewd. 5 Acute: keen sight. 6 Exceptionally intelligent. 7 Characterized by intensity, force, or zest: a *keen* appetite. See synonyms under ACUTE, ARDENT, ASTUTE, CLEVER, EAGER¹, FINE¹, KNOWING, SAGACIOUS, SHARP, VIVID. [OE *cēne*] — **keen′ly** *adv.* — **keen′ness** *n.*
keen² (kēn) *n.* A wailing cry; dirge. — *v.i.* To wail loudly over the dead. [<Irish *caoine* <*caoinim* I wail] — **keen′er** *n.*

keep (kēp) *v.* **kept, keep·ing** *v.t.* 1 To have and retain possession or control of; hold. 2 To withhold knowledge of, as a secret. 3 To manage or conduct: to *keep* a shop. 4 To have charge of; tend: to *keep* bar. 5 To care for; guard or defend from harm: May God *keep* you. 6 To be faithful to the conditions of; fulfil, as a promise or contract. 7 To maintain by action or conduct: to *keep* silence. 8 To cause to continue in some condition or state; preserve unchanged: *Keep* the home fires burning. 9 To make regular entries in: to *keep* a diary. 10 To set down in writing; maintain a written record of: to *keep* accounts. 11 To have regularly for sale: to *keep* groceries. 12 To provide for or maintain, as with food or lodging. 13 To have in one's employ or for one's use or pleasure. 14 To celebrate or observe, especially with rites or ceremony, as a holiday. 15 To conduct, as a meeting. 16 To detain or restrain; prevent: What *kept* you? 17 To hold prisoner; confine. 18 To remain; hold to: *Keep* your present course. 19 To hold or maintain in the same position or state as before: *Keep* your seat. — *v.i.* 20 To continue in a condition, place, or action: They *kept* firing; *Keep* to the right-hand side. 21 To remain; stay: often with *up, down, in, out, off, away,* etc. 22 To remain sound, fresh, etc.: This fruit *keeps* till spring. 23 *Colloq.* To be in session: School *keeps* till three o'clock. — **to keep back** 1 To restrain. 2 To withhold. — **to keep in with** *Colloq.* To remain in the good graces of. — **to keep on** To continue; persist. — **to keep time** 1 To indicate time correctly, as a clock. 2 To make movements in unison or concord with others. 3 To count or observe rhythmic accents. — **keep track of** (or **tabs on**) To continue to be informed about. — **to keep up** 1 To keep pace with; not fall behind. 2 To maintain in good condition or repair. 3 To continue; go on with. 4 To maintain and renew knowledge or information concerning: usually with *with* or *on.* 5 To cause to stay awake or out of bed. — *n.* 1 Means of subsistence; livelihood. 2 The donjon of a medieval castle; hence, a castle; fortress. 3 That in which something is kept. — **for keeps** *Colloq.* For permanent keeping; for good; for ever. [OE *cēpan* observe]
Synonyms (verb): carry, celebrate, conduct, continue, defend, detain, fulfil, guard, hold, maintain, obey, observe, preserve, protect, refrain, restrain, retain, support, sustain, withhold. *Keep,* signifying generally to have and *retain* in possession, is the terse, strong Old English term for many acts which are more exactly discriminated by other words. We *keep, observe,* or *celebrate* a festival; we *keep* or *hold* a prisoner in custody; we *keep* or *preserve* silence, *keep* the peace, *preserve* order—*preserve* being the more formal word; we *keep* or *maintain* a horse, a servant, etc.; a man *supports* his family; we *keep* or *obey* a commandment, *keep* or *fulfil* a promise. In the expressions to *keep* a secret, *keep* one's own counsel, *keep* faith or *keep* the faith, such words as *preserve* or *maintain* could not be substituted without loss. A person *keeps* a shop or store, *conducts* or carries on a business; he *keeps* or *carries* a certain line of goods; we may *keep* or *restrain* one from folly, crime, or violence; we *keep* from or *refrain* from evil, ourselves. *Keep* in the sense of *guard* or *defend* implies that the defense is effectual. Compare CELEBRATE, OCCUPY, PRESERVE, RESTRAIN, RETAIN. *Antonyms:* see synonyms for ABANDON.
keep·er (kē′pər) *n.* 1 One who or that which keeps; specifically, the overseer of a prison; the guardian of an insane person; the caretaker of a wild animal; any guardian. 2 A device for keeping something in place, as the socket into which a bolt slides. 3 One who observes or obeys: a *keeper* of promises. 4 That which keeps well, without spoiling, as fruit. 5 The armature of a magnet; also, the soft iron bar placed across the poles of a horseshoe magnet to prevent loss of magnetism.
keep·ing (kē′ping) *n.* 1 Custody, charge, or possession. 2 Right relation or proportion;

harmony; congruity: The act was in *keeping* with his mood. **3** Maintenance; support.

keep·sake (kēp'sāk') *n.* Anything kept, or given to be kept, for the sake of the giver; a memento.

kees·hond (kās'hond, kēs'-) *n. pl.* **·hond·en** (-hon'dən) A breed of dog of Arctic or sub-Arctic origin, long popular in Holland, ash-gray in color and having a short, closely knit body, straight legs, wedge-shaped head, thick feathery coat, and curly tail. [< Du. *Kees,* a nickname for *Cornelius* + *hond* a dog; so called from the first breeder]

KEESHOND
(About 20 inches
high at the shoulder)

keeve (kēv) *n.* A large vat. [OE *cȳf*]

Kee·wa·tin (kē·wä'tin) A district of the Northwest Territories, Canada; 228,160 square miles.

kef (kāf) *n.* **1** A condition marked by voluptuous and dreamy repose and the passive enjoyment of languor. **2** Indian hemp, smoked to produce this condition: also spelled *keef, kief.* [< Arabic *kaif* good humor]

kef·ir (kef'ər) *n.* A kind of fermented milk resembling kumiss: used in the Caucasus. Also spelled *kephir.* [< Caucasian]

keg (keg) *n.* A small, strong barrel, usually of 5- to 10-gallon capacity. [< earlier *cag* < ON *kaggi*]

keg·ler (keg'lər) *n. Colloq.* One who bowls; a bowler. [< G *kegel* ninepin]

Keigh·ley (kēth'lē) A municipal borough in western Yorkshire, England.

Kei Islands (kā) An Indonesian island group between Ceram and the Aru Islands; total 555 square miles: also *Kai Islands.*

Kei·jo (kā·jō) The Japanese name for SEOUL.

keir (kir) See KIER.

keist·er (kēs'tər) *n. U.S. Slang* A box, trunk, suitcase, or the like: also spelled *keyster, kiester.* Also **keest'er.** [? < Yiddish < G *kiste* a box]

Kei·tel (kīt'l), **Wilhelm,** 1882–1946, German marshal in World War II.

Keith (kēth), **Sir Arthur,** 1866–1955, English anthropologist.

keit·lo·a (kīt'lō·ə, kāt'-) *n.* A South African two-horned rhinoceros. [< native name]

Ke·ku·lé von Stra·do·nitz (kā'kōō·lā fôn shträ'dō·nits), **Friedrich August,** 1829–96, German chemist.

Ke·lan·tan (kə·län·tän') One of the States of Malaya, in the northern part; 5,746 square miles; capital, Kota Bharu.

Kel·lar (kel'ər), **Harry,** 1849–1922, U.S. magician.

Kel·ler (kel'ər), **Helen Adams,** 1880–1968, U.S. writer and lecturer; blind and deaf from infancy.

Kel·ly (kel'ē), **Howard Atwood,** 1858–1943, U.S. gynecological surgeon.

ke·loid (kē'loid) *n. Pathol.* A fibrous tumor in the connective tissue of the skin, of various shapes and sizes, and usually caused by injury: also spelled *cheloid.* [< Gk. *kēlē* tumor + -OID]

kelp (kelp) *n.* **1** Any large coarse seaweed (family *Laminariaceae*); specifically, the California sea palm (*Postelsia palmaeformis*). **2** The ashes of seaweeds: formerly the source of soda as used in glassmaking and soapmaking, now a source chiefly of iodine. —**giant kelp** A very large, tough, and massive seaweed (*Macrocystis pyrifera*), belonging to the brown algae: it is found mainly on the Pacific coast of the United States, and has been known to reach a length of 700 feet. [ME *culp*; origin uncertain]

kel·pie (kel'pē) *n. Scot.* A malevolent water sprite, supposed to haunt fords in the form of a horse. Also **kel'py.**

kel·son (kel'sən) See KEELSON.

kelt (kelt) *n. Scot.* Undyed cloth of black and white wool mixed.

Kelt (kelt), **Kelt·ic** (kel'tik) See CELT, etc.

kel·ter (kel'tər) *n. Brit. Dial.* Working order; kilter.

Kel·vin scale (kel'vin) *Physics* The absolute scale of temperature, based on the average kinetic energy per molecule of a perfect gas. Zero is equal to −273° Celsius or −459.4° Fahrenheit. [after William Thompson, 1824–1907, Lord *Kelvin,* English physicist]

Ke·mal A·ta·türk (ke·mäl' ä·tä·türk'), 1881–1938, Turkish general; president 1923–38: known as *Mustapha Kemal.*

Kem·ble (kem'bəl), **Frances Anne,** 1809–93, English actress: called "Fanny Kemble." — **John Philip,** 1757–1823, English tragedian; uncle of the preceding.

Kem·pis (kem'pis), **Thomas à,** 1380–1471, German mystic, reputed author of the *Imitation of Christ.*

ken (ken) *v.* **kenned** or **kent, ken·ning** *v.t.* **1** *Scot.* To know; have knowledge of. **2** *Scot. Law* To recognize as heir. **3** *Obs.* To see. — *v.i.* **4** *Scot. & Brit. Dial.* To have understanding. —*n.* Reach of sight or knowledge; cognizance.

Ke·nai Peninsula (kē'nī) An extension of southern Alaska into the Gulf of Alaska; 150 miles long.

kench (kench) *n.* A bin for salting fish or skins. —*v.t. Dial.* To place in a salting bin. [Var. of dial. E *canch* a trench]

Ken·dal (ken'dəl) *n.* A coarse woolen cloth of green color made at Kendal, England; also, the color of this cloth. Also **Kendal green.**

Keng·tung (keng'tŏŏng) The easternmost and largest of the Shan States, Upper Burma; 12,405 square miles; capital, Kengtung.

Ken·il·worth (ken'əl·wûrth) An urban district in central Warwickshire, England; site of the ruins of **Kenilworth Castle** where Leicester entertained Queen Elizabeth I, 1575.

Kenilworth ivy A scrophulariaceous herb (*Cymbalaria muralis*) of delicate growth.

Ké·ni·tra (kā·nē·trá') The former name of Port-Lyautey.

Ken·nan (ken'ən), **George Frost,** born 1904, U.S. diplomat; writer on Russian affairs.

Ken·ne·bec (ken'ə·bek) A river in central Maine, flowing about 150 miles SW to the Atlantic.

Ken·ne·dy (ken'ə·de), **John Fitzgerald,** 1917–1963, 35th president of the United States, 1961–63; assassinated. —**Robert Francis,** 1925–68, U.S. Senator; assassinated.

Kennedy, Cape A cape of eastern Florida, site of a rocket and missile launching installation: formerly *Cape Canaveral.*

ken·nel¹ (ken'əl) *n.* **1** A house for a dog or for a pack of hounds; also, the pack. **2** *pl.* A professional establishment where dogs are bred, raised, boarded, trained, etc. **3** The hole or lair of a fox or like beast. **4** A vile lodging. —*v.* **·neled** or **·nelled, ·nel·ing** or **·nel·ling** *v.t.* To keep or confine in or as in a kennel. —*v.i.* To lodge or take shelter in a kennel. [< F *chenil* < L *canis* a dog; formed on analogy with *ovile* a sheepfold < *ovis* a sheep]

ken·nel² (ken'əl) *n.* The gutter of a street; channel. [Var. of obs. *cannel* a channel]

ken·nel³ (ken'əl) See CANNEL.

Ken·nel·ly (ken'əl·ē), **Arthur Edwin,** 1861–1939, U.S. electrical engineer.

Ken·nel·ly–Heav·i·side layer (ken'əl·ē·hev'ē·sīd) See HEAVISIDE LAYER.

Ken·ne·saw Mountain (ken'ə·sô) A national monument in NW Georgia; scene of a decisive Union victory in the Civil War, 1864.

Ken·neth (ken'əth) A masculine personal name. [< Celtic, handsome]

ken·ning¹ (ken'ing) *n. Scot.* **1** The smallest recognizable portion. **2** Recognition.

ken·ning² (ken'ing) *n.* In early Germanic and Scandinavian literature, a poetical periphrasis used instead of a simple name of a thing, as "oar-steed" for "ship." [< ON *kennungar* symbols]

Ken·ny (ken'ē), **Elizabeth,** 1886–1952, Australian nurse; developed a physiotherapy for poliomyelitis: known as *Sister Kenny.*

ke·no (kē'nō) *n.* A game of chance played by drawing numbers from a container and covering with counters the corresponding numbers on cards. The player who first covers a row of five numbers is the winner. Also called *bingo, lotto.* [< F *quine* five winners]

ken·o·gen·e·sis (ken'ə·jen'ə·sis, kē'nə-) See CENOGENESIS.

Ke·no·sha (kə·nō'shə) A city on Lake Michigan in SE Wisconsin.

ke·no·sis (ki·nō'sis) *n. Theol.* Christ's action in putting aside his divinity during the Incarnation, *Phil.* ii 5–8. [< Gk. *kenōsis* an emptying < *kenoein* empty]

ke·not·ic (ki·not'ik) *adj.* Of or pertaining to the doctrine of kenosis. —*n.* One who believes in the doctrine of kenosis.

ken·o·tron (ken'ə·tron) *n.* A unidirectional, two-electrode thermionic tube, which acts as a rectifier of high-voltage alternating currents. [< Gk. *kenōsis* emptying +(ELEC)TRON]

Ken·sing·ton (ken'zing·tən) A metropolitan borough of western London.

kent¹ (kent) *Scot.* Past tense and past participle of KEN. Also **kend** (kend).

Kent (kent) A county in SE England; 1,525 square miles; county town, Maidstone.

Kent (kent), **James,** 1763–1847, U.S. jurist. — **Rockwell,** 1882–1971, U.S. artist.

Kent·ish (ken'tish) *adj.* Of or pertaining to Kent. —*n.* The Old English and Middle English dialects of Kent.

kent·ledge (kent'lej) *n. Naut.* Permanent pig-iron ballast. [? < QUINTAL + -AGE]

Ken·tuck·y (kən·tuk'ē) A south central State of the United States; 40,395 square miles; capital, Frankfort; entered the Union June 1, 1792: nickname *Bluegrass State.* Abbr. KY —**Ken·tuck'i·an** *adj. & n.*

Kentucky bluegrass A grass (*Poa pratensis*) common in temperate and cold regions: valuable for forage.

Kentucky boat A large flat-bottomed river boat, usually towed or propelled by oars, formerly used for transporting freight. Also **Kentucky ark, Kentucky flat.**

Kentucky coffee tree A tall leguminous tree (*Gymnocladus dioicus*) having seeds, called **Kentucky coffee beans,** often used as a substitute for coffee.

Kentucky Derby A famous American horse race, run at Churchill Downs, Louisville, Ky., since 1875.

Kentucky River A river in Kentucky, flowing 259 miles NW to the Ohio River.

Ken·ya (kēn'yə, ken'-) A republic of the Commonwealth of Nations in eastern Africa; 224,960 square miles; capital, Nairobi: formerly *East African Protectorate.*

Kenya, Mount An extinct volcanic cone in central Kenya, the second highest mountain in Africa; 17,040 feet.

Ken·yat·ta (ken·yä'tə), **Jomo,** 1893?–1978, black African leader; prime minister of Kenya 1963–64; president 1964–78.

Ke·o·kuk (kē'ə·kuk) A city in SE Iowa on the Mississippi.

Ke·os (kē'os) A Greek island in the Cyclades: ancient *Ceos:* medieval *Zea:* also *Kea.*

kep (kep) *v.t. Scot.* To catch; stop.

keph·a·lin (kef'ə·lin) See CEPHALIN.

Ke·phal·le·ni·a (ke'fä·lə·nē'ə) See CEPHALONIA.

keph·ir (kef'ər) See KEFIR.

kep·i (kep'ē) *n.* A flat-topped military cap with vizor. [< F *képi* < dial. G *käppi,* dim. of *kappe* a cap]

Kep·ler (kep'lər), **Johannes,** 1571–1630, German astronomer; formulated **Kepler's laws,** relative to the motions of planets.

kept (kept) Past tense and past participle of KEEP.

ker (kûr) *n.* **1** In Greek religion, a spirit or soul of one dead; sometimes, a malignant spirit. **2** The personification of fate. [< Gk. *Kēr*]

Ker·ak (ker'äk) A town of south central Jordan, near the Dead Sea.

Ke·ra·la (kā'rʊ·lʊ) A constituent State of extreme SW India on the Malabar Coast, consisting of most of the former State of Travencore-Cochin and of the Malabar district and other former sections of Madras State; 15,035 square miles; capital, Trivandrum.

ke·ram·ic (kə·ram'ik), **ke·ram·ics** See CERAMIC, etc.

ker·a·tin (ker'ə·tin) *n. Biochem.* A highly insoluble albuminous compound containing sulfur that forms the essential ingredient of horny tissue, as of horns, claws, nails, etc. — **ke·rat·i·nous** (kə·rat'ə·nəs) *adj.*

ker·a·ti·tis (ker'ə·tī'tis) *n. Pathol.* Inflammation of the cornea.

kerato– *combining form* **1** Horn: *keratogenous.* **2** Cornea of the eye: *keratoplasty.* Also, before vowels, **kerat–.** [< Gk. *keras, keratos* horn]

ker·a·to·con·junc·ti·vi·tis (ker'ə·tō·kən·jungk'tə·vī'tis) *n. Pathol.* Inflammation of the cornea and conjunctiva; shipyard eye.

ker·a·tog·e·nous (ker′ə-toj′ə-nəs) adj. Promoting the growth of horn.

ker·a·toid (ker′ə-toid) adj. Resembling keratin or horn; horny.

Ker·a·tol (ker′ə-tōl, -tol) n. A pyroxylin-coated waterproof cloth resembling leather: a trade name.

ker·a·to·plas·ty (ker′ə-tō-plas′tē) n. Surg. The operation of transplanting corneal tissue; plastic surgery of the cornea. — **ker′a·to·plas′tic** adj.

ker·a·tose (ker′ə-tōs) adj. Pertaining to or characterized by horny tissue, as certain sponges.

kerb (kûrb), **kerb·stone** (-stōn) See CURB, etc.

Kerch (kûrch) A port in the Crimea at the end of **Kerch Peninsula**, an eastern extension of the Crimea on **Kerch Strait** which connects the Sea of Azov with the Black Sea.

ker·chief (kûr′chif) n. A square of linen, silk, or other fabric used to cover the head or neck, or as a handkerchief. [ME keverchef, kerchef <OF couvrechef < covrir cover + chef head] — **ker′chiefed** adj.

Ke·ren·sky (kə-ren′skē, Russian kyer′in-skē), **Alexander Feodorovich,** 1881–1970, Russian revolutionary leader; prime minister, July–Nov. 1917; removed by Bolsheviks.

kerf (kûrf) n. 1 The channel made by a saw, or the width of such a channel. 2 A cut of a cloth-shearing machine. 3 The act or process of cutting. [OE cyrf a cutting]

Ker·gue·len Islands (kûr′gə-lən) An archipelago in the southern Indian Ocean, comprising a dependency of Madagascar; 2,700 square miles; the chief island, **Kerguelen** (1,318 square miles), is also called *Desolation Island*.

Ke·rin·chi (kə-rin′chē), **Mount** A peak of western Sumatra; 12,467 feet: also *Indrapura.*

Ker·kheh (kär′khe) See KARKHEH.

Ker·ky·ra (ker′kē-rä) The Greek name for CORFU.

Ker·mad·ec Islands (kər-mad′ek) An island group NE of New Zealand, comprising a dependency of New Zealand; 13 square miles.

Ker·man (kûr′män, ker′-) 1 A former province of SE Iran: ancient *Carmania.* 2 A city in SE Iran; former capital of Kerman: also *Kirman.*

Ker·man·sha (ker′män-shä′) A city in western Iran. Also **Ker′man·sha·han′** (-hän′).

ker·mes (kûr′mēz) n. The dried bodies of the females of a cochineal-like scale insect (genus Kermes), used as a red dyestuff. [<Arabic qirmiz. Related to CRIMSON.]

kermes oak A small evergreen oak (*Quercus coccifera*) of the Mediterranean region, infested by the kermes insect. Also **ker′mes.**

ker·mess (kûr′mis) n. 1 In Flanders, etc., a periodical outdoor festival. 2 An indoor or outdoor festival imitative of the Flemish. Often spelled *kirmess.* Also **ker′mis.** [<Du. kermis < kerk misse church mass]

kern[1] (kûrn) n. 1 Archaic An Irish irregular, light-armed foot soldier. 2 Archaic A body of such soldiers. 3 A peasant; churl. Also **kerne.** [<Irish ceithern a band of soldiers]

kern[2] (kûrn) n. Printing That part of a type which overhangs the shaft or shank, as of an italic *f.* — v.t. To make (type) with a kern. [<F carne projecting angle]

Kern (kûrn), **Jerome David,** 1885–1945, U.S. composer.

ker·nel (kûr′nəl) n. 1 A grain or seed; the edible part of a nut. 2 A hard concretion of flesh. 3 The central part of anything; nucleus; gist. — v.i. To envelop as a kernel. ◆ Homophone: colonel. [OE cyrnel, dim. of corn a seed]

Kern River (kûrn) A river in southern central California, flowing 155 miles SW from the Sierra Nevada.

ker·o·sene (ker′ə-sēn) n. A mixture of hydrocarbons distilled from crude petroleum and used for burning in lamps: also called *coal oil.* [<Gk. kēros wax + -ENE]

Kerr (kär), **Archibald John,** 1882–1951, Baron Inverchapel, British diplomat.

Ker·ry (ker′ē) A county of SW Munster, Ireland; 1,815 square miles; county town, Tralee.

Ker·ry (ker′ē) n. pl. ·ries One of an Irish breed of cattle raised in County Kerry.

Kerry blue terrier See under TERRIER.

ker·sey (kûr′zē) n. 1 A smooth, lightweight, ribbed woolen cloth. 2 pl. Kinds of kersey; also trousers of kersey. [from *Kersey,* village in England]

ker·sey·mere (kûr′zē-mir) n. Cassimere.

kes·trel (kes′trəl) n. A European falcon (*Falco tinnunculus*), resembling the American sparrow hawk and noted for its hovering habits. [Var. of ME castrel <OF cresserelle]

ketch[1] (kech) n. A fore-and-aft rigged, two-masted vessel: similar to a yawl but having the mizzen- or jiggermast forward of the rudder post. [Earlier cache. Related to CATCH, v.]

ketch[2] (kech) n. A hangman. [after Jack Ketch]

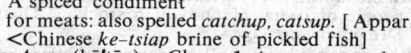

GAFF–RIGGED KETCH

Ketch·i·kan (kech′i-kan) A port of entry in SE Alaska.

ketch·up (kech′əp) n. A spiced condiment for meats: also spelled *catchup, catsup.* [Appar. <Chinese *ke-tsiap* brine of pickled fish]

ke·tene (kē′tēn) n. Chem. 1 A pungent, colorless gas, $H_2C:CO$, obtained by decomposing acetone, ethyl acetate, or acetic anhydride with intense heat. 2 Any of a group of organic compounds of the form $R_2C:CO$. [<KET(ONE) + -ENE]

keto- combining form Chem. Ketone; related to ketone bodies. Also, before vowels, **ket-,** as in ketosis. [<KETONE]

ke·to·e·nol tautomerism (kē′tō-ē′nôl) Chem. Tautomerism in which certain organic compounds may occur in both the keto and enol forms.

ke·tone (kē′tōn) n. Chem. One of a class of reactive organic compounds in which the carbonyl group unites with two hydrocarbon radicals, a single bivalent radical, or derivatives. The simplest member of the class is acetic ketone or acetone. [<G keton <F acétone acetone] — **ke·ton·ic** (ki-ton′ik) adj.

ke·tose (kē′tōs) n. Chem. Any of a class of monosaccharides containing a ketone group.

ke·to·sis (kē-tō′sis) n. Pathol. Excessive formation or secretion of ketones in the body, as in acidosis, diabetes, etc.

Ket·ter·ing (ket′ər-ing), **Charles Franklin,** 1876–1958, U.S. electrical engineer and inventor.

ket·tle (ket′l) n. 1 A metallic vessel for stewing or boiling; a teakettle. 2 A tin pail. 3 A hole in the bottom of a stream or pond where carp lie in winter. 4 A kettle-shaped cavity, as in rock or glacial drift: also **kettle hole.** 5 A kettledrum. [OE cetel]

ket·tle·drum (ket′l-drum′) n. 1 A drum having a brass hemispherical shell and parchment head, and sounded by soft-headed elastic drumsticks. 2 An informal afternoon party.

Keu·ka Lake (kyoo′kə, kə-yoo′-) One of the Finger Lakes in west central New York.

kev·el (kev′əl) n. Naut. A belaying cleat or peg: usually in pairs. [<AF keville a pin, peg <LL clavicula bar of a door, orig. dim. of L clavis a key]

Kew (kyoo) A borough of Richmond and suburb of London, in Surrey, England.

Ke·wee·naw Peninsula (kē′wə-nô) A Michigan headland extending 60 miles NE into Lake Superior to form **Keweenaw Bay.**

Kew·pie (kyoo′pē) n. A chubby, cherubic doll, made of chalkstone or plastic: a trade name.

kex (keks) n. A hollow stalk; a weed. [Origin unknown]

key[1] (kē) n. 1 A detachable instrument for turning the catch or bolt of a lock forwards or backwards in order to lock or unlock. 2 An instrument for holding and turning a screw, nut, valve, or the like, as for winding a clock. 3 Anything serving to disclose, open, or solve something. 4 Something that opens or prepares a way. 5 A gloss, table, or group of notes interpreting certain symbols, ciphers, problems, etc. 6 Any one of the finger levers in typewriters, typesetting machines, etc. 7 Electr. A circuit-breaker or -opener operated by the fingers, as in a telegraph-sending apparatus. 8 Music a In musical instruments, a lever to be pressed by the finger. b A system of tones, according to which a piece of music is written, in which all the notes of a scale bear a definite and recognized relationship to some particular note (the keynote or tonic): the *key* of C. 9 Tone or pitch of the voice. 10 Tone or style of expression. 11 Mech. a A wedge, cotter, bolt, or pin used to secure various parts together. b One of various implements, as a tightening wedge, for fixing a collar to a shaft. 12 Archit. A keystone (def. 1). 13 In building, any special surfacing or surface for holding plaster in place. 14 The roughness on the unfinished face of a veneer giving stronger adherence to the glue. 15 Bot. A key fruit; samara. — v.t. 1 To fasten with or as with a key. 2 To wedge tightly or support firmly with a key, wedge, etc. 3 To complete (an arch) by adding the keystone. 4 To provide with keys. 5 Music To regulate the pitch or tone of. — **to key up** 1 To raise the pitch of. 2 To cause excitement, anticipation, etc., in. — adj. Of chief or decisive importance: a *key* position. ◆ Homophone: quay. [OE cæg]

key[2] (kē) n. A low island, especially one of coral, along a coast: usually *cay* in the Gulf of Mexico and the West Indies: rarely *kay.* ◆ Homophone: quay. [Var. of CAY]

Key (kē), **Francis Scott,** 1780?–1843, American lawyer; wrote *The Star-Spangled Banner.*

key·board (kē′bôrd′, -bōrd′) n. A row of keys as in a piano or typewriter; also, the range or arrangement of the keys, as of an organ, piano, etc.

key bugle A bugle having keys, and a compass of two octaves including semitones.

keyed (kēd) adj. 1 Having keys: said of musical instruments, etc. 2 Brought to a tension, as a musical string. 3 Tuned, as a musical instrument. 4 Secured by a keystone or key.

key fruit Bot. A dry, indehiscent, winged fruit, as that of the ash or elm; a samara.

key·hole (kē′hōl′) n. A hole for a key, as in a door or lock.

Key Lar·go (kē lär′gō) The largest island of the Florida Keys; 28 miles long.

key log The log caught or wedged in a log jam that must be released to break the jam.

key man 1 A person without whose work or direction something could not go on; an indispensable person. 2 A telegraph operator.

Keynes (kānz), **John Maynard,** 1883–1946, English economist.

key·note (kē′nōt′) n. 1 Music The tonic of a key, from which it is named: also **key tone.** 2 A basic idea, fact, principle, or sentiment. — v.t. ·not·ed, ·not·ing 1 To sound the keynote of. 2 To give the essential points of, as a political platform.

key·not·er (kē′nō′tər) n. The person selected to present the basic issues, especially of a political platform.

key–plug (kē′plug′) n. That part of a cylinder lock which receives the key, permitting it to turn when all the tumblers are in the release position. See illustration under LOCK.

Keys (kēz) n. pl. The 24 members of the House of Keys, the elective branch of the legislature of the Isle of Man.

Key·ser·ling (kī′zər-ling), **Count Hermann Alexander,** 1880–1946, German social philosopher and writer.

key signature Music The number of sharps or flats following the clef sign at the beginning of each staff, to indicate in what key the music is to be played.

keyst·er (kēs′tər) See KEISTER.

key·stone (kē′stōn′) n. 1 Archit. The uppermost and last-set stone of an arch, which completes it and locks its members together. 2 The fundamental element, as of a science or doctrine.

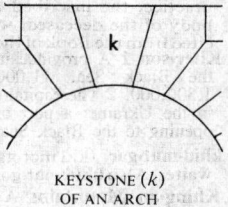

KEYSTONE (k) OF AN ARCH

Keystone State Nickname of PENNSYLVANIA.

key·way (kē′wā′) *n. Mech.* **1** The groove or recess in a shaft or wheel hub for the insertion of key: also called **key bed.** **2** The opening in a cylinder lock to receive the key.

Key West A port on **Key West Island,** westernmost of the Florida Keys.

K.G.B. In the former Soviet Union, a division of the Ministry of State Security. The K.G.B. was created in 1954 for internal and external espionage and policing, renowned for its meticulous and far-reaching methods of information-gathering. There were 17 divisions within the K.G.B., including the border guard, counterintelligence, and the secret police. [*Russian* K(omitet) G(osudarstvennoy) B(ezopasnosti)]

Kha·ba·rovsk 1 A mountainous territory (kray) in southeastern Russia, bordering the Sea of Okhotsk, and the territory of Amur; 965,400 square miles. **2** The capital of the Khabarovsk region; pop. 615,000, on the southwestern edge of the territory, near the disputed border with China.

khad·dar (kud′ər) *n.* Homespun cotton cloth made in India: also **khadi** (kä′dē). [< Hind. *khādar*]

Kha·kas·sia A republic within Russia, in the south central region of Siberia; capital, Abakan; 24,000 square miles, pop. 600,000. Formerly **the Khakass Autonomous Region** of the Soviet Union.

khak·i (kak′ē, kä′kē) *adj.* Of the color of dust; having a neutral tannish-brown or olive-drab color. —*n.* A light olive-drab or brownish cotton cloth. [< Hind. *khākī* dusty]

kha·lif (kā′lif, kal′if) See CALIPH.

Kha·lil (khä·lēl′), **El** The Arabic name for HEBRON.

Khal·kis (khäl·kēs′) The Greek name for CHALCIS.

kham·sin (kam′sin, kam·sēn′) *n. Meteorol.* A hot wind from the Sahara that prevails in Egypt before the vernal equinox; simoom. Also **kam·sean′**: sometimes spelled *kamsin.* [< Arabic *khamsīn* < *khamsūn* fifty; so called because it occurs for a period of 50 days]

khan[1] (kän, kan) *n.* An Oriental inn surrounding a courtyard. [< Arabic *khān* an inn]

khan[2] (kän, kan) *n.* In various Oriental countries, a ruler, chief, etc.; now a title of respect for any dignitary. See CHAM. [< Persian *khān* prince]

khan·ate (kän′āt, kan′-) *n.* The jurisdiction of a khan; a principality.

Kha·nia (khä·nyä′) The Greek name for CANEA.

khan·jar (khän′jär) See CANJIAR.

Khan·ka, Lake A lake on the China-Russian border, 1,700 square miles; in the territory (okrug) of Primor′ye. The country borders bisect the lake.

Khan·ty-Man·si An autonomous region (okrug) in Russia; capital, Khanty-Mansiysk; 200,000 square miles; pop. 1,300,000.

Khar·kiv 1 An eastern province in the Ukraine; 12,100 square miles, pop. 3,200,000. **2** The capital of the province of Kharkiv, pop. 1,700,000.

Khar·toum (kär·to͞om′) A city near the confluence of the Blue Nile with the White Nile; capital of Sudan. Also **Khar·tum′.**

Kha·si (kä′sē) **and Jain·ti·a** (jīn′tē·ə) **Hills** An autonomous district of western Assam, India; 6,141 square miles; capital, Shillong.

Kha·tan·ga Gulf A gulf on the western coast of the Laptev Sea, north of Siberia, Russia.

Khay·yám (kī·äm′), **Omar** See OMAR KHAYYAM.

khed·ah (ked′ə) See KEDDAH.

khe·dive (kə·dēv′) *n.* The title of the Turkish viceroy of Egypt from 1867 to 1914. [< Persian *khidīv* king]

Khe·lat (kə·lät′) See KALAT.

khen·em stone (ken′əm) In ancient Egyptian practice, the inscribed amulet placed on the body of the deceased, while passages were recited from the Book of the Dead.

Kher·son 1 A province in the Ukraine bordering the Black Sea, 11,000 square miles; pop. 1,300,000. **2** The capital of the Kherson province in the Ukraine; a port on the Dnieper near the opening to the Black Sea.

khid·mut·gar (kid′mət·gär) *n. Hindi* A male waiter. Also **khid′mat·gar.**

Khing·an Mountains A range of mountains in northeastern China, bordering Mongolia and China. The range is divided into the **Great Khingan Mountains** to the west and the **Little Khingan Mountains** to the east.

Khi·u·ma The former name of the island province of Hiiumaa, Estonia; 14 miles from the mainland in the Baltic Sea; 395 square miles; pop. 11,500.

Khi·va A city in Uzbekistan; former capital of an independent khanate.

Khmer *n.* **1** One of the ethnic groups of Cambodia, accounting for 95 percent of the population of the country. The other ethnic groups in Cambodia are the Chinese, Cham, and other Asian nationalities. **2** The traditional language of the Khmer population and the official language of Cambodia.

Khmer Republic The former name of Cambodia (1970–1975) a republic in SW Indochina; 53,668 square miles; capital, Phnom Penh; Also **the State of Kampuchia.**

Khnum (khno͞om) The ram-headed god associated with ancient Elephantine in Egypt; in early Egypt, the ram and other animals were considered as actual gods associated with particular cities.

Khoi·san (koi′sän) *n.* A family of languages spoken by Negroid tribes in SW Africa, including Bushman and Hottentot.

Kholm (khôlm) The Russian name for CHELM.

Khond (kond) *n.* **1** A member of an aboriginal hill people of India, of Dravidian stock. **2** Their Dravidian language.

Kho·ra·san (khō′rä·sän′) A province of NE Iran. Also **Khu′ra·san′**(kho͞o′-).

Khor·ram·shahr (kho͞or′räm·shär′) A port on the Shatt al Arab in SW Iran.

Kho·tan (kō′tän′) A town and oasis in SW Sinkiang province, China: Chinese *Hotien.*

Khrush·chev (khro͞osh′chef), **Nikita,** 1894–1971, U.S.S.R. official; first secretary of the Communist Party 1953–1964; chairman of the Council of Ministers (premier) 1958–1964.

Khu·fu (ko͞o′fo͞o) See CHEOPS.

Khu·zi·stan (kho͞o′zē·stän′) A province of SW Iran, corresponding to ancient Elam: formerly *Arabistan.*

Khy·ber Pass (kī′bər) A mountain pass on the India-Pakistan border; over 30 miles long: also *Khaiber Pass.*

Kia·mu·sze A city in the province of Manchuria, China; also **Chiamussu.**

Ki·an (kē·än′) A city in western Kiansi province, China.

Kiang·ling (jyäng′ling′) A city on the Yangtze in southern Hupeh province, China: formerly *Kingchow.*

Kiang·si (jyäng′shē′) A province in SE China; 65,000 square miles; capital, Nanchang.

Kiang·su (jyäng′sō′) A province in eastern China; 35,000 square miles; since 1949 divided administratively into **North Kiangsu**; 24,000 square miles; capital, Yangchow; and **South Kiangsu;** 11,000 square miles; capital, Wusih.

Kiao·chow (jyou′chou′) A former German leased territory on the SE coast of Shantung, China; 400 square miles.

kiaugh (kyäkh) *n. Scot.* Trouble; toil; worry.

Kia·yi (jyä′yē′) See CHIAYI.

kib·blings (kib′lingz) *n. pl.* Small bits or strips cut from fish, used as bait by Newfoundland fishermen. [Cf. dial. E *kibble* grind coarsely]

kib·butz (ki·bo͞ots) *n. pl.* **·butz·im** (**·**bo͞o tsēm′) An Israeli collective or communal settlement, esp. a cooperative farm.

kibe (kīb) *n.* **1** A chap or crack in the flesh; an ulcerated chilblain. **2** A sore on the hoof of a sheep. [Cf. Welsh *cibi* a chilblain]

Ki·bei (kē′bā′) *n. pl.* **·bei** A citizen or citizens of the United States of Japanese parentage, born in America but educated in Japan. Compare ISSEI, NISEI. [< Japanese]

kib·itz (kib′its) *v.i. Colloq.* To act as a kibitzer. [Back formation < KIBITZER]

kib·itz·er (kib′it·sər) *n. Colloq.* One who meddles with other persons' affairs; specifically, a person who, although not a player, makes suggestions and gives gratuitous advice to card-players. [< Yiddish]

kib·lah (kib′lä) *n.* The direction toward which Moslems kneel and bow in prayer indicated by a niche on the wall in each mosque in Islam. See KAABA. [Arabic *qiblah* something placed opposite < *qabala* be opposite]

ki·bosh (kī′bosh) *n. Slang* Nonsense or humbug. —**to put the kibosh on** To put a stop to; do for. [Prob. < Yiddish]

kick (kik) *v.i.* **1** To strike out with the foot or feet; give a blow with the foot, as in swimming, propelling the ball in football, etc. **2** To strike out with the foot habitually: This horse *kicks.* **3** To recoil, as a firearm. **4** *Colloq.* To object; complain. —*v.t.* **5** To strike with the foot. **6** To drive or impel by striking with the foot. **7** To strike in recoiling. **8** In football, to score (a goal) by a kick. —**to kick about** (or **around**) **1** To abuse; neglect. **2** *Colloq.* To roam from place to place. **3** To be neglected; go unnoticed. **4** *Colloq.* To give thought or consideration to; discuss. —**to kick back 1** To recoil violently or unexpectedly, as a gun. **2** *Colloq.* To pay (part of a commission, salary, etc.) to someone in a position to grant privilege, power, etc., usually as a bribe. —**to kick in 1** *Colloq.* To contribute or participate by contributing. **2** *Slang* To die. —**to kick off 1** In football, to put the ball in play by kicking it toward the opposing team. **2** *Slang* To die. —**to kick oneself** To have remorse or regret. —**to kick out** *Colloq.* To exclude or eject violently or suddenly, as with a kick. —**to kick the bucket** *Slang* To die. —**to kick up** *Slang* To make or stir up (trouble, confusion, etc.). —**to kick upstairs** To give an apparent promotion to (someone) in order to remove from a position of actual power. —*n.* **1** A blow with the foot; also, ability or power to kick. **2** The recoil of a firearm. **3** In football, one who kicks; also, a turn at kicking. **4** *Slang* An act of violent opposition or objection. **5** Something that stimulates or excites, as the alcoholic content of drink. **6** Effective action or power; energy; vim; pep. **7** *Slang* Stimulation; pleasure; thrill. **8** The depression in the bottom of a molded bottle. **9** *Slang* A pocket. —**on a kick** *Slang* Intensely but temporarily interested in a particular subject or activity; He's on a silent-movie *kick.* [ME *kike;* origin unknown]

Kick·a·poo (kik′ə·po͞o) *n.* One of a tribe of Algonquian Indians, formerly of northern Illinois: now on reservations in Kansas, Oklahoma, and Mexico.

kick·back (kik′bak′) *n.* **1** A recoil; repercussion; any reaction to something said or done. **2** Money comprising part of a commission, fee, etc., returned by prior agreement or coercion, often illegal or unethical.

kick·er (kik′ər) *n.* **1** One who or that which kicks. **2** *Slang* A surprising element or turn of events.

kick-off (kik′ôf′, -of′) *n.* **1** In football, the kick with which a game or half is begun. **2** Any beginning.

kick plate A metal plate affixed to the bottom portion of a door to protect its surface. Also **kicking plate.**

kick·shaw (kik′shô) *n.* **1** Something fantastic or trifling; a nameless trifle. **2** Any unsubstantial, fancy, or unrecognizable dish of food. Also **kick′shaws.** [Alter. of F *quelque chose* something]

kick·y (kik′ē) *adj.* **kick·i·er, kick·i·est** *Slang* Stimulating; exciting.

kid[1] (kid) *n.* **1** A young goat. **2** Leather, or, in the plural, gloves or shoes made from goatskin. **3** The meat of a young goat. **4** *Colloq.* A child or infant; youngster. **5** Formerly, a white servant in the American colonies indentured for four or five years. —*adj.* **1** Made of kidskin. **2** *Colloq.* Younger: my *kid* brother. —*v.t. & v.i.* **kid·ded, kid·ding 1** To give birth to (young): said of goats. **2** *Slang* To make fun of (someone); tease jokingly. **3** *Slang* To deceive or try to deceive (someone); humbug. [< ON *kidh*] —**kid′der** *n.*

kid[2] (kid) *n.* **1** A small tub for sailors' rations. **2** On fishing vessels, a small wooden tub to hold fish when caught. [? Var. of KIT[1]]

Kidd (kid), **William,** 1650?–1701, British sea captain and pirate; hanged: called "Captain Kidd."

Kid·der·min·ster (kid′ər·min′stər) *n.* A two-ply ingrain carpet, showing warp and filling on each side. [from *Kidderminster,* England, where first made]

kid·dy (kid′ē) *n. pl.* **kid·dies** *Slang* A small child.

kid glove A glove made of kidskin or similar material. —**with kid gloves** In a tactful or gingerly manner.

kid-glove (kid′gluv′) *adj.* **1** Wearing or requiring kid gloves; hence, socially formal. **2** Over-nice; too fastidious to use the hands for work.

kid·nap (kid′nap) *v.t.* **·naped** or **·napped, ·nap·ing** or **·nap·ping 1** To seize and carry off (someone) by force or fraud, usually so as to

demand a ransom. **2** To steal (a child). [<KID[1] (def. 4) + *nap*, dial. var. of NAB] —**kid′·nap′· er, kid′nap·per** *n.*

kid·ney (kid′nē) *n.* **1** *Biol.* One of a pair of bean-shaped glandular organs situated at the back of the abdominal cavity, close to the spinal column in man and other vertebrates. The kidneys serve in the excretion of waste products through a fine network of tubules to the ureters and thence to the bladder. ◆ Collateral adjective: *renal.* **2** Temperament. [Origin uncertain]

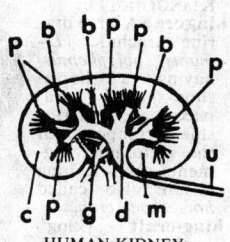

HUMAN KIDNEY
Longitudinal Section
p. Pyramids.   *u.* Ureter.
g. Papillae.   *d.* Pelvis.
c. Cortical portion.
b. Bertin's columns.

kidney bean 1 The kidney-shaped seed of a plant of the bean family (*Phaseolus vulgaris*); French bean; haricot. **2** The plant itself. **3** The scarlet runner.

kidney ore A variety of hematite found in compact, kidney-shaped masses.

kidney stone 1 Nephrite. **2** A hard mineral formed in the kidney or bladder.

kidney vetch A European herb (*Anthyllis vulneraria*) having cloverlike flower heads, commonly yellow: once reputed useful in kidney troubles and for stanching wounds.

Ki·dron (kē′drən, kid′rən) See KEDRON.

kid·skin (kid′skin) *n.* **1** Leather tanned from the skin of a young goat, used for gloves, shoes, etc. **2** The fur, used for coats.

kief (kēf) See KEF.

Kiel (kēl) A port in NW Germany, capital of Schleswig-Holstein, on the **Kiel Canal**, extending 61 miles from the Baltic Sea to the North Sea.

Kiel·ce (kyel′tse) A city in SE central Poland. *Russian* **Kel·tsy** (kel′tsi).

Kien (jyen) The chief river of Kweichow province, China, flowing 700 miles east to the Yangtze.

kier (kir) *n.* A cylindrical tank or vat in which fabric materials are boiled, cleaned, and bleached: also spelled *keir.* [Prob. <ON *ker* tub]

Kier·ke·gaard (kir′kə·gôr), **Sören Aabye**, 1813–55, Danish philosopher and theologian.

kie·sel·guhr (kē′zəl·gŏŏr) *n.* A fine, variously colored earth, derived from the accumulated deposits of the cell walls of diatoms, used as an absorbent for dynamite, as a polishing powder, etc.; diatomite. [<G *kiesel* flint + *guhr* sediment]

kie·ser·ite (kē′zər·īt) *n.* A white, friable, slightly soluble hydrous magnesium sulfate, $MgSO_4 \cdot H_2O$. [after D. G. *Kieser*, German mineralogist]

kiest·er (kēs′tər) See KEISTER.

Ki·ev (kē·ev′, kē′yev; *Russian* kē′yef) A city on the Dnieper; of the Ukraine, historical capital of the princes of Kiev.

kike (kīk) *n. Slang* A Jew: a vulgar and offensive term of contempt. [Origin uncertain]

Ki·ku·yu (ki·kōō′yōō) *n. pl.* **·yu 1** One of a Bantu tribe of British East Africa in the area of Mount Kenya. **2** The Bantu language of this tribe.

Ki·lau·e·a (kē′lou·ā′ə) An active crater on Mauna Loa volcano, Hawaii Island.

Kil·dare (kil·dâr′) A county in central Leinster province, eastern Ireland; 654 square miles; county town, Kildare.

kil·der·kin (kil′dər·kin) *n.* **1** A cask with the capacity of half a barrel. **2** An old English measure of 18 gallons. [<MDu. *kinderkin* little child]

ki·lim (ki·lēm′) *n.* A tapestry-woven type of rug or spread made in the Caucasus, Turkey, and other parts of the Near East. [<Turkish *kilīm* <Persian]

Ki·li·man·ja·ro (kil′i·män·jä′rō) The highest mountain of Africa, in NE Tanganyika; 19,565 feet.

Kil·ken·ny (kil·ken′ē) A county of southern Leinster province, Ireland; 796 square miles; county town, Kilkenny.

Kilkenny cats In Irish legend, two cats said to

have fought till only their tails remained: supposed to refer to a contest between Kilkenny and Irishtown.

kill[1] (kil) *v.t.* **1** To deprive of life; cause the death of; slay. **2** To slaughter for food; butcher. **3** To destroy; put an end to: to *kill* love with hatred. **4** To destroy the active qualities of; neutralize: to *kill* lye. **5** To spoil the effect of; offset, as a color. **6** To cancel; cross out: to *kill* a paragraph. **7** To stop, as an engine or electric current. **8** To pass (time) aimlessly. **9** *Colloq.* To overwhelm with strong emotion, laughter, etc. **10** In tennis, to strike (the ball) to the opponent's court with such force that it cannot be returned. —*v.i.* **11** To slay or murder. **12** To suffer or undergo death; die: These plants *kill* easily. —*n.* **1** An animal killed as prey. **2** The act of killing, especially in hunting. —**in at the kill** Present at the climax of a chase or other undertaking. [ME *cullen, killen;* origin uncertain]

Synonyms (verb) : assassinate, butcher, destroy, dispatch, execute, massacre, murder, slaughter, slay. To *kill* is simply to *destroy* life, whether human, animal, or vegetable, with no suggestion of how or why. *Assassinate, execute, murder,* apply only to the taking of human life; to *murder* is to *kill* with premeditation and malicious intent; to *execute* is to *kill* in fulfilment of a legal sentence; to *assassinate* is to *kill* by assault; this word is chiefly applied to the *killing* of public or eminent persons through political motives, whether secretly or openly. To *slay* is to *kill* by a blow, or by a weapon. *Butcher* and *slaughter* apply primarily to the *killing* of cattle; to *butcher* when the *killing* is especially brutal; soldiers mown down in a hopeless charge are said to be *slaughtered* when no brutality on the enemy's part is implied. To *dispatch* is to *kill* swiftly and in general quietly, always with intention, with or without right.

kill[2] (kil) *n.* A creek, stream, or channel: an element in many U.S. geographical names: *Schuylkill.* [<Du. *kil*]

Kil·lar·ney (ki·lär′nē) An urban district of central County Kerry in SW Ireland near the three **Lakes of Killarney.**

kill·deer (kil′dir) *n. pl.* **·deers** or **·deer** A North American ring plover (*Oxyechus vociferus*), common in the Mississippi Valley. Also **kill′dee** (-dē). [Imit.; from its cry]

kill·er (kil′ər) *n.* **1** A destroyer of life; a slayer. **2** A murderer or an assassin. **3** A delphinoid cetacean of the genus *Orcinus* ; the **killer whale** of northern seas, especially *Orcinus orca* of the North Atlantic.

Kil·lie·cran·kie (kil′ē·krang′kē) A pass in the Grampians, Scotland; scene of Scottish victory over British forces, 1689.

kil·li·fish (kil′i·fish) *n. pl.* **·fish** or **·fish·es** One of a family (*Cyprinodontidae*) of widely distributed small fishes (*Fundulus* and related genera), found in fresh or brackish waters. [Appar. KILL[2] + FISH]

kil·li·ki·nick (kil′ē·ki·nik′) See KINNIKINIC.

kill·ing (kil′ing) *n.* **1** The act of taking life; murder. **2** *Colloq.* A phenomenal profit resulting from bold speculation; a financial coup. **3** Any great success. —*adj.* **1** Slaying; that kills. **2** *Slang* Very amusing.

kill·kid (kil′kid′) *n.* Lambkill.

kill·joy (kil′joi) *n.* One who spoils pleasure; a gloomy person.

kil·lock (kil′ək) *n. Naut.* A small anchor; specifically, a heavy stone in a wooden frame used as an anchor by small boats. Also **kil′lick.** [Origin unknown]

Kil·mar·nock (kil·mär′nək) A burgh in northern Ayrshire, Scotland.

Kil·mer (kil′mər), **Joyce,** 1886–1918, U.S. poet and editor; killed in World War I.

kiln (kil, kiln) *n.* An oven or furnace for baking, burning, or drying industrial products, as for burning bricks. [OE *cylne* <L *culina* kitchen]

kiln-dry (kil′drī′, kiln′-) *v.t.* **·dried, ·dry·ing** To dry in a kiln.

kil·o (kil′ō, kē′lō) *n. pl.* **kil·os** Kilogram: an abbreviated form.

kilo- *prefix* One thousand (times a given unit): used chiefly in the metric system of weights

and measures: *kilogram, kilocalorie.* [<F <Gk. *chilioi* a thousand]

kil·o·cal·o·rie (kil′ə·kal′ə·rē) *n.* A great calorie: equal to one thousand calories.

kil·o·gram (kil′ə·gram) *n.* A measure of weight equal to 1,000 grams. See METRIC SYSTEM. Also **kil′o·gramme.**

kil·o·gram-me·ter (kil′ə·gram·mē′tər) *n.* A unit of work, the equivalent of the force expended in raising one kilogram one meter vertically: about 7.2 foot-pounds. Also **kil′o·gram-me′· tre.**

kil·o·hertz (kil′ə·hûrts) *n.* The unit of electrical frequency equal to one thousand cycles per second: formerly called *kilocycle.*

kil·o·li·ter (kil′ə·lē′tər) *n.* A measure of capacity equal to 1,000 liters. See METRIC SYSTEM. Also **kil′o·li′tre.**

kil·o·me·ter (kil′ə·mē′tər, ki·lom′ə·tar) *n.* A measure of length equal to 1,000 meters. See METRIC SYSTEM. Also **kil′o·me′tre.**

kil·o·met·ric (kil′ə·met′rik) *adj.* Of, pertaining to, or expressed in terms of kilometers. Also **kil′o·met′ri·cal.**

kil·o·ton (kil′ə·tun) *n.* **1** A weight of 1,000 tons. **2** A unit equivalent to the explosive power of 1,000 tons of TNT; used in expressing the energy of atomic and thermonuclear weapons.

kil·o·watt (kil′ə·wät) *n.* One thousand watts: a unit of electrical power.

kil·o·watt-hour (kil′ə·wät·our′) *n.* The work done or the energy resulting from one kilowatt acting for one hour: equal to approximately 1.34 horsepower-hours.

Kil·pat·rick (kil·pat′rik), **Hugh Judson**, 1836–1881, U.S. general.

kilt (kilt) *n.* A short pleated skirt worn by Scottish Highland men. —*v.* **1** To make broad, vertical pleats in; pleat. **2** *Scot.* To tuck up, as the skirts of a dress. [Prob. <Scand. Cf. Dan. *kilte* tuck up.] —**kilt′ing** *n.*

KILT
a. Tartan. *b.* Kilt.
c. Sporran.

kilt·ed (kil′tid) *adj.* **1** Attired in a kilt. **2** Made with pleats, as a dress. **3** Tucked up, as a skirt.

kil·ter (kil′tər) *n.* U.S. Dial. Proper or working order: My radio is out of *kilter.* Also, *Brit. Dial.,* **kelter.**

kilt·ie (kil′tē) *n. Scot.* **1** One wearing a kilt. **2** A Highland soldier. Also **kilt′y.**

kilt·ing (kil′ting) *n.* A series of flat pleats, each of which partly overlaps the preceding one.

Ki·lung (kē′lŏŏng′) See KEELUNG.

Kim·ber·ley (kim′bər·lē) Capital city in Northern Cape Province, Republic of South Africa.

kim·ber·lite (kim′bər·līt) *n.* A biotite-bearing, commonly porphyritic, variety of peridotite. The residual clay resulting from its decomposition is the diamond-bearing "blue ground" of Kimberley.

kim·mer (kim′ər) *n. Scot.* **1** A gossip. **2** A young girl.

ki·mo·no (kə·mō′nə, ki·mō′nō) *n. pl.* **·nos** A Japanese loose robe fastened with a sash: imitated as an Occidental woman's negligée. [<Japanese]

kin (kin) *n.* **1** Relationship; consanguinity. **2** Collectively, relatives by blood. **3** *Obs.* A group of persons having a common ancestor; clan; tribe. —*adj.* Of the same blood or ancestry; hence, related; kindred. [OE *cyn.* Akin to KIND[2].]

Synonyms (noun): affinity, alliance, birth, blood, consanguinity, descent, family, kind, kindred, race, relationship. *Kind* is broader than *kin,* denoting the most general *relationship,* as the whole human species in *mankind, humankind,* etc; *kin* denotes direct *relationship* that can be traced through either blood or marriage, preferably the former: either of these words may signify collectively all persons of the same blood or members of the same family, relatives, or relations. *Affinity* denotes *relationship* by marriage, *consanguinity* denotes *relationship* by blood. There are no true antonyms of *kin* or *kindred,* except those by negatives, since strangers, aliens, foreigners, and foes may still be *kin* or *kindred.* See KINDRED.

-kin *suffix* Little; small: *lambkin.* [<MDu. *-kijn, -ken*]
Kin·a·ba·lu (kin′ə·bə·lōō′) The highest mountain in Borneo, in British North Borneo; 13,455 feet.
kin·aes·the·sia (kin′is·thē′zhə, -zhē·ə), **kin·aes·the·sis** (kin′is·thē′sis) See KINESTHESIA, etc.
kin·ase (kin′ās, kī′nās) *n. Biochem.* A ferment capable of activating another ferment, as zymogen. [<KIN(ETIC) + -ASE]
Kin·caid (kin·kād′) An archeological site in southern Illinois where ceremonial temple mounds are found, thought to date from 1300 to 1700 B.C.
Kin·car·dine (kin·kär′din) A county in eastern Scotland on the North Sea; 383 square miles; county town, Stonehaven: also *The Mearus.* Also **Kin·car′dine·shire** (-shir).
Kin·chin·jun·ga (kin′chin·jung′gə) A former name for KANCHENJUNGA.
Kin·chow (kin′chou′, *Chinese* jin′jō′) See CHINCHOW.
kind[1] (kīnd) *adj.* **1** Having gentleness, tenderness, or goodness of heart; humane; kindly; also, proceeding from or expressing goodheartedness: *kind* words. **2** Gentle or tractable, as an animal. **3** *Archaic* Affectionate; loving. **4** *Obs.* Characteristic; native. See synonyms under AMIABLE, AMICABLE, CHARITABLE, FRIENDLY, GOOD, HUMANE, PLEASANT, PROPITIOUS. [OE *gecynde*]
kind[2] (kīnd) *n.* **1** Essential or distinguishing quality; sort. **2** A number of persons or things of the same character; a class. **3** A modification or variety of a given sort of thing; a species. **4** *Obs.* Nature in general, or natural disposition. See synonyms under AFFINITY, KIN, SORT. **—in kind 1** With something of the same sort: to repay a blow *in kind.* **2** Specifically, in produce instead of money: to pay taxes *in kind.* **—of a kind 1** Of the same sort or variety. **2** Of imperfect quality; of sorts; poetry *of a kind.* [OE *cynd.* Akin to KIN.]
kin·der·gar·ten (kin′dər·gär′tən) *n.* A school for little children in which instructive diversions, object lessons, and healthful games are prominent features. [<G <*kinder* children + *garten* garden]
kin·der·gart·ner (kin′dər·gärt′nər) *n.* A kindergarten teacher or pupil. Also **kin′der·gar′·ten·er** (-gär′tən·ər)· [<G]
kin·der·spiel (kin′dər·shpēl′) *n. German* A dramatic piece or entertainment performed by children.
kind–heart·ed (kīnd′här′tid) *adj.* Having a kind and sympathetic nature. **—kind′–heart′·ed·ly** *adv.* **—kind′–heart′ed·ness** *n.*
kin·dle[1] (kin′dəl) *v.* **·dled, ·dling** *v.t.* **1** To cause (a flame, fire, etc.) to burn; light. **2** To set fire to; ignite. **3** To excite or inflame, as the feelings or passions. **4** To make bright or glowing as if with flame. **—***v.i.* **5** To take fire; start burning. **6** To become excited or inflamed. **7** To become bright or glowing. See synonyms under BURN[1]. [ON *kynda*]
kin·dle[2] (kin′dəl) *v.t.* & *v.i.* **·dled, ·dling** To give birth to (young). **—***n. Dial.* Progeny. [ME *kindlen.* Akin to KIND[2].]
kin·dler (kind′lər) *n.* **1** One who or that which kindles, illumines, or animates. **2** A piece of light wood or artificial composition used in kindling fires.
kind·less (kīnd′lis) *adj.* **1** *Poetic* Heartless; unkind. **2** *Obs.* Unnatural. **—kind′less·ly** *adv.*
kin·dling (kind′ling) *n.* **1** Material with which a fire is started or kindled. **2** The act of starting a fire or causing to burn. **3** The act of arousing emotion, ambition, etc.
kind·ly (kīnd′lē) *adj.* **·li·er, ·li·est 1** Having or manifesting kindness; sympathetic. **2** Having a favorable or grateful effect; beneficial. **3** *Obs.* Proper to its kind; natural; native; akin. **—***adv.* **1** In a kind manner or spirit; good-naturedly. **2** *Obs.* By nature; naturally. See synonyms under FRIENDLY, PLEASANT, PROPITIOUS. **—kind′li·ness** *n.*
kind·ness (kīnd′nis) *n.* **1** The quality of being kind; good will; kindly disposition. **2** A kind act; a favor. **3** A kindly feeling. See synonyms under BENEVOLENCE, MERCY.
kind of Somewhat.
kin·dred (kin′drid) *adj.* **1** Of the same family; related by blood; akin. **2** Of a like nature or character; congenial. **—***n.* **1** Relationship; consanguinity. **2** Collectively: relatives by blood; kind. **3** Affinity. [Earlier *kynred* <OE *cyn* family + *-ræden* state]
Synonyms (noun): kin, kinfolk, kinsmen, relations, relatives. *Kin* and *kindred* are used to denote both relationship and the persons related. See AFFINITY, KIN. Compare FAMILY.
kine (kīn) *n. Archaic* Cattle: plural of COW[1].
kin·e·mat·ics (kin′ə·mat′iks) *n. pl. (construed as singular)* That branch of mechanics treating of the motion of bodies in the abstract and without reference to the action of forces. [<Gk. *kinēma, -atos* movement < *kineein* move] **—kin′e·mat′ic** or **·i·cal** *adj.* **—kin′e·mat′i·cal·ly** *adv.*
kin·e·mat·o·graph (kin′ə·mat′ə·graf, -gräf) See CINEMATOGRAPH.
kin·e·phan·tom (kin′ə·fan′təm) *n.* The illusion of reversed motion in a fast-moving object, as the spokes of a wheel in a motion picture. [<KINE(MATOGRAPH) + PHANTOM]
kin·e·scope (kin′ə·skōp) *n.* **1** A vacuum tube attached to a prepared screen against which a beam of electrons reproduces the images sent out from a television transmitter. **2** A filmed record of a television program made with such a device: also **kin·e** (kin′ē). [<KINE(MATOGRAPH) + -SCOPE]
ki·ne·si·at·rics (ki·nē′sē·at′riks) *n.* The treatment of disease by muscular movement or exercise. [<Gk. *kinēsis* motion + -IATRICS]
ki·ne·sim·e·ter (ki·nə·sim′ə·tər) *n.* An instrument for measuring the motion of a part. Also **ki·ne·si·om·e·ter** (ki·nē′sē·om′ə·tər).
ki·ne·si·ther·a·py (ki·nē′si·ther′ə·pē) *n. Med.* A mode of treating disease by muscular movements. [<Gk. *kinēsis* motion + THERAPY]
kin·es·the·si·a (kin′is·thē′zhə, -zhē·ə) *n. Psychol.* The perception or consciousness of one's own muscular movements: often spelled *kinaesthesia.* Also **kin′es·the′sis** (-thē′sis). [<NL <Gk. *kineein* move + *aisthēsis* perception] **—kin′es·thet′ic** (-thet′ik) *adj.*
ki·net·ic (ki·net′ik) *adj.* **1** Producing motion; motor. **2** Consisting in or depending upon motion; active: distinguished from *potential*: *kinetic* energy. [<Gk. *kinētikos* < *kineein* move]
kinetic lead *Mil.* In gunnery, the correction made for the relative motion of a target when the lead angle is computed.
ki·net·ics (ki·net′iks) *n. pl. (construed as singular)* That branch of dynamics treating of the production or modification of motion in bodies.
kinetic theory *Physics* Any theory of the constitution of bodies which explains their properties by the motion of their particles, especially that according to which the elasticity of gases is due to the rapid motion of their molecules, which dart about in straight lines with an average velocity that increases with the temperature, until deflected by encounters with one another or with the walls of the containing vessel. This theory has been found capable of explaining nearly all the phenomena of gases, and is now generally accepted.
kin·folk (kin′fōk′) *n. pl.* Relatives collectively; kin. Also **kin′folks:** also *kinsfolk, kinspeople.* See synonyms under KINDRED.
king (king) *n.* **1** The sovereign male ruler of a kingdom. ◆ Collateral adjective: *regal.* **2** One who or that which is preeminent among others of the same kind or class; a leader; chief; head. **3** A person or thing of great importance, position, or power: a *king* of finance. **4** A playing card bearing the semblance of a king. **5** In chess, the principal piece; in checkers, a piece that has reached the adversary's king row, and may then be moved in any direction. [OE *cyng*]
King (king), **Charles Glen,** 1878–1956, U.S. chemist. **—Ernest Joseph,** 1878–1956, U.S. admiral; Chief of Naval Operations in World War II. **—Martin Luther, Jr.,** 1929–1968, U.S. leader of nonviolent civil rights movement for Negroes; winner of Nobel peace prize in 1964; assassinated. **—Rufus,** 1775–1827, U.S. statesman and diplomat. **—William Lyon Mackenzie,** 1874–1950, Canadian premier, 1921–26, 1926–1930, 1935–48.
king apple A kind of winter apple.
King Arthur See ARTHUR.
king·bird (king′bûrd′) *n.* An American tyrant flycatcher (genus *Tyrannus*).
king·bolt (king′bōlt′) *n.* A vertical central bolt attaching the body of a vehicle to the fore axle and serving as a pivot in turning.
King Charles spaniel See under SPANIEL.
King·chow (king′jō′) A former name for KIANGLING.
king crab A large marine arachnid *(Limulus polyphemus)* having a horseshoe-shaped carapace, a posterior shield composed of the abdominal segments, and a long telson: also called *horseshoe crab.*

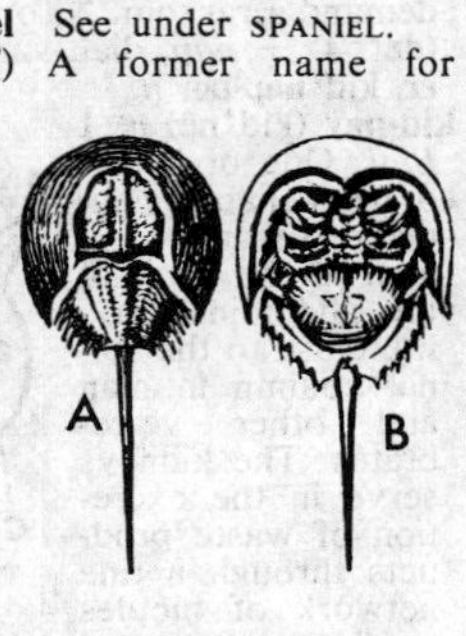

KING CRAB
A. Shell, or carapace, seen from above.
B. Under side, showing legs and telson.

king·craft (king′·kraft′, -kräft′) *n.* The craft or calling of kings; kingly statesmanship.
king·cup (king′kup′) *n.* **1** Any of several buttercups, especially the bulbous buttercup *(Ranunculus bulbosus)* and the creeping buttercup *(R. repens).* **2** The common marsh marigold.
king·dom (king′dəm) *n.* **1** The territory, people, state, or realm ruled by a king or a queen; a monarchy. **2** The spiritual dominion of God on earth. **3** Any separate field of independent authority, action, or influence; sphere. **4** One of the three primary divisions of natural objects known as the *animal, vegetable,* and *mineral kingdoms.*
king·fish (king′fish′) *n. pl.* **·fish** or **·fish·es 1** One of various American food fishes (genus *Menticirrhus*), especially *M. saxatilis,* common on the northern Atlantic coast. **2** The opah. **3** The cero. **4** *U.S. Slang* A vainglorious person.
king·fish·er (king′fish′ər) *n.* Any of several non-passerine birds (family *Alcedinidae*), generally crested, with straight, deeply cleft bill, which feed on fish; especially, the **eastern belted kingfisher** of the United States *(Megaceryle alcyon).*
King George's Falls See AUGHRABIES FALLS.
King Horn In certain medieval English and French romances, an exiled prince who falls in love and after many hardships wins his bride.
King James Bible See under BIBLE.
King Lear See LEAR.
king·let (king′lit) *n.* **1** A little or unimportant king. **2** Any of several small birds, resembling the warblers, especially the American **golden-crowned kinglet** *(Regulus satrapa)* and the **ruby-crowned kinglet** *(Regulus calendula).*
king·ly (king′lē) *adj.* **·li·er, ·li·est** Pertaining to or worthy of a king; regal; kinglike. **—***adv.* In a regal or kingly way; royally. **—king′li·ness** *n.*
Synonyms (adj.): august, kinglike, majestic, princely, regal, royal. *Royal* denotes that which actually belongs or pertains to a monarch; *regal* denotes that which in outward state is appropriate for a king; a subject may assume *regal* magnificence in residence, dress, and equipage. *Kingly* denotes that which is worthy of a king in personal qualities, especially of character and conduct; *princely* is especially used of treasure, expenditure, gifts, etc., as *princely* munificence, a *princely* fortune, where *royal* would change the sense. See IMPERIAL. *Antonyms*: beggarly, contemptible, inferior, mean, poor, servile, slavish, vile.
King·man Reef (king′mən) The northernmost atoll of the Line Islands, administered (1934) by the United States Navy.
king–of–arms (king′uv·ärmz′) *n.* In Great Britain, one of a body of officials instituted in 1484 to examine and inquire concerning rights and titles in heraldry.
king·palm (king′päm′) *n.* Any of a genus *(Archontophoenix)* of tropical and subtropical forest feather palms.
king·pin (king′pin′) *n.* **1** A kingbolt. **2** In tenpins, the foremost pin of a set arranged in order for playing: also called *headpin.* **3** In ninepins, the center pin. **4** *Slang* A person of first importance.
king·post (king′pōst′) *n.* A single vertical strut supporting the apex of a triangular truss and resting on a crossbeam. Also **king post.**
king row In checkers, the row of squares nearest to either of the players.

Kings (kingz) Either of two books of the Old Testament chronicling the history of the Jewish kings.

king salmon The quinnat, or North Pacific salmon.

king's bench See under COURT.

Kings Canyon National Park A mountainous region in the Sierra Nevada, east central California; 708 square miles; noted for its giant sequoia trees; established 1940.

king's counsel In the British Empire, barristers who are designated as counsel of the crown and cannot afterward plead against the crown without permission: also *queen's counsel.*

king's English See under ENGLISH.

king's evidence See STATE'S EVIDENCE.

king's evil Scrofula: once supposed to be curable by a monarch's touch.

king·ship (king'ship) *n.* **1** Royal state; kinghood. **2** Government by a king. **3** The person of a king.

Kings·ley (kingz'lē), **Charles,** 1819–75, English novelist. —**Henry,** 1830–76, novelist; brother of Charles. —**Sidney,** born 1906, U.S. playwright.

King's Lynn A municipal borough of western Norfolk, England: also *Lynn, Lynn Regis.*

Kings Mountain A ridge in NW South Carolina; scene of an American victory in the Revolutionary War, 1780.

king snake A large harmless colubrine snake (*Lampropeltis getulus*) of the southern United States that kills other snakes and feeds largely on rats and mice.

king's silver A soft, very pure silver formerly used for costly dishes and plate.

King·ston (king'stən, kingz'tən) **1** A port, capital of Jamaica, British West Indies. **2** A city on the Hudson River in SE New York. **3** A city in SE Ontario, Canada.

King·ston–on–Thames (king'stən·on'temz', kingz'tən) A municipal borough in NE Surrey, England; site of the King's Stone on which the West Saxon kings were crowned and of the last battle of the Civil War, 1648. Also **King'ston–up·on'–Thames'.**

King·ston–up·on–Hull (king'stən·ə·pon'hul', kingz'tən-) See HULL.

Kings·town (king'stən, kingz'toun) Capital of St. Vincent in the Windward Islands.

king's yellow A vivid yellow pigment, formerly obtained from orpiment, now also made synthetically from arsenic trisulfide: also called *Chinese yellow.*

King·te·chen (jing'du'jun') The former name of FOWLIANG.

king·truss (king'trus') *n.* A truss, as in roofing, having a kingpost.

king·wood (king'wŏŏd') *n.* **1** A Brazilian tree (*Dalbergia cearensis*) prized for its wood of fine texture having handsome dark–violet stripings. **2** The wood of this tree.

kink[1] (kingk) *n.* **1** An abrupt bend, twist, loop, or tangle, as in a wire rope. **2** A tightly twisted curl, as in hair or wool. **3** A mental quirk or prejudice. **4** An original, novel, or clever way of doing something. **5** A fashion or fad. **6** A hindrance, obstruction, or difficulty. **7** A crick; cramp. See synonyms under WHIM. —*v.t.* & *v.i.* To form or cause to form a kink or kinks. [<Du., twist, curl]

kink[2] (kingk) *n. Scot.* **1** A violent or convulsive laughing fit. **2** The whoop in whooping cough. —*v.i.* **1** To laugh violently or convulsively. **2** To gasp, as in laughing or coughing.

kink·a·jou (king'kə·jōō) *n.* A nocturnal, arboreal, raccoon-like carnivore (genus *Potos,* family *Procyonidae*) of the warmer parts of South and Central America, having large eyes, soft woolly fur, and a long prehensile tail. [<F *quincajou* < Tupian]

KINKAJOU
(Up to 3 feet long including the tail)

kink·y (king'kē) *adj.* **kink·i·er, kink·i·est** **1** Full of kinks; snarled. **2** Closely or tightly curled, as hair. **3** *Slang* Odd; queer; eccen-

tric. **4** *Slang* Involving or appealing to unconventional or perverted sexual tastes. **5** *Slang* Unconventional in a sophisticated way. —**kink'i·ly** *adv.* —**kink'i·ness** *n.*

kin·ni·ki·nic (kin'ē·kə·nik') *n.* **1** The leaves or bark of certain plants, as the willow and sumac, prepared for smoking. **2** Any plant so used. Also **kin'ni·kin·nic', kin'ni·kin·nick'**: sometimes *killikinnick.* [<Algonquian, that which is mixed]

Kin·ross (kin·rôs'), A county of east central Scotland; 82 square miles; county town, Kinross. Also **Kin·ross·shire** (-shir).

Kin·sey (kin'zē), **Alfred,** 1894–1956, U.S. zoologist; especially known for his statistical reports on sexual behavior in the United States.

kins·folk (kinz'fōk'), **kins·peo·ple** (kinz'pē'pəl) See KINFOLK.

Kin·sha·sa (kēn·shä'sä) The capital of Zaire.

kin·ship (kin'ship) *n.* Relationship, especially by blood.

kins·man (kinz'mən) *n. pl.* **·men** (-mən) A blood relation. —**kins'wom·an** (-wŏŏm'ən) *n. fem.*

Synonyms: connection, relative, relation. *Kinsman* is preferred in certain cases, on the ground of greater clearness, to *relative, relation, connection.* A man's *relative* or *relation* is one who is related to him, either by blood, as a brother (a *kinsman*), or by law, as a brother-in-law (not a *kinsman*), or, loosely, by some other bond. *Connection* is still more vague and unsatisfactory. The same applies to *kinswoman.* See KINDRED.

Kio·ga (kyō'gə) See KYOGA, LAKE

ki·osk (kē·osk', kē'osk, kī'-) *n.* An open ornamental summerhouse in Turkey now imitated in other countries and modified to serve as a booth, news–stand, bandstand, or the like. [< Turkish *kiŭshk*]

Kio·to (kyō'tō) See KYOTO.

Ki·o·wa (kī'ə·wä, -wə) *n.* One of a fierce tribe of Plains Indians of the Kiowan linguistic stock, formerly inhabiting parts of Nebraska and Wyoming. Also **Ki'o·way** (-wā).

Ki·o·wan (kī'ə·wən) *n.* A North American Indian linguistic stock consisting of the Kiowas.

kip[1] (kip) *n.* **1** The untanned skin of a calf. **2** The untanned skin of an adult of any small breed of cattle. **3** A collection of such skins composed of a specific number. Also **kip'·skin'** (-skin'). [Origin uncertain]

kip[2] (kip) *n. Slang* **1** A lodging house. **2** A bed there. **3** *Obs.* A brothel. [Cf. Dan. *horekippe* brothel]

Kip·chak (kip·chäk') *n.* **1** One of the Mongol Tatars of the Golden Horde, who established a kingdom in Europe and Asia in the 13th century, with its capital Sarai on the lower Volga. **2** One of a group of tribes inhabiting Turkestan. **3** The Turkic language of the Kipchaks.

Kip·ling (kip'ling), **Rudyard,** 1865–1936, English author and poet.

kip·per (kip'ər) *n.* **1** A salmon or herring cured by kippering. **2** The male salmon during the spawning season. —*v.t.* To cure, as fish, by splitting, salting, and drying or smoking. [? OE *cypera* spawning salmon]

Kirch·hoff (kirkh'hôf), **Gustav Robert,** 1824–1887, German physicist.

Kir·ghiz *n. pl.* **-ghiz** or **-ghiz·es** (also **Kyr·gyz**) **1** One of a Turkic people of Mongolian descent, dwelling in the Asian region, south of Kazakhstan. **2** The Turkic language of the Kirghiz.

Kir·ghiz·stan (also **Kyr·gyz·stan; the Kyrgyz Republic**) A republic in central Asia, a member of the Commonwealth of Independent States; 76,042 square miles; capital, Bishkek (formerly Frunze); pop. 4,500,000; formerly the **Kirghiz Soviet Socialist Republic** (1936–1991).

Kirghiz Range A vast mountain range bordering south Kazakhstan and covering Kirghizstan.

Ki·rin (kē'rin') A province of east central Manchuria; 45,000 square miles.

Kir·jath–Ar·ba (kûr'jath·är'bə) The ancient name for HEBRON.

kirk (kûrk) *n.* **1** *Scot.* A church or the church. **2** The established Presbyterian Church of Scotland, as distinguished from the

Roman Catholic Church, the Church of England, or the Episcopal Church.

Kirk·cal·dy (kər·kôl'dē, -kô'dē) A port on the Firth of Forth in southern Fifeshire, Scotland.

Kirk·cud·bright (kər·kōō'brē) A county in SW Scotland; 899 square miles; capital, Kircudbright. Also **Kirk·cud'bright·shire** (-shir).

Kirk·la·re·li (kərk·lä'rə·lē) A town in northern Turkey in Europe: scene of a Bulgarian victory over the Turks, 1912. Formerly **Kirk–ki·lis·sa** (kirk'kē·lē·sä').

Kirk·man (kûrk'mən) *n. pl.* **·men** (-mən) A member of the Church of Scotland.

Kir·kuk (kir·kook') A city in NE Iraq.

Kirk·wall (kûrk'wôl, -wəl) A port, county seat of Orkney county, Scotland.

Kir·man (kir·män') *n.* A type of Persian rug having naturalistic floral patterns and soft, rich coloring. [from *Kerman,* Iran, where originally made]

Kir·man (kir·män') See KERMAN.

kir·mess (kûr'mis) See KERMESS.

kirn[1] (kûrn, kirn) *n. Scot.* The last sheaf of the harvest; hence, a harvest celebration. [Origin obscure]

kirn[2] (kûrn, kirn) *n. Scot.* Churn.

kirn·milk (kûrn'milk', kirn'-) *n. Scot.* Buttermilk.

Ki·rov **1** A city on the Vyatka river in west central Russia. **2** The territory (oblast) around the Vyatka river and Severnyye Uvaly (the northern hills).

Ki·ro·va·bad (also **Gyandzha, Gäncä**) The second largest city in Azerbaijan, in the Caucasus region; formerly (1830–1920) Elisavetpol, (1921–1935) Gandzha.

Kirsch (kirsh) *n.* A brandy distilled from the fermented juice of cherries and their pits, originally from Germany and Alsace. Also **Kirsch'·was'ser** (-väs'ər).

kirs·ten (kûr'sən) *v.t. Scot.* To christen. Also **kir'sen.** —**kirs'ten·ing** *adj.*

kir·tle (kûrt'l) *n.* A garment with a skirt; a frock or mantle. [OE *cyrtel,* prob. ult. <L *curtus* short] —**kir'tled** *adj.*

kish (kish) *n.* Graphite which forms on the top of molten iron high in carbon. [<G *kies* gravel, pyrites]

Ki·shi·nev (kish'i·nef, *Russian* kē·shē·nyôf') The capital of the Moldavian S.S.R.: Rumanian *Chisinău.*

Kis·ka (kis'kə) An island in the Rat Island group of the Aleutian Islands, SW Alaska.

Kis·lev (kis'lef) *n.* A Hebrew month: also called *Chisleu.* Also **Kish'lev, Kis'lev.** See CALENDAR (*Hebrew*).

kis·met (kiz'met, kis'-) *n.* Appointed lot; fate. [<Turkish <Arabic *qisma* <*qasama* divide]

Kis·pest (kish'pesht) A city in north central Hungary SE of Budapest.

kiss (kis) *n.* **1** An affectionate salutation by contact of the lips. **2** A gentle touch. **3** One of various forms of confectionery. [< *v.*] —*v.t.* & *v.i.* **1** To touch with the lips, as in greeting or love. **2** To touch slightly. **3** *Printing* To touch: said of printed characters. See synonyms under CARESS. [OE *cyssan* kiss] —**kiss'er** *n.*

kissing bug **1** A hemipterous insect (*Reduvius personatus*) which occasionally bites man on the lips or cheeks: also called *masked hunter.* **2** One of several other bloodsucking insects, as the sharp–beaked *Melanolestes picipes.*

kist (kist) *n. Scot.* A chest, box, or coffin. —**kist'ful** *n.*

Kist·na (kist'nə) A river in southern India, flowing 800 miles across the Deccan: also *Krishna.*

kist·vaen (kist'vīn) *n.* An ancient, box–shaped sepulchral chamber smaller than a dolmen, made of flat stones: sometimes spelled *cistvaen.* Also **kist.** [Welsh *cist faen* <*cist* coffin + *faen* stone]

kit[1] (kit) *n.* **1** A tub, pail, or box for packing. **2** A small pail. **3** A collection of articles and appliances for any special purpose; an outfit; also, a group of persons; especially, a political constituency. **4** A collection of persons or things; the whole lot: the whole *kit* and caboodle of them. Compare CABOODLE. [<MDu. *kitte*]

kit[2] (kit) *n.* A kitten.

kit³ (kit) *n.* A small, three-stringed violin, used from the 16th to the 18th century: also *kit violin.* [Origin unknown]

Kit (kit) Diminutive of CATHERINE, CHRISTOPHER.

Ki·ta·za·to (kē·tä·zä·tō), **Shibamiro**, 1852–1931, Japanese bacteriologist and pathologist; discoverer of the bacilli of bubonic plague and of dysentery. Also **Ki·ta·sa·to.**

kitch·en (kich′ən) *n.* **1** A room specially set apart and containing the necessary utensils for cooking food. **2** A culinary department. [OE *cycene*, ult. <L *coquina* <*coquere* cook]

kitch·en·er (kich′ən·ər) *n.* **1** *Brit.* A cookstove. **2** A kitchen employee; also, one who has charge of a kitchen; chef.

Kitch·en·er (kich′ən·ər), **Horatio Herbert**, 1850–1916, first Earl of Khartoum; English statesman and field marshal.

kitch·en·ette (kich′ən·et′) *n.* A small kitchen.

kitchen garden A garden in which vegetables and, sometimes, fruits are grown for home use.

kitchen midden *Anthropol.* A mound composed of shells, bones, rude stone implements, and other refuse of primitive or prehistoric dwellings. [Trans. of Dan. *kökkenmödding*]

kitchen police *Mil.* Enlisted men detailed to perform routine kitchen chores; also, such duty. Abbr. *K.P.*

kitch·en·ware (kich′ən·wâr′) *n.* Kitchen utensils.

kite (kīt) **1** Any of certain birds of prey of the hawk family (*Falconidae*), having long, pointed wings and a forked tail. Some species are scavengers, as the **pariah kite** (genus *Milvus*) of India. **2** A light frame, usually of wood, covered with paper or some light fabric, to be flown in the air at the end of a long string. **3** *Naut.* One of several light

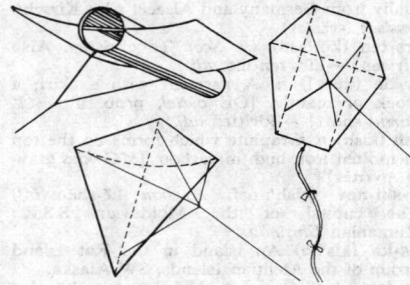

TYPES OF KITES (*def.* 2)

sails for use in a very light wind, as skysails. **4** In commerce, any negotiable paper not representing a genuine transaction but so employed as to obtain money, sustain credit, etc.; also, a bank check which is drawn with insufficient funds on deposit to secure the advantage of the time period prior to collection: considered to be a malpractice. **5** A shrewd and greedy bargainer; a sharper. — **to fly one's own kite** To tend to one's own affairs. — *v.* **kit·ed, kit·ing** *v.i.* **1** To soar or fly like a kite; move along swiftly. **2** In commerce, to obtain money or credit by the use of kites. — *v.t.* **3** In commerce, to issue as a kite. [OE *cȳta*]

kite balloon See under BALLOON.

kith (kith) *n. Scot. & Brit. Dial.* One's friends, acquaintances, or associates.

kith and kin Friends and relatives.

Ki·thai·ron (kē′the·rôn′) The Greek name for CITHAERON.

kith·a·ra (kith′ə·rə) *n.* A cithara.

kithe (kīth) *v.i. & v.t. Scot.* To recognize; show; make or become known: also spelled *kythe.*

kit·ling (kit′ling) *n. Scot.* A young cat; kitten.

kitsch (kich) *n.* Art or literary works, etc., having broad popular appeal and little aesthetic merit. [<G]

kit·tel (kit′l) *n.* A white cotton gown worn by orthodox Jews for solemn occasions and as a burial garment. [<G, a smock]

kit·ten (kit′n) *n.* A young cat or other feline animal. — *v.t. & v.i.* **·tened, ·ten·ing** To give birth to (kittens). [<OF *chitoun*, dim. of *chat* a cat]

kit·ten·ish (kit′ən·ish) *. adj.* Playfully coy. — **kit′ten·ish·ly** *adv.* — **kit′ten·ish·ness** *n.*

kit·ti·wake (kit′ē·wāk) *n.* A gull of northern seas (genus *Rissa*), having the hind toe rudimentary. [Imit.]

kit·tle (kit′l) *adj. Scot.* Skittish; ticklish.

kit·tool (ki·tōol′) *n.* A stiff, elastic fiber from the leaves of the fishtail palm (*Caryota urens*) of Ceylon and India: used for machine brushes. Also **kit·tul′.** [<Singhalese *kitūl* <Skt. *hintāla* marshy date tree]

Kitt·redge (kit′rij), **George Lyman**, 1860–1941, U.S. educator, author, editor, and scholar.

kit·ty¹ (kit′ē) *n. pl.* **·ties 1** In certain card games, the pool to which each player contributes a percentage of his winnings, used to cover expenses, the cost of refreshments, etc.: also called *widow.* **2** Hence, money pooled for any specific purpose. **3** In certain card games, a hand or part of a hand left over after a deal, which may be used by the highest bidder. [Cf. obs. *kidcote* a prison]

kit·ty² (kit′ē) *n. pl.* **·ties 1** A kitten. **2** A pet name for a cat.

Kit·ty (kit′ē) Diminutive of CATHERINE.

kit·ty-cor·nered (kit′ē-kôr′nərd) See CATER-CORNERED.

Kitty Hawk A village on Albermarle Sound, North Carolina: here Wilbur and Orville Wright made the first sustained airplane flight in the United States, December, 1903.

kit violin See KIT³.

Kiung·shan (kyōōng′shän′, *Chinese* jyōōng′· shän′) A city in northern Hainan, Kwangtung province, China. Former name: **Kiung′chow′** (-chou′, *Chinese* -jō′).

Kiu·shu (kyōō·shōō) See KYUSHU.

ki·va (kē′və) *n.* A room built in a Pueblo dwelling or beneath it, devoted to secret religious ceremonies, tribal councils, etc., entered by an opening in the roof. [<Hopi]

kiv·er¹ (kiv′ər) *v.t. & n. Scot.* Cover; shelter.

kiv·er² (kiv′ər) *n.* A shallow keeve.

Ki·vu (kē′vōō), **Lake** A lake in east central Africa on the Belgian Congo border; 1,110 square miles.

Ki·wa·ni·an (kə·wä′nē·ən, -wô′-) *n.* A member of a Kiwanis Club.

Ki·wa·nis Clubs (kə·wä′nis, -wô′-) A chain of clubs of businessmen in the United States and Canada, having the slogan "Service": originated, 1914; organized, 1915. [<N. Am. Ind. *keewanis* make oneself known]

ki·wi (kē′wē) *n.* **1** A flightless bird of New Zealand, the apteryx: named from its cry. **2** *Mil. Slang* An air force officer who does not make flights. **3** *Austral.* A New Zealander. [Imit.]

Kiz·il-Ir·mak (ki·zil′ir·mäk′) A river in central Asia Minor, flowing 715 miles SW to the Black Sea: ancient *Halys.*

Ki·zil Kum (ki·zil′ kōōm′) See KYZYL KUM.

Kjö·len (khœ′lən) A range of mountains between Norway and Sweden; highest point about 6,900 feet.

Kla·gen·furt (klä′gən·fŏŏrt) A city in southern Austria, capital of Carinthia.

Klai·pe·da (klī′pe·dä) The Lithuanian name for MEMEL.

Klam·ath (klam′əth) *n.* **1** One of a tribe of North American Indians of Lutuamian linguistic stock, formerly occupying the Klamath Lake and River region in Oregon, now on Klamath reservation, Oregon. **2** The language of the Klamath Indians: term usually extended also to the Modoc dialect.

Klam·ath River (klam′əth) A river in southern Oregon and NW California, flowing 263 miles from **Upper Klamath Lake** to the Pacific.

Klan (klan) See KU KLUX.

Klans·man (klanz′mən) *n. pl.* **·men** (-mən) A member of the Ku Klux Klan.

Kla·ra (klä′rä) German and Swedish form of CLARA.

Klau·sen·burg (klou′zen·bŏŏrkh) The German name for CLUJ.

klax·on (klak′sən) *n.* **1** An early type of automobile horn. **2** A low horn, especially one used on shipboard for sounding an alarm. Also **klaxon horn.** [<Gk. *klazein* make a harsh sound]

Klea·gle (klē′gəl) *n.* An organizer of Ku Klux Klans.

Klé·ber (klā·bâr′), **Jean Baptiste**, 1753–1800, French general.

Klebs–Löff·ler bacillus (klebz′lœf′lər) The diphtheria bacillus. [after Edwin *Klebs*, 1834–1913, and Friedrich August Johannes *Löffler*, 1852–1915, German bacteriologists]

Klee (klā, klē), **Paul**, 1879–1940, Swiss painter.

Kleen·ex (klē′neks) *n.* A soft paper tissue, used as a handkerchief, etc.: a trade name.

Klein (klīn), **Felix**, 1849–1925, German mathematician.

Klein bottle *Math.* A surface having only one side and no edges, constructed by inserting the smaller end of a tapering tube through one side of its larger end, then spreading the smaller end to join and coincide with the larger. [after Felix *Klein*]

Kleist (klīst), **Heinrich von**, 1777–1811, German dramatist.

kleft (kleft) *n.* One of a group of patriotic Greek mountaineers who organized into brigands and bands and carried out robberies to aid the cause of Greek independence from Turkish rule. [<Gk. *kleptes* a thief <*kleptein* steal]

klep·to·ma·ni·a (klep′tə·mā′nē·ə) *n.* An uncontrollable, morbid propensity to steal: also spelled *cleptomania.* [<Gk. *kleptein* steal + -MANIA] — **klep′to·ma′ni·ac** (-mā′nē·ak) *n.*

klet·ter·schuh·e (klet′ər·shōō′ə) *n. pl. German* Rope-soled shoes used in mountaineering.

Kle·ve (klā′və) The German name for CLEVES.

klieg light (klēg) A powerful incandescent floodlight, rich in actinic rays: used in making motion pictures. [after A. *Kliegl*, 1872–1927, and his brother John, 1869–1959, U.S. stage-lighting pioneers born in Germany]

Kling·sor (kling′zôr, -zōr) In Wagner's *Parsifal*, a magician who in revenge for his exclusion from the knighthood of the Grail attempts to corrupt the knights by his arts, and, after failing to tempt Parsifal, is destroyed.

klip·spring·er (klip′spring·ər) *n.* A small, agile African antelope (*Oreotragus oreotragus*) inhabiting mountainous regions from Ethiopia to the Cape of Good Hope. [<Du., lit., cliff-springer]

Klon·dike (klon′dīk) A region in NW Canada in the basin of the **Klondike River**, a tributary of the Yukon River, flowing 100 miles west.

kloof (klōōf) *n. Afrikaans* A mountain pass or cleft; a gorge or narrow valley.

Klop·stock (klôp′shtôk), **Friedrich Gottlieb**, 1724–1803, German poet.

Klu·ane (klōō·än′), **Lake** A lake in SW Yukon near the Alaska border; 184 square miles.

Kluck (klōōk), **Alexander von**, 1846–1934, German general.

klys·tron (klis′tron, -trən, klī′stron, -strən) *n.* A vacuum tube for generating a powerful, high-frequency radio beam by means of a flow of electrons rhythmically accelerated and retarded between cavities within which electrical oscillations are produced. [<Gk. *kleistos* closed + (ELEC)TRON]

knack (nak) *n.* **1** The trick of doing a thing readily and well. **2** Cleverness; adroitness. **3** A clever device. — *v.t. & v.i. Rare* To strike sharply. [Cf. ME *knack* a sharp blow]

knack·er (nak′ər) *n. Brit.* A dealer in, and slaughterer of, old horses. [Origin uncertain]

knack·wurst (näk′wûrst) *n.* A short, thick sausage, often highly seasoned: also *knock-wurst.* [<G <*knacken* sputter, crackle + *wurst* sausage]

knag (nag) *n. Scot.* A knot or knob.

knag·gy (nag′ē) *adj.* **·gi·er, ·gi·est** Full of knots; rough.

knap¹ (nap) *v.t. & v.i.* **knapped, knap·ping 1** *Archaic* To break in pieces; snap. **2** *Rare* To bite sharply; nibble. — *n.* A sharp cracking noise. [Imit.]

knap² (nap) *n. Scot.* A knob or mound.

knapping hammer A long-handled steel hammer for breaking stones.

knap·sack (nap′sak) *n.* A case or bag of leather or canvas worn strapped across the shoulders, for carrying equipment or supplies; especially, a soldier's traveling case. [<Du. *knapzak* <*knappen* bite + *zak* a sack]

knap·weed (nap′wēd′) *n.* **1** A common European meadow plant (*Centaurea nigra*) naturalized in the United States, with heads of purple flowers: also called *bullweed.* **2** Any of various other species of *Centaurea.* [Earlier *knopweed* <obs. *knop* a knob + WEED]

knar (när) *n.* A knot on a tree or in wood. [Akin to Du. *knar* stump, knot] — **knarred**, **knar′ry** *adj.*

knave (nāv) *n.* **1** A dishonest person; rogue. **2** A playing card, the jack. **3** *Archaic* A male servant. ◆ Homophone: *nave.* [OE *cnafa* servant]

knav·er·y (nā′vər·ē) *n. pl.* **·er·ies 1** Deceitfulness; trickery. **2** An instance of this; knavish action or behavior. **3** *Archaic* Mischievous quality; roguery.

knav·ish (nā′vish) *adj.* Of, pertaining to, or characteristic of a knave. —**knav′ish·ly** *adv.*

knead (nēd) *v.t.* **1** To mix and work, as dough or clay, into a uniform mass, usually by pressing, turning, etc., with the hands. **2** To work upon by thumps or squeezes of the hands; massage. **3** To make by or as by kneading. ◆ Homophone: *need.* [OE *cnedan*]—**knead′. er** *n.*

knee (nē) *n.* **1** *Anat.* The joint, or the region about the joint of the human leg, midway between the hip joint and the ankle. **2** A region considered similar to the knee of man: in the hind leg of horses, dogs, and similar animals, the stifle joint; in the foreleg, the carpal joint at the top of the cannon bone: said of hoofed beasts. **3** In birds, the joint at the top of the tarsus. **4** A plate, usually triangular, for connecting or joining structural members. **5** Anything like or suggesting a knee; also, in clothing, the part covering the knee. **6** Any of the upward projections, spurlike or angular, from the roots of swamp trees, especially the bald cypress. —*v.t.* To touch or strike with the knee. —*v.i. Obs.* To kneel. [OE *cnēow*]

KNEE JOINT
c.Crucial ligament.
f.Femur.
lp.Ligamentum patellae.
p.Patellae.
pl.Posterior ligament.
t.Tibia.

knee action A method of suspending the front wheels of an automotive vehicle so that each wheel can move up and down independently of the other.

knee breeches Breeches extending from the waist to a point just below the knee. Also **knee-smalls** (nē′smôlz′).

knee·cap (nē′kap′) *n.* **1** The patella. **2** A protective covering or padding for the knee: also **knee′pad′.**

knee-deep (nē′dēp′) *adj.* **1** Rising to the knee. **2** Sunk to the knee.

knee-high (nē′hī′) *adj.* Reaching as high as the knees.

knee-hole (nē′hōl′) *adj.* Having a recessed space for the knees: a *kneehole* desk.

knee-jerk (nē′jûrk′) *adj. Colloq.* Acting in a way that displays unthinking acceptance of preconceived ideas or stereotypes: *knee-jerk* liberals.

knee jerk A reflex action of the lower leg caused by a sudden, brisk tapping of the tendon just below the kneecap.

knee joint 1 *Anat.* The articulation between the femur and the tibia, which includes the patella. **2** A joint made or stiffened by a knee, as in shipbuilding. **3** A toggle joint.

kneel (nēl) *v.i.* **knelt** or **kneeled, kneeling** To fall or rest on the bent knee or knees. [OE *cnēowlian*]—**kneel′er** *n.*

knee-pad (nē′pad′) *n.* A protective covering for the knee or for the stocking at the knee.

knee·pan (nē′pan′) *n.* The patella; the kneecap.

knee·piece (nē′pēs′) *n.* In medieval armor, a covering strapped to the leg as protection for the knee and adjacent parts.

knell (nel) *n.* **1** The tolling of a bell, as in announcing a death. **2** An omen of death, rain, or failure. —*v.i.* **1** To sound a knell; toll, as mourning. **2** To give a sad or warning sound. —*v.t.* **1** To summon or proclaim by or as by a knell. [OE *cnyll* <*cnyllan* knock]

Knel·ler (nel′ər), **Sir Godfrey**, 1646–1723, English painter born in Germany; original name *Gottfried Kneller*.

knelt (nelt) Past tense and past participle of KNEEL.

Knes·set (knes′et) *n.* The single-chamber Constituent Assembly or Parliament of the Republic of Israel (*Knesseth Israel*), established by the Constitution of December, 1948. [<Hebrew]

knew (nōō, nyōō) Past tense of KNOW.

knibb·lack (nib′lak) *n. Scot.* A small round stone; a lump; knob. Also **knibb′loch** (-lôkh).

Knick·er·bock·er (nik′ər·bok′ər) *n.* **1** A descendant of one of the early Dutch settlers in New York State. **2** A New Yorker. [after Diedrich, *Knickerbocker*, typical Dutch character, fictitious author of Irving's *History of New York*]

knick·er·bock·ers (nik′ər·bok′ərz) *n. pl.* Wide short breeches gathered below the knee; knickers.

knick·ers (nik′ərz) *n. pl.* **1** Knickerbockers. **2** A woman's or girl's undergarment, similar to bloomers.

knick-knack (nik′nak) *n.* A trifling article; trinket; trifle: also spelled *nick-nack.* [Varied reduplication of KNACK]

knife (nīf) *n. pl.* **knives** (nīvz) **1** A cutting instrument with one or more sharp-edged, often pointed, blades, commonly set in a handle. **2** An edged blade forming a part of an implement or machine. **3** A weapon such as a cutlas or sword. —*v.t.* **knifed, knif·ing 1** To stab or cut with a knife. **2** *U.S. Slang* To work against with underhand methods. [OE *cnīf*]

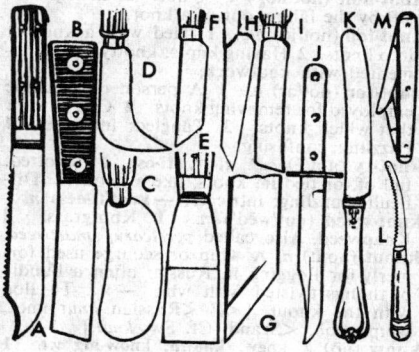

KNIVES
A. saw—back fish knife.
B. Hacking knife.
C. Paperhanger's knife.
D. Oilcloth knife.
E. Putty knife.
F. Woodcarver's knife.
G. Blade of mat—knife.
H. Felt knife.
I. Paring knife.
J. Hunting knife.
K. Table knife.
L. Paring or fruit knife.
M. Folding pocket knife or penknife.

knife-edge (nīf′ej′) *n.* **1** An edge sharpened like that of a knife. **2** A wedge of steel with a fine edge, serving as a fulcrum, as for a balance beam or a pendulum. **3** The girdle of a gem.

knife pleat A very narrow pleat, pressed to sharpness; usually in the plural.

knife switch *Electr.* A switch consisting of one or more knifelike blades which make contact between flat springs.

knight (nīt) *n.* **1** In medieval times, a gentleman bred to the profession of arms, and admitted with special ceremonies to honorable military rank. **2** *Brit.* The holder of a title next below that of baronet, entitling him to use *Sir* before his given name. **3** A champion or devoted follower, as of a cause; any man devoted to the service of a woman, principle, etc. **4** A member of any society in which the official title of knight obtains. **5** A chessman bearing a horse's head and moving one square in any direction, then one diagonally, without regard to intervening pieces. —*v.t.* To make (someone) a knight. ◆ Homophone: *night.* [OE *cniht* boy, servant] —**knight′age** *n.* ◆ Such terms as *knight banneret, knight baronet, knight companion,* and *Knight Templar* are each two nouns in apposition. In the plural each word often takes the inflection: *Knight Templars,* etc.

knight bachelor *pl.* **knights bachelors** In England, a knight of the most ancient but lowest order of knighthood.

knight errant *pl.* **knights errant** A medieval knight who went forth to redress wrongs or seek adventures.

knight-er·rant·ry (nīt′er′ən·trē) *n. pl.* **·ries 1** The customs and practices of the knights errant; chivalry. **2** Quixotic behavior.

knight·head (nīt′hed′) *n. Naut.* One of two timbers rising from the keel of a vessel and supporting the bowsprit between them.

knight·hood (nīt′hōōd) *n.* **1** The character, dignity, rank, or vocation of a knight. **2** Knights collectively. **3** Chivalry.

knight·ly (nīt′lē) *adj.* **1** Pertaining to a knight; chivalrous. **2** Composed of knights: a *knightly* order. —**knight′li·ness** *n.*

Knights Hospitalers of St. John of Jerusalem See HOSPITALER.

Knights of Columbus A fraternal and benevolent society of American Roman Catholic men: founded 1882.

Knights of Labor A national organization of laboring men in the United States, active between 1869 and 1917.

Knights of Malta, Knights of Rhodes See HOSPITALER.

Knights of the Round Table The body of knights comprising King Arthur's court. See ROUND TABLE.

Knights of the White Camelia One of various local, secret organizations of the southern United States that rose after the Civil War, dedicated to maintain white supremacy.

Knight Templar *pl.* **Knights Templars** *for def.* **1; Knights Templar** *for def.* **2. 1** A member of a great military order founded in 1119 for the defense of the Latin kingdom of Jerusalem and for the protection of pilgrims, and known as the **Knights of the Temple,** or **Knights Templars,** from the fact that their headquarters was once next to the so-called Temple of Solomon in Jerusalem. **2** A Free-mason of an order claiming descent from the medieval order of Knights Templars.

knish (kə·nish′) *n.* A small square or round of dough filled with potatoes, meat, kasha, etc., and baked or fried. [<Yiddish]

knit (nit) *v.* **knit** or **knit·ted, knit·ting** *v.t.* **1** To form (a fabric or garment) by interlocking loops of a single yarn or thread by means of needles. **2** To fasten or unite closely and firmly. **3** To draw (the brows) together into wrinkles; contract. —*v.i.* **4** To make a fabric by interweaving a yarn or thread. **5** To become closely and firmly united; grow together, as broken bones. **6** To come together in wrinkles; contract. [OE *cnyttan.* Akin to KNOT.]

knit·ter (nit′ər) *n.* **1** One who knits. **2** A knitting machine.

knit·ting (nit′ing) *n.* **1** The act of one who or that which knits. **2** The fabric produced by knitting.

knitting needle A straight, slender rod, pointed at one or both ends, used in hand knitting.

knives (nīvz) Plural of KNIFE.

knob (nob) *n.* **1** A rounded protuberance, bunch, or boss. **2** A rounded handle, as of a door. **3** A rounded mountain; knoll. [ME *knobbe,* prob. <MLG. Cf. Flemish *knobbe.*] —**knobbed** (nobd) *adj.* —**knob′like′** *adj.*

knob·by (nob′ē) *adj.* **·bi·er, ·bi·est** Full of knobs; also, knoblike. —**knob′bi·ness** *n.*

knob·ker·rie (nob′ker·ē) *n.* A round-headed stick used as a club and a missile in southern Africa. [<Afrikaans *knopkirie*]

knock (nok) *v.t.* **1** To give a heavy blow to; hit. **2** To strike (one thing) against another; bring into collision. **3** To drive or impel by striking: to *knock* a ball over a fence. **4** To make or cause by striking: to *knock* a hole in a wall. **5** *U.S. Slang* To find fault with; carp at. —*v.i.* **6** To strike a blow or blows, as with the fist or a club. **7** To come into collision; bump. **8** To make a pounding or clanking noise, as an engine. **9** *U.S. Slang* To find fault; carp. —**to knock about (or around) 1** To strike repeatedly; hit from side to side. **2** To wander from place to place. **3** To treat neglectfully; abuse. —**to knock down 1** To take apart for convenience in shipping or storing. **2** In auctions, to sell to the highest bidder. **3** *U.S. Slang* To embezzle a part of money passing through one's hands. —**to knock off 1** To leave off; stop,

as work, talking, etc. **2** To deduct. **3** To do or make quickly or easily. **4** *U.S. Slang* To kill; also, to overwhelm or defeat. — **to knock out 1** In boxing, to defeat (an opponent) by striking him to the ground for a count of ten. **2** To render unconscious or exhausted. — **to knock out of the box** In baseball, to hit the pitches of (an opposing pitcher) so often as to cause his removal from the game. — **to knock together** To build or make roughly or hurriedly. — **to knock up 1** *Brit.* To rouse, as by knocking on the door. **2** *Brit. Colloq.* To tire out; exhaust. **3** *U.S. Slang* To make pregnant. — *n.* **1** A sharp blow; a rap; also, a knocking. **2** *Mech.* **a** The noise produced in machinery or in engines when the operating parts are defective, badly worn, or poorly adjusted. **b** In an internal-combustion engine, the metallic explosive sounds due to uneven or improperly timed combustion. **3** *U.S. Colloq.* Hostile criticism; an adverse comment. [OE *cnocian*]

knock·a·bout (nok′ə-bout′) *adj.* **1** Characterized by knocking about, noisiness, or roughness. **2** Adapted for or suitable to any kind of rough usage. **3** Adaptable to all kinds of labor. — *n. Naut.* A small, partially decked yacht, carrying a mainsail and jib rigged fore-and-aft. Compare RACE-ABOUT.

knock·down (nok′doun′) *adj.* **1** Having sufficient force to fell or overthrow. **2** Constructed so as to be easily taken down, or apart, or so that the parts can be readily put together. — *n.* **1** A blow that fells; also, the act of felling. **2** Any prefabricated unassembled article.

knocked-on-at·om (nokt′on′at′əm) *n. Physics* An atom in a solid substance which recoils after the impact of a high-energy particle, often with sufficient energy to displace other atoms.

knock·er (nok′ər) *n.* **1** One who knocks. **2** A hinged metal hammer fastened to a door as a means of signaling for admittance.

knock-knee (nok′nē′) *n.* **1** An inward curvature of the legs that causes the knees to knock together in walking. **2** *pl.* Such knees. — **knock′-kneed′** *adj.*

knock-off hub (nok′ôf′, -of′) In automobiles, the system by which a wheel is affixed to an axle by an eared screw cap, enabling rapid removal and replacement of the wheel.

knock·out (nok′out′) *adj.* Rendering insensible, as a blow at the angle of the jaw; overpowering. — *n.* **1** A knockout blow; also, a prizefight that has been ended by such a blow. **2** *Slang.* An overwhelmingly attractive or successful person or thing.

knockout drops Drops of some powerful narcotic, as chloral hydrate, used to produce unconsciousness, often for criminal purposes.

knock·wurst (näk′wûrst) See KNACKWURST.

knoll[1] (nōl) *n.* A small round hill; a mound; also, a hilltop. [OE *cnoll* hill]

knoll[2] (nōl) *Archaic v.t.* **1** To proclaim or call by ringing a bell. **2** To sound, as a knell. — *v.i.* **3** To sound a knell; toll. — *n.* The tolling of a bell; knell. [Var. of KNELL]

knop (nop) *n.* A knob; an ornamental boss or stud. [Prob. var. of KNOB]

knosp (nosp) *n. Archit.* A flower bud, or a budlike ornament. [<MHG *knospe* bud]

Knos·sos (nos′əs) See CNOSSUS.

knot[1] (not) *n.* **1** An intertwining of the parts of one or more ropes, cords, etc., so that they will not slip. **2** An ornamental bow of silk, lace, etc. **3** Anything that resembles a knot. **4** A hard, gnarled portion of the trunk of a tree at the insertion of a branch; especially, such a gnarled knob of a pine tree, used for kindling or firewood. **5** *Bot.* **a** A node or joint in a stem; also, a protuberance or swelling. **b** *pl.* Any of several diseases of trees, characterized by such swellings. **6** A cluster or group, as of persons. **7** *Naut.* **a** A division of a log line, marked by pieces of cloth or knotted string at equal distances, and used to determine the rate of a ship's motion. **b** A speed of a nautical mile in an hour. **c** A nautical mile. **8** A knob. **9** A bond or association or union. **10** Something not easily solved; a difficulty; problem. **11** An enlargement of a muscle or of the bone beneath it; a swollen gland or nerve. **12** The red-breasted sandpiper. See REDBREAST. — **French knot** A decorative knot made by twisting or winding a thread several times around a needle and

then pushing the latter through the coil. — *v.* **knot·ted, knot·ting** *v.t.* **1** To tie in a knot; form a knot or knots in. **2** To secure or fasten by a knot. **3** To form knobs, bosses, etc., in. — *v.i.* **4** To form a knot or knots. **5** To tie knots for fringe. [OE *cnotta*]

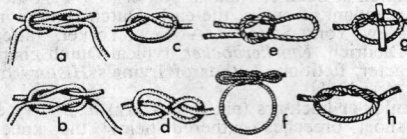

KNOTS

a.	Square or reef knot.	*e.* Single bowknot.
b.	Granny knot.	*f.* Double bowknot.
c.	Overhand knot.	*g.* Boat knot.
d.	Figure-8 knot.	*h.* Surgeon's knot.

knot[2] (not) *n.* A migratory sandpiper (*Calidris canutis*) breeding in Arctic regions. [Origin unknown]

knot·grass (not′gras′, -gräs′) *n.* **1** A widely distributed polygonaceous herb (*Polygonum aviculare*) with jointed stems and small greenish flowers. **2** Any of several other grasses, as the wild oat (*Avena fatua*). Also called *birdgrass*.

knot·hole (not′hōl′) *n.* A hole, as in a plank, left by the falling out of a knot.

knot·ted (not′id) *adj.* **1** Tied with a knot or into knots. **2** Having knots; knotty. **3** Ornamented with knotwork.

knot·ter (not′ər) *n.* **1** A person or machine employed for removing knots. **2** One who or that which knots. **3** Tangled; intricate. **4** Puzzling; confusing.

knot·ty (not′ē) *adj.* **·ti·er, ·ti·est** **1** Knotted; full of, or tied in, knots; like a knot. **2** Difficult; puzzling; intricate. — **knot′ti·ness** *n.*

knot·weed (not′wēd′) *n.* **1** Knotgrass. **2** Knapweed. Also called *persicary, smartweed.*

knout (nout) *n.* A whip or scourge used formerly for flogging in Russia: often a bundle of thongs twisted with wire. — *v.t.* To flog with the knout. [<F <Russian *knut* knot, whip, prob. <Scand. Cf. Sw. *knut.*]

know (nō) *v.* **knew, known, know·ing** *v.t.* **1** To perceive or understand clearly or with certainty; apprehend as objectively true: to *know* the truth. **2** To have information or intelligence of: to *know* the enemy's plans. **3** To be acquainted with; have experience of or familiarity with: Do you *know* each other? **4** To recognize; identify; also, to distinguish between: to *know* peas from beans. **5** To have practical skill in or knowledge of: often with *how:* Do you *know* how to ski? **6** *Archaic* To have sexual intercourse with. — *v.i.* **7** To have knowledge: often with *of:* Do you *know* of any better reason? **8** To be or become aware or cognizant. — *n.* The fact or condition of knowing; knowledge. — **in the know** *Colloq.* Having full, or more than usual, information. [OE *cnāwan*] — **know′a·ble** *adj.* & *n.* — **know′er** *n.*

Synonyms (verb): apprehend, ascertain, cognize, comprehend, discern, discover, discriminate, distinguish, experience, learn, perceive, realize, recognize, understand. See LEARN. Compare synonyms for KNOWLEDGE. *Antonyms:* Compare synonyms for IGNORANT.

know-how (nō′hou′) *n. Colloq.* Knowledge of how to perform a complicated operation or procedure; technical skill.

know·ing (nō′ing) *adj.* **1** Perceptive; astute; shrewd; also, possessing sly, covert, or secret knowledge: a *knowing* look. **2** Conscious; intentional. **3** Having knowledge or information. — **know′ing·ness** *n.*

Synonyms: acute, astute, clever, cunning, discerning, intelligent, keen, penetrating, sagacious, sharp, shrewd. A *knowing* look, air, etc., indicates the possession of reserved knowledge which the person could impart if he chose. *Knowing* has often a slightly invidious sense. We speak of a *knowing* rascal, meaning *cunning* or *shrewd* within a narrow range, but a *knowing* child has more knowledge than would be looked for at his years, perhaps more than is quite desirable, although to speak of a child as *intelligent* is altogether complimentary. See ASTUTE, CLEVER, INTELLIGENT, WISE[2]. *Antonyms:* dull, gullible, senseless, silly, simple, stolid, stupid, undiscerning, unintelligent.

know·ing·ly (nō′ing·lē) *adv.* **1** With knowledge. **2** Shrewdly; slyly. **3** Intentionally; on purpose: Who would *knowingly* commit a crime?

know-it-all (nō′it·ôl′) *n. Colloq.* A person affecting knowledge in almost all subjects. Also **know′-all′.**

knowl·edge (nol′ij) *n.* **1** A result or product of knowing; information or understanding acquired through experience; practical ability or skill. **2** Information; learning; specifically, the cumulative culture of the human race. **3** The clear and certain apprehension of truth; assured rational conviction. **4** The act, process, or state of knowing; cognition. **5** Any object of knowing or mental apprehension; that which is or may be known; the knowable; also actual or possible range of information. **6** Specific information; notification; notice. **7** *Archaic* Sexual intercourse. [OE *cnawlæc* < *cnāwan* know]

Synonyms: acquaintance, apprehension, cognition, cognizance, comprehension, erudition, experience, information, intelligence, intuition, learning, light, lore, perception, recognition, scholarship, science, wisdom. *Knowledge* is all that the mind knows, from whatever source derived or obtained, or by whatever process; the aggregate facts, truths, or principles acquired or retained by the mind, including alike the *intuitions* native to the mind and all that has been learned respecting phenomena, causes, laws, principles, literature, etc. We say of a studious man that he has a great store of *knowledge,* or of an intelligent man of the world, that he has a fund of varied *information.* We speak of *perception* of external objects, *apprehension* of intellectual truth. Simple *perception* gives a limited *knowledge* of external objects, merely as such; the *cognition* of the same objects is a *knowledge* of them in some relation; *cognizance* is the formal or official *recognition* of something as an object of *knowledge;* we take *cognizance* of it. *Intuition* is primary *knowledge* antecedent to all teaching or reasoning; *experience* is *knowledge* that has entered directly into one's own life; as, a child's *experience* that fire will burn. See ACQUAINTANCE, EDUCATION, LEARNING, SCIENCE, WISDOM. *Antonyms:* ignorance, illiteracy, inexperience, misapprehension, misconception, misunderstanding, rudeness, unfamiliarity.

knowl·edge·a·ble (nol′ij·ə·bəl) *adj. Colloq.* Having knowledge; knowing; shrewd.

known (nōn) Past participle of KNOW. — *adj.* Apprehended mentally; recognized; understood; especially, recognized by all as the truth.

know-noth·ing (nō′nuth′ing) *n.* An uneducated or ignorant person; an ignoramus.

Know-noth·ing (nō′nuth′ing) *n.* A member of a party in U.S. politics (1853–56), which aimed at excluding foreign-born persons from the government, and at making it difficult for them to become citizens: so called because, in its original form as a secret society, its members professed to "know nothing" about it when questioned. — **Know′-noth′ing·ism** *n.*

known quantity *Math.* A quantity whose value is stated: generally denoted by one of the earlier letters of the alphabet, *a, b, c,* etc.

Knox (noks), **Henry,** 1750–1806, American Revolutionary general. — **John,** 1505?–72, Scottish Protestant reformer, theologian, and historian. — **(William) Frank(lin),** 1874–1944, U.S. publisher; secretary of the navy, 1940–1944.

Knox·ville (noks′vil) A city on the Tennessee River in eastern Tennessee.

knub·bly (nub′lē) *adj.* Having protuberances; gnarled. [<*knubble,* dim. of *knub,* var. of KNOB]

knuck·le (nuk′əl) *n.* **1** One of the joints of the fingers, or the region about it; especially, one of the joints connecting the fingers to the rest of the hand. **2** The knee or ankle joint of certain animals, used as foods. **3** The central tubular projection of a hinge through which the pin passes. **4** In shipbuilding, an angular fitting of timbers. **5** *pl. U.S.* A children's game of marbles. — **brass knuckles** A device of metal, fitting over the knuckles, used as a protection for them in striking and to add force to the blow; also **knuck′le-dust′er.** — *v.i.* **knuck·led, knuck·ling** To hold the knuckles on the

ground in shooting a marble. — **to knuckle down 1** To apply oneself seriously and assiduously. **2** To yield; submit; give in: also **knuckle under.** [ME *knokel* <LG. Cf. G *knöchel*, dim. of *knochen* bone.]

knuckle bone 1 A huckle bone, as of a sheep; also, in man, one of the bones of the fingers. **2** *pl.* A children's game.

knuck·led (nuk′əld) *adj.* Jointed.

knuckle joint 1 The joint formed at a knuckle. **2** A hinge joint in which a projection in one part lies between two projections of the other part.

knur (nûr) *n.* A knot or knob. [ME *knorre, knurre* <MDu. knorre]

knurl (nûrl) *n.* **1** A hard substance or protuberance; knot; lump. **2** One of a series of small ridges on the edge of a thumbscrew to facilitate manual turning. **3** *Scot.* A hunchbacked dwarf. [? Dim. of KNUR] — **knurled, knurl′y** *adj.*

Knut (knŏŏt) See CANUTE.

KO (kā′ō′) See KAYO.

ko·a·la (kō·ä′lə) *n.* An arboreal marsupial of Australia (*Phascolarctos cinereus*), having cheek pouches, large ears, gray woolly fur, and no external tail. It feeds on the leaves and buds of the eucalyptus, but descends at night to dig up and eat roots. [<native Australian name]

KOALA
(About 2 feet 9 inches in length)

kob (kob, kōb) *n.* **1** A large antelope (genus *Kobus* or *Adenota*), with elongated horns, ringed at the base, and a long tufted tail, as the waterbuck. **2** Any of the several smaller related antelopes, as a reedbuck: all natives of southern Africa. Also **ko·ba** (kō′bə). [<Senegalese]

KOB (*Kobus kob*)
(About 3 feet high at the shoulder)

Ko·be (kō′be) A port in southern Honshu, Japan.

Kö·ben·havn (kœ′- pən·houn′) Danish name for COPENHAGEN.

Ko·blenz (kō′blents) See COBLENZ.

ko·bold (kō′bold, -bōld) *n.* In German folklore, an underground being inhabiting mines and caves; goblin; gnome. [<G; ult. origin unknown]

Ko·burg (kō′bŏŏrkh) See COBURG.

Koch (kôkh), **Robert,** 1843–1910, German physician and bacteriologist; discovered pathogenic bacteria of tuberculosis and cholera.

Koch·er (kôkh′ər), **Emil Theodor,** 1841–1917, Swiss physician and surgeon.

Ko·chi (kō′chē) A city in central Shikoku, Japan.

Kock (kôk), **Paul de,** 1794–1871, French novelist and dramatist.

Ko·da·chrome (kō′də·krōm) *n.* A full-color photographic film: a trade name.

Ko·dak (kō′dak) *n.* A small portable camera carrying a roll of sensitized film upon which a series of negatives can be quickly made: a trade name. — *v.t.* & *v.i.* To photograph with a Kodak.

Ko·di·ak bear (kō′dē·ak) See KADIAK BEAR.

Ko·di·ak Island (kō′dē·ak) An island in the Gulf of Alaska off Alaska Peninsula; over 5,000 square miles: also *Kadiak.*

Ko·dok (kō′dok) The modern name for FASHODA.

ko·el (kō′əl) *n.* A cuckoo (genus *Eudanamys*) native to Australia, India, and the East Indies; the coee bird. [<Hind. <Skt. *kokila*]

Koen·raad (kœn′rät) Dutch form of CONRAD.

Koff·ka (kôf′kä), **Kurt,** 1886–1941, U.S. psychologist born in Germany.

Ko·fu (kō·fōō) A city on central Honshu island, Japan.

Ko·hel·eth (kō·hel′ith) **1** The preacher: often identified with Solomon. *Eccles.* i 1–2. **2** The book of Ecclesiastes. [<Hebrew *qôheleth*]

Koh·i·nor (kō′i·nōŏr′) A famous Indian diamond, weight (cut) about 106 carats; one of the British crown jewels since the annexation of Punjab, 1849. Also **Koh′i·noor′, Koh′i·nur′.** [<Persian *kōhinūr* mountain of light]

kohl (kōl) *n.* In Eastern countries, a powder of antimony used to darken the edges of the eyes. [<Arabic *kuhl.* Akin to ALCOHOL.]

Köh·ler (kœ′lər), **Wolfgang,** 1887–1959, U.S. psychologist born in Germany.

kohl·ra·bi (kōl′rä·bē, kōl·rä′-) *n. pl.* **·bies** A variety of cabbage with an edible turnipshaped stem. [<G <Ital. *cavoli rope* (*pl.*) <L *caulis* cabbage + *rapa* turnip]

Koi·ne (koi·nā′) *n.* **1** The common form of Greek, an outgrowth of the Attic dialect with many Ionic elements, used throughout the Greek world from the time of the conquests of Alexander to the sixth century A.D. Koine was the literary language of Aristotle and Plutarch, and was used in the Septuagint and the New Testament; in its spoken form it became the basis of virtually all modern Greek dialects. **2** Any mixed language that becomes the lingua franca of a region: also *koine.* [<Gk. *koinē* (*dialektos*) common (language)]

Ko·kand (kô·känt′) A city in eastern Uzbek S.S.R.

Ko·ko·mo (kō′kə·mō) A city in north central Indiana.

Ko·ko Nor (kō′kō′ nôr′) A salt lake in NE Tsinghai province, China; 2,300 square miles: also *Kuku Nor.*

kok·sa·ghyz (kōk′sa·gēz′) *n.* A dandelionlike plant (*Taraxacum kok-saghyz*) native to Turkestan, the roots of which yield latex and inulin: cultivated as a source of rubber. [<Russian <Turkish *kök* a root + *sagiz* rubber]

Ko·ku·ra (kō·kōō·rä) A port in northern Kyushu island, Japan.

ko·la (kō′lə), **ko·la·nut** (-nut′) See COLA, etc.

Ko·la Peninsula (kō′lə) A projection of NW U.S.S.R. between the Barents Sea and the White Sea; 50,000 square miles; 250 miles long.

Ko·lar Gold Fields (kō·lär′) A city of eastern Mysore State, India.

Kol·ha·pur (kōl′hä·pōŏr′) **1** A former Deccan State in Bombay State, India. **2** A city in southern Bombay State, formerly the capital of Kolhapur.

Kolhapur and the Deccan States A former (1933–1947) political agency of princely states in western India.

ko·lin·sky (kə·lin′skē, kō-) *n.* Any of several minks of northern China and Russia; especially, *Mustela siberica,* the Siberian mink; also, the fur of any of these: sometimes called *Tartar Sable.* [<Russian *kolinski* of Kola, a peninsula abounding in minks]

kol·khoz (kōl·khôz′) *n.* A collective farm in the U.S.S.R. [<Russian *kol*(*lektivnoe*) collective + *khoz*(*aistvo*) farm, household]

Kol·lon·tai (ko·lon·tī′), **Aleksandra,** 1872–1952, U.S.S.R. revolutionary and diplomat; also **Kol·lon·tay′.**

Koll·witz (kôl′vits), **Käthe,** 1867–1945, German painter, etcher, and lithographer.

Köln (kœln) The German name for COLOGNE.

Ko·lozs·vár (kō′lōzh·vär) The Hungarian name for CLUJ.

Ko·lusch·an (kə·lush′ən) *n.* A linguistic stock of North American Indians of SE Alaska, consisting of the 18 Tlingit tribes. Also **Ko·lush′.** [<Russian *kalyuschka* piece of wood (inserted in the nether lip)]

Kol·y·ma (kol·ē·mä′) A river in NE Yakut Autonomous S.S.R., flowing 1,335 miles north to the East Siberian Sea. Also **Kol·i·ma′.**

Kolyma Range A mountain system in northern Khabarovsk territory; highest point, over 6,000 feet.

Kom·an·dor·ski Islands (kom′än·dôr′skē) An island group in the SW Bering Sea: also *Commander Islands.*

Ko·ma·ti (kə·mä′tē) A river in southern Africa,

flowing 500 miles NE to the Indian Ocean.

ko·mat·ik (kō·mad′ik) *n. Canadian* An Eskimo sled: also spelled *comatik.* [<Eskimo]

Ko·men·ský (kô′men·skē) See COMENIUS.

Ko·mi Autonomous S.S.R. (kō′mē) An administrative division of NE European Russian S.F.S.R.; 156,000 square miles; capital, Syktyvkar: formerly *Zyrian Autonomous Region.*

Kom·in·tern (kŏm′in·tûrn) See COMINTERN.

ko·mon·dor (kō′mon·dôr) *n.* A breed of working dog used in Hungary for ten centuries; tall, sturdy, and having a wide muzzle and long, thick, white coat. [<Magyar]

Kom·so·molsk (kom′so·môlsk′) A city in eastern European Russian S.F.S.R. on the Amur.

Kon·a·kri (kon′ə·krē) See CONAKRY.

Kon·go (kong′gō) The German name for the CONGO.

Kö·nig·grätz (kœ′nik·grets) The German name for HRADEC KRÁLOVÉ.

Kö·nigs·berg (kœ′nikhs·berkh) The former German name for KALININGRAD.

ko·ni·ol·o·gy (kō′nē·ol′ə·jē) See CONIOLOGY.

Kon·stan·tin (kōn′stän·tēn′) German form of CONSTANTINE.

Kon·stanz (kōn′stänts) German form of CONSTANT.

Kon·stanz (kōn′stänts) The German name for CONSTANCE.

Kon·stan·ze (kōn·stän′tsə) German form of CONSTANCE.

Kon·ya (kôn′yä) A city in SW central Turkey in Asia: ancient *Iconium.* Also **Kon′ia.**

Koo (kōō), **V. K. Wellington,** born 1887, Chinese statesman and diplomat; original name *Ku Wei-chün.*

Kooch Behar (kōōch′ bi·här′) A former name for COOCH BEHAR.

koo·doo (kōō′dōō) *n.* A large, striped African antelope (genus *Strepsiceros*), grayish-brown in color: also spelled *kudu.* [<Hottentot *kudu*]

kook (kōōk) *n. Slang* An unconventional, eccentric, or unbalanced person. [? <CUCKOO] — **kook′i·ness** *n.* — **kook′y** *adj.*

GREATER KOODOO
(Up to 5 feet high at the shoulder)

kook·a·bur·ra (kōōk′ə·bûr′ə) *n.* A large, insectivorous Australian kingfisher; the laughing jackass. [<native Australian]

koo·ra·jong (kōō′rə·jong) See KURRAJONG.

Koo·te·nay (kōō′tə·nā) A river rising in Kootenay National Park in SE British Columbia; 543 square miles; established 1920; flowing through northern Montana and Idaho, thence through Kootenay Lake, a lake 75 miles long in SE British Columbia, to the Columbia River; total length 450 miles, of which 276 are in Canada. Also, in the United States, Koo′te·nai.

kop (kop) *n.* In South Africa, a hill; headland. [<Afrikaans <Du., a head]

ko·peck (kō′pek) *n.* A small copper coin of Russia; one one-hundredth of a ruble: also spelled *copeck.* Also **ko′pek.** [<Russian *kopeïka* <*kopye* lance]

koph (kōf) *n.* The nineteenth Hebrew letter. See ALPHABET. [<Hebrew *qoph*]

kop·je (kop′ē) *n.* In South Africa, a hillock. [<Afrikaans *kopje,* dim. of *kop* kop]

kor (kôr, kōr) See HOMER². [<Hebrew *kōr,* lit., round vessel]

Ko·ran (kō·rän′, -ran′) *n.* The Moslem sacred scripture, written in Arabic and professing to record the revelations of Allah (God) to Mohammed: also *Alcoran, Alkoran.* [<Arabic *Qur'ān,* lit., book <*quar'a* read]

Kor·do·fan (kôr′dō·fän′) A province of central Sudan; 146,930 square miles; capital, El Obeid.

Ko·re·a (kō·rē′ə, kō-) A peninsula of eastern Asia; 85,228 square miles; 1910–45 Japanese *Chosen;* divided (1948) into: **1** the **Republic of Korea (South Korea);** 36,760 square miles; capital, Seoul; and **2** the **Democratic People's Republic of Korea (North Korea);** 46,968 square miles; capital, Pyongyang.

Korea Bay An arm of the Yellow Sea between the Liaotung Peninsula, NE China, and the

western coast of North Korea. Also **East Korea Bay.** Formerly **Bay of Chosen.**

Ko·re·an (kô·rē'ən, kō-) *adj.* Belonging or relating to Korea (Chosen) or its inhabitants. —*n.* **1** An inhabitant or a native of Korea. **2** The agglutinative language of Korea, somewhat similar to Japanese.

Korea Strait The passage from the Sea of Japan to the East China Sea between Korea and Japan.

Ko·rit·sa (kô'r·6ē·tsä') A city in SE Albania. *Albanian* **Kor·çë** (Kô'chə).

Kor·ne·lis (kôr·nā'lis) Dutch form of CORNELIUS.

Korn·gold (kôrn'gōlt), **Erich Wolfgang,** 1897–41957, U.S. composer born in Austria.

Kor·o·len·ko (k336 r'ē·leng'kō, *Russian* Kô·rô·lyen'kə), **Vladimir Galaktionovich,** 1853-1921, Russian novelist.

ko·ru·na (kô·rōō'nä) *n.* The monetary unit of Czechoslovakia. See CROWN (money). [<Czech <L *corona* crown]

Ko·rze·niow·ski (kô'zhe·nyôfa'skē), **Teodor Józef Konrad** See CONRAD, JOSEPH.

Kor·zyb·ski (kôr·zib'skē), **Alfred Habdank,** 1879–1950, U.S. scientist and originator of general semantics; born in Poland.

kos (kos) *n.* A Hebrew measure of capacity of about four cubic inches. [<Hebrew, cup]

Kos (kos, kôs) The second largest island of the Dodecanese group; 114 square miles: Italian *Coo*: also *Cos.*

Kos·ci·us·ko (kos'ē·us'kō), **Thaddeus,** 1746–1817, Polish patriot in the American Revolution. Also Polish **Tadeusz Koś·ciusz·ko** (kosh·chōōsh'kô).

Kos·ci·us·ko (kos'ē·us'kō), **Mount** A mountain in SE New South Wales; highest peak in Australia; 7,316 feet.

ko·sher (kō'shər) *adj.* **1** Permitted by the Jewish ceremonial law; clean; pure: said usually of food. **2** *Slang* All right; good; legitimate. —*n.* A kosher shop, also, the food sold there. —*v.t.* (kosh'ər) To make kosher. Also spelled *kasher.* [<Hebrew *kāshēr* fit, proper]

Ko·ši·ce (kô'shē·tse) A city in SE Slovakia, Czechoslovakia: German *Kaschau,* Hungarian *Kassa.*

Kos·so·vo (kô'sô·vô) A region of southern Serbia, Yugoslavia; scene of Turkish victories over the Serbs, 1389, and Hungarians, 1448. Also **Ko'so·vo.**

Kos·suth (kos'ōōth, ko·sōōth'; *Hungarian* kô'shōōt), **Ferenc,** 1841–1914, Hungarian politician; son of Louis. —**Louis,** 1802–94, Hungarian patriot: led insurrection, 1848.

Kos·tro·ma A region (okrug) in north central European Russia bordering the Volga river.

Ko·sy·gin (ko·sig'n) **Alexei Nikolayevich,** born 1904–1980, Soviet statesman; chairman of the Council of Ministers (premier) 1964–.

Ko·ta·ba·ru (kō'tə·bä 'rōō) The capital of West Irian, a port in the NE part: formerly *Hollandia.*

Ko·ta Bha·ru The capital of Kelantan, Malaysia. Also **Kota Ba'roe** or **Ba'ru.**

Kot·ka (kôt'kä) A port in SE Finland, on the Gulf of Finland.

ko·to (kō'tō) *n.* A Japanese musical instrument with 13 strings, plucked with 3 plectra fastened to the thumb, index, and middle finger of the right hand, while the left adjusts the strings. [<Japanese]

Ko·tor (kô'tôr) A port in western Montenegro, Yugoslavia, on the **Gulf of Kotor,** an inlet of the Adriatic in SW Yugoslavia: Italian *Cattaro.*

Kot·ze·bue (kôt'sə·bōō), **August Friedrich Ferdinand von,** 1761–1819, German dramatist.

Kot·ze·bue Sound (kot'sə·byōō) An inlet of the Chukchi Sea in NW Alaska.

kou·miss (kōō'mis), **kou·mys** See KUMISS.

Kous·se·vitz·ky (kōō'sə·vit'skē), **Serge,** 1874–1951, Russian orchestral conductor active in the United States.

kous·so (kōōs'ō) See CUSSO.

Kov·no (kôv'nō) The Russian name for KAUNAS.

Ko·weit (kō·wāt') See KUWAIT.

Kow·loon (kou'lōōn') The chief port of Hong Kong on **Kowloon Peninsula** (3 square miles) NE of Hong Kong Island.

kow·tow (kou'tou', kō'-) *n.* A Chinese form of obeisance: kneeling and touching the forehead to the ground before a superior. —*v.i.* **1** To make such obeisance. **2** To act in an obsequious or servile manner. Also **ko·tow** (kō'-

tou'). [<Chinese *k'o-t'ou,* lit., knock the head]

Kra (krä), **Isthmus of** A neck of land in SE Asia, 40 miles wide at its narrowest point, connecting the Malay Peninsula with Burma and Thailand.

kraal (kräl) *n.* **1** A village or group of native huts in South Africa, usually surrounded by a stockade. **2** The social unit such a community represents. **3** An enclosure for cattle. Also spelled *craal.* [<Afrikaans, village, pen <Pg. *curral* pen for cattle. Related to CORRAL.]

Krae·pe·lin (krä'pə·lin), **Emil,** 1856–1926, German psychiatrist.

Krafft-E·bing (kräft'ā'bing), **Baron Richard von,** 1840–1902, German neurologist and psychiatrist.

kraft (kraft, kräft) *n.* A tough, usually dark-brown paper, made from high-grade sulfate wood pulp. [<G, strength]

Krag (krag) *n.* A bolt-action repeating rifle formerly used in the U.S. Army: in full, **Krag-Jör·gen·sen rifle** (-jûr'gən·sən). [after O. *Krag* and E. *Jörgensen,* Norwegian inventors]

krait (krīt) *n.* An extremely venomous dull-bluish snake (genus *Bungarus*), especially the **banded krait** (*B. fasciatus*) of the Malay Peninisula, India, and Borneo. [<Hind. *karait*]

Kra·ka·to·a (krä'kə·tō 'ä) A volcanic island in the Strait of Sunda, between Java and Sumatra, Malay Archipelago; major eruption, 1883. Also **Kra'ka·tau'** (-tou').

kra·ken (krä'kən, krä'-P) *n.* A fabulous sea monster of Norwegian seas. [<Norw.]

Kra·ków (krä'kōōf) The Polish name for CRACOW. *Russian* **Kra·kov** (krä'kôf).

kra·ko·wi·ak (krə·kō'vē ·ak) See CRACOVIENNE.

Kras·no·dar 1 A territory of southern European Russia on the Sea of Azov and the Black Sea; 32,800 square miles. **2** The capital of the Krasnodar okrug; formerly Ekaterinodar.

Kras·no·yarsk 1 A territory of central Siberian Russia; 928,000 square miles. **2** Its capital, a city on the Yenisei, pop. 900,000.

K-ra·tion (kā'rash'ən, -rā'shən) *n.* A highly condensed emergency ration provided for soldiers of the U.S. Army.

Kre·feld (krā'felt) A city on the Rhine in North Rhine–Westphalia, West Germany.

Kreh·biel (krā'bēl), **Henry,** 1854–1923, U.S. music critic, author, and editor.

Kreis·ler (krīs'lər), **Fritz,** 1875–1962, U.S. violinist and composer born in Austria.

Kre·men·chug (kre'min·chōōk') A city in central Ukrainian S.S.R. on the Dnieper river.

krem·lin (krem'lin) *n.* The citadel of a Russian town. [<F <Russian *kreml'* citadel]

Krem·lin (krem'lin) **1** The citadel of Moscow, enclosing the former palace of the Czar. **2** The government of the U.S.S.R.

Krem·nitz white (krem'nits) See CREMNITZ WHITE.

kreu·zer (kroit'sər) *n.* Any of several former small silver or copper coins of Austria and Germany. Also **kreut'zer.** [<G <*kreuz* cross]

Krieg (krēg) *n.* German War.

krieg·spiel (krēg'spēl) *n.* A game in which figures representing troops, guns, etc., are moved about a model of the terrain in simulation of actual military maneuvers: used in the instruction or practice of military tactics. [<G *kriegspiel,* lit., war game]

Kriem·hild (krēm'hild, *Ger.* krēm'hilt) In the *Nibelungenlied,* the wife of Siegfried and sister of King Gunther; rival of Brunhild. Also **Kriem·hil·de** (krēm·hil'dē).

krim·mer (krim'ər) *n.* A fur resembling Persian lamb prepared from fleece of lambs raised mostly in the Crimean Peninsula. [<G *krimmer* <*Krim* Crimea]

kris (krēs) *n.* A dagger with a wavy blade used in Malaysia: also spelled *crease, creese, cris.* [<Malay]

KRIS WITH SHEATH

Krish·na (krish'nə) **1** A celebrated Hindu deity, an incarnation of Vishnu. **2** See KISTNA. —**Krish'na·ism** *n.*

Kris·pin (kris·pēn') Swedish form of CRISPIN. Also *Dutch* **Kris·pijn** (krēs'pīn).

Kriss Krin·gle (kris kring'gəl) St. Nicholas; Santa Claus. [<G *Christkindl,* dim. of *Christkind* Christ child]

Kris·ti·a·ni·a (kris'chē·a'nē·ə) The former name of OSLO.

Kris·tian·sand (kris'chən·sand, *Norwegian* kris·tyän·sän') A port on the Skagerrak, SW Norway.

Kris·to·fer (kris'tə·fer) Swedish form of CHRISTOPHER.

Kri·voi Rog (krē·voi' rôk') A city in SE Ukrainian S.S.R.

Krk (kûrk) The largest of the Yugoslav islands in the northern Adriatic; 165 square miles: Italian *Veglia.*

Krogh (krôg), **August,** 1874–1946, Danish physiologist.

Kró·lew·ska Hu·ta (krōō·lef'skähōō'tä) A former name of CHORZOW.

kro·na (krō'nə, *Sw.* krōō'nə) *n. pl.* **kro·nor** (krō'nôr) The Swedish monetary unit, equivalent to 100 öre. [<Sw.]

kro·ne (krō'nə) *n.* **1** *pl.* **kro·ner** (krō'nər) A gold coin, the monetary unit of Norway and Denmark, equivalent to 100 öre: also called *crown.* **2** *pl.* **kro·nen** (krō'nən) Any of several former European gold coins, equivalent in Germany to 10 marks, in Austria-Hungary to 100 heller. [<Dan.]

Kro·nos (krō'nos) In Greek mythology, the youngest of the Titans, son of Uranus and Gaea, who deposed his father, married his sister, Rhea, and was himself deposed by his son Zeus, who threw him into Tartarus with the other Titans: identified with the Roman *Saturn* : also spelled *Cronus.*

Kron·stadt (krōn'shtät) **1** A Russian port and naval base on an island in the Gulf of Finland, 14 miles west of Leningrad. *Russian* **Kron'·shtadt. 2** The German name for STALIN.

kroon (krōōn) *n. pl.* **kroons** or **kroo·ni** (krōō'nē) The monetary unit of Estonia. [<Estonian *kron*]

Kro·pot·kin (krə·pot'kin, *Russian* krô·pôt'·kēn), **Prince Peter Alexeivich,** 1842–1921, Russian geographer, anarchist, and author.

kru·bi (krōō'bē) *n.* A giant plant (*Amorphophallus titanum*) of the arum family native in Sumatra, with tuberous roots and a malodorous vaselike spathe that may grow to a diameter of 8 feet and a height of 12 feet or more: regarded as the largest flower in the world: also called *grubi.* Also **kru'but** (-but). [<native name]

Kru·ger (krōō'gər, *Afrikaans* krü'gər), **Stephanus Johannes Paulus,** 1825–1904, Boer statesman; president of the South African Republic, 1883–1900: called "Oom Paul."

Kruger National Park A game preserve lying in Eastern and Northern Transvaal provinces, Republic of South Africa; about 8,650 square miles; established 1926.

Kru·gers·dorp (krōō'gərz·dôrp, *Afrikaans* krü'·gərs·dôrp') A town, in Gauteng, Republic of South Africa.

krul·ler (krul'ər) See CRULLER.

Krupp (krup, *Ger.* krōōp) A German family of steel and munition manufacturers at Essen, Germany, notably **Alfred,** 1812–87; his son **Friedrich Alfred,** 1854–1902; and **Bertha,** 1886–1957, daughter of the preceding.

kry·o·lite (krī'ə·līt), **kry·o·lith** (-lith) See CRYOLITE.

kryp·ton (krip'ton) *n.* A colorless, insert, gaseous element (symbol Kr) of the zero group in the periodic table, isolated by Ramsay in 1898. See ELEMENT. [<NL <Gk. *krypton,* neut. of *kryptos* hidden]

K-se·ries (kā'sir'ē) *Physics* The group of shorter wavelengths in the typical X-ray spectrum of an element, believed to be caused by the transition of electrons to the quantum number of one.

Kshat·ri·ya (kshat'rē·yə) *n.* The warrior caste of the Aryan Hindus; a member of the caste. Also **Kshat'ru·ya** (-rōō-). [<Skt. *kṣatriya* <*kṣatra* rule]

Kua·la Be·lait A city in Brunei, capital of the district of Belait.

Kua·la Lum·pur A city in the SW part of Malaysia, capital of Malaysia, and a federal territory in Malaysia; pop. 1,300,000.

Kua·la Treng·ga·nu A city on the South China Sea, capital of Trengganu, a State of Malaysia; pop. 750,000.

Kuan Yin (kwän yin) A Chinese Buddhistic goddess: often called the Goddess of Mercy: also spelled *Kwan Yin*, or, in Japanese, *Kwannon*.

Ku·ban (kŏō·bän′) A river in Georgian S.S.R., flowing 584 miles north to the Black Sea.

Ku·blai Khan (kŏō′blī kän′), 1214–94, founder of the Mongol dynasty of China. Also *Kubla Khan*.

ku·chen (kŏō′khən) *n.* A yeast dough coffee cake. [<G]

Ku·ching (kŏō′ching) The capital of Sarawak, Malaysia.

ku·dos (kyoo′dos) *n.* Glory; credit; praise. [<Gk. *kydos* glory]

ku·du (kŏō′dŏō) See KOODOO.

Ku·dus (kŏō′dŏōs) A town of central Java. *Dutch* **Koe′does**.

kud·zu·vine (kŏōd′zŏō·vīn′) *n.* A hairy, fragrant climbing vine of China and Japan (*Pueraria thunbergiana*). A fiber from the inner bark is used by the Japanese for fabrics and cordage. [<Japanese]

Kuen·lun (kŏōn′lŏōn′) See KUNLUN.

Ku·fic (kyŏō′fik) *adj.* Relating to Kufa, an ancient Arabian city on the Euphrates, or to the primitive Arabic characters used by its writers, and in which the Koran was originally written. — *n.* The Arabic alphabet, as written at Kufa. Also spelled *Cufic*.

Ku·fra (kŏō′frä) A group of oases in the center of the Libyan Desert, southern Cyrenaica, Libya. *Italian* **Cu′fra**.

Kuhn (kŏōn), **Richard,** 1900–1967, Austrian chemist.

Kui·by·shev (kwē′bi·shef) A city on the Volga river in SW Russian S.F.S.R.: formerly *Samara*.

Ku·ke·naam (kŏō′kə·näm) A mountain (8,620 feet) and waterfall (dropping 2,000 feet) on the British Guiana–Venezuela boundary: also *Cuquenán*.

Ku Klux Klan (kyŏō′ kluks′ klan′) *n.* **1** A secret society in the southern United States after the Civil War, aiming to prevent Negro ascendancy. **2** A modern secret society, founded in 1915 at Atlanta, Ga., aiming at arbitrary regulation of life by white Protestants: also **Ku–Klux Klan.** **3** A member of either society. [Alter. of Gk. *kyklos* a circle] — **Ku′ Klux′ Klan′ner.**

Ku·ku Nor (kŏō′kŏō′ nôr′) See KOKO NOR.

Ku·la Gulf (kŏō′lə) A section of the SW Pacific in the Solomon Islands off New Georgia.

ku·lak (kŏō′lak, kyŏō′-, kŏō·lak′, kyŏō-) *n.* A well-to-do Russian peasant employing hired labor: the object of particular liquidation by the Soviet government after the Bolshevik revolution. [<Russian, lit., fist, tight–fisted man <Estonian]

Kul·tur (kŏōl·tŏōr′) *n.* Progress, achievement, and efficiency, in all phases, practical or theoretical, of political, economic, social, scientific, or artistic life. [<G]

Kul·tur·kampf (kŏōl·tŏōr′kämpf) *n.* The abortive political struggle initiated by Bismarck in 1872, between the German imperial government and the Roman Catholic Church, which had for its main issue the control by the state of educational and ecclesiastical appointments. [<G, culture–conflict]

Ku·lun (kŏō′lŏōn′) The Chinese name for ULAN BATOR.

Ku·ma·mo·to (kŏō·mä·mō·tō) A port on the west coast of Kyushu island, Japan.

Ku·ma·si (kŏō·mä′sē) A city in south central Ghana, the former capital of Ashanti: formerly *Coomassie*.

Kum·chon (kŏōm·chon) A city of South Korea. *Japanese* **Kin·sen** (kin·sen).

ku·miss (kŏō′mis) *n.* Fermented mare's milk, used by the Tatar tribes of central Asia, or a drink made in imitation of it: often spelled *koumiss, koumys.* Also **ku′mys.** [<Russian *kumys* <Tatar *kumix*]

küm·mel (kim′əl, *Ger.* kü′məl) *n.* A German or Russian liqueur flavored with aniseed, cumin, or caraway. [<G, caraway seed <L *cuminum*]

kum·mer·bund (kum′ər·bund) See CUMMERBUND.

kum·quat (kum′kwot) *n.* **1** A small citrus tree (genus *Fortunella*) cultivated in China, Japan, and the United States. **2** Its acid,

plumlike, orange–colored fruit. Also spelled *cumquat.* [Cantonese alter. of Mandarin *chin-chü,* lit., golden orange]

Kun (kŏōn), **Béla,** 1886–1938?, Hungarian Communist leader; premier 1919.

Kun·dry (kŏōn′drē) In Wagner's *Parsifal,* a beautiful woman, slave of Klingsor, doomed to eternal penitence for having laughed at Christ while he carried the cross. She is redeemed from sin by Parsifal.

Ku·ne·ne (kŏō·nā′nə) See CUNENE.

Ku·ners·dorf (kŏō′nərs·dôrf) A village in western Poland, 4 miles east of Frankfort on the Oder; scene of a decisive defeat of Frederick the Great 1759. *Polish* **Ku·no·wi·ce** (kŏō′nō·vē′tse).

Kung (kŏōng), **Hsiang–hsi,** born 1881, Chinese statesman.

K′ung Fu–tse (kŏōng′ fŏō′tse′) See CONFUCIUS.

Ku·nie (kŏō′nye) See ISLE OF PINES, New Caledonia.

Ku·ni·yo·shi (kŏō·nē·yō·shē), **Yasuo,** 1893–1953, U. S. painter born in Japan.

Kun·lun (kŏōn′lŏōn′) A series of mountain ranges in northern Tibet and southern Sinkiang; highest altitude, 25,340 feet: also *Kuenlun.*

Kun·ming (kŏōn′ming′) The capital of Yunnan province, China: formerly *Yunnan.*

Kun·san (kŏōn·sän) A port of South Korea. *Japanese* **Gun·zan** (gŏōn·zän).

kunz·ite (kŏōnts′īt) *n.* A lilac–colored variety of spodumene, used as a gemstone: found at Pala, California. [after G. F. *Kunz,* 1856–1932, U. S. mineralogist]

Kuo·min·tang (kwō′min′tang′) *n.* The nationalist party of China, founded in 1912 by Sun Yat-sen and led since 1927 by Chiang Kai-shek; defeated and ousted by the Chinese Communists following the Chinese civil war (1945–49). It retains control of Taiwan. [<Chinese *kuo* nationalist + *min* people's + *tang* party]

Ku·pang (kŏō·päng′) A port of SW Timor, capital of Indonesian Timor.

Ku·pre·a·nof (kŏō′prē·ä′nôf) An island in the Alexander Archipelago, SE Alaska.

Ku·ra (kŏō′rä) A river in Transcaucasia, flowing 940 miles NE to the Caspian Sea: ancient *Cyrus.* Also **Kur** (kŏōr).

kur·bash (kŏōr′bash) *n.* A whip of heavy hide, used as an instrument of torture by the Turks. [<Turkish *qirbāch*]

Kurd (kûrd, kŏōrd) *n.* One of a Moslem people dwelling chiefly in Kurdistan.

Kurd·ish (kûr′dish, kŏōr′-) *adj.* Of or pertaining to the Kurds, their culture, or language. — *n.* The Iranian language of the Kurds.

Kur·di·stan (kûr′di·stan, kŏōr′di·stän) A region in NW Iran, NE Iraq, and SE Turkey in Asia.

Ku·re (kŏō·re) A city in SW Hondo island, Japan.

Kurg (kŏōrg) See COORG.

Ku·ri·a Mu·ri·a Islands (kŏō′rē·ə mŏō′rē·ə) A group of five islands off the SE Oman coast in the Arabian Sea, considered part of Aden Colony; 28 square miles.

Ku·rile Islands (kŏō·rēl′, kŏō′ril) A chain of Russian islands between the southern tip of Kamchatka and the main islands of Japan; 5,700 square miles: Japanese *Chishima Retto.* Also **Ku′ril Islands, Ku′riles.**

Ku·ril·i·an (kŏō·ril′ē·ən) *adj.* Of or pertaining to the Kurile Islands or their inhabitants. — *n.* A native of the Kurile Islands.

Kur·land (kŏōr′lənd) See COURLAND.

Ku·ro·shi·wo (kŏō·rō·shē·wō) See JAPAN CURRENT under CURRENT.

kur·ra·jong (kûr′ə·jong) *n.* Any of various Australian trees of the families *Sterculiaceae* and *Malvaceae* whose leaves are valued as fodder; especially, the **black kurrajong** (*Brachychiton populneum*), whose bark yields a durable, tough fiber: also spelled *currajong, koorajong.* [< native name]

Kursk (kŏōrsk) A city in SW Russian S.F.S.R.

kur·to·sis (kər·tō′sis) *n. Stat.* The relative degree of curvature near the mode of a frequency curve, as compared with that of a normal curve of the same variance. [<Gk. *kyrtos* curved + -OSIS]

Ku·ru·su (kŏō·rŏō·sŏō), **Saburo,** 1883–1954, Japanese diplomat.

Kush (kush), **Kush·it·ic** (kŏōsh·it′ik) See CUSH, etc.

Kus·ko·kwim River (kus′kə·kwim) A river in western Alaska, flowing 600 miles SW to **Kuskokwim Bay,** an inlet of the Bering Sea.

kus·so (kus′ō) See CUSSO.

Kutch (kŏōch, kuch) See CUTCH.

Kut–el–A·ma·ra (kŏōt′el·ə·mä′rə) A city on the Tigris in eastern Iraq. Also **Kut** (kŏōt), **Kut–al–I·ma·ra** (kŏōt′äl·i·mä′rə).

Ku·tu·zov (kŏō·tŏō′zôf), **Mikhail Ilarionovich,** 1745–1813, Russian field marshal; defeated Napoleon at Smolensk (1812).

ku·vasz (kŏō′väsh) *n.* A breed of large, powerful working dog with a thick, white coat. [<Magyar]

Ku·wait (kŏō·wīt′) A sheikdom in NE Arabia; 1,930 square miles; capital, Kuwait: also *Koweit.* — **Ku·wait′i** *n. & adj.*

Kux·ha·ven (kŏōks′hä·fən) See CUXHAVEN.

Kuyp (koip) See CUYP.

Kuz·netsk Basin (kŏōz·nyetsk′) The richest coal basin in the U.S.S.R., comprising a region along the Tom in the south central Russian S.F.S.R. in Asia. Shortened form **Kuz·bas** (kŏōz·bäs′).

kvass (kväs, kvas) *n.* A Russian fermented drink resembling sour beer, made from rye, barley, etc. [<Russian *kvas*]

Kwa·ja·lein (kwä′jə·lān) An atoll in the Marshall Islands; 6 square miles. Also **Kwa′ja·long** (-lông).

Kwang·chow (kwäng′chō′, *Chinese* gwäng′jō′) The Chinese name for CANTON.

Kwang·cho·wan (kwäng′chō′wän′, *Chinese* gwäng′jō′wän′) The French name for CHANKIANG.

Kwang·si (kwang′sē′, *Chinese* gwäng′sē′) A province of SE China; 85,000 square miles; capital, Kweilin.

Kwang·tung (kwang′tŏōng′, *Chinese* gwän′dŏōng′) A province in SE China; 85,000 square miles; capital, Canton.

Kwan·non (kwän·nōn) See KUAN YIN. Also **Kwan Yin** (kwän yin).

Kwan·tung Leased Territory (kwan′tŏōng′, *Chinese* gwän′dŏōng′) A region on the southern tip of Liaotung Peninsula, SE Manchuria, leased, 1905–1945, by Japan; 1,337 square miles. *Japanese* **Kan·to** (kän·tō).

kwash·i·or·kor (kwäsh′ē·ôr′kôr′) *n. Pathol.* A nutritional disease prevalent among children in South Africa and elsewhere, characterized by swelling of the hands, feet, and face and the appearance of discolored blotches on the body. It is associated with a carbohydrate diet low in proteins and amino acids. Also called *Johnny red.* [< native name]

Kwei·chow (kwā′chou′, *Chinese* gwä′jō′) A province in southern China; 65,000 square miles; capital, Kweiyang.

Kwei·lin (kwā′lin′, *Chinese* gwä′lin′) The capital of Kwangsi province, China.

Kwei·sui (kwā′swā′, *Chinese* gwä′swä′) The capital of Suiyuan province, northern China.

Kwei·yang (kwā′yang′, *Chinese* gwä′yäng′) The capital of Kweichow province, China.

ky·a·nite (kī′ə·nīt) See CYANITE.

ky·an·ize (kī′ən·īz) *v.t.* **·ized, ·iz·ing** To impregnate, as wood, with mercuric chloride so as to prevent decay. Also, *Brit.* **ky′an·ise.** [< after J. H. *Kyan,* 1774–1850, Irish inventor] — **ky′an·i·za′tion** (-ə·zā′shən, -ī·zā′-) *n.*

kyar (kyär) See COIR.

Kyd (kid), **Thomas,** 1558–94, English dramatist.

kye (kī) *n. pl. Scot.* Kine.

Ky·klops (kī′klops) See CYCLOPS.

ky·lix (kī′liks) *n. pl.* **ky·li·kes** (kī′li·kēz) A shallow, circular, earthenware drinking cup, having small handles at the sides and resting on a slender, moderately high foot: used chiefly at banquets in ancient Greece: also spelled *cylix.* [<Gk., cup]

KYLIX

ky·mo·graph (kī′mə·graf, -gräf) *n.* **1** *Med.* An instrument for recording wavelike oscillations, composed of a revolving tambour on which a stylus records pulse waves, muscular contractions, respiratory

movements, and the like. **2** *Aeron.* A device for recording the oscillations of an aircraft in flight. Also **ky′mo·graph′i·on** (-ē·on): sometimes spelled *cymograph.* [<Gk. *kyma* wave + -GRAPH] — **ky′mo·graph′ic** *adj.*

Kym·ric (kim′rik), **Kym·ry** (kim′rē) See CYM-RIC, etc.

Kyn·e·wulf (kin′ə·wŏŏlf, kün′-) See CYNEWULF.

Kyo·ga (kyō′gə), **Lake** A lake in central Uganda in the middle course of the Victoria Nile: also *Kioga.*

Kyong·song (kyông·sông) See SEOUL.

Kyo·to (kyō·tō) A city on SW Honshu island, Japan; the third largest city and the capital of the Japanese Empire until 1868: also *Kioto.*

ky·pho·sis (kī·fō′sis) *n. Pathol.* Backward curvature of the spine; humpback. [<NL <Gk. *kyphōsis* <*kyphos* humpbacked] — **ky·phot·ic** (kī·fot′ik) *adj.*

Kyr·i·e e·le·i·son (kir′i·ē i·lā′i·sən) *Eccl.* **1** An ancient petition used in eucharistic rites and other offices: **a** In the Greek Church, a response made by the people to prayers said in the liturgy. **b** In the Roman Catholic Church, a part of a short litany said or chanted immediately after the introit of the mass. **2** In the Anglican Church, a translation of this, said or chanted during the Eucharist. **3** A musical setting for this petition. [<LL <Gk. *Kyrie eleēson* Lord, have mercy]

kyr·i·o·log·ic (kir′ē·ə·loj′ik) See CURIOLOGIC.

kyte (kīt) *n. Scot.* The belly.

kythe (kīth) See KITHE.

Ky·the·ra (kē′thē·rä) A Greek island south of the Peloponnesus; 108 square miles: Latin *Cythera,* Italian *Cerigo.*

Kyu·shu (kyōō·shōō) The southernmost of the five principal islands of Japan; 16,247 square miles: also *Kiushu.*

Ky·zyl Kum (ki·zil′ kōōm′) A desert area in Kazakh and Uzbek S.S.R., extending SE from the Aral Sea: also *Kizil Kum.*

L

l, L (el) *n. pl.* **l's, L's** or **ls, Ls** or **ells** (elz) **1** The 12th letter of the English alphabet: from Phoenician *lamed,* Greek *lambda,* Roman *L.* **2** The sound of the letter *l,* normally a voiced alveolar continuant. See ALPHABET. —**symbol 1** The Roman numeral 50: see under NUMERAL. **2** *Chem.* Lithium (L). **3** Anything shaped like an **L**.

la[1] (lä) *n. Music* The sixth tone of the diatonic scale. [<Ital. <Med. L. See GAMUT.]

la[2] (lä, lô) *interj.* Look! O!: an exclamation expressing surprise, emphasis, etc. Also spelled *law.* [OE *lā.* Doublet of LO.]

L.A. (el′ā′) *Colloq.* Los Angeles.

laa·ger (lä′gər) *n.* A defensive enclosure formed by wagons or otherwise; camp. — *v.t. & v.i.* To camp in or form into a laager. Also spelled *lager.* [<Afrikaans <Du. *leger* a camp]

Laa·land (lô′län) A Danish island in the Baltic Sea; 479 square miles; chief city, Maribo: also *Lolland.*

lab·an (lab′ən) See LEBEN.

La·ban (lā′bən) Brother of Rebecca; father of Rachel and Leah. *Gen.* xxix 10–30.

lab·a·rum (lab′ə·rəm) *n. pl.* **·ra** (-rə) **1** The form of the Roman military standard adopted by Constantine, bearing the cross and the monogram of Christ. **2** An ecclesiastical banner borne in processions. [<LL <Gk. *labaron;* ult. origin unknown]

lab·da·num (lab′də·nəm) See LADANUM.

lab·e·fac·tion (lab′ə·fak′shən) *n.* The act of making or becoming weak or tottering; decay; downfall. Also *Archaic* **lab′e·fac·ta′tion** (-fak·tā′shən). [<L *labefactus,* pp. of *labefacere* cause to totter <*labare* totter, fall to pieces + *facere* make]

la·bel (lā′bəl) *n.* **1** A slip, as of paper, affixed to something and bearing an inscription to indicate its character, ownership, etc. **2** *Archit.* A projecting molding or dripstone over a wall opening. — *v.t.* **·beled** or **·belled,** **·bel·ing** or **·bel·ling 1** To mark with a label; attach a label to. **2** To classify; designate. [<OF, a ribbon, ? <OHG *lappa* a rag] — **la′bel·er** or **la′bel·ler** *n.*

la·bel·lum (lə·bel′əm) *n. pl.* **·la** (-ə) **1** *Bot.* The lip or lower petal of an orchid, often enlarged or variously shaped. **2** *Entomol.* Part of the proboscis of a dipterous insect. [<NL <L, dim. of *labrum* a lip]

la·bi·a (lā′bē·ə) Plural of LABIUM.

la·bi·al (lā′bē·əl) *adj.* **1** Of or pertaining to the lips: a *labial* vein. **2** *Phonet.* Formed, articulated, or modified by the lips, as (p), (b), (m), (w), or the rounded vowels (ō) and (ōō). **3** Having edges or lips, as an organ pipe. **4** Pertaining to the labia. — *n.* **1** *Phonet.* A labial sound. **2** An appliance designed to correct stammering. **3** An organ pipe with lips. [<Med. L *labialis* <L *labium* a lip]

la·bi·al·ize (lā′bē·əl·īz′) *v.t.* **·ized, ·iz·ing** *Phonet.* **1** To make labial; give a labial sound to. **2** To modify (a vowel) by rounding the lips; round. — **la′bi·al·ism, la′bi·al·i·za′tion** *n.*

la·bi·a ma·jo·ra (lā′bē·ə mə·jô′rə) *Anat.* The external mucous folds of the vulva. [<NL <L, lit., the larger lips]

labia mi·no·ra (mi·nô′rə) *Anat.* The inner mucous folds of the vulva. [<NL <L, lit., the smaller lips]

La·bi·a·tae (lā′bē·ā′tē) *n. pl.* A family of widely distributed herbs and shrubs with characteristically square stems, opposite leaves, and whorled flowers: it includes mint, hyssop, thyme, and many other aromatic and medicinal plants. [<NL <*labiatus* LABIATE]

la·bi·ate (lā′bē·āt, -it) *adj. Bot.* **1** Having lips or liplike parts, as a calyx or corolla. **2** Belonging to the *Labiatae.* Also **la′bi·at·ed.** [<NL *labiatus* <L *labium* a lip]

La·biche (la·bēsh′), **Eugène Marin,** 1815–88, French dramatist.

la·bile (lā′bil) *adj.* **1** Prone to undergo chemical change or alteration of atomic structure; unstable. **2** Having a tendency to glide from place to place; smoothly flowing or passing along. **3** Liable to err, slip, or fall. **4** Being free and uncontrolled: said of the emotions. [<L *labilis* <*labi* slip, fall] — **la·bil′i·ty** *n.*

labio- *combining form* Related to, or formed by the lips and (another organ): *labiodental.* [<L *labium* a lip]

la·bi·o·den·tal (lā′bē·ō·den′təl) *Phonet. adj.* Formed with the lower lip and the upper front teeth, as *f* and *v* in English. — *n.* A sound so formed. Also *dentilabial.*

la·bi·o·na·sal (lā′bē·ō·nā′zəl) *Phonet. adj.* Produced with the lips closed and the voiced breath passing through the nose, as *m.* — *n.* A sound so formed.

la·bi·o·ve·lar (lā′bē·ō·vē′lər) *Phonet. adj.* Produced with the lips rounded and partially closed and the back of the tongue near or against the velum, as *w.* — *n.* A sound so formed.

la·bi·um (lā′bē·əm) *n. pl.* **·bi·a** (-bē·ə) **1** A lip or liplike organ or part. **2** *pl.* The folds of the external genitals of the mammalian female. **3** *Entomol.* A movable sclerite between the maxillae of an insect, forming the lower surface of the mouth; the lower lip. [<L, a lip]

la·bor (lā′bər) *n.* **1** Physical or mental exertion, particularly for some useful or desired end; toil; work. **2** That which requires exertion or effort; a task. **3** The working class collectively. **4** Parturition; travail. **5** Any stress or difficulty. **6** *Naut.* Heavy rolling and pitching of a vessel. — **Department of Labor** An executive department of the U. S. government, since 1913 (from 1903 to 1913 part of the Department of Commerce and Labor) headed by the Secretary of Labor and charged with matters pertaining to the welfare of wage earners, especially in regard to wages, working conditions, and opportunities for employment. Also **Labor Department.** See synonyms under BUSINESS, INDUSTRY, TASK, TOIL[1], WORK. — *v.i.* **1** To do work; toil; strive to accomplish a work or purpose. **2** To move with difficulty or painful exertion. **3** To roll or pitch, as a ship in a heavy sea. **4** To be hindered, burdened, or oppressed: to *labor* under a misapprehension. **5** To suffer the pains of childbirth; be in travail. — *v.t.* **6** To work at laboriously; develop in great detail: to *labor* a point. **7** *Archaic* or *Poetic* To till; cultivate. Also, *Brit., labour.* [<OF *labor, labour* <L *labor, -oris* toil, distress]

lab·o·ra·to·ry (lab′rə·tôr′ē, -tō′rē; *Brit.* lə·bor′ə·trē) *n. pl.* **·ries 1** A building or room fitted up for conducting scientific experiments, analyses, or similar work. **2** A department, as in a factory, for research, testing, and experimental technical work. [<Med. L *laboratorium* <L *laborare* labor <*labor, -oris* labor]

Labor Day In most States of the United States, a legal holiday, usually the first Monday in September, originally set aside as a holiday in honor of labor.

la·bored (lā′bərd) *adj.* Performed laboriously; elaborate; strained: a *labored* joke.

la·bor·er (lā′bər·ər) *n.* One who performs physical or manual, especially unskilled, labor.

la·bo·ri·ous (lə·bôr′ē·əs, -bō′rē-) *adj.* **1** Requiring much labor; toilsome. **2** Diligent; industrious. See synonyms under ARDUOUS, DIFFICULT, WEARISOME. — **la·bo′ri·ous·ly** *adv.* — **la·bo′ri·ous·ness** *n.* [<OF *laborios* <L *laboriosus* <*labor* labor]

la·bor·ite (lā′bər·īt) *n.* One who supports labor interests, especially in politics. Also *Brit.* **la′bour·ite.**

la·bor om·ni·a vin·cit (lā′bôr om′nē·ə vin′sit) *Latin* Labor conquers all things.

la·bor-sav·ing (lā′bər·sā′ving) *adj.* Doing away with, or diminishing the need for, manual work.

labor union A union of workers organized to better working conditions and advance mutual interests; a trade union.

la·bour (lā′bər), **la·bour·er** (lā′bər·ər), etc. British spelling of LABOR, etc.

La·bour·ite (lā′bər·īt) *n.* A member of a Labour party in Great Britain or the Commonwealth.

Labour Party 1 In Great Britain, a political party drawing its chief support from the working class and committed to socialistic reform. Organized in the later 19th century, by the 1920's it had supplanted the Liberal Party as the chief opposition to the Conservative Party. **2** A similar party in other members of the Commonwealth.

Lab·ra·dor (lab′rə·dôr) **1** A territory of eastern Canada, comprising a dependency of Newfoundland; 110,000 square miles; capital, Battle Harbor. **2** The peninsula of NE North America between the Saint Lawrence River and Hudson Bay; 530,000 square miles.

Labrador auk See PUFFIN.

lab·ra·dor·ite (lab′rə·dôr′īt) *n.* A triclinic lime-soda feldspar exhibiting a brilliant play of colors. [from *Labrador,* where originally found + -ITE[1]]

Labrador Sea A part of the North Atlantic between Labrador and SW Greenland.

Labrador tea An evergreen shrub (*Ledum groenlandicum*) of the northern regions, having white flowers and rust-colored leaves used for tea.

la·bret (lā′bret) *n.* A stud or plug of hard material, as stone, worn as an ornament in a hole pierced in the lip by various primitive peoples. [Dim. of LABRUM]

la·broid (lā′broid) *adj.* Of or pertaining to a family (*Labridae*) of fishes including the wrasses, tautog, etc. — *n.* A labroid fish. [< NL *Labroidea* <*Labrus* a genus of the family

Labridae <L *labrus* a kind of fish < *labrum* a lip]

la·brum (lā'brəm, lab'rəm) *n.* *pl.* **·bra** (-brə) **1** A lip (especially an outer lip) or a liplike part. **2** *Entomol.* A usually movable sclerite situated between the mandibles of an insect; the upper lip. **3** *Zool.* The outer lip of a univalve shell. [<L, a lip]

La Bru·yère (là brü·yâr'), **Jean de**, 1645–96, French writer and moralist.

La·bu·an (lä'boo·än') An island off the NW coast of Borneo, a part of Sabah; 30 square miles; chief town, Victoria.

la·bur·num (lə·bûr'nəm) *n.* Any of a genus (*Laburnum*) of deciduous Old World trees, especially the **golden-chain laburnum** (*L. anagyroides*), having pendulous racemes of yellow flowers and hard, dark wood: it yields a poisonous alkaloid used in medicine as a purgative and emetic. [<NL <L; ult. origin unknown]

lab·y·rinth (lab'ə·rinth) *n.* **1** A confusing network of passages, as in a building; a maze of intricate paths, as in a park or garden. **2** Hence, any perplexing combination. **3** *Anat.* The winding passages of the internal ear. [<LABYRINTH] — **lab'y·rin'thine** (-thin, -thēn) or **thi·an** or **·thic** or **·thi·cal** *adj.* — **lab'y·rin'thi·cal·ly** *adv.*

THE LABYRINTH OF MINOS

Lab·y·rinth (lab'ə·rinth) In Greek mythology, the maze used to confine the Minotaur, constructed by Daedalus for Minos of Crete. [<L *labyrinthus* <Gk. *labyrinthos*; ult. origin unknown]

lac[1] (lak) *n.* **1** A resinous substance exuded from an East Indian lac insect (*Tachardia lacca*) and used in making varnishes, etc. Compare SHELLAC. **2** The sap of certain trees or plants used for varnish. **3** Lacquer. [<Hind. *lākh* <Prakrit *lakkha* <Skt. *lākshā*]

lac[2] (lak) See LAKH.

lac[3] (lak) *n.* Milk. [<NL <L]

Lac·ca·dive Islands (lak'ə·dīv) A group of 14 coral reefs and islands in the SE Arabian Sea off the Malabar Coast, comprising a Union Territory of India; total, long thought to be about 80 square miles; the Indian government figure is 10 square miles; headquarters at Kozhikode in Kerala, India.

lac·case (lak'ās) *n.* A copper-protein enzyme which oxidizes phenols, found in the lacquer tree and other plants. [<NL *lacc(a)* lacquer + -ASE]

lac·cate (lak'āt) *adj.* *Bot.* Having a varnished appearance, as the leaves of certain plants. [<NL *lacc(a)* lacquer + -ATE[1]]

lac·co·lith (lak'ə·lith) *n.* *Geol.* A mass of intrusive lava spreading out between strata and lifting the overlying rocks into domes. Also **lac'co·lite** (-līt). [<Gk. *lakkos* a reservoir + -LITH[1]] — **lac'co·lith'ic, lac'co·lit'ic** (-lit'ik) *adj.*

lace (lās) *n.* **1** A cord or string for fastening together the parts of a shoe, a corset, etc.; any string. **2** A delicate network of threads of linen, silk, cotton, etc., arranged in figures

TYPES OF LACE

Alencon	Battenberg	Blonde Pointe
Mechlin	Honiton	d'Angleterre

or patterns; also, any ornamental cord or braid. **3** A dash of spirits, as in tea or coffee. — *v.* **laced, lac·ing** *v.t.* **1** To fasten or draw together by tying the lace or laces of. **2** To pass (a cord or string) through hooks, eye-

lets, etc., as a lace. **3** To trim with or as with lace. **4** To compress the waist of (a person) by tightening laces, as of a corset. **5** To intertwine or interlace. **6** To streak, as with color. **7** To add a dash of spirits to a beverage. **8** *Colloq.* To beat; thrash. — *v.i.* **9** To be fastened by means of a lace. — **to lace into** To strike or attack with or as with a heavy blow or blows. [<OF *laz, las* orig. a noose <L *laqueus* a noose, trap. Akin to LASH, LATCH.]

Lac·e·dae·mon (las'ə·dē'mən) See SPARTA.

Lac·e·dae·mo·ni·an (las'ə·di·mō'nē·ən) *adj.* & *n.* Spartan; Laconian.

lace·ground (lās'ground') *n.* A foundation of lacelike net; a réseau.

lac·er (lā'sər) *n.* **1** One who laces. **2** A dash of spirits added to a beverage.

lac·er·ate (las'ər·āt) *v.t.* **·at·ed, ·at·ing** **1** To tear raggedly, as the flesh. **2** To hurt; injure, as the feelings. See synonyms under REND. — *adj.* Rent; jagged; torn. [<L *laceratus*, pp. of *lacerare* tear < *lacer* mangled] — **lac'er·a·ble** *adj.* — **lac'er·a'tion** *n.* — **lac'er·a'tive** *adj.*

La·cer·ta (lə·sûr'tə) *n.* **1** *Astron.* A northern constellation near Cepheus. See CONSTELLATION. **2** *Zool.* A genus of Old World lizards typical of the family *Lacertidae*, especially the common green lizard (*L. viridis*) of southern Europe. [<L, a lizard]

lac·er·til·i·an (las'ər·til'ē·ən) *n.* One of a suborder of reptiles (*Lacertilia*) which includes lizards, chameleons, and related limbless forms. — *adj.* Of or pertaining to the *Lacertilia*: also **la·cer·ti·an** (lə·sûr'shē·ən, -shən). [<NL *Lacertilia* <L *lacertus, lacerta* a lizard]

lace·wing (lās'wing') *n.* Any of certain insects (order *Neuroptera*) having four lacy wings and shiny eyes, especially the green lacewing (genus *Chrysopa*) or the brown lacewing (genus *Hemerobius*), the larvae of which destroy insects. For illustration see INSECT (beneficial).

lace·wood (lās'wood') *n.* **1** The American sycamore. **2** The silky oak (*Cardwellia sublimis*) of Queensland, Australia. **3** The wood of either of these trees, used for furniture, cabinetwork, and veneering.

lace·work (lās'wûrk') *n.* **1** Lace. **2** Any open-work resembling lace.

lach·es (lach'iz) *n.* *Law* Inexcusable delay in asserting a right. [<AF *laches, lachesse*, OF *laschesse* < *lasche* negligent < *laschier* slacken <L *laxare* < *laxus* lax]

Lach·e·sis (lak'ə·sis) One of the three Fates. [<L <Gk., lit., a lot < *lanchanein* obtain by lot or fate]

La·chish (lā'kish) A Biblical locality south of Jerusalem, a Canaanite capital, II *Kings* xiv 19.

Lach·lan River (läk'lən) A river in south central New South Wales, Australia, flowing 922 miles SW to the Murrumbidgee River.

lach·ry·mal (lak'rə·məl), **lach·ry·ma·tor** (lak'rə·mā'tər), etc. See LACRIMAL, etc.

lac·ing (lā'sing) *n.* **1** The act of fastening, as with a lace. **2** Lace (def. 1). **3** A connecting or strengthening member; crosspiece. **4** *Colloq.* A thrashing. **5** Any ornamental braid, as of gold or silver.

lacing course A band of dressed stone inset into a rough-hewn stone wall to form a horizontal line in an otherwise unrelieved design.

la·cin·i·ate (lə·sin'ē·āt, -it) *adj.* **1** Bordered with fringe; fringed. **2** *Bot.* Slashed or cut irregularly into narrow lobes or segments; fringed; incised, as flower petals. Also **la·cin'i·at·ed, la·cin'i·ose** (-ōs). [<NL *lacinia* a slash in a leaf or petal <L, a flap) + -ATE[1]]

lack (lak) *v.t.* **1** To be without; have none or too little of. **2** To be short by; require: It *lacks* two months till summer. — *v.i.* **3** To be wanting or deficient; be missing. — *n.* **1** The state of being needy. **2** Want; deficiency; failure. [ME *lac*, prob. <MLG *lak* deficiency]

lack·a·dai·si·cal (lak'ə·dā'zi·kəl) *adj.* Affectedly sentimental; languishing; listless. Also **lack'a·dai'sy** (-dā'zē) [<*lackadaisy*, alter. of LACKADAY] — **lack'a·dai'si·cal·ly** *adv.* — **lack'a·dai'si·cal·ness** *n.*

lack·a·day (lak'ə·dā') *interj.* *Archaic* Alack!: an exclamation expressing grief or regret. [Aphetic var. of ALACKADAY. See ALACK.]

lack·ey (lak'ē) *n.* **1** A male servant; a footman; menial. **2** Any servile attendant or

follower. — *v.t.* & *v.i.* To attend or act as a lackey. Also LACQUEY. [<OF *laquay* <Sp. *lacayo,* ? <Arabic *luka'* servile]

lack·lus·ter (lak'lus'tər) *adj.* Wanting luster; dim. — *n.* A lack of luster; dullness; also, that which wants luster. Also *Brit.* **lack'lus'tre**.

lac·mus (lak'məs) See LITMUS.

La·co·ni·a (lə·kō'nē·ə) A region and ancient country in the SE Peloponnesus, Greece; 1,500 square miles; capital, Sparta: Modern Greek *Lakonía.* Also **La·con·i·ca** (lə·kon'i·kə). — **La·co'ni·an** *adj.* & *n.*

la·con·ic (lə·kon'ik) *adj.* Using or consisting of few words; short and forceful; concise; pithy. Also **la·con'i·cal.** See synonyms under TERSE. [<L *Laconicus* <Gk. *Lakonikos* <*Lakōn* a Spartan; with ref. to the habitual terseness of Spartan speech] — **la·con'i·cal·ly** *adv.*

lac·o·nism (lak'ə·niz'əm) *n.* **1** A brief and sententious manner of expression. **2** A terse, pointed phrase; laconic expression. Also **la·con·i·cism** (lə·kon'ə·siz'əm).

La Co·ru·ña (lä kō·roo'nyä) See CORUÑA, LA.

lac·quer (lak'ər) *n.* **1** A quick-drying varnish made from pyroxylin or other resin, nitrocellulose, and sometimes a pigment, dissolved in a volatile solvent. **2** Varnished woodwork, often inlaid: Chinese *lacquer,* Japanese *lacquer:* also **lac'quer·work'.** **3** A resinous varnish susceptible of a fine polish, obtained from the lacquer tree (*Toxicodendron verniciifluum*) of China and Japan. **4** Decorative work, as on leather lacquered in imitation of enamel. — *v.t.* To coat or varnish with lacquer. Also **lack'er.** [<MF *lacre* a kind of sealing wax <Pg. < *lacca* gum lac <Hind. *lākh* LAC[1]; infl. in form by F *lacque* LAC[1]] — **lac'quer·er** *n.*

lacquer red Any of various shades of vermilion characteristic of Chinese lacquer.

lac·ri·mal (lak'rə·məl) *adj.* **1** Of or pertaining to tears. **2** Pertaining to or related to tear-producing organs. — *n.* A lacrimatory. Also spelled *lachrymal.* [<Med. L *lacrimalis, lacrymalis* <L *lacrima* a tear]

lac·ri·mar·y (lak'rə·mer'ē) *adj.* Pertaining to, containing, or meant to contain tears: also *lacrimatory.* Also spelled *lachrymary.* [<L *lacrima*]

lac·ri·ma·tion (lak'rə·mā'shən) *n.* **1** The act of shedding tears. **2** The secretion of tears. [<L *lacrimatio, -onis* < *lacrimatus,* pp. of *lacrimare* shed tears < *lacrima* a tear]

lac·ri·ma·tor (lak'rə·mā'tər) *n.* Any of various chemicals which, on being released from shells, bombs, or other containers, provoke a copious flow of tears, with irritation of the eyes: also called *tear gas.* [<L *lacrima* a tear + -ATOR]

lac·ri·ma·to·ry (lak'rə·mə·tôr'ē, -tō'rē) *n.* *pl.* **·ries** A small, narrow-necked glass bottle of a type found in ancient tombs, formerly supposed to have contained the tears of mourners. — *adj.* Lacrimary. Also spelled *lachrymatory.* [<Med. L *lacrimatorium* <L, neut. of *lacrimatorius* of tears < *lacrima* a tear]

LACRIMATORY

lac·ri·mose (lak'rə·mōs) *adj.* Shedding, or given to shedding, tears; tearful: also spelled *lachrymose.* [<L *lacrimosus* < *lacrima* a tear] — **lac'ri·mose'ly** *adv.*

la·crosse (lə·krôs', -kros') *n.* A ball game of American Indian origin, played by two teams of ten men each: the object of each side is to advance the ball across the field with a long, racketlike implement (the *crosse*) between the opponents' goal posts. [<F *la crosse,* lit., the crozier, hooked stick]

La Crosse (lə krôs', -kros') A city on the Mississippi in western Wisconsin.

lac·tal·bu·min (lak'tal·byoo'min) *n.* *Biochem.* A water-soluble protein found in milk. [<LACT- + ALBUMIN]

lac·tam (lak'tam) *n.* *Chem.* Any of a series of organic ring compounds containing the CO·NH group and formed by the elimination of water from the carboxyl and amino groups. [<LACT- + AM(INO)]

Lac·tan·ti·us (lak·tan'shəs), **Lucius Caecilius,**

Latin Christian author of the fourth century.

lac·ta·ry (lak′tər·ē) *adj.* Of or pertaining to milk. [<*lactarius* <*lac, lactis* milk]

lac·tase (lak′tās) *n. Biochem.* An enzyme present in the digestive juices, in certain yeasts, etc., and capable of changing lactose into glucose and galactose.

lac·tate (lak′tāt) *v.i.* **·tat·ed, ·tat·ing 1** To form or secrete milk. **2** To suckle young. —*n.* A salt or ester of lactic acid. —**lac·ta′·tion** *n.*

lac·te·al (lak′tē·əl) *adj.* Pertaining to or like milk; conveying a milklike fluid: also **lac′te·an, lac′te·ous.** —*n. Anat.* One of the lymphatic vessels that take up and convey the chyle. [<L *lacteus* <L *lac, lactis* milk]

lac·tes·cence (lak·tes′əns) *n.* The quality of being milklike; milkiness. Also **lac·tes′cen·cy.**

lac·tes·cent (lak·tes′ənt) *adj.* **1** Milklike; becoming milky. **2** Having or secreting a milky juice. [<L *lactescens, -entis,* ppr. of *lactescere,* inceptive of *lactere* be milky <*lac, lactis* milk]

lac·tic (lak′tik) *adj.* **1** Of, pertaining to, or derived from milk. **2** *Chem.* Designating a limpid sirupy acid, **lactic acid,** $C_3H_6O_3$, with a very bitter taste, contained in sour milk, and the result of lactic fermentation in many compounds.

lac·tif·er·ous (lak·tif′ər·əs) *adj.* **1** Conveying or containing milk or milky fluid; lacteal. **2** Yielding a milky juice, as certain plants. [<LL *lactifer* milk-bearing <L *lac, lactis* milk + *-fer* -FEROUS]

lacto- *combining form* Milk: *lactogenic.* Also before vowels, **lact-.** [<L *lac, lactis* milk]

lac·to·ba·cil·lus (lac′tō·bə·sil′əs) *n. pl.* **·cil·li** (-sil′ī) Any aerobic, rod-shaped bacterium of a genus *(Lactobacillus)* which forms lactic acid, especially *L. acidophilus,* used in the dairy industry and in fermentation processes. [<NL <L *lac, lactis* milk + BACILLUS]

lac·to·fla·vin (lak′tō·flā′vin) See RIBOFLAVIN.

lac·to·gen·ic (lak′tō·jen′ik) *adj.* **1** Stimulating the milk glands. **2** Designating a hormone, as prolactin, which stimulates the secretion of milk.

lac·to·glob·u·lin (lak′tō·glob′yə·lin) *n.* A globulin of milk.

lac·tom·e·ter (lak·tom′ə·tər) *n.* A hydrometer for determining the density or richness of milk.

lac·tone (lak′tōn) *n. Chem.* One of a class of organic anhydrides in which the molecule of water is derived from hydroxyl and carboxyl, both contained in the same radical, with the etherification in the same radical, with the etherification of the acid part by the alcoholic part. [<LACT- + -ONE] —**lac·ton·ic** (lak·ton′ik) *adj.*

lac·to·pro·te·in (lak′tō·prō′tē·in, -tēn) *n.* A protein derived from milk.

lac·to·scope (lak′tə·skōp) *n.* An instrument for determining the purity or richness of milk.

lac·tose (lak′tōs) *n. Biochem.* A white, odorless, cyrstalline disaccharide, $C_{12}H_{22}O_{11}\cdot H_2O$, present in milk; milk sugar. [<LACT(O)- + -OSE[2]]

lac·tu·ca·ri·um (lak′tōō·kâr′ē·əm) *n.* The wild lettuce *(Lactuca virosa)* or its inspissated milky juice, used as a sedative. [<NL <L *lactuca* lettuce]

La Cum·bre (lä kōōm′brā) See USPALLATA.

la·cu·na (lə·kyōō′nə) *n. pl.* **·nas** or **·nae** (-nē) **1** A space from which something is wanting or has been omitted; hiatus; gap. **2** A small pit, hollow, or depression; a gap or small opening. **3** *Anat.* One of the cavities in which lie the osteoblasts of bone. Also **la·cune′** (-kyōōn′). [<L, a hole, pool <*lacus* a basin, pond]

la·cu·nar (lə·kyōō′nər) *adj.* **1** Of or pertaining to a lacuna. **2** Containing or having lacunae: also **la·cu′nal.** —*n. pl.* **la·cu·nars** or **lac·u·nar·i·a** **(lak′yōō·nâr′ē·ə)** *Archit.* **1** A sunken panel or coffer in a ceiling or a soffit. **2** A ceiling or a soffit having sunken panels or compartments. —**lac·u·nar·y** (lak′yōō·ner′ē) *adj.*

la·cu·nose (lə·kyōō′nōs) *adj.* Marked by shallow depressions. [<L *lacunosus* <*lacuna.* See LACUNA.]

la·cus·trine (lə·kus′trin) *adj.* **1** Of or pertaining to a lake. **2** Found in or growing in lakes, as certain plants. **3** Formed in or near lakes, as geological deposits. Also **la·cus′tral, la·cus′tri·an.** [<L *lacus* a lake]

lac·y (lā′sē) *adj.* **lac·i·er, lac·i·est 1** Lacelike. **2** Of lace. —**lac′i·ly** *adv.* —**lac′i·ness** *n.*

lad (lad) *n.* A boy or youth; companion; fellow. Also **lad′die.** [<ME *ladde,* ? ult. <ON]

La·dakh (lə·däkh′) A district of eastern Kashmir; 45,762 square miles; capital, Leh

lad·a·num (lad′ə·nəm) *n.* A dark-colored, brittle, bitter resin from various species of the rockrose (genus *Cistus*): often spelled *labdanum.* See LAUDANUM. [<L *ladanum, ledanum* <Gk. *ladanon, lēdanon* <*lēdon* mastic]

lad·der (lad′ər) *n.* **1** A device of wood, rope, etc., for climbing and descending: usually a series of rounds, supported at their ends by long sidepieces; also, any means of ascending. **2** A run in a stocking or other knit fabric. **3** *Mil.* A three-round burst fired rapidly from a gun pointing in the same direction but with the second and third rounds at a decreased range. [OE *hlǣdder*]

lad·der-back (lad′ər·bak′) *n.* A chair back constructed with two posts connected by horizontal slats; also, a chair having such a back.

ladder stitch An embroidery stitch giving a ladder effect.

lade (lād) *v.* **lad·ed, lad·ed** or **lad·en, lad·ing** *v.t.* **1** To load with a burden or cargo; also, to load as a cargo. **2** To weight down; burden; oppress. **3** To dip or lift (a liquid) in or out with a ladle or dipper. —*v.i* **4** To receive cargo. **5** To dip or lift a liquid. See synonyms under LOAD. [OE *hladan* load]

lad·en[1] (lād′n) Alternative past participate of LADE. —*adj.* Burdened: *laden* with care.

lad·en[2] (lād′n) *v.t.* & *v.i.* **lad·ened, lad·en·ing** To lade. [Var. of LADE]

La·dies′ Aid Society (lā′dēz) **1** A women's organization founded during the Civil War to make and send clothing, bandages, etc., to the soldiers. **2** Any of various women's societies engaged in raising money for church purposes.

ladies′ room In a public building, a room or rooms provided with toilet facilities for women.

la·dies-tress·es (lā′dēz·tres′iz) See LADY-TRESSES.

La·din lə·dēn′) *n.* **1** A Rhaeto-Romanic dialect spoken in the Engadine and Friuli regions of Switzerland and northern Italy. **2** One who speaks Ladin. [<L *Latinus* Latin]

la·ding (lā′ding) *n.* **1** The act of loading. **2** A load or cargo.

la·di·no (lə·dē′nō *n. SW U.S.* A horse that is cunning as well as vicious and unmanageable. [<Sp., cunning, crafty]

La·di·no lä·dē′nō *n.* **1** A Spanish dialect, with many Hebrew elements, spoken by Turkish and other Sephardic Jews. **2** In Latin America, a mestizo. [<Sp., wise, learned, <L *Latinus* Latin]

Lad·is·laus (lad′is·lôs) A masculine personal name. Also **Lad′is·las** (-läs). [<Slavic, ruling with fame]

—**Ladislaus I —Ladislaus I**, 1040?–95, king of Hungary 1077–95; canonized, 1192.

la·dle (lād′l) *n.* **1** A cup-shaped vessel, with a long handle, for dipping or conveying liquids. **2** A milwheel float. —*v.t.* **·dled, ·dling** To dip up and carry in a ladle. [OE *hlǣdel* <*hladan* lade] —**la′dler** *n.*

La·do·ga (lä′dô·gä), **Lake** The largest lake in Europe, in NW European U.S.S.R.; 7,100 square miles. *Finnish* **Laa·tok·ka** (lä′tôk·kä).

La·don (lā′dən) In Greek mythology, the never-sleeping dragon guarding the golden apples of the Hesperides.

la·drone (lə·drōn′) *n.* A mercenary soldier; robber; rascal. [<Sp. *ladrón,* <L *latro, -onis* a robber]

La·drone Islands (lə·drōn′) See MARIANAS ISLANDS. Also **La·drones′.**

la·dro·nism (lə·drō′niz·əm) *n.* **1** Brigandage; plunder. **2** Resistance by ladrones.

la·dy (lā′dē) *n. pl.* **·dies 1** A refined and well-bred woman; a gentlewoman. **2** A woman of superior position in society; a woman of good family and recognized social standing. **3** Any woman: in the plural, used as a form of address. **4** The woman who is at the head of or has authority over a household or an estate: the *lady* of the house; the mistress of a family or manor. **5** A sweetheart; ladylove. **6** *Colloq.* Wife: the colonel's *lady.* —*adj.* **1** Of or like a lady; becoming to a lady. **2** Female: a *lady* doctor. ◆ *Lady* is here a genteelism, as it is in such compounds as *saleslady. Woman* is the more appropriate word to indicate the feminine gender of these occupational terms: a *woman* doctor, a *saleswoman,* etc. [OE *hlǣfdīge,* lit., bread-kneader <*hlāf* bread, loaf + *-dige,* a stem akin to *dāh* dough]

La·dy (lā′dē) *n.* **1** In Great Britain, the title belonging to the wife of any peer below the rank of duke; also given by courtesy to the daughters of dukes, marquises, and earls, and to the wives of lords, baronets, and knights: correlative to *Lord* or *Sir.* **2** The Virgin Mary: usually with *Our.*

la·dy·bell (lā′dē·bel′) *n.* An Erect perennial herb (genus *Adenophora)* having fleshy roots and bell-shaped, usually violet, flowers: often confused with the bellflower.

la·dy·bird (lā′dē·bûrd′) *n.* A small, convex, brightly-colored beetle *(Adalia bipunctata),* usually red spotted with black, or black spotted with red. It feeds on aphids and other small insects. Also **lady beetle, la′dy·bug′** (-bug′). For illustration see INSECT (beneficial).

Lady Day A day observed in honor of the Virgin Mary; specifically, the feast of the Annunciation, March 25: one of the quarter days in England.

la·dy·fin·ger (lā′dē·fing′gər) *n.* **1** A small sponge cake: so called from its shape. **2** A very small firecracker.

la·dy-in-wait·ing (lā′dē·in·wā′ting) *n. pl.* **la·dies-in-wait·ing** A lady of the British royal household in attendance at court.

la·dy-kill·er (lā′dē·kil′ər) *n. Colloq.* A man supposed to be peculiarly fascinating to women.—**la′dy-kill′ing** *adj.* & *n.*

la·dy·kin (lā′di·kin) *n.* A little lady. [Dim. of LADY]

la·dy·like (lā′dē·līk′) *adj.* **1** Like or suitable to a lady; gentle; delicate. **2** Effeminate.

la·dy·love (lā′dē·luv′) *n.* A woman who is beloved; sweetheart.

Lady of the Lake See VIVIEN.

la·dy·palm (lā′dē·päm′) *n.* A low, reedlike fan palm (genus *Rhaphis)* with broad leaves and yellowish flowers, native to southern China.

la·dy·ship (lā′dē·ship) *n.* The rank or condition of a lady: used as a title, with *her* or *your.*

la·dy·slip·per (lā′dē·slip′ər) *n.* **1** Any of a genus *(Cypripedium)* of orchids resembling a slipper; especially, in the United States, the common wild species. *C. calceolus pubescens* and *C. parviflorum.* **2** The moccasin flower. Also **la′dy's-slip′per.**

SHOWY LADYSLIPPER (Up to 2 feet tall)

lady's man A man fond of the company of women and attentive to them. Also **ladies′ man.**

La·dy·smith (lā′dē·smith) A town in Kwa Zulu/Natal province, Republic of South Africa; besieged by Boers 1899–1900.

la·dy-smock (lā′dē·smok′) *n.* The cuckoo flower. Also **la′dy's-smock′.**

la·dy′s-thumb (lā′dēz·thum′) *n.* Persicary.

la·dy-tress·es (lā′dē·tres′iz) *n.* A hardy terrestrial orchid (genus *Spiranthes*) of wide distribution, having slender stems and small flowers in more or less twisted spikes: also spelled *ladies-tresses.* Also **la′dy's-tress′es.**

La·e (lä′ā) A port, chief city of the Territory of New Guinea.

Laën·nec (lā·nek′), **René Théophile Hyacinthe,** 1781–1826, French physician; invented the stethoscope.

La·er·tes (lā·ûr′tēz) **1** In the *Odyssey,* a king of Ithaca; father of Odysseus. **2** In Shakespeare's *Hamlet,* brother of Ophelia and son of Polonius.

Lae·ta·re Sunday (lē·târ′ē) *n.* The fourth Sunday in Lent: Mid-Lent Sunday: so called from the first word in the introit of the mass of that day. [<L. imperative sing. of *laetari* rejoice <*laetus* joyful]

laevo- See LEVO-.

La Farge (lə färj′), **John,** 1835–1910, U.S. painter.

La·fay·ette (lä′fē·et′, laf′ē·et′; *Fr.* là·fà·yet′), **Marquis de,** 1757–1834, Marie Joseph Paul Yves Roch Gilbert Motier, French general and patriot; served in the American Revolutionary army. Also **La Fay·ette′.**

La Fol·lette (lə fol′it), **Robert Marion,** 1855–

1925, U.S. political leader; U.S. senator 1906–1925.

La Fon·taine (lä fon·tān′, *Fr.* là fôṅ·ten′), **Jean de**, 1621–95, French fabulist and poet.

lag[1] (lag) *v.i.* **lagged, lag·ging** 1 To move slowly; stay or fall behind; loiter. 2 In billiards, to shoot one's cue ball to the end rail so that it will rebound to the head rail, the player whose ball stops nearest the end rail winning first place in the order of play. 3 In marbles, to throw one's taw as near as possible to a line on the ground in order to decide the order of play. See synonyms under LINGER. — *n.* 1 Retardation of movement for any cause. 2 The retardation of magnetization in respect of a magnetizing force. 3 In billiards and marbles, an act of lagging. [? Var. of LACK]

lag[2] (lag) *n.* 1 A stave of a barrel, cask, drum, etc. 2 A piece forming part of a lagging. — *v.t.* **lagged, lag·ging** To provide or cover with lags or lagging. [Prob. <ON *lögg* rim of a barrel]

lag[3] (lag) *v.t.* **lagged, lag·ging** *Slang* 1 To arrest. 2 To send to penal servitude. — *n. Slang* 1 A convict. 2 A period of penal servitude. [Prob. <LEG, with ref. to fetters]

lag·an (lag′ən) *n.* In maritime law, goods cast from a vessel in peril, but to which a buoy or float is attached as evidence of ownership: also spelled *ligan*. Compare FLOTSAM, JETSAM. [<AF <Gmc.: prob. akin to ON *lögn* a net laid in the sea]

La·gash (lä′gash) An ancient Sumerian city in southern Babylonia: also *Shirpula.*

Lag b'O·mer (läg′ bō′mər) A Jewish festival, the 18th day of Iyyar. [<Hebrew, lit., 33rd (day) of the omer (the 49 days from the second day of Passover to the first of Shabuoth)]

la·ger (lä′gər) *n.* 1 Beer containing few hops, and stored for several months before use: also **lager beer.** 2 Laager. [<G *lager-bier*, lit., store beer, < *lager* a storehouse + *bier* beer]

La·ger·kvist (lä′yər·kvist), **Pär,** born 1891, Swedish novelist and dramatist.

La·ger·lof (lä′yər·lœf), **Selma,** 1858–1940, Swedish novelist.

lag·gard (lag′ərd) *n.* One who lags; a loiterer. — *adj.* Falling behind; loitering; slow; tardy. [<LAG[1] + -ARD] — **lag′gard·ly** *adv.* — **lag′gard·ness** *n.*

lag·gen (lag′ən) *n. Dial. & Scot.* 1 The angle formed by the bottom and side of a wooden dish. 2 The bottom hoop, as of a cask. 3 *pl.* Barrel staves. Also **lag′gin.** [<ON *lögg*; infl. in form by LAGGING]

lag·ger (lag′ər) *n.* 1 One who lags. 2 *Slang* A convict serving or having served a term of penal servitude.

lag·ging (lag′ing) *n.* 1 Strips of wood used for various purposes, as to form a jacketing for a steam cylinder, to support an arch of masonry while in construction, to brace the beams of a floor, etc. 2 The action of covering. [<LAG[2]]

La Gio·con·da (lä jō·kôn′dä) See MONA LISA.

la·gniappe (lan·yap′, lan′yap) *n. Dial.* A small present given to the purchaser of an article by a merchant or storekeeper; a gratuity: also spelled *lanyappe.* Also **la·gnappe′.** [<dial. F (Creole) <F *la* the + Sp. *ñapa* a lagniappe <Quechua *yapa*]

La·go·a dos Pa·tos (lə·gō′ə thŏŏsh pä′tōos) See PATOS, LAGOA DOS.

La·go di Gar·da (lä′gō dē gär′dä) See GARDA.

Lag·o·mor·pha (lag′ə·môr′fə) *n. pl.* An order of gnawing mammals regarded as differing from the rodents in dentition and in structure of the jaws, including rabbits, hares, and pikas. [<NL <Gk. *lagōs* a hare + *morphē* form]

la·goon (lə·gŏŏn′) *n. Geog.* 1 A body of shallow salt water, as a bay or inlet, separated from but connecting with the sea. 2 A body of shallow fresh water, as a pond or lake, usually connecting with a river or lake. 3 A depression in high tablelands of the western United States. Also **la·gune′.** [<F *lagune* <Ital. *laguna* <L *lacuna.* See LACUNA.]

Lagoon Islands A former name for the EL-LICE ISLANDS.

lag·oph·thal·mos (lag′of·thal′məs) *n. Pathol.* A morbid condition in which the eyes cannot be completely closed; also called *hare's-eye.*

[<NL <Gk. *lagophthalmos* hare-eyed, unable to close the eyes < *lagōs* a hare + *ophthalmos* an eye] — **lag′oph·thal′mic** *adj.*

La·gos (lä′gōs, lä′gos) 1 A port on the Gulf of Guinea, capital of Nigeria. 2 A former British colony, amalgamated with Nigeria since 1906.

La·grange (lə·gränj′, *Fr.* là·gränzh′), **Joseph Louis,** 1736–1813, French mathematician and astronomer.

La Gran·ja (lä gräng′hä) See SAN ILDEFONSO.

Lag·ting (läg′ting) *n.* The upper house of the Norwegian parliament. [<Norw. *lag* society, law + *ting* parliament]

La Guai·ra (lä gwī′rä) The port of Caracas in northern Venezuela. Also **La Guay′ra.**

La Guar·di·a (lə gwär′dē·ə), **Fiorello,** 1882–1947, U.S. politician and mayor of New York 1934–45.

La Hague (lə häg′, *Fr.* là àg′) See HAGUE, LA.

La Hogue (lä ōg′) See SAINT-VAAST-LA-HOGUE.

La·hore (lə·hōr′) 1 A commissioner's division of West Pakistan; 9,119 square miles. 2 The leading city of this division, capital of the province of West Pakistan; capital of the former province of the Punjab, Pakistan, 1947–55; capital of the former province of the Punjab, British India, 1849–1947.

Lai·bach (lī′bäkh) The German name for LJUBLJANA.

la·ic (lä′ik) *adj.* Pertaining to the laity: also **la′i·cal.** — *n.* A layman. [<LL *laicus* <Gk. *laikos* < *laos* the people] — **la′i·cal·ly** *adv.*

la·i·cize (lä′ə·sīz) *v.t.* **-cized, ·ciz·ing** To secularize. — **la′i·ci·za′tion** *n.*

laid (lād) Past tense and past participle of LAY[1]. — *adj.* Covered with close, fine, parallel watermarked lines: *laid* paper.

laigh (lākh) *Scot. adj.* Low. — *n.* A hollow. Also **laich.**

l'Ai·glon (lā·glôṅ′) Son of Napoleon I. [<F, lit., the eaglet]

Lai·ka (lī′kə) *n.* 1 A breed of dog of Siberian Arctic origin, of medium size and white or gray coloring, noted for its sturdiness and intelligence. 2 The name of a dog of this breed sent aloft in the second U.S.S.R. artificial earth satellite in November, 1957.

lain (lān) Past participle of LIE[1].

lair[1] (lâr) *n.* 1 The resting place or den of a wild animal. 2 *Scot.* Any place for resting; a bed. 3 A burial plot. — *v.i.* 1 To rest in a lair; make a lair. — *v.t.* 2 To place in a lair. 3 To serve as a lair for. [OE *leger* bed. Akin to LIE[1].]

lair[2] (lâr) *n. Scot.* Lore; learning.

laird (lârd) *n. Scot.* A lord; also, the proprietor of a landed estate; occasionally, merely a landlord. — **laird′ly** *adj.* — **laird′ship** *n.*

lais·sez–faire (les′ā·fâr′) *n.* 1 The let-alone principle; in economics, absolutely uncontrolled industrial and commercial competition; non-interference. 2 Indifference. Also **lais′ser–faire′.** [<F, lit., let do <*laissez,* imperative of *laisser* let + *faire* do, make]

lais·sez–pas·ser (les′ā pä·sā′) *n.* A permit. [<F, lit., let pass <*laissez,* imperative of *laisser* let + *passer* pass]

laith (lāth) *Scot.* Loath; reluctant. — **laith′ly** *adv.*

la·i·ty (lä′ə·tē) *n. pl.* **·ties** 1 The people as distinguished from the clergy. 2 Those outside a certain profession. [<LAY[2] + -ITY]

La·ius (lā′yəs) In Greek legend, a king of Thebes, husband of Jocasta, who was unwittingly killed by his son Oedipus. He is said to have introduced homosexual love into Greece.

lake[1] (lāk) *n.* 1 A considerable inland body of water or natural enclosed basin serving to drain the surrounding country. ♦ Collateral adjective: *lacustrine.* 2 A small artificial pond; also, a pool of any liquid: a *lake* of wine. [Fusion of OE *lac* a stream, pool and OF *lac* a basin, pond, lake <L *lacus.* Akin to LEACH, LEAK.]

lake[2] (lāk) *n.* 1 A deep red pigment made by combining some animal (as cochineal) or vegetable (as madder) coloring matter with a metallic oxide, usually that of aluminum or tin. 2 The color of this pigment. 3 Any insoluble metallic compound yielding variously colored pigments by the chemical interaction of mordant and dye. [Var. of LAC[1]]

lake[3] (lāk) *v.t.* **laked, lak·ing** 1 To separate the hemoglobin from the red corpuscles of (blood). 2 To make red in color, as the blood. [<LAKE[2] (from the red color of the corpuscles)] — **lak′ing** *n.*

Lake (lāk), **Simon,** 1866–1945, U.S. engineer, naval architect and submarine builder.

Lake District A region in Cumberland, Lancashire, and Westmoreland counties, England, containing the principal English lakes. Also **Lake Country, Lake Land.**

lake dweller An inhabitant of a lake dwelling; a lacustrian.

lake dwelling A habitation erected on piles over the waters of a lake, as in prehistoric Switzerland.

lake herring A herringlike whitefish or cisco (genus *Leucichthys*) of the Great Lakes.

Lake of Geneva See GENEVA, LAKE OF.

Lake of the Woods A lake between the northern part of Minnesota and Manitoba and Ontario provinces, Canada; 1,485 square miles.

Lake Poets The English poets Coleridge, Wordsworth, and Southey, who lived for a while in the English Lake District.

lak·er (lā′kər) *n.* 1 A lake fish; especially, the lake trout of America. 2 One connected with a lake, or lakes, as a visitor to a lake, or a vessel engaged in lake trade. [<LAKE[1]]

Lake Success A village in SE New York on Long Island; headquarters of the United Nations Security Council, 1946–50.

lake trout Any of various salmonoid fishes, especially, in North America, the namaycush. Also **lake salmon.**

lakh (lak) *n.* The sum of 100,000; 100,000 rupees; a great number: also spelled *lac.* [<Hind. *lākh* <Skt. *laksha* 100,000]

La·ko·ni·a (lä·kō·nye′ä) The modern Greek name for LACONIA.

lak·y[1] (lā′kē) *adj.* Like a lake. [<LAKE[1]]

lak·y[2] (lā′kē) *adj.* Of or pertaining to the pigment lake. [<LAKE[2]]

lak·y[3] (lā′kē) *adj.* Transparent: said of blood in which the red corpuscles have been made colorless. [<LAKE[3]]

la·li·a·try (lə·lī′ə·trē) *n.* The branch of medicine which studies disorders of speech. [<NL <Gk. *lalia* speech + -IATRY]

La Lí·ne·a (lä lē′nä·ä) A port of southern Spain. Also **La Lí·ne·a de la Con·cep·ción** (thä lä kōn′·thep·thyōn′)

Lal·lan (lal′ən) *Scot. adj.* Of or pertaining to the Lowlands of Scotland; Lowland. — *n.* The Lowland Scottish dialect. Also **Lal′land.**

lal·la·tion (la·lā′shən) *n.* An imperfect pronunciation of *r* which makes it sound like *l;* lambdacism; babbling speech. [<L *lallatus,* pp. of *lallare* sing "la la" or a lullaby]

l'Al·le·gro (lä·lā′grō) *Italian* The merry or cheerful one; the joyous man: title of a poem by Milton.

La·lo (là·lō′), **Édouard Victor Antoine,** 1823–1892, French composer.

lal·o·neu·ro·sis (lal′ō·nŏŏ·rō′sis, -nyōŏ-) *n. Psychiatry* A nervous disorder affecting speech. [<NL <Gk. *laleein* talk, chatter + NEUROSIS]

lal·o·pa·thol·o·gy (lal′ō·pa·thol′ə·jē) *n.* The branch of medicine which deals with speech disorders. [<Gk. *laleein* talk, chatter + PATHOLOGY]

lal·o·pho·bi·a (lal′ō·fō′bē·ə) *n.* A morbid fear of speaking. [<NL <Gk. *laleein* talk, chatter + -PHOBIA]

lam[1] (lam) *v.t.* **lammed, lam·ming** *Slang* To beat; thrash; punish. [? <ON *lamdha,* pt. of *lemja* thresh. Akin to LAME.]

lam[2] (lam) *Slang v.i.* **lammed, lam·ming** To run away; flee hastily. — *n.* Sudden flight. — **on the lam** In flight; fleeing. — **to take it on the lam** To flee hastily; run away. [Prob. <*lammas,* alter. of *nammus,* ? alter. of Sp. *vamos* let us be off, infl. in form by G *nehmen* take]

la·ma[1] (lä′mə) *n.* 1 A priest or monk of Lamaism ranking high in the hierarchy. 2 A title of courtesy given to all monks of Lamaism. See DALAI LAMA. [<Tibetan *blama* < *bla* above]

la·ma[2] (lä′mə) See LLAMA: an erroneous use.

La·ma·ism (lä′mə·iz′əm) *n.* The religious system of Tibet and Mongolia, a variety of Northern Buddhism, introduced into Tibet in the 7th century, and essentially modified

by Sivaism and native Shamanistic beliefs and practices. [<LAMA[1] + -ISM] — **La′ma·ist** *n.* — **La′ma·is′tic** *adj.*

La Man·cha (lä män′chä) A generally arid region of south central Spain.

La Manche (lȧ mänsh) The French name for the ENGLISH CHANNEL.

La·marck (lȧ·märk′), **Chevalier de,** 1744–1829, Jean Baptiste Pierre Antoine de Monet, French naturalist; pioneer of the theory of evolution of species by adaptation to environments and by the inheritance of acquired characteristics.

La·marck·i·an (lə·märk′ē·ən) *adj.* Of or pertaining to Jean de Lamarck, or to Lamarckism. — *n.* A believer in Lamarckism.

La·marck·ism (lə·märk′iz·əm) *n. Biol.* The theory of descent or evolution propounded by Lamarck, which assumes that species have become developed by the efforts of an organism to adapt itself to new conditions, and by the inheritance of the changes thus produced: often applied to belief in the inheritability of acquired characteristics.

La·mar·tine (lȧ·mȧr·tēn′), **Alphonse Marie Louis de Prat de,** 1790–1869, French poet.

la·ma·ser·y (lä′mə·ser′ē) *n. pl.* **·ser·ies** A Buddhist monastery or convent of Tibet or Mongolia. [<F *lamaserie* < *lama* a lama]

lamb (lam) *n.* **1** A young sheep; also, its flesh. **2** Any gentle or innocent person. **3** An unsophisticated person; simpleton. **4** An inexperienced and gullible speculator in stocks. — **the Lamb** Christ. — *v.i.* To give birth: said of sheep. [OE] — **lamb′like′, lamb′ish** *adj.*

Lamb (lam), **Charles,** 1775–1834, English essayist and critic: pen name *Elia.* — **Mary,** 1764–1847, sister of Charles; co-author with him of *Tales from Shakespeare.* — **William** See MELBOURNE, VISCOUNT.

lam·baste (lam·bāst′) *v.t.* **·bast·ed, ·bast·ing** *Slang* **1** To beat or thrash. **2** To scold; castigate. [<LAM[1] + BASTE[3]] — **lam·bast′ing** *n.*

lamb·da (lam′də) *n.* The eleventh letter and seventh consonant of the Greek alphabet (Λ, λ). See ALPHABET. [<Phoenician *lamed*]

lamb·da·cism (lam′də·siz′əm) *n.* A disorder of speech in which the sufferer cannot pronounce the letter *l* correctly. See LALLATION. [<L *lambdacismus* <Gk. *lambdakismos* < *lambdakizein* pronounce lambda imperfectly < *lambda* LAMBDA]

lamb·doid (lam′doid) *adj.* Resembling in form the Greek letter lambda (Λ): said of the suture between the occipital and the two parietal bones of the skull. Also **lamb·doi′dal.**

lam·bent (lam′bənt) *adj.* **1** Playing with a soft, undulatory movement; gliding; flickering. **2** Softly radiant. **3** Touching lightly but brilliantly: *lambent* wit. [<L *lambens, -entis,* ppr. of *lambere* lick] — **lam′ben·cy, lam′bent·ness** *n.* — **lam′bent·ly** *adv.*

lam·bert (lam′bərt) *n. Physics* The cgs unit of brightness; the uniform brightness of a perfect diffusing surface emitting or reflecting light at the rate of one lumen per square centimeter. [after J. H. *Lambert,* 1728–1777, German physicist]

Lam·beth (lam′bəth) A metropolitan borough of SW London.

Lambeth Palace The official London residence of the archbishop of Canterbury.

lamb·kill (lam′kil′) *n.* A North American shrub *(Kalmia angustifolia)* with deep-pink flowers and narrow leaves said to be poisonous to animals: also called *killikid, sheep laurel.*

lamb·kin (lam′kin) *n.* A little lamb; figuratively, a cherished child. Also **lamb′ie.** [Dim. of LAMB]

lamb lettuce Corn salad.

Lamb of God Christ, by analogy with the paschal lamb. *John* i 29.

lam·boys (lam′boiz) *n. pl.* Flexible steel plates worn skirtlike from the waist of 15th century armor. [? Alter. of JAMBEAUX]

lam·bre·quin (lam′bər·kin, -brə-) *n.* **1** A draped strip, as of cloth or leather, hanging from the casing above a window, doorway, etc. **2** An ornamental covering for a helmet. [<F <Du. *lamperkin,* dim. of *lamper* a veil]

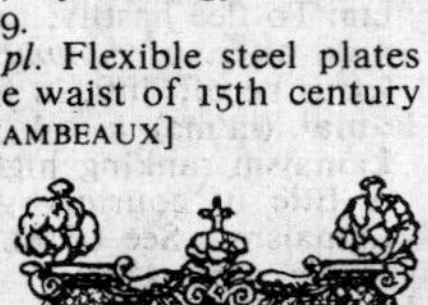

LAMBREQUIN *(def. 1)*

lamb·skin (lam′skin′) *n.* A lamb's skin, especially when dressed, as for glovemaking.

lamb's wool The wool of lambs used in the manufacture of various textile fabrics.

lamb's-wool (lamz′wo͝ol) *n.* A drink made of hot ale with sugar, nutmeg, and roasted apples.

lam·dan (läm′dən) *n.* A person learned in Jewish lore. [<Hebrew]

lame[1] (lām) *adj.* **1** Crippled or disabled, especially in the legs. **2** Hence, inefficient; halting. **3** Sore; painful: a *lame* back. — *v.t.* **lamed, lam·ing** To make lame; cripple. [OE *lama.* Akin to LAM[1].] — **lame′ly** *adv.* — **lame′·ness** *n.*

lame[2] (lām) *n.* A thin plate of metal; specifically one used in making armor. [<F <L *lamina* a lamina]

la·mé (la·mā′) *n.* A fabric woven of flat gold or silver thread, often brocaded, sometimes mixed with silk or other fiber. [<F, orig. pp. of *lamer* laminate < *lame* a lame[2]]

la·med (lä′med) The twelfth Hebrew letter. Also **la′medh.** See ALPHABET. [<Hebrew, lit., a whip, club]

lame duck *Colloq.* **1** A helpless or disabled person. **2** On the stock exchange, one who cannot fulfil his contracts. **3** *U.S.* A member of a legislature, especially of Congress, whose term continues some time after his defeat for reelection.

la·mel·la (lə·mel′ə) *n. pl.* **·lae** (-ē) **1** A thin plate, scale, or lamina, as in the gills of bivalves, or in bone. **2** *Bot.* A gill of a mushroom, one of the thin plates attached to the under side of the cap. [<NL <L, dim. of *lamina* a lamina]

lam·el·lar (lə·mel′ər, lam′ə·lər) *adj.* Scalelike; composed of thin layers or scales. Also **lam·el·late** (lam′ə·lāt, lə·mel′āt), **lam′el·lat′ed.** — **lam′el·la′tion** *n.*

la·mel·li·branch (lə·mel′i·brangk) *n.* One of a class *(Pelecypoda,* formerly *Lamellibranchiata)* of mollusks, having bivalve shells enclosing a mantle within which is the compressed body of the organism, including clams, mussels, and oysters. — *adj.* Of or pertaining to this class. [<NL *lamellibranchia,* name of this class <L *lamella* LAMELLA + Gk. *branchia* gills, pl. of *branchion* a fin] — **la·mel′li·bran′·chi·ate** (-brang′kē·āt, -it) *adj.* & *n.*

la·mel·li·corn (lə·mel′i·kôrn) *adj. Entomol.* **1** Terminating in leaflike joints, as the antennae of certain beetles. **2** Having such antennae. **3** Of or pertaining to a division of beetles *(Lamellicornia)* having a lateral leaflike expansion on each of the terminal antennal segments, as the scarab beetle. — *n.* One of the lamellicorn beetles. [<NL *lamellicornis* <L *lamella* LAMELLA + *cornu* a horn]

la·mel·li·form (lə·mel′i·fôrm) *adj.* Having the form of a thin plate, scale, or lamella; scalelike; lamellar.

la·mel·li·ros·tral (lə·mel′i·ros′trəl) *adj. Ornithol.* Of or pertaining to a group of birds having lamellar ridges on the inner edges of the bills, as ducks, swans, and geese. Also **la·mel′li·ros′trate** (-trāt). [<NL *lamellirostris* <L *lamella* LAMELLA + *rostrum* a beak]

lamelli- *combining form* Lamellae; resembling lamellae: *lamellibranch.* [<L *lamella* a plate]

la·mel·loid (lə·mel′oid, lam′ə·loid) *adj.* Of or resembling a plate or lamella. [<LAMELL(A) + -OID]

la·mel·lose (lə·mel′ōs, lam′ə·lōs) *adj.* Composed of or full of thin plates, scales, or lamellae; lamelliform. [<LAMELL(A) + -OSE[1]]

la·ment (lə·ment′) *v.t.* To feel or express sorrow for; bewail. — *v.i.* To feel or express sorrow; mourn; grieve. — *n.* **1** The expression of grief; lamentation. **2** A plaintive song or melody. See synonyms under MOURN. [<L *lamentari* < *lamentum* a wailing, weeping] — **la·ment′er** *n.*

lam·en·ta·ble (lam′ən·tə·bəl) *adj.* **1** Expressing sorrow; mournful: a *lamentable* cry. **2** Exciting regret or dissatisfaction; despicable; deplorable: a *lamentable* failure. See synonyms under PITIFUL. — **lam′en·ta·bly** *adv.*

lam·en·ta·tion (lam′ən·tā′shən) *n.* The act of lamenting or bewailing; utterance of profound regret or grief; a wailing cry.

Lam·en·ta·tions (lam′ən·tā′shəns) A lyrical poetic book of the Old Testament, attributed to Jeremiah the prophet; also, the music to which a portion of it is sung in the Roman Catholic Church at Tenebrae.

la·mi·a (lā′mē·ə) *n.* A female demon or vampire; witch. [<L, a witch sucking children's blood <Gk., a fabulous monster]

La·mi·a (lā′mē·ə) In Greek mythology, a queen of Libya, beloved of Zeus, who was robbed of her children by Hera and took revenge by killing the children of others.

lam·i·na (lam′ə·nə) *n. pl.* **·nae** (-nē) or **·nas** **1** A thin scale or sheet. **2** A layer or coat lying over another, as in bone, minerals, armor, etc. **3** *Bot.* The blade or flat expanded portion of a leaf, or the blade of a petal. [<L]

lam·i·nar·i·a (lam′ə·nâr′ē·ə) *n.* Any member of a genus *(Laminaria)* of brown algae, especially the giant kelp. [<NL <L *lamina* a leaf] — **lam·i·nar·i·a·ceous** (lam′ə·nâr′ē·ā′shəs) *adj.*

lam·i·nate (lam′ə·nāt) *v.* **·nat·ed, ·nat·ing** *v.t.* **1** To beat, roll, or press, as metal, into thin sheets. **2** To cut or separate into thin sheets. **3** To make, as plastic materials or plywood, of layers united by the action of heat and pressure. **4** To cover with thin sheets or laminae. — *v.i.* **5** To become separated into sheets or laminae. — *adj.* Consisting of or disposed in laminae: also **lam′i·nal, lam′i·nar, lam′i·nar′y, lam′i·nat′ed.** [<NL *laminatus* laminated <L *lamina* a leaf] — **lam′·i·na·ble** *adj.* — **lam′i·na′tion** *n.*

lam·i·nif·er·ous (lam′ə·nif′ər·əs) *adj.* Bearing or composed of laminae.

lam·i·ni·tis (lam′ə·nī′tis) *n.* Inflammation of the laminae of a horse's hoof; founder. [<NL <L *lamina* a leaf, layer + *-itis* -ITIS]

lam·i·nose (lam′ə·nōs) *adj.* Laminate. Also **lam′i·nous** (-nəs). [<LAMIN(A) + -OSE[1]]

Lam·mas (lam′əs) *n.* **1** A Roman Catholic festival celebrated on August 1; the feast of Peter's Chains. **2** Quarter day in Scotland, and half-quarter day in England, falling on August 1. Also **Lammas day.** [OE *hlāfmæsse* bread feast < *hlāf* bread, loaf + *mæsse* a mass]

Lam·mas·tide (lam′əs·tīd′) *n.* The season of Lammas. [<LAMMAS + TIDE[1] (def. 4)]

lam·mer·gei·er (lam′ər·gī′ər) *n.* The great bearded vulture *(Gypaëtus barbatus),* native to the mountains of Asia, southern Europe, and North Africa. Also **lam′mer·geir** (-gir), **lam′mer·gey′er.** [<G *lämmergeier,* lit., lamb-vulture < *lämmer,* pl. of *lamm* a lamb + *geier* a vulture]

Lam·mer·muir Hills (lam′ər·mo͝or′, lam′ər·mo͝or) A range of low hills in SE Scotland; highest point, 1,733 feet. Also **Lam′mer·moor′ Hills.**

lam·my (lam′ē) *n. pl.* **·mies** A sailor's quilted woolen jumper. Also **lam′mie.** [? < *lammy,* var. of *lambie,* affectionate dim. of LAMB]

La·mont (lə·mont′), **Thomas William,** 1870–1948, U. S. banker.

La·motte-Fou·qué (lȧ·môt′fo͞o·kā′) See FOUQUÉ.

lamp (lamp) *n.* **1** A vessel in which oil is burnt through a wick; hence, any device employing a flame, incandescent wire, or the like, for furnishing an artificial light, or a similar device for heating. ◆ Collateral adjective: *lucernal.* **2** Anything that gives out light, actually or metaphorically. **3** A flash, as of lightning. **4** A heavenly body. **5** A torch. **6** *pl. Slang* The eyes. — *v.t. Slang* To look at. [<OF *lampe* <L *lampas* <Gk. < *lampein* shine]

lam·pad (lam′pad) *n.* A lamp or torch; candlestick. [<Gk. *lampas, lampados* < *lampein* shine]

lam·pas[1] (lam′pəs) *n.* Inflammation and swelling of the fleshy bars in the roof of a horse's mouth. Also **lam′pers** (-pərs). [<F <OF, throat]

lam·pas[2] (lam′pəs) *n.* Any elaborately patterned fabric; specifically, a fabric similar to damask, but in many colors, used as furniture covering. [<F; origin uncertain]

lamp·black (lamp′blak′) *n.* Fine carbon deposited from smoke or smoky flame: used as a pigment, in printer's ink, etc.: also called *carbon black.*

Lam·pe·du·sa (läm′pe·do͞o′zä) The largest of the Pelagie Islands between Malta and Tunisia: ancient *Lopadusa.*

lam·per·eel (lam′pər·ēl′) *n.* **1** A lamprey: also **lam′preel** (-prēl). **2** An eelpout or mutton fish. [? < *lampre,* var. of LAMPREY + EEL]

lam·pi·on (lam′pē·ən) *n.* A small lamp. [<F <Ital. *lampione* a carriage or street lamp, aug. of *lampa* <L *lampas* LAMP]

lamp·light (lamp′līt′) *n.* Light emitted by lamps; artificial light.

lamp·light·er (lamp′līt′ər) *n.* **1** A person who lights lamps, especially gas street lamps. **2** That by which a lamp is lighted, as a torch, or an electric device.

lam·poon (lam·pōōn′) *n.* A written satire designed to bring a person into ridicule or contempt; a pasquinade. See synonyms under RIDICULE. —*v.t.* To abuse or satirize in a lampoon. [< MF *lampon* < *lampons* let's drink (a drinking-song refrain) < *lamper* guzzle] —**lam·poon′er, lam·poon′ist** *n.* —**lam·poon′er·y** *n.*

lamp·post (lamp′pōst′) *n.* A post supporting a lamp in a street, park, etc.

lam·prey (lam′prē) *n.* An eel-like carnivorous cyclostome (*Petromyzon* and related genera) having in the adult stages a circular suctorial mouth, with sharp rasping teeth on its inner surface, and well-developed eyes. [< OF *lampreie* < Med. L. *lampreda, lampetra* < L *lambere* lick + *petra* rock < Gk.; supposedly so called because they cling to rocks with their mouths]

lamp shell *Zool.* A brachiopod: so called from its resemblance to an old Roman oil lamp.

lamp·wick (lamp′wik′) *n.* A wick for a lamp.

lam·yik (läm′yik) *n.* A piece of parchment issued by the Dalai Lama of Tibet to serve as a passport permitting a Westerner to enter the Forbidden City of Lhasa: also called *red arrow letter.* [< Tibetan]

lan′ (lan) *n. Scot.* Land.

la·na·i (lä·nä′ē) *n. Hawaiian* A veranda or porch.

La·na·i (lä·nä′ē) An island in the central Hawaiian Islands; 156 square miles.

Lan·ark (lan′ərk) A county in south central Scotland; 853 square miles; capital, Lanark. Also **Lan′ark·shire** (-shir).

la·na·ry (lā′nə·rē) *n. pl.* **·ries** A place for storing wool. [< L *lanaria,* fem. of *lanarius* of wool < *lana* wool]

la·nate (lā′nāt) *adj.* **1** Woolly. **2** *Bot.* Provided or covered with long, fine, wool-like hairs. Also **la′nat·ed.** [< L *lanatus* < *lana* wool]

Lan·ca·shire (lang′kə·shir) A county in NW England; 1,875 square miles; capital, Lancaster. Also **Lan·cas·ter** (lang′kəs·tər).

Lan·cas·ter (lang′kəs·tər) A royal house of England, reigning from 1399 to 1461, and descended from John of Gaunt, fourth son of Edward III. The three Lancastrian kings were Henry IV, Henry V, and Henry VI. See YORK, and WARS OF THE ROSES in table under WAR.

Lan·cas·te·ri·an (lang′kəs·tir′ē·ən) *adj.* Pertaining to the system introduced in primary schools by Joseph Lancaster, 1778–1838, of England, in which advanced pupils taught those below them.

Lan·cas·tri·an (lang·kas′trē·ən) *adj.* Belonging or relating to the House of Lancaster. —*n.* **1** An adherent of the House of Lancaster, as opposed to the Yorkists, especially in the Wars of the Roses. **2** A native or inhabitant of Lancashire.

lance (lans, läns) *n.* **1** A long shaft with a spearhead, used as a thrusting weapon; any long, slender spear, or something resembling one. **2** A lancet. **3** A thrust with a lance or lancet. **4** One who uses a lance; lancer. **5** In pyrotechnics, a small paper case for white or colored fire. **6** A whaler's spear for killing the whale after its capture with the harpoon and line. —*v.t.* **lanced, lanc·ing 1** To pierce with a lance. **2** To cut or open with a lancet. [< OF < L *lancea* a light spear < Celtic]

lance corporal See under CORPORAL².

lance·let (lans′lit, läns′-) *n.* Any of several species of small fishlike translucent animals (genus *Branchiostoma*) having a notochord and other vertebrate characteristics, which burrow in the sand of warm sea beaches; an amphioxus. [Dim. of LANCE]

Lan·ce·lot (lan′sə·lot, län′-; *Fr.* län·slō′) A masculine personal name: often spelled *Launcelot.* Also *Pg.* **Lan·ce·lo·te** (län·sə·lō′tē).

—**Lancelot of the Lake** In Arthurian romance, the bravest and ablest of the knights of the

Round Table; lover of Guinevere; father of Galahad. Also **Lancelot du Lac.** [< F, servant]

lan·ce·o·late (lan′sē·ə·lit, -lāt) *adj.* **1** Shaped like the head of a lance or spear. **2** *Bot.* Tapering, as some leaves. Also **lan′ce·o·lar** (-lər), **lan′ce·o·lat′ed.** [< LL *lanceolatus* < *lanceola* a small lance, dim. of *lancea* LANCE]

lanc·er (lan′sər, län′-) **1** One who lances; a cavalry soldier armed with a lance. **2** *pl.* A quadrille, or square dance for eight or sixteen couples; also, the music for it: also **lan′ciers** (-sərz).

lance sergeant See under SERGEANT.

lan·cet (lan′sit, län′-) *n.* **1** A surgeon's two-edged cutting or bloodletting instrument with one or more small blades. **2** *Archit.* **a** A lancet-shaped or acutely pointed window: also **lancet window. b** An acutely pointed arch: also **lancet arch. 3** A small lance. [< F *lancette,* dim. of *lance* < OF, LANCE]

lan·cet·ed (lan′sit·id, län′-) *adj.* Having lancet windows or arches.

lancet fish 1 An ocean fish (genus *Alepisaurus*) with large, lancetlike teeth. **2** A surgeon fish.

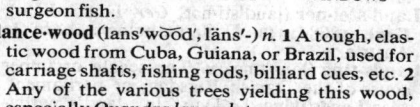

LANCET WINDOWS

lance·wood (lans′wood′, läns′-) *n.* **1** A tough, elastic wood from Cuba, Guiana, or Brazil, used for carriage shafts, fishing rods, billiard cues, etc. **2** Any of the various trees yielding this wood, especially *Oxandra lanceolata.*

Lan·chow (lan′chou′, *Chinese* län′jō′) Capital of Kansu province, NW China: formerly *Kaolan.*

Lan·ci·lot·to (län′chē·lôt′tō) Italian form of LANCELOT.

lan·ci·nate (lan′sə·nāt) *v.t.* **·nat·ed, ·nat·ing** To strike through; pierce, as with pain. [< L *lancinatus,* pp. of *lancinare* tear to pieces]

lan·ci·na·tion (lan′sə·nā′shən) *n.* **1** Shooting or acute pain. **2** A tearing away; laceration.

land (land) *n.* **1** The solid substance composing the material part of the earth, considered in its entirety. **2** A country or district, large or small, especially considered as a place of human habitation, or as distinguished by events or facts of interest. **3** Ground or soil considered with reference to its use, value, condition, etc.: real estate: *farm land* ; *coal land.* **4** *Law* Any tract of ground whatever, together with all its appurtenances; also, a share or interest in land, tenements, or any hereditament, both corporeal and incorporeal. ◆ Collateral adjective: *predial.* **5** Any unindented space in a surface marked with indentations, as a level space between the furrows of millstone, or a space on the bore of a rifle between two grooves. **6** In economic discussion, those resources which are supplied by nature, as distinguished from the developments and improvements resulting from human labor. —*v.t.* **1** To put ashore; transfer from a vessel to the shore. **2** To bring to rest on land or water: He *landed* the plane at Washington. **3** To bring to some point, condition, or state: His words *landed* him in trouble. **4** In fishing, to bring (a fish) from the water or into a net, boat, etc.; catch. **5** *Colloq.* To obtain or secure; win, as a position. **6** *Colloq.* To deliver, as a blow. —*v.i.* **7** To go or come ashore, as from a boat. **8** To touch at a port; come to land: said of ships. **9** To descend and come to rest, as after flight; come down: The bird *landed* in the tree. **10** To come to some place, condition, or state; arrive; end: The swindlers soon *landed* in jail. See synonyms under ARRIVE, REACH. [OE]

Synonyms (noun) : continent, country, district, earth, ground, region, shore, soil. *Antonyms* : deep, flood, ocean, sea, surge, water, wave.

-land *combining form* **1** A region of a certain kind: *woodland.* **2** The country of: *Scotland.* **3** A specified place or realm: *cloudland.* An inhabitant of any of these places is denoted by the combining form **-lander.** [< LAND]

land agent 1 A real-estate agent. **2** One who helps settlers get title to their claims.

lan·dau (lan′dô, -dou) *n.* **1** A type of closed automobile body the rear top of which may be raised or lowered. **2** A four-wheeled covered carriage with a double top that can be removed or folded back. [from *Landau,* a Bavarian city where it was first made]

TWO TYPES OF THE LANDAU
a. Closed top.
b. Open top.

lan·dau·let (lan′dô·let′) *n.* **1** An automobile body with rear section enclosed and the top collapsible. **2** A small landau. Also **lan′dau·lette′.** [Dim. of *landau*]

land bank 1 A bank taking mortgages on land in exchange for currency notes; especially, the **Massachusetts Land Bank** of 1740. **2** One of twelve U.S. government banks organized in 1916 to make mortgage loans on land.

land claim 1 A claim to a piece of land based on conformity to the legal requirements for settlement and title. **2** The land claimed, and the paper entitling the claimant to the land.

lande (land) *n.* A level sandy region unfit for cultivation and covered with heath or broom, as along the seacoast in SW France. [< F < OF *launde* < Breton *lann* < Celtic. Doublet of LAWN.]

land·ed (lan′did) *adj.* **1** Having an estate in land. **2** Consisting in land.

land·fall (land′fôl′) *n.* **1** Property in land immediately transferred by the death of its owner. **2** A landslide. **3** A sighting of or coming to land.

land·fill (land′fil′) *n.* **1** The disposal of garbage, trash, excavated earth, etc., by depositing in a site, often used to build up swampy or shoreline areas. **2** Materials so used. **3** A site where such deposits are made.

land·form (land′fôrm′) *n.* A physical feature of the earth's surface, such as a plateau, an isthmus, a mountain, etc.

land-grant (land′grant′, -gränt′) *n.* Government land granted to a railroad, educational institution, etc.

land·grave (land′grāv′) *n.* A title of superior distinction borne by certain German counts or Grafen. [< MHG *lantgrave* < *lant, land* land + *grave, grafa* count]

land·gra·vi·ate (land·grā′vē·it, -āt) *n.* The territory, office, authority, or jurisdiction of a landgrave. Also **land′gra·vate** (-grā·vāt). [< Med. L *landgraviatus* < *landgravio* a count < MLG *landgrave* LANDGRAVE]

land·hold·er (land′hōl′dər) *n.* A landowner.

land·ing (lan′ding) *n.* **1** The act of going or placing ashore from any kind of craft or vessel: the *landing* of passengers; also, the act of coming or falling to earth, as of an airplane. **2** The place where any kind of craft lands; a wharf; pier. **3** *Archit.* The place at the head of a staircase, or a platform interrupting a flight of stairs.

landing area 1 A landing field. **2** A jump area.

landing beam *Aeron.* A short-wave radio beam transmitted from a landing field to an aircraft pilot in order to facilitate safe landing.

landing craft One of several types of military vessels especially designed for the landing of men and materiel upon a hostile shore.

landing field A tract of ground properly surfaced for the landing and take-off of aircraft.

landing gear *Aeron.* The under-structure of an aircraft designed to carry the load when resting or running on the surface of land or water, and also to buffer the shock of landing.

landing ramp A broad gangplank to permit the rapid landing of men and supplies from a landing craft.

landing strip A narrow, surfaced runway for the landing and take-off of aircraft.

Lan·dis (lan′dis), **Kenesaw Mountain,** 1866–1944, U.S. jurist and baseball commissioner.
land·la·dy (land′lā′dē) *n. pl.* **·dies** A woman who keeps an inn or boarding house, or who lets her property; also, the wife of a landlord.
länd·ler (lent′lər) *n.* An Austrian country dance in slow triple time, probably the precursor of the waltz; also, music for this dance: also called *Tyrolienne.* [<G < dial. G *Landl* upper Austria, dim. of *land* land]
land·less (land′lis) *adj.* Destitute of property in lands.
land·locked (land′lokt′) *adj.* **1** Surrounded and protected by land. **2** Living in or confined to landlocked water: said especially of a normally anadromous fish: *landlocked* salmon.
land·lop·er (land′lō′pər) *n.* A tramp; vagabond. Also **land′loup′er** (-lou′pər,-lōō′-). [<Du. *landlooper* < *land* land + *loopen* run]
land·lord (land′lôrd′) *n.* **1** A man who keeps an inn or hotel. **2** A man who owns and lets real estate. **3** In England, the lord of a manor. [OE *landhlāford* < *land* land + *hlāford* lord]
land·lord·ism (land′lord′iz·əm) *n.* **1** Action, conduct, or opinions peculiar to a landlord; a landlord's authority, or the view that landed interests should be paramount. **2** The system under which land is owned by persons to whom tenants pay a fixed rent.
land·lub·ber (land′lub′ər) *n.* An awkward or inexperienced person on board a ship; a raw sailor. [<LAND + LUBBER]
land·man (land′mən) *n. pl.* **·men** (-mən) One who lives or serves on land.
land·mark (land′märk′) *n.* **1** A fixed object serving as a boundary mark to a tract of land, or as a guide to seamen, etc. **2** A prominent or memorable object in the landscape. **3** A distinguishing fact, event, etc. See synonyms under BOUNDARY. [OE *landmearc* < *land* land + *mearc* boundary]
landmark beacon A beacon light, other than an airport or airway beacon, that serves to indicate a definite geographical location.
land mine See under MINE[1].
land office A U.S. government office of the Department of the Interior for the transaction of business pertaining to the public lands. Officially, **General Land Office.**
land–of·fice business (land′ô′fis, -of′is) *U.S. Colloq.* A flourishing business conducted at a rapid pace.
Land of Nod (nod) See NOD, LAND OF.
Land of Promise **1** Canaan, promised to Abraham by God. *Gen.* xv 18. **2** Any longed-for place of happiness or improvement.
Land of the Midnight Sun Norway.
Land of the Rising Sun Japan.
Lan·dor (lan′dər, -dôr), **Walter Savage,** 1775–1864, English poet and prose writer.
land·own·er (land′ō′nər) *n.* One who owns real estate. **— land′own′er·ship** *n.* **— land′·own′ing** *n.* & *adj.*
land pike *U.S.* **1** The hellbender (def. 1). **2** An inferior breed of hog.
land·plane (land′plān′) *n. Aeron.* An airplane designed to rise from and alight on land.
land–poor (land′po͝or′) *adj.* Owning much land which yields an income insufficient to meet its expenses.
land power A nation having military strength on land: opposed to *sea power.*
land·scape (land′skāp) *n.* **1** A stretch of country as seen from a single point. **2** A picture representing natural scenery. Also *Obs.* **land′skip** (-skip). **—** *v.* **·scaped, ·scap·ing** *v.t.* To improve or change the natural features or appearance of, as a park or garden. **—** *v.i.* To be a landscape gardener. [<Du. *landschap* < *land* land + *-schap* -SHIP]
landscape architect One who draws up, coordinates, and supervises the execution of plans for converting a given area of land into a unified ornamental development.
landscape gardener One who plans, executes, and supervises operations for the horticultural improvement of private or public grounds.
land·scap·ist (land′skā·pist) *n.* **1** A painter of landscapes. **2** A landscape gardener.
land scrip *U.S.* **1** A landholding certificate issued to a person or company. **2** In connection with land grants made for higher education, a certificate granted to a State having insufficient public lands, entitling it to its share of such lands in other States.
Land·seer (land′sir), **Sir Edwin Henry,** 1802–1873, English painter.
Land's End A cape on the SW coast of Cornwall, the westernmost point of England. Also **Lands End.**
land side The side, as of a seashore house, toward the land.
land·side (land′sīd′) *n.* The flat side of a plowshare, away from the furrow.
land·slide (land′slīd′) *n.* **1** The slipping of a mass of land from a higher to a lower level. **2** The land that has slipped down: also **land′slip′**. **3** *Colloq.* An overwhelming plurality of votes for one political party or candidate in an election.
Lands·mål (läns′mōl) *n.* One of the two official forms of Norwegian, based on an arbitrary consolidation of Norwegian dialects: also called *New Norwegian.* Compare RIKSMÅL. [<Norw., lit., country's language < *land* country + *mål* language]
lands·man (landz′mən) *n. pl.* **·men** (-mən) **1** One who lives on the land. **2** *Naut.* An inexperienced sailor, as one on his first voyage or one rated below an ordinary seaman: opposed to *seaman.*
land speculator One who buys and sells land; specifically, one who profits illegally in the buying and selling of unsettled government lands.
Land·stei·ner (land′stī·nər, *Ger.* länt′shtī·nər), **Karl,** 1868–1943, U.S. pathologist born in Austria.
Lands·ting (läns′ting) *n.* The senate or upper house of the Danish Rigsdag, or parliament. Also **Lands′thing.** [<Dan., lit., land's parliament < *land* land + *t(h)ing* parliament]
Land·sturm (länt′shto͝orm) *n.* **1** A general levy in time of war, as made in various European countries. **2** The final reserve forces of a nation, called out in cases of great emergency or for home-defense. [<G, lit., landstorm < dial. G (Swiss), trans. of F *levée en masse,* general levy of troops]
Land·tag (länt′täkh) *n.* The general legislative assembly in a German state. [<G <MHG *lanttac,* lit., land–day < *land, lant* land + *tag, tac* day]
land·ward (land′wərd) *adj.* & *adv.* Being, facing, or going toward the land. Also **land′·wards.**
Land·wehr (länt′vār) *n.* An emergency military force of various European countries. [<G < *land* land + *wehr* defense < *wehren* defend]
lane[1] (lān) *n.* **1** A narrow way or path, confined between fences, walls, hedges, or similar boundaries: distinguished from an *alley,* which is ordinarily between buildings and in city or town, while the *lane* is rural. **2** Any narrow way, passage, or similar course; a prescribed route or passage, as for steamers: a shipping *lane.* See synonyms under ROAD. [OE *lanu* lane]
lane[2] (lān) *adj. Scot.* Alone. **— his lane, my lane, their lane,** etc. Himself alone, myself alone, themselves alone, etc.
lane·ly (lān′lē) *adj. Scot.* Lonely.
lane route One of the routes prescribed for trans–Atlantic steamers in northern waters, being different for eastward– and westward–bound vessels to avoid collisions: also called *ocean–lane route.*
Lan·franc (lan′frangk), 1005–89, Benedictine prior; archbishop of Canterbury.
lang (lang) *adj. Scot.* Long.
Lang (lang), **Andrew,** 1844–1912, Scottish critic, essayist, historian, poet, and translator. **— Cosmo Gordon,** 1864–1945, English prelate; archbishop of Canterbury, 1928–42.
Lang·er·hans (läng′ər·häns), **Islands of** See ISLANDS OF LANGERHANS.
Lang·land (lang′lənd), **William,** 1330?–1400?, English poet. Also **Lang′ley** (-lē).
lang·lauf (läng′louf) *n.* A cross–country run, especially in skiing. [<G < *lang* long + *lauf* a course < *laufen* run]
lang·läuf·er (läng′loi·fər) *n.* A cross–country skier. [<G < *langlauf* LANGLAUF]
lang·ley (lang′lē) *n.* A unit of solar radiation, equal to 1 small calorie per square centimeter of surface per unit of time. [after S. P. *Langley*]
Lang·ley (lang′lē), **Samuel Pierpont,** 1834–1906, U.S. astronomer, scientist, inventor; student of mechanical flight.
Lang·muir (lang′myo͝or), **Irving,** 1881–1957, U. S. chemist.
Lan·go·bar·di (lang′gō·bär′dē) *n. pl.* The Lombards. [<L, prob. <OHG *lang* long + *bart* beard] **— Lan′go·bar′dic** *adj.*
Lan·gre·o (läng·grā′ō) A mining region of NW Spain.
lang·shan (lang′shan) *n.* A breed of large domestic fowl introduced from China. [< Chinese, from *Langshan,* lit., wolf hill, a town near Shanghai]
lang·syne (lang′sīn′, -zīn′) *adv. Scot.* Long since; long ago: used also as a noun. See AULD LANG SYNE.
Lang·ton (lang′tən), **Stephen,** died 1228, English patriot and archbishop of Canterbury.
Lang·try (lang′trē), **Lily,** 1852–1929, *née* Emily Charlotte Le Breton, English actress: called the "Jersey Lily."
lan·guage (lang′gwij) *n.* **1** The expression and communication of emotions or ideas between human beings by means of speech and hearing, the sounds spoken or heard being systematized and confirmed by usage among a given people over a period of time. **2** Transmission of emotions or ideas between any living creatures by any means. **3** The words forming the means of communication among members of a single nation or group at a given period; tongue: the French *language.* **4** The impulses, capacities, and powers which induce and make possible the creation and use of all forms of human communication by speech and hearing. **5** The vocabulary or technical expressions used in a specific business, science, etc.: the *language* of mathematics. **6** One's characteristic manner of expression or use of speech. [<OF *langage* < *langue* tongue <L *lingua* tongue, language. Akin to TONGUE.]
Synonyms: barbarism, dialect, diction, expression, gibberish, idiom, patois, speech, tongue, vernacular. *Language* originally signified only the *expression* of thought by spoken words; it has now acquired the broader interpretation of the *expression* of thought by any means. *Speech* denotes the power of articulate utterance; we can speak of the *language* of animals, but not of their *speech.* A *tongue* is the *speech* or *language* of some one people, country, or race. A *dialect* is a special mode of speaking a *language* peculiar to some locality or class; a *barbarism* is a usage that is felt to be substandard. *Idiom* refers to the construction of phrases and sentences, and the way of forming or using words; it is the peculiar mold in which each *language* casts its thought. The great difficulty of translation lies in giving the thought expressed in one *language* in the *idiom* of another. A *dialect* may be used by the highest as well as the lowest within its range; a *patois* is usually illiterate, belonging to the lower classes; those who speak a *patois* understand the cultured form of their own *language,* but speak only their own form; often a *patois* is a kind of linguistic enclave, as the dialect of the French–Canadians in rural Quebec, or the speech of the Cajuns in Louisiana.
language arts Those elementary–school subjects, especially, reading, spelling, literature, and composition, both written and oral, that deal with the acquisition of facility in one's native language.
Langue·doc (läṅg·dôk′) A region and former province in southern France, between the Loire and the Pyrenees.
langue d'oc (läṅg dôk′) The form of Old French spoken south of the Loire in the Middle Ages, surviving in modern Provençal: so called from the use of the word *oc* for "yes." [<OF, lit., language of *oc* <Provençal: *oc* yes <L *hoc* this (thing)]
langue d'o·ïl (läṅg dô·ēl′) The form of Old French spoken north of the Loire during the Middle Ages, from which modern French developed: so called from the use of the word *oui* or *oïl* for "yes". [<OF, lit., language of *oïl* <L *hoc illi* this for that < *hoc this* + *ille* that]
lan·guet (lang′gwet) *n.* A little tongue or something resembling a tongue in structure or function. Also **lan′guette.** [<F *languette,* dim. of *langue* tongue. See LANGUAGE.]
lan·guid (lang′gwid) *adj.* **1** Indisposed to physical exertion; affected by weakness or fatigue. **2** Wanting in interest or animation;

listless. 3 Lacking in force or quickness of movement. See synonyms under FAINT, SICKLY. [< L *languidus* faint, weak < *languere* languish] — **lan′guid·ly** *adv.* —**lan′guid·ness** *n.*

lan·guish (lang′gwish) *v.i.* **1** To become weak or feeble; be or grow faint or listless. **2** To live or be in unfavorable circumstances so as to be weakened by them: to *languish* in a dungeon. **3** To affect a look of sentimental longing or melancholy. **4** To pine with love or desire. —*n.* **1** A tender look. **2** The act or state of languishing. [< OF *languiss-*, stem of *languir* < L *languescere*, inceptive of *languere* be weary, languish] —**lan′guish·er** *n.*

lan·guish·ing (lang′gwish·ing) *adj.* **1** Lacking interest or force. **2** Sentimentally pensive. **3** Becoming weak or listless. —**lan′guish·ing·ly** *adv.*

lan·guish·ment (lang′gwish·mənt) *n.* **1** The state of being languid. **2** Sentimental languor or tenderness.

lan·guor (lang′gər) *n.* **1** Lassitude of body or depression of mind, as from exertion; weakness. **2** An atonic debility or prostration. **3** Amorous dreaminess. **4** The absence of activity; dulness. **5** A state of premature decay in plants. [< OF < L *languor, languoris* < *languere* languish] — **lan′·guor·ous** *adj.* —**lan′guor·ous·ly** *adv.* — **lan′·guor·ous·ness** *n.*

lan·gur (lung·gŏŏr′) *n.* A long-tailed Asian monkey (genus *Presbytis*), noted for its remarkable leaping power; as, the common langur or hanuman and the Himalayan langur. [< Hind. *langūr* < Skt. *lāṅgūlin*, lit., having a tail]

lan·iard (lan′yərd) See LANYARD.

la·ni·ar·y (lā′nē·er′ē, lan′ē-) *adj.* Adapted for tearing, as the canine teeth. —*n. pl.* **·ar·ies** A canine tooth. [< L *laniarius* pertaining to a butcher < *lanius* a butcher < *laniare* tear]

La·nier (lə·nir′), **Sidney,** 1842–81, U.S. poet.

la·nif·er·ous (lə·nif′ər·əs) *adj.* Bearing wool: often **la·nig′er·ous** (-nij′-). [< L *lanifer* < *lana* wool + *-fer* -FEROUS]

lan·i·tal (lan′ə·tal) *n.* A substance originally produced in Italy from casein, similar to wool in chemical composition and use. [< Ital. *lan(a)* wool + *Ital(ia)* Italy]

lank (langk) *adj.* **1** Lean; shrunken. **2** Long, straight, and thin: *lank* hair. **3** *Obs.* Languid. See synonyms under GAUNT, MEAGER. [OE *hlanc* flexible] —**lank′ly** *adv.* —**lank′ness** *n.*

Lan·kes·ter (lang′kəs·tər), **Sir Edwin Ray,** 1847–1929, English zoologist and comparative anatomist.

lank·y (lang′kē) *adj.* **lank·i·er, lank·i·est** Tall; thin; shrunken. [< LANK + -Y] —**lank′i·ly** *adv.* —**lank′i·ness** *n.*

lan·ner (lan′ər) *n.* **1** A falcon of southern Europe and Asia, especially *Falco biarmicus.* **2** In falconry, the female of this falcon. [< OF *lanier,* ? ult. < L *laniarius.* See LANIARY.]

lan·ner·et (lan′ər·et) *n.* In falconry, the male of the lanner. [< OF *laneret,* dim. of *lanier* LANNER]

lan·o·lin (lan′ə·lin) *n.* An unctuous fatty mixture of the ethers of cholesterin with fatty acids, obtained from various keratin tissues, as the wool of sheep, valuable in pharmacy as a vehicle for substances intended to be applied to the skin: also called *wool fat.* Also **lan′o·line** (-lin, -lēn). [< L *lan(a)* wool + *ol(eum)* oil + -IN]

la·nose (lā′nōs) *adj.* Woolly; resembling wool. [< L *lanosus* < *lana* wool]

lans·downe (lanz′doun) *n.* A material made of silk or similar fiber and wool mixed. [? from *Lansdown,* a town in England]

Lan·sing (lan′sing) The capital of Michigan.

lans·que·net (lans′kə·net) *n.* A card game for any number of players, in which all bets are made on single cards and must be covered by the banker. [< F < G *landsknecht* a (mercenary) foot soldier < *land* country + *knecht* servant]

lant (lant) *n.* Urine, particularly if stale: used as a detergent in wool-scouring. [OE *hland* urine]

lan·ta·na (lan·tā′nə, -tä′-) *n.* Any of a genus (*Lantana*) of mainly tropical American shrubs of the verbena family bearing spikes or umbels of red, orange, lilac, or white flowers. [< NL, viburnum]

lan·tern (lan′tərn) *n.* **1** A transparent case, as on a lamp post or of portable character, for enclosing and protecting a light. **2** *Archit.* A tower or the like, as on a roof or dome, open below and admitting light from the sides; also, a small tower, pavilion, or pinnacle placed on the apex of a dome or crowning another tower. **3** One of various mechanisms likened to a lantern. **4** A lighthouse. **5** A magic lantern. **6** One of the street lamps of Paris, used as gallows during the French Revolution. Also *Obs.* **lant·horn** (lant′hôrn′, lan′tərn). [< F *lanterne* < L *lanterna* < Gk. *lamptēr* < *lampein* shine]

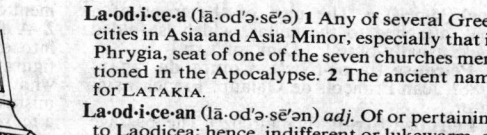

LANTERN ON CHURCH TOWER

lantern fish Any of various small, large-eyed marine fishes bearing rows of phosphorescent organs along the under parts of their bodies.

lantern fly A homopterous insect (family *Fulgoridae*) formerly supposed to produce light from a large protuberant snout.

lan·tern-jawed (lan′tərn·jôd′) *adj.* Having long, thin jaws; hence, having a thin visage.

lantern wheel *Mech.* A lantern-shaped device performing the work of a pinion, in which a circle of bars between two heads takes the place of pinion teeth: sometimes called *trundle.* Also **lantern pinion.**

lan·tha·nide series (lan′thə·nīd) *Physics* The group of rare-earth elements beginning with lanthanum and ending with lutetium, atomic numbers 57 to 71, characterized by closely related properties and great difficulty of separation. [< LANTHAN(UM) + *-ide*, var. of -ID[2]]

lan·tha·num (lan′thə·nəm) *n.* A dark lead-gray metallic element (symbol La) of the lanthanide series. See ELEMENT. [< NL < Gk. *lanthanein* lie concealed]

lan·tho·pine (lan′thə·pēn) *n.* A white crystalline alkaloid, $C_{23}H_{25}O_4N$, obtained from opium. [< Gk. *lanth(anein)* lie hidden + OP(IUM) + -INE[2]]

Lan·tsang (län′tsäng′) The Chinese name for the MEKONG.

la·nu·gi·nous (lə·nōō′jə·nəs, -nyōō′-) *adj.* Woolly or downy. Also **la·nu′gi·nose** (-nōs). [< L *lanuginosus* < *lanugo, -inis* down < *lana* wool]

la·nu·go (lə·nōō′gō, -nyōō′-) *n. Biol.* A downy growth; specifically, the soft, rudimentary hair found on the body of a child at birth. [< L, down < *lana* wool]

lan·yappe (lan·yap′) See LAGNIAPPE.

lan·yard (lan′yərd) *n.* **1** *Naut.* A small rope used on a ship, especially, a four-stranded hemp rope, especially one rove through deadeyes and used in setting up riggings. **2** A cord used in firing certain kinds of cannon. **3** A stout cord worn around the neck, especially by sailors, and used for attaching a knife: called a **knife lanyard.** Also spelled *laniard.* [Alter. of obs. *lanyer* < OF *lasniere* a thong < *lasne* a noose; infl. in form by *yard*[1] a spar]

Lan·za·ro·te (län′thä·rō′tä) Northeasternmost of the Canary Islands; 310 square miles.

Lan·ze·lot (län′tsə·lôt) German form of LANCELOT.

La·o (lä′ō) *n.* **1** A Buddhistic people living in Laos and northern and eastern Thailand. **2** Their Thai language.

La·oag (lä·wäg′) A port in NW Luzon, Philippines.

La·oc·o·on (lā·ok′ə·won, -ō·won) In Greek legend, a priest of Apollo who warned the Trojans against the wooden horse of the Greeks, and was destroyed with his two sons by two serpents sent by Athena or Apollo.

La·od·a·mi·a (lā·od′ə·mī′ə) In the *Iliad,* the wife of Protesilaus, the first Greek killed at Troy, who died from grief at his loss, after persuading the gods to grant him three more hours of life in which to be with her. Also **La·o·da·mei·a** (lā′ə·də·mī′ə).

La·od·i·ce·a (lā·od′ə·sē′ə) **1** Any of several Greek cities in Asia and Asia Minor, especially that in Phrygia, seat of one of the seven churches mentioned in the Apocalypse. **2** The ancient name for LATAKIA.

La·od·i·ce·an (lā·od′ə·sē′ən) *adj.* Of or pertaining to Laodicea; hence, indifferent or lukewarm, as in religion *Rev.* iii 14–22. —*n.* **1** An inhabitant of one of the eight Greek cities named Laodicea. **2** An indifferent or lukewarm Christian; hence, any indifferent or lukewarm person.

La·oighis (lā′ish) A county of western Leinster province, Ireland; 664 square miles; county town, Maryborough: also *Leix.*

La·om·e·don (lā·om′ə·don) In Greek legend, the founder of Troy and father of Priam.

Laon (läṅ) A city in northern France.

La·os (lä′os, lā′ōs) A constitutional monarchy in NW Indochina; 91,400 square miles; capital, Vientiane; royal residence, Luang Prabang.

Lao-tse (lou′dzu′), 604?–531? B.C., Chinese philosopher and mystic, founder of Taoism; also **Lao-tze** and **Lao-tzu.**

lap[1] (lap) *n.* **1** That part of the body below the waist on which, when in a sitting posture, one may conveniently support anything; the upper and front surface of the thighs or knees: to hold a child on one's *lap.* **2** The clothing that covers the front of the thighs when one sits down. **3** By extension, a place for supporting or fostering: fortune's *lap.* **4** A loose fold or flap of a garment; a skirt. **5** That part of a substance which extends over another; also, the length of such extension: the *lap* of a shingle. **6** One course around a race track, usually an even fraction of a mile. **7** A piece of soft metal, wood, or leather, usually in the form of a rotating disk, used in cutting gems and polishing hard metal. **8** The state of overlapping. —*v.* **lapped, lap·ping** *v.t.* **1** To fold and lay over; wrap around something. **2** To lay (one thing) partly over or beyond another: to *lap* weatherboards. **3** To reach or extend partly over or beyond; overlap: These doors *lap* each other. **4** To take upon or as upon the lap; surround with love, care, etc.: *lapped* in idleness and luxury. **5** To grind or polish (a gem) with a lap. **6** To get one or more laps ahead of (an opponent) in a race. —*v.i.* **7** To be folded; wrap. **8** To lie partly upon or beside something else; overlap. **9** To lie beyond or into something else: One wall *laps* into the other. [OE *læpa, lappa* a fold or hanging part of a garment]

lap[2] (lap) *v.t.* & *v.i.* **lapped, lap·ping 1** To take (a liquid) into the mouth with the tongue: said of animals. **2** To wash against (the shore, etc.) with a slight, rippling sound: said of water. —*n.* **1** The act of lapping, as with the tongue; a lick. **2** The sound of lapping, or a similar sound. **3** *Colloq.* That which is licked up, as pap or a drink, especially a weak or diluted drink. [Prob. fusion of OE *lapian* lap and OF *laper* lick < Gmc.] —**lap′per** *n.*

La Pal·ma (lä päl′mä) See PALMA (sense 2).

La Pam·pa (lä päm′pä) An interior province of central Argentina; 55,103 square miles; capital, Santa Rosa.

laparo- *combining form Med.* The flanks or loins; the wall of the abdomen. Also, before vowels, **lapar-.** [< Gk. *lapara* flank]

lap·a·ros·co·py (lap′ə·ros′kə·pē) *n. Surg.* The examination of the abdominal cavity by means of a narrow instrument inserted through an incision.

lap·a·rot·o·my (lap′ə·rot′ə·mē) *n. Surg.* The operation of opening the abdomen by incision in the loin. [< LAPARO- + -TOMY]

La Paz (lä päz′, *Sp.* lä päs′) A city in western Bolivia; the de facto capital, although Sucre is nominally the capital.

lap·board (lap′bôrd′, -bōrd′) *n.* A flat wide board sometimes having a cavity on one edge hollowed out to fit the waist: used especially by tailors, etc., or over the arms of a chair, as a table.

lap-dis·solve (lap′di·zolv′) *n.* In motion pictures, the gradual change of one scene into another, as by lapping two exposures on the same strip of film.

lap dog A dog small enough to be held on the lap.

la·pel (lə·pel′) *n.* The part of the front of a coat, attached to the collar, which is folded back: usually plural. [Dim. of LAP[1]]

La Pé·rouse (là pā·rōōz′), **Comte de,** 1741–1788?, Jean François de Galaup, French navigator.

La Pé·rouse Strait (là pā·rōōz′) The passage from the Sea of Okhotsk to the Sea of Japan between Sakhalin and Hokkaido.

lap·ful (lap′fŏŏl′) *n.* As much as the lap can hold.

lap·i·dar·i·an (lap′ə·dâr′ē·ən) *adj.* Of or relating to stones; written on stones: a *lapidarian* inscription. [<L *lapidarius* <*lapis, -idis* a stone]

lap·i·dar·y (lap′ə·der′ē) *adj.* **1** Pertaining to stones or the art of working in precious stones. **2** Inscribed upon or cut in stone. —*n. pl.* **·dar·ies 1** One who cuts, engraves, and sets precious stones. **2** A connoisseur in lapidary work or gems; lapidist. [<L *lapidarius* LAPIDARIAN]

lap·i·date (lap′ə·dāt) *v.t.* **·dat·ed, ·dat·ing 1** To hurl stones at. **2** To stone to death. [<L *lapidatus,* pp. of *lapidare* <*lapis, -idis* a stone] —**lap′i·da′tion** *n.*

la·pid·i·fy (lə·pid′ə·fī) *v.t.* & *v.i.* **·fied, ·fy·ing** To turn to stone; petrify. [<F *lapidifier* <Med. L *lapidificare* <L *lapis, -idis* a stone + *facere* make] —**lap·i·dif·ic** (lap′ə·dif′ik) or **·i·cal** *adj.* —**la·pid′i·fi·ca′tion** *n.*

la·pil·lus (lə·pil′əs) *n. pl.* **·li** (-ī) A small fragment of lava ejected from a volcano. [<L, dim. of *lapis* a stone]

lap·in (lap′in, *Fr.* là·paṅ′) *n.* A rabbit; also, its fur. [<F]

la·pis (lā′pis, lap′is) *n. pl.* **lap·i·des** (lap′ə·dēz) A stone: used in Latin phrases. [<L]

lap·is laz·u·li (lap′is laz′yōō·lī) **1** A rich blue complex mixture of minerals, originally used to produce ultramarine and by the ancients for decoration, and believed to be their sapphire. **2** The color of this substance. [<NL <L *lapis* a stone + Med. L *lazuli,* genitive of *lazulus* azure <Arabic *lāzaward.* See AZURE.]

Lap·i·thae (lap′ə·thē) *n. pl. of* **Lap·ith** (lap′·ith) In Greek mythology, a wild tribe of Thessaly who, at the wedding of their king Pirithous, fought and overcame the centaurs, after the latter had attempted to carry off the bride and other women present at the feast. Also **Lap′i·thæ.**

lap–joint (lap′joint′) *v.t.* To join together by a lap joint.

lap joint A joint in which a layer of material laps over another, as in shingling. —**lap–joint·ed** (lap′join′tid) *adj.*

La·place (là·plàs′), **Marquis de,** 1749–1827, Pierre Simon, French astronomer and mathematician. —**La·pla′ci·an** *adj.*

Lap·land (lap′land) A region of northern Europe on the Barents Sea, largely within the Arctic Circle. See LAPP. —**Lap′land·er** *n.*

La Pla·ta (lä plä′tä) A port in eastern Argentina, capital of Buenos Aires province. See also PLATA, RÍO DE LA.

Lapp (lap) *n.* **1** One of a Mongoloid people inhabiting Lapland, of short stature, and markedly brachycephalic: also called *Saami.* Formerly nomadic and dependent upon reindeer herds for food and clothing, the Lapps are now settled largely in Sweden and Norway. Also **Lap′land′er. 2** The Finno–Ugric language of the Lapps. [<Sw.]

lap·per[1] (lap′ər) *n.* **1** One who laps or folds. **2** One who polishes with a lap. **3** A lapping machine.

lap·per[2] (lap′ər) See LOPPER.

lap·pet (lap′it) *n.* **1** A small lap or flap used for ornamenting a garment, etc. **2** *Ornithol.* A fleshy process pendent from the head of a bird; a wattle. **3** A lobe, as of the ear. **4** A portion of anything that hangs loose. **5** The guard of a keyhole. [Dim. of LAP[1]]

lap·sa·tion (lap·sā′shən) *n.* In insurance, a lapsing.

lapse (laps) *v.i.* **lapsed, laps·ing 1** To pass slowly or by degrees; slip; sink: to *lapse* into a coma. **2** To deviate from virtue or truth; fail in duty or accuracy. **3** To pass or elapse, as time. **4** To become void, usually by disuse or neglect: The agreement *lapsed.* **5** *Law* To pass or be forfeited to another because of the negligence, failure, or death of the holder. See synonyms under FALL. —*n.* **1** An insensible or gradual slipping, gliding, or passing away; imperceptible movement onward or downward: the *lapse* of ages. **2** A fall to a lower form or state; a falling into decay or ruin, as a building: used also figuratively. **3** A slight deviation from what is right, proper, or just; a slip or mistake through lack of care or attention: a *lapse* in conduct; *lapse* of the pen. **4** Failure or miscarriage, as through fault or negligence: a *lapse* of justice. **5** *Law* The defeat of a right or privilege through fault, failure, or neglect, as, to perform certain conditions of a testamentary bequest. **6** Apostasy. [<L *lapsus* a slip <*labi* glide, slip] —**laps′a·ble, laps′i·ble** *adj.* —**laps′er** *n.*

lapse rate *Meteorol.* The rate of decrease of temperature with vertical height above the earth.

lap·si (lap′sī) *n. pl. Latin* Apostates among the early Christians.

lap·stone (lap′stōn′) *n.* A stone, held in the lap, on which a shoemaker hammers leather.

lap·strake (lap′·strāk′) *adj.* Built with planks overlapping and riveted together; clinker–built, as a boat. —*n.* A boat so built. Also **lap′streak′** (-strēk′). [<LAP[1] + STRAKE]

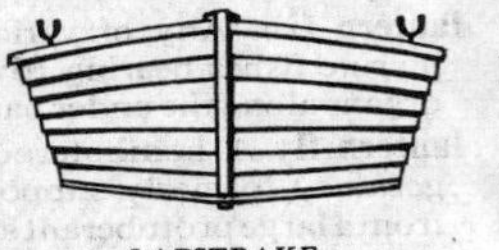
LAPSTRAKE
Flat–bottom rowboat.

lap·sus (lap′səs) *n. Latin* A slip; a mistake.

lap·sus cal·a·mi (lap′səs kal′ə·mī) *Latin* A slip of the pen.

lap·sus lin·guae (lap′səs ling′gwē) *Latin* A slip of the tongue.

lap·sus me·mo·ri·ae (lap′səs mə·mō′ri·ē) *Latin* A slip of the memory.

Lap·tev Sea (läp′tyif) An arm of the Arctic Ocean north of the Yakut S.S.R.: formerly *Nordenskjöld Sea. Russian* **More Lap·te·vykh** (läp′tyə·vēk).

La·pu·ta (lə·pyōō′tə) In Swift's *Gulliver's Travels,* a flying island peopled by philosophers.

lap·wing (lap′wing′) *n.* A ploverlike bird *(Vanellus vanellus)* having the plumage of the upper parts lustrous or metallic and the head crested. Its flight is heavy and flopping; its shrill note resembles the sound *pee–weet.* [OE *hlēapwince* <*hleapan* leap + *wince,* prob. <*wincan* totter; so called from its awkward manner of flight; infl. in form by LAP[1] and WING]

Lar (lär) The singular of LARES.

La·rache (lä·räsh′) A port in western Spanish Morocco: Arabic *El Araish.*

Lar·a·mie (lar′ə·mē) A city in SE Wyoming on the **Laramie River,** a river flowing 216 miles NE to the North Platte through northern Colorado and SE Wyoming.

lar·board (lär′bərd, -bôrd′, -bōrd′) *adj* & *adv. Naut.* Being or going on or toward the left side of a ship as one faces the bow. —*n.* The left–hand side of a ship: now replaced by *port.* [ME *laddebord,* lit., prob., lading side <OE *hladan* lade + *bord* side; infl. in form by STARBOARD]

lar·ce·ner (lär′sə·nər) *n.* A thief; one who commits larceny. Also **lar′ce·nist.**

lar·ce·ny (lär′sə·nē) *n. pl.* **·nies** *Law* The unlawful abstraction, without claim of right, of the personal goods of another with intent to defraud the owner; theft. The distinction between **grand larceny** and **petit** (or **petty) larceny,** based on the value of the stolen property, has been abolished in England and most of the United States. [<AF *larcin,* OF *larrecin* <L *latrocinium* theft <*latrocinari* rob <*latro* robber] —**lar′ce·nous** *adj.* —**lar′·ce·nous·ly** *adv.*

larch (lärch) *n.* **1** Any one of several cone–bearing, deciduous trees of the pine family (genus *Larix*). **2** The strong, durable wood of this tree. [<G *lärche* <MHG *lerche* <L *larix, laricis*]

lard (lärd) *n.* The semisolid oil of hog's fat after rendering. —*v.t.* **1** To prepare lean meat or poultry by inserting strips of bacon or fat before cooking. **2** To cover or smear with lard or grease. **3** To mix with something so as to enrich or improve; interlard. [<OF, bacon <L *lardum* lard] —**lard′y** *adj.*

lar·da·ce·in (lär·dā′sē·in, -sēn) *n.* A fatty protein compound produced in waxy or albuminoid degeneration. [<LARD + -ACE(OUS) + -IN]

lar·da·ceous (lär·dā′shəs) *adj.* **1** Of the nature of lard. **2** Pertaining to or indicative of lardacein; fatty or waxy.

lar·der (lär′dər) *n.* A room where articles of food are kept before cooking; pantry; hence, the provisions of a household. [<AF *larder,* OF *lardier* <Med. L *lardarium,* orig., a storehouse for bacon <L *lardum* lard]

larder beetle A small, blackish–and–gray beetle *(Dermestes lardarius)* about 1/3 inch long, whose larva feeds on dried meats, etc. For illustration see INSECT (injurious).

Lard·ner (lärd′nər), **Ring(gold) (Wilmer),** 1885–1933, U. S. author.

lard oil A heavy oil expressed from lard.

lar·don (lär′dən) *n.* A thin slice of bacon or pork for larding meat. Also **lar·doon** (lär·dōōn′). [<F <*lard.* See LARD.]

Lar·es (lâr′ēz, lā′rēz) *n. pl. of* **Lar** (lär) Tutelary deities of ancient Rome, adopted from the Etruscans, and worshiped as spirits of departed ancestors presiding over the households of their descendants: associated with the *Penates.*

lares and pe·na·tes (pə·nā′tēz) The household gods; hence, one's home and cherished belongings.

large (lärj) *adj.* **larg·er, larg·est 1** Absolutely or relatively great or ample as regards size, dimensions, quantity, number, extent, range, etc.; big; great; spacious; ample; extensive: opposed to *little* or *small.* **2** Having unusual breadth of sympathy or comprehension: a *large* heart or mind. **3** Favorable in direction; fair: said of a wind when it is abeam. **4** Characterized by fullness: said of the pulse. **5** *Obs.* Prodigal of words, gifts, or money; lavish. **6** *Obs.* Unrestrained in liberty or morals. **7** *Obs.* Complete; full. —**at large** (Formerly with the possessive pronoun: *at his large.*) **1** To the fullest extent; in full. **2** Free or unrestrained in movement; at liberty: The thief is still *at large.* **3** Not included within particular limitations; in general; for all. **4** Elected from a State as a whole rather than from a particular congressional or electoral district: a congressman *at large.* —*adv.* **1** *Naut.* Before the wind, or with the wind on the quarter. **2** *Colloq.* Boastfully. [<OF <L *larga,* fem. of *largus* abundant] —**large′·ness** *n.*

Synonyms (adj.): abundant, ample, big, broad, bulky, capacious, coarse, colossal, commodious, considerable, enormous, extensive, gigantic, grand, great, huge, immense, long, massive, spacious, vast, wide. *Large* denotes extension in more than one direction, and beyond the average of the class to which the object belongs; we speak of a *large* surface or a *large* solid, but of a *long* line. A *large* man is a man of more than ordinary size; a *great* man is a man of remarkable ability. *Big* is a more emphatic word than *large,* but ordinarily less elegant. *Antonyms*: diminutive, inconsiderable, infinitesimal, insignificant, limited, little, mean, microscopic, minute, narrow, paltry, petty, scanty, slender, slight, small, tiny, trifling, trivial.

large–heart·ed (lärj′här′tid) *adj.* Generous. —**large′–heart′ed·ness** *n.*

large·ly (lärj′lē) *adv.* **1** In a large manner. **2** To a great extent; generally. **3** Generously; abundantly; copiously. **4** Pompously.

large–mind·ed (lärj′mīn′did) *adj.* Liberal in ideas; not narrow–minded. —**large′–mind′ed·ness** *n.*

large–scale (lärj′skāl′) *adj.* Of large size or scope.

lar·gess (lär′jis, -jes) *n.* **1** A gift; gratuity. **2** Liberality; bounty. Also **lar′gesse.** See synonyms under GIFT. [<F *largesse* <L *largus* abundant]

lar·ghet·to (lär·get′ō) *Music adj.* Slow; in a time not quite so slow as *largo*: a direction to the performer. —*n.* A musical movement requiring moderately slow time. [<Ital., dim. of *largo* LARGO]

lar·ghis·si·mo (lär·gis′i·mō) *adj. Music* Very slow. [<Ital., superl. of *largo* LARGO]

larg·ish (lär′jish) *adj.* Somewhat large.

lar·go (lär′gō) *adj.* & *adv. Music* Slow; broad; majestic. —*n. pl.* **·gos** A movement in slow time. [<Ital., slow, large <L *largus* abundant]

lar·i·at (lar′ē·ət) *n.* **1** A rope, especially of horsehair, for tethering animals. **2** A lasso. —*v.t.* To fasten or catch with a lariat. [<Sp. *la reata* <*la* the + *reata* rope]

lar·ine (lar′in, lā′rīn) *n.* One of a subfamily

(*Larinae*) of longipennate birds, having the upper mandible as long as the lower and with a single sheath; a gull or tern. — *adj.* Of or pertaining to the *Larinae*. [<NL <LL *larus* a gull <Gk. *laros*]

La Rio·ja (lä ryō′hä) A province of western Argentina; 35,691 square miles; capital, La Rioja.

La·ri·sa (lä′rē·sä) The chief city of Thessaly, Greece. Also **La·ris·sa** (lə·ris′ə).

la·rith·mics (lə·rith′miks) *n.* The scientific study and analysis of human populations in their quantitative aspects: distinguished from *eugenics*. [<Gk. *laos* people + *arithmos* a number] — **la·rith′mic** *adj.*

lark[1] (lärk) *n.* **1** Any of numerous small singing birds (family *Alaudidae*), as the European skylark (*Alauda arvensis*). **2** One of various other birds, as a titlark or meadowlark. [OE *lāferce, lǣwerce*]

lark[2] (lärk) *n.* A hilarious time; frolic; humorous adventure. — *v.i.* To play pranks; frolic. [<dial. E (Northern) *lake* play, fusion of ON *leika* leap and OE *lācan* frolic; infl. in form by LARK[1]] — **lark′er** *n.* — **lark′some** *adj.*

lark·spur (lärk′spûr) *n.* Any of several showy herbs of the crowfoot family (genus *Delphinium*) with alternate, palmately divided leaves, and loose, terminal clusters of irregular, spurred, white, pink, lavender, or blue flowers. — **scarlet larkspur** A species of larkspur (*Delphinium cardinale*) that grows wild in California. [<LARK[1] + SPUR]

larkspur blue A light, bright blue, the color of some larkspurs.

lark·y (lär′kē) *adj.* **lark·i·er**, **lark·i·est** *Colloq.* High-spirited and carefree; frolicsome: a *larky* adventure.

La Roche·fou·cauld (lä rôsh·fōo·kō′), **Duc François de**, 1613–80, Prince de Marcillac, French writer and politician.

La Ro·chelle (lä rō·shel′) A port city of western France on the Bay of Biscay; Huguenot stronghold, besieged and taken by Cardinal Richelieu, 1627–28.

La·rousse (lä·rōos′), **Pierre Athanase**, 1817–1875, French grammarian and encyclopedist.

lar·ri·gan (lar′ə·gən) *n.* A moccasin made of prepared oiled leather: used chiefly by lumbermen. [<dial. E (Canadian); origin unknown]

lar·ri·kin (lar′ə·kin) *Chiefly Austral. adj.* Boisterously rude; rowdyish. — *n.* A rough, disorderly fellow; rowdy. [<dial. E (Australian), prob. <*Larry*, nickname for LAWRENCE]

lar·rup (lar′əp) *Colloq. v.t.* To beat; thrash. — *n.* A blow. [<dial. E (East Anglian), ? <Du. *larpen* thrash]

Lar·ry (lar′ē) Diminutive of LAWRENCE.

Lars (lärs) Swedish form of LAWRENCE.

lar·um (lar′əm) *Archaic* An alarm. [Aphetic var. of ALARUM]

lar·va (lär′və) *n. pl.* **·vae** (-vē) **1** *Biol.* The early form of any animal when it is unlike the parent, or undergoes a metamorphosis. **2** *Entomol.* The first stage of an insect after leaving the egg, preceding the pupa, as a caterpillar, a grub, or a maggot. **3** In ancient Roman superstition, an evil spirit; a ghost, a mask] — **lar′val** *adj.*

lar·vate (lär′vāt, -vit) *adj.* Clothed or concealed as if with a mask: said of certain diseases. Also **lar′vat·ed.** [<L *larvatus* <*larva* a mask]

lar·vi·pos·i·tor (lär′və·poz′ə·tər) *n. Entomol.* In certain dipterous insects, the modified ovipositor. [<LARVA + L *positor* a placer <*positus*, pp. of *ponere* put, place]

la·ryn·gal (lə·ring′gəl) *adj.* Originating in the larynx.

la·ryn·ga·phone (lə·ring′gə·fōn) *n.* A type of microphone which picks up and transmits voice vibrations by direct contact with the throat of the speaker: used to minimize interference by external sounds. [<*larynga-*, var. of LARYNGO- + -PHONE]

la·ryn·ge·al (lə·rin′jē·əl, -jəl) *adj.* **1** Of, pertaining to, or near the larynx: also **la·ryn′ge·an. 2** Attacking the larynx, as a disease. **3** Adapted or used for treating the larynx, as an instrument. [<NL *laryngeus* <Gk. *larynx, laryngos* larynx]

la·ryn·gis·mus (lar′ən·jiz′məs) *n.* **1** *Pathol.* Spasm of the muscles of the glottis. **2** A disease of horses caused by paralysis of muscles of the larynx; roaring. [<NL <Gk.

laryngismos shouting <*laryngizein* shout <*larynx, laryngos* larynx] — **lar′yn·gis′mal** *adj.*

laryngismus strid·u·lus (strid′yə·ləs) *Pathol.* A disease of children marked by laryngeal spasms and a strident breathing; false or spasmodic croup. [<NL, lit., rattling laryngismus]

lar·yn·gi·tis (lar′ən·jī′tis) *n. Pathol.* Inflammation of the larynx. — **lar′yn·git′ic** (-jit′ik) *adj.*

laryngo- *combining form* The larynx; pertaining to the larynx: *laryngoscope.* Also, before vowels, **laryng-.** [<Gk. *larynx, laryngos* the larynx]

lar·yn·gol·o·gy (lar′ing·gol′ə·jē) *n.* Scientific knowledge of the larynx, its functions and diseases. — **lar·yn·go·log·i·cal** (lə·ring′gō·loj′i·kəl) *adj.* — **lar′yn·gol′o·gist** *n.*

la·ryn·go·scope (lə·ring′gə·skōp) *n.* An instrument for inspecting the larynx. — **la·ryn′go·scop′ic** (-skop′ik) *adj.*

lar·yn·gos·co·py (lar′ing·gos′kə·pē) *n.* Examination by means of the laryngoscope.

lar·yn·got·o·my (lar′ing·got′ə·mē) *n. Surg.* The operation of cutting into the larynx. [<Gk. *laryngotomia* <*larynx, laryngos* the larynx + *tomē* a cutting <*temnein* cut]

lar·ynx (lar′ingks) *n. pl.* **la·ryn·ges** (lə·rin′jēz) or **lar·ynx·es** *Anat.* The organ of voice in mammals and most other vertebrates, situated at the upper part of the trachea, consisting of a cartilaginous box across which are stretched the vocal cords whose vibrations produce sound. [<Gk. *larynx, laryngos* the larynx]

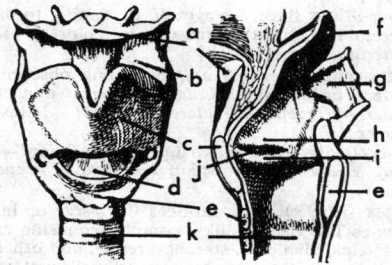

HUMAN LARYNX
Left: front view.   Right: side view.
a. Hyoid bone.   *f.* Epiglottis.
b. Thyrohyoid ligament. *g.* Thyrohyoid membrane.
c. Thyroid cartilage.   *h.* Vocal chord.
d. Cricothyroid ligament. *i.* Vocal chord.
e. Cricoid cartilage.   *j.* Laryngeal ventricle.
                          k. Trachea.

La·sa (lä′sä′) The Chinese name for LHASA.

La Salle (lä säl′), **Sieur Robert Cavelier de**, 1643–87, French explorer.

Las Be·la (lus bā′lə) A princely state of SE Baluchistan, West Pakistan; 7,043 square miles; capital, Bela.

las·car (las′kər) *n.* An East Indian native, serving as a sailor. [<Hind. *lashkar* army (used for *lashkari* belonging to the army, a soldier) <Persian <Arabic *al-'askar* the army]

Las Ca·sas (läs kä′säs), **Bartolomé de**, 1474–1566, Spanish historian and missionary to the American Indians: called "Apostle of the Indies."

las·civ·i·ous (lə·siv′ē·əs) *adj.* **1** Having wanton desires; lustful; lewd. **2** Tending to produce sensual desires. See synonyms under BRUTISH. [<LL *lasciviosus* <L *lascivia* wantonness <*lascivus* sportive, lustful] — **las·civ′i·ous·ly** *adv.* — **las·civ′i·ous·ness** *n.*

la·ser (lā′zər) *n.* An optical maser.

lash (lash) *n.* **1** A thong on a whip handle; a whip. **2** A stroke with or as with a whip. **3** A sharp, sarcastic remark. **4** An eyelash. **5** Any heavy blow, as of waves beating the shore. — *v.t.* **1** To strike, punish, or urge forward with or as with a whip. **2** To throw or move quickly or suddenly, as from side to side: to *lash* the tail. **3** To beat or dash against with force or violence: The waves *lashed* the pier. **4** To attack or criticize severely; berate. **5** To arouse the emotions of, as with words. **6** To bind or tie with or

as with a lashing. — *v.i.* **7** To move quickly or violently; dash. — **to lash out 1** To strike out violently or wildly. **2** To break into angry or vehement speech. [<Prob. fusion of MLG *lasch* a flap and OF *laz* a cord; infl. in form and sense by OF *lachier* fasten. Akin to LACE, LATCH.]

lash·er[1] (lash′ər) *n.* One who or that which lashes.

lash·er[2] (lash′ər) *n.* **1** Slack water, as above a weir. **2** The weir itself. [<LASH (*v.* def. 7) + -ER[1]]

lash·ing (lash′ing) *n.* **1** A fastening made by passing a rope, cord, or the like, around two or more objects. **2** The rope used to do this. **3** A whipping.

Lash·io (läsh′yō) The capital of Shan State and Northern Shan States, Upper Burma.

Lash·kar (lush′kər) The winter capital of Madhya Bharat State, India.

lash–up (lash′up′) *n. Colloq.* A temporary connection or contrivance.

Las·ki (las′kē), **Harold J(oseph)**, 1893–1950, English political scientist.

La Sou·fri·ère (lä sōo·frē·âr′) A volcano on St. Vincent, Windward Islands, The West Indies; 4,048 feet; dormant since 1903: also *Soufrière.* Also **La Grande Soufrière.**

Las Pal·mas (läs päl′mäs) See PALMAS, LAS.

La Spe·zia (lä spä′tsyä) A port on the Gulf of Spezia: also *Spezia.*

lass (las) *n.* **1** A young woman; girl. **2** A sweetheart. **3** *Scot.* A servant-girl; maid. [<Scand. Cf. OSw. *lösk kona* an unmarried woman.]

Las·salle (lä·säl′), **Ferdinand Johann Gottlieb**, 1825–64, German socialist.

Las·sen Volcanic National Park (las′ən) An area of lava formations in northern California containing **Lassen Peak** (10,453 feet), the only active volcano in the United States; 161 square miles; established, 1916.

las·sie (las′ē) *n.* A little girl; a lass. Also **las′sock** (-ək). [Dim. of LASS]

las·si·tude (las′ə·tōod, -tyōod) *n.* A state of disinclination to exertion; languor; weariness; debility. [<F <L *lassitudo* <*lassus* faint]

las·so (las′ō) *n. pl.* **·sos** or **·soes** A long rope or leather thong, with a running noose, for catching horses and cattle. — *v.t.* To catch with a lasso. [<Sp. *lazo* <L *laqueus* a snare] — **las′so·er** *n.*

lasso cell A nematocyst.

last[1] (last, läst) *adj.* **1** Being at the end; latest; hindmost; final. **2** Next before the present; most recent. **3** Least fit or likely; most remote. **4** Beyond or above all others; utmost. **5** Beneath all others. — *adv.* **1** After all others in time or order. **2** At a time next preceding the present: He was *last* seen heading west. **3** In conclusion; finally. — *n.* **1** The end; conclusion. **2** The final appearance, experience, or mention: We'll never hear the *last* of this. — **at last** At length; at the end; finally. [OE *latost*, superl. of *læt* late, slow] — **last′ly** *adv.*

last[2] (last, läst) *v.i.* **1** To remain in existence; continue to be; endure. **2** To continue unchanged or unaltered; persevere. **3** To be as much as or more than needed; hold out: Will our supplies *last* through the winter? — *n.* Ability to endure; stamina. [OE *læsten* follow a track, continue, accomplish. Akin to LAST[3].] — **last′er** *n.*

last[3] (last, läst) *n.* A shaped form, usually of wood, on which to make a boot or shoe. — *v.t.* To fit to or form on a last. [OE *læst* a boot, shoemaker's last <*last* a footstep, track. Akin to LAST[2].] — **last′er** *n.*

last[4] (last, läst) *n.* **1** A weight or measure varying for different articles, but often reckoned as 80 bushels. **2** One or two tons, usually 4,000 pounds: a unit in estimating ship capacity. [OE *hlæst* a load <*hladan* lade]

Las·tex (las′teks) *n.* A fine, round, rubber thread, manufactured in strands and wound with rayon, cotton, silk, or wool: a trade name. [<(E)LAS(TIC) + TEX(TILE)]

last·ing[1] (las′ting, läs′-) *adj.* Continuing; durable; permanent. See synonyms under PERMANENT, PERPETUAL. — *n.* Endurance; continuance. [<LAST[2]] — **last′ing·ly** *adv.* — **last′ing·ness** *n.*

last·ing² (las′ting, läs′-) *n.* **1** A fabric used for the uppers of shoes, etc. **2** The operation of stretching an upper on a shoemaker's last. [< LAST³]

Last Judgment See under JUDGMENT.

Last Supper The last meal of Jesus Christ with his disciples before the Crucifixion.

last word **1** The final say, as in a dispute. **2** The latest or most modern fashion, style, advancement, etc.

Las Ve·gas (läs vā′gəs) The second largest city of Nevada, in the SE part; famous for its gambling casinos.

Lász·ló (läs′lō) Hungarian form of LADISLAUS.

lat (lät) *n. pl.* **lats** or **la·tu** (lä′to͞o) The monetary unit of Latvia. [< Lettish *lats* < *Latvia* Latvia]

Lat·a·ki·a (lat′ə·kē′ə) *n.* A fine grade of tobacco developed in Turkey. [from *Latakia;* so called because produced near there]

La·ta·ki·a (lä′tä·kē′ä) **1** A province of western Syria, on the Mediterranean; 2,433 square miles. **2** Its capital, the chief Syrian port: ancient *Laodicea*: French *Lattaquié.*

la·ta·ni·a (lə·tā′nē·ə) *n.* The palmetto or cabbage palm of the southern United States. [< NL < F *lattanier* < Cariban *aláttani*]

latch¹ (lach) *n.* A catch for fastening a door, lid, shutter, etc., commonly not requiring any special key. See synonyms under LOCK¹ — *v.t.* & *v.i.* To fasten by means of a latch; close. —**to latch on to** *Slang* **1** To fasten (oneself) to. **2** To obtain; get. [OE *laeccan, laeccean* seize. Akin to LACE, LASH.]

latch² (lach) *v.t.* See LEACH.

latch·et (lach′it) *n.* A lace, thong, or strap that fastens a shoe or sandal. Also **shoe latchet.** [< OF *lachet,* dial. var. of *lacet,* dim. of *las, laz.* See LACE.]

latch·key (lach′kē′) *n.* A key for releasing a latch, especially on an outside or front door.

latchkey child A child who comes home after school to an empty house, the parent or parents being still at work.

latch·string (lach′string′) *n.* A string fastened to a latch and passed through a hole above it to the outside: used for lifting a latch.

late (lāt) *adj.* **lat·er** or **lat·ter, lat·est** or **last** **1** Coming after the appointed time; tardy. **2** Far advanced toward the end or close; at or continuing to an advanced hour. **3** Recent or comparatively recent: often implying a subsequent change. **4** Deceased, especially recently deceased. —*adv.* **1** After or beyond the usual proper or appointed time; after delay; at or until an advanced hour. **2** Not long ago; recently. **3** After a while; in course of time: contrasted with *soon* or *early* : We rue our follies soon or *late* : more frequently used in the comparative degree. —**of late** In time not long past or near present; recently. [OE *lœt* late, slow] —**late′ness** *n.*

lat·ed (lā′tid) *adj.* Belated.

la·teen (la·tēn′) *adj. Naut.* Designating a rig common in the Mediterranean, having a triangular sail (**lateen sail**) suspended from a long yard set obliquely to the mast. [< F *(voile) latine* Latin (sail), fem. of *latin* < L *Latinus*]

la·teen-rigged (la·tēn′rigd′) *adj. Naut.* Having a lateen sail or sails.

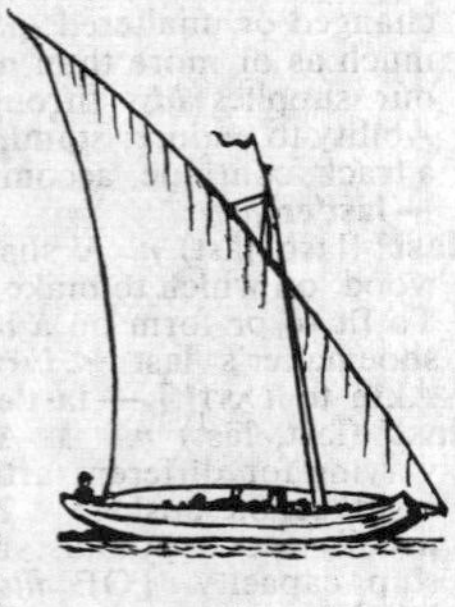

LATEEN SAIL
Shown on a dhow.

Late Greek See under GREEK.

Late Latin See under LATIN.

late·ly (lāt′lē) *adv.* Not long ago; recently.

la·ten·si·fi·ca·tion (lə·ten′sə·fə·kā′·shən) *n. Phot.* The technique of making a fogging exposure after the initial exposure, in order to bring out shadow details and increase the effective emulsion speed of some negative materials. [< LATEN(CY) + (INTEN)SIFICATION]

la·tent (lā′tənt) *adj.* **1** Not visible or apparent; hidden; dormant. **2** *Psychol.* Potentially capable of being expressed, as an emotion or attitude. **3** *Bot.* Undeveloped, as a concealed bud. [< L *latens, -entis,* ppr. of *latere* be hidden] —**la′ten·cy** *n.* —**la′tent·ly** *adv.*

latent heat *Physics* The amount of heat required to change the state of a unit mass of a body, either from solid to liquid or from liquid to vapor, without changing the temperature of the body.

latent image *Phot.* The invisible image produced by the action of light on the silver halide or other grains of a photographic emulsion before development of the film.

latent period **1** *Pathol.* The interval between the incubation period of a disease and its outbreak. **2** *Physiol.* Elapsed time between a stimulus and its response.

lat·er (lā′tər) *adv.* At a subsequent time; hereafter.

lat·er·al (lat′ər·əl) *adj.* **1** Pertaining to, proceeding from, or directed toward the side. **2** *Biol.* Situated on one or both sides of the median plane of a body, limb, or organ: opposed to *medial.* [< L *lateralis* < *latus, lateris* a side] —**lat′er·al·ly** *adv.*

lat·er·al-cut (lat′ər·əl·kut′) *adj.* Having sound-producing lines indented in a horizontal plane by the recording instrument of a phonograph: said of a recording: distinguished from *hill-and-dale.*

lateral pass See under PASS.

Lat·er·an (lat′ər·ən) **1** The basilica of St. John Lateran, the cathedral church of the pope as bishop of Rome, ranking above all other churches in the Roman Catholic world. **2** The palace, formerly a papal residence and now a museum, adjacent to the basilica. [< L *Lateranus,* name of a Roman family]

lat·er·ite (lat′ər·īt) *n.* A red, ferruginous, porous clay of tropical regions. [< L *later* a brick + -ITE¹] —**lat′er·it′ic** (-it′ik) *adj.*

lat·er·i·tious (lat′ər·ish′əs) *adj.* Pertaining to or resembling brick; brick-red in color. [< L *lateritius* < *later* a brick]

la·tes·cent (lə·tes′ənt) *adj.* Becoming obscure, latent, or hidden. [< L *latescens, -entis,* ppr. of *latescere,* inceptive of *latere* be hidden] —**la·tes′cence** *n.*

lat·est (lā′tist) Alternative superlative of LATE. —*adj.* & *adv.* **1** Most recent. **2** *Archaic* & *Poetic* Last.

la·tex (lā′teks) *n. pl.* **lat·i·ces** (lat′ə·sēz) or **la·tex·es** The viscid, milky, complex emulsion of proteins, alkaloids, starches, resins, and other substances secreted by the cells of certain plants, as the milkweed, rubber tree, poppy, dandelion, etc. [< L, a liquid]

lath (lath, läth) *n.* **1** A thin strip of wood or metal, as one of a number nailed to studs or beams and serving to support a coat of plaster, or on rafters to support shingles or slates. **2** An angle-iron forming the support for an iron roof. **3** Laths taken collectively; lathwork. **4** Figuratively, a thin, slender, or delicate person or thing. —*v.t.* To cover or line with laths. [Prob. fusion of OE *lætt* and OE *læth* (assumed); ? infl. in form by Welsh *llath*] —**lath′er** *n.*

lathe¹ (lāth) *n.* **1** A machine for shaping articles in which an object is mounted and rotated, while a tool is thrust against the work, shaping it down, usually to some circular form. **2** In a loom, the swinging beam which beats up the weft. **3** A potter's wheel. —*v.t.* **lathed, lath·ing** To form or shape on a lathe. [Prob. < MDu. *lade*]

lathe² (lāth) *n.* An English administrative district, now existing only in Kent, composed of several hundreds. [OE *læth*]

lath·er (lath′ər) *n.* **1** Foam or froth of soapsuds. **2** Foam of profuse sweating, as of a horse. —**in a lather** *Colloq.* In a state of intense excitement or agitation. —*v.t.* **1** To cover with lather. **2** *Colloq.* To flog; thrash. —*v.i.* **3** To become covered with lather. **4** To form lather. [OE *lēathor* washing soda, soap. Akin to LAVE.] —**lath′er·er** *n.* —**lath′er·y** *adj.*

lath·ing (lath′ing, läth′-) *n.* **1** The act or process of covering with laths. **2** The foundation of laths on which plaster may be laid; the material for such foundation. **3** Any work with laths or like material.

lathing hatchet A hatchet with a narrow blade, for cutting and attaching wooden laths. See illustration under HATCHET.

lath·work (lath′wûrk′, läth′-) *n.* Lathing.

lath·y (lath′ē, läth′ē) *adj.* **lath·i·er, lath·i·est** Like a lath; long and slender.

La·tian (lā′shən) *adj.* Of or pertaining to ancient Latium in Italy; Latin.

lat·i·ces (lat′ə·sēz) Plural of LATEX.

lat·i·cif·er·ous (lat′ə·sif′ər·əs) *adj.* Containing or conveying latex. [< L *latex, laticis* a liquid + -FEROUS]

lat·i·clave (lat′ə·klāv) *n.* **1** A broad vertical purple stripe down the tunics of ancient Romans of senatorial rank. **2** A tunic thus marked. [< LL *laticlavium, laticlavus* < *latus* broad + *clavus* a purple stripe]

lat·i·fo·li·ate (lat′ə·fō′lē·it, -āt) *adj. Bot.* Having broad leaves. Also **lat′i·fo′li·ous.** [< NL *latifoliatus* < L *latus* broad + *folia* a leaf]

lat·i·fun·di·um (lat′ə·fun′dē·əm) *n. pl.* **·di·a** (-dē·ə) A large landed property. [< L < *latus* wide + *fundus* an estate]

Lat·i·mer (lat′ə·mər), **Hugh,** 1485?–1555, English Protestant churchman; burned at the stake.

Lat·in (lat′n) *adj.* **1** Pertaining to ancient Latium, its inhabitants, their culture, or language. **2** Pertaining to or denoting the peoples or countries, as France, Italy, and Spain, whose languages and cultures are derived from the ancient Roman civilization. **3** Of or belonging to the Western or, since the Reformation, the Roman Catholic Church, as distinguished from the Greek Church. —*n.* **1** One of the people of ancient Latium. **2** A member of any of the modern Latin peoples. **3** A member of the Western or Roman Catholic Church: used especially in the Greek Church. **4** The Indo-European, Italic language of ancient Latium and Rome: extensively used in western Europe until modern times as a language of learning, and still retained as the official language of the Roman Catholic Church. —**Old Latin,** the language before the first century B.C., as preserved in early inscriptions and the comedies of Plautus. —**Classical Latin,** the literary language of the period 80 B.C. to A.D. 200, standardized by such writers as Cicero, Caesar, Livy, Vergil, Tacitus, and Juvenal. Abbr. *L* —**Late Latin,** the language from 200–600, including the patristic writings. Abbr. *LL* —**Low Latin,** the language of any period after the classical, as Medieval Latin, especially as influenced and modified by other continental languages. —**Medieval Latin,** the language used by the writers of the Middle Ages, from 600–1500: also called *Middle Latin.* Abbr. *Med. L* —**New Latin,** a form of the language, based on Latin and Greek elements, developed since the Renaissance and used chiefly in scientific and taxonomic terms. Abbr. *NL* —**Vulgar Latin,** the popular speech of the Romans in all stages of the language from about A.D. 200 through the medieval period: the chief source of the Romance languages. [< L *Latinus* of Latium, Latin]

Latin alphabet A set of letters containing, originally, 20 characters derived from the Western Greek alphabet (in turn, developed from the Phoenician) with the later addition of G, Y, and Z. The English alphabet, descendent from the Latin, has the added characters J, U, and W. Also called *Roman alphabet.*

Latin America Those countries of the western hemisphere south of the Rio Grande, in which the official languages are derived from Latin. See SPANISH AMERICA. —**Lat′in-A·mer′·i·can** *adj.*

Latin American A native or inhabitant of Latin America.

Lat·in·ate (lat′ən·āt) *adj.* Resembling or derived from Latin.

Latin Church That part of the Catholic Church which accepts the pope as supreme authority on earth, and uses Latin for the liturgy of the mass. Compare UNIAT.

Latin cross See under CROSS.

La·tin·ic (lə·tin′ik) *adj.* Of Latin.

Lat·in·ism (lat′ən·iz′əm) *n.* An idiom peculiar to or imitating Latin. —**Lat′in·is′tic** *adj.*

Lat·in·ist (lat′ən·ist) *n.* One versed in Latin.

La·tin·i·ty (lə·tin′ə·tē) *n.* Latin style or idiom.

Lat·in·ize (lat′ən·īz) *v.* **·ized, ·iz·ing** *v.t.* **1** To translate into Latin. **2** To make Latin in customs, thought, etc. **3** To cause to resemble the Roman Catholic Church, as in dogma or ritual. **4** To transliterate into Latin characters, as a Greek word. —*v.i.* **5** To use Latin words, forms, etc. [< L *latinizare* < *Latinus* Latin] —**Lat′in·i·za′tion** *n.* —**Lat′in·iz′er** *n.*

la·ti·no (la·tē′nō) *n. pl.* **·nos** *Often cap.* A Latin American. [< Am. Sp. < Sp., L]

Latin Quarter A section of Paris on the left (south) bank of the Seine, known for the large

number of artists and students who live there.

lat·i·ros·tral (lat′ə·ros′trəl) *adj.* *Ornithol.* Having a broad beak, as certain birds. [<NL *Latirostres,* former group name for the swallows <L *latus* broad + *rostrum* a beak]

lat·ish (lā′tish) *adj.* Rather late.

lat·i·tude (lat′ə·to͞od, -tyo͞od) *n.* **1** *Geog.* Distance on the earth's surface northward or southward from the equator measured in degrees of the meridian; angular distance reckoned on a meridian. **2** *Astron.* The angular distance of a heavenly body above the plane of the ecliptic, as viewed from some point. **3** A region or place with reference to its distance north or south of the equator. **4** Figuratively, one's proper place or environment. **5** Extent of deviation from what is regular or customary; independence or liberty of action or conduct. **6** Laxity. **7** Strength of application; range or scope. [<L *latitudo* breadth < *latus* broad] — **lat′i·tu′di·nal** *adj.*

lat·i·tu·di·nar·i·an (lat′ə·to͞o′də·nâr′ē·ən, -tyo͞o′-) *adj.* Broad, tolerant, or lax in religious principles. — *n.* **1** One who is extremely tolerant or lax in religious principles; a freethinker; liberal. **2** One who departs from the strict standards of orthodoxy. [<L *latitudo, -inis* LATITUDE + -ARIAN] — **lat′i·tu′di·nar′i·an·ism** *n.*

Lat·i·tu·di·nar·i·an (lat′ə·to͞o′də·nâr′ē·ən. -tyo͞o′-) *n.* One of a party of English churchmen of the 17th century who advocated the union of the dissenters with the established church.

La·ti·um (lā′shē·əm) A region and ancient country in central Italy; original home of the Latins. *Italian* **La·zio** (lä′tsyō).

La·to·na (lə·tō′nə) In Roman mythology, the mother of Diana and Apollo: identified with the Greek *Leto.*

la·tri·a (lə·trī′ə) *n.* In the Roman Catholic Church, that supreme worship which can be lawfully given to God only: distinguished from *dulia* and *hyperdulia.* [<LL *latria* <Gk. *latreia* service, worship < *latreuein* work for hire, worship < *latris* a hired servant]

la·trine (lə·trēn′) *n.* A privy, especially in a camp, barracks, hospital, etc. [<F <L *latrina* a bath, a privy < *lavatrina* < *lavare* wash]

La·trobe (lə·trōb′), **Benjamin Henry,** 1764–1820, American architect born in England.

-latry *combining form* Worship of; excessive devotion to: *idolatry.* [<Gk. *latreia* worship]

Lat·ta·quié (là·tà·kyā′) The French name for LATAKIA.

lat·ten (lat′n) *n.* Metal in thin sheets, especially (and originally) brass. [<OF *laton, leiton,* prob. <MHG *latta* a thin plate, a lath. Akin to LATH.]

lat·ter (lat′ər) *adj.* **1** Of more recent date; modern. **2** *Obs.* Latest or last. — **the latter** The second of two mentioned persons or things: opposed to *the former.* [OE *lætra,* compar. of *læt* late] — **lat′ter·ly** *adv.*

lat·ter-day (lat′ər·dā′) *adj.* Belonging to the present; recent; modern.

Latter-day Saint A Mormon.

lat·ter·most (lat′ər·mōst′) *adj.* Last; latest.

lat·tice (lat′is) *n.* **1** Open-work of metal or wood, formed by crossing or interlacing strips or bars; also, anything made of such work, as a window, a blind, or a screen: also called *latticework.* **2** That which resembles a lattice: a *lattice* of branches. **3** *Her.* A bearing of vertical and horizontal bars crossing one another. **4** *Physics* A space lattice. **5** *Telecom.* A network of lines indicating fixed positions in a radio or radar system. — *v.t.* **lat·ticed, lat·tic·ing** **1** To furnish or enclose with a lattice. **2** To arrange or interlace like latticework. [<OF *lattis* < *latte* a lath <MHG. Akin to LATH.]

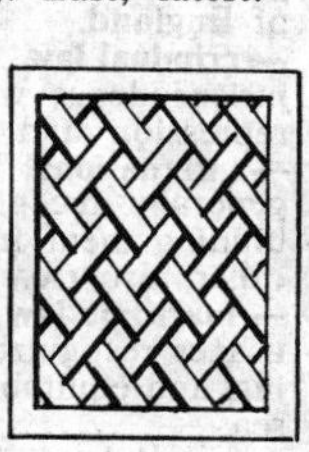

LATTICE

lat·tice·work (lat′is·wûrk′) *n.* **1** Lattice (def. 1). **2** In embroidery, stitching in an outline resembling a lattice: done on solid material, and used as a background.

lat·tic·ing (lat′is·ing) *n.* **1** The act of making or furnishing with lattice. **2** In bridge-building, a system of timbers or bars crossing in such a manner as to connect and strengthen the two channels of a strut and cause them to act as one construction.

la·tus rec·tum (lā′təs rek′təm) *Math.* The chord drawn through a focus of a plane curve perpendicular to its major axis. [<NL, a

Lat·vi·a A republic on the Baltic Sea in NE Europe; 24,900 square miles; capital, Riga; pop. 2,700,000. Formerly the **Latvian Soviet Socialist Republic** (1940–1991).

Lat·vi·an (lat′vē·ən) *adj.* Of or pertaining to Latvia, its inhabitants, or their language. — *n.* **1** A Lett. **2** The Lettish language.

laud (lôd) *n.* **1** Praise or commendation; extolment. **2** The part of divine worship that consists chiefly of praise; also, a song of praise or honor. **3** *pl.* A religious service consisting of the psalms immediately following matins, and constituting with the latter the first of the seven canonical hours: sometimes **Lauds.** See synonyms under PRAISE. — v.t. To praise; extol. [<OF *laude* <L *laus, laudis* praise] — **laud′er** *n.*

Laud (lôd), **William,** 1573–1645, archbishop of Canterbury; supporter of Charles I; impeached and beheaded.

laud·a·ble (lô′də·bəl) *adj.* **1** Worthy of approval; praiseworthy. **2** Healthy or promotive of health or healing; salubrious; normal: said of pus or bodily juices. — **laud′a·ble·ness, laud′a·bil′i·ty** *n.* — **laud′a·bly** *adv.*

lau·da·nine (lô′də·nēn) *n.* *Chem.* A white, crystalline alkaloid from opium, $C_{20}H_{25}O_4N$, belonging pharmacologically to the codeine group. [<LAUDAN(UM) + -INE²]

lau·da·num (lô′də·nəm) *n.* **1** Tincture of opium. **2** Formerly, a preparation in which opium predominated. [<NL <Med. L, var. of L *ladanum* LADANUM]

lau·da·tion (lô·dā′shən) *n.* The act of praising; praise.

laud·a·to·ry (lô′də·tôr′ē, -tō′rē) *adj.* Eulogizing; praising: also **laud′a·tive.** — *n.* *pl.* **·ries** A panegyric. [<L *laudatorius* <L *laudare* praise, celebrate]

Lau·der (lô′dər), **Sir Harry,** 1870–1950, Scottish singer and comedian.

Lau·e (lou′ə), **Max von,** 1879–1960, German physicist.

laugh (laf, läf) *v.i.* **1** To express amusement, hilarity, derision, etc., by expressions of the face and by a series of explosive sounds made in the chest and throat. **2** To be or appear gay or lively. — *v.t.* **3** To express by laughter. **4** To move or influence by laughter or ridicule: He *laughed* himself out of his worries. — **to laugh at** **1** To express amusement concerning. **2** To make light of; belittle. — **to laugh away** To drive off or away by laughter. — **to laugh in** (or **up**) **one's sleeve** To be secretly amused although outwardly serious. — **to laugh off** To dismiss with a laugh; treat lightly or scornfully. — **to laugh on** (or **out of**) **the other** (or **wrong**) **side of the mouth** To feel sudden disappointment or annoyance after mirth or supposed triumph. — *n.* **1** The act or sound of laughter. **2** *Colloq.* Anything provoking or producing laughter. [OE *hlæhhan*] — **laugh′er** *n.*

laugh·a·ble (laf′ə·bəl, läf′-) *adj.* Ridiculous; exciting laughter; humorous; ludicrous. — **laugh′a·ble·ness** *n.* — **laugh′a·bly** *adv.*

laugh·ing (laf′ing, läf′-) *adj.* Fit to be laughed at: a *laughing* matter.

laughing gas Nitrous oxide, N_2O, an anesthetic with exhilarating effect when inhaled: used in dental surgery.

laughing goose The white-fronted goose (*Anser albifrons*) of western North America: also called *harlequin brant.*

laughing gull The black-headed gull (*Larus atricilla*) of the Atlantic coast of North America.

laughing jackass The kookaburra.

laugh·ing·ly (laf′ing·lē, läf′-) *adv.* With a laugh, laughter, or merriment.

laugh·ing·stock (laf′ing·stok′, läf′-) *n.* A butt for ridicule.

laugh·ter (laf′tər, läf′-) *n.* **1** The sound or action of laughing. **2** Any exclamation or expression indicating merriment or derision. ◆ Collateral adjective; *risible.* [OE *hleahtor* < root of *hlæhhan* laugh]

Synonyms: cachinnation, fun, giggling, glee, hilarity, jollity, merriment, mirth, rejoicing, snickering, tittering. *Antonyms*: distress, frowning, gloom, glowering, groaning, lowering, mourning, sadness, sorrow, tears, wailing, weeping.

launce (lôns) *n.* The sand eel: also spelled *lance.*

Laun·ce·lot (lôn′sə·lot, län′-) See LANCELOT.

launch¹ (lônch, länch) *v.t.* **1** To cause to move from land into water for the first time, as a ship on completion of its hull. **2** To put into the water; set afloat, as a boat or log. **3** To make a beginning of; set in motion: to *launch* an enterprise. **4** To start (someone) on a career, course, etc. **5** To give a start to the flight or course of, as a rocket, torpedo, or airplane. **6** To hurl or throw, as a spear. — *v.i.* **7** To put or go to sea: usually with *out* or *forth.* **8** To start on a career, course, etc. **9** To begin something with vehemence or urgency; plunge: He *launched* into a tirade. — **to launch out** **1** To strike out suddenly or wildly. **2** To be vehement or reckless. **3** To start; commence. — *n.* **1** The act of launching. **2** The movement of a ship, boat, etc., from the land into the water; especially, the sliding over ways of a newly built vessel from the stocks into the water; also, the spot where a ship is built, and the tackle used in launching it. **3** The start of a bird for flight. [<AF *lancher,* OF *lancier* < *lance* LANCE]

launch² (lônch, länch) *n.* **1** The largest of the boats carried by a warship, used for transporting men and supplies. **2** A large, open boat, propelled by steam or electricity, and used as a pleasure craft. [<Sp. *lancha,* prob. <Malay *lanca* a three-masted boat < *lancār* speedy]

launch·er (lôn′chər, län′-) *n.* **1** One who or that which launches. **2** Any mechanical device or installation for launching rockets, guided missiles, satellites, etc.

launching pad The platform from which a rocket or guided missile is fired.

laun·der (lôn′dər, län′-) *v.t.* **1** To wash and iron, as clothing. — *v.i.* **2** To wash and iron laundry. **3** To undergo washing and ironing. — *n.* A trough or gutter, as of wood, for conveying water. [Contraction of ME *lavender* a laundress <OF *lavendier* a washerwoman < LL *lavandarius,* ult. <L *lavare* wash] — **laun′der·er** *n.*

laun·dress (lôn′dris, län′-) *n.* A woman who works in a laundry; washerwoman.

laun·dro·mat (lôn′drə·mat, län-) *n.* *U.S.* A commercial establishment where the customer brings laundry to be washed and dried in coin-operated automatic machines. [<*Laundromat,* a trade name]

laun·dry (lôn′drē, län′-) *n.* *pl.* **·dries** **1** A place for washing and ironing clothes. **2** Articles sent to a laundry for washing and ironing. **3** *Obs.* A laundress. [Alter. of obs. *lavendry* <OF *lavenderie* < *lavendier.* See LAUNDER.] — **laun′dry·man** (-mən) *n.* — **laun′dry·wom′an** (-wo͝om′ən) *n. fem.*

Laun·fal (lôn′fəl), **Sir** In romances by Thomas Chestre and James Russell Lowell, a knight of the Round Table.

Lau·ra (lô′rə, *Ger., Ital.* lou′rä) A feminine personal name. Also *French* **Laure** (lōr). [<L *laurus* the laurel]
— **Laura** The idealized lady to whom Petrarch's sonnets were addressed: identified with **Laura de Noves,** 1307–48, wife of Hugues de Sade of Avignon.

lau·ra·ceous (lô·rā′shəs) *adj.* Belonging to a family (*Lauraceae*) of aromatic and medicinal trees and shrubs, the laurels, which includes sassafras and cinnamon, mostly natives of warm climates. [<NL <L *laurus* the laurel]

lau·re·ate (lô′rē·it) *adj.* **1** Crowned or decked with laurel, as a mark of distinction or honor. **2** Deserving of distinction; preeminent, especially as a poet; also, relating to or distinctive of poets. **3** Made of laurel or in imitation of laurel. — *n.* **1** In England, the poet officially invested with the title of poet laureate by the crown. **2** In former times, a poet publicly crowned with laurel in recognition of his merit. See under POET. — *v.t.* (-rē·āt) **·at·ed, ·at·ing** **1** To crown with a laurel

wreath. 2 To make poet laureate. [<L *laureatus* crowned with laurel < *laurea* a laurel tree or crown, orig. fem. of *laureus* made of laurel < *laurus* laurel] — **lau′re·ate·ship′** *n.* — **lau′re·a′tion** *n.*

lau·rel (lôr′əl, lor′-) *n.* 1 An evergreen shrub (*Laurus nobilis*) of the Mediterranean area, with aromatic, lance-shaped leaves, yellowish flowers, and succulent, cherrylike fruit: also called **bay laurel, Grecian laurel, noble laurel:** also called *bay.* 2 Any other species of the genus *Laurus.* 3 An American evergreen shrub of either of two genera, as the mountain laurel (*Kalmia latifolia*) or the great laurel (*Rhododendron maximum*). 4 In England, a species of evergreen cherry tree (genus *Prunus*) with flowers in racemes and inedible fruit. 5 *pl.* A crown or wreath of laurel, indicating honor or high merit; hence, honor or distinction. 6 A salmon that has passed the summer in fresh water. — **to rest on one's laurels** To be content with what one has already achieved or accomplished. — *v.t.* **·reled** or **·relled, ·rel·ing** or **·rel·ling** 1 To wreathe or crown with laurel. 2 To honor. [<OF *laurier, lorier* < *lor* <L *laurus* a laurel]

Lau·rence (lôr′əns, lor′-) See LAWRENCE. Also *Du.* **Lau·rens** (lou′rens), *Fr.* **Lau·rent** (lō·räṅ′), *Ger.* **Lau·renz** (lou′rents), *Lat.* **Lau·ren·tius** (lô·ren′shəs).

Lau·ren·cin (lô·räṅ·saṅ′), **Marie,** 1885–1956, French painter.

Lau·ren·tian (lô·ren′shən) *adj.* 1 Of or pertaining to the St. Lawrence River. 2 *Geol.* Pertaining to the ancient Archean rocks underlying the Algonquian rocks of North America.

Laurentian Mountains A crescent-shaped range extending from the Saint Lawrence River to the Arctic Ocean and forming the watershed between Hudson Bay and the Saint Lawrence; highest peak, 3,905 feet. Also **Lau·ren·tides** (lô·räṅ·tēd′).

Laurentian Plateau See CANADIAN SHIELD.

lau·ric (lô′rik) *adj. Biochem.* Designating a fatty acid, $C_{11}H_{23}COOH$, found as a glyceride in spermaceti, laurel oil, etc. [<L *laurus* laurel + -IC]

Lau·rie (lô′rē) Diminutive of LAURA, LAURENCE.

Lau·rier (lô·ryā′), **Sir Wilfred,** 1841–1919, French-Canadian statesman.

Lau·rin·da (lô·rin′də) Latin form of LAURA.

Lau·rus (lô′rəs) *n.* A genus of evergreen trees of the family *Lauraceae.* [<L, laurel tree]

lau·rus·tine (lô′rəs·tin) *n.* A southern European shrub (*Viburnum tinus*) having oblong leaves hairy on the underside and fragrant white or pink flowers appearing in winter. Also **lau·rus·ti·nus** (lô′rəs·tī′nəs). [<NL *laurustinus* <L *laurus tinus* < *laurus* laurel + *tinus* a plant]

Lau·sanne (lō·zän′) A Swiss city on the northern shore of Lake Geneva, capital of Vaud canton.

laus De·o (lôs dē′ō) *Latin* Praise be to God.

la·va (lä′və, lav′ə) *n.* 1 Melted rock, issuing from a volcanic crater or a fissure in the earth's surface. 2 Such rock when solidified. [<Ital., orig. a stream of rain < *lavare* wash <L]

la·va·bo (lə·vā′bō) *n. pl.* **·boes** 1 In the Anglican and Roman Catholic churches, the washing of the hands by the celebrant after the offertory, during the Eucharist. 2 That part of Psalm xxvi which is recited by the priest while washing the hands: from the opening word. 3 A small linen towel used to wipe the priest's hands in this rite. 4 A stationary washbowl or lavatory with running water; also, in monasteries, the room in which this is placed. [<L, I shall wash, 1st person sing. future of *lavare* wash]

lav·age (lav′ij, *Fr.* là·vàzh′) *n. Med.* A cleansing, especially the washing out or irrigation of an organ, as the stomach. [<F < *laver* wash <L *lavare*]

La·val (là·vàl′), **Pierre,** 1883–1945, premier of France 1931–32, 1935–36; premier of Vichy government 1942–44; executed for treason.

la·va–la·va (lä′və·lä′və) *n.* A loincloth or waistcloth of printed calico worn by natives of Samoa and other islands of the Pacific. [<Samoan]

lav·a·liere (lav′ə·lir′) *n.* A piece of jewelry, consisting of a necklace and pendant. Also **lav′a·lier′.** [<F *la vallière* a sort of necktie, ? after Louise de *La Vallière,* 1644–1710, mistress of Louis XIV]

La·va·ter (lä′vä·tər, lä·vä′-), **Johann Kaspar,** 1741–1801, Swiss poet, theologian, and physiognomist.

la·va·tion (la·vā′shən) *n.* A washing. Also **lave·ment** (lāv′mənt). [<L *lavatio, -onis* < *lavare* wash]

lav·a·to·ry (lav′ə·tôr′ē, -tō′rē) *n. pl.* **·ries** 1 An apartment for washing; a place where anything is washed; specifically, a room in a public or semipublic place, as in a school or hotel, provided with appliances for washing and usually with urinals and toilets. 2 *Med.* A wash for a diseased part; lotion. 3 *Eccl.* A piscina; also, a water drain in a sacristy where the priest washes his hands before vesting. — *adj.* Washing. [<LL *lavatorium* a place for washing < *lavare* wash]

lave[1] (lāv) *v.t.* & *v.i.* **laved, lav·ing** 1 To wash; bathe. 2 To flow along or against as if washing. [Fusion of OE *lafian* wash, pour and OF *laver* wash, both <L *lavare* wash. Akin to LATHER.]

lave[2] (lāv) *n. Scot.* The rest; remainder. [OE *laf*]

lav·en·der (lav′ən·dər) *n.* 1 An aromatic shrub (genus *Lavandula*) of the mint family, especially the Old World **spike lavender** (*L. officinalis*), the source of oil of lavender. 2 Its characteristic perfume. 3 The dried flowers and leaves of this plant, used to scent linen, etc. 4 The color of lavender flowers, a pale lilac. — *adj.* Of, pertaining to, or like lavender. [<AF *lavendre* <Med. L *lavendula, livendula,* ? <L *livere* be bluish < *lividus* blue; infl. in form by *lavare* wash, because used as a perfume in baths]

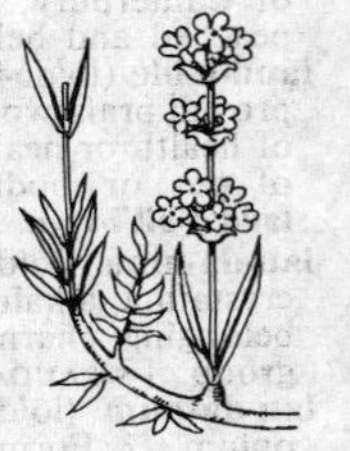

SPIKE LAVENDER (Plant from 2 to 3 feet tall)

la·ver[1] (lā′vər) *n.* 1 A large basin or other receptacle to wash in; specifically, in Solomon's temple and the ancient Jewish tabernacle, a large vessel of bronze at which the priests washed their hands and feet before sacrifices. 2 That which laves. [<LAVE[1]]

la·ver[2] (lā′vər) *n.* Any edible purple seaweed (genus *Porphyra*) or a dish prepared from it. Also **red laver.** [<L, a water plant]

La·veran (là·vräṅ′), **Charles Louis Alphonse,** 1845–1922, French pathologist; discovered the plasmodium that causes malarial fever.

lav·er·ock (lav′ər·ək, lāv′rək) *n. Scot.* The lark. Also **lav·rock** (lav′rək).

La·ver·y (lā′vər·ē, lav′ər·ē), **Sir John,** 1856–1941, English painter.

La·vin·i·um (lə·vin′ē·əm) In classical geography, a city in Latium founded by Aeneas.

lav·ish (lav′ish) *adj.* 1 Bestowed, expended, or existing in profusion; superabundant. 2 Spending extravagantly; prodigal. 3 Wild or unrestrained. — *v.t.* To give or bestow profusely or generously; squander. See synonyms under SQUANDER. [<OF *lavasse, lavache* a downpour of rain <Provençal *lavaci* <L *lavatio* a lavation] — **lav′ish·er** *n.* — **lav′ish·ly** *adv.* — **lav′ish·ness** *n.*

lav·ish·ment (lav′ish·mənt) *n.* A lavishing prodigality.

La·voi·sier (là·vwà·zyā′), **Antoine Laurent,** 1743–94, French chemist; identified and named oxygen; guillotined.

la·vol·ta (lə·vol′tə) *n.* An old dance for two persons consisting of lively, bounding steps. Also **la·volt′, la·vol′to.** [<Ital. < *la* the + *volta* a turn <L *volutus,* pp. of *volvere* turn]

La·von·gai (lä·vông′gī) An island in the Bismarck Archipelago; 460 square miles: formerly *New Hanover.*

law[1] (lô) *n.* 1 A rule of conduct, recognized by custom or by formal enactment, which a community considers as binding upon its members. 2 A system or body of such rules. 3 The condition of society when such rules are observed: to establish *law* and order. 4 The body of rules relating to a specified subject: criminal *law;* statute *law.* 5 Statute and common law, as opposed to equity. 6 An enactment of a legislature, as opposed to a constitution. 7 Remedial justice as administered by the courts: to resort to the *law.* 8 The branch of knowledge concerned with jurisprudence: to study *law.* 9 The vocation of an attorney, solicitor, etc.: to practice *law.* 10 The legal profession as a whole. 11 The Mosaic system of rules recorded in the Pentateuch. 12 A rule of conduct having divine origin; also such rules, collectively. 13 An imperative rule or command: His word is *law.* 14 Any rule of conduct or procedure: the *laws* of hospitality; the *laws* of poetry. 15 In science and philosophy, a statement of the manner or order in which a defined group of natural phenomena occur under certain conditions: also called *law of nature.* 16 *Math.* The rule or formula by which certain functions vary or according to which certain operations are performed. 17 An allowance made or a start given to a competitor in a race or to a hunted animal. — **the law** The police, personifying legal force. — *v.t.* & *v.i.* To proceed against (someone) at law. — *adj.* Of or pertaining to law or the law. [OE *lagu* <ON *lag* something laid or fixed, in pl., law. Akin to LAY[1].]

Synonyms (noun): canon, code, command, commandment, decree, edict, enactment, formula, mandate, order, ordinance, principle, regulation, rule, statute. *Law* in its ideal is the statement of a *principle* of right in mandatory form, by competent authority, with adequate penalty for disobedience; in common use the term is applied to any legislative act, however imperfect or unjust. *Command* and *commandment* are personal and particular; as, the *commands* of a parent; the Ten *Commandments.* An *edict* is the act of an absolute sovereign or other authority; we speak of the *edict* of an emperor, the *decree* of a court. A *mandate* is specific for an occasion or a purpose; a superior court issues its *mandate* to an inferior court to send up its records (see MANDATE). *Statute* is the recognized legal term for a specific *law; enactment* is the more vague and general expression. We speak of algebraic or chemical *formulas,* municipal *ordinances,* military *orders,* army *regulations,* ecclesiastical *canons,* the *rules* of a business house. *Law* is often used, also, for a recognized *principle,* whose violation is attended with injury or loss that acts like a penalty; as, the *laws* of business; the *laws* of nature. In more strictly scientific use, a natural *law* is simply a recognized system of sequences or relations; as Kepler's *laws* of planetary distances. See JUSTICE, LEGISLATION.

— **canon law** See CANON LAW.

— **ceremonial law** Law pertaining to the religious ceremonies of the Jews, as given in the Old Testament.

— **civil law** 1 The body or system of jurisprudence which the people of a state or nation establish for their government as citizens. 2 The body of Roman law, received by the governments of continental Europe as the foundation of their jurisprudence; also so received in the State of Louisiana.

— **common law** A system of jurisprudence originating in custom or usage, as distinguished from statutory law: the *common law* of England.

— **criminal law** The branch or department of jurisprudence which relates to crimes, their repression and punishment.

— **international law** The rules of conduct generally recognized by civilized states as binding them in their conduct toward each other: also LAW OF NATIONS.

— **maritime law** The body of principles and usages recognized by commercial nations as just and equitable in regulating affairs on the sea.

— **moral law** The divinely prescribed law regarding moral conduct; the law of right; especially, the Decalog.

— **Mosaic law** The Law of Moses.

— **natural law** 1 The rule of civil conduct deducible from the common reason and conscience of mankind: the *natural law* of self-defense. 2 A law of nature. See LAW (def. 15).

— **organic law** The fundamental law of a state; a constitution.

— **parliamentary law** The body of rules recognized or ordained for preserving order and regulating the modes of procedure and course of debate in legislative or deliberative bodies.

— **Roman Law** See CIVIL LAW.

law[2] (lô) *adj. Scot.* Low.

law[3] (lô) *interj.* An exclamation expressing

astonishment, admiration, etc. [Fusion of *law*, var. of LA[2] and *law*, alter. of LORD, used as an exclamation]

Law (lô), **(Andrew) Bonar,** 1858–1923, English statesman. **—John,** 1671–1729, Scottish financier. **—William,** 1686–1761, English devotional writer.

law-a·bid·ing (lô′ə·bī′ding) *adj.* Obedient to or abiding by the law.

law–break·er (lô′brā′kər) *n.* One who violates the law; a criminal. **—law′–break′ing** *n.* & *adj.*

Lawes (lôz), **Henry,** 1596–1662, English composer. **—Lewis Edward,** 1883–1947, U.S. penologist.

law·ful (lô′fəl) *adj.* **1** Permitted or not forbidden by law; legitimate: *lawful* acts. **2** Constituted by law; enforceable at law: *lawful* claims. **3** Valid, or regarded as valid: said of a marriage; also, born of such a marriage: said of offspring. **4** Having full legal rights. See synonyms under JUST, RIGHT. **—law′ful·ly** *adv.* **—law′ful·ness** *n.*

law·giv·er (lô′giv′ər) *n.* One who makes or enacts a law or laws; a legislator. **—law′giv′·ing** *adj.* & *n.*

law–hand (lô′hand′) *n.* The handwriting used in or characteristic of old legal documents; also, manuscripts written in this hand.

la·wi·ne (lä·vē′nə) *n. pl.* **·nen** (-nən) An avalanche. Also *lauwine.* [<G <LL *labina.* See AVALANCHE.]

law·less (lô′lis) *adj.* **1** Not subject or obedient to law of any sort; unruly; disobedient. **2** Without the sanction or authority of law; contrary to law: *lawless* measures. **3** Not formed or constructed according to law or rule; irregular: *lawless* verses. **4** Beyond the reach, or not within the province, of law. **5** Without the protection of law; outlawed: a *lawless* fugitive. **—law′less·ly** *adv.* **—law′less·ness** *n.*

law·mak·ing (lô′mā′king) *n.* The enacting of laws; legislation. **—law′mak′er** *n.*

Law·man (lô′mən) See LAYAMON.

law merchant **1** The body of commercial usages or rules recognized by civilized nations as regulating the rights of persons engaged in trade. **2** Commercial and mercantile law.

lawn[1] (lôn) *n.* **1** A piece of ground with grass kept closely mown. **2** A glade between woods. [Var. of LAUNDE] **—lawn′y** *adj.*

lawn[2] (lôn) *n.* **1** Fine thin linen or cotton fabric. **2** A fine clay sieve. [Earlier *laune (lynen)* Laon (linen) <*Laon* Laon, where it was formerly made]

lawn bowling See BOWLS.

lawn·mow·er (lôn′mō′ər) *n.* A machine for clipping the grass of lawns, either power-driven or propelled by hand, and equipped with spiral blades rotating against a horizontal bar, or rotary cutting blades.

lawn tennis See TENNIS.

Law of Moses The Pentateuch; Mosaic law.

law of nations International law.

law of parsimony *Philos.* A regulative principle in the interpretation of scientific data, requiring that of several equiprobable assumptions, hypotheses, or theories regarding a given phenomenon or group of phenomena, the simplest and least cumbersome is to be preferred. Also called *Ockham's razor.*

Law·rence (lôr′əns, lor′-) A masculine personal name. [<L, prob. a laurel]
—Lawrence, Saint Christian martyr of the third century.

Law·rence (lôr′əns, lor′-) A city on the Merrimac River in NE Massachusetts.

Law·rence (lôr′əns, lor′-), **D(avid) H(erbert),** 1885–1930, English novelist and poet.
—Ernest Orlando, 1901–58, U.S. physicist.
—Sir Thomas, 1769–1835, English painter.
—T(homas) E(dward), 1888–1935, English soldier, archeologist, adventurer, and writer: known as *Lawrence of Arabia*: changed his surname to *Shaw* after 1927.

law·ren·ci·um (lô·ren′sē·əm) *n.* A very short-lived radioactive element (symbol Lw), originally produced by bombarding californium with the nuclei of a boron isotope.

law·sone (lô′sōn) *n.* The red coloring matter extracted from the leaves and twigs of the henna plant: used as a hair dye and as a constituent of henna. [after Dr. John *Lawson,* died about 1712, Scottish naturalist]

law·suit (lô′sōōt′) *n.* A proceeding in a court of law for redress of wrongs, or for enforcement of right.

law·yer (lô′yər) *n.* **1** One who practices law; an attorney or solicitor. **2** A member of any branch of the legal profession. **3** In the New Testament, an expositor of the Mosaic law. **4** *U.S.* The black-necked stilt *(Himantopus mexicanus)*: also called *longshanks.* **5** The American burbot. **6** The bowfin: also called *mudfish* and *grindle.* **7** *Brit. Dial.* A long briar or bramble. [<LAW[1] + -YER]

lax (laks) *adj.* **1** Lacking tenseness or firmness; slack; yielding. **2** Not stringent or energetic; remiss; weak in control. **3** Wanting exactness of meaning or application. **4** *Med.* Loose: said of the bowels. **5** *Bot.* Not having the parts close together: a *lax* flower cluster. **6** *Phonet.* Formed with a relatively relaxed tongue and jaw, as (i) and (ōō); wide: opposed to *tense.* See synonyms under VAGUE. [<L *laxus* loose] **—lax′i·ty, lax′ness** *n.* **—lax′ly** *adv.*

lax·a·tion (lak·sā′shən) *n.* The act of loosening, or the state of being loosed; relaxation.

lax·a·tive (lak′sə·tiv) *n. Med.* A gentle purgative. **—***adj. Med.* **1** Having power to open or loosen the bowels, as a medicine; gently purgative. **2** Subject to or characterized by diarrhea: *laxative* bowels, a *laxative* disease. [<F, fem. of *laxatif* <L *laxativus* < *laxare.* See LAXATION.]

lay[1] (lā) *v.* **laid, lay·ing** *v.t.* **1** To cause to lie; place prostrate or at length; deposit. **2** To put or place: Don't *lay* a hand on me. **3** To strike or beat down; overthrow; destroy: to *lay* a city in ashes. **4** To cause to settle or subside, as dust, a storm, etc. **5** To calm or allay, as doubts. **6** To place in regular order or proper position: to *lay* title. **7** To think out; devise; arrange: to *lay* plans. **8** To attribute or ascribe: to *lay* blame. **9** To give importance to; put: to *lay* emphasis on something. **10** To bring forward; advance, as a claim. **11** To bring forth from the body and deposit, as an egg. **12** To construct; build, as a foundation. **13** To make (a table) ready for a meal. **14** To bury; inter. **15** To impose, as taxes, punishment, etc.; assess. **16** To spread over a surface: to *lay* a fixative. **17** To strike with or apply, as in punishment: He *laid* the whip across the culprit's back. **18** To locate: The scene is *laid* in the boudoir. **19** To set or prepare, as a trap. **20** To place as a wager or bet. **21** To twist strands so as to form (rope). **22** *Mil.* To aim (a cannon). **23** *U.S. Slang* To have sexual intercourse with; seduce. **—***v.i.* **24** To bring forth and deposit eggs. **25** To make a bet or bets. **26** *Naut.* To go to a specified position: *Lay* aloft to hand sail! **27** To lie; recline: an incorrect use. See synonyms under PUT[1]. **—to lay about one** **1** To deal blows on all sides. **2** To exert oneself to the utmost. **—to lay away** **1** To store up; save. **2** To bury. **—to lay before** To put forward or present, as a report. **—to lay by** To lay away (def. 1). **—to lay down** **1** To give up or relinquish; sacrifice. **2** To state or proclaim: to *lay down* the law. **3** To bet. **—to lay for** To wait to attack or harm. **—to lay hold of** To seize or grasp. **—to lay in** To procure and store. **—to lay into** To attack vigorously. **—to lay it on** *Colloq.* To be extravagant or exorbitant, as in praise or demands. **—to lay off** **1** To take off and put aside, as clothes. **2** To survey; mark off. **3** *U.S. Colloq.* To dismiss from a job, usually temporarily. **4** *U.S. Colloq.* To take a rest; stop working. **5** *U.S. Slang* To stop annoying, teasing, etc. **—to lay on** **1** To put on; apply, as color. **2** To beat or strike; attack. **—to lay out** **1** To spend. **2** To prepare for burial. **3** *Slang* To strike prostrate or unconscious. **4** To set forth the details of: to *lay out* the plot of a novel. **—to lay over** To stop, as for a rest, on a journey. **—to lay siege to** To besiege. **—to lay up** **1** To make a store of. **2** To confine, as by illness or injury. **—***n.* **1** The manner in which something lies or is placed; relative arrangement: the *lay* of the land. **2** *Slang* A line of work; particular business or field of activity. **3** A definite quantity of yarn or thread. **4** The swinging beam or batten of a loom. **5** The direction or amount of twist given to the strands of a rope. **6** A profit or share of profits; a price; specifically, a share of the profits of a whaling or sealing voyage, according to an arrangement made before sailing. [OE *lecgan* make lie < pt. of *licgan* lie[1]. Akin to LAW[1].]

lay[2] (lā) *adj.* Pertaining to the laity; non-professional; inexperienced. [<OF *lai* <Med. L *laicus* <Gk. *laïkos* < *laos* the people]

lay[3] (lā) Past tense of LIE[1].

lay[4] (lā) *n.* A song, ballad, or narrative poem; also, any melody or melodious utterance. [<OF *lai,* prob. <Gmc.]

lay·a·bout (lā′ə·bout′) *n. Chiefly Brit.* A lazy, idle person; a good-for-nothing.

Lay·a·mon (lā′ə·mən, lä′yə-) English priest and poet chronicler of the 13th century; author of *Brut,* a long, Middle English history of Britain from the legendary Brutus to Cadwallader, A.D. 689. Also *Lawman.*

Lay·ard (lā′yərd, lârd), **Sir Austen Henry,** 1817–94, English diplomat and archeologist.

lay·a·way (lā′ə·wā′) *n.* An agreement to make a series of payments to buy merchandise that is delivered when fully paid for. Also **layaway plan.**

lay brother **1** A layman. **2** A brother in a monastery, serving under vows and wearing the dress of the order, but not in holy orders.

lay–by (lā′bī′) *n. pl.* **–bys** **1** *Brit.* A roadside area where vehicles may turn off, as for repairs or parking. **2** In New Zealand, a layaway.

lay communion **1** The communion of the laity at the Lord's table. **2** The condition of being in communion with the church as a layman only.

lay–days (lā′dāz′) *n. pl.* **1** In commerce, the days allowed a ship's lessee for loading and discharging cargo. **2** In marine insurance, the days (usually not beyond 30) while a ship lies idle in port without fires, for which return of insurance premium may be demanded. [<LAY[1] + pl. of DAY]

lay·er (lā′ər) *n.* **1** One who or that which lays. **2** A single horizontal thickness of a course, stratum, or coat. **3** *Bot.* A shoot or twig laid in the ground to take root without being detached from the parent plant. **4** In leatherwork, a welt. **5** In tanning, a pit in which hides are soaked in layers. **6** An artificial oyster bed. **—***v.t. Bot.* To propagate by layers. [<LAY[1] + -ER[1]] **—lay′·er·ing** *n.*

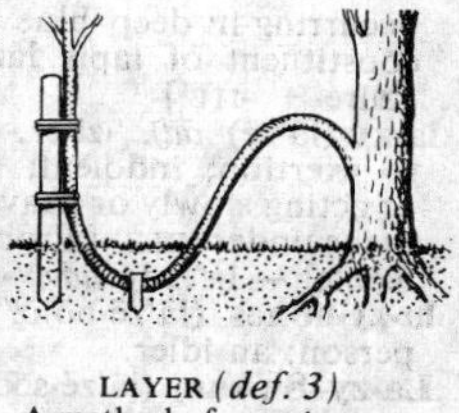

LAYER *(def. 3)*
A method of securing new plants from old stock.

lay·er·age (lā′ər·ij) *n. Bot.* The propagation of plants by rooting parts of them.

layer cake A cake made in layers, having a sweetened filling or icing between layers, and usually frosted.

lay·ered (lā′ərd) *adj.* Having or covered with layers; arranged in layers.

lay·ette (lā·et′) *n.* A full equipment of clothes, bedding, etc., for a newly born child. [<F, dim. of *laie* a packing box, drawer <Flemish *laeye* <MDu. *lade* a chest, trunk. Akin to LADE.]

lay figure **1** A jointed model of the human body that can be arranged, as by artists, to hang drapery upon. **2** A mere puppet; a tool of others. [<Earlier *layman* (<Du. *leeman* < *led* a limb + *man* man) + FIGURE]

lay·man (lā′mən) *n. pl.* **·men** (-mən) One of the laity; a man not belonging to the clergy or other profession or body of experts. **—lay′·wom′an** (-wōōm′ən) *n. fem.* [<LAY[2] + MAN]

lay–off (lā′ôf′, -of′) *n.* The act of discharging or firing workmen or employees; also, a discontinuance, as of work.

lay–out (lā′out′) *n.* **1** *Slang* That which is laid out; a set of articles set out or provided; an outfit; a spread. **2** The space dragged over by a seine in fishing. **3** A laying out or planning, as of a piece of work, a campaign, etc.; a design; an arrangement. **4** In faro, the thirteen cards of a suit laid face upward at the beginning of the game. **5** The make-up of a book, magazine, etc. Also **lay·out.**

lay-o·ver (lā′ō′vər) *n.* A stopover.
la·zar (lā′zər, laz′ər) *n.* One afflicted with a loathsome disease; a leper. [<Med. L *lazarus,* after LAZARUS (*Luke* xiv 20)]
laz·a·ret·to (laz′ə·ret′ō) *n. pl.* **·tos** **1** A pest-house or pest ship; also, a hospital. **2** A quarantine building. **3** A storeroom near a vessel's stern. Also **laz′a·ret′, laz′a·rette′, la·zar·house** (lā′zər·hous′, laz′ər-). [<Ital. *lazzaretto* < dial. Ital. (Venetian) *lazareto, nazareto* < (Santa Madonna di) *Nazaret,* a Venetian church used as a plague hospital in the 15th c.; infl. in form by *lazzaro* a leper <Med. L *lazarus.* See LAZAR.]
Laz·a·rist (laz′ə·rist) *n.* A member of a Roman Catholic order founded in 1624 by St. Vincent de Paul for rural mission work in France. Called *Vincentian* in the United States. Also **Laz′a·rite** (-rit). [<F *lazariste,* from *(Collège de St.) Lazare,* a school at Paris, where the order was established <L *Lazarus* Lazarus]
la·zar·like (lā′zər·līk′, laz′ər-) *adj.* Covered with sores; leprous. Also **la′zar·ly.**
Laz·a·rus (laz′ə·rəs) A masculine personal name. Also *Fr.* **La·zare** (là·zàr′), *Ital.* **Laz·za·ro** (läd′dzä·rō). [<Hebrew, God has helped]
—**Lazarus** A brother of Martha and Mary, raised from the dead by Christ. *John* xi 1.
—**Lazarus** A sick beggar in the parable of the rich and the poor man. *Luke* xvi 20.
Laz·a·rus (laz′ə·rəs), **Emma,** 1849–87, U. S. poet and philanthropist.
laze (lāz) *v.* **lazed, laz·ing** *v.i.* To be lazy; loaf; idle. —*v.t.* To pass (time) in idleness. —*n.* Idleness; laziness. [Back formation <LAZY]
laz·u·li (laz′yŏŏ·lī) See LAPIS LAZULI.
lazuli finch The indigo bunting.
laz·u·lite (laz′yŏŏ·līt) *n.* A vitreous, azure-blue, brittle phosphate of aluminum and magnesium, crystallizing in the monoclinic system. [<Med. L *lazulus* lazuli + -ITE[1]]
laz·u·rite (laz′yŏŏ·rīt) *n. Mineral.* A silicate of sodium and aluminum containing sulfur and occurring in deep-blue crystals: the principal constituent of lapis lazuli. [<Med. L *lazur* azure + -ITE[1]]
la·zy (lā′zē) *adj.* **·zi·er, ·zi·est** **1** Indisposed to exertion; indolent; slothful. **2** Moving or acting slowly or heavily; sluggish. See synonyms under IDLE. [Prob. <MLG *lasich* loose, feeble] —**la′zi·ly** *adv.* —**la′zi·ness** *n.*
la·zy·bones (lā′zē·bōnz′) *n. Colloq.* A lazy person; an idler.
La·zy–Su·san (lā′zē·sōō′zən) *n.* A revolving stand for condiments, bread, butter, etc., usually placed in the center of the table.
la·zy–tongs (lā′zē·tongz′) *n. pl.* Tongs consisting of a series of diagonal levers pivoted together in the middle and at the ends, by which device the tongs can be extended by a simple movement of scissorslike handles so as to pick up objects at a distance.

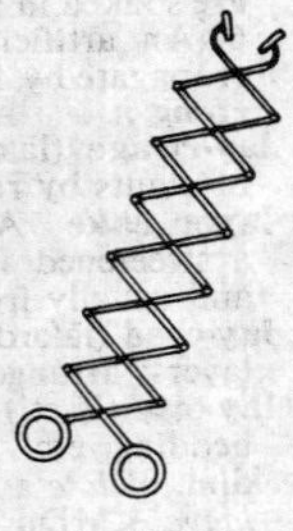

LAZY–TONGS

laz·za·ro·ne (laz′ə·rō′nā, *Ital.* läd′dzä·rō′nā) *n. pl.* **·ro·ni** (-rō′nē, *Ital.* -rō′nē) A Neapolitan beggar. [<Ital., aug. of *lazzaro* a leper <Med. L *lazarus* a lazar]
L–bar (el′bär′) *n.* A steel bar shaped like an **L**.
-le *suffix* Repeatedly: used to form frequentative verbs, but often without appreciable force: *sparkle, haggle.* [OE *-lian*]
lea[1] (lē) *n.* A grassy field or plain. ◆ Homophone: *lee.* [OE *lēah,* orig. open ground in a wood]
lea[2] (lē) *n.* A varying measure of yarn: 80 yards in worsted, 120 yards in cotton and silk, and 300 yards in linen: also spelled *lay.* ◆ Homophone: *lee.* [Back formation <earlier *leas,* taken as pl., prob. <F *lier* <L *ligare* bind]
leach (lēch) *v.t.* **1** To cause (a liquid) to percolate through something. **2** To percolate a liquid through (ashes, etc.) so as to remove the soluble portions. **3** To remove (soluble portions) by means of a percolating liquid. **4** *Metall.* To dissolve (metals or minerals) out of ore by cyanide or chlorine solutions, acids, etc. —*v.i.* **5** To lose soluble matter by percolation. **6** To be removed by percolations. —*n.* **1** Wood ashes, through which water is passed to carry away the soluble portions. **2** The vessel in which ashes, etc., are leached: also **leach tub.** **3** The act or process of leaching. **4** The solution obtained by leaching. Also spelled *latch.* ◆ Homophone: *leech.* [OE *leccan* wet, irrigate. Akin to LAKE[1], LEAK.] —**leach′er** *n.*
leach·y (lē′chē) *adj.* **leach·i·er, leach·i·est** Pervious; porous.
Lea·cock (lē′kok), **Stephen Butler,** 1869–1944, Canadian economist and humorist.
lead[1] (lēd) *v.* **led, lead·ing** *v.t.* **1** To go with or ahead of so as to show the way; guide. **2** To draw along; guide by or as by pulling: to *lead* a person by the hand. **3** To serve as a direction or route for: The path *led* them to a valley. **4** To cause to go in a certain course of direction, as wire, water, etc. **5** **a** To direct the affairs or actions of; be the leader of, as an army or expedition. **b** To direct the playing or performance of: to *lead* an orchestra. **6** To have the first or foremost place among: He *led* the field by ten feet. **7** To influence or control the opinions, thoughts, actions, etc., of; induce: His experiments *led* him to these conclusions. **8** To live or experience; pass: to *lead* a happy life. **9** To begin or open: to *lead* a discussion. **10** In card games, to begin a round of play with: He *led* the ace. **11** In hunting, to aim a weapon or missile ahead of (a moving target). —*v.i.* **12** To act as guide; conduct. **13** To have leadership or command; be in control. **14** To be guided: The horse *leads* easily. **15** To be first or in advance. **16** To afford a way or passage; reach or extend: The road *led* into a swamp. **17** In card games, to make the first play. **18** In boxing, to strike at an opponent, especially in testing his defense: to *lead* with a left. —**to lead off** To make a beginning; start. —**to lead on** To entice or tempt, especially to extravagance or error. —**to lead one a merry chase** (or **dance**) To cause someone trouble or confusion by unpredictable actions. —**to lead the way** **1** To act as guide. **2** To take the initiative. —**to lead to** To result in; cause: His carelessness *led to* his downfall. —**to lead with one's chin** *U.S. Slang* To expose oneself to unnecessary harm. —*n.* **1** Position in advance or at the head; priority. **2** The distance, time, etc., by which anything precedes. **3** The act of leading or conducting; guidance: to give a novice a *lead* in hunting; a clue or hint. **4** In cards, etc., the right to play first in a round; the card, piece, or suit played first. **5** A way or passage; especially, an open channel or passage through ice. **6** A lode or vein of ore; also, an old river bed where gold has been found. **7** In drama, the principal part; the actor who performs in such a part. **8** *Naut.* The course of a rope. **9** *Electr.* A main electrical conductor. **10** In shooting a gun, the act of aiming ahead of a moving target. **11** In baseball, the distance from base of a runner ready to run to the next base. **12** A leash for leading a dog. **13** In journalism, the opening of a news story with a summary of its contents. —*adj.* Acting as leader: the *lead* dog. [OE *lǣden* cause to go]
Synonyms (verb): conduct, convey, direct, escort, excel, guide, head, outstrip, precede, surpass. See ACTUATE, DRAW, INFLUENCE, PERSUADE, PRECEDE. *Antonyms*: ape, chase, copy, follow, imitate, obey, pursue, succeed.
lead[2] (led) *n.* **1** A soft, heavy, inelastic, malleable, ductile, bluish-gray metallic element (symbol Pb) in the fourth group of the periodic table, most commonly occurring in the sulfide mineral, galena. **2** Any one of various articles made of lead or its alloys. **3** *Printing* A thin strip of type metal or brass used in composition. **4** *Naut.* A weight of lead used in sounding at sea. **5** Leaden sheets or plates used for covering roofs. **6** One of the cames in a diamond-paned window. **7** Graphite: also called **black lead.** **8** A mixture of lead carbonate and hydrated lead oxide: also called **white lead.** **9** *Colloq.* Projectiles from firearms; bullets. —*v.t.* **1** To cover, weight, fasten, treat, or fill with lead. **2** To glaze, as porcelain, with powdered metallic ore. **3** *Printing* To separate (lines of type) with leads. **4** To construct (a window) with leaden cames. —*v.i.* **5** To become filled or clogged with lead: said of rifle grooves. [OE *lēad,* prob. <Celtic] —**lead′y** *adj.*
lead acetate *Chem.* A white, soluble, crystalline salt, $Pb(C_2H_3O_2)_2 \cdot 3H_2O$, made by the action of acetic acid on litharge. From the sweet taste of the solution it is named *sugar of lead.*
lead arsenate *Chem.* A white, heavy, poisonous crystalline compound, $Pb_3(AsO_4)_2$: used as a constituent of insecticides.
lead azide *Chem.* A white to brownish crystalline compound, PbN_6: used as a substitute for mercury fulminate in explosives.
Lead·beat·er's possum (led′bē′tərz) An arboreal marsupial *(Gymnobelideus leadbeateri)* of Australia, related to the flying phalangers; thought to be extinct until rediscovered in 1961.
lead carbonate Cerusite.
lead chromate Chrome yellow.
lead dioxide *Chem.* The compound PbO_2 prepared as a dark-brown, amorphous powder: used in the manufacture of storage batteries.
lead·en (led′n) *adj.* **1** Made of lead; also, of the dull-gray color of lead. **2** Heavy; dull or sluggish; also, base in quality. —**lead′en·ly** *adv.* —**lead′en·ness** *n.*
lead·er (lē′dər) *n.* **1** One who leads or conducts; a guide; commander. **2** *Music* A director or conductor of an orchestra; also, the player of the first or principal instrument in an orchestra or band; in an orchestra, usually the head of the first violins. **3** That which leads, or occupies a chief place, as the foremost horse of a team, etc. **4** A tendon or sinew. **5** In journalism, the chief editorial article of a newspaper. **6** An article of merchandise offered at a special price to attract customers. **7** *Printing* A horizontal row of printed dots or hyphens, or a dot or hyphen of such a row, used to guide the eye, as from one side of a page to the other. **8** In fishing, a short line of gut, nylon, etc., attaching the hook or lure to the line. **9** A pipe to carry water from the roof or upper part of a building to the ground. See synonyms under CHIEF, MASTER.
lead·er·ship (lē′dər·ship) *n.* The office or position of a leader; guidance. See synonyms under PRECEDENCE.
lead glass (led) Flint glass. See under GLASS.
lead–in (lēd′in′) *n.* A wire connecting the antenna of a radio with the receiving set: also, *Brit., down-lead.*
lead·ing (lē′ding) *adj.* **1** Having priority or influence; chief. **2** Attention-getting, as, a *leading* display. **3** Furnishing a lead or precedence. See synonyms under FIRST. —*n.* A directing or guiding influence; specifically, spiritual guidance. —**lead′ing·ly** *adv.*
leading article **1** An editorial; also, the first article, as in a magazine. **2** Leader (def. 6).
leading edge *Aeron.* The forward edge of an airfoil or propeller blade.
leading strings **1** Strings to support children learning to walk. **2** Guidance or restraint.
lead line (led) A line for taking soundings.
lead–off (lēd′ôf′, -of′) *n.* **1** A beginning; the first of a succession or series. **2** The opening or attacking movement in any bout of skill or strength, competitive game, etc. **3** The player who leads off.
lead pencil (led) A pencil, usually of graphite mixed with clay for hardness, and incased in wood, paper, or the like.
lead plant (led) A low shrub *(Amorpha canescens)* of the southern and southwestern United States, with lead-gray leaves and twigs.
lead poisoning (led) *Pathol.* Poisoning caused by the slow, continuous absorption of lead by the tissues of the body: marked by nutritional disturbances, anemia, paralysis, and cerebral disorders: also called *plumbism.*
leads·man (ledz′mən) *n. pl.* **·men** (-mən) *Naut.* A sailor who heaves the lead.
lead tetraethyl *Chem.* A colorless, heavy, inflammable, extremely poisonous, liquid hydrocarbon, $Pb(C_2H_5)_4$, prepared by the action of ethyl chloride on a lead sodium alloy: used as an anti-knock agent in internal-combustion engines.
lead time (lēd) **1** *Mil.* **a** The time required to move from the planning and development stage of a new aircraft, ship, weapon, etc., to active production for use. **b** The calculation based on target distance and speed that determines the point of aim of a projectile or missile. **2** The interval between one stage in a sequence of industrial operations or

commercial procedures and a subsequent one.
lead·wort (led'wûrt') *n.* Plumbago.
leaf (lēf) *n. pl.* **leaves** (lēvz) **1** A lateral photosynthetic appendage of the stem of a plant, commonly broad, flat, thin, and of a green color. ◆ Collateral adjective: *foliar*. **2** Foliage collectively; leafage; specifically, the leaves of the tobacco or the tea plant when gathered for curing or sale. **3** A single division of a folded sheet of paper or the like, as in a book, or a single unfolded piece; also, what is written or printed on a leaf. **4** A hinged, folding, sliding, or removable part or section, as of a table, door, gate, screen, or folding fan. **5** A very thin sheet or plate of metal, as gold; also, one of marble, horn, etc. **6** A layer or fold of fat, especially over the kidneys of a hog. **7** One of the thin, flat strips of metal composing a spring of an automobile. **8** A petal: incorrect, but popularly used. — **to turn over a new leaf** To change one's ways or conduct, especially for the better. — *adj.* Of, pertaining to, suggestive of, or occurring in, a leaf or leaves. — *v.i.* To put forth or produce leaves. — *v.t.* To turn or run through the pages of a book: often with *through.* ◆ Homophone: *lief.* [OE *lēaf*]

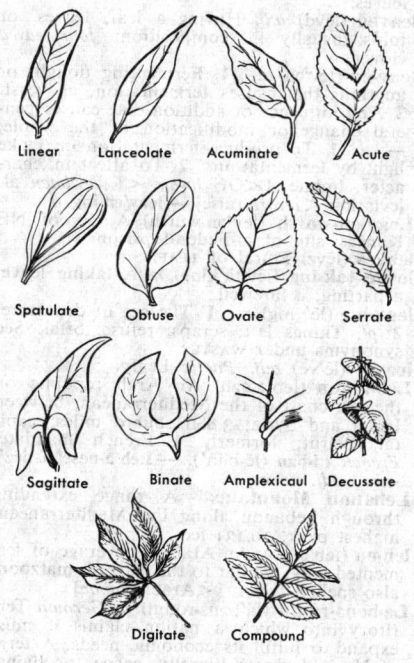

Linear   Lanceolate   Acuminate   Acute

Spatulate   Obtuse   Ovate   Serrate

Sagittate   Binate   Amplexicaul   Decussate

Digitate   Compound

TYPES OF TREE LEAVES

leaf·age (lēf'fij) *n.* Leaves collectively; foliage.
leaf beet Chard (def. 2).
leaf beetle Any of a family (*Chrysomelidae*) of usually small, bright-colored beetles which are found, both in the larval and the adult stages, on leaves.
leaf blight Any of various plant diseases, chiefly of fungous origin, having a conspicuously damaging effect on leaves, especially those affecting pome fruits.
leaf bud A bud that develops into a leafy branch without flowers.
leaf curl A destructive plant disease caused by various fungi of the family *Exoascaceae*, which attack certain forest and fruit trees, as the oak, poplar, and peach, with serious deformation of the leaves: also called *witch broom.* Also **leaf blister.**
leaf fat **1** A layer of fat about the kidneys of swine, from which is obtained leaf lard. **2** Folds of fat over the kidneys of other animals.
leaf·hop·per (lēf'hop'ər) *n.* Any of a family (*Cicadellidae*) of homopterous leaping insects which suck the juices of various plants.

leaf insect Phyllium.
leaf lard Lard made from leaf fat; also, the leaves themselves.
leaf·less (lēf'lis) *adj.* Having or bearing no leaves.
leaf·let (lēf'lit) *n.* **1** A little leaf. **2** *Bot.* One of the separate divisions of a compound leaf. **3** A small printed leaf; a tract; also, a folding circular having several unsewed or unstitched pages in one strip; a folder. **4** A leaflike part. [Dim. of LEAF]
leaf miner The larva of a tineid moth, or of a beetle, fly, or other insect, which feeds on the leaves of plants and trees.
leaf roll **1** A virus disease of the potato, characterized by a pronounced upward curling of the leaves and by a reduction in the size of the tubers. **2** Any of various other plant diseases having a similar effect upon the leaves.
leaf roller The larva of certain small moths, especially of the family *Tortricidae*, that rolls itself up in the leaves of the plant it attacks.
leaf spot A disease of apples, pears, quinces, and other fruits, caused by a sac fungus (*Physalospora malorum*) and resulting in widespread damage: also called *black rot, fruit rot.*
leaf spring *Mech.* A spring made of one or more flat plates or strips: distinguished from a spiral spring.

LEAF SPRING

leaf·stalk (lēf'stôk') *n.* A petiole.
leaf·y (lē'fē) *adj.* **leaf·i·er, leaf·i·est** **1** Having or full of leaves; consisting of or characterized by leaves. **2** Producing broad leaves. **3** Like a leaf or leaves. **4** Existing in thin sheets or layers; laminate.
league[1] (lēg) *n.* **1** A measure of distance, varying from about 2.42 to 4.6 English statute miles. The English **land league** contains approximately 3 statute miles, or 4.82 kilometers; the **marine league** in common use equals 3 geographic miles, or 5.56 kilometers. **2** In Texas, an old Spanish land measure equaling about 4,438 acres; a square league. [< OF *legue* < LL *leuga, leuca* a Gaulish mile < Celtic]
league[2] (lēg) *n.* **1** An alliance of persons or states for mutual support in a common cause. **2** Any close connection or union; as, a commercial *league.* **3** An association of baseball, football, basketball, or other teams which play among themselves. See synonyms under ALLIANCE. — *v.t. & v.i.* **leagued, lea·guing** To join in a league; combine. [< OF *ligue* < Ital. *liga, lega* < *legare* bind < L *ligare*] — **lea·guer** (lē'gər) *n.*
League of Nations An international organization established January 10, 1920, primarily for the preservation of peace under the Covenant of the League in the Treaty of Versailles; formally dissolved April 18, 1946, when its functions, library, and buildings were turned over to the United Nations.
lea·guer (lē'gər) *Archaic n.* **1** A siege. **2** The camp of a besieging force; also, any military camp. — *v.t.* To beleaguer; besiege. [< Du. *leger* a camp]
Le·ah (lē'ə) A feminine personal name. [< Hebrew, weary]
— **Leah** The elder daughter of Laban; one of the wives of Jacob. *Gen.* xxix 16.
Lea·hy (lā'hē), **William Daniel,** 1875-1959, U. S. admiral of the fleet 1944-48.
leak (lēk) *n.* **1** An opening, mechanical or otherwise, that permits the unintended entrance or escape of a fluid, of electric current, etc. **2** Hence, anything which permits the unintentional loss or accrual of something: a *leak* in the espionage system. **3** Leakage. — **to spring a leak** To spring open, part, or crack, so as to let a fluid in or out. — *v.i.* **1** To let a liquid, etc., enter or escape undesignedly, as through a hole or crack. **2** To pass in or out accidentally: often with *in* or *out.* **3** To become known despite efforts at secrecy: usually with *out:* Our plans *leaked* out. — *v.t.* **4** To let (a liquid, etc.) enter or escape undesignedly. **5** To dis-

close (information, etc.) without authorization. ◆ Homophone: *leek.* [< ON *leka* drip. Akin to LEACH, LAKE[1].] — **leak'y** *adj.*
leak·age (lē'kij) *n.* **1** The act of leaking. **2** The quantity that leaks. **3** An allowance for loss by leaking.
leakage current *Electr.* A stray current, generally weak, which escapes through inadequate or defective insulation.
leal (lēl) *adj. Scot.* **1** True-hearted; loyal; faithful. **2** True; actual. — **leal'ly** *adv.* — **leal·ty** (lēl'əl·tē) *n.*
lean[1] (lēn) *v.* **leaned** or **leant, lean·ing** *v.i.* **1** To incline from an erect position: The tower is *leaning.* **2** To incline against or rest on something for support: to *lean* against a tree. **3** To depend or rely: with *on* or *upon:* to *lean* on friendship. **4** To have a mental tendency or inclination: to *lean* toward an opinion. — *v.t.* **5** To cause to incline from an erect position. **6** To place (one thing) against another for support: to *lean* a ladder against a house. — *n.* A leaning; inclination. ◆ Homophone: *lien.* [Fusion of OE *hleonian* lean and OE *hlænen* cause to lean]
Synonyms (verb): bear, confide, depend, recline, rely, repose, rest, trust. See REST[1].
lean[2] (lēn) *adj.* **1** Free from or lacking fat; lank; thin. **2** Lacking in richness, productiveness, or other desirable qualities: *lean* ore, a *lean* harvest. **3** Manifesting thinness, or attended by want. See synonyms under MEAGER. — *n.* Flesh or muscle without fat: *lean* meat. ◆ Homophone: *lien.* [OE *hlæne* thin] — **lean'ly** *adv.* — **lean'ness** *n.*
Le·an·der (lē·an'dər) **1** A masculine personal name. Also *Fr.* **Lé·an·dre** (lā·än'dr'), *Ital., Sp.* **Le·an·dro** (*Ital.* lā·än'drō, *Sp.* -thrō). **2** In Greek legend, the lover of Hero. [< Gk., lion man]
lean·ing (lē'ning) *adj.* Inclining from the vertical: a *leaning* tower. — *n.* An inclination; bias; tendency.
Le·a·nor (lā'ä·nôr') Spanish form of ELEANOR.
leant (lent) Alternative past tense and past participle of LEAN.
lean-to (lēn'tōō') *n. pl.* **-tos** (-tōōz') **1** A building having a single-pitched roof with its apex against an adjoining wall. **2** A rude shelter consisting of branches or planks which slope from a crossbar to the ground. — *adj.* Having rafters, as a roof, which slope in only one direction.
leap (lēp) *v.* **leaped** or **leapt, leap·ing** *v.i.* **1** To jump from the ground with the feet in the air, as from one place or position to another. **2** To move suddenly by or as by jumps or jumping: to *leap* aboard; to *leap* to a conclusion. — *v.t.* **3** To clear by jumping over: to *leap* a barrier. **4** To cause to leap: to *leap* a horse over a hedge. — *n.* **1** The act of leaping; a bound. **2** The space passed over in leaping. [OE *hlēapan*] — **leap'er** *n.*
Synonyms (verb): bounce, bound, caper, dance, frisk, gambol, hop, jump, skip, spring, vault.
leap·frog (lēp'frôg', -frog') *n.* A game in which one player puts his hands on the back of another, who is stooping over, and leaps over him. — *v.* **-frogged, -frog·ging** *v.t.* **1** To jump over as in the game of leapfrog. **2** *Mil.* To bypass (an enemy position), the capture of which is considered strategically unnecessary. — *v.i.* **3** To jump as in the game of leapfrog.
leaping evil Louping ill.
leapt (lept, lēpt) Alternative past tense and past participle of LEAP.
leap year In the Julian and Gregorian calendars, a year of 366 days, an additional day being added to February to allow for the difference in length between the common and the astronomical years. Every year exactly divisible by four, or, in centesimal years, exactly divisible by 400, is a leap year.
lear[1] (lir) *n. Scot.* Learning; lore; also, a lesson.
lear[2] (lir) See LEER[2].
lear[3] (lir) See LEER[3].
Lear (lir) Legendary king of Britain mentioned by Geoffrey of Monmouth, Layamon, Holinshed, etc.; hero of Shakespeare's *King Lear.*

Lear (lir), **Edward,** 1812–88, English humorist.

lea-rig (lē′rig′, lā′-) *n. Scot.* A grassy ridge, particularly on the outskirts of a plowed field.

learn (lûrn) *v.* **learned** or **learnt, learn·ing** *v.t.* **1** To acquire knowledge of or skill in by observation, study, instruction, etc. **2** To find out; gain acquaintance with; ascertain: to *learn* the facts. **3** To fix in the mind; memorize. **4** To become practiced in: to *learn* bad habits. — *v.i.* **5** To gain knowledge; acquire skill. **6** To be informed; hear. [OE *leornian.* Akin to LORE[1].] — **learn′er** *n.*

Synonyms: acquire, commit, get, inform, instruct, know, master, memorize, perceive, teach, train. *Learn* refers to the process of getting knowledge, *know* to the result. What we once thoroughly *learn* we *know.* See ACQUIRE, GAIN, KNOW. Compare KNOWLEDGE. *Antonyms*: forget, lose, miss, pass.

learn·ed (lûr′nid) *adj.* Possessed of learning; erudite. — **learn′ed·ly** *adv.*

learn·ing (lûr′ning) *n.* **1** Knowledge obtained by study or from instruction; scholarship; erudition. **2** The act of acquiring knowledge or skill. **3** *Psychol.* The modification of behavior following upon and induced by interaction with the environment and as a result of experiences leading to the establishment of new patterns of response to external stimuli.

Synonyms: education, erudition, instruction, knowledge, lore, scholarship, study, training, tuition. *Learning* may be acquired by one's unaided industry, but any full *education* must be the result in great part of *instruction, training,* and personal association. *Study* is emphatically what one does for himself, and in which *instruction* and *tuition* can only point the way. *Lore* is used only in poetic style, for accumulated *knowledge,* as of a people or age, or in a general sense for *learning* or *erudition. Information* is *knowledge* of fact, real or supposed, derived from persons, books, or observation; it is regarded as casual and haphazard. *Learning* is much higher, being wide and systematic *knowledge,* the result of long, assiduous *study*; *erudition* is recondite *learning* secured only by extraordinary industry, opportunity, and ability. See EDUCATION, KNOWLEDGE, SCIENCE, WISDOM. *Antonyms*: ignorance, illiteracy. See synonyms for IGNORANT.

lease[1] (lēs) *n.* The system of crossing warp threads during weaving. [Appar. var. of LEASH, in this sense]

lease[2] (lēs) *v.t.* **leased, leas·ing** **1** To grant the temporary possession and profits of, as lands or tenements, usually for a specified rent; let. **2** To take possession of or hold under a lease. — *n.* **1** A contract for the letting of land, etc., for rent; also, such letting. **2** Any tenure by permission, or its duration. [<AF *les,* OF *lais* a letting < *laissier* let, leave <L *laxare* loosen < *laxus* loose] — **leas′a·ble** *adj.*

lease·back (lēs′bak′) *n.* The sale of real property to a buyer who as part of the same transaction leases it to the seller: short for *sale and lease back.*

lease·hold (lēs′hōld′) *adj.* Held by lease. — *n.* A tenure held by a lease. — **lease′hold′er** *n.*

leash (lēsh) *n.* **1** A line or thong, as for holding a dog, etc. **2** A brace and a half; three creatures of like kind, as greyhounds; three in general. — *v.t.* To hold or secure by a leash. [<OF *lesse, laisse* <L *laxa,* fem. of *laxus* loose]

leas·ing (lē′sing) *n. Brit. Dial.* Lying or a lie; falsehood. [OE *lēasung* < *lēasian* tell lies < *lēas* destitute of, false]

least (lēst) *adj.* Smallest in size, value, etc.; minimal. — *n.* That which is least. — *adv.* In the lowest or smallest degree. [OE *lǣst, lǣsest,* superl. of *lǣssa* less]

least action *Physics* That property of a dynamic system having a constant total energy whereby any change in its configuration will take place with a minimum of action among and between its constituent particles.

least common denominator See under DENOMINATOR.

least energy *Physics* The tendency of a dynamic system to remain in stable equilibrium only under those conditions for which the potential energy of the system is at a minimum.

least flycatcher See under FLYCATCHER.

least sandpiper See under SANDPIPER.

least squares *Math.* A method of deducing the most probable value of a quantity from a set of observations or measurements, in accordance with the principle that the sum of the squares of all the errors is at a minimum.

least·wise (lēst′wīz′) *adv. Colloq.* At least. Also **least′ways′** (-wāz′).

leath·er (leth′ər) *n.* **1** The skin or hide of an animal, when tanned or dressed for use. **2** A piece, part, or article consisting or made of leather, as a football. — *v.t.* **1** To cover or furnish with leather. **2** *Colloq.* To beat or flog with or as with a leather strap. [OE *lether*] — **leath′er·y** *adj.* — **leath′er·i·ness** *n.*

leath·er·back (leth′ər·bak′) *n.* The soft-shelled turtle (*Dermochelys coriacea*) living in warm seas, and notable for its flexible, leathery carapace. It sometimes exceeds 1,000 pounds in weight.

leath·er·board (leth′ər·bôrd′, -bōrd′) *n.* An imitation leather sole made from scraps of leather assembled and pressed into sheets: also called *fiber leather.*

leath·er·coat (leth′ər·kōt′) *n.* A russet apple.

leath·er·craft (leth′ər·kraft′, -kräft′) *n.* The handicraft of designing and making things of leather.

Leath·er·ette (leth′ər·et′) *n.* An imitation leather, used chiefly in bookbinding, upholstering, etc.: a trade name.

leath·er·head (leth′ər·hed′) *n.* **1** *Slang* A stupid person; blockhead. **2** The friarbird.

leath·ern (leth′ərn) *adj.* Made of leather. [OE *letheren* < *lether* leather]

leath·er·neck (leth′ər·nek′) *n. Slang* A member of the U. S. Marine Corps.

leath·er·oid (leth′ər·oid) *n.* A material with leatherlike qualities, made by treating vegetable fiber with certain chemicals.

leath·er·stock·ing (leth′ər·stok′ing) *n.* A person who wears leather stockings; hence, a frontiersman. — *adj.* Characteristic of, or about, pioneers and pioneer life: *leatherstocking* customs or stories.

Leath·er·stock·ing (leth′ər·stok′ing) Natty Bumppo, the hero of J. F. Cooper's *Leather-stocking Tales.*

leath·er·wood (leth′ər·wo͝od′) *n.* A low, thymelaeaceous, North American shrub or bush (*Dirca palustris*) with white, soft wood, tough, fibrous bark, and small, yellow flowers: also called *moosewood.*

leath·er·work (leth′ər·wûrk′) *n.* **1** The process of preparing or tooling leather. **2** An ornamental pattern tooled in leather.

leath·er·work·er (leth′ər·wûr′kər) *n.* One who prepares or ornaments leather. — **leath′er·work′ing** *n.*

leave[1] (lēv) *v.* **left, leav·ing** *v.t.* **1** To go or depart from; quit. **2** To allow to remain behind or continue as specified; abandon: to *leave* work undone; to *leave* a plow in a field. **3** To place or deposit so as to allow to remain behind: to *leave* word. **4** To cause to remain after departure, cessation, healing, etc.: The war *left* its mark. **5** To refer or entrust to another for doing, deciding, etc.: I *leave* the matter to you. **6** To sever or terminate connection, employment, etc., with: to *leave* a job. **7** To have as a remainder: Three minus two *leaves* one. **8** To have remaining after death: to *leave* a large family. **9** To give by will; bequeath. **10** To desist from; stop: usually with *off.* — *v.i.* **11** To depart or go away; set out. **12** To desist; cease: with *off*: He *left* off where I began. See synonyms under ABANDON. — **to leave out** To omit from consideration; fail to include. [OE *lǣfan,* lit., let remain] — **leav′er** *n.*

◆ **leave, let** *Leave* and *let,* often confused, are not synonyms. *Leave* means to go away or depart, *let* to permit. Perhaps because the noun *leave* has "permission" as one of its meanings, popular usage endows the verb *leave* with the sense "permit," and tries to make it interchangeable with *let* in such expressions as *Let me go.* But the substitution of *leave* for *let* violates established idiom, for while *let* can be followed by the infinitive without "to," *leave* cannot: *Leave it to him to decide* or *Leave the decision to him,* but never *Leave him decide. Leave me go* is readily recognized as violating both sense and idiom, and is hence considered illiterate. So with *Leave me be.* This last is synonymous with *Leave me alone,* widespread in children's speech as a replacement for the standard English *Let me alone,* which has the idiomatic meaning "Don't bother me" or "Stop bothering me." In this case, and in this case only, *Leave it alone* may be regarded as having acquired fair colloquial standing, with two reservations. It is only in the imperative that *leave* is here admissible as a substitute for *let*; in declined forms, the idiomatic sense does not carry over. *They left him alone* does not mean *They let him alone.* The second reservation follows from this. In formal English, *Leave me alone* means "Go away so that I may be alone." Solitude may insure freedom from annoyance, but asking *to be left alone* is not the same as demanding *to be let alone.*

leave[2] (lēv) *n.* **1** Permission given to do something otherwise forbidden or unlawful. **2** Liberty to go or to be absent. **3** A departure; parting. **4** Permission granted an officer of a military service or to enlisted naval personnel to be absent from duty: also **leave of absence.** See synonyms under PERMISSION. — **to take leave** **1** To depart; go away. **2** To abandon; quit: with *of*: He *took leave* of his senses. [OE *lēaf* permission]

leave[3] (lēv) *v.i.* **leaved, leav·ing** To put forth leaves.

leaved (lēvd) *adj.* Having a leaf, leaves, or folds: usually in composition: *four-leaved* clover.

leav·en (lev′ən) *n.* **1** Fermenting dough, or anything that causes fermentation, as yeast. **2** Any influence or addition that causes general change or modification of the whole. — *v.t.* **1** To produce fermentation in; make light by fermentation. **2** To affect in character; imbue. [<OF *levain* <L *levamen* alleviation < *levare* raise] — **leav′en·ing** *n.*

Leav·en·worth (lev′ən·wûrth) A city of NE Kansas; site of a Federal prison.

leaves (lēvz) Plural of LEAF.

leave-tak·ing (lēv′tā′king) *n.* A taking leave; a parting; a farewell.

leav·ing (lē′ving) *n.* **1** The act of departure. **2** *pl.* Things left; scraps; refuse; offal. See synonyms under WASTE.

leav·y (lē′vē) *adj. Poetic* Leafy.

Leb·a·non (leb′ə·nən) An Arab republic on the east coast of the Mediterranean, between Israel and Syria; 3,880 square miles; capital, Beirut; formerly a French mandate. *French* **Li·ban** (lē·bäṅ′). — **Leb′a·nese′** (-nēz′, -nēs′) *adj.* & *n.*

Lebanon Mountains A range extending through Lebanon along the Mediterranean; highest peak, 10,131 feet.

leb·en (leb′ən) *n.* An Arabian beverage of fermented milk, similar to the Turkish matzoon: also spelled *laban.* [<Arabic *laban*]

Le·bens·raum (lā′bəns·roum) *n. German* Territory into which a nation claims it must expand to fulfill its economic needs. A term of Nazi ideology; literally, space for living. See GEOPOLITICS.

Le Bour·get (lə bo͝or·zhe′) A suburb of NE Paris; site of an important airport.

Le·brun (lə·brœṅ′), **Charles,** 1619–90, French historical painter. Also **Le Brun.**

Lec·ce (let′chā) A city in Apulia, SE Italy.

Lech (lekh) A river in Austria and Germany, flowing 175 miles NE to the Danube.

lech·er (lech′ər) *n.* A habitually lewd or excessively sensual man. [<OF *lecheor* < *lechier* live in debauchery, lick <OHG *leccōn* lick]

lech·er·ous (lech′ər·əs) *adj.* Given to or characterized by lewdness or lust. — **lech′er·ous·ly** *adv.* — **lech′er·ous·ness** *n.*

lech·er·y (lech′ər·ē) *n.* **1** Free indulgence in lust; gross sensuality. **2** Selfish pleasure. [<OF *lecherie, licherie* < *lecheor* LECHER]

lec·i·thin (les′ə·thin) *n. Biochem.* A brownish-yellow, waxy, phosphorized fat contained in the cell tissue of many plants and animals, especially the brain, nerves, egg yolk, and protoplasm: used in medicine as a tonic and nutrient. [<Gk. *lekithos* an egg's yolk + -IN]

lec·i·thin·ase (les′ə·thin·ās′) *n.* Any of several enzymes capable of hydrolyzing lecithin. [< LECITHIN + -ASE]

Leck·y (lek′ē), **William Edward Hartpole,** 1838–1903, English historian.

Le·conte de Lisle (lə·kôṅt′ də lēl′), **Charles Marie René,** 1818–94, French poet.

Le Cor·bu·sier (lə kôr·bü·zyā′) Pseudonym of *Charles Edouard Jeanneret,* 1887–1965, Swiss architect, painter, and writer.

Le Creu·sot (lə krœ·zō′) A town in east central France.

lec·tern (lek′tərn) *n.* **1** A reading desk, in some churches, from which various services are chanted or read. **2** A reading stand, as on a rostrum. [<OF *lettrun* <LL *lectrum* <L *lectus,* pp. of *legere* read]

lec·tion (lek′shən) *n.* **1** A lesson appointed to be read in church service. **2** A variation in the text of an author. [<OF *lectiun* <L *lectio, -onis* < *lectus,* pp. of *legere* read]

lec·tion·ar·y (lek′shən·er′ē) *n. pl.* **·ar·ies** A book or a table of lessons for church service. [<Med. L *lectionarium* <L *lectio* LECTION]

lec·tor (lek′tər) *n.* A reader; specifically, one who reads lessons in a church or lectures in a university. [<L, a reader < *lectus,* pp. of *legere* read]

lec·tu·al (lek′chōō·əl) *adj.* **1** Of or pertaining to a bed or couch. **2** Confining one to his bed: a *lectual* disease. [<LL *lectualis* <L *lectus* a bed, couch]

lec·ture (lek′chər) *n.* **1** A discourse delivered aloud for instruction or entertainment. **2** A formal reproof; reprimand. — *v.* **·tured, ·tur·ing** *v.t.* **1** To deliver lectures to; instruct by lecturing. **2** To rebuke or castigate authoritatively or at length. — *v.i.* **3** To give a lecture. [<L *lectura* an act of reading < *lectus,* pp. of *legere* read] — **lec′tur·er** *n.*

lec·ture·ship (lek′chər·ship) *n.* The office or rank of lecturer.

led (led) Past tense and past participle of LEAD[1].

Le·da (lē′də) In Greek mythology, the wife of Tyndareus and by him mother of Clytemnestra; by Zeus, who appeared to her in the form of a swan, she was the mother of Helen and of Castor and Pollux.

ledge (lej) *n.* **1** A shelf upon which articles can be laid. **2** Something resembling a shelf, as a shelflike ridge of rock, or a shelflike projection from a building. **3** A rocky outcrop or reef. **4** A metal-bearing rock stratum; a lode or vein. [ME *legge,* prob. < root of *leggen* LAY[1]] — **ledg′y** *adj.*

ledg·er[1] (lej′ər) *n.* **1** The principal book of accounts of a business establishment, in which all the transactions of each day are entered under appropriate heads so as to show the debits and credits of each account. **2** A bar, stone, or the like, that is made to lie flat or stay in a fixed position. **3** A horizontal piece fastened to a timber scaffolding to sustain the putlogs. **4** A horizontal stone slab over a grave. **5** Ledger tackle or ledger bait: also spelled *leger.* [ME *legger,* prob. < *leggen* LAY[1]; infl. by MDu. *legger* lay]

ledg·er[2] (lej′ər) *adj.* Remaining or lying in a place: *ledger* bait. Also *leger.* [See LEDGER[1]]

ledger bait A fishing bait lying at the bottom of the water: also spelled *leger bait.*

ledger board The horizontal board forming the top rail of a fence, the handrail of a stairway, etc.

ledger tackle Any form of floating tackle the lower portion of which lies on the bottom: also *leger line, leger tackle.* Also **ledger line.**

lee[1] (lē) *n.* **1** The direction opposite that from which the wind comes; the side sheltered, or that shelters, from wind. **2** A shelter afforded by any object in a wind. — *adj.* Pertaining to the side opposite to that from which the wind comes: a *lee* shore. ◆ Homophone: *lea.* [OE *hlēo* a shelter]

lee[2] (lē) *n. Scot.* A falsehood; lie. ◆ Homophone: *lea.*

Lee (lē) A Virginia family prominent in American history, including **Richard Henry,** 1732–1794, his brother **Francis Lightfoot,** 1734–97, Revolutionary statesmen and signers of the Declaration of Independence; **Henry,** 1756–1818, Revolutionary soldier and statesman: known as *Light-Horse Harry Lee;* his son **Robert Edward,** 1807–70, commander in chief of the Confederate army; **Fitzhugh,** 1835–1905, Confederate general, nephew of Robert Edward Lee.
— **Charles,** 1731–82, American Revolutionary general; court-martialed and dismissed.
— **Sir Sidney,** 1859–1926, English editor and scholar.

Lee (lē), **T(sung) D(ao),** born 1926, U.S. physicist born in China.

lee·an·gle (lē′ang′gəl) *n. Austral.* A heavy war club, with the head bent to a shape much like a miners' pick: also spelled *liangle.*

lee·board (lē′bôrd′, -bōrd′) *n. Naut.* A board lowered on the lee side of a vessel and acting as a keel or centerboard to keep it from drifting to leeward.

leech[1] (lēch) *n.* **1** Any one of a class (*Hirudinea*) of carnivorous, aquatic, bloodsucking annelid worms; especially, the **medicinal leech** (*Hirudo medicinalis*), formerly used for drawing blood, which can ingest three times its weight in blood. **2** Hence, one who appropriates or filches the substance or wealth of others. **3** *Archaic* A physician; doctor. **4** A blood-drawing apparatus: also **artificial leech.** — *v.t.* **1** To bleed with leeches. **2** *Obs.* To treat with medicine; heal. ◆ Homophone: *leach.* [OE *lǣce,* orig. a physician] — **leech′er** *n.*

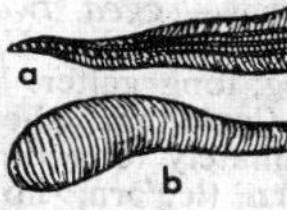

LEECH
a. Common. *b.* Medicinal.
(Vary in size from 1 to 18 inches)

leech[2] (lēch) *n. Naut.* **1** The edge of a square sail. **2** The after edge of a fore-and-aft sail. ◆ Homophone: *leach.* [ME *lich,* ? <Scand. Cf. ON *lik* a boltrope.]

Leeds (lēdz) A city and county borough in central Yorkshire, England.

leek (lēk) *n.* A culinary herb (*Allium porrum*) of the lily family, closely allied to the onion. ◆ Homophone: *leak.* [OE *lēac*]

leer[1] (lir) *n.* A sly look or glance expressing immodest desire, malicious intent, etc. — *v.i.* To look with a leer. [OE *hlēor* a cheek, face; hence "a glance over one's cheek"]

leer[2] (lir) *n.* An oven for annealing glass: also spelled *lear, lehr.* [Origin unknown]

leer[3] (lir) *adj. Brit. Dial.* Empty: also spelled *lear.* [OE *lǣre* (assumed from *lǣrnes* emptiness)]

leer·ing·ly (lir′ing·lē) *adv.* With a leer. [< LEER[1]]

leer·y (lir′ē) *adj. Slang* Shrewd and sly; suspicious; wary. [<LEER[1] + -Y]

lees (lēz) *n. pl.* The settlings of liquor; sediment; dregs. [Pl. of obs. *lee* <OF *lie* < Med. L *lia,* prob. <Celtic]

lee shore The shore on the lee side of a ship, toward which the wind blows the ship. — **on a lee shore** In danger or difficulties.

lee·some (lē′səm) *adj. Scot.* Pleasant; agreeable.

leet (lēt) *n.* In England, a former court of jurisdiction for petty offenses: also called *courtleet.* [<AF *lete;* ult. origin uncertain]

lee tide A tide running with the wind

Leeu·war·den (lā′vär·dən) A city in northern Netherlands, capital of Friesland province.

Leeu·wen·hoek (lā′vən·hōōk), **Anton van,** 1632–1723, Dutch naturalist and microscopist; discovered the red blood corpuscles and the capillary circulation of blood.

lee·ward (lē′wərd, lōō′ərd) *adj. Naut.* Pertaining to the direction in which the wind blows. — *n.* The direction toward which the wind blows: opposed to *windward.* — *adv.* Toward the lee: also **lee′ward·ly.**

Lee·ward Islands (lē′wərd) **1** A northern group of West Indian islands in the Lesser Antilles, extending SE from Puerto Rico to the Windward Islands. **2** A former British colony in this group, divided into the four colonies (former federated presidencies) of (1) Antigua, (2) St. Christopher, Nevis and Anguilla, (3) Montserrat, these three being members of The West Indies, and (4) the British Virgin Islands; 422.5 square miles; former capital, St. John's, on Antigua. **3** See SOCIETY ISLANDS.

lee·way (lē′wā′) *n.* **1** *Naut.* The lateral drift of a vessel to leeward. **2** The falling behind or away from a set course. **3** *Colloq.* Extra margin, space, time, money, etc.

left[1] (left) Past tense and past participle of LEAVE[1].

left[2] (left) *adj.* **1** Pertaining to that side of the body which is toward the north when one faces the rising sun: opposite to *right.* **2** Situated on the left-hand side; sinistral. **3** Designating that side or bank of a river which is on the left facing the direction of flow. — *n.* **1** The left side. **2** Anything on or toward that side of the human body which normally contains the lower portion of the heart. **3** In European countries, the more radical political parties, seated to the left of the presiding officer in a deliberative assembly: also **The Left.** — *adv.* On or to the left. [OE (Kentish), weak, worthless, as in *lyftādl* paralysis]

Left Bank A district of Paris along the left (south) bank of the Seine, famous for its many artist and student inhabitants.

left-hand (left′hand′) *adj.* **1** Situated on the left side; sinistral. **2** Turning, opening, or swinging to the left.

left-hand·ed (left′han′did) *adj.* **1** Having the left hand or arm stronger or more dexterous than the right. **2** Done with the left hand; turning or moving from right to left or oppositely to the motion of the hands of a clock: a *left-handed* screw. **3** Adapted for use by the left hand, as a tool. **4** Clumsy; awkward. **5** Without sincerity; indirect: a *left-handed* compliment. **6** Morganatic: from the giving to the bride of the left hand instead of the right by the bridegroom in a morganatic marriage. — **left′-hand′ed·ly** *adv.* — **left′-hand′·ed·ness** *n.*

left-hand·er (left′han′dər) *n.* **1** One who is left-handed. **2** A left-handed blow.

left·ism (lef′tiz·əm) *n.* The advocacy of radical or ultraliberal policies. — **left′ist** *n.* & *adj.*

left·o·ver (left′ō′vər) *n.* A part not used or consumed. — *adj.* Remaining unconsumed.

left wing **1** A political party or group advocating radical or liberal politics. **2** That part of any group advocating radical liberal policies. Also **Left Wing.** — **left′-wing′** *adj.* — **left′-wing′er** *n.*

left·y (lef′tē) *n. Slang* A left-handed person: especially applied to a baseball pitcher or batter.

leg (leg) *n.* **1** A limb of an animal used for supporting the body and for walking; especially, in man, the part of the lower limb between knee and ankle. ◆ Collateral adjective: *crural.* **2** Something that resembles a leg: the *leg* of a table, etc. **3** Hence, anything that gives support. **4** That portion of a garment or stocking which covers the leg. **5** *Naut.* The distance run by a vessel on one tack. **6** Any appreciable section of a journey. **7** That portion of a cricket field which would be included between an imaginary line drawn at right angles from the batsman's left leg to the boundary and a line drawn from the batsman's middle wicket to the boundary. **8** *Archaic* An obeisance. — **a leg to stand on** A tenable or logical basis for argument. — **to pull one's leg** *Slang* To fool or make fun of someone. — **on one's last legs** On the verge of death or collapse. — **to shake a leg** *Slang* To make haste; hurry. — *v.i.* **legged, leg·ging** *Colloq.* To walk; run: often with *it.* [<ON *leggr*]

leg·a·cy (leg′ə·sē) *n. pl.* **·cies** **1** Something left by will; a bequest. **2** Hence, anything, as a characteristic, derived from an ancestor. [<OF *legacie,* orig. a legateship <Med. L *legatia* the district of a legate <L *legatus.* See LEGATE.]

le·gal (lē′gəl) *adj.* **1** Created or permitted by law. **2** Of, pertaining to, or connected with law: the *legal* mind. **3** In conformity with law; lawful: a *legal* rate of interest. **4** Capable of being remedied by a resort to law, as distinguished from equity. **5** Characteristic of those who practice law: He has a *legal* approach to all situations. **6** *Theol.* **a** Relating to or founded upon the Mosaic law. **b** Pertaining to the doctrine of salvation by works rather than by grace. — *n. pl.* Investments legally open to trustees, fiduciaries, etc. [< OF *legal* <L *legalis* < *lex, legis* law. Doublet of LOYAL.]

legal cap Ruled writing paper, about 8 1/2 x 13 inches, made up in pads gummed at the top for lawyers' use.

add,āce,câre,pälm; end,ēven; it,īce; odd,ōpen,ôrder; tōōk,pōōl; up,bûrn; ə = a in *above,* e in *sicken,* i in *clarity,* o in *melon,* u in *focus;* yōō = u in *fuse;* oi,oil; ou,pout; ch,check; g,go; ng,ring; th,thin; th,this; zh,vision. Foreign sounds à,œ,ü,kh,ṅ; and ◆: see page xx. < from; + plus; ? possibly.

le·ga·lis ho·mo (li·gā'lis hō'mō) *Latin* A lawful or legal person.

le·gal·ism (lē'gəl·iz'əm) *n.* **1** Close adherence to law; strict conformity to law. **2** *Theol.* The doctrine of salvation by works, as distinguished from that by grace. **3** The tendency to observe the letter rather than the spirit of the law. **— le'gal·ist** *n.* **— le'gal·is'tic** *adj.*

le·gal·i·ty (li·gal'ə·tē) *n. pl.* **·ties** **1** The condition of being legal. **2** The distinctive spirit of the legal profession. **3** Adherence or conformity to law.

le·gal·ize (lē'gəl·īz) *v.t.* **·ized, ·iz·ing** To make legal; sanction. Also *Brit.* **le'gal·ise.** **— le'gal·i·za'tion** (-ə·zā'shən, -ī·sā'-) *n.*

Le Gal·lienne (lə gal'yən, gal·yen'), **Richard,** 1866–1947, English poet and journalist. **— Eva,** born 1899, U. S. actress; daughter of the preceding.

legal memory *Law* The period through which things past are accepted in law as definitely affecting present rights or principles.

legal separation *Law* See A MENSA ET THORO.

legal tender Coin or other money that may legally be offered in payment of a debt, and that may not be refused by a creditor.

leg·ate (leg'it) *n.* **1** A person accredited by one state or nation as its diplomatic representative to the court or government of another state or nation; an ambassador; envoy. **2** A representative of the pope in various functions, political or ecclesiastical. **3** In ancient Roman history: **a** An ambassador sent from ancient Rome to a foreign nation, or one sent by a foreign nation to Rome. **b** A person accompanying a Roman general into the field as adviser, or a subordinate in command. **c** A governor of a province **4** A district governed by a legate; specifically, formerly one of the six provinces of the Romagna. See synonyms under DELEGATE. [<OF *legat* <L *legatus,* pp. of *legare* send as a deputy, bequeath] **— leg'ate·ship** *n.* **— leg'a·tine** (-tin, -tīn), **leg·an·tine** (-ən·tin, -tīn) *adj.*

leg·a·tee (leg'ə·tē') *n.* The recipient of a legacy. [< *legate, v.* bequeath <L *legatus,* pp. of *legare* bequeath]

le·ga·tion (li·gā'shən) *n.* **1** The act of deputing or delegating. **2** A diplomatic mission, or the persons composing it. **3** The official residence or place of business of the chief of a diplomatic mission. **4** The office or rank of a legate. [<L *legatio, -onis* < *legare* send]

le·ga·to (li·gä'tō) *adj.* & *adv.* *Music* In a smooth, connected manner: opposed to *staccato.* [<Ital., lit., bound, pp. of *legare* bind <L *ligare*]

le·ga·tor (li·gā'tər, leg'ə·tôr') *n.* One who makes a will; a testator. [<L < *legatus,* pp. of *legare* bequeath]

leg–by (leg'bī') *n.* In cricket, a run made upon a ball which glances off the batsman's body (exclusive of the hand or wrist). Also **leg'–bye'.**

leg·end (lej'ənd) *n.* **1** An unauthenticated story from early times, preserved by tradition and popularly thought to be historical. **2** Such narratives, collectively. **3** A chronicle of the life of a saint, originally to be read aloud in religious services or at meals. **4** Loosely, the fame of a person or place: the Woodrow Wilson *legend.* **5** An inscription or motto on a coin or monument. **6** A caption for an illustration; an explanatory description or key to a map or chart. **7** *Music* A composition intended to describe or relate a story, without words. See synonyms under FICTION.**— local legend** A story, current in a definite region, which explains some local custom, geographical feature, name, etc., as of lovers' leaps, outlaws, haunted places, buried treasure, etc. [<OF *legende* <Med. L *legenda* things read, neut. pl. of L *legendus* to be read, gerundive of *legere* read]

leg·en·dar·y (lej'ən·der'ē) *adj.* **1** Of or pertaining to a legend. **2** Quasi–historical or traditional. **3** Celebrated in or known from legends.

Le·gen·da Au·re·a (li·jen'də ô'rē·ə) The Golden Legend.

Le·gen·dre (lə·zhän'dr'), **Adrien Marie,** 1752–1833, French mathematician.

leg·er (lej'ər) See LEDGER².

Lé·ger (lā·zhā'), **Fernand,** 1881–1955, French painter.

leger bait, etc. See LEDGER BAIT, etc.

leg·er·de·main (lej'ər·də·mān') *n.* **1** Sleight of hand. **2** Any deceptive adroitness; any artful trick. [<F *léger de main,* lit., light of hand < *léger* light (<L *levis*) + *de* of (<L, from) + *main* hand <L *manus*] **— leg'er·de·main'ist** *n.*

leger lines Short lines added above or below a musical staff to increase its range. [< *leger,* var. of LEDGER¹ + *lines,* pl. of LINE]

le·ges (lē'jēz) Plural of LEX.

leg·ged (leg'id, legd) *adj.* Having a specified kind or number of legs: usually in combination: *bow–legged, two–legged,* etc.

leg·ging (leg'ing) *n.* *Usually pl.* A covering for the leg; long gaiter.

leg·gy (leg'ē) *adj.* **·gi·er, ·gi·est** Having disproportionately long or conspicuous legs.

leg·horn¹ (leg'ərn, -hôrn) *n.* **1** A fine plait of leghorn straw, used for making bonnets and hats. **2** A bonnet or hat made of this plait. **—** *adj.* Made of leghorn straw. [from *Leghorn*]

leg·horn² (leg'hôrn, leg'ərn) *n.* A hardy Mediterranean breed of domestic fowls. [from *Leghorn*]

Leg·horn (leg'hôrn) A port on the Ligurian Sea, central Italy: Italian *Livorno.*

leghorn straw The straw of a variety of wheat (*Triticum aestivum*) or of spelt.

leg·i·ble (lej'ə·bəl) *adj.* **1** That can be deciphered or read with ease. **2** That can be discovered or discerned from evident indications. [<LL *legibilis* <L *legere* read] **— leg'i·bil'i·ty, leg'i·ble·ness** *n.* **— leg'i·bly** *adv.*

le·gion (lē'jən) *n.* **1** A division of the ancient Roman army, consisting of ten cohorts of infantry, with an auxiliary force of 300 cavalry: altogether between 4,200 and 6,000 men. **2** One of various other military organizations of other countries. **3** *pl.* Military force. **4** A great number; multitude. **5** *Zool.* A taxonomic category, no longer used. [<OF *legiun* <L *legio -onis* < *legere* choose, levy an army]

le·gion·ar·y (lē'jən·er'ē) *adj.* **1** Pertaining to a legion. **2** Innumerable. **—** *n. pl.* **·ar·ies** A soldier of a legion.

legionary ant See DRIVER ANT.

le·gion·naire (lē'jən·âr') *n.* **1** A legionary. **2** A member of the American Legion. Also *Fr.* **lé·gion·naire** (lā·zhə·nâr'). [<F *légionnaire* < *légion* (<OF *legiun* LEGION) + *-aire* -ARY]

Legion of Honor An order of merit instituted by Napoleon in 1802 as a reward for civil and military services.

Legion of Merit A decoration established in 1942 and awarded to personnel of the armed forces of the United States and its allies who have distinguished themselves by exceptionally meritorious conduct and fidelity.

leg·is·late (lej'is·lāt) *v.* **·lat·ed, ·lat·ing** *v.i.* To make a law or laws. **—** *v.t.* To bring about or effect by legislation. [Back formation < LEGISLATOR]

leg·is·la·tion (lej'is·lā'shən) *n.* **1** Enactment of laws, or business incidental thereto. **2** The laws enacted by a legislative power. [<LL *legislatio, -onis* < *legis,* genitive of *lex* a law + *latio, -onis* a bringing, proposing < *latus,* pp. to *ferre* bring]

Synonyms: code, economy, jurisprudence, law, polity. A *code* is a system of *laws*; *jurisprudence* is the science of *law,* or a system of *laws* scientifically considered, classed, and interpreted; *legislation,* primarily the act of legislating, denotes also the body of statutes enacted by a legislative body; an *economy* is a body of *laws* and regulations, with the entire system, political or religious, especially the latter, of which they form a part; as, the *code* of Draco, Roman *jurisprudence,* British *legislation,* the Mosaic *economy.* The Mosaic *economy* is known also as the Mosaic *law,* and we speak of the English common *law,* or the *law* of nations. *Polity* differs from *economy* as applying to the system itself, while *economy* applies to the method of administration or to the system as administered. See LAW¹.

leg·is·la·tive (lej'is·lā'tiv) *adj.* **1** Having the power to legislate; that makes or enacts laws: distinguished from *administrative* and *judicial.* **2** Of, pertaining to, or suitable to legislation. **3** Of or pertaining to a legislature. **—** *n.* The law–making power in government. **— leg'is·la'tive·ly** *adv.*

leg·is·la·tor (lej'is·lā'tər) *n.* **1** One who legislates; a lawgiver. **2** A member of a legislature. [L, proposer of a law < *lex, legis* a law + *lator* < *latus,* pp. to *ferre* bring] **— leg·is·la·to·ri·al** (lej'is·lə·tôr'ē·əl, -tō'rē-) *adj.* **— leg'is·la'tress** (-tris), **leg'is·la'trix** (-triks) *n. fem.*

leg·is·la·ture (lej'is·lā'chər) *n.* A body of men empowered to make laws for a country or state; the legislative body of a state or territory. See CONGRESS.

le·git·i·mate (lə·jit'ə·mit) *adj.* **1** Having the sanction of law or custom; authorized; lawful; also, genuine. **2** Born in wedlock. **3** Based strictly on hereditary rights or sovereignty. **4** Following in regular or natural sequence; logically deduced. See synonyms under AUTHENTIC. **—** *v.t.* (lə·jit'ə·māt) **·mat·ed, ·mat·ing** **1** To make legitimate. **2** To justify. [<Med. L *legitimatus,* pp. of *legitimare* declare to be lawful <L *legitimus* lawful < *lex, legis* a law] **— le·git'i·ma·cy, le·git'i·mate·ness** *n.* **— le·git'·i·mate·ly** *adv.* **— le·git'i·ma'tion** *n.*

legitimate drama **1** Any drama spoken and acted on the stage: opposed to motion pictures, television, etc. **2** Formerly, drama conforming to certain literary and dramatic principles; not burlesque or melodrama.

le·git·i·mist (lə·jit'ə·mist) *n.* One who supports legitimate authority or supports a certain authority as legitimate; specifically, in France, a supporter of the claims of the elder branch of the Bourbon family. Also **le·git'i·ma·tist.** [<F *légitimiste* < *légitime* legitimate <L *legitimus.* See LEGITIMATE.] **— le·git'i·mism** *n.*

le·git·i·mize (lə·jit'ə·mīz) *v.t.* **·mized, ·miz·ing** **1** To make legitimate. **2** To make acceptable or tolerable: to assert that some TV programs *legitimize* violence. Also **le·git'i·ma·tize. — le·git'i·mi·za'tion** *n.*

leg·len (leg'lən) *n.* *Scot.* A milk pail.

leg·less (leg'lis) *adj.* Having no legs.

leg·man (leg'man') *n. pl.* **·men** (-men') **1** A reporter who collects data for a news story outside the editorial offices, as from interviews, obtaining official statements and documents, etc. **2** An office assistant or subordinate employed to do various errands.

leg–of–mut·ton (leg'ə·mut'n) *adj.* Shaped like a leg of mutton, as a sail or sleeve.

Le·gree (lə·grē'), **Simon** See SIMON LEGREE.

leg·ume (leg'yōōm, lə·gyōōm') *n.* **1** The fruit or seed of any leguminous plant, as peas and beans. **2** A one–celled, two–valved seed vessel formed of a single dehiscent carpel having the seeds arranged along the inner or ventral suture. [<F *légume* <L *legumen,* lit., a gatherable thing < *legere* gather]

le·gu·min (lə·gyōō'min) *n.* *Biochem.* A globulin present in peas and other leguminous seeds. [<LEGUM(E) + -IN]

le·gu·mi·nous (lə·gyōō'mə·nəs) *adj.* **1** Of or pertaining to legumes, or to a large, widely distributed family (*Leguminosae*) of plants, the pea or bean family, bearing legumes. **2** Producing legumes. Also **le·gu'mi·nose** (-nōs). [<L *legumen, -inis* a legume + -OUS]

leg·work (leg'wûrk') *n.* *Colloq.* The physical activity incidental to doing research.

Leh (lā) The capital of Ladakh, Kashmir.

Le Ha·vre (lə ä'vr') See HAVRE, LE.

Le·hár (lā'här), **Franz,** 1870–1948, Austrian composer of operettas.

Le·high River (lē'hī) A river in eastern Pennsylvania, flowing 100 miles south and east to the Delaware River.

Leh·man (lē'mən, lā'-), **Herbert Henry,** 1878–1963, U. S. banker and statesman.

Leh·man Caves National Monument (lē'·mən) An area of subterranean chambers and tunnels in the Snake Mountains, eastern Nevada; 640 acres; established as a national monument in 1922.

Leh·mann (lā'mən, *Ger.* lā'män), **Lotte,** born 1888, German soprano. **— Rosamond,** born 1904?, English novelist.

Lehm·bruck (lām'brōōk), **Wilhelm,** 1881–1919, German sculptor.

lehr (lâr) See LEER².

le·hu·a (lā·hōō'ä) *n.* **1** A tree (*Metrosideros tremuloides*) of the myrtle family, native in the Pacific Islands, having vivid red flowers and a hard wood. **2** The blossom of this tree. **3** Its wood. [<Hawaiian]

lei¹ (lā, lā'ē) *n.* In the Hawaiian Islands, a garland or wreath of showy flowers and leaves, as hibiscus blossoms, or of feathers: usually worn around the neck or as an ornamental headdress. [<Hawaiian]

lei² (lā) Plural of LEU.

Leib·nitz (līp'nits), **Baron Gottfried Wilhelm von,** 1646–1716, German philosopher and

mathematician. Also **Leib′niz.** — **Leib·nitz′·i·an** *adj.* & *n.*

Leices·ter (les′tər) *n.* A variety of long-wooled sheep originally developed in Leicester.

Leices·ter (les′tər) A county in central England; 832 square miles; county town, Leicester. Also **Leices′ter·shire** (-shir).

Leices·ter (les′tər), **Earl of,** 1533–88, Robert Dudley, politician and general; favorite of Queen Elizabeth I.

Lei·den (līd′n) See LEYDEN.

Leif Ericson See ERICSON.

Leigh·ton (lā′tən), **Lord Frederick,** 1830–96, English painter.

Lein·ster (len′stər) A province of SE Ireland on the Irish Sea; 7,580 square miles.

lei·ot·ri·chous (li·ot′rə·kəs) *adj.* Lissotrichous. [<NL *Leiotrichi* the smooth-haired (division of mankind) <Gk. *leios* smooth + *thrix, trichos* hair]

Leip·zig (līp′sik, -sig; *Ger.* līp′tsikh) A city in the former state of Saxony, southern East Germany.

leish·man·i·a·sis (līsh′mən·ī′ə·sis) *n. Pathol.* Any disease caused by parasitic protozoans of the genus *Leishmania*, especially the tropical disease kala-azar. Also **leish′man·i′o·sis.** [after Sir William B. *Leishman*, 1865–1926, English army surgeon]

leis·ter (lēs′tər) *n.* A three-pronged fishing spear. — *v.t.* To spear with a leister. [<ON *liōstr* < *liōsta* strike] — **leis′ter·er** *n.*

lei·sure (lē′zhər, lezh′ər) *n.* **1** Freedom from the demands of work or duty. **2** Spare time; time available for some particular purpose. — *adj.* **1** Free or unoccupied. **2** Having leisure: the *leisure* class. [<OF *leisir* be permitted <L *licere*]

lei·sure·ly (lē′zhər·lē, lezh′ər-) *adj.* Done at leisure; deliberate; slow. — *adv.* At leisure, deliberately. — **lei′sure·li·ness** *n.*

Leith (lēth) A port on the Firth of Forth in SE Scotland; incorporated since 1920 in the city of Edinburgh.

Leith·a (lī′tä) A river in eastern Austria and NW Hungary, flowing 112 miles north and east to the Danube.

leit·mo·tif (līt′mō·tēf′) *n. Music* A representative theme used to indicate a certain person, attribute, or idea, in an opera or other composition. Also **leit′mo·tiv** (-tēf′). [<G *leitmotiv* < *leiten* lead + *motiv* <Med. L *motivus*. See MOTIVE.]

Lei·trim (lē′trim) A county of NE Connacht province, Ireland; 589 square miles; county town Carrick-on-Shannon.

Leix (lāks) See LAOIGHIS.

Lek (lek) The northern branch of the Rhine delta in central Netherlands.

Le·ly (lē′lē), **Sir Peter,** 1618–80, Dutch painter born in Germany and active in England.

Le·mai·tre (lə·me′tr′), **François Élie Jules,** 1853–1914, French critic. — **Abbé Georges Edouard,** born 1894, Belgian physicist and astronomer.

lem·an (lem′ən, lē′mən) *n. Archaic* A sweetheart of either sex; especially, a mistress. Also **lem′man.** [ME *lemman, leofmon* <OE *leof* beloved + *mann* a man]

Le·man (lē′mən), **Lake** The Lake of Geneva. French *Lac Le·man* (låk lā·män′).

Le Mans (lə mäŋ′) A city in NW France.

Le Mans start In automobile racing, a method of starting contestants by lining the cars diagonally on one side of the track, the drivers standing on the other; at a signal the drivers run to their cars, start them, and proceed onto the track. [from *Le Mans*; because traditionally used at an annual automobile race held there]

Lem·berg (lem′berkh) The German name for Lvov.

lem·ma [1] (lem′ə) *n. pl.* **lem·mas** or **lem·ma·ta** (lem′ə·tə) **1** A subject or theme assumed for treatment, as in verse. **2** *Logic* **a** A subsidiary proposition employed as auxiliary in demonstrating another one. **b** A proposition assumed to be true. [<L <Gk. *lēmma* something taken, a premise < *lēmm-*, stem of *lambanein* take]

lem·ma [2] (lem′ə) *n. Bot.* A small, chaffy bract inside and above the glumes in a spikelet of grass. [<Gk. *lemma* a husk < *lepein* peel]

lem·ming (lem′ing) *n.* Any of several small arctic rodents (genera *Lemmus, Dicrostonyx,* and *Myopus*) with a short tail and furry feet. One European species is noted for recurrent migrations in vast numbers, often terminated by drowning in the ocean. [<Norw.]

LEMMING
(About 4 inches long)

Lem·ni·an (lem′nē·ən) *adj.* Of or pertaining to Lemnos. — *n.* A native or inhabitant of Lemnos.

Lemnian bole A white or grayish-yellow variety of aluminous earth. Also **Lemnian earth.**

Lemnian smith Hephaestus, whose forge was said to be in the volcanic regions of Lemnos.

Lem·nos (lem′nəs) A Greek island in the NE Aegean Sea; 184 square miles: also *Limnos.*

lem·nis·cate (lem′nis·kāt, -kit) *n. Math.* The plane curve in the shape of a figure eight traced by the foot of a perpendicular drawn from the origin to a tangent to a rectangular hyperbola: the locus of the vertex of a triangle when the product of the two adjacent sides is maintained equal to 1/4 of the fixed, opposite side. Also called **Bernoulli's lemniscate.** [<NL *lemniscata,* orig. fem. of L *lemniscatus* adorned with ribbons < *lemniscus.* See LEMNISCUS.]

[Diagram of lemniscate in polar coordinates, with angles 90°, 180°, 0°, 270° marked]

LEMNISCATE
A symmetrical tracing in polar coordinates.

lem·nis·cus (lem·nis′kəs) *n. pl.* **·nis·ci** (-nis′ī) **1** *Anat.* A bundle or fillet of nerve fibers in the medulla and pons. **2** *Zool.* One of a pair of club-shaped organs at the base of the proboscis of certain parasitic worms (class *Acanthocephala*). [<NL <L, a ribbon <Gk. *lēmniskos*]

lem·on (lem′ən) *n.* **1** An oval citrus fruit with a bright-yellow skin containing the essential **oil of lemon,** and very acid pulp and juice. **2** The small or medium-sized evergreen tree (*Citrus medica* and *C. lemon*) of the rue family that produces this fruit. **3** The color of the rind of lemon; bright yellow. **4** *U.S. Slang* Something disappointing, worthless, or unpleasant. — *adj.* **1** Flavored with or containing lemon: *lemon* pie. **2** Lemon-colored. [<OF *limon* <Sp. *limón* <Arabic *laimūn* <Persian *līmūn.* Related to LIME².]

lem·on·ade (lem′ən·ād′) *n.* A drink made of lemon juice, water, and sugar. [<F *limonade* < *limon* LEMON]

lemon geranium A common garden flower (*Pelargonium limoneum*) related to the geranium, having the odor of lemons.

lemon grass An Old World tropical grass (*Cymbopogon citratus*) whose leaves yield an oil used as a flavoring and in perfumery.

lemon squash *Brit.* Lemonade.

lemon verbena A tropical American shrub (*Lippia citriodora*) with white flowers and lanceolate leaves having an odor of lemon.

lem·on·wood (lem′ən·wŏŏd′) *n.* **1** The yellowish-white, tough, flexible wood of a Central American tree (*Calycophyllum candidissimum*), used for fishing rods, bow staves, etc. **2** The tree itself. Also called *degame.*

lemon yellow **1** A pigment consisting of a mixture of barium and chromic acid ground in water or oil. **2** Lead chromate.

lem·pi·ra (lem·pē′rä) *n.* The gold monetary unit of Honduras. [<Am. Sp., after *Lempira,* an Indian chief who fought the Spanish]

Lem·u·el (lem′yŏŏ·əl) A masculine personal name. [<Hebrew, belonging to God]

le·mur (lē′mər) *n.* A small, arboreal, mostly nocturnal mammal with fox-like face and soft fur, found chiefly in Madagascar, related to the monkeys, and belonging to a class or suborder (*Lemuroidea*) which, with the *Tarsioidea,* is believed to represent the ancestral primate form. [<NL <L *lemures* ghosts; with ref. to their nocturnal habits]

RING-TAILED LEMUR
(About 2 feet long; tail: 2 feet)

lem·u·res (lem′yŏŏ·rēz) *n. pl.* In Roman religion, the shades or spirits of the dead; ghosts; specters. On the ninth of May a festival, the **Le·mu·ri·a** (lə·myŏŏr′ē·ə), was held to appease these departed spirits. [<L]

Le·mu·ri·a (lə·myŏŏr′ē·ə) A hypothetical continent, supposedly submerged beneath the Indian Ocean, thought by E. Haeckel to be the original home of lemuroid primates.

lem·u·roid (lem′yŏŏ·roid) *adj.* Of or pertaining to the lemurs. — *n.* A lemur. Also **lem′u·rine** (-rīn, -rin).

Le·na (lē′nə) Diminutive of HELEN and of MAGDALENE.

Le·na (lē′nə, *Russian* lyä′nə) The easternmost and longest river of Siberian Russian S.F.S.R., flowing 2,648 miles north to the Laptev Sea.

Len·a·pe (len′ə·pē) *n.* The generic name of the Algonquian tribes in Pennsylvania, New Jersey, and vicinity; the Delawares: also called *Leni-Lenape, Lenni-Lenape.* [Short for Algonquian (Lenape) *Leni-lenape,* lit., a real man < *leni* real + *lenape* a man]

Le·nard rays (lā′närt) *Physics* Cathode rays that stream into the atmosphere through a metallic window of a vacuum tube known as a **Lenard tube** or a Coolidge cathode-ray tube. [after Philipp von *Lenard,* 1862–1947, German physicist]

Le·nau (lā′nou), **Nikolaus,** 1802–1850, pseudonym of *Nikolaus Niembsch von Strehlenau,* Austrian lyric poet.

Len·clos (län·klō′), **Ninon de,** 1620–1705, French beauty and wit: real name *Anne L'Enclos.*

lend (lend) *v.* **lent, lend·ing** *v.t.* **1** To grant the temporary use of without further compensation than the understanding that the thing or its equivalent will be returned. **2** To grant the temporary use of, as money, for a compensation. **3** To impart; furnish: The thought *lends* beauty to the poem. **4** To accommodate (oneself or itself): The statement *lends* itself to interpretation. — *v.i.* **5** To make a loan or loans. — **to lend a hand** To give assistance. — **to lend an ear** To hearken. [OE *lǣnan* < *lǣn* a loan. Akin to LOAN.] — **lend′er** *n.*

lend–lease (lend′lēs′) *n.* In World War II, the furnishing of goods and services to any country whose defense was deemed vital to the defense of the United States, under the terms of the **Lend–Lease Act** passed by Congress March 11, 1941.

le·net·ic (lə·net′ik) *adj. Ecol.* Of, pertaining to, or designating plant or animal communities inhabiting still waters. Also **le·nit′ic** (-nit′-). [<L *lenis* smooth]

L'En·fant (län·fän′), **Pierre Charles,** 1754–1825, French architect; planned the city of Washington, D.C.

length (lengkth) *n.* **1** Extension from end to end; hence, usually, the greatest dimension of a surface or body, as distinguished from *breadth* or *width.* **2** Distance measured along a line from end to end. **3** The state of being long. **4** Extent in point of time. **5** A specific or understood distance; a thing of known extent: a boat's *length.* **6** Power of extension; reach; extent; the distance reached or that may be reached. **7** In classical prosody, quantity. **8** *Phonet.* **a** The period required for the pronunciation of a vowel. **b** The quality of a vowel. — **at length** **1** After an interval of

expectation; finally; at last. **2** At full length; without omission or contraction. [OE *lengthu* < *lang* long]

length·en (lengk′thən) *v.t.* & *v.i.* To make or become longer. See synonyms under PROTRACT, STRETCH.

length·wise (lengkth′wīz′) *adv.* In a longitudinal direction. Also **length′ways′** (-wāz′).

length·y (lengk′thē) *adj.* **length·i·er, length·i·est** Having length; unduly long. **— length′i·ly** *adv.* **— length′i·ness** *n.*

le·ni·ent (lē′nē·ənt, lēn′yənt) *adj.* **1** Of merciful disposition; gentle; mild; indulgent. **2** *Archaic* Soothing; emollient. See synonyms under CHARITABLE. [<L *leniens, -entis,* ppr. of *lenire* soothe < *lenis* soft, mild] **— le′ni·en·cy, le′ni·ence** *n.* **— le′ni·ent·ly** *adv.*

Len·i–Len·a·pe (len′ē·len′ə·pē), **Len·ni–Len·a·pe** See LENAPE.

Le·nin (len′in, *Russian* lye′nyin), **Nikolai,** 1870–1924, Russian revolutionary; leader of Bolshevik party; chief leader of the Russian Revolution and head of the Soviet government 1917–24: real name *Vladimir Ilyich Ulianov.*

Le·ni·na·kan The former name of Gyumri, a city in NW Armenia; pop. 163,00; formerly **Aleksandropol.**

Le·nin·grad The former name of Saint Petersburg, a city in NW Russia on the Gulf of Finland; capital of the Russian Empire, 1712–1917; the name has been changed through history: **Saint Petersburg** (1703–1914; 1993–), **Petrograd** (1914–1924), **Leningrad** (1924–1993).

Lenin Peak A mountain on the Kirghiz–Tadzhik border, the second highest in the Soviet Union; 23,382 feet.

le·nis (lē′nis) *adj. Phonet.* Weakly articulated, with little or no aspiration: said especially of stop consonants, and opposed to *fortis.* — *n. pl.* **le·nes** (lē′nēz) **1** A lenis consonant. **2** In Greek grammar, the smooth breathing *(spiritus lenis).* Also **le·ne** (lē′nē). [<L, smooth, soft]

len·i·tive (len′ə·tiv) *adj.* Having the power or tendency to allay pain or mitigate suffering. — *n.* That which soothes or mitigates; an aperient medicine; a laxative. [<Med. L *lenitivus* <L *lenitus,* pp. of *lenire* soothe]

len·i·ty (len′ə·tē) *n.* The state or quality of being lenient. [<OF *lenité* <L *lenitas, -tatis* softness < *lenis* soft]

le·no (lē′nō) *n.* **1** A type of weave with paired and twisted warp yarns. **2** A loose, open fabric of such a weave. [<F *linon* < *lin* flax]

Le·no·ra (lə·nôr′ə, -nō′rə) See ELEANOR. Also *Ger.* **Le·no·re** (lā·nō′rə), *Fr.* **Le·noir** (lə·nwär′).

Le·nor·mant (lə·nôr·män′), **François,** 1837–1883, French scholar and archeologist.

lens (lenz) *n.* **1** A piece of glass or other transparent substance, bounded by two surfaces, of different curvature, generally spherical, or by one spherical or curved, and one plane surface, by which rays of light may be made to converge or to diverge. ◆ Collateral adjective: *lenticular.* **2** Any device for concentrating or dispersing radiation by refraction. **3** A biconvex transparent body situated behind the iris of the eye. See illustration under EYE. **— crown lens** The convex portion in an achromatic lens. [<L *lens, lentis* a lentil; so called from the similarity in form]

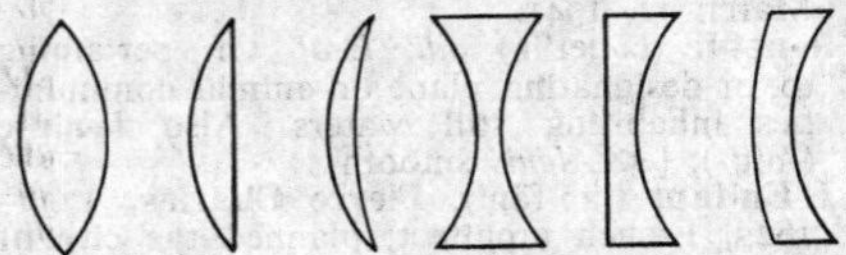

LENS

a. Convexo–convex. *d.* Concavo–concave.
b. Plano–convex. *e.* Plano–concave.
c. Convexo–concave. *f.* Concavo–convex.

lent (lent) Past tense and past participle of LEND.

Lent (lent) *n.* **1** *Eccl.* A fast of forty days (excluding Sundays), observed annually from Ash Wednesday till Easter as a season of penitence and self–denial. **2** *Obs.* In the Middle Ages, a period of fasting at any time of the year: St. Martin's *Lent,* observed from Martinmas (November 11) till Christmas. [Short for *Lenten,* OE *lencten, lengten* the spring] **— Lent′en** *adj.*

len·ta·men·te (len′tä·men′tā) *adv. Music* Slowly. [<Ital. < *lento* LENTO]

len·tan·do (len·tän′dō) *adj.* & *adv. Music* Becoming slower by degrees; rallentando. [<Ital., ppr. of *lentare* become slow < *lento* LENTO]

lent·en (len′tən) *adj.* **1** Plain; spare; meager. **2** Cold or chary. [OE *lencten* spring, Lent; with ref. to the traditional meagerness of Lenten fare]

len·ti·cel (len′tə·sel) *n. Bot.* A loose, lens–shaped mass of cells belonging to the corky layer of plants, constituting a break in the continuity of the epidermis and permitting an interchange between gases within the plant and the external air. [<F *lenticelle* <NL *lenticella,* dim. of L *lens, lentis* a lentil]

len·tic·u·lar (len·tik′yə·lər) *adj.* **1** Resembling a double–convex lens; lens–shaped. **2** Of or pertaining to a lens. **3** *Meteorol.* Designating an ovoid–shaped cloud with usually clean edges, found at all levels and characterized by a tendency to remain stationary for long intervals, despite constant evaporation. [<LL *lenticularis* < *lenticula,* dim. of L *lens, lentis* a lentil. See LENS.]

len·ti·form (len′tə·fôrm) *adj.* Lens–shaped. [<L *lens, lentis* a lentil + -FORM. See LENS.]

len·tig·i·nose (len·tij′ə·nōs) *adj.* Pertaining to lentigo; freckled; dusty. Also **len·tig′i·nous** (-nəs). [<LL *lentiginosus* <L *lentigo, -ginis* a freckle < *lens, lentis* a lentil]

len·ti·go (len·tī′gō) *n. pl.* **·tig·i·nes** (-tij′ə·nēz) **1** A freckle. **2** *Med.* A freckly condition of the skin. [<L < *lens, lentis* a lentil]

len·til (len′təl) *n.* **1** An Old World leguminous plant *(Lens culinaris)* with pale–blue flowers and broad pods containing edible seeds. **2** The seed itself. [<F *lentille* <L *lenticula,* dim. of *lens, lentis* a lentil]

len·tis·si·mo (len·tis′i·mō) *adj.* & *adv. Music* Very slow; very slowly. [<Ital., superl. of *lento* LENTO]

len·to (len′tō) *adj.* & *adv. Music* Slow; slowly. [<Ital. <L *lentus*]

len·toid (len′toid) *adj.* Lens–shaped; lenticular. [<L *lens, lentis* a lentil + -OID. See LENS.]

len·tor (len′tôr) *n.* Extreme slowness of movement or function; sluggishness: heart *lentor.* [<F *lenteur* <L *lentor* < *lentus* slow]

l'en·voi (len′voi, *Fr.* län·vwà′) See ENVOY. Also **l'en′voy.**

Le·o (lē′ō) A masculine personal name; the appellation of thirteen popes, and six Byzantine emperors. [<L, a lion]

— Leo I, 390?–461, pope 440–461; defended Rome against Attila: called "Leo the Great."

— Leo III, 675?–741; emperor of Byzantium 717–741: called "The Isaurian."

— Leo III, 750?–816, pope 795–816; crowned Charlemagne as emperor; canonized.

— Leo X, 1475–1521, pope 1513–21: real name Giovanni de' Medici.

— Leo XIII, 1810–1903, pope 1878–1903: real name Gioacchino Pecci.

Le·o (lē′ō) **1** The fifth sign of the zodiac, which the sun enters about July 21. **2** A constellation containing the Sickle and the bright star Regulus. See CONSTELLATION. [<NL <L, a lion]

Le·on (lē′on) A masculine personal name. [<L, a lion]

Le·ón (lā·ôn′) **1** A region and former kingdom in NW Spain, part of an ancient kingdom; 20,504 square miles. **2** A province of NW Spain; 5,432 square miles; capital, León. **3** A city in Guanajuato state, central Mexico: officially **León de los Al·da·mas** (thā lōs äl·thä′mäs). **4** The second largest city and former capital of Nicaragua.

Leon·ard (len′ərd, *Du.* lā′ō·närt) A masculine personal name. Also *Fr.* **Lé·o·nard** (lā·ō·nàr′), *Ital., Sp.* **Le·o·nar·do** (lā′ō·när′dō, *Sp.* -thō), *Ger.* **Le·on·hard** (lā′ōn·härt), *Lat.* **Le·o·nar·dus** (lē′ə·när′dəs). [<Gmc., strong as a lion]

Le·o·nar·desque (lē′ə·när·desk′) *adj.* Resembling or pertaining to the style of Leonardo da Vinci.

Le·o·nar·do da Vin·ci (lā′ō·när′dō dä vēn′·chē), 1452–1519, Italian painter, sculptor, architect, engineer, musician, scientist, and natural philosopher.

Le·on·ca·val·lo (lā·ôn′kä·väl′lō), **Ruggiero,** 1858–1919, Italian composer.

Le·o·nid (lē′ə·nid) *n.* One of the meteors that form a shower about November 14 in a modified form every year, but especially brilliant at intervals of approximately 33 years: their radiant point is in the constellation Leo. [<F <NL *Leo, Leonis* the constellation LEO + *-id* -ID[1]]

Le·on·i·das (lē·on′ə·dəs) A masculine personal name. [<Gk., lionlike]

— Leonidas I, died 480 B.C., king of Sparta, killed at Thermopylae.

le·o·nine (lē′ə·nīn, -nin) *adj.* Pertaining to or like a lion; fierce; powerful; majestic. [<OF *leonin* <L *leoninus* < *leo, leonis* a lion]

Le·o·nine (lē′ə·nīn, -nin) *adj.* **1** Belonging or relating to any of the thirteen popes named Leo. **2** Designating a medieval Latin verse, or an English verse resembling it, in which the final syllable of a line rimes with the one in the middle: so called after Leo of St. Victor, a medieval monk who used such rimes in his verse. [<L *leoninus*]

Le·o·no·ra (lē′ə·nôr′ə, -nō′rə; *Ital.* lā′ō·nō′rä) See ELEANOR. Also **Le·o·nore** (lē′ə·nôr, -nōr; *Ger.* lā′ō·nō′rə).

le·on·ti·a·sis (lē′on·tī′ə·sis) *n. Pathol.* A morbid thickening of the facial bones, giving a leonine appearance: seen in leprosy, elephantiasis, and certain other diseases. [<NL <Gk. < *leōn, leontos* a lion + -IASIS]

leop·ard (lep′ərd) *n.* **1** A ferocious, carnivorous mammal of the cat family *(Felis* or *Panthera pardus)* of Asia and Africa, of a pale fawn color, spotted with dark brown or black. A black variety, but having detectable spots, is often called a *panther.* **2** Any similar cat, such as the **American leopard** or jaguar, the **hunting leopard** or cheetah, the **snow leopard** or ounce. **3** *Her.* A lion passant gardant. **4** *Brit.* A gold coin of the reign of Edward III; a half–florin. [<OF <LL *leopardus* <Gk. *leopardos* < *leōn* a lion + *pardos* a panther] **— leop′ard·ess** *n. fem.*

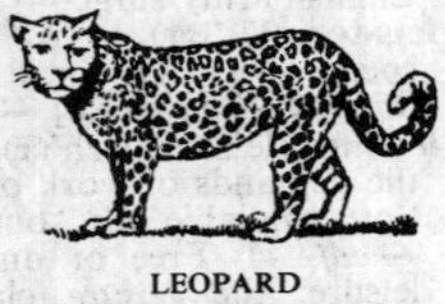

LEOPARD
(About 2 1/2 feet high at the shoulder; length: 7 feet over–all)

leopard cat The American ocelot *(Felis pardalis).*

Le·o·par·di (lā′ō·pär′dē), **Count Giacomo,** 1798–1837, Italian poet.

leopard moth A European moth *(Zeuzera pyrina)* introduced into the United States; its larvae are destructive borers in trees and shrubs.

Le·o·pold (lē′ə·pōld, *Ger.* lā′ō·pōlt) A masculine personal name. Also *Fr.* **Lé·o·pold** (lā·ō·pôld′), *Ital., Sp.* **Le·o·pol·do** (*Ital.* lā′ō·pōl′dō, *Sp.* -thō), *Lat.* **Le·o·pol·dus** (lē′ə·pōl′dəs). [<Gmc., bold for the people]

— Leopold I, 1640–1705, Holy Roman Emperor 1658–1705.

— Leopold I, 1790–1865, king of the Belgians 1831–65.

— Leopold II, 1747–92, Holy Roman Emperor 1790–92.

— Leopold II, 1835–1909, king of the Belgians, 1865–1909; exploiter of the Belgian Congo.

— Leopold III, born 1901, king of the Belgians 1934–51; German prisoner of war 1944; exiled 1945.

Leopold II, Lake A lake in the western Belgian Congo; 900 square miles.

Le·o·pold·ville (lē′ə·pōld·vil′) A former name for KINSHASA.

le·o·tard (lē′ə·tärd) *n.* **1** A short, close–fitting, sleeveless garment, low at the neck, and fitted between the legs: worn by acrobats, etc. **2** A modern adaptation of this, having a high neck and covering the body to the wrist and ankle: used by dancers as practice clothes. [after *Léotard,* 19th c. French aerialist]

Le·pan·to (le·pän′tō) The Italian name for NAUPAKTOS; scene of a European naval victory over the Turks, 1571.

Lepanto, Gulf of The Italian name for the GULF OF CORINTH.

Lepanto, Straits of The former name for RION STRAIT.

Le·pa·ya (lye′pə·yə) See LIEPAJA.

lep·er (lep′ər) *n.* One afflicted with leprosy. [< obs. *leper* leprosy <OF *lepre, liepre* <L *lepra* <Gk., orig. fem. of *lepros* scaly < *lepos* a scale < *lepein* peel]

lepido- *combining form* Scale or flake: *lepidolite.* Also, before vowels, **lepid-.** [<Gk. *lepis, lepidos* a scale]

le·pid·o·lite (li·pid′ə·līt, lep′ə·dō·līt′) *n.* A lithium-bearing variety of mica. [<Gk. *lepis, -idos* a scale + -LITE]

lep·i·dop·ter·an (lep′ə·dop′tər·ən) *n.* Any of an order *(Lepidoptera)* of insects having four wings covered with minute scales, and undergoing a complete metamorphosis through the egg, caterpillar, pupa, and imago stages; butterflies and moths. — *adj.* Of or pertaining to the *Lepidoptera.* [<NL, order name < *lepidopteron* LEPIDOPTERON] — **lep′i·dop′ter·al, lep′i·dop′ter·ous** *adj.*

lep·i·dop·ter·on (lep′ə·dop′tər·ən) *n. pl.* **·ter·a** (-tər·ə) Any lepidopterous insect; a moth or butterfly. [<NL <Gk. *lepis, -idos* a scale + *pteron* a wing]

lep·i·do·si·ren (lep′ə·dō·sī′rən) *n.* One of a genus *(Lepidosiren)* of primitive, eel-like lungfishes, as *L. paradoxa* of South America. [<LEPIDO- + SIREN (def. 3)]

lep·i·dote (lep′ə·dōt) *adj. Bot.* Scurfy with minute scales. [<NL *lepidotus* <Gk. *lepidōtos* < *lepis, lepidos* a scale]

Lep·i·dus (lep′ə·dəs), **Marcus Aemilius,** died 13 B.C., Roman triumvir with Antony and Octavian (Augustus).

Le·pon·tine Alps (li·pon′tin) The central part of the Alps between southern Switzerland and northern Italy.

lep·o·rid (lep′ə·rid) *n.* One of a family *(Leporidae)* of gnawing mammals belonging to the order *Lagomorpha* or suborder *Duplicidentata;* a rabbit or hare. — *adj.* Of or pertaining to the *Leporidae.* [<NL *Leporidae,* family name <L *lepus, leporis* a hare]

lep·o·ride (lep′ə·rid) *n.* The hybrid offspring of the European hare and rabbit; a Belgian hare. [<F *léporide* <L *lepus, leporis* a hare]

lep·o·rine (lep′ə·rīn, -rin) *adj.* Like or pertaining to hares. [<L *leporinus* < *lepus, leporis* a hare]

lep·re·chaun (lep′rə·kôn) *n.* In Irish folklore, a fairy cobbler who, if caught and held, must reveal the location of treasure. [<Irish *lupracān* <OIrish *luchorpan* < *lu* little + *corpān,* dim. of *corp* body <L *corpus, -oris*]

lep·ro·sar·i·um (lep′rə·sâr′ē·əm) *n.* A leper colony or hospital. [<NL <LEPROS(Y) + (SANIT)ARIUM]

lep·rose (lep′rōs) *adj. Bot.* Having a scurfy appearance; scalelike; leprous: usually said of crustaceous lichens. [<L *leprosus* < *lepra.* See LEPER.]

lep·ro·sy (lep′rə·sē) *n. Pathol.* A chronic, endemic, communicable disease characterized by nodular skin lesions, nerve paralysis, and physical mutilation: caused by the microorganism *Mycobacterium* or *Bacillus leprae.* Also *Hansen's disease.* [<OF *leprosie,* prob. <LL *leprosus* <L *lepra.* See LEPER.]

lep·rous (lep′rəs) *adj.* **1** Affected with leprosy; unclean. **2** Scalelike; scurfy; covered with scales; leprose. Also **lep′er·ous** (-ər·əs). [<OF *lepros, leprous* <LL *leprosus* <L *lepra.* See LEPER.] — **lep′rous·ly** *adv.* — **lep′rous·ness** *n.*

-lepsy *combining form* Seizure; attack: *catalepsy.* Also **-lepsia.** [<Gk. *lepsis* a seizure < *lambanein* seize]

lepto- *combining form Biol.* Fine; slender; small: *leptorrhine.* Also, before vowels, **lept-.** [<Gk. *leptos* slender]

lep·tome (lep′tōm) *n.* Phloem. [<Gk. *leptos* fine, delicate]

lep·ton[1] (lep′ton) *n. pl.* **·ta** (-tə) A coin of modern Greece, valued at 1/100 drachma. [<Gk. *lepton (nomisma),* lit., a small coin, neut. of *leptos* small, fine]

lep·ton[2] (lep′ton) *n. Physics* An atomic particle of very small mass as the electron, positron, neutrino, or antineutron. [<Gk., neut. of *leptos* fine]

lep·tor·rhine (lep′tə·rīn, -rin) *adj.* Having a narrow or slender nose. [<LEPTO- + Gk. *rhis, rhinos* nose]

lep·to·so·mat·ic (lep′tə·sō·mat′ik) *adj.* Denoting a person having a light, lean, narrow body.

lep·to·tene (lep′tə·tēn) *adj. Biol.* Designating a stage in cell meiosis in which the nuclear substance assumes the form of delicate threads. [<LEPTO- + Gk. *tainia* a ribbon]

Le·pus (lē′pəs) *n.* **1** The genus of mammals (family *Leporidae*) which includes most of the hares and rabbits. **2** A southern constellation, the Hare. See CONSTELLATION. [<L, a hare]

Lé·ri·da (lā′rē·thä) A city in NE Spain: ancient *Ilerda.*

Ler·mon·tov (lyer′mən·tôf), **Mikhail Yurevich,** 1814–41, Russian poet.

Ler·na (lûr′nə) A marshy district in the NE Peloponnesus.

Le·sage (lə·säzh′), **Alain René,** 1668–1747, French novelist and dramatist.

Les·bi·an (lez′bē·ən) *n.* **1** A native or inhabitant of Lesbos. **2** A homosexual woman: so called from the alleged homosexuality of Sappho and her followers. — *adj.* **1** Of or pertaining to Lesbos or to Lesbians. **2** *Rare* Erotic. [<L *Lesbius* <Gk. *Lesbios* <*Lesbos* Lesbos, the home of Sappho]

Les·bi·an·ism (lez′bē·ən·iz′əm) *n.* Homosexuality among women.

Les·bos (lez′bəs, -bos) A Greek island off NW Turkey; 623 square miles: also *Mytilene.*

Les Cayes (lā kā′) A port of SW Haiti: also *Aux Cayes, Cayes.*

Les·caze (les·käz′), **William,** born 1896, U.S. architect born in Switzerland.

Le·sche·tiz·ky (le′shə·tit′skē), **Teodor,** 1830–1915, Polish pianist, teacher, and composer.

lèse-ma·jes·té (lez′mà·zhes·tā′) *n.* In some European countries, an offense against the sovereign power; treason. In England, the term **lese-maj·es·ty** (lēz′maj′is·tē) has been replaced by *treason.* [<F <L *laesa majestas* < *laesa,* fem. of *laesus,* pp. of *laedere* injure + *majestas* MAJESTY]

Les·ghi·an (lez′gē·ən) *n.* One of a group of mountain people of Dagestan, U.S.S.R. Also spelled *Lezghian.*

le·sion (lē′zhən) *n.* **1** A hurt; loss; injury. **2** *Pathol.* Any morbid change in function or structure of an organ or tissue. [<F *lésion* <L *laesio, -onis* < *laesus,* pp. of *laedere* injure]

Le·so·tho (le·sōō′tōō, -sō′thō) An independent member of the Commonwealth of Nations consisting of an enclave in the eastern part of South Africa; 11,716 sq. mi.; capital, Maseru: formerly *Basutoland.*

less (les) Comparative of LITTLE. — *adj.* **1** Smaller; not as large or much. **2** Of slighter consequence; inferior in age, rank, etc. **3** Fewer: used with collective nouns. *Less* refers to quantity, measure, or degree; *fewer* refers to number. — *n.* **1** A smaller part or quantity. **2** The smaller (of things compared); the younger (of persons). — *adv.* In an inferior degree; not as much. — *prep.* Minus; by the subtraction or omission of: a year *less* a month, nine *less* six. [OE *lǣssa*]

-less *suffix* **1** Deprived or destitute of; without: *harmless.* **2** Beyond the range of (the action of the main element): *countless.* [OE *-leas* < *leas* free from]

Les Saintes (lā saṅt′) An island group comprising a dependency of Guadeloupe; 5 1/2 sq. mi. *French* **Îles des Saintes** (ēl dā saṅt′).

les·see (les·ē′) *n.* One to whom a lease is made; one holding property by lease. [<AF *lessee,* OF *lessé,* pp. of *lesser, laissier.* See LEASE[2].]

less·en[1] (les′ən) *v.t.* **1** To make less; decrease. **2** To make little of; disparage. — *v.i.* **3** To become less. ◆ Homophone: *lesson.* See synonyms under ABATE, ALLAY, ALLEVIATE, IMPAIR. — **less′en·er** *n.* — **less′en·ing** *adj.* & *n.*

less·en[2] (les′ən) *conj. Dial.* Unless.

Les·seps (les′əps, *Fr.* le·seps′), **Count Ferdinand de,** 1805–94, French engineer; built the Suez Canal.

less·er (les′ər) *adj.* Less; smaller; inferior.

Lesser Antilles See ANTILLES.

Lesser Bear The constellation Ursa Minor.

Lesser Dog The constellation Canis Minor.

lesser doxology See DOXOLOGY, GLORIA.

Lesser Slave Lake A lake in central Alberta, Canada; 461 square miles.

Lesser Sunda Islands An island group in the Malay Archipelago, including Bali, Lombok, Sumbawa, Sumba, Flores, Timor, and the Solor Islands, together with adjacent smaller islands, and comprising the province of Nusa Tenggara, Indonesia and Portuguese Timor; about 28,600 square miles.

Lesser Wallachia See OLTENIA.

Les·sing (les′ing), **Gotthold Ephraim,** 1729–1781, German dramatist and critic.

les·son (les′ən) *n.* **1** A specific exercise to be learned or recited at one time; task assigned by a teacher. **2** Instruction; an instance of instruction. **3** *pl.* A course of instruction. **4** A set portion of any work or writing suitable for reading at one time; a reading; specifically, a portion of Scripture read or appointed to be read in divine service. **5** Knowledge gained by experience. **6** A reprimand; lecture. See synonyms under TASK. — *v.t.* **1** To give a lesson or lessons to. **2** To rebuke; scold. ◆ Homophone: *lessen.* [<OF *lecon* <L *lectio, -onis* a reading. Doublet of LECTION.]

les·sor (les′ôr, les·ôr′) *n.* One who grants a lease or demises a property. [<AF < *lesser, laissier.* See LESSEE.]

lest (lest) *conj.* **1** In order that . . . not; so that . . . not; for fear that: We hid it *lest* he should see it. **2** That: following expressions indicating alarm or anxiety: We were worried *lest* the money run out. [OE *(thy) lǣs the* (by the) less that]

let[1] (let) *v.* **let, let·ting** *v.t.* **1** To allow; permit: He won't *let* her do it. **2** To allow to go, come, or pass: They would not *let* us on board. **3** To cause; make: She disliked him and *let* him know it. **4** To cause to escape or be released: to *let* blood. **5** To grant the temporary possession or occupancy of, as a room or house, for rent or other compensation: often with *out.* **6** To assign, as a contract, for performance. **7** As an auxiliary verb, *let* is used to express command or suggestion: *Let* him come. — *v.i.* **8** To be rented or leased. — **to let alone** (or **be**) To refrain from disturbing, bothering, or tampering with. See note under LEAVE. — **to let down 1** To allow to descend; lower. **2** To relax; reduce effort or concentration. **3** *Colloq.* To disappoint. — **to let fly** To hurl, as a missile. — **to let loose 1** To free; liberate. **2** *Colloq.* To act unrestrainedly. — **to let off 1** To discharge or reduce, as pressure. **2** *Colloq.* To excuse from an engagement, duty, or penalty; dismiss. — **to let on** *Colloq.* **1** To pretend. **2** To reveal; allow to be known. — **to let out 1** To release; allow to go, escape, etc. **2** To reveal; divulge. **3** To make larger by releasing a part previously fastened: to *let out* a seam. **4** *Colloq.* To dismiss or be dismissed, as a school. — **to let up** To slacken; abate. — **to let up on** *Colloq.* To reduce or cease applying pressure or harsh measures to. — **to let well enough alone** To refrain from tampering with what is regarded as unfavorable to change or already satisfactory. [OE *lǣtan*]

let[2] (let) *n.* **1** Anything that obstructs or hinders; an obstacle; impediment: usually in the phrase "without *let* or hindrance." **2** In tennis, rackets, fives, ping-pong, etc., a served ball which touches the net in passing over. — *v.t. Archaic* **let** or **let·ted, let·ting** To hinder or impede; obstruct. [OE *lettan,* lit., make late]

-let *suffix of nouns* **1** Small; little: *kinglet.* **2** A band or small article for: *bracelet.* [<OF *-let, -lette* < *-el* (<L *-ellus*) + *-et,* dim. suffixes]

let alone Without mentioning; to say nothing of: He can't even float, *let alone* swim.

let-down (let′doun′) *n.* **1** Abatement or slackening; decrease, as of speed or energy. **2** *Colloq.* Disillusionment; disappointment.

le·thal (lē′thəl) *adj.* **1** Causing death; deadly; fatal. **2** Pertaining to death. [<L *lethalis* < *lethum, letum* death] — **le′thal·ly** *adv.*

le·thal·i·ty (lē·thal′ə·tē) *n.* **1** The quality of being lethal. **2** The degree of destructiveness produced by the action of a bomb, warhead, or similar weapon.

le·thar·gic (li·thär′jik) *adj.* Pertaining to, resembling, or affected by lethargy; drowsy; apathetic; dull; sleepy. Also **le·thar′gi·cal.** — **le·thar′gi·cal·ly** *adv.*

leth·ar·gize (leth′ər·jīz) *v.t.* **·gized, ·giz·ing** To make lethargic.

leth·ar·gy (leth′ər·jē) *n. pl.* **·gies 1** *Pathol.* A state of morbid and prolonged sleep; stupor. **2** A state of inaction, indifference, or dulness; apathy. See synonyms under

APATHY, STUPOR. [<OF *lethargie* <LL *lethargia* <Gk. *lēthargia* <*lēthargos* forgetful <*lēthē* oblivion]

Le·the (lē′thē) **1** In Greek and Roman mythology, the river of forgetfulness, one of the five rivers surrounding Hades. **2** Oblivion; forgetfulness. [<Gk. *lēthē* oblivion] — **Le·the·an** (li·thē′ən) *adj.*

le·thif·er·ous (li·thif′ər·əs) *adj.* Deadly; lethal; fatal. [<L *lethifer* <*lethum, letum* death + *ferre* carry]

Le·ti·cia (lā·tē′syä) A town in extreme SE Colombia; capital of Amazonas commissionary; claimed by Peru but awarded to Colombia in 1934.

Le·ti·ti·a (li·tish′ē·ə, -tish′ə) A feminine personal name. Also *Ital.* **Le·ti·zi·a** (lā·tēt′sē·ä), *Lat.* **Lae·ti·ti·a** (lē·tish′ē·ə). [<L, joy]

Le·to (lē′tō) In Greek mythology, the mother by Zeus of Apollo and Artemis: identified with the Roman *Latona.*

Lett (let) *n.* **1** One of a people inhabiting Latvia and adjacent Baltic regions. **2** Lettish.

let·ter (let′ər) *n.* **1** A mark or character used to represent a sound or articulation of human speech; a character of the alphabet; a primary element of written speech; also, a type bearing such a character, or, collectively, printer's type or a style of type. **2** A school insigne of cloth to be worn on a sweater, customarily awarded by a school or college to its distinguished athletes. **3** A written or printed communication from one person to another; especially, a missive longer than a note; an epistle. **4** A document certifying a grant of authority, right, privilege, or the like, made to the person named therein: often in the plural: *letters* dimissory, *letters* patent. **5** The literal or exact meaning or requirement of the words used: the *letter* of the law. **6** *pl.* Literary culture; learning; knowledge; erudition; also, literature in the aggregate or in general: the domain of *letters.* **7** *Music* A tone, note, key, or degree designated or symbolized by a letter of the alphabet. — **man of letters** A man who follows literature as a profession; also, a man of learning; a scholar. — *v.t.* To inscribe or write with letters. [<OF *lettre* <L *littera* a letter of the alphabet, in pl., an epistle] — **let′ter·er** *n.*

Synonyms (noun): character, emblem, mark, sign, symbol, type.

let·ter·box (let′ər·boks′) *n.* A receptacle for posting letters.

let·ter–car·ri·er (let′ər·kar′ē·ər) *n.* A postman; one who carries and delivers letters.

let·ter–drop (let′ər·drop′) *n.* A small opening in a mailbox, post office, etc., through which letters are dropped.

let·tered (let′ərd) *adj.* **1** Versed in letters; learned; literary; educated. **2** Inscribed or marked with letters.

let·ter·gram (let′ər·gram) *n.* A telegraphic communication, slower than a regular telegram and sent at a reduced rate. See DAY LETTER, NIGHT LETTER. [<LETTER + (TELE)GRAM]

let·ter·head (let′ər·hed′) *n.* A printed heading at the top of a sheet of letter paper, or a sheet that bears such a heading.

let·ter–high (let′ər·hī′) *adj.* Type-high.

let·ter·ing (let′ər·ing) *n.* **1** The act, process, or business of marking or stamping with letters or of making letters. **2** Letters collectively; an inscription.

let·ter·man (let′ər·man′) *n.* *pl.* **·men** (-men′) *U.S.* An athlete to whom a letter has been awarded.

letter of advice A letter giving special information, as from a consignor to a consignee, from an agent to a principal, or from drawer to drawee of a bill of exchange.

letter of credence The document accrediting an envoy to a foreign power.

letter of credit A commercial instrument issued by a merchant or banker authorizing the bearer to draw money or obtain goods up to a certain amount from other bankers or merchants.

letter of marque A commission issued by a government authorizing a private person to take the property of a foreign state; especially, a document licensing an individual to arm a vessel and prey upon enemy merchant shipping. Also **letter of marque and reprisal.**

letter paper Paper for business or personal correspondence, usually a size of writing paper 8 1/2 x 11 or 8 x 10 inches.

let·ter–per·fect (let′ər·pûr′fikt) *adj.* **1** Having thoroughly memorized (something, as a speech, dramatic role, etc.); knowing by heart. **2** Accurate as to spelling, etc.: said of a manuscript, proof, etc.

let·ter·press (let′ər·pres′) *n.* Letters and words printed; the printed text of a book. — *adj.* Printed from type or plates with a raised surface, as distinguished from matter printed by lithography, gravure, and offset printing.

let·ter·shop (let′ər·shop′) *n.* An establishment that furnishes a service for duplicating, addressing, or mailing letters in quantity.

letters of administration *Law* A document issued by a court authorizing a certain person named therein to administer or settle the estate of one who has died without making a will.

letters patent An open document, under seal of the government, granting some special right, authority, privilege, or property, or conferring some title; especially, a document giving to the person named the exclusive right to use, make, or sell some invention.

letters testamentary *Law* A document issued to an executor of a will authorizing him to be executor.

Let·tic (let′ik) *adj.* Of or pertaining to the language of the Letts. — *n.* Lettish.

Let·tish (let′ish) *adj.* Of or pertaining to the Letts or their language. — *n.* The language of the Letts, belonging to the Baltic branch of the Balto-Slavic languages; Latvian: spoken in Latvia, Lithuania, and East Prussia.

let·tre de ca·chet (let′r′ də kà·she′) *French* In French history, a sealed, secret, royal letter ordering arrest and imprisonment without trial.

let·tuce (let′is) *n.* **1** A garden herb *(Lactuca sativa)* whose crisp, edible leaves are used as a salad. **2** Any of several similar plants. [<OF *laitues,* pl. of *laitue* <L *lactuca* <*lac, lactis* milk; with ref. to its milky juice]

let–up (let′up′) *n.* *Colloq.* Abatement; cessation; intermission.

le·u (lā′o͞o) *n.* *pl.* **lei** (lā) A silver coin, the monetary unit of Rumania, equivalent to 100 bani. Also **ley.** [<Rumanian, lit., a lion <L *leo*]

Leu·cas (lo͞o′kəs) The Latin name for LEVKAS. Also **Leu·ca′di·a** (lo͞o·kā′dē·ə).

leu·cine (lo͞o′sin, -sēn) *n.* *Biochem.* A white, crystalline amino acid, $C_6H_{13}NO_2$, produced in the decomposition of proteins during pancreatic digestion. Also **leu′cin** (-sin). [<Gk. *leukos* white + -INE[2]]

leu·cite (lo͞o′sīt) *n.* A white potassium-aluminum silicate found in igneous rocks. [<Gk. *leukos* white + -ITE[1]]

leuco– See LEUKO–.

leu·co·crat·ic (lo͞o′kō·krat′ik) *adj.* *Geol.* Characterized by the predominance of light-colored minerals, as certain igneous rocks: opposed to *melanocratic.* [<LEUCO- + Gk. *krat(eein)* rule + -IC]

leu·co·cyte (lo͞o′kə·sīt) *n.* *Biol.* The most commonly occurring type of the white or colorless blood corpuscle: a large, nucleated ameboid cell formed in red bone marrow, constituting an important agent in protection against infectious diseases. Also *leukocyte.* [<LEUCO- + -CYTE] — **leu′co·cyt′ic** (-sit′ik) *adj.*

leu·co·ma·ine (lo͞o·kō′mə·ēn, -in) *n.* *Biochem.* One of various nitrogen compounds normally present in animal tissues as products of metabolism: related to uric acid and creatine, and sometimes toxic. [<LEUCO- + (PTO)MAINE]

leu·co·mel·a·nous (lo͞o′kō·mel′ə·nəs) *adj.* Having a light or fair complexion, with dark eyes and hair. Also **leu′co·me·lan′ic** (-mə·lan′ik). [<LEUCO- + Gk. *melas, melanos* black]

leu·co·plas·tid (lo͞o′kō·plas′tid) *n.* *Bot.* One of the colorless granules embedded in the protoplasmic mass of active vegetable cells, forming points about which the starch accumulates. Also **leu′co·plast.**

leu·co·poi·e·sis (lo͞o′kō·poi·ē′sis) *n.* *Physiol.* The production of leucocytes. [<NL <LEUCO(CYTE) + Gk. *poiēsis* a making <*poieein* make] — **leu′co·poi·et′ic** (-et′ik) *adj.*

leu·co·sin (lo͞o′kə·sin) *n.* *Biochem.* A simple protein found in wheat. [<Gk. *leukos* white + -IN]

leu·co·stic·te (lo͞o′kō·stik′tē) *n.* A fringilline bird *(Leucosticte tephrocotis littoralis),* the rosy finch of the NW United States. [<NL *Leucosticte,* genus name <Gk. *leukos* white + *stiktos* pricked]

Leuc·tra (lo͞ok′trə) An ancient city of Boeotia, Greece, SW of Thebes; scene of the Theban defeat of the Spartans, 371 B.C.

leud (lo͞od) *n.* *pl.* **leuds** or **leu·des** (lo͞o′dēz) A feudal vassal in the Frankish kingdoms. [<Med. L *leudes* <OHG *liudi, liuti*]

leuk (lo͞ok) *v.t.* & *v.i.* *Scot.* To look.

leu·ke·mi·a (lo͞o·kē′mē·ə) *n.* *Pathol.* A disordered and generally fatal condition of the blood and bloodmaking tissues, characterized by a marked and persistent excess in the number of leucocytes, accompanied by hyperactivity of the lymph glands, internal hemorrhage, anemia, and exhaustion. Also **leu·kae′mi·a.** — **leu·ke′mic** *adj.*

leuko– *combining form* Whiteness; lack of color: *leukoderma*: also spelled *leuco–.* Also, before vowels, **leuk–.** [<Gk. *leukos* white]

◆ *Leuko–,* though used interchangeably with *leuco–,* is preferred for most medical and many biological terms.

leu·ko·cyte (lo͞o′kə·sīt) See LEUCOCYTE.

leu·ko·cy·the·mi·a (lo͞o′kō·sī·thē′mē·ə) *n.* Leukemia. [<NL <Gk. *leukos* white + *kytos* vessel + *haima* blood]

leu·ko·cy·to·sis (lo͞o′kō·sī·tō′sis) *n.* *Pathol.* An abnormal increase in the number of leucocytes in the blood. — **leu′ko·cy·tot′ic** (-tot′ik) *adj.*

leu·ko·der·ma (lo͞o′kō·dûr′mə) *n.* *Pathol.* Defective pigmentation of the skin, occurring in white patches. [<LEUKO- + Gk. *derma* skin] — **leu′ko·der′mic** *adj.*

leu·ko·ma (lo͞o·kō′mə) *n.* *Pathol.* An opaque and whitish condition of the cornea. [<NL <Gk. *leukōma* <*leukos* white]

leu·ko·pe·ni·a (lo͞o′kō·pē′nē·ə) *n.* *Pathol.* An abnormal reduction in the number of white blood corpuscles in the blood. [<NL <Gk. *leukos* white + *penia* poverty <*penesthai* be poor] — **leu′ko·pe′nic** *adj.*

leu·kor·rhe·a (lo͞o′kə·rē′ə) *n.* *Pathol.* A whitish morbid discharge from the vagina. Also **leu′cor·rhe′a, leu′cor·rhoe′a.** [<NL <Gk. *leukos* white + *rheein* flow]

Leu·pold (loi′pōlt) German form of LEOPOLD.

Leu·tze (loit′sə), **Emanuel,** 1816–68, American historical painter born in Germany.

lev (lef) *n.* *pl.* **lev·a** (lev′ə) A copper coin, the monetary unit of Bulgaria, equivalent to 100 stotinki. [<Bulgarian, lit., a lion <OSlavic *livu,* ult. <Gk. *leōn, -ontos*]

Lev·al·loi·si·an (lev′ə·loi′zē·ən) *adj.* *Anthropol.* Denoting a culture stage of the Lower Paleolithic following the Acheulean and merging with the Mousterian. [after the *Levallois* flake, a type of flint tool first found near Levallois-Perret]

Le·val·lois–Per·ret (lə·vȧ·lwȧ′pe·re′) A NW suburb of Paris, France.

le·vant[1] (lə·vant′) *n.* **1** Morocco leather from the Levant: also **Levant morocco.** **2** Levanter. — *adj.* Made of Levant morocco.

le·vant[2] (lə·vant′) *v.i.* *Brit.* To decamp; abscond. [<Sp. *levantar* lift <*levar* <L *levare* raise] — **le·vant′er** *n.*

Le·vant (lə·vant′) **1** The coast of the eastern Mediterranean from western Greece to western Egypt. **2** The non-European coastlands along the eastern shore of the Mediterranean. [<F <Ital. *levante* <L *levans, -antis,* pp. of *levare* raise]

Levant dollar See under DOLLAR.

le·vant·er (lə·van′tər) *n.* An easterly gale in the Mediterranean: also called *levant.*

le·van·tine (lə·van′tin, lev′ən·tīn, -tēn) *n.* A stout, closely woven, reversible silk fabric.

Le·van·tine (lə·van′tin, lev′ən·tīn, -tēn) *adj.* **1** Pertaining to the Levant; eastern; Oriental. **2** Pertaining to the descendants of Europeans in the East. — *n.* A native or naturalized inhabitant of the Levant, especially one of European descent.

Levant States The parts of Syria under French mandate, 1920–44, comprising Syria, Lebanon, Latakia, and Jebel ed Druz.

le·va·tor (lə·vā′tər) *n.* *pl.* **lev·a·to·res** (lev′ə·tôr′ēz, -tō′rēz) or **le·va·tors** **1** *Anat.* A muscle that raises an organ or part. **2** *Surg.* An instrument for lifting up the depressed part in a fracture of the skull or in trephining. [<LL, a raiser <L *levare* raise]

lev·ee[1] (lev′ē) *n.* **1** An embankment beside

a stream, to prevent overflow. **2** A steep natural bank. —*v.t.* To furnish with a levee or levees; embank. [<F *levée,* pp. fem. of *lever* raise <L *levare*]

lev·ee² (lev′ē, lə·vē′) *n.* **1** A morning reception or assembly at the house of a sovereign or great personage. **2** In Great Britain, a formal reception held shortly after midday by the sovereign at which only men are received. **3** A reception or promiscuous assembly of callers or guests; especially, a reception given by the president of the United States. [<F *levé,* an arising, var. of *lever* < *se lever* arise <L *levare* raise]

lev·el (lev′əl) *adj.* **1** Having a flat and even surface; without inequalities; strictly conforming to the surface of a body of still water; also, approximately flat. **2** Conforming to a horizontal plane; not sloping. **3** Being in the same line or plane with something else. **4** Equal to something or someone else in importance, rank, or degree. **5** Aimed or moving in a direct line; hence, straightforward; honest. **6** Well-balanced; having good judgment. **7** Even in tone, color, etc. **8** Denoting a surface everywhere at right angles to the line in which a force acts, so that motion upon it causes no gain or loss of energy. —**one's level best** *Colloq.* One's very best. —*n.* **1** A line or surface wholly at right angles to the vertical. **2** A horizontal line, surface, plane, or position; also, an approximately horizontal surface, as a plain. **3** The mean altitude of something: sea *level.* **4** Degree of moral, intellectual, or social elevation; rank; specifically, an equal rank: The men were on a *level* mentally. **5** The line in which anything is aimed. **6** A device for ascertaining, or for adjusting something to, a horizontal line or plane by noting the position of a bubble contained within a sealed tube of alcohol or other liquid: used by builders and surveyors, with or without a microscope. **7** Differences in altitude thus measured. **8** A section of a canal from one lock to another. —**on the level** *U.S. Colloq.* Without equivocation; in a fair, honest manner. —*v.* **lev·eled** or **lev·elled, lev·el·ing** or **lev·el·ling** *v.t.* **1** To make flat; give a flat or horizontal surface to: often with *off.* **2** To reduce to the ground; demolish; raze. **3** To bring or reduce to a common condition, state, etc. **4** To make horizontal, as with a level (def. 6). **5** To aim or direct, as a rifle, the eyes, etc. **6** To make even and uniform, as colors. **7** In surveying, to ascertain the vertical contours of (ground). —*v.i.* **8** To aim a weapon directly at a mark or target. **9** To bring persons or things to a common state or condition. —**to level off** *Aeron.* To fly a plane parallel with the ground, as before landing. —*adv.* **1** In a right or level line; direct; straight. **2** In an even manner; steadily. [<OF *livel, nivel* <L *libella,* dim. of *libra,* balance] —**lev′el·ly** *adv.* —**lev′el·ness** *n.*
Synonyms (adj.): even, flat, horizontal, plain, plane, smooth. We speak of a *horizontal* line, a *flat* morass, a *level* road, a *plain* country, a *plane* surface (especially in the scientific sense). That which is *level* may not be *even,* and that which is *even* may not be *level;* a *level* road may be very rough; a slope may be *even.* See FLAT, HORIZONTAL, SMOOTH. *Antonyms:* broken, hilly, inclined, irregular, rolling, rugged, slanting, sloping, uneven.

lev·el·er (lev′əl·ər) *n.* **1** One who or that which levels. **2** One who would destroy social distinctions; specifically, **Leveler,** a member of an English political body during the rule of Oliver Cromwell. **3** A scraping implement used in grading, or a device for leveling. Also **lev′el·ler.**

lev·el-head·ed (lev′əl-hed′id) *adj.* **1** Having sound common sense; not flighty or impulsive. **2** Steady; reliable: said of a horse. —**lev′el-head′ed·ness** *n.*

lev·el·ing (lev′əl·ing) *n.* **1** The reduction of uneven surfaces to a level. **2** The reduction of unequal ranks or conditions to a common level. **3** In surveying, the operation of ascertaining the comparative levels of different points of land, so as to lay out a grade. Also **lev′el·ling.**

leveling rod A graduated pole bearing a marker: used by surveyors to mark a level, being sighted through a leveling instrument. Also **levelling rod.**

Le·ven (lē′vən), **Loch** A lake in Kinross County, east central Scotland; 8 square miles; on an island are the ruins of **Lochleven Castle,** where Mary Queen of Scots was imprisoned.

lev·er (lev′ər, lē′vər) *n.* **1** A mechanical device, consisting of a rigid structure, often a straight bar, turning freely on a fixed point or fulcrum, and serving to impart pressure or motion from a source of power to a resistance; one of the six so-called mechanical powers. **2** Any one of various tools on the principle defined above, as a starting bar for a marine engine. **3** Any means of exerting effective power. —*v.t. & v.i.* To move with or use a lever. [<OF *leveour,* lit., a lifter < *lever* raise <L *levare*]

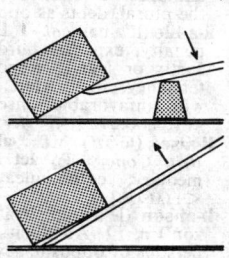
TWO PRINCIPAL TYPES OF LEVERS
Above: First class.
Below: Second class.

Le·ver (lē′vər), **Charles James,** 1806–72, Irish novelist.

lev·er·age (lev′ər·ij, lē′vər-) *n.* **1** The mechanical advantage gained by use of a lever. **2** Increased power or advantage. **3** The arrangement by which the power of a lever is controlled.

lev·er·et (lev′ər·it) *n.* A young hare; a hare less than a year old. [<AF, OF *levrete,* dim. of *levre* a hare <L *lepus, leporis*]

Le·ver·ku·sen (lā′vər·kōō′zən) A town in North Rhine–Westphalia, West Germany.

Le·ver·rier (lə·ve·ryā′), **Urbain Jean Joseph,** 1811–77, French astronomer.

Le·vi (lē′vī) A masculine personal name. — **Levi** The third son of Jacob, or the tribe descended from him. [<Hebrew, joining]

lev·i·a·ble (lev′ē·ə·bəl) *adj.* That may be levied or levied upon or seized. [<LEVY¹ + -ABLE]

le·vi·a·than (lə·vī′ə·thən) *n.* **1** A large aquatic but unidentified animal mentioned in the Scriptures: possibly a crocodile or other large reptile (*Job* xli 1), a serpent (*Isa.* xxvii 1), or a whale (*Ps.* civ 26). **2** Hence, any large animal, as a whale. **3** By extension, something huge and colossal, as a ship of unusual size. [<LL <Hebrew *liwyāthān*]

Le·vi·a·than (lə·vī′ə·thən) The title of a work by Thomas Hobbes which develops the analogy between the human body and human society and expounds the monarchic principle; hence, the political organism; the state.

lev·i·gate (lev′ə·gāt) *v.t.* **·gat·ed, ·gat·ing 1** To reduce to a fine powder, as by grinding between hard surfaces. **2** To make a smooth paste of. —*adj.* Made smooth; polished. [<L *levigatus,* pp. of *levigare* polish < *levis* smooth + *agere* make] —**lev′i·ga′tion** *n.* —**lev′i·ga′tor** *n.*

lev·in (lev′in) *n. Archaic* Lightning. [ME *levene,* prob. <Gmc.]

lev·i·rate (lev′ə·rāt, lē′və·rit) *n.* The ancient custom of marriage between a man and the widow of his brother, required by the Mosaic law when there was no male issue and when the two brothers had been residing on the same family estate. [<L *levir* a husband's brother + -ATE¹] —**lev′i·rat′i·cal** (-rat′i·kəl) *adj.*

Le·vis (lē′vīz) *n. pl.* Tight-fitting, heavy denim trousers, with narrow legs and with rivets inserted at points of greatest strain: a trade name. Also **Levi Strauss·es** (strou′siz). [after *Levi* Strauss, U.S. manufacturer]

lev·i·tate (lev′ə·tāt) *v.* **·tat·ed, ·tat·ing** *v.i.* To rise and float in the air, as from lightness or buoyancy. —*v.t.* To cause to rise and float in the air. [<L *levis* light, on analogy with *gravitate*] —**lev′i·ta′tor** *n.*

lev·i·ta·tion (lev′ə·tā′shən) *n.* **1** The act of making light, or the state of being light; buoyancy, whether physical or spiritual. **2** The illusion of suspending heavy objects or the human body in the air without support.

Le·vite (lē′vīt) *n.* One of the tribe or family of Levi, especially a descendant of Levi, acting as assistant to the priests of the tribe in the services of the sanctuary. *Num.* xviii 6.

Le·vit·i·cal (lə·vit′i·kəl) *adj.* Pertaining to the Levites, to the law, or the book of Leviticus. Also **Le·vit′ic.**

Le·vit·i·cus (lə·vit′i·kəs) The third book of the Old Testament, containing ceremonial laws. [<L *Leviticus (liber)* <Gk. *Leuitikon (biblion),* lit., the Levitical (book)]

lev·i·ty (lev′ə·tē) *n.* **1** Lightness of humor or temperament; lack of mental gravity; want of seriousness or earnestness. **2** Frivolity; volatility; also, fickleness. **3** The state or quality of being light; especially, the quality of relative lightness. **4** A supposed tendency to rise in spite of gravity. [<L *levitas, -tatis* < *levis* light]
Synonyms: flightiness, frivolity, giddiness, inconstancy, lightness, thoughtlessness, vanity. *Antonyms:* earnestness, gravity, seriousness, sobriety, steadiness, thoughtfulness.

Lev·kas (lef·käs′) A Greek island, northernmost of the Ionian chain and often identified with the Homeric Ithaca; 114 square miles: Italian *Santa Maura:* Latin *Leucadia, Leucas.*

levo– *combining form* Turned or turning to the left: used especially in chemistry and physics: *levorotatory.* Also spelled *laevo-.* [<L *laevus* left]

le·vo·duc·tion (lē′vō·duk′shən) *n.* Movement toward the left: said of the eye. [<LEVO- + L *ductus,* pp. of *ducere* lead]

le·vo·ro·ta·to·ry (lē′vō·rō′tə·tôr′ē, -tō′rē) *adj. Physics* Rotating the plane of polarization from right to left: opposed to *dextrorotatory:* also called **le′vo·gy′rate** (-jī′rāt). —**le′vo·ro·ta′tion** *n.*

lev·u·lin (lev′yə·lin) *n. Biochem.* A colorless amorphous compound resembling starch. It readily decomposes into levulose. [<LEVUL-(OSE) + -IN]

lev·u·lin·ic (lev′yə·lin′ik) *adj. Chem.* Denoting an odorless, colorless acid, $C_5H_8O_3$, extracted from the nucleic acid of the thymus gland and also obtained synthetically by heating levulose and certain other sugars with concentrated hydrochloric acid.

lev·u·lose (lev′yə·lōs) *n.* Fructose. [<L *laevus* left + -UL(E) + -OSE²]

lev·y¹ (lev′ē) *v.* **lev·ied, lev·y·ing** *v.t.* **1** To impose and collect by authority or force, as a tax, fine, etc. **2** To enlist or call up (troops, etc.) for military service. **3** To prepare for, begin, or wage (war). —*v.i.* **4** To make a levy. **5** *Law* To seize property by judicial writ in order to fulfil a judgment: usually with *on.* —*n. pl.* **lev·ies 1** The act of exacting or collecting by compulsion. **2** That which is levied, as money or troops. [<OF *levée,* pp. fem. of *lever* raise <L *levare*] —**lev′i·er** *n.*

lev·y² (lev′ē) *n. pl.* **lev·ies** The Spanish real, equal to 12 1/2 cents: once current in the United States as *elevenpence.* [Short for ELEVENPENCE]

levy in mass A levy of all men capable of military service and within the control of the power making the levy.

lev·y·ist (lev′ē·ist) *n.* One who advocates a levy on capital.

lewd (lōōd) *adj.* **1** Characterized by lust; lustful; carnal; licentious. **2** Morally depraved; vicious; wicked. **3** *Obs.* Low; unlearned. See synonyms under IMMODEST. [OE *lǣwede* lay, unlearned, ? fusion of *L laicus* LAY² and OE *lǣwan* betray] —**lewd′ly** *adv.* —**lewd′ness** *n.*

Lew·es (lōō′is) The county town of East Sussex; scene of Simon de Montfort's victory over Henry III, 1264.

Lew·es (lōō′is), **George Henry,** 1817–78, English philosopher and critic.

Lew·es River (lōō′is) The upper course of the Yukon River in southern Yukon, Canada, flowing 338 miles north.

lew·is (lōō′is) *n.* A dovetailed tenon made in several parts and inserted into a corresponding mortise in a heavy stone, for the purpose of attaching a hoisting gear. Also **lew′is·son** (-ən). [? <LEWIS, proper name]

Lew·is (lōō′is) See LOUIS.

Lew·is (lo͞o′is), **Cecil Day,** 1904–1972, English poet. — **G(ilbert) N(ewton),** 1875–1946, U.S. chemist. — **John L(lewellyn),** 1880–1969, U.S. labor leader. — **Matthew Gregory,** 1775–1818, English novelist and dramatist: known as *Monk Lewis.* — **Meriwether,** 1774–1809, U.S. explorer. See CLARK, WILLIAM. —**(Percy) Wyndham,** 1884–1957, British painter and writer. — **Sinclair,** 1885–1951, U.S. novelist.

Lewis gun A small automatic machine-gun. [after Col. Isaac N. *Lewis,* 1858–1931, U.S. inventor]

lew·is·ite (lo͞o′is·īt) *n. Chem.* An oily, colorless to light-amber liquid, $C_2H_2Cl_3As$, having a faint odor of geraniums. Used in chemical warfare it combines the vesicant effects of mustard gas with the toxic action of arsenic. Also called *chlorvinylchlorarsine.* [after W. L. *Lewis,* 1878–1943, U.S. chemist]

Lew·i·sohn (lo͞o′ə·sən), **Adolph,** 1849–1938, U.S. philanthropist born in Germany. — **Ludwig,** 1883–1955, U.S. novelist and critic.

Lew·is·ton (lo͞o′is·tən) A city on the Androscoggin River in SW Maine.

Lew·is–with–Har·ris (lo͞o′is·with·har′is) An island, the largest and northernmost of the Outer Hebrides, Scotland; 825 square miles.

lex (leks) *n. pl.* **le·ges** (lē′jēz) Law: used in numerous Latin phrases. [<L]

lex·i·cal (lek′si·kəl) *adj.* **1** *Ling.* Relating to the meaning of the words of a language, as distinguished from their syntactical function. **2** Pertaining to a lexicon or to lexicography. [<Gk. *lexikos* pertaining to words <*lexikon* LEXICON]

lex·i·cog·ra·phy (lek′sə·kog′rə·fē) *n.* The art or process of compiling lexicons or dictionaries. [<NL *lexicografia* <Gk. *lexikographos* one who writes a lexicon <*lexikon* lexicon + *graphein* write] — **lex′i·cog′ra·pher** *n.* — **lex′i·co·graph′ic** (-kō·graf′ik) or **·i·cal** *adj.*

lex·i·con (lek′sə·kon) *n.* **1** An alphabetically arranged book setting forth the meanings and etymology of the words of a language; a dictionary: specifically applied to dictionaries of Latin, Greek, or Hebrew. **2** All the morphemes in any language. [<Gk. *lexikon,* neut. of *lexikos* pertaining to words <*lexis* way of speaking <*legein* say, speak]

Lex·ing·ton (lek′sing·tən) **1** A city in NE central Kentucky. **2** A town in eastern Massachusetts; scene of the first battle of the Revolutionary War, April 19, 1775.

lex lo·ci (leks′ lō′sī) *Latin* The law of the place.

lex non scrip·ta (leks′ non skrip′tə) *Latin* Unwritten law; the common law.

lex scrip·ta (leks′ skrip′tə) *Latin* The written or statute law.

lex ta·li·o·nis (leks′ tal′ē·ō′nis) *Latin* The law of retaliation.

Ley·den (lī′dən) A city in SW Netherlands: also *Leiden.*

Leyden jar *Electr.* A condenser for static electricity, consisting of a glass jar coated inside and out with tinfoil nearly to the top. Also **Leyden vial.** [from *Leyden,* where it was invented]

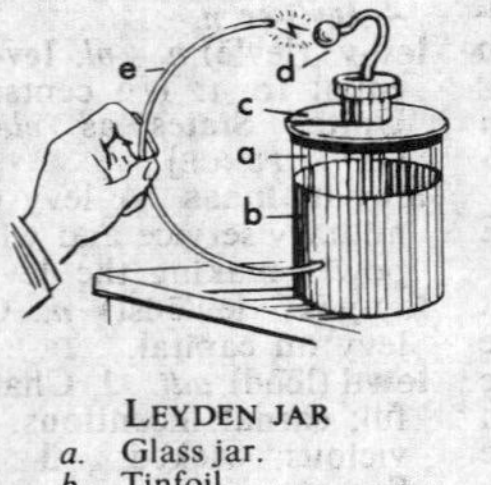

LEYDEN JAR
a. Glass jar.
b. Tinfoil.
c. Ebonite stopper.
d. Brass rod and ball.
e. Discharging wire.

Ley·te (lā′tā) An island in the Visayan Islands, Philippines; 2,785 square miles.

Leyte Gulf An inlet of the Pacific in the eastern Philippines between Leyte and Samar; scene of a United States naval victory over Japanese forces in World War II, October, 1944.

Ley·ton (lāt′n) A municipal borough in SW Essex county, England.

Lez·ghi·an (lez′gē·ən) See LESGHIAN.

Lha·sa (lä′sä) The capital of Tibet, near the southern border; seat of the Dalai Lama: Chinese *Lasa.* Also **Lhas′sa.**

Lhasa ap·so (äp′sō) A small, long-haired, ancient breed of dog, native to Tibet, used as watchdogs in lamaseries: also called *Tibetan lion dog.* [<LHASA + Tibetan *abso seng kye* bark lion sentinel dog]

Lhé·vinne (lā·vēn′), **Josef,** 1874–1944, Russian pianist.

li (lē) *n.* A Chinese unit of length, approximately one-third of a mile. [<Chinese *li*]

li·a·bil·i·ty (lī′ə·bil′ə·tē) *n. pl.* **·ties** **1** The state of being liable, or exposed to some accidental or incidental result or occurrence: *liability* to disease. **2** The condition of being responsible for a possible or actual loss, penalty, evil, expense, or burden: *liability* for damages. **3** That for which one is liable; in the plural, debts as opposed to *assets.*

li·a·ble (lī′ə·bəl) *adj.* **1** Exposed, as to damage, penalty, expense, burden, etc.: with *to.* **2** Justly or legally responsible. **3** Having a tendency, inclination, or likelihood; likely: with unfavorable sense. See synonyms under APT, LIKELY. [<F *lier* <L *ligare* bind]

li·aise (lē·āz′) *v.i.* **·aised, ·ais·ing** *Chiefly Brit. Colloq.* To act as an agent or intermediary; communicate. [Back formation <LIAISON]

li·ai·son (lē′ā·zon′, lē·ā′zon, lē′ə·zon; *Fr.* lē·ā·zôṅ′) *n.* **1** An illicit intimacy between two persons of opposite sex; intrigue. **2** A bond or union: a *liaison* of the intellect. **3** In cookery, a thickening used in sauces, soups, etc., as yolks of eggs beaten with cream. **4** In speaking or reading French, the carrying over in pronunciation of a final consonant to a succeeding word beginning with a vowel or silent *h,* as in *Est-il un homme?* Applied also to such sound-unions in certain other languages. **5** Unity of action, as between distant fighting forces or between an executive officer and his subordinates, maintained by various forms of contact and communication. —*adj.* Pertaining to one who or that which serves to maintain unity of action, as between an executive officer and his subordinates, or between parts of an army, etc.: a *liaison* officer. [<F <L *ligatio* <*ligare* bind]

Liá·kou·ra (lyä′ko͞o·rä) The former name for PARNASSUS.

li·an·a (lē·an′ə, -ä′nə) *n.* A twining or climbing plant of tropical forests, with ropelike, woody stems. Also **li·ane** (lē·än′). [<F *liane,* earlier *viorne* <L *viburnum* viburnum; infl. in F by *lier* bind <L *ligare*]

Liao (lyou) A river flowing 900 miles south through southern Manchuria to the Gulf of Liaotung. *Chinese* **Liao Ho.**

Liao·ning (lyou′ning′) Formerly, the southernmost of the three original provinces of Manchuria; divided, 1934, 1949: formerly *Shengking.*

Liao·noing (lyou′noing′) A province of southern Manchuria, NE China; 65,000 square miles; capital, Shenyang.

Liao·si (lyou′shē′) A former province of SW Manchuria, NE China; 21.676 square miles; capital, Chinchow.

Liao·tung (lyou′do͝ong′) A former province of southern Manchuria, NE China; 39,758 square miles; capital, Antung; extending south as **Liaotung Peninsula,** dividing the northern Yellow Sea into the Bay of Chosen and the **Gulf of Liaotung.** See KWANTUNG.

Liao·yang (lyou′yäng′) A city in western Liaonoing province, NE China.

li·ar (lī′ər) *n.* One who intentionally utters falsehood, or is given to lying. [OE *leogere*]

Li·ard (lē′ärd) A river of SE Yukon Territory, NE British Columbia, and SW Northwest Territories, Canada, flowing about 550 miles north to the Mackenzie River.

Li·as (lī′əs) *n. Geol.* The lowest of the rock series comprised in the Jurassic system of Europe. [<F *liais,* kind of limestone; ult. origin unknown] — **Li·as·sic** (lī·as′ik) *adj.* & *n.*

lib (lib) *n. Slang* Liberation (def. 2). — **lib′ber** *n.*

li·ba·tion (lī·bā′shən) *n.* **1** Liquid poured out, as in honor of a deity; also, the act of so pouring liquid. **2** Humorously, a drinking; potation. [<F <L *libatio, -onis* <*libare* pour out (as an offering)]

Li·bau (lē′bou) The German name for LIEPAJA. *Russian* **Li·ba·va** (lē·bä′və).

Lib·by (lib′ē) Diminutive of ELIZABETH.

li·bec·cio (lē·bet′chō) *n.* A Mediterranean wind blowing from the southwest. Also *Obs.* **li·bec′chio** (-bek′yō). [<Ital. <L *Libs, Libis* <Gk. *Lips, Libos* southwest wind]

li·bel (lī′bəl) *n.* **1** Anything tending to degrade or asperse character or reputation. **2** *Law* Slander written and published; the act or crime of publishing it; also, a false publication damaging to property or business. **3** *Law* The written allegation of the plaintiff in a suit before a court of admiralty or an ecclesiastical court. **4** Any publicly circulated slanderous document. —*v.t.* **·beled** or **·belled, ·bel·ing** or **·bel·ling** **1** To publish a libel concerning; defame. **2** In admiralty law, to bring suit against, as a ship or cargo. See synonyms under ASPERSE. [<OF <L *libellus,* dim. of *liber* book] — **li′bel·er** or **li′bel·ler, li′bel·ist** or **li′bel·list** *n.*

li·bel·ant (lī′bəl·ənt) *n.* One who institutes a libel or suit in admiralty. Also **li′bel·lant.** [<F *libellant,* ppr. of *libeller* institute a suit]

li·bel·ee (lī′bəl·ē′) *n.* The party against whom a suit in admiralty is filed. Also **li′bel·lee′.**

li·bel·lu·la (lī·bel′yo͞o·lə) *n.* Any of a genus (*Libellula*) of typical dragonflies. [<NL <L *libellulus,* reduplicated dim. of *liber* book; from its resemblance to a book when in flight]

li·bel·ous (lī′bəl·əs) *adj.* Containing that which defames or libels; defamatory; slanderous. Also **li′bel·lous.**

li·ber (lī′bər) *n. pl.* **li·bri** (lī′brī) **1** A book, as a volume of public records of deeds, mortgages, etc. **2** *Bot.* The bast or inner bark of exogenous plants. [<L, book, inner bark (which was once used to write upon)]

lib·er·al (lib′ər·əl, lib′rəl) *adj.* **1** Possessing or manifesting a free and generous heart; bountiful. **2** Appropriate or fitting for a broad and enlightened mind: a *liberal* education; *liberal* arts. **3** Free from narrowness, bigotry, or bondage to authority or creed, as in religion; inclined to democratic or republican ideas, as opposed to monarchical or aristocratic, as in politics; broad; popular; progressive. **4** Bestowed without stint; abundant. **5** Not restricted to the literal meaning: a *liberal* construction. **6** Free by or from birth; hence, of high character; refined; independent. **7** *Obs.* Unduly free; licentious. See synonyms under AMPLE, CHARITABLE, GENEROUS. —*n.* Any person who advocates liberty of thought, speech, or action; one who is opposed to conservatism: distinguished from *radical.* Also **lib′er·al·ist.** [<OF <L *liberalis* pertaining to a freeman <*liber* free] — **lib′er·al·is′tic** *adj.* — **lib′er·al·ly** *adj.*

Lib·er·al (lib′ər·əl, lib′rəl) *n.* A member of the Liberal Party in Great Britain, Canada, or Australia.

liberal arts See under ART[1].

lib·er·al·ism (lib′ər·əl·iz′əm) *n.* **1** An attitude toward social, economic, political, and ecclesiastical policies, favoring gradual reform and ordered change rather than reaction or revolution and opposed equally to arbitrary censorship and undue license in dealing with ideas. **2** A doctrine often equated with laissez-faire economics, holding to free trade and to minimum interference by the state with economic activities: contrasted to SOCIALISM, SYNDICALISM, and COMMUNISM. **3** In political theory, adherence to policies of gradual reform through parliamentary procedure, the upholding of civil liberties as central in a free society, and a belief in the doctrine of progress: opposed to *conservatism.* **4** *Eccl.* **a** In 19th century Roman Catholic church polity, a movement opposed to ultramontanism, and favoring the formulation of doctrines and practices governing the relation of theology to social ethics; opposing promulgation of the infallibility doctrine with broad participation by laity, clergy, and prelacy in formulating the social and economic policies of the state. **b** In Protestant church bodies, an attitude favoring the use of the methods of historical criticism on the Bible, wide leeway for individual interpretation of creeds, doctrines, and ritual, and latitude as to methods of church government and congregational organization: opposed to *fundamentalism.* **5** Loosely, general opposition to conservatism and reaction in any field.

lib·er·al·i·ty (lib′ə·ral′ə·tē) *n. pl.* **·ties** **1** The quality of being liberal or generous. **2** A gift; donation. See synonyms under BENEVOLENCE.

lib·er·al·ize (lib′ər·əl·īz′) *v.t.* & *v.i.* **·ized, ·iz·ing** To make or become liberal. —**lib′er·al·i·za′tion** (lib′ər·əl·ə·zā′shən, -ī·zā′, lib′rəl-) *n.* — **lib′er·al·iz′er** *n.*

Liberal Party **1** In Great Britain, the political party formed by the coalition of Whigs and Radicals about 1832 and opposed to the Conservative Party. Since 1918 its power

declined with the rise of the Labour Party. 2 One of the principal political parties of Canada. 3 One of the principal political parties of Australia.

lib·er·ate (lib′ə·rāt) *v.t.* **·at·ed, ·at·ing 1** To set free; release from bondage. 2 To release from chemical combination. 3 *Colloq.* To free from oppression or from conventions considered oppressive. [<L *liberatus*, pp. of *liberare* free <*liber* free] —**lib′er·a′tor** *n.*

lib·er·a·tion (lib′ər·ā′shən) *n.* 1 The act of liberating, or the state of being liberated. 2 A political and social movement formed to promote the interests of a group regarded as the object of unfair discrimination or bias: women's *liberation.* —**lib′·er·a′tion·ist** *n.*

Li·be·rec (lē′be·rets) A city in northern Bohemia, Czechoslovakia: German *Reichenberg.*

Li·be·ri·a (lī·bir′ē·ə) A republic on the west coast of Africa; 43,000 square miles; capital, Monrovia. —**Li·be′ri·an** *adj.* & *n.*

lib·er·tar·i·an (lib′ər·târ′ē·ən) *n.* 1 One who believes in the freedom of the will. 2 One who maintains the principles and doctrines of liberty, particularly in thought and conduct. 3 An adherent of libertarianism. —*adj.* Of or pertaining to the doctrine of the libertarians.

lib·er·tar·i·an·ism (lib′ər·târ′ē·ən·iz′əm) *n.* A theory of government which holds that the state is subordinate to the individual. It may range from anarchism to democracy.

lib·er·tine (lib′ər·tēn) *n.* 1 One who does not restrain his desires or appetites; a debauchee. 2 In ancient Rome, a manumitted slave, a freedman, or the child of such a person. —*adj.* 1 Dissolute; licentious. 2 Freed from slavery; manumitted. [<L *libertinus* <*libertus* freedman <*liber* free]

lib·er·tin·ism (lib′ər·tēn·iz′əm) *n.* 1 Unrestrained indulgence in licentious practices. 2 An extreme exercise of freedom in thought or opinion, especially on religious subjects. Also **lib′er·tin·age** (-ij).

lib·er·ty (lib′ər·tē) *n. pl.* **·ties 1** The state of being exempt from the domination of others or from restricting circumstances; freedom. 2 A special exemption; franchise; privilege; in the U.S. Navy, permission to be absent from one's ship or station for a short period. 3 Unusual or undue freedom or familiarity. 4 The possession and exercise of the right of self-government. 5 The power of voluntary choice; freedom from necessity. 6 A place or district within which certain immunities or privileges are enjoyed; specifically, in England, a district within a county, exempt from the jurisdiction of the sheriff. —**at liberty** Free; unconfined; having permission (to do something). —**civil liberty** Freedom of the individual citizen from government control, restraint of, or interference with, his property, opinions, or affairs, except as the public good may require. —**individual liberty** Freedom from restraint in the performance of rights outside of government control. —**political liberty** The right to participate in the election of rulers and the making and administration of laws. [<F *liberté* <L *libertas, -tatis* <*liber* free]

Synonyms: emancipation, freedom, independence, license. In general terms, it may be said that *freedom* is absolute, *liberty* relative; *freedom* is the absence of restraint, *liberty* is the removal or avoidance of restraint. The two words are constantly interchanged; the slave is set at *liberty*, or gains his *freedom*. *Independence* is said of states or nations, *freedom* and *liberty* of individuals. *Liberty* keeps strictly to the thought of being clear from restraint or compulsion; *freedom* takes a wider range, applying to other oppressive influences; we speak of *freedom* from annoyance or intrusion. *License* is a permission or privilege granted by adequate authority, a bounded *liberty*; in the wider sense, *license* is an ignoring and defiance of all that should restrain. See PERMISSION, RIGHT. *Antonyms*: captivity, compulsion, constraint, imprisonment, necessity, obligation, oppression, serfdom, servitude, slavery, superstition.

Liberty Bell The bell in Independence Hall, Philadelphia, rung July 4, 1776, when the Declaration of Independence was adopted; cracked 1835.

liberty cap A close-fitting, soft cap, with elongated crown, usually folded over: originally worn by freedmen in ancient Rome, and adopted as a symbol of liberty in the French Revolution: also called *Phrygian cap.*

Liberty Island A small island off the southern tip of Manhattan, New York; site of the Statue of Liberty: formerly *Bedloe's Island.*

Liberty Ship A U.S. merchant ship of about 10,000 tons displacement: designed for rapid manufacture and built in large numbers during World War II.

Lib·i·a (lib′ē·ə) See LIBYA.

li·bid·i·nous (li·bid′ə·nəs) *adj.* Lustful; lewd. [<F *libidineux* <L *libidinosus* <*libido, -inis* lust <*libet, lubet* it pleases] —**li·bid′i·nous·ly** *adv.* —**li·bid′i·nous·ness** *n.*

li·bi·do (li·bī′dō, -bē′-) *n. Psychoanal.* 1 The instinctual craving or drive behind all human activities, the repression of which leads to psychoneuroses. 2 Psychic energy, especially that associated with sexual instinct. [<L, lust] —**li·bid′i·nal** (-bid′ə·nəl) *adj.*

li·bra (lī′brə *for def. 1,* lē′brä *for defs. 2 and 3*) *n.* 1 The Roman pound, equivalent to 327 grams. 2 The Spanish and Portuguese pound of sixteen ounces. 3 A gold coin of Peru, equal to ten soles. [<L, pound]

Li·bra (lī′brə) 1 The Balance, the seventh sign of the zodiac which the sun enters about Sept. 21. 2 *Astron.* A zodiacal constellation. See CONSTELLATION. [<L, a balance]

li·brar·i·an (lī·brâr′ē·ən) *n.* 1 A person in charge of a library. 2 A person qualified by training for library service. —**li·brar′i·an·ship′** *n.*

li·brar·y (lī′brer·ē, -brə·rē) *n. pl.* **·brar·ies 1** A collection of books, pamphlets, etc., kept for reading and consultation; especially, such a collection arranged to facilitate reference, as by classification and indexing. 2 A building, an apartment, or a series of apartments containing such a collection: the *Library* of Congress. 3 A series of books having some characteristic in common issued by the same publisher. 4 A collection of books for recreation or study belonging to a private individual: a doctor's *library.* 5 A commercial establishment for selling or hiring out books. —**circulating library** A library from which books can be taken away under certain restrictions: also **lending library**: distinguished from a **reference library**, where books may be consulted but not carried away. [<OF *librarie* <L *librarium* <*liber, libri* book]

Library of Congress The national library of the United States in Washington, D.C.; established 1800.

li·brate (lī′brāt) *v.i.* **li·brat·ed, li·brat·ing 1** To move back and forth, as a balance before coming to rest; oscillate. 2 To be poised; hover. [<L *libratus*, ppr. of *librare* balance <*libra* balance] —**li′bra·to′ry** (-brə·tôr′ē, -tō′rē) *adj.*

li·bra·tion (lī·brā′shən) *n.* 1 The act of balancing or librating; balance; equipoise. 2 *Astron.* An apparent slow swinging motion of a body on each side of its mean position, as in the *libration* of the moon.

li·bret·tist (li·bret′ist) *n.* A writer of librettos.

li·bret·to (li·bret′ō) *n. pl.* **·tos** or **·ti** (-ē) A book containing the words of an opera, or the words themselves. [<Ital., little book, dim. of *libro* <L *liber*]

Li·bre·ville (lē′brə·vēl) A port on the west coast of equatorial Africa, capital of Gabon Republic.

li·bri·form (lī′brə·fôrm) *adj. Bot.* Having the form of liber or bast. [<L *liber, libri* liber (def. 2) + -FORM]

Lib·y·a (lib′ē·ə) 1 The ancient Greek and Roman name for all of North Africa except Egypt. 2 A constitutional monarchy (1951) in North Africa on the Mediterranean; formerly an Italian colony; 679,358 square miles; capitals, Tripoli and Bengasi. *Italian* **Lib′i·a.**

Lib·y·an (lib′ē·ən) *adj.* Pertaining to Libya, its inhabitants, or their language. —*n.* 1 A native or inhabitant of Libya. 2 The extinct Hamitic language spoken in ancient Libya, including the Numidian and Mauretanian dialects.

Libyan Desert A part of the Sahara Desert extending through eastern Libya, western Egypt, and NW Sudan.

Lib·y·co-Ber·ber (lib′i·kō·bûr′bər) *n.* A branch of the Hamitic subfamily of the Hamito-Semitic language family, consisting of ancient Libyan and the modern Berber dialects.

lice (līs) Plural of LOUSE.

li·cense (lī′səns) *n.* 1 Authority or liberty granted to do or omit an act; specifically, in law, a permission, as for manufacturing a patented article or for the sale of intoxicants. 2 A written or printed certificate of a legal permit. 3 Unrestrained liberty of action; abuse of privilege; disregard of propriety. 4 Allowable deviation from established rule; variation from a standard for a purpose: poetic *license.* See synonyms under LIBERTY, PERMISSION, RIGHT. —*v.t.* **·censed, ·cens·ing** To grant a license to or for; give permission to; authorize. See synonyms under PERMIT. Also **li′cence.** [<OF *licence* <L *licentia* <*licens, licentis*, ppr. of *licere* be permitted] —**li′cens·a·ble** *adj.* —**li′cens·er** or **li′cenc·er** or *Law* **li′cen·sor** *n.*

li·cen·see (lī′sən·sē′) *n.* One to whom a license is granted. Also **li′cen·cee′.**

li·cen·ti·ate (lī·sen′shē·it, -āt) *n.* 1 A person licensed, as by a university, to practice a certain profession: a *licentiate* in dental surgery. 2 In some Continental universities, a person holding a degree intermediate between bachelor and doctor. [<Med. L *licentiatus*, pp. of *licentiare* allow, license <L *licentia* LICENSE]

li·cen·tious (lī·sen′shəs) *adj.* 1 Exceeding the limits of propriety; wanton; lewd. 2 Careless of rule and accuracy, especially in literary matters. [<F *licentieux* <L *licentiosus*] —**li·cen′tious·ly** *adv.* —**li·cen′tious·ness** *n.*

li·chee (lē′chē) See LITCHI.

li·chen (lī′kən) *n.* 1 A flowerless plant (class or group *Lichenes*) commonly growing flat upon a surface, as of a rock, and composed of loose cellular tissue, a slender white-celled epiphytic ascomycetous or (rarely) basidiomycetous fungus, and a number of globular greenish or bluish algal cells upon which the fungal cells prey. 2 *Pathol.* Any of several papular skin diseases. —*v.t.* To cover with lichens. [<L <Gk. *leichēn*, prob. <*leichein* lick] —**li′chen·a′ceous** (-ā′shəs), **li′chen·ous, li′chen·ose** (-ōs) *adj.*

li·chen·in (lī′kən·in) *n. Biochem.* A white gelatinous carbohydrate, $C_6H_{10}O_5$, obtained from Iceland moss; moss starch. [<LICHEN + -IN]

li·chen·ol·o·gy (lī′kən·ol′ə·jē) *n.* The science or study of lichens. —**li′chen·ol′o·gist** *n.*

Lich·field (lich′fēld) A city in SE Staffordshire, England; birthplace of Samuel Johnson.

lich·gate (lich′gāt′) *n.* A churchyard gate covered with a roof under which a bier may stand. [OE *līc* corpse + GATE]

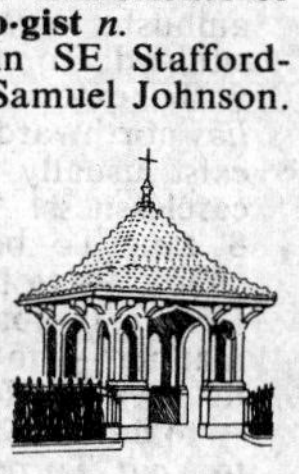

LICHGATE
Little Church Around the Corner, New York.

licht (likht) *n., adj., v.t.* & *v.i. Scot.* Light (in all senses).

lic·it (lis′it) *adj.* Lawful. [<L *licitus* <*licere* be allowed] —**lic′it·ly** *adv.*

lick (lik) *v.t.* 1 To pass the tongue over the surface of. 2 To bring to a specified state or condition by passing the tongue over: to *lick* a surface clean. 3 To take in by the tongue; lap up. 4 To move or pass lightly over or about: The waves *licked* the base of the cliff. 5 *Colloq.* **a** To defeat; overcome. **b** To thrash; beat. —*v.i.* 6 To move quickly or lightly: The flame *licked* up in the grate. —**to lick into shape** *Colloq.* To put in proper form or condition. —**to lick one's chops** To show pleased anticipation. —**to lick up** To consume or devour entirely. —*n.* 1 A stroke of the tongue in licking. 2 The application of something, as if by a stroke of the tongue, or something so applied: a *lick* of paint. 3 As much as can be taken up by the tongue at one stroke or lap. 4 A deposit of salt frequented by animals that lick it. 5 A camping place along a trail near a pond, pool, or creek. 6 *Colloq.* A stroke, blow, or whack: a *lick*

on the ear; also, in the plural, in baseball, an inning at bat. 7 *Slang* A spurt of speed or energy; exertion. [OE *liccian* lick]

lick·er·ish (lik′ə·rish) *adj.* 1 *Archaic* Tempting or enticing the appetite. 2 Eager to taste or enjoy. 3 Lustful. Also spelled *liquorish.* [Var. of LECHEROUS] —**lick′er·ish·ly** *adv.* —**lick′er·ish·ness** *n.*

lick·e·ty-split (lik′ə·tē·split′) *adv. Slang* At full speed. Also **lick′e·ty-cut′** (-kut′).

lick·ing (lik′ing) *n.* 1 A lapping with the tongue. 2 *Colloq.* A whipping; castigation; also, a defeat.

Lick·ing River (lik′ing) A river in eastern Kentucky, flowing 320 miles NW to the Ohio River.

lick·spit·tle (lik′spit′l) *n.* A servile flatterer.

lic·o·rice (lik′ə·ris, -rish) *n.* 1 A perennial leguminous herb *(Glycyrrhiza glabra)* of southern and central Europe. 2 Its root, used in medicine and confection. 3 The inspissated juice of the root. Also spelled *liquorice.* [<AF *licorys,* OF *licoresse* <LL *liquiritia,* alter. of Gk. *glycyrrhiza* < *glykys* sweet + *rhiza* root]

lic·tor (lik′tər) *n.* One of the officers or guards attending the chief Roman magistrates: they bore the fasces as a symbol of office. [<L, prob. < *ligare* tie]

ROMAN LICTOR

lid (lid) *n.* 1 A cover closing an aperture, as of a receptacle, movable to afford access to the inside. 2 An eyelid. 3 *Bot.* A top, as that of a pyxis or the capsule of a moss, which separates by a transverse dividing line; an operculum. 4 *Slang* A hat. [OE *hlid*] —**lid′ded** *adj.*

Lid·dell Hart (lid′əl härt′), **Basil Henry,** born 1895, English military authority.

Li·di·a (lē′dē·ä) Italian form of LYDIA.

Li·di·ce (lē′di·tse) A village in west central Bohemia, Czechoslovakia, destroyed 1942 by the Germans in World War II.

lid·less (lid′lis) *adj.* 1 Having no lid, as a pot or kettle. 2 Without eyelids; hence, watchful; sleepless.

Li·do (lē′dō) An Italian island on the Adriatic, separating the Lagoon of Venice from the Gulf of Venice; fashionable bathing resort.

lie[1] (lī) *v.i.* **lay, lain, ly·ing** 1 To rest or place oneself prone or at full length, as on a bed: often with *down*: He is *lying* down. 2 To be on or rest against a surface: The sign is *lying* next to the wall. 3 To be or continue in or as in a specified condition or position: to *lie* in ambush: to *lie* at a disadvantage. 4 To be situated: Rome *lies* in a plain of central Italy. 5 To extend in some direction: Our route *lies* northward. 6 To have source or cause; exist: usually with *in*: His trouble *lies* in his carelessness. 7 To be buried, as in a tomb. 8 *Law* To be maintainable, as a criminal charge. —**to lie** (or **lay**) **down on the job** *U.S. Colloq.* To loaf; do something in a desultory manner. —**to lie in** To be in childbed. —**to lie in wait (for)** To wait in ambush (for). —**to lie low** *Slang* To go into hiding. —**to lie to** *Naut.* To remain nearly stationary with the bow as near the wind as possible. —**to lie with** *Archaic* To have sexual intercourse with. —*n.* 1 The position or arrangement in which a thing lies; manner of lying; lay. 2 The lair of an animal. [OE *licgan*]

lie[2] (lī) *n.* 1 An untruth; falsehood. 2 Anything that deceives or creates a false impression. 3 An accusation of lying: to give him the *lie.* —**white lie** An untruth uttered or implied in deference to conventionality, expediency, or courtesy; a fib. —**to give the lie to** 1 To accuse of lying. 2 To expose as false; belie. —*v.* **lied, ly·ing** *v.i.* 1 To make untrue statements knowingly, especially with intent to deceive. 2 To give an erroneous or misleading impression: Figures do not *lie.* —*v.t.* 3 To bring or obtain by lying: He *lied* his way out of trouble. [OE *lyge*]

Synonyms (noun): deceit, deception, fabrication, falsehood, untruth. A *lie* is the uttering of what one knows to be false with intent to deceive. The novel or drama is not a *lie,* because not meant to deceive; the ancient teaching that the earth was flat was not a *lie,* because not then known to be false. *Untruth* is more than lack of accuracy, implying always lack of veracity; but it is a somewhat milder and more dignified word than *lie.* See DECEPTION, FRAUD. *Antonyms*: fact, truth, veracity.

Lie (lē), **Jonas Lauritz,** 1833–1908, Norwegian novelist. —**Jonas,** 1880–1940, U. S. painter, born in Norway. —**Trygve,** 1896–1968, Norwegian statesman; first secretary general of the United Nations.

Lie·big (lē′bikh), **Baron Justus von,** 1803–73, German chemist; founded agricultural chemistry.

Lieb·knecht (lēp′knekht), **Karl,** 1871–1919, German journalist and socialist leader; shot by the monarchists.

Liech·ten·stein (lik′tən·stīn, *Ger.* lēkh′tən·shtīn) A sovereign principality of central Europe between Switzerland and Austria; 62 square miles; capital, Vaduz.

Lied (lēd, *Ger.* lēt) *n. pl.* **Lied·er** (lē′dər) *German* A reflective lyric poem or ballad set to music, expressing a single sentiment or emotion in a series of stanzas.

Lie·der·kranz (lē′dər·kränts) *n.* 1 A singing society. 2 A group of songs. 3 A soft cheese with a strong flavor and odor: a trade name. [<G, lit., garland of songs]

lie detector A psychogalvanometer or similar instrument whose records are assumed to indicate the guilt or innocence of the person under questioning to whom it is applied.

lief (lēf) *adv.* Willingly; freely; as willingly as not: I had as *lief* stay as go: often used to imply preference: as *lief* die as live dishonored. —*adj. Archaic* 1 Dear; dearly loved; pleasing. 2 Willing; glad. ◆ Homophone: *leaf.* [OE *lēof* dear]

lief·er (lē′fər) *adv.* More gladly or willingly; rather.

liege (lēj) *adj.* 1 Bound in vassalage to a lord. 2 Having the right to the service and allegiance of a vassal; sovereign; supreme. 3 Faithful; loyal. —*n.* 1 A vassal; also, a citizen. 2 A liege lord; a feudal sovereign or superior. [<OF <Med. L *ligius* free < *laeticus* free < *letus* freedman <OHG *ledig* free]

Liége (lyezh) A city in eastern Belgium. *Flemish* **Luik** (loik).

liege·man (lēj′mən) *n. pl.* **·men** (-mən) A feudal vassal; a loyal servitor.

Lieg·nitz (lēg′nits) A city in SW Poland, formerly in Lower Silesia, Germany. *Polish* **Leg·ni·ca** (leg·nē′tsä).

lien (lēn, lē′ən) *n.* A legal claim on property, as security for a debt. ◆ Homophone: *lean.* [<F, band <L *ligamen* < *ligare* tie]

li·e·nal (lī·ē′nəl) *adj.* Of or pertaining to the spleen. [<L *lien* spleen]

li·en·ter·y (lī′ən·ter′ē) *n. Pathol.* Diarrhea characterized by the discharge of undigested food. [<Med. L *lienteria* <Gk. *leienteria* < *leios* smooth + *enteron* intestine] —**li′en·ter′ic** *adj.*

Lie·pa·ja (lye′pä·yä) The second largest city of Latvia: German *Libau*: also *Lepaya.*

li·erne (lē·ûrn′) *n. Archit.* A crossrib or a branch rib in Gothic vaulting. [<F]

lieu (lōō) *n.* Place; stead: in the phrase *in lieu of.* [<F <L *locus.* Doublet of LOCUS.]

lieu·ten·ant (lōō·ten′ənt, *Brit. Army* lef·ten′·ənt) *n.* 1 An officer who fills the place of a superior in the latter's absence or acts for him under his direction; deputy. 2 In the U. S. Army, Air Force, and Marine Corps, a commissioned officer holding either of two ranks, **first** or **second lieutenant,** the former ranking next below a captain. 3 In the U. S. Navy and Coast Guard, a commissioned officer holding either of two ranks, **lieutenant** or **lieutenant (junior grade),** the former ranking next below a lieutenant commander and the latter next above an ensign. 4 A police officer next above a sergeant and below a captain. [<F *lieutenant* < *lieu* place + *tenant,* ppr. of *tenir* hold] —**lieu·ten′an·cy** *n.*

lieutenant colonel, lieutenant commander, lieutenant general See under COLONEL, etc.

lieutenant governor 1 An officer authorized to perform the duties of a governor during his absence or disability, or to take his place in case of death or resignation. 2 Occasionally, in the British Empire, a subordinate governor, who is acting governor of a territory under a governor general. —**lieu·ten′·ant-gov′er·nor·ship′** *n.*

life (līf) *n. pl.* **lives** (līvz) 1 That state in which animals and plants exist which distinguishes them from inorganic substances and from dead organisms: characterized by metabolism and growth, reproduction, and internally initiated adaptations to the environment. 2 That vital existence, the loss of which means death: to give one's *life.* 3 The period of animate existence from birth until death, or a part of it. 4 Any conscious and intelligent existence: the *life* here and hereafter. 5 Energy and animation; spirit; vivacity: to put *life* into an enterprise. 6 A source of liveliness, animation, etc.: to be the *life* of the party. 7 That which keeps something alive; the source or essence of existence. 8 A living being; a person: Many *lives* were lost. 9 Living things in the aggregate: plant *life.* 10 In art, a living figure or semblance: a picture drawn from *life.* 11 The course of active human existence; human affairs: daily *life* in the city. 12 A certain manner or way of living: the *life* of a recluse. 13 *Theol.* A state of spiritual attainment or awareness following conversion. 14 A biography. 15 The duration of efficiency or usefulness of anything: the *life* of a machine. —**for life** For the remainder of one's existence, until death: to hold office *for life.* —*adj.* 1 Of or pertaining to life or a life. 2 Lasting for a lifetime, or from a given point until death: a *life* sentence. 3 In art, studying from a living model: a *life* class. [OE *līf*]

Synonym: vitality. *Life* is the state of actual living; *vitality* is the power of living or the capacity of maintaining *life*; as, Reptiles have remarkable *vitality. Life* may also be used for the vital principle; as, the *life* of a seed. See WARMTH. *Antonyms*: death, decease, dissolution.

life belt *n.* A life preserver in the form of a belt.

life·blood (līf′blud′) *n.* 1 The blood necessary to life; vital blood. 2 Anything giving strength or energy or as indispensable as blood.

life·boat (līf′bōt′) *n.* A strong, buoyant boat used in abandoning ship, saving castaways, etc.

life·buoy (līf′boi′, -bōō′ē) *n.* A life preserver, usually in the shape of a ring: also *life ring.*

life class A class in which artists draw from living models.

life cycle The entire series of processes comprehended in the life of an organism from the ovum.

life expectancy The probable length of life of a person, varying according to age, sex, physical condition, occupation, and prevailing environmental factors. Compare LIFE SPAN.

life·ful (līf′fo͝ol) *adj.* Full of vitality; outgoing. —**life′ful·ly** *adv.* —**life′ful·ness** *n.*

life·guard (līf′gärd′) *n.* An expert swimmer hired by a bathing resort, pool, etc., to protect the safety of bathers.

Life Guards *Brit.* The two cavalry regiments serving to protect the lives of the British sovereigns.

life history *Biol.* The complete train of phenomena characterizing the existence and growth of an organism from its inception to its decease.

life insurance Insurance on the life of oneself or of another. Also **life assurance.** See under INSURANCE.

life jacket A life preserver in the form of a jacket.

life·less (līf′lis) *adj.* 1 Destitute of life, either naturally or by deprivation; dead; inanimate. 2 Wanting in energy, power, vigor, or spirit; torpid; dull. 3 Exhibiting none of the signs of life; apparently dead: She fell *lifeless* at his feet. 4 Uninhabited by men or animals. —**life′less·ly** *adv.* —**life′less·ness** *n.*

Synonyms: dead, deceased, defunct, dull, extinct, inanimate, inert, spiritless, torpid. *Dead* primarily applies to a once-living organism from which life has departed: this original meaning controls the derived senses; *inanimate* primarily applies to that which never had life. *Lifeless* may be used in either connection, and may be also used of that which exhibits none of the signs of life. The derived meanings of these words are many. A picture, a statue, a poem, an actor's rendering of his part may be spoken of as *lifeless*; we speak of a *dead* book, *dead* capital, a *dead* wall, and even of a *dead* (that is, a dull or nonresonant) sound. *Deceased* is in formal and approved use as a euphemism for *dead*; *defunct* is used to mean finished or *extinct* as

well as *dead*. *Extinct* implies cessation of vitality or force: an *extinct* volcano. See DEAD, FLAT. *Antonyms:* active, alive, animated, live, living, stirring, vigorous.

life·like (līf′līk′) *adj.* Resembling that which is living; true to life; realistic. — **life′like′·ness** *n.*

life line 1 A rope shot to a wrecked ship by which a heavier line for a breeches buoy may be rigged. **2** A line attached to a buoy, mast, etc., which may be clung to, as by bathers, sailors in stormy weather, etc. **3** A line for raising and lowering a diver. **4** Any route for transporting vital supplies. **5** In palmistry, a line about the base of the thumb which allegedly foretells facts of a person's life.

life·long (līf′lông′, -long′) *adj.* Lasting or continuing through life.

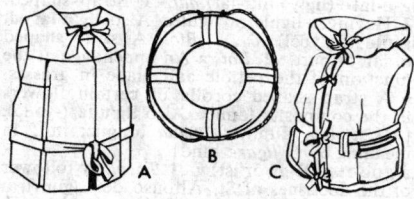

LIFE PRESERVERS
A. Solid block cork. *B.* Cork ring buoy.
C. Collar-type life jacket.

life peer *Brit.* A peer whose rank and title expire at his death.

life preserver 1 A buoyant device, often inflatable, in the form of a belt, jacket, ring, etc., used to keep a person afloat in water. **2** *Brit.* A loaded cane or other weapon for self-defense.

lif·er (lī′fər) *n. Slang* **1** One serving a prison sentence for life. **2** The life sentence.

life raft A raftlike structure for saving life in time of shipwreck; especially, a collapsible rubber boat equipped with oars and an apparatus permitting rapid inflation.

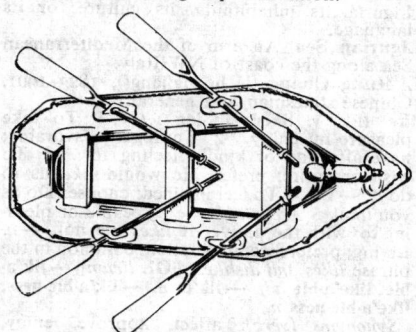

INFLATABLE LIFE RAFT
Capacity, 7 men; weight, 50 pounds.

life ring A lifebuoy.

Life–Sav·ing Service (līf′sā′ving) A former U.S. government service in charge of life–saving stations: since 1915 its activities have been performed by the U.S. Coast Guard.

life·sav·er (līf′sā′vər) *n.* **1** One who saves a life; especially, a trained person stationed at a bathing beach, or the like, to prevent loss of life by drowning. **2** A life preserver. — **life′–sav′ing** *n. & adj.*

life-saving station One of a system of U.S. Coast Guard stations or headquarters along the coasts and lakeshores, equipped to rescue shipwrecked or drowning persons.

life–size (līf′sīz′) *adj.* Of natural size; of the size of the object portrayed. Also **life′–sized′.**

life span The extreme length of life regarded as biologically possible in any plant or animal, or in the species to which it belongs. Compare LIFE EXPECTANCY.

life style Style (def. 6).

life table A statistical table arranged to show the number of people in a population who will survive to a given age and the probable life expectancy of a person at that or any other age: also called *mortality table.*

life·time (līf′tīm′) *n.* The whole period of a life. — *adj.* Lasting for the duration of a life: a *lifetime* job.

life·work (līf′wûrk′) *n.* The work of a lifetime; the work to which one is devoted.

Lif·fey (lif′ē) A river in eastern Ireland, flowing 50 miles through Dublin to Dublin Bay.

lift¹ (lift) *v.t.* **1** To raise from a lower to a higher position or place; hoist; elevate. **2** To hold up; support or display in the air. **3** To raise to a higher degree or condition; exalt. **4** To make clearly audible; shout: to *lift* a cry. **5** To subject (the face) to plastic surgery, usually so as to impart beauty or restore an appearance of youth: She had her face *lifted.* **6** *Colloq.* To take surreptitiously; steal; plagiarize. **7** *U.S.* To pay off, as a mortgage. **8** In golf, to pick up (the ball), as from an unfavorable position, and concede the prescribed penalty. — *v.i.* **9** To put forth effort in order to raise something: All together now, *lift!* **10** To rise; yield to upward pressure. **11** To rise or disperse; dissipate: The fog *lifted.* — *n.* **1** The act of lifting or raising. **2** The distance through which something rises or is raised. **3** The amount of weight lifted. **4** Exaltation or stimulation of the mind or feelings. **5** A rise in condition; promotion. **6** Elevated carriage or position: the *lift* of her chin. **7** Assistance by lifting or raising. **8** A ride in a vehicle offered to a pedestrian, taking him part or all of the way to his destination. **9** A machine, device, or the like that lifts or assists in lifting, as a hoisting machine. **10** *Brit.* An elevator in a building. **11** *Mining* **a** A set of pumps. **b** A vertical slice of ore removed in one series of operations. **c** The difference in height between one level and another. **12** In shoemaking, any layer of leather or other material forming the heel. **13** *Aeron.* The vertical component of the aerodynamic pressure upon an aircraft. **14** An elevation of ground. [< ON *lypta* raise in the air. Akin to LOFT.] — **lift′er** *n.*

lift² (lift) *n. Brit. Dial.* The sky.

lift·off (lift′ôf′, -of′) *n. Aerospace* The vertical ascent of a rocket or spacecraft from its launching pad.

lift pump A pump for lifting a liquid to its own level: distinguished from *force pump.*

lig·a·ment (lig′ə·mənt) *n.* **1** *Anat.* A band or sheet of firm, compact, fibrous tissue, closely binding related structures, as bones, etc., together; especially one connecting or investing the opposed surfaces of a joint. **2** A band or connecting tie; that which binds together. [< L *ligamentum* band < *ligare* bind] — **lig′a·men′tous, lig′a·men′tal, lig′a·men′ta·ry** *adj.*

li·gan (lī′gən) See LAGAN.

li·gate (lī′gāt) *v.t.* **·gat·ed, ·gat·ing** To bind with a ligature; bandage. [< L *ligatus,* pp. of *ligare* bind, tie]

li·ga·tion (lī·gā′shən) *n.* **1** The act of tying or binding up, especially an artery; also, the condition of being bound. **2** Something used in tying; bandage.

lig·a·ture (lig′ə·chər) *n.* **1** Anything that constricts, or serves for binding or tying. **2** *Surg.* A thread or wire tied around a blood vessel to arrest bleeding or used for removing a tumor. **3** A ligation; the act of binding. **4** *Printing* Two or more connected letters, as fi, ffi, œ; also, in writing, the character used to indicate the connection (‿). Compare DIGRAPH. **5** *Music* A slur; notes joined by a slur. — *v.t.* **·tured, ·tur·ing** To bind or compress with a ligature. [< F < L *ligatura* < *ligatus,* pp. of *ligare* bind]

li·geance (lī′jəns, lē′-) *n.* **1** *Law* The jurisdiction or territory of a sovereign. **2** *Obs.* Allegiance. [< OF *ligeance* < *lige* liege; infl. by L *ligare* bind]

light¹ (līt) *n.* **1** *Physics* **a** That form of radiant energy that stimulates the organs of sight, having wavelengths ranging from about 3900 to 7700 angstrom units and propagated at a speed of about 186,300 miles a second. **b** Ultraviolet or infrared light. Also called *luminous energy.* **2** The natural condition or medium that permits vision; luminosity: opposed to *darkness.* **3** The sensation produced by exciting the organs of vision, as the eye, optical nerves, and visual centers of the

brain. **4** Mental or spiritual illumination. **5** A source of light, as the sun, moon, a flame, lamp, beacon, etc.; also, an emission of light. **6** That which admits light; a window or pane. **7** The state of being visible, known, or exposed: to come to *light.* **8** Daytime; daylight; dawn. **9** The point of view from which, or circumstances in which, a thing is seen or considered; aspect. **10** A part of a picture representing an illuminated object. **11** The power of vision; perception by eyesight. **12** Something with which to enkindle or make a blaze or light: a *light* for a pipe. **13** One who is noteworthy or eminent; a model. — **accidental light** In art, light coming from some other source than that of the chief light; a cross light. — **in the light of** In view of; considering. — **pick-up light** An anti-aircraft searchlight working alone or in coordination with a locator system to spot aircraft targets. — *adj.* **1** Full of light; not dark; bright. **2** Of a faint or pale color. — *v.* **light·ed** or **lit, light·ing** *v.t.* **1** To set burning, as wood, a lamp, etc.; ignite; kindle, as a fire. **2** To make light; illuminate. **3** To brighten or animate. **4** To guide or conduct with light: The fires *lighted* him home. — *v.i.* **5** To take fire; start burning. **6** To become bright or luminous: usually with *up.* [OE *lēoht*] — **light′er** *n.* — **light′less** *adj.*

◆ **lighted, lit** Either form is acceptable as the past tense and past participle of *light,* but *lighted* is probably more common as the past participle and is the usual form for the attributive adjective: The moon *lighted* (or *lit*) my path; I have already *lighted* (or *lit*) the oven; a *lighted* cigarette. In figurative use, the more common form is *lit:* Her face was *lit* with joy.

Synonyms (noun): blaze, flame, flare, flash, flicker, glare, gleam, glimmer, glisten, glistening, glitter, glow, illumination, incandescence, scintillation, sheen, shimmer, shine, shining, sparkle, twinkle, twinkling. A *flame* is both hot and luminous; if it contains few solid particles it will yield little *light,* but it may afford intense heat, as in the case of a hydrogen *flame.* A *blaze* is an extensive, brilliant *flame.* Light is the general term for any luminous effect discernible by the eye, from the faintest phosphorescence to the *blaze* of the sun. A *flare* is a wavering *flame* or *blaze,* a *flash* is a *light* that appears and disappears in an instant. The *glare* and *glow* are steady, the *glare* painfully bright, the *glow* subdued. *Shine* and *shining* refer to a steady or continuous emission of *light; sheen* is faint *shining,* usually by reflection. *Glimmer, glitter,* and *shimmer* denote wavering *light.* A *gleam* is not wavering, but transient or intermittent; a *glitter* is a hard *light;* the *glitter* of burnished arms. A *sparkle* is a sudden *light,* as of sparks thrown out; *scintillation* is the more exact and scientific term for the actual emission of sparks, also the figurative term for what suggests such emission: *scintillations* of wit or of genius. *Illumination* is wide-spread, brilliant *light,* as when all the windows of a house are lighted. The *light* of *incandescence* is intense and white like that from metal at a white heat. See KNOWLEDGE. *Antonyms:* blackness, dark, darkness, dimness, dusk, gloom, gloominess, obscurity, shade, shadow.

light² (līt) *adj.* **1** Having little weight; of small weight by comparison; not heavy: *light* as air. **2** Easy to carry, handle, move, etc.; not taxing to the muscles or digestive organs; not burdensome: a *light* task; *light* food. **3** Free from that which encumbers; not heavily loaded: *light* troops. **4** Of no great consequence; lacking gravity; trivial. **5** Lacking in intensity or effect; moderate. **6** Free from anxiety, trouble or distress; cheerful. **7** Not in full possession of the senses; flighty; delirious: *light* in the head. **8** Below the proper or usual weight: *light* coin. **9** Well-leavened and raised; not soggy: *light* bread. **10** Loose or sandy: a *light* soil. **11** Characterized by levity; without dignity or substantial character; also, loose in morals. **12** Handling or touching with slight force; hence, easy; graceful; active; nimble: a *light* touch; a *light* style. **13** Suitable for easy work. **14** Free from clumsiness or heaviness in appearance

or construction: *light* tracery. **15** Having no metrical stress: said of a syllable or vowel. **16** In Sanskrit grammar, having a short vowel: said of a syllable. **17** *Meteorol.* Designating air (No. 1) or a breeze (No. 2) on the Beaufort scale. **— to make light of** To treat or consider as trifling. — *v.i.* **light·ed** or **lit, light·ing 1** To descend and settle down after flight, as a bird; land. **2** To happen or come, as by chance or accident: with *on* or *upon.* **3** To get down, as from a horse or carriage; dismount. **4** To fall; strike, as a blow. **— to light into** *Slang* **1** To attack; assail. **2** To scold; castigate. **— to light out** *U.S. Slang* To depart in haste. — *adv.* Lightly; cheaply; easily. [OE *lēoht, līht*] **— light′ly** *adv.*

light·en[1] (līt′n) *v.t.* **1** To make light or more light. **2** To enlighten, as the mind. **3** *Rare* To send forth like lightning. — *v.i.* **4** To become light or more light. **5** To flash or shine. **6** To flash lightning.

light·en[2] (līt′n) *v.t.* **1** To make less heavy. **2** To reduce the load of: to *lighten* ship. **3** To make less burdensome or oppressive. **4** To relieve from distress; gladden. — *v.i.* **5** To become less heavy. See synonyms under ALLAY, ALLEVIATE.

light·er[1] (lī′tər) *n.* A device for lighting a cigarette, cigar, or pipe.

light·er[2] (lī′tər) *n.* A bargelike vessel used in loading or unloading ships lying at a distance from a wharf, or in transporting goods in bulk for short distances. — *v.t.* & *v.i.* To transport (goods) by lighter. [<Du. *lichter* < *lichten* make light, unload < *licht* light]

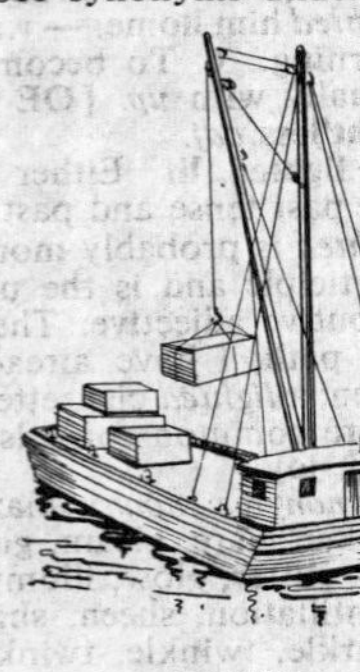

LIGHTER

light·er·age (lī′tər·ij) *n.* **1** The price for unloading a ship by lighters, or for the use of lighters. **2** The removal or conveying of a cargo by lighters.

light·er-than-air (lī′tər·thən·âr′) *adj.* *Aeron.* Having a specific gravity less than that of air: said especially of aircraft of the aerostat type, as a balloon or dirigible.

light·face (līt′fās′) *n.* *Printing* Type having light, thin lines.

light–fin·gered (līt′fing′gərd) *adj.* Addicted to petty theft; thievish; pilfering.

light–fog (līt′fôg′, -fog′) *n.* *Phot.* A blur of light, by accident or design, fogging a negative.

light–foot·ed (līt′fo͝ot′id) *adj.* Nimble in running or dancing; having a light step. **— light′–foot′ed·ly** *adv.*

light–head·ed (līt′hed′id) *adj.* **1** Silly; frivolous. **2** Dizzy; delirious. **— light′–head′ed·ly** *adv.* **— light′–head′ed·ness** *n.*

light–heart·ed (līt′här′tid) *adj.* Free from care; gay. See synonyms under MERRY. **— light′–heart′ed·ly** *adv.* **— light′–heart′ed·ness** *n.*

light heavyweight A boxer or wrestler weighing between 161 and 175 pounds.

light·horse·man (līt′hôrs′mən) *n.* *pl.* **·men** (-mən) A cavalryman bearing light arms and equipment.

light·house (līt′hous′) *n.* A tower equipped with high-powered lamps, erected at a point of danger to guide seamen by night.

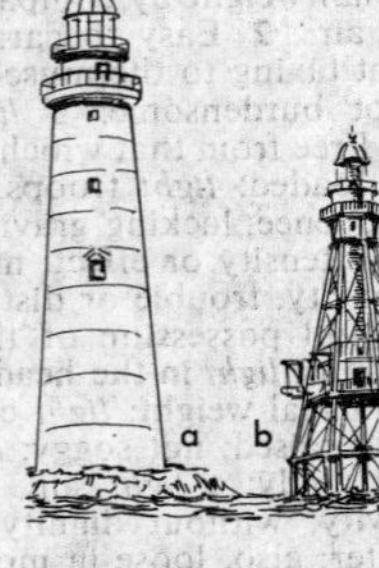

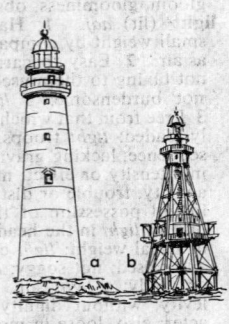

LIGHTHOUSE
a. Stone and steel construction.
b. Screwpile ocean lighthouse.

light·ing (lī′ting) *n.* **1** Illumination. **2** A distribution of light, as on a face or in a picture. **3** An arrangement of lights, especially on a stage.

light·ly (līt′lē) *adv.* **1** With little weight, force, pressure, or effect. **2** Without heaviness of spirit; airily; cheerily. **3** With levity; carelessly; heedlessly; also, frivolously, wantonly, or irreverently. **4** In a slight degree; slightly; mildly. **5** For slight reasons. **6** Nimbly; with light or swift step or motion. **7** Easily; readily. — *v.t.* *Scot.* To make light of; slight.

light–mind·ed (līt′mīn′did) *adj.* Lacking seriousness or strength of mind; foolish. **— light′–mind′ed·ly** *adv.* **— light′–mind′ed·ness** *n.*

light·ness (līt′nis) *n.* **1** The state, quality, or condition of being light. **2** That attribute of a color which identifies it as equivalent to some member of the series of grays between black and white: also called *brilliance.* Compare BRIGHTNESS, HUE, SATURATION. See COLOR.

light·ning (līt′ning) *n.* **1** A sudden flash of light caused by the discharge of electricity between two electrified regions of cloud, or between a cloud and the earth. **2** The discharge itself. **— ball lightning** A luminous, electrically charged sphere, usually less than a foot across, which sometimes appears during a thunderstorm, moving slowly and generally discharging on contact. **— chain lightning** Lightning discharged in swift, long strokes, forked or jagged in appearance. — *adj.* Fast; rapid: a *lightning* movement. [Earlier *lightening* < *lighten* flash]

lightning arrester A device for preventing damage to electrical equipment by carrying off excess voltage due to lightning or other electric disturbance.

lightning bug A firefly.

lightning rod A sharp-pointed metallic conductor used to protect buildings from lightning by carrying an electric current harmlessly to the ground. Also **lightning conductor.**

light–o'–love (līt′ə·luv′) *n.* **1** An old dance tune. **2** A coquettish or wanton woman.

light ratio *Astron.* The constant numerical factor 2.512 by which stars of successive apparent magnitudes differ from each other in brightness.

light red High-quality burnt ocher, used as a permanent pigment; loosely, any calcined ocher or certain iron oxides. **— light–red** *adj.*

lights (līts) *n. pl.* Lungs, especially of mammals. [ME *lihtes*; so called from their light weight]

light·ship (līt′ship′) *n.* A vessel, having warning lights, signals, etc., moored in dangerous waters as a guide to ships.

light·some[1] (līt′səm) *adj.* **1** Light; playful. **2** Graceful. **3** Nimble. **4** Frivolous. **— light′some·ly** *adv.* **— light′some·ness** *n.*

light·some[2] (līt′səm) *adj.* Full of light; luminous. **— light′some·ly** *adv.* **— light′some·ness** *n.*

light·stand (līt′stand′) *n.* A small table on which to set a light.

light·struck (līt′struk′) *adj.* Exhibiting a light-fog.

light·weight (līt′wāt′) *n.* **1** A boxer or wrestler weighing between 127 and 135 pounds. **2** *Slang* An unimportant, incompetent, or stupid person. — *adj.* **1** Having little weight; trivial. **2** Pertaining to lightweights.

light·wood (līt′wo͝od′) *n.* **1** Resinous pine, commonly the heart of the yellow pine. **2** The resinous knots of pine used for kindling.

light–year (līt′yir′) *n.* *Astron.* The distance that light traverses in one year, approximately six trillion miles: used as a unit in measuring the distance of stars. Compare PARSEC.

lign·al·oes (līn·al′ōz, lig·nal′-) *n.* **1** A fragrant, resinous Oriental wood (*Aquilaria agallocha*); aloe weed. **2** Aloes, the drug. [<OF <L *lignum aloes* wood of aloes]

lig·ne·ous (lig′nē·əs) *adj.* Composed of or like wood; woody. [<L *ligneus* < *lignum* wood]

ligni– *combining form* Wood: *lignivorous.* Also, before vowels, **lign–.** Also **ligno–.** [<L *lignum* wood]

lig·ni·form (lig′nə·fôrm) *adj.* Having the form or appearance of wood.

lig·ni·fy (lig′nə·fī) *v.t.* & *v.i.* **·fied, ·fy·ing** To convert into or become wood. [<LIGNI- + -FY] **— lig′ni·fi·ca′tion** *n.*

lig·nin (lig′nin) *n.* *Bot.* An organic substance which, with cellulose, forms the chief part of woody tissue. Also **lig′nose** (-nōs). [<LIGN(I)- + -IN]

lig·nite (lig′nīt) *n.* A compact, carbonized vegetable substance often retaining fibrous structure, forming an imperfect fuel intermediate between peat and true coal; brown coal. [<F] **— lig·nit′ic** (-nit′ik) *adj.*

lig·niv·o·rous (lig·niv′ə·rəs) *adj.* Wood-eating, as certain insects. [<LIGNI- + -VOROUS]

lig·no·cel·lu·lose (lig′nō·sel′yə·lōs) *n.* *Bot.* The substance making up the woody and fibrous parts of plants, consisting of lignin combined with cellulose.

lig·nose (lig′nōs) *n.* One of the constituents of lignin. [<L *lignosus* < *lignum* wood]

lig·num·vi·tae (lig′nəm·vī′tē) *n.* **1** A small tropical American tree (*Guaiacum officinale*). **2** Its greenish-brown, hard, heavy wood. **3** Any of certain related American trees, as the **bastard lignumvitae** (*G. sanctum*). [<NL <L, wood of life]

Li·gny (lē·nyē′) A village in central Belgium; scene of a French victory over the Prussians two days before Waterloo, 1815.

lig·ro·in (lig′rō·in) *n.* *Chem.* A distillate of petroleum used as a solvent and illuminant; petroleum naphtha. Also **lig′ro·ine.** [Origin unknown]

lig·u·late (lig′yə·lit, -lāt) *adj.* **1** Strap-shaped. **2** Having a ligule or ligules. Also **lig′u·lat′ed.**

lig·ule (lig′yo͞ol) *n.* **1** *Biol.* A strap-shaped organ or part. **2** *Bot.* **a** An appendage at the junction of the petiole and blade in grasses. **b** A strap-shaped corolla of certain flowers in the composite family. Also **lig′u·la** (-yə·lə). [<L *ligula,* dim. of *lingua* tongue; infl. in meaning by L *ligare* bind]

Li·guo·rist (lē·gwôr′ist) *n.* **1** *Theol.* A follower of the doctrines of St. Alfonso de Liguori; a probabilist. **2** A Redemptorist. Also **Li·guo′·ri·an.**

lig·ure (lig′yo͝or) *n.* A precious stone, possibly the jacinth, worn by the high priest of ancient Israel. *Exod.* xxviii 19. [<LL *ligurius* <Gk. *ligyrion* <Hebrew *leshem*]

Li·gu·ri·a (li·gyo͝or′ē·ə) A region of northern Italy on the Mediterranean; 2,098 square miles.

Li·gu·ri·an (li·gyo͝or′ē·ən) *n.* **1** A member of a tribe who, in ancient times, inhabited central and northern Italy and parts of Switzerland, France, and Spain. **2** The extinct, primarily Indo-European language of the Ligurians, probably closely related to Italic and Celtic. **3** An inhabitant of modern Liguria. **4** The dialect of Italian spoken in modern Liguria. — *adj.* Of or pertaining to ancient or modern Liguria, its inhabitants, its culture, or its language.

Ligurian Sea An arm of the Mediterranean Sea along the coast of NW Italy.

Li Hung–Chang (lē ho͝ong′jäng′), 1823–1901, Chinese statesman and general.

like[1] (līk) *v.* **liked, lik·ing** *v.t.* **1** To take pleasure in; enjoy. **2** To regard favorably; have affection or kindly feeling for. **3** To wish or desire; prefer: He would *like* us to do it. — *v.i.* **4** To feel inclined; choose: Do as you *like*! **5** *Archaic* To be agreeable or pleasing to: with the dative: It *likes* me not. — *n.* Liking; preference; inclination: common in the phrase *likes and dislikes.* [OE *līcian*] **— lik′a·ble, like′a·ble** *adj.* **— lik′er** *n.* **— lik′a·ble·ness, like′a·ble·ness** *n.*

Synonyms (verb): affect, approve, enjoy, esteem, fancy, love, relish. See LOVE. *Antonyms*: see synonyms under ABHOR.

like[2] (līk) *adj.* **1** Resembling; similar in qualities, appearance, etc. **2** Bearing a close or faithful resemblance, as a portrait. **3** *Math.* Identical: *like* angles. **4** Nearly identical; equivalent: Take a *like* amount of plaster. **5** In golf, having played the same number of strokes: said of competing players. **6** *Dial.* Likely to; expected: We are *like* to meet no more. **7** *Dial.* On the point or verge of; about to: I am *like* to cry when I think of her. **— like..., like...** As the one is, so the other will be: *like* father, *like* son. — *adv.* **1** In the manner of; as if: To run *like* mad. **2** *Colloq.* Likely: *Like* as not we'll meet again. — *prep.* **1** Similar to; resembling: You look *like* your father. **2** Characteristic of; expected from: That's just *like* your impudence! **3** In the mood or frame of mind for: to feel *like* sleeping. **4** So as to indicate, promise, or presage: to look *like* rain. **— like anything** (or **blazes, the devil,** etc.) *Colloq.* With great speed, force, violence, or vehemence. — *n.* That which is similar or equivalent to, or of the same nature as, something else. **— the like** (or **likes**) of: *Colloq.* Any thing or person like. — *v.i.* *Dial.* To come near or be on the point of: used in the past and past perfect tenses with the perfect infinitive: He *liked* (or *had liked*) to have died. — *conj.* **1** *Colloq.* As; in the manner that: It all happened

like you said. **2** *Colloq.* As if: It looks *like* he's going to fall. [OE *gelīc*]

◆**like, as, as if** *Like* is unacceptable as a conjunction at the formal level of writing, where factual clauses of comparison are introduced by *as,* contrary–to–fact ones by *as if* with the subjunctive. At the informal level, because it signals a coming comparison much more strongly than the rather neutral *as, like* is in widespread use. It has good colloquial standing, except with die–hard sticklers for correctness, in idiomatic expressions where it serves both as an adverb to round out a phrasal verb, and as a conjunction governing a finite verb: It looks *like* we're in for trouble; It sounds *like* a train's coming, and I'll have to run for it. In the last, the almost imperceptible gradation from the formally correct *That sounds like a train coming* to the informal *It sounds like a train's coming* shows why any ironclad prohibition of *like* as a conjunction at the informal level is ill–advised. The effort to ban it has frightened the timid into substituting *as* for *like* in adjectival or prepositional uses where *like* is idiomatic. Nor has the attempted ban deterred novelists and playwrights, whose trade demands a good ear for the way people actually speak, from representing their literate characters as making rather free use in dialog of *like* as a conjunction, usually, however, with a regard for idiom.

–like *suffix of adjectives* Resembling or similar to: *childlike, wavelike.* [<LIKE]

◆ Compounds containing *–like* are usually written solid, but hyphenated when three *l*'s occur together, as in *shell–like,* or when two *l*'s occur in a confusing sequence of letters, as in *eel–like.*

like·li·hood (līk′lē·ho͝od) *n.* **1** The character of being likely. **2** Probability or a probability: There is some *likelihood* of his coming. Also **like′li·ness.** See synonyms under PROBABILITY.

like·ly (līk′lē) *adj.* **·li·er, ·li·est 1** Apparently true or real; plausible; probable. **2** Reasonably to be expected; liable. **3** Apt to please; promising. **4** Well adapted for the purpose. — *adv.* Probably.

Synonyms: (*adj.*): apt, credible, liable, presumable, probable, reasonable. *Apt* implies a natural fitness or tendency: An impetuous person is *apt* to speak hastily. *Liable* refers to a contingency regarded as unfavorable: The ship was *liable* to founder at any moment. *Likely* refers to a contingent event regarded as very probable: An industrious worker is *likely* to succeed. *Credible* signifies readily to be believed: a *credible* narrative; *likely* in such connection is used ironically to signify the reverse: a *likely* story! A thing is *presumable* which, from what is known, may be taken for granted in advance of proof. *Reasonable* in this connection signifies such as the reason can be satisfied with, independently of external grounds for belief or disbelief. Compare APPARENT, PROBABLE. *Antonyms*: doubtful, dubious, improbable, incredible, questionable, unlikely.

like–mind·ed (līk′mīn′did) *adj.* Similarly disposed in opinion or tastes.

lik·en (lī′kən) *v.t.* To represent as similar; compare. See synonyms under COMPARE.

like·ness (līk′nis) *n.* **1** The state or quality of being like; a resemblance. **2** A portrait; representation. **3** Counterfeit form; guise. See synonyms under ANALOGY, APPROXIMATION, DUPLICATE, IMAGE, PICTURE.

like·wise (līk′wīz′) *adv.* **1** In like manner. **2** Also; moreover.

li·kin (lē′kēn′) *n.* A Chinese provincial transit duty. [<Chinese *li–chin*]

lik·ing (lī′king) *n.* Inclination due to some attraction; preference.

li·lac (lī′lək, -lək) *n.* **1** An ornamental flowering shrub (genus *Syringa*) having fragrant purplish or white flowers. The species best known in America are the **common lilac** (*S. vulgaris*), which has light rosy–purple flowers and is the State flower of New Hampshire, and the **Persian lilac** (*S. persica*), a smaller shrub with white or purplish flowers. **2** The light rosy–purple color of the common lilac flower. [<Sp. <Arabic *līlak, laylak* <Persian *līlak* bluish, var. of *nīlak,* dim. of *nīl* blue]

lil·i·a·ceous (lil′ē·ā′shəs) *adj.* Of or pertaining to a large, widely distributed family (*Liliaceae*) of monocotyledonous, mostly perennial herbs and shrubs, characterized by radially symmetrical flowers and bulbous rootstocks; designating the lily family. [<LL *liliaceus* <L *lilium* lily]

Lil·i·an (lil′ē·ən) A feminine personal name. Also **Lil′li·an.** [<L, lily]

lil·ied (lil′ēd) *adj.* **1** Like lilies. **2** Covered or decorated with, or abounding in, lilies.

Lil·i·en·thal (lil′ē·ən·thôl′), **David Eli,** born 1899, U. S. civil administrator.

Lil·ith (lil′ith) **1** In Babylonian legend, a female demon who inhabited ruins. **2** In Hebrew folklore, Adam's first wife. **3** In medieval folklore, a famous witch. [<Hebrew *Līlīth* <Assyrian–Babylonian *līlītu* of the night]

Li·li·u·o·ka·la·ni (lē·lē′o͞o·ō·kä·lä′nē), **Lydia Kamehameha,** 1838–1917, queen of the Hawaiian Islands 1891–93.

Lille (lēl) A city in northern France: formerly *Lisle.*

Lil·li·bul·le·ro (lil′ē·bə·lâr′ō) *n.* An English revolutionary song ridiculing the appointment of Talbot of Tyrconnell as lieutenant of Ireland in 1686. It helped foment the revolution of 1688. [An arbitrary formation]

Lil·li·put (lil′i·put, -pət) In Swift's *Gulliver's Travels,* a country inhabited by a race of diminutive people.

Lil·li·pu·tian (lil′i·pyo͞o′shən) *adj.* Pertaining to the fictitious kingdom of Lilliput or to its inhabitants; very small. — *n.* **1** An inhabitant of Lilliput. **2** A very small person, especially, a self–important one.

lilt (lilt) *n.* **1** A brisk, merry song. **2** Rhythmic movement or flow. **3** A buoyant manner of walking. — *v.t.* & *v.i.* To sing or speak in a light, rhythmic manner. [ME *lulte.* Cf. Du. *lul* pipe.]

lil·y (lil′ē) *n. pl.* **lil·ies 1** Any of numerous ornamental liliaceous plants (genus *Lilium*) having a bulbous root, erect stem, and large, showy, erect or nodding flowers; especially, the **madonna lily** (*L. candidum*) and the **goldband lily** (*L. auratum*). **2** A fleur–de–lis. **3** Any of numerous plants resembling the true lilies: *waterlily; daylily.* — *adj.* White and soft; pale and delicate, like a lily. [OE *lilie* <L *lilium,* prob. <Gk. *leirion*]

lily iron A harpoon with a detachable head.

lil·y–liv·ered (lil′ē·liv′ərd) *adj.* Cowardly.

lil·y–of–the–Nile (lil′ē·uv·thə·nīl′) *n.* **1** The calla. **2** The African lily.

lil·y–of–the–val·ley (lil′ē·uv·thə·val′ē) *n. pl.* **lil·ies–of–the–val·ley** A low, smooth, stemless lilywort (*Convallaria majalis*) with two oblong leaves and nodding, fragrant, cup–shaped flowers.

lil·y–white (lil′ē·hwīt′) *adj.* **1** White as a lily. **2** Pure; unsullied: often used ironically: hard to believe in her *lily–white* innocence. **3** Composed of or admitting white people only: a *lily–white* country club.

lil·y·wort (lil′ē·wûrt′) *n.* Any plant of the lily family.

Li·ma (lē′mə) **1** A department in west central Peru; 15,048 square miles. **2** Its capital, the capital and largest city of Peru.

Li·ma bean (lī′mə) **1** A variety of climbing bean (*Phaseolus limensis*). **2** Its large flat seeds, a common article of food. [after *Lima,* Peru]

lim·a·cine (lim′ə·sīn, -sin) *adj.* **1** Of or pertaining to a family (*Limacidae*) of gastropods; the slug family. **2** Sluglike. [<L *limax, limacis* slug]

lim·a·çon (lim′ə·son) *n. Math.* The curve traced by a point fixed on a secant of a fixed circle, the circumference of which touches the origin, as the secant revolves about the origin. Also called **Pascal's limaçon.**

limb[1] (lim) *n.* **1** One of the jointed parts of the animal body, as a leg, arm, or wing. **2** A branch of a tree. **3** A person or thing forming a part of something else; an arm or branch of anything; member: *limb* of the law. **4** *Colloq.* A roguish young person; a mischievous child. — **out on a limb** *Colloq.* At a great disadvantage. — *v.t.* To dismember. ◆ Homophone: *limn.* [OE *lim*] — **limb′less** *adj.*

limb[2] (lim) *n.* **1** An edge or part, as of a disk; specifically, the edge of the disk of the moon or other heavenly body. **2** The graduated portion of a leveling rod or instrument for determining angles. ◆ Homophone: *limn.* [<F *limbe* <L *limbus* edge]

lim·bate (lim′bāt) *adj. Bot.* Bordered, as a leaf or flower having the margin of a different color from the rest. [<LL *limbatus* <L *limbus* border]

limbed (limd) *adj.* Possessing limbs: often used in compounds: strong–*limbed.*

lim·ber[1] (lim′bər) *adj.* **1** Easily bent; pliant; flexible. **2** Lithe and agile; nimble; supple: said of persons or their movements. See synonyms under SUPPLE. — *v.t.* & *v.i.* To make or become limber: often with *up.* [Origin uncertain] — **lim′ber·ly** *adv.* — **lim′ber·ness** *n.*

lim·ber[2] (lim′bər) *n.* **1** *Mil.* A two–wheeled, detachable vehicle at the forepart of a gun carriage, used to transport ammunition. **2** *Naut.* A lengthwise gutter on each side of the keelson to permit water to pass into the pump well. — *v.t.* & *v.i.* To attach a limber to (a gun): often with *up.* [Origin uncertain. Cf. F *limonière* < *limon* shaft.]

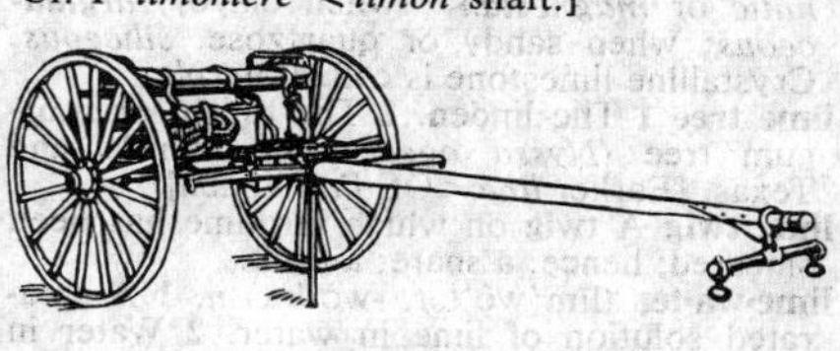

GUN LIMBER

lim·bic (lim′bik) *adj.* Of, pertaining to, or forming a border. [<LIMBUS]

lim·bo (lim′bō) *n.* **1** *Theol.* A region on the edge of hell to which are consigned the souls of the righteous who died before the coming of Christ (**limbo patrum,** or **limbo of the fathers**) and the souls of infants who died before baptism (**limbo infantum,** or **limbo of the infants**). **2** A place of neglect or oblivion to which unwanted or worthless persons or things are relegated and forgotten. **3** A place of confinement; a prison. [<L *limbus* border, *in limbo* on the border]

Lim·burg (lim′bûrg, *Du., Flemish* lim′bœrkh) **1** A province of NE Belgium; 930 square miles; capital, Hasselt. Also **Lim·bourg** (lan̈·bo͞or′). **2** A province of SE Netherlands; 839 square miles; capital, Maastricht.

Lim·burg·er cheese (lim′bûr·gər) A soft, white cheese with a strong odor, originally made at Limburg, Belgium. Also **Lim′burg cheese, Lim′burg·er.**

lim·bus (lim′bəs) *n.* A border or interface, especially if marked by a difference in color or structure between the adjoining parts. [<L, border]

lime[1] (līm) *n.* A white, earthlike calcium oxide, CaO. It is produced artificially by calcining calcium carbonate, as limestone, marble, or seashells, yielding the anhydrous calcium–oxide quicklime, which with water forms **slaked lime.** It also readily absorbs moisture from the air, forming **air–slaked lime.** — *v.t.* **limed, lim·ing 1** To apply lime to. **2** To catch with or as with birdlime; ensnare. **3** To cement. [OE *līm*]

lime[2] (līm) *n.* **1** A small tree (*Citrus aurantifolia*) of the rue family, native in tropical regions. **2** Its small, green, lemonlike, acid fruit. [<F <Sp. *lima* <Arabic *limah.* Related to LEMON.]

lime·ade (līm·ād′) *n.* A drink made of lime juice, water, and sugar.

Lime·house (līm′hous′) A district of Stepney, east London, on the Thames, largely inhabited by sailors and dock workers.

lime·kiln (līm′kil′, -kiln′) *n.* A kiln for burning lime from limestone or seashells. Also **lime kiln.**

lime·light (līm′līt′) *n.* **1** A powerful light originally produced by burning lime, now often replaced by the electric spotlight: thrown on the stage to make actors more prominent. **2** That part of a theater stage illuminated by a limelight or spotlight. **3** Publicity; notoriety.

li·men (lī′mən) *n. pl.* **li·mens** or **lim·i·na** (lim′·ə·nə) A threshold (def. 3). [<L, threshold]

lim•er•ick (lim′ər•ik) *n.* A humorous verse of five anapestic lines, of which the first, second, and fifth lines are three-stress and rime, and the third and fourth lines are two-stress and rime. [after LIMERICK]

Lim•er•ick (lim′ər•ik) 1 A county in central Munster province, Ireland; 1,037 square miles. 2 Its capital, a port on the Shannon River. Irish Gaelic *Luimneach.*

Li•mes (lī′mēz) *n.* 1 A system of fortifications built by the Romans under Vespasian and Trajan to protect the provinces of southern Germany and Rhaetia against the Germans: about 336 miles long. Also **Li′mes Ger•man•i•cus** (jər•man•i•kəs). 2 (*Ger.* lē′mes) An elaborate series of fortifications built by Germany in 1938–39, opposing the French Maginot line and extending from the Swiss border along the French, Belgian, and Dutch frontiers: also *Siegfried Line, Westwall.* [<L *limes* border]

lime•stone (līm′stōn′) *n.* A rock composed wholly or in part of calcium carbonate. When containing magnesium carbonate, it is *dolomitic* or *magnesian* ; when clayey, *argillaceous*; when sandy or quartzose, *siliceous.* Crystalline limestone is called *marble.*

lime tree 1 The linden. 2 The tupelo or sourgum tree *(Nyssa ogeche)* of Florida and Texas. [Earlier *line* <OE *lind* linden]

lime twig A twig on which birdlime has been smeared; hence, a snare; a trick.

lime•wa•ter (līm′wô′tər, -wot′ər) *n.* 1 A saturated solution of lime in water. 2 Water in which slaked lime has been dissolved. Also **lime water.**

lime•y (lī′mē) *n.* Slang 1 A British sailor: from the former practice of averting scurvy on long voyages by eating limes. Also **lime′ juic′er.** 2 Any Englishman, sometimes taken to be offensive.

li•mic•o•line (li•mik′ə•lin) *adj.* Shore-dwelling: said of certain wading birds, as plovers and snipes. Also **li•mic′o•lous.** [<LL *limicola* dweller in mud <*limus* mud + *colere* dwell]

lim•i•nal (lim′ə•nəl) *adj.* Relating to or at the threshold, entrance, or beginning. [<L *limen* threshold]

lim•it (lim′it) *n.* 1 A line, point, or boundary beyond which something ceases to extend, operate, avail, etc. 2 That which is limited or has bounds; ;a district; period. 3 That which impedes or hinders; a check. 4 *Math.* A definite quantity or value which a series is conceived or proved to approach but never reach. 5 In certain games, as of cards, the largest amount which may be wagered at one time: used with the definite article, especially in poker. See synonyms under BOUNDARY, END, MARGIN. **—off limits** A locality or area forbidden to military personnel except on official business. **—three-mile limit** A distance of three geographic miles from the shore line seaward, allowed by international law for teroritorial jurisdiction. —*v.t.* To set a bound or bounds to; keep within a limit; restrict. [<L *limes, limites*] **—lim′it•a•ble** *adj.* **—lim•i•ta•tive** (lim′ə•tā′tiv) *adj.* **—lim′it•er** *n.* **—lim′it•less** *adj.*

Synonyms (verb) : bound, check, circumscribe, confine, define, hinder, impede, repress, restrain, restrict. See CIRCUMSCRIBE, SCRIMP.

lim•i•tar•y (lim′ə•ter′ē) *adj.* 1 Forming or marking a limit or boundary; limiting. 2 Limited.

lim•i•ta•tion (lim′ə•tā′shən) *n.* 1 The act of limiting. 2 Restriction; circumscription. 3 *Law* A restrictive condition or stipulation; also, a period of time fixed by law within which certain acts are to be performed to render them valid. [<L *limitatio, -onis*]

lim•it•ed (lim′it•id) *adj.* 1 Confined to certain limits; in law, restricted within prescribed limits. 2 Circumscribed, as a government, a monarchy, etc.; held in check by a constitution. 3 Making only a few specific stops, carrying only a certain +number of passengers, and usually charging extra fare: a *limited* train. 4 Restricted to use on or within certain dates: a *limited* ticket. 5 *Brit.* Restricted in liability to the amount invested in stock of a business: a *limited* company.

lim•it•ed-slip differential (lim′it•id•slip′) An automobile differential-gear system so designed that in the event of one driving wheel losing its traction, the power is transmitted to the other wheel.

limit load *Engin.* The load which may safely be carried by a given structure under normal conditions.

limn (lim) *v.t.* 1 To draw or paint; delineate. 2 To describe in words. 3 To decorate, as manuscripts; illuminate. ◆ Homophone: *limb.* [ME *limnen* <*luminen* <OF *enluminer* <L *illuminare.* Doublet of ILLUMINATE.] **—lim•ner** (lim•nər) *n.* **—lim•ning** (lim′ning) *n.*

lim•net•ic (lim•net′ik) *adj. Ecol.* Pertaining to or dwelling in lakes, as certain plants and animals. Also **lim•nic•o•lous** (lim•nik′ ə•ləs). [<Gk. *limnētēs* marsh-dwelling <*limnē* pool]

lim•nol•o•gy (lim•nol′ə•jē) *n.* The scientific study of bodies of fresh water in all their aspects, with special reference to plant and animal life. [<Gk. *limnē* pool + -LOGY]

Lim•nos (lēm′nôs) See LEMNOS.

Li•moges (lē•mōzh′, *Fr.* lē•môzh′) A city in west central France.

Limoges ware A type of fine porcelain manufactured at Limoges, France.

lim•o•nene (lim′ə•nēn) *n. Chem.* One of three isomeric terpenes, $C_{10}H_{16}$, occurring in various essential oils, and having a lemonlike odor. [<NL *Limonum* lemon + -ENE]

li•mo•nite (lī′mə•nīt) *n.* A stalactitic, fibrous, silky, brown or yellow ferric hydroxide; bog ore. [<Gk. *leimōn* meadow + -ITE²] **—li′mo•nit′ic** (-nit′ik) *adj.*

Li•mou•sin (lē•moo•zaṅ′) A region and former province of central France.

lim•ou•sine (lim′ə•zēn′, lim′ə•zēn) *n.* A large automobile, originally with a closed compartment for three to five passengers, and the roof projecting over the driver's seat; later, with each compartment separately enclosed. [<F, from *Limousin*]

limp¹ (limp) *v.i.* 1 To walk with a halting or irregular gait, as in favoring an injured leg or foot. 2 To proceed in a defective or irregular manner: His logic *limps.* —*n.* The step of a lame person; a halt. [Prob. OE *limpan* occur, walk lamely. Cf. OE *lempheal*t lame.] **—limp′er** *n.*

limp² (limp) *adj.* 1 Lacking stiffness; limber. 2 Lacking positiveness or firmness. [Origin uncertain. Cf. ON *limpa* indisposition, weakness.] **—limp′ly** *adv.* **—limp′ness** *n.*

lim•pet (lim′pit) *n.* A small, edible gastropod with a spirally coiled shell, found clinging to rocks. [OE *lempedu* <LL *lampreda* lamprey]

lim•pid (lim′pid) *adj.* Characterized by liquid clearness; transparent; lucid; clear. See synonyms under CLEAR, TRANSPARENT. [<L *limpidus* clear] **—lim•pid•i•ty** (lim•pid′ə•tē), **lim′•+pid•ness** *n.* **—lim′pid•ly** *adv.*

limp•kin (limp′kin) *n.* A courlan of Florida and tropical America. [<LIMP¹ + -KIN; from its walk]

Lim•po•po (lim•pō′pō) A river forming northern border of the Republic of South Africa's North West and Northern Transvaal provinces, flowing 995 miles partially through Mozambique into the Indian Ocean.

limp•sy (limp′sē) *adj.* **•si•er, •si•est** Limp; flimsy.

lim•u•loid (lim′yə•loid) *adj.* Pertaining to or resembling the king crab. —*n.* A king crab. [<LIMULUS]

lim•u•lus (lim′yə•ləs) *n. pl.* **L•li** A king crab. [<L, dim. of *limus* sidelong, askance]

lim•y (lī′mē) *adj.* **lim•i•er, lim•i•est** 1 Containing or covered with lime. 2 Resembling lime. 3 Smeared with birdlime.

lin (lin) *n.* Scot. 1 A waterfall. 2 A precipice or ravine. Also spelled *lyn.* [OE *hlynn* torrent]

Li•na (lē′nə, lī′nə) Diminutive of CAROLINE.

lin•age (lī′nij) *n.* 1 The number of printed lines, as of text or advertising matter, contained in a book or magazine. 2 Alinement. Also spelled *lineage.*

lin•al•o•ol (lin•al′ō•ōl, lin′ə•lool′) *n. Chem.* An unsaturated, open-chain alcohol, $C_{10}H_{17}OH$, found in the essential oils of certain plants, as the bergamot. [<*linaloa,* a scented Mexican wood <Sp. *linaloe.* Cf. LIGNALOES.]

Li•na•res (lē•nä′rās) A city in southern Spain.

linch•pin (linch′pin′) *n.* A pin through the end of an axle, to keep a wheel in place. [OE *lynis* linchpin + PIN]

Lin•coln (ling′kən), **Abraham,** 1809–1865, 16th president of the United States during the Civil War, 1861–65; issued Proclamation of Emancipation; assassinated. **—Benjamin,** 1733–1810, American Revolutionary general and statesman.

Lin•coln (ling′kən) 1 A maritime county in eastern England; 2,664 square miles; county seat, Lincoln. Also **Lin′coln•shire** (-shir); shortened form **Lincs** (lingks). 2 The capital of Nebraska.

Lincoln's Birthday The anniversary of Abraham Lincoln's birth, February 12: a legal holiday in many States of the United States.

Lincoln's Inn See INNS OF COURT.

l'in•con•nu (laṅ•kô•nü′) *French* The unknown.

Lind (lind), **Jenny,** 1820–87, Swedish coloratura soprano: called "the Swedish Nightingale."

Lind•bergh (lind′bûrg), **Charles Augustus,** 1902–74, U.S. aviator; made the first nonstop solo flight from New York to Paris, 1927.

lin•den (lin′dən) *n.* A tree (genus *Tilia*) with soft white wood, cordate leaves, and cream-colored flowers; especially, the **American linden** *(T. Yamericana),* used for making furniture. Also called *basswood, lime tree.* [OE, orig. adj. < *lind* linden, lime tree]

Lin•des•nes (lin′dəs•nes) See NAZE, THE.

Lind•say (lin′zē), **Sir David,** 1490–1555, Scottish poet: also spelled *Lyndsay.* **—(Nicholas) Vachel,** 1879–1931, U.S. poet.

Lind•sey (lin′zē), **Benjamin Barr,** 1869–1943, U.S. jurist and reformer.

line¹ (līn) *n.* 1 A string or cord. 2 *Naut.* A rope, cord, or wire used for a specific purpose. 3 A wire or cable conducting power or telecommunication signals between two stations. 4 A fishing line. 5 Any slender mark or stroke, as drawn with a pen, pencil, tool, etc. 6 Something resembling the long mark or trace made by a pen or tool; band; seam; furrow. 7 In art: **a** The representation of form by the use of strokes, instead of by shading or coloring. **b** *pl.* The distinguishing features of the composition of a painting or drawing. 8 *Music* One of the parallel horizontal strokes that form a musical staff. 9 In various games, as football, baseball, tennis, etc., a mark of division or outline on the field, diamond, court, etc. 10 In television, one horizontal trace of the electron beam across the screen. 11 A thin furrow or wrinkle on the face or hands. 12 *Geom.* The trace, straight or curved, made by a moving point; an extent of length conceived without breadth or thickness. 13 A boundary or limit: the Mason-Dixon *Line.* 14 Contour; outline: the broken *line* of the shore. 15 *Geog.* **a** The equator. **b** Any circle, arc, or boundary conceived for purposes of plotting the earth's surface: the date *line.* 16 A row of persons or things: The people stood in *line.* 17 Agreement; accord: to bring all the factions into *line.* 18 A course of action, thought, procedure, etc.: a *line* of argument; the *line* of duty. 19 Plan of construction or procedure: an argument based on political *lines. P* 20 A course of movement; route: the *line* of march. 21 A branch of activity; a business or vocation: the advertising *line.* 22 The compass of one's ability, talent, etc.: Such jokes are not in his *line.* 23 A series of persons each of whom is the next descendant or heir of the one preceding. 24 A row of printed or written words bounded by the margins of a page or column. 25 A short letter; a note. 26 A verse (def. 1). 27 *pl.:* The words of a play or of an actor's part. 28 In advertising, a measure of column space equaling 1/14 inch. 29 A railroad track or roadbed. 30 Any system of public transportation: a steamship *line.* 31 A pipe or system of pipes conveying a fluid: a gas *line.* 32 *Mil.* **a** A series of fortifications presenting an extended front: Maginot *line.* **b** A trench or rampart. **c** A row of soldiers standing abreast, as distinguished from *column.* 33 *Naut.* An arrangement of ships in a certain order. 34 *Mil.* The combatant forces, as distinguished from the special services and the staff. 35 *Nav.* The class of officers having command of combat operations. 36 In football: **a** The linemen, collectively. **b** The line of scrimmage: see LINE OF SCRIMMAGE under SCRIMMAGE. 37 A variety of goods of a certain class or type, carried by a store or offered by an advertiser. 38 *pl. Colloq.* Marriage-lines. 39 *Colloq.* **a** A glib manner of speech. **b** A

few words or a speech intended to sway or influence. See synonyms under BOUNDARY, MARK. **— in line for** In succession for; ready for. **— in line with** In accord with. **— *v.* lined, lin·ing** *v.t.* **1** To mark with lines; put lines upon. **2** To place in a line; bring into alinement or conformity: often with *up.* **3** To form a line along: Police *lined* the side of the road. **4** To place something in a line along: to *line* a wall with archers. **5** In baseball, to bat (the ball) in a line drive. **— *v.i.* 6** To form a line; assume position or place: usually with *up.* **— to line out** In baseball: **a** To be retired by batting a line drive to a fielder. **b** To get (a hit) by batting a line drive which is not caught or fielded. **— to line up 1** To form a line. **2** To bring into line. **3** To organize for or against some activity, issue, etc. [OE *līne* cord; infl. by F *ligne* <L *linea* linen thread <*linum* flax]

line[2] (līn) *v.t.* **lined, lin·ing 1** To apply a covering or layer, usually of different material, to the inside surface of. **2** To serve as an inner covering or layer for: Lockers *lined* the wall. **3** To fill or supply: to *line* one's pockets with bribes. **— *n.* 1** The fiber of flax. **2** Linen. [OE *līn* flax]

lin·e·age[1] (lin′ē·ij) *n.* Ancestral line of consanguinity; pedigree; family. [<OF *lignage* <L *linea* line]

line·age[2] (lī′nij) See LINAGE.

lin·e·al (lin′ē·əl) *adj.* **1** Of the nature of an ancestral line or lineage; ascending or descending in a direct line: distinguished from *collateral.* **2** Made with lines. [<L *linealis* <*linea* line] **— lin′e·al·ly** *adv.*

lin·e·a·ment (lin′ē·ə·mənt) *n.* A distinguishing line or mark; a feature. [<L *lineamentum* <*linea* line]

lin·e·ar (lin′ē·ər) *adj.* **1** Pertaining to or composed of lines. **2** Very narrow and elongate: a *linear* leaf. **3** Denoting a measurement in one dimension. **4** *Math.* Pertaining to an equation of the first degree. [<L *linearis*]

linear measure Measurement by length; a unit or system of units for measuring length, as in the following table of the principal customary standards. See also METRIC SYSTEM.

1 mil	=	0.001 inch (in.)
12 inches	=	1 foot (ft.)
3 feet	=	1 yard (yd., yds.)
6 feet	=	1 fathom (fath.)
5.5 yards	=	1 rod (rd.)
40 rods	=	1 furlong (fur.)
5280 feet	=	1 mile (mi.)
1760 yards	=	1 mile

lin·e·ate (lin′ē·it, -āt) *adj.* Marked with lines. Also **lin′e·at′ed.** [<L *lineatus*]

lin·e·a·tion (lin′ē·ā′shən) *n.* **1** A drawing of lines; delineation. **2** A contour or outline.

line·back·er (līn′bak′ər) *n.* In football, a defensive player whose normal position is just behind the line of scrimmage.

line–breed (līn′brēd′) *v.t. Genetics* To interbreed (successive generations) to one ancestor of a given line in order to develop selected characteristics. **— line′–breed′ing** *n.*

line drive In baseball, a ball batted with such force as to travel almost parallel to the ground.

Line Islands (līn) A Pacific island group south of Hawaii, divided between the United States and Great Britain; 112 square miles: also *Equatorial Islands.*

line·man (līn′mən) *n. pl.* **·men** (-mən) **1** In surveying, a man who carries the tape, line, or chain. **2** A man employed about the line of a railway, telegraph, or telephone, especially in making repairs. **3** In football, one of the players stationed along the line of scrimmage, consisting of the center and the right and left guards, tackles, and ends.

lin·en (lin′in) *n.* **1** A fabric woven from the fibers of flax. **2** Articles made of linen, or made formerly of linen but now often of cotton: bed *linen,* table *linen,* body *linen.* **— *adj.*** Made of the textile fiber of flax: *linen* cloth. [OE *līnen* made of flax <*līn* flax]

line of force *Physics* A line in a field of force every point on which coincides with the field intensity.

line of scrimmage See under SCRIMMAGE.

line of sight The straight line joining the eye of an observer and a target or other observed object.

line of vision The straight line joining the central fovea of the retina and the point to which vision is directed.

lin·e·o·late (lin′ē·ə·lāt′) *adj.* Minutely lineate. Also **lin′e·o·lat′ed.** [<L *lineola,* dim. of *linea* line + -ATE[1]]

lin·er[1] (lī′nər) *n.* **1** A ship, aircraft, etc., operated commercially by a specific line. **2** A person or thing that marks or traces lines. **3** In baseball, a line drive.

lin·er[2] (lī′nər) *n.* **1** One who makes linings. **2** A lining, or a piece used in forming a lining.

line–rid·er (līn′rī′dər) See FENCE–RIDER.

lines·man (līnz′mən) *n. pl.* **·men** (-mən) **1** In many games, as in tennis, the official watching the lines of the court. **2** In football, the official supervising the sidelines and marking the distances gained or lost in each play.

line squall *Meteorol.* A squall or series of squalls occurring along a squall line and usually marked by sudden changes in wind direction.

line storm *Dial.* An equinoctial.

line–up (līn′up′) *n.* **1** The formation of players in any game, such as football, hockey, etc., when drawn up for action. **2** An array of people united by some aim. **3** A mustering of criminal suspects by police for identification and questioning.

lin·ey (lī′nē) See LINY.

ling[1] (ling) *n.* **1** A codlike food fish (*Molva molva*) of the North Atlantic. **2** The Lake Ontario burbot (*Lota maculosa*). [? <Du. *leng* or OE *lengu* length]

ling[2] (ling) *n.* The heath or heather. [<ON *lyng*]

–ling[1] *suffix of nouns* **1** Little; young; petty: *duckling*: often used contemptuously: *princeling.* **2** A person or thing related to or characterized by: *worldling.* [OE]

–ling[2] *suffix* Forming adverbs: **1** (from nouns) Toward: *sideling.* **2** (from adjectives) Being; becoming: *darkling.* Also **–lings.** [OE *-ling, -linga*]

lin·ga (ling′gə) *n.* A phallus or phallic symbol, used extensively in the cult worship of Siva. Also **lin′gam** (-gəm). [<Skt. *lingam,* lit., symbol]

Lin·ga·yen Gulf (ling′gä·yen′) An inlet of the South China Sea in western Luzon, Philippines.

lin·ger (ling′gər) *v.i.* **1** To stay on as if reluctant to leave; delay going. **2** To move slowly; saunter; loiter: to *linger* on the way. **3** To dwell upon, as from enjoyment or persistence. **4** To continue in life or existence; endure: often with *on*: The sound *lingers* on in my memory. **— *v.t.* 5** To protract; drag out. **6** To pass (time) in lingering: with *away* or *out.* [Earlier *lenger,* freq. of OE *lengen* delay. Akin to LONG.] **— lin′ger·er** *n.*

Synonyms: crawl, creep, dawdle, delay, drag, flag, halt, hesitate, lag, loiter, saunter, wait. *Antonyms*: see synonyms for ACCELERATE.

lin·ge·rie (län′zhə·rē, *Fr.* laṅ·zhrē′) *n.* Women's underwear: originally of laced linen, now of silk, rayon, nylon, etc. [<F *lingerie,* collective noun formed from *linge* linen]

lin·ger·ing (ling′gər·ing) *adj.* Protracted; slow; dilatory.

Ling·ga Archipelago (ling′gə) An Indonesian island group, including **Lingga Island** (319 square miles) off the east coast of Sumatra; 842 square miles.

lin·go (ling′gō) *n. pl.* **lin·goes 1** Language, especially if strange or unintelligible. **2** The specialized vocabulary and idiom of a profession, class, etc.: medical *lingo.* See synonyms under SLANG. [<Pg. <L *lingua* tongue]

lin·gua (ling′gwə) *n. pl.* **·guae** (-gwē) **1** The tongue. **2** A language. [<L]

lin·gua·den·tal (ling′gwə·den′təl) *adj.* & *n. Phonet.* Interdental. Also **lin·gui·den·tal** (ling′gwi·den′təl).

lin·gua fran·ca (ling′gwə frang′kə) **1** A mixture of French, Spanish, Italian, Greek, and Arabic, spoken in the Mediterranean ports: often called *Sabir.* **2** Any mixed jargon used as a commercial or trade language, such as pidgin English, Chinook jargon, etc. [<Ital., lit., language of the Franks; prob. infl. by *franco* rough and ready]

lin·gual (ling′gwəl) *adj.* Pertaining to the tongue or the use of the tongue in utterance. **— *n.*** *Phonet.* A sound pronounced chiefly with the tongue, as (t), (d), and (l). [<Med. L *lingualis*]

Lin·guet·ta (lĕng·gwet′tä), **Cape** The Italian name for CAPE GLOSSA.

lin·gui·form (ling′gwi·fôrm) *adj.* Tongue-shaped. [<L *lingua* + -FORM]

lin·guist (ling′gwist) *n.* **1** One who knows many languages. **2** An authority in linguistics. [<L *lingua* + -IST]

lin·guis·tic (ling·gwis′tik) *adj.* **1** Of or pertaining to language. **2** Pertaining to linguistics. Also **lin·guis′ti·cal. — lin·guis′ti·cal·ly** *adv.*

linguistic atlas Dialect atlas.

linguistic form Any unit of speech that has meaning, as a sentence, phrase, word, combining form, affix, etc.

lin·guis·tics (ling·gwis′tiks) *n.* The science of language, its origin, structure, modifications, etc., including among its studies the fields of phonetics, phonemics, morphology, syntax, and semantics: usually divided into **historical** (or *diachronic*) **linguistics,** the study of the evolution of languages and linguistic phenomena; **descriptive** (or *synchronic*) **linguistics,** the study of a language or languages at a given stage of development; **comparative linguistics,** the comparison and contrast of related languages; **geographical linguistics** (or **linguistic geography**), the classification of the distribution of languages and dialects on a regional basis.

linguistic stock 1 An original language and all the languages and dialects derived from it. **2** All the people speaking languages or dialects derived from one original: The Shawnee Indians belong to the Algonquian *linguistic stock.*

lin·gu·late (ling′gyə·lāt) *adj.* Having the shape of a tongue; linguiform; ligulate. [<L *lingula,* dim. of *lingua* tongue]

ling·y (ling′ē) *adj.* Covered with ling or heather.

lin·i·ment (lin′ə·mənt) *n.* A liquid preparation for external use, for bruises, inflammation, etc. [<LL *linimentum* <L *linire* anoint]

li·nin (lī′nin) *n.* **1** *Chem.* A white, bitter, crystalline compound, $C_{23}H_{22}O_9$, found in the purging flax (*Linum catharticum*). **2** *Biol.* A fiber of the nuclear reticulum of the cell that has little affinity for dyes; an achromatic thread of the nucleus: contrasted with *chromatin.* [<L *linum* + -IN]

lin·ing (lī′ning) *n.* **1** The act of one who lines. **2** A covering of the inner surface of a thing; also, material suitable for such use. **3** Contents.

link[1] (lingk) *n.* **1** One of the loops of which a chain is made; hence, something which connects separate things; a tie. **2** A hinge. **3** A single constituent part of a continuous series. **4** *Mech.* A connecting rod which transmits power from one part of a machine to another. **5** A length of 7.92 inches, or 20.11 centimeters, used in surveying. **6** *Colloq.* A section of a chain of sausages. **7** One of the component parts of a mechanical device formed of a number of identical or similar units. **8** *Chem.* A bond. **9** Links (def. 2). **— *v.t.* & *v.i.*** To join or connect by or as by links; unite. See synonyms under UNITE. [ME *linke* <Scand.; cf. Icel. *hlekkr,* Sw. *länk* a link. Akin to OE *hlencan* twist.]

link[2] (lingk) *n.* A torch. [Origin uncertain]

link[3] (lingk) *v.i. Scot.* & *Brit. Dial.* To walk lightly and quickly; trip.

link·age (ling′kij) *n.* **1** The act of linking, or the state of being linked. **2** *Mech.* A series or system of links and connecting rods for transmitting power, especially as used in automotive vehicles. **3** *Electr.* A relation between a magnetic line of force and the conductive coil that forms its vehicle. **4** *Biol.* Inheritance of the kind in which the genes, usually in the same chromosome, tend to act together as a unit or **linkage group** in the general process of segregation. **5** A pantograph.

link block *Mech.* The block sliding in or on a link, actuated thereby, and operating on the valve stem in link motion, either directly or through other members.

link·boy (lingk′boi′) *n.* A boy or man em-

ployed to light the way, by means of a link or torch, for pedestrians on dark streets. Also **link, link′man** (-mən).

linked (lingkt) *adj.* **1** Joined together. **2** *Biol.* Exhibiting linkage.

link hinge *Mech.* A hinge having the two leaves permanently attached to a link permitting free rotation. See illustration under HINGE.

link motion *Mech.* An assemblage of parts for operating the valves of locomotive and similar engines, its essential feature being a slotted bar, which is driven by one or two eccentrics.

Lin·kö·ping (lin′chœ·ping) A city of SE Sweden.

links (lingks) *n. pl.* **1** Flat or undulating land. **2** A golf course: sometimes construed as singular. [OE *hlinc* slope]

Link trainer *Aeron.* A ground device equipped to train airplane pilots for instrument flight: a trade name.

link·up (lingk′up′) *n.* **1** A linking together; contact: the *linkup* of space vehicles. **2** A pooling or combining, as of resources or efforts.

link·work (lingk′wûrk′) *n.* A fabric consisting of links joined together; a chain.

Lin·lith·gow (lin·lith′gō) A burgh in east central Scotland, county town of West Lothian.

Lin·lith·gow·shire (lin·lith′gō·shir) A former name for WEST LOTHIAN.

linn (lin) *n.* The linden tree. [<LINDEN]

Lin·nae·us (li·nē′əs), **Carolus,** 1707–78, Swedish naturalist and taxonomist; Latinized form of **Karl von Lin·né** (lē·nā′).

Lin·ne·an (li·nē′ən) *adj.* Pertaining to Linnaeus, especially to his binomial system of classifying plants and animals according to genus and species. Also **Lin·nae′an.**

lin·net (lin′it) *n.* **1** One of various singing birds, as the common European **gray** or **gorse linnet** (genus *Carduelis*), the male of which in summer has the breast and crown bright crimson. **2** The house finch (*Carpodacus mexicana*) of the western United States. [<OF *linette* <L *linum* flax; from its feeding on flax seeds]

Lin·nhe (lin′ē), **Loch** An inlet on the west coast of Scotland between Inverness and Argyll.

lin·o·le·ic (lin′ə·lē′ik, li·nō′lē·ik) *adj. Chem.* Of or denoting a colorless to yellow, oily, fatty acid, $C_{18}H_{32}O_2$, found in linseed oil, cottonseed oil, and other vegetable oils. [< LINOLEUM]

li·no·le·um (li·nō′lē·əm) *n.* A preparation of linseed oil hardened by oxidizing. When mixed with ground cork and pressed upon canvas or burlap, it is used as a floor covering. [<L *linum* flax + *oleum* oil]

Li·no·type (lī′nə·tīp) *n.* A machine which casts a complete line of type on a single body: a trade name. **— li′no·typ′er, li′no·typ′·ist** *n.*

lin·sang (lin′sang) *n.* A long-tailed, East Indian viverrine mammal (genus *Prionodon*) related to but smaller than the genet. [< Javanese *linsang*]

lin·seed (lin′sēd′) *n.* Flaxseed. [OE *linsǣd*]

linseed oil A yellowish drying oil made from flaxseed.

lin·sey–wool·sey (lin′zē·wŏŏl′zē) *n.* **1** A cloth made of linen and wool or cotton and wool mixed. **2** *Obs.* Nonsense; jargon. **—** *adj.* Made of linen and wool. [ME *lynsy-wolsye* < *lynsy* (? < *lin* linen + *saye* cloth) + WOOL]

lin·stock (lin′stok) *n.* Formerly, an iron-shod pike with a crotch designed to hold a rope match for firing a gun. [<Du. *lontstok* < *lont* match + *stok* stick]

lint (lint) *n.* **1** The soft down of raveled or scraped linen; also, downy feathers. **2** A net; netting. **3** Cotton fiber. [<L *linteum* linen cloth < *linum* flax] **— lint′y** *adj.*

lin·tel (lin′təl) *n.* A horizontal top piece, as of a doorway or window opening. [<OF <LL *lintellus, limitellus,* dim. of *limes, limites* limit]

lint·er (lin′tər) *n.* A machine for removing linters from cotton seeds after they have been ginned.

lint·ers (lin′tərz) *n. pl.* A mixture of cotton fuzz and fibers left behind on the cotton gin: used as batting, for stuffing upholstery, and in the manufacture of rayon.

lint·white (lint′hwīt′) *n.* The European gray linnet. [OE *līnetwige,* lit., flax-plucker]

lin·y (lī′nē) *adj.* **lin·i·er, lin·i·est 1** Like a line. **2** Full of, or marked with, lines or streaks. Also spelled *liney.*

Lin Yu·tang (lin′yōō′täng′), born 1895, Chinese writer and philologist active in the United States.

Linz (lints) A city on the Danube, the capital of Upper Austria.

li·on (lī′ən) *n.* **1** A large, yellowish-brown or tawny, carnivorous mammal (*Panthera leo*) of the cat family, native to Africa and SW Asia, the adult male having a long mane. **2** Figuratively, a man of conspicuous courage; one of leonine character or mien. **3** An object of peculiar interest and curiosity; a prominent or notable person. **4** A former gold coin of Scotland. **— mountain lion** The puma. **— to twist the lion's tail** To make anti-British statements: from the lion on the heraldic shield of England. [<F <L *leo* <Gk. *leōn*]

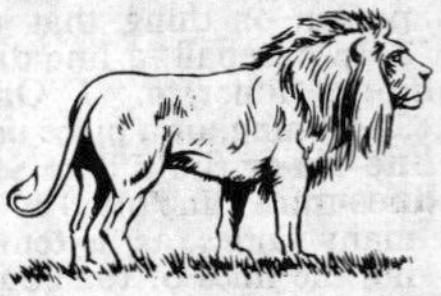

LION
(About 3 feet high at the shoulder; length: 10 feet over-all)

Li·on (lī′ən) The zodiacal sign or the constellation Leo. See CONSTELLATION.

Lion, Gulf of the A wide bay of the Mediterranean Sea in the southern coast of France. *French* **Golfe du Lion** (lē·ôn′).

lion dog 1 In Chinese and Japanese art and sculpture, a stylized lion, distorted so that the body resembles that of a dog, used as a symbol of good luck: also *Foo dog.* **2** Any of several breeds of small dog, as the Lhasa apso or Pekingese, having a leonine head.

li·on·ess (lī′ən·is) *n.* A female lion. [<OF *lionnesse*]

li·on·et (lī′ən·et) *n.* A small or young lion; a lion cub. [<OF]

li·on·heart (lī′ən·härt′) *n.* A person of exceptional bravery; especially, **Lionheart,** as a nickname of Richard I of England. See COEUR DE LION. **— lion′heart′ed** *adj.*

li·on·ize (lī′ən·īz) *v.t.* **·ized, ·iz·ing** To treat or regard as a celebrity. **— li′on·i·za′tion** *n.*

lip (lip) *n.* **1** One of the two folds of flesh that bound the mouth and cover the teeth. ◆ Collateral adjective: *labial.* **2** Hence, from the use of these organs in speaking, speech; especially, impertinent speech; sauciness. **3** Anything having the appearance or purpose of a lip, as of a cup, bell, crater, wound, etc. **4** An embouchure. **5** Any structure that bounds an orifice, slit, or groove. **6** *Bot.* Either of the two large lobes of a bilabiate corolla or calyx; also, in orchids, a labium. **— to keep a stiff upper lip** To keep up one's courage; be stoical. **—** *v.* **lipped, lip·ping** *v.t.* **1** To touch with the lips; apply the lips to. **2** *Archaic* To utter with the lips; whisper. **3** In golf, to hit the ball so that it strikes the edge of (the cup) without dropping in. **—** *v.i.* **4** To adjust the lips to the mouthpiece of a wind instrument for playing. **—** *adj.* **1** Of or pertaining to the lips or a lip. **2** Characterized by or made with the lips. **3** Made with the lips only; superficial; insincere: *lip* service. [OE *lippa*]

Lip·a·ri Islands (lip′ə·rē, *Ital.* lē′pä·rē) A group of volcanic islands off the NE coast of Sicily; 45 square miles. Italian *Isole Eolie*: also *Aeolian Islands.*

lip·a·roid (lip′ə·roid) *adj.* Fatty; resembling fat. [<Gk. *liparos* fat, greasy + -OID]

lip·ase (lip′ās, lī′pās) *n.* A fat-splitting enzyme.

li·pec·to·my (li·pek′tə·mē) *n. Surg.* An operation for the removal of excess fatty tissue. [<LIP(O)- + -ECTOMY]

lip·id (lip′id, lī′pid) *n. Biochem.* Any of a large class of organic substances which include the true fats and certain related compounds, as waxes and sterols. They are insoluble in water and have a typical greasy feel. Also **lip·ide** (lip′īd, lī′pīd).

Li Po (lē′ bō′), 700?–762, Chinese poet: also *Li T'ai-po.*

lipo– *combining form* **1** Fat; fatty: *lipotropic.* **2** A lipid: *lipoprotein.* Also, before vowels, **lip–.** [<Gk. *lipos* fat]

lip·o·ca·ic (lip′ō·kā′ik) *n. Biochem.* A hormonelike substance extracted from raw pancreas and having the power to regulate the fat metabolism of the liver. [<LIPO- + Gk. *kaiein* burn]

lip·o·chrome (lip′ō·krōm) *n. Biochem.* Any of a class of pigments, including the carotenoids, found in natural fats, as butter or egg yolk.

lip·o·cyte (lip′ō·sīt) *n. Biol.* A fat-bearing cell.

lip·oid (lip′oid) *n. Biochem.* A fat that is not decomposed by alkalis, as cholesterol.

li·pol·y·sis (li·pol′ə·sis) *n.* The breakdown and decomposition of fat. [<LIPO- + -LYSIS] **— lip·o·lyt·ic** (lip′ō·lit′ik) *adj.*

li·po·ma (li·pō′mə) *n. Pathol.* A tumor, generally painless and benign, made up of fat cells. [<LIP(O)- + -OMA] **— li·pom·a·tous** (li·pom′ə·təs) *adj.*

lip·o·pro·te·in (lip′ō·prō′tē·in, -tēn) *n. Biochem.* Any of a class of proteins found in combination with lipids, as in blood, egg yolk, milk, etc.

li·pot·ro·py (li·pot′rə·pē) *n.* An affinity for fats or oils or for fatty tissue. Also **li·pot′ro·pism. — lip·o·trop·ic** (lip′ō·trop′ik) *adj.*

Lip·pe (lip′ə) A former state of NW Germany, now included in North Rhine-Westphalia; 469 square miles; capital, Detmold.

lipped (lipt) *adj.* **1** Having a lip, lips, or a structure resembling lips. **2** *Bot.* Labiate.

lip·pen (lip′ən) *v.t.* & *v.i. Scot.* To trust.

Lip·pi (lip′ē, *Ital.* lēp′pē), **Filippo,** 1406?–69, Florentine painter and monk: known as *Fra Lippo Lippi.* **— Filippino,** 1457?–1504, Florentine painter; son of the preceding.

Lip·pi·zan·er (lip′it·sä′nər) *n.* One of a breed of generally white horses developed in Austria and often ridden in dressage exhibitions.

Lipp·mann (lēp·màn′), **Gabriel,** 1845–1921, French physicist.

Lipp·mann (lip′mən), **Walter,** 1889–1974, U.S. journalist and author.

lip–read (lip′rēd′) *v.t. & v.i.* **–read, –read·ing** To interpret (speech) from the position assumed by the lips and mouth for each word.

lip–read·ing (lip′rē′ding) *n.* Interpretation of speech from the position of the lips and mouth of the speaker: practiced especially by the deaf. **— lip′–read′er** *n.*

lip service Service that is professed but not intended or performed.

lip·stick (lip′stik′) *n.* A small, colored cosmetic stick of creamy texture, used to tint lips.

Lip·ton (lip′tən), **Sir Thomas Johnston,** 1850–1931, English merchant and yachtsman.

li·quate (lī′kwāt) *v.t.* **·quat·ed, ·quat·ing 1** To liquefy; melt. **2** *Metall.* To separate (a metal) from its impurities by the application of heat. [<L *liquatus,* pp. of *liquare* melt] **— li·qua·tion** (lī·kwā′shən) *n.*

liq·ue·fac·tion (lik′wə·fak′shən) *n.* **1** The operation of liquefying. **2** The state of being liquefied. **— liq′ue·fa′cient** (-fā′shənt) *adj.* & *n.*

liq·ue·fi·er (lik′wə·fī′ər) *n.* An apparatus devised for the liquefaction of gases.

liq·ue·fy (lik′wə·fī) *v.t.* & *v.i.* **·fied, ·fy·ing** To convert into or become liquid; melt. See synonyms under MELT. [<L *liquefacere* < *liquere* be liquid + *facere* make] **— liq′ue·fi′a·ble** *adj.*

li·ques·cent (li·kwes′ənt) *adj.* **1** Melting. **2** Having a tendency to melt or to become liquid. [<L *liquescens, -entis,* ppr. of *liquescere,* incept. of *liquere* become liquid] **— li·ques′cence, li·ques′cen·cy** *n.*

li·queur (li·kûr′) *n.* A sweetened alcoholic beverage, usually served after dinner, made by flavoring a spirit with aromatic ingredients, such as fruit, seeds, or herbs, before the distillation process; a cordial. [<F <OF *licur.* Doublet of LIQUOR.]

liq·uid (lik′wid) *adj.* **1** Flowing, or capable of flowing; being a liquid. **2** Limpid; clear. **3** *Physics* Composed of molecules having free movement among themselves, but without a separative tendency like that of gases. **4** Flowing smoothly; mellifluous: *liquid* tones. **5** Containing or suggesting liquid; watery. **6** *Phonet.* Pronounced with a smoothly flowing sound; vowel-like, as (l) and (r). **7** Easily or quickly converted into cash: *liquid* assets. See synonyms for FLUID. **—** *n.* **1** *Physics* A substance in that state in which the particles move freely among themselves and remain in one mass; a fluid which differs from a gas in not diffusing through the entire volume of a containing vessel. **2** *Phonet.* The consonants (l) and (r). [<F *liquide* <L *liquidus* < *liquere* be liquid] **— li·quid·i·ty** (li·kwid′ə·tē), **liq′uid·ness** *n.* **— liq′uid·ly** *adv.*

liquid air An intensely cold mixture of nitrogen and oxygen, existing only at temperatures below the boiling point of its components, and brought to a liquid condition by a reduction of temperature and an increase of pressure: chiefly used as a refrigerant.

liq·uid·am·bar (lik'wid·am'bər) n. 1 Any of a genus (*Liquidambar*) of balsamiferous trees of eastern Asia and Atlantic North America; especially, the American sweetgum. 2 The balsam yielded by such trees: used in medicine and the arts; copalm. [<NL]

liq·ui·date (lik'wə·dāt) v. **·dat·ed, ·dat·ing** v.t. 1 *Law* **a** To determine and settle the liabilities of (an estate, firm, etc.) and apportion the assets. **b** To determine and settle the amount of, as indebtedness or damages. 2 To pay or settle, as a debt. 3 To convert into cash. 4 To destroy or annihilate; do away with. 5 *Slang* To murder. — v.i. 6 To settle one's debts; go into liquidation. [< Med. L *liquidatus*, pp. of *liquidare* make liquid or clear <L *liquidus* liquid] — **liq'ui·da'· tor** n.

liq·ui·da·tion (lik'wə·dā'shən) n. The act of liquidating or the state of being liquidated. — **to go into liquidation** To cease from transacting business and gather in assets, settle debts, and divide surpluses, if any.

liquid crystal *Chem.* A substance intermediate in state between liquid and solid, having the fluidity of a liquid and the optical anisotropy of a crystalline solid.

liquid fire Burning oil or other inflammable chemicals: used in warfare, as from flame-throwers.

liquid measure A unit or system of units for measuring liquids, as in the following table of principal customary standards. See also METRIC SYSTEM.

4 gills	=	1 pint (pt., pts.)	
2 pints	=	1 quart (qt., qts.)	
4 quarts	=	1 gallon (gal., gals.)	
60 minims (min., ♍)	=	1 fluid dram (fl. dr., ʒ)	
8 fluid drams	=	1 fluid ounce (fl. oz., ʒ)	
16 fluid ounces	=	1 pint	

liq·uo·crys·tal·line (lik'wō·kris'tə·lin, -līn) adj. Designating that state of a liquid which exhibits properties similar to those of a crystal; mesomorphic.

liq·uor (lik'ər) n. 1 Any alcoholic or intoxicating liquid; especially, one that is distilled. 2 One of various solutions; specifically, an aqueous solution of a non-volatile substance: distinguished from a sirup, infusion, or decoction. 3 A liquid of any sort, as blood, milk, etc. — v.t. 1 To treat with liquor (def. 2). 2 *Slang* To supply or ply with alcoholic liquor: often with *up*. — v.i. 3 *Slang* To drink alcoholic liquor, especially in quantity: usually with *up*. [<OF *licor, licur* <L *liquor*. Doublet of LIQUEUR.]

liq·uo·rice (lik'ə·ris, -rish) See LICORICE.

liq·uor·ish (lik'ə·rish) See LICKERISH.

li·ra (lir'ə, *Ital.* lē'rä) n. pl. **li·re** (lir'ə, *Ital.* lē'rā) 1 The monetary unit of Italy, a small coin equivalent to 100 centesimi. 2 A gold coin of Turkey equivalent to 100 piasters: also called *Turkish pound*. [<Ital. <L *libra* pound]

Li·ri (lē'rē) A river in south central Italy, flowing 98 miles south to the Gulf of Gaeta. Ancient **Li·ris** (lir'is).

lir·i·o·den·dron (lir'ē·ō·den'drən) n. pl. **·dra** (-drə) Any of a genus (*Liriodendron*) of Asian and North American trees of the magnolia family; especially, the tuliptree of the United States. [<NL <Gk. *leirion* lily + *dendron* tree]

lir·i·pipe (lir'ə·pīp) n. In medieval dress, the long tail of a clerical tippet; hence, any long scarf or streamer attached to a headdress. Also **lir'i·poop** (-pōōp). [<Med. L *liripipium*; ult. origin uncertain]

Li·sa (lē'sə, -zə, lī'-) Diminutive of ELIZABETH. Also **Li'za**.

Lis·bon (liz'bən) A port on the Tagus, capital of Portugal. *Portuguese* **Lis·bo·a** (lēzh·bō'ä).

LIRIPIPE

Li·sette (lē·zet') French diminutive of ELIZABETH.

lisle (līl) n. 1 A fine, hard-twisted cotton thread, formerly linen: used in knitting gloves, stockings, etc. 2 Any fabric made of lisle thread. [from *Lisle*, now Lille, France]

Lisle (lēl) A former spelling of LILLE.

lisp (lisp) n. 1 A speech defect or affectation in which the sibilants (s) and (z) are pronounced with the tongue between the teeth so that the sounds produced are like (th) in *thank* and (th) in *this*. 2 The act or habit of speaking with a lisp. 3 The sound of a lisp. — v.t. & v.i. 1 To pronounce or speak with a lisp. 2 To speak imperfectly or in a childlike manner. [OE *wlispian*] — **lisp'er** n.

lis pen·dens (lis pen'denz) *Law Latin* A suit pending; during the pendency of a suit: Land bought of a defendant *lis pendens* is taken subject to the judgment afterward rendered.

lis·some (lis'əm) adj. Lithesome. Also **lis'som**. See synonyms under SUPPLE. [Alter. of LITHESOME] — **lis'some·ness** n.

lis·sot·ri·chous (li·sot'rə·kəs) adj. Having straight hair. [<Gk. *lissos* smooth + *thrix, trichos* hair]

list¹ (list) n. A series of words, numbers, names, etc., as on a strip of paper; a roll or catalog. — v.t. To place on or in a list or catalog, especially in alphabetical or numerical order. [<OF *liste* <OHG *līsta*]

list² (list) n. 1 The selvage or edge of a woven textile fabric. 2 Selvages, collectively. 3 A strip of fabric. 4 A colored stripe. 5 A narrow strip of wood cut from a plank. 6 *Agric.* A ridge or furrow made with a lister in cultivating corn. 7 pl. The palisades bounding a piece of ground used as a jousting field; hence, the field itself. — **to enter the lists** To accept a challenge; enter a contest or discussion. — v.t. 1 To cover with lists of cloth. 2 To sew or arrange in strips or stripes. 3 *Agric.* **a** To plow by means of a lister. **b** To plant by means of a lister. 4 In carpentry, to remove the rough edge of, as a board. [OE *liste*]

list³ (list) v.t. & v.i. 1 To lean or incline to one side; careen, as a ship. 2 *Archaic* To wish or choose; please. — n. 1 A careening; leaning or inclination of a ship to one side. 2 *Archaic* Desire; wish. [OE *lystan* < *lust* desire]

list⁴ (list) v.t. & v.i. *Poetic* To listen to or listen. See synonyms under LISTEN. [OE *hlystan* < *hlyst* hearing]

List (list), **Siegmund Wilhelm Walther,** born 1880, German field marshal in World War II.

listed security A stock or bond that has been admitted to the roster of approved securities by a stock exchange, thus becoming available for trading on the exchange.

lis·tel (lis'təl) n. *Archit.* A small square molding; a list. [<F <Ital. *listello*, dim. of *lista* list²]

lis·ten (lis'ən) v.i. 1 To make an effort to hear; give ear. 2 To pay attention; give heed or compliance, as to warning or advice. — n. The act of listening. [OE *hlysnan*] — **lis'ten·er** n.

Synonyms (verb): attend, hark, harken, hear, heed, list⁴. To *hear* is simply to become conscious of sound, to *listen* is to make a conscious effort to *hear*. We may *hear* without *listening*, as words suddenly uttered in an adjoining room; or we may *listen* without *hearing*, as to a distant speaker. In *listening* the ear is intent upon the sound; in *attending* the mind is intent upon the thought; but *listening* implies some attention to the meaning or import of the sound. To *heed* is not only to *attend*, but to remember and observe. *Harken* is nearly obsolete. Antonyms: ignore, neglect, scorn, slight.

listening post 1 A concealed position near enemy lines from which an observer may transmit to his own forces information or warning of hostile action. 2 A station equipped with sound-locating devices for warning against the approach of enemy aircraft or sea vessels. 3 A radio station equipped to pick up short-wave messages from different countries.

list·er¹ (lis'tər) n. *Agric.* A double-moldboard plow for throwing up ridges, as in beet- or corn-culture: it simultaneously throws a deep furrow, plants the seed, and covers it with earth. Also called *middle-breaker*. [<LIST² + -ER¹]

list·er² (lis'tər) n. One who makes a list or lists; specifically, a tax appraiser.

Lis·ter (lis'tər), **Joseph,** 1827–1912, Baron Lister of Lyme Regis, English surgeon; founder of antiseptic surgery.

Lister bag See LYSTER BAG.

Lis·ter·ine (lis'tə·rēn', lis'tə·rēn) n. Proprietary name for a weak antiseptic solution. [after Sir Joseph *Lister*]

list·ing (lis'ting) n. 1 The compiling of a list. 2 A place on a list.

list·less (list'lis) adj. Inattentive; heedless of what is passing; indifferent; languid; lacking energy. See synonyms under FAINT, INATTENTIVE. [OE *lust* desire + -LESS] — **list'less·ly** adv. — **list'less·ness** n.

list mill A power-driven wheel covered with cloth on which gemstones are buffed or polished.

list price The price of goods as published in price lists or catalogs.

Liszt (list), **Franz,** 1811–86, Hungarian composer and pianist.

lit¹ (lit) Alternative past tense and past participle of LIGHT¹ and LIGHT².

lit² (lit) n. The gold monetary unit of Lithuania. Also *Lithuanian* **li·tas** (lē'täs).

lit·a·ny (lit'ə·nē) n. pl. **·nies** 1 *Eccl.* A liturgical form of prayer, consisting of a series of different supplications said by the clergy, to which the choir or people repeat the same response. 2 Any solemn prayer. See synonyms under prayer. — **the Litany** In the Book of Common Prayer, a general supplication in this form. [<OF *letanie* <LL *litania* <Gk. *litaneia* < *litaneuein* pray]

li·tchi (lē'chē) n. 1 A Chinese tree (*Litchi chinensis*) of the soapberry family, producing small, thin-shelled, edible fruits called **litchi nuts**. 2 The fruit of this tree. Also spelled *lichee, lychee*. [<Chinese *li-chih*]

lit de jus·tice (lē də zhü·stēs') *French* Literally, bed of justice; the seat which the king of France occupied when holding a formal session of the parliament; hence, the session itself.

-lite combining form Mineral. Stone; stonelike: *cryolite*. Also spelled *-lyte*. [<F, var. of *-lithe* <Gk. *lithos* stone]

li·te pen·den·te (lī'tē pen·den'tē) *Latin* During the trial.

li·ter (lē'tər) n. A measure of capacity in the metric system, equal to the volume of one kilogram of water at 4° C. and 760 mm. atmospheric pressure, or to 1.0567 liquid quarts. See METRIC SYSTEM. Also *litre*. [<F *litre* <Gk. *litra* pound]

lit·er·a·cy (lit'ər·ə·sē) n. The state or condition of being literate.

lit·er·al (lit'ər·əl) adj. 1 According to the letter or verbal statement; not figurative or metaphorical. 2 Following the exact words or construction: a *literal* translation. 3 Consisting of or expressed by letters. 4 Matter-of-fact; unimaginative: said of persons. 5 Exact as to fact or detail; not exaggerated. See synonyms under VERBAL. ◆ Homophone: *littoral*. [<OF <LL *literalis, litteralis* < *littera* letter]

lit·er·al·ism (lit'ər·əl·iz'əm) n. 1 Close adherence to the exact word or sense, often to the point of unimaginativeness. 2 In the fine arts, a tendency to represent without idealizing; realistic representation or depiction. — **lit'er·al·ist** n.

lit·er·al·ize (lit'ər·əl·īz') v.t. **·ized, ·iz·ing** To make literal; interpret or accept literally.

lit·er·al·ly (lit'ər·ə·lē) adv. 1 In a literal manner. 2 *Colloq.* In a manner of speaking; figuratively: used for emphasis: He was *literally* green with envy.

lit·er·ar·y (lit'ə·rer'ē) adj. 1 Of or pertaining to letters or used in literature. 2 Versed in or devoted to literature. 3 Engaged or occupied in the field of literature: a *literary* man. [<L *litterarius*]

lit·er·ate (lit'ər·it) adj. 1 Able to read and write. 2 Having a knowledge of letters or literature; educated. 3 Literary. — n. 1 Anyone able to read and write. 2 One versed

in letters or literature. [<L *litteratus* < *littera* letter]

lit·e·ra·ti (lit′ə·rä′tē, -rā′tī) *n. pl.* Men of letters; scholars. [<L]

lit·e·ra·tim (lit′ə·rā′tim, -rä′-) *adv.* Letter for letter; with exact literalness; literally. [<L]

lit·er·a·tor (lit′ə·rā′tər) *n.* A literary man. [<L]

lit·er·a·ture (lit′ər·ə·chŏŏr, lit′rə·chər) *n.* **1** The written or printed productions of the human mind collectively. **2** Written works which deal with themes of permanent and universal interest, characterized by creativeness and grace of expression, as poetry, fiction, essays, etc.: distinguished from works of scientific, technical, or journalistic nature; belles-lettres. **3** The writings that pertain to a particular epoch, country, language, subject, or branch of learning: ancient *literature*; the *literature* of chemistry. **4** The act or occupation of a literary man; literary work. **5** Acquaintance with letters or books; learning. **6** *Music* The total number of compositions for a particular instrument or ensemble. **7** Any printed matter used or distributed for advertising or political purposes, etc.: campaign *literature*. [<L *litteratura* < *littera* letter]

Synonyms: belles-lettres, books, publications, writings. *Literature* is collective, referring to all that has been written in some land or age, or in some department of human knowledge: the *literature* of Greece; the *literature* of art. *Literature*, used absolutely, denotes *belles-lettres, i.e.*, the works collectively that embody taste, feeling, loftiness of thought, and purity and beauty of style, as poetry, history, fiction, and dramatic compositions. In the broad sense we speak of the *literature* of science; in the narrower sense, we speak of *literature* and science as distinct departments of knowledge. *Literature* is also used to signify literary pursuits or occupations: to devote one's life to *literature*. Compare KNOWLEDGE.

lith (lith) *n. Archaic* A limb; joint; segment: usually in the phrase **lith and limb.** [OE]

-lith *combining form* Stone; rock: *monolith*. [<Gk. *lithos* a stone]

lith·arge (lith′ärj, li·thärj′) *n.* Yellow lead monoxide, PbO, made by heating lead in a current of air: used in glassmaking, as a pigment, cement, etc. [<F *litarge* <L *lithargyrus* <Gk. *lithargyros* silver scum < *lithos* stone + *argyros* silver]

lithe (līth) *adj.* Bending easily or gracefully; supple. See synonyms under SUPPLE. [OE, soft] **—lithe′ly** *adv.* **—lithe′ness** *n.*

li·the·mi·a (li·thē′mē·ə) *n. Pathol.* An excess of urates and uric acid in the blood. Also **li·thae′·mi·a.** [<LITH(O)- + -EMIA] **—li·the′mic** *adj.*

lithe·some (līth′səm) *adj.* Lithe; nimble; lissome.

lith·i·a (lith′ē·ə) *n.* A white, caustic compound, Li_2O, that dissolves slowly in water to form lithium hydrate; lithium oxide. [<NL <Gk. *lithos* stone]

li·thi·a·sis (li·thī′ə·sis) *n. Pathol.* The formation of stones or calculi in the body. [<NL <Gk. < *lithos* stone]

lithia water A natural mineral water containing lithium salts.

lith·ic (lith′ik) *adj.* **1** Of, pertaining to, or having calculus or stone in the bladder. **2** Of or pertaining to stone. **3** *Chem.* Of or pertaining to lithium. [<Gk. *lithikos* of stone]

lith·i·um (lith′ē·əm) *n.* A soft, silver-white, metallic element (symbol Li) belonging to the first group of the periodic table. It is the lightest of the metals and is found only in combination. See ELEMENT. [<NL <Gk. *lithos* stone]

litho- *combining form* Stone; related to stone: *lithophilous*. Also, before vowels, **lith-.** [<Gk. *lithos* stone]

lith·o·graph (lith′ə·graf, -gräf) *v.t.* To produce or reproduce by lithography. **—*n.*** A lithographic print. [<LITHO- + -GRAPH] **—li·thog·ra·pher** (li·thog′rə·fər) *n.* **—lith′o·graph′ic** or **·i·cal** *adj.* **—lith′o·graph′i·cal·ly** *adv.*

li·thog·ra·phy (li·thog′rə·fē) *n.* The art of producing printed matter from a stone or stones on which the design or matter to be printed has been made in a soapy ink, grease pencil, or other suitable material. Zinc and aluminum are now widely substituted for stone.

lithographic stone A yellowish, compact, fine-grained, slaty limestone used in lithography. Also **lithographic slate.**

lith·oid (lith′oid) *adj.* Of or resembling stone; having stony structure or texture. Also **li·thoi·dal** (li·thoid′l).

li·thol·o·gy (li·thol′ə·jē) *n.* **1** The science that treats of rocks as mineral masses, especially with reference to their structure. **2** The branch of medicine which treats of calculi in the body. [<LITHO- + -LOGY] **—lith·o·log·ic** (lith′ə·loj′ik) or **·i·cal** *adj.* **—li·thol′o·gist** *n.*

lith·o·marge (lith′ə·märj) *n.* A mixture of hydrous aluminum silicates, related to kaolin. [<LITHO- + L *marga* marl]

lith·o·phane (lith′ə·fān) *n.* Ornamentation impressed in porcelain or glass, as in a lampshade, made visible by light passing through it. [<LITHO- +Gk. *-phaneia, phainein* appear]

li·thoph·i·lous (li·thof′ə·ləs) *adj.* **1** Stone-loving. **2** *Ecol.* Living among, beneath, or on stones: said of insects and plants preferring a stony habitat. [<LITHO- + -PHILOUS]

lith·o·phyte (lith′ə·fīt) *n.* **1** *Zool.* A calcareous or stony polyp or plantlike organism, as a coral. **2** *Bot.* A plant that lives on stony or rocky surfaces in air or under water. **—lith′o·phyt′ic** (-fit′ik) *adj.*

lith·o·pone (lith′ə·pōn) *n.* A mixture of barium sulfate and zinc sulfide, used as a white paint and in the manufacture of rubber tires, linoleums, etc. [<LITHO- + L *ponere* place]

lith·o·sphere (lith′ə·sfir) *n.* The rigid crust of rock surrounding the inner viscous material of the earth and similar bodies in the solar system.

li·thot·o·my (li·thot′ə·mē) *n. Surg.* The operation of removing stones from the bladder by incision into the organ. [<LL *lithotomia* <Gk. < *lithos* stone + *temnein* cut] **—lith·o·tom·ic** (lith′·ə·tom′ik) or **·i·cal** *adj.* **—li·thot′·o·mist** *n.*

lith·o·tint (lith′ə·tint) *n.* **1** The art of producing pictures in color tints from lithographic stones. **2** A picture so produced.

li·thot·ri·ty (li·thot′rə·tē) *n. Surg.* The operation of reducing stone in the bladder to fine, easily voided fragments. Also **li·thot′rip·sy** (-rip·sē). [<LITHO- + L *tritus*, pp. of *terere* rub, grind]

Lith·u·a·ni·a (lith′ōō·ā′nē·ə) Southernmost of the Baltic States of NE Europe; since 1940 formally **Lithuanian Soviet Socialist Republic,** a constituent republic of the U.S.S.R.; 25,200 square miles; capital, Vilna. *Lithuanian* **Lie·tu·va** (lye·tōō′vä).

Lith·u·a·ni·an (lith′ōō·ā′nē·ən) *adj.* Of or pertaining to Lithuania, its people, or their language. **—*n.*** **1** A native or inhabitant of Lithuania. **2** The Balto-Slavic language of the Lithuanians, belonging to the Baltic branch.

lith·y (lī′thē) *adj.* **lith·i·er, lith·i·est** *Archaic* Lithe; flexible; willowy.

lit·i·gant (lit′ə·gənt) *adj.* Disposed to litigate; engaged in litigation. **—*n.*** A party to a lawsuit. [<F]

lit·i·gate (lit′ə·gāt) *v.* **·gat·ed, ·gat·ing** *v.t.* To bring before a court of law for decision or settlement; contest at law. **—*v.i.*** To carry on a lawsuit. [<L *litigatus*, pp. of *litigare* < *lis, litis* lawsuit + *agere* do, act] **—lit′i·ga·ble** (-gə·bəl) *adj.* **—lit′i·ga′tor** *n.*

lit·i·ga·tion (lit′ə·gā′shən) *n.* The act of carrying on a suit in a law court; a judicial contest; hence, any controversy that must be decided upon evidence.

li·ti·gious (li·tij′əs) *adj.* **1** Inclined to litigation; hence, quarrelsome. **2** Subject to litigation or contention; controvertible; disputable: a *litigious* right. **3** Of or pertaining to litigation: *litigious* form. [<F *litigieux* <L *litigiosus* < *litigium* litigation] **—li·tig′ious·ly** *adv.* **—li·tig′ious·ness** *n.*

lit·mus (lit′məs) *n.* A blue dyestuff made by fermenting certain coarsely powdered lichens. It is turned red by acids and remains blue when treated with an alkali. Also called *lacmus*. [<AF *lytemoise* <ON *litmose* lichen used in dyeing < *litr* color + *mosi* moss]

litmus paper Unsized paper dipped into a solution of litmus, and used to test solutions for acidity.

lit·o·ral (lit′ər·əl) See LITTORAL.

li·to·tes (lī′tə·tēz, -tō-, lit′ə-) *n.* A rhetorical figure in which an assertion is made by means of negation or understatement; ironic understatement. Example: a fact of no small importance (*i.e.*, of very great importance). See MEIOSIS. [<NL <Gk. *litotēs* < *litos* simple, spare]

li·tre (lē′tər) See LITER.

lit·ter (lit′ər) *n.* **1** The offspring borne at one time by a cat, sow, or other multiparous animal. **2** A stretcher used for conveying sick or wounded. **3** A couch carried on shafts protruding at each end, and used for the transportation of people of wealth or importance. **4** Straw, hay, or other similar material, used as bedding for horses, cattle, etc. **5** Waste materials, shreds, and fragments scattered about; a clutter; a state of disorder. **6** The upper part of a forest floor which is not in an advanced state of decomposition. See synonyms under FLOCK. **—*v.t.*** **1** To bring forth young: said of animals. **2** To furnish, as cattle, with litter. **3** To cover or strew with or as with litter: often with *up*: to *litter* a room with toys. **4** To throw or spread about carelessly. **—*v.i.*** **5** To give birth to a litter of young. [<OF *litiere* < Med. L *lectaria* <L *lectus* bed] **—lit′ter·y** *adj.*

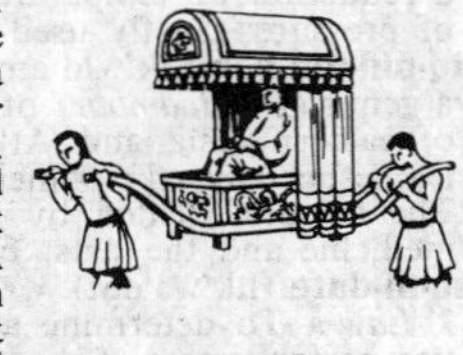

LITTER
Late Roman period.

lit·te·rae hu·ma·ni·o·res (lit′ə·rē hyōō·mā′nē·ō′rēz) *Latin* Humanistic studies; classical literature, history, and philosophy.

lit·ter·a·teur (lit′ər·ə·tûr′) *n.* One who is by profession engaged in literature. [<F]

lit·ter·bug (lit′ər·bug′) *n. Colloq.* A person who is careless in disposing of garbage, waste, and litter; one who violates or ignores street-cleaning regulations.

lit·tle (lit′l) *adj.* **less** or *Colloq.* **lit·tler, least** or *Colloq.* **lit·tlest** **1** Of a size, amount, quantity, etc., below the ordinary; diminutive; small. **2** Below the usual amount; restricted. **3** Below the normal distance or time; short; brief. **4** Below the standard in respect to dignity or consequence; insignificant; petty; hence, mean; narrow: a *little* quarrel, a *little* nature. **5** Lacking in ability, efficiency, or force; weak. **6** Smaller than other like things. **7** Being in the early years of life: when I was *little*. **—*n.*** A small quantity, space, time, degree, etc. **—*adv.*** **less, least** **1** In a small degree; slightly. **2** Not at all: used before a verb: She *little* knows how much I care. [OE *lȳtel* < *lȳt* small] **—lit′tle·ness** *n.*

Synonyms (adj.): brief, contemptible, diminutive, feeble, inconsiderable, insignificant, mean, microscopic, minute, narrow, paltry, petty, short, slender, slight, small, tiny, trifling, trivial, unimportant. See INSIGNIFICANT, MINUTE[2], SMALL.

Little America An Antarctic base for exploring expeditions, on the Ross Shelf Ice south of the Bay of Wales; established by Admiral Byrd, 1929.

Lit·tle (lit′l), **Malcolm** See MALCOLM X.

Little Armenia See CILICIA.

Little Bear See under BEAR.

Little Big·horn River (big′hôrn′) A river in Wyoming and Montana, flowing 90 miles north to the Bighorn River; scene of Custer's defeat by Indians, 1876.

little boy A young boy, usually one between the ages of two and ten or eleven.

Little Colorado River A river flowing 315 miles north through Arizona to the Colorado River in the Grand Canyon.

Little Dipper See URSA MINOR.

Lit·tle-end·i·an (lit′l·en′dē·ən) *n.* One who disputes about trifles: from Swift's *Gulliver's Travels*, in which a religious party of this name in Lilliput maintained that eggs should be broken at the little end. See BIG-ENDIAN.

Lit·tle-Eng·land·er (lit′l·ing′glən·dər) *n.* In the 19th century, one of those opposed to the territorial expansion of the British Empire and to imperial federation.

Little Fox The northern constellation, Vulpecula.

little girl A young girl, usually one between the ages of two and ten or eleven.

Little Go The preliminary examination for the B.A. degree at Cambridge University, England: also called *Previous Examination*.

little hours In the Roman Catholic Church,

the offices of prime, tierce, sext, and nones.

Little John One of Robin Hood's lieutenants.

Little Kar·roo (kə·rōō′) See SOUTHERN KARROO.

Little Missouri River A river in the NW United States, flowing 560 miles NE to the Missouri.

lit·tle·neck clam (lit′l·nek′) The young of the hardshell clam or quahaug: much esteemed as a food. Also **lit′tle·neck′**. [from *Little Neck*, Long Island]

Little Office In the Roman Catholic Church, an office of lessons and hymns in honor of the Virgin Mary.

Little Rho·dy (rō′dē) Nickname of RHODE ISLAND.

Little Rock The capital of Arkansas.

Little Russia A name formerly applied to the Ukraine region, and often extended to include adjacent areas in Poland and Rumania.

Little Russian See under RUSSIAN.

Little St. Bernard Pass See under ST. BERNARD.

little theater A small theater, usually composed of an artists' group, college students, etc., producing plays which are often experimental and innovative: often used attributively to denote a movement in the 1920's involving the growth of these theaters.

Lit·tle·ton (lit′əl·tən), **Sir Thomas,** 1407?–81, English jurist; author of earliest printed treatise on English law.

lit·to·ral (lit′ər·əl) *n.* A shore and the country contiguous to it. —*adj.* Pertaining to the shore. Also spelled *litoral.* ◆ Homophone: *literal.* [<L *littoralis* < *litus, -oris* +6 seashore]

li·tur·gics (li·tûr′jiks) *n.* The doctrine, history, or science of liturgies.

lit·ur·gist (lit′ər·jist) *n.* 1 One who uses or advocates liturgical forms of worship. 2 One versed in liturgics. 3 One who leads in reciting the liturgy.

lit·ur·gy (lit′ər·jē) *n. pl.* **·gies** 1 A collection of prescribed forms for public worship; a ritual; specifically, in the Roman Catholic Church, the mass. 2 In the Greek Church, the Eucharist: also **Divine Liturgy.** [<F *liturgie* <Med. L *liturgia* <Gk. *leitourgia* public duty, ult. <*laos* people + *ergon* work] —**li·tur·gic** (li·tûr′jik) or **·gi·cal** *adj.* —**li·tur′gi·cal·ly** *adv.*

lit·u·us (lit′yŏŏ·əs) *n. pl.* **·u·i** (lit′yŏŏ·ī) *Math.* A polar curve traced by a point moving so that the square of its distance from the pole varies inversely as its polar angle: it is trumpet-shaped, asymptotic to the polar axis, and approaches the pole as a limit. [<L, crooked staff, curved trumpet]

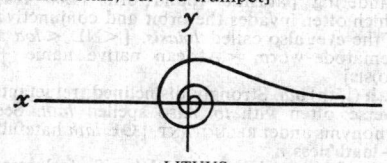

LITUUS

Lit·vi·nov (lit·vē′nôf), **Maxim,** 1876–1951, Soviet Russian statesman and diplomat.

Liu Shao-chi (lyōō′ shou′chē′), 1898?-1973, Chinese Communist leader, chairman of the People's Republic of China 1959–1973.

Li·ut·prand (lē′ŏŏt·pränd), 922?–972?, Lombard prelate, diplomat, and historian: also *Luitprand.*

liv·a·ble (liv′ə·bəl) *adj.* 1 Worth living; fit to be lived. 2 Agreeable or fit for living in or with. Also **live′a·ble.**

live (liv) *v.* **lived, liv·ing** *v.i.* 1 To be alive; have life. 2 To continue in life; remain alive: As long as you *live.* 3 To endure or persist; last: This day will *live* in infamy. 4 To maintain life; subsist: to *live* on a pittance. 5 To depend for food; feed: with *on* or *upon :* to *live* on carrion. 6 To dwell; abide. 7 To pass life in a specified manner: to *live* frugally. 8 To enjoy a varied and active life. 9 To escape destruction; stay afloat: No boat can *live* in that surf. —*v.t.* 10 To pass: to *live* the life of a saint. 11 To manifest or practice in one's life: to *live* a lie. —**to live down** To live in such a manner as to expiate (a crime), forget or cause to be forgotten (shame),or mature beyond (folly). —**to live high** To live luxuriously. —**to live in** To

reside at one's place of employment. —**to live on** To depend on parasitically, as for one's maintenance. —**to live out** To reside away from one's place of employment. —**to live through** To have experience of and survive. —**to live up to** To fulfil the hopes, terms, or character of. —**to live well** 1 To live luxuriously. 2 To live virtuously. —**to live with** 1 To dwell with as a lodger or companion. 2 To cohabit with: also **to live together.** —*adj.* (līv) 1 Possessing life; living; alive; quick: opposed to *dead* and *inanimate;* hence, ready for use; operative; effective. 2 Burning or glowing; a *live* coal. 3 Of present interest and importance; vital: a *live* book or topic. 4 Possessing liveliness, interest, or animation; alert; energetic: a *live* man of business. 5 *Printing* Ready for printing; kept for use: *live* copy. 6 Of or pertaining to living beings. 7 Containing an unexploded charge: said of munitions, etc.: a *live* shell. 8 Swarming with, or caused by a great number of living creatures. 9 Charged with electricity; carrying a current: a *live* wire. 10 Unwrought; pure; vivid: *live* rock or color. 11 Having motion or power to impart motion, as a part of a machine. See synonyms under ALIVE. [OE *lifian* live]

Synonyms (verb): continue, endure, exist, feed (with *on* or *upon*), subsist, survive. See ABIDE. *Antonyms:* see synonyms for DIE.

-lived *combining form* Having a (specified kind of) life or life span or (a given number of) lives: long-*lived,* nine-*lived.* [<LIFE]

live-for-ev·er (līv′fər·ev′ ər) *n.* A garden herb (*Sedum telephium*) of the orpine family, with greenish-white or purple flowers: naturalized in the United States.

live-in (liv′in′′) *adj.* Living at the home or other place where one works: a *live-in* housekeeper.

live·li·hood (līv′lē·hŏŏd) *n.* Means of subsistence; regular maintenance; employment; living.

live·long (liv′lông′, -long′) *adj.* That lives long or is tediously slow in passing; whole; entire: the *livelong* day. [ME *lefe longe,* lit., lief long; *lief,* here orig. intens., was later confused with *live*]

live·ly (līv′lē) *adj.* **·li·er, ·li·est** 1 Full of energy or of animation; stimulating; brisk; vivacious. 2 Intensely alive or active in the mind; animated; also, enlivening. 3 Striking to the senses; forcible; vivid. 4 In games, reactive; responsive to impact; rebounding: said of a ball: opposed to *dead.* 5 *Obs.* Lifelike. See synonyms under ACTIVE, AIRY, ALIVE, CHEERFUL, GOOD, MERRY, NIMBLE, RACY, SPRIGHTLY, VIVACIOUS, VIVID . —**live′li·ly** *adv.* —**live′li·ness** *n.*

li·ven (lī′vən) *v.t. & v.i.* To make or become lively or cheerful: often with *up.*

Liv·ens projector (liv′ənz) A type of mortar for the discharge of gas-containing projectiles: usually employed in large numbers to give a high concentration of gas. [after Capt. W. H. *Livens,* born 1889, British army officer]

live oak 1 One of several evergreen trees of the oak family native in the United States, especially *Quercus virginiana.* 2 The hard, durable wood of this tree.

liv·er[1] (liv′ər) *n.* 1 The largest glandular organ of vertebrates, in man situated just under the diaphragm and on the right side: it secretes bile, and is of great importance in metabolism. ◆ Collateral adjective: *hepatic.* 2 A digestive gland in invertebrates usually functioning as a pancreas, and consisting of cecal tubes. 3 The liver of certain animals, used as food. [OE *lifer*]

liv·er[2] (liv′ər) *n.* One who lives; a dweller.

liver extract A concentrated extract of mammalian liver, used in the treatment of anemia.

liver fluke Any of various trematode worms parasitic in the bile ducts of sheep, cows, pigs, and sometimes man, especially *Fasciola hepatica,* associated with the black disease of sheep.

liv·er·ied (liv′ər·ēd) *adj.* Dressed in livery, as a servant.

liv·er·ish (liv′ər·ish) *adj.* Feeling or exhibiting symptoms of disordered liver.

liv·er-leaf (liv′ər·lēf′) *n.* Hepatica.

liver of sulfur See HEPAR.

liver ore 1 A variety of cinnabar. 2 A brownish variety of cuprite.

Liv·er·pool (liv′ər·pōōl) A port and county borough of SW Lancashire, England, on the Mersey estuary. —**Liv·er·pud·li·an** (liv′ər·pud′·lē·ən) *adj. & n.*

liv·er·stone (liv′ər·stōn) *n.* A form of barite which yields an unpleasant odor when heated or rubbed.

liv·er·wort (liv′ər·wûrt) *n.* Any mosslike plant belonging to the family *Hepaticae,* but differing from true mosses in always having bilateral stems, vertically ranked leaves, and a capsule which opens by two or four valves.

liv·er·wurst (liv′ər·wûrst) *n.* A sausage made of or containing ground liver. [<G *leberwurst*]

liv·er·y (liv′ər·ē) *n. pl.* **·er·ies** 1 A particular dress or uniform worn by servants. 2 The distinctive dress of any association or organization. 3 Formerly, the dress or badge peculiar to a retainer of a feudal baron or knight. 4 Any characteristic dress, covering or outward appearance: trees in the *livery* of spring. 5 The stabling and care of horses for compensation, as at a boarding stable. 6 *Law* Delivery, as of lands. 7 *U.S.* A livery stable. [<OF *livree* gift of clothes by a master to a servant <*livrer* deliver, free <L *liberare* free <*liber* free]

livery cupboard A cupboard or stand formerly used in a dining-room to hold the liveries or rations.

liv·er·y·man (liv′ər·ē·mən) *n. pl.* **·men** (-mən) 1 A man who keeps a livery stable. 2 A freeman of the City companies or guilds of London, England.

livery stable A stable where horses and vehicles are kept for hire.

lives (līvz) Plural of LIFE.

live steam Steam supplied direct from a boiler, before doing or while doing its work in a cylinder: distinguished from *exhaust steam.*

live·stock (līv′stok′) *n.* Domestic animals kept for farm purposes, especially marketable animals, as cattle, horses, and sheep.

live wire 1 A wire carrying an electric current. 2 *Colloq.* An energetic person; a hustler.

liv·id (liv′id) *adj.* Black-and-blue, as contused flesh; lead-colored; ashy-pale. [<F *livide* <L *lividus* <*livere* be livid] —**liv′id·ly** *adv.* —**liv′id·ness, li·vid·i·ty** (li·vid′ə·tē) *n.*

liv·ing (liv′ing) *adj.* 1 Having life or vitality; live: opposed to *dead;* pertaining to the living. 2 Actually operative or efficient; also, quickening or vivifying. 3 Flowing, as water: distinguished from *stagnant.* 4 Ignited; flaming: said of coal, etc. 5 Filled with or true to life; vivacious; lively; animated. 6 Enough to sustain life or live on: a *living* wage. See synonyms under ALIVE. —*n.* 1 Livelihood. 2 In the Church of England, a benefice, or the revenue derived from it. 3 Manner of life. 4 Those who live; formerly, also, he who lives: with the definite article. 5 The fact of existing, or of dwelling in a certain place. 6 The action of existing or of passing one's life in a specified manner. 7 *Obs.* An estate; property; possessions.

living death A condition so wretched as scarcely to deserve the name of life.

living picture A tableau vivant.

liv·ing-room (liv′ing·rōōm′, -rŏŏm′) *n.* A room designed and furnished for the general occupancy of a family.

living space Lebensraum.

Liv·ing·ston (liv′ing·stən), **Robert R.,** 1746–1813, American Revolutionary statesman: helped draw up the Declaration of Independence.

Liv·ing·stone (liv′ing·stən), **David,** 1813–73, Scottish explorer and missionary in Africa.

Liv·ing·stone (liv′ing·stən) A town on the Zambezi, the former capital of Northern Rhodesia; now in Zambia.

living wage A wage that will enable a person to support himself and his family in reasonable security.

Li·vo·ni·a (li·vō′nē·ə) A region and former province of Russia in NE Europe, divided in 1918 between Latvia and Estonia. —**Li·vo′·ni·an** *adj. & n.*

Li·vor·no (li·vôr′nō) The Italian name for LEGHORN.

li·vre (lē′vər) *n.* An old French money of account, originally equal in value to a pound of silver. [<F <L *libra* pound]

Liv·y (liv′ē) Anglicized name of Titus Livius, 59 B.C.–A.D. 17, Roman historian.

lix·iv·i·ate (lik·siv′ē·āt) *v.t.* **·at·ed**, **·at·ing** To leach. [<L *lixivius* made into lye < *lix* ashes, lye] **—lix·iv′i·al** *adj.*

lix·iv·i·a·tion (lik·siv′ē·ā′shən) *n.* The process of extracting a soluble alkali or saline compound from a mixture by washing; leaching.

lix·iv·i·um (lik·siv′ē·əm) *n.* **1** A solution of alkaline salts, as lye. **2** A solution obtained by leaching. [<L <*lix* ashes, lye]

liz·ard (liz′ərd) *n.* **1** Any of various reptiles (suborder *Sauria*), as an agama, basilisk, chameleon, gecko, glass snake, horned toad, iguana, monitor, or skink. Lizards commonly have an elongate, scaly body, a long tail, and four legs, but the latter may be reduced to two or may be rudimentary or absent. **2** Any four-legged reptile of similar form. **3** A kind of low sledge for hauling logs, stones, etc. [<OF *laisard* <L *lacerta*]

LIZARD
a. Varanus (from 4 to 12 feet in length).
b. Chameleon (up to 18 inches in length).

Lizard, The A promontory in SW Cornwall, England; its extremity, **Lizard Head** or **Lizard Point**, is the southernmost point of Great Britain.

lizard fish 1 An elongate marine fish (family *Synodontidae*), having a lizardlike head. **2** The saury.

Liz·zie (liz′ē) Diminutive of ELIZABETH.

Lju·blja·na (lyōō′blyä·nä) A city in NW Yugoslavia, capital of Slovenia: German *Laibach*.

lla·ma (lä′mə, *Sp.* lyä′mä) *n.* A South American woolly-haired, humpless, cameloid ruminant (genus *Auchenia* or *Lama*), usually white or spotted with brown or black; the guanaco: used as a beast of burden in the Andes. [<Sp. <Quechua]

LLAMA
(From 3 1/2 to 4 feet at the shoulder)

Llan·daff (lan′daf, lan·daf′) A suburb of Cardiff in SE Glamorganshire, Wales; site of a 12th century cathedral.

Llan·dud·no (lan·dud′nō, -did′-) A resort town in NE Carnarvonshire, Wales.

Lla·nel·ly (la·nel′ē) A port in SE Carmarthenshire, Wales.

lla·no (lä′nō, *Sp.* lyä′nō) *n. pl.* **·nos** A flat, treeless plain, as the wide, grassy tracts of northern South America. [<Sp., plain, flat <L *planus*]

Lla·no Es·ta·ca·do (lä′nō es′tə·kä′dō, *Sp.* lyä′-

nō es′tä·kä′dō) A barren plateau region in western Texas and SE New Mexico south of the Great Plains: also *Staked Plain*. [<Sp., staked plain]

Llew·el·lyn (lōō·el′ən) A masculine personal name. [<Celtic, lightning]

Lloyd (loid) A masculine personal name. [<Celtic, gray]

Lloyd George (loid jôrj), **David**, 1863–1945, Earl of Dwyfor, British statesman; prime minister 1916–22.

Lloyd's (loidz) *n.* A corporation of English underwriters of marine insurance for the collection and distribution of maritime intelligence and the protection of their common interests and credit: started in 1688 in a London coffee house by Edward Lloyd.

Lloyd's Register An annual list of the seagoing vessels of all nations, their age, tonnage, etc., classified according to seaworthiness.

lo (lō) *interj.* Behold! observe!: used mainly in the phrase *Lo and behold*! [OE *lā*]

loach (lōch) *n.* A small, fresh-water, cyprinoid fish of the Old World (family *Cobitidae*), related to the minnow. [<F *loche*]

load (lōd) *n.* **1** That which is laid upon anything for conveyance; a burden; specifically, as much as can be carried, or as is customarily carried. **2** That which is borne with difficulty; hence, figuratively, a grievous mental burden. **3** The charge of a firearm. **4** A weight of various amounts. **5** The resistance overcome by a motor or engine in driving machinery. **6** Downward pressure on a structure: when caused by gravity alone, it is called **dead load**; when caused by gravity increased by the stresses of transverse motion, it is called **live load**. **7** The power delivered by a machine or apparatus, especially an electric generator. **8** *Slang* An excess of alcoholic liquor. **9** *pl. Colloq.* A great plenty; abundance: *loads* of time. **—to get a load of** *U.S. Slang* To listen to or look at. *—v.t.* **1** To put something on or into to be carried. **2** To place (a load) in or on a carrier. **3** To supply with something excessively or in abundance: to *load* one with honors. **4** To weigh down or oppress; burden. **5** To charge (a firearm) with ammunition. **6** To take on (a load, cargo, etc.). **7** To make heavy on one side or end by adding extra weight: to *load* dice or a whip. **8** To add a substance to for the purpose of falsifying; adulterate; doctor: to *load* silk with gum. **9** In insurance, to increase (a premium) by the addition of loading. See LOADING (def. 4). *—v.i.* **10** To take on or put on a load or cargo. **11** To charge a firearm with ammunition. **12** To be charged with ammunition: The new gun *loads* through the breech. ◆ Homophone: *lode*. [OE *lād* way, journey, act of carrying goods. Doublet of LODE.] **—load′er** *n.*

Synonyms (*noun*): burden, cargo, charge, clog, encumbrance, freight, incubus, pack, weight. A *burden* is what one has to bear, and is used chiefly of that which is borne by a living agent. A *load* is what is laid upon a person, animal, or conveyance, or what is customarily so imposed: as, a *load* of coal. *Weight* measures the pressure due to gravity. A ship's *load* is called distinctively a *cargo*, or it may be known as *freight* or *lading*. *Freight* denotes merchandise in or for transportation. A *load* to be fastened upon a horse or mule is called a *pack*. See WEIGHT. *Synonyms* (*verb*): burden, charge, cumber, lade, oppress.

load displacement *Naut.* A ship's displacement when fully loaded.

load·ed (lō′did) *adj.* **1** Filled or laden. **2** Weighted, as fraudulent dice. **3** Charged with ammunition. **4** Charged with special implication: a *loaded* question. **5** *Slang* Intoxicated. **6** *Slang* Wealthy.

load factor *Electr.* The ratio of the average load of a generating station to the maximum or peak load.

load·ing (lō′ding) *adj.* Arranged so that it may be loaded (in a specified way): used in compounds: a *breechloading* cannon. *—n.* **1** Anything added to a substance for the purpose of giving it weight or body. **2** In art, a heavy charge of opaque color. **3** A load or burden; lading. **4** In insurance, an addition to the premium to cover expenses, fluctuations in the death rate, etc. **5** The act or operation of furnishing with a load.

loading coil *Electr.* An inductance coil connected in a circuit to increase its period of oscillation.

load line *Naut.* **1** A line drawn on the plan of a ship to indicate the maximum mean draft to which it may be submerged by the weight of its cargo or under various conditions. **2** The Plimsoll mark. **3** The line of intersection of the surface of the water with a ship's side under any given load.

load·star (lōd′stär′), **load·stone** (lōd′stōn′) See LODESTAR, LODESTONE.

loaf[1] (lōf) *v.i.* **1** To hang about or saunter lazily or aimlessly; idle time away. **2** To neglect one's work. *—v.t.* **3** To spend (time) idly: with away. [Back formation <LOAFER]

loaf[2] (lōf) *n. pl.* **loaves** (lōvz) A shaped mass, as of bread, cake, etc., intended to be cut. [OE *hlāf* bread]

loaf·er (lō′fər) *n.* **1** One who loafs; an idler. **2** A casual shoe resembling a moccasin. [Cf. G *landläufer* an idler, loiterer, Du. *landloper* a vagrant]

loam (lōm) *n.* **1** A non-coherent mixture of sand and clay, containing organic matter. **2** A mixture of sand and clay, usually with straw or the like: used in foundry work to make molds, in plastering walls, plugging holes, etc. **3** *Archaic* Any soil; especially, fertile earth. *—v.t.* To coat or fill with loam. [OE *lām*] **—loam′y** *adj.*

loan (lōn) *n.* **1** Something lent, especially a sum of money lent at interest. **2** The act of lending; a lending. **3** Permission to use: a *loan* of credit. *—v.t. & v.i.* To lend. ◆ Homophone: *lone*. [OE *lān*]

Lo·an·da (lō·än′dä) A former spelling of LUANDA.

Loan·gwa (lwäng′gwä) See LUANGWA.

loan·ing (lō′ning) *n. Scot.* **1** A lane. **2** A milking place. Also **loan**, **loan′in**.

loan office 1 A pawnshop. **2** An office where loans are arranged, the accounts kept, and interest paid to lenders. **3** Formerly, an office set up in certain states by the Revolutionary Continental government to handle subscriptions to government loans.

loan-shark (lōn′shärk′) *U.S. Colloq.* One who lends money at a usurious or illegal rate of interest.

loan word A word adopted from another language and partly or completely naturalized phonetically or morphologically, as the English word *chauffeur*, taken from the French.

lo·a·sis (lō′ə·sis) *n. Pathol.* A species of filariasis common in West Africa, caused by a wandering parasitic roundworm (*Loa loa*) which often invades the orbit and conjunctiva of the eye: also called *loiasis*. [<NL <*loa* trematode worm <African native name + -(o)SIS]

loath (lōth) *adj.* Strongly disinclined; reluctant; averse: often with *to*. Also spelled *loth*. See synonyms under RELUCTANT. [OE *lāth* hateful] **—loath′ness** *n.*

loathe (lōth) *v.t.* **loathed**, **loath·ing** To feel great hatred or disgust for; abhor; detest. See synonyms under ABHOR. [OE *lāthian* be hateful] **—loath′er** *n.*

loath·ful (lōth′fəl) *adj.* Exciting abhorrence; hateful; detestable. **—loath′ful·ly** *adv.* **—loath′ful·ness** *n.*

loath·ing (lō′thing) *n.* Extreme dislike or disgust; aversion. See synonyms under ANTIPATHY.

loath·ly (lōth′lē) *adj.* Loathsome; repulsive. *—adv.* With reluctance; not willingly. [OE *lāthlice*] **—loath′li·ness** *n.*

loath·some (lōth′səm) *adj.* Exciting revulsion or disgust. **—loath′some·ly** *adv.* **—loath′some·ness** *n.*

loaves (lōvz) Plural of LOAF.

lob (lob) *v.* **lobbed**, **lob·bing** *v.t.* **1** To pitch or strike (a ball, etc.) in a high, arching curve, as in tennis or cricket. *—v.i.* **2** To move clumsily or heavily. **3** To lob a ball. *—n.* **1** In tennis, a stroke that sends the ball high into the air. **2** In cricket, a slow, underhand ball. **3** A soft, thick, lumpy mixture. **4** A worm for bait. [? Imit.] **—lob′ber** *n.*

Lo·ba·chev·ski (lō·bä·chef′skē), **Nikolai**, 1793–1856, Russian mathematician.

lo·bar (lō′bər, -bär) *adj.* **1** Of a lobe or lobes. **2** *Pathol.* Of, pertaining to, or describing acute febrile pneumonia affecting one or more lobes of the lungs. [<NL *lobaris*]

lo·bate (lō′bāt) *adj.* Composed of lobes; lobelike. Also **lo′bat·ed.** [<NL *lobatus*] **— lo′bate·ly** *adv.* **— lo·ba′tion** *n.*

lob·by (lob′ē) *n. pl.* **·bies 1** A hall, vestibule, or corridor on the main floor of a large public building, as a theater or hotel; a lounge; foyer. **2** The part of an assembly-room of a legislative or deliberative body not appropriated to the official use of members, and to which outsiders have free entry. **3** *U. S.* The persons or groups of persons who accost or solicit legislators in order to influence the action of a legislative body in the interest of a special group, industry, etc.: so called because supposed to frequent lobbies. **4** A cold-storage chamber for the temporary storage of ice. **—** *v.* **·bied, ·by·ing** *v.i.* To attempt to influence a legislator or legislators in favor of one's own interests. **—** *v.t.* To attempt to obtain passage or defeat of (a bill, etc.) by such means. [<Med. L *lobia.* Doublet of LODGE, *n.,* LOGE, LOGGIA.]

lob·by·ism (lob′ē·iz′əm) *n. U. S.* The practice of lobbying. **— lob′by·ist** *n.*

lobe (lōb) *n.* **1** A protuberance, especially globular, as of an organ or part. **2** The soft lower extension of the external ear. **3** A principal division of a molar tooth. [<F <Gk. *lobos*]

lo·bec·to·my (lō·bek′tə·mē) *n. Surg.* The operation of removing a lobe, as of the brain, lung, etc. [<LOBE + -ECTOMY]

lobed (lōbd) *adj.* **1** Lobate; having lobes. **2** *Bot.* Having divisions that extend not more than half-way from the margin to the center and rounded lobes or sinuses: said of leaves, petals, etc.

lo·be·li·a (lō·bē′lē·ə, -bēl′yə) *n.* Any of a large genus *(Lobelia)* of herbaceous plants with showy flowers either axillary or in bracted racemes. [<NL, after Matthias de *Lobel,* 1538–1616, Flemish botanist]

lo·be·line (lō′bə·lēn) *n. Chem.* A white, crystalline alkaloid, $C_{22}H_{27}O_2N$, from the seeds of Indian tobacco. Its hydrochloride is used as a respiratory stimulant. [<LOBEL(IA) + -INE[2]]

Lo·ben·gu·la (lō′beng·gyōō′lə, lō·beng′gyə·lə), 1833–94, king of the Matabele.

lob·lol·ly (lob′lol·ē) *n. pl.* **·lies** *U. S.* **1** *Colloq.* A mudhole; oozy mire. **2** A loblolly bay or pine. [< dial. E *lob* bubble + *lolly* broth]

loblolly bay A tree *(Gordonia lasianthus)* with smooth, shining, lanceolate leaves and showy white flowers, growing in southern U. S. coastal swamps.

loblolly boy *Obs.* A ship's surgeon's assistant and dispenser. [obs. nautical slang *loblolly* medicine + boy]

loblolly pine See under PINE.

lo·bo (lō′bō) *n. pl.* **·bos** The timber wolf *(Canis nubilus),* of the western United States. [<Sp., wolf]

lo·bot·o·my (lō·bot′ə·mē) *n. Surg.* The operation of cutting into or across a lobe, especially of the brain. [<Gk. *lobos* a lobe + -TOMY]

lob·scouse (lob′skous) *n.* A dish consisting of salt meat, vegetables, and biscuit. Also **lob·scourse** (-skôrs, -skōrs). [Origin unknown]

lob·ster (lob′stər) *n.* **1** A marine crustacean (genus *Homarus*) much used as food, having a large first pair of ambulatory legs, which form the claws, and compound eyes carried on flexible stalks. **2** One of various other long-tailed crustaceans, as a spiny lobster or crayfish. [OE *loppestre* lobster, grasshopper <L *locusta* lobster, locust; infl. in form by *loppe* spider. Doublet of LOCUST.]

lobster pot A trap consisting of a cage with netting at the ends for catching lobsters.

lobster shift A work shift during the latter part of the night; a graveyard shift.

lob·ule (lob′yōōl) *n.* A small lobe, or lobe made small by separation from a larger lobe. [<NL *lobulus,* dim. of *lobus* a lobe] **— lob′u·lar, lob′u·late** (-lit, -lāt) *adj.*

lob·worm (lob′wûrm′) See LUGWORM.

lo·cal (lō′kəl) *adj.* **1** Pertaining to a prescribed place or a limited portion of space. **2** Restricted to or characteristic of a particular place. **3** Pertaining to place in general. **4** *Med.* Relating to or affecting a specific part or organ of the body: said of a disease or injury, or of the remedies used. **5** Relating to a locus. **—** *n.* **1** A subway or suburban train that stops at all the stations. **2** A local branch or unit of a trade union or fraternal organization. **3** An item of local interest in a newspaper. [<F <L *localis* < *locus* place] **— lo′cal·ly** *adv.*

local anesthesia Anesthesia restricted in action to a specific part of the body.

local color In literature and art, the presentation of the characteristic manners, speech, dress, scenery, etc., of a certain period or region so as to achieve a sense of realism.

lo·cale (lō·kal′, -käl′) *n.* Locality; specifically, a spot considered with reference to surrounding features or circumstances. [<F]

local government 1 Independent government in local affairs by the small political entity of a limited region. **2** The governing head or body of such a locality.

lo·cal·ism (lō′kəl·iz′əm) *n.* **1** A manner of acting or speaking particular to a place; local custom or idiom. **2** A word, a meaning of a word, a pronunciation, etc., peculiar to a locality, rather than in general usage. **3** Provincialism. **4** The state or condition of being local; influence exerted by a particular place.

lo·cal·i·ty (lō·kal′ə·tē) *n. pl.* **·ties 1** A definite region in any part of space; geographical position. **2** Restriction to a particular place. See synonyms under NEIGHBORHOOD, PLACE. [<F *localité* <LL *localitas, -tatis*]

lo·cal·ize (lō′kəl·īz) *v.t.* **·ized, ·iz·ing 1** To make local; limit or assign to a specific area or locality. **2** To determine the place of origin of. Also *Brit.* **lo′cal·ise. — lo′cal·i·za′·tion** *n.*

local option The privilege granted to a political division, as a county or town, of determining whether something, especially the sale of intoxicants, shall be permitted within its limits.

local time See under TIME.

Lo·car·no (lō·kär′nō) A town on Lago Maggiore in SE central Switzerland; scene of an international conference on political problems following World War I, 1925.

lo·cate (lō′kāt, lō·kāt′) *v.* **·cat·ed, ·cat·ing** *v.t.* **1** To discover the position or source of; find. **2** To assign place or locality to: to *locate* a scene in a valley. **3** *U. S.* To establish in a place; situate: My office is *located* in Portland. **4** *U. S.* To survey, set, or designate the site or boundaries of, as a mining claim. **—** *v.i.* **5** *Colloq.* To establish oneself or take up residence; settle. See synonyms under SET. [<L *locatus,* pp. of *locare* < *locus* place]

lo·ca·tion (lō·kā′shən) *n.* **1** The act of locating, or the state of being located. **2** The exact position in space; place. **3** A plot of ground defined by boundaries; a mining claim. **4** *Law* A renting or letting for hire; also, the establishment or fixing of the boundaries of a tract of land. **5** A site selected for staging a scene in a motion picture. **6** Any one of five minor civil divisions in New Hampshire. See synonyms under PLACE. [<L *locatio, -onis*]

loc·a·tive (lok′ə·tiv) *adj.* **1** *Gram.* In certain inflected languages, as Latin, Greek, and Sanskrit, designating the case of the noun denoting place where or at which. **2** *Anat. & Zool.* Indicating relative position in a series. **—** *n. Gram.* **1** The locative case. **2** A word in this case. [<L *locatus,* pp. of *locare* locate; on analogy with L *vocativus* vocative]

lo·ca·tor (lō′kā·tər) *n.* **1** One who or that which locates. **2** One who locates land under the land laws, or is entitled to locate it. **3** *Law* One who lets a thing or services for hire. [<L]

locator card 1 A card bearing all essential facts about a person, especially an enlisted man or officer. **2** A similar card describing an article in a military depot.

loch (lokh, lok) *n. Scot.* **1** A lake. **2** A bay, or arm of the sea.

loch·an (lokh′ən) *n. Scot.* A little loch; pond.

lo·chi·a (lō′kē·ə, lok′ē·ə) *n. pl. Med.* The discharges from the vaginal passages after childbirth, continuing from two to three weeks. [<NL <Gk. *lochia,* neut. pl. of *lochios* pertaining to childbirth < *lochos* childbirth] **— lo′chi·al** *adj.*

Loch·in·var (lok′in·vär, lokh′-) The young hero of a ballad in Scott's *Marmion* who abducts his sweetheart just before she is to be wedded to another.

lo·ci (lō′sī) Plural of LOCUS.

lock[1] (lok) *n.* **1** A device to fasten an object; specifically, one for so securing a door, drawer, or the like, as to prevent its being opened, except by a special key or combination. **2** A spring mechanism for exploding the charge of a firearm. **3** A section of a canal, etc., enclosed by gates at either end, within which the water level may be varied to raise or lower vessels from one level to another. **4** An intermingling or fastening together; hence, a hold, hug, or grapple in wrestling. **5** A lockup. **6** One of various mechanical devices for fixing something so that it may remain in place. **7** An airlock. **8** A device to prevent a carriage wheel from turning, as in descending a hill. **9** The oblique position of the fore axle with relation to the hind axle of a vehicle when turning or swerving. **— combination lock** A lock which can be opened only by combining its dial-operated tumblers in a certain sequence. **— cylinder lock** A lock fitted with a cylinder having a control element which can be actuated only by a key whose particularly shaped surface engages with the tumblers and sets them to the exact position for unlocking. **—** *v.t.* **1** To secure or fasten by means of a lock. **2** To shut, confine, or exclude by means of a lock: with *in, up,* or *out.* **3** To join or unite securely; interlock; link: to *lock* arms. **4** To make immovable, as by jamming or by a lock. **5** To provide (a canal, etc.) with a lock or locks. **6** To move (a ship) through a waterway by means of locks. **—** *v.i.* **7** To become locked or fastened. **8** To become joined or linked. **9** To become jammed immovably. **10** To proceed by means of locks: said of ships. **11** To turn (wheels) under a carriage body. [OE *loc* fastening, enclosure]

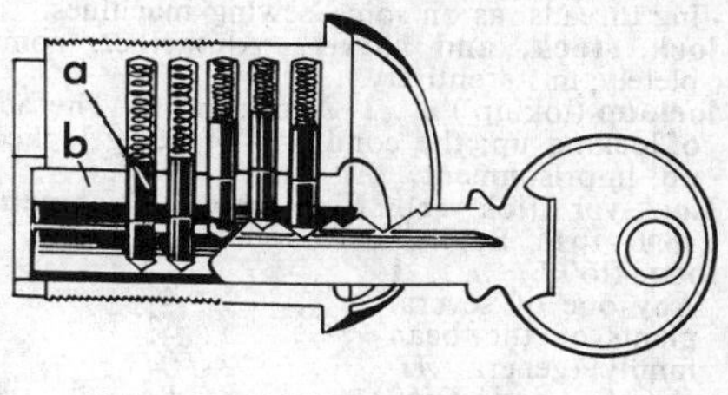

CYLINDER LOCK
Insertion of the proper key raises all the tumblers *(a)* to the exact position required to release the key-plug *(b),* thus permitting the key to turn (here partly inserted).

Synonyms (noun): bar, bolt, catch, clasp, fastening, hasp, hook, latch. A *bar* is a piece of wood or metal, usually of considerable size, by which an opening is obstructed, a door held fast, etc. A *bar* may be movable or permanent; a *bolt* is a movable rod or pin of metal sliding in a socket, and adapted for securing a door or window. A *lock* is an arrangement by which an enclosed *bolt* is shot forward or backward by a key, or other device; the *bolt* is the essential part of the *lock.* A *latch* or *catch* is an accessible *fastening* designed to be easily movable, and simply to secure against accidental opening of the door, cover, etc. A *hasp* is a metallic strap that fits over a staple, calculated to be secured by a padlock; a simple *hook* that fits into a staple is also called a *hasp.* A *clasp* is a *fastening* that can be sprung into place, to draw and hold the parts of some object firmly together, as the *clasp* of a book.

lock[2] (lok) *n.* **1** A tuft of hair; ringlet; tress. **2** *pl.* A head of hair. **3** A small quantity of hay, wool, etc. [OE *locc*]

lock·age (lok′ij) *n.* **1** Material going to form the lock of a canal. **2** The difference in level between the locks of a canal. **3** The toll levied for passing through a lock.

Locke (lok), **David Ross,** 1833–88, U. S. political satirist; pseudonym *Petroleum V. Nasby.* **— John,** 1632–1704, English philosopher and essayist.

lock·er (lok′ər) *n.* **1** One who or that which

locks. **2** A closet or receptacle fastened with a lock.

lock·et (lok′it) *n.* A small case, suspended on a necklace or chain, often holding a portrait. [<OF *locquet,* dim. of *loc* latch <Gmc.]

lock·fast (lok′fast′, -fäst′) *adj.* Securely held by some locked contrivance.

Lock·hart (lok′ərt, -härt), **John Gibson,** 1794–1854, Scottish writer and biographer.

lock·jaw (lok′jô′) *n. Pathol.* A spasmodic contraction of the muscles of the lower jaw; trismus. See TETANUS.

lock nut *Mech.* **1** An auxiliary nut used to prevent the loosening of another. **2** A nut that automatically locks when screwed tight.

lock–out (lok′out′) *n.* The closing of a factory or other place of business by employers to bring employees on strike to terms. Also **lock′out′**. Compare STRIKE.

lock·ram (lok′rəm) *n.* A coarse, cheap linen. [after *Locronan,* a village in Brittany]

locks·man (loks′mən) *n. pl.* **·men** (-mən) A warden; turnkey.

lock·smith (lok′smith′) *n.* A maker or repairer of locks. **— lock′smith′er·y, lock′smith′ing** *n.*

lock step A marching step in which each marcher follows as closely as possible the one in front of him.

lock stitch A stitch made by two interlocking threads, as on some sewing machines.

lock, stock, and barrel Altogether; completely; in its entirety.

lock·up (lok′up′) *n.* **1** A prison. **2** The act of locking up; the condition of being locked up; imprisonment.

Lock·yer (lok′yər), **Sir Joseph Norman,** 1836–1920, English astronomer.

loco (lō′kō) *n.* **1** Any one of several plants of the bean family (genera *Astragalus* and *Oxytropis*), often poisonous to livestock, and found in the western and SW United States: also called *crazyweed.* **2** Loco disease. — *adj. Slang* Crazy; insane. — *v.t.* **1** To poison with locoweed. **2** *U.S. Slang* To render insane. [<Sp., insane]

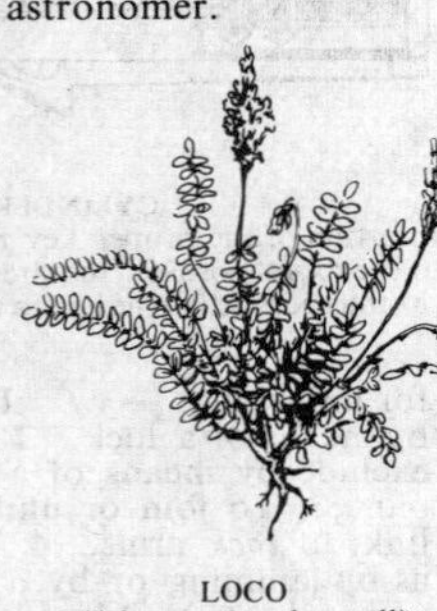

LOCO
(About 12 inches tall)

lo·co ci·ta·to (lō′kō sī·tā′tō) *Latin* In the place cited. Abbr. *loc. cit.*

loco disease An ailment attacking horses or other animals that have eaten the loco. It affects the brain, causing slowness of gait, loss of flesh, defective vision, delirium, and eventually, death: generally curable by careful and prolonged dieting.

Lo·co·fo·co (lō′kō·fō′kō) *n. pl.* **·cos 1** The extreme section of the Democratic party of 1835, known as the Equal Rights party. **2** Any adherent of that party. [after *Locofoco,* trade name for a friction match; from the use of these matches to light the candles at one of their early meetings]

lo·co·mo·bile (lō′kə·mō′bil) *adj.* Self-propelling.

lo·co·mo·tion (lō′kə·mō′shən) *n.* The act or power of moving from one place to another. [<L *loco* from a place + *motio, -onis* movement]

lo·co·mo·tive (lō′kə·mō′tiv) *adj.* **1** Pertaining to locomotion. **2** Moving from one place to another. **3** Possessed of the power of moving. — *n.* A self-propelling electric, diesel, or steam engine on wheels, especially one for use on a railway.

lo·co·mo·tor (lō′kə·mō′tər) *adj.* Of or pertaining to locomotion. — *n.* One who or that which has the power of locomotion.

locomotor ataxia *Pathol.* A disease of the spinal cord, characterized by unsteadiness and inability to coordinate locomotor and other voluntary movements; tabes dorsalis.

lo·co·weed (lō′kō·wēd′) *n.* Loco (def. 1).

Lo·cri (lō′krī, lok′rī) *n. pl.* The people of Locris.

Lo·cris (lō′kris, lok′ris) An ancient state of eastern and central Greece, divided into **Eastern Locris,** NW of Boeotia, and **Western Locris,** north of the Gulf of Corinth. **— Lo′cri·an** *adj.*

loc·u·lus (lok′yə·ləs) *n. pl.* **·li** (-lī) A small cavity or chamber; a cell. [<L, dim. of *locus* place] **— loc′u·lar, loc′u·late** (-lāt, -lit), **loc′u·lat′ed** *adj.*

lo·cum te·nens (lō′kəm tē′nenz) *Chiefly Brit.* A temporary representative or substitute. [<L, holding the place <*locus* place + *tenens,* ppr. of *tenere* hold]

lo·cus (lō′kəs) *n. pl.* **·ci** (-sī) **1** A place; locality; area. **2** *Math.* A surface or curve regarded as traced by a line or point moving under specified conditions; any figure made up wholly of points or lines that satisfy given conditions. **3** A figure formed by the foci of a series of pencils of light. **4** A passage in a writing. **5** *pl.* A series of passages, as from the Scriptures, classified for reading or study; any book containing such passages. **6** *Genetics* The linear position of a gene on a chromosome. [<L. Doublet of LIEU.]

lo·cus clas·si·cus (lō′kəs klas′ə·kəs) *Latin* An illustrative or authoritative passage from a standard work.

lo·cus si·gil·li (lō′kəs si·jil′ī) *Latin* The place of the seal; abbreviated in legal documents, *L. S.*

lo·cust[1] (lō′kəst) *n.* **1** Any of a family (*Locustidae*) of widely distributed orthopterous insects resembling grasshoppers but having short antennae, especially those of migratory habits (*Locusta, Pachytylus, Melanoplus,* and related genera), which are destructive of grain and vegetation in many parts of the world. **2** A cicada or harvest fly. [<OF *locuste* <L *locusta.* Doublet of LOBSTER.]

lo·cust[2] (lō′kəst) *n.* **1** A North American tree (*Robinia pseudoacacia*) of the bean family, with a rough bark, odd-pinnate leaves, and loose, slender racemes of fragrant, white flowers; also, its wood. **2** Any of several other trees with similar pods, as the carob tree. **3** The honey locust. [<NL *locusta;* orig. applied to the carob pod from its fancied resemblance to the insect]

lo·cus·ta (lō·kus′tə) *n. Bot.* A spikelet in grasses. [<NL. See LOCUST[2].]

lo·cu·tion (lō·kyōō′shən) *n.* **1** A mode of speech. **2** An idiom; phrase. [<L *locutio, -onis* a speaking <*loqui* speak]

loc·u·to·ry (lok′yə·tôr′ē, -tō′rē) *n. pl.* **·ries** A place for conversation; specifically, a reception room in a monastery or convent. [<Med. L *locutorium* <L *locutor* speaker <*loqui* talk]

lode (lōd) *n.* **1** A somewhat continuous, unstratified, metal-bearing vein. **2** A tabular deposit of valuable mineral between definite boundaries of associated rock. **3** A reach of water, as in a canal. ◆ Homophone: *load.* [OE *lād* way, journey. Doublet of LOAD.]

lode·star (lōd′stär′) *n.* A guiding star; the polestar: also spelled *loadstar.*

lode·stone (lōd′stōn′) *n.* A variety of magnetite that shows polarity and acts like a magnet when freely suspended: also spelled *loadstone.*

Lo·de·wijk (lō′də·vīk) Dutch form of LOUIS. Also *Ital.* **Lo·do·vi·co** (lō′dō·vē′kō).

lodge (loj) *v.* **lodged, lodg·ing** *v.t.* **1** To furnish with temporary living quarters; house. **2** To rent a room or rooms to; take as a paying guest. **3** To serve as a shelter or dwelling for. **4** To deposit for safekeeping or storage. **5** To place or implant, as by throwing, thrusting, etc.: I *lodged* an arrow in the tree. **6** To place (a complaint, information, etc.) before proper authority. **7** To confer or invest (power, etc.). **8** To beat down (crops): said of rain, storms, etc. — *v.i.* **9** To take temporary shelter or quarters; pass the night. **10** To live in a rented room or rooms. **11** To become fixed in some place or position: The bullet *lodged* in his leg. See synonyms under ABIDE, ACCOMMODATE. — *n.* **1** A small house affording temporary accommodations; a hut. **2** A small dwelling appurtenant to a manor house, park, or the like. **3** The lair of a wild animal, especially of a group of beavers; also, collectively, the beavers themselves. **4** A local subdivision of a secret society, or its meeting place. **5** *U. S.* Among the American Indians, a small hut or tepee of skins, bark, and poles; also, its inhabitants. [<OF *logier* <*loge* <Med. L *lobia, laubia* porch, gallery <OHG *louba* <*loub* foliage; *n.,* doublet of LOBBY, LOGE, LOGGIA]

Lodge (loj), **Henry Cabot,** 1850–1924, U. S. politician and historian. **— Sir Oliver (Joseph),** 1851–1940, English physicist, author, and investigator of psychic phenomena. **— Thomas,** 1558?–1625, English dramatist and novelist.

lodge pole A pole used in building an American Indian lodge.

lodge–pole pine (loj′pōl′) A tall, slender tree (*Pinus contorta latifolia*) of the western United States.

lodg·er (loj′ər) *n.* Something or someone that lodges; especially, one who occupies a rented room or rooms in the house of another.

lodg·ing (loj′ing) *n.* **1** A place of temporary abode. **2** *pl.* A room or rooms hired as a place of residence in the house of another. **3** Accommodation, as a room: to include board and *lodging.*

lodging house A house other than a hotel where lodgings are let.

lodg·ment (loj′mənt) *n.* **1** The act of lodging or the state of being lodged. **2** A foothold gained in some place. **3** Lodgings; accommodation; a lodging house. Also **lodge′ment.**

Lo·di (lō′dē) A city in northern Italy; scene of Napoleon's defeat of the Austrians, 1796.

Łódź (wōōj) A city in central Poland. *Russian* **Lodz** (lôts′y′).

lo′e (lōō) *v.* & *n. Scot.* Love. Also spelled *loo.*

Loeb (lōb, *Ger.* lœp), **Jacques,** 1859–1924, U. S. physiologist born in Germany. — **James,** 1867–1933, U. S. philanthropist and banker, born in Germany; endowed the publication of the Loeb Classical Library.

loess (lō′is, lœs) *n. Geol.* A pale, yellowish clay or loam forming deposits along river valleys, etc., in Asia, Europe, and North America. [<G <*lösen* pour, dissolve]

Loe·wi (lœ′vē), **Otto,** 1873–1961, U. S. pharmacologist born in Germany.

Lo·fo·ten Islands (lō·fō′tən) A group of islands off the NW coast of Norway; 550 square miles.

loft (lôft, loft) *n.* **1** A low story directly under a roof. **2** A large storeroom. **3** An elevated floor or gallery within a large building, as a church or barn. **4** An incline on the face of a golf club tending to cause elevation in the trajectory of the ball; also, a stroke which lifts the ball high in the air. **5** A place for keeping pigeons; hence, a flock of pigeons. — *v.t.* **1** To provide with a loft. **2** In golf: **a** To give loft to (a club). **b** To strike (a ball) so that it rises or travels in a high arc. — *v.i.* **3** In golf, to strike the ball so that it rises in a high arc. [OE <ON, upper room, air, sky. Akin to LIFT.]

loft·er (lôf′tər, lof′-) *n.* In golf, an iron club used for lofting the ball. Also **lofting iron.**

loft·y (lôf′tē, lof′-) *adj.* **loft·i·er, loft·i·est** Elevated, as in position, character, language, or quality; exalted; haughty; stately. See synonyms under EMINENT, GRAND, HIGH, SUBLIME. **— loft′i·ly** *adj.* **— loft′i·ness** *n.*

log (lôg, log) *n.* **1** A bulky piece of timber cut down and cleared of branches. **2** Figuratively, a dull, stupid person. **3** *Naut.* A device for showing the speed of a vessel, consisting of a triangular board, the **log chip** or **ship,** weighted on one edge and attached to a line, the **log line,** that runs out from a reel, the **log reel,** on shipboard. **4** A record of the daily progress of a vessel and of the events of a voyage. **5** Any record of performance, as of an engine, oil well, aircraft, etc. — *v.* **logged, log·ging** *v.t.* **1** To cut (trees) into logs. **2** To cut down the trees of (a region) for timber. **3** *Naut.* **a** To enter in a logbook. **b** To travel (a specified distance) as shown by a log. **c** To travel at (a specified speed). — *v.i.* **4** To cut down trees and transport logs for sawing into lumber. [ME *logge,* prob. <Scand. Cf. ON *lāg,* Dan. *laag* felled tree.]

log– Var. of LOGO–.

Lo·gan (lō′gən), **Mount** A peak in SW Yukon Territory, Canada, the second highest in North America; 19,850 feet.

lo·ga·ni·a·ceous (lō·gā′nē·ā′shəs) *adj.* Designating or pertaining to a family (*Loganiaceae*) of poisonous herbs, shrubs, and trees, with opposite, entire, stipulate leaves and a cymose inflorescence of regular, perfect, four- or five-parted flowers. [<NL, after James *Logan,* 1674–1751, Irish botanist]

lo·gan·ber·ry (lō′gən·ber′ē) *n. pl.* **·ries 1** A hybrid plant (*Rubus loganobaccus*) obtained by crossing the red raspberry with the blackberry: cultivated for its edible fruit. **2** The

fruit itself. [after J. H. *Logan* of California, the originator]

log·a·oe·dic (lŏg′ə·ē′dik, lōg′-) *adj.* Prose-poetic; partaking of the nature of prose and poetry: applied to a meter composed of cyclic dactyls and trochees. — *n.* A logaoedic verse. [<LL *logaoedicus* <Gk. *logaoidikos* < *logos* speech + *aoidē* song]

log·a·pha·si·a (lŏg′ə·fā′zhē·ə, -zhə, lōg′-) *n. Psychiatry* Inability to communicate ideas in speech. [<Gk. *logos* speech + APHASIA]

log·a·rithm (lŏg′ə·rĭth′əm, lōg′-) *n. Math.* 1 The exponent of the power to which a fixed number, called the base, must be raised in order to produce a given number. For example, in decimal logarithms the base is 10 and the logarithm of 100 is 2 because 10 raised to the second power is 100; the logarithm of 1000 is 3 because 10 raised to the third power is 1000, and so on. 2 In a former and broader sense, one of any series of numbers whose members correspond, each to each, with the natural numbers, but are in arithmetical progression when the latter are in geometrical, so that, if the products of two sets of numbers are equal, the sums of the corresponding logarithms are also equal. [<NL <Gk. *logos* word, ratio + *arithmos* number] — **log′a·rith′mic** or **·mi·cal** *adj.* — **log′a·rith′mi·cal·ly** *adv.*

logarithmic curve *Math.* A curve traced by a point with ordinates increasing arithmetically and abscissas increasing geometrically. It is asymptotic to the negative axis of the dependent variable and passes through the coordinate (1,0) or (0,1) depending on which coordinate is assumed as the variable.

logarithmic spiral *Math.* The polar curve traced by a point moving so that the angle subtended between its radius vector and a tangent to the curve is equal to the modulus; a polar curve traced by a point with a polar angle proportional to the logarithm of the distance from the point to the pole: also called *equiangular spiral, logistic spiral.*

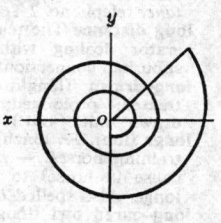

LOGARITHMIC SPIRAL
o. Origin.
x., y. x-axis, *y*-axis.

log·book (lŏg′bŏŏk′, lōg′-) *n.* The book in which the official record of a ship or aircraft is entered; also, a book containing a similar record of performance of a small military unit. Also **log book.**

log cabin A small, rough house built of logs. Also **log house, log hut.**

log carriage The carriage in a sawing machine that moves the log back and forth before the saw.

loge (lōzh) *n.* A box in a theater; booth; stall. [<F <OF. Doublet of LOBBY, LODGE, *n.,* LOGGIA.]

log·gan (lŏg′ən, lōg′-) *n.* A large boulder so balanced as to rock easily; a rocking stone. Also **lo·gan** (lō′gən), **loggan stone.** [< dial. E rock, move to and fro]

log·ger (lŏg′ər, lōg′-) *n.* 1 A person engaged in logging; a lumberjack. 2 A machine used for loading logs on flat cars.

log·ger·head (lŏg′ər·hed′, lōg′-) *n.* 1 A blockhead; dunce. 2 A large marine turtle (*genus Caretta*) of tropical Atlantic waters. 3 The loggerhead shrike. See under SHRIKE. 4 A post on the gunwale of a whaleboat around which the line is turned to retard the motion of a harpooned whale. — **at loggerheads** Engaged in a quarrel; unable to agree. [< dial. E *logger* log tied to a horse's leg to impede movement + HEAD]

log·gi·a (lŏj′ē·ə, lō′jä; *Ital.* lôd′jä) *n.* A covered gallery or portico having a colonnade on one or more sides, open to the air: compare PORCH, VERANDA. [<Ital. <OF *loge.* Doublet of LOBBY, LODGE, *n.,* LOGE.]

log·ging (lŏg′ing, lōg′-) *n.* The business or occupation of felling timber and transporting logs to a mill or market.

log·i·a (lŏg′ē·ə) *n. pl.* of **log·i·on** (lŏg′ē·on) Collections of sayings attributed to a relig-

ious leader; especially, **Logia,** the maxims, doctrines, or truths ascribed to Jesus in the four Gospels; also, the agrapha, or collection of sayings ascribed to Jesus, but not found in the Bible. [<Gk., pl. of *logos* word]

log·ic (lŏj′ik) *n.* 1 The normative science which investigates the principles of valid reasoning and correct inference, either from the general to the particular, **deductive logic;** or from the particular to the general, **inductive logic.** Compare FORMAL LOGIC, SYMBOLIC LOGIC. 2 The basic principles of reasoning developed by and applicable to any field of knowledge: the *logic* of science. 3 Effective or convincing force: The *logic* of his argument is unassailable. 4 The system of thought or ideas governing conduct, belief, behavior, etc.: the *logic* of business enterprise. [<F *logique* <L *logica* <Gk. *logikē* (*technē*) logical (art) < *logikos* of speaking or reason < *logos* word, speech, thought]

log·i·cal (lŏj′i·kəl) *adj.* 1 Relating to or of the nature of logic. 2 Conformed to the laws of logic; consistent in point of reasoning: a *logical* conclusion. 3 Capable of or characterized by clear reasoning; versed in the principles of logic: a *logical* writer. — **log′i·cal·ly** *adv.* — **log′i·cal′i·ty** (-kal′ə·tē), **log′i·cal·ness** *n.*

-logical *combining form* Of or related to a (specified) science or study: *biological, geological, zoological.* [<-LOG(Y) + -ICAL]

logical positivism A movement in philosophy devoted to unifying the sciences, chiefly by creation of a unified terminology in which the statements of any science are expressible. Also called **logical empiricism.**

lo·gi·cian (lō·jish′ən) *n.* One versed in logic.

lo·gis·tic (lō·jis′tik) *adj.* 1 Of, pertaining to, or skilled in calculation. 2 Of or pertaining to proportion. 3 Sexagesimal. 4 Of or pertaining to logistics. Also **lo·gis′ti·cal.** — *n.* 1 The art of calculation; common practical arithmetic. 2 Sexagesimal arithmetic. [< Med. L *logisticus* <Gk. *logistikos* < *logizesthai* reckon < *logos* word, calculation]

lo·gis·tics (lō·jis′tiks) *n. pl.* (*construed as singular*) 1 The branch of military science that embraces the details of moving, evacuating, and supplying armies. 2 Logistic. [<F *logistique* < *logis* quarters, lodging < *loger* quarter <OF *logier.* See LODGE.]

logistic spiral Logarithmic spiral.

log jam A mass of logs that have become jammed in their course down a stream.

logo– *combining form* Word; speech: *logomachy.* Also, before vowels, *log–.* [<Gk. *logos* word, speech]

log·o·gram (lŏg′ə·gram, lōg′-) *n.* 1 An abbreviation or other sign representing a word, as $ for *dollar.* 2 A form of versified word puzzle. — **log′o·gram·mat′ic** *adj.*

log·o·graph (lŏg′ə·graf, -gräf, lōg′-) *n.* 1 A character, or combination of characters, used to represent a word; logogram. 2 A logotype. — **log′o·graph′ic** or **·i·cal** *adj.*

lo·gog·ra·phy (lō·gog′rə·fē) *n.* 1 *Printing* The use of logotypes. 2 The art of reporting speeches in longhand by several reporters, each taking down a few words in succession.

log·o·griph (lŏg′ə·grif, lōg′-) *n.* 1 A word riddle, in which it is required to discover some word by a recombination of the letters or elements of various given words or by guessing and combining other words which (when correctly arranged) form the word to be guessed. 2 Any anagram or puzzle which involves an anagram. [<LOGO- + Gk. *griphos* riddle] — **log′o·griph′ic** *adj.*

lo·gom·a·chy (lō·gom′ə·kē) *n. pl.* **·chies** 1 Strife over mere words; verbal contention. 2 Any of various games in which letters are arranged into words. [<Gk. *logomachia* <

logos word + *machē* a battle] — **lo·gom′a·chist** *n.*

log·on (lŏg′on, lōg′-) *n.* An elementary tone signal, of whatever frequency and intensity, distinguishable as such by the human ear: used especially in the quantitative study and analysis of auditory capacity. [<Gk. *logon,* accusative of *logos* word, utterance]

lo·gop·a·thy (lō·gop′ə·thē) *n. Pathol.* Any disorder affecting the speech. [<LOGO- + -PATHY]

Log·os (lŏg′os, lōg′-) *n.* 1 In classical Greek and neo-Platonic philosophy, the cosmic reason giving order, purpose, and intelligibility to the world. 2 The creative Word of God, the second person of the Trinity, incarnate as Jesus Christ, identified with the cosmic reason. *John* i 1–14. [<Gk., word]

lo·go·tech·nics (lō′gō·tek′niks) *n.* The theory, art, and practice of forming new words, especially with reference to specific requirements in science, technology, medicine, etc. [<Gk. *logotechnēs* an artificer of words + -ICS; coined (1954) by R. W. Brown, U. S. geologist] — **lo′go·tech′ni·cal** *adj.*

log·o·thete (lŏg′ə·thēt, lōg′-) *n.* In Byzantine history, any one of several officials, especially, the imperial auditor or accountant. [<Med. L *logotheta* <Gk. *logothetēs* < *logos* word, account + *tithenai* set]

log·o·type (lŏg′ə·tīp, lōg′-) *n. Printing* A type bearing a syllable, a word, or words. Compare LIGATURE (def. 4).

log·o·typ·y (lŏg′ə·tī′pē, lōg′-) *n.* The use of logotypes.

log-roll (lŏg′rōl′, lōg′-) *v.t.* To obtain passage of (a bill) by log-rolling. — *v.i.* To engage in log-rolling. Also **log′roll.** [Back formation <LOG-ROLLING]

log-rolling (lŏg′rō′ling, lōg′-) *n.* 1 Handling and removing of logs, as in clearing land. 2 *U.S.* A combining of politicians for mutual assistance on their separate projects. 3 Birling. — **log′-roll′er** *n.*

Lo·gro·ño (lō·grō′nyō) A city on the Ebro in northern Spain.

log scale A table showing the amount of lumber in board measure one inch thick contained in a round log of given length and diameter.

-logue *combining form* Speech; recitation; discourse: *monologue.* Also **-log.** [<Gk. *logos* word, speech]

log·way (lŏg′wā′, lōg′-) *n.* 1 An inclined chute or slide up which logs are moved from the water to the sawmill: also called *gangway.* 2 A corduroy road.

log·wood (lŏg′wŏŏd′, lōg′-) *n.* 1 A Central American tree (*Haematoxylon campechianum*). 2 Its heavy, reddish wood: used as a dyestuff.

log·work (lŏg′wûrk′, lōg′-) *n.* 1 The service of keeping a ship's log. 2 A structure of logs.

lo·gy (lō′gē) *adj.* **·gi·er, ·gi·est** *U.S. Colloq.* Dull; heavy; lethargic. [? <Du. *log* heavy]

-logy *combining form* 1 The science or study of: *biology, conchology.* 2 A list or compilation of: *anthology, martyrology.* [<Gk. *-logia* < *logos* word, study < *legein* speak]

Lo·hen·grin (lō′ən·grin) In German medieval romances, son of Parsifal and a knight of the Grail: first mentioned in Wolfram von Eschenbach's *Parzival;* subject of an opera by Wagner.

loi·a·sis (loi′ə·sis) See LOASIS.

Loi·kaw (loi′kô′) The capital of Karenni State, Upper Burma.

loin (loin) *n.* 1 The part of the body between the lower rib and hip bone. ◆ Collateral adjective: *lumbar.* 2 The forepart of the hindquarters of beef, lamb, veal, etc., with the flank removed. — **to gird one's loins** To prepare for action. [<OF *loigne, logne* <L *lumbus*]

loin·cloth (loin′klôth′, -kloth′) *n.* A piece or strip of cloth worn about the loins and hips; a waistcloth; breechcloth.

loir (lwär) *n.* A large European dormouse (*Glis glis*). [<F <L *glis, gliris*]

Loire (lwär) The longest river in France, flowing 620 miles NW from the Cévennes to the Bay of Biscay.

loi·ter (loi′tər) *v.i.* 1 To remain or pause idly or aimlessly; loaf. 2 To travel in a leisurely manner and with frequent pauses; linger on the way; dawdle. — *v.t.* 3 To pass (time) idly;

LOGGIA

with *away.* [<Du. *leuteren* shake, totter, dawdle]—**loi'ter·er** *n.* —**loi'ter·ing** *adj. & n.*

Lo·ki (lō'kē) In Norse mythology, a god who created disorder and mischief: he appears occasionally as a helper but mostly as an enemy of the gods. [<ON]

loll (lol) *v.i.* **1** To lie or lean in a relaxed or languid manner; lounge. **2** To hang loosely; droop. —*v.t.* **3** To permit to droop or hang, as the tongue. —*n.* **1** The act of lolling. **2** An indolent person. [Cf. MDu. *lollen* sleep] —**loll'er** *n.*

Loll·and (lôl'än) See LAALAND.

Lol·lard (lol'ərd) *n.* The name applied to a follower of John Wyclif, an English religious reformer and precursor of Protestantism. Also **Lol'ler.** [<MDu. *lollaerd,* lit., grumbler, mumbler (of prayers) <*lollen* mumble, doze]

lol·li·pop (lol'ē·pop) *n.* A lump or piece of hard candy attached to the end of a stick. Also **lol'ly·pop.** [Prob.<dial. E *lolly* tongue + POP[1]]

lol·lop (lol'əp) *v.i. Colloq.* **1** To lounge; sprawl. **2** To move with leaps or jumps. [< LOLL]

lol·ly (lol'ē) *n. pl.* **·lies** *Brit.* **1** A piece of candy, especially hard candy. **2** *Colloq.* Ice cream, flavored ices, etc., frozen on a stick. **3** *Slang* Money. [Short for LOLLIPOP]

Lo·ma·mi (lō·mä'mē) A tributary of the Congo in SE and central Zaïre, flowing 900 miles north.

Lo·mas de Za·mo·ra (lō'mäs thā sä·mō'rä) A city in greater Buenos Aires, Argentina.

Lo·max (lō'maks), **Alan,** born 1915, U.S. folklorist. —**John Avery,** 1872?–1948, U.S. folklorist, father of the preceding.

Lombard (lom'bərd, -bärd, lum'-) *n.* **1** One of a Germanic tribe that established a kingdom, the modern Lombardy, in northern Italy, 568–774. **2** A native or inhabitant of Lombardy. [< OF <Ital. *Lombardo* <LL *Longobardus,* ? < OHG *lang* long +*bart* beard] —**Lom·bar'dic** *adj.*

Lom·bard (lom'bärd, -bərd, lum'-), **Peter,** 1100?–60, Italian theologian.

Lombard Street 1 A street in London where many banks and financial offices are located. **2** Figuratively, the world of London finance and financiers.

Lom·bar·dy (lom'bər·dē, lum'-) A region of northern Italy; 9,190 square miles; capital, Milan; formerly an independent kingdom. *Italian* **Lom·bar·di·a** (lôm·bär'dē·ä).

Lombardy poplar See under POPLAR.

Lom·blem (lom·blem') One of the Lesser Sunda Islands east of Alor, the largest of the Solor group; 499 square miles: also *Kawula.*

Lom·bok (lom·bok') One of the Lesser Sunda Islands east of Bali; 1,825 square miles; capital, Mataram.

Lombok Strait A channel connecting the Indian Ocean with the Java Sea between Bali and Lombok.

Lom·bro·so (lôm·brō'sō), **Cesare,** 1836–1909, Italian criminologist.

Lo·mé (lô·mā') A port on the Gulf of Guinea, capital of Togo.

lo·ment (lō'ment) *n. Bot.* An indehiscent legume with constrictions or transverse articulations between the seeds, as a peanut. Also **lo·men·tum** (lō·men'təm). [<L *lomentum* bean meal <*lotum,* pp. of *lavare* wash; because used as a cosmetic wash in antiquity] —**lo'men·ta'ceous** (-tā'shəs) *adj.*

Lo·mond (lō'mənd), **Loch** The largest lake of Scotland, in Dumbarton and Stirling counties; 23 miles long.

Lon·don (lun'dən), **Jack,** 1876–1916, U.S. author.

Lon·don (lun'dən) **1** A city and administrative county near the mouth of the Thames, England, capital of the United Kingdom and chief city of the British Empire. **The City of London** represents London within its ancient boundaries and is the business and financial center: often called *the City;* 1 square mile. The **County of London** comprises the cities of London and Westminster and 28 metropolitan boroughs; administered by the **London County Council;** 117 square miles. **Greater London,** embracing the City and Metropolitan Police Districts, comprises the County of London, County of Middlesex, and parts of Surrey, Hertford, Essex, and Kent, an area roughly within a radius of 15 miles from Charing Cross; 693 square miles. *Ancient* **Lon·din·i·um** (lən·din'ē·əm). **2** A city on the Thames in SW Ontario, Canada.

Lon·don·der·ry (lun'dən·der'ē) A county of Ulster, Northern Ireland; 801 square miles; county town, Londonderry: also *Derry.*

lone (lōn) *adj.* **1** Standing by itself; isolated. **2** Unaccompanied; solitary. **3** Single; unmarried; widowed. **4** Lonesome. **5** Lonely; unfrequented. ◆ Homophone: *loan.* [Aphetic var. of ALONE] —**lone'ness** *n.*

lone hand *n.* In some card games, a person playing without aid from a partner; also, the hand he plays.

lone·ly (lōn'lē) *adj.* **·li·er, ·li·est 1** Deserted or unfrequented by human beings; sequestered: a *lonely* dell or gorge. **2** Solitary or addicted to solitude; living in seclusion. **3** Sad from lack of sympathy or friendship; lonesome; forlorn. See synonyms under SOLITARY. —**lone'li·ly** *adv.* —**lone'li·ness** *n.*

lon·er (lō'nər) n. *U.S. Colloq.* One who prefers to live or work alone.

lone·some (lōn'səm) *adj.* **1** Depressed or sad because of loneliness. **2** Lonely or secluded; so sequestered as to cause uneasiness: a *lonesome* forest. See synonyms under SOLITARY. —**lone'some·ly** *adv.* —**lone'some·ness** *n.*

Lone Star State Nickname of TEXAS.

long[1] (lông, long) *adj.* **1** Having relatively great linear extension; not short: opposed to *short,* and distinguished from *broad* and *wide.* **2** Having relatively great extension in time; lasting. **3** Extended either in space or time to a specified degree: an hour *long,* a foot *long.* **4** Continued in a series to a great extent: a *long* list of grievances. **5** Delayed unexpectedly or unduly; dilatory. **6** Far-reaching; extending far in prospect or into the future; far away in time. **7** Holding for a rise, as stocks. **8** Denoting measure, weight, quantity, etc., in excess of a standard: a *long* five minutes. **9** *Phonet.* **a** Relatively more prolonged in sound: The sound (ē) is *longer* in *seed* than in *seat.* **b** Conventionally, indicating the sounds of *a, e, i, o, u* as they are pronounced in *mate, scene, nice, dote, fuse* (in diacritical systems, often written with a macron), as opposed to the "short" sounds of *bat, fed, pit, rot, cup*: in the early Old English period, each of these letters indicated a long or a short vowel sound of similar quality but different duration; this distinction no longer exists and the designation is now an arbitrary one. **10** In classical prosody, requiring relatively more time to pronounce: said of syllables containing a long vowel (*eta, omega,* etc.), a diphthong, or a vowel followed by two consonants or a double consonant. **11** In English prosody, accented. —*n.* **1** The whole extent of a thing; something that is characterized by length: used elliptically. **2** In medieval music, a note equal to four or sometimes six whole notes. **3** A long syllable. **4** *pl.* Those who have purchased securities or commodities and are holding them for an advance in price: opposed to *shorts.* —**the long and the short** The whole; the entire sum and substance. —*adv.* **1** To or at a great extent or period. **2** For a length of time. **3** Through the whole extent or duration. **4** At a point of duration far distant: *long* before or after. —**as** (or **so**) **long as** Under condition that; since. —**before long** Soon. —**for long** For a long time. —**so long** *Colloq.* Good-by. [OE *lang, long*]

Long, meaning "for a long time," may appear as a combining form in hyphemes:

long–accustomed	**long–living**
long–agitated	**long–lost**
long–awaited	**long–neglected**
long–borne	**long–past**
long–breathed	**long–planned**
long–buried	**long–possessed**
long–cherished	**long–projected**
long–contended	**long–protracted**
long–continued	**long–resounding**
long–delayed	**long–settled**
long–deserted	**long–sought**
long–desired	**long–standing**
long–enduring	**long–suffered**
long–established	**long–suffering**
long–expected	**long–term**
long–experienced	**long–threatened**
long–felt	**long–time**
long–forgotten	**long–wandering**
long–hidden	**long–wedded**
long–kept	**long–wished**
long–lasting	**long–withheld**

long[2] (lông, long) *v.i.* To have a strong or yearning desire; wish earnestly. [OE *langian* grow long]

long[3] (lông, long) *v.i. Obs.* **1** To be fitting or proper. **2** To belong. [Aphetic form of OE *gelang* dependent on]

Long (lông, long), **Crawford Williamson,** 1815–78, U.S. surgeon; pioneer in use of ether anesthesia in surgery. —**Huey,** 1893–1935, U.S. lawyer and politician.

lon·gan (long'gən) *n.* **1** A Chinese and East Indian tree *(Euphoria longan)* of the soapberry family. **2** Its small, edible fruit, resembling the litchi. [<NL *longanum* <Chinese *lung–yen* dragon's–eye]

lon·ga·nim·i·ty (long'gə·nim'ə·tē) *n.* Disposition to endure patiently. [<LL *longanimitas* <*longus* long + *animus* mind]

long·boat (lông'bōt', long'-) *n. Naut.* The largest boat carried on a sailing vessel.

long·bow (lông'bō', long'-) *n.* A bow of great length drawn and discharged by hand: distinguished from the *crossbow.*—**to draw, use,** or **pull the longbow** To overstate; exaggerate.

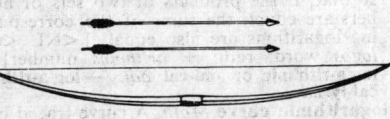

LONGBOW AND ARROWS

long·cloth (lông'klôth', long'kloth) *n.* A fine, soft, cotton cloth garment.

long–dis·tance (lông'dis'təns, long'-) *adj.* & *adv.* **1** Connecting distant places: a *long–distance* telephone. **2** To or from a distant place.

long distance The telephone exchange or operator dealing with other than local or suburban connections.

long–drawn (lông'drôn', long'-) *adj.* Protracted; prolonged; tedious. Also **long'–drawn'–out'** (-out').

longe (lunj, *Fr.* lôṅzh) *n.* A long rein used in training horses. —*v.t.* **longed, longe·ing** To cause (a horse) to circle at the end of a longe. Also spelled *lunge.* [<F]

long–eared owl (lông'ird', long'-) See under OWL.

lon·ge·ron (lon'jər·ən, *Fr.* lôṅzh·rôṅ) *n. Aeron.* A main longitudinal member of the body of an airplane. [<F]

lon·gev·i·ty (lon·jev'ə·tē) *n.* **1** Great age, or length of life. **2** The tendency to live long. [<L *longaevitas, -tatis* <*longaevus* long–lived < *longus* long + *aevum* age]

longevity pay Additional pay for long service given to members of the U.S. armed forces. Also called *fogy pay.*

long face An expression of the face indicating exaggerated sadness. —**long–faced** (lông'fāst', long'-) *adj.*

Long·fel·low (lông'fel·ō, long'-), **Henry Wadsworth,** 1807–82, U.S. poet.

Long·ford (lông'fərd, long'-) A county in NW Leinster Province, Ireland; 403 square miles; county town, Longford.

long green *U.S. Slang* Paper money.

long·hair (lông'hâr', long'-) *n. U.S. Slang* **1** A person interested in classical rather than popular music. **2** A man or boy with long hair, esp. a hippie. —*adj.* Of or pertaining to classical rather than popular music. —**long'hair, long'haired** *adj.*

long·hand (lông'hand', long'-) *n.* Ordinary handwriting with the words spelled in full: distinguished from *shorthand.*

long·head (lông'hed', long'-) *n.* A dolichocephalic person. —**long'head'ed** *adj.* —**long'·head'ed·ly** *adv.* —**long'head'ed·ness** *n.*

long head *Colloq.* Shrewdness; foresight; common sense. —**long'–head'ed** *adj.*

long·horn (lông'·hôrn', long'-) *n.* **1** One of a breed of domestic cattle with long horns: also **Texas longhorn. 2** *Entomol.* A longicorn beetle. **3** In the western United States, a seasoned inhabitant who knows the ways and cannot be tricked: opposed to *tenderfoot.*

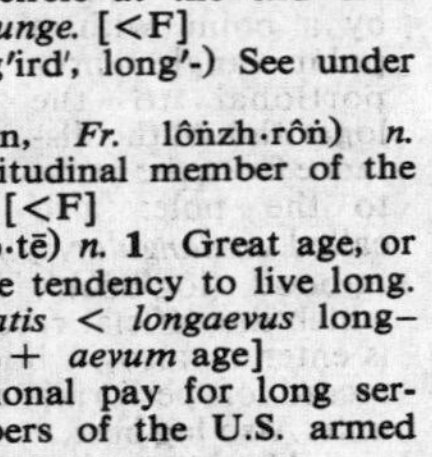

TEXAS LONGHORN

long house Among North American Indians, especially the Iroquois, a council house or community dwelling sometimes 100 to 200 feet long.

longi– *combining form* Long: *longipennate.* [<L *longus* long]

lon·gi·corn (lon′ji·kôrn) *n. adj.* 1 Having long antennae. 2 Of or pertaining to a family of beetles (*Cerambycidae*), usually with long, filiform antennae: the larvae are woodborers. [<LONGI– + L *cornu* horn]

lon·gi·lin·e·al (lon′ji·lin′ē·əl) *adj. Anthropol.* Designating a physical type characterized by length and relative slenderness of body; dolichomorphic: opposed to *brevilineal.*

long·ing (lông′ing, long′-) *n.* An eager, strong, or earnest craving. See synonyms under APPETITE, DESIRE. — **long′ing·ly** *adv.*

Lon·gi·nus (lon·jī′nəs), **Dionysius Cassius,** 213?–273, Greek Platonic philosopher.

lon·gi·pen·nate (lon′ji·pen′āt) *adj. Ornithol.* Having long wings or feathers, as certain birds. Also **lon′gi·pen′nine** (-pen′ēn, -īn).

lon·gi·ros·tral (lon′ji·ros′trəl) *adj. Ornithol.* Having a long bill, as the ibis and related birds. Also **lon′gi·ros′trate** (-trāt, -trit).

long·ish (lông′ish, long′-) *adj.* Rather long.

Long Island An island of SE New York just east of the mouth of the Hudson; 1,723 square miles; separated from Connecticut by **Long Island Sound**, a sheltered arm of the Atlantic 90 miles long.

lon·gi·tude (lon′ji·tōōd, -tyōōd) *n.* 1 *Geog.* Distance east or west on the earth's surface, measured by the angle which the meridian through a place makes with some standard meridian, as that of Greenwich or Paris. Longitude may be expressed either in time (**longitude in time**) or in degrees (**longitude in arc**). 2 *Astron.* The angular distance from the vernal equinox to the intersection with the ecliptic of the perpendicular from a heavenly body: usually termed **celestial longitude,** and distinguished as *geocentric* when the earth's center is assumed as the central point, and *heliocentric* when the sun's center is taken as the central point. 3 *Math.* The angle the radius vector makes with the initial meridian axis in the spherical coordinate system. [<F <L *longitudo* <*longus* long]

lon·gi·tu·di·nal (lon′ji·tōō′də·nəl, -tyōō′-) *adj.* 1 Pertaining to longitude or length. 2 Running lengthwise. 3 *Biol.* Of, pertaining to, or extending along the cephalocaudal axis. — **lon′gi·tu′di·nal·ly** *adv.*

long johns (jonz) *Slang* Ankle-length, fitted underdrawers of knitted fabric.

long jump In sports, the broad jump.

long·leaf pine (lông′lēf′, long′-) The southern yellow or Georgia pine (*Pinus palustris*), important as a source of turpentine.

long·lin·er (lông′lī′nər) *n. Canadian* A type of fishing vessel using a long line with many baited hooks.

long·lin·er·man (lông′lī′nər·mən, long′-) *n. Canadian* A fisherman on a longliner.

long–lived (lông′livd′, -livd′, long′-) *adj.* Having a long life. — **long′–lived′ness** *n.*

long measure Linear measure.

long moss Spanish moss.

long·neck (lông′nek′, long′-) *n.* The pintail duck.

Lon·go·bar·di (long′gō·bär′dē) *n. pl.* The Lombards (def. 1). [<LL] — **Lon′go·bar′di·an, Lon′go·bard** *adj.*

long pig Human flesh, as prepared for a cannibal feast: Maori and Polynesian term.

long–range (lông′rānj′, long′-) *adj.* 1 Designed to shoot or move over distances: a *long–range* projectile. 2 Taking account of, or extending over, a long span of future time: *long–range* plans.

long run An extended series of occurrences. — **in the long run** After the whole course of events; eventually.

long·shanks (lông′shangks′, long′-) *n.* The black–necked stilt (*Himantopus mexicanus*).

long·shore (lông′shôr′, -shōr′, long′-) *adj.* Belonging, living, or working along a shore or waterside. [Aphetic var. of ALONGSHORE]

long·shore·man (lông′shôr′mən, -shōr′, long′-) *n. pl.* **·men** (-mən) One who loads and unloads vessels; a stevedore.

long shot *Colloq.* 1 A bet made with little

chance of winning and hence at great odds. 2 Something backed at great odds, as a horse. — **not by a long shot** Decidedly not; not at all.

long–sight·ed (lông′sī′tid, long′-) *adj.* 1 Seeing far or to a great distance; sagacious. 2 Far–sighted; hypermetropic. — **long′–sight′ed·ness** *n.*

long·some (lông′səm, long′-) *adj.* Very long; hence, irksome; tedious. [OE *langsum*]

Longs Peak (lôngz, longz) A mountain in Rocky Mountain National Park, north central Colorado; 14,255 feet.

long·spur (lông′spûr′, long′-) *n.* A fringilline bird (genera *Calcarius* and *Rhynchophanes*) with elongated hind claws, found in the arctic regions and Great Plains of North America.

long–sta·ple (lông′stā′pəl, long′-) *adj.* Having a long fiber: said of cotton.

Long·street (lông′strēt, long′-), **James,** 1821–1904, American Confederate general.

long–suf·fer·ing (lông′suf′ər·ing, long′-) *adj.* Enduring injuries for a long time; patient; forbearing. — *n.* Patient and forbearing endurance of injuries or offense: also **long′–suf′fer·ance.**

long–tom (lông′tom′, long′-) *n.* A cradle used by miners for washing gold–bearing dirt.

Long Tom 1 A long swivel gun mounted on the decks of old sailing vessels. 2 A long–range coastal gun. 3 *Slang* Any large cannon having a long range. [<*long Tom Turk*; 19th century naval slang]

long–wind·ed (lông′win′did, long′-) *adj.* Continuing for a long time in speaking or writing; hence, tedious; lacking conciseness. — **long′wind′ed·ly** *adv.* — **long′wind′ed·ness** *n.*

long·wise (lông′wīz′, long′-) *adv.* Lengthwise. Also **long′ways′** (-wāz′).

Long·xu·yen (loung′swē′un) A city in southern Vietnam.

loo¹ (lōō) *n.* 1 A game of cards resembling euchre, played by several persons with three or five cards apiece. 2 The deposit made in the pool in the game of loo. 3 The fact of failing to take a trick at loo. — *v.t.* To subject to a forfeit at loo. [Short for *lanterloo* <F *lanturelu,* name of the game; orig. a vaudeville refrain]

loo² (lōō) See LO'E.

loo·by (lōō′bē) *n. pl.* **·bies** *Colloq.* 1 A lubber; a lout. 2 The ruddy duck. [? Akin to LUBBER]

loof¹ (lōōf) See LUFF.

loof² (lōōf) *n. Scot.* The palm of the hand.

loo·fah (lōō′fə) *n.* 1 Any of a genus (*Luffa*) of Old World, tropical, cucurbitaceous herbs with the male flowers in racemes and the female solitary. 2 The ovate or oblong fruit of this herb, fibrous within, and often used to filter oil and grease from condensed steam, as well as for cleaning and scrubbing. Also **loo′fa.** Also called *dishcloth gourd, vegetable sponge, luffa.* [<Arabic *lūfah*]

look (lŏŏk) *v.i.* 1 To direct the eyes toward something in order to see. 2 To direct or turn one's attention or consideration. 3 To search; make examination or inquiry: to *look* through a desk. 4 To appear to be; seem: He *looks* trustworthy. 5 To have a specified direction or view; front: This house *looks* over the park. 6 To expect: with an infinitive: I didn't *look* to find you home. — *v.t.* 7 To turn or direct the eyes upon: He *looked* her up and down. 8 To express by looks: to *look* one's hatred. 9 To give the appearance of being (a specified age). 10 To influence by looks: to *look* someone into silence. — **to look after** To take care of. — **to look daggers (at)** To scowl; glare (at). — **to look down on** To regard condescendingly or contemptuously. — **to look for** 1 To search for. 2 To expect. — **to look forward to** To anticipate pleasurably. — **to look in** (or **in on**) To make a short visit to. — **to look into** To examine; make inquiry. — **to look like** 1 To have the appearance of being; resemble. 2 To indicate the probability of: It *looks like* rain. — **to look on** 1 To be a spectator. 2 To consider; regard. — **to look out** To be on the watch; take care. — **to look over** To examine; scrutinize. — **to look to** 1 To attend to. 2 To turn to, as for help, advice, etc. — **to look up** 1 To search for and find, as in a file, dictionary, etc. 2 *Colloq.* To discover the where-

abouts of and make a visit to. 3 *Colloq.* To improve; become better. — **to look up to** To have respect for. — *n.* 1 The act of looking or seeing with voluntary attention: I will take a *look* at it. 2 *pl.* The appearance of the face or figure; cast of countenance. 3 Aspect; expression. 4 Appearance in general, either to the eye or understanding: I do not like the *look* of the thing. See synonyms under AIR, MANNER. [OE *locian*]

Synonyms (*verb*): behold, contemplate, descry, discern, gaze, glance, inspect, regard, scan, see, stare, survey, view, watch. To *see* is simply to become conscious of an object of vision; to *look* is to make a conscious and direct endeavor to *see.* To *behold* is to fix the sight and the mind with distinctness and consideration upon something that has come to be clearly before the eyes. We may *look* without *seeing,* as in darkness, and we may *see* without *looking,* as in the case of a flash of lightning. To *gaze* is to *look* intently, long, and steadily. To *glance* is to *look* casually or momentarily. To *stare* is to *look* with a fixed intensity. To *scan* is to *look* at minutely, to note every visible feature. To *inspect* is to go below the surface, study item by item. *View* and *survey* are comprehensive, *survey* expressing the greater exactness of measurement. *Watch* brings in the element of time; we *watch* for a movement or change.

look·er (lŏŏk′ər) *n.* 1 One who looks or watches. 2 *U.S. Slang* A handsome or good–looking person.

look·er–on (lŏŏk′ər·on′) *n. pl.* **look·ers–on** A spectator; onlooker.

look–in (lŏŏk′in′) *n. Slang* 1 A hasty, casual glance or visit. 2 *U.S. Colloq.* A chance: If he fights the champion, he hasn't a *look–in.*

look·ing–glass (lŏŏk′ing·glas′, -gläs′) *n.* A mirror.

look–out (lŏŏk′out′) *n.* 1 The act of watching or looking out; especially, careful or alert watchfulness. 2 A post of observation; also, the person or the group on watch in or at such a post. 3 One engaged in the U.S. Forest Service to detect fires. 4 One assigned to watch for enemy aircraft, tanks, or troop movements. 5 Prospect; outlook; chances of good or bad to come: a good *look–out* ahead. 6 *Colloq.* Concern; care: It's your own *look–out.*

Look·out Mountain (lŏŏk′out′) A ridge in SE Tennessee, near Chattanooga; scene of a Civil War battle, 1863.

look–see (lŏŏk′sē′) *n. Slang* An inspection or survey: Have a *look–see.* [Orig. Pidgin English]

loom¹ (lōōm) *v.i.* 1 To appear or come into view indistinctly, as from below the horizon or through a mist, especially so as to seem large or ominous. 2 To appear to the mind as threatening or portentous: Great difficulties *loom* ahead. 3 To shine. — *n.* A gradual, vague appearance of something, as of a ship in the fog. [Origin uncertain. Cf. Sw. *loma* move slowly (toward).]

loom² (lōōm) *n.* 1 A machine in which yarn or thread is woven into a fabric, by the crossing of threads called chain or warp, running lengthwise, with others called weft, woof, or filling. See illustration on page following. 2 The art or technique of working with a loom; the occupation of a weaver; weaving. 3 *Naut.* **a** The shaft of an oar, as distinguished from the blade. **b** That part of an oar between the rowlock and the handle. [OE *gelōma* tool]

loom³ (lōōm) *n.* 1 A guillemot. 2 A loon (def. 1). [<ON *lomr*]

loom·ing (lōō′ming) *n.* A mirage that elevates and elongates a figure, especially when viewed across the water.

loon¹ (lōōn) *n.* 1 A diving, fish–eating waterfowl (genus *Gavia*), with short tail feathers and webbed feet. 2 A guillemot. — **common loon** The great northern diver (*Gavia immer*). [See LOOM³]

LOON
(Length 31 to 36 inches)

loon² (lōōn) *n.* 1 A worthless, demented, or

stupid person; a lout; dolt. **2** A rogue; scamp. **3** *Obs.* A menial. Also *Obs. & Scot. loun, lown.* [Cf. Du. *loen* stupid fellow G *lümmel* lout]

HAND LOOM
The two sets of warp threads (*a, a*), alternately raised and lowered by the heddle (*b, b*), form between them a tunnel of threads called the shed (*c*). Through this shed the shuttle (*d*) is passed, carrying across the weft thread (*e*), which is beaten against the finished fabric by the movable comblike frame or reed (*f*). When the heddle is shifted, the two sets of warp reverse position, binding the weft into the fabric and opening another shed.

loon·y (lōō'nē) *Slang. adj.* **1** Lunatic or demented. **2** Foolish; somewhat crazy; erratic; silly. — *n. pl.* **loon·ies** A demented or daft person. Also spelled *luny.* [<LUNATIC]

loop¹ (lōōp) *n.* **1** A fold or doubling, as of a string or rope, so as to form an eye or a bend through which something may be passed; a noose; bight; hence, a curve or bend of any kind. **2** A stitch used in crocheting and knitting. **3** *Electr.* A complete magnetic or electrical circuit. **4** A curve in a railroad, carried completely around to reach a different level; also, a branch from the main line, returning to it after making a détour. **5** One of the basic patterns by which fingerprints are classified and identified, consisting of one or more ridges whose terminal points are on or toward the same side of the design. **6** *Aeron.* A complete, vertical, circular turn made by an airplane in flight. **7** *Physics* The part of a vibrating string, column of air, or standing wave system which is between two nodes; an antinode. — **to loop the loop** To make a vertical, circular turn, as an airplane in flight. — *v.t.* **1** To form a loop or loops in or of. **2** To fasten, connect, or encircle by means of a loop or loops. **3** *Aeron.* To fly (an aircraft) in a loop or loops. — *v.i.* **4** To make a loop or loops. **5** To move by forming loops, as a measuring worm. [Cf. Irish *lub* loop]

loop² (lōōp) *n.* Iron of pasty consistency ready for rolling. [<F *loupe*]

loop³ (lōōp) *n.* Any small window or aperture; a loophole. [Cf. MDu. *lupen* lie in wait, peer]

Loop, The The principal business, financial, hotel, and theatrical district of downtown Chicago, near the lake front.

loop buttonhole A loop of crochet, cord, or fabric serving as a buttonhole.

loop·er (lōō'pər) *n.* **1** A bodkinlike instrument for making loops. **2** A measuring worm.

loop·hole (lōōp'hōl') *n.* **1** A narrow opening through which small arms are fired. **2** A means of escape, or place of observation. — *v.t.* **-holed, -hol·ing** To furnish with loopholes. [<LOOP² + HOLE]

loop stitch A stitch composed of a series of loops, the last one finished with a knot; also called *picot stitch.*

loop·y (lōō'pē) *adj.* **1** Having or full of loops. **2** *Slang* Crazy. **3** *Scot.* Shrewd; sly.

loose (lōōs) *adj.* **loos·er, loos·est** **1** Not fastened or confined; not bound or attached; unbound or untied; freed from normal bonds or restraint: *loose* tresses; to be *loose* from old habits. **2** Lax in power, character, qual-

ity, principle, or conduct; careless; slovenly; slack; relaxed; wanton; dissolute: *loose* bond, *loose* conduct. **3** Not precise or exact; vague; indefinite; rambling; unconnected: *loose* reasoning; a *loose* style. **4** Not close, compact, dense, tight, or crowded; lacking union of parts; slackly joined or tied; not compact in frame: a *loose* knot or bond; a *loose* array; a fabric of *loose* texture; a man of *loose* build. **5** Not tight; open: said of a cough when expectoration is without difficulty, or of an abnormal laxity of the bowels. **6** Designating a stable or stall in which the animals are kept untied. See synonyms under IMMORAL, VAGUE, VULGAR, WANTON. — **on the loose** At liberty; at large; unconfined. — *adv.* In a loose manner; to play fast and loose. — *v.* **loosed, loos·ing** *v.t.* **1** To set free, as from bondage, penalty, etc. **2** To untie or undo, as a knot or rope. **3** To make less tight; loosen; slacken. **4** *Naut.* To cast off; release, as a boat from its moorings. **5** To let fly; shoot or discharge, as arrows. — *v.i.* **6** To become loose. **7** To loose something. [<ON *lauss*] — **loose'ly** *adv.* — **loose'ness** *n.*

loose–joint·ed (lōōs'join'tid) *adj.* **1** Having joints not tightly articulated; hence, able to move with more than ordinary freedom. **2** Ungainly.

loose–leaf (lōōs'lēf') *adj.* Designed for the easy insertion and removal of pages: a *loose-leaf* notebook.

loos·en (lōō'sən) *v.t.* **1** To untie or undo, as bonds or chains. **2** To set free; release. **3** To make less tight, firm, or compact: to *loosen* the stones of a wall. **4** To effect laxity in the action of (the bowels). **5** To relax the strictness of, as discipline. — *v.i.* **6** To become loose or looser. See synonyms under RELAX. — **loos'en·er** *n.*

loose sentence A sentence that is grammatically complete before its end: All compound sentences are *loose sentences.*

loose-strife (lōōs'strīf') *n.* **1** Any one of various plants, mostly with four-cornered branches and regular or irregular flowers, as the **common loosestrife** (*Lysimachia vulgaris*) of the primrose family or the **purple loosestrife** (*Lythrum salicaria*) of the family *Lythraceae.* **2** Any plant of the loosestrife family. [<LOOSE + STRIFE; direct trans. of L *lysimachia* <Gk. *lysimachion* <*lyein* loose + *machē* battle]

loo·some (lōō'səm) *adj. Scot.* Lovable.

loot¹ (lōōt) *v.t.* **1** To plunder, as a conquered city; pillage. **2** To carry off as plunder. — *v.i.* **3** To engage in plundering. — *n.* **1** Booty taken from a sacked city by a victorious army; plunder. **2** Anything unlawfully taken, as by one in an official position. [<Hind. *lūt* <Skt. *luṇṭ*] — **loot'er** *n.*

loot² (lōōt) *Scot.* Past tense of LET¹.

looves (lōōvz) Plural of LOOF.

lop¹ (lop) *v.t.* **lopped, lop·ping** **1** To cut or trim the branches, twigs, etc., from, as a tree. **2** To cut off, as branches or twigs. — *n.* A cutting from a tree; specifically, the trimmings or small twigs and branches not measured as timber; fagot. [Origin unknown] — **lop'per** *n.*

lop² (lop) *v.* **lopped, lop·ping** *v.i.* **1** To droop or hang down. **2** To hang or move about in an awkward or slouching manner. — *v.t.* **3** To permit to droop or hang down. — *adj.* Drooping. [Origin unknown]

Lo·pa·du·sa (lō'pə·dōō'sə, -dyōō'-) An ancient name for LAMPEDUSA.

lope (lōp) *v.t. & v.i.* **loped, lop·ing** To run or cause to run with a steady, swinging stride. — *n.* A slow, easy gallop. [<ON *hlaupa* leap, run] — **lop'er** *n.*

lop-eared (lop'ird') *adj.* Having drooping or pendulous ears.

Lo·pe de Ve·ga (lō'pā thā vā'gä) See VEGA, LOPE DE.

lopho– *combining form* Crest; crested. Also, before vowels, **loph–.** [<Gk. *lophos* crest]

lo·pho·branch (lō'fō·brangk, lof'ō-) *adj.* Of or pertaining to a division of teleost fishes (*Lophobranchii*), especially an order with imperfect branchial arches and tuftlike gill elements, including pipefishes and sea horses. — *n.* One of the *Lophobranchii.* [<LOPHO– + Gk. *branchion* gill] — **lo'pho·bran'chi·ate** (-kē·it, -āt) *adj. & n.*

lo·phot·ri·chous (lō·fot'ri·kəs) *adj. Zool.* Having a tuft of cilia at one pole of the cell:

characteristic of some micro-organisms. Also **lo·pho·trich·ic** (lō'fō·trik'ik, lof'ō-). [<LOPHO– + Gk. *thrix, trichos* hair]

lop·per (lop'ər) *v.t. & v.i. Scot.* To curdle: also spelled *lapper.*

lop·py (lop'ē) *adj.* **·pi·er, ·pi·est** **1** Limp; pendulous; hanging down. **2** Choppy: said of water.

lop–sid·ed (lop'sī'did) *adj.* Heavy or hanging down on one side; lacking in symmetry. — **lop'–sid'ed·ly** *adv.* — **lop'–sid'ed·ness** *n.*

lo·qua·cious (lō·kwā'shəs) *adj.* Given to continual talking; chattering. See synonyms under GARRULOUS. [<L *loquax, loquacis* <*loqui* talk] — **lo·qua'cious·ly** *adv.* — **lo·qua'cious·ness, lo·quac·i·ty** (lō·kwas'ə·tē) *n.*

lo·quat (lō'kwot, -kwat) *n.* **1** A low-growing, pomaceous tree (*Eriobotrya japonica*), cultivated for its fruit, a small, yellow pome. **2** This fruit. [Cantonese alter. of Chinese *lu–chü* rush orange]

lo·qui·tur (lok'wi·tər) *Latin* He or she speaks.

lo·ran (lôr'an, lō'ran) *n.* A navigation system by which a ship or an aircraft may accurately determine its position by noting the time intervals between radio pulse signals transmitted from a network of ground stations and recorded on an oscilloscope. [<LO(NG) RA(NGE) N(AVIGATION)]

Lor·ca (lôr'kä) A city in Murcia, SE Spain.

Lor·ca (lôr'kä), **Federico García** See *García Lorca, Federico.*

lord (lôrd) *n.* **1** One possessing supreme power and authority; a ruler. **2** A title of respect, formerly given to any superior, as by a wife to a husband: still sometimes humorously so used. **3** In feudal law, the owner of a manor under grant from the crown; a landlord. **4** A title of honor or nobility in Great Britain, given generally to men noble by birth or ennobled by patent. This includes **lords spiritual** (archbishops and bishops), who are members of the House of Lords, and also **lords temporal:** marquises, earls, viscounts, and barons. The formal titles are as follows: *Baron* X, the *Marquis* of X, the *Earl* of X, *Viscount* X; informally all are addressed *Lord* X. The given name is mentioned only to distinguish holders of the same title at different periods. Where the names are homonymous, the locality of the peerage is stated, as *Viscount Grey of Fallodon,* who was spoken of as *Lord Grey.* The title is given by courtesy to the eldest sons of dukes, marquises, and earls, who each take by courtesy also an inferior title held by the father, frequently the second title, and to the younger sons of dukes and marquises, prefixed to their Christian name and surname; in these cases the Christian names must always be mentioned, coming after "Lord," to distinguish among brothers: *Lord* Robert Cecil. It is also a title of office, such as the *Lord* Lieutenant, the *Lord* Chancellor, *Lord* Privy Seal, *Lords* of the Treasury, Admiralty, Bedchamber. **5** In astrology, a controlling planet. — *v.t.* To invest with the title of lord. — **to lord it (over)** To act in a domineering or arrogant manner. [OE *hlāford, hlāfweard,* lit., bread keeper <*hlāf* loaf + *weard* keeper, ward] — **lord'less** *adj.* — **lord'like** *adj.*

Lord (lôrd) **1** God. **2** Jesus Christ. Also *Our Lord.*

Lord Advocate The principal public prosecutor in Scotland.

lord–and–la·dy (lôrd'ənd·lā'dē) *n. pl.* **lord–and–la·dies** The harlequin duck.

Lord Howe Island (hou) An Australian dependency NE of Sydney; 5 square miles.

lord·ing (lôr'ding) *n.* **1** A lordling. **2** *Obs.* Lord; master.

lord lieutenant 1 The chief executive officer of a county in England. **2** Until 1922, the English viceroy in Ireland.

lord·ling (lôrd'ling) *n.* A little lord; petty chieftain: generally used contemptuously.

lord·ly (lôrd'lē) *adj.* **·li·er, ·li·est** **1** Of, pertaining to, or like a lord; becoming a lord; lofty; noble; insisting on compliance: a *lordly* presence. **2** Characterized by undue loftiness; insolent: a *lordly* air or demeanor. See synonyms under IMPERIOUS. — *adv.* In a lordly manner. — **lord'li·ness** *n.*

Lord of Hosts Jehovah; God.

Lord of Misrule Formerly, a person chosen to preside over the revels, festivities, and

sports in English royal or aristocratic households.

lor·do·sis (lôr·dō′sis) *n. Pathol.* Inward curvature of a bone; specifically, curvature of the spine with the convexity forward. Also **lor·do′ma** (-mə). [<NL <Gk. *lordōsis* < *lordos* bent backward] — **lor·dot′ic** (-dot′ik) *adj.*

lords-and-la·dies (lôrdz′ənd·lā′dēz) *n.* 1 The cuckoo pint or wakerobin. 2 The jack-in-the-pulpit.

Lord's Day Sunday; the Sabbath. [Trans. of L *dies dominica*]

lord·ship (lôrd′ship) *n.* 1 The state or quality of a lord; hence, the title by which noblemen (excluding dukes), bishops, and judges in England are addressed or spoken of, preceded by *your* or *his.* 2 The jurisdiction of a lord; seigniory; domain; manor. 3 The dominion, power, or authority of a lord; hence, sovereignty in general; supremacy. [OE *hlafordscipe.* See LORD.]

Lord's Prayer The prayer taught by Jesus to his disciples. *Matt.* vi 9–13.

Lord's Supper *Eccl.* 1 The Eucharist; the Holy Communion. 2 The Last Supper.

Lord's Table The altar or table on which the elements of the Eucharist are laid during and after consecration.

lore[1] (lôr, lōr) *n.* 1 The body of traditional, popular, often anecdotal knowledge about a particular subject. 2 Learning or erudition. 3 *Archaic* Any special instruction; also, a lesson or the act of teaching. See synonyms under LEARNING, WISDOM. [OE *lar*]

lore[2] (lôr, lōr) *n.* 1 *Ornithol.* The side of a bird's head between the eye and the beak. 2 *Zool.* A corresponding part in fishes and reptiles. [<L *lorum* strap, thong]

Lo·re·lei (lôr′ə·lī, *Ger.* lō′rə·lī) In German folklore, a siren on a rock in the Rhine, who lured boatmen to shipwreck by her singing: also called *Lurlei.* [<G]

Lo·ren·gau (lō′rən·gou) A port on Manus island, chief city of the Admiralty Islands.

Lo·rentz (lō′rents), **Hendrik Antoon,** 1853–1928, Dutch physicist.

Lo·renz (lō·rents′) Danish and German form of LAWRENCE. Also **Lo·ren·zo** (lə·ren′zō; *Ital.* lō·ren′tsō, *Sp.* lō·ren′thō).

Lo·renz (lō′rents), **Adolf,** 1854–1946, Austrian orthopedic surgeon.

lor·gnette (lôr·nyet′) *n.* 1 A pair of eyeglasses with an ornamental handle into which they may be folded when not in use. 2 A long-handled opera glass. [<F < *lorgner* spy, peer <OF *lorgne* squinting]

lor·gnon (lôr·nyôṅ′) *n. French* 1 A monocle. 2 A lorgnette.

lo·ri·ca (lō·rī′kə) *n. pl.* **·cae** (-kē) 1 An ancient Roman cuirass or corselet. 2 *Zool.* A protective covering or shell, as in infusorians or rotifers. [<L < *lorum* thong]

lor·i·cate (lôr′ə·kāt, lor′-) *v.t.* **·cat·ed, ·cat·ing** To cover with a protective coating. — *adj.* Covered with a lorica or shell. [<L *loricatus,* pp. of *loricare* clothe in mail, harness < *lorica* corselet] — **lor′i·ca′tion** *n.*

Lo·rient (lô·ryäṅ′) A port of NW France on the Bay of Biscay.

lor·i·keet (lôr′ə·kēt, lor′-) *n.* Any of certain small Polynesian parrots resembling the lory. [<LORY + (PARA)KEET]

Lo·rin·da (lô·rin′də, lə-) See LAURA.

lo·ris (lôr′is, lō′ris) *n.* A small, arboreal, nocturnal, Asian lemur (genera *Loris* and *Nycticebus*), having the index finger small. *Loris gracilis* is the **slender loris** of southern India and Ceylon; *Nycticebus tardigradus* is the slow lemur or **East Indian loris.** [<F <Flemish *lorrias* lazy, the sloth]

lorn (lôrn) *adj.* 1 *Archaic* Without kindred or friends; forlorn. 2 *Obs.* Lost. [OE *loren,* pp. of *lēosan* lose. Akin to FORLORN.]

Lorne (lôrn), **Firth of** An arm of the Atlantic separating Mull island from the Scottish mainland.

Lor·rain (lô·raṅ′), **Claude** Pseudonym of *Claude Gelée,* 1600–82, French painter.

Lor·raine (lô·rān′, lō-, lə-; *Fr.* lô·ren′) A region and former province of eastern France; after the Franco-Prussian War part of Alsace-Lorraine; restored to France, 1919: German *Lothringen.* See ALSACE-LORRAINE.

lor·ry (lôr′ē, lor′ē) *n. pl.* **·ries** 1 A low, four-wheeled, platform wagon. 2 *Brit.* A similar motor vehicle for carrying heavy loads; a truck. [Prob. dial. E *lurry* pull, tug]

lo·ry (lō′rē, lôr′ē) *n. pl.* **·ries** Any of certain parrots of Australasia (genera *Lorius, Apnosmictus,* and others) with brilliant, scarlet plumage, long bill, and tongue ending in a form of brush. [<Malay *lūrī*]

Los An·ge·les (lôs an′jə·lēz, ang′gə·ləs, los) A port in southern California, the fourth largest city in the United States: also *Colloq. L.A.* A native of Los Angeles is known as an *Angeleno.*

Lo·schmidt number (lō′shmit) *Physics* 1 The number of molecules in 1 cubic centimeter of an ideal gas at 0° C. and normal atmospheric pressure, equal to 2.687 x 10^{19}. 2 The Avogadro number. [after Joseph *Loschmidt,* 1821–95, Austrian physicist]

lose (lo͞oz) *v.* **lost, los·ing** *v.t.* 1 To part with, as by accident or negligence, and be unable to find; mislay. 2 To fail to keep, control, or maintain: to *lose* one's footing; to *lose* one's mind. 3 To be deprived of; suffer the loss of, as by accident, death, removal, etc.: to *lose* a leg. 4 To fail to gain or win: to *lose* a prize; to *lose* a battle. 5 To fail to utilize or take advantage of; miss: to *lose* a chance. 6 To fail to see or hear; miss: I *lost* not a word of the speech. 7 To fail to keep in sight, memory, etc.: We *lost* him in the crowd. 8 To cease to have: to *lose* one's sense of duty. 9 To squander; waste, as time. 10 To wander from so as to be unable to find: to *lose* the path. 11 To outdistance or elude, as runners or pursuers. 12 To cause the loss of: His rashness *lost* him his opportunity. 13 To bring to destruction or death; ruin: usually in the passive: All hands were *lost.* — *v.i.* 14 To suffer loss. 15 To be defeated. — **to lose heart** To become discouraged. — **to lose oneself** 1 To lose one's way, as in a wood. 2 To disappear or hide: The thief *lost himself* in the crowd. 3 To become engrossed. 4 To become confused or bewildered. — **to lose one's heart (to)** To fall in love (with). — **to lose out** *U.S. Colloq.* To fail or be defeated. — **to lose sight of** 1 To fail to keep in sight. 2 To take no notice of; ignore or forget. [Fusion of OE *losian* be lost and *lēosan* lose] — **los′a·ble** *adj.*

lo·sel (lō′zəl, lo͞o′zəl, loz′əl) *adj.* Inclined to idleness and waste. — *n.* A worthless fellow. [OE *losen,* pp. of *losian* be lost]

los·er (lo͞o′zər) *n.* One who loses or fails to win in any transaction; a defeated contestant.

losh (losh) *interj. Scot.* An exclamation of surprise or deprecation. [Euphemistic alter. of LORD; cf. GOSH]

los·ing (lo͞o′zing) *n.* 1 The act or fact of letting go, missing, lacking, or being deprived. 2 *pl.* Money lost, especially in gambling. — *adj.* 1 That incurs loss: a *losing* business. 2 Not winning; defeated: the *losing* team.

loss (lôs, los) *n.* 1 The act or state of losing; failure to keep or win; privation: *loss* of fortune or friends. 2 *Usually pl.* That which is lost, or its amount: His *losses* were great; The *losses* of the army were severe. 3 The state of being lost, or of having suffered destruction: the *loss* of a ship at sea. 4 Useless application; futile expenditure; waste. 5 Injury or diminution of value within the limits provided in an insurance policy, or the sum payable on that account. 6 *Physics* That part of electrical or mechanical energy which is expended in overcoming friction, etc., and from which no productive work is obtained. — **at a loss** 1 At so low a price as to result in a loss. 2 In confusion or doubt; perplexed. — **dead loss** An irremediable loss; one without hope of salvage, insurance, or any mitigation. — **to bear a loss** 1 To sustain a loss bravely. 2 To make good a loss. [OE *los*]

Synonyms: damage, defeat, deprivation, destruction, detriment, disadvantage, failure, forfeiture, injury, misfortune, privation, waste. See INJURY.

lost (lôst, lost) *adj.* 1 Not to be found or recovered; parted with; missing; left, as by accident, in a forgotten place: *lost* goods or friends. 2 Not won, gained, used, or enjoyed; missed; wasted: *lost* opportunity. 3 Ruined physically, morally, or spiritually; damned; destroyed. 4 Having wandered from the way; also, abstracted: *lost* in thought; bewildered; perplexed. 5 No longer known or used: a *lost* art. — **to be lost upon** (or **on**) To have no effect upon (a person).

lost cause Any cause that cannot possibly succeed; specifically, in American history, the cause of the Confederate States.

lost motion Slackness in a mechanical connection resulting in an appreciable difference between the travel of the driving and the driven elements.

lost tribes Those members of the ten northern, or Israelitish, Hebrew tribes that were taken into Assyrian captivity (II *Kings* xvii 6), believed never to have returned.

lot (lot) *n.* 1 Anything, as a die or piece of paper, used in determining something by chance; also, the fact or process of deciding something in such manner. 2 The share that comes to one as the result of drawing lots. 3 The part in life that comes to one without his planning; chance; fate. 4 A collection or parcel of things separated from others: The auctioneer sold the goods in ten *lots.* 5 A parcel or quantity of land, as surveyed and apportioned for sale or other special purpose: a city *lot,* a wood *lot.* 6 *Colloq.* A kind of person: He is a bad *lot.* 7 *Often pl. Colloq.* A great quantity or amount; a number of things, collectively: a *lot* of money, *lots* of trouble. ◆ *Lot* or *lots* is construed as a singular if attributed to a singular word, plural if to a plural word: A *lot* of money was hidden, but, A *lot* of diamonds were hidden. 8 A proportion of taxes allotted to one. 9 A motion-picture studio and the space it uses. See synonyms under FLOCK. — *adv.* Very much: a *lot* worse. — *v.* **lot·ted, lot·ting** *v.t.* 1 To divide, as land, into lots. 2 To apportion by lots; allot. — *v.i.* 3 To cast lots. [OE *hlot*]

Lot (lot) A nephew of Abraham, who with his wife and daughters escaped the destruction of Sodom. His wife, disobeying a warning, looked back at the city and became a pillar of salt. *Gen.* xi 27, xix.

Lot (lôt) A river in south central France, flowing 300 miles west from the Cévennes to the Garonne: ancient *Oltis.*

lo·tah (lō′tə) *n. Anglo-Indian* A small, round pot, usually of brass or copper, used in India for drinking and ablution. Also **lo′ta.**

lote (lōt) *n.* The lotus. [<LOTUS]

loth (lōth) *adj.* Loath.

Lo·thair (lō·thâr′, *Fr.* lō·târ′) A masculine personal name. Also *Ger.* **Lo·thar** (lō·tär′), *Ital.* **Lo·tha·rio** (lō·tä′ryō). [<Gmc., famous warrior]

— **Lothair I,** 795–855, Holy Roman Emperor 840–55.

— **Lothair the Saxon,** 1060?–1137, Holy Roman Emperor 1133–37.

Lo·thar·i·o (lō·thâr′ē·ō) In Nicholas Rowe's *The Fair Penitent,* a young Genoese nobleman and gay rake; hence, a seducer.

Lo·thi·ans (lō′thē·ənz), **The** A division of SE Scotland including East Lothian, Midlothian, and West Lothian.

Loth·ring·en (lōt′ring·ən) The German name for LORRAINE.

Lo·ti (lō·tē′), **Pierre** Pseudonym of *Louis Marie Julien Viaud,* 1850–1923, French novelist.

lo·tion (lō′shən) *n.* 1 A medicated liquid for the skin, eyes, or any diseased or bruised part, for cleansing or healing. 2 *Archaic* A bathing or washing. [<L *lotio, -onis* washing < *lavare* wash]

Lo·toph·a·gi (lō·tof′ə·jī) *n. pl.* In the *Odyssey,* a people living on the northern coast of Africa who lived a life of indolence and forgetfulness induced by eating the fruit of the lotus: some of Odysseus' followers ate with them, and forgot their friends, homes, and native land. [<Gk. *lōtophagoi* < *lōtos* lotus + *phagein* eat]

Lot·ta (lot′ə), **Lot·tie** (lot′ē), **Lot·ty** Diminutives of CHARLOTTE.

lot·ter·y (lot′ər·ē) *n. pl.* **·ter·ies** A distribution of, or scheme for distributing, prizes as determined by chance or lot, especially where such chances are allotted by sale of

tickets; hence, any chance disposition of any matter. [<Ital. *lotteria* <*lotto* lottery, lot <F *lot* <Gmc.]

lot·to (lot'ō) *n.* A game of chance played with cards and disks: also called *keno.* Also **lo·to** (lō'tō). [<Ital. See LOTTERY.]

Lot·to (lôt'tō), **Lorenzo,** 1480?–1556, Venetian painter.

lo·tus (lō'təs) *n.* **1** One of various Old World plants of the waterlily family, noted for their large floating leaves and showy flowers; especially, the **white** and **blue lotus** of the Nile (respectively *Nymphaea lotus,* and *N. caerulea*); also, the **sacred lotus** of India *Nelumbium nelumbo*) with fragrant pink or rose flowers. **2** The lotus tree. **3** Any of a genus (*Lotus*) of herbs or shrubs of the bean family. **4** *Archit.* A representation or conventionalization of the lotus flower, bud, or leaves. Also **lo'tos.** [<L <Gk. *lōtos*]

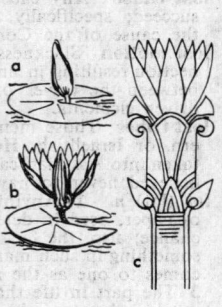

LOTUS
a. Bud and leaf.
b. Blossom and leaf.
c. Stylized lotus in Egyptian architecture and ornament.

lo·tus–eat·er (lō'təs-ē'tər) *n.* In the *Odyssey,* one who lives in irresponsible enjoyment from eating the fruit of the lotus tree; hence, a voluptuary. See LOTOPHAGI.

lotus tree The common jujube.

Loua·la·ba (lwä·lä·bä') The French spelling of LUALABA.

loud (loud) *adj.* **1** Striking the auditory nerves with great force; having great volume or intensity of sound; noisy. **2** Making a great noise. **3** Pressing or urgent; clamorous: a *loud* demand. **4** Conspicuous or ostentatious without taste or refinement; vulgarly showy; flashy. —*adv.* With loudness; loudly. [OE *hlūd*] —**loud'ly** *adv.* —**loud'ness** *n.*

loud·en (loud'n) *v.t. & v.i.* To make or become louder.

loud–mouthed (loud'mouthd, -moutht') *adj.* Possessed of a loud voice; offensively clamorous or talkative.

loud·speak·er (loud'spē'kər) *n.* An electromagnetic device for amplifying the sounds transmitted by radio, public-address system, or the like.

lough (lokh) *n. Irish* **1** A loch; lake or pool. **2** A partially landlocked arm of the sea.

lou·is (lōō'ē) *n.* **1** A French gold coin worth twenty francs. **2** An old French gold coin worth about twenty-three francs, used through the reigns of Louis XIII–Louis XVI. Also *louis d'or.* [<F, after *Louis* XIII]

Lou·is (lōō'is, *Fr.* lōō·ē') A masculine personal name. Also spelled *Lewis.* [<Gmc., famed warrior]

—**Louis I,** 778–840, Holy Roman Emperor 814–840; son and successor of Charlemagne: called "le Débonnaire."

—**Louis VIII,** 1187–1226, king of France 1223–26.

—**Louis IX,** 1214–70; king of France 1226–70; defeated and captured by the Saracens at Mansûra 1249; canonized 1297 as *Saint Louis.*

—**Louis XI,** 1423–83, king of France 1461–1483; made the power of the throne paramount.

—**Louis XIII,** 1601–43, king of France 1610–1643; son of Henry IV.

—**Louis XIV,** 1638–1715, king of France 1643–1715; son of the preceding: called "Le Grand Monarque," "le roi soleil."

—**Louis XV,** 1710–74, king of France 1715–1774; great-grandson of the preceding; ceded Canada to Great Britain.

—**Louis XVI,** 1754–93, king of France 1774–1792; grandson of Louis XV; dethroned by the revolution and guillotined.

—**Louis XVIII,** 1755–1824, brother of Louis XVI; king of France April, 1814–March, 1815, and June, 1815–24.

—**Louis Napoleon** See NAPOLEON III.

—**Louis Philippe,** 1773–1850, king of France 1830–48; abdicated: known as *The Citizen King.*

Lou·is (lōō'is), **Joe,** born 1914, U.S. heavyweight boxing champion 1937–49; real name *Joseph Louis Barrow.*

Lou·i·sa (lōō·ē'zə) A feminine personal name. Also **Lou·ise** (lōō·ēz'). [See LOUIS]

Lou·is·burg (lōō'is·bûrg) A town on the eastern coast of Cape Breton Island, Canada; captured from the French by British forces in 1745 and 1758. Also **Lou·is·bourg.**

lou·is d'or (lōō'ē dôr') A louis. [<F, gold louis]

Lou·ise (lōō·ēz'), **Lake** A lake in Banff National Park, SW Alberta, Canada.

Lou·i·si·ade Archipelago (lōō·ē'zē·ād') A Papuan island group SE of New Guinea; 980 square miles.

Lou·i·si·an·a (lōō·ē'zē·an'ə) One of the United States, fronting south on the Gulf of Mexico; 48,523 square miles; capital, Baton Rouge; comprised of portions of West Florida and of the Louisiana Purchase of 1803, it entered the Union April 8, 1812; nickname, *Pelican State* or *Creole State*: abbr. LA —**Lou·i'si·an'i·an, Lou·i'si·an'an** *adj. & n.*

Louisiana Purchase The French colonial territory in west central North America, purchased from France by the United States in 1803 for $15,000,000: the land between the Mississippi River and the Rocky Mountains, the Gulf of Mexico and Canada.

Lou·is–Qua·torze (lōō'ē·kà·tôrz') *adj.* Designating the style of architecture, interior decoration, and furniture which characterized the period of Louis XIV in France (1643–1715), marked by baroque architectural forms and ornate and grandiose decorative treatment employing animal and mythological forms richly carved. [<F]

Lou·is–Quinze (lōō'ē·kanz') *adj.* Designating the style of architecture, decoration, and furniture characteristic of the period of Louis XV (1715–74), marked by the culmination of the rococo as expressed in flowing lines, rounded forms, and graceful shell, flower, and other ornaments. [<F]

Lou·is–Seize (lōō'ē·sez') *adj.* Designating a style of architecture, decoration, and furniture which characterized the period of Louis XVI (1774–93): a reaction against the Louis-Quinze period, marked by simple, rectilinear forms, and using symmetrical Greco–Roman wreaths, birds, etc., as ornaments, or Greek egg–and–anchor or leaf motifs, achieving a plain internal decoration. [<F]

Lou·is–Treize (lōō'ē·trez') *adj.* Designating the style of architecture, decoration, and furniture which characterized the period of Louis XIII (1610–43), marked by Renaissance forms, rich inlaid ornaments, geometric panels and deep moldings, and carving in the Flemish style. [<F]

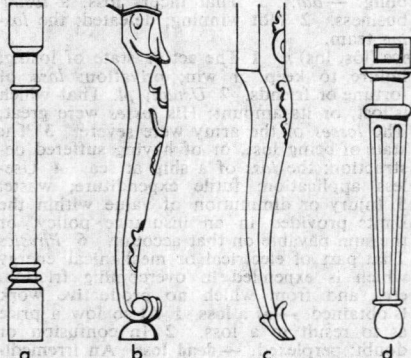

PERIOD STYLES ILLUSTRATED BY CHAIR LEGS
a. Louis XIII. *b.* Louis XIV. *c.* Louis XV. *d.* Louis XVI.

Lou·is·ville (lōō'ē·vil) A city on the Ohio River in Kentucky.

loun (loun) *adj. Scot.* Lown.

lounge (lounj) *v.* **lounged, loung·ing** *v.i.* **1** To lie, lean, move, etc., in an idle or lazy manner. **2** To pass time indolently. —*v.t.* **3** To spend or pass indolently, as time. —*n.* **1** act of lounging. **2** A room in a hotel, club, etc., for lounging. **3** A couch with little or no back; any sofa. [Origin unknown]

loung·er (loun'jər) *n.* One who lounges; an idler.

loup[1] (loup, lōōp) *v.t. & v.i.* **lap** or **loup·en, loup·ing** *Scot. & Brit. Dial.* To leap. [<ON *hlaupa*]

loup[2] (lōō) *n.* A light mask or half-mask made of silk: worn at masquerades. [<F]

loup–cer·vier (lōō·ser·vyā') *n. French* The Canada lynx (*Lynx canadensis*). [<L *lupus cervarius* lynx <*lupus* wolf + *cervarius* stag-hunting <*cervus* stag]

loupe (lōōp) *n.* A small magnifying glass; a lens, especially one adapted for the use of jewelers and watchmakers. [<F]

loup–ga·rou (lōō·gà·rōō') *n. pl.* **loups–ga·rous** (lōō·gà·rōō') A werewolf. [<F *loup* wolf (<L *lupus*) + *garou* werewolf <Gmc.]

LOUPE
Made to be used as an eyepiece.

loup·ing ill (lou'ping, lō'-) *Scot.* An infectious virus disease of sheep; leaping evil. Also **loup ill.**

Loup River (lōōp) A river in east central Nebraska, flowing 300 miles east to the Platte River.

lour (lour), **lour·ing** (lour'ing), **lour·y** (lour'ē) See LOWER[1], etc.

Lourdes (lōōrd) A town in SW France; shrine and grotto of the Virgin (*Our Lady of Lourdes*).

Lou·ren·ço Mar·ques (lō·ren'sō mär'kəs, *Pg.* lō·rãñ'sōō mär'kish) A port on Delagoa Bay, capital of Mozambique.

louse (lous) *n. pl.* **lice** (līs) **1** A small, flat-bodied, wingless insect (order *Anoplura*) living as an external parasite on birds or mammals, especially the crab louse (*Phthirus pubis*) and the human body louse (genus *Pediculus*). **2** One of various other insects parasitic on other animals or plants, as the biting bird louse (order *Mallophaga*) and the plant louse. For illustrations see under INSECTS (injurious). **3** *Slang* A contemptible person. —*v.t. & v.i. U.S. Slang* To ruin; bungle: with *up.* [OE *lūs*]

louse·wort (lous'wûrt') *n.* Any one of a genus (*Pedicularis*) of scrophulariaceous woodland herbs; wood betony.

lous·y (lou'zē) *adj.* **lous·i·er, lous·i·est 1** Infested with lice; pedicular. **2** *Slang* Dirty. **3** *Slang* Contemptible; foul; mean. **4** *Slang* Having plenty (of): usually with *with*: *lousy* with money.

lout[1] (lout) *n.* An awkward fellow; clown; boor. [? <ON *lutr* bent, stooped]

lout[2] (lout) *v.i. Obs.* To bow or curtsy; bend; stoop. [OE *lūtan* bow]

Louth (louth) A county of NE Leinster province, Ireland; 317 square miles; county town, Drogheda.

lou·ther (lōō'thər) *v.i. Scot.* To plod, as in mire or wet snow.

lout·ish (lou'tish) *adj.* Clumsy; awkward; boorish. —**lout'ish·ly** *adv.* —**lout'ish·ness** *n.*

Lou·vain (lōō·vän', *Fr.* lōō·van') A city in central Belgium. *Flemish* Leu·ven (lœ'vən, -və).

lou·ver (lōō'vər) *n.* **1** A window, as in a belfry tower, designed for ventilation and having slats (**louver boards**) sloped to keep out the rain: also **lou'ver–win'dow** (-win'dō). **2** A lantern-like cupola or turret on the roof of a medieval dwelling. **3** Any of several narrow openings, or the slatted piece having these, serving as outlets for heated air. [<OF *lover*]

LOUVER
a. Construction set in gable (*b*).

Lou·vre (lōō'vr') An ancient royal palace in Paris, made a museum in the 18th century.

Lou·ÿs (lōō·ē', *Fr.* lwē), **Pierre,** 1870–1925, French writer.

lov·a·ble (luv'ə·bəl) *adj.* Worthy of love; amiable; also, evoking love. See synonyms under AMIABLE, LOVELY. Also **love'a·ble.** —**lov'a·bil'i·ty, lov'a·ble·ness** *n.* —**lov'a·bly** *adv.*

lov·age (luv'ij) *n.* A European herb (*Levisticum officinale*) of the parsley family: used sometimes as a domestic remedy. [<OF *luvesche* <LL *levisticum,* alter. of L *ligusticum,* neut. of *ligusticus* Ligurian]

love (luv) *n.* **1** A strong, complex emotion or feeling causing one to appreciate, delight in,

and crave the presence or possession of another and to please or promote the welfare of the other; devoted affection or attachment. **2** Specifically, such feeling between husband and wife or lover and sweetheart. **3** One who is beloved; a sweetheart. **4** Sexual passion, or the gratification of it. **5** A very great interest or fondness: *love* of learning. **6** In tennis, a score of nothing. — **for the love of** For the sake of; in loving remembrance of: used in adjurations, solemn oaths, etc. — **for love or money** For any consideration; under any circumstances. — **in love** Experiencing love; enamored. — **no love lost between** No affection or liking between. — *v.* **loved,** **lov·ing** *v.t.* **1** To feel love or affection for. **2** To take pleasure or delight in; like very much. **3** To caress. — *v.i.* **4** To feel love, especially for one of the opposite sex; be in love. See synonyms under ADMIRE, LIKE. [OE *lufu*]

Synonyms (noun): affection, attachment, attraction, charity, devotion, esteem, feeling, fondness, friendship, liking, passion, regard, tenderness. *Affection* is kindly feeling, deep, tender, and constant, going out to some person or object, being less fervent and ardent than *love*. *Love* is the yearning or outgoing of soul toward something that is regarded as excellent, beautiful, or desirable; *love* may be briefly defined as strong and absorbing *affection* for and *attraction* toward a person or object. *Love* is more intense, absorbing, and tender than *friendship*, more intense, impulsive, and perhaps passionate than *affection*; we speak of fervent *love*, but of deep or tender *affection*, or of close, firm, strong *friendship*. *Love* is used specifically for personal *affection* between the sexes, and can never properly denote mere animal passion, which is expressed by such words as appetite, desire, lust. One may have *love* for animals, inanimate objects, or for abstract qualities that enlist the affections, as we speak of *love* for a horse or a dog, for mountains, woods, ocean, or of *love* of nature, and *love* of virtue. *Love* of articles of food is better expressed by *liking*, as *love*, in its full sense, denotes something spiritual and reciprocal, such as can have no place in connection with objects that minister merely to the senses. See ATTACHMENT, FRIENDSHIP. *Antonyms:* see synonyms for ANTIPATHY, ENMITY, HATRED.

Love (luv) A personification of love; Cupid or Eros.
love affair A romantic attachment between two people not married to each other.
love apple The tomato.
love·bird (luv'bûrd') *n.* One of several small parrots (genera *Agapornis* and *Psitta*) often kept as cage birds: so called from the affection they appear to show for their mates.
love feast 1 A common devotional meal partaken of by early Christians, originally culminating in the Eucharist; agape. **2** A somewhat similar celebration observed in some modern churches, as the Methodist and Moravian. **3** A banquet held in common rejoicing over something.
love game In tennis, a game in which the winner has lost no point.
love-in-a-mist (luv'in-ə-mist') *n.* A European ranunculaceous garden plant (*Nigella damascena*) with blue flowers.
love-in-i-dle·ness (luv'in-ī'dəl-nis) *n.* The pansy.
love-knot (luv'not') *n.* A knot tied in pledge of love and constancy, or representation of it, as in jewelry.
Love·lace (luv'lās), **Richard,** 1618–58, English poet.
love·less (luv'lis) *adj.* Having no love; unloving; also, not lovable. — **love'less·ly** *adv.* — **love'less·ness** *n.*
love-lies-bleed·ing (luv'līz'blē'ding) *n.* Any of several species of amaranth.
love·lock (luv'lok') *n.* A separate lock of hair worn curled and tied with ribbons; especially such a lock as worn formerly by courtiers.
love·lorn (luv'lôrn) *adj.* Forsaken by or pining for a lover.
love·ly (luv'lē) *adj.* **·li·er, ·li·est 1** Possessing mental or physical qualities that inspire admiration and love; charming. **2** Beautiful.

3 Attractive; inviting. **4** *Colloq.* Delightful; pleasing: We had a *lovely* visit with them. **5** *Obs.* Affectionate; loving. [OE *luflic*] — **love'·li·ness** *n.*
Synonyms: amiable, beautiful, charming, delectable, delightful, enchanting, lovable, pleasing, sweet, winning, winsome. See AMIABLE, BEAUTIFUL.
love·mak·ing (luv'mā'king) *n.* The act of making love; wooing; courtship.
love potion A magic draft or drink designed to arouse love toward a certain person in the one who drinks.
lov·er (luv'ər) *n.* **1** One who loves; a warm admirer; devoted friend. **2** One who is in love; specifically, a paramour: in the singular now used only of the man. **3** One who enjoys or is strongly attracted by some object or diversion. — **lov'er·ly** *adj.* & *adv.*
Lov·er (luv'ər), **Samuel,** 1797–1868, Irish novelist.
love seat A double chair or small sofa for two persons in Queen Anne and later styles.
love set In tennis, a set in which the winner has not lost a game.
love·sick (luv'sik') *adj.* **1** Languishing with love. **2** Indicating or expressing such a condition: a *lovesick* serenade. — **love'sick'ness** *n.*
love·some (luv'səm) *adj. Obs.* **1** Inspiring love; lovable. **2** Expressing love; loving.
love·vine (luv'vīn') *n.* The dodder.
lov·ing (luv'ing) *adj.* **1** Affectionate; devoted; kind: *loving* friends or brothers. **2** Indicative of love or kind feeling: *loving* looks and words. See synonyms under AMIABLE, CHARITABLE. — **lov'ing·ly** *adv.* — **lov'ing·ness** *n.*
loving cup 1 A wine cup, usually with two or more handles, meant to be passed from hand to hand around a circle of friends; a parting cup. **2** A trophy presented to the winner of an athletic or other kind of contest.
lov·ing-kind·ness (luv'ing-kīnd'nis) *n.* Kindness that comes from personal attachment; specifically, the loving care of God for his people.
low¹ (lō) *adj.* **1** Having relatively little upward extension; not high or tall. **2** Having relatively little elevation; raised only slightly above a recognized level: a *low* bridge; near the horizon: a *low* moon. **3** Situated below a recognized level; deep; depressed. **4** Having less than the normal or regular height, or less height than something taken as a standard; descending from the usual level. **5** Cut so as to expose the neck; décolleté. **6** Of sounds having depth of pitch; deep; also, having little volume or strength; soft. **7** Being less than the usual rate, amount, or reckoning; scant: *low* wages or interest. **8** Being little in degree, number, grade, station, quality, character, etc.; humble; moderate. **9** Being below the proper standard in refinement, moral character, principle, or condition; lacking pride, principle, force, dignity, or worth; vulgar; weak: *low* spirits; *low* standards of morality. **10** Dead; prostrate: He lies *low*. **11** *Phonet.* Pronounced with the tongue low and flat; open: said of vowels: opposed to *high*. **12** Little advanced in civilization or organic evolution. **13** Badly nourished; lacking in vigor; also, not nourishing; plain: a *low* diet. **14** *Mech.* Giving the least speed: *low* gear. **15** *Geog.* Pertaining to latitudes near the equator. **16** *Eccl.* **a** Pertaining to broad evangelical doctrine. **b** Denoting a service shorn of elaborate ritual: a *low* mass. **17** *Bot.* Growing close to the ground: a *low* herb. See synonyms under BASE, COMMON, HUMBLE, VULGAR. — *adv.* **1** In a low way; in or to a low position; not on high. **2** At a low price; cheap. **3** In a humble rank or degraded condition. **4** So as not to be loud in sound; softly; also, at a low pitch. **5** In such a path that the declination or the altitude is small; near the equator or the horizon. — **to lie low 1** To be dead or prostrate. **2** To be or remain in hiding. **3** To hold one's tongue till the proper moment; wait. — *n.* **1** A low area. **2** The first gear or speed of an automobile: Put it in *low*. [OE *lah* <ON *lagr*] — **low'·ness** *n.*
low² (lō) *n.* The moo or bellow of cattle: also **low'ing.** — *v.i.* To bellow, as cattle; moo. — *v.t.* To utter by lowing. [OE *hlowan*]

low³ (lō) *n. Scot.* A glowing fire; blaze. Also **lowe.**
Low (lō), **David,** 1891–1963, English cartoonist.
Low Archipelago See TUAMOTU ARCHIPELAGO.
low area *Meteorol.* A region of low atmospheric pressure.
low-ar·e·a storm (lō'âr'ē-ə) A cyclone.
low-born (lō'bôrn') *adj.* Of humble birth.
low·boy (lō'boi') *n.* A table, often a dressing table, with drawers, similar to the lower part of a highboy.
low-bred (lō'bred') *adj.* Vulgar; ill-bred.
low-brow (lō'brou') *Colloq. n.* A person of uncultivated tastes; a non-intellectual: an uncomplimentary term. — *adj.* Of or suitable for such a person: also **low'browed'.** — **low'brow'·ism** *n.*
Low-Church (lō'chûrch') *adj.* Of or belonging to a group (**Low Church**) in the Anglican Church which stresses evangelical doctrine and is, in general, opposed to extreme ritualism. — **Low-Church·man** (lō'chûrch'mən) *n.*
low comedy Comedy in which both subject matter and presentation are in the broad style of farce or burlesque; comedy characterized by slapstick and lively physical action rather than by witty dialog.
Low Countries The region of NW Europe comprising the Netherlands, Belgium, and Luxemburg.
low-down¹ (lō'doun') *n. Slang* Inside or secret information; the truth of a matter.
low-down² (lō'doun') *adj. Colloq.* Degraded; mean.
low-down·er (lō'dou'nər) *n. Dial.* A poor white.
Low·ell (lō'əl) A distinguished Massachusetts family, descendants of **John,** 1743–1802, jurist, including **James Russell,** 1819–91, poet, essayist, editor, and diplomat; **Percival,** 1855–1916, astronomer; **Abbott Lawrence,** 1856–1943, educator; president of Harvard University 1909–33; brother of Percival; **Amy,** 1874–1925, poet and critic; sister of Percival.
Low·ell (lō'əl) A city on the Merrimac River in NE Massachusetts.
low·er¹ (lou'ər) *v.i.* **1** To look angry or sullen; scowl. **2** To appear dark and threatening, as the weather. — *n.* A scowl; a gloomy aspect. Also spelled *lour.* [Cf. G *lauern* lurk]
low·er² (lō'ər) Comparative of LOW. — *adj.* **1** Inferior in position, in value or rank; situated below something else: a *lower* berth. **2** *Geol.* Older; designating strata normally beneath the newer (and upper) rock formations. — *n.* That which is beneath something above; specifically, a lower berth. — *v.t.* **1** To bring to a lower position or level; let down, as a window. **2** To reduce in degree, quality, amount, etc.: to *lower* prices. **3** To bring down in estimation, rank, etc.; humble or degrade. **4** To change, as a sound, to a lower pitch or volume. — *v.i.* **5** To become lower; sink; decrease. See synonyms under ABASE, ABATE, DISPARAGE, WEAKEN.
Lower Austria An autonomous province of NE Austria; 7,097 square miles; capital, Vienna. *German* **Nie·der·ös·ter·reich** (nē'dər-œs'tə·rīkh).
Lower Burma See BURMA, UNION OF.
Lower California A peninsula of NW Mexico separating the Gulf of California from the Pacific; about 760 miles long; 55,634 square miles: divided into **Northern Territory;** 27,655 square miles; capital, Mexicali; and **Southern Territory;** 27,979 square miles; capital, La Paz. Spanish *Baja California.*
Lower Canada A former name for the province of QUEBEC.
low·er-case (lō'ər·kās') *adj. Printing* Describing the small letters of a font of type which are kept in the low case (see CASE); small letters. — *v.t.* **-cased, -cas·ing** To set as or change to lower-case letters. [From their being kept in the lower two cases of type]
lower class The socially or economically inferior group in society. — **low·er-class** (lō'ər·klas', -kläs') *adj.*
low·er-class·man (lō'ər-klas'mən, -kläs'-) *n. pl.* **-men** (-mən) A freshman or a sophomore.
Lower Cretaceous *Geol.* The older part of the

Cretaceous period, or its representative rocks or fossils. See CRETACEOUS.

lower criticism The method of critical investigation which seeks to determine the original wording of a text: also called *textual criticism*. Compare HIGHER CRITICISM.

Lower Franconia An administrative division of NW Bavaria, West Germany; 3,277 square miles; capital, Würzburg: formerly *Mainfranken*. *German* **Un·ter·fran·ken** (o͝on′tər·fräng′kən).

Lower House The popular division of a legislative body; in the United States, the House of Representatives, as opposed to the Upper House or Senate; in Great Britain, the House of Commons, as opposed to the House of Lords.

low·er·ing (lou′ər·ing) *adj.* **1** Overcast with clouds; gloomy; threatening. **2** Frowning or sullen. Also spelled *louring*. **—low′er·ing·ly** *adv.* **—low′er·ing·ness** *n.*

low·er·most (lō′ər·mōst′) *adj.* Lowest.

Lower Saxony A state of north central West Germany; 18,279 square miles; capital, Hanover. *German* **Nie·der·sach·sen** (nē′dər·zäk′sən).

Lower Silurian *Geol.* The former name for ORDOVICIAN.

lower world 1 The abode of the dead; hell; Hades. Also **lower regions. 2** The earth.

low·er·y (lou′ər·ē) *adj.* Cloudy; threatening storm: also spelled *loury*.

Lowes (lōz), **John Livingston,** –1945, U.S. scholar, critic, and educator.

lowest common multiple See under MULTIPLE.

Lowes·toft (lōs′tôft, -təft) *n.* A variety of porcelain originally made at Lowestoft, England.

Lowes·toft (lōs′tôft, -təft) A municipal borough and port in eastern Suffolk, England.

Low German See under GERMAN.

low–key (lō′kē′) *adj.* Having a low degree of intensity; relatively pale or quiet; understated. Also **low–keyed** (lō′kēd′).

low·land (lō′lənd) *adj.* Pertaining to or characteristic of a low or level country. —*n.* (*also* lō′land′) *Usually pl.* Land lower than the adjacent country; level land. **—The Lowlands** The less elevated districts lying in the south and west of Scotland. **—Low′land′er** *n.*

Low·land (lō′lənd) *adj.* Pertaining to or belonging to The Lowlands. —*n.* (*also* lō′land′) The speech or dialect of the Scotch Lowlands.

Low Latin See under LATIN.

low·ly (lō′lē) *adj.* **·li·er, ·li·est 1** Situated or lying low, as land. **2** Having low rank or importance; unpretending; humble. See synonyms under HUMBLE. —*adv.* **1** In a manner appropriate to humble life; rudely; meanly. **2** In a meek or modest manner. **—low′li·ness** *n.*

low mass The ordinary form of mass without music.

low–mind·ed (lō′mīn′did) *adj.* Having low or mean thoughts, sentiments, or motives; base.

lown[1] (loun) *adj. Scot.* Sheltered; tranquil. **—lown′ly** *adv.*

lown[2] (lo͞on) See LOON[2].

low–necked (lō′nekt′) *adj.* Cut low in the neck; décolleté: said of a garment.

low–pitched (lō′picht′) *adj.* **1** Low in tone, key, or range of tone, as a voice. **2** Having little angular elevation: said of a roof.

low–pres·sure (lō′presh′ər) *adj.* **1** Requiring a low degree of pressure. **2** Having a condenser, as an engine. **3** *Meteorol.* Designating an atmospheric pressure below that which is normal at sea level.

low relief Bas-relief.

low–spir·it·ed (lō′spir′it·id) *adj.* Lacking spirit or animation; despondent; melancholy. **—low′–spir′it·ed·ly** *adv.* **—low′–spir′it·ed·ness** *n.*

Low Sunday The Sunday following Easter.

low–ten·sion (lō′ten′shən) *adj. Electr.* Having or characterized by a low electric potential, as a battery, magneto, or vacuum tube.

low–test (lō′test′) *adj.* Possessing a relatively high boiling point, as gasoline.

low tide The furthest recession of the tide at any point; also, the time of its occurrence. Also **low water.**

low–wa·ter (lō′wô′tər, -wot′ər) *adj.* Pertaining to low tide or its time or measure of recession.

lox[1] (loks) *n.* Smoked salmon. [<Yiddish <G *lachs* salmon]

lox[2], **LOKS** (loks) *n.* Liquid oxygen.

lox·o·drom·ic (lok′sə·drom′ik) *adj.* Pertaining to oblique sailing on the rhumb line. Also **lox′o·drom′i·cal.** [<Gk. *loxos* oblique + *dromos* a running]

lox·o·drom·ics (lok′sə·drom′iks) *n. pl.* (construed as singular) The art of oblique sailing. Also **lox·od·ro·my** (lok·sod′rə·mē).

loy·al (loi′əl) *adj.* **1** Constant and faithful in any relation implying trust or confidence; bearing true allegiance to constituted authority. **2** Professing or indicative of faithful devotion. **3** *Obs.* Legitimate. See synonyms under FAITHFUL. [<OF *loial, leial* <L *legalis.* Doublet of LEGAL.] **—loy′al·ism** *n.* **—loy′al·ly** *adv.*

loy·al·ist (loi′əl·ist) *n.* One who adheres to and defends his sovereign or state.

Loy·al·ist (loi′əl·ist) *n.* **1** One who was loyal to the British crown during the American Revolution. **2** One who was loyal to the Union during the Civil War. **3** One who was loyal to the Republican Constitution during the Spanish Civil War.

loy·al·ty (loi′əl·tē) *n. pl.* **·ties** Devoted allegiance. See synonyms under ALLEGIANCE, FIDELITY. [<OF *loialte*]

Loyalty Islands A dependency of New Caledonia; total, 740 square miles. *French* **Îles Loy·au·té** (ēllwä·yō·tā′).

Lo·yo·la (loi·ō′lə, *Sp.* lō·yō′lä), **Ignatius of,** 1491–1556, Spanish soldier and priest; founder, with Francisco Xavier, of the Society of Jesus (the Jesuits); canonized in 1622: original name *Iñigo de Oñez y Loyola.* **—Loy·o·lism** (loi′ə·liz′əm) *n.*

loz·enge (loz′inj) *n.* **1** *Math.* A rhombus with all sides equal, having two acute and two obtuse angles. **2** A small medicated or sweetened tablet, originally diamond-shaped. [<OF *losenge,?* <L *lapis, -idis* stone]

LP (el′pē′) *adj.* Designating a phonograph record pressed with microgrooves and played at a speed of 33⅓ revolutions per minute. —*n.* A long-playing phonograph record: a trade name. [< *l(ong)-p(laying)*]

LSD (el′es′dē′) *n.* A drug that produces states similar to those of schizophrenia, used in medicine and illicitly as a hallucinogen. See LYCSERGIC ACID. Also **LSD–25.** [<*l(y)s(ergic acid) d(iethylamide)*]

Lu·a·la·ba (lo͞o′ä·lä′bä) The upper course of the Congo, flowing 400 miles north: French *Loualaba.*

Lu·an·da (lo͞o·än′də) A port, capital of Angola: formerly *Loanda, São Paulo de Loanda.*

Luang Pra·bang (lwäng prä·bäng′) A city of north central Laos; royal residence.

Luang·wa (lwäng′gwä) A river in eastern Zambia, flowing 500 miles SW to the Zambesi: formerly *Loangwa.*

lu·au (lo͞o′ou) *n.* A Hawaiian outdoor feast, esp. one that features roast pig. [< Hawaiian *lu'au*]

Lu·bang Islands (lo͞o·bäng′) A Philippine island group off NE Mindoro; 88 square miles.

lub·ber (lub′ər) *n.* An awkward, ungainly fellow; specifically, a landsman on shipboard. [Origin uncertain. Cf. ON *lubba* short.] **—lub′·ber·li·ness** *n.* **—lub′ ber·ly** *adj. & adv.*

lubber line *Aeron.* A fixed line in an aircraft compass, gyro, direction finder, or similar instrument, parallel to the longitudinal axis of the aircraft and used as a base line.

lubber's hole *Naut.* A hole through the floor of a platform or top at the head of a lower mast by which sailors can go aloft without climbing over the rim by the futtock shrouds.

Lü·beck (lo͞o′bek, *Ger.* lü′bek) A city in northern West Germany.

Lu·blin (lo͞o′blin, *Polish* lyo͞o′blēn) A city in eastern Poland Russian *Lyublin.*

lu·bra (lo͞o′brə) *n. Austral.* A young aboriginal female. [<native Australian]

lu·bric (lo͞o′brik) *adj. Obs.* Lubricous. Also **lu′·bri·cal.** [<L *lubricus* slippery]

lu·bri·cant (lo͞o′brə·kənt) *adj.* Lubricating. —*n.* Anything that lubricates, as grease.

lu·bri·cate (lo͞o′brə·kāt) *v.t.* **·cat·ed, ·cat·ing 1** To apply grease, oil, or other lubricant to so as to reduce friction and wear. **2** To make slippery or smooth. [<L *lubricatus,* pp. of *lubricare* make slippery <*lubricus* slippery] **—lu′bri·ca′tion** *n.* **—lu′bri·ca′tive** *adj.*

lu·bri·ca·tor (lo͞o′brə·kā ′tər) *n.* **1** One who or that which lubricates. **2** A device, as an oil cup, by which a lubricant is fed or applied to a bearing surface.

lu·bric·i·ty (lo͞o·bris′ə·tē) *n.* **1** The state of being slippery; hence, shiftiness; instability; evanescence. **2** Lewdness. **3** Power for lubrication. [<F *lubricité* <L *lubricitas* <*lubricus* slippery]

lu·bri·cous (lo͞o′brə·kəs) *adj.* **1** Smooth and slippery. **2** Elusive; unstable. **3** Lascivious; lewd; wanton. Also **lu·bri·cious** (lo͞o·brish′əs). [<L *lubricus*]

lu·bri·fac·tion (lo͞o′brə·fak′shən) *n.* The act or process of lubricating or making slippery or smooth. [<L *lubricus* smooth + *factus,* pp. of *facere* make]

Lu·bum·ba·shi (lo͞o·bo͝om′bä ·shē) The capital of Katanga province, Republic of the Congo.

Luc (lük) French form of LUKE. Also *Ital.* **Lu·ca** (lo͞o′kä), **Lu·cas** (*Dan., Du., Ger., Sw.* lo͞o′·käs; *Lat.* lo͞o′kəs), *Hungarian* **Lu·cáts** (lo͞o′·käch). [<L, light]

Lu·can (lo͞o′kən), 39–65, Roman poet: full name *Marcus Annaeus Lucanus.*

Lu·ca·ni·a (lo͞o·kā′nē·ə) The ancient name for BASILICATA.

lu·carne (lo͞o·kärn′) *n.* A dormer or garret window; also, a small window or light in a spire. [<F; ult. origin uncertain. Cf. OHG *lukka* opening.]

Luc·ca (look′kä) A city in Tuscany, north central Italy.

luce (lo͞os) *n.* A fish, the pike, especially when fully grown. [<OF *lus* <L *lucius*]

Luce (lüs) French form of LUCIUS.

Luce (lo͞os), **Clare Boothe,** born 1903, U.S. dramatist and diplomat; wife of Henry R. **—Henry Robinson,** 1898–1967, U.S. editor and publisher.

lu·cent (lo͞o′sənt) *adj.* Showing radiance or brilliance; shining; luminous. [<L *lucens, -entis,* ppr. of *lucere* shine] **—lu′cen·cy** *n.*

lu·cer·nal (lo͞o·sûr′nəl) *adj.* Relating to a lamp or to any artificial light. [<L *lucerna* lamp <*lux* light]

lu·cerne (lo͞o·sûrn′) *n.* A tall, cloverlike herb of the pea family *(Medicago sativa),* used for forage: now commonly called *alfalfa, purple medic.* Also **lu·cern′.** [<F *luzerne*; ult. origin unknown]

Lu·cerne (lo͞o·sûrn′, *Fr.* lü·sern′) A canton of central Switzerland; 580 square miles; capital, Lucerne (German *Luzern*) on **Lake of Lucerne,** a lake in north central Switzerland; 44 square miles: also **Lake of the Four Forest Cantons** (German *Vierwaldstättersee*).

lu·ces (lo͞o′sēz) Plural of LUX.

Lu·cia (lo͞o′shə; *Ger.* lo͞o′tsē·ə, *Ital.* lo͞o·chē′ä, *Lat.* lo͞o′shē·ə, *Pg.* lo͞o′sē·ə, *Sp.* lo͞o·thē′ä) A feminine personal name: also *Lucy.* Also *Fr.* **Lu·cie** (lü·sē′, *Du.* lo͞ov′sē·ä). [<L, light]

Lu·cian (lo͞o′shən), 125?–210?, Greek satirist. Also **Lu·ci·a·nus** (lo͞o′shē·ā′·nəs).

lu·cid (lo͞o′sid) *adj.* **1** Intellectually bright and clear; mentally sound; sane. **2** Easily understood; perspicuous; clear. **3** Giving forth light; shining. **4** Translucent; pellucid. **5** Smooth and shining. See synonyms under CLEAR, SANE, TRANSPARENT. [<L *lucidus* <*lucere* shine] **—lu·cid·i·ty** (lo͞o·sid′ə·tē), **lu′·cid·ness** *n.* **—lu′cid·ly** *adv.*

lu·ci·fer (lo͞o′sə·fər) *n.* A friction match. —*adj.* Emitting light. [after *Lucifer*]

Lu·ci·fer (lo͞o′sə·fər) **1** The planet Venus as the morning star. **2** Satan, especially as the leader of the revolt of the angels before his fall from heaven. [<L, light-bearer <*lux, lucis* light + *ferre* bear] **—Lu·cif·er·ous** (lo͞o·sif′ər·əs) *adj.*

lu·cif·er·ase (lo͞o·sif′ə·rās) *n.* Biochem. An enzyme present in fireflies and in certain other luminous organisms: it oxidizes luciferin to produce light. [<L *lucifer* light-bearing + -ASE]

lu·cif·er·in (lo͞o·sif′ər·in) *n.* Biochem. A water-soluble, heat-stable protein which produces heatless light, as in fireflies. [<L *lucifer* light-bearing + -IN]

lu·cif·er·ous (lo͞o·sif′ər·əs) *adj.* Emitting light. [<L *lucifer* light-bearing + -OUS]

lu·ci·form (lo͞o′sə·fôrm) *adj.* Having the nature or appearance of light. [< L *lux, lucis* light + -FORM]

Lu·ci·na (lo͞o·sī′nə) In Roman mythology, the goddess presiding over childbirth. [< L *lucina,* fem. of *lucinus* bringing to the light <*lux, lucis* light]

Lu·cin·da (lo͞o·sin′də) See LUCY.

Lu·cite (lo͞o′sīt) *n.* A thermoplastic, transparent acrylic resin, easily machined into various shapes and having the property of transmitting light around curves and corners: a trade name.

Lu·cius (lo͞o′shəs; *Ger.* lo͞o′tsē·o͞os, *Fr.* lü·sē·üs′) A masculine personal name. Also *Ital.*

Lucio (lōō'chō, *Pg.* lōō'sy;oo *Sp.* lōō'thyō), [<L, light]

lu·ci·vee (lōō'sə·vē) *n.* The loup-cervier. Also **lu'ci·fee** (-fē). [Alter. of LOUP-CERVIER]

luck (luk) *n.* 1 That which happens by chance; fortune or lot. 2 Happy chance; good fortune; success. [Prob. <MDu. *luk, geluk*]

luck·less (luk'lis) *adj.* Having no luck. —**luck'·less·ly** *adv.*

Luck·ner (luk'nər, *Ger.* lōōk'nər), **Count Felix von**, 1881–1966, German naval officer; known as the *Sea Devil.*

Luck·now (luk'nou) A city in central Uttar Pradesh, India; the capital of the State; British forces were besieged here during the Sepoy Rebellion, 1857.

luck·y[1] (luk'ē) *adj.* **luck·i·er, luck·i·est** 1 Favored by fortune; fortunate; successful. 2 Productive of luck; auspicious; favorable: said of events and things: a *lucky* penny or circumstance. See synonyms under AUSPICIOUS, FORTUNATE, HAPPY, WELL. —**luck'i·ly** *adv.* —**luck'i·ness** *n.*

luck·y[2] (luk'ē) *n. pl.* **luck·ies** *Scot.* A grandam or aged woman; goody; sometimes part of a person's name: *Lucky* Macpherson. Also **luck'ie.**

luck·y[3] (luk'ē) *adv. Scot.* More than sufficiently: *lucky* hot.

lu·cra·tive (lōō'krə·tiv) *adj.* Productive of wealth; highly profitable. See synonyms under PROFITABLE [<L *lucrativus* <*lucratus*, pp. of *lucrari* gain <*lucrum* wealth] —**lu'cra·tive·ly** *adv.* —**lu'cra·tive·ness** *n.*

lu·cre (lōō'kər) *n.* Money, especially as the object of greed; gain. See synonyms under WEALTH. [<F <L *lucrum* gain]

Lu·cre·tia (lōō·krē'shə, *Ger.* lōō·krā'tsē·ə) A feminine personal name. Also *Fr.* **Lu·crèce** (lü·kres'), *Ital.* **Lu·cre·zia**, **Sp.* **Lu·cre·ci·a** (lōō·krā'thē·ä). [<L, wealth] —**Lucretia** In Roman legend, the wife of Collatinus who killed herself after she had been violated by Sextus Tarquinius; subject of a poem by Shakespeare.

Lu·cre·tius (lōō·krē'shəs, -shē·əs), 96?–55 B.C. Roman poet and philosopher: full name *Titus Lucretius Carus.*

lu·cu·brate (lōō'kyōō·brāt) *v.i.* **·brat·ed, ·brat·ing** 1 To study or write laboriously, as at night. 2 To write in a learned manner. [<L *lucubratus*, pp. of *lucubrare* work by artificial light <*lux, lucis* light]

lu·cu·bra·tion (lōō'ky·brā'shən) *n.* 1 Close and earnest meditation or study. 2 The product of deep meditation or earnest study; a literary composition; often, a pedantic or over-elaborated work. [<L *lucubratio, -onis*] —**lu'cu·bra'tor** *n.* —**lu'cu·bra·to'ry** (-brətôr'ē, -tō'rē) *adj.*

lu·cu·lent (lōō'kyōō·lənt) *adj.* 1 Full of light; brilliant. 2 Clearly evident; lucid. [<L *luculentus*]

Lu·cul·lus (lōō·kul'əs), **Lucius Licinius**, 110?–57? B.C., Roman consul, proverbial for his wealth and luxury. —**Lu·cul'lan, Lu·cul·le·an** (lōō'kə·lē'ən), **Lu·cul'li·an** *adj.*

lu·cus a non lu·cen·do (lōō'kəs ā non lōō·sen'-dō) *Latin* Literally, a grove because it is *not* light: in allusion to an ancient absurd derivation of *lucus*, grove, from *lucere*, be light. Hence, something absurdly reasoned out.

Lu·cy (lōō'sē) Variant of LUCIA.

Lucy Sto·ner (stō'nər) An advocate of women's rights; especially one advocating the retention of maiden names by married women. [after *Lucy Stone*, 1818–93, U.S. woman suffragist.]

Lud·dite (lud'it) *n.* One of a band of workmen who joined in riots (1811–16) for the destruction of machinery, under the belief that its introduction reduced wages and increased unemployment: called who after Ned Lud, a feeble-witted mechanic who destroyed several stocking-frames: in English industrial history.

Lu·den·dorff (lōō'dən·dôrf), **Erich von**, 1865–1937, German general in World War I.

Lü·der·itz (lü'dər·its) A port in SW Namibia: formerly *Angra Pequeña.*

Lud·hi·a·na (lōō'dē·ä'nə) A city in central Punjab, India.

lu·di·crous (lōō'də·krəs) *adj.* Calculated to excite laughter; incongruous; droll; ridiculous. See synonyms under ABSURD, HUMOROUS,

QUEER, RIDICULOUS. [<L *ludicrus* <*ludere* play] —**lu'di·crous·ly** *adv.* —**lu'di·crous·ness** *n.*

Lu·do·vi·ka (lōō'dō·vē'kä) German and Swedish form of LOUISE.

Lud·wig (*Ger.* lōōt'vikh, *Sw.* lōōd'vig) German and Swedish form of LOUIS. Also *Latin* **Lu·do·vi·cus** (lōō'dō·vē'kəs). —**Ludwig II**, 1845–86, king of Bavaria, 1864–1886; patron of the arts; declared insane; committed suicide.

Lud·wigs·ha·fen (lōōt'viks·hä·fən) A city in the Rhineland Palatinate, West Germany. Also **Lud'wigs·ha'fen-am-Rhein** (-äm·rīn').

lu·es (lōō'ēz) *n.* 1 Formerly, an infectious or pestilential disease. 2 Plague. 3 Syphilis. [<L, plague, discharge <*luere* flow] —**lu·et·ic** (lōō·et'ik) *adj.*

luff (luf) *n. Naut.* 1 The sailing of a ship close to the wind. 2 The rounded part of a vessel's bow. 3 The foremost edge of a fore-and-aft sail. —*v.i. Naut.* 1 To bring the head of a vessel nearer the wind; sail near the wind. 2 To bring the head of a vessel into the wind, with the sails shaking. Also spelled *loof.*

luf·fa (luf'ə) See LOOFAH.

Luft·waf·fe (lōōft'väf'ə) *n. German* The German air force, as organized by the Nazi regime in 1939. [<G. lit., air weapon]

lug[1] (lug) *n.* 1 The lobe of the ear; the ear. 2 Hence, an earlike projection such as an ear or handle for carrying or supporting, or for insertion of a handle, ring, pole, etc.; the *lugs* of a kettle. 3 The loop at the side of the saddle of a harness which holds the shaft. [Origin uncertain. Cf. Sw. *lugg* foreclock.]

lug[2] (lug) *n.* 1 The act or exertion of lugging; anything that is moved with slowness and difficulty. 2 A shallow box or container, 13 ½ by 16 inches inside dimensions, for carrying fruit or vegetables. 3 *Naut.* A square sail bent to a yard and having no boom: also *lugsail.* 4 *Slang* An exaction, especially of money for political uses. —*v.t.* **lugged, lug·ging** 1 To carry or pull with effort; drag. 2 *Colloq.* To bring, as irrelevant topics, into a conversation, discussion, etc.; introduce unreasonably. [Prob. <Scand. Cf. Sw. *lugga* pull by the hair.]

lug[3] (lug) *n.* A lugworm. [Origin uncertain. Cf. LG *lug* slow, heavy.]

Lug (lōō) In old Irish mythology, one of the Tuatha De Danann, the god of light and sun, patron of the arts; father of Cuchulain. Also transliterated **Lugh.** [<Irish **Lugh**, lit., swift, active]

Lug·aid (lōō'ē) In Old Irish mythology, a king of Munster who joined forces with Maeve, Queen of Connacht, in the Cattle Raid of Cuailgne; also, his son, who later slew Cuchulain.

Lu·gansk (lōō·gänsk') An industrial city of eastern Ukrainian S.S.R.: formerly (1935–58) called *Voroshilovgrad.*

luge (lōōj) *n.* A short, stout sled; also called *toboggan.* [<F <dial. F]

Lu·ger (lōō'gər) *n.* A German automatic pistol widely used in Europe as a military sidearm: manufactured in various calibers, most commonly 7.65 mm, and 9 mm.: also called *Parabellum* in Europe. [after Georg *Luger*, 19th c. German engineer]

lug·gage (lug'ij) *n.* 1 Anything burdensome or heavy to carry. 2 Baggage. [<LUG[2]]

lugged (lugd) *adj. Scot.* Having ears or earlike appendages.

lug·ger (lug'ər) *n.* A one-, two-, or three-masted vessel having lugsails only. [<LUG(SAIL) + -ER[2]]

lug·gie (lug'ē, lōōg'ē, lōō'gē) *n. Scot.* A small wooden dish with lugs or ears.

Lu·go (lōō'gō) A city in Galicia, NW Spain.

lug·sail (lug'səl, -sāl') *n.* Lug[2] (def. 3).

lu·gu·bri·ous (lōō·gōō'brē·əs, -gyōō'-) *adj.* 1 Exhibiting or producing sadness; doleful. 2 Exaggeratedly solemn or sad. See synonyms under SAD. [<L

lugubris <*lugere* mourn] —**lu·gu'·bri·ous·ly** *adv.* —**lu·gu'·bri·ous·ness** *n.*

lug·worm (lug'wûrm') *n.* An annelid worm (genus *Arenicola*) with two rows of tufted gills on the back, living in the sand of seashores; much used for bait: also called *lobworm.*

Lu·i·gi (lōō·ē'jē) Italian form of LOUIS. Also *Sp.* **Lu·is** (lōō·ēs'), *Pg.* **Luis** (lōō·ēs')

Lu·i·gia (lōō·ē'jä) Italian form of LOUISA.

Luim·neach (lim'nəkh) The Gaelic name for LIMERICK.

Lu·i·ni (lōō·ē'nē), **Bernardino**, 1470?–1530?, Italian painter.

Lu·i·sa (lōō·ē'sä) Italian and Spanish form of LOUISA. Also *Ger.* **Lu·i·se** (lōō·ē'zə), *Pg.* **Lu·i·za** (lōō·ēzə).

Lu·it·pold (lōō'it·pōlt) Old German form of LEOPOLD.

Luke lōōk A masculine personal name. [<L, light] —**Luke, Saint** Physician and companion of St. Paul; traditionally thought to be author of the third gospel and of *The Acts of the Apostles.*

luke·warm (lōōk'wôrm') *adj.* 1 Moderately warm; tepid. 2 Hence, not ardent or hearty; indifferent. [Prob. OE *hlēow* warm. Cf. LG *luk* tepid.] —**luke'warm'ly** *adv.* —**luke'warm'ness** *n.*

Lü·le·bur·gaz (lü'lə·bŏōr·gäz', -gäz') A town in central Turkey in Europe; scene of a battle of the First Balkan War, 1912. Also **Lu'le Bur·gas'.**

lull (lul) *v.t.* 1 To soothe or quiet; put to sleep. 2 To calm; allay, as suspicions. —*v.i.* 3 To become calm. —*n.* 1 An abatement of noise or violence; an interval of calm or quiet. 2 That which lulls or soothes. See synonyms under TRANQUILIZE. [Pro. <Sw. *lulla* sing to sleep; ult. imit.]

lull·a·by (lul'ə·bī) *n. pl.* **·bies** 1 A song to lull a child to sleep; a cradlesong; also, the music for such a song. 2 *Obs.* A goodnight or farewell. [<LULL]

Lul·ly (lü·lē'), **Jean Baptiste**, 1633?–87, French composer born in Italy. Also **Lul·li'**. —**Lul·ly** (lul'ē), **Raymond**, 1235?–1315, Spanish ecclesiastic and philosopher.

lu·lu (lōō'lōō) *n. Slang* Anything of an exceptional or outstanding nature, as a difficult examination, a beautiful person, etc. [Prob. reduplication of *Lou*, the familiar form of LOUISE]

lum (lum) *n. Brit. Dial. & Scot.* A chimney.

lu·ma·chelle (lōō'mə·kel) *n.* A variety of limestone containing fragments of shells, fossils, etc., sometimes brilliantly iridescent. Also **lu'ma·chel, lu'ma·chel'la** (-kel'ə). [<Ital. *lumachella*, dim. of *lumaca* snail <L *limax, limacis*]

lum·ba·go (lum·bā'gō) *n. Pathol.* Rheumatic pain in the lumbar region of the back; backache. [<L <*lumbus* loin]

lum·bar (lum'bər, -bär) *adj.* Pertaining to or situated near the loins. —*n.* A lumbar vertebra or nerve. [<NL *lumbaris* <L *lumbus* loin]

lum·ber[1] (lum'bər) *n.* 1 *U.S. & Can.* Timber sawed into board, planks, etc. 2 Disused articles laid aside. 3 Hence, rubbish. *adj.* Made of, pertaining to, or dealing in, lumber. —*v.t.* 1 *U.S. & Can.* To cut down (timber); also, to cut down the timber of (an area). 2 To fill or obstruct with useless articles. 3 To heap in disorder. —*v.i.* 4 *U.S. & Can.* To cut down or saw timber for marketing. [Var. of *Lombard* in obs. sense of "money-lender, pawnshop"; hence, stored articles] —**lum'ber·er** *n.*

lum·ber[2] (lum'bər) *v.i.* 1 To move or proceed in a heavy or awkward manner. 2 To move with a rumbling noise. —*n.* A rumbling noise. [Origin uncertain. Cf. Sw. *lomra* resound, *loma* walk heavily.]

lum·bered (lum'bərd) *adj.* Having the timber cut off: said of land.

lum·ber·ing[1] (lum'bər·ing) *n.* The business of felling and shaping timber into logs, boards, etc.

lum·ber·ing[2] (lum'bər·ing) *adj.* Clumsily huge and heavy; moving heavily; rumbling. —**lum'ber·ing·ly** *adv.* —**lum'ber·ing·ness** *n.*

lum·ber·jack (lum'bər·jak) *n.* 1 A lumberman.

LUGGER

2 A boy's or man's short, straight jacket of heavy warm material: originally made in imitation of coats worn by lumbermen: also **lum′ber·jack′et** (-jak′it). [<LUMBER[1] + *jack* man, boy]
lum·ber·man (lum′bər·mən) *n. pl.* **·men** (-mən) A person engaged in the business of lumbering.
lum·ber–room (lum′bər·ro͞om′, -ro͝om′) *n.* A room for lumber or useless articles.
lum·ber·some (lum′bər·səm) *adj.* Cumbersome.
lum·ber·yard (lum′bər·yärd′) *n.* A yard for the storage or sale of lumber.
lum·bri·ca·lis (lum′brə·kā′lis) *n. pl.* **·les** (-lēz) *Anat.* **1** One of the four vermiform muscles in the palm of the hand. **2** One of four similar muscles in the sole of the foot. [<NL <L *lumbricus* worm] — **lum′bri·cal** *adj.*
lum·bri·coid (lum′brə·koid) *adj.* **1** Of or pertaining to the common earthworm (genus *Lumbricus*). **2** Pertaining to or designating a roundworm (*Ascaris lumbricoides*) parasitic in the intestines of man. — *n.* The roundworm. [<L *lumbricus* earthworm + -OID]
lu·men (lo͞o′mən) *n. pl.* **·mens** or **·mi·na** (-mə·nə) **1** A passageway or opening. **2** *Biol.* The inner cavity of a cell or tubular organ, as a gland. **3** *Physics* A unit for measuring luminous flux, equal to the flow through a steradian from a uniform point source of one international candle. [<L, light]
lum·head (lum′hed′) *n. Scot.* A chimney top.
Lu·mi·nal (lo͞o′mə·nəl, -nôl) Proprietary name for a brand of phenobarbital.
lu·mi·nance (lo͞o′mə·nəns) See BRIGHTNESS (def. 2).
lu·mi·nar·y (lo͞o′mə·ner′ē) *n. pl.* **·nar·ies** **1** Any body that gives light; specifically, one of the heavenly bodies as a source of light. **2** One who enlightens men or makes clear any subject. **3** Any light or source of illumination. [<OF *luminaire* <LL *luminarium* candle, torch < *lumen* light]
lu·mi·nesce (lo͞o′mə·nes′) *v.i.* **·nesced, ·nesc·ing** To become luminescent. [Back formation <LUMINESCENT]
lu·mi·nes·cence (lo͞o′mə·nes′əns) *n.* A light-emission not directly attributable to the heat that produces incandescence, as *bioluminescence.*
lu·mi·nes·cent (lo͞o′mə·nes′ənt) *adj.* Emitting or capable of emitting light apart from incandescence or high temperature. [<L *lumen* light + -ESCENT]
lu·mi·nif·er·ous (lo͞o′mə·nif′ər·əs) *adj.* Producing or conveying light. [<L *lumen* light + -FEROUS]
lu·mi·nos·i·ty (lo͞o′mə·nos′ə·tē) *n. pl.* **·ties** **1** The quality of being luminous. **2** Something luminous. **3** *Physics* The ratio of the luminous flux of an object to the corresponding radiant flux, expressed in lumens per watt.
lu·mi·nous (lo͞o′mə·nəs) *adj.* **1** Giving or emitting light; shining. **2** Full of light; well lighted; bright. **3** Perspicuous; lucid. See synonyms under BRIGHT, VIVID. [<L *luminosus* <*lumen* light] — **lu′mi·nous·ly** *adj.* — **lu′mi·nous·ness** *n.*
luminous energy Light.
luminous flux *Physics* The time rate of the flow of visible light, expressed in lumens.
luminous intensity *Physics* The luminous flux emitted from a point source of light per spheradian.
lu·mis·ter·ol (lo͞o·mis′tər·ōl) *n.* A sterol, $C_{28}H_{44}O$, resulting from the ultraviolet irradiation of ergosterol. [< *lumi-* (<L *lumen* light) + (ERGO)STEROL]
lum·mox (lum′əks) *n. U. S. Colloq.* A stupid, heavy, clumsy person. [Cf. G *lümmel* lout]
lump[1] (lump) *n.* **1** A shapeless mass of inert matter, especially a small mass. **2** A mass of things thrown together. **3** A protuberance. **4** A stupid person. **5** A heavy, ungainly person. See synonyms under MASS. — **in a** (or **the**) **lump** All together; with no distinction. — *v.t.* **1** To put together in one mass, group, etc. **2** To consider or treat collectively: to *lump* facts. **3** To make lumps in or on. — *v.i.* **4** To become lumpy; raise in lumps. **5** To move or fall heavily. [<ME, prob. <Scand. Cf. Dan. *lumpe* a lump.]
lump[2] (lump) *v.t. Colloq.* To put up with; endure (something disagreeable): You may like it or *lump* it. [Origin uncertain]
lump·er (lum′pər) *n.* **1** One who lumps. **2** A stevedore.
lump·fish (lump′fish′) *n. pl.* **·fish** or **·fish·es** A fish of northern seas (*Cyclopterus lumpus*), oval in shape and with the skin studded with three lateral rows of tubercles. Also **lump′suck′·er** (-suk′ər). [So called from its bulk]
lump·ish (lum′pish) *adj.* Like a lump; stupid. — **lump′ish·ly** *adv.* — **lump′ish·ness** *n.*
lump sum A full and single sum.
lump·y (lum′pē) *adj.* **lump·i·er, lump·i·est** **1** Full of lumps. **2** Lumpish or gross. **3** Running in confused, pounding waves that do not break: a *lumpy* sea. — **lump′i·ly** *adv.* — **lump′i·ness** *n.*
lumpy jaw Actinomycosis.
lu·na (lo͞o′nə) *n.* In alchemy, silver. [<L, the moon]
Lu·na (lo͞o′nə) In Roman mythology, the goddess of the moon and of months: identified with the Greek *Selene.* [<L]
lu·na·cy (lo͞o′nə·sē) *n. pl.* **·cies** **1** An intermittent form of insanity: formerly supposed to depend on the changes of the moon. **2** In forensic psychiatry and law, mental unsoundness to the point of irresponsibility. **3** Wild foolishness; wanton and senseless conduct. See synonyms under INSANITY. [<LUNATIC]
Luna moth A large North American moth (*Tropaea luna*), having light-green wings with long tails and lunate spots. [So called from the crescent-shaped spots on its wings]

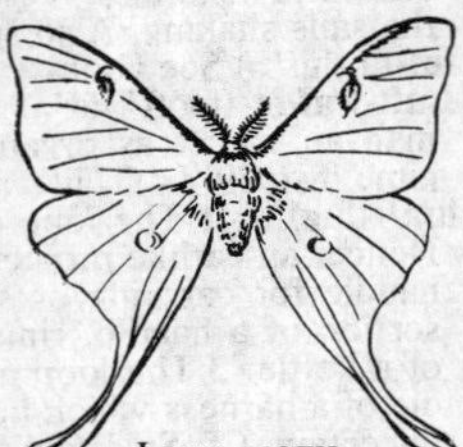

LUNA MOTH
(Wingspread from 4 1/2 to 6 inches)

lu·nar (lo͞o′nər) *adj.* **1** Of or pertaining to the moon; crescented or orbed; like the moon. **2** Measured by revolutions of the moon. **3** In alchemy and medicine, of or pertaining to silver. [<L *lunaris* < *luna* the moon]
lunar caustic *Chem.* Silver nitrate formed into pencils and used for cauterizing. [<LUNA]
lunar day The period of the moon's rotation on its axis.
lu·nar·i·an (lo͞o·nâr′ē·ən) *adj.* Pertaining to the moon. — *n.* **1** A supposed inhabitant of the moon. **2** An investigator of the moon. [<L *lunaris*]
lunar module *Aerospace* A part of a space vehicle designed to land astronauts on the moon and lift them off to link up with the command module. Also **lunar excursion module.**
lunar month See under MONTH.
lu·na·ry (lo͞o′nər·ē) *adj.* Connected with the moon; lunar. — *n.* A fern, the moonwort. [<L *lunaris*]
lunar year Twelve lunar months.
lu·nate (lo͞o′nāt) *adj.* Crescent-shaped. Also **lu′nat·ed.** [<L *lunatus*]
lu·na·tic (lo͞o′nə·tik) *adj.* **1** Affected with lunacy. **2** Characteristic of or resembling lunacy; crazy; insane. Also **lu·nat·i·cal** (lo͞o·nat′i·kəl). See synonyms under INSANE. — *n.* An insane person. [<LL *lunaticus* <L *luna* moon]
lu·na·tion (lo͞o·nā′shən) *n. Astron.* The interval between two returns of the new moon, averaging 29.53059 days. [<Med. L *lunatio, -onis* <L *luna* the moon]
lunch (lunch) *n.* **1** A light meal between other meals, as between breakfast and dinner. **2** Food provided for a lunch. — *v.i.* To eat lunch. — *v.t.* To furnish lunch for. [Short for LUNCHEON] — **lunch′er** *n.*
lunch·eon (lun′chən) *n.* **1** A bit of food taken between meals. **2** A lunch. [? Blend of dial. E *lunch* a lump of food + obs. *nuncheon* afternoon snack]
lunch·eon·ette (lun′chən·et′) *n.* A place or counter where light lunches can be obtained.
lunch·room (lunch′ro͞om′, -ro͝om′) *n.* A restaurant serving light meals and refreshments.
Lun·dy's Lane (lun′dēz) A region near Niagara Falls, Ontario; scene of a battle (1814) in the War of 1812.
lune[1] (lo͞on) *n.* **1** *Geom.* A figure bounded by two arcs of circles. **2** The moon. ◆ Homophone: *loon.* [<F <L *luna* the moon]
lune[2] (lo͞on) *n.* A leash used in hawking. ◆ Homophone: *loon.* [<OF *loigne* leash < Med. L *longea* <L *longus* long]
Lü·ne·burg (lü′nə·bo͝orkh) A city in Lower Saxony, West Germany.
Lü·nen (lü′nən) A city in North Rhine-Westphalia, West Germany.
lunes (lo͞onz) *n. pl. Archaic* Outbreaks of lunacy; mad freaks. [<Med. L *luna* moon, fit of lunacy]
lu·nette (lo͞o·net′) *n.* **1** Something shaped like a half-moon. **2** *Mil.* A fieldwork or a detached work formed by two parallel flanks, two faces meeting in a salient angle, with an open gorge. **3** *Archit.* An arched opening in the side of a long vault formed by the intersection with it of a smaller vault, as for a window. **4** A ring on the tongue or trail plate of a vehicle, for attaching to a limber, motor truck, or other towing vehicle. Also **lu·net** (lo͞o′nit). [<F, dim. of *lune* moon]
Lu·né·ville (lü·nā·vēl′) A town in NE France; the Treaty of Lunéville, effecting peace between Austria and France, was signed here in 1801.
lung (lung) *n. Anat.* **1** Either of the two saclike organs of respiration in air-breathing vertebrates. ◆ Collateral adjective: *pulmonary.* **2** An analogous organ in invertebrates. [OE *lungen*]
lunge[1] (lunj) *n.* **1** A sudden pass or thrust; specifically, a long thrust with a sword or a bayonet. **2** A sudden forward lurch; plunge. — *v.* **lunged, lung·ing** — *v.i.* **1** To make a lunge or pass; thrust. **2** To move with a lunge. — *v.t.* **3** To thrust with or as with a lunge. [Aphetic var. of obs. *allonge* <F *allonger* prolong <L *ad* to + *longus* long]
lunge[2] (lunj) See LONGE.
lung·er (lung′ər) *n. Slang* A person having tuberculosis of the lungs.
lung·fish (lung′fish′) *n. pl.* **·fish** or **·fish·es** A dipnoan.
lun·gi (lung′gē) *n.* **1** In India, a loincloth. **2** The material from which it is made: also used for scarfs and turbans. Also **lun′gee.** [<Hind.]
Lung·ki (lo͝ong′kē′) A port of southern Fukien province, China: formerly *Changchow.*
lung·worm (lung′wûrm′) *n.* Any of several nematode worms parasitic in the lungs of animals, especially the common lungworm (genus *Dictyocaulus*) of horses, cattle, and sheep.
lung·wort (lung′wûrt′) *n.* **1** A European herb (genus *Pulmonaria*) of the borage family, having white blotches on the leaves. **2** The Virginia cowslip.
luni– *combining form* Of or pertaining to the moon; lunar. [<L *luna* moon]
lu·ni·so·lar (lo͞o′ni·sō′lər) *adj.* Of or resulting from the combined action of the sun and moon.
lu·ni·ti·dal (lo͞o′ni·tīd′l) *adj.* Relating to the tides as produced by the moon's attraction.
lunitidal interval The interval between the moon's passage of the meridian and lunar high tide.
lunk·head (lungk′hed′) *n. Slang* A slow-witted person. [Prob. alter. of LUMP + HEAD] — **lunk′head′ed** *adj.*
lunt (lunt, lo͝ont) *n. Scot.* **1** A whiff of smoke. **2** A slow-burning match or torch.
Lunt (lunt), **Alfred,** born 1893, U. S. actor.
lu·nu·la (lo͞o′nyə·lə) *n. pl.* **·lae** (-lē) **1** A crescentic structure or appearance. **2** The whitish area at the base of the nails: also **lu′nule** (-nyo͞ol). **3** A lune (arc). [<L, diminutive of *luna* the moon]
lu·nu·lar (lo͞o′nyə·lər) *adj.* Having the form of a small crescent. [<LUNULA]
lu·nu·late (lo͞o′nyə·lāt, -lit) *adj.* **1** Having or approaching a crescent form. **2** Having crescentic markings. Also **lu′nu·lat′ed.**
lu·ny (lo͞o′nē) See LOONY.
Lu·per·ca·li·a (lo͞o′pər·kā′lē·ə, -kāl′yə) *n. pl.* A Roman festival celebrated on February 15, in honor of a rustic deity, **Lu·per·cus** (lo͞o·pûr′·kəs) or *Faunus,* at which after various ceremonies the priests ran half-clothed through the streets. Also **Lu′per·cal** (-kal). [<L, neut. pl. of *Lupercalis* of Lupercus <*Lupercus* Faunus < *lupus* wolf]
Lu·per·ci (lo͞o′pər·sī) *n. pl.* The priests of Lupercus or Faunus. [<L]
lu·pine[1] (lo͞o′pīn) *adj.* **1** Of or pertaining to a wolf; like a wolf; wolfish. **2** Pertaining to the group of canines that includes dogs and wolves. [<L *lupinus* < *lupus* wolf]
lu·pine[2] (lo͞o′pin) *n.* A plant of the bean family (genus *Lupinus*) bearing terminal racemes of mostly blue or purple flowers, as the **white lupine** of the Old World (*L. albus*) whose seeds are edible. Also **lu′pin** (-pin). [<F *lupin*

<L *lupinus* wolflike: reason for the name unknown]

lu·pu·lin (lōō′pyə·lin) *n.* **1** A brittle crystalline compound forming the active principle of hops. **2** A yellow aromatic powder contained in the fruit of hops, and used medicinally as a sedative. [<NL *lupulus* the hop, dim. of L *lupus*]

lu·pus (lōō′pəs) *n. Pathol.* A chronic tuberculous skin disease with warty nodules, generally about the nose. Also **lupus vul·ga·ris** (vul·gar′is). [<L, wolf]

Lu·pus (lōō′pəs) The Wolf, a constellation. See CONSTELLATION. [<L]

lurch[1] (lûrch) *v.i.* **1** To roll suddenly to one side, as a ship at sea. **2** To move unsteadily; stagger. —*n.* A sudden swaying or rolling to one side: hence; any sudden swinging movement. [Origin uncertain]

lurch[2] (lûrch) *n.* In cribbage, the state of a player who has made 30 holes or less while his opponent has won with 61; also a game thus won. —**to leave in the lurch** To leave in an embarrassing position. —*v.i.* In cribbage, piquet, and similar games, to win a double game. [<F *lourche*, name of a game <*lourche* deceived <Gmc. Cf. MDu. *lurz* left-handed, unlucky.]

lurch[3] (lûrch) *v.t.* & *v.i. Obs.* To swindle; cheat. [Var. of LURK]

lurch·er (lûr′chər) *n.* **1** One who lies in wait or lurks: a lurking thief; poacher. **2** A crossbred dog that hunts by scent and in silence.

lur·dan (lûr′dən) *Archaic adj.* Stupid; incapable. —*n.* A stupid person; blockhead. Also **lur′dane.** [<OF *lourdin* <*lourd* heavy]

lure (lōōr) *n.* **1** A device resembling a bird and sometimes baited with food: fastened to a falconer's wrist and used to recall the hawk. **2** In angling, an artificial bait; also, a decoy for animals. **3** Anything that invites by the prospect of advantage or pleasure. —*v.t.* **lured, lur·ing** **1** To attract or entice; allure. **2** To recall (a hawk) with a lure. See synonyms under ALLURE, DRAW. [<OF *leurre* <MHG *louder* bait] —**lur′er** *n.*

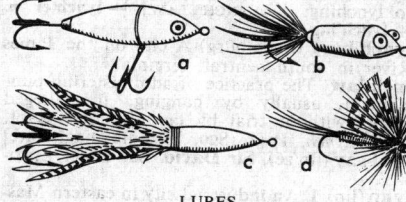

LURES
a. Wood or plastic lure. *c.* Feather lure.
b. Floating cork lure. *d.* Dry fly.

lu·rid (lōōr′id) *adj.* **1** Giving a ghastly or dull-red light; dismal. **2** Of a dingy, dirty-brown color. **3** Violent; terrible; sensational: a *lurid* crime. **4** Pale; wan; sallow; ghastly. [<L *luridus* sallow] —**lu′rid·ly** *adv.* —**lu′rid·ness** *n.*

lurk (lûrk) *v.i.* **1** To lie hidden, as in ambush. **2** To exist unnoticed or unsuspected. **3** To move secretly or furtively; slink. —*n. Austral. Slang* A dodge; scheme; racket. [Origin uncertain. Cf. Norw. *lurka* sneak off.] —**lurk′er** *n.* —**lurk′ing·ly** *adv.*

Lur·lei (lōōr′lī) See LORELEI.

Lu·sa·ka (lōō·sä′kə) The capital of Zambia.

Lu·sa·tia (lōō·sä′shə) A region of SE Germany and SW Poland between the Elbe and the Oder. *German* **Lau·sitz** (lou′zits).

lus·cious (lush′əs) *adj.* **1** Very grateful to the sense of taste; rich, sweet, and delicious; pleasing to any sense or to the mind. **2** Sweet and rich to excess. See synonyms under DELICIOUS, SWEET. [? blend of LUSH and DELICIOUS] —**lus′cious·ly** *adv.* —**lus′cious·ness** *n.*

lush[1] lush *adj.* **1** Full of juice or succulence; fresh and luxuriant: also, having abundant growth. **2** Easily plowed and mellow, as ground. [? Var. of dial. E *lash* soft and watery <OF *lasche* <L *laxus* loose] —**lush′ness** *n.*

lush[2] (lush) *Slang n.* **1** Intoxicating, or strong alcoholic beverage. **2** A drunken man: also

lush′er. —*v.t.* & *v.i.* To drink (alcoholic liquor). [Origin unknown]

Lu·shun (lü′shoōn′) The Chinese name for PORT ARTHUR.

lush·y (lush′ē) *adj. Slang* Drunk.

Lu·si·ta·ni·a (lōō′sə·tā′nē·ə) An ancient name for PORTUGAL.

Lu·si·ta·ni·a (lōō′sə·tā′nē·ə) *n.* A British passenger ship torpedoed and sunk by a German submarine off the coast of Ireland May 7, 1915, with loss of 1,198 lives including 128 Americans.

Lu·si·ta·ni·an (lōō′sə·tā′nē·ən) *adj.* Of or pertaining to Lusitania. —*n.* A native or inhabitant of Lusitania.

lust (lust) *n.* **1** Vehement or longing affection or desire. **2** Inordinate desire for carnal pleasure. **3** *Obs.* Pleasure; inclination. See synonyms under APPETITE. —*v.i.* To have passionate or inordinate desire, especially sexual desire. [OE, pleasure]

lus·ter (lus′tər) *n.* **1** Natural or artificial brilliancy or sheen; refulgence; gloss. **2** Brilliancy of beauty, of character, or of achievements; splendor. **3** A glaze, varnish, or enamel applied to porcelain in a thin layer, and giving it a smooth, glistening surface: common in the phrase *metallic luster.* **4** A dress material having a highly finished surface. **5** A source or center of light; specifically, a branched candelabrum, chandelier, or the like. **6** *Mineral.* The quality of the surface of a mineral as regards the kind and intensity of the light it reflects. —*v.* **·tered** or **·tred, ·ter·ing** or **·tring** *v.t.* To give a luster or gloss to. —*v.i.* To be or become lustrous. Also **lus′tre.** [<F *lustre* <Ital. *lustro* <*lustrare* shine <L <*lustrum* purification]

lus·ter·ware (lus′tər·wâr′) *n.* Pottery treated with metallic luster.

lust·ful (lust′fəl) *adj.* **1** Having carnal or sensual desire. **2** *Archaic* Vigorous; lusty. —**lust′ful·ly** *adv.* —**lust′ful·ness** *n.*

lust·hood (lust′hoōd) *n. Archaic* Vigor of body; brawny strength. Also **lust′i·head** (-hed).

lus·tral (lus′trəl) *adj.* **1** Pertaining to or used in purification. **2** Pertaining to a lustrum. [<L *lustralis* <*lustrum* purification]

lus·trate (lus′trāt) *v.t.* **·trat·ed, ·trat·ing** To make pure by propitiatory offering or ceremony. [<L *lustratus*, pp. of *lustrare* purify by propitiatory offerings <*lustrum* purification]

lus·tra·tion (lus·trā′shən) *n.* The ancient rite of purification and expiation. [<L *lustratio, -onis*]

lus·trous (lus′trəs) *adj.* Having luster; shining; also, illustrious. See synonyms under BRIGHT. —**lus′trous·ly** *adv.* —**lus′trous·ness** *n.*

lus·trum (lus′trəm) *n.* **1** A lustration or purification: the solemn ceremony of purification of the entire Roman people made every five years. **2** A period of five years. [<L, ? <*luere* wash]

lust·y (lus′tē) *adj.* **lust·i·er, lust·i·est** **1** Full of vigor and health; able-bodied; robust. **2** *Obs.* Jolly; merry. **3** *Obs.* Agreeable; delightful. **4** *Obs.* Lustful. —**lust′i·ly** *adv.* —**lust′i·ness** *n.*

lu·sus na·tu·rae (lōō′səs nə·toōr′ē, -tyoōr′ē) A strange and abnormal natural production; a freak or sport of nature: also **lu′sus.** [<L, joke of nature]

Lut (loōt) See DASHT-I-LUT.

lu·ta·nist (lōō′tə·nist) *n.* One who plays the lute. Also **lu′te·nist.**

lute[1] (loōt) *n.* A stringed musical instrument having a large, pear-shaped body like a mandolin, played by plucking the strings with the fingers. —*v.t.* & *v.i.* To play on the lute. [<OF *leüt* <Pg. *laut* <Arabic *al′ūd* the piece of wood]

lute[2] (loōt) *n.* **1** A cementlike composition used to exclude air, as around pipe joints. **2** In brick-

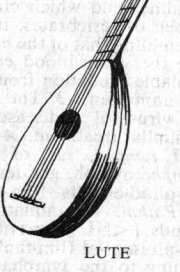

LUTE

making, a scraper having a cutting edge to smooth the surface of a drying yard. Also **lut′ing.** —*v.t.* **lut·ed, lut·ing** To seal with lute. [<OF *lut* <L *lutum* mud] —**lu·ta′tion** *n.*

lu·te·al (lōō′tē·əl) *adj. Anat.* Pertaining to or similar to the cells of the corpus luteum. [<L *luteus* yellow]

lu·te·in (lōō′tē·in, -tēn) *n. Biochem.* A yellow pigment, $C_{48}H_{56}O_2$, found in egg yolks, fat cells, and in the corpus luteum. [<L *luteum* egg yolk <*luteus* yellow] —**lu′te·in′ic** *adj.*

lu·te·o·lin (lōō′tē·ə·lin) *n. Chem.* A yellow crystalline compound, $C_{15}H_{10}O_6$, obtained from dyer's-broom, and used as a dyestuff. [<F *lutéoline* <NL (*Reseda*) *luteola* dyer's weed <L *luteolus* yellowish <*luteus* yellow]

lu·te·ous (lōō′tē·əs) *adj.* Of golden-yellowish color. [<L *luteus* <*lutum* weed used by dyers]

Lu·te·tia (lōō·tē′shə) Ancient name for PARIS. Also **Lu·te′tia Pa·ri·si·o·rum** (pə·rē′sē·ō′rəm).

lu·te·tium (lōō·tē′shəm) *n.* A metallic element (symbol Lu) of the lanthanide series, isolated from ytterbium. See ELEMENT. [from LUTETIA]

lu·te·um (lōō′tē·əm) See CORPUS LUTEUM.

Lu·ther (lōō′thər, *Ger.* loō′tər) A masculine personal name. Also *Latin* **Lu·ther·us** (lōō′tə·rəs). [<Gmc., famous warrior]

Lu·ther (lōō′thər), **Martin**, 1483–1546, German monk, theologian, and leader of the Reformation; excommunicated in 1520 by Pope Leo X; composed many Lutheran hymns and translated the Bible into German.

Lu·ther·an (lōō′thər·ən) *n.* A follower or disciple of Luther; a member of the Lutheran Church. —*adj..* **1** Pertaining to or believing in Martin Luther or his doctrines. **2** Pertaining to the Lutheran Church or its doctrines. —**Lu′ther·an·ism** *n.*

Lutheran Church A Protestant denomination founded in Germany by Martin Luther in the 16th century. Its chief doctrine is justification by faith alone. The Lutheran churches in America are grouped in three principal bodies: the **American Lutheran Church, Evangelical Lutheran Synodical Conference of North America,** and **United Lutheran Church in America.** See also MISSOURI SYNOD.

lu·thern (lōō′thərn) *n.* A lucarne. [? Alter. of LUCARNE]

Lu·ton (lōō′tən) A municipal borough of southern Bedford, England.

Lu·tu·a·mi·an (lōō′toō·ā′mē·ən) *n.* An independent linguistic stock of North American Indians, having two divisions, Klamath and Modoc, formerly dwelling in California and Oregon: now inhabiting reservations in Oregon and Oklahoma. Both dialects were most commonly known as *Klamath.*

Lüt·zen (lü′tsən) A town in the former state of Saxony-Anhalt, East Germany; scene of battles in the Thirty Years' War (1632) and the Nopoleonic Wars (1813).

Lu·wi·an (lōō′ē·ən) *n.* An extinct language of Asia Minor of which few inscriptions remain: considered to be closely related to Hittite. —*adj.* Of this language. Also **Lu·vi·an** (lōō′·vē·ən).

lux (luks) *n. pl.* **lux·es** or **lu·ces** (lōō′sēz) *Physics* The unit of illumination in the metric system, equivalent to the illumination on a surface of one square meter on which there is a uniformly distributed flux of one lumen. [<L, light]

lux·ate (luk′sāt) *v.t.* **·at·ed, ·at·ing** To put out of joint; dislocate. [<L *luxatus*, pp. of *luxare* dislocate <*luxus* dislocated] —**lux·a′tion** *n.*

luxe (lōōks, luks; *Fr.* lüks) *n.* Superfine quality; luxury: usually with *de*: edition *de luxe.* [<F <L *luxus* extravagance]

Lux·em·burg (luk′səm·bûrg, *Fr.* lük·sän·boōr′) **1** A constitutional grand duchy between Belgium, France, and Germany; 999 square miles; capital, Luxemburg. **2** A province of SE Belgium; 1,795 square miles; capital, Arlon. Also **Lux′em·bourg.**

Lux·em·burg (loōk′səm·boōrkh), **Rosa,** 1870–1919, German socialist leader.

lux·me·ter (luks′mē′tər) *n.* An instrument that measures illumination in terms of luxes.

lux mun·di (luks mun′dī) *Latin* Light of the world.

Lux·or (luk′sôr, loōk′-) A city on the Nile in Upper Egypt on the southern part of the

site of ancient Thebes. *Arabic* **El Uk·sor** (al o͝ok′so͞or).

lux·u·ri·ance (lug·zho͝or′ē·əns, luk·sho͝or′-) *n.* Excessive growth; exuberance; lushness. Also **lux·u′ri·an·cy.**

lux·u·ri·ant (lug·zho͝or′ē·ənt, luk·sho͝or′-) *adj.* **1** Exhibiting or characterized by luxuriance in growth; also, fertile, as soil. **2** Exuberant in fancy, invention, etc.; abundant, extravagant, or excessive in action or speech; ornate, florid, or rich in design. See synonyms under FERTILE. [<L *luxurians, -antis,* ppr. of *luxuriare.* See LUXURIATE.] **—lux·u′ri·ant·ly** *adv.*

lux·u·ri·ate (lug·zho͝or′ē·āt, luk·sho͝or′-) *v.i.* **·at·ed, ·at·ing** **1** To take great pleasure; indulge oneself fully. **2** To live sumptuously. **3** To grow profusely. [<L *luxuriatus,* pp. of *luxuriare* be fruitful, abound <*luxuria.* See LUXURY.] **—lux·u·ri·a′tion** *n.*

lux·u·ri·ous (lug·zho͝or′ē·əs, luk·sho͝or′-) *adj.* **1** Pertaining or administering to luxury; voluptuous. **2** Supplied with luxuries. [<L *luxuriosus*] **—lux·u′ri·ous·ly** *adv.* **—lux·u′ri·ous·ness** *n.*

lux·u·ry (luk′shər·ē, *occasionally* lug′zhər·ē) *n. pl.* **·ries** **1** A free indulgence in the pleasures that gratify the senses. **2** Anything that ministers to comfort or pleasure that is expensive or rare, but is not necessary to life, health, subsistence, etc.; a delicacy. [<OF *luxurie* <L *luxuria* <*luxus* extravagance]

Lu·zern (lo͞o·tsern′) The German name for LUCERNE.

Lu·zon (lo͞o·zon′, *Sp.* lo͞o·sōn′) The largest of the Philippines; 40,420 square miles; capital, Manila.

Luzon Strait The channel connecting the Pacific and the South China Sea: divided into the Bashi, Balintang, and Babuyan Channels.

Lvov (lvôf) A city in Ukrainian S.S.R.: German *Lemberg. Polish* **Lwów** (lvo͞of).

-ly[1] *suffix of adjectives* Like; characteristic of; pertaining to: *manly, godly.* Compare -LIKE. [OE *-lic*]

-ly[2] *suffix of adverbs* **1** In a (specified) manner: used to form adverbs from adjectives, or (rarely) from nouns: *brightly, busily.* **2** Occurring every (specified interval): *hourly, yearly.* [OE *-lice* <*-lic* -LY[1]]

◆ In cases where an adjective already ends in *-ly,* the forms of the adjective and adverb are often identical: He spoke *kindly.* Occasionally, *-ly* is added to *-ly* (which is then changed to *-li*), as in *surlily,* but this is generally avoided as awkward. In the case of words derived from French adjectives in *-le,* the ending is dropped before adding *-ly,* as in *nobly, possibly.*

Lya·khov Islands (lyä′khôf) A southern group of the New Siberian Islands in Yakut Autonomous S.S.R.; total, 2,660 square miles.

Ly·all·pur (lī′əl·po͝or) A city in Punjab, West Pakistan.

ly·ard (lī′ərd) *adj. Scot.* Silver-gray or streaked with gray. Also **ly′art** (-ərt). [<OF *liart*]

Lyau·tey (lyō·tā′), **Louis Hubert,** 1854–1934, French marshal and colonial administrator.

Lyau·tey (lyō·tā′), **Port** See PORT-LYAUTEY.

ly·can·thrope (lī′kən·thrōp, lī·kan′thrōp) *n.* **1** A werewolf. **2** One afflicted with lycanthropy. [<Gk. *lykanthrōpos* <*lykos* wolf + *anthrōpos* a man]

ly·can·thro·py (lī·kan′thrə·pē) *n.* **1** The supposed power of turning a human being into a wolf or of becoming a wolf, by magic or witchcraft. **2** Belief in werewolves. **3** *Psychiatry* A mania in which the patient imagines himself to be a wolf or some other wild animal. [<Gk. *lykanthrōpia*] **—ly′can·throp′ic** (-throp′ik) *adj.*

Ly·ca·on (lī·kā′on) In Greek mythology, a king of Arcadia and father of Callisto, who, when Zeus sought his hospitality disguised as a poor man, tested the god's divinity by offering him human flesh as food: Zeus transformed him into a wolf. [<Gk. *Lykaōn* <*lykos* wolf]

Ly·ca·o·ni·a (lī′kā·ō′nē·ə, lik′ə-) An ancient district in the SE part of Phrygia, Asia Minor.

ly·cée (lē·sā′) *n. French* A public classical secondary school in France qualifying its students for a university; a lyceum. [<F <L *lyceum.* See LYCEUM.]

ly·ce·um (lī·sē′əm) *n. pl.* **·ce·ums** or **·ce·a** (-sē′ə) **1** An association for popular instruction by lectures, a library, debates, etc.; also, its building or hall. **2** An intermediate classical school. [<LYCEUM]

Ly·ce·um (lī·sē′əm) A grove near Athens in which Aristotle taught. [<L <Gk. *Lykeion* <*lykeios,* ? wolf-slaying, epithet of Apollo (whose temple was near this grove)]

ly·chee (lē′chē) See LITCHI.

lych·nis (lik′nis) *n.* Any plant of the genus *Lychnis* of erect ornamental herbs. *L. chalcedonica* is the scarlet lychnis, and *L. coronaria* the rose campion. [<L <Gk.]

Lyc·i·a (sis′ē·ə, lish′ə) An ancient country on the SW coast of Asia Minor; a Roman province.

Lyc·i·an (lish′ē·ən, lish′ən) *adj.* Belonging or relating to ancient Lycia. **—** *n.* **1** A member of the people that inhabited Lycia. **2** Their language, believed to be related to Hittite.

Lyc·i·das (lis′ə·dəs) **1** In Virgil's *Eclogue* iii, a shepherd. **2** Subject of an elegy (1637) by Milton.

Ly·co·me·des (lī′kə·mē′dēz) In Greek legend, a king of Scyros; son of Apollo and guardian of Achilles.

ly·co·pod (lī′kə·pod) *n.* A plant of the clubmoss family. [<Gk. *lykos* wolf + -POD; after the resemblance of the root to a claw]

ly·co·po·di·um (lī′kə·pō′dē·əm) *n.* **1** A plant (genus *Lycopodium*) of erect or creeping evergreen pteridophytes, the clubmosses. **2** An inflammable fine yellow powder, the spores of clubmosses. [<NL]

Ly·cur·gus (lī·kûr′gəs) A traditional Spartan lawgiver of the ninth century B.C.

Lyd·da (lid′ə) A town and site of Israel's chief airport in central Israel. *Arabic* **Ludd** (lo͝od). *Hebrew* **Lud** (lo͝od).

lyd·dite (lid′īt) *n.* A high explosive, chiefly of picric acid: used for torpedo and other shells which on explosion kill by shock or suffocation from its deadly fumes. [from *Lydd,* town in England, where first manufactured]

Lyd·gate (lid′gāt, -git), **John,** 1370?–1451?, English poet.

Lyd·i·a (lid′ē·ə; *Dan., Du.* lē′dē·ä, *Greek* lē·dē′ä) A feminine personal name. Also *Fr.* **Ly·die** (lē·dē′). [<Gk., Lydian girl]

Lyd·i·a (lid′ē·ə) An ancient country of western Asia Minor on the Aegean.

Lyd·i·an (lid′ē·ən) *adj.* **1** Belonging or relating to ancient Lydia in Asia Minor, famous for wealth, luxury and music; also, pertaining to its inhabitants. **2** By extension, effeminate; gentle: in reference to Lydian accomplishments and culture; also, sensuous or voluptuous. **—** *n.* **1** One of the people of ancient Lydia. **2** Their language, probably related to Hittite. **3** One of the modes in early music.

lye (lī) *n.* **1** A solution leached from ashes, or derived from a substance containing alkali: used in making soap, preparing hominy, etc. **2** A lixivium. [OE *lēah*]

Ly·ell (lī′əl), **Sir Charles,** 1797–1875, English geologist.

ly·ing[1] (lī′ing) *n.* The practice of telling lies; untruthfulness. See synonyms under DECEPTION. **—** *adj.* Addicted to, conveying, or constituting falsehood; mendacious; false. **—ly′·ing·ly** *adv.*

ly·ing[2] (lī′ing) Present participle of LIE[1]. **—** *adj.* Being in a horizontal position; prostrate.

ly·ing-in (lī′ing·in′) *n.* The confinement of women during childbirth; parturition. **—** *adj.* Of or pertaining to childbirth: a *lying-in* home or hospital.

Lyl·y (lil′ē), **John,** 1554–1606, English dramatist and novelist. See EUPHUISM.

lymph (limf) *n.* **1** A transparent, colorless, alkaline fluid which circulates in the lymph vessels of vertebrates. It consists of a plasma resembling that of the blood and of corpuscles like the white blood corpuscles. **2** The coagulable exudation from the blood vessels in inflammation. **3** The virus, or a culture of the virus, of a disease, used in vaccination or similar treatment. **4** *Obs.* A spring; water. [<L *lympha,* var. of *limpa* water, ? <Gk. *nymphē* nymph, goddess of moisture]

lym·phad·e·ni·tis (lim·fad′ə·nī′tis, lim′fə·də-) *n. Pathol.* Inflammation of the lymphatic glands. [<NL <LYMPH(O)- + ADEN(O)- + -ITIS]

lym·phan·gi·al (lim·fan′jē·əl) *adj.* Of or pertaining to the lymphatic vessels; lymphatic. [<LYMPH(O)- + ANGI(O)- + -AL[1]]

lym·phat·ic (lim·fat′ik) *adj.* **1** Pertaining to, containing, or conveying lymph. **2** Caused by or affecting the lymphatic glands. **3** Having a phlegmatic temperament. **—** *n.* A vessel that conveys lymph into the veins; an absorbent vessel. [<NL <L *lymphaticus* frantic, frenzied, trans. of Gk. *nympholēptos* caught by nymphs]

lym·pha·tism (lim′fə·tiz′əm) *n.* **1** Lymphatic temperament. **2** *Pathol.* An unhealthy condition due to an excess of lymphatic tissue. [<LYMPHATIC]

lym·pha·ti·tis (lim′fə·tī′tis) *n. Pathol.* Inflammation in any part of the lymphatic system. [<LYMPHAT(O)- + -ITIS]

lymphato- *combining form* Lymphatic. Also, before vowels, **lymphat-.**

lym·pha·tol·y·sis (lim′fə·tol′ə·sis) *n. Pathol.* Dissolution or breakdown of lymphatic tissue. [<LYMPHATO- + -LYSIS] **—lym·pha·to·lyt·ic** (lim′fə·tō·lit′ik) *adj.*

lymph cell A lymphocyte.

lymph gland *Anat.* One of the nodular bodies about the size of a pea, found in the course of the lymphatic vessels, composed of a reticulum containing lymphoid cells.

lympho- *combining form* Lymph; of or pertaining to lymph or the lymphatic system: *lymphocyte.* Also, before vowels, **lymph-.** [See LYMPH]

lym·pho·cyte (lim′fə·sīt) *n. Anat.* A variety of nucleated, colorless leucocyte in the lymphatic glands of all vertebrate animals, resembling a small white blood corpuscle.

lym·pho·cy·to·sis (lim′fə·sī·tō′sis) *n. Pathol.* An excess of lymphocytes in the blood. **—lym′pho·cy·tot′ic** (-tot′ik) *adj.*

lym·phoid (lim′foid) *adj.* Of, pertaining to, or resembling lymph or a lymphatic gland. [<LYMPH + -OID]

lymphoid tissue Tissue constituting the lymph glands; adenoid tissue.

lym·phor·rhe·a (lim′fə·rē′ə) *n. Pathol.* A flow of lymph from ruptured lymph vessels.

lyn (lin) See LIN.

lyn·ce·an (lin·sē′ən) *adj.* **1** Pertaining to or characteristic of the lynx. **2** Lynx-eyed; sharp-sighted. [<L *lynceus* <Gk. *lynkeios* <*lynx* lynx]

lynch (linch) *v.t.* To kill by mob action, as by hanging or burning. **—** *adj.* Of or relating to lynching. [<LYNCH LAW] **—lynch′er** *n.* **—lynch′ing** *n.*

Lynch·burg (linch′bûrg) A city on the James River in south central Virginia.

lynch law The practice of administering punishment, usually by hanging, for alleged crimes without trial by law. [? after Capt. Wm. *Lynch,* 1742–1820, Virginia magistrate]

Lynd·say (lin′zē), **Sir David** See under LINDSAY.

Lynn (lin) **1** An industrial city in eastern Massachusetts. **2** See KING'S LYNN.

Lynn Canal A fiord in the mainland of SE Alaska near Alexander Archipelago.

Lynn Re·gis (rē′jis) See KING'S LYNN.

lynx (lingks) *n.* Any of several wildcats (genus *Lynx*) of Europe and North America, with short tails, tufted ears, and relatively long limbs; especially, the Canadian lynx (*L. canadensis*) and the North American bay lynx (*L. rufus*). [<L *lynx, lyncis* <Gk. *lynx*]

Lynx (lingks) A northern constellation. See CONSTELLATION.

lynx-eyed (lingks′īd′) *adj.* Having acute sight.

lyo- *combining form* A loosening; dissolution: *lyophilic.* Also, before vowels, **ly-.** [<Gk. *lyein* loosen]

Ly·on (lī′ən), **Mary,** 1797–1849, U. S. educator; founder of Mt. Holyoke College.

Ly·on·nais (lē·ô·nā′) A region and former province of east central France. Also **Ly·o·nais′.**

ly·on·naise (lī′ə·nāz′, *Fr.* lē·ô·nez′) *adj.* Made with finely sliced onions; especially, designating a method of preparing potatoes with fried onions. [<F, fem. of *lyonnais* of Lyon]

Ly·on·nesse (lī′ə·nes′) In Arthurian legend, a region lying between Cornwall and the Scilly Islands, supposed to have sunk into the sea.

Ly·ons (lī′ənz, *Fr.* lē·ôn′) A city of east central France at the confluence of the Rhône and the Saône; the third largest city of France. Also **Ly·on′.** **—Ly·on·nais′** *adj.*

ly·o·phil·ic (lī′ə·fil′ik) *adj. Chem.* Pertaining to or designating a colloidal system either phase of which is more or less freely soluble

in the other. [<LYO- + Gk. *philos* loving]

ly·o·pho·bic (lī′ə·fō′bik) *adj. Chem.* Resisting solution: said of colloidal systems neither phase of which will freely dissolve in the other. [<LYO- + Gk. *phobos* fear]

ly·o·sorp·tion (lī′ə·sôrp′shən) *n. Chem.* The adsorption of a solvent film upon the surface of suspended particles. [<LYO- + (AD)SORPTION]

ly·o·trop·ic (lī′ə·trop′ik, -trō′pik) *adj. Chem.* 1 Designating a series of ions, radicals, or salts arranged according to their influence on certain colloidal, physiological, or catalytic phenomena. 2 Having an affinity for entering into solution.

Ly·ra (lī′rə) An ancient constellation representing the lyre of Hermes or of Orpheus; the Harp. It contains the bright star Vega. See CONSTELLATION. [<L <Gk.]

ly·rate (lī′rāt) *adj. Bot.* Lyre-shaped, as a pinnatifid leaf having its upper lobes largest. Also **ly′rat·ed**. [<NL *lyratus*] — **ly′rate·ly** *adv.*

lyre (līr) *n.* An ancient harplike stringed instrument, having a hollow body and two horns bearing a crosspiece between which and the body were stretched the strings, generally seven. [<L *lyra* <Gk.]

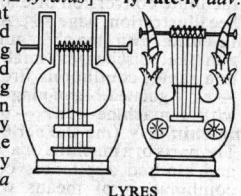

LYRES

Lyre (līr) The constellation Lyra.

lyre·bird (līr′bûrd′) *n.* An Australian passerine bird (genera *Menura* and *Harriwhitea*) having the tail feathers of the males arranged in lyre shape.

lyr·ic (lir′ik) *adj.* 1 Originally, belonging to a lyre; hence, adapted for singing to a lyre. 2 Characterizing verse expressing the poet's personal emotions or sentiments; songlike: distinguished from *epic, dramatic.* 3 Pertaining to the writing of such verse; having written lyric poetry. 4 Musical; singing or to be sung. 5 *Music* Light, graceful, and having a flexible quality: opposed to *dramatic:* said of the voice in singing. Also **lyr′i·cal.** — *n.* 1 A lyric poem; a song. 2 *Usually pl.* The words of a song, especially as distinguished from the music. [<L *lyricus* <Gk. *lyrikos* <*lyra* a lyre] — **lyr′i·cal·ly** *adv.*

lyr·i·cism (lir′ə·siz′əm) *n.* 1 Lyrical quality;

a lyric composition. 2 Emotional expression, as of enthusiasm.

lyr·i·cist (lir′ə·sist) *n.* 1 One who writes the words of a song or the lyrics for a musical play. 2 A lyric poet.

lyric poetry Any form of poetry giving expression to the poet's personal emotions or sentiments. It includes the *sonnet,* the *elegy, ode, song, psalm, hymn,* etc.

ly·ri·form (lī′rə·fôrm) *adj.* Shaped like a lyre.

lyr·ism (lir′iz·əm) *n.* 1 Lyre-playing; hence, the singing of lyrics, or music in general. 2 Lyricism. [<F *lyrisme*]

lyr·ist (lir′ist) *n.* 1 One who plays the lyre. 2 A lyric poet. [<L *lyristes* <Gk. *lyristēs* <*lyrixein* play on a lyre]

Lys (lēs) A river in northern France and western Belgium, flowing 130 miles NE to the Scheldt. *Flemish* **Lei′e** (lī′ə).

Ly·san·der (lī·san′dər), died 395 B.C., Spartan general.

lyse (līs) *v.t. & v.i.* **lysed, lys·ing** To undergo or cause to undergo lysis. [<Gk. *lysis* loosening]

Ly·sen·ko (li·seng′kō, *Russian* lē′sin·kə), **Tro·fim,** born 1898, U.S.S.R. biologist and agronomist: also *Lisenko.*

Ly·sen·ko·ism (li·seng′kō·iz′əm) *n.* The theory regarding the nature and processes of inheritance which challenges the formal genetics of Mendel, Weismann, and Morgan, claiming especially that the genes may be permanently modified by somatic influences, thus permitting a selective inheritance of acquired characteristics. [after T. *Lysenko*]

ly·ser·gic acid (li·sûr′jik) *n. Biochem.* A crystalline alkaloid, $C_{16}H_{16}N_2O_2$, derived from ergot, of which it is the chief toxic principle, and forming the base of **lysergic acid di·eth·yl·am·ide-25** (dī′eth·əl·am′īd), or LSD. [< LYS- + *erg(ot)* + -IC]

lysi- *combining form* A loosening: *lysigenetic.* Also, before vowels, **lys-.** [<Gk. *lysis* a loosening]

Lys·i·as (lis′ē·əs), 458?–378? B.C., Athenian orator.

ly·si·ge·net·ic (lī′sə·jə·net′ik) *adj. Biol.* Produced or producing by the breakdown or absorption of intermediate or contiguous cells: said of certain intercellular spaces or of their mode of formation. Also **ly′si·gen′ic, ly·sig·e·nous** (lī·sij′ə·nəs). — **ly′si·ge·net′i·cal·ly** *adv.*

Ly·sim·a·chus (lī·sim′ə·kəs), 361?–281 B.C., Macedonian general under Alexander the Great; king of Thrace.

ly·sim·e·ter (lī·sim′ə·tər) *n.* An instrument for determining the solubility of substances.

ly·sin (lī′sin) *n.* A substance capable of destroying bacteria, blood corpuscles, etc. [< LYS(I)- + -IN]

ly·sine (lī′sēn, -sin) *n. Biochem.* An important amino acid, $C_6H_{14}O_2N_2$, produced on the hydrolysis of various proteins. Also **ly′sin.** [<LYS(I)- + -INE²]

Ly·sip·pus (li·sip′əs) Greek sculptor of the fourth century B.C. — **Ly·sip′pan** *adj.*

ly·sis (lī′sis) *n.* 1 *Pathol.* The gradual disappearing of a disease. Compare CRISIS. 2 *Biochem.* The process of disintegration or destruction of cells. [<NL <Gk., loosening < *lyein* loose, dissolve]

-lysis *combining form* A loosing, dissolving, etc.: *hydrolysis, paralysis.* [<Gk., loosening < *lyein* loose, dissolve]

lys·sa (lis′ə) *n.* Hydrophobia; rabies. [<Gk., frenzy, madness]

lys·so·pho·bi·a (lis′ə·fō′bē·ə) *n. Psychiatry* A morbid fear of insanity. [<Gk. *lyssa* madness + -PHOBIA] — **lys′so·pho′bic** *adj.*

Lys·ter bag (lis′tər) A portable, waterproof bag for supplying disinfected drinking water to troops: also spelled *Lister bag.* [after W.J.L. *Lyster,* 1869–1947, U.S. Army surgeon]

Lys·tra (lis′trə) An ancient town of Lycaonia.

-lyte¹ *combining form* A substance decomposed by a (specified) process: *electrolyte.* [<Gk. *lytos* loosened, dissolved < *lyein* loosen]

-lyte² *combining form* — LITE.

-lytic *combining form* Loosing; dissolving: used in adjectives corresponding to nouns in *-lysis: hydrolytic paralytic.* [<Gk. *lytikos* loosing < *lysis* a loosening]

lyt·ta (lit′ə) *n. pl.* **lyt·tae** (lit′ē) *Anat.* A vermiform cartilage or fibrous band on the under surface of the tongue in carnivores, as the dog. [<L, a worm said to grow under a dog's tongue and cause madness <Gk., madness]

Lyt·ton (lit′ən), **Earl of,** 1831–91, Edward Robert Bulwer-Lytton, son of Lord Lytton; English poet and diplomat; pseudonym *Owen Meredith.* — **Lord,** 1803–73, Edward George Earle Lytton Bulwer-Lytton, first Baron Lytton, English novelist.

Lyu·blin (lyŏŏ′blin) The Russian name for LUBLIN.

M

m, M (em) *n. pl.* **m's, M's** or **ms, Ms** or **ems** (emz) 1 The 13th letter of the English alphabet: from Phoenician *mem,* Greek *mu,* Roman *M.* 2 The sound of the letter *m,* usually a voiced, bilabial nasal. See ALPHABET. — *symbol* 1 The Roman numeral 1,000. See under NUMERAL. 2 *Printing* An em.

ma (mä, mô) *n.* Mama; mother. [Short for MAMA]

ma'am (mam, mäm, *unstressed* məm) *n.* 1 A respectful address to women, corresponding to *sir* in the case of men. 2 A dame; mistress: used in combination: a *schoolma'am.* 3 *Brit.* A term of respectful address used to the queen or to a royal princess. [Contraction of MADAM]

Maar·tens (mär′tənz), **Maarten** Pen name of Joost Marius Willem Van der Poorten-Schwartz, 1858–1915, Dutch novelist; wrote in English.

Maas (mäs) The Dutch name for the MEUSE.

Maas·tricht (mäs′trikht, mäs′trikht′) See MAESTRICHT.

Mab (mab), **Queen** In English folklore, the queen of the fairies.

Ma·bel (mā′bəl) A feminine personal name. Also *Irish* **Mab,** *Fr.* **Ma·belle** (mà·bel′), *Lat.* **Ma·bil·i·a** (mə·bil′ē·ə). [Short for AMABEL]

Mab·i·no·gi·on (mab′ə·nō′gē·ən) *n.* A collec-

tion of eleven medieval Welsh romances translated by Lady Charlotte Guest in 1838–1849. [<Welsh *mabinogion,* pl. of *mabinogi* bardic instructional material < *mabinog* a bard's apprentice]

Mac- *prefix* In Scottish and Irish names, son of: *MacDougal,* son of Dougal: abbr. *Mc, Mᶜ,* or *M′.* See also MC-. [<Scottish Gaelic and Irish, son]

ma·ca·bre (mə·kä′brə, -bər) *adj.* Suggestive of death; gruesome; frightful. Also **ma·ca′ber.** [<F <OF (*danse*) *macabré* (dance) of death, prob. alter. of *Macabé* <LL *Maccabaeus,* ? a character in a morality play]

ma·ca·co (mə·kä′kō) *n. pl.* **·cos** Any one of various lemurs, especially the black lemur of Madagascar (*Lemur macaco*). [<Pg. < Tupian *macaco, macaca* a monkey]

mac·ad·am (mə·kad′əm) *n.* 1 Broken stone for macadamizing a road. 2 A macadamized road. [after John L. *McAdam,* 1756–1836, British engineer]

mac·ad·am·ize (mə·kad′ə·mīz) *v.t.* **·ized, ·iz·ing** To pave with small consolidated broken stone on a soft or hard, but drained and convex, substratum. — **mac·ad′am·i·za′tion** *n.* — **mac·ad′am·iz′er** *n.*

Ma·cao (mə·kou′, -kä′ō) A Portuguese overseas province at the mouth of the Canton

River, comprising a peninsula of an island in the delta (often called **Macao Island**) and three small offshore islands, the **Tai·pa Islands** (tī′pä′) and **Co·lo·a·ne** (kōō·lō′ə·nē); total, 6 square miles; capital, Macao, on Macao Island. *Portuguese* **Ma·cáu** (mə·kou′).

ma·caque (mə·käk′) *n.* An Old World monkey (genus *Macaca*) with stout body, short tail, cheek pouches, and pronounced muzzle. [<F <Pg. *macaco.* See MACACO.

MACAQUE
(Body length: 2 to 3 feet, depending on species)

mac·a·ro·ni (mak′ə·rō′nē) *n. pl.* **·nis** or **·nies** 1 An edible paste of wheat flour made into slender tubes. Compare SPAGHETTI, VERMICELLI. 2 A medley. 3 One of a body of Revolutionary soldiers from Maryland who wore a showy uniform. 4 An English dandy of the 18th century who affected the tastes and fashions prevalent in Continental society; a fop. Also **mac′ca·ro′ni.** [<

Ital. *maccaroni, maccheroni,* pl. of *macherone* groats <LGk. *makaria* a broth with barley groats <Gk., blessedness <*makar* blessed]

mac·a·ron·ic (mak′ə·ron′ik) *adj.* **1** Consisting of a burlesque medley of real or coined words from various languages; hence, jumbled; mixed. **2** Pertaining to or like macaroni. Also **mac′a·ron′i·cal.** [<NL *macaronicus* <Ital. *maccheronico* <*maccheroni* MACARONI]

mac·a·roon (mak′ə·ro͞on′) *n.* A small cooky of ground almonds or almond paste, white of egg, and sugar; also, an imitation of this made with coconut. [<MF *macaron* <Ital. *maccarone,* var. of *macherone* MACARONI]

Mac·Ar·thur (mək·är′thər), **Douglas,** 1880–1964, U. S. general in World War II; commander in chief in the Pacific and in Japan.

Ma·cas·sar (mə·kas′ər) A port and the largest city of Celebes, on **Macassar Strait,** a channel between Borneo and Celebes: also *Makassar.*

Ma·cas·sar oil (mə·kas′ər) **1** A volatile oil distilled from the flowers of ylang-ylang, and originally obtained from Macassar. **2** A substitute made from perfumed castor oil, etc.: used as a hair dressing.

Ma·cau·lay (mə·kô′lē), **Thomas Babington,** first Baron Macaulay of Rothley, 1800–59, English historian, essayist, statesman.

ma·caw (mə·kô′) *n.* A large tropical American parrot (genus *Ara*), with a long tail, harsh voice, and brilliant plumage. [<Pg. *macao,* prob. <Tupian *maca(vuana)*]

Mac·beth (mək·beth′), died 1057, king of Scotland; hero of Shakespeare's tragedy of the same name.

Mac·ca·bees (mak′ə·bēz) A family of Jewish patriots who, beginning in the reign of Antiochus IV (175–164 B.C.), led a revolt against Syrian religious oppression, which resulted in the deliverance and freedom of Judea; also, four books written in Hebrew and translated into Greek, treating of Jewish oppression and persecution from 222 to 135 B.C. The first two books are regarded as canonical by Roman Catholics, but all as apocryphal by Protestants. [<LL *Machabaei,* pl. of *Machabaeus* <Gk. *Makkabaios,* prob. <Aramaic *maggābā* a hammer]

Mac·ca·be·us (mak′ə·bē′əs), **Judas,** died 160? B.C., Jewish patriot; leader against the Seleucids. **—Mac′ca·be′an** *adj.*

mac·chia (mak′yə) See MAQUIS.

Mac·don·ald (mək·don′əld), **George,** 1824–1905, Scottish novelist and poet. **—James Ramsay,** 1866–1937, English labor leader and statesman; prime minister 1924, 1929–35.

Mac·Don·ough (mək·don′ō), **Thomas,** 1783–1825, U. S. naval officer in the War of 1812.

Mac·Dow·ell (mək·dou′əl), **Edward Alexander,** 1861–1908, U. S. composer.

Mac·Duff (mək·duf′) A character in Shakespeare's *Macbeth,* who kills Macbeth.

mace[1] (mās) *n.* **1** A club-shaped staff of office borne before officials or displayed on the table of a legislative body. **2** A medieval steel war club, often with spiked metal head, for use against armor. **3** A person who carries a mace, as in a ceremony. **4** A curriers' knobbed mallet for softening hides. **5** A flat-headed form of billiard cue, formerly used on pocket tables. [<OF *masse, mace.* Cf. LL *matteola* a mallet.]

mace[2] (mās) *n.* An aromatic spice made from the covering of nutmeg seed. [<OF *macis* <L *macir* <Gk. *maker* a spicy bark from India]

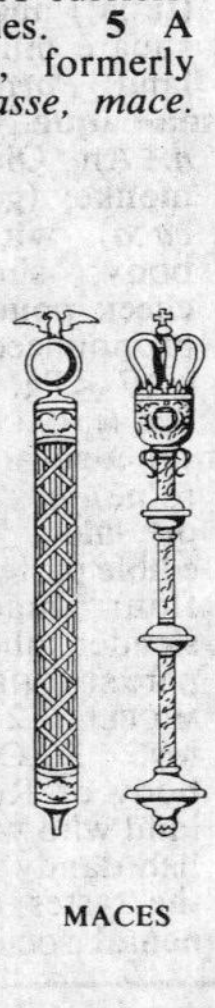

MACES

Mace (mās) *n.* A chemical solution similar to tear gas that temporarily blinds or incapacitates one when sprayed in the face, used as a weapon. **—** *v.t.* **Maced, Mac·ing** To spray with Mace. [<Chemical *Mace,* a trade name]

mace·bear·er (mās′bâr′ər) *n.* An official who carries a mace, as in a procession.

mac·é·doine (mas′i·dwän′, *Fr.* mȧ·sā·dwȧn′) *n.* A dish of mixed vegetables or fruits, served as a salad or dessert; also, any mixture; medley; olio. [<F, a type of parsley <OF *(perresel) macedoine* Macedonian (parsley)]

Mac·e·do·ni·a (mas′ə·dō′nē·ə) A region of SE Europe in the southern Balkan peninsula on the Aegean, divided among Bulgaria, Greece, and Yugoslavia; the ancient Greek kingdom of **Mac·e·don** (mas′ə·don) under Alexander the Great became a leading world power in the fourth century B.C. **—Mac′e·do′ni·an** *adj.* & *n.*

Ma·cei·ó (mä′sā·ô′) A port on the Atlantic, capital of Alagoas state, eastern Brazil.

mac·er (mā′sər) *n.* **1** A macebearer. **2** In Scotland, an officer who attends the courts and executes their orders. [<OF *maissier* <*masse, mace* mace]

mac·er·ate (mas′ə·rāt) *v.* **·at·ed, ·at·ing** *v.t.* **1 a** To reduce to a soft mass by soaking. **b** To separate the soft parts of by soaking; digest. **2** To make thin; emaciate. **—** *v.i.* **3** To undergo maceration. [<L *maceratus,* pp. of *macerare* make soft, knead] **—mac′er·at′er, mac′er·a′tor** *n.*

mac·er·a·tion (mas′ə·rā′shən) *n.* The process or action of steeping a solid material in liquid so as to soften it or break down its structure; digestion.

mach (mak, mäk) See MACH NUMBER.

Ma·cha·do y Mo·ra·les (mä·chä′thō ē mō·rä′·lās), **Gerardo,** 1871–1939, president of Cuba 1925–33.

mach effect (mak, mäk) *Physics* **1** Any effect produced by an object moving at transonic or supersonic speeds, as a shock wave. **2** The aggregate of such effects.

ma chère (mȧ shâr′) *French fem.* My dear.

ma·chet·e (mə·shet′ē, mə·shet′; *Sp.* mä·chā′tā) *n.* A heavy knife or cutlas used both as an implement and as a weapon by the natives of tropical America. [<Sp., dim. of *macho* an ax, a hammer <L *marculus,* dim. of *marcus* a hammer]

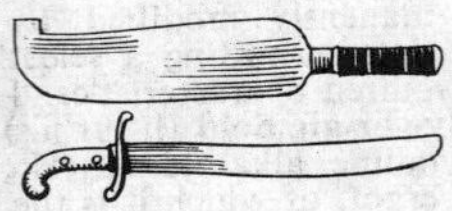

SPANISH MACHETES

Mach·i·a·vel·li (mäk′ē·ə·vel′ē, *Ital.* mä′kyä·vel′·lē), **Niccolò,** 1469–1527, Florentine statesman and writer on government.

Mach·i·a·vel·li·an (mak′ē·ə·vel′ē·ən) *adj.* Of or pertaining to Niccolò Machiavelli, or to the unscrupulous doctrines of political opportunism associated with his name. **—** *n.* A follower of Machiavelli.

Mach·i·a·vel·li·an·ism (mak′ē·ə·vel′ē·ən·iz′əm) *n.* The theory and practice of power politics elaborated from Machiavelli's *The Prince:* envisaging (1) seizure, maintenance, and extension of absolute power by the nicely graduated use of guile, fraud, force, and terror; (2) control by the ruler of all avenues of communication, thus facilitating the deliberate molding of public opinion; (3) the employment for surveillance and terrorist activities of subordinates who can be disowned and liquidated by the ruler, who thus escapes the blame for their atrocities.

ma·chic·o·late (mə·chik′ə·lāt) *v.t.* **·lat·ed, ·lat·ing** To furnish with machicolations. [<Med. L *machicolatus,* pp. of *machicolare*]

ma·chic·o·la·tion (mə·chik′ə·lā′shən) *n.* **1** *Archit.* An opening between a wall and a parapet, to permit missiles or boiling liquids to be dropped upon an assailing enemy. **2** The act of showering missiles on an attacking party through such openings.

ma·chin·a·ble (mə·shē′nə·bəl) *adj. Metall.* Capable of being shaped, cut, or polished by high-speed machine tools, as certain metals and alloys. **—ma·chin′a·bil′i·ty** *n.*

mach·i·nate (mak′ə·nāt) *v.t.* & *v.i.* **·nat·ed, ·nat·ing** To plan or devise; scheme, especially with evil intent. [<L *machinatus,* pp. of *machinari* contrive <*machina* MACHINE]

mach·i·na·tion (mak′ə·nā′shən) *n.* The act of contriving a secret or hostile plan; also, such a plan; plot. See synonyms under ARTIFICE. **—mach′i·na′tor** *n.*

ma·chine (mə·shēn′) *n.* **1** Any combination of mechanisms for utilizing, modifying, applying, or transmitting energy, whether simple, as a lever and fulcrum, pulley, etc., or complex, as a Fourdrinier papermaking apparatus. **2** An automobile; also, any other mechanical vehicle, as a bicycle, airplane, etc. **3** In many trades or vocations, the construction principally used or typical of the trade. **4** One who acts in a mechanical manner; a robot. **5** An ancient theatrical contrivance, originating in Greece, for the creation of stage effects: also applied to such portions of the plot of a work of fiction as are introduced for the sake of effect. **6** The organization of the powers of any complex body: the *machine* of government; specifically, an organization within a political party, controlled by practical politicians, in which discipline and subordination are maintained chiefly by the use of patronage, as in the distribution of offices and contracts. **7** Formerly, a military engine. **—** *adj.* **1** Pertaining to, for, produced by, or producing a machine or machinery: *machine* knitting, *machine* shop, etc. **2** Typified by the application or predominance of machines: *machine* age. **3** Mechanical; lacking in originality or uniqueness. **—** *v.t.* **·chined, ·chin·ing** To shape, mill, make, etc., by machinery. [<F <L *machina* <Gk. *mēchanē* <*mēchos* a contrivance] **—ma·chin′al** *adj.*

machine element One of various simple mechanisms, as the lever,. pulley, cam, gearwheel, etc., which, alone or in combination, facilitate conversion of energy to useful work. See illustration, page 763. Also **simple machine.**

ma·chine-gun (mə·shēn′gun′) *n.* An automatic gun that discharges small-arms ammunition in a rapid, continuous fire: also **machine gun.** **—** *v.t.* **-gunned, -gun·ning** To fire at or shoot with a machine-gun. **—ma·chine′-gun′ner** *n.*

ma·chin·er·y (mə·shē′nər·ē) *n. pl.* **·er·ies 1** The parts of a machine or a number of machines and kindred appliances collectively. **2** Any combination of means working together; a complex system of appliances; the arrangements for effecting a specific end. **3** The supernatural or other means by which the catastrophe of a classical drama was brought about; hence, the incidents and events introduced to build up the plot in a work of fiction.

machine shop A workshop for making or repairing machines.

machine tool A power-driven tool, partly or wholly automatic in action, as a lathe, used for cutting and shaping the parts of a machine.

ma·chin·ist (mə·shē′nist) *n.* A maker or repairer of machines; one expert in their design or construction, or in using metalworking tools.

ma·chis·mo (mä·chēz′mō, -chiz′-) *n.* Maleness or masculinity, especially when associated with strong or exaggerated pride in or a conspicuous display of the qualities, attitudes, etc., considered characteristically masculine. [<Sp. <*macho* male]

mach·me·ter (mak′mē′tər, mäk′-) *n. Aeron.* An instrument for determining the speed of airplanes, especially with reference to the mach number. [<MACH (NUMBER) + -METER]

mach number (mak, mäk) A number expressing the speed of an object moving through a fluid medium in relation to the speed of sound in the same medium: in aeronautics it is the ratio of the air speed to the speed of sound in the undisturbed medium, a mach number of 1 indicating a speed equal to the speed of sound. Also *mach.* [after Ernst *Mach,* 1838–1916, Austrian physicist]

ma·cho (mä′chō) *n. pl.* **·chos** (-chōs) A virile man, especially one who takes excessive pride in his virility. **—** *adj.* Of or characteristic of a macho. [<Sp., male]

ma·chree (mə·krē′) *n.* My heart; my love: a term of endearment. [<Irish <*mo* my + *croidhe* heart <OIrish *cride*]

Ma·chu·pic·chu (mä′cho͞o·pēk′cho͞o) A ruined pre-Incan city in south central Peru. Also **Machu Picchu.**

-machy *combining form* A fight between, or by means of: *logomachy.* [<Gk. *-machia* <*machē* a battle]

Ma·cie (mā′sē), **James Lewis** See SMITHSON, JAMES.

mac·in·tosh (mak′ən·tosh) See MACKINTOSH.

Mack·en·sen (mäk′ən·zən), **August von,** 1849–1945, German field marshal in World War I.

Mac·Ken·zie (mə·ken′zē) **1** A district in the Northwest Territories, Canada; 527,490 square miles. **2** A river in NW Canada, flowing generally north 2,514 miles to the Beaufort Sea.

Mac·Ken·zie (mə·ken′zē), **Sir Alexander,** 1755–1820, Scottish explorer in North America.

mack·er·el (mak′ər·əl) *n.* **1** An Atlantic food fish *(Scomber scombrus),* steel-blue above with blackish bars, and silvery beneath. **2** Some scombroid fish resembling it, as the

Spanish mackerel (*Scomberomorus maculatus*). [<OF *makerel*; ult. origin unknown]
mackerel gull The common tern.
mackerel sky *Meteorol.* A cloud formation with numerous detached cloudlets resembling the markings on a mackerel's back.
Mack·i·nac (mak′ə·nô), **Straits of** A channel between Lake Michigan and Lake Huron; 4 miles wide at the narrowest point.
Mack·i·nac Island (mak′ə·nô) A resort city on the southern end of Mackinac Island in the Straits of Mackinac. Also **Mackinac.**

Mackinaw cloth A heavy-napped woolen fabric, or one having cotton or rayon mixed in the yarns: the two sides may be different colors, sometimes in plaids: used for lumbermen's jackets, sport clothes, windbreakers, etc.
Mackinaw coat A thick, short, double-breasted coat with a plaid pattern.
Mackinaw trout See NAMAYCUSH.
mack·in·tosh (mak′ən·tosh) *n.* **1** A waterproof overgarment or cloak. **2** Thin rubber-coated cloth. Also *macintosh.* [after Charles

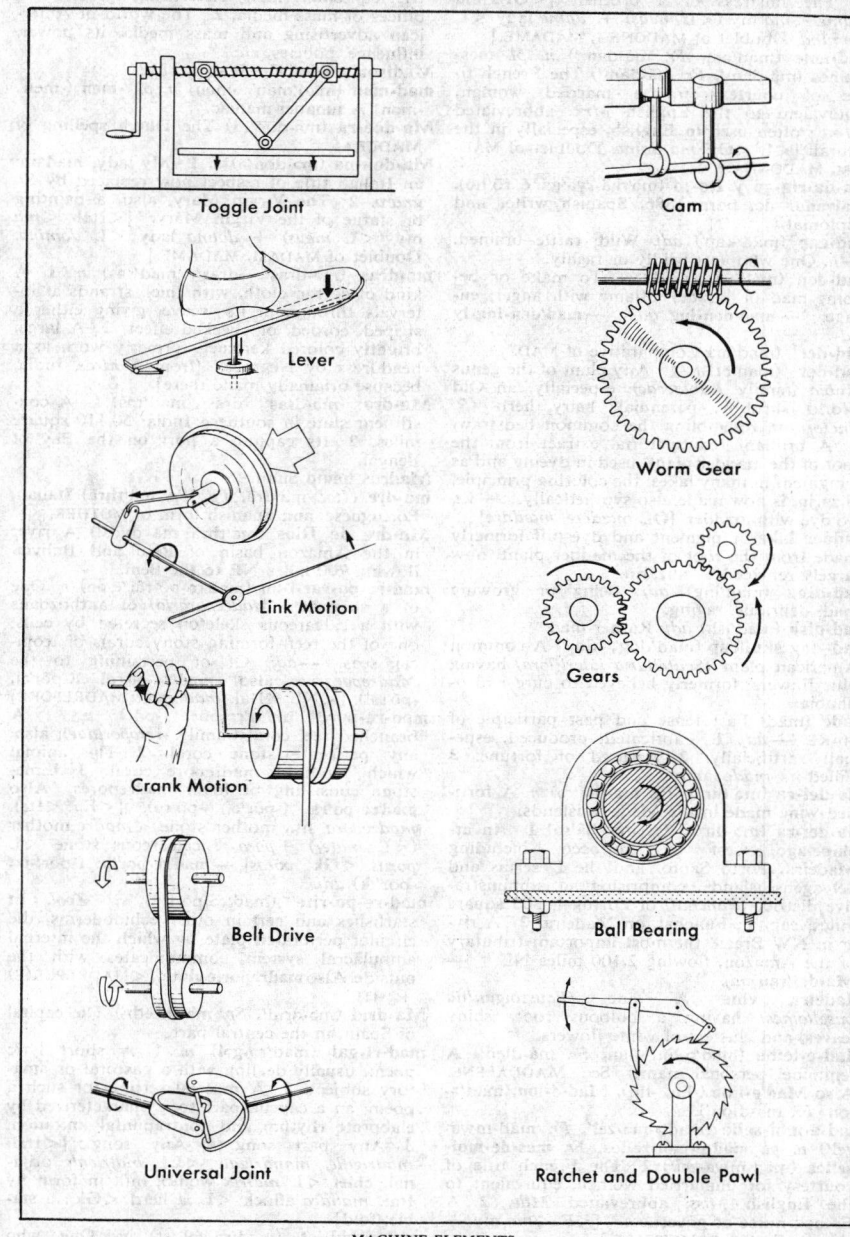

Toggle Joint

Lever

Link Motion

Crank Motion

Belt Drive

Universal Joint

Cam

Worm Gear

Gears

Ball Bearing

Ratchet and Double Pawl

MACHINE ELEMENTS

mack·i·naw (mak′ə·nô) A shortened form of MACKINAW BLANKET, MACKINAW BOAT, MACKINAW COAT. [<dial. F (Canadian) *Mackinac* <*Michilimackinac* Mackinac Island <Algonquian (Ojibwa) *mitchimakinak* a large turtle]
Mackinaw blanket A thick, heavy blanket formerly used by Indians and traders of the western United States.
Mackinaw boat A large, sharp-ended, flat-bottomed bateau, sometimes equipped with sails, and formerly used on the northern Great Lakes.

Macintosh, 1766–1843, Scottish chemist, inventor of the cloth]
mack·le (mak′əl) *n.* A spot or blemish; also, a blurred impression. — *v.t. & v.i.* **mack·led, mack·ling** To print with a blurred or double image; blur; blot. Also spelled *macule.* [<F *macule* <L *macula* a spot]
Mac·lar·en (mə·klar′ən), **Ian** Pseudonym of John Watson, 1850–1907, Scottish author.
Mac·Lau·rin (mə·klôr′in), **trisectrix of** See TRISECTRIX OF MACLAURIN.
mac·le (mak′əl) *n.* **1** A twin crystal, especially of a diamond. **2** Chiastolite. **3** A

mackle. **4** Mascle. [F <OF *mascle* <Med. L *mascula* mesh of net <L *macula* spot]
Mac·Leish (mək·lēsh′), **Archibald,** born 1892, U.S. poet.
Mac·leod (mə·kloud′), **Fiona** Pseudonym of William Sharp.
— **John James Rickard,** 1876–1935, Scottish physiologist.
Ma·clu·ra (mə·klŏŏr′ə) *n.* The Osage orange. [<NL, after Wm. *Maclure,* 1763–1840, U.S. geologist born in Scotland]
Mac·Ma·hon (mȧk·mȧ·ôn′), **Marie Edmé Patrice Maurice de,** 1808–93, Duke of Magenta, French marshal; president of France 1873–79.
Mac·Mil·lan (mək·mil′ən), **Donald Baxter,** born 1874, U.S. Arctic explorer.
Mac·mil·lan (mək·mil′ən), **Harold,** born 1894, British statesman; prime minister 1957–.
Mac·Mon·nies (mək·mon′ēz), **Frederick William,** 1863–1937, U.S. sculptor.
Ma·con (mā′kən) A city in central Georgia.
Mâ·con (mȧ·kôn′) *n.* A wine produced in the neighborhood of Mâcon, France.
Mac·Pher·son (mək·fûr′sən), **James,** 1736–1796, Scottish writer. See OSSIAN.
Mac·quar·ie River (mə·kwôr′ē, -kwor′ē) A river in central New South Wales, Australia, flowing 590 miles NW to the Darling River.
mac·ra·mé (mak′rə·mā) *n.* A fringe, lace, or trimming of knotted thread or cord; knotted work. [Appar. <Turkish *maqramah* a towel <Arabic *miqramah* a veil]
Mac·rea·dy (mə·krē′dē), **William Charles,** 1793–1873, English tragedian.
mac·ren·ceph·a·ly (mak′ren·sef′ə·lē) *n.* *Pathol.* Hypertrophy of the brain. [<MACR(O)- + ENCEPHAL(O)- + -Y¹] — **mac′ren·ce·phal′ic** (-sə·fal′ik), **mac′ren·ceph′a·lous** *adj.*
macro- *combining form* Large or long in size or duration: *macrocephaly, macrobiosis.* Also, before vowels, **macr-.** [<Gk. *makros* large]
mac·ro·bi·o·sis (mak′rō·bī·ō′sis) *n.* Longevity. [<NL <Gk. *makros* long + *bios* life] — **mac′ro·bi·ot′ic** (-ot′ik) *adj.*
mac·ro·bi·ot·ics (mak′rō·bī·ot′iks) *n.pl.* (construed as sing.) A dietetic regimen advocating the use of whole-grain cereals, the avoidance of meat, etc. [<MACRO- + BIOTIC]
mac·ro·ceph·a·ly (mak′rō·sef′ə·lē) *n.* Excessive size of the head. [<MACRO- + Gk. *kephalē* head] — **mac′ro·ce·phal′ic** (-sə·fal′ik) *adj. & n.* — **mac′ro·ceph′a·lous** *adj.*
mac·ro·chem·is·try (mak′rō·kem′is·trē) *n.* The chemistry of large-scale operations or of reactions visible to the naked eye. — **mac′ro·chem′i·cal** (-i·kəl) *adj.*
mac·ro·cli·mate (mak′rō·klī′mit) *n.* *Meteorol.* The general climate prevailing over a large area considered as a unit. Compare MICROCLIMATE. — **mac′ro·cli·mat′ic** (-klī·mat′ik) *adj.*
mac·ro·cosm (mak′rə·koz′əm) *n.* **1** The great world; the universe: opposed to *microcosm.* **2** The whole of any sphere or department of nature or knowledge to which man is related. [<OF *macrocosme* <Med. L *macrocosmus* <Gk. *makros* long, great + *kosmos* world] — **mac′ro·cos′mic** *adj.*
mac·ro·cyst (mak′rə·sist) *n.* *Biol.* **1** An enlarged cyst. **2** *Bot.* A large reproductive cell in certain fungi.
mac·ro·cyte (mak′rə·sīt) *n.* An abnormally large erythrocyte. [<MACRO- + (ERYTHRO)-CYTE]
mac·ro·dome (mak′rə·dōm) See under DOME.
mac·ro·e·co·nom·ics (mak′rō·ē′kə·nom′iks, -ek′ə-) *n.* Economics studied in terms of large aggregates of data whose mutual relationships are interpreted with reference to the behavior of the system as a whole: developed by John Maynard Keynes. — **mac′ro·e′co·nom′ic** *adj.*
mac·ro·ga·mete (mak′rō·gə·mēt′, -gam′ēt) *n.* *Biol.* The female of two conjugating gametes: so called from its being the larger. Compare MICROGAMETE. [<MACRO- + GAMETE]
mac·rog·a·my (mə·krog′ə·mē) *n.* *Biol.* Conjugation between gametes similar in structure to the original vegetative cells.
mac·ro·graph (mak′rə·graf, -gräf) *n.* A drawing or illustration of an object as seen with the unaided eye.
ma·crog·ra·phy (mə·krog′rə·fē) *n.* **1** Examination with the unaided eye. **2** Extremely large writing: contrasted with *micrography.*

ma·crom·e·ter (mə·krom′ə·tər) *n.* A range-finding instrument similar to a sextant, for measuring distant objects.

mac·ro·me·te·or·ol·o·gy (mak′rō·mē′tē·ə·rol′ə·jē) *n.* The meteorology of large areas; world meteorology; also, the study of climatic phenomena over extended periods of time. Compare MICROMETEOROLOGY.

mac·ro·mol·e·cule (mak′rə·mol′ə·kyo͞ol) *n.* A giant molecule, as that of a protein, rubber, cellulose, starch, etc. **—mac′ro·mo·lec′u·lar** (-yə·lər) *adj.*

mac·ro·mor·phol·o·gy (mak′rō·môr·fol′ə·jē) *n.* The gross anatomy of plants.

ma·cron (mā′krən, -kron) *n.* A straight line (-) over a vowel to show that it has a long sound, as, ā: opposed to *breve* (˘). [<Gk. *makron,* neut. of *makros* long]

mac·ro·nu·cle·us (mak′rō·no͞o′klē·əs, -nyo͞o′-) *n. pl.* **·cle·i** (-klē·ī) *Biol.* The larger of two nuclei in certain protozoans, as *Paramecium.*

mac·ro·nu·tri·ent (mak′rō·no͞o′trē·ənt, -nyo͞o′-) *n.* A chemical nutrient required in large amounts for plant growth and vitality.

mac·ro·phys·ics (mak′rō·fiz′iks) *n.* The physics of masses, or of large bodies. **—mac′ro·phys′i·cal** *adj.*

mac·ro·po·di·an (mak′rə·pō′dē·ən) *n.* Any of a family *(Macropodidae)* of marsupials, especially those having six sharp upper incisors and two larger lower ones, enlarged saltatorial hind legs, and long tail: including wallabies and kangaroos. *—adj.* Of or pertaining to the *Macropodidae*: also **ma·crop·o·dine** (mə·krop′ə·din, -dīn), [<NL <Gk. *makropous, -podos* long-footed <*makros* long + *pous, podos* a foot]

ma·crop·si·a (mə·krop′sē·ə) *n. Pathol.* A condition of the eyes in which objects appear larger than they really are: often called *megalopsia.* Also **ma·cro′pi·a** (-krō′pē·ə). [<NL <Gk. *makros* large + *ōps, ōpos* eye]

mac·ro·scop·ic (mak′rə·skop′ik) *adj.* Visible to the naked eye. Also **mac′ro·scop′i·cal.**

mac·ro·spe·cies (mak′rə·spē′shēz) *n. Biol.* A species of which the members exhibit a large range of variation. Compare MICROSPECIES.

mac·ro·spo·ran·gi·um (mak′rō·spə·ran′jē·əm) See MEGASPORANGIUM.

mac·ro·spore (mak′rə·spôr, -spōr) *n.* **1** *Bot.* A megaspore. **2** *Biol.* One of the larger of the two kinds of anisospores in ameboid protozoans.

mac·ro·struc·ture (mak′rə·struk′chər) *n.* The structure of metal as observed with the naked eye or under low magnification on a polished or etched surface. **—mac′ro·struc′tur·al** *adj.*

mac·ro·therm (mak′rə·thûrm) *n.* A tropical plant, or one requiring much heat and moisture for survival: also called *megatherm.*

ma·cru·ran (mə·kro͝or′ən) *n.* One of a suborder *(Macrura)* of crustaceans with well-developed, elongated abdomens, including shrimps, prawns, lobsters, and crayfishes. [<NL <Gk. *makros* long + *oura* tail] **—ma·cru′ral, ma·cru′roid, ma·cru′rous** *adj.*

mac·ta·tion (mak·tā′shən) *n.* The killing of a sacrificial victim. [<L *mactatio, -onis* < *mactatus,* pp. of *mactare* kill]

mac·u·la (mak′yə·lə) *n. pl.* **·lae** (-lē) **1** A spot, as of color on the skin. **2** *Astron.* A dark spot on the sun's surface. **3** A fleck; blotch. [<L, a spot]

mac·u·late (mak′yə·lāt) *v.t.* **·lat·ed, ·lat·ing** To spot or blemish; stain. *—adj.* (-lit) Spotted; stained. [<L *maculatus,* pp. of *maculare* < *macula* a spot]

mac·u·la·tion (mak′yə·lā′shən) *n.* **1** The act of spotting, or a spotty condition. **2** The marking of a spotted animal or plant. **3** A soiling; defilement.

mac·ule (mak′yo͞ol) See MACKLE.

mad (mad) *adj.* **mad·der, mad·dest 1** Mentally deranged; insane. **2** Subject to an overpowering emotion; excited intensely or beyond self-control: *mad* with jealousy or grief. **3** *Colloq.* Angry; furious; enraged. **4** Rabid; having hydrophobia; hence, uncontrollable. **5** Proceeding from or indicating a disordered mind; rash: a *mad* project. **6** Tumultuous or uncontrollable in movement or action: said of things: a *mad* torrent. **7** Reckless; heedless. *—n. Slang* Anger; a fit of temper. **—to have a mad on** *Slang* To be angry. [Aphetic var. of OE *gemǣd, gemǣded,* pp. of *gemǣdan* make mad <*gemād* insane] **—mad′ly** *adv.* **—mad′·ness** *n.*

Mad·a·gas·car A country off the east coast of Africa, and the world's fourth largest island, in the Indian Ocean; land that was originally rainforest, now deforested; 227,600 square miles; capital, Antananarivo; pop.13,000,000. French **Grande-Ile. Grande-Terre.** Formerly **Malagasy Republic.** —_*adj. & n.* **Madagascan, Malagasy.**

mad·am (mad′əm) *n. pl.* **mes·dames** (mā·däm′, *Fr.* mā·dȧm′) *for def.* **1**; **mad·ams** *for def.* **2. 1** My lady; mistress: a title of courtesy originally addressed to a woman of rank or high position, but now used to any woman, as at the beginning of a letter. Compare SIR. See MA'AM. **2** The mistress of a brothel. [<OF *ma dame* <*ma* my (<L *meus*) + *dame* lady <L *domina.* Doublet of MADONNA, MADAME.]

mad·ame (mad′əm, *Fr.* mȧ·dȧm′) *n. pl.* **mes·dames** (mā·däm′, *Fr.* mā·dȧm′) The French title of courtesy for a married woman, equivalent to the English *Mrs.*: abbreviated *Mme.*; often used in English, especially in the plural. [<F <OF *ma dame.* Doublet of MADAM, MADONNA.]

Ma·da·ria·ga y Ro·jo (mä′thä·ryä′gä ē rō′hō), **Salvador de,** born 1886, Spanish writer and diplomat.

mad·cap (mad′kap′) *adj.* Wild; rattle-brained. *—n.* One who acts wildly or rashly.

mad·den (mad′n) *v.t. & v.i.* To make or become mad or insane; inflame with anger; enrage. **—mad′den·ing** *adj.* **—mad′den·ing·ly** *adv.*

mad·der[1] (mad′ər) Comparative of MAD.

mad·der[2] (mad′ər) *n.* **1** Any plant of the genus *Rubia* (family *Rubiaceae*); especially, an Old World shrubby, perennial, hairy herb *(R. tinctorum),* resembling the common bedstraw. **2** A brilliant red tinctorial extract from the root of the madder plant, used in dyeing and as a pigment in many lakes: the coloring principle, alizarin, is now made also synthetically. *—v.t.* To dye with madder. [OE *mædere, mæddre*]

madder lake A pigment and dyestuff formerly made from the root of the madder plant, now largely replaced by alizarin.

mad·ding (mad′ing) *adj.* Being or growing mad; delirious; raging.

mad·dish (mad′ish) *adj.* Rather mad.

mad-dog skullcap (mad′dôg′, -dog′) A common American plant *(Scutellaria lateriflora)* having blue flowers: formerly believed to cure hydrophobia.

made (mād) Past tense and past participle of MAKE. *—adj.* **1** Fabricated; produced, especially artificially. **2** Assured of fortune. **3** Filled in: *made* land.

Ma·dei·ra (mə·dir′ə, *Pg.* mə·thā′rə) *n.* A fortified wine made in the Madeira islands.

Ma·dei·ra (mə·dir′ə, *Pg.* mə·thā′rə) **1** An archipelago west of Morocco, including Madeira, Porto Santo, and the Desertas and Selvagens islands, comprising an administrative district *(Funchal)* of Portugal; 305 square miles; capital, Funchal, on Madeira. **2** A river in NW Brazil, the most important tributary of the Amazon, flowing 2,100 miles NE. **—Ma·dei′ran** *adj.*

Madeira vine A vine *(Boussingaultia baselloides)* having a bulbous root, shiny leaves, and clusters of white flowers.

Mad·e·leine (mad′ə·lin, -lān, *Fr.* mȧ·dlen′) A feminine personal name. See MAGDALENE. Also **Mad′e·line** (-lin, -līn), **Mad·e·lon** (mad′ə·lon, *Fr.* mȧ·dlôn′).

mad·e·moi·selle (mad′ə·mə·zel′, *Fr.* mȧd·mwȧ·zel′) *n. pl.* **mad·e·moi·selles,** *Fr.* **mes·de·moi·selles** (mād·mwȧ·zel′) **1** The French title of courtesy for unmarried women, equivalent to the English *Miss*: abbreviated *Mlle.* **2** A French nurse or governess. [<F <*ma* my + *demoiselle.* See DEMOISELLE.]

Ma·de·ro (mä·thā′rō), **Francisco Indalecio,** 1873–1913, president of Mexico 1911–13.

made-up (mād′up′) *adj.* **1** Artificial; fictitious. **2** Complete; finished. **3** With make-up or cosmetics applied.

mad·house (mad′hous′) *n.* **1** A lunatic asylum. **2** A place of confusion, turmoil, and uproar; bedlam.

Ma·dhya Bha·rat (mu′dyə bä′rət) A former constituent state in west central India, formed in 1948 by merger of Gwalior and the states of Central India, most of which became merged into Madhya Pradesh, November 1, 1956; 46,710 square miles; capitals, Lashkar and Indore.

Ma·dhya Pra·desh (mu′dyə prə·dāsh′) A constituent State in central India on the northern Deccan Plateau; 171,201 square miles; capital, Bhopal: formerly *Central Provinces and Behar.*

Mad·i·son (mad′ə·sən) The capital of Wisconsin.

Mad·i·son (mad′ə·sən), **Dolly,** 1768–1849, *née* Payne, wife of James; celebrated as a hostess. **—James,** 1751–1836, president of the United States 1809–17.

Madison Avenue 1 A street running north and south through Manhattan borough of New York City, center of a commercial district containing many advertising agencies and offices of mass media. **2** The world of American advertising and mass media, its power, influence, policies, etc.

Madison's War The War of 1812.

mad·man (mad′man′, -mən) *n. pl.* **·men** (-men′, -mən) A lunatic; maniac.

Ma·doe·ra (mə·do͞o′rä) The Dutch spelling of MADURA.

Ma·don·na (mə·don′ə) *n.* **1** My lady; madam: an Italian title of respect now replaced by *Signora.* **2** The Virgin Mary; also, a painting or statue of the Virgin Mary. [<Ital. <*ma* my (<L *meus*) + *donna* lady <L *domina.* Doublet of MADAM, MADAME.]

ma·dras (mə·dras′, -dräs′, mad′rəs) *n.* **1** A kind of cotton cloth, with thick strands at intervals throughout its weave, giving either a striped, corded, or checked effect. **2** A large, brightly colored kerchief, formerly worn as a headdress by Negroes. [from *Madras,* India, because originally made there]

Ma·dras (mə·dras′, -dräs′, mad′rəs) **1** A constituent state in southern India; 50,110 square miles. **2** Its capital, a port on the Bay of Bengal.

Madras hemp Sunn.

ma·dre (*Ital.* mä′drā, *Pg., Sp.* mä′thrā) Italian, Portuguese, and Spanish form of MOTHER.

Ma·dre de Dios (mä′thrā thā dyōs′) A river in the Amazon basin of Peru and Bolivia, flowing 700 miles NE to the Beni.

mad·re·po·rar·i·an (mad′rə·pô·râr′ē·ən) *n.* One of a suborder *(Madreporaria)* of anthozoans with a calcareous skeleton secreted by cells; one of the reef-forming stony corals of tropical seas. *—adj.* Of or pertaining to the *Madreporaria*: also **mad′re·po′ral** (-pôr′əl, -pō′rəl). [<NL <Ital. *madrepora* MADREPORE]

mad·re·pore (mad′rə·pôr, -pōr) *n.* **1** A branched reef coral (family *Acroporidae*); also, any perforate stone coral. **2** The animal which produces madrepore coral. **3** Limestone consisting of fossil madrepores. Also **mad′re·po′ra** (-pôr′ə, -pō′rə). [<F <Ital. *madrepora,* lit., mother stone <*madre* mother (<L *mater*) +*poro,* ? calcareous stone <L *porus* <Gk. *pōros*] **—mad′re·por′ic** (-pôr′·ik, -por′ik) *adj.*

mad·re·po·rite (mad′rə·pô·rīt′) *n. Zool.* In starfishes and certain other echinoderms, the circular perforated plate by which the internal ambulacral system communicates with the outside. Also **madreporic plate.** [<MADREPOR(E) + -ITE[1]]

Ma·drid (mə·drid′, *Sp.* mä·thrēth′) The capital of Spain, in the central part.

mad·ri·gal (mad′rə·gəl) *n.* **1** A short lyric poem, usually dealing with a pastoral or amatory subject. **2** A musical setting for such a poem; an a capella part song characterized by elaborate rhythm and contrapuntal imitation. **3** Any part song **4** Any song. [<Ital. *madrigale, mandrigale* <LL *matricale* original, chief <L *matrix* womb; infl. in form by Ital. *mandra* aflock <L, a herd <Gk., a stable, fold]

mad·ri·gal·ist (mad′rə·gəl·ist) *n.* One who writes, or performs in, madrigals.

ma·dri·lène (mad′rə·len′, *Fr.* mȧ·drē·len′) *n.* A consommé flavored with tomato and served hot or cold. [<F <Sp. *Madrileño* of Madrid]

Mad·ri·le·ño (mä′dri·lā′nyō) *n. pl.* **-ños.** One who was born or lives in Madrid.

ma·dro·ña (mə·drō′nyə) *n.* A large evergreen tree *(Arbutus menziesii)* of northern California with shining oval or oblong leaves, dense racemes of white flowers, and dry, yellow, edible berries, called **madroña apples.** Also **ma·dro′ño** (-nyō). [<Sp. *madroño*]

mad·stone (mad′stōn′) *n.* A stone formerly believed to cure hydrophobia.

Ma·du·ra (mä·do͞o′rä) An Indonesian island in the Java Sea; 2,112 square miles including offshore islands: Dutch *Madoera.*

Madura foot Mycetoma.

Ma·du·rai (mäj′ŏŏ·rī, mə·dŏŏr′ī) A city in southern Madras State, India: also *Mathurai*. Formerly **Ma·du·ra** (mäj′ŏŏ·rə, mə·dŏŏr′ə).

Mad·u·rese (mäj′ŏŏ·rēz′, -rēs′) *adj.* Of or pertaining to Madurai, its people, or their language. —*n. pl.* **·rese 1** A native or inhabitant of Madurai and eastern Java. **2** The Indonesian language of the Madurese.

Ma·du·ro (mə·dŏŏr′rō) *adj.* Matured; that is, of full strength and color: said of cigars. —*n.* Such a cigar. [<Sp. <L *maturus*]

mad·wom·an (mad′wŏŏm′ən) *n. pl.* **·wom·en** (-wim′in) An insane woman; lunatic.

mad·wort (mad′wûrt′) *n.* Any of various shrubs or herbs of the mustard family (genera *Alyssum* or *Lobularia*) with small alternate leaves and small yellow or white flowers in terminal racemes or clusters. [? Trans. of NL *Alyssum*, genus name <L <Gk. *alysson* <a- not + *lyssa* rabies]

mae (mā) *adj. & adv. Scot.* More.

Mae·an·der (mē·an′dər) See MEANDER. Also **Mæ·an′der**.

Mae·ce·nas (mi·sē′nəs), **Gaius Cilnius**, 73?-8 B.C., Roman statesman; friend and patron of Horace and Vergil; hence, any patron of the arts.

mael·strom (māl′strəm) *n.* Any irresistible movement or influence: from the **Maelstrom**, a whirlpool or current off the NW coast of Norway. [<Du. *maelstrom, maalstroom* <*malen* grind, whirl round + *stroom* a stream]

mae·nad (mē′nad) *n.* **1** A female votary or priestess of Dionysius; a bacchante. **2** Any woman beside herself with frenzy or excitement. Also spelled *menad*. [<L *Maenas, -adis* <Gk. *mainas* frenzied <*mainesthai* rave] —**mae·nad′ic** *adj.*

Mae Nam (ma′ näm′) See CHAO PHRAYA.

ma·es·to·so (mäs′es·tō′sō) *adj. & adv. Music* With majesty; stately. [<Ital., majestic <L *majestas* greatness]

Maes·tricht (mäs′trikht) A city in southern Netherlands, capital of Limburg province: also *Maastricht*.

ma·es·tro (mä·es′trō, mī′strō) *n.* A master in any art, especially in music. [<Ital., a master <L *magister*]

Mae·ter·linck (mā′tər·lingk), **Maurice**, 1862–1949, Belgian poet, dramatist, and essayist.

Mae West (mā) An inflatable vestlike life preserver used by aviators downed at sea in World War II. [after *Mae West*, born 1892, U.S. actress]

Maf·e·king (maf′ə·king) A town in Northwest province, Republic of South Africa.

maf·fick (maf′ik) *v.i. Brit.* To celebrate uproariously. [Back formation <*mafficking* <MAFEKING, taken as a ppr.; from the extravagant celebration of the relief of the British garrison at Mafeking, May 17, 1900]

Ma·fi·a (mä′fē·ä, maf′ē·ə) *n.* A Sicilian secret society, characterized by hostility to and deliberate flouting of the law and its representatives; also, any similar organization of Italians and Sicilians believed to exist in other countries; Black Hand. Also **Maf′fi·a.** Compare CAMORRA. [<Ital. *maffia*; ult. origin uncertain]

ma·fi·o·so (mä′fē·ō′sō, -zō, maf′ē-) *n. pl.* **·si** (-sē, -zē) *Sometimes cap.* A member of the Mafia. [<Ital. <MAFIA]

ma foi (ma fwä′) *French* My faith; upon my word: an interjection.

mag (mag) *n. Brit. Slang* A halfpenny. [<dial. E *make* a halfpenny; infl. in form by *meg*, orig. a guinea]

Mag (mag) Diminutive of MARGARET.

Ma·gal·la·nes (mä′gä·yä′näs) See PUNTA ARENAS.

mag·a·zine (mag′ə·zēn′, mag′ə·zēn) *n.* **1** A house, room, or receptacle in which anything is stored; a depot; warehouse; specifically, a strong building for storing gunpowder and other military stores; also, a storeroom for gunpowder and shells aboard ship. **2** A receptacle in which the supply of reserve cartridges of a repeating rifle is placed; also, a case in which cartridges are carried. **3** A periodical publication containing sketches, stories, essays, etc. **4** A reservoir or supply chamber in a battery, camera, or the like. —*v.t.* **·zined,**

·zin·ing To store up for future use. [<MF *magasin* <OF *magazin* <Arabic *makhāzin*, pl. of *makhzan* a storehouse <*khazana* store up]

magazine gun A quick-firing small arm fitted with a case carrying a supply of reserve cartridges. See MAGAZINE (def. 2). Also **magazine pistol** or **rifle.**

mag·a·zin·ist (mag′ə·zē′nist) *n.* A contributor to or editor of a magazine. —**mag′a·zin′ism** *n.*

mag·da·len (mag′də·lin) *n.* A reformed prostitute. Also **mag′da·lene** (-lēn). [after *Mary Magdalene*]

Mag·da·le·na (mäg′dä·lā′nä) A river in Colombia, flowing 1,060 miles north to the Caribbean Sea.

Mag·da·lene (mag′də·lēn, *Ger.* mäg′dä·lā′nə) A feminine personal name. Also **Mag′da·len, Mag·da·le·na** (mag′də·lē′nə, *Du., Pg., Sp., Sw.* mäg′dä·lā′nä). [<LL <Gk. *Magdalēnē*, lit., of Magdala <*Magdala* Magdala, a town on the Sea of Galilee] —**the Magdalene** Mary Magdalene.

Mag·da·le·ni·an (mag′də·lē′nē·ən) *adj. Anthrophol.* Describing an advanced culture stage of the upper Paleolithic in western Europe, immediately preceding the Mesolithic period: it is noted especially for its delicate carvings in bone and ivory and for the brilliant realism of its polychrome cave paintings. [<F *magdalenien*, from *La Madeleine* in west central France, where artifacts were found]

Mag·da·len Islands (mag′də·lin) An island group in the Gulf of Saint Lawrence, eastern Quebec province, Canada; total, 102 square miles. *French* **Iles Ma·de·leine** (ēl mȧ·dlen′).

Mag·de·burg (mag′də·bûrg, *Ger.* mäg′də·bŏŏrkh) A city in central Germany, on the Elbe.

mage (māj) *n.* A magician. [<F <L *magus.* See MAGI.]

Ma·ge·lang (mä′gə·läng′) A town in central Java.

Ma·gel·lan (mə·jel′ən), **Fernando**, 1480–1521, Portuguese navigator in the Spanish service. —**Mag·el·lan·ic** (maj′ə·lan′ik) *adj.*

Magellan, Strait of The channel between the Atlantic and the Pacific separating the South American mainland from Tierra del Fuego.

Magellanic clouds *Astron.* Two aggregations of star clusters and nebulae near the south pole of the heavens, looking like detached fragments of the Milky Way. See under COALSACK.

Ma·gen·die (mȧ·zhän·dē′), **François**, 1783–1855, French physician and physiologist.

ma·gen·ta (mə·jen′tə) *n.* **1** A somewhat glaring red coal-tar dyestuff derived from aniline: also called *aniline red* and *fuchsia.* **2** The color given by the pigment, a strong purplish-rose or purplish-red. [from *Magenta;* so called because discovered just after the French victory (1859)]

Ma·gen·ta (mä·jen′tä) A town in Lombardy, northern Italy; scene of a French victory over Austrian forces, 1859.

Ma·gers·fon·tein (mä′gərs·fôn·tān′) A locality of Northern Cape Province, Republic of South Africa; scene of a Boer victory in the South African War.

Mag·gio·re (mäd·jô′rā), **Lago** A lake in northern Italy and Switzerland; 65 square miles.

mag·got (mag′ət) *n.* **1** The larva of a fly; a footless insect larva; a grub. **2** A whim; fancy. [Prob. alter. of ME *maddock, mathek* <ON *mathkr* a worm]

mag·got·y (mag′ət·ē) *adj.* **1** Infested with maggots; flyblown. **2** Whimsical.

Ma·gi (mā′jī) *n. pl.* of **Ma·gus** (mā′gəs) **1** The priestly caste of the Medes and Persians. **2** Specifically, the three 'wise men' who came 'from the east' to Bethlehem to pay homage to the infant Jesus. *Matt.* ii 1. [<L, pl. of *magus* <Gk. *magos* <Persian *magu* a priest, a magician] —**Ma′gi·an** *adj. & n.*

Ma·gi·an·ism (mā′jē·ən·iz′əm) *n.* The creed and cult of the Magi.

mag·ic (maj′ik) *n.* **1** Any supernatural art; sorcery; necromancy. **2** Sleight of hand. **3** Any agency that works with wonderful effect. See synonyms under SORCERY. —**black magic** Any of the branches of magic which invoke the aid of demons or spirits, as witchcraft or diabolism. —**like magic** As if by magic; instantly. —*adj.* **1** Of the nature of magic; used in magic; possessing supernatural powers; sorcerous. **2** Acting like magic. [<OF *magique* <LL *magica (ars)* magic (art) <Gk. *magikē (technē)* <*magikos* of the Magi]

mag·i·cal (maj′i·kəl) *adj.* Pertaining to or produced by or as by magic. ◆ The adjective *magic* is applied more commonly to the powers, influences, or practices, while *magical* is more frequently used of the effects of magic: *magic* arts, a *magic* wand, but *magical* effect, a *magical* result. —**mag′i·cal·ly** *adv.*

ma·gi·cian (mə·jish′ən) *n.* An expert in magic arts; sorcerer; wizard.

magic lantern A device for throwing magnified pictures upon a screen in a darkened room by means of a light placed behind a lens or lenses.

ma·gilp (mə·gilp′) *n.* A mixture used as a vehicle for oil colors, usually composed of a pale drying oil and a turpentine varnish, such as mastic: also spelled *megilp.* Also **ma·gilph′** (-gilf′). [? after *McGilp,* a surname]

Ma·gi·not line (mazh′ə·nō, *Fr.* mȧ·zhē·nō′) A system of French fortifications along the German frontier, built during 1925–1935. [after André *Maginot,* 1877–1932, French statesman]

mag·is·te·ri·al (maj′is·tir′ē·əl) *adj.* **1** Of or pertaining to a magistrate or magistracy; like or befitting a master; commanding; authoritative. **2** Hence, having an air of authority; dictatorial. **3** Domineering; pompous. **4** Pertaining to a chemist's or alchemist's magistery. See synonyms under DOGMATIC. [<Med. L *magisterialis* <LL *magisterius* <L *magister* a master] —**mag′is·te′ri·al·ly** *adv.* —**mag′is·te′ri·al·ness** *n.*

mag·is·te·ri·um (maj′is·tir′ē·əm) *n.* The authority of the church to teach dogmatically; a Roman Catholic usage. [<L, the office of a master <*magister* a master]

mag·is·ter·y (maj′is·ter′ē, -tər·ē) *n. pl.* **·ter·ies 1** An authoritative statement or exposition; a magisterial decree. **2** A fundamental master principle of nature; also, a panacea. **3** In alchemy, the power to transmute metals or the product of transmutation. **4** A compound, as a precipitate, formed when two liquids are mixed, and differing in character from either: a term used by the older chemists and preserved in the phrase *magistery of bismuth.* [<Med. L *magisterium* the philosopher's stone <L. See MAGISTERIUM.]

mag·is·tra·cy (maj′is·trə·sē) *n. pl.* **·cies 1** The office or dignity of a magistrate. **2** The district under a magistrate's jurisdiction. **3** Magistrates collectively.

mag·is·tral (maj′is·trəl) *adj.* **1** Like a magistrate; imperious or pedagogical; magisterial. **2** In pharmacy, specially compounded or prescribed; not kept in stock. **3** Having sovereign power as a medicine. **4** Chief; main: the *magistral* line. —*n. Mil.* The line from which the positions of the various members of a fortification are determined: also **magistral line.** [<F <L *magistralis* <*magister* a master]

mag·is·trate (maj′is·trāt, -trit) *n.* **1** One clothed with public civil authority; an executive or judicial officer. **2** Usually, when unqualified, a minor local justice. [<L *magistratus* magisterial office <L *magister* a master]

mag·is·tra·ture (maj′is·trə·chŏŏr) *n.* **1** Magistracy; government. **2** The term of a magistrate's office. **3** Magistrates collectively. [<F <*magistrat* <L *magistratus.* See MAGISTRATE.]

Ma·gle·mo·si·an (mä′glə·mō′zē·ən) *adj.* Of or

relating to the special phases or aspects of the Mesolithic forest culture of northern Europe as indicated by discoveries at Maglemose, Denmark.

mag·ma (mag′mə) *n. pl.* **·ma·ta** (-mə·tə) **1** Any soft, doughy mixture of organic and mineral materials. **2** *Geol.* The molten mass from which igneous rocks are formed. **3** The residue obtained after expressing the juice from fruits. [<L <Gk. < root of *massein* knead] **— mag·mat·ic** (mag·mat′ik) *adj.*

Mag·na Car·ta (mag′nə kär′tə) **1** The Great Charter of English liberties, delivered June 19, 1215, by King John, at Runnymede, on the demand of the English barons: first document of the English constitution. **2** Any fundamental constitution that secures personal liberty and civil rights. Also **Mag′na Char′ta,** the erroneous but common form. [<Med. L, lit., Great Charter]

mag·na cum lau·de (mag′nə kum lô′dē, mäg′·nä kōōm lou′də) See under CUM LAUDE.

mag·na·flux test (mag′nə·fluks) A method for the detection of defects in metals and in engine parts by noting the arrangement of the particles of a magnetic powder scattered over the magnetized surface. [<MAGN(ETIC) + -a- + FLUX]

Magna Grae·ci·a (grē′shē·ə) See GRAECIA MAGNA. Also **Mag′na Græ′ci·a.**

mag·na·nim·i·ty (mag′nə·nim′ə·tē) *n. pl.* **·ties** **1** The quality of being magnanimous; greatness of soul; generosity in sentiment or conduct toward others; exaltation above mean or petty motives. **2** A magnanimous deed.

mag·nan·i·mous (mag·nan′ə·məs) *adj.* **1** Elevated in soul; scorning what is mean or base. **2** Dictated by magnanimity; unselfish: *magnanimous* candor. See synonyms under GENEROUS. [<L *magnanimus* <*magnus* great + *animus* mind, soul] **— mag·nan′i·mous·ly** *adv.* **— mag·nan′i·mous·ness** *n.*

mag·nate (mag′nāt) *n.* A person of rank or importance; a noble or grandee; one notable or powerful in any sphere: an industrial *magnate.* [<LL *magnas, -atis* <*magnus* great]

mag·ne·sia (mag·nē′zhə, -shə, -zē·ə) *n. Chem.* Magnesium oxide, MgO, a light, white, earthy powder, used in medicine as an antacid laxative, in glassmaking, etc. It can be made by burning magnesium or by igniting certain of the magnesium salts. **— milk of magnesia** A milk-white aqueous suspension of magnesium hydroxide, $Mg(OH)_2$: used as a laxative and antacid. [<Med. L <Gk. *Magnēsia (lithos)* (stone) of Magnesia <*Magnēsia* Magnesia (def. 2)] **— mag·ne′sian, mag·ne′sic** *adj.*

Mag·ne·sia (mag·nē′zhə, -shə) **1** An ancient city of Lydia, western Asia Minor, on the site of modern Manissa; scene of the defeat of Antiochus the Great by the two Scipios, 190 B.C. Also **Magnesia ad Si·py·lum** (ad sip′ə·lum). **2** In classical geography, the coastal district of Thessaly south of the Vale of Tempe, part of which forms a nome of modern Greece.

mag·ne·site (mag′nə·sīt) *n.* A massive, granular carbonate of magnesium, $MgCO_3$. [<MAGNES(IA) (ALBA) + -ITE[1]]

mag·ne·si·um (mag·nē′zē·əm, -zhē-, -shē-) *n.* A light, malleable, ductile, silver-white, metallic element (symbol Mg), used to produce a brilliant light by its combustion, and also as an alloy metal. It occurs abundantly in combination, as in magnesite and dolomite. See ELEMENT. [<NL, magnesia]

magnesium light A brilliant and intense light obtained by the combustion of magnesium: used in signaling, pyrotechnics, etc.

mag·net (mag′nit) *n.* **1** A lodestone. **2** Any mass of a material capable of attracting magnetic or magnetized bodies. Magnets are natural when, like lodestones, they are found already magnetized, or artificial when magnetism has been given to them by placing them in the field of another magnet or in that caused by an electric current. See ELECTROMAGNET. **3** Figuratively, a person or thing exercising a strong attraction. [<OF *magnete* <L *magnes, magnetis* <Gk. *Magnēs (lithos)* Magnesian (stone), i.e., a magnet <*Magnēsia* Magnesia (def. 2)]

mag·net·ic (mag·net′ik) *adj.* **1** Pertaining to a magnet or magnetism. **2** Able to attract or be attracted by a lodestone. **3** Capable of exerting or responding to magnetic force. **4** Pertaining to terrestrial magnetism. **5** Possessing personal attractiveness or magnetism. *— n.* A substance that has or may be given a magnetic field, as iron, steel, nickel, cobalt. **— mag·net′i·cal·ly** *adv.*

magnetic chart A chart indicating the variations in the earth's magnetic field for a given area.

magnetic equator An irregular, unstable line on the earth's surface, encircling it nearly midway between the magnetic poles, where a free magnetic needle has no tendency to dip; the aclinic line. It coincides nearly with the terrestrial equator. See ACLINIC.

magnetic field That region in the neighborhood of a magnet or current-carrying body in which magnetic forces are observable.

magnetic flux *Physics* The flux of magnetic intensity through a surface: expressed in maxwells or webers.

magnetic head *Electronics* A device for recording and playback by which magnetized particles on a moving tape are impressed with a pattern analogous to that of incident sound waves.

magnetic hysteresis That property of a magnetic material by virtue of which the magnetic induction depends upon the previous conditions of magnetization.

magnetic induction *Physics* The magnetic flux per unit of area at a point on a surface: expressed in gauss or in webers per square meter.

magnetic latitude Latitude as measured from the magnetic equator.

magnetic lens *Physics* An assembly of coils and electromagnets so arranged as to produce a magnetic field which will constrain a stream of charged particles to follow a prescribed path.

magnetic meridian A grid line indicating any of the horizontal components of the earth's magnetic field and which passes through the magnetic poles.

magnetic mine An underwater mine containing a sensitive device which, in the presence of any large mass of magnetic material, as a ship, senses the change in the magnetic field and actuates an electrical circuit which detonates the mine.

magnetic moment A measure of the magnetizing force exerted by a magnetized body or electric current.

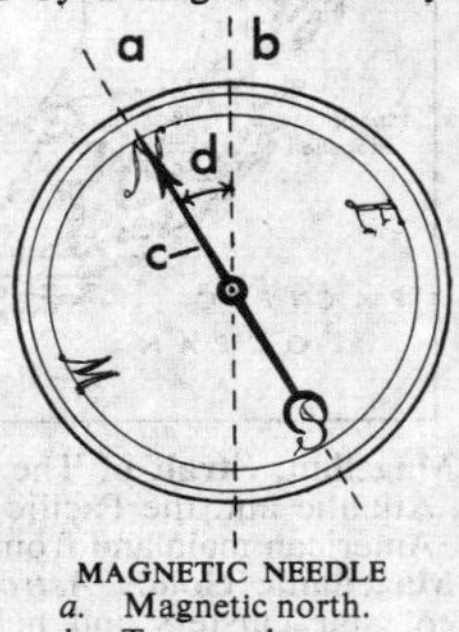

MAGNETIC NEEDLE
a. Magnetic north.
b. True north.
c. Magnetic needle.
d. Angle of variation.

magnetic needle A freely movable, needle-shaped piece of magnetized material which tends to point to the north and south (magnetic) poles of the earth.

magnetic north That direction on the earth's surface toward which one end of the magnetic needle tends to point.

magnetic pole **1** Either of the poles of a magnet; more specifically, those points on the earth's surface where the lines of magnetic force are vertical, called the **North** and **South Magnetic Poles.** These slowly change position and do not coincide with the geographical poles. **2** A pole of a magnet.

magnetic pyrites See PYRRHOTITE.

mag·net·ics (mag·net′iks) *n. pl. (construed as singular)* The science of magnetism.

magnetic signature The specific magnetic susceptibility of a material, product, or structure: said especially of the change of field in the neighborhood of ships exposed to the danger of sensitive magnetic mines.

magnetic speaker A loudspeaker.

magnetic storm A sudden disturbance of the magnetic field surrounding the earth, occurring simultaneously over areas of the earth and apparently connected with sunspots.

magnetic tape *Electronics* A thin ribbon of paper or plastic, one side of which is coated with particles of iron oxide which form magnetic patterns corresponding to the electromagnetic impulses of a tape recorder.

mag·net·ism (mag′nə·tiz′əm) *n.* **1** The specific properties of a magnet, regarded as an effect of molecular interaction. **2** The science that treats of the laws and conditions of magnetic phenomena: also *magnetics.* **3** The amount of magnetic moment in a magnetized body. **4** The sympathetic personal quality that attracts or interests. **5** Mesmerism. Compare ANIMAL MAGNETISM.

mag·net·ite (mag′nə·tīt) *n.* A massive, granular, isometric, black iron oxide, Fe_3O_4; lodestone; an important ore of iron. [<MAGNET + -ITE[1]] **— mag′net·it′ic** (-tit′ik) *adj.*

mag·net·i·za·tion (mag′nə·tə·zā′shən) *n.* The amount of magnetism in or the magnetic moment of a material.

mag·net·ize (mag′nə·tīz) *v.t.* **·ized, ·iz·ing** **1** To communicate magnetic properties to. **2** To attract by strong personal influence; captivate. **3** *Obs.* To hypnotize. Also *Brit.,* **mag′net·ise. — mag′net·iz′a·bil′i·ty** *n.* **— mag′net·iz′a·ble** *adj.* **— mag′net·iz′er** *n.*

magnetizing force A vector quantity that measures the capacity of magnetized bodies or electric currents to produce magnetic induction. Symbol, H.

mag·ne·to (mag·nē′tō) *n. pl.* **·tos** Any magnetoelectric machine in which the rotation of a coil of wire between the poles of a permanent magnet induces a current of electricity in the coil; especially, a type of alternator, widely used as a means of igniting the explosive mixtures used in internal-combustion engines, as in automobiles. Also **mag·ne·to·dy·na·mo** (mag·nē′tō·dī′nə·mō), **mag·ne·to·gen·er·a·tor** (mag·nē′tō·jen′ə·rā′tər). [Short for *magnetoelectric machine*]

magneto– *combining form* Magnetic; magnetism: *magnetomotive.*

mag·ne·to·chem·is·try (mag·nē′tō·kem′is·trē) *n.* The science which treats of the interrelations between magnetic and chemical phenomena. **— mag·ne′to·chem′i·cal** *adj.*

mag·ne·to·e·lec·tric·i·ty (mag·nē′tō·i·lek·tris′·ə·tē) *n.* **1** Electricity generated by the inductive action of a magnet. **2** The science that treats of the principles and phenomena of such electricity. **— mag·ne′to·e·lec′tric, mag·ne′to·e·lec′tri·cal** *adj.*

mag·ne·to·graph (mag·nē′tə·graf, -gräf) *n.* A recording magnetometer.

mag·ne·to·hy·dro·dy·nam·ic (mag·nē′tō·hī′·drō·dī·nam′ik) *adj. Physics* Of, pertaining to, or characterized by the interaction of electromagnetic, mechanical, thermal, and hydrodynamic forces, as by an electric arc in the generation of a plasma jet.

mag·ne·tol·y·sis (mag′nə·tol′ə·sis) *n.* Chemical action in a substance placed in a magnetic field: analogous to electrolysis. [<MAGNETO- + -LYSIS] **— mag·net·o·lyt·ic** (mag·net′ə·lit′ik) *adj.*

mag·ne·tom·e·ter (mag′nə·tom′ə·tər) *n.* An instrument for measuring the intensity and direction of magnetic forces. **— mag′ne·tom′·e·try** *n.*

mag·ne·to·mo·tive (mag·nē′tō·mō′tiv, mag′·nə·tō-) *adj.* **1** Acting magnetically. **2** Characterizing a force producing magnetic flux: distinguished from *electromotive.*

mag·ne·ton (mag′nə·ton) *n. Physics* A unit of magnetic moment: The Bohr magneton has the value of 9.27×10^{-21} erg gauss^{-1}.

mag·ne·to–op·tics (mag·nē′tō·op′tiks) *n.* The study of the behavior of light waves in a magnetic field. **— mag·ne′to–op′tic, mag·ne′to–op′ti·cal** *adj.*

mag·ne·to·scope (mag·nē′tə·skōp, -net′ə-) *n.* An instrument designed to indicate the presence of magnetic force lines without measuring them.

mag·ne·to·sphere (mag·nē′tə·sfir) *n.* A region of the atmosphere extending beyond the exosphere to about 40,000 miles and forming a continuous band of ionized particles trapped by the earth's magnetic field. Compare VAN ALLEN RADIATION.

mag·ne·to·stric·tion (mag·nē′tō·strik′shən) *n. Physics* The mechanical deformation produced in certain materials when subjected to the action of a magnetic field.

mag·ne·tron (mag′nə·tron) *n. Electronics* A vacuum tube in which the flow of electrons is subject to the control of an external magnetic field. [<MAGNET + (ELEC)TRON]

magni– *combining form* **1** Great; large: *magnirostrate,* large-beaked. **2** *Zool.* Long: *magnicaudate,* long-tailed. [<L *magnus* great]

mag·nif·ic (mag·nif′ik) *adj.* **1** Illustrious; magnificent; sumptuous. **2** Strikingly vast or dignified; imposing. **3** Of language, exalted; sublime; also, pompous; grandiloquent. Also **mag·nif′i·cal.** [<F *magnifique* <L *magnificus* <*magnus* great + *fic-*, stem of *facere* make] — **mag·nif′i·cal·ly** *adv.*

Mag·nif·i·cat (mag·nif′ə·kat) *n.* The hymn or canticle of the Virgin Mary, beginning with the word *Magnificat* in the Latin version. *Luke* i 46–55. [<L, it magnifies]

mag·ni·fi·ca·tion (mag′nə·fə·kā′shən) *n.* **1** The act, process, or degree of magnifying. **2** The state of being magnified. **3** Magnifying power. **4** The act of extolling or glorifying. [<L *magnificatio, -onis* <*magnificare* <*magnificus.* See MAGNIFIC.]

mag·nif·i·cence (mag·nif′ə·səns) *n.* **1** The state or quality of being magnificent; the exhibition of greatness of action, character, intellect, wealth, or power; brilliant or imposing appearance; display of splendor. **2** A title of courtesy in medieval Rome. [<OF <L *magnificentia* <*magnificus* noble. See MAGNIFIC.]

mag·nif·i·cent (mag·nif′ə·sənt) *adj.* **1** Grand or majestic in appearance, quality, character, or action; extremely fine or good; befitting the great, as in deeds, manners, or surroundings; great in effect, promise, or import: a *magnificent* prospect, pearl, plan, etc.; also, exalted; imposing: *magnificent* language. **2** Exhibiting magnificence; characterized by splendor: sometimes used as a title: Suleiman the *Magnificent.* See synonyms under GRAND, IMPERIAL, SUBLIME. [<OF <LL *magnificens,* var. of *magnificus.* See MAGNIFIC.] — **mag·nif′i·cent·ly** *adv.*

mag·nif·i·co (mag·nif′ə·kō) *n. pl.* **·coes 1** A noble of the Venetian republic: an old title. **2** A lordly personage; one who affects state or splendor. [<Ital. <L *magnificus.* See MAGNIFICENCE.]

mag·ni·fy (mag′nə·fī) *v.t.* **·fied, ·fy·ing 1** To increase the apparent size of, as by a microscope. **2** To increase the size of; enlarge. **3** To cause to seem greater or more important. **4** *Archaic* To extol; exalt. See synonyms under AGGRAVATE, INCREASE, PRAISE. [<OF *magnifier* <L *magnificare* <*magnificus.* See MAGNIFICENCE.] — **mag′ni·fi′a·ble** *adj.* — **mag′ni·fi′er** *n.*

mag·nil·o·quent (mag·nil′ə·kwənt) *adj.* Of bombastic, pompous style; vainglorious. [<L *magnus* great + *loquens, -entis,* ppr. of *loqui* speak] — **mag·nil′o·quence** *n.* — **mag·nil′o·quent·ly** *adv.*

Mag·ni·to·gorsk (mäg′nē·tô·gôrsk′) A city on the Ural in Russian S.F.S.R.

mag·ni·tude (mag′nə·tood, -tyood) *n.* **1** Great size or extent; grandeur; importance. **2** *Math.* That which is conceived of as measurable. **3** The property of having size or extent. **4** *Astron.* A measure of the relative brightness of a star, ranging from one for the brightest to six for those just visible to the naked eye. The standard of reference is the polestar, with a brightness 2.512 times greater than the one next below it; magnitudes greater than one on the scale are expressed as minus quantities. Compare LIGHT RATIO. **5** Largeness in respect to relation or effect. [<L *magnitudo* <*magnus* large]

Synonyms: bigness, bulk, dimension, extent, greatness, hugeness, immensity, largeness, size, vastness. *Antonyms:* diminutiveness, littleness, pettiness, slightness, smallness.

mag·no·li·a (mag·nō′lē·ə, -nōl′yə) *n.* **1** Any of a genus (*Magnolia*) of trees or shrubs with large, fragrant, and often showy flowers. **2** The blossom of the evergreen magnolia (*M. grandiflora*), the State flower of Louisiana and of Mississippi. [<NL, genus name, after Pierre *Magnol,* 1638–1715, French botanist]

mag·no·li·a·ceous (mag·nō′lē·ā′shəs) *adj.* Of or pertaining to a family (*Magnoliaceae*) of polypetalous trees or shrubs, the magnolia family, often aromatic, with alternate, undivided, feather-veined leaves, and large, solitary, axillary or terminal flowers with calyx and corolla colored alike, in three or more rows of three each. [<NL *Magnoliaceae,* family name <*Magnolia* MAGNOLIA]

magnolia warbler The black-and-yellow

---

warbler (*Dendroica magnolia*) of North America.

mag·num (mag′nəm) *n.* A wine bottle of twice the ordinary size, holding about two quarts; also, the quantity such a bottle will hold. [<L, neut of *magnus* great]

magnum o·pus (ō′pəs) *Latin* The chief work of an artist; a masterpiece; literally, great work.

Mag·nus effect (mag′nəs) *Physics* The deflecting effect upon the normal path of a rotating cylinder or sphere caused by the transverse forces of wind or air currents circulating around it. [after H. G. *Magnus,* 1802–70, German physicist]

mag·nus hitch (mag′nəs) A knot used to fasten a rope to a spar, etc., similar to a clove-hitch but having one more turn. [Prob. <L *magnus* large]

Ma·gog (mā′gog) See GOG AND MAGOG.

ma·got (mȧ·gō′) *n.* The Barbary ape. [<F, ? <*Magog* MAGOG]

Mag·ot·ty-bay bean (mag′ə·tē·bā′) A leguminous vine (*Chamaecrista fasciculata*) common on eastern American shores. [? from *Magothy* River, Maryland]

mag·pie (mag′pī) *n.* **1** A corvine bird (genus *Pica*), having a long, graduated tail. The common **European magpie** (*P. pica* or *caudata*) has iridescent black plumage with white scapulars, belly, sides, flanks, and inner web of flight feathers: often tamed and taught to speak words, and noted for its thievishness. The **American magpie** (*P. hudsonia*) is a variety of the European magpie. *P. nuttali* is the **yellow-billed magpie** of California. **2** An Australian crow shrike resembling a magpie. **3** A chatterbox; a garrulous gossip. [<*Mag,* diminutive of MARGARET, + PIE²]

Mag·say·say (mäg·sī′sī), **Ramón,** 1907–57, president of the Philippines 1953–57.

ma·guey (mag′wā, *Sp.* mä·gā′ē) *n.* **1** Any of various Mexican agave plants with fleshy leaves and edible cabbage-like heads, especially the century plant (*Agave americana*) and the pulque agave (*A. atrovirens*). **2** A fiber plant (genus *Furcraea*) related to the agave. **3** The fiber of these plants. [<Sp., prob. <Taino]

MAGUEY
(Leaves up to 6 feet long; 8 to 10 inches broad)

Ma·gus (mā′gəs) Singular of MAGI.

Mag·yar (mag′yär, *Hungarian* mud′yär) *n.* **1** One of a people who invaded and conquered Hungary at the end of the ninth century; a Hungarian. **2** The Finno-Ugric language of Hungary. — *adj.* Of or pertaining to the Magyars or their language.

Mag·yar·or·szág (mud′yär·ôr′säg) The Hungarian name for HUNGARY.

Ma·ha·bha·ra·ta (mə·hä′bä′rə·tə) An ancient Hindu epic, written in Sanskrit and thought to date from 300 B.C., recounting the dynastic wars of two related families over a kingdom in northern India. This large work, probably the longest in the world, and the *Râmâyana* are the two great epics of ancient India. Also **Ma·ha′bha′ra·tam.** [<Skt. *Mahábhárata,* lit., the great story]

ma·hal·a (mə·hal′ə) *n.* In the western United States and Canada, an Indian squaw. [<N. Am. Ind. *muk′ela*]

Ma·hal·la el Ku·bra (mə·hal′ə el kōō′brə) A city in the Nile delta. Also **Ma·hal′la.**

Ma·han (mə·han′), **Alfred Thayer,** 1840–1914, U. S. admiral and naval historian.

Ma·ha·na·di (mə·hä′nə·dē) A river in eastern India, flowing 512 miles to the Bay of Bengal.

ma·ha·ra·ja (mä′hə·rä′jə, *Hind.* mə·hä′rä′jə) *n.* **1** A great Hindu prince; the title of some native rulers. **2** A prominent religious teacher of the Hindus. Also **ma′ha·ra′jah.** [<Hind. <Skt. *mahárája* <*maha* great + *rája* a king]

ma·ha·ra·ni (mä′hə·rä′nē, *Hind.* mə·hä′rä′nē) *n.* A Hindu princess; the wife of a maharaja. Also **ma′ha·ra′nee.** [<Hind. <*maha* great + *rání* a queen]

---

ma·hat·ma (mə·hat′mə, -hät′-) *n.* In theosophy or esoteric Buddhism, an adept of the highest order; literally, great-souled one: a title of respect. [<Skt. *mahátman* <*maha* great + *átman* soul] — **ma·hat′ma·ism** *n.*

Mah·di (mä′dē) *n.* The Moslem messiah, or one claiming the title; specifically, Mohammed Ahmed, 1843–85, who led a revolt in the Sudan, 1883. [<Arabic *mahdīy,* lit., he who is guided aright, pp. of *hadā* lead rightly] — **Mah′dism** *n.* — **Mah′dist** *adj. & n.*

Ma·hé (mä·hā′) A free city and former French settlement in SW Madras, India, on the Arabian Sea; 23 square miles.

Mahé Island The principal island in the Seychelles group in the western Indian Ocean; 56 square miles.

Ma·hi·can (mə·hē′kən) *n.* One of a tribe of North American Indians of Algonquian linguistic stock formerly occupying the territory from the Hudson River to Lake Champlain; later, one of an Algonquian tribe between the Hudson River and Narragansett Bay, dialectally divided into the *Mohegans* of the Thames and lower Connecticut rivers, and the *Mohicans,* occupying both banks of the Hudson. [<Algonquian, lit., a wolf]

mah jong (mä′jong′, jông′) A game of Chinese origin, usually for four persons, played with 144 tiles marked in suits, dice, and counters. Also **mah jongg.** [<dial. Chinese <Chinese *ma ch'iao,* lit., a house sparrow; from the design on one of the tiles]

Mah·ler (mä′lər), **Gustav,** 1860–1911, Austrian composer and conductor.

mahl·stick (mäl′stik′, môl′-) *n.* A staff with a ball at one end, used by painters to steady the hand while using the brush. Also spelled *maulstick.* [<Du. *maalstok* <*malen* paint + *stok* a stick]

Mah·moud (mä·mōōd′, mä′mōōd) Persian form of MOHAMMED. Also **Mah·mud′.** — **Mahmoud II,** 1785–1839, sultan of Turkey; defeated (1829) in Greek war for independence.

ma·hog·a·ny (mə·hog′ə·nē) *n.* **1** A large tropical American tree (genus *Swietenia*), with fine-grained, hard, reddish wood much used for cabinetwork. **2** The wood itself. **3** One of various other trees yielding a similar wood, as African mahogany (*Khaya ivorensis*); also its wood. **4** Acajou. **5** Any of the various shades of brownish-red or reddish-brown of the finished wood. — *adj.* **1** Of or pertaining to, or consisting of mahogany. **2** Of a mahogany color. [< obs. Sp. *mahogani,* prob. <Arawakan]

Ma·hom·et (mə·hom′it) See MOHAMMED.

Ma·hom·e·tan (mə·hom′ə·tən), etc. See MO-HAMMEDAN, etc.

Ma·hón (mə·hōn′, *Sp.* mä·ōn′) The chief city and port of Minorca, Balearic Islands: formerly *Port Mahón.*

Ma·hound (mə·hound′, -hōōnd′) *n.* **1** The prophet Mohammed. **2** *Scot.* Satan; an evil spirit. [<OF *Mahon, Mahum* <*Mahomet* Mohammed]

ma·hout (mə·hout′) *n.* The keeper and driver of an elephant. [<Hind. *mahāut, mahāvat* <Skt. *mahāmātra,* lit., great in measure]

Mah·rat·i (mä·rat′ē) See MARATHI.

Mah·rat·ta (mə·rat′ə) *n.* One of a Hindu people of SW and central India. Also spelled *Maratha.* [<Hind. *Marhaṭa* <Marathi *Maraṭhi* <Skt. *Mahārāṣṭra,* lit., great country]

Mäh·ren (mā′rən) The German name for MO-RAVIA.

Mäh·risch–Os·trau (mā′rish·ôs′trou) The German name for MORAVSKÁ OSTRAVA.

ma huang (mä hwäng′) A Chinese species of joint fir. [<Chinese]

Mai·a (mä′yə, mī′ə) **1** In Greek mythology, the eldest of the Pleiades, mother by Zeus of Hermes. **2** In Roman mythology, a goddess of growth and spring: identified with the Greek *Maia* and the *Bona Dea.* Also **Maia Ma·jes·ta** (mə·jes′tə).

maid (mād) *n.* **1** Any unmarried woman; virgin; girl; lass. **2** A female servant: also **maidservant.** [Short for MAIDEN]

mai·dan (mī·dän′) *n.* In Persia and India, a public plaza or parade ground; hence, an open space. [<Persian *maidán*]

Mai·da·nek (mī′də·nek) During World War II,

---

a Nazi concentration and extermination camp near Lublin, Poland.

maid·en (mād′n) n. 1 An unmarried woman, especially if young; a maid; virgin. 2 Something untried or unused, as a race horse that has never won an event. 3 A rude kind of beheading machine used in Scotland in the 16th and 17th centuries. —adj. 1 Pertaining to or suitable for a maiden. 2 Virgin; unmarried. 3 Initiatory; unused; untried. 4 Of or pertaining to the first use or experience: a *maiden* voyage. 5 Pure; sinless. [OE *mægden*, prob. dim. of *mægeth* a virgin] —**maid′en·li·ness** n. —**maid′en·ly** adj. & adv.

maid·en·hair (mād′n·hâr′) n. A very delicate and graceful fern (genus *Adiantum*) with an erect black stem, common in damp, rocky woods. Also **maidenhair fern.**

maidenhair tree The ginkgo.

maid·en·head (mād′n·hed′) n. 1 The hymen. 2 Maidenhood; virginity.

maid·en·hood (mād′n·hŏŏd′) n. The state of being a maiden; freshness; purity; virginity. Also **maid′hood.**

maiden name A woman's surname before marriage.

Maid Marian 1 The sweetheart and companion of Robin Hood. 2 A character in morris dances and other ancient sports: at first a May queen, later a grotesque buffoon, often impersonated by a boy.

maid of honor 1 An unmarried lady attendant upon an empress, queen, or princess: usually of noble birth. 2 The chief unmarried attendant of a bride at a wedding ceremony.

maid·ser·vant (mād′sûr′vənt) n. A female servant.

Maid·stone (mād′stən, -stōn) The county town of Kent, England.

Mai·du·gu·ri (mī·dōō′gŏŏr·ē) A city in NE Nigeria, capital of Bornu province.

ma·ieu·tic (mā·yōō′tik) adj. Helping to bring forth ideas and truths from the mind of a pupil by a series of pertinent questions: said of the Socratic method. Also **ma·ieu′ti·cal.** [< Gk. *maieutikos*, lit., obstetric < *maieuesthai* act as a midwife < *maia* a midwife]

mai·gre (mā′gər) adj. Not consisting of flesh or its juices: said of dishes used by Roman Catholics on days of abstinence; hence, of or appropriate for a fast. —n. A large marine food fish, the European *Sciaena aquila*. [< OF. See MEAGER.]

mai·hem (mā′hem) See MAYHEM.

Mai·kop (mī′kôp) A city in the NW Caucasus mountains, Russian S.F.S.R. Also **May′kop.**

mail[1] (māl) n. 1 The governmental system for handling letters, etc., by post. 2 Letters, magazines and other printed matter, parcels, etc., consigned and sent from place to place under a governmental post-office system. 3 The collection or delivery of postal matter at a specified time: My letter missed the *mail*. 4 Letters, papers, etc., received by, or for, a person: Your *mail* is on the table. 5 A conveyance, as a train, plane, etc., for carrying postal matter. —adj. Pertaining to or used in the process of conveying or handling mail. —v.t. To send by mail, as letters; deposit in a mailbox or at a post office; post. ◆ Homophone: *male*. [< OF *male* < OHG *malha* a wallet] —**mail′a·ble** adj.

mail[2] (māl) n. 1 Armor of chains, rings, or scales: often called **chain mail.** 2 Any strong covering or defense, as the shell of a turtle. —**coat of mail** A hauberk. —v.t. To cover with or as with mail. ◆ Homophone: *male*. [< OF *maille* < L *macula* spot, mesh of a net]

mail[3] (māl) n. Scot. & Brit. Dial. That which is paid; rent; wages. Also **maill.** ◆ Homophone: *male*. [OE *māl* < ON, speech, agreement; infl. in sense by ON *māle* contract, stipend]

mail·bag (māl′bag′) n. A bag or pack in which mail is transported.

mail·box (māl′boks′) n. 1 A box in which letters, etc., are posted for collection. 2 A box into which private mail is put when delivered. Also **mail box.**

CHAIN MAIL ARMOR

mail car A railroad car for carrying mail.

mail·catch·er (māl′kach′ər) n. A mechanical device for transferring mailbags to or from a moving train.

mailed (māld) adj. 1 Covered or armed with mail. 2 Zool. Having a defensive armor, as scales. [< MAIL[2]]

mailed fist Menace of attack or violence; especially, menace of aggressive war.

mail·er (mā′lər) n. 1 A mail boat. 2 An addressing machine: also **mailing machine.** 3 One who mails a letter.

mail·gram (māl′gram′) n. U.S. A message transmitted electronically between place of origin and destination, converted to written form, and delivered in the next scheduled distribution of mail. [< MAIL + (TELE)GRAM]

mail·ing (mā′ling) n. 1 The act of sending mail. 2 The mail sent at one time. 3 Scot. A rented piece of ground; farm; homestead: also **mail′en.**

mailing list A list of names, as of individuals, organizations, etc., to which advertising circulars, announcements, solicitations, and the like, are sent.

Mail·lol (má·yôl′), **Aristide,** 1861–1944, French sculptor.

mail·lot (mī·yō′) n. A tightly fitting garment which covers the torso, used by dancers, acrobats, and swimmers. [< F, dim. of *máille* knitted material, lit., mail[2]]

mail·man (māl′man′, -mən) n. pl. **·men** (-men′, -mən) A letter-carrier; postman.

mail order An order for goods, sent and filled through the agency of the mail. —**mail-or·der** (ôr′dər) adj.

mail train 1 A railway train that carries mail. 2 A train of wagons that formerly carried mail in the western United States.

maim (mām) v.t. To deprive of the use of a bodily part; mutilate; disable. —n. Rare A crippling; mutilation; maiming. See MAYHEM. [< OF *mahaigner, mayner*, ult. origin uncertain] —**maim′er** n.

Mai·mon·ides (mī·mon′ə·dēz), 1135–1204, Spanish rabbi, theologian, and philosopher: also called *Moses ben Maimon.*

main[1] (mān) n. 1 A chief conduit or conductor, as for conveying gas, water, etc. 2 The mainland. 3 *Poetic* The ocean. 4 Violent effort; strength: chiefly in the phrase *with might and main.* 5 The chief part; the most important point. —**in** (or **for**) **the main** For the most part; on the whole. —adj. 1 First or chief in size, rank, importance, strength, extent, etc.; principal; chief; leading: the *main* building, the *main* line of a railroad, with which branch lines connect. 2 undivided; unqualified; full: by *main* force. 3 Designating any broad extent or expanse, as of land or sea. 4 *Naut.* Near or connected with the mainsail or mainmast. 5 *Brit. Dial.* Considerable; remarkable. 6 *Obs.* Vast; mighty; powerful. —adv. *Brit. Dial.* Very; greatly; extremely. ◆ Homophone: *mane.* [OE *mægen*] —**main′ly** adv.

main[2] (mān) n. 1 A match of several battles at cockfighting. 2 A hand or throw of dice; also, a number selected by the caster before he throws the dice in games of hazard and craps. ◆ Homophone: *mane.* [? < MAIN[1], as in *main chance*]

main[3] (mān) Scot. v.i. To moan. —n. A moan. ◆ Homophone: *mane.*

Main (mān, Ger. mīn) A river in western Germany, flowing 305 miles west to the Rhine.

main deck *Naut.* The chief deck of a vessel; on a warship, the topmost deck stretching from stem to stern; on a merchantman, the deck between and below the poop and forecastle decks.

main drag U.S. Slang The principal street or section of a city.

Maine (mān), **Sir Henry James,** 1822–88, English jurist.

Maine (mān) 1 A State of the NE United States bordering on Canada and the Atlantic; 32,562 square miles; capital, Augusta; entered the Union March 15, 1820; nickname, *Pine-Tree State*: abbr. ME 2 An ancient province of western France.

Maine (mān) A U.S. battleship, blown up in Havana harbor, Feb. 15, 1898, with the loss of 260 lives: one of the events precipitating the Spanish–American War.

Main-fran·ken (mīn′frang′kən) The former name of Lower Franconia, 1938–45.

main·land (mān′land, -lənd) n. A principal body of land; a continent, as distinguished from an island. —**main′land·er** n.

Main·land (mān′lənd) 1 Pomona Island. 2 The largest of the Shetland Islands, Scotland; 406 square miles.

main·line (mān′līn′) n. A main road, railroad line, etc. —v.t. & v.i. **·lined, ·lin·ing** Slang To inject (a narcotic drug, especially heroin) directly into a vein. —**main′lin·er** n.

Main Line A traditionally wealthy and fashionable residential district outside of Philadelphia.

main·mast (mān′məst, -mast′, -mäst′) n. *Naut.* The principal mast of a vessel: ordinarily, the second mast from the bow.

main·sail (mān′səl, -sāl′) n. *Naut.* A sail bent to the main yard, or one carried on the mainmast: in a square-rigged vessel, called the **main course.**

main sequence *Astron.* The area of the Hertzsprung–Russell diagram that includes the sun and the majority of stars.

main·sheet (mān′shēt′) n. *Naut.* The sheet by which the mainsail is trimmed and set.

main·spring (mān′spring′) n. 1 The principal spring of a mechanism, as of a watch. 2 The most efficient cause or motive.

main·stay (mān′stā′) n. 1 *Naut.* The rope from the mainmast head forward, used to steady the mast in that direction. 2 A chief support or dependence.

main·stream (mān′strēm′) n. The main or middle course or direction: in the *mainstream* of American political thought.

Main Street The principal business street of a small town: a symbol of its manners, customs, culture, typical thinking, etc.

main·tain (mān·tān′) v.t. 1 To carry on or continue; engage in, as a correspondence. 2 To keep unimpaired or in proper condition: to *maintain* roads; to *maintain* a reputation. 3 To supply with food or livelihood; support; pay for. 4 To uphold; claim to be true. 5 To assert or state; affirm. 6 To hold or defend, as against attack. See synonyms under AFFIRM, ALLEGE, ASSERT, JUSTIFY, KEEP, PRESERVE, RETAIN, SUPPORT. [< OF *maintenir* < L *manu tenere*, lit., hold in one's hand < *manu*, ablative of *manus* hand + *tenere* hold]

main·te·nance (mān′tə·nəns) n. 1 The act of maintaining. 2 Means of support. 3 *Law* The officious intermeddling in a suit, by assisting or maintaining either party, with money or otherwise. [< OF *maintenance* < *maintenir* MAINTAIN]

Main·te·non (mant·nôn′), **Marquise de,** 1635–1719, Françoise d'Aubigné; second wife of Louis XIV of France.

main·top (mān′top′) n. *Naut.* A platform at the head of the lower section of the mainmast.

main·top·gal·lant·mast (mān′tə·gal′ənt·məst, mast′, -mäst′, -top-) n. *Naut.* On a square-rigged vessel, the mast next above the mainmast.

main·top·mast (mān′top′məst) n. *Naut.* 1 On a square-rigged vessel, the mast next above the maintopgallantmast. 2 On a fore-and-aft-rigged ship, the mast next above the mainmast.

main yard *Naut.* The lower yard on the mainmast.

Mainz (mīnts) A city on the Rhine, capital of Rhineland-Palatinate, West Germany: French *Mayence.*

ma·iol·i·ca (mä·yol′ē·kä) See MAJOLICA.

mai·o·sis (mī·ō′sis) See MEIOSIS (def. 1).

mair (mâr) adj. & n. Scot. More.

maist (māst) adj., n., & adv. Scot. Most.

mais·ter (mās′tər) n. Scot. Master.

Mai·sur (mī·sŏŏr′) See MYSORE.

Mait·land (māt′lənd), **Frederic William,** 1850–1906, English jurist and historian.

maî·tre (me′tr′) n. French Master.

maî·tre d' (mā′trə dē′) pl. **maî·tre d's** (dēz′) A headwaiter. [Short for MAÎTRE D'HOTEL]

maître d'hô·tel (dō·tel′) French 1 The proprietor or manager of a hotel. 2 A headwaiter; steward. 3 A sauce of melted butter, parsley, and lemon juice or vinegar.

maize (māz) n. 1 A tall, stout food and forage plant (*Zea mays*). 2 Its grain; Indian corn. 3 A light, soft shade of yellow; any of the various yellow tints of ripe corn. ◆ Homophone: *maze*. [< Sp. *maíz* < Taino *mahiz*]

maize·bird (māz′bûrd′) n. A bird that feeds on Indian corn, as the red-winged blackbird.

ma·jes·tic (mə·jes′tik) *adj.* Having or exhibiting majesty; stately; royal, august. Also **ma·jes′ti·cal.** See synonyms under AWFUL, GRAND, IMPERIAL, KINGLY, SUBLIME. — **ma·jes′ti·cal·ly** *adv.* — **ma·jes′ti·cal·ness** *n.*

maj·es·ty (maj′is·tē) *n. pl.* **·ties** Exalted dignity; stateliness; grandeur; especially, **His, Her,** or **Your Majesty,** a title given to monarchs. [<OF *majesté* <L *majestas, -tatis* (related to *majus,* neut. compar. of *magnus* great)]

ma·jol·i·ca (mə·jol′i·kə, -yol′-) *n.* A kind of Italian pottery, glazed and decorated, usually in rich colors and Renaissance designs; any glazed Italian pottery; faience. Also spelled *maiolica.* [<Ital. *maiolica,* prob. < *Majolica,* early name of MAJORCA, where formerly made]

ma·jor (mā′jər) *adj.* **1** Greater in number, quantity, or extent. **2** Greater in dignity or importance; of primary consideration; principal; leading. **3** *Music* **a** Designating a chord or interval greater by a half-step than the preceding minor. **b** Containing a major third, sixth, and seventh. See INTERVAL. **4** *Logic* Designating the first premise of a syllogism, or the premise containing the first proposition. **5** *Law* Being of legal age. — *n.* **1** An officer in the U.S. Army, Air Force, or Marine Corps ranking next above a captain and next below a lieutenant colonel. **2** *Law* One who is of legal age. **3** *Music* A major key, chord, or interval. **4** *U.S.* The specialized course of study in a definite field which a college or university student follows to obtain his degree. **5** *U.S.* A student who follows a (specified) course of study: an English *major.* — *v.i.* To pursue a definite field of study: with *in:* to *major* in history. [<L, compar. of *magnus* great. Doublet of MAYOR.]

Ma·jor·ca (mə·jôr′kə) The largest of the Balearic Islands; 1,352 square miles; capital, Palma: Spanish *Mallorca.* — **Ma·jor′can** *adj.* & *n.*

ma·jor·do·mo (mā′jər·dō′mō) *n. pl.* **·mos** **1** The chief steward of a royal household. **2** A butler. **3** *SW U.S.* The overseer of a ranch. [<Sp. *mayordomo* <Med. L *major domus* chief of a house < *major* an elder (<L, greater) + *domus* a house]

major general See under GENERAL.

ma·jor·i·ty (mə·jôr′ə·tē, -jor′-) *n. pl.* **·ties** **1** More than half of a given number or group; the greater part. **2** The amount or number by which one group of things exceeds another group; excess. **3** The age at which the laws of a country permit a person to manage his or her own affairs: in most States of the United States, the age of 21 years. **4** The rank or commission of a major. **5** In U.S. politics, more than half of the people; more than half of the votes cast. **6** The number of votes cast for a candidate over and above the number cast for his nearest opponent; a plurality. **7** The party having the most power in a legislature. [<MF *majorité* <L *majoritas, -tatis* < *major.* See MAJOR.]

major key *Music* A key based on the tones of a major scale, the intervals being a half-step larger than minor intervals.

major league In baseball, either of the two main groups of professional teams in the United States. — **ma′jor-league′** *adj.*

major mode See under MODE.

major scale See under SCALE.

major suit In bridge, either of the sets of spades and hearts: so called from their higher point value.

major term See under TERM.

ma·jus·cule (mə·jus′kyōōl) *n.* A capital letter; especially, a large initial letter, as in old manuscripts. [<F <L *majuscula (littera),* fem. of *majusculus* somewhat larger, dim. of *major.* See MAJOR.] — **ma·jus′cu·lar** *adj.*

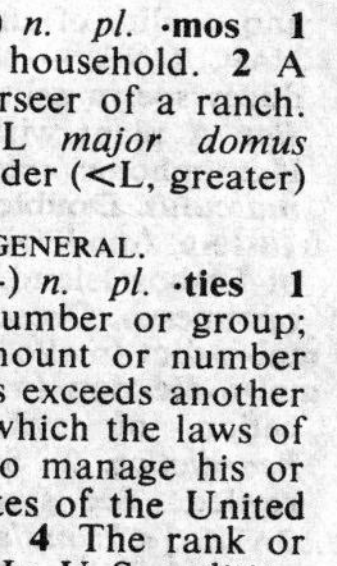

MAJUSCULE

mak (mak) *v.t.* & *v.i. Scot.* To make.

Ma·kas·sar (mə·kas′ər) See MACASSAR.

Ma·ka·te·a (mä′kä·tā′ə) An island dependency of Tahiti in the Society Islands.

make[1] (māk) *v.* **made, mak·ing** *v.t.* **1** To bring about the existence of by the shaping or combining of materials; produce; build; construct; fashion. **2** To bring about; cause: Don't *make* trouble. **3** To bring to some state or condition; cause to be: The wind *made* him cold. **4** To appoint or assign; elect: They *made* him captain. **5** To form or create in the mind, as a plan. **6** To compose or create, as a poem or piece of music. **7** To understand or infer to be the meaning or significance; interpret; think: What do you *make* of it? **8** To put forward; advance: to *make* an offer. **9** To present, as for record; utter or express: to *make* a declaration. **10** To obtain for oneself; earn; accumulate: to *make* a fortune. **11** To amount to; add up to: Four quarts *make* a gallon. **12** To bring the total to: That *makes* five attempts. **13** To develop into; become: He *made* a good soldier. **14** To accomplish; effect or form: to *make* an agreement. **15** To estimate to be; reckon: He *made* the height twenty feet. **16** To induce or force; compel: He *made* me do it! **17** To draw up, enact, or frame, as laws, testaments, etc. **18** To prepare for use, as a bed. **19** To afford or provide: This brandy *makes* good drinking. **20** To be the essential element or determinant of: Stone walls do not a prison *make.* **21** To cause the success of: His speech *made* him politically. **22** To traverse; cover: to *make* fifty miles before noon. **23** To travel at the rate of: to *make* fifty miles per hour. **24** To arrive at; reach: to *make* Boston. **25** To board before departure: to *make* a train. **26** To earn so as to count on a score: to *make* a touchdown. **27** *Electr.* To complete (a circuit). **28** *Colloq.* To win a place on: to *make* the team. **29** In card games: **a** To declare as trump. **b** To capture a trick with (a card). **c** To shuffle: to *make* the deck. **30** In bridge, to win (a bid). **31** *U.S. Slang.* To seduce. — *v.i.* **32** To cause something to assume a specified condition: to *make* ready; to *make* fast. **33** To act or behave in a certain manner: to *make* merry. **34** To start: They *made* to go. **35** To go or extend in some direction: with *to* or *toward.* **36** To flow, as the tide; rise, as water. — **to make as if** (or **as though**) To pretend. — **to make away with** **1** To carry off; steal. **2** To get rid of; destroy. — **to make believe** To pretend. — **to make do** To get along with what is available, especially with an inferior substitute. — **to make for** **1** To go toward. **2** To attack; assail. **3** To have effect on; contribute to. — **to make heavy weather** *Naut.* To roll and pitch, as a ship in a storm. — **to make it** To succeed in doing something. — **to make off** To leave suddenly; run away. — **to make off with** To steal. — **to make out** **1** To see; discern. **2** To comprehend; understand. **3** To establish by evidence. **4** To fill out; draw up, as a bank draft. **5** To be successful; manage. — **to make over** **1** To put into new form; renovate. **2** To transfer title or possession of. — **to make up** **1** To compose; compound, as a prescription. **2** To be the parts of; comprise: These elements *make up* the structure. **3** To settle differences and become friendly again: to kiss and *make up.* **4** To devise; invent; fabricate: to *make up* an answer. **5** To supply what is lacking in. **6** To compensate for; atone for. **7** To settle; decide: to *make up* one's mind. **8** *Printing* To arrange, as lines, into columns or pages. **9** To put cosmetics on (the face). **10** In education, to repeat (an examination or course one has failed), or take (an examination) one has missed. — **to make up to** *Colloq.* To make a show of friendliness and affection toward; flatter. — *n.* **1** The manner in which parts or qualities are grouped to constitute a whole; constitution; structure; shape. **2** The operation or product of manufacture; brand: a new *make* of automobile. **3** The amount produced; yield. **4** The closing or completion of an electrical circuit. **5** A declaration (def. 3). — **on the make** *Slang* **1** Greedy for profit; interested only in making money. **2** Eager for amorous conquest. [OE *macian*]

Synonyms (verb): become, cause, compel, compose, constitute, constrain, construct, create, do, effect, establish, execute, fabricate, fashion, force, frame, get, manufacture, occasion, perform, reach, require, shape. *Make* is essentially causative; to the idea of cause all its various senses may be traced (compare synonyms for CAUSE *noun*). To *make* is to *cause* to exist, or to *cause* to exist in a certain form or in certain relations; it thus includes the idea of *create. Make* includes also the idea of *compose, constitute;* as, The parts *make* up the whole. Similarly, to *cause* a voluntary agent to do a certain act is to *make* him do it, or *compel* him to do it, *compel* fixing the attention more on the process, *make* on the accomplished fact. See COMPEL, GET, PRODUCE, REACH. *Antonyms:* see synonyms for ABOLISH, BREAK, DEMOLISH.

make[2] (māk) *n. Obs.* A mate. [OE *gemaca*]

make-and-break (māk′ənd·brāk′) *n. Electr.* A device for making and breaking an electrical circuit.

make-be·lieve (māk′bi·lēv′) *adj.* Pretended; unreal. — *n.* A mere pretense; sham. Also **make′-be·lief′** (-lēf′).

make-fast (māk′fast′, -fäst′) *n. Naut.* An iron ring or other object to which a boat is made fast.

make·less (māk′lis) *adj. Obs.* **1** Without a mate. **2** Matchless. [<MAKE[2] + -LESS]

make·peace (māk′pēs′) *n.* A peacemaker.

mak·er (mā′kər) *n.* **1** One who makes. **2** A manufacturer. **3** *Law* One who signs a promissory note. **4** *Archaic* A poet.

Mak·er (mā′kər) *n.* God, as the creator of the universe.

-maker *combining form* One who or that which produces: *glassmaker.* [<MAKE]

make-read·y (māk′red′ē) *n. Printing* The operation of leveling up and adjusting a type form on a press so that all parts of it will give a clear, clean, and uniform impression when printed.

make·shift (māk′shift′) *adj.* Having the character of or being a temporary resource: also **make′shift′y.** — *n.* Something adopted as a temporary contrivance in any emergency.

make-up (māk′up′) *n.* **1** The arrangement or combination of the parts of which anything is composed; an aggregate of qualities. **2** *Printing* The arrangement of composed type in pages, columns, or forms, as in imposition. **3** The costumes, wigs, cosmetics, etc., used to assume a theatrical role; also, the art of applying or assuming them. **4** Lipstick, powder, rouge, etc., applied to a woman's face.

make·weight (māk′wāt′) *n.* **1** That which is thrown into a scale to increase weight. **2** Any person or thing made use of to fill up a deficiency.

Ma·ke·yev·ka A city in the Donbas, eastern Ukraine.

Ma·khach·ka·la A port on the Caspian Sea, capital of Dagestan in Russia.

Ma·kin (mä′kin, mug′in) See BUTARITARI.

mak·ing (mā′king) *n.* **1** The act of causing, fashioning, or constructing; workmanship. **2** That which contributes to improvement or success: He has the *making* of a fine character. **3** A quantity of anything made at one time; batch. **4** *Often pl.* The materials or ingredients required to make something. **5** Composition; structure; make.

-making *combining form* Act of causing or producing; creating or causing to be: *paper-making.* [<MAKE]

mal- *prefix* Bad; ill; evil; wrong; defective; imperfect; uneven: signifying also simple negation, and forming words directly from Latin and mediately through French: opposed to *bene-, eu-.* [<F *mal-* <L *male-* < *malus* bad]

Many words containing the prefix *mal-* are self-explaining, the prefix simply adding the meaning defective or evil:

maladaptation	**malconstruction**
maladjustment	**malexecution**
maladminister	**malinfluence**
malconformation	**malnutrition**

Mal·a·bar (mal′ə·bär) A district of SW India extending 450 miles NW from Cape Comorin to the Madras-Bombay border. Also **Malabar Coast.**

Ma·lac·ca (mə·lak′ə) A port on the Strait of Malacca and the capital of the **Settlement of**

Malacca, a State of Malaya, formerly under British protection; 633 square miles. *Malay* **Ma·lak'a.**

Malacca, Strait of A channel between the Malay Peninsula and Sumatra connecting the Andaman Sea and the South China Sea.

Malacca cane A walking stick made from the wood of an Asian rattan palm *(Calamus rotang).* [from *Malacca*]

ma·la·ceous (mə·lā'shəs) *adj.* Designating a family *(Malaceae)* of trees, including the apple, pear, quince, etc. See POMACEOUS. [<NL, family name <L *malum* an apple <Gk. *mēlon*]

Mal·a·chi (mal'ə·kī) A masculine personal name. [<Hebrew *malākhī*, lit., my messenger] —**Malachi** A minor Hebrew prophet of the fifth century B.C.; also, the book containing his prophecies.

mal·a·chite (mal'ə·kīt) *n.* A green basic cupric carbonate, $CuCO_3 \cdot Cu(OH)_2$, found usually massive, rarely in crystals, and sometimes as an incrustation. It is one of the ores of copper. [<OF *melochite*, ult. <L *malache* a mallow <Gk. *malachē*; so called because resembling mallow leaves in color]

malachite green A pigment made of malachite, having an intense bluish–green color. Compare BICE GREEN.

malaco– *combining form* Soft; mucilaginous: *malacopterous.* Also, before vowels, **malac–.** [<Gk. *malakos* soft]

mal·a·coid (mal'ə·koid) *adj.* Having a soft texture.[<MALAC(O)- + -OID]

mal·a·col·o·gy (mal'ə·kol'ə·jē) *n.* The branch of zoology that treats of mollusks. [MALACO- + -LOGY]

mal·a·cop·ter·ous (mal'ə·kop'tər·əs) *adj.* Having soft fins, as certain fishes. [<MALACO- + -PTEROUS]

mal·a·cos·tra·can (mal'·ə·kos'trə·kən) *n.* Any of a division or subclass *(Malacostraca)* of crustaceans, embracing crabs, lobsters, crayfish, etc. —*adj.* Of or pertaining to the *Malacostraca:* also **mal'a·cos'tra·cous.** [<NL *Malacostraca,* subclass name <Gk. *malakostrakos* soft–shelled <*malakos* soft + *ostrakon* a shell]

mal·ad·dress (mal'ə·dres') *n.* Awkwardness or rudeness in speech or manner; lack of politeness or tact. [<F *maladresse* <*maladroit* MALADROIT]

mal·ad·just·ed (mal'ə·jus'tid) *adj.* **1** Imperfectly adjusted. **2** *Psychol.* Poorly adapted to one's environment through conflict between personal desires and external circumstances. —**mal'ad·just'ment** *n.*

mal·ad·min·is·ter (mal'əd·min'is·tər) *v.t.* To administer badly or dishonestly.

mal·ad·min·is·tra·tion (mal'əd·min'is·trā'shən) *n.* Bad management, as of public affairs.

mal·a·droit (mal'ə·droit') *adj.* Clumsy or blundering. See synonyms under AWKWARD. [<F <*mal-* MAL- +*adroit* clever] —**mal'a·droit'ly** *adv.* —**mal'a·droit'ness** *n.*

mal·a·dy (mal'ə·dē) *n. pl.* **·dies 1** A disease, especially when chronic or deep–seated; sickness; illness. **2** Any disordered condition. See synonyms under DISEASE. [<OF *maladie* <LL *male habitus* <L *male* ill + *habitus,* pp. of *habere* have]

ma·la fi·de (mā'lə fī'dē) *Latin* In bad faith.

Mal·a·ga (mal'ə·gə) *n.* **1** A rich, sweet white wine made in Málaga, Spain. **2** A white, sweet grape of the muscat variety, grown in Spain and California.

Mál·a·ga (mal'ə·gə, *Sp.* mä'lä·gä) A port on the Mediterranean in Andalusia, southern Spain.

Mal·a·gas·y (mal'ə·gas'ē) *adj.* Of or pertaining to Madagascar, its inhabitants, or their language. —*n.* **1** A native of Madagascar. **2** The Indonesian language of Madagascar.

Malagasy Republic The former name of Madagascar (1958–1974); comprising the island of Madagascar; 227,602 square miles; capital, Tananarive.

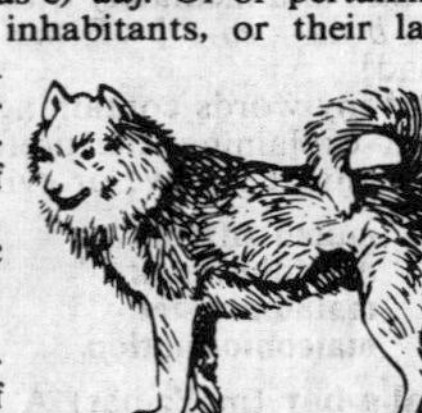

ESKIMO MALAMUTE
(From 22 to 25 inches high at the shoulder)

mal·aise (mal·āz', *Fr.* mȧ·lez') *n.* Uneasiness; indisposition. [<F <*mal* ill + *aise* EASE]

Ma·lai·ta (mə·lā'tə) One of the British Solomon Islands; 2,500 miles.

ma·la·mute (mä'lə·myōōt, mal'ə-) *n.* A large sled dog of Alaska, having a compact body, a thick, long coat, usually gray or black–and–white, a broad head, straight, big–boned forelegs, and well–cushioned feet. Also spelled *malemute, malemiut.* [Orig., name of an Innuit tribe, alter. of Eskimo (Malamute) *Mahlemut* <*Mahle,* the tribe's name +*mut* a village]

Ma·lan (mə·län'), **Daniel François,** 1874–1959, South African prime minister 1948–54.

mal·an·ders (mal'ən·dərz) *n. pl.* A scaly disease on the hock and at the bend of the knee of the foreleg of a horse: also spelled *mallenders.* Compare SALLENDERS. [<OF *malandre* a sore in a horse's knee <L *malandria*]

Ma·lang (mä·läng') A city in eastern Java.

mal·a·pert (mal'ə·pûrt) *adj.* Bold or forward; impudent; saucy. —*n.* A saucy person. [<OF <*mal-* MAL- + *apert, espert* clever, able <L *expertus.* See EXPERT.] —**mal'a·pert'ly** *adv.* —**mal'a·pert'ness** *n.*

mal·ap·por·tion·ment (mal'ə·pôr'shən·mənt, -pōr'-) *n.* Unfair apportionment of representatives in a legislature.

Mal·a·prop (mal'ə·prop), **Mrs.** A character in Sheridan's *The Rivals,* who uses words inappropriately. [<MALAPROPOS]

mal·a·prop·ism (mal'ə·prop·iz'əm) *n.* The incorrect or inappropriate use of a word; a verbal blunder. [after Mrs. *Malaprop*] —**mal'a·pro'pi·an** (-prō'pē·ən) *adj.*

mal·ap·ro·pos (mal'ap·rə·pō') *adj.* Out of place; not appropriate. [<F *mal à propos* not to the point <*mal* ill + *à* to + *propos* purpose] —**mal'ap·ro·po'ism** *n.*

ma·lar (mā'lər) *adj. Anat.* Relating to or being in or near the cheek. —*n.* The cheek bone. [<NL *malaris* <L *mala* jaw, cheek]

ma·lar·i·a (mə·lâr'ē·ə) *n.* **1** *Pathol.* A disease caused by any of certain animal parasites (genus *Plasmodium*), which are introduced into the system by the bite of the infected anopheles mosquito and invade the red corpuscles of the blood, causing intermittent chills and fever. **2** Any foul or unwholesome air, as from decomposition; miasma; mephitis. [<Ital. *mal'aria, mala aria,* lit., bad air] —**ma·lar'i·al, ma·lar'i·an, ma·lar'i·ous** *adj.*

ma·lar·i·o·ther·a·py (mə·lâr'ē·ō·ther'ə·pē) *n. Med.* The treatment of cerebrospinal syphilis by inoculation with the parasite causing tertian malaria. [MALARI(A) + *-o-* +THERAPY]

ma·lar·ky (mə·lär'kē) *n. Slang* Insincere or senseless talk; bunk. Also **ma·lar'key.** [? <an Irish personal name]

mal·as·sim·i·la·tion (mal'ə·sim'ə·lā'shən) *n.* Imperfect or faulty assimilation.

mal·ate (mal'āt, mā'lāt) *n. Chem.* A salt or ester of malic acid. [<MAL(IC) + -ATE[3]]

Ma·la·wi (mä'lä·wē) An independent member of the Commonwealth of Nations in SE Africa; 49,177 square miles; capital, Zomba: formerly *Nyasaland.*

Ma·lay (mā'lā, mə·lā') *n.* **1** A member of the dominant race in Malaysia; a Malayan. **2** The language spoken on the Malay Peninsula and widely used as a lingua franca throughout the East Indies, belonging to the Indonesian subfamily of Austronesian languages. **3** A variety of domestic fowl. —*adj.* Of or pertaining to the Malays; Malayan.

Ma·lay·a (mə·lā'ə) A federation of eleven states in the Commonwealth of Nations, now incorporated in Malaysia, including the former Federated Malay States and Unfederated Malay States, the two settlements of Malacca and Penang on the southern Malay Peninsula, and adjacent islands; 50,600 square miles; capital, Kuala Lumpur: formerly **Malayan Union.** Also **Malaya.**

Mal·a·ya·lam (mal'ə·yä'ləm) *n.* The language of the Malabar coast, India, related to Tamil, and belonging to the Dravidian family of languages.

Ma·lay·an (mə·lā'ən) *adj.* **1** Malay. **2** Indonesian. —*n.* **1** A Malay (def. 1). **2** An Indonesian. **3** The Indonesian subfamily of Austronesian languages.

Malay Archipelago An island group in the Indian and Pacific oceans SE of Asia, including Java, Borneo, Sumatra, Celebes, Timor, the Lesser Sunda Islands, and the Philippines; about 773,000 square miles: also the *East Indies, Malaysia.*

Ma·lay·o–Pol·y·ne·sian (mə·lā'ō·pol'ə·nē'zhən, -shən) *adj.* **1** Of or pertaining to the brown peoples of the Indian and Pacific oceans, including Malays and Polynesians. **2** Designating the languages of these peoples. —*n.* The Austronesian family of languages. [<MALAY + *-o-* + POLYNESIAN]

Malay Peninsula The southernmost peninsula of Asia, including the Federation of Malaya and part of Thailand.

Ma·lay·sia (mə·lā'zhə, -shə) **1** A federation of fourteen states in the Commonwealth of Nations, including Malaya, Sabah, and Sarawak; 127,334 square miles; capital, Kuala Lumpur. **2** The Malay Archipelago. —**Ma·lay'sian** *adj. & n.*

Mal·colm (mal'kəm) A masculine personal name. [<Celtic, servant of (St.) Columba]

Mal·colm X (mal'kəm eks) Name adopted by *Malcolm Little,* 1925–65, U.S. political and religious leader, active in the Black Muslim movement; assassinated.

mal·con·tent (mal'kən·tent) *adj.* Discontented, as with a government or economic system; dissatisfied; uneasy. —*n.* A person dissatisfied with the existing state of affairs; one rebellious against authority. [<OF <*mal-* MAL- + *content* CONTENT]

mal de dents (mȧl də däṅ') *French* Toothache.

mal de mer (mȧl də mâr') *French* Seasickness.

mal·dis·tri·bu·tion (mal'dis·trə·byōō'shən) *n.* Unfair or uneven distribution of people or goods.

Mal·dive Islands (môl'dīv, mal'-) An independent republic in the Indian Ocean; 12 islands SW of Sri Lanka; 115 square miles; capital, Malé.

mal du pays (mȧl dü pā·ē') *French* Homesickness.

male (māl) *adj.* **1** Pertaining to the sex that begets young; masculine. **2** Made up of men or boys. **3** *Bot.* Having stamens, but no pistil; also, adapted to fertilize, but not to produce fruit, as stamens. **4** Denoting some implement or object, as a gage or plug, which fits into a corresponding part known as *female.* **5** Indicating superiority of strength and quality of anything. See synonyms under MASCULINE. —*n.* **1** An organism that produces sperm cells; a male person or animal. **2** *Bot.* A plant with only staminate flowers. ◆ Homophone: *mail.* [<OF *male, mascle* <L *masculus.* Doublet of MASCULINE.]

Ma·le·a (mə·lē'ə), **Cape 1** The SE extremity of Lesbos Island. **2** The SE extremity of Peloponnesus, Greece, on the Aegean.

mal·e·dict (mal'ə·dikt) *adj. Obs.* Accursed.

mal·e·dic·tion (mal'ə·dik'shən) *n.* **1** An invocation of evil; a cursing: opposed to *benediction.* **2** Slander. **3** The state of being reviled. See synonyms under IMPRECATION, OATH. [<L *maledictio, -onis* <*maledictus,* pp. of *maledicere* <*male* ill +*dicere* speak] —**mal'e·dic'to·ry** *adj.*

mal·e·fac·tor (mal'ə·fak'tər) *n.* One who commits a crime. [<L <*malefactus,* pp. of *malefacere* <*male* ill + *facere* do] —**mal'e·fac'tion** *n.* —**mal'e·fac'tress** *n. fem.*

male fern A fern *(Dryopteris filixmas)* used in medicine as a vermifuge.

ma·lef·ic (mə·lef'ik) *adj.* Occasioning evil or disaster. [<L *maleficus* <*malefacere.* See MALEFACTOR.]

ma·lef·i·cent (mə·lef'ə·sənt) *adj.* Causing or doing evil or mischief; harmful: opposed to *beneficent.*[<L *maleficus* MALEFIC]

ma·le·ic (mə·lē'ik) *adj. Chem.* Pertaining to or designating a white, crystalline, astringent acid, $C_4H_4O_4$, prepared by the catalytic oxidation of benzene: used as a dye for fabrics, etc. [<F *maléique* <*malique* MALIC]

Ma·lé Island (ma'lā) The capital of the Maldive Islands.

Ma·le·ku·la (mal'ə·kōō'lə) An island of the New Hebrides group; 980 square miles.

ma·le·mute (mä'lə·myōōt, mal'ə-), **ma·le·miut** See MALAMUTE.

Mal·en·kov (mal'ən·kôv, mə·len'-; *Russian* mä'·lyin·kôf), **Georgi,** born 1902, U.S.S.R. leader; premier 1953–55.

mal·en·ten·du (mȧl·äṅ·täṅ·dü') *n. French* Misunderstanding.

Mal·e·ven·tum (mal'ə·ven'təm) The ancient name for BENEVENTO.

ma·lev·o·lent (mə·lev'ə·lənt) *adj.* Having an evil disposition toward others; ill–disposed. See synonyms under MALICIOUS. [<OF <L *malevolens, -entis* <*male* ill + *volens, -entis,* ppr. of *velle* wish, will] —**ma·lev'o·lence** *n.* —**ma·lev'o·lent·ly** *adv.*

mal·fea·sance (mal·fē′zəns) n. Law The performance of some act which is unlawful or wrongful or which one has specifically contracted not to perform: said usually of official misconduct. Compare MISFEASANCE, NONFEASANCE. [<AF malfaisance <OF malfaisant < mal ill + faisant, ppr. of faire de <L facere]

mal·fea·sant (mal·fē′zənt) adj. Guilty of malfeasance. —n. A person guilty of malfeasance.

mal·for·ma·tion (mal′fôr·mā′shən) n. Any irregularity, anomaly, or abnormal deformation in the structure of an organism. [<MAL- + FORMATION]

mal·formed (mal·fôrmd′) adj. Badly formed or made; deformed.

mal·func·tion (mal·fungk′shən) n. Physiol. Impairment or disturbance of any bodily function; dysfunction.

Mal·gache (mál·gásh′) n. & adj. French Madagascan.

mal·gré (mál·grā′) prep. French In spite of; notwithstanding. Also, Obs., maugre.

malgré lui (lwē) French In spite of himself or herself.

Mal·herbe (má·lerb′), François de, 1555–1628, French poet.

Ma·li (mä′lē) A landlocked, independent republic in west Africa; 464,873 miles; capital, Bamako; formerly French Sudan, an overseas territory. —**Ma′li** adj. & n.

mal·ic (mal′ik, mā′lik) adj. 1 Of, pertaining to, or obtained from apples. 2 Chem. Pertaining to or designating a deliquescent crystalline acid, $C_4H_6O_5$, with a pleasant taste: contained in the juice of many sour fruits and some plants, and also made synthetically. [< F malique <L malum an apple]

mal·ice (mal′is) n. 1 A disposition to injure another; evil intent; spite; ill will. 2 Law A wilfully formed design to do another an injury: also **malice aforethought**. See synonyms under ENMITY, HATRED. [<OF <L malitia; malus bad]

ma·li·cious (mə·lish′əs) adj. 1 Harboring malice, ill will, or enmity; spiteful. 2 Resulting from or prompted by malice. [<OF malicios <L malitiosus <malitia MALICE] —**ma·li′cious·ly** adv. —**ma·li′cious·ness** n.

Synonyms: bitter, evil-disposed, evil-minded, hostile, ill-disposed, ill-natured, invidious, malevolent, malign, malignant, mischievous, rancorous, resentful, spiteful, venomous, virulent. The malevolent person wishes ill to another; the malicious person has the desire and intent to do evil, if possible, to another. The malign or malignant spirit has a deep, intense, and insatiable hostility, such as is indicated by rancorous or venomous, with or without active desire or intent to injure. Spiteful is a feeble word indicating the desire or intent to inflict petty, exasperating annoyance or injury. Compare ACRIMONY, BITTER, ENMITY, HATRED. Antonyms: amiable, amicable, beneficent, benevolent, benign, benignant, friendly, good-natured, kind, kind-hearted, kindly, sympathetic, tender, well-disposed.

ma·lign (mə·līn′) v.t. To speak slander of. See synonyms under ABUSE, ASPERSE, REVILE. —adj. 1 Having an evil disposition toward others; ill-disposed; malevolent: opposed to benign. 2 Tending to injure; pernicious. See synonyms under MALICIOUS. [<OF malignier, maliner plot, deceive <L malignare contrive maliciously <malignus evil-disposed <malus evil] —**ma·lign′ly** adv. —**ma·lign′er** n.

ma·lig·nant (mə·lig′nənt) adj. 1 Having or manifesting extreme malevolence or enmity. 2 Evil in nature, or tending to do great harm; also, malcontent. 3 Pathol. So aggravated as to threaten life: opposed to benign: a malignant tumor. 4 Boding ill; baleful; threatening. —n. A person of extreme enmity or evil intentions. [<L malignans, -antis, ppr. of malignare. See MALIGN.] —**ma·lig′nance, ma·lig′nan·cy** n. —**ma·lig′nant·ly** adv.

ma·lig·ni·ty (mə·lig′nə·tē) n. pl. ·ties 1 The state or quality of being malign; violent animosity. 2 Destructive tendency; virulence. 3 Often pl. An evil thing or event. See synonyms under ACRIMONY, ENMITY, HATRED.

ma·lines (mə·lēn′, Fr. má·lēn′) n. 1 Lace made in Malines, Belgium; also called Mechlin lace. 2 A gauzelike veiling for trimming hats: also **ma·line′**. [<F, from Malines Mechlin]

Ma·lines (má·lēn′) The French name for MECHLIN.

ma·lin·ger (mə·ling′gər) v.i. To feign sickness or incapacity, especially so as to avoid work or duty. [<F malingre sickly <mal bad (<L malus) + OF heingre lean] —**ma·lin′ger·er** n.

Ma·li·now·ski (má′li·nôf′skē), **Bronislaw Kasper**, 1884–1942, U.S. anthropologist born in Poland.

mal·i·son (mal′ə·zən, -sən) n. Archaic A malediction; curse. [<OF <L maledictio MALEDICTION]

mal·kin (mô′kin, môl′-, mal′-) n. Obs. 1 A kitchenmaid; a slattern. 2 A scarecrow representing a woman. 3 A cat. 4 Scot. A hare. Also spelled maukin. [Dim. of MATILDA, MAUD]

mall[1] (môl, mal) n. 1 A maul. 2 A war hammer. —v.t. To maul. [Var. of MAUL]

mall[2] (môl, mal, mel) n. 1 The game pall-mall, or a place in which it is played. 2 A level, shaded walk. [Short for PALL-MALL]

mal·lard (mal′ərd) n. 1 The common wild duck (Anas platyrhynchos), or, formerly, its drake. 2 Any wild duck. 3 Obs. The domesticated duck. [<OF malart <masle MALE]

Mal·lar·mé (má·lár·mā′), **Stéphane**, 1842–98, French poet.

mal·le·a·ble (mal′ē·ə·bəl) adj. 1 Capable of being hammered or rolled out without breaking; ductile. 2 Hence, susceptible to the shaping power of surrounding influences; pliant. [<OF <L malleare MALLEATE] —**mal′le·a·bil′i·ty, mal′le·a·ble·ness** n. —**mal′le·a·bly** adv.

malleable iron 1 Cast iron that has been rendered tough and malleable by long-continued high heating and slow cooling. 2 Wrought iron; forged iron.

mal·le·ate (mal′ē·āt) v.t. ·at·ed, ·at·ing To shape into a plate or leaf by beating; hammer. [<L malleatus, pp. of malleare <malleus a hammer] —**mal′le·a′tion** n.

mal·lee (mal′ē) n. Austral. 1 Any one of several scrubby species of eucalyptus of South Australia and Victoria; especially, Eucalyptus dumosa and E. oleosa. 2 Brushwood composed of such trees.

mal·le·in (mal′ē·in) n. Biochem. A poisonous, yellowish-white compound, obtained from the active metabolic products of the bacillus of glanders, used for the diagnosis of that disease. Also **mal′le·ine** (-in, -ēn). [<L malle(us) glanders + -IN]

mal·le·muck (mal′ə·muk) n. The southern albatross, fulmar, petrel, or other closely related bird. [<Du. mallemok <mol foolish + mok a gull]

mal·len·ders (mal′ən·dərz) See MALANDERS.

mal·le·o·lus (mə·lē′ə·ləs) n. pl. ·o·li (-ə·lī) Anat. A hammer-shaped bony process on each side of the ankle. [<L, dim. of malleus a hammer] —**mal·le′o·lar** adj.

mal·let (mal′it) n. 1 A wooden hammer or light maul. 2 A light hammer, frequently of metal. 3 A long-handled wooden hammer used in the game of croquet. 4 A wooden-headed Malacca cane or stick used in the game of polo. [<OF maillet, dim. of mail a MAUL]

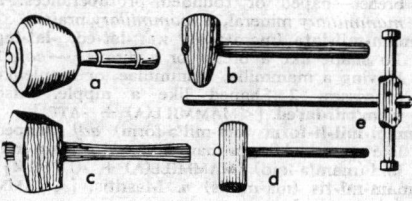

MALLETS
a. Mason's mallet.   b. Bossing mallet.
c. Carpenter's mallet.   d. Tinsmith's mallet.
e. Calking mallet.

mal·le·us (mal′ē·əs) n. pl. ·le·i (-lē·ī) Anat. The club-shaped outermost ossicle of the middle ear, articulating with the incus. See illustration under EAR. [<L, a hammer]

Mal·lor·ca (mä·lyôr′kä) The Spanish spelling of MAJORCA.

mal·low (mal′ō) n. 1 Any plant of the genus Malva. The most common in the United States is the **running** or **dwarf mallow** (M. rotundifolia), a spreading herb with roundish leaves, small, pale-pink flowers, and flat, disklike fruit: the leaves are used in brewing a medicinal tea. 2 Any part of the mallow family: Indian mallow. [OE mealuwe <L malva. Double of MAUVE.]

mallow rose See ROSEMALLOW.

malm (mäm) n. 1 A soft, friable, whitish limestone. 2 A whitish calcareous loam occurring in the southern counties of England; marl. [OE mealm(stan) sandstone or limestone]

Mal·mé·dy (mál·mā·dē′) A town on the Belgian-German frontier; awarded to Belgium under the Versailles Treaty.

Malmes·bur·y (mämz′bər·ē), **William of,** 1095?–1143?, English monk and historian.

Mal·mö (mal′mō, Sw. mäl′mœ) A port in SW Sweden.

malm·sey (mäm′zē) n. A rich sweet wine made in the Canary Islands, Madeira, Spain, and Greece. [<Med. L malmasia <Gk. Monembasia Monemvasia, Greece, a small Laconian coastal town formerly exporting wine]

mal·nu·tri·tion (mal′nōō·trish′ən, -nyōō-) n. Faulty or inadequate nutrition.

ma·lo (mä′lō) n. A loin cloth or girdle worn by Hawaiian men, formerly made of tapa, now of brightly dyed cotton fabrics. [<Hawaiian, cloth]

mal·oc·clu·sion (mal′ə·klōō′zhən) n. Dent. Faulty closure of the upper and lower teeth. [<MAL- + OCCLUSION]

mal·o·dor (mal·ō′dər) n. An offensive odor.

mal·o·dor·ous (mal·ō′dər·əs) adj. Having a disagreeable smell, literally or figuratively; obnoxious. —**mal·o′dor·ous·ly** adv. —**mal·o′dor·ous·ness** n.

ma·lon·ic (mə·lon′ik, -lō′nik) adj. Chem. Of, pertaining to, or designating a white, crystalline acid, $CH_2(CO_2H)_2$ obtained chiefly by oxidizing malic acid. [<F malonique <malique MALIC]

mal·o·nyl·u·re·a (mal′ə·nil·yŏŏr′ē·ə) n. Barbituric acid. [<MALON(IC) + -YL +UREA]

Mal·o·ry (mal′ər·ē), **Sir Thomas,** died 1470?, English author and translator; compiled the Morte d'Arthur, a collection of stories about King Arthur translated from the French.

mal·pais (mal′pīs) n. SW U.S. Bad land; specifically, land having an under layer of basaltic lava. [<Sp. mal, malo bad (<L malus) + país a country <L patria]

Mal·pi·ghi (mäl·pē′gē), **Marcello,** 1628–94, Italian anatomist. —**Mal·pigh′i·an** (-pig′ē·ən) adj.

mal·pigh·i·a·ceous (mal·pig′ē·ā′shəs) adj. Of or pertaining to a family (Malpighiaceae) of trees, shrubs, or, more rarely, herbs, with hermaphrodite flowers, mostly native to the tropics. [<NL Malpighiaceae, family name < Malpighia, genus name, after Marcello Malpighi]

Malpighian bodies Anat. A tuft of blood vessels at the commencement of the uriniferous tubules in the kidney. Also **Malpighian capsules** or **corpuscles.** [after Marcello Malpighi]

Malpighian layer Anat. The deeper, softer layer of the epidermis, comprising the active cells.

Malpighian tubes Entomol. The tubular portions of the excretory organ of an insect. Also **Malpighian vessels.**

Mal·pla·quet (mál·plá·ke′) A village in northern France; scene of Marlborough's victory over the French, 1709.

mal·po·si·tion (mal′pə·zish′ən) n. Pathol. A wrong or faulty position, as of the fetus. —**mal·posed** (-pōzd′) adj.

mal·prac·tice (mal·prak′tis) n. 1 Improper or illegal practice, as in medicine or surgery. 2 Improper or immoral conduct. —**mal·prac·ti·tion·er** (mal′prak·tish′ən·ər) n.

Mal·raux (mál·rō′), **André,** 1901–1976, French novelist and art critic.

malt (môlt) n. 1 Grain, usually barley, softened by water, artificially germinated and then dried: rich in carbohydrates and proteins and essential in brewing and as a nutrient. 2 Slang Malt liquor; beer or ale. —v.t. 1 To cause (grain) to germinate artificially, by moisture and heat, and become malt. 2 To treat with

malt, or extract of malt. —*v.i.* **3** To be changed into or become malt: said of grain. **4** To convert grain into malt. [OE *mealt.* Akin to MELT.]

Mal·ta (môl′tə) **1** A republic in the Mediterranean, comprising the **Maltese Islands;** Malta, Gozo, and Comino; 122 square miles; capital, Valletta. **2** The largest of these islands; 95 square miles: ancient *Melita.*

Malta fever Undulant fever.

mal·tase (môl′tās) *n. Biochem.* A digestive enzyme which hydrolyzes maltose into dextrose. [<MALT + -ASE]

malted milk 1 A powder made of dehydrated milk and malted cereals, soluble in milk or water. **2** The beverage made with this powder.

Mal·tese (môl·tēz′, -tēs′) *adj.* Of or pertaining to Malta, its inhabitants, or their language, or to the Knights of Malta. —*n. pl.* **·tese 1** A native of Malta; the people of Malta collectively. **2** The language of Malta, a dialectal Arabic with elements of Italian. **3** A Maltese cat or dog.

Maltese cat A domestic cat with long, silky, bluish-gray hair.

Maltese cross See under CROSS.

Maltese dog An ancient breed of toy spaniel, originating in Malta, with a long, silky, white coat.

mal·tha (mal′thə) *n.* **1** A thick mineral pitch, formed by drying petroleum. **2** A variety of ozocerite. **3** Any similar preparation used as a cement, stucco, or mortar. [<L <Gk., a mixture of wax and pitch]

malt house A building in which grains are malted and other preparations made for use in the brewer's trade.

Mal·thus (mal′thəs), **Thomas Robert,** 1766–1834, English political economist.

Mal·thu·si·an (mal·thōō′zē·ən, -zhən) *adj.* Of or pertaining to the theory of T. R. Malthus that population increases faster than the means of support and, unless checked by sexual restraint, is restricted only by famine, pestilence, war, etc. —*n.* A believer in the theories of Malthus. —**Mal·thu′si·an·ism** *n.*

malt liquor A fermented liquor, esp. beer or ale made from malt.

malt·ose (môl′tōs) *n. Biochem.* A hard, white, dextrorotatory, crystalline sugar, $C_{12}H_{22}O_{11}\cdot H_2O$, formed by the action of amylase on starch. [<MALT + -OSE[2]]

mal·treat (mal·trēt′) *v.t.* To treat badly or unkindly; abuse. See synonyms under ABUSE. [<F *maltraiter* <*mal-* MAL- + *traiter* <OF *traitier* TREAT] —**mal·treat′ment** *n.*

malt·ster (môlt′stər) *n.* A maker of or dealer in malt.

malt·y (môl′tē) *adj.* **malt·i·er, malt·i·est** Of, pertaining to, containing, or resembling malt.

mal·va·ceous (mal·vā′shəs) *adj.* Pertaining or belonging to the mallow family *(Malvaceae)* of herbs, shrubs, or trees, with alternate palmately nerved leaves and regular flowers, including althea, cotton, okra, etc. [<LL *malvaceus* < *malva* a mallow]

mal·va·si·a (mal′və·sē′ə) *n.* Malmsey wine; also, the kind of grape from which malmsey wine is made. [<Ital. *Malvasia,* alter. of Gk. *Monembasia.* See MALMSEY.] —**mal′va·si′an** *adj.*

Mal·vern Hill (mal′vərn) A plateau near Richmond, Virginia; scene of a Confederate defeat in the Civil War, 1862.

Malvern Hills A range in western England on the Worcester-Hereford border; highest point, 1,307 feet.

mal·ver·sa·tion (mal′vər·sā′shən) *n.* Evil or corrupt conduct; misconduct, as in public office. [<MF <*malverser* <L *male versari* < *male* wrongly, ill + *versari* behave, passive freq. of *vertere* turn]

mal·voi·sie (mal′voi·zē, -və-) *n.* Malmsey. [<OF *malvesia* <Ital. *malvasia* MALVASIA; refashioned after F *malvoisie*]

Mal·vo·li·o (mal·vō′lē·ō) In Shakespeare's *Twelfth Night,* the pompous majordomo of Olivia.

ma·ma (mä′mə, mə·mä′) *n.* Mother: a term of familiar address and endearment. Also **mam′·ma.** [Repetition of infantile syllable *ma*]

mam·ba (mäm′bə) *n.* Any of certain long, venomous, arboreal snakes (genus *Dendraspis*) of southern Africa; especially, the common olive-green or black mamba *(D. angusticeps).* [< Zulu *in-amba*]

mam·bo (mäm′bō) *n. pl.* **·bos** A form of popular music, derived from Cuban Negro styles, achieving its effects by syncopation of a four-beat rhythmic pattern, with accents on the second and fourth beats.

ma·melle (ma·mel′) *n.* In western United States, a rounded hillock. [F, breast]

mam·e·luke (mam′ə·lōōk) *n.* In Moslem countries, a male slave. [<F *mameluk* <Arabic *mamlūk* a slave, orig. pp. of *malaka* possess]

Mam·e·luke (mam′ə·lōōk) *n.* A member of a famous military caste, originally composed of slaves, which dominated Egypt from 1254 to 1811. Also **Mam′a·luke.**

ma·mey (mä·mā′, -mē′) *n.* **1** A tropical American tree *(Mamea americana)* bearing edible, yellow fruits resembling the pomelo in size and shape: also **mamey de Santo Domingo. 2** A fruit of this tree: also **mamey apple. 3** The sapodilla or marmalade tree. Also **mam·mee** (mä·mā′, -mē′). [<Sp. <Taino]

mam·ma (mam′ə) *n. pl.* **·mae** (-ē) The milk-secreting organ of a mammal; a breast, udder, or bag. [<L, breast]

mam·mal (mam′əl) *n.* A vertebrate animal whose female suckles its young. [< MAMMALIA]

Mam·ma·li·a (ma·mā′lē·ə) *n. pl.* A class of vertebrates whose females have milk-secreting mammae to nourish their young, including man, all warm-blooded quadrupeds, seals, cetaceans, and sirenians. [<NL <LL *mammalis* of the breast <L *mamma* breast]

mam·ma·lif·er·ous (mam′ə·lif′ər·əs) *adj.* Containing remains of mammals, as geological strata. [<MAMMALI(A) + -FEROUS]

mam·mal·o·gy (ma·mal′ə·jē) *n.* The branch of zoology that treats of the *Mammalia.* [< MAMMAL + -LOGY]

mam·ma·ry (mam′ər·ē) *adj.* Of, pertaining to, or of the nature of a mamma or breast, or the mammae.

mammary gland The milk gland, which in a female forms the bulk of the breast or mamma. The mammary glands occur in both the male and female in all mammals, but are rudimentary in the male.

mam·mate (mam′āt) *adj.* Having mammae or breasts. Also **mam′me·at′ed** (-ē·ā′tid). [<L *mammatus* <*mamma* breast]

mam·ma·tus (ma·mā′təs) *n. Meteorol.* A cloud form characterized by pouchlike protuberances along the lower surface: noted especially in stratocumulus and cumulonimbus clouds. [< L. See MAMMATE.]

mam·mer (mam′ər) *v.i. Brit. Dial.* To stammer; hesitate; be confused. [Prob. imit.]

mam·mer·ing (mam′ər·ing) *n.* A state of doubt or perplexity.

mam·met (mam′it) See MAUMET.

mam·mie (mam′ē) See MAMMY.

mam·mif·er·ous (ma·mif′ər·əs) *adj.* Having mammae or breasts; mammalian. [<MAMM(A) + -(I)FEROUS]

mam·mil·la (ma·mil′ə) *n. pl.* **·lae** (-ē) *Anat.* A nipple or teat, or some nipplelike or teat-shaped structure or protuberance. [<L *mamilla, mammilla,* dim. of *mamma* breast]

mam·mil·lar·y (mam′ə·ler′ē) *adj.* **1** Of, pertaining to, or resembling a mammilla or a mamma. **2** Studded with or composed of breast-shaped or rounded protuberances: a *mammillary* mineral, a *mammillary* prairie.

mam·mil·late (mam′ə·lāt) *v.t.* **·lat·ed, ·lat·ing** To shape like a breast or a nipple. —*adj.* **1** Having a mammilla, mammillae, or nipplelike processes. **2** Shaped like a nipple. Also **mam′mil·lat′ed.** [<MAMMILL(A) + -ATE[1]]

mam·mil·li·form (ma·mil′ə·fôrm) *adj.* Shaped like or resembling a mammilla. Also **mam·mil·loid** (mam′ə·loid). [MAMMILL(A) + -(I)FORM]

mam·mi·tis (ma·mī′tis) *n.* Mastitis. [<MAMM(A) + -ITIS]

mam·mock (mam′ək) *n. Archaic* A fragment; scrap. [<dial. E; ult. origin uncertain]

mam·mo·gram (mam′ə·gram) *n.* An X-ray photograph of the breast or breasts.

mam·mog·ra·phy (mə·mog′rə·fē) *n.* X-ray examination of the breast or breasts. [<L *mamma* breast + Gk. *graphein* write]

mam·mol·o·gy (ma·mol′ə·jē) *n.* Mammalogy. [<MAMM(ALIA) + -(O)LOGY]

mam·mon (mam′ən) *n.* **1** Riches; wealth. **2** Worldliness; avarice. *Matt.* vi 24; *Luke* xvi 9. [<LL <Gk. *mammōnas* <Aramaic *māmōnā* riches, prob. ult. < *ʼāman* trust]

Mam·mon (mam′ən) **1** The personification of riches, avarice, and worldly gain. **2** In Milton's *Paradise Lost,* one of the fallen angels.

mam·mon·ism (mam′ən·iz′əm) *n.* Devotion to the acquisition of wealth; worldliness. —**mam′·mon·ist, mam′mon·ite** *n.*

mam·moth (mam′əth) *n.* **1** A large, once very abundant, extinct northern elephant *(Mammuthus primigenius)* of the Pleistocene, closely resembling the Indian elephant, with coarse outer hair, close woolly under hair, and enormous, usually curved tusks: its remains have been found in Alaska and Siberia. **2** The extinct imperial elephant *(M. imperator)* which ranged west of the Mississippi River. —*adj.* Huge; colossal. [<Russian *mammot, mamant*]

WOOLLY MAMMOTH
(About 9 feet high at the shoulder)

Mammoth Cave National Park A series of underground caverns in SW Kentucky, noted for their remarkable onyx formations; 79 square miles; established, 1936.

mam·my (mam′ē) *n. pl.* **·mies 1** Mother; mama. **2** A Negro nurse or foster mother of white children, especially in the Southern U.S. Also spelled *mammie.* [Dim. of MAMA]

man (man) *n. pl.* **men** (men) **1** A member of the genus *Homo* (family *Hominidae,* class *Mammalia*), the most highly developed of the primates, differing from other animals in having erect posture, extraordinary development of the brain, and the power of articulate language: only existing species, *Homo sapiens.* Earlier forms include the following: CRO-MAGNON MAN, GRIMALDI MAN, HEIDELBERG MAN, MIDLAND MAN, MODJOKERTO MAN, NEANDERTHAL MAN, RHODESIAN MAN, SOLO MAN, WADJAK MAN. **2** The human race. **3** Any one, indefinitely. **4** An adult male of the human kind: distinguished from *woman, boy,* and *youth.* **5** The male part of the race collectively. **6** A male person who is manly; also, manhood. **7** An adult male servant, dependent, or vassal. **8** A piece, figure, disk, etc., used in playing certain games, as chess or checkers. **9** A ship or vessel: used in composition: a *man-*of-war; an *Indiaman.* **10** A husband; lover; *man* and wife; Her *man* is dead. **11** Fellow: used in direct address: Hey, *man,* look at this! —**the Man** *U.S. Slang* A white man regarded as a representative of the establishment, as a police officer or a boss. —**to a man** Every one. —**to be one's own man** To be independent. —*v.t.* **manned, man·ning 1** To supply with men: to *man* a fort. **2** To take stations at, on, or in for work, defense, etc.: *Man* the pumps! —**to man oneself** To prepare or brace oneself, as for an ordeal. [OE *mann*]

Man may appear as a combining form in hyphemes or in solidemes, meaning "of, by, for, or like a man":

man-baiting	**man-hating**
man-bodied	**man-high**
man-born	**man-hunt**
man-catching	**man-hunting**
man-changed	**mankiller**
man-created	**mankilling**
man-degrading	**man-made**
man-destroyer	**man-minded**
man-destroying	**man-ridden**
man-devised	**man-shaped**
man-eating	**man-size**
man-enslaved	**man-stealing**
man-fearing	**man-taught**
man-grown	**mantrap**
man-hater	**man-worthy**

Man (man), **Isle of** One of the British Isles in the Irish Sea between Northern Ireland and England; 220 square miles; capital Douglas: ancient *Mona*: a native of the island is known as a *Manxman.*

ma·na (mä′nə) *n.* Among Pacific islanders, the supernatural power or force that works through a person or an inanimate object.

man-a·bout-town (man′ə·bout′toun′) *n.* A man who frequents night clubs, theaters, restaurants, bars, etc.; hence, a sophisticate.

man·a·cle (man′ə·kəl) *n.* **1** *Usually pl.* One of a connected pair of metallic instruments for confining or restraining the hands; a hand-

cuff. **2** Anything that constrains or fetters. —*v.t.* **·cled, ·cling 1** To put manacles on. **2** To hamper; constrain. [<OF *manicle* <L *manicula,* dim. of *manus* hand]

man·age (man′ij) *v.* **·aged, ·ag·ing** *v.t.* **1** To direct or conduct the affairs or interests of: to *manage* a business. **2** To control the direction, operation, etc., of, as a machine. **3** To cause to do one's bidding, as by persuasion or flattery. **4** To bring about or contrive: to *manage* to do something. **5** To handle or wield, as a weapon or implement. **6** To train (a horse) in the exercises of a manège. —*v.i.* **7** To carry on or conduct business or affairs. **8** to contrive to get along: I'll *manage.* See synonyms under GOVERN, REGULATE. —*n. Obs.* **1** Management. **2** Behavior. **3** Manège; a riding school. [<Ital. *maneggiare* handle, train horses, ult. <L *manus* a hand]

man·age·a·ble (man′ij·ə·bəl) *adj.* Capable of being managed; tractable; docile. See synonyms under DOCILE. —**man′age·a·bil′i·ty, man′age·a·ble·ness** *n.* —**man′age·a·bly** *adv.*

man·age·ment (man′ij·mənt) *n.* **1** The act, art, or manner of managing, controlling, or conducting. **2** The skilful use of means to accomplish a purpose. **3** Managers or directors collectively. See synonyms under CARE, OVERSIGHT.

man·ag·er (man′ij·ər) *n.* **1** One who manages; especially, one who has the control of a business or a business establishment; a director. **2** An adroit schemer; intriguer. See synonyms under MASTER, SUPERINTENDENT. —**man′ag·er·ship** *n.*

man·ag·er·ess (man′ij·ər·is, -ij·ris; *Brit.* man′ij·ər·es′) *n.* Chiefly Brit. A female manager.

man·a·ge·ri·al (man′ə·jir′ē·əl) *adj.* Of, pertaining to, or characteristic of a manager or management. —**man′a·ge′ri·al·ly** *adv.*

Ma·na·gua (mä·nä′gwä) The capital of Nicaragua, on **Lake Managua,** a lake in SW Nicaragua (390 square miles).

man·a·kin (man′ə·kin) *n.* **1** Any of numerous small tropical American birds (family *Pipridae)* of brilliant plumage. **2** A manikin. [Orig. var. of MANIKIN]

Ma·na·ma (mä·nä′mä) The capital of the Bahrein Islands, on Bahrein.

ma·ña·na (mä·nyä′nä) *n. & adv. Spanish* Tomorrow. —**land of mañana** Land of perpetual procrastination.

Man·a·sa·ro·war (man′ə·sə·rō′ər) A lake in SW Tibet; 200 square miles.

Ma·nas·sas (mə·nas′əs) A town in NE Virginia; scene of two battles of Bull Run in the Civil War, July 21, 1861, and Aug. 29–30, 1862.

Ma·nas·seh (mə·nas′ə) A masculine personal name. [<Hebrew, causing to forget] —**Manasseh** A son of Joseph (*Gen.* xli 51); also, a tribe of Israel descended from him. —**Manasseh** King of Judah, in the seventh century B.C.; restored idol-worship.

man·at·arms (man′ət·ärmz′) *n. pl.* **men·at·arms** (men′-) A soldier; especially, a heavily armed soldier of medieval times.

man·a·tee (man′ə·tē′) *n.* A sirenian (genus *Trichechus*) of the tropical Atlantic shores and rivers; a sea cow. [<Sp. *manati* <Cariban *manattoui*]

MANATEE
(From 8 to 12 feet in length over—all)

Ma·naus (mä·nous′) A city on the Rio Negro in NW Brazil, capital of Amazonas. Formerly **Ma·ná·os** (mä·nä′ōs).

ma·nav·e·lins (mə·nav′ə ·linz) *n. pl. Naut. Slang* Odds and ends; leftover scraps. Also **ma·nav′i·lins.** [Var. of nautical slang *manarvelings* <*manarvel* steal small stores]

Man·ches·ter (man′ches·tər, -chis-) **1** A county borough and city in Lancashire, England. A native of Manchester is known as a *Mancunian.* **2** A city in southern New Hampshire.

man·chet (man′chit) *n. Archaic* A small loaf of fine white bread. [ME *manchett,* ? dim.

<OF *(painde)maine* <L *panis dominicus,* lit., lord's bread]

man·child (man′chīld′) *n. pl.* **·chil·dren** (-chil′drən) A male child.

man·chi·neel (man′chi·nēl′) *n.* A tropical American tree *(Hippomane mancinella)* having an acrid, milky, poisonous sap. [<F *mancenille* <Sp. *manzanilla,* dim. of *manzana* an apple <L *(mala) matiana* (apples) of Matius <*Matius,* a Roman culinary author]

Man·chu (man·chōō′, man′chōō) *n.* **1** One of a Mongoloid people that conquered China in 1643 and established the dynasty overthrown in 1912. **2** The language of this people, belonging to the Manchu-Tungusic subfamily of Altaic languages. —*adj.* Of or pertaining to Manchuria, its people, or its language. Also **Man·choo′.** [< Manchu, lit., pure] —**Man·chu′ri·an** (-chōōr′ē·ən) *adj. & n.*

Man·chu·kuo (man′chōō′kwō′, *Chinese* män′·jō′kwō′) A former empire in NE Asia, 1932–45, established under Japanese auspices; comprising Manchuria and the Chinese province of Jehol and part of Chahar in Inner Mongolia; about 503,013 square miles; capital, Hsinking. Also **Man′chou′kuo′.**

Man·chu·ri·a (man·chōōr′ē·ə) A major division of NE China; 585,000 square miles; capital, Mukden. See MANCHUKUO. —**Man·chu′ri·an** *adj. & n.*

Man·chu-Tun·gus·ic (man·chōō′tŏŏn·gŏŏz′ik) *n.* A subfamily of the Altaic languages, consisting of Manchu and Tungus.

man·cip·i·um (man·sip′ē·əm) *n.* In ancient Roman law, the legal status of a person conveyed by the paterfamilias to another by the ceremony of mancipation. If emancipated from the mancipium, the person became again subject to paternal power and so remained, unless sold three times, when the authority of the paterfamilias ceased. [<L <*manceps* a buyer < *manus* a hand + *capere* take]

man·ci·ple (man′sə·pəl) *n.* A steward, as of an English college. [<OF *manciple, mancipe* <L *mancipium* MANCIPIUM]

Man·cu·ni·an (man·kyōō′nē·ən) *n.* A native of Manchester, England. [< Med. L *Mancunium* Manchester]

man·cus (mang′kəs) *n.* An Anglo-Saxon monetary unit worth thirty pence. [OE]

-mancy *combining form* Divining, foretelling, or discovering by means of: *necromancy.* [<Gk. *manteia* power of divination]

Man·da·lay (man′də·lā, man′də·lā′) A city on the Irrawaddy in central Burma.

man·da·mus (man·dā′məs) *n.* Law A writ originally (in England) of royal prerogative, now a writ of right, issued by courts of superior jurisdiction and directed to subordinate courts, corporations, or the like, commanding them to do something therein specified: modified by statute from the ordinary common law form in jurisdiction. —*v.t. Colloq.* To command by or serve with a mandamus. [<L, we command < *mandare.* See MANDATE.]

Man·dan (man′dan) *n.* **1** One of a tribe of North American Indians of Siouan stock, of the NW United States. **2** The Siouan language of this tribe.

man·da·rin (man′də·rin) *n.* **1** An official of the Chinese Empire, either civil or military: a title used by foreigners indiscriminately. The recognized official grades under the Empire were nine, each rank being distinguished by its official specific regalia, a conspicuous part of which is the **mandarin button. 2** Any of certain small Chinese oranges, having a loose skin and very sweet pulp; a tangerine. **3** An orange or reddish-yellow dye. [<Pg. *mandarim* <Malay *mantrī* a minister of state <Hind. <Skt. *mantrin* a counselor <*mantra* counsel]

Man·da·rin (man′də·rin) *n.* **1** The Chinese language of North China, in the Peking dialect now the official language of the country. **2** Formerly, the court language of the Chinese Empire.

mandarin duck A crested duck *(Aix galericulata)* , with variously colored plumage.

man·da·ta·ry (man′də·ter′ē) *n. pl.* **·tar·ies** One to whom a charge is given; an agent. See MANDATE (def. 2).

man·date (man′dāt, -dit) *n.* **1** An authoritative requirement, as of a sovereign; a command; order; charge. **2** A charge to a nation, author-

izing the government, administration, and development of conquered territory, given by a congress or league of nations, to which the grantee is responsible; also, the territory given in charge. **3** A judicial command directed to an officer of the court to enforce an order of that court; a precept from an appellate court directing what a subordinate court shall do in an appealed case. **4** A rescript of the pope ordering that the person named shall have the first vacant benefice in the gift of the person addressed. **5** An instruction from an electorate to the legislative body, or its representative, to follow a certain course of action. See synonyms under LAW. —*v.t.* (-dāt) **·dat·ed, ·dat·ing** To assign (a colony or other territory) to a specific nation under a mandate. [<L *mandatum,* pp. neut. of *mandare* command <*manus* hand + *dare* give (to)]

man·da·tor (man·dā′tər) *n.* One who gives a mandate; a director. [<L < *mandatus,* pp. of *mandare.* See MANDATE.]

man·da·to·ry (man′də·tôr′ē, -tō′rē) *adj.* Expressive of positive command; obligatory. —*n. pl.* **·ries 1** A mandatary. **2** A mandate.

Man·de·an (man·dē′ən) *n.* **1** A member of an ancient sect of Gnostics, Christians of St. John, still existing in Mesopotamia, who combine Judaism, Mohammedanism, and Christianity with the ancient Babylonian worship. **2** The Aramaic dialect used in the writings of the Mandeans. —*adj.* Of or pertaining to the Mandeans or their doctrines. Also **Man·dae′an.** [<Mandean *mandayyā,* lit., having knowledge (<*mandā* knowledge), trans. of Gk. *gnostikoi* Gnostics] —**Man·de′ism** *n.*

Man·de·la (man·de′lə) **Nelson Rolihlahla,** 1918–, first black president of Republic of South Africa (1994–).

man·del·ic (man·del′ik) *adj.* Pertaining to or designating a white crystalline acid, $C_8H_8O_3$, used in medicine as a urinary antiseptic. [<G *mandel* an almond]

Man·de·ville (man′də·vil), **Bernard,** 1670?–1733, English author born in Holland. —**Sir John,** 1300?–72, pseudonym of a reputed English traveler whose *Narrative of Travels* appeared in Latin and French, 1357–71, and in English in the 15th century.

man·di·ble (man′də·bəl) *n. Biol.* **1** The lower jaw bone, or its equivalent. **2** Either the upper or the lower part of the beak of a bird, or of the beak of a cephalopod. **3** Either one of the upper or outer pair of jaws in an insect. **4** The operculum of a polyzoan. [<LL *mandibula* jaw <L *mandere* chew]

man·dib·u·lar (man·dib′yə·lər) *adj.* Of, pertaining to, or formed by a mandible: the *mandibular* arch of the fetal skull. Also **man·dib′u·lar′y** (-ler′ē). — *n.* The lower jaw, or mandible. [<LL *mandibul(a)* MANDIBLE + -AR]

man·dib·u·late (man·dib′yə·lit, -lāt) *adj.* Having mandibles adapted for biting and chewing: said of certain insects. —*n.* Any insect having chewing jaws.

Man·din·go (man·ding′gō) *n. pl.* **·gos** or **·goes 1** One of a Negroid people of western Sudan, Africa. **2** Any of the Sudanic languages of the Mandingos. —**Man·din′gan** *adj. & n.*

man·do·la (man·dō′lə) *n.* A large mandolin. [<Ital. *mandola, mandora* <L *pandura.* See BANDORE.]

man·do·lin (man′də·lin, man′də·lin′) *n.* A stringed musical instrument with an almond-shaped body and metal strings arranged like those of a violin. [<F *mandoline* <Ital. *mandolino,* dim. of *mandola* MANDOLA] —**man′do·lin′ist** *n.*

man·drake (man′drāk) *n.* **1** A short-stemmed Old World plant *(Mandragora officinarum)* of the nightshade family, with narcotic properties. **2** Its fleshy roots, sometimes having a fancied resemblance to the human form. **3** The May apple. Also **man·drag·o·ra** (man·drag′ər·ə). [Alter. of ME *mandrag(g)e,* <OE *mandragora* <LL <L *mandragoras* <Gk.; infl. in form by folk etymology <MAN + DRAKE² a dragon]

man·drel (man′drəl) *n. Mech.* **1** A shaft or spindle on which an object may be fixed for rotation. **2** A smooth, hard, cylindrical or conical core about which wire may be coiled or metal or glass forged. **3** A pattern or form

against which metalwork is pressed in spinning. Also **man′dril.** [Prob. alter. of F *mandrin* a lathe]

man·drill (man′dril) *n.* A large, ferocious West African baboon (genus *Papio*), having large canine teeth and bony prominences on the cheeks striped with blue and scarlet. [<MAN + DRILL[3]]

MANDRILL
(About 30 inches at the shoulder: length 3 to 4 feet)

man·du·cate (man′jo͞o·kāt) *v.t.* **·cat·ed, ·cat·ing** *Rare* To chew; masticate. [<L *manducatus*, pp. of *manducare* chew]

Man·dy (man′dē) Diminutive of AMANDA.

mane (mān) *n.* The long hair growing on and about the neck of some animals, as the horse, lion, etc. ◆ Homophone: *main.* [OE *manu*] **— maned** *adj.* **— mane′less** *adj.*

man-eat·er (man′ē′tər) *n.* **1** A cannibal. **2** An animal that devours, likes to devour, or is supposed to devour human flesh; especially, a tiger or a lion. **3** A large shark with trenchant teeth; especially, *Carcharodon carcharias.*

ma·nège (ma·nezh′) *n.* **1** The art of training and riding horses. **2** A school of horsemanship; riding school; also, a school for the training of horses. **3** The style and movements of a trained horse. Also **ma·nege′.** [<F <Ital. *maneggio* < *maneggiare.* See MANAGE.]

ma·nes (mā′nēz) *n. pl.* **1** In ancient Roman religion, the spirits of the dead; especially, the spirits of dead ancestors. **2** Deified ancestral spirits collectively. [<L, ? orig. pl. of *manis* good]

Ma·nes (mā′nēz), 216?–276?, Persian prophet; founder of Manicheism: also called *Manicheus.*

Ma·net (ma·nā′, *Fr.* mà·ne′), **Édouard,** 1832–1883, French painter.

Man·e·tho (man′ə·thō) An Egyptian priest and writer of the third century B.C.

ma·neu·ver (mə·no͞o′vər, -nyo͞o′-) *n.* **1** A movement or change of position, as of troops or war vessels. **2** Any dexterous or artful proceeding. **—** *v.t.* **1** To put, as troops, through a maneuver or maneuvers. **2** To put, bring, make, etc., by a maneuver or maneuvers. **3** To manipulate; conduct adroitly. **—** *v.i.* **4** To perform a maneuver or maneuvers. **5** To use tricks or stratagems; manage adroitly. Also spelled *manoeuver, manoeuvre.* [<F *manoeuvre* <OF *maneuvre* <LL *manopera* < *manoperare* <L *manu operari* work with the hand < *manus* hand + *operari.* See OPERATE. Doublet of MAINOR, MANURE.] **— ma·neu′ver·a·bil′i·ty** or **·vra·bil′i·ty** *n.* **— ma·neu′ver·a·ble** or **·vra·ble** *adj.* **— ma·neu′ver·er** *n.*

ma·neu·vers (mə·no͞o′vərz, -nyo͞o′-) *n. pl.* Large-scale military exercises involving the use of great numbers of troops under conditions simulating actual battle conditions; war games.

man·fash·ion (man′fash′ən) *adv.* **1** In a manly, confident, straightforward way. **2** Astride: to ride *manfashion.*

man Friday A person devoted or subservient to another, like Robinson Crusoe's servant of that name; a factotum.

man·ful (man′fəl) *adj.* Having a manly spirit; characterized by courage and perseverance; sturdy. See synonyms under MANLY, MASCULINE. **— man′ful·ly** *adv.* **— man′ful·ness** *n.*

mang (mang) *prep. Scot.* Among.

Man·ga·lore (mang′gə·lôr′, -lōr′) A port of western Madras, SW India.

Man·gan (mang′gən), **James Clarence,** 1803–1849, Irish poet.

man·ga·nate (mang′gə·nāt) *n. Chem.* A salt of manganic acid, such as those of sodium, potassium, and barium. [<MANGAN(IC) + -ATE[3]]

man·ga·nese (mang′gə·nēs, -nēz) *n. Chem.* A hard, brittle, metallic element (symbol Mn). In color, it is grayish-white tinged with red; it rusts like iron, but is not magnetic; it is widely distributed (in combination) in nature, and forms an important component of certain alloys, such as manganese steel. See ELEMENT. [<F *manganèse* <Ital. *manganese,* alter. of Med. L *magnesia* MAGNESIA]

manganese dioxide Pyrolusite.

manganese spar **1** Rhodonite. **2** Rhodochrosite.

manganese steel A very hard, ductile steel containing from 12 to 14 percent of manganese.

man·gan·ic (mang·gan′ik) *adj. Chem.* Of, pertaining to, containing, or obtained from manganese in its highest valence, as manganic acid, H_2MnO_4, known chiefly by its salts. [<MANGAN(ESE) + -IC]

man·ga·nite (mang′gə·nīt) *n.* **1** A dark, steel-gray to iron-black orthorhombic manganese hydroxide, MnO(OH). **2** *Chem.* Any salt obtained from certain hydroxides of manganese, and regarded as an acid.

man·ga·nous (mang′gə·nəs) *adj.* Of, pertaining to, or containing manganese in its lowest valence.

Man·ga·re·va (mäng′ä·rā′vä) **1** Largest of the Gambier Islands. **2** The Gambier Islands.

mange (mānj) *n.* An itching skin disease of dogs and other domestic animals, caused by burrowing parasitic mites. Also **the mange.** [<OF *manjue* an itch, eating < *manjuer, mangier.* See MANGER.]

man·gel-wur·zel (mang′gəl·wûr′zəl, -wûrt′səl) *n.* A large-rooted European beet (*Beta vulgaris*), fed to cattle. Also **man′gel.** [<G < *mangoldwurzel* < *mangold* a beet + *wurzel* a root]

man·ger (mān′jər) *n.* A trough or box, for feeding horses or cattle. [<OF *mangeoire, mangeure* < *mangier* eat <L *manducare* chew]

man·gle[1] (mang′gəl) *v.t.* **·gled, ·gling** **1** To disfigure or mutilate, as by cutting, bruising, or crushing; lacerate. **2** To mar or ruin; spoil: to *mangle* a word. See synonyms under REND. [<AF *mangler, mahangler,* appar. freq. of OF *mahaigher* MAIM]

man·gle[2] (mang′gəl) *n.* A machine for smoothing fabrics by pressing them between rollers. **—** *v.t.* **·gled, ·gling** To smooth with a mangle. [<Du. *mangel* <MDu. *mange* <Ital. *mangano* <LL *manganum* <Gk. *manganon* a pulley, a war machine. Doublet of MANGONEL.]

man·gler (mang′glər) *n.* One who or that which mangles.

man·go (mang′gō) *n. pl.* **·goes** or **·gos** **1** The edible, fleshy fruit of a tropical tree allied to the sumac. **2** The tree (*Mangifera indica,* family *Anacardiaceae*) producing the fruit. **3** A pickled green muskmelon. [<Pg. *manga* <Malay *mañga* <Tamil *mān-kāy* < *mān* a mango tree + *kāy* a fruit]

man·go·nel (mang′gə·nel) *n.* A military engine formerly used for throwing stones and other missiles. [<OF, dim. of LL *manganum.* Doublet of MANGLE[2].]

man·go·steen (mang′gə·stēn) *n.* **1** The red-dish-brown fruit of an East Indian tree, about the size of an apple, having a thick, fleshy rind, and a white, juicy pulp. **2** The tree (*Garcinia mangostana*) producing this fruit. [<Malay *mangustan*]

man·grove (mang′grōv, man′-) *n.* **1** A tropical tree (genus *Rhizophora,* especially *R. mangle*) which throws out many aerial roots from the lower branches and stem, forming dense thickets. **2** A shrub of the vervain family, as the **black mangrove** (*Avicennia marina*). [<Sp. *mangle* <Taino; infl. in form by GROVE]

mangrove cuckoo A cuckoo (*Coccyzus minor*) frequenting mangroves of the West Indies, Florida, etc.

man·gy (mān′jē) *adj.* **·gi·er, ·gi·est** **1** Affected with the mange. **2** Figuratively, poverty-stricken; squalid. **— man′gi·ly** *adv.* **— man′gi·ness** *n.*

man·han·dle (man′han′dəl) *v.t.* **·dled, ·dling** **1** To move by manpower without mechanical aids. **2** To handle with roughness, as in anger.

Man·hat·tan (mən·hat′ən, man-) *n.* **1** A cocktail made of whisky and vermouth, often with a dash of bitters and a cherry. **2** One of a tribe of Algonquian North American Indians, formerly inhabiting Manhattan Island.

Man·hat·tan Island (mən·hat′ən, man-) An island in SE New York at the mouth of the Hudson River; 22 square miles; comprising **Manhattan** borough of New York City.

man·hole (man′hōl′) *n.* An opening through which a man may enter a boiler, conduit, sewer, etc., for making repairs.

man·hood (man′ho͝od) *n.* **1** Manly qualities collectively; manliness; courage. **2** The state of being of age; man's estate. **3** The state of being a man, or a human being as distinguished from other animals or beings. **4** Men collectively: the *manhood* of the nation.

man-hour (man′our′) *n.* A unit of measure equal to the amount of work one man can do in one hour.

ma·ni·a (mā′nē·ə, mān′yə) *n.* **1** Madness. **2** *Psychiatry* Exaggerated melancholia alternating periodically with an exaggerated sense of well-being, accompanied by excessive activity (both mental and physical): also called *manic-depressive psychosis.* **3** A strong, ungovernable desire; also, colloquially, a craze: a *mania* for rare books. See synonyms under FRENZY, INSANITY. [<L <Gk., madness < *mainesthai* rage. Akin to MANTIC.]

-mania *combining form* An exaggerated, persistent, or irrational craving for or infatuation with. [<Gk. *mania* madness] Below are some examples.

agromania	open country
bibliomania	books
cratomania	power
dipsomania	alcohol
kleptomania	stealing
megalomania	greatness, fame
mythomania	telling lies
nostomania	one's home
nymphomania	men
plutomania	wealth
pyromania	setting fires
toxicomania	poisons

ma·ni·ac (mā′nē·ak) *adj.* Having a mania; raving. See synonyms under INSANE. **—** *n.* A person wildly or violently insane; a madman. [<LL *maniacus* <L *mania* MANIA] **— ma·ni·a·cal** (mə·nī′ə·kəl) *adj.* **— ma·ni′a·cal·ly** *adv.*

-maniac *combining form* Forming adjectives (often used as nouns) from nouns in *-mania*: *kleptomaniac.*

man·ic (man′ik, mā′nik) *adj.* Pertaining to, like, or affected by mania. [<MAN(IA) + -IC]

man·ic-de·pres·sive (man′ik·di·pres′iv) *adj. Psychiatry* Denoting a mental disorder characterized by sudden fluctuations of depression and excitement. **—** *n.* One who suffers from this disorder.

Man·i·chee (man′ə·kē) *n.* A follower of the Persian Manes. [<LL *Manichaeus* <LGk. *Manichaios* Manes]

Man·i·che·ism (man′ə·kē′iz·əm) *n.* A dualistic religious philosophy developed by the Persian Manes and his followers in which goodness, typified as light, God, or the soul, is represented as in conflict with evil, typified by darkness, Satan, or the body: taught from the third to the seventh century. Also **Man′i·chae′ism. — Man′i·che′an, Man′i·chae′an** *adj.* & *n.*

man·i·cure (man′ə·kyo͝or) *n.* **1** The care or treatment of the hands and fingernails. **2** *Obs.* A manicurist. **—** *v.t.* & *v.i.* **·cured, ·curing** To take care of or treat (the hands and nails). [<F <L *manus* hand + *cura* care]

man·i·cur·ist (man′ə·kyo͝or′ist) *n.* One who cares for or treats the hands and fingernails.

man·i·fest (man′ə·fest) *n.* **1** In shipping and transportation: **a** An itemized account of a carrier's cargo, showing ports of lading, consignees, etc. **b** The list of passengers, cargo, etc., for an airplane flight. **c** A detailed list of the cars of a train. **d** A fast freight train, or perishable goods on it. **2** *Obs.* A manifesto. **—** *v.t.* **1** To make plain to sight or understanding; reveal; display. **2** To prove; be evidence of. **3** To show the manifest of (a shipment). **—** *adj.* Plainly apparent to sight or understanding; evident; plain. [<L *manifestus* evident, lit., struck by the hand] **— man′i·fest′ly** *adv.*

Synonyms (adj.): apparent, bare, clear, conspicuous, distinct, evident, glaring, indubitable, obvious, open, overt, palpable, patent, plain, transparent, unmistakable, visible. See CLEAR, EVIDENT, NOTORIOUS, OVERT. *Antonyms*: concealed, covert, dark, hidden, impalpable, impenetrable, imperceptible, invisible, latent, obscure, occult, secret, undiscovered, unimagined, unknown, unseen.

man·i·fes·ta·tion (man′ə·fes·tā′shən) *n.* **1** The act of manifesting or making plain; the state or fact of being manifested; disclosure or display; a revelation. **2** Hence, a public or

collective act by a government or party in order to emphasize its power, determination, or special views. **3** A revealing agency. **4** In spiritualism, the materialization of a spirit. See synonyms under MARK[1], SIGN. — **man'i·fes'tant** n.

man·i·fes·to (man'ə·fes'tō) n. pl. ·toes A public, official, and authoritative declaration making announcement or explanation of intentions, motives, or principles of actions. [<Ital. <L manifestus. See MANIFEST.]

man·i·fold (man'ə·fōld) v.t. **1** To make more than one copy of at once, as with carbon paper on a typewriter. **2** To multiply. — adj. **1** Of great variety; numerous. **2** Manifested in many ways, or including many acts or elements; complex; being so in many ways or for many reasons. **3** Existing in great abundance. **4** Comprising or uniting several parts or channels of the same kind, as a pipe with several outlets. See synonyms under COMPLEX, MANY. — n. **1** A copy made by manifolding. **2** Math. A number of objects related under one system. **3** A tube with one or more inlets and two or more outlets; a T branch, as the pipe between carburetor and engine, in internal-combustion engines with more than one cylinder. [OE manigfeald varied, numerous] — **man'i·fold·ly** adv. — **man'i·fold·ness** n.

man·i·fold·er (man'ə·fōl'dər) n. **1** One who or that which manifolds. **2** A machine or apparatus for making manifold copies, as of a document.

Ma·ni·hi·ki (mä'nē·hē'kē) An island of the South Pacific administered by New Zealand with the Cook Islands: also Humphrey Island.

man·i·hot (man'ē·hot) n. Any of a large genus (Manihot) of tropical American, mainly Brazilian, herbs or woody plants of the spurge family. Brazilian or Ceará rubber is the product of M. glaziovi. [<NL <F <Tupian mandioca manioc root]

man·i·kin (man'ə·kin) n. **1** A model of the human body, showing its structure. **2** A dressmaker's assistant or lay figure wearing new costumes so as to display them for sale: also spelled mannequin. **3** A little man; dwarf. Also spelled manakin, mannikin. [<Du. manneken, dim. of man man]

ma·nil·a (mə·nil'ə) n. **1** A cheroot made in Manila. **2** The fiber of the abaca (Musa textilis), a tall, perennial herb of the same genus as the banana: also Manila hemp, **ma·nil'la**.

Ma·nil·a (mə·nil'ə, Sp. mä·nē'lä) A port on SW Luzon; former capital of the Philippines.

Manila Bay A landlocked inlet of the China Sea in SW Luzon, Philippines.

Manila paper A heavy, light-brown paper originally made of Manila hemp, now made of various fibers.

Manila rope Rope made of Manila hemp.

man·i·oc (man'ē·ok, mä'nē-) n. The bitter or sweet cassava. [<F <Tupian mandioca manioc root]

man·i·ple (man'ə·pəl) n. **1** Eccl. A band worn on the left arm as a vestment by the clergy of the Roman Catholic and sometimes the Anglican Church. **2** A subdivision of the Roman legion containing 60 or 120 men. [<OF maniple, manipule <L manipulus a handful <manus hand + base of plere fill]

ma·nip·u·lar (mə·nip'yə·lər) adj. **1** Pertaining to manipulation or handling. **2** Pertaining to a maniple. [<L manipularis <manipulus a MANIPLE; infl. in sense by MANIPULATION]

ma·nip·u·late (mə·nip'yə·lāt) v.t. ·lat·ed, ·lat·ing **1** To handle, operate, or use with or as with the hands, especially with skill. **2** To influence or control artfully or deceptively; to manipulate stocks. **3** To change or alter (figures, accounts, etc.), usually fraudulently. [Back formation <MANIPULATION <F, ult. <L manipulus a MANIPLE] — **ma·nip'u·la'tion** n. — **ma·nip'u·la'tive, ma·nip'u·la·to'ry** adj. — **ma·nip'u·la'tor** n.

Ma·ni·pur (mun'i·pŏor) A Union Territory of NE India, bordering on Burma; 8,628 square miles; capital, Imphal.

Man·i·pu·ri (mun'i·pŏor'ē) n. A native or inhabitant of Manipur.

ma·nis (mā'nis) n. A pangolin. [<NL, sing. <L manes MANES]

Ma·nis·sa (mä'nē·sä', mä'nē·sä) A city in eastern Turkey in Asia, on the site of ancient Magnesia. Also **Ma'ni·sa'**.

man·i·to (man'ə·tō) n. Among the Algonquian Indians, the unfathomable spirit or power behind life and the universe. See WAKANDA. Also **man·i·tou** (man'ə·tōō), **man'i·tu.** — **Kitchi Manito** Great Spirit. [<Algonquian (Massachuset) manitto he is a god]

Man·i·to·ba (man'ə·tō'bə, -tō·bä') A province in central Canada; 246,512 square miles; capital, Winnipeg. — **Man'i·to'ban** adj. & n.

Manitoba, Lake A lake in SW Manitoba; 67 square miles.

Manitoba maple Canadian The box elder.

Man·i·tou·lin Island (man'ə·tōō'lin) A Canadian island in Lake Huron, south central Ontario; 1,600 square miles.

Ma·ni·za·les (mä'nē·sä'läs) A city in west central Colombia.

man·kind (man'kīnd', man'kīnd') n. **1** The whole human species. **2** (man'kīnd') Men collectively as distinguished from women. Synonyms: humanity, humankind, man, men. See HUMANITY.

man·like (man'līk') adj. Like a man; having the qualities proper to the human race, to the male sex, to manly character. See synonyms under MANLY, MASCULINE.

man·ly (man'lē) adj. ·li·er, ·li·est Possessing the characteristics of a true man, as strength, frankness, and intrepidity. — adv. Archaic In a manner befitting a man. — **man'li·ly** adv. — **man'li·ness** n.

Synonyms: manful, manlike, mannish. Manlike may mean only having the outward appearance or semblance of a man, or it may be substantially equivalent to manly. Manly refers to all the qualities and traits worthy of a man; manful especially to the valor and prowess that become a man; we speak of a manful struggle; manly decision; we say manly gentleness, or tenderness; we could not say manful tenderness. Mannish is a depreciatory word referring to the mimicry or parade of some superficial qualities of manhood; as, a mannish woman. See MASCULINE.

Mann (man), Horace, 1796–1859, U.S. educator.

Mann (män), Heinrich, 1871–1950, German novelist active in the United States. — Thomas, 1875–1955, German novelist active in the United States; brother of the preceding.

man·na (man'ə) n. **1** The miraculously supplied food on which the Israelites subsisted in the wilderness. Exodus xvi 14–36. **2** Divine or spiritual nourishment. **3** A sweetish substance obtained from incisions in the stems of various trees or shrubs, especially the stems of the flowering ash (Fraxinus ornus and F. rotundifolia) of southern Europe. It is a mild laxative. [OE <LL <Gk. <Aramaic mannā <Hebrew mān]

Mann Act (man) A bill prohibiting the interstate transportation of women and girls for immoral purposes, enacted by Congress in June, 1910: also called White-slave Act. [after James Robert Mann, 1856–1922, U.S. congressman]

Man·nar (mə·när'), Gulf of An inlet of the Indian Ocean between southern Madras and Ceylon.

man·ne·quin (man'ə·kin) See MANIKIN (def. 2).

man·ner (man'ər) n. **1** The way of doing anything; method of procedure; mode. **2** The demeanor or bearing peculiar to one; personal carriage; mien; address. **3** pl. General modes of life or conduct; especially, social behavior. **4** pl. Polite, civil, or well-bred behavior. **5** Usual or ordinary practice; habit; custom; also, characteristic style in literature or art. **6** Sort or kind. **7** Character; guise. — **to the manner born** Familiar with something from birth. — Homophone: manor. [<AF manere, OF maniere, ult. <L manuarius of the hand <manus hand]

Synonyms: appearance, aspect, carriage, demeanor, deportment, fashion, habit, look, mien, mode, practice, style, way. See ADDRESS, AIR, BEHAVIOR, CUSTOM, SYSTEM.

man·nered (man'ərd) adj. **1** Having (specified) manners: often used in combination: ill-mannered. **2** Affected.

Man·ner·heim (män'ər·hīm), Baron Carl

Gustaf Emil von, 1867–1951, Finnish soldier and statesman.

man·ner·ism (man'ər·iz'əm) n. **1** Characteristic or marked adherence to an unusual or affected manner, style, or peculiarity. **2** A peculiarity of manner, as in behavior or speech.

man·ner·ist (man'ər·ist) n. A person addicted to mannerism; an imitator; specifically, an artist or writer whose work is marked by a persistent or extreme adherence to some style, manner, etc., as one of the school of painters of the 16th and 17th centuries who unduly emphasized and imitated the style of Michelangelo and other Italian painters.

man·ner·less (man'ər·lis) adj. Lacking manners; ill-mannered.

man·ner·ly (man'ər·lē) adj. Well-behaved; polite. — adv. With good manners; politely. — **man'ner·li·ness** n.

man·ners–bit (man'ərz·bit') n. A small amount left on a plate by a guest at table, for the sake of good manners, as indicating that the serving was abundant.

Mann·heim (man'hīm) A city on the Rhine in NW Baden–Württemberg, West Germany.

man·ni·kin (man'ə·kin) See MANIKIN.

Man·ning (man'ing), Henry Edward, 1808–92, English Roman Catholic cardinal and writer. — **William Thomas,** 1866–1949, U.S. Episcopalian divine; bishop of New York 1921–46.

man·nish (man'ish) adj. Resembling, characteristic of, or suitable to a man; aping manhood; masculine. See synonyms under MANLY, MASCULINE. [OE menisc] — **man'nish·ly** adv. — **man'nish·ness** n.

man·ni·tol (man'ə·tōl, -tol) n. Biochem. A slightly sweet crystalline alcohol, $C_6H_{14}O_6$, found widely distributed in nature, as in celery, sponges, sea grasses, and especially in the dried sap of the flowering ash. Also **man'nite** (-īt). [<MANNA (def. 3) + -ITE[3] + -OL[1]] — **man·nit'ic** (man·nit'ik) adj.

man·nose (man'ōs) n. A hexose, $C_6H_{12}O_6$, obtained by the oxidation of mannitol. [<MANN(ITOL) + -OSE]

man·o·cry·om·e·ter (man'ō·krī·om'ə·tər) n. An instrument for determining the variations in the freezing or melting point of substances with changes in pressure. [<Gk. manos thin, rare + kryos an icy cold + -METER]

Ma·no·el (mä'nō·el') Portuguese form of EMMANUEL.

ma·noeu·ver (mə·nōō'vər, -nyōō'-), **ma·noeu·vre** See MANEUVER.

Man of Destiny Napoleon I: so regarded by himself.

man of God **1** A saint, prophet, etc.; a holy man. **2** A clergyman.

Man of Sorrows A name supposed to allude to the Messiah (Isa. liii 3); hence, Jesus Christ.

man of straw One put forward as an irresponsible tool or as a fraudulent surety.

man–of–war (man'əv·wôr', man'ə-) n. pl. **men–of–war** (men'-) **1** A naval vessel armed for active hostilities. **2** The Portuguese man–of–war. Also **man'–o'–war'**.

man–of–war bird or **hawk** A frigate bird.

ma·nom·e·ter (mə·nom'ə·tər) n. An instrument for measuring pressure, as of gases and vapors; usually, a U–tube. [<Gk. manos thin, rare + -METER] — **man·o·met·ric** (man'ə·met'rik) or **·ri·cal** adj.

Ma·non Les·caut (má·nôn' les·kō') Promiscuous heroine of Prévost's novel Histoire du Chevalier Des Grieux et de Manon Lescaut.

man·or (man'ər) n. **1** Brit. A nobleman's or gentleman's landed estate. **2** In old English law, a tract or district of land granted by the king to one as lord, with authority to exercise jurisdiction over it by a court–baron. **3** In Anglo–Saxon times, a thane's or lord's estate, composed of the land and of a part of the agricultural capital employed to till it, as well as the laborers, beasts, implements, etc., and having on it a community of serfs or villeins; later, an estate complying with the minimum requirements entitling the lord of the manor to hold a court–baron. **4** U.S. A tract of land originally granted as a manor and let by the proprietor to tenants in perpetuity or for a long term. See synonyms under HOUSE. — Homophone: manner. [<OF manoir a

dwelling, orig. a verb [<L *manere* remain] —**ma·no·ri·al** (mə·nôr′ē·əl, -nō′rē-) *adj.*

man·or-house (man′ər·hous′) *n.* The residence of the lord of the manor. Also **man′ or-seat′** (-sēt′).

man·pow·er (man′pou′ər) *n.* **1** Power supplied by the physical strength of a man or men. **2** The normal rate at which a man can work, generally equal to 1/10 horsepower. **3** The strength of all the men available for any service; specifically, the warpower of a nation in terms of the number of men available for military service, industry, agriculture, etc.

man·qué (män·kā′) *adj. French* Defective; falling short of what is intended. —**man·quée′** *adj.* fem.

man·rope (man′rōp′) *n. Naut.* A rope serving as a hand railing to a gangway, ladder, etc., on board ship.

man·sard (man′särd) *n.* **1** A roof with a double pitch on all sides; also **mansard roof. 2** A room within such a roof; an attic. [<F *mansarde*, after François *Mansard*, 1598–1666, French architect who revived it]

manse (mans) *n.* **1** A clergyman's house, especially a Scottish Presbyterian minister's house; a parsonage. **2** A landholder's residence. [<Med. L *mansa, mansus.* See MANSION.]

man·ser·vant (man′sûr′vənt) *n.* An adult male servant.

Mans·field (manz′fēld, mans′-) A municipal borough of Nottinghamshire, England.

Mans·field (manz′fēld, mans′-), **Katherine** Pseudonym of Kathleen Beauchamp Murry, 1888–1923, British author born in New Zealand. —**Richard,** 1854–1907, U.S. actor born in England.

Mans·field (manz′fēld, mans′-), **Mount** The highest peak of the Green Mountains, Vermont; 4,393 feet.

Man·ship (man′ship), **Paul,** Born 1885, U.S. sculptor.

man·sion (man′shən) *n.* **1** A large or handsome dwelling; specifically, the house of the lord of a manor; a manor-house. **2** In astrology, one of the 12 divisions of the heavens; a house. **3** According to Oriental and medieval astronomers, one of the 28 divisions of the heavens occupied by the moon on successive days. **4** *Archaic* Any place of abode. **5** A small compartment, abode, or dwelling in a larger house or enclosure. **6** *pl. Brit.* An apartment house. See synonyms under HOUSE. [<OF <L *mansio, -onis* a dwelling < *mansus,* pp. of *manere* remain, dwell. Doublet of MENAGE.]

man-sized (man′sīzd′) *adj. Colloq.* Of a size appropriate for a man; large.

man·slaugh·ter (man′slô′tər) *n.* The killing of man by man; especially, such killing without malice.

man·slay·er (man′slā′ər) *n.* One who commits homicide. —**man′slay′ing** *n.*

man·sue·tude (man′swə·tood, -tyood) *n.* Accustomed gentleness or mildness; tameness. [<L *mansuetudo, -inis* <*mansuetus,* pp. of *mansuesere* tame <*manus* hand + *suescere* accustom]

man·swear (man′swâr′) *v.i.* **·swore, ·sworn, ·swear·ing** *Obs.* To swear falsely. [OE *mānswerian* <*mān* wickedness + *swerian* swear]

mant (mänt) *v.t. & v.i. Scot.* To stammer. —**mant′er** *n.*

man·ta (man′tə) *n.* **1** A coarse cotton cloth used by the lower classes of Spanish America for clothing; specifically, a woman's shawl or other article of clothing made of such material. **2** In the Rocky Mountains, the canvas covering of the load of a pack-animal. **3** A devilfish. **4** *Obs.* A mantelet. [<Sp., a blanket <LL *mantum* a cloak, back formation <*mantellum.* See MANTLE.]

man·teau (man′tō, *Fr.* mä ́n·tō′) *n. pl.* **·teaus** (-tōz) or **·teaux** (*Fr.* -tō′) **1** A cloak or mantle worn by women; any mantle. **2** *Obs.* A woman's gown; a mantua. [<F <OF *mantel* MANTLE]

man·tel (man′təl) *n.* The facing about a fireplace, including the shelf above it; also, the shelf. ◆Homophone: *mantle.* [Var. of MANTLE; infl. in meaning by F *manteau* a mantelpiece]

man·tel·et (man′təl·et, mant′lit) *n.* **1** A small mantle or short cloak. **2** *Mil.* A screen or shield, as in an embrasure, to protect the defenders; a movable roof to protect a besieging party; also, a shield or protection, made of metal, rope, or wood, placed at openings, portholes, etc., to protect the gunner from

bullets or smoke. **3** In target-shooting, a bulletproof enclosure for observation. **4** A movable shelter used by hunters. Also spelled *mantlet.* [<OF, dim. of *mantel.* See MANTLE.]

man·tel·let·ta (man′təl·let′ə) *n.* In the Roman Catholic Church, a sleeveless vestment reaching almost to the knees, worn by bishops and various church dignitaries. [<Ital., dim. of *mantello* <L *mantellum.* See MANTLE.]

man·tel·piece (man′təl·pēs′) *n.* A mantel shelf.

man·tel·tree (man′təl·trē′) *n.* A wooden mantel; also, the arch of a mantel.

man·tic (man′tik) *adj.* Relating to divination, soothsaying, or the supposed inspired condition of a soothsayer; prophetic: *mantic* frenzy. [<Gk. *mantikos* <*mantis* a prophet. Akin to MANIA.]

-mantic *combining form* Used to form adjectives corresponding to nouns ending in *-mancy:* necromantic. [<Gk. *mantikos* prophetic < *manteia* divination]

man·til·la (man·til′ə) *n.* **1** A woman's light scarf or head covering of lace, as worn in Spain, Mexico, Italy, etc. **2** Any short mantle. [<Sp., dim. of *manta* MANTA]

man·tis (man′tis) *n. pl.* **·tis·es** or **·tes** (-tēz) A carnivorous, orthopterous, long-bodied insect (family *Mantidae*) with large eyes and movable head, which assumes a position with its forelegs folded as if in prayer. Also called *praying mantis.* For illustration see INSECTS (beneficial). [<Gk., a prophet, also a kind of insect]

man·tis·sa (man·tis′ə) *n. Math.* The decimal or fractional part of a logarithm: so named as being added to the integral part or characteristic. [<L, a makeweight, trifling addition, ? <Etruscan]

mantis shrimp A squill. Also **mantis crab.**

man·tle (man′təl) *n.* **1** A loose garment, usually without sleeves, worn over the other garments; a cloak. **2** Anything that clothes or envelops; hence, whatever covers or conceals; a *mantle* of darkness. **3** *Zool.* **a** The variously modified flap or folds of the membranous covering of a mollusk. It secretes the shell. **b** The back, scapulars, and folded wings of a bird, when distinguished by color, as in gulls. **c** The soft external body-wall in the tunic of ascidians. **4** The outer covering of a wall. **5** The outer masonry of a blast furnace. **6** A sheath of clay laid over a wax model, forming a mold when the wax is melted out. **7** A mantel. **8** A hood of network fabric, generally cylindrical, of the salts of certain rare refractory earths with high radiating power, as cerium oxide, intended to give light by incandescence, as in the flame of a Bunsen burner, or in the Welsbach burner. —*v.* **·tled, ·tling** *v.t.* **1** To cover with or as with a mantle; conceal. —*v.i.* **2** To overspread or cover the surface of something. **3** To be or become covered, overspread, or suffused. **4** To spread out one wing at a time over the corresponding outstretched leg: said of hawks. ◆Homophone: *mantel.* [Fusion of OE *mentel* and OF *mantel,* both <L *mantellum, mantelum* a cloak, cloth, towel]

mant·let (mant′lit) See MANTELET.

man·tu·a (man′choo·ə, -too·ə) *n.* A woman's loose cloak, worn about 1700. [Alter. of *manteau;* infl. in form by *Mantua*]

Man·tu·a (man′choo·ə, -too·ə) A city on the Mincio, Lombardy, Italy; birthplace of Vergil. Italian **Man·to·va** (män′tō·vä). —**Man′tu·an** *n. & adj.*

Ma·nu·a Islands (mä·noo′ä) An island group in American Samoa; 22 square miles.

man·u·al (man′yoo·əl) *adj.* **1** Done, made, or used by the hand; of, relating to, or affecting the hand; *manual* employments. **2** *Law* Actually possessed; in one's own hands. **3** Resembling a manual; designed to be retained for reference: said of a book. — *n.* **1** A compact volume; handbook of instruction or directions. **2** A keyboard, as of an organ. **3** A systematic exercise in the handling of some military weapon. [<OF *manuel* <L *manualis* <*manus* hand] —**man′u·al·ly** *adv.*

manual alphabet A series of manual signs or gestures representing the letters of the written alphabet, used by the deaf as a substitute for vocal speech. See illustration.

manual training In U.S. schools, training of pupils in carpentry, woodworking, etc.

ma·nu·bri·um (mə·noo′brē·əm, -nyoo′-) *n. pl.* **·bri·a** (-brē·ə) **1** *Anat.* Some part or process like or likened to a handle; especially, the an-

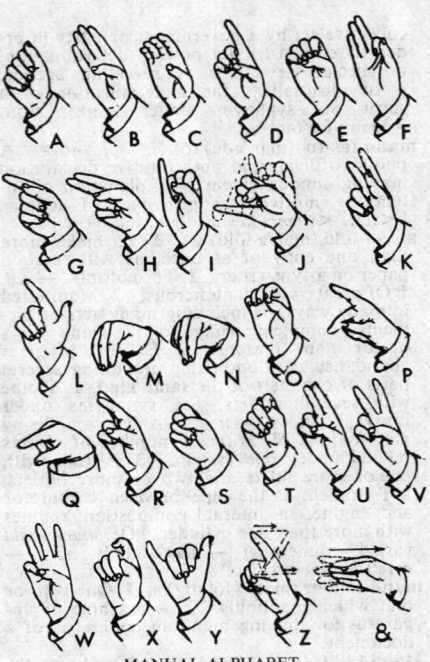

MANUAL ALPHABET

terior part of the sternum in man and many mammals: also called *episternum.* **2** *Mech.* A handle or haft, as of an organ stop. [<L, a handle, <*manus* hand] —**ma·nu′bri·al** *adj.*

Ma·nu·el (mä′noo·el′) Portuguese and Spanish form of EMMANUEL.

man·u·fac·to·ry (man′yə·fak′tər·ē) *n. pl.* **·ries** A place or establishment where anything is manufactured; a factory. [<MANUFACTURE; on analogy with FACTORY]

man·u·fac·ture (man′yə·fak′chər) *v.t.* **·tured, ·tur·ing 1** To make or fashion by hand or machinery, especially in large quantities. **2** To work into useful form, as wool or steel. **3** To create by artifice; invent falsely; concoct. **4** To produce in a mechanical way, as art, poetry, etc. See synonyms under MAKE[1], PRODUCE. —*n.* **1** The production of goods by hand or by industrial art or processes. **2** Anything made by industrial art or processes; manufactured articles collectively. **3** The making or contriving of anything. [<MF <Med. L *manufactura* <L *manus* hand + *factura* a making <*factus,* pp. of *facere* make] —**man′u·fac′tur·er** *n.* —**man′u·fac′tur·ing** *adj.*

man·u·mit (man′yə·mit′) *v.t.* **·mit·ted, ·mit·ting** To free from bondage, as a slave; emancipate; liberate. [<L *manumittere* <*manu emittere,* lit., send forth from one's hand <*manus* hand + *emittere* <*ex* away from + *mittere* send] —**man′u·mis′sion** (-mish′ən) *n.*

ma·nure (mə·noor′, -nyoor′) *n.* Any substance, as dung, decaying animal or vegetable matter, or certain minerals, applied to fertilize soil. —*v.t.* **·nured, ·nur·ing** To apply manure or other fertilizer to, as soil. [<AF *maynoverer* work with the hands, OF *manouvrer* < LL *manoperare.* Doublet of MANEUVER, MAINOR.] —**ma·nur′er** *n.*

ma·nus (mä′nəs) *n. pl.* **ma·nus** **1** *Anat.* The hand, or the corresponding terminal part of a limb in vertebrates, as a forefoot, claw, hoof, or the like. **2** In ancient Roman law, authoritative control: said of persons rather than of things, as of the wife or children being *in manu* (literally, in the hand) of the husband or father. [<L, hand]

Ma·nus (mä′noos) Largest of the Admiralty Islands; 633 square miles.

man·u·script (man′yə·skript) *n.* **1** Matter written by hand with a pen or the like; a composition in handwriting or typewriting, as distinguished from a printed one. Abbr. *MS.,* plural *MSS.* **2** A roll or book written before the invention of printing. —*adj.* Written by hand. [<Med. L *manuscriptus* <L *manus* hand + *scriptus,* pp. of *scribere* write]

Ma·nu·ti·us (mə·noo′shē·əs, -shəs, -nyoo′-),

Aldus, 1450–1515, Italian printer; inventor of italic letters.

man·ward (man'wərd) *adv.* To or toward man. Also **man'wards.**

man·wise (man'wīz') *adv.* After the manner of a man or of men.

Manx (mangks) *adj.* Pertaining to the Isle of Man, its people, or their language. —*n.* **1** The people of the Isle of Man collectively: with *the.* **2** The Gaelic language of the Manx, virtually extinct. [<ON *manskr* of the Isle of Man, ult. <Celtic]

Manx cat (mangks) A variety of domestic cat having no tail.

Manx·man (mangks'-mən) *n. pl.* **·men** (-mən) A native of the Isle of Man.

man·y (men'ē) *adj.* **more, most** Constituting a large number; numerous. —*n.* **1** A large number: *Many* of those present left early. **2** The masses; crowd; multitude: with *the.* —*pron.* A large number of persons or things. [OE *manig*]

MANX CAT
Named after the Isle of Man, this cat is common throughout Russia and the Far East.

◆ *Many* followed by *a, an,* or *another* indicates a great number thought of singly: *Many a* man has had to find this out for himself. The phrase *a great many* is idiomatic; it resembles a collective noun, but takes only a plural verb: *A great many* are involved.

Synonyms (adj.): divers, frequent, manifold, multifarious, multiplied, multitudinous, numerous, sundry, various. *Antonyms:* few, infrequent, rare, scarce, uncommon.

man·y·plies (men'i·plīz') *n. Zool.* The third stomach of a ruminant, whose lining membrane is raised into many closely set, longitudinal folds; omasum. [<MANY + *plies,* pl. of PLY[1], *n.*]

Man·za·na·res (män'thä·nä'räs) A river in central Spain, flowing 55 miles SE past Madrid to a tributary of the Tagus.

man·za·nil·la (man'zə·nil'ə, *Sp.* män·thä·nē'lyä) *n.* **1** A pale, dry sherry with low alcoholic content. **2** A bitter olive usually stuffed with pimentos. [<Sp., orig. name of several carduaceous plants, dim. of *manzana* an apple. See MANCHINEEL.]

Man·za·nil·lo (män'sä·nē'yō) A port in SE Cuba.

man·za·ni·ta (man'zə·nē'tə, *Sp.* män'sä·nē'tä) *n.* Any one of several shrubs or small trees (genus *Arctostaphylos*) of the western United States, including the bearberry. [<Sp., dim. of *manzana* an apple. See MANCHINEEL.]

Man·zi·kert (man'zi·kûrt) A village in eastern Turkey NW of Lake Van; scene of the decisive defeat of the Byzantine Empire by the Seljuk Turks, 1071.

Man·zo·ni (män·dzō'nē), **Alessandro,** 1785–1873, Italian novelist and poet.

Mao·ism (mou'iz'əm) *n.* The militant communist doctrines or practices of Mao Tse-tung, characterized especially by a rejection of the possibility of coexistence with capitalistic states. —**Mao'ist** *n.*

Ma·o·ri (mä'ō·rē, mou'rē) *n.* **1** One of an aboriginal, light-brown people of New Zealand, chiefly Polynesian, mixed somewhat with Melanesian. **2** The Polynesian language of these people. —*adj.* Of or pertaining to the Maoris or their language.

Mao Tse-tung (mou' dzu'dŏong'), 1893–1976, Chinese Communist leader; chairman of the People's Republic of China 1949–59.

map (map) *n.* **1** A representation on a plane surface of any region, as of the earth's surface; a chart. **2** Figuratively, any exact delineation. **3** *Slang* The face. —**off the map** Out of existence; out of the running. —*v.t.* **mapped, map·ping 1** To make a map of. **2** To plan in detail: often with *out.* [<OF *mappe-(monde)* <Med. L *mappa (mundi)* map (of the world) <L, cloth, napkin]

Map (map), **Walter,** 1140?–1209?, Welsh author: also called **Ma·pes** (mā'pēz).

ma·ple (mā'pəl) *n.* **1** Any of a large genus

(Acer) of deciduous trees of the north temperate zone, with opposite leaves and a fruit of two joined samaras. **2** Its wood, which is hard, light in color, and of close grain. **3** The amber–yellow color of the finished wood. **4** The flavor of the sap of the sugar maple. —**hard maple 1** The sugar maple. **2** The black maple (*A. nigrum*). [OE *mapel(trēow), mapul(der)* a maple (tree)]

ma·qui (mä'kē) *n.* An ornamental evergreen shrub (*Aristotelia macqui*), used in Chile in making musical instruments. A medicinal wine is made from its purple acid berries. [<Sp. <Araucan]

ma·quis (mä·kē') *n.* A zone of shrubby, mostly evergreen plants in the Mediterranean region, transitional between steppe and forest growths: known as cover for game or bandits: also called *macchia.* [<F <Ital. *macchia* a thicket, orig. a spot <L *macula* small spot]

Ma·quis (mä·kē') *n. pl.* **·quis** The military branch of the French Underground, originally guerrilla bands, named for the maquis, chaparral–like brush of the Mediterranean coasts where they were first organized; by extension, the whole French Forces of the Interior, or French Underground, which developed after the fall of France in World War II.

mar (mär) *v.t.* **marred, mar·ring 1** To do harm to; impair or ruin. **2** To injure so as to deface; disfigure. See synonyms under HURT. —*n.* A disfiguring mark; blemish; injury. [OE *merran, mierran* hinder, injure] —**mar'·rer** *n.*

Mar (mär), **Earl of,** 1675–1732, John Erskine, Scottish politician and rebel, defeated by Argyle at Dunblane, 1715.

mar·a·bou (mar'ə·bōo) *n.* **1** A stork of the genus *Leptoptilos,* especially the African marabou (*L. crumeniferus*), whose soft, white, lower tail and wing feathers are used in millinery. **2** The adjutant bird. **3** A plume from the marabou. **4** A delicate white silk that can be dyed without being freed from gum. Also **mar'a·bout** (-bōot). [<F *marabou, marabout.* See MARABOUT.]

Mar·a·bout (mar'ə·bōot) *n.* A Moslem hermit or holy man of northern Africa, revered as a saint by the Berbers. [<F *marabout* <Arabic *murābit* a hermit]

MARABOU
(From 3 to 4 feet high at the shoulder)

ma·ra·ca (mə·rä'kə, *Pg.* mä·rä'kä) *n.* A percussion instrument made of a gourd or gourd–shaped rattle with beans or beads inside it. [<Pg. *maracá* <Tupian]

Ma·ra·cai·bo (mä'rä·kī'bō) A port and the second largest city of Venezuela, on the narrows between Lake Maracaibo (5,000 square miles) in NW Venezuela and the Gulf of Maracaibo (also *Gulf of Venezuela*), an inlet of the Caribbean in Venezuela and Colombia.

Mar·a·can·da (mar'ə·kan'də) Ancient name for SAMARKAND.

Ma·ra·cay (mä'rä·kī') A city in northern Venezuela.

Ma·rah (mā'rə, mâr'ə) *n.* Bitter water: used in allusion to the meaning in *Exodus* xv 23. [<Hebrew *mārāh,* fem. of *mar* bitter]

mar·a·na·tha (mar'ə·nath'ə) See ANATHEMA MARANATHA.

Ma·ran·hão (mä'rə·nyouɴ') A state of NE Brazil on the Atlantic; 129,270 square miles; capital, São Luis de Maranhão.

Ma·ra·ñón (mä'rä·nyōn') One of the main sources of the Amazon in Peru, flowing 1,000 miles north.

ma·ran·ta (mə·ran'tə) *n.* Starch from arrowroot. [after Bartolommeo *Maranta,* died 1554, Italian physician and botanist]

ma·ras·ca (mə·ras'kə) *n.* A small, wild cherry (*Prunus cerasus marasca*) of the Dalmatian mountains. [<Ital., aphetic var. of *amarasca*

< *amaro* bitter <L *amarus*]

mar·a·schi·no (mar'ə·skē'nō) *n.* A cordial distilled from the fermented juice of the marasca and flavored with the cracked pits. [<Ital. < *marasca* MARASCA]

maraschino cherries Cherries preserved in maraschino liqueur.

ma·ras·mus (mə·raz'məs) *n. Pathol.* A gradual and continuous wasting away of the body; emaciation, especially in infants and the aged. [<NL <Gk. *marasmos* <*marainein* waste]— **ma·ras'mic** *adj.*

Ma·rat (má·rá'), **Jean Paul,** 1743–93, French revolutionary leader; killed by Charlotte Corday.

Ma·ra·tha (mə·rä'tə) See MAHRATTA.

Ma·ra·thi (mə·rä'tē) *n.* The Indic language of the Mahratta of India: also spelled *Mahrati.*

mar·a·thon (mar'ə·thon) *n.* **1** A footrace of 26 miles, 385 yards: a feature of the Olympic games: so called from a messenger's legendary run from Marathon to Athens to announce the Athenian victory over the Persians, 490 B.C. **2** Any endurance contest.

Mar·a·thon (mar'ə·thon) A plain in Attica, Greece, on the Aegean; scene of decisive victory of the Athenians over the Persians, 490 B.C.

ma·raud (mə·rôd') *v.i.* To rove in search of plunder; make raids for booty. —*v.t.* To invade for plunder; raid. —*n.* A foray. [<F *marauder* <*maraud* a rogue]—**ma·raud'er** *n.*

mar·a·ve·di (mar'ə·vā'dē) *n.* A former Spanish coin of little value. [<Sp. *maravedí* <Arabic *murābitīn,* a Moorish dynasty of Spain, 1087–1147]

mar·ble (mär'bəl) *n.* **1** A compact, granular, partly crystallized limestone, occurring in many colors, valuable for building or ornamental purposes. ◆ Collateral adjective: *marmoreal.* **2** A sculptured or inscribed piece of this stone. **3** A small ball made of this stone, or of baked clay, glass, or porcelain. **4** *pl.* A boys' game played with such balls. **5** Marbling (def. 1). —*v.t.* **bled, ·bling** To color or vein in imitation of marble, as book edges.—*adj.* **1** Made of or like marble. **2** Without feeling; cold. See synonyms under PALE[2]. [<OF *marble, marbre* <L *marmor* <Gk. *marmaros,* lit., sparkling–stone, orig. stone; infl. in sense by *marmairein* sparkle]

marble cake A cake made of light and dark batter mixed to give a marblelike appearance.

mar·bled (mär'bəld) *adj.* Veined, clouded, or variegated like marble.

mar·ble·ize (mär'bəl·īz) *v.t.* **·ized, ·iz·ing** *U.S.* To marble.

mar·ble·wood (mär'bəl·wŏod') *n.* **1** A large East Indian tree (*Diospyros marmorata*) of the ebony family, yielding a variegated wood. **2** Its wood.

mar·bling (mär'bling) *n.* **1** A marking, mottling, or coloring resembling that of marble. **2** The act or method of imitating marble.

mar·bly (mär'blē) *adj.* **1** Resembling or containing marble. **2** Still or rigid like marble.

Mar·burg (mär'bûrg, *Ger.* mär'bŏorkh) A city in west central Hesse, West Germany. Also **Mar'burg an der Lahn** (än der län').

marc (märk) *n.* **1** Solid refuse remaining from grapes or other fruit after pressing. **2** A brandy distilled from this. **3** Any insoluble residue after a substance has been treated with a solvent. [<F, prob. <*marcher* tread, press (grapes). See MARCH[1].]

Marc (märk), **Franz,** 1880–1916, German painter.

mar·ca·site (mär'kə·sīt) *n.* **1** A pale, bronze–yellow, orthorhombic iron disulfide, FeS[2]; white iron pyrites. It is a dimorphous form of pyrites. **2** An ornament made of crystallized white pyrites or of highly polished steel. [<Med. L *marcasita,* prob. <Arabic *marqashīṭā* <Aramaic]

mar·cel (mär·sel') *v.t.* **·celled, ·cel·ling** To dress (the hair) in even, continuous waves by means of special irons. [after M. *Marcel,* 19th c. French hairdresser]—**mar·cel'ler** *n.*

marcel wave In hairdressing, a style of dressing the hair in tiers of even, continuous waves.

Mar·cel·la (mär·sel'ə) A feminine personal name.

Mar·cel·lus (mär·sel'əs) A masculine personal

name; diminutive of MARCUS. Also *Fr.* **Mar·cel** (mår·sel′), *Ital.* **Mar·cel·lo** (mär·chel′lō).
—**Marcellus, Marcus Claudius,** 268?–208 B.C., Roman general in the Second Punic War.

mar·ces·cent (mär·ses′ənt) *adj.* **1** Withering; withered. **2** *Bot.* Withering without falling off, as the corollas of heaths, etc. [<L *marcescens, -entis,* ppr. of *marcescere,* inceptive of *marcere* be faint, languid] —**mar·ces′cence** *n.*

march[1] (märch) *n.* **1** Movement together on foot and in time, as of soldiers; a stately, dignified walk. **2** A movement, as of soldiers, from one stopping place to another. **3** The distance thus passed over. **4** Onward progress: the *march* of events. **5** A piece of music suitable for regulating the movements of persons marching. —*v.i.* **1** To move with measured, regular steps, as a soldier; proceed in step, as troops. **2** To walk in a solemn or dignified manner. **3** To proceed steadily; advance. —*v.t.* **4** To cause to march. [<MF *marche* < *marcher* walk, orig. trample, ult. <LL *marcus* a hammer <L *marculus*] —**march′er** *n.*

march[2] (märch) *n.* **1** A region or district lying along a boundary line; frontier. **2** *pl.* The border regions of England and Wales, or of England and Scotland. **3** *Scot.* The boundary or boundary marks between lands or estates. See synonyms under BOUNDARY. [<OF *marche* < Gmc. Akin to MARK[1], MARGIN.]

March The third month of the year, containing 31 days. [<AF *marche,* OF *marz* <L *Martius (mensis)* (month) of Mars <*Mars* the god Mars]

March (märkh) A river in Czechoslovakia forming part of the boundary between Czechoslovakia and Austria and flowing 180 miles NW to the Danube: Czech *Morava.*

Marche (mårsh) A region and former province of central France.

Mär·chen (mer′khən) *n. pl.* **Mär·chen** *German* A story; especially, a fairy tale or folk tale.

march·er (mär′chər) *n.* **1** An officer who defended a march. **2** One who resides in a march. [<MARCH[2]]

Mar·ches (mär′chiz), **The** A region of central Italy; 3,741 square miles; capital, Ancona. *Italian* **Le Mar·che** (lā mär′kā).

mar·che·sa (mär·kā′zä) *n. pl.* **·che·se** (-kā′zā) *Italian* A marchioness.

mar·che·se (mär·kā′zā) *n. pl.* **·che·si** (-kā′zē) *Italian* A nobleman of the rank of a marquis.

Mar·ches·van (mär·khesh′vən) See HESHWAN.

March hare A hare in the breeding season: regarded as a symbol of madness from the supposed wildness of hares at this time.

mar·chion·ess (mär′shən·is) *n.* **1** The wife or widow of a marquis. **2** A woman having in her own right the rank corresponding to that of a marquis. [<Med. L *marchionissa,* fem. of *marchio, -onis* a captain of the marches < *marca* march[2] <Gmc.]

march·land (märch′land′) *n.* Land along the boundaries of adjacent countries; borderland. [<MARCH[2] + LAND]

march·pane (märch′pān′) *n.* Marzipan. [<MF *marcepain* <Ital. *marzapane* MARZIPAN]

Mar·ci·a (mär′shē·ə, -shə) A feminine personal name.

Mar·co Po·lo (mär′kō pō′lō) See POLO, MARCO.

Mar·co·ni (mär·kō′nē) *adj.* Pertaining to or designating the system of wireless telegraphy, developed by Guglielmo Marconi.

Mar·co·ni (mär·kō′nē), **Guglielmo,** 1874–1937, Italian inventor of wireless telegraphy.

Marconi rig In yachting, a type of rig consisting of a triangular sail mounted on a tall mast and having no gaff and a relatively short boom: so called from the resemblance of the mast and its stays to a radio mast. Compare GAFF RIG.

mar·cot·tage (mär′kō·täzh′) *n.* A method for the vegetative propagation of plants in which a part of the stem or branch is packed with moss until roots have formed and the treated part is ready for independent growth. [<F < *marcotter* plant layers <*marcotte* a layer (def. 3) <L *mergus* a vine layer, a diver <*mergere* dip, bury]

Mar·cus (mär′kəs) See MARK. Also *Fr.* **Marc** (mårk), *Ital.* **Mar·co** (mär′kō). [<L, of MARS]
—**Marcus Antonius** See ANTONY, MARK.
—**Marcus Aurelius** See under AURELIUS.

Mar·cus Island (mär′kəs) A North Pacific island east of the Volcano Islands, administered by the United States; one square mile; held (1899–1945) by Japan as **Mi·na·mi To·ri Shi·ma** (mē·nä·mē tō·rē shē·mä).

Mar del Pla·ta (mär thel plä′tä) A city in SE Buenos Aires province, Argentina.

Mar·di gras (mär′dē grä′) Shrove Tuesday; last day before Lent: celebrated as a carnival in certain cities. [<F., lit., fat Tuesday]

Mar·duk (mär′dook) In Babylonian mythology, the chief deity, originally a local sun-god.

mare[1] (mâr) *n.* The female of the horse and other equine animals. [OE *mēre,* fem. of *mearh* a horse]

mare[2] (mâr) *n.* A hag or goblin supposed to produce nightmare; also, nightmare. [OE. Akin to MAR.]

mar·e[3] (mâr′ē) *n. pl.* **mar·i·a** (mâr′ē·ə) Any of a number of dark, seemingly flat areas of the moon's surface. [<L, sea; because of their resemblance to seas]

ma·re clau·sum (mâr′ē klô′səm) *Latin* A closed sea; a sea subject to one nation: distinguished from an *open sea,* which is free to all.

Mare Island (mâr) An island in San Pablo Bay, north California; site of U.S. Navy yard.

ma·rem·ma (mə·rem′ə) *n. pl.* **·me** (-ē) **1** A fertile, marshy, but unhealthful piedmont region near the sea, as in Tuscany, Italy. **2** The miasmatic exhalations of such a region. [<Ital.< L *maritimus* MARITIME]

Ma·ren·go (mə·reng′gō) A village in Piedmont, NW Italy; scene of Napoleon's defeat of the Austrians, 1800.

ma·re nos·trum (mâr′ē nos′trəm) *Latin* Our sea: the Roman name for the Mediterranean.

mare's-nest (mârz′nest′) *n.* A seemingly important discovery that proves worthless, imaginary, or false.

mare's-tail (mârz′tāl′) *n.* **1** *Meteorol.* Long, fibrous, cirrus clouds, supposed to indicate rain. **2** A perennial aquatic herb *(Hippuris vulgaris)* with entire lineal leaves in whorls.

Mar·ga·ret (mär′gə·rət) **1** A feminine personal name. Also **Mar·ger·y** (mär′jər·ē), *Lat.* **Mar·ga·re·ta** (mär′gə·rē′tə), *Du.* **Mar·ga·re·tha** (mär′gä·rē′tä), *Ger.* **Mar·ga·re·the** (mär′gə·rā′tə), *Pg.* **Mar·ga·ri·da** (mär′gə·rē′thə) *Lat., Ital.* **Mar·ga·ri·ta** (mär′gä·rē′tä), *Ital.* **Mar·ghe·ri·ta** (mär′ge·rē′tä), *Fr.* **Mar·gue·rite** (mår·gə·rēt′). [<Gk., pearl] **2** In Goethe's *Faust,* Margarethe, the heroine: also *Gretchen.*
—**Margaret of Anjou,** 1430–82, wife of Henry VI of England; a leader of the Lancastrians in the Wars of the Roses.
—**Margaret of Navarre,** 1492–1549, queen of Navarre, 1544–49.
—**Margaret of Valois,** 1553–1615, wife of Henry of Navarre; divorced: also known as *Margaret of France.*

mar·gar·ic (mär·gar′ik, -gär′-) *adj.* Of, pertaining to, or resembling pearl; pearly. Also **mar·ga·rit·ic** (mär′gə·rit′ik). [<F *margarique* <Gk. *margaron* a pearl]

margaric acid A white, crystalline, fatty acid, $C_{17}H_{34}O_2$, obtained from the wax of lichens or made synthetically. [<F *margarique* MARGARIC; with ref. to the pearly luster of its crystals]

mar·ga·rine (mär′jə·rin, -rēn, -gə-) *n.* A blend of refined, edible vegetable oil or meat fat, or a combination of both, churned with cultured skim milk to the consistency of butter. Also called *oleomargarine.* [<the early mistaken belief that it contained a derivative of margaric acid]

mar·ga·ri·ta (mar′gə·rē′tə) *n.* A cocktail made of tequila, lime or lemon juice, and an orange liqueur.

mar·ga·rite (mär′gə·rīt) *n.* **1** A hydrated silicate of calcium and aluminum. **2** Minute spherical crystals arranged as a beadlike pattern in glassy igneous rocks. **3** *Obs.* A pearl. [<OF <L *margarita* a pearl. See MARGARET.]

Mar·gate (mär′git) A municipal borough, port, and resort in NE Kent, England.

mar·gay (mär′gā) *n.* One of various South and Central American striped and spotted wild cats; especially, the long-tailed *Felis tigrina* [<F <*margaia* <Pg. *maracajá* <Tupian *mbaracaïa*]

marge[1] (märj) *n. Archaic* A margin. [<MF < L *margo* a margin]

marge[2] (märj) *n. Brit. Colloq.* Margarine.

mar·gin (mär′jin) *n.* **1** A bounding line; border; verge; brink; edge. **2** An allowance, provision, or reservation for contingencies or changes, as of time or money. **3** Range or scope; provision for increase or progress. **4** The difference between the cost of an article and its selling price. **5** A sum of money or other security deposited with a broker to protect him against loss in buying and selling for his principal; also, the difference in value between the security and the loan. **6** The difference between price and cost of production; in the adjustment of the relations of capital and labor, the minimum profit which will enable an undertaking to continue active. **7** The part of a page left blank around the body of printed or written text. —*v.t.* **1** To furnish with a margin; form a margin or border to; border. **2** To enter, place, or specify on the margin of a page, as a note or comment. **3** In commerce, to deposit a margin upon; hold by giving an addition to or a deposit upon a margin. [<L *margo, -inis.* Akin to MARK[1], MARCH[2].]

Synonyms (noun): beach, border, boundary, brim, brink, confines, edge, limit, lip, marge, shore, skirt, verge. See BANK, BOUNDARY.

mar·gi·nal (mär′jə·nəl) *adj.* **1** Pertaining to or constituting a margin. **2** Written, printed, or placed on the margin. **3** *Psychol.* Relating to the fringe of consciousness. **4** *Econ.* Operating or furnishing goods at a rate barely meeting the costs of production. **5** Of a nature that barely qualifies as useful, productive, or necessary. —**mar′gi·nal·ly** *adv.*

mar·gi·na·li·a (mär′jə·nā′lē·ə, nāl′yə) *n. pl.* **1** Marginal notes. **2** *Zool.* Spicules forming a collar around the osculum of a sponge. [< NL, neut. pl. of *marginalis* marginal <L *margo, -inis* a margin]

mar·gi·nate (mär′jə·nāt) *v.t.* **·nat·ed, ·nat·ing** To provide with a margin or margins. —*adj. Biol.* Having a margin, especially one of a distinct character, appearance, or color: also **mar′·gi·nat′ed.** [<L *marginatus,* pp. of *marginare* <*margo, -inis* a margin] —**mar′gi·na′·tion** *n.*

mar·grave (mär′grāv) *n.* **1** A hereditary German title of nobility, corresponding to *marquis.* **2** Formerly, the lord or governor of a German mark, march, or border. **3** A hereditary title of certain princes of the Holy Roman Empire. [<MDu. *markgrave* < MHG *marcgrave* <*mark* a march[2] + *graf* a count]

mar·gra·vi·ate (mär·grā′vē·it) *n.* The territory of a margrave. Also **mar·gra·vate** (mär′grə·vāt). [<Med. L *margravius,* ? <MHG *marcgrave* a margrave]

mar·gra·vine (mär′grə·vēn) *n.* The wife or widow of a margrave. [<Du. *markgravin,* fem. of *markgraaf* <MDu. *markgrave* a margrave]

mar·gue·rite (mär′gə·rēt′) *n.* A flower of the composite family, as the common garden daisy and the oxeye daisy of the fields; also, a chrysanthemum, *Chrysanthemum frutescens.* [<F, a pearl, daisy, from a proper name. See MARGARET.]

Ma·ri·a (mə·rī′ə, -rē′ə; *Du., Ger., Ital., Sp., Sw.* mä·rē′ä; *Hungarian* mä′rē·ä) A feminine personal name. See also MARY. Also **Mar·i·an** (mar′ē·ən), **Ma·rie** (mə·rē′; *Dan.* mä·rē′e, *Fr.* må·rē′), **Mar·i·on** (mar′ē·ən). [See MARY]
—**Maria de 'Medici,** 1573–1642, wife of Henry IV of France. Also *Marie de Médicis.*
—**Maria Theresa,** 1717–80, wife of Francis I, Holy Roman Emperor.
—**Marie Antoinette,** 1755–93, wife of Louis XVI of France; guillotined.
—**Marie Louise,** 1791–1847, wife of Napoleon I; empress of the French.

ma·ri·a·chi (mär·ē·ä′chē) *n.* **1** A wandering band of Mexican street musicians. **2** The musicians, usually made up of singers and guitarists. **3** The music they play. [<Mexican Sp.]

ma·ri·age de con·ve·nance (må·ryäzh′ də kôṅ·väns) *French* A marriage of convenience; an advantageous marriage; not a love match.

Mar·i·an (mâr′ē·ən) *n.* **1** A worshiper or devotee of the Virgin Mary. **2** An adherent of Mary I, queen of England, or a defender of Mary Queen of Scots. —*adj.* **1** Of or pertaining to the Virgin Mary, or characterized by a special devotion to her. **2** Pertaining to Queen Mary of England, or to Mary Queen of Scots.

Mar·i·an (mar′ē·ən) A feminine personal name. See MARIA.

Ma·ri·na·o (mä′ryä·nä′ō) A city in western Cuba.

Ma·ri·a·nas Islands (mä′rē·ä′näs) An archipelago in the western Pacific Ocean, including Guam, Saipan, Tinian, and Rota; comprising part of the United Nations Trust Territory of the Pacific Islands (excluding Guam); total, 450 square miles; Japanese mandate, 1919–1944: formerly *Ladrones.* Also **Ma′ri·a′na** or **Ma′ri·an′ne Islands** (-rē·än′ə).

Ma·ri·anne (mâr′ē·an′) 1 A feminine personal name. 2 The French Republic, as personified on coins, etc.

Ma·ri·a Ther·e·si·o·pel (mä·rē′ä ter·ā′zē·ō′pel) A German name for SUBOTICA.

Ma·ri Autonomous S.S.R. (mä′rē) An administrative division of central European Russian S.F.S.R.; 8,900 square miles; capital, Ioshkar-Ola.

Ma·rie (mə·rē′) See MARIA.

Ma·rie Ga·lante (mà·rē′ gà·länt′) An island dependency of Guadeloupe; 60 square miles. Also **Ma·rie′–Ga·lante′.**

Ma·ri·gna·no (mä′rē·nyä′nō) A former name for MELEGNANO.

mar·i·gold (mar′ə·gōld) *n.* 1 A plant of the composite family (genus *Tagetes*), with golden–yellow flowers; especially, the French marigold (*T. patula*), and the Aztec or African marigold (*T. erecta*). 2 The calendula. 3 The marsh marigold. [<MARY, prob. with ref. to the Virgin Mary + GOLD]

marigold yellow The bright orange–yellow color of various marigolds.

mar·i·hua·na (mar′ə·wä′nə, *Sp.* mä′rē·hwä′nä) *n.* The hemp plant (*Cannabis sativa*), whose dried leaves and flower tops yield a narcotic smoked in cigarettes. Also **ma′ri·jua′na.** [<Am. Sp. *marihuana, mariguana,* ? blend of N. Am. Ind. name and Sp. *Maria Juana* Mary Jane, a personal name]

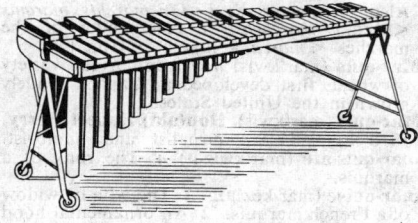

MODERN MARIMBA

ma·rim·ba (mə·rim′bə) *n.* A form of xylophone sometimes having calabash resonators. [< Bantu *marimba, malimba,* pl. of *limba,* a kind of musical instrument]

Ma·rin (mä′rin), **John,** 1870–1953, U.S. painter.

ma·ri·na (mə·rē′nə) *n. Naut.* A basin or safe anchorage for small vessels; especially, one at which provisions, supplies, etc., may be obtained. [<Ital., a seacoast <L *marinus* MARINE]

Ma·ri·na (mä·rē′nä) See ESPÍRITO SANTO.

mar·i·nade (mar′ə·nād′) *n.* 1 A brine pickle sometimes flavored with wine, spices, and herbs, in which meat or fish are placed before cooking, to improve their flavor. 2 Pickled meat or fish. [<F <Sp. *marinada* <*marinar* pickle in brine <*marino* marine <L *marinus* MARINE]

mar·i·nate (mar′ə·nāt) *v.t.* **·nat·ed, ·nat·ing** 1 To soak in oil and vinegar or brine preparatory to cooking; prepare with marinade. 2 To allow, as salad, to soak in French dressing before serving. [<MARIN(ADE) + -ATE[1]]

Ma·rin·du·que (mä′rin·dōō′kā) An island of the Philippines south of Luzon; 346 square miles.

ma·rine (mə·rēn′) *adj.* 1 Of or pertaining to the sea or matters connected with the sea; maritime. 2 Native to, existing in, or formed by the sea. 3 Intended for use at sea or in navigation; nautical; naval: *marine* currents, *marine* law, a *marine* almanac. 4 Employed on shipboard. See synonyms under NAUTICAL. — *n.* 1 A soldier trained for

service at sea and on land; a member of the Marine Corps: also **Marine.** 2 Shipping, or shipping interests generally. See MERCHANT MARINE. 3 A picture or painting of the sea. [<OF *marin* <L *marinus* <*mare, maris* a sea]

Marine Corps A branch of the U.S. Navy made up of combat troops, air forces, etc., under their own officers: the oldest organized military or naval body in the United States, authorized 1775: officially, the *United States Marine Corps.*

mar·i·ner (mar′ə·nər) *n.* One who navigates or assists in navigating a ship; a sailor. [<AF <L *marinus* marine]

Mariner's Medal A medal awarded to any seaman who is wounded or suffers from exposure owing to enemy action while serving on a ship during a war.

Ma·ri·nism (mar′ə·niz′əm) *n.* An ornate and flamboyant literary style, of the type cultivated by the Italian poet **Giambattista Ma·ri·ni** (mä·rē′nē), 1569–1625.

Mar·i·ol·a·try (mâr′ē·ol′ə·trē) *n.* Worship of the Virgin Mary: an opprobrious term: also spelled *Maryolatry.* [<*Mario-* (<MARY) + -LATRY] — **Mar′i·ol′a·trous** *adj.*

Mar·i·ol·o·gy (mâr′ē·ol′ə·jē) *n.* The whole body of religious belief and dogma relating to the Virgin Mary. Also spelled *Maryology.* [< *Mario-* (<MARY) + -LOGY]

Mar·i·on (mar′ē·ən) A masculine or feminine personal name. [<F, dim. of *Marie* MARY]

Mar·i·on (mar′ē·ən), **Francis,** 1732–95, American Revolutionary general: called "the Swamp Fox."

mar·i·o·nette (mar′ē·ə·net′) *n.* A puppet moved by strings. [<F *marionnette,* dim. of *Marion,* dim. of *Marie* MARY; prob. orig. a small image of the Virgin Mary]

Mar·i·po·sa (mar′ə·pō′zə) A county in central California, containing Yosemite Valley; 1,455 square miles.

Mariposa lily Any of a genus (*Calochortus*) of showy, colorful, liliaceous Mexican and Californian plants. Also **Mariposa tulip.**

mar·ish (mar′ish) *Obs. adj.* Marshy; boggy; growing in marshes, as plants. — *n.* A marsh; fen. [<OF *marais, mareis* <Med. L *mariscus* a marsh <Gmc.]

Mar·ist (mâr′ist) *adj.* 1 Of, pertaining to, or dedicated to the Virgin Mary. 2 Of or pertaining to the Marist Fathers, or to institutions founded by them. — *n.* A member of a Roman Catholic order devoted specifically to instruction and foreign missions: also **Marist Fathers.** [<(the VIRGIN) MAR(Y) + -IST]

Ma·ri·tain (mà·rē·tan′), **Jacques,** 1882–1973, French philosopher.

mar·i·tal (mar′ə·təl) *adj.* 1 Of or pertaining to marriage. 2 Of or pertaining to a husband. [<L *maritalis* <*maritus* a husband, orig. married] — **mar′i·tal·ly** *adv.*

mar·i·time (mar′ə·tīm) *adj.* 1 Situated on or near the sea. 2 Pertaining to the sea or matters connected with the sea; marine. 3 Characterized by pursuits, interests, or power at sea; nautical. See synonyms under NAUTICAL. [<F <L *maritimus* <*mare, maris* a sea]

Maritime Alps The part of the Alps between France and Italy, extending to the Mediterranean coast.

Maritime Provinces The provinces of New Brunswick, Nova Scotia, and Prince Edward Island on the Atlantic seaboard of eastern Canada.

Ma·ri·tza (mä·rē′tsä) A river in SE Europe, flowing 300 miles SE to the Aegean. Also **Ma·ri′tsa.** *Turkish* **Me·riç** (me·rēch′), *Greek* **Év·ros** (ev′ros).

Mar·itz·burg (mar′its·bûrg) A popular name for PIETERMARITZBURG.

Ma·ri·u·pol (mä·ryōō′pôl) The former name for ZHDANOV.

Mar·i·us (mâr′ē·əs), **Gaius,** 157–86 B.C., Roman general and consul.

Mar·i·vaux (mà·rē·vō′), **Pierre Carlet de Chamblain de,** 1688–1763, French dramatist and novelist.

mar·jo·ram (mär′jər·əm) *n.* Any of several perennial herbs of the mint family (genus *Majorana*), with nearly entire leaves, dense oblong spikes of–flowers, and colored bracts. *M. hortensis* is the **sweet marjoram,** used for seasoning in cookery. [<OF *majorane* <Med. L *majorana,* ? ult. <L *amaracus* <Gk. *amarakos*]

mark[1] (märk) *n.* 1 A visible trace, impression, or sign produced or left on any substance, as a line, scratch, dot, scar, spot, stain, or blemish; any physical peculiarity produced by drawing, indenting, stamping, or other process or agency. 2 A symbol or character, as a stamp, brand, or device, made on or attached to something to identify, distinguish, or call attention; a trademark. 3 A cross or other character made instead of a signature by one who cannot write. 4 A letter of the alphabet, number, or character by which excellence, defect, or quality is registered, as on a student's paper or record. 5 A symbol, written or printed: a *mark* of interrogation. 6 An object serving to guide, direct, or point out, as a boundary, a course, or a place in a book. 7 That which indicates the presence or existence of something; a characteristic; an evidence; a symptom. 8 That which is aimed at, or toward which effort is directed; something shot, fired, or thrown at, as a target; that which one strives to attain or achieve; a goal. 9 A proper bound or limit; standard. 10 Distinction; eminence: a person of *mark.* 11 A license to make reprisals. See LETTER OF MARQUE. 12 A person easily duped: an easy *mark.* 13 *Naut.* A strip of cloth or the like knotted or twisted into a lead line at intervals to indicate fathoms of depth. 14 An observing or noting; heed. 15 In medieval times, a piece of land held in common by a body of kindred freemen. 16 *Archaic* A boundary; limit. — **beside the mark** Pointless. — **bless the mark! save the mark!** Ejaculations of deprecation, irony, scorn, or humorous surprise: used originally of a good, then ironically of a bad, marksman. — **to make one's mark** To succeed. — **of mark** Famous; noteworthy; important. — **up to the mark** Up to standard; in good health or condition, etc. — *v.t.* 1 To make a mark or marks on. 2 To trace the boundaries of; limit. 3 To indicate by a mark or sign: X *marks* the spot. 4 To make or produce by writing, drawing, etc. 5 To be a characteristic of; typify. 6 To designate as if by marking; destine: He was *marked* for death. 7 To pay attention to; notice; remark. 8 To make known; manifest; show: to *mark* displeasure with a frown. 9 To apply a price, identification, etc., to. 10 To give marks or grades to; grade. — *v.i.* 11 To take notice; pay attention. 12 To keep score or count. 13 To make a mark or marks. See synonyms under INSCRIBE. Compare CIRCUMSCRIBE. — **to mark down** 1 To note down by writing or making marks. 2 To put a lower price on, as for a sale. — **to mark time** 1 To keep time by moving the feet but not advancing. 2 To pause in action or progress temporarily, as while awaiting developments. — **to mark up** 1 To make marks on; scar. 2 To increase the price of. [OE *mearc,* orig. boundary. Akin to MARGIN, MARCH[2].]

Synonyms (noun): badge, characteristic, fingerprint, footprint, impress, impression, indication, line, manifestation, print, sign, stamp, symbol, token, trace, track, vestige. See AIM, CHARACTERISTIC, LETTER, SIGN, TRACE.

mark[2] (märk) *n.* 1 The former monetary unit of Germany, a silver coin equivalent to 100 pfennige and valued at 23.8 cents: superseded in 1924 by the **reichs·mark** (rīkhs′märk′) and, after World War II, by the **deut·sche·mark** (doi′chə·märk′) in West Germany and the **ost·mark** (ôst′märk′) in East Germany. 2 A former silver coin of Scotland and England, worth 13s. 4d. 3 A former European unit of weight, equal to 256.27 grains. 4 A markka. [OE *marc* a unit of weight, prob. <LL *marca,* ? <Gmc. ? Akin to MARK[1].]

Mark (märk) A masculine personal name. Also *Greek* **Mar·kos** (mär′kos), *Ger., Sw.* **Mar·kus** (mär′kōōs). [<L, of Mars]

— **Mark** The evangelist who wrote the second of the gospel narratives in the New Testament; also, the Gospel by him. Also **Saint Mark.**

— **Mark Antony** See under ANTONY.

marked (märkt) *adj.* Brought prominently to

notice; distinguished; prominent. — **mark·ed·ly** (mär′kid-lē) *adv.* — **mark′ed·ness** *n.*

marked man One who is singled out by others, as for suspicion, vengeance, etc.

mark·er (mär′kər) *n.* **1** That which marks; specifically, a bookmark, a milestone, a gravestone, etc. **2** A scorekeeper. **3** A device for tracing the lines of a tennis court or other playing ground. **4** *Slang* A written promise to pay a specified amount, used as currency in gambling, speculation, etc.

mar·ket (mär′kit) *n.* **1** A place where merchandise is exposed for sale; specifically, an open space or a large building in a town or city, generally with stalls or designated positions occupied by different dealers, especially such a place for the sale of provisions: also **market place. 2** A private store for the sale of provisions: a meat *market.* **3** The state of trade as determined by prices, supply, and demand; traffic: a brisk *market.* **4** A locality or country where anything can be bought or sold; a place where any commodity is in demand: the South American *markets.* **5** A gathering of people for selling and buying, especially of a particular commodity: the wheat *market.* **6** The value of a thing as determined by the price it will bring; value in general; worth. — *v.t.* **1** To take or send to market for sale; sell. — *v.i.* **2** To deal in a market; sell or buy. **3** To buy food. [OE <AF <L *mercatus,* orig. pp. of *mercari* trade < *merx, mercis* merchandise. Doublet of MART[1]]

nar·ket·a·ble (mär′kit-ə-bəl) *adj.* **1** Suitable for sale; in demand. **2** Current in markets. **3** Of or pertaining to trading. — **mar′ket·a·bil′i·ty** *n.*

mar·ket·er (mär′kit-ər) *n.* One who buys or sells in a market.

market order An order to a broker to buy or sell at the current market price.

market price See under PRICE.

mar·ket–ripe (mär′kit-rīp′) *adj.* Not quite ripe: said of slightly unripe fruits picked to reach the market in salable condition.

market value The price which may be expected for a given commodity, security, or service under the conditions of a given market: distinguished from *normal value,* which is the average of values over a long period.

Mark·ham (mär′kəm), **(Charles) Edwin,** 1852–1940, U.S. poet.

Markham, Mount An Antarctic peak on the west edge of Ross Shelf Ice; 15,100 feet.

mark·ing (mär′king) *n.* **1** A mark or an arrangement of marks; characteristic coloring. **2** The act of making a mark.

mark·ka (märk′kä) *n.* The monetary unit of Finland. [<Finnish <Sw. *mark* <ON *mörk.* Akin to MARK[2].]

marks·man (märks′mən) *n. pl.* **·men** (-mən) **1** One skilled in hitting the mark, as with a rifle or other weapon. **2** In the U.S. Army, the lowest of three grades for skill in the use of small arms. **3** The soldier having this grade. Compare SHARPSHOOTER, EXPERT. — **marks′man·ship** *n.* — **marks′wom′an** *n. fem.*

Mark Twain (märk twān) Pseudonym of Samuel Langhorne Clemens, 1835–1910, U.S. humorist and novelist.

mark–up (märk′up′) *n.* **1** A raising of price. **2** The amount of price increase. **3** The sum added to cost, in computing selling price, to cover overhead and profit. **4** *Printing* The placement on copy of editorial directions for the printer or engraver.

marl[1] (märl) *v.t. Naut.* To wrap with marline, tying each turn with a hitch. [<Du. *marlen,* appar. freq. <MDu. *merren* tie]

marl[2] (märl) *n.* **1** An earthy deposit containing lime, clay, and sand, used as fertilizer. **2** A soft, earthy, crumbling stratum of varying composition. — *v.t.* To fertilize or spread with marl. [<OF *marle* <LL *margila,* dim. of L *marga,* ? <Celtic]

Marl·bor·ough (märl′bûr-ō, -bər-ə) A municipal borough in eastern Wiltshire, England.

Marl·bor·ough (märl′bûr-ō, -bər-ə), **Duke of,** 1650–1722, John Churchill; English general who defeated the French at Blenheim, Aug. 13, 1704.

marled (märld) *adj. Scot.* Variegated; marbled; mottled.

mar·lin[1] (mär′lin) *n.* Any of various deep-sea game fishes of the genus *Makaira;* especially, *M. ampla* of the Atlantic and the black or

striped marlins of the Pacific. [<MARLINE- (SPIKE); so called because of its shape]

mar·lin[2] (mär′lin) *n. U.S. Dial.* A curlew. [Alter. of obs. *marling,* var. of MERLIN]

mar·line (mär′lin) *n. Naut.* A small rope of two strands loosely twisted together: used for winding ropes, cables, etc. [<Prob. fusion of Du. *marlijn* (<*marren* tie + *lijn* a line) and E *marling* a binding <Du. <*marlen,* freq. of *marren*]

mar·line·spike (mär′lin-spīk′) *n. Naut.* A sharp-pointed iron pin used in splicing ropes. Also **mar′lin·spike′, mar′ling·spike′** (-ling-).

MARLINESPIKES

marl·ite (märl′īt) *n.* A variety of marl that differs from common marl by remaining solid on exposure to air. [<MARL[2] + -ITE[1]] — **mar·lit·ic** (mär-lit′ik) *adj.*

Mar·lowe (mär′lō), **Christopher,** 1564–93, English dramatist. — **Julia** Stage name of *Sarah Frost Sothern,* 1866–1950, U.S. actress born in England; wife of E. H. Sothern.

marl·y (mär′lē) *adj.* Resembling or of the nature of marl; abounding in marl. Also **mar·la·ceous** (mär-lā′shəs).

mar·ma·lade (mär′mə-lād) *n.* A preserve made by boiling the pulp and part of the rind or skin of fruits, usually citrus fruits, with sugar to the consistency of jam. [<MF *marmelade* <Pg. *marmelada* <*marmelo* a quince <L *melimelum* <Gk. *melimēlon* <*meli* honey + *mēlon* an apple]

marmalade tree A tall, tropical American, sapotaceous evergreen tree *(Achras zapota).* It bears plumlike fruits used chiefly for preserving. Also called *sapodilla.*

Mar·ma·ra (mär′mə-rə), **Sea of** A sea between Europe and Asia, leading by the Bosporus to the Black Sea, and by the Dardanelles to the Aegean: ancient *Propontis.* Also **Mar·mo·ra** (mär′mə-rə, mär-môr′ə, -mō′rə).

Mar·mi·on (mär′mē-ən), **Lord** The hero of *Marmion, A Tale of Flodden Field,* a romantic poem by Sir Walter Scott.

mar·mite (mär-mēt′) *n.* A small, lidded ceramic or enameled cooking pot. [<F, a pot, kettle]

Mar·mo·la·da (mär′mō-lä′dä) The highest mountain in the Dolomites, northern Italy; 10,964 feet.

mar·mo·re·al (mär-môr′ē-əl, -mō′rē-) *adj.* Pertaining to, made of, or resembling marble. Also **mar·mo′re·an** (-môr′ē-, -mō′rē-). [<L *marmoreus* <*marmor* MARBLE]

mar·mo·set (mär′mə-zet) *n.* **1** A small Central and South American monkey (family *Callithricidae*) with soft, woolly hair and a long hairy tail. **2** A related species, Goeldi's marmoset *(Callimico goeldii).* **3** The tamarin. **4** The ouistiti. [<OF *marmouset* a grotesque figure, prob. ult. <Gk. *mormō, -ous* a she-monster, bogey; with ref. to its appearance]

MARMOSET
(About the size of a large squirrel)

mar·mot (mär′mət) *n.* **1** A stout, short-tailed, burrowing rodent of mountain regions (genus *Marmota*). The species found in North America is known as a *woodchuck* or *ground hog.* **2** A related rodent, as the prairie dog. [<F *marmotte,* fusion of OF *marmotte* a monkey and Romansch *murmont* a marmot <L *mus, muris* a mouse + *mons, montis* a mountain]

Marne (märn) A river in NE France, flowing 325 miles NW to the Seine; scene of two decisive battles of World War I, 1914, 1918.

Ma·roc (mà-rôk′) The French name for MOROCCO.

Ma·ro·ni (mə-rō′nē) A river in the Guianas, flowing 450 miles north to the Atlantic. Dutch **Ma·ro·wij·ne** (mä-rō-wī′nə).

ma·roon[1] (mə-rōōn′) *v.t.* **1** To put ashore and abandon on a desolate island or coast. **2** To abandon; leave helpless. [< *n.* (def. 1)] — *n.* **1** One of a class of Negroes, chiefly fugitive slaves or their descendants, living wild in the mountains of some West Indies islands and of Guiana. **2** *Rare* A person left alone on an island; a marooned person. [<F *marron* a maroon (def. 1) <Sp. *cimarron* wild]

ma·roon[2] (mə-rōōn′) *n.* **1** A dull, dark–red color. **2** A coal–tar dyestuff. — *adj.* Having a dull, dark–red color. [<F *marron* a chestnut, chestnut color <Ital. *marrone*]

Ma·ros (mô-rōsh′) The Hungarian name for the MURES.

mar·plot (mär′plot′) *n.* One who, by meddling, mars or frustrates a design or plan.

marque (märk) *n.* A license of reprisal upon an enemy, as at sea in wartime: chiefly in the phrase *letter of marque.* [<F, mark, imprint, stamp <Provençal *marca* seizure <*marcar* seize as a pledge <*marc* a pledge <Gmc. Akin to MARK[1].]

mar·quee (mär-kē′) *n.* **1** A large field tent, especially one for an officer, or one used at lawn entertainments. **2** An awning or roof-like structure over the entrance to a hotel, theater, or other building. [<MARQUISE a canopy, mistaken as pl. <F]

Mar·que·san (mär-kā′sən) *adj.* Of the Marquesas Islands, the inhabitants, or their language. — *n.* **1** A native of the Marquesas Islands. **2** Their Polynesian language.

Mar·que·sas Islands (mär-kā′säs) A group of islands in French Oceania, in the South Pacific north of the Tuamotu group; 480 square miles. Also **Mar·que′zas Islands.** French *Îles Mar·quises* (ēl mår·kēz′).

Marquesas Keys A group of Florida islets west of Key West.

mar·quess (mär′kwis) See MARQUIS.

mar·que·try (mär′kə-trē) *n.* Inlaid work of wood often interspersed with stones, ivory, etc., especially as used in the decoration of furniture. Also **mar′que·te·rie.** [<MF *marqueterie* <*marqueter* variegate, inlay < *marque* a mark[1], ult. <Gmc.]

Mar·quette (mär-ket′), **Jacques,** 1636–75, French Jesuit priest and missionary who explored Canada: called "Père Marquette."

mar·quis (mär′kwis, *Fr.* mår·kē′) *n.* The title of a nobleman next in rank below a duke. Also, *Brit., marquess.* [<OF *marchis, marquis* <Med. L *marchensis* a commander of the marches <*marca* a march[2] <Gmc.]

Mar·quis (mär′kwis) *n.* An important variety of wheat, first developed in Canada, widely grown in the United States.

Mar·quis (mär′kwis), **Don(ald) Robert Perry,** 1878–1937, U.S. journalist and humorist.

mar·quis·ate (mär′kwiz-it) *n.* The rank of a marquis.

mar·quise (mär-kēz′) *n.* **1** The wife or widow of a French marquis. **2** An ornamental hood over a door; a marquee. **3** In gem-cutting, a pointed oval form, especially for diamonds. **4** A ring set with an oval cluster of gemstones. [<F, fem. of *marquis* a marquis]

MARQUISE

mar·qui·sette (mär′ki-zet′, -kwi-) *n.* A lightweight, open-mesh fabric of cotton, silk, rayon, or nylon, or a combination of these, used for curtains and women's and children's garments. [<F, dim. of *marquise* a marquise]

Marquis of Queensberry Rules A widely observed boxing code devised in 1869 by John Sholto Douglas (1844–1900), eighth Marquis of Queensberry.

Mar·ra·kesh (mä-rä′kesh) **1** A city in SW Morocco: formerly *Morocco.* **2** A region of SW Morocco; 45,725 square miles. Also **Mar·ra′kech.**

mar·ram (mar′əm) *n.* **1** Beachgrass. **2** A dune overgrown and bound together by this grass. [<ON *maralmr* < *marr* a sea + *halmr* haulm]

mar·riage (mar'ij) *n.* **1** The act of marrying, or the state of being married; specifically, a compact entered into by a man and a woman, to live together as husband and wife; wedlock. ◆ Collateral adjectives: *hymeneal, marital.* **2** A wedding; a nuptial celebration: with *of* or *between.* **3** Figuratively, any close union. **4** In pinochle, the king and queen of any suit. [<OF *mariage,* ult. <L *maritus* a husband] Synonyms: matrimony, nuptials, union, wedding, wedlock. *Matrimony* denotes the state of those united in the *marriage* relation; *marriage* denotes primarily the act of so uniting, but is much used also for the state. *Wedlock,* a word of specific legal use, is the Saxon term for the state or relation denoted by *matrimony. Wedding* denotes the ceremony, with any attendant festivities, by which two persons are united as husband and wife, *nuptials* being the more formal and stately term to express the same idea. Antonyms: bachelorhood, celibacy, divorce, maidenhood, virginity, widowhood.

mar·riage·a·ble (mar'ij·ə·bəl) *adj.* Fitted by age, physical condition, etc., for marriage; nubile. — **mar'riage·a·bil'i·ty,** **mar'riage·a·ble·ness** *n.*

marriage lines *Brit.* A marriage certificate.
mar·ried (mar'ēd) *adj.* **1** Pertaining to marriage; connubial; conjugal: the *married* state. **2** Having a spouse; united by or as by matrimony; wedded: a *married* man.
mar·ron (mar'ən, *Fr.* mȧ·rôn') *n.* A chestnut, especially when used as food and in confectionery. [<F. See MAROON².]
marron gla·cé (glȧ·sā') *French* A candied chestnut.
mar·row¹ (mar'ō) *n.* **1** A soft vascular tissue found in the central cavities of bones. **2** The interior substance of anything; essence; pith. [OE *mearg, mearh*] — **mar'row·y** *adj.*
mar·row² (mar'ō) *v.t. & v.i. Scot. & Brit. Dial.* To associate; marry. [? <Scand. Cf. ON *margr* friendly, lit., many.]
mar·row·bone (mar'ō·bōn') *n.* **1** A bone containing marrow. **2** *pl.* One's knees: used humorously. **3** *pl.* Crossbones, the piratical emblem.
mar·row·fat (mar'ō·fat') *n.* A large, rich pea. Also **marrow pea.**
marrow squash A variety of squash having an ovoid, fine-grained body; vegetable marrow.
Mar·rue·cos (mär·rwä'kōs) The Spanish name for MOROCCO.
mar·ry¹ (mar'ē) *v.* **·ried, ·ry·ing** *v.t.* **1** To join as husband and wife in marriage. **2** To take in marriage. **3** To give in marriage. **4** To unite closely. **5** *Naut.* To fasten end to end, as ropes, without increasing the diameter. — *v.i.* **6** To take a husband or wife. [<OF *marier* <L *maritare* <*maritus* a husband, married] — **mar'ri·er** *n.*
mar·ry² (mar'ē) *interj. Archaic* An exclamation of surprise or asseveration: a euphemistic variant of *Mary!* or *by Mary!* [Alter. of MARY; with ref. to the Virgin Mary]
Mar·ry·at (mar'ē·it, -at), **Frederick,** 1792–1848, English naval captain and novelist.
Mars (märz) *n. Obs.* In medieval alchemy, iron. [after *Mars,* the planet]
Mars (märz) **1** In Roman mythology, the god of war: identified with the Greek *Ares:* formerly called *Mavors.* **2** *Astron.* The fourth planet in order of distance from the sun, from which its mean distance is 141,500,-000 miles, its least distance from the earth being about 35,000,000 miles. Mars has two satellites, a diameter of about 4,230 miles, a diurnal rotation of 24 hours, 37 minutes, 22.67 seconds, and a year of 686.9 days.
Mar·sa·la (mär·sä'lä) *n.* A light, sweet white wine originally made in Marsala.
Mar·sa·la (mär·sä'lä) A port of western Sicily.
Marse (märs) *n. U.S. Dial.* Master: formerly used by Negro slaves. Also **Mars.** [Alter. of MASTER]
Mar·seil·lais (mär'sə·lāz', *Fr.* mȧr·sā·ye') *adj.* Of or pertaining to Marseille, or to its inhabitants. — *n.* A native or inhabitant of Marseille. [<F <*Marseille* Marseille] — **Mar·seil·laise** (mär'sə·lāz', *Fr.* mȧr·sā·yez') *n. & adj. fem.*
Marseillaise The national anthem of the

French Republic, written in 1792 by Rouget de Lisle. [<F, fem. of *Marseillais* MARSEILLAIS]
mar·seille (mär·sāl') *n.* A thick cotton fabric having a raised weave, similar to piqué. Also **mar·seilles** (mär·sālz'). [from *Marseille,* France]
Mar·seille (mär·sā'y') A port on the Gulf of the Lion; the second largest city in France. Also **Mar·seilles** (mär·sā', -sälz').
marsh (märsh) *n.* A tract of low, wet land; swamp. ◆ Collateral adjective: *paludal.* [OE *mersc, merisc.* Akin to MORASS.] — **marsh'y** *adj.* — **marsh'i·ness** *n.*
Marsh (märsh), **Othniel Charles,** 1831–1899, U.S. paleontologist.
mar·shal (mär'shəl) *n.* **1** An officer authorized to regulate ceremonies, preserve order, etc. **2** An official of the United States courts; also, the head of the police force or fire department in some cities. **3** In some European countries, a military officer of high rank; a field marshal. **4** In medieval times, a groom or master of the horse; later, as an officer of the king, a judge in courts of chivalry, etc. — *v.t.* **·shaled** or **·shalled, ·shal·ing** or **·shal·ling 1** To arrange or dispose in order, as facts. **2** To array or draw up, as troops for battle. **3** To lead; usher. ◆ Homophone: *martial.* [<OF *mareschal* <Med. L *mariscalcus* <OHG *marah-scalh,* lit., a horse-servant <*marah* a horse + *scalh* a servant] — **mar'shal·cy, mar'shal·ship** *n.* — **mar'shal·er, mar'shal·ler** *n.*
Mar·shall (mär'shəl), **Alfred,** 1842–1924, English economist. — **George Catlett,** 1880–1959, chief of staff of U.S. Army in World War II; secretary of state 1947–49. — **John,** 1755–1835, U.S. statesman; jurist; secretary of state 1800–01; chief justice of United States 1801–1835.
Mar·shall Islands (mär'shəl) An island group in the NW Pacific, including Bikini, Eniwetok, Kwajalein, Jaluit, and other islands, comprising part of the United Nations Trust Territory of the Pacific Islands; total, 65 square miles; capital, Jaluit; Japanese mandate, 1920–1944.
Marshall Plan A post-World War II recovery program of U.S. financial aid to certain European countries, initiated June, 1947.
Mar·shal·sea (mär'shəl·sē) *Brit.* **1** The court (abolished 1849) held by the marshal of the royal household, originally to administer justice to the sovereign's domestic servants. **2** A debtors' prison in Southwark, abolished in 1842. [Var. of *marshalcy* <AF *mareschalcie* <Med. L *marisalcia* <*mariscalcus* a marshal]
marsh bluebill A ring-necked duck.
marsh elder 1 Any of a genus (*Iva*) of American salt-marsh plants, especially the high-water shrub (*I. frutescens*) of the SE United States: also called *sumpweed.* **2** The guelder-rose.
marsh frog A pickerel frog.
marsh gas Methane.
marsh hare In Louisiana, the muskrat.
marsh harrier An Old World hawk (*Circus aeruginosus*) with a yellowish head and predominantly dark-brown plumage: it nests on swampy ground and feeds largely on frogs, snakes, and small waterfowl.
marsh hawk An American hawk (*Circus hudsonius*) inhabiting marshes where it preys on snakes, frogs, etc.
marsh hen 1 The northern clapper rail (*Rallus longirostris crepitans*), which inhabits saltwater marshes along the American Atlantic coast. **2** The American coot (*Fulica americana*).
marsh·mal·low (marsh'mal'ō, -mel'ō) *n.* **1** A plant of the mallow family (*Althaea officinalis*) growing in marshy places. **2** A sweetmeat formerly made from the root of this plant; now a confection made of starch, corn sirup, and gelatin, coated with powdered sugar.
marsh marigold A showy swamp plant (*Caltha palustris*) of the crowfoot family, having bright-yellow flowers, found in swamps and wet meadows: also called *cowslip.*
marsh poisoning Impaludism.
marsh rosemary A seaside perennial herb (*Limonium carolinianum*), with a strongly astringent root: used medicinally. **2** The moorwort.
Mar·si·an (mär'sē·ən) *adj.* Of or pertaining to the **Mar·si** (mär'sī), a people of ancient Italy.

— *n.* **1** One of the Marsi. **2** Their language, belonging to the Sabellian branch of the Italic languages.
Mar·si·van (mär'sē·vän') See MERZIFON.
Mar·ston (mär'stən), **John,** 1575?–1634, English dramatist and satirist.
Mar·ston Moor (mär'stən) An area in central Yorkshire, England, where Cromwell defeated the Royalists July 2, 1644.
mar·su·pi·al (mär·soo'pē·əl) *n.* Any member of an order (*Marsupialia*) of mammals, as the kangaroos, opossums, wombats, etc., whose females typically lack a placenta, carrying their young in a marsupium. — *adj.* **1** Having a marsupium. **2** Of or pertaining to the *Marsupialia,* or of the nature of a marsupium or pouch. [<NL *marsupialis* <L *marsupium.* See MARSUPIUM.] — **mar·su'pi·a'li·an** (-ā'lē·ən), **mar·su'pi·an** *adj. & n.*
marsupial mouse Any of several small marsupials of Australia, as the **fat-tailed marsupial mouse** (*Sminthopsis crassicaudata*), or the **yellow-footed marsupial mouse** (*Antechinus flavipes*).
mar·su·pi·um (mär·soo'pē·əm) *n. pl.* **·pi·a** (-pē·ə) A pouchlike invagination; specifically, a brood pouch or external receptacle for carrying young, as on the abdomen of marsupials. [<L, a pouch, purse <Gk. *marsypion,* dim. of *marsipos*]
Mars yellow A pigment consisting chiefly of hydrous oxide of iron and aluminum; iron yellow. Other pigments in the same group are **Mars orange, Mars red, Mars violet.**
Mar·sy·as (mär'sē·əs) In Greek mythology, a satyr and flute-player, who was defeated in a musical contest and flayed alive by Apollo.
mart¹ (märt) *n.* **1** A market. **2** *Archaic* A fair; also, traffic; trading. [<MDu. *markt, mart* <L *mercatus.* Doublet of MARKET.]
mart² (märt) *n. Scot.* An animal slaughtered at Martinmas.
Mar·ta (mär'tä) Italian and Spanish form of MARTHA.
Mar·ta·ban (mär'tə·bän') A triangular inlet of the Andaman Sea in SE Burma.
mar·ta·gon (mär'tə·gon) See under LILY.
mar·tel·lo tower (mär·tel'ō) A circular tower of masonry, formerly erected on coasts for defense against invasion. Also **mar·tel'lo.** [from Cape *Mortella,* in Corsica, where such a tower was erected; infl. in form by Ital. *martello* a hammer]
mar·ten (mär'tən) *n.* **1** A weasel-like, fur-bearing carnivorous mammal (genus *Martes*) having arboreal habits, as the American pine marten (*M. americana*), and the large, sturdy fisher marten (*M. pennanti*). **2** The fur of a marten, often dyed and sold as an inferior sable. [<OF *martrine* of the marten <*martre* a marten <WGmc.]

MARTEN
(Species vary from 1 1/2 to 2 1/2 feet in body size)

mar·tens·ite (mär'tənz·īt) *n. Metall.* A constituent of rapidly quenched steel, consisting of iron and up to two percent of carbon. [after Prof. A. *Martens,* German metallurgist + -ITE¹] — **mar'ten·sit'ic** (-tən·zit'ik) *adj.*
Mar·tha (mär'thə, *Dan., Du., Ger., Sw.* mär'tä) A feminine personal name. Also *Fr.* **Marthe** (märt). [<Aramaic, a lady] — **Martha** Friend of Jesus, and sister of Lazarus and Mary, who served Jesus at Bethany (*Luke* x 40); hence, figuratively, a houseworker.
Martha's Vineyard An island off SE Massachusetts; 20 miles long.
mar·tial (mär'shəl) *adj.* **1** Pertaining to, connected with, or suggestive of war or military operations: opposed to *civil: court martial.* **2** Warlike; brave; characteristic of a warlike person. See synonyms under WARLIKE. ◆ Homophone: *marshal.* [<OF <L *martialis* pertaining to Mars <*Mars, Martis* Mars] — **mar'tial·ism** *n.* — **mar'tial·ist** *n.* — **mar'tial·ly** *adv.*
Mar·tial (mär'shəl) *adj.* **1** Pertaining to the god

Mars. 2 In astrology, under the evil influence of the planet Mars. 3 *Astron.* Martian.

Mar·tial (mär′shəl), 40?–100?, Latin epigrammatist: full name *Marcus Valerius Martialis.*

martial law Military jurisdiction exercised by a government temporarily governing the civil population of a locality through its military forces, without the authority of written law, as necessity may require.

Mar·tian (mär′shən) *adj.* 1 *Astron.* Pertaining to the planet Mars. 2 Martial (defs. 1 and 2). —*n.* One of the supposed inhabitants of Mars. [<L *Martius* <*Mars, Martis* Mars]

mar·tin (mär′tən) *n.* 1 Any of certain birds of the swallow family, having a tail less forked than the common swallows; specifically, the **purple martin** *(Progne subis),* the **sand martin** or bank swallow *(Riparia riparia),* etc. 2 Some bird likened to a true martin, as a kingbird or chimney swift. [<F, prob. <*Martin* MARTIN]

Mar·tin (mär′tən; *Fr.* mȧr·taṅ′, *Ger.* mär′tēn) A masculine personal name. Also **Mar·tyn** (mär′tən), *Du.* **Mar·tijn** (mär′tīn), *Pg.* **Mar·ti·nho** (mär·tē′nyoo), *Ital., Sp.* **Mar·ti·no** (mär·tē′nō), *Lat.* **Mar·ti·nus** (mär·tī′nəs). [<L *Martinus* warlike]

—**Martin, Saint,** 315?–399?, bishop of Tours. See MARTINMAS.

Mar·tin (mär′tən), **Homer Dodge,** 1836–97, U.S. painter.

Mar·tin du Gard (mȧr·taṅ′ dü gȧr′), **Roger,** 1881–1958, French novelist.

Mar·ti·neau (mär′tə·nō), **Harriet,** 1802–76, English writer. —**James,** 1805–1900, English theologian and writer; brother of the preceding.

mar·ti·net (mär′tə·net′) *n.* A strict disciplinarian, especially military or naval: often used in derogatory sense. [after General *Martinet,* 17th c. French drillmaster]

Mar·ti·net (mȧr·tē·ne′), **André,** born 1908, French linguist.

mar·tin·gale (mär′tən·gāl) *n.* 1 A forked strap for holding down a horse's head by connecting the head gear with the bellyband. 2 *Naut.* A vertical spar under the bowsprit used in guying the stays. Also **mar′tin·gal** (-gal). [<F <Provençal *martengalo,* appar. fem. of *martengo* an inhabitant of Martigues, a town in Provence; ? with ref. to tight hose or breeches worn there]

mar·ti·ni (mär·tē′nē) *n.* A cocktail made of gin and dry vermouth, usually served with a green olive or a twist of lemon peel. [after *Martini* and Rossi, a company making vermouth]

Mar·ti·ni (mär·tē′nē), **Simone di,** 1283–1344, Sienese painter.

Mar·ti·nique (mär′ti·nēk′) An island in the Lesser Antilles, comprising an overseas department of France; 427 square miles; capital, Fort-de-France.

Mar·tin·mas (mär′tən·məs) *n.* The feast of St. Martin, November 11. [<Saint *Martin* + -MAS]

mart·let (märt′lit) *n.* 1 A martin. 2 *Her.* A martin or swallow without feet: used as a bearing, crest, or mark of cadency. [<F *martelet,* alter. of *martinet,* dim. of *martin* a martin; ? infl. in form by *roitelet* a wren]

mar·ton·ite (mär′tən·īt) *n.* Bromacetone.

mar·tyr (mär′tər) *n.* 1 One who submits to death rather than forswear his religion; specifically, one of the early Christians who suffered death for their religious principles. 2 One who dies or suffers for principles, or sacrifices all for a cause: a *martyr* to science. 3 One who suffers much or long, as from ill health or misfortune: a *martyr* to rheumatism. —*v.t.* 1 To put to death as a martyr. 2 To torture; persecute or torment. [OE <LL < Gk. *martyr,* Aeolic form of *martys, martyros* a witness]

mar·tyr·dom (mär′tər·dəm) *n.* 1 The condition or fate of a martyr. 2 Protracted or extreme suffering. [OE *martyrdōm*]

mar·tyr·ize (mär′tər·īz) *v.* **·ized, ·iz·ing** *v.t.* To make a martyr of. —*v.i.* To become a martyr. —**mar′tyr·i·za′tion** *n.* —**mar′tyr·iz′er** *n.*

mar·tyr·ol·o·gy (mär′tə·rol′ə·jē) *n. pl.* **·gies** A historical record of martyrs. [<Med. L *martyrologium* <LGk. *martyrologion* <*martyr* martyr + Gk. *logos* word, account] —**mar·tyr·o·log·ic** (mär′tər·ə·loj′ik) or **·i·cal** *adj.* —**mar′tyr·ol′o·gist** *n.*

mar·vel (mär′vəl) *v.* **·veled** or **·velled, ·vel·ing** or **·vel·ling** *v.i.* To be filled with wonder, surprise, etc.: We *marveled* at the young pianist's precocious brilliance. —*v.t.* To wonder at or about: with a clause as object. —*n.* 1 That which excites wonder; a prodigy. 2 The emotion of wonder. 3 A miracle. See synonyms under PRODIGY. [<OF *merveillier* <*merveille* a wonder <L *mirabilia,* neut. pl. of *mirabilis* wonderful <*mirari* wonder at]

Mar·vell (mär′vəl), **Andrew,** 1621–78, English poet and satirist.

mar·vel-of-Pe·ru (mär′vəl·əv·pə·rōō′) *n.* The four-o'clock.

mar·vel·ous (mär′vəl·əs) *adj.* 1 Exciting astonishment; singular; wonderful. 2 Pertaining to the supernatural; miraculous. Also **mar′vel·lous.** See synonyms under EXTRAORDINARY. —**mar′vel·ous·ly, mar′vel·lous·ly** *adv.* —**mar′vel·ous·ness, mar′vel·lous·ness** *n.*

Mar·war (mär′wär) See JODHPUR.

Marx (märks), **Karl,** 1818–83, German socialist, revolutionary leader and writer on economics; author of *Das Kapital.* —**Marx′i·an** *adj. & n.*

Marx·ism (märk′siz·əm) *n.* The body of doctrine formulated by Karl Marx and Friedrich Engels in systematic form, including economic determinism, class conflicts leading inevitably to revolution in the transition from feudalism to capitalism and thence to communism under the dictatorship of the proletariat, and the predicted ultimate triumph of world communism as a result of destructive rivalries among the capitalist-imperialist powers.

Marx·ism-Len·in·ism (märk′siz·əm·len′in·iz′əm) *n.* The philosophy of history and politics based upon the works of Karl Marx and Nikolai Lenin, stressing Lenin's recension of Marxism in order to make it applicable to backward agrarian countries. —**Marx′ist-Len′in·ist** *n.*

Marx·ist (märk′sist) *adj.* 1 Of or pertaining to Karl Marx or his theories; Marxian. 2 Like or developed from the theories of Karl Marx: *Marxist* socialism. —*n.* A follower of Karl Marx; specifically, an adherent of Marxist socialism.

Mar·y (mâr′ē) A feminine personal name. Also *Polish* **Mar·ya** (mär′yä). See also MARIA. [< Hebrew, bitter]

—**Mary** The mother of Jesus: also *Virgin Mary.*

—**Mary** The sister of Lazarus and Martha.

—**Mary I,** 1516–58, queen of England, 1553–1558: known as *Mary Tudor* or *Bloody Mary.*

—**Mary II,** 1662–94, queen of England 1689–1694, ruling jointly with her husband, William III.

—**Mary Magdalene** A disciple from Magdala out of whom Jesus cast seven devils. *Luke* viii 2. She is often identified with the penitent sinner whom Jesus forgave. *Luke* vii 36–50.

—**Mary Queen of Scots,** 1542–87, queen of Scotland 1542–67; beheaded: also *Mary Stuart.*

Mary Jane (jān) 1 A low-heeled, usually patent-leather slipper with an ankle strap, worn especially by young girls. 2 *Slang* Marihuana. [def. 2 <folk etymology]

Mar·y·land (mâr′i·lənd, mer′i-) An eastern State of the United States, on Chesapeake Bay; 12,327 square miles; capital, Annapolis; entered the Union April 28, 1788, one of the original thirteen States; nickname, *Cockade State* or *Old Line State*: abbr. MD

Maryland yellowthroat See under YELLOWTHROAT.

Mar·y·le·bone (mâr′i·lə·bōn′, mâr′lə·bən, *Brit.* mal′ə·bōn′) A metropolitan borough of NW London, England: also *St. Marylebone.*

Mar·y·ol·a·try (mâr′ē·ol′ə·trē), **Mar·y·ol·o·gy** (-ol′ə·jē) See MARIOLATRY, etc.

mar·zi·pan (mär′zə·pan) *n.* A confection of grated almonds, sugar, and white of eggs, usually made into a paste and molded into various shapes: formerly known as *marchpane.* [<G <Ital. *marzapane,* orig. a small box, a dry measure, a weight <Med. L *matapanus* a Venetian coin stamped with an enthroned Christ <Arabic *mauthabān* a seated king, a coin <*wathaba* sit]

-mas *combining form* Mass; a (specified) festival or its celebration: *Christmas.* [<MASS[2]]

Ma·sac·cio (mä·sät′chō), 1402–28, Florentine painter: real name *Tommaso Guidi.*

Ma·san (mä·sän) A port in southern Korea. Formerly **Ma·sam·po** (mä·säm·pō).

Ma·sa·ryk (mä′sä·rik), **Jan,** 1886–1948, Czechoslovak diplomat and politician. —**Tomás,** 1850–1937, philosopher; first president of Czechoslovakia 1918–35; father of the preceding.

Mas·ba·te (mäz·bä′tā) One of the Visayan Islands, Philippines; 1,262 square miles.

Mas·ca·gni (mäs·kä′nyē), **Pietro,** 1863–1945, Italian composer.

mas·ca·longe (mas′kə·lonj) See MUSKELLUNGE.

mas·car·a (mas·kar′ə) *n.* A cosmetic preparation used to darken the eyelashes, usually black, brown, or blue. [<Sp. *máscara* a mask <Arabic *maskharah* a buffoon]

Mas·ca·rene Islands (mas′kə·rēn) An island group, including Réunion and Mauritius, in the Indian Ocean.

mas·cle (mas′kəl) *n.* 1 A lozenge-shaped plate used in scale armor. 2 *Her.* A lozenge voided. Also spelled *macle.* [<OF. See MACLE.]

mas·con (mas′kon, mäs-) *n.* Any of the dense concentrations of mass in the moon's lithosphere which cause irregularities in the gravitational field surrounding the moon. [<MAS(S) + CON(CENTRATION)]

mas·cot (mas′kot, -kət) *n.* 1 A person, animal, or thing thought to bring good luck. 2 *Brit.* An ornament on the radiator of an automobile. [<F *mascotte* <Provençal *mascot,* dim. of *masco* a sorcerer, lit., a mask]

mas·cu·line (mas′kyə·liṅ) *adj.* 1 Having the distinguishing qualities of the male sex, or pertaining to males; specially suitable for men; manly: opposed to *feminine.* 2 *Gram.* Being of the male gender. 3 *Bot.* Male; staminate. —*n.* 1 A male person; that which is of the male sex. 2 *Gram.* The masculine gender or a word of this gender: opposed to *feminine* and *neuter.* [<OF *masculin* <L *masculinus* <*masculus* male <*mas.* Doublet of MALE.] —**mas′cu·line·ly** *adv.* —**mas′cu·lin′i·ty, mas′cu·line·ness** *n.*

Synonyms (adj.): male, manful, manlike, manly, mannish, virile. *Male* is applied to the sex, *masculine* to the qualities, especially to the stronger, hardier, and more imperious qualities that distinguish the *male* sex; as applied to women, *masculine* has often the depreciatory sense of unwomanly, rude, or harsh; as, a *masculine* face or voice, or the like; still one may say in a commendatory way, she acted with *masculine* courage or decision. *Masculine* may apply to the distinctive qualities of the *male* sex at any age; *virile* applies to the distinctive qualities of mature manhood only, as opposed not only to *feminine* or *womanly* but to *childish,* and is thus an emphatic word for *sturdy, intrepid,* etc. See also under MANLY. *Antonyms:* see synonyms for FEMININE.

Mase·field (mās′fēld), **John,** 1878–1967, English poet, novelist, and dramatist; poet laureate 1930–1967.

ma·ser (mā′zər) *n. Physics* Any of various devices that generate electromagnetic waves of precise frequency or that amplify such waves while maintaining frequency and phase, by using the excess energy of a resonant atomic or molecular system. [Acronym derived from *m(icrowave) a(mplification by) s(timulated) e(mission of) r(adiation)*]

mash (mash) *n.* 1 A soft, pulpy mass. 2 A mixture of meal, bran, etc., and water, fed warm to cattle. 3 Crushed or ground grain or malt, infused in hot water to produce wort. 4 In winemaking, the crushed grapes before fermentation begins. —*v.t.* 1 To crush or beat into a mash or pulp. 2 To convert into mash, as malt or grain, by infusing in hot water. [OE *māsc(wyrt)* mashwort, infused malt]

mash·er (mash′ər) *n.* 1 One who or that which mashes. 2 *Slang* A man who persistently annoys women unacquainted with him, as by attempting familiarities, etc.

Mash·er·brum (mush′ər·broom) A peak in the Karakoram mountain system, Kashmir; 25,600 feet. Also **Mash′ar·brum.**

Mash·had (mȧsh·hȧd′) See MESHED.

mash·ie (mash′ē) *n.* An iron golf club with a deep, short blade and much loft: used in approaching. See illustration under GOLF CLUB. Also **mash′y.** [? Alter. of F *massue* a club < LL *mattiuca* (assumed), prob. <Celtic]

mash·lin (mash′lin) *n. Scot.* Mixed grain.

Ma·sho·na·land (mə·shō′nə·land) A region of Southern Rhodesia; 80,344 square miles.

Mas·i·nis·sa (mas′ə·nis′ə), 238–148 B.C., king of Numidia; ally of Scipio against the Carthaginians.

mas·jid (mus′jid) *n. Arabic* A Moslem mosque.

mask[1] (mask, mäsk) *n.* 1 A cover or disguise, as for the features; a protective appliance for the face or head: a gas *mask*. 2 A subterfuge. 3 A cast of the face taken just after death. 4 A play or dramatic performance, in vogue in the 16th and 17th centuries, in which the actors were masked and represented allegorical or mythological subjects, originally in dumb show, but later in dialog, poetry, and song; also, a dramatic composition written for such a play: also spelled *masque*. 5 A masquerade: also spelled *masque*. 6 A masker. 7 An artistic covering for the face, used by Greek and Roman actors in comedy and tragedy. 8 *Archit.* A reproduction of a face or a face and neck, used as a gargoyle, a keystone of an arch, etc. 9 *Mil.* A screen of brush or the like for hiding a battery or any military operation from the enemy; camouflage. 10 *Zool.* Any formation about the head suggesting a mask; specifically, the enlarged lower lip of a larval dragonfly. 11 A fox's or dog's head. See synonyms under PRETENSE. —*v.t.* 1 To cover (the face, head, etc.) with a mask. 2 To hide or conceal with or as with a mask; disguise. —*v.i.* 3 To put on a mask; assume a disguise. [< F *masque* < Ital. *maschera, mascara* < Arabic *maskharah* a buffoon]

Synonyms (verb): cloak, conceal, cover, disguise, dissemble, hide, masquerade, pretend, screen, shroud, veil. See HIDE. *Antonyms:* betray, communicate, declare, disclose, divulge, exhibit, expose, publish, reveal, show, tell.

MASKS
a. Greek tragedy.   *c.* Tibetan ceremonial.
b. Greek comedy.   *d.* Ancient Shinto.
         e. Domino.

mask[2] (mask, mäsk) *v.t. & v.i. Brit. Dial.* To infuse or be infused. [Var. of MASH]

masked (maskt, mäskt) *adj.* 1 Having the face covered with or as with a mask; disguised. 2 Personate. 3 *Zool.* Having markings resembling a mask, as various pupae of insects.

masked or **mask ball** A ball at which the dancers wear masks or dominos.

masked hunter The kissing bug.

mas·keg (mas′keg) See MUSKEG.

mask·er (mas′kər, mäs′-) *n.* One who wears a mask: also spelled *masquer*.

mask·ing (mas′king, mäs′-) *n. Scot.* A crushing into a mash.

masking tape An adhesive tape used to protect those parts of a surface not to be painted, sprayed, or otherwise treated.

mas·ki·nonge (mas′kə·nonj) See MUSKELLUNGE.

mas·lin (maz′lin) *n. Brit. Dial.* 1 Mixed grain, especially wheat and rye. 2 Bread made from such mixture. 3 A mixture; potpourri. [< OF *mesteillon* < LL *mistilio, -onis,* ult. < L *mixtus,* pp. of *miscere* mix]

mas·o·chism (mas′ə·kiz′əm) *n. Psychiatry* A condition in which sexual gratification depends on being dominated, cruelly treated, beaten, etc. [after Leopold von Sacher-*Masoch,* 1835–95, Austrian novelist, who described this condition] —**mas′o·chist** *n.* — **mas′o·chis′tic** *adj.*

ma·son (mā′sən) *n.* One who lays brick and stone in building; also, a stonecutter. —*v.t.* To build of masonry. [< OF *masson, maçon* < Med. L *matio, macio, -onis,* prob. < Gmc.]

Ma·son (mā′sən) *n.* A member of the order of Freemasons. —**Ma·son·ic** (mə·son′ik) *adj.*

Ma·son (mā′sən), **James Murray,** 1798–1871, Confederate statesman; with John Slidell, seized on board the British steamer *Trent,* 1861. —**Walt,** 1862–1939, U.S. humorist and poet.

mason bee A solitary bee (*Chalicodoma muraria*) of southern Europe which builds its nest of sand, clay, etc.

Ma·son–Dix·on line (mā′sən·dik′sən) The boundary between Pennsylvania and Maryland as surveyed by the Englishmen Charles Mason and Jeremiah Dixon in 1763–67: before the Civil War it was regarded as dividing Slave States from Free States, and is still used to distinguish the North from the South. Also **Mason and Dixon's line.**

Ma·son·ite (mā′sən·īt) *n.* A tough, dense, moisture-resistant fiberboard made from wood fibers exploded under high steam pressure: widely used as a building and construction material: a trade name.

Mason jar A glass jar having a tightly fitting screw top, used for canning and preserving: patented by John L. Mason of New York in 1857.

ma·son·ry (mā′sən·rē) *n. pl.* **·ries** 1 The art or work of building with brick or stone. 2 That which is built by masons or of materials which masons use.

Ma·son·ry (mā′sən·rē) *n.* Freemasonry.

Ma·so·ra (mə·sō′rə) *n.* 1 A collection of criticisms and marginal notes to the Old Testament, made by Jewish writers before the tenth century. 2 The tradition relied on by the Jews to preserve the Old Testament text from corruption. Also **Ma·so′rah.** [< Hebrew (modern) *māsōrah* < Hebrew *māsōreth* tradition, orig., bond (of the covenant)] —**Mas·o·ret·ic** (mas′ə·ret′ik) or **·i·cal,** *adj.* —**Mas′o·rete** (-rēt), **Mas′o·rite** (-rīt) *n.*

Mas·pe·ro (mäs′pə·rō, *Fr.* más·pə·rō′), **Gaston Camille Charles,** 1846–1916, French Egyptologist.

Mas·qat (mus′kat, mäs′kät) See MUSCAT.

masque (mask, mäsk), **mas·quer** (mas′kər, mäs′-) See MASK[1] (defs. 4 and 5), MASKER.

mas·quer·ade (mas′kə·rād′, mäs′-) *n.* 1 A social party composed of persons masked and costumed; also, the costumes and disguises worn on such an occasion. 2 A false show or disguise. 3 Formerly, a form of dramatic representation. —*v.i.* **·ad·ed, ·ad·ing** 1 To take part in a masquerade. 2 To wear a mask or disguise. 3 To disguise one's true character; assume a false appearance. See synonyms under MASK[1]. [Alter. of F *mascarade* < Sp. *mascarada* < *máscara* a mask. See MASCARA.] —**mas′quer·ad′er** *n.*

mass[1] (mas, mäs) *n.* 1 An assemblage of things that collectively make one quantity. 2 A body of concrete matter; a lump. 3 The principal part of anything. 4 Extent of volume; bulk; size. 5 *Physics* The measure or expression of the inertia of a body, as indicated by the acceleration imparted to it when acted upon by a given force: it is the quotient of the weight of a body divided by the acceleration due to gravity. —*adj.* 1 Of, for, or consisting of the public in general. 2 Done on a large scale: *mass* production. —**the masses** The common people. See synonyms under MOB[1]. —*v.t. & v.i.* To form into a mass; assemble. [< OF *masse* < L *massa,* prob. < Gk. *maza* a barley cake]

Synonyms (noun): aggregate, body, bulk, heap, lump, matter, substance, total, totality, whole. See AGGREGATE, HEAP, THRONG.

mass[2] (mas, mäs) *n. Eccl.* 1 The eucharistic liturgy in the Roman Catholic and some Anglican churches, regarded as a commemoration or repetition of Christ's sacrifice on Calvary. 2 A celebration of this. See HIGH MASS, LOW MASS. 3 A musical setting for the fixed portions of this liturgy, as the Credo, Sanctus, Kyrie eleison, etc. Also **Mass.** —**black mass** 1 A mass for the dead: so called because the celebrant wears black vestments. 2 A ceremony performed in so-called worship of Satan as a burlesque of the Christian mass. [OE *mæsse* < LL *messa* dismissal < L *missa,* pp. fem. of *mittere* send, dismiss < *ite, missa est* go, you are dismissed; said by the priest after the Eucharist is ended]

Mas·sa·chu·set (mas′ə·chōō′sit) *n.* 1 One of a large and important tribe of North American Indians of Algonquian linguistic stock, formerly inhabiting the region around Massachusetts Bay. 2 The language of this tribe. Also **Mas′sa·chu′sett.** [< Algonquian (Massachuset) *Massa-adchu-es-et,* lit., at the big hill < *massa* big + *wadchu* hill + *es,* dim. suffix + *et* at the]

Mas·sa·chu·setts (mas′ə·chōō′sits) A NE State of the United States on the Atlantic; 8,266 square miles; capital, Boston; entered the Union Feb. 6, 1788, one of the thirteen original States; nickname, *Bay State:* abbr. MA

Massachusetts Bay A wide inlet of the Atlantic on the eastern coast of Massachusetts, extending from Cape Ann to Cape Cod.

mas·sa·cre (mas′ə·kər) *n.* The indiscriminate killing of human beings, as in savage warfare; slaughter. —*v.t.* **·cred** (-kərd), **·cring** To kill indiscriminately or in great numbers; slaughter. [< MF < OF *maçacre, macecle,* ? < *mache–col* butcher < *macher* smash + *col* neck < L *collum*] —**mas′sa·crer** *n.*

Synonyms (noun): butchery, carnage, havoc, slaughter. A *massacre* is the indiscriminate killing in numbers of the unresisting or defenseless; *butchery* is the killing of men rudely and ruthlessly as cattle are killed in the shambles. *Havoc* may not be so complete as *massacre,* nor so coldly brutal as *butchery,* but is more widely spread and furious; it is destruction let loose, and may be applied to organizations, interests, etc., as well as to human life. *Carnage* refers to widely scattered or heaped up corpses of the slain; *slaughter* is similar in meaning, but refers more to the process, and *carnage* to the result.

mas·sage (mə·säzh′) *n.* A system of remedial treatment consisting of kneading, rubbing, and otherwise manipulating a part or the whole of the body with the hands. —*v.t.* **·saged, ·sag·ing** To treat by massage. [< F < *masser* massage < *masse* mass < L *massa,* ? < Gk. *massein* knead] —**mas·sag′er, mas·sag′ist** *n.* —**mas·sa·geuse** (mas′ə·zhoez′) *n. fem.*

mas·sa·sau·ga (mas′ə·sô′gə) *n.* The pigmy rattlesnake (*Sistrurus miliarius*) of the southern United States, seldom exceeding 20 inches in length, and living in dry, warm areas: also called *ground rattlesnake.* [< Ojibwa name of a river in Ontario, Canada]

Mas·sa·soit (mas′ə·soit), died 1661, American Indian chief of Massachusetts; friendly with the Pilgrims of Plymouth Colony.

Mas·sa·wa (mäs·sä′wä) The chief port of Eritrea, on the Red Sea; former capital of Eritrea. Formerly **Mas·so′wa.**

mass bell The Sanctus bell.

mass communication The simultaneous dissemination of a single item of information, advertising, propaganda, etc., to the largest possible audience by the use of mass media.

mass defect *Physics* The difference between the mass number of a nuclide and its nucleon mass.

mas·sé (ma·sā′) *n.* In billiards, a stroke with a cue held perpendicularly, causing the cue ball to return in a straight line or to describe a curve. Also **massé shot.** [< F < *masser* make a massé shot < *masse* billiard cue, lit., a mace]

Mas·sé·na (mà·sā·nà′), **André,** Prince d'Essling, 1758–1817, French marshal under Napoleon I.

Mas·se·net (mas′nā′, *Fr.* más·ne′), **Jules Émile Frédéric,** 1842–1912, French composer.

mas·se·ter (ma·sē′tər) *n. Anat.* A masticatory muscle connected with the lower jaw. [< NL < Gk. *masētēr* chewer < *masasthai* chew] —**mas·se·ter·ic** (mas′ə·ter′ik), **mas′se·ter′ine** (-ēn, -īn) *adj.*

mas·seur (ma·sûr′, *Fr.* mà·sœr′) *n. French* A man who practices or gives massage. —**masseuse** (ma·sōōz′, -sōōs′; *Fr.* mà·sœz′) *n. fem.*

mas·si·cot (mas′ə·kot) *n.* 1 Lead monoxide: a rare mineral associated with galena. 2 A yellowish paint pigment similar to litharge. [< F < Sp. *mexacote* < Arabic *shabb qubti* Coptic alum]

mas·sif (mas′if, *Fr.* mà·sēf′) *n. Geol.* 1 The dominant, central mass of a mountain ridge more or less defined by longitudinal or transverse valleys. 2 A diastrophic block of the earth's crust, isolated by boundary faults. [< F]

Mas·sif Cen·tral (má·sēf' sän·tral') A plateau region of central France, covering one sixth of the country's surface.

Mas·si·mi·lia·no (mäs'sē·mē·lyä'nō) Italian form of MAXIMILIAN.

Mas·sine (mä·sēn'), **Léonide**, born 1896, Russian ballet dancer and choreographer.

Mas·sin·ger (mas'ən·jər), **Philip**, 1583–1640, English dramatist.

mas·sive (mas'iv) adj. 1 Constituting a large mass; ponderous; large: a massive forehead. 2 Belonging to the total mass of anything. 3 Being without definite form, as a mineral; amorphous. 4 Geol. Homogeneous: said of certain rock formations. 5 Figuratively, imposing in scope or degree; having considerable magnitude. See synonyms under LARGE. [<F massif] — **mas'sive·ly** adv. — **mas'sive·ness** n.

Massive Mount The second highest peak in the Rocky Mountains, in central Colorado; 14,418 feet. Also **Massive Mountain.**

mass media Newspapers, magazines, paperbound books, radio, television, and motion pictures, considered as means of reaching a very wide public audience.

mass meeting A large public gathering for the discussion of some topic, usually political.

mass number Physics 1 The whole number nearest the mass of any isotope of an element: 3 and 4 are mass numbers of the isotopes of helium. 2 The number of protons and neutrons in an atom: distinguished from atomic number.

mas·so·ther·a·py (mas'ō·ther'ə·pē) n. Treatment by massage. [<Gk. massein knead + THERAPY] — **mas'so·ther'a·peu'tic** (-ther'ə·pyōō'tik) adj.

mass–pro·duce (mas'prə·dōōs', -dyōōs') v.t. ·duced, ·duc·ing To manufacture or produce by machinery (goods or articles) in great numbers or quantities. — **mass production**

mass ratio The ratio of the total mass of a rocket to its mass after the expenditure of fuel, calculated at approximately 2.72 to 1 for a rocket designed to travel at the exhaust velocity of its fuel.

mass spectrograph Physics An instrument for determining the relative masses of electrically charged particles by passing a stream of them through a magnetic field and noting the variable deflections from a straight path.

mass·y (mas'ē) adj. **mass·i·er, mass·i·est** Consisting of a mass or masses; big; bulky. — **mass'i·ness** n.

mast¹ (mast, mäst) n. 1 Naut. A pole or spar of round timber or tubular iron or steel, set upright in a sailing vessel to sustain the yards, sails, etc. 2 The upright pole of a derrick. 3 Any large, upright pole. — **before the mast** Occupying the position of, or serving as, a common sailor: from the fact that common sailors were quartered forward of the foremast. — v.t. To furnish with a mast or masts. [OE mæst] — **mast'less** adj.

mast² (mast, mäst) n. The fruit of the oak, beech, and other trees; acorns, etc. [OE mæst mast, fodder]

mast– Var. of MASTO–.

mas·ta·ba (mas'tə·bə) n. In ancient Egypt, an oblong building used as a mortuary chapel and place of offerings, with sloping sides and flat top, covering the mouth of a sepulchral pit. Also **mas'ta·bah**. [<Arabic maṣṭabah bench]

MASTABA
Of solid masonry, except for a small chapel and (unconnected) shaft to the mummy chamber.

mas·tax (mas'taks) n. Zool. The pharynx or gizzard of a rotifer. [<Gk., mouth, jaws < masasthai chew]

mas·tec·to·my (mas·tek'tə·mē) n. Surg. The operation of removing the breast. [<MAST- + -ECTOMY]

mas·ter (mas'tər, mäs'-) n. 1 A male person who has authority over others, as the principal of a school, an employer, the head of a household, the owner of a domestic animal, etc. 2 One who has control or disposal of something; an owner. 3 In the U.S. merchant marine, the captain of a vessel. 4 One who is familiar with all the details of an art, profession, science, or trade. 5 One who has

charge of some special thing, place, or business. 6 A young gentleman. 7 An honorary title; specifically, **Master,** a scholastic title and rank between bachelor and doctor. 8 Law Any of various officers of the court who assist the judges by hearing evidence, reporting, etc.: a master in chancery. 9 Scot. The courtesy title of a viscount's (or baron's) eldest son. 10 One who has disciples or followers; a religious leader. 11 One who gains the victory; a victor. — **the** (or **our**) **Master** Christ. —v.t. 1 To overcome or subdue; bring under control; defeat. 2 To become expert in: to master Greek. 3 To control or govern as a master. See synonyms under CONQUER, GAIN, LEARN, SUBDUE. — adj. Having the mastery; chief; controlling. [Fusion of OE magister and OF maistre, both <L magister, orig. a double compar. of magnus great] — **mas'ter·dom** n. — **mas'ter·hood** n. — **mas'ter·less** adj.

Synonyms (noun): boss, captain, chief, commander, despot, director, employer, foreman, governor, head, leader, lord, manager, monarch, overseer, owner, prince, principal, proprietor, schoolmaster, sovereign, teacher. See CHIEF, SUPERINTENDENT, VICTOR. Antonyms: assistant, attendant, dependent, drudge, inferior, menial, retainer, serf, servant, servitor, slave, subaltern, subordinate, valet, waiter.

mas·ter–at–arms (mas'tər·ət·ärmz', mäs'-) n. pl. **mas·ters–at–arms** A petty officer who maintains discipline and order on a naval vessel.

master builder 1 A contractor who employs men to build. 2 One who has charge of building operations; a foreman or architect.

mas·ter·ful (mas'tər·fəl, mäs'-) adj. 1 Having the power or characteristics of a master; domineering; arbitrary. 2 Showing mastery, as of an art, science, situation, etc. — **mas'ter·ful·ly** adv. — **mas'ter·ful·ness** n.

master hand 1 One skilled in his craft; an expert. 2 Great skill; expertness.

master key A key that will unlock two or more locks each of which has its own key that fits no other lock.

mas·ter·ly (mas'tər·lē, mäs'-) adj. Characteristic of a master; befitting a master. — adv. In a masterly manner; as befits a master. — **mas'ter·li·ness** n.

master mason A skilled mason.

Master Mason A Freemason of the third degree.

mas·ter·mind (mas'tər·mīnd', mäs'-) n. A person of great intelligence and executive ability. — v.t. To plan and direct (a project) skilfully: to mastermind a plot.

Master of Arts 1 A degree given by a college or university to a person who has completed a prescribed course of graduate study in the humanities, social sciences, etc. 2 A person who has received this degree. Abbr. M.A., A.M.

master of ceremonies A person presiding over an entertainment or dinner and introducing the performers or speakers: also, emcee.

Master of Science 1 A degree given by a college or university to a person who has completed a prescribed course of graduate study in science. 2 A person who has received this degree. Abbr. M.S., M.Sc.

mas·ter·piece (mas'tər·pēs', mäs'-) n. A work or piece of art or literature done with consummate skill or showing the hand of a master; a supreme accomplishment; chef-d'oeuvre. [after G meisterstück]

Mas·ters (mas'tərz, mäs'-), **Edgar Lee**, 1869–1950, U.S. poet.

mas·ter·ship (mas'tər·ship, mäs'-) n. 1 The state, personality, or character of a master; also, mastery. 2 Masterly skill; preeminence.

mas·ter·sing·er (mas'tər·sing'ər, mäs'-) See MEISTERSINGER.

mas·ter·stroke (mas'tər·strōk', mäs'-) n. A masterly or decisive action or achievement.

mas·ter·work (mas'tər·wûrk', mäs'-) n. A masterpiece.

mas·ter·work·man (mas'tər·wûrk'mən, mäs'-) n. pl. **·men** (-mən) A skilled workman, craftsman, or artist; also, a foreman or overseer over workmen.

mas·ter·wort (mas'tər·wûrt', mäs'-) n. 1 Any of several herbs of the parsley family, especially those of the genus Astrantia. 2 A European plant (Peucedanum ostruthium), formerly used as a pot herb.

mas·ter·y (mas'tər·ē, mäs'-) n. 1 The condition of having power and control; dominion. 2 The knowledge or skill of a master. 3 Superiority in a contest; victory. See synonyms under VICTORY.

mast·head (mast'hed', mäst'-) n. 1 Naut. a The top of a lower mast. b The head or top of a mast to which a flag is raised. c A sailor acting as look-out at the masthead. 2 That section of a newspaper or other periodical, published in each edition, stating the ownership, officers, and staff conducting it, the advertising, editorial, and publishing offices, etc. — v.t. 1 To raise to or display at the masthead, as a flag. 2 To send to a masthead for punishment.

mas·tic (mas'tik) n. 1 A small Mediterranean evergreen tree (Pistacia lentiscus) of the cashew family. 2 The aromatic resin obtained from this tree, used as a varnish and in medicine as a styptic. 3 A quick-drying cement. [<F <LL mastichum <Gk. mastichē]

mas·ti·cate (mas'tə·kāt) v.t. ·cat·ed, ·cat·ing 1 To crush or grind (food) for swallowing; chew. 2 To reduce, as rubber, to a pulp by crushing or kneading. [<LL masticatus, pp. of masticare chew <Gk. mastichaein gnash the teeth < mastax jaw] — **mas'ti·ca'tion** n. — **mas'ti·ca'tor** n.

mas·ti·ca·to·ry (mas'tə·kə·tôr'ē, -tō'rē) adj. 1 Of, pertaining to, or used in mastication. 2 Adapted for chewing: the masticatory mouth of a bee. — n. pl. **·ries** A substance chewed to increase the secretion of saliva.

mas·tiff (mas'tif, mäs'-) n. One of an old English breed of large hunting dogs, with a thick-set, heavy body, straight forelegs, a broad skull, drooping ears, and pendulous lips. [<OF mastin <L mansuetus gentle < pp. of mansuescere tame < manus hand; infl. in form by OF mestif mongrel]

MASTIFF
(About 30 inches high at the shoulder)

mas·ti·goph·o·ran (mas'ti·gof'ər·ən) n. Any one of a class of protozoa (Mastigophora), many of which are parasitic in man and other animals, characterized by the presence of one or more whiplike organs of locomotion called flagellae. — adj. Of or pertaining to the Mastigophora. [<Gk. mastix, mastigos whip + phoros bearing < pherein bear]

mas·ti·tis (mas·tī'tis) n. 1 Pathol. Inflammation of the mammary gland. 2 Garget. [<MAST- + -ITIS]

masto– combining form Med. The breast or the mammary gland. Also, before vowels, mast–, as in mastitis. [<Gk. mastos the breast]

mas·to·don (mas'tə·don) n. A primitive elephantlike mammal (order Proboscidea), distinguished from elephants and mammoths chiefly by its molar teeth; especially, the extinct, shaggy-haired Mammut americanus once common in North America. [< NL <MAST- + Gk. odous, odontos tooth; from the nipple-shaped projections on its teeth]

MASTODON
(About 9 feet high at the shoulder)

mas·toid (mas'toid) adj. Anat. 1 Designating a process of the temporal bone behind the ear for the attachment of muscles. 2 Pertaining to or situated near this process. 3 Nipplelike; breastlike. — n. The mastoid process. [<Gk. mastoeidēs <mastos breast + eidos form]

mas·toid·ec·to·my (mas'toid·ek'tə·mē) n. Surg. Excision of mastoid cells or of the mastoid process. [<MASTOID + -ECTOMY]

mas·toid·i·tis (mas'toid·ī'tis) n. Pathol. Inflammation of the mastoid process. [<MASTOID + -ITIS]

mas·tur·bate (mas'tər·bāt) v.i. ·bat·ed, ·bat·ing To perform masturbation. [<L masturbatus, pp. of masturbari; ult. origin uncertain]

mas·tur·ba·tion (mas'tər·bā'shən) n. Sexual

self-gratification; onanism: also called *self-abuse.* [<L *masturbatio, -onis*] **—mas′tur·ba′tor** *n.*

Ma·su·ri·a (mə·zŏŏr′ē·ə, -sŏŏr′-) A region of NE Poland on the U. S. S. R. border, containing the many **Masurian Lakes:** Polish *Mazury.* *German* **Ma·su·ren·land** (mä·zōō′rən·länt).

ma·su·ri·um (mə·sŏŏr′ē·əm) *n.* A supposed metallic element whose place in the periodic table is now occupied by technetium. [from *Masuria,* where first found]

mat[1] (mat) *n.* **1** A flat article, woven or plaited, or made of some perforated or corrugated material, to be laid on a floor, and on which to wipe one's shoes or feet. **2** Any flat piece of lace, plaited straw, leather, etc., used as a floor covering, table protection, ornament, etc. **3** Any dense or twisted growth, as of hair or rushes. *—v.* **mat·ted, mat·ting** *v.t.* **1** To cover with or as with mats. **2** To knot or entangle into a mat. *—v.i.* **3** To become knotted or entangled together. [OE *matt(e)* <LL *matta*]

mat[2] (mat) *n.* **1** A lusterless, dull, or roughened surface; also, a tool for producing such a surface. **2** *Printing* A sheet of papier-mâché or wood fiber for recording the impression of type or cuts in stereotyping; a matrix. **3** A border of white cardboard, serving as the frame, or part of the frame, of a picture. *—v.t.* **mat·ted, mat·ting** To produce a dull surface on, as metal or glass. *—adj.* Presenting a lusterless surface. Also *matte.* [OF, defeated, overcome <Arabic *māt*]

Mat·a·be·le (mat′ə·bē′lē) *n. pl.* **·be·le** or **·be·les** (-bē′lēz) One of a Zulu people who were driven across the Vaal by the Boers in 1837 and occupied the region north of the Limpopo, later known as Matabeleland.

Mat·a·be·le·land (mat′ə·bē′lē·land′) A region in southwest Zimbabwe between the Limpopo and Zambezi rivers; 69,989 square miles.

mat·a·dor (mat′ə·dôr) *n.* **1** In bullfighting, the man who kills the bull with a thrust of a sword. **2** In various card games, one of the highest trumps. [<Sp., killer <*matar* slay]

Ma·ta·mo·ros (mä′tä·mō′rōs) A city near the mouth of the Rio Grande in NE Mexico.

Mat·a·nus·ka Valley (mat′ə·nōōs′kə) A region of southern Alaska, site of an experimental colonization project by the United States government in 1935.

Ma·tan·zas (mä·tän′säs) **1** A province in western Cuba; 3,260 square miles. **2** Its capital, a port.

Ma·ta·pan (mä′tä·pän′), **Cape** The southernmost point of the Greek mainland: also *Cape Tainaron.*

match[1] (mach) *n.* **1** One similar or equal in appearance, position, quality, or character; a suitable or fit associate; also a possible mate. **2** A person or thing that is the equal of another in ability, strength, character, position, etc.; one able to cope with or oppose another; a peer. **3** A contest of skill, strength, etc., between persons or animals. **4** A counterpart; facsimile; also, either of two things harmonizing or corresponding. **5** A marriage or mating, or an agreement to marry or pair; a pairing or coupling. *—v.t.* **1** To be similar to or in accord with in quality, degree, etc.: His looks *match* his mood; The hat *matches* the coat. **2** to make or select as equals or as suitable for one another: to *match* pearls. **3** To place together as mates or companions; marry. **4** To cause to correspond: adapt: *Match your efforts to your salary.* **5** To compare so as to decide superiority; test: to *match* wits. **6** to set (equal opponents) in opposition: to *match* boxers. **7** To equal; oppose successfully: No one could *match* him. *—v.i.* **8** To be equal, similar, or corresponding; suit. **9** To be married; mate. [OE *gemæcca* companion] **—match′a·ble** *adj.* **—match′er** *n.*

match[2] (mach) *n.* **1** Any article manufactured for the purpose of starting or communicating a fire; specifically, a splinter of soft wood or a piece of waxed thread or cardboard tipped with a combustible composition that ignites by friction. **2** A fuse of cotton wicking prepared to burn quickly or slowly, and used for firing cannon. [<OF *mesche* wick, prob. <L *myxa* wick of a candle]

match·board (mach′bôrd′, -bōrd′) *n.* A board, specially cut with a groove along one edge and a tongue along the other, for close joining on floors, ceilings, etc.

match·book (mach′bŏŏk′) *n.* A small paper folder containing safety matches, with a strip of specially prepared surface at one end for striking them.

match·box (mach′boks′) *n.* a small box for containing matches.

matched (macht) *adj.* Having a tongue on one edge and a groove on the other: said of boards.

match·less (mach′lis) *adj.* That cannot be matched or equaled; peerless. **—match′less·ly** *adv.* **—match′less·ness** *n.*

match·lock (mach′lok′) *n.* **1** An old type of musket fired by placing a lighted match against the powder in the pan. **2** The gunlock on such a musket.

match·maker[1] (mach′mā′kər) *n.* One who makes plans, or schemes, to bring about a marriage. **2** One who arranges matched games or contests. **—match′mak′ing** *adj. & n.*

match·maker[2] (mach′mā′kər) *n.* One who makes matches for lighting. **—match′mak′ing** *adj. & n.*

match·mark (mach′märk′) *n.* A distinguishing mark placed on separable parts of machinery as a guide for assembling. *—v.t.* To put a matchmark upon.

match play In golf, a form of competitive play in which the score is computed by totaling the number of holes won or lost by each side.

match player A golfer who competes in match play.

match point In tennis and similar games, the final point needed to win a match.

match·stick (mach′stik′)′ *n.* A piece of wood tipped with sulfur and used as a match.

match·wood (mach′wŏŏd′) *n.* **1** Wood suitable for making matches; also, splinters. **2** *Obs.* A combustible substance used as tinder; touchwood.

mate[1] (māt) *n.* **1** A companion or associate; comrade. **2** One that is paired or coupled with another, as in matrimony; also, the male or female of animals paired for propagation. **3** An equal in a contest; a match. **4** An officer of a merchant vessel, ranking next below the captain. **5** *Nav.* An assistant to a warrant officer; a petty officer: the boatswain's *mate.* See synonyms under ASSOCIATE. *—v.* **mat·ed, mat·ing** *v.t.* **1** To join as mates or a pair; match; marry. **2** To pair for breeding, as animals. **3** To associate; couple. *—v.i.* **4** To match; marry. **5** To pair. **6** To consort; associate. [<MLG <*gemate* <*ge* together + *mat* meat, food. Prob. akin to MEAT.] **—mate′less** *adj.*

mate[2] (māt) *v.t.* **mat·ed, mat·ing 1** In chess, to checkmate. **2** To defeat or confound. *—n.* A checkmate. *—Interj.* Checkmate. [<CHECKMATE]

ma·té (mä′tā, mat′ā) *n.* **1** An infusion of the leaves of a Brazilian holly *(Ilex paraguariensis),* much used as a beverage in South America: also called *Paraguay tea, yerba.* **2** The Paraguay tea plant. [<Sp. <Quechua *mati* calabash (in which it was steeped)]

mat·e·lote (mat′ə·lōt) *n.* A Stew of fish in wine and oil, with herb seasoning. Also **mat′e·lotte** (-lot). [<F <*matelot* sailor]

Ma·te·o (mä·tā′ō) Spanish form of MATTHEW.

ma·ter (mā′tər, mä′-) *n. Latin* Mother.

mater do·lo·ro·sa (dō′lə·rō′sə) *Latin* Sorrowful mother: in art or music, the Virgin Mary as the sorrowing mother.

ma·ter·fa·mil·i·as (mā′tər·fə·mil′ē·əs) *n. Latin* The mother of a family; a matron.

ma·te·ri·al (mə·tir′ē·əl) *n.* **1** That of which anything is composed or may be constructed; matter considered as a component part of something. **2** Collected facts, impressions, ideas, or notes containing them, and sketches, etc., that may be used in completing a literary or an artistic production. **3** Matter regarded as the amorphous substratum of reality. **4** The tools, instruments, articles, etc., for doing something. See also MATERIEL. **5** A cloth or fabric. *—adj.* **1** Pertaining to matter; having a corporeal existence; physical. **2** Pertaining to matter in a corporeal relation; affecting the physical nature; also, pertaining to the body or the appetites; corporeal; sensuous; sensual. **3** Pertaining to the subject matter; essential; important. **4** Pertaining to matter as opposed to form. **5** Consisting of, relating to, or composed of matter regarded as the primary substance of the physical universe. **6** Replete with matter or good sense. See synonyms under IMPORTANT, PHYSICAL. [<LL *materialis* <L *materia* matter, stuff]

ma·te·ri·al·ism (mə·tir′ē·əl·iz′əm) *n.* **1** The doctrine that the facts of experience are all to be explained by reference to the reality, activities, and laws of physical or material substance. **2** Undue regard for material interests.

ma·te·ri·al·ist (mə·tir′ē·əl·ist) *n.* **1** A believer in the doctrine of materialism; also, a believer in the existence of matter. **2** One who takes interest exclusively, chiefly, or excessively in the material or bodily necessities and comforts of life. **—ma·te′ri·al·is′tic** *adj.* **—ma·te′·ri·al·is′ti·cal·ly** *adv.*

ma·te·ri·al·i·ty (mə·tir′ē·al′ə·tē) *n. pl.* **·ties 1** The quality or state of being material; physical as distinguished from psychical being. **2** Substance; matter; a material thing; a body. Also **ma·te′ri·al·ness.**

ma·te·ri·al·ize (mə·tir′ē·əl·īz′) *v.* **·ized, ·iz·ing** *v.t.* **1** To give material or actual form to; represent as material. **2** To cause (a spirit, etc.) to appear in visible form. **3** To make materialistic. *—v.i.* **4** To assume material or visible form; appear. **5** To take form or shape; be realized: Our plans never *materialized.* **—ma·te′ri·al·i·za′tion** *n.* **—ma·te′ri·al·iz′er** *n.*

ma·te·ri·al·ly (mə·tir′ē·əl·ē) *adv.* **1** In a material and important manner. **2** In essence or substance. **3** From a physical point of view; physically.

ma·te·ri·a med·i·ca (mə·tir′ē·ə med′i·kə) *Med.* **1** The branch of medical science that relates to medicinal substances, their nature, uses, effects, etc. **2** The substances employed as remedial agents. [<Med. L <*materia* matter + *medica,* fem. of *medicus* medical]

ma·te·ri·el (mə·tir′ē·el′) *n. Mil.* **1** All nonexpendable ordnance, transport, and equipment of an army. **2** All material things of an army except personnel. Also *French* **ma·té·riel** (má·tā·ryel′). [<F, material]

ma·te·ri·es mor·bi (mə·tir′i·ēz môr′bī) *Latin* The morbid substances, organisms, etc., which cause disease.

ma·ter·nal (mə·tûr′nəl) *adj.* **1** Pertaining to a mother; motherly. **2** Connected with or inherited from one's mother; coming through the relationship of a mother. [<F *maternel* <L *maternus* <*mater* a mother] **—ma·ter′·nal·ly** *adv.*

ma·ter·nal·ize (mə·tûr′nəl·īz) *v.t.* **·ized, ·iz·ing** To make maternal.

ma·ter·ni·ty (mə·tûr′nə·tē) *n. pl.* **·ties 1** The condition of being a mother. **2** The qualities of a mother; motherliness. [<F *maternité* <L *maternitas*]

maternity hospital A hospital for the care of women during childbirth and of newborn babies; lying-in hospital.

mate·ship (māt′ship) *n.* **1** The state or condition of being a mate or companion. **2** The position or authority of one holding the office of mate.

ma·tey (mā′tē) *Brit. Colloq. adj.* Friendly; chummy. *—n.* Friend; chum.

math[1] (math) *n.* A mowing, or that obtained by mowing: now rare except in *aftermath.* [OE *mǣth*]

math[2] (math) *n. Colloq.* Mathematics.

math·e·mat·i·cal (math′ə·mat′i·kəl) *adj.* **1** Pertaining to or of the nature of mathematics. **2** Rigidly exact or precise. Also **math′e·mat′ic.** [<L *mathematicus* <Gk. *mathēmatikos* disposed to learn, mathematical <*mathēma* learning <*manthanein* learn] **—math′e·mat′·i·cal·ly** *adv.*

mathematical expectation *Stat.* The probability of the occurrence of a given event multiplied by the amount of money offered or wagered on its occurrence.

mathematical logic Symbolic logic.

math·e·ma·ti·cian (math′ə·mə·tish′ən) *n.* One versed in mathematics.

math·e·mat·ics (math′ə·mat′iks) *n.* The logical study of quantity, form, arrangement, and magnitude; especially, the methods for disclosing, by the use of rigorously defined concepts and self-consistent symbols, the properties and exact relations of quantities and magnitudes, whether in the abstract, **pure mathematics**, or in their practical connections, **applied mathematics**.

MATHEMATICAL SYMBOLS

+	Plus or positive; sign of addition
−	Minus or negative; sign of subtraction
±	Plus or minus
∓	Minus or plus
× or ·	Multiplied by
÷ or :	Divided by
= or ::	Equals; is equal to; as
≠ or ≉	Does not equal
≅	Approximately equal; congruent
>	Greater than
<	Less than
≥	Greater than or equal to
≤	Less than or equal to
∽	Similar to; equivalent
∴	Therefore
∵	Since or because
≡	Identical; identically equal to
∝	Directly proportional to; varies directly as
∞	Infinity
$\sqrt{}$	Square root
$\sqrt[n]{}$	*n*th root
e or ε	Base (2.718···) of natural system of logarithms
Σ	Summation of
∫	Integral of
$\int_b^a$	Integral between limits of *a* and *b*
≐ or →	Approaches as a limit
$f(x), F(x), \phi(x)$	Function of *x*
Δ	Increment of, as Δ *y*
d	Differential, as *dy*
$\dfrac{dy}{dx}$, or $f'(x)$	Derivative of $y = f(x)$ with respect to *x*
δ	Variation, as δ *y*
π	pi; ratio of circumference of circle to diameter
n! or $\lfloor n$	Factorial *n* or *n* factorial
∠, ∠s	Angle, angles
⊥, ⊥s	Perpendicular to, perpendiculars
‖, ‖s	Parallel to, parallels
△, ⟁	Triangle, triangles
∟, ∟s	Right angle, right angles
▱, ▱s	Parallelogram, parallelograms
▭, ▭s	Rectangle, rectangles
□, □s	Square, squares
○ or ⊙	Circle, circumference
′	Minutes of arc; prime; minutes of time; feet
″	Seconds of arc; double prime; seconds of time; inches

Math·er (math′ər), **Cotton,** 1663?–1728?, American clergyman and writer. — **Increase,** 1639–1723, American clergyman and writer; father of Cotton.

Ma·thi·as (mä·tē′äs) German form of MAT-THIAS. Also *Sp.* **Ma·ti·as** (mä·tē′äs).

Ma·thieu (mà·tyœ′) French form of MATTHEW.

Ma·thu·ra (mu′tŏŏr·ə) A city in western Uttar Pradesh, India, sacred to Hindus as the birthplace of Krishna: formerly *Muttra.*

Ma·thu·rai (mə·tŏŏr′ī) See MADURAI.

ma·ti·co (mə·tē′kō) *n.* A tropical American shrub (*Piper angustifolium*) of the pepper family: its hairy leaves yield a volatile oil having stimulant and hemostatic properties. [<Sp., dim. of *Mateo* Matthew]

Ma·til·da (mə·til′də; *Ital.* mä·tēl′dä, *Sw.* mä·til′dä) A feminine personal name. Also **Ma·thil·da** (mə·til′də, *Du.* ma·til′dä), **Ma·thil·de** (*Dan.* mä·til′de, *Fr.* mà·tēld′), **Ma·til·de** (*Ger.* mä·tēl′də, *Sp.* mä·tēl′dä). [<Gmc., mighty in battle]
— **Matilda,** 1102–67, daughter of Henry I of England; disputed the English throne with Stephen of Blois: known as *Maud.*
— **Matilda of Flanders,** died 1083, wife of William the Conqueror.

mat·in (mat′in) *n.* **1** *pl. Eccl.* The first of the canonical hours, usually said at midnight. **2** *pl.* In the Anglican Church, Morning Prayer. **3** Figuratively, any morning song, as of a bird. **4** *Obs.* Morning. — *adj.* Of or belonging to the morning: also **mat′in·al.** Also spelled *mattin.* [<OF *matin* early <L *matutinus* (*tempus*) (time) of the morning, appar. <*Matuta* goddess of morning]

mat·i·née (mat′ə·nā′) *n.* An entertainment or reception held in the daytime; specifically, a theatrical or cinematic performance given in the afternoon. Also **mat′i·nee′.** [<F <*matin* morning. See MATIN.]

mat·ing (mā′ting) *n.* The act of pairing or matching.

Ma·tisse (mà·tēs′), **Henri,** 1869–1954, French painter.

mat–knife (mat′nīf′) *n. pl.* **–knives** (-nīvz′) A knife having the edge ground at an angle, used for cutting engravings, heavy paper, artist's matboard, etc. See illustration under KNIFE.

Ma·to Gros·so (mat′ə grō′sō, *Pg.* mä′tŏŏ grō′-sŏŏ) A state of central and western Brazil, the second largest state in Brazil; 487,489 square miles; capital, Cuiabá: formerly *Matto Grosso.*

mat·rass (mat′rəs) *n.* **1** A long–necked, round–bodied glass vessel for distilling and digesting. See BOLTHEAD (def. 1). **2** A thin, hard glass tube used in blowpipe analysis. Also spelled *mattrass.* [<F *matras* bolt]

matri– *combining form* Mother: *matricide.* [<L *mater, matris* mother]

ma·tri·arch (mā′trē·ärk) *n.* A woman holding the position corresponding to that of a patriarch in her family or tribe. [<MATRI- + (PATRI)ARCH] — **ma′tri·ar′chal** *adj.* — **ma′tri·ar′chal·ism** *n.*

ma·tri·ar·chate (mā′trē·är′kit) *n.* Matriarchal government; a system of matriarchalism. [< MATRIARCH + -ATE²]

ma·tri·ar·chy (mā′trē·är′kē) *n. pl.* **·chies** A social organization having the mother as the head of the family, in which descent, kinship, and succession are reckoned through the mother, instead of the father; also, government by women. — **ma′tri·ar′chic** *adj.*

ma·tri·ces (mā′trə·sēz, mat′rə-) Plural of MATRIX.

mat·ri·cide (mat′rə·sīd) *n.* **1** The killing of one's mother. **2** One who kills his mother. [<L *matricidium* <*mater, matris* mother +

caedere kill; def. 2 <L *matricida*] — **mat′ri·ci′dal** *adj.*

mat·ri·cli·nous (mat′rə·klī′nəs) *adj. Biol.* Showing hereditary characteristics inclined to the maternal side: opposed to *patriclinous.* Also **mat′ro·cli′nous, mat′ro·cli′nal.**

ma·tric·u·lant (mə·trik′yə·lənt) *n.* A candidate or applicant for matriculation.

ma·tric·u·late (mə·trik′yə·lāt) *v.t. & v.i.* **·lat·ed, ·lat·ing** To enrol in a college or university as a candidate for a degree. — *n.* One who is so enrolled. [<Med. L *matriculatus,* pp. of *matriculare* enrol <*matricula,* dim. of *matrix* womb, origin, public roll <*mater* mother] — **ma·tric′u·la′tion** *n.* — **ma·tric′u·la′tor** *n.*

mat·ri·lin·e·al (mat′rə·lin′ē·əl) *adj.* Pertaining to or describing descent or derivation through the female line. Compare PATRILINEAL.

mat·ri·lo·cal (mat′rə·lō′kəl) *adj. Anthropol.* Denoting residence of a married couple in the wife's community, as in certain clan societies. Compare PATRILOCAL.

mat·ri·mo·ni·al (mat′rə·mō′nē·əl) *adj.* Pertaining to matrimony. — **mat′ri·mo′ni·al·ly** *adv.*
— *Synonyms:* bridal, conjugal, connubial, hymeneal, hymenean, nuptial, sponsal, spousal. *Antonyms:* celibate, single, unespoused, unwedded.

mat·ri·mo·ny (mat′rə·mō′nē) *n. pl.* **·nies** **1** The union of a man and a woman in marriage; wedlock. **2** A card game played by any number of persons; also, a combination of king and queen in this and certain other games. See synonyms under MARRIAGE. [<L *matrimonium* <*mater, matris* mother]

matrimony vine The boxthorn.

ma·trix (mā′triks) *n. pl.* **ma·tri·ces** (mā′trə-sēz, mat′rə-) **1** That which contains and gives shape or form to anything. **2** The womb. **3** *Biol.* Intercellular substance; hence, the formative cells from which a structure grows. **4** A mold in which anything is cast or shaped, or that which encloses like a mold. **5** *Printing* A papier–mâché, plaster, or other impression of a form, from which a plate for printing may be made. **6** *Geol.* The impression or mold of the exterior of a crystal or other mineral left in the containing rock when the object is removed, or the mass in which a fossil, gemstone, mineral, etc., is embedded. **7** *Math.* A rectangular array of symbols or terms enclosed between parentheses or double vertical bars to facilitate the study of relationships. **8** The material used as a filler between the fragments of a shrapnel projectile. [<L, womb, breeding animal <*mater, matris* mother]

ma·tron (mā′trən) *n.* **1** A married woman; mother; also, a woman of established age and dignity. **2** A housekeeper, or a female superintendent, as of an institution. [<OF *matrone* <L *matrona* <*mater, matris* mother] — **ma′tron·al** *adj.* — **ma′tron·like′** *adj.*

ma·tron·age (mā′trən·ij) *n.* **1** The condition of being a matron. **2** Matronly attention or care. **3** Matrons collectively.

ma·tron·ize (mā′trən·īz) *v.t.* **·ized, ·iz·ing** **1** To render matronlike. **2** To chaperon.

ma·tron·ly (mā′trən·lē) *adj.* Of or like a matron; elderly. — *adv.* In a matronly manner. — **ma′tron·li·ness** *n.*

matron of honor A married woman acting as chief attendant to a bride at her wedding. See MAID OF HONOR.

mat·ro·nym·ic (mat′rō·nim′ik) See METRONYMIC.

Ma·trûh (mə·trōō′) A Mediterranean port of western Egypt: also *Mersa Matrûh.*

Ma·tsu·ya·ma (mä·tsŏŏ·yä·mä) A port on NW Shikoku island, Japan.

Matt (mat) Diminutive of MATTHEW.

matte¹ (mat) *n. Metall.* An impure metallic product containing sulfur, obtained in smelting sulfide ores, as of copper, lead, etc. [<F]

matte² (mat) See MAT².

mat·ted (mat′id) *adj.* **1** Covered with mats or matting. **2** Tangled like the fibers of a mat. — **mat′ted·ly** *adv.* — **mat′ted·ness** *n.*

mat·ter (mat′ər) *n.* **1** That which makes up the substance of anything, especially of material things. **2** The material of which a thing is composed. **3** *Physics* That aspect of reality conceived as existing prior to and independently of the mind and to have characteristics susceptible to precise measurement in terms of extension, force, mass, radiation, and energy. **4** That which constitutes the

essence or substance of a particular thing. **5** Something not exactly conceived or stated; an indefinite, often a comparatively small, amount. **6** A subject for discussion or feeling. **7** Something of moment and importance. **8** A condition of affairs, especially if unpleasant or unfortunate; case; difficulty; trouble: What's the *matter*? **9** The thought, or material of thought. **10** *Pus.* **11** *Philos.* The as yet undifferentiated substratum of those properties and changes of which the human senses take cognizance and which, by their differentiation and combination in an infinite variety of forms, constitute the separate existences and characteristic qualities of physical things. **12** *Printing* Type that is set or composed; also, material to be set up; copy. **13** Written or printed documents sent by mail. See synonyms under MASS[1], TOPIC. — *v.i.* **1** To be of concern or importance; signify. **2** To form or discharge pus; suppurate. [<F *matière* <L *materia* stuff]

Mat·ter·horn (mat′ər-hôrn, *Ger.* mä′ter-hôrn) A mountain in the Alps on the Swiss–Italian border: 14,780 feet: French *Mont Cervin.*

mat·ter-of-course (mat′ər-əv-kôrs′, -kōrs′) *adj.* Following or accepting as an expected conclusion or as a natural or logical result.

mat·ter-of-fact (mat′ər-əv-fakt′) *adj.* Closely adhering to facts; straightforward.

mat·ter-of-fact·ly (mat′ər-əv-fakt′lē) *adv.* In a matter-of-fact manner; straightforwardly. — **mat′ter-of-fact′ness** *n.*

Mat·thew (math′yōō) A masculine personal name. Also *Lat.* **Mat·thae·us** (mə-thē′əs, *Dan.* mä-tä′əs), *Ger., Sw.* **Mat·thä·us** (mä-tā′ōōs), *Du.* **Mat·the·us** (mä-tā′əs), *Ital.* **Mat·te·o** (mät-tā′ō). [<Hebrew, gift of God] — **Matthew** One of the Twelve Apostles, author of the first Gospel; also, the Gospel by him. Also **Saint Matthew.** — **Matthew of Paris,** 1200–59?, English monk and chronicler.

Mat·thews (math′yōōz), **(James) Brander,** 1852–1929, U.S. scholar, author, and educator.

Mat·thi·as (mə-thī′əs, *Fr.* mȧ-tē-ȧs′) A masculine personal name. Also *Du.* **Mat·thijs** (mä-tīs′). [See MATTHEW] — **Matthias** The apostle chosen by lot to succeed Judas Iscariot. *Acts* i 23–26.

mat·tin (mat′in) See MATIN.

mat·ting (mat′ing) *n.* **1** A woven fabric of fiber, straw, etc., used as a floor covering, etc. **2** The act or process of making mats. **3** A dull, flat surface effect, as in gilding, etc.

mat·tock (mat′ək) *n.* A pickaxlike tool for digging and grubbing, having blades instead of points. [OE *mattuc*]

MATTOCK

Mat·to Gros·so (mat′ə grō′sō, *Pg.* mä′tōō grō′sōō) A former spelling of MATO GROSSO.

mat·toid (mat′oid) *n.* A person mentally unbalanced in one way or on one subject. [<Ital. *mattoide* <*matto* mad <L *mattus* intoxicated]

mat·trass (mat′rəs) See MATRASS.

mat·tress (mat′rəs) *n.* **1** A casing of ticking or other strong fabric filled with hair, cotton, or rubber, and used as a bed. **2** A mat woven of brush, poles, etc., used in protecting embankments, forming dikes, jetties, etc. [<OF *materas* <Ital. *materasso* <Arabic *maṭraḥ* place where something is thrown]

mat·u·rate (mach′ōō-rāt, mat′yōō-) *v.i.* **·rat·ed, ·rat·ing 1** To ripen or mature. **2** *Med.* To suppurate; form pus. [<L *maturatus,* pp. of *maturare* ripen <*maturus* ripe, fully developed] — **mat′u·ra′tive** *adj.*

mat·u·ra·tion (mach′ōō-rā′shən, mat′yōō-) *n.* **1** *Med.* The formation of pus. **2** The process of ripening or coming to maturity; ripeness. **3** *Biol.* The final stages in the preparation of gametes for fertilization, during which reduction to one half in the number of chromosomes in the germ cells occurs; meiosis.

ma·ture (mə-choor′, -toor′, -tyoor′) *adj.* **1** Completely developed; perfectly ripe: *mature* grain; as applied to persons, fully developed

in character and powers: a *mature* thinker. **2** Highly developed; approaching perfection. **3** Thoroughly elaborated or arranged; fully digested or considered; complete in detail: a *mature* scheme. **4** Due and payable; having reached its time limit: a *mature* bond. **5** *Geol.* Designating the maximum complexity and diversity of earth features, as achieved by the forces of erosion at full vigor; also, adjusted to local surroundings, as the course of a river. See synonyms under RIPE. — *v.* **·tured, ·tur·ing** *v.t.* **1** To cause to ripen or come to maturity; bring to full development. **2** To perfect; complete. — *v.i.* **3** To come to maturity or full development; ripen. **4** To become due, as a note. [<L *maturus* of full age]

ma·tur·i·ty (mə-choor′ə-tē, -toor′-, -tyoor′-) *n.* **1** The state or condition of being mature: also **ma·ture′ness. 2** Full development, as of the body. **3** The time at which a thing matures: a note payable at *maturity.* [<F *maturité* <L *maturitas*]

ma·tu·ti·nal (mə-tōō′tə-nəl, -tyōō′-) *adj.* Pertaining to morning; before noon; early. [<L *matutinalis* <*matutinus* early in the morning <*Matuta,* goddess of morning] — **ma·tu′ti·nal·ly** *adv.*

mat·zo (mät′sə, -sō) *n. pl.* **mat·zoth** (mät′sōth, -sōs) or **mat·zos** (-səs, -səz) **1** Unleavened bread in the form of wafers, eaten by Jews at Passover. **2** A wafer of unleavened bread. [<Hebrew *matstsôth,* pl. of *matstsāh* unleavened]

mat·zoon (mat-sōōn′) See YOGURT.

Mau·beuge (mō-bœzh′) A city in northern France.

Maud (môd) A feminine personal name; also, diminutive of MAGDALENE and MATILDA. Also **Maude.**

maud·lin (môd′lin) *adj.* **1** Made foolish by liquor. **2** Foolishly and tearfully affectionate. [<*Maudlin* <OF *Maudelene, Madeleine* (Mary) Magdalen, who was often depicted with eyes swollen from weeping]

Maugham (môm), **(William) Somerset,** 1874–1965, English novelist and dramatist.

mau·gre (mô′gər) *prep.* Obsolete form of MALGRÉ. [<OF]

Mau·i (mou′ē) The second largest of the Hawaiian Islands; 728 square miles.

mau·kin (mô′kin) See MALKIN.

maul (môl) *n.* A heavy mallet for driving wedges, piles, etc. — *v.t.* **1** To beat and bruise; batter. **2** To handle roughly; manhandle; abuse. **3** *U.S.* To split by means of a maul and wedges, as logs or rails. Also spelled *mall.* [<OF *mail* <L *malleus* hammer. ? Akin to L *molere* grind into pieces, crush.] — **maul′er** *n.*

Maul·main (môl-mān′) See MOULMEIN.

maul·stick (môl′stik′) See MAHLSTICK.

STEEL FENCE-POST MAUL

Mau Mau (mou′ mou′) *pl.* **Mau Mau** or **Mau Maus** A member of a secret organization of Kikuyu tribesmen, active from 1952 in terrorist activities directed against European colonists in Kenya, Africa. [< native name]

mau·met (mô′mit) *n.* **1** *Obs.* An idol: from the early belief that the Moslems worshiped images of Mohammed. **2** *Brit. Dial.* A scarecrow; a doll. Also spelled *mammet.* [Contraction of MAHOMET] — **mau′met·ry** *n.*

maun (môn) *v.i. Scot.* Must.

mau·na (mô′nə) *Scot.* Must not. Also **maun′na.**

Mau·na Ke·a (mou′nä kā′ä) An extinct volcano on Hawaii; highest mountain in the Hawaiian Islands; 13,825 feet.

Mau·na Lo·a (mou′nä lō′ä) An active volcano on Hawaii; 13,675 feet.

maund (mônd) *n.* A unit of weight used in India, varying from 24.7 to 82.28 lbs. avoirdupois. [<Hind. *mān*]

maun·der (môn′dər) *v.i.* **1** To talk in a wandering or incoherent manner; drivel. **2** To move dreamily or idly. [? Freq. of obs. *maund* beg; infl. in meaning by MEANDER] — **maun′der·er** *n.*

maun·dy (môn′dē) *n.* The religious ceremony of washing the feet of others, especially of in-

feriors: in commemoration of the washing of the disciples' feet by Christ; hence, **Maundy,** the service connected with such ceremony. [<OF *mandé* <L *mandatum* command; from the use of *mandatum* at the beginning of the ceremony. See MANDATE.]

Maundy Thursday The day before Good Friday, commemorating the Last Supper of Christ with his disciples, at which he washed their feet. [See MAUNDY]

Mau·pas·sant (mō-pȧ-sän′), **(Henri René Albert) Guy de,** 1850–93, French writer.

Mau·re·ta·ni·a (môr′ə-tā′nē-ə) An ancient country of North Africa, including the northern part of modern Morocco and the western part of Algeria.

Mau·re·ta·ni·an (môr′ə-tā′nē-ən) *adj.* Pertaining to ancient Mauretania or its inhabitants. — *n.* **1** One of the ancient people of Mauretania. **2** The Libyan dialect spoken by these people.

Mau·ri·ac (mô-ryȧk′), **François,** 1885–1970, French novelist.

Mau·rice (mə-rēs′, môr′is, mor′is; *Fr.* mô-rēs′) A masculine personal name. Also *Sp.* **Mau·ri·cio** (mou-rē′thyō), *Ital.* **Mau·ri·sio** (mou-rē′syō) or **Mau·ri·zio** (mou-rē′tsyō), **Mau·ri·ti·us** (*Du.* mou-rē′sē-əs, *Lat.* mou-rish′əs), *Du.* **Mau·rits** (mou′rits). [<L, Moorish] — **Maurice,** 1521–53, Elector of Saxony; secured religious freedom in Germany. — **Maurice of Nassau,** 1567–1625, Prince of Orange; Dutch general; son of William the Silent.

Mau·ri·ta·ni·a (môr′ə-tā′nē-ə), **Islamic Republic of** An independent republic of the French Community, on the coast of west Africa; 418,120 square miles; capital, Nouakchott; formerly a French overseas territory. — **Mau′·ri·ta′ni·an** *adj. & n.*

Mau·ri·ti·us (mô-rish′ē-əs) An island in the Indian Ocean east of Madagascar; 720 square miles; comprising with its dependencies a British crown colony (804 square miles); capital, Port Louis. *French* **Mau·rice** (mô-rēs′). — **Mau·ri′ti·an** *adj. & n.*

Mau·rois (mô-rwä′), **André** Pseudonym of Émile Herzog, 1885–1967, French biographer and novelist.

Mau·ry (mô′rē), **Matthew Fontaine,** 1806–1873, U.S. naval officer and oceanographer.

Maur·ya (mour′yə) An Indian dynasty, 325?–184? B.C., founded by *Chandragupta I.*

Mau·ser (mou′zər) *n.* A magazine rifle having great range and high muzzle velocity; also, a type of automatic pistol: a trade name. [after P. P. *Mauser,* 1838–1914, German inventor]

mau·so·le·um (mô′sə-lē′əm) *n. pl.* **·le·ums** or **·le·a** (-lē′ə) A large, stately tomb. [<L <Gk. *Mausōleion,* tomb of King Mausolus of Caria, erected by Queen Artemisia at Halicarnassus about 350 B.C. See SEVEN WONDERS OF THE WORLD.] — **mau′so·le′an** *adj.*

mauve (mōv) *n.* **1** A purple pigment and dye derived from mauvein. **2** Any of various purplish-rose shades. [<F, mallow <L *malva.* Doublet of MALLOW.]

mauve·in (mō′vin) *n. Chem.* A coal-tar violet dyestuff, $C_{27}H_{24}N_4$, obtained by oxidizing aniline: the first aniline dye of commerce. Also **mauve·ine** (mō′vin, -vēn). [<MAUVE]

mav·er·ick (mav′ər-ik) *n.* **1** *U.S.* An unbranded or orphaned animal, particularly a calf, legitimately belonging to the first one to brand it. **2** *Colloq.* A person with no attachments or affiliations, especially political ones. [after Samuel A. *Maverick,* 1803–1870, Texas lawyer, who did not brand his cattle]

ma·vis (mā′vis) *n.* The European song thrush or throstle (genus *Turdus*). [<F *mauvis*]

Ma·vors (mā′vôrz) An early name for Mars, the Roman god of war.

ma·vour·neen (mə-vōor′nēn, -vôr′-) *n.* My darling: an expression of affection. Also **ma·vour′nin.** [<Irish *mo muirnín*]

maw[1] (mô) *n.* **1** The craw of a bird. **2** The stomach. **3** The air bladder of a fish. **4** The gullet, jaws, or mouth of a voracious mammal or fish. [OE *maga* stomach]

maw[2] (mô) *v.t. Scot.* To mow, as hay.

mawk·ish (mô′kish) *adj.* **1** Productive of disgust or loathing; sickening or insipid. **2** Char-

acterized by false or feeble sentimentality; lacking in strength or vigor. See synonyms under FLAT. [<obs. *mawk* a maggot] — **mawk′ish·ly** *adv.* — **mawk′ish·ness** *n.*

Maw·son (mô′sən), **Sir Douglas**, 1882–1958, Australian explorer.

Max (maks) A masculine personal name; originally a diminutive of MAXIMILIAN.

max·i (maks′ē) *n. pl.* **max·is** A long skirt or coat, usually reaching to the ankle.

max·il·la (mak·sil′ə) *n. pl.* **·lae** (-ē) **1** *Anat.* The upper jaw bone in vertebrates. **2** *Zool.* One of the pair or pairs of jaws behind the mandibles of an arthropod. [<L, dim. of *mala* jaw]

max·il·lar·y (mak′sə·ler′ē, mak·sil′ər·ē) *adj.* Of, pertaining to, or situated near the jaw or a maxilla: a *maxillary* artery. — *n. pl.* **·lar·ies** A maxilla or jaw bone.

max·il·li·ped (mak·sil′ə·ped) *n. Zool.* **1** One of the limbs of certain crustaceans, modified to serve as masticatory organs, and situated behind the maxillae. **2** One of a pair of poisonous claws situated near the mouth of a centipede. [<L *maxilla* jaw bone + -PED]

max·im (mak′sim) *n.* A brief statement of a practical principle or proposition; a proverbial saying. See synonyms under ADAGE, RULE. [<F *maxime* <L *maxima* (*sententia, propositio*) greatest (authority, premise), fem. of *maximus*. See MAXIMUM.]

Max·im (mak′sim), **Hiram Percy**, 1869–1936, U.S. inventor, son of Sir Hiram. — **Sir Hiram Stevens**, 1840–1916, U.S. inventor, civil, mechanical, and electrical engineer; became a British subject. — **Hudson**, 1853–1927, U.S. mechanical engineer and inventor; brother of Sir Hiram.

max·i·mal (mak′sə·məl) *adj.* Greatest; highest. See MAXIMUM.

Max·i·mal·ist (mak′sə·məl·ist) *n.* One of a former party or faction of extremist Russian revolutionists: distinguished from *Minimalist*.

Maxim gun A water-cooled machine-gun which utilizes the recoil of each shot to fire the next: invented by Sir Hiram S. Maxim.

Max·i·mil·ian (mak′sə·mil′yən, *Ger., Sw.* mäk′-si·mē′lē·än) A masculine personal name. Also *Sp.* **Max·i·mil·i·a·no** (mäk′sē·mē′lē·ä′nō), **Max·i·mil·i·a·nus** (*Du.* mäk·sē·mē′lē·ä′nəs, *Lat.* mak′si·mil′ē·ä′nəs), *Pg.* **Max·i·mil·i·ão** (mäk′si·mē′lē·oun′), *Fr.* **Max·i·mi·lien** (mȧk·sē·mē·lyaṅ′). [<L, greatest *Aemilius*.]

— **Maximilian I**, 1459–1519, Holy Roman Emperor 1493–1519.
— **Maximilian II**, 1527–76, Holy Roman Emperor 1564–76.
— **Maximilian (Ferdinand Joseph)**, 1832–67, archduke of Austria; emperor of Mexico 1864–67; executed.

max·im·ite (mak′sim·īt) *n.* A picric-acid high explosive used as a bursting charge for projectiles: invented by Hudson Maxim.

max·i·mize (mak′sə·mīz) *v.t.* **·mized**, **·miz·ing** To make as great as possible; increase to the maximum; intensify. — **max′i·mi·za′tion** *n.*

max·i·mum (mak′sə·məm) *n. pl.* **·ma** (-mə) **1** The greatest quantity, amount, degree, or magnitude that can be assigned. **2** *Math.* **a** A value of a varying quantity that is greater than any neighboring value. **b** The highest possible of all the values which a variable or a function can express; the point at which a varying quantity ceases to increase and begins to decrease. **3** *Astron.* The moment of greatest brightness in a variable star, or its magnitude at such time. — *adj.* **1** As large or great as possible. **2** Pertaining to a maximum: *maximum* weight. [<L *maximus*, superl. of *magnus* great]

ma·xi·xe (mə·shē′shä, mȧk·sēks′) *n.* A Brazilian dance to the two-step. [<Brazilian Pg.]

Max Mül·ler (mäks mül′ər), **Friedrich** See MÜLLER.

max·well (maks′wel) *n.* The practical cgs unit of magnetic flux, equal to the flux through one square centimeter normal to a magnetic field with an intensity of one gauss. [after James Clerk *Maxwell*]

Max·well (maks′wel), **James Clerk**, 1831–79, Scottish physicist.

Maxwell's demon *Physics* An imaginary being of molecular proportions, devised by James Clerk Maxwell to illustrate the kinetic theory of gases.

may¹ (mā) *v.* Present: *sing.* **may**, **may** (*Archaic*

may·est or **mayst**), **may**, *pl.* **may**; past: **might** A defective verb now used only in the present and past tenses as an auxiliary followed by the infinitive without *to*, or elliptically with the infinitive understood, to express: **1** Permission or allowance: *May* I go? You *may.* **2** Desire or wish: *May* your tribe increase! **3** Contingency, especially in clauses of result, concession, purpose, etc.: He died that we *might* live. **4** Possibility: You *may* be right. **5** *Law* Obligation or duty: the equivalent of *must* or *shall.* **6** *Obs.* Ability; power: now usually *can.* ◆ See usage note under CAN. [OE *mæg*]

may² (mā) *n.* The English hawthorn (*Crataegus oxyacantha*), with white, rose, or crimson flowers. Also **may′bush** (-boŏsh′). [<MAY, because it blooms in this month]

May (mā) **1** The fifth month of the year, containing 31 days. **2** The prime of life; youth. **3** May Day festivities. [<OF *mai* <L (*mensis*) *Maius* (month of) May, prob. <*Maia*, goddess of growth; so called because regarded as a month of growth]

May (mā) A feminine personal name: contraction of MARY.

May (mā), **Cape** The southernmost point in New Jersey between the Atlantic and Delaware Bay.

Ma·ya (mä′yə) **1** In Hindu religion, Devi, mother of the world; the personified active will of the Creator. **2** In Hindu philosophy, illusion, often personified as a maiden. [<Skt. *māyā* illusion]

Ma·ya (mä′yə) *n.* **1** One of a tribe of Central American Indians, the most important tribe of the Mayan linguistic stock, still comprising a large percentage of the population of Yucatán, northern Guatemala, and British Honduras. They were the first Indians to develop writing and an accurate astronomical calendar. **2** The language of the Mayas, in its historical and modern forms. — *adj.* Of or pertaining to the Mayas, their culture, or their language.

Ma·ya·güez (mä′yä·gwäs′) A port in western Puerto Rico.

Ma·yan (mä′yən) *adj.* Of the Mayas, their culture, or their language. — *n.* **1** A Maya. **2** A family of Central American Indian languages, including Maya and Quiché.

May apple 1 The ovoid, oblong, yellowish fruit of a North American herb (*Podophyllum peltatum*). **2** The herb itself, of which the rhizomes yield podophyllin. Also called *mandrake root.*

Ma·ya·ri iron (mä·yä′rē) An iron made from Cuban ores, containing small percentages of chromium, vanadium, nickel, titanium, and certain other elements: used in high-grade machine castings. [from *Mayari*, a Cuban town]

MAY APPLE
a. Flower.
b. Fruit.

May basket A little basket of flowers left at the door of a friend as a May Day token.

may·be (mā′bē) *adv.* Perhaps; possibly. [<(*it*) *may be*]

May·bird (mā′bûrd′) *n.* **1** In the southern United States, the bobolink. **2** In the eastern United States, the redbreast (def. 3).

May·bug (mā′bug′) *n.* **1** The cockchafer. **2** The June beetle. Also **May′bee′tle** (-bēt′l).

May·day (mā′dā′) *n.* The international radiotelephone call for immediate help sent out by an aircraft or ship in distress. [<F *m'aidez* help me]

May Day The first day of May, traditionally celebrated as a spring festival by crowning a May Queen, dancing around a Maypole, etc.: commemorated in many countries as a labor holiday.

Ma·yence (mȧ·yäṅs′) The French name for MAINZ.

Ma·yenne (mȧ·yen′), **Duc de**, 1554–1611, Charles of Lorraine; French general; defeated by Henry IV.

May·er (mī′ər), **Julius Robert von**, 1814–78, German physicist.

may·est (mā′ist) May: obsolescent or poetic second person singular, present tense of MAY: with *thou*. Also spelled *mayst.*

May·fair (mā′fâr) A fashionable residential district of the West End, London.

may·flow·er (mā′flou′ər) *n.* **1** The trailing arbutus, State flower of Massachusetts. **2** *Brit.* The hawthorn or may; also, the marsh marigold. **3** Any of various other plants which blossom in the spring.

Mayflower The ship on which the Pilgrims came to America in 1620.

may·fly (mā′flī′) *n. pl.* **·flies 1** An ephemerid insect, which in the nymphal state inhabits water and is long-lived, and in the adult state merely propagates its kind and then dies. **2** An artificial fly in imitation of this insect. **3** *Brit.* A caddis fly.

may·hap (mā′hap) *adv. Archaic* It may chance or happen; very likely; peradventure; perhaps. Also **may′hap′pen** (-ən). [<(*it*) *may hap*(*pen*)]

may·hem (mā′hem) *n.* **1** *Law* The offense of depriving a person by violence of any limb, member, or organ, or causing any mutilation of the body. Also spelled *maihem.* **2** Egregious disorder or damage. [<OF *mehaing, mahaigne.* Related to MAIM.]

May·ing (mā′ing) *n.* The celebration of May Day.

May·kop (mī·kôp′) See MAIKOP.

May·o (mā′ō) A maritime county of western Connacht, Ireland; 2,084 square miles; county town, Castlebar.

May·o (mā′ō), **Charles Horace**, 1865–1939, U.S. surgeon. — **William James**, 1861–1939, surgeon, brother of the preceding.

Ma·yon (mä·yôn′) An active volcano in SE Luzon, Philippines; 7,916 feet.

may·on·naise (mā′ə·nāz′, mī′-) *n.* A sauce or dressing made by beating together raw egg yolk, butter or olive oil, lemon juice or vinegar, and condiments. [<F, ? <*Mahón*, Balearic port]

may·or (mā′ər, mâr) *n.* The chief magistrate of a city, borough, or municipal corporation. [<F *maire* <L *major* greater. Doublet of MAJOR.] — **may′or·al** *adj.*

may·or·al·ty (mā′ər·əl·tē, mâr′əl-) *n. pl.* **·ties** The office or term of a mayor. [<OF *mairalté*]

Ma·yotte (mȧ·yôt′) Easternmost of the Comoro Islands, NW of Madagascar; 140 square miles.

May·pole (mā′pōl′) *n.* A pole decorated with flowers and ribbons, around which dancing takes place on May Day.

may·pop (mā′pop) *n.* **1** The passionflower (*Passiflora incarnata*) of the southern United States. **2** The small yellow fruit of this plant. [Alter. of N. Am. Ind. *maracock.* Cf. Tupian *maracujá.*]

May Queen A young girl crowned with flowers in May Day festivities.

mayst (māst) See MAYEST.

May·thorn (mā′thôrn′) *n.* The hawthorn.

May·time (mā′tīm′) *n.* The month of May. Also **May′tide** (-tīd′).

may·weed (mā′wēd′) *n.* A strong-scented, acrid weed (*Anthemis cotula*) of the composite family, bearing white-rayed flowers on a yellow disk; stinking camomile. [Alter. of *maidweed* < *maytheweed* <OE *magothe* + WEED]

May wine Any still, white wine flavored with steeped orange and pineapple slices and woodruff: named for the month of May, in which the woodruff flowers.

Maz·a·gan (maz′ə·gan′) A port in western Morocco.

maz·ard (maz′ərd) *n. Obs.* **1** A mazer. **2** The skull; the head. Also **maz′zard**. [Var. of MAZER]

Maz·a·rin (maz′ə·rin, *Fr.* mȧ·zȧ·raṅ′), **Jules**, 1602–61, French cardinal and statesman; prime minister under Louis XIV: real name *Giulio Mazzarini.*

Maz·a·rine (maz′ə·rēn) *adj.* Of or pertaining to Cardinal Mazarin, or named from him.

Mazarine blue A deep, rich blue: named after Cardinal Mazarin.

Maz·a·ru·ni (maz′ə·roō′nē) A river in northern British Guiana, flowing 350 miles NE to the Essequibo.

Ma·za·tlán (mä′sä·tlän′) A port in NW Mexico, on the Gulf of California.

Maz·da·ism (maz′də·iz′əm) *n.* Zoroastrianism. Also **Maz′de·ism**. [<OPersian *Aura mazda* the principle of good]

maze (māz) *n.* **1** An intricate network of paths or passages; a labyrinth. **2** Embarrassment; uncertainty; perplexity. — *v.t. Archaic* To daze or stupefy; bewilder. ◆ Homophone: *maize.* [<AMAZE] — **maz′y** *adj.* — **maz′i·ly** *adv.* — **maz′i·ness** *n.*

Ma·zep·pa (mə·zep′ə), **Ivan Stephanovich**,

1644–1709, a Cossack chief; hero of a poem by Byron.

ma·zer (māʹzər) *n.* A bowl, goblet, or drinking cup made of hard wood. Also *mazard.* [<OF *masere* maple wood <Gmc.] .

ma·zu·ma (mə·zooʹmə) *n. U.S. Slang* Money. [<Yiddish *m'zumon* "the ready necessary"]

ma·zur·ka (mə·zûrʹkə, -zoorʹ-) *n.* 1 A lively Polish round dance resembling the polka. 2 The music for such a dance. Also **ma·zourʹka.** [<Polish, woman from Mazovia, a province in Poland]

Ma·zu·ry (mä·zooʹrē) The Polish name for Msuria.

ma·zut (mə·zootʹ) *n.* The residue from the distillation of Russian petroleum: used as a fuel oil. Also **ma·zoutʹ.** [<Russian]

maz·zard cherry (mazʹərd) The fruit of the European wild sweet cherry (*Prunus avium*). [Earlier *mazer* maple wood; appar. from the hardness of the wood]

Maz·zi·ni (mät·tsēʹnē), **Giuseppe,** 1805–72, Italian patriot and revolutionary; aided Garibaldi to unite Italy.

Mba·ba·ne (mbä·bäʹnä) The capital of Swaziland.

M'bo·mu (mboʹmoo) See Bomu.

Mc– See also Mac.

Mc·A·doo (makʹə·doo), **William Gibbs,** 1863–1941, U.S. lawyer and statesman; secretary of the treasury 1913–18.

Mc·Car·thy·ism (mə·kärʹthē·izʹəm) *n.* 1 The practice of making public and sensational accusations of disloyalty or corruption, usually with little or no proof or with doubtful evidence. 2 The practice of conducting sensational inquisitorial investigations, ostensibly to expose subversion, especially pro-Communist activity. [after Joseph *McCarthy*, 1909–1957, U.S. Senator]

Mc·Clel·lan (mə·klelʹən), **George Brinton,** 1826–85, Union general in the Civil War.

Mc·Col·lum (mə·kolʹəm), **Elmer Verner,** 1879–1967, American physiological chemist.

Mc·Cor·mack (mə·kôrʹmik), **John,** 1884–1945, U.S. tenor born in Ireland.

Mc·Cor·mick (mə·kôrʹmik), **Cyrus Hall,** 1809–1884, U.S. inventor of the reaping machine. —**Joseph Medill,** 1877–1925, U.S. newspaper publisher.

Mc·Coy (mə·koiʹ), **the** (**real**) *U.S. Slang* The authentic person or thing. [Appar. from an episode, existing in many versions, in which a celebrated American boxer, Kid McCoy, spectacularly established his identity]

Mc·Dou·gal (mək·dooʹgəl), **William,** 1871–1938, U.S. psychologist born in England.

Mc·Guf·fey (mə·gufʹē), **William Holmes,** 1800–1873, U.S. educator; author of a series of children's readers.

Mc·In·tire (makʹən·tīr) *adj.* Pertaining to or naming the finely carved furniture and architectural embellishments in the neo-classic taste by Samuel McIntire, 1757–1811, woodcarver of Salem, Mass.

Mc·In·tosh (makʹən·tosh) *n.* A red variety of early autumn apple. Also **McIntosh red.** [after John *McIntosh* of Ontario, who discovered it in the 18th century]

Mc·Kin·ley (mə·kinʹlē), **Mount** A peak in central Alaska, highest in North America, 20,300 feet.

Mc·Kin·ley (mə·kinʹlē), **William,** 1843–1901, president of the United States, 1897–1901; assassinated.

Mc·Mas·ter (mək·masʹtər, -mäsʹ-), **John Bach,**1852–1932, U.S. historian.

M–Day (emʹdāʹ) *n. Mil.* Mobilization day; the day the Department of Defense orders mobilization for war.

Mdi·na (mə·dēʹnə) The Maltese name for Città Vecchia.

me (mē) *pron.* The objective case of *I.*
◆ **It's me, etc.** Anyone who answers the question "Who's there?" by saying "It's me" is using acceptable colloquial idiom. Here *It is I* would seem stilted, although at the formal level of writing it is expected: They have warned me that *it is I*, and not he, who will have to bear the brunt of the criticism. After a finite impersonal form of the verb *to be*, as *it is*, *it was*, etc., a personal pronoun should, according to prescriptive grammar, be in the same case as the subject: the nominative; ac-

cordingly, at the formal level, we find *It is he, It is we, It is they,* etc. Since only the personal and relative pronouns retain different inflected forms for the nominative and objective cases, the rule might appear to be invented to cover this one exceptional situation. The normal subject-verb-object order of the English sentence creates a strong expectation that what follows the verb will be in the objective case, and perhaps for this reason popular usage has long favored *It's me* over the formal *It is I.* British and American playwrights in recent years have also represented their characters, and not only the uneducated speakers among them, as saying *It's him, It's her, It's them,* etc. In spite of the exact parallel in construction with *It's me,* these expressions are not yet condoned to the same extent, even at the colloquial level.

me·a cul·pa (mēʹə kulʹpə) *Latin* My fault; my blame.

mead¹ (mēd) *n.* A liquor of fermented honey and water to which malt, yeast, and spices are added; metheglin. See Hydromel. ◆ Homophone: *meed.* [OE *meodu*]

mead² (mēd) *n. Poetic* A meadow. ◆ Homophone: *meed.* [OE *mæd*]

Mead (mēd), **Lake** A reservoir formed by Hoover Dam in Boulder Canyon of the Colorado River in Arizona and Nevada; 246 square miles; largest artificial lake in the world. See Black Canyon.

Mead (mēd), **Margaret,** 1901–1978, U.S. anthropologist.

Meade (mēd), **George Gordon,** 1815–72, Union general in the Civil War, born in Spain.

mead·ow (medʹō) *n.* A tract of low or level land, producing grass for hay. [OE *mæ dwe,* oblique case of *moed*] —**meadʹ ow·y** *adj.*

mead·ow·beau·ty (medʹō·byoo 'tē) *n. pl.* **·ties** Any of a genus (*Rhexia*) of low-growing herbs, usually with four-parted purple flowers; especially, the common species (*R. virginica*).

meadow bird The bobolink.

meadow hen The American bittern.

mead·ow·lark (medʹō·lärk') *n.* An American songbird (genus *Sturnella*) related to the blackbird; especially, the southern meadowlark (*S. magna*), brownish or grayish above, marked with black and yellow beneath.

meadow lily The Canada lily.

meadow mouse The field mouse.

meadow rue Any species of the genus *Thalictrum* of the crowfoot family, having leaves like those of rue.

mead·ow·sweet (medʹō·swēt') *n.* 1 A shrub of the rose family (genus *Spiraea*); especially, *S. salicifolia,* having alternate simple or pinnate leaves and white or rose-colored flowers: also **meadow queen.** 2 Any plant of a related genus (*Filipendula*).

meadow weed Wild oat (def. 1).

mea·ger (mēʹgər) *adj.* 1 Deficient or destitute of quantity or quality; scanty; inadequate. 2 Deficient in or scantily supplied with fertility, strength, or richness. 3 Wanting in flesh; thin; emaciated. Also **meaʹgre.** [<OF *maigre* <L *macer* lean] —**meaʹ ger·ly** *adv.* —**meaʹger·ness** *n.*
Synonyms: barren, emaciated, feeble, gaunt, jejune, lank, lean, poor, skinny, spare, starved, starveling, tame, thin. See Gaunt. *Antonyms:* bonny, bouncing, burly, chubby, corpulent, fat, fleshy, hearty, obese, plump, portly, stout.

meal¹ (mēl) *n.* 1 Comparatively coarsely ground grain. 2 Unbolted wheat flour; chop. 3 A powder produced by grinding; any powdery, meal-like material; sulfur *meal.* [OE *melu*]

meal² (mēl) *n.* 1 The portion of food taken at one time; a repast. 2 Its occasion or time. ◆ Collateral adjective: *prandial.* [OE *mæl* measure, time, meal]

–meal *suffix* The quantity taken at one time or the unit of measurement: now obsolete except in *piecemeal.* [OE *-mælum,* oblique case of *mæl* measure, time]

meal·ie (mēʹlē) *n.* 1 An ear of maize. 2 *pl.* Maize; Indian corn. [<Afrikaans *mielie* <Pg. *milho* millet <L *milium*]

meal·time (mēlʹtīm') *n.* The habitual time for eating a meal.

meal·worm (mēlʹwûrm') *n.* 1 The larva of a beetle (*Tenebrio molitor*) destructive to flour, meal, etc. 2 A meal-bred grub prepared as bait for ground fishing.

meal·y (mēʹlē) *adj.* **meal·i·er, meal·i·est** 1 Having a resemblance to or the qualities or taste of meal; farinaceous. 2 Overspread or besprinkled with or as with meal; pale-colored; of anemic appearance. 3 Having the appearance of being covered with meal; farinose. 4 Mealy-mouthed. 5 Friable; floury: said of the endosperm of malt. 6 Flecked with white spots: said of cattle. 7 Smooth-flavored; harsh to the taste: said of tea. —**mealʹi·ness** *n.*

meal·y·bug (mēʹlē·bug') *n.* Any of a large cosmopolitan family (*Pseudococcidae*) of coccids whose soft, oval bodies are usually covered with a mealy wax secretion: they include many of the most destructive plant pests.

meal·y–mouthed (mēʹlē-moutht', -mouth') *adj.* Unwilling to express adverse opinions plainly; euphemistic; insincere.

mean¹ (mēn) *v.* **meant, mean·ing** *v.t.* 1 To have in mind as a purpose or intent: I *meant* to visit him. 2 To intend or design for some purpose, destination, etc.: Was that remark *meant* for me? 3 To intend to express or convey: That's not what I *meant.* 4 To have as the particular sense or significance: denote; portend: Those clouds mean snow. —*v.i.* 5 To have disposition or intention; be disposed: He *means* well. 6 To be of specified importance or influence: Her beauty *means* everything to her. See synonyms under Import, Purpose. ◆ Homophone: *mien.* [OE *mænan* tell, wish, intend]

mean² (mēn) *adj.* 1 Low in grade, quality, or condition; of humble antecedents; lowly; also, indicative of or suited to low rank; poor; inferior; shabby. 2 *Colloq.* Disagreeable; unpleasant; unkind; wicked. 3 Ignoble in mind, character, and spirit; lacking magnanimity or honor; base; petty; also, miserly; stingy. 4 Worthy of no respect; slight or contemptible. 5 Of little value or efficiency. 6 Not fit for cultivation: said of land. 7 Vicious or unmanageable: said of horses. 8 *Colloq.* Irritable; ashamed; paltry; also, ill: to feel *mean.* See synonyms under Bad, Base, Common, Insignificant, Little, Small, Vulgar. ◆ Homophone: *mien.* [OE (*ge*)*mæne* common, ordinary] —**meanʹly** *adv.* —**meanʹness** *n.*

mean³ (mēn) *n.* 1 The middle state between two extremes; hence, moderation; avoidance of excess; medium: the happy *mean.* 2 *Math.* A quantity having an intermediate value between two extremes, or between several quantities: the arithmetical *mean.* 3 *pl.* The medium through which anything is done; instrumentality: used often with singular construction: a *means* to an end. 4 *pl.* Money or property as a procuring medium; wealth. 5 A plan of procedure. 6 *Logic* The middle term in a syllogism. 7 *Obs.* An intermediary; mediator. See synonyms under Agent. —**arithmetical mean** The quotient of the sum of two or more quantities divided by the number of quantities; the average. —**by all means** Without hesitation; certainly. —**by any means** 1 In any manner possible; somehow; at all. 2 By all means. —**by no manner of means** Most certainly not; not for any consideration; on no account whatever: also **by no means.** —**geometric** (or **geometrical**) **mean** The square root of the product of two given numbers. —**golden mean** A wise moderation; the avoidance of extremes. —*adj.* 1 Intermediate as to position between extremes. 2 Intermediate as to size, degree, or quality; medium; average. 3 Intermediate as to time; intervening. 4 Having an intermediate value between two extremes or among several values; average: the *mean* distance covered daily. ◆ Homophone: *mien.* [<OF *meien* <L *medianus* <*medius* middle. Doublet of Median, Mesne, Mizzen.]

me·an·der (mē·anʹdər) *v.i.* 1 To wind and turn in a course. 2 To wander aimlessly. —*n.* 1 A tortuous or winding course; hence, a maze; perplexity. 2 The Greek key or fret pattern. [<Meander] —**me·anʹder·er** *n.* —**me·anʹder·ing, me·anʹdrous** *adj.*

Me·an·der (mē·anʹdər) The ancient name for

the MENDERES, proverbial for its windings: also *Maeander.*

mean·ing (mē′ning) *n.* **1** That which is intended; object; intention; aim. **2** That which is signified; significance; sense; acceptation; import; connotation. See synonyms under PURPOSE. — *adj.* **1** Having purpose or intention: usually in combination: well–*meaning.* **2** Significant; suggestive. — **mean′ing·ful** *adj.* — **mean′ing·ful·ly** *adv.* — **mean′ing·less** *adj.* — **mean′ing·less·ly** *adv.* — **mean′ing·less·ness** *n.* — **mean′ing·ly** *adv.*

mean latitude Middle latitude.

mean sun *Astron.* A fictitious sun considered to be moving uniformly with respect to the equator: a concept used to facilitate the computation of time.

meant (ment) Past tense and past participle of MEAN[1].

mean·time (mēn′tīm′) *n.* Intervening time or occasion. — *adv.* In or during the meantime.

mean time See under TIME. Also **mean solar time.**

mean·while (mēn′hwīl′) *n.* & *adv.* Meantime.

Mearns (mûrnz), **The** See KINCARDINE.

mea·sle (mē′zəl) *n.* **1** The larva *(Cysticercus)* of a certain tapeworm (genus *Taenia*) found in meat and generally producing measles in swine. **2** Any excrescence upon a plant or tree. [See MEASLES]

mea·sled (mē′zəld) *adj.* Affected with measles.

mea·sles (mē′zəlz) *n.* **1** An acute, highly contagious, generally self–immunizing virus disease affecting children and sometimes adults: it is characterized by chills, fever, severe coryza, and an extensive eruption of small red macules; rubeola. **2** Any of various eruptive diseases of a similar character: used with a qualifying adjective: French *measles.* **3** A disease affecting swine and cattle, caused by the presence of larval tapeworms in the flesh. — **French measles, German measles** Rubella. [ME *maseles,* pl. of *masel* a blister <LG. Cf. MDu. *masel* spot on the skin.]

mea·sly (mēz′lē) *adj.* **·sli·er, ·sli·est** **1** Affected with measles. **2** Containing tapeworm larvae: said of meat. **3** *Slang* Not fit to be touched; beneath contempt; also, mean; skimpy; stingy; scanty.

meas·ur·a·ble (mezh′ər·ə·bəl) *adj.* **1** Capable of being measured or of computation. **2** Limited; moderate: *measurable* severity. — **meas′·ur·a·bil′i·ty, meas′ur·a·ble·ness** *n.* — **meas′·ur·a·bly** *adv.*

meas·ure (mezh′ər) *n.* **1** The extent or dimensions of anything. **2** A standard of measurement. **3** Hence, any standard of criticism, comparison, judgment, or award. **4** A series of measure units; a system of measurements: dry *measure.* See WEIGHT. **5** An instrument or vessel of measurement. **6** The act of measuring; measurement. **7** A quantity measured, or regarded as measured. **8** Reasonable limits; moderation: beyond *measure*; also, degree; reasonable proportion: A *measure* of allowance should be made. **9** A certain proportion; relative extent. **10** A specific act or course; transaction; specifically, a legislative bill. **11** That which makes up a sum or total. **12** Any quantity regarded as a unit and standard of comparison with other quantities; a quantity of which some other given quantity forms an exact multiple. **13** *Music* **a** That division of time by which melody and rhythm are regulated; rate of movement; time. **b** The portion of music contained between two bar lines; bar. **14** In prosody, meter; a rhythmical period. **15** A slow and stately dance or dance movement. **16** *pl. Geol.* A series of related rock strata, having some common feature. — *v.* **·ured, ·ur·ing** *v.t.* **1** To take or ascertain the dimensions, quantity, capacity, etc., of, especially by means of a measure. **2** To set apart, mark off, etc., by measuring: often with *off* or *out.* **3** To estimate by comparison; judge; weigh: to *measure* a risk. **4** To serve as the measure of. **5** To bring into competition or comparison. **6** To traverse as if measuring; travel over. **7** To adjust; regulate: *Measure* your actions to your aspirations. — *v.i.* **8** To make or take measurements. **9** To yield a specified measurement: The table *measures* six by four feet. **10** To admit measurement. — **to measure one's length** To fall prostrate at full length. — **to measure out** To distribute or allot by measure. — **to measure swords** **1** To fight with swords. **2** To fight or contend as in a debate. — **to measure up to** To fulfil, as expectations. [<F *mesure* <L *mensura* < *metiri* measure] — **meas′ur·er** *n.*

meas·ured (mezh′ərd) *adj.* **1** Ascertained, adjusted, or proportioned by rule. **2** Uniform; slow and stately; rhythmical; deliberate. **3** In moderation; held in restraint; guarded. — **meas′ured·ly** *adv.* — **meas′ured·ness** *n.*

meas·ure·less (mezh′ər·lis) *adj.* Incapable of measurement; unlimited; immense. See synonyms under INFINITE.

meas·ure·ment (mezh′ər·mənt) *n.* **1** The process or result of measuring anything; mensuration. **2** The amount, capacity, or extent determined by measuring. **3** A system of measuring units.

measuring worm A geometrid.

meat (mēt) *n.* **1** The flesh of animals used as food: sometimes limited to the flesh of mammals, as opposed to fish or fowl; also, any animal killed for food: to hunt one's *meat.* **2** Anything eaten for nourishment; victuals; hence, that which nourishes. **3** The edible part of anything. **4** A meal; especially, dinner; the main meal. **5** The essence, gist, or pith: the *meat* of an essay. **6** *Slang* Anything one does with special ease or pleasure; forte. ◆ Homophones: *meet, mete.* [OE *mete*] — **meat′less** *adj.*

Meath (mēth, mēth) A county of NE Leinster province, Ireland; 903 square miles; county town, Trim.

meat packing *U.S.* The commercial slaughtering of meat–producing animals and the processing, packaging, and distribution of meat and meat products. — **meat packer**

me·a·tus (mē·ā′təs) *n. pl.* **·tus** or **·tus·es** *Anat.* A conspicuous passage or canal: the auditory *meatus.* [<L, a passage < *meare* go]

meat·y (mē′tē) *adj.* **meat·i·er, meat·i·est** **1** Full of or resembling meat. **2** Having strength; nourishing. **3** Significant; pithy. — **meat′i·ness** *n.*

Meaux (mō) A city in north central France.

me·ca·te (mā·kä′tā) *n. SW U.S.* A rope made of maguey fiber, or sometimes of plaited horsehair: used for tying horses. [<Sp. < Nahuatl]

mec·ca (mek′ə) *n.* **1** A place visited by many people; any attraction. **2** The object of one's aspiration, yearning, or effort. [from *Mecca*]

Mec·ca (mek′ə) The capital of Hejaz and one of the capitals of Saudi Arabia; birthplace of Mohammed and a holy city of Islam to which Moslems make pilgrimages: also *Mekka.*

me·chan·ic (mə·kan′ik) *n.* **1** One engaged in mechanical employment; an artisan; handicraftsman. **2** *Obs.* A mean or lowly fellow. See synonyms under ARTIST. — *adj.* **1** Pertaining to mechanics; mechanical. **2** Involving manual labor or skill. [<L *mechanicus* <Gk. *mēchanikos* < *mēchanē* a machine]

me·chan·i·cal (mə·kan′i·kəl) *adj.* **1** Pertaining to mechanics; in accordance with the laws of mechanics. **2** Produced by a machine. **3** Operated by mechanism. **4** Operating as if by a machine or machinery. **5** Doing or done involuntarily, by mere force of habit. **6** Automatic; not instinct with life; artificial. **7** Failing to show independence of thought; slavish. **8** Skilled in the use of tools and mechanisms. — **me·chan′i·cal·ly** *adv.* — **me·chan′i·cal·ness** *n.*

mech·a·ni·cian (mek′ə·nish′ən) *n.* One who understands the science of mechanics; a designer of machinery.

me·chan·ics (mə·kan′iks) *n. pl.* **1** The branch of physics that treats of the phenomena caused by the action of forces on material bodies, including statics and kinetics: construed as singular. **2** The science of machinery and of its practical applications: construed as singular. **3** The mechanical or technical aspects: construed as plural.

Me·chan·ics·ville (mə·kan′iks·vil) A hamlet 7 miles NE of Richmond, Virginia; site of a battle (June 26, 1862) in the Civil War.

mech·a·nism (mek′ə·niz′əm) *n.* **1** The parts of a machine collectively; machinery in general. **2** A system which constitutes a working agency. **3** Technique; mechanical execution or action. **4** The theory that the forces that produce organic growth are the same physical and chemical agencies that operate in the inorganic world, differing from them only in degree: opposed to *vitalism.* **5** *Psychol.* The mental processes, conscious or unconscious, by which certain actions are effected. See synonyms under TOOL. — **mech′·a·nis′tic** *adj.* — **mech′a·nis′ti·cal·ly** *adv.*

mech·a·nist (mek′ə·nist) *n.* **1** A mechanician. **2** A believer in philosophical mechanism.

mech·a·ni·za·tion (mek′ə·nə·zā′shən, -nī-) *n.* **1** The act or process of applying machinery to the performance of specified operations. **2** The aggregate results of such application. **3** *Mil.* The maximum coordinated utilization of power–driven equipment, mechanized armament, and automatic weapons in the service of the combat personnel.

mech·a·nize (mek′ə·nīz) *v.t.* **·nized, ·niz·ing** **1** To make mechanical. **2** To convert (an industry, etc.) to machine production. **3** *Mil.* To equip with tanks, trucks, etc. — **mech′a·nized** *adj.*

mech·a·no·ther·a·py (mek′ə·nō·ther′ə·pē) *n. Med.* The treatment of disease by mechanical means, as massage. [< *mechano-* (<MECHANIC) + THERAPY]

Mech·lin (mek′lin) *n.* A lace with bobbin ground and designs outlined by thread or flat cord, made in Malines (Mechlin), Belgium: also called *malines.*

Mech·lin (mek′lin) A town of north central Belgium: French *Malines. Flemish* **Mech·e·len** (mekh′ə·lən).

Meck·len·burg (mek′lən·bûrg, *Ger.* mek′lən·bŏŏrkh) A former state of northern Germany on the Baltic, comprising the former grand duchies of **Meck′len·burg–Schwe·rin′** (-shvā·rēn′), **Meck′len·burg–Stre′litz** (-shtrā′lits), and western Pomerania; 8,856 square miles; capital, Schwerin; divided, July 1952, into several districts of East Germany.

mec·on·ism (mek′ə·niz′əm, mē′kə-) *n. Pathol.* Addiction to opium; poisoning by opium. [<Gk. *mēkōn* a poppy]

me·cop·ter·ous (mə·kop′tər·əs) *adj.* Of, pertaining or belonging to an order *(Mecoptera)* of slender, predacious insects with biting mouth parts and long, narrow wings. [<NL <Gk. *mēkos* length + *pteron* wing]

med·al (med′l) *n.* A small piece of metal, bearing a device, usually commemorative of some event or deed of bravery, scientific research, or literary production, etc. — *v.t.* **·aled** or **·alled, ·al·ing** or **·al·ling** To confer a medal upon. ◆ Homophone: *meddle.* [<F *médaille* <Ital. *medaglia,* ult. <L *metallum.* Doublet of METAL.] — **me·dal·lic** (mə·dal′ik) *adj.*

Medal for Merit A medal awarded by the United States to civilians for exceptional services in times of peace or war.

med·al·ist (med′l·ist) *n.* **1** A collector, engraver, or designer of medals. **2** The recipient of a medal awarded for services or merit. **3** In golf, the winner at medal play. Also **med′·al·list.**

me·dal·lion (mə·dal′yən) *n.* **1** A large medal; also, a subject painted, engraved, etc., and set in a circular or oval frame or design: used as decorative elements in carpets, lace, etc. **2** Any one of several ancient Greek silver coins. [<F *médaillon* <Ital. *medaglione,* aug. of *medaglia* MEDAL] — **me·dal′lion·ist** *n.*

Medal of Honor The highest U. S. decoration, awarded to a member of the armed forces who risked his life in action beyond the call of duty. It is awarded in the name of Congress and usually presented personally by the president. Also called *Congressional Medal of Honor.*

medal play In golf, a form of competitive play in which the score is computed by counting only the total number of strokes played by each competitor in playing the designated number of holes.

Me·dan (me·dän′) A town in NE Sumatra.

med·dle (med′l) *v.i.* **·dled, ·dling** **1** To take part in or concern oneself with something without need or request: often with *in* or *with.* **2** *Obs.* To mix; mingle. See synonyms under INTERPOSE, MIX. ◆ Homophone: *medal.* [<OF *medler, mesdler,* var. of *mesler,* ult. <L *miscere* mix] — **med′dler** *n.* — **med′dling** *adj.* & *n.*

med·dle·some (med′l·səm) *adj.* Given to meddling; officiously inclined; interfering; intrusive. — **med′dle·some·ly** *adv.* — **med′dle·some·ness** *n.*

Synonyms: impertinent, intrusive, meddling, obtrusive, officious. The *meddlesome* person interferes unasked in the affairs of others; the *intrusive* person thrusts himself uninvited into their company or conversation; the *obtrusive* person thrusts himself or his opinions

conceitedly and undesirably upon their notice; the *officious* person thrusts his services, unasked and undesired, upon others. Compare ACTIVE, INQUISITIVE, INTERPOSE. *Antonyms*: modest, reserved, retiring, shy, unassuming, unobtrusive.

Mede (mēd) *n.* One of an ancient Asiatic people who flourished in Media in the sixth century B.C.

Me·de·a (mə·dē′ə) In Greek legend, a sorceress of Colchis who aided Jason to obtain the Golden Fleece and, when deserted by him for Creusa, killed her rival and her own children and fled to Athens.

Me·del·lín (mā′thā·yēn′) A city in NW Colombia.

med·e·vac (med′ə·vak′) *n.* The evacuation of the wounded, as from battle sites, usually by helicopter. [< *med(ical) evac(uation)*]

me·di·a (mē′dē·ə) *n. pl. of* **medium** 1 Means of disseminating information, entertainment, etc., such as books, newspapers, radio, television, motion pictures, and magazines. 2 In advertising, all means of communication that carry advertisements, including billboards, direct mail, catalogs, radio, etc.

Me·di·a (mē′dē·ə) An ancient country of SW Asia, corresponding to the NW Iranian plateau. — **Me′di·an** *adj.* & *n.*

me·di·a·cy (mē′dē·ə·sē) *n.* 1 The state or quality of being mediate. 2 Mediation.

me·di·ae·val (mē′dē·ē′vəl, med′ē-), **me·di·ae·val·ism,** etc. See MEDIEVAL, etc

me·di·al (mē′dē·əl) *adj.* 1 Of or pertaining to the middle, in position or character or in calculation; mean. 2 Nearer the median plane of a body: opposed to *lateral.* 3 Designating a letter neither initial nor final. — *n. Phonet.* Any of a group of voiced stops (b, d, g), conceived as intermediate between the voiceless stops (p, t, k) and the rough or aspirate group (bh, dh, gh, ph, th, kh). [<LL *medialis* <L *medius* middle] — **me′di·al·ly** *adv.*

me·di·an (mē′dē·ən) *adj.* 1 Pertaining to the middle, or situated in the median plane. 2 *Stat.* Of, pertaining to, or designating that point in a series of values which divides the series into two groups, each containing the same number of entries: 8 is the *median* point of the series 2, 5, 8, 10, 13. [<L *medianus* < *medius* middle. Doublet of MEAN[3], MESNE, MIZZEN.] — **me′di·an·ly** *adv.*

median plane That plane that divides a body longitudinally into symmetrical halves.

me·di·as·ti·num (mē′dē·as·tī′nəm) *n. pl.* **·na** (-nə) *Anat.* 1 A median partition or septum separating two cavities of the body. 2 The partition between the two pleural sacs of the chest, extending from the sternum to the thoracic vertebrae and downward to the diaphragm. [<NL <Med. L *mediastinus* medial < *medius*] — **me′di·as·ti′nal** *adj.*

me·di·ate (mē′dē·āt) *v.* **·at·ed, ·at·ing** *v.t.* 1 To settle or reconcile by mediation, as differences. 2 To bring about or effect by mediation. 3 To serve as the medium for effecting (a result) or conveying (an object, information, etc.). — *v.i.* 4 To act between disputing parties in order to bring about a settlement, compromise, etc. 5 To occur or be in an intermediate relation or position. See synonyms under INTERPOSE. — *adj.* (-it) 1 Acting as an intervening agency; indirect. 2 Occurring or effected as a result of indirect or median agency. 3 Intermediate. [<LL *mediatus*, pp. of *mediare* stand between, mediate] — **me′di·ate·ly** *adv.* — **me′di·ate·ness** *n.* — **me′di·a′tive** *adj.* — **me′di·a′tor** *n.* — **me′di·a·to′ri·al** (-tôr′ē·əl, -tō′rē·əl), **me′di·a·to′ry** *adj.*

me·di·a·tion (mē′dē·ā′shən) *n.* 1 The act of mediating; intercession; interposition. 2 A friendly intervention in the disputes of others, with their consent, for the purpose of adjusting differences. See CONCILIATION.

med·ic[1] (med′ik) *n.* Any one of several plants of the bean family (genus *Medicago*), especially the lucerne or alfalfa. [<L *medicus* <Gk. *Mēdikē (poa)* Median (grass) <*Mēdos* a Mede]

med·ic[2] (med′ik) *n. Colloq.* 1 A doctor, physician, or intern. 2 A medical corpsman.

med·i·ca·ble (med′ə·kə·bəl) *adj.* Capable of relief by medicine; curable.

Med·i·caid (med′i·kād′) *n. U.S.* A tax–supported health insurance program for low–income people.

med·i·cal (med′i·kəl) *adj.* 1 Pertaining to medicine or its practice. 2 Having curative properties. [<F *médicale* <LL *medicalis* <L *medicus* a physician] — **med′i·cal·ly** *adv.*

medical examiner 1 *Law* An official legally designated to examine the bodies of those dead as a result of violence or crime, to perform autopsies, and to establish the proximate cause and circumstances of the death. 2 A doctor authorized by a life insurance company to determine the physical fitness of a prospective insurant.

medical jurisprudence The branch of medicine and related sciences which deals with questions involving the applications of the civil and criminal law; forensic medicine. See under JURISPRUDENCE.

med·i·ca·ment (med′ə·kə·mənt, mə·dik′ə-) *n.* 1 Any substance for the alleviation of disease or wounds. 2 A healing agency. [<L *medicamentum* < *medicare.* See MEDICATE.] — **med′i·ca·men′tal** *adj.*

med·i·care (med′i·kâr′) *n. Often cap. U.S.* A health insurance program supported in part by government funds, serving especially the aged.

med·i·cate (med′ə·kāt) *v.t.* **·cat·ed, ·cat·ing** 1 To treat medicinally. 2 To tincture or impregnate with medicine. [<L *medicatus*, pp. of *medicare* heal < *medicus* a physician] — **med′i·ca′tive, med′i·ca·to′ry** (-kə·tôr′ē, -tō′rē) *adj.*

med·i·ca·tion (med′ə·kā′shən) *n.* 1 Any substance used to treat disease, heal wounds, etc.; a medicine. 2 The act or process of medicating.

Med·i·ce·an (med′ə·sē′ən, -chē′-) *adj.* Of or pertaining to the Medici.

Med·i·ci (med′ə·chē, *Ital.* mā′dē·chē) A family of Florentine bankers who became rulers of Tuscany, patrons of the arts, literature, etc. Among its members were **Catherine de' Medici,** 1519–89, queen of Henry II of France, who planned the St. Bartholomew's Day Massacre; **Cosimo (Cosmo) de' Medici,** 1389–1464; **Cosimo (Cosmo) de' Medici,** 1519–74, first Grand Duke of Tuscany: called "Cosimo the Great"; **Lorenzo de' Medici,** 1448?–92, prince of Florence, statesman, educator, patron of art, literature, and printing: known as *Lorenzo the Magnificent*; **Maria de' Medici** (see under MARIA); **Giovanni de' Medici** (see LEO X).

me·dic·i·nal (mə·dis′ə·nəl) *adj.* Adapted to cure or mitigate disease. — **me·dic′i·nal·ly** *adv.*

med·i·cine (med′ə·sin) *n.* 1 A substance possessing, or reputed to possess, curative or remedial properties. 2 The healing art; the science of the preservation of health and of treating disease for the purpose of cure, specifically, as distinguished from surgery or obstetrics. 3 Among North American Indians, any agent or influence used to prevent or cure ills or to invoke supernatural protection or aid, varying from actual remedies (cinchona, etc.) to fetishes, prayers, and symbolic rites (**medicine dance, medicine song,** etc.); specifically, among the Algonquians, any mystery. See MANITO. 4 *Colloq.* Something distasteful or unpleasant: to give someone a dose of his own *medicine.* 5 *Obs.* Something used for other than healing purposes, as the philosopher's stone, elixirs, poisons, love philters, etc. — **to take one's medicine** To endure necessary hardship, discomfort, or punishment, or to do something unpleasant but required. [<L *medicina* < *medicus* physician < *mederi* heal]

medicine ball A large, heavy, leather–covered ball, thrown and caught for physical exercise.

medicine lodge A lodge in a North American Indian village, used for ritualistic, religious ceremonies.

medicine man Among North American Indians, one professing supernatural powers of healing and of invoking the spirits; a shaman.

med·i·co (med′ə·kō) *n. pl.* **·cos** *Colloq.* A doctor or a medical student. [<Ital., a physician]

medico– *combining form* Pertaining to medical science and: *medico–legal.* Also, before vowels, **medic–.** [<L *medicus* a physician]

me·di·e·val (mē′dē·ē′vəl, med′ē-) *adj.* Belonging to or descriptive or characteristic of the Middle Ages: also spelled *mediaeval.* [<L *medius* middle + *aevum* age] — **me′di·e′val·ly** *adv.*

Medieval Greek See under GREEK.

me·di·e·val·ism (mē′dē·ē′vəl·iz′əm, med′ē-) *n.* The spirit or practices of the Middle Ages; the flavor or general tone of medieval life; devotion to the institutions, ideas, or traits of the Middle Ages; also, any custom, idea, etc., surviving from the Middle Ages. — **me′di·e′val·ist** *n.*

Medieval Latin See under LATIN.

Me·di·na (mə·dē′nə) A Moslem holy city in Hejaz, western Saudi Arabia; goal of Mohammed's Hegira and the place of his tomb.

medio– *combining form* Middle. Also, before vowels, **medi–.** [<L *medius* middle]

me·di·o·cre (mē′dē·ō′kər, mē′dē·ō′kər) *adj.* Of only middle quality; ordinary; commonplace. [<L *mediocris* < *medius* middle]

me·di·oc·ri·ty (mē′dē·ok′rə·tē) *n. pl.* **·ties** 1 Commonplace ability or condition. 2 A commonplace person.

med·i·tate (med′ə·tāt) *v.* **·tat·ed, ·tat·ing** *v.i.* To engage in continuous and contemplative thought; muse; cogitate. — *v.t.* To think about doing; plan; intend: to *meditate* mischief. See synonyms under CONSIDER, DELIBERATE, MUSE. [<L *meditatus,* pp. of *meditari* muse, ponder] — **med′i·tat′er, med′i·ta′tor** *n.* — **med′i·ta′tive** *adj.* — **med′i·ta′tive·ly** *adv.*

med·i·ta·tion (med′ə·tā′shən) *n.* The act of meditating; the turning or revolving of a subject in the mind; continuous thought; contemplation. See synonyms under REFLECTION, THOUGHT.

med·i·ter·ra·ne·an (med′ə·tə·rā′nē·ən) *adj.* Enclosed nearly or wholly by land, as a sea or other large body of water; landlocked. [<L *medius* middle + *terra* earth]

Med·i·ter·ra·ne·an (med′ə·tə·rā′nē·ən) *adj.* 1 Of or pertaining to the Mediterranean Sea. 2 Inhabiting the shores of the Mediterranean. — *n.* 1 The Mediterranean Sea. 2 One who lives in a Mediterranean country, or belongs to the Mediterranean race. — **Key of the Mediterranean** Gibraltar.

Mediterranean fever Undulant fever.

Mediterranean race A subdivision of the Caucasoid race, regarded as designating the peoples inhabiting the shores of the Mediterranean Sea, including the ancient Iberian, Ligurian, Pelasgian, and Hamitic stocks and their modern descendants.

Mediterranean Sea An arm of the Atlantic Ocean comprising a great inland sea between Europe, Asia Minor, and Africa; 965,000 square miles.

me·di·um (mē′dē·əm) *n. pl.* **·di·ums** *(always for def 5)* or **me·di·a** (-dē·ə) 1 An intermediate quality, degree, or condition; mean. 2 A surrounding or enveloping element; condition of life; environment. 3 Any substance, as air, through or in which something may move or an effect be produced: Air is a *medium* of sound. 4 An intermediate means or agency; instrument: Radio is an advertising *medium.* 5 A person believed to be in communication with or controlled by the personality of someone deceased. 6 In painting, a liquid which gives fluency to the pigment. 7 A mathematical mean. 8 *Bacteriol.* A substance sterilized by heat in which bacteria, viruses, and other micro–organisms are developed: also **culture medium.** 9 A size of paper, usually 18 x 23 inches, between demy and royal. — **circulating medium** A money currency. — *adj.* 1 Intermediate in quantity, quality, position, size, or degree; middle. 2 Mediocre. [<L, orig. neut. sing. of *medius* middle]

medium bomber See under BOMBER.

me·di·um·is·tic (mē′dē·əm·is′tik) *adj.* Of or pertaining to spiritualist mediums or to their practices.

me·dji·di·e (me·jē′dē·e) *n.* 1 A modern Turkish silver coin equivalent to 19 piasters. 2 A Turkish gold coin, the lira. [<Turkish *mejīdī*]

med·lar (med′lər) *n.* 1 A small, European tree *(Mespilus germanica)* of the rose family. 2 Its edible fruit, hard and bitter when ripe, but agreeably acid when it begins to decay. [<OF *medler,* var. of *meslier* < *mesle* fruit of the medlar <L *mespila* <Gk. *mespilē*]

add,āce,câre,pälm; end,ēven; it,īce; odd,ōpen,ôrder; tŏŏk,pōōl; up,bûrn; ə = a in *above,* e in *sicken,* i in *clarity,* o in *melon,* u in *focus*; yōō = u in *fuse*; oi,oil; ou,pout; ch,check; g,go; ng,ring; th,thin; th,this; zh,vision. Foreign sounds à,œ,ü,kh,ṅ; and ◆: see page xx. < from; + plus; ? possibly.

med·ley (med′lē) *n.* **1** A mingled and confused mass of ingredients, usually incongruous; a heterogeneous group; jumble. **2** A composition of different songs or parts of songs arranged to run as a continuous whole. **3** A cloth woven from yarn of mingled colors: properly including blue and black. **4** In sports, a relay race in which all legs are not the same, as in distance or in swimming stroke used. —*adj.* **1** Mixed; confused. **2** Of mixed colors; motley. [<OF *medlee*, orig. fem. pp. of *medler*. See MEDDLE.]

Mé·doc (mā·dōk′) *n.* A red wine originally made in Médoc, France.

Mé·doc (mā·dôk′) A region of SW France.

me·dul·la (mə·dul′ə) *n. pl.* **·lae** (-ē) **1** *Anat.* **a** The inner portion of an organ or part, distinguished from the cortex. **b** The marrow of long bones. **c** The pith of a hair. **d** The spinal cord: also **medulla spi·na·lis** (spī·nā′lis). **2** The ganglion of the brain which, connecting with the spinal cord, controls breathing, swallowing, circulation, etc.: also **medulla ob·lon·ga·ta** (ob′lông·gä′tə). **3** *Bot.* The inner central columnar mass of parenchymatous tissue in the stems and roots of certain plants; also, in lichens, the middle layer of tissue composing the thallus, and in fungi proper, the central tissue within the rind of the fungus body. [< L <*medius* middle] —**med·ul·lar·y** (med′ə·ler′ē, mi·dul′ər·ē), **me·dul′lar** *adj.*

medullary rays 1 *Anat.* Extensions of the tubules of the kidney into the cortical substance. **2** *Bot.* The vertical bands or plates of cellular (parenchymatous) tissue, proceeding from the pith to the surface, and characteristic of the species of exogenous plants.

medullary sheath Myelin. See illustration under EXOGEN.

med·ul·lat·ed (med′ə·lā′tid, mi·dul′ā·tid) *adj.* Provided with a medullary sheath: said of nerve fibers.

me·du·sa (mə·dōō′sə, -zə, -dyōō′-) *n. pl.* **·sas** or **·sae** (-sē, -zē) A jellyfish. [<L] —**me·du′·san** *adj.*

Me·du·sa (mə·dōō′sə, -zə, -dyōō′-) One of the Gorgons, killed by Perseus who gave her head to Athena.

me·du·soid (mə·dōō′soid, -zoid, -dyōō′-) *adj.* Resembling a medusa or jellyfish. —*n.* **1** A medusa–shaped gonophore of a hydrozoan. **2** Any medusa.

Med·way (med′wā) A river rising in SE Surrey and NE Sussex, England, and flowing 70 miles NE through western Kent to the Thames estuary at Sheerness.

meed (mēd) *n. Archaic* **1** A well–deserved reward; recompense. **2** A present, gift, or bribe. ◆ Homophone: **mead**. [OE *mēd*]

meek (mēk) *adj.* **1** Of gentle and long–suffering disposition. **2** Submissive; compliant; lacking spirit or backbone. **3** Humble; lowly. **4** *Obs.* Gentle; indulgent; kind; compassionate. See synonyms under HUMBLE, PACIFIC. —*adv.* Meekly. [<ON *miukr* gentle, soft] —**meek′ly** *adv.* —**meek′ness** *n.*

meer (mir) *n. Scot.* Mare.

meer·schaum (mir′shəm, -shôm, -shoum) *n.* **1** A soft, light, compact, heat–resisting magnesium silicate, $H_4Mg_2Si_3O_{10}$, used for carving into tobacco pipes, cigar holders, and the like; sepiolite. It is closely related to talc. **2** A pipe made from this material. [<G <*meer* sea + *schaum* foam]

Mee·rut (mē′rət) A city in NW Uttar Pradesh, India.

meet[1] (mēt) *v.* **met, meet·ing** *v.t.* **1** To come upon; encounter. **2** To make the acquaintance of; be introduced to. **3** To be at the place of arrival of: We *met* him at the station. **4** To come into contact, conjunction, or intersection with; join: where the path *meets* the road. **5** To keep an appointment with. **6** To come into the view, hearing, etc., of: A ghastly sight *met* our eyes. **7** To experience; undergo: to *meet* bad weather. **8** To oppose in battle; fight with. **9** To face or counter: to *meet* a blow with a blow. **10** To deal with; refute or cope with: to *meet* an accusation. **11** To comply with; act or result in conformity with, as expectations or wishes. **12** To pay, as a bill. —*v.i.* **13** To come together, as from opposite or different directions. **14** To come together in contact, conjunction, or intersection; join. **15** To assemble. **16** To make acquaintance or be introduced. **17** To come together in conflict or opposition; contend. **18** To agree. —**to meet up with** *U.S. Colloq.* **1** To encounter. **2** To experience; undergo. —**to meet with 1** To come upon; encounter. **2** To deal or confer with. **3** To experience. **4** To be the subject or recipient of. —*n.* **1** An assembling together of huntsmen; also, the company or rendezvous. **2** An athletic contest: a track meet. ◆ Homophones: *meat, mete*. [OE *mētan*]

meet[2] (mēt) *adj.* Suitable, as to an occasion; adapted; fit. See synonyms under APPROPRIATE, BECOMING. —*adv. Obs.* Meetly; suitably. ◆ Homophones: *meat, mete*. [OE *gemǣte*] —**meet′ly** *adv.* —**meet′ness** *n.*

meet·ing (mē′ting) *n.* **1** A coming together. **2** An assembly of persons; specifically, a congregation of the Friends or Quakers; also, their meeting house. See synonyms under ASSEMBLY, COLLISION, COMPANY.

meeting house 1 A house used for public meetings, especially for public worship. **2** A place of worship used by the Friends.

mega– *combining form* **1** Great; large; powerful: *megaphone*. **2** In the metric system, electricity, etc., a million, or a million times, as in the following:

megabar	mega–erg	megampere
megacycle	megafarad	megavolt
megadyne	megameter	megohm

Also, before vowels, **meg–**. [<Gk.*megas* large]

meg·a·ce·phal·ic (meg′ə·sə·fal′ik) *adj.* Large-headed; specifically, having a cranial capacity above the average. Also **meg′a·ceph′a·lous** (-sef′ə·ləs).

meg·a·death (meg′ə·deth) *n.* The death of one million persons: a term used in reference to nuclear warfare. [<MEGA-+ DEATH]

Me·gae·ra (mə·jir′ə) In Greek mythology, one of the three Furies. Also **Me·gæ′ra.** [<L < Gk. *Megaira*<*magairein* grudge]

meg·a·ga·mete (meg′ə·gə·mēt′, -gam′ēt) *n.* A macrogamete.

meg·a·hertz (meg′ə·hûrtz′) *n.* A unit of frequency equal to one million cycles per second.

meg·a·lith (meg′ə·lith) *n. Archeol.* A huge stone, especially one used in prehistoric monuments. —**meg·a·lith′ic** *adj.*

megalo– *combining form* Big; indicating excessive or abnormal size: *megalocephalic*. Also, before vowels, **megal–**. [<Gk. *megas, megalou* big]

meg·a·lo·car·di·a (meg′ə·lō·kär′dē·ə) *n. Pathol.* Morbid enlargement of the heart. [<MEGALO- + Gk. *kardia* heart]

meg·a·lo·ceph·a·ly (meg′ə·lō·sef′ə·lē) *n.* **1** Unusual largeness of the head. **2** *Pathol.* Progressive enlargement of the cranium. Also **meg·a·lo·ce·pha′li·a** (-sə·fā′lē·ə). [<MEGALO- + Gk. *kephalē* head] —**meg·a·lo·ce·phal′ic** (-sə·fal′ik), **meg·a·lo·ceph′a·lous** *adj.*

meg·a·lo·ma·ni·a (meg′ə·lō·mā′nē·ə, -mān′yə) *n.* **1** *Psychiatry* A mental disorder in which the subject thinks himself great or exalted; delusions of grandeur, power, etc. **2** A tendency to magnify and exaggerate. —**meg·a·lo·ma′ni·ac** *adj.* & *n.* —**meg·a·lo·ma·ni′a·cal** (-mə·nī′ə·kəl) *adj.*

meg·a·lop·o·lis (meg′ə·lop′ə·lis) *n.* A densely populated urban area including one or more major cities. [<MEGALO- + Gk. *polis* city] —**meg·a·lo·pol′i·tan** (meg′ə·lō·pol′ə·tan) *n.*

meg·a·lop·si·a (meg′ə·lop′sē·ə) *n.* Macropsia.

Meg·a·lop·ter·a (meg′ə·lop′tər·ə) *n. pl.* An order of soft–bodied insects with large wings, long antennae, chewing mouth parts, and aquatic larvae; alderflies and hellgrammites or dobson flies. [<MEGALO- + Gk. *pteron* wing] —**meg′a·lop′ter·ous** *adj.*

meg·a·lo·saur (meg′ə·lə·sôr′) *n. Paleontol.* A gigantic, terrestrial, carnivorous dinosaur (genus *Megalosaurus*) of the suborder *Therapoda*. [< MEGALO- + Gk. *sauros* lizard] —**meg′a·lo·saur′i·an** *adj.* & *n.*

Meg·an·thro·pus (meg·an′thrə·pəs) *n. Zool.* An extinct giant hominoid primate of the Pleistocene, represented by massive fossile jawbones found in 1939 and 1941 in central Java. [<NL <Gk. *megas* great + *anthrōpos* man]

meg·a·phone (meg′ə·fōn) *n.* A funnel–shaped device for amplifying or directing sound. —*v.t. & v.i.* **·phoned, ·phon·ing** To address or speak through a megaphone.

meg·a·pod (meg′ə·pod) *adj.* Having large feet, as certain Australian jungle birds.

Meg·a·ra (meg′ər·ə) An ancient city in east central Greece, capital of Megaris. —**Me·gar·i·an** (mə·gâr′ē·ən), **Me·gar·ic** (mə·gar′ik) *adj.*

Meg·a·ris (meg′ə·ris) A mountainous region of ancient Greece on the isthmus between the Peloponnesus and northern Greece.

meg·a·spo·ran·gi·um (meg′ə·spə·ran′jē·əm) *n. pl.* **·gi·a** (-jē·ə) *Bot.* A sporangium which bears only megaspores: also called *macrosporangium*.

meg·a·spore (meg′ə·spôr, -spōr) *n. Bot.* A large, asexual spore developed by certain seed plants, and giving rise always to a female gamete; the embryo sac of a seed plant: also called *macrospore*.

meg·a·spo·ro·phyll (meg′ə·spôr′ə·fil, -spō′rə-) *n. Bot.* A leaf or sporophyll which produces only megasporangia.

me·gass (mə·gas′, -gäs′) *n.* Bagasse. Also **me·gasse′**.

meg·a·there (meg′ə·thir) *n. Paleontol.* A gigantic, extinct, slothlike edentate (genus *Megatherium*), associated with the Pleistocene in North America. [<MEGA- + Gk. *thērion* wild animal]

MEGATHERE
(Fossils indicate length up to 20 feet)

meg·a·therm (meg′ə·thûrm) *n.* A macrotherm.

meg·a·ton (meg′ə·tun′) *n.* A unit of nuclear explosive power equal to one million tons of TNT.

meg·a·tron (meg′ə·tron) *n.* A compact, sturdy type of vacuum tube designed to increase the range of wave frequencies and power in radio, television, and other electronic fields. [<MEGA- + (ELEC)TRON]

meg·a·vi·ta·min (meg′ə·vī′tə·min) *adj.* Pertaining to the treatment of disease by the administering of very large vitamin dosage: *megavitamin therapy*.

Megh·na (meg′nə) A river in East Pakistan, flowing 132 miles SW to the Bay of Bengal.

Me·gid·do (mə·gid′ō) An ancient city of NW Palestine at the western edge of the Plain of Jezreel.

me·gilp (mə·gilp′) See MAGILP.

me·grim (mē′grim) *n.* **1** A headache confined to one side of the head, characterized by nausea and vomiting; migraine. **2** *pl.* Dulness; depression of spirits. **3** A whim or fad. [< F *migraine*]

Me·hem·et A·li (mə·hem′et ä′lē, me·met′), 1769–1849, viceroy of Egypt 1805–48. Also known as *Mohammed Ali*.

Mei·ji (mā·jē) *n.* The reign, 1867–1912, of the Emperor Mutsuhito, 1852–1912, of Japan, regarded as a historic era. [<Japanese, lit., enlightened peace]

mei·kle (mē′kəl) See MICKLE.

Meik·le·john (mik′əl·jon), **Alexander,** 1872–1964, U.S. educator born in England.

Mei·nin·gen (mī′ning·ən) A town in the former state of Thuringia, SW East Germany.

Mein Kampf (min kämpf′) A book by Adolf Hitler, outlining his political philosophy and personal history, and setting forth his plans for the German domination of Europe. [<G, my battle]

mei·ny (mā′nē) *n.* **1** *Obs.* An army or retinue; attendants; household; crew. **2** *Scot.* A multitude or throng. Also **mei′nie.** [<OF *mesnee, meyné*, ult.<L *mansio* a dwelling. See MANSION.]

mei·o·sis (mī·ō′sis) *n.* **1** *Biol.* That process in the division of germ cells by which the number

of chromosomes is reduced from the double or *diploid* number typical of somatic cells to the halved or *haploid* number characteristic of gametes: distinguished from *mitosis*: also spelled *maiosis.* 2 In rhetoric, understatement, often giving the effect of irony or humor, by representing a fact, thing, deed, etc., as being smaller than it really is: also spelled *miosis.* [<Gk. *meiōsis* lessening] — **mei·ot′ic** (-ot′ik) *adj.*

Meis·sen (mī′sən) A city on the Elbe in SE East Germany in the former state of Saxony.

Meissen ware A kind of porcelain or chinaware made in Meissen, Germany.

Meis·so·nier (mā·sô·nyā′), **Jean Louis Ernest,** 1815–91, French painter.

Meis·ter·sing·er (mīs′tər·sing′ər, *Ger.* mīs′tər·zing′ər) *n. pl.* **·sing·er** *German* One of the burgher poets and musicians of Germany in the 14th, 15th, and 16th centuries, the successors of the minnesingers: often called *mastersinger.* — **Die Meistersinger von Nürnberg** Title of a comic opera by Richard Wagner.

Meit·ner (mīt′nər), **Lise,** 1878–1968, German physicist.

Mé·ji·co (mā′hē·kō) The Spanish name for MEXICO.

Mek·ka (mek′ə) See MECCA.

Mek·nès (mek·nes′) A city in NW Morocco: formerly *Mequinez.*

Me·kong (mā·kong′) A river in SE Asia, flowing 2,600 miles south to the China Sea: Chinese *Lantsang.*

mel (mel) *n.* Honey; especially the pure, clarified honey used in the preparation of certain drugs. [<L]

mel·a·mine (mel′ə·mēn, -min) *n. Chem.* A transparent, colorless, crystalline compound, $C_3N_6(NH_2)_3$, the amide of cyanuric acid: combined with cellulose pulp and formaldehyde, it produces a synthetic resin of good qualities. [< *mel (am),* a chemical compound + AMINE]

melan– Var. of MELANO–.

mel·an·cho·li·a (mel′ən·kō′lē·ə) *n. Psychiatry* Mental disorder characterized by excessive brooding and depression of spirits: typical of manic–depressive psychoses. [<L. See MELANCHOLY.] — **mel′an·cho′li·ac** *adj. & n.*

mel·an·chol·y (mel′ən·kol′ē) *adj.* 1 Morbidly gloomy; sad; dejected. 2 Suggesting or promoting sadness. 3 Somberly thoughtful; pensive. — *n.* 1 Low spirits; despondency; depression. 2 Melancholia. 3 Pensive contemplation; serious and sober reflection. 4 *Archaic* The dark, acrid, and viscous substance once believed to be secreted by the kidneys and to be responsible for gloomy dejection of spirits; one of the humors. [<F *melancolie* <L *melancholia* <Gk. < *melas, -anos* black + *cholē* bile] — **mel′an·chol′ic** *adj.* — **mel′an·chol′i·cal·ly** *adv.*

Me·lanch·thon (mə·langk′thən), **Philipp,** Grecized name of Philipp Schwarzert, 1497–1560, religious reformer and scholar; associate of Luther. Also **Me·lanc′thon.**

mel·a·ne·mi·a (mel′ə·nē′mē·ə) *n. Pathol.* A morbid excess of black pigment in the blood: noted chiefly in pernicious anemia. Also **mel′·a·nae′mi·a.** [<MELAN- + Gk. *haima* blood] — **mel′a·ne′mic** *adj.*

Mel·a·ne·sia (mel′ə·nē′zhə, -shə) The islands of the western Pacific south of the Equator, comprising one of the three main divisions of the Pacific Islands; total, 60,000 square miles.

Mel·a·ne·sian (mel′ə·nē′zhən, -shən) *n.* 1 One of the native people of Melanesia, having dark skins and thick, kinky beards and hair: believed to be a mixture of Papuan, Polynesian, and Malay stocks. 2 A branch of the Oceanic subfamily of the Austronesian family of languages, including the languages spoken in the Solomon, Loyalty, and Admiralty islands, Fiji, the New Hebrides, New Caledonia, etc., and the Micronesian group of the Caroline, Gilbert, and Marshall islands. — *adj.* Of or pertaining to Melanesia, its native inhabitants, or their languages.

mé·lange (mā·länzh′) *n. French* A mixture or medley; also, a literary miscellany.

me·la·ni·an (mə·lā′nē·ən) *adj. Anthropol.* Having dark or black pigmentation: said of Negroes, Melanesians, etc. [<F *mélanien* <Gk. *melas, -anos* black]

me·lan·ic (mə·lan′ik) *adj.* 1 Relating to or resembling melanosis or melanism; melanoid. 2 Black; melanian.

mel·a·nin (mel′ə·nin) *n. Biochem.* The brownish–black pigment contained in animal tissues, as the skin and hair, formed by the action of the enzyme tyrosinase upon tyrosine.

mel·a·nism (mel′ə·niz′əm) *n.* 1 Abnormal development of dark coloring matter in the skin, feathers, etc.: opposed to *albinism.* 2 Excessive darkness, as of the eyes, hair, skin, etc., due to extreme pigmentation. — **mel′a·nis′tic** *adj.*

mel·a·nite (mel′ə·nīt) *n.* A black variety of garnet.

melano– *combining form* Black; dark–colored: *melanosis.* Also, before vowels, *melan–.* [< Gk. *melas, melanos* black]

Mel·a·noch·ro·i (mel′ə·nok′rō·ī) *n. pl.* Caucasians having fair skins and dark hair. [< MELAN- + Gk. *ōchros* pale] — **Mel′a·noch′·roid** *adj.*

mel·an·o·crat·ic (mel′ən·ō·krat′ik) *adj. Geol.* Of or pertaining to those igneous rocks characterized by a predominance of dark or ferromagnesian minerals: opposed to *leucocratic.*

mel·a·noid (mel′ə·noid) *adj.* 1 Looking black or having a dark appearance. 2 Of the nature of melanosis.

mel·a·no·ma (mel′ə·nō′mə) *n. Pathol.* A black–pigmented tumor. [<MELAN- + -OMA]

mel·a·no·sis (mel′ə·nō′sis) *n. Pathol.* An organic disease in which pigment is deposited in the skin and other tissues; black degeneration. — **mel′a·not′ic** (-not′ik) *adj.*

mel·a·nous (mel′ə·nəs) *adj.* Having dark or black skin and hair: opposed to *xanthous.*

mel·an·tha·ceous (mel′ən·thā′shəs) *adj.* Of or pertaining to a former family *(Melanthaceae)* of monocotyledonous plants in the lily order, distinguished from lilies by the absence of bulbs: it included plants of the genera *Colchicum* and *Veratrum.* [<NL <Gk. *melas, -anos* black + *anthos* flower]

mel·a·phyre (mel′ə·fīr) *n.* Any igneous porphyry with a dark groundmass. [<F <Gk. *melas* black + F *(por)phyre* porphyry]

Mel·ba (mel′bə), **Dame Nellie,** 1861–1931, Australian operatic soprano: real name *Helen Mitchell Armstrong.*

Melba toast Thinly sliced bread toasted until brown and crisp.

Mel·bourne (mel′bərn) A port and capital of Victoria, Australia.

Mel·bourne (mel′bərn), **Viscount,** 1779–1848, William Lamb, English statesman; prime minister 1834, 1835–41.

Mel·chi·or (mel′kē·ôr) One of the three Magi.

Mel·chis·e·dec (mel·kiz′ə·dek) 1 In Old Testament history, a priest; king of Salem. *Gen.* xiv 18. 2 Of or denoting the greater priesthood of the Mormon Church. Also **Mel·chiz′·e·dek.**

meld (meld) *v.t. & v.i.* In pinochle and other card games, to announce or declare (a combination of cards in the hand), for inclusion in one's total score. — *n.* A group of cards to be declared, or the act of declaring them. [<G *melden* announce]

mel·der (mel′dər) *n. Scot.* The quantity of grain ground at one time; a grist.

Mel·e·a·ger (mel′ē·ā′jər) In Greek mythology, the son of Oeneus and Althaea, who slew the Calydonian boar and in a quarrel over the spoils killed his mother's brothers: Althaea took revenge by burning the log she had removed from the hearth at his birth, when it had been prophesied that her son would die after it was consumed.

mê·lée (mā′lā, mā·lā′; *Fr.* me·lā′) *n.* A general hand–to–hand fight; an affray. [<F <OF *meslee,* var. of *medlee.* See MEDLEY.]

Me·le·gna·no (mā′lā·nyä′nō) A town in northern Italy SE of Milan; scene of French victory over Swiss, 1515: formerly *Marignano.*

me·li·a·ceous (mē′lē·ā′shəs) *adj.* Of or pertaining to a family *(Meliaceae)* of trees and shrubs of the order *Geraniales,* mainly native to the warm portions of Asia and America; the mahogany family, including the Spanish cedar (genus *Cedrela*). [<NL <Gk. *melia* an ash tree]

mel·ic (mel′ik) *adj.* Suitable for singing, or meant to be sung: said of poetry. In ancient Greek poetry it is the successor of the elegiac and iambic forms of verse and includes the Aeolian or single–voice lyric, and the Dorian or choral lyric. — *n.* Melic poetry. Compare ELEGIAC and IAMBIC. [<Gk. *melikos* < *melos* song]

Me·lil·la (mā·lē′lyä) A Spanish possession on the NW coast of Africa, constituting a port and enclave in eastern Morocco.

mel·i·lot (mel′ə·lot) *n.* Any one of several sweet–smelling, cloverlike herbs of the genus *Melilotus,* especially the **sweet clover** *(M. officinalis)* and the **Bokhara clover** *(M. alba).* [<OF *melilot* <LL *melilotus* <Gk. *melilōtos* < *meli* honey + *lōtos* a lotus]

mel·i·nite (mel′ə·nīt) *n.* An explosive of great power and similar to lyddite, yielded by combining guncotton with picric acid. [<Gk. *mēlinos* yellow]

mel·io·rate (mēl′yə·rāt) *v.t. & v.i.* **·rat·ed, ·rat·ing** To improve, as in quality or condition; ameliorate. See synonyms under AMEND. [<LL *melioratus,* pp. of *meliorare* improve < *melior* better] — **mel′io·ra·ble** *adj.* — **mel′·io·ra′tive** *adj.* — **mel′io·ra′tor** *n.*

mel·io·ra·tion (mēl′yə·rā′shən) *n.* 1 A betterment. 2 *Ling.* An improvement or elevation in the meaning of a word, as in *nice* (formerly "foolish"): opposed to *pejoration.*

mel·io·rism (mēl′yə·riz′əm) *n.* 1 The improvement of society by bettering man's physical being and environment instead of by ethical or religious means. 2 A modified optimism, teaching that the world is neither the best nor the worst possible, but is susceptible of improvement through the increase of good as man evolves. Compare OPTIMISM and PESSIMISM. [<L *melior* better] — **mel′io·rist** *adj. & n.* — **mel′io·ris′tic** *adj.*

mel·ior·i·ty (mēl·yôr′ə·tē, -yor′-) *n.* The state of being better; superiority.

mel·is·mat·ic (mel′is·mat′ik) *adj. Music* Florid and ornate in phrasing. [<NL *melisma* song <Gk.]

Me·lis·sa (mə·lis′ə, *Ital.* mā·lēs′sä) A feminine personal name. Also *Fr.* **Mé·lisse** (mā·lēs′) or **Mé·lite** (mā·lēt′). [<Gk., bee]

Mel·i·ta (mel′ə·tə) The ancient name for MALTA.

Mel·i·to·pol (mel′ə·tô′pəl) A city in southern Ukrainian S.S.R.

mell (mel) *v.t. & v.i. Obs.* 1 To mix; mingle. 2 To meddle. [<OF *meller,* var. of *mesler.* See MEDDLE.]

mel·lif·er·ous (mə·lif′ər·əs) *adj.* Producing or bearing honey. Also **mel·lif′ic.** [<L *mellifer* honey–bearing < *mel* honey + *ferre* bear]

mel·lif·lu·ous (mə·lif′lo͞o·əs) *adj.* 1 Sweetly or smoothly flowing; dulcet; honeyed. 2 Flowing like or as with honey. Also **mel·lif′lu·ent.** [<L *mellifluus* < *mel* honey + *fluere* flow] — **mel·lif′lu·ence, mel·lif′lu·ous·ness** *n.* — **mel·lif′lu·ous·ly, mel·lif′lu·ent·ly** *adv.*

mel·liph·a·gous (mə·lif′ə·gəs) *adj.* Feeding on honey, as certain animals and birds: often **mel·liv′o·rous** (-liv′ər·əs). Also **me·liph′a·gous.** [<Gk. *meli* honey + *phagein* to eat]

mel·lite (mel′īt) *n.* 1 Any medicated preparation containing honey. 2 The mineral honeystone. [<L *mel* honey + -ITE[1]]

Mel·lon (mel′ən), **Andrew William,** 1855–1937, U. S. banker, secretary of the treasury 1921–1932.

mel·lo·phone (mel′ō·fōn) *n.* A circular althorn. [<MELLOW + -PHONE]

mel·low (mel′ō) *adj.* 1 Soft by reason of ripeness; well–matured; not bitter or acid: *mellow* fruit; *mellow* wine. 2 Of a rich or delicate quality: *mellow* tints; *mellow* tones. 3 Companionable; jolly. 4 Made jovial by liquor. 5 Soft and friable, as soil. See synonyms under RIPE. — *v.t. & v.i.* To make or become mellow; ripen; soften. [ME *melwe,* ? <OE *melu* meal. Akin to Flemish *meluw* soft, tender.] — **mel′low·ly** *adv.* — **mel′low·ness** *n.*

me·lo·de·on (mə·lō′dē·ən) *n.* A small reed organ or harmonium. [<Gk. *melōdia* melody]

me·lo·di·a (mə·lō′dē·ə) *n.* An organ stop having wood pipes and a tone nearly like the clarabella; a stopped diapason. [<LL]

me·lod·ic (mə·lod′ik) *adj.* Pertaining to or containing melody; melodious. — **me·lod′i·cal·ly** *adv.*

me·lod·ics (mə·lod′iks) n. pl. (construed as singular) The branch of musical science relating to the pitch of tones and the principles of melody.

me·lo·di·ous (mə·lō′dē·əs) adj. Agreeable to the ear; producing or characterized by melody; tuneful. — **me·lo′di·ous·ly** adv. — **me·lo′di·ous·ness** n.

mel·o·dize (mel′ə·dīz) v. **·dized**, **·diz·ing** v.t. 1 To make melodious. 2 To compose melody for. — v.i. 3 To make melody or melodies. — **mel′o·diz′er**, **mel′o·dist** n.

mel·o·dra·ma (mel′ə·drä′mə, -dram′ə) n. 1 Originally, a drama with a romantic story or plot, sensational incidents, and usually including some music and song. 2 Any sensational and emotional drama, usually having a happy ending. 3 Behavior or language of a theatrical nature. [<F mélodrame <Gk. melos song + drama drama] — **mel′o·dram′a·tist** n.

mel·o·dra·mat·ic (mel′ə·drə·mat′ik) adj. Of, pertaining to, or like melodrama; sensational. — **mel′o·dra·mat′i·cal·ly** adv.

mel·o·dra·mat·ics (mel′ə·drə·mat′iks) n. pl. Melodramatic behavior.

mel·o·dy (mel′ə·dē) n. pl. **·dies** 1 Pleasing sounds or an agreeable succession of such sounds. 2 Musical sounds or quality, as in the words of a poem. 3 A poem written or suitable for being set to music. 4 Music a A succession of simple tones, usually in the same key, constituting, in combination, a rhythmic whole: distinguished as a formal element from harmony and rhythm. b The chief part or voice in a harmonic composition; the air. [<OF melodie <LL melodia <Gk. melōidia choral song <melōidos melodious <melos song + aoidos singer]

Synonyms: harmony, music, symphony, unison. Harmony is simultaneous; melody is successive; harmony is the correspondence of two or more notes sounded at once, melody the succession of a number of notes continuously following one another. A melody may be wholly in one part; harmony must be of two or more parts. Accordant notes of different pitch sounded simultaneously produce harmony; unison is the simultaneous sounding of two or more notes of the same pitch. Tones sounded at the interval of an octave are also said to be in unison, but this is not literally exact. Music may denote the simplest melody or the most complex and perfect harmony. A symphony (apart from its technical orchestral sense) is any pleasing consonance of musical sounds, vocal or instrumental. Compare METER², SONG, TUNE. Antonyms: discord, dissonance.

Me·lo·i·dae (mə·lō′ə·dē) n. pl. A family of coleopterous insects with plump cylindrical bodies; the blister beetles. [<NL <meloē oil beetle; ult. origin unknown] — **mel·oid** (mel′oid) adj. & n.

Mel·o·lon·thi·nae (mel′ə·lon·thī′nē) n. pl. A subfamily of beetles (family Scarabaeidae) including the cockchafers and June beetles. [<NL <Gk. mēlolonthē cockchafer] — **mel′o·lon′thine** (-thīn, -thin) adj. & n.

mel·o·ma·ni·a (mel′ə·mā′nē·ə, -mān′yə) n. An excessive or morbid fondness for music. [<Gk. melos song + -MANIA] — **mel′o·ma′ni·ac** n.

mel·on (mel′ən) n. A trailing plant of the gourd family, or its fruit. There are two genera, the muskmelon and the watermelon, each with numerous varieties. [<F <LL melo, melonis <L melopepo <Gk. mēlopepōn apple-shaped melon <mēlon apple + pepōn melon]

mel·on·ite (mel′ən·īt) n. A reddish-white, granular nickel telluride, Ni₂Te₃; tellurnickel. [from Melones mine, Calif., where found]

Me·los (mē′los) See MILO.

Mel·pom·e·ne (mel·pom′ə·nē) The Muse of tragedy. [<Gk. Melpomenē, lit., the songstress <melpein sing]

Mel·rose (mel′rōz) A burgh of SE Scotland; site of a ruined Cistercian abbey, founded 1136.

melt (melt) v.t. & v.i. **melt·ed**, **melt·ed** (Archaic **mol·ten**), **melt·ing** 1 To reduce or change from a solid to a liquid state by heat; fuse. 2 To dissolve, as in water. 3 To disappear or cause to disappear; dissipate: often with away. 4 To blend by imperceptible degrees; merge. 5 To make or become softened in feeling or attitude. — n. 1 Something melted. 2 A single

operation of fusing. 3 The amount of a single fusing. [OE meltian. Akin to MALT.] — **melt′·a·ble** adj. — **melt′a·bil′i·ty** n. — **melt′er** n.

Synonyms (verb): dissolve, fuse, liquefy, thaw. Antonyms: congeal, freeze, harden, indurate, solidify.

melt·age (mel′tij) n. 1 The process of melting. 2 The amount resulting from melting.

melting point The temperature at which a specified solid substance becomes liquid.

melting pot 1 A vessel in which things are melted; crucible. 2 A country, city, or region in which immigrants of various racial and cultural backgrounds are assimilated.

mel·ton (mel′tən) n. A heavy woolen cloth with a short nap: used for overcoats. [after Melton Mowbray, England]

melt·wa·ter (melt′wô′tər, -wot′ər) n. The whitish water from melting glaciers.

Me·lun·geon (mə·lun′jən) n. One of a darkskinned people of mixed white, Negro, and Indian stock, living in the mountains of Tennessee. [? <F mélange mixture]

mel·vie (mel′vē) v.t. Scot. To cover with meal.

Mel·ville (mel′vil) **Herman**, 1819–91, U.S. novelist and poet.

Melville Bay An inlet of Baffin Bay in NW Greenland.

Melville Island 1 The largest of the Parry Islands, in the Arctic Ocean, Northwest Territories, Canada; 16,503 square miles. 2 An Australian island comprising part of Northern Territory, Australia; 2,400 square miles.

Melville Lake A lake in SE Labrador; 120 miles long.

Melville Peninsula A peninsula in Northwest Territories, Canada, between the Gulf of Boothia and Foxe Basin; 24,156 square miles; 250 miles long.

Mel·vin (mel′vin) A masculine personal name. [OE, high protector]

mem (mem) n. The thirteenth Hebrew letter. See ALPHABET. [<Hebrew mēm, lit., water]

mem·ber (mem′bər) n. 1 A person belonging to an incorporated or organized body, society, etc.: a Member of Congress, a member of a club. 2 A limb or other functional organ of an animal body. 3 A part or element of a structural or composite whole, distinguishable from other parts or elements, as a part of a sentence, syllogism, period, or discourse, or any necessary part of a structural framework, as a tie rod, post, or strut in the truss of a bridge. 4 A subordinate classificatory part: A species is a member of a genus. 5 Bot. A part of a plant considered with reference to position and structure, but regardless of function. 6 Math. a Either side of an equation. b A set of figures or symbols forming part of a formula or number. c Any one of the items forming a series. See synonyms under PART, TERM. [<OF membre <L membrum limb]

mem·ber·ship (mem′bər·ship) n. 1 The state of being a member. 2 The members of an organization, collectively.

mem·brane (mem′brān) n. 1 A thin, pliable, sheetlike layer of animal or vegetable tissue serving as a cover, connection, or lining. 2 A piece of parchment. [<L membrana, lit., limb coating <membrum member] — **mem′bra·nous** (-brə·nəs), **mem′bra·na′ceous** (-nā′shəs) adj.

membrane bone Anat. A bone developed in membrane, as one of those of the vault of the skull.

Mem·el (mem′əl, Ger. mā′məl) 1 A territory of western Lithuanian S.S.R.; 1,026 square miles. 2 Its capital, a port on the Baltic Sea: Lithuanian Klaipeda. 3 The German name for the NEMAN.

me·men·to (mə·men′tō) n. pl. **·toes** or **·tos** 1 A hint or reminder to awaken memory; souvenir; memorial. 2 Eccl. Either of the two prayers in the canon of the mass in which the living and the departed are respectively mentioned. [<L, remember, imperative of meminisse remember]

memento mo·ri (môr′ī) Latin An emblem or reminder of death, as a skull, etc.: literally, remember that you must die.

Mem·ling (mem′ling) **Hans**, 1430–95, Flemish painter. Also **Mem·linc** (mem′lingk).

Mem·non (mem′non) 1 In Greek legend, a king of the Ethiopians killed by Achilles and made immortal by Zeus. 2 A statue of Amenhotep III at Thebes, Egypt, associated with Memnon by the Greeks and said to emit a

musical note when touched by the sun at dawn. — **Mem·no·ni·an** (mem-nō′nē·ən) adj.

mem·o (mem′ō) n. pl. **mem·os** Colloq. A memorandum.

mem·oir (mem′wär) n. 1 An account of something deemed worthy of record; especially, one addressed to a public institution or scientific society. 2 pl. The reminiscences of a person, either general or relating to a particular period, published together. 3 A biographic memorial. See synonyms under HISTORY. [<F mémoire <L memoria memory. Doublet of MEMORY.] — **mem′oir·ist** n.

mem·o·ra·bil·i·a (mem′ə·rə·bil′ē·ə) n. pl. Things worthy of memory, or an account of them. [<L, neut. pl. of memorabilis memorable]

mem·o·ra·ble (mem′ər·ə·bəl) adj. Worthy to be remembered; noteworthy. [<L memorabilis] — **mem′o·ra·bil′i·ty**, **mem′o·ra·ble·ness** n. — **mem′o·ra·bly** adv.

mem·o·ran·dum (mem′ə·ran′dəm) n. pl. **·dums** or **·da** (-də) 1 Something to be remembered; hence, a brief note of a thing or things to be remembered. 2 Law A brief written outline of the terms of a transaction. 3 An informal letter. 4 A statement of goods sent from a consignor to a consignee. See synonyms under RECORD. [<L, a thing to be remembered]

me·mo·ri·al (mə·môr′ē·əl, -mō′rē-) adj. 1 Commemorating the memory of a deceased person or of any event. 2 Contained within one's memory: distinguished from immemorial. — n. 1 Something designed to keep in remembrance a person, event, etc. 2 A summary or presentation of facts usually made the ground of a petition or remonstrance. 3 Law A memorandum filed for record. See synonyms under HISTORY, RECORD, TRACE. [<OF <L memorialis]

Memorial Day Decoration Day.

me·mo·ri·al·ist (mə·môr′ē·əl·ist, -mō′rē-) n. 1 One who writes memoirs. 2 One who writes, signs, or presents a memorial.

me·mo·ri·al·ize (mə·môr′ē·əl·īz′, -mō′rē-) v.t. **·ized**, **·iz·ing** 1 To commemorate. 2 To present a memorial to. Also Brit. **me·mo′ri·al·ise′**. — **me·mo′ri·al·i·za′tion** n.

mem·o·rize (mem′ə·rīz) v.t. **·rized**, **·riz·ing** To commit to memory; learn by heart. See synonyms under LEARN. — **mem′o·ri·za′tion** n. — **mem′o·riz′er** n.

mem·o·ry (mem′ər·ē) n. pl. **·ries** 1 The mental process or faculty of representing in consciousness an act, experience, or impression, with recognition that it belongs to time past. 2 The experiences of the mind taken in the aggregate, and considered as influencing present and future behavior. 3 The accuracy and ease with which a person can retain and recall past experiences. 4 That which is remembered, as an act, event, person, or thing. 5 The period of time covered by the faculty of remembrance: beyond the memory of man. 6 The state of being remembered; posthumous reputation: The memory of Washington will endure. 7 That which reminds; a memorial; a memento. 8 The information storage unit of a computer. [<OF memorie <L memoria <memor mindful. Doublet of MEMOIR.]

Synonyms: recollection, remembrance, reminiscence, retrospect, retrospection. Memory is the faculty by which knowledge is retained or recalled; memory is a retention of knowledge within the grasp of the mind, while remembrance is the having what is known consciously before the mind. Either may be voluntary or involuntary. Recollection involves volition, the mind making a distinct effort to recall something, or fixing the attention actively upon it when recalled. Reminiscence is a half-dreamy memory of scenes or events long past; retrospection is a distinct turning of the mind back upon the past, bringing long periods under survey. Antonyms: forgetfulness, oblivion, obliviousness.

Mem·phi·an (mem′fē·ən) adj. Of or pertaining to ancient Memphis, Egypt, or to its inhabitants.

Mem·phis (mem′fis) 1 A port on the Mississippi River in SW Tennessee. 2 The ancient capital of Egypt on the Nile above the apex of its delta.

Mem·phre·ma·gog (mem′frə·mā′gog), **Lake** A lake in northern Vermont and southern Quebec; 30 miles long.

mem·sah·ib (mem′sä·ib) n. Anglo-Indian A

European lady or mistress: a name given by native servants. [< MA·AM + Arabic *sāhib* master]

men¹ (men) *v. t. & v. i. Scot.* To mend.

men² (men) Plural of MAN.

men·ace (men′is) *v.* **·aced, ·ac·ing** *v.t.* **1** To threaten with evil or harm. **2** To make threats of. —*v.i.* **3** To make threats; appear threatening. See synonyms under THREATEN. —*n.* A threat; something which threatens; an impending evil. [< OF *manace* < L *minacia* < *minax, -acis* threatening < *minari* threaten] —**men′ac·er** *n.* —**men′ac·ing·ly** *adv.*

me·nac·me (mə·nak′mē) *n. Physiol.* The reproductive period of a woman's life, during which menstruation occurs. [< Gk. *mēn* month + *akmē* peak]

me·nad (mē′nad), **me·nad·ic** (mə·nad′ik) See MAENAD, etc.

mé·nage (mā·näzh′, *Fr.* mā·nàzh′) *n.* **1** The persons of a household, collectively; a domestic establishment. **2** Household management. Also **me·nage′.** [< F < L *mansio, -onis* house. Doublet of MANSION.]

me·nag·er·ie (mə·naj′ər·ē) *n.* **1** A collection of wild animals kept for exhibition. **2** The enclosure in which they are kept. [< F]

Men·ai Strait (men′ī) A channel between the island of Anglesey and the mainland in NW Wales.

Me·nam (me·näm′) See CHAO PHRAYA.

Me·nan·der (mə·nan′dər), 343?–291? B.C., Greek comic dramatist.

me·nar·che (mə·när′kē) *n. Physiol.* The commencement of menstrual function in women. [< Gk. *mēn* month + *archē* beginning]

Men·cius (men′shəs), 372?–289? B.C., Chinese philosopher: Latin form of Chinese *Meng-tse.*

Menck·en (meng′kən), **H(enry) L(ouis),** 1880–1956, U.S. author and editor.

mend (mend) *v.t.* **1** To make sound or serviceable again by repairing; patch. **2** To correct errors or faults in; reform; improve: *Mend* your ways. **3** To correct (some defect). —*v.i.* **4** To become better, as in health; improve. —*n.* **1** The act of repairing or patching. **2** A mended portion of a garment. —**on the mend** Recovering health; recuperating; convalescing. [Apheticform of AMEND] —**mend′a·ble** *adj.* —**mend′er** *n.*

men·da·cious (men·dā′shəs) *adj.* **1** Addicted to lying; falsifying. **2** Characterized by deceit; false. [< L *mendax, -acis* lying] —**men·da′cious·ly** *adv.* —**men·da′cious·ness** *n.*

men·dac·i·ty (men·das′ə·tē) *n.* Lying; falsity. [< L *mendacitas, -tatis*]

Men·del (men′dəl), **Gregor Johann,** 1822–1884, Austrian monk and botanist; founder of the science of genetics.

Men·de·ley·ev (men′də·lā′əf), **Dmitri Ivanovich,** 1834–1907, Russian chemist; discovered the periodic law. Also **Men′de·lé′eff.**

men·de·le·vi·um (men′də·lē′vē·əm) *n. Chem.* The short-lived radioactive element (symbol Md) of atomic number 101 and mass number 256. [after Dmitri Ivanovich *Mendeleyev*]

Men·de·li·an (men·dē′lē·ən) *adj.* **1** Of or pertaining to Gregor Mendel. **2** Relating to or in accordance with Mendel's laws.

Men·del·ism (men′dəl·iz′əm) *n.* The theory of heredity as put forth by Mendel. Also **Men·de′li·an·ism.**

Mendel's laws *Genetics* Principles formulated by Gregor Mendel as a result of experiments in breeding garden peas. They state that certain contrasting characters of cross-bred parents, as color height, etc., are inherited by the hybrid offspring through determining factors which act as units, and that subsequent cross-bred generations manifest these characters in varying combinations from dominant to recessive, each combination being present in a definite proportion of the total number of offspring.

Men·dels·sohn (men′dəl·sən, *Ger.* men′dəl·zōn), **Moses,** 1729–86, German Jewish theologian and philosopher.

Men·dels·sohn-Bar·thol·dy (men′dəl·sən·bär·tōl′dē, *Ger.* men′dəl·zōn·bär·tól′dē), **Felix,** 1809–47, German composer and musician; grandson of Moses Mendelssohn. Also **Men′dels·sohn.**

Men·de·res (men′də·res′) **1** A river in western Turkey in Asia, flowing SW to the Aegean: an-

cient *Meander.* **2** A river in NW Turkey in Asia, flowing NW across the plain of ancient Troy to the Dardanelles: ancient *Scamander.*

men·di·cant (men′də·kənt) *adj.* **1** Begging; depending on alms for a living. **2** Pertaining to or like a beggar. —*n.* **1** A beggar. **2** A begging friar. [< L *mendicans, -antis,* ppr. of *mendicare* beg < *mendicus* needy] —**men′di·can·cy, men·dic′i·ty** (men·dis′ə·tē) *n.*

men·di·go (men′di·gō) The splake.

mend·ing (men′ding) *n.* Articles to be mended.

Men·do·ci·no (men′də·sē′nō), **Cape** The westernmost point of California.

Men·do·za (men·dō′sä) A province of western Argentina; 58,239 square miles; capital, Mendoza.

Men·do·za (men·dō′thä), **Pedro de,** 1487?–1537, Spanish explorer who founded Buenos Aires and Asunción.

mends (mendz) *n. pl. Brit. Dial.* Amends. —**to the mends** *Brit. Dial.* Over and above.

Men·e·la·us (men′ə·lā′əs) In Greek legend, a son of Atreus, brother of Agamemnon, and a king of Sparta; after his wife Helen was abducted by Paris, Menelaus led the Greek princes against Troy, where he defeated Paris; reconciled with Helen, after eight years of wandering, he returned with her to Sparta.

Men·e·lik II (men′e·lik), 1844–1913, emperor of Abyssinia 1889–1910; defeated Italians at Aduwa, 1896.

me·ne, me·ne, tek·el, u·phar·sin (mē′nēmē′ nētek′əl yōō·fär′sin) *Aramaic* Numbered, numbered, weighed, (and) divided: in the Bible, the words that appeared on the wall at Belshazzar's feast, and which Daniel interpreted to mean that God had judged and doomed Belshazzar's kingdom. *Dan.* vi 24–28.

Me·nén·dez de A·vi·les (mā·nen′däth thää·vē′läs), **Pedro,** 1519–74, Spanish captain, founder of St. Augustine, Florida.

Me·nes (mē′nēz) Traditionally the first Egyptian king; founder of the first dynasty of Egypt in the fifth millennium B.C. Also **Me·ni** (mē′nē).

Meng-tse (mung′dzu′) See MENCIUS.

Meng·tze (mung′dzu′) A city in SE Yunnan province, China.

men·ha·den (men·hād′n) *n.* A herringlike fish (*Brevoortia tyrannus*) found along the North Atlantic coast of the United States: it is the source of **menhaden oil,** used in industry, and of fertilizer. [Alter. of Algonquian *munnawhat* fertilizer]

men·hir (men′hir) *n.* A prehistoric sepulchral or battle monument consisting of a single tall stone, usually left rough. [< F < Celtic (Breton) *men* stone + *hir* long]

me·ni·al (mē′nē·əl, mēn′yəl) *adj.* **1** Pertaining or appropriate to servants. **2** Servile. See synonyms under BASE². —*n.* **1** One doing servile work: generally in contempt. **2** Figuratively, a person of low or servile nature. [< AF < OF *meisniee, maisnie* household < LL *mansionata* < L *mansio* house] —**me′ni·al·ly** *adv.*

Mé·nière's disease (mā·nyârz′) *Pathol.* Progressive deafness of one ear, with vertigo, tinnitus, nausea, and vomiting. [after Prosper *Ménière,* 1799–1862, French physician]

me·nin·ges (mə·nin′jez) *n. pl.* of **me·ninx** (mē′ ningks) *Anat.* The membranes (the dura mater, pia mater, and arachnoid) enveloping the brain and spinal cord. [< NL < Gk. *mēninx, mēningos* membrane] —**me·nin′ge·al** *adj.*

men·in·gi·tis (men′ən·jī′tis) *n. Pathol.* Inflammation of the enveloping membranes of an organ, especially those of the brain and spinal cord. Certain forms are caused by infection with diplococcus bacterium (*Neisseria intracellularis*). —**men·in·git′ic** (-jit′ik) *adj.*

me·nis·cus (mə·nis′kəs) *n. pl.* **·nis·cus·es** or **·nis·ci** (-nis′ī) **1** Any crescent-shaped body. **2** *Optics* A lens convex on one side and concave on the other. **3** *Anat.* A disklike body of fibro-cartilage found in some joints of the body exposed to concussion. **4** *Physics* The surface or upper part of a liquid column made convex or concave by capillarity. [< L < Gk. *mēniskos* crescent, dim. of *mēnē* the moon]

men·i·sper·ma·ceous (men′ē·spər·mā′shəs) *adj.* Designating a family (*Menisper-*

MENISCUS LENSES

maceae) of mostly tropical, woody or herbaceous climbing plants having alternate leaves and small dioecious flowers, and yielding substances of narcotic and toxic properties; the moonseed family. [< NL *menispermaceae* < Gk. *mēnē* moon + *sperma* seed]

Men·non·ite (men′ən·īt) *n.* A member of a Protestant denomination that grew out of the Anabaptist movement in the 16th century, and still flourishes in Europe and the United States: named after Menno Simons, 1496?–1561, a leader of the sect in the Netherlands. They are opposed to the taking of oaths, the holding of public office, and military service.

me·no (mā′nō) *adv. Music* Less. [< Ital. < L *minus*]

me·nol·o·gy (mə·nol′ə·jē) *n.* **1** A calendar of the months; especially, one having a record of events by month. **2** A register or collection of lives of the saints arranged according to months and days of the month, as in the Greek Church. [< Gk. *mēn* month + -LOGY]

me·nom·i·nee (mə·nom′ə·nē) *n. Canadian* Wild rice. [< Algonquian (Cree)]

men·o·pause (men′ə·pôz) *n. Physiol.* Final cessation of the menses; change of life: opposed to *menarche.* [< Gk. *mēn* month + *pauein* cause to cease]

Me·nor·ca (mā·nôr′kä) The Spanish name for MINORCA.

men·or·rha·gi·a (men′ə·rā′jē·ə) *n. Pathol.* Excessive menstruation [< Gk. *mēn* month + -RRHAGIA]

Me·not·ti (mə·not′ē), **Gian Carlo,** born 1911, U.S. composer and librettist.

Men·sa (men′sə) A southern constellation. See CONSTELLATION.

men·sal¹ (men′səl) *adj.* Belonging to or used at the table. [< L *mensalis* < *mensa* table]

men·sal² (men′səl) *adj.* Monthly. [< L *mensis* month]

mensch (mensh) *n. pl.* **men·schen** *Colloq.* A genuine, respected, honored person. [< Yiddish < Ger., person]

mense (mens) *n. Scot. & Brit. Dial.* Dignified conduct or manner; decorum. [OE *mensk* < ON *mennska* humanity] —**mense′ful** *adj.*

men·ses (men′sēz) *n. pl. Physiol.* A periodical bloody flow from the uterus of a female mammal, resulting when an ovum is not fertilized, and occuring in women about once every lunar month; the menstrual flow. [< L, pl. of *mensis* month]

Men·she·vik (men′shə·vik) *n. pl.* **·vi·ki** (-vē′kē) or **·viks** A member of the conservative element in the Russian Social Democratic Party. Compare BOLSHEVIK, MAXIMALIST. Also **Men′she·vist.** [< Russian *menshe* smaller, minority] —**Men′she·vism** *n.*

mens le·gis (menz lē′jis) *Latin* The spirit of the law.

mens sa·na in cor·po·re sa·no (menz sā′nəin kôr′pə·rēsä′nō) *Latin* A sound mind in a sound body.

men·stru·al (men′strōō·əl) *adj.* **1** *Physiol.* Pertaining to the menses or to a menstruum. **2** Continuing a month; occurring monthly. Also **men′stru·ous.**

men·stru·ate (men′strōō·āt) *v.i.* **·at·ed, ·at·ing** To discharge the menses. [< L *menstruatus,* pp. of *menstruare menstruus* monthy < *mensis* month] —**men·stru·a′tion** *n.*

men·stru·um (men′strōō·əm) *n. pl.* **·stru·ums** or **·stru·a** (-strōō·ə) The medium in which a substance is dissolved; a solvent.

men·su·ra·ble (men′shər·ə·bəl) *adj.* **1** That can be measured. **2** Mensural. [< LL *mensurabilis* < *mensurare* measure < *mensura.* See MEASURE.] —**men·su·ra·bil′i·ty** *n.*

men·su·ral (men′shər·əl) *adj.* **1** Pertaining to measure. **2** *Music* Characterized by a fixed rhythm and measure.

men·su·rate (men′shə·rāt) *v.t.* **·rat·ed, ·rat·ing** *Rare* To measure the dimensions or quantity of. [< L *mensuratus,* pp. of *mensurare < mensura.* See MEASURE.]

men·su·ra·tion (men′shə·rā′shən) *n.* **1** The act, art, or process of measuring. **2** The branch of mathematical science that has to do with measurement, as of lines, surfaces, or volume. **3** The result of measuring; measure.

[<LL *mensuratio, -onis*] — **men'su·ra'tive** *adj.*

-ment *suffix of nouns* **1** The concrete result of; a thing produced by: *achievement.* **2** The instrument or means of: *atonement.* **3** The process or action of: *government.* **4** The quality, condition, or state of being: *astonishment.* [<F <L *-mentum*]

men·tal¹ (men'təl) *adj.* **1** Pertaining to the mind: contrasted with *corporeal.* **2** Effected by or due to the mind, especially without the aid of written symbols. [<F <LL *mentalis* <L *mens, mentis* mind] — **men'tal·ly** *adv.*

men·tal² (men'təl) *adj.* Of, pertaining to, or situated near the chin: the *mental point.* — *n.* A plate or scale of the chin, as in snakes. [<L *mentum* chin]

mental age See under AGE.

mental blindness A mental condition in which images conveyed by the optic nerves are not properly recognized: also called *mind-blindness, psychic blindness.*

mental deafness A form of deafness in which sounds and words are heard but cannot be interpreted: also called *mind-deafness, psychic deafness.*

mental deficiency *Psychiatry* Lack of one or more mental capacities and functions present in the normal individual, usually to the point of disqualifying from full participation in ordinary life; feeble-mindedness. The principal types, in order of increasing deficiency, are moronism, imbecility, and idiotism.

mental healing The curing of any disorder, ailment, or disease by concentrating the mind either directly on the healing forces in nature, or on the denial of the discomforts experienced.

mental hygiene The scientific study and rational application of all methods that will restore, preserve, promote, and improve mental health, especially in relation to the normal functioning of the personality as a whole.

men·tal·i·ty (men·tal'ə·tē) *n. pl.* **·ties** **1** The sum of the mental faculties or powers; mental activity. **2** Cast or habit of mind.

Mental Science New Thought.

Men·ta·wai Islands (men·tä'wī) An Indonesian island group off the west coast of Sumatra; 2,354 square miles. Also **Men·ta'wei** (-wā).

men·tha·ceous (men·thā'shəs) *adj.* Designating or pertaining to a genus (*Mentha*) of odorous perennial herbs of the mint family, with opposite leaves and small flowers, including the peppermint, spearmint, etc. [<L *mentha* mint + -ACEOUS]

men·thane (men'thān) *n. Chem.* Any one of three isomeric, saturated hydrocarbons, C_{10}-H_{20}, corresponding to cymenes: parent substance for several of the terpenes. [<MENTHOL + -ANE²]

men·thene (men'thēn) *n. Chem.* A colorless, liquid, oily hydrocarbon, $C_{10}H_{18}$, derived from the oil of peppermint. [<L *mentha* mint + -ENE]

men·thol (men'thôl, -thōl, -thol) *n. Chem.* A white, waxy, crystalline alcohol, $C_{10}H_{19}OH$, obtained from and having the odor of oil of peppermint: used as a flavoring agent, in perfumery, and in medicine as an anodyne for neuralgia and similar ailments. [<L *mentha* mint + -OL¹]

men·tho·lat·ed (men'thə·lā'tid) *adj.* Treated with, containing, or impregnated with menthol.

men·ti·cide (men'tə·sīd) *n.* The undermining and destruction of a person's mental powers by deliberate intent and with the use of all available psychological means. [<L *mens, mentis* mind + -CIDE]

men·tion (men'shən) *v.t.* To speak of incidentally or briefly; refer to in passing; specify or name. See synonyms under ALLUDE, INFORM. — *n.* The act of mentioning; casual allusion; notice: used especially in the phrase *to make mention of.* [<OF <L *mentio, -onis* <*mens, mentis* mind] — **men'tion·a·ble** *adj.* — **men'tion·er** *n.*

Men·ton (män·tôn') A resort town on the Italian border of the French Riviera. *Italian* **Men·to·ne** (män·tō'nā).

men·tor (men'tər, -tôr) *n.* A wise and trusted teacher, guide, and friend; an elderly monitor or adviser. [<MENTOR] — **men·to'ri·al** (-tôr'ē-əl, -tō'rē-) *adj.*

Men·tor (men'tər, -tôr) In the *Odyssey*, the sage guardian of Telemachus, appointed by

---

Odysseus before he departed for the Trojan War. [<Gk., lit., adviser]

men·tum (men'təm) *n.* **1** The chin. **2** *Entomol.* The distal sclerite of the labium or lower lip of insects.

men·u (men'yōō, mān'-; *Fr.* mə·nü') *n.* A bill of fare or the dishes included in it. [<F, small, detailed <L *minutus.* See MINUTE².]

Men·u·hin (men'yōō·in), **Yehudi,** born 1917, U. S. violinist.

me·ow (mē·ou', myou) See MEW². [Imit.]

me·per·i·dine hydrochloride (mə·per'ə·dēn, -din) A white, odorless, crystalline compound, $C_{15}H_{22}ClO_2$, used in medicine as an analgesic and sedative; Demerol.

Me·phis·to·phe·le·an (mə·fis'tə·fē'lē·ən) *adj.* Of, pertaining to, or like Mephistopheles; cynical; crafty; sardonic; fiendish. Also **Me·phis'to·phe'li·an.**

Meph·is·toph·e·les (mef'is·tof'ə·lēz) **1** In medieval legend, a devil to whom Faust sold his soul for wisdom and power. **2** A crafty, sardonic fiend; a diabolical person. Also **Me·phis·to** (mə·fis'tō).

mer– Var. of MERO–.

Me·rak (mē'rak) The star Beta in the constellation Ursa Major; the smaller of the two stars composing the Pointers toward the pole-star.

mer·can·tile (mûr'kən·til, -tīl) *adj.* **1** Pertaining to or characteristic of merchants. **2** Conducted or acting on business principles; commercial. [<F <Ital. <L *mercans, -antis,* pp. of *mercari* traffic. See MERCHANT.]

mercantile agency An institution which collects, records, and furnishes to regular clients full information about the financial standing, credit ratings, etc., of individuals and firms.

mercantile paper Negotiable instruments for the payment of money, given in course of business, as bills of exchange, promissory notes, etc.: also called *commercial paper.*

mercantile system A theory in political economy that wealth consists not in labor and its products, but in the quantity of silver and gold in a country, and hence that mining, the exportation of goods, and the importation of gold should be encouraged by the state.

mer·can·til·ism (mûr'kən·til·iz'əm) *n.* **1** The spirit or theory of mercantile life or trade in general. **2** The mercantile system. — **mer'can·til·ist** *n. & adj.* — **mer'can·til·is'tic** *adj.*

mer·cap·tan (mər·kap'tan) *n.* Thiol. [<G <Med. L *mer(curium) captan(s)* seizing mercury]

mer·cap·tide (mər·kap'tīd) *n.* The metal salt of a mercaptan or thiol, obtained by replacing the sulfur hydrogen constituent with a metal.

mer·cap·to (mər·kap'tō) *n.* Sulfhydryl. [See MERCAPTAN]

Mer·ca·tor (mər·kā'tər, *Flemish* mer·kà'tôr), **Gerhard,** 1512–94, Flemish geographer and cartographer.

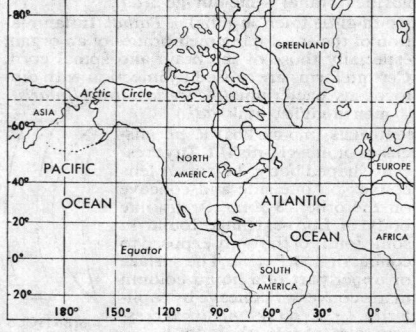

MERCATOR'S PROJECTION

Mercator's projection A system of making maps in which the meridians are represented by parallel straight lines, and the parallels

---

of latitude by lines perpendicular to the meridians, and at increasing intervals, so as to preserve the actual ratio between the increments of longitude and latitude at every point. It is accurate at the equator, but areas become increasingly distorted toward the poles.

Mer·ced River (mər·sed') A river in central California, flowing 150 miles SW to the San Joaquin.

mer·ce·nar·y (mûr'sə·ner'ē) *adj.* **1** Influenced by desire for gain or reward; greedy; venal. **2** Serving for pay or profit; hired: *mercenary* soldiers. **3** Pertaining to or resulting from sordidness. See synonyms under VENAL¹. — *n. pl.* **·nar·ies** A person working or serving only or chiefly for pay; a hired soldier in foreign service. See synonyms under AUXILIARY. [<L *mercenarius* <*merces* reward, hire] — **mer'ce·nar'i·ly** *adv.* — **mer'ce·nar'i·ness** *n.*

mer·cer (mûr'sər) *n. Brit.* **1** Formerly, a dealer in small wares. **2** A dealer in cloth or silks. [<F *mercier* <L *merx, mercis* wares]

mer·cer·ize (mûr'sə·rīz) *v.t.* **·ized, ·iz·ing** To treat (cotton fabrics) with caustic soda or potash, so as to increase their color-absorbing qualities and impart a silky gloss. [after John *Mercer,* 1791–1866, English inventor] — **mer·cer·i·za·tion** (mûr'sər·ə·zā'shən, -ī·zā'shən) *n.*

mer·cer·y (mûr'sər·ē) *n. pl.* **·cer·ies** *Brit.* A mercer's wares or place of business. [<OF *mercerie*]

mer·chan·dise (mûr'chən·dīz, -dīs) *n.* **1** Anything movable customarily bought and sold for profit. **2** *Obs.* Mercantile dealings; commerce; trade: hence, gain or advantage. — *v.t. & v.i.* **·dised, ·dis·ing** To barter; trade; buy and sell. **2** To promote the sale of (an article) through advertising, etc. Also **mer'chan·dize.** [<F *marchandise.* See MERCHANT.] — **mer'chan·dis'er** *n.*

mer·chant (mûr'chənt) *n.* **1** A person who buys and sells commodities as a business or for profit; a trader. **2** A shopkeeper; storekeeper. — *adj.* Of or pertaining to merchants or merchandise; commercial. [<OF *marchant* <L *mercari* traffic, buy <*merx, mercis* wares]

mer·chant·a·ble (mûr'chən·tə·bəl) *adj.* That can be bought or sold.

merchant iron Wrought iron converted into marketable bars or rods of various sizes and shapes: often used for making hooks, chains, and rivets, and in reinforcing concrete.

mer·chant·man (mûr'chənt·mən) *n. pl.* **·men** (-mən) **1** A trading or merchant vessel. **2** *Archaic* A merchant.

merchant marine **1** All the vessels of a nation, collectively, both publicly and privately owned, engaged in commerce and trade. **2** The officers and men employed on these vessels.

mer·ci (mer·sē') *interj. French* Thank you.

Mer·ci·a (mûr'shē·ə, -shə) An ancient Anglo-Saxon kingdom of central England, later annexed to Wessex.

Mer·ci·an (mûr'shē·ən, -shən) *adj.* Of or pertaining to Mercia, its people, or their dialect. — *n.* **1** An inhabitant of Mercia. **2** The dialect of Old English spoken in Mercia: the forerunner of the Midland dialects.

mer·ci beau·coup (mer·sē' bō·kōō') *French* Thank (you) very much.

Mer·cier (mer·syā'), **Désiré Joseph,** 1851–1926, Belgian cardinal.

mer·ci·ful (mûr'sə·fəl) *adj.* **1** Full of mercy; compassionate. **2** Characterized by or indicating mercy. — **mer'ci·ful·ly** *adv.* — **mer'ci·ful·ness** *n.*

Synonyms: benignant, clement, compassionate, forgiving, gentle, gracious, humane, pitiful, pitying, tender, tender-hearted. The *merciful* man is disposed to withhold or mitigate the suffering even of the guilty; the *compassionate* man sympathizes with and desires to relieve actual suffering, while one who is *humane* would forestall and prevent the suffering which he sees to be possible. See CHARITABLE, GOOD, HUMANE, PROPITIOUS.

mer·ci·less (mûr'sə·lis) *adj.* Having or showing no mercy. See synonyms under BARBAROUS, IMPLACABLE. — **mer'ci·less·ly** *adv.* — **mer'ci·less·ness** *n.*

mer·cu·ri·al (mər·kyŏŏr'ē·əl) *adj.* **1** Pertaining to the god Mercury; hence, lively; volatile. **2** Of or relating to quicksilver. — *n.* A preparation containing mercury. [<L *mercurialis*

<Mercurius Mercury] — **mer·cu′ri·al·ly** adv. — **mer·cu′ri·al·ness** n.

mer·cu·ri·al·ism (mər·kyŏŏr′ē·əl·iz′əm) n. Pathol. The condition produced by excessive use of medicines containing mercury; mercury poisoning.

mer·cu·ri·al·ize (mər·kyŏŏr′ē·əl·īz′) v.t. ·ized, ·iz·ing 1 To make mercurial. 2 To treat with mercury. — **mer·cu′ri·al·i·za′tion** n.

mer·cu·ric (mər·kyŏŏr′ik) adj. Chem. Of, pertaining to, or containing mercury in its highest valence.

mercuric chloride Corrosive sublimate. Also **mercury chloride.**

mercuric oxide Chem. A compound, HgO, obtained from mercuric nitrate by heat, forming both red and yellow powders which, with lard, are used in making ointments for certain skin diseases.

mercuric sulfide Chem. A compound, HgS, found native as cinnabar, or artificially produced as a black or a vermilion powder by the action of hydrogen sulfide on mercury salts.

Mer·cu·ro·chrome (mər·kyŏŏr′ə·krōm) n. Proprietary name of an iridescent, green, crystalline mercury compound, C$_{20}$H$_8$Br$_2$Na$_2$·Hg, turning red in an aqueous solution, which is used as a germicide and as a moderately active local antiseptic. [<MERCURY + -CHROME]

mer·cu·rous (mər·kyŏŏr′əs) adj. Chem. Of, pertaining to, or containing mercury in its lowest valence: mercurous chloride, mercurous oxide, etc.

mer·cu·ry (mûr′kyə·rē) n. pl. ·ries 1 A heavy, silver-white metallic element (symbol Hg), liquid at ordinary temperatures; quicksilver. See ELEMENT. 2 The quicksilver in a thermometer or barometer, as indicating temperature, etc. 3 A messenger. 4 An Old World plant (genus Mercurialis), especially M. annua, the annual or French mercury, used in medicine, and M. perennis, the perennial (or dog's) mercury, which is poisonous.

Mer·cu·ry (mûr′kyə·rē) 1 In Roman mythology, the herald and messenger of the gods, god of commerce, eloquence, and skill, and patron of messengers, travelers, merchants, and thieves: identified with the Greek Hermes. 2 Astron. The planet of the solar system nearest the sun, from which its mean distance is about 36,000,000 miles. It is the smallest of the major planets, having a diameter of about 3,000 miles, and revolving about the sun in 88 of our days.

mer·cu·ry-va·por lamp (mûr′kyə·rē·vā′pər) A glass tube or bulb containing mercury vapor made luminous by the passage of an electric discharge. Its light is a source of ultraviolet rays.

Mer·cu·ti·o (mər·kyŏŏ′shē·ō) In Shakespeare's Romeo and Juliet, a witty and brave young nobleman; friend of Romeo.

mer·cy (mûr′sē) n. pl. ·cies 1 The act of treating an offender with less severity than he deserves; also, forbearance to injure others when one has power to do so. 2 The act of relieving suffering, or the disposition to relieve it; compassion. 3 A providential blessing. [<OF <L merces, mercedis hire, payment, reward; with ref. to the heavenly reward for compassion]
Synonyms: benevolence, benignity, blessing, clemency, compassion, favor, forbearance, forgiveness, gentleness, grace, kindness, lenience, leniency, lenity, mildness, pardon, pity, tenderness. Mercy is the exercise of less severity than one deserves, or in a more extended sense, the granting of kindness or favor beyond what one may rightly claim. Clemency is a colder word than mercy signifying mildness and moderation in the use of power where severity would have legal sanction; it often denotes a habitual mildness of disposition on the part of the powerful, and is a matter rather of good nature or policy than of principle. Leniency or lenity denotes an easy-going avoidance of severity; these words are more general and less magisterial than clemency. Grace is favor, kindness, or blessing shown to the undeserving; forgiveness, mercy, and pardon are exercised toward the ill-deserving. Pardon remits the outward penalty which the

offender deserves; forgiveness dismisses resentment or displeasure from the heart of the one offended. Mercy is also used in the wider sense of refraining from harshness or cruelty toward those who are in one's power without fault of their own; as, They besought the robber to have mercy. See LENITY, PITY. Antonyms: cruelty, hardness, harshness, implacability, justice, penalty, punishment, revenge, rigor, severity, sternness, vengeance.

mercy killing Euthanasia.

mercy seat 1 In ancient Jewish ritual, the golden lid of the ark of the covenant whence God gave his oracles to the high priest, and upon which was sprinkled the blood of the yearly atonement. 2 Figuratively, the throne of God.

mere¹ (mir) adj. 1 Such as is mentioned and no more; nothing but. 2 Obs. Absolute; entire; unqualified. See synonyms under PURE. [<L merus unmixed, bare]

mere² (mir) n. 1 A pond; pool. 2 Scot. The sea. [OE mere]

mere³ (mir) n. Brit. A boundary line. [OE gemǣre]

-mere combining form Zool. A part or division: blastomere. [<Gk. meros part]

Mer·e·dith (mer′ə·dith), George, 1828–1909, English novelist and poet. — Owen See LYTTON.

mere·ly (mir′lē) adv. 1 Without including anything else; only; solely. 2 Obs. Absolutely; wholly. See synonyms under BUT¹.

mer·e·tri·cious (mer′ə·trish′əs) adj. 1 Deceitfully or artificially attractive; vulgar; tawdry. 2 Pertaining to a harlot; wanton. [<L meretricius <meretrix, -icis prostitute <merere earn, gain] — **mer′e·tri′cious·ly** adv. — **mer′e·tri′cious·ness** n.

Me·rezh·kov·ski (mi′rish·kôf′skē), Dmitri, 1865–1941, Russian novelist and critic. Also **Me′rej·kow′ski.**

mer·gan·ser (mər·gan′sər) n. A fish-eating duck (subfamily Merginae), with toothlike processes along the upper edge of the bill, and the head usually crested, as the hooded merganser (Lophodytes cucullatus) of North America. [<NL <L mergus diver <mergere plunge + anser goose]

merge (mûrj) v.t. & v.i. merged, merg·ing To combine or be combined so as to lose separate identity; blend. See synonyms under UNITE. [<L mergere dip, immerse] — **mer′gence** n.

Mer·gen·tha·ler (mûr′gən·thä′lər, Ger. mer′gən·tä′lər), Ottmar, 1854–99, U.S. inventor of the Linotype, born in Germany.

merg·er (mûr′jər) n. 1 Law The extinguishment of a lesser estate, right, or liability in a greater one. 2 One who or that which merges. 3 A combination of a number of commercial interests or companies in one.

Mer·gui Archipelago (mər·gwē′) An island group in the Andaman Sea off the Tenasserim coast of Lower Burma, to which they belong.

Mé·ri·da (mā′rē·thä) A city in SE Mexico, capital of Yucatán state.

me·rid·i·an (mə·rid′ē·ən) n. 1 Obs. Noontime; midday. 2 The highest or culminating point of anything; the zenith: the meridian of life. 3 Astron. A great circle passing through the poles and zenith of the celestial sphere at any point; the celestial meridian. 4 Geog. a A great circle drawn from any point on the earth's surface and passing through both poles. b The half-circle so drawn between the poles, called a meridian of longitude, or geographic meridian. 5 A line on a surface of revolution in the same plane as its axis. — adj. 1 Of or pertaining to noonday: meridian heat. 2 Pertaining to or at the highest or culminating point; brightest: meridian fame. 3 Of or pertaining to a meridian. [<OF meridien <L meridianus <meridies noon, south <medidies <medius middle + dies day]

me·rid·i·o·nal (mə·rid′ē·ə·nəl) adj. 1 Of or pertaining to the meridian. 2 Relating to southern climates or people: meridional customs. 3 Approximating a direction north and south. 4 Situated or lying in the south; southerly. — n. An inhabitant of a southern country; specifically, a resident of southern France. [<OF <LL meridionalis southern] — **me·rid′i·o·nal′i·ty** n. — **me·rid′i·o·nal·ly** adv.

Mé·ri·mée (mā·rē·mā′), Prosper, 1803–70, French novelist and historian.

me·ringue (mə·rang′) n. The beaten white of eggs sweetened, baked, and used to garnish pastry; also, pastry so garnished. [<F <G meringe, lit., cake of Mehringen (in Germany)]

me·ri·no (mə·rē′nō) n. pl. ·nos 1 A superior breed of sheep, originating in Spain, and having very fine, closely set, silky wool. See SHEEP. Also **Merino sheep.** 2 The wool of this sheep. 3 A fabric made of merino wool. 4 A kind of knitted goods used for underwear. — adj. 1 Pertaining to merino sheep or their wool. 2 Made of merino wool. [<Sp.]

Mer·i·on·eth·shire (mer′ē·on′ith·shir) A county of NW Wales; 660 square miles; county town, Dolgelley. Also **Mer′i·on′eth.**

mer·i·stem (mer′ə·stem) n. Bot. Plant tissue in process of formation; vegetable cells in a state of active division and growth, as those at the apex of growing stems and roots. [<Gk. meristos divided <merizein divide <meros part] — **mer′i·ste·mat′ic** (-stə·mat′ik) adj.

me·ris·tic (mə·ris′tik) adj. Divided into parts; segmented. [<Gk. meristos]

mer·it (mer′it) n. 1 Often pl. The quality or fact of deserving, especially of deserving well; desert: Does his merit justify the reward? 2 Worth or excellence; quality: A man of merit. 3 That which deserves esteem, praise, or reward; a commendable act or quality: the merit of silence. 4 pl. The actual rights or wrongs of a matter considered exclusively of extraneous details or technicalities: to decide a case on its merits. 5 Reward, recompense, or, sometimes, punishment received or deserved; a token or award of excellence. See synonyms under WORTH. — v.t. To earn as a reward or punishment; deserve. [<OF merite <L meritum <meritus, pp. of merere deserve] — **mer′it·ed** adj. — **mer′it·ed·ly** adv.

mer·i·toc·ra·cy (mer′ə·tok′rə·sē) n. pl. ·ra·cies 1 A system or society in which talent, intellectual achievements, and excellence of performance are considered worthier of reward than race, sex, social status, or wealth. 2 The leaders produced by such a system or society. — **mer·i·to·crat** (mer′ə·tə·krat′) n. — **mer·i·to·crat·ic** (mer′ə·tə·krat′ik) adj.

mer·i·to·ri·ous (mer′ə·tôr′ē·əs, -tō′rē-) adj. Deserving of reward; praiseworthy. — **mer′i·to′ri·ous·ly** adv. — **mer′i·to′ri·ous·ness** n.

merit system A system adopted in the U.S. Civil Service whereby appointments and promotions are made on the basis of the merit and fitness of the appointee, ascertained through qualifying examinations.

merle (mûrl) n. The European blackbird (Turdus merula). Also **merl.** [<F <L merula blackbird]

mer·lin (mûr′lin) n. A small European falcon (Falco columbarius aesalon); also, a related American species, the pigeon hawk (F. columbarius). [<OF esmerillon, dim. of esmeril]

Mer·lin (mûr′lin) In the Arthurian cycle and other medieval legends, a magician and prophet who built the Round Table for King Arthur. [<Med. L Merlinus <Welsh Myrrdin, lit., sea fortress]

mer·lon (mûr′lən) n. Mil. The solid part of a battlement, between the embrasures. See illustration under BATTLEMENT. [<F <Ital. merlone, aug. of merlo battlement]

mer·maid (mûr′mād′) n. A legendary marine creature having as its upper part the head and body of a lovely woman and as its lower part the scaled body and tail of a fish. Also **mer′maid′en.** [<MERE² + MAID]

mer·man (mûr′man′) n. pl. ·men (-men′) A legendary marine creature, having as its upper part the head and body of a man and as its lower part the scaled body and tail of a fish. [<MERE² + MAN]

mero- combining form Part; partial; incomplete: meroplankton. Also, before vowels, **mer-.** [<Gk. meros a part, division]

mer·o·blast (mer′ə·blast) n. A meroblastic ovum. [<MERO- + Gk. blastos sprout]

mer·o·blas·tic (mer′ə·blas′tik) adj. Biol. Undergoing partial or incomplete segmentation, with formation of food yolk, as in the eggs of birds: opposed to holoblastic. — **mer′o·blas′ti·cal·ly** adv.

Mer·o·ë (mer'ō-ē) The ancient capital of Ethiopia on the Nile in northern Sudan; an archeological site of extensive ruins and groups of pyramids partly excavated.

mer·o·gen·e·sis (mer'ə-jen'ə-sis) n. Biol. Segmentation; reproduction by the formation of parts. [<MERO- + GENESIS] — **mer'o·ge·net'ic** (-jə-net'ik) adj.

Me·rom (mē'rəm), **Waters of** See LAKE HULA.

Mer·o·pe (mer'ə-pē) In Greek mythology, one of the Pleiades, not seen by the naked eye with the other six among the stars, supposedly having hidden herself from shame for loving a mortal: called the lost Pleiad.

mer·o·plank·ton (mer'ə-plangk'tən) n. Biol. Plankton found only at certain times or in certain seasons of the year.

-merous suffix Zool. Having (a specified number or kind of) parts: trimerous, pentamerous (often written 3-merous, 5-merous, etc.). [<Gk. meros a part, division]

Mer·o·vin·gi·an (mer'ə-vin'jē-ən, -jən) adj. Designating or pertaining to the first royal Frankish dynasty, founded by Clovis I in 486, and lasting until 751. — n. A member of the Merovingian dynasty. Also **Mer'o·win'gi·an**. [<L Merovingi, descendants of Merovaeus, a legendary Frankish king]

mer·o·zo·ite (mer'ə-zō'īt) n. Zool. One of the mature spores liberated in the sporulating stage of certain protozoa, as the parasite causing malaria (Plasmodium). [<MERO- + (SPORO)-ZO(A) + -ITE¹]

Mer·ri·am (mer'ē·əm), **John Campbell**, 1869-1945, U. S. paleontologist.

Mer·ri·mack (mer'ə-mak) n. The U. S. first armored warship, a Confederate vessel; fought the Monitor at Hampton Roads, 1862: Confederate name Virginia.

THE MERRIMACK: 4,636 TONS; DRAFT 23 FEET
Originally the U.S.S. Merrimack, later renamed C.S.S. Virginia.

Mer·ri·mac River (mer'ə-mak) A river in New Hampshire and Massachusetts, flowing 110 miles to the Atlantic. Also **Mer'ri·mack**.

mer·ri·ment (mer'i-mənt) n. The act of making merry; mirth; celebration. See synonyms under ENTERTAINMENT, HAPPINESS, LAUGHTER, SPORT.

mer·ry (mer'ē) adj. ·ri·er, ·ri·est 1 Inclined to mirth and laughter; full of fun; lively. 2 Of or pertaining to mirth or scenes of mirth; jovial and sportive; mirthful. 3 Inciting to mirth, cheerfulness, and gay spirits; fitted or calculated to enliven; exhilarating; bracing. 4 Colloq. Slightly tipsy; high. 5 Obs. Jibing; sarcastic. [OE myrige pleasant] — **mer'ri·ly** adv. — **mer'ri·ness** n.

Synonyms: blithe, blithesome, facetious, frolicsome, gay, glad, gladsome, gleeful, hilarious, jocose, jocund, jolly, jovial, joyous, lighthearted, lively, mirthful, sportive. See CHEERFUL, HAPPY, JOCOSE, VIVACIOUS, WANTON. Antonyms: see synonyms for SAD.

mer·ry–an·drew (mer'ē-an'drōō) n. A clown or buffoon.

Mer·ry del Val (mer'rē thel väl'), **Alfonso Marquis de**, 1864-1943, Spanish diplomat born in London. — **Rafael**, 1865-1930, cardinal; papal secretary of state 1903-1914: born in London.

mer·ry–go–round (mer'ē-gō-round') n. 1 A revolving platform fitted with wooden horses, boatlike vehicles, etc., on which people ride for amusement, usually to music; a carousel. 2 A whirl, as of pleasure.

mer·ry·mak·ing (mer'ē-mā'king) adj. Frolicking. — n. Festivity; frolic. See synonyms under FROLIC, REVEL, SPORT. — **mer'ry·mak'er** n.

mer·ry·thought (mer'ē-thôt') n. Brit. The wishbone of a fowl's breast.

Mer·sa Ma·trûh (mər·sa' mə·trōō') See MATRÛH.

Mer·sey (mûr'zē) A river between Cheshire and Lancashire, NW England, flowing 70 miles NW to the Irish Sea: its estuary is 16 miles long and forms Liverpool harbor.

Mer·sin (mər·sēn') See IÇEL.

Mer·thyr Tyd·fil (mûr'thər tid'vil) A county borough in NE Glamorganshire, Wales.

Mer·zi·fon (mer'zē-fôn') A town in north central Turkey in Asia: also Marsivan. Also **Mer'si·van'** (-vän').

mes– Var. of MESO-.

me·sa (mā'sə, Sp. mā'sä) n. A high, broad, and flat tableland with sharp, usually rocky, slopes descending to the surrounding plain, common in the SW United States. [<Sp. <L mensa table]

Me·sa·bi Range (mə·sä'bē) A long, narrow range of iron-ore-producing hills in NE Minnesota.

mé·sal·li·ance (mā·zal'ē·əns, Fr. mā·zà·lyäns') n. A marriage with one of inferior position; misalliance. [<F]

Mesa Verde National Park (mā'sə vûrd') An area in SW Colorado containing ruins of prehistoric cliff-dwellings; 80 square miles; established as a national park in 1906.

mes·cal (mes·kal') n. 1 A spineless cactus (Lophophora williamsii), native to the SW United States and northern Mexico. Its tops, which are often called mescal buttons, grow but little above the ground, contain a narcotic stimulating substance, and are chewed by the Indians, especially during the performance of religious ceremonies. 2 A mescal maguey. 3 An intoxicating liquor distilled from pulque. [<Sp. mezcal <Nahuatl mexcalli]

mes·ca·line (mes'kə-lēn, -lin) n. Chem. A white, crystalline alkaloid, $C_{11}H_{17}O_3N$, extracted from mescal buttons. It has narcotic and tetanic properties, and induces powerful color hallucinations: also spelled mezcaline. [<MESCAL]

mescal maguey Any plant from which the liquor mescal is obtained, especially the pulque agave (Agave atrovirens).

mes·dames (mā·däm', Fr. mā·dàm') Plural of MADAME.

mes·de·moi·selles (mād·mwà·zel') French Plural of MADEMOISELLE.

me·seems (mē·sēmz') v., impersonal Archaic It seems to me.

mes·en·ceph·a·lon (mes'en-sef'ə-lon) n. Anat. The central division of the brain; the midbrain. [<NL <MES- + ENCEPHALON] — **mes·en·ce·phal·ic** (mes·en'sə-fal'ik) adj.

mes·en·chyme (mes'eng-kim) n. Biol. The portion of the mesoderm that produces the connective tissues of the body, the blood vessels, lymphatic system, and heart. It is cellular in structure, and in some of the lower forms of life is the same as mesoblast. Also **mes·en·chy·ma** (mes·eng'kə-mə). [<NL mesenchyma <MES- + Gk. en- in + chein pour] — **mes·en'chy·mal**, **mes'en·chym'a·tous** (-kim'ə-təs) adj.

mes·en·ter·i·tis (mes·en'tə-rī'tis) n. Pathol. Inflammation of the mesentery. [<MESENTER(ON) + -ITIS]

mes·en·ter·on (mes·en'tər-on) n. pl. ·ter·a (-tər·ə) Biol. 1 The middle portion of the primitive intestinal cavity, lined with endoderm: distinguished from the buccal and anal parts, which are lined with ectoderm. 2 The midgut. [<MES- + ENTERON] — **mes·en'ter·on'ic** (-tə·ron'ik) adj.

mes·en·ter·y (mes'ən-ter'ē) n. pl. ·ter·ies Anat. A fold of the peritoneum that invests an intestine and connects it with the abdominal wall; especially, the fold investing the small intestine. Also **mes'en·te'ri·um** (-tir'ē·əm). [<Med.L mesenterium <Gk. mesenterion < mesos middle + enteron intestine] — **mes'en·ter'ic** adj.

Me·se·ta (mā·sā'tä) The entire interior of Spain, covering almost three fourths of the country and comprising an immense plateau with Madrid at its center.

mesh (mesh) n. 1 One of the open spaces between the cords of a net or the wires of a sieve: often expressed numerically in terms of a unit area: a 100-mesh screen. 2 pl. Such cords or wires collectively. 3 Anything that entangles or involves. 4 Mech. The engagement of gear teeth. — v.t. & v.i. 1 To make or become entangled, as in a net. 2 To make or become engaged, as gear teeth. [Cf. OE max a net and MDu. maesche a mesh] — **mesh'y** adj.

Me·shach (mē'shak) Babylonian captive. Dan. iii. See SHADRACH.

Me·shed (me·shed') A walled city and Moslem shrine in NE Iran: also Mashhad. Also **Meshhed** (mesh·hed').

mesh·work (mesh'wûrk') n. A combination of meshes; network.

me·si·al (mē'zē-əl, mes'ē·əl) adj. Situated in or directed toward the middle: the mesial plane of the body. Also **me'si·an**. [<Gk. mesos middle] — **me'si·al·ly** adv.

mes·ic¹ (mes'ik, mē'zik) adj. Bot. Pertaining to or characterized by a medium moisture supply, as in certain plants. [<Gk. mesos middle]

mes·ic² (mes'ik, mē'sik) adj. Physics Of, pertaining to, characteristic of, or produced by mesons. [<MESON²]

me·sit·y·lene (mə·sit'ə-lēn, -lin) n. Chem. A colorless, liquid hydrocarbon, C_9H_{12}, made by heating acetone with concentrated sulfuric acid. [<mesityl a hypothetical organic radical (<Gk. mesitēs mediator + -YL) + -ENE]

mes·i·tyl oxide (mes'i-təl) Chem. A colorless hydrocarbon, $C_6H_{10}O$, used as a solvent for nitrocellulose and certain gums and resins. [See MESITYLENE]

mes·mer·ism (mes'mə-riz'əm, mez'-) n. 1 The theory, as exemplified by Franz Anton Mesmer, 1733-1815, that one person can produce in another an abnormal condition resembling sleep, during which the mind of the subject is passively responsive to the will of the operator: now identified with hypnotism. Compare ANIMAL MAGNETISM. 2 Personal magnetism. — **mes·mer·ic** (mes·mer'ik, mez-), **mes·mer'i·cal** adj. — **mes·mer'i·cal·ly** adv. — **mes'mer·ist** n.

mes·mer·ize (mes'mə-rīz, mez'-) v.t. ·ized, ·iz·ing To hypnotize. Also Brit. **mes'mer·ise**. — **mes'mer·i·za'tion** n. **mes'mer·iz'er** n.

mesn·al·ty (mē'nəl-tē) n. The estate of a mesne lord. Also **mesn·al·i·ty** (mē·nal'ə-tē). [<MF mesnalte]

mesne (mēn) adj. Law Being between two periods or extremes; intermediate; intervening. [<MF, alter. of AF meen <L medianus mean. Doublet of MEAN³, MEDIAN, MIZZEN.]

mesne lord One holding lands as an intermediate between a superior lord and a subordinate tenant.

meso– combining form 1 Situated in the middle: mesocarp. 2 Intermediate in size or degree: mesognathous. Also, before vowels, mes–. [<Gk. mesos middle]

mes·o·blast (mes'ə-blast, mē'sə-) n. Biol. The middle germinal layer of the embryo. See MESENCHYME. [<MESO- + Gk. blastos sprout] — **mes'o·blas'tic** adj.

mes·o·carp (mes'ə-kärp, mē'sə-) n. Bot. The middle layer of a pericarp.

mes·o·ce·phal·ic (mes'ō-sə-fal'ik, mē'sō-) adj. Anat. 1 Intermediate in head form; having a cephalic index of from 76.0 to 80.9. 2 Having a medium cranial capacity. 3 Of or pertaining to the mesocephalon. Also **mes'o·ceph'a·lous** (-sef'ə-ləs). — **mes'o·ceph'a·ly** n.

mes·o·ceph·a·lon (mes'ə-sef'ə-lon, mē'sə-) n. The pons Varolii.

mes·o·crat·ic (mes'ə-krat'ik, mē'sə-) adj. Geol. Having the dark constituents slightly in excess of the light ones: said of certain igneous rocks.

mes·o·derm (mes'ə-dûrm, mē'sə-) n. 1 Biol. The middle germ layer of the embryo, from which are developed the muscular, vascular, and osseous systems. 2 Bot. The middle layer of the wall of a moss and capsule. — **mes'o·der'mal**, **mes'o·der'mic** adj.

mes·o·gas·tri·um (mes'ə-gas'trē·əm, mē'sə-) n. Biol. One of the two mesenteries in the stomach of an embryo; also, the region of the umbilicus. [<MESO- + Gk. gastēr belly] — **mes'o·gas'tric** adj.

me·sog·na·thous (mə·sog'nə·thəs) adj. Having moderately projecting jaws; also, having a facial profile angle of 98° to 103°. Also **mes·og·nath·ic** (mes'əg-nath'ik). [<MESO- + -GNATHOUS] — **me·sog'na·thism**, **me·sog'na·thy** n.

mes·o·kur·to·sis (mes'ō-kər-tō'sis, mē'sō-) n. Stat. The symmetrical kurtosis characterizing the region near the mode of a normal probability curve. — **mes'o·kur'tic** (-kûr'tik) adj.

Mes·o·lith·ic (mes'ə-lith'ik, mē'sə-) adj. Anthropol. Pertaining to or describing that period of human culture immediately following the Magdalenian stage of the Paleolithic, characterized by small, delicately worked microliths and an economy transitional between food gathering and a settled agriculture. Also called Epipaleolithic, Miolithic. [<MESO- + LITH(O)- + -IC]

me·sol·o·gy (mə·sol'ə-jē) n. The study of the environment in its relations to organisms;

ecology. [<MESO- + -LOGY] **—mes′o·log′ic, mes′o·log′i·cal** (mes′ə·loj′i·kəl) *adj.*

Mes·o·lon·ghi (mes′ō·lông′gē) See MISSOLONGHI.

mes·o·mor·phic (mes′ə·môr′fik, mē′sə-) *adj.* **1** *Physics* Of or pertaining to a state of matter intermediate between the true liquid and the crystal; liquo–crystalline: also **mes′o·mor′·phous. 2** Designating a physical type developed predominantly from the mesodermal layer of the embryo; the muscular or athletic type. Compare ECTOMORPHIC, ENDOMORPHIC.

mes·on[1] (mes′on, mē′son) *n.* **1** The plane that divides the body longitudinally into two halves; the median or mesial plane. **2** *Music* Loosely, a tetrachord. [<NL <Gk. *mesos* middle]

mes·on[2] (mes′on, mē′son) *n. Physics* Any of a group of short–lived, unstable atomic particles having a mass intermediate between that of the electron and the proton. They are believed to be a product of cosmic–ray disintegration and may be electrically neutral or carry either a positive or negative charge. The principal types are the mu–meson and pi–meson. [< Gk. *mesos* middle]

mes·o·neph·ros (mes′ə·nef′rəs, mē′sə-) *n. Biol.* The middle of three tubular organs found in connection with the primitive genitourinary apparatus, and formed later than the pronephros; the mid–kidney or Wolffian body. It is the permanent kidney in some animals, as amphibians. [<NL <MESO-+ Gk. *nephros* kidney] **—mes′o·neph′ric** *adj.*

mes·o·pause (mez′ō·pôz) *n.* A transition zone between the mesosphere and the ionosphere, beginning at a height of about 50 miles.

mes·o·phyll (mes′ə·fil, mē′sə-) *n. Bot.* The soft, inner, parenchymatous tissue of a leaf; the cellular portion lying between the upper and lower epidermis. Also **mes′o·phyl, mes′o·phyl′·lum.** [<MESO- + Gk. *phyllon* leaf]

mes·o·phyte (mes′ə·fīt, mē′sə-) *n. Bot.* A plant requiring medium conditions of moisture and dryness, intermediate between a hydrophyte and a xerophyte. **—mes′o·phyt′ic** (-fit′ik) *adj.*

mes·o·plast (mes′ə·plast, mē′sə-) *n. Biol.* A cell nucleus. [<MESO- + Gk. *plastos* formed] **—mes′o·plas′tic** *adj.*

Mes·o·po·ta·mi·a (mes′ə·pə·tā′mē·ə) An ancient country of Asia comprising the region about the lower Tigris and the lower Euphrates, included in modern Iraq. [<Gk. <*mesos* middle +*potamos* river] **—Mes′o·po·ta′mi·an** *n. & adj.*

mes·or·rhine (mes′ə·rīn, -rin, mē′sə-) *adj.* Having a relatively broad, high–bridged nose. [< MESO- +Gk. *rhis, rhinos* nose]

mes·o·sere (mes′ə·sir, mē′sə-) *n. Bot.* The flora and major plant development of the Mesozoic era. [<MESO- +L *serere* sow, plant]

mes·o·sphere (mes′ō·sfir) *n.* A layer of the atmosphere lying between the stratopause and mesopause.

mes·o·the·li·um (mes′ə·thē′lē·əm, mē′sə-) *n. Biol.* **1** The portion of the mesoderm and the tissues derived from it that in vertebrates forms two principal layers, visceral and parietal, and produces the epithelium of the peritoneum and pleurae, the striated muscles, etc. **2** Epithelium when mesoblastic in origin. [< NL <MESO-+ (EPI)THELIUM] **—mes′o·the′·li·al** *adj.*

mes·o·ther·mal (mes′ə·thûr′məl, mē′sə-) *adj.* Possessing or pertaining to medium warmth. Also **mes′o·ther′mic.**

mes·o·tho·rax (mes′ə·thôr′aks, -thō′raks, mē′ sə-) *n. Entomol.* The middle one of the three segments of the thorax in insects, bearing the anterior wings and the middle legs. **—mes′o·tho·rac′ic** (-thô·ras′ik, -thō·ras′ik) *adj.*

mes·o·tho·ri·um (mes′ə·thôr′ē·əm, -thō′rē-, mē′sə-) *n. Physics* Either of two isotopes resulting from the radioactive disintegration of thorium, intermediate between thorium and radiothorium.

mes·o·tron (mes′ə·tron, mē′sə-) *n. Physics* Meson. [<MESO- + (ELEC)TRON]

Mes·o·zo·ic (mes′ə·zō′ik, mē′sə-) *n. Geol.* The era between the Paleozoic and the Cenozoic, including the Triassic, Jurassic, and Cretaceous periods: characterized by the dominance of the reptiles, the rise of flowering plants, and the beginnings of archaic mammals. — *adj.* Of or pertaining to this era. [<MESO- + -ZOIC]

mes·quite (mes·kēt′, mes′kēt) *n.* Either of two spiny, deep-rooted shrubs or small trees of the pea family, found in the southwestern United States, and extending southward to Peru. The **honey mesquite** *(Prosopis glandulosa* or *juliflora)* yields sweet algarroba pods used for cattle fodder; the **screw-pod mesquite** *(Strombocarpa odorata),* or screwbean, has edible spiral pods. Also spelled *mezquite, muskit.* Also **mes·quit′.** [< Sp. *mezquite* <Nahuatl *mizquitl*]

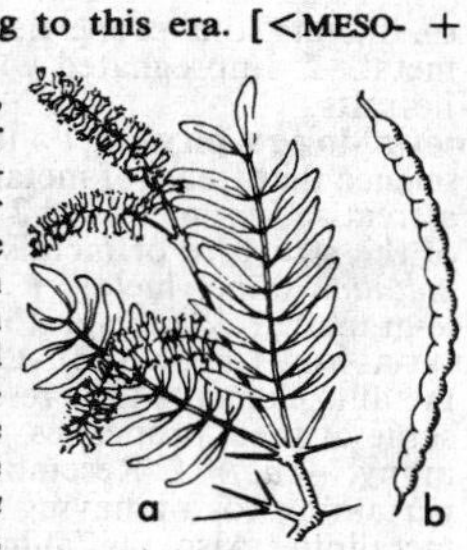

MESQUITE
a. Flower.
b. Fruit (edible).

mess (mes) *n.* **1** A quantity of food sufficient for one meal or for a particular occasion: a *mess* of beans; also, a portion of soft, partly liquid food, as pottage. **2** A number of persons who habitually take their meals together, as on board ship or in military units; also, a meal taken by them. **3** The sum or total of a haul of fish. **4** A state of disorder; especially, a condition of unclean confusion. **5** A confusing and embarrassing situation. **6** An unpleasant or unclean concoction; confused jumble. *—v.i.* **1** To busy oneself; dabble: often with *around* or *about.* **2** To make a mess; bungle: often with *up.* **3** To interfere; meddle: often with *around.* **4** To eat with a mess (def. 2). *—v.t.* **5** To make a mess of; muddle; botch: often with *up.* **6** To make dirty; be foul: often with *up.* **7** To provide meals for. [<OF *mes* <L *missus* course at a meal, orig. pp. of *mittere* send] **—mess′y** *adj.* **—mess′i·ly** *adv.* **—mess′i·ness** *n.*

mes·sage (mes′ij) *n.* **1** A communication, as of information, sent in any way. **2** A formal communication from a chief executive to a legislative body, not delivered in person: a *message* from the president to Congress. **3** An errand; the carrying out of a mission; a messenger's business. **4** An utterance divinely inspired; hence, any important communication embodying a truth, principle, or advice. **5** A television or radio commercial. [<OF < Med. L *missaticum* <*missus,* pp. of *mittere*]

message center *Mil.* An agency attached to a headquarters or command post, and charged with the receipt, transmission, and delivery of messages.

Mes·sa·li·na (mes′ə·lī′nə), **Valeria,** executed A.D. 48, third wife of Emperor Claudius; notorious for profligacy.

mes·sa·line (mes′ə·lēn′, mes′ə·lēn) *n.* A lightweight, lustrous, twilled silk fabric.

Mes·sa·pi·an (mə·sā′pē·ən) *n.* **1** A member of an ancient people inhabiting SE Italy. **2** The Indo–European language of the Messapians, possibly related to ancient Illyrian. *—adj.* Of or pertaining to the Messapians or their language.

Mes·se·ne (me·sē′nē) A town in SW Peloponnesus, Greece, capital of ancient Messenia. Also **Mes·si′ni.**

mes·sen·ger (mes′ən·jər) *n.* **1** One sent with a message or on an errand; one employed to carry messages; specifically, a bearer of official dispatches. **2** A forerunner; herald. [ME *messanger, messanger* <OF *messagier* <*message* MESSAGE: the *n* is non–historic]

Mes·se·ni·a (me·sē′nē·ə) A region of SW Peloponnesus, Greece, on the Ionian Sea, comprising an ancient country. Also **Mes·si′·ni·a.**

Mes·ser·schmitt (mes′ər·shmit), **Wilhelm,** 1898–1978, German aircraft designer.

mess hall A building or room where meals are regularly eaten, as by a military group.

Mes·si·ah (mə·sī′ə) *n.* **1** The Anointed One; the Christ: the name for the promised deliverer of the Hebrews, assumed by Jesus, and given to him by Christians: with *the.* **2** Loosely, a looked–for liberator of a country or people. Also **Mes·si′as.** [<LL *Messias* <Gk. <Aramaic *mĕshīhā,* Hebrew *māshīah* anointed] **—Mes·si′ah·ship** *n.* **—Mes·si·an·ic** (mes′ē·an′ik) *adj.*

Mes·si·dor (me·sē·dôr′) See under CALENDAR (Republican).

mes·sieurs (mes′ərz, *Fr.* mā·syœ′) *n. pl.* of *Fr.* **mon·sieur** (mə·syœ′) Sirs; gentlemen: in English in the contracted form *Messrs.,* used as plural of *Mr.*

mes·sin (mes′in) *n. Scot.* A lap dog; hence, an insignificant person. Also **mes′san.**

Mes·si·na (mə·sē′nə, *Ital.* mās·sē′nä) A port in NE Sicily on the **Strait of Messina,** the channel between Italy and Sicily, two miles wide at its narrowest point.

Mes·sines (me·sēn′) A village in western Belgium, scene of two battles in World War I, 1914 and 1917.

mess jacket A man's short, tailored jacket, usually white and terminating exactly at the waistline: worn on semiformal occasions.

mess kit A small, compactly arranged unit containing cooking and eating utensils: used by soldiers and campers.

mess·mate (mes′māt′) *n.* An associate at a mess, especially onboard ship.

mes·suage (mes′wij) *n. Law* A dwelling house with its belongings, outhouses, garden, etc. [< OF *mesuage,* prob. alter. of *mesnage.* See MÉNAGE.]

Mes·ta (mes′tä) A river in SW Bulgaria and NE Greece, flowing 150 miles SE to the Aegean. *Greek* **Nes·tos** (nes′tos).

mes·tee (mes·tē′) *n.* The offspring of a white person and a quadroon; an octoroon: also spelled *mustee.* [<Sp. *mestizo* mongrel, hybrid]

mes·ti·zo (mes·tē′zō) *n. pl.* **·zos** or **·zoes** Any one of mixed blood; in Mexico and the western United States, a person of Spanish and Indian blood. Also **mes·te′so, mes·ti′no** (-nō). [<Sp. <LL *mixticius* <L *mixtus,* pp. of *miscere* mix] **—mes·ti′za** (-zə) *n. fem.*

Meš·tro·vić (mesh′trô·vich), **Ivan,** 1883–1962, Yugoslav sculptor.

met (met) Past tense and past participle of MEET[1].

met– Var. of META–.

meta– *prefix* **1** Changed in place or form; reversed; altered: *metamorphosis.* **2** *Anat. & Zool.* Behind; after; on the farther side of; later: often equivalent to *post–* or *dorso–*: *metathorax, metaplasis.* **3** With; alongside: *metabiosis.* **4** Beyond; over; transcending: *metaphysics, metapsychology.* **5** *Chem.* **a** A modification, usually polymeric, of. **b** A derivative of: *metaprotein.* **c** A derivative of an acid anhydride, formed by withdrawal of one or more water molecules: distinguished from *ortho–*: *metaphosphoric* acid. **d** A benzene derivative in which the substituted atoms or radicals occupy the positions 1, 3: abbr. *m–.* Compare ORTHO–, PARA–. See BENZENE RING. Also, before vowels and *h, met–.* [<Gk. < *meta* after, beside, with]

met·a·bi·o·sis (met′ə·bī·ō′sis) *n. Biol.* The condition of dependence of one organism upon another. [<META- + Gk. *bios* life] **—met′a·bi·ot′ic** (-ot′ik) *adj.*

met·a·bol·ic (met′ə·bol′ik) *adj.* **1** Of, pertaining, to, or exhibiting metabolism: *metabolic* processes. **2** Pertaining to or undergoing change, transformation, or metamorphosis. Also **met′a·bol′i·cal.** [<Gk. *metabolikos*]

me·tab·o·lism (mə·tab′ə·liz′əm) *n. Biol.* The aggregate of all physical and chemical processes constantly taking place in living organisms, including those which use energy to build up assimilated materials (anabolism) and those which release energy by breaking them down (catabolism). Also **me·tab′o·ly** (-ə·lē). [<Gk. *metabolē* <*meta-* beyond + *ballein* throw]

me·tab·o·lite (mə·tab′ə·līt) *n.* A chemical product of metabolism.

me·tab·o·lize (mə·tab′ə·līz) *v.t. & v.i.* **·lized, ·liz·ing** To subject to or change by metabolism.

met·a·car·pal (met′ə·kär′pəl) *adj.* Of or pertaining to the metacarpus. *—n.* One of the bones of the metacarpus.

met·a·car·pus (met′ə·kär′pəs) *n. Anat.* The part of the fore– or thoracic limb between the carpus or wrist and the phalanges or bones of the finger. It consists in man of five bones. [< NL <Gk. *metakarpion* <*meta-* beyond + *karpos* wrist]

met·a·cen·ter (met′ə·sen′tər) *n. Physics* That point in a floating body slightly displaced from equilibrium through which the resultant upward pressure of the fluid always passes; the center of gravity of the unsubmerged portion of a floating body. Also **met′a·cen′tre.** — **met′a·cen′tric** *adj.*

met·a·chem·is·try (met′ə·kem′is·trē) *n.* The chemistry of elements and compounds which yield exceptionally large amounts of energy in relation to their mass. — **met′a·chem′i·cal** *adj.*

met·a·chro·ma·tism (met′ə·krō′mə·tiz′əm) *n.* An alteration in color; specifically, such alteration due to heating or cooling. — **met′a·chro·mat′ic** (-krō·mat′ik) *adj.*

Met·a·com·et (met′ə·kom′it) Indian name of American Indian chief, King Philip.

met·a·gal·ax·y (met′ə·gal′ək·sē) *n. pl.* **·ax·ies** *Astron.* The entire material universe, regarded especially as a system including all the galaxies.

met·age (mē′tij) *n.* **1** Measurement. **2** The price charged for measurement. **3** A general term for the tolls formerly exacted by the corporation of London over a part of the Thames above and below the city. [<METE[1]]

met·a·gen·e·sis (met′ə·jen′ə·sis) *n. Biol.* A type of reproduction in which a series of generations of unlike forms comes between the egg and the parent type; alternation of generations. — **met′a·ge·net′ic** (-jə·net′ik) *adj.*

me·tag·na·thous (mə·tag′nə·thəs) *adj. Ornithol.* Having the points of the mandibles crossing each other, as in the crossbill. [< META- + -GNATHOUS] — **me·tag′na·thism** *n.*

met·ag·nos·tic (met′ag·nos′tik) *adj.* Beyond the knowledge, whether of the sense or the understanding, of man as he is at present constituted; metaphysical. — *n.* A person holding a belief in the existence of a Supreme Being who transcends human knowledge. [<META- + Gk. *gnōstikos* knowing] — **met′ag·nos′ti·cism** *n.*

met·al (met′l) *n.* **1** An element that forms a base by combining with a hydroxyl group or groups. It is usually hard, heavy, lustrous, malleable, ductile, tenacious, and a good conductor of heat and electricity. **2** A composition of some metallic element; also, an alloy: generally with a qualifying word. **3** Cast iron while melted. **4** Broken stone for road surfaces or for railway ballast: also called **road metal.** **5** *Her.* Gold *(or)* or silver *(argent)* tincture. **6** Molten glass. **7** The weight of the projectiles that a warship's guns can throw at once. **8** *Printing* Type metal; also, composed type. **9** The constituent material of anything; essential quality. — **noble metal** A metal that does not readily oxidize in the open air, as gold, silver, and platinum. — **white metal** Any one of the various white alloys, such as pewter, used for making ornaments, small castings, etc; specifically, a soft, smooth, malleable, copper–zinc alloy of exceptional antifrictional properties used to form the bearing surface in the crankshaft and connecting–rod bearings in most internal–combustion engines. — *adj.* Consisting of or pertaining to metal. — *v.t.* **·aled** or **·alled**, **·al·ing** or **·al·ling** To furnish or cover with metal. ◆ Homophone: *mettle.* [<OF <L *metallum* mine <Gk. *metallon.* Doublet of MEDAL.]

met·a·lin·guis·tics (met′ə·ling·gwis′tiks) *n.* An area of linguistic study concerned with the interrelationship of the structure and meaning of the language of a society and other aspects of its culture, such as the social system.

met·al·ist (met′l·ist) *n.* **1** One who works with or has special knowledge of metals. **2** An advocate of metallic money as against a paper currency. Also **met′al·list.**

met·al·ize (met′l·īz) *v.t.* **·ized, ·iz·ing** To turn into or treat with metal. Also **met′al·lize,** *Brit.* **met′al·ise.**

me·tal·lic (mə·tal′ik) *adj.* **1** Being, containing, yielding, or having the characteristics of a metal: a *metallic* voice; *metallic* luster. **2** Pertaining to a metal. — **me·tal′li·cal·ly** *adv.*

metallic soap A soapy, waxlike material made by combining the salts of certain metals, as lead or aluminum, with various fatty acids: used in the textile, varnish, and paint industries.

met·al·lif·er·ous (met′ə·lif′ər·əs) *adj.* Yielding or containing metal.

met·al·line (met′ə·lin, -līn) *adj.* **1** Relating to, having the properties of, or resembling metal. **2** Impregnated with metals or metallic salts.

met·al·log·ra·phy (met′ə·log′rə·fē) *n.* **1** The science that treats of metallic substances; also, a treatise on metals. **2** Microscopic study of the structure of metals and alloys. [<Gk. *metallon* mine, metal + -GRAPHY] — **me·tal·lo·graph·ic** (mə·tal′ə·graf′ik) *adj.*

met·al·loid (met′ə·loid) *n.* One of those nonmetallic elements that resemble the metals in some of their properties, as arsenic and antimony. — *adj.* **1** Resembling a metal. **2** Of, pertaining to, or having the properties of a metalloid. Also **met′al·loi′dal.**

me·tal·lo·ther·a·py (mə·tal′ō·ther′ə·pē) *n.* Medical treatment by the use of metals, especially metal salts. [<Gk. *metallon* mine, metal + THERAPY]

met·al·lur·gy (met′ə·lûr′jē) *n.* The art or science of extracting a metal or metals from ores, as by smelting, reducing, refining, alloying, electrolysis, etc. [<NL *metallurgia* <Gk. *metallourgos* working in mines < *metallon* mine + *-ergos* working] — **met′al·lur′gic** or **·gi·cal** *adj.* — **met′al·lur′gi·cal·ly** *adv.* — **met′·al·lur′gist** *n.*

met·al·work (met′l·wûrk′) *n.* **1** Articles made of metal. **2** Metalworking.

met·al·work·ing (met′l·wûr′king) *n.* The making or the business of making things out of metal. — **met′al·work′er** *n.*

met·a·math·e·mat·ics (met′ə·math′ə·mat′iks) *n.* That branch of mathematics which is concerned with the formalized and rigorously logical treatment of pure symbols, having regard only to internal consistency and the establishment of absolute proofs of the validity of a given set of axioms, postulates, theorems, etc., within a mathematical system. — **met′a·math′e·mat′i·cal** *adj.*

met·a·mer (met′ə·mər) *n. Chem.* A compound or substance exhibiting metamerism. [<META- + Gk. *meros* part] — **met′a·mer′ic** (-mer′ik) *adj.*

met·a·mere (met′ə·mir) *n. Biol.* One of the series of homologous segments that form the body of a chordate or articulate animal, as a worm; a somite. Also **me·tam·er·on** (mə·tam′·ər·on). [<META- + -MERE] — **met′a·mer′ic, me·tam′er·al** *adj.* — **met′a·mer′i·cal·ly** *adv.*

me·tam·er·ism (mə·tam′ə·riz′əm) *n.* **1** *Chem.* A variety of isomerism in which the compounds have not only the same percentage of composition, but also the same molecular weight. **2** *Biol.* Disposition in metameres; the state of being a metamere; also, an example of this. Also **me·tam′er·y.**

met·a·mor·phic (met′ə·môr′fik) *adj.* **1** Producing metamorphism. **2** Pertaining to, caused by, or exhibiting metamorphism. Also **met′a·mor′phous.**

met·a·mor·phism (met′ə·môr′fiz·əm) *n.* **1** *Geol.* The changes in the composition and texture of rocks caused by earth forces accompanied by heat, pressure, moisture, etc. **2** Any metamorphosis. [See METAMORPHOSIS]

met·a·mor·phop·si·a (met′ə·môr·fop′sē·ə) *n. Pathol.* A defect in vision which makes objects appear distorted. [<NL <Gk. *metamorphōsis* transformation + *ōps* eye]

met·a·mor·phose (met′ə·môr′fōz) *v.t.* **·phosed, ·phos·ing** **1** To change the form of; transmute. **2** To change by metamorphism. Also **met′a·mor′phize.** See synonyms under CHANGE. [<F *métamorphoser*]

met·a·mor·pho·sis (met′ə·môr′fə·sis) *n. pl.* **·pho·ses** (-fə·sēz) **1** A passing from one form or shape into another; transformation with or without change of nature: especially applied to change by means of witchcraft, sorcery, etc. **2** Complete transformation of character, purpose, circumstances, etc.; also, a person or thing metamorphosed. **3** *Biol.* A change in form, structure, or function in an organism resulting from development; transformation; specifically, the series of marked external changes through which an individual passes after leaving the egg and before attaining sexual maturity, as the larva, pupa, and imago of an insect. Compare METAGENESIS. **4** *Bot.* The varied development of plant organs of the same morphological value, such development resulting from their adaptations of different functions: also **met′a·mor′phy.** **5** *Pathol.* A morbid change of the elements of tissues into another form of structure. **6** The changes in form going on in living tissues, blood corpuscles, etc. [<L <Gk. *metamorphōsis* < *metamorphoein* transform < *meta-* beyond + *morphē* form]

met·a·neph·ros (met′ə·nef′ros) *n. Biol.* The posterior one of three similar tubular organs in connection with the genitourinary apparatus. It develops into the permanent kidney. [<NL <META- + Gk. *nephros* kidney]

met·a·phase (met′ə·fāz) *n. Biol.* The middle stage of mitotic cell division, during which the chromosomes split along the equatorial plane between the two poles of the spindle. [<META- + -PHASE]

met·a·phor (met′ə·fôr, -fər) *n.* A figure of speech in which one object is likened to another by speaking of it as if it were that other: distinguished from *simile* by not employing any word of comparison, such as "like" or "as." See synonyms under ALLEGORY, SIMILE. — **mixed metaphor** Figurative language in which incongruous, and often contradictory, metaphors are used; confusion of figurative with plain statement. [<F *métaphore* <L *metaphora* <Gk. < *metapherein* < *meta-* beyond, over + *pherein* carry] — **met′a·phor′·ic** (-fôr′ik, -for′ik) or **·i·cal** *adj.* — **met′a·phor′·i·cal·ly** *adv.*

met·a·phos·phate (met′ə·fos′fāt) *n. Chem.* A salt of metaphosphoric acid.

met·a·phos·phor·ic acid (met′ə·fos·fôr′ik,-for′·ik) *Chem.* The glacial phosphoric acid of commerce, HPO_3, usually sold in the form of transparent sticks. It is obtained by heating orthophosphoric acid.

met·a·phrase (met′ə·frāz) *v.t.* **·phrased, ·phras·ing** **1** To translate word for word. **2** To alter the wording of. — *n.* **1** A literal translation. **2** A phrase in response; retort. **3** A school exercise consisting in the rendering of a piece of poetry into prose or of prose into verse. [<Gk. *metaphrasis* < *metaphrazein* paraphrase < *meta-* beyond + *phrazein* phrase]

met·a·phrast (met′ə·frast) *n.* One who renders poetry into prose or prose into poetry, or changes the meter of verse. [<Gk. *metaphrastēs*] — **met′a·phras′tic** or **·ti·cal** *adj.*

met·a·phys·ic (met′ə·fiz′ik) *n.* Metaphysics. — *adj.* Metaphysical.

met·a·phys·i·cal (met′ə·fiz′i·kəl) *adj.* **1** Of or pertaining to metaphysics. **2** Treating of or versed in metaphysics. **3** Beyond or above the physical or experiential; pertaining to or being of the essential nature of reality; transcendental. **4** Dealing with abstractions; apart from, or opposed to, the practical. **5** Designating certain poets of the 17th century, notably Cowley and Donne, whose verses were characterized by complex, intellectualized imagery: term originating with Dr. Samuel Johnson. [See METAPHYSICS] — **met′a·phys′i·cal·ly** *adv.*

metaphysical healing Christian Science.

met·a·phy·si·cian (met′ə·fi·zish′ən) *n.* One skilled or versed in metaphysics. Also **met′a·phys′i·cist.**

met·a·phys·ics (met′ə·fiz′iks) *n. pl. (construed as singular)* **1** The systematic study or science of the first principles of being and of knowledge; the doctrine of the essential nature and fundamental relations of all that is real. **2** Speculative philosophy in the wide sense. **3** The principles of philosophy as applied to the methodology of any particular science. **4** Mental science in general; psychology. **5** In popular use, abstruse and bewildering discussion. Also *metaphysic.* [<Med. L *metaphysica* <Med. Gk. < *ta meta ta physika* the (works) after the physics; in ref. to Aristotle's ontological treatises, which came after his *Physics*]

met·a·pla·si·a (met′ə·plā′zhē·ə) *n. Biol.* The direct transformation of one kind of tissue into another, as cartilage into bone. [<NL <Gk. *meta-* beyond + *plassein* mold]

me·tap·la·sis (mə·tap′lə·sis) *n. Biol.* The period of completed growth in the life cycle of an organism; maturity. [<NL]

met·a·plasm (met′ə·plaz′əm) *n.* **1** *Biol.* The lifeless, non–protoplasmic material of a cell, as inclusions of fats and carbohydrates. **2** A reversal or change in the order of the letters or syllables of a word. [<L *metaplasmus* <Gk. *metaplasmos* < *meta-* beyond + *plassein* mold] — **met′a·plas′mic** *adj.*

met·a·po·di·um (met′ə·pō′dē·əm) *n. pl.* **·di·a** (-dē·ə) **1** The posterior part of the foot in

gastropods and pteropods. **2** The metacarpus and metatarsus of quadrupeds. Also **met·a·pode** (-pōd), **met·a·pod** (-pod).

met·a·pro·te·in (met′ə·prō′tē·in, -tēn) *n. Biochem.* A protein resulting from the action of acids and alkalis and soluble in weak solutions of either but not in solutions of neutral salts.

met·a·psy·chics (met′ə·sī′kiks) *n.* Parapsychology.

met·a·psy·chol·o·gy (met′ə·sī·kol′ə·jē) *n.* **1** Psychology restricted to philosophical speculations on the origin, structure, function, purpose, etc., of the mind. **2** *Psychoanal.* The investigation and study of mental processes from three points of view: the dynamic, topographical, and economic. — **met′a·psy′·cho·log′i·cal** (-sī′kə·loj′i·kəl) *adj.*

met·a·psy·cho·sis (met′ə·sī·kō′sis) *n.* Interchange of mental influence or action without a recognized physical medium.

met·a·so·ma·to·sis (met′ə·sō′mə·tō′sis) *n. Geol.* That form of metamorphism by means of which a rock or mineral undergoes chemical change through the action of external materials. Also **met′a·so′ma·tism** (-sō′mə·tiz′əm). [< META- + SOMAT(O)- + -OSIS]

met·a·some (met′ə·sōm) *n. Geol.* A mineral which has developed individually within ·another mineral. [< META- + -SOME²]

met·a·sta·ble (met′ə·stā′bəl) *adj. Physics & Chem.* Denoting an apparent state of equilibrium, as in supersaturated solutions. — **met′a·sta·bil′i·ty** (-stə·bil′ə·tē) *n.*

me·tas·ta·sis (mə·tas′tə·sis) *n. pl.* **·ses** (-sēz) **1** Change of one thing into another. **2** Metabolism. **3** *Pathol.* The transfer of a disease or of its manifestations from one part of the body to another. **4** In rhetoric, a rapid change from one point to another. [< L < Gk. <*methistanai* place differently, change < *meta-* after + *histanai* place] — **met′a·stat′ic** (-stat′ik) *adj.* — **met′a·stat′i·cal·ly** *adv.*

METEOROLOGY SYMBOLS

,	Drizzle		⇼	Duststorm; Sandstorm
●	Rain		⟨	Lightning
✳	Snow		⌒	Rainbow
≡	Fog		○	Smoke
∪	Frost		∞	Haze
▽	Showers		∧	Squalls
℞	Thunderstorms		0	Exceptional visibility
↔	Ice crystals or ice needles		⸹	Signs of tropical storm
▲	Sleet		○	Cloudless sky
⌔	Aurora		◐	Partly cloudy sky
⩊	Lunar corona		◑	Cloudy sky
⊕	Solar corona		⬤	Overcast sky
⌒	Dew			

WIND DIRECTION

↓	North		↑	South
↓↙	NNE		↑↖	SSE
↙	NE		↖	SE
↘	NW		↗	SW
↓↘	NNW		↑↗	SSW
←	East		→	West
←↘	ESE		→↗	WSW
←↙	ENE		→↖	WNW

me·tas·ta·size (mə·tas′tə·sīz) *v.i.* **·sized, ·siz·ing** *Pathol.* To shift or spread from one part of the body to another: said specifically of malignant growths.

met·as·then·ic (met′əs·then′ik) *adj. Biol.* Having the posterior or lower part of the body well developed, as a kangaroo. [< META- + STHENIC]

met·a·syph·i·lis (met′ə·sif′ə·ləs) *n. Pathol.* **1** Congenital syphilis, with typical degenera-

---

tive changes, but without localized external lesions. **2** Parasyphilis. — **met′a·syph′i·lit′ic** (-sif′ə·lit′ik) *adj.*

met·a·tar·sal (met′ə·tär′səl) *adj.* Of or pertaining to the metatarsus. — *n.* One of the bones of the metatarsus. See illustration under FOOT.

met·a·tar·sal·gi·a (met′ə·tär·sal′jē·ə) *n. Pathol.* Neuralgia in the middle of the foot. [< METATARS(US) + -ALGIA]

met·a·tar·sus (met′ə·tär′səs) *n. pl.* **·si** (-sī) *Anat.* The part of the hind or pelvic limb between the tarsus or ankle and the phalanges or bones of the toe. In man it consists of five bones. [< NL < META- + TARSUS]

met·a·the·ri·an (met′ə·thir′ē·ən) *n.* Any one of a subclass (*Metatheria*) of mammals whose young are born immature and are carried in a pouch until fully developed; one of the marsupials, as a kangaroo, opossum, or bandicoot. — *adj.* Of or pertaining to the *Metatheria.* [< META- + Gk. *thērion* beast]

me·tath·e·sis (mə·tath′ə·sis) *n. pl.* **·ses** (-sēz) **1** The transposition of letters, syllables, or sounds in a word. **2** *Chem.* A substitution, as the replacing or exchange of one or more radicals or groups in a compound; double decomposition or mutual exchange. **3** *Surg.* The operation of removing a morbific substance from one place to another for relief, as by pushing a calculus lodged in the urethra back into the bladder. **4** Any change or reversal of conditions. [< LL < Gk. < *metatithenai* transpose < *meta-* over + *tithenai* place] — **met·a·thet′ic** (met′ə·thet′ik) or **·i·cal** *adj.*

met·a·tho·rax (met′ə·thôr′aks, -thō′raks) *n. Entomol.* The hindmost of the three segments of the thorax in insects, bearing the hind wings and the third pair of legs. — **met′a·tho·rac′ic** (-thô·ras′ik, -thō-) *adj.*

met·a·troph·ic (met′ə·trof′ik) *adj.* Saprophytic. [< META- + Gk. *trophikos* feeding, nursing]

me·tat·ro·phy (mə·tat′rə·fē) *n. Pathol.* A wast-

---

ing away because of disordered nutrition. Also **met·a·tro·phi·a** (met′ə·trō′fē·ə). [< MET- + ATROPHY]

Me·tau·ro (mā·tou′rō) A river in central Italy, flowing 207 miles NE to the Adriatic; at its delta the Romans defeated the Carthaginians under Hasdrubal, 207 B.C. Ancient **Me·tau·rus** (me·tô′rus).

Me·tax·as (mə·tak′səs, *Greek* me′täk·säs′),

Joannes, 1871–1941, Greek soldier and statesman.

met·a·xy·lem (met′ə·zī′ləm) *n. Bot.* The thick–walled cell portion in the woody tissues of plants, developed outside the primary xylem. [< META- + XYLEM]

met·a·zo·an (met′ə·zō′ən) *n.* Any member of a primary division (*Metazoa*) of the animal kingdom, whose cells become differentiated into at least an outer and an inner wall, including all animals higher than protozoans. Also **met′a·zo′on.** — *adj.* Of or pertaining to the metazoans: also **met′a·zo′ic.** [< META- + Gk. *zōion* animal]

Metch·ni·koff (mech′ni·kôf), **Elie,** 1845–1916, Russian physiologist and bacteriologist: also known as *Ilya Ilich Metchnikoff.*

mete¹ (mēt) *v.t.* **met·ed, met·ing 1** To allot or distribute by measure; apportion: usually with *out.* **2** *Obs.* To measure. — *n. Obs.* Measure. ◆ Homophones: *meat, meet.* [OE *metan* measure]

mete² (mēt) *n. Obs.* A boundary line; limit; confine: usually in the phrase *metes and bounds.* ◆ Homophones: *meat, meet.* [< OF < L *meta* goal, boundary]

met·em·pir·i·cal (met′em·pir′i·kəl) *adj.* Lying beyond the bounds of experience, as intuitive principles; not derived from experience; transcendental; a priori: opposed to *empirical.* Also **met′em·pir′ic.**

met·em·pir·i·cism (met′em·pir′ə·siz′əm) *n.* The science of pure reason; metaphysics proper; hence, with some, transcendental philosophy. Also **met′em·pir′ics.**

me·tem·psy·cho·sis (mə·temp′sə·kō′sis, met′·əm·sī-) *n.* Transmigration of souls from body to body. [< LL < Gk. *metempsychōsis* < *metempsychoein* < *meta-* over + *empsychoein* animate < *en-* in + *psychē* soul, life]

met·en·ceph·a·lon (met′en·sef′ə·lon) *n. pl.* **·la** (-lə) *Anat.* **1** The fifth cerebral vesicle of the brain and the parts derived therefrom, comprising the medulla oblongata and the posterior part of the roof of the fourth ventricle. **2** The part of the brain consisting of the cerebellum and pons Varolii. [< NL < MET- + ENCEPHALON] — **met′en·ce·phal′ic** (-sə·fal′·ik) *adj.*

me·te·or (mē′tē·ər, -ôr) *n.* **1** *Astron.* A luminous phenomenon, produced by a small mass of matter from the celestial spaces which strikes the earth's atmosphere with great velocity and is dissipated by heat: when not very brilliant, called a *shooting star.* **2** A meteoroid. **3** *Obs.* Any phenomenon of the atmosphere: **aerial meteors** (winds, hurricanes, etc.), **aqueous meteors** (rain, snow, etc.), **igneous meteors** (lightning, shooting stars, etc.), **luminous meteors** (aurora, rainbow, etc.). [< Med. L *meteorum* < Gk. *meteōron* thing in the air < *meteōros* high in the air < *meta-* beyond + *eōra* suspension]

Meteor Crater A depression caused by a meteor in central Arizona; 600 feet deep, 4,000 feet in diameter: also *Diablo Crater.*

me·te·or·ic (mē′tē·ôr′ik, -or′ik) *adj.* **1** Relating to meteors. **2** Meteorological. **3** Transitorily brilliant: a *meteoric* career. Also **me′te·or′i·cal.** — **me′te·or′i·cal·ly** *adv.*

me·te·or·ite (mē′tē·ə·rīt′) *n.* **1** A fallen meteor; a mass of stone or iron that has fallen upon the earth from outer space. **2** A meteoroid. — **me′te·or·it′ic** (-ə·rit′ik) *adj.*

me·te·or·o·graph (mē′tē·ər·ə·graf′, -gräf′, mē′·tē·ôr′ə-, -or′ə-) *n.* A self-recording instrument, frequently attached to a kite or balloon, by which several meteorological elements are plotted in the form of a diagram. [< F *météorographe*]

me·te·or·oid (mē′tē·ə·roid) *n. Astron.* One of innumerable small particles of matter moving through the celestial spaces, which, when they encounter the earth's atmosphere, form meteors or shooting stars.

me·te·or·ol·o·gy (mē′tē·ə·rol′ə·jē) *n.* **1** The science that treats of atmospheric phenomena, especially those that relate to weather. **2** The character of the weather and of atmospheric changes of any particular place. [< Gk. *meteōrologia* < *meteōros* high in the air + *logos* discourse] — **me′te·or′o·log′ic** (-ôr′ə·loj′ik), **me′te·or′o·log′i·cal** *adj.* — **me′te·or′o·log′i·cal·ly** *adv.* — **me′te·or·ol′o·gist** *n.*

---

meteor shower *Astron.* The apparent passage of a group of meteors upon entering the earth's atmosphere.

me·ter[1] (mē′tər) *n.* **1** An instrument, apparatus, or machine for measuring fluids, gases, electric currents, grain, etc., and recording the results obtained. **2** Any person or thing that measures; specifically, one of several officers appointed to measure certain commodities, as for tolls. —*v.t.* To measure or test by means of a meter. [< METE[1]]

me·ter[2] (mē′tər) *n.* **1** The fundamental unit of length in the metric system, originally defined as one ten-millionth of the distance on the earth's surface from the pole to the equator; 39.37 inches. In practice, it is the distance between two fiducial lines marked on the platinum-iridium International Prototype Meter deposited at Sèvres, France. See METRIC SYSTEM. **2** A measured verbal rhythm, the structure of verse; a definite arrangement of groups of syllables in a line, having a time unit and a regular beat; also, a specific arrangement of words, or a specific sequence of such lines in a stanza. **3** The character of a musical composition as being divisible into measures equal in time and length, and similar in rhythmic pattern. Also spelled *metre.* [< F *mètre* < L *metrum* measure < Gk. *metron*]

Synonyms : euphony, measure, rhythm, verse. *Euphony* is agreeable linguistic sound, however produced; *meter, measure,* and *rhythm* denote agreeable succession of sounds in the utterance of connected words; *euphony* may apply to a single word or even a single syllable; the other words apply to lines, sentences, paragraphs, etc.; *rhythm* and *meter* may be produced by accent only, as in English, or by accent and quantity combined, as in Greek or Italian; *rhythm* or *measure* may apply either to prose or to poetry, or to music, dancing, etc.; *meter* is more precise than *rhythm,* applies only to poetry, and denotes a measured *rhythm.* A *verse* is strictly a metrical line, but the word is often used as synonymous with stanza. *Verse,* in the general sense, denotes metrical writing; as, prose and *verse.* Compare MELODY, POETRY.

-meter *combining form* **1** That (instrument or unit) by which a thing is measured: *calorimeter.* **2** Measure according to or containing (the main element): *hexameter.* [< L *metrum* < Gk. *metron* measure]

me·ter·age (mē′tər·ij) *n.* **1** The act or result of measuring. **2** The charge for measurement.

met·es·trus (met·es′trəs) *n. Biol.* The period of sexual quiescence following estrus in female mammals: often spelled *metoestrus, metoestrum.* Also **met·es′trum.** [< NL < MET- + ESTRUS] —**met·es′trous** *adj.*

meth·ac·ry·late (meth·ak′rə·lāt) *n. Chem.* An ester of methacrylic acid.

meth·a·cryl·ic acid (meth′ə·kril′ik) *Chem.* A colorless acid, $C_4H_6O_2$, the esters of which are extensively used in the making of plastics. [< METH(YL) + ACRYLIC]

meth·a·done (meth′ə·dōn) *n.* A synthetic opiate used as an analgesic and experimentally as a substitute for heroin in the treatment of addicts. Also **meth′a·don** (-don). [< *(di)meth(yl) a(mino) d(iphenylheptan)one*]

meth·am·phet·a·mine (meth′am·fet′ə·mēn,-min) *n. Chem.* A compound, $C_{10}H_{15}N{\cdot}HCl$, related to the amphetamines, that allays hunger and stimulates the central nervous system. [< METH- + AMPHETAMINE]

meth·ane (meth′ān) *n. Chem.* A colorless, inflammable gas, CH_4, the simplest of the saturated hydrocarbons, formed by decomposition of vegetable matter, or artificially by dry distillation of certain organic matter, or by chemical treatment of certain metal compounds, as aluminum carbide. It is an important component of illuminating gas: often called *marsh gas.* [< METH(YL) + -ANE[2]]

methane series *Chem.* A group of saturated aliphatic hydrocarbons having the general formula C_nH_{2n+2}, and identified by the ending *-ane* : also called *alkanes.*

meth·a·nol (meth′ə·nōl, -nol) *n. Chem.* Methyl alcohol; a colorless, volatile, inflammable liquid, CH_3OH, obtained by the destructive distillation of wood or by catalytic treatment of hydrogen and carbon monoxide: highly toxic and widely used in industry and the arts: also called *carbinol, wood alcohol.* [< METHANE + -OL[1]]

meth·a·qua·lone (meth′ə·kwā′lōn) *n.* An addictive drug, $C_{16}H_{14}N_2O$, used as a sedative; Quaalude.

Meth·e·drine (meth′ə·drēn) *n.* Proprietary name for a brand of methamphetamine.

me·theg·lin (mə·theg′lin) *n.* A fermented drink made of water and honey; mead. [< Welsh *meddyglyn* < *meddyg* doctor (< L *medicus*) + *llyn* juice, liquor]

met·he·mo·glo·bin (met·hē′mə·glō′bin, -hem′ə-) *n. Biochem.* A stable, brown-red, crystalline compound formed by the decomposition of blood and by oxidation of hemoglobin. Also **met·hae′mo·glo′bin.** [< MET- + HEMOGLOBIN]

me·the·na·mine (mə·thē′nə·mēn, -min) *n. Chem.* An organic compound, $C_6H_{12}N_4$, crystallized from a mixture of formalin and ammonia: used in the vulcanization of rubber, in making synthetic resins, and as an antiseptic: also called *Urotropin, hexamethylenamine, hexamethylenetetramine.* [< *methene* (< METHYL + -ENE) + AMINE]

me·thinks (mē·thingks′) *v., impersonal Obs.* It seems to me; I think. [OE *me thyncth* < *thyncan* seem]

me·thi·o·nine (mə·thī′ə·nēn, -nin) *n. Biochem.* An amino acid, $C_5H_{11}O_2NS$, containing sulfur and closely related to cystine: obtained from various proteins. [< ME(THYL) + THIO- + -INE[2]]

metho- *combining form Chem.* Used to indicate the presence of a methyl group in a compound. Also, before vowels, **meth-,** as in *methane,* [< METHYL]

meth·od (meth′əd) *n.* **1** A general or established way or order of doing anything, or the means or manner by which it is presented or taught. **2** Orderly and systematic arrangement, as of ideas and topics, etc.; the design or plan of a speaker or of an author. **3** The arrangement of natural bodies according to their common characteristics. See synonyms under MANNER, RULE, SYSTEM. [< F *méthode* < L *methodus* < Gk. *methodos* < *meta-* after + *hodos* way]

me·thod·i·cal (mə·thod′i·kəl) *adj.* **1** Given to or characterized by orderly arrangement. **2** Arranged with method. Also **me·thod′ic.** —**me·thod′i·cal·ly** *adv.* —**me·thod′i·cal·ness** *n.*

meth·od·ist (meth′əd·ist) *n.* An observer of method or order. —**meth′od·ism** *n.* —**meth′od·is′tic, meth′od·is′ti·cal** *adj.*

Meth·od·ist (meth′əd·ist) *n.* A member of any one of the Protestant churches that have grown out of the religious movement begun at Oxford University in the first half of the 18th century, in which John Wesley as a leader was associated with Charles Wesley, George Whitefield, and others. The largest Methodist body in the United States is the **Methodist Church,** formed by the union of the **Methodist Episcopal Church,** the **Methodist Episcopal Church, South,** and the **Methodist Protestant Church.** —*adj.* Pertaining to, belonging to, like, or typical of this church or its doctrines. [< METHOD + -IST] —**Meth′od·ism** *n.* —**Meth′od·is′tic, Meth′od·is′ti·cal** *adj.*

meth·od·ize (meth′əd·īz) *v.t.* **·ized, ·iz·ing** To reduce or subject to method; systematize. Also *Brit.* **meth′od·ise.** See synonyms under REGULATE. —**meth′od·i·za′tion** *n.*

meth·od·ol·o·gy (meth′ə·dol′ə·jē) *n.* **1** The science of method or of arranging in due order. **2** The division of pure logic that treats of the methods of directing the means of thinking to the end of clear and connected thinking. [< Gk. *methodos* method + -LOGY]

me·thought (mē·thôt′) *v., impersonal Obs.* It seemed to me; I thought.

Me·thu·se·lah (mə·thōō′zə·lə) The son of Enoch; a Hebrew patriarch reputed to have lived 969 years. *Gen.* v 27.

meth·yl (meth′əl) *n. Chem.* An organic radical, CH_3, existing only in combination, as in methyl alcohol, etc. It is univalent, and forms esters with acids. [< METHYLENE] —**me·thyl·ic** (mə·thil′ik) *adj.*

methyl acetate *Chem.* A liquid product, $CH_3CO_2CH_3$, of wood alcohol or wood vinegar, used as a solvent or a flavoring material.

meth·yl·al (meth′əl·al) *n. Chem.* A colorless, volatile, inflammable liquid, $C_3H_8O_2$, with a pungent taste and the odor of chloroform, used in medicine and in the making of perfumery and artificial resins: also called *formal.* [< METHYL + AL(COHOL)]

methyl alcohol Methanol.

meth·yl·am·ine (meth′əl·am′ēn, -in) *n. Chem.* A colorless, gaseous, inflammable amine, CH_3NH_2, with a strong fishy odor, contained in the products of the decomposition of certain organic compounds, and also made synthetically from ammonia by replacement of hydrogen by methyl. [< METHYL + AMINE]

meth·yl·ate (meth′əl·āt) *v.t.* **·at·ed, ·at·ing** *Chem.* To mix or saturate with methyl or methanol. —*n.* A compound derived from methanol by replacing the hydrogen of the hydroxyl group with an element or radical of equal valence: potassium *methylate.* [< METHYL + -ATE] —**meth′yl·a′tion** *n.*

methylated spirit *Chem.* A mixture of ethyl alcohol with ten percent of methanol: used in the arts, unfit for drinking.

methyl chloride *Chem.* A gas, CH_3Cl, which on compression becomes a colorless liquid of ethereal odor yielding a poisonous vapor: used as a refrigerant and fire extinguisher.

meth·yl·cho·lan·threne (meth′əl·kō·lan′thrēn) *n. Biochem.* A yellow, crystalline hydrocarbon, $C_{21}H_{16}$, extracted from bile acids and also prepared synthetically: believed to be strongly carcinogenic. [< METHYL + CHOL(E)- + ANTHR(ACINE) + -ENE]

meth·yl·di·chlor·ar·sine (meth′əl·dī′klôr·är′·sēn, -sin) *n. Chem.* A colorless liquid compound, CH_3AsCl_2, adapted for chemical warfare as a vesicant and lung irritant. [< METHYL + DI- + CHLOR- + ARSINE]

meth·yl·ene (meth′əl·ēn) *n. Chem.* A bivalent organic radical, CH_2, derived from methane. [< F *méthyline* < Gk. *methyl* wine + *hylē* wood]

methylene blue *Chem.* A dark, blue-green aniline dye, $C_{16}H_{18}N_3ClS{\cdot}3H_2O$, having medicinal properties in the treatment of diphtheria, malaria, etc., and as an antidote in cyanide poisoning: used also as a chemical indicator and bacteriological stain.

meth·yl·gua·ni·dine (meth′əl·gwä′nə·dēn, -din) *n. Biochem.* A ptomaine, $C_2H_7N_3$, derived from creatinine and from certain foods, as spoiled fish. [< METHYL + GUANADINE]

methyl methacrylate *Chem.* A polymerized methacrylate forming transparent thermosetting plastics resembling glass in their optical properties. [See METHACRYLIC]

meth·yl·naph·tha·lene (meth′əl·naf′thə·lēn) *n. Chem.* A methyl compound, $C_{10}H_7CH_3$, occurring in two isomeric forms, one of which is used in the determination of cetane numbers. [< METHYL + NAPHTHALENE]

methyl orange *Chem.* An azo dyestuff used chiefly as an indicator in alkalimetry; a brilliant orange-yellow powder, readily soluble in water, colored red on the addition of acids.

meth·yl·ros·an·i·line (meth′əl·roz·an′ə·lēn, -lin) *n.* Gentian violet. [< METHYL + ROSANILINE]

me·tic·u·lous (mə·tik′yə·ləs) *adj.* Careful about trivial matters; finical; particular. [< F *méticuleux* < L *meticolosus* fearful < *metus* fear] —**me·tic′u·los′i·ty** (-los′ə·tē) *n.* —**me·tic′u·lous·ly** *adv.*

mé·tier (mā·tyā′) *n. French* Trade; profession.

mé·tif (mā·tēf′) *n. pl.* **·tifs** (-tēfs′) or **·tis** (-tēs′) *French* A person of mixed blood; especially, a person half French and half American Indian. Also **me·tiff′.**

met·o·chy (met′ə·kē) *n. Entomol.* The relationship of mutual tolerance without mutual aid existing between ants and their neutral insect guests. [< Gk. *metochē* sharing < *metochein* share in]

met·o·don·ti·a·sis (met′ō·don·tī′ə·sis) *n. Dent.* **1** Abnormal or imperfect dentition. **2** Faulty teething. [< NL < MET- + Gk. *odontiaein* cut teeth + -IASIS]

met·oes·trus (met·es′trəs), **met·oes·trum** See METESTRUS.

Me·ton·ic cycle (mə·ton′ik) A period of 19 Julian years, amounting to nearly 235 lunar revolutions, at the conclusion of which the phases of the moon recur at the same time of the year. [after *Meton,* Athenian astronomer of the fifth century B.C.]

met·o·nym (met′ə·nim) *n.* A word used as a substitute for another. [See METONYMY]

me·ton·y·my (mə·ton′ə·mē) *n.* A figure of speech that consists in the naming of a thing by one of its attributes, as "the crown prefers" for "the king prefers." [< L *metonymia* < Gk. *metōnymia* < *meta-* altered + *onyma* name] —**met·o·nym·ic** (met′ə·nim′ik), **met′o·nym′i·cal** *adj.* —**met′o·nym′i·cal·ly** *adv.*

me·too·ism (mē'tōō'iz'əm) n. The practice of representing as one's own the popular or successful policies of another, especially a political rival. — **me'·too'er** n.

met·o·pe¹ (met'ə-pē) n. Archit. 1 A square slab, sculptured or plain, between triglyphs in a Doric frieze. 2 Originally, the opening supposed to have been left by primitive Greek builders between the ends of adjoining ceiling beams. [<L metopa <Gk. metopē < meta- between + opē opening]

met·o·pe² (met'ə-pē) n. Anat. The face, forehead, or frontal surface. [Gk. metōpon forehead < meta- between + ōps eye] — **me·top·ic** (mə-top'ik) adj.

me·tox·e·ny (mə-tok'sə-nē) n. Heteroecism. [<Gk. meta- among, after + xenos host]

metr– Var. of METRO–.

me·tral·gi·a (mə-tral'jē-ə) n. Pathol. Pain in the womb. [<METR(O)-¹ + -ALGIA]

Met·ra·zol (met'rə-zōl, -zol) n. Proprietary name of a synthetic drug, $C_6H_{10}N_4$, used in medicine as a heart stimulant and in the shock treatment of certain nervous and mental disorders.

me·tre (mē'tər) See METER².

met·ric (met'rik) adj. 1 Pertaining to the meter as a unit of measurement or to the metric system. 2 Metrical (def. 1). [<L metricus <Gk. metrikos]

met·ri·cal (met'ri-kəl) adj. 1 Relating to meter or versification; composed in poetic measures; rhythmical. 2 Metric (def. 1). — **met'ri·cal·ly** adv.

metrical stress The emphasis required by the meter of a poem: opposed to rhetorical stress.

metric centner A quintal.

metric hundredweight A weight of 50 kilograms.

me·tri·cian (mə-trish'ən) n. 1 One versed in metrics. 2 A composer of verse.

met·rics (met'riks) n. pl. (construed as singular) 1 The mathematical theory of measurement. 2 The art of metrical composition.

metric system A decimal system of weights

met·ri·fy (met'rə-fī) v.t. & v.i. ·fied, ·fy·ing 1 To write in meter, versify. 2 To convert to the metric system or metric units.

me·trist (mē'trist, met'rist) n. One versed in meters or skilled in metrical composition; a versemaker. [<Med. L metrista]

me·tri·tis (mə-trī'tis) n. Pathol. Inflammation of the womb. — **me·trit'ic** (-trit'ik) adj.

met·ro (met'rō) n. pl. ·ros Often cap. In European countries, an underground railway; subway. [<F métro < chemin de fer) métro-(politain) metro(politan railroad); in England <METRO(POLITAN DISTRICT RAILWAY)]

metro–¹ combining form The uterus; pertaining to the uterus: metropathic. Also, before vowels, **metr–**. [<Gk. metra the uterus]

metro–² combining form Measure: metrology. Also, before vowels, **metr–**. [<Gk. metron a measure]

me·trol·o·gy (mə-trol'ə-jē) n. The science that treats of systems of weights and measures or of measure. [<METRO-² + -LOGY] — **met·ro·log·i·cal** (met'rə-loj'i·kəl) adj. — **me·trol'o·gist** n

met·ro·nome (met'rə-nōm) n. An instrument for indicating and marking exact time in music, consisting usually of a reversed pendulum whose period of vibration is regulated by a shifting weight. [<METRO-² + Gk. nomos law] — **met'ro·nom'ic** (-nom'ik) adj.

METRONOME

me·tro·nym·ic (mē'trə-nim'ik, met'rə-) adj. Pertaining to or derived from the name of one's mother or female ancestors: also **me·tron·y·mous** (mə·tron'ə·məs). — n. 1 A name taken from the mother's side or derived from the maternal name: also **me'tro·nym.** Compare PATRONYMIC. 2 A metronymic designation. [<Gk. mētrōnymikos <mētēr mother + onyma name]

met·ro·path·ic (met'rə-path'ik) adj. Pathol. Of

me·tror·rha·gi·a (mē'trə-rā'jē·ə, met'rə-) n. Pathol. Uterine hemorrhage, especially when not menstrual. [<METRO-¹ + -RRHAGIA]

-metry combining form The process, science, or art of measuring: geometry. [<Gk. metria <metron a measure]

Met·su (met'sü), **Gabriel**, 1630-67, Dutch painter. Also **Met'zu.**

Met·ter·nich (met'ər·nikh), **Prince**, 1773-1859, Klemens Wenzel Nepomuk Lothar von Metternich, Austrian statesman and diplomat.

met·tle (met'l) n. The stuff or material of which a thing is composed; especially, constitutional temperament or disposition; specifically, courage; ardor. See synonyms under COURAGE. — **on one's mettle** Aroused to one's utmost or best efforts. ◆ Homophone: metal. [Var. of METAL]

met·tle·some (met'l·səm) adj. Having courage or spirit; ardent; fiery. Also **met'tled.**

me·tump (mə-tump') n. Canadian A tumpline.

Metz (mets, Fr. mes) A city in NE France on the Moselle.

me·um (mē'əm) pron. Latin Mine; belonging to me: used in the phrase **meum and tuum**, mine and thine.

Meurthe (mûrt) A river in NE France, flowing 105 miles NW to the Moselle.

Meuse (myōoz, Fr. mœz) A river in western Europe, flowing 580 miles north from France to the North Sea: Dutch Maas.

mew¹ (myōo) n. 1 A cage for molting birds; an enclosure; pen for fattening or breeding; also, any place of concealment. 2 pl. A stable; specifically, the stables in London in which the royal horses are kept: so called because built on the site of the mews or cages of the royal hawks. — v.t. 1 To confine in or as in a mew; immure or conceal: often with up. 2 Obs. To change (feathers); molt. — v.i. 3 Obs. To molt. [<OF muer change <L mutare]

mew² (myōo) v.i. To cry as a cat. — n. The ordinary plaintive cry of a cat. Also spelled miaou, miaow, meow. [Imit.]

METRIC SYSTEM

Length		Equivalents			Weight or Mass		Equivalents			Capacity		Equivalents		
		Metric		U.S.			Metric		U. S.			Metric		U. S.
millimeter	(mm)	.001	m	.03937 in.	milligram	(mg)	.001	g	.0154 gr.	milliliter	(ml)	.001	l	.033 fl. oz.
centimeter	(cm)	.01	m	.3937 in.	centigram	(cg)	.01	g	.1543 gr.	centiliter	(cl)	.01	l	.338 fl. oz.
decimeter	(dm)	.1	m	3.937 in.	decigram	(dg)	.1	g	1.543 gr.	deciliter	(dl)	.1	l	3.38 fl. oz.
METER	(m)	1	m	39.37 in.	GRAM	(g)	1	g	15.43 gr.	LITER	(l)	1	l	1.056 li. qts.
dekameter	(dkm)	10	m	10.93 yds.	dekagram	(dkg)	10	g	.3527 oz. av.	dekaliter	(dkl)	10	l	.283 bu.
hectometer	(hm)	100	m	328.08 ft.	hectogram	(hg)	100	g	3.527 oz. av.	hectoliter	(hl)	100	l	2.837 bu.
kilometer	(km)	1000	m	.6213 mi.	kilogram	(kg)	1000	g	2.2 lbs. av.	kiloliter	(kl)	1000	l	264.18 gal.

Area		Equivalents			Volume		Equivalents		
		Metric		U. S.			Metric		U. S.
sq. millimeter	(mm²)	.000001	ca	.00155 sq. in.	cu. millimeter	(mm³)	.001	cm³	.016 minim
sq. centimeter	(cm²)	.0001	ca	.155 sq. in.	cu. centimeter	(cc, cm³)	.001	dm³	.061 cu. in.
sq. decimeter	(dm²)	.01	ca	15.5 sq. in.	cu. decimeter	(dm³)	.001	m³	61.023 cu. in.
CENTARE	(ca, m²)	1	m²	10.76 sq. ft.	STERE	(s, m³)	1	m³	1.307 cu. yds.
sq. dekameter	(dkm²)	100	ca	.0247 acre	cu. dekameter	(dkm³)	1000	m³	1307.942 cu. yds.
Also are	(a)			2.47 acres	cu. hectometer	(hm³)	1,000,000	m³	1,307,942.8 cu. yds.
sq. hectometer	(hm²)	10,000	ca	.386 sq. mi.	cu. kilometer	(km³)	1,000,000,000	m³	0.24 cu. mile
Also hectare	(ha)								
sq. kilometer	(km²)	1,000,000	ca						

Other prefixes occasionally used are: MICRO—one millionth; MYRIA—10,000 times; MEGA—1,000,000 times

and measures having as fundamental units the gram and the meter. From the gram are derived measures of weight, and from the meter measures of length; measures of surface are based on the square meter and measures of capacity on the liter. The table shown above gives the basic and derived units of the metric system, together with abbreviations and a list of equivalent values in customary U. S. standards; originating in a report to the French Academy (1791) it was legalized in France, Nov. 2, 1801; now universally used in scientific measurement.

metric ton A unit of weight, equal to 1,000 kilograms, 0.984 long ton, or 1.023 short tons.

met·ri·fi·ca·tion (met'rə-fə-kā'shən) n. The adoption of the metric system or the conversion to metric units from those of another system. Also Brit. **met·ri·ca·tion** (met'ri-kā'shən).

or pertaining to disorders of the uterus. [< METRO-¹ + Gk. pathos suffering] — **me·trop·a·thy** (mə·trop'ə·thē) n.

me·trop·o·lis (mə-trop'ə-lis) n. 1 A chief city, either the capital or the largest or most important city of a state or country. 2 The seat of a metropolitan bishop. 3 In ancient Greece, the mother city of a colony. [<Gk. métropolis city <mētēr mother + polis city]

met·ro·pol·i·tan (met'rə-pol'ə-tən) n. 1 An archbishop who exercises a limited authority over the bishops of the same ecclesiastical province. 2 A citizen of the mother city, as opposed to a colonist. 3 One who lives in a metropolis; also, one who has the manners and the ideas, or practices the customs, of a metropolis. — adj. Pertaining to a metropolis or to a metropolitan. [<LL metropolitanus]

mew³ (myōo) n. A European sea gull. Also **mew gull.** [OE mǣw; imit.]

Me·war (mā·wär') See UDAIPUR (def. 1).

mewl (myōol) v.i. To cry, as an infant. — n. An infant's cry or crying. [Freq. of MEW²]

Mex·i·can (mek'sə-kən) n. 1 A native or inhabitant of Mexico. The inhabitants are chiefly of mestizo and native Indian blood, with a minority of white persons of Spanish ancestry. 2 The Nahuatl or Aztec language. — adj. Pertaining to Mexico, its inhabitants, or their language.

Mexican bean beetle A ladybird (Epilachna varivestis) with spotted wings, which feeds on the leaves and green pods of beans. For illustration see INSECTS (injurious).

Mexican broomroot Zacatón.

Mexican chickpea A leguminous herb of western Asia and tropical America (Cicer

arietinum) with short inflated pods containing seeds used as food and in coffee blends: also called *garbanzo.*

Mexican hairless An ancient breed of small dog found in Mexico, hairless excepting a tuft on the head and a fuzzy growth toward the end of the tail: also called *biche.*

Mexican saddle A heavy leather saddle, having a high pommel and cantle and, usually, wooden stirrups.

MEXICAN HAIRLESS
(From 11 to 13 inches high at the shoulder)

Mexican War See table under WAR.

Mex·i·co (mek'sə·kō) 1 A republic in southern North America between the Pacific and the Caribbean and the Gulf of Mexico, administratively divided into 29 states; 760,373 square miles. 2 Its capital, the largest city in the republic and capital of the **Federal District of Mexico** (573 square miles) in the center of the country: also **Mexico City.** 3 A state in central Republic of Mexico; 8,267 square miles; capital, Toluca. Spanish *Méjico.*

Mexico, Gulf of An arm of the Atlantic; nearly enclosed by the United States, Mexico, and Cuba; 700,000 square miles.

Mey·er (mī'ər), **Adolf,** 1866–1950, U.S. psychiatrist. —**Kuno,** 1858–1919, German Celtic scholar.

Mey·er·beer (mī'ər·bār), **Jakob,** 1791–1864, German composer.

Mey·er·hof (mī'ər·hōf), **Otto,** 1884–1951, German physiologist.

Meyn·ell (men'əl), **Alice,** *née* Thompson, 1847–1922, English poet and essayist.

mez·ca·line (mez'kə·lēn, -lin) See MESCALINE.

me·ze·re·on (mə·zir'ē·ən) *n.* 1 A low, Old World shrub (*Daphne mezereum*) with clusters of sweet-smelling, lilac-purple flowers: cultivated in the United States. 2 Mezereum (def. 1). [< Med. L < Arabic *māzariyān* camellia]

me·ze·re·um (mə·zir'ē·əm) *n.* 1 The dried bark of any of the *Daphne* species: used in medicine as an irritant and vesicant, and in the treatment of syphilis, rheumatism, and various skin diseases. 2 Mezereon (def. 1).

mez·qui·te (mes·kē'tā) See MESQUITE.

me·zu·zah (mə·zōō'zə, me·zōō'zä) *n. pl.* **·zoth** (-zōth) In Judaism, a parchment inscribed with the passages *Deut.* vi 4–9 and xi 13–21, to be rolled up in a case or tube and affixed to the doorpost of a dwelling, as the passages command. Also **me·zu'za.** [< Hebrew *mezūzāh* doorpost]

mez·za·nine (mez'ə·nēn, -nin) *n. Archit.* 1 A low-ceilinged story between two main ones, especially between the ground floor and the one above it. Also **mezzanine floor, mezzanine story.** 2 In a theater, the first balcony or the front rows of the first balcony. [< F < Ital. *mezzanino,* dim. of *mezzano* middle < L *medianus*]

mez·zo (met'sō, med'zō, mez'ō) *adj.* Half; medium; moderate. [< Ital. < L *medius* middle]

mez·zo-re·lie·vo (met'sō·ri·lē'vō) *n. pl.* **·vos** Half relief; a piece of sculpture in which the rounded figures project half-way from the background material; demi-relief. See RELIEF. [< Ital. *mezzo rilievo.* See MEZZO and RELIEF.]

mez·zo-ri·lie·vo (med'zō·rē·lyä'vō) *n. pl.* **mez·zi·ri·lie·vi** (-vē) *Italian* Mezzo-relievo.

mezzo soprano A voice lower than a soprano and higher than a contralto; also, a person possessing, or a part written for, such a voice.

mez·zo·tint (met'sō·tint, med'zō-, mez'ō-) *n.* 1 A method of copperplate engraving, producing an even gradation of tones, like a photograph. 2 An impression so produced. —*v.t.* To engrave in or represent by mezzotint. [< Ital. *mezzotinto* < *mezzo* middle + *tinto* painted] —**mez'zo·tint'·er** *n.*

mho (mō) *n.* The practical unit of electrical conductance, being the reciprocal of the ohm. [< OHM reversed]

mi (mē) *n. Music* 1 The third note of the diatonic scale. 2 The note E. [< Ital. See GAMUT.]

Mi·am·i (mī·am'ē) *n.* A member of an Algonquian tribe of North American Indians formerly located between the Miami and Wabash rivers. [< N. Am. Ind.]

Miami A city on Biscayne Bay, southern Florida.

Miami Beach A resort city on an island between the Atlantic and Biscayne Bay, southern Florida.

Miami River A river in SW Ohio, flowing 160 miles SW to the Ohio River: also *Great Miami River.*

mi·a·na bug (mē·ä'nə) The tampan. [from *Miana,* an Iranian town]

mi·aou, mi·aow (mē·ou') See MEW².

mi·ar·o·lit·ic (mī·ar'ə·lit'ik) *adj. Geol.* Of, pertaining to, or designating a form of igneous rock containing small cavities into which fully developed crystals have projected. [< Ital. *miarola* a granite found near Baveno, Italy + Gk. *lithos* stone]

mi·as·ma (mī·az'mə, mē-) *n. pl.* **·mas** or **·ma·ta** (-mə·tə) Polluting exhalations; the poisonous effluvium once supposed to rise from putrid matter, swamps, and marshy ground, especially at night. Also **mi'asm.** [< NL < Gk., pollution < *miainein* stain, defile] —**mi·as'mal, mi·as·mat·ic** (mī'az·mat'ik), **mi·as'mic** *adj.*

mi·aul (mē·ôl', -oul') *v.i.* To cry as a cat; mew. —*n.* The mewing of a cat. [Imit.]

mib (mib) *n.* 1 A marble. 2 *pl.* The game of marbles. [? Alter. of MARBLE]

mi·ca (mī'kə) *n.* Any of a class of silicates, crystallizing in the monoclinic system and having eminently perfect basal cleavage, affording thin, tough laminae or scales, colorless to jet-black, transparent to translucent, and of widely varying chemical composition. The better grades are extensively used for electrical insulation; the transparent varieties are loosely called *isinglass.* [< L, crumb; infl. by *micare* glitter]

mi·ca·ceous (mī·kā'shəs) *adj.* 1 Of, pertaining to, consisting of, or containing mica. 2 Resembling mica; laminated; sparkling: also used figuratively: a *micaceous* literary style.

mica diorite A variety of diorite in which mica replaces hornblende.

Mi·cah (mī'kə) A masculine personal name. [< Hebrew, like Jehovah] —**Micah** A Hebrew prophet of the eighth century B.C.; also, the book of the Old Testament bearing his name.

Mi·caw·ber (mə·kô'bər), **Wilkins** In Dickens's *David Copperfield,* an improvident family man, always waiting for "something to turn up."

mice (mīs) Plural of MOUSE.

mi·celle (mi·sel') 1 *Biol.* One of the theoretical structural units which are said to make up organized bodies. 2 *Chem.* The structural unit of a colloid, composed of an aggregate of molecules having crystalline properties and able to change in size without chemical alteration. Also **mi·cell', mi·cel'la** (-sel'ə). [< NL *micella,* dim. of L *mica* crumb, grain] —**mi·cel'lar** *adj.*

Mi·chael (mī'kəl; *Ger.* mī'khä·el, *Lat.* mī'kə·el) A masculine personal name. Also Polish **Mi·chal** (mē'khäl), Russian **Mi·cha·il** (mē·kä·ēl), Fr. **Mi·chel** (mē·shel'), Ital. **Mi·che·le** (mē·kā'·lā). [< Hebrew, who is like God] —**Michael** An archangel. *Rev.* xii 7. In Milton's *Paradise Lost,* he expels Adam and Eve from Paradise. In Moslem mythology, one of the four archangels, called the champion of the faith. —**Michael I,** born 1921, king of Rumania 1927–30, 1940–47.

Mich·ael·mas (mik'əl·məs) The feast of St. Michael, Sept. 29; a quarterly rent day in England. [< MICHAEL + -MAS]

Michaelmas daisy 1 A European blue aster (*Aster tripolium*). 2 Any of several North American asters, wild and cultivated.

Mi·chel·an·ge·lo (mī'kəl·an'jə·lō), 1475–1564, Italian sculptor, painter, architect, and poet. Also **Mi'chael An'ge·lo:** full name **Mi·chel·an·ge·lo Buo·nar·ro·ti** (mē'kel·än'je·lō bwô'när·rô'tē).

Miche·let (mēsh·le'), **Jules,** 1798–1874, French historian.

Mi·chel·son (mī'kəl·sən), **Albert Abraham,** 1852–1931, U.S. physicist born in Germany.

Mich·i·gan (mish'ə·gən) A north central State of the United States: 57,980 square miles; capital, Lansing; entered the Union Jan. 26, 1837; nickname, *Wolverine State*: abbr. MI —**Mich'i·gan·ite'** (-īt'), **Mich'i·gan'der** (-gan'dər) *n.*

Michigan, Lake The only one of the Great Lakes entirely within the United States, lying between Michigan and Wisconsin; 22,400 square miles.

Mi·cho·a·cán (mē·chō·ä·kän') A maritime state of SW Mexico; 23,200 square miles; capital, Morelia.

Mick (mik) *n. Slang* An Irishman: a contemptuous usage. [< MICHAEL]

mick·ey finn (mik'ē fin') *Slang* A drugged drink. Also **mick'ey, Mick'ey Finn.** [Origin unknown]

mick·le (mik'əl) *Obs.* or *Scot. adj.* 1 Large; great. 2 Much; many. —*n.* 1 A large amount or quantity; abundance. 2 By corruption, a small amount or quantity. Also spelled *meikle.* [OE *micel*]

Mic·mac (mik'mak) *n. pl.* **·mac** or **·macs** One of a tribe of North American Indians of Algonquian linguistic stock located in Nova Scotia, New Brunswick, and Newfoundland. [< N. Am. Ind., lit., allies]

mi·cra (mī'krə) Plural of MICRON.

mi·cri·fy (mī'krə·fī) *v.t.* **·fied, ·fy·ing** To make small or insignificant. [< MICR(O)- + -(I)FY]

micro- *combining form* 1 In the metric and other systems of measurement, the one-millionth part of (the specified unit):

microampere	microfarad	micromho
microangstrom	microhenry	micromicron
microbar	microhm	microphot
microcoulomb	microjoule	microvolt
microcurie	microlux	microwatt

2 An apparatus or instrument which enlarges in size or volume: *microphone.* 3 Exceptionally or abnormally small: *micro-organism.* 4 Microscopic; using or requiring a microscope:

microbotany	micropathology
microgeology	micropetrography
microhistology	micropetrology
micromechanics	microphysiography
micrometallurgy	microphysiology
micromineralogy	microzoology

Also, before vowels, sometimes **micr-.** [< Gk. *mikros* small]

mi·cro·a·nal·y·sis (mī'krō·ə·nal'ə·sis) *n.* The chemical analysis and identification of minute quantities. —**mi·cro·an·a·lyst** *n.* —**mi·cro·an·a·lyt'i·cal** (-an'ə·lit'i·kəl) *adj.* —**mi·cro·an·a·lyt'i·cal·ly** *adv.*

mi·cro·bar·o·graph (mī'krō·bar'ə·graf, -gräf) *n. Meteorol.* An instrument which records the lesser fluctuations of atmospheric pressure.

mi·crobe (mī'krōb) *n.* A microscopic organism; especially, a pathogenic bacterium. Also **mi·cro·bi·on** (mī·krō'bē·on). [< F < Gk. *mikros* small + *bios* life] —**mi·cro'bi·al, mi·cro'bi·an, mi·cro'bic** *adj.*

mi·cro·bi·cide (mī·krō'bə·sīd) *n.* Any substance or agent that destroys microbes; a germ-killer. [< MICROBE + -CIDE] —**mi·cro'bi·ci'dal** *adj.*

mi·cro·bi·ol·o·gy (mī'krō·bī·ol'ə·jē) *n.* The scientific study of the structure, development, function, and mode of action of micro-organisms, as bacteria, viruses, molds, etc., especially with regard to their significance in health and disease. —**mi·cro·bi·o·log·i·cal** (mī'krō·bī'ə·loj'i·kəl) *adj.* —**mi·cro·bi·ol'o·gist** *n.*

mi·cro·bi·o·ta (mī'krō·bī·ō'tə) *n. pl. Ecol.* The microscopic plant and animal organisms of a region. [< NL < MICRO- + BIOTA] —**mi·cro·bi·ot'tic** (-ot'ik) *adj.*

mi·cro·ceph·a·ly (mī'krō·sef'ə·lē) *n.* Abnormal smallness of the head; imperfect development of the cranium. Also **mi·cro·ce·pha'li·a** (-sə·fā'lē·ə). [< MICRO- + Gk. *kephalē* head] —**mi·cro·ce·phal'ic** (-sef'ik), **mi·cro·ceph'a·lous** *adj.*

mi·cro·chem·is·try (mī'krō·kem'is·trē) *n.* The chemistry of very small objects or quantities, especially those requiring the use of the microscope. —**mi·cro·chem'i·cal** *adj.*

mi·cro·chip (mī'krō·chip') *n.* A chip (def. 8).

mi·cro·cir·cuit (mī'krō·sûr'kət) *n.* An electronic circuit made up of very tiny components.

mi·cro·cli·mate (mī'krō·klī'mit) *n. Meteorol.* The climate of a very small area, as of a forest, meadow, lake, wheat field, etc., with special reference to local variations from the general climate of a region. Compare MACRO-

CLIMATE. —**mi·cro·cli·mat·ic** (mī′krō·klī·mat′·ik) adj.

mi·cro·cline (mī′krə·klīn) n. A grayish, reddish, greenish, or green translucent potash feldspar, $KAlSi_3O_8$, crystallizing in the triclinic system. See FELDSPAR.

mi·cro·coc·cus (mī′krə·kok′əs) n. pl. ·coc·ci (-kok′sī) Any member of a genus (Micrococcus) of spherical bacteria occurring in irregular masses or in plates. They are generally Gram-positive, and feed either on living or on dead matter. [<NL]

mi·cro·cop·y (mī′krə·kop′ē) n. pl. ·cop·ies A reduced photographic copy, as of a letter, manuscript, etc.

mi·cro·cosm (mī′krə·koz′əm) n. 1 A little world; the world or universe on a small scale; hence, man, as if combining in himself all the elements of the great world: opposed to macrocosm. 2 A little community. Also **mi′·cro·cos′mos** (-koz′məs), **mi′cro·cos′mus**. [<F microcosme <LL microcosmus <Gk. mikros kosmos, lit., little world] —**mi′cro·cos′mic**, **mi′cro·cos′mi·cal**, **mi′cro·cos′mi·an** adj.

microcosmic salt Chem. A white crystalline salt, sodium ammonium hydrogen phosphate, $Na(NH_4)HPO_4·4H_2O$, used to identify metallic oxides in lead tests.

mi·cro·crys·tal·line (mī′krō·kris′tə·lin, -lēn) adj. 1 Cryptocrystalline. 2 Having a crystalline structure visible only under a microscope.

mi·cro·cyte (mī′krə·sīt) n. Pathol. A small red blood corpuscle found in cases of anemia.

mi·cro·dis·sec·tion (mī′krō·di·sek′shən) n. Dissection, as of tissue, under the microscope.

mi·cro·dont (mī′krə·dont) adj. Having unusually small teeth. Also **mi·cro·don′tous**. [<MICR(O)- + Gk. odous, odontos tooth]

mi·cro·e·co·nom·ics (mī′krō·ē′kə·nom′iks, -ek′ə-) n. Economics studied in terms of individual areas of the economy, esp. a company or a family.

mi·cro·e·lec·tron·ics (mī′krō·i·lek′tron′iks) n. Branch of electronics that deals with the miniaturization of circuits and components.

mi·cro·fiche (mī′krō·fēsh) n. A sheet of microfilm. [<F <MICRO- + fiche card]

mi·cro·film (mī′krō·film) n. 1 A photograph, as of a printed page, document, or other object, highly reduced for ease in transmission and storage, and capable of reenlargement or reading by suitable optical devices. 2 A microphotograph. —**mi′cro·film′ing** n.

mi·cro·form (mī′krō·fôrm′) n. A method of reproducing images greatly reduced in size, as on microfilm.

mi·cro·fos·sil (mī′krō·fos′əl) n. The fossilized remains of an extremely minute organism, usually of submarine origin and of value in the study of early geological conditions and biological development.

mi·cro·ga·mete (mī′krō·gə·mēt′, -gam′ēt) n. Biol. The male of two conjugating gametes: so called from its being the smaller one. Compare MACROGAMETE.

mi·cro·gram (mī′krə·gram) n. A unit of weight in the metric system, equal to one thousandth of a milligram. Also **mi′cro·gramme**.

mi·cro·graph (mī′krə·graf, -gräf) n. 1 A pantograph instrument for minute writing, drawing, or engraving. 2 A picture of an object as seen through a microscope. 3 An instrument for recording and photographically magnifying very small movements, as those of a diaphragm. —**mi′cro·graph′ic** adj.

mi·crog·ra·phy (mī·krog′rə·fē) n. 1 The description or study of microscopic objects. 2 The art or habit of writing very minutely. 3 Very minute handwriting. Contrasted with macrography.

mi·cro·groove (mī′krə·grōōv) n. 1 A fine groove or channel, especially as cut in the surface of a long-playing phonograph record. 2 A phonograph record having such grooves. —adj. Having microgrooves.

mi·cro·in·cin·er·a·tion (mī′krō·in·sin′ə·rā′shən) n. A method for the study of the inorganic constituents of cells and tissues by burning the organic materials and examining the residue under the microscope.

mi·cro·lec·i·thal (mī′krə·les′ə·thəl) adj. Alecithal. [<MICRO- + Gk. lekithos yolk]

mi·cro·li·ter (mī′krə·lē′tər) n. A metric unit of capacity, equal to one thousandth of a millili-

ter. Also **mi′cro·li′tre**.

mi·cro·lith (mī′krə·lith) n. Anthropol. A small, flint implement of the late Paleolithic, Mesolithic, and Neolithic culture periods. —**mi′cro·lith′ic** adj.

mi·crol·o·gy (mī·krol′ə·jē) n. 1 The branch of science that treats of microscopic objects or is dependent on microscopic investigations. 2 Undue attention to minute and unimportant matters. [<MICRO- + -LOGY]

mi·cro·me·te·or·ol·o·gy (mī′krō·mē′tē·ə·rol′ə·jē) n. The study of climatic conditions in very small areas or localities. Compare MACROMETEOROLOGY.

mi·crom·e·ter (mī·krom′ə·tər) n. 1 An instrument for measuring very small distances or dimensions. 2 A caliper or gage arranged to allow of minute measurements. [<MICRO- + METER] —**mi·cro·met·ri·cal** (mī′krə·met′ri·kəl), **mi′cro·met′ric** adj. —**mi′cro·met′ri·cal·ly** adv. —**mi·crom′e·try** n.

MICROMETER

micrometer caliper A caliper or gage having a micrometer screw.

micrometer screw A screw with fine and very accurately cut threads, and a circular, graduated head, which shows the amount of advancement or retraction of the screw: used in making fine measurements, often to .0001 of an inch.

mi·cro·mil·li·me·ter (mī′krō·mil′ə·mē′tər) n. 1 The one-millionth part of a millimeter, or the one-billionth part of a meter $(1 \times 10^{-9}$ m.). 2 One millimicron.

mi·cro·min·i·a·tur·ize (mī′krō·min′ē·ə·chər·īz, -min′ə-) v.t. ·ized, ·iz·ing. To reduce the size of, as the parts of electronic circuits, to a scale smaller than miniature. —**mi′cro·min′i·a·tur′i·za′tion** n.

mi·cron (mī′kron) n. pl. ·cra (-krə) The one-thousandth part of a millimeter, or the one-millionth part of a meter (symbol μ). Also spelled mikron. [<NL <Gk. mikron, neut. of mikros small]

Mi·cro·ne·sia (mī′krə·nē′zhə, -shə) One of the three main divisions of Pacific islands, in the western Pacific north of the equator.

Mi·cro·ne·sian (mī′krə·nē′zhən, -shən) n. 1 A native of Micronesia. The Micronesians are a mixed race of Melanesian, Polynesian, and Malay stocks, but have shorter stature and darker skins than the Polynesians. 2 A group of Melanesian languages of the Austronesian family, spoken in the Caroline, Gilbert, and Marshall islands. —adj. Of or pertaining to Micronesia, its people, or their languages.

mi·cron·ize (mī′krən·īz) v.t. ·ized, ·iz·ing To comminute (a substance) into particles not more than a few microns in diameter. [<MICRON + -IZE] —**mi′cron·i·za′tion** n.

mi·cro·nu·cle·us (mī′krō·nōō′klē·əs, -nyōō′-) n. pl. ·cle·i (-klē·ī) Biol. A small nucleus, especially the smaller of two nuclei, as in infusorians.

mi·cro·nu·tri·ent (mī′krō·nōō′trē·ənt, -nyōō′-) n. A substance essential in the nourishment of animals and plants but only in small amounts or in low concentration, as certain minerals. —adj. Of or pertaining to such a substance.

mi·cro–or·gan·ism (mī′krō·ôr′gən·iz′əm) n. Any extremely small plant or animal organism, especially one visible only in an optical or electron microscope, as a bacterium, protozoan, or virus.

mi·cro·pa·le·on·tol·o·gy (mī′krō·pā′lē·ən·tol′ə·jē) n. The study of microscopic fossils in relation to their geologic and ecological environment, especially those forms found in core samples from submarine depths. —**mi′cro·pa′le·on′to·log′ic** (-pā′lē·on′tə·loj′ik) or **·i·cal** adj. —**mi′cro·pa′le·on·tol′o·gist** n.

mi·cro·par·a·site (mī′krō·par′ə·sīt) n. A parasitic micro-organism.

mi·cro·phone (mī′krə·fōn) n. A device for amplifying sounds by the electromagnetic conversion of sound waves impinging upon a sensitive diaphragm. It forms the principal element of a telephone transmitter, and is the

first component of any sound–reproducing system, as in radio broadcasting, sound films, etc. —**mi′cro·phon′ic** (-fon′ik) adj.

mi·cro·pho·to·graph (mī′krō·fō′tə·graf, -gräf) n. 1 A microscopic photograph of any object, as a writing, picture, etc. Compare PHOTOMICROGRAPH. 2 Microfilm. —**mi′cro·pho′to·graph′ic** adj. —**mi′cro·pho·tog′ra·phy** (-fə·tog′rə·fē) n.

mi·cro·pho·tom·e·ter (mī′krō·fō·tom′ə·tər) n. An instrument for the measurement of very small luminous intensities, and for the comparative study of spectral lines. —**mi′cro·pho′to·met′ric** (-fō′tə·met′rik) adj. —**mi′cro·pho·tom′e·try** n.

mi·cro·phys·ics (mī′krə·fiz′iks) n. 1 That branch of physics which investigates the structure, characteristics, and behavior of microscopic particles of matter. 2 Nucleonics.

mi·cro·phyte (mī′krə·fīt) n. A microscopic plant, generally parasitic. —**mi′cro·phy′tal**, **mi′cro·phyt′ic** (-fit′ik) adj.

mi·cro·pla·si·a (mī′krə·plā′zhē·ə, -zē·ə) n. Pathol. A condition of arrested development; dwarfism.

mi·cro·print (mī′krə·print) n. A microphotograph reproduced in a print that may be examined or read by means of a magnifying glass.

mi·cro·proc·ess·or (mī′krō·pros′əs·ər) n. Electronic processor located in a quarter–inch square silicon chip, which can carry out the functions of an ordinary computer or processor.

mi·cro·si·a (mī·krop′sē·ə) n. Pathol. A defect in vision causing objects to appear unusually small. Also **mi·cro′pi·a** (-krō′pē·ə). [<NL <MICR(O)- + -OPSIS] —**mi·crop′tic** (-tik) adj.

mi·cro·pyle (mī′krə·pīl) n. 1 Bot. The aperture in the coats of a plant ovule through which the pollen tube penetrates. 2 Biol. An aperture in the vitelline membrane of the ovum, serving to admit a spermatozoon. [<MICRO- + Gk. pylē gate] —**mi′cro·py′lar** adj.

mi·cro·py·rom·e·ter (mī′krō·pī·rom′ə·tər) n. An optical instrument for observing the temperature, etc., of minute light– or heat–radiating bodies.

mi·cro·rock·et (mī′krō·rok′it) n. A miniature rocket used for testing a proposed full–scale model.

mi·cro·scope (mī′krə·skōp) n. An optical instrument consisting of a single lens or a combination of lenses for magnifying objects too small to be seen or clearly observed by the naked eye. [<NL microscopium]

mi·cro·scop·ic (mī′krə·skop′ik) adj. 1 Pertaining to a microscope or to microscopy. 2 Made with or as with a microscope. 3 Exceedingly minute; visible only under the microscope: opposed to macroscopic. See synonyms under LITTLE. Also **mi′cro·scop′i·cal**. —**mi′cro·scop′i·cal·ly** adv.

Mi·cro·sco·pi·um (mī′krə·skō′pē·əm) n. A southern constellation. See CONSTELLATION. [<NL]

mi·cros·co·py (mī·kros′kə·pē, mī′krə·skō′pē) n. The art or practice of examining objects with a microscope. —**mi·cros′co·pist** n.

mi·cro·sec·ond (mī′krō·sek′ənd) n. One millionth of a second: used especially in timing the action of subatomic particles in nuclear physics.

mi·cro·seism (mī′krə·sīz′əm) n. Geol. A very slight tremor or vibration of the earth's crust, detectable only by a microseismometer. [<MICRO- + Gk. seisma shaking] —**mi′cro·seis′mic**, **mi′cro·seis′mi·cal** adj.

mi·cro·seis·mom·e·ter (mī′krō·sīz·mom′ə·tər, -sīs-) n. An apparatus for indicating the direction, duration, and intensity of microseisms. Also **mi′cro·seis′mo·graph** (-sīz′mə·graf, -gräf, -sīs′-). [<MICROSEISM + (O)METER]

mi·cro·some (mī′krə·sōm) n. Biol. A minute corpuscle embedded in the protoplasm of an active cell. The great number of these corpuscles contributes to the granular appearance of protoplasm. Also **mi′cro·so′ma** (-sō′mə).

mi·cro·spe·cies (mī′krə·spē′shēz) n. Biol. A species having definite but slight variability; also, a species distributed within the confines of a limited area.

mi·cro·spec·tro·scope (mī′krō·spek′trə·skōp) n. A combination of the microscope and spectroscope for observing the absorptive spectrum of a minute body.

mi·cro·spo·ran·gi·um (mī′krō·spə·ran′jē·əm)

n. pl. **·gi·a** (-jē·ə) *Bot.* A sporangium producing or containing microspores, as in the pollen sac of the anther in seed plants.

mi·cro·spore (mī′krə·spôr, -spōr) *n. Bot.* A small, asexually produced spore in seed plants, male in function.

mi·cro·spo·ro·phyll (mī′krə·spôr′ə·fil, -spō′rə·) *n. Bot.* A sporophyll producing microsporangia.

mi·cros·to·mous (mī·kros′tə·məs) *adj.* Having an unusually small mouth. Also **mi·cro·stom·a·tous** (mī′krō·stom′ə·təs). [<MICRO- + -STOMOUS]

mi·cro·tome (mī′krə·tōm) *n.* An instrument for making very thin sections for microscopic observations. — **mi′cro·tom′ic** (-tom′ik) or **-i·cal** *adj.* — **mi·crot·o·mist** (mī·krot′ə·mist). — **mi·crot′o·my** *n.*

mi·cro·wave (mī′krə·wāv) *n.* A high-frequency electromagnetic wave having a wavelength of from 1 millimeter to about 30 centimeters.

mi·cru·rgy (mī′krûr·jē) *n.* A highly refined precision technique for the microdissection, study, and investigation of living protoplasm, usually in the form of single cells, as bacteria, amebae, etc. [<MICR(O)- + -URGY] — **mi·crur·gic** (mī·krûr′jik) or **-gi·cal** *adj.* — **mi′crur·gist** *n.*

mic·tu·rate (mik′chə·rāt) *v.i.* **·rat·ed, ·rat·ing** To urinate. [<MICTURITION; an erroneous formation]

mic·tu·ri·tion (mik′chə·rish′ən) *n.* The act of urination. [<L *micturitus*, pp. of *micturire*, desiderative of *mingere* pass water]

mid[1] (mid) *adj.* **1** Middle. **2** *Phonet.* Produced with the tongue in a relatively midway position between high and low: said of certain vowels, as (ō) in *boat.* — *n. Archaic* The middle. [OE *midd*]

mid[2] (mid) *prep.* Amid; among: a poetical usage.

mid- *combining form* Middle; middle point or part of:

mid–act	midmonth
mid–African	midmonthly
midafternoon	midmorning
mid–April	mid–mouth
mid–arctic	mid–movement
mid–Asian	mid–nineteenth
mid–August	mid–November
midautumn	mid–ocean
midaxillary	mid–October
mid–block	mid–oestral
mid–breast	mid–orbital
mid–Cambrian	mid–Pacific
mid–career	mid–part
midcarpal	mid–period
mid–century	mid–periphery
mid–channel	mid–pillar
mid–chest	midpit
mid–continent	mid–Pleistocene
mid–course	mid–position
mid–court	midrange
mid–crowd	mid–refrain
mid–current	mid–region
mid–December	mid–Renaissance
mid–diastolic	mid–river
mid–dish	mid–road
middorsal	mid–sea
mid–eighteenth	midseason
mid–Empire	midsentence
mid–European	mid–September
midevening	mid–Siberian
midfacial	mid–side
mid–February	mid–sky
mid–field	mid–slope
mid–flight	mid–sole
midforenoon	midspace
mid–forty	mid–span
midfrontal	midstory
mid–hour	midstout
mid–ice	midstreet
mid–incisor	mid–stride
mid–Italian	mid–styled
mid–January	mid–sun
mid–July	mid–swing
mid–June	mid–tap
mid–lake	midtarsal
midleg	mid–Tertiary
mid–length	mid–thigh
mid–life	mid–thoracic
mid–line	mid–tide
mid–link	mid–time
mid–lobe	mid–totality
midmandibular	mid–tow
mid–March	mid–town
mid–May	mid–value

midventral	mid–water
mid–volley	midwintry
mid–walk	mid–world
mid–wall	midyear
mid–watch	mid–zone

mid-air (mid′âr′) *n.* The middle or midst of the air.

Mi·das (mī′dəs) In Greek legend, a king of Phrygia to whom Dionysus granted the power of turning whatever he touched into gold; when his food and even his daughter were thus transmuted, he prayed to have the power taken back.

mid-At·lan·tic (mid′ət·lan′tik) *n.* The middle part of the Atlantic Ocean.

mid-brain (mid′brān′) *n.* The mesencephalon.

mid-Can·a·da line (mid′kan′ə·də) A chain of radar stations in Canada along the 55th and 56th parallels, maintained by the Canadian government.

mid-day (mid′dā′) *n.* Noon.

mid-den (mid′n) *n.* **1** A kitchen midden. **2** *Brit. Dial.* A dunghill or heap of refuse. [ME *midding* <Scand. Cf. Dan. *mödding* < *mög* dung, muck + *dynge* heap (of dung).]

mid-dle (mid′l) *adj.* **1** Occupying a position equally distant from the extremes; mean. **2** Occupying any intermediate position. **3** *Gram.* In Greek and Sanskrit, designating a voice of the verb which indicates action by the subject for his own sake. See VOICE. — *n.* **1** The part or point equally distant from the extremities. ◆ Collateral adjective: *median.* **2** Something that is intermediate. **3** The middle voice. See synonyms under CENTER. — *v.t.* **·dled, ·dling** *Naut.* To fold or double in the middle. [OE *middel*]

middle age The time of life between youth and old age, commonly between 40 and 60. — **mid′dle-aged′** (-ājd′) *adj.*

Middle Ages The period in European history between classical antiquity and the Renaissance: usually regarded as extending from the downfall of Rome, in 476, to about 1450.

Middle America That part of Latin America north of South America and south of the United States; specifically, the six Central American states as well as Mexico, Cuba, Haiti, and the Dominican Republic.

Middle Atlantic States New York, New Jersey, and Pennsylvania.

mid-dle-break-er (mid′l·brā′kər) *n. Agric.* A lister. Also **mid′dle-bust′er** (-bus′tər).

mid-dle-brow (mid′l·brou′) *n.* A person who has conventional or middle–class tastes, interests, opinions, etc.

middle C *Music* The note written on the first leger line above the bass staff and the first leger line below the treble staff; also, the corresponding tone or key.

middle class The class of a society that occupies a position between the laboring class and the very wealthy or the nobility. — **mid′·dle-class′** (-klas′, -kläs′) *adj.*

Middle Congo See CONGO REPUBLIC.

Middle Dutch See under DUTCH.

middle ear *Anat.* The tympanum: occasionally applied to the tympanum, the mastoid cells, and the Eustachian tube.

Middle East See under EAST.

Middle English See under ENGLISH.

Middle French See under FRENCH.

Middle High German See under GERMAN.

Middle Kingdom 1 The former Chinese Empire, regarded as occupying the center of the world: later considered as the 18 provinces of China proper. **2** A kingdom of ancient Egypt, 2400–1580 B.C., having first Heracleopolis, then Thebes, for its capital: also **Middle Empire**.

Middle Latin See MEDIEVAL LATIN under LATIN.

middle latitude The latitude midway between two places on the same hemisphere: also called *mean latitude.*

Middle Low German See under GERMAN.

mid-dle-man (mid′l·man′) *n. pl.* **·men** (-men′) **1** One who acts as an agent; one who buys in bulk from producers and resells. **2** The actor in the middle of a line of minstrel performers who propounds questions to the endmen; the interlocutor. **3** Any intermediary.

mid-dle-most (mid′l·mōst′) *adj.* **1** Situated exactly in the middle. **2** Being in the midst of; hence, very intimate. Also *midmost.*

mid-dle-of-the-road (mid′l·əv·thə·rōd′) *adj.* Tending toward neither side or extreme; moderate, especially in politics. Also **mid·dle–road·ing** (mid′l·rō′ding).

middle of the road A moderate position.

mid-dle-of-the-road·er (mid′l·əv·thə·rō′dər) *n.* One who endorses a moderate course, especially in politics. Also **mid′dle–road′er.**

mid-dle-piece (mid′l·pēs′) *n. Biol.* The part lying between the nucleus and the flagellum of a spermatozoon.

Middle Persian See under PERSIAN.

Mid-dles-brough (mid′lz·brə) A port and county borough in NE Yorkshire, England.

Mid-dle-sex (mid′l·seks) A county of SE England, comprising the NW part of London; 232 square miles.

Middle States The eastern States of the United States between New England and the South: New York, New Jersey, Pennsylvania, Delaware, and Maryland.

Middle Temple See INNS OF COURT.

Mid-dle-ton (mid′l·tən), **Arthur**, 1742–87, South Carolina patriot; signer of Declaration of Independence. — **Thomas**, 1570?–1627, English dramatist.

mid-dle-weight (mid′l·wāt′) *n.* A boxer or wrestler weighing between 147 and 160 pounds.

Middle West That section of the United States between the Rockies and the Alleghenies and north of the Ohio River and the southern borders of Kansas and Missouri: also *Midwest.* Also **middle west.** — **Middle Western**

mid-dling (mid′ling) *adj.* **1** Of middle rank, condition, size, or quality. **2** In tolerable but not good health; in fair health. — *n.* **1** *pl.* The coarser part of ground wheat, as distinguished from flour and bran: formerly used only for feed, but now manufactured into the best brand of flour, since it contains most gluten. **2** Pork or bacon cut from between the shoulder and ham of a hog. **3** A quality of cotton on which prices are based. [<MID + -LING[2]]

mid-dling-ly (mid′ling·lē) *adj.* Tolerably. Also **mid′dling.**

mid-dy (mid′ē) *n. pl.* **·dies** *Colloq.* A midshipman.

middy blouse A woman's or child's blouse not closely fitted and having a wide collar similar to that of a sailor's blouse.

Mid-gard (mid′gärd) In Norse mythology, the earth, middlemost of several worlds, and girdled by a great serpent: also spelled *Mithgarth.* Also **Mid′garth** (-gärth). [<ON *Mithgarther* < *mithr* mid + *garthr* yard, house]

midge (mij) *n.* **1** A gnat or small fly; especially, a small, long-legged, dipterous insect of the family *Ceratopogonidae* that does not bite and has aquatic larvae. For illustration see INSECTS (injurious). **2** A small person; dwarf. [OE *mycge*]

midg·et (mij′it) *n.* **1** An extremely small person. **2** Anything very small of its kind. — *adj.* Small; diminutive. [Dim. of MIDGE]

mid-gut (mid′gut′) *n. Anat.* The primitive intestinal cavity, formed by the closure of the body walls of the embryo.

mid-i (mid′ē) *n. pl.* **mid·is** A shirt, dress, or coat with a hemline at mid–calf. [< MIDDLE]

Mi·di (mē·dē′) *French* Southern France.

Mid·i·an·ite (mid′ē·ən·īt′) *n.* One of an ancient nomadic tribe of NW Arabia, descended from Midian, a son of Abraham. *Gen.* xxv 2. [< Hebrew *Midhyān* name of a son of Abraham] — **Mid′i·an·it′ish** *adj.*

mi·di·nette (mē′dē·net′) *n. fem. French* A young working girl, so called because she leaves the shop at noon for lunch.

mid-i-ron (mid′ī′ərn) *n.* An iron golf club with a loft intermediate between that of the cleek and that of the mashie.

mid-land (mid′lənd) *adj.* **1** In the interior country. **2** Surrounded by the land; mediterranean. — *n.* The interior of a country.

Mid-land (mid′lənd) *n.* The dialects of Middle English spoken in London and the Midland counties of England; especially, **East Midland**, the direct predecessor of Modern English.

Mid-lands (mid′ləndz) *n. pl.* A region comprising the middle counties of England, generally coextensive with Anglo-Saxon Mercia.

Mid-lo-thi-an (mid·lō′thē·ən) A county in SE Scotland; 366 square miles; county town, Edinburgh.

mid-most (mid′mōst′) *adj.* Middlemost. — *n.*

The midmost part of anything. — *adv.* In the midst or middle. [OE *mydmest*]

mid·night (mid′nīt′) *n.* Twelve o'clock at night; the middle of the night. — *adj.* Pertaining to, occurring in, or like the middle of the night; dark.

midnight blue A very dark blue, almost black.

midnight sun The sun visible at midnight as a result of the fact that the latitude of the place from which it is viewed is greater than the polar distance of the sun, or above 66 degrees.

mid·noon (mid′no͞on′) *n.* The middle of the day; noon.

mid–point (mid′point′) *n.* A point at the middle.

Mid·rash (mid′rash, -räsh) *n. pl.* **Mid·rash·im** (mid·rash′im, -räsh′-) or **Mid·rash·oth** (mid·rash′ōth, -räsh′-) Jewish exegetical treatises on the Old Testament, dating from the 4th to the 12th century; specifically, the Haggadah. [< Hebrew, explanation]

mid·rib (mid′rib′) *n. Bot.* The primary vein, or rib, of a leaf, usually running from apex to base.

mid·riff (mid′rif) *n.* The diaphragm. [OE *midhrif* < *midd* mid + *hrif* belly]

mid·ship (mid′ship′) *adj. Naut.* At or pertaining to the middle of a vessel's hull.

mid·ship·man (mid′ship′mən) *n. pl.* **·men** (-mən) **1** A student training at the United States Naval Academy for commissioning as an officer. **2** *Brit.* In the Royal Navy: **a** An officer ranking between a naval cadet and the lowest commissioned officer. **b** Formerly, one of a class of youths performing minor duties on shipboard as training for commissioning as officers. [<*amidshipman*; so called from being amidships when on duty]

mid·ships (mid′ships) *adv.* Amidships. — *n. pl.* The midship timbers.

midst (midst) *n.* The central part; middle: often with the implication of being surrounded, beset, or hard pressed: in the *midst* of duties or dangers. See synonyms under CENTER. Compare synonyms for AMID. — **in our, your,** or **their midst** In the midst of, or among, us, you, or them. — *prep.* Amidst. — *adv.* In the middle. [OE *midd* + adverbial *-s* + intrusive or superlative *-t*]

mid·stream (mid′strēm′) *n.* The middle of a stream.

mid·sum·mer (mid′sum′ər) *n.* **1** The middle of summer. **2** Popularly, the time of the summer solstice, about June 21. — *adj.* Like, or occurring in, the middle of the summer.

mid–term (mid′tûrm′) *adj. & adv.* In the middle of the term. — *n.* **1** The middle of the term. **2** *Colloq.* A mid–term examination, as at a college.

mid–Vic·to·ri·an (mid′vik·tôr′ē·ən, -tō′rē-) *adj.* Of or characteristic of the middle period of Queen Victoria's reign in England, or the period approximately 1850–80. — *n.* **1** A British person belonging to this era. **2** A person of markedly Victorian ideas or tastes.

mid·way (mid′wā′, -wā′) *adj.* Being in the middle of the way or distance. — *n.* (mid′wā′) **1** The middle or the middle course. **2** The space, at a fair or exposition, assigned for the display of exhibits and along which the various amusements are situated. — *adv.* Half–way. [OE *midweg*]

Midway Islands Two islets in the North Pacific NW of Honolulu, belonging to the United States and under jurisdiction of the U.S. Navy; 2 square miles; scene of one of the decisive battles of World War II, June, 1942.

mid·week (mid′wēk′) *n.* The middle of the week. — *adj.* In the middle of the week. — **mid′week′ly** *adv.*

Mid·week (mid′wēk′) *n.* In the Society of Friends, Wednesday.

Mid·west (mid′west′) *n.* The Middle West. — **Mid′west′ern** *adj.*

Mid·west·ern·er (mid′wes′tər·nər) *n.* A person from the Middle West.

mid·wife (mid′wīf′) *n. pl.* **·wives** (-wīvz′) A woman who assists women in childbirth. [OE *mid* with + *wif* wife]

mid·wife·ry (mid′wī′fər·ē, -wif′rē) *n.* Obstetrics.

mid·win·ter (mid′win′tər) *n.* **1** The middle of winter. **2** Popularly, the winter solstice, about Dec. 21.

mid·years (mid′yirz′) *n. pl.* Examinations given in the middle of a school or college year.

mien (mēn) *n.* The external appearance or manner of a person; carriage; bearing. See synonyms under AIR[1], MANNER. ◆ Homophone: *mean.* [? Aphetic form of DEMEAN; infl. by F *mine* <Celtic (Breton) *min* beak, muzzle]

miff (mif) *Colloq. v.t.* To cause to be irritated or offended. — *v.i.* To take offense. — *n.* A huff. [Origin uncertain. Cf. G *muffen* sulk.]

mif·fy (mif′ē) *adj. Colloq.* **1** Supersensitive; easily offended. **2** Delicate: said of plants. — **mif′fi·ness** *n.*

Mig (mig) *n.* A type of jet fighter plane of the Soviet air force. [< *Mi(koyan)* and *G(urevich)*, Soviet aircraft designers] Also **MIG.**

might[1] (mīt) Past tense of MAY[1]. Both *may* and *might* are now considered subjunctives with present or future sense, the difference between the two being one of degree rather than of time. *May* implies a greater probability than *might,* the latter indicating possibility but less likelihood: He *might* be on time, but don't depend on it. As a request for permission, *might* is felt to be more hesitant in approach: *Might* we expect your reply by Tuesday? *Might* I come to dinner some evening?

might[2] (mīt) *n.* **1** Ability to do anything requiring force or power; strength. **2** The possession of great resources; intensity of will; ability. See synonyms under POWER. — **with might and main** With utmost endeavor; with one's whole strength. ◆ Homophone: *mite.* [OE *meaht, miht*]

might·i·ly (mī′tə·lē) *adv.* **1** With might; with great force, energy, or earnestness. **2** To a great degree; greatly; very much: I wanted *mightily* to go.

might·i·ness (mī′tē·nis) *n.* The state or quality of being mighty or powerful.

might·y (mī′tē) *adj.* **might·i·er, might·i·est** **1** Possessed of might; powerful; strong. **2** Of unusual bulk, consequence, etc. **3** Momentous; wonderful: a *mighty* host. See synonyms under POWERFUL. — *adv. Colloq.* Very; to a great degree; very much: a *mighty* fine person.

mi·gnon (min′yon, *Fr.* mē·nyôṅ′) *adj.* Delicately small; dainty. [<F <Gmc. Cf. OHG *minna* love. Doublet of MINION.] — **mi·gnonne** (min′yon, *Fr.* mē·nyôn′) *adj. fem.*

mi·gnon·ette (min′yən·et′) *n.* A North African annual plant *(Reseda odorata)* having wedge–shaped leaves, greenish, fragrant flowers with fringed petals, and bladdery seed vessels open at the top. [<F]

mi·graine (mī′grān) *n.* A form of recurrent paroxysmal headache, usually confined to one side of the head, and associated with various gastric and nervous disturbances. See MEGRIM. [<F <LL *hemicrania* <Gk. *hēmikrania* < *hēmi* half + *kranion* skull]

mi·grant (mī′grənt) *adj.* Migratory. — *n.* A migratory bird or other animal or person. [<L *migrans, -antis,* ppr. of *migrare* roam]

mi·grate (mī′grāt) *v.i.* **·grat·ed, ·grat·ing** **1** To move from one country, region, etc., to settle in another. **2** To move periodically from one region or climate to another, as birds or fish. See synonyms under EMIGRATE. [<L *migratus,* pp. of *migrare*] — **mi′gra·tor** *n.*

mi·gra·tion (mī·grā′shən) *n.* **1** The act of migrating. **2** The totality of persons or animals migrating, or the time occupied in migrating. **3** *Chem.* The removal or shifting of one or more atoms from one position in the molecule to another. **4** *Physics* The drift or movement of ions, under the influence of electromotive force, toward one or the other electrode. [<L *migratio, -onis*] — **mi·gra′tion·al** *adj.* — **mi·gra′tion·ist** *n.*

mi·gra·to·ry (mī′grə·tôr′ē, -tō′rē) *adj.* **1** Pertaining to migration. **2** Given to migrating. **3** Roving; nomadic.

Mi·guel (mē·gel′) Portuguese and Spanish form of MICHAEL. Also *Hungarian* **Mi·ha·ly** (mē′·hä·lē), *Sw.* **Mi·ka·el** (mē′kä·äl).

mi·ka·do (mi·kä′dō) *n.* The sovereign of Japan: a title used chiefly by foreigners. [<Japanese *mi* august + *kado* door]

mike (mīk) *n. Colloq.* A microphone. [Short for MICROPHONE]

Mike (mīk) Diminutive of MICHAEL.

Mi·khai·lo·vić (mē·khī′lō·vich), **Draja,** 1893–1946, Serb guerrilla leader in Yugoslavia in World War II; executed.

Mi·klós (mē′klōsh) Hungarian form of NICHOLAS.

mi·kron (mī′kron) See MICRON.

mil (mil) *n.* **1** A unit of length or diameter, equal to one thousandth of an inch or to 25.4001 microns. **2** A milliliter, or one cubic centimeter. **3** *Mil.* **a** A unit of angular measure equal to 1/6400 of a circle, or about 0.0560 degree. **b** A unit of angular measure equal to 0.001 radian. **4** A former monetary unit of Palestine, equal to one thousandth of a pound; also, the coin having this value. [<L *mille* thousand]

mi·la·dy (mi·lā′dē) *n.* An English noblewoman; a gentlewoman: a Continental term used of such a woman. Also **mi·la′di.** [<F <E *my lady*]

mil·age (mī′lij) See MILEAGE.

Mi·lan (mi·lan′, -län′, mil′ən) The second largest city of Italy, in Lombardy. *Italian* **Mi·la·no** (mē·lä′nō).

Mil·an·ese (mil′ən·ēz′, -ēs′) *adj.* Pertaining to Milan, in Italy. — *n. pl.* **·ese** A native or inhabitant of Milan; the people of Milan.

Mi·laz·zo (mē·lät′sō) A port in NE Sicily: site of ancient *Mylae.*

milch (milch) *adj.* Giving milk, as a cow. [OE *milc, meolc* milk]

milch·y (mil′chē) *adj.* Milky.

mild (mīld) *adj.* **1** Moderate in action or disposition. **2** Expressing kindness; calm. **3** Moderate in effect or degree. **4** Not of strong flavor. **5** *Metall.* Designating strong and tough but malleable steel containing only a small percentage of carbon. See synonyms under BLAND, CHARITABLE, PACIFIC. [OE *milde*] — **mild′ly** *adv.* — **mild′ness** *n.*

mild·en (mīl′dən) *v.t. & v.i.* To make or become mild.

mil·dew (mil′do͞o, -dyo͞o) *n.* **1** Any of a family *(Erysiphaceae)* of ascomycetous parasitic fungi that attack a great variety of plants, as hops, cherries, roses, etc. **2** A fungous disease of plants, particularly one caused by a fungus that makes a superficial downy coating on the diseased part of the host plant. **3** Any mold on walls, food, clothing, etc. — *v.t. & v.i.* To affect or be affected with mildew. [OE *mildēaw* honeydew] — **mil′dew·y** *adj.*

Mil·dred (mil′drid) A feminine personal name. [OE, moderate power]

mile (mīl) *n.* A measure of distance (see STATUTE MILE below) in the United States, Great Britain, and Ireland, and in all British possessions; remotely derived from the ancient Roman mile, which was about 1,620 yards or 4,860 feet. — **air mile** A nautical mile by air. — **geographical, nautical,** or **sea mile** One sixtieth of a degree of the earth's equator, or 6,080.2 feet. That of the United States is now the international nautical mile, equal to 6,076.103 feet or 1,852 meters. — **statute mile** The legal mile of the United States, Great Britain, etc., 5,280 feet, or 1,609.35 meters. [OE *mīl* <LL *milia, millia* <L *mille passuum* thousand paces]

mile·age (mī′lij) *n.* **1** The entire length or amount of anything that is or may be measured in miles, especially when stated in miles; aggregate number of miles of track, wire, etc., traversed, made, or used. **2** Compensation reckoned at so much a mile, allowed in lieu of expenses of travel. **3** The rate a mile paid by one traveling in a car, or using a car for any purpose. **4** Number of miles traveled by an automobile, etc., as estimated for each gallon of fuel used. **5** Length of service, quality of performance, etc.; use. Also spelled *milage.*

mileage ticket A ticket entitling the holder to transportation for a specific number of miles.

mil·er (mī′lər) *n.* A person or horse trained to race a mile.

Miles (mīlz) A masculine personal name. [< Gmc., warrior, or L, soldier]

Mi·le·sian (mī·lē′zhən, -shən) *adj.* Of Miletus. — *n.* A native or citizen of Miletus.

Mi·le·sian (mī·lē′zhən, -shən) *n.* **1** In ancient Irish legend, one of the sons or people of Miledh, the mythical ancestor of all the Irish, who migrated from Asia Minor and wandered, via Spain, to Ireland; hence, one of the first Celtic settlers of Ireland. **2** An Irishman.

mile·stone (mīl′stōn′) *n.* **1** A post, pillar, or stone set up to indicate distance in miles from a given point: also **mile′post′** (-pōst′). **2** An important event or turning point in a person's life.

MILESTONE
A 17th century stone, Brooklyn, N. Y.

Mi·le·tus (mī·lē′təs) An ancient port in western Asia Minor.
mil·foil (mil′foil) *n.* Yarrow. [< OF <L *millefolium* < *mille* thousand + *folium* leaf]
Mil·ford Ha·ven (mil′fərd hā′vən) A port in southern Pembroke, Wales.
Mil·haud (mē·yō′), **Darius,** 1892–1974, French composer.
mil·i·ar·i·a (mil′ē·âr′ē·ə) *n. Pathol.* An acute inflammatory disease of the sweat glands marked by an eruption of vesicles and papulae of the size of a pinpoint or larger; miliary fever; the millet-seed rash. [< NL, fem. of L *miliarius.* See MILIARY.]
mil·i·a·ri·sion (mil′ē·ə·rizh′ən) *n.* A silver coin introduced by Constantine and valued at one thousandth of the gold pound; the chief silver coin of the early Middle Ages. Also **mil′i·a·rense′** (-rens′), **mil′i·a·ren′sis** (-ren′sis). [<L *milia,* pl. of *mille* thousand]
mil·i·ar·y (mil′ē·er′ē, mil′yə·rē) *adj.* **1** Like millet seeds. **2** Accompanied by a rash of pimples the size of a millet seed. **3** *Pathol.* Designating a form of tuberculosis caused by the discharge into one or more organs of minute bacillary tubercles originating elsewhere in the body. [<L *miliarius* < *milium* millet]
Mil·i·cent (mil′ə·sənt) A feminine personal name. Also **Mil′li·cent.** [<Gmc., power to work]
mi·lieu (mē·lyœ′) *n.* Surroundings; environment. [<F <OF *mi* middle (<L *medius*) + *lieu* place <L *locus*]
mil·i·tant (mil′ə·tənt) *adj.* **1** Pertaining to conflict with opposing powers or influences. **2** Of a warlike or combative tendency; aggressive. **—*n.*** A combative person; a soldier. [<L *militans, -antis,* ppr. of *militare* be a soldier] **— mil′i·tan·cy** *n.* **— mil′i·tant·ly** *adv.*
mil·i·ta·rism (mil′ə·tə·riz′əm) *n.* **1** A system emphasizing and aggrandizing the military spirit and the need of constant preparation for war. **2** A desire to foster the maintenance of a powerful military position. **— mil′i·ta·rist** *n.* **— mil′i·ta·ris′tic** *adj.* **— mil′i·ta·ris′ti·cal·ly** *adv.*
mil·i·ta·rize (mil′ə·tə·rīz′) *v.t.* **·rized, ·riz·ing** **1** To imbue with militarism. **2** To convert to a military system. **— mil′i·ta·ri·za′tion** (-rə·zā′shən, -rī-) *n.*
mil·i·tar·y (mil′ə·ter′ē) *adj.* **1** Pertaining to armed forces or to warfare; martial; warlike. **2** Done or carried on by force of arms: distinguished from *civil.* See synonyms under WARLIKE. **—*n.*** A body of armed men or soldiers; soldiery. See synonyms under ARMY. [<F *militaire* <L *militaris* < *miles, militis* soldier] **— mil′i·tar′i·ly** *adv.*
military academy A school for boys or young men combining military training and academic education; specifically, the U. S. Military Academy at West Point, New York.
military attaché An army officer attached to his country's embassy or legation in a foreign country.
military governor An army or navy officer serving (usually temporarily) as the civil governor of a state or territory under martial law.
military intelligence **1** Information, of whatever character and however obtained, that is of military value to a country in peace or war. **2** The branch or division of a government engaged in obtaining, interpreting, and using such information.
military mast A strong mastlike structure on a warship, designed to carry a turret, observation tower, etc.
military police *Mil.* A body of soldiers charged with police duties among troops.
mil·i·tate (mil′ə·tāt) *v.i.* **·tat·ed, ·tat·ing** To have influence: with *against,* or, more rarely, *for.* [<L *militatus,* pp. of *militare* be a soldier < *miles, militis*]
mi·li·tia (mə·lish′ə) *n.* **1** A body of citizens enrolled and drilled in military organizations other than the regular military forces, and called out only in emergencies. **2** *U.S.* All able-bodied male citizens between eighteen and forty-five years of age not members of the regular military forces. **— organized militia** *U.S.* The National Guard, Organized Reserves, the Naval Reserve, and the Marine Corps Reserve. [<L, military service < *miles, militis*] **— mi·li′tia·man** (-mən) *n.*
mil·i·um (mil′ē·əm) *n. Pathol.* A skin disease characterized by small yellowish globules. [<L, millet; after the resemblance of the globules to millet seed]
Mil·i·um (mil′ē·əm) *n.* A genus of millet grass. [<NL]
milk (milk) *n.* **1** The opaque, whitish liquid secreted by the mammary glands of female mammals for the nourishment of their young; especially, cow's milk, drunk or used by human beings. ◆ Collateral adjectives: *galactic, lacteal.* **2** The sap of certain plants. **3** Any one of various emulsions. **—*v.t.*** **1** To draw milk from the mammary glands of. **2** To draw (milk). **3** To draw off as if by milking; extract: to *milk* sap from a tree. **4** To draw or extract something from: to *milk* someone of information. **5** To exploit; take advantage of. **—*v.i.*** **6** To yield milk. [OE *meolc, milc*]
milk adder The house snake.
milk-and-wa·ter (milk′ən·wô′tər, -wot′ər) *adj.* **1** Weak and vacillating; namby-pamby. **2** Mawkish; sentimental.
milk·ber·ry (milk′ber′ē) *n.* The snowberry.
milk·er (mil′kər) *n.* **1** One who or that which milks; specifically, a mechanical device for milking cows. **2** A domestic animal, especially a cow, that is milked or that gives milk.
milk fever **1** *Pathol.* A fever attending the secretion of milk about the third day after childbirth. **2** A similar disease of milk cows.
milk·fish (milk′fish′) *n. pl.* **·fish** or **·fish·es** A large, toothless, silvery fish (genus *Chanos*) allied to the herring, especially *C. chanos* of South Pacific waters.
milk leg **1** *Pathol.* A painful white swelling of the leg of a parturient woman. **2** A chronic swelling of a horse's leg, caused by inflammation of the lymphatic vessels.
milk-liv·ered (milk′liv′ərd) *adj.* Cowardly; timorous.
milk·maid (milk′mād′) *n.* A dairymaid.
milk·man (milk′man′) *n. pl.* **·men** (-men′) **1** One who delivers milk from door to door. **2** A man who milks cows.
milk of magnesia See under MAGNESIA.
Milk River A river in Canada and Montana, flowing 625 miles east to the Missouri.
milk run *U.S. Slang* In the air force, a regularly repeated mission.
milk shake A drink made of chilled, flavored milk, and sometimes ice-cream, shaken or whipped until frothy.
milk sickness *Pathol.* A disease caused by drinking the milk or eating the dairy products of cows that have fed on certain poisonous plants: marked by vomiting, intestinal disturbances, and trembling.
milk snake The house snake. Also called *milk adder.*
milk·sop (milk′sop′) *n.* An effeminate man; a sissy.
milk·stone (milk′stōn′) See GALALITH.
milk sugar The sugar contained in milk; lactose.
milk tooth A tooth of the deciduous or first dentition.
milk·vetch (milk′vech′) *n.* The ground plum: so called from the supposed increase in the secretion of milk by goats feeding upon it.
milk·weed (milk′wēd′) *n.* **1** One of a genus *(Asclepias)* of plants having a milky juice. **2** Any of several similar or related plants.
milkweed butterfly The monarch butterfly.
milk white A bluish-white color, like the color of skimmed milk.
milk·wort (milk′wûrt′) *n.* **1** Any of a genus *(Polygala)* of plants with varicolored, showy flowers: so called from the fancied property of increasing the secretion of milk in nursing women; specifically, the **orange milkwort** *(P. lutea)* of the SE United States. **2** The sea milkwort.
milk·y (mil′kē) *adj.* **milk·i·er, milk·i·est** **1** Containing or like milk. **2** Yielding milk. **3** Very mild; spiritless. **4** Containing young or spawn: said of oysters. Also spelled *milchy.* **— milk′·i·ly** *adv.* **— milk′i·ness** *n.*
Milky Way *Astron.* A luminous band encircling the heavens, composed of distant stars and nebulae not separately distinguishable to the naked eye; the Galaxy.
mill[1] (mil) *n.* **1** A machine by means of which grain is ground for food. **2** Any one of various kinds of machines that transform raw material by other processes than grinding: often in combination: a *sawmill;* planing *mill.* **3** A machine for reducing to small or smaller proportions hard substances of any kind. **4** A building fitted up with the machinery requisite for a factory: often in combination: *powdermill.* **5** A hardened steel roller, bearing a design in relief, by which a printing plate or a die may be made by pressure. **6** A milling cutter. **7** *Slang* A pugilistic combat; set-to. **8** A raised or ridged edge or surface made by milling. **9** A machine for crushing or grinding vegetable substances in order to express the juice. **— to go through the mill** To receive or undergo the experiences or hardships needed to acquire a certain degree of skill or wisdom. **—*v.t.*** **1** To grind, shape, polish, roll, etc., in or with a mill. **2** To raise and indent the edge of (a coin). **3** To cause to move with a circular motion. **4** To beat or whip to a froth, as chocolate. **5** *Slang* To strike or thrash; beat. **—*v.i.*** **6** To move slowly in a circle, as cattle. **7** *Slang* To fight or box. [OE *myln, mylen* <LL *molina* <L *mola* millstone]
mill[2] (mil) *n.* **1** A thousandth part. **2** *U.S.* The thousandth part of a dollar, or the tenth part of a cent. [<L *mille* thousand]
Mill (mil), **James,** 1773–1836, Scottish historian, philosopher, and political economist. **— John Stuart,** 1806–73, English philosopher; political economist; son of the preceding.
Mil·lais (mi·lā′), **Sir John Everett,** 1829–96, English painter.
Mil·lay (mi·lā′), **Edna St. Vincent,** 1892–1950, U.S. poet.
mill·board (mil′bôrd′, -bōrd′) *n.* Heavy pasteboard used for the covers of books; imitation pressboard.
mill·cake (mil′kāk′) *n.* **1** The by-product left after the oil has been extracted from linseed. **2** The cake formed by mixing and pressing together the materials of gunpowder previous to granulation.
mill car A railroad flat car upon which heavy hoisting apparatus is mounted.
mill cinder The slag from the puddling furnaces of a steel-rolling mill.
mill·dam (mil′dam′) *n.* **1** A barrier thrown across a watercourse to raise its level sufficiently to turn a millwheel. **2** The pond formed by such a barrier.
milled (mild) *adj.* **1** Passed through, cut by, or mixed in a mill. **2** Having the edges fluted or grooved: said of coins.
mil·le·fi·o·ri (mil′ə·fē·ôr′ē, -ō′rē) *n. Italian* An ancient mosaic glass, later made in Venice, having a flowerlike pattern; literally, a thousand flowers.
mil·le·nar·i·an (mil′ə·nâr′ē·ən) *adj.* Of or pertaining to a thousand; specifically, relating to the millennium. **—*n.*** One who believes in the millennium. **— mil′le·nar′i·an·ism** *n.*
mil·le·nar·y (mil′ə·ner′ē) *adj.* Of or pertaining to a thousand; millenarian; millennial. **—*n. pl.*** **·nar·ies** **1** The space of a thousand years; the millennium. **2** A millenarian. [<LL *millenarius* <L *milleni* a thousand each < *mille* thousand]
mil·len·ni·al (mi·len′ē·əl) *adj.* Of or pertaining to the millennium or to any period of a thousand years. **—*n.*** A thousandth anniversary. **— mil·len′ni·al·ist** *n.* **— mil·len′ni·al·ly** *adv.*
mil·len·ni·um (mi·len′ē·əm) *n. pl.* **·ni·a** (-ē·ə) **1** A period of a thousand years. **2** The thousand years of the kingdom of Christ on earth. *Rev.* xx 1–5. **3** Hence, by extension, any period of happiness, beneficial government or the like. [<NL < *mille* thousand + *annus* year]
mil·le·ped (mil′ə·ped), **mil·le·pede** (mil′ə·pēd) See MILLIPEDE.
mil·le·pore (mil′ə·pôr, -pōr) *n. Zool.* A coral-like hydrozoan (genus *Millepora*) with numerous cavities in the enclosing and often bulky limestone structure. Also **mil·lep·o·ra** (mə·lep′ər·ə). [<F *millépore* < *mille* thousand + *pore* pore]
mill·er (mil′ər) *n.* **1** One who keeps or tends a mill, particularly a gristmill. **2** A milling machine. **3** A mothmiller.

Mil·ler (mil′ər), **Arthur,** born 1915, U. S. playwright. — **Henry,** born 1891, U. S. author. — **Joaquin** Pseudonym of Cincinnatus Heine Miller, 1839–1913, U. S. poet. — **Joe,** 1684–1738, English comedian: real name *Josias Miller.* — **William,** 1782–1849, U. S. Adventist; founder of the Millerites.

Mille·rand (mēl·räṅ′), **Alexandre,** 1859–1943, French statesman; president 1920–24.

mil·ler·ite (mil′ər·īt) *n.* A metallic, brass-yellow, brittle nickel sulfide, NiS, crystallizing in the hexagonal system. [after W. H. *Miller,* 1801–80, English mineralogist]

Mil·ler·ite (mil′ər·īt) *n.* A follower of William Miller, who announced in 1831 that Christ's second coming and the end of the world would be in 1843. — **Mil′ler·ism** *n.*

miller's thumb A small, fresh-water fish (family *Cottidae*) with broad, flattened head and spiny fins.

Mil·les (mil′əs), **Carl,** 1875–1955, Swedish sculptor active in the United States.

mil·les·i·mal (mi·les′ə·məl) *adj.* Pertaining to thousandths. — *n.* A thousandth. [<L *millesimus* < *mille* thousand]

mil·let (mil′it) *n.* **1** A grass (*Panicum miliaceum*), or its seed, cultivated in the United States for forage, but in the Old World from earliest times, and still in some parts of Europe, as a cereal. **2** One of various other grasses, or their seed, as the **foxtail** or **Italian millet** (*Setaria italica*), **pearl millet** (*Pennisetum glaucum*), etc. [<F, dim. of *mil* <L *milium*]

Mil·let (mē·le′), **Jean François,** 1814–75, French artist.

mill finish A surface finish produced on sheet and plate steel characteristic of the ground finish that is present on the rollers used in fabrication.

mill·hand (mil′hand′) *n.* A worker in a mill.

milli– *combining form* **1** A thousand: *millipede.* **2** In the metric and other systems of measurement, the thousandth part of (a specified unit):

milliampere	**millicurie**	**millilux**
milliangstrom	**millifarad**	**milliphot**
milliare	**millihenry**	**millistere**
millibar	**millilambert**	**millivolt**

[<L *mille* a thousand]

mil·liard (mil′yərd) *n.* A thousand millions; usually, in the United States, called a billion. [<F <Pg. *milhar* thousand]

mil·li·ar·y (mil′ē·er′ē) *adj.* Pertaining to a Roman mile. — *n. pl.* **·ar·ies** A Roman milestone, set up at intervals of 1,000 paces. [<L *milliarius*]

mil·lier (mē·lyā′) *n.* A metric ton, 1,000 kilograms. [<F]

mil·li·gram (mil′ə·gram) *n.* The thousandth part of a gram. See METRIC SYSTEM. Also **mil′·li·gramme.** [<F *milligramme*]

Mil·li·kan (mil′ə·kən), **Robert Andrews,** 1868–1955, U. S. physicist.

mil·li·li·ter (mil′ə·lē′tər) *n.* The thousandth part of a liter. See METRIC SYSTEM. Also **mil′·li·li′tre.** [<F *millilitre*]

mil·li·me·ter (mil′ə·mē′tər) *n.* The thousandth part of a meter. See METRIC SYSTEM. Also **mil′·li·me′tre.** [<F *millimètre*]

mil·li·mi·cron (mil′ə·mī′kron) *n.* A thousandth of a micron, or a millionth of a millimeter; also, ten angstroms (symbol m, also μ).

mil·li·mol (mil′ə·mol) *n.* The thousandth part of a mol. Also **mil′li·mole** (-mōl). [<MILLI- + MOL]

mil·line (mil·līn′) *n.* The rate of cost for placing an advertisement of one agate line before a million readers. [<MILL(ION) + LINE]

mil·li·ner (mil′ə·nər) *n.* **1** A person employed in making, trimming, or selling bonnets, women's hats, etc. **2** *Obs.* A dealer in small wares: a haberdasher. [<*Milaner* an inhabitant of Milan, in Italy; hence, a man from Milan who imported silks and the like]

mil·li·ner·y (mil′ə·ner′ē, -nər·ē) *n.* **1** The articles made or sold by milliners. **2** The occupation or establishment of a milliner. [<MILLINER]

mill·ing (mil′ing) *n.* **1** The operating of a mill or mills, as in the grinding of meal or metals, the preparation of cloth, etc. **2** A milled surface, as of a coin, or the act or process of producing it: distinguished from *reeding.* **3** The slow, round-and-round motion of or as of a herd of cattle. [<MILL, *v.*]

mil·lion (mil′yən) *n.* **1** The cardinal number equivalent to ten hundred thousand or to a thousand thousand, or the symbols (1,000,000) representing it; ten to the sixth power. **2** Elliptically, a thousand thousand of the ordinary units of account, as dollars, francs, or pounds: He is worth a *million.* **3** An indefinitely great number. — **the million** The common people. [<OF <Ital. *millione* (now *milione*), aug. of *mille* thousand]

mil·lion·aire (mil′yən·âr′) *n.* One whose possessions are valued at a million or more, as of dollars, pounds, etc. Also **mil′lion·naire′.** [<F *millionaire*]

mil·lion·fold (mil′yən·fōld′) *adj.* A million times the quantity. — *adv.* In a millionfold proportion; a million times in amount: with the indefinite article *a,* construed as a plural.

mil·lionth (mil′yənth) *adj.* **1** Being last in a series of a million: an ordinal numeral. **2** Being one of a million equal parts: a *millionth* part. — *n.* One part in a million equal parts; one divided by one million.

mil·li·pede (mil′ə·pēd) *n.* A herbivorous, slow-moving arthropod (class *Diplopoda*) having a rounded body marked by numerous segments, from nearly all of which issue two pairs of appendages: also spelled *milleped, millepede.* Also **mil′li·ped** (-ped). [<L *millepeda* < *mille* thousand + *pes, pedis* foot]

mill·pond (mil′pond′) *n.* **1** A body of water dammed up to run a mill. **2** A body of water adjoining a sawmill where logs are floated until sawn.

mill·race (mil′rās′) *n.* The sluice through which the water runs to a millwheel.

mill·run (mil′run′) *n.* **1** A millrace. **2** A certain amount of ore tested for content or quality by the process of milling. **3** The mineral yielded by the test.

mill–run (mil′run′) *adj.* Average; just as it comes from the mill; not selected: also *run-of-the-mill.*

Mills bomb (milz) A highly explosive grenade weighing about 1 1/2 pounds and usually thrown by hand. Also **Mills grenade.** [after Sir Wm. *Mills,* 1856–1932, British inventor]

mill·stone (mil′stōn′) *n.* **1** One of a pair of thick, heavy, stone disks for grinding something, as grain. **2** That which pulverizes or bears down. **3** A heavy or burdensome weight. *Matt.* xvii 6.

mill town A town whose center of activity is a mill or group of mills, and whose population is employed, for the most part, in the mill or mills.

mill·wheel (mil′hwēl′) *n.* The waterwheel that drives a mill.

mill·work (mil′wûrk′) *n.* Carpentry work delivered from a mill ready for installation or use.

mill·wright (mil′rīt′) *n.* One who plans, builds, or fits out mills; also, a machinist who sets up shafting, etc.

Milne (miln), **A(lan) A(lexander),** 1882–1956, English playwright, novelist, and writer of children's books.

Mil·ner (mil′nər), **Sir Alfred,** 1854–1925, first Viscount Milner; British administrator in South Africa.

mi·lo (mī′lō) *n.* A non-saccharin sorghum similar to millet. [<Bantu *maili*]

Mi·lo (mī′lō) A renowned Greek athlete, about 520 B.C.

Mi·lo (mē′lō) The southwesternmost island in the Cyclades group; 61 square miles: also *Melos.* Also **Mi′los** (-lôs).

mil·o·maize (mil′ō·māz) *n.* See MILO.

mi·lord (mi·lôrd′) *n.* An English nobleman; a gentleman: a Continental term used of such a man. [<F <E *my lord*]

Milque·toast (milk′tōst) See CASPAR MILQUETOAST.

mil·reis (mil′rās) *n.* **1** A former Brazilian monetary unit, equivalent to 1,000 reis. **2** A former Portuguese monetary unit, superseded in 1911 by the escudo. [<Pg., lit., a thousand reis]

milt[1] (milt) *n.* The spleen. [OE *milte* spleen]

milt[2] (milt) *n.* **1** The sperm of a fish. **2** The spermatic organs of a fish when filled with seminal fluid; the soft roe. — *v.t.* To impregnate (fish roe) with milt. [OE *milte*]

milt·er (mil′tər) *n.* **1** A male fish. **2** The milt of a fish.

Mil·ti·a·des (mil·tī′ə·dēz) Athenian general; defeated the Persians at Marathon, 490 B.C.

Mil·ton (mil′tən), **John,** 1608–74, English poet.

Mil·ton·ic (mil·ton′ik) *adj.* Of, pertaining to, or like the poet Milton or his works or style; sublime; majestic. Also **Mil·to′ni·an** (-tō′nē·ən).

Mil·town (mil′toun) *n.* Proprietary name for a synthetic drug used in pill form as a tranquilizer.

Mil·wau·kee (mil·wô′kē) A port on Lake Michigan in SE Wisconsin.

Mil·yu·kov (mē·lyo͞o′kôf), **Pavel Nikolaevich,** 1859–1943, Russian politician and historian.

mim (mim) *Brit. Dial.* Demure; precise. [Imit.]

mime (mīm) *n.* **1** A mimic play or farce or the dialog for this; a dramatic representation, akin to comedy, mimicking real persons or events: a favorite amusement among the Greeks and Romans. **2** An actor in a mime; hence, a mimic; clown, buffoon. — *v.* **mimed, mim·ing** *v.t.* To mimic; imitate. — *v.i.* To play the mimic; play a part with gestures and usually without words. [<L *mimus* <Gk. *mimos*] — **mim′er** *n.*

Mim·e·o·graph (mim′ē·ə·graf′, -gräf′) *n.* An apparatus in which a thin fibrous paper coated with paraffin is used as a stencil for reproducing copies of written or typewritten matter: a trade name. — *v.t.* To reproduce by means of a Mimeograph. [<Gk. *mimeisthai* imitate + -GRAPH]

mi·me·sis (mi·mē′sis, mī-) *n.* **1** Imitation or representation of the supposed speech, characteristic dialect, carriage, or gestures of an individual or a people, as in art and literature. **2** *Biol.* Mimicry. [<NL <Gk. *mimēsis* imitation]

mi·met·ic (mi·met′ik, mī-) *adj.* **1** Quick to mimic; imitative. **2** Relating to mimicry or mimesis. **3** Mimic (*adj.* def. 1). Also **mi·met′i·cal.** [<Gk. *mimētikos*] — **mi·met′i·cal·ly** *adv.*

mim·ic (mim′ik) *v.t.* **·icked, ·ick·ing** **1** To imitate the speech or actions of, as in ridicule. **2** To copy closely; ape. **3** To have or assume the color, shape, etc., of; simulate: Some insects *mimic* leaves. See synonyms under IMITATE. — *n.* **1** One who is given to mimicry; a mimic actor; buffoon. **2** A copy; imitation. — *adj.* **1** Of the nature of mimicry; imitative; mimetic: a *mimic* gesture. **2** Copying the real; simulated; mock: a *mimic* court. [<L *mimicus* <Gk. *mimikos* < *mimos* mime] — **mim′i·cal** *adj.* — **mim′ick·er** *n.*

mim·ic·ry (mim′ik·rē) *n. pl.* **·ries** **1** The act of imitating, especially for sport; also, a thing produced as a copy. **2** *Zool.* An imitative superficial resemblance in one animal to another or to its immediate environment, for purposes of concealment or protection. Compare PROTECTIVE COLORATION. See synonyms under CARICATURE.

Mi·mir (mē′mir) In Norse mythology, the giant who kept the **Mi·mis·brun·nen** (mē′mis·bro͝on′·ən), or well of wisdom, flowing from the root of Ygdrasil, and for a draft from which Odin bartered his eye. Also **Mi′mer.**

mi·mo·sa (mi·mō′sə, -zə) *n.* **1** Any plant of a large genus (*Mimosa*) of tropical herbs, shrubs, or trees of the bean family, with feathery, bipinnate foliage, and clusters of small flowers; especially, the sensitive plant. **2** A light yellow: the color of certain varieties of mimosa. [<NL <L *mimus* mime; from its supposed mimicry of animal life] — **mim·o·sa·ceous** (mim′ō·sā′shəs, mī′mō-) *adj.*

Min (min) **1** A river in Fukien province, China, flowing 350 miles SE to the China Sea. **2** A river in Szechwan province, China, flowing 500 miles south to the Yangtze.

min' (mīn) *v.* & *n. Scot.* Mind.

mi·na[1] (mī′nə) *n. pl.* **·nae** (-nē) or **·nas** An ancient Greek and Asian weight or sum of money, equal to 100 drachmas. [<L <Gk. *mna*]

mi·na[2] (mī′nə) See MYNA. Also **mi′nah.**

mi·na·cious (mi·nā′shəs) *adj.* Threatening; of a menacing character. [<L *minax, minacis.* See MENACE.] — **mi·na′cious·ly** *adv.* — **mi·na′·cious·ness, mi·nac·i·ty** (mi·nas′ə·tē) *n.*

min·a·ret (min′ə·ret′) *n.* A high, slender tower attached to a Moslem mosque, surrounded by one or more balconies, from which is sounded the stated summons to prayer. [<Sp. *minarete* <Turkish *manārat* <Arabic *manārah* lamp, lighthouse <*minār* candlestick]

MINARET
A. Shown in relation to mosque.
B. Detail showing the balcony.

Mi·nas Basin (mī′nəs) The NE arm of the Bay of Fundy, Nova Scotia; connected by the **Minas Channel** (24 miles long) with the Bay of Fundy.

Mi·nas de Rí·o·tin·to (mē′näs thä rē′ō·tēn′tō) A town in SW Spain; site of copper mines since Roman times: also **Ríotinto.**

Mi·nas Ge·rais (mē′nəzh zhə·rīs′) An inland state in eastern Brazil; 224,701 square miles; capital, Bello Horizonte. Formerly **Minas Geraes.**

min·a·to·ry (min′ə·tôr·ē, -tō′rē) *adj.* Threatening, as with destruction or punishment. Also **min′a·to′ri·al.** [<OF *minatoire* <LL *minatorius* <*minatus,* pp. of *minari* threaten] — **min′a·to′ri·al·ly, min′a·to′ri·ly** *adv.*

mince (mins) *v.* **minced, minc·ing** *v.t.* **1** To cut or chop into small bits, as meat. **2** To subdivide minutely. **3** To diminish the force or strength of; moderate: He didn't *mince* words with her. **4** To say or do with affected primness or elegance. — *v.i.* **5** To walk with short steps or affected daintiness. **6** To speak or behave with affected primness. — *n.* **1** Mincemeat. **2** *Rare* An affectation. [<OF *mincier;* ult. <L *minuere* lessen, make smaller] — **minc′er** *n.* — **minc′ing·ly** *adv.*

minced oath (minst) A mild or weak oath: "Egad" is a *minced oath.*

mince·meat (mins′mēt′) *n.* **1** Meat chopped very fine. **2** A mixture of chopped meat, fruit, spices, etc., used in mince pie.

mince pie A pie made of mincemeat.

minc·ing-horse (min′sing·hôrs′) *n.* A heavy block of hardwood usually mounted on legs, used for chopping meats or vegetables.

minc·ing-spade (min′sing·spād′) *n.* A knife-edged spade used in whaling, for chopping or mincing blubber.

Min·cio (mēn′chō) A river in northern Italy, flowing 115 miles from Lake Garda to the Po. Ancient **Min·cius** (min′shəs).

mind (mīnd) *n.* **1** The aggregate of all conscious and unconscious processes originating in and associated with the brain, especially those pertaining to cognition, intelligence, and intellect. **2** Memory; remembrance: to bear in *mind.* **3** Opinion; way of thinking: to change one's *mind.* **4** Desire; inclination: to have a *mind* to leave. **5** Mental disposition, character, or temper: a liberal *mind*; a cheerful *mind.* **6** Intellectual power or capacity. **7** The faculty of cognition and intellect, as opposed to the will and emotions: a noble heart and a cultivated *mind.* **8** A person, regarded as having intellect: the great *minds* of our time. **9** Sanity; sound mentality: to lose one's *mind.* **10** *Philos.* The spirit of intelligence pervading the universe: opposed to *matter.* **11** In Christian Science, God: also **Divine Mind.** — **a month's mind** The monthly commemoration, usually the first, of a person's death. — **on one's mind** Occupying one's thoughts. — **to speak one's mind** To declare one's opinions freely or candidly. — **to take one's mind off** To turn one's thoughts from. — *v.t.* **1** To pay attention to; occupy oneself with: *Mind* your own business. **2** To be careful or wary concerning: *Mind* your step. **3** To give heed to, as commands; obey. **4** To care for; tend. **5** To be concerned about; regard with annoyance; dislike: Do you *mind* the noise? **6** To be aware of; notice; perceive. **7** *Colloq.* To remember: sometimes used reflexively. **8** *Archaic* To remind. **9** *Obs.* To intend; purpose. — *v.i.* **10** To pay attention; take notice; watch. **11** To be obedient. **12** To be concerned; care: I don't *mind.* **13** To be careful. [OE *gemynd*] — **mind′er** *n.*

Synonyms (noun): brain, consciousness, disposition, instinct, intellect, intelligence, reason, sense, soul, spirit, thought, understanding. *Mind* includes all the powers of sentient being apart from the physical factors in bodily faculties and activities; in a limited sense, *mind* is nearly synonymous with *intellect,* but includes *disposition,* or the tendency toward action, as appears in the phrase "to have a *mind* to work." The *intellect* is that assemblage of faculties which is concerned with knowledge, as distinguished from emotion and volition. *Understanding* is chiefly used of the reasoning powers: the *understanding* is distinguished by many philosophers from *reason* in that *reason* is the faculty of the high cognitions or a priori truth. *Thought,* the act, process, or power of thinking, is often used to denote the thinking faculty, and especially the *reason.* The *instinct* of animals is held to be of the same nature as the *intellect* of man, but inferior and limited; yet the apparent difference is very great. Human *instincts* denote tendencies independent of reasoning or instruction. As the seat of mental activity, *brain* is often used as a synonym for *mind, intellect, intelligence. Sense* is used as denoting clear mental action, good judgment, acumen; as, He is a man of *sense,* or, he showed good *sense. Consciousness* includes all that a sentient being perceives, knows, thinks, or feels, from whatever source. See GENIUS, SOUL, UNDERSTANDING. *Antonyms:* body, brawn, matter.

Min·da·na·o (min′də·nä′ō) The southernmost and second largest island in the Philippines; 36,537 square miles.

Mindanao Sea Part of the Pacific bounded by Mindanao to the south and by Leyte, Bohol, Cebu, and Negros to the north.

mind-blind·ness (mīnd′blīnd′nis) *n.* Mental blindness.

mind-cure (mīnd′kyŏŏr′) *n.* **1** The treatment and cure of disease, especially of neuroses, by direct influence upon the mind of the patient and without the use of drugs. **2** Psychotherapy.

mind-deaf·ness (mīnd′def′nis) *n.* Mental deafness.

mind·ed (mīn′did) *adj.* **1** Disposed. **2** Having a specified kind of mind: evil-*minded.*

Min·del (min′dəl) See GLACIAL EPOCH.

mind·ful (mīnd′fəl) *adj.* Keeping in mind; heeding; having knowledge (of); aware. See synonyms under THOUGHTFUL. — **mind′ful·ly** *adv.* — **mind′ful·ness** *n.*

mind·less (mīnd′lis) *adj.* **1** Devoid of intelligence. **2** Not giving heed or attention; careless. — **mind′less·ly** *adv.* — **mind′less·ness** *n.*

Min·do·ro (min·dō′rō) An island in the central Philippines; 3,759 square miles.

mind-read·ing (mīnd′rē′ding) *n.* **1** The ascertaining of the thoughts or purpose of some other mind by the interpretation of voluntary or involuntary muscle movements or facial expressions. **2** Telepathy. — **mind′-read′er** *n.*

Mind·szen·ty (mind′sen·tē) **Joseph,** born 1892, Hungarian Roman Catholic cardinal, imprisoned by the Nazis in 1944 and by the Communist regime in Hungary 1948–56.

mine[1] (mīn) *n.* **1** An excavation for digging out some useful product, as ore or coal. **2** Any deposit of such material suitable for excavation. **3** An underground tunnel dug beneath an enemy's fortifications, as for the placement of an explosive charge. **4** A case containing such a charge buried in the earth, or floating on or near, or anchored beneath, the surface of the water. **5** Any productive source of supply. **6** A burrow made by an insect. — **bounding mine** A land mine set just beneath the surface of the ground and designed to rise a few feet in the air before exploding its charge of shrapnel and fragments. — **land mine** A high-explosive or chemical mine, actuated by the weight of a person, troops, or vehicles. — *v.* **mined, min·ing** *v.t.* **1** To dig (coal, ores, etc.) from the earth. **2** To dig into (the earth, etc.) for coal, ores, etc. **3** To make by digging, as a tunnel; burrow. **4** To dig a tunnel under, as for placing an explosive mine; sap. **5** To attack or destroy by slow or secret means; undermine. **6** To place an explosive mine or mines in or under: to *mine* a harbor. — *v.i.* **7** To dig in a mine for coal, ores, etc.; work in a mine. **8** To make a tunnel, etc., by digging; burrow. **9** To place explosive mines. [<OF <Celtic. Cf. Irish *mein* vein of metal.] — **min′er** *n.*

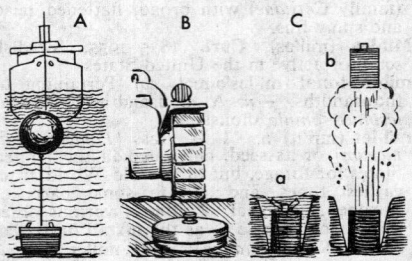

MINES
A. Marine mine anchored in harbor entrance.
B. Buried anti-tank mine.
C. Anti-personnel mine *(a)*; inner canister rises and explodes *(b).*

mine[2] (mīn) *pron.* **1** The possessive case of *I* employed predicatively; belonging or pertaining to me: That book is *mine.* **2** The things or persons belonging or pertaining to me: His work is better than *mine*; Fortune has been good to me and *mine.* — **of mine** Belonging or relating to me; my: the double possessive. — *pronominal adj. Archaic* My: *mine* eyes. [OE *mīn*]

mine detector An electromagnetic instrument for detecting the presence and locating the position of mines.

mine field An area in water or on land systematically planted with mines.

mine layer An auxiliary naval vessel, of submarine or surface type, provided with special equipment for the laying of mines.

min·er·al (min′ər·əl) *n.* **1** A naturally occurring, homogeneous substance or material formed by inorganic processes and having a characteristic set of physical properties, a definite range of chemical composition, and a·molecular structure usually expressed in crystalline forms. **2** Any inorganic substance, as ore, a rock, or a fossil. — **accessory minerals** Those components or minerals forming so small a part of a rock or occurring so rarely as not to be included in its description. — *adj.* **1** Pertaining to, consisting of, or resembling minerals. **2** Impregnated with mineral constituents. [<OF <Med. L *minerale,* neut. sing. of *mineralis* of a mine <*minera* a mine]

mineral butter *Chem.* Antimony trichloride, SbCl$_3$, a colorless, translucent, poisonous, crystalline substance: used as a mordant and reagent, and in the manufacture of certain dyes.

mineral carbon Graphite.

mineral charcoal A pulverulent substance showing patterned traces of vegetable origin but consisting mainly of carbon: it occurs in thin layers in bituminous coal.

min·er·al·ize (min′ər·əl·īz′) *v.* **·ized, ·iz·ing** *v.t.* **1** To convert from a metal to a mineral, as iron to rust. **2** To convert to a mineral substance; petrify. **3** To impregnate with minerals or other inorganic substances. — *v.i.* **4** To observe, study, and collect minerals. Also **min·er·al·o·gize** (min′ə·ral′ə·jīz), *Brit.* **min′er·al·ise.** — **min′er·al·i·za′tion** *n.*

min·er·al·iz·er (min′ər·əl·īz′ər) *n.* **1** An element that combines with a metal to form an ore, as sulfur. **2** A volatile or other substance, as boron or water, that facilitates the recrystallization of rocks.

mineral jelly See PETROLATUM.

mineral kingdom The great division of nature

which comprises all inorganic and non-living materials, as rocks, metals, minerals, etc. Compare ANIMAL KINGDOM, VEGETABLE KINGDOM.

min·er·al·o·gy (min′ə·ral′ə·jē) *n.* The science of minerals. **—min′er·a·log′i·cal** (-ər·ə·loj′i·kəl) *adj.* **—min′er·a·log′i·cal·ly** *adv.* **—min′er·al′o·gist** *n.*

mineral oil Any of various oils derived from inorganic matter, especially petroleum and its products: used as a fuel, in medicine as a laxative, etc.

mineral pitch Asphalt.

mineral tar Maltha.

mineral water Any natural water containing one or more minerals in solution, especially one impregnated with salts or gases having therapeutic properties.

mineral wax Ozocerite.

mineral wool A fibrous, fluffy material resembling wool in appearance, and made by subjecting molten silicate, molten slag, or other similar materials to a steam blast and cooling rapidly to prevent crystallization: used as packing and as an insulator: also called *rock wool, slag wool.* Compare GLASSWOOL.

Mi·ner·va (mi·nûr′və) In Roman mythology, the goddess of wisdom, handicraft, and technical dexterity: identified with Greek *Athena.*

min·e·stro·ne (min′ə·strō′nē) *n.* A thick vegetable soup containing vermicelli, barley, etc., in a meat broth.

mine sweeper 1 A naval vessel equipped for the detection, destruction, and removal of marine mines. **2** A heavy roller attached to the front of a tank for exploding land mines.

mine thrower A trench mortar.

Ming (ming) *n.* In Chinese history, the last ruling dynasty (1368–1644) of truly Chinese origin: noted for the artistic works, as porcelains, produced during its rule. [<Chinese, lit., luminous]

min·gle (ming′gəl) *v.* **min·gled, min·gling** *v.t.* **1** To mix or unite together; blend. **2** To join or combine; bring into close relation. *—v.i.* **3** To be or become mixed, united, or closely joined. **4** To enter into company; mix or associate, as with a crowd. **5** To take part; become involved, as in a dispute. See synonyms under MIX. [<Freq. of OE *mengan*] **—min′gler** *n.*

Min·how (min′hō′) A former name for FOOCHOW.

min·i (min′ē) *n. pl.* **min·is 1** A miniskirt. **2** *Colloq.* Anything smaller or shorter than others of its class. *—adj.* **·i·er, ·i·est** Very small or miniaturized. [<MINI-]

mini- *combining form* Small; tiny: *miniskirt.* [<L *minimus* least, smallest]

min·i·a·ture (min′ē·ə·chər, min′ə·chər) *n.* **1** A painting of small dimensions and delicate workmanship, usually a portrait, or the art of executing such paintings on ivory, metal, or vellum, in water-colors or oils. **2** A portrayal of anything on a small scale; hence, reduced dimensions or extent. **3** *Obs.* Lettering in red; rubrication, as of medieval manuscripts. See synonyms under PICTURE. *—adj.* Much smaller than reality; very small. [<F <Ital. *miniatura* <Med. L <L *miniare* paint red <*minium* red lead, ? <Iberian; later infl. in meaning by L *minuere* lessen]

min·i·a·tur·ize (min′ē·ə·chər·īz′, min′ə·chər·īz′) *v.t.* **·ized, ·iz·ing** To reduce the size of, as the parts of an instrument or machine. **—min′i·a·tur′i·za′tion** *n.*

min·i·bike (min′ē·bīk′) *n.* A small motorcycle with a single seat.

min·i·cam (min′ə·kam) *n.* A small, portable camera, usually one using 35-mm. film.

min·i·com·put·er (min′ē·kəm·pyōō′tər) *n.* A small, inexpensive electronic computer.

Min·i·é ball (min′ē·ā, min′ē; *Fr.* mē·nyā′) A conical rifle ball with hollow base and a plug driven in by the explosion of the charge to expand the lead and fill the grooves of the rifling: formerly used in the **Minié rifle,** specially designed for it. [after Capt. Claude Etienne *Minié,* 1814–79, French inventor]

min·i·fy (min′ə·fī) *v.t.* **·fied, ·fy·ing 1** To make small or less. **2** To lessen the worth or importance of. [<L *minor* less + -FY]

min·i·kin (min′ə·kin) *adj. Obs.* Of small size or delicate form. *—n. Rare* Something very minute or delicate, as the smallest size of pin. [<Du. *minneken,* dim. of *minne* love]

min·im (min′im) *n.* **1** An apothecaries' fluid measure; roughly, one drop, or one sixtieth of a fluid dram: in the United States, 0.06 cubic centimeter; in England, 0.059 cubic centimeter. **2** *Music* A half note. **3** An extremely small creature; a pigmy. **4** A down-stroke in writing, as in forming the letter *n.* **5** *Printing* A size of type, about 7-point, between nonpareil and brevier. *—adj.* Extremely small. [<F *minime* <L *minimus* least, smallest. Doublet of MINIMUM.] **—min′i·mal** *adj.*

Min·i·mal·ist (min′ə·məl·ist) *n.* One belonging to the more conservative branch of the former Russian Social Democrats: distinguished from *Maximalist.*

min·i·mize (min′ə·mīz) *v.t.* **·mized, ·miz·ing 1** To reduce to the smallest possible amount or degree. **2** To regard or represent at a minimum. Also *Brit.* **min′i·mise. —min′i·miz′er** *n.* **—min′i·mi·za′tion** *n.*

min·i·mum (min′ə·məm) *adj.* Consisting of or showing the least possible amount or degree; being a minimum. *—n. pl.* **·ma** (-mə) or **·mums 1** The least possible quantity, amount, or degree. **2** A value of a function that is less than any value which immediately precedes and follows it. **3** The lowest degree, variation, etc., as of temperature, recorded. [<L, neut. of *minimus.* Doublet of MINIM.] **—min′i·mal** *adj.*

minimum wage 1 A wage fixed by law or agreement as the smallest amount an employer may offer an employee in a specific group. **2** A living wage.

min·ing (mī′ning) *n.* **1** The act, process, or business of extracting coal, ores, etc., from mines. **2** The act of laying explosive mines.

mining camp A temporary settlement around or near a mine.

min·ion (min′yən) *n.* **1** A servile favorite or follower: a term of contempt. **2** *Printing* A size of type, about 7-point. **3** A saucy girl or woman; minx. **4** *Obs.* One who is beloved; a paramour. *—adj. Rare* Dainty; delicate; fine. [<F *mignon.* Doublet of MIGNON.]

min·i·scule (min′əs·kyōōl) *adj.* Minuscule.

min·ish (min′ish) *v.t.* & *v.i. Obs.* To make or become less; diminish. [<F *menuisier* make small <L *minutus,* pp. of *minuere* lessen]

min·i·skirt (min′i·skûrt′) *n.* A short skirt worn by women with the hemline well above the knee. Also **min′i-skirt′.** [<MINI- + SKIRT]

min·is·ter (min′is·tər) *n.* **1** The chief of an executive department of a government. **2** One commissioned to represent his government in diplomatic intercourse with another government. **3** One who is authorized to preach the gospel and administer the ordinances of the church; a clergyman. **4** One who acts in subservience to the will of another; a servant; agent. **5** One who promotes or dispenses. *—v.i.* **1** To give attendance or aid; provide for the wants or needs of someone. **2** To be conducive; contribute. *—v.t.* **3** To administer or apply. **4** *Archaic* To supply; furnish. See synonyms under SERVE. [<OF *ministre* <L *minister* an attendant <*minor* less; after L *magister* master <*magis* greater]

min·is·te·ri·al (min′is·tir′ē·əl) *adj.* **1** Of or pertaining to a minister of the gospel or the ministry; clerical. **2** Of or pertaining to a minister or executive staff in civil government. **3** *Law* Pertaining to an act or duty performed according to the mandate of legal authority, so that the agent is not accountable for its propriety or consequences: opposed to *judicial.* **4** Instrumental; causative. [<F *ministériel*] **—min′is·te′ri·al·ly** *adv.*

min·is·te·ri·al·ist (min′is·tir′ē·əl·ist) *n.* In English politics, one who supports the ministry.

minister plenipotentiary See PLENIPOTENTIARY.

minister resident See under RESIDENT.

min·is·trant (min′is·trənt) *adj.* Ministering. *—n.* One who ministers. [<L *ministrans, -antis,* ppr. of *ministrare* serve]

min·is·tra·tion (min′is·trā′shən) *n.* **1** The act of performing service as a minister. **2** Any religious ceremonial. [<L *ministratio, -onis*] **—min′is·tra′tive** *adj.*

min·is·try (min′is·trē) *n. pl.* **·tries 1** The body of officials in charge of the administration of the departments of a government. In the United States it is selected by the president with the advice and consent of the Senate, and is called the *Cabinet.* **2** An executive department of government. **3** Ministers of the gospel collectively, or their office. **4** The act of ministering, or the state or office of a minister; ministration; service. [<L *ministerium*]

Min·i·track (min′i·trak′) *n.* A sensitive electronic system for tracking the paths of earth satellites by the timing of radio signals received by ground stations: a trade name.

min·i·um (min′ē·əm) *n.* **1** A vivid opaque red lead oxide, Pb_3O_4: used chiefly as a pigment. **2** Cinnabar. [<L]

min·i·ver (min′ə·vər) *n.* **1** A fur or mixture of furs used in the Middle Ages for trimming. **2** Any white fur, as ermine. [<OF *menu vair,* lit., little spotted (fur)]

mink (mingk) *n.* **1** An amphibious, slender-bodied, carnivorous mammal (genus *Mustela*), related to the weasel and valued for its soft, thick, glossy, brown fur. **2** The fur of this mammal. [<Scand. Cf. Sw. *menk.*]

Min·kow·ski (ming·kôf′skē), **Hermann,** 1864–1909, Russian mathematician.

Min·ne·ap·o·lis (min′ē·ap′ə·lis) A city on the Mississippi in SE central Minnesota.

Min·ne·ha·ha (min′ē·hä′hä) In Longfellow's *The Song of Hiawatha,* a Dakota Indian maiden, the wife of Hiawatha.

min·ne·sing·er (min′ə·sing′ər) *n.* A lyric poet of medieval Germany. Compare TROUBADOUR. [<G *minne* love + *singer* singer]

Min·ne·so·ta (min′ə·sō′tə) A State in the north central United States bordering on Canada and Lake Superior; 84,682 square miles; capital, St. Paul; entered the Union May 11, 1858; nickname, *Gopher State*: abbr. MN **—Min′ne·so′tan** *n.* & *adj.*

Min·ne·wit (min′ə·wit), **Peter** See MINUIT, PETER.

Min·nie (min′ē) A feminine personal name. [<G, love]

min·now (min′ō) *n.* **1** A small European cyprinoid fish *(Phoxinus phoxinus).* **2** One of various other small fishes; especially, in the United States, a fish of the carp family. **3** The young of various fishes. Also **min′nie.** [OE *myne* small fish; prob. infl. in meaning by F *menu* small]

Mi·no·an (mi·nō′ən) *adj.* **1** Of or pertaining to an advanced Bronze Age civilization that flourished in Crete from about 3000 to 1100 B.C. **2** Denoting two types of linear script using pictographic and syllabic signs, found on clay tablets at Minos's palace at Cnossus, Nestor's palace at Pylos, and other Greek and Cretan sites, and dating from the 17th to 13th centuries B.C.: **Linear A** is thought to be Akkadian on the basis of a tentative decipherment made in 1957; **Linear B,** deciphered in 1952, is an Achaean dialect of Greek.

mi·nor (mī′nər) *adj.* **1** Less in number, quantity, or extent: opposed to *major.* **2** Of secondary consideration. **3** *Music* **a** Higher than the corresponding major interval by a semitone. **b** Characterized by minor intervals, scales, or tones. **c** In a minor key; sad; plaintive. **4** *Logic* Designating a minor term. *—n.* **1** One below the age when full civil and personal rights can be exercised. **2** *Logic* A minor term or minor premise. See SYLLOGISM. **3** *Music* A minor key, interval, etc. **4** Hence, a pathetic or plaintive quality, as in literature or art. **5** *U.S.* A branch of study for degree candidates in colleges and universities, usually related to but requiring less time than a major; a secondary subject of study. **6** In English public schools, the younger of two namesakes; junior. ◆ Homophone: *miner.* [<L]

Mi·nor·ca (mi·nôr′kə) *n.* One of a breed of domestic fowls resembling Leghorns. [from *Minorca*]

Mi·nor·ca (mi·nôr′kə) Second largest of the Balearic islands; 264 square miles. Spanish *Menorca.*

Mi·nor·can (mi·nôr′kən) *n.* A native or inhabitant of Minorca. *—adj.* Of or pertaining to Minorca or its people.

Mi·nor·ite (mī′nə·rīt) *n.* A Franciscan. Also

Mi′nor·ist. [< Med. L *(Fratres) Minores* Lesser (Brethren), original name of the order]
mi·nor·i·ty (mə·nôr′ə·tē, -nor′-, mī-) *n. pl.* **·ties 1** The smaller in number of two parts or parties: opposed to *majority.* **2** The state of being a minor; legal infancy. **3** A group comprising less than half of a population and differing from the others and especially from a larger predominant group, as in race, religion, political affiliation, etc.: also **minority group.** [< F *minorité*]
minor key *Music* A key or mode based on the minor scale and characterized by the use of the minor third, and producing a plaintive or mournful effect. See THIRD *n.*
minor league Any professional sports league not having the standing of a major league. **—mi′nor-league′** *adj.*
minor mode See under MODE.
minor scale See under SCALE.
minor suit In bridge, diamonds or clubs.
minor term *Logic* The subject of both the minor premise and the conclusion of a syllogism.
Mi·nos (mī′nəs, -nos) In Greek mythology, a king of Crete, son of Zeus and husband of Pasiphae, who became a judge of the lower world after his death. [< Gk. *Minōs*]
Min·o·taur (min′ə·tôr) In Greek mythology, the offspring, half man and half bull, of Pasiphae and a white bull sent by Poseidon to Minos, who confined it in the Labyrinth where it was annually fed human flesh until killed by Theseus. See ANDROGEUS. [< L *Minotaurus* < Gk. *Minōtauros* < *Minōs* Minos + *tauros* bull]
Minsk 1 The capital of the Republic of Belarus, in Eastern Europe: pop. 900,000; **2** the central and largest province in Belarus.
min·ster (min′stər) *n.* A monastery church; in Great Britain, often a cathedral: often used in combination: *Axminster.* [OE *mynster* < LL *monasterium.* Doublet of MONASTERY.]
min·strel (min′strəl) *n.* **1** Originally, in the Middle Ages, a retainer whose business it was to play musical instruments for the entertainment of his lord. **2** A wandering musician who composed and sang to the harp; one of a class of vagrant musicians and mountebanks, repressed by Henry IV. **3** A performer in a minstrel show. **4** *Poetic* A poet; singer; musician. See synonyms under POET. [< OF *menestrel* < LL *ministerialis* servant, jester < L *minister* attendant]
minstrel show A comic variety show of songs, dances, jokes, etc., given by a company of performers in blackface.
min·strel·sy (min′strəl·sē) *n. pl.* **·sies 1** The occupation of a minstrel. **2** Ballads or lyrics collectively. **3** A troupe of minstrels. [< AF *menestralcie,* OF *menestralsie*]
mint[1] (mint) *n.* **1** A place where the coin of a country is manufactured. **2** Figuratively, an abundant supply of anything: used especially of money. **3** Figuratively, the source of a fabrication or invention. *—v.t.* **1** To make (money) by stamping; coin. **2** To invent or fabricate, as a word. *—adj.* Unused; in original condition: a *mint* stamp. [OE *mynet* coin < L *moneta* mint < *Moneta* epithet of Juno, whose temple at Rome was used as a mint. Doublet of MONEY.] **—mint′er** *n.*
mint[2] (mint) *n.* Any one of several aromatic herbs of the genus *Mentha,* of the family *Labiatae;* especially, spearmint and peppermint, used medicinally. [OE *minte* < L *menta, mentha* < Gk. *mintha*]
mint[3] (mint) *v.t. Scot.* To hint; intend.
mint·age (min′tij) *n.* **1** The act of minting, or that which is minted; coinage; also, figuratively, the act of fabricating or coining. **2** The duty paid for coining. **3** The authorized impression placed upon a coin.
mint julep A drink made of brandy or whisky mixed with crushed ice and sugar and flavored with fresh mint.
min·u·end (min′yōō·end) *n.* The number from which another is to be subtracted: opposed to *subtrahend.* [< L *minuendus* to be lessened, gerundive of *minuere* lessen]
min·u·et (min′yōō·et′) *n.* **1** A slow, stately dance for couples in triple measure: introduced in France in the 17th century. **2** A musical composition suited to this dance: often as a movement in a sonata or symphony. [< F *menuet,* dim. of *menu* small < L *minutus*]
Min·u·it (min′yōō·it), **Peter,** 1580?–1641, third governor of New Netherlands (New York): originally known as *Peter Minnewit.*
mi·nus (mī′nəs) *prep.* **1** Lessened, or requiring to be lessened by; less: 10 *minus* 5. **2** *Colloq.* Deprived of; lacking: *minus* a hat. *—adj.* **1** Lying or reckoned in that one of two opposite directions arbitrarily assumed as negative. **2** Negative: A debt may be treated as a *minus* quantity. *—n.* **1** A minus sign. **2** A minus quantity. [< L, neut. of *minor*]
mi·nus·cule (mi·nus′kyōōl) *n.* **1** A semi-uncial cursive script, developed by the monks out of the uncial in the 7th–9th centuries and forming the basis of the modern small Roman and Greek letters; hence, any small or lower-case letter. **2** Any very small thing. *—adj.* **1** Of, pertaining to, like, or composed of minuscules. **2** Very small; miniature. [< L *minusculus,* dim. of *minor* less]
minus sign A sign (−) denoting subtraction, or reckoning or measuring in the negative direction.
min·ute[1] (min′it) *n.* **1** The 60th part of an hour; also, a moment; hence, any short, indefinite period of time. **2** The 60th part of a degree: a unit of angular measure indicated by the sign(′), and called a *minute* of arc. **3** A brief note or summary in writing of something to be remembered; memorandum; specifically, in the plural, an official record of the proceedings of any deliberative body. *—v.t.* **·ut·ed, ·ut·ing 1** To make a minute or brief note of; record. **2** To time to the minute. [< F < Med. L *minuta (pars)* small (part), minute < L *minutus* small]
mi·nute[2] (mī·nōōt′, -nyōōt′, mi-) *adj.* **1** Exceedingly small; hence, unimportant; trifling. **2** Attending to small things; critically careful; very exact. [< L *minutus* small, little, orig. pp. of *minuere* lessen] **—mi·nute′ness** *n.*
Synonyms: circumstantial, comminuted, critical, detailed, diminutive, exact, fine, little, particular, precise, slender, tiny. That is *minute* which is of exceedingly limited dimensions, as a grain of dust. That which is broken up into *minute* particles is said to be *comminuted*; things may be termed *fine* which would not be termed *comminuted*; as, *fine* sand; *fine* gravel; but, in using an adverb, we say a substance is finely *comminuted.* An account extended to very *minute* particulars is *circumstantial, detailed, particular,* and examination so extended is *critical, exact, precise.* See FINE, LITTLE, PRECISE, SMALL. *Antonyms*: see synonyms for LARGE.
min·ute gun (min′it) A gun fired at intervals of a minute as a sign of distress, or of mourning as at a funeral.
min·ute hand (min′it) The hand of a timepiece that marks the minutes.
min·ute·ly[1] (min′it·lē) *adj.* & *adv.* At intervals of a minute.
mi·nute·ly[2] (mī·nōōt′lē, -nyōōt′-, mi-) *adv.* In a minute manner; very finely, closely, or exactly.
min·ute·man (min′it·man′) *n. pl.* **·men** (-men′) A man ready for service at a minute's notice: specifically applied to certain militiamen and armed citizens in the American Revolution.
min·u·the·sis (min′yə·thē′sis) *n. Physiol.* Diminished response of a sense organ due to continuous stimulation. [< LL < Gk. *minythēsis* a lessening < *minytheein* decrease]
mi·nu·ti·a (mi·nōō′shē·ə, -shə, -nyōō′-) *n. pl.* **·ti·ae** (-shi·ē) *Chiefly pl.* Small or unimportant details. [< L]
minx (mingks) *n.* A saucy, forward girl or woman. [Prob. < LG *minsk* impudent woman]
mi·o·car·di·a (mī′ə·kär′dē·ə) *n. Physiol.* Contraction of the heart; systole. [< NL < Gk. *meiōn* less + *kardia* heart]
Mi·o·cene (mī′ə·sēn) *adj.* Pertaining to or designating a geological epoch near the end of the Tertiary period, associated with a great development of modern mammals: also **Mi′o·cen′ic** (-sen′ik), See chart under GEOLOGY. *—n.* The Miocene epoch or series. [< Gk. *meiōn* less + *kainos* recent]
Mi·o·lith·ic (mī′ə·lith′ik) *adj. Anthropol.* Mesolithic. [< Gk. *meiōn* less + -LITH[1] + -IC]
mi·o·sis (mī·ō′sis) *n.* **1** *Pathol.* **a** The period in the course of a disease when the symptoms begin to diminish. **b** Excessive contraction of the pupil of the eye: also spelled *myosis.* **2** Meiosis. [< Gk. *myein* close + -OSIS] **—mi·ot′ic** (-ot′ik) *adj.*
mi·o·ther·mic (mī′ə·thûr′mik) *adj.* Of or pertaining to those temperature conditions now prevailing on earth, especially as compared with past geological periods. [< Gk. *meiōn* less + *thermē* heat]
miq·ue·let (mik′ə·let) *n.* **1** A Spanish infantryman detailed for escort duty. **2** *Obs.* A partisan; a bandit of the Pyrenees. [< F < Sp. *miquelete*]
Mi·que·lon (mik′ə·lon, *Fr.* mē·kə·lôn′) An island off southern Newfoundland; 83 square miles. See under SAINT PIERRE.
mir (mir) *n.* A Russian local community, with common land apportioned by lot. [< Russian]
Mi·ra·beau (mē·rà·bō′), **Comte de,** 1749–91, Gabriel Honoré de Riquetti, French Revolutionary orator, writer, and statesman.
mi·ra·bi·le dic·tu (mi·rab′ə·lē dik′tōō, -tyōō) *Latin* Wonderful to relate.
mir·a·bil·i·a (mir′ə·bil′ē·ə) *n. pl. Latin* Miracles; wonders.
mir·a·cle (mir′ə·kəl) *n.* **1** Any wonderful or amazing thing, fact, or event; a wonder. **2** An event in the natural world, but out of its established order, possible only by the intervention of divine power. **3** A medieval dramatic representation of religious subjects: also **miracle play:** see MYSTERY[1] (def. 10). See synonyms under PRODIGY. [< F , < L *miraculum* < *mirari* wonder < *mirus* wonderful]
mi·rac·u·lous (mi·rak′yə·ləs) *adj.* **1** Effected by direct divine agency; supernatural. **2** Surpassingly strange; wonderful. **3** Possessing the power to work miracles; wonder-working. See synonyms under SUPERNATURAL. [< F *miraculeux* < Med. L *miraculosus* < L *miraculum*] **—mi·rac′u·lous·ly** *adv.* **—mi·rac′u·lous·ness** *n.*
mir·a·dor (mir′ə·dôr′, -dōr′-) *n. Archit.* A balcony or oriel window. [< Sp. < *mirar* behold < L *mirari* wonder]
Mir·a·flo·res Lake (mir′ə·flôr′əs, -flō′rəs) An artificial lake in southern Canal Zone, linking Gaillard Cut with the Pacific section through **Miraflores Locks.**
mi·rage (mi·räzh′) *n.* **1** An optical illusion, as of an oasis or a sheet of water in the desert, or ships seen inverted in the air. It occurs when the lower strata of air are at a very different temperature from the higher strata, so that images are seen as by reflection. **2** Anything that falsely appears to be real. [< F < *se mirer* be reflected, look at oneself < L *mirari* wonder at]
Mi·ran·da (mi·ran′də) A feminine personal name. [< L, admirable]
—Miranda In Shakespeare's *Tempest,* the heroine; daughter of Prospero.
mir·bane oil (mûr′bān) Nitrobenzene. [Prob. a fanciful formation]
mire (mīr) *n.* Wet, yielding earth; swampy ground; deep mud or slush. *—v.* **mired, mir·ing** *v.t.* **1** To cause to sink or become stuck in or as in mire. **2** To defile; soil. *—v.i.* **3** To sink in mire; bog down. [< ON *mýrr* swampy ground] **—mir′y** *adj.* **—mir′i·ness** *n.*
mir·ex (mir′eks) *n.* A persistent, toxic chlorinated hydrocarbon, $C_{10}Cl_{12}$, formerly used widely as a pesticide against fire ants. Also **Mir′ex.**
Mir·i·am (mir′ē·əm) A feminine personal name. [< Hebrew, bitter]
—Miriam Sister of Moses and Aaron. *Ex.* xv 20.
mirk[1] (mûrk), **mirk·i·ly,** etc. See MURK, etc.
mirk[2] (mûrk) *Scot. adj.* Dark, gloomy. *—n.* Darkness.
mir·mil·lon (mir·mil′ən) *n.* One of a class of ancient Roman gladiators armed with sword and shield and characterized by the figure of a fish on the helmet. See illustration under GLADIATOR. [< L *mirmillo* < Gk. *mormyros* sea fish]
Mi·ró (mē·rō′), **Joan,** born 1893, Spanish painter.
mir·ror (mir′ər) *n.* **1** An object having a nearly perfect reflecting surface; a looking-glass. **2** *Optics* A speculum. **3** Whatever reflects or clearly represents; an exemplar. **4** A crystal used by diviners. *—v.t.* To reflect or show an image of, as in a mirror. [< OF *mirour* < LL *mirare* look at < L *mirari* wonder at, admire]
mir·ror·scope (mir′ər·skōp) *n.* **1** A mirror used to reflect a design so as to permit of rapid reproduction, as by artists. **2** A projector (def. 3).

mir·ror·stone (mir'ər·stōn') *n.* Mica, especially of the muscovite variety.

mirth (mûrth) *n.* 1 Pleasurable feelings, or gaiety of spirits, manifested in jesting and laughter; social merriment; jollity. 2 *Obs.* Pleasure; joy. See synonyms under HAPPINESS, LAUGHTER, SPORT. [OE *myrth, myrgth* < *myrig* pleasant, merry]

mirth·ful (mûrth'fəl) *adj.* Merry. See synonyms under CHEERFUL, HAPPY, MERRY, VIVACIOUS. — **mirth'ful·ly** *adv.* — **mirth'ful·ness** *n.*

mirth·less (mûrth'lis) *adj.* Lacking mirth or merriment; joyless. — **mirth'less·ly** *adv.* — **mirth'less·ness** *n.*

mir·za (mir'zä) *n.* A Persian title, placed before a name to denote a scholar and after a name to denote a prince. [<Persian, contraction of *mīrzādah* < *mīr* prince (<Arabic *amīr* ruler) + *zādah* son of]

mis-[1] *prefix* Bad; amiss; wrongly. [OE *mis-* wrong; infl. in meaning by ME *mes-* MIS-[2]] *Mis-* may appear as a prefix in hyphemes or solidemes; for examples, see the list of self-explanatory words at the foot of the page.

mis-[2] *prefix* Bad; amiss; not: found with negative or depreciatory force in words borrowed from Old French; *misadventure, miscreant.* [<OF *mes-* <L *minus* less]

mis-[3] Var. of MISO-.

mis·ad·ven·ture (mis'əd·ven'chər) *n.* An unlucky chance; misfortune. See synonyms under ACCIDENT, MISFORTUNE. [<OF *mesaventure*]

mis·ad·ven·tured (mis'əd·ven'chərd) *adj. Obs.* Unfortunate.

mis·al·li·ance (mis'ə·lī'əns) *n.* An undesirable alliance, as marriage with one of inferior station or character. [<F *mésalliance*]

mis·an·thrope (mis'ən·thrōp, miz'-) *n.* One who entertains aversion to or distrust of his fellow men. Also **mis·an·thro·pist** (mis·an'thrə·pist). [<Gk. *misanthrōpos* hating mankind < *misein* hate + *anthrōpos* a man] — **mis·an·throp'ic** (-throp'ik) or **·i·cal** *adj.* — **mis·an·throp'i·cal·ly** *adv.*

mis·an·thro·py (mis·an'thrə·pē) *n.* Hatred or distrust of mankind.

mis·ap·ply (mis'ə·plī') *v.t.* **·plied, ·ply·ing** 1 To use or apply incorrectly or inefficiently. 2 To use or apply wrongly or dishonestly.

mis·ap·pro·pri·ate (mis'ə·prō'prē·āt) *v.t.* **·at·ed, ·at·ing** To use or take improperly or dishonestly; misapply. — **mis'ap·pro'pri·a'tion** *n.*

mis·be·come (mis'bi·kum') *v.t.* **·came, ·come, ·com·ing** To be unbecoming or not befitting to.

mis·brand (mis·brand') *v.t.* To label or brand incorrectly or falsely.

mis·call (mis·kôl') *v.t.* 1 To call by a wrong name; misname. 2 *Brit. Dial.* To revile; abuse.

mis·car·riage (mis·kar'ij) *n.* 1 *Med.* A premature delivery of a non-viable fetus; abortion. 2 Failure to reach or to bring to an expected result, destination, or conclusion.

mis·car·ry (mis·kar'ē) *v.i.* **·ried, ·ry·ing** 1 To fail of an intended effect; go wrong. 2 To bring forth a fetus prematurely; have a miscarriage; abort.

mis·ce·na·tion (mis'i·jə·nā'shən) *n. Biol.* Interbreeding of races, especially intermarriage or interbreeding between white and Negro or white and Oriental races. [<L *miscere* mix + *genus* race] — **mis'ce·ge·net'ic** (-jə·net'ik) *adj.*

mis·cel·la·ne·a (mis'ə·lā'nē·ə) *n. pl.* A miscellaneous collection; especially, literary miscellanies. [<L]

mis·cel·la·ne·ous (mis'ə·lā'nē·əs) *adj.* Consisting of several kinds; variously mixed; also, many-sided; promiscuous; varied. See synonyms under HETEROGENEOUS. [<L *miscellaneus* < *miscellus* mixed < *miscere* mix] — **mis'cel·la'ne·ous·ly** *adv.* — **mis'cel·la'ne·ous·ness** *n.*

mis·cel·la·nist (mis'ə·lā'nist, -lə·nist) *n.* A composer of miscellanies.

mis·cel·la·ny (mis'ə·lā'nē) *n. pl.* **·nies** 1 *Often pl.* A collection of literary compositions on various subjects. 2 Any miscellaneous collection. [Anglicized var. of MISCELLANEA]

mis·chance (mis·chans', -chäns') *n.* An instance of ill-luck; a mishap. See synonyms under CATASTROPHE, MISFORTUNE. [<OF *mescheance*]

mis·chief (mis'chif) *n.* 1 Any occurrence attended with evil or injury; troublesome or damaging action or its result; damage; vexation. 2 Any annoying or vexatious action or course of conduct; a prank; also, the spirit or mood leading to such acts. 3 A prankish person. See synonyms under INJURY. [<OF *meschef* bad result < *meschever* come to grief < *mes-* MIS- (<L *minus* less) + *chief* head, end <L *caput* head]

mis·chief–mak·er (mis'chif·mā'kər) *n.* One who causes mischief, especially by instigating ill–feeling between others. — **mis'chief–mak'ing** *adj. & n.*

mis·chie·vous (mis'chi·vəs) *adj.* 1 Inclined to mischief; of a prankish nature. 2 Injurious. See synonyms under BAD, MALICIOUS, NOISOME, PERNICIOUS. — **mis'chie·vous·ly** *adv.* — **mis'chie·vous·ness** *n.* [<AF *meschevous*]

mis·ci·ble (mis'i·bəl) *adj.* 1 Capable of being mixed. 2 Suitable for mixing. [<L *miscere* mix] — **mis'ci·bil'i·ty** *n.*

mis·col·late (mis·kə·lāt') *v.t.* **·lat·ed, ·lat·ing** In bookbinding, to assemble (sheets or signatures) in wrong sequence. — **mis'col·la'tion** *n.*

mis·col·or (mis·kul'ər) *v.t.* 1 To give a wrong color to. 2 To misrepresent. Also *Brit.* **mis·col'our.**

mis·con·ceive (mis'kən·sēv') *v.t. & v.i.* **·ceived, ·ceiv·ing** To conceive wrongly; misunderstand. — **mis'con·ceiv'er** *n.* — **mis'con·cep'tion** (-sep'shən) *n.*

mis·con·duct (mis'kən·dukt') *v.t.* 1 To behave (oneself) improperly. 2 To mismanage. — *n.* (mis·kon'dukt) 1 Improper conduct; bad behavior. 2 *Law* Adultery. 3 Mismanagement.

mis·con·stru·al (mis'kən·strōō'əl) *n.* 1 An erroneous interpretation. 2 The act of putting a false meaning upon something said or done by another. 3 Misunderstanding or the result of a misunderstanding.

mis·con·strue (mis'kən·strōō') *v.t.* **·strued, ·stru·ing** To interpret erroneously; put a false or unwarranted meaning to; misunderstand. — **mis'con·struc'tion** (-struk'shən) *n.*

mis·cre·ance (mis'krē·əns) *n. Archaic* The condition or quality of adhering to a false faith; heresy. [<OF *mescreant* disbelieving, ppr. of *mescroire* < *mes-* mis- (<L *minus* less) + *croire* believe <L *credere*]

mis·cre·an·cy (mis'krē·ən·sē) *n. Archaic* 1 The condition or act of a miscreant; villainy. 2 Miscreance.

mis·cre·ant (mis'krē·ənt) *n.* 1 A vile wretch; an evil-doer. 2 *Archaic* An unbeliever; infidel. — *adj.* 1 Villainous; conscienceless. 2 *Archaic* Unbelieving; infidel. [<OF *mescreant* unbelieving]

mis·cue (mis·kyōō') *n.* In billiards, a stroke spoiled in effect by a slipping of the cue. — *v.i.* **·cued, ·cu·ing** 1 To make a miscue. 2 In the theater, to miss one's cue; to answer another's cue.

mis·deed (mis·dēd') *n.* A wrong or improper act. See synonyms under OFFENSE, SIN. [OE *misdǣd*]

mis·de·mean·ant (mis'di·mē'nənt) *n.* One who is guilty of a misdemeanor or misconduct. — **first–class misdemeanant** In English law, one of a class of prisoners guilty of misdemeanor, but not subjected to the same prison regulations as a criminal, nor considered as a person convicted of a crime.

mis·de·mean·or (mis'di·mē'nər) *n.* 1 Misbehavior; a misdeed. 2 *Law* Any offense less than a felony. In England the distinction between a felony and a misdemeanor is still maintained. In the United States this distinction has, in most States, either been abolished or is treated in a manner that makes it of no practical value. Compare FELONY. Also *Brit.* **mis·de·mean'our.** See synonyms under OFFENSE.

mis·do (mis·dōō') *v.t. & v.i.* **·did, ·done, ·do·ing** To do wrongly; bungle. [OE *misdon*] — **mis·do'er** *n.* — **mis·do'ing** *n.*

mis·doubt (mis·dout') *v.t. Archaic* 1 To doubt; call in question. 2 To fear; suspect. — *v.i.* 3 To be in doubt; suspect. — *n.* 1 Doubt; wavering; irresolution. 2 Suspicion; apprehension.

mise (mīz) *n.* 1 *Law* The issue pleaded in a writ of right. 2 *Law* Expenses; specifically, the costs and charges in an action. 3 The adjustment of a dispute by arbitration or compromise. [<AF <OF *mis* put, laid out, pp. of *mettre* <L *mittere* send]

mise en scène (mēz än sen') *French* The setting of a play on the stage; hence, general or visible surroundings.

Mi·se·no (mē·zā'nō), **Cape** A promontory in southern Italy between the Bay of Naples and the Gulf of Gaeta. Ancient **Mi·se·num** (mī·sē'nəm).

mi·ser (mī'zər) *n.* One who saves and hoards avariciously. [<L *miser* wretched]

mis·er·a·ble (miz'ər·ə·bəl, miz'rə-) *adj.* 1 Wretchedly unhappy. 2 Of mean quality; bad; valueless: sometimes expressing contempt. 3 Producing, proceeding from, or exhibiting misery; pitiable: *miserable* weather; a *miserable* groan. See synonyms under PITIFUL, SAD. — *n. Obs.* A miserable person. [<OF <L *miserabilis* pitiable < *miserari* pity < *miser* wretched] — **mis'er·a·ble·ness** *n.* — **mis'er·a·bly** *adv.*

mis·e·re·re (miz'ə·râr'ē, -rir'ē) *n.* In church stalls, a small wooden bracket affixed perpendicularly to the bottom of the seat and designed to afford support to the worshiper when the seat is turned up: also called *misericorde.*

Mis·e·re·re (miz'ə·râr'ē, -rir'ē) *n.* 1 The 51st psalm, so called from the opening words in the Latin version. 2 A musical setting of this psalm. [<L, imperative of *misereri* have mercy]

mis·er·i·corde (miz'ər·i·kôrd', mi·zer'i·kôrd) *n.* 1 A small dagger used in the Middle Ages to give the death stroke to a fallen knight. 2 Formerly, a dispensation from fasting given to a member of a monastic order. 3 An apartment in a monastery serving as a refectory for monks who had received such dispensation. 4 Miserere. Also **mis'er·i·cord'.** [<OF <L *misericordia* < *misereri* have pity + *cor, cordis* heart]

mis·er·i·cor·di·a (miz'ə·ri·kôr'dē·ə) *Latin* Pity; compassion; mercy.

mi·ser·ly (mī'zər·lē) *adj.* Of or like a miser; grasping; mean. See synonyms under AVARICIOUS. — **mi'ser·li·ness** *n.*

mis·er·y (miz'ər·ē) *n. pl.* **·er·ies** 1 Extreme distress or suffering, especially as a result of poverty; wretchedness; also, a cause of wretchedness. 2 *Dial.* A cause of pain: a

misaccent	misadvise	misanalyze	misassay	misbandage	mischaracterization	miscoinage
misaccentuation	misaffection	misanswer	misassent	misbegin	mischaracterize	miscollocation
misachievement	misaffirm	misapparel	misassert	misbelove	mischarge	miscommand
misacknowledge	misagent	misappear	misassign	misbestow	mischristen	miscommit
misact	misaim	misappearance	misassociate	misbetide	miscipher	miscommunicate
misadapt	misalienate	misappellation	misassociation	misbias	miscitation	miscompare
misadaptation	misalinement	misappoint	misatone	misbill	miscite	miscomplain
misadd	misallegation	misappointment	misattribute	misbind	misclaim	miscomplaint
misaddress	misallege	misappraise	misattribution	misbuild	misclaiming	miscompose
misadjust	misallotment	misappraisement	misauthorization	miscanonize	misclass	miscomputation
misadmeasurement	misallowance	misapprehensible	misauthorize	miscensure	misclassification	miscompute
misadministration	misalphabetize	misascribe	misaver	miscenter	misclassify	miscon
misadvice	misalter	misascription	misaward	mischallenge	miscoin	misconclusion

misery in the back. See synonyms under MISFORTUNE, PAIN. [<OF *miserie* <L *miseria* < *miser* wretched]

mis·fea·sance (mis·fē′zəns) *n. Law* The performance of a lawful act in an unlawful or culpably negligent manner. Compare MALFEASANCE, NONFEASANCE. [<OF *mesfaisance* < *mesfaire* do wrong < *mes-* mis- + *faire* do <L *facere*] **— mis·fea′sor** *n.*

mis·fire (mis·fīr′) *n.* The failure to discharge or explode when desired: said of a firearm, explosive, or internal-combustion engine. **—** *v.i.* **·fired, ·fir·ing** To fail to explode or be fired.

mis·fit (mis·fit′) *v.t.* & *v.i.* **·fit·ted, ·fit·ting** To fail to fit or make fit. **—** *n.* **1** Something that fits badly. **2** (mis′fit′) A person who does not adjust or adapt himself readily to his surroundings. **3** The act or condition of fitting badly.

mis·for·tune (mis·fôr′chən) *n.* **1** Adverse or ill fortune. **2** An unlucky chance or occurrence; calamity.

Synonyms: adversity, affliction, bereavement, blow, calamity, chastening, chastisement, disappointment, disaster, distress, failure, hardship, harm, ill, misadventure, mischance, misery, mishap, reverse, ruin, sorrow, stroke, trial, tribulation, trouble, visitation. *Misfortune* is usually of lingering character or consequences, and such as the sufferer is not deemed directly responsible for; as, He had the *misfortune* to be born blind. Any considerable *disappointment, failure,* or *misfortune,* as regards outward circumstances, as loss of fortune, position, and the like, when long continued or attended with enduring consequences, constitutes *adversity.* For the loss of friends by death we commonly use *affliction* or *bereavement. Calamity* and *disaster* are used of sudden and severe *misfortunes.* We speak of the *misery* of the poor, the *hardships* of the soldier. *Affliction, chastening, trial,* and *tribulation* all suggest some disciplinary purpose of God with beneficent design. *Affliction* may be keen and bitter, but brief; *tribulation* is long and wearing. Compare ACCIDENT, ADVERSITY, BLOW, CATASTROPHE, LOSS. *Antonyms*: blessing, boon, comfort, consolation, gratification, happiness, joy, pleasure, prosperity, relief, success, triumph.

mis·give (mis·giv′) *v.* **·gave, ·giv·ing** *v.t.* To make fearful, suspicious, or doubtful: My heart *misgives* me. **—** *v.i.* To be apprehensive.

mis·giv·ing (mis·giv′ing) *n.* A feeling of doubt, premonition, or apprehension. See synonyms under ANXIETY, DOUBT, FEAR.

mis·guide (mis·gīd′) *v.t.* **·guid·ed, ·guid·ing** To guide wrongly in action or thought; mislead. **— mis·guid′ance** *n.* **— mis·guid′er** *n.*

mi·shan·ter (mi·shan′tər) *n. Scot.* Misfortune; ill-luck; misadventure.

mis·hap (mis′hap, mis·hap′) *n.* An unfortunate accident; slight misfortune. See synonyms under ACCIDENT, CATASTROPHE, MISFORTUNE. [<MIS-[1] + HAP]

mish·mash (mish′mash′, -mosh′) *n.* A medley; hotch-potch. **—** *v.t.* To make a hotch-potch of; jumble. Also **mish′-mash′.** [Reduplication of MASH]

Mish·na (mish′nə) *n. pl.* **Mish·na·yoth** (mish′·nä·yōth′) **1** The first part of the Talmud, consisting of a collection of traditions and decisions made by Rabbi Juda, called the Holy (born about A.D. 150), summing up all previous rabbinical labors. **2** A paragraph of this collection. **3** The opinion of any notable expounder of the Jewish law; also, the sum and substance of his teachings. Also **Mish′nah.** [<Hebrew *mishnāh* repetition, oral law < *shānāh* repeat, teach] **— Mish·na·ic** (mish·nā′ik), **Mish′nic** or **·ni·cal** *adj.*

mis·in·form (mis′in·fôrm′) *v.t.* To give false or erroneous information to. **— mis′in·for·ma′tion** *n.* **— mis′in·form′er, mis′in·form′ant** *n.*

mis·in·ter·pret (mis′in·tûr′prit) *v.t.* To interpret wrongly; misunderstand. **— mis′in·ter′pre·ta′tion** *n.* **— mis′in·ter′pret·er** *n.*

Mi·sio·nes (mē·syō′nās) A national territory in NE Argentina; 11,514 square miles; capital, Posadas.

mis·join·der (mis·join′dər) *n. Law* The uniting of things or persons that should not be united: the *misjoinder* of parties in action: contrasted with *non-joinder.*

mis·kal (mis·käl′) *n.* An Oriental weight equivalent to 4.7 grams in Persia, and to 4.8 grams in Turkey. [<Arabic *mithqāl* weight]

Mis·kolc (mēsh′kōlts) A city in NE Hungary. Formerly **Mis′kolcz.**

mis·lay (mis·lā′) *v.t.* **·laid, ·lay·ing** To lay in a place not remembered; misplace. See synonyms under DISPLACE. **— mis·lay′er** *n.*

mis·lead (mis·lēd′) *v.t.* **·led, ·lead·ing** To direct wrongly; lead astray or into error. **— mis·lead′er** *n.* **— mis·lead′ing** *adj.* **— mis·lead′·ing·ly** *adv.*

mis·leared (mis·lird′) *adj. Scot.* Ill-bred or ill-taught.

mis·like (mis·līk′) *v.t.* **1** To dislike. **2** To displease. **—** *n.* Dislike; aversion; disapproval. **— mis·lik′er** *n.* **— mis·lik′ing** *n.* **— mis·lik′·ing·ly** *adv.*

mis·man·age (mis·man′ij) *v.t.* & *v.i.* **·aged, ·ag·ing** To manage badly or improperly. **— mis·man′age·ment** *n.* **— mis·man′ag·er** *n.*

mis·mar·riage (mis·mar′ij) *n.* An unhappy, incongruous, or inharmonious marriage.

mis·no·mer (mis·nō′mər) *n.* **1** A name wrongly applied; an inapplicable designation. **2** A misnaming; specifically, the giving of a wrong name to a person in a legal document. [<AF <OF *mesnommer* call by the wrong name < *mes-* wrongly + *nomer* <L *nominare* name]

miso- *combining form* Hating: *misogynist.* Also, before vowels, *mis-.* [<Gk. *misein* hate]

mis·og·a·my (mis·og′ə·mē) *n.* Hatred of marriage. [<MISO- + -GAMY] **— mis·og′a·mist** *n.*

mis·og·y·ny (mis·oj′ə·nē) *n.* Hatred of woman: opposed to *philogyny.* [<Gk. *misogynia* < *misein* hate + *gynē* woman] **— mis·og′y·nist** *n.* **— mis·og′y·nous** *adj.*

mis·ol·o·gy (mis·ol′ə·jē) *n.* Hatred of discussion or inquiry; aversion to enlightenment. [<Gk. *misologia* < *misein* hate + *logos* discourse] **— mis·ol′o·gist** *n.*

mis·o·ne·ism (mis′ō·nē′iz·əm, mī′sō-) *n.* Hatred of change, innovation or novelty. [<MISO- + Gk. *neos* new] **— mis′o·ne′ist** *n.*

mis·pick·el (mis′pik·əl) *n.* Arsenopyrite. [<G; ult. origin unknown]

mis·play (mis·plā′) *n.* In games, a wrong play; hence, any bad move.

mis·plead (mis·plēd′) *v.t.* & *v.i.* **·plead·ed** or **·pled, ·plead·ing** *Law* To plead erroneously.

mis·print (mis·print′) *v.t.* To print incorrectly. **—** *n.* (mis′print′, mis·print′) An error in printing.

mis·pri·sion (mis·prizh′ən) *n.* **1** *Law* Concealment of a crime, especially of treason or felony; also, loosely, contempt or high misdemeanor. **2** *Archaic* Misconception; misunderstanding. [<OF *mesprision* mistake < *mesprendre* do wrong, take amiss < *mes-* mis- + *prendre* take <L *prehendere*]

mis·rep·re·sent (mis′rep·ri·zent′) *v.t.* To give an incorrect or false representation of. See synonyms under PERVERT. **— mis′rep·re·sen·ta′tion** *n.* **— mis′rep·re·sen′ta·tive** *adj.* & *n.*

mis·rule (mis·rōōl′) *v.t.* **·ruled, ·rul·ing** To rule unwisely or unjustly; misgovern. **—** *n.* **1** Bad or unjust rule or government. **2** Disorder or confusion.

miss[1] (mis) *n.* **1** A young girl: chiefly colloquial, or in trade use: clothing for *misses.* **2** *Often cap.* A title used in speaking to an unmarried woman or girl: used without the name. [Contraction from MISTRESS]

miss[2] (mis) *v.t.* **1** To fail to hit or strike. **2** To fail to meet, catch, obtain, accomplish, see, hear, perceive, etc.: to *miss* the point. **3** To fail to attend, keep, perform, etc.: to *miss* church. **4** To overlook or fail to take advantage of, as an opportunity. **5** To discover or feel the loss or absence of. **6** To escape; avoid: He just *missed* being wounded. **—** *v.i.* **7** To fail to hit; strike wide of the mark. **8** To be unsuccessful; fail. **— to miss fire 1** To fail to discharge: said of firearms. **2** To be unsuccessful; fail. **—** *n.* **1** The act of missing; a failure to hit, find, attain, succeed, etc. **2** *Obs.* Loss; want. [OE *missan*]

Miss (mis) *n.* A title of address used with the name of a girl or an unmarried woman.

mis·sal (mis′əl) *n.* **1** The book containing the service for the celebration of mass throughout the year; a mass book. **2** Loosely, an illuminated black-letter or manuscript book of early date resembling the old mass books. ◆ Homophone: *missile.* [<Med. L *missale,* neut. of *missalis (liber)* mass (book) <LL *missa* mass]

mis·say (mis·sā′) *v.t.* & *v.i.* **·said, ·say·ing** *Archaic* To say (something) wrongly or incorrectly.

mis·sel thrush (mis′əl) A large European thrush *(Turdus viscivorus)* that feeds largely on mistletoe berries. Also **mis′sel.** [OE *mistel* mistletoe]

mis·shape (mis·shāp′) *v.t.* **·shaped, ·shaped** or **·shap·en, ·shap·ing** To shape badly; deform.

mis·shap·en (mis·shā′pən) *adj.* Shaped badly; deformed.

mis·sile (mis′əl) *n.* **1** Any object, especially a weapon, intended to be thrown or discharged; a projectile. **2** A guided missile. **—** *adj.* Such as may be thrown or hurled. ◆ Homophone: *missal.* [<L *missilis* < *missus,* pp. of *mittere* send]

mis·sile·man (mis′əl·mən) *n. pl.* **·men** (-mən) One who is skilled in the practical details of missilery, rocketry, and spacemanship.

mis·sile·ry (mis′əl·rē) *n.* The science and art of missiles, their design, construction, launching, range, and destructive capacities.

miss·ing (mis′ing) *adj.* Absent from the proper or accustomed place; lost; gone: said specifically of soldiers who are absent but whose fate has not been definitely ascertained. **— to turn up missing** To be absent; fail to arrive or be found.

missing link 1 Something lacking to make complete a chain or series. **2** *Biol.* A hypothetical form of life assumed to be intermediate in development between man and the anthropoid apes.

mis·sion (mish′ən) *n.* **1** The act of sending, or the state of being sent, as on some errand. **2** The sending forth of men with authority to preach or spread the gospel; authority so given by God or the church. **3** The business or service on which one is sent. **4** That which one is or feels destined to accomplish; the destined or chosen end of one's efforts. **5** An effort to spread, or the work of spreading, religious teaching. **6** A single field or locality covered by missionary work; the body of missionaries there established; a missionary station; also, any educational, religious, or welfare center for the underprivileged in a city. **7** *Eccl.* A regularly organized church and congregation not having the status of a parish in canon law; a quasi-parish. **8** The office of a foreign ambassador or envoy. **9** The persons sent on any errand or service. **10** *Mil.* A definite task assigned to an individual or unit of the armed services. **11** *Aeron.* A flight operation of a single aircraft or formation.

---

misconfer	**miscultivated**	**misdesire**	**misdraw**	**misenjoy**	**misexplain**	**misfond**
misconfident	**misculture**	**misdetermine**	**misdrive**	**misenrol**	**misexplanation**	**misform**
misconfiguration	**miscurvature**	**misdevise**	**miseat**	**misenter**	**misexplication**	**misformation**
misconjecture	**miscut**	**misdevoted**	**misecclesiastic**	**misentitle**	**misexposition**	**misframe**
misconjugate	**misdaub**	**misdevotion**	**misedit**	**misentry**	**misexpound**	**misgage**
misconjugation	**misdecide**	**misdiet**	**miseducate**	**misenunciation**	**misexpress**	**misgesture**
misconjunction	**misdecision**	**misdispose**	**miseducation**	**misevent**	**misexpression**	**misgraft**
misconsecrate	**misdeclaration**	**misdisposition**	**miseducative**	**misexample**	**misexpressive**	**misgrave**
misconsequence	**misdeclare**	**misdistinguish**	**miseffect**	**misexecute**	**misfashion**	**misground**
miscook	**misdefine**	**misdistribute**	**misencourage**	**misexecution**	**misfather**	**misgrow**
miscookery	**misdeliver**	**misdistribution**	**misendeavor**	**misexpectation**	**misfault**	**misgrown**
miscopy	**misdelivery**	**misdivide**	**misenforce**	**misexpend**	**misfield**	**misguess**
miscredulity	**misdentition**	**misdower**	**misengrave**	**misexpenditure**	**misfile**	**mis-hallowed**

—*adj.* **1** Pertaining to or belonging to a mission. **2** Like the early Spanish architecture and simple furniture of the missions of the SW United States. —*v.t.* **1** To send on a mission. **2** To establish a mission in. [<L *missio, -onis* <*missus,* pp. of *mittere* send] —**mis′sion·al** *adj.*

mis·sion·ar·y (mish′ən·er′ē) *n. pl.* **·ar·ies** **1** A person sent to propagate religion or to do educational or charitable work in some place where his church has no self-supporting local organization; hence, one who spreads any new system or doctrine. **2** A person sent on a mission; a messenger; ambassador. —*adj.* Pertaining to missions.

Missionary Baptist A Baptist who believes in or contributes to missionary work: opposed to *Primitive Baptist.*

Missionary Ridge A ridge of hills about 1,000 feet high in Tennessee and Georgia; a Civil War battleground, 1863.

Mis·sis·sip·pi (mis′ə·sip′ē) A State in the south central United States on the Gulf of Mexico; 47,716 square miles; capital, Jackson; entered the Union Dec. 10, 1817: nickname *Bayou State.* Abbr. MS

Mis·sis·sip·pi·an (mis′ə·sip′ē·ən) *adj.* **1** Relating to the Mississippi River or to the State. **2** *Geol.* Relating to the earlier of the two geological periods or systems in the American Carboniferous division of the Paleozoic era. See chart under GEOLOGY. —*n.* **1** One born or residing in Mississippi. **2** The Lower Carboniferous or Mississippian geological formation.

Mississippi River A river in the central United States, flowing 2,350 miles south to the Gulf of Mexico; from the headwaters of the Missouri River, flowing 3,892 miles to the Gulf of Mexico.

Mississippi scheme A plan formulated by the Scottish economist, John Law, in which a company was formed to exploit and monopolize all the land drained by the Mississippi, the Ohio, and the Missouri rivers. Subsequent mismanagement of minting rights which were granted the company led to wild speculation, panic, and inflation, causing the failure of the company in 1720. Also called **Mississippi bubble.**

Mississippi Sound An arm of the Gulf of Mexico bordering Louisiana, Mississippi, and Alabama.

mis·sive (mis′iv) *n.* That which is sent; especially a letter; a message in writing. —*adj.* Sent or designed to be sent. [<Med. L *missivus* <L *missus,* pp. of *mittere* send]

miss–lick (mis′lik) *n. Colloq.* A cut made by an

ax or knife off the true line; hence, any mistake.

Mis·so·lon·ghi (mis′ə·lông′gē) A port in west central Greece; here Byron died, April 29, 1824, during the Greek struggle for independence from Turkish rule: Greek *Mesolonghi.*

Mis·sou·ri (mi·zŏŏr′ē) *n. pl.* **·ri** One of a tribe of North American Indians of the Siouan family, formerly inhabiting northern Missouri, now in Oklahoma with the Otoe.

Mis·sou·ri (mi·zŏŏr′ē, -zŏŏr′ə) A State in the west central United States west of the Mississippi; 69,674 square miles; capital, Jefferson City; entered the Union Aug. 10, 1821: nickname, *Ozark State* or *Show Me State*: abbr. MO —**to be from Missouri** To be on the alert against deception; be skeptical. —**Mis·sou′ri·an** *adj. & n.*

Missouri River The longest river of the United States and chief tributary of the Mississippi, flowing 2,714 miles from the Rocky Mountains to the Mississippi River near St. Louis.

Missouri skylark A pipit of the North American plains (*Anthus spraguei*): also called *Sprague's pipit.*

Missouri Synod A leading conservative Lutheran body in the Lutheran Synodical Conference, first organized in 1847 and characterized by a strict adherence to traditional Lutheran doctrines: officially called *The Lutheran Church–Missouri Synod.*

mis·spell (mis·spel′) *v.t. & v.i.* **·spelled** or **·spelt,** **·spell·ing** To spell incorrectly.

mis·state (mis·stāt′) *v.t.* **·stat·ed,** **·stat·ing** To state wrongly or falsely.

mis·step (mis·step′) *n.* A false or wrong step; error.

mis·sus (mis′əz) *n. Colloq.* Mistress; wife. Also **mis′sis.** [Alter. of MISTRESS]

miss·y (mis′ē) *n. pl.* **miss·ies** Miss: a colloquial or diminutive form.

mist (mist) *n.* **1** An aggregation of fine drops of water in the atmosphere at or near the earth's surface, floating or falling very slowly: used either synonymously with *fog* or distinguished from it, as being less dense, or as consisting of drops large enough to fall perceptibly but slowly. **2** *Meteorol.* A very thin fog in which the horizontal visibility is greater than 1,100 yards. **3** Water vapor condensed on and dimming a surface. **4** Any colloidal suspension of a liquid in a gas. **5** Anything that dims or darkens; that which obscures physical or mental vision. —*v.i.* **1** To be or become dim or misty; blur. **2** To rain in very fine drops. —*v.t.* **3** To make dim or misty; blur. [OE]

mis·take (mis·tāk′) *n.* An error in action, judgment, perception, or impression; a blunder. See synonyms under ERROR. —*v.* **·took, ·tak·en, ·tak·ing** *v.t.* **1** To understand wrongly; acquire a wrong conception of; misinterpret. **2** To take (a person or thing) to be another; fail to identify correctly: to *mistake* friends for enemies. —*v.i.* **3** To make a mistake. [<ON *mistaka*] —**mis·tak′a·ble** *adj.*

mis·tak·en (mis·tā′kən) *adj.* **1** Characterized by mistake; incorrect; wrong. **2** Being in error; wrong in opinion or judgment. See synonyms under ABSURD. —**mis·tak′en·ly** *adv.* —**mis·tak′en·ness** *n.*

Mis·tas·si·ni Lake (mis′tä·sē′nē) A lake in central Quebec, Canada; 840 square miles.

Mis·ter (mis′tər) *n.* **1** Master: a title of address prefixed to the name and to some official titles of a man: commonly written *Mr.*: *Mr.* Darwin; *Mr.* Chairman. **2** Official salutation in addressing a warrant officer, flight officer, or a cadet in the U.S. Military Academy at West Point, and, in some practice,

officers below the rank of captain. In the Navy it is directed to those of all ranks below that of commander; in the Maritime Service it is applicable to all ranks below the captain of the ship. [Var. MASTER]

mist–flow·er (mist′flou′ər) *n.* A tall perennial herb (*Eupatorium coelestinum*) of the composite family, with coarsely toothed leaves and clusters of light–blue or violet flowers.

Mis·ti (mēs′tē), El See EL MISTI.

mis·tle·toe (mis′əl·tō)

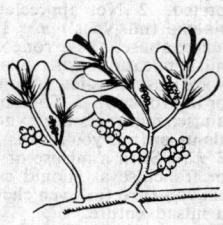

n. **1** A European evergreen parasitic shrub (*Viscum album*) with yellowish-green leaves and inconspicuous flowers, succeeded by glutinous white berries: found on various deciduous trees. **2** An American plant (*Phoradendron flavescens*) related to this shrub: the State flower of Oklahoma. [OE *misteltan* mistletoe twig]

MISTLETOE

mis·took (mis·tŏŏk′) Past tense of MISTAKE. Also *Scot.* **mis·teuk** (-tyŏŏk′).

mis·tral (mis′trəl, *Fr.* mēs·trál′) *n.* **1** A cold, dry, and violent northwest Alpine wind blowing from the Ebro to the Gulf of Genoa and also through the southern provinces of France. **2** A worsted dress fabric with twisted warp and weft threads woven to give a nubbed effect. [<F, lit., master wind <L *magistralis* <*magister* master]

Mis·tral (mēs·trál′), **Frédéric Joseph Étienne,** 1830–1914, Provençal poet and lexicographer. —**Gabriela,** 1889–1957, Chilean poet; real name *Lucila Godoy de Alcavaga.*

mis·treat (mis·trēt′) *v.t.* To treat badly or unkindly; abuse. —**mis·treat′ment** *n.*

mis·tress (mis′tris) *n.* **1** A woman in authority or control, or to whom service is rendered; a female head, chief, or owner, as of a country household, an institution, or an estate; also a female schoolteacher. **2** A woman who unlawfully, or without marriage, fills the place of a wife; also, a woman beloved and courted; a sweetheart. **3** A woman who is well skilled in or has mastered anything. **4** *Scot.* A married woman or wife. [<OF *maistresse,* fem. of *maistre.* See MASTER.]

Mis·tress (mis′tris) *n.* A title of address formerly applied to both married and unmarried women: now generally supplanted by *Mrs.* for married and *Miss* for unmarried women.

Mistress of the Adriatic Venice.

Mistress of the Seas Great Britain.

Mistress of the World Rome: when its empire embraced the known world.

mis·tri·al (mis·trī′əl) *n.* A trial of a lawsuit that is void because of errors; also, a trial of a lawsuit in which the jury cannot agree on a verdict.

mis·trust (mis·trust′) *n.* Lack of trust or confidence. —*v.t. & v.i.* To regard (someone or something) with suspicion or doubt; distrust. See synonyms under DOUBT, SUSPECT. —**mis·trust′er** *n.* —**mis·trust′ful** *adj.* —**mis·trust′ful·ly** *adv.* —**mis·trust′ful·ness** *n.*

mis·tryst (mis·trist′) *v.t. Scot.* **1** To fail to keep an engagement with. **2** To perplex.

mist·y (mis′tē) *adj.* **mist·i·er, mist·i·est** **1** Containing, characterized by, or accompanied by mist. **2** Dimmed or obscured by or as by mist; hence, lacking clearness or perspicuity; confused; indistinct; vague. See synonyms

mis–hear	misincite	misinter	mislive	misnatured	mispagination	misphrase
mis–hearer	misinclination	misinterment	mislocate	misnavigation	mispaint	mispoint
mis–heed	misincline	misintimation	mislocation	misnumber	misparse	mispoise
mis–hit	misinfer	misjoin	mislodge	misnurture	mispart	mispolicy
mis–hold	misinference	miskeep	mismark	misnutrition	mispassion	misposition
mishumility	misinflame	miskindle	mismeasure	misobservance	mispatch	mispossessed
misidentification	misingenuity	mislabel	mismeasurement	misobserve	mispen	mispractice
misidentify	misinspired	mislabor	mismeet	misoccupy	misperceive	misprejudiced
misimagination	misinstruct	mislanguage	mismenstruation	misopinion	misperception	mispresent
misimagine	misinstruction	mislearn	misminded	misordination	misperform	misprincipled
misimpression	misinstructive	mislie	mismingle	misorganization	misperformance	misproceeding
misimputation	misintend	mislight	mismotion	misorganize	mispersuade	misproduce
misimpute	misintention	mislikeness	misnarrate	mispage	misperuse	mispronounce

under THICK. — **mist′i·ly** adv. — **mist′i·ness** n.

mis·un·der·stand (mis′un·dər·stand′, mis·un′-) v.t. & v.i. **·stood**, **·stand·ing** To understand wrongly; misinterpret.

mis·un·der·stand·ing (mis′un·dər·stan′ding, mis·un′-) n. **1** A misapprehension; mistake as to meaning or motive. **2** A disagreement; dissension. See synonyms under QUARREL.

mis·un·der·stood (mis′un·dər·stŏŏd′, mis·un′-) adj. **1** Not comprehended; wrongly interpreted. **2** Not appreciated at true worth.

mis·use (mis·yōōs′) n. **1** Ill-treatment; violence; abuse. **2** Erroneous or improper use; misapplication. Also **mis·us′age**. — v.t. (mis·yōōz′) **·used**, **·us·ing 1** To use or apply wrongly or improperly. **2** To subject to ill-treatment; abuse; maltreat. See synonyms under ABUSE. **mis·us·er** (mis·yōō′zər) n. **1** One who misuses. **2** Law Such a misuse or abuse of a privilege or franchise as should cause its forfeiture.

mis·ven·ture (mis·ven′chər) n. An ill venture; a misadventure.

Mi·tau (mē′tou) The German name for JELGAVA. Russian **Mi·ta·va** (mē′tə·və).

Mitch·ell (mich′əl), **John**, 1870–1919, U.S. labor leader. — **Maria**, 1818–89, U.S. astronomer. — **Silas Weir**, 1829–1914, U.S. physician and novelist. — **William**, 1879–1936, U.S. general; advocate of air power; called "Billy Mitchell."

Mitch·ell (mich′əl), **Mount** A peak in the Black Mountains, NW North Carolina; the highest point in the United States east of the Mississippi; 6,684 feet.

mite[1] (mīt) n. Any of various small arachnids (order Acarina) of both terrestrial and aquatic habits: many of them are parasitic on men, animals, plants, and stored grain, as the itch mite, cheese mite, etc. ♦ Homophone: might. [OE mīte] — **mit′y** adj.

mite[2] (mīt) n. **1** A very small amount or particle. **2** Any very small coin or sum of money: the widow's mite. Mark xii 42. See synonyms under PARTICLE. ♦ Homophone: might. [<Du. mijt]

mi·ter (mī′tər) n. **1** A headdress worn by various church dignitaries, as popes, archbishops, bishops, and abbots: a tall ornamental cap terminating in two peaks; hence, the office or dignity of a bishop, etc. **2** The official headdress of the ancient Jewish high priest. **3** A headdress resembling a bishop's miter, worn in the 15th century by women. **4** The junction of two bodies at an equally divided angle, as at the corner of a picture frame: also **miter joint.** — v.t. **1** To confer a miter upon; raise to the rank of bishop. **2** To make or join with a miter joint. Also **mitre.** [<OF mitre <L mitra <Gk., belt, turban] — **mi′ter·er** n.

ECCLESIASTICAL MITER

miter box A box having a bottom and sides, but no top or ends, the sides having kerfs or sawguides in which wooden strips may be sawed to accurate miters.

mi·ter·wort (mī′tər·wûrt′) n. Any of a genus (Mitella) of low, slender, mainly North American perennial herbs of the saxifrage family, having small miter-shaped flowers. Also **mi′tre·wort′**.

Mit·ford (mit′fərd), **Mary Russell**, 1787–1855, English author.

mith·er (mith′ər) n. Scot. Mother.

Mith·gar·thr (mith′gär·thər) See MIDGARD.

Mith·ra (mith′rə) **1** The ancient Persian god of light and truth. **2** In the Zoroastrian belief, a god often acting as the mediator between the Supreme God and man. Also

Mith′ras (-rəs). [<L <Gk. Mithras <OPersian Mithra] — **Mith·ra·ic** (mith·rā′ik) adj. — **Mith·ra′i·cism** n. — **Mith·ra′ism** n. — **Mith′·ra·is′tic** adj.

Mith·ri·da·tes VI (mith′rə·dā′tēz), 132?–63 B.C., king of Pontus; defeated by Pompey: known as Mithridates the Great.

Mith·ri·dat·ic (mith′rə·dat′ik) adj. Of or pertaining to any of several kings of Pontus named Mithridates, especially Mithridates VI.

mith·ri·dat·ism (mith′rə·dā′tiz·əm) n. Immunity against poisons secured by the administration of gradually increasing doses: so called from King Mithridates VI of Pontus, who is said to have immunized himself by this method. [<obs. mithridiate an antidote against poison <LL mithridatium <Mithridateus of Mithridates] — **mith′ri·dat′ic** (-dat′ik) adj.

mi·ti·cide (mī′tə·sīd) n. A chemical agent destructive of mites: also called acaricide. [<miti- (<MITE[1]) + -CIDE]

mit·i·gate (mit′ə·gāt) v.t. & v.i. **·gat·ed**, **·gat·ing** To make or become milder, less harsh, or less severe; moderate. See synonyms under ABATE, ALLAY, ALLEVIATE, AMEND, PALLIATE, RELAX. [<L mitigatus, pp. of mitigare <mitis mild + agere do, drive] — **mit′i·ga·ble** adj. — **mit′·i·gant** adj. & n. — **mit′i·ga′tion** n. — **mit′i·ga′tive** adj. — **mit′i·ga′tor** n. — **mit′i·ga·to′ry** (-gə·tôr′ē, -tō′rē) adj. & n.

mi·tis casting (mī′tis, mē′-) **1** The process of making castings of wrought iron of which the melting point has been lowered by the addition of a small amount of aluminum. **2** A casting so made. [<L mitis mild + CASTING]

mi·to·chon·dri·a (mī′tə·kon′drē·ə) n. Chondriosome. [<NL <Gk. mitos thread + chondros cartilage, granule]

mi·to·sis (mī·tō′sis) n. Biol. The series of changes in indirect cell division by which the chromatin of the nucleus is modified into a double set of chromosomes that splits longitudinally, one set going to each nuclear pole of the spindle before final division into two fully mature daughter cells. Compare MEIOSIS. [<NL <Gk. mitos thread + -OSIS] — **mi·tot·ic** (mī·tot′ik) adj. — **mi·tot′i·cal·ly** adv.

mi·trail·leur (mē·trà·yœr′) n. **1** A soldier who operates a mitrailleuse. **2** A mitrailleuse. [<F <mitrailler fire grapeshot <mitraille grapeshot, small coins <OF mitre, mite small coin]

mi·trail·leuse (mē·trà·yœz′) n. **1** A kind of breechloading machine-gun of grouped barrels for the rapid firing of small missiles. **2** Any machine-gun. [<F]

mi·tral (mī′trəl) adj. **1** Pertaining to or resembling a miter. **2** Of or pertaining to the mitral valve.

mitral valve Anat. A membranous valve between the left auricle and the left ventricle of the heart: it prevents the flow of blood into the auricle.

mi·tre (mī′tər) See MITER.

mitt (mit) n. **1** A glove, often of lace or knitwork, that does not extend over the fingers. **2** A mitten; specifically, in baseball, a heavy padded mitten used by the catcher and the first baseman. **3** pl. Slang The hands. [<MITTEN]

mit·ten (mit′n) n. **1** A covering for the hand, encasing the four fingers together and the thumb separately. **2** A mitt. **3** pl. Slang The hands; also, boxing gloves. [<F mitaine]

mit·ti·mus (mit′ə·məs) n. **1** Law An order by a magistrate committing a prisoner to jail. **2** A dismissal. [<L, we send <mittere send]

mitz·vah (mits′vä) n. pl. **·voth** (-vōth) A command of God; hence, the fulfilment of such a command, regarded as a special privilege; especially, a function of the synagog ceremonial or an act promoting the welfare of

the Jews. Also **mits′vah.** [<Hebrew mitzwah commandment]

Mi·vart (mī′vərt, miv′ərt), **St. George Jackson**, 1827–1900, English biologist.

mix (miks) v. **mixed** or **mixt**, **mix·ing** v.t. **1** To put together in one mass or compound; blend. **2** To make by combining ingredients: to mix dough. **3** To combine or join: to mix business with pleasure. **4** To cause to associate or mingle: to mix social classes together. **5** To crossbreed. — v.i. **6** To be mixed or blended. **7** To associate; get along. **8** To take part; become involved. — **to mix up 1** To blend thoroughly. **2** To confuse; bewilder. **3** To implicate or involve. — n. **1** The act or effect of mixing. **2** A mixture, expecially a commercial mixture of prepared ingredients: a cake mix. **3** A proportion, as of things that make up a mixture; specifically, the proportion of certain substances or raw materials before their subjection to a fabricating or manufacturing process: a mix of cement. **3** Telecom. The correct blending of the sound input of two or more microphones. **4** A combination of various elements; mixture: a movie providing a heady mix of violence, sex, and glamour. [Back formation <MIXED] — **mix′a·ble, mix′i·ble** adj.

Synonyms (verb): amalgamate, associate, blend, combine, commingle, commix, compound, confuse, fuse, incorporate, join, meddle, mingle, unite. Compare COMPLEX, HETEROGENEOUS.

mixed (mikst) adj. **1** Mingled in a body or mass; joined together; associated; blended: generally of different or even incongruous elements: a mixed metaphor. **2** Containing persons of both sexes: a mixed school, mixed foursome, etc. **3** Mentally confused, as with liquor. **4** Law Designating statutes which concern both persons and property; also, designating property which is not altogether real nor personal, but a compound of both. **5** Bot. Denoting inflorescence which combines cymose and racemose. [<F mixte <L mixtus, pp. of miscere mix]

mixed bag A mixture or assortment of miscellaneous elements.

mixed economy A combination of laissez-faire with governmentally planned and/or controlled economy.

mixed marriage Marriage between persons of different religions or races.

mixed number See under NUMBER.

mixed train A train transporting both passengers and freight.

mixed-up (mikst′up′) adj. Confused or disordered.

mix·en (mik′sən) n. Archaic A dunghill; compost heap. [OE mixen < meox dung]

mix·er (mik′sər) n. **1** One who or that which mixes; a machine or device for mixing. **2** Colloq. A person with reference to his ability to mix socially or get along well in groups.

mix·o·troph·ic (mik′sə·trof′ik) adj. Biol. Pertaining to or designating plants and animals capable of feeding on both inorganic and dead organic material, as certain flagellate protozoa. [<Gk. mixis mingling + trophē food]

mix·ture (miks′chər) n. **1** The act of mixing. **2** Something resulting from mixing; admixture. **3** Something added as an ingredient. **4** A pharmaceutical preparation consisting of an aqueous solution in which is suspended an insoluble compound: intended for internal use. **5** A commingling of two or more substances in varying proportions, in which the ingredients retain their individual chemical properties, and from which they may be separated, unaltered, by mechanical means. Compare COMPOUND. [<F <L mixtura <miscere mix]

---

misproportion	misrate	misreform	misresemblance	mis–sheathed	misstroke	misthread
misproposal	misread	misregulate	misresolved	mis–ship	misstyle	misthrive
mispropose	misrealize	misrehearsal	misresult	misshod	missuggestion	misthrow
misprovide	misreason	misrehearse	misreward	mis–sing	missuit	mistitle
misprovidence	misreceive	misrelate	misrime	missolution	missummation	mistouch
misprovoke	misrecital	misrelation	misseason	missort	mis–sway	mistranscribe
mispunctuate	misrecite	misreliance	misseat	missound	misswear	mistranscription
mispunctuation	misrecognition	misrely	mis–see	misspace	missyllabication	mistranslate
mispurchase	misrecognize	misrender	mis–seed	misspeak	missyllabify	mistranslation
mispursuit	misrecollect	misrepeat	missemblance	misstart	mistaught	mistune
misqualify	misrefer	misreposed	mis–send	missteer	mistend	mistutor
misquote	misreference	misreprint	mis–sense	misstop	misterm	misunion
misraise	misreflect	misrepute	missentence	misstrike		misyoke

mix-up (miks′up′) *n.* **1** A confusion; muddle. **2** *Colloq.* A fight.

Mi·ya·za·ki (mē·yä·zä ·kē) A city on SE Kyushu island, Japan.

Mi·zar (mī′zər, mē′-) The star Zeta, second from the end in the handle of the Dipper, constellation of Ursa Major: the faint star close to it is *Alcor.* [<Arabic *mī′zar* veil, cloak]

miz·zen (miz′ən) *n. Naut.* **1** A mizzenmast. **2** A triangular sail set on the mizzen. —*adj.* Of or pertaining to the mizzen or mizzenmast. Also **miz′en.** [<F *misaine* <Ital. *mezzana,* fem. of *mezzano* middle < L *medianus.* Doublet of MEIDIAN, MEAN,[3] MESNE.]

miz·zen·mast (miz′ən·məst, -mast′, -mäst′) *n. Naut.* **1** The mast next abaft the mainmast. **2** The shorter of the two masts of a ketch or yawl.

Mjol·nir (myol′nir) *n.* In Norse mythology, Thor's terrible hammer. Also **Mjoll′nir, Mjöll·nir** (myœl′nir), **Mjol′ner.**

mks The meter-kilogram-second system of units for the measurement of physical quantities. It differs from the cgs system in using the international standards of length and mass instead of their submultiples, the centimeter and the gram.

mne·me (nē′mē) *n.* A hypothetical unit of memory assumed to exist in all animal cells. [<Gk. ′*mnēmē* memory]

mne·mon·ic (ni·mon′ik) *adj.* Pertaining to, aiding, or designed to aid the memory. Also **mne·mon′i·cal.** [<Gk. *mnēmonikos* <*mnēmōn* mindful <*mnasthai* remember]

mne·mon·ics (ni·mon′iks) *n.* The science of memory improvement. Also **mne·mo·tech·nics** (nē′mō·tek′niks).

Mne·mos·y·ne (nē·mos′ə·nē, -moz′-) In Greek mythology, the goddess of memory and mother (by Zeus) of the Muses. [<L <Gk. *mnēmosynē* memory <*mnasthai* remember]

-mo *suffix Printing* Folded into a (specified) number of leaves: said of a sheet of paper: 12 *mo* or *duodecimo.* Also shown by the symbol (°), as in 12°. [<L *-mo,* as in the phrase *induodecimo* twelvefold]

mo·a (mō′ə) *n.* A large, flightless, extinct bird (family *Dinornithiformes*) of New Zealand, having enormous legs with at least three toes; especially, the largest species (*Dinornis robustus*). [<native name]

Mo·ab (mō′ab) An ancient country in the upland area east of the Dead Sea.

Mo·ab·ite (mō′əb·īt) *n.* One of the descendants of Moab, son of Lot. *Gen.* xix 37. —**Mo·ab·it·ess** (mō′əb·īt′is) *n.* fem.

Moabite Stone A stone slab with a Moabite inscription, dating from 850 B.C.; discovered, 1868.

moan (mōn) *n.* **1** A low mournful sound indicative of grief or pain. **2** A similar sound: the *moan* of the wind. **3** *Obs.* Lamentation; complaint. —*v.i.* **1** To utter moans of grief or pain. **2** To make a low, mournful sound, as wind in trees. —*v.t.* **3** To lament; bewail. [Cf. OE *mænan* lament, moan]

moat (mōt) *n.* A defensive ditch on the outside of a fortress wall. —*v.t.* To surround with or as with a moat. ◆Homophone: *mote.* [<OF *mote* embankment]

mob[1] (mob) *n.* **1** A turbulent or lawless crowd or throng; a rabble. **2** The lowest class of people; the masses; populace. **3** *Austral.* A herd, as of sheep or cattle. **4** *Slang* A gang, as of thieves. —*v.t.* **mobbed, mob·bing 1** To attack in a mob; crowd around and annoy. **2** To crowd into, as a hall. [<L *mob(ile vulgus)* movable crowd] —**mob′ber** *n.* —**mob′bish** *adj.* —**mob′bish·ly** *adv.*

Synonyms (noun): canaille, crowd, masses, people, populace, rabble.

mob[2] (mob) *n.* A cap or headdress formerly worn by women and girls and usually tied under the chin. Also **mob′cap′.** [<Du. *mop* coif, cap]

mo·bile (mō′bəl, -bēl) *adj.* **1** Characterized by freedom of movement; movable. **2** Changing easily in expression or in state of mind; changeable. **3** Moving or flowing freely. **4** That can be easily and quickly moved, as military units. **5** Designating a mobile. —*n.* (mō′bēl) A form of sculpture arranged so that its movable parts, suspended or balanced on rods, wires, etc., describe kinetic rather than static patterns. [<F <L *mobilis* movable] —**mo·bil·i·ty** (mō·bil′ə·tē) *n.*

Synonyms: changeable, changing, expressive, fickle, movable, sensitive, variable, volatile. See ACTIVE. *Antonyms:* dull, fixed, immovable, still, stolid, unchanging, unvarying.

Mo·bile (mō·bēl′) A port of Alabama, on **Mobile Bay,** an arm of the Gulf of Mexico in SW Alabama.

mobile home *U.S.* A movable living unit, originally conceived of as a trailer but now designed more like a ranch house, which can be connected to utilities and is often put on a foundation as a permanent dwelling.

Mobile River A river in SW Alabama flowing 45 miles south from the confluence of the Tombigbee and Alabama rivers to Mobile Bay at Mobile.

mo·bi·lize (mō′bə·līz) *v.* **·lized, ·liz·ing** *v.t.* **1** To make ready for war, as an army, industry, etc. **2** To assemble for use; organize. **3** To make mobile; put into circulation or use. —*v.i.* **4** To get ready for war. Also *Brit.* **mo′bi·lise.** [<F *mobiliser*] —**mo·bi·li·za′tion** (-lə·zā′shən, -lī·zā′-) *n.*

Mö·bi·us surface (mœ′bē·o͞os) *Geom.* A surface both sides of which may be completely traversed without crossing either edge: made by joining the half-twisted ends of a rectangular strip of paper or other flexible material. Also **Möbius strip.** [after August Ferdinand *Möbius,* 1790–1868, German mathematician and astronomer]

mob law Lynch law.

mo·ble (mob′əl) *v.t. Archaic* To cover with a cap or mob. [<MOB[2]]

mob·oc·ra·cy (mob·ok′rə·sē) *n. pl.* **·cies 1** Lawless control of public affairs by the mob or populace. **2** The mob considered as the dominant class. [<MOB[1] + -(O)CRACY]

mob·o·crat (mob′ə·krat) *n.* One who favors mobocracy; a demagog. —**mob′o·crat′ic, mob′o·crat′i·cal** *adj.*

mob·ster (mob′stər) *n. Slang* A gangster.

moc·ca·sin (mok′ə·sin) *n.* **1** A foot covering made of soft leather or buckskin; worn by North American Indians; also, a soft shoe or slipper. **2** A dark-colored, obscurely blotched, venomous snake (genus *Agkistrodon*) of the southern United States. *A. piscivorus* is the **water moccasin.** [<Algonquian *mohkisson*]

MOCCASIN
(Average length about 4 feet; largest speciments to 6 feet)

moccasin flower Any one of certain orchids of the genus *Cypripedium,* common in the United States, especially the showy ladyslipper (*C. reginae*), State flower of Minnesota.

mo·cha (mō′kə) *n.* **1** A choice coffee, originally grown in Arabia. **2** A rich, coffee-flavored icing, or a cake flavored with it. **3** A fine sheepskin leather used for making gloves. **4** A dark, dull, grayish-brown color. [from *Mocha*]

Mo·cha (mō′kə) A port of Yemen, in SW Arabia: also *Mokha.*

mock (mok) *v.t.* **1** To treat or address scornfully or derisively; hold up to ridicule. **2** To ridicule by imitation of action or speech; mimic derisively. **3** To deceive; delude. **4** To defy; make futile. **5** *Poetic* To imitate; counterfeit. —*v.i.* **6** To express or show ridicule, scorn, or contempt; scoff. —*adj.* Merely imitating the reality; sham. —*n.* An act of mocking; a jeer; mockery. [<OF *mocquer*] — **mock′er** *n.* —**mock′ing·ly** *adv.*

Synonyms (verb): banter, chaff, deride, flout, gibe, insult, jeer, taunt. See IMITATE, MISLEAD, SCOFF. Compare COUNTERFEIT.

mock·er·y (mok′ər·ē) *n. pl.* **·er·ies 1** Derisive or contemptuous mimicry. **2** A false show; sham. **3** A butt of ridicule. **4** Labor in vain. See synonyms under BANTER, SCORN.

mock-he·ro·ic (mok′hi·rō′ik) *adj.* Imitating or satirizing the heroic manner, style, attitude, or character. —*n.* **1** Any writing using the grand style as a comic expedient. **2** *pl.* Affectation of the grand manner in expressing trivialities.

mock·ing·bird (mok′ing·bûrd′) *n.* **1** A bird (*Mimus polyglottos*) common in the southern and eastern United States, noted for its rich song and powers of imitating the calls of other birds. **2** One of various other birds that mock, as the catbird.

mocking thrush The thrasher.

mocking wren 1 The Carolina wren. **2** Bewick's wren. See under WREN.

mock moon A paraselene.

mock orange Any of a genus (*Philadelphus*) of ornamental shrubs of the saxifrage family: also called *syringa.*

mock sun A parhelion.

mock title See HALF-TITLE.

mock-tur·tle soup (mok′tûr′təl) Soup prepared from calf's head or other meat, and somewhat resembling green-turtle soup.

mock-up (mok′up′) *n.* **1** A model, usually full-scale, of a proposed structure, machine, apparatus, etc. **2** An airplane, etc., constructed for purposes of study, testing, or training of personnel.

Moc·te·zu·ma (môk′tä·so͞o ′mä) See MONTEZUMA.

mod (mod) *adj.* Bold, flamboyant, and unconventional, as in dress or behavior. —*n. Sometimes cap.* One who dresses or behaves in a flamboyant or unconventional manner. [<MODERN]

mo·dal (mōd′l) *adj.* **1** Of or denoting a mode or manner, especially a mode of grammar, a mode in music, or a mode of logical statement. **2** Characterized by form or manner without reference to matter or substance. **3** Pertaining to or designating a statistical mode. —**mo′dal·ly** *adv.*

mo·dal·i·ty (mō·dal′ə·tē) *n. pl.* **·ties 1** Modal character; the fact or quality of being modal. **2** *Logic* The character of a proposition as expressing or asserting a sequence of necessity (including impossibility) or of contingency (including probability and possibility).

Mod·der (mod′ər) A river in Orange Free State Province, Republic of South Africa, flowing 225 miles NW to the Riet.

mode (mōd) *n.* **1** Manner of being, doing, etc.; way; method. **2** Prevailing style; common fashion. **3** *Gram.* Mood. **4** *Music* A method of dividing an octave by placing the steps and half-steps of which it is composed in certain arbitrary relations. In the **major mode,** tones are arranged as given in the major scale; in the **minor mode,** as in the minor scale. **5** *Psychol.* A faculty or phenomenon of mind considered as a state of consciousness. **6** *Philos.* The manner of a thing's existence so far as it is not essential. **7** *Logic* **a** The style of the connection between the antecedent and the consequent of a proposition. **b** The arrangement of the propositions of a syllogism according to their quantity and quality. **8** *Stat.* That value, magnitude, or score which occurs the greatest number of times in a given series of observations: also called *norm.* **9** *Geol.* The actual mineral composition of a rock, expressed in percentages by weight: distinguished from *norm.* **10** A light bluish-gray color. **11** *Physics* One of a set of forms of motion of a dynamic system, having the properties that the variation with time is either harmonic or exponential and that any form of motion of the system can be represented as a superposition of members of the set. See synonyms under MANNER, SYSTEM. [< L *modus* measure, manner]

mod·el (mod′l) *n.* **1** An object, usually in miniature, representing accurately something to be made or already existing; more rarely, a plan or drawing: a *model* of a building. **2** A person who poses for painters, sculptors, etc. **3** A thing or person to be imitated or

patterned after; that which is taken as a pattern or an example. **4** A person employed to wear articles of clothing to display them to customers. **5** That which strikingly resembles something else; an approximate copy or image. —*v.* **·eled** or **·elled, ·el·ing** or **·el·ling** *v.t.* **1** To plan or fashion after a model or pattern. **2** To make a model of. **3** To fashion; make. **4** To display by wearing, as a coat or hat. —*v.i.* **5** To make a model or models. **6** To pose or serve as a model (defs. 2 and 4). **7** To assume the appearance of natural form. —*adj.* Serving or used as a model; suitable for a model; worthy to be imitated. [<F *modèle* <Ital. *modello,* dim. of *modo* <L *modus* measure, manner] —**mod′·el·er, mod′el·ler** *n.*

Synonyms (noun): archetype, copy, design, ectype, example, facsimile, image, imitation, mold, original, pattern, prototype, replica, representation, type. A *pattern* must be closely followed in its minutest particulars by a faithful copyist; a *model* may allow a great degree of freedom. A sculptor may idealize his living *model*; his workmen must exactly copy in marble or metal the *model* he has made in clay. The *archetype* is the original form, actual or ideal, in accordance with which existing things are made; a *prototype* is either the original or an authenticated copy that has the authority of the original. See EXAMPLE, IDEA, IDEAL.

Model T An early model of automobile manufactured by Henry Ford in great numbers: also called *tin lizzie.*

Mo·de·na (mō′dā·nä) A city in north central Italy.

mod·er·ate (mod′ər·it) *adj.* **1** Keeping or kept within reasonable limits; not extreme, excessive, or radical; also, mild; temperate; calm; reasonable; gentle. **2** Not strongly partisan: said of political and religious parties, and their tenets or views. **3** Medium; fair; also, mediocre. **4** Slow in thought, speech, or action. **5** *Meteorol.* Designating a breeze (No. 4) or a gale (No. 7) on the Beaufort scale. See synonyms under GRADUAL, MODEST, SLOW, SOBER. —*n.* A person of moderate views, opinions, or practices; especially, a member of a political or religious party which is not strongly partisan. —*v.* (mod′ə·rāt) **·at·ed, ·at·ing** *v.t.* **1** To reduce the violence, severity, etc., of; make less extreme; restrain. **2** To preside over. —*v.i.* **3** To become less intense or violent; abate. **4** To act as moderator. See synonyms under ABATE, ALLAY, ALLEVIATE, TEMPER, TRANQUILIZE. [<L *moderatus,* pp. of *moderare* regulate < *modus* measure] —**mod′er·ate·ly** *adv.* —**mod′er·ate·ness** *n.* —**mod′er·a′tion** *n.*

mod·e·ra·to (mod′ə·rä′tō) *adj.* & *adv. Music* In moderate time; moderately. [<Ital.]

mod·er·a·tor (mod′ə·rā′tər) *n.* **1** One who restrains or regulates. **2** The presiding officer of a meeting; also, the presiding officer in Presbyterian and Congregational courts. **3** *Physics* A substance, as graphite or beryllium, used to control the rate of a nuclear chain reaction in an atomic–energy reactor. —**mod′er·a′tor·ship** *n.*

mod·ern (mod′ərn) *adj.* **1** Pertaining to the present or recent period; not ancient. **2** *Obs.* Commonplace; common; trite. —*n.* **1** A person of modern times, or modern views or characteristics: also **mod′ern·er.** **2** *Printing* A style of type face characterized by contrasting heavy down–strokes and thin cross–strokes. [<LL *modernus* recent <L *modo* just now] —**mod′ern·ly** *adv.* —**mo·der·ni·ty** (mo·dûr′nə·tē), **mod′ern·ness** *n.*

Synonyms (adj.): fresh, late, new, novel, recent. *Modern* history pertains to any period since the Middle Ages; *modern* literature, *modern* architecture, etc., are not strikingly remote from the styles and types prevalent today. That which is *late* is somewhat removed from the present, but not far enough to be called old. That which is *recent* is very close to the present, but not quite so sharply distinguished from the past as *new.* See NEW.

mod·ern·ism (mod′ərn·iz′əm) *n.* **1** Something characteristic of modern as distinguished from former or classical times; a modern idiom or practice. **2** Modern character, methods, or mental attitude. **3** The humanistic tendency in religious thought to supplement old theological creeds and dogmas by new scientific and philosophical learning and thus to place emphasis on practical ethics and world–wide social justice: distinguished from *fundamentalism.* —**mod′ern·ist** *n.* —**mod′ern·is′tic** *adj.*

mod·ern·ize (mod′ərn·īz) *v.t.* & *v.i.* **·ized, ·iz·ing** To make or become modern in ideas, standards, methods, etc. —**mod′ern·i·za′tion** *n.* —**mod′ern·iz′er** *n.*

mod·est (mod′ist) *adj.* **1** Restrained by a sense of propriety or humility. **2** Characterized by reserve, propriety, or purity; decorous; chaste. **3** Free from excess; moderate. [<F *modeste* <L *modestus* moderate < *modus* measure] —**mod′est·ly** *adv.*

Synonyms: chaste, decent, decorous, humble, moderate, proper, pure, retiring, unassuming, unobtrusive, unostentatious, unpretending, unpretentious, virtuous. See HUMBLE.

mod·es·ty (mod′is·tē) *n.* Decent reserve and propriety; delicacy; decorum.

Synonyms: backwardness, bashfulness, coldness, constraint, coyness, diffidence, reserve, shyness, timidity, unobtrusiveness. *Bashfulness* is a shrinking from notice without assignable reason. *Coyness* is a half encouragement, half avoidance of offered attention, and may be real or affected. *Diffidence* is self–distrust; *modesty,* a humble estimate of oneself in comparison with others or with the demands of some undertaking. *Modesty* has also the specific meaning of a sensitive shrinking from anything indelicate. *Shyness* is a tendency to shrink from observation; *timidity,* a distinct fear of criticism, error, or failure. *Reserve* is holding oneself aloof from others, or holding back one's feelings from expression, or one's affairs from communication to others. Compare ABASH, PRIDE, RESERVE, TACITURN. *Antonyms*: abandon, arrogance, assumption, assurance, boldness, conceit, confidence, egotism, forwardness, frankness, freedom, haughtiness, impudence, indiscretion, loquaciousness, loquacity, pertness, sauciness, self–conceit, self–sufficiency, sociability.

mod·i·cum (mod′i·kəm) *n. pl.* **·cums** or **·ca** (-kə) **1** A moderate amount; a little. **2** A small thing or person. [<L < *modus* measure]

mod·i·fi·ca·tion (mod′ə·fə·kā′shən) *n.* **1** The act of modifying, or the state of being modified. **2** *Biol.* Variation in plants and animals, specifically by localized changes in an organism due to external influences and not inheritable. Compare MUTATION. **3** That which results from modifying. —**mod·i·fi·ca·to·ry** (mod′ə·fə·kā′tər·ē) *adj.*

mod·i·fi·er (mod′ə·fī′ər) *n.* **1** One who or that which qualifies, changes, limits, or varies. **2** *Gram.* A word, phrase, or clause that alters, restricts, or varies the application of another word or group of words, as an adjective or adverb. See also UNIT MODIFIER.

mod·i·fy (mod′ə·fī) *v.* **·fied, ·fy·ing** *v.t.* **1** To make somewhat different in form, character, etc.; vary. **2** To reduce in degree or extent; moderate. **3** *Gram.* To qualify the meaning of; restrict; limit. **4** *Ling.* To alter (a vowel) by umlaut. —*v.i.* **5** To be or become modified; change. See synonyms under CHANGE, TEMPER. [<F *modifier* <L *modificare* < *modus* measure + *facere* make] —**mod′i·fi′a·ble** *adj.*

Mo·di·glia·ni (mō′dē·lyä′nē), **Amedeo,** 1884–1920, Italian painter and sculptor.

mo·dil·lion (mō·dil′yən) *n. Archit.* An enriched block or horizontal bracket used in series under a Corinthian or Composite cornice: sometimes, with less ornament, under one of the Roman Ionic order. [<F *modillon* <Ital. *modiglione*]

mo·di·o·lus (mō·dī′ə·ləs) *n. pl.* **·li** (-lī) *Anat.* The central stem round which wind the passages of the cochlea of the internal ear. [<L, bucket on a water wheel < *modus* measure]

mod·ish (mō′dish) *adj.* Conformable to the current mode, fashion, or usage; stylish. —**mod′·ish·ly** *adv.* —**mod′ish·ness** *n.*

mo·diste (mō·dēst′) *n.* A woman who makes or deals in fashionable articles, especially of women's dress or millinery. [<F]

Mo·djes·ka (mō·jes′kə), **Helena,** 1840–1909, Polish actress active in the United States.

Mo·djo·ker·to Man (mō′jō·kâr′tō) A primitive hominid identified from the fossil skull of an infant found in 1931 in Pleistocene deposits near Modjokerto, Java: it bears anatomical resemblances both to Pithecanthropus and to Neanderthal man.

Mo·doc (mō′dok) *n.* A North American Indian of a small, nearly extinct tribe of Lutuamian linguistic stock, formerly living in California, now on reservations in Oregon and Oklahoma. See LUTUAMIAN.

mo·do et for·ma (mō′dō et fôr′mə) *Latin* In manner and form.

Mo·dred (mō′drid) In Arthurian legend, King Arthur's treacherous nephew (or son). During Arthur's absence Modred usurped the throne: after Arthur's return they killed each other in battle.

mod·u·lar (moj′ŏŏ·lər) *adj.* **1** Of, like, or pertaining to a module or modulus. **2** Composed of modules: *modular* homes.

mod·u·late (moj′ŏŏ·lāt) *v.* **·lat·ed, ·lat·ing** *v.t.* **1** To vary the tone, inflection, or pitch of. **2** To regulate or adjust; temper; soften. **3** *Music* To change or cause to change to a different key. **4** To intone or sing. **5** *Electronics* To alter the frequency or amplitude of (a radio carrier wave). —*v.i.* **6** *Electronics* To alter the frequency or amplitude of a carrier wave. **7** *Music* To change from one key to another by using a transitional chord common to both. [<L *modulatus,* pp. of *modulari* regulate < *modulus* MODULE] —**mod′u·la·to′ry** (-lə·tôr′ē, -tō′rē) *adj.*

mod·u·la·tion (moj′ŏŏ·lā′shən) *n.* **1** The act of modulating, or the state of being modulated; specifically, a musical inflection of the voice; change in pitch. **2** *Music* A change from one key to another by the use of a transitional chord common to both. **3** *Telecom.* The process of varying the frequency, amplitude, intensity, or phase of a carrier wave so as to conform with a transmitted signal wave.

mod·u·la·tor (moj′ŏŏ·lā′tər) *n.* **1** One who or that which modulates. **2** *Telecom.* A tube or valve for effecting modulation. **3** A musical chart showing the relations of tones and scales.

mod·ule (moj′ŏŏl) *n.* **1** A standard or unit of measurement. **2** *Archit.* A measure of proportion among the parts of a classical order, the size of the diameter or semidiameter of the base of a column shaft usually being taken as a unit. **3** A standard structural component repeatedly used, as in a building, computer, etc.: cubic *modules* used in the design of a table. **4** A preassembled, self–contained unit, often a component or subassembly of a larger structure: a housing *module*; a lunar *module.* **5** *Obs.* A mere image. [<L *modulus* < *modus* measure. Doublet of MOLD[1].]

mod·u·lor (moj′ŏŏ·lôr) *n.* A system of industrial design based upon the ideal proportions of the human body: units derived from the basic dimensions can be assembled to secure maximum harmony and utility. —*adj.* Of or characterized by such design.

mod·u·lus (moj′ŏŏ·ləs) *n. pl.* **·li** (-lī) **1** *Physics* A number, coefficient, or quantity that measures a force, function, or effect: *modulus* of elasticity: sometimes abbreviated to *M* or μ. See CONGRUENT. **2** *Math.* The logarithm of *e* to the base 10 ($\log_{10}e$): Napierian logarithms are multiplied by this factor to convert them to logarithms to the base 10. [<L, dim. of *modus* a measure]

mo·dus (mō′dəs) *n. Latin* Mode; manner.

modus op·er·an·di (op′ə·ran′dī) *Latin* A manner of operation.

modus vi·ven·di (vi·ven′dī) *Latin* A manner of living; especially, a temporary arrangement pending a final settlement.

moe (mō) *adj.* & *adv. Obs.* More.

mo·el·lon (mō′əl·on) *n.* **1** A form of rubble masonry used as a filling in the facing walls of a structure. **2** Dégras (def. 1). [<F, alter. of OF *moilon*; ? infl. by F *moelle* pith]

Moe·rae (mē′rē) See MOIRAI. Also **Mœ′ræ.**

Moe·ro (mwe·rō′) The French spelling of MWERU.

Moe·si·a (mē′shē·ə) An ancient country and former Roman province in SE Europe south of the Danube. Also **Mœ′si·a.**

Moe·so·goth (mē′sə·goth) *n.* A member of the Gothic tribe that settled in Moesia. —**Moe′·so·goth′ic** *adj.*

mo·fette (mō·fet′) *n.* **1** A noxious emanation of gas from a fissure; a gas spring. **2** An opening in the earth from which noxious gas escapes, as from a volcano. Also **mof·fette′.** [<F <Ital. *mofetta* < *muffare* decay <G *muff* mold]

mo·fus·sil (mə·fus′əl) *n. Anglo–Indian* The

country as distinguished from the residencies and the towns.

Mog·a·di·shu (mog′ə·dish′ōō) The chief port and capital of Somalia, on the Indian Ocean. *Italian* **Mo·ga·di·scio** (mō′gä·dē′shō).

Mog·a·dor (mog′ə·dôr′, -dōr′; *Fr.* mô·gȧ·dôr′) A port on the Atlantic coast of SW Morocco.

mo·gen Da·vid (mō′gən dä′vid, duv′id) A mystic device formed by the intertwining of two equilateral triangles; the six-pointed star: used as a symbol of Judaism. Also called *star of David, shield of David, Solomon's seal.* [<Hebrew, star of David]

Mo·gi·lev (mō′gi·lef, *Russian* mô′gē·lyôf′) A city in SW Belorussian S.S.R., on the Dnieper. Also **Mo·hi·lev** (mô′hē·lyôf′).

mo·gul (mō′gul, mō·gul′) *n.* **1** Any great or pretentious personage; autocrat: also **great mogul. 2** A type of freight locomotive with three pairs of coupled drivers and one pair of leading truck wheels.

Mo·gul (mō′gul, mō·gul′) *n.* A Mongol; Mongolian; specifically, one of the Mongol conquerors of Hindustan, or a follower of Genghis Khan in the 13th century. Also **Mo·ghul′.** — **the Great** or **Grand Mogul** The former Mongol emperor of Delhi. [<Persian *mugal* a Mongol]

Mo·hács (mō′häch) A city on the Danube in southern Hungary; scene of a decisive Turkish victory over the Hungarians, 1526.

mo·hair (mō′hâr) *n.* **1** The hair of the Angora goat. **2** A smooth, wiry fabric made of mohair filling and cotton warp: often called *brilliantine.* **3** A fabric of cut or uncut loops with cotton or wool back and mohair pile: used chiefly for upholstery. [Earlier *mocayare* <Arabic *mukhayyar*, infl. in form by *hair*]

Mo·ham·med (mō·ham′id), 570–632, Arabian religious and military leader; founder of Islam and author of the *Koran*: also spelled *Mahomet.* Also **Mo·hom′ed.** — **Mohammed II,** 1430?–81, sultan of Turkey 1451–81; captured Constantinople, 1453.

Mohammed Ali See MEHEMET ALI.

Mo·ham·me·dan (mō·ham′ə·dən) *adj.* Pertaining to Mohammed or to his religion and institutions. — *n.* A follower of Mohammed or believer in Islam; a Muslim. Also *Mahometan, Muhammadan.*

Mo·ham·me·dan·ism (mō·ham′ə·dən·iz′əm) *n.* The religion founded by Mohammed; Islam.

mo·har·ra (mō·här′ə) See MOJARRA.

Mo·har·ran (mə·här′ən) See MUHARRAM.

Mo·ha·ve (mō·hä′vē) *n.* A member of a tribe of North American Indians of Yuman linguistic stock, formerly living along the Colorado River. — *adj.* Of or pertaining to this tribe. Also spelled *Mojave.*

Mohave Desert See MOJAVE DESERT.

Mo·hawk (mō′hôk) *n.* **1** One of a tribe of North American Indians of Iroquoian stock, one of the original tribes of the Five Nations, formerly ranging from the Mohawk River Valley, New York, to the St. Lawrence: now in Canada, New York, and Wisconsin. **2** The Iroquoian language of this tribe. **3** A Mohock. [<N. Am. Ind. Cf. Narragansett *mohowaicuck*, lit., they eat animate things, hence, eaters of human flesh; so named by enemy tribes.]

Mohawk River A river in central New York, flowing 140 miles SE to the Hudson.

Mo·he·gan (mō·hē′gən) *n.* One of a tribe of North American Indians of Algonquian linguistic stock, the eastern branch of the Mahican group: formerly occupying the region from the lower Connecticut and Thames rivers northward to Massachusetts. See MAHICAN. [<Algonquian *maingan* wolf]

Mo·hen·jo-Da·ro (mō·hen′jō-dä′rō) A site of Indus Valley civilization in NW Sind, West Pakistan.

Mo·hi·can (mō-hē′kən) *n.* One of a warlike tribe of North American Indians belonging to the Algonquian linguistic stock, and formerly dwelling along both banks of the Hudson. See MAHICAN.

Mo·hock (mō′hok, -hôk) *n.* One of a band of lawless rowdies, often aristocratic rakes, who frequented the streets of London early in the 18th century. Also **Mo′hawk.** [Var. of MOHAWK]

Mo·hole (mō′hōl′) *n.* A hole drilled or to be drilled through the ocean floor to the Mohorovicic discontinuity.

Mo·hor·o·vic·ic discontinuity (mə·hôr′ə·vis′ik, -vich′ik) *n. Geol.* A rock layer forming a boundary between the earth's crust and mantle about 6 to 25 miles deep. Also **Mo·ho** (mō′. hō′). [after Andrija *Mohorovic̆*, Yugoslavian scientist]

Mohs scale (mōz) *Mineral.* A qualitative scale in which the hardness of a mineral is determined by its ability to scratch, or be scratched by, any one of 10 standard minerals arranged in the following increasing order of hardness: 1, talc; 2, gypsum; 3, calcite; 4, fluorite; 5, apatite; 6, feldspar; 7, quartz; 8, topaz; 9, corundum; 10, diamond. [after Friedrich *Mohs*, 1773–1839, German mineralogist who conceived it]

moi·dore (moi′dôr, -dōr) *n.* A former Portuguese or Brazilian gold coin. [Pg. *moeda d'ouro* coin of gold <L *moneta* money + *aurum* gold]

moi·e·ty (moi′ə·tē) *n. pl.* **·ties 1** A half. **2** A small portion. [<F *moitié* <L *medietas* < *medius* half]

moil (moil) *v.i.* To work hard; toil; drudge. — *n.* **1** A soiling; defilement; spot. **2** Confusion; vexation; trouble. **3** *Scot.* Toil; drudgery. [<OF *moillier, muiller* wet <L *mollis* soft; infl. in meaning by *toil*] — **moil′er** *n.* — **moil′ing·ly** *adv.*

Moi·rai (moi′rī) In Greek mythology, the three birth goddesses, identified with the Fates: also spelled *Moerae.*

moi·ré (mwä·rā′) *adj.* Having a wavelike or watered appearance, as certain fabrics. — *n.* **1** A corded silk or rayon fabric, having a wavy or watered pattern produced by passing the fabric between engraved cylinders which press the design into the material: also **moire** (mwär). **2** The finish or effect of this process on certain fabrics. [<F <*moirer* watered silk <*moire* watered silk <MOHAIR]

Mo·ïse (mō·ēz′) French form of MOSES. Also *Ital.* **Mo·i·se** (mō′ē·zä′), *Sp.* **Mo·i·ses** (mō′ē·säs′, *Pg.* mō·ē·zesh′).

Mois·san (mwä·sän′), **Henri,** 1852–1907, French chemist.

moist (moist) *adj.* **1** Having slight sensible wetness; damp; humid. **2** Tearful: *moist eyes.* **3** Marked by the presence of pus, phlegm, etc. [<OF *moiste* <a fusion of L *musteus* dew + *mucidus* moldy <*mucus* mucus] — **moist′ly** *adv.* — **moist′ness** *n.*

mois·ten (mois′ən) *v.t. & v.i.* To make or become moist. — **mois′ten·er** *n.*

mois·ture (mois′chər) *n.* Slight sensible wetness; a small amount of liquid exuding from, diffused through, or resting on a substance; dampness. [<OF *moisteur*]

mo·jar·ra (mə·här′ə) *n.* A large salt-water fish (genus *Gerres*), similar to a bass, inhabiting mostly tropical waters: also spelled *moharra.* [<Sp.]

Mo·ja·ve (mō·hä′vē) See MOHAVE.

Mojave Desert An arid region comprising part of the Great Basin in southern California; 15,000 square miles: also *Mohave Desert.*

Mo·ji (mō·jē) A port on northern Kyushu island, Japan.

Mo·kha (mō′kə) See MOCHA.

Mo·ki (mō′kē) See MOQUI.

Mok·po (môk·pō) A port of SW Korea. *Japanese* **Mop·po** (mop·pō).

mol (mōl) *n. Chem.* The gram-molecule; that weight of a substance, expressed in grams, which is equal numerically to its molecular weight: also spelled *mole.* [<G]

mo·la (mō′lə) *n. pl.* **·lae** (-lē) Mole⁴. [<L]

mo·lal (mō′ləl) *adj. Chem.* **1** Pertaining to the mol or gram-molecule. **2** Designating a solution which has a concentration equivalent to one mol of the solute in 1,000 grams of the solvent. Compare MOLAR¹. [<MOL + -AL] — **mo·lal·i·ty** (mō·lal′ə·tē) *n.*

mo·lar¹ (mō′lər) *adj.* **1** *Physics* Pertaining to a mass; acting on or exerted by a mass, as force. **2** *Chem.* Having or containing a gram-molecular weight or mol; specifically, denoting a solution containing one mol of solute to the liter. Compare MOLAL. [<MOL + -AR] — **mo·lar·i·ty** (mō·lar′ə·tē) *n.*

mo·lar² (mō′lər) *n.* A grinding tooth with flattened crown, situated behind the canine and

incisor teeth. — *adj.* **1** Grinding, or adapted for grinding. **2** Pertaining to a molar. [<L *molaris* <*mola* mill]

mo·las·ses (mə·las′iz) *n.* A viscid, dark-colored liquor drained off from raw cane or beet sugar; treacle. [<Pg. *melaço* <L *mellaceus* honeylike <*mel* honey]

mold¹ (mōld) *v.t.* **1** To work into a particular shape or form; model; shape. **2** To shape or cast in or as in a mold; make on a mold. **3** In founding, to form a mold of or from. **4** To ornament with molding. See synonyms under BEND, GOVERN, INFLUENCE. [<*n.*] — *n.* **1** A matrix for shaping anything in a fluid or plastic condition: distinguished from *cast.* **2** Hence, that after which something else is patterned, or the thing that is molded. **3** Form; nature; also, kind; character. **4** The physical form; shape: now applied to the human form. **5** A molding, or number of moldings. See synonyms under MODEL. Also spelled *mould.* [<OF *modle* <L *modulus* < *modus* measure, limit. Doublet of MODULE.] — **mold′a·ble** *adj.* — **mold′er** *n.*

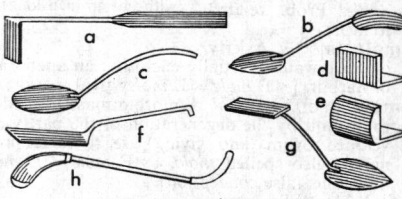

IRON-MOLDER'S TOOLS
a. Lifter. *e.* Half-round corner.
b. Taper and square. *f.* Yankee.
c. Oval or dog-tail. *g.* Heart and square.
d. Square corner. *h.* Flange and bead.

mold² (mōld) *n.* **1** Any fungous growth on food, clothing, walls, etc., especially such growths as form a woolly or furry coating on decaying vegetable matter or in moist, warm places. **2** Any of various fungi producing such growths. **3** Mustiness; decay. — *v.t. & v.i.* To become or cause to become moldy. Also spelled *mould.* [<obs. *moul* grow moldy <Scand. Cf. Dan. *mugle* grow moldy.]

mold³ (mōld) *n.* **1** Earth that is fine and soft, and rich in organic matter. **2** The constituent material of anything; earthy material; matter. **3** The earth; ground; hence, a grave. — *v.t.* To cover with mold. Also spelled *mould.* [OE *molde* earth]

Mold (mōld) County town of Flintshire, Wales.

Mol·dau (môl′dou) The German name for the VLTAVA.

Mol·da·vi·a (mol·dā′vē·ə) A historical province of eastern Rumania; 14,690 square miles. Also **Mol·do·va** (môl·dō′vä).

Mol·da·vi·an (mol·dā′vē·ən) *adj.* Of or relating to Moldavia. — *n.* **1** A native or naturalized inhabitant of Moldavia. **2** The Rumanian language of the Moldavians.

Moldavian Soviet Socialist Republic A constituent republic of SW European U.S.S.R.; 13,000 square miles; capital, Kishinev.

mol·da·vite (mol′də·vīt) *n.* **1** A dull-green natural glass resembling obsidian and thought to be of meteoritic origin. **2** A variety of ozocerite found in Moravia. [from the *Moldau,* near which it is found]

mold·board (mōld′bôrd′, -bōrd′) *n.* **1** *Agric.* The curved metal plate of a plow, by which the earth is turned over and pulverized. **2** A similar part of a machine for building roads: also spelled *mouldboard.* [<MOLD³ + BOARD]

mold·er (mōl′dər) *v.i.* To decay gradually and turn to dust; crumble; waste away. — *v.t.* To cause to crumble. Also spelled *moulder.* See synonyms under DECAY. [Freq. of obs. *mold* crumble]

-mol·der *combining form* One who molds or fashions (a specific thing): *glass-molder, iron-molder.* [<MOLD¹]

mold fungus A fungus which causes mold; specifically, any of an order (*Mucorales*) of phycomycetous fungi, as the common bread mold (*Rhizopus nigricans*).

mold·ing (mōl′ding) *n.* **1** The act of shaping with or as with a mold. **2** Anything made in or as in a mold. **3** *Archit.* **a** A more or less ornamental strip on some part of a structure.

b A cornice or other depressed or projecting decorative member on a surface or angle of any part of a building. Also spelled *moulding.*

mold·warp (mōld′wôrp) *n. Brit. Dial.* The European mole. Also spelled *molewarp, mouldwarp.* [OE *molde* soil + *weorpan* throw up]

mold·y (mōl′dē) *adj.* **mold·i·er, mold·i·est** Covered with mold; hence, old; musty: also spelled *mouldy.* **—mold′i·ness** *n.*

mole[1] (mōl) *n.* **1** A small permanent spot on the skin; a birthmark. **2** A stain or spot, as in a garment. [OE *māl*]

mole[2] (mōl) *n.* A small, insectivorous mammal (family *Talpidae*) with velvety fur, minute eyes, and very broad forefeet adapted for digging and forming extensive underground excavations. [ME *molle* <MLG. Cf. MDu. *molle.* Prob. related to MOLD[1].]

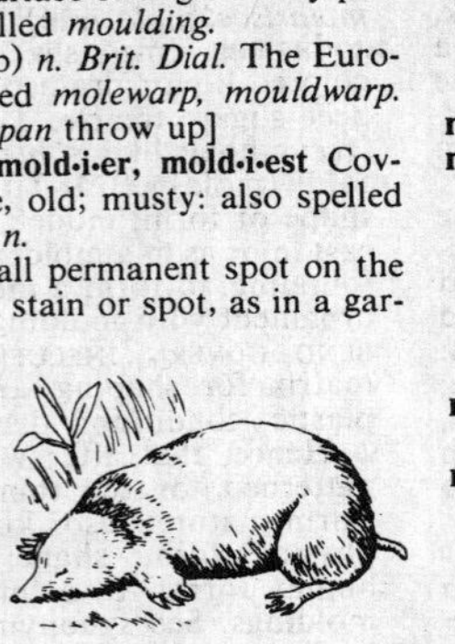

COMMON MOLE
(About 5 1/2 inches long, with tail an inch long)

mole[3] (mōl) *n.* A jetty or breakwater, partially enclosing an anchorage or harbor. [<F *môle* <L *moles* great mass]

mole[4] (mōl) *n. Pathol.* A morbid mass formed in the womb by the degeneration of the partly developed ovum, and giving rise to false pregnancy: also spelled *mola.* [<F *môle* <L *mola* millstone, false conception]

mole[5] (mōl) See MOL.

Mo·lech (mō′lek) See MOLOCH.

mole cricket **1** A burrowing cricket (family *Gryllotalpidae*) with a soft, cylindrical body and broad, stout, molelike front legs, found in some sandy soils. For illustration see INSECTS (injurious). **2** Any of several related species.

mo·lec·u·lar (mə·lek′yə·lər) *adj.* **1** Of, pertaining to, or consisting of molecules. **2** Resulting from the action of molecules: *molecular* changes. [<NL *molecularis*]

molecular film A layer of a substance having a thickness of one molecule: also called *monolayer.*

molecular volume *Chem.* The molecular weight of a substance divided by its density under specified conditions, usually the boiling point and normal atmospheric pressure.

molecular weight *Chem.* The sum of the weights of the constituent atoms of a molecule; specifically, the weight of a molecule of any gas or vapor as compared with some standard gas, such as oxygen.

mol·e·cule (mol′ə·kyōōl) *n.* **1** *Physics* The smallest part of an element, substance, or compound that can exist freely in the solid, liquid, or gaseous state and still retain its composition and properties. **2** Any small particle. See synonyms under PARTICLE. [<F *molécule* <NL *molecula,* dim. of L *moles* mass]

mole·hill (mōl′hil′) *n.* A small heap or ridge of earth raised by a burrowing mole.

mole·skin (mōl′skin′) *n.* **1** The skin of a mole. **2** A heavy, twill fabric, usually cotton, having a thick, soft nap resembling moleskin: used chiefly for coats, jackets, etc.

mo·lest (mə·lest′) *v.t.* To annoy or harm by interference; disturb injuriously. See synonyms under ABUSE, PERSECUTE. [<OF *molester* <L *molestare* <*molestus* troublesome <*moles* mass, burden] **—mo·les·ta·tion** (mō′les·tā′shən, mol′es·tā′shən) *n.* **—mo·lest′er** *n.*

mole·warp (mōl′wôrp) See MOLDWARP.

Mol·fet·ta (môl·fet′tä) A port in Apulia, SE Italy, on the Adriatic.

Mo·lière (mô·lyâr′) Pseudonym of Jean Baptiste Poquelin, 1622–73, French dramatist.

moll (mol) *n. Slang* **1** A girl; a sweetheart. **2** The mistress of a thief or vagrant. **3** A prostitute. [<MOLL]

Moll (mol) Diminutive of Mary. [<*Molly,* dim. of MARY]

mol·lah (mol′ə) *n.* A Moslem complimentary title of address given to religious dignitaries; also, a judge. Also spelled *moolah, mullah.* [<Turkish *mulla* <Arabic *mawla* master, sir]

mol·le (mō·lā′) *n.* The sharp, astringent condiment extracted from the drupes of a tropical American pepper tree *(Schinus molle).*

mol·les·cent (mə·les′ənt) *adj.* Producing softness; softening. [<L *mollescens, -entis*] **—mol·les′cence** *n.*

Moll Flan·ders (flan′dərz) The heroine of Daniel Defoe's novel *Moll Flanders* (1722), one of the first English fictional works to express a note of social criticism.

mol·lient (mol′yənt) See EMOLLIENT.

mol·li·fy (mol′ə·fī) *v.t.* **·fied, ·fy·ing** **1** To make less angry; soothe; pacify; appease. **2** To reduce the violence or intensity of. See synonyms under ALLAY, TEMPER. [<F *mollifier* <LL *mollificare* <L *mollis* soft + *facere* make] **—mol′li·fi′a·ble** *adj.* **—mol′li·fi·ca′tion** *n.* **—mol′li·fi′er** *n.* **—mol′li·fy′ing·ly** *adv.*

mol·li·ti·es (mə·lish′i·ēz) *n. Pathol.* A softening of an organ or tissue. [<L]

mol·lus·cum (mə·lus′kəm) *n. Pathol.* Any of various skin diseases, especially, **molluscum con·ta·gi·o·sum** (kən·tā′jē·ō′səm), caused by a filtrable virus and characterized by the formation of hard skin tubercles, usually on the face. [<NL]

mol·lusk (mol′əsk) *n.* Any member of a large phylum *(Mollusca)* of mostly marine invertebrates having a soft, unsegmented body protected usually by a calcareous shell and including snails, oysters, cuttlefish, squids, whelks, limpets, etc. Also mol lusc. [<F. *mollusque* <L *molluscus (nux)* soft, thin-shelled (nut) <*mollis* soft] **—mol·lus·can** (mə·lus′kən) *adj.* & *n.* **—mol·lus′cous** *adj.*

mol·ly·cod·dle (mol′ē·kod′l) *n.* Any excessively pampered or protected person; one who is coddled or coddles himself; a sissy. —*v.t.* **·dled, ·dling** To pamper; coddle. [<*Molly,* dim. of MARY, + CODDLE] **—mol′ly·cod′dler** *n.*

Mol·ly Ma·guire (mol′ē mə·gwīr′) **1** One of a secret society that terrorized inhabitants of the coal regions of eastern Pennsylvania (1867–77). **2** Originally, one of a secret society in Ireland organized (1843) to prevent evictions by terrorizing officers of the law. [So called because the members were often disguised as women]

Mol·nár (mōl′när), **Ferenc,** 1878–1952, Hungarian playwright.

mo·loch (mō′lok) *n.* A spiny Australian lizard (genus *Moloch*), resembling the horned toad. [<NL *Moloch,* genus name <MOLOCH]

Mo·loch (mō′lok) **1** In the Bible, a god of the Ammonites and Phoenicians to whom human sacrifices were offered. **2** Any system or principle involving merciless sacrifice: also spelled *Molech.* [<LL <Gk. <Hebrew *Mōlekh* a king]

Mo·lo·kai (mō′lə·kī′) An island in the central Hawaiian Islands; 260 square miles.

Mo·lo·tov (mô′lə·tôf) A former name for PERM.

Mo·lo·tov (mô′lə·tôf), **Vyacheslav Mikhailovich,** born 1890, U.S.S.R. statesman: original name *Skryabin.*

Molotov breadbasket A container filled with small incendiary bombs which are designed to scatter over a large area when dropped from aircraft.

Molotov cocktail See FRANGIBLE GRENADE under GRENADE.

molt (mōlt) *v.t.* & *v.i.* To cast off or shed (feathers, horns, skin, etc.) in preparation for replacement by new growth. —*n.* The molting process or season. Also spelled *moult.* [ME *mouten,* OE *bimūtian* exchange for <L *mutare* change] **—molt′er** *n.*

mol·ten (mōl′tən) Archaic past participle of MELT. —*adj.* **1** Reduced to fluid by heat; melted. **2** Made by molding; cast.

molten sea See BRAZEN SEA.

Molt·ke (môlt′kə), **Count Helmuth Karl Bernhard von,** 1800–91, Prussian field marshal. — **Helmuth Johannes Ludwig von,** 1848–1916, German general in World War I; nephew of preceding.

mol·to (môl′tō) *adv. Music* Much; very: *molto* adagio. [<Ital. <L *multum* much]

Mo·luc·ca Islands (mə·luk′ə) A widely scattered island group, comprising a province of Indonesia, between Celebes and New Guinea: 33,315 square miles: formerly *Spice Islands. Malay* **Ma·lu·ku** (mä·lōō′kōō). Also **Mo·luc′cas.**

mo·ly (mō′lē) *n. pl.* **·lies** **1** A mythical plant of magic virtues, with a white flower and a black root: mentioned in the *Odyssey.* **2** A European wild garlic. **3** Molybdenum. [<L <Gk. *mōly*]

mo·lyb·date (mə·lib′dāt) *n. Chem.* A salt of molybdic acid.

mo·lyb·de·nite (mə·lib′də·nīt) *n.* A scaly, metallic, lead-gray, soft molybdenum disulfide, MoS_2: an important ore of molybdenum.

mo·lyb·de·num (mə·lib′də·nəm, mol′ib·dē′·nəm) *n.* A silvery-white, very hard metallic element (symbol Mo, atomic number 42) widely distributed in various minerals, used in alloys and essential in trace amounts to plant nutrition. See PERIODIC TABLE. [<NL <L. *molybdaena* lead, galena <Gk. *molybdaina* <*molybdos* lead]

mo·lyb·dic (mə·lib′dik) *adj. Chem.* Of, pertaining to, or containing molybdenum. especially in its higher valence.

mo·lyb·dous (mə·lib′dəs) *adj. Chem.* Of or pertaining to molybdenum, especially in its lower valence.

mom (mom) *n. U.S. Colloq.* Mother. [<MAMA]

Mom·ba·sa (mom·bä′sə, -bas′ə) A port in SE Kenya on **Mombasa Island** (7 square miles), separated from the mainland by Mombasa harbor.

mome (mōm) *n. Obs.* A stupid fellow; also, a buffoon. [? <MUM[1]]

mo·ment (mō′mənt) *n.* **1** A very short period of time; an instant; also, a point of time; definite period. **2** The present time. **3** Consequence or importance, as in influencing judgment or action. **4** *Stat.* The arithmetic mean of the deviations in a frequency distribution, each deviation being raised to the same power. **5** *Physics* **a** The product of a quantity and its distance to some significant related point: *moment* of area, *moment* of mass, etc. **b** The measure of a force with reference to its effect in producing rotation: also called *torque.* **6** The thing originating or causing; principle of movement or development; a moving force. See synonyms under WEIGHT. [<F <L *momentum* movement. Doublet of MOMENTUM.]

mo·men·tar·i·ly (mō′mən·ter′ə·lē, mō′mən·ter′·ə·lē) *adv.* **1** For a moment. **2** From moment to moment. **3** At any moment. Also **mo′ment·ly.**

mo·men·tar·y (mō′mən·ter′ē) *adj.* Lasting but a moment. **—mo′men·tar′i·ness** *n.*

mo·men·tous (mō·men′təs) *adj.* Of great importance; weighty. See synonyms under IMPORTANT, SERIOUS. **—mo·men′tous·ly** *adv.* **—mo·men′tous·ness** *n.*

mo·men·tum (mō·men′təm) *n. pl.* **·ta** (-tə) or **·tums** **1** *Mech.* The impetus of a moving body. **2** *Physics* The quantity of motion in a body as measured by the product of its mass and velocity. **3** An essential or constituent element. **4** *Music* An eighth rest. [<L. Doublet of MOMENT.] **—mo·men′tal** *adj.*

mom·ism (mom′iz·əm) *n.* Dominance of feminine values in a society, attributed to undue prolongation of maternal influence: a derogatory term. [<MOM + -ISM; coined by Philip Wylie, 1902–1971, U.S. author]

Momm·sen (mom′sən, -zən; *Ger.* mom′zən), **Theodor,** 1817–1903, German historian.

Mom·son lung (mom′sən) A respiratory device to aid persons to escape from a sunken submarine: invented by Rear Admiral Charles B. Momson, born 1896, U.S. Navy.

Mo·mus (mō′məs) In Greek mythology, the god of blame and mockery. [<L <Gk. *mōmos* blame, ridicule]

mon (mon) *n. Scot.* Man.

Mon (mōn) *n.* **1** One of the dominant native peoples of the Pegu region in Burma. **2** The Austro-Asiatic language of the Mons. Also *Peguan.*

mon- *combining form* Var. of MONO-.

Mo·na (mō′nə) The ancient name for the ISLE OF MAN. Also **Mo·na·pi·a** (mō·nä′pē·ə).

mon·ac·e·tin (mon·as′ə·tin) *n.* A colorless or pale-yellow, hygroscopic liquid, $C_5H_{10}O_4$, obtained by heating glycerol with glacial acetic acid: it is used as a solvent for basic dyes, and in making certain explosives: also spelled *monoacetin.* [<MON- + *acetin* a liquid ester of acetic acid]

mon·a·chism (mon′ə·kiz′əm) *n.* The monastic manner of life; monasticism. [<L *monachus* monk + -ISM] **—mon′a·chal** (-kəl) *adj.*

mon·ac·id (mon·as′id) See MONOACID.

Mon·a·co (mon′ə·kō, mə·nä′kō; *Fr.* mô·nà·kō′) An independent principality on the Mediterranean in SE France; 370 acres. **—Mon′a·can** *adj.*

mon·ad (mon′ad, mō′nad) *n.* **1** An indestructible unit; a simple and indivisible substance. **2** A minute, simple, single-celled organism, especially a flagellate infusorian. **3** In metaphysics, the one inseparable spirit in mankind

manifesting itself in each person; also, the one inseparable spirit in nature. —*adj.* Of, pertaining to, or consisting of a monad: also **mo·nad'ic** or **·i·cal.** [< LL *monas, monadis* < Gk. *monas* a unit < *monos* alone]

mon·a·del·phous (mon'ə-del'fəs) *adj. Bot.* Having the stamens united by their filaments into a single set or tube, as in plants of the mallow family. Also **mon'a·del'phi·an.** [< MON- + Gk. *adelphos* brother]

mon·ad·ism (mon'ad·iz'əm, mō'nad-) *n.* A theory of monads in philosophy or physics. —**mon'ad·is'tic** *adj.*

mo·nad·nock (mə-nad'nok) *n. Geog.* An isolated hill or mass of rock rising above a peneplain. [from Mt. *Monadnock*]

Mo·nad·nock (mə-nad'nok), **Mount** An isolated peak in SW New Hampshire; 3,165 feet.

Mon·a·ghan (mon'ə-gən, -hən) A county of Ulster province, Ireland; 498 square miles; county seat, Monaghan.

Mo·na Li·sa (mō'nə lē'zə) A portrait by Leonardo da Vinci of a Neapolitan woman: also called *La Gioconda.*

mon a·mi (môn nȧ·mē') *French* My friend.

mo·nan·drous (mə-nan'drəs) *adj.* 1 Having one male or husband at a time. 2 *Bot.* Having one stamen to the flower. [< Gk. *monandros* < *mono-* single + *anēr, andros* male, man]

mo·nan·dry (mə-nan'-drē) *n.* 1 The custom or practice of having only one husband at a time. 2 *Bot.* The condition of possessing only one perfect stamen, as in certain orchids. [< Gk. *monandria.* See MONANDROUS.]

mo·nan·thous (mə-nan'thəs) *adj. Bot.* Having but one flower: said of a peduncle or a whole plant. [< MON- + Gk. *anthos* flower]

mon·arch (mon'ərk) *n.* 1 A sovereign, as a king or emperor; in modern times, usually, a hereditary constitutional sovereign; originally, the sole ruler of a nation. 2 One who or that which surpasses others of the same kind. 3 A large, orange-brown butterfly (*Danaus menippe*) whose larva feeds on milkweed: also called *milkweed butterfly.* See synonyms under MASTER. [< LL *monarcha* < Gk. *monarchēs* < *monarchos* ruling alone < *monos* alone + *archein* rule] —**mo·nar·chal** (mə-när'kəl) *adj.* —**mo·nar'chal·ly** *adv.*

mo·nar·chi·an·ism (mə-när'kē·ən·iz'əm) *n.* A heretical doctrine of the second and third centuries which denied any real distinction between the persons of the Trinity. [< LL *monarchianus* < *monarchia* sovereignty of a single person < *monarcha* MONARCH] —**mo·nar'chi·an·is'tic** *adj.*

mo·nar·chi·cal (mə-när'ki·kəl) *adj.* Pertaining to, governed by, or favoring a monarch or monarchy. Also **mo·nar'chi·al, mo·nar'chic.** —**mo·nar'chi·cal·ly** *adv.*

mon·arch·ism (mon'ərk·iz'əm) *n.* Monarchical preferences or principles. —**mon'arch·ist** *n.* —**mon'arch·is'tic** *adj.*

mon·ar·chy (mon'ər·kē) *n. pl.* **·chies** 1 Government by a monarch; sovereign control. 2 A government or territory ruled by a monarch. — **absolute monarchy** A government in which the will of the monarch is positive law; a despotism. —**constitutional** or **limited monarchy** A monarchy in which the power and prerogative of the sovereign are limited by constitutional provisions. [< LL *monarchia* < Gk.]

Mo·nar·da (mə-när'də) *n.* A genus of aromatic American herbs of the mint family, with toothed leaves and large flowers in showy clusters; including the horsemint and Oswego tea. [< NL, after N. *Monardes*, 1493–1588, Spanish botanist]

mon·as (mon'əs, mō'nəs) *n.* A monad. [< Gk.]

mon·as·ter·y (mon'əs·ter'ē) *n. pl.* **·ter·ies** A dwelling place occupied in common by persons, especially monks, under religious vows of seclusion; also, the community of persons living in such a place. See synonyms under CLOISTER. [< LL *monasterium* < Gk. *monastērion* < *monastēs* a monk < *monazein* be alone < *monos* alone. Doublet of MINSTER.]

mo·nas·tic (mə-nas'tik) *adj.* 1 Pertaining to religious seclusion. 2 Characteristic of monasteries or their inhabitants; monkish. Also **mon·as·te·ri·al** (mon'əs·tir'ē·əl), **mo·nas'ti·cal.** — *n.* A

monk or other religious recluse. [< F *monastique* < Med. L *monasticus* < Gk. *monastikos*] —**mo·nas'ti·cal·ly** *adv.*

mo·nas·ti·cism (mə-nas'tə·siz'əm) *n.* The monastic life; asceticism.

mon·a·tom·ic (mon'ə-tom'ik) *adj. Chem.* 1 Consisting of a single atom, as the molecules of certain elements. 2 Containing one replaceable or reactive atom. 3 Monovalent.

mon·au·ral (män·ôr'·əl, mon'-) *adj.* 1 Pertaining to, designed for, or characterized by the perception of sound by one ear only. 2 Designating the transmission or reproduction of sound through a single channel.

mon·ax·i·al (mon·ak'sē·əl) *adj.* Having but one axis; uniaxial.

mon·a·zite (mon'ə-zīt) *n.* A resinous, brownish-red or brown phosphate of the rare-earth metals, chiefly cerium, lanthanum, and didymium: an important source of thorium. [< G *monazit* < Gk. *monazein* be alone < *monos* alone]

mon cher (môn shâr') *French* My dear. —**ma chère** (má shâr') *fem.*

Monck (mungk), **George** See MONK, GEORGE.

Monc·ton (mungk'tən) A city in SE New Brunswick, Canada.

Mon·day (mun'dē, -dā) *n.* The second day of the week. [OE *mōn(an)dæg* day of the moon; trans. of L *lunae dies*]

monde (môṅd) *n. French* The world; society. [< F < L *mundus* world]

Mond process (mond) *Metall.* A method for obtaining pure nickel by passing a stream of carbon monoxide over powdered nickel oxide and separating it from the resulting nickel-carbonyl vapor. [after Ludwig *Mond*, 1839–1909, English chemist born in Germany]

Mon·dri·an (môn'drē·än), **Piet,** 1872–1944, Dutch painter.

mo·ne·cious (mə-nē'shəs, mō-) See MONOECIOUS.

Mo·né·gasque (mō'nə·gask, *Fr.* mô·nā·gȧsk') *French* A citizen of Monaco.

Mo·nel metal (mō·nel') A corrosion-resistant nickel alloy of copper, iron, and manganese, reduced from ore of the same composition: used for industrial equipment, machine parts, etc.: a trade name. [after Ambrose *Monel*, d. 1921, U.S. manufacturer]

mo·ner·on (mə-nir'ən) *n. pl.* **·a** An organism that lacks a cellular nucleus, including bacteria and blue-green algae. [< NL < Gk. *monos* alone]

Mo·net (mō·ne'), **Claude,** 1840–1926, French painter.

mon·e·tar·ism (mon'ə·tə·riz'əm, mun'-) *n.* The theory that the economy of a country is determined chiefly by the amount of money available. —**mon'e·tar·ist** *adj., n.*

mon·e·tar·y (mon'ə·ter'ē, mun'-) *adj.* Pertaining to money, finance, or currency; consisting of money; pecuniary. See synonyms under FINANCIAL. [< L *monetarius* of a mint < *moneta* mint. See MINT.] —**mon'e·tar'i·ly** *adv.*

mon·e·tize (mon'ə·tīz, mun'-) *v.t.* **·tized, ·tiz·ing** 1 To legalize as money. 2 To give a standard value to (a metal) as currency. 3 To coin into money. Also *Brit.* **mon'e·tise.** [< L *moneta* mint, money] —**mon'e·ti·za'tion** *n.*

mon·ey (mun'ē) *n. pl.* **mon·eys** or **mon·ies** 1 Anything that serves as a common medium of exchange in trade, as coin or notes. ◆Collateral adjective: *pecuniary.* 2 Legal tender for debts. 3 Purchasing power; credit; bank deposits, etc.; a denomination of value or unit of account. 4 Wealth; property. 5 *pl.* Cash payments or receipts. 6 A system of coinage. —**call money** Money loaned on security, or deposited in a bank, subject to repayment on demand of the lender. —**hard money** Metallic currency or specie. [< OF *moneie* < L *moneta.* Doublet of MINT.]

Synonyms : bills, bullion, capital, cash, coin, currency, funds, gold, notes, property, silver, specie. Money is the authorized medium of exchange; coined *money* is called *coin* or *specie.* What are termed in England *banknotes* are in the United States commonly called *bills* : a five-dollar *bill.* Cash is *specie* or *money* in hand, or paid in hand: the *cash* account; the *cash* price. In the legal sense, *property* is not *money*, and *money* is not *property*; for *property* is that which has inherent value, while *money*, as such, has but

representative value, and may or may not have intrinsic value. *Bullion* is either *gold* or *silver* uncoined or the coined metal considered without reference to its coinage, but simply as merchandise, when its value as *bullion* may be very different from its value as *money.* The word *capital* is used chiefly of accumulated *property* or *money* invested in productive enterprises or available for such investment. Compare PROPERTY, WEALTH.

mon·ey·bags (mun'ē·bagz') *n. Slang* 1 A rich man. 2 Wealth.

mon·ey·chang·er (mun'ē·chān'jər) *n.* A person who changes money at a prescribed rate. Also **mon'ey·deal'er** (-dē'lər), **mon'ey·job' ber** (-job'ər).

money cowry See COWRY.

mon·eyed (mun'ēd) *adj.* 1 Possessed of money; wealthy. 2 In the form of money. Also spelled *monied.*

mon·ey·lend·er (mun'ē·len'dər) *n.* A person whose business is the lending of money at interest.

mon·ey·mak·ing (mun'ē·mā'king) *adj.* 1 Bent upon and successful in accumulating wealth. 2 Likely to bring in money; profitable. — *n.* The acquisition or procurement of money or wealth. —**mon'ey·mak'er** *n.*

money market The market in which money is the commodity bought and sold; the sphere of financial operations.

money of account A monetary denomination used in keeping accounts, but not represented by a coin, as the mill of the United States.

money order An order for the payment of a specified sum of money; specifically, such an order issued at one post office or telegraph office and payable at another.

mon·ey·wort (mun'ē·wûrt') *n.* A trailing herb (*Lysimachia nummularia*) of the primrose family with solitary yellow flowers and rounded leaves. [< MONEY + WORT; trans. of NL *Nummularia* < *nummus* a coin]

mon·ger (mung'gər, mong'-) *n.* 1 *Brit.* A dealer or trader: chiefly in compounds: *fishmonger.* 2 One who engages in discreditable matters: chiefly in compounds: a *scandalmonger.* [OE *mangere* < *mangian* traffic]

Mon·gol (mong'gəl, -gol, -gōl,) *adj.* Of or pertaining to Mongolia or its inhabitants. —*n.* 1 A member of any of the native tribes of Mongolia; specifically, a Mongol (eastern Mongolia), a Buriat (Siberia), or an Eleut or Kalmuck (western Mongolia). 2 The Mongolian language of any of these peoples. 3 Any member of the Mongoloid race. [< Mongolian *mong* brave]

Mon·go·lia (mong·gō'lē·ə, mon-) A region of east central Asia south of Asiatic Russian S.F.S.R., east and north of China's Sinkiang-Uigur Autonomous Region, west of most of former Manchuria and the rest of NE China, and north of central China; about 1,000,000 square miles; divided into: (1) the **Mongolian People's Republic** (formerly *Outer Mongolia*), an independent country in the northern and western part; 590,966 square miles; capital, Ulan Bator; (2) *Inner Mongolia*, a region of northern China, including the former provinces of Ningsia, Suiyuan, Chahar, and Jehol and western (former) Manchuria, most of which region now comprises: (3) the *Inner Mongolian Autonomous Region*, an autonomous division of central northern China, including parts of western (former) Manchuria, and former Chahar and Jehol provinces and all of former Suiyuan province; over 400,000 square miles; capital, Huhehot (formerly *Kweisui*).

Mon·go·li·an (mong·gō'lē·ən, -gōl'yən, mon-) *adj.* 1 Of or pertaining to Mongolia, its people, or their languages; Mongol. 2 Exhibiting Mongolism. — *n.* 1 A native of Mongolia. 2 A subfamily of the Altaic languages, including the languages of the Mongols.

Mon·gol·ic (mong·gol'ik, mon-) *adj.* Of or peculiar to the Mongols; Mongolian. —*n.* Any of the Mongolian languages.

Mon·gol·ism (mong'gəl·iz'əm) *n.* Down syndrome.

Mon·go·loid (mong'gə·loid) *adj.* 1 *Anthropol.* Of or pertaining to the racial group native to Asia and North America, including Malaysians, Eskimos, and some Native Americans.

Characteristics include broad noses, high cheek bones, and dark eyes with marked epicanthic folds. **2** Resembling a Mongol or a Mongolian. **3** Characterized by Mongolism. —*n.* A member of the Mongoloid race.

mon·goose (mong′gōōs, mung′-) *n. pl.* **·goos·es** A small, ferretlike mammal (family *Viverridae*) which fearlessly attacks and kills venomous snakes; especially, the **Indian mongoose** (*Herpestes nyula*): often written *mungoose*. [< Marathi *mungūs*]

MONGOOSE

mon·grel (mung′grəl, mong′-) *n.* **1** The progeny of crossed breeding; sometimes restricted to the progeny of artificial varieties: distinguished from a *hybrid*; specifically, a dog of mixed breed. **2** Any incongruous mixture. —*adj.* Of mixed breed or origin; specifically, of a word or language made up of other words or languages: often a term of contempt. [< obs. *mong* mixture < OE *gemang* +-*rel*, dim. suffix]

mon·grel·ize (mung′grə·līz′, mong′-) *v.t.* **·ized,** **·iz·ing** To mix, esp. racial characteristics.

'mongst (mungst) *prep.* Amongst: an aphetic form.

mon·ied (mun′ēd) See MONEYED.

Mon·i·er–Wil·liams (mun′ē·ər·wil′yəmz, mon′-), Sir Monier, 1819–99, English Sanskrit scholar.

mon·i·ker (mon′ə·kər) *n. Slang* **1** A name; a signature. **2** A tramp's initials or other mark of identification. Also **mon′ick·er.** [Prob. blend of MONOGRAM and MARKER]

mon·i·li·a·sis (mon′ə·lī′ə·sis) *n. Pathol.* A disease caused by infection with any of various gasforming fungi (family *Moniliaceae*). Also **mon′i·li′o·sis.** [< NL < L *monile* necklace +-IASIS; from the alternating swellings and constrictions caused by it]

mo·nil·i·form (mō·nil′ə·fôrm) *adj. Biol.* Resembling a string of beads; contracted or jointed at regular intervals so as to resemble a necklace. [< L *monile* necklace +-FORM]

mon·ish (mon′ish) *v.t. Obs.* To admonish. [See ADMONISH.]

mon·ism (mon′iz·əm, mō′niz·əm) *n.* **1** The doctrine of cosmology that attempts to explain the phenomena of the cosmos by one principle of being or ultimate substance: opposed to philosophical *dualism* and *pluralism*. **2** Any theory that refers many different facts to a single principle. **3** See MONOGENESIS (Def. 1). [< NL *monismus* < Gk. *monos* single]—**mon′ist** *n.* —**mo·nis′tic** or **·ti·cal** *adj.* —**mo·nis′ti·cal·ly** *adv.*

mo·ni·tion (mō·nish′ən) *n.* **1** Friendly counsel given by way of warning and implying caution or reproof; admonition. **2** Indication; notice. **3** *Law* A summons or citation in civil and admiralty practice. [< F < L *monitio, -onis* < *monitus*, pp. of *monere* warn]—**mon·i·tive** (mon′ə·tiv) *adj.*

mon·i·tor (mon′ə·tər) *n.* **1** One who advises or cautions. **2** A senior pupil placed in charge of a dormitory or class. **3** Something that warns or advises; a reminder. **4** *Nav.* An ironclad vessel having a low, flat deck and low freeboard, and fitted with a blister and with one or more turrets carrying heavy guns; specifically, the first vessel of the type, "The Monitor." See MERRIMAC. **5** *Zool.* Any of several large carnivorous lizards (family *Varanidae*) of the Old World tropics; especially, the East Indian kabara-goya (*Varanus salvator*), which reaches a length of seven feet. **6** *Mining* A contrivance, consisting of nozzle and holder, whereby the direction of a stream can be readily changed. **7** *Telecom.* **a** A high-fidelity loudspeaker in the control-room of a radio studio, used to insure adequate sound transmission. **b** A receiver for listening to a sta-

tion's broadcasts to check on quality and frequency of transmission, compliance with laws, material transmited, etc. —*v.t.* **1** *Telecom.* To listen to (a station, broadcast, etc.) with or as with a monitor. **2** To have charge of (a person or group) as a monitor. **3** To keep watch over or check as a means of control: to *monitor* tax returns. [< L *monitus.* See MONITION.]

mon·i·to·ri·al (mon′ə·tôr′ē·əl, -tō′rē-) *adj.* **1** Pertaining to a monitor or to instruction by monitors. **2** Monitory.

mon·i·to·ry (mon′ə·tôr′ē, -tō′rē) *adj.* Conveying monition; admonitory: a *monitory* look. —*n.* An ecclesiastical monition. [< L *monitorius.* See MONITION]

monitory letter A papal letter of monition.

monk (mungk) *n.* **1** Formerly, a religious hermit. **2** One of a company of men vowed to separation from the world and to poverty, celibacy, and religious duties; a member of a monastic order. **3** *Printing* An area on a printed page or sheet containing too much ink: opposed to *friar.* [OE *munuc* < LL *monachus* < Gk. *monachos* < *monos* alone]—**monk′ish** *adj.* —**monk′ish·ly** *adv.*

Monk (mungk), **George,** 1608–70, Duke of Albemarle; English soldier. Also spelled *Monck.*

monk·er·y (mungk′ər·ē) *n. pl.* **·er·ies 1** Monastic life, ways, or beliefs: generally used opprobriously. **2** A monastery or its inmates.

mon·key (mung′kē) *n.* **1** Any of a group of primates (suborder *Anthropoidea*) having elongate limbs, hands and feet adapted for grasping, and a highly developed nervous system, including marmosets, baboons, and macaques, but not the anthropoid apes. **2** Any primate below man, especially the smaller arboreal forms, as lemurs and tarsiers. **3** A person regarded as a monkey, as a mischievous child. **4** One of various small articles or contrivances; especially, an iron block or ram with a catch, used in pile-driving by hoisting and dropping. —*v.t.* To play or trifle; fool; meddle: often with *with* or *around with.* [? < MLG *Moneke*, name of the son of Martin the Ape in *Reynard the Fox.* Cf. MF *monne*, Sp. *mona* a female ape.]

monkey bread See BAOBAB.

monkey business *Slang* Foolish tricks; deceitful or mischievous behavior; folly.

monkey chatter In electronics slang, garbled speech, music, or other sound signals in radio reception, caused by interference of adjoining frequencies with the carrier wave of the desired channel.

monkey cup An East Indian pitcherplant; any species of the genus *Nepenthes.*

monkey flower Any one of various figworts of the genus *Mimulus*, especially the cultivated species, *M. luteus* with yellow flowers, and *M. cardinalis* with red: so called from the gaping or grimacing appearance of the corolla.

monkey gaff *Naut.* A gaff attached to the mizzentopmast of a vessel for the display of signals.

monkey jacket **1** A short jacket of coarse material, worn especially by sailors. **2** *Slang* A dinner jacket.

monkey jar A large, undecorated earthenware jar, used for cooling drinking water.

monkey pot **1** The hard, woody, pot- or urnshaped fruit of several tropical American trees of the family *Lecythidaceae*, especially *Lecythis ollaria* and *L. zabucajo*; also, the plant, the fruit of which has a circular lid which, when the nutlike seeds are ripe, separates with a cracking sound. **2** A barrel-shaped melting pot used in making flint glass.

monkey puzzle A large Chilean tree (*Araucaria araucana*) yielding a hard, durable, yellowish-white wood and edible seeds.

mon·key·shines (mung′kē·shīnz′) *n. pl. U.S. Slang* Frolicsome tricks like a monkey's; pranks. [< MONKEY + SHINE, *n.* (def. 4)]

monkey wrench A wrench having an adjustable jaw for grasping a nut, bolt, or the like.

monk·fish (mungk′fish′) *n. pl.* **·fish** or **·fish·es 1** The angelfish. **2** The angler. [So called from a hoodlike protuberance suggesting a monk's cowl]

Mon-Khmer (mōn′kmer′) *n.* A subfamily of the Austro–Asiatic family of languages, spoken

chiefly in Indochina, including Mon, Khmer, and the Annamese dialects.

monk·hood (mungk′hŏŏd) *n.* **1** The character or condition of a monk. **2** Monks collectively. [OE *munukhade*]

monks·hood (mungks′hŏŏd′) *n.* **1** A plant of the genus *Aconitum*, especially the poisonous *A. napellus*, having the upper sepal arched at the back like a hood. **2** Aconite.

Mon·mouth (mon′məth) **1** A county in western England on the border of Wales; 546 square miles; county town, Monmouth. Also **Mon′mouth·shire** (-shir). **2** A county in east central New Jersey; site of the Revolutionary War battle of **Monmouth Courthouse,** June 28, 1778.

Mon·mouth (mon′məth), **Duke of,** 1649–85, James Scott, an illegitimate son of Charles II of England, who claimed the throne and led an insurrection against James II; beheaded.

MONKS-HOOD
(Plants from 1 to 6 feet tall, varying with species)

mon·o (mon′ō) *adj.* Monophonic (def. 1). —*n.* Mononucleosis.

mono- *combining form* **1** Single; one. **2** *Chem.* Denoting the presence in a compound of a single atom, or an equivalent of the element or radical to the name of which it is prefixed: *monobasic.* Also, before vowels, **mon-.** [< Gk. < *monos* single, alone]

mon·o·ac·e·tin (mon′ō·as′ə·tin) See MONACETIN.

mon·o·ac·id (mon′ō·as′id) *adj. Chem.* Possessing one hydroxyl group that can replace the hydrogen of an acid: said of bases: also spelled *monacid.* Also **mon′o·a·cid′ic** (-ə·sid′ik).

mon·o·ba·sic (mon′ə·bā′sik) *adj. Chem.* Possessing but a single hydrogen atom replaceable by a metal or positive radical: applied to acids.

Mo·noc·a·cy River (mə·nok′ə·sē) A river in Pennsylvania and northern Maryland which rises near Gettysburg and flows 60 miles SW to the Potomac; scene of Civil War battle in 1864 near Frederick, Maryland.

mon·o·carp (mon′ə·kärp) *n. Bot.* A plant that yields fruit only once before dying.

mon·o·car·pel·lar·y (mon′ə·kär′pə·ler′ē) *adj. Bot.* Consisting of a single carpel.

mon·o·car·pous (mon′ə·kär′pəs) *adj. Bot.* Having a gynoecium composed of a single carpel.

Mo·noc·er·os (mə·nos′ər·əs) A southern constellation, the Unicorn. See CONSTELLATION. [< NL < Gk. *mono-* single +*keras* horn]

mon·o·chā·si·um (mon′ə·kā′ze·əm, -zhē-) *n. Bot.* A uniparous cyme; a cyme having only one lateral axis. [< NL < Gk. *mono-* single +*chasis* division]—**mon′o·cha′si·al** *adj.*

mon·o·chlo·ride (mon′ə·klôr′īd, -klō′rīd) *n. Chem.* A chloride which contains one chlorine atom in each molecule.

mon·o·chord (mon′ə·kôrd) *n.* **1** A single chord or string on which intervals can be marked in mathematical ratios, the vibrations giving the notes in the musical scale. **2** An acoustical instrument with one string and a movable bridge, used for measuring intervals. [< Med. L *monochordus* < Gk. *mono-* single *chordē* string]

mon·o·chro·mat·ic (mon′ə·krō·mat′ik) *adj.* Of one color. Also **mon′o·chro′ic.** [< Gk. *monochrō matikos*]—**mon′o·chro·mat′i·cal·ly** *adv.*

mon·o·chrome (mon′ə·krōm) *n.* A painting or the art of painting in a single color, or different shades of a single color. —*adj.* Monochromatic. [< Gk. *monochrōmos*]—**mon′o·chro′mic,** **mon′o·chro′mi·cal** *adj.*

mon·o·cle (mon′ə·kəl) *n.* An eyeglass for one eye. [< F < LL *monoculus* one-eyed < Gk. *monos* single +L *oculus* eye]—**mon′o·cled** *adj.*

mon·o·cli·nal (mon′ə·klī′nəl) *adj. Geol.* Having an inclination in only one direction, or composed of rock strata so inclined. —*n.* A monocline. —**mon′o·cli′nal·ly** *adv.*

mon·o·cline (mon′ə·klīn) *n. Geol.* A stratum or fold of rocks inclined in only one direction. [< MONO- +Gk. *klinein* incline]

mon·o·clin·ic (mon′ə·klin′ik) *adj.* Pertaining to or designating a crystal system having two oblique axes and a third perpendicular to both.

mon·o·cli·nous (mon'ə·klī'nəs) *adj. Bot.* Containing both androecium and gynoecium in the same flower; bisexual; hermaphrodite.

mon·o·clo·nal antibody (mon'ō·clō'nəl) An antibody produced by cloning a specific hybridoma.

mo·no·coque (mô·nô·kôk') *n. French Aeron.* An airplane construction having a shell-shaped fuselage or nacelle in which the skin carries the main stresses.

mon·o·cot·y·le·don (mon'ə·kot'ə·lēd'n) *n.* Any of a great subclass (*Monocotyledones*) of seed plants (*Angiospermae*) bearing one cotyledon in the embryo, including palms, orchids, lilies, and grasses. Compare DICOTYLEDON. Also **mon'·o·cot.** —**mon'o·cot'y·le'do·nous** *adj.*

mon·o·crat (mon'ə·krat) *n.* A person in favor of rule by a monarch: term used by Thomas Jefferson about 1790 to mean a Federalist sympathizer with England in the war between England and France. —**mon'o·crat'ic** *adj.* —**mo·noc·ra·cy** (mə·nok'rə·sē) *n.*

mon·oc·u·lar (mə·nok'yə·lər) *adj.* 1 One-eyed. 2 Of or pertaining to one eye. Also **mo·noc'·u·lous.** [See MONOCLE]

mon·o·cul·ture (mon'ə·kul'chər) *n. Agric.* The use of a given tract of land for the intensive cultivation of only one crop or product, as cotton, wool, tobacco, etc.

mon·o·cy·cle (mon'·ə·sī'kəl) *n.* A one-wheeled vehicle.

mon·o·cyte (mon'ə·sīt) *n. Physiol.* A large, white blood corpuscle with a horseshoe-shaped nucleus surrounded by clear cytoplasm.

mon·o·dac·ty·lous (mon'ə · dak'tə · ləs) *adj. Zool.* Having only one toe, finger, or claw. Also **mon'o·dac'tyl.** [< Gk. *monodaktylos* < *monos* single + *daktylos* finger]

Mon·o·del·phi·a (mon'ə·del'fē·ə) See EUTHERIA.

mon·o·dra·ma (mon'ə·drä'mə, -dram'ə) *n.* A drama written for or acted by a single performer.

mon·o·dy (mon'ə·dē) *n. pl.* **·dies** 1 Any melancholy literary composition with a single emotional motive; especially, a poem on the death of a friend. Compare THRENODY. 2 In Greek tragedy, the lyric solo, usually of a somber character; hence, a dirge. 3 *Music* **a** A composition in which one vocal part predominates, or the style of such a composition; homophony; opposed to *polyphony.* **b** A song for a single voice, with instrumental accompaniment. 4 A monotonous sound; unvarying tone: the *monody* of waves. [< LL *monodia* < Gk. *monōidia* < *monōidos* singing alone < *monos* alone + *aedein* sing] —**mo·nod·ic** (mə·nod'ik), **mo·nod'i·cal** *adj.* —**mo·nod'i·cal·ly** *adv.* —**mon'o·dist** *n.*

mo·noe·cious (mə·nē'shəs) *adj. Bot.* Having male and female organs in the same individual, as stamens and pistils in separate blossoms on the same plant. Also spelled *monecious, monoicous.* Also **mo·ne'cian.** [< MON- + Gk. *oikos* house]

mo·nog·a·mist (mə·nog'ə·mist) *n.* 1 One who has only one living spouse: opposed to *bigamist* and *polygamist.* 2 One who does not practice or believe in second marriage after the death of the first spouse: opposed to *digamist.* —**mo·nog'a·mis'tic** *adj.*

mo·nog·a·mous (mə·nog'ə·məs) *adj.* 1 Pertaining to monogamy: *monogamous* practices. 2 Having only one spouse; holding to monogamy. 3 Having or paired with but one mate, as certain birds. 4 *Biol.* Having flowers with the anthers united. [< LL *monogamus*] —**mo·nog'a·mous·ly** *adv.*

mo·nog·a·my (mə·nog'ə·mē) *n.* 1 The principle or practice of single marriage: opposed to *bigamy* and *polygamy.* 2 The habit of pairing with or having but one mate. [< F *monogamie* < LL *monogamia* < Gk. < *monos* single + *gamos* marriage]

mon·o·gen·e·sis (mon'ə·jen'ə·sis) *n. Biol.* 1 Oneness of origin; the doctrine of the descent of all living organisms from a single cell. Compare POLYGENESIS. 2 Asexual reproduction. 3 Direct development of an ovum into an organism which resembles the parent. 4 Monogenism. [< NL]

mon·o·ge·net·ic (mon'ə·jə·net'ik) *adj.* 1 Pertaining to or exhibiting monogenesis or monogenism. 2 Asexual. 3 *Geol.* Resulting from one genetic process, as a group of mountains. 4 Giving only one color to textile fabrics: said of dyestuffs.

mon·o·gen·ic (mon'ə·jen'ik) *adj.* 1 *Biol.* Having but one method of reproduction, specifically asexual reproduction. 2 *Geol.* Having parts all of the same nature: said of certain rocks.

mo·nog·e·nism (mə·noj'ə·niz'əm) *n.* The doctrine that the whole human race is of one blood or species. [< MONO- + -GEN + -ISM] —**mo·nog'e·nist** *n.*

mo·nog·e·nous (mə·noj'ə·nəs) *adj.* Asexual. [< MONO- + -GENOUS]

mo·nog·e·ny (mə·noj'ə·nē) *n.* 1 Monogenesis. 2 Monogenism. ✦ Homophone: *monogeny.*

mon·o·gram (mon'ə·gram) *n.* 1 A character consisting of two or more letters interwoven into one, as the initials of several names. 2 A single character in writing, or a mark representing a word. [< LL *monogramma* < Gk. *monos* single + *gramma* letter] —**mon'o·gram·mat'ic** (-grə·mat'ik) *adj.*

mon·o·graph (mon'ə·graf, -gräf) *n.* A description or systematic exposition of one thing or class of things; a dissertation or treatise written in great detail. —**mo·nog·ra·pher** (mə·nog'rə·fər) *n.* —**mon'o·graph'ic** *adj.* —**mo·nog'ra·phy** *n.*

mo·nog·y·ny (mə·noj'ə·nē) *n.* The custom or practice of having only one wife at a time. Compare MONANDRY. ✦ Homophone: *monogeny.* [< MONO- + Gk. *gynē* woman] —**mo·nog'y·nist** *n.* —**mo·nog'y·nous** *adj.*

mon·o·hy·brid (mon'ō·hī'brid) *n. Biol.* A hybrid offspring of parents differing in one characteristic.

mon·o·hy·drate (mon'ō·hī'drāt) *n. Chem.* The union of a single molecule of water with an element or a compound.

mon·o·hy·dric (mon'ō·hī'drik) *adj. Chem.* Possessing a single hydroxyl radical.

mo·noi·cous (mə·noi'kəs) See MONOECIOUS.

mo·nol·a·try (mə·nol'ə·trē) *n.* Worship of some one of several gods: distinguished from *monotheism.* [< MONO- + -LATRY] —**mo·nol'a·ter, mo·nol'a·trist** *n.* —**mo·nol'a·trous** *adj.*

mon·o·lay·er (mon'ō·lā'ər) *n.* A molecular film.

mon·o·lith (mon'ə·lith) *n.* 1 A single piece or block of stone fashioned or placed by art, particularly one notable for its size. 2 Something like a monolith, as in size, structure, aspect, or quality.

mon·o·lith·ic (mon'ə·lith'ik) *adj.* 1 Of or resembling a monolith. 2 Single in character, as a political movement or ideology; marked by uniformity.

mon·o·log (mon'ə·lôg, -log) *n.* 1 That which is spoken by one person alone; especially, a dramatic soliloquy, or a story or drama told or performed by one person; also, a lengthy speech by one person, occurring in the course of conversation. 2 A literary composition, or a poem, written as a soliloquy. Also **mon'o·logue.** [< F *monologue* < Gk. *monologos* speaking alone < *monos* alone + *logos* discourse] —**mon'o·log'ic** (-loj'ik) or **·i·cal** *adj.* —**mo·nol·o·gist** (mə·nol'ə·jist) *n.*

mon·o·ma·ni·a (mon'ə·mā'nē·ə, -mān'yə) *n.* 1 A mental disorder characterized by obsession with one idea. 2 The unreasonable pursuit of one idea; a craze. [< NL] —**mon'o·ma'ni·ac** *n.* —**mon'o·ma·ni'a·cal** (-mə·nī'ə·kəl) *adj.*

mon·o·mer (mon'ə·mər) *n. Chem.* The structural unit of a polymer: either a single molecule or a substance consisting of identical molecules. [< MONO- + Gk. *meros* part]

mon·o·mer·ic (mon'ə·mer'ik) *adj.* 1 Having or consisting of a single piece. 2 *Zool.* Derived from one segment or part. [< MONOMER]

mo·nom·er·ous (mə·nom'ər·əs) *adj. Bot.* Having a single member in each whorl or circular series: said of a flower. Sometimes written *1-merous.* [< MONO- + -MEROUS]

mon·o·met·al·ism (mon'ō·met'əl·iz'əm) *n.* The theory or system of a single metallic standard in coinage. Also **mon'o·met'al·lism.** —**mon'o·met'·al·ist** *n.*

mon·o·me·tal·lic (mon'ō·mə·tal'ik) *adj.* 1 Consisting of a single metal: a *monometallic* currency. 2 Of or pertaining to monometalism.

mo·nom·e·ter (mə·nom'ə·tər) *n.* 1 A line of verse having one metrical foot. 2 Verse consisting of monometers. [< MONO- + METER²]

mon·o·met·ric (mon'ō·met'rik) *adj.* Isometric.

mo·no·mi·al (mō·nō'mē·əl) *adj.* Consisting of a single term: a *monomial* expression. —*n. Math.* An expression consisting of a single term. [< MONO- + *-nomial,* as in *binomial;* an irregular formation]

mon·o·mo·lec·u·lar (mon'ō·mə·lek'yə·lər) *adj. Chem.* Having a thickness of one molecule.

mon·o·mor·phic (mon'ə·môr'fik) *adj.* 1 *Biol.* Of the same or an essentially similar type of structure; also, having the same form throughout successive stages of development. 2 *Bot.* Forming similar spores: said of fungi. Also **mon'o·mor'·phous.**

Mo·non·ga·he·la River (mə·nong'gə·hē'lə) A river in West Virginia and western Pennsylvania, flowing 128 miles NE to the Allegheny River at Pittsburgh.

mon·o·nu·cle·o·sis (mon'ō·nōō·klē·ō'sis,-nyōō'-) *n. Pathol.* See INFECTIOUS MONONUCLEOSIS. [< NL < MONO- + NUCLE(US) + -OSIS]

mon·o·pet·al·ous (mon'ə·pet'əl·əs) *adj. Bot.* 1 Gamopetalous. 2 Having corollas actually consisting of a single laterally placed petal: applicable to a few flowers.

mo·noph·a·gous (mə·nof'ə·gəs) *adj.* Monotrophic. [< MONO- + -PHAGOUS]

mon·o·pho·bi·a (mon'ə·fō'bē·ə) *n. Psychiatry* Morbid fear of solitude.

mon·o·phon·ic (mon'ə·fon'ik) *adj.* 1 Of, pertaining to, or functioning in the reproduction of sound through a single channel. 2 *Music* Of or pertaining to a monody.

mon·oph·thong (mon'əf·thông, -thong) *n. Phonet.* 1 A vowel, or single vowel sound. 2 A vowel digraph, or two written vowels with a simple sound. [< MONO- + Gk. *phthongos* sound] —**mon'oph·thon'gal** *adj.*

mon·o·phy·let·ic (mon'ō·fī·let'ik) *adj.* 1 *Zool.* Of or pertaining to a single phylum. 2 *Biol.* Derived from one parent form.

mon·o·phyl·lous (mon'ō·fil'əs) *adj. Bot.* Having or composed of one leaf.

Mo·noph·y·site (mə·nof'ə·sīt) *n.* One of a Christian sect originating in the fifth century which affirms that Christ had but one nature, the divine alone or a single compounded nature, and not two natures so united as to preserve their distinctness. [< LGk. *monophysitēs* < *monos* single + *physis* nature] —**Mon·o·phy·sit·ic** (mon'ō-fi-sit'ik) *adj.* —**Monoph'y·sit'ism** *n.*

mon·o·plane (mon'ə·plān) *n. Aeron.* An airplane with only one supporting surface: distinguished from *biplane* and *triplane.*

mon·o·ple·gi·a (mon'ə·plē'jē·ə) *n. Pathol.* Paralysis of one part of the body. [< NL] —**mon'o·ple'gic** *adj.*

mon·o·pode (mon'ə·pōd) *n.* 1 Anything sustained by one foot; particularly, one of a fabulous Ethiopian race with only one leg. 2 A monopodium. —*adj.* One-footed: also **mo·nop·o·dous** (mə·nop'ə·dəs). [< LL *monopodius* < Gk. *monos* single + *pous, podos* foot]

mon·o·po·di·al (mon'ə·pō'dē·əl) *adj.* 1 Of or pertaining to a monopode. 2 *Bot.* Having but one main or primary axis, as ordinary plants. —**mon'o·po'di·al·ly** *adv.*

mon·o·po·di·um (mon'ə·pō'dē·əm) *n. pl.* **·di·a** (-dē·ə) *Bot.* A stem or axis of growth, as in the pine and other conifers, formed by the continued development of a terminal bud, all branches originating as lateral appendages.

mon·o·pole (mon'ə·pōl) *n. Physics.* A hypothetical particle carrying a single magnetic pole and representing the basic unit of magnetism.

mo·nop·o·lize (mə·nop'ə·līz) *v.t.* **·lized, ·liz·ing** 1 To obtain or exercise a monopoly of. 2 To assume exclusive possession or control of: to *monopolize* one's time. Also *Brit.* **mo·nop'o·lise.** —**mo·nop'o·liz'er** *n.*

MONOCYCLE

of a commodity, as allows prices to be raised. 2 A combination or company controlling a monopoly. 3 Exclusive possession or control of anything. 4 That which is the subject of a monopoly. 5 *Law* An exclusive license from the government for buying, selling, making, or using anything, and now granted only in case of patents and copyrights. [< L *monopolium* < Gk. *monopōlion* < *monos* alone + *pōlein* sell] — **mo·nop′o·lism** *n.* —**mo·nop′o·list** *n.* & *adj.* — **mo·nop′o·lis′tic** *adj.*

mon·o·pro·pel·lant (mon′ō·prə·pel′ənt) *n.* A liquid rocket propellant consisting of fuel and oxidizer mixed and ready for ignition in the combustion chamber: applied also to solid fuels.

mo·nop·so·ny (mə·nop′sə·nē) *n. Econ.* A condition of the market in which there is only one buyer for the product of a number of sellers. [< MON- + Gk. *opson* market]

mon·o·rail (mon′ō·rāl) *n.* 1 A single rail serving as a track for cars either suspended from it or balanced upon it by means of gyroscopes. 2 A railway using such a track.

mon·o·sac·cha·ride (mon′ə·sak′ə·rīd, -rid) *n. Biochem.* Any of a class of simple sugars which cannot be decomposed by hydrolysis, as glucose and fructose.

mon·o·sep·a·lous (mon′ə·sep′ə·ləs) *adj. Bot.* Having the sepals more or less united by their edges into a tube: also, more properly, *gamosepalous*: applied also to those rare cases in which the calyx actually consists of a single laterally placed sepal.

mon·o·sil·ane (mon′ə·sil′ān) *n. Chem.* Silane.

mon·o·so·di·um glu·ta·mate (glōō′tə·māt) The sodium salt of glutamic acid $C_5H_8O_4NaN$, sometimes used in cooking as a flavor enhancer.

mon·o·some (mon′ə·sōm) *n. Genetics* The unpaired sex or X-chromosome.

mon·o·sper·mous (mon′ə·spûr′məs) *adj. Bot.* One-seeded. Also **mon′o·sper′mal.**

mon·o·stich (mon′ə·stik) *n.* A composition of one verse; especially, an epigram.

mon·o·stome (mon′ə·stōm) *adj. Zool.* Having a single sucker or mouth: also **mo·nos·to·mous** (mə·nos′tə·məs). —*n.* An animal with but a single mouth or sucker.

mo·nos·tro·phe (mə·nos′trə·fē) *n.* A metrical composition containing only one kind of strophe. [< MONO- + STROPHE] —**mon·o·stroph·ic** (mon′ə·strof′ik) *adj.*

mon·o·stroph·ics (mon′ə·strof′iks) *n. pl.* Monostrophic verses.

mon·o·sty·lous (mon′ə·stī′ləs) *adj. Bot.* Having only one style. [< MONO- + Gk. *stylos* pillar]

mon·o·syl·la·bism (mon′ə·sil′ə·biz′əm) *n.* The state or quality of being monosyllabic; addiction to the use of words having but one syllable.

mon·o·syl·la·ble (mon′ə·sil′ə·bəl) *n.* A word of one syllable. —**mon·o·syl·lab·ic** (-si·lab′ik) *adj.* — **mon′o·syl·lab′i·cal·ly** *adv.*

mon·o·the·ism (mon′ə·thē·iz′əm) *n.* The doctrine that there is but one God. [< MONO- + Gk. *theos* god] —**mon′o·the′ist** *n.* —**mon′o·the·is′tic** or **·ti·cal** *adj.* —**mon′o·the·is′ti·cal·ly** *adv.*

mon·o·ther·mi·a (mon′ə·thûr′mē·ə) *n. Med.* A condition of uniform temperature, as in the body. [< NL < Gk. *monos* single + *thermē* heat] —**mon′o·ther′mic** *adj.*

mon·o·tint (mon′ə·tint) *n.* A monochrome.

mon·o·tone (mon′ə·tōn) *n.* 1 Sameness of utterance or tone; monotony in the style of composition or speech, or something composed in such style. 2 A single musical tone unvaried in pitch or key; also, a chant in such a tone; an intoning.

mo·not·o·nous (mə·not′ə·nəs) *adj.* 1 Not varied in inflection, cadence, or pitch. 2 Tiresomely uniform. See synonyms under TEDIOUS. [< Gk. *monotonos*] —**mo·not′o·nous·ly** *adv.* —**mo·not′o·nous·ness** *n.*

mo·not·o·ny (mə·not′ə·nē) *n.* 1 The state or quality of being monotonous; irksome uniformity or lack of variety; also, sameness of tone; want of variety in cadence or inflection. 2 *Math.* **a** Continual increase or decrease of a quantity, function, etc. **b** Absence of either increase or decrease. [< Gk. *monotonia* < *monos* single + *tonos* tone] —**mon·o·ton·ic** (mon′ə·ton′ik) *adj.*

mon·o·treme (mon′ə·trēm) *n.* Any member of the lowest order of mammals *(Monotremata)*, without true teeth in the adult stage and having a single opening for the genitourinary and digestive organs, as in duckbills and echidnas. [< MONO- + Gk. *trēma* hole] —**mon′o·trem′a·tous** (-trem′ə·təs), **mon′o·tre′mous** *adj.*

mo·not·ri·chous (mə·not′rə·kəs) *adj.* Having only one polar flagellum, as certain bacteria: also **mon·o·trich·ic** (mon′ə·trik′ik). [< MONO- + Gk. *thrix, trichos* hair]

mon·o·troph·ic (mon′ə·trof′ik) *adj.* Subsisting on or requiring only one kind of food; monophagous. [< MONO- + Gk. *trophē* food]

mo·not·ro·py (mə·not′rə·pē) *n.* The property, possessed by certain substances, tissues, or organs, of occurring in only one stable form. [< MONO- + -TROPY] —**mon·o·trop′ic** (mon′ə·trop′ik) *adj.*

mon·o·type (mon′ə·tīp) *n.* 1 *Biol.* The only representative of its kind, as a species of a genus or the like. 2 *Printing* A print from a metal plate on which a design, painting, etc., has been made.

Mon·o·type (mon′ə·tīp) *n. Printing* A machine which automatically casts and sets type in single characters or units: a trade name. Compare LINOTYPE.

mon·o·typ·ic (mon′ə·tip′ik) *adj.* 1 Containing but one representative; having only one type: a *monotypic* genus. 2 Being a monotype.

mon·o·va·lence (mon′ə·vā′ləns) *n. Chem.* Univalence. Also **mon′o·va′len·cy.** —**mon′o·va′lent** *adj.*

mon·ox·ide (mon·ok′sīd, mə·nok′-) *n. Chem.* A compound containing a single atom of oxygen in each molecule.

Mon·roe (mən·rō′), **James,** 1758–1831, president of the United States 1817–25.

Monroe Doctrine The doctrine, essentially formulated by President Monroe in his message to Congress (December 2, 1823), that any attempt by European powers to interfere in the affairs of the American countries or to acquire territory on the American continents would be regarded by the United States as an unfriendly act.

Mon·ro·vi·a (mən·rō′vē·ə) The capital of Liberia, a port on the Atlantic.

mons (monz) *n. pl.* **mon·tes** (mon′tēz) *Anat.* The rounded fatty eminence at the lower part of the abdomen, covered with hair in the adult: the **mons pu·bis** (pyōō′bis) of the male, or the **mons ven·er·is** (ven′ər·is) of the female. [< L, hill, mountain]

Mons (môns) A city in SW Belgium, capital of Hainaut province.

mon·sei·gneur (mon·sen·yûr′, mon·sēn′yər; *Fr.* môn·se·nyœr′) *n. pl.* **mes·sei·gneurs** (me·se·nyœr′) My lord: a title given to princes of the church and formerly to the higher nobility of France. [< F < *mon* my + *seigneur* lord < L *senior* older. See SENIOR.]

mon·sieur (mə·syûr′, *Fr.* mə·syœ′) *n. pl.* **mes·sieurs** (mes′ərz, *Fr.* me·syœ′) 1 The French title of courtesy for men, equivalent to *Mr.* and *sir*; abbreviated, M., *pl.* MM. It is capitalized when used with a proper name. 2 A Frenchman. [< F < *mon* + *sieur,* short for *seigneur.* See MONSEIGNEUR.]

mon·si·gnor (mon·sēn′yər, *Ital.* môn′sē·nyōr′) *n. pl.* **·gnors** or *Ital.* **·gno·ri** (-nyō′rē) A title of honor of certain prelates and Roman Catholic officials, as of the papal court: abbreviated *Mgr.* Also **mon·si·gno·re** (môn′sē·nyō′rā). [< Ital. *monsignore* < F *monseigneur.* See MONSEIGNEUR.]

mon·soon (mon·sōōn′) *n. Meteorol.* 1 A wind that blows more or less steadily along the Asiatic coast of the Pacific, in winter from the northeast **(dry monsoon),** in summer from the southwest **(wet monsoon).** 2 A trade wind. [< MDu. *monssoen* < Pg. *monção* < Arabic *mausim* season]

mon·ster (mon′stər) *n.* 1 A fabulous animal, compounded of various brute forms. 2 A being that is greatly malformed; anything hideous or abnormal in structure and appearance; a teratism. 3 One abhorred because of his unnatural or inhuman character. 4 A very large person, animal, or thing. See synonyms under PRODIGY. —*adj.* Extraordinary or enormous in size or numbers; huge. [< OF *monstre* < L *monstrum* divine omen, monster < *monere* warn]

mon·strance (mon′strəns) *n.* In Roman Catholic ritual, a sacred vessel in which the consecrated Host is exposed for adoration: also called *ostensorium, ostensory.* [< OF < Med. L *monstrantia* < L *monstrare* show]

mon·stros·i·ty (mon·stros′ə·tē) *n. pl.* **·ties** 1 Anything unnaturally huge, malformed, or distorted. 2 The character of being monstrous.

mon·strous (mon′strəs) *adj.* 1 Deviating greatly from the natural or normal; unnatural in form or structure. 2 Of extraordinary size or number; excessive; huge: a *monstrous* beast or multitude. 3 Inspiring abhorrence, hate, incredulity, etc., in a remarkable degree; hateful; hideous; incredible; intolerable: a *monstrous* cruelty. See synonyms under ABSURD, EXTRAORDINARY, FLAGRANT. —*adv. Archaic* Extremely. [< OF *monstreux* < L *monstrosus* < *monstrum.* See MONSTER.] —**mon′strous·ly** *adv.* —**mon′strous·ness** *n.*

mon·tage (mon·täzh′) *n.* 1 A picture made by superimposing several different pictures so as to blend into one another, or so as to show figures upon a desired background; a composite picture; also, the process of composing such a picture. 2 In motion pictures, a swiftly run sequence of images or pictures illustrating a sequence of associated ideas; the dizzy revolving of several images around a central, focused image or picture to signify the passage of time or the like. 3 The section of a motion picture using this method. [< F]

Mon·ta·gu (mon′tə·gyōō), **Lady Mary Wortley,** 1689–1762, English writer.

Mon·ta·gue (mon′tə·gyōō) The family of Romeo, in Shakespeare's *Romeo and Juliet.*

Mon·taigne (mon·tān′, *Fr.* môn·ten′y′), **Michel Eyquem de,** 1533–92, French essayist.

Mon·tan·a (mon·tan′ə) A State in the NW United States bordering on Canada; 147,138 square miles; capital, Helena; entered the Union Nov. 8, 1889; nickname, *Treasure State*: abbr. MT —**Mon·tan′an** *adj.* & *n.*

mon·tan·ic (mon·tan′ik) *adj.* Of or pertaining to mountains; mountainous. Also **mon·tane** (mon′tān). [< L *montan(us)* + -IC]

Mon·ta·nism (mon′tə·niz′əm) *n.* The doctrine of an ascetic Christian sect of the second century, founded by Montanus of Phrygia. —**Mon′ta·nist** *n.* —**Mon′ta·nis′tic** or **·ti·cal** *adj.*

mon·tan wax (mon′tən) A hydrocarbon wax of high melting point extracted from lignite, used as insulation and in making polishes, candles, phonograph records, etc. [< L *montanus* of the mountain]

Mon·tauk Point (mon′tôk) The easternmost point of New York, a promontory at the tip of the southern peninsula of Long Island.

Mont Blanc (mont blangk′, *Fr.* môn blän′) The highest mountain of the Alps, on the French-Italian border; 15,780 feet.

Mont·calm (mont·käm′, *Fr.* môn·kälm′), **Joseph Louis,** 1712–59, Marquis de Saint Véran, French general; fell in defense of Quebec against the British under Wolfe.

mont-de-pié·té (môn·də·pyā·tā′) *n. French* A pawnshop authorized and controlled by the state to lend money to the poor; literally, mount of piety: originated in Italy in the 15th century. Also *Italian* **mon·te di pie·tà** (môn′tā dē pyā·tä′).

mon·te (mon′tē) *n.* 1 A Spanish gambling game of cards. 2 A table on which, or a place where, monte is played. 3 The money stacked in front of the dealer to pay off stakes: also **monte bank** [< Sp., lit., mountain; in ref. to the pile of unplayed cards]

Mon·te Car·lo (mon′tē kär′lō, *Ital.* môn′tā kär′lō) A resort town in Monaco, on the Mediterranean.

Monte Cassino See CASSINO.

mon·teith (mon·tēth′) *n.* An ornamental punch bowl. [from *Monteigh,* a surname]

Mon·te·mez·zi (môn′tā·med′dzē), **Italo,** 1875–1952, Italian composer.

Mon·te·ne·gro (mon′tə·nē′grō) A constituent republic of southern Yugoslavia; formerly a kingdom; 5,343 square miles; capital, Titograd. *Serbo-Croatian* **Cr·na Go·ra** (tsûr′nä gō′rä). — **Mon′te·ne′grin** *adj.* & *n.*

Mon·te·rey (mon′tə·rā′) A city in western California on **Monterey Bay,** an inlet of the Pacific south of San Francisco.

Mon·ter·rey (mon′tə·rā′, *Sp.* mōn′ter·rā′) A city in NE Mexico, capital of Nuevo León state; captured by United States troops (September, 1846) in the Mexican War.

Mon·tes·pan (mon′tə·span′, *Fr.* môn·tes·pän′),

Marquise de, 1641–1707, Françoise Athénaïs de Rochechouart, mistress of Louis XIV of France.

Mon·tes·quieu (mon′təs·kyoo′, *Fr.* môn′tes·ky′), **Baron de la Brède et de,** 1689–1755, Charles Louis de Secondat, French jurist and philosophical writer on history and government.

Mon·tes·so·ri (mon′tə·sôr′ē, sō′rē; *Ital.* môn′·tes·sō′rē), **Maria,** 1870–1952, Italian educator.

Montessori method A system of teaching small children by training their sense perceptions, and by guiding rather than controlling their activity.

Mon·teux (mon·tü′), **Pierre,** 1875–1964, French conductor.

Mon·te·ver·di (mon′tə·vûr′dē, *Ital.* môn′tā·ver′·dē), **Claudio,** 1567–1643, Italian composer.

Mon·te·vid·e·o (mon′tə·vi·dā′ō, -vid′ē·ō; *Sp.* môn′tā·vē·thä′ō) A port on the Rio de la Plata, capital of Uruguay.

Mon·te·zu·ma (mon′tə·zoo′mə), 1479?–1520, last Aztec emperor of Mexico; dethroned by Cortez: also **Moctezuma.**

Mont·fort (mont′fərt, *Fr.* môn·fôr′), **Simon de,**1160?–1218, French crusader. **—Simon de,** 1208?–65, Earl of Leicester, English general and statesman; son of the preceding.

mont·gol·fi·er (mont·gol′fē·ər) *n.* A hot-air balloon. [after the *Montgolfier* brothers]

Mont·gol·fi·er (mont·gol′fē·ər, *Fr.* môn·gôl·fyā′), **Jacques Étienne,** 1745–99, and **Joseph Michel,** 1740–1810, French inventors, brothers, whose hot-air balloon was the first to make a successful ascent (1783).

Mont·gom·er·y (mont·gum′ər·ē) **1** The capital of Alabama, in the east central part of the State on the Alabama River. **2** A county in central Wales; 797 square miles; county town, Montgomery: also **Mont·gom′er·y·shire** (-shir).

Mont·gom·er·y (mont·gum′ər·ē, mən-), **Sir Bernard Law,**1887–1976, first Viscount Montgomery of Alamein, English field marshal in World War II. **—Richard,** 1736?–75, general in the Continental Army; killed at Quebec.

month (munth) *n.* **1** A unit of time, originally equal to the interval between two new moons, afterward called a **lunar month,** and equal on the average to 29.53 days. **2** One of the 12 parts into which the calendar year is divided, called a **calendar month;** loosely, thirty days or four weeks. **3** The twelfth part of a solar year: also **solar month.** ◆ **Collateral adjective:** *mensal.* [OE *mōnath.* Akin to MOON.]

month·ly (munth′lē) *adj.* **1** Continuing a month, or done in a month. **2** Happening once a month. **3** Pertaining to the menses. —*adv.* Once a month. —*n. pl.* **·lies 1** A periodical published once a month. **2** *pl.* The menses.

monthly meeting In the Society of Friends, a meeting held once a month, by two or more neighboring congregations, for worship and business; also, the organized unit composed of these congregations.

Mon·ti·cel·lo (mon′tə·sel′ō, -chel′ō) The estate and residence of Thomas Jefferson about 3 miles east of Charlottesville, Virginia.

Mont·mar·tre (môn·mär′tr′) A northern district of Paris, famous for its night clubs.

Mont·mo·ren·cy River (mont′mə·ren′sē) A river in southern Quebec, Canada, flowing 60 miles south to the St. Lawrence River; near its mouth is **Montmorency Falls,** 275 feet high.

Mont·pel·ier (mont·pēl′yər) The capital of Vermont.

Mont·pel·lier (môn·pe·lyā′) A city in southern France.

Mont·re·al (mon′trē·ôl′) A city in southern Quebec, Canada, on **Montreal Island** at the confluence of the St. Lawrence and Ottawa rivers. *French* **Mont·ré·al** (môn·rā·äl′).

Mon·treux (môn·tr′) A resort in western Switzerland on the eastern shore of Lake Geneva.

Mon·trose (mon·trōz′, mont·rōz′,) **Marquis of,** 1612–50, James Graham, Scottish royalist leader; executed.

Mont Saint Mi·chel (môn san mē·shel′) A rocky islet, site of a famous ancient fortress and abbey, in **Mont Saint Michel Bay,** an inlet of the Gulf of Saint Malo in northern France.

Mont·ser·rat (mont′sə·rat′) **1** An island in the Leeward Islands, a British colony, member of

The West Indies; 37.5 square miles. **2** A mountain in NE Spain, 4,054 feet; site of the 11th century Benedictine **Montserrat Monastery.**

mon·u·ment (mon′yə·mənt) *n.* **1** Something erected to perpetuate the memory of a person or of an event. **2** A notable structure, deed, production, etc., worthy to be considered as a memorial of the past, or of some event of person. **3** A stone or other permanent mark serving to indicate an angle or boundary. **4** A tomb. **5** *Obs.* A statue; effigy. [<F <L *monumentum* <L *monere* remind]

mon·u·men·tal (mon′yə·men′təl) *adj.* **1** Pertaining to or like a monument. **2** Serving as a monument; memorial; impressive; conspicuous; enduring. **3** Spectacular; excessive: a *monumental* fraud. [<L *monumentalis*] —**mon′u·men′tal·ly** *adv.*

mon·u·men·tal·ize (mon′yə·men′təl·īz) *v.t.* **·ized, ·iz·ing** To establish a lasting record or memorial of.

mon·y (mon′ē) *adj. Scot.* Many. Also **mon′ie.**

-mony *suffix* of nouns The condition, state, or thing resulting from: *parsimony.* [<L *-monia, -monium*]

Mon·za (môn′tsä) A city in Lombardy, Italy.

mon·zo·nite (mon′zə·nīt) *n.* A coarse-grained igneous rock containing approximately equal amounts of orthoclase and plagioclase, with inclusions of colored silicates. [from Mount *Monzoni,* in the Tirol] —**mon′zo·nit′ic** (-nit′·ik) *adj.*

moo (moo) *v.i.* To low as or like a cow. —*n.* The lowing noise made by a cow. [Imit.]

mooch (mooch) *Slang v.t.* **1** To obtain without paying; beg; cadge: to *mooch* a drink. **2** To steal. —*v.i.* **3** To loiter about; skulk; sneak. Also spelled *mouch.* [Var. of dial. *miche* pilfer <OF *muchier* hide, skulk] —**mooch′er** *n.*

mood¹ (mood) *n.* **1** Temporary or capricious state of mind in regard to passion or feeling; humor; disposition. **2** *pl.* Fits of morose or sullen behavior; the state of being moody: to have *moods.* **3** *Obs.* Anger. See synonyms under FANCY, TEMPER. [OE *mō d*]

mood² (mood) *n.* **1** *Gram.* The manner in which the action or condition expressed by a verb is stated, whether as actual, doubtful, commanded, etc. The English moods proper are the indicative, subjunctive, and imperative. The infinitive is sometimes also classed as a mood. Certain verb-phrases are likewise loosely called moods, as those formed by *may, might, can, could* (potential), *should, would* (conditional), *must, ought* (obligative). Also *mode.* **2** *Logic* Mode. **3** *Music* Mode. [Var. of MODE]

mood·y (moo′dē) *adj.* **mood·i·er, mood·i·est 1** Given to or expressive of capricious moods. **2** Petulant; sullen; melancholy. See synonyms under MOROSE. — **mood′i·ly** *adv.* —**mood′i·ness** *n.*

Mood·y (moo′dē), **Dwight Lyman,** 1837–99, U.S. evangelist. —**William Vaughn,** 1869–1910, U.S. poet and dramatist.

mool (mool) *Scot. n.* **1** Dirt; dust. **2** The grave. —*v.t.* **1** To crumble. **2** To bury.

moo·lah (moo′lə) See MOLLAH.

moo·ley (moo′lē) *n.* A cow without horns. See MULEY.

moon (moon) *n.* **1** A celestial body revolving around the earth from west to east in a lunar month of 29.53 days or a sidereal month of 27.33 days; mean diameter, 2,160 miles; mean distance from the earth, 238,900 miles. In mass, the earth is 81.5 times greater than the moon; in volume, 49 times greater. **2** A satellite revolving about any planet. See under PLANET. **3** A lunar month. **4** Something resembling a moon or crescent. **5** Moonlight. —**dark of the moon** That period of time between the full moon and the new moon. —**man in the moon** The fancied appearance of a face in the disk of the full moon, caused by the shadows, lines, spots, etc., on its surface. —*v.i. Colloq.* To stare or wander about in an abstracted or listless manner. —*v.t.* To pass (time) thus. [OE *mōna.* Akin to MONTH.]

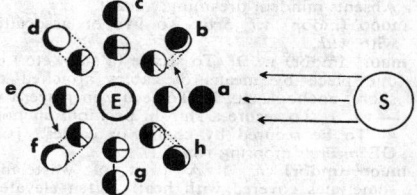

PHASES OF THE MOON
E. Earth.   S. Sun.
a. New.   *b.* Crescent.   *c.* 1st Quarter.
d. Gibbous.   *e.* Full.   *f.* Gibbous.
g. 3rd Quarter.   *h.* Crescent.

Moon, Mountains of the See RUWENZORI.

moon·beam (moon′bēm′) *n.* A ray of moonlight.

moon·blind (moon′blind′) *adv.* **1** Purblind; feeble-sighted. **2** Moon-struck. **3** Affected with moonblindness.

moon·blind·ness (moon′blind′nis) *n.* **1** A form of blindness erroneously attributed to moonlight; nyctalopia. **2** A periodic inflammation of the eyes of horses.

moon·calf (moon′kaf′, -käf′) *n.* **1** A stupid person; dolt; idiot. **2** A monster; deformity. [With ref. to the supposed bad influence of the moon]

moon·craft (moon′kraft′, -kräft′) *n.* A spacecraft designed to travel to the moon.

moon·eye (moon′ī′) *n.* **1** An eye affected with moonblindness. **2** Moonblindness.

moon·eyed (moon′īd′) *adj.* **1** Having moon-eyes. **2** Moonblind (def. 3). **3** Having eyes wide open, as with amazement, awe, etc.

moon·fish (moon′fish′) *n. pl.* **·fish** or **·fish·es 1** Any of various carangoid fishes found on either coast of the western hemisphere, having a silvery or yellowish, much compressed body, especially *Vomer setipinnis:* also called *horsefish.* **2** The opah. **3** The Mexican top minnow (*Platypoecilus maculatus*).

moon·flow·er (moon′flou′ər) *n.* Any of a genus (*Calonyction*) of perennial climbing herbs of the morning-glory family; especially, *C. aculeatum* (formerly genus *Ipomoea*), bearing fragrant, white flowers which open at night.

moon·glade (moon′glād′) *n.* The silvery reflection of moonlight on water.

moon·light (moon′līt′) *n.* The light of the moon. —*adj.* Pertaining to or illuminated by moonlight. —*v.i. Colloq.* To work at a job in addition to one's regular job. —**moon′ light′·er, moon′light′ing** *n.*

moon·lit (moon′lit′) *adj.* Lighted by the moon.

moon·quake (moon′kwāk′) *n.* A trembling or shaking of the moon's surface analogous to an earthquake. [<MOON + (EARTH)QUAKE]

moon·rise (moon′rīz′) *n.* The appearing of the moon above the horizon, or the time when it appears.

moon·seed (moon′sēd′) *n.* A North American climbing plant of the genus *Menispermum,* of the family *Menispermaceae:* so called from its crescent-shaped seeds.

moon·set (moon′set′) *n.* The setting, or the time of setting, of the moon; specifically, the

moment at which it passes below the horizon.

moon·shine (mōōn′shīn′) *n.* **1** Moonlight. **2** Something visionary or unreal; pretence; nonsense. **3** *Colloq.* Smuggled or illicitly distilled spirits. **—moon′shin′y** *adj.*

moon·shin·er (mōōn′shī′nər) *n. Colloq.* An illicit distiller; smuggler.

moon·stone (mōōn′stōn′) *n.* A whitish, cloudy feldspar, valued as a gemstone.

moon–struck (mōōn′struk′) *adj.* Affected by or as by the moon; lunatic; deranged. Also **moon′–strick′en** (-strik′ən).

moon·wort (mōōn′wûrt′) *n.* **1** The herb honesty. **2** Any fern of the genus *Botrychium,* especially *B. lunaria.* [Trans. of Med. L *lunaria* <L *luna* moon]

moon·y (mōō′nē) *adj.* **moon·i·er, moon·i·est** **1** Moon–struck. **2** Moonlit. **3** Like moonlight, or giving out light resembling moonlight. **4** Round or crescent–shaped. **5** Absent–minded; dreaming; vacant.

moop (mōōp) *v.i. Scot.* To live or associate: with *with.*

moor[1] (mŏŏr) *v.t.* **1** To secure (a ship, etc.) in one place by means of cables attached to shore, anchors, etc. **2** To secure in place; fix. *—v.i.* **3** To secure a ship in position; anchor. **4** To be secured by chains or cables. [Cf. OE *mǣrels* mooring rope]

moor[2] (mŏŏr) *n.* **1** A tract of wasteland sometimes covered with heath, often elevated and frequently marshy and abounding in peat. **2** A tract of land on which game is preserved for shooting. [OE *mōr*] **—moor′ish** *adj.*

Moor (mŏŏr) *n.* **1** A person of mixed Berber and Arab blood, inhabiting Morocco and the southern Mediterranean coast. **2** Any North African native; specifically, a Saracen or a Spanish descendant of the Saracens. **3** A Mohammedan of India. [<F *more, maure* < L *Maurus* Moor, Mauritanian <Gk. *Mauros*] **—Moor′ish** *adj.*

moor·age (mŏŏr′ij) *n.* A mooring place.

moor·cock (moor′kok′) *n.* The male of the red grouse.

Moore (mŏŏr, môr, mōr), **George,** 1852–1933, Irish novelist, critic, and dramatist. **—Henry,** 1898–1978, English sculptor. **—John Bassett,** 1860–1947, U.S. jurist. **—Marianne Craig,** 1887–1972, U.S. poet. **—Thomas,** 1779–1852, Irish poet.

Mo·o·re·a (mō′ō·rā′ə) The second largest island in the Windward group of the Society Islands; 50 square miles.

moor·fowl (mŏŏr′foul′) *n.* The red grouse.

moor·hen (mŏŏr′hen′) *n.* **1** The female of the moorfowl. **2** The water hen *(Gallinula chloropus).* **3** The American coot.

moor·ing (mŏŏr′ing) *n.* **1** The act of securing a vessel. **2** *Chiefly pl.* The place where a vessel is moored. **3** *Chiefly pl.* Anything by which an object is fastened.

mooring mast The tower to which a dirigible or blimp is secured when not in flight: also **mooring tower.**

moor·land (mŏŏr′land′) *n.* A moor or marsh. *—adj.* Having marshy properties. **—moor′·land′er** *n.*

moor·wort (mŏŏr′wûrt′) *n.* A low, smooth shrub *(Andromeda polifolia)* of the heath family, with narrow, thick, evergreen leaves, growing in wet bogs.

moor·y (mŏŏr′ē) *adj.* **moor·i·er, moor·i·est** Of the nature of moorland; marshy.

moose (mōōs) *n. pl.* **moose** **1** A large, heavily built mammal *(Alces americana)* of the deer family, found in northern North America: the male bears huge, palmate antlers. **2** The northern European elk. [<Algonquian (Massachuset) *moos* he strips off; because it eats the bark of trees]

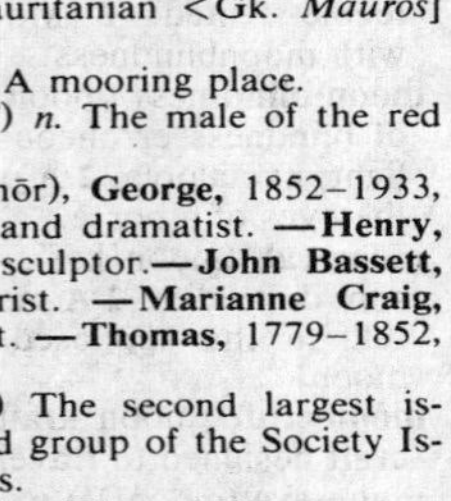

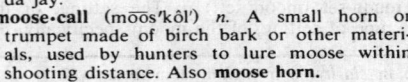

MOOSE
(Up to nearly 7 feet high at the shoulder; weight to 1,000 pounds)

moose·bird (mōōs′·bûrd′) *n.* The Canada jay.

moose·call (mōōs′kôl′) *n.* A small horn or trumpet made of birch bark or other materials, used by hunters to lure moose within shooting distance. Also **moose horn.**

moose·flow·er (mōōs′flou′ər) *n.* Trillium: also called *wakerobin.*

moose·grass (mōōs′gras′, -gräs′) *n.* Ground hemlock.

Moose·head Lake (mōōs′hed) The largest lake in Maine, source of the Kennebec River; 36 miles long; 120 square miles.

moose·wood (mōōs′wŏŏd′) *n.* Leatherwood.

moot (mōōt) *n.* **1** In Anglo–Saxon times, the meeting of freemen and farmers for the discussion or debate of local affairs. **2** Hence, discussion or argument; especially, in modern usage, discussion of a mock lawsuit for the sake of practice. **3** The place where a meeting is held. *—v.t.* **1** To debate; discuss. **2** To argue (a case) in a moot court. *—adj.* Still open to discussion; intended for discussion: a *moot* point. [OE *mōt* assembly, court] **—moot′er** *n.*

moot court A court for the trial of a fictitious suit by law students.

mop[1] (mop) *n.* **1** A piece of cloth, or the like, attached to a handle: used for washing floors. **2** Any loosely tangled bunch or mass, as of hair. *—v.t.* **mopped, mop·ping** To rub or wipe with or as with a mop. **—to mop up** **1** To take up with or as with a mop. **2** *Mil.* To wipe out remnants of enemy resistance in (captured areas). **—to mop (up) the floor with** *Slang* To defeat easily and decisively. [Origin uncertain. Cf. F. *mappe* napkin <L mappa.]

mop[2] (mop) *n.* **1** A wry mouth; grimace. **2** A pouting or petted young person; a young girl. [<*v.*] *—v.i.* To make a wry face; grimace. [Cf. Du. *moppen* pout]

mope (mōp) *v.* **moped, mop·ing** *v.i.* To be gloomy, listless, or dispirited. *—v.t.* To make gloomy or dispirited. *—n.* **1** One who mopes. **2** *pl.* Dejection; depression. [Prob. <Scand. Cf. Sw. *mopa* sulk, Dan. *maabe* be stupid, unaware.] **—mop′er** *n.* **—mop′ish** *adj.* **—mop′·ish·ly** *adv.* **—mop′ish·ness** *n.*

mo·ped (mō′ped) *n.* A heavy–duty bicycle equipped with an engine. [<*mo(tor)* +*ped (al)*]

mop·pet (mop′it) *n.* **1** A rag doll or one made of cloth. **2** A child; youngster. [Dim. of ME *moppe* rag doll, ? <L *mappa* napkin]

mop–up (mop′up′) *n. Colloq.* An ending or wiping out.

mo·quette (mō·ket′) *n.* A woolen fabric with a velvety pile, used for carpets and upholstery. [<F; ult. origin uncertain]

Mo·qui (mō′kē) *n.* A Hopi Indian: also spelled *Moki.*

mo·ra (môr′ə, mō′rə) *n. pl.* **mo·rae** (môr′ē, mō′rē) or **mo·ras** **1** In civil law, delay, especially if unjustifiable; default. **2** In prosody, a unit of meter, the common short foot, usually indicated by the breve. [<L, delay]

mo·ra·ceous (mô·rā′shəs, mō-) *adj.* Denoting or belonging to a family *(Moraceae)* of mostly tropical herbs, shrubs, and trees of the order *Urticales,* including the mulberry, common fig, hop, hemp, etc. [<L *morus* mulberry]

Mo·rad·a·bad (mō·rad′ə·bad, mō·rad′ä·bäd′) A city in north central Uttar Pradesh State, northern India.

mo·raine (mə·rān′, mō-) *n. Geol.* A ridge or heap of earth, stones, etc., carried by a glacier and deposited on adjacent ground, either along the course or at the edges of the glacier, as a **medial** or **lateral moraine,** or at its lower terminus, as a **terminal moraine.** [<dial. F] **—mo·rain′al, mo·rain′ic** *adj.*

mor·al (môr′əl, mor′-) *adj.* **1** Pertaining to character and behavior from the point of view of right and wrong, and obligation of duty; pertaining to rightness and duty in conduct. **2** Conforming to right conduct; actuated by a sense of the good, true, and right; good; righteous; virtuous. **3** Concerned with the principles of right and wrong; ethical: *moral* philosophy; *moral* values. **4** Acting or suited to act through man's intellect or sense of right: often opposed to *physical*: *moral* support. **5** *Logic* Probable as opposed to demonstrative: *moral* proof. **6** Of or pertaining to the science or doctrine of human nature as fitted for conduct. Most writers on modern philosophy use the term to cover the entire sphere of human conduct which comes under the distinctions of right and wrong. **7** Attempting or serving to inculcate or convey a moral; moralizing: a *moral* writer. **8** Of or influencing morals or morale: *moral* force. **9** Capable of understanding the difference between right and wrong: a *moral* agent. *—n.* **1** The lesson taught by a fable or the like. **2** *pl.* Conduct or behavior; ethics. [<F <L *moralis* <*mos, moris* custom; in the pl., manners, morals] **—mor′al·ly** *adv.*

Synonyms (adj.): dutiful, ethical, excellent, faithful, good, honest, honorable, incorruptible, just, pious, religious, right, righteous, true, upright, virtuous, worthy. *Antonyms:* see synonyms for IMMORAL.

mo·rale (mə·ral′, -räl′, mô-) *n.* **1** State of mind with reference to confidence, courage, hope, etc.: used especially of a number of persons associated in some enterprise, as troops, workers, etc. **2** Obs. Morality. [<F. See MORAL.]

moral hazard In insurance, a risk resulting from doubt as to the honesty of the person insured.

moral insanity Mental deficiency amounting to the incapacity to distinguish between right and wrong, or characterized by compulsions to perform unsocial, irresponsible, or criminal acts: a legal term variously interpreted in different statutes.

mor·al·ism (môr′əl·iz′əm, mor′-) *n.* The belief in a morality divested of all religious character.

mor·al·ist (môr′əl·ist, mor′-) *n.* **1** A teacher of morals. **2** One who practices morality without religion. **—mor′al·is′tic** *adj.*

mo·ral·i·ty (mə·ral′ə·tē, mô-) *n. pl.* **·ties** **1** The doctrine of man's moral duties; ethics. **2** Virtuous conduct; rectitude; chastity. **3** The quality of being morally right. **4** A lesson inferred; a moral. **5** Conformity, or degree of conformity, to conventional rules, without or apart from inspiration and guidance by religion or other spiritual influences. **6** A form of allegorical drama of the 15th and 16th centuries in which the characters were personified virtues, vices, mental attributes, etc. See synonyms under VIRTUE. [<L *moralitas, -tatis* <*moralis.* See MORAL.]

mor·al·ize (môr′əl·īz, mor′-) *v.* **·ized, ·iz·ing** *v.i.* **1** To make moral reflections; talk about morality. *—v.t.* **2** To explain in a moral sense; derive a moral from. **3** To improve the morals of. Also *Brit.* **mor′al·ise.** **—mor′al·i·za′tion** *n.* **—mor′al·iz′er** *n.*

moral philosophy Ethics.

moral victory A defeat that is accounted a victory on the moral level, as when the righteousness of a defeated cause has been clearly established.

mo·rass (mə·ras′, mô-, mō-) *n.* A tract of low-lying, soft, wet ground; marsh. [<Du. *moeras,* earlier *marasch* <OF *maresc* <Med. L *mariscus* <Gmc. Ult. akin to MARSH.]

mor·a·to·ri·um (môr′ə·tôr′ē·əm, -tō′rē-, mor′-) *n. pl.* **·ri·a** (-ē·ə) or **·ri·ums** *Law* An emergency act of legislation or a government edict authorizing a debtor or bank to suspend payments for a given period; also, the period during which it is, or is to be, in force. [<NL <LL *moratorius.* See MORATORY.]

mor·a·to·ry (môr′ə·tôr′ē, -tō′rē, mor′-) *adj.* Pertaining or intended to delay: particularly applied to legislation in the nature of a moratorium. [<LL *moratorius* <L *morari* delay <*mora* delay]

Mo·ra·va (mô′rä·vä) **1** The Czech name for the river MARCH. **2** The Czech name for MORAVIA.

Mo·ra·vi·a (mô·rā′vē·ə, mō-) A central region of Czechoslovakia; 8,219 square miles; a former Austrian crownland: German *Mähren,* Czech *Morava.*

Mo·ra·vi·an (mô·rā′vē·ən, mō-) *adj.* Pertaining to Moravia or the Moravians. *—n.* **1** A native of Moravia. **2** One of a Christian sect founded by disciples of John Huss in Moravia (15th century), and now in Germany, Britain, and America. The sect is also known as the *Renewed Church of the United Brethren* or *Unity of the Brethren.*

Moravian Gap A mountain pass between the Carpathians and the Sudeten in central Europe.

Mo·rav·ská O·stra·va (mô′räf·skä ôs′trä·vä) A city of northern Moravia, Czechoslovakia: German *Mährisch–Ostrau:* also *Ostrava.*

mo·ray (môr′ā, mō·rā′) *n.* A brightly colored, voracious, savage eel of the family *Muraenidae,* inhabiting tropical and subtropical waters, especially among coral reefs: also called *murry.* The Mediterranean moray *(Muraena helena)* is esteemed as a food fish.

A related species is the **banded moray** (*Gymnothorax waialuoe*) of Hawaiian waters. [? <Pg. *moreia* <L *muraena*.]

Mor·ay (mûr′ē, *Scot.* mûr′ā) A county of NE Scotland; 476 square miles; county town, Elgin. Formerly *Elgin.* Also **Mor′ay·shire** (-shir).

mor·bid (môr′bid) *adj.* **1** Being in a diseased or abnormal state. **2** Caused by or denoting a diseased condition of body or mind. **3** Taking an excessive interest in matters of a gruesome or unwholesome nature; also, apprehensive; suspicious. **4** Grisly; gruesome: a *morbid* story. **5** Of or pertaining to disease; pathological: *morbid* anatomy. [<L *morbidus* <*morbus* disease] —**mor′bid·ly** *adv.* —**mor′bid·ness** *n.*

mor·bi·dez·za (môr′bē-ded′dzä) *n. Italian* In painting, delicacy or softness of flesh tints.

mor·bid·i·ty (môr·bid′ə·tē) *n.* **1** The condition of being morbid or diseased. **2** The rate of disease or proportion of diseased persons in a community: compare MORTALITY (def. 3).

mor·bif·ic (môr·bif′ik) *adj.* Producing disease. Also **mor·bif′i·cal.** —**mor·bif′i·cal·ly** *adv.*

mor·bil·li (môr·bil′ī) *n. pl.* The measles. [< Med. L, pl. of *morbillus,* dim. of *morbus* disease]

mor·bil·li·form (môr·bil′ə·fôrm) *adj.* Resembling measles. [<MORBILLI + -FORM]

mor·bil·lous (môr·bil′əs) *adj.* Relating to or affected with measles.

mor·ceau (môr·sō′) *n. pl.* **·ceaux** (sō′) *French* A small bit or fragment; also, a short composition, as of music or poetry.

mor·da·cious (môr·dā′shəs) *adj.* Biting, or given to biting; hence, sarcastic. [<L *mordax, -acis* <*mordere* bite] —**mor·da′cious·ly** *adv.* —**mor·dac′i·ty** (-das′ə·tē) *n.*

mor·dan·cy (môr′dən·sē) *n.* Pungency; the quality of being biting or sarcastic. **2** Acting as a mordant. —*v.t.* To treat or imbue with a mordant. [<OF]

mor·dant (môr′dənt) *n.* **1** Any substance, such as tannic acid or aluminum hydroxide, which, by combining with a dyestuff to form an insoluble compound (lake), serves to produce a fixed color in a textile fiber. **2** The corrosive used in etching. —*adj.* **1** Biting; pungent; sarcastic. **2** Acting as a mordant. —*v.t.* To treat or imbue with a mordant. [<OF]

Mor·de·cai (môr′də·kī) In the Old Testament, Esther's cousin, instrumental in saving the Jews from extermination. *Esth.* ii 15.

mor·dent (môr′dənt) *n. Music* The rapid alternation of a tone with the tone immediately below it or the character indicating it: a form of trill. Also **mor·den·te** (môr·den′tā). —**inverted mordent** The rapid alternation of a note with one above it: a pralltriller. [<G < Ital. *mordente,* ppr. of *mordere* bite <L]

Mor·dred (môr′drid) See MODRED.

Mord·vin·i·an Autonomous Soviet Socialist Republic (môrd·vin′ē·ən) An administrative division of central European Russian S.F.S.R.; 10,080 square miles; capital, Saransk: also **Mor·do·vi·an Autonomous S.S.R.** (môr·dō′vē·ən).

more (môr, mōr) *adj. superlative* **most 1** Greater in amount, extent, or degree: comparative of *much: more* water. **2** Greater in number: comparative of *many.* **3** Greater in rank or dignity. **4** Added to some former number; extra. —*n.* **1** A greater quantity, amount, etc. **2** Something that exceeds something else. —*adv.* **1** To a greater extent or degree. **2** In addition; further; again: usually qualified by *any, never,* a numeral, etc.: I cannot walk any *more.* [OE *māra*]

More (môr, mōr), **Hannah,** 1745–1833, English religious writer. —**Paul Elmer,** 1864–1937, U.S. critic and essayist. —**Sir Thomas,** 1478?–1535, lord chancellor of England; author; beheaded; canonized, 1935.

Mo·re·a (mô·rē′ə, mō-) A former name for PELOPONNESUS.

Mo·reau (mô·rō′), **Jean Victor,** 1761–1813, French Republican general.

mo·reen (mə·rēn′) *n.* A sturdy, ribbed, cotton, wool, or wool and cotton fabric, often with a watered or embossed finish, used for hangings and upholstery. [Prob. <MOIRE + -*een,* as in *velveteen*]

mo·rel[1] (mə·rel′) *n.* An edible mushroom of

the genus *Morchella,* somewhat resembling a sponge on the end of a stalk. [<MF *morille,* ult. <Gmc. Cf. OHG *morhila* little carrot.]

mo·rel[2] (mə·rel′) *n.* The black nightshade (*Solanum nigrum*). Also **mo·relle′.** [<OF *morele* <Med. L *morella,* ? <LL *maurella,* a kind of plant]

Mo·re·lia (mō·rā′lyä) A city of south central Mexico, capital of Michoacán state.

mo·rel·lo (mə·rel′ō) *n.* A variety of cultivated cherry, with a dark–red skin, flesh, and juice: used in cooking and preserving. [<Flemish *marelle,* aphetic var. of *amarelle* <Ital. *amarello,* dim. of *amaro* bitter <L *amarus*]

Mo·re·los (mō·rā′lōs) A state in southern Mexico; 1,916 square miles; capital, Cuernavaca.

more·o·ver (môr·ō′vər, mōr-) *adv.* Beyond what has been said; further; besides; likewise.

mo·res (môr′ēz, mō′rēz) *n. pl. Sociol.* **1** Those established, traditional customs or folkways regarded by a social group as essential to its preservation and welfare. **2** The accepted conventions of a group or community. [<L, pl. of *mos, moris* custom]

Mo·res·net (mō·rez·ne′) A mining district on the Belgian–German frontier; ceded to Belgium under the Treaty of Versailles, 1919.

Mo·resque (mô·resk′, mə-) *adj.* Moorish; decorated in the style of the Moors. —*n.* Decorative work, by means of interlacings, relief, etc., highly colored and gilded. Compare MORISCO (def. 3). [<F <Ital. *moresco* <L *Maurus* Mauritanian]

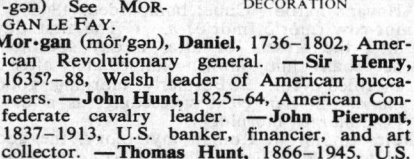

MORESQUE PANEL DECORATION

Mor·gain (môr′gān, -gən) See MORGAN LE FAY.

Mor·gan (môr′gən), **Daniel,** 1736–1802, American Revolutionary general. —**Sir Henry,** 1635?–88, Welsh leader of American buccaneers. —**John Hunt,** 1825–64, American Confederate cavalry leader. —**John Pierpont,** 1837–1913, U.S. banker, financier, and art collector. —**Thomas Hunt,** 1866–1945, U.S. zoologist.

mor·ga·nat·ic (môr′gə·nat′ik) *adj.* Designating a legitimate marriage between a male member of certain royal families of Europe and a woman of inferior rank, in which the titles and estates of the husband are not shared by the wife or their children. Also **mor′ga·nat′i·cal.** [<NL *morganaticus* <LL (*matrimonium ad*) *morganaticum* (wedding with) morning gift < OHG *morgengeba* morning gift (in lieu of a share in the estate)] —**mor′ga·nat′i·cal·ly** *adv.*

Morgan horse A breed of horse of Arabian strain descendent from the stallion *Justin Morgan* (died 1821): noted for its powerful frame, gentle disposition, and versatility. [after *Justin Morgan,* owner of the original horse]

mor·gan·ite (môr′gən·īt) *n.* A rose–pink variety of beryl, used as a semiprecious gemstone. [after John Pierpont *Morgan*]

Morgan le Fay (lə fā′) In Arthurian legend, the fairy half–sister of Arthur. She appears in Carlovingian romance as *Fata Morgana.* [< OF *Morgain la fée* Morgan the fairy]

mor·gen (môr′gən) *n. pl.* **·gen** or **·gens** A land measure formerly used by the Dutch, and still employed in South Africa: equal to about two acres. [<Du. & G, morning; hence, area plowed in one morning]

Mor·gen·thau (môr′gən·thô), **Henry,** 1891–1967, U.S. secretary of the Treasury 1934–1945.

morgue (môrg) *n.* **1** A place where bodies of the dead are kept until identified or claimed. **2** In a newspaper editorial office, the department in charge of filed items and biographical material: used for obituary notices, etc. [<F, orig., the name of the Paris building used for this purpose]

Mo·ri·ah (mə·rī′ə) A hill in Jerusalem; site of Solomon's temple. II *Chron.* iii 1.

mor·i·bund (môr′ə·bund, -bənd, mor′-) *adj.* Dying; at the point of death. [<L *moribundus*

<*mori* die] —**mor′i·bun′di·ty** *n.* —**mor′i·bund·ly** *adv.*

mo·rin (môr′in, mō′rin) *n.* A crystalline compound, $C_{15}H_{10}O_7$, obtained from old fustic: used as a yellow dyestuff and as a reagent for aluminum. [<F *morine* <L *morum* mulberry]

mo·ri·on[1] (môr′ē·on, mō′rē-) *n.* A kind of open helmet without vizor worn by men–at–arms: also spelled **morrion.** [<OF <Sp. *morrión* <*morra* crown of the head]

mo·ri·on[2] (môr′ē·on, mō′rē-) *n.* A dark, sometimes nearly black, variety of smoky quartz. [<F <LL, a misreading of L *mormorion*]

Mo·ris·co (mə·ris′kō) *adj.* Moorish. —*n. pl.* **·cos** or **·coes 1** One of the Moors who remained in Spain after the conquest of Granada in 1492; a Moor. **2** A morris dance or dancer. **3** The Moresque style of architecture or decoration. [<Sp. <*Moro* Moor]

Mo·ri·son (môr′ə·sən, mor′-), **Samuel Eliot,** 1887–1976, U.S. historian.

mo·ri·tu·ri te sa·lu·ta·mus (môr′i·tyŏŏr′ē tē sal′yŏŏ·tā′məs) *Latin* We (who are) about to die salute thee: salutation of the gladiators to the Roman emperor.

Mo·ritz (mō′rits) Danish, Swedish, and German form of MAURICE.

Mor·land (môr′lənd), **George,** 1763–1804, English painter.

Mor·ley (môr′lē), **Christopher,** 1890–1957, U.S. writer. —**John,** 1838 – 1923, first Viscount Morley of Blackburn, English statesman and man of letters.

Mor·mon (môr′mən) *n.* **1** A member of a religious sect officially styled "The Church of Jesus Christ of Latter–day Saints," founded in the U.S. by Joseph Smith in 1830: also **Mor′mon·ist, Mor′mon·ite. 2** In Mormon belief, a prophet and sacred historian of the fourth century A.D. who wrote, on golden tablets, a history of an early American people. The tablets, called the **Book of Mormon,** one of the holy books of the Mormon faith, were found by Joseph Smith near Palmyra, New York, and translated and published by him in 1830. —**Mor′mon·ism** *n.*

Mormon Bible The Book of Mormon. See under MORMON.

Mormon Church The Church of Jesus Christ of Latter–day Saints.

Mormon State Nickname of UTAH.

Mormon trail The trail taken by the Mormons, 1847, from Iowa to Utah.

morn (môrn) *n. Poetic* The morning. [OE *morgen*]

Mor·nay (môr·nā′), **Philippe de,** 1549–1623, Seigneur du Plessis, French Huguenot leader; minister of Henry IV: also known as *Duplessis–Mornay.*

morn·ing (môr′ning) *n.* **1** The early part of the day; the time from midnight to noon, or from sunrise to noon; hence, any early stage. **2** The dawn: often personified as **Morning,** the goddess Eos or Aurora. —*adj.* Pertaining to or occurring in the early part of the day. ◆ Collateral adjective: *matutinal.* [< MORN; by analogy with EVENING]

morn·ing–glo·ry (môr′ning·glôr′ē, -glō′rē) *n. pl.* **·ries 1** A twining plant (genus *Ipomoea*) with funnel–shaped flowers of various colors. **2** Any one of many convolvulaceous plants.

morning gun A gun fired at reveille on military posts as a signal for raising the flag.

Morning Prayer In the Anglican church, the order for public worship in the morning.

morning sickness Vomiting and nausea in the morning, common in early pregnancy.

morn·ing–star (môr′ning·stär′) *n.* A weapon made of a metal ball set with spikes and chained to a handle; a mace.

morning star Any of the planets Jupiter, Mars, Saturn, Mercury, or especially Venus, when rising shortly before the sun.

Mo·ro (môr′ō, mō′rō) *n. pl.* **·ros 1** A member of one of the Moslem tribes of the southern Philippines. **2** The Indonesian language of the Moros. [<Sp., a Moor]

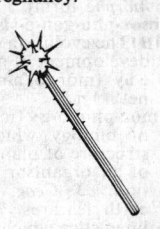

MORNING–STAR

Mo·roc·co (mə·rok′ō) **1** A kingdom on the Atlantic and Mediterranean coasts of NW

Africa; 160,000 square miles; capital, Rabat: French *Maroc*, Spanish *Marruecos*. **2** A former name for MARRAKESH. *Arabic* **El Maghreb el Ag·sa** (al mä′greb al äg′sä). **— Mo·roc′can** *adj.* & *n.*

morocco leather A fine leather made from goatskin tanned with sumac. Also **mo·roc′co.**

Mo·ro Gulf (môr′ō, mō′rō) A large northern inlet of the Celebes Sea in SW Mindanao.

mo·ron (môr′on, mō′ron) *n.* A person whose mental capacity has been arrested during development and who represents mentally the condition of a child of from 8 to 12 years of age. [<Gk. *mōron*, neut. of *mōros* dull, sluggish] **— mo·ron·ic** (mô·ron′ik, mō-) *adj.* **— mo·ron′i·cal·ly** *adv.*

mo·ron·ism (môr′on·iz′əm, mō′ron-) *n.* The mildest degree of feeble–mindedness, rated above imbecility and idiocy. Also **mo·ron·i·ty** (mō·ron′ə·tē, mō-).

Mor·o·pus (môr′ə·pəs, mor′-) *n. Paleontol.* A genus of extinct North American chalicotheres of the Tertiary period having a skull similar to that of the horse, slender legs, and hoofs modified into three large claws. [<NL <Gk. *mōros* sluggish + *pous* foot]

mo·rose (mə·rōs′) *adj.* Having a surly temper; sullen; gloomy. [<L *morosus* < *mos, moris* manner, habit] **— mo·rose′ly** *adv.* **— mo·rose′·ness, mo·ros·i·ty** (-ros′ə·tē) *n.*

Synonyms (adj.): acrimonious, bitter, churlish, crabbed, crusty, dogged, gloomy, gruff, ill–humored, ill–natured, moody, severe, sour, splenetic, sulky, sullen, surly. The *sullen* and *sulky* are discontented and resentful; *sullen* denotes more of pride, *sulky* more of resentful obstinacy. The *morose* are bitterly dissatisfied with the world in general, and disposed to vent their ill nature upon others. The *sullen* and *sulky* are for the most part silent; the *morose* growl out bitter speeches. A *surly* person is in a state of latent anger, resenting approach as intrusion, and ready to take offense at anything. See AUSTERE. Compare ACRIMONY. *Antonyms*: amiable, benignant, bland, complaisant, friendly, genial, gentle, good–natured, indulgent, kind, mild, pleasant, sympathetic, tender.

mor·phal·lax·is (môr′fə·lak′sis) *n. Biol.* The regeneration of parts of a living organism by the gradual transformation of other parts. [<Gk. *morphē* form + *allaxis* exchange]

mor·pheme (môr′fēm) *n. Ling.* The smallest lexical unit of a language, as a word, root, affix, or inflectional ending. *Man, run, pro–, –ess, –ing, ouch,* etc., are morphemes. [<F *morphème* <Gk. *morphē* form]

Mor·phe·us (môr′fē·əs, -fyōōs) In Greek mythology, the god of dreams, son of Hypnos, god of sleep. [<L <Gk. *morphē* form; from the shapes he calls up in dreams] **— Mor′·phe·an** *adj.*

mor·phic (môr′fik) *adj.* Morphologic.

–morphic *combining form* Having the form or shape of: *anthropomorphic.* [<Gk. *morphē* form]

mor·phine (môr′fēn) *n. Chem.* A bitter, white, crystalline, narcotic alkaloid, $C_{17}H_{19}NO_3{\cdot}H_2O$, contained in opium and used for alleviating pain. Also **mor′phi·a** (-fē·ə). [<F <L *Morpheus* god of sleep]

mor·phin·ism (môr′fin·iz′əm) *n. Pathol.* A morbid condition of the system produced by an excessive dose or habitual use of morphine.

morpho– *combining form* Form; shape: *morpholysis.* Also, before vowels, **morph–.** [<Gk. *morphē* form]

mor·pho·gen·e·sis (môr′fō·jen′ə·sis) *n. Biol.* **1** The evolution of forms of structure. **2** The development of organic forms. Also **mor·phog·e·ny** (môr·foj′ə·nē). **— mor′pho·ge·net′ic** (-jə·net′ik) *adj.*

mor·phol·o·gy (môr·fol′ə·jē) *n.* **1** That branch of biology which treats of the form and structure of plants and animals. **2** The form of an organism considered apart from function. **3** *Geog.* The study of the forms of earth features. **4** *Ling.* **a** The branch of linguistics which deals with morphemes, their arrangement in words, and the changes they undergo in various grammatical constructions. **b** The arrangement, composition, and inflection of the morphemes of a language. [<MORPHO- + -LOGY] **— mor·pho·log·ic** (môr′·fə·loj′ik) or **·i·cal** *adj.* **— mor′pho·log′i·cal·ly** *adv.* **— mor·phol′o·gist** *n.*

mor·phol·y·sis (môr·fol′ə·sis) *n.* The breakdown of form or structure. [<MORPHO- + -LYSIS]

mor·pho·sis (môr·fō′sis) *n. Biol.* The order or mode of formation of an organ or organism. [<Gk. *morphōsis* shaping < *morphē* form] **— mor·phot′ic** (-fot′ik) *adj.*

–morphous *combining form* Having a (specified) form: often equivalent to *–morphic*: *anthropomorphous.* [<Gk. *morphē* form]

Mor·rig·u (môr′ē·ōō) In Old Irish mythology, a war goddess, described as attending the battlefield in the form of a demoniacal raven. She helped the Tuatha De Danann defeat the Fomorians. Also **Mor·ri·gan** (môr′ē·ən).

mor·ri·on (môr′ē·on, mō′rē-) See MORION[1].

mor·ris (môr′is, mor′-) *n.* **1** An old English rustic dance, in which the performers took the part of Robin Hood and other characters in English folklore. **2** A dance by a single dancer with castanets. Also **mor′rice, morris dance.** [Earlier *morys, morish* Moorish]

Mor·ris (môr′is, mor′-), **Gouverneur,** 1752–1816, American statesman; financier. **— Robert,** 1734–1806, American statesman, financier, and philanthropist; signer of the Declaration of Independence. **— William,** 1834–96, English painter, craftsman, poet, and socialist; invented the **Morris chair,** an armchair with an adjustable back.

Mor·ris Jes·up (môr′is jes′əp, mor′is), **Cape** The world's northernmost point of land, at the northern extremity of Greenland; 440 miles from the North Pole.

Mor·ri·son (môr′ə·sən, mor′-), **Herbert Stanley,** 1888–1965, English Labour party leader and politician.

Mor·ri·son (môr′ə·sən, mor′-), **Mount** The highest mountain of Taiwan; 13,599 feet. *Chinese* **Sin·kao** (shin′kou′), *Japanese* **Ni·i·ta·ka** (nē·ē·tä·kä).

mor·ro (môr′ō, mor′ō; *Sp.* môr′rō) *n. pl.* **mor·ros** (môr′ōz, mor′-; *Sp.* môr′rōs) A round hill. [<Sp.]

Morro Castle A fort defending the entrance to Havana harbor, Cuba; bombarded, 1898.

mor·row (môr′ō, mor′ō) *n.* **1** The first day after the present or after a day specified; hence, any time following immediately after a specified event. **2** Formerly, morning: good *morrow.* **—** *adj.* Next succeeding, as a day. [OE *morgen* morning]

Mors (môrs) In Roman mythology, the god of death: identified with the Greek *Thanatos.* [<L, death]

Morse (môrs), **Philip McCord,** born 1903, U. S. physicist. **— Samuel Finley Breese,** 1791–1872, U. S. artist and inventor; constructed (1832–35) the first practical telegraph.

INTERNATIONAL MORSE CODE

LETTERS

a	• –	**j**	• – – –	**s**	• • •
b	– • • •	**k**	– • –	**t**	–
c	– • – •	**l**	• – • •	**u**	• • –
d	– • •	**m**	– –	**v**	• • • –
e	•	**n**	– •	**w**	• – –
f	• • – •	**o**	– – –	**x**	– • • –
g	– – •	**p**	• – – •	**y**	– • – –
h	• • • •	**q**	– – • –	**z**	– – • •
i	• •	**r**	• – •		

NUMERALS

1	• – – – –	**4**	• • • • –	**8**	– – – • •
2	• • – – –	**5**	• • • • •	**9**	– – – – •
3	• • • – –	**6**	– • • • •	**0**	– – – – –
		7	– – • • •		

PUNCTUATION

Period	• – • – • –
Comma	– – • • – –
Semicolon	– • – • – •
Question mark	• • – – • •
Exclamation	– – – •
Colon	– – – • • •
Apostrophe	• – – – – •
Hyphen	– • • • • –
Fraction bar	– • • – •
Parenthesis	– • – – • –
Quotation marks	• – • • – •
Double dash	– • • • –

Morse code **1** A system of telegraphic signals invented by S. F. B. Morse, comprised of dots and dashes or short and long flashes representing the letters of the alphabet and used in transmitting messages. **2** International Morse code. Also **Morse alphabet.**

mor·sel (môr′səl) *n.* **1** A bit of food; bite. **2** A small piece of anything. [<OF, dim. of *mors* bite <L *morsus* < *mordere*]

Morse telegraph A telegraph employing the dot–and–dash or Morse code, recording the signals on a continuous paper strip. The first commercial system was set up between Baltimore and Washington in 1844.

mort[1] (môrt) *n.* **1** *Obs.* Death. **2** A flourish on the hunting horn, announcing the death of game. Also **morte.** [<F *mort* <L *mors, mortis* < *mori* die]

mort[2] (môrt) *n. Brit. Dial.* A great quantity or number. [? < *mortal* (def. 6)]

mort[3] (môrt) *n. Brit. Dial.* A salmon in its third year. [Orig. unknown]

mor·tal (môr′təl) *adj.* **1** Subject to death; hence, pertaining to humanity; human. **2** Causing, or that may or will cause, death; fatal. **3** *Theol.* Incurring the penalty of eternal death, as a sin: opposed to *venial.* **4** Marking the end of life. **5** Subject to fatal injury, as a vital organ. **6** *Colloq.* Extreme: a *mortal* fright; also, long and tedious. **7** Deadly in malice or purpose; inveterate: a *mortal* foe. **—** *n.* Whatever is mortal or subject to death; a human being. **—** *adv. Colloq.* Very; exceedingly: *mortal* tired. [<OF <L *mortalis* < *mors, mortis* death]

mor·tal·i·ty (môr·tal′ə·tē) *n.* **1** The quality of being mortal. **2** Death. **3** Frequency of death; the proportion of deaths in a specified number of the population; the death rate. **4** Humanity; mankind. [<OF *mortalité* <L *mortalitas*]

mortality table A life table.

mor·tal·ly (môr′təl·ē) *adv.* **1** Fatally. **2** After the manner of a mortal. **3** Extremely.

mortal mind In Christian Science, nothing, claiming to be something, for Mind is immortal; a belief that life, substance, and intelligence are in and of matter: the opposite of Spirit and therefore the opposite of God, or good.

mor·tar[1] (môr′tər) *n.* **1** A strong bowl–like vessel in which substances are crushed or pounded with a pestle. **2** *Mil.* A piece of ordnance with a large bore for firing heavy shells at low muzzle velocity and great angles of elevation that they may drop upon the object aimed at. **3** *Mining* A tublike cast–iron receptacle with grated sides, in which ore is stamped. **4** Any of several devices for hurling pyrotechnic shells or bombs and also life lines. [OE *mortere* <L *mortarium*]

mor·tar[2] (môr′tər) *n.* **1** A building material prepared by mixing lime, plaster of Paris, or cement, with sand, water, and sometimes other materials. It is used in masonry, plastering, etc. **2** Loosely, a cement. **—** *v.t.* To plaster or join with mortar. [<OF *mortier* <L *mortarium*]

mor·tar·board (môr′tər·bôrd′, -bōrd′) *n.* **1** A square board with a handle, on which a mason holds mortar. **2** The academic cap: so called from the four–cornered piece forming its crown.

mortar hoe A hoe with openings in the blade, used for mixing mortar, cement, etc. See illustration under HOE.

mort·gage (môr′gij) *n.* **1** *Law* An estate in land created by conveyance coupled with a condition of defeasance on the performance of some stipulated condition, as the payment of money. **2** A lien upon land or other property as security for the performance of some obligation, to become void on such performance. **3** The act of conveying, or the instrument effecting the conveyance. **4** A state or condition of being pledged as security for a debt like that of a mortgage of property. **— first mortgage** A mortgage having precedence as a lien over all other mortgages. **—** *v.t.* **·gaged, ·gag·ing** **1** To make over or pledge (property) by mortgage. **2** To pledge. [<F, dead pledge]

mort·ga·gee (môr′gi·jē′) *n.* The person to whom a mortgage is given; the holder of a mortgage.

mort·ga·gor (môr′gi·jər) *n.* A person who mortgages his property to another as security for a loan. Also **mort′gag·er.**

mor·tice (môr′tis) See MORTISE.

mor·ti·cian (môr·tish′ən) *n.* A funeral director; undertaker. [<L *mors, mortis* death + -ICIAN]

mor·ti·fi·ca·tion (môr′tə·fə·kā′shən) *n.* **1** The state of being humbled or depressed by disappointment or chagrin. **2** *Pathol.* The death

of one part of an animal body, as from gangrene, while the rest is still alive. **3** In religion, the act of subduing the passions and appetites by fasting, penance, or painful severities inflicted on the body. **4** That which mortifies or causes humiliation. See synonyms under CHAGRIN. [<LL *mortificatio, -onis*]

mor·ti·fy (môr′tə·fī) *v.* **·fied, ·fy·ing** *v.t.* **1** To affect with humiliation, shame, or chagrin; humiliate. **2** To discipline or punish (the body, passions, etc.) by fasting, penance, or other ascetic practices. **3** *Pathol.* To cause mortification in (a part of the body). — *v.i.* **4** To practice ascetic self-discipline. **5** *Pathol.* To undergo mortification; become gangrenous. [<OF *mortifier* <LL *mortificare* <L *mors, mortis* death + *facere* make] — **mor′ti·fi·er** *n.* — **mor′ti·fy′ing·ly** *adv.*

Mor·ti·mer (môr′tə·mər), **Roger de,** 1287?–1330, Earl of March; Welsh rebel, favorite of Isabella, queen of Edward II of England.

mor·tise (môr′tis) *n.* **1** A space hollowed out, as in a timber, to receive a tenon or the like. **2** Figuratively, adhering power; firmness. — *v.t.* **·tised, ·tis·ing** **1** To cut or make a mortise in. **2** To join by a tenon and mortise. Also spelled *mortice.* [<OF *mortaise* < Arabic *murtazza* joined, fixed in]

MORTISE AND TENON
a. Mortise.
b. Tenon.

mort·main (môrt′mān) *n. Law* The state of lands and tenements held by one that cannot alienate them, as a religious corporation; inalienable tenure or possession. The term is applied in some of the United States to statutes restricting the right of religious corporations to hold land. [<OF *mortemain* <Med. L *mortua manus* dead hand]

Mor·ton (môr′tən), **William Thomas Green,** 1819–68, U. S. dentist; pioneer in use of ether as an anesthetic.

mor·tu·ar·y (môr′chōo·er′ē) *adj.* Pertaining to the burial of the dead; also, relating to or reminiscent of the dead. — *n. pl.* **·ar·ies** **1** In old English law, a gift claimed by or given to a parish minister on the death of a parishioner. **2** A place for the temporary reception of the dead; dead house. [<L *mortuarius* belonging to the dead]

mor·u·la (môr′yoo·lə, -oo-) *n. pl.* **·lae** (-lē) *Biol.* The compact, spherical mass of cells formed by an ovum in the early stages of its development; the mulberry body. [<NL, dim. of L *morum* mulberry] — **mor′u·lar** *adj.*

mo·sa·ic (mō·zā′ik) *n.* **1** Inlaid work composed of bits of stone, glass, etc., forming a pattern or picture. **2** A piece of inlaid work of this kind, or anything resembling such work. **3** *Phot.* An assemblage of aerial photographs pieced together and joined at the margins so as to form a single, continuous picture of a terrain. **4** The plate covered with minute, photosensitive granules which is mounted in the image-scanning element of an electron television camera. — *adj.* Of, pertaining to, or resembling mosaic; tessellated; inlaid. — *v.t.* **·icked, ·ick·ing** **1** To make as if by combining in a mosaic. **2** To decorate with mosaic. [<OF *mosaicq* <Med. L *musaicus* <Gk. *mouseios* of the Muses, artistic <*Mousa* Muse] — **mo·sa·i·cist** (mō·zā′ə·sist) *n.*

Mo·sa·ic (mō·zā′ik) *adj.* Of or pertaining to Moses or his laws. Also **Mo·sa′i·cal.** [<NL *Mosaicus* <L *Moses* Moses]

mosaic disease One of several destructive and infectious diseases of plants caused by a filtrable virus and characterized by a pale, mottled appearance of the foliage: tobacco *mosaic*; potato *mosaic.*

mosaic gold 1 An alloy of copper and zinc; ormolu varnish. **2** Stannic sulfide.

Mo·san·der (mōō·sän′dər), **Carl Gustav,** 1797–1858, Swedish chemist.

Mos·by (mōz′bē), **John Singleton,** 1833–1916, American Confederate soldier and author.

mos·ca·tel (mos′kə·tel′) See MUSCATEL (def. 2).

mos·chate (mos′kāt, -kit) *adj.* Having the odor of musk. [<NL *moschatus* <Med. L *moschus* musk]

mos·cha·tel (mos′kə·tel′, mos′kə·tel) *n.* A low perennial herb (*Adoxa moschatellina*) with greenish flowers and having a musky odor; muskroot. [<F *moscatelle* <Ital. *moscatella*]

Mos·cow The capital of Russia; pop. 9,000,000. The former capital of the Soviet Union. *Russian* **Mos·kva** (mos·kvä′).

Mose·ley (mōz′lē), **Henry Gwyn–Jeffreys,** 1887–1915, English physicist.

Mo·selle (mō·zel′) *n.* A light, dry wine made in the valley of the Moselle, chiefly in the region from Trier to Traben-Trarbach.

Mo·selle (mō·zel′) A river in NE France, Luxemburg, and western Germany, flowing 320 miles NE to the Rhine at Coblenz. *German* **Mo·sel** (mō′zel).

Mo·ses (mō′zis, -ziz; *Ger., Sw.* mō′ses) A masculine personal name. [<Egyptian, child, son] — **Moses** In the Old Testament, the younger son of Amram and Jochebed, who led the Israelites out of Egypt into the Promised Land, received the Ten Commandments from God, and gave laws to the people; hence, a leader; legislator.

Moses (mō′zis, -ziz), **Anna Mary,** 1860–1961, U. S. painter: called "Grandma Moses."

mo·sey (mō′zē) *v.i. U. S. Slang* **1** To saunter, or stroll; shuffle along. **2** To go away; move off. [? <VAMOOSE]

Mos·kva A river in Russia, flowing 315 miles to the Oka.

Mos·lem (moz′ləm, mos′-) *n. pl.* **·lems** or **·lem** A Muslim. —*adj.* Muslim. —**Mos′lem·ism** *n.*

Mos·ley (mōz′lē), **Sir Oswald,** born 1896, English politician.

mosque (mosk) *n.* A Muslim temple of worship. Also **mosk.** [<F *mosquée* <Ital. *moschea* <Arabic *masjid* < *sajada* prostrate oneself, pray]

mos·qui·to (məs·kē′tō) *n. pl.* **·toes** or **·tos** **1** A two-winged, dipterous insect (family *Culicidae*), having (in the female) a long proboscis capable of puncturing the skin for extracting blood. The infections of malaria and yellow fever are spread by the bite of certain species. For illustration see INSECTS (injurious). **2** Any of various other gnats or flies inflicting a similar puncture. Also spelled *musquito.* [<Sp., dim. of *mosca* fly <L *musca*] — **mos·qui′tal** *adj.*

mosquito boat A patrol torpedo boat.

mosquito fleet *Naut. Slang* An assemblage of small craft.

mosquito hawk 1 A nighthawk. **2** A dragonfly.

mosquito net A fine netting or gauze placed in windows, over beds, etc., to keep out mosquitoes.

mosquito netting A coarsely meshed fabric used to make mosquito nets.

moss[1] (môs, mos) *n.* **1** A delicate, bryophytic plant (class *Musci*), growing on the ground, decaying wood, rocks, trees, etc., having a stem and distinct leaves, and producing capsules which open by an operculum and contain spores unmixed with elaters. **2** Any of several other cryptogamous plants, as certain lichens, clubmosses, etc. — *v.t.* To cover with moss. [<MOSS[2]] — **moss′y** *adj.* — **moss′i·ness** *n.*

moss[2] (môs, mos) *n.* A bog; peat bog. [OE *mos*]

moss agate A variety of quartz containing mineral oxides, as manganese dioxide, arranged in mosslike forms.

moss·back (môs′bak′, mos′-) *n.* **1** An old fish or turtle on whose back is a growth of algae or the like. **2** One who is out of touch with the progress of the times; a conservative or reactionary person; especially, an extreme conservative in politics. **3** During the American Civil War, in the South, one who avoided conscription by hiding.

moss–backed (môs′bakt′, mos′-) *adj.* **1** Having moss or mosslike growth on the back. **2** Behind the times; reactionary.

Möss·bau·er effect (mœs′bou′ər) The absorption of gamma rays emitted from a radioactive isotope by nuclei of the same isotope, with resonance between the emitting and absorbing nuclei, both of which are anchored in crystals. It is used in the exact determination of wavelengths, time intervals, the red shift, and in testing various concepts of relativity and quantum theory. [after Rudolf L. *Mössbauer,* born 1929, U.S. physicist born in Germany]

moss·board (môs′bôrd′, -bōrd′, mos′-) *n.* A type of pasteboard made principally of peat moss and used in the preparation of surgical dressings.

moss·bunk·er (môs′bungk·ər, mos′-) *n.* The menhaden. Also **moss′bank·er.** [Alter. of Du. *marskanker*]

moss green Any of various shades of dull yellowish green.

moss·grown (môs′grōn′, mos′-) *adj.* Overgrown with moss; hence, very ancient.

moss hag *Scot.* A pit or slough in a moss or bog, where the moss or peat has been cut away.

mos·so (môs′sō) *adj. Music* Rapid; literally, moved. [<Ital., pp. of *movere* move <L]

moss pink A plant (*Phlox subulata*) of the eastern United States, occurring in several varieties which form mats close to the ground and have white, pink, or purplish flowers. Also **moss phlox.**

moss rose 1 A cultivated variety of the rose (*Rosa centifolia muscosa*) with a mossy calyx and stem. **2** Portulaca.

moss starch Lichenin.

moss–troop·er (môs′trōō′pər, mos′-) *n.* One of the marauders who infested the mossy marshes between Scotland and England prior to the union of the two kingdoms; hence, a bandit or undisciplined soldier.

most (mōst) *adj.* **1** Consisting of the greatest number: superlative of *many.* **2** Consisting of the greatest amount or quantity: superlative of *much.* **3** *Obs.* Greatest in size, rank, or age. — *n.* **1** The greater number; the larger part: the *most* of my belongings. **2** Greatest amount, value, or advantage; utmost degree, extent, or effect. — *adv.* **1** In the highest degree, or in the greatest number or quantity. **2** *Dial.* Almost. **3** Greatest, as in amount or degree: used with adjectives and adverbs to form the superlative degree. [OE *mǣst*]

-most *suffix* Most: added to adjectives, adverbs, and prepositions to form superlatives: *outmost.* [OE *-mest* <*-ma* + *-est,* superlative suffixes]

Mos·tar A city in central Bosnia and Herzegovina; an historic region of Herzogovina, named for the Stari Most bridge that spanned the Neretva River from 1566 until it was destroyed during the civil war in Yugoslavia in 1993.

most·ly (mōst′lē) *adv.* For the most part; principally.

Mo·sul (mō·sōōl′) The second largest city of Iraq, on the Tigris opposite the site of ancient Nineveh. Also **Mo·sul′.**

Mosz·kow·ski (môsh·kôf′skē), **Moritz,** 1854–1925, Polish composer born in Germany.

mot[1] (mō) *n.* A witty or pithy saying; bon mot. [<F, word <LL *muttum* uttered sound <*muttire* murmur]

mot[2] (mot) *n.* A bugle note, or its mark in music. [<OF]

mote[1] (mōt) *v.* **1** *Archaic* May; might. **2** *Obs.* Must. ◆ Homophone: *moat.* [OE *mōt* it is permitted]

mote[2] (mōt) *n.* A minute particle; speck. ◆ Homophone: *moat.* [OE *mot* atom]

mo·tel (mō·tel′) *n.* A hotel for motorists, usually comprising private cabins and garage or parking facilities. [<MO(TOR) + (HO)TEL]

mo·tet (mō·tet′) *n. Music* A contrapuntal, polyphonic song of a sacred nature, usually unaccompanied. Also **mo·tet′to.** [<OF, dim. of *mot* word. See MOT[1].]

moth (môth, moth) *n. pl.* **moths** (môthz, mōths, mothz, moths) Any of various typically nocturnal, lepidopterous insects (division *Heterocera*), distinguished from butterflies by their stout bodies and smaller, usually dull-colored wings, which fold laterally across the abdomen. The larvae of the gipsy moth, silkworm, etc., feed on plants; those of the clothes moth (family *Tineidae*) feed on textiles, clothing, and furs. [OE *moththe*]

moth ball A ball of camphor or naphthalene, for the protection of clothing, etc., from moths. — **in moth balls** In protective storage.

moth–ball (môth′bôl, moth′–) *Mil. & Nav. adj.* Designating ships or military equipment laid up in reserve and covered or coated with protective materials. — *v.t.* To put in reserve and protective storage.

moth·eat·en (môth′ēt′n, moth′–) *adj.* Eaten by moths; hence, used up or worn out: also *mothy.*

moth·er[1] (muth′ər) *n.* 1 A female parent. 2 That which has produced or given birth to anything. 3 An abbess or other nun of rank or dignity. 4 An elderly woman or matron: a familiar title. — *v.t.* 1 To care for as a mother. 2 To bring forth as a mother; produce. 3 To admit or claim parentage, authorship, etc., of. — *adj.* 1 Native: *mother* tongue. 2 Holding a maternal relation. [OE *mōdor*]

moth·er[2] (muth′ər) *n.* 1 A slimy film composed of bacteria and yeast cells that forms on the surface of fermenting liquids and is active in the production of vinegar: also called *mother–of–vinegar.* 2 Dregs; lees. — *v.i.* To become mothery, as vinegar. [Special use of MOTHER[1]] — **moth′er·y** *adj.*

Mother Car·ey's chicken (kâr′ēz) The petrel; especially, the storm petrel. [Alter. of L *mater cara* dear mother, an epithet of the Virgin Mary]

mother cell A cell which by division produces other cells.

Mother Goose 1 The imaginary narrator of a volume of folk tales, compiled in French by Charles Perrault in 1697. 2 The imaginary compiler of a collection of nursery rimes of English folk origin, first published in London about 1760 by John Newbery.

moth·er·hood (muth′ər·hood) *n.* The state of being a mother.

Mother Hub·bard (hub′ard) 1 The main character in an old nursery rime. 2 A woman's loose, flowing gown, unconfined at the waist.

moth·er–in–law (muth′ər·in·lô′) *n.* *pl.* **moth·ers–in–law** 1 The mother of one's spouse. 2 *Brit. Dial.* A stepmother.

moth·er·land (muth′ər·land′) *n.* The land of one's ancestors; native land; mother country.

moth·er·less (muth′ər·lis) *adj.* Having no mother.

mother liquor The liquid remaining after the substances in solution have been deposited by crystallization or precipitation.

mother lode *Mining* 1 *Cap.* The great gold-bearing quartz vein in California, traced by its outcrop from Mariposa to Amador. 2 Any principal vein in a mining region.

moth·er·ly (muth′ər·lē) *adj.* 1 Resembling a mother: a *motherly* woman. 2 Pertaining to or becoming to a mother: *motherly* authority, *motherly* care. — *adv.* In the manner of a mother. — **moth′er·li·ness** *n.*

Mother of God A title officially given to the Virgin Mary at the Council of Ephesus in 431.

moth·er–of–pearl (muth′ər·əv·pûrl′) *n.* The hard, iridescent internal layer of certain shells, as of pearl oysters, abalones, and mussels; nacre.

Mother of the Gods Rhea.

moth·er–of–vin·e·gar (muth′ər·əv·vin′ə·gər) See MOTHER[2].

Mother's Day A memorial day in honor of mothers, observed annually in the United States on the second Sunday in May. See FATHER'S DAY.

mother tongue 1 One's native language. 2 A language from which another language has sprung.

Moth·er·well and Wish·aw (muth′ər·wel ənd wish′ô) A burgh on the Clyde in Lanarkshire, Scotland; formerly two towns.

mother wit Inherent, natural, or native intelligence; common sense.

moth·er·wort (muth′ər·wûrt′) *n.* An Old World herb (*Leonurus cardiaca*) of the mint family, with lanceolate, toothed leaves, and small, purplish flowers: now common in the U.S. [So called because once thought to be valuable in the treatment of diseases of the womb]

moth·mill·er (môth′mil′ər, moth′–) *n.* 1 A pale moth with floury wings; a miller. 2 *Colloq.* Any moth.

moth·proof (môth′proof′, moth′–) *adj.* Resistant to the attack of moths. — *v.t.* **·proofed, ·proof·ing** To render (textiles) resistant to moths.

moth·y (môth′ē, moth′ē) *adj.* **moth·i·er, moth·i·est** Moth-eaten.

mo·tif (mō·tēf′) *n.* 1 The underlying idea or main feature or element in literary, musical, or artistic work. 2 In the decorative arts, a distinctive element of design. Also **mo·tive** (mō′tiv). [<F]

mo·tile (mō′til) *adj.* 1 *Biol.* Having the power of spontaneous motion, as certain minute organisms. 2 Causing motion. [<L *motus*, pp. of *movere* move] — **mo·til′i·ty** *n.*

mo·tion (mō′shən) *n.* 1 Change of position in reference to an assumed point or center; a shifting movement. 2 The interaction of parts in a mechanism to produce a particular result. 3 A formal proposition in a deliberative assembly. 4 A significant movement of the limbs, eyes, etc.; a gesture: She made *motions* to him. 5 An impulse to action; incentive. 6 *Music* Melodic progression. 7 *Law* An application to a court to obtain an order or rule directing some act to be done. 8 A mechanism. 9 *Obs.* A puppet or puppet show. — **perpetual motion** Continuous mechanical motion, especially as applied to machines which are claimed to do useful work without the expenditure of equivalent amounts of work upon them. — *v.i.* To make a gesture of direction or intent, as with the hand. — *v.t.* To direct or guide by a gesture. [<F <L *motio, -onis* <*motus*, pp. of *movere* move] — **mo′tion·al** *adj.* — **mo′tion·less** *adj.* — **mo′tion·less·ly** *adv.*

Synonyms (noun): act, action, change, move, movement, passage, transit, transition. *Motion* may be either abstract or concrete, more frequently the former; *movement* is always concrete, that is, considered in connection with the thing that moves or is moved; thus we speak of the *movements* of the planets, but of the laws of planetary *motion;* of military *movements,* but of perpetual *motion. Motion* is *change* of place or position in space; *transition* is a passing from one point or position in space to another. *Move* is used chiefly of contests or competition, as in chess or politics: as, It is your *move;* a shrewd *move* of the opposition. We speak of mental or spiritual *acts* or processes, or of the laws of mental *action,* but a formal proposal of *action* in a deliberative assembly is termed a *motion. Action* is a more comprehensive word than *motion.* See ACT, TOPIC. *Antonyms:* quiescence, quiet, repose, rest.

motion picture 1 A sequence of pictures, each slightly different from the last, photographed by a special camera on a single strip of film, for projection on a screen, giving the optical illusion of continuous, ordered movement: also called *cinema, movie, moving picture.* 2 A photoplay. — **mo′tion–pic′ture** *adj.*

motion sickness Nausea and sometimes vomiting caused by the effect of certain complex movements on the semicircular canals of the inner ear, typically experienced in a moving vehicle, ship, or airplane.

motion study The detailed observation and analysis of the different movements involved in the performance of a given repetitive task, with a view to lessening the fatigue and increasing the efficiency of the workers.

mo·ti·vate (mō′tə·vāt) *v.t.* **·vat·ed, ·vat·ing** To provide with a motive; instigate; induce.

mo·ti·va·tion (mō′tə·vā′shən) *n.* Causative factor; incentive; drive. — **mo′ti·va′tion·al** *adj.*

motivation research The use of psychological or other social-science concepts and techniques in marketing, advertising, and public-opinion research to investigate the conscious or subliminal causes of consumer behavior, and the motives that lead to a favorable or unfavorable response.

mo·tive (mō′tiv) *n.* 1 That which incites to motion or action. 2 A predominant idea; design. — *adj.* 1 Having power to move; causing motion. 2 Relating to a motive or motives. — *v.t.* **·tived, ·tiv·ing** 1 To motivate; prompt. 2 To relate to the leading idea or motif in a work of art, etc. [<OF *motif* <Med. L *motivus* <*motus,* pp. of *movere* move]

Synonyms (noun): consideration, ground, incentive, incitement, inducement, influence, reason. *Motive* may signify either a mental impulse, or something external that is an object of desire, and so an *inducement* or *incitement* to action. Compare CAUSE, IMPULSE, PURPOSE, REASON.

motive power 1 The power, or means of

generating power, by which motion is imparted to an object, machine, etc. 2 Figuratively, an impelling force.

mo·tiv·i·ty (mō·tiv′ə·tē) *n.* The power of producing motion; motive energy.

mot juste (mō zhüst′) *French* The precise word; exactly the right expression.

mot·ley (mot′lē) *adj.* 1 Variegated in color; particolored. 2 Composed of heterogeneous elements. 3 Clothed in varicolored garments. — *n.* 1 A dress of various colors, such as was formerly worn by court jesters. 2 A jester or fool in motley garments. 3 A medley, as of colors. [ME *motteley;* origin uncertain]

Mot·ley (mot′lē), **John Lothrop,** 1814–77, U.S. historian.

mot·mot (mot′mot) *n.* One of a family of birds, the *Momotidae,* of the warmer parts of America, related to the kingfishers; a sawbill. The middle pair of tail feathers is usually elongated and racket-shaped. [Imit. of its note]

MOTLEY
(*n. def. 1*)

mo·to·fa·cient (mō′tə·fā′shənt) *adj. Physiol.* Producing motion: said especially of muscles whose contraction results in a definite movement. [<L *motus* motion, moving <*movere* move + *faciens, -entis,* ppr. of *facere* make, cause]

mo·tor (mō′tər) *n.* 1 One who or that which produces motion, as a machine, nerve, etc. 2 An internal-combustion engine, especially one operating on gasoline. 3 A motorcar or motorcycle. 4 An electric motor. — **rotary motor** An internal-combustion engine having multiple radial cylinders rotating about a fixed crankshaft. — *adj.* 1 Causing, producing, or imparting motion. 2 Transmitting impulses from the nerve centers to the muscles. 3 Pertaining to consciousness of motion. — *v.i.* To travel or ride in an automobile. [<L <*motus,* pp. of *movere*] — **mo′tor·ing** *adj. & n.*

mo·tor·boat (mō′tər·bōt′) *n.* A boat propelled by an internal-combustion engine, or by an electric motor.

mo·tor·bus (mō′tər·bus′) *n.* A power-driven omnibus. Also **motor coach.**

mo·tor·cade (mō′tər·kād) *n.* A procession of motorcycles or automobiles. [<MOTOR + (CAVAL)CADE]

mo·tor·car (mō′tər·kär′) *n.* An automobile.

mo·tor·cy·cle (mō′tər·sī′kəl) *n.* A two-wheeled vehicle, sometimes having an attached sidecar with a third wheel, propelled by an internal-combustion engine. — *v.i.* **·cled, ·cling** To travel or ride on a motorcycle. — **mo′tor·cy′clist** *n.*

motor drive A power unit consisting of an electric motor and auxiliaries, used to operate a machine or group of machines.

mo·tor·drome (mō′tər·drōm) *n.* An enclosure, course, or track where motor-driven vehicles of various kinds are tested in competition or otherwise.

motor generator A device for transforming electrical power by permanently connecting, usually on a common bedplate, a motor and a generator; a dynamotor.

motor home *U.S.* An automotive vehicle equipped with living accommodations and resembling a trailer but built on a single chassis.

mo·tor·ist (mō′tər·ist) *n.* One who drives an automobile; one who travels by automobile.

mo·to·ri·um (mō·tôr′ē·əm, -tō′rē-) *n. Physiol.* 1 That portion of the nervous system which controls the motor apparatus. 2 Any center of a motor function. [<NL <L *motor* a mover]

mo·tor·ize (mō′tər·īz) *v.t.* **·ized, ·iz·ing** 1 To equip with a motor or motors. 2 To equip with motor-propelled vehicles in place of horses and horse-drawn vehicles. — **mo′tor·i·za′tion** *n.*

mo·tor·man (mō′tər·mən) *n. pl.* **·men** (-mən) One who operates a motor, as on a street car or an electric locomotive.

motor oil A high-grade lubricating oil, designed for the exacting requirements of internal-combustion engines.

motor scooter See SCOOTER (def. 2).

mo·tor·ship (mō′tər·ship′) *n.* A vessel, as a

passenger ship, of which the principal motive power is derived from an internal-combustion oil or gas engine.

motor spirit Any fuel adapted for spark-ignition, internal-combustion engines; specifically, coal or petroleum distillates blended with suitable additions, as alcohol.

motor transport *Mil.* Any motor vehicle used for transport only: distinguished from *combat vehicle.*

motor vehicle 1 Any vehicle operated by a motor or engine. 2 A vehicle adapted to be pulled by another, as a trailer.

Mott (mot), **John Raleigh,** 1865-1955, U.S. clergyman and leader in the Y.M.C.A. — **Lucretia,** 1793-1880, *née* Coffin, U.S. social reformer.

Mot·ta (môt'tä), **Giuseppi,** 1871-1940, Swiss lawyer and statesman.

motte (mot) *n. Dial.* A small growth of trees on a prairie. Also **mott.** [<Sp. *mata* clump, grove]

mot·tet·to (môt·tet'tō) *n.* Italian Motet.

Mot·teux (mô·tœ'), **Peter Anthony,** 1663-1718, English dramatist and translator, born in France.

mot·tle (mot'l) *v.t.* **·tled, ·tling** To mark with spots or streaks of different colors or shades; blotch. — *n.* 1 The spotted, blotched, or variegated appearance of any mottled surface, as of wood or marble. 2 One of a number of spots or blotches on any surface. [<MOTLEY]

mot·tled (mot'ld) *adj.* Marked with spots of different color or shades of color; blotched; variegated.

mot·to (mot'ō) *n. pl.* **·toes** or **·tos** 1 An expressive word or pithy sentence enunciating some guiding principle, rule of conduct, or the like; a phrase inscribed on something or prefixed to a literary composition as somehow indicative of its qualities. 2 A piece of paper printed with a motto or sentiment and wrapped around a small piece of candy; also, the piece of candy enclosed. See synonyms under ADAGE. [<Ital. <F *mot.* See MOT.]

mot·ty (mot'ē) *adj. Scot.* Abounding in motes. Also **mot'tie.**

mou' (moo) *n. Scot.* The mouth.

mouch (mooch) See MOOCH.

mou·choir (moo·shwàr') *n. French* A pocket handkerchief.

mou·die (mou'dē) *n. Scot.* A mole; also, a molecatcher. Also **mou'di·wort** (-wûrt).

moue (moo) *n.* A pouting grimace expressive of disdain or distaste. [<F]

mouf·lon (moof'lon) *n.* A hairy wild sheep; specifically, *Ovis musimon* of the mountains of Corsica and Sardinia, the males with very large and curved horns. Also **mouf'flon.** [<F <dial. Ital. *muffolo* <*muffione* <LL *mufro, -onis*]

mouil·lé (moo·yā') *adj.* Given a palatalized pronunciation, as *ll* in the French name *Villon.* [<F, pp. of *mouiller* moisten]

mou·jik (moo·zhēk') See MUZHIK.

Mouk·den (mook'den', mook'dən, mook'-) See MUKDEN.

moul (mool) *v.t. & v.i. Obs.* or *Brit. Dial.* To make or become moldy.

mou·lage (moo·läzh') *n.* 1 A cast, in plaster of Paris or other similar material, of an object or of its impressed outlines on a surface: frequently used in criminal identification, as of footprints, tire marks, etc. 2 A synthetic, rubberlike, plastic material used in making casts. [<F]

mould (mōld), **moult** (mōlt), etc. See MOLD, etc.

mould goose The musk duck.

mould·warp (mōld'wôrp) See MOLDWARP.

mou·lin (moo·lan') *n.* A nearly vertical shaft in a glacier, formed by the surface water trickling through a crevice. [<F, mill <LL *molina.* See MILL.]

mou·line (moo·lēn') *n.* 1 The circular swing of a saber. 2 The drum of a winch, capstan, or the like; a windlass mechanism. 3 A form of turnstile. Also **mou·li·net** (moo'lē·net). [<F, dim. of *moulin* mill]

Mou·lins (moo·lan') The capital of Allier department, central France.

Moul·mein (mool·mān') A port on the Andaman Sea in Lower Burma, chief town of Tenasserim: also *Maulmain.*

mouls (moolz) *Scot.* See MOOLS.

moult (mōlt), **moult·ing,** etc. *Brit.* Molt, etc.

Moul·ton (mōl'tən), **Forest Ray,** 1872-1952, U.S. astronomer.

Moul·trie (mool'trē, moo'-, mōl'-), **William,** 1730-1805, American Revolutionary general; builder and defender (1776) of Fort Moultrie, Charleston Harbor, South Carolina.

mound¹ (mound) *n.* 1 A heap or pile of earth, either natural or artificial; hillock. 2 One of the earthworks built by the Mound Builders for burial or fortification. 3 In baseball, the slightly raised ground from which the pitcher pitches the ball. See synonyms under RAMPART. — *v.t.* 1 To fortify or enclose with a mound. 2 To heap up in a mound. [Origin uncertain]

mound² (mound) *n.* A jeweled ball or globe, often surmounted by a cross, forming part of the regalia of a king or emperor: an emblem of sovereignty; an orb. [<F *monde* <L *mundus* world]

MOUND²

Mound Builder One of the aboriginal people who built the burial mounds and fortifications found in the Mississippi basin and adjoining regions: the ancestors of the North American Indians dwelling in that region at the time of the first European explorers.

Mounds·ville (moundz'vil) A city in NW West Virginia; site of a conical Indian mound.

mount¹ (mount) *v.t.* 1 To ascend by climbing; go up, as stairs. 2 To climb upon; ascend and seat oneself on, as a horse. 3 To put on horseback. 4 To furnish with a horse or horses. 5 To set or place in an elevated position: to *mount* a plaque on a wall. 6 To place in position for use or operation, as a cannon or engine. 7 To put in or on a support, frame, etc., as for exhibition: to *mount* a butterfly. 8 To furnish, as a play, with scenery, costumes, etc. 9 To copulate with a female: said of male animals. 10 In microscopy: a To place or fix (a sample) on a slide. b To prepare (a slide) for examination. 11 *Mil. & Nav.* To carry or be equipped with: a ship *mounting* thirty-two guns. 12 To put on (clothing), especially for display. 13 *Mil.* To stand or post (guard). 14 *Mil.* To prepare for and begin: to *mount* an offensive. — *v.i.* 15 To rise or ascend; go up. 16 To increase in number, amount, or degree: often with *up:* The bills *mounted* up. 17 To get on horseback. 18 To get up on or on top of something. — *n.* 1 That upon or by which anything is prepared or equipped for use, exhibition, ornament, preservation, or examination. 2 The card, etc., upon which a drawing or photograph is mounted. 3 The parts and appliances by which a gun is attached to its carriage. 4 The glass slide and its adjuncts upon which a microscopic subject is secured for examination. 5 A saddle horse or other animal used for riding: by extension, a bicycle. 6 The act of riding a horse in a race; also, the privilege or opportunity of doing so. 7 A style of mounting. [<OF *monter* <L *mons, montis* mountain] — **mount'a·ble** *adj.* — **mount'er** *n.*

mount² (mount) *n.* 1 An elevation of the earth's surface; a mountain; a hill. When used as part of a proper name it usually precedes the specific application: *Mount* Washington. 2 *Obs.* A raised fortification commanding the surrounding country. 3 In palmistry, one of seven fleshy protuberances in the palm of the hand. [OE *munt* <L *mons* mountain]

moun·tain (moun'tən) *n.* 1 A natural elevation of the earth's surface, rising more or less abruptly to a small summit area, attaining an elevation greater than that of a hill, and standing either in a single mass or forming part of a series. 2 Any large heap or pile resembling this. 3 Something of great magnitude. — **the Mountain** A name given to the ultra-revolutionary party of the French National Assembly or Convention in 1793, from the fact that its members occupied the highest seats in the chamber. — *adj.* 1 Of, pertaining to, or living or growing on mountains. 2 Like or suggesting a mountain or mountains. [<OF

montaigne <L *montanus* mountainous <*mons, montis* mountain]

mountain ape *Paleontol.* Oreopithecus.

mountain ash 1 Any of various American deciduous shrubs (genus *Sorbus*), having alternate simple or pinnate leaves, white flowers, and vivid red fruit, especially *S. americana.* 2 The rowan.

mountain avens A small evergreen plant (*Dryas octopetala*) of the rose family, growing in arctic and alpine regions.

mountain cat 1 The cougar. 2 The bobcat.

mountain chain A series of mountains connected and having some common characteristics.

mountain cork A variety of asbestos occurring in light, flexible sheets which will float on water. Also **mountain leather.**

mountain cranberry The mountain cowberry (*Vaccinium vitis-idaea minus*), having edible red berries, evergreen leaves, and pink or red flowers.

mountain dew *Slang* Illicitly distilled whiskey.

moun·tain·eer (moun'tən·ir') *n.* 1 An inhabitant of a mountainous district. 2 One who climbs mountains. — *v.i.* To climb mountains.

mountain goat The Rocky Mountain goat; a goat antelope.

mountain laurel In the eastern United States, the low-growing calicobush (*Kalmia latifolia*), an evergreen shrub with white or pink flowers; State flower of Connecticut and Pennsylvania. The foliage is poisonous to livestock.

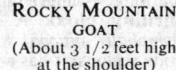

ROCKY MOUNTAIN GOAT
(About 3 1/2 feet high at the shoulder)

mountain lion The puma or cougar.

moun·tain·ous (moun'tən·əs) *adj.* 1 Full of mountains. 2 Huge. — **moun'tain·ous·ly** *adv.*

mountain range 1 One of the components of a mountain chain, usually a group of more or less parallel ridges of similar origin, structure, etc. 2 A land area dominated by such a group of mountains, characterized by great variations in elevation above sea level.

mountain rat A pack rat.

mountain sheep The bighorn.

mountain sickness *Pathol.* A form of anoxemia accompanied by nausea, due to insufficient oxygen consumption at high altitudes, especially on mountains.

Mountains of the Moon See RUWENZORI.

mountain specter The specter of the Brocken.

Mountain Standard Time See STANDARD TIME. Abbr. M.S.T.

Mount·bat·ten (mount·bat'n), **Lord Louis,** born 1900, English admiral in World War II: originally *Prince Louis Francis Battenberg.*

Mount Des·ert (dez'ərt, di·zûrt') An island in Acadia National Park off the SE coast of Maine; 100 square miles.

moun·te·bank (moun'tə·bangk) *n.* 1 A vendor of quack medicines at fairs, who usually mounts a platform or wagon to sell his wares. 2 Hence, a charlatan. See synonyms under QUACK. — *v.i.* To play the mountebank. [<Ital. *montimbanco* <*monta* mount + *in* on + *banco* bench]

mount·ed (moun'tid) *adj.* Elevated on or equipped with horses: *mounted* police.

Mount·ie (moun'tē) See MOUNTY.

mount·ing (moun'ting) *n.* 1 The act of mounting; elevation. 2 A mount, as of a picture. 3 The act of preparing for use, etc.

Mount McKinley National Park A region in south central Alaska; 3,030 square miles; established as a national park in 1917.

Mount Rainier National Park A region in the Cascade Mountains of west central Washington; 378 square miles; established as a national park in 1899.

Mount Rob·son Provincial Park (rob'sən) A national park in eastern British Columbia, Canada, near the Alberta border; 65 miles long, 10 to 20 miles wide.

Mount Ver·non (vûr'nən) The home and burial place of George Washington; 15 miles below

Washington, D.C., on the Potomac River.

Moun·ty (moun′tē) *n. pl.* **·ties** *Colloq.* A member of the Royal Canadian Mounted Police: also spelled *Mountie.*

mourn (môrn, mōrn) *v.i.* **1** To feel or express grief or sorrow. **2** To display the conventional signs of grief after someone's death; wear mourning. —*v.t.* **3** To grieve or sorrow for (someone dead). **4** To grieve over or lament (misfortune, failure, etc.); bewail; deplore. **5** To utter in a sorrowful manner. [OE *murnan*]

Synonyms: bemoan, bewail, deplore, grieve, lament, regret, rue, sorrow. Mourning is thought of as prolonged; grief or regret may be transient. One may *grieve* or *mourn, regret, rue,* or *sorrow* without a sound; he *bemoans* with suppressed and often inarticulate sounds of grief; *bewails* with passionate utterance, whether of inarticulate cries or of spoken words; he *laments* in plaintive or pathetic words.

mourn·er (môr′nər, mōr′-) *n.* **1** One who mourns; specifically, one who attends a funeral. **2** A penitent at a revival meeting.

mourner's bench *U.S.* A bench near the preacher reserved for penitents at a revival meeting: also called *anxious seat.*

mourn·ful (môrn′fəl, mōrn′-) *adj.* **1** Indicating or expressing sorrow. **2** Oppressed with grief. **3** Exciting sorrow. See synonyms under PITIFUL, SAD. —**mourn′ful·ly** *adv.* —**mourn′ful·ness** *n.*

mourn·ing (môr′ning, mōr′-) *n.* **1** The act of sorrowing or expressing grief; lamentation; sorrow. **2** The symbols or outward manifestations of grief, as the use of symbolical colors in dress, the draping of buildings or doors, and the half-masting of flags. —*adj.* Relating to or expressive of mourning. —**mourn′ing·ly** *adv.*

mourning cloak A brownish-black butterfly *(Nymphalis antiopa)* widely distributed in temperate regions: it has a row of dark spots just inside the yellow border on the upper side of the wings: also called *Camberwell beauty.*

mourning dove The Carolina turtledove *(Zenaidura macroura),* common in North America: so called for its plaintive note.

mourning warbler A warbler of the eastern United States *(Oporonis philadelphia)* also called for its plaintive note.

mouse (mous) *n. pl.* **mice** (mīs) **1** One of various small rodents frequenting human habitations throughout the world, as the common **house mouse** *(Mus musculus).* ◆ Collateral adjective: *murine.* **2** Any of various similar animals, as the American **harvest mouse** (genus *Reithrodontomys*), or the **lemming mouse** (genus *Synaptomys*). **3** *Slang* A young woman. **4** *Slang* A discolored swelling of the eye, caused by a blow or bruise. **5** *Naut.* A swelling worked on a rope to prevent its slipping; also, a mousing. —*v.* (mouz) **moused, mous·ing** *v.i.* **1** To hunt or catch mice. **2** To hunt for something cautiously and softly; prowl. —*v.t.* **3** To hunt for, as a cat hunts mice. **4** *Naut.* To secure (a hook) with mousing. **5** *Obs.* To rend as a cat does a mouse. [OE *mūs,* pl. *mȳs.*]

mouse·bane (mous′bān′) *n.* Aconite.

mouse·bird (mous′bûrd′) *n.* **1** An African bird (genus *Colius*) with a conical bill, long medial tail feathers, and soft plumage. **2** A shrike.

mouse-ear (mous′ir′) *n.* **1** Any one of various plants whose leaves resemble the ears of a mouse; especially, the European hawkweed *(Hieracium pilosella).* **2** The forget-me-not.

mouse gray A medium shade of gray, the color of the fur of the common house mouse.

mous·er (mou′zər) *n.* **1** An animal that catches mice; especially, a cat. **2** A person who goes about stealthily.

mouse·tail (mous′tāl′) *n.* One of a genus *(Myosurus)* of plants of the crowfoot family: so called from its slender spike.

mouse·trap (mous′trap′) *n.* A trap for catching mice.

mous·ing (mou′zing) *n.* **1** The act of hunting mice. **2** *Naut.* A lashing or shackle passed around the shank and point of a hook, to prevent its spreading or unhooking. —*adj.* **1** Given to catching mice; prowling. **2** Thorough; careful; patient, as a cat hunting a mouse.

mous·que·taire (mo͞os′kə·târ′) *n.* **1** A member of one of the two companies of mounted musketeers forming the bodyguard of the French kings between 1622 and 1786. **2** A woman's cloth cloak with large buttons: in fashion about 1855. **3** A long glove of kid or silk, loose about the wrist: worn by women [<F, musketeer]

mous·sa·ka (mo͞o′sə·kä′) *n.* A baked dish of the Middle East made of alternating layers of ground meat and eggplant, served with a cheese sauce.

mousse (mo͞os) *n.* A light, frozen dessert made of whipped cream, white of egg, sugar, and flavoring extract, sometimes with the beaten yolks of eggs and gelatin; also, a similar dish made with finely ground meat, fish, or vegetables: lobster *mousse.* [<F]

mousse·line (mo͞os·lēn′) *n.* **1** Fine French muslin. **2** A thin glass blown to resemble lace. [<F. See MUSLIN.]

mousse·line-de-soie (mo͞os·lēn′də·swä′) *n. French* A plain-weave silk chiffon fabric, often figured; silk muslin.

Mous·sorg·sky (mo͞o·sôrg′skē), **Modest Petrovich,** 1835–81, Russian composer: also *Mussorgsky.*

mous·tache (məs·tash′, mus′tash) See MUSTACHE.

Mous·te·ri·an (mo͞o·stir′ē·ən) *adj. Anthropol.* Pertaining to or describing the culture stage of the Middle Paleolithic, represented in western Europe by artifacts of stone and other materials believed to indicate the social forms of the Neanderthal race of hunters. [<F *moustérien* <*Le Moustier,* a village in France where such remains were found]

mous·y (mou′sē, -zē) *adj.* **mous·i·er, mous·i·est** **1** Infested with or inhabited by mice. **2** Of, pertaining to, or like a mouse; having the color or smell of a mouse. **3** Like a mouse in appearance or manner; pallid; timid. Also **mous′ey.**

mouth (mouth) *n. pl.* **mouths** (mouthz) **1** The orifice at which food is taken into the body; the entrance to the alimentary canal; the cavity between the lips and throat. ◆ Collateral adjective: *oral.* **2** The human mouth as the channel of speech. **3** A wry face; grimace. **4** That part of a stream where its waters are discharged; also, the entrance to a harbor. **5** The opening for discharge in the muzzle of a firearm. **6** The slit in an organ pipe, from which the wind passes against the lip; also, the edge of the opening in a flute or similar instrument, against which the performer's breath is directed. **7** The opening of a vessel by which it is emptied or filled. **8** The entrance or opening into a cavity, mine, etc. **9** The space or opening between the jaws of a vice. —**down in** (or **at**) **the mouth** Disconsolate; dejected. —**to fix one's mouth for** To get ready for. —*v.t.* (mouth) **1** To utter in a forced or affected manner; declaim. **2** To seize or take in the mouth. **3** To caress or fondle with the mouth. **4** To accustom (a horse) to the bit. —*v.i.* **5** To speak in a forced or affected manner. **6** To distort the mouth; grimace. [OE *mūth*] —**mouth′er** (mou′thər) *n.*

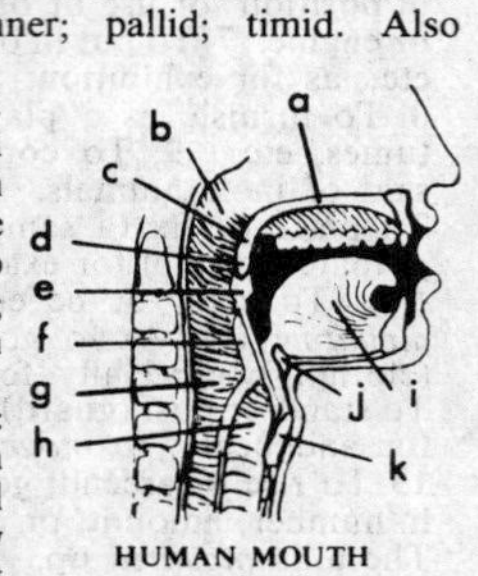

HUMAN MOUTH
a. Hard palate.
b. Pharynx.
c. Soft palate.
d. Uvula.
e. Tonsil.
f. Epiglottis.
g. Esophagus.
h. Trachea
i. Tongue.
j. Hyoid bone.
k. Larynx.

mouthed (mouthd, moutht) *adj.* **1** Having a mouth: used in composition, to denote a characteristic of the mouth or of speech: a hard-*mouthed* horse. **2** Provided with a mouth.

mouth·ful (mouth′fo͝ol′) *n. pl.* **·fuls** (-fo͝olz′) **1** As much as can be or is usually put into or held in the mouth at one time. **2** A small quantity.

mouth organ **1** A harmonica. **2** A set of panpipes.

mouth·piece (mouth′pēs′) *n.* **1** That part of any instrument, tool, etc., that is applied to the mouth. **2** One who speaks for others. **3** *Slang* A criminal lawyer.

mouth-to-mouth (mouth′tə·mouth′) *adj.* Pertaining to or designating a first-aid technique in which the lungs of a nonbreathing subject are repeatedly and forcibly filled with air from the mouth of the operator, which is closely applied to the mouth of the subject at each insufflation.

mouth·y (mou′thē, -thē) *adj.* **mouth·i·er, mouth·i·est** **1** Garrulous. **2** Addicted to grimaces in speaking. —**mouth′i·ly** *adv.* —**mouth′i·ness** *n.*

mou·ton (mo͞o′ton) *n.* Processed lambskin or sheepskin used in various types of apparel, especially coats. [<F, sheep]

mou·ton·née (mo͞o′tə·nā′) *French adj. Geog.* Having the form of a sheep's back: said of rocks, etc. Also **mou′ton·néed′.**

mov·a·ble (mo͞o′və·bəl) *adj.* **1** Capable of being moved in any way, as from one place, position, or posture to another; susceptible of transposition: *movable* property. **2** Capable of being moved in respect of time; recurring at varying intervals. See synonyms under MOBILE. —*n.* **1** Anything that can be moved; especially, anything that may be readily moved or is adapted for moving. **2** *pl.* House furniture of a movable nature; also, personal property, as distinguished from real or fixed property. Also **move′a·ble.** —**mov′a·ble·ness, mov′a·bil′i·ty** *n.* —**mov′a·bly** *adv.*

movable kidney A floating kidney.

move (mo͞ov) *v.* **moved, mov·ing** *v.i.* **1** To change place or position; pass or go from one place to another. **2** To change one's residence. **3** To make progress; advance; proceed. **4** To live or associate; be active: to *move* in cultivated circles. **5** To operate or revolve; work: said of machines, etc. **6** *Colloq.* To depart; go or start: often with *on.* **7** To take action; begin to act. **8** To be disposed of by sale. **9** To make an application, appeal, or proposal: to *move* for adjournment. **10** To evacuate: said of the bowels. **11** In chess, checkers, etc., to make a move. —*v.t.* **12** To change the place or position of; carry, push, or pull from one place to another. **13** To set or keep in motion; stir or shake. **14** To rouse, influence, or impel to some action; prompt; actuate. **15** To affect with passion, sympathy, etc.; stir; excite. **16** To offer for consideration, action, etc.; propose, especially formally. **17** To cause (the bowels) to evacuate. See synonyms under ACTUATE, CARRY, CONVEY, INFLUENCE, PERSUADE, STIR[1]. —*n.* **1** The act of moving; movement. **2** An act in the carrying out of a plan. **3** In games, the changing of the place of a piece. —**to get a move on** To hurry; get going. See synonyms under MOTION. [<AF *mover,* OF *moveir* <L *movere*]

move·ment (mo͞ov′mənt) *n.* **1** The act of changing place or of moving in any way; any change of position. **2** A series of actions, incidents, or ethical impulses tending toward some end: the temperance *movement.* **3** An effect resembling motion, as in a picture. **4** *Mech.* A particular arrangement of related parts accomplishing a motion: the *movement* of a watch. **5** *Music* **a** The pace or speed at which a piece or section of music sounds best. **b** One of the sections of a larger work, as of a symphony. **c** Melodic progression. **6** Rhythm; meter. **7** The act of emptying the bowels; also, the state of being or the matter so emptied. **8** An elemental part of action in military or naval evolution or maneuver. See synonyms under ACT, MOTION.

mov·er (mo͞o′vər) *n.* **1** One who or that which moves; specifically, one engaged in the business of moving household goods and other possessions. **2** A tenant farmer who moves away as soon as the soil is exhausted.

mov·ie (mo͞o′vē) *n. Colloq.* **1** A motion picture. **2** A motion-picture theater. **3** *pl.* The motion-picture industry. **4** *pl.* A showing of motion pictures. [Contraction of *moving picture*]

mov·ie-go·er (mo͞o′vē·gō′ər) *n. Colloq.* One who attends motion-picture showings regularly or frequently. —**mov′ie-go′ing** *n.*

mov·ing (mo͞o′ving) *adj.* **1** Causing to move; impelling to act; influencing; instigating; persuading. **2** Exciting the susceptibilities; affecting; touching. —**mov′ing·ly** *adv.* —**mov′ing·ness** *n.*

moving picture A motion picture.

moving platform A platform operated by an endless belt or several such side by side,

moving at graduated speeds, carrying along passengers or merchandise. Also **moving sidewalk.**

moving staircase An escalator.

mow[1] (mō) v. **mowed, mowed** or **mown, mowing** v.t. **1** To cut down, as grain, with a scythe or machine. **2** To cut the grain or grass of, as a field or lawn. **3** To cut down or kill rapidly or indiscriminately: with *down.* —v.i. **4** To cut down grass or grain. [OE *māwan*] —**mow′er** n.

mow[2] (mō, mou) v.i. To make faces; grimace. [< n.] —n. A grimace. [< OF *moue*]

mow[3] (mou) n. Hay or grain stored in a barn; also, the place of storage. —v.t. To store in a mow. [OE *mūga*]

mown (mōn) adj. Cut down, as by mowing.

mox·a (mok′sə) n. A cottony material, used, when ignited, as a counterirritant or cautery, prepared in China and Japan from certain species of *Artemisia,* especially *A. moxa.* **2** A substance for similar use obtained from other sources. **3** Any of the plants producing this material. [< Japanese *mogusa* a caustic < *moe kusa* burning herb]

moy·en âge (mwà·yen äzh′) *French* The Middle Ages.

Moy·zesz (moi′zesh) Polish form of MOSES. Also **Mo·zes** (*Dan.* mō′zes, *Hungarian* mō′zesh).

Mo·zam·bique (mō′zam·bēk′) **1** A Portuguese overseas province in SE Africa; 297,731 square miles; capital, Lourenço Marques: also *Portuguese East Africa.* **2** A port of northern Mozambique, on **Mozambique Channel,** a strait of the Indian Ocean between Madagascar and SE Africa. *Portuguese* **Mo·cam·bi·que** (mōō′səm·bē′kə).

Moz·ar·ab (mōz·âr′əb) n. A member of a Christian congregation in Spain that maintained a modified form of its religion after the Moslem conquest. [< Sp. *Mozárabe* < Arabic *musta′rib* would-be Arab]

Mo·zart (mō′tsärt, -zärt), **Wolfgang Amadeus,** 1756–91, Austrian composer.

mo·zet·ta (mō·zet′ə) n. A hooded jacket worn by the prelates of the Roman Catholic Church. Also **moz·zet′ta.** [< Ital.]

Moz·za·rel·la (môd′dzä·rel′lä) n. A soft Italian curd cheese, originally made of buffalo's milk: used mainly in cooking. [< Ital.]

Mr. (mis′tər) n. pl. **Messrs.** (mes′ərz) A title prefixed to the name of a man: a contracted form of *Mister.*

Mrs. (mis′iz) n. pl. **Mmes.** (mā·däm′) A title prefixed to the name of a married woman: a contracted form of *Mistress.*

Ms. (miz) n. pl. **Ms.'s** (miz′əz) A title prefixed to the name of a woman: a contracted form of *Mistress.*

MSG (em′es′jē′) n. Monosodium glutamate.

mu (myoo, moo) n. **1** The twelfth letter in the Greek alphabet (M, μ): equivalent to *m.* As a numeral it denotes 40. **2** The micron (symbol μ).

muc- Var. of MUCO-.

much (much) adj. **more, most 1** Great in quantity or amount. **2** *Obs.* Many in number. —n. **1** A considerable quantity. **2** A remarkable or important thing. —adv. **1** In a great degree. **2** For the most part; nearly. [ME *muchel,* OE *mycel*] —**much′ness** n.

mu·cic (myoo′sik) adj. *Chem.* Of, pertaining to, or designating a crystalline acid, $C_6H_{10}O_8$, formed by the oxidation of milk sugar, various gums, etc. [< F *mucique* < L *mucus* mucus]

mu·cid (myoo′sid) adj. Moldy; also, slimy; mucilaginous. [< L *mucidus* < *mucere* be moldy] —**mu′cid·ness** n.

mu·ci·lage (myoo′sə·lij) n. **1** A gummy or slimy substance obtained from the seeds, bark, or roots of various plants by infusion in water. **2** A solution of vegetable gum or mucus in water, especially when intended as an adhesive. [< F < LL *mucilago* < *mucere* be moldy, musty < *mucus* mucus]

mu·ci·lag·i·nous (myoo′si·laj′ə·nəs) adj. **1** Of, pertaining to, or like mucilage; soft, slimy, and viscid. **2** Producing mucilage, as glands. [< F *mucilagineux*] —**mu′ci·lag′i·nous·ness** n.

mu·cin (myoo′sin) n. *Biochem.* A glycoprotein secreted by the mucous membranes. [< F *mucine* < *mucus* mucus] —**mu′cin·ous** adj.

muck (muk) n. **1** Moist manure containing decomposed vegetable matter. **2** A nasty mess; filth. **3** Vegetable mold combined with earth. — v.t. **1** To fertilize with manure. **2** *Colloq.* To make dirty; pollute. **3** To remove muck from. [ME *muk* < Scand. Cf. ON *myki* dung, *moka* shovel manure.]

Muck (mook), **Karl,** 1859–1940, German conductor, active in the United States.

muck·er (muk′ər) n. *Brit. Slang* A coarse, rude person. [Cf. G *mucker* a low person]

muck·le (muk′əl) *Scot.* adj. Much. —n. A large quantity.

muck·rake (muk′rāk′) v.i. **·raked, ·rak·ing** To search for or expose real or alleged corruption on the part of political officials, businessmen, etc. [Back formation < MUCKRAKER, used in 1906 by President Theodore Roosevelt, in allusion to the "man with the muckrake" in Bunyan's *Pilgrim's Progress*] —**muck′rak′er** n. — **muck′rak′ing** n.

muck rake A rake used in collecting muck or dung.

muck·worm (muk′wûrm′) n. **1** The larva of a beetle (*Ligyrus gibbosus*) common in dung heaps. **2** *Slang* A miser.

muck·y (muk′ē) adj. **muck·i·er, muck·i·est** Foul; nasty. —**muck′i·ly** adv. —**muck′i·ness** n.

muco- *combining form* Mucus; mucus and: *mucopurulent:* also, before vowels, *muc-.* Also **muci-.** [< L *mucus* mucus]

mu·coid (myoo′koid) adj. Like mucus. —n. *Biochem.* A compound glycoprotein similar to mucin, found in connective tissue, in cysts, in the vitreous humor, etc. [< MUC- + -OID]

mu·co·pro·te·in (myoo′kō·prō′tē·in, -tēn) n. *Biochem.* A glycoprotein combining a protein with a carbohydrate group.

mu·co·pu·ru·lent (myoo′kō·pyoor′ə·lənt, -yə·lənt) adj. Relating to or consisting of both mucus and purulent matter.

Mu·co·ra·les (myoo′kō·rā′lēz) n. pl. An order of fungi (class *Phycomycetes*) which includes several mold species, as the common bread mold. [< NL]

mu·co·sa (myoo·kō′sə) n. pl. **·sae** (-sē) *Anat.* A mucous membrane. [< NL, fem. of L *mucosus* mucous] —**mu·co′sal** adj.

mu·cous (myoo′kəs) adj. **1** Secreting mucus. **2** Pertaining to or resembling mucus. Also **mu′cose** (-kōs). [< L *mucosus* slimy < *mucus*] — **mu·cos′i·ty** (-kos′ə·tē) n.

mucous membrane *Anat.* A membrane secreting or producing mucus, that lines passages communicating with the exterior, as the alimentary canal, air passages, etc.

mu·cro (myoo′krō) n. pl. **mu·cro·nes** (myoo·krō′nēz) *Biol.* A small, sharp process or part, as the point of a leaf; a spine. [< NL < L, point of a sword]

mu·cro·nate (myoo′krə·nāt) adj. *Biol.* Having a short, straight point, as a leaf, feather, etc.: also **mu′cro·nat·ed.** [< L *mucronatus* < *mucro* point of a sword]

mu·cus (myoo′kəs) n. **1** *Biol.* A viscid animal substance, as that secreted by the mucous membranes. **2** *Bot.* A gummy substance in plants. [< L]

mud (mud) n. **1** Wet and sticky earth; mire. **2** *Colloq.* Slander; abuse; detraction of character: to sling *mud* at someone. —v.t. **mud·ded, mud·ding** To soil or cover with mud. [? < MLG *mudde*]

mud boat 1 A scow or barge used in dredging: also **mud scow. 2** A kind of low sledge with wide runners used for hauling logs over swampy ground.

mud·cap (mud′kap′) v.t. **·capped, ·cap·ping 1** To cap with mud. **2** To cover (a charge of high explosive) with mud before detonating it above an exposed mass of rock. —**mud′cap′ping** n.

mud·cat (mud′kat′) n. A large catfish of the Mississippi valley.

mud dauber 1 Any of various wasps (family *Sphecidae*) that build mud cells in which their larvae develop. For illustration see INSECTS (beneficial). **2** A swallow that builds a nest of mud.

mud·dle (mud′l) v. **·dled, ·dling** v.t. **1** To mix in confusion; jumble. **2** To confuse mentally; bewilder. **3** To make muddy or turbid; roil. **4** To stir or mix, as a drink. —v.i. **5** To act in a con-

fused or ineffective manner. —**to muddle through** *Brit.* To achieve one's object despite one's own confusion and mistakes; succeed despite oneself. —n. **1** A muddy or dirty condition. **2** A mixed or confused condition, as of the mind; a mess. [< MUD + freq. suffix]

mud·dle·head·ed (mud′l·hed′id) adj. Mentally confused; addle-brained.

mud·dler (mud′lər) n. **1** A stick for churning or stirring liquids. **2** One who muddles.

mud drum An enclosed container placed at the bottom of any manufacturing or power apparatus, as a boiler, for the purpose of collecting insoluble waste matter, sludge, etc.

mud·dy (mud′ē) adj. **·di·er, ·di·est 1** Bespattered with mud; turbid. **2** Mentally confused. **3** Consisting of mud; earthy; gross; impure. **4** Dull; cloudy: a *muddy* complexion, *muddy* weather. See synonyms under FOUL, THICK. —v.t. & v.i. **·died, ·dy·ing** To become or cause to become muddy. —**mud′di·ly** adv. —**mud′di·ness** n.

mud eel An eel-shaped amphibian having very small forelegs and no hind legs, that buries itself in the mud; especially, *Siren lacertina* of the swamps of the southern United States: also called *congo* and *siren.*

mud·fish (mud′fish′) n. pl. **·fish** or **·fish·es** Any of various fishes that inhabit stagnant or muddy water, as the bowfin, killifish, etc.

mud flat A low-lying strip of ground covered with mud, especially one between high and low tide.

mud·guard (mud′gärd′) n. A guard over the wheel of a vehicle to protect from splashing mud.

mud hen 1 The American coot (*Fulica americana*). **2** The Florida gallinule (*Gallenula chloropus*). **3** The clapper rail. See under RAIL[2].

mud·lark (mud′lärk′) n. *Brit. Colloq.* One who works or dabbles in mud; a street urchin.

mud·pot (mud′pot′) n. A geyser which ejects mud. Also **mud geyser.**

mud·pup·py (mud′pup′ē) n. pl. **·pies 1** The hellbender. **2** A tailed amphibian with bushy, persistent, external gills, especially *Necturus maculosus,* found in the large lakes of North America.

MUDPUPPY
(From 12 to 17 inches long)

mud·sill (mud′sil′) n. **1** The foundation timber of a structure placed directly on the ground. **2** *U.S. Dial.* A person of low social state or condition.

mud·sling·ing (mud′sling′ing) n. The practice of casting malicious slurs at an opponent, especially in a political campaign. —**mud′sling′er** n.

mud·stone (mud′stōn′) n. A gray, sandy shale that readily decomposes into mud.

mud·suck·er (mud′suk′ər) n. A California fish related to the goby (*Gillichthys mirabilis*), much used as bait.

mud turtle Any of various turtles inhabiting muddy rivers in different parts of the world, especially the small common variety of the United States (genus *Kinosternon*).

mu·ez·zin (myoo·ez′in) n. In Moslem countries, a crier from a minaret or other part of the mosque who calls the faithful to prayer. Also **mu·ed′din** (-ed′in). [< Arabic *mu′adhdhin* < *adhana* call]

muff[1] (muf) v.t. & v.i. **1** To perform (some act) clumsily; blunder. **2** In baseball, to fail to hold (the ball) in attempting a catch. —n. **1** A bungling action; in baseball, etc., a failure to catch the ball. **2** A bungler. **3** A stupid fellow; dolt. [Origin unknown]

muff[2] (muf) n. A covering of fur or cloth, usually cylindrical, into which the hands are thrust from opposite ends to keep them warm. [< Du. *mof* < F *moufle*]

muf·fin (muf′in) n. A light, quick bread, baked in small cup-shaped tins, and usually eaten hot with butter; also, a small, flat yeast bread: also called *English muffin.* [Origin uncertain. Cf. OF *moufflet* soft (bread).]

---

muf·fin·eer (muf'in·ir') **1** A metal cruet with a perforated top for sprinkling salt or sugar on muffins. **2** A covered dish to keep muffins, etc., hot.

muffin stand A small tiered stand used in tea service for holding and passing cakes, sandwiches, etc.

muf·fle (muf'əl) *v.t.* **·fled**, **·fling** **1** To wrap up in a blanket, scarf, etc., as for warmth or concealment. **2** To prevent from seeing, hearing, or speaking by wrapping the head. **3** To deaden the sound of by or as by wrapping: to *muffle* a cry. **4** To deaden (a sound). — *n.* **1** Something used for muffling. **2** A clay oven for firing pottery without direct exposure to flame. **3** The naked upper lip and nose of ruminants and certain other mammals. [<OF *moufle* heavy leather or fur mitten]

muf·fler (muf'lər) *n.* **1** Anything used for wrapping up or muffling; specifically, a scarf worn about the neck; also, a veil or scarf worn by women. **2** A device to reduce noise, as from the exhaust of an internal–combustion engine. **3** A mitten. [<MUFFLE]

muf·ti¹ (muf'tē) *n.* In Moslem countries, an expounder of religious law. [<Arabic <*āftá* expound the law]

muf·ti² (muf'tē) *n.* Civilian dress; plain clothes, especially when worn by one who normally wears a uniform. [<MUFTI¹; prob. from the fact that a mufti is a civil official]

mug¹ (mug) *n.* **1** A drinking cup, usually cylindrical, with a handle and no lip. **2** That which is contained in a mug. [Cf. Sw. *mugg*, Norw. *mugga*]

mug² (mug) *Slang n.* **1** The human face or mouth. **2** A grimace. **3** A photograph of the face of a suspect: also **mug shot. 4** A criminal. — *v.* **mugged, mug·ging** *v.t.* **1** To photograph (someone), especially for official purposes. **2** To assault, usually with the intent to rob. — *v.i.* **3** To make faces; grimace. [<MUG¹; prob. from the fact that drinking mugs were often shaped to resemble a face] — **mug'ger** *n.*

mug·ger (mug'ər) *n.* A crocodile (*Crocodilus palustris*) of India and the East Indies, with a broad snout: it grows to a length of about 12 feet. Also **mug'gar, mug'gur.** [<Hind. *magar* <Skt. *makara* sea monster]

mug·ging (mug'ing) *n.* *Slang* Assault, often with the intention of robbery, usually by attacking the victim from behind and locking an arm around his throat. [<MUG²]

mug·gins (mug'inz) *n.* **1** One of several card games in which exposed cards are matched or suits are built. **2** A variant in the game of dominoes. **3** *Brit. Slang* A foolish person. [Prob. < *Muggins*, a surname used in arbitrary allusion to *mug* (slang) a card-sharper's dupe]

mug·gy (mug'ē) *adj.* **·gi·er, ·gi·est** Warm, moist, and close; sultry. [<dial. E *mug* drizzle, prob. <ON *mugga* drizzling mist] — **mug'gi·ness** *n.*

mug·wort (mug'wûrt') *n.* An aromatic bitter herb (*Artemisia vulgaris*) of the composite family, sometimes used in folk medicine as a diaphoretic and emmenagog.

mug·wump (mug'wump) *n.* *U.S.* **1** A Republican who bolted the party candidate, James G. Blaine, in the presidential election of 1884. **2** Anyone who claims the right of independent action, especially in politics; an independent. [<Algonquian *mugquomp* great man, chief] — **mug'wump·er·y, mug'wump·ism** *n.*

Mu·ham·ma·dan (moo·ham'ə·dən), etc. See MOHAMMEDAN, etc.

Mu·har·ram (moo·har'əm) *n.* A Mohammedan month; also, the first ten days of the month, a period of lamentation. See CALENDAR (Mohammedan). Also spelled *Moharran.* [<Arabic *muharram* sacred, the first month of the year]

Mühl·bach (mül'bäkh), **Luise** Pen name of *Klara Mundt,* 1814–73, German novelist.

Muh·len·berg (myoo'lən·bûrg), **Frederick Augustus Conrad,** 1750–1801, American politician and clergyman; member of the Continental Congress. — **John Peter,** 1746–1807, American Revolutionary general.

Müh·len·berg (myoo'lən·bûrg, *Ger.* mü'lən·berkh), **Heinrich,** 1711–87, German clergyman, chief founder of Lutheranism in the United States.

muh·ly grass (myoo'lē) Any of a genus (*Muhlenbergia*) of mostly perennial, wiry grasses growing in the SW United States and Mexico, as the **ring muhly** (*M. torreyi*), and **spike muhly** (*M. wrighti*), valued as forage plants for livestock. [after Dr. G. H. E. *Muhlenberg,* 1753–1815, American botanist]

Mu·hu (moo'hoo) An Estonian island in the Baltic; 79 square miles. Also *Russian* **Mu·khu** (moo'khoo).

muir (myoor) *n. Scot.* A moor; heath.

Muir (myoor), **John,** 1838–1914, U.S. naturalist.

mu·i·ra·pu·a·ma (moo·ē'rä·poo·ä'mä) *n.* The dried stems and roots of a Brazilian plant (*Liriosma ovata*), reputed to have properties as a nerve stimulant and aphrodisiac. [<Pg. <Tupian]

Muir Glacier (myoor) A glacier in the St. Elias Mountains, Alaska; 350 square miles.

mu·jik (moo·zhēk', moo'zhik) See MUZHIK.

Muk·den (mook'den', mook'dən, mook'-) Former name of SHENYANG.

Mu·ker·ji (moo'ker·jē'), **Dhan Gopal,** 1890–1936, East Indian writer, active in the United States.

muk·luk (muk'luk) *n.* **1** An Alaskan Eskimo boot of seal or other animal skin, made so that the fur is inside. **2** *pl.* Sport or lounging shoes of the soft moccasin type. [<Alaskan Eskimo *makliak, muklok* large seal]

mu·la·da (moo·lä'thä) *n. SW U.S.* A drove of mules.

mu·lat·to (mə·lat'ō, myoo-, -lä'tō) *n. pl.* **·toes** A person having one white and one Negro parent; loosely, anyone having white and Negro blood. — *adj.* **1** Of or pertaining to a person of such descent. **2** Of a light-brown color. [<Sp. *mulato* of mixed breed < *mulo* mule <L *mulus*]

mul·ber·ry (mul'ber'ē, -bər·ē) *n. pl.* **·ries** **1** The edible, berrylike fruit of a tree (genus *Morus*) whose leaves are valued for silkworm culture, especially the white mulberry (*M. alba*). **2** A deep purplish-red, the color of a mulberry. [ME *mulberie,* dissimilated var. of *murberie,* OE *morberie* <L *morum* mulberry + OE *berie* a berry]

mulberry body The morula.

mulch (mulch) *n.* Any loose material, as straw, placed about the stalks of plants to protect their roots. — *v.t.* To cover with mulch. [ME *molsh.* Cf. dial. *G molsch* soft, decaying.]

mulct (mulkt) *v.t.* **1** To punish (a person) by a fine or penalty. **2** To deprive of something fraudulently or deceitfully; cheat. — *n.* A fine, or similar penalty. [<L *mulctare* < *mulcta, multa* a fine]

mule¹ (myool) *n.* **1** A hybrid between the ass and horse, especially between a jackass and a mare, as distinguished from a hinny. **2** Any hybrid or cross, especially one that is sterile. **3** A spinning machine which draws, stretches, and twists at one operation: also called *spinning mule, jenny, spinning jenny:* also **mule'-jen'ny** (-jen'ē). **4** A person having the stubborn qualities of a mule. **5** A small electric engine or tractor for towing canal boats. [<F <L *mulus*]

mule² (myool) *n.* A backless lounging slipper. [<MF <L *mulleus* red slipper]

mule deer The black-tailed deer (genus *Odocoileus*), of the western United States, having long ears.

mule–driv·er (myool'drī'vər) *n.* One who drives mules.

mule–skin·ner (myool'skin'ər) *n. U.S. Colloq.* A mule-driver.

mu·le·teer (myoo'lə·tir') *n.* A mule-driver. [<F *muletier* < *mulet* mule]

mule train A train of mules carrying packs; also, a train of heavy freight wagons drawn by mules.

mu·ley (myoo'lē, mool'ē, moo'lē) *adj.* Hornless: said of cattle. — *n.* A hornless cow. Also spelled *mooley, mulley.* [<Irish *maol, moile* hornless, dismantled]

Mul·ha·cén (moo'lä·thän') A mountain in SE Spain, in the Sierra Nevada; the highest peak in Spain; 11,411 feet. Also **Mu·ley–Ha·cén** (moo·lä'ä·thän').

Mül·heim–an–der–Ruhr (mül'hīm–än·dər–roor') A city on the Ruhr in western North Rhine-Westphalia, West Germany. Also **Mül'heim.**

Mul·house (mül·ōoz') A city in eastern France near the German border. *German* **Mül·hau·sen** (mül'hou·zən).

mu·li·eb·ri·ty (myoo'lē·eb'rə·tē) *n.* The state of being a woman; womanliness. [<LL *muliebris* womanly < *mulier* woman]

mul·ish (myoo'lish) *adj.* Resembling a mule; stubborn. See synonyms under OBSTINATE. — **mul'ish·ly** *adv.* — **mul'ish·ness** *n.*

mull¹ (mul) *v.t.* To heat and spice, as wine or beer. [<MULSE]

mull² (mul) *v.t.* To ponder; cogitate: usually with *over.* [<obs. *mull* grind, OE *myl* dust]

mull³ (mul) *n.* **1** A thin, soft, cotton, rayon, or silk dress goods. **2** A variety of soft, thin muslin used as a base for medicated ointments, as mulla. [Short for *mulmull* <Hind. *malmal.*]

mull⁴ (mul) *n.* A horn snuffbox. [Var. of *mill* (in a Scottish use); orig., a snuffbox in which tobacco could be ground to a powder by a mechanism]

Mull (mul) An island in NW Argyllshire, Scotland, the largest of the Inner Hebrides; 351 square miles.

mul·la (mul'ə) *n. Med.* An ointment having a base of lard and salt, spread on a piece of mull.

mul·lah (mul'ə, mool'ə) See MOLLAH.

mul·len (mul'ən) *n.* **1** A tall, stout, woolly herb (*Verbascum thapsus*) of the figwort family, the **great mullen. 2** Any plant of the same genus, as the **moth mullen** (*V. blattaria*). Also **mul'lein.** [<AF *moleine* <OF *mol* soft <L *mollis*]

mull·er (mul'ər) *n.* **1** A pestlelike implement with which to mix paints. **2** A mechanical pulverizer or grinder. [<obs. *mull* pulverize, OE *myl* dust]

Mul·ler (mul'ər), **Hermann Joseph,** born 1890, U.S. geneticist.

Mül·ler (mül'ər), **(Friedrich) Max,** 1823–1900, English philologist and Orientalist born in Germany. — **Johannes Peter,** 1801–58, German physiologist.

mul·let¹ (mul'it) *n. pl.* **·lets** or **·let** **1** A food fish (family *Mugilidae*), usually greenish or copper-colored, with silvery sides, found on warm coasts. *Mugil cephalus* is the **striped mullet** of both coasts of the Atlantic. **2** A food fish (family *Mullidae*): often called *surmullet. Mullus barbatus* is the highly esteemed European **red mullet.** [<OF *mulet* <L *mullus* red mullet]

mul·let² (mul'it) *n. Her.* A star of five or more points. [<OF *molette* rowel]

mul·let–head (mul'it·hed') *n.* A fresh-water fish having a flat head.

mul·let–head·ed (mul'it·hed'id) *adj. Slang* Stupid.

mul·ley (mool'ē, moo'lē) See MULEY.

mul·li·gan (mul'i·gən) *n. Slang* **1** A stew, originally made by tramps, composed of odds and ends of food: also **mulligan stew. 2** In golf, an extra shot, especially a tee shot, after an inept first shot. [< *Mulligan,* Irish surname]

mul·li·ga·taw·ny (mul'i·gə·tô'nē) *n.* A strongly flavored soup of meat and curry. [<Tamil *milagu–tannīr* pepper water]

mul·li·grubs (mul'ə·grubz) *n. Slang* An acute colicky pain; colic; hence, the blues. [A grotesque arbitrary formation]

Mul·lin·gar (mul'in·gär') The county town of Westmeath, Ireland.

mul·lion (mul'yən) *n. Archit.* A vertical dividing piece between window lights or panels. — *v.t.* To furnish with or divide by means of mullions. [Prob. metathetic var. of earlier *monial* <OF *moinel, monial;* ult. origin unknown] — **mul'lioned** *adj.*

mul·lock (mul'ək) *n.* An accumulation of waste rock about a mine; refuse earth; a waste dump. [< obs. *mull* dust + -OCK] — **mul'lock·y** *adj.*

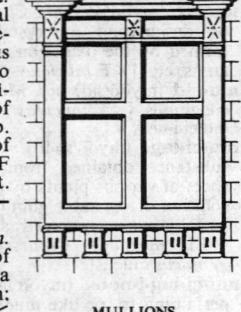

MULLIONS

Mu·lock (myoo'lok), **Miss** See CRAIK, DINAH MARIA.

mulse (muls) *n.* Wine heated and sweetened. [<L *mulsum,* pp. of *mulcere* sweeten]

Mul·tan (mool·tän') A city in southern Punjab, West Pakistan.

multi– *combining form* **1** Much; many; consisting of many; as in:

multiangular	multilobed
multiareolate	multilobular
multiarticulate	multilobulate
multiarticulated	multimedial
multiaxial	multimetallic
multiblade	multimillion
multibladed	multimolecular
multibranchiate	multination
multicamerate	multinational
multicapital	multinervate
multicapitate	multinodal
multicapsular	multinodous
multicarinate	multinodular
multicellular	multiovular
multicentral	multiovulate
multicentric	multipartisan
multicharge	multiperforate
multichord	multiperforated
multichrome	multipersonal
multiciliate	multipinnate
multiciliated	multipointed
multicircuit	multipolar
multicoil	multiracial
multicolor	multiradial
multiconductor	multiradiate
multicore	multiradicate
multicourse	multiramified
multicrystalline	multiramose
multidenominational	multiramous
multidentate	multirate
multidenticulate	multireflex
multidenticulated	multirooted
multidigitate	multisaccate
multidimensional	multisacculate
multidirectional	multisegmental
multidisciplinary	multisensitivity
multiethnic	multiseptate
multifaced	multiserial
multifaceted	multiserially
multifactorial	multiseriate
multiflagellate	multishot
multiflorous	multispermous
multiflue	multispicular
multifocal	multispiculate
multifoliate	multispindle
multifurcate	multispinous
multigranulate	multispiral
multigyrate	multispired
multihead	multistaminate
multihearth	multistoried
multihued	multistratified
multi–infection	multistriate
multijet	multisulcate
multilamellar	multisulcated
multilaminar	multisyllable
multilaminate	multiterminal
multilaminated	multititular
multilevel	multitoed
multilighted	multituberculate
multilineal	multituberculated
multilinear	multitubular
multilingual	multivaned
multilobar	multivoiced
multilobate	multivolumed

2 Having more than two (or sometimes, more than one); as in:

multicostate	multimammae
multicuspid	multimammate
multicuspidate	multimotor
multicylinder	multinuclear
multielectrode	multinucleate
multiengine	multinucleolar
multiexhaust	multinucleolate
multiflow	multispeed

3 Many times over: *multimillionare.* **4** *Med.* Affecting many; as in:

multiarticular	multiganglionic
multifamilial	multiglandular

Also, before vowels, sometimes **mult–**. [< L *multus* much]

mul·ti·cip·i·tal (mul'ti·sip'ə·təl) *adj. Bot.* Many–headed: said of plants with many stems from one root. [<MULTI– + L *caput* head]

mul·ti·col·ored (mul'ti·kul'ərd) *adj.* Exhibiting or made up of many colors.

mul·ti·far·i·ous (mul'tə·fâr'ē·əs) *adj.* Having great diversity or variety. [< L *multifarius*] — **mul'ti·far'i·ous·ly** *adv.* — **mul'ti·far'i·ous·ness** *n.*

mul·ti·fid (mul'tə·fid) *adj. Bot.* Cut into many lobes or segments, as a leaf. Also **mul·tif·i·dous** (mul·tif'ə·dəs). [<MULTI– + -FID]

mul·ti·foil (mul'tə·foil) *n. Geom.* A plane figure made of the congruent arcs of circles which are symmetrically arranged along the sides of a regular polygon.

mul·ti·fold (mul'tə·fōld) *adj.* Many times doubled; manifold.

mul·ti·form (mul'tə·fôrm) *adj.* Having many forms, shapes, or appearances. See synonyms under COMPLEX. [< L *multiformis*] — **mul'ti·form'i·ty** *n.*

Mul·ti·graph (mul'tə·graf, -gräf) *n.* A typesetting and printing machine in which the type is moved from a typesetting drum to a printing chamber: a trade name.

mul·ti·lat·er·al (mul'ti·lat'ər·əl) *adj.* **1** Having many sides. **2** *Govt.* Involving more than two nations: a *multilateral* trade agreement.

mul·ti·me·di·a (mul'ti·mē'dē·ə) *adj.* Relating to or using two or more media, especially a combination apprehended by different senses, as sight and hearing.

mul·ti·mil·lion·aire (mul'ti·mil'yən·âr') *n.* A person having a fortune of several or many millions of dollars, pounds, francs, etc.

mul·ti·no·mi·al (mul'ti·nō'mē·əl) *adj.* Polynomial. [<MULTI– + (BI)NOMIAL]

mul·tip·a·ra (mul·tip'ə·rə) *n. pl.* **·rae** (-rē) A woman who has borne more than one child, or who is parturient the second time. [<NL < L *multiparus*]

mul·tip·a·rous (mul·tip'ə·rəs) *adj.* **1** Giving birth to many at one time. **2** Having borne more than one child. [<MULTI– + -PAROUS]

mul·ti·par·tite (mul'ti·pär'tīt) *adj.* **1** Divided into many parts. **2** *Govt.* Multilateral (def. 2).

mul·ti·pede (mul'tə·pēd) *n.* A many–footed animal or insect. — *adj.* Having many feet. Also **mul'ti·ped** (-ped).

mul·ti·phase (mul'tə·fāz) *adj.* Polyphase.

mul·ti·plane (mul'tə·plān) *n. Aeron.* An airplane with two or more supporting surfaces, one above another.

mul·ti·ple (mul'tə·pəl) *adj.* **1** Containing or consisting of more than one; repeated more than once; manifold. **2** *Electr.* Having two or more conductors or pieces of apparatus, such as lamps, connected in parallel: a *multiple* circuit. — *n. Math.* The product of a given number and its factor. — **common multiple** Any number which is exactly divisible by two or more numbers, not including itself. — **lowest common multiple** The smallest number divisible by each of two or more numbers: 12 is the *least common multiple* of 2, 3, 4, and 6: often abbr. *L.C.M.* Also **least common multiple.** [<F < L *multiplex*]

multiple allele *Genetics* One of three or more alleles, only two of which may pass from the parents to a normal diploid offspring.

multiple factors *Genetics* Two or more distinct genes which are believed to act as a unit or with cumulative effect in the transmission of certain plant and animal characteristics, as size, pigmentation, color of eyes, etc.

multiple fruit *Bot.* A fruit consisting of numerous smaller fruits, each developed from a single flower, as the pineapple: also called *collective fruit.*

multiple myeloma *Pathol.* A malignant tumor of the bone marrow occurring at numerous sites.

multiple neuritis *Pathol.* Neuritis involving several nerves simultaneously.

multiple sclerosis *Pathol.* Sclerosis occurring in patches in the brain or spinal cord or both, and characterized by tremors, failure of coordination, and various nervous and mental symptoms.

multiple star *Astron.* A system of three or more stars revolving around a common gravitational center.

mul·ti·plet (mul'tə·plit) *n. Physics* Two or more spectral lines very close together in an atomic spectrum and associated with different energy characteristics of the atom. [<MULTIPLE]

mul·ti·plex (mul'tə·pleks) *adj.* **1** Multiple; manifold. **2** *Telecom.* Designating a system for the simultaneous transmission of two or more messages in either or both directions over the same wire, as in telegraphy or te-

lephony. **3** *Phot.* Designating a method based upon the stereoscopic principle: three cameras are used, together with auxiliary equipment designed to facilitate the construction of accurate maps. — *v.t. & v.i. Telecom.* To send (two or more messages) at the same time over the same wire. [<L <*multus* much + stem of *plicare* fold]

mul·ti·pli·cand (mul'tə·plə·kand') *n.* A number multiplied, or to be multiplied, by another. [<L *multiplicandus* to be multiplied, gerundive of *multiplicare*. See MULTIPLY.]

mul·ti·pli·cate (mul'tə·plə·kāt) *adj.* Consisting of or being many or more than one. [<L *multiplicatus*, pp. of *multiplicare* multiply]

mul·ti·pli·ca·tion (mul'tə·plə·kā'shən) *n.* **1** The process of multiplying. **2** The process of finding the sum (the *product*) of a number (the *multiplicand*) repeated a given number of times (the *multiplier*). Opposed to *division.* [<OF < L *multiplicatio, -onis*]

mul·ti·pli·ca·tive (mul'tə·plə·kā'tiv) *adj.* Tending to multiply; indicating multiplication. — **mul'ti·pli·ca'tive·ly** *adv.*

mul·ti·plic·i·ty (mul'tə·plis'ə·tē) *n.* The condition of being manifold or various; hence, a large number. [<LL *multiplicitas, -tatis* <L *multiplex*]

mul·ti·pli·er (mul'tə·plī'ər) *n.* **1** One who or that which multiplies or increases in quantity, or causes something else to multiply or increase. **2** *Math.* The number by which a quantity is multiplied. **3** *Physics* An instrument or mechanical device for increasing or intensifying an effect. **4** *Electr.* An open spiral coil in a wireless telegraph receiver which has the effect of exalting the potential oscillations.

mul·ti·ply (mul'tə·plī) *v.* **·plied, ·ply·ing** *v.t.* **1** To increase the quantity, amount, or degree of; make more numerous. **2** *Math.* To perform the operation of multiplication upon. — *v.i.* **3** To become more in number, amount, or degree; increase. **4** *Math.* To perform the operation of multiplication. See synonyms under PROPAGATE. — *adv.* So as to be numerous; in many ways. [<OF *multiplier* <L *multiplicare* < *multiplex*. See MULTIPLEX.] — **mul'ti·pli'a·ble** *adj.*

mul·ti·pro·pel·lant (mul'ti·prə·pel'ənt) *n.* A rocket propellant consisting of two or more chemicals separately fed into the combustion chamber. — *adj.* Of or pertaining to such a propellant.

mul·ti·pur·pose (mul'ti·pûr'pəs) *adj.* Adapted to more than one use or type of service.

mul·ti·range (mul'tə·rānj) *adj.* Having a wide range of operations or performance, as certain precision instruments.

mul·ti·sec·tion (mul'ti·sek'shən) *adj.* Having or occupying more than one section.

mul·ti·stage (mul'tə·stāj) *adj.* **1** Having or characterized by a number of definite stages in the completion of a process or action. **2** Having several sections, each of which fulfils a given task before burnout: said especially of a rocket or ballistic missile.

mul·ti·tude (mul'tə·tōōd, -tyōōd) *n.* **1** The state of being many or numerous. **2** A large gathering; concourse. **3** A large number of things. See synonyms under ARMY, ASSEMBLY, COMPANY, THRONG. — **the multitude** The common people. [<OF < L *multitudo* <*multus* much, many]

mul·ti·tu·di·nous (mul'tə·tōō'də·nəs, -tyōō'-) *adj.* Consisting of a vast number. See synonyms under MANY. [<L *multitudo, -inis* + crowd + -OUS] — **mul'ti·tu'di·nous·ly** *adv.* — **mul'ti·tu'di·nous·ness** *n.*

mul·ti·va·lent (mul'ti·vā'lənt) *adj. Chem.* Having three or more valences. — **mul'ti·va'lence** *n.*

mul·ti·valve (mul'tə·valv) *n.* A shell with many valves. — *adv.* Having many valves. — **mul'·ti·val'vu·lar** (-val'vyə·lər) *adj.*

mul·ti·verse (mul'tə·vûrs) *n. Philos.* The plurality of worlds as conceived in or projected by the mind: contrasted with *universe.* [<MULTI– + (UNI)VERSE]

mul·ti·ver·si·ty (mul'ti·vûr'sə·tē) *n. pl.* **·ties** A very large university with a student enrollment of many thousands, offering instruction and graduate study in many fields and often on a number of campuses. [< MULTI– + (UNI)VERSITY]

mul·tiv·o·cal (mul·tiv'ə·kəl) *adj.* Having various meanings. —*n.* A word that has more than one signification. [< MULTI- + VOCAL]

mul·ti·vol·tine (mul'ti·vol'tin, -tēn) *adj. Entomol.* Having many broods of offspring in a year, as certain insects. [< MULTI- + Ital. *volta* turn]

Mult·no·mah Falls (mult·nō'mə) A waterfall in NW Oregon in a small tributary of the Columbia River; about 850 feet high.

mul·toc·u·lar (mul·tok'yə·lər) *adj.* 1 Having two or more eyes. 2 Having eyes divisible, like those of a fly, into facets. [< MULT(I)- + OCULAR]

mul·tum in par·vo (mul'təm in pär'vō) *Latin* Much in little.

mul·ture (mul'chər) *n.* 1 A grinding of grain. 2 The grain ground or the toll paid for the grinding. [< OF *moulture* < Med. L *molitura* < L *molere* grind]

mum[1] (mum) *v.i.* mummed, mum·ming *Obs.* To be silent. —*adj.* Silent; saying nothing. —*n.* Silence; *Mum's* the word. —*interj.* Hush! Be quiet! [Imit.]

mum[2] (mum) *v.i.* mummed, mum·ming To play or act in a mask, as at Christmas; be a mummer. Also **mumm.** [< MUM[1]. Cf. MDu. *mommen* mask, OF *momer* act in a dumb show.]

mum[3] (mum) *n.* A strong sweet beer, first brewed in Germany by Christian Mumme, 1492.

mum[4] (mum) Corruption of MADAM, MA'AM.

mum[5] (mum) *n. Colloq.* A chrysanthemum.

mum·ble (mum'bəl) *v.t. & v.i.* ·bled, ·bling 1 To speak or utter in low, indistinct tones; mutter. 2 *Rare* To chew slowly and ineffectively, as with toothless gums. —*n.* A low, mumbling speech; mutter. [ME *momelen*, freq. of obs. *mum* make inarticulate sounds. Cf. G *mummeln*.] — **mum'bler** *n.* —**mum'bling** *adj.* —**mum'bling·ly** *adv.*

mum·ble-the-peg (mum'bəl·thə·peg') *n.* A boy's game played with a jackknife, which is tossed and flipped in various ways so as to stick into the ground: so called because the player who failed was originally required to draw a peg out of the ground with his teeth. Also **mum'ble-peg'**, **mum·ble·ty-peg** (mum'bəl·tē·peg'). [< MUMBLE. *v.* (def. 2) + PEG]

mum·bo jum·bo (mum'bō jum'bō) 1 Any object of superstitious homage; a fetish. 2 Incantation. [< MUMBO JUMBO]

Mum·bo Jum·bo (mum'bō jum'bō) Among certain tribes of the western Sudan, a village god or presiding genius, who protects the village from evil and terrifies the women and keeps them in subjection. [< Mandingo *mama dyambo*]

mu·mes·on (myoo'mes'on, -mē'son) *n. Physics.* A muon. [< MU + MESON]

mum·mer (mum'ər) *n.* 1 One who acts or makes sport in a mask. 2 An actor.

mum·mer·y (mum'ər·ē) *n. pl.* ·mer·ies 1 A masked performance. 2 Hypocritical parade of ritual. [< MF *mommerie* dumb show]

mum·mi·fy (mum'ə·fī) *v.* ·fied, ·fy·ing *v.t.* To make a mummy; preserve by drying. —*v.i.* To dry up; shrivel. Also **mummy**. [< F *momifier* < Med. L *mumia* < Arabic *mūmiyā* < Persian *mūm* wax] —**mum'mi·form** *adj.* —**mum'mi·fi·ca'tion** *n.*

mum·my (mum'ē) *n. pl.* ·mies 1 A body embalmed in the ancient Egyptian manner; also, any dead body which is very well preserved. 2 A person or thing that is dried up and withered. 3 *Obs.* The dried flesh of mummies; dead meat. —*v.t. & v.i.* ·mied, ·my·ing To mummify. [< F *momie* < Med. L *mumia* < Arabic *mūmiyā* < Persian *mūm* wax] —**mum'mi·form** *adj.*

mummy cloth 1 The fabric in which a mummy is enwrapped. 2 A crêpelike fabric of cotton, silk, rayon, or wool.

mump·ish (mum'pish) *adj.* Sullen; sulky; morose; petulant. [< obs. *mump* mutter, ? < Du. *mompelen* mumble]

mumps (mumps) *n. pl. (construed as singular) Pathol.* An acute, contagious, febrile disease of viral origin, characterized by inflammation and swelling of the facial glands, and occasionally of the ovaries and testicles: also called *parotitis*. [Pl. of obs. *mump* grimace.]

mun[1] (mun) *n. Brit. Dial.* Man.

mun[2] (mun, moon) *v. Scot. & Brit. Dial.* Must.

Mu·na (moo'nə) An Indonesian island SE of Celebes; 659 square miles. *Dutch* **Moe·na** (moo'nə).

munch (munch) *v.t. & v.i.* To chew steadily

and noisily. [ME *monchen, manchen*. Prob. ult. imit.] —**munch'er** *n.*

Mun·chau·sen (mun·chô'zən, mun'chou'zən), **Baron**, 1720–97, Hanoverian nobleman, whose extravagant stories of his exploits formed the basis of the *Tales of Munchausen*, collected by Rudolf Erich Raspe. Also **Münch·hau·sen** (münkh'hou'zən). —**Mun·chau'sen·ism** *n.*

Mün·chen-Glad·bach (mün'khən gläd'bäkh) A city in central western North Rhine-Westphalia, West Germany; the twin city of Rheydt.

Mun·cie (mun'sē) A city in central Indiana.

Mun·da (moon'də) *n.* A subfamily of the Austro-Asiatic family of languages, spoken in central India and along the southern slope of the Himalayas.

mun·dane (mun'dān, mun·dān') *adj.* Pertaining to the world; worldly. [< F *mondain* < L *mundanus* < *mundus* world] —**mun'dane·ly** *adv.* —**mun'dane·ness** *n.*

Mun·de·lein (mun'də·līn), **George William**, 1872–1939, U.S. cardinal.

mun·dic (mun'dik) *n. Brit. Dial.* Pyrite. [? < Celtic (Cornish) *maen tag* pretty stone]

mun·dun·go (mun·dung'gō) *n. Archaic* A black malodorous tobacco. Also **mun·dun'gus**. [Jocular alter. of Sp. *mondongo* tripe]

mun·go (mung'gō) *n.* The waste produced from hard-spun or felted cloth. Compare SHODDY. [? < *mung*, var. of obs. *mong* mixture]

mun·goose (mung'goos) See MONGOOSE.

Mu·nich (myoo'nik) A city on the Isar, capital of Bavaria, SE West Germany. *German* **Mün·chen** (mün'khən).

mu·nic·i·pal (myoo·nis'ə·pəl) *adj.* 1 Pertaining to a town or city or its local government; also, having local self-government. 2 Pertaining to the internal government of a state or nation. [< L *municipalis* < *municipium* town possessing right of self-government < *municeps* free citizens < *munia* official duties + *capere* take] —**mu·nic'i·pal·ly** *adv.*

municipal borough See under BOROUGH.

municipal corporation An incorporated town.

mu·nic·i·pal·ism (myoo·nis'ə·pəl·iz'əm) *n.* Municipal government as opposed to central government; also, the theory of this.—**mu·nic'i·pal·ist** *n.*

mu·nic·i·pal·i·ty (myoo·nis'ə·pal'ə·tē) *n. pl.* ·ties 1 An incorporated borough, town, or city. 2 In Cuba and some other Latin-American countries, an administrative area somewhat like a county. [< F *municipalité*]

mu·nic·i·pal·ize (myoo·nis'ə·pəl·īz) *v.t.* ·ized, ·iz·ing 1 To place within municipal authority or transfer to municipal ownership. 2 To make a municipality of. —**mu·nic'i·pal·i·za'tion** *n.*

municipal ownership Ownership by a municipality: said especially of public services, as electricity, waterworks, etc.

mu·nif·i·cent (myoo·nif'ə·sənt) *adj.* Extraordinarily generous or bountiful; liberal. See synonyms under GENEROUS. [< L *munificens, -entis* < *munificus* < *munus* gift + *facere* make] —**mu·nif'i·cence, mu·nif'i·cen·cy** *n.* —**mu·nif'i·cent·ly** *adv.*

mu·ni·ment (myoo'nə·mənt) *n.* 1 That which supports or defends. 2 *Law* Any deed, record, or instrument by which title to property may be defended or evidenced: usually in the plural. 3 Any means of defending. [< OF < L *munimentum* fortification, support < *munire* fortify]

mu·ni·tion (myoo·nish'ən) *n.* 1 Ammunition and all necessary war materiel: usually in the plural. 2 The requisites for any undertaking. 3 *Obs.* A fort; stronghold. —*v.t.* To furnish with munitions. [< F < L *munitio, -onis* < *munire* fortify]

mun·nion (mun'yən) *n.* A mullion.

Mun·ro (mun·rō'), **Hector Hugh** See SAKI.

Mun·sell color system (mun·sel') A system for the classification and identification of colors by means of reference to the three standard factors of hue, chroma (saturation), and value (lightness). [after Albert H. *Munsell*, 1858–1918, U.S. artist]

Mun·sey (mun'sē), **Frank Andrews**, 1854–1925, U.S. publisher.

Mun·ster (mun'stər) A province in southern Ireland; 9,317 square miles.

Mün·ster (mün'stər) A city in northern North

Rhine-Westphalia, western West Germany. Also **Mün·ster-in-West·fa·len** (-ēn-vest·fä'lən).

Mün·ster·berg (mün'stər·berkh), **Hugo**, 1863–1916, U.S. philosopher and psychologist born in Germany.

munt (munt) *v.t. & v.i. Scot.* To mount.

Mun·te·ni·a (mun·tē'nē·ə, *Rumanian* moon·tā'nyä) The eastern region of Walachia, Rumania; 20,070 square miles: also *Greater Walachia*.

Mun·the (mun'te), **Axel**, 1857–1949, Swedish physician and writer.

munt·jac (munt'jak) *n.* Any of various small, short-legged deer (genus *Muntiacus*) of east Asia, the males having short, two-pronged horns on long pedicles; especially, *M. muntjak* of Java. Also **munt'iak**. [< Javanese *mënjaṅan*]

mu·on (myoo'on) *n. Physics* An unstable subatomic particle bearing an electric charge and having a mass approximately 210 times that of an electron.

Muo·nio (mwô'nyô) A river rising in Lapland near the meeting point of the Norwegian, Swedish, and Finnish borders and flowing 180 miles SE and south along the Swedish-Finnish border, to its confluence with the Torne.

Mur (moor) A river in Austria, Hungary, and Yugoslavia, flowing 300 miles east to the Drava. *Hungarian* **Mu·ra** (moo'rä).

mu·rae·na (myoo·rē'nə) *n.* An eel; moray. [< L *muraena*, a fish < Gk. *myraina* sea eel, lamprey]

mu·ral (myoor'əl) *adj.* 1 Pertaining to or supported by a wall. 2 Resembling a wall. —*n.* A painting or decoration on a wall. [< L *muralis* < *murus* wall]

mu·ral·ist (myoor'əl·ist) *n.* A painter of murals.

Mu·ra·sa·ki (moo·rä·sä·kē), **Lady**, Japanese novelist and poet of the eleventh century.

Mu·rat (moo·rät') A river in east central Turkey, flowing 380 miles west to the Euphrates. Also **Mu·rad** (-räd').

Mu·rat (mü·ra'), **Joachim**, 1771–1815, French general; marshal of France 1804; king of Naples 1808–15; brother-in-law of Napoleon.

Mur·chi·son Falls (mûr'chə·sən) A series of three waterfalls in the lower Victoria Nile; 400 feet high.

Mur·chi·son River (mûr'chə·sən) A river in Western Australia, flowing 440 miles SW to the Indian Ocean.

Mur·cia (mûr'shə, moor'-; *Sp.* moor'thyä) 1 A region and former kingdom of southern Spain; 10,108 square miles. 2 Its former capital, a city in SE Spain.

mur·der (mûr'dər) *v.t.* 1 To kill (a human being) with premeditated malice. 2 To kill in a barbarous or inhuman manner; slaughter. 3 To spoil by bad performance, etc.; mangle; butcher. See synonyms under KILL. —*n.* The unlawful and intentional killing of one human being by another. —**murder will out** Murder cannot be concealed. [Fusion of OE *morthor* + OF *murdre*, both < Gmc.] —**mur'der·er** *n.* —**mur'der·ess** *n. fem.*

mur·der·ous (mûr'dər·əs) *adj.* 1 Pertaining to murder; destructive. 2 Given to murder. 3 Characterized by murder. See synonyms under SANGUINARY. —**mur'der·ous·ly** *adv.* —**mur'der·ous·ness** *n.*

mure (myoor) *v.t.* mured, mur·ing To immure; confine. —*n. Obs.* A wall. [< F *murer*, ult. < L *murus* wall]

Mu·res (moo'resh) A river of NW Rumania and SE Hungary, flowing 550 miles from the Carpathians to the Tisza: Hungarian *Maros*. Also **Mu'resh**.

mu·rex (myoor'eks) *n. pl.* **mu·ri·ces** (myoor'ə·sēz) or **rex·es** A rough-shelled marine gastropod (genus *Murex*) of warm seas, especially *M. trunculus* and *M. brandaris*, from whose large mucus gland a purple dye was obtained in ancient times. [< L, purple fish]

mu·rex·ide (myoo·rek'sid) *n. Chem.* The ammonium hydrogen salt, $C_8H_8O_6N_6·H_2O$, of purpuric acid: formerly used to produce pink, purple, or red dyes, now displaced by aniline colors. [< MUREX + -IDE]

Mur·free (mûr'frē), **Mary Noailles** See CRADDOCK.

Mur·frees·bor·o (mûr'frēz·bûr'ō) A city in central Tennessee; site of the Civil War battle of Stones River, December 31, 1862, and January 2, 1863.

mur·geon (mûr'jən) *n. Scot.* A smirk; a grimace.

mu·ri·ate (myŏor′ē·āt) Former name for CHLORIDE.

mu·ri·at·ed (myŏor′ē·ā′tid) adj. 1 Salted; pickled. 2 Archaic Treated with or containing a chloride or hydrochloric acid.

mu·ri·at·ic (myŏor′ē·at′ic) adj. Hydrochloric. [< L muriaticus pickled < muria brine]

mu·ri·cate (myŏor′ə·kit) adj. Biol. Rough, with short, hard, tubercular excrescences. [< L muricatus murex–shaped, pointed < murex]

Mu·ri·el (myŏor′ē·əl) A feminine personal name. [< Gk., myrrh]

mu·ri·form (myŏor′ə·fôrm) adj. Bot. Regularly arranged like bricks in a wall: said of cells in plants. Also **mu′rine** (-ēn). [< L murus wall + -FORM]

Mu·ril·lo (myŏo·ril′ō, Sp. mŏo·rē′lyō), **Bartolomé Esteban,** 1618–82, Spanish painter.

mu·rine (myŏor′īn, -in) adj. Of or pertaining to a family (Muridae) or a subfamily (Murinae) of rodents, embracing true mice and rats. — n. One of the Murinae or Muridae. [< L murinus < mus, muris a mouse]

murk (mûrk) adj. Murky; dark. — n. Darkness; gloom. Also spelled mirk. [< ON myrkr darkness] — **murk′ly** adv.

murk·y (mûr′kē) adj. murk·i·er, murk·i·est Darkened, thickened, or obscured; hazy; gloomy; obscure: also spelled mirky. See synonyms under DARK. — **murk′i·ly** adv. — **murk′i·ness** n.

Mur·man Coast (mŏor′män′) The Arctic coast of the Kola Peninsula in NW U.S.S.R.: also Norman Coast.

Mur·mansk (mŏor′mänsk′) A port of the western Murman Coast; world's largest city north of the Arctic Circle.

mur·mur (mûr′mər) n. 1 A low sound continually repeated. 2 A complaint uttered in a half-articulate voice. 3 An abnormal, rasping sound heard in certain morbid conditions: a heart murmur. — v.i. 1 To make a murmur. 2 To complain in a low tone; mutter. — v.t. 3 To utter in a low tone. See synonyms under BABBLE, COMPLAIN. [< OF < L] — **mur′mur·er** n. — **mur′mur·ing** adj. — **mur′mur·ing·ly** adv.

mur·mur·ous (mûr′mər·əs) adj. Characterized or accompanied by murmurs. — **mur′mur·ous·ly** adv. — **mur′mur·ous·ness** n.

Mu·ro·ran (mŏo·rō·rän′) A port on SW Hokkaido island, Japan.

mur·phy (mûr′fē) n. pl. **·phies** Slang A potato. [from an Irish surname]

Mur·phy (mûr′fē), **Frank,** 1890–1949, U.S. jurist, associate justice of the Supreme Court 1940–49. — **William Parry,** born 1892, U.S. physician.

mur·ra (mûr′ə) n. Latin A material of ancient Rome which has been variously supposed to be Chinese jade, porcelain, iridescent glass, or artificially colored chalcedony. Also **mur′rha.**

mur·rain (mûr′in) n. 1 A malignant contagious fever affecting domestic animals, as anthrax. 2 Any plague or pestilence. See RINDERPEST. — adj. Affected with murrain. [< OF morine < L mori die]

Mur·ray (mûr′ē), **Gilbert,** 1866–1957, English classical scholar. — **Sir James Augustus Henry,** 1837–1915, Scottish philologist and lexicographer. — **John,** 1778–1843, English publisher; first published works of Byron, Jane Austen, etc. — **Lindley,** 1745–1826, U.S. grammarian. — **Philip,** 1866–1952, U.S. labor leader. — **William,** 1705–93, Earl of Mansfield; English jurist.

Murray River The principal river of Australia, forming part of the boundary between Victoria and New South Wales and flowing 1,600 miles to the Indian Ocean.

murre (mûr) n. pl. **murres** or **murre** 1 The foolish guillemot. 2 The razor-billed auk. Also **murr.** [Origin uncertain]

murre·let (mûr′lit) n. Any of certain small sea birds (family Alcidae) of the islands of the North Pacific. [Dim. of MURRE]

mur·rey (mûr′ē) adj. Of a purplish-red or mulberry color. — n. 1 Her. The tincture sanguine. 2 A dark purplish red. [< OF moree < L morum mulberry]

mur·rine (mûr′in, -īn) adj. Of, pertaining to, or consisting of murra. Also **mur′rhine.** [< L murrinus]

murrine glass Glassware having a transparent ground with embedded flowers, ribbons, etc., of colored glass.

Mur·rum·bid·gee (mûr′əm·bij′ē) A river in New South Wales, Australia, rising in the Great Dividing Range and flowing 1,050 miles north to the Murray River.

mur·ry (mûr′ē) See MORAY.

Mur·vie·dro (mŏor·vyä′thrō) A former name for SAGUNTO.

mu·sa·ceous (myŏo·zā′shəs) adj. Pertaining to or designating a family (Musaceae) of monocotyledonous plants including the common banana, proceeding from rootstocks, with stems composed of sheathing leafstalks and flowers bursting through spathes. [< NL Musaceae < Musa, genus name < Arabic mawzah banana]

Mus Al·lah (mŏos′ ä·lä′) See STALIN PEAK (def. 3).

mus·ca (mus′kə) n. pl. **mus·cae** (mus′sē) A fly; any of a genus (Musca) of dipterous insects of the family Muscidae, including the housefly. [< L, fly] — **mus·cid** (mus′id) adj. & n.

Mus·ca (mus′kə) A southern constellation, the Fly. See CONSTELLATION. [< NL]

mus·ca·dine (mus′kə·din, -dīn) n. The fox grape or scuppernong (Vitis or Muscadinia rotundifolia) of the southern United States. [< Provençal muscade, fem. of muscat. See MUSCAT.]

mus·cae vol·i·tan·tes (mus′sē vol′ə·tan′tēz) Minute specks or motes apparently moving before the eye, caused by defects or impurities in the vitreous humor of the eye, etc. [< L, flying flies]

mus·ca·rine (mus′kə·rēn, -rin) n. Chem. A deliquescent, extremely poisonous, white, crystalline alkaloid, $C_8H_{13}O_3N$, found in certain fungi, as the fly agaric, and in putrefying fish. [< NL muscarius of flies < L musca fly]

mus·cat (mus′kat, -kət) n. 1 One of several varieties of musk–flavored Old World grapes. 2 A sweet, white wine made from such grapes. [< F < Provençal < Ital. moscato < LL muscus musk]

Mus·cat (mus·kat′) A port on the Gulf of Oman, capital of Muscat and Oman: also Masqat.

Muscat and Oman An independent sultanate of SE Arabia on the Gulf of Oman; 82,000 square miles; capital, Muscat: also Oman.

mus·ca·tel (mus′kə·tel′) n. 1 A rich, sweet wine made from the muscat grape. 2 The muscat grape: also spelled moscatel. Also **mus′ca·del′** (-del′). [< OF, dim. of muscat. See MUSCAT.]

mus·cle (mus′əl) n. 1 Anat. An organ composed of tissue arranged in bundles of fibers, by whose contraction bodily movements are effected. Two principal types are known: striated (striped), involved in voluntary movements, and smooth (unstriped), acting independently of the will. The heart muscle belongs anatomically between the two. 2 The tissue of the muscular organs. 3 Muscular strength. — v.i. **·cled, ·cling** To push in or ahead by sheer physical strength. ◆ Homophone: mussel. [< F < L musculus, lit., little mouse, dim. of mus. Doublet of MUSSEL.]

mus·cle-bound (mus′əl·bound′) adj. Affected with a form of muscular hypertrophy char-

acterized by lack of elasticity in a muscle: caused by excessive exercise in training.

mus·cled (mus′əld) adj. Having or supplied with muscles.

muscle fiber Physiol. A muscle cell consisting of a soft contractile substance enclosed in a tubular sheath.

muscle plasma Physiol. The liquid that can be expressed from muscle tissue: it clots spontaneously and is sometimes injected intravenously as a restorative and stimulant.

muscle sense Physiol. The perception of muscular movement derived from the functioning of afferent nerves connected with muscle tissue, skin, joints, and tendons.

Muscle Shoals Rapids in the Tennessee River, NW Alabama; site of the Wilson Dam.

muscle spindle Anat. One of various groups of muscle fibers enclosed in a sheath of connective tissue and terminating in sensory organs.

muscle sugar Inositol.

mus·coid (mus′koid) adj. Mosslike. — n. A mosslike plant. [< L muscus moss + -OID]

mus·co·va·do (mus′kə·vā′dō) n. A raw brown sugar obtained by evaporating the juice of sugarcane and draining off the molasses. Also **mus′ca·va′da** (-də), **mus′co·vade** (-vād). [< Sp. mascabado unrefined, pp. of mascabar diminish, var. of menoscabar < menos (< L minus) + cabo head (< L caput)]

mus·co·vite (mus′kə·vīt) n. The most common and important white or potash mica, $KAl_2(OH)_2AlSi_3O_{10}$. [< earlier Muscovy glass]

Mus·co·vite (mus′kə·vīt) n. An inhabitant of Muscovy or ancient Russia; hence, a Russian. — adj. Of or pertaining to Muscovy or to Russia; Russian. — **Mus′co·vit′ic** (-vit′ik) adj.

mus·co·vy (mus′kə·vē) n. pl. **·vies** A large greenish–black duck (Cairina moschata) of America from Mexico to Brazil, now widely domesticated. Also **muscovy duck.** [Alter. of MUSK DUCK.]

Mus·co·vy (mus′kə·vē) Archaic Russia.

mus·cu·lar (mus′kyə·lər) adj. 1 Pertaining to or depending upon muscles. 2 Possessing strong muscles; powerful. 3 Accomplished by muscle or muscles. — **mus′cu·lar′i·ty** (-lar′ə·tē) n. — **mus′cu·lar·ly** adv.

muscular dystrophy Pathol. One of various diseases of undetermined cause, characterized by wasting of muscles and often terminating in physical helplessness.

mus·cu·la·ture (mus′kyə·lə·chŏor) n. 1 The disposition or arrangement of muscles in a part or organ. 2 The muscle system as a whole. Also **mus′cu·la′tion.** [< F]

muse[1] (myŏoz) n. Something regarded as the source of artistic inspiration; the inspiring power of a poet or of poetry. [< MUSE]

muse[2] (myŏoz) v.t. & v.i. **mused, mus·ing** To consider thoughtfully or at length; ponder; meditate. — n. 1 The act or state of musing; reverie. 2 Wonder. [< OF muser] — **mus′er** n. — **muse′ful** adj.

Synonyms (verb): brood, cogitate, consider, contemplate, deliberate, dream, meditate, ponder, reflect, ruminate, stew, study, think. Compare REFLECTION.

THE MUSES—FROM A SARCOPHAGUS IN THE LOUVRE, PARIS

A. Clio. *B.* Thalia. *C.* Erato. *D.* Euterpe. *E.* Polyhymnia. *F.* Calliope. *G.* Terpsichore. *H.* Urania. *I.* Melpomene.

Muse (myŏoz) In Greek mythology, any of the nine goddesses presiding over poetry, the arts, sciences, etc.: Calliope, Clio, Erato,

Euterpe, Melpomene, Polyhymnia, Terpsichore, Thalia, and Urania. [<F <L *Musa* <Gk. *Mousa* a Muse, eloquence, music]

mu·sette (myōō·zet') *n.* **1** Any melody of soft, pastoral character written in imitation of bagpipe airs. **2** A small bagpipe formerly popular in France. **3** A variety of small oboe. **4** A small leather or canvas knapsack or wallet, used especially by soldiers, and carried by a strap worn over the shoulder: also **musette bag.** [<F, dim. of *muse* a bagpipe]

mu·se·um (myōō·zē'əm) *n.* **1** A place preserving and exhibiting works of nature, art, curiosities, etc.; also, any collection of such objects. **2** Any place where curiosities, freaks, monstrosities, etc., are exhibited. [<L <Gk. *mouseion* temple of the Muses <*Mousa*]

mush[1] (mush) *n.* **1** Thick porridge, made by boiling meal or flour in water or milk. **2** Anything soft and pulpy. **3** *Colloq.* Sentimentality. [Var. of MASH]

mush[2] (mush) *v.i.* In Alaska and the Canadian Arctic, to travel on foot, especially over snow with a dog sled. — *interj.* Get along! a call of the drivers of a dog team. [Prob. <*mush on,* alter. of F (Canadian) *marchons,* the cry of voyageurs and trappers to their dogs] — **mush'er** *n.*

mush·mel·on (mush'mel'ən) See MUSKMELON.

mush·room (mush'·rōōm, -rŏŏm) *n.* **1** A large, rapidly growing fungus of the order *Agaricales,* consisting of an erect stalk and a caplike expansion: certain poisonous varieties are called *toadstools,* but the distinction is not scientifically correct. The best-known edible mushrooms are of the genus *Agaricus,* especially the **field mushroom,** *A. campestris.* **2** An object or excrescence of similar shape. — *v.i.* **1** To grow or spread rapidly, like a mushroom: The town *mushroomed* overnight. **2** To expand at one end into a mushroomlike shape: said of bullets. — *adj.* **1** Pertaining to or made of mushrooms. **2** Sudden in growth and rapid in decay; ephemeral; upstart. [<OF *mouscheron* <*mousse* moss]

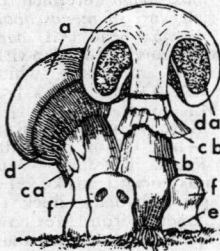

AGARIC MUSHROOM
a. Pileus, entire and cut.
b. Stipe in velum.
ca. Ruptured velum.
d. Gills.
cb. Velum forming ring.
da. Cross-section of gill.
e. Mycelium.
f.f. Young mushrooms.

mush·y (mush'ē) *adj.* **mush·i·er, mush·i·est** **1** Soft; pulpy. **2** *Colloq.* Sentimental; romantic. — **mush'i·ly** *adv.* — **mush'i·ness** *n.*

mu·sic (myōō'zik) *n.* **1** The science and art of the rhythmic combination of tones, vocal or instrumental, embracing melody and harmony. **2** A composition, or mass of compositions, conceived or executed according to musical rule or spirit. **3** Any rhythmic succession or combination of sounds, especially if pleasing to the ear; also, the sensations or emotions thus produced. **4** A band of musicians; an orchestra. See synonyms under MELODY. — **absolute music** Pure or abstract music wholly self-sufficient without representation or dependence on title, program, etc.: opposed to the pictorial or descriptive **program music.** — **to face the music** To take the consequences courageously and without complaint; accept facts. [<F *musique* <L *musica* <Gk. *mousikē* (*technē*) musical (art) <*Mousa* a Muse]

mu·si·cal (myōō'zi·kəl) *adj.* **1** Pertaining to music. **2** Capable of producing or appreciating music; fond of music. **3** Melodious. — *n.* **1** A musical comedy. **2** *Colloq.* A musicale. — **mu'si·cal·ly** *adv.* — **mu'si·cal·ness** *n.*

musical chairs A marching game played to music, in which the contestants circle around a row of opposite-facing chairs, one less than the number of players. When the music stops, each marcher rushes for a chair, one person for whom there is no chair being eliminated. On each round, a chair is removed until finally only one remains, the contestant reaching it first being declared the winner. Also called "Going to Jerusalem."

musical comedy A kind of theatrical performance, characterized by music, songs, dances, jokes, and elaborate costumes, staging, and settings, usually based on a tenuous plot: also *musical.*

mu·si·cale (myōō'zə·kal', *Fr.* mü·zē·kàl') *n.* An informal concert or private recital: also *musical.* [<F]

music box A case containing a mechanism that reproduces melodies.

music hall 1 A public hall or building devoted to musical entertainments. **2** *Brit.* A vaudeville house.

music house A firm that publishes music.

mu·si·cian (myōō·zish'ən) *n.* One skilled in music; especially, a professional performer. [<OF *musicien*]

mu·si·cian·ly (myōō·zish'ən·lē) *adj.* Exhibiting musical taste, learning, or skill.

music of the spheres The harmony produced by the movements of the celestial spheres: a conception of Pythagorean philosophy.

mu·si·col·o·gist (myōō'zə·kol'ə·jist) *n.* One engaged in or versed in musicology.

mu·si·col·o·gy (myōō'zə·kol'ə·jē) *n.* The scientific and historical study of music as an art and as a craft.

music stand 1 A rack to hold sheet music for a performer. **2** A bandstand.

mus·ing (myōō'zing) *adj.* Thoughtful; dreamy; preoccupied. — **mus'ing·ly** *adv.*

musk (musk) *n.* **1** A soft, reddish-brown, powdery secretion of a penetrating odor, obtained from the preputial follicles or **musk bag** of the male musk deer. It is used by perfumers and in medicine. **2** A similar substance from some other animals, as the muskrat or civet. **3** *Chem.* Any of several organic compounds used to replace natural musk. **4** Muskroot. **5** The odor of musk. [<OF *musc* <LL *muscus* <Gk. *moschos* <Persian *mushk* (prob. akin to Skt. *mushka* testicle, dim. of *mus* a mouse)]

musk beaver The muskrat.

musk beetle A large European beetle (*Aromia moschata*) of a bronze-green color, and having a musky odor suggesting roses.

musk cat 1 A civet. **2** *Obs.* A perfumed, effeminate man; a dandy.

musk deer A small hornless deer (*Moschus moschiferus*) of central and eastern Asia, of which the male has a musk-secreting gland.

musk duck 1 A muscovy. **2** An Australian duck (*Biziura lobata*), with a dislike appendage on the chin, and having a musky odor in the breeding season: also called *mould goose.*

MUSK DEER
(From 17 to 20 inches high; color brown speckled with gray or buff)

mus·keg (mus'keg) *n.* **1** A rocky basin filled by successive deposits of unstable material, as leaves, muck, and moss, incapable of sustaining much weight. **2** A swamp. Also spelled *maskeg.* [<Chippewa *muskig* grassy bog]

muskeg moss An absorbent, sterilized swamp moss (genus *Sphagnum*) used as a surgical dressing.

mus·kel·lunge (mus'kə·lunj) *n. pl.* **·lunge** *n.* A large North American pike (*Esox masquinongy*), valued as a game fish: also spelled *mascalonge, maskinonge.* [<Algonquian *maskinonge* <*mas* great + *kinonge* pike]

mus·ket (mus'kit) *n.* A smoothbore military hand gun; specifically, a hand gun for infantry, now superseded by the rifle. [<OF *mosquet* gun, hawk <Ital. *moschetto* hawk <L *musca* fly]

mus·ket·eer (mus'kə·tir') *n.* A soldier armed with a musket; hence, a foot soldier. [<F *mousquetaire*]

mus·ket·ry (mus'kit·rē) *n.* **1** Muskets collectively. **2** The science of the operation of small arms.

Mus·kho·ge·an (mus·kō'gē·ən, mus'kō·gē'ən) *n.* One of the principal North American Indian linguistic stocks, well advanced in culture, including the Chickasaw, Choctaw, Creek, and Seminole tribes, formerly inhabiting the Gulf region of the SE United States. Also **Mus·ko·gi·an** (mus·kō'gē·ən).

mus·kit (mus·kēt') See MESQUITE.

musk·mel·on (musk'mel'ən) *n.* **1** The juicy, edible, gourdlike fruit of a trailing herb (*Cucumis melo*) of the melon family; cantaloup. **2** The plant bearing this fruit. Also, *Colloq.,* *mushmelon.*

musk ox A shaggy, hollow-horned ruminant (*Ovibos moschatus*) combining the characteristics of the sheep and ox and emitting a strong odor of musk: now restricted to Greenland and the North American continent.

MUSK OX
(About 4 feet high at the shoulder)

musk·rat (musk'rat') *n. pl.* **·rats** or **·rat** A North American aquatic rodent (*Ondatra zibethica*) yielding a valuable fur and secreting a substance with a musky odor: sometimes called *musquash.*

musk·root (musk'rōōt', -rŏŏt') *n.* The musky, spongy root of a plant (*Ferula sumbul*) of the parsley family, from Russian Turkestan: employed medicinally as a stimulant and anti-spasmodic. Also called *sumbul.*

MUSKRAT
(About 22 inches over-all in length)

musk rose A cultivated climbing rose (*Rosa moschata*) from Europe, with large white flowers in panicled clusters.

musk turtle A small turtle (*Sternotherus odoratus*) of the eastern United States and Canada, distinguished by bright-yellow lines on each side of the head.

musk·y (mus'kē) *adj.* **musk·i·er, musk·i·est** Like musk; smelling of musk. — **musk'i·ly** *adv.* — **musk'i·ness** *n.*

Mus·lim (muz'lim, mŏŏz'-, mŏŏs'-) *n. pl.* **·lims** or **·lim** A believer in Islam; Mohammedan. — *adj.* Of or pertaining to Islam or the Muslims. Also called *Moslem:* also **Mus'lem.** [<Arabic, one who submits <*aslama* surrender (to God)] — **Mus'lim·ism** *n.*

mus·lin (muz'lin) *n.* Any of several varieties of plain-weave cotton cloth ranging from thin batiste and nainsook to heavy sheetings such as longcloth and percale. [<F *mousseline* <Ital. *mussolino,* dim. of *mussolo* muslin < *Mussolo* Mosul, city in Iraq where made.

mus·lin-kail (muz'lin-kāl') *n. Scot.* A thin broth containing greens and shelled barley.

mus·quash (mus'kwosh) *n.* The muskrat. [<N. Am. Ind., it is red]

mus·qui·to (mus·kē'tō) See MOSQUITO.

muss (mus) *v.t. U.S. Colloq.* To make messy or untidy; rumple; crumple: often with *up.* — *n. Colloq.* **1** A state of disorder or disturbance; mess. **2** Confused struggle or tumult; squabble. [Alter. of MESS]

mus·sel (mus'əl) *n.* **1** A small bivalve mollusk, especially the common edible mussel (*Mytilus edulis*). **2** One of several other fresh-water mollusks, of the genera *Anodonta, Unio,* and others, whose shells are made into buttons, etc. ◆ Homophone: *muscle.* [OE *musle* <L *musculus,* dim. of *mus* mouse. Doublet of MUSCLE.]

Mus·sel·shell River (mus'əl·shel) A river in central Montana, flowing 292 miles NE to the Missouri.

Mus·set (mü·se'), **(Louis Charles) Alfred de,** 1810–57, French poet, dramatist, and novelist.

Mus·so·li·ni (mŏŏs'ə·lē'nē, *Ital.* mōōs'sō·lē'nē), **Benito,** 1883–1945, Italian Fascist leader; premier 1922–43; executed: called "Il Duce" (the leader).

Mus·sul·man (mus'əl·mən) *n. pl.* **·mans** (-mənz) or **·men** (-mən) A Muslim; Mohammedan. — *adj.* Belonging or relating to the Moslems. [<Persian & Turkish *musulmân* <Arabic *muslimūn,* pl. of *muslim*]

muss·y (mus'ē) *U.S. Colloq. adj.* **muss·i·er, muss·i·est** Disarranged; rumpled; slightly soiled. — **muss'i·ly** *adv.* — **muss'i·ness** *n.*

must[1] (must) *v.* A defective verb now used only as an auxiliary followed by the infinitive without *to,* or elliptically with the infinitive understood, to express: **1** Obligation or compulsion: *Must* you go? I *must.* **2** Requirement: You *must* be healthy to be accepted. **3** Probability or supposition: You *must* be tired. **4** Conviction or certainty: War *must* follow. ◆ A past conditional is formed by

placing the following verb in the perfect infinitive: *He must have gone.* —*n.* **1** Anything that is required or vital. **2** A news item or other material that must be printed: usually marked *must.* —*adj.* Important and essential: a *must* book. [OE *moste,* pt. of *mōtan* may]

must[2] (must) *n.* Mustiness; mold. —*v.t.* & *v.i. Obs.* To make or become musty. [Back formation < MUSTY[1]]

must[3] (must) *n.* **1** The expressed unfermented juice of the grape. **2** Unfermented potato pulp. [OE < L *mustum (vinum)* new wine]

must[4] (must) *n.* **1** A state of dangerous frenzy, related to sexual excitement, associated with adult male animals, especially elephants. **2** An elephant in this condition. —*adj.* Being in a state of must. Also spelled *musth.* [< Hind. *mast* drunk, lustful]

must[5] (must) *n. Scot.* Musk, especially in the form of hair powder.

mus·tache (məs·tash′, mus′tash) *n.* **1** The growth of hair on the upper lip of men: occasionally used in the plural, in reference to its two parts. **2** The hair or bristles growing near the mouth of an animal. **3** An old soldier: a brave old *mustache*: a gallicism. Also **mus·ta′chio** (-tä′shō): sometimes spelled *moustache.* [< F *moustache* < Ital. *mostaccio* face < Med. L *mustacia* < Gk. *mystax* upper lip < *mastax* mouth, jaws] —**mus·tached** (məs·tasht′) *adj.*

Mus·ta·fa (mo͞os′tä·fä), **Kemal Pasha** See KEMAL.

Mus·tagh (mo͞os·tä′) See KARAKORAM.

mus·tang (mus′tang) *n.* **1** The wild horse of the American plains. **2** One of these horses broken to the saddle; a cow pony. [< Sp. *mesteño,* obs. *mestengo,* lit., belonging to a cattlemen's association, wild < *mesta* association, group < L *mixtus,* pp. of *miscere* mix]

mustang grape A vine *(Vitis candicans)* of the SW United States, having light-colored pungent berries or grapes.

mus·tard (mus′tərd) *n.* **1** Either of two species of *Brassica,* **white mustard** *(B. hirta)* and **black mustard** *(B. nigra),* both annual herbs with yellow flowers and pods of roundish seeds. **2** The pungent seed of the mustard, crushed and adapted for use as a condiment or as a medicinal rubefacient and diuretic. **3** A strong, dark-yellow color, the color of ground mustard. [< OF *moustarde* < L *mustum* must[3]; from once having been prepared with must]

mustard gas *Chem.* An oily amber liquid, dichlorethyl sulfide, $C_4H_8Cl_2S$, having an odor of mustard or garlic, and used in warfare because of its powerful blistering effect.

mustard oil A fixed oil of unpleasant odor extracted from mustard seeds and used in making soap, as a lubricant, etc.

mustard plaster A plaster of powdered mustard and flour used as a counterirritant and rubefacient.

mus·tee (mus·tē′, mus′tē) See MESTEE.

mus·te·line (mus′tə·lin, -līn) *adj.* Pertaining to a family *(Mustelidae)* of fur-bearing, predacious mammals which includes weasels, skunks, badgers, otters, wolverines, and martens. [< L *mustelinus* < *mustela* weasel]

mus·ter (mus′tər) *v.t.* **1** To summon or assemble (troops, etc.), as for service, review, or roll call. **2** To collect or summon: often with *up:* to *muster* up one's courage. —*v.i.* **3** To come together or assemble, as troops for service, review, etc. —**to muster in** To enrol as military recruits. —**to muster out** To collect or assemble, as troops, for discharge from military service. See synonyms under CONVOKE. —*n.* **1** An assemblage, especially of troops for parade or review. **2** A muster roll. **3** A specimen; pattern; sample. **4** An imposing gathering; array. —**to pass muster** To pass inspection; hence, to be acceptable or accepted. [< OF *mostrer* exhibit < L *monstrare* show]

mus·ter-mas·ter (mus′tər·mas′tər, -mäs′-) *n.* An officer who inspects troops, their equipment, etc.

muster roll The official list or roll of officers and men in a military troop or a ship's crew.

musth (must) See MUST[4].

must·y[1] (mus′tē) *adj.* **must·i·er, must·i·est** **1** Having a moldy odor; ill-flavored; fetid; stale. **2** Without life, sparkle, or flavor. **3** Without life or energy; listless; apathetic. See synonyms under TRITE. [? Alter. of earlier *moisty* < MOIST] —**must′i·ly** *adv.* —**must′i·ness** *n.*

must·y[2] (mus′tē) *n.* Formerly, a cheap quality of snuff having a musty flavor.

mu·ta·ble (myo͞o′tə·bəl) *adj.* Capable of changing; liable to change; hence, fickle; unstable. See synonyms under FICKLE. [< L *mutabilis* < *mutare* change] —**mu′ta·ble·ness, mu′ta·bil′i·ty** *n.* —**mu′ta·bly** *adv.*

mu·ta·gen (myo͞o′tə·jən) *n.* Any agent that increases the incidence of mutation in germ plasm. [< L *mutare* change + -GEN] —**mu·ta·gen·ic** (myo͞o′tə·jen′ik) *adj.*

mu·ta·gen·e·sis (myo͞o′tə·jen′ə·sis) *n.* The initiation of mutation.

Mu·tan·kiang (mo͞o′dän′jyäng′) A city in eastern Manchuria.

mu·tant (myo͞o′tənt) *n.* **1** That which admits of or undergoes mutation or change. **2** *Biol.* A plant or animal organism differing from its parents in one or more characteristics that are inheritable; a sport. [< L *mutans, -antis,* ppr. of *mutare* change]

mu·tate (myo͞o′tāt) *v.t.* & *v.i.* **·tat·ed, ·tat·ing** To undergo or subject to change, especially by mutation. [< L *mutatus,* pp. of *mutare* change] —**mu′ta·tive** *adj.*

mu·ta·tion (myo͞o·tā′shən) *n.* **1** The act or process of change; alteration; variation. **2** Modification of one vowel by another; umlaut. See UMLAUT. **3** *Biol.* A sudden, well-marked, transmissible variation in the organism of a plant or animal, especially as resulting from new combinations of genes and chromosomes and as distinguishable from cumulative evolutionary changes over a long period. **4** Change; hence, succession and serial succession; consecutive order. See synonyms under CHANGE. [< L *mutatio, -onis*] —**mu·ta′tion·al** *adj.*

mu·ta·tis mu·tan·dis (myo͞o·tā′tis myo͞o·tan′dis) *Latin* The necessary changes having been made.

mutch (much) *n. Scot.* A woman's close-fitting cap; also, a man's nightcap; a child's cap.

mutch·kin (much′kin) *n. Scot.* A liquid measure containing three quarters of one imperial pint.

mute (myo͞ot) *adj.* **1** Uttering no word or sound; silent. **2** *Law* Refusing to plead upon arraignment. **3** Lacking the power of speech; dumb. **4** *Phonet.* Of or pertaining to a stop consonant. See synonyms under TACITURN. —*n.* **1** One who is silent; especially, a person who refuses or is unable to speak; a person who is dumb by reason of deafness or other infirmity: also called *deaf-mute.* **2** An undertaker's assistant. **3** *Law* A prisoner who refuses to plead on arraignment. **4** *Phonet.* A stop consonant, as (b), (p), (t), (d). **5** A device to silence, muffle, or deaden the tone of a musical instrument. —*v.t.* **mut·ed, mut·ing** To deaden or muffle the sound of (a musical instrument). [< L *mutus* dumb] —**mute′ly** *adv.* —**mute′ness** *n.*

mu·ti·cous (myo͞o′tə·kəs) *adj. Biol.* Without a point; unarmed; defenseless: said especially of certain plants and animals. Also **mu′tic, mu′ti·cate** (-kāt). [< L *muticus,* var. of *mutilus* docked, curtailed. See MUTILATE.]

mu·ti·late (myo͞o′tə·lāt) *v.t.* **·lat·ed, ·lat·ing** **1** To deprive (a person, animal, etc.) of a limb or essential part; maim. **2** To damage or injure by the removal of an important part or parts: to *mutilate* a speech. [< L *mutilatus,* pp. of *mutilare* maim < *mutilus* docked, maimed] —**mu′ti·la′tion** *n.* —**mu′ti·la′tive** *adj.* —**mu′ti·la′tor** *n.*

mu·ti·neer (myo͞o′tə·nir′) *n.* One who takes part in mutiny: also *Obs.* **mu·tine** (myo͞o′tin). —*v.i.* To mutiny. [< MF *mutinier* < *mutin.* See MUTINY.]

mu·ti·nous (myo͞o′tə·nəs) *adj.* Disposed to mutiny; seditious. See synonyms under REBELLIOUS, RESTIVE, TURBULENT. —**mu′ti·nous·ly** *adv.* —**mu′ti·nous·ness** *n.*

mu·ti·ny (myo͞o′tə·nē) *n. pl.* **·nies** **1** Rebellion against constituted authority; insubordination; especially, a revolt of soldiers or sailors against their officers or commander. **2** *Obs.* Tumult; discord; strife. See synonyms under REVOLUTION. —*v.i.* **·nied, ·ny·ing** To revolt against constituted authority, as in the army or navy; take part in a mutiny. [< F *mutiner* rebel < OF *mutin, meutin* riotous < *muete* riot < L *motus,* pp. of *movere*]

mut·ism (myo͞o′tiz·əm) *n.* **1** Inability or refusal to utter articulate sounds: often associated with certain mental disorders. **2** Muteness. [< F *mutisme*]

Mu·tsu·hi·to (mo͞o·tso͞o·hē·tō), 1852–1912, emperor of Japan 1867–1912.

mutt (mut) *n. Slang* **1** A cur; mongrel dog. **2** A stupid person; blockhead. Also **mut.** [< MUTT(ONHEAD)]

mut·ter (mut′ər) *v.i.* **1** To speak in a low, indistinct tone and with compressed lips, as in complaining or talking to oneself. **2** To complain; grumble. **3** To make a low, rumbling sound. —*v.t.* **4** To say in a low, indistinct tone. —*n.* An imperfect utterance; murmur. [Prob. imit. Cf. dial. G *muttern* and L *muttire.*] —**mut′ter·er** *n.* —**mut′ter·ing** *n.* & *adj.* —**mut′ter·ing·ly** *adv.*

mut·ton (mut′n) *n.* **1** The flesh of sheep as food. **2** Humorously, a sheep. [< F *mouton* < Celtic. Cf. O Irish *molt* ram, Welsh *mollt* Breton *maout.*] —**mut′ton·y** *adj.*

mutton chop **1** A piece of mutton from the rib for broiling or frying. **2** *Printing* An em quad or em rule. —**mut′ton-chop′** (-chop′) *adj.*

mut·ton·chops (mut′n·chops′) *n. pl.* Burnsides or side whiskers shaped like mutton chops.

mut·ton·fish (mut′n·fish′) *n. pl.* **·fish** or **·fish·es** **1** The eelpout. **2** An abalone *(Haliotis iris)* said to taste like mutton. **3** The pargo or other snapper found from Florida to Brazil. **4** The mojarra.

mutton ham *Naut.* A small sail shaped like a leg of mutton, used on small fishing boats: also *mutton-leg.*

mut·ton·head (mut′n·hed′) *n. Slang* A stupid, dense person. [< MUTTON (def. 2) + HEAD; from the traditional stupidity of sheep] —**mut′ton-head′ed** (-hed′id) *adj.*

mut·ton-leg (mut′n·leg′) *n.* **1** A woman's dress sleeve, very full at the top: so called because shaped like a leg of mutton. **2** Mutton ham.

Mut·tra (mu′trə) The former name for MATHURA.

mu·tu·al (myo͞o′cho͞o·əl) *adj.* **1** Pertaining reciprocally to both of two; reciprocally related or bound; reciprocal in action or effect. **2** Shared or experienced alike; common. [< F *mutuel* < LL *mutualis* < L *mutuus* < *mutare* change] —**mu′tu·al·ly** *adv.* —**mu′tu·al′i·ty** *n.*

Synonyms: common, correlative, interchangeable, joint, reciprocal. That is *common* to which two or more persons have the same or equal claims, or in which they have equal interest or participation; that is *mutual* which is freely interchanged; that is *reciprocal* in respect to which one act or movement is met by a corresponding act or movement in return. *Antonyms*: detached, disconnected, dissociated, distinct, disunited, separate, separated, severed, sundered, unconnected, unreciprocated, unshared.

mutual fund An investment company which provides diversification and professional management for the pooled capital of the investors, paying out to its shareholders as mutual owners virtually all earnings including realized capital gains except for management fees and administrative costs, thus remaining tax free in its own operations. The shares of an **open-end mutual fund** are redeemable at the option of the stockholder at the net asset value of the portfolio calculated daily, and its shares are generally sold continually with a distribution charge on purchase. The shares are not listed on the stock exchange. A **closed-end mutual fund** has fixed capitalization, the shares not being offered or redeemable.

mutual insurance **1** A method of insurance based upon a reciprocal contract whereby various persons engage to indemnify each other against certain designated losses. **2** Popularly, the system of a company in which policyholders receive a certain share of the profits: also **mutual plan.**

add,āce,câre,pälm; end,ēven; it,īce; odd,ōpen,ôrder; to͝ok,po͞ol; up,bûrn; ə = a in *above,* e in *sicken,* i in *clarity,* o in *melon,* u in *focus*; yo͞o = u in *fuse,* oi,oil; ou,pout; ch,check; g,go; ng,ring; th,thin; th,this; zh,vision. Foreign sounds à,œ,ü,kh,ṅ; and ◆: see page xx. < from; + plus; ? possibly.

mu·tu·al·ism (myōō′chōō·əl·iz′əm) n. Biol. Symbiosis advantageous to both or all parties concerned.

mu·tu·al·ize (myōō′chōō·əl·īz) v.t. & v.i. ·ized, ·iz·ing 1 To make or become mutual. 2 To put (a firm or corporation) on the basis of majority employee or consumer ownership of common stock. —mu′tu·al·i·za′tion n.

mu·tule (myōō′chool) n. Archit. One of a series of rectangular blocks under a Doric corona, with dependent droplike ornaments called guttae. [< F < L mutulus modillion]

muu-muu (mōō′mōō′) n. A long, loose gown for women, originally worn in Hawaii. [< Hawaiian]

mu·zhik (mōō·zhēk′, mōō′zhēk) n. A Russian peasant in Czarist times: also spelled moujik, mujik. Also **mu·zjik′**. [< Russian]

Muz·zey (muz′ē), **David Saville**, 1870–1965, U.S. historian.

muz·zle (muz′əl) n. 1 The projecting snout of an animal. 2 A guard or covering for an animal's snout to prevent biting or eating. 3 The front end of a firearm. —v.t. ·zled, ·zling 1 To put a muzzle on. 2 To restrain from speaking, expressing opinions, etc.; gag. [< OF musel < Med. L musellum, dim. of LL musus snout] —muz′zler n.

muz·zle·load·er (muz′əl·lō′dər) n. A firearm loaded through the muzzle. —muz′zle·load′ing adj.

muzzle velocity The velocity of a bullet or projectile at the instant of leaving the muzzle of a gun.

muz·zy (muz′ē) adj. Colloq. Muddled; hence, stupid.

MVD The secret police of Soviet Russia. [< Russian < M(inisterstvo) V(nutrennikh) D(el) Ministry of Internal Affairs]

Mwe·ru (mwā′rōō) A lake between SE Belgian Congo and Northern Rhodesia; 173 square miles: French Moero.

my (mī) pronominal adj. 1 The possessive case of the pronoun I employed attributively; belonging or pertaining to me: my house. 2 An adjective used in forms of address in customary phrases: my lord; also used in expressions of endearment: my boy. —interj. An exclamation of surprise: oh my! [OE mīn]

my- Var. of MYO-.

my·al·gi·a (mī·al′jē·ə) n. Pathol. Pain in a muscle; cramp. [< NL < MY- + -ALGIA] —my·al′gic adj.

my·a·sis (mī′ə·sis) See MYIASIS.

my·as·the·ni·a (mī′as·thē′nē·ə) n. Pathol. Muscular debility, accompanied by general and usually progressive exhaustion but without marked sensory disturbance or atrophy. [< NL < MY- + ASTHENIA]

Myc·a·le (mik′ə·lē), **Mount** A peak in SW Turkey on the mainland opposite Samos; scene of a Greek naval victory over the Persians, 479 B.C.

my·ce·li·um (mī·sē′lē·əm) n. Bot. The thallus or vegetative portion of a fungus, consisting of threadlike tubes, or hyphae. See illustration under MUSHROOM. Also **my′cele** (-sēl). [< NL < Gk. mykēs mushroom] —my·ce′li·al, my·ce′li·an adj. —my·ce′li·oid, my·ce′li·oid (mī′sə·loid) adj.

My·ce·nae (mī·sē′nē) An ancient city in NE Peloponnesus, Greece; excavated 1876–77. Also **My·ce′næ**.

My·ce·nae·an (mī′sə·nē′ən) adj. Of or pertaining to Mycenae or to a civilization of which it was the center, existing in parts of Greece, Asia Minor, Sicily, and neighboring countries before the advance of the Hellenes, and thought to have been at its height about 1400 B.C.

-mycete combining form Bot. A member of a class of fungi: corresponding in use to class names in -mycetes: Basidiomycete. See -MYCETES.

-mycetes combining form Bot. Used to form class names of fungi: Basidiomycetes. [< Gk. mykēs, mykētos fungus]

my·ce·to·gen·ic (mī·sē′tō·jen′ik) adj. Produced or caused by a fungus. Also **my·ce′to·ge·net′ic** (-jə·net′ik), **my′ce·tog′e·nous** (-toj′ə·nəs). [< Gk. mykēs, mykētos mushroom + -GENIC]

my·ce·to·ma (mī′sə·tō′mə) n. pl. ·to·ma·ta (-tō′mə·tə) Pathol. A tumor or tumorlike growth caused by a fungus, as Madura foot. [< Gk. mykēs, mykētos fungus + -OMA]

my·ce·to·zo·an (mī·sē′tō·zō′ən) A myxomycete. [< Gk. mykēs, mykētos fungus + -ZOA]

myco- combining form Fungus: mycology. Also before vowels, **myc-**. [< Gk. mykēs fungus]

my·co·bac·te·ri·um (mī′kō·bak·tir′ē·əm) n. pl. ·ri·a (-ē·ə) One of a genus (Mycobacterium) of slender, typically aerobic bacteria difficult to stain, including the bacterium of tuberculosis and that of leprosy. [< MYCO- + BACTERIUM]

my·col·o·gy (mī·kol′ə·jē) n. 1 The science of ngi. 2 The fungous life of a region. [< MYCO- + -LOGY] —my·co·log·ic (mī′kə·loj′ik) or ·i·cal adj. —my·col′o·gist n.

my·cor·rhi·za (mī′kə·rī′zə) n. Bot. A subterranean hyphal mass or mycelium often found on the roots of certain trees, especially of the oak, heath, and pine families. Also **my′co·rhi′za**. [< MYCO- + Gk. rhiza root] —my·cor·rhi′zic adj.

my·co·sis (mī·kō′sis) n. Pathol. 1 A fungous growth within the body. 2 A disease or morbid condition caused by a fungous growth, as ringworm. [< MYC(O) + -OSIS] —my·cot′ic (-kot′ik) adj.

my·co·tro·phism (mī′kō·trō′fiz·əm) n. Bot. The nutrition of the higher plants by the aid of fungi on their roots and in their leaves; nourishment by mycorrhiza. [< MYCO- + Gk. trophē nutrition] —my·co·tro′phic adj.

my·dri·a·sis (mi·drī′ə·sis, mī-) n. Pathol. An abnormal or prolonged dilation of the pupil of the eye. [< LL < Gk.]

myd·ri·at·ic (mid′rē·at′ik) adj. Med. Relating to or causing dilation of the pupil. —n. A drug that dilates the pupil, as belladonna.

my·e·len·ceph·a·lon (mī′ə·len·sef′ə·lon) n. Anat. The afterbrain; the posterior part of the rhombencephalon or that portion of the medulla oblongata lying behind the pons Varolii and cerebellum. [< MYEL(O) + ENCEPHALON]

my·e·lin (mī′ə·lin) n. Biochem. A semisolid, fatlike substance that surrounds the axillary portion of medullated nerve fibers; the medullary sheath. Also **my′e·line** (-lēn, -lin). [< Gk. myelos marrow]

my·e·li·tis (mī′ə·lī′tis) n. Pathol. 1 Inflammation of the spinal cord. 2 Inflammation of the bone marrow. [< MYEL(O) + -ITIS]

myelo- combining form Anat. 1 The bone marrow. 2 The spinal cord. Also, before vowels, **myel-**. [< Gk. myelon marrow]

my·e·loid (mī′ə·loid) adj. Anat. 1 Pertaining to, from, or resembling marrow. 2 Of or pertaining to the spinal cord. [< MYEL(O) + -OID]

my·e·lo·ma (mī′ə·lō′mə) n. pl. ·mas or ·ma·ta (-mə·tə) Pathol. A tumor composed of bone marrow cells. [< MYEL- + -OMA]

My·ers (mī′ərz), **F(rederic) W(illiam) H(enry)**, 1843–1901, English philosopher and writer.

my·i·a·sis (mī′yə·sis) n. Pathol. Any of various diseases caused by flies or maggots. [< NL < Gk. myia fly + -(o)SIS]

Myit·kyi·na The capital of Kachin State, Myanmar.

My·lae (mī′lē) The ancient name for MILAZZO; scene of a Roman naval victory over Carthage, 260 B.C. Also **My′læ**.

my·lo·nite (mī′lə·nīt) n. Geol. A hard, compact rock having a banded or streaky appearance, produced by the crushing and reforming of earth material under extreme pressure. [< Gk. mylōn mill]

my·na (mī′nə) n. One of various Oriental, starlinglike birds of the genera Acridotheres and Eulabes. Eulabes religiosa, the common myna of India, is often tamed and taught to speak words: sometimes spelled mina, minah. Also **my′nah**. [< Hind. mainā]

MYNA
(About 9 inches over all)

myn·heer (mīn·hâr′, -hir′) n. Sir; Mr.: a Dutch title of address; hence, a Dutchman. [< Du. mijn heer, lit., my lord]

myo- combining form Muscle; of or pertaining to muscle: myology. Also, before vowels, **my-**. [< Gk. mys, myos a muscle]

my·o·car·di·al (mī′ō·kär′dē·əl) adj. Anat. Of or pertaining to the heart muscle. [< MYO- + Gk. kardia heart]

my·o·car·di·o·gram (mī′ō·kär′dē·ə·gram) n. The record made by a myocardiograph.

my·o·car·di·o·graph (mī′ō·kär′dē·ə·graf, -gräf) n. An instrument for registering the muscular action of the heart.

my·o·car·di·tis (mī′ō·kär·dī′tis) n. Pathol. Inflammation of the myocardium. [< NL] —my′o·car·dit′ic (-dit′ik) adj.

my·o·car·di·um (mī′ō·kär′dē·əm) n. Anat. The muscular tissue of the heart. [< NL < MYO- + Gk. kardia heart]

my·o·gen·ic (mī′ō·jə·net′ik) adj. Physiol. Originating in muscle or in muscle tissue. Also **my′o·gen′ic**, **my·og′e·nous** (mī·oj′ə·nəs).

my·o·gram (mī′ə·gram) n. The record made by a myograph.

my·o·graph (mī′ə·graf, -gräf) n. An instrument for recording and showing muscular movement.

my·og·ra·phy (mī·og′rə·fē) n. A scientific description of muscles.

my·oid (mī′oid) adj. Resembling a muscle or muscle tissue.

my·ol·o·gy (mī·ol′ə·jē) n. The study of the structure, functions, and diseases of the muscles. [< MYO- + -LOGY] —my·o·log·ic (mī′ə·loj′ik) or ·i·cal adj. —my·ol′o·gist n.

my·o·ma (mī·ō′mə) n. pl. ·ma·ta (-mə·tə) Pathol. A muscular tumor. [< MY- + -OMA] —my·om′a·tous (-om′ə·təs) adj.

my·o·mec·to·my (mī′ō·mek′tə·mē). n. Surg. The removal of a myoma. [< MYOMA + -ECTOMY]

my·op·a·thy (mī·op′ə·thē) n. Pathol. Disease of a muscle. Also **my·o·path·i·a** (mī′ō·path′ē·ə) [< MYO- + -PATHY] —my′o·path′ic adj.

my·ope (mī′ōp) n. One who is near-sighted. Also **my′ops** (-ops). [< F < LL myops < Gk. myōps < myein close + ōps an eye]

my·o·pi·a (mī·ō′pē·ə) n. Pathol. Defect in vision so that objects can be seen distinctly only when very near the eye; near-sightedness due to focusing of images in front of instead of on the retina. Also **my·o·py** (mī′ə·pē). [< NL] —my·op′ic (-op′ik) adj.

my·o·scope (mī′ə·skōp) n. Med. An instrument for observing the contraction of muscles.

my·o·sin (mī′ə·sin) n. A globulin constituting about half of the protein in muscle and combining with actin to form actomyosin. [< Gk. mys, myos muscle]

my·o·sis (mī·ō′sis) See MIOSIS.

my·o·so·tis (mī′ə·sō′tis) n. Any of a genus of plants (Myosotis) of the borage family; especially, M. scorpioides, having branched racemes of blue or pink flowers. Also **my′o·sote** (-sōt). [< NL < Gk., lit., mouse ear < mys, myos a mouse + ous, ōtos ear]

my·ot·ic (mī·ot′ik) adj. Of, pertaining to, or having miosis. —n. A drug causing contraction of the pupil of the eye.

My·ra (mī′rə) An ancient city in Lycia, Asia Minor, Acts xxvii 5.

myria- combining form 1 Very many; of great number: myriapod. 2 In the metric system, ten thousand: myriagram. Also, before vowels, **myri-**. [< Gk. myrios < myrioi ten thousand]

myr·i·ad (mir′ē·əd) adj. Composed of a very large indefinite number; innumerable. —n. 1 A vast indefinite number. 2 Ten thousand. [< Gk. myrias, myriados < myrios numberless]

myr·i·a·gram (mir′ē·ə·gram′), **myr·i·a·li·ter** (-lē′tər), **myr·i·a·me·ter** (mē′tər) n. In the metric system, 10,000 grams, liters, or meters.

myr·i·a·pod (mir′ē·ə·pod) n. One of a class of arthropods (Myriapoda) whose bodies are made up of a varying number of segments, each of which bears one or two pairs of jointed appendages: includes the centipedes and millipedes. — **myr·i·ap·o·dan** (mir′ē·ap′ə·dən) adj. & n. — **myr·i·ap′o·dous** adj.

my·ri·ca (mi·rī′kə) n. The dried bark of the wax-myrtle root, used in medicine as an alterative and emetic. [< L < Gk. myrikē tamarisk]

my·ris·tic (mi·ris′tik) adj. 1 Of, pertaining to, or containing the principle of nutmeg. 2 Chem. Designating a white crystalline acid, $C_{14}H_{28}O_2$, contained in nutmeg butter and similar vegetable sources. [< NL nux myristica nutmeg genus < Gk. myrizein anoint]

myrmeco- combining form Ant; pertaining to ants: myrmecophagous. Also, before vowels, **myrmec-**. [< Gk. myrmēx, myrmēkos ant]

myr·me·col·o·gy (mûr′mə·kol′ə·jē) n. The department of entomology that treats of ants. [< MYRMECO- + -LOGY] —myr′me·co·log′i·cal (-kə·loj′i·kəl) adj. —myr′me·col′o·gist n.

myr·me·coph·a·gous (mûr′mə·kof′ə·gəs) adj. Feeding on ants. [< MYRMECO- + -PHAGOUS]

myr·mi·don (mûr′mə·don, -dən) n. A faithful adherent; also, a follower or underling of rough or desperate character, who executes the commands of his master without question

or scruple; especially, a petty officer of the law. [< MYRMIDON]

Myr·mi·don (mûr′mə·don, -dən) *n.* One of a warlike people of ancient Thessaly, represented as followers of Achilles in the Trojan War. [< Gk. *Myrmidones*] —**Myr′mi·do′ni·an** (-dō′nē-ən) *adj.*

my·rob·a·lan (mī·rob′ə·lən, mi-) *n.* **1** Any of the prunelike fruits of several tropical plants (genus *Terminalia*), formerly much used by tanners and calico printers. **2** The weeping plum of the western Mediterranean region (*Phyllanthus emblica*). **3** The myrobalan plum of SW Asia (*Prunus cerasifera*), having a sweet, very juicy fruit. [< F < Arabic < Gk. *myrobalanos* < *myron* juice, ointment + *balanos* nut]

My·ron (mī′rən) A Greek sculptor of the fifth century B.C. —**My·ron′ic** (-ron′ik) *adj.*

my·ro·sin (mī′rə·sin, mir′ə·sin) *n. Biochem.* An enzyme found in the seeds of black and white mustard: it hydrolyzes the glycosides. [< Gk. *myron* ointment]

myrrh (mûr) *n.* **1** An aromatic gum resin that exudes from several trees or shrubs of Arabia and Abyssinia: used in medicine. **2** Any shrub or tree that yields this gum, especially *Commiphora myrrha* and *C. abyssinica.* [OE *murra* < L *myrrha* < Gk. < Semitic. Cf. Arabic *myrr*, Hebrew *mōr.*]

myr·rhin (mûr′in, mir′-) *n. Biochem.* A resinous principle found in myrrh. Also **myr′rhine.**

myr·ta·ceous (mûr·tā′shəs) *adj.* Pertaining to or designating a family (*Myrtaceae*) of trees or shrubs, the myrtle family, widely distributed in tropical and semitropical countries, and including many valuable aromatic resin- and timber-producing genera, as *Pimenta*, *Eucalyptus*, *Caryophyllus*, etc. [< NL *Myrtaceae* < L *myrtus* a myrtle tree]

myr·tle (mûr′təl) *n.* **1** A tree or shrub of the genus *Myrtus;* especially, *M. communis* of southern Europe, originally from Asia. It is a bushy shrub or small tree with glossy evergreen leaves, fragrant white or rose-colored flowers, and black berries. **2** One of various other plants like the common myrtle. Among the ancients it was sacred to Venus. **3** The periwinkle (*Vinca minor*); also, the California laurel (*Umbellularia californica*). [< F *myrtille* bilberry < Med. L *myrtillus* myrtle, dim. of L *myrtus* < Gk. *myrtos* < Semitic. Cf. Persian *mûrd.*]

Myr·tle (mûr′təl) A feminine personal name. [< MYRTLE]

myrtle warbler A small insectivorous bird (*Dendroica coronata*) of North America, with blue-gray or black-and-yellow back.

my·sel (mi·sel′) *pron. Scot.* Myself; by myself. Also **my·sell′.**

my·self (mī·self′) *pron.* **1** I; me: the emphatic form of *I* and *me*, used in the nominative with *I* in apposition: I *myself* will see to it; I'll write it *myself;* also, in poetical nominative use as a simple subject: *Myself* hath often heard; also used as the object of a verb either direct or indirect: I deceived *myself* (reflexive); She invited Helen, Jeff, and *myself* (compound object); I got it for *myself* (object of a preposition). **2** Normal condition of mind or body: I feel *myself* again. [OE *mē sylf*]

My·si·a (mish′ē·ə) An ancient region of NW Asia Minor on the Aegean and the Sea of Marmara.

My·sore (mī·sôr′, -sōr′) **1** A constituent State of southern India on the southern Deccan Plateau; 74,326 square miles; capital, Bangalore. **2** The former dynastic capital of Mysore State. Also *Maisur.*

mys·ta·gog (mis′tə·gôg, -gog) *n.* An interpreter of religious mysteries; an initiator into mysteries; teacher. Also **mys′ta·gogue.** [< L *mystagogus* < Gk. *mystagōgos* < *mystēs* an initiate + *agōgos* leader < *agein.* See MYSTERY.] —**mys′ta·gog′ic** (-goj′ik) *adj.* —**mys′ta·go′gy** (-gō′jē) *n.*

mys·te·ri·ous (mis·tir′ē·əs) *adj.* Involved in or implying mystery; unexplained; obscure. [< L *mysterium*] —**mys·te′ri·ous·ly** *adv.* —**mys·te′ri·ous·ness** *n.*

Synonyms: abstruse, cabalistic, dark, enigmatic, hidden, incomprehensible, inexplicable, inscrutable, mystic, mystical, obscure, occult, recondite, secret, transcendental, unfathomable, unfathomed, unknown. That is *mysterious* in the true sense which is beyond human comprehension; that is *mystic* or *mystical* which has associated with it some *hidden* or *recondite* meaning. See DARK, SECRET. *Antonyms:* see synonyms for CLEAR.

mys·ter·y[1] (mis′tər·ē) *n. pl.* **·ter·ies** **1** Something unknown or incomprehensible in its nature; an inexplicable phenomenon. **2** Secrecy or obscurity: an event wrapped in *mystery.* **3** A secret: the *mysteries* of freemasonry. **4** Any affair or event so concealed or unexplained as to excite awe or curiosity: a murder *mystery.* **5** A literary or dramatic piece relating such an affair. **6** *Theol.* A truth known only through faith or revelation and incomprehensible to the human reason. **7** *Eccl.* **a** A sacrament, especially the Eucharist. **b** *pl.* The eucharistic elements. **8** *pl.* In classical antiquity, certain religious rites to which only selected worshipers were admitted. **9** *pl.* A cult practicing such rites. **10** A medieval dramatic performance based on Scriptural events or characters: also **mystery play.** [< L *mysterium* < Gk. *mystērion* secret worship, secret thing < *mystēs* an initiate into the mysteries < *myein* shut, shut the eyes]

mys·ter·y[2] (mis′tər·ē) *n. pl.* **·ter·ies** *Archaic* A trade; occupation. [< Med. L *misterium* < L *ministerium* service, office; infl. in form by L *mysterium*]

mys·tic (mis′tik) *adj.* **1** Pertaining to a mystery of the faith. **2** Spiritually symbolic. **3** Of or designating an occult or esoteric rite, practice, etc. **4** Of mysterious meaning or character; mysterious. —*n.* **1** One who professes a knowledge of spiritual truth or a feeling of union with the divine, reached through contemplation or intuition. **2** A practicer of occult or mystical rites. [< L *mysticus* < Gk. *mystikos* pertaining to secret rites < *mystēs* an initiate]

mys·ti·cal (mis′ti·kəl) *adj.* **1** Having a spiritual character or reality beyond the comprehension of human reason. **2** Relating to mystics or mysticism. **3** Mystic (defs. 2 and 3).

mys·ti·cism (mis′tə·siz′əm) *n.* **1** The belief that knowledge of divine truth or the soul's union with the divine is attainable by spiritual insight or ecstatic contemplation without the medium of the senses or reason. **2** Any theory advancing intense meditative and intuitive methods of thought or conduct. **3** Vague or obscure speculation involving confused or fanciful thinking.

mys·ti·fy (mis′tə·fī) *v.t.* **·fied, ·fy·ing** **1** To confuse, especially deliberately; perplex or bewilder; hoax. **2** To treat as obscure or mysterious. See synonyms under PERPLEX.

[< F *mystifier*] —**mys′ti·fi·ca′tion** *n.* —**mys′ti·fi′er** *n.* —**mys′ti·fy′ing** *adj.* —**mys′ti·fy′ing·ly** *adv.*

mys·tique (mis·tēk′) *n. French* The mythical and enigmatic character of a person, idea, or thing, as a focus of popular veneration: the *mystique* of Stalin.

myth (mith) *n.* **1** A story, presented as historical, dealing with the cosmological and supernatural traditions of a people, their gods, culture, heroes, religious beliefs, etc. **2** A popular fable or folk tale. **3** A parable; allegory. See synonyms under FICTION. [< LL *mythos* < Gk. word, speech, story]

myth·i·cal (mith′i·kəl) *adj.* **1** Pertaining to myth; legendary. **2** Fictitious. Also **myth′ic.** —**myth′i·cal·ly** *adv.*

myth·i·cize (mith′ə·sīz) *v.t.* **·cized, ·ciz·ing** To convert into or explain as a myth.

mytho- *combining form* Myth; myth and: *mythography.* Also, before vowels, **myth-.** [< Gk. *mythos* a legend]

my·thog·ra·phy (mi·thog′rə·fē) *n.* **1** The collecting of myths; descriptive mythology. **2** Expression of mythic characters or ideas in art form. [< MYTHO- + -GRAPHY] —**my·thog′ra·pher** *n.*

my·thol·o·gize (mi·thol′ə·jīz) *v.* **·gized, ·giz·ing** *v.i.* To narrate, classify, or explain myths. —*v.t.* To mythicize. Also *Brit.* **my·thol′o·gise.** [< F *mythologiser*] —**my·thol′o·gist, my·thol′o·giz′er** *n.*

my·thol·o·gy (mi·thol′ə·jē) *n. pl.* **·gies** **1** The myths and legends of a people concerning creation, gods, and heroes. **2** The scientific collection and study of myths; study of the beliefs of mankind; also, a volume of myths. [¶ < LL *mythologia* < Gk., telling of tales < *mythos* legend + *logos* discourse] —**myth·o·log·i·cal** (mith′ə·loj′i·kəl), **myth′o·log′ic** *adj.* —**myth′o·log′i·cal·ly** *adv.*

myth·o·ma·ni·a (mith′ə·mā′nē·ə, -mān′yə) *n.* A compulsive tendency to tell lies.

myth·o·pe·ic (mith′ə·pē′ik) *adj.* Mythmaking; relating to a supposed stage of human culture when all natural phenomena are explained by myths. Also **myth′o·poe′ic.** [< Gk. *mythopoios* < *mythos* legend + *poieein* make] —**myth′o·pe′ist** *n.*

Myt·i·le·ne (mit′ə·lē′nē) **1** Lesbos. **2** A seaport on SE Lesbos, capital of the Aegean Islands division of Greece: formerly *Kastro.* Also **Myt′i·li′ni.**

myx·e·de·ma (mik′sə·dē′mə) *n. Pathol.* A disease associated with hypotrophy of the thyroid gland and characterized by dryness and wrinkling of the skin, swelling of the face, and progressive mental deterioration. Also **myx′oe·de′ma.** [< NL < MYX(O)- + EDEMA] —**myx′e·dem′ic** (-dem′ik), **myx′e·dem′a·tous** (-dem′ə·təs) *adj.*

myxo- *combining form* Slimy; like mucus. Also, before vowels, **myx-.** [< Gk. *myxa* mucus]

myx·o·ma (mik·sō′mə) *n. pl.* **·ma·ta** (-mə·tə) *Pathol.* A soft, elastic tumor composed of mucous tissue. [< NL < MYX(O)- + -OMA] —**myx·om·a·tous** (-som′ə·təs) *adj.*

myx·o·my·cete (mik′sō·mī·sēt′) *n.* One of the slime molds (*Myxomycetes*), a class of fungi exhibiting both plant and animal characteristics and classified by some authorities as *Mycetozoa.* They consist of masses of naked protoplasm with ameboid movements, and are chiefly saprophytic, living on dead and decaying matter. [< MYXO- + -MYCETE] —**myx′o·my·ce′tous** *adj.*

N

n, N (en) *n. pl.* **n's, N's** or **ns, Ns, ens** (enz) **1** The 14th letter of the English alphabet: from Phoenician *nun*, Greek *nu*, Roman *N.* **2** The sound of the letter *n*, a voiced, alveolar nasal. See ALPHABET. —*symbol* **1** *Printing* An en: see

EN. **2** *Chem.* Nitrogen (symbol N). **3** *Math.* An indefinite number.

Na *Chem.* Sodium (symbol Na). [< NL *natrium*]

nab[1] (nab) *v.t.* **nabbed, nab·bing** *Colloq.* **1** To catch or arrest, as a criminal. **2** To take or seize

suddenly. [Cf. Norw., Sw. *nappa* snatch]

nab[2] (nab) *n.* **1** *Geog.* A projecting part of a hill or rock; a peak, promontory, or summit. **2** *Mech.* A projection or spur on the bolt of a lock. [< ON *nabbi* a knoll]

Nab·a·te·an (nab′ə·tē′ən) *n.* **1** One of an ancient Arabic people dwelling east and southeast of Palestine, independent from 312 B.C. to A.D. 106, when they submitted to Roman rule. **2** The language of these people, belonging to the Aramaic subgroup of the Northwest Semitic languages.

Na·blus (nä·blo͞os′) The chief town of Samaria, western Jordan, on the site of ancient *Sechem,* rebuilt by Hadrian as *Neapolis.*

na·bob (nā′bob) *n.* **1** A European who has become rich in India; hence, any rich man. **2** A nawab, viceroy, or governor in India under the old Mogul empire. [<Hind. *nawwāb* <Arabic *nuwwab,* pl. of *nā'ib* a deputy] **—na′bob·er·y** *n.* **—na′bob·ish** *adj.*

Na·both (nā′both) In the Bible, the owner of a vineyard which Ahab coveted and, with the aid of Jezebel, unlawfully procured. I *Kings* xxi.

nac·a·rat (nak′ə·rat) *n.* **1** Bright red-orange color. **2** A fine linen or crêpe fabric dyed this color. [<F, appar. <Sp. *nacarado* <*nacar* nacre]

na·celle (nə·sel′) *n.* Aeron. **1** The basket suspended from a balloon. **2** The framework below the envelope of a dirigible balloon, which carries the motor, passengers, etc. **3** An enclosed shelter for housing the cargo or power plant and sometimes the personnel of an airplane. [<F]

na·cho (nä′chō) *n. pl.* **-chos** A tortilla chip covered with beans, hot peppers, etc., then sprinkled with cheese. [<Sp.]

na·cre (nā′kər) *n.* Mother-of-pearl. [<F]

na·cre·ous (nā′krē·əs) *adj.* **1** Of, like, or producing nacre. **2** Iridescent; pearly.

na·da (nä′də) *n.* In East Indian music, the term for a esthetically agreeable sound, as distinct from noise, grinding, clanging, etc.

na·dir (nā′dər, -dir) *n.* **1** The point of the celestial sphere directly beneath the place where one stands: opposed to *zenith.* **2** Figuratively, the lowest possible point: the *nadir* of melancholy. [<F <Arabic *nadir (es-semt)* opposite (the zenith)]

nae (nā) *adj. Scot.* No; none.

nae·thing (nā′thing) *n. Scot.* Nothing.

nae·void, nae·vus (nē′void), (nē′vəs) See NEVOID, NEVUS.

Na·fud (na·fo͞od′) A desert area in northern Saudi Arabia: also *Nefud.*

nag[1] (nag) *v.* **nagged, nag·ging** *v.t.* To torment with constant faultfinding, scolding, and urging. —*v.i.* To scold, find fault, or urge continually. —*n.* One who nags, especially a woman. [<Scand. Cf. Sw. *nagga* vex.] **—nag′·ger** *n.* **—nag′ging** *adj.* **—nag′ging·ly** *adv.*

nag[2] (nag) *n.* **1** A pony or small horse. **2** An old or inferior horse. **3** *Archaic* A worthless person; jade. [ME *nagge;* origin uncertain]

Na·ga Hills (nä′gə) A series of hill ranges between NE India and western Burma.

na·ga·na (nə·gä′nə) *n.* A disease of cattle and horses caused by trypanosomes introduced into the blood by the tsetse fly. [<Zulu]

Na·ga·ri (nä′gə·rē) *n.* **1** Any one of a group of vernacular alphabets in India. **2** Devanagari.

Na·ga·sa·ki (nä·gä·sä·kē) A port on western Kyushu island, Japan; largely destroyed by an atomic bomb dropped by U.S. airmen on August 9, 1945.

Nä·ge·li (nā′gə·lē), **Karl Wilhelm von,** 1817–1891, Swiss botanist.

Na·gor·no-Ka·ra·bakh Autonomous Region (nä·gôr′nə·kä′rä·bäkh′) An administrative division of SW Azerbaijan S.S.R.; 1,700 square miles.

Na·go·ya (nä·gō·yä) A city on southern Honshu island, Japan, on Ise Bay.

Nag·pur (näg′po͝or) A city in NE Bombay State, India, former capital of Madhya Pradesh State.

Nag·y·va·rad (nôd′y′·vä ′rôd) Hungarian name for ORADEA.

Na·ha (nä·hä) Chief city of Okinawa island and headquarters of the U.S. military government of the Ryukyu Islands.

Na·hua (nä′wä) *n. pl.* **Na·hua** One of a group of civilized Indian peoples of Mexico and Central America belonging to the Uto-Aztecan linguistic stock, including the Aztecs, Toltecs, etc.

Na·hua·tl (nä′wät′l) *n.* The Uto-Aztecan language of the Aztecs, including many dialects. —*adj.* Designating or pertaining to this language.

Na·hua·tlan (nä′wät·lən) *n.* A branch of the Uto-Aztecan linguistic family of North American Indians, including the Aztec dialects. —*adj.* Of or pertaining to this linguistic branch.

Na·huel Hua·pí (nä·wel′ wä ·pē′) A lake on the eastern slope of the Andes in western Argentina near the Chilean border; 210 square miles.

Na·hum (nā′əm, -hum) A Hebrew prophet; also, the book of the Old Testament containing his prophecies. [<Hebrew, consolation]

nai·ad (nā′ad, nī′-) *n. pl.* **·ads** or **·a·des** (-ə·dēz) **1** In classical mythology, one of the water nymphs who were believed to dwell in and preside over fountains, lakes, brooks, and wells. **2** *Bot.* A plant of the pondweed family (genus *Naias*). **3** The nymph stage in the life cycle of certain insects: applied especially to aquatic forms. [<Gk. *Naias, -ados.* Related to Gk. *naein* flow.]

nai·ant (nā′ənt) See NATANT.

Na·i·du (nä′i·do͞o), **Sarojini,** 1879–1949, Hindu poet and reformer.

na·if (nä·ēf′) *adj. French* Masculine form of NAIVE. Also **na·ïf′.**

naig (näg) *n. Scot.* A nag; riding horse. Also **naig′ ie.**

nail (nāl) *n.* **1** A thin horny plate on the end of a finger or toe. **2** A claw, talon, or hoof. **3** A slender piece of metal having a point and a head, and used for driving into or through wood, etc., as for fastening pieces together. **4** A measure of length, 2 1/4 inches. **5** A callosity on the inner side of a horse's leg. **—on the nail** *Colloq.* **1** Right away; immediately. **2** At the exact spot or moment. **3** Of immediate interest or importance; under discussion. —*v.t.* **1** To fasten or fix in place with a nail or nails. **2** To close up or shut in by means of nails. **3** To secure by decisive or prompt action: to *nail* a contract. **4** To fix firmly or immovably: Terror *nailed* him to the spot. **5** To succeed in hitting or striking. **6** *Colloq.* To catch or seize; intercept. **7** *Colloq.* To detect and expose, as a lie or liar. [OE *nægel*]

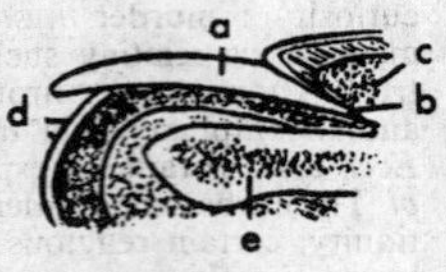

HUMAN FINGERNAIL
Longitudinal section
a. Nail.
b. Matrix.
c. Nailfold.
d. Epidermis.
e. Phalanx.

nail bed *Anat.* That portion of the true skin upon which the nail rests.

nail·brush (nāl ′brush′) *n.* A brush with stiff bristles, used for cleaning the hands and fingernails.

nail file A fine, flat file used for manicuring the fingernails.

nail·fold (nāl′fōld′) *n. Anat.* The duplication of the skin that surrounds the edges of a nail; cuticle.

nail polish A lacquer applied to the nails to give a glossy finish, made from soluble cotton treated with various organic compounds, as toluene, ethyl acetate, ethanol, etc., and usually colored by the addition of dyes. Also **nail enamel.**

nain·sook (nān′so͝ok, nan′-) *n.* A soft, lightweight cotton fabric, heavier than batiste: used for lingerie and infants' wear. [<Hind. *nainsukh,* lit., pleasure of the eye]

Nai·paul (nī′pôl;), **V.S.,** born 1932, West Indian novelist, educated in Trinidad and England. Full name, **Vidiadhar Surajprasad Naipaul.**

Nairn (nârn) A county in NE Scotland; 163 square miles; county town, Nairn. Also **Nairnshire** (nârn′shir, -shər).

Nai·ro·bi (nī·rō′bē) The capital of Kenya in eastern Africa.

na·ive (nä·ēv′) *adj.* **1** Ingenuous; artless; without sophistication. **2** Not consciously logical; uncritical. Also **na·ïve′.** See synonyms under CANDID. [<F, fem. of *naïf* <L *nativus* natural. Doublet of NATIVE.] **—na·ive′ly** *adv.* **—na·ive′ness** *n.*

na·ive·té (nä·ēv′tā′, nä·ēv′tā) *n.* The state or quality of being naive. Also **na·ïve′té′, na·ive·ty** (nä·ēv′tē).

Najd (näjd) See NEJD.

Na·jin (nä·jēn) A port of Northern Korea. *Japanese* **Ra·shin** (rä·shēn).

na·ked (nā′kid) *adj.* **1** Having no clothes or garments on; nude. **2** Having no covering, or lacking the usual covering. **3** Unsheathed; bare, as a sword. **4** Unsaddled, as a horse. **5** Having no defense or protection; exposed. **6** Being without means of sustenance, etc.; destitute; bare; also, stripped. **7** Being without concealment or excuse. **8** Without addition or adornment; plain; evident; mere. **9** Without some accessory, qualification, belonging, etc., which is customary or natural. **10** *Law* Having no consideration or inducement; unconfirmed; not validated. **11** *Bot.* **a** Not enclosed in an ovary or case. **b** Without a pericarp: said of seeds. **c** Destitute of leaves: said of stalks. **d** Having no hairs; smooth: said of leaves. **12** *Zool.* Lacking fur, hair, scales, or feathers. [OE *nacod*] **—na′ked·ly** *adv.* **—na′ked·ness** *n.*

naked eye The eye unaided by optical instruments.

Na·khi·che·van Autonomous S.S.R. (nä ′·khē·che·vän′) **1** A republic forming part of the Azerbaijan S.S.R.; 2,100 square miles. **2** Its capital and chief city, on the Araxes.

Nak·tong (näk·tông) The largest river of Korea, flowing 326 miles to Korea Strait near Pusan.

Nal·chik (näl′chik) The capital of Kabardian Autonomous S.S.R.

nam (näm, nam) Past tense of NIM.

nam·a·ble (nā′mə·bəl) *adj.* **1** Capable of being named. **2** Memorable; worthy of being mentioned. Also **name′a·ble. —nam′a·bil′i·ty, name′a·bil′i·ty** *n.*

Na·man·gan (nä′män·gän′) A city in eastern Uzbek S.S.R.

Na·ma·qua·land (nə·mä′ kwə·land) A coastal region of SW Africa, divided by the Orange River into **Great Namaqualand** in Namibia and **Little Namaqualand** in Northern Cape Province, Republic of South Africa. Also **Na′ma·land.**

nam·ay·cush (nam′ə·kush, -ā -) *n.* The great lake trout *(Cristivomer namaycush)* of North America; the Mackinaw trout: also spelled *naymacush.* [<Algonquian (Cree) *namekus* trout]

nam·by-pam·by (nam′bē·pam′bē) *adj.* Weakly sentimental; insipid; inane. — *n. pl.* **-pam·bies** **1** Writing, talk, or action of a feebly sentimental or finical character. **2** A person given to such talk or action. [<nickname of Ambrose Philips, 1671–1749, English poet; with ref. to his feeble, sentimental verse]

name (nām) *n.* **1** The distinctive appellation by which a person or thing is known. **2** A descriptive or arbitrary appellation; designation; title. **3** General reputation; eminence; fame. **4** A person, cause, thing, or class, or the claims of authority thereof, as represented by the name. **5** An opprobrious appellation. **6** A race or family, as having a common descent and patronymic. **7** A memorable person, character, or thing: great *names* in music. **8** Mere sound or simulation, in distinction from substance or reality: a wife in *name* only. **—by the name of** Named. —*v.t.* **named, nam·ing 1** To give a name to; entitle; style; term. **2** To mention or refer to by name; cite. **3** To designate for some particular purpose or office; nominate; appoint. **4** To give the name of; identify: *Name* the capital of Peru. **5** To set or specify, as a price or requirement. [OE *nama*] **—nam′er** *n.*

Synonyms (noun) : agnomen, appellation, cognomen, denomination, designation, epithet, style, title. *Name* in the most general sense includes all other words of this group; in the more limited sense a *name* is personal, an *appellation* is descriptive, a *title* is official. In the phrase William the Conqueror, king of England, William is the man's *name,* which belongs to him personally; Conqueror is the *appellation* which he won by his acquistion of England; king is the *title* denoting his royal rank. An *epithet* is given to mark some assumed characteristic, good or bad. *Designation* may be used in the sense of *appellation,* but is far broader and more general in meaning. One's personal *name,* as John or Mary, is given in infancy, and is often called the given or Christian, or first *name.* The *cognomen* is the family *name* which belongs to one by right of birth or marriage. In modern use, *style* is the legal *designation* by which a person or house is known in official or business

relations. A *denomination* is a specific, and especially a collective name; the term is applied to a separate religious organization, also to money or notes of a certain value; as, The sum was in notes of the *denomination* of one thousand dollars. See TERM.

name-day (nām′dā′) *n.* The day of the saint for whom one is named.

name·less (nām′lis) *adj.* 1 Having no name; unnamed. 2 Having no fame or reputation; illegitimate; obscure; anonymous. 3 Not suitable or fit to be spoken of. 4 Not to be named; inexpressible; indescribable. —**name′·less·ly** *adv.* —**name′·less·ness** *n.*

name·ly (nām′lē) *adv.* That is to say; to wit; videlicet.

name·plate (nām′plāt′) *n.* A piece of wood, metal, or plastic with a name inscribed on it.

name·sake (nām′sāk) *n.* One who is named after or has the same name as another.

Nam·hoi (näm′hoi′) A city in central Kwangtung province, SE China: formerly *Fatshan.*

Na·mib·ia (nə·mi′bē·ə) A country in SW Africa on the Atlantic Ocean, capital Windhoek, formerly German Southwest Africa.

Nam·po (näm′pō′) See CHINNAMPO.

Nam Tso (näm′tsō′) The largest lake of Tibet, NW of Lhasa; elevation, 15,180 feet;′ 950 square miles: Mongolian *Tengri Nor.*

Na·mur (nä·moor′, *Fr.* nà·mûr′) A city in south central Belgium. Flemish **Na·men** (nä′mən).

Nan (nän) A river in northern Thailand, flowing 500 miles south to the Chao Phraya.

nan·a (nan′ə, nä′nä) *n.* Grandmother.

Nan·chang (nän′chäng′) The capital city of Kiangsi province, SE China.

Nan·cy (nan′sē) Diminutive of ANN.

Nan·cy (nan′si, *Fr.* nän·sē′) A city of NE France, chief city of Lorraine.

Nan·da De·vi (nun′dä dā′vē) A mountain in northern Uttar Pradesh, India; 25,645 feet.

nane (nän) *adj.* & *pron. Scot.* None; no one.

Nan·ga Par·bat (nung′gə pûr′bət) A mountain in NW Kashmir; 26,660 feet.

nan·keen (nan·kēn′) *n.* 1 A buff-colored Chinese cotton fabric. 2 *pl.* Clothes made of nankeen. Also **nan·kin′.** [from *Nanking,* where originally made]

Nan·king (nan′king′, nän′-) A port on the Yangtze, fomer capital of Kiangsu province; capital of China, 1928–37.

Nanking porcelain Any of various types of fine Chinese porcelain painted in blue on white: also called *blue-and-white.* Also **Nankeen porcelain.**

Nan Ling (nän′ ling′) A mountain chain in SE China, on the northern border of Kwangtung province.

Nan·ning (nän′ning′) A city of southern China, former capital of Kwangsi province.

nan·ny (nan′ē) *n. pl.* **·nies** *Colloq.* 1 A female goat: also **nanny goat.** 2 *Brit.* A child's nurse. [from *Nanny,* a personal name]

Nan·ny (nan′ē) Diminutive of ANN.

nano- *combining form* 1 One billionth part of: *nanosecond.* 2 Microscopic; very small: *nanoplankton.*

nan·o·gram (nan′ə·gram) *n.* One billionth of a gram.

ɲan·o·me·ter (nan′ə·mē′tər) *n.* One billionth of a meter.

na·no·plank·ton (nä′nə·plangk′tən, nan′ə-) *n.* Floating plant and animal organisms of microscopic size. Also **nan′ no·plank′ton** (nan′·ə-). [<Gk. *nanos* dwarf + PLANKTON]

na·no·sec·ond (nan′ə·sek′ənd, nä′nə-) *n.* One billionth of a second.

Nan·sei Islands (nän·sā) See RYUKYU ISLANDS.

Nan·se·mond River (nan′sə·mond) A river in SE Virginia, flowing 25 miles north to the James River estuary near Hampton Roads.

Nan·sen (nän′sən), **Fridtjof,** 1861–1930, Norwegian Arctic explorer and naturalist.

Nan Shan (nän′ shän′) A mountain range in Tsinghai and Kansu provinces, China.

Nan·tas·ket Beach (nan·tas′kit) A resort village of eastern Massachusetts, on Massachusetts Bay south of Boston.

Nantes (nants, *Fr.* nänt) A city of western France, on the Loire. —**Edict of Nantes** An order granting freedom of conscience to Protestants, issued by Henry IV of France in 1598 and revoked in 1685 by Louis XIV.

Nan·tuck·et (nan·tuk′it) An island and summer resort off the SE coast of Massachusetts; 57 square miles. —**Nan·tuck′et·er** *n.*

Nan·tung (nän′toong′) A city of northern Kiangsu province; China: formerly *Tungchow.*

Na·o·mi (nā·ō′mē, nā′ə·mē, -mī) A feminine personal name. [< Hebrew, pleasant] —**Na·omi** In the Bible, the mother-in-law of Ruth. *Ruth* i 2.

na·os (nā′os) *n. Archit.* The principal chamber or body of an ancient Greek temple, usually containing a statue of the deity; a cella. [<Gk., a temple]

nap¹ (nap) *n.* A short sleep; doze. —*v.i.* **napped, nap·ping** 1 To take a nap; doze. 2 To be unprepared or off one's guard. [OE *hnappian* doze] —**nap′per** *n.*

nap² (nap) *n.* 1 The short fibers on the surface of flannel, etc., forming a soft surface lying smoothly in one direction. 2 A covering resembling this, as upon some plants or insects. —*v.t.* **napped, nap·ping** To raise a nap on. [<MDu. *noppe*]

nap³ (nap) See NAPOLEON (def. 2).

na·palm (nā′päm) *n.* A jellied mixture of aluminum soap powder and oil or gasoline, used as an incendiary in bombs, flame-throwers, etc. — *v.t.* & *v.i.* To attack or burn with napalm. [< *na(phthenic)* and *palm(itic) acids*]

nape (nāp) *n.* 1 The back of the neck, especially its upper part. ◆Collateral adjective: *nuchal.* 2 The back of a fish next to the head. [Origin uncertain]

na·per·y (nā′pər·ē) *n. pl.* **·per·ies** An article of household linen, as napkins, tablecloths, etc., or such linen collectively. [<OF *naperie* <*nape.* See NAPKIN.]

Naph·ta·li (naf′tə·lī) The sixth son of Jacob. *Gen.* xxx 8.

naph·tha (naf′thə, nap′-) *n.* 1 A volatile mixture of low-boiling hydrocarbons between gasoline and benzine, obtained by distilling petroleum: used as a solvent, cleaning fluid, fuel, etc., and in the making of varnishes. 2 Petroleum. [<L <Gk., prob. <Persian *naft* petroleum]

naph·tha·lene (naf′thə·lēn, nap′-) *n. Chem.* A white, solid, aromatic hydrocarbon, $C_{10}H_8$, obtained from coal-tar distillates and crystallizing in white platelets: its derivatives are used in the making of dyestuffs: also called *tar camphor.* Also **naph′tha·line** (-lin, -lēn).

naph·thal·ic acid (naf·thal′ik, nap-) Former name for PHTHALIC ACID.

naph·thene (naf′thēn, nap′-) *n. Chem.* Any of a group of saturated ring hydrocarbons having the general formula C_nH_{2n}, especially those obtained from Russian and Galician petroleum.

naph·thol (naf′thōl, -thol, nap′-) *n. Chem.* 1 Either of two isomeric compounds, the alpha and beta, $C_{10}H_7OH$, derived from naphthalene by replacing an atom of hydrogen by the hydroxyl group; specifically, the beta variety. 2 Any one of a class of naphthalene derivatives containing the hydroxyl group. Also **naph′tol** (-tōl, -tol). [<NAPHTH(ALENE) + -OL²]

naph·tho·lism (naf′thə·liz′əm, nap′-) *n. Pathol.* Poisoning caused by excessive or prolonged use of naphthol.

Na·pier (nā′pē·ər, nə·pir′), **Sir Charles James,** 1782–1853, British general. —**John,** 1550–1617, Scottish mathematician; invented logarithms. —**Robert Cornelis,** 1810–80, Lord Napier of Magdala, British general.

Na·pier·i·an logarithms (nə·pir′ē·ən) *Math.* The logarithmic system employing the base *e*: (2.71828 . . .): also called *natural logarithms.* Also **Na·pe′ri·an.**

na·pi·form (nā′pə·fôrm) *adj. Bot.* Turnipshaped; large above and small or slender below: a *napiform* rootstock. [<L *napus* turnip + -(I)FORM]

nap·kin (nap′kin) *n.* 1 A small cloth, as of linen, for use at table, etc. 2 *Brit.* A diaper. 3 *Scot.* A handkerchief. [ME *napekyn,* dim. of OF *nape* <L *mappa* a cloth]

Na·ples (nā′pəlz) A port in SW Italy on the **Bay of Naples,** a semicircular inlet of Tyrrhenian Sea in SW Italy: Greek *Parthenope, Neapolis.* Italian **Na·po·li** (nä′pō·lē).

nap·less (nap′lis) *adj.* 1 Made without a nap. 2 Threadbare.

Naples yellow A semi-opaque, permanent pigment in various shades of yellow consisting of lead antimoniate. Inferior grades are mixtures of ocher, zinc oxide, or cadmium yellow.

Na·po (nä′pō) A river in NE Ecuador and north central Peru, flowing 550 miles SE to the Amazon.

na·po·le·on (nə·pō′lē·ən, *Fr.* nà·pô·là·ôn′) *n.* 1 A former French gold coin, equivalent to 20 francs. 2 A card game: the highest bidder names trumps and, if he takes the tricks he has bid, receives from each adversary one chip for each trick; also, the taking of all the tricks in this game by one player: also called *nap.* 3 A pastry composed of layers of puff pastry filled with cream of custard. [after *Napoleon* Bonaparte]

Na·po·le·on (nə·pō′lē·ən) A masculine personal name. Also *Fr.* **Na·po·lé·on** (nà·pô·lā·ô n′), *Ital.* **Na·po·le·o·ne** (nä·pō′lā·ô′nä). [<F <Gk., of the new city] — **Napoleon** See BONAPARTE.

Na·po·le·on·ic (nə·pō′lē·on′ik) *adj.* 1 Belonging or relating to Napoleon Bonaparte, his conquests, etc. 2 Belonging or relating to Napoleon III.

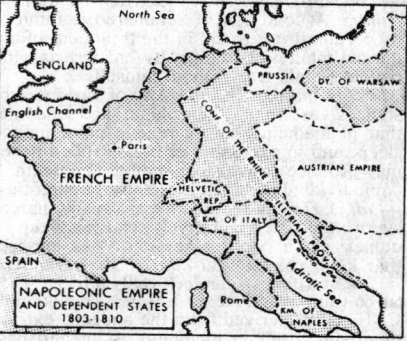

Napoleonic Wars See table under WAR.

nappe (nap) *n.* 1 *Geol.* A recumbent anticline, a portion of which has been thrust over other rocks. 2 *Engin.* The sheet of water overlying the top of a weir. 3 *Geom.* In a cone, one of the two conical surfaces divided by the vertex. [<F, a sheet]

nap·per (nap′ər) *n.* An implement or machine that raises a nap on fabrics.

nap·py¹ (nap′ē) *adj.* **·pi·er, ·pi·est** Having or characterized by a nap, or abundance of nap.

nap·py² (nap′ē) *adj.* **·pi·er, ·pi·est** 1 Inclined to fall asleep; drowsy. 2 Tending to produce drowsiness or intoxication; hence, slightly intoxicated. —*n. Scot.* Strong ale or beer.

nap·py³ (nap′ē) *n. pl.* **·pies** A round earthen or glass dish with flat bottom and sloping sides. Also **nap′pie.** [OE *hæp* bowl]

na·prap·a·thy (nə·prap′ə·thē) *n.* The treatment of disease by the manipulative correction of the disordered ligaments and connective tissues by which the disease is assumed to be caused. [<Czech *napra(va)* correction + -PATHY] —**nap′ra·path** *n.*

Nar·ba·da (nər·bud′ə) A river of central India, flowing about 775 miles west to the Gulf of Cambay: fomerly *Nerbudda.*

Nar·bonne (nár·bôn′) A town in southern France; formerly a port on the Gulf of the Lion: ancient **Nar·bo Mar·ti·us** (när′bō mär′shəs).

narc (nark) *n. Slang.* A police officer or federal treasury agent who investigates narcotics crimes.

nar·ce·ine (när′si·ēn, -in) *n. Chem.* A silky, bitter, crystalline alkaloid, $C_{23}H_{27}NO_8$, contained in the aqueous extract of opium from which the morphine has been separated. Also **nar·ce′ia, nar′ce·in.** [<L *narce* torpor (<Gk. *narkē*) + -INE²]

nar·cis·sism (när·sis′iz·əm) *n.* 1 *Psychoana.* Sexual excitement or gratification derived from contemplation of the self: an arrested or regressive stage. 2 Self-love; excessive interest in or admiration for oneself. Also **nar′cism** (när′siz·əm). —**nar·cis′sist** *n.* — **nar′·cis·sis′tic** *adj.*

nar·cis·sus (när·sis′əs) *n.* 1 One of a genus

(*Narissus*) of bulbous flowering plants of the amaryllis family, including the daffodil and jonquil. 2 A flower or bulb of this genus. *N. poeticus* is the **poet's narcissus.**

Nar·cis·sus (när·sis'əs) In Greek mythology, a youth who caused the death of Echo by spurning her love: in punishment Nemesis caused him to pine away and die for love of his own image in a pool, and changed him into the narcissus.

narco— *combining form* Torpor; insensibility: *narcomania.* Also, before vowels, **narc—.** [<Gk. *narkē* numbness]

nar·co·lep·sy (när'kə·lep'sē) *n. Pathol.* A condition marked by an uncontrollable desire for sleep or by sudden attacks of drowsiness: sometimes associated with petit mal. — **nar'·co·lep'tic** *adj.*

nar·co·ma·ni·a (när'kō·mā'nē·ə, -mān'yə) *n. Psychiatry* 1 A morbid craving to seek relief from pain, principally through the use of narcotics. 2 Psychotic alcoholism. — **nar'co·ma'·ni·ac** *adj.*

nar·co·sis (när·kō'sis) *n.* Deep sleep or unconsciousness produced by a drug. Also **nar·co'ma** (-kō'mə).

nar·co·syn·the·sis (när'kō ·sin'thə·sis) *n. Psychiatry* A condition of seminarcosis induced by certain drugs to aid in the treatment of abnormal mental conditions by encouraging the patient to talk freely about himself.

nar·cot·ic (när·kot'ik) *n.* 1 Any of various substances, as opium, morphine, and codeine, that in medicinal doses relieve pain, induce sleep, and in excessive or uncontrolled doses may produce convulsions, coma, and death. 2 An individual addicted to the use of narcotics. —*adj.* 1 Having the quality of causing narcosis or stupor. 2 Figuratively, causing sleep or dulness, as a book or sermon. Also **nar·cose** (när'kōs), **nar·cot'i·cal** *adj.* [<Gk. *narkōtikos* <*narkē* torpor] — **nar·cot'i·cal·ly** *adv.*

nar·co·tine (när'kə·tēn, -tin) *n.* An alkaloid, $C_{22}H_{23}O_7N$, derived from the aqueous extract of opium: used in medicine as an antispasmodic and tonic. Also **nar'co·tin** (-tin).

nar·co·tism (när'kə·tiz' əm) *n.* 1 Stupor due to narcotics. 2 Any method or influence inducing narcosis. 3 A morbid tendency to sleep. 4 Addiction to narcotics.

nar·co·tize (när'kə·tīz) *v.t.* **·tized, ·tiz·ing** To bring under the influence of a narcotic; stupefy. — **nar'co·ti·za'tion** *n.*

nard (närd) *n.* 1 Spikenard (the plant, oil, or ointment). 2 Any one of several aromatic plants or roots (mostly species of valerian) formerly used in medicine. [<OF *narde* <L *nardus* <Gk. *nardos,* prob. <Semitic] — **nard'ine** (när'dēn, -din) *adj.*

Na·ren·ta (nä·ren'tä) The Italian name for the NERETVA.

nar·es (nâr'ēz) *n. pl.* of **nar·is** (nâr'is) *Anat.* 1 Openings into the nose or nasal passages. 2 The nostrils. [<L, nostrils]

Na·rew (nä'ref) A river in western Belorussian S.S.R. and NE Poland, flowing 275 miles NW to the Vistula. Russian **Na·rev'.**

nar·ghi·le (när'gə·li) *n.* An Oriental tobacco pipe by which the smoke is drawn through water by means of a long tube. See HOOKAH. Also **nar'gi·le, nar'gi·leh.** [<Persian *nārgīleh cf1* <*nārgīl* a coconut; because originally made of coconut shell]

nark (närk) *n. Brit. Slang* An informer; stool pigeon. [<Romany *nāk* a nose]

Nar·kom·vnu·del (när·kom' vnoo·dyel) *n.* People's Commissariat for Internal Affairs, U.S.S.R.: originally *Cheka,* later OGPU: abbreviated *NKVD.* [<Russian *Nar(odni) Kom(misariat) Vnu(trennikh) Del*]

Nar·ra·gan·set (nar'ə·gan' sit) *n.* 1 One of a tribe of North American Indians of Algonquian stock, formerly inhabiting Rhode Island. 2 The Algonquian language of this tribe. 3 One of a breed of small, robust, sure-footed horses, originally bred in Rhode Island, and valued as saddle horses: also **Nar'ra·gan'sett.**

Nar·ra·gan·sett Bay (nar'ə·gan'sit) An inlet of the Atlantic Ocean in SE Rhode Island.

nar·rate (nar·rāt', nar'āt) *v.t.* **·rat·ed, ·rat·ing** To tell or relate as a story; give an account of. See synonyms under RELATE. [<L *narratus,* pp. of *narrare* relate] — **nar·ra'tor, nar·rat'er** *n.* — **nar'ra·to'ry** (-tôr'ē, -tō'rē) *adj.*

nar·ra·tion (na·rā'shən) *n.* 1 The act of narrating the particulars of an event or series of

events. 2 That which is narrated; narrative. See synonyms under HISTORY, REPORT.

nar·ra·tive (nar'ə·tiv) *n.* 1 An orderly, continuous account of an event or series of events. 2 The act or art of narrating. See synonyms under HISTORY, REPORT, STORY[1]. —*adj.* Pertaining to narration. — **nar'ra·tive·ly** *adv.*

nar·row (nar'ō) *adj.* 1 Having comparatively little distance from side to side. 2 Limited in extent or duration; circumscribed; small. 3 Illiberal; bigoted. 4 Limited in means or resources; straitened. 5 Niggardly; parsimonious. 6 Barely accomplished, attained, or sufficient: *a narrow* escape. 7 Scrutinizing closely. 8 *Phonet.* Tense. See synonyms under LITTLE, SCANTY, SMALL. —*v.t. v.i.* To make or become narrower, as in width or scope. —*n.* 1 *Usually pl.* A narrow passage; strait; also, the narrowest part of an isthmus or cape. 2 A narrow part of a street, or of a valley or pass. —**The Narrows** 1 A strait connecting Upper New York Bay with Lower New York Bay between the western end of Long Island and Staten Island. 2 The narrowest part of the Dardanelles. [OE *nearu*] — **nar'row·ness** *n.*

nar·row-gage (nar'ō·gāj') *adj.* 1 Denoting a width of railroad track less than the standard gage. 2 *Colloq.* Petty; illiberal; narrow-minded. —*n.* 1 A railroad having a gage narrower than 4 feet 8 1/2 inches. 2 A train for a narrow-gage railroad.

nar·row·ly (nar'ō·lē) *adv.* 1 With little breadth, width, or distance from side to side. 2 With small extent or duration; contractedly; restrictedly. 3 Barely; hardly.

nar·row-mind·ed (nar'ō·mīn' did) *adj.* Of contracted mental scope; also, illiberal or bigoted. — **nar'row-mind'ed·ly** *adv.* — **nar'row-mind'ed·ness** *n.*

har·thex (när'theks) *n. Archit.* A porch, vestibule, or division of a church or basilica before the entrance proper. [<L <Gk. *narthēx,* orig. a plant with a hollow stalk]

Nar·va (när'vä) A city in NE Estonia.

Nar·vá·ez (när·vä'eth), **Pánfilo de,** 1480?–1528, Spanish general; defeated by Cortés in Mexico; explored Florida.

Nar·vik (när'vik) A port in northern Norway.

nar·whal (när'wəl, -hwəl) *n.* A large, arctic cetacean (*Monodon monoceros*) of the family *Delphinidae,* having in the male a long, straight, spiraled tusk: valued for its oil and ivory. Also **nar'wal, nar'whale'.** [<Dan. or Sw. *narhval*]

NARWHAL
a. Head of male showing tusk.
b. The female.
(From 12 to 16 feet in body length;
the spiraled tusk from 6 to 8 feet)

nar·y (nâr'ē) *adj. Dial.* Never a; not one: opposite of *ary.*

na·sal[1] (nā'zəl) *adj.* 1 Of or pertaining to the nose. 2 *Phonet.* Pronounced with the voiced breath passing partially or wholly through the nose, as in (m), (n), and (ng), and the French nasal vowels. —*n. Phonet.* A nasal sound. [<NL *nasalis* <L *nasus* the nose] — **na·sal·i·ty** (nā·zal' ə·tē) *n.*

na·sal[2] (nā'zəl) *n.* A nosepiece. [<OF *nasal, nasel* <L *nasus* nose]

nasal index A number expressing the ratio of the greatest breadth of the nose (multiplied by 100) to the length: it is greater when measured on the face than on the skull, and varies with age.

na·sal·ize (nā'zəl·īz) *v.* **·ized, ·iz·ing** *v.t.* To give a nasal sound to. —*v.i.* To pronounce oral sounds in the manner of nasals; talk through the nose. — **na' sal·i·za'tion** *n.*

nas·cent (nas'ənt, nā'sənt) *adj.* Beginning to exist or develop. [<L *nascens,* ppr. of *nasci* be born] — **nas' cence, nas'cen·cy** *n.*

nascent state *Chem.* The uncombined condi-

tion of an atom or radical when recently set free from a compound and ready to enter into combination with some other atom or radical. Also **nascent condition.**

nase·ber·ry (nāz'ber'ē) *n. pl.* **·ries** The plumlike fruit of the sapodilla. [<Sp. *níspero* medlar]

Nase·by (nāz'bē) A village in Northamptonshire, central England; site of decisive defeat of loyalists by Cromwell, 1645.

Nash (nash), **Ogden,** 1902–1971, U.S. poet and humorist. —**Thomas,** 1567–1601, English pamphleteer, poet, and dramatist: also **Nashe.**

Nash·u·a (nash'ōō·ə) A city in southern New Hampshire, on the Merrimac River.

Nash·ville (nash'vil) The capital of Tennessee, on the Cumberland River.

Nashville warbler The common warbler of eastern North America (*Vermivora ruficapilla*), having an olive-green back and yellow breast.

na·si·on (nā'zē·on) *n. Anat.* The point at the root of the nose where the frontal and two nasal bones meet. [<NL <L *nasus* nose] — **na'si·al** *adj.*

Nas·myth (nāz'mith, nā'smith, naz'mith), **Alexander,** 1758–1840, Scottish portrait painter.

naso— *combining form* Nose; nasal and: *nasofrontal.* [<L *nasus* nose]

na·so·fron·tal (nā'zō·frun'təl) *adj. Anat.* Of or pertaining to the nasal and frontal bones.

na·so·phar·ynx (nā'zō·far'ingks) *n. Anat.* The upper part of the pharynx, above and behind the soft palate. — **na'so·pha·ryn'ge·al** (-fə·rin' jē·əl) *adj.*

na·so·scope (nā'zō·skōp) *n.* A small electric lamp for examining the nasal cavity.

Nas·sau (nas'ô) 1 (*Ger.* nä'sou) A former duchy in western Germany, now included in Hesse. 2 A port on New Providence Island, capital of the Bahama Islands.

Nassau Range A mountain system of west central New Guinea; highest peak, 16,400 feet.

Nas·ser (näs'ər, nas'-), **Gamal Abdel,** 1918–1970, prime minister of Egypt 1953– 56; president 1956–58; president of the United Arab Republic 1958–1970. Real surname *Abdel-Nasser.*

Nast (nast), **Thomas,** 1840–1902, U.S. political cartoonist born in Germany.

nas·tic (nas'tik) *adj. Bot.* Pertaining to or designating an automatic response in plants whose direction and character is determined by internal cellular pressure. [<Gk. *nastos* tight-pressed]

—nastic *combining form* Nastic toward or by: *epinastic.*

na·stur·tium (na·stûr'shəm) *n.* 1 A plant of the geranium family (genus *Tropaeolum*) with funnel-shaped flowers, commonly yellow, orange, scarlet, or crimson. 2 A rich yellow or reddish-orange color. [<L, cress <*nasus* the nose + *tortus,* pp. of *torquere* twist (from the pungent odor of the plant).

nas·ty (nas'tē) *adj.* **·ti·er, ·ti·est** 1 Filthy or offensive dirty. 2 Morally filthy; indecent. 3 Nauseating; disgusting to the senses; disagreeable: the *nasty* task of cleaning a chicken coop. 4 Difficult to handle or deal with; vexatious; annoying: a *nasty* turn of events. 5 Painful; serious; bad: a *nasty* cut. 6 Ill-natured: a *nasty* brat; a *nasty* trick. See synonyms under FOUL. [Cf. Sw. *naskug* filthy] — **nas'ti·ly** *adv.* — **nas'ti·ness** *n.*

—nasty *combining form* A generalized automatic response to a (specified) stimulus: *epinasty.* [<Gk. *nastos* close-pressed]

na·tal (nāt'l) *adj.* 1 Pertaining to one's birth; dating from birth. 2 *Poetic* Native. [<L *natalis* <*nasci* be born]

Na·tal (nä·täl') Portuguese and Spanish forms of NOEL.

Na·tal (nə·tal') 1 A former province in the eastern section of the Republic of South Africa; 35,284 square miles; alternating capitals Umlundi and Pietermaritzburg. Now: Kwa Zulu/Natel province. 2 A port in NE Brazil, capital of Rio Grande do Norte state.

na·tal·i·ty (nə·tal'ə·tē) *n.* The birth rate in a given community or place.

Na·tan (nä·tän') Spanish form of NATHAN.

Na·ta·na·el (nä′tä·nä·el′) Spanish form of NATHANIEL.

na·tant (nā′tənt) *adj.* Floating or swimming at the surface. [< L *natans, -antis,* ppr. of *natare* swim]

na·ta·tion (nā·tā′shən) *n.* The art of swimming or floating. [< L *natatio, -onis* < *natare* swim] — **na·ta′tion·al** *adj.*

na·ta·to·ri·al (nā′tə·tôr′ē·əl, -tō′rē-) *adj.* Swimming, or adapted for swimming. Also **na′ta·to′ry.**

na·ta·to·ri·um (nā′tə·tôr′ē·əm, -tō′rē-) *n. pl.* **·to·ri·ums** or **·to·ri·a** (-tôr′ē·ə, -tō′rē·ə) A swimming pool.

Natch·ez (nach′iz) *n.* One of a tribe of North American Indians of Muskhogean linguistic stock, formerly occupying the lower Mississippi Valley; overcome by the French in 1729–1730; later merged with Creek.

Natch·ez (nach′iz) A port on the Mississippi River in SW Mississippi.

na·tes (nā′tēz) *n. pl.* The buttocks. [< L]

Na·than (nā′thən; *Fr.* nà·tän′, *Ger.* nä′tän) A masculine personal name. [< Hebrew, given; a gift]
—**Nathan** A prophet who called King David to account for the death of Uriah. II *Sam.* xii 1.

Na·than (nā′thən), **George Jean,** 1882–1958, U.S. editor and dramatic critic. —**Robert,** born 1894, U.S. novelist.

Na·than·a·el (nə·than′ē·əl, -than′yəl) A disciple of Jesus. *John* xxi 2.

Na·than·i·el (nə·than′ē·əl, -than′yəl; *Du., Ger.* nä·tä′nē·el; *Fr.* nà·tà·nyel′) A masculine personal name. Also **Na·than·a·el** (nə·than′ē·əl, -than′yəl). [< Hebrew, gift of God]

nathe·less (nāth′lis, nath′-) *adv. Archaic* Nevertheless. Also **nath·less** (nath′lis).

na·tion (nā′shən) *n.* **1** A people as an organized body politic, usually associated with a particular territory and possessing a distinctive cultural and social way of life. **2** An aggregation of people of common origin and language. **3** A race; tribe; specifically, a tribe of American Indians or the territory occupied by them. See synonyms under PEOPLE. [< F < L *natio, -onis* breed, race < *nasci* be born]

Na·tion (nā′shən), **Carry Amelia,** 1846–1911, *née* Moore, Kansan temperance reformer: also *Carrie Nation.*

na·tion·al (nash′ən·əl) *adj.* **1** Belonging to a nation as a whole: opposed to *local.* **2** Of, pertaining to, or characteristic of a nation as distinguished from other nations. **3** Patriotic. **4** Authorized by a national government. —*n.* One who is a member of a nation. —**na′tion·al·ly** *adv.*

national bank 1 *U.S.* A commercial bank formerly authorized by statute to issue circulating notes secured by government bonds, and now exercising the ordinary functions of a bank of deposit and discount, with double liability of shareholders for all debts. **2** A bank associated with the national finances, such as the Bank of France.

national committee A committee which heads a political party of the United States: it consists of two delegates from each State serving for four years.

national convention In the United States, a convention of representatives of a political party elected at State and Territory primaries, held to decide upon party policy and to nominate candidates for president and vice president of the nation.

national debt The debt owed by any state; especially, the funded debt.

National Geographic Society A scientific society founded in 1888 in Washington, D.C.

National Guard *U.S.* An organized land or air force maintained by a State, a Territory, or the District of Columbia, usually in conjunction with but not under the direct control of the U.S. Army or Air Force. Its units or personnel operate on a semiactive basis as part of the militia except in national emergencies or under special circumstances, when they may be called into Federal service.

National Guard of the United States Those members and units of the National Guard that have taken an oath of appointment in the Federal service and are thereby constituted as a component part of the United States Army.

na·tion·al·ism (nash′ən·əl·iz′əm) *n.* **1** Devotion to the nation as a whole; patriotism. **2** A system demanding national conduct of all industries. **3** A world order founded on the right of each nation to determine its policies unhindered by others: opposed to *internationalism.* **4** A demand for national independence. **5** A national custom, trait, etc. —**na′tion·al·ist** *adj.* & *n.* — **na′tion·al·is′tic** *adj.* —**na′tion·al·is′ti·cal·ly** *adv.*

na·tion·al·i·ty (nash′ən·al′ə·tē) *n. pl.* **·ties 1** The quality of being national; national independence. **2** A nation. **3** A connection with a particular nation, as by citizenship.

na·tion·al·ize (nash′ən·əl·īz) *v.t.* **·ized, ·iz·ing 1** To place under the control or ownership of a nation. **2** To give a national character to. **3** To make into a nation. Also *Brit.* **na′tion·al·ise.** — **na′tion·al·i·za′tion** *n.* —**na′tion·al·iz′er** *n.*

National Labor Relations Board A U.S. government board established in 1935 to insure the rights of employees to self-organization and bargaining through the enforcement of codes detailing unfair labor practices and through the conducting of investigations and bargaining elections.

National Military Establishment See DEPARTMENT OF DEFENSE under DEFENSE.

national park A tract of U.S. government land withdrawn by special Act of Congress from settlement, occupancy, or sale, for the benefit and enjoyment of the public: preserved and maintained by the Federal government because of its historical interest, great natural beauty, or the value of its forests, wildlife, etc.

National Road See CUMBERLAND ROAD.

National Socialism The doctrines of the Nazi party. See NAZI.

Nation of Islam See under BLACK MUSLIM.

na·tion-wide (nā′shən·wīd′) *adj.* Throughout the entire nation.

na·tive (nā′tiv) *adj.* **1** Born or produced in a region or country in which one lives; indigenous: opposed to *foreign, exotic.* **2** Of or pertaining to one's birth or to its place or circumstances. **3** Natural rather than acquired; inborn; inherited. **4** Of or pertaining to natives; conferred by or peculiar to natives: usually applied to non-European peoples. **5** Natural to any one or any thing. **6** Plain, simple, unaffected, unadorned; untouched by art. **7** Occurring in nature in a pure state: *native* copper. **8** *Obs.* Related to birth; near; closely connected. —*n.* **1** One born in, or any product of, a given country or place; an aborigine. **2** Livestock common to a country or region. **3** In astrology, one born under a star or its aspect. [< F *natif* < L *nativus* < *nasci* be born. Doublet of NAIVE.] —**na′tive·ly** *adv.* — **na′tive·ness** *n.*
Synonyms (adj.): indigenous, innate, natal, natural, original. *Native* denotes that which belongs to one by birth; *natal* that which pertains to the event of birth; *natural* denotes that which rests upon inherent qualities of character or being. We speak of one's *native* country, or of his *natal* day; of *natural* ability, *native* genius. See INHERENT, NATURAL, PRIMEVAL, RADICAL. *Antonyms*: acquired, alien, artificial, assumed, foreign.

native bear *Austral.* The koala.

na·tive-born (nā′tiv·bôrn′) *adj.* Born in the region or country specified.

Native States See INDIAN STATES.

na·tiv·ism (nā′tiv·iz′əm) *n.* **1** Partiality in favor of native-born citizens in preference to foreign-born. **2** The doctrine of innate ideas. —**na′tiv·ist** *n.* —**na′tiv·is′tic** *adj.*

na·tiv·i·ty (nā·tiv′ə·tē, nə-) *n. pl.* **·ties 1** The coming into life or the world; birth. **2** A horoscope. **3** The condition of being born a serf or villein. **4** The condition of being a native. —**the Nativity** The birth of Jesus.

NATO (nā′tō) North Atlantic Treaty Organization.

na·tri·um (nā′trē·əm) *n.* Sodium: so called in pharmacy and formerly in chemistry. [< NL < F *natron* NATRON]

nat·ro·lite (nat′rə·līt, nā′trə-) *n.* A white or colorless, orthorhombic, hydrous sodium-aluminum zeolite occurring in prismatic, needlelike crystals: also called *needlestone.*

na·tron (nā′tron) *n.* A brittle, vitreous, white, alkaline, hydrous sodium carbonate, $Na_2CO_3 \cdot 10H_2O$, crystallizing in the monoclinic system. [< F < Sp. *natrón* < Arabic *natrūn, nitrūn* < Gk. *nitron* niter]

nat·ty (nat′ē) *adj.* **·ti·er, ·ti·est** Smart; spruce; tidy. See synonyms under NEAT[1]. [? Akin to NEAT[1]] —**nat′ti·ly** *adv.* —**nat′ti·ness** *n.*

Na·tu·na (nə·to͞o′nə) See BUNGURAN ISLANDS.

nat·u·ral (nach′ər·əl) *adj.* **1** Of or pertaining to one's nature or constitution; innate; inborn; also, indigenous; native. **2** Of or pertaining to a particular nature; derived from nature; hence, exhibiting kindly feeling or affection. **3** Of or pertaining to nature; belonging or pertaining to the existing order of things: *natural* law; normal. **4** Coming within common experience; having to do with objects in the order of nature: opposed to *supernatural.* **5** Not forced or artificial; without affectation or exaggeration; lifelike. **6** Produced by nature; not artificial: a *natural* bridge. **7** Connected by ties of consanguinity; being such by birth: a *natural* brother. **8** Belonging to the inferior nature; not spiritual; animal. **9** Born out of wedlock; illegitimate. **10** *Music* Not sharped nor flatted: G *natural*; specifically, denoting the key of C, which is without flats or sharps in the signature. **11** *Math.* Designating an actual number in contradistinction to a logarithm: a *natural* sine, *natural* cosine, *natural* tangent, etc. See synonyms under INHERENT, NATIVE, NORMAL, PHYSICAL, RADICAL. —*n.* **1** *Music* **a** A note on a line or a space that is affected by neither a sharp nor a flat. **b** A character (♮) which acts upon a sharped degree of the staff as a flat and upon a flatted degree as a sharp. **2** In keyboard musical instruments, a white key. **3** One born without the usual powers of reason or understanding; a born fool. **4** *Colloq.* A person or thing admirably suited for some purpose, or obviously destined for success. [< F *naturel* < L *naturalis* < *natura* nature] —**nat′u·ral·ness** *n.*

Natural Bridge A rock-and-earth natural bridge over Cedar Creek in western Virginia; span, 90 feet; width, 50–100 feet; height, 215 feet.

Natural Bridges National Monument A region in SE Utah containing three natural bridges; 4 square miles; established, 1908.

natural childbirth Childbirth conducted as a relaxed, relatively painless natural function.

natural gas Any gaseous hydrocarbon, consisting chiefly of methane, generated naturally in subterranean oil deposits: used as a fuel.

natural gender See under GENDER.

natural history The observation and study of the facts of the material universe as distinguished from man: commonly restricted to zoology, botany, geology, mineralogy, etc.

nat·u·ral·ism (nach′ər·əl·iz′əm) *n.* **1** Action or thought derived from or identified with exclusively natural desires and instincts. **2** In literature, art, etc.: **a** Adherence to observed nature; specifically, the principles of Zola, de Maupassant, and others who attempted to apply "scientific" objectivity to their treatment of life, without imposing judgments of value or avoiding what is considered ugly. **b** The qualities of a work of art resulting from such doctrines. **3** *Philos.* The doctrine that phenomena are derived from natural causes and can be explained by scientific laws: opposed to *supernaturalism.* **4** *Theol.* The doctrine that religion does not depend on supernatural revelation, but may be derived from the natural world.

nat·u·ral·ist (nach′ər·əl·ist) *n.* **1** One versed in natural sciences, as a zoologist or botanist. **2** An adherent of naturalism.

nat·u·ral·is·tic (nach′ər·əl·is′tik) *adj.* **1** In accordance with nature; not conventional or ideal. **2** According to the doctrines of naturalism. **3** Pertaining to naturalists.

nat·u·ral·i·za·tion (nach′ər·əl·i·zā′shən, -ī·zā′-) *n.* The act or process of admitting an alien to citizenship.

naturalization papers Documents recording an alien's application for citizenship or verifying the conferment of citizenship.

nat·u·ral·ize (nach′ər·əl·īz) *v.* **·ized, ·iz·ing** *v.t.* **1** To confer the rights and privileges of citizenship upon, as an alien. **2** To adopt (a foreign word, custom, etc.) into the common use of

a country or area. **3** To adapt (a foreign plant, animal, etc.) to the environment of a country or area. **4** To explain by natural laws: to *naturalize* a miracle. **5** To make natural; free from conventionality. —*v.i.* **6** To become as if native; adapt. Also *Brit.* **nat'u·ral·ise. —nat'u·ral·iz'er** *n.*

natural law A rule of conduct supposed to be inherent in man's nature and discoverable by reason alone.

natural logarithms Napierian logarithms.

nat·u·ral·ly (nach'ər·əl·ē) *adv.* **1** Without effort; spontaneously. **2** Without affectation or exaggeration. **3** As might have been expected; of course. **4** In a lifelike or natural manner.

natural philosophy **1** Natural history. **2** The physical sciences taken collectively.

natural resource Any of those sources of wealth provided by nature, as soil, forests, minerals, water supply, water power, and wild game.

natural sciences The sciences treating of the physical universe, taken collectively and in distinction from the mental and moral sciences and from abstract mathematics.

natural selection *Biol.* The process whereby individual variations of peculiarities that are of advantage in a certain environment tend to become perpetuated in the race; survival of the fittest.

na·ture (nā'chər) *n.* **1** The character, constitution, or essential traits of a person, thing, or class, especially if original rather than acquired. **2** The physical or psychic constitution or character of persons or things, whether native or acquired: often personified in poetry or figurative prose. **3** The entire material universe and its phenomena. **4** The system of natural existences, forces, changes, and events, regarded as distinguished from, or exclusive of, the supernatural: Man is included in *nature.* **5** The sum of physical or material existences and forces in the universe. **6** The constitution or inherited or habitual condition and tendencies of man. **7** *Theol.* The unregenerate state; character unchanged by grace. **8** *Obs.* Generative energy; genesis; birth. See synonyms under CHARACTER, SORT, TEMPER. [< F < L *natura* < *natus*, pp. of *nasci* be born]

-natured *combining form* Possessing a (specified) nature, disposition, or temperament: ill-*natured.* [< NATURE (def. 1)]

na·tur·op·a·thy (nā'chə·rop'ə·thē) *n. Med.* A system of therapy which avoids drugs in favor of such physical agencies as sunshine, air, water, exercise, etc. [< NATURE + -(O)PATHY] —**na·tur'o·path** (nə·chŏŏr'ə·path) *n.* —**na·tur'o·path'ic** *adj.*

Nau·cra·tis (nô'krə·tis) An ancient Greek city in the Nile delta, Egypt. Also **Nau'kra·tis.**

naught (nôt) *n.* **1** Not anything; nothing. **2** A cipher; zero; the character 0. —*adj.* **1** Of no value or account. **2** *Obs.* Bad; wicked; also, poor in quality. —*adv.* Not in the least. Also spelled *nought.* [OE *nāwiht* < *nā* not + *wiht* thing]

naugh·ty (nô'tē) *adj.* **·ti·er, ·ti·est** **1** Perverse and disobedient; wayward; mischievous. **2** *Obs.* Corrupt; wicked. See synonyms under BAD. [< NAUGHT] —**naugh'ti·ly** *adv.* —**naugh'ti·ness** *n.*

nau·ma·chy (nô'mə·kē) *n. pl.* **·chies** **1** In ancient Rome, a fight between ships for the amusement of the people; also, an artificial basin for the convenience of such battles. **2** A naval battle; especially, a mock sea fight. Also —**nau·ma·chi·a** (nô·mā'kē·ə). [< L < Gk. *naumachia* sea fight < *naus* ship + *machē* fight]

Nau·pak·tos (nô·pak'təs, näf'päk·tôs) A town on the northern shore of the Gulf of Corinth, west central Greece: Italian *Lepanto*: also *Navpaktos.*

nau·path·i·a (nô·path'ē·ə) *n.* Seasickness. [< NL < Gk. *naus* a ship + *path-*, stem of *paschein* suffer]

nau·pli·us (nô'plē·əs) *n. pl.* **·pli·i** (-plē·ī) *Zool.* A larval stage of certain crustaceans, with body unsegmented, a median eye, and three pairs of legs which correspond to the anterior and posterior antennae and the mandibles of the adult. [< L, a kind of shellfish]

Na·u·ru (nä·ōō'rōō) A Pacific island just south of the equator and west of the Gilbert Islands, comprising a United Nations Trust Territory administered by Australia; 8 square miles.

nau·sea (nô'zhə, -zē·ə, -shə, -sē·ə) *n.* **1** Sickness of the stomach, producing dizziness and an impulse to vomit. **2** A feeling of loathing in general. [< L < Gk. *nausia* < *naus* ship]

nau·se·ate (nô'zhē·āt, -zē, -shē-, -sē-) *v.t.* & *v.i.* **·at·ed, ·at·ing** To affect with or feel nausea or disgust. —**nau'se·a'tion** *n.*

nau·seous (nô'zhəs, -shəs) *adj.* **1** Nauseating; disgusting. **2** *Colloq.* Affected with nausea; queasy. —**nau'seous·ly** *adv.* —**nau'seous·ness** *n.*

Nau·sic·a·a (nô·sik'ā·ə, -i·ə) In the *Odyssey,* the daughter of King Alcinous, who by the contrivance of Athena finds the shipwrecked Odysseus and guides him to her father, from whom he receives aid to return to Ithaca.

nautch (nôch) *n.* In India, an entertainment featuring dancing girls **(nautch girls).** [< Hind. *nāch* dance]

nau·ti·cal (nô'ti·kəl) *adj.* Pertaining to ships, seamen, or navigation. Also **nau'tic.** [< Gk. *nautikos* < *naus* ship] —**nau'ti·cal·ly** *adv.*

Synonyms: marine, maritime, naval, ocean, oceanic. *Marine* signifies belonging to the ocean, *maritime* bordering on or connected with the ocean; as, *marine* products; *marine* animals; *maritime* nations; *maritime* laws. *Naval* refers to the armed force of a nation on the sea, and on lakes and rivers; *nautical* denotes primarily anything connected with sailors, or with ships or navigation; as, a *nautical* almanac. *Oceanic* is especially applied to that which is suggestive of an *ocean.*

nautical mile See under MILE.

nau·ti·lus (nô'tə·ləs) *n. pl.* **·lus·es** or **·li** (-lī) **1** Any of a family of cephalopod mollusks containing a single surviving genus *(Nautilus)* found in southern seas and having a natant spiral shell containing a series of empty chambers lined with mother-of-pearl that are successively secreted and then sealed off as the animal outgrows them. **2** The paper nautilus. [< L < Gk. *nautilos,* sailor]

CHAMBERED NAUTILUS
Cross-section
(The shell up to 10 inches across)

Nautilus The first atomic-powered submarine, launched by the U.S. Navy: made the first undersea crossing of the North Pole on August 3, 1958.

Nav·a·ho (nav'ə·hō) *n. pl.* **·hos** or **·hoes** One of a tribe of North American Indians of Athapascan stock, now living on reservations in Arizona, New Mexico, and Utah. Also **Nav'a·jo.**

Nav·a·jo Mountain (nav'ə·hō) A peak in southern Utah; 10,416 feet.

na·val (nā'vəl) *adj.* **1** Pertaining to ships and a navy: distinguished from *civil.* **2** Having a navy; relating to the navy. See synonyms under NAUTICAL. ◆ Homophone: *navel.* [< L *navalis* < *navis* ship]

naval academy A school where men are trained as naval officers; specifically, the U.S. Naval Academy at Annapolis, Maryland.

naval auxiliary A launch or auxiliary vessel, as a tanker.

naval brass *Metall.* A type of brass containing a small percentage of tin to increase hardness and resistance to corrosion: used for marine fittings, etc.

naval stores Rosin and its products, as turpentine, pine oil, etc.; also, tar, pitch, asphalt, and other similar materials formerly or still used by shipbuilders.

na·var (nā'vär) *n.* A method of improving the efficiency of aircraft navigation by the use of an interlocking system of radar beacons operating from ground stations with receivers in aircraft. [< NAV(IGATION) A(ND) R(ANGING)]

Na·va·ri·no (nä'vä·rē'nō) The medieval name for PYLOS.

Na·varre (nə·vär', *Fr.* nȧ·vȧr') **1** A region and former kingdom in northern Spain and SW France. **2** One of the Basque provinces, in northern Spain; 4,024 square miles; capital, Pamplona. *Spanish* **Na·var·ra** (nä·vär'rä).

nave[1] (nāv) *n. Archit.* The main body of a cruciform church, between the side aisles, and usually having a clerestory. ◆ Homophone: *knave.* [< OF < L *navis* ship]

nave[2] (nāv) *n.* **1** The central part or hub of a wheel. **2** *Obs.* The navel. ◆ Homophone: *knave.* [OE *nafu*]

na·vel (nā'vəl) *n.* **1** The depression on the abdomen where the umbilical cord was attached. **2** A central part or point. ◆ Homophone: *naval.* [OE *nafela* < *nafu* nave[2]]

na·veled (nā'vəld) *adj.* Having a navel; set as in a navel or hollow. Also **na'velled.**

navel orange An orange, usually seedless, having a small secondary fruit and a rind marked at the apex with a navel-like depression.

na·vel·wort (nā'vəl·wûrt') *n.* **1** A low herb (genus *Omphalodes*) of the borage family, native in Europe and Asia, with alternate leaves and blue or white flowers resembling forget-me-nots: also **na'vel·seed'.** **2** A succulent herb *(Umbilicus pendulinus)* with yellowish or greenish tubular flowers. **3** Any of various other plants, as the pennywort or the water milfoil.

nav·i·cert (nav'ə·sûrt) *n. Brit.* A safe-conduct authorizing a merchant vessel of a friendly or neutral nation to pass through a naval blockade. [< L *navis* ship + CERT(IFICATE)]

na·vic·u·lar (nə·vik'yə·lər) *adj.* **1** Boat-shaped; scaphoid. **2** Pertaining to a boat. —*n. Anat.* **1** A bone on the radial side of the wrist; also, the bone in front of the astragalus in the foot: also **na·vic'u·la're** (-lâr'ē). See illustration under FOOT. **2** A large bone behind the joint between the second and third phalanges of a horse's foot. [< LL *navicularis* < L *navis* ship]

na·vic·u·lar·thri·tis (nə·vik'yə·lär·thrī'tis) *n.* Inflammation of the navicular bone of the foot of a horse. Also **navicular disease.**

nav·i·gate (nav'ə·gāt) *v.* **·gat·ed, ·gat·ing** *v.t.* **1** To travel over, across, or on by ship or aircraft. **2** To steer; direct the course of. —*v.i.* **3** To travel by means of ship or aircraft. **4** To steer or manage a ship or aircraft. **5** To plot a course for a ship or aircraft. [< L *navigatus,* pp. of *navigare* < *navis* a boat + *agere* drive] —**nav·i·ga·ble** (nav'ə·gə·bəl) *adj.* —**nav'i·ga·bly** *adv.* —**nav'i·ga·bil'i·ty, nav'i·ga·ble·ness** *n.*

nav·i·ga·tion (nav'ə·gā'shən) *n.* **1** The act of navigating. **2** The art of ascertaining the position and directing the course of vessels at sea or of aircraft in flight. —**nav'i·ga'tion·al** *adj.*

nav·i·ga·tor (nav'ə·gā'tər) *n.* **1** One who navigates, or directs the course of a ship, aircraft, etc. **2** A person skilled in navigation.

Navigators' Islands See SAMOA.

Nav·pak·tos (näf'päk·tôs). See NAUPAKTOS.

nav·vy (nav'ē) *n. pl.* **·vies** *Brit.* A laborer on canals, railways, etc. [< NAVIGATOR, in obsolete sense of "one employed in digging canals"]

na·vy (nā'vē) *n. pl.* **·vies** **1** The entire marine military force of a country, under the control of a government department, and including vessels, men in the service, yards, etc. **2** The entire shipping of a country engaged in trade and commerce; the merchant marine. **3** A fleet of ships, as of merchantmen. —**United States Navy** The U.S. naval force administered by the Department of the Navy under the Department of Defense and including the Regular Navy, the Naval Reserve, the United States Marine Corps, and the United States Coast Guard when operating as a component of the Navy. [< OF *navie* < L *navis* ship]

navy bean The common, small, dried, white bean: so called from its common use in the U.S. Navy.

navy blue Any of various shades of dark blue. Also **navy.** —**na'vy-blue'** *adj.*

Navy Cross A decoration in the form of a bronze cross awarded by the U.S. Navy for extraordinary heroism or service in war.

navy gray A medium bluish-gray: adopted in World War II for the color of work uniforms of officers in the U.S. Navy. —**na'vy-gray'** *adj.*

navy yard A government-owned dockyard for the construction, repair, equipment, or care of warships.

na·wab (nə·wôb') *n. Anglo-Indian* A Moslem ruler or viceroy in India; by courtesy, any person of rank and distinction. See NABOB. [< Hind. *nawwāb* nabob]

Nax·os (nak'səs) The largest island of the Cyclades group; 169 square miles. Formerly **Nax·i·a** (nak'sē·ə).

nay (nā) *adv.* **1** No: indicating negation. **2** Not only so, but also: He is a good, *nay,* an excellent man. —*n.* **1** A negative vote or voter: opposed to *yea.* **2** A negative; denial. [< ON *nei* < *ne* not + *ei* ever]

Na·ya·rit (nä′yä·rēt′) A maritime state in western Mexico; 10,547 square miles; capital, Tepic.

nay·ma·cush (nā′mə·kush) See NAMAYCUSH.

Naz·a·rene (naz′ə·rēn) *n.* **1** An inhabitant of Nazareth: applied specifically to Christ, **the Nazarene,** or disparagingly to the early Christians by opponents. **2** One of a sect of Jewish Christians (first to fourth century) that observed the Jewish ritual, but did not require its observance by Gentile Christians: they believed in the divinity of Christ and the apostleship of Paul. —*adj.* Of or pertaining to Nazareth or the Nazarenes. Also **Naz′a·re′an** (-rē′ən).

Naz·a·reth (naz′ə·rith) An ancient town in Lower Galilee, northern Israel; scene of Christ's childhood.

Naz·a·rite (naz′ə·rīt) *n.* **1** A Hebrew who had assumed certain vows, including total abstinence, leaving the hair uncut, and refraining from touching a dead body. *Numbers* vi. **2** Erroneously, a Nazarene. Also **Naz′i·rite.** [< Gk. *Nazaritēs* < Hebrew *nāzar* abstain] —**Naz′a·rit′ic** (-rit′ik), **Naz′i·rit′ic** *adj.*

Naze (nāz), **The 1** A cape at the southern extremity of Norway: Norwegian *Lindesnes.* **2** A headland on the NE coast of Essex, England.

Na·zi (nä′tsē, nat′sē, na′zē) *n.* A member of the National Socialist German Workers Party, founded in 1919 on fascist principles and dominant from 1933 to 1945 in Germany under the dictatorship of Hitler, where it followed the principles of extreme nationalism, racism, totalitarian direction of all cultural, political, and economic activity, and militarization, while urging a destiny of world leadership for Germany. —*adj.* Of or pertaining to the Nazis or their party. [< G, short for *Nationalsozialistische (Partei)* National Socialist (Party)]

Na·zi·fy (nä′tsə·fī, nat′sə-) *v.t.* **·fied, ·fy·ing** To subject to Nazi influence or control; cause to be Nazi-like. —**Na′zi·fi·ca′tion** *n.*

Na·zim·o·va (nə·zim′ə·və), **Alla,** 1879–1945, Russian actress active in the United States.

Na·zism (nä′tsiz·əm, nat′siz-) *n.* The doctrines or practices of the Nazi party. Also **Na·zi·ism** (nä′tsē·iz′əm, nat′sē-).

Nb *Chem.* Niobium (symbol Nb).

Nd *Chem.* Neodymium (symbol Nd).

Ne *Chem.* Neon (symbol Ne).

Ne·an·der·thal man (nē·an′dər·täl, -thôl, -thol; *Ger.* nā·än′dər·täl) A relatively advanced protohuman species *(Homo neanderthalensis)* first identified from fragments of a fossil skeleton discovered in 1856 in cave deposits of the Neander valley near Düsseldorf. It is regarded as typical of a race of ancient cave-dwellers who preceded modern man, developing the Mousterian stone culture in western Europe. [< G *Neanderthal* Neander valley]

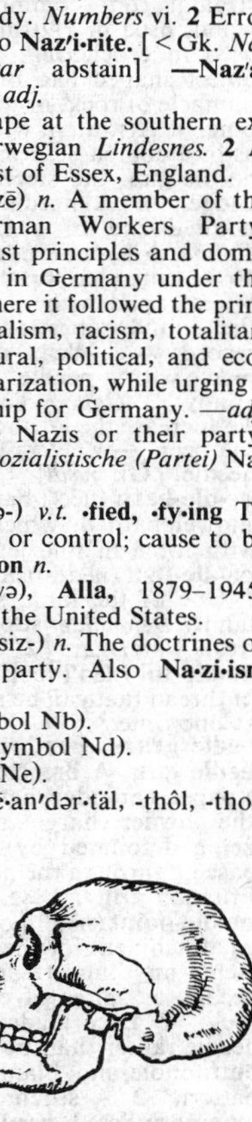

NEANDERTHAL SKULL

neap[1] (nēp) *adj.* Designating the tide occurring one or two days after the first and third quarters of the moon. —*n.* **1** A neap tide. **2** The lowest ebb. [OE *nēp-* in *nēpflod* low tide]

neap[2] (nēp) *n. U.S. Dial.* A wagon tongue [? < Scand. Cf. dial. Norw. *neip* forked pole.]

Ne·ap·o·lis (nē·ap′ə·lis) **1** The Greek name for SHECHEM, Samaria. **2** A Greek name for NAPLES.

Ne·a·pol·i·tan (nē′ə·pol′ə·tən) *adj.* Of or pertaining to Naples. —*n.* A native or resident of Naples.

near (nir) *adj.* **1** Not distant in place, time, or degree; nigh; contiguous. **2** Closely related by blood or affection; familiar. **3** Closely touching one's interests. **4** In riding or driving, placed on the left: opposed to *off.* **5** Following or imitating closely; literal: a *near* copy; also, resembling or substituted for: *near* beer. **6** Penurious or miserly; stingy. **7** Short or speedy; tending to lessen a distance: a *near* way. **8** Avoiding by a narrow margin; close: a *near* escape. See synonyms under ADJACENT. —*adv.* **1** At little distance; not remote in place, time, or degree. **2** Nearly; almost; approximately. **3** In a close relation; intimately. **4** *Naut.* Close to the wind. **5** Stingily; parsimoniously. —*v.t.* & *v.i.* To come or draw near (to); approach. —*prep.* Close by or to. See synonyms under AT. [OE *nēar,* comp. of *nēah* NIGH] —**near′ness** *n.*

near beer Any imitation beer of little or no alcoholic content.

near·by (nir′bī′) *adj.* & *adv.* Close at hand; adjacent.

Ne·arc·tic (nē·ärk′tik) *adj.* Of or pertaining to a zoogeographic region including the northern part of the New World, or the realm embracing temperate and arctic North America with Greenland. [< NE(O)- + ARCTIC]

Near East See under EAST.

Near Islands (nir) The westernmost group of the Aleutian Islands.

near·ly (nir′lē) *adv.* **1** Within a little; almost. **2** With a close regard to one's interest. **3** At no great distance; closely; narrowly. **4** Stingily.

near rime In prosody, a more or less radical substitute for rime, including such devices as assonance and consonance: also called *paraphone, half rime, oblique rime.*

near-sight·ed (nir′sī′tid) *adj.* Able to see distinctly at short distances only; myopic. —**near′-sight′ed·ly** *adv.* —**near′-sight′ed·ness** *n.*

neat[1] (nēt) *adj.* **1** Characterized by strict order, tidiness, and cleanliness. **2** Well-proportioned; trim; shapely. **3** Suited in character to a required purpose; hence, adroit; clever. **4** Clear of extraneous matter; free from admixture; undiluted: a glass of brandy *neat.* **5** Remaining after every deduction; net. [< AF *niet,* OF *net* < L *nitidus* shining] —**neat′ly** *adv.* —**neat′ness n.**

Synonyms: clean, cleanly, dapper, natty, nice, orderly, prim, spruce, tidy, trim. That which is *clean* is simply free from soil or defilement of any kind. Things are *orderly* in relation to other things; a room or desk is *orderly* when every article is in place; a person is *orderly* who habitually keeps things so. *Tidy* denotes that which conforms to propriety in general; an unlaced shoe may be perfectly *clean,* but is not *tidy. Neat* refers to that which is *clean* and *tidy,* with nothing superfluous, conspicuous, or showy; we speak of plain but *neat* attire; the same idea of freedom from the superfluous appears in the phrases "a *neat* speech," "a *neat* turn," "a *neat* reply," etc. A *clean* cut has no ragged edges; a *neat* stroke just does what is intended. *Nice* is stronger than *neat,* implying value and beauty; a cheap, coarse dress may be perfectly *neat,* but would not be termed *nice. Spruce* is applied to the show and affectation of neatness with a touch of smartness. *Trim* denotes a certain shapely and elegant firmness, often with suppleness and grace. *Prim* applies to a precise, formal, affected nicety. *Dapper* is *spruce* with the suggestion of smallness and slightness; *natty,* a diminutive of *neat,* suggests minute elegance, with a tendency toward the exquisite; as, a *dapper* man in a *natty* business suit. See BECOMING. *Antonyms*: dirty, disorderly, dowdy, negligent, rough, rude, slouchy, slovenly, soiled, untidy.

neat[2] (nēt) *n. Obs.* **1** Bovine cattle collectively. **2** A single bovine animal. —*adj.* Pertaining to bovine animals: *neat* cattle. [OE *nēat*]

'neath (nēth) *prep. Poetic* Beneath.

neat·herd (nēt′hûrd′) *n.* A herdsman.

neat's-foot oil (nēts′fŏŏt′) A pale yellow oil obtained by boiling the feet of neat cattle: used as a lubricant and softening agent for leather.

neb (neb) *n.* **1** The beak or bill, as of a bird; nose; snout. **2** The tip end of a thing; nib, as of a pen. **3** *Scot.* The face; also, the mouth. [OE *nebb*]

Neb·i·im (neb′i·ēm′, *Hebrew* nə·vē′im) *n. pl.* The second of the three divisions of the Hebrew scriptures known as the Prophets, as distinguished from the Law (Torah), etc.

Ne·bo (nē′bō), **Mount** A mountain in Moab from which Moses saw the Promised Land. *Deut.* xxxii 49. See PISGAH.

Ne·bras·ka (nə·bras′kə) A State in the north central United States; 77,237 square miles; capital, Lincoln; entered the Union Feb. 9, 1867; nickname, *Tree Planter State*: abbr. NE —**Ne·bras′kan** *adj.* & *n.*

Neb·u·chad·nez·zar (neb′yŏŏ·kəd·nez′ər) A Chaldean king of Babylon, 604?–561? B.C.; conquered Jerusalem and destroyed the Temple. *Dan.* i 1. Also **Neb′u·chad·rez′zar** (-rez′ər).

neb·u·la (neb′yə·lə) *n. pl.* **·lae** (-lē) or **·las 1** *Astron.* A luminous celestial body of cloudlike appearance and vast extent, composed of gaseous or stellar matter in various degrees of density. **2** *Pathol.* **a** A speck on the cornea; visual opacity. **b** Cloudiness of the urine. [< L, vapor, mist] —**neb′u·lar** *adj.*

nebular hypothesis *Astron.* A hypothesis that the solar system existed originally in the form of a nebula which, by cooling, condensing, and revolving, was formed into the sun and into rings of matter which later were consolidated into the planetary bodies.

neb·u·lize (neb′yə·līz) *v.t.* **·lized, ·liz·ing 1** To spray, as a wound or a morbid surface, with medicated liquid. **2** To reduce to a spray; atomize. —**neb′u·li·za′tion** *n.* —**neb′u·liz′er** *n.*

neb·u·lose (neb′yə·lōs) *adj.* Cloudlike; clouded.

neb·u·los·i·ty (neb′yə·los′ə·tē) *n.* **1** Nebulousness. **2** A misty or nebulous appearance; also, nebulous matter; a nebula.

neb·u·lous (neb′yə·ləs) *adj.* **1** Having its parts confused or mixed; hazy; indistinct: a *nebulous* idea. **2** Like a nebula. —**neb′u·lous·ly** *adv.* —**neb′u·lous·ness** *n.*

nec·es·sar·i·an·ism (nes′ə·sâr′ē·ən·iz′əm) *n.* The philosophical doctrine that acts of volition are predetermined by the force of inner motives; determinism; fatalism; necessity. Also **ne·ces′·si·tar′i·an** —**nec′es·sar′i·an,** **ne·ces·si·tar·i·an** (nə·ses′ə·târ′ē·ən) *adj.* & *n.*

nec·es·sar·y (nes′ə·ser′ē) *adj.* **1** Being such in its nature or conditions that it must exist, occur, or be true; inevitable. **2** Absolutely needed to accomplish a desired result; essential; requisite. **3** Compulsory: a *necessary* action. **4** Being such that it must be believed. **5** *Archaic* Rendering useful and intimate service. —*n. pl.* **·sar·ies 1** That which is indispensable; an essential requisite: used usually in the plural: the *necessaries* of life. **2** That which is subject to the law of necessity: The *necessary* is opposed to the contingent. **3** A watercloset; privy. [< L *necessarius* necessary] —**nec′es·sar′i·ly** *adv.* —**nec′es·sar′i·ness** *n.*

Synonyms (adj.): compulsory, essential, indispensable, inevitable, needed, needful, required, requisite, unavoidable, undeniable. That which is *essential* belongs to the essence of a thing, so that the thing cannot exist in its completeness without it; that which is *indispensable* may be only an adjunct, but it is one that cannot be spared. That which is *requisite* is so in the judgment of the person requiring it. Food is *necessary,* death is *inevitable*; a *necessary* conclusion satisfies a thinker; an *inevitable* conclusion silences opposition. *Needed* and *needful* are more concrete than *necessary,* and respect an end to be attained, while *necessary* may apply simply to what exists; we speak of a *necessary* inference; *necessary* food is what one cannot live without, while *needful* food is that without which we cannot enjoy comfort, health, and strength. *Antonyms*: casual, contingent, needless, non-essential, optional, unnecessary, useless, worthless.

ne·ces·si·tate (nə·ses′ə·tāt) *v.t.* **·tat·ed, ·tat·ing 1** To make necessary, unavoidable, or certain. **2** To compel. See synonyms under COMPEL. [< Med. L. *necessitatus,* pp. of *necessitare* compel < *necessitas, -tatis* necessity] —**ne·ces′si·ta′tion** *n.* —**ne·ces′si·ta′tive** *adj.*

ne·ces·si·tous (nə·ses′ə·təs) *adj.* Extremely needy; destitute; poverty-stricken. —**ne·ces′·si·tous·ly** *adv.* —**ne·ces′si·tous·ness** *n.*

ne·ces·si·ty (nə·ses′ə·tē) *n. pl.* **·ties 1** The quality of being necessary: Food is a *necessity* for growth. **2** That which is unavoidable or

necessary, as in physical, moral, or logical sequence; a state of things rendering something inevitable. 3 That which is indispensably requisite to an end desired: often in the plural: the *necessities* of life; also, the fact of being indispensable; indispensableness. 4 The condition of being in want; poverty. 5 The doctrine that all events are necessarily determined. It embraces physical determinism, or fatalism, and philosophical or rational determinism, thus precluding chance or free will. — **of necessity** Necessarily; unavoidably. [<L *necessitas, -tatis*]

Synonyms: compulsion, destiny, emergency, essential, exigency, extremity, fatality, fate, indispensability, indispensableness, need, requirement, requisite, unavoidableness, urgency, want. An *essential* is something, as a quality or element, that belongs to the essence of something else so as to be inseparable from it in its normal condition, or in any complete idea or statement of it. *Need* and *want* always imply a lack; but *necessity* simply denotes the exclusion of any alternative either in thought or fact. See PREDESTINATION, WANT. Compare NECESSARY. *Antonyms*: choice, contingency, doubt, doubtfulness, dubiousness, fortuity, freedom, option, possibility, uncertainty.

Nech·es River (nech′iz) A river in eastern Texas, flowing 416 miles SE to the head of Sabine Lake.

neck (nek) *n.* 1 *Anat.* **a** The part of an animal that connects the head with the trunk. **b** Any similarly constricted portion of an organ or part: the *neck* of the femur. ◆ Collateral adjective: *cervical.* 2 The narrowed part of an object, particularly if near one end. 3 Something likened to a neck, from its position, shape, etc. 4 The narrow part of a bottle. 5 A narrow passage of water connecting two larger bodies. 6 A peninsula, isthmus, or cape. 7 That part of a garment which is close to the neck. 8 That part of a stringed musical instrument of the banjo class between the head and the body, and bearing the frets, if any. 9 *Archit.* The upper part of the shaft of a column, immediately below the capital. 10 The diminished part of a shaft, axle, etc., where it rests in a bearing. — *v.i.* 1 *U.S. Slang* To make love by kissing and caressing. — *v.t.* 2 *U. S. Slang* To make love to (someone) in such a manner. 3 To behead or strangle, as a chicken. [OE *hnecca*]

neck and neck Keeping evenly abreast; keeping up with each other.

Neck·ar (nek′är) A river in Baden-Württemberg, southern West Germany, flowing 228 miles NE, NW, and west from the Black Forest to the Rhine at Mannheim.

neck·band (nek′band′) *n.* 1 The part of a garment that fits around the neck: the *neckband* of a shirt or dress. 2 A band around the neck.

neck·cloth (nek′klôth′) *n.* A folded cloth worn around the neck and collar; a cravat. Compare STOCK (def. 24).

Neck·er (nek′ər, *Fr.* ne·kâr′), **Jacques,** 1732–1804, French statesman; minister of finance of Louis XVI; born in Switzerland.

neck·er·chief (nek′ər·chif) *n.* A kerchief for the neck.

neck·ing (nek′ing) *n.* 1 *Archit.* An ornamental treatment, as a sculptured band, a hollow, etc., of the neck of a column; also, a gorgerin. 2 Any necklike stem. 3 *Slang* Kissing and caressing in lovemaking.

neck·lace (nek′lis) *n.* An ornament, as of precious stones, precious metal, beads, or the like, worn around the neck.

neck of the woods *U.S. Colloq.* A region or neighborhood.

neck–or–noth·ing (nek′ôr·nuth′ing) *adj.* Risking everything; desperate.

neck·tie (nek′tī′) *n.* 1 A band or scarf passing round the neck or collar and tying in front under the chin; any bow or tie worn under the chin. 2 *U.S. Slang* A halter. — **necktie sociable** or **party** *U.S. Slang* A lynching.

neck·wear (nek′wâr′) *n.* 1 Any article worn around the throat. 2 Ties, cravats, collars, mufflers, etc., collectively.

neck·yoke (nek′yōk′) *n.* 1 A yoke for the neck. 2 A crosspiece to connect the forward end of the tongue of a vehicle with the harness.

nec·rec·to·my (nek·rek′tə·mē) *n. Surg.* The removal of dead matter. [<NECR(O) + -ECTOMY]

ne·cre·mi·a (ne·krē′mē·ə) *n. Pathol.* A diminishing vitality of the blood. Also **ne·crae′mi·a.** [<NECR(O)- + -EMIA]

nec·ren·ceph·a·lus (nek′rən·sef′ə·ləs) *n. Pathol.* Softening of the brain. [<NECR(O)- + Gk. *enkephalos* brain]

necro– *combining form* Corpse; dead matter: *necropolis.* Also, before vowels, **necr–.** [<Gk. *nekros* a corpse]

nec·ro·bac·il·lo·sis (nek′rō·bas′ə·lō′sis) *n.* An infective disease of cattle, sheep, horses, elk, and swine due to invasion of the body by a micro–organism *(Actinomyces necrophorus)* which produces large areas of gangrenous and necrotic tissue.

nec·ro·bi·o·sis (nek′rō·bī·ō′sis) *n. Pathol.* Progressive decay and death of an organ or tissue. [<NECRO- + Gk. *bios* life] — **nec′ro·bi·ot′ic** (-ot′ik) *adj.*

nec·ro·gen·ic (nek′rə·jen′ik) *adj.* Originating or living in dead matter. Also **ne·crog·e·nous** (ne·kroj′ə·nəs).

ne·crol·o·gy (ne·krol′ə·jē) *n. pl.* **·gies** 1 A list of persons who have died in a certain place or time. 2 A treatise on or an account of the dead. 3 Formerly, a register of those for whose souls prayer was to be offered. [<NECRO- + Gk. *logos* a list, register] — **nec·ro·log·ic** (nek′rə·loj′ik), **nec′ro·log′i·cal** *adj.* — **nec′ro·log′i·cal·ly** *adv.* — **ne·crol′o·gist** *n.*

nec·ro·man·cy (nek′rə·man′sē) *n.* 1 Divination by means of pretended communication with the dead. 2 Black magic; sorcery. See synonyms under SORCERY. — **nec′ro·man′cer** *n.* — **nec′ro·man′tic** *adj.*

nec·ro·ma·ni·a (nek′rō·mā′nē·ə, -mān′yə) *n.* A morbid preoccupation with death or interest in dead persons. — **nec′ro·ma′ni·ac** (-nē·ak) *n.*

ne·croph·a·gous (ne·krof′ə·gəs) *adj.* Subsisting on carrion. [<NECRO- + -PHAGOUS]

nec·ro·phile (nek′rə·fīl, -fil) *n.* One who has a morbid attraction, usually of an erotic nature, to corpses. — **nec′ro·phil′i·a, ne·croph·i·lism** (ne·krof′ə·liz′əm), **ne·croph′i·ly** *n.*

nec·ro·pho·bi·a (nek′rō·fō′bē·ə) *n.* A morbid fear of death or of dead bodies. — **nec′ro·pho′bic** *adj.*

ne·crop·o·lis (ne·krop′ə·lis) *n.* A cemetery, especially one belonging to an ancient city. [<NECRO- + Gk. *polis* city]

nec·rop·sy (nek′rop·sē) *n. pl.* **·sies** An examination of a dead body; an autopsy. Also **ne·cros·co·py** (ne·kros′kə·pē). [<NECRO- + -OPSY]

ne·crose (ne·krōs′, nek′rōs) *v.t.* & *v.i.* **·crosed, ·cros·ing** To affect with or suffer from necrosis.

ne·cro·sis (ne·krō′sis) *n.* 1 *Pathol.* The death of a part of the body, as of a bone; mortification; gangrene. 2 *Bot.* A gradual decay in trees or plants. [<Gk. *nekrōsis* deadness] — **ne·crot′ic** (-krot′ik) *adj.*

necrotic enteritis An intestinal disorder of swine marked by extensive ulceration.

ne·crot·o·my (ne·krot′ə·mē) *n.* 1 The dissection of a dead body. 2 *Surg.* The excision of dead bone. [<NECRO- + -TOMY] — **nec·ro·tom·ic** (nek′rə·tom′ik) *adj.* — **ne·crot′o·mist** *n.*

nec·tar (nek′tər) *n.* 1 In Greek mythology, the drink of the gods. 2 Hence, any especially sweet drink: applied specifically to certain spiced or honeyed wines. 3 *Bot.* The saccharine substance secreted by some plants and forming the base of natural honey. [<L <Gk. *nektar*] — **nec·tar·e·an** (nek·târ′ē·ən) *adj.* — **nec·tar′e·ous** *adj.*

nec·tar·if·er·ous (nek′tə·rif′ər·əs) *adj.* Nectar- or honey–bearing.

nec·tar·ine (nek′tə·rēn′, nek′tə·rēn) *n.* A variety of peach having a smooth, waxy skin without down and a firm, aromatic pulp. — *adj.* Sweet and delicious.

nec·ta·ry (nek′tər·ē) *n. pl.* **·ries** 1 *Bot.* The organ or part of a plant that secretes nectar. 2 *Entomol.* One of the small, abdominal honey tubes of an aphid. — **nec·tar′i·al, nec·tar′e·al** (-târ′ē·əl) *adj.*

Ned (ned) Diminutive of EDWARD. Also **Ned′dy.** — **to raise Ned** *U.S. Colloq.* To start trouble or a disturbance.

ned·dy (ned′ē) *n. Brit. Dial.* 1 A donkey: usually as a proper or pet name. 2 A simpleton.

Ne·der·land (nā′dər·länt) The Dutch name for the NETHERLANDS.

née (nā) *adj.* Born: noting the maiden name of a married woman: Madame d'Arblay, *née* Burney. [<F, pp. of *naître* be born <L *nasci*]

nee·bour (nē′bər) *n. Scot.* A neighbor.

need (nēd) *v.t.* 1 To have need or want of; require. — *v.i.* 2 To be in want. 3 *Archaic* To be necessary: It *needs* not. 4 To be obliged or compelled: in this sense *need* is used as an uninflected auxiliary verb only in negative and interrogative sentences, followed by the infinitive without *to*: He *need* not go; *Need* he come? — *n.* 1 A lack of something requisite or desirable; hence, indigence; poverty: He was in *need.* 2 A situation of want or peril. 3 The thing needed. See synonyms under NECESSITY, POVERTY, WANT. ◆ Homophone: *knead.* [OE *nīed, nēd*] — **need′er** *n.*

need·ful (nēd′fəl) *adj.* 1 Needed; requisite; necessary. 2 Needy. — **need′ful·ly** *adv.* — **need′ful·ness** *n.*

Need·ham (nē′dəm), **John Turberville,** 1713–1781, English naturalist.

need·i·ness (nē′di·nis) *n.* The state of being in want; poverty.

nee·dle (nēd′l) *n.* 1 A small, slender, pointed instrument containing an eye at the head, or, in sewing machines, at the point, to carry thread through a fabric in sewing. 2 The straight rod, commonly of wire, bone, or wood, used in knitting; also, the hooked rod used in crocheting. 3 Any instrument or object shaped like or used as a needle, as a pinnacle of rock, or a leaf, such as that of the pine. 4 A straight wire, balanced and pivoted, as in a compass; a magnetic needle. 5 In a needle gun, the steel bolt that fires the cartridge. 6 A needle valve. 7 The sharp-pointed end of a hypodermic syringe. 8 *Colloq.* A hypodermic needle. 9 An obelisk. 10 A thin, sharp–pointed piece of steel, etc., often tipped with diamond, etc., to transmit the sound vibrations from a phonograph record. — *v.* **·dled, ·dling** *v.t.* 1 To sew or pierce with a needle. 2 *Colloq.* To heckle or annoy. 3 *Colloq.* To goad; prod. 4 *Colloq.* To increase the alcoholic content of: to *needle* the beer. — *v.i.* 5 To sew or work with a needle. [OE *nǣdl*]

nee·dle·bath (nēd′l·bath′, -bäth′) *n.* A form of shower bath in which the water is projected with force in fine jets.

nee·dle·fish (nēd′l·fish′) *n. pl.* **·fish** or **·fish·es** 1 One of the long, slender sea fishes of the family *Belonidae*, superficially resembling the fresh–water gar. 2 The pipefish.

nee·dle·ful (nēd′l·fo͝ol′) *n. pl.* **·fuls** The length of thread that can be suitably used in a needle at one time.

needle grass Feather grass.

needle gun A breechloading small arm firing a paper cartridge having the primer between the powder charge and the bullet, the primer being detonated by a needlelike firing pin passing through the powder: introduced in the Prussian army, 1842.

nee·dle·point (nēd′l·point′) *n.* 1 A sharp–pointed attachment for the leg of a drawing instrument; anything resembling the point of a needle, as spires of cathedrals or crystals of rock. 2 Lace made entirely with a sewing needle rather than bobbins, and worked with buttonhole and blanket stitches on a paper pattern. 3 A stitch used in needle tapestry, or embroidered needle tapestry itself.

need·less (nēd′lis) *adj.* Useless; not required. — **need′less·ly** *adv.* — **need′less·ness** *n.*

nee·dle·stone (nēd′l·stōn′) *n.* Natrolite.

needle valve *Mech.* 1 A valve having a conoidal opening closed by a plug of similar shape: designed to control accurately the flow of a liquid, as in a carbureter. 2 A valve with a conoidal plug fitting into a cylindrical opening: designed to give a large increase in opening with a slight increase in lift.

nee·dle·wom·an (nēd′l·wo͝om′ən) *n. pl.* **·wom·en** (-wim′in) A seamstress.

nee·dle·work (nēd′l·wûrk′) *n.* 1 Work done with a needle; sewing; specifically, embroidery. 2 The business of sewing with a needle. — **nee′dle·work′er** *n.*

needs (nēdz) *adv.* Necessarily; indispensably: often with *must.*

need·y (nē′dē) *adj.* **need·i·er, need·i·est** Being in need, want, or poverty; necessitous. — **need′i·ly** *adv.*

Ne·en·ga·tu (nye·eng′gə·to͞o′) *n.* Tupi, the northern branch of the Tupian linguistic stock: widely used in the Amazon region.

neep (nēp) *n. Scot.* & *Brit. Dial.* A turnip.

ne'er (nâr) *adv.* Never: a contraction.

ne'er-do-well (nâr′dōō·wel′) *n.* A useless, unreliable person. —*adj.* Useless; good-for-nothing. Also **ne'er′-do-good′** (-gŏŏd′), *Scot.* **ne'er′-do-weel′** (-wēl′).

Neer·win·den (nār·vin′dən) A village in eastern Belgium; scene of English defeat by the French, 1693, and Austrian victory over the French, 1793.

neeze (nēz) *v.i.* Obs. To sneeze. [Cf. ON *hnjosa* sneeze]

ne·far·i·ous (ni·fâr′ē·əs) *adj.* Wicked in the extreme; heinous. See synonyms under CRIMINAL, FLAGRANT, INFAMOUS, SINFUL. [<L *nefarius* <*nefas* a crime <*ne-* not + *fas* a divine command, right] —**ne·far′i·ous·ly** *adv.* —**ne·far′i·ous·ness** *n.*

Ne·fer·ti·ti (ne′fər·tē′tē) Egyptian queen of the 14th century B.C., wife of Ikhnaton: also *Nofretete.*

Ne·fud (ne·fŏŏd′) See NAFUD.

ne·gate (ni·gāt′, nē′gāt) *v.t.* **·gat·ed, ·gat·ing 1** To make ineffective; nullify. **2** To deny the existence of. [<L *negatus,* pp. of *negare* deny]

ne·ga·tion (ni·gā′shən) *n.* **1** The act of denying or of asserting the falsity of a proposition; denial in general. **2** Absence of anything affirmative or definite; voidness; nullity.

neg·a·tive (neg′ə·tiv) *adj.* **1** Containing contradiction or denial; expressing negation: opposed to *affirmative.* **2** Characterized by denial or refusal: a *negative* reply. **3** Exhibiting or characterized by absence of that which is essential to positive or affirmative character: the opposite of *positive.* **4** *Phot.* Exhibiting the reverse; showing dark for light and light for dark: a *negative* plate or film. **5** *Math.* **a** Denoting a direction or quality the opposite of another assumed as positive: usually denoted by the minus sign (−). **b** Less than zero; to be subtracted; minus: said of quantities. **6** *Geom.* Situated or measured downward from the axis of *X* or to the left of the axis of *Y.* **7** *Electr.* Denoting a type of electricity characterized by an excess of electrons on a charged body: opposed to *positive.* It is similar to that produced on a resinous object after rubbing with wool. **8** *Biol.* Describing a plant or animal response directed away from or in opposition to a stimulus. **9** *Med.* Indicating the absence of a suspected condition, or the absence of certain bacteria. See synonyms under PASSIVE. —*n.* **1** A proposition, word, or act expressing refusal or denial: My request received a *negative.* **2** The side of a question that denies; also, a negative decision. **3** The right to veto. **4** A photograph having the lights and shades reversed, used for printing positives. **5** *Gram.* A particle employing or expressing denial. The principal negative is *not.* **6** *Electr.* **a** Negative or frictional electricity. **b** The negative plate of a voltaic cell. **7** *Math.* A negative sign or quantity. —**double negative** *Gram.* The use of two negatives in the same statement, as in "I didn't see nobody." ◆This usage is a descendant of a formation native to the Germanic languages and was regularly used in Old and Middle English to intensify negation. It survives in Modern English, but is now considered substandard on analogy with Latin, where a double negative becomes an affirmative. Such statements as "I am not unhurt," however, are standard English, and have the effect of weak affirmatives. —*v.t.* **·tived, ·tiv·ing 1** To deny; contradict. **2** To refuse to sanction or enact; veto. **3** To prove to be false; disprove. **4** To neutralize; counteract. [<L *negativus* <*negare* deny] —**neg′a·tive·ly** *adv.* —**neg′a·tive·ness, neg·a·tiv·i·ty** (neg′ə ·tiv′ə·tē) *n.*

negative income tax Payment by the government to those whose incomes fall below a specified level, regarded as a means of replacing or supplementing welfare payments.

neg·a·tiv·ism (neg′ə·tiv·iz′əm) *n.* **1** The beliefs or attitude of any negative thinker; atheism, agnosticism, etc. **2** The denial of traditional beliefs without proposing constructive substitutes. **3** *Psychol.* A type of behavior characterized by resistance to suggestion: when the subject fails to do what he is expected or asked to do, such behavior is known as **pas·sive negativism;** when the subject does the opposite, **active** or **command negativism.** —**neg′a·tiv·ist** *n.* — **neg′a·tiv·is′tic** *adj.*

neg·a·to·ry (neg′ə·tôr′ē, -tō′rē) *adj.* Signifying negation.

Neg·ev (neg′ev, ne·gev′) A triangular desert region in southern Israel; 4,700 square miles. Also **Neg·eb** (neg′eb, nə·geb′).

neg·lect (ni·glekt′) *v.t.* **1** To disregard; ignore. **2** To fail to give proper attention to or take proper care of: to *neglect* one's business. **3** To fail to do or perform through carelessness or oversight; leave undone. —*n.* **1** The act of neglecting, or the state of being neglected. **2** Habitual want of attention or care; negligence. [<L *neglectus,* pp. of *negligere* <*nec-* not + *legere* gather, pick up] —**neg·lect′a·ble** *adj.* —**neg·lect′er** *n.*

Synonyms (noun): carelessness, default, disregard, failure, heedlessness, inadvertence, inattention, indifference, neglectfulness, negligence, oversight, remissness, slackness, slight. *Neglect* is the failing to take such care, show such attention, pay such courtesy, etc., as may be rightfully or reasonably expected. *Negligence* may be used in almost the same sense, but with a slighter force; but it is often used to denote the quality or trait of character of which the act is a manifestation, or to denote the habit of neglecting that which ought to be done. *Negligence* in dress implies want of care as to its arrangement, tidiness, etc.; *neglect* of one's garments would imply leaving them exposed to defacement or injury, as by dust, moths, etc. See SLIGHT. *Antonyms*: see synonyms under CARE.

neg·lect·ful (ni·glekt′fəl) *adj.* Exhibiting or indicating neglect. See synonyms under INATTENTIVE. —**neg·lect′ful·ly, neg·lect′ing·ly** *adv.* —**neg·lect′ful·ness** *n.*

neg·li·gée (neg′li·zhā′, neg′li·zhā; *Fr.* nā·glē·zhā′) *n.* **1** A woman's soft, flowing, usually decorative dressing gown. **2** Any informal, careless, or incomplete attire. —*adj.* Of a woman, appearing careless in dress. [<F *négligée,* orig. pp. of *négliger* neglect]

neg·li·gence (neg′lə·jəns) *n.* **1** The act of neglecting. **2** An act or instance of neglect. **3** Disregard for outward appearances or for conventionalities. See synonyms under NEGLECT.

neg·li·gent (neg′lə·jənt) *adj.* **1** Apt to omit what ought to be done; neglectful. **2** Unconventional. See synonyms under INATTENTIVE. [<L *negligens, -entis,* ppr. of *negligere* NEGLECT] —**neg′li·gent·ly** *adv.*

neg·li·gi·ble (neg′lə·jə ·bəl) *adj.* That can be disregarded; inconsiderable; trifling; of little importance or size. —**neg′li·gi·bil′i·ty, neg′li·gi·ble·ness** *n.* —**neg′li·gi·bly** *adv.*

ne·go·ti·a·ble (ni·gō′shē·ə·bəl, -shə·bəl) *adj.* **1** That can be negotiated. **2** *Law* Transferable to a third person, as for the payment of debts. **3** That can be managed, overcome, or successfully dealt with. —**ne·go′ti·a·bil′i·ty** *n.* —**ne·go′ti·a·bly** *adv.*

negotiable instruments Instruments, such as bills of exchange, notes, checks, drafts, bills of lading, etc., covered by the Negotiable Instrument Law in effect in most States of the United States.

ne·go·ti·ant (ni·gō′shē·ənt) *n.* One who negotiates; a negotiator.

ne·go·ti·ate (ni·gō′shē·āt) *v.* **·at·ed, ·at·ing** *v.i.* **1** To treat or bargain with others in order to reach an agreement. —*v.t.* **2** To procure, arrange, or conclude by mutual discussion: to *negotiate* an agreement. **3** To transfer for a value received; sell; assign, as a note or bond. **4** To surmount, cross, or cope with (some obstacle). See synonyms under TRANSACT. [<L *negotiatus,* pp. of *negotiari* trade <*negotium* business] —**ne·go′ti·a′tion** *n.* —**ne·go′ti·a′tor** *n.* —**ne·go′ti·a·to′ry** *adj.*

Ne·gress (nē′gris) *n.* A black woman or girl; usually taken to be offensive.

Ne·gril·lo (ni·gril′ō) *n. Anthropol.* A member of a people belonging to a group of dark-skinned peoples of small stature that live in Africa. See NEGRITO. [< Sp., dim. of *negro* black]

Ne·gri Sem·bi·lan (nā′grē sem·bē·län′) A state in SW Federation of Malaya; 2,550 square miles; capital, Seremban.

Ne·gri·to (ni·grē′tō) *n.* pl. **·tos** or **·toes** *Anthropol.* A member of a people belonging to a group of dark-skinned peoples of small stature that live in Oceania and the southeastern part of Asia. [< Sp., dim. of *negro* black] —**Ne·grit′ic** (-grit′ik) *adj.*

ne·gri·tude (nē′grə·tōōd′, -tyōōd′) *n. Often cap.* **1** An awareness of and pride in black African culture and heritage. **2** Black African culture. **3** The state or condition of being black. Also *French* **né·gri·tude** (nā′grə·tüd′). [<F *négritude* <*négre* black <L *niger* black]

Ne·gro (nē′grō) *n. pl.* **·groes 1** A member of the black race distinguished from members of other races by usually inherited physical and physiological characteristics, without regard to language or culture, *esp.* a member of a people belonging to the African branch of the black race; sometimes taken to be offensive. **2** A person of Negro descent, sometimes taken to be offensive. [<Sp. <L *niger* black]

Ne·gro (nā′grō), **Río** See Río NEGRO.

Ne·groid (nē′groid) *adj.* **1** *Anthropol.* Pertaining to or characteristic of the Negro, or black race. **2** Resembling, related to, or characteristic of Negroes or blacks. —*n.* A person of Negro descent or having some Negro characteristics.

Ne·gro·ness (nē′grō·nis) *n.* The fact or condition of being a Negro.

Neg·ro·pon·te (neg′rō·pôn′tā) The Italian name for EUBOEA.

Ne·gros (nā′grōs) One of the Visayan Islands, fourth largest of the Philippines; 4,905 square miles.

ne·gus (nē′gəs) *n.* A drink made of wine, water, and lemon juice, sweetened. [after Col. Francis *Negus,* died 1732, who concocted it]

Ne·gus (nē′gəs) *n.* The title of the kings of Abyssinia.

Ne·he·mi·ah (nē′hə·mi′ə) **1** A Hebrew statesman and historian. **2** A book of the Old Testament attributed to him, recounting the rebuilding of Jerusalem. [<Hebrew *Nechhemiah* comforted of Jehovah]

Neh·ru (nārōō), **Ja·wa·har·lal** (jə·wä′hər·läl), 1889–1964, Indian nationalist leader; prime minister 1947–1964. —**(Pandit) Motilal,** 1861–1931, Indian nationalist; father of preceding.

neif (nēf) See NIEVE.

neigh (nā) *v.i.* To utter the cry of a horse; whinny. —*n.* A whinny. [OE *hnǣgan*]

neigh·bor (nā′bər) *n.* **1** One who lives near another. **2** One who is near by chance. **3** Friend; stranger: a colloquial and friendly term of address. **4** A fellow man. — *adj.* Close at hand; adjacent. —*v.t.* **1** To live or be near to or next to; adjoin: Ohio *neighbors* Indiana. **2** To bring near to or in close association. —*v.i.* **3** To be in proximity; lie close. **4** To live nearby; be neighborly. Also *Brit.* **neigh′bour.** [OE *nēahgebur* <*nēah* near + *gebur* farmer]

neigh·bor·hood (nā′bər·hŏŏd) *n.* **1** The region near where one is or resides; vicinity. **2** The people collectively who dwell in the vicinity. **3** Nearness; the condition of standing in the relation of a neighbor. **4** Friendly relations; neighborliness. **5** A district considered with reference to a given characteristic. — **in the neighborhood of** About; near.

Synonyms: district, locality, vicinage, vicinity. See APPROXIMATION.

neigh·bor·ing (nā′bər·ing) *adj.* Adjacent; near.

neigh·bor·ly (nā′bər·lē) *adj.* Appropriate to a neighbor; sociable. See synonyms under AMICABLE, FRIENDLY. — **neigh′bor·li·ness** *n.*

Neil·son (nēl′sən), **William Allan,** 1869–1946, U.S. educator born in Scotland, president of Smith College 1917–39.

Neis·se (nī′sə) A river in Czechoslovakia, East Germany, and Poland, flowing 140 miles to the Oder: Polish *Nysa.*

Neis·ser (nī′sər), **Albert Ludwig Siegmund,** 1855–1916, German dermatologist; discoverer of the gonococcus.

neis·ser·o·sis (nī′sə·rō′sis) *n.* Pathol. Gonococcus infection. [after A. L. S. *Neisser*]

neist (nēst) *adj., adv., & prep. Brit. Dial.* Next; nearest: also, *Scot., niest.*
nei·ther (nē′thər, nī-) *adj.* Not either. —*pron.* Not the one nor the other. —*conj.* **1** Not one nor the other: followed by correlative *nor*: He will *neither* go nor send. **2** Not at all: an intensive now replaced by *either* except in incorrect usage: He has no strength, nor sense *neither.* **3** Nor yet. [OE *nother;* infl. in form by EITHER]
Nejd (nejd) A province of Saudi Arabia comprising a viceroyalty of the country; 450,000 square miles; capital, Riyadh: also *Najd.*
nek·ton (nek′ton) *n.* The aggregate of marine organisms actively swimming on or near the surface of the sea. [<NL <Gk. *nektos* swimming] **—nek·ton′ic, nek·ter′ic** (-ter′ik) *adj.*
Ne·le·us (nē′lē·əs) In Greek legend, a son of Poseidon and king of Pylos, father of twelve sons, all of whom save Nestor were slain by Hercules.
Nell (nel), **Nel·lie, Nel·ly** (nel′ē) Diminutives of HELEN.
nel·son (nel′sən) *n.* A wrestling hold in which the arms are thrust under the opponent's armpits from behind, and the hands gripped at the back of his neck: also called **full nelson.** The **half, quarter,** and **three-quarter nelson** are variants of this fundamental hold.
Nel·son (nel′sən), **Viscount Horatio,** 1758–1805, English admiral; hero of Trafalgar: known as *Lord Nelson.*
Nel·son River (nel′sən) A river in NE Manitoba province, Canada, flowing 400 miles NE from Lake Winnipeg to Hudson Bay.
ne·lum·bo (ni·lum′bō) *n. pl.* **·bos** One of a genus *(Nelumbium)* of aquatic herbs of the waterlily family. *N. pentapetalum* is the water chinkapin and *N. nelumbo* is the sacred lotus of India. [<NL <Singhalese *nelumbu*]
Ne·man (nye′mən) A river in Belorussian S.S.R. and Lithuania, flowing 597 miles west to the Courland Lagoon: Polish *Nieman,* Lithuanian *Nemunas,* German *Memel.*
nem·a·thel·minth (nem′ə·thel′minth) *n.* One of a phylum or class *(Nemathelminthes)* of worms having a threadlike, unsegmented body with papillae or spines at the anterior extremity, as the nematodes and acanthocephalans; the roundworms. —*adj.* Pertaining to these worms. Also **nem′a·tel′minth** (-tel′-). [<NL <Gk. *nēma, -atos* thread + *helmins* a worm]
nemato- *combining form* Thread; filament: *nematocyst*: also, before vowels, **nemat-.** Also **nema-.** [<Gk. *nēma, -matos* thread]
nem·a·to·cyst (nem′ə·tō·sist′) *n. Zool.* One of the stinging cells in jellyfishes, polyps, and other hydrozoans, in the interior of which is coiled a long filament whose instantaneous release causes paralysis of the organism it touches: also called *lasso cell, nettle cell.* **—nem′a·to·cys′tic** *adj.*
nem·a·tode (nem′ə·tōd) *n.* Any of a phylum or class *(Nematoda)* of roundworms having a mouth and intestinal canal, some of which, as the hookworm, are intestinal parasites in man and other animals. [<NL <Gk. *nēma, -atos* a thread]
Ne·me·a (nē′mē·ə, nə·mē′ə) A valley in ancient Argolis, Greece; celebrated for the **Nemean games,** one of the four great pan-Hellenic festivals. **—Ne·me′an** *adj.*
Nemean lion In Greek legend, a fierce lion which Hercules strangled.
ne·mer·te·an (ni·mûr′tē·ən) *n.* One of a phylum or class *(Nemertea)* of flatworms, mostly marine and non-parasitic, with skin ciliated, proboscis retractile, and muscular, vascular, and nervous systems characteristically developed: often brilliantly colored. —*adj.* Of or pertaining to the *Nemertea.* [<NL <Gk. *Nēmertēs,* one of the Nereids] **—ne·mer′ti·an, ne·mer′tine, ne′mer·tin′e·an** *adj. & n.*
nem·e·sis (nem′ə·sis) *n.* Retributive justice; retribution. [<L <Gk. <*nemein* distribute]
Nem·e·sis (nem′ə·sis) In Greek mythology, the goddess of retributive justice or vengeance. [Prob. <*nemein* allot, distribute]
ne·mi·ne con·tra·di·cen·te (nem′ə·nē kon′·trə·di·sen′tē) *Latin* No one speaking in opposition; hence, unanimously.
ne·mi·ne dis·sen·ti·en·te (nem′ə·nē di·sen′·shē·en′tē) *Latin* No one dissenting; hence, unanimously.
ne·mo me im·pu·ne la·ces·sit (nē′mō mē im·pyōō′nē lə·ses′it) *Latin* No one attacks me with impunity: motto of Scotland.
nem·o·ral (nem′ər·əl) *adj.* Pertaining to a wood, grove, or the like. [<L *nemoralis* <*nemus, nemoris* a grove]
nem·o·rose (nem′ə·rōs) *adj. Bot.* Inhabiting groves or open woodland places: said especially of plants.
Ne·mu·nas (nye′mōō·näs) The Lithuanian name for the NEMAN.
neo- *combining form* **1** New; recent; a modern or modified form of: *Neo-Platonism.* **2** *Geol.* Denoting the most recent subdivision of a period: *Neocene.* Also, before vowels, usually **ne-.** [<Gk. <*neos* new]
ne·o·ars·phen·am·ine (nē′ō·ärs′fen·am′in, -fen·ə·mēn′) *n. Chem.* A modified compound of arsphenamine, $C_{13}H_{13}O_4N_2SAs_2Na$, used in the treatment of syphilis and certain other diseases.
Ne·o-Cath·o·lic (nē′ō·kath′ə·lik, -kath′lik) *adj.* **1** Of or pertaining to a school in the Anglican church in avowed sympathy with Roman Catholic doctrine and ritual. **2** In France, pertaining to a school of liberal Catholicism opposed to ultramontanism. —*n.* A member of either of these schools. **—Ne′o-Ca·thol′i·cism** (-kə·thol′ə·siz′əm) *n.*
Ne·o·cene (nē′ə·sēn) *adj. Geol.* Of or pertaining to the later of the two epochs into which the Tertiary period was at one time divided, or to the corresponding series of strata. —*n.* The Neocene epoch. [<NEO- + Gk. *kainos* new]
Ne·o-Chris·ti·an·i·ty (nē′ō·kris′chē·an′ə·tē) *n.* A rationalistic interpretation of Christianity.
ne·o·clas·sic (nē′ō·klas′ik) *adj.* Of, pertaining to, or denoting neo-classicism. Also **ne′o·clas′si·cal.**
ne·o·clas·si·cism (nē′ō·klas′ə·siz′əm) *n.* **1** A revival of classical style in literature, art, etc. **2** In the later 17th and the 18th centuries, an esthetic and philosophical movement which sought to recover the classical spirit of order and moderation: characterized by close adherence to rules and conventional forms, restraint in the expression of emotion, and an emphasis on the typical and general rather than the individual or eccentric. **—ne′o·clas′si·cist** *n.*
ne·o·cul·tu·ra·tion (nē′ō·kul′chə·rā′shən) *n.* The creation and establishment of new cultural forms, especially as a result of transculturation.
Ne·o-Dar·win·ism (nē′ō·där′win·iz′əm) *n. Biol.* Darwinism as modified and extended by more recent students, who accept the theory of natural selection as sufficient to account for evolution, and deny, as in the case of Weismann especially, the inheritance of acquired characters. See NEO-LAMARCKISM, WEISMANNISM. **—Ne′o-Dar·win′i·an** (-där·win′ē·ən) *adj. & n.* **—Ne′o-Dar′win·ist** *n.*
ne·o·dym·i·um (nē′ō·dim′ē·əm) *n.* A metallic element (symbol Nd, atomic number 60) found in combination with cerium and other elements of the lanthanide series. See PERIODIC TABLE. [<NEO- + (DI)DYMIUM]
Ne·o·gae·a (nē′ō·jē′ə) *n.* A zoogeographical region including the western hemisphere or New World. [<NEO- + Gk. *gaia* earth] **—Ne′o·gae′an** *adj.*
ne·o·ge·ic (nē′ō·jē′ik) *adj.* Of or belonging to the western hemisphere or New World: opposed to *gerontogeic.*
Ne·o·gene (nē′ō·jēn) *adj. Geol.* Of or pertaining to the Upper Tertiary and the Quaternary periods in the Cenozoic geological era: includes the Miocene, Pliocene, Pleistocene, and Holocene epochs. [<Gk. *neogenēs* newborn]
ne·o·gen·ic (nē′ō·jen′ik) *adj.* Newly formed: said especially of rocks and minerals. Also **ne′o·ge·net′ic** (-jə·net′ik).
Ne·o-He·bra·ic (nē′ō·hē·brā′ik) *n.* That form of the Hebrew language used in post-Biblical Jewish literature. *–adj.* Pertaining to post-Biblical Hebrew.
ne·o·im·pres·sion·ism (nē′ō·im·presh′ən·iz′əm) *n.* The doctrines and methods of a group of artists of the 19th century, based on a more strictly scientific practice of impressionist technique. Compare IMPRESSIONISM, POINTILLISM, POST-IMPRESSIONISM. **—ne′o·im·pres′sion·ist** *n. & adj.*
Ne·o-La·marck·ism (nē′ō·lə·märk′iz·əm) *n. Biol.* Lamarckism as revived, modified, and extended by students who hold to the inheritance of acquired habits as a potent influence in evolution. **—Ne′o-La·marck′i·an** *adj. & n.* **—Ne′o-La·marck′ist** *n.*
Ne·o-Lat·in (nē′ō·lat′n) *n.* **1** One of a group of peoples whose language is derived from Latin. **2** New Latin: see under LATIN.
ne·o·lith (nē′ə·lith) *n.* A Neolithic implement.
Ne·o·lith·ic (nē′ə·lith′ik) *adj. Anthropol.* Of or pertaining to the period of human culture following the Mesolithic: characterized by a great variety of polished stone implements and the development of new social forms based upon primitive techniques in weaving, spinning, and potterymaking, and the introduction of a settled agriculture exploiting many new domesticated plants. [<Gk. *neos* new + *lithos* stone]
ne·ol·o·gism (nē·ol′ə·jiz′əm) *n.* **1** A new word or phrase. **2** The use of new words or new meanings for old words. **3** A new doctrine in theology. **—ne·ol′o·gis′tic, ne·ol′o·gis′ti·cal** *adj.*
ne·ol·o·gist (nē·ol′ə·jist) *n.* **1** A person who invents or employs new words. **2** A person who adopts new views in theology.
ne·ol·o·gy (nē·ol′ə·jē) *n. pl.* **·gies** A neologism. [<NEO- + Gk. *logos* word] **—ne·o·log·i·cal** (nē′ə·loj′i·kəl) *adj.* **—ne′o·log′i·cal·ly** *adv.*
Ne·o-Mal·thu·sian (nē′ō·mal·thōō′zhən, -zē·ən) *n.* An advocate of birth control: so called from Malthus' belief that population is always checked at a level proportionate to the available means of subsistence. —*adj.* Pertaining to birth control. **—Ne′o-Mal·thu′sian·ism** *n.*
ne·o·morph (nē′ə·môrf) *n.* A newly acquired organ or part. Also **ne′o·mor′phism.**
ne·o·my·cin (nē′ə·mī′sin) *n.* An antibiotic related to streptomycin, used in the local treatment of certain skin and eye infections.
ne·on (nē′on) *n.* A colorless, odorless, chemically inactive gaseous element (symbol Ne, atomic number 10) found in the atmosphere in a ratio of about 15 parts per million. See PERIODIC TABLE. [<NL <Gk. *neos* new]
ne·o·na·tal (nē′ō·nā′təl) *adj.* Of or pertaining to newborns: *neonatal* care.
ne·o·nate (nē′ō·nāt) *n.* A newborn infant. [<NEO- + L *natus* born]
ne·o·pho·bi·a (nē′ə·fō′bē·ə) *n.* Morbid fear of the new or unfamiliar. **—ne′o·phobe** *n.***—ne′o·pho′bic** *adj.*
ne·o·phyte (nē′ə·fīt) *n.* **1** A recent convert. **2** A novice of a religious or mystic order. **3** Any novice or beginner. **4** *Bot.* A new or recently introduced plant species; an exotic. [<Gk. *neophytos* novice]
ne·o·plasm (nē′ə·plaz′əm) *n. Pathol.* A growth or formation of tissue resulting from morbid action; a tumor.
ne·o·plas·ty (nē′ə·plas′tē) *n.* Plastic surgery for the restoration of old or the formation of new parts. **—ne′o·plas′tic** *adj.*
Ne·o-Pla·ton·ism (nē′ō·plā′tən·iz′əm) *n.* An Alexandrian system of philosophy of the third century, commingling Jewish and Christian ideas with doctrines of Plato and other Greek philosophers and Oriental mysticism. **—Ne′o-Pla·ton′ic** (-plə·ton′ik) *adj.* **—Ne′o-Pla′ton·ist** *n.*
ne·o·prene (nē′ə·prēn) *n. Chem.* A synthetic rubber obtained in a variety of types from chloroprene, and produced by the combination of hydrogen with acetylene gas. [<NEO-+ (CHLORO) PRENE]
Ne·op·tol·e·mus (nē′op·tol′ə·məs) In Greek legend, a son of Achilles who fought in the Trojan War, killed Priam and Astyanax, sacrificed Polyxena on Achilles' grave, carried off Andromache, and later married Hermione: also known as *Pyrrhus.*
Ne·o·sal·var·san (nē′ō·sal′vər·san) *n.* Proprietary name for a brand of neoarsphenamine.
Ne·o-Scho·las·ti·cism (nē′ō·skə·las′tə·siz′əm) *n.* The revival in modern times of Scholasticism, specifically that of Thomas Aquinas, incorporating new elements to make it applicable to contemporary problems.
Ne·o·sho River (nē·ō′shō) A river in Kansas and Oklahoma, flowing 460 miles SE to the Arkansas River.
ne·o·style (nē′ə·stīl) *n.* A contrivance for making several copies of a document; a cyclostyle.
ne·o·ter·ic (nē′ə·ter′ik) *adj.* Recent in origin; new. Also **ne′o·ter′i·cal.** —*n.* One of modern times; a modern. [<Gk. *neōterikos* youthful] **—ne′o·ter′i·cal·ly** *adv.*

ne·ot·er·ism (nē·ot′ə·riz′əm) *n.* That which is new, modern, or recently introduced; the coinage of new words, or a newly coined word. —**ne·ot′er·ist** *n.* —**ne·ot′er·is′tic** *adj.*

Ne·o·trop·i·cal (nē′ō·trop′i·kəl) *adj.* Of, pertaining to, or designating the zoogeographical region of the New World that includes Central and South America and the adjacent islands.

ne·o·type (nē′ə·tīp) *n.* In systematics, any specimen of a plant or animal chosen to replace the original specimen when all type material has been lost or destroyed.

Ne·o·zo·ic (nē′ə·zō′ik) *adj. Geol.* **1** Of or pertaining to the Mesozoic and Cenozoic geological eras, as contrasted with the Paleozoic. **2** The Cenozoic era.

nep (nep) *n.* Small knots in cotton fiber produced by uneven growth of the plant or by friction in process machinery. [Cf dial. E *nap* a knob, button]

Nep (nep) Contraction of NEW ECONOMIC POLICY: also written **NEP.**

Ne·pal (ni·pôl′) An independent kingdom between Tibet and India; 56,000 square miles; capital, Katmandu. —**Nep·a·lese** (nep′ə·lēz′, ·lēs′) *adj. & n.*

ne·pen·the (ni·pen′thē) *n.* **1** A drug or potion supposed by the ancient Greeks to banish pain and sorrow. **2** Any agent causing oblivion. [< L < Gk. *nēpenthēs* free from sorrow < *nē-* not + *penthos* sorrow] —**ne·pen′the·an, ne·pen′thic** *adj.*

ne·pen·thes (ni·pen′thēz) *n.* One of a genus (*Nepenthes*) of mainly East Indian herbs or half-shrubby plants, the East Indian pitcher plants. [< NL < Gk. *nēpenthēs* NEPENTHE]

ne·per (nā′pər) *n.* A unit of power-level difference or of attenuation in electrical communication circuits: equal to 8.686 decibels. [after John *Napier*]

NEPENTHES
(Pitchers from 4 to 10 inches long)

Neph·e·le (nef′ə·lē) In Greek legend, the wife of Athamas, mother of Phrixus and Helle, who after her husband set her aside for another, sent her children away on a ram with golden fleece. See PHRIXUS.

neph·e·line (nef′ə·lin) *n.* A colorless or variously colored hexagonal sodium aluminum silicate, NaAlSiO₄. Also **neph′e·lite.** [< Gk. *nephelē* cloud]

neph·e·lin·ite (nef′ə·lin·īt′) *n.* A dark-gray volcanic rock composed of the minerals nepheline, augite, and magnetite. Also **neph′e·lin·yte′.**

neph·e·lom·e·ter (nef′ə·lom′ə·tər) *n.* An instrument used for the measurement of light transmitted or scattered by translucent substances: also used for the determination of the quantity of matter suspended in a liquid. [< Gk. *nephelē* cloud + -METER] —**neph′e·lo·met′ric** (nef′ə·lō·met′rik) *adj.* —**neph′e·lom′e·try** *n.*

neph·ew (nef′yōō, *esp. Brit.* nev′yōō) *n.* **1** The son of a sister or a brother; by extension, a grandnephew. **2** An unlawfully begotten son: a euphemism. **3** *Obs.* A descendant; grandchild; also, a cousin. [< F *neveu* < L *nepos* grandson, nephew]

nepho- *combining form* Cloud; pertaining to the clouds: *nephology.* Also, before vowels, **neph-.** [< Gk. *nephos* cloud]

neph·o·gram (nef′ə·gram) *n. Meteorol.* A cloud picture made by a nephograph.

neph·o·graph (nef′ə·graf, ·gräf) *n. Meteorol.* An electrically operated camera for photographing clouds, with special reference to their position in the sky.

ne·phol·o·gy (ni·fol′ə·jē) *n.* The branch of meteorology that treats of clouds. —**neph·o·log·i·cal** (nef′ə·loj′i·kəl) *adj.*

neph·o·scope (nef′ə·skōp) *n. Meteorol.* An instrument for indicating the direction and velocity of winds by observations of cloud drift.

ne·phral·gi·a (ni·fral′jē·ə, ·jə) *n. Pathol.* Pain in the kidney or kidneys. [< NEPHR(O)- + -ALGIA]

ne·phrec·to·my (ne·frek′tə·mē) *n. Surg.* The excision of a kidney. [< NEPHR(O)- + -ECTOMY]

neph·ric (nef′rik) *adj.* Of, pertaining to, or situated near the kidneys; renal. [< Gk. *nephros* kidney]

ne·phrid·i·um (ni·frid′ē·əm) *n. pl.* **·phrid·i·a** (-frid′ē·ə) *Biol.* **1** One of the series of primitive excretory organs that afterward develop into uriniferous tubules, as in annelid worms, mollusks, and other invertebrates. **2** The embryonic tube which develops into the kidney in vertebrates. [< NL < Gk. *nephridios* pertaining to the kidneys] —**ne·phrid′i·al** *adj.*

neph·rism (nef′riz·əm) *n. Pathol.* General ill health due to chronic kidney disease.

neph·rite (nef′rīt) *n.* A very hard, compact, white to dark-green mineral: formerly worn as a remedy for diseases of the kidney. Compare JADE¹. [< G *nephrit* < Gk. *nephros* a kidney]

ne·phrit·ic (ni·frit′ik) *adj.* **1** Pertaining to, affecting, or affording relief to the kidneys. **2** Affected with nephritis. **3** Of the nature of nephrite. Also **ne·phrit′i·cal.** —*n.* Any medicine applicable to disease of the kidney.

ne·phri·tis (ni·frī′tis) *n. Pathol.* **1** Inflammation of the kidneys. **2** Bright's disease.

nephro- *combining form* A kidney; pertaining to the kidneys: *nephropathy.* Also, before vowels, **nephr-.** [< Gk. *nephros* kidney]

ne·phrog·e·nous (ni·froj′ə·nəs) *adj.* Originating in or caused by the kidney. Also **neph·ro·gen·ic** (nef′rə·jen′ik). [< NEPHRO- + -GENOUS]

neph·roid (nef′roid) *adj.* Shaped like a kidney.

ne·phrol·y·sis (ni·frol′ə·sis) *n.* **1** *Pathol.* The breakdown of kidney substance due to the action of poisons. **2** *Surg.* The separation of an inflamed kidney from morbid adhesions. [< NEPHRO- + -LYSIS] —**neph·ro·lyt·ic** (nef′rə·lit′ik) *adj.*

ne·phrop·a·thy (ni·frop′ə·thē) *n.* Any disease of the kidney. —**neph·ro·path·ic** (nef′rə·path′ik) *adj.*

ne·phro·sis (ni·frō′sis) *n. Pathol.* Disease of the kidney, especially any disease characterized by degenerative lesions of the renal tubules. —**ne·phrot′ic** (-frot′ik) *adj.*

ne·phrot·o·my (ni·frot′ə·mē) *n. Surg.* Incision of the kidney.

ne plus ul·tra (nē′ plus ul′trə) *Latin* The extreme or utmost point; hence, perfection; literally, nothing more beyond.

Ne·pos (nē′pos, nep′os), **Cornelius,** Roman historian and biographer of the first century B.C.

nep·o·tism (nep′ə·tiz′əm) *n.* Favoritism, especially governmental patronage, extended toward relatives. [< F *népotisme* < Ital. *nepotismo* < L *nepos* a grandson, nephew] —**ne·pot·ic** (ni·pot′ik) *adj.* —**nep′o·tist** *n.*

Nep·tune (nep′tōōn, -tyōōn) **1** In Roman mythology, son of Saturn and Ops, god of the sea: identified with the Greek *Poseidon.* **2** By personification, the ocean. **3** *Astron.* The eighth planet from the sun, discovered in 1846 by Galle of Berlin. Its mean distance from the sun is 2,793,000,000 miles; period of revolution, about 165 years; diameter, about 27,700 miles. It has two satellites. See PLANET.

Nep·tu·ni·an (nep·tōō′nē·ən, -tyōō′-) *adj.* **1** Of or pertaining to Neptune or his domain, the sea. **2** *Geol.* **a** Formed in or by the agency of water: said of rocks. **b** Of or pertaining to the theory of the aqueous origin of certain rocks: opposed to the *Plutonic* theory. —**Nep′tun·ist** *adj. & n.*

nep·tu·ni·um (nep·tōō′nē·əm, -tyōō′-) *n.* A radioactive element (symbol Np, atomic number 93) existing in minute amount in uranium ores and produced in gram quantities in nuclear reactors. See PERIODIC TABLE.

neptunium series *Physics* A sequence of radioactive elements beginning with plutonium of mass 241 and continuing through successive disintegrations to the stable isotope bismuth 209: named from its longest-lived member, neptunium 237, with a half-life of 2.2 × 10⁶ years.

Ner·bud·da (nər·bud′ə) A former spelling of NARBADA.

Ne·re·id (nir′ē·id) *pl.* **Ne·re·i·des** (ni·rē′ə·dēz) or **Ne·re·ids** In Greek mythology, one of the fifty daughters of Nereus and Doris, sea nymphs who attend Poseidon.

ne·re·is (nir′ē·is) *n.* Any of a genus (*Nereis*) of burrowing annelid worms having a long, flattened body and a distinct head: common near the seashore: also called *clamworm.* [< NL < Gk., a Nereid]

Ne·ret·va (ne′ret·vä) A river in the Dinaric Alps, Herzegovina, and Dalmatia, flowing 135 miles NW to the Adriatic: Italian *Narenta.*

Ne·reus (nir′ōōs, -ē·əs) In Greek mythology, a sea god, father of the Nereides.

Ne·ri (nā′rē), **Saint Philip,** 1515–95, Italian priest; founded the Congregation of the Oratory; canonized, 1622.

ne·rit·ic (ni·rit′ik) *adj.* Of or pertaining to the coastline or to shallow water. [< L *nerita* mussel < Gk. *nēritēs*]

Nernst (nernst), **Walther Hermann,** 1864–1941, German physicist and chemist.

Ne·ro (nir′ō), 37–68, Nero Claudius Caesar Drusus Germanicus, Roman emperor 54–68: original name *Lucius Domitius Ahenobarbus.* —**Ne·ro′ni·an, Ne·ron·ic** (ni·ron′ik) *adj.*

ner·o·li (ner′ə·lē) *n.* The essential oil distilled from orange blossoms: an isomer of geraniol used in perfumery. [after Princess *Neroli,* an Italian noblewoman said to have discovered it]

Ner·va (nûr′və), **Marcus Cocceius,** 32?–98, Roman emperor 96–98.

ner·vate (nûr′vāt) *adj.* Provided with nerves or veins; having nerves.

ner·va·tion (nûr·vā′shən) *n.* The arrangement or disposition of nerves, as in plants and insects. Also **ner·va·ture** (nûr′və·chŏŏr).

nerve (nûrv) *n.* **1** A cordlike structure, composed of delicate filaments, by which impulses are transmitted to or from different parts of the body. ◆ Collateral adjective: *neural.* **2** A tendon: used only in the phrase, *to strain every nerve.* **3** Anything likened to a nerve, as a rib or vein of a leaf or of an insect's wing. **4** Active strength or vigor; coolness; intrepidity. **5** *pl.* Nervous excitability; a nervous attack. —*v.t.* **nerved, nerv·ing** To give strength, vigor, or courage to. [< L *nervus* sinew] —**nerv′al** *adj.*

nerve-block (nûrv′blok′) *n.* A method of surgical anesthesia in which sensation is cut off from definite nerves.

nerve canal *Dent.* The narrow cavity in a tooth for passage of the nerve to the pulp.

nerve cell *Physiol.* **1** The cell body of a neuron. **2** An individual cell of the nervous system.

nerve center *Anat.* An aggregation of nerve cells controlling a particular sense or function, as hearing, respiration, etc.

nerve fiber One of the essential threadlike units of which a nerve is composed.

nerve impulse *Physiol.* A wave of chemical and electrical change propagated along a nerve fiber and serving as a stimulus to body movements and activities.

nerve·less (nûrv′lis) *adj.* **1** Destitute of nerve or force; strengthless; unnerved. **2** Having no nerves. —**nerve′less·ly** *adv.* —**nerve′less·ness** *n.*

nerve net *Zool.* The primitive, reticulated nervous system of coelenterates, as in the hydra: its reactions to stimuli affect the entire organism.

nerve-rack·ing (nûrv′rak′ing) *adj.* Extremely irritating or exasperating to one's nerves. Also **nerve′wrack·ing.**

ner·vi·duct (nûr′və·dukt) *n. Anat.* A passage in a bone for a nerve. [< L *nervus* a nerve + *ductus,* pp. of *ducere* lead]

ner·vine (nûr′vēn, -vīn) *adj.* **1** Pertaining to the nerves. **2** Calming or quieting to the nerves. —*n.* Any medicine acting on the nerves.

nerv·ing (nûr′ving) *n.* A veterinary operation for the excision of a part of a nerve trunk when in a state of chronic inflammation.

ner·vos·i·ty (nûr·vos′ə·tē) *n.* The state of being nervous; the tendency or disposition to exhibit nervous tension.

ner·vous (nûr′vəs) *adj.* **1** Affected or caused by the condition or action of the nerves: *nervous* prostration. **2** Easily disturbed or agitated, owing to weak nerves; excitable; timid. **3** Abounding in nerve or nerve force; vigorous; sinewy; nervy; also, highly strung. **4** Terse; crisp, as literary style. **5** Of or

pertaining to the nerves or nervous system. [<L *nervosus* sinewy] — **ner′vous·ly** *adv.* — **ner′vous·ness** *n.*

nervous prostration Neurasthenia.

nervous system *Biol.* The organized aggregate of all the nerve cells and nerve tissues of the higher animals, centralized in the spinal cord and brain of vertebrates. It has the functions of coordinating, controlling, and regulating responses to stimuli, directing behavior, and, in man, conditioning the phenomena of consciousness.

ner·vu·ra·tion (nûr′vyə·rā′shən) *n.* The arrangement or disposition of nervures.

ner·vure (nûr′vyŏor) *n. Biol.* A principal vein, as on a leaf or an insect's wing. Also **ner′vule** (-vyŏol). [<F <L *nervus* sinew]

nerv·y (nûr′vē) *adj.* **nerv·i·er**, **nerv·i·est** **1** Exhibiting force or strength; sinewy. **2** Full of nerve or courage; brave. **3** *Slang* Displaying brazen assurance; cool; impudent. **4** *Brit.* Nervous; jumpy; excitable.

nes·cience (nesh′əns, -ē·əns) *n.* The state of not knowing; ignorance, especially that due either to the nature of the human mind or of external things. [<LL *nescientia* ignorance <*ne*- not + *scire* know] — **nes′cient** *adj. & n.* — **nes′cient·ist** *n.*

ness (nes) *n.* A promontory or cape: frequently used as a termination in the proper name of a headland: *Dungeness*; *Sheerness*. [OE *næs*]

-ness suffix of nouns **1** State or quality of being: *darkness*. **2** An example of this state or quality: to do someone a *kindness*. [OE *-nis(s)*, *-nes(s)*]

Nes·sel·rode (nes′əl·rōd, *Russian* nyi′sil·rô′de), **Count Karl Robert**, 1780–1862, Russian diplomat.

Nes·sel·rode pudding (nes′əl·rōd) A custard made with preserved fruits and nuts, and flavored with rum: used as a pie filling. [after Count K. R. *Nesselrode*]

Nes·sler's reagent (nes′lərz) *Chem.* An aqueous solution of mercuric iodide, potassium iodide, and caustic potash: used in testing for ammonia. Also **Nessler's solution.** [after Julius *Nessler*, 1827–1905, German chemist]

Nes·sus (nes′əs) In Greek legend, a centaur who tried to abduct Deianira and was slain by her husband Hercules. The shirt of Nessus, steeped in his blood by Deianira, who believed it to be a charm to preserve her husband's love, caused the death of Hercules when he put it on.

nest (nest) *n.* **1** The habitation prepared by a bird for the hatching of its eggs and the rearing of its young. **2** The bed or home of

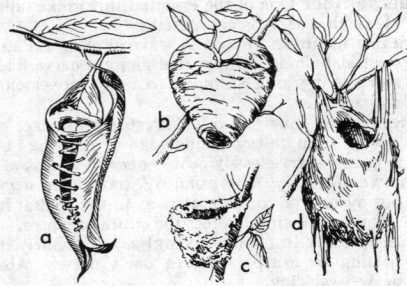

TYPES OF NESTS

　　a. Tailorbird. 　　*c.* Hummingbird.
　　b. Hornet. 　　*d.* Oriole.

certain fish, insects, turtles, mice, etc. **3** Any cozy place or abode; a retreat. **4** A haunt of anything bad, vulgar, or unpleasant; a den; also, those occupying it: a *nest* of brigands. **5** A series or set of similar things fitting into each other: a *nest* of bowls. **6** A connected set of small gearwheels, springs, or the like. **7** An isolated deposit of any ore or mineral in a rock. **8** A center of enemy resistance in battle: a machine-gun *nest*. — *v.t.* **1** To place in or as in a nest. **2** To pack or place one inside another. — *v.i.* **3** To build or occupy a nest. **4** To hunt for nests. [OE]

n'est–ce pas (nes pä′) *French* Isn't that so?

nest egg 1 A natural or artificial egg kept in a nest to attract a fowl. **2** Something laid by, as a sum of money, as a nucleus for future accumulation or for emergencies.

nest·er (nes′tər) *n. U.S. Dial.* A farmer seeking to settle on land used by cattlemen: a term of opprobrium.

nes·tle (nes′əl) *v.* **·tled**, **·tling** *v.i.* **1** To lie closely or snugly; cuddle; snuggle. **2** To settle down in comfort and pleasure. **3** To lie as if sheltered; be half-hidden. **4** *Rare* To nest. — *v.t.* **5** To place or press lovingly or fondly. **6** To place in or as in a nest. [OE *nestlian*] — **nes′tler** *n.*

nest·ling (nest′ling, nes′-) *n.* A bird too young to leave the nest; hence, a young child. — *adj.* Recently hatched.

Nes·tor (nes′tər) **1** In Greek legend, a king of Pylos and one of the Argonauts, the oldest and wisest Greek chief in the Trojan War. **2** Any wise old man.

Nes·to·ri·an·ism (nes·tôr′ē·ən·iz′əm, -tō′rē-) *n. Theol.* The doctrine that Christ had two distinct natures, the divine and human, subsisting independently. — **Nes·to′ri·an** *n. & adj.*

Nes·to·ri·us (nes·tôr′ē·əs, -tō′rē-) Fifth century Syrian patriarch of Constantinople, condemned and banished as a heretic.

net[1] (net) *n.* **1** An open fabric, woven or tied with meshes, for the capture of fishes, birds, etc. ◆ Collateral adjective: *reticular.* **2** An openwork fabric, as lace. **3** Something constructed with meshes, as a tennis net. **4** In tennis and similar games, a returned ball which does not go over the net. — *v.t.* **net·ted, net·ting 1** To catch in or as in a net; ensnare. **2** To make into a net. **3** To cover or enclose with a net. **4** In tennis, etc., to hit (the ball) into the net. — *adj.* **1** Manufactured or formed of netting, or resembling netting. **2** Captured or snared in a net. [OE]

net[2] (net) *adj.* **1** Free from everything extraneous; obtained after deducting all expenses. **2** Not subject to any discount or deduction. — *n.* A net profit, amount, weight, etc. — *v.t.* **net·ted, net·ting** To earn or yield as clear profit. [<F. See NEAT.]

net·ground (net′ground′) *n.* A foundation of net or meshes.

neth·er (neth′ər) *adj.* Situated at the lowest part; especially, pertaining to the parts beneath the heavens or the earth. [OE *neothera* under]

Neth·er·lands (neth′ər·ləndz) A country of NW Europe, first part of the Kingdom of the Netherlands; 12,425 square miles of land, 15,780 square miles with interior waters; capital, Amsterdam; seat of government, The Hague. Also, popularly, *Holland.* Dutch *Nederland.* — **Neth′er·land′er** *n.* — **Neth′er·land′ish** *adj.*

Netherlands, Kingdom of the A united kingdom comprising three equal and autonomous parts, the Netherlands, the Netherlands Antilles and Surinam, and the non-autonomous overseas territory of Netherlands New Guinea; 231,872 square miles; capital, Amsterdam.

Netherlands Antilles Part of the Kingdom of the Netherlands, comprising three islands north of Venezuela: *Aruba, Bonaire,* and *Curaçao,* each island largely autonomous; and a fourth largely autonomous unit comprising three islands in the Leeward Islands group: *Saba, Sint Eustatius,* and *Sint Maarten;* total, 336 square miles; capital, Willemstad, on Curaçao: also *Dutch West Indies, Netherlands West Indies.*

Netherlands East Indies Formerly, the island colonial possessions of the Netherlands in the Malay Archipelago: also *Dutch East Indies.* Also **Netherlands Indies.**

Netherlands Guiana See SURINAM.

Netherlands New Guinea A Netherlands overseas territory, comprising the western half of the island of New Guinea and several adjacent islands; now incorporated into Indonesia as West Irian: also *Dutch New Guinea.*

Netherlands Timor See TIMOR.

Netherlands West Indies See NETHERLANDS ANTILLES.

neth·er·most (neth′ər·mōst′) *adj.* Lowest.

neth·er·ward (neth′ər·wərd) *adv.* In a descending course; downward.

nether world The world of the shades or dead; specifically, the world of punishment after death; hell, conceived as being beneath the earth.

Né·thou (nā·tōo′), **Pic de** The French name for ANETO, PICO DE.

net knot *Biol.* A relatively large and thickened mass of chromatin in the nucleus of a cell.

ne·tsu·ke (nā·tsŏo·kā) *n. Japanese* A small, carved or wrought toggle or button attached to a pipe case, etc.

Net·tie (net′ē) Diminutive of ANTOINETTE. Also **Net′ty.**

net·ting (net′ing) *n.* **1** A fabric of openwork; a net; network. **2** The act or operation of making net. **3** The act, practice, or right of using nets, as in fishing.

net·tle[1] (net′l) *n.* **1** An herb of the genus *Urtica,* with opposite leaves, inconspicuous, greenish, imperfect flowers, and minute stinging hairs. The stinging is due to the irritating watery juice discharged by the hairs when broken. **2** Any of the various plants of some other genus of the nettle family. **3** Any of various plants of the same or some other family, having some real or fancied resemblance to the nettle genus. **4** A condition of irritation. — *v.t.* **·tled, ·tling 1** To sting as the nettle does. **2** To annoy or irritate; provoke. See synonyms under PIQUE[1]. [OE *netle*] — **net′tler** *n.*

net·tle[2] (net′l) *n. Naut.* A small rope made by tightly twisting two or three yarns. Also **net′·tle-stuff** (-stuf′). [Var. of *knettle* <*knit*]

nettle cell A nematocyst.

nettle rash Urticaria. Also **nettle fever.**

net ton A short ton.

net·work (net′wûrk′) *n.* **1** A fabric of openwork; netting. **2** A system of interlacing lines, tracks, or channels. **3** Any complex arrangement of interconnected electrical circuits. **4** *Telecom.* A chain of broadcasting stations.

Neu·châ·tel (nœ′shə·tel′, *Fr.* nœ·shà·tel′) **1** A canton in western Switzerland in the Jura; 309 square miles. **2** Its capital, a town on the north shore of the **Lake of Neuchâtel** (24 miles long; 4 to 5 miles wide). *German* **Neu·en·burg** (noi′ən·bŏork).

Neuf·châ·tel (nœ′shə·tel′, *Fr.* nœ·shà·tel′) *n.* A soft, white cheese produced in Neufchâtel, a town in northern France.

Neuil·ly–sur–Seine (nœ·yē′sür·sen′) A suburb of NW Paris, France.

neuk (nyōok) *n. Scot.* Nook; corner.

neume (nōom, nyōom) *n. Music* **1** One of various symbols in a system of notation first devised to aid rote singers of the Gregorian chants, indicating direction of the melody and later including the musical pitch and accents: also spelled **neum. 2** *pl.* This system. [<LL *neuma* song <Gk. *pneuma* breath, sigh]

Neu·Meck·len·burg (noi′mek′lən·bŏork) A former name for NEW IRELAND.

Neu·pest (noi′pest) The German name for UJPEST.

Neu–Pom·mern (noi′pom′ərn) Former name of NEW BRITAIN.

Ne·u·quén (nā′ŏo·kān′) **1** A national territory of west central Argentina; 36,429 square miles; capital, Neuquén. **2** A river in this territory, flowing about 320 miles SE to the Río Negro.

neur– Var. of NEURO-.

neu·ral (nŏor′əl, nyŏor′-) *adj.* **1** Of or pertaining to the nerves or nervous system: the *neural* axis. **2** Of, pertaining to, or situated on the side that contains the axis of the central nervous system; in vertebrates, the dorsal side. [<Gk. *neuron* nerve]

neu·ral·gi·a (nŏo·ral′jē·ə, -jə, nyŏo-) *n. Pathol.* An acute, paroxysmal pain along the course and over the local distribution of a nerve. [<NEUR- + -ALGIA] — **neu·ral′gic** *adj.*

neu·ras·the·ni·a (nŏor′əs·thē′nē·ə, -thēn′yə, nyŏor′-) *n.* **1** *Pathol.* Derangement of the nervous system with depression of vital force; nervous prostration. **2** *Psychoanal.* A neurosis characterized by physical disorder, as headache, constipation, etc., originated by inadequate expression of the libido. [<NL <Gk. *neuron* a nerve + *asthenia* weakness] — **neu·ras·then′ic** (-then′ik) *adj. & n.*

Neu·rath (noi′rät), **Baron Konstantin von,** 1873–1956, German diplomat.

neu·ra·tion (nŏo·rā′shən, nyŏo-) *n.* Nervation.

neu·rax·is (nŏo·rak′sis, nyŏo-) *n. Anat.* The brain and spinal cord; the axon. [<NEUR- + AXIS] — **neu·rax′i·al** *adj.*

neu·rax·on (nŏo·rak′sən, nyŏo-) *n. Anat.* The process of a nerve cell that forms the axial cylinder of a nerve; axon. [<NEUR- + AXON]

neu·rec·to·my (nŏo·rek′tə·mē, nyŏo-) *n. Surg.* The excision of a nerve. [<NEUR- + -ECTOMY]

neu·ren·ter·ic (nŏor′ən·ter′ik, nyŏor′-) *adj. Biol.* Of or pertaining to the neural and the

enteric tubes of the embryo: the *neurenteric* canal, the tube connecting the caudal end of the neural tube with the digestive tract of the embryo.

neu·ri·lem·ma (nŏŏr′ə·lem′ə, nyoor′-) *n. Anat.* The delicate sheath of a nerve fiber: also spelled *neurolemma*. Also **neu′ri·lem′a.** [< NL < Gk. *neuros* nerve + *eilēma* sheath]

neu·ri·tis (nŏŏ·rī′tis, nyoo-) *n. Pathol.* Inflammation of a nerve. —**neu·rit′ic** (-rit′ik) *adj.*

neuro- *combining form* Nerve; pertaining to a nerve: *neurocyte* : also, before vowels, *neur-.* Also **neuri-.** [< Gk. *neuron* sinew, nerve]

neu·ro·blast (nŏŏr′ə·blast, nyoor′-) *n. Biol.* 1 A cell with a large oval nucleus in the spinal cord of the early embryo. Prolongations of such cells form the nerve fibers. 2 A part of the nervous system of an insect resulting from histolysis in the larva. 3 An embryonic cell that develops into a nerve cell.

neu·ro·cele (nŏŏr′ə·sēl, nyoor′-) *n. Anat.* The system of central communicating cavities (ventricles and passages) found in the spinal cord and brain. Also **neu′ro·coele.**

neu·ro·chem·is·try (nŏŏr′ō·kem′ə·strē) *n.* That branch of chemistry that has to do with chemicals, esp. the neurotransmitters, that affect the nervous system.

neu·ro·cyte (nŏŏr′ə·sīt, nyoor′-) *n.* A nerve cell together with its processes.

neu·rog·li·a (nŏŏ·rog′lē·ə, nyoo-) *n. Anat.* The supporting tissue of the central nervous system, composed of finely branched ectodermic cells within thin interlacing processes. [< NL < Gk. *neuro-* nerve + *glia* glue]

neu·ro·hy·po·phy·sis (nŏŏr′ō·hī·pof′ə·sis, nyoor′-) *n. pl.* **·ses** (-sēz). The posterior lobe of the pituitary gland together with the stalk of gray matter that connects it with the brain.

neu·roid (nŏŏr′oid, nyoor′-) *adj.* Nervelike.

neu·ro·lem·ma (nŏŏr′ə·lem′ə, nyoor′-) *n.* 1 The retina. 2 Neurilemma.

neu·rol·o·gy (nŏŏ·rol′ə·jē, nyoo-) *n.* The science of the nervous system in health and disease. —**neu·ro·log·i·cal** (nŏŏr′ə·loj′i·kəl, nyoor′-) *adj.* —**neu·rol′o·gist** *n.*

neu·rol·y·sis (nŏŏ·rol′ə·sis, nyoo-) *n.* 1 The destruction of nerve tissue. 2 Liberation of a nerve from morbid adhesions. 3 Relief of nerve tension by stretching. 4 Nervous exhaustion through over stimulation. —**neu·ro·lyt·ic** (nŏŏr′ə·lit′ik, nyoor′-) *adj.*

neu·ro·ma (nŏŏ·rō′mə, nyoo-) *n. pl.* **·ma·ta** (-mə·tə) *Pathol.* A tumor developing from a nerve. [< NL < Gk. *neuros* nerve + *-ōma* a growth]

neu·ron (noor′on, nyoor′-) *n.* 1 *Biol.* A nerve cell with all its processes and extensions. 2 *Entomol.* A vein or costa of an insect's wing. Also **neu′rone** (-ōn). [< NL < Gk. *neuros* nerve] —**neu·ron·ic** (nŏŏ·ron′ik, nyŏŏ-) *adj.*

neu·ro·path (nŏŏr′ə·path, nyoor′-) *n. Psychiatry* One suffering from or subject to nervous disorders; a neurotic. —**neu·ro·path′ic, neu·ro·path′i·cal** *adj.* —**neu·ro·path′i·cal·ly** *adv.*

neu·ro·pa·thol·o·gy (nŏŏr′ō·pə·thol′ə·jē, nyoor′-) *n.* The pathology of the nervous system. —**neu′ro·pa·thol′o·gist** *n.*

neu·ro·phys·i·ol·o·gy (nŏŏr′ō·fiz′ē·ol′ə·jē, nyoor′-) *n.* The physiology of the nervous system. —**neu′ro·phys′i·o·log′i·cal** (-fiz′ē·ə·loj′i·kəl) *adj.* —**neu′ro·phys′i·ol′o·gist** *n.*

neu·ro·psy·chi·a·try (nŏŏr′ō·sī·kī′ə·trē, nyoor′-) *n.* The study and treatment of diseases involving both neurological and mental factors; the pathology of nervous disorders combined with psychiatry. —**neu′ro·psy·chi·at′ric** (-sī′kē·at′rik) *adj.* —**neu′ro·psy·chi′a·trist** (-sī·kī′ə·trist) *n.*

neu·ro·psy·chol·o·gy (nŏŏr′ō·sī·kol′ə·jē, nyoor′-) *n.* The study of the relationships existing between the mind and the nervous system. —**neu′ro·psy′cho·log′i·cal** (-sī′kə·loj′i·kəl) *adj.*

neu·ro·psy·cho·sis (nŏŏr′ō·sī·kō′sis, nyoor′-) *n. Psychiatry* Mental disorder arising from a nervous disorder.

neu·rop·ter (nŏŏ·rop′tər, nyoo-) *n.* Any of an order (*Neuroptera*) of insects having four similar, net-veined wings, chewing mouth parts, and active carnivorous larvae, as ant-lions, etc. [< NL < Gk. *neuros* sinew, nerve + *pteron* wing] —**neu·rop′ter·al** *adj.* —**neu·rop′·ter·an** *adj. & n.*

neu·rop·ter·oid (nŏŏ·rop′tə·roid, nyoo-) *adj.* Like the *Neuroptera.* —*n.* A neuropteroid insect.

neu·rop·ter·ous (nŏŏ·rop′tər·əs, nyoo-) *adj.* 1 Of or pertaining to the *Neuroptera.* 2 Having net-veined wings.

neu·ro·sis (nŏŏ·rō′sis, nyoo-) *n. pl.* **·ses** (-sēz) *Psychiatry* A disorder of the psychic or mental functions without lesion of nerves and of less severity than a psychosis. —**neu·ro′sal** *adj.*

neu·rot·ic (nŏŏ·rot′ik, nyoo-) *adj.* 1 Pertaining to or suffering from neurosis. 2 *Colloq.* Having a morbid nature or tendency. 3 Pertaining to a nerve or the nervous system. —*n.* 1 A person afflicted with neurosis. 2 Disease of the nerves.

neu·rot·o·my (nŏŏ·rot′ə·mē, nyoo-) *n.* 1 *Surg.* The division or severing of a nerve, to relieve pain. 2 The dissection of the nervous system, as for study. [< NEURO- + -TOMY] —**neu·ro·tom·ic** (nŏŏr′ə·tom′ik, nyoor′-) *adj.* —**neu·rot′o·mist** *n.*

neu·ro·trans·mit·ter (nŏŏr′ō·tranz·mit′ər, nyoor′-) *n.* A chemical agent (such as acetylcholine, norepinephrine) which transmits a nerve impulse across a synapse.

Neu·satz (noi′zäts) The German name for NOVI SAD.

Neuse River (nŏŏs, nyōōs) A river in eastern North Carolina, flowing 300 miles SE to Pamlico Sound.

Neus·tri·a (nōōs′trē·ə, nyōōs′-) The western part of the Frankish Empire of the sixth century, comprising the region of modern France between the Meuse and the Loire.

neu·ter (nŏŏ′tər, nyōō′-) *adj.* 1 *Gram.* a Neither masculine nor feminine in gender. Compare GENDER. b *Rare* Intransitive; neither active nor passive; middle: said of verbs in classical languages. 2 *Biol.* Sexless; having functionless or imperfectly developed sex organs, as certain plants and animals. 3 *Obs.* Neutral. —*n.* 1 An animal of no apparent sex, as a worker bee. 2 A eunuch. 3 A castrated animal. 4 *Gram.* a The neuter gender. b A word in this gender. 5 A neutral in warfare or other conflict. [< MF *neutre* < L *neuter* < *ne-* not + *uter* either]

neu·tral (nŏŏ′trəl, nyōō′-) *adj.* 1 Refraining from interference in a contest; not taking the part of either or any belligerent: a *neutral* power. 2 Belonging to neither of two contestants; belonging to a neutral power: *neutral* forces. 3 Having no decided character; indefinite; middling. 4 Having no decided color; predominantly brownish or grayish. 5 *Biol.* Sexless; neuter. 6 *Bot.* Lacking pistils or stamens. 7 *Chem.* Lacking decided acid or alkaline qualities. 8 *Electr.* Neither positive nor negative. 9 *Phonet.* Pronounced with the tongue in a relaxed, mid-central position, as the *a* in *about.* —*n.* One who or that which is neutral. [< L *neutralis* < *neuter* neuter] —**neu′tral·ly** *adv.*

neu·tral·ism (nŏŏ′trəl·iz′əm, nyōō′-) *n.* A political doctrine holding that abstention from alliance with ideologic or economic power blocs in international relations serves a country's best interests. —**neu′tral·ist** *n.*

neu·tral·i·ty (nŏŏ·tral′ə·tē, nyōō-) *n. pl.* **·ties** 1 The state of being a neutral nation during a war. 2 The state of being neither good nor bad; indifference. 3 *Chem.* The condition of being neither acid nor basic. 4 The character of being neutral: the *neutrality* of a ship.

neu·tral·i·za·tion (nŏŏ′trəl·ə·zā′shən, -ī·zā′-, nyōō′-) *n.* 1 Act of neutralizing or state of being neutralized. 2 *Ling.* The temporary suspension of a relevant feature in two phonemes, as /t/ and /d/ in *latter* and *ladder.*

neu·tral·ize (nŏŏ′trəl·īz, nyōō′-) *v.t.* **·ized, ·iz·ing** 1 To counteract or destroy by opposite force or influence; nullify; counterbalance. 2 To declare (a nation, area, etc.) to be neutral and not involved in hostilities. 3 *Chem.* To make neutral or inert. 4 *Electr.* To render electrically inert; void of electricity. 5 *Mil.* To render incapable of effective action. Also *Brit.* **neu′tral·ise.** —**neu′tral·iz′er** *n.*

neutral oil A light lubricating oil from petroleum, generally mixed with animal or vegetable oils.

neu·tri·no (nŏŏ·trē′nō, nyŏŏ-) *n. pl.* **·nos** *Physics* An atomic particle associated with the radioactive emission of beta rays, carrying no electric charge and having a mass comparable to that of the electron.

neu·tron (nŏŏ′tron, nyŏŏ′-) *n. Physics* An electrically neutral particle of the atom, having a mass approximately equal to that of the proton.

neutron bomb A thermonuclear bomb designed to release intense radiation in order to destroy life and spare property.

neutron star A hypothetical celestial body of small radius and great density representing a terminal stage in the evolution of a star of mass comparable to that of the sun.

neu·tro·pe·ni·a (nŏŏ′trə·pē′nē·ə, nyŏŏ′-) *n. Pathol.* A blood disorder marked by a sharp reduction in the number of leucocytes; agranulocytosis. [< NEUTRO(PHILE) + Gk. *penia* dearth]

neu·tro·phile (nŏŏ′trə·fīl, -fil, nyŏŏ′-) *adj.* Stainable with neutral dyes: said of bacteria and leucocytes. Also **neu′tro·phil′** (-fil), **neu′tro·phil′ic.**

Neuve–Cha·pelle (nœv·shä·pel′) A village in northern France, the center of severe fighting in World War I, 1914–15.

Ne·va (nē′və, *Russian* nyi·vä′) A river in NW U.S.S.R., flowing 46 miles from Lake Ladoga to its delta at Leningrad on the Gulf of Finland.

Ne·vad·a (nə·vad′ə, -vä′də) A State in the western United States; 110,540 square miles; capital, Carson City; entered the Union Oct. 31, 1864; nickname, *Sagebrush State* : abbr. NV —**Ne·vad′an** *adj. & n.*

né·vé (nā·vā′) *n.* The consolidated snow on the summit of a mountain, composed of roundish grains, resembling sand: a transition stage in the formation of glacier ice. [< dial. F (Swiss), glacier, ult. < L *nix, nivis* snow]

nev·er (nev′ər) *adv.* 1 Not at any time: also used in composition to form adjectives: *never*-ending. 2 Not at all; positively not: used emphatically: *Never* fear. [OE *næfre* < *ne* not + *æfre* ever]

nev·er·more (nev′ər·môr′, -mōr′) *adv.* Never again.

nev·er·nev·er (nev′ər·nev′ər) *n. Austral.* Wild, remote country; desert lands.

Ne·vers (nə·vâr′) A city on the Loire in central France.

never so To an extent or degree beyond the actual or conceivable; no matter how: *never so* great.

nev·er·the·less (nev′ər·thə·les′) *conj. & adv.* None the less; however; yet. See synonyms under BUT[1], NOTWITHSTANDING.

Nev·in (nev′in), **Ethelbert,** 1862–1901, U.S. composer.

Ne·vis (nē′vis, nev′is) See ST. CHRISTOPHER, NEVIS, AND ANGUILLA.

Nev·ski (nev′skē, nef′-), **Alexander** See ALEXANDER NEVSKI.

ne·vus (nē′vəs) *n. pl.* **·vi** (-vī) A birthmark, or congenital mole on man or animal: also spelled *naevus.* [< L *naevus* blemish] —**ne′void** (-void) *adj.*

new (nŏŏ, nyŏŏ) *adj.* 1 Recently come into existence or use; lately made; recently settled or recently opened to settlement: *new* country. 2 Lately discovered; also, recently become important or well known. 3 Beginning or recurring afresh; renewed: the *new* moon. 4 Changed in essence, constitution, force, etc.: usually for the better: I feel a *new* man. 5 Another; different from that heretofore known or used. 6 Recently come from any place or out of any condition. 7 Unaccustomed; unfamiliar: a horse *new* to the saddle. 8 Specifically, named for another: used in place names, to distinguish a place from its namesake: *New* Zealand, *New* Orleans. —*adv.* Newly; recently. [OE *nēowe*] —**new′ness** *n.*

New Amsterdam The capital of the Dutch colony of New Netherland; in 1664 renamed *New York.*

New·ark (nŏŏ′ork, nyŏŏ′-) A city in NE New Jersey on **Newark Bay,** an estuary at the confluence of the Hackensack and Passaic rivers.

New Bedford A city on Buzzards Bay, SE Massachusetts.

new blue Ultramarine.

New·bolt (nōō′bōlt, nyōō′-), **Sir Henry John,** 1862–1938, English poet and historian.

new·born (nōō′bôrn, nyōō′-) adj. Newly born; in the first few days or weeks of life. —n. A newborn infant or animal.

New Britain The largest island in the Bismarck Archipelago; 14,600 square miles; chief city, Rabaul: formerly Neu–Pommern.

New Brunswick A province of SE Canada on the Bay of Fundy; 27,985 square miles; capital, Fredericton: abbr. N.B.

New·burg (nōō′bûrg, nyōō′-) See À LA NEWBURG.

New Caledonia An island in the SW Pacific east of Australia; 8,548 square miles; with its dependencies, the Loyalty Islands, the Isle of Pines, and other smaller adjacent islands, it comprises a French overseas territory; total, 9,401 square miles; capital, Nouméa: French Nouvelle Calédonie.

New Castile A region of central Spain. Spanish Cas·til·la la Nue·va (käs·tē′lyä lä nwä′vä).

New·cas·tle·up·on·Tyne (nōō′kas·əl·ə·pon′· tīn′, nyōō′-) A port in SE Northumberland, England, and its county seat: also **Newcastle, Newcastle–on–Tyne.** —**to carry coals to Newcastle** To take goods to a place where they already abound; hence, to waste one's labor.

New Church See SWEDENBORGIANISM.

New·chwang (nōō′chwäng′) A town in SW Liotung province, Manchuria.

New·comb (nōō′kəm, nyōō′-), **Simon,** 1835–1909, U.S. astronomer.

new·com·er (nōō′kum′ər, nyōō′-) n. One who has recently arrived.

new deal 1 A dealing of cards with a new deck. **2** Any new system designed to do away with old ills and to promote reform.

New Deal The policies and principles of the administration under President Franklin D. Roosevelt, embracing various social, economic, and political measures through legislative and administrative change; also, the Roosevelt administration.

New Dealer A supporter of the measures advocated by the New Deal.

New Delhi The capital of India in Delhi State, and administrative center just SW of Delhi.

New Democratic Party The socialist party of Canada: until 1961 called Cooperative Commonwealth Federation.

New Economic Policy The policy adopted in 1921 as a temporary measure by the government of the Soviet Union, permitting to a limited extent private ownership in minor industries, restoring free trade in agricultural production of labor, and establishing a system of pay for services rendered in place of the uniform wage rate. Also Nep, NEP.

new·el (nōō′əl, nyōō′-) n. **1** A post from which the steps of a winding stair radiate. **2** A post at the end of a stair or hand rail. [< OF nouel stone of a fruit < LL nucale < L nut]

New England The NE section of the United States, including Maine, New Hampshire, Vermont, Massachusetts, Rhode Island, and Connecticut. —**New Englander**

NEWEL

New England aster A perennial aster (Aster novae–angliae) having purple flowers and growing wild throughout eastern North America.

new–fan·gled (nōō′fang′gəld, nyōō′-) adj. **1** Of new fashion: generally in depreciation: newfangled notions **2** Rare Fond of novelty. —**new′–fan′gled·ness** n.

new–fash·ioned (nōō′fash′ənd, nyōō′-) adj. Made in a new style; recently become fashionable.

New Forest A partly wooded region in SW Hampshire, England; about 145 square miles.

New·found·land (nōō′fənd·lənd, nyōō′-) n. A large dog of a breed originating in Newfoundland, characterized by a broad head, square muzzle, and thick, usually black coat.

New·found·land (nōō′fənd·land′, nyōō′-) The easternmost province of Canada, comprising the island of Newfoundland (42,734 square miles) and its dependency, Labrador, on the mainland; total, 152,734 square miles; capital, St. John's —**New·found′land·er** (-found′-) n.

New France The region discovered and settled by the French in North America, including Canada, the Great Lakes region, and Louisiana, from 1534 to 1763.

New·fy (nōō′fē, nyōō′-) n. pl. ·fies Canadian Slang A Newfoundlander.

New·gate (nōō′git, -gāt, nyōō′-) A prison in London, destroyed 1902.

New Georgia An island group in the British Solomon Islands; total, 2,000 square miles; also, the chief island of this group.

New Granada A Spanish viceroyalty in NW South America, later divided into the republics of Ecuador, Colombia, Panama, and Venezuela.

New Guin·ea (gin′ē) The world's second largest island, north of Australia in the Malay Archipelago; 304,200 square miles: also Papua: Indonesian I·ri·an (ē′rē·än) divided into West Irian, and Territory of Papua and New Guinea.

New Guinea, Territory of A United Nations Trust Territory, comprising NE New Guinea, the Bismarck Archipelago, and Bougainville and Buka in the Solomon Islands; about 93,000 square miles; administrative center, Port Moresby: became part of the Territory of Papua and New Guinea, 1949.

New Hampshire A State of the NE United States; 9,304 square miles; capital, Concord; entered the Union June 21, 1788, one of the thirteen original States; nickname, Granite State: abbr. NH

New Hanover A former name for LAVONGAI.

New Harmony A socialistic community in SW Indiana established in 1825 by Robert Owen.

New Haven A city on Long Island Sound in Connecticut; site of Yale University.

New Hebrides An island group in the SW Pacific north of New Caledonia and west of Fiji, comprising an Anglo–French condominium; 5,700 square miles; capital, Vila.

New High German See HIGH GERMAN under GERMAN.

New Ireland An island of the Bismarck Archipelago; 3,340 square miles; formerly Neu–Mecklenburg.

new·ish (nōō′ish, nyōō′-) adj. Rather new.

New Jersey A State of the eastern United States on the Atlantic; 7,836 square miles; capital, Trenton; entered the Union Dec. 18, 1787, one of the thirteen original States; nickname, Garden State: abbr. NJ —**New Jerseyite**

New Jerusalem The city of God; heaven. Rev. xxi 2.

New Jerusalem Church See SWEDENBORGIANISM.

New Latin See under LATIN.

New London A port in SE Connecticut on Long Island Sound; site of a naval base.

new·ly (nōō′lē, nyōō′-) adv. **1** In a new or recent manner; lately. **2** In a different way; so as to be or appear new; afresh.

new·ly–wed (nōō′lē·wed′, nyōō′-) n. A person recently married.

New·man (nōō′mən, nyōō′-), **Cardinal John Henry,** 1801–90, English author and theologian.

new·mar·ket (nōō′mär·kit, nyōō′-) n. **1** A long, close–fitting coat for outdoor wear: also **Newmarket coat. 2** A game of cards resembling the game of stops.

New·mar·ket (nōō′mär·kit, nyōō′-) A town in West Sussex, England; a horse–racing center since the 17th century.

New Mexico A State of the SW United States on the Mexican border; 121,666 square miles; capital, Santa Fe; entered the Union Jan. 6, 1912; nickname, Sunshine State: abbr. NM —**New Mexican**

new moon That phase of the moon when it is directly between the earth and the sun, its disk then being invisible; also, the first visible crescent of the disk.

new–mown (nōō′mōn′, nyōō′-) adj. Recently cut or mown.

New Netherland The Dutch colony in North America, 1613–1664, near the mouth of the Hudson River; capital, New Amsterdam.

New Norwegian Landsmål.

New Order The system of regimentation imposed on Germany after 1933, and later on the countries conquered by the Axis powers.

New Or·le·ans (ôr′lē·ənz, ôr·lēnz′, ôr′lənz) A port of SE Louisiana on the Mississippi: a native of the city is sometimes known as an Orleanian. —**New Or·lean·i·an** (ôr·lē′nē·ən)

new penny A penny (def. 3).

New·port (nōō′pôrt, -pōrt, nyōō′-) **1** A city of SE Rhode Island on Narragansett Bay; site of a United States naval base. **2** A municipal borough of Hampshire, England, on the Isle of Wight. **3** A county borough and port of Monmouthshire, England, on the Severn estuary.

Newport News A city on the James River in SE Virginia.

New Providence Island The chief island of the Bahamas; 58 square miles.

New Quebec See UNGAVA.

new–rich (nōō′rich′, nyōō′-) adj. Newly rich; hence, showy; pretentious.

new rich Those who have recently acquired riches. Also, French, nouveaux riches.

news (nōōz, nyōōz) n. pl. (construed as singular) **1** Fresh information concerning something that has recently taken place. **2** A newspaper. **3** Anything new or strange. See synonyms under TIDINGS. [Trans. of OF noveles < LL nova new (things)]

news agency 1 A business concern that deals in and distributes newspapers and other periodicals. **2** An agency that sells news items to newspapers, etc.: also called news bureau.

New Sar·um (sâr′əm) See SALISBURY.

news·boy (nōōz′boi, nyōōz′-) n. A boy who sells or delivers newspapers.

news·cast (nōōz′kast′, -käst′, nyōōz′-) n. A radio news program. —v.t. & v.i. To broadcast (news). —news′cast′er n.

news–gath·er·er (nōōz′gath′ər·ər, nyōōz′-) n. One who collects news.

news–hawk (nōōz′hôk′, nyōōz′-) n. U.S. Colloq. A journalist with a sharp eye for news.

New Siberian Islands An archipelago off the Arctic coast of the Yakut S.S.R.; total, 11,000 square miles.

news·mag·a·zine (nōōz′mag·ə·zēn, nyōōz′-) n. A periodical, especially a weekly, that summarizes the news and reports current events of general interest.

news·man (nōōz′man′, -mən, nyōōz′-) n. pl. ·men (-men′, -mən) A man who delivers or sells newspapers; also, a newspaper reporter.

New South Wales A state of SE Commonwealth of Australia; 309,433 square miles; capital, Sydney.

New Spain The former Spanish possessions, comprising a viceroyalty, in the SW United States, Central America north of Panama, the West Indies, and the Philippines.

news·pa·per (nōōz′pā′pər, nyōōz′-) n. A publication issued for general circulation at frequent intervals; a public print that circulates news, etc. —**news′pa′per·man′** (-man′, -mən) n.

news·print (nōōz′print′, nyōōz′-) n. The thin, unsized paper on which the ordinary daily or weekly newspaper is printed.

news·reel (nōōz′rēl′, nyōōz′-) n. A motion picture, usually of short duration, showing events of current interest.

news–stand (nōōz′stand′, nyōōz′-) n. A stand or stall at which newspapers and periodicals are offered for sale.

New Style See GREGORIAN CALENDAR under CALENDAR.

New Sweden A Swedish colony in North America, 1638–55, on the Delaware River below Trenton.

news·worth·y (nōōz′wûr′thē, nyōōz′-) adj. Important enough to be written up in a newspaper; considered to be of current interest.

news·y (nōōz′zē, nyōōz′-) adj. Colloq. Full of news.

newt (nōōt, nyōōt) n. One of various small, semiaquatic, salamander–like amphibians, chiefly of the genus Triturus. [Earlier ewt, evet, OE efete; in ME an ewt was taken as a newt]

NEWT
(From 3 1/2 to 20 inches in length, varying with the species)

New Territories A leased section of Hong Kong colony on the Chinese mainland north of Kowloon peninsula; 359 square miles.

New Testament 1 The promises of God to man as revealed in the life and teachings of

Christ. **2** That portion of the Bible containing the life and teachings of Christ, including the Gospels, the Epistles, the Acts of the Apostles, and the Revelation of St. John the Divine.

New Thought A modern religious philosophy stressing "God in man" and the power of right thinking over disease and failure: also called *Higher Thought, Mental Science, Practical Christianity.*

new·ton (nōō′tən, nyōō′-) *n. Physics* A unit of force in the mks system, equal to 100,000 dynes, or that force which will impart to a mass of 1 kilogram an acceleration of 1 meter per second per second. [after Isaac *Newton*]

New·ton (nōō′tən, nyōō′-), **Sir Isaac,** 1642–1727, English philosopher, mathematician, and physicist; formulated the basic laws of dynamics, the law of gravitation, and the elements of differential calculus. —**New·to·ni·an** (nōō·tō′nē·ən, nyōō-) *adj.*

new town A planned, new community, often under government auspices or with government support, consisting of various types of housing, schools, parks, and sometimes local industries.

New World The western hemisphere.

new year The year just begun or just about to begin.

New Year The first day of the year; in the Gregorian calendar, January 1. Also **New Year's Day.** Compare CALENDAR.

New Year's Eve The evening of December 31.

New York 1 A State of the NE United States on the Atlantic; 49,576 square miles; capital, Albany; entered the Union July 26, 1788; one of the thirteen original States; nickname, *Empire State*: abbr. NY **2** A port at the mouth of the Hudson River in SE New York, divided into the five boroughs of the Bronx, Brooklyn, Manhattan, Queens, and Richmond, comprising the largest city of the United States; 365 square miles: also *Greater New York.*

NEW YORK HARBOR

New York Bay An inlet of the Atlantic Ocean at the mouth of the Hudson River, forming **New York Harbor** and divided by the Narrows into **Upper New York Bay** and **Lower New York Bay.**

New York·er (yôr′kər) An inhabitant of New York; specifically, a native or resident of New York City.

New York State Barge Canal A waterway system of central New York, connecting the Hudson River with Lake Erie and with Lake Champlain; total length, 525 miles.

New Zea·land (zē′lənd) A self-governing member of the Commonwealth of Nations, comprising a group of islands, principally North Island and South Island, in the South Pacific SE of Australia; 103,416 square miles, excluding island territories; capital, Wellington.

New Zea·land·er (zē′lən·dər) *n.* A resident of New Zealand; formerly, a Maori.

Nex·ö (nek′sœ), **Martin Andersen,** 1869–1954, Danish novelist born in Germany.

next (nekst) *adj.* **1** Being nearest to, in time, space, order, rank, etc.; immediately succeeding or preceding. **2** Almost: *next* to impossible. See synonyms under ADJACENT, IMMEDIATE. —*adv.* In the nearest time, place, or rank; especially, immediately succeeding: when I *next* meet her. —*prep.* Nearest to. [OE *nēahst,* superl. of *nēah* nigh]

next-door (neks′dôr′, -dōr′) *adj.* In the next house: a *next-door* neighbor.

next door 1 The nearest or adjacent house. **2** In the next house: the lady *next door.*

next friend *Law* A person who, as the nearest friend, appears to prosecute an action in behalf of someone under legal disability, as a minor child, etc.

next of kin 1 *Law* The kindred of a person who would share in his estate according to the statutes of distribution. **2** The person most closely related to one.

nex·us (nek′səs) *n. pl.* **·us·es** or **·us** A bond or tie between the several members of a group or series; link. [< L < *nectere* tie]

Ney (nā), **Michel,** 1769–1815, French marshal under Napoleon; executed.

Ney·sha·pur (nā′shä·pōōr′) See NISHAPUR.

Nez Per·cé (nez′ pûrs′, *Fr.* nā per·sā′) One of a tribe of North American Indians of Shahaptian stock, formerly dwelling in Idaho, Oregon, and Washington. [< F, pierced nose]

Nga·mi (ngä′mē), **Lake** A marsh region of NW Bechuanaland Protectorate, formerly a lake covering 20,000 square miles.

Ngan·dong man (ngän′dong) Solo man.

Ni *Chem.* Nickel (symbol Ni).

ni·a·cin (nī′ə·sin) *n.* Nicotinic acid.

Ni·ag·a·ra Falls (nī·ag′ər·ə, -rə) **1** A city on the Niagara River, western New York. **2** See under NIAGARA RIVER.

Niagara River A river between Ontario province, Canada, and New York State, flowing 34 miles from Lake Erie to Lake Ontario; in its course occurs **Niagara Falls,** a cataract divided by Goat Island into the American Falls, 167 feet high and 1,000 feet wide, and Horseshoe Falls on the Canadian side, 160 feet high and 2,500 feet wide.

Nia·mey (nyä·mā′) A port on the Niger, capital of the Republic of Niger.

Ni·as (nē′äs) An Indonesian island off the western coast of Sumatra; 1,569 square miles.

Ni·as·sus (nī·as′əs) Ancient name of NISH.

nib (nib) *n.* **1** A projecting, pointed part. **2** A beak of a bird; neb. **3** The point of a pen. **4** The point of anything. —*v.t.* **nibbed, nib·bing 1** To furnish with a nib. **2** To sharpen or mend the nib or point of. [Var. of NEB]

nib·ble (nib′əl) *v.* **·bled, ·bling** *v.t.* **1** To eat (food) with small, quick bites. **2** To bite gently or cautiously, as bait. —*v.i.* **3** To bite off or eat little bits. **4** To take gentle or cautious bites: usually with *at.* —*n.* The act of nibbling; a little bite. [Cf. LG *nibbelen*] —**nib′bler** *n.*

Ni·be·lung (nē′bə·lōōng) *n. pl.* **·lungs** or **·lung·en** (-lōōng′ən) **1** In Teutonic mythology, one of the children of the mist, a dwarf people who held a magic ring and hoard of gold, which were wrested from them by Siegfried. **2** In the *Nibelungenlied,* one of the Burgundian kings.

Ni·be·lung·en·lied (nē′bə·lōōng′ən·lēt′) The lay of the Nibelungs, a Middle High German epic poem written by an unknown author during the early 13th century, embodying legends of the Burgundian kings which were based on various compilations; the source of Wagner's operatic cycle, *The Ring of the Nibelung.*

nib·lick (nib′lik) *n.* A golf club with a slanted iron head for lifting the ball out of bunkers, long grass, etc. See illustration under GOLF CLUB. [Origin uncertain]

Ni·cae·a (nī·sē′ə) **1** An ancient town of Bithynia in Asia Minor on the site of modern Iznik. **2** An ancient name for NICE. —**Council of Nicaea** A council held at Nicaea, Asia Minor, A.D. 325, which condemned Arianism and promulgated the Nicene Creed. —**Ni·cae′an** *adj. & n.*

Nic·a·ra·gua (nik′ə·rä′gwə) A republic of Central America; 57,143 square miles; capital, Managua.

Nicaragua, Lake The largest lake of central America, in SW Nicaragua; 3,100 square miles.

Nic·a·ra·guan (nik′ə·rä′gwən) *adj.* Of or pertaining to Nicaragua. —*n.* A native of Nicaragua.

Ni·ca·ri·a (nyi·kä·rē′ə) A former name for ICARIA. Also **Ni′ka·ri′a.**

nic·co·lite (nik′ə·līt) *n.* A usually massive, brittle, metallic, pale copper-red nickel arsenide, NiAs, crystallizing in the hexagonal system: also called *copper nickel.* [< NL *niccolum* nickel]

nice (nīs) *adj.* **nic·er, nic·est 1** Characterized by discrimination and judgement; acute; discerning. **2** Refined and pure in tastes or habits; refined; hence, overparticular; dainty; modest; fastidious; scrupulous. **3** Requiring careful consideration, discrimination, or treatment; delicate; subtle. **4** Exactly fitted or adjusted; accurate. **5** Delicately constructed; hence, easily disarranged or injured; fragile; tender. **6** Agreeable or pleasant in any way: a wide use. **7** Agreeable socially; respectable: *nice* people. See synonyms under CHOICE, FINE[1], NEAT[1], PRECISE, TASTEFUL. ◆ Homophone: *gneiss.* [< OF, stupid < L *nescius* ignorant < *ne-* not + *scire* know] —**nice′ly** *adv.* —**nice′ness** *n.*

Nice (nēs) A port of SE France: ancient *Nicaea,* Italian *Nizza.* —**Ni·çoise** (nē·swäz′) *adj. & n.*

Ni·cene (nī′sēn, nī·sēn′) *adj.* Pertaining to Nicaea, in Asia Minor: also spelled *Nicaean.*

Nicene Creed *Eccl.* **1** A Christian confession of faith, adopted against the Arian heresy by the first Council of Nicaea, A.D. 325. **2** A similar creed, later attributed to the Council of Constantinople, A.D. 381, and accepted by the Greek Church: also called *Constantinopolitan* or *Niceno-Constantinopolitan Creed.* **3** A modification of this, containing a clause referring to the Holy Spirit, adopted by the Council of Toledo, A.D. 589.

ni·ce·ty (nī′sə·tē) *n. pl.* **·ties 1** The quality of being nice. **2** A delicate point or distinction; refinement of criticism; subtlety. **3** A rare or delicious thing; delicacy. **4** Fastidiousness. **5** *Obs.* Coyness; shyness. [< OF *niceté* folly < *nice.* See NICE.]

niche (nich) *n.* **1** A recessed space or hollow; specifically, a recess in a wall for a statue or the like. **2** Hence, any position specially adapted to its occupant. —*v.t.* **niched, nich·ing** To put in a niche. [< F < *nicher* nest, ult. < L *nidus* a nest]

NICHE

nich·er (nikh′ər) See NICKER[2].

Nich·o·las (nik′ə·ləs) A masculine personal name. Also *Lat.* **Ni·co·la·us** (nik′ō·lā′əs), *Fr.* **Ni·co·las** (nē·kō·lä′), *Ital.* **Nic·co·lò** (nēk′kō·lô′), *Pg.* **Ni·co·láo** (nē′kō·lä′ōō), *Sp.* **Ni·co·lás** (nē′kō·läs′), *Ger.* **Ni·ko·laus** (nē′kō·lous), *Russian* **Ni·co·lai** (nē′kō·lī′). [< Gk., victory of the people]

—**Nicholas, Saint** Fourth century prelate, bishop of Myra; patron saint of Russia, seamen, and children. In Dutch nursery lore, the Santa Claus who brings presents to children on Christmas Eve. See SANTA CLAUS.

—**Nicholas I,** 1796–1855, czar of Russia 1825–55.

—**Nicholas II,** 1868–1918, czar of Russia 1894–1917; executed.

—**Nicholas V,** 1397–1455, real name Tommaso Parentucelli, pope 1447–55.

—**Nicholas of Cusa,** 1401–64, German prelate and scholar.

Nich·ol·son (nik′əl·sən), **Sir Francis,** 1655–1728, British colonial administrator.

nicht wahr (nikht vär′) *German* Isn't that so?

Ni·ci·as (nish′ē·əs) Athenian general; killed at Syracuse, 413 B.C.

nick (nik) *n.* **1** A slight cut, chip, or indentation in the surface or edge of anything. **2** A score or tally: from the use of notched sticks for keeping tally. **3** A point of time; critical moment. **4** *Printing* A groove on the shank of a type character to aid in correct alinement. —*v.t.* **1** To make a nick or nicks in; notch. **2** To record or tally by making nicks. **3** To cut through or into. **4** *Slang* To cheat or trick. **5** To hit or catch at the exact moment; guess or understand exactly. **6** *Brit. Slang* To arrest; catch. [Origin uncertain] —**nick′er** *n.*

Nick (nik) The devil. Also **Old Nick.** [Nickname of NICHOLAS]

nick·el (nik′əl) *n.* **1** A hard, malleable, metallic element (symbol Ni, atomic number 28), widely used in metallurgy and the arts. See PERIODIC TABLE. **2** A five-cent coin of the United States, of a nickel-and-copper alloy. —*v.t.* To plate with nickel. [< Sw. < G *(kupfer)nickel,* lit., copper demon; because its ore looks like copper but contains none]

nick·el·bloom (nik′əl·blōōm′) *n.* Annabergite.

nickel carbonyl *Chem.* A yellow, volatile, highly poisonous liquid, $Ni(CO)_4$, obtained by passing carbon monoxide over finely divided nickel. Also **nickel tetracarbonyl.**
nick·el·ic (nik′əl·ik) *adj.* Of, pertaining to, or containing nickel, especially trivalent nickel.
nick·el·if·er·ous (nik′əl·if′ər·əs) *adj.* Containing nickel, as ore.
nick·el·o·de·on (nik′əl·ō′dē·ən) *n.* **1** An early type of motion-picture theater charging an admission fee of five cents. **2** An automatic slot machine, such as a cinematograph or a phonograph, which performs when a nickel is inserted. [<NICKEL (def. 2) + *odeon,* var. of ODEUM]
nick·el·ous (nik′əl·əs) *adj.* Of, pertaining to, or containing nickel, especially bivalent nickel.
nick·el-plate (nik′əl·plāt′) *v.t.* **-plat·ed, -plat·ing** To cover with nickel by electroplating. **—nick′el-plat′ed** *adj.*
nickel plate A thin layer of nickel deposited on the surface of objects by electrolysis.
nickel silver German silver.
nick·er[1] (nik′ər) *n.* A seed of the nickernut tree, used by children in games resembling marbles. Also **nick′er·nut.** [? < Du. *knikker* a marble]
nick·er[2] (nik′ər) *n.* & *v.i.* **1** Neigh. **2** Laugh. Also, *Scot., nicher.* [Imit.]
nick·er·nut tree (nik′ər·nut) **1** A tropical American climbing shrub *(Caesalpinia crista)* with prickly, oval pods bearing seeds or nuts called *nickernuts* or *bonducnuts.* **2** The Kentucky coffee tree. [? <NICKER[1], from the use of its seeds as marbles]
nick·nack (nik′nak′) See KNICK-KNACK.
nick·name (nik′nām′) *n.* **1** A familiar name, sometimes a diminutive, as Tom for Thomas. **2** A descriptive or facetious name given to a person, place, or thing in derision, affection, or acclaim, as Longshanks, Honest Abe, Empire State, etc. —*v.t.* **·named, ·nam·ing 1** To give a nickname to. **2** To misname. [ME *ekename* a surname; later *an ekename* was taken as *a nickname*]
Nic·o·bar Islands (nik′ə·bär′) See under ANDAMAN AND NICOBAR ISLANDS. Also **Nic′o·bars′.**
Nic·o·de·mus (nik′ə·dē′məs) A ruler of the Jews and disciple of Christ. *John* iii 1.
Nic·o·lay (nik′ə·lā), **John George,** 1832–1901, U.S. biographer.
Ni·colle (nē·kôl′), **Charles Jean Henri,** 1866–1936, French physician and bacteriologist.
Nic·ol prism (nik′əl) *Optics* A set of two prisms of Iceland spar cemented together: used for producing plane-polarized light. Also **nic′ol.** [after Wm. *Nicol,* 1768?–1851, Scottish physicist]
Nic·ol·son (nik′əl·sən), **Harold,** born 1886, English biographer and diplomat.
Ni·cop·o·lis (ni·kop′ə·lis, nī-) An ancient city of southern Epirus, Greece.
Nic·o·si·a (nik′ə·sē′ə) The capital of Cyprus, in the north central part.
nic·o·tine (nik′ə·tēn, -tin) *n.* A poisonous, colorless, oily, liquid alkaloid, $C_{10}H_{14}N_2$, with a very acrid taste, contained in the leaves of tobacco. Also **nic′o·tin.** [after Jean *Nicot,* 1530–1604, French courtier, who introduced tobacco into France from Portugal] **—nic·o·tin·ic** (nik′ə·tin′ik) *adj.*
nicotinic acid The anti-pellagra factor of the vitamin B complex; a colorless, crystalline, water-soluble compound, $C_6H_5NO_2$, present in liver, kidney, muscle meats, fish, milk, and green vegetables, and also made by the oxidation of nicotine: also called *niacin.*
nic·o·tin·ism (nik′ə·tin·iz′əm) *n.* The morbid effects resulting from the excessive use of tobacco.
Nic·the·roy (nē′tə·roi′) A former spelling of NITERÓI.
nic·ti·tate (nik′tə·tāt) *v.i.* **·tat·ed, ·tat·ing** To wink. Also **nic′tate.** [<Med. L *nictitatus,* pp. of *nictitare,* freq. of L *nictare* wink]
nictitating membrane The third or lateral eyelid, in birds, crocodiles, etc., springing from the inner and anterior border of the eye.
nic·ti·ta·tion (nik′tə·tā ′shən) *n.* **1** The act of winking. **2** *Pathol.* Rapid and involuntary winking due to nervous derangement. Also **nic·ta′tion.**
Ni·da·ros (nē′dä·rōs) A former name for TRONDHEIM.
nid·der·ing (nid′ər·ing) *n. Archaic* A coward. —*adj.* Cowardly; base. Also **nid′er·ing.** [Alter. of ME *nithing* a villain; misread in early text]
nide (nīd) *n.* A nest or brood of young pheasants. —*v.i.* **nid·ed, nid·ing** *Rare* To nest. [<L *nidus* nest]
ni·dic·o·lous (ni·dik′ə·ləs) *adj.* Remaining in the nest for some time after hatching: said of birds. [<L *nidus* nest + *colere* inhabit]
nid·i·fy (nid′ə·fī) *v.i.* **·fied, ·fy·ing** To build a nest. Also **nid′i·fi·cate′.** [<L *nidificare* <*nidus* a nest + *facere* make] **—nid′i·fi·ca′tion** *n.*
ni·dus (nī′dəs) *n. pl.* **·di** (-dī) **1** A place for the natural deposit of eggs, especially of insects, spiders, etc. **2** A place in an organism adapted to the development of some germ or parasite; hence, a center of infection. [<L]
Nie·buhr (nē′bo͝or), **Barthold Georg,** 1776–1831, German historian, philologist, and critic. **—Reinhold,** 1892–1971, U.S. Protestant theologian.
niece (nēs) *n.* The daughter of a brother or sister; also, the daughter of a brother-in-law or sister-in-law. [<OF, ult. <L *neptis* niece, granddaughter]
ni·el·lo (nē·el′ō) *n. pl.* **·li** (-ī) **1** The art of decorating metal plates by incising designs upon them and then filling in the incised lines with a black alloy. **2** A work produced by this method: also **ni·el′lo-work′. 3** A black alloy used in this work. [<Ital. <L *nigellus* blackish <*niger* black] **—ni·el′list** *n.*
Niel·sen (nēl′sən), **Carl,** 1865–1931, Danish composer.
Nie·men (nē′mən, *Polish* nye′men) The Polish name for the NEMAN.
Nie·möl·ler (nē′mœl·ər), **Martin,** born 1892, German anti-Nazi Protestant leader.
Nier·stein·er (nir′stī·nər, -shtī-) *n.* A full-bodied, white Rhine wine.
niest (nēst) See NEIST.
Nie·tzsche (nē′chə), **Fredrich Wilhelm,** 1844–1900, German philosopher.
Nie·tzsche·ism (nē′chi·iz′əm) *n.* The principles propounded in the philosophy of Nietzsche; especially, the doctrine of the development of the superman. Also **Nie′tzsche·an·ism. —Nie′tzsche·an** *adj.* & *n.*
Ni·eu·port (nē′o͞o·pōrt) A town in western Belgium; scene of Dutch victory over Spanish forces, 1600. Also **Ni′euw·poort.**
nieve (nēv) *n. Scot. Brit. Dial.* The fist or hand. Also spelled *neif.*
nif·fer (nif′ər) *Scot. v.t.* To barter; exchange. —*n.* An exchange or barter.
Nif·l·heim (niv′əl·hām) The lowest of the nine worlds of Norse mythology, the world of fog or mist; the northern limit of cold and darkness. Also **Nif′el·heim.** [<ON <*nifl* fog + *heimr* world]
nif·ty (nif′tē) *adj.* **·ti·er, ·ti·est** *Slang* Stylish; pleasing.
Ni·ger (nī′jər, -gər) A river of western Africa, flowing 2,600 miles from near the Sierra Leone border through French West Africa and Nigeria to the Gulf of Guinea.
Ni·ger (nī′jər, -gər), **Republic of** An independent republic of the French Community in north central Africa; 458,975 square miles; capital, Niamey: formerly a French overseas territory.
Ni·ge·ri·a (nī·jir′ē·ə) An independent state of the British Commonwealth, in west Africa, including the northern part of the former British Cameroons; 356,093 square miles; capital, Lagos: formerly a British dependency. **—Ni·ge′ri·an** *adj.* & *n.*
Ni·ger seed (nī′jər, -gər) Ramtil.
nig·gard (nig′ərd) *n.* A parsimonious person. —*v.t.* & *v.i. Obs.* To act or treat in a niggardly manner. —*adj.* Niggardly. [Cf. ON *hnöggr* stingy]
nig·gard·ly (nig′ərd·lē) *adj.* Meanly covetous or avaricious; parsimonious; stingy. —adv. In the manner of a niggard. **—nig′ gard·li·ness** *n.*
nig·ger (nig′ər) *n.* **1** a black person; usually taken as an offensive term of contempt or racial slur. **2** a member of any dark-skinned people; usually taken as an offensive term of contempt or racial slur. **3** a member of any socially disadvantaged group of people. [Earlier *neger* <F *nègre* <Sp. *negro* BLACK]
nig·ger·head (nig′ər·hed′) *n.* **1** A stone or boulder, especially one having nodules. **2** The black-eyed Susan. **3** *Naut.* A spool about which a hauling rope is wound; a bollard.
nig·gle (nig′əl) *v.i.* **·gled, ·gling 1** To occupy oneself with trifles; be too precise. **2** To putter; trifle. [Cf. dial. Norw. *nigla*]
nig·gling (nig′ling) *n.* **1** Work that is too detailed or meticulous. **2** In art, overelaborate or too detailed a treatment. —*adj.* **1** Fussy; overelaborate. **2** Mean; pretty; trite. **3** Troublesome; annoying. **—nig′gling·ly** *adv.*
nigh (nī) *adj.* **nigh·er, nigh·est** or, formerly, **next 1** Being close by; near in time or place. **2** On the left: used of a team. **3** Closely allied in kinship; intimate. **4** Most convenient; direct. See synonyms under ADJACENT. —*adv.* **1** Not remote in time or place; closely by; near. **2** Almost; nearly. —*prep.* Close to; near. —*v.t.* & *v.i. Rare* To draw near; approach. [OE *neah, neh*]
night (nīt) *n.* **1** The period during which the sun is below the horizon from sunset to sunrise. ◆Collateral adjective: *nocturnal.* **2** The close of day; evening. **3** A condition of darkness, or gloom; sorrow; misfortune. **4** Death. ◆Homophone: *knight.* [OE *niht*]
night·bird (nīt′bûrd′) *n.* A bird that flies or sings by night.
night blindness Nyctalopia.
night-bloom·ing cereus (nīt′blo͞o′ ming) See CEREUS.
night·cap (nīt′kap′) *n.* **1** A headcovering to be worn in bed. **2** *Colloq.* A drink of liquor taken just before going to bed. **3** *Colloq.* The final event in a day's program of sports competition; specifically, in baseball, the second game of a double-header.
night·chair (nīt′châr′) *n.* A commode (def. 3).
night·clothes (nīt′klōz′, -klōthz′) *n. pl.* Clothes to be worn in bed.
night club A restaurant open at night, providing entertainment, food, and drink.
night·crawl·er (nīt′krô′lər) *n. U.S. Colloq.* Any large earthworm that emerges at night. See NIGHTWALKER (def. 3).
night·fall (nīt′fôl′) *n.* The close of day.
night·glass (nīt′glas′, -gläs′) *n.* A spyglass or telescope arranged with concentrating lenses for use at night, especially at sea.
night·gown (nīt′goun′) *n.* A long, loose gown worn in bed. Also **night′dress′.**
night·hawk (nīt′hôk′) *n.* **1** An American goatsucker (genus *Chordeiles*) of nocturnal habits, related to the whippoorwill. **2** The nightjar. **3** One who works or stays up at night.
night heron A bird (genus *Nycticorax*) of somewhat nocturnal habits, having a comparatively short, stout bill. **—black-crowned night heron** One of two forms of night herons (*N. nycticorax*) found in North America.
night·in·gale (nī′tən·gāl, nī′ting-) *n.* **1** A small, Old World, migratory bird (genus *Luscinia*), of the thrush family *(Turdidae),* noted for the melodious night song of the male. **2** The bulbul [OE *nihtegale,* lit., night-singer]
Night·in·gale (nī′tən·gāl, nī′ting-), **Florence,** 1820–1910, English nurse born in Italy; served in the military hospitals during the Crimean War; regarded as the founder of modern nursing service.
night·jar (nīt′jär′) *n.* A goatsucker, especially the common European species (*Caprimulgus europaeus).*
night latch A spring latch operated from the outside by a key and from the inside by a knob or the like. Also **night lock.**
night letter A lettergram sent during the night, usually at a reduced rate.
night·long (nīt′lông′, -long′) *adj.* Lasting through the night.
night·ly (nīt′lē) *adj.* **1** Pertaining to night or to every night; occuring at night or every night. **2** Dark; having the appearance of night. —*adv.* By night; every night.
night·mare (nīt′mâr) *n.* **1** A sensation of oppression or suffocation during sleep, with terrifying dreams and apparent inability to move or speak. **2** Hence, any oppressive influence. **3** An evil spirit formerly supposed to suffocate people during sleep; an incubus. [<NIGHT + MARE[2]] **—night′mar·ish** *adj.*
night owl 1 An owl especially nocturnal in habits. **2** Nighthawk (def. 3).
night raven 1 The nightjar. **2** The night heron.
night rider In the southern United States, any of a band of masked, mounted men who perform lawless acts of violence at night, generally to punish, intimidate, etc.

nights (nīts) *adv.* At night.

night school A school that holds classes during the evening, especially for those who cannot attend day school.

night·shade (nīt'shād) *n.* **1** Any one of a genus (*Solanum*) of flowering plants; especially, the **common** or **black nightshade** (*S. nigrum*), a weedlike plant with white flowers and black berries, reputed poisonous, but used medicinally, and the **climbing** or **woody nightshade** (*S. dulcamara*). **2** The belladonna or **deadly nightshade**. **3** The henbane. **— enchanter's nightshade** A low, inconspicuous herb (genus *Circaea*) growing in damp woods.

BLACK NIGHTSHADE
a. Spray showing blossom *(b)* and fruit *(c).*

night·shirt (nīt'shûrt') *n.* A loose, shirtlike garment worn in bed, usually by men or boys.

night soil The contents of privies, cesspools, etc., usually removed at night.

night spot *U.S. Colloq.* A night club.

night·stick (nīt'stik') *n.* A long, stout club carried by policemen, especially at night.

night sweats *Pathol.* Excessive sweating during sleep, often associated with phthisis.

night table A bedside table or stand.

night terrors *Med.* A disorder of children resembling nightmare, with fits of semiconscious screaming; pavor nocturnus.

night·tide (nīt'tīd') *n.* Nighttime.

night·time (nīt'tīm') *n.* The time from sunset to sunrise, or from dark to dawn.

night·walk·er (nīt'wô'kər) *n.* **1** One who walks in his sleep. **2** One who frequents the streets at night. **3** A large angleworm.

night watch 1 A guard for night duty. **2** A watch period of the night hours.

night watchman A person hired to keep watch and be on guard at night.

night·y (nīt'ē) *n. pl.* **night·ies** *Colloq.* A nightgown.

nig·nog (nig'nog') *n. Brit. Slang* A dark-skinned person, as an Indian, Pakistani, or Negro: an offensive and derogatory term. [Prob. reduplication of NIG(GER)]

ni·gres·cence (nī-gres'əns) *n.* The process of becoming black, or the blackness so produced. [< L *nigrescere* grow black < *niger* black] **— ni·gres'cent** *adj.*

nig·ri·fy (nig'rə-fī) *v.t.* **·fied**, **·fy·ing** To make black. [< L *nigrificare* < *niger* black + *facere* make] **— nig'ri·fi·ca'tion** *n.*

Ni·gri·ti·a (nī-grish'ē-ə) A former name for the region of the SUDAN.

Ni·gri·ti·an (nī-grish'ē-ən) *adj.* **1** Of or pertaining to Nigritia. **2** Negro. **—** *n.* A Negro.

nig·ri·tude (nig'rə-tōōd, -tyōōd) *n.* Blackness; darkness. [< L *nigritudo* < *niger* black]

nig·ro·sine (nig'rə-sēn, -sin) *n. Chem.* Any of a group of deep blue or black dyes obtained from aniline and its homologs. [< L *niger* black + -OS(E)[1] + -INE[2]]

ni·hil (nī'hil, nī'-) *n.* Nothing; nil. [< L]

ni·hil ad rem (nī'hil ad rem) *Latin* Nothing to the point.

ni·hil·ism (nī'əl·iz'əm, nī'hil·) *n.* **1** The doctrine that nothing exists or can be known; also, the rejection of religious and moral creeds, known as **ethical nihilism**. **2** A political doctrine holding that the existing structure of society should be destroyed; specifically, a movement in Russia in the 19th century advocating the overthrow of the social order and many revolutionary reforms, resulting in violence and terrorism. **3** Loosely, any revolutionary propaganda involving violence. **— ni'hil·ist** *n.* **— ni'hil·is'tic** *adj.*

ni·hil·i·ty (nī·hil'ə·tē, ni-) *n.* Nothingness.

Ni·hon (nē'hōn) See JAPAN.

Ni·i·ga·ta (nē·ē·gä·tä) A port on NW Honshu island, Japan.

Ni·i·ha·u (nē'ē·hä'ōō) An island in the NW Hawaiian Islands: 72 square miles.

Ni·jin·sky (nə·jin'skē, *Russian* ni·zhēn'skē), **Vaslav**, 1890–1950, Russian ballet dancer and choreographer.

Nij·me·gen (nī'mā·gən, *Du.* nī'mā·khən) A city on the Waal in eastern Netherlands; site of a peace conference, 1678: German *Nimwegen.*

-nik *suffix* One associated, concerned, or connected with: *peacenik.* [< Russ., noun suffix]

Ni·ke (nī'kē) In Greek mythology, the winged goddess of victory: identified with the Roman Victoria.

Nik·ko (nēk·kō) A town and religious center on central Honshu island, Japan.

Ni·ko·la·ev (nē'kō·lä'yef) A port on the Bug estuary in SW Ukrainian S.S.R.: formerly *Vernoleninsk.*

Ni·ko·lay·evsk (nē'kō·lä'yefsk) A city near the mouth of the Amur in SE Russian S.F.S.R. Also **Ni·ko·lay·evsk–on–A·mur'** (-on·ä·mōōr').

nil (nil) *n.* Nothing. [< L, contraction of *nihil* nothing]

nil des·pe·ran·dum (nil des'pə·ran'dəm) *Latin* Nothing to be despaired of; never despair.

Nile (nīl) The longest river in Africa, rising in Lake Victoria and flowing 3,485 miles north to the Mediterranean; between Lake Victoria and Lake Albert it is known as the **Victoria Nile**; between Lake Albert and the Sudan as the **Albert Nile** (Arabic *Bahr-el-Jebel*); between Lake No and Khartoum as the **White Nile** (Arabic *Bahr-el-Abiad*); at Khartoum it receives the **Blue Nile** (Arabic *Bahr-el-Azraq*), a tributary flowing 850 miles from Ethiopia, and is known as the Nile (Arabic *Bahr-en-Nil*) for the rest of its course. **— Battle of the Nile** A British naval victory over the French, near the mouth of the Nile on August 1, 1798.

Nile green Any of several light-green tints.

nil·gai (nil'gī) *n.* A large, short-maned Indian antelope (*Boselaphus tragocamelus*) with the hind legs much shorter than the fore: often spelled *nylghai, nylghau.* Also **nil'gau** (-gô), **nil'ghai, nil'ghau** (-gô). [< Persian *nīlgāu* < *nīl* blue + *gāu* cow]

Nil·gi·ri Hills (nil'gi·rē) A mountainous plateau district in Madras State, India; highest peak, 8,640 feet. Also **The Nil'gi·ris.**

nill (nil) *v.t. & v.i. Archaic* To be unwilling. [OE *nillan* < *ne-* not + *willan* will]

nil ni·si bo·num (nil nī'sī bō'nəm) *Latin* Short for DE MORTUIS NIL NISI BONUM.

Ni·lom·e·ter (nī·lom'ə·tər) *n.* A gage for measuring the height of water in the Nile. [< Gk. *Neilometrion < Neilos* Nile + *metron* measure] **— Ni·lo·met·ric** (nī'lō·met'rik) *adj.*

Ni·lot·ic (nī·lot'ik) *adj.* **1** Of, pertaining to, or characteristic of the Nile or the peoples native to the Nile basin. **2** Of or pertaining to a subfamily of Sudanic languages spoken by any of these peoples, including Dinka and Fula.

nim (nim) *v.t.* **nam** or **nimmed**, **no·men** or **nome**, **nim·ming** *Obs.* To take; steal. [OE *niman*]

nim·ble (nim'bəl) *adj.* **·bler**, **·blest 1** Light and quick in motion or action; agile. **2** Intellectually alert or acute; keen; quick-witted. **3** Circulating freely, as money. **4** Indicating a ready mind; clever: a *nimble* answer. [OE *numel* quick at learning] **— nim'ble·ness** *n.* **— nim'bly** *adv.*

Synonyms: active, agile, alert, brisk, bustling, lively, prompt, quick, speedy, sprightly, swift. *Nimble* refers to lightness, freedom, and quickness of motion within a somewhat narrow range, with readiness to turn suddenly to any point; *swift* applies commonly to sustained motion over greater distances; a pickpocket is *nimble*-fingered, a dancer *nimble*-footed; an arrow, a race horse, or an ocean steamer is *swift.* We speak of *nimble* wit,

swift destruction. *Alert*, which is a synonym for *ready*, sometimes comes near the meaning of *nimble* or *quick*, from the fact that the ready, wide-awake person is likely to be lively, quick, speedy. See ACTIVE, ALERT, SPRIGHTLY. *Antonyms:* clumsy, dilatory, dull, heavy, inactive, inert, slow, sluggish, unready.

nim·bus (nim'bəs) *n. pl.* **·bus·es** or **·bi** (-bī) **1** A dark, heavy, rain-bearing cloud; also **nim·bo·stra·tus** (nim'bō·strā'təs, -strat'əs). See CLOUD. **2** A halo or bright disk encircling the head, as of Jesus, saints, etc., in pictures, on medallions, etc. **3** A cloud of glory or surrounding aura of light in which the gods were supposed to be clothed when appearing upon earth; hence, any atmosphere or aura of fame, glamour, etc., surrounding a person. [< L, rain cloud]

Nîmes (nēmz, *Fr.* nēm) A city in southern France. Formerly **Nismes** (nēm).

ni·mi·e·ty (ni·mī'ə·tē) *n.* Redundancy; excess. [< LL *nimietas, -tatis < nimis* too much] **— nim·i·ous** (nim'ē·əs) *adj.*

nim·i·ny–pim·i·ny (nim'ə·nē·pim'ə·nē) *adj.* Affectedly nice or delicate; effeminate. [Imit.]

Nim·itz (nim'its), **Chester William**, 1885–1966, U.S. admiral; in command of U.S. Pacific Fleet in World War II.

Nim·rod (nim'rod) Grandson of Ham; a mighty hunter. *Gen.* x 8.

Nim·rud (nim·rōōd') The modern name for the site of ancient KALAKH.

Nim·u·e (nim'ōō·ā) See under VIVIAN.

Nim·we·gen (nim'vā·gən) The German name for NIJMEGEN.

Ni·na (nī'nə, nē'-) Diminutive of ANN.

Ni·ña (nē'nə, *Sp.* nē'nyä) *n.* One of the three ships of Columbus on his maiden voyage to America.

nin·com·poop (nin'kəm·pōōp) *n.* A foolish or silly person; simpleton. [Origin unknown]

nine (nīn) *n.* **1** The cardinal number preceding ten and following eight, or any of the symbols (9, ix, IX) representing this number. **2** Anything containing nine members or units, as a playing card with nine pips; specifically, a baseball team. **— the Nine The Muses.** **—** *adj.* Being or consisting of one more than eight; thrice three; novenary. [OE *nigon*]

nine·fold (nīn'fōld') *adj. & adv.* Nine times as many or as great; nonuplicate.

nine–men's–mor·ris (nīn'menz·môr'is, -mor'-) *n.* A game played on a diagram marked out on the ground, or on a board. Each player, having five, nine, or twelve (according to the number playing) counters or pieces, endeavors to place three in a row, upon doing which he takes one of his opponent's pieces.

nine·pence (nīn'pəns) *n. Brit.* **1** The sum of nine pennies. **2** A coin of this value, no longer minted.

nine·pin (nīn'pin') *n.* One of the pins in the game of ninepins.

nine·pins (nīn'pinz') *n. pl. (construed as singular)* A game similar to tenpins, in which nine large wooden pins are employed.

nine·teen (nīn'tēn') *adj.* Being nine more than ten. **—** *n.* The sum of ten and nine; also, its symbols (19, xix, XIX). **— nine'teenth'** (-tēnth') *adj. & n.*

nine·ty (nīn'tē) *adj.* Being nine times ten. **—** *n. pl.* **·ties** The sum of ten and eighty: a cardinal numeral; also, its symbols (90, xc, XC). **— nine'ti·eth** *adj. & n.* **— nine'ty·fold'** *adj. & adv.*

Nin·e·veh (nin'ə·və) An ancient city on the Tigris, capital of Assyria: Latin *Ninus.* **— Nin'e·vite** (-vīt) *n.*

Ning·po (ning'pō') A treaty port in NE Chekiang province, China.

Ning·sia (ning'shyä') **1** A former province of NW China in the region of Inner Mongolia; created 1928 from part of Kansu province; remerged with Kansu 1954; 106,150 square miles; capital Yinchwan. **2** See YINCHWAN. Also **Ning'hsia.**

nin·ny (nin'ē) *n. pl.* **·nies** A simpleton; dunce. [? Short for *an innocent*]

ni·non (nē'non) *n.* A kind of firm chiffon used for lingerie, neckwear, dresses, etc.: often called *triple voile.* [< F]

Ni·non (nē·nôn') A French form of ANN.

ninth (nīnth) *adj.* **1** Next in order after the eighth: the ordinal of *nine.* **2** Being one of

nine equal parts. —*n.* **1** One of nine equal parts; the quotient of a unit divided by nine. **2** *Music* **a** An interval of an octave and a second, or a note separated from another by this interval. **b** The two notes written or sounded together. —*adv.* In the ninth order, place, or rank: also, in formal discourse, **ninth′ly.**

Ni·nus (nī′nəs) **1** In Assyrian legend, the founder of Nineveh and husband of Semiramis. **2** The Latin name for NINEVEH.

Ni·o·be (nī′ə·bē) In Greek mythology, the daughter of Tantalus and wife of Amphion, whose children were killed by Apollo and Artemis after she had vaunted her superiority to their mother Leto: the weeping Niobe was turned by Zeus into a stone from which tears continued to flow.

NIOBE
After copy of a statue attributed to Scopas in the Uffizi, Florence.

ni·o·bi·um (nī·ō′bē·əm) *n.* A soft, lustrous white metallic element (symbol Nb, atomic number 41) valuable as an alloying element: formerly called *columbium.* See PERIODIC TABLE.

ni·o·bous (nī·ō′bəs) *adj. Chem.* Denoting a compound which contains trivalent niobium.

Ni·o·brar·a River (nī′ə·brâr′ə) A river in eastern Wyoming and northern Nebraska, flowing 431 miles east to the Missouri.

Ni·os (nē′os) See Ios.

nip[1] (nip) *v.* **nipped, nip·ping** *v.t.* **1** To compress tightly between two surfaces or points; squeeze; bite. **2** To sever or remove by pinching or clipping, as shoots. **3** To check or destroy the growth or development of. **4** To affect painfully or injuriously; benumb: said of cold **5** *Slang* To steal; pilfer. **6** *Slang* To snatch; take. —*v.i.* **7** *Brit. Colloq.* To move nimbly or rapidly: with *off, away, in,* etc. —*n.* **1** The act of compressing sharply. **2** A biting, pinching, or clipping off; also, whatever is pinched off; hence, a pinch. **3** A sudden blight, as by frost. **4** A sharp saying; cutting remark; gibe. [Cf. Du. *nijpen* nip]

nip[2] (nip) *n.* A small dram, especially of strong drink. —*v.t.* & *v.i.* To drink (liquor) in sips. [< earlier *nipperkin,* measure holding about a half pint]

ni·pa (nī′pə, nē′-) *n.* **1** Any of a genus *(Nipa)* of palms of tropical SE Asia. One species *(N. fruticans)* has feathery leaves, used for weaving, thatching, etc., and bunches of edible fruit. **2** An alcoholic beverage made from this palm. [< NL < Malay *nīpah*]

nip and tuck A case of near equality, as between to runners; neck and neck.

niph·a·blep·si·a (nif′ə·blep′sē·ə) *n.* Snow blindness. Also **niph·o·typh·lo·sis** (nif′ə·tif·lō′sis). [< NL < Gk. *nipha* (accusative sing.) snow + *ablepsia* blindness]

Nip·i·gon (nip′ə·gon), **Lake** A lake in west central Ontario, Canada, north of Lake Superior; 1,870 square miles.

Nip·is·sing (nip′ə·sing), **Lake** A lake in east central Ontario, Canada, midway between Georgian Bay and the Ottawa River; 330 square miles.

nip·per[1] (nip′ər) *n.* **1** One who nips. **2** One of various pincers for nipping. **3** An incisor, as of a horse. **4** A great claw, as of a crab. **5** A heavy, padded, woolen mitten or glove, used by New England fishermen.

nip·per[2] (nip′ər) *n. Brit. Colloq.* A small boy.

nip·ping (nip′ing) *adj.* Pinching; biting; cutting; sarcastic. **—nip′ping·ly** *adv.*

nip·ple (nip′əl) *n.* **1** The pigmented cone-shaped process of the breast containing the milk duct; a pap; teat. **2** A protuberance to receive a percussion cap. **3** A small tubular pipefitting. **4** A tip, usually of rubber, for a nursing bottle. [Earlier *neble,* ? dim. of NEB]

Nip·pon (nip′on, ni·pon′; *Japanese* nēp·pōn) See JAPAN. **—Nip′pon·ese′** (-ēz′, -ēs′) *adj.* & *n.*

Nip·pur (ni·po͝or′) An ancient Sumerian city of southern Babylonia, the earliest religious capital of the area.

nip·py (nip′ē) *adj.* **·pi·er, ·pi·est 1** Biting; sharp; acid; sarcastic. **2** Active; vigorous; alert. **nip′pi·ly** *adv.*

nir·va·na (nir·vä′nə,nər·van′ə) *n.* **1** In Hinduism, a "blowing out" of the spark of life; hence, spiritual reunion with Brahma; bliss. **2** In Buddhism, the ideal and goal of all religious effort: freedom from passion and delusion, and absorption of the individual into the supreme spirit; complete enlightenment. **3** The attainment of complete freedom from all mental, emotional, and psychic tension. [< Skt. *nirvāṇa* a blowing out < *nirvā* blow]

Ni·san (nī′san, nis′ən; *Hebrew* nē·sän′) A Hebrew month: also called *Abib.* See CALENDAR (Hebrew). Also **Nis′san.**

Ni·sei (nē·sā) *n. pl.* **·sei** or **·seis** An American citizen of immigrant Japanese parentage who was born and educated in the United States. Compare ISSEI, KIBEI.

Nish (nēsh) A city in SE central Serbia, Yugoslavia: ancient *Niassus. Serbo-Croatian* **Nis.** Formerly **Nis·sa** (nis′ə).

Ni·sha·pur (nē′shä·po͝or′) A city in NE Iran: also *Neyshapur.*

Ni·shi·no·mi·ya (nē·shē·nō·mī·yä) A city on Osaka Bay, Honshu island, Japan.

ni·si (nī′sī) *conj. Law* Unless: used after the word *order, rule, decree,* etc., signifying that it shall become effective at a certain time, unless before the time named it is modified or avoided. [< L < *ni* not + *si* if]

ni·si pri·us (nī′sī prī′əs) *Law* Literally, unless sooner; hence, a general designation suggestive of the trial of civil causes before a judge and jury.

Ni·sen hut (nis′ən) A portable, insulated structure of inverted U-sections for the shelter of troops, chiefly in arctic areas. Compare QUONSET HUT. [after P.N. *Nissen,* 1871–1930, Canadian Army engineer]

Ni·stru (nē′stro͞o) The Rumanian name for the DNIESTER.

ni·sus (nī′səs) *n. pl.* **·sus** *Latin* The exercise of power in acting or attempting to act; an effort, endeavor, or exertion.

nit (nit) *n.* **1** The egg of a louse or other insect. **2** The immature insect itself. **3** A small speck. **4** *Scot.* A nut. [OE *hnitu*] **—nit′ty** *adj.*

nit·chie (nich′ē) *n. Canadian* An Indian: an offensive term.

nite (nīt) *n.* A non-standard variant spelling of NIGHT.

ni·ter (nī′tər) *n.* **1** A crystalline white salt; saltpeter; potassium or sodium nitrate. **2** *Obs.* Natron. Also **ni′tre.** [< F *nitre* < L *nitrum* < Gk. *nitron* natron]

Ni·te·rói (nē′tə·roi′) A city on Guanabara Bay, SE Brazil, capital of Rio de Janeiro state: formerly *Nictheroy.*

nit·id (nit′id) *adj.* **1** *Bot.* Shining; glossy, as many leaves and seeds. **2** *Obs.* Lustrous; bright, as metal. [< L *nitidus* < *nitere* shine]

nit-pick (nit′pik′) *Colloq. v.t.* **1** To fuss over, especially with the aim of picking out petty faults. —*v.i.* **2** To engage in nit-picking. Also **nit′pick.** [Back formation < NIT-PICKING] **—nit′-pick·er** *n.*

nit-pick·ing (nit′pik·ing) *n. Colloq.* A fussing over trivial details, often with the aim of finding fault.

nitr- Var. of NITRO-.

ni·tra·mine (nī′trə·mēn, -min) *n. Chem.* Any of a class of compounds in which a nitro group is attached directly to a trivalent nitrogen atom: also *nitroamine.*

ni·trate (nī′trāt) *v.t.* **·trat·ed, ·trat·ing** *Chem.* To treat or combine with nitric acid or a compound; to change into a nitro derivative. —*n.* **1** A salt or ester of nitric acid: silver *nitrate.* **2** Sodium or potassium nitrate. [< L *nitratus* mixed with natron < *nitrum* niter] **—ni·tra′tion** *n.*

ni·tric (nī′trik) *adj. Chem.* **1** Of, pertaining to, or obtained from nitrogen. **2** Containing nitrogen in the higher state of valence.

nitric acid *Chem.* A colorless, highly corrosive liquid, HNO_3, sometimes formed in the atmosphere in small quantities, but usually made by decomposing sodium or potassium nitrate with sulfuric acid.

nitric bacteria See NITROBACTERIUM.

nitric oxide *Chem.* A colorless, gaseous compound, NO, liberated when certain metals are dissolved in nitric acid.

ni·tride (nī′trīd, -trid) *n. Chem.* A compound of nitrogen with some more positive element, as boron, phosphorus, and any of the metals. Also **ni′trid** (-trid).

ni·tri·fi·ca·tion (nī′trə·fə·kā′shən) *n. Chem.* **1** The method or act of nitrifying. **2** The conversion of ammonium salts into nitrites and nitrates, especially by soil bacteria.

ni·tri·fi·er (nī′trə·fī′ər) *n. Chem.* A substance containing nitrogen that aids in the process of nitrification.

ni·tri·fy (nī′trə·fī) *v.t.* **·fied, ·fy·ing** *Chem.* **1** To combine with nitrogen. **2** To convert, by oxidation, into nitric or nitrous acid or into nitrates or nitrites. **3** To treat or impregnate (soil, etc.) with nitrates. [< F *nitrifier*] **—ni′tri·fi′a·ble** *adj.*

ni·trile (nī′tril, -trēl, -trīl) *n. Chem.* Any of a group of cyanogen compounds, yielding ammonia upon saponification, and corresponding to the formula RCN, in which R is an organic radical. Also **ni′tril** (-tril).

ni·trite (nī′trīt) *n. Chem.* A salt of nitrous acid.

nitro- *combining form* **1** *Chem.* **a** Containing the univalent radical NO_2: *nitrophenol.* **b** Of or containing nitrogen in some other form: *nitroglycerin.* **2** Nitrifying: *nitrobacterium.* Also before vowels, *nitr-.* Also **nitri-.** [< L *nitrum* natron]

ni·tro·am·ine (nī′trō·am′ēn, -in) *n.* Nitramine.

ni·tro·bac·te·ri·um (nī′trō·bak·tir′ē·əm) *n. pl.* **·ri·a** (-ē·ə) Any of various soil bacteria involved in the process of nitrification, especially the nitrous group (genus *Nitrosomonas*), which converts ammonia into nitrites, and the nitric group (genus *Nitrobacter*), which oxidizes nitrites into nitrates. Also **nitric** or **nitrous bacterium.**

ni·tro·ben·zene (nī′trō·ben′zēn, -ben·zēn′) *n. Chem.* A yellow, oily compound, $C_6H_5NO_2$, formed by the nitration of benzene: also called *mirbane oil.*

ni·tro·cel·lu·lose (nī′trō·sel′yə·lōs) *n.* Cellulose nitrate.

ni·tro·chlo·ro·form (nī′trō·klôr′ə·fôrm, -klō′·rə-) *n.* Chlorpicrin.

ni·tro·cot·ton (nī′trō·kot′n) *n.* Guncotton.

ni·tro·ga·tion (nī′trō·gā′shən) *n.* A method of increasing soil fertility by the addition to irrigation water of anhydrous ammonia in controlled amounts. [< NITRO- + (IRRI)GATION]

ni·tro·gen (nī′trə·jən) *n.* An odorless, colorless, gaseous element (symbol N, atomic number 7) forming 78 percent of the atmosphere by volume and constituting a key element in the substance of living organisms. See PERIODIC TABLE. [< NITRO- + -GEN]

nitrogen balance *Biochem.* The relation between the nitrogen intake and the nitrogen output of a human body. An excess of intake gives a plus balance, an excess of output a minus balance.

nitrogen cycle *Biol.* The sequence of physical and chemical processes by which atmospheric nitrogen is taken into the soil, utilized by plants and animals, and eventually returned to the atmosphere.

nitrogen equilibrium *Physiol.* That condition of the body in which the nitrogen intake and output are equal.

nitrogen fixation 1 The conversion of atmospheric nitrogen into nitrates by soil bacteria, either free-living or in symbiotic relations with the roots of certain leguminous plants. **2** The production of nitrogen compounds, as for fertilizers and explosives, by various electrochemical processes utilizing free nitrogen. **—ni′tro·gen-fix′ing** *adj.*

nitrogen iodide *Chem.* A chocolate-colored powder, $N_2H_3I_3$, explosive when dry.

ni·trog·en·ize (nī·troj′ən·īz, nī′trə·jən·īz′) *v.t.* **·ized, ·iz·ing** To treat or combine with nitrogen.

nitrogen narcosis *Pathol.* A deranged, sometimes fatal nervous and mental condition resembling that of alcoholic intoxication, caused by the action of nitrogen inhaled by divers at excessive depths below the surface of the water.

ni·trog·e·nous (nī·troj′ə·nəs) *adj.* Pertaining to or containing nitrogen. Also **ni·tro·ge·ne·ous** (nī′trō·jē′nē·əs).

ni·tro·glyc·er·in (nī′trō·glis′ər·in) *n. Chem.* A colorless to pale-yellow, oily liquid, $C_3H_5(ONO_2)_3$, made by nitrating glycerol: an explosive and propellant, commonly combined, as with infusorial earth, to form dynamite and reduce the danger of its explosion by percussion. It is sometimes used in medicine. Also **ni′tro·glyc′er·ine.** [< NITRO- + GLYCERIN]

nitro group *Chem.* The univalent NO_2 radical.

ni·tro·hy·dro·chlo·ric acid (nī′trō·hī′drə·klôr′·ik, -klō′rik) Aqua regia.

ni·tro·jec·tion (nī′trō·jek′shən) *n.* The process

of injecting anhydrous ammonia gas directly into the soil as a means of increasing soil fertility. [<NITRO- + (IN)JECTION]

ni·trol·ic (nī·trol′ik) *adj. Chem.* Noting a class of acids derived from nitroparaffin by the action of nitrous acid and having the general formula RCN_2O_3H.

ni·trom·e·ter (nī·trom′ə·tər) *n.* An apparatus or instrument used for the determination of nitrogen in some of its combinations when contained in mixtures. [<NITRO- + -METER]

ni·tro·par·af·fin (nī′trō·par′ə·fin) *n. Chem.* Any derivative of the methane series in which hydrogen has been replaced by a nitro group.

ni·tro·phe·nol (nī′trō·fē′nōl, -nol) *n. Chem.* Any of a group of phenol compounds derived by the replacement of one or more hydrogen atoms by the nitro group: used in the making of dyestuffs.

ni·troph·i·lous (nī·trof′ə·ləs) *adj.* **1** Obtaining nutriment from nitrogenous soil. **2** Growing in a soil rich in nitrates.

ni·tro·phyte (nī′trə·fīt) *n.* A plant growing in a soil rich in nitrogen.

ni·tros·a·mine (nī·tros′ə·mēn, -min) *n. Chem.* Any of a group of organic compounds containing the bivalent radical N·NO. Also **ni·tros′a·min** (-min). [<NITROS(O)- + -AMINE]

nitroso- *combining form Chem.* Of or containing nitrosyl. Also, before vowels, **nitros-**. [<NL *nitrosus* <L, of natron <*nitrum* natron]

ni·tro·starch (nī′trō·stärch′) *n. Chem.* An explosive compounded of starch and sulfuric and nitric acids.

ni·tro·syl (nī·trō′sil, nī′trə·sēl′, nī′trə·sil) *n. Chem.* The univalent radical NO; known only in its combinations.

ni·trous (nī′trəs) *adj. Chem.* Of, pertaining to, or derived from nitrogen: especially applied to those compounds of nitrogen containing less oxygen than the nitric compounds. [<L *nitrosus* full of natron <*nitrum* natron]

nitrous acid *Chem.* An unstable compound, HNO_2, occurring only in solution.

nitrous oxide Laughing gas.

nit·ty-grit·ty (nit′ē·grit′ē) *U.S. Slang. n.* The basic question or details; the heart of the matter. —*adj.* Down-to-earth; basic.

nit·wit (nit′wit′) *n.* A silly or stupid person.

Ni·u·a·fo·o (nē·ōō′ä·fô′ō) The northernmost island of the Tonga group.

Ni·u·e (nē·ōō′ā) An island dependency of New Zealand SE of Samoa and east of Tonga; 100 square miles: also *Savage Island.*

ni·val (nī′vəl) *adj.* Pertaining to the snow; also, growing under the snow. [<L *nivalis* <*nix, nivis* snow]

niv·e·ous (niv′ē·əs) *adj.* Snowy; like snow.

Ni·ver·nais (nē·ver·nā′) A region and former province of central France.

Ni·vôse (nē·vōz′) See CALENDAR (Republican).

nix[1] (niks) *n.* In Teutonic mythology, a water spirit appearing in male or female form, and sometimes appearing as part fish. [<G *nix*] **—nix′ie** *n. fem.*

nix[2] (niks) *Slang n.* **1** Nothing. **2** No. —*adv.* No. —*interj.* Stop! Watch out!: an exclamation urging someone to stop saying or doing something. —*v.t.* To forbid or disagree with: He *nixed* our suggestions on the matter. [<G *nichts* nothing]

Nix·on (niks·ən), **Richard Milhous,** born 1913, U.S. statesman; vice president of the United States 1953–61; 37th president of the United States 1969–74; resigned.

ni·zam (ni·zäm′, -zam′, nī-) *n. pl.* **·zam** A Turkish regular soldier. [<Turkish *nizām* <Arabic <*nazāma* govern]

Ni·zam (ni·zäm′, -zam′, nī-) *n.* The title of the native ruler of Hyderabad, India.

Ni·zam·ate (ni·zäm′āt, -zam′-, -it) *n.* The territory governed by the Nizam.

Nizh·ni Nov·go·rod (nēzh′nē nôv′gə·rot) A former name for GORKI.

Nizh·ni Ta·gil (nēzh′nē tä·gēl′) A city in the central Urals in western Siberian Russian S.F.S.R.

Niz·za (nēt′tsä) The Italian name for NICE.

Njord (nyôrd) In Norse mythology, one of the Vanir, god of the winds and sea, father of Frey and Freya. Also **Njorth** nyôrth).

NKVD See NARKOMVNUDEL.

no[1] (nō) *adv.* **1** Nay; not so: opposed to *yes.* **2** Not at all; not in any wise: used with comparatives: *no* better than the other. **3** *Scot.* Not. **4** Not: used to express an alternative after *or*: whether or *no.* —*adj.* Not any; not one: *No* seats are left. —*n. pl.* **noes 1** A negative reply; a denial: He will not take *no* for an answer. **2** A negative vote or voter: The *noes* have it. [OE *na* <*ne* not + *a* ever]

no[2] (nō) *n.* The classical drama of Japan, traditionally tragic or noble in theme, requiring masks and elaborate costumes, stylized gesture, music, and dancing. Compare KABUKI. Also spelled *noh.*

No *Chem.* Nobelium (symbol No).

No (nō), **Lake** A lake on the White Nile in south central Sudan; 40 square miles.

no-ac·count (nō′ə·kount′) *adj. Slang* Worthless: also spelled *no-'count.*

No·a·chi·an (nō·ā′kē·ən) *adj.* Of or pertaining to Noah or to his times: the *Noachian* flood. Also **No·ach′ic** (-ak′ik), **No·ach′i·cal** (-ak′-).

No·ah (nō′ə, *Ger.* nō′ä) A masculine personal name. Also *Du.* **No·ach** (nō′äkh), *Fr.* **No·é** (nō·ā′), *Sw.* **No·a** (nō′ä). [<Hebrew, rest] **— Noah** In the Old Testament, a patriarch who, at the command of God, built an ark to save his family and "two of every sort of living thing" from the Flood. *Gen.* vi 14-22.

nob[1] (nob) *n.* **1** *Slang* The head. **2** In cribbage, the jack of trumps. [Var. of KNOB]

nob[2] (nob) *n. Brit. Slang* A person of social distinction; nobleman. [? Special use of NOB[1] (def.1)]

no-ball (nō′bôl′) *n.* In cricket, a ball unfairly bowled.

nob·ble (nob′əl) *v.t.* **·bled, ·bling** *Brit. Slang* **1** To drug or disable (a horse) to prevent its winning a race. **2** To gain or influence by bribery or other underhand means. **3** To steal or cheat; swindle. **4** To catch. [Origin uncertain] **—nob′bler** *n.*

nob·by (nob′ē) *adj.* **·bi·er, ·bi·est** *Brit. Slang* Fit for a nob; hence, elegant or flashy; showy; stylish. [<NOB[2]]

No·bel (nō·bel′), **Alfred Bernhard,** 1833–96, Swedish industrialist and philanthropist; inventor of dynamite; founded by his will the **Nobel Prizes,** awarded annually to those whose work in physics, chemistry, medicine, literature, economics, and furtherance of the world's peace is thought of most benefit to humanity.

no·be·li·um (nō·bē′lē·əm) *n.* A synthetic, radioactive metallic element (symbol No, atomic number 102) of the actinide series, having seven isotopes, the most stable of which has an atomic mass of 255 and a half-life of three minutes. See PERIODIC TABLE.

Nob Hill A fashionable district of San Francisco, California.

No·bi·le (nō′bē·lā), **Umberto,** 1885–1978, Italian aeronautical engineer and Arctic explorer.

no·bil·i·ar·y (nō·bil′ē·er′ē, -bil′yə·rē) *adj.* Of or pertaining to the nobility. [<F *nobiliaire* <L *nobilis* noble]

nobiliary particle A preposition used as a prefix to a family name, indicating the noble birth of the person concerned, as *de* or *von.*

no·bil·i·ty (nō·bil′ə·tē) *n. pl.* **·ties 1** The state of being noble, as in character or rank. **2** A class composed of nobles; in Great Britain, the peerage. **3** High-mindedness; magnanimity. **4** Great moral excellence. **5** Noble lineage. [<OF *nobilité* <L *nobilitas, -tatis* <*nobilis* noble]

no·ble (nō′bəl) *adj.* **·bler, ·blest 1** Exalted in character or quality; excellent; worthy. **2** Characterized by or indicative of virtue or magnanimity; high-minded. **3** Of or pertaining to an aristocracy; of lofty lineage; aristocratic. **4** Imposing in appearance; magnificent; grand. **5** Precious; pure: said of minerals and metals. **6** Chemically resistant or inert, as helium. **7** In falconry, long-winged, as a true falcon: see IGNOBLE. See synonyms under AWFUL, GENEROUS, HIGH, ILLUSTRIOUS, IMPERIAL. —*n.* **1** A person having hereditary title, rank, and privileges; in England, a peer; a member of the Second Estate, as distinct from the clergy and commoners. **2** An old English gold coin weighing 120 grains (1351). [<F <L *nobilis* noble, well-known. Related to L *noscere* know.] **—no′bly** *adv.*

no·ble·man (nō′bəl·mən) *n. pl.* **·men** (-mən) A man of noble rank; in England, a peer.

noble metal *Chem.* A metal which strongly resists oxidation and the action of acids, especially gold and platinum.

no·ble·ness (nō′bəl·nis) *n.* The quality of being noble; nobility.

no·blesse (nō·bles′) *n.* **1** *Obs.* Noble birth; nobleness. **2** The body of the nobility.

no·blesse o·blige (nō·bles′ ō·blēzh′) *French* Those of birth, wealth, or social position should behave generously or nobly toward others; literally, nobility obliges.

no·ble·wom·an (nō′bəl·wŏŏm′ən) *n. fem. pl.* **·wom·en** (-wim′in) A woman of noble rank.

no·bod·y (nō′bod′ē, -bəd·ē) *pron.* Not anybody. —*n. pl.* **·bod·ies** A person of no importance or influence.

no·cent (nō′sənt) *adj. Rare* **1** Injurious; hurtful. **2** Guilty. [<L *nocens, -entis,* ppr. of *nocere* harm]

no·ci·as·so·ci·a·tion (nō′sē·ə·sō′sē·ā′shən, -sō′·shē-) *n. Physiol.* The loss of nerve force resulting from overstimulation of nociceptors or from shock or exhaustion. [<L *nocere* harm + ASSOCIATION]

no·ci·cep·tor (nō′sē·sep′tər) *n. Physiol.* A sense organ or receptor which responds to and transmits painful stimuli. Compare BENECEPTOR. [<NL <L *nocere* injure + *-ceptor,* as in *receptor*] **—no′ci·cep′tive** *adj.*

nock (nok) *n.* **1** The notch on the butt end of an arrow. **2** The notch on the horn of a bow for securing the bowstring. —*v.t.* **1** To notch, as an arrow or bow. **2** To fit (an arrow) to the bowstring, as for shooting. [ME *nocke,* prob. <Scand. Cf. dial. Sw. *nokke* notch.]

noc·tam·bu·la·tion (nok·tam′byə·lā′shən) *n.* Somnambulism. Also **noc·tam′bu·lism.** [<L *nox, noctis* night + *ambulare walk*]

noc·tam·bu·list (nok·tam′byə·list) *n.* A somnambulist.

nocti- *combining form* By or at night: *noctiflorous.* Also, before vowels, **noct-.** [<L *nox, noctis* night]

noc·ti·flo·rous (nok′tə·flôr′əs, -flō′rəs) *adj. Bot.* Blooming at night. [<L *nox* night + *florere* flower]

noc·ti·lu·ca (nok′tə·lōō′kə) *n.* Any bioluminescent marine flagellate of the genus *Noctiluca,* found in warm seas, where its abundant presence gives the waves a brilliantly colored phosphorescent luminosity. [<NL <L *nox, noctis* night + *lucere* shine]

noc·ti·lu·cent (nok′tə·lōō′sənt) *adj. Meteorol.* Luminous by night: said especially of certain high altitude clouds visible at night by reflected sunlight.

noc·ti·pho·bi·a (nok′tə·fō′bē·ə) *n.* Nyctophobia.

noc·tu·id (nok′chōō·id) *n.* Any of a large family *(Noctuidae)* of medium-sized moths, especially those with stout bodies and shining eyes, as the army worm and the cutworm, whose larvae are very destructive pests. —*adj.* Of or pertaining to the *Noctuidae.* [<NL <L *noctua* night owl] **—noc′tu·id′e·ous** (-id′ē·əs) **noc·tu′id·ous, noc·tu·oid** (nok′chōō·oid) *adj.*

noc·tule (nok′chōōl) *n.* A large bat *(Nyctalus noctula)* of Europe.

noc·tur·nal (nok·tûr′nəl) *adj.* **1** Pertaining to night; occurring or active at night. **2** Seeking food by night, as animals. **3** Having blossoms that open by night. Opposed to *diurnal.* **—noc·tur′nal·ly** *adv.*

noc·turne (nok′tûrn) *n.* **1** In painting, a night scene. **2** *Music* A composition of a romantic, dreamy nature regarded as appropriate to night. [<F <L *nocturnus* nightly]

noc·u·ous (nok′yōō·əs) *adj.* Causing harm; noxious. [<L *nocuus* injurious <*nocere* harm] **—noc′u·ous·ly** *adv.* **—noc′u·ous·ness** *n.*

nod (nod) *n.* A forward and downward motion of the head, more or less quick or jerky; also, a similar motion of the top of anything, as a tree. [<*v.*] —*v.* **nod·ded, nod·ding** *v.i.* **1** To make a brief forward and downward movement of the head, as in agreement, invitation, etc. **2** To let the head fall forward briefly and involuntarily, as when drowsy; be sleepy. **3** To be inattentive or careless; make an error. **4** To incline the top or upper part as if nodding: said of trees, flowers, etc. —*v.t.* **5** To bend (the head) forward and downward

briefly. 6 To express or signify by nodding: to *nod* approval. 7 To affect in a specified manner by nodding: He *nodded* me from the room. [Cf. G *notteln* shake] —**nod′der** *n.*

Nod (nod), **Land of 1** The land east of Eden in which Cain settled after killing Abel. *Gen.* iv 16. 2 Sleep.

no·dal (nōd′l) *adj.* Of or pertaining to a node or nodes.

nod·dle (nod′l) *n. Colloq.* The head: a humorous use. [<NOD]

nod·dy (nod′ē) *n. pl.* **·dies 1** A dunce; a fool. 2 A light, two-wheeled, one-horse vehicle. 3 One of several terns (subfamily *Sterninae*), especially *Anous stolidus* of the Atlantic coast. [<NOD]

node (nōd) *n.* **1** A knot or knob; swelling. **2** *Bot.* The joint or knob on the stem of a plant, from which leaves, buds, or other structures grow. **3** *Math.* A point at which a curve cuts or crosses itself. **4** *Astron.* Either of the two points at which the intersection of the planes of two orbits, especially those of a satellite and its primary, pierces the celestial sphere; specifically, the point where the orbit of a heavenly body intersects the ecliptic. The node encountered by a body in its northward passage is called its **ascending node;** in its southward passage, the **descending** or **setting node. 5** *Anat.* A firm, flattened tumor on a bone, tendon, or the like. **6** The plot of a story or drama. **7** *Physics* A stationary point, line, or plane in a vibrating body where the amplitude of a wave is virtually zero. [<L *nodus* knot] —**no·dal** (nōd′l) *adj.*

nod·i·cal (nod′i·kəl, nō′di-) *adj. Astron.* Of or pertaining to the nodes.

no·dose (nō′dōs, nō·dōs′) *adj.* Having nodes or knots; knobby. [<L *nodosus* full of knots < *nodus* a knot] —**no·dos·i·ty** (nō·dos′ə·tē) *n.*

nod·u·lar (noj′ə·lər) *adj.* Relating to, shaped like, or containing nodules.

nod·ule (noj′o͞ol) *n.* **1** A little knot, lump, or node. **2** *Bot.* A tubercle. [<L *nodulus,* dim. of *nodus* a knot] —**nod′uled** *adj.*

nod·u·lose (noj′ə·lōs) *adj.* Having nodules. Also **nod′u·lous** (-ləs).

no·dus (nō′dəs) *n.* **1** A knot. **2** Node (def. 5). **3** A difficulty; complexity; knotty point. [<L]

No·el (nō′əl) A masculine personal name. Also *Fr.* **No·ël** (nō·el′). [<L, Christmas]

No·ël (nō·el′) *n.* **1** Christmas. **2** A carol: also spelled *Nowel.* [<OF <L *natalis* birthday]

no·e·mat·ic (nō′ə·mat′ik) *adj.* Of or pertaining to mental processes. [<Gk. *noema* thought]

no·e·sis (nō·ē′sis) *n.* **1** Comprehension by the intellect alone. **2** Cognition, especially as applied to sources of self-evident knowledge. [<Gk. *noēsis* intelligence< *noeein* think]

no·et·ic (nō·et′ik) *adj.* Pertaining to the mind; intellectual. [<Gk. *noētikos* intelligent]

no–fault (nō′fôlt′) *adj.* **1** Describing or pertaining to a form of motor vehicle insurance that insures the policyholder against his own loss rather than against loss to others he may have caused, and in which the assignment of blame is ordinarily irrelevant. **2** Not based on the assignment of blame: *no–fault* divorce.

nog[1] (nog) *n.* **1** A peg or a square or oblong block of wood. **2** A wooden pin driven through a wall. [? Var. of ME *knag* a peg < LG]

nog[2] (nog) *n.* **1** A strong ale. **2** Eggnog. Also **nogg.** [<dial. E]

nog·gin (nog′in) *n.* **1** A small mug, or its contents. **2** A liquid measure equal to about a gill. **3** *Slang* A person's head. [Origin uncertain]

nog·ging (nog′ing) *n.* **1** Pieces of wood inserted in a masonry wall, to stiffen it, or upon which to nail finishing material. **2** Brick filling in the interstices of a frame wall. [<NOG[1]]

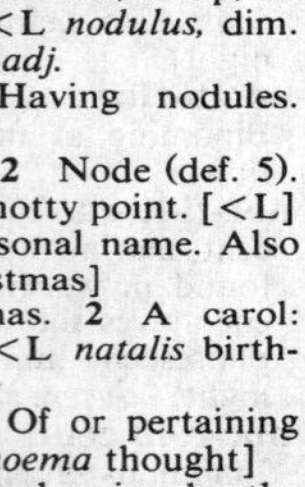
NOGGING
As seen in half-timbered gable.

no go An impasse; balk. Also **no–go** (nō′gō′) *n.*

No·gu·chi (nō·go͞o·chē), **Hideyo,** 1876–1928, Japanese bacteriologist active in the United States.

Noh (nō) See No.

no–hit (nō′hit′) *adj.* Pertaining to a baseball game in which a pitcher allows no base hits to the other team.

no–hit·ter (nō′hit′ər) *n.* A no–hitgame in baseball.

no·how (nō′hou′) *adv. Illit.* In no way; not by any means.

noil (noil) *n.* **1** Short-staple fibers combed out from long-staple during the combing process in preparing wool or cotton yarns. **2** Waste silk produced in the manufacture of spun silk. [Origin uncertain]

noise (noiz) *n.* **1** A sound of any kind, especially a loud or a disturbing sound. **2** In communications, the confused sound caused by discordant vibrations or undesirable random voltages in a channel. **3** *Obs.* Clamor; discussion; gossip. —*v.* **noised, nois·ing** *v.t.* **1** To spread by rumor or report; often with *about* or *abroad.* —*v.i.* **2** To be noisy; make a noise. **3** To talk in a loud and voluble manner. [<OF *noyse;* ult. origin uncertain]
Synonyms: blare, clamor, clatter, din, hubbub, jangle, outcry, racket, rattle, roar, tumult, uproar. See SOUND[1], TUMULT. *Antonyms:* calmness, noiselessness, peace, quiet, silence.

noise·less (noiz′lis) *adj.* Causing or making no noise; silent. —**noise′less·ly** *adv.* —**noise′·less·ness** *n.*

noise level In acoustics, that value of noise which may be expressed in decibels with reference to a specified frequency range.

noise·mak·er (noiz′mā′kər) *n.* **1** A horn, bell, or other device for making noise at celebrations. **2** One who or that which makes noise.

noi·some (noi′səm) *adj.* **1** Very offensive, particularly to the sense of smell. **2** Injurious; noxious. [<*noy,* aphetic var. of ANNOY + -SOME] —**noi′some·ly** *adv.*—**noi′some·ness** *n.*
Synonyms: deadly, deleterious, destructive, detrimental, fetid, foul, harmful, hurtful, insalubrious, mischievous, noxious, pernicious, pestiferous, pestilential, poisonous, unhealthful, unwholesome. *Noxious* is a stronger word than *noisome,* as referring to that which is injurious or *destructive. Noisome* denotes that which is disgusting, especially to the sense of smell; as, the *noisome* stench of *noxious* gases. *Antonyms:* beneficial, healthful, invigorating, salubrious, salutary, wholesome.

nois·y (noi′zē) *adj.* **nois·i·er, nois·i·est 1** Making a loud noise. **2** Characterized by noise. —**nois′i·ly** *adv.* —**nois′i·ness** *n.*
Synonyms: blatant, blustering, boisterous, brawling, clamorous, obstreperous, riotous, tumultuous, turbulent, uproarious, vociferous. *Antonyms:* dumb, hushed, inaudible, mute, noiseless, quiet, silent, still.

no–knock (nō′nok′) *adj.* Designating the lawful entry by force, without warning, into a suspect's living quarters by police officers.

no·lens vo·lens (nō′lenz vō′lenz) *Latin* Unwilling or willing; undecided; willy–nilly.

no·li–me–tan·ge·re (nō′lī·mē·tan′jə·rē) *n.* **1** A warning not to touch or meddle with. **2** Touch–me–not (def. 1). **3** The squirting cucumber. **4** A picture showing Jesus as he appeared to Mary Magdalene after his resurrection: so called from his words of warning to her. **5** Any person or thing not to be touched or interfered with. **6** *Pathol.* Rodent ulcer. [<L *noli me tangere* touch me not]

noll (nol, nôl) *n. Obs.* The head. [OE *hnoll* crown of the head]

nol·le pros·e·qui (nol′ē pros′ə·kwī) *Law* An entry of record in a civil or criminal case, to signify that the plaintiff or prosecutor will not press it. Abbr. *nol. pros.* [<L, be unwilling to prosecute]

no·lo con·ten·de·re (nō′lō kən·ten′də·rē) *Law* A plea by a defendant in a criminal action, which, while not an admission of guilt, has the same legal effect as regards the proceedings on the indictment. Such a plea does not debar a defendant from denying the truth of the charges in any other proceedings arising out of the same matter. [<L, I am unwilling to contend]

nol–pros (nol′pros′) *v.t.* **–prossed, –pros·sing** *Law* To subject to a nolle prosequi. [Short for NOLLE PROSEQUI]

nom (nôn) *n. French* Name.

nom– Var. of NOMO–.

no·ma (nō′mə) *n. Pathol.* Gangrenous inflammation of the mouth, especially in young children. [<NL <Gk. *nomē*< *nomein* feed]

no·mad (nō′mad, nom′ad) *adj.* Nomadic. —*n.* A rover; one of an unsettled, wandering people, tribe, or race. [<L *nomas, -adis* <Gk. *nomas* <*nomein* pasture, feed] —**no′mad·ism** *n.*

no·mad·ic (nō·mad′ik) *adj.* **1** Pertaining to nomads; roaming. **2** Unsettled. Also **no·mad′i·cal.** —**no·mad′i·cal·ly** *adv.*

no man's land 1 Waste or unowned land; specifically, a plot of land situated beyond the limits of the north wall of the City of London, where executions took place in the 14th century. **2** In warfare, the land between the opposing armies.

nom·arch (nom′ärk) *n.* The governor of a nomarchy or nome. [<Gk. *nomarchēs* < *nomos* province + *archein* rule]

nom·ar·chy (nom′är·kē) *n. pl.* **·chies** A province of modern Greece; a nome.

nom·bles (nom′bəlz, num′-) See NUMBLES.

nom·bril (nom′bril) *n. Her.* The navel point, between the fess point and the base point on an escutcheon. See illustration under ESCUTCHEON. [<F <OF *lombril,* ult. <L *umbilicus* navel]

nom de guerre (nôn də gâr′) *French* An assumed name; a pseudonym; literally, a war name.

nom de plume (nom′ də plo͞om′, *Fr.* nôn də plüm′) A pen name; a writer's assumed name. [<F *nom* a name + *de* of + *plume* a pen]

nome[1] (nōm) *n.* A province or department of ancient Egypt or modern Greece. Also, **Greek,** *nomos.* [<Gk. *nomos* province]

Nome (nōm) A city in western Alaska; 12 miles west of **Cape Nome,** a promontory of the southern Seward Peninsula.

no·men·cla·tor (nō′mən·klā′tər) *n.* **1** One who assigns or announces names. **2** One who gives names; a scientific classifier. [<L <*nomen* name + *calare* call]

no·men·cla·ture (nō′mən·klā′chər, nō·men′klə-) *n.* A system of names, as used in any art or science, or by any recognized group, school, system, or authority. [<L *nomenclatura* list of names]

nom·i·nal (nom′ə·nəl) *adj.* **1** Of or pertaining to a name or names. **2** Existing in name only; not actual: a *nominal* peace. **3** So slight or inconsiderable as to be hardly worth naming; trifling: a *nominal* sum. **4** Consisting of or containing names: a *nominal* roll. **5** Assigned to a person by name, as stocks or shares. **6** *Gram.* **a** Pertaining to or like a noun or nouns. **b** Functioning as a noun or nouns. [<L *nominalis* <*nomen* name]

nom·i·nal·ism (nom′ə·nəl·iz′əm) *n. Philos.* The doctrine that abstract or generic conceptions, or universals, have no basis or representation in reality but are names only, and that only individual objects exist: opposed to *realism.* Compare CONCEPTUALISM. —**nom′i·nal·ist** *adj. & n.* —**nom′i·nal·is′tic** *adj.*

nom·i·nal·ly (nom′ə·nəl·ē) *adv.* In a nominal manner; in name only: opposed to *really, actually.*

nominal wages See REAL WAGES.

nom·i·nate (nom′ə·nāt) *v.t.* **·nat·ed, ·nat·ing 1** To name as a candidate for elective office. **2** To appoint to some office or duty. **3** *Obs.* To name; entitle. —*adj.* **1** Nominated. **2** Having a legal or particular name. [<L *nominatus,* pp. of *nominare* <*nomen, -inis* a name] —**nom′i·na′tor** *n.*

nom·i·na·tion (nom′ə·nā′shən) *n.* **1** The act of nominating; the fact or condition of being nominated. **2** The power of appointment, as of a clergyman to a benefice. —**direct nomination** A method of nominating candidates for office by the direct votes of the people instead of by means of a representative convention.

nom·i·na·tive (nom′ə·nə·tiv, nom′ə·nā′tiv) *adj.* **1** *Gram.* Designating the case of the subject of a finite verb, or of a word agreeing with, or in apposition to the subject; in English grammar, subjective. **2** Appointed by nomination; nominated. **3** Bearing the name of a person, as an invitation or a share of stock. —*n. Gram.* **1** The nominative case. **2** A word in this case.

nom·i·nee (nom′ə·nē′) *n.* **1** One who receives a nomination. **2** A designated person on whose life another's annuity depends.

no·mism (nō′miz·əm) *n.* Strict adherence to religious or moral law. [<Gk. *nomos* law] —**no·mis·tic** (nō·mis′tik) *adj.*

nomo– *combining form* Law; custom; usage: *nomocracy.* Also, before vowels, *nom–.* [<Gk. *nomos* law]

no·mo·gen·e·sis (nō′mə·jen′ə·sis) *n. Biol.* The doctrine which attributes all evolutionary change in plants and animals to the operation of predetermined and unchanging laws. —**no′·mo·ge·net′ic** (-jə·net′ik) *adj.*

no·mo·graph (nō′mə·graf, -gräf) *n.* **1** *Math.* A graph consisting of graduated scales for two or more interrelated variables, so arranged that a straight line joining given values of the two known variables will cut the scale of the third variable at the value sought; an isopleth. Also called **no′mo·gram.** **2** Any graphic representation of numerical relations.

no·mog·ra·phy (nō·mog′rə·fē) *n.* **1** The art of drafting laws, or a treatise on that art. **2** *Math.* A method for the graphic representation on a plane surface of the relations between two or more variables; the science and technique of graphic computation. —**no·mo·graph·ic** (nō′mə·graf′ik) or **·i·cal** *adj.*

no·mol·o·gy (nō·mol′ə·jē) *n.* **1** The science that treats of law and lawmaking. **2** The branch of any science that treats of the laws that explain its phenomena, as in biology, psychology, etc. — **nom·o·log·i·cal** (nom′ə·loj′i·kəl) *adj.* — **no·mol′o·gist** *n.*

no more 1 Dead; gone. **2** Nothing more: I'll say *no more.* **3** No longer: It rains *no more.* **4** Never again: She'll sing *no more.* **5** Not to any greater extent: We could *no more* see than the blind. **6** Neither: I did not speak, *no more* did he.

no·mos (nō′mos) See NOME.

nom·o·thet·ic (nom′ə·thet′ik) *adj.* **1** Giving or enacting laws. **2** Nomistic. **3** Pertaining to a science of universal or general laws. Also **nom′o·thet′i·cal.** [< Gk. *nomothetikos* < *nomos* law + *tithēnai* establish]

No·mu·ra (nō·mōō·rä), **Kichisaburo,** 1877–1964, Japanese admiral and diplomat.

-nomy *combining form* The science or systematic study of: *astronomy, economy.* [< Gk. *nomos* law]

non- *prefix* Not. [< L *non* not]
♦ Non- is the Latin negative adverb adopted as an English prefix. It denotes in general simple negation or absence of, as in *non-attendance,* lack of attendance. Compare UN- and IN-, which are more commonly antithetical and emphatic. Numerous words beginning with *non-* are self-explaining, as in the following partial list:

non-absolute	non-conducive
non-absorbable	non-Congressional
non-absorbent	non-connivance
non-abstainer	non-connotative
non-acceptance	non-consent
non-accomplishment	non-consideration
non-acquaintance	non-consumption
non-acquiescence	non-contagious
non-action	non-contentiously
non-active	non-conversion
non-adherence	non-crystallized
non-adherent	non-currency
non-adjacent	non-deliquescent
non-admission	non-delivery
non-adult	non-development
non-aggression	non-discrimination
non-aggressive	non-distribution
non-agreement	non-divisibility
non-agricultural	non-doctrinal
non-alcoholic	non-eficient
non-alienating	non-elastic
non-alienation	non-electric
non-aligned	non-empirical
non-arrival	non-entry
non-Aryan	non-equation
non-attached	non-equilibrium
non-attendance	non-essential
non-attention	non-eternal
non-believing	non-eternity
non-belligerent	non-European
non-Biblical	non-excusable
non-budding	non-execution
non-canonical	non-exempt
non-Catholic	non-exercise
non-Christian	non-existence
non-church	non-existent
non-citizen	non-existing
non-coincident	non-expert
non-collegiate	non-explosive
non-colonial	non-extant
non-combustible	non-factual
non-communicant	non-fatal
non-Communist	non-fiction
non-competitive	non-fictional
non-complaisance	non-financial
non-conception	non-fiscal

non-flammable	non-recognition
non-freedom	non-rectangular
non-freeman	non-regimented
non-fulfilment	non-reigning
non-Hellenic	non-relative
non-householder	non-reproductive
non-human	non-resemblance
non-identity	non-resinous
non-improvement	non-resistant
non-inflammable	non-resisting
non-instruction	non-scheduled
non-interference	non-scientific
non-interrupted	non-sectarian
non-liberation	non-sensitive
non-literary	non-sentient
non-luminous	non-separable
non-magnetic	non-sexual
non-marital	non-sexually
non-material	non-society
non-materiality	non-specie
non-member	non-spiritous
non-membership	non-sporting
non-metalliferous	non-standard
non-modulated	non-subscriber
non-natural	non-subscribing
non-nitrogenous	non-supporter
non-nutritive	non-supporting
non-observance	non-syllabic
non-officially	non-sympathizer
non-operative	non-sympathy
non-orthodox	non-tax
non-oxidating	non-technical
non-parallel	non-terminating
non-parasitic	non-toxic
non-paying	non-truth
non-payment	non-understanding
non-performance	non-validity
non-poisonous	non-venomous
non-professional	non-volatile
non-profit	non-volition
non-protection	non-voluntary
non-Protestant	non-vortical
non-publication	non-voter
non-punishment	non-voting
non-reactive	non-worker
non-recital	non-working

non·age (non′ij, nō′nij) *n.* The period of legal minority; immaturity. [< NON- + AGE]

non·a·ge·nar·i·an (non′ə·jə·nâr′ē·ən, nō′nə-) *adj.* Pertaining to the nineties in age. —*n.* A person between the ages of ninety and a hundred. [< L *nonagenarius* of ninety]

non·a·gon (non′ə·gon) *n.* A nine-sided polygon. [< L *nonus* ninth + Gk. *gōnia* angle]

non·ane (non′ān) *n.* *Chem.* A liquid hydrocarbon, C_9H_{20}, of the methane series. [< L *nonus* ninth; because ninth in the series]

no·na·no·ic acid (nō′nə·nō′ik) Pelargonic acid.

non·ap·pear·ance (non′ə·pir′əns) *n.* Failure to appear, especially failure to appear in court in answer to a summons.

non·bore·safe (non′bôr′sāf, -bōr′-) *adj. Mil.* Designating a type of fuze that does not have a safety device to prevent explosion of the burster charge of a projectile while it is in the bore of the gun.

nonce (nons) *n.* Present time or occasion. —**for the nonce** For the present time or occasion. [ME *for then ones* for the one (occasion), misread as *for the nones*]

nonce word A word coined for one occasion.

non·cha·lance (non′shə·ləns, non′shə·läns′) *n.* Jaunty indifference or unconcern.

non·cha·lant (non′shə·lənt, non′shə·länt′) *adj.* Without concern; casual; indifferent. [< F, orig. ppr. of *nonchaloir* < L *non calere* not be warm, be indifferent] —**non′cha·lant·ly** *adv.*

non·com (non′kom′) *Colloq. adj.* Non-commissioned. —*n.* A non-commissioned officer.

non·com·bat·ant (non′kəm·bat′ənt, -kom′bə·tənt, -kum′-) *n.* **1** One who is not a combatant; especially, one attached to a military force but whose duties do not require that he fight, as a chaplain or medical officer. **2** Anyone not connected with the military service in time of war; a civilian.

non·com·mis·sioned (non′kə·mish′ənd) *adj.* Not holding a military commission.

non-commissioned officer See under OFFICER.

non·com·mit·tal (non′kə·mit′l) *adj.* Not committal; not having or expressing a decided opinion. —**non′·com·mit′tal·ly** *adv.*

non·com·pli·ance (non′kəm·plī′əns) *n.* Failure or neglect to comply. —**non′·com·pli′ant** *adj. & n.*

non com·pos men·tis (non kom′pəs men′tis) *Latin* Not of sound mind; mentally unbalanced: often shortened to **non compos.**

non·con·cur (non′kən·kûr′) *v.t.* **-curred, ·cur·ring** To reject, as a bill or resolution.

non·con·duc·tor (non′kən·duk′tər) *n.* A substance or material that offers resistance to the passage of some form of energy: a *non-conductor* of heat or electricity; an insulator or dielectric. —**non′·con·duct′ing** *adj.*

non·con·form·ist (non′kən·fôr′mist) *n.* One who does not conform to established usage, as in religion; specifically, a person, especially a Protestant clergyman, refusing to conform to the Book of Common Prayer where the Church of England is established by law; a dissenter. — **non′con·form′ing** *adj.* —**non′con·for′mi·ty** (-fôr′mə·tē) *n.*

non con·stat (non kon′stat) *Latin* It does not follow.

non·co·op·er·a·tion (non′kō·op′ə·rā′shən) *n.* Refusal to cooperate; specifically, civil resistance to a government through disobedience, boycotting of institutions, etc. —**non′·co·op′er·a·tive** (kō·op′rə·tiv, -ə·rā′tiv) *adj.* —**non′·co·op′er·a′tion·ist** *n.* —**non′·co·op′er·a′tor** *n.*

non·de·script (non′di·skript) *adj.* Not distinctive enough to be described. —*n.* A person or thing of no particular type, kind, or character: often used disparagingly. [< NON- + L *descriptus,* pp. of *describere.* See DESCRIBE.]

non·dis·junc·tion (non′dis·jungk′shən) *n. Biol.* The failure of paired chromosomes to separate during cell mitosis.

non·dis·tinc·tive (non′dis·tingk′tiv) *adj.* **1** Not distinctive. **2** *Ling.* Non-relevant.

non·du·ty (non′dōō′tē, -dyōō′-) *adj. Mil.* Designating the status of an enlisted man or officer who, for any reason, is not available for duty with his unit or command.

none (nun) *pron.* **1** Not one; no one. **2** No or not one specifically named person or thing: A bad book is better than *none.* **3** Not any: That is *none* of her business. **4** (*construed as pl.*) Not any (of the persons or things specified): *None* of them have their drawings finished; *None* of the apples are rotten. —*adv.* In no respect; not at all: *none* the worse for wear. —*adj. Archaic* Not one; no one; no: generally before a vowel: *none* other gods before me. [OE *nān* < *ne* not + *ān* one]

non·ef·fec·tive (non′i·fek′tiv) *adj.* **1** Not effective; inoperative. **2** Unfitted or unavailable for active service or duty in the army or navy: a *non-effective* officer. —*n.* A soldier or sailor unfitted for active service or duty, because of sickness, wounds, or the like.

non·e·go (non·ē′gō, -eg′ō) *n. pl.* **·gos 1** Whatever is not the self, or not of or pertaining to the conscious self; more especially, the object of the conscious ego as opposed to or set over against the ego. **2** The objective or material world.

non·en·ti·ty (non·en′tə·tē) *n. pl.* **·ties 1** A person or thing of no account; a nobody. **2** The negation of being; non-existence. [NON- + ENTITY]

nones (nōnz) *n. pl.* **1** The ninth day before the ides in the Roman calendar. **2** The canonical office, originally recited at 3 p.m., or the ninth hour by ancient Roman reckoning. [< OF < L *nonae* < *nonus* ninth < *novem* nine]

non est (non est) *Latin* It is not; it is wanting; it does not exist.

none·such (nun′such′) *n.* **1** A person or thing having no equal; an unexampled thing: also spelled *nonsuch.* **2** An annual leguminous herb (*Medicago lupulina*) with numerous yellow flowers and pods that turn black: also called *black medic.*

none·the·less (nun′thə·les′) *adv.* In spite of everything; nevertheless. Also **none the less.**

non-Eu·clid·e·an (non′yōō·klid′ē·ən) *adj. Math.* Designating a geometry dealing with a space in which the axioms and postulates of Euclid do not necessarily hold.

non·ex·pend·a·ble (non′ik·spen′də·bəl) *adj.* Designating articles of public property for which there is responsibility and accountability: said especially of war materials which

are not consumed or destroyed by the mere act of use.

non·fea·sance (non·fē′zəns) *n. Law* The nonperformance of some act which one is bound by legal or official duty to perform. Compare MALFEASANCE, MISFEASANCE. **— non·fea′sor** *n.*

non·fer·rous (non·fer′əs) *adj.* Pertaining to or designating any metal other than or not containing iron, as copper, tin, platinum, etc.

non·fi·nite (non·fī′nīt) *adj. Gram. & Logic* **1** Indefinite; at any unspecified time. **2** Limitless but finite, as a Möbius surface. **3** Endless; starting from the point specified and continuing indefinitely in one direction. **4** Infinite; without limits as to space or time. Example: *Continuing* and *extending*, as gerunds or verbal nouns, are called *non-finite* forms or infinitives in *-ing* by the older grammarians of English. **5** *Theol.* Eternal. Example: God *is* (now, ever was, and always will be). The word *is* here exhibits the eternal aspect of the *non-finite* verb. **6** Transcendent: where time is merely another dimension in the space-time continuum. Example: In the statement "Mass implies inertia," the verb *implies* exhibits the transcendent aspect of the *non-finite* tense, indicating that the relationship mass-energy is always true in the space-time multiverse.

non-frat·er·ni·za·tion (non·frat′ər·nə·zā′shən, -nī·zā′-) *n.* A policy pursued by the U.S. Army during and after World War II, forbidding the association of occupying military forces with civilians.

non-ha·la·tion film (non′hā·lā′shən) Film that has been opaqued to prevent reflection.

non-hy·gro·scop·ic (non·hī′grə·skop′ik) *adj.* Having little or no tendency to absorb moisture: a *non-hygroscopic* gunpowder.

no·nil·lion (nō·nil′yən) *n.* A cardinal number: in the French and American system of numeration, denoted by 1 followed by thirty ciphers; in the English system, 1 with fifty-four ciphers. [<F <L *nonus* ninth (< *novem* nine) + F *million* a million] **— no·nil′lionth** (-yənth) *adj.*

non-in·duc·tive (non′in·duk′tiv) *adj. Electr.* Not inductive: applied to a resistance that offers no greater opposition to a varying than to an unvarying current.

non-in·ter·course (non·in′tər·kôrs, -kōrs) *n.* No intercourse: commonly applied to a legal or diplomatic prohibition of commercial intercourse.

Non-Intercourse Act In U.S. history, an Act of Congress, passed in 1809, forbidding all commercial intercourse with England and France.

non-in·ter·ven·tion (non′in·tər·ven′shən) *n.* The state or condition of not interfering; refusal to intervene.

non-in·ter·ven·tion·ist (non′in·tər·ven′shən·ist) *n.* One who advocates a policy of non-intervention.

non-join·der (non·join′dər) *n. Law* An omission to join, as by a person who should be one of a party in an action. Compare MISJOINDER.

non·ju·ror (non·jŏŏr′ər) *n.* **1** A clergyman in England who refused to take the oath of allegiance to William and Mary after the revolution of 1688. **2** A Scottish Presbyterian who refused the oath abjuring the Stuart Pretenders. [<NON- + JUROR, in obs. sense "one who takes an oath"]

non-le·thal (non·lē′thəl) *adj.* Not capable of causing death: a *non-lethal* drug or chemical agent; non-toxic.

non li·cet (non lī′sit) *Latin* It is not lawful.

non li·quet (non lī′kwit, lik′wit) *Latin* The case is not clear.

non-met·al (non·met′l) *n. Chem.* Any element (as oxygen, nitrogen, carbon, sulfur, arsenic, and iodine) which has acid rather than basic properties, and is incapable of forming cations in solution.

non-me·tal·lic (non′mə·tal′ik) *adj.* **1** Not metallic. **2** Pertaining to a non-metal.

non-mor·al (non·môr′əl, -mor′-) *adj.* Having no relation to morals or to ethical conceptions and ideals; not moral or immoral. **— non′-mo·ral′i·ty** (-mō·ral′ə·tē, -mə-) *n.*

non-mo·tile (non·mō′til) *adj.* Incapable of motion of itself.

Non·ni (non′nē′) A river of central Manchuria, flowing 740 miles south to the Sungari.

non-nu·cle·at·ed (non·nōō′klē·ā′tid, -nyōō′-) *adj. Biol.* Not having a nucleus, as a cell.

no-no (nō′nō′) *n. pl.* **-nos** *Colloq.* Something forbidden or very undesirable.

non-ob·jec·tive art (non′əb·jek′tiv) Art that does not attempt to represent the recognizable form or effect of objects as they appear in nature.

non ob·stan·te (non ob·stan′tē) *Latin* Notwithstanding; in spite of.

non om·nis mo·ri·ar (non om′nis môr′ē·är) *Latin* My work will live; literally, I shall not wholly die.

non·pa·reil (non′pə·rel′) *adj.* Of unequaled excellence. **—** *n.* **1** Something of unequaled excellence. **2** *Printing* **a** A size of type between agate and minion: the former and now seldom used name for 6-point type. **b** A 6-point slug. **3** One of various birds of brilliant coloring of the southern United States, especially the painted bunting. **4** A variety of russet apple. [<OF < *non* not (<L) + *pareil* equal <LL *pariculus*, dim. of L *par* equal]

non-par·ous (non·par′əs) *adj.* Not having borne children.

non-par·tic·i·pat·ing (non′pär·tis′ə·pā′ting) *adj.* Not participating, nor conveying the right to participate, in the surplus or profits of an insurance company; pertaining to insurance in which the policyholders are not allowed to participate in the profits.

non-par·ti·san (non·pär′tə·zən) *adj.* Not pertaining or adhering to any established party.

non-pay (non′pā′) *adj.* Designating the status of an enlisted man or officer whose pay is canceled for periods of unauthorized absence.

non·plus (non·plus′, non′plus) *v.t.* **·plused** or **·plussed, ·plus·ing** or **·plus·sing** To bring to a nonplus; baffle; perplex. **—** *n.* A mental standstill; perplexity, especially as causing silence or indecision. [<L *non plus* no further < *non* not + *plus* more]

non pos·su·mus (non pos′ə·məs) *Latin* We cannot; we are not able.

non-pro·duc·tive (non′prə·duk′tiv) *adj.* Not producing: a labor term designating clerical workers, inspectors, etc. **— non′pro·duc′tive·ness** *n.*

non-pros (non·pros′) *v.t.* **-prossed, -pros·sing** *Law* To enter judgment against (a plaintiff who fails to prosecute). [Short for NON PROSEQUITUR]

non pro·seq·ui·tur (non prō·sek′wi·tər) *Law* A judgment entered at common law against a plaintiff who fails to prosecute. Compare NOLLE PROSEQUI. [<L, lit., he does not prosecute]

non-rel·e·vant (non′rel′ə·vənt) *adj.* **1** Not relevant. **2** *Ling.* Denoting those features of a phoneme which do not function to differentiate it from other phonemes in a language, as aspiration in English.

non-rep·re·sen·ta·tion·al (non′rep′ri·zen·tā′·shən·əl) *adj.* Not representational; specifically, denoting a form of art that does not attempt to represent the recognizable form or effect of objects as they appear in nature.

non-res·i·dent (non·rez′ə·dənt) *adj.* Not resident in a place: a *non-resident* landlord. **—** *n.* One not permanently residing in, or systematically absent from, a particular place. **— non-res′i·dence, non-res′i·den·cy** *n.*

non-re·straint (non′ri·strānt′) *n.* Absence of restraint; especially, the treatment of insane persons without using a straitjacket or other physical restraint.

non·rig·id (non·rij′id) *adj. Aeron.* Denoting an airship whose form is maintained by the internal pressure in the gas chambers and ballonets.

non·sense (non′sens, -səns) *n.* **1** That which is without sense, or without good sense; meaningless or ridiculous language; absurd behavior. **2** Things of no importance. **— non·sen′si·cal** *adj.* **— non·sen′si·cal·ly** *adv.* **— non·sen′si·cal·ness** *n.*

non seq·ui·tur (non sek′wə·tər) The fallacy of irrelevant conclusion; an inference that does not follow from the premises. [<L, it does not follow]

non-sked (non′sked′) *Colloq. adj.* Non-scheduled: applied especially to passenger airplane service offered without scheduled flying times and at rates lower than those of the regular scheduled airlines. **—** *n.* Something not operating on or holding to a schedule. [Short for *non-scheduled*]

non·skid (non′skid′) *adj.* Having the surface treaded or corrugated to reduce skidding: said of tires.

non·stop (non′stop′) *adj.* Making, having made, or scheduled to make no stops: a *nonstop* flight; *nonstop* train.

non-stri·at·ed (non·strī′ā·tid) *adj.* Void of striations; without stripes, as muscle fibers.

non·such (nun′such′) See NONESUCH.

non·suit (non′sōōt′) *Law v.t.* To order the dismissal of the suit of. **—** *n.* **1** The abandonment of a suit. **2** A judgment dismissing a suit, when the plaintiff either abandons it or fails to establish a cause of action. [<AF *nonsute*, OF *nonsuite* <*non* not (<L) + *suite*. See SUIT.]

non-sup·port (non′sə·pôrt′, -pōrt′) *n.* Failure or neglect to provide for the support of dependents.

non-un·ion (non·yōōn′yən) *adj.* **1** Not belonging to a trade union. **2** Not employing or recognizing any trade union or its members. **—** *n.* Lack of union or joining: said specifically of broken bones that do not knit properly.

non-un·ion·ism (non·yōōn′yən·iz′əm) *n.* Non-adherence or opposition to the establishment or the principles of trade unions. **— non-un′ion·ist** *n.*

non·u·ple (non′yə·pəl) *adj.* Consisting of nine; having nine parts or members; ninefold; also, taken by nines. **—** *n.* A number or sum nine times as great as another. [<F <L *nonus* ninth; on analogy with *quadruple, quintuple,* etc.]

non·u·pli·cate (non·yōō′plə·kit) *adj.* **1** Ninefold. **2** Raised to the ninth power. [<L *nonus* ninth; on analogy with *duplicate*]

non-us·er (non·yōō′zər) *n. Law* A continued omission to assert or exercise some right or privilege, whereby the right or privilege is lost.

non-vi·a·ble (non·vī′ə·bəl) *adj.* Having no capacity to survive independently: said especially of a fetus.

non-violent (non′vī′ə·lənt) *adj.* **1** Free from violence: a *non-violent* demonstration. **2** Not given to or believing in violence. **— non′-vi′o·lence** *n.* **— non′-vi′o·lent·ly** *adv.*

non-white (non′hwīt′) *adj.* **1** Not white. **2** Being other than Caucasian. **—** *n.* A non-white person, as a Negro.

noo·dle[1] (nōōd′l) *n. Slang* **1** A simpleton: also **noo′dle·head′**. **2** The head. [Origin unknown]

noo·dle[2] (nōōd′l) *n.* A thin strip of dried dough, usually made with egg. [<G *nudel*]

nook (nŏŏk) *n.* A narrow and retired place, as in an angle; a recess, as in a garden. [ME *noke* corner, ? <Scand.]

noon (nōōn) *n.* **1** That time of day when the sun is on the meridian; the middle of the day; in an exact sense, 12 o'clock in the daytime. **2** The highest point of any period or career: the *noon* of life. **3** Originally, the ninth hour after sunrise, or about 3 o'clock p.m; midway between 12 o'clock and sunset; hence, the canonical hour of nones. **4** *pl.* A noontime repast. [OE *non* <L *nona (hora)* ninth (hour)]

noon·day (nōōn′dā′) *n.* The middle of the day. **—** *adj.* Pertaining to midday.

no one Not anyone; no person.

noon·ing (nōō′ning) *n. Archaic* **1** A rest taken at noon. **2** A midday meal. **3** Noon.

noon mark Formerly, a mark made in a familiar place, on a floor, doorstep, etc., where a certain shadow fell at noon; hence, noon.

noon·tide (nōōn′tīd′) *n.* **1** The time of midday. **2** The period of culmination: the *noontide* of glory. **3** The position of the moon at midnight; midnight. **—** *adj.* Of, occurring at, or characteristic of noon: *noontide* glory. Also **noon′time′** (-tīm′).

noose (nōōs) *n.* **1** A loop furnished with a running knot, as in a hangman's halter or a snare; slipknot. **2** Anything that restricts one's freedom. **—** *v.t.* **noosed, noos·ing 1** To capture or secure with a noose. **2** To make a noose in or with. [<Provençal *nous* <L *nodus* a knot]

Noot·ka fir (nōōt′kə) *Canadian* The Douglas fir.

Nootka Sound An inlet of the Pacific in western Vancouver Island, Canada.

no·pal (nō′pəl) *n.* **1** Any one of various cacti (especially genus *Nopalea*), as *N. cochenillifer*, used for rearing the cochineal insect. **2** A prickly pear. [<Sp. <Nahuatl *nopalli*]

nope (nōp) *adv. Slang* No.

nor[1] (nôr) *conj.* And not; likewise not. ◆ *Nor* is used, chiefly, as a correlative of a preceding negative, usually *neither* or *not.* It may be used, as for poetical effect, without a correlative: We sat still, *nor* stirred. In older writing and in poetry, it often appears as an introductory negative instead of *neither:* He heeded *nor* praise *nor* blame. [Contraction of ME *nother* neither]

nor[2] (nôr) *conj. Brit. Dial.* Than: He does better *nor* you.

nor- *combining form Chem.* A normal or a parent compound. [< NORMAL]

No·ra (nôr′ə, nō′rə) A feminine personal name; diminutive of ELEANOR, HONORA, LEONORA. Also **No′rah.**

no·ra·ghe (nə-rä′gā) See NURAGH.

Nord (nôr) The northernmost department of France, on the Belgian border; 2,229 square miles; capital, Lille.

Nor·dau (nôr′dou), **Max Simon,** 1849–1923, German physician, author, and Zionist leader born in Hungary: original surname *Südfeld.*

Nor·den·skjöld (nōōr′dən-shœld), **Baron Nils Adolf Erik,** 1832–1901, Swedish Arctic explorer.

Nor·den·skjöld Sea (nōōr′dən-shœld) A former name for the LAPTEV SEA.

Nord·hau·sen (nôrt′hou-zən) A city in the former state of Thuringia, western East Germany.

Nordhausen acid Fuming sulfuric acid. [from *Nordhausen,* where formerly made]

Nor·dic (nôr′dik) *adj. Anthropol.* Pertaining or belonging to the blond-haired subdivision of the Caucasian ethnic stock, inhabiting Scandinavia, Scotland, and England, and to other Germanic peoples of northwestern Europe. —*n.* A member of this subdivision. [< F *nordique* < *nord* north]

Nord·kyn (nōr′kün), **Cape,** A cape in northern Norway on the Arctic Ocean, the northernmost point of the European mainland. Compare NORTH CAPE.

Nore (nōr), **The** An anchorage, lighthouse, and sandbank in the Thames estuary, SE England.

nor′·east·er (nôr-ēs′tər) See NORTHEASTER.

nor·ep·i·neph·rine (nôr′ep′ə-nef′rin, -rēn) *n.* A hormone, $C_6H_3(OH)_2 \cdot CHOH \cdot CH_2 \cdot NH_2$, that as a transmitter of nerve signals and as a vasoconstrictor.

Nor·folk (nôr′fək) **1** A county of eastern England; 2,054 square miles; county town, Norwich. **2** A port on the Elizabeth River south of Hampton Roads in SE Virginia; site of a United States naval base.

Norfolk Island An island dependency of Australia north of New Zealand; 13 square miles.

Norfolk jacket A loose-fitting jacket, with side pockets, belt and two box pleats at the back and front, worn in shooting, fishing, etc. Also **Norfolk coat.**

Nor·ge (nôr′gə) The Norwegian name for NORWAY.

nor·gine (nôr′jēn, -jin) *n.* Algin.

no·ri·a (nō′rē-ə) *n.* An undershot water wheel having buckets on its rim: utilized to raise water in the Levant, Spain, etc.: introduced from ancient Persia, and often called *Persian wheel.* [< Sp. < Arabic *nā′ūrah*]

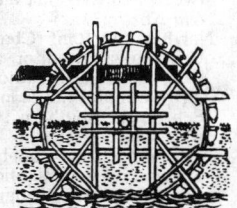

NORIA

Nor·i·cum (nôr′i-kəm, nor′-) An ancient country and Roman province south of the Danube, corresponding to southern Austria.

Nor·land (nôr′lənd) *n. Poetic* Northland; also, northlander. —**Nor′land·er** *n.*

norm (nôrm) *n.* **1** A rule or authoritative standard; a model, type, pattern, or value considered as representative of a specified group. **2** *Psychol.* The average or median of performance in a given function or test, regarded as a standard for the group concerned. **3** *Stat.* The mode. **4** *Geol.* The theoretical standard of chemical composition of igneous rocks, expressed in terms of

oxides: distinguished from *mode.* [< L *norma* rule]

Nor·ma (nôr′mə) A southern constellation. See CONSTELLATION.

Nor·ma (nôr′ma) A feminine personal name. [< L, pattern]

nor·mal (nôr′məl) *adj.* **1** In accordance with an established law or principle; conforming to a type or standard; regular; natural. **2** Constituting a standard; model. **3** *Math.* Of, pertaining to, or constituting a normal; perpendicular. **4** Average; mean. **5** *Chem.* **a** Denoting a molecular structure based on an unbranched chain of carbon atoms. **b** Denoting a salt containing no replaceable hydrogen or hydroxide radical. **c** Denoting an aqueous solution containing one gram equivalent of the active solute in one liter of solution. **6** *Biol.* Designating a condition not exposed to or modified by special experimental treatment. **7** *Psychol.* Well adjusted to the outside world; without undue mental tensions. —*n.* **1** *Math.* **a** A perpendicular; specifically, a perpendicular to a curve or curved surface; a straight line perpendicular to a tangent line or plane at the point of tangency. **b** The intercept, on the normal line, between the curve and either the X-axis or the center of curvature. **2** A common or natural condition. **3** A usual or accepted rule or process. **4** The average or mean value of observed quantities. **5** An abbreviated expression for normal temperature, volume, etc. [< L *normalis* < *norma* rule] —**nor·mal·i·ty** (nôr·mal′ə-tē) *n.* —**nor′mal·ly** *adv.* —**nor′mal·ness** *n.*

Synonyms (adj.): common, natural, ordinary, regular, typical, usual. That which is *natural* is according to nature; that which is *normal* is according to the standard or rule which is observed or claimed to prevail in nature; a deformity may be *natural,* symmetry is *normal;* the *normal* color of the crow is black, while the *normal* color of the sparrow is gray, but one is as *natural* as the other. *Typical* refers to such an assemblage of qualities as makes the specimen, genus, etc., a type of some more comprehensive group, while *normal* is more commonly applied to the parts, qualities, etc, of a single object; the specimen was *typical;* color, size, and other characteristics *normal.* The *regular* is that which is steady and constant, as opposed to that which is fitful and changeable; the *normal* action of the heart is *regular.* That which is *common* or *usual* is shared by a great number of persons or things. See COMMON, GENERAL, NATURAL, USUAL. *Antonyms:* abnormal, exceptional, irregular, monstrous, rare, uncommon, unprecedented, unusual.

normal class *Mineral.* The class of highest symmetry in each crystal system; the holohedral class.

nor·mal·cy (nôr′məl-sē) *n.* The state or quality of being normal; normality. Compare NORMAL *n.* (def. 2).

normal distribution *Stat.* The frequency of occurrence of a given series of data for each change in an independent variable: usually represented by a bell-shaped curve.

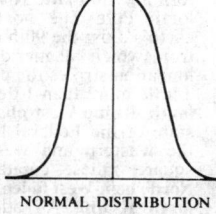

NORMAL DISTRIBUTION CURVE

nor·mal·ize (nôr′məl-īz) *v.t.* **-ized, ·iz·ing** **1** To make normal; reduce to a standard or normal state or form. **2** *Metall.* To heat (steel) above its critical range and hold it at a given temperature for a stated time before allowing it to cool in still air. —**nor′mal·i·za′tion** *n.* —**nor′mal·iz′er** *n.*

normal school A school for the training of secondary school graduates to become teachers.

normal spin *Aeron.* A tailspin which is continued voluntarily by the pilot.

normal value The average of values over a long period.

Nor·man (nôr′mən) *adj.* Pertaining to Normandy or to the Normans. —*n.* **1** A native of

Normandy. See ANGLO-NORMAN, NORSEMAN, NORTHMAN. **2** Norman French. [< OF *Normans,* plural of *Normant* Northman]

Nor·man (nôr′mən) A masculine personal name. [< Gmc., northman]

Nor·man (nôr′mən) An erroneous name for PERCHERON.

Nor·man (nôr′mən), **Montagu Collet,** 1871–1950, first Baron Norman of St. Clare, English financier.

Norman architecture The form assumed by Romanesque architecture in Normandy and as developed in England: characterized by the round arch, barrel vault, and massive construction. Also **Norman style.**

Norman Coast See MURMAN COAST.

Norman Conquest The subjugation of England by William of Normandy after the Battle of Hastings in 1066.

Nor·man·dy (nôr′mən-dē) A region and former province of NW France, comprising Cotentin peninsula and the region to the SE and east.

Norman French The dialect of French spoken by the Norman conquerors in England: also called *Anglo-French, Anglo-Norman.*

Nor·man·ize (nôr′mən-īz) *v.t. & v.i.* To make or become Norman in style, customs, character, etc. —**Nor′man·i·za′tion** *n.*

nor·ma·tive (nôr′mə-tiv) *adj.* Pertaining to, based upon, or establishing a norm, especially a norm assumed to have the prescriptive value of a standard or rule of usage: *normative* grammar. Distinguished from *empirical.* [< NORM + -ATIVE]

normative science A department of knowledge which studies the phenomena and principles of human conduct with a view to establishing standards of value and norms of procedure, as politics, ethics, and esthetics: distinguished from *descriptive science, exact science.*

Norn (nôrn) *n. pl.* **Nor·nir** (nôr′nir) In Norse mythology, one of the three giant goddesses, Urd, Verdandi, and Skuld (past, present, and future), who disposed of the destinies of men and gods.

nor·nic·o·tine (nôr·nik′ə-tēn, -tin) *n. Chem.* A colorless, liquid alkaloid, $C_9H_{12}N_2$, found in the leaves of certain varieties of tobacco and having about half the toxicity of nicotine. [< NOR- + NICOTINE]

Nor·ris (nôr′is, nor′-), **Charles Gilman,** 1881–1945, U.S. novelist; brother of Frank. —**Frank,** 1870–1902, U.S. novelist and journalist. —**George William,** 1861–1944, U.S. statesman and legislator; senator from Nebraska 1913–43. —**Kathleen,** 1880–1966, U.S. novelist; wife of Charles.

Nor·ris Reservoir (nôr′is, nor′-) An artificial lake (53 square miles) formed by Norris Dam, the first major dam (1936) of the Tennessee Valley Authority.

Norr·kö·ping (nôr′chœ·ping) A port in SE Sweden.

Norse (nôrs) *adj.* **1** Scandinavian. **2** West Scandinavian, i.e., Norwegian, Icelandic, and Faroese. —*n.* **1** The Scandinavians or West Scandinavians collectively: with *the.* **2** The Scandinavian or North Germanic group of the Germanic languages; specifically, the language of Norway. **3** The West Scandinavian languages. —**Old Norse** The ancestor of the North Germanic languages, best represented in the literature of the period (before 1500) by Old Icelandic; Old Scandinavian. *Abbr.* ON [Prob. < Du. *Noorsch* a Norwegian, var. of *Noordsch* < *noord* north + *-sch* -ISH]

Norse·man (nôrs′mən) *n. pl.* **·men** (-mən) A Scandinavian of Viking times.

north (nôrth) *n.* **1** One of the four cardinal points of the compass; the direction on the left side of a person facing the rising sun, and opposite to the *south.* For this and other points of the compass, see illustration under COMPASS CARD. **2** Any region north of a given point. **3** *Poetic* The north wind. —*adj.* **1** Lying toward or in the north; northern; boreal. **2** Issuing from or inhabiting the north. **3** Facing or proceeding toward the north. —*adv.* Toward the north; northward. [OE]

North (nôrth) *n.* **1** That portion of the United States north of Maryland, the Ohio River, and

---

add,āce,câre,pälm; end,ēven; it,īce; odd,ōpen,ôrder; tŏŏk,pōōl; up,bûrn; ə = a in *above,* e in *sicken,* i in *clarity,* o in *melon,* u in *focus* ; yōō = u in *fuse,* oi,oil; ou,pout; ch,check; g,go; ng,ring; th,thin; ŧħ,this; zh,vision. Foreign sounds à,œ,ü,kh,ṅ; and ◆: see page xx. < from; + plus; ? possibly.

Missouri: the Free States opposed to the Confederacy (the South) in the Civil War. **2** The part of England north of the Humber.

North (nôrth), **Christopher** See WILSON, JOHN. —**Lord Frederick,** 1732–92, second earl of Guilford, British prime minister at the start of the American Revolution. —**Sir Thomas,** 1535–1603?, English author.

North Albanian Alps A mountain group at the southern end of the Dinaric Alps on the Albanian-Yugoslav border; highest peak, 8,714 feet.

North America The northern continent of the western hemisphere; 8,443,600 square miles. —**North American** adj. & n.

North American Indian An Indian of any of the tribes formerly inhabiting North America north of Mexico, now the United States and Canada.

North·amp·ton (nôr·thamp'tən) **1** A county in south central England; 914 square miles; county town, Northampton. Also **North·amp'ton·shire** (-shir). **2** A city in western Massachusetts.

North Borneo a former British crown colony comprising the northern part of Borneo and adjacent islands; now incorporated in Malaysia as Sabah: also *British North Borneo.*

north·bound (nôrth'bound') adj. Going northward. Also **north'bound'.**

North Brabant A province of southern Netherlands; 1,894 square miles; capital, s'Hertogenbosch.

north by east One point east of north on the mariner's compass. See COMPASS CARD.

north by west One point west of north on the mariner's compass. See COMPASS CARD.

North Cape A cape on a Norwegian island in the Barents Sea, popular considered the northernmost point of Europe. Compare NORDKYN, CAPE.

North Car·o·li·na (kar'ə·lī'nə) A SE State of the United States on the Atlantic; 52,712 square miles; capital, Raleigh; entered the Union Nov. 21, 1789, one of the thirteen original States; nickname, *Tarheel State:* abbr. NC —**North Car'o·lin'i·an** (-lin'ē·ən)

North Channel A strait between Scotland and NE Ireland connecting the Irish Sea with the Atlantic; 13 miles wide at the narrowest point.

North·cliffe (nôrth'klif), **Viscount,** 1865–1922, Alfred Charles William Harmsworth, English newspaper publisher.

North Da·ko·ta (də·kō'tə) A north central State of the United States bordering on Canada; 70,665 square miles; capital, Bismarck; entered the Union Nov. 2, 1889; nickname, *Flickertail State:* abbr. ND —**North Da·ko'·tan**

north·east (nôrth'ēst', in nautical usage nôr'ēst') n. That point on the mariner's compass midway between north and east; any region lying toward that point on the horizon. —adj. From the northeast. —adv. Toward the northeast. —**north'east'er·ly** adj. & adv. —**north'east'ern** adj. —**north'east'ward** adj. & adv. —**north'·east'ward·ly, north'east' wards** adv.

northeast by east One point east of northeast on the mariner's compass. See COMPASS CARD.

northeast by north One point north of northeast on the mariner's compass. See COMPASS CARD.

Northeast Corridor The regional corridor along the eastern coast of the United States from Boston to Washington, D.C., including Philadelphia and New York City.

north·east·er (nôrth'ēs'tər, in nautical usage nôr·ēs'tər) n. **1** A gale from the northeast. **2** A waterproof hat with sloping brim worn by fishermen and other mariners in stormy weather. Also spelled *nor'easter.*

Northeast Passage A water route from the Atlantic to the Pacific along the northern coast of Europe and Asia.

north·er (nôr'thər) n. A cold windstorm from the north; specifically, a wind blowing over Texas to the Gulf of Mexico. —**north'er·ly** adj. & adv. —**north'er·li·ness** n.

north·ern (nôr'thərn) adj. Pertaining to the north or the North. —n. **1** A northerner. **2** *Poetic* A north wind. [OE *northerne*] —**north'ern·most** adj.

Northern Car, The See CAR.

Northern Caucasus Region lying north of the

Caucasus Mountains in southern European Russia. See CAUCASUS.

Northern Cir·cars (sûr·kärz') An historic region in the northern part of Madras, India.

Northern Cross The northern constellation Cygnus, so called from the cross formed by its principal stars.

Northern Crown Corona Borealis.

Northern Dvina See DVINA.

north·ern·er (nôr'thər·nər) n. One born or residing in the north.

North·ern·er (nôr'thər·nər) n. One from the North, as distinguished from a Southerner.

northern hemisphere The half of the earth north of the equator.

Northern Ireland See IRELAND.

Northern Kar·roo (kə·rōō') The highest (up to 10,000 feet) plateau region of the Republic of South Africa, in Western Cape Province.

northern lights The aurora borealis.

Northern Rhodesia See ZAMBIA.

Northern Spy A large, yellow-and-red variety of apple.

Northern Territories A former British protectorate in western Africa, included since 1957 in Ghana.

Northern Territory A region of north central Australia; 523,620 square miles; capital, Darwin.

North Germanic See under GERMANIC.

North Holland A province of NW Netherlands; 1,016 square miles; capital, Haarlem.

north·ing (nôr'thing, -thing) n. **1** *Nav.* Difference of latitude, measured toward the north, between any position and the last one determined. **2** *Astron.* North declination. **3** Deviation toward the north.

North Island The northernmost of the principal islands of New Zealand; 44,281 square miles.

North Korea See under KOREA.

north·land (nôrth'lənd) n. A land in the north. —adj. Of or pertaining to a northern land or lands. [OE] —**north'land·er** n.

North·man (nôrth'mən) n. pl. **·men** (-mən) A Scandinavian; especially, in history, a Scandinavian of the Viking period. Compare NORMAN, NORSEMAN. [OE]

north-north·east (nôrth'nôrth'ēst', in nautical usage nôr'nôr'ēst') adj., adv., & n. Midway between north and northeast. See COMPASS CARD.

north-north·west (nôrth'nôrth'west', in nautical usage nôr'nôr'west') adj., adv., & n. Midway between north and northwest. See COMPASS CARD.

North·olt (nôr'thōlt) A town in Middlesex, 11 miles NW of London: site of a major international airport.

North Ossetia A constituent republic in southern European Russia on the northern slope of the Caucasus; 3,100 square miles; capital, Vladikavkaz; pop. 650,000.

North Platte River A river in northern Colorado, SE Wyoming, and western Nebraska, flowing 680 miles NE to join the South Platte, forming the Platte River.

North Pole The northern extremity of the earth's axis; the 90th degree of north latitude, from which all meridians are south. Its prolongation strikes the celestial sphere at a point a little more than 1 degree from Polaris.

North Rhine-West·pha·lia (rīn'west·fāl'yə) A state of the Federal Republic of Germany, in the western and west central parts; 13,108 square miles; capital Düsseldorf. *German* **Nord·rhein-West·fa·len** (nôrt'rīn·vest·fä'lən).

North Riding An administrative division of northern Yorkshire, England; 2,127 square miles.

North River The estuary of the Hudson River which flows between New York and New Jersey.

Nor·throp (nôr'thrəp), **John Howard,** born 1891, U.S. biochemist.

North Sea The arm of the Atlantic Ocean between Great Britain and the continent of Europe; 600 by 350 miles; formerly *German Ocean.*

North Star Polaris, the polestar.

North·um·ber·land (nôr·thum'bər·lənd) A county of northern England; 2,019 square miles; county town, Newcastle-upon-Tyne.

North·um·bri·a (nôr·thum'brē·ə) An ancient Anglo-Saxon kingdom, extending from the Humber to the Firth of Forth.

North·um·bri·an (nôr·thum'brē·ən) adj. **1** Of

---

the ancient English kingdom of Northumbria, its people, or their dialect. **2** Of the modern county of Northumberland in England, its people, or their dialect. —n. **1** A native or inhabitant of Northumbria. **2** The Old English dialect of these people. **3** A native or inhabitant of Northumberland. **4** The peculiarities of speech of modern Northumbrians.

North Vietnam 1 The Democratic Republic of Vietnam, comprising the former French protectorate of Tonkin and the northern part of the former Empire of Annam; 63,344 square miles; capital, Hanoi. **2** Tonkin alone, a former kingdom and French protectorate; 44,670 square miles; capital, Hanoi.

north·ward (nôrth'wərd) adv. Toward the north. Also **north'wards.** —adj. Directed or lying toward the north. —n. The northward direction or point of the compass. —**north'·ward·ly** adj. & adv.

north·west (nôrth'west', in natural usage nôr'·west') n. **1** That point on the mariner's compass lying midway between north and west; any region situated toward that point on the horizon. **2** The NW region of the United States when its western boundary was the Mississippi. **3** The NW part of the United States. **4** The NW part of Canada. —**Old Northwest** The Northwest Territory. —adj. From the northwest. —adv. Toward the northwest. —**north'west'er·ly** adj. & adv. —**north'west'ern** adj. —**north'west'ward** adj. & adv. —**north'west'ward·ly, north'west' wards** adv.

northwest by north One point north of northwest on the mariner's compass. See COMPASS CARD.

northwest by west One point west of northwest on the mariner's compass. See COMPASS CARD.

north·west·er (nôrth'wes'tər, in nautical usage nôr'wes'tər) n. A gale which blows from the northwest.

North-West Frontier Province A former province of West Pakistan on the Afghanistan border, included in West Pakistan province October, 1955; a province of British India, 1901–47; 13,560 square miles; with tribal areas and princely states, 39,259 square miles; capital, Peshawar.

Northwest Passage A water route from the Atlantic to the Pacific along the northern coast of America.

Northwest Semitic See under SEMITIC.

Northwest Territories A region and administrative unit of northern Canada east of Yukon Territory and north of Hudson Strait, Hudson Bay, and the provinces of Manitoba, Saskatchewan, Alberta, and British Columbia; 1,304,903 square miles including fresh water.

Northwest Territory A region awarded to the United States by Britain in 1973, extending from the Great Lakes to the Ohio River between Pennsylvania and the Mississippi: also *Old Northwest.*

Nor·ton (nôr'tən) **Charles Eliot,** 1827–1908, U.S. educator, editor, and author. —**Thomas,** 1532–84, English author.

Norton Sound (nôr'tən) An arm of the Bering Sea on the southern shore of Seward Peninsula, western Alaska.

Nor·um·be·ga (nôr'əm·bē'gə) The old name of a region on the Atlantic coast of North America, mentioned in maps and writings of the 16th and 17th centuries.

Nor·way (nôr'wā) A kingdom of northern Europe, in the western part of the Scandinavian peninsula; 119,240 square miles; capital, Oslo: Norwegian *Norge.*

Norway maple A tall European maple (*Acer platanoides*), an excellent shade tree.

Norway pine The red pine (*Pinus resinosa*) of the eastern United States.

Norway spruce See under SPRUCE.

Nor·we·gian (nôr·wē'jən) adj. Of or pertaining to Norway, its inhabitants, or their language. —n. **1** A native of Norway. **2** The North Germanic language of Norway. See LANDSMÅL, RIKSMÅL. Abbr. *Norw.* [<Med. L *Norwegia, Norvegia* Norway <ON *Nôrvegr* <*northr* north + *vegr* way]

Norwegian Sea That part of the Atlantic off the coast of Norway.

nor'·west·er (nôr·wes'tər) n. An oilskin coat

worn by mariners in stormy weather. [Contraction of NORTHWESTER]

Nor·wich (nôr′ij, -ich, nor′-) A city, county borough, and county town of Norfolk, England.

nose (nōz) *n.* **1** That part of the face of an animal containing the nostrils and the organ of smell. ◆ Collateral adjectives: *nasal, rhinal.* **2** The power or sense of smelling; scent. **3** That which resembles a nose; a ship's prow; the frontal tapering end of a torpedo; a spout; nozzle, etc. **4** The working end of a tool; also, the threaded end of a lathe or milling–machine spindle. **—on the nose** *Slang* Exactly; precisely. **—*v.* nosed, nos·ing** *v.t.* **1** To perceive or discover by or as by the sense of smell; scent. **2** To examine or touch with the nose; sniff. **3** To make (one's way) carefully and with the front end forward. **—*v.i.* 4** To smell; sniff. **5** To pry; meddle. **6** To move, especially carefully. **—to nose out** To defeat by a small margin. **—to nose over** To turn over on its nose, as an airplane. [OE *nosu,* orig. the two nostrils]

nose·band (nōz′band′) *n.* That part of a bridle passing over the nose of a horse and attached to the cheek pieces.

nose·bleed (nōz′blēd′) *n.* **1** Bleeding from the nose; epistaxis. **2** Any of various plants, as the wakerobin, Indian paintbrush, or milfoil.

nose cone The conical and separable forward section of a missile or rocket, designed to carry a warhead, instruments, etc.

nose·dive (nōz′dīv′) *n.* **1** *Aeron.* A steep downward plunge of an airplane. **2** Any sudden descent or crash. **—*v.i.* ·dived, ·div·ing** To plunge downward.

nose·gay (nōz′gā′) *n.* A bouquet. [<NOSE + GAY, in obs. senses "a bright object, a pretty flower"]

nose–heav·y (nōz′hev′ē) *adj. Aeron.* Denoting the condition of an airplane in which the nose tends to sink when the longitudinal control is released unless corrected by trim controls.

nose·piece (nōz′pēs′) *n.* **1** Any protective covering for the nose. **2** An attachment on a microscope to permit the use of two or more objectives without disturbing the focus. **3** The narrow band fitting across the nose in a pair of spectacles.

nose wheel *Aeron.* A third landing wheel attached under the nose of some types of airplane.

nosh (nosh) *Colloq. n.* A snack; tidbit. **—*v.i.*** To eat a snack. **—*v.t.*** To munch on. [<Yiddish] **—nosh′er** *n.*

no–show (nō′shō′) *n.* One who makes a reservation for an airplane flight but fails to claim his seat at the time of take–off.

nos·ing (nō′zing) *n.* **1** That part of a stair tread projecting beyond the riser; also, a shield for the edge of a stair tread. **2** *Archit.* A nose–shaped molding or dripstone. [<NOS(E) + -ING[1]]

noso– *combining form* Disease: *nosogenesis.* [< Gk. *nosos* a disease]

no·so·gen·e·sis (nō′sə·jen′ə·sis) *n.* pathogenesis.

no·so·ge·og·ra·phy (nō′sō·jē·og′rə·fē) *n.* The study of the geographical factors and distribution of diseases. [<NOSO- + GEOGRAPHY] **—no′so·ge′o·graph′ic** (-jē′ə·graf′ik) *adj.*

no·sog·ra·phy (nō·sog′rə·fē) *n.* A description and classification of diseases. **—no·sog′ra·pher** *n.*

no·sol·o·gy (nō·sol′ə·jē) *n.* **1** The branch of medical science that treats of the systematic classification of diseases. **2** A list or classification of this kind. **3** The special characteristics of a particular disease; also, opinions regarding it. [<NL *nosologia* <Gk. *nosos* adisease + *-logia* -LOGY] **—nos·o·log·i·cal** (nos′·ə·loj′i·kəl) *adj.* **—no·sol′o·gist** *n.*

no·so·ma·ni·a (nō′sə·mā′nē·ə,-mān′yə) *n. Psychiatry* Extreme hypochondria; the morbid conviction of suffering from some particular disease. [<NOSO- +-MANIA]

nos·tal·gi·a (nos·tal′jē·ə, -jə) *n.* **1** Severe or poignant homesickness. **2** Any longing for something far away or long ago. **3** *Psychiatry* Prolonged, often morbid fixation of one's thoughts on home, family, and friends. [< NL <Gk. *nostos* a return home + *algos* a pain] **—nos·tal′gic** *adj.*

nos·toc (nos′tok) *n.* Any of a genus *(Nostoc)* of fresh–water algae having a definite, globose or variously expanded, gelatinous or membranaceous thallus. They form greenish masses in fresh water, in damp places, and on stones. [<NL; coined by Paracelsus]

nos·tol·o·gy (nos·tol′ə·jē) *n.* The doctrines or science relating to the phenomena of extreme old age or second childhood; geriatrics. [< Gk. *nostos* a return home + -LOGY] **—nos·to·log·ic** (nos′tə·loj′ik) *adj.*

nos·to·ma·ni·a (nos′tə·mā′nē·ə, -mān′yə) *n. Psychiatry* Intense or excessive nostalgia. [< NL <Gk. *nostos* a return home + *mania* madness]

nos·top·a·thy (nos·top′ə·thē) *n. Psychiatry* An acute, often morbid fear of returning to one's home or to familiar scenes: the opposite of *nostalgia.* [<Gk. *nostos* a return home + -PATHY] **—nos·to·path·ic** (nos′tə·path′ik) *adj.*

Nos·tra·da·mus (nos′trə·dā′məs), 1503–66, French physician, astrologer, and prophet: original name *Michel de Notredame.*

nos·tril (nos′trəl) *n.* One of the anterior openings in the nose. [OE *nosthyrl* <*nos(u)* nose + *thyrel* a hole<*thurh* through]

nos·trum (nos′trəm) *n.* **1** A favorite remedy; patent medicine; quack recipe. **2** Anything savoring of quackery: political *nostrums.* [< L *nostrum,* neut. of *noster* our own; because prepared by those selling it]

nos·y (nō′zē) *adj. Colloq.* **1** Prying; snooping; inquisitive. **2** Stinking; malodorous.

not (not) *adv.* In no manner, or to no extent or degree: used in negation, prohibition, or refusal. [ME, contraction of NOUGHT]

not– Var. of NOTO–.

no·ta be·ne (nō′tə bē′nē) *Latin* Note well; take notice: abbr. *N.B.*

no·ta·bil·i·ty (nō′tə·bil′ə·tē) *n. pl.* **·ties 1** Notableness. **2** A person of distinction.

no·ta·ble (nō′tə·bəl, *also for def.* 2 not′ə·bəl) *adj.* **1** Worthy of note; remarkable; distinguished. **2** Eminently careful, thrifty, or skillful, as in housekeeping. **—*n.*** One who or that which is worthy of note, distinguished, or eminent. [<OF <L *notabilis* <*notare* note < *nota* a mark] **—no′ta·ble·ness** *n.* **—no′ta·bly** *adv.*

No·ta·ble (nō′tə·bəl) *n.* In France before the Revolution, one of the persons summoned by the king to a deliberative assembly in national crises.

no·ta·rize (nō′tə·rīz) *v.t.* **·rized, ·riz·ing** To attest to or authenticate as a notary. **—no′ta·ri·za′tion** *n.*

no·ta·ry (nō′tə·rē) *n. pl.* **·ries 1** An officer empowered to authenticate contracts, administer oaths, take depositions, etc.: also **notary public. 2** Formerly, a scrivener, or one who drew up legal papers. [<AF *notarie,* OF *notaire* <L *notarius* a shorthand writer, a clerk <*notare.* See NOTABLE.] **—no·tar·i·al** (nō·târ′ē·əl) *adj.*

no·ta·tion (nō·tā′shən) *n.* **1** The process of designating by figures, etc. **2** Any system of signs, figures, or abbreviations employed for convenience in any science or art, especially algebraic, arithmetical, or musical characters. [<L *notatio, -onis* <*notare.* See NOTABLE.] **—no·ta′tion·al** *adj.*

notch (noch) *n.* **1** A hollow cut or mark made in anything; a nick; indentation; especially, a mark or nick cut into the handle of a gun or other weapon to record each person killed. **2** A narrow, short defile. **3** *Colloq.* A degree: He is a *notch* above the others. **—*v.t.* 1** To make a notch or notches in. **2** To record by means of notches; tally. [Prob. <ME *an oche* a notch <OF *oche, osche* <*oschier* notch] **—notch′er** *n.*

note (nōt) *n.* **1** That by which anything may be known; an outward sign. **2** A mark or character used in writing or printing to indicate or call attention to something: a *note* of interrogation (?) or exclamation (!). **3** A brief comment appended to text. **4** A brief record or summary; a memorandum. **5** A complete record or report: Make a *note* of that statement. **6** An official communication in writing from one government to another. **7** A brief letter; a billet. **8** *Logic* A distinctive mark or character of an object such as its qualities afford. **9** Notice; observation. **10** An account or bill. **11** High importance, estimation, or repute; distinction: something of *note.* **12** *Music* **a** An oval character in musical notation, either solid or formed in outline, used to indicate the length of a tone, and also, as placed on a staff, to point out, in conjunction with the signature, the pitch and relative position in a scale system. **b** Loosely, any musical sound: The first *notes* of the fiddles were

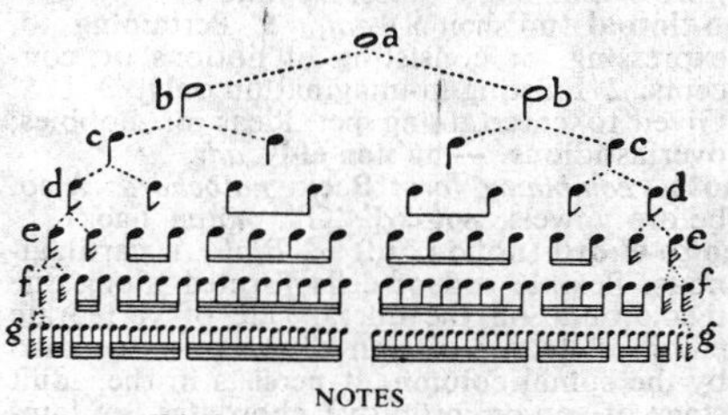

NOTES

a. Whole note. *b.* Half note. *c.* Quarter note. *d.* Eighth note. *e.* Sixteenth note. *f.* Thirty–second note. *g.* Sixty–fourth note.

heard. **c** A key of the keyboard. **13** *Physics* Tone (def. 2): the preferable word in this sense. **14** A melodious or vocal sound, as of a bird; voice; tone. **15** Manner of speaking. **16** A signed promise by one party to another to pay a certain sum of money at a specified time: a promissory *note*; a bank *note.* **17** The general tone, coloring, or quality of a painting. See synonyms under REMARK, SIGN, SOUND. **—*v.t.* not·ed, not·ing 1** To take notice or note of; observe; remark. **2** To set down, as in writing; make a note of. **3** To mention specially or separately in the course of writing. **4** To annotate. **5** To set down in musical notation. [<OF <L *nota* a mark, orig. pp. fem. of *noscere* know] **—not′er** *n.*

note·book (nōt′bo͝ok′) *n.* **1** A book in which to enter memoranda. **2** A book in which notes of hand are registered; billbook.

not·ed (nō′tid) *adj.* Well known by reputation or report. See synonyms under EMINENT, ILLUSTRIOUS. **—not′ed·ly** *adv.*

note·less (nōt′lis) *adj.* **1** Not noted; unobserved; obscure. **2** Unmusical.

note of hand A promissory note.

note paper Paper for writing notes or letters.

note·wor·thy (nōt′wûr′thē) *adj.* Worthy of note; remarkable; significant. **—note′wor′thi·ly** *adv.* **—note′wor′thi·ness** *n.*

noth·ing (nuth′ing) *n.* **1** Not any being or existence; also, not any particular thing, act, or event; no thing: opposed to *thing, anything, something*: He has *nothing.* **2** A state of non–existence; nothingness; hence, insignificance or unimportance: to rise from *nothing.* **3** A person or thing of slight significance, consideration, or value; any trifle. **4** A cipher; zero; naught. **—*adv.*** In no degree; to no extent; not at all.

noth·ing·ness (nuth′ing·nis) *n.* **1** A state of non–existence. **2** Worthlessness; utter insignificance. **3** A trifle; nothing. **4** Unconsciousness; also, death.

no·tice (nō′tis) *v.t.* **·ticed, ·tic·ing 1** To pay attention to or take cognizance of; remark or observe. **2** To treat courteously or with favor. **3** To mention; refer to or comment on. **4** To serve with a notice; notify. [<*n.*] **—*n.* 1** The act of noticing or observing; attention: to take *notice* of. **2** Announcement; information; warning. **3** Respectful treatment; civility. **4** An order communicated to one; especially, a formal written or printed notification, instruction, or warning, as of the termination or intended termination of an agreement; also, a public communication openly displayed. **5** A short literary advertisement or review: a book *notice.* [<F <L *notitia* celebrity] **—no′tice·a·ble** *adj.* **—no′tice·a·bly** *adv.*

no·ti·fi·ca·tion (nō′tə·fə·kā′shən) *n.* **1** The act of notifying. **2** Notice given. **3** The writing that gives information.

no·ti·fy (nō′tə·fī) *v.t.* **·fied, ·fy·ing 1** To give notice to; inform. **2** *Brit.* To give information of; make known. See synonyms under

ANNOUNCE, INFORM[1]. [<OF *notifier* <L *notificare* < *notus* known + *facere* make] —**no′ti·fi′er** *n.*

no·tion (nō′shən) *n.* **1** A mental apprehension; an idea. **2** Loosely, an opinion; a hastily formed theory. **3** Intention; inclination. **4** *pl. U.S.* Miscellaneous, small, useful articles, such as ribbons, thread, pins, needles, hairpins, etc. See synonyms under IDEA, THOUGHT[1]. [<L *notio, -onis* < *noscere* know]

no·tion·al (nō′shən·əl) *adj.* **1** Pertaining to, expressing, or consisting of notions or concepts. **2** Existing in imagination only. **3** *U.S.* Given to entertaining pet ideas or hobbies; overfastidious. —**no′tion·al·ly** *adv.*

noto– *combining form* Back: *notochord.* Also, before vowels, **not–**. [<Gk. *nōton* back]

no·to·chord (nō′tə·kôrd) *n. Biol.* A cartilaginous, flexible rod of cells formed along the median line on the dorsal side of vertebrate embryos, in a situation afterwards occupied by the spinal column. It persists in the adult stage of certain primitive chordates, as lampreys and tunicates.

No·to·gae·a (nō′tə·jē′ə) *n.* A zoogeographical realm including the Australian and Neotropical regions. [<Gk. *notos* south + *gaia* earth] —**No′to·gae′al, No′to·gae′an, No′to·gae′ic** *adj.*

no·to·ri·e·ty (nō′tə·rī′ə·tē) *n. pl.* **·ties** **1** The character of being notorious. **2** Common knowledge or talk. **3** One who or that which is notorious. See synonyms under FAME. [<F *notoriété* <Med. L *notorius* making known. See NOTORIOUS.]

no·to·ri·ous (nō·tôr′ē·əs, -tō′rē-) *adj.* Being publicly known and the subject of general unfavorable remark. [<Med. L *notorius* < *notus* known, orig. pp. of *noscere* know] —**no·to′ri·ous·ly** *adv.*

Synonyms: egregious, evident, known, manifest, obvious, open, overt, patent, plain, undeniable, undenied, undisputed, unquestionable, well-known.

no·tor·nis (nō·tôr′nis) *n.* A ratite bird (genus *Notornis*) of New Zealand and neighboring islands, with rudimentary wings. [<NL <Gk. *notos* south + *ornis* bird]

No·tre Dame (nō′trə däm′, nō′tər dām′; *Fr.* nô′tr′ däm′) **1** *French* Our Lady (Mary, mother of Jesus). **2** A famous early Gothic cathedral in Paris, built 1163–1257.

no–trump (nō′trump′) *n.* In bridge, a bid or a declaration calling for play without a trump suit. —*adj.* Without a trump suit; denoting a hand suitable for playing without a trump suit. —**no′–trump′er** *n.*

Not·ta·way River (not′ə·wā) A river in western Quebec, Canada, flowing 205 miles NW to Hudson Bay.

Not·ting·ham (not′ing·əm) A county of north central England; 844 square miles; county town, Nottingham: shortened form **Notts.** Also **Not′ting·ham·shire** (-shir′).

no·tun·gu·late (nō·tung′gyə·lāt) *n. Paleontol.* Any member of an extinct order (*Notungulata* or *Notoungulata*) of herbivorous mammals of the Tertiary, whose principal habitat was South America. —*adj.* Of or pertaining to the *Notungulata.* Also **no′to·un′gu·late** (nō′tō·ung′gyə·lāt). [<NOTO- + UNGULATE]

not·with·stand·ing (not′with·stan′ding, -with-) *adv.* All the same; nevertheless: Though imprisoned, he escaped *notwithstanding.* —*prep.* In spite of: He left *notwithstanding* your orders. —*conj.* In spite of the fact that; although.

Synonym (prep.): despite. *Notwithstanding* simply states that circumstances shall not be or have not been allowed to withstand; *despite* refers primarily to personal and perhaps spiteful opposition; as, he failed *notwithstanding* his good intentions; or, he persevered *despite* bitter hostility.

Synonyms (conj.): although, but, howbeit, however, nevertheless, still, though, yet. *However* simply waives discussion and (like the archaic *howbeit*) says, "be that as it may, this is true"; *nevertheless* concedes the truth of what precedes, but claims that what follows is none the less true; *notwithstanding* marshals the two statements face to face, admits the one and its seeming contradiction to the other, while insisting that it cannot, after all, withstand the other. *Yet* and *still* are weaker than *notwithstanding,* while stronger than *but.* *Though* and *although* make as little as possible of the concession, dropping it, as it were, incidentally; as, "*though* we are guilty, thou art good"; to say "we are guilty, *but* thou art good," would make the concession of guilt more emphatic. See BUT[1].

notwithstanding that Although.

Nou·ak·chott (nōō·āk·shôt′) The capital of the Islamic Republic of Mauritania.

nou·gat (nōō′gət, *Fr.* nōō·gä′) *n.* A confection consisting usually of a honey or sugar paste mixed with chopped almonds, pistachios, etc. [<F <Provençal, ult. <L *nux, nucis* a nut]

nought (nôt) See NAUGHT.

Nou·mé·a (nōō·mē′ə, -mā′ə) A port, capital of New Caledonia.

nou·me·nal (nōō′mə·nəl, nou′-) *adj.* Of or pertaining to noumena or the noumenon: opposed to *phenomenal.* —**nou′me·nal·ly** *adv.* —**nou′me·nal·ism** *n.* —**nou′me·nal·ist** *n.*

nou·me·non (nōō′mə·non, nou′-) *n. pl.* **·me·na** (-mə·nə) *Philos.* **1** An object of intuition by the reason or understanding, as something transcending perception through the senses: opposed to *phenomenon.* **2** The unknown ground or cause of phenomena, regarded as necessarily assumed by the mind, but the real nature of which is wholly transcendent; the unknowable thing in itself. [<NL <Gk., orig. ppr. passive of *noeein* think]

noun (noun) *Gram. n.* **1** A word used as the name of a thing, quality, or action existing or conceived by the mind; a substantive. A **proper noun** is the name of an individual person, place, or thing, as *Paul, Nicole, Venice, Rover, U.S.S. Nautilus,* etc.; a **common noun** is the name an individual object has in common with others of its class, as *man, city, hill*; a **collective noun** is one expressing a collection or aggregate of individuals, as *assembly, army*; an **abstract noun** is one indicating a quality, as *goodness, beauty.* **2** Anything that can be used as subject, object, or appositive, as a substantive clause. —*adj.* Of or pertaining to a noun or nouns: also **noun′al.** [<AF, OF *nun* <L *nomen* name] —**noun′al·ly** *adv.*

nour·ish (nûr′ish) *v.t.* **1** To furnish material to sustain the life and promote the growth of (a living organism). **2** Hence, to support; maintain. **3** To furnish with knowledge; educate. See synonyms under CHERISH. [<OF *noriss-*, stem of *norir* <L *nutrire* nourish] —**nour′ish·a·ble** *adj.* —**nour′ish·er** *n.* —**nour′ish·ing** *adj.*

nour·ish·ment (nûr′ish·mənt) *n.* **1** Nutriment. **2** The act of nourishing or the state of being nourished. **3** That which promotes growth in any way. See synonyms under FOOD, NUTRIMENT.

nous (nōōs, nous) *n. Philos.* **1** Mind, as employed in thinking, feeling, or willing. **2** The higher reason; emanation of the divine principle. [<Gk. *nous, noos* mind]

nous ver·rons (nōō ve·rôn′) *French* We shall see.

nou·veau riche (nōō·vō′ rēsh′) *French pl.* **nou·veaux riches** (nōō·vō′ rēsh′) One recently become rich; a parvenu.

nou·veau·té (nōō·vō·tā′) *n. French* A new thing; a novelty.

Nou·velle Ca·lé·do·nie (nōō·vel′ kà·lā·dō·nē′) The French name for NEW CALEDONIA.

no·va (nō′və) *n. pl.* **·vae** (-vē) or **·vas** *Astron.* A star which suddenly flares up in the heavens and fades away again to its former magnitude after a period of a few weeks or months. [<L *novus* new]

no·vac·u·lite (nō·vak′yə·līt) *n.* An extremely fine-grained sedimentary siliceous rock used for hones; whetstone. [<L *novacula* razor]

No·va Gô·a (nô′və gō′ə) A city in Gôa, capital of Portuguese India: also *Pangim, Panjim.*

No·va·lis (nō·vä′lis) Pseudonym of *Friedrich von Hardenberg,* 1772–1801, German poet.

No·va Lis·bo·a (nô′və lēzh·bō′ə) Capital-elect of Angola: formerly *Huambo.*

No·va·ra (nō·vä′rä) A city in Piedmont, northern Italy. Ancient **No·va′ri·a** (-rē·ä).

No·va Sco·tia (nō′və skō′shə) A maritime province of eastern Canada; 21,068 square miles; capital, Halifax: French *Acadia* (1605–1713). —**No′va Sco′tian** *adj.* & *n.*

No·va·tians (nō·vā′shənz) See CATHARI.

no·va·tion (nō·vā′shən) *n.* **1** *Law* A substitution of a new engagement, indebtedness, obligation, creditor, or debtor for an existing one. **2** A making anew; creation; inception. [<L *novatio* making new < *novare* make new < *novus* new]

No·va·ya Zem·lya (nô′və·yə zim·lyä′) An Arctic archipelago in European U.S.S.R. separating the Kara and Barents seas; 35,000 square miles.

nov·el (nov′əl) *n.* **1** A fictional prose narrative of considerable length, representing characters and events as if in real life by a plot or scheme of action of greater or less complexity. **2** The particular type of literature exemplified by fiction of this character: with the definite article: Dostoevsky is one of the fathers of the modern *novel.* **3** In Roman law, a new constitution or decree supplemental to a decree. **4** *Usually pl.* A novella. See synonyms under FICTION. —*adj.* Of recent origin; new, strange, or unusual. See synonyms under FRESH, MODERN, NEW. [Fusion of Ital. *novella* a novel and OF *novel* new, both <LL *novellus* <L *novus* new] —**nov′el·ly** *adj.*

nov·el·ette (nov′əl·et′) *n.* A short novel.

nov·el·ist (nov′əl·ist) *n.* A writer of novels.

nov·el·is·tic (nov′əl·is′tik) *adj.* Of, pertaining to, characteristic of, or found in novels. —**nov′el·is′ti·cal·ly** *adv.*

nov·el·ize (nov′əl·īz) *v.t.* **·ized, ·iz·ing** To put into the form of a novel. —**nov′el·i·za′tion** *n.*

no·vel·la (nō·vel′lä) *n. pl.* **·le** (-lā) *Italian* A short tale or narrative, usually with a moral, often of satirical nature: typified by the stories in Boccaccio's *Decameron.*

Nov·els (nov′əlz) *n. pl.* In civil law: **1** The amendments and supplementary laws to the Justinian Code decreed by Justinian and his immediate successors: in Latin, *Novellae Constitutiones.* **2** Similar decrees proclaimed by other Roman emperors.

nov·el·ty (nov′əl·tē) *n. pl.* **·ties** **1** The quality of being novel. **2** Something novel or unusual; especially, a small manufactured article or trinket for personal adornment: usually in the plural. **3** An innovation. See synonyms under CHANGE.

No·vem·ber (nō·vem′bər) The eleventh month of the year, containing 30 days. [<L *November* ninth month < *novem* nine]

no·ve·na (nō·vē′nə) *n.* In the Roman Catholic Church, a devotion consisting of a prayer said on nine successive days, asking for some special blessing. [<LL <L *novem* nine]

nov·e·nar·y (nov′ə·ner′ē) *adj.* Relating to the number nine. [<L *novenarius* < *novem* nine]

no·ven·ni·al (nō·ven′ē·əl) *adj.* Occurring every ninth year. [<L *novennis* < *novem* nine + *annus* year]

no·ver·cal (nō·vûr′kəl) *adj.* Of, pertaining to, or suitable for a stepmother. [<L *noverca* stepmother]

Nov·go·rod (nôv′gə·rot) A city of NW Russian S.F.S.R. on the Volkhov.

nov·ice (nov′is) *n.* **1** A beginner in any business or occupation; an untried or inexperienced person; tyro. **2** *Eccl.* **a** One who enters a religious house or community on probation. **b** One who has been recently converted. **3** In competitive games, etc., a person or animal entered in a class in which he or it has not already won an award. [<F <L *novicius* new < *novus*] —**nov′ice·hood** (-hŏŏd) *n.*

No·vi Sad (nô′vē säd′) A city on the Danube in NE Yugoslavia, capital of the autonomous province of Vojvodina, northern Serbia: German *Neusatz.*

no·vi·ti·ate (nō·vish′ē·it, -āt) *n.* **1** The state of being a novice. **2** *Eccl.* **a** The period of probation of a novice in a religious order. **b** The part of a monastic establishment inhabited by novices. Also **nov·ice·ship** (nov′is·ship). **3** A novice. Also **no·vi′ci·ate.**

No·vo·cain (nō′və·kān) *n.* Proprietary name for a brand of procaine, used as a local anesthetic: less toxic than cocaine. Also **No′vo·caine.**

No·vo Kuz·netsk (nô′vō kŏŏz·netsk′) A former name for STALINSK.

No·vo·ros·siisk (nô′və·ro·sēsk′) A port on the Black Sea in SW European Russian S.F.S.R.

No·vo·si·birsk (nô′və·si·birsk′) A city in SW Asian Russian S.F.S.R. on the Ob.

no·vus or·do se·clo·rum (nō′vəs ôr′dō sə·klôr′əm, -klō′rəm) *Latin* A new order of the ages: motto on the Great Seal of the United States.

now (nou) *adv.* **1** At once. **2** At or during the present time. **3** Nowadays. **4** In the immediate past: He said so just *now.* **5** In the immediate future: He is going just *now.* **6** In such circumstances; things being as they are: *Now* we can be sure of getting home. **7** At

this point in the proceedings, narrative, etc.: The war was *now* virtually over. See synonyms under IMMEDIATELY, YET. —*conj.* Since; seeing that: *Now* the books have arrived, I must stay here and read them. —*n.* The present time, moment, or occasion. ◆ *Now* is often used as an expletive, as in command, remonstrance, etc.: Come *now,* don't make me insist! [OE *nū*]

now·a·days (nou'ə·dāz') *adv.* In the present time or age.

now and again Occasionally; from time to time. Also **now and then.**

no·way (nō'wā') *adv.* In no way, manner, or degree. Also **no'ways'.**

Now·el (nō·el') *Archaic* See NOËL.

no·where (nō'hwâr') *adv.* In no place; not anywhere. —*n.* No place. Also *U.S. Dial.* **no'wheres'.**

no·whith·er (nō'hwith'ər) *adv.* Toward no definite place.

no·wise (nō'wīz') *adv.* In no manner or degree.

nowt (nout) *n. Scot.* **1** An ox. **2** Figuratively, a stupid or clumsy person.

Nox (noks) In Roman mythology, the goddess of night: identified with the Greek *Nyx.*

nox·ious (nok'shəs) *adj.* Causing, or tending to cause, injury to health or morals; pernicious. See synonyms under BAD, INIMICAL, NOISOME, PERNICIOUS. [< L *noxius* < *nocere* hurt] —**nox'ious·ly** *adv.* —**nox'ious·ness** *n.*

noy·ade (nwȧ·yȧd') *n. French* Execution by drowning, especially as practiced during the Reign of Terror (1793–94) in Nantes, France.

Noy·on (nwȧ·yôṅ') A town in northern France; scene of Charlemagne's coronation; birthplace of Calvin.

noz·zle (noz'əl) *n.* **1** A projecting spout or pipe for discharge, as of a teapot, or the muzzle of a gun barrel, etc.; specifically, a rigid tube or vent, commonly tapering, at the end of a flexible tube, as a hose. **2** An inlet or outlet pipe. Also **noz'le.** [Dim. of NOSE]

Np *Chem.* Neptunium (symbol Np).

nth (enth) *adj.* **1** Representing an ordinal equivalent to *n.* **2** Infinitely or indefinitely large or small: raised to the *nth* degree.

nu (nōō, nyōō) *n.* The thirteenth letter in the Greek alphabet (Ν, ν): equivalent to English *n.* As a numeral it denotes 50. [< Gk. *ny*]

nu·ance (nōō·äns', nōō'äns, nyōō'-; *Fr.* nü·äṅs') *n.* A shade of difference in tone or color; hence, a slight degree of difference in anything perceptible to the mind. [< F < *nuer* shade, ult. < L *nubes* a cloud]

nub (nub) *n.* **1** A protuberance; knob. **2** The core of a matter; pith or point: the *nub* of the story. [Earlier *knub.* Related to KNOB.]

Nu·ba (nōō'bä) *n.* **1** A Nubian. **2** One of a Negro tribe of the central Sudan, related to the Nubians. **3** The language of the Nuba peoples, related to the Sudanic languages: also called *Berberi.*

nub·bin (nub'in) *n. U.S.* An imperfectly developed ear of maize; hence, anything small and stunted. [< NUB]

nub·ble (nub'əl) *n. Dial.* **1** A protuberance; nub. **2** An island formed like a knob. [Dim. of NUB] —**nub'bly** *adj.*

nu·bi·a (nōō'bē·ə, nyōō'-) *n.* A soft, light scarf or covering for the head, worn by women. [< L *nubes* cloud]

Nu·bi·a (nōō'bē·ə, nyōō'-) A region and ancient country of NE Africa in the northern Sudan and southern Egypt, between the Red Sea and the Sahara.

Nu·bi·an (nōō'bē·ən, nyōō'-) *adj.* Of or pertaining to Nubia, its people, or their language. —*n.* **1** A native of Nubia; specifically, a member of any of the Negroid tribes formerly ruling the territory between Egypt and Abyssinia. **2** The Sudanic language of the Nubians. **3** A Nubian horse or goat.

Nubian Desert A sandstone plateau in NE Sudan between the Nile valley and the Red Sea.

nu·bile (nōō'bil, nyōō'-) *adj.* Of suitable age to marry; marriageable. [< L *nubilis* < *nubere* wed] —**nu·bil'i·ty** *n.*

nu·bi·lous (nōō'bə·ləs, nyōō'-) *adj.* **1** Cloudy; foggy. **2** Obscure; indefinite. Also **nu'bi·lose** (-lōs). [< L *nubilus* < *nubes* cloud]

nu·cel·lus (nōō·sel'əs, nyōō-) *n. pl.* **·li** (-ī) *Bot.* The body or essential part of a plant ovule, within which the embryo and its covering are developed. [< NL < L *nucella,* dim. of *nux, nucis* a nut] —**nu·cel'lar** *adj.*

nu·cha (nōō'kə, nyōō'-) *n. pl.* **·chae** (-kē) The nape or back of the neck. [< LL < Arabic *nukhā'* spinal marrow] —**nu'chal** *adj.*

nu·cle·ar (nōō'klē·ər, nyōō'-) *adj.* **1** Of, pertaining to, forming, of the nature of, or depending upon a nucleus or nuclei. Also **nu'cle·al. 2** Of or employing the energy of the nucleus of the atom: *nuclear* weapons.

nuclear family A family consisting of parents and child or children considered as a discrete group.

nuclear fission *Physics* See under FISSION.

nuclear fusion *Physics* See under FUSION.

nuclear medicine The use of radioisotopes for diagnostic and therapeutic purposes in medicine.

nuclear physics That branch of physics which investigates the atomic nucleus.

nuclear plate *Biol.* Equatorial plate.

nuclear submarine A submarine driven by steam produced in a reactor using fissionable material as fuel: also called *atomic submarine.* Also **nuclear-powered submarine.**

nu·cle·ase (nōō'klē·ās, nyōō'-) *n. Biochem.* An enzyme which hydrolyzes nucleic acids.

nu·cle·ate (nōō'klē·āt, nyōō'-) *adj.* Having a nucleus. Also **nu'cle·at'ed.** —*v.t.* & *v.i.* **·at·ed, ·at·ing** To form or gather into a nucleus. —**nu'·cle·a'tion** *n.*

nu·cle·ic (nōō·klē'ik, nyōō-) *adj. Biochem.* Designating a group of complex, non-crystalline acids present in organic nuclear material, as yeast, chromatin, the thymus gland, etc. They contain carbohydrates combined with phosphoric acids and bases derived from purine or pyrimidine.

nucleic acid *Biochem.* A complex acid derived from nuclein and nucleoproteins: it plays an important role in digestion and metabolism.

nu·cle·in (nōō'klē·in, nyōō'-) *n. Biochem.* A colorless, amorphous protein containing nucleic acid, and found as a normal constituent of cell nuclei.

nu·cle·o·late (nōō'klē·ə·lāt', nyōō'-) *adj.* Having nucleoli. Also **nu'cle·o·lat'ed.**

nu·cle·o·lus (nōō·klē'ə·ləs, nyōō-) *n. pl.* **·li** (-lī) *Biol.* A dense body or bodies composed mostly of RNA found within the nucleus of a typical cell; plasmosome. [< LL, dim. of *nucleus.* See NUCLEUS.] —**nu·cle'o·lar** *adj.*

nu·cle·on (nōō'klē·on, nyōō'-) *n. Physics* One of the particles composing the nucleus of an atom, the proton, or the neutron, regarded as a single variety of particle existing in either of two states.

nu·cle·on·ics (nōō'klē·on'iks, nyōō'-) *n.* The practical applications of nuclear physics in any field of science, engineering, and technology, especially in relation to the development of atomic energy. —**nu'cle·on'ic** *adj.*

nucleon number *Physics* Mass number.

nu·cle·o·plasm (nōō'klē·ə·plaz'əm, nyōō'-) *n. Biol.* The more fluid part of the nucleus of a cell; karyoplasm. —**nu'cle·o·plas'mic** *adj.*

nu·cle·o·pro·te·in (nōō'klē·ə·prō'tē·in, -tēn, nyōō'-) *n. Biochem.* Any of a class of substances found in the nuclei of plant and animal cells, and containing one or more protein molecules combined with nucleic acid.

nu·cle·o·side (nōō'klē·ə·sīd', nyōō'-) *n. Biochem.* A glycoside derived from nucleic acid by removing the phosphoric acid from a nucleotide, leaving the carbohydrate in combination with the purine or pyrimidine derivative.

nu·cle·o·tide (nōō'klē·ə·tīd', nyōō'-) *n.* Biochem. One of several compounds derived from nucleic acid by hydrolysis and consisting of phosphoric acid combined with a sugar and a purine or pyrimidine derivative.

nu·cle·us (nōō'klē·əs, nyōō'-) *n. pl.* **·cle·i** (-klē·ī) **1** A center of development; central mass; kernel. **2** *Biol.* A complex, spheroidal body surrounded by a thin membrane and embedded in the protoplasm of most plant and animal cells. It contains the chromatin which is essential in the processes of heredity, and is the directive center of all the vital activities of the cell, as assimilation, metabolism, growth, and reproduction. **3** *Physiol.* A group of nerve cells within the nervous system from which the nerve fibers originate. **4** *Zool.* The apex, or earliest formed part of a shell; also, the central part, as of an operculum, around which additional parts are formed. **5** *Astron.* The starlike point seen in the head of a comet, and at the center of a nebula. **6** *Physics* The central core of an atom, believed to contain its effective mass and to have a positive charge balanced by the negative charge of the surrounding electrons. Its principal components are the proton and neutron. [< L, a kernel, dim. of *nux, nucis* a nut]

nu·clide (nōō'klīd, nyōō'-) *n. Physics* A particular nuclear species as characterized by the atomic number and the mass number.

nude (nōōd, nyōōd) *adj.* **1** Without clothing or covering; naked; bare. **2** *Law* Naked; lacking an essential legal requisite. —*n.* **1** A nude figure, as in painting or sculpture. **2** The state of being unclad: to appear in the *nude.* **3** Any of several light beige or pinkish-beige tints. [< L *nudus* naked, bare] —**nude'·ly** *adv.* —**nude'ness** *n.*

nudge (nuj) *v.* **nudged, nudg·ing** *v.t.* To touch or push gently, as with the elbow, in order to attract attention, convey a meaning, etc. —*v.i.* To give a nudge. —*n.* The act of nudging; a gentle push, as with the elbow. [? Akin to dial. Norw. *nugga* push]

nudi- *combining form* Naked; bare; without covering: *nudicaudate.* [< L *nudus* naked]

nu·di·branch (nōō'di·brangk, nyōō'-) *n.* Any of various brightly colored marine gastropods (suborder Nudibranchia) lacking shells and true gills in the adult stage. Also called *sea slug.* [< NUDI- + Gk. *branchia* gills] —**nu'di·bran'chi·ate** (-brang'kē·it) *adj.* & *n.*

nu·di·cau·lous (nōō'di·kô'ləs, nyōō'-) *adj. Bot.* Having naked or leafless stems.

nu·die (nōō'dē, nyōō'dē) *n. Slang.* A moving picture, play, or publication showing nude people or figures.

nud·ism (nōō'diz·əm, nyōō'-) *n.* The doctrine or practice of living in the state of nudity for hygienic reasons. —**nud'ist** *n.*

nu·di·ty (nōō'də·tē, nyōō'-) *n. pl.* **·ties 1** The state of being nude. **2** A naked part; anything unclad.

Nu·e·ces River (nōō·ā'sās) A river in southern Texas, flowing 315 miles SE to **Nueces Bay,** an arm of Corpus Christi Bay.

Nue·vo Le·ón (nwā'vō lā·ōn') A state in NE Mexico; 25,136 square miles; capital, Monterrey.

nu·ga·to·ry (nōō'gə·tôr'ē, -tō'rē, nyōō'-) *adj.* **1** Having no power; inoperative. **2** Having no worth or meaning; insignificant. See synonyms under USELESS. [< L *nugatorius* < *nugae* trifles, nonsense] —**nu'ga·to'ri·ly** *adv.* —**nu'·ga·to'ri·ness** *n.*

nug·get (nug'it) *n.* A lump; specifically, a lump of precious metal, usually gold, found in a free state. [? dim. of dial. E *nug* lump]

nug·get·y (nug'it·ē) *adj.* **1** Found in the form of nuggets. **2** Nugget-shaped.

nui·sance (nōō'səns, nyōō'-) *n.* **1** That which annoys, vexes, or harms. **2** *Law* That which by its use or existence works annoyance or damage to another. See synonyms under ABOMINATION. [< F < *nuire* harm < L *nocere*]

nuisance tax A small tax paid by the consumer and considered a nuisance by both the collector and the payer.

Nu·ku·a·lo·fa (nōō'kōō·ä·lō'fä) Capital of the Tonga Islands.

Nu·ku Hi·va (nōō'kōō hē'vä) The largest island of the Marquesas group; 46 square miles.

Nu·kus (nōō·kōōs') Capital of Kara-Kalpak Autonomous S.S.R.

null (nul) *adj.* **1** Of no legal force or effect; void: especially in the phrase **null and void. 2** Having no existence. **3** Of no avail; useless; nugatory. **4** Lacking distinction or individuality; negative. **5** Zero. See synonyms under USELESS. —*n.* **1** Something that has no force or no meaning; a cipher. **2** *Telecom.* A cone of silence. [< L *nullus* no, none]

nul·lah (nul'ə) *n. Anglo-Indian* The dry bed of a small stream, or the stream itself; a gorge or ravine. [< Hind. *nālā*]

nul·li·fi·ca·tion (nul'ə·fə·kā'shən) *n.* The act of nullifying; in U.S. history, the claim of right

by a State to refuse obedience to the laws of the United States, as by South Carolina in 1832. —**nul′li·fi·ca′tion·ist, nul′li·fi·ca′tor** *n.*

nul·li·fid·i·an nul′ə·fid′ē·ən) *adj.* Having no religious faith. —*n.* One who has no religious faith. [< L *nullus* no + *fides* faith]

nul·li·fy (nul′ə·fī) *v.t.* **·fied, ·fy·ing 1** To bring to nothing; render ineffective or valueless. **2** To deprive of legal force or effect; make void; annul. See synonyms under ABOLISH, ANNUL, CANCEL. [< LL *nullificare* < *nullus* none + *facere* make] —**nul′li·fi′er** *n.*

nul·lip·a·ra (nu·lip′ər·ə) *n. pl.* **·a·rae** (-ə·rē) A woman who has never given birth to a child. Compara PRIMIPARA, MULTIPARA. [< L *nullus* none + *parere* bring forth] —**nul·li·par·i·ty** (nul′ə·par′ə·tē) *n.* **nul·lip′a·rous** *adj.*

nul·li·pore (nul′ə·pôr, -pōr) *n. Bot.* A red-spored, coral-like, lime-secreting seaweed (family *Rhodophyceae*); a coralline. [< L *nullus* not any + *porus* pore] —**nul′li·po′rous** *adj.*

nul·li·ty (nul′ə·tē) *n. pl.* **·ties 1** The state of being null. **2** A nonentity. **3** *Law* A void act or instrument. [< F *nullité* < L *nullitas, -tatis* < *nullus* none]

Nu·ma Pom·pil·i·us (nōō′mə pom·pil′ē·əs, nyōō′-) The legendary second king of Rome, 715–675 B.C.

numb (num) *adj.* Destitute, wholly or partially, of the power of sensation or of motion; benumbed. —*v.t.* To make numb. [Orig. pp. of NIM; *b* added on analogy with *dumb, lamb*] —**numb′ly** *adv.* —**numb′ness** *n.*

Synonyms (adj.): benumbed, deadened, dull, insensible, narcotized, paralyzed, stupefied, torpid. *Antonyms*: feeling, impressionable, sensitive, sentient.

num·bat (num′bat) *n. Austral.* The banded anteater. [< native Australian]

num·ber (num′bər) *n.* **1** One of a series of symbols or words used in classifying or arranging quantities; a numeral: Nine is a *number.* When a definite number is mentioned, the sign meaning number (#) is often used, followed by a numeral: R.F.D. #2: abbr. *no.*, or *No.*, from Latin *numero,* by number. See below for principal kinds of number. **2** A collection of units or individuals, whether large or small; an indefinite aggregation: often in the plural: a *number* of facts; large *numbers of people.* **3** *pl.* The science of numerals; arithmetic. **4** The character or quality of being numerous; Reliance is placed more on spirit than on *number.* **5** One of a numbered series, as of a periodical: the May *number* of "The Atlantic"; one of the parts of a literary, artistic, or musical work issued in parts. **6** One of the divisions or movements of a piece of music or of a musical or dancing program. **7** One of a numbered group. **8** *Often pl.* Poetic measure; rhythm; hence, verse or verses. **9** *Gram.* The form of inflection of a noun, pronoun, adjective, or verb, that indicates whether one thing or more is meant. English has the singular and the plural number. Greek and Sanskrit have in addition a dual number. See DUAL, PLURAL, SINGULAR. **10** *Colloq.* An article of merchandise numbered in a catalog; hence, any article, although unnumbered: This is our most popular *number.* —**by the numbers** *Mil.* A preparatory drill command to indicate that each subsequent movement is to be carried out step by step as its number is ordered. —**to get** (or **have**) **someone's number** *Colloq.* To have insight into a person's motives, character, etc. —*v.t.* **1** To determine the total number of; count; reckon. **2** To assign a number to; designate by a number or numbers. **3** To include as one of a collection or group. **4** To amount to; total: We *number* fifty men. **5** To set or limit the number of: Your days are *numbered.* —*v.i.* **6** To make a count; total. **7** To be included, as in a group. [< F *nombre* < L *numerus*] —**num′ber·er** *n.*

—**abstract number** Any number considered without reference to any particular object: distinguished from *concrete number.*

—**algebraic number** Any number which is the solution of an algebraic equation having integer coefficients.

—**amicable number** Either of two numbers, as 220 and 284, one of which is the sum of all the divisors of the other except itself.

—**cardinal number** Any number that directly expresses the number of digits under consideration as 1, 2, 3 . . . 8, etc.

—**composite number** Any integer exactly divisible by one or more integers other than itself or 1: opposed to *prime number.*

—**compound number** A number containing more than one unit or denomination, as feet and inches.

—**concrete number** A number applied to particular objects, as, four men; ten dollars; distinguished from *abstract number.*

—**defective number** A number which is greater than the sum of all its divisors except itself.

—**denominate number** A number expressing units of a specified kind, as, pounds, bushels, miles, etc.

—**irrational number** A number which cannot be expressed as an integer or the quotient of integers, as $\sqrt{2}$ $\sqrt{5}$, π, etc.

—**mixed number** A number, as 3 1/2, 5 3/4, which is the sum of an integer and a fraction.

—**ordinal number** A number that shows the order of a unit in a given series, as, first, second, third, etc.

—**perfect number** A number, as 6, 28, 496, which is equal to the sum of all its aliquots except itself. Compare *amicable number.*

—**polygonal number** The sum of an arithmetical progression that has the property of corresponding numerically to the number of points required to form a group of successively larger, regular polygons in accordance with a certain rule, as, 3, 6, 10, 15 . . .

—**prime number** A number divisible without remainder by no whole number except itself and unity: opposed to *composite number.*

—**Pythagorean numbers** Any set of three integers, as 3, 4, 5, satisfying the Pythagorean theorem.

—**rational number** A number which can be expressed as an integer or as a quotient of integers.

—**real number** Any rational or irrational number that does not contain an even root of a negative number.

—**sphenic number** A number product of three unequal prime factors.

—**square number** A number, as 1, 4, 9, 16, which is the square of some integer.

—**transcendental number** A number which is not an algebraic number, as π.

—**triangular number** A polygonal number which, apart from 1, is generated by making an array of dots in the form of an equilateral triangle, as 3, 6, 10, 15.

num·ber·less (num′bər·lis) *adj.* **1** Very numerous; innumerable; countless. **2** Having no number. See synonyms under INFINITE.

number one *Colloq.* **1** Oneself. **2** Anything of the best quality. **3** *Brit.* A ship's officer ranking next below the captain, equivalent to the executive officer in the U.S. Navy.

Num·bers (num′bərz) The fourth book of the Pentateuch, giving the two censuses of Israel.

numbers pool A lottery, in which wagers are laid on the appearance of some particular, unpredictable number, as the last digits in the parimutuel racing totals of a given day: also called *policy racket.* Also **numbers game.**

numb·fish (num′fish′) *n. pl.* **·fish** or **·fish·es** An electric ray.

num·bles (num′bəlz) *n. pl. Archaic.* The entrails of a deer; especially, the edible organs, as heart, liver, etc.: also spelled *nombles.* [< OF *nombles,* ult. < L *lumbulus,* dim. of *lumbus* a loin]

numb·skull (num′skul′) See NUMSKULL.

nu·men (nōō′mən, nyōō′-) *n. pl.* **·mi·na** (-mə·nə) **1** In ancient Roman religion, a local divinity or presiding spirit. **2** An indwelling force or spirit that animates or guides. [< L, divine nod < *nuere* to nod.]

nu·mer·a·ble (nōō′mər·ə·bəl, nyōō′-) *adj.* That can be numbered.

nu·mer·ral (nōō′mər·əl, nōō′-) *n.* **1** A symbol, character, or letter, alone or in combination with others, used to express a number. **2** A word that expresses number or is used in numerating or counting. —**Arabic numerals** The symbols, 1, 2, 3, 4, 5, 6, 7, 8, 9, 0, based on the decimal system and in general use since the tenth century. —**Roman numerals** The letters used until the tenth century as symbols in arithmetical notation. The basic letters are I(1), V(5), X(10), L(50), C(100), D(500), and M(1000), and intermediate and higher numbers are formed according to the following rules: Any symbol following another of equal or greater value adds to its value, as II = 2, XI = 11; any symbol preceding one of greater value substracts from its value, as IV = 4, IX = 9, XC = 90; when a symbol stands between two of greater value, it is subtracted from the second and the remainder added to the first, as XIV = 14, LIX = 59. —*adj.* **1** Used in expressing a number. **2** Pertaining to number. [< L *numeralis* < *numerus* number] —**nu′mer·al·ly** *adv.*

nu·mer·ar·y (nōō′mə·rer′ē, nyōō′-) *adj.* Pertaining to numbers.

nu·mer·ate (nōō′mə·rāt, nōō′-) *v.t.* **·at·ed, ·at·ing 1** To enumerate; count. **2** To read, as a numerical expression, according to some system of numeration. [< L *numeratus,* pp. of *numerare* number < *numerus* a number]

nu·mer·a·tion (nōō′mə·rā′shepn, nyōō′-) *n.* **1** The act or art of reading or naming numbers, or a system of reading or naming them, especially those written decimally and according to the Arabic notation. Compare NOTATION. For numbers above and including 1,000,000,000 there are two systems in use: the French, used commonly in the United States, and the English. In the former, the above number is read *one billion;* in the latter, *one thousand million.* In general, in the former the successive names *billion, trillion,* etc., apply to the results obtained by multiplying 1,000 twice, thrice, etc., by itself; in the latter to those obtained by multiplying 1,000 by itself four times, six times, etc. **2** Enumeration.

nu·mer·a·tor (nōō′mə·rā′tər, nyōō′-) *n.* **1** *Math.* In a common fraction, the term which stands above or to the left of the line and denotes how many of the parts of a unit (expressed by the denominator) are taken. **2** One who or that which numbers.

nu·mer·i·cal (nōō·mer′i·kəl, nyōō-) *adj.* **1** Pertaining to or denoting number. **2** Numerable. **3** Represented by or consisting of numbers or figures, as in arithmetic, and not by letters, as in algebra. **4** *Math.* **a** Signifying that numbers have the place of letters: opposed to *literal.* **b** Designating a quantity considered opposed to *algebraic.* [< NL *numericus* < L *numerus* a number] —**nu·mer′i·cal·ly** *adv.*

.**nu·mer·ol·o·gy** (nōō′mə·rol′ə·jē, nyōō′-) *n.* **1** The science of numbers. **2** A system that purports to explain the occult influence of numbers, as those of the day of one's birth, the month in the year, and the year in the calendar, on life. —**nu′mer·o·log′i·cal** *adj.*

nu·mer·os·i·ty (nōō′mə·ros′ə·tē, nyōō′-) *n.* **1** The state or condition of being numerous. **2** In symbolic logic, that property of a set, collection, or class which is defined by a cardinal number: the *numerosity* of a triplet, triad, or trilogy is 3.

nu·mer·ous (nōō′mər·əs, nyōō′-) *adj.* Consisting of a great number of units; being many. See synonyms under FREQUENT, MANY. —**nu′·mer·ous·ly** *adv.* —**nu′mer·ous·ness** *n.*

Nu·mid·i·a (nōō·mid′ē·ə, nyōō-) An ancient kingdom and Roman province in northern Africa, roughly corresponding to Algeria.

Nu·mid·i·an (nōō·mid′ē·ən, nyōō-) *adj.* Of or pertaining to ancient Numidia or its inhabitants. —*n.* **1** One of the ancient people of Numidia. **2** The Libyan dialect spoken by these people.

Numidian crane The demoiselle.

Numidian marble The yellow, pink, or red marbles found generally in northern Africa; especially those of Mauretania.

nu·mi·nous (nōō′mə·nəs, nyōō′-) *adj.* **1** Of or pertaining to a numen. **2** Evoking awe or reverence. **3** Mysterious; inscrutable. [< L *numen, -inis.* See NUMEN.]

nu·mis·mat·ic (nōō′miz·mat′ik, -mis-, nyōō′-) *adj.* Pertaining to or consisting of coins or medals. Also **nu′mis·mat′i·cal.** [< F *numismatique* < L *numisma, -atis* a coin < Gk. *nomisma* < *nomizein* sanction]

nu·mis·mat·ics (nōō′miz·mat′iks, -mis-, nyōō′-) *n. pl.* (*construed as singular*) The science of coins and medals. Also **nu·mis·ma·tol·o·gy** (nōō·miz′mə·tol′ə·jē, -mis′-, nyōō-). —**nu·mis′·ma·tist, nu·mis′ma·tol′o·gist** *n.*

num·mu·lar (num′yə·lər) *adj.* **1** Of or pertaining to coins or money: also **num·ma·ry** (num′ər·ē). **2** Resembling coins: *nummular* sputa. Also **num′mu·lar′y, num′mu·lat′ed.** [< L *nummulus,* dim. of *nummus* a coin

num·mu·la·tion (num′yə·lā′shən) *n.* The arrangement of red blood corpuscles in columns

like stacked-up coins, as seen under the microscope.

num·mu·lite (num′yə·līt) *n. Paleontol.* A large foraminifer of a nearly extinct family characteristic of the older Tertiary: preserved fossil forms show it as having a thin, coinlike shell. [<L *nummulus* small coin] — **num′mu·lit′ic** (-lit′ik) *adj.*

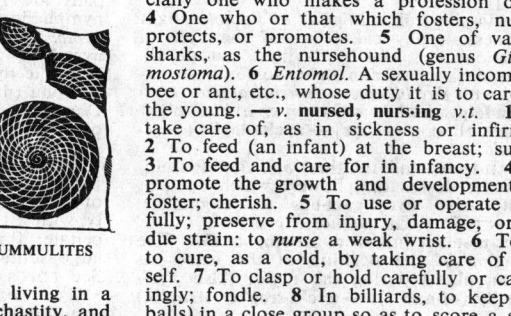

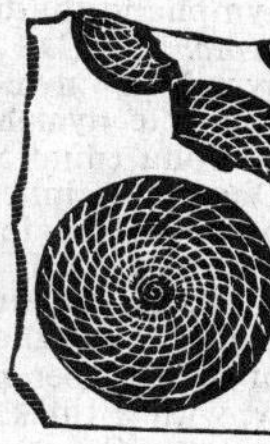
NUMMULITES

num·skull (num′skul) *n.* A blockhead; a dunce: also spelled *numbskull.*

nun[1] (no͞on, no͝on) *n.* The fourteenth Hebrew letter.

nun[2] (nun) *n.* **1** A woman devoted to a religious life, and living in a convent under vows of poverty, chastity, and obedience. **2** One of various birds, as the nunbird. **3** *Naut.* A conical or cone-shaped buoy made of metal: also **nun buoy.** [OE *nunne* <L *nonna,* fem. of *nonnus* an old man] — **nun′nish** *adj.*

Nun (no͞on) A principal outlet of the Niger in southern Nigeria.

nun·bird (nun′bûrd′) *n.* A South American bird (genus *Monasa*) having black plumage, usually with white about the head: also called *trappist.*

nunc di·mit·tis (nungk′ di·mit′is) *Latin* A dismissal; departure; permission to depart.

Nunc dimittis 1 The song or canticle of Simeon (*Luke* ii 29–32): so called from the first two words of the Latin version. **2** An English translation of this canticle. **3** A musical setting for this. [<L, now let depart]

nun·ci·a·ture (nun′shē·ə·cho͝or) *n.* The office or term of office of a nuncio. [<Ital. *nunziatura* < *nunzio* NUNCIO]

nun·ci·o (nun′shē·ō) *n. pl.* **·ci·os 1** An ordinary ambassador of the pope to a foreign court or government: distinguished from *legate.* **2** Any messenger. Also **nun′ci·us** (-shē·əs). [<Ital. *nunzio* <L *nuntius* a messenger]

nun·cle (nung′kəl) *n. Dial.* An uncle. [< *an uncle,* taken as *a nuncle*]

nun·cu·pa·tive (nung′kyə·pā′tiv, nung·kyo͞o′pə·tiv) *adj. Law* Oral as distinguished from written: said especially of a will. Also **nun′cu·pa·to′ry** (-pə·tôr′ē, -tō′rē). [<LL *nuncupativus* < *nuncupare* call by name]

Nun·ea·ton (nun·ē′tən) A municipal borough of NE Warwick, England.

nun·na·tion (nu·nā′shən) *n.* The addition of the letter *n* to a word, as in the declension of Arabic nouns. [<Arabic *nūn,* the letter *n*]

nun·ner·y (nun′ər·ē) *n. pl.* **·ner·ies** A convent for nuns. See synonyms under CLOISTER.

nun's-veil·ing (nunz′vā′ling) *n.* A soft, thin, untwilled woolen fabric, used for veiling and as a dress material.

Nu·per·caine (no͞o′pər·kān, nyo͞o′-) *n.* Proprietary name for a white, crystalline, odorless compound, $C_{20}H_{29}N_3O_2$, used as a local anesthetic with an action similar to that of cocaine or procaine.

nup·tial (nup′shəl) *adj.* Pertaining to marriage or the marriage ceremony. See synonyms under MATRIMONIAL. [<L *nuptialis* < *nuptus,* pp. of *nubere* marry] — **nup′tial·ly** *adv.*

nuptial flight *Entomol.* The mating flight of many insects, as ants and gnats, during which conspicuous swarming may occur.

nup·tials (nup′shəlz) *n. pl.* (*construed as singular*) The marriage ceremony or state. See synonyms under MARRIAGE.

nu·ragh (no͞o′räg) *n.* One of a class of prehistoric stone structures numerous in Sardinia: also spelled *noraghe.* Also **nu·ra′ghe** (-rä′gā). [< dial. Ital. *nuraghe*]

Nu·rem·berg (no͝or′əm·bûrg, nyo͝or′-) A city of northern Bavaria, West Germany. *German* **Nürn·berg** (nürn′berkh).

Nu·ris·tan (no͝or′is·tan) A mountainous district of NE Afghanistan; 5,000 square miles: formerly *Kafiristan.*

nurl (nûrl) *v.t.* To mill or roughen, as the rim of a coin. [Var. of KNURL]

nurse (nûrs) *n.* **1** A female servant who takes care of young children: in the case of one who suckles an infant, called a wet-nurse; otherwise, less frequently, a drynurse. **2** One who suckles a babe. **3** A person who cares for the sick, wounded, or enfeebled, especially one who makes a profession of it. **4** One who or that which fosters, nurses, protects, or promotes. **5** One of various sharks, as the nursehound (genus *Ginglymostoma*). **6** *Entomol.* A sexually incomplete bee or ant, etc., whose duty it is to care for the young. — *v.* **nursed, nurs·ing** *v.t.* **1** To take care of, as in sickness or infirmity. **2** To feed (an infant) at the breast; suckle. **3** To feed and care for in infancy. **4** To promote the growth and development of; foster; cherish. **5** To use or operate carefully; preserve from injury, damage, or undue strain: to *nurse* a weak wrist. **6** To try to cure, as a cold, by taking care of oneself. **7** To clasp or hold carefully or caressingly; fondle. **8** In billiards, to keep (the balls) in a close group so as to score a series of caroms. — *v.i.* **9** To act or serve as a nurse. **10** To take nourishment from the breast. **11** To suckle an infant. See synonyms under CHERISH. [Earlier *nurice* <OF <LL *nutricia* <L *nutrix* < *nutrire* nourish, foster] — **nurs′er** *n.*

nurse·maid (nûrs′mād′) *n.* A girl or woman employed to care for children.

nurs·er·y (nûr′sər·ē) *n. pl.* **·er·ies 1** A room in a house set apart for the occupation and use of children; also, a playroom. **2** A place where trees, shrubs, etc., are raised for sale or transplanting. **3** The place where anything is fostered, bred, or developed; hence, any condition that promotes growth. **4** *Obs.* The act of nursing; also, that which is nursed.

nurs·er·y·man (nûr′sər·ē·mən) *n. pl.* **·men** (-mən) One who owns or manages a nursery for the cultivation of trees and shrubs.

nursery rime A simple story, riddle, proverb, etc., presented in rimed verse or jingle for children.

nursing bottle A small, graduated bottle fitted with a rubber nipple, for feeding infants.

nursing home A small private hospital.

nurs·ling (nûrs′ling) *n.* An infant; also, anything that is carefully tended or supervised. Also **nurse′ling.**

nur·ture (nûr′chər) *n.* **1** The act of nourishing. **2** That which nourishes or fosters; education. **3** *Biol.* The aggregate of environmental conditions and influences acting on an organism subsequent to birth. Compare NATURE. — *v.t.* **·tured, ·tur·ing 1** To feed or support; nourish; rear; foster. **2** To bring up or train; educate. [<OF *nurture,* var. of *nourriture* <LL *nutritura* <L *nutrire* nourish] — **nur′tur·er** *n.*

Synonyms (noun): breeding, discipline, education, instruction, schooling, teaching, training, tuition. *Breeding* and *nurture* include *teaching* and *training*, especially as directed by and dependent upon home life and personal association; *breeding* having reference largely to manners with such qualities as are deemed distinctively characteristic of high birth; *nurture* (literally *nourishing*) having more direct reference to moral qualities, not overlooking the physical and mental. See EDUCATION, CHERISH, TEACH.

Nu·sa Teng·ga·ra (no͞o′sə teng·gä′rə) A province of Indonesia, comprising all of the Lesser Sunda Islands, exclusive of Portuguese Timor; 61,995 square miles; capital, Singaradja, on Bali.

nut (nut) *n.* **1** *Bot.* **a** A fruit consisting of a kernel or seed enclosed in a woody shell, as in the hazelnut, beechnut, or chestnut; also, the kernel of such fruit, especially when edible. **b** A hard, indehiscent, one-seeded pericarp resulting from a compound ovary. **2** *Mech.* A small block of metal having an internal screw thread so that it may be fitted upon a bolt, screw, or the like. **3** A person or matter difficult to deal with; a problem. **4** *Slang* The head. **5** *Slang* A crazy or irresponsible person. **6** The ridge at the upper end of the neck of stringed instruments, serving to elevate the strings; also, the adjustable end of a fiddle bow. — *v.i.* **nut·ted, nut·ting** To seek or gather nuts. [OE *hnutu*] — **nut′ter** *n.*

nu·tant (no͞o′tənt, nyo͞o′-) *adj. Bot.* Nodding; drooping: said especially of flowers. [<L *nutans, -antis,* ppr. of *nutare* nod]

nu·ta·tion (no͞o·tā′shən, nyo͞o-) *n.* **1** *Astron.* The periodic inequalities in the motion of the axis and pole of the earth around the pole of the ecliptic as a center. **2** *Bot.* A spontaneous rotatory movement, as of young growing parts of plants. **3** The act of nodding the head. [<L *nutatio, -onis* < *nutare* nod] — **nu·ta′tion·al** *adj.*

nut·crack·er (nut′krak′ər) *n.* **1** *Chiefly pl.* A device for cracking nuts. **2** One of certain crowlike birds (genus *Nucifraga*), as the common Old World nutcracker (*N. caryocatactes*), or **Clark's nutcracker** (*N. columbiana*) of the coniferous forests of western North America. **3** A nuthatch.

nut·gall (nut′gôl′) *n.* A nut-shaped gall, as on an oak tree; an oak apple.

nut·grass (nut′gras′, -gräs′) *n.* A perennial herb (*Cyperus rotundus*) of the sedge family bearing nutlike tubers: also called *cocograss.*

nut·hatch (nut′hach′) *n.* A small, short-tailed bird (family *Sittidae*) related to the titmouse, having a slender bill as long as the head and feeding on nuts and insects.

nut·let (nut′lit) *n.* **1** A diminutive nut. **2** The stone in a drupe.

nut·meg (nut′meg) *n.* **1** The aromatic kernel of the fruit of various tropical trees (genus *Myristica*), especially of the nutmeg tree (*M. fragrans*) of the Molucca Islands. **2** The tree itself. [ME *notemuge,* partial trans. of OF *nois mugue* < *nois* nut + *mugue* musk <L *muscus*]

nutmeg flower Fennelflower.

Nutmeg State Nickname of CONNECTICUT.

nut pick A small sharp-pointed instrument for picking out the kernels of nuts.

nu·tri·a (no͞o′trē·ə, nyo͞o′-) *n.* **1** The coypu. **2** Its soft, brown fur, often dyed to resemble beaver. [<Sp., an otter <L *lutra*]

nu·tri·ent (no͞o′trē·ənt, nyo͞o′-) *adj.* **1** Giving nourishment. **2** Conveying nutrition. — *n.* **1** Something that nourishes. **2** A drug or other substance which acts upon the nutritive processes of an organism. [<L *nutriens, -entis,* ppr. of *nutrire* nourish]

nutrient solution A solution containing, in correct proportions and strength, the various chemical substances required for plant growth: used in hydroponics.

nu·tri·ment (no͞o′trə·mənt, nyo͞o′-) *n.* **1** That which nourishes; food. **2** That which promotes development. [<L *nutrimentum* < *nutrire* nourish] — **nu′tri·men′tal** *adj.*

Synonyms: aliment, food, meat, nourishment, provision, sustenance. *Nourishment* and *sustenance* apply to whatever can be introduced into the system as a means of sustaining life; we say of a convalescent: He is taking *nourishment. Aliment* is similar in meaning, but less frequent in use. *Nutriment* and *nutrition* have more of scientific reference to the vitalizing principles of various *foods*; thus, wheat is said to contain a great amount of *nutriment.* Compare FOOD.

nu·tri·tion (no͞o·trish′ən, nyo͞o-) *n.* **1** The aggregate of all the processes by which food is assimilated, growth promoted, and waste repaired in living organisms. **2** Nutriment. See synonyms under FOOD. [<L *nutrire*] — **nu·tri′tion·al** *adj.* — **nu·tri′tion·al·ly** *adv.*

nu·tri·tion·ist (no͞o·trish′ən·ist, nyo͞o-) *n.* One who specializes in the processes and problems of nutrition.

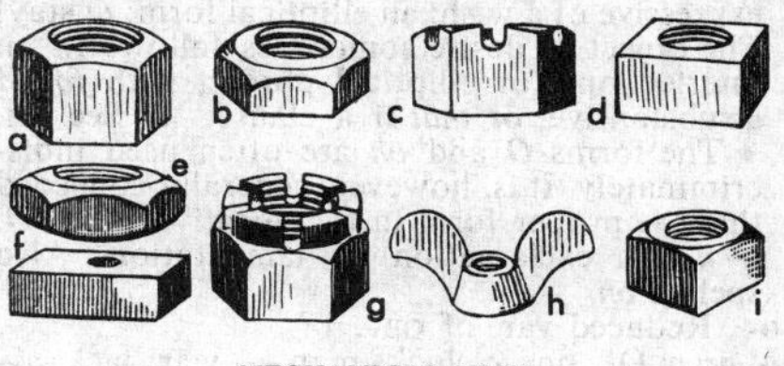

MECHANICAL NUTS

a. Hexagonal, soft. *b.* Lock. *c.* Hexagonal, slotted. *d.* Square, plain. *e.* Double-cupped. *f.* Joint, untapped. *g.* Castle. *h.* Thumb. *i.* Square, chamfered.

nu·tri·tious (no͞o·trish′əs, nyo͞o-) *adj.* Nourishing; promoting nutrition; trophic. — **nu·tri′tious·ly** *adv.* — **nu·tri′tious·ness** *n.*

nu·tri·tive (no͞o′trə·tiv, nyo͞o′-) *adj.* **1** Having nutritious properties. **2** Of or relating to

nutrition. — **nu′tri·tive·ly** adv. — **nu′tri·tive·ness** n.

nuts (nuts) Slang adj. **1** Crazy; demented. **2** Madly in love: with about. **3** Extremely enthusiastic: with about: He's nuts about baseball. — interj. An exclamation of scorn, disapproval, etc. [<NUT]

nut·shell (nut′shel′) n. The shell of a nut. — **in a nutshell** In brief and concise statement or form.

Nut·tall (nut′ôl), **George Henry Falkiner**, 1862–1937, U.S. biologist.

nut·ter (nut′ər) n. One who gathers nuts.

nut·ty (nut′ē) adj. **·ti·er**, **·ti·est** **1** Abounding in nuts. **2** Having the flavor of nuts. **3** Slang Crazy; also, madly in love; very enthusiastic. — **nut′ti·ly** adv. — **nut′ti·ness** n.

nut·wood (nut′wŏŏd′) n. **1** Any tree bearing nuts, as walnut, hazel, hickory, etc. **2** The wood of such a tree.

nux vom·i·ca (nuks′ vom′i·kə) **1** The flattened, disklike, silky, poisonous seed of an Indian tree (Strychnos nux-vomica). It contains several alkaloidal poisons, principally strychnine and brucine. **2** The tree producing this fruit. [<Med. L <nux a nut + vomere vomit]

nuz·zle (nuz′əl) v. **·zled**, **·zling** v.i. **1** To root or dig with the nose or snout, as a hog does. **2** To nestle or snuggle; lie close. — v.t. **3** To rub with the nose; push the nose against. **4** To root up with the nose or snout. [Freq. of NOSE, v.]

ny·an·za (nī·an′zə) n. A sheet of water; lake; also, a river feeding a lake. [<Bantu]

Nya·sa (nyä′sä, nī·as′ə), **Lake** A lake in eastern Africa between Nyasaland and Mozambique; 11,000 square miles. Formerly **Nyas′sa.**

Nya·sa·land (nyä′sä·land, nī·as′ə-) A former British protectorate in SE Africa. See MALAWI.

nyc·ta·gi·na·ceous (nik′tə·ji·nā′shəs) adj. Bot. Of or pertaining to a family of plants (Nyctaginaceae) widely distributed in warm and tropical lands, including the bougainvillea; the four-o'-clock family. [<NL <Nyctago,

-inis, former genus name <Gk. nyx, nyktos night]

nyc·ta·lo·pi·a (nik′tə·lō′pē·ə) n. Pathol. Night blindness; a physical defect of the eyes in which one sees well by daylight, but poorly in the dark or in dim light: sometimes confused with day blindness or hemeralopia. Also **nyc′ta·lo′py.** [<NL <Gk. nyx, nyktos night + alaos blind + ōps eye] — **nyc′ta·lop′ic** (-lop′ik) adj.

nyc·tan·thous (nik·tan′thəs) adj. Bot. Pertaining to or designating flowers which open at night. Also **nyc·ti·gam·ous** (nik′tə·gam′əs). [<NYCT(O) + Gk. anthos flower]

nyc·tit·ro·pism (nik·tit′rə·piz′əm) n. Bot. The changing of the position of the leaves of certain plants during the night. Also **nyc′ti·nas′ty** (-ti·nas′tē). — **nyc′ti·trop′ic** (-trop′ik) adj.

nycto– combining form Night; nocturnal: nyctophobia. Also, before vowels, **nyct–.** Also **nycti–.** [<Gk. nyx, nyktos night]

nyc·to·pho·bi·a (nik′tə·fō′bē·ə) n. Morbid fear of night or of darkness: also called noctiphobia, scotophobia. — **nyc′to·pho′bic** adj.

Nye (nī), **Edgar Wilson**, 1850–96, U.S. humorist: known as Bill Nye.

nyet (nyet) adv. Russian No.

Nyí·regy·há·za (nye′redy′·hä′zô) A city in NE Hungary.

nyl·ghai (nil′gī), **nyl·ghau** (nil′gô) See NILGAI.

Ny·lon (nī′lon) n. A synthetic thermoplastic polyamide derivative from coal, air, and water, which may be formed into fibers, bristles, sheets, and other forms which, when drawn, are characterized by extreme toughness, elasticity, and strength: a trade name.

ny·lons (nī′lonz) n. pl. Stockings made of Nylon.

nymph (nimf) n. **1** In Greek and Roman mythology, a beautiful maiden belonging to a class of lesser divinities inhabiting groves, forests, fountains, springs, mountains, the ocean, etc. **2** Hence, an attractive girl; a lovely young woman. **3** Entomol. **a** The young of an insect which undergoes incom-

plete metamorphosis, at which stage the wing pads are first evident. **b** One of various nymphalid butterflies, as a fritillary. [<L nympha <Gk. nymphē nymph, bride] — **nymph′al**, **nym·phe·an** (nim·fē′ən) adj. — **nymph′ic**, **nymph′i·cal** adj.

nym·pha (nim′fə) n. pl. **·phae** (-fē) **1** Anat. One of the inner folds of the mucous membrane of the female pudenda. **2** A nymph (def. 3a). [<L <Gk. nymphē a bride]

nym·phae·a·ceous (nim′fē·ā′shəs) adj. Pertaining to or designating a family (Nymphaeaceae) of aquatic, perennial herbs, the waterlily family, with a thick, horizontal rootstock, mainly peltate, floating or submersed leaves, and large solitary flowers living in fresh water. See LOTUS. [<NL <L nymphaea waterlily <Gk. nymphaia]

nym·pha·lid (nim′fə·lid) n. Any of a family (Nymphalidae) of medium to large butterflies, often brightly colored, including the emperor, tortoise-shell, and admiral butterflies. [<NL <L nympha a nymph]

nympho– combining form Nymph; bride: nymphomania. Also, before vowels, **nymph–.** [<Gk. nymphē a nymph]

nym·pho·lep·sy (nim′fə·lep′sē) n. **1** A kind of ecstasy or frenzy, said to have taken possession of one who looked upon a nymph. **2** An emotional state caused by an unrealizable desire. [<Gk. nympholeptos frenzied < nymphē a nymph + lambanein take] — **nym′pho·lept** (-lept) n. — **nym′pho·lep′tic** adj.

nym·pho·ma·ni·a (nim′fə·mā′nē·ə, -mān′yə) n. Psychiatry A morbid and ungovernable sexual desire in women. — **nym′pho·ma′ni·ac** adj. & n.

Ny·sa (nē′sä) The Polish name for the NEISSE.

nys·tag·mus (nis·tag′məs) n. Pathol. A spasmodic movement of the eyes, rotatory or from side to side. [<Gk. nystagmos drowsiness < nystazein nod in sleep, grow drowsy] — **nys·tag′mic** adj.

Nyx (niks) In Greek mythology, the goddess of night: identified with the Roman Nox.

O

o, O (ō) n. pl. **o's, O's**, or **os, Os**, or **oes** (ōz) **1** The 15th letter of the English alphabet: from Phoenician ayin, which was a consonant, through Greek omicron and omega, and Roman O. **2** Any sound of the letter o. See ALPHABET. — symbol **1** Math. Zero or naught: called also round O. **2** Chem. Oxygen (symbol O). **3** Anything shaped like an O; an oval or circle; a spot or spangle: Giotto's O. See appendix (ABBREVIATIONS).

O (ō) interj. **1** An exclamation prefixed to an expression of address, as a sign of the vocative, used especially in earnest appeal or exhortation, or in prayer to the Deity, to emphasize the feeling or passion conveyed by the words. A note of exclamation usually follows the vocative word, phrase, or clause: O Lord! O my countrymen! **2** An ejaculation expressive of a wish: an elliptical form: O stay! The object of desire sometimes follows in an interjectional or elliptical phrase, with for if a substantive, or that if a clause. **3** See OH. ♦ The forms O and oh are often used indiscriminately. It is, however, generally conceded that the proper form in the vocative use is O. — n. An exclamation or lamentation. Also spelled oh.

o– Reduced var. of OB–.

o' prep. Of: one o'clock, man–o'–war, jack–o'–lantern.

O' A descendant of: O'Conor: a patronymic prefix commonly used in Irish surnames, equivalent to the English and Scandinavian suffixes -son, -sen. Compare MAC, FITZ. [<Irish ó grandson, descendant]

oaf (ōf) n. **1** Originally, a misshapen bantling left in place of a pretty child supposed to be stolen by fairies; a changeling. **2** A simpleton; a stupid, lubberly person. [Earlier auf <ON alfr elf. Akin to ELF.]

oaf·ish (ō′fish) adj. Stupid; doltish. — **oaf′ish·ly** adv. — **oaf′ish·ness** n.

O·a·hu (ō·ä′hŏŏ) The island in the north central

Hawaiian Islands on which Honolulu is located; 589 square miles.

oak (ōk) n. **1** A hardwood, acorn-bearing tree or shrub (genus Quercus) of the beech family, valued for the hardness, strength, and durability of its timber. ♦ Collateral adjective: quercine. **2** The wood or timber of the oak. **3** One of various other plants having a resemblance or relation to the oak: Jerusalem oak. **4** A stout door: so called because usually made of oak. **5** Any of various shades of finished oak wood. **6** The leaves of the oak, as in a garland: used as a crown: in ancient Rome, the reward of a hero who saved the life of a fellow man. **7** Oaken woodwork or furniture. — **quartered oak** Oaken boards cut by quarter–sawing, and exhibiting a striking grain. — **to sport one's oak** To exclude visitors by closing the outer door of one's apartment: English university slang. [OE āc]

oak apple A gall produced on an oak by an insect: also called nutgall. Also **oak gall.**

oak·en (ō′kən) adj. Made of oak.

Oak·ham (ō′kəm) The county town of Rutland county, England.

Oak·land (ōk′lənd) A port on San Francisco Bay, California.

oak–leaf cluster (ōk′lēf′) A bronze decoration given to holders of certain U.S. military medals in recognition of acts meriting a second award of the same medal. It represents a small twig bearing 4 oak leaves and 3 acorns.

Oak·ley (ōk′lē), **Annie** See ANNIE OAKLEY.

Oak Ridge A town in eastern Tennessee; site of an atomic research center.

oak·um (ō′kəm) n. Hemp fiber obtained by untwisting old rope: used in calking, etc. [OE acuma, var. of acumba <a– off, without + cemban comb[1]]

oar (ôr, ōr) n. **1** A wooden implement for propelling or, occasionally, for steering a boat, consisting of a long shaft with a blade at one end. **2** An oarsman. **3** An oarlike

appendage in certain worms. — v.t. **1** To propel with or as with oars; row. **2** To make (one's way) or traverse (water) with or as with oars. — v.i. **3** To proceed by or as by rowing; row. ♦ Homophone: ore. [OE ār] — **oar′less** adj.

oared (ôrd, ōrd) adj. **1** Having oars for propulsion. **2** Having oarlike feet or swimming appendages.

oar·fish (ôr′fish′, ōr′-) n. pl. **·fish** or **·fish·es** Any of several fishes (genus Regalecus) of northern seas, with oarlike dorsal rays and a length of up to twenty feet.

oar·lock (ôr′lok′, ōr′-) n. A device on the side of a boat for keeping an oar in place; rowlock. [OE ārloc <ār oar + loc lock, enclosure]

oars·man (ôrz′mən, ōrz′-) n. pl. **·men** (-mən) One who rows.

oars·man·ship (ôrz′mən·ship, ōrz′-) n. The art of rowing; skill in rowing.

o·a·sis (ō·ā′sis, ō′ə·sis) n. pl. **·ses** (-sēz) **1** An area in a waste or desert made fertile by ground water or by surface irrigation. **2** Any place providing relief or refreshment; refuge: a small city park that provided an oasis of quiet amidst the street noises. [<L <Gk. Oasis, a city in the Libyan Desert <Egyptian]

oast (ōst) n. A kiln for drying hops or malt. [OE āst a kiln]

oat (ōt) n. **1** Usually pl. A cereal grass (Avena sativa) extensively cultivated for its edible grain. **2** A musical pipe made from a stem of the oat; a shepherd's pipe; hence, a pastoral song. — **to feel one's oats 1** To feel lively; have a sense of vitality. **2** To feel important. — **to sow one's wild oats** To indulge in the follies or excesses to which youth is liable. [OE āt]

oat·cake (ōt′kāk′) n. A cake of oatmeal, usually rolled thin and baked hard. Also **oat cake.**

oat·en (ōt′n) adj. **1** Made of oats or oatmeal,

or of the straw of oats. 2 Sounded on a pipe made from a stem of oat.

Oates (ōts), **Titus**, 1649–1705, English impostor who fabricated a supposed Catholic conspiracy to massacre Protestants, burn London, and kill the king; convicted of perjury; pardoned.

oat·grass (ōt′gras′, -gräs′) *n.* **1** Any uncultivated kind of oats. **2** Any of various oatlike grasses.

oath (ōth) *n. pl.* **oaths** (ōthz) **1** A solemn attestation in support of a declaration or a promise, by an appeal to God or to some person or thing regarded as high and holy; also, the declaration or promise so supported. **2** *Law* Such an attestation or affirmation of the truth of a statement as renders liable to punishment for perjury one who wilfully thus asserts what is not true. **3** The form of words in which such attestation is made. **4** A frivolous and blasphemous use of the name of the Deity or of any sacred name or object, as in appeal or ejaculation. **5** An imprecation lightly or humorously used. [OE *āth*]

Synonyms: adjuration, affidavit, anathema, ban, blasphemy, curse, denunciation, execration, imprecation, malediction, profanity, reprobation, swearing, vow. In the highest sense, as in a court of justice, "an *oath* is a reverent appeal to God in corroboration of what one says"; an *affidavit* is a sworn statement made in writing in the presence of a competent officer; an *adjuration* is a solemn appeal to a person in the name of God to speak the truth. An *oath* is made to man in the name of God; a *vow* is usually made to God. In the lower sense, an *oath* may be mere *blasphemy* or profane *swearing*. *Anathema, curse, execration,* and *imprecation* are modes of invoking vengeance or retribution from a superhuman power upon the person against whom they are uttered. *Anathema* is a solemn ecclesiastical condemnation of a person or of a proposition. *Curse* may be just and authoritative; as, the *curse* of God; or, it may be wanton and powerless. *Execration* expresses most of personal bitterness and hatred; *imprecation* refers to the coming of the desired evil upon the person against whom it is uttered. *Malediction* is a general wish of evil, a less usual but very expressive word. Compare TESTIMONY. *Antonyms*: benediction, benison, blessing

oat·meal (ōt′mēl′) *n.* **1** The meal of oats. **2** Porridge made of it. Also **oat meal.**

Oa·xa·ca (wä·hä′kä) A state in SW Mexico on the Pacific; 36,355 square miles; capital, Oaxaca. Also **Oa·xa′ca de Juá·rez** (thā hwä′·räs).

Ob (ōb) A river of western Asian Russian S.F.S.R., flowing 2,500 miles NW to the **Ob Gulf,** an inlet of the Kara Sea 500 miles long.

ob– *prefix* **1** Toward; to; facing: *obvert.* **2** Against; in opposition to: *object, obstruct.* **3** Over; upon: *obliterate.* **4** Completely: *obdurate.* **5** Inversely: *obovate*: prefixed to adjectives in scientific Neo-Latin and English terms. Also: *o–* before *m,* as in *omit; oc–* before *c,* as in *occur; of–* before *f,* as in *offend; op–* before *p,* as in *oppress.* [<L *ob* toward, for, against]

O·ba·di·ah (ō′bə·dī′ə) A masculine personal name. [<Hebrew, servant of the Lord]
— **Obadiah** A minor prophet living in the sixth century B.C.; also, the book of the Old Testament containing his prophecies.

ob·bli·ga·to (ob′lə·gä′tō, *Ital.* ôb′blē·gä′tō) *adj.* **1** That cannot be dispensed with; necessary. **2** *Music* Referring to parts or accompaniments essential to the performance of a composition. — *n. pl.* **·tos** or **·ti** (-tē) *Music* A part or accompaniment, usually written for a single instrument. [<Ital. *obbligato, obligato* <L *obligatus,* pp. of *obligare.* See OBLIGE.]

ob·cor·date (ob·kôr′dāt) *adj. Bot.* Inversely heart-shaped, as the leaves of some plants. [<OB- + CORDATE]

ob·du·ra·cy (ob′dyə·rə·sē) *n.* Obstinacy; obdurateness.

ob·du·rate (ob′dyə·rit, -rāt) *adj.* **1** Unmoved by feelings of humanity or pity; inexorable. **2** Perversely impenitent. **3** Unyielding; stubborn. See synonyms under HARD, OBSTINATE. [<L *obduratus,* pp. of *obdurare* harden < *ob–* against + *durare* harden < *durus* hard] — **ob′·du·rate·ly** *adv.* — **ob′du·rate·ness** *n.*

o·be (ō′bē), **o·be·ah** (ō′bē·ə) See OBI.

o·be·di·ence (ō·bē′dē·əns, ə·bē′-) *n.* **1** Submission to command, prohibition, law, or duty. **2** The fact of being obeyed, or having subjects obedient to one. **3** *Eccl.* Sphere of authority, or those acknowledging it. See synonyms under ALLEGIANCE, SUBMISSION.

o·be·di·ent (ō·bē′dē·ənt, ə·bē′-) *adj.* Complying with or submitting to a behest, law, etc.; habitually yielding to authority; submissive; dutiful. See synonyms under DOCILE, OBSEQUIOUS. [<OF *obedient* <L *obediens, -entis,* ppr. of *obedire* OBEY] — **o·be′di·ent·ly** *adv.*

O·beid (ō·bād′), **El** Capital of Kordofan province, Sudan.

o·bei·sance (ō·bā′səns, ō·bē′-) *n.* An act of courtesy or reverence, consisting of bowing or a bending of the knee; a bow or courtesy; homage; deference. [<OF *obeissance* < *obeissant,* ppr. of *obeir* OBEY] — **o·bei′sant** *adj.*

ob·e·lisk (ob′ə·lisk) *n.* **1** A square shaft with pyramidal top, usually monumental. The Egyptian obelisks are always monolithic and slightly tapering. **2** *Printing* The dagger sign (†) used as a mark of reference; obelus. [<L *obeliscus* <Gk. *obeliskos,* dim. of *obelos* a spit, pointed pillar] — **ob·e·lis′cal, ob′e·lis′koid** *adj.*

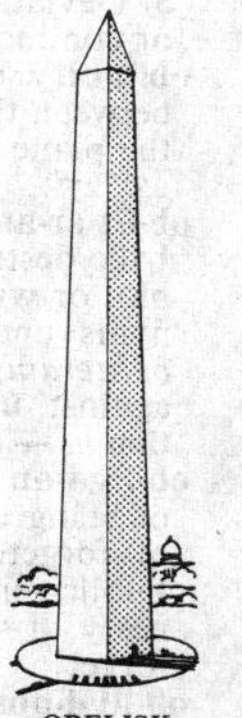

OBELISK
Washington Monument, Washington, D.C. (555 feet, 5 1/2 inches high)

ob·e·lize (ob′ə·līz) *v.t.* **·lized, ·liz·ing** To mark with an obelus. [<Gk. *obelizein* mark with an obelus < *obelos* an obelus]

ob·e·lus (ob′ə·ləs) *n. pl.* **·li** (-lī) **1** A critical mark, as — or ÷, used in ancient manuscripts to designate a suspected reading or to indicate a spurious passage. **2** *Printing* Obelisk. [<L <Gk. *obelos* a spit, obelisk, critical mark]

O·ber·am·mer·gau (ō′bər·äm′ər·gou) A village in Upper Bavaria, West Germany; noted for its Passion play, presented once a decade, performed by the villagers.

O·ber·hau·sen (ō′bər·hou′zən) A city in North Rhine-Westphalia, West Germany.

O·ber·land (ō′bər·länt) A mountainous region of central Switzerland, specifically the **Bernese Oberland** (*Bernese Alps).*

O·ber·on (ō′bə·ron) In medieval legend, folklore, and Shakespeare's *Midsummer Night's Dream,* the king of the fairies, husband of Titania.

o·bese (ō·bēs′) *adj.* Very corpulent. See synonyms under CORPULENT. [<L *obesus* fat, orig. pp. of *obedere* devour < *ob–* completely + *edere* eat] — **o·bese′ly** *adv.*

o·bes·i·ty (ō·bē′sə·tē, ō·bes′ə-) *n. Pathol.* An excessive accumulation of fat in the body; morbid corpulency. Also **o·bese′ness.**

o·bey (ō·bā′, ə·bā′) *v.t.* **1** To do the bidding of; be obedient to. **2** To carry into effect; execute, as a command. **3** To act in accordance with; be guided by: to *obey* the law. — *v.i.* **4** To be obedient. [<OF *obeir* <L *obedire,* var. of *oboedire* give ear, obey < *ob–* in the direction of + *audire* hear] — **o·bey′er** *n.*

Synonyms: comply, defer, keep, observe, submit, yield. See FOLLOW, KEEP, SERVE. *Antonyms*: contemn, defy, disobey, infringe, refuse, resist, violate. See synonyms for GOVERN.

ob·fus·cate (ob·fus′kāt, ob′fəs-) *v.t.* **·cat·ed, ·cat·ing** **1** To confuse or perplex; bewilder. **2** To darken or obscure. [<L *obfuscatus,* pp. of *obfuscare* darken, obscure < *ob–* against + *fuscare* darken < *fuscus* dark] — **ob′fus·ca′·tion** *n.*

o·bi[1] (ō′bē) *n.* **1** A kind of sorcery practiced by the Negroes of the West Indies and SE United States: a revival or survival of African magic rites, specializing in poisons and the power of terror. **2** A charm or fetish used in these magical practices. Also called *obe, obeah.* [Var. of *obeah* < native West African name] — **o′bi·ism** *n.*

o·bi[2] (ō′bē) *n.* A broad sash with a bow in the back, worn by Japanese women: also spelled *obe.* [<Japanese *ōbi*]

O·bi Islands (ō′bē) An Indonesian island group NW of Ceram; 1,069 square miles: also *Ombi.*

o·bi·it (ō′bē·it) *Latin* He (or she) died.

o·bit (ō′bit, ob′it) *n.* **1** The death or date of death of a person; also, an obituary. **2** A ceremony or service commemorating a death. [<OF <L *obitus* a going down, a death < *obire* go down, die < *ob–* down + *ire* go]

ob·i·ter dic·tum (ob′ə·tər dik′təm) *Latin pl.* **ob·i·ter dic·ta** (dik′tə) A remark by the way or in passing. See DICTUM.

o·bit·u·ar·y (ō·bich′ōō·er′ē) *adj.* Pertaining to the death of a person. — *n. pl.* **·ar·ies** A published notice of a death; a biographical sketch of one recently deceased. [<Med. L *obituarius* <L *obitus.* See OBIT.]

ob·ject[1] (əb·jekt′) *v.i.* **1** To offer arguments or opposition; dissent. **2** To feel or state disapproval; be averse. — *v.t.* **3** To offer as opposition or criticism; charge. See synonyms under OPPOSE. [<L *objectus,* pp. of *objicere* < *ob–* towards, against + *jacere* throw] — **ob·jec′tor** *n.*

ob·ject[2] (ob′jikt, -jekt) *n.* **1** Anything that lies within the cognizance of the senses; especially, anything tangible or visible; any material thing. **2** That which is affected or intended to be affected by feeling or action. **3** That on which one sets his mind as an end; purpose; aim. **4** *Gram.* A noun or pronoun to which the action of a transitive verb is directed, or which receives or endures the effect of this action. A **direct object** receives the direct action of the verb, as in the sentence "He ate the pie," *pie* is the direct object of *ate*; an **indirect object** receives the secondary action of the verb, as in "She gave him the pie," *him* is the indirect object of *gave.* **5** *Colloq.* A person of pitiable or ridiculous aspect; any sight that evokes laughter, disgust, pity, etc. See synonyms under AIM, DESIGN, PURPOSE, REASON. [<Med. L *objectum* something thrown in the way <L *objectus.* See OBJECT[1].]

object ball In billiards or pool, the ball which the player purposes to hit with his cue ball.

object glass *Optics* A lens or combination of lenses for focusing the rays of light passing through it; in a telescope or microscope, the lens nearest the object; in a camera or projector, the lens that makes the image of the object. Also **object lens.**

ob·jec·ti·fy (əb·jek′tə·fī) *v.t.* **·fied, ·fy·ing** To present, as in form or character, from an external viewpoint; make objective. [<OBJECT[2] + -(I)FY] — **ob·jec′ti·fi·ca′tion** *n.*

ob·jec·tion (əb·jek′shən) *n.* **1** The act of objecting. **2** An impediment raised; a dissenting argument; an adverse fact.

ob·jec·tion·a·ble (əb·jek′shən·ə·bəl) *adj.* Deserving of disapproval; offensive. — **ob·jec′·tion·a·bil′i·ty** *n.* — **ob·jec′tion·a·bly** *adv.*

ob·jec·tive (əb·jek′tiv) *adj.* **1** Of or belonging to an object; having the nature of an object or being that which is thought of or perceived, as opposed to that which thinks or perceives; outside the mind: opposed to *subjective.* **2** Directed to or pertaining to an object or end: an *objective* goal. **3** Having independent existence apart from experience or thought; substantive; self-existent. **4** Directing the mind or activity toward external things without reference to personal sensations; also, resulting from such direction; hence, representing things as they are; unbiased by thoughts, emotions, opinions, etc.: said of an artist, a writer, etc., or of his habits of thought. **5** Made up of objects represented precisely as they are, without idealization; realistic: said of a work of art, as a picture. **6** *Gram.* Denoting the case of the object of a transitive verb or of a preposition; accusative. — *n.* **1** *Gram.* **a** The objective or accusative case. **b** A word in this case. **2** *Optics* An object glass. **3** A result to be achieved or a point to be reached in any military action; the assigned goal of a mission. [<Med. L *objectivus* < *objectum.* See OBJECT[2].] — **ob·jec′tive·ly** *adv.*

ob·jec·tiv·ism (əb·jek′tə·viz′əm) *n.* **1** The power that enables an author or artist to treat subjects objectively, or apart from his own personality. **2** The tendency to give prominence to the facts of sense perception; the theory that human knowledge is based on the external world rather than within the ego. — **ob·jec′tiv·ist** *n.* — **ob·jec′tiv·is′tic** *adj.*

ob·jec·tiv·i·ty (ob′jek·tiv′ə·tē) *n.* **1** The state or relation of being objective. **2** Material reality. Also **ob·jec′tive·ness.**

ob·ject·less (ob′jikt·lis, -jekt-) *adj.* **1** Without aim; purposeless. **2** Having no corresponding object or concrete representation.

object lesson **1** A lesson in which the object to be known, or a representation of it, is shown to the eye. **2** The exemplification of a principle or moral in a concrete form or striking instance.

ob·jet d'art (ôb·zhe′ dàr′) *French pl.* **ob·jets d'art** (ôb·zhe′) Any work of artistic value.

ob·jur·gate (ob′jər·gāt, əb·jûr′-) *v.t.* **·gat·ed, ·gat·ing** To rebuke severely; scold sharply; berate. [<L *objurgatus,* pp. of *objurgare* rebuke < *ob-* against + *jurgare* scold] **— ob′·jur·ga′tion** *n.* **— ob′jur·ga′tor** *n.* **— ob·jur′ga·to′ri·ly** *adv.* **— ob·jur′ga·to′ry** *adj.*

ob·lan·ce·o·late (ob·lan′sē·ə·lit, -lāt′) *adj. Bot.* Lance-shaped, but tapering toward the base, as the leaves of certain plants. [<OB- inversely + LANCEOLATE]

ob·late[1] (ob′lāt, ob·lāt′) *adj.* Flattened at the poles: opposed to *prolate.* [<NL *oblatus* < *ob-* against, inversely + L *(pro)latus* lengthened out] **— ob′late·ly** *adv.*

ob·late[2] (ob′lāt, ob·lāt′) *adj.* Consecrated; dedicated; devoted to a religious life. *— n.* A person so devoted, as in a monastery or to certain religious work. [<Med. L *oblatus* <L, pp. to *offerre* OFFER]

ob·la·tion (ob·lā′shən) *n.* **1** The act of offering or anything offered in worship, especially the elements of the Eucharist. **2** Hence, any grateful and solemn offering. **3** In canon law, any property given to a church. [<OF, an offering, sacrifice <Med. L *oblatio, -onis* <L < *oblatus.* See OBLATE[2].] **— ob·la′tion·al** *adj.* **— ob·la·to·ry** (ob′lə·tôr′ē, -tō′rē) *adj.*

ob·li·gate (ob′lə·gāt) *v.t.* **·gat·ed, ·gat·ing** To bind or compel, as by contract, conscience, promise, etc. *— adj.* (ob′lə·git, -gāt) **1** Bound or restricted. **2** *Biol.* Having only one life condition: distinguished from *facultative.* [<L *obligatus,* pp. of *obligare* OBLIGE]

ob·li·ga·tion (ob′lə·gā′shən) *n.* **1** The act of obligating or state of being obligated; also, the duty, promise, etc., by which one is bound. **2** The constraining power of conscience or law. **3** A requirement imposed by the customs of society or the laws of propriety and expediency; what one owes in return for a service, benefit, kindness, favor, etc. **4** A binding legal agreement, contract, bond, etc., bearing a penalty. **5** The condition of being indebted for an act of kindness, a service received, etc.; also, the kindness or service. See synonyms under DUTY. **— ob′li·ga′tor** *n.*

ob·li·ga·tive (ob′lə·gā′tiv) *adj.* Implying or expressing obligation: distinguished from *facultative.*

ob·lig·a·to·ry (ə·blig′ə·tôr′ē, -tō′rē, ob′lə·gə-) *adj.* **1** In civil or moral law, binding. **2** Of the nature of, or constituting a duty or obligation; imperative.

o·blige (ə·blīj′) *v.t.* **o·bliged, o·blig·ing** **1** To obligate; constrain. **2** To place under an obligation, as for a favor or kindness. **3** To do a favor or service for. See synonyms under ACCOMMODATE, BIND, COMPEL. [<OF *obliger, obligier* bind by oath or promise <L *obligare,* orig. tie around < *ob-* towards + *ligare* bind] **— o·blig′er** *n.*

ob·li·gee (ob′lə·jē′) *n.* One who is obliged; specifically, *Law,* the person in whose favor an obligation is entered into or incurred: opposed to *obligor.*

o·blig·ing (ə·blī′jing) *adj.* Disposed to do favors; accommodating; kind. See synonyms under GOOD, PLEASANT, POLITE. **— o·blig′ing·ly** *adv.* **— o·blig′ing·ness** *n.*

ob·li·gor (ob′lə·gôr′, ob′lə·gôr) *n. Law* The person who is bound to perform an obligation.

ob·lique (ə·blēk′, *in military usage* ə·blīk′) *adj.* **1** Deviating from the perpendicular or from a right line by any angle except a right angle; neither perpendicular nor horizontal; slanting. **2** Differing from a right angle; either acute or obtuse: said of angles. **3** Evasive; indirect; not straightforward; disingenuous. **4** Not in the direct line of descent; collateral. **5** *Bot.* Unequal-sided, as a leaf. **6** *Gram.* Having to do with cases other than the nominative and vocative. **7** *Anat.* Designating several muscles whose fibers run obliquely: the external *oblique* muscle of the abdomen. *— n.* **1** One of the oblique muscles. **2** An oblique line. **3** A veering to the right or left less than ninety degrees, as in sailing. *— v.i.* **·liqued, ·li·quing** **1** To deviate from the perpendicular; slant. **2** *Mil.* To march or advance in an oblique direction. [<L *obliquus* < *ob-* against, completely + *liquis* slanting, awry] **— ob·lique′ly** *adv.* **— ob·lique′ness** *n.*

ob·lique-an·gled (ə·blēk′ang′gəld) *adj.* Having the angles oblique: an *oblique-angled* triangle.

oblique case *Gram.* Any case other than the nominative or vocative.

oblique coordinates See CARTESIAN COORDINATE SYSTEM.

oblique rime Near rime.

oblique sailing Navigation along a course lying at an oblique angle to the meridian.

ob·liq·ui·ty (ə·blik′wə·tē) *n. pl.* **·ties** **1** Oblique quality or state. **2** Inclination from a vertical or horizontal line or plane; also, the amount or the angle of such inclination. **3** Deviation from right or moral principles or conduct. **— ob·liq′ui·tous** *adj.*

obliquity of the ecliptic *Astron.* The angle between the plane of the earth's equator and the plane of the ecliptic: equal to a mean of 23° 27′.

ob·lit·er·ate (ə·blit′ə·rāt) *v.t.* **·at·ed, ·at·ing** **1** To destroy utterly; leave no trace of. **2** To blot or wipe out; erase, as writing. See synonyms under ABOLISH, ANNUL, CANCEL. [<L *obliteratus,* pp. of *obliterare* blot out < *ob-* against, upon + *litera* a letter] **— ob·lit′er·a′tion** *n.* **— ob·lit′er·a′tive** *adj.* **— ob·lit′er·a′tor** *n.*

ob·liv·i·on (ə·bliv′ē·ən) *n.* **1** The state or fact of being utterly forgotten. **2** The act or fact of forgetting completely; forgetfulness. **3** Public remission and pardon of offense; amnesty. [<OF <L *oblivio, -onis* < *oblivisci* forget]

ob·liv·i·ous (ə·bliv′ē·əs) *adj.* **1** Forgetful, or given to forgetfulness. **2** Lost in thought; abstracted. **3** Inducing forgetfulness. See synonyms under ABSTRACTED. **— ob·liv′i·ous·ly** *adv.* **— ob·liv′i·ous·ness** *n.*

ob·long (ob′lông, -long) *adj.* **1** Longer in one dimension than in another: applied most commonly to rectangular objects somewhat elongated. **2** Having one principal axis longer than the other or others. **3** *Bot.* Bluntly elliptical, as a leaf. *— n.* A figure having greater length than breadth; a long rectangle. [<L *oblongus* somewhat long < *ob-* towards + *longus* long]

ob·lo·quy (ob′lə·kwē) *n. pl.* **·quies** **1** The state of one who is under odium or disgrace or spoken ill of. **2** Vilification; defamation; calumny. **3** *Obs.* A cause of disgrace or reproach. See synonyms under SCANDAL. [<LL *obloquium* a contradiction < *obloqui* < *ob-* against + *loqui* speak]

ob·nox·ious (əb·nok′shəs) *adj.* **1** Of a character to give offense or excite aversion; odious; objectionable. **2** *Law* Liable or answerable; amenable. **3** *Obs.* Subject; exposed: *obnoxious* to punishment. See synonyms under SUBJECT. [<L *obnoxiosus* < *obnoxius* exposed to harm, liable < *ob-* towards + *noxa* an injury] **— ob·nox′ious·ly** *adv.* **— ob·nox′ious·ness** *n.*

ob·nu·bi·la·tion (ōb·nōō′bə·lā′shən, -nyōō′-) *n. Psychiatry* A nebulous or clouded state of consciousness, as just before syncope or epileptic seizures. [< obs. *obnubilate* overcloud <L *obnubilatus,* pp. of *obnubilare* < *ob-* over + *nubilare* make cloudy < *nubila* clouds]

o·boe (ō′bō, ō′boi) *n.* A wooden double-reed wind instrument with a high, penetrating, melancholy tone. [<Ital. <F *hautbois* HAUTBOY] **— o′bo·ist** *n.*

ob·o·lus (ob′ə·ləs) *n. pl.* **·li** (-lī) **1** A weight and a silver coin of ancient Greece; one sixth of a drachma. **2** A medieval silver coin of Hungary and Bohemia. Also **ob·ol** (ob′əl). See DIOBOL. [<L <Gk. *obolos*]

ob·o·vate (ob·ō′vāt) *adj. Bot.* Inversely ovate, as certain leaves. [<OB- inversely + OVATE]

ob·o·void (ob·ō′void) *adj. Bot.* Solidly obovate, with the broader end upward or outward. [<OB- inversely + OVOID]

O·bre·gón (ō′brā·gōn′), **Alvaro,** 1880–1928, president of Mexico 1920–24, 1928; assassinated.

O'Bri·en (ō·brī′ən), **Edward Joseph,** 1890–1941, U.S. editor.

ob·scene (əb·sēn′, ob-) *adj.* **1** Offensive to chastity or decency. **2** Offensive to the senses; foul. See synonyms under FOUL, IMMODEST, VULGAR. [<F *obscène* <L *obscenus, obscaenus* ill-omened, filthy < *obs-,* var. of *ob-* towards + *caenum* filth] **— ob·scene′ly** *adv.*

ob·scen·i·ty (əb·sen′ə·tē, -sē′nə-, ob-) *n. pl.* **·ties** Obscene quality of act, thought, speech, or representation; gross indecency; unchaste action; lewdness. Also **ob·scene′ness.** See synonyms under INDECENCY.

ob·scur·ant (əb·skyŏŏr′ənt) *n.* One who obscures; specifically, one who opposes education, popular enlightenment, and freedom of thought. Also **ob·scur′ant·ist.** [<G *obskurant* <L *obscurans, -antis,* ppr. of *obscurare* darken] **— ob·scur′ant·ism** *n.* **— ob·scu·ra·tion** (ob′skyə·rā′shən) *n.*

ob·scure (əb·skyŏŏr′) *adj.* **·scur·er, ·scur·est** **1** Dim; dark; dusky; gloomy. **2** Not clear to the mind; vague; abstruse. **3** Faintly marked; hard to discern; undefined. **4** Remote or apart; hidden from view or notice; hence, little known; lowly: *obscure* birth. *— v.t.* **·scured, ·scur·ing** **1** To darken or cloud; dim. **2** To hide from view; conceal. **3** To make unintelligible; confuse: to *obscure* an issue. **4** To make indefinite in sound, as a vowel. *— n.* Indistinctness of outline or color. [<OF *obscur, oscur* <L *obscurus,* lit., covered over] **— ob·scure′ly** *adv.* **— ob·scure′ness** *n.*

Synonyms (adj.): abstruse, ambiguous, complicated, dark, difficult, dim, indistinct, involved, profound, unintelligible. That is *obscure* which the eye or mind cannot clearly see or understand. If the matter is *abstruse,* as if removed from the usual way of thinking, it is *difficult* to comprehend. The matter may be *complicated* by the intertwining of its many parts, or it may be so deep as to be *profound.* The expression of the thought may be *ambiguous,* as if looking in two ways, or *involved* and confused in form, or it may be *unintelligible* to the mind. Sometimes it is *dark, dim,* and *indistinct* by reason of lack of light or want of transparency.

ob·scu·ri·ty (əb·skyŏŏr′ə·tē) *n. pl.* **·ties** **1** The state or quality of being obscure. **2** Dimness; darkness. **3** Lack of distinctness or perspicuity. **4** The condition of being unknown to fame. **5** An unknown or obscure person, place, or thing.

ob·se·crate (ob′sə·krāt) *v.t.* **·crat·ed, ·crat·ing** *Rare* To supplicate; beseech. [<L *obsecratus,* pp. of *obsecrare* beseech < *ob-* on account of + *sacrare* make sacred < *sacer* sacred] **— ob′·se·cra′tion** *n.* **— ob′se·cra′to·ry** (-krā′tər·ē) *adj.*

ob·se·qui·ous (əb·sē′kwē·əs) *adj.* **1** Sycophantic or adulatory in manner; cringing; servile. **2** *Rare* Promptly obedient. [<L *obsequiosus* compliant < *obsequium* compliance < *obsequi* comply with < *ob-* towards + *sequi* follow] **— ob·se′qui·ous·ly** *adv.* **— ob·se′qui·ous·ness** *n.*

Synonyms: attentive, compliant, cringing, deferential, fawning, flattering, obedient, servile, slavish, submissive, sycophantic. See BASE[2], SUPPLE. *Antonyms:* independent, self-assertive, self-respecting. See synonyms for AUSTERE.

ob·se·quy (ob′sə·kwē) *n. pl.* **·quies** *Usually pl.* The last office for the dead; a funeral service. [<AF *obsequie* <Med. L *obsequiae,* pl., funeral, rites, fusion of LL *exequiae* funeral rites and L *obsequium* dutiful service. See OBSEQUIOUS.]

ob·serv·a·ble (əb·zûr′və·bəl) *adj.* **1** That can be observed; manifest. **2** Notable. **3** Customary; demanding observance. **— ob·serv′a·ble·ness** *n.* **— ob·serv′a·bly** *adv.*

ob·ser·vance (əb·zûr′vəns) *n.* **1** The act of observing, as a custom or ceremony; compliance, as with law or duty. **2** Any common custom, form, rite, etc. **3** Heedful attention; observation. **4** *Eccl.* **a** The rule or constitution of a religious order. **b** The order, or the house of such an order. **5** *Archaic* Obsequious compliance. See synonyms under FORM, SACRAMENT. [<OF <L *observantia* attention, reverence, < *observans, -antis,* ppr. of *observare* OBSERVE]

ob·ser·vant (əb·zûr′vənt) *adj.* **1** Carefully attentive; habitually noting. **2** Strict in observing rules; heedful of duties. **3** Obedient; attentive. [<F, orig. ppr. of *observer* OBSERVE] **— ob·ser′vant·ly** *adv.*

Ob·ser·van·tine (ob·zûr′vən·tin, -tēn) *n.* A member of the branch of the Franciscan order which observes the original rule strictly,

especially with regard to the vow of poverty. Also **Ob·ser′vant.** [<F *Observantin* < *observant*, ppr. of *observer* OBSERVE]

ob·ser·va·tion (ob′zər·vā′shən) *n.* **1** The act, faculty, or habit of observing; the fact of being observed. **2** Scientific scrutiny of a natural phenomenon, for experiment, verification, or measurement and calculation; also, the record of such an examination and the data connected with it: an astronomical or meteorological *observation*: in this sense distinguished from *experimentation.* **3** Experience or knowledge acquired by observing. **4** An incidental remark. **5** *Obs.* Observance. See synonyms under REMARK. **— to take** (or **work out) an observation** *Naut.* To calculate the latitude and longitude from angular measurements of the altitude and position of the sun or other celestial body. **— ob′ser·va′tion·al** *adj.*

observation car A railway car with a rear section either open or glass-enclosed, used for passenger sight-seeing or for track inspection of the right-of-way.

observation post Any point, open or concealed, in which an observer may gather information of a specified nature; especially, in wartime, a station for directing gunfire, watching enemy action, etc.

ob·ser·va·to·ry (əb·zûr′və·tôr′ē, -tō′rē) *n. pl.* **·ries 1** A building designed and equipped for the systematic observation of natural phenomena: an astronomical *observatory.* **2** A tower built for obtaining a panoramic view. [<NL *observatorium* <L *observatus*, pp. of *observare* OBSERVE]

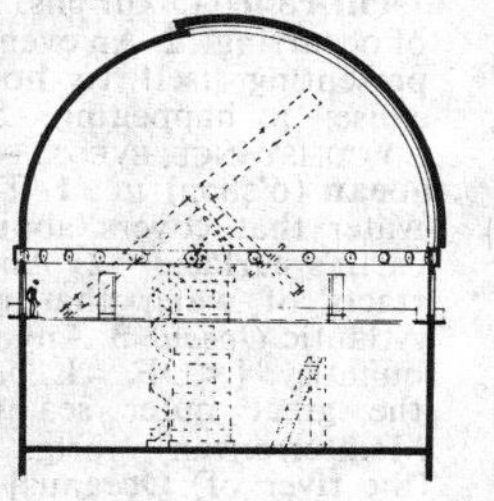

OBSERVATORY
Schematic plan.

ob·serve (əb·zûrv′) *v.* **·served, ·serv·ing** *v.t.* **1** To notice by the sense of sight; see. **2** To watch attentively; keep under surveillance: to *observe* enemy troop movements. **3** To make methodical observation of, as for scientific purposes: to *observe* sunspots. **4** To abide by the restrictions or provisions of: to *observe* a fast. **5** To celebrate or solemnize (an occasion), as with appropriate festivities or ceremony. **6** To say as a comment or opinion; mention. **—** *v.i.* **7** To make a remark; comment: often with *on* or *upon.* **8** To take notice. **9** To act as an observer. See synonyms under CELEBRATE, EXAMINE, FOLLOW, OBEY. [<OF *observer* <L *observare* watch < *ob-* towards + *servare* keep, watch] **— ob·serv′ing** *adj.* **— ob·serv′ing·ly** *adv.*

ob·serv·er (əb·zûr′vər) *n.* **1** One who observes; specifically, in modern warfare, one who observes the effect of artillery fire on the enemy, one who keeps a look-out for enemy aircraft, or one who makes meteorological observations. **2** A member of the crew of a military aircraft that makes reconnaissance flights.

ob·sess (əb·ses′) *v.t.* To occupy or trouble the mind of to an excessive degree; preoccupy; harass; haunt. [<L *obsessus*, pp. of *obsidere* besiege < *ob-* towards, against + *sedere* sit] **— ob·ses′sive** *adj.* **— ob·ses′sor** *n.*

ob·ses·sion (əb·sesh′ən) *n.* **1** A vexing or haunting, as by an evil spirit or morbidly dominant idea; the fact of being thus haunted; also, that which dominates or afflicts anyone in such manner. **2** *Psychiatry* A compulsive idea or emotion associated with the subconscious and exerting a more or less persistent influence upon conduct and behavior; also, the compulsion itself.

ob·sid·i·an (əb·sid′ē·ən, ob-) *n.* A glassy, volcanic rock, usually black and having the composition of rhyolite but containing few or no individualized crystals. [<L *obsidianus*, alter. of *obsianus*, after *Obsius*, a Roman said by Pliny to be its discoverer]

ob·sid·i·o·nal (əb·sid′ē·ə·nəl) *adj.* **1** Of or pertaining to a siege. **2** Pertaining to or contracted during trench warfare: *obsidional* infection. [<L *obsidionalis* < *obsidio, -onis* < *obsidere* besiege. See OBSESS.]

ob·so·les·cent (ob′sə·les′ənt) *adj.* Growing obsolete. [<L *obsolescens, -entis*, ppr. of *obsolescere* grow old < *ob-* against + *solere* be accustomed, use] **— ob′so·les′cence** *n.* **— ob′so·les′cent·ly** *adv.*

ob·so·lete (ob′sə·lēt) *adj.* **1** Gone out of use, as a word or phrase, a style, fashion, etc.; of a discarded type or fashion. **2** *Biol.* Imperfectly developed; atrophied; suppressed or lacking: said of markings, parts, organs, etc. [<L *obsoletus* grown old, worn out, pp. of *obsolescere.* See OBSOLESCENT.] **— ob′so·lete′ly** *adv.* **— ob′so·lete′ness** *n.* **— ob′so·let′ism** *n.*

Synonyms: ancient, antiquated archaic, disused, obsolescent, old, out-of-date, rare. Some of the most *ancient* words are not *obsolete.* A word is *obsolete* which has quite gone out of use; a word is *archaic* or *obsolescent* which is falling out of use; *archaic* is also applied to a word which is *obsolete* in general usage but which survives in special texts, as the Bible, hymnals, poetry, etc.; a word is *rare* if there are few present instances of its use. See OLD. *Antonyms*: see synonyms for FRESH, MODERN, NEW.

ob·sta·cle (ob′stə·kəl) *n.* That which stands in the way; a hindrance or obstruction in either a physical or a moral sense. See synonyms under BARRIER, IMPEDIMENT. [<OF <L *obstaculum* < *obstare* stand before, withstand < *ob-* before, against + *stare* stand]

ob·ste·tri·cian (ob′stə·trish′ən) *n.* A medical and surgical specialist in childbirth.

ob·stet·rics (əb·stet′riks) *n.* The branch of medical science relating to pregnancy and childbirth; midwifery. [Orig. pl. of *obstetric, adj.*, <L *obstetricus* < *obstetrix, -icis* a midwife < *obstare.* See OBSTACLE.] **— ob·stet′ri·cal, ob·stet′ric** *adj.* **— ob·stet′ri·cal·ly** *adv.*

ob·sti·na·cy (ob′stə·nə·sē) *n. pl.* **·cies 1** Persistent and usually unreasonable adherence to one's own opinion or purpose; stubbornness. **2** The quality of being difficult to subdue or remedy: said especially of ailments. **3** Stubborn action.

ob·sti·nate (ob′stə·nit) *adj.* **1** Persistently and unreasonably resolved in a purpose or opinion; stubborn. **2** Hard to control or cure. [<L *obstinatus* stubborn < *obstinare* persist < *obstare.* See OBSTACLE.] **— ob′sti·nate·ly** *adv.* **— ob′sti·nate·ness** *n.*

Synonyms: contumacious, decided, determined, dogged, firm, fixed, headstrong, heady, immovable, indomitable, inflexible, intractable, mulish, obdurate, opinionated, persistent, pertinacious, refractory, resolute, resolved, stubborn, unflinching, unyielding. The *headstrong* person is not to be stopped in his own course of action, while the *obstinate* and *stubborn* is not to be driven to another's way. The *headstrong* act; the *obstinate* and *stubborn* may simply refuse to stir. *Stubborn* is the term most frequently applied to animals and inanimate things. *Refractory* implies more activity of resistance; the *stubborn* horse balks; the *refractory* animal plunges, rears, and kicks; metals that resist ordinary processes of reduction are termed *refractory.* One is *obdurate* who adheres to his purpose in spite of appeals that would move any tender-hearted person. *Contumacious* refers to a proud and insolent defiance of authority, as of the summons of a court. *Pertinacious* applies to that which is active and aggressive; *pertinacious* demand is contrasted with *obstinate* refusal. The *unyielding* conduct which we approve we call *decided, firm, inflexible, resolute*; that which we condemn we are apt to term *headstrong, obstinate, stubborn.* See INFLEXIBLE, PERVERSE. *Antonyms*: amenable, complaisant, compliant, docile, irresolute, obedient, pliable, pliant, submissive, teachable, tractable, undecided, wavering, yielding.

ob·sti·pant (ob′stə·pənt) *n. Med.* A drug or other substance that induces obstipation.

ob·sti·pa·tion (ob′stə·pā′shən) *n. Med.* Persistent or intractable constipation. [<L *obstipatio, -onis* a stopping up, ult. < *ob-* against + *stipare* press together]

ob·strep·er·ous (əb·strep′ər·əs) *adj.* Making a great disturbance; clamorous; boisterous; unruly. See synonyms under NOISY, TURBULENT. [<L *obstreperus* < *obstrepere* make noise against < *ob-* against + *strepere* roar] **— ob·strep′er·ous·ly** *adv.* **— ob·strep′er·ous·ness** *n.*

ob·struct (əb·strukt′) *v.t.* **1** To stop or impede movement through (a way or passage) by obstacles or impediments; barricade; choke; clog. **2** To block or retard the progress or way of; impede; check. **3** To come or be in front of so as to hide from sight. [<L *obstructus*, pp. of *obstruere* block up < *ob-* against + *struere* pile, build] **— ob·struct′er, ob·struc′tor** *n.* **— ob·struc′tive** *adj.* **— ob·struc′tive·ly** *adv.* **— ob·struc′tive·ness** *n.*

Synonyms: arrest, bar, barricade, check, choke, clog, embarrass, hinder, impede, interrupt, oppose, retard, stay, stop. To *obstruct* is literally to build up against: The road is *obstructed* by fallen trees. We may *hinder* one's advance by following and clinging to him; we *obstruct* his course by standing in his way. Anything that makes one's progress slower, whether from within or from without, *impedes, checks, hinders, retards*, or *stays*; an obstruction to one's progress is always from without. To *arrest* is to cause to stop suddenly; *obstructing* the way may have the effect of *arresting* progress. See CHECK, HINDER, OPPOSE. *Antonyms*: accelerate, advance, aid, clear, facilitate, forward, free, further, open, promote.

ob·struc·tion (əb·struk′shən) *n.* **1** A hindrance; obstacle. **2** The act of preventing progress; the state of being obstructed. See synonyms under BARRIER, IMPEDIMENT.

ob·struc·tion·ist (əb·struk′shən·ist) *n.* One who obstructs; especially, one who opposes reform, or who delays the progress of business, as in a legislature. **— ob·struc′tion·ism** *n.*

ob·stru·ent (ob′stroo̅·ənt) *adj. Med.* Causing obstruction or impediment, as of the stomach. **—** *n.* A medicine that obstructs. [<L *obstruens, -entis*, ppr. of *obstruere.* See OBSTRUCT.]

ob·tain (əb·tān′) *v.t.* **1** To gain possession of, especially by effort; acquire; get. **2** *Archaic* To arrive at; reach. **—** *v.i.* **3** To be customary or prevalent; hold good: Chivalry *obtained* until the Renaissance. **4** *Archaic* To succeed; prevail. [<OF *obtenir* <L *obtinere* < *ob-* against + *tenere* hold, keep] **— ob·tain′a·ble** *adj.* **— ob·tain′er** *n.* **— ob·tain′ment** *n.*

Synonyms: acquire, earn, gain, get, procure, receive, secure, win. When one *gets* the object of his desire, he is said to *obtain* it, whether he has *gained* or *earned* it or not. *Win* denotes contest, with a suggestion of chance or hazard; in popular language, a person is often said to *win* a lawsuit, but in legal phrase he is said to *gain* his suit, case, or cause. One *obtains* a thing commonly by some direct effort of his own, he *procures* it commonly by the intervention of someone else; he *secures* what has seemed uncertain or elusive, when he *gets* it firmly into his possession or under his control. Compare GAIN, GET, PURCHASE.

ob·tect (ob·tekt′) *adj. Entomol.* Covered with a hard chitinous case, as the pupa of most flies. Also **ob·tect′ed.** [<L *obtectus*, pp. of *obtegere* < *ob-* over + *tegere* cover]

ob·test (ob·test′) *v.t.* **1** To beseech; implore. **2** To invoke as a witness. **—** *v.i.* **3** To protest. [<L *obtestari* call to witness < *ob-* on account of + *testari* bear witness] **— ob·tes·ta·tion** (ob′tes·tā′shən) *n.*

ob·trude (əb·tro͞od′) *v.* **ob·trud·ed, ob·trud·ing** *v.t.* **1** To thrust or force (oneself, an opinion, etc.) upon others without request or warrant. **2** To push forward or out; eject. **—** *v.i.* **3** To intrude oneself. [<L *obtrudere* < *ob-* towards, against + *trudere* thrust] **— ob·trud′er** *n.*

ob·tru·sion (əb·tro͞o′zhən) *n.* The act of obtruding or the thing obtruded; an instance of obtruding. [<LL *obtrusio, -onis* < *obtrusus*, pp. of *obtrudere* OBTRUDE]

ob·tru·sive (əb·tro͞o′siv) *adj.* Tending to obtrude; obtruding; pushing; intruding. See synonyms under MEDDLESOME. **— ob·tru′sive·ly** *adv.* **— ob·tru′sive·ness** *n.*

ob·tund (ob·tund′) *v.t.* To make blunt or dull; deaden, as pain. [<L *obtundere* blunt < *ob-* against + *tundere* beat] **— ob·tund′ent** *adj. & n.*

ob·tu·rate (ob′tyə·rāt, -tə-) *v.t.* **·rat·ed, ·rat·ing 1** To close or stop up (an opening or hole). **2** In ordnance, to close or seal (a gun breech)

to prevent the escape of gas in firing. [<L *obturatus,* pp. of *obturare* stop up] **—ob′tu·ra′tion** *n.* **—ob′tu·ra′tor** *n.*

ob·tuse (əb·tōōs′, -tyōōs′) *adj.* **1** *Bot.* Blunt or rounded at the extremity, as a leaf or petal: opposed to *acute.* **2** Dull intellectually or emotionally; stupid; insensible. **3** Heavy, dull, and indistinct, as a sound. See synonyms under BLUNT. [<L *obtusus* blunt, dulled, orig. pp. of *obtundere.* See OBTUND.] **—ob·tuse′ly** *adv.* **—ob·tuse′ness** *n.*

obtuse angle See under ANGLE.

ob·verse (ob·vûrs′, ob′vûrs) *adj.* **1** Turned toward or facing one: opposed to *reverse.* **2** Inverse; narrower at the base than at the apex: an *obverse* leaf. **3** Corresponding to something else as its counterpart. **—***n.* (ob′·vûrs) **1** That side of a coin or medal upon which the face or main device is struck: opposed to *reverse;* that side of any object which is meant to be seen; the front as opposed to the back. **2** *Logic* The counterpart of any truth, fact, or statement. [<L *obversus,* pp. of *obvertere* OBVERT] **—ob·verse′ly** *adv.*

ob·ver·sion (ob·vûr′shən, -zhən) *n.* **1** A turning down or toward. **2** *Logic* A form of immediate inference in which the positive and negative or antecedent and consequent terms of a proposition are reversed in such a way that the converse or transverse forms can be legitimately inferred from the original proposition; conversion.

ob·vert (ob·vûrt′) *v.t.* **1** To turn the front, principal, or a different side of (a thing) toward another. **2** *Logic* To infer the obverse, or contradictory predicate of (a proposition). [<L *obvertere* <*ob-* towards, against, down + *vertere* turn]

ob·vi·ate (ob′vē·āt) *v.t.* **·at·ed, ·at·ing** To meet or provide for, as an objection or difficulty, by effective measures; clear away; prevent. [<L *obviatus,* pp. of *obviare* meet, withstand <*ob-* against + *via* a way] **—ob′vi·a′tion** *n.* **—ob′vi·a′tor** *n.*

ob·vi·ous (ob′vē·əs) *adj.* **1** Immediately evident without further reasoning or investigation; palpably true; manifest. **2** *Obs.* Standing or placed in the way. See synonyms under CLEAR, EVIDENT, MANIFEST, NOTORIOUS. [<L *obvius* in the way, obvious <*ob-* against + *via* a way] **—ob′vi·ous·ly** *adv.* **—ob′vi·ous·ness** *n.*

ob·vo·lute (ob′və·lōōt) *adj. Bot.* Overlapping: said of the margins of leaves or petals in vernation which are mutually infolded one within another. Compare CONVOLUTE. [<L *obvolutus,* pp. of *obvolvere* wrap around <*ob-* upon + *volvere* roll] **—ob′vo·lu′tion** *n.* **—ob′vo·lu′·tive** *adj.*

oc– Assimilated var. of OB–.

oc·a·ri·na (ok′ə·rē′nə) *n.* A small musical instrument in the shape of a sweet potato, usually of terra cotta, with a mouthpiece and finger holes. It yields soft, sonorous notes. [<Ital., dim. of *oca* a goose <L *auca;* so called with ref. to its shape]

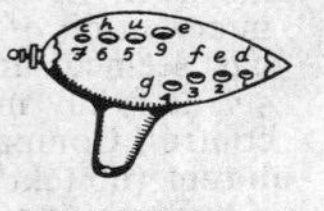

OCARINA

O'Ca·sey (ō·kā′sē), **Sean,** 1880–1964, Irish playwright.

Oc·cam (ok′əm) See OCKHAM.

oc·ca·sion (ə·kā′zhən) *n.* **1** A particular event, or juncture of events, considered simply as exciting notice or interest; especially, an important event or celebration. **2** An event or juncture of affairs that presents some reason, motive, or opportunity for action; an opportunity permitting or a reason requiring action; cause: no *occasion* for haste. **3** A determinative condition, as opposed to the main or principal cause. **4** A need or exigency. **5** *pl. Obs.* Needs. **6** *Obs.* Any matter of business requiring attention. See synonyms under CAUSE, OPPORTUNITY. **—by occasion of** In consequence of; by reason of. **—on occasion** On suitable opportunity; at need; now and then. **—to take occasion** To avail oneself of the opportunity. **—***v.t.* To cause or bring about; cause accidentally or incidentally. See synonyms under MAKE, PRODUCE. [<L *occasio, -onis* a falling towards, an opportunity <*occidere* fall down <*ob-* towards, down + *cadere* fall]

oc·ca·sion·al (ə·kā′zhən·əl) *adj.* **1** Occurring at irregular intervals. **2** Belonging or suitable to some special occasion. **3** Happening casually or incidentally. See synonyms under INCIDENTAL.

oc·ca·sion·al·ism (ə·kā′zhən·əl·iz′əm) *n. Philos.* The doctrine that mind is not responsible for changes in the body, or vice versa, but that the Divine Spirit intervenes to produce the apparent interaction. **—oc·ca′sion·al·ist** *n.*

oc·ca·sion·al·ly (ə·kā′zhən·əl·ē) *adv.* In an occasional manner; more or less frequently at irregular times or intervals.

oc·ci·dent (ok′sə·dənt) *n.* The west: opposed to *orient.* [<OF <L *occidens, -entis* sunset, the west, orig. ppr. of *occidere* fall. See OCCASION.]

Oc·ci·dent (ok′sə·dənt) **1** The countries west of Asia; specifically, Europe. **2** The western hemisphere. Opposed to *Orient.*

oc·ci·den·tal (ok′sə·den′təl) *adj.* Of or belonging to the West, or the countries constituting the Occident: opposed to *oriental.* **—***n.* One born or living in a western country. Also **Oc′ci·den′tal.**

Oc·ci·den·tal·ism (ok′sə·den′təl·iz′əm) *n.* The spirit, life, and culture of the people of the Occident. **—Oc′ci·den′tal·ist** *n.*

oc·ci·den·tal·ize (ok′sə·den′təl·īz) *v.t.* **·ized, ·iz·ing** To render occidental in spirit, culture, character, etc. **—oc′ci·den′tal·i·za′tion** *n.*

oc·cip·i·tal (ok·sip′ə·təl) *adj.* **1** Pertaining to the occiput. **2** Pertaining to the occipital bone. **—***n.* The occipital bone. [<Med. L *occipitalis* <L *occiput, -itis* OCCIPUT]

occipital bone *Anat.* The hindmost bone of the skull between the parietal and temporal bones.

occipito– *combining form Anat.* Occipital; occipital and: *occipitofrontal,* pertaining to the occiput and the forehead. [<L *occiput* back of the head]

oc·ci·put (ok′sə·put, -pət) *n. pl.* **·cip·i·ta** (-sip′·ə·tə) *Anat.* The lower back part of the skull. [<L, back of the head <*ob-* against + *caput* head]

oc·clude (ə·klōōd′) *v.* **·clud·ed, ·clud·ing** *v.t.* **1** To shut up or close, as pores or openings. **2** To shut in, out, or off. **3** *Chem.* To take up, either on the surface or internally, but without change of properties: Palladium *occludes* hydrogen. **—***v.i.* **4** *Dent.* To meet so that the corresponding cusps fit closely together: said of the teeth of the upper and lower jaws. [<L *occludere* shut <*ob-* against, upon + *claudere* close] **—oc·clu′dent** *adj.* **—oc·clu·sion** (ə·klōō′zhən) *n.* **—oc·clu′sive** (-siv) *adj.*

oc·clud·er (ə·klōō′dər) *n. Optics* A device to shut off vision.

oc·cult (ə·kult′, ok′ult) *adj.* **1** Of, pertaining to, or designating those mystic arts involving magic, divination, astrology, alchemy, or the like. **2** Not divulged; secret. **3** Beyond human understanding; mysterious. See synonyms under MYSTERIOUS, SECRET. **—***n.* Occult arts or sciences. **—***v.t.* **1** To hide or conceal from view. **2** *Astron.* To hide or conceal by occultation. **—***v.i.* **3** To become hidden or concealed from view. [<L *occultus,* pp. of *occulere* cover over, hide] **—oc·cult′ly** *adv.* **—oc·cult′ness** *n.*

oc·cul·ta·tion (ok′ul·tā′shən) *n.* **1** The act of occulting, or the state of being occulted. **2** *Astron.* Concealment of one celestial body by another interposed in the line of vision, as of a star or planet by the moon, or of a satellite by a planet. Compare ECLIPSE. **3** A disappearance from view or notice.

oc·cult·er (ə·kul′tər) *n.* A device used in a telescope to screen a light.

oc·cult·ism (ə·kul′tiz·əm) *n.* **1** The theory or practice of occult arts or sciences. **2** Belief in occult or supernatural powers. **—oc·cult′ist** *n.*

oc·cu·pan·cy (ok′yə·pən·sē) *n.* The act of occupying; a taking possession; also, the time during which anything is occupied. See synonyms under OCCUPATION.

oc·cu·pant (ok′yə·pənt) *n.* **1** One who occupies. **2** A tenant. [<L *occupans, -antis,* ppr. of *occupare.* See OCCUPY.]

oc·cu·pa·tion (ok′yə·pā′shən) *n.* **1** One's regular, principal, or immediate business. **2** The state of being busy. **3** The possession and holding of land by military force; the occupancy and holding of a nation by an army of another. **4** Occupancy. [<OF <L *occupatio, -onis* a seizing <*occupatus,* pp. of *occupare.* See OCCUPY.]

Synonyms: occupancy, possession, tenure, use. See BUSINESS, EXERCISE, WORK. *Antonyms:* dispossession, ejectment, eviction, resignation, vacating.

oc·cu·pa·tion·al (ok′yə·pā′shən·əl) *adj.* Of, pertaining to, or caused by, an occupation: *occupational* statistics; *occupational* diseases. **—oc′cu·pa′tion·al·ly** *adv.*

occupational therapy *Med.* The treatment of nervous, mental, or physical disabilities by means of work adapted to favor recovery and normal readjustment to external conditions.

oc·cu·py (ok′yə·pī) *v.t.* **·pied, ·py·ing** **1** To take and hold possession of, as by conquest. **2** To fill or take up (space or time): The estate *occupies* ten acres. **3** To inhabit; dwell in. **4** To hold; fill, as an office or position. **5** To busy or engage; employ: He *occupies* himself with trifles. [<OF *occuper* <L *occupare* seize, take possession of <*ob-* against + *capere* take] **—oc′cu·pi′er** *n.*

Synonyms: busy, employ, engage, fill, have, hold, keep, possess, preoccupy, use. See ENTERTAIN, HAVE, INTEREST, POSSESS.

oc·cur (ə·kûr′) *v.i.* **·curred, ·cur·ring** **1** To happen; come about. **2** To be found or met with; appear: Trout *occur* in this lake. **3** To present itself; come to mind: The theory just *occurred* to me. See synonyms under HAPPEN. [<L *occurrere* run to or against, befall <*ob-* towards, against + *currere* run]

oc·cur·rence (ə·kûr′əns) *n.* **1** The act or fact of occurring. **2** An event considered as simply presenting itself to notice without obvious cause; a happening. See synonyms under CIRCUMSTANCE, EVENT. **—oc·cur′rent** *Rare adj.*

o·cean (ō′shən) *n.* **1** The great body of salt water that covers about two thirds of the earth's surface. **2** Any one of the greater tracts of water that cover the globe: the Atlantic *Ocean.* **3** Any unbounded expanse or quantity. [<OF <L *oceanus* <Gk. *ōkeanos* the great outer sea (as opposed to the Mediterranean), orig. *Ōkeanos (potamos)* (the river of) Oceanus]

o·cean·ad (ō′shən·ad) *n.* An ocean-dwelling plant. [<OCEAN + -AD[1]]

ocean gray A light silvery-gray color used on ships of the U. S. Navy in World War II.

O·ce·an·i·a (ō′shē·an′ē·ə) The islands of the Pacific, including Melanesia, Micronesia, and Polynesia, sometimes including the Malay Archipelago and Australasia. Also **O′ce·an′·i·ca.** **—O′ce·an′i·an** *adj. & n.*

o·ce·an·ic (ō′shē·an′ik) *adj.* Relating to, or living in, the ocean; pelagic.

O·ce·an·ic (ō′shē·an′ik) *n.* A subfamily of the Austronesian family of languages, including the Melanesian languages of the Solomon Islands, Fiji, New Caledonia, the New Hebrides, etc., and the Micronesian group.

O·ce·a·nid (ō·sē′ə·nid) In Greek mythology, one of the 3,000 sea nymphs, daughters of Oceanus and Tethys. [<Gk. *Ōkeanis, -idos*]

Ocean Island A Pacific island west of the Gilbert group, comprising part of the Gilbert and Ellice Islands colony; 2 square miles.

o·cean–lane route (ō′shən·lān′) See LANE ROUTE.

o·ce·an·og·ra·phy (ō′shē·ən·og′rə·fē, ō′shən-) *n.* The branch of physical geography that treats of oceanic life and phenomena. [<OCEAN + -(O)GRAPHY] **—o′ce·an·og′ra·pher** *n.* **—o′ce·an·o·graph′ic** (-ə·graf′ik) or **·i·cal** *adj.* **—o′ce·an·o·graph′i·cal·ly** *adv.*

o·ce·an·oph·i·lous (ō′shē·ən·of′ə·ləs) *adj. Biol.* Living in the ocean, as a plant or animal. [<OCEAN + -(O)PHILOUS]

O·ce·a·nus (ō·sē′ə·nəs) **1** In Greek mythology, a Titan, husband and brother of Tethys, father of the Oceanids and all river gods. **2** In classical geography, the mighty stream said to encircle the habitable world.

oc·el·lat·ed (os′ə·lā′tid) *adj.* **1** Having an ocellus or ocelli (of color), as in the tail of a peacock. **2** Resembling an ocellus. **3** Spotted. Also **oc′el·late.** [<L *ocellatus* small-eyed <*ocellus.* See OCELLUS.] **—oc′el·la′tion** *n.*

o·cel·lus (ō·sel′əs) *n. pl.* **·li** (-ī) **1** *Biol.* A minute simple eye, as of many invertebrates. **2** A spot of color surrounded by a ring or rings of color as in the tail of a peacock. [<L, dim. of *oculus* eye] **—o·cel′lar** *adj.*

o·ce·lot (ō′sə·lot, os′ə-) *n.* A large Central and South American cat (*Felis pardalis*) of a prevailing yellowish- or reddish-gray, with black-edged blotches. [<F, short for Nahuatl *tlaocelotl* <*tlalli* a field + *ocelotl* a jaguar]

o·cher (ō′kər) *n.* **1** A native earth varying

from light yellow to deep orange or brown, and consisting of iron trioxide and water with varying proportions of clay in impalpable subdivision, largely used as a pigment. **2** Any metallic oxide occurring in an earthy or finely divided form. **3** A dark-yellow color derived from or compared to ocher. —**red ocher** A red, ferruginous native ocher: also called *Indian red*, *Venetian red*. Also **o′chre.** [< OF *ocre* < L *ochra* < Gk. *ōchra* yellow ocher < *ōchros* pale yellow] —**o′cher·ous, o·chre·ous** (ō′krē·əs), **o′cher·y, o′chry** adj.

och·le·sis (ok·lē′sis) *n. Pathol.* Any disease caused by overcrowding. [< NL < Gk. *ochlēsis* a disturbance < *ochlein* move, disturb < *ochlos* a crowd]

och·loc·ra·cy (ok·lok′rə·sē) *n. pl.* **·cies** Rule of the multitude; government by the populace; mob rule. [< MF *ochlocratie* < Gk. *ochlokratia* mob rule < *ochlos* a crowd + *krateein* rule] —**och′lo·crat** *n.* —**och·lo·crat·ic** (ok′lə·krat′ik) *adj.*

och·lo·pho·bi·a (ok′lə·fō′bē·ə) *n.* Morbid fear of crowds; demophobia. [< Gk. *ochlos* a crowd + -PHOBIA]

och·one (ə·khōn′) *interj.* Alas: a cry of grief. [< Irish *ochoin*]

o·chroid (ō′kroid) *adj.* Of the color of ocher.

Ochs (oks), **Adolph,** 1858–1935, U.S. newspaper publisher.

ock *suffix of nouns* Small; little: now often without perceptible force: *hillock.* [OE *-oc, -uc*]

Ock·ham (ok′əm), **William of,** 1285?–1349?, English Franciscan and scholastic philosopher: known as the *Invincible Doctor.* Also spelled *Occam.*

Ockham's razor *Philos.* **1** A leading tenet of nominalism formulated by william of Ockham and stating that terms, concepts, and assumptions must not be multiplied beyond necessity. **2** The law of parsimony.

o′clock (ə·klok′) Of, according to, or by the clock.

Oc·mul·gee River (ōk·mul′gē) A river in central Georgia, flowing 225 miles east to the Altamaha.

O′Con·nell (ō·kon′əl), **Daniel,** 1775–1847, Irish nationalist statesman and orator: called "the Liberator."

O′Con·nor (ō·kon′ər), **Flannery,** 1925–64, American short-story writer. —**Frank** Pseudonym of *Michael O′Donovan,* 1903–1966, Irish short-story writer. —**Thomas Power,** 1848–1929, Irish politician and journalist: known as *Tay Pay.*

o·co·til·lo (ō′kə·tēl′yō, Sp. ō′kō·tē′yō), *n.* The candlewood tree of California and Mexico. [< Sp., dim. of *ocote* Mexican pine < Nahuatl *ocotl*]

oc·re·a (ok′rē·ə, ō′krē·ə) *n. pl.* **oc·re·ae** (ok′ri·ē, ō′kri·ē) **1** *Bot.* **a** A stipule or combined pair of stipules forming a legging-shaped sheath about the stem of a plant. **b** A thin sheath around the seta of a moss: erroneously written *ochrea.* **2** *Ornithol.* A sheath, as the boot of a bird. [< L, a legging, a greave]

oc·re·ate (ok′rē·it, -āt, ō′krē-) *adj.* **1** Having ocreae. **2** *Ornithol.* Booted: said of the tarsi of certain birds.

oct-, octa- See OCTO-.

oc·ta·chord (ok′tə·kôrd) *n.* **1** A musical instrument with eight strings. **2** A diatonic scale of eight tones. [< LL *octochordus* < Gk. *oktachordos* < *okta-* eight + *chordē* a string] —**oc′ta·chor′dal** *adj.*

oc·tad (ok′tad) *n.* **1** A series of eight. **2** *Chem.* An atom, radical, or element that has a combining power of eight. **3** In ancient notation, a group of eight figures arranged similarly to successive powers of ten. [< L *octas, -adis* < Gk. *oktas, -ados* a group of eight < *oktō* eight] —**oc·tad′ic** *adj.*

oc·ta·gon (ok′tə·gon) *n.* A plane figure with eight sides and eight angles. [< L *octagonos* < Gk. *oktagōnos* < *okta-* eight + *gōnia* an angle]

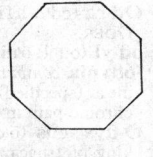
OCTAGON

oc·tag·o·nal (ok·tag′ə·nəl) *adj.* Eight-sided and eight-angled. —**oc·tag′o·nal·ly** *adv.*

oc·ta·he·dral (ok′tə·hē′drəl)

adj. Having eight equal plane faces.

oc·ta·he·drite (ok′tə·hē′drīt) See ANATASE.

oc·ta·he·dron (ok′tə·hē′drən) *n. pl.* **·dra** (-drə) A solid figure bounded by eight plane faces. [< Gk. *oktaedron,* orig. neut. of *oktaedros* eight-sided < *okta-* eight + *hedra* a seat]

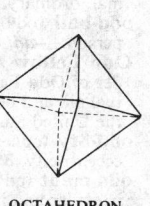
OCTAHEDRON

oc·tam·er·ous (ok·tam′ər·əs) *adj. Bot.* Having the parts in eights, as a flower with eight-members in each set of organs: frequently written *8-merous.* [< Gk. *oktameres* < *okta-* eight + *meros* a part]

oc·tam·e·ter (ok·tam′ə·tər) *adj.* In prosody, having eight measures or metrical feet. —*n.* A verse of eight feet. [< L *octameter* < Gk. *oktametros* < *okta-* eight + *metron* a measure]

oc·tan (ok′tən) *adj.* Recurring on the eighth day: an *octan* fever. [< F *octane, octaine*]

oc·tane (ok′tān) *n.* **1** Any of several isomers in the methane series having the empirical formula C_8H_{18}. **2** The normal isomer of octane, a colorless liquid which is used as a solvent. **3** Octane number. [< OCT- + -ANE]

octane number A measure of the antiknock properties of a motor fuel as determined in a standard internal-combustion engine in comparison with standard fuels consisting of normal heptane containing increasing percentages of isooctane, the antiknock effect increasing with increased isooctane content.

oc·tan·gle (ok′tang·gəl) *n.* An octagon. [< LL *octangulus* < *octo* eight + *angulus* an angle]

oc·tan·gu·lar (ok·tang′gyə·lər) *adj.* Eight-angled and eight-sided; octagonal.

Oc·tans (ok′tanz) A southern constellation. See CONSTELLATION. Also **Oc′tant** (-tənt). [< NL. See OCTANT.]

oc·tant (ok′tənt) *n.* **1** An eighth part of a circle; an arc subtending an angle of 45 degrees. **2** *Astron.* The position in the heavens that is one eighth of a circle distant from conjunction or quadrature; one of the four positions of the moon midway between new or full moon and quarters. **3** An instrument resembling a sextant but having an arc of only 45 degrees: used for measuring the angular height of the sun, moon, and other celestial bodies as an aid in navigation. **4** *Geom.* One of the eight trihedral compartments of space formed by three planes with the three axes, *x, y,* and *z,* of a Cartesian coordinate system as edges. [< LL *octans* an eighth part < L *octo* eight] —**oc·tant′al** (-tan′təl) *adj.*

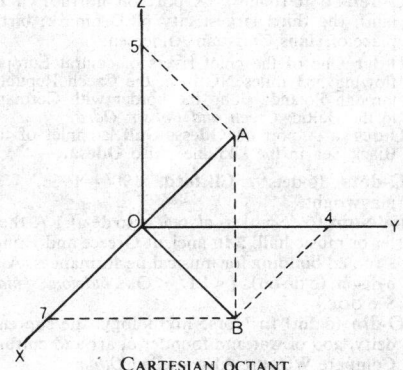
CARTESIAN OCTANT
O. Origin. Coordinates of *A*: $x = 4$, $y = 7$, $z = 5$; of *B*; $x = 4$, $y = 7$.

oc·ta·pla (ok′tə·plə) *n.* **1** A Bible written or printed in eight languages or containing eight versions. **2** Any polyglot book in eight languages. [< Gk. *oktapla,* neut. pl. of *oktaploos* eightfold]

oc·tar·chy (ok′tär·kē) *n. pl.* **·chies** **1** A government headed by eight persons. **2** A country under eight rulers. **3** A group of eight allied governments. [< OCT- + -ARCHY]

oc·tave (ok′tiv, -tāv) *n.* **1** *Music* **a** The interval between any note and that given by twice as many or by half as many vibrations

in a second. **b** A note at this interval above or below any other, considered in relation to that other. **c** Two notes at this interval, sounded together; also, the resulting consonance. **d** An organ stop giving tones an octave higher than those normally corresponding to the keys played. **2** The eighth day from a feast day, beginning with the feast day as one; also, the lengthening of a festival so as to include a period of eight days. **3** Any group or series of eight. **4** In prosody, the first eight lines in an Italian sonnet, or a stanza of eight lines. —*adj.* **1** Composed of eight. **2** In prosody, composed of eight lines. **3** *Music* Producing tones an octave higher. Also **oc·ta·val** (ok·tā′vəl, ok′tə-) *adj.* [< OF < L *octava,* fem. of *octavus* eighth < *octo* eight]

Oc·ta·vi·a (ok·tā′vē·ə, *Ger., Sp.* ōk·tä′vē·ä) A feminine personal name. Also *Fr.* **Oc·ta·vie** (ôk·tä·vē′) or **Oc·tave** (ôk·täv′). [See OCTAVIUS.] —**Octavia,** died 11 B.C., sister of Augustus and wife of Mark Antony.

Oc·ta·vi·an (ok·tā′vē·ən) Augustus Caesar: so called from 45–27 B.C.

Oc·ta·vi·us (ok·tā′vē·əs) A masculine personal name. Also **Oc·ta·vi·a·nus** (ok·tā′vē·ā′nəs), **Oc·ta·vus** (ok·tā′vəs, ok·tə·vəs), *Fr.* **Octave** (ôk·täv′) or **Oc·ta·vien** (ôk·tä·vyaN′), *Sp.* **Oc·ta·vio** (ōk·tä′vyō). [< L, eighth]

oc·ta·vo (ok·tā′vō, -tä′-) *n. pl.* **·vos** The page size ($6 \times 9\frac{1}{2}$ inches except where otherwise specified) of a book made up of printer's sheets folded into eight leaves; also, a book consisting of pages of this size: often called *eightvo* and written *8vo* or *8°.* —*adj.* In octavo; consisting of pages of this size. [< L *(in)* octavo *(in)* an eighth *(of a sheet)*]

oc·ten·ni·al (ok·ten′ē·əl) *adj.* **1** Recurring at intervals of eight years. **2** Occupying periods of eight years. [< L *octennium* a period of eight years < *octo* eight + *annus* a year] —**oc·ten′ni·al·ly** *adv.*

oc·tet (ok·tet′) *n.* **1** A musical composition for eight parts or eight performers. **2** A choir of eight voices, or an orchestra of eight performers. **3** Any group of eight; especially, the first eight lines of an Italian sonnet; octave (def. 4). **4** *Physics* A group of eight electrons in the shell of an atom. Also **oc·tette′.** [< L *octo* eight; on analogy with *duet*]

oc·til·lion (ok·til′yən) *n.* A cardinal number: in the French and American systems, represented by a figure 1 with 27 ciphers annexed; in the English system by a figure 1 with 48 ciphers. [< MF < L *octo* eight; on analogy with *million*] —**oc·til′lionth** (-yənth) *adj. & n.*

octo- *combining form* Eight: *octopus:* also, before vowels, *oct-.* Also *octa-.* [< L *octo* and Gk. *oktō* eight]

Oc·to·ber (ok·tō′bər) **1** The tenth month of the year (the eighth of the Roman year), containing 31 days. **2** Ale or cider made in October. [< L, the eighth (month) < *octo* eight]

October Revolution See RUSSIAN REVOLUTION under REVOLUTION.

Oc·to·brist (ok·tō′brist) *n.* One of that faction in the Russian Duma which supported the czar in reform measures proposed in October, 1905. The proposals were only partly carried out and the party soon disappeared, its remnants supporting monarchical ideas, so that the term came to designate a reactionary.

oc·to·dec·i·mo (ok′tə·des′ə·mō) *n. pl.* **·mos** The page size (approximately $4 \times 6\frac{1}{2}$ inches) of a book made up of printer's sheets folded into 18 leaves; also, a book consisting of pages of this size: often called *eighteenmo* and written *18mo* or *18°.* —*adj.* In octodecimo; consisting of pages of this size. [< L *(in)* octodecimo *(in)* an eighteenth *(of a sheet)*]

oc·to·ge·nar·i·an (ok′tə·jə·nâr′ē·ən) *adj.* Being eighty or from eighty to ninety years of age: also **oc·tog·e·nar·y** (ok·toj′ə·nerē). —*n.* A person between eighty and ninety years of age. [< L *octogenarius* < *octogeni* eighty each < *octoginta* eighty]

oc·to·he·dral (ok′tə·hē′drəl) See OCTAHEDRAL.

oc·to·lat·er·al (ok′tə·lat′ər·əl) *adj.* Eight-sided. [< OCTO- + LATERAL]

oc·to·nar·y (ok′tə·ner·ē) *adj.* **1** Of or pertaining to the number eight. **2** Having eight parts or members. —*n. pl.* **·nar·ies** **1** In prosody, an octave. **2** An ogdoad. [< L *octonarius*

containing eight < *octoni* eight at a time < *octo* eight]

oc·to·pus (ok′tə·pəs) *n. pl.* **·pus·es** or **·pi** (-pī) or **oc·top·o·des** (ok·top′ə·dēz) **1** Any of the marine cephalopod mollusks of the genus *Octopus*, having no shell, a soft, domed head with large eyes and the mouth on the underside surrounded by eight long, partially webbed tentacles bearing two rows of suckers. Also called *devilfish.* **2** Figuratively, any organized power regarded as of far-reaching capacity for harm; specifically, a powerful business organization; a trust. [< NL < Gk. *oktapous* eight-footed < *okta-* eight + *pous* a foot]

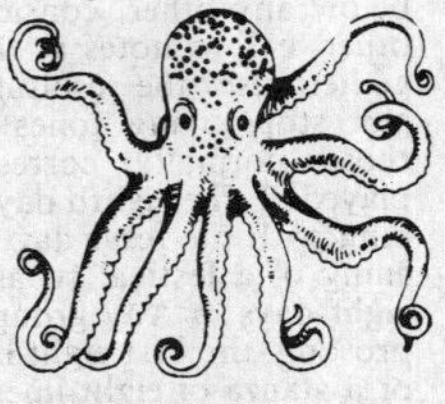

OCTOPUS
(Varies according to species, from a 6-inch to a 32-foot span over-all)

oc·to·roon (ok′tə·rōōn′) *n.* A person who is one-eighth Negro: the offspring of a white person and a quadroon. [< L *octo* eight + (QUAD)ROON]

oc·to·syl·lab·ic (ok′tə·si·lab′ik) *adj.* **1** Composed of eight syllables, as a line of verse. **2** Containing lines of eight syllables. —*n.* An octosyllabic line or verse. [< LL *octosyllabus* < L < Gk. *oktasyllabos* < *okta-* eight + *syllabē* a syllable]

oc·troi (ok′troi, *Fr.* ôk·trwȧ′) *n.* **1** A government grant or privilege given a person or company; especially, a trade monopoly so conferred. **2** A tax levied at the gates of a city on articles of trade. **3** The gate where it is collected; also, the service of collection. [< F < *octroyer, ottroyer* grant < LL *auctorizare* < L *auctor* an author < *augere* increase]

oc·tu·ple (ok′tōō·pəl, -tyōō-, ok·tōō′pəl, -tyōō′-) *adj.* **1** Consisting of eight parts or copies. **2** Multiplied by eight. —*v.t.* **·pled, ·pling** To multiply by eight. —*n.* A number or sum eight times as great as another. [< L *octuplus* eightfold < *octo* eight] **—oc′tu·ply** *adv.*

oc·u·lar (ok′yə·lər) *adj.* Pertaining to, like, derived from, or connected with the eye; visual. —*n.* The lenses forming the eyepiece of an optical instrument. [< L *ocularis* < *oculus* eye] **—oc′u·lar·ly** *adv.*

oc·u·list (ok′yə·list) *n.* One skilled in treating diseases of the eye; an opthalmologist. [< MF *oculiste* < L *oculus* eye]

oculo- *combining form* Eye; of or pertaining to the eye: *oculomotor.* Also, before vowels, **ocul-.** [< L *oculus* the eye]

oc·u·lo·mo·tor (ok′yə·lə·mō′tər) *Anat. adj.* Causing or connected with movement of the eye: the *oculomotor* nerve. —*n.* The oculomotor or third cranial nerve, which supplies most of the muscles that move the eyeball.

O·cyp·e·te (ō·sip′ə·tē) One of the Harpies.

od (od, ōd) *n.* A hypothetical force formerly supposed by some to pervade all nature: assumed to account for the phenomena of magnetism, chemical action, mesmerism, etc.: also *odyl.* [< G; coined by Baron Karl von Reichenbach, 1788–1869, German chemist] **—od·ic** (od′ik, ō′dik) *adj.*

Od (od) *n.* & *interj. Archaic* God: a euphemism used in oaths. Also **Odd.** [Alter. of GOD]

OD (ō′dē′) *n. pl.* **OD's** A narcotic overdose. *v.i.* **OD'd, OD'ing** To become ill, or die, from a narcotic overdose.

o·da·lisk (ō′də·lisk) *n.* A female slave or concubine in an Oriental harem. Also **o′da·lisque.** [< F *odalisque* < Turkish *ōdaliq* chambermaid < *ōdah* a chamber]

odd (od) *adj.* **1** Not even; leaving a remainder when divided by two. **2** Marked with an odd number. **3** Left over after a division. **4** Additional to any round number; thrown in or mentioned without exact enumeration: two hundred and *odd* miles; extra: an *odd* fork. **5** Occasional; causal: to work at *odd* jobs. **6** Peculiar; singular; queer; eccentric. **7** Single: an *odd* slipper. —*n.* In golf, an advantage of one or more strokes given to a less skilful player over his opponent. [< ON *odda-* odd, third < *oddi* a point of land, triangle, odd number] **—odd′ly** *adv.* **—odd′·ness** *n.*

Synonyms (adj.): anomalous, bizarre, comical, droll, eccentric, extraordinary, fantastic, fantastical, grotesque, peculiar, quaint, queer, rare, strange, uncommon, unique, unmatched, unusual, whimsical. See QUEER, RARE[1]. *Antonyms*: common, conventional, customary, even, normal, ordinary, usual.

odd·ball (od′bôl′) *n. Slang* An odd or eccentric person. —*adj.* Habitually odd or eccentric.

Odd Fellow A member of the Independent Order of Odd Fellows, a secret society for the mutual aid and benefit of the members: organized in the United States, 1819.

odd·i·ty (od′ə·tē) *n. pl.* **·ties 1** Singularity. **2** An eccentricity. **3** Something odd or peculiar.

odd·ment (od′mənt) *n.* **1** That which is only an irregular and incidental and not an essential part of some course or system; something left over. **2** *Printing* A constituent part of a book other than the text, as the title page, index, etc. **3** *pl.* Small belongings; odds and ends.

odd-pin·nate (od′pin′āt, -it) *adj. Bot.* Pinnate with a single leaflet at the end, as the locust leaf.

odds (odz) *n. pl. (sometimes construed as singular)* **1** An equalizing allowance based on the apparent chances of success of an opponent or contestant. **2** The amount or proportions by which one's bet differs from that of another: The *odds* are three to two. **3** The balance of probability that something will happen or be found to be the case. **4** In a contest of any sort, a difference to the advantage of one side: the *odds* in one's favor. **5** In a contest, the advantage of one side over the opposing side. **—at odds** At variance; disagreeing. **—to give** (or **lay**) **odds** To offer to bet with someone on terms apparently favorable to him. **— to take odds** To agree to a wager on terms apparently favorable to the other person.

odds and ends Fragments; miscellaneous articles.

odds-on (odz′on′) *adj.* Considered as having the best chance of winning.

ode (ōd) *n.* **1** In classical prosody, a lyric poem intended to be sung or chanted, exemplified by the **Pindaric ode,** consisting of three stanzas (strophe, antistrophe, and epode), and the **Horatian ode,** consisting of one stanzaic form throughout. **2** In modern usage, a lyric poem, rimed or unrimed, of lofty tone, treating progressively one dignified theme, often in the form of an address. [< MF < LL *ode, oda* < Gk. *ōidē, aoidē* a song < *aeidein* sing] **—od·ic** (ō′dik) *adj.*

-ode[1] *combining form* Way; path: *anode, cathode.* [< Gk. *hodos* a way]

-ode[2] *suffix* Like; resembling; having the nature of: *phyllode.* [< Gk. *-ōdēs* < *eidos* form]

O·den·burg (ō′dən·bōōrkh) The German name for SOPRON.

O·den·se (ō′thən·sə) A port on north Fyn Island, the third largest city of Denmark: birthplace of Hans Christian Andersen.

O·der One of the chief rivers of central Europe, flowing 563 miles NE from the Czech Republic through Poland, along the border with Germany to the Baltic: *Czech and Polish: Odra.*

O·des·sa A port on **Odessa Gulf,** an inlet of the Black Sea in the Ukraine. Also **Odesa.**

O·dets (ō·dets′), **Clifford,** 1906—1963, U.S. playwright.

o·de·um (ō′dē·əm) *n. pl.* **o·de·a** (ō′dē·ə) **1** A theater or music hall. **2** In ancient Greece and Rome, a roofed building for musical performances. Also **o·de·on** (ō′dē·on). [< LL < Gk. *ōideion* < *ōidē.* See ODE.]

O·din (ō′din) In Norse mythology, the supreme deity, god of war and founder of art and culture. Compare WODEN. Also spelled *Othin.*

o·di·ous (ō′dē·əs) *adj.* **1** Exciting hate, repugnance, or disgust. **2** Regarded with aversion or disgust. See synonyms under FOUL, INFAMOUS. [< AF < L *odiosus* < *odium.* See ODIUM.] **—o′di·ous·ly** *adv.* **—o′di·ous·ness** *n.*

o·di·um (ō′dē·əm) *n.* **1** The state of being odious; offensiveness; opprobrium. **2** A feeling of extreme repugnance, disgust, or hate. See synonyms under SCANDAL. [< L, hatred < *odisse* hate]

O·do·a·cer (ō′dō·ā′sər), 434?–493, German ruler of Italy 476–493: also *Ottokar.*

O·do·ar·do (ō′dō·är′dō) Italian form of EDWARD.

o·do·graph (ō′də·graf, -gräf) *n.* **1** A pedometer. **2** An odometer. **3** An automatic, portable map-making device designed to work from a moving vehicle. [< Gk. *hodos* a way + -GRAPH]

O·do·graph (ō′də·graf, -gräf) *n.* An instrument for automatically recording to correct scale the course of a ship at sea: a trade name.

o·dom·e·ter (ō·dom′ə·tər) *n.* An appliance for measuring distance traveled, as a mechanical registering attachment to the wheel of a vehicle: also spelled *hodometer.* [< Gk. *hodometros* < *hodos* a way, a road + *metron* a measure]

o·dom·e·try (ō·dom′ə·trē) *n.* Measurement by odometer.

O·don (ō·dôn′) French form of OTTO. Also *Hungarian* **O·dön** (œ′dœn).

o·don·a·tous (ō·don′ə·təs) *adj.* Of or pertaining to an order *(Odonata)* of slender, long-bodied, generally large, predatory insects with four equal, net-veined wings, including the dragonflies and damsel flies. [< NL < Gk. *odous, odontos* a tooth]

o·don·tal·gi·a (ō′don·tal′jē·ə, -jə) *n. Pathol.* Toothache. [< Gk. < *odous, odontos* a tooth + *algos* a pain] **—o′don·tal′gic** *adj.*

odonto- *combining form* Tooth; of the teeth: *odontology.* Also, before vowels, **odont-.** [< Gk. *odous, odontos* a tooth]

o·don·to·blast (ō·don′tə·blast) *n. Anat.* A tooth cell that produces dentine. **—o·don′to·blas′tic** *adj.*

o·don·to·glos·sum (ō·don′tə·glos′əm) *n.* Any of a large genus *(Odontoglossum)* of tropical American epiphytic orchids with thick, fleshy leaves and large flowers with free, spreading sepals. [< NL < Gk. *odous, odontos* a tooth + *glossa* a tongue]

o·don·to·graph (ō·don′tə·graf, -gräf) *n.* **1** *Mech.* An instrument for correctly laying out gear teeth. **2** *Dent.* A device for showing irregularities occurring in the surface of tooth enamel.

o·don·toid (ō·don′toid) *adj.* **1** Toothlike. **2** Of or pertaining to the odontoid bone or process.

odontoid process *Anat.* A toothlike or peglike projection from the body of the axis or second vertebra of the neck, upon which the atlas rotates: found in mammals and birds. Also **odontoid peg.**

o·don·tol·o·gy (ō′don·tol′ə·jē) *n.* The body of scientific knowledge that relates to the structure, health, and growth of the teeth. [< ODONTO- + -LOGY] **—o·don·to·log·i·cal** (ō·don′·tə·loj′i·kəl) *adj.* **—o·don′to·log′i·cal·ly** *adv.* **—o′don·tol′o·gist** *n.*

o·don·to·phore (ō·don′tə·fôr, -fōr) *n. Zool.* **1** A protrusible, ribbonlike organ covered with teeth for rasping, etc., and connected with the mouth of cephalous mollusks. **2** The radula, tongue, or lingual ribbon. [< Gk. *odontophoros* bearing teeth < *odous, odontos* tooth + *-phoros* bearing < *pherein* bear] **—o·don·toph·o·ral** (ō′don·tof′ər·əl) *adj.* **—o′don·toph′o·rine** (-rin, -rēn) *adj.* & *n.* **—o′don·toph′·o·rous** *adj.*

o·don·to·scope (ō·don′tə·skōp) *n.* A small dental mirror, used by a dentist to examine the teeth. [< ODONTO- + -SCOPE]

o·dor (ō′dər) *n.* **1** That quality of a material substance that renders it perceptible to the sense of smell; scent. **2** Regard or estimation: to be in bad *odor.* **3** A perfume; incense. See synonyms under SAVOR, SMELL. Also *Brit.* **o′dour.** [< AF *odour,* OF *odor* < L *odor, -oris*]

o·dor·if·er·ous (ō′də·rif′ər·əs) *adj.* Diffusing an odor. [< L *odorifer* < *odor, -oris* an odor + *ferre* bear] **—o′dor·if′er·ous·ly** *adv.* **—o′dor·if′er·ous·ness** *n.*

o·dor·less (ō′dər·lis) *adj.* Having no odor. **—o′dor·less·ly** *adv.* **—o′dor·less·ness** *n.*

o·dor·ous (ō′dər·əs) *adj.* Having an odor; fragrant. **—o′dor·ous·ly** *adv.* **—o′dor·ous·ness** *n.*

Od·ra (ôd′rä) The Czech and Polish name for the ODER.

od·yl (od′il, ō′dil) *n.* An od. Also **od′yle.**

-odynia *combining form Med.* Pain; chronic pain in a (specified) part of the body: *osteodynia,* chronic pain in a bone. [< Gk. *odynē* pain]

O·dys·seus (ō·dis′yōōs, -ē·əs) In Greek legend, king of Ithaca, one of the Greek leaders in the Trojan War, figuring in the *Iliad* and hero of the *Odyssey;* Ulysses.

Od·ys·sey (od′ə·sē) *n.* **1** An ancient Greek epic poem attributed to Homer, describing the wanderings of Odysseus during the ten

years after the fall of Troy. 2 A long, wandering journey: often **od′ys·sey.** — **Od′ys·sey′·an** *adj.*

oe– See also words beginning E–.

Oe·a (ē′ə) The Phoenician name for TRIPOLI. Also **Œ′a.**

oe·cist (ē′sist) *n.* 1 In ancient Greece, the founder of a colony. 2 *pl.* The founders of Australian colonies. [<Gk *oikistēs* <*oikos* home]

oec·u·men·i·cal (ek′yōō·men′i·kəl, *Brit.* ē′kyōō·men′i·kəl) See ECUMENICAL.

Oe–Cus·se (ō·kōō′sē) See AMBENO.

oe·de·ma (i·dē′mə) See EDEMA.

Oed·i·pus (ed′ə·pəs, ē′də-) In Greek legend, the son of Laius and Jocasta, who, abandoned by them at birth because of an oracle and raised by the king of Corinth, eventually returned to Thebes. After guessing the riddle of the sphinx and accidentally killing his father, he unwittingly married his mother and became king of Thebes; discovering his relationship to Jocasta, he blinded himself and died in exile. Also **Œd′i·pus.** [<L <Gk. *Oidipous,* lit., swollen-footed]

Oedipus complex *Psychoanal.* A strong, typically unconscious attachment to the parent of opposite sex, with antagonism toward the other: productive of various neurotic disorders when it persists unresolved into adult life. Compare ELECTRA COMPLEX.

Oeh·len·schlä·ger (œ′lən·shlā′gər), **Adam,** 1779–1850, Danish poet and dramatist: also spelled *Öhlenschläger.*

oeil-de-boeuf (œ′y′də·bœf′) *n. pl.* **oeils-de-boeuf** (œ′y′-) A circular or oval window; a bull's-eye. [<F, lit., eye of an ox]

oeil·lade (œ·yàd′) *n. French* A glance; an ogle.

Oe·ne·us (ē′nē·əs) In Greek mythology, a king of Calydon and father of Meleager, who neglected a sacrifice to Artemis, causing her to send a boar to devastate his country. See CALYDONIAN BOAR. Also **Œ′ne·us.**

oe·nol·o·gy (ē·nol′ə·jē) See ENOLOGY.

oe·no·mel (ē′nə·mel, en′ə-) *n.* 1 A beverage of wine and honey. 2 Hence, anything combining sweetness and strength. Also spelled *oinomel.* [<LL *oenomeli* <Gk. *oinomeli* < *oinos* wine + *meli* honey]

Oe·no·ne (ē·nō′nē) In Greek mythology, a nymph of Mount Ida; wife of Paris, who deserted her for Helen of Troy. Also **Œ·no′ne.**

o'er (ôr, ōr) *prep. & adv. Poetic* Over.

oer·sted (ûr′sted) *n.* The cgs unit of magnetic intensity, equal to a force of 1 dyne exerted on a unit magnetic pole. [after Hans C. *Oersted,* 1777–1851, Danish physicist]

oe·soph·a·gus (i·sof′ə·gəs), etc. See ESOPHAGUS, etc.

oes·trin (es′trin, ēs′-) See ESTROGEN.

oes·trum (es′trəm, ēs′-), **oes·trus** (es′trəs, ēs′-) See ESTRUM, ESTRUS.

Oe·ta (ē′tə) A mountain chain in east central Greece; highest peak, 7,063 feet. *Greek* **Oi·te** (oi′tā).

oeu·vre (œ′vr′) *n. pl.* **oeu·vres** (œ′vr′) *French* 1 A work, as of art or literature. 2 The totality of works, as of an author.

of (uv, ov; *unstressed* əv) *prep.* 1 Coming from; originating at or from: Anne *of* Cleves; an actor *of* noble birth. 2 Associated or connected with; included among: Is he *of* your party? 3 Located at: the Leaning Tower *of* Pisa. 4 Away or at a distance from: within six miles *of* home. 5 Named; specified as: the city *of* Newark; a fall *of* ten feet. 6 Characterized by: a man *of* strength. 7 With reference to; as to: quick *of* wit. 8 About; concerning: Good is said *of* him. 9 Because of: dying *of* pneumonia. 10 Possessing: a man *of* means. 11 Belonging to: the lid *of* a box. 12 Pertaining to: the majesty *of* the law. 13 Composed of: a ship *of* steel. 14 Containing: a glass *of* water. 15 Taken from; from the number or class of: six *of* the seven conspirators. 16 So as to be without: relieved *of* anxiety; despoiled *of* ornaments. 17 Proceeding from; produced by: the plays *of* Shakespeare; the work *of* a vanished hand. 18 Directed toward; exerted upon: the massacre *of* the innocents; a love *of* opera. 19 During or at a specified time or occasion: He came *of* a Sunday; *of* recent years. 20 Set aside for or devoted to: a program *of* Lieder. 21 Before; until: used in telling time: ten minutes *of* ten. 22 *Archaic* By: loved *of* all men. [OE, var. of *af, æf* away from]

of– Assimilated var. of OB–.

o·fay (ō′fā) *n. U.S. Slang* A white person: a contemptuous term. [? Pig latin for FOE]

of course 1 In the usual order or procedure; naturally; as expected. 2 Doubtless; certainly.

off (ôf, of) *adj.* 1 Farther or more distant; remote: an *off* chance. 2 In a (specified) circumstance or situation: to be well *off.* 3 Not in accordance with the facts; wrong: Your reckoning is *off.* 4 Not in the usual health or condition; not up to standard: an *off* season for roses. 5 Not in existence; no longer considered active or effective: The deal is *off.* 6 Away from work; not on duty: He spent his *off* hours at the rink. 7 In riding or driving, on the right: opposed to *near:* Pass on the *off* side. 8 *Naut.* Seaward; farther from the coast. 9 In cricket, to the left of a bowler: said of the side of the field facing the batsman. —*adv.* 1 To a distance; so as to be away: My horse ran *off.* 2 To or at a (specified) future time: Your engagement is another week *off.* 3 To or at a (specified) distance: The inn is a mile *off.* 4 So as to be no longer in place, connection, etc.: Take *off* your hat. 5 So as to be no longer functioning, continuing, or in operation: Turn the lights *off.* 6 So as to be away from one's work, duties, etc.: to take the day *off.* 7 So as to be completed, exhausted, etc.: to kill *off* one's enemies; to drink *off* a draught. 8 So as to deviate from or be below what is regarded as standard: His game was *off.* 9 *Naut.* Away from land, a ship, the wind, etc.: Keep her four points *off.* —**off with . . . !** Take off! Remove!: *Off with* his head! —**off with you!** Go away! Leave! —**right** (or **straight**) **off** Forthwith; immediately. —**to be off** 1 To leave; depart. 2 *Colloq.* To be insane. —*prep.* 1 So as to be separated, detached, distant, or removed from (a position, source, etc.): Take your feet *off* the table; twenty miles *off* course. 2 Not engaged in or occupied with; relieved from: *off* duty. 3 Extending away or out from; no longer on: *off* Broadway. 4 So as to deviate from or be below (what is regarded as standard): to be *off* one's game. 5 On or from (the material or substance of): living *off* nuts and berries. 6 *Colloq.* No longer using, engaging in, or advocating: to be *off* drinking. 7 *Naut.* Opposite to and seaward of: the battle *off* the eastern cape. —*n.* 1 The state or condition of being off. 2 In cricket, the offside (of the field). [ME, orig. stressed var. of OF]

of·fal (ôf′əl) *n.* 1 Those parts of a butchered animal that are rejected as worthless. 2 Rubbish or refuse of any kind. See synonyms under WASTE. [ME *ofall* <OFF + FALL]

Of·fa·ly (of′ə·lē) A county in Leinster province, central Ireland; 771 square miles; county town, Tullamore.

off and on Now and then; intermittently.

off–beat (ôf′bēt′, of′-; *for adj.* 2 *esp.* ôf′bēt′, of′-) *n. Music* Any secondary or weak beat in a measure. —*adj.* 1 *Music* Having primary accents in 4/4 time on the second and fourth beats. 2 *Slang* Unconventional; out of the ordinary.

off–Broad·way (ôf′brôd′wā, of′-) *adj.* 1 Not situated in the Broadway entertainment district of New York City: an *off-Broadway* theater. 2 Designating a play regarded as experimental, noncommercial, etc. —*n.* Any area in New York City in which off-Broadway plays are produced. —*adv.* In an off-Broadway theater or play.

off·cast (ôf′kast′, -käst′, of′-) *adj.* Rejected; cast off. —*n.* Anything thrown away or rejected.

off chance A bare possibility.

off–col·or (ôf′kul′ər, of′-) *adj.* 1 Unsatisfactory in color, as a gem. 2 Bad, indelicate, or indecent by implication; of doubtful virtue. Also *Brit.* **off–col′our.**

Of·fen·bach (ôf′ən·bäk, of′-; *Ger.* ôf′ən·bäkh) A city on the Main in southern Hesse, West Germany.

Of·fen·bach (ôf′ən·bäk, of′-; *Fr.* ô·fen·bàk′), **Jacques,** 1819–80, French composer born in Germany.

of·fence (ə·fens′) The usual British spelling of OFFENSE.

of·fend (ə·fend′) *v.t.* 1 To give displeasure or offense to; displease; affront; anger. 2 To affect (the taste, eyes, etc.) with displeasure. 3 *Obs.* To transgress or violate. —*v.i.* 4 To give displeasure or offense; be offensive. 5 To commit an offense or crime; sin. See synonyms under AFFRONT, PIQUE[1]. [<OF *offendre* strike against <L *offendere* < *ob-* against + *fendere* hit, thrust] —**of·fend′er** *n.*

of·fense (ə·fens′) *n.* 1 The act of offending; any sin, wrong, or fault. 2 That which injures the feelings or causes displeasure; that which provokes. 3 The state of being offended; umbrage; anger. 4 Assault or attack: a weapon of *offense.* 5 A cause of sin or stumbling. Also, *Brit., offence.* [<OF <L *offensa* a striking against, orig. pp. fem. of *offendere.* See OFFEND.]

of·fen·sive (ə·fen′siv) *adj.* 1 Serving, adapted, or intended to give offense; displeasing; annoying. 2 Causing unpleasant sensations; disagreeable. 3 Serving as a means of attack. 4 Injurious. See synonyms under FOUL, ROTTEN, VULGAR. —*n.* Aggressive methods, operations, or attitude: with the definite article. —**of·fen′sive·ly** *adv.* —**of·fen′sive·ness** *n.*

of·fer (ô′fər, of′ər) *v.t.* 1 To present for acceptance or rejection; tender. 2 To suggest for consideration or action; propose. 3 To present with solemnity or in worship; make an offering of. 4 To show readiness to do or attempt; propose or threaten: to *offer* battle. 5 To attempt to do or inflict; hence, to do or inflict: to *offer* insult or resistance. 6 To suggest as payment; bid. 7 To present for sale. —*v.i.* 8 To present itself; appear: No opportunity *offered.* 9 To make an offering in worship or sacrifice. —*n.* 1 The act of offering; a proffer or proposal. 2 An attempt or endeavor to do something. See synonyms under PROPOSAL. [OE *offrian* offer a sacrifice <L *offerre* present < *ob-* before + *ferre* bring; infl. in meaning by OF *offrir* offer] —**of′fer·er, of′fer·or** *n.*

Synonyms (verb): adduce, allege, bid, exhibit, extend, present, proffer, propose, tender, volunteer. What one *offers* he brings before another for acceptance or rejection. *Proffer* is a more formal and deferential word, with a suggestion of contingency; as, to *proffer* one's services; the worshiper *offers,* but does not *proffer* sacrifice. See ALLEGE.

of·fer·ing (ô′fər·ing, of′ər-) *n.* 1 The act of making an offer. 2 That which is offered; sacrifice; any gift. 3 A contribution at a religious service.

of·fer·to·ry (ô′fər·tôr′ē, -tō′rē, of′ər-) *n. pl.* **·ries** *Eccl.* 1 *Usually cap.* A section of the eucharistic liturgy, usually following the saying of the creed, during which the bread and wine to be consecrated are offered, and the alms of the congregation are collected. 2 Any collection taken during a religious service; also, the part of a service when it is taken. 3 An antiphon, hymn, or anthem sung during the offertory. 4 A prayer of oblation said by the celebrant over the bread and wine to be consecrated. [<Med. L *offertorium* an offering <LL *offertus,* pp. of L *offerre.* See OFFER.]

off·hand (ôf′hand′, of′-) *adv.* Without preparation; unceremonious or unceremoniously; extempore. —*adj.* Done, said, or made extemporaneously. Also **off′hand′ed.** —**off′hand′·ed·ly** *adv.*

of·fice (ô′fis, of′is) *n.* 1 A particular duty, charge, or trust; an employment undertaken by commission or authority; a post or position held by an official or functionary; specifically, a position of trust or authority under a government: the *office* of premier. 2 That which is performed, assigned, or intended to be done by a particular thing, or that which anything is fitted to perform; function; service. 3 A place, building, or series of rooms in which some particular branch of the public service is conducted: the Patent *Office,* Post *Office;* also, the persons conducting such business; specifically, the head of the department and his immediate assistants: The Executive *Office* serves the president. In the United States the term is applied to those branches of the government business ranking next to

the departments, the chiefs of which are not cabinet members; in Great Britain, to all branches of government business over which a secretary of state presides and to certain other departments having their chiefs in the cabinet: the War *Office,* Home *Office.* **4** A room or building in which a person transacts his business or carries on his stated occupation: distinguished from *shop, store, studio,* etc.: the lawyer's *office.* **5** *pl. Brit.* The outbuildings devoted to culinary or other domestic purposes. **6** The persons collectively, as an association or corporation, whose headquarters are in an office: The *office* has telegraphed me to return. **7** *Eccl.* A prescribed religious or devotional service, particularly that for the canonical hours, or the service itself: the divine *office*; specifically, the daily service of the breviary, morning and evening prayer, the mass, communion, etc. **8** A ceremony; rite. **9** *pl.* A proffered action of any kind; especially, a service: reinstated through the good *offices* of a friend. See synonyms under DUTY. [<AF <L *officium* a service, prob. <*opus* a work + *facere* do, make]

office boy A boy hired to run errands or do odd jobs in an office.

of·fice-hold·er (ôf′is·hōl′dər, of′-) *n.* One who holds an office under a government.

office hours The number of hours one works in an office; also, the hours an office is open for business.

of·fi·cer (ôf′ə·sər, of′ə-) *n.* **1** One elected or appointed to office, as in a company, a society, or an ecclesiastical body, or one filling some other semipublic position, as by appointment. **2** One appointed to a certain military or naval rank and authority, specifically by commission. **3** In the merchant marine, etc., the captain or any of the mates. **4** A member of the constabulary or police force. **5** In corporate bodies and other organizations, one who holds a position entailing certain duties, as secretary or treasurer, as distinguished from an employee. **—commissioned officer** An officer who receives a commission, ranking, in the U.S. Army, from second lieutenant to general, and in the U.S. Navy from ensign to admiral. **—line officer** An officer of a combat branch of the service; officer of the line. **—non-commissioned officer** An officer appointed from the military ranks by an authorized commanding officer. The non-commissioned grades rank from corporal through master sergeant. **—warrant officer** In the U.S. Army, Navy, Air Force, Marine Corps, and Coast Guard, an officer without a commission, but having authority by virtue of a certificate or warrant. His rank is superior to that of a non-commissioned officer. See table under GRADE. *—v.t.* **1** To furnish with officers. **2** To command; direct; manage. [<AF *officer,* OF *officier* <Med. L *officarius* <L *officium* OFFICE]

officer of the day An officer, in a military body, responsible for a 24-hour period for the safety of the command, its property, maintenance of order, and performance of the guard in a post, camp, or station.

officer of the guard In a military body, an officer responsible to the officer of the day for the maintenance of discipline and performance of guard duty in a camp, post, or station.

of·fi·cial (ə·fish′əl) *adj.* **1** Pertaining to or holding an office or public trust. **2** Derived from the proper office or officer; authoritative. **3** In pharmacy, authorized to be used in medicine. **4** Formal; studied; ceremonious. *—n.* One holding an office or performing duties of a public nature. [<OF <L *officialis* <*officium* OFFICE] **—of·fi′cial·dom** *n.* **—of·fi′cial·ly** *adv.* **—of·fi′cial·ness** *n.*

of·fi·cial·ism (ə·fish′əl·iz′əm) *n.* **1** Official state, condition, or system. **2** Rigid adherence to official forms.

of·fi·cial·ize (ə·fish′ə·līz) *v.t.* **-ized, -iz·ing** To make official. **—of·fi′cial·i·za′tion** *n.*

of·fi·ci·ant (ə·fish′ē·ənt) *n.* One who conducts or officiates at a religious service, office, or ceremony; celebrant. [<Med. L *officians, -antis,* ppr. of *officiare.* See OFFICIATE.]

of·fi·ci·ar·y (ə·fish′ē·er′ē) *n. pl.* **·ar·ies** A body of officials. *—adj.* Pertaining to or holding an office.

of·fi·ci·ate (ə·fish′ē·āt) *v.i.* **·at·ed, ·at·ing 1** To act or serve as a priest or minister; conduct a service. **2** To perform the duties or functions of an office. **3** In sports, to act as a referee, umpire, etc. [<Med. L *officiatus,* pp. of *officiare* perform divine service <L *officium* OFFICE] **—of·fi′ci·a′tion** *n.* **—of·fi′·ci·a′tor** *n.*

of·fic·i·nal (ə·fis′ə·nəl) *adj.* **1** Prepared and on hand, as drugs. **2** Employed in the arts or as a medicine. *—n.* Any drug or medicine kept ready for sale. [<Med. L *officinalis* <L *officina* workshop, contraction of *opificina* <*opifex* workman <*opus* work + *facere* do]

of·fi·cious (ə·fish′əs) *adj.* **1** Unduly forward in offering one's services. **2** Obtrusive and interfering; meddling with what is not one's concern. **3** *Obs.* Disposed to serve or oblige; friendly. See synonyms under MEDDLESOME. [<L *officiosus* obliging <*officium* OFFICE] **—of·fi′cious·ly** *adv.* **—of·fi′cious·ness** *n.*

off·ing (ô′fing, of′ing) *n. Naut.* **1** That part of the visible sea offshore but beyond anchorage. **2** A position some distance offshore. **—in the offing 1** In sight and not very distant. **2** Soon to happen, arrive, etc.

off·ish (ô′fish, of′ish) *adj.* Inclined to be distant in manner; aloof. **—off′ish·ness** *n.*

off-line (ôf′līn′, of′-) *adj.* Associated with, but not directly controlled by, an electronic computer.

off-load (ôf′lōd′, of′-) *v.t.* & *v.i.* To unload.

off-peak (ôf′pēk′, of′-) *adj.* Below the maximum: an *off-peak* load in a power plant.

off-print (ôf′print′, of′-) *v.t.* To reprint (an excerpt). *—n.* A reproduction or separate printing of an article or paragraph printed in some publication.

off-put·ting (ôf′pŏŏt′ing, of′-) *adj.* Putting one off; causing hostility, indifference, etc.

off·scour·ing (ôf′skour′ing, of′-) *n.* That which is scoured off; something vile or despised.

off·set (ôf′set′, of′-) *n.* **1** Anything regarded or advanced as a counterbalance or equivalent; set-off. **2** *Geol.* A spur or branch from a range of mountains or hills. **3** *Bot.* A short lateral branch of a plant that takes root where it rests on the soil, thus serving for propagation. **4** A line drawn from a curved or irregular main line at right angles to an auxiliary line, to assist in measuring areas or in plotting. **5** A ledge or set-off in a wall; also, a fence spur set at right angles to the main fence. **6** A terrace; especially, a terrace on a hill or mountain side. **7** *Archit.* A comparatively thin place in the length of a wall; also, a recess below the general plane of a wall; a sunk panel. **8** A bend in a pipe bringing one part out of, but parallel with, the line of another part. **9** *Printing* **a** The smut or smear of a freshly printed sheet on the surface of the sheet in contact with it. **b** An impression made by the offset printing method. **10** A descendant; offspring; offshoot. *—adj.* **1** *Printing* Of or pertaining to offset printing. **2** *Archit.* Of or pertaining to a ledge, panel, frame or the like not flush with a surface into which it is set. *—v.* (ôf′set′, of′-) **·set, ·set·ting** *v.t.* **1** To compensate for, as by balancing or opposing with an equivalent; counterbalance. **2** To transfer (an impression) from one surface to another. **3** *Printing* **a** To print by offset printing. **b** To smudge or mark with an offset. **4** *Archit.* To make an offset in. *—v.i.* **5** To make an offset, as in printing. **6** To branch off; project as an offset.

offset printing A method of printing from a lithographic surface to a rubber-surfaced cylinder, and thence onto the paper.

off·shoot (ôf′shŏŏt′, of′-) *n.* **1** *Bot.* A side shoot or branch from the main stem of a plant. **2** Anything that branches off from the parent stock or is regarded as a side issue.

off·shore (ôf′shôr′, -shōr′, of′-) *adj.* **1** Moving or directed away from the shore. **2** Situated or occurring at some distance from the shore. *—adv.* **1** At a distance from the shore. **2** From or away from the shore.

off·side (ôf′sīd′, of′-) *adv.* **1** At or on the wrong side. **2** In football, out of play: said of a player in certain contingencies when he gets in front of the ball during a scrimmage, or when the ball has been last touched by his own side behind him. **3** In hockey, in the attacking zone ahead of the puck.

off·sid·er (ôf′sī′dər, of′-) *n. Austral.* A friend; partner; follower; hanger-on.

off·spring (ôf′spring′, of′-) *n.* **1** That which springs from or is the progeny of any person, animal, or plant. **2** A child or children; issue. [OE *ofspring* <*of* of, off + *springan* spring]

off-stage (ôf′stāj′, of′-) *n.* The area behind or to the side of a stage, out of view of the audience.*—adj.* In or from this area: *off-stage* dialog. *—adv.* To this area: He went *off-stage.*

off-track (ôf′trak′, of′-) *adj.* Not carried on at the racetrack: *off-track* betting.

off-white (ôf′hwīt′, of′-) *n.* Oyster-white

O'Fla·her·ty (ō·fla′hər·tē), **Liam,** born 1896, Irish novelist and short-story writer.

oft (ôft, oft) *adv. Archaic* & *Poetic* Often. *—adj. Obs.* Frequent. [OE]

oft·en (ôf′ən, of′-) *adv.* On frequent or numerous occasions; repeatedly. *—adj. Obs.* Repeated; frequently occurring. [Var. of ME *ofte,* OE *oft*]

oft·en·times (ôf′ən·tīmz′, of′-) *adv.* Frequently; often. Also *Archaic* **oft·times** (ôf′tīmz′, of′-).

O·ga·sa·wa·ra Ji·ma (ō·gä·sä·wä·rä jē·mä) The Japanese name for the BONIN ISLANDS.

Og·den (og′dən) A city in northern Utah.

Og·den (og′dən), **Charles Kay,** 1889–1957, English psychologist, educator, and semanticist.

og·do·ad (og′dō·ad) *n.* **1** The number eight. **2** Anything constructed of eight parts, individuals, or members; any group of eight. [<LL *ogdoas, -adis* <Gk. *ogdoas, -ados* <*oktō* eight]

o·gee (ō′jē, ō·jē′) *n. Archit.* **1** A molding having in section a reverse or long S-curve. **2** Such a curve used in any construction. **3** An arch with two such curves meeting at the apex: called **ogee arch.** [Appar. alter. of OF *ogive* OGIVE]

og·ham (og′əm) *n.* **1** An ancient British and Irish script of the fifth and sixth centuries having an alphabet of 20 characters (lines, dots, or notches) arranged along an arris, and ascribed to the god Ogma: found cut into the edges of tombstones and pillars. **2** An inscription in that script; also, any one of the characters used. Also **og′am.** [<Irish <OIrish *ogam,* after *Ogma,* its mythical inventor] **—o·gham·ic** (ō·gam′ik) *adj.*

o·give (ō′jīv, ō·jīv′) *n.* **1** *Archit.* **a** A diagonal rib of a vaulted arch or bay. **b** A pointed arch. **2** *Stat.* A frequency curve any of whose ordinates expresses a percentage or number of observations less than or more than the corresponding abscissa. **3** The tapering forward part of a projectile: also called *head.* [<OF *ogive, augive, orgive.* ? ult. <Arabic *auj* a summit] **—o·gi′val** *adj.*

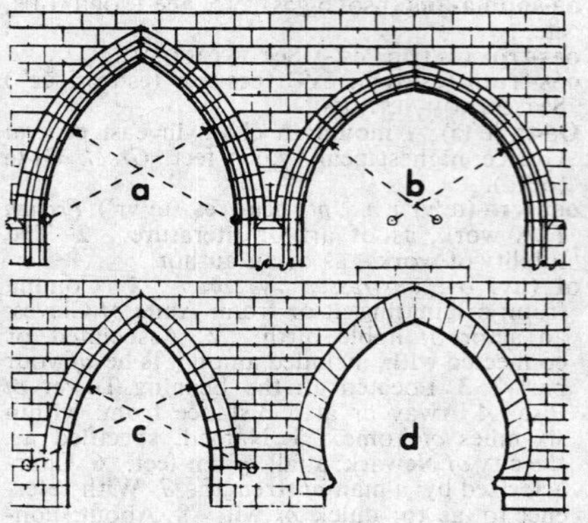

OGIVES
a. Equilateral. *b.* Dropped.
c. Lancet. *d.* Moorish.

o·gle (ō′gəl) *v.* **o·gled, o·gling** *v.t.* **1** To look at with admiring or impertinent glances. **2** To stare at; look at. *—v.i.* **3** To look or stare in an admiring or impertinent manner. *—n.* An amorous or coquettish look. [Prob. <LG *oegelen, ogelen,* freq. of *oegen* look at <*oege* an eye] **—o′gler** *n.*

O·gle·thorpe (ō′gəl·thôrp), **James Edward,** 1696–1785, British general; founder of the colony of Georgia.

OGPU (og′pōō) *n.* Formerly, the Russian Soviet secret police: superseded by the *Narkomvnudel,* which was in turn replaced by the

MVD. Also called *Gay-Pay-Oo*. [<Russian *O(b'yedinennoye) G(osudarstvennoye) P(oliticheskoye) U(pravlenie)* Unified Government Political Administration]

O'Gra·dy (ō·grā′dē), **Standish James,** 1846–1928, Irish historian.

o·gre (ō′gər) *n.* **1** In fairy tales, a man-eating giant or monster. **2** A person regarded as resembling this. [<F; prob. coined by Perrault] —**o′gre·ish, o′grish** *adj.* —**o′gress** *n.* fem.

O·gyg·i·a (ō·jij′ē·ə) In the *Odyssey*, Calypso's island.

oh (ō) *interj.* **1** An exclamation expressing surprise, sudden emotion, etc. **2** See O (*interj.*)

O. Hen·ry (ō hen′rē) Pseudonym of *William Sydney Porter*, 1862–1910, U.S. short-story writer.

O'Hig·gins (ō·hig′ənz, *Sp.* ō·ē′gēns), **Bernardo,** 1778–1842, Chilean soldier and statesman: called "the Liberator of Chile."

O·hi·o (ō·hi′ō) A north central State of the United States, on Lake Erie; 41,222 square miles; capital, Columbus; entered the Union March 1, 1803; nickname, *Buckeye State*: abbr. OH —**O·hi′o·an** *adj. & n.*

Ohio River A river in the east central United States, flowing 981 miles SW from the junction of the Allegheny and Monongahela rivers in western Pennsylvania to the Mississippi.

Öh·len·schlä·ger (œ′lən·shlā′gər), **Adam** See OEHLENSCHLÄGER.

Ohm (ōm) *n.* The unit of electrical resistance. The international ohm is the resistance at 0°C. of a uniform column of mercury having a mass of 14.4521 grams. It is equal to 1.000495 absolute ohms. [after G. S. *Ohm*] —**ohm′ic** *adj.*

Ohm (ōm), **Georg Simon,** 1787–1854, German physicist.

ohm·age (ō′mij) *n.* Electrical resistance of a conductor, expressed in ohms.

ohm·me·ter (ōm′mē′tər) *n.* A galvanometer having a dial or scale graduated to ohms and fractions of ohms, for measuring the resistance of a conductor.

o·ho (ō·hō′) *interj.* An exclamation expressing astonishment, exultation, etc.

O·hře (ôr′zhe) The Czech name for the EGER.

–oid *suffix* Like; resembling; having the form of: *ovoid, hydroid*. [<F *-oïdes* <L *-oides* <Gk. *-oeidēs* <*eidos* form]

–oidea *combining form Zool.* Used to form the names of classes or superfamilies: *Asteroidea, Echinoidea.* [<Gk. *-oeidēs* resembling <*eidos* form]

oil (oil) *n.* **1** A greasy or unctuous, generally combustible liquid, of vegetable, animal, or mineral origin, insoluble in water but sometimes soluble in alcohol, and always in ether: variously used as food, for lubricating, illuminating, and fuel, and in the manufacture of soap, candles, cosmetics, perfumery, etc. **2** Petroleum. **3** An oil paint; also, an oil painting. **4** Anything of an oil consistency **5** Fawning or flattering speech; an apology or excuse. — *v.t.* **1** To smear, lubricate, or supply with oil. **2** To bribe; flatter. [<AF *olie*, OF *oile* <L *oleum* oil]

Oil may appear as a combining form in hyphemes or solidemes, or as the first element in two-word phrases; as in:

oil-bearing	oil-forming
oil box	oil-fueled
oil-bright	oil gage
oil-burning	oil gas
oil camp	oil groove
oil-carrying	oil harden
oil-containing	oil-hardened
oil crane	oil-hardening
oil cup	oil-heater
oil derrick	oilhole
oil-dispensing	oil industry
oil distiller	oil-insulated
oil-distributing	oil-laden
oil drill	oil-ladened
oil-driven	oil-land
oil engine	oil-lit
oil-fed	oil-press
oil-filled	oil producer
oil-finding	oil-producing
oil-finished	oilproof
oil-fired	oilproofing
oil-pumping	oil stove
oil-refiner	oil tanker
oil refining	oil tar
oil-regulating	oil-tempered
oil-rich	oil-testing
oil-saving	oil-thickening
oil-secreting	oiltight
oilskinned	oiltightness
oilsmelling	oil tube
oil-soaked	oilway
oil-stained	oil-yielding

oil·bird (oil′bûrd′) *n.* The guacharo.

oil burner 1 A furnace or heating unit that operates on oil fuel. **2** An atomizer for spraying oil into such a furnace.

oil·cake (oil′kāk′) *n.* The mass of compressed seeds of cotton, flax, etc., or coconut pulp from which oil has been expressed.

oil·can (oil′kan′) *n.* A can for holding lubricating or fuel oil.

oil·cloth (oil′klôth′, -kloth′) *n.* A cotton fabric coated on one side with a preparation of vegetable oils and pigments mixed with a clay filler, and sometimes ornamented with printed patterns: used for table, shelf, wall, or floor coverings, for bags, luggage, waterproofing, etc.

oil color A pigment ground in linseed or other oil, used chiefly by artists.

oil·er (oi′lər) *n.* **1** One who or that which oils; specifically, one who oils engines or machinery. **2** Any automatic device for oiling machinery. **3** A coat of oilskin. **4** A vessel for the transportation of oil.

oil field An oil-producing area, especially one under active exploitation.

oil gland 1 *Bot.* An oil-secreting gland, as in some plants. **2** *Ornithol.* The gland at the rump of a bird that secretes oil for the dressing of the plumage; the uropygial gland.

oil of lavender A yellow, fragrant oil distilled from the blossoms of lavender, especially the spike lavender: used in medicine and perfumery. Also called **oil of spike.**

oil of turpentine See under TURPENTINE.

oil of vitriol Sulfuric acid.

oil of wintergreen Wintergreen (def. 2).

oil painting 1 The art of painting in oils. **2** A painting done in pigments mixed in oil.

oil·paper (oil′pā′pər) *n.* Paper treated with oil for transparency and resistance against moisture and dryness.

oil pool An accumulation of petroleum in sedimentary rocks, usually associated with characteristic geological features.

Oil Rivers The Niger delta, Nigeria; governed by Britain as the **Oil Rivers Protectorate,** 1890–93.

oil shale A compact, typically laminated, brown or black sedimentary shale impregnated with petroleum in varying proportions.

oil·skin (oil′skin′) *n.* Cloth made waterproof with drying oil, or a garment of such material.

oil slick A smooth area on the surface of water caused by a film of oil.

oil·stone (oil′stōn′) *n.* A smooth stone, used when moistened with oil for sharpening tools.

oil well A well or boring for petroleum.

oil·y (oi′lē) *adj.* **oil·i·er, oil·i·est 1** Pertaining to or containing oil. **2** Smeared, rubbed, soaked, or coated with oil. **3** Smooth or deceitfully affable. — **oil′i·ly** *adv.* —**oil′i·ness** *n.*

oi·nol·o·gy (oi·nol′ə·jē) See ENOLOGY.

oi·no·mel (oi′nə·mel) See OENOMEL.

oint·ment (oint′mənt) *n.* A fatty preparation, with which a medicine has been incorporated; an unguent. [<OF *oignement*, ult. <L *unguentum* an unguent; infl. in form by obs. *oint* anoint <F, pp. of *oindre* <L *unguere*]

Oir·each·tas (er′əkh·thəs) *n. pl.* The combined legislatures of Ireland, consisting of the President, Dail Eireann (the representative assembly) and the Seanaid (the senate). [<Irish, assembly]

Oise (wäz) A river of Belgium and NE France, flowing 187 miles SW to the Seine.

O·je·da (ō·hā′thä), **Alonzo,** 1468?–1515?, Spanish explorer; accompanied Columbus on his second voyage.

O·jib·wa (ō·jib′wä) *n. pl.* **·wa** or **·was 1** One of a tribe of North American Indians of Algonquian linguistic stock, formerly inhabiting the regions around Lake Superior; Chippewa. **2** The Algonquian language of this tribe. Also **O·jib′way.** [<Algonquian (Ojibwa) *Ojibway* roast till puckered <*ojib* pucker + *ub-way* roast; with ref. to their puckered moccasin seams]

OK (ō′kā′) *interj., adj., & adv.* All correct; all right: expressing approval, agreement, etc. —*v.t.* (ō·kā′) **OK'd, OK'ing** To sign with an *OK*; endorse; approve. Also **O.K., o′kay′; o′keh′.** [<The Democratic *O.K.* Club, organized in 1840 to support President Martin Van Buren, nicknamed *Old Kinderhook*, from *Kinderhook*, N.Y., his birthplace]

o·ka (ō′kə) *n.* **1** A weight used in Turkey, Egypt, Bulgaria, etc., equal to about 2.828 lbs. **2** A unit of capacity, equal to about one liter. [<Ital. *oca, occa* <Turkish *ōqah* <Arabic *ūqivah* <Gk. *oungia* an ounce <L *uncia*]

O·ka (ō·kä′) **1** A river of the west central European Russian S.F.S.R., flowing 918 miles east to the Volga at Gorki. **2** A river in SW Buryat-Mongol S.S.R., flowing 500 miles north to the Angara.

O·ka·no·gan River (ō′kə·nō′gən) A river in northern Washington and southern British Columbia, Canada, flowing 115 miles south to the Columbia River.

o·ka·pi (ō·kä′pē) *n.* An African ruminant (*Okapia johnstoni*) related to the giraffe, but with a smaller body and a shorter neck. [< native Sudanic name]

O·ka·ya·ma (ō·kä·yä′mä) A port on SW Honshu island, Japan.

OKAPI
(From 5 to 5½ feet high at the shoulder)

O·kee·cho·bee (ō′kē·chō′bē), **Lake** A lake in south central Florida; 730 square miles; 35 miles long, 30 miles wide.

Okeechobee Waterway See CROSS-FLORIDA WATERWAY.

O'Keeffe (ō·kēf′), **Georgia,** 1887–1986, U.S. painter.

O·ke·fi·no·kee Swamp (ō′kə ·fə·nō′kē) A swamp in NE Florida and SE Georgia; 700 square miles. Also **O·kee·fe·no·kee** (ō′kē·fə·ō′kē).

O'Kel·ley (ō·kel′e), **Sean Thomas,** 1883–1965, Irish political leader; president of Ireland 1945–1959.

O·ken (ō′kən), **Lorenz,** 1779–1851, German naturalist and philosopher.

O·khotsk (ō·kotsk′, *Russian* ō·khôtsk′), **Sea of** A NW arm of the Pacific west of Kamchatka and the Kurile Islands.

O·kie (ō′kē) *n. U.S. Slang* **1** An inhabitant of Oklahoma. **2** A migrant farmworker; originally, one from Oklahoma or other parts of the Dust Bowl forced by drought, mortgage foreclosure, etc., to leave his land or to seek work elsewhere. [Dim. of *Oklahoman*]

O·ki·na·wa (ō′ki·nä′wä) The largest of the Ryukyu Islands; 467 square miles; attacked and captured by United States forces, 1945, in World War II: formally returned to Japan, May 15, 1972.

O·kla·ho·ma (ō′klə·hō′mə) A State in the south central United States; 69,919 square miles; capital, Oklahoma City; entered the Union Nov. 16, 1907; nickname *Sooner State*: abbr. OK — **O′kla·ho′man** *adj. & n.*

Oklahoma City The capital of Oklahoma.

O·ko·vang·go (ō′kō·vang′gō) A river in SW central Africa, flowing 1,000 miles south and east from central Angola to the **Okovanggo Basin,** a marsh in Botswana: Portuguese *Cubango*. Also **Okovango.**

o·kra (ō′krə) *n.* **1** A tall annual herb (*Hibiscus* or *Abelmoschus esculentus*) of the mallow family. **2** Its green mucilaginous pods, used in soups and stews, or as a vegetable. **3** Gumbo. [<Ashanti]

O·ku·ma (ō·kōō′mä), **Marquis Shigenobu,** 1838–1922, Japanese statesman.

O·ku·si (ō·kōō′sē) See AMBENO.

-ol[1] *suffix Chem.* Denoting an alcohol or phenol: *methanol, glycerol.* [<(ALCOH)OL]

-ol[2] *suffix Chem.* Var. of -OLE[1], as in *benzol.*

O·laf (ō′ləf; *Dan., Norw.* ō′läf, *Sw.* ōō′läf) A masculine personal name; also, the name of a number of Scandinavian kings. Also **O·lav** (ō′lav, *Norw.* ō′läv, -läf), *Lat.* **O·la·us** (ō·lā′əs; *Dan.* ō·lä′ōōs, *Ger.* ō·lous′, *Sw.* ōō·lä′ōōs). [<Scand., lit., left by his ancestors]
— Olaf I, 969?–1000, king of Norway 995?–1000: one of the heroes of the *Heimskringla*: known as *Olaf Trygvesson.*
— Olaf II, 995?–1030, king of Norway 1016?–1028; canonized; patron saint of Norway.

O·land (œ′länd) A Swedish island in the Baltic Sea; 519 square miles; chief town, Borgholm.

O·lav V (ō′läv, ō′läf), born 1903, king of Norway 1957–.

old (ōld) *adj.* **old·er** or **eld·er, old·est** or **eld·est** 1 Having lived or existed in a certain state for a long time: said of things liable to decay: an *old* elm; having lived beyond the middle period of life; aged: opposed to *young.* 2 Exhibiting discretion and judgment or deportment like a mature and experienced person. 3 Having some specified age: used after the noun expressing time or age: a child two months *old.* 4 Having been made, used, or known for a long time: opposed to *new, fresh, recent,* or *modern*; belonging to an early or remote period of history or development; ancient; antique: the *old* Greeks, *old* coins; also, belonging to a period long past or just preceding the present; not the latest; previous; former. 5 Belonging to the former of two or the earliest of several things: the *Old* Testament. 6 Long cultivated; not newly tilled: *old* land; not of this year's harvest: *old* corn. 7 Worthless on account of age or repeated use; shabby; worn-out: an *old* coat; also, stale; trite: an *old* joke. 8 Continued or established for a long time; known or used long; familiar: used often as an epithet of kindness or friendship: an *old* comrade. 9 Having had long experience or practice; hence, crafty; cunning: an *old* offender, an *old* hand at farming. 10 A general term of endearment or kindly familiarity: *old* boy. 11 In physical geography, in the later stages of a cycle of development: said of topographic forms, streams, etc. 12 Signifying the primeval character of the devil: the *old* enemy. 13 *Colloq.* More than enough; plentiful; great; wonderful: a great *old* racket. *— n.* 1 Past time: days of *old.* 2 A long time; long standing: my friend of *old.* [OE *ald*] **— old′ness** *n.*
Synonyms (adj.): aged, ancient, antiquated, antique, decrepit, elderly, gray, hoary, immemorial, obsolete, olden, patriarchal, remote, senile, time-honored, time-worn, venerable. That is termed *old* which has existed long, or which existed long ago. *Olden* is a statelier form of *old*, and is applied almost exclusively to time, not to places, buildings, persons, etc. As regards periods of time, the familiar are also the near; thus, the *old* times are not too far away for familiar thought and reference; the *olden* times are more remote, *ancient* times still further removed. *Aged* applies chiefly to long-extended human life. *Decrepit, gray,* and *hoary* refer to the effects of age on the body exclusively; *senile* upon the mind also; as, a *decrepit* frame, *senile* garrulousness. One may be *aged* and neither *decrepit* nor *senile. Elderly* is applied to those who have passed middle life, but scarcely reached *old* age. *Remote* primarily refers to space, but is extended to that which is far-off in time; as, at some *remote* period. See ANCIENT[1], OBSOLETE, PRIMEVAL. Compare ANTIQUE. *Antonyms*: compare synonyms for NEW, YOUTHFUL.

Old Bailey The former sessions house, or criminal court, in London; replaced (1906) by the Central Criminal Court.

Old Baldy A peak in southern Colorado, in the Sangre de Cristo Mountains; 14,125 feet: also *Baldy.*

Old·bridge (ōld′brij) A village in NE County Meath, Ireland; scene of the Battle of the Boyne, 1690.

Old Castile A region of central Spain. *Spanish* **Cas·til·la la Vie·ja** (käs·tē′lyä lä vyā′hä).

Old·cas·tle (ōld′kas·əl, -käs·əl), **Sir John** See LORD COBHAM.

Old Colony Plymouth Colony.

old country The native land of any emigrant.

Old Dart *Austral.* England.

Old Dominion Nickname of VIRGINIA.

old·en (ōl′dən) *adj.* Old; ancient. See synonyms under ANCIENT[1], OLD.

Old·en·burg (ōl′dən·bûrg, *Ger.* ōl′dən·bŏŏrkh) 1 A former state of NW Germany, included after 1945 in Lower Saxony; 2,084 square miles. 2 Its former capital.

Old English See under ENGLISH.

old-fan·gled (ōld′fang′gəld) *adj.* Having a fondness for what is old-fashioned. [<OLD + FANGLED; on analogy with NEW-FANGLED]

old-fash·ioned (ōld′fash′ənd) *adj.* 1 Having the characteristics or customs of former times; antiquated; old-time. 2 Having the notions or ways of an old person. See synonyms under ANTIQUE.

old fo·gy (fō′gē) A person of extremely conservative or old-fashioned ideas. Also **old fo′gey.**

old-fo·gy·ish (ōld′fō′gē·ish) *adj.* Of, pertaining to, or like an old fogy; extremely conservative or behind the times. Also **old′-fo′gey·ish.**

Old French See under FRENCH.

Old Glory The flag of the United States.

old guard The conservative element in a community, political party, etc.

Old Guard The imperial guard formed by Napoleon I in 1804, composed of veterans of three campaigns. [Trans. of F *Vieille Garde*; so called in contrast with *Jeune Garde* Young Guard, formed 1810]

Old·ham (ōl′dəm) A county borough in SW Lancashire, England.

Old Harbour Bay A Caribbean inlet in southern Jamaica: also *Portland Bight.*

Old Hickory Nickname of Andrew Jackson.

Old High German See under GERMAN.

Old Icelandic See under ICELANDIC.

Old Irish See under IRISH.

Old Ironsides The U.S. frigate *Constitution*: in allusion to the hardness of her planking.

old·ish (ōl′dish) *adj.* Somewhat old.

old lady *Slang* 1 One's wife. 2 One's mother.

Old Latin See under LATIN.

old-light (ōld′līt′) *adj.* Favoring old principles; in Scottish ecclesiastical history denoting a party which favored union between church and state. *— n.* One who maintains old-light principles.

old-line (ōld′līn′) *adj.* Traditional; conservative; following a beaten path.

Old Line State Nickname of MARYLAND.

old maid An elderly single woman; a spinster. **— old′-maid′ish** *adj.*

old man *Slang* 1 One's father. 2 One's husband. 3 Any man in a position of authority, as one's employer, the captain of a vessel, etc.; especially, the senior officer on board a ship. 4 Old Mr. —: *Old Man* Brown. 5 A term of address, as to a friend. 6 Among North American Indians, a wise man.

old-man's beard (ōld′manz′) 1 Spanish moss. 2 The fringe tree. 3 The black gum.

Old Nick The devil.

Old Norse See under NORSE.

Old Northwest See NORTHWEST TERRITORY.

Old Orchard Beach A summer resort on the coast of SW Maine.

Old Persian See under PERSIAN.

Old Pretender See STUART, JAMES EDWARD.

Old Prussian See under PRUSSIAN.

old rose Any of various shades of grayish or purplish red.

Old Sar·um (sâr′əm) An ancient ruined city in SE Wiltshire, England.

Old Saxon See under SAXON.

Old Scandinavian See OLD NORSE under NORSE.

old sledge See SEVEN-UP.

Old South The South before the Civil War.

old squaw A sea duck *(Clangula hyemalis)* of the northern hemisphere: also called *oldwife.*

old·ster (ōld′stər) *n. Colloq.* A person of advanced years; an old or elderly person.

Old Stone Age The Paleolithic period of human culture.

old·style (ōld′stīl′) *n. Printing* A style of type first used in the 18th century, the downstrokes and the cross-strokes being of nearly the same thickness. Compare MODERN.

old-style (ōld′stīl′) *adj.* Of a former style.

Old Style See GREGORIAN CALENDAR under CALENDAR.

Old Testament The first of the two main divisions of the Bible, containing the books of the old or Mosaic covenant, and including the historical books, the prophets, and the books of wisdom.

old-time (ōld′tīm′) *adj.* Of long standing.

old-tim·er (ōld′tī′mər) *n. Colloq.* 1 One who has been a member, resided in a place, or filled a position for a long time. 2 An old-fashioned person.

Ol·du·vai Gorge (ōl·dōō·vī′, ōl′dōō·vī) A gorge about 100 miles southeast of Lake Victoria in Tanzania, the site of many fossils of extinct mammals, including *Zinjanthropus*, believed to be a forerunner of early man.

old·wife (ōld′wīf′) *n.* 1 Any of several fishes found in West Indian waters, as the parrotfish, the spot, alewife, menhaden, etc. 2 The old squaw.

old-wom·an·ish (ōld′wŏŏm′ən·ish) *adj.* Characteristic of an old woman; fussy.

old-world (ōld′wûrld′) *adj.* 1 Of or pertaining to the Old World or eastern hemisphere; not American. 2 Prehistoric; antique.

Old World The eastern hemisphere.

-ole[1] *suffix Chem.* 1 Denoting a heterocyclic compound having five members in the ring and two hetero atoms: *pyrrole.* 2 Denoting certain aldehydes and ethers. Also spelled *-ol.* [<L *oleum* oil]

-ole[2] *suffix* Small; little: *nucleole, petiole.* [<L *-olus*, a diminutive suffix]

o·le·a·ceous (ō′lē·ā′shəs) *adj.* Designating a family *(Oleaceae)* of shrubs and trees; the olive family. It includes many widely distributed plants, including the lilac, jasmine, and ash. [<NL <L *olea* an olive tree]

o·le·ag·i·nous (ō′lē·aj′ə·nəs) *adj.* Pertaining to oil; oily. [<F *oléagineux* <L *oleaginus* pertaining to the olive < *olea* an olive tree] **— o′le·ag′i·nous·ly** *adv.* **— o′le·ag′i·nous·ness** *n.*

o·le·an·der (ō′lē·an′dər) *n.* An Old World evergreen ornamental shrub *(Nerium oleander)* with leathery leaves yielding a poisonous glycoside with medicinal properties, and clusters of fragrant, rose or white flowers. [<MF *oléandre* <Med. L *oleander* <LL *lorandrum*, ? alter. of L *rhododendron* RHODODENDRON]

o·le·as·ter (ō′lē·as′tər) *n.* An ornamental shrub or small tree *(Elaeagnus angustifolia)* of western Asia and southern Europe, with fragrant, yellow flowers; the Russian wild olive. [<L < *olea* an olive tree]

o·le·ate (ō′lē·āt) *n. Chem.* A salt or ester of oleic acid.

o·lec·ra·non (ō·lek′rə·non, ō′lə·krā′non) *n. Anat.* The curved process of the ulnar bone, marking its juncture with the humerus; the point of the elbow. [<Gk. *ōlekranon*, contraction of *ōlenokranon* head or point of the elbow < *ōlenē* elbow + *kranion* head, skull] **— o·lec′ra·nal** *adj.*

o·le·fi·ant (ō′lə·fī′ənt, ō·lē′fē·ənt) *adj.* Producing oil. [<F *(gaz) oléfiant* olefiant (gas), ppr. of *oléfier* make oil <L *oleum* oil + *facere* make]

olefiant gas Ethylene.

o·le·fin (ō′lə·fin) *n.* Alkene. [<OLEF(IANT) + -IN] **— o′le·fin′ic** *adj.*

o·le·ic (ō·lē′ik, ō′lē-) *adj.* Of, pertaining to, or derived from oil. [<L *oleum* oil + -IC]

oleic acid *Chem.* An oily compound, $C_{17}H_{33}CO_2H$, contained as an ester in most mixed oils and fats, and obtained by saponification with an alkali.

o·le·in (ō′lē·in) *n. Chem.* A colorless liquid glyceride of oleic acid, the chief constituent of fatty oils: also *elain.* Also **o·le·ine** (ō′lē·in, ō′li·ēn). [<F *oléine* <L *oleum* oil]

O·lek·ma (o·lyek′mə) A river in southern Yakut Autonomous S.S.R., flowing 794 miles north to the Lena.

O·le·nek (o·lyi·nyôk′) A river in NW Yakut Autonomous S.S.R., flowing 1,500 miles north and east to the Laptev Sea.

o·le·o (ō′lē·ō) Short for OLEOMARGARINE.

oleo- *combining form* 1 Oil; of oil: *oleoresin.* 2 Olein; oleic: *oleomargarine.* [<L *oleum* oil]

o·le·o·graph (ō′lē·ə·graf′, -gräf′) *n.* 1 A chromolithograph imitating an oil painting. 2 The pattern assumed by a drop of oil placed on water. [<OLEO- + -GRAPH] **— o·le·og·ra·pher** (ō′lē·og′rə·fər) *n.* **— o′le·o·graph′ic** *adj.* **— o′le·og′ra·phy** *n.*

o·le·o·mar·ga·rine (ō′lē·ō·mär′jə·rin, -rēn, -gə-) *n.* Margarine. [<OLEO- + MARGARINE]

oleo oil Beef tallow, obtained as a yellow liquid consisting of olein with a small amount

of palmitin: used in making margarine, soap, and as a base for some lubricants.

o·le·o·res·in (ō′lē·ō·rez′in) n. 1 A native compound of an essential oil and a resin. 2 A pharmaceutical preparation consisting of a fixed or volatile oil containing a resin and sometimes other active matter in solution.

O·lé·ron (dô·lā·rôn′), **Ile d'** The largest island in the Bay of Biscay, belonging to France; 68 square miles.

ol·fac·tie (ol·fak′tē) n. Physiol. A unit of measurement of olfactory sensation, equal to the lowest perceptible concentration of a given scent. Also **ol·fac′ty.** [Coined by Dr. Zwaardemaker, 19th c. Dutch scientist, inventor of the olfactometer]

ol·fac·tion (ol·fak′shən) n. The act, sense, or process of smelling; scent. [<L olfactus. See OLFACTORY.]

ol·fac·tom·e·ter (ol′fak·tom′ə·tər) n. An instrument for measuring the keenness of the sense of smell. [<OLFACTO(RY) + -METER]

ol·fac·to·ry (ol·fak′tər·ē, -trē) adj. Pertaining to the sense of smell. —n. pl. **·ries** 1 Usually pl. The organ of smell. 2 The capacity to smell. [<L olfactus, pp. of olfacere smell <olere have a smell + facere make]

Ol·ga (ol′gə, Russian ôl′gä) A feminine personal name. [<Russian <Scand., holy]

o·lib·a·num (ō·lib′ə·nəm) n. A gum resin; Oriental frankincense. [<Med. L <LL libanum <Gk. libanos <Arabic al-lubān frankincense]

Ol·i·fants River (ol′ə·fənts) A river in the Republic of South Africa and Mozambique, flowing 350 miles NE to the Limpopo river.

ol·i·garch (ol′ə·gärk) n. A ruler in an oligarchy. [<Gk. oligarchēs <oligos few + archein rule]

ol·i·gar·chy (ol′ə·gär′kē) n. pl. **·chies** A form of government in which supreme power is restricted to a few [Prob. <Med. L oligarchia <Gk. <oligarchēs. See OLIGARCH.] —**ol′i·gar′chic, ol′i·gar′chal, ol′i·gar′chi·cal** adj. **oligo-** combining form Small; few; scanty: oligocythemia. Also, before vowels, **olig-.** [<Gk. oligos few]

Ol·i·go·cene (ol′ə·gō·sēn′) n. Geol. The third in order of age of the geological epochs or series comprised in the Lower Tertiary system. —adj. Of or pertaining to the Oligocene. [<OLIGO- + Gk. kainos new, recent]

ol·i·go·chaete (ol′ə·gō·kēt′) n. One of a class (Oligochaeta) of fresh-water and terrestrial hermaphroditic annelid worms, including the earthworms, which lack a distinct head. —adj. Of or pertaining to the Oligochaeta. Also **ol′i·go·chete′.** [<NL <Gk. oligos few + chaitē bristle, mane; so called because it has a small number of bristly locomotive organs]—**ol′i·go·chae′tous** (-kē′təs) adj.

ol·i·go·clase (ol′ə·gō·klās′) n. A massive, vitreous, whitish, triclinic soda-lime feldspar. [<OLIGO- + Gk. klasis a fracture <klaein break]

ol·i·go·chro·me·mi·a (ol′ə·gō·krō·mē′mē·ə) n. Pathol. A deficiency of hemoglobin in the blood. [<NL oligochromaemia <Gk. oligos few + chrōma color + haima blood]

ol·i·go·cy·the·mi·a (ol′ə·gō·sī·thē′mē·ə) n. Pathol. A deficiency or diminution of the red blood corpuscles. Also **ol·i·go·cy·thae′mi·a.** [<NL oligocythaemia <Gk. oligos few + kytos hollow, a cell + haima blood]

ol·i·go·gen·ics (ol′ə·gō·jen′iks) n. Limitation in the number of children; birth control. [<OLIGO- + (EU)GENICS]

ol·i·go·phre·ni·a (ol′ə·gō·frē′nē·ə) n. Arrested mental development. [<NL <Gk. oligos little + phrēn mind] —**ol′i·go·phren′ic** (-fren′ik) adj.

ol·i·gop·o·ly (ol′ə·gop′ə·lē) n. pl. **·lies** A form of monopoly in which the effective control of a market is exercised by a limited number of competitive sellers. [<OLIGO- + (MONO)POLY]

ol·i·gop·so·ny (ol′ə·gop′sə·nē) n. pl. **·nies** A market condition in which the purchase of goods and services is restricted to a few buyers. [<OLIG(O)- + Gk. opsōnein buy victuals]

ol·i·go·syn·thet·ic (ol′ə·gō·sin·thet′ik) adj. 1 Based upon or derived from a few essential components. 2 Ling. Describing a language whose lexicon is composed of relatively few roots.

o·li·o (ō′lē·ō) n. pl. **o·li·os** 1 A miscellaneous collection, as of musical pieces or numbers; a medley. 2 An olla podrida; a seasoned meat and vegetable stew. [<OLLA]

Ol·i·phant (ol′ə·fənt), **Margaret,** 1828–97, née Wilson, English novelist.

ol·i·va·ceous (ol′ə·vā′shəs) adj. Olive-green. [<NL olivaceus <L oliva an olive]

ol·i·var·y (ol′ə·ver′ē) adj. Like an olive, especially in shape. 2 Anat. Relating to the **olivary body,** an olive-shaped eminence containing a nucleus of gray matter, found at either side of the medula oblongata. [<L olivarius belonging to olives <oliva an olive]

ol·ive (ol′iv) n. 1 An evergreen tree (Olea europaea) with leathery leaves, hard yellow wood, and an oily fruit. 2 The fruit of the olive tree. 3 A dull, medium yellowish-green color, like that of the unripe olive: also called **olive green.** 4 An olive branch. —adj. 1 Pertaining to the olive. 2 Having a dull yellowish-green color. [<OF <L oliva an olive]

Ol·ive (ol′iv) See OLIVIA.

olive branch 1 A branch of the olive tree, as an emblem of peace. 2 pl. Offspring; children: alluding to Psalms cxxviii 3.

olive drab 1 Any of several shades of greenish-brown. 2 A woolen material of this color, used for uniforms by the United States Army. —**ol′ive-drab′** (-drab′) adj.

olive oil Oil expressed from olives: used in making salad dressings, soap, etc.

Ol·i·ver (ol′ə·vər) A masculine personal name. Also Du., Ger., Sw. **O·li·vier** (ō′li·vēr′, Fr. ō·lē·vyā′), Ital. **O·li·vie·ro** (ō′lē·vyâ′rō), Pg. **O·li·vei·ro** (ō′lē·vā′rōō), Sp. **O·li·ve·ri·o** (ō′lē·vā′rē·ō). [Prob. <Gmc., army of the elves] —**Oliver** A paladin of Charlemagne's court.

Olives, Mount of A hill just east of Jerusalem: Matt. xvi 1. Also **O·li·vet** (ol′ə·vet, -vit).

O·liv·i·a (ō·liv′ē·ə, Du., Ger., Ital., Sw. ō·lē′·vyä) A feminine personal name. Also Fr. **O·li·vie** (ō·lē·vē′). [<L, olive tree] —**Olivia** In Shakespeare's Twelfth Night, a countess courted by Orsino.

ol·i·vine (ol·ə·vēn, -vin) n. 1 Chrysolite. 2 Green garnet: used as a gem. [<L oliva an Olive + -INE²]

ol·la (ol′ə, Sp. ô′lyä, ô′yä) n. 1 A wide-mouthed pot or jar, usually of earthenware. 2 An olla podrida. [<Sp. <L olla a pot]

ol·la po·dri·da (ol′ə po·drē′də, Sp. ô′lyä pō·thrē′thä, ô′yä) 1 A dish of meat and vegetables, usually highly seasoned, cooked together. 2 Any heterogeneous mixture or miscellany. [<Sp., lit., a putrid pot <olla an olla + podrida putrid <L putridus]

ol·o·gy (ol′ə·jē) n. pl. **·gies** Colloq. A science or branch of learning: a humorous term. [<-LOGY]

O·lo·mouc (ô′lô·mōts) A city in north central Moravia, Czechoslovakia. German **Ol·mütz** (ôl′müts).

Ol·sztyn (ôl′shtin) A city in NE Poland; formerly in East Prussia: German Allenstein.

Olt (ôlt) A river in Rumania, flowing 348 miles SW to the Danube. Also **Ol·tul** (ôl′tōōl).

Oltenia (ol·tē′nē·ə, Rumanian ì·tā′nyä) The western part of Wallachia: also Lesser Wallachia.

Ol·tis (ol′tis) The ancient name for the LOT.

o·ly·koek (ō′lē·kōōk) n. U.S. Dial. A Dutch cake made like a cruller. [<Du. oliekoek a doughnut]

O·lym·pi·a (ō·lim′pē·ə) 1 An ancient city on a plain near Ellis in western Peloponnesus, Greece; scene of the Olympic games. 2 A port on Puget Sound; capital of Washington.

O·lym·pi·ad (ō·lim′pē·ad) n. 1 The interval of four years between two successive celebrations of the Olympic games, by which intervals the ancient Greeks reckoned time: sometimes erroneously used to designate the games or their celebration. 2 The modern Olympic games. [<MF Olympiade <L Olym-

pias, -adis <Gk. Olympias, -ados <Olympios OLYMPIAN]

O·lym·pi·an (ō·lim′pē·ən) adj. 1 Pertaining to the great gods of Olympus or to Mount Olympus itself; hence, of eminent, godlike power, excellence, or manner. 2 Pertaining to Olympia or to the Olympic games. Also **O·lym′pic.** 3 Grandly disinterested, and likely to be impractical: an Olympian proposal to eliminate crime. —n. 1 One of the higher gods of Greek mythology, twelve in number, who dwelt on Mount Olympus. 2 A contestant in the Olympic games. 3 A resident or native of Olympia. [<LL Olympianus <L Olympius <Gk. Olympios <Olympia Olympia, the Olympic games]

Olympic games 1 Athletic games and races held at the chief ancient Pan-Hellenic festival, which was celebrated every four years at Olympia in honor of Zeus. See OLYMPIAD. 2 A modern revival of the old contests, held every four years at some city chosen for this event, beginning with Athens in 1896. Also **Olympian games, Olympics.**

Olympic National Park A heavily forested region, 1,305 square miles; established 1938; in the **Olympic Mountains,** part of the Coast Range in NW Washington; highest peak, **Mount Olympus,** 7,954 feet.

Olympic Peninsula A peninsula bounded by Puget Sound, the Pacific, and Juan de Fuca Strait, including the Olympic Mountains.

O·lym·pus (ō·lim′pəs) 1 The highest mountain of Greece, between Thessaly and Macedonia on the Aegean, regarded in Greek mythology as the home of the Olympian gods; 9,570 feet. Also **Mount O·lym′pus.** 2 Any abode of gods; also, the sky; heaven.

O·lyn·thus (ō·lin′thəs) An ancient city in SE Macedonia; destroyed 348 B.C. by Philip of Macedon. —**O·lyn′thi·ac** (-thē·ak) adj.

Om (ōm) n. 1 In Hinduism, a mystic ejaculation representing the name of the Supreme Being, uttered on solemn occasions of invocation to Brahma. 2 In modern occultism, the spiritual essence. [<Skt.] **-oma** suffix Med. Tumor; morbid growth: carcinoma. [<Gk. -ōma]

O·magh (ō′mə) The county town of Country Tyrone, Northern Ireland.

O·ma·ha (ō′mə·hä, -hô) n. One of the Siouan tribe of North American Indians now living in Nebraska. [<Siouan (Omaha), lit., those going upstream]

O·ma·ha (ō′mə·hä, -hô) A city on the Missouri River in eastern Nebraska.

Omaha Beach A name given to that part of the Normandy coast where units of the United States Army landed on June 6, 1944, during the Allied invasion of France, World War II.

O·man (ō′man, ō·man′, ō·män′) 1 The coastal region of the eastern promontory (**Oman Promontory**) of the Arabian peninsula. 2 Muscat and Oman. See TRUCIAL OMAN.

Oman, Gulf of A NW arm of the Arabian Sea between the Oman section of the Arabian peninsula and Iran.

O·man (ō′mən) **Sir Charles William,** 1860-1946, English historian.

Omar Khay·yám (ō′mär kī·äm′, ō′mər), died 1123?, Persian poet and astronomer; author of the Rubáiyát.

o·ma·sum (ō·mā′səm) n. pl. **·sa** (-sə) The manyplies or third stomach of a ruminant; the psalterium. [<NL <L, bullock's tripe, paunch]

O·may·yad (ō·mī′ad) See OMMIAD.

om·ber (ōm′bər) n. A gambling game played with 40 cards, popular in the 18th century; also, the player undertaking to win the pool in this game. Also **om′bre.** [<F ombre <Sp. hombre a man <L homo, hominis]

Om·bi Islands (om′bē) See OBI ISLANDS.

ombro- combining form Rain: ombrophilous. Also, before vowels, **ombr-.** [<Gk. ombros rain]

om·broph·i·lous (om·brof′ə·ləs) adj. Bot. Relating to or characterizing plants able to withstand much rain. [<OMBRO- + -PHILOUS] —**om·bro·phile** (om′brə·fil, -fil) n.

om·buds·man (om·budz′mən) n. pl. **·men** (-mən) A governmental official appointed to receive and report grievances against the government. [<Sw.]

OLIVE
a. Flowering branch.
b. Floret.
c. Olive (fruit).

Om·dur·man (om'dŏŏr·män') A city on the White Nile, opposite Khartoum in central Sudan.

-ome combining form Bot. Group; mass; body: caulome. [< Gk. -ōma. See -OMA.]

o·me·ga (ō·mē'gə, ō·meg'ə, ō'meg·ə) n. The twenty-fourth and last letter and seventh vowel in the Greek alphabet (Ω, ω); figuratively, the end; the last. It corresponds to English long o. As a numeral it denotes 800. Compare ALPHA, OMICRON. [< Gk. ō mega great o]

om·e·let (om'ə·lit, om'lit) n. A dish of eggs, etc., beaten together and cooked in a frying pan. Also **om'e·lette.** [< F omelette < OF amelette < alemette, lit., a thin plate < alemelle < la lemelle, lamelle < L lamella. See LAMELLA.]

o·men (ō'mən) n. A phenomenon or incident regarded as a prophetic sign. See synonyms under SIGN. —v.t. To foretell as or by an omen; presage; preshadow. [< L]

o·men·tum (ō·men'təm) n. pl. **·ta** (-tə) Anat. A free fold of the peritoneum passing between certain of the viscera. The **small omentum** passes from the lesser curvature of the stomach to the liver; the **great omentum** from the lower border of the stomach to the transverse colon, lying in front of the intestines like an apron. [< NL < L, a membrane enclosing the bowels] —**o·men'tal** adj.

o·mer (ō'mər) n. A Hebrew measure of capacity; the tenth of an ephah. [< Hebrew 'ōmer]

Om·fre·do (ōm·frā'dō) Italian form of HUMPHREY.

om·i·cron (om'ə·kron, ō'mə-) n. The fifteenth letter and fifth vowel of the Greek alphabet (O, o): equivalent to English short o. As a numeral it denotes 70. Also **om'i·kron.** [< Gk. o mikron little o]

om·i·nous (om'ə·nəs) adj. 1 Of the nature of or marked by an omen or by a presentiment of evil; portentous; ill-omened: ominous fears. 2 Serving as an omen in general; prognostic. [< L ominosus < omen, ominis an omen] —**om'i·nous·ly** adv. —**om'i·nous·ness** n

Om·ish (om'ish) See AMISH.

o·mis·si·ble (ō·mis'ə·bəl) adj. That can be omitted; subject to omission.

o·mis·sion (ō·mish'ən) n. 1 The act of omitting or state of being omitted or neglected. 2 Anything omitted or neglected. 3 Neglect or failure to do something that can and should be done; also, an instance of this. See synonyms under ERROR. [< L omissio, -onis < omissus, pp. of omittere OMIT] —**o·mis·sive** (ō·mis'iv) adj. —**o·mis'sive·ly** adv.

o·mit (ō·mit') v.t. **o·mit·ted, o·mit·ting** 1 To leave out; fail to include. 2 To fail to do, make, etc.; neglect or forbear. [< L omittere let go < ob- down, away + mittere send]

om·ma·tid·i·um (om'ə·tid'ē·əm) n. pl. **·tid·i·a** (-tid'ē·ə) Zool. One of the simple elements of a compound eye, as in arthropods. [< NL, dim. of Gk. omma, -atos eye] —**om'ma·tid'i·al** adj.

om·mat·o·phore (ə·mat'ə·fôr, -fōr) n. Zool. An eyestalk, as of a snail. [< NL ommatophorus < Gk. omma, -atos eye + -phoros bearing < pherein bear] —**om·ma·toph·o·rous** (om'ə·tof'ər·əs) adj.

Om·mi·ad (ō·mī'ad) n. pl. **Om·mi·ads** or **Om·mi·a·des** (ō·mī'ə·dēz) A member of a dynasty of early Moslem caliphs who ruled at Damascus 661–750, and in southern Spain 756–1031. Also spelled Omayyad. [after Omayyah, great-grandfather of the first caliph of the dynasty]

omni- combining form All; totally: omnipotent. [< L all]

om·ni·a bo·na bo·nis (om'nē·ə bō'nə bō'nis) Latin All things (are) good to the good.

om·ni·a vin·cit a·mor (om'nē·ə vin'sit ā'môr) Latin Love conquers all things.

om·ni·bear·ing (om'nə·bâr'ing) n. The bearing of an omnirange.

om·ni·bus (om'nə·bəs, -bus) n. 1 A long passenger vehicle sometimes with two decks; a bus. 2 A printed anthology, either of works by a single author or of short stories, poems, etc., of the same general type: an omnibus of Westerns; a Conrad omnibus. 3 An omnibus box. —adj. Covering a full collection of objects or cases: an omnibus bill. [< F < L, for all, dat. pl. of omnis all]

omnibus bar A bus bar.

omnibus bill Any legislative bill or act, or section thereof, containing miscellaneous unrelated provisions.

omnibus box A large box or loge on a level with the stage of a theater.

om·ni·di·rec·tion·al (om'ni·di·rek'shən·əl) adj. Telecom. Capable of or adapted for operating equally well in all directions, as a radio transmitter or antenna.

om·ni·far·i·ous (om'nə·fâr'ē·əs) adj. Of all varieties, forms, or kinds. [< L omnifarius < omnis all + fari speak]

om·nif·er·ous (om·nif'ər·əs) adj. Producing all kinds. [< L omnifer < omnis all + ferre bear]

om·nif·ic (om·nif'ik) adj. All-creating. [< Med. L omnificus < omnis all + facere make]

om·nip·a·rous (om·nip'ər·əs) adj. Producing or bearing all things. [< LL omniparus < omnis all + parere produce]

om·nip·o·tence (om·nip'ə·təns) n. 1 Unlimited and universal power, as a divine attribute; hence, **Omnipotence** God. 2 Unlimited power within a certain sphere, or of a certain kind. Also **om·nip'o·ten·cy.**

om·nip·o·tent (om·nip'ə·tənt) adj. Almighty; not limited in authority or power. —**The Omnipotent** God. [< OF < L omnipotens, -entis < omnis all + potens, -entis able, powerful] —**om·nip'o·tent·ly** adv.

om·ni·pres·ence (om'nə·prez'əns) n. The quality of being everywhere present at the same time; ubiquity. [< Med. L omnipraesentia < omnipraesens, -entis < omnis all + praesens, -entis present] —**om·ni·pres'ent** adj.

om·ni·range (om'nə·rānj) n. Aeron. A network of very-high-frequency radio beams emitted simultaneously in all directions from a system of ground stations, permitting aircraft pilots to chart their courses and positions anywhere within range of the network. [< L omnis all + RANGE]

om·nis·cience (om·nish'əns) n. 1 Infinite knowledge: an attribute of God; hence, **Omniscience** God. 2 Loosely, very extensive knowledge. Also **om·nis'cien·cy.**

om·nis·cient (om·nish'ənt) adj. Knowing all things; all-knowing. —**The Omniscient** God. [< NL omnisciens, -entis < omnis all + sciens, -entis, ppr. of scire know] —**om·nis'cient·ly** adv.

om·ni·um-gath·er·um (om'nē·əm·gath'ər·əm) n. A miscellaneous collection; a medley. [< L omnium, genitive pl. of omnis all + GATHER + L -um, neut. suffix]

om·niv·o·rous (om·niv'ə·rəs) adj. 1 Eating food of all kinds indiscriminately; hence, greedy. 2 Eating both animal and vegetable food: said of bears, crows, etc. [< L omnivorus < omnis all + vorare devour] —**om·niv'o·rous·ly** adv. —**om·niv'o·rous·ness** n.

O·mo·lon (o'mə·lôn') A river in Asian Russian S.F.S.R., flowing 715 miles north to the Kolyma.

o·mo·pha·gi·a (o'mə·fā'jē·ə) n. The eating of raw flesh. Also **o·moph·a·gy** (ō·mof'ə·jē). [< NL < Gk. ōmophagia < ōmos raw + phagein eat] —**o·mo·phag·ic** (ō'mə·faj'ik), **o·moph·a·gous** (ō·mof'ə·gəs) adj. —**o·moph·a·gist** (ō·mof'ə·jist) n.

O'More (ō·môr'), **Rory** Name of three Irish rebel chieftains of the 16th century: also Rory O'more.

Om·pha·le (om'fə·lē) In Greek mythology, a Lydian queen in whose service Hercules, dressed as a woman, spun wool and did other womanly tasks for three years, in order to expiate a murder.

om·pha·los (om'fə·ləs) n. 1 A round stone in the temple of Apollo at Delphi, supposed by the ancient Greeks to mark the middle point of the earth. 2 The central boss of a shield. 3 A central point; hub. [< Gk., navel]

Omsk (ômsk) A city on the Irtish in western Asiatic Russian S.F.S.R.

on (on, ôn) prep. 1 In contact with the upper surface of; above and supported by: lying on the ground. 2 In contact with any surface or part of: a blow on the head. 3 So as to be suspended from: a puppet on a string. 4 Directed or moving along the course of: Be on your way. 5 Near; adjacent to: the town on the river bank; the store on your right. 6 Within the duration of: He arrived on my birthday. 7 At the moment or point of: on the hour; at the time of: He withdrew on my speaking thus. 8 In a state or condition of: on fire; on record. 9 By means of; with the support of: on wheels; on all fours. 10 Using as a means of sustenance, activity, etc.: living on fruit. 11 Accumulated with; in addition to: thousands on thousands of them. 12 Sustained or con-

firmed by; with the authority of: committed on purpose; I swear to it on my honor. 13 In the interest or favor of: betting on a horse. 14 Concerning; about: a work on economics. 15 Engaged in; occupied or connected with: on a journey; on duty all night. 16 As a consequence or result of: making a profit on tips. 17 In accordance with or relation to; in terms of: measured on the Centigrade scale. 18 Directed, tending, or moving toward or against: making war on the enemy. 19 Following after: disease on the heels of famine. 20 Colloq. With; accompanying, as about one's person: Do you have five dollars on you? 21 Colloq. At the expense of; paid by: The joke is on them; drinks on the house. See synonyms under ABOVE, AT. —**to have something on** U.S. Colloq. To have knowledge, possess evidence, etc., against (a person). —adv. 1 In or into a position or condition of contact, adherence, covering, etc.: He put his hat on. 2 In the direction of something: He looked on while they played. 3 In advance; ahead, in space or time: a collision head on ; later on. 4 In continuous course or succession: The music went on. 5 In or into operation, performance, or existence: to turn the electricity on. —**and so on** And like what has gone before; et cetera. —**on and on** Without interruption; continuously. —**to be on to** To be aware of or informed about (someone, something, etc.); understand. —adj. 1 In operation, progress, or application: The play is on; The brake is on. 2 Near; located nearer. 3 In cricket, indicating or pertaining to the side of the wicket and field where the batsman stands. —n. 1 The state or fact of being on. 2 In cricket, the on side of the field or wicket. [OE on, an]

On (on) The Egyptian name for HELIOPOLIS.

on·a·ger (on'ə·jər) n. pl. **·gers** or **·gri** (-grī) 1 A wild ass (Equus onager) of central Asia. 2 A medieval military engine by which stones were hurled with a slinglike device. [< L, a wild ass < Gk. onagros < onos an ass + agrios wild]

on·a·gra·ceous (on'ə·grā'shəs) adj. Pertaining to or designating a family (Onagraceae) of plants of temperate climates; the evening-primrose family. [< NL < L onagra, fem. of onager ONAGER]

o·nan·ism (ō'nən·iz'əm) n. 1 Withdrawal before orgasm; incomplete coitus. 2 Masturbation. [after Onan. See Gen. xxxviii 9.] —**o'nan·ist** n. —**o·nan·is'tic** adj.

once (wuns) adv. 1 One time, without repetition. 2 During some past time. 3 At any time; ever; also, at some future time. —adj. Former; formerly existing; quondam. —conj. As soon as; whenever. —n. One time. —**all at once** All of a sudden. —**at once. 1** Simultaneously. **2** Immediately. —**once for all** Finally. —**once in a while** Occasionally. —**this once** On this occasion only. [ME ones, OE anes, genitive of an one]

once-o·ver (wuns'ō'vər) n. Slang 1 A quick glance or survey. 2 A brief but comprehensive application of labor or study.

On·cid·i·um (on·sid'ē·əm) n. A large, varied genus of tropical American orchids with few leaves, and a loose raceme of striking flowers. They are among the most prized of cultivated orchids, O. papilio, the butterfly orchid, being one of the best-known. [< NL < Gk. onkos an arrow's barb; so called from the form of the lower petal]

on·co·gene (on'kō·jēn') n. Any gene implicated in the development of a tumor. [< Gk. onkos tumor + GENE]

on·co·gen·e·sis (on'kō·jen'ə·sis) n. The formation and development of tumors. —**on·co·gen'ic** adj. —**on'co·ge·nic'i·ty** n.

on·col·o·gy (on·kol'ə·jē) n. The science of tumors. [< Gk. onkos bulk, a tumor + -LOGY] —**on·co·log·ic** (on'kə·loj'ik), **·i·cal** adj. —**on·col'o·gist** n.

on·com·ing (on'kum'ing) adj. Approaching. —n. An approach.

on·do·gram (on'də·gram) n. The record made by an ondograph. [< F onde a wave (< L unda) + -(o)GRAM]

on·do·graph (on′də·graf, -gräf) *n.* An instrument by which electric wave forms, especially those of alternating currents, are recorded autographically. [< F *onde* a wave (< L *unda*) + -(O)GRAPH]
on·dom·e·ter (on·dom′ə·tər) *n.* A meter for registering the frequency of electromagnetic waves. [< F *onde* a wave (< L *unda*) + -(O)METER]
one (wun) *adj.* **1** Being a single individual or object; being a unit. **2** Being an individual or thing thought of as indefinite. **3** Designating a person, thing, or group as contrasted with another; this; that. **4** Single in kind; the same; closely united or alike. **5** Unitary. —*n.* **1** A single unit; the cardinal number preceding two; also, a symbol (1, i, I) representing this number. **2** A single thing or person. —*pron.* **1** Someone or something; anyone or anything. **2** One of certain persons or things already mentioned. **—all one** Of the same or of no consequence. **—at one** In harmony; the same. **—one another** Each other: said of an action or relation involving two or more persons or things reciprocally: They love *one another.* **—one by one** Singly and in succession. **—one day** Some indefinite day or period in the past or future. [OE *ān*]
-one *suffix Chem.* Denoting an organic compound of the ketone group: *acetone.* [< Gk. *-ōnē,* fem. patronymic]
O·ne·ga (ō·neg′ə), **Lake** The second largest lake in Europe, in NW European Russian S.F.S.R.; about 3,880 square miles.
one-horse (wun′hôrs′) *adj.* **1** Drawn or adapted to be worked by one horse. **2** *Colloq.* Of inferior resources or capacity; small; unimportant: a *one-horse* town.
O·nei·da (ō·nī′də) *n.* A member of a tribe of North American Indians of Iroquoian stock.
Oneida Lake A lake in central New York; 20 miles long; 80 square miles.
O'Neill (ō·nēl′), **Eugene Gladstone,** 1888–1953, U.S. playwright.
o·nei·rism (ō·nī′riz·əm) *n. Psychol.* A psychic condition induced by or resembling dreams but prolonged into the waking period. Compare HYPNOPOMPIC. [< Gk. *oneiros* a dream]
oneiro- *combining form* Dream; of dreams: *oneiromancy*: also *oniro-*. Also, before vowels, **oneir-.** [< Gk. *oneiros* a dream]
o·nei·ro·crit·ic (ō·nī′rə·krit′ik) *adj.* Pertaining to or professing power to interpret dreams: also **o·nei′ro·crit′i·cal.** —*n.* One who interprets dreams. [< Gk. *oneirokritikos* pertaining to the interpretation of dreams < *oneiros* a dream + *kritikos* able to discern < *krinein* judge] **—o·nei′ro·crit′i·cal·ly** *adv.*
one-lin·er (wun′lī′nər) *n. Colloq.* A brief remark, meant to be humorous, clever, critical, etc., often used by a comedian in a performance.
one·ness (wun′nis) *n.* **1** Singleness; unity; sameness. **2** Agreement; concord. **3** Quality of being unique. See synonyms under UNION.
one-night stand (wun′nīt′) *U.S.* A town or theater in which a traveling show gives a performance on one night only; also, the performance itself.
on·er·ous (on′ər·əs) *adj.* **1** Burdensome or oppressive. **2** *Law* Legally liable for an obligation or subject to a burden: opposed to *gratuitous.* See synonyms under ARDUOUS, DIFFICULT. [< OF *onereus* < L *onerosus* < *onus, oneris* a burden] **—on′er·ous·ly** *adv.* **—on′er·ous·ness** *n.*
on·er·y (on′ər·ē) See ORNERY.
one·self (wun′self′, wunz′-) *pron.* One's own self or personality; himself or herself.
one-sid·ed (wun′sī′did) *adj.* **1** Of or pertaining to but one side; hence, partial; unfair; inadequate. **2** Unequal-sided, as elm leaves. **3** Unilateral. **—one′-sid′ed·ly** *adv.* **—one′-sid′ed·ness** *n.*
one·step (wun′step′) *n.* **1** A round dance consisting of a long step in two-four time. **2** The ragtime music for such a dance.
one-time (wun′tīm′) *adj.* Former; quondam.
one-track (wun′trak′) *adj. Colloq.* Limited to a single idea or pursuit: a *one-track* mind.
one-up·man·ship (wun′up′mən·ship′) *n. Colloq.* The practice or technique of trying to gain an advantage over another.
one-way (wun′wā′) *adj.* **1** Moving in one direction only: *one-way* traffic. **2** Permitting traffic in one direction only.
On·froi (ôṅ·frwȧ′) French form of HUMPHREY.
Ong·jin (ông·jin) A city of central Korea. *Japanese* **O·shin** (ō·shin).
on·go·ing (on′gō′ing) *adj.* Going on, continuing, or progressing.
on·ie (on′ē) See ONY.
on·ion (un′yən) *n.* **1** A field-grown edible bulb of an herb *(Allium cepa)* of the lily family; a succulent vegetable remarkable for its pungent odor and taste. **2** One of various allied plants. [< OF *oignon* < L *unio, -onis* unity, a pearl, an onion. Doublet of UNION.]
On·ions (un′yənz), **Charles Talbut,** 1873–1965, English philologist and lexicographer.
on·ion·skin (un′yən·skin′) *n.* A thin, translucent paper.
oniro- See ONEIRO-.
on-line (on′līn′, ôn′-) *adj.* Directly connected to, and controlled by, an electronic computer.
on·look·er (on′lo͝ok′ər, ôn′-) *n.* One who looks on; a spectator.
on·look·ing (on′lo͝ok′ing, ôn′-) *adj.* **1** Looking on. **2** Looking forward.
on·ly (ōn′lē) *adv.* **1** Without another or others; singly. **2** In one manner or for one purpose alone. **3** In full; wholly. **4** Solely; merely; exclusively: limiting a statement to a single defined person, thing, or number. —*adj.* **1** Alone in its class; having no fellow or mate; sole; single; solitary: an *only* child. **2** Standing alone by reason of excellence. See synonyms under SOLITARY. —*conj.* Except that; but. [OE *ānlīc* < *ān* one + *-lic* -LY]
on·ly-be·got·ten (ōn′lē·bi·got′n) *adj.* Begotten as the sole issue or undisputed and incontestable heir: the *only-begotten* Son of God.
O·no·fre·do (ō′nō·frā′dō) Italian form of HUMPHREY.
on·o·mas·tic (on′ə·mas′tik) *adj.* **1** Of or pertaining to a name. **2** *Law* Designating a signature of an instrument the body of which is in another handwriting, or the instrument itself. [< Gk. *onomastikos* of naming < *onomastos* named < *onomazein* name < *onoma* a name]
on·o·mas·tics (on′ə·mas′tiks) *n. pl. (construed as sing.)* The study of the origin and evolution of proper names.
on·o·mat·o·ma·ni·a (on′ə·mat′ə·mā′nē·ə, -mān′yə, ō·nom′ə·tə-) *n.* A morbid dread of some particular word or name, or an irresistible impulse to repeat it. [< NL < Gk. *onoma, -atos* a name + *mania* madness]
on·o·mat·o·poe·ia (on′ə·mat′ə·pē′ə, ō·nom′ə·tə-) *n.* **1** The formation of words in imitation of natural sounds, as *crack, splash,* or *bow-wow.* **2** An imitative word. **3** The selection and use of such words. Also **on′o·mat′o·po·e′sis** (-pō·ē′sis), **on′o·mat′o·py** (-mat′ə·pē). [< L < Gk. *onomatopoiia* the making of words < *onoma, -atos* name + *poieein* make] **—on′o·mat′o·poe′ic** or **·i·cal, on′o·mat′o·po·et′ic** (-pō·et′ik) *adj.* **—on′o·mat′o·po·et′i·cal·ly** *adv.*
On·on·da·ga (on′ən·dô′gə, -dä′-) *n.* **1** One of a tribe of North American Indians of Iroquoian stock formerly living in New York and Ontario. **2** *Geol.* A limestone formation of the lower portion of the Devonian period. [< Iroquoian *onont-a′gē,* lit., on top of the hill] **—On′on·da′gan** *adj.*
Onondaga Lake A salt lake in central New York; 5 miles long.
on·rush (on′rush′, ôn′-) *n.* An onward rush or flow.
on·set (on′set′, ôn′-) *n.* **1** An impetuous attack; assault, as of troops. **2** An attack, as of fever; seizure, as of passion. **3** A setting about; outset. See synonyms under ATTACK.
on·shore (on′shôr′, -shōr′, ôn′-) *adv. & adj.* To, toward, or on the shore.
on-side (on′sīd′, ôn′-) *adv.* Not off-side; in position to legally play.
on·slaught (on′slôt′, ôn′-) *n.* A violent hostile assault. See synonyms under AGGRESSION, ATTACK. [Earlier *anslacht,* prob. < Du. *annslag* a striking at, attempt < *slagen* strike; refashioned after *draught, slaughter,* etc.]
on-stage (on′stāj′, ôn′-) *adj.* On stage, visible to the audience. —*adv.* To an area on stage visible to the audience.
On·tar·i·o (on·târ′ē·ō) A province in SE Canada between the Great Lakes and Hudson Bay; 412,582 square miles; capital, Toronto: abbr. *Ont.* **—On·tar′i·an** *adj. & n.*
Ontario, Lake The smallest and easternmost of the five Great Lakes; 7,540 square miles.
on-the-job (on·thə·job′, ôn-) *adj.* Pertaining to skills acquired, especially under guidance, while actually doing the job, as distinguished from formal preparation before employment: *on-the-job* training.
on·to (on′to͞o, ôn′-) *prep.* **1** Upon the top of; to and upon: The cat jumped *onto* the table. **2** *Colloq.* Aware of; informed about: I'm *onto* your tricks. Also written **on to.**
onto- *combining form* Being; existence: *ontogeny.* Also, before vowels, **ont-.** [< Gk. *ōn, ontos,* ppr. of *einai* be]
on·tog·e·ny (on·toj′ə·nē) *n. Biol.* The history of the development of the individual organism: distinguished from *phylogeny.* Also **on·to·gen·e·sis** (on′tō·jen′ə·sis). [< ONTO- + -GENY] **—on·to·ge·net·ic** (on′tō·jə·net′ik), **on′to·gen′ic** (-jen′ik) *adj.* **—on·tog′e·nist** *n.*
on·to·log·i·cal (on′tə·loj′i·kəl) *adj.* Pertaining to ontology. Also **on′to·log′ic.** **—on′to·log′i·cal·ly** *adv.*
ontological argument The metaphysical a priori argument that the real objective existence of God is necessarily involved in the existence of the very idea of God.
on·tol·o·gism (on·tol′ə·jiz′əm) *n.* The doctrine that man has an immediate and certain knowledge of God, and that this knowledge is the foundation and guaranty of all his knowledge: opposed to *psychologism.*
on·tol·o·gy (on·tol′ə·jē) *n.* The science of real being; the philosophical theory of reality; the doctrine of the universal and necessary characteristics of all existence. Compare METAPHYSICS, PHILOSOPHY. [< NL *ontologia* < Gk. *ōn, ontos* being + *-logia* < *logos* word, study] **—on·tol′o·gist** *n.*
o·nus (ō′nəs) *n.* A burden or responsibility; a duty. [< L]
o·nus pro·ban·di (ō′nəs prō·ban′dī) *Latin* The burden of proof; the responsibility of proving: generally resting upon the party holding the affirmative side of an issue.
on·ward (on′wərd, ôn′-) *adv.* **1** In the direction of progress; forward; ahead. **2** On in time. Also **on′wards.** —*adj.* Moving or leading forward or ahead.
on·y (on′ē) *adj. & pron. Scot.* Any: also spelled *onie.*
on·yx (on′iks) *n.* A cryptocrystalline variety of quartz consisting of layers of different colors, usually in even planes; a variety of chalcedony. [< Gk., a nail, onyx]
onyx glass Cameo glass.
oo (o͞o) *n. Scot.* Wool.
oo- combining form **1** Egg; pertaining to eggs: *oology.* **2** *Biol.* An ovum; *oogenesis.* [< Gk. *ōon* an egg]
o·o·cyte (ō′ə·sīt) *n. Biol.* **1** An egg which has not reached full development. **2** An immature female gamete, as in certain protozoans. [< OO- + -CYTE]
oo·dles (o͞od′lz) *n. pl. Slang* A great deal; many; more than plenty. [< dial. E (Irish) *oodle,* var. of HUDDLE, *n.*]
o·og·a·my (ō·og′ə·mē) *n. Biol.* The union of two gametes of different size and form, called egg and sperm cells. Compare ISOGAMY. [< OO- + -GAMY] **—o·og′a·mous** *adj.*
o·o·gen·e·sis (ō′ə·jen′ə·sis) *n. Biol.* The origin and development of the ovum. Also **o·og·e·ny** (ō·oj′ə·nē). **—o′o·ge·net′ic** (-jə·net′ik) *adj.*
o·o·go·ni·um (ō′ə·gō′nē·əm) *n. pl.* **·ni·a** (-nē·ə) **1** *Bot.* The female reproductive organ in thallophytic plants, a large spherical cell or sac within which the oospheres, or egg cells, are developed. **2** *Biol.* A cell whose divisions give rise to oocytes. Also **o·o·gone** (ō′ə·gōn). [< NL < Gk. *ōon* an egg + *gonos* offspring]
o·o·lite (ō′ə·līt) *n.* A granular variety of limestone made up of nearly spherical concretions about some minute, preexisting particles, and resembling in texture the roe of a fish: used for building. [< F *oölithe* < Gk. *ōon* an egg + *lithos* a stone] **—o′o·lit′ic** (-lit′ik) *adj.*
O·o·lite (ō′ə·līt) *n. Geol.* The upper part of the Jurassic system in England.
o·ol·o·gy (ō·ol′ə·jē) *n.* The branch of ornithology that treats of eggs. [< OO- + -LOGY]

—o·o·log·ic (ō′ə-loj′ik), o′o·log′i·cal *adj.* —o·ol′o·gist *n.*

oo·long (oo′lông) *n.* A variety of dark tea that is partly fermented before being dried. [< dial. Chinese < Chinese *wu-lung* < *wu* black + *lung* a dragon]

oo·mi·ak (oo′mē·ak) See UMIAK.

o·o·my·cete (ō′ə-mī·sēt′) *n.* One of a subclass (*Oomycetes*) of fungi producing sexual and nonsexual spores: it includes the water molds and downy mildews. [< NL < Gk. *ōon* an egg + *mykēs, mykētos* a mushroom] —o′o·my·ce′tous *adj.*

o·o·phore (ō′ə-fôr, -fōr) *n.* [< OO- + -PHORE] —o·o·phor·ic (ō′ə-fôr′ik) *adj.*

o·o·pho·rec·to·my (ō′ə-fə-rek′tə-mē) *n.* Ovariotomy. [< OOPHOR(O) + -ECTOMY]

o·o·pho·ri·tis (ō′ə-fə-rī′tis) *n. Pathol.* Inflammation of an ovary or the ovaries, sometimes with inflammation of the Fallopian tubes. [< OOPHOR(O) + -ITIS]

oophoro- *combining form* Ovary; ovarian. Also before vowels, *oor-.* [< Gk. *ōophoros* egg-bearing]

o·o·phyte (ō′ə-fīt) *n. Bot.* The stage in the life history of mosses, ferns, and liverworts, during which sexual organs are developed: one of the examples of the alternation of generations; the gametophyte. [< OO- + -PHYTE] —o′o·phyt′ic (-fit′ik) *adj.*

oo·ra·li (oo′ə-rä′lē) *n.* Urare.

Oor·du (oor′doo) See URDU.

o·o·sperm (ō′ə-spûrm) *n.* 1 A fertilized ovum. 2 Oospore.

o·o·sphere (ō′ə-sfir) *n. Bot.* In algae and fungi, the egg cell prior to fertilization.

o·o·spore (ō′ə-spôr, -spōr) *n. Bot.* The fertilized and fully developed oosphere, produced within an oogonium. [< OO- + SPORE] —o·o·spor·ic (ō′ə-spôr′ik, -spor′ik), o·os·po·rous (ō-os′pər-əs) *adj.*

o·o·the·ca (ō′ə-thē′kə) *n. pl.* **·cae** (-sē) 1 *Entomol.* The egg case of certain insects, as of a cockroach. 2 *Bot.* In ferns, a sporangium. [< NL < Gk. *ōon* an egg + *thēkē* a case] —o′o·the′cal *adj.*

ooze¹ (ooz) *v.* oozed, ooz·ing *v.i.* 1 To flow or leak out slowly or gradually, as through pores or small holes; seep; percolate. 2 To exude moisture. 3 To escape or disappear: His courage *oozed* away. —*v.t.* 4 To give off or exude. [< *n.*] —*n.* 1 A slow, gradual leak; gentle flow: the *ooze* of a small spring. 2 That which oozes. 3 An infusion or decoction of a tanniferous substance, such as oak bark, used in tanning. —*adj.* 1 Designating calfskin, sheepskin, goatskin, or other hide susceptible of a soft, velvety finish on the flesh side. 2 Denoting this kind of finish, or the process by which it is produced: *ooze* calf; *ooze* leather. [OE *wōs* sap, juice; infl. in meaning by OE *wāse* mire, dirt]

ooze² (ooz) *n.* 1 Slimy mud or moist, spongy soil. 2 A deposit of calcareous matter found on the ocean bottom and largely made up of the remains of foraminifers. 3 The fibers on the surface of unfinished cotton thread. 4 A piece of muddy or marshy ground; bog; fen. 5 Seaweed. [OE *wāse* mire, marsh]

oo·zy¹ (oo′zē) *adj.* **·zi·er, ·zi·est** Slowly leaking; gently dripping. —oo′zi·ness *n.*

oo·zy² (oo′zē) *adj.* **·zi·er, ·zi·est** Containing, composed of, or like mud or ooze; slimy. —oo′zi·ly *adv.* —oo′zi·ness *n.*

o·pac·i·fy (ō-pas′ə-fī) *v.* **·fied, ·fy·ing** *v.t.* 1 To cause to become opaque. —*v.i.* 2 To become opaque; lose transparency, as the lens of the eye. —o·pac′i·fi·ca·tion (ō-pas′ə·fə-kā′shən) *n.*

o·pac·i·ty (ō-pas′ə-tē) *n. pl.* **·ties** 1 The state of being opaque; obscurity. 2 That which is opaque. 3 *Physics* Imperviousness to light or other forms of radiation. Compare TRANSMITTANCE. [< MF *opacité* < L *opacitas* < *opacus*. See OPAQUE.]

o·pah (ō′pə) *n.* A large fish (genus *Lampris*) of warm seas, noted for the brilliancy of its colors. [< Ibo *úbá*]

o·pal (ō′pəl) *n.* An amorphous, variously colored, hydrous silica, softer and less dense than quartz. The **precious** (or **noble**) **opal** presents a peculiar play of delicate colors, and is valued as a gemstone. The **fire** (or **flame**) **opal** shows its colors disposed in streaks: often called *girasol.* [< L *opalus* < Gk. *opallios* < Skt. *upala* a precious stone]

o·pal·esce (ō′pəl·es′) *v.t.* **·esced, ·esc·ing** To exhibit opalescence.

o·pal·es·cence (ō′pəl·es′əns) *n.* An iridescent play of pearly or milky colors, as in an opal. —o′pal·es′cent, o′pal·ine (-ēn, -in) *adj.*

o·paque (ō-pāk′) *adj.* 1 Impervious to light; not translucent. 2 Loosely, imperfectly transparent. 3 Imervious to reason; unintelligent. 4 Impervious to radiant heat, electric radiation, etc. 5 Having no luster; dull. 6 Unintelligible; obscure: an *opaque* style. 7 *Obs.* Dark; lying in shadow. See synonyms under DARK. —*n.* 1 Opacity; that which is opaque. 2 An opaque substance used to block out portions of a photographic negative or positive. —*v.t.* o·paqued, o·paqu·ing 1 To make opaque. 2 To block out parts of with opaque, as a photographic negative or positive. [< L *opacus* shaded, darkened; after F *opaque*] —o·paque′ly *adv.* —o·paque′ness *n.*

op art (op) A style of art of the 1960's characterized by complex geometric patterns designed to create optical distortions, illusions, and the like. [< *optical art*]

ope (ōp) *v.t. & v.i.* oped, op·ing *Poetic & Archaic* To open. [ME, short for OPEN]

o·pen (ō′pən) *adj.* 1 Affording approach, view, passage, or access because of the absence or removal of barriers, restrictions, etc.; unobstructed: The new road is *open* for traffic; *open* country. 2 Public; unbounded; accessible to all: the *open* market; in *open* competition; the *open* sea. 3 Unconcealed; overt; not secret or hidden: *open* hostility. 4 Expanded; unfolded: an *open* flower. 5 Exposed; not enclosed or covered over; unprotected: an *open* car. 6 Ready for business, appointment, etc.: an *open* day in the schedule. 7 Not settled or decided; pending: an *open* account; an *open* question. 8 Ready and free for engagement, employment, etc.; available: The job is still *open.* 9 Ready to consider proof or argument; unbiased; receptive: often with *to:* an *open* mind; *open* to conviction. 10 Generous; liberal: He gives with an *open* hand. 11 *Phonet.* a Pronounced with a wide opening above the tongue; low: said of vowels, as the *a* in *father:* opposed to *close.* b Ending in a vowel or diphthong: said of a syllable. 12 Frank; ingenuous; not deceptive: *open* and aboveboard. 13 Eager or willing to receive: with *open* arms. 14 In hunting or fishing, without prohibition: *open* season. 15 Liable to attack, robbery, temptation, etc. 16 Having openings, holes, or perforations, as woven goods or needlework; porous. 17 Mild; free from fog, mist, or ice: an *open* winter; *open* weather; *open* water in northern seas. 18 *Printing* a Widely spaced, as a line on a page. b Widely leaded or containing many breaks; fat: said of composed or printed matter. 19 *Music* Not stopped by the finger, as a string, or having the top uncovered, as an organ pipe; also, produced by an open string or pipe: said of a note, tone, etc. 20 Unrestricted by union regulations in the employment of labor: an *open* shop. 21 *U.S. Colloq.* Not under control in the sale of intoxicants, gambling, or vice: an *open* town. 22 Out of doors. 23 *U.S.* Of or designating a policy of admitting students for matriculation to a college or university without regard to their academic preparedness, thus providing an opportunity for members of disadvantaged groups to obtain university degrees: *open* admissions. 24 In the elementary grades, of or characterized by an educational environment designed to encourage self-motivated learning by giving children freedom to move from one small group to another within and sometimes beyond the limits of the classroom: *open* classrooms. See synonyms under BLUFF², CANDID, EVIDENT, MANIFEST, NOTORIOUS, OVERT. —*v.t.* 1 To set open or ajar, as a door; unclose; unfasten. 2 To make passable; free from obstacles. 3 To make or force (a hole, passage, etc.). 4 To remove the covering, lid, etc., of: to *open* a package. 5 To expand, as for viewing; unroll; unfold, as a map. 6 To make an opening or openings into: to *open* an abscess. 7 To make or declare ready for commerce, use, etc.: to *open* a store. 8 To make or declare public or free of access, as a park; make available for settlement. 9 To make less compact; expand: to *open* ranks. 10 To make more receptive to ideas or sentiments; enlighten: to *open* the mind. 11 To bare the secrets of; divulge; reveal: to *open* one's heart. 12 To begin; commence, as negotiations. 13 *Law* To undo or recall (a judgment or order) so as to permit its validity to be questioned. —*v.i.* 14 To become open. 15 To come apart or break open; rupture: The wound *opened* again. 16 To come into view; spread out; unroll. 17 To afford access or view: The door *opened* on a courtyard. 18 To become receptive or enlightened. 19 To begin; be started: The season *opened* with a ball. 20 In the theater, to begin a season or tour. —*n.* Any wide space not enclosed, obstructed, or covered, as by woods, rocks, etc.; open land or water: usually with the definite article: in the *open.* [OE. Akin to UP.] —o′pen·ly *adv.* —o′pen·ness *n.*

o·pen-air (ō′pən·âr′) *adj.* 1 Out of doors; taking place in an open field or street: an *open-air* service. 2 Relating to the plein-air school of painters.

o·pen-and-shut (ō′pən·ənd·shut′) *adj.* Simple; obvious; easily determinable.

open chain *Chem.* An organic compound in which the carbon atoms are disposed in a chain open at both ends, as in aliphatic compounds.

o·pen-cut (ō′pən·kut′) *adj.* Open-pit.

open door 1 The policy of giving to all nations the same commercial privileges in a dependency, or recently conquered territory, as those exercised by the dominant country: used attributively in such phrases as **open-door policy, open-door principle,** etc. 2 Opportunity for free trade. 3 Admission to all without charge.

o·pen-end (ō′pən·end′) *adj.* Having a capitalization that is not fixed but subject to fluctuation as shares are sold or redeemed: A mutual fund is an *open-end* investment trust.

o·pen·er (ō′pən·ər) *n.* 1 An instrument for opening anything firmly closed: usually in combination: a can-*opener.* 2 A person who opens or is employed to open: usually in combination: a pew-*opener.* 3 In poker and similar games: a The player who opens the jackpot. b *pl.* Cards of sufficient value, as a pair of jacks, to enable the player to open a pot.

o·pen-eyed (ō′pən·īd′) *adj.* Having the eyes open; wary; watchful; also, amazed: in *open-eyed* wonder.

o·pen-faced (ō′pən·fāst′) *adj.* 1 Possessing a countenance suggestive of frankness, simplicity, and honesty. 2 Having a face uncovered by a casing, as a watch.

o·pen-hand·ed (ō′pən·han′did) *adj.* Giving freely; liberal. See synonyms under GENEROUS. —o′pen-hand′ed·ly *adv.* —o′pen-hand′ed·ness *n.*

o·pen-heart·ed (ō′pən·här′tid) *adj.* Disclosing the thoughts and intentions plainly; frank; candid. —o′pen-heart′ed·ly *adj.* —o′pen-heart′ed·ness *n.*

o·pen-hearth (ō′pən·härth′) *adj. Metall.* 1 Having a shallow or open hearth: said of furnaces used in making steel by the Siemens - Martin process. 2 Made in a shallow or open hearth: said of steel.

OPEN—HEARTH FURNACE

open house 1 A house extending hospitality to all who wish to come. 2 An occasion when a school, factory, institution, clubhouse, etc., is open to visitors, as for inspection, observation, etc.

o·pen·ing (ō′pən·ing) *n.* 1 The act of becoming open or of causing to be open. 2 Something that is open; a vacant or unobstructed space, as within barriers or boundaries; a hole, passage, or gap; a space. 3 A tract in a forest where trees are lacking or thinly scattered. 4 An aperture in a wall; especially, one for the admission of light or air. 5 The first part or stage, as of a period, act, or process; a beginning; prelude. 6 In chess, checkers, etc., a specific mode of beginning the game; the series of opening moves. 7 An opportunity for action, especially in business. See synonyms under BEGINNING, BREACH, ENTRANCE¹, HOLE, OPPORTUNITY.

o·pen-mind·ed (ō′pən·mīn′did) *adj.* Free from prejudiced conclusions; amenable to reason; receptive. — **o′pen-mind′ed·ly** *adv.*
o·pen-mouthed (ō′pən·mouthd′, -moutht′) *adj.* 1 Having the mouth open; gaping, as in wonder or surprise. 2 Noisy; clamorous.
o·pen-pit (ō′pən·pit′) *adj.* Designating a mine dug directly into the surface, with the pit open to the air.
open range An unfenced area of grazing country.
o·pen-ses·a·me (ō′pən·ses′ə·mē) *n.* An unfailing means or formula for opening secret doors and gaining entrance. [From the story of *Ali Baba and the Forty Thieves* where the door of the robbers' cave opened only at the magic conjuration *"open sesame"*]
open shop An establishment in which union labor and non-union labor are employed: opposed to *closed shop.*
open stove A stove having the firebox open to the room; a Franklin stove.
open syllable See under SYLLABLE.
open timber A forest having no undergrowth.
o·pen·work (ō′pən·wûrk′) *n.* Any product of art or handicraft with many small openings.
op·er·a (op′ər·ə, op′rə) *n.* 1 A form of drama in which music is a dominant factor, made up of arias, recitatives, choruses, etc., with orchestral accompaniment, scenery, acting, and sometimes dance: the principal types are **comic opera,** in which there is spoken dialog and the story ends happily; **grand opera,** a dramatic composition generally with a serious or tragic theme, of which the plot is elaborated as in a play and the dialog is set to music throughout; **light opera,** in which the plot has humorous situations, a happy ending, and some spoken dialog. 2 A particular musical drama or its music or libretto; also, its representation. 3 The theater in which operas are given. 4 Plural of OPUS. [<Ital. <L, a work, labor < *opus, operis* work] — **op·er·at·ic** (op′ə·rat′ik) *adj.* — **op′er·at′i·cal·ly** *adv.*
op·er·a·ble (op′ər·ə·bəl) *adj.* Capable of treatment by surgical operation. — **op′er·a·bil′i·ty** *n.*
o·pé·ra bouffe (ô·pā·rà bo͞of′) *French* A farcical comic opera. Also *Ital.* **o·pe·ra buf·fa** (ô′pā·rä bo͞of′fä).
o·pé·ra co·mique (ô·pā·rà kô·mēk′) *French* Comic opera.
opera glass A binocular telescope of small size, suitable for use at the theater. Also **opera glasses.**
opera hat A tall hat, the crown of which is extended by springs and is capable of being collapsed into an approximately flat form.
opera house A theater specially adapted for performance of operas; loosely, any theater.
op·er·and (op′ər·and) *n. Math.* Any quantity or symbol upon which an operation is performed: also called *faciend.* [<L *operandum,* neut. gerundive of *operari.* See OPERATE.]
op·er·ant (op′ər·ənt) *adj.* 1 Producing a specified effect. 2 *Psychol.* Designating conditioning by which desired behavior is elicited by rewards that reinforce appropriate responses. — **op′er·ant·ly** *adv.*
op·er·ate (op′ə·rāt) *v.* **·at·ed, ·at·ing** *v.i.* 1 To act or function, especially with force or influence; work. 2 To bring about or produce the proper or intended effect. 3 To perform a surgical operation. 4 To deal in securities, stocks, etc., especially speculatively. 5 To carry on a military or naval operation: usually with *against.* — *v.t.* 6 To control the working or function of, as a machine. 7 To manage or conduct the affairs of: to *operate* a railroad. 8 To bring about or cause. [<L *operatus,* pp. of *operari* work, have an effect < *opus, operis* a work] — **op′er·at′a·ble** *adj.*
op·er·a·tion (op′ə·rā′shən) *n.* 1 The act or process of operating; the exertion or action of any form of power or energy. 2 A method of exercising or applying force; a mode of action. 3 A single specific act or transaction, especially in the stock market. 4 A course or series of acts to effect a certain purpose; process. 5 The state of being in action: The machinery is in *operation.* 6 *Surg.* Any systematic manipulation upon the body, performed either with or without instruments, to restore disunited or deficient parts, to remove diseased or injured parts, or to extract foreign matter. 7 *Math.* **a** The act of making a change in the value or form of a quantity. **b** The change itself as indicated by symbols or rules: distinguished from the process by which such change is accomplished. 8 Some special kind of activity; manner of action; a vital or natural process of activity. 9 A military or naval campaign.
Synonyms: action, agency, effect, execution, force, influence, performance, procedure, result. *Operation* is *action* resulting in change, whether produced by the *agency* or *action* of an intelligent agent or of a material substance or *force*; as, military *operations*; the *operation* of a medicine. *Performance* and *execution* denote intelligent *action,* considered with reference to the actor or to that which he accomplishes; *performance* accomplishing the will of the actor, *execution* often the will of another. Compare ACT, EXERCISE. *Antonyms*: failure, inaction, ineffectiveness, inefficiency, inutility, powerlessness.
op·er·a·tion·al (op′ə·rā′shən·əl) *adj.* 1 Pertaining to an operation. 2 Organized or prepared to carry out assigned tasks, especially of a military character. 3 Fit or ready for some specified use. 4 In actual service, as a machine, aircraft, etc.
operations research The application of scientific method, engineering procedures, and technical skills to insure maximum efficiency in the conduct of planned operations in industry and government, both in war and in peace. Also called **operational research.**
op·er·a·tive (op′ər·ə·tiv, -ə·rā′tiv) *adj.* 1 Exerting force or influence. 2 Moving or working efficiently; effective. 3 Connected with operations: *operative* surgery. 4 Concerned with practical work, mechanical or manual. 5 Engaged in practical activity, as a workman or mechanic. — *n.* 1 A person employed as a skilled worker, as in a mill or factory, etc.; an artisan. 2 *Colloq.* A detective; one who works secretly. See synonyms under ARTIST. — **op′er·a·tive·ly** *adv.*
op·er·a·tor (op′ə·rā′tər) *n.* 1 One who operates; any skilled worker; specifically, one who works a telephone switchboard, one who receives or sends messages on a telegraph, or one who works a typesetting machine. 2 A broker who acts for others in trading in speculative securities. 3 The owner and director of a coal mine, oil field, or other large industrial organization. 4 *Math.* A symbol that briefly indicates a mathematical process. See synonyms under AGENT.
o·per·cu·lum (ō·pûr′kyo͞o·ləm) *n. pl.* **·la** (-lə) *Biol.* 1 A lid, cover, or lidlike part or organ, as of the orifice of the capsule in mosses, of certain capsules (as a pyxis) in flowering plants, of the hair follicles, etc. 2 A horny or shelly plate in many gastropods, serving to close the aperture when the animal is retracted. 3 In fishes, the gill cover; specifically, the hindmost and uppermost bone of the gill cover. 4 In the king crab, the plate that covers the abdominal limbs. 5 The labrum of certain dipterous insects. 6 A part of the cerebral cortex. Also **o·per·cele** (ō·pûr′sēl), **o·per′·cule** (-kyo͞ol). [<L, a covering, lid < *operire* cover] — **o·per′cu·lar** *adj.* — **o·per′cu·late, o·per′cu·lat′ed** *adj.*
o·pe·re ci·ta·to (op′ə·rē si·tā′tō) *Latin* In the work cited, or quoted: abbr. *op. cit.*
op·e·ret·ta (op′ə·ret′ə) *n.* A short, humorous opera with dialog. [<Ital., dim. of *opera*]
op·er·ose (op′ə·rōs) *adj.* Laborious; also, industrious. [<L *operosus*] — **op′er·ose′ly** *adv.*
O·phel·ia (ō·fēl′yə) A feminine personal name. Also *Fr.* **O·phé·lie** (ō·fā·lē′). [Prob. <Gk., a help]
— **Ophelia** In Shakespeare's *Hamlet,* the daughter of Polonius; in love with Hamlet.
oph·i·cleide (of′ə·klīd) *n.* A brass wind instrument resembling a cornet: now replaced in orchestras by the tuba. [<F *ophicléide* <Gk. *ophis* serpent + *kleis, kleidos* key]
o·phid·i·an (ō·fid′ē·ən) *n.* One of a suborder of limbless reptiles (*Ophidia*), with mandibular rami connected only by an elastic ligament, and having no pectoral arch; a serpent; snake. — *adj.* Of or pertaining to the *Ophidia,* or to snakes; snakelike. [<NL <Gk. *ophis* a snake]
oph·i·dism (of′ə·diz′əm) *n.* Poisoning by the venom of a snake. Also **oph·i·di·a·sis** (of′ə·dī′ə·sis).
ophio- *combining form* Serpent; of or pertaining to serpents: *ophiolatry.* Also, before vowels, **ophi-.** [<Gk. *ophis* a serpent]
oph·i·ol·a·try (of′ē·ol′ə·trē) *n.* Serpent worship. [<OPHIO- + -LATRY] — **oph′i·ol′a·trous** *adj.*
oph·i·ol·o·gy (of′ē·ol′ə·jē) *n.* The branch of zoology that treats of serpents; herpetology. [<OPHIO- + -LOGY] — **oph′i·o·log′i·cal** (-ə·loj′i·kəl) *adj.* — **oph′i·ol′o·gist** *n.*
O·phir (ō′fər) In the Bible, a land rich in gold from which Solomon obtained his wealth. I *Kings* x 11.
oph·ite (of′īt, ō′fīt) *n.* A greenish altered diabase of the late Mesozoic age occurring in the Pyrenees. [<L *ophites* <Gk. *ophitēs (lithos)* a serpentine (stone) < *ophis* a serpent]
o·phit·ic (ō·fit′ik) *adj. Mineral.* Characterized by feldspar crystals in a matrix of augite crystals.
Oph·i·u·chus (of′ē·yo͞o′kəs, ō′fē-) A northern constellation, the Serpent-holder or Doctor. See CONSTELLATION. [<L <Gk. *ophiouchos* < *ophis* a serpent + *echein* hold]
oph·thal·mi·a (of·thal′mē·ə) *n. Pathol.* Inflammation of the eye, its membranes, or its lids. Also **oph·thal′my.** [<LL <Gk. *ophthalmos* an eye]
oph·thal·mic (of·thal′mik) *adj.* Of, for, or pertaining to the eye: an *ophthalmic* ointment.
oph·thal·mi·tis (of′thal·mī′tis) *n. Pathol.* Inflammation of the eye, including the outer and internal structures.
ophthalmo- *combining form* Eye; pertaining to the eyes: *ophthalmology.* Also, before vowels, **ophthalm-.** [<Gk. *ophthalmos* the eye]
oph·thal·mol·o·gy (of′thal·mol′ə·jē) *n.* The science dealing with the structure, functions, and diseases of the eye. — **oph·thal′mo·log′ic** (-mə·loj′ik) or **·i·cal** *adj.* — **oph′thal·mol′o·gist** *n.*
oph·thal·mo·scope (of·thal′mə·skōp) *n.* An optical instrument having a concave mirror with a hole in its center, for illuminating and viewing the center of the eye. — **oph·thal′mo·scop′ic** (-skop′ik) or **·i·cal** *adj.* — **oph·thal·mos·co·py** (of′thal·mos′kə·pē) *n.*

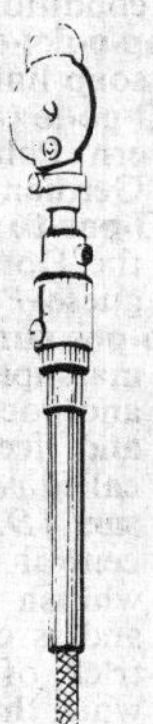
OPTHALMOSCOPE

-opia *combining form Med.* A (specified) defect of the eye, or condition of sight: *myopia.* Also spelled *-opy.* [<Gk. *-ōpia* < *ōps, ōpos* the eye]
o·pi·ate (ō′pē·it, -āt) *n.* 1 Medicine containing opium; a narcotic. 2 Something inducing sleep. — *adj.* Consisting of opium; tending to induce sleep. — *v.t.* (-āt) **·at·ed, ·at·ing** 1 To treat with opium or an opiate. 2 To deaden; dull. [<Med. L *opiatus,* pp. of *opiare* treat with opium <L *opium* OPIUM]
o·pine (ō·pīn′) *v.t.* & *v.i.* **o·pined, o·pin·ing** To hold or express as an opinion; think; conjecture: now usually humorous. [<MF *opiner* <L *opinari* think]
o·pin·ion (ə·pin′yən) *n.* 1 A conclusion or judgment held with confidence, but falling short of positive knowledge. 2 *Often pl.* A settled judgment or conviction on some subject, as religion or politics. 3 Favorable judgment or estimation; reputation. 4 Specifically, an estimate of the excellence or value of a person or a thing; also, a common or prevailing sentiment; public opinion. 5 *Law* The formal announcement of the conclusions of a court in a case before it; also, the conclusion of an attorney touching the merits of a submitted case: to take the *opinion* of counsel. [<OF <L *opinio, -onis* < *opinari* think]
Synonyms: belief, conviction, decision, determination, doctrine, estimate, idea, impression, judgment, notion, persuasion, sentiment, view. An *opinion* is a general conclusion held as probable, but without full certainty; a *conviction* is sustained by such evidence as removes all doubt from the believer's mind; a *persuasion* is a confident *opinion,* involving the heart as well as the intellect. In religion,

a *doctrine* is a statement of *belief* regarding a single point; a *creed* is a summary statement of *doctrines*. Such a system of *doctrines* is often called a faith; as, the Anglican or Lutheran faith. Compare BELIEF, FAITH, IDEA, THOUGHT[1].

o·pin·ion·at·ed (ə·pin′yən·ā′tid) *adj.* Unwarrantably attached to one's own opinion; obstinate. See synonyms under DOGMATIC, OBSTINATE. —**o·pin′ion·at′ed·ness** *n.*

o·pin·ion·a·tive (ə·pin′yən·ā′tiv) *adj.* **1** Opinionated. **2** Of the nature of opinion. **3** Relating to an opinion; doctrinal. —**o·pin′ion·a′·tive·ly** *adv.* —**o·pin′ion·a′tive·ness** *n.*

op·is·thog·na·thous (op′is·thog′nə·thəs) *adj.* Having receding jaws: opposed to *prognathous.* [<Gk. *opisthen* behind + *gnathos* jaw] —**op′is·thog′na·thism** (-nə·thiz′əm) *n.*

o·pis·tho·graph (ə·pis′thə·graf, -gräf) *n.* An ancient manuscript having writing on the back as well as on the front; also, a slab inscribed on both sides; especially, a mural slab whose back has been used for a later inscription, the front being turned to the wall. [<Gk. *opisthographos* written on the back or cover < *opisthen* behind + *graphein* write] —**o·pis′·tho·graph′ic** *adj.*

op·is·thot·o·nos (op′is·thot′ə·nəs) *n. Pathol.* A rigid muscular spasm of the neck and back, arching the body backward, as in tetanus. [<Gk. < *opisthen* behind + *tonos* tension < *teinein* stretch]

o·pi·um (ō′pē·əm) *n.* A milky exudation from the unripe capsules of the **opium poppy** (*Papaver somniferum*), containing a mixture of about 20 alkaloids, the most important of which is morphine. It is a powerful narcotic, with a sticky, gumlike body, bitter taste, and heavy odor. [<L <Gk. *opion* opium, dim. of *opos* vegetable juice]

opium den A room or place, usually illegal, for opium-smoking.

o·pi·um·ism (ō′pē·əm·iz′əm) *n. Pathol.* **1** Addiction to the use of opium. **2** A morbid condition due to such addiction.

op·o·del·doc (op′ə·del′dok) *n.* A camphorated soap liniment. [? <Gk. *opos* vegetable juice]

O·po·le (ô·pô′le) A port on the Oder in southern Poland; until 1945, in Upper Silesia, Germany. *German* **Op·peln** (ôp′əln).

O·por·to (ō·pôr′tō) A port of NW Portugal on the Douro, 3 miles from its mouth: Portuguese *Pôrto.*

o·pos·sum (ə·pos′əm, pos′əm) *n.* An American marsupial (genus *Didelphis*) of largely arboreal and nocturnal habits, having a prehensile tail and feet adapted for grasping: popularly called *possum.* The **common** (or **Virginia**) **opossum** (*D. virginiana*), which ranges from the central United States to Brazil, has a soft, whitish-gray pelage, with black ears and feet, and is esteemed as food. It is noted for its trick of feigning death, or *playing possum,* when threatened with danger. [<Algonquian (Virginian) *apasum,* lit., a white beast]

opossum shrimp A crustacean (family *Mysidae*) which carries its eggs in a pouch beneath the thorax.

Op·pen·heim (op′ən·hīm), **E(dward) Phillips,** 1866–1946, English novelist.

Op·pen·heim·er (op′ən·hī′mər), **J. Robert,** 1904–1967, U. S. physicist.

Op·per (op′ər), **Frederick Burr,** 1857–1937, U.S. cartoonist.

op·pi·dan (op′ə·dən) *adj.* Relating to a town; civic. —*n.* At Eton College in England, a student who boards in town: distinguished from *colleger.* [<L *oppidanus* a townsman, orig. adj. < *oppidum* a town]

op·pi·late (op′ə·lāt) *v.t.* **·lat·ed, ·lat·ing** *Med.* To block or obstruct; constipate. [<L *oppilatus,* pp. of *oppilare* stop up < *ob-* against + *pilare* ram down < *pilus* a pestle] —**op′pi·lant** *adj.* —**op′pi·la′tion** *n.*

op·po·nent (ə·pō′nənt) *n.* One who opposes another, as in battle or debate; antagonist. See synonyms under ENEMY. —*adj.* **1** Acting against something or someone; opposing. **2** *Anat.* Bringing one part, as of a muscle, into opposition to another. **3** Standing in front; opposite. [<L *opponens, -entis,* ppr. of *opponere* set against < *ob-* against + *ponere* place] —**op·po′nen·cy** *n.*

op·por·tune (op′ər·tōōn′, -tyōōn′) *adj.* Meeting some requirement; especially seasonable or timely. See synonyms under AUSPICIOUS, CONVENIENT. [<MF, fem. of *opportun* seasonable, exposed <L *opportunus* suitable, lit., at the port < *ob-* before + *portus* a harbor] —**op′·por·tune′ly** *adv.* —**op′por·tune′ness** *n.*

op·por·tu·nist (op′ər·tōō′nist, -tyōō′-) *n.* One who governs his course by opportunities or circumstances rather than by fixed principles or by regard for consistency or consequences. —**op′por·tu·nis′tic** (-tōō·nis′tik, -tyōō-) *adj.* —**op′por·tu′nism** *n.*

op·por·tu·ni·ty (op′ər·tōō′nə·tē, -tyōō′-) *n. pl.* **·ties** **1** A fit or convenient time; favorable occasion. **2** *Obs.* Opportuneness. **3** *Obs.* Importunity: an erroneous use.

Synonyms: convenience, occasion, opening, season. *Occasion* in the popular sense is a conjunction of circumstances which seems to require or inclines to or is fit for certain action; an *opportunity* is a conjunction of circumstances which makes certain action possible, with probability of success, advantage or gratification; as, I had *occasion* to interfere; I found an *opportunity* for a good investment.

op·pos·a·ble (ə·pō′zə·bəl) *adj.* **1** Capable of being placed opposite: said especially of the thumb. **2** That can be opposed. —**op·pos′a·bil′i·ty** *n.*

op·pose (ə·pōz′) *v.* **·posed, ·pos·ing** *v.t.* **1** To act or be in opposition to; resist; combat; fight. **2** To set in opposition or contrast: to *oppose* love to hatred. **3** To place before or in front. —*v.i.* **4** To act or be in opposition. [<OF *opposer, oposer* <L *ob-* against + OF *poser.* See POSE[1].] —**op·pos′er** *n.*

Synonyms: check, combat, confront, contradict, contravene, defy, face, object, obstruct, oppugn, resist, withstand. See CONTEND, CONTRAST, DISPUTE, HINDER[1], OBSTRUCT, REPEL. *Antonyms*: see synonyms for AID.

op·posed (ə·pōzd′) *adj.* **1** Set or placed in front or before; opposite. **2** Being in opposition, as in principle, meaning, purpose, etc. See synonyms under ALIEN, CONTRARY, INIMICAL, RELUCTANT.

op·pose·less (ə·pōz′lis) *adj.* Not to be opposed with effect; irresistible.

op·po·site (op′ə·zit) *adj.* **1** Situated or placed on the other side, or on each side, of an intervening space or thing; contrary in position: *opposite* ends of the room. **2** Facing or moving the other way; contrary: *opposite* directions. **3** Contrary in tendency or character; diametrically different: *opposite* opinions; the *opposite* sex. **4** *Bot.* **a** Arranged (as similar parts or organs) in pairs, so that the whole diameter of some intervening body separates them, as leaves on a stem. **b** Having one part or organ immediately before, or vertically over, another, as a stamen before a petal. See synonyms under CONTRARY. —*n.* **1** Something or someone that is opposite, opposed, or contrary. **2** An antonym. **3** *Obs.* An antagonist. —*adv.* In an opposite or complementary direction or position. —*prep.* **1** Across from; facing. **2** Complementary to, as in theatrical roles: He played *opposite* her. [<OF <L *oppositus,* pp. of *opponere.* See OPPONENT.] —**op′po·site·ly** *adv.* —**op′po·site·ness** *n.*

op·po·si·tion (op′ə·zish′ən) *n.* **1** The act of opposing or resisting; antagonism. **2** The state of being opposite or opposed; antithesis; also, a position confronting another or a placing in contrast. **3** That which is or furnishes an obstacle to some result: The stream flows without *opposition.* **4** *Often cap.* The political party opposed to the ministry or administration in power. **5** *Astron.* **a** The relative position of two heavenly bodies 180° apart in geometric longitude. **b** The position of a body opposite to the sun designated by the symbol ☍; as, ☍ ♂ ☉, *opposition* of Mars to the sun. **6** *Ling.* A state of contrast between any one phoneme and all the other phonemes in a language, as, /p/ is said to be in *bilateral opposition* to /b/ on the basis of the distinctive feature of voice, and in *multilateral opposition to* /d/ on the basis of the distinctive features of voice and place of articulation. **7** *Logic* The relation between two propositions which have the same subject and predicate but differ in quantity or quality or in both. See synonyms under AMBITION, ANTIPATHY, COLLISION, COMPETITION, EMULATION. —**in opposition** In the position of being opposed or hostile to a political party or measure: The Democratic party is *in opposition.* [<OF <L *oppositio, -onis* < *oppositus.* See OPPOSITE.] —**op′po·si′tion·al** *adj.* —**op′po·si′tion·ist** *n.* —**op′po·si′tion·less** *adj.*

op·pos·i·tive (ə·poz′ə·tiv) *adj.* Placed or capable of being placed in contrast. —**op·pos′i·tive·ly** *adv.* —**op·pos′i·tive·ness** *n.*

op·press (ə·pres′) *v.t.* **1** To burden or keep in subjugation by harsh and unjust use of force or authority; tyrannize. **2** To lie heavy upon physically or mentally; weigh down; depress; dispirit. **3** *Obs.* To crush or trample; overwhelm. See synonyms under ABUSE, LOAD, PERSECUTE. [<OF *oppresser, apresser* <Med. L *oppressare,* freq. of L *opprimere* crush < *ob-* against + *premere* press] —**op·pres′sor** *n.*

op·pres·sion (ə·presh′ən) *n.* **1** The act of oppressing. **2** Subjection to unjust hardships; tyranny. **3** Mental depression; languor; dulness of spirits. **4** A sense of weight or of constriction. **5** That which oppresses or is hard to bear; privation; hardship; cruelty.

op·pres·sive (ə·pres′iv) *adj.* **1** Characterized by, tending to, or disposed to practice oppression; burdensome; tyrannical. **2** Producing a sense of depression, physical or mental. See synonyms under HARD, HEAVY. —**op·pres′·sive·ly** *adv.* —**op·pres′sive·ness** *n.*

op·pro·bri·ous (ə·prō′brē·əs) *adj.* **1** Consisting of contemptuous abuse; imputing disgrace. **2** Shameful; disgraceful; odious; held in dishonor. [<OF *opprobrieus* <LL *opprobriosus* <L *opprobrium* OPPROBRIUM] —**op·pro′bri·ous·ly** *adv.* —**op·pro′bri·ous·ness** *n.*

op·pro·bri·um (ə·prō′brē·əm) *n.* **1** The state of being scornfully reproached; ignominy. **2** Reproach mingled with disdain. **3** A cause of disgrace or reproach. [<L, a disgrace < *opprobrare* reproach < *ob-* against + *probum* an infamy]

op·pugn (ə·pyōōn′) *v.t.* To assail or oppose with argument; call in question; controvert. See synonyms under OPPOSE. [<L *oppugnare* < *ob-* against + *pugnare* fight < *pugna* a fight] —**op·pugn′er** *n.*

op·pug·nant (ə·pug′nənt) *adj.* **1** Opposing in a hostile manner. **2** Combative. —**op·pug′·nan·cy, op·pug′nance** *n.*

Ops (ops) In Roman mythology, the wife of Saturn, goddess of the harvest: identified with the Greek *Rhea.*

-opsia *combining form Med.* A (specified) type or condition of sight: *macropsia.* Also spelled *-opsy.* [<NL <Gk. *opsis* sight]

-opsis *combining form Biol.* A thing having a (specified) appearance: often used in describing fruits: *caryopsis, coreopsis* [<Gk. *opsis* sight, appearance]

op·so·ma·ni·a (op′sə·mā′nē·ə, -mān′yə) *n.* A morbid craving for rich foods and delicate fare. [<NL <Gk. < *opson* cooked meat, dainties + *mania* madness]

op·son·ic (op·son′ik) *adj.* Of or pertaining to opsonin.

opsonic index *Bacteriol.* The ratio of the quantity of bacteria destroyed by phagocytes in the blood serum of any individual to that destroyed in a normal serum.

op·son·i·fy (op·son′ə·fī) *v.t.* **·fied, ·fy·ing** To render (bacteria) susceptible to phagocytosis by the action of opsonins. [<OPSON(IN) + -(I)FY] —**op·son′i·fi·ca′tion** *n.*

op·so·nin (op′sə·nin) *n. Bacteriol.* A component of blood serum which acts upon invading cells or bacteria, so as to assist in their absorption by the phagocytes. [<Gk. *opson* cooked meat + -IN]

op·son·ize (op′sən·īz) *v.t.* **·ized, ·iz·ing** To opsonify.

-opsy Var. of -OPSIS.

opt (opt) *v.i.* To choose; decide. [<F *opter* <L *optare* choose, wish]

op·ta·tive (op′tə·tiv) *adj.* **1** Expressing or indicative of desire or choice. **2** *Gram.* Denoting that mood in Greek and certain other languages which expresses wish or desire. —*n. Gram.* **1** The optative mood. **2** A word or construction in this mood. [<MF, fem. of *optatif* <LL *optativus* <L *optare* wish] —**op′·ta·tive·ly** *adv.*

op·tic (op′tik) *adj.* **1** Pertaining to the eye or to vision. **2** Optical. —*n. Colloq.* An eye. [<MF *optique* <Med. L *opticus* <Gk. *optikos* < *optos* seen < *ops-,* fut. stem of *horaein* see, behold]

op·ti·cal (op′ti·kəl) *adj.* **1** Pertaining to optics. **2** Of or pertaining to eyesight. **3** Designed to assist or improve vision. —**op′ti·cal·ly** *adv.*

optical activity The capacity to rotate the plane of polarization of light.

optical art Op art (which see).

optical fibers Fibers of clear plastic, often in bundles, that transmit light and sharp images along any desired path.

optical glass See under GLASS.

optical maser *Physics* A type of maser that can enormously amplify light. Also called *laser*.

optic angle The angle formed at either eye by two lines drawn from the extremities of an object of vision, varying with the distances of the object beheld.

optic axis 1 One of the directions along which a ray of light undergoes no double refraction within a crystal. 2 The axis of the eye corresponding with the line of vision passing through the center of the lens and cornea.

optic disk *Anat.* The expanded portion of the optic nerve as it enters the retina.

op·ti·cian (op·tish′ən) *n.* One who makes or deals in optical goods. [<F *opticien* <Med. L *optica* OPTICS]

optic nerve *Anat.* The special nerve of vision, connecting the retina with the cerebral centers. See illustration under EYE.

op·tics (op′tiks) *n.* The science that treats of the phenomena of light, vision, and sight. [<OPTIC; trans. of Med. L *optica* <Gk. *ta optika* optical matters]

optic thalamus *Anat.* A large, ovoid mass of gray matter at the side of the third ventricle at the base of the brain, connected with the origin of the optic nerve.

op·ti·mal (op′tə·məl) *adj.* Of, pertaining to, indicating, or characterized by an optimum.

op·ti·me (op′tə·mē) *n.* In Cambridge University, England, one who has attained the second, **Senior optime**, or third, **Junior optime**, grade in mathematical honors. See WRANGLER (def. 2). [<L *optimus* best]

op·ti·mism (op′tə·miz′əm) *n.* 1 The doctrine that everything is ordered for the best; also, the doctrine that the universe is constantly tending toward a better state. 2 Disposition to look on the bright side of things: opposed to *pessimism*. [<F *optimisme* <L *optimus* best] — **op′ti·mist** *n.* — **op′ti·mis′tic** or **·ti·cal** *adj.* — **op′ti·mis′ti·cal·ly** *adv.*

op·ti·mize (op′tə·mīz) *v.* **·mized**, **·miz·ing** *v.t.* 1 *Technol.* To plan or prepare plans for (industrial production) in order to secure maximum efficiency. 2 To make the most of. — *v.i.* 3 To be optimistic. 4 To work toward obtaining an optimum.

op·ti·mum (op′tə·məm) *n.* *pl.* **·ma** (-mə) **·mums** 1 The condition or degree producing the best result. 2 The combination of conditions, as of food, etc., that produces the best average result in the growth and development of organisms. 3 The most favorable degree, conditions, etc. — *adj.* Producing or conducive to the best results. [<L, neut. of *optimus* best]

op·tion (op′shən) *n.* 1 The right, power, or liberty of choosing; discretion; the exercise of such right, power, or liberty. 2 The purchased privilege of either buying or selling something at a specified price within a specified time. 3 A thing that is or can be chosen. See synonyms under ALTERNATIVE. [<MF <L *optio, -onis* <*optare* choose]

op·tion·al (op′shən·əl) *adj.* Depending on choice; elective. — *n.* A study or course to be chosen from two or more offered; an elective. — **op′tion·al·ly** *adv.*

op·tom·e·ter (op·tom′ə·tər) *n.* An optical instrument for measuring the range of vision of the eye, and its peculiarities as a refracting medium. [<OPT(IC) + -(O)METER]

op·tom·e·trist (op·tom′ə·trist) *n.* One who is skilled in optometry.

op·tom·e·try (op·tom′ə·trē) *n.* The profession or occupation of measuring vision and prescribing corrective lenses to compensate for visual defects.

op·u·lence (op′yə·ləns) *n.* 1 Wealth; affluence. 2 Luxuriance. Also **op′u·len·cy.** See synonyms under COMFORT.

op·u·lent (op′yə·lənt) *adj.* 1 Possessing great wealth. 2 Exuberant; profuse. [<L *opulentus* <*opulens, -entis* <*ops, opis* power, wealth] — **op′u·lent·ly** *adv.*

o·pun·ti·a (ō·pun′shē·ə) *n.* One of a large genus (*Opuntia*) of mainly tropical American cacti, the prickly pears, having a usually flattened, much-branched stem and tubular yellow, red, or purple flowers. [<NL *L Opuntia* (*herba*) (a plant) native to Opus <*Opus, Opuntis*, a city in ancient Locris <Gk. *Opous*]

o·pus (ō′pəs) *n.* *pl.* **op·er·a** (op′ər·ə, op′rə) A literary or musical work or composition. [<L, a work]

o·pus·cule (ō·pus′kyool) *n.* A small or unimportant work. [<OF <L *opusculum*, dim. of *opus* a work]

-opy See -OPIA.

o·quas·sa (ō·kwas′ə) *n.* A small lake trout (*Salvelinus oquassa*) of Maine, with a bluish-black body. [from *Oquassa* Lake in Maine; ult. <Algonquian]

OPUNTIA
The fruit of some species is edible.

or¹ (ôr, *unstressed* ər) *conj.* 1 Introducing an alternative: stop *or* go; red *or* white. 2 Offering a choice of a series: Will you take milk *or* coffee *or* chocolate? 3 Introducing an equivalent: the culinary art *or* art of cookery. 4 Indicating uncertainty: He lives in Chicago *or* thereabouts. 5 Introducing the second alternative of a choice limited to two: with *either* or *whether*: It must be either black *or* white; I don't care whether he goes *or* not. 6 *Poetic* Either; whether: *or* in the heart *or* in the head. [ME, contraction of *other, auther* either, OE *āther*; infl. in meaning by OE *oththe* or]

or² (ôr) *adv., prep.,* & *conj. Obs.* or *Scot.* Before; ere: chiefly in the phrase, **or ever,** before ever; ere. [OE *ār*, var. of *ǣr* earlier, before]

or³ (ôr) *n. Her.* Gold: represented in engraving by a white surface powdered with dots. [<MF *L aurum* gold]

-or¹ *suffix* The person or thing performing the action expressed in the root verb: *competitor.* See note under -ER¹. [<AF -*our*, OF -*or* <L -*or*, -*ator*]

-or² *suffix* The quality, state, or condition of: *favor.* [<OF <L]

or·ach (ôr′əch, -′-) *n.* Any of various plants (genus *Atriplex*), especially the **garden orach** or mountain spinach (*A. hortensis*), a tall, hardy annual, formerly common in England as a pot herb. Also **or′ache.** [<AF *arasche,* OF *arroche* <L *atriplex, -plicis* <Gk. *atraphaxys, -yos*]

or·a·cle (ôr′ə·kəl, or′-) *n.* 1 The seat of the worship of some ancient divinity, as of Apollo at Delphi, where prophecies were given out by the priests in answer to inquiries. 2 A prophecy thus given. 3 The deity whose prophecies were given. 4 A person of unquestioned wisdom or knowledge, or something regarded as of infallible authority. [<OF <L *oraculum* <*orare* speak, pray <*os, oris* mouth]

o·rac·u·lar (ô·rak′yə·lər, ō-) *adj.* 1 Pertaining to an oracle. 2 Obscure; enigmatical. 3 Prophetic. — **o·rac′u·lar′i·ty** *n.* — **o·rac′u·lar·ly** *adv.* — **o·rac′u·lar·ness** *n.*

O·ra·dea (ō·rä′dyä) A city in NW Rumania: German *Grosswardein,* Hungarian *Nagyvárad.* Also **Oradea Ma·re** (mä′rě)

o·ral (ô′rəl, ō′rəl) *adj.* 1 Uttered through the mouth; consisting of spoken words. 2 Pertaining to or situated at or near the mouth. 3 *Psychoanal.* a Of or relating to the earliest stage of psychosexual development of the child in which interest in and gratification from feeding, sucking, and biting are dominant. b Of, pertaining to, or characterized by qualities in the adult, as aggressiveness or gregariousness, regarded as typifying this stage of development. Compare ANAL, GENITAL. 4 *Zool.* Designating the side of the body on which the mouth is placed. 5 Of, pertaining to, or using speech. 6 Taken or administered by mouth. 7 *Phonet.* Pronounced through the mouth with the nasal passage closed; nonnasal: opposed to *nasal.* See synonyms under VERBAL. — *n.* An oral examination, as in a college. [<L *os, oris* mouth] — **o′ral·ly** *adv.*

O·ran (ō·ran′, *Fr.* ô·rän′) A port on Oran Bay, a semicircular inlet of the Mediterranean in NW Algeria.

o·rang (ō·rang′) *n.* An orang-utan.

or·ange (ôr′inj, or′-) *n.* 1 A large, round, juicy fruit (technically a berry) of a low, much-branched, evergreen tree (genus *Citrus*), with a reddish-yellow rind enclosing membranous divisions and a refreshing, sweetish or subacid pulp. 2 Any of the trees yielding this fruit, as the Spanish sour orange (*C. aurantium*), the sweet orange (*C. sinensis*). 3 Any of many related species, such as the trifoliate orange (*Poncirus trifoliata*). 4 The kumquat. 5 The osage orange. 6 A reddish-yellow color; also, a pigment of this color. — **mandarin orange** A mandarin (def. 2). — *adj.* 1 Reddish-yellow. 2 Pertaining to an orange. [<OF <Provençal *auranja* (infl. by *aur* gold), earlier (*n*)*aranja* <Sp. *naranja* <Arabic *nāranj* <Persian *nārang*]

Or·ange (ôr′inj, or′-; *Fr.* ô·ränzh′) 1 A former principality of western Europe, now a part of SE France, although the title has remained with the Dutch princes of Orange. 2 Its former capital, a city of Vaucluse department, SE France.

or·ange·ade (ôr′inj·ād′) *n.* A beverage made of orange juice, sugar, and water. [<F]

orange blossom The white blossom of the orange tree: much worn by brides: State flower of Florida.

Orange Free State A province of the east central Republic of South Africa; 49,866 square miles; capital, Bloemfontein; a Boer republic until 1900; known as **Orange River Colony** from 1900 to 1910. *Afrikaans* **O·ran·je Vry·staat** (ō·rän′yə frä′stät).

Or·ange·ism (ôr′inj·iz′əm, or′-) *n.* The principles of the Orangemen; Irish Protestantism. Also **Or′ang·ism.** — **Or′ange·ist, Or′ang·ist** *n.*

Or·ange·man (ôr′inj·mən, or′-) *n.* *pl.* **·men** (-mən) A member of a secret society founded in northern Ireland in 1795 for the purpose of upholding Protestant ascendancy and succession in England: named in honor of William, Prince of Orange.

orange pekoe A finely sifted grade of black tea of India, Ceylon, and Java.

Orange Range A mountain system in central Netherlands New Guinea, the eastern section of the Snow Mountains; highest point, 15,585 feet.

Orange River A river in Lesotho, Republic of South Africa, and South-West Africa, flowing 1,300 miles SW, NW, and west from NE Lesotho to the Atlantic and forming the southern boundaries of Orange Free State and South-West Africa.

or·ange·ry (ôr′inj·rē, or′-) *n.* *pl.* **·ries** A place for cultivating orange trees; an orange grove or greenhouse.

or·ange·wood (ôr′inj·wood′, or′-) *n.* The finegrained, yellowish wood of the orange tree: used in lathe work and in dentistry.

o·rang·u·tan (ō·rang′ə·tan, -ō·tan) *n.* *pl.* **·tans** or **·tan** A large, anthropoid ape (genus *Pongo* or *Simia*) of Borneo and Sumatra, about 4 1/2 feet in height, having brownish-red hair, brown skin, small ears, doglike teeth, narrow lips, and long arms reaching to the ankles: also called *orang.* Also **o·rang′-ou·tang** (-ə-tang, -ōō-tang). [<Malay *oraṅ utan* <*oraṅ* a man + *utan* a forest]

o·rate (ô·rāt′, ō-rāt′, ō′rāt, ō·rāt′) *v.i.* **o·rat·ed, o·rat·ing** To deliver an oration; speechify: chiefly humorous. [<L *oratus,* pp. of *orare.* See ORATION.]

o·ra·tion (ô·rā′shən, ō·rā′-) *n.* 1 An elaborate public speech. 2 A graduation speech. See synonyms under SPEECH. [<L *oratio, -onis* <*oratus,* pp. of *orare* pray, speak <*os, oris* mouth. Doublet of ORISON.]

or·a·tor (ôr′ə·tər, or′-) *n.* 1 One who delivers an oration; an eloquent public speaker. 2 A high school or college student chosen to make a speech. 3 *Law* The complainant in a chancery proceeding; a petitioner in chancery. [<AF *oratour* <L *orator* <*orare.* See ORATION.] — **or′a·tor·ship′** *n.*

or·a·tor·i·cal (ôr′ə·tôr′ə·kəl, -tō′rə-, or′-) *adj.* Of, like, or characteristic of oratory or an orator. — **or′a·tor′i·cal·ly** *adv.*

or·a·to·ri·o (ôr′ə·tôr′ē·ō, -tō′rē·ō, or′-) *n.* *pl.* **·os** A musical composition, usually on a

sacred theme, for solo voices, chorus, and orchestra, dramatic in that it tells a connected story, though without scenery or acting. [<Ital., lit., a small chapel <L *oratorium.* See ORATORY[2].]

or·a·to·ry[1] (ôr′ə·tôr′ē, -tō′rē, or′-) *n. pl.* **·ries** **1** The art of public speaking; eloquence. **2** Eloquent language. See synonyms under SPEECH. [<L *oratoria (ars)* the oratorical (art), orig. fem. of *oratorius* < *orator* ORATOR]

or·a·to·ry[2] (ôr′ə·tôr′ē, -tō′rē, or′-) *n. pl.* **·ries** **1** A place for prayer; a private chapel. **2** One of various congregations of priests in the Roman Catholic Church, who live together without vows, primarily for the purpose of teaching. [<LL *oratorium (templum)* (a temple) for prayer, orig. neut. of *oratorius* of prayer < *orator* one who prays < *oratus.* See ORATION.]

O·ra·zio (ō·rät′syō) Italian form of HORATIO.

orb (ôrb) *n.* **1** A rounded mass; a sphere or globe. **2** A circle or orbit; anything circular. **3** A sphere topped by a cross: symbolic of royal power. **4** *Obs.* The plane of the orbit or the orbit of a planet. — *v.t.* **1** To shape into a sphere or circle. **2** *Poetic* To enclose; encircle. [<L *orbis* a circle]

or·bic·u·lar (ôr·bik′yə·lər) *adj.* **1** Having the form of an orb or orbit. **2** Well-rounded. **3** *Bot.* Circular, as a leaf or petal. [<L *orbicularis* < *orbiculus,* dim. of *orbis* a circle] — **or·bic′u·lar′i·ty** (-lar′ə·tē) *n.*

or·bic·u·late (ôr·bik′yə·lit, -lāt) *adj.* Made into or taking the form of an orb or orbit; orbicular. Also **or·bic′u·lat′ed.** — **or·bic′u·late·ly** *adv.*

Synonyms: circular, globular, spherical, spheroidal.

or·bit (ôr′bit) *n.* **1** *Astron.* The path in space along which a celestial body moves about its center of attraction. **2** *Anat.* One of the two cavities of the skull containing the eyes. **3** *Ornithol.* The eyelid and skin surrounding the eye of a bird. **4** *Physics* The assumed path of an electron around the atomic nucleus. **5** A range of influence or action: the *orbit* of imperialism. — *v.t.* To cause to move in an orbit, as an artificial satellite. — *v.i.* To move in an orbit. [<L *orbita* track of a wheel, an orbit < *orbis* a wheel, a circle] — **or′bi·tal** *adj.*

orbital cavity *Anat.* The bony socket enclosing and protecting the eyeball in the skull of vertebrates.

orbital decay The progressive spiraling change from elliptical to circular in the orbit of an artificial satellite whose velocity is gradually diminished by the residual air resistance encountered at perigee.

orbital index The maximum height of the orbital cavity multiplied by 100 and divided by the orbital width.

orc (ôrk) *n.* A grampus or some other cetacean: also spelled *ork.* [ME *orgue* <L *orca,* a kind of whale]

Or·ca·gna (ôr·kä′nyä), **Andrea,** 1308?–68, Florentine painter: original name *Andrea di Cione.*

or·ce·in (ôr′sē·in) *n. Chem.* A reddish-brown coloring matter, $C_{28}H_{24}N_2O_7$, obtained from orcinol by the action of aqueous ammonia and air. It is the tinctorial principle of archil. [<ORC(INOL) + -EIN]

or·chard (ôr′chərd) *n.* A plantation of trees grown for their products, as fruit, nuts, oils, etc.; also, the enclosure or ground containing them. [OE *orceard* < *ort-geard* a garden < *ort* (? <Med. L *ortus* a garden <L *hortus*) + *geard* a yard, enclosure]

or·chard·ist (ôr′chərd·ist) *n.* One who cultivates trees in orchards for their products. Also **or′chard·man** (-mən).

orchard oriole A common oriole *(Icterus spurius)* of eastern North America, smaller and having less brilliant plumage than the Baltimore oriole.

or·ches·tra (ôr′kis·trə) *n.* **1** A band of musicians playing together, especially a symphony orchestra; also, the instruments on which they play. **2** In theaters, the place immediately before the stage, occupied by the musicians; by extension, the main floor. **3** In the ancient Greek and Roman theaters, the approximately semicircular space from which the tiers of seats rose, in the Greek theater reserved for the chorus, and in the Roman theater reserved for the seats of the senators and other distinguished men. [<L <Gk. *orchēstra,* lit., a dancing space < *orcheesthai* dance] — **or·ches·tral** (ôr·kes′trəl) *adj.* — **or·ches′tral·ly** *adv.*

or·ches·trate (ôr′kis·trāt) *v.t.* & *v.i.* **·trat·ed, ·trat·ing** **1** To compose or arrange (music) for an orchestra. **2** To arrange or bring about, as by manipulation or careful planning: to *orchestrate* economic growth. **3** To bring into harmony: to *orchestrate* wilderness areas with urban centers.

or·ches·trat·ed (ôr′kis·trā′tid) *adj.* Planned to achieve a desired effect, often with the conspiratorial or cooperative contributions of various parties: a carefully *orchestrated* attack on the press.

or·ches·tra·tion (ôr′kis·trā′shən) *n.* **1** The arrangement of music for performance by an orchestra. **2** The act of orchestrating, or the state of being orchestrated; planned or harmonious arrangement.

or·chid (ôr′kid) *n.* **1** Any of a widely distributed family *(Orchidaceae)* of terrestrial or epiphytic monocotyledonous plants having thickened, bulbous roots and often very showy and distinctive flowers. **2** Any of various delicate, rosy-purple colors. [<NL <L *orchis,* an orchid <Gk., orig. a testicle; so called because of the shape of its tubers]

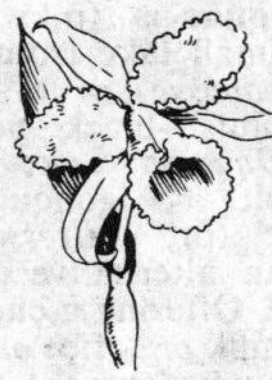

ORCHID FLOWER

or·chi·da·ceous (ôr′ki·dā′shəs) *adj.* Of, pertaining to, or belonging to the orchid family.

orchido- *combining form* **1** *Bot.* Orchid; pertaining to orchids: *orchidology.* **2** *Med.* Orchio-. Also, before vowels, **orchid-.** [<ORCHID]

or·chid·ol·o·gy (ôr′ki·dol′ə·jē) *n.* The study and cultivation of orchids. — **or′chid·ol′o·gist** *n.*

or·chil (ôr′kil) *n.* **1** A purple or blue dye obtained from archil. **2** Archil. [<OF *orcheil, orchel* ARCHIL]

orchio- *combining form* Testicle; pertaining to the testicles. Also before vowels, **orchi-.** [<Gk. *orchis* a testicle]

or·chis (ôr′kis) *n.* Any plant of the genus *Orchis* having dense spikes of small flowers, frequently of striking shape and structure. [<NL <L, ORCHID]

or·chi·tis (ôr·kī′tis) *n. Pathol.* Inflammation of the testicle. Also **or·chei′tis, or·chi·di·tis** (ôr′ki·dī′tis). — **or·chit′ic** (-kit′ik) *adj.*

or·ci·nol (ôr′sə·nōl, -nol) *n. Chem.* A colorless crystalline compound, $C_7H_8O_2$, derived from certain lichens, as archil, and aloes. Also **or′cin.** [<Ital. *orc(ello)* archil + -IN + -OL[1]]

Or·cus (ôr′kəs) In Roman mythology: **1** The abode of the dead. **2** Pluto or Dis, the god of the underworld and lord of the dead.

Or·czy (ôr′tsē), **Baroness,** 1865–1947, English novelist born in Hungary. Also **Emmuska Orczy.**

or·dain (ôr·dān′) *v.t.* **1** To order or decree; enact; establish. **2** To predestine; destine: said of God, fate, etc. **3** To invest with ministerial or priestly functions. See synonyms under INSTALL, INSTITUTE. [<OF *ordener* <L *ordinare* order < *ordo, -inis* an order] — **or·dain′er** *n.*

or·deal (ôr·dēl′, -dē′əl, ôr′dēl) *n.* **1** A severe test of character or endurance; a trying course of experience. **2** A medieval form of judicial trial in which the accused was subjected to physical tests, as carrying or walking over burning objects or immersing the hand in scalding water, the result being considered a divine judgment of guilt or innocence. See synonyms under PROOF. [OE *ordāl, ordēl* a judgment < *or-* out + *dǣl* a deal; infl. in meaning by L *ordela* an ordeal <Gmc.]

ordeal bean Calabar bean.

or·der (ôr′dər) *n.* **1** Methodical and harmonious arrangement, as of successive things or as of military units in a formation. **2** Proper or working condition; available state. **3** A command or authoritative regulation. **4** *Law* Any direction of a court made to be entered of record in a cause, and not included in the final judgment. **5** A written commission or instruction to supply, purchase, or sell something. **6** Established use or customary procedure. **7** Established or existing state of things. **8** A class or body of persons united by some common bond, as for mutual insurance, protection, aid, social culture, etc.: the *Order* of Odd Fellows; a monastic or religious body: an *order* of mendicant friars. **9** A group of persons upon whom a government or sovereign has conferred an honor or dignity, and who are thus entitled to affix to their names designated initials and to wear specific insignia; also, the insignia worn as a sign of membership in such a group. **10** Social rank. **11** A class or kind of a common degree of excellence. **12** *Usually pl. Eccl.* **a** Any of the various grades or degrees of the Christian ministry: also **holy orders, sacred orders.** In the Anglican Church, there are three orders: bishops, priests, and deacons. The Greek Church recognizes in addition subdeacons and readers. In the Roman Catholic Church, there are seven orders: priests (including bishops), deacons, subdeacons (the **major orders**), acolytes, exorcists, readers, and doorkeepers (the **minor orders**). **b** The rank or position of an ordained clergyman. **c** The rite or sacrament of ordination. **d** A liturgical form for a service or the performance of a rite: the *order* of confirmation. **13** *Archit.* **a** The general character of a column and its parts as distinguishing a style of architecture; a style of architecture. Usually there are considered to be five orders of classical architecture — Doric, Ionic, Corinthian, Tuscan, and Composite. **b** A column with its entablature. **14** *Biol.* A taxonomic category ranking next below the class, and above the family. **15** *Math.* A number expressing the degree of complexity of an algebraic expression. **16** *Gram.* The sequence of words in a sentence or construction. **17** The position of the rifle as a result of the command *order arms.* **18** Any one of the ancient nine grades of angels. **19** *Obs.* Suitable care; preparation: usually in the phrase *to take order.* — **in order** **1** In accordance with rule; hence, apt; appropriate. **2** Neat; tidy. — **in order that** So that; to the end that. — **in order to** For the purpose of; to the end that. — **in short order** Quickly; without delay. — **on order** Ordered but not yet delivered. — **on the order of** Similar to. — **out of order** **1** Not in proper sequence or arrangement. **2** Not in good working condition. **3** Not in accord with established rule or procedure: a senator ruled *out of order.* **4** Uncalled-for; improper: The insinuation was *out of order.* — **to order** According to the buyer's specifications: a shirt made *to order.* — *v.t.* **1** To give a command or direction to. **2** To command to go, come, etc.: They *ordered* him out of the city. **3** To give an order that (something) be done; prescribe. **4** To give an order for: to *order* a new suit. **5** To put in orderly or systematic arrangement; regulate. **6** To ordain: He was *ordered* deacon. — *v.i.* **7** To give an order or orders. — **to order arms** *Mil.* To bring a rifle perpendicularly against the right side, with the butt on the ground. See synonyms under DICTATE, REGULATE. [<OF *ordre* <L *ordo, -inis* a row, series, an order] — **or′der·er** *n.* — **or′der·less** *adj.*

Synonyms (noun): command, direction, directive, injunction, instruction, prohibition, requirement. *Instruction* implies more superiority of knowledge, *direction* more of authority; a teacher gives *instructions* to his pupils, an employer gives *directions* to his workmen; but the *instructions* of a superior regarding action are viewed as specific *commands.* A *directive* conveys all three of these — *instructions* for action, *directions* for procedure, and *command* for performance. *Order* is more absolute still; soldiers and railroad employees have simply to obey the *orders* of their superiors. *Command* is a loftier word less frequent in common life: the *commands* of God. A *requirement* is imperative, but not always formal; it may be in the nature of things; as, the *requirements* of the position. *Prohibition* is a *command* not to do; *injunction* is now oftenest so used, especially as the *requirement* by legal authority that certain action be temporarily suspended or refrained from.

or·der·ing (ôr′dər·ing) *n.* **1** The act of directing, commanding, or disposing. **2** The act or process of arrangement, or the state of being arranged. **3** Right administration. **4** The act of ordination. **5** The act of arranging for procurement, purchase, or delivery of something.

or·der·ly (ôr′dər·lē) *adj.* **1** Having regard for arrangement; methodical; systematic. **2**

Peaceful. 3 Characterized by order. 4 Pertaining to orders. See synonyms under NEAT[1]. —*n. pl.* **·lies 1** A soldier or non-commissioned officer detailed to carry orders for superior officers. **2** A hospital attendant. —*adv.* According to the rules of order; methodically; regularly; properly. **—or'der·li·ness** *n.*

or·di·nal[1] (ôr'də·nəl) *adj.* **1** Denoting position in an order or succession. **2** Pertaining to an order, as of plants, animals, etc. —*n.* An ordinal number. See under NUMBER. [<LL *ordinalis* <L *ordo, -inis* an order]

or·di·nal[2] (ôr'də·nəl) *n. Eccl.* **1** A book of rites for clerical ordinations, episcopal consecrations, etc. **2** An ordo. [<Med. L *ordinale* <LL *ordinalis.* See ORDINAL[1].]

or·di·nance (ôr'də·nəns) *n.* **1** An authoritative rule; an order, decree, or law of a municipal body. **2** A religious rite or ceremony. **3** *Archit.* A system of arrangement. **4** A law or command of God, or a decree of fate. **5** *Obs.* Order, as arrangement, disposition, rank, position, array, provision, or preparation. **6** *Obs.* The act of devising, arranging, or contriving plans; a design or device. See synonyms under LAW[1], SACRAMENT. [<OF *ordenance* < Med. L *ordinantia* <L *ordinans, -antis,* ppr. of *ordinare* ORDAIN]

or·di·nand (ôr'də·nand) *n.* A candidate for ordination. [<L *ordinandus,* gerundive of *ordinare* ORDAIN]

or·di·nant (ôr'də·nənt) *adj.* Exercising authority; ruling.

or·di·nar·i·ly (ôr'də·ner'ə·lē, ôr'də·nâr'ə·lē) *adv.* **1** In ordinary cases; commonly; usually: *Ordinarily,* he walks to work. **2** In the usual manner. **3** To the usual extent; normally.

or·di·nar·y (ôr'də·ner'ē) *adj.* **1** Of common or everyday occurrence; customary; usual. **2** According to an established order; regular; normal. **3** Common in rank or degree; of average merit or consequence; commonplace. **4** Having immediate or ex-officio jurisdiction, as a judge. See synonyms under COMMON, GENERAL, HABITUAL, NORMAL, USUAL. —*n. pl.* **·nar·ies 1** That which is usual or common. **2** *Brit.* A meal provided regularly at a fixed price. **3** *Brit.* An eating house where such meals are served. **4** *Law* One who exercises jurisdiction in his own right, and not by delegation. **5** *U.S.* In some States, a judge exercising probate jurisdiction. **6** *Eccl.* **a** A rule or book prescribing the form for saying mass. **b** The practically unchangeable part of the mass: opposed to the *proper.* **7** An early type of bicycle with a large front wheel and a small rear wheel. **8** *Her.* A charge of the simplest kind, usually bounded between simple lines, as a chief, pale, fess, chevron, bend, cross, saltire, or quarter. **—in ordinary 1** In actual and constant service. **2** *Naut.* Out of commission; laid up:, said of a ship. [<L *ordinarius* regular, usual <*ordo, -inis* an order] **—or'di·nar'i·ness** *n.*

or·di·nate (ôr'də·nit) *adj.* **1** Characterized by order; regular. **2** *Biol.* Arranged in a regular row or rows, as spots on an insect's body or wings. —*n. Math.* **1** The distance of any point from the axis of abscissas, measured on a line parallel to the axis of ordinates in a coordinate system. **2** The line or number indicating such distance. [<L *ordinatus,* pp. of *ordinare* ORDAIN]

or·di·na·tion (ôr'də·nā'shən) *n.* **1** *Eccl.* The rite of consecration to the ministry. **2** The state of being ordained, regulated, or settled. **3** Arrangement of things in order; array. **4** Natural or proper order.

ord·nance (ôrd'nəns) *n. Mil.* **1** All kinds of weapons and their appliances used in war. **2** Cannon or artillery. [Contraction of ORDINANCE]

Ordnance Department A branch of the armed services responsible for the design, manufacture, procurement, maintenance, issue, and efficiency of ordnance.

or·do (ôr'dō) *n. pl.* **·di·nes** (-də·nēz) *Eccl.* **1** A book containing directions for the portions of the mass and the daily office which vary according to the calendar. **2** A book of rubrics for administering the sacraments and for other ceremonies. [<L, order]

or·don·nance (ôr'də·nəns, *Fr.* ôr·dô·näns) *n.* **1** A right arranging of parts, as in a picture, so as to produce the best effect. **2** A law or ordinance; specifically, in French law, a code of laws on any subject. [<F <OF *ordenance* ORDINANCE]

Or·do·vi·ces (ôr'də·vī'sēz, ôr·dov'ə·sēz) *n. pl.* An ancient Celtic tribe in Wales. [<L]

Or·do·vi·cian (ôr'də·vish'ən) *adj.* **1** *Geol.* Of, pertaining to, or designating a geological period of the Paleozoic era, following the Cambrian and preceding the Silurian. **2** Of or pertaining to the Ordovices. —*n.* An epoch of the Paleozoic era: sometimes called *Lower Silurian.* [<L *Ordovices* the Ordovices]

or·dure (ôr'jər, -dyoor) *n.* Excrement; feces. [<OF <*ord* foul, nasty <L *horridus* HORRID]

Or·dzho·ni·kid·ze (ôr'jon·i·kēd'zə) A former name for DZAUDZHIKAU.

ore (ôr, ōr) *n.* **1** A natural substance containing an economically valuable metal, and sometimes forming part of a rock. **2** Loosely, a natural substance containing a non-metallic mineral: sulfur *ore.* ◆Homophone: *oar.* [OE *ār, ǣr* brass, copper; infl. in meaning by OE *ōra* unwrought metal]

ö·re (œ'rə) *n. pl.* **ö·re** A Scandinavian bronze coin, equaling 1/100 krone in Norway and Denmark, and 1/100 krona in Sweden. [<Norw., Dan., and Sw.]

o·re·ad (ôr'ē·ad, ō'rē-) *n.* **1** In classical mythology, a mountain nymph. **2** A sun-loving plant; a heliophyte. [<L *oreas, -adis* <Gk. *oreias, -ados* <*oros* a mountain]

Ö·re·bro (œ'rə·brōō') A city in south central Sweden; the country's foremost paper-manufacturing center; site of many medieval buildings.

o·rec·tic (ō·rek'tik) *adj. Philos.* Of or pertaining to the appetites or desires; appetent; motive. Also **o·rec'tive.** [<Gk. *orektikos* appetitive <*orektos* stretched out, longed for <*oregein* stretch out, desire]

ore dressing *Metall.* The mechanical separation of valuable metals and minerals from the ores in which they occur.

o·reg·a·no (ō·reg'ə·nō) *n.* Origan. [<Sp. *orégano* <L *origanum* ORIGAN]

Or·e·gon (ôr'ə·gon, -gən, or'-, ôr'ē·gən) A State of the western United States on the Pacific; 96,981 square miles; capital, Salem; entered the Union Feb. 14, 1859; nickname, *Beaver State:* abbr. OR **—Or'e·go'ni·an** (gō'nē·ən) *adj. & n.*

Oregon Country A name used between 1818 and 1846 for the region of the NW United States including the present States of Washington, Oregon, Idaho, and parts of Montana and Wyoming.

Oregon fir The Douglas fir. Also **Oregon pine.**

Oregon grape A thornless evergreen shrub *(Mahonia aquifolium)* of the barberry family, with dark-blue berry clusters resembling grapes: the State flower of Oregon.

Oregon jargon Chinook.

Oregon Trail A former route extending from the Missouri River about 2,000 miles NW to the Columbia River in Oregon: used by pioneers, 1804–1846.

ore house A building in which mined ore is stored. Also **ore shed.**

o·re·ide (ō'rē·id) See OROIDE.

O·rel (ō·rel', *Russian* o·ryôl') A city on the Oka in west central European Russian S.F.S.R.

Ore Mountains The English name for the ERZGEBIRGE.

O·ren·burg (ō'rən·boorkh) A former name for CHKALOV.

O·ren·se (ō·ren'sā) **1** A province of Galicia, NW Spain; 2,694 square miles. **2** Its capital, a city of great antiquity, occupied by the Romans and noted since their time for its warm sulfur springs.

O·re·o·pith·e·cus (ôr'ē·ō·pith'ə·kəs, ō'rē-) *n.* A primate of the Miocene or Pliocene epochs, identified in 1872 from a group of fossilized bones discovered in brown coal deposits in Tuscany: of uncertain evolutionary rank but possibly ancestral to the hominid family. Also called *mountain ape.* [<NL <Gk. *oros, oreos* a mountain + *pithēkos* an ape]

ore shoot That portion of an ore deposit which is exceptionally rich in metal content.

O·res·tes (ô·res'tēz, o-) In Greek legend, the son of Agamemnon and Clytemnestra who, aided by his sister Electra, killed his mother and Aegisthus, her lover, to avenge his father's murder; he was then pursued by the Furies until Athena granted him absolution. In another version he expiated his guilt by carrying off an image of Artemis from Tauris to Greece with the aid of his sister Iphigenia. [<L <Gk. *Orestes* <*oros, oreos* a mountain]

Ö·re·sund (œ'rə·soon) The strait between Zealand (Denmark) and Sweden, connecting the Kattegat with the Baltic; 87 miles long; average width 17 miles, at its narrowest, 2½ miles: also *The Sound.*

o·rex·is (o·rek'sis) *n.* Appetite; craving. [<Gk., a desire <*oregein.* See ORECTIC.]

Or·fa·ni (ôr·fä'nē), **Gulf of** See STRYMONIC GULF.

Or·fi·la (ôr·fe·lå'), **Matthieu Joseph Bonaventure,** 1787–1853, French chemist; founder of toxicology.

or·fray (ôr'frā) See ORPHREY.

or·gan (ôr'gən) *n.* **1** A musical wind instrument consisting of a collection of pipes made to sound by means of compressed air from bellows and played upon by means of keys: also **pipe organ. 2** An electronic musical instrument not employing pipes or wind, designed to give the sounds and timbres of a pipe organ. **3** A musical instrument resembling or having some mechanism resembling the pipe organ: a reed *organ;* a barrel *organ.* **4** Any part of an organism, plant, or animal performing some definite function: the digestive *organs.* **5** An instrument or agency for communication of the views of a person or party; especially, a newspaper or periodical published in the interest of some political party or religious denomination. [Fusion of OE *organa* and OF *organe,* both <L *organum* an instrument, engine, organ <Gk. *organon* a tool, a musical instrument]

or·gan·dy (ôr'gən·dē) *n. pl.* **·dies** A very thin, crisp, transparent, cotton muslin, plain or figured, used for dresses, collars, cuffs, etc. Also **or'gan·die.** [<F *organdi;* ult. origin uncertain]

or·gan-grind·er (ôr'gən·grīn'dər) *n.* The player of a hand organ; specifically, a street musician playing a hand organ.

or·gan·ic (ôr·gan'ik) *adj.* **1** Of, pertaining to, or of the nature of animals and plants. **2** Affecting an organ or organs of an animal or plant: *organic* diseases. **3** Serving the purpose of an organ. **4** *Chem.* Of or pertaining to compounds containing carbon as an essential ingredient. **5** Inherent in or pertaining to the organization or fundamental structure; structural; constitutional. **6** Of or characterized by systematic coordination of parts; organized; systematized. **7** *Law* Designating that system of laws or principles forming the foundation of a government. **8** *Agric.* Pertaining to the use of compost, manure, peat moss, and other natural fertilizers in the cultivation of farms and gardens. Also **or·gan'i·cal.** See synonyms under RADICAL. **—or·gan'i·cal·ly** *adv.*

organic chemistry The branch of chemistry that relates to carbon compounds.

organic disease *Pathol.* A disease that affects some particular organ in its structure, as distinguished from its function.

or·gan·i·cism (ôr·gan'ə·siz'əm) *n.* **1** *Med.* The doctrine that all diseases are caused by specific lesions of one or more organs. **2** *Biol.* The theory of living processes as the result of the activity of all the organs considered as an autonomous, integrated system. **3** *Sociol.* The concept of society as an organism, of which beliefs, ideas, customs, etc., are component parts. **—or·gan'i·cist** *n.*

organic law 1 The law by which a government outlines and establishes its own political structure. **2** An act of Congress providing a form of government for a territory.

or·gan·ism (ôr'gən·iz'əm) *n.* **1** An animal or plant internally organized to maintain vital activities. **2** Anything that is analogous in structure and function to a living thing: the social *organism.* **—or'gan·is'mal** *adj.*

or·gan·ist (ôr'gən·ist) *n.* **1** One who plays the organ. **2** In the Middle Ages, a singer who

accompanied the plain song with another part. See ORGANUM (def. 2).

or·gan·i·za·tion (ôr′gən·ə·zā′shən, -ī·zā′-) *n.* **1** The act of organizing, or the state of being organized; also, that which is organized. **2** An animal or vegetable organism. **3** A number of individuals systematically united for some end or work: a military *organization.* **4** The officials, committeemen, etc., who control a political party: also called *machine.* **5** Any combination of parts. Also *Brit.* **or′gan·i·sa′tion.**

or·gan·ize (ôr′gən·īz) *v.* **·ized, ·iz·ing** *v.t.* **1** To bring together or form as a whole or combination, as for a common objective. **2** To arrange systematically; order. **3** To furnish with organic structure. **4 a** To enlist (workers) in a trade union. **b** To unionize the workers of (a factory, etc.). —*v.i.* **5** To form or join an organization. Also *Brit.* **or′gan·ise.** See synonyms under INSTITUTE. [<Med. L *organizare* <L *organum* ORGAN] **—or′gan·iz′a·ble** *adj.* **—or′gan·iz′er** *n.*

organo- *combining form* **1** *Biol.* Related to anorgan, or to the organs of the body: *organogenesis.* **2** *Chem.* Organic: *organometallic.* [<Gk. *organon* an instrument, organ]

organ of Corti A complex structure in the human ear directly involved with the perception of sound: discovered by Alfonso Corti.

or·ga·no·gen·e·sis (ôr′gə·nō·jen′ə·sis) *n. Biol.* The development of organs in animals and plants. **—or′ga·no·ge·net′ic** (-jə·net′ik) *adj.*

or·ga·nog·ra·phy (ôr′gə·nog′rə·fē) *n.* Scientific description of organs; descriptive organology. **—or′ga·no·graph′ic** (-nō·graf′ik) or **·i·cal** *adj.*

or·ga·no·lep·tic (ôr′gə·nō·lep′tik) *adj. Physiol.* **1** Having an effect upon one of the organs of sense, as taste or smell. **2** Of or pertaining to sense impressions and their evaluation: applied especially to laboratory tests of food, flavors, and odors. [<F *organoleptique* <Gk. *organon* organ + *lep-*, stem of *lambanein* take]

or·ga·nol·o·gy (ôr′gə·nol′ə·jē) *n.* The branch of biology that treats of organs of the body. **—or′ga·no·log′ic** (-nō·loj′ik) or **·i·cal** *adj.* **—or′ga·nol′o·gist** *n.*

or·ga·no·me·tal·lic (ôr′gə·nō·mə·tal′ik) *adj. Chem.* Designating or pertaining to a compound of metal and carbon.

or·ga·non (ôr′gə·non) *n. pl.* **·na** (-nə) or **·nons** A system of rules and principles considered as an instrument of guidance, as of knowledge or thought. Also *organum.* [<Gk., organ]

or·ga·no·sil·i·con (ôr′gə·nō·sil′ə·kon) *n. Chem.* Any of an important class of compounds or polymers containing silicon and carbon; a ilicone.

or·ga·no·ther·a·py (ôr′gə·nō·ther′ə·pē) *n. Med.* The treatment of disease by remedies derived from animal organs. Also **or′ga·no·ther′a·peu′tics** (-ther′ə·pyōō′tiks).

organ pipe One of the long tubes of a pipe organ, in which a column of air is made to vibrate so as to produce a tone of definite pitch.

or·ga·num (ôr′gə·nəm) *n. pl.* **·na** (-nə) or **·nums 1** An organon. **2** In medieval music, a part sung as an accompaniment to the melody or plain song at an interval of a fourth or a fifth above or below it; also, this method of part singing. [<L, ORGAN]

or·gan·za (ôr·gan′zə) *n.* A sheer, crisp fabric used for evening dresses, trimming, etc. [Origin uncertain]

or·gan·zine (ôr′gən·zēn) *n.* **1** A silk thread made of several single threads twisted together; thrown silk. **2** A fabric made of organzine. [<F *organsin* <Ital. *organzine;* ult. origin unknown]

or·gasm (ôr′gaz·əm) *n.* **1** Immoderate or extreme excitement or behavior. **2** *Physiol.* The acme of excitement at the culmination of the sexual act, followed by detumescence. [<F *orgasme* <Gk. *orgasmos* a swelling <*orgaein* swell, be excited] **—or·gas·mic** (ôr·gaz′mik), **or·gas·tic** (ôr·gas′tik) *adj.*

or·geat (ôr′zhat, *Fr.* ôr·zhá′) *n.* A sirup made from barley water and sugar flavored with almonds, orange flowers, etc. [<MF <Provençal *orjat* <*ordi, orge* barley <L *hordeum*]

Or·get·o·rix (ôr·jet′ə·riks) Helvetian chief of the first century B.C. who opposed Julius Caesar.

or·gi·as·tic (ôr′jē·as′tik) *adj.* Pertaining to or resembling the Greek orgies; hence, marked by wild revelries. Also **or′gi·ac, or′gic.** [<Gk. *orgiastikos* <*orgatēs* a celebrator of an orgy <*orgiazein* celebrate orgies]

or·gone (ôr′gōn) *n.* In the psychobiology of Wilhelm Reich, biological energy, accumulated from the environment and discharged gradually in all activity but suddenly in the orgasm: identified with the libido, as defined by Freud and, tentatively, with the ether of older physical theories.

or·gy (ôr′jē) *n. pl.* **·gies. 1** Wild or wanton revelry; a drunken carousal; debauch. **2** Any immoderate or excessive indulgence in something; an *orgy* of reading. **3** *pl.* The secret rites in honor of certain ancient Greek and Roman deities, as Dionysus, marked by ecstatic or frenzied songs and dances. [Earlier *orgies,* pl. <MF <L *orgia* <Gk., secret rites]

or·i·bi (ôr′ə·bē, or′-) *n. pl.* **·bis** or **·bi** A small, dun-colored African antelope (genus *Ourebia*), about two feet high at the shoulder: also spelled *ourebi.* [<Afrikaans <Hottentot *arab*]

or·i·chalc (ôr′i·kalk, or′-) *n.* In ancient Greece, an alloy of copper and zinc, resembling gold; brass. Also **or′i·chalch.** [<L *orichalcum* <Gk. *oreichalkon,* lit., mountain copper <*oros, oreos* a mountain + *chalkos* copper, brass]

o·ri·el (ôr′ē·əl, ō′rē-) *n. Archit.* A bay window; especially, one built out from a wall and resting on a bracket or similar support. [<OF *oriol* a porch, gallery, ? <Med. L *oriolum;* ult. origin unknown]

o·ri·ent (ôr′ē·ənt, ō′rē-) *n.* **1** The east; opposed to *occident.* **2** The eastern sky; also, dawn; sunrise. **3** The iridescent luster of a pearl. —*v.t.* **1** To cause to face or turn to the east. **2** To place or adjust, as a map, in exact relation to the points of the compass. **3** To adjust according to first principles or recognized facts or truths; adapt (oneself) mentally to a situation. **4** To adjust in relation to something else: His experience *oriented* his ideas toward science. —*adj.* **1** Resembling sunrise; bright. **2** Ascending. [<OF <L *oriens, -entis* rising sun, east, orig. ppr. of *oriri* rise]

O·ri·ent (ôr′ē·ənt, ō′rē-) The East; Asia, especially eastern Asia: opposed to *Occident.*

o·ri·en·tal (ôr′ē·en′təl, ō′rē-) *adj.* **1** *Astron.* Eastern; appearing or being in the eastern sky: said of stars and planets. **2** Specially bright, clear, and pure: said of gems. **3** Noting a variety of precious corundum, especially sapphire, marked by colors suggestive of other gems: an *oriental* amethyst, *oriental* aquamarine, *oriental* emerald, *oriental* topaz. **—o′ri·en′tal·ly** *adv.*

O·ri·en·tal (ôr′ē·en′təl, ō′rē-) *adj.* **1** Of or pertaining to the Orient; eastern. **2** Magnificent; gorgeous; sumptuous: *Oriental* luxury. **3** Designating a zoogeographical realm or region which includes India, southern Asia, the East Indies, and the Philippine Islands. —*n.* An inhabitant of Asia; an Asian. Opposed to *Occidental.* Also **o′ri·en′tal.**

O·ri·en·tal·ism (ôr′ē·en′təl·iz′əm, ō′rē-) *n.* **1** An Oriental quality or character of thought, speech or manners, or the disposition to adopt such a quality or character. **2** Knowledge of or proficiency in Oriental languages, literature, etc. Also **o′ri·en′tal·ism. —O′ri·en′tal·ist** *n.*

O·ri·en·tal·ize (ôr′ē·en′təl·īz, ō′rē-) *v.t.* & *v.i.* **·ized, ·iz·ing** To make or become Oriental. Also *Brit.* **O′ri·en′tal·ise.**

Oriental rug A rug or carpet hand-woven in one piece in the Orient.

oriental topaz A yellow form of corundum used as a gemstone.

o·ri·en·tate (ôr′ē·en·tāt′, ō′rē-) *v.* **·tat·ed, ·tat·ing** *v.t.* To orient —*v.i.* To face or turn eastward or in some specified direction; be oriented. [<F *orienter* <OF *orient* ORIENT]

o·ri·en·ta·tion (ôr′ē·en·tā′shən, ō′rē-) *n.* **1** The act of orienting, or the state of being oriented. **2** Position, or the determining of position, with relation to the points of the compass. **3** The determination or adjustment of one's position with reference to circumstances, ideals, etc. **4** *Psychol.* Awareness of one's own temporal, spatial, and personal relationships. **5** *Archit.* The construction of a church upon an east-west axis, so as to have the altar in the eastern end. **6** The homing instinct, as in pigeons. **7** *Chem.* The particular disposition of the constituent atoms in a compound, especially as determined by electrical forces.

O·ri·en·te (ôr′ē·en′tā, ō′rē-) **1** A province of eastern Cuba; 14,132 square miles; capital, Santiago de Cuba: formerly *Santiago de Cuba.* **2** A region and former province of Ecuador, comprising all its territory east of the Andes.

o·ri·en·ted (ôr′ē·en·tid, ō′rē-, -ən·tid) *adj.* **1** Directed toward; interested in: *oriented* to the arts. **2** Directed or centered: used in combination: *child-oriented.*

or·i·fice (ôr′ə·fis, or′-) *n.* A small opening into a cavity; an aperture. See HOLE. [<MF <LL *orificium* <L *os, oris* mouth + *facere* make]

or·i·flamme (ôr′ə·flam, or′-) *n.* **1** The red banner of the abbey of St. Denis, used as a battle standard by the kings of France until the 15th century. **2** *Her.* A blue banner charged with three fleurs-de-lis of gold. **3** Any flag or standard. Also spelled *auriflamme.* [<F <OF *oriflambe* <Med. L *auriflamma* <L *aurum* gold + *flamma* a flame]

or·i·ga·mi (ôr′i·gä′mē) *n.* The ancient Japanese art of folding single sheets of paper into animal and other forms, usually without the aid of scissors or paste. [<Japanese]

or·i·gan (ôr′ə·gən, or′-) *n.* The wild marjoram *(Origanum vulgare),* an important source of carvacrol: its fragrant leaves are esteemed as a seasoning. Also spelled *oregano.* [<OF <L *origanum* <Gk. *origanon,* an herb like marjoram <*oros, oreos* a mountain + *ganos* brightness, joy]

Or·i·gen (ôr′ə·jen, -jən, or′-), 185?–254?, Greek theologian.

or·i·gin (ôr′ə·jin, or′-) *n.* **1** The commencement of the existence of anything. **2** A primary source; cause. **3** Parentage; ancestry. **4** *Anat.* The relatively fixed point of attachment of a muscle. Compare INSERTION. **5** *Math.* **a** The point at which the axes of a Cartesian coordinate system intersect; the point where the ordinate and abscissa equal zero. **b** The point in a polar coordinate system where the radius vector equals zero. See illustration under QUADRANT, OCTANT. See synonyms under BEGINNING. [Appar. <OF *origine* <L *origo, -inis* a rise, beginning]

o·rig·i·nal (ə·rij′ə·nəl) *adj.* **1** Of or belonging to the beginning, origin, or first stage of existence of a thing. **2** Immediately produced by one's own mind and thought; not copied or produced by imitation. **3** Able to produce works requiring thought, without copying or imitating those of others; creative; inventive. See synonyms under AUTHENTIC, FIRST, NATIVE, PRIMEVAL, RADICAL, TRANSCENDENTAL. —*n.* **1** The first form of anything. **2** The language in which a book is first written. **3** A person of unique character or genius; also, an eccentric. **4** Originator; also, origin. See synonyms under IDEAL, MODEL.

o·rig·i·nal·i·ty (ə·rij′ə·nal′ə·tē) *n. pl.* **·ties 1** The power of originating inventiveness. **2** The quality of being original or novel.

o·rig·i·nal·ly (ə·rij′ə·nəl·ē) *adv.* **1** At the beginning. **2** In a new and striking manner.

original sin *Theol.* The natural corruption and depravity inherent in mankind because of Adam's first sinful disobedience.

o·rig·i·nate (ə·rij′ə·nāt) *v.* **·nat·ed, ·nat·ing** *v.t.* To bring into existence; create, initiate. —*v.i.* To come into existence; have origin; arise. See synonyms under INSTITUTE, PRODUCE, PROPAGATE. **—o·rig′i·na′tion** *n.* **—o·rig′i·na′tive** *adj.* **—o·rig′i·na′tive·ly** *adv.* **—o·rig′i·na′tor** *n.*

o·ri·na·sal (ôr′ə·nā′zəl, or′-) *adj.* **1** *Anat.* Of or pertaining to the mouth and nose: the *orinasal* duct. **2** *Phonet.* Pronounced with the nasal and oral passages both open, as the French nasal vowels. —*n. Phonet.* An orinasal vowel. [<L *os, oris* mouth + NASAL]

O·ri·no·co (ôr′ə·nō′kō, or′-) A river in Venezuela, flowing about 1,700 miles NW and north to the Atlantic Ocean.

o·ri·ole (ôr′ē·ōl, ō′rē-) *n.* **1** Any of a family *(Oriolidae)* of black-and-yellow passerine birds of the Old World, related to the crows; the common **European** (or **golden**) **oriole** *(Oriolus oriolus)* is bright yellow with sharply contrasting black wings and tail, and builds a hanging nest. **2** One of various black-and-yellow American songbirds (family *Icteridae*) building a hanging nest; especially, the Baltimore oriole and the orchard oriole. [<OF *oriol* <Med. L *oriolus* <L *aureolus,* dim. of *aureus* golden <*aurum* gold]

O·ri·on (ō·rī′ən) **1** In Greek and Roman mythology, a giant hunter who pursued the

Pleiades and was killed by Diana: he was placed among the stars by her as a constellation. 2 *Astron.* An equatorial constellation, noted for its group of three stars in a line (the Sword Belt or Girdle), and for its two bright stars, Betelgeuse and Rigel. See CONSTELLATION.

O·ris·ka·ny (ō·ris′kə·nē) A village on the Mohawk River in central New York; scene of a battle in the Revolutionary War, 1777.

or·i·son (ôr′i·zən, or′-) *n. Usually pl.* A devotional prayer. See synonyms under PRAYER. [<OF *oreisun, orison* <L *oratio, -onis* a prayer. Doublet of ORATION.]

O·ris·sa (ō·ris′ə) A constituent State of east central India on the NW Bay of Bengal; 60,136 square miles; capital, Bhubaneswar.

O·ri·ya (ō·rē′yä) *n.* One of the major Indic languages of India, closely related to Bengali.

O·ri·za·ba (ō′rē·sä′bä) A city in Veracruz state, Mexico, SE of Pico de Orizaba.

Orizaba, Pico de An inactive volcano in Veracruz state, the highest point in Mexico; 18,700 feet: also *Citlatépetl.*

ork (ôrk) See ORC.

Or·khon (ôr′kon) A river in north central Mongolian People's Republic, flowing 700 miles east and north to the Selenga. Also **Or′hon** (-hon).

Ork·ney Islands (ôrk′nē) An island group and county of northern Scotland off the NE tip of the mainland; 376 square miles; capital, Kirkwall. Also **Ork′neys.**

Or·lan·do (ôr·lan′dō) A masculine personal name. See ROLAND.

Or·lan·do (ôr·län′dō), **Vittorio Emanuele,** 1860–1952, Italian statesman; premier 1917–1919.

orle (ôrl) *n. Her.* A subordinary bearing consisting of a band, half the width of a bordure, extending round the shield near the edge. [<F <OF *urle, ourle,* dim. <L *ora* a border]

Or·lé·a·nais (ôr·lā·à·ne′) A region and former province in north central France on both sides of the Loire.

Or·le·an·ism (ôr′lē·ən·iz′əm) *n.* Adherence to the Orléans family.

Or·le·an·ist (ôr′lē·ən·ist) *n.* A supporter of the Orléans branch of the French royal family descended from the younger brother of Louis XIV. —*adj.* Of or pertaining to Orleanists or Orleanism.

Or·lé·ans (ôr·lā·äṅ′) Name of a cadet branch of the Valois and Bourbon houses of France, many members of which have been prominent in French history from the 14th century. — **Louis Philippe Joseph d',** 1747–93, revolutionary and egalitarian; guillotined: known as *Philippe Égalité.*

Or·lé·ans (ôr·lā·äṅ′) A city of north central France, on the Loire.

Or·lon (ôr′lon) *n.* A synthetic fiber woven from an acrylic resin: it has high resistance to heat, light, and chemicals and is widely used as a textile material: a trade name.

or·lop (ôr′lop) *n. Naut.* The lowest deck of a ship, especially of a warship. [<Du. *overloop,* orig. a covering <*over* over + *loopen* run; so called because it covers the hold]

Or·ly (ôr·lē′) A SE suburb of Paris; site of an international airport.

or·mer (ôr′mər) *n.* 1 An ear shell; especially, *Haliotis tuberculata,* an edible univalve mollusk of the Channel Islands. 2 An abalone. [<dial. F (Channel Islands) <F *ormier,* contraction of *oreille de mer,* lit., ear of the sea; so called with ref. to its shape]

or·mo·lu (ôr′mə·lōō) *n.* Gilt or bronzed metallic ware, or lustrous bronze, used in decorating furniture, etc. [<F *or moulu,* lit., ground gold <*or* gold (<L *aurum*) + *moulu,* pp. of *moudre* grind <L *molere*]

Or·muz (ôr′muz, ôr·mōōz′) See HORMUZ.

Or·muzd (ôr′muzd) In Zoroastrian religion, the principle of good, source of light, and creator of the world: opponent of Ahriman, the evil deity: called *Ahura Mazda* in the Avesta. Also **Or′mazd** (-mäzd). [<Persian *Ormazd,* ult. <Avestan *Ahura-Mazda,* lit., wise lord]

or·na·ment (ôr′nə·mənt) *n.* 1 A part or an addition that contributes to the beauty or elegance of a thing. 2 Ornamentation in the abstract, or ornaments collectively. 3 Any thing or person considered as a source of honor or credit. 4 A mark of distinction; decoration. 5 *Music* A decorative note or notes not necessary to the melody; an appoggiatura. —*v.t.* (ôr′nə·ment) To adorn with ornaments; embellish. See synonyms under ADORN, GARNISH. [<OF *ornement* <L *ornamentum* equipment, ornament <*ornare* adorn] — **or′na·ment′er** *n.*

or·na·men·tal (ôr′nə·men′təl) *adj.* Serving to adorn. —*n.* An ornamental object, especially a plant meant for decorative purposes. — **or′·na·men′tal·ly** *adv.*

or·na·men·ta·tion (ôr′nə·men·tā′shən) *n.* 1 The act of adorning, or the state of being adorned. 2 Ornamental things collectively; that with which something is ornamented.

or·nate (ôr·nāt′) *adj.* 1 Ornamented to a marked degree; artistically elaborate, as a literary style. 2 Ornamented; decorated. [<L *ornatus,* pp. of *ornare* adorn] — **or·nate′ly** *adv.* — **or·nate′ness** *n.*

or·ner·y (ôr′nər·ē, ôrn′rē) *adj. U.S. Dial.* 1 Mean; low; also, unruly; stubborn. 2 Common; ordinary. [Alter. of ORDINARY] — **or′·ner·i·ness** *n.*

or·nis (ôr′nis) *n.* Avifauna. [<G <Gk., a bird]

or·nith·ic (ôr·nith′ik) *adj.* Of or pertaining to birds. [<Gk. *ornithikos* birdlike <*ornis, ornithos* a bird]

or·ni·thine (ôr′nə·thēn, -thin) *n. Biochem.* An amino acid, $C_5H_{12}O_2N_2$, found in the urine of birds; a product of arginine. [<Gk. *ornis, ornithos* a bird + -INE[2]]

or·ni·this·chi·an (ôr′nə·this′kē·ən) *Paleontol. adj.* Belonging to an order (*Ornithischia*) of birdlike, chiefly amphibious dinosaurs of the Jurassic and Cretaceous periods, including the iguanodon. —*n.* A member of this order. [<NL <Gk. *ornis, ornithos* a bird + *ischion* a hip]

ornitho- *combining form* Bird; of or related to birds: *ornithology.* Also, before vowels, **ornith-.** [<Gk. *ornis, ornithos* a bird]

Or·ni·tho·gae·a (ôr′nə·thō·jē′ə) *n.* A zoogeographical realm including New Zealand and Polynesia, characterized by extinct and existing avifauna not found elsewhere. Also **Or′·ni·tho·ge′a.** [<NL <Gk. *ornis, ornithos* a bird + *gaia* earth, land] — **Or′ni·tho·gae′an** or **·ge′an** *adj.*

or·ni·thoid (ôr′nə·thoid) *adj.* Resembling a bird or birds.

or·ni·thol·o·gy (ôr′nə·thol′ə·jē) *n.* The branch of zoology that treats of birds. [<ORNITHO- + -LOGY] — **or′ni·tho·log′ic** (-thə·loj′ik) or **·i·cal** *adj.* — **or′ni·tho·log′i·cal·ly** *adv.* — **or′ni·thol′o·gist** *n.*

or·ni·thoph·i·lous (ôr′nə·thof′ə·ləs) *adj. Bot.* Bird-loving: said of flowers that are adapted for or depend upon birds (usually hummingbirds) to transfer the pollen from the stamens to the stigma; bird-pollinated. [<ORNITHO- + -PHILOUS]

or·ni·tho·pod (ôr′nə·thō·pod, ôr·nī′-) *Paleontol. n.* One of an extinct order (*Ornithischia*) of bipedal dinosaurians of herbivorous habits. —*adj.* Of or pertaining to this order. [<NL *Ornithopoda* <Gk. *ornis, ornithos* a bird + *pous, podos* a foot]

or·ni·thop·ter (ôr′nə·thop′tər) *n.* A theoretical type of aircraft sustained and propelled by an upward and downward movement of the wings, as in the flight of a bird: also called *orthopter.* [<ORNITHO- + Gk. *pteron* a wing]

or·ni·tho·rhyn·chus (ôr′nə·thō·ring′kəs) *n. pl.* **·chi** (-kī) An egg-laying mammal with a duck-like bill; a duckbill. [<NL <Gk. *ornis, ornithos* a bird + *rhynchos* a beak] — **or′ni·tho·rhyn′chous** *adj.*

or·ni·tho·sis (ôr′nə·thō′sis) *n.* An infectious virus disease of turkeys, chickens, and other birds not of the parrot family: it resembles psittacosis and is transmissible to man.

oro-[1] *combining form* Mouth; oral: *oropharynx.* [<L *os, oris* the mouth]

oro-[2] *combining form Geol.* Mountain; of mountains: *orography.* [<Gk. *oros* a mountain]

or·o·ban·cha·ceous (ôr′ō·bang·kā′shəs, or′-) *adj.* Designating a genus (*Orobanche*) typical of a family (*Orobanchaceae*) of low, leafless, parasitic, yellowish or brownish herbs lacking chlorophyll; the broomrapes. [<NL <L, broomrape <Gk. *orobanchē* <*orobos* a kind of vetch + *anchein* throttle]

o·rog·e·ny (ô·roj′ə·nē, ō-) *n. Geol.* The process of mountain formation. [<ORO-[2] + -GENY] — **or·o·gen·ic** (ôr′ə·jen′ik, or′-) *adj.*

o·rog·ra·phy (ô·rog′rə·fē, ō-) *n.* The branch of physiography that treats of the development and relations of highlands and mountain ranges. [<ORO-[2] + -GRAPHY] — **or·o·graph·ic** (ôr′ə·graf′ik, or′-) or **·i·cal** *adj.*

o·ro·ide (ôr′ō·īd, ō′rō-) *n.* An alloy of copper, zinc, tin, and other metals, having a golden luster: also spelled *oreide.* [<F *or* gold (<L *aurum*) + Gk. *eidos* form]

o·rol·o·gy (ô·rol′ə·jē, ō-) *n.* The study of mountains. [<ORO-[2] + -LOGY] — **or·o·log·i·cal** (ôr′ə·loj′i·kəl, or′-) *adj.* — **o·rol′o·gist** *n.*

o·rom·e·ter (ô·rom′ə·tər, ō-) *n.* An aneroid barometer having, in addition to the usual scale, a second system of graduations giving elevations above sea level corresponding to barometric pressure; a mountain barometer. [<ORO-[2] + -METER] — **or·o·met·ric** (ôr′ə·met′·rik, or′-) *adj.*

O·ron·tes (ô·ron′tēz, ō-) A river of NW Syria and southern Turkey, flowing 240 miles north from the Anti-Lebanon mountains to the Mediterranean.

o·ro·phar·ynx (ôr′ō·far′ingks, ō′rō-) *n. pl.* **·pha·ryn·ges** (-fə·rin′jēz) or **·phar·ynx·es** *Anat.* That part of the pharynx behind the mouth; the pharynx proper. [<ORO-[1] + PHARYNX]

O·ro·si·us (ə·rō′shē·əs), **Paulus** Fifth century Spanish theologian and author.

o·ro·tund (ôr′ə·tund, ō′rə-) *adj.* 1 Full, clear, rounded, and resonant: said of the voice or utterance. 2 Pompous; inflated, as a manner of speech. —*n.* An orotund quality of voice: also **o′ro·tun′di·ty.** [<L *ore rotundo* with well-turned speech, lit., with a round mouth <*os, oris* mouth + *rotundus* round]

O·roz·co (ō·rōs′kō), **José Clemente,** 1883–1949, Mexican painter.

Or·pen (ôr′pən), **Sir William,** 1878–1931, Irish painter.

or·phan (ôr′fən) *n.* A child whose parents are dead. —*adj.* 1 Having lost one or (more commonly) both parents: said of a child. 2 Pertaining to a child so bereaved. —*v.t.* To bereave of parents or of a parent; make an orphan of. [<LL *orphanus* <Gk. *orphanos,* lit., bereaved] — **or′phan·hood** (-hŏŏd) *n.*

or·phan·age (ôr′fən·ij) *n.* 1 The state of being an orphan. 2 An institution for orphans.

Orphans' Court In some States of the United States, a court having jurisdiction over the estates of deceased persons and guardianship of orphans; also, a probate court.

Or·phe·us (ôr′fē·əs) In Greek mythology, a musician who could charm beasts and even rocks and trees by his singing to the lyre. When his wife Eurydice died he was permitted to lead her back to earth from Hades provided he would not look at her: he failed in the test and was later killed by the Thracian women who were enraged at his mourning for Eurydice. — **Or′phe·an** *adj.*

Or·phic (ôr′fik) *adj.* 1 Belonging, relating, or similar to Orpheus or his works. 2 Of or pertaining to Orphism; hence, oracular; mysterious. Also **Or′phi·cal.** [<L *Orphicus* <Gk. *Orphikos* <*Orpheus* Orpheus]

Orphic mysteries Esoteric doctrines and rites practiced by the worshipers of Dionysus Zagreus, claiming Orpheus as their founder.

Or·phism (ôr′fiz·əm) *n.* The system of the Orphic mysteries.

or·phrey (ôr′frē) *n.* 1 Gold embroidery, or any costly embroidery. 2 A band of gold embroidery or other rich material put on certain ecclesiastical vestments. Also spelled *orfray.* [<OF *orfreis* <Med. L *aurifrisium* <L *auriphrygium* <*aurum* gold + *Phrygius* Phrygian]

or·pi·ment (ôr′pə·mənt) *n.* An easily cut, pearly, lemon-yellow, native arsenic trisulfide, As_2S_3, used as a pigment and as a dyestuff. [<OF <L *auripigmentum* gold pigment]

or·pine (ôr′pin) *n.* 1 An Old World species of stonecrop (*Sedum telephium*) with tuberous root, stout erect stem, ovate leaves, and white or purple flowers in dense tufts: naturalized in the United States. 2 A Mediterranean herb (*Telephium imperati*) of the pink family, with

prostrate stems and white flowers in terminal clusters. Also **or′pin.** [< OF *orpin* < *orpiment* ORPIMENT]

Or·ping·ton (ôr′ping·tən) *n.* A variety of domestic fowl originating in Orpington, a village in Kent, England.

or·ra (ôr′ə, or′ə) *adj. Scot.* **1** Odd, in the sense of extra and occasional; incidental: an *orra* job. **2** Employed for odd jobs, as on a farm. **3** Composed of or belonging to the riff-raff; low; despicable: an *orra* gathering.

or·re·ry (ôr′ə·rē, or′-) *n. pl.* **·ries** A mechanical apparatus for exhibiting the relative motions and positions of the members of the solar system; a cosmoscope. [after the fourth Earl of *Orrery,* Charles Boyle, 1676–1731, English statesman for whom an early copy of the machine was made]

or·rhol·o·gy (ô·rol′ə·jē, ō-) *n.* Serology. [< Gk. *orrhos* serum + -LOGY]

or·ris (ôr′is, or′-) *n.* Any of the several species of *Iris* having a scented root, especially *I. florentina,* of which the dried rootstock is used in medicine, perfumery, etc. Also **or′rice.** [Prob. alter. of Ital. *ireos* < L *iris* IRIS]

or·seille (ôr·sāl′) *n.* Archil. [< F < OF *orchel* ARCHIL]

Or·si·no (ôr·sē′nō) In Shakespeare's *Twelfth Night,* the duke of Illyria, who marries Viola, the heroine.

ort (ôrt) *n. Usually pl.* A worthless leaving, as of food after a meal. [< Prob. < Du. *ooraete* remains of food]

Or·te·gal (ôr′tā·gäl′), **Cape** A headland of NW Spain.

Or·te·ga y Gas·set (ôr·tā′gä ē gä·set′), **José,** 1883–1955, Spanish philosopher and author.

Or·ten·si·a (ôr·ten′sē·ä) Italian form of HORTENSE.

or·tet (ôr′tet) *n. Bot.* The plant from which a clon is derived. [< L *ortus* an origin, a rising < *oriri* rise]

or·thi·con (ôr′thə·kon) *n.* A sensitive television camera tube which uses low-velocity electrons in scanning and can pick up scenes under all lighting conditions or by infrared radiations. Also **image orthicon.** [< ORTH(O)- + ICON(OSCOPE)]

ortho- *combining form* **1** Straight; upright; in line: *orthotropic.* **2** At right angles; perpendicular: *orthorhombic.* **3** Correct; proper; right: *orthography.* **4** *Med.* The correction of irregularities or deformities of: *orthodontia.* **5** *Chem.* **a** A compound, usually an acid, containing the greatest possible number of hydroxyl groups: distinguished from *meta-.* **b** A benzene derivative in which the substituted atoms or radicals occupy the positions 1, 2: abbr. *o-.* Compare META-, PARA-. See BENZENE RING. Also, before vowels, **orth-.** [< Gk. < *orthos* straight]

or·tho axis (ôr′thō) *Mineral.* That axis in a crystal of the monoclinic system which is perpendicular to the other two axes.

or·tho·bi·o·sis (ôr′thō·bī·ō′sis) *n.* Sound and correct living; living in accordance with proper hygienic principles.

or·tho·cen·ter (ôr′thō·sen′tər) *n. Geom.* The point at which the three altitudes of a triangle intersect.

or·tho·ce·phal·ic (ôr′thō·sə·fal′ik) *adj.* Having a head in which the ratio between the vertical and transverse diameters is from 70 to 75. Also **or′tho·ceph′a·lous** (-sef′ə·ləs). **—or′tho·ceph′a·ly** *n.*

or·tho·chro·mat·ic (ôr′thō·krō·mat′ik) *adj. Phot.* Maintaining natural relations of light and shade, especially by the use of films or plates treated to give correct values to the greens and yellows: also called *isochromatic.* **—or′tho·chro′ma·tism** (-krō′mə·tiz′əm) *n.*

or·tho·clase (ôr′thō·klās, -klāz) *n.* A brittle, colorless to flesh-colored or gray mineral consisting mainly of potassium feldspar, $KAlSi_3O_8$, crystallized in the monoclinic system. [< ORTHO- + Gk. *klasis* a fracture < *klaein* break]

or·tho·clas·tic (ô′thō·klas′tik) *adj.* Having right-angled cleavages, as orthoclase.

or·tho·cy·mene (ôr′thō·sī′mēn) *n. Chem.* One of the three isomeric forms of cymene.

or·tho·dome (ôr′thə·dōm) *n.* A domelike surface parallel to one of the axes in a monoclinic crystal. **—or′tho·dom′ic** (-dom′ik) *adj.*

or·tho·don·tia (ôr′thə·don′shə, -shē·ə) *n.* The branch of dentistry which is concerned with the prevention and correction of irregularities and faulty positions of the teeth. [< NL < Gk. *orthos* right, straight + *odous, odontos* a tooth] **—or′tho·don′tic** (-don′tik) *adj.* **—or′tho·don′tist** *n.*

or·tho·dox (ôr′thə·doks) *adj.* **1** Correct or sound in doctrine; holding the commonly accepted faith, established doctrines, etc.: opposed to *heterodox.* **2** Conforming to the Christian faith as formulated in the early ecumenical creeds. **3** Approved; accepted. [< MF *orthodoxe* < LL *orthodoxus* < Gk. *orthodoxos* having right opinion < *orthos* right + *doxa* opinion < *dokeein* think] **—or′tho·dox′ly** *adv.*

Or·tho·dox (ôr′thə·doks) *adj.* Pertaining to the Greek Church.

Orthodox Church The Greek Church.

Orthodox Judaism Judaism as practiced by those who hold that both the Scriptures and the oral laws are divinely authoritative and that traditional rituals are to be faithfully observed. Compare CONSERVATIVE JUDAISM, REFORM JUDAISM.

or·tho·dox·y (ôr′thə·dok′sē) *n. pl.* **·dox·ies** **1** Belief in estblished doctrine. **2** Agreement with accepted standards, established doctrines, ideas, etc. **—or′tho·dox′i·cal** *adj.*

or·tho·e·pist (ôr·thō′ə·pist, ôr′thō·ə·pist) *n.* An authority on pronunciation. **—or·tho·e·pis·tic** (ôr′thō·ə·pis′tik) *adj.*

or·tho·e·py (ôr·thō′ə·pē, ôr′thō·ep′ē) *n.* **1** The art of correct pronunciation. **2** Pronunciation in general. [< Gk. *orthoepeia* correctness of diction < *orthos* right + *epos* a word] **—or·tho·ep·ic** (ôr′thō·ep′ik) or **·i·cal** *adj.*

or·thog·a·my (ôr·thog′ə·mē) *n.* **1** *Bot.* Immediate or direct self-fertilization of the ovary, as by the stamens of the same flower; autogamy. **2** Normal bisexual union. **—or·tho·gam·ic** (ôr′thō·gam′ik), **or·thog′a·mous** *adj.*

or·tho·gen·e·sis (ôr′thō·jen′ə·sis) *n. Biol.* The doctrine that the phylogenetic evolution of organisms takes place systematically in a definite direction and not accidentally in many directions; variation predetermined by the germ plasm. **—or′tho·ge·net′ic** (-jə·net′ik) *adj.*

or·thog·na·thous (ôr·thog′nə·thəs) *adj.* Having the lower jaw in line with the upper; having straight jaws. Also **or·thog·nath·ic** (ôr′thog·nath′ik). [< ORTHO- + -GNATHOUS] **—or·thog′na·thism, or·thog′na·thy** *n.*

or·thog·o·nal (ôr·thog′ə·nəl) *adj.* Having or determined by right angles; perpendicular. [< F *orthogonale* < *orthogone* a right triangle < LL *orthogonium* < Gk. *orthogōnios* < *orthos* right + *gōnia* an angle] **—or·thog′o·nal·ly** *adv.*

or·tho·graph·ic (ôr′thə·graf′ik) *adj.* **1** Relating to orthography; also, correctly spelled. **2** Pertaining to right lines or angles. Also **or′tho·graph′i·cal.** **—or′tho·graph′i·cal·ly** *adv.*

orthographic projection A map projection in which the lines lie at right angles to the plane of projection.

or·thog·ra·phy (ôr·thog′rə·fē) *n. pl.* **·phies** **1** A mode or system of spelling, especially of spelling correctly or according to usage. **2** The science that treats of letters and spelling. **3** The art or act of drawing in correct architectural projection. **—or·thog′ra·pher, or·thog′ra·phist** *n.*

or·tho·hy·dro·gen (ôr′thō·hī′drə·jən) *n. Chem.* An unstable form of hydrogen in which the molecules consist of two hydrogen atoms spinning in the same direction, thus giving improperly alined poles. Compare PARAHYDROGEN. [< ORTHO- in line + HYDROGEN]

or·tho·ki·net·ic (ôr′thō·ki·net′ik) *adj.* Pertaining to or having movement in one direction, as molecules or particles.

or·tho·pe·dics (ôr′thə·pē′diks) *n.* The branch of surgery which is concerned with the correction of skeletal and spinal deformities, especially in children. Also **or′tho·pae′dics.** [< F *orthopédique* < *orthopédie* orthopedics < Gk. *orthos* right + *paideia* training of children < *pais, paidos* child] **—or′tho·pe′dic** *adj.*

or·tho·pe·dist (ôr′thə·pē′dist) *n.* A physician specializing in orthopedics.

or·thoph·o·ny (ôr·thof′ə·nē) *n.* The art of speaking correctly. [< ORTHO- + -PHONY] **—or·tho·phon·ic** (ôr′thə·fon′ik) *adj.*

or·tho·phos·phor·ic (ôr′thō·fos·fôr′ik, -for′-) *adj. Chem.* Designating common phosphoric acid, H_3PO_4, a colorless, syrupy liquid with acid taste: used in medicine and the arts.

or·tho·pod (ôr′thə·pod) *n.* An orthopedist.

or·tho·psy·chi·a·try (ôr′thō·sī·kī′ə·trē) *n.* The study, investigation, and treatment of incipient mental disorders and the less extreme aberrations of behavior; mental hygiene. **—or′·tho·psy′chi·at′ric** (-sī′kē·at′rik) or **·ri·cal** *adj.* **—or′tho·psy·chi′a·trist** *n.*

or·thop·ter (ôr·thop′tər) See ORNITHOPTER.

or·thop·ter·an (ô·thop′tər·ən) *n.* Any of an order *(Orthoptera)* of insects with membranous hind wings and coriaceous, usually straight fore wings, including locusts, crickets, grasshoppers, cockroaches, etc. *—adj.* Of or pertaining to the *Orthoptera.* Also **or·thop′ter·on.** [< NL < Gk. *orthos* straight + *pteron* a wing] **—or·thop′ter·al, or·thop′ter·ous** *adj.*

or·thop·tic (ôr·thop′tik) *adj.* **1** Of, pertaining to, or characterized by normal binocular vision. **2** Designating a method of correcting defective vision by muscular exercise of the eyes. [< ORTH(O)- + OPTIC]

or·thop·tics (ôr·thop′tiks) *n. pl. (construed as singular)* The treatment of defects in binocular vision and of poor visual habits, especially by training in eye movements.

or·tho·rhom·bic (ôr′thə·rom′bik) *adj.* Pertaining to a crystal system assumed to contain three unequal axes at right angles.

or·tho·scop·ic (ôr′thə·skop′ik) *adj.* **1** Having correct vision. **2** Constructed so as to correct optical distortion: an *orthoscopic* eyepiece of a telescope.

or·tho·stat·ic (ôr′thə·stat′ik) *adj.* Of or relating to an upright standing position.

or·thos·ti·chy (ôr·thos′tə·kē) *n. pl.* **·chies** *Bot.* A vertical row or rank: applied to an arrangement of organs on an axis, as leaves or flowers. [< ORTHO- + Gk. *stichos* a row] **—o·thos′ti·chous** *adj.*

or·tho·trop·ic (ôr′thə·trop′ik) *adj. Bot.* Growing vertically: said of developing plant organs that grow nearly vertically, either upward or downward. **—or·thot·ro·pism** (ôr·thot′rə·piz′əm) *n.*

or·thot·ro·pous (ôr·thot′rə·pəs) *adj. Bot.* Growing straight: said of an ovule in which the nucellus is straight. Also **or·thot′ro·pal.** [< NL *orthotropus* < Gk. *orthos* straight + *trepein* turn] **—or·thot′ro·py** *n.*

Ort·ler Range (ôrt′lər) A division of the Alps in northern Italy; highest peak, 12,792 feet.

or·to·lan (ôr′tə·lən) *n.* **1** An Old World bunting *(Emberiza hortulana)* reddish-green above with blackish spots, and with a greenish-gray head: highly esteemed as a table delicacy. **2** Any of several other birds, as the reedbird or bobolink of the United States. [< F < Provençal < Ital. *ortolano* a gardener < L *hortulanus* < *hortulus,* dim. of *hortus* a garden; so called because it frequents gardens]

O·ru·ro (ō·rōō′rō) A city of west central Bolivia.

Or·vie·to (ôr·vyā′tō) A city in central Italy: ancient *Urbs Vetus.*

Or·well·i·an (ôr·wel′ē·ən) *adj.* Of, relating to, or like the writings of George Orwell (1903–50), British novelist and political satirist.

-ory[1] *suffix of nouns* A place or instrument for (performing the action of the main element): *dormitory, lavatory.* [< OF *-oire, -orie* < L *-orium;* or directly < L]

-ory[2] *suffix of adjectives* Related to; like; resembling: *amatory, laudatory.* [< OF *-oire* < L *-orius;* or directly < L]

Or·yok·ko (ō·ryôk·kō) The Japanese name for the YALU.

o·ryx (ôr′iks, or′-, ō′riks) *n.* A long-horned African antelope (genus *Oryx*), as the gemsbok. [< NL < L < Gk., a pickax, a kind of antelope; so called from its pointed horns]

os[1] (os) n. pl. **o·ra** (ôr′ə, ō′rə) *Anat.* A mouth or opening into the interior of an organ. [< L]

os[2] (os) *n. pl.* **os·sa** (os′ə) *Anat.* A bone. ob < L]

os[3] (ōs) *n. pl.* **o·sar** (ō′sär) *Geol.* A sinuous ridge of glacial sand and gravel, deposited by a stream flowing beneath; an esker: also spelled *ose.* [< Sw. *ås* a ridge, a chain of hills]

Os *Chem.* Osmium (symbol Os).

O·sage (ō′sāj) *n.* One of a tribe of North American Indians of southern Siouan stock, formerly inhabiting the region between the Missouri and Arkansas rivers: now living in Oklahoma. [< Siouan (Osage) *Wazhazhe* war people]

Osage orange A showy, spreading, moraceous tree *(Maclura pomifera)* native to

Arkansas and adjacent regions, having alternate, entire, glossy leaves and a large inedible aggregate fruit somewhat like an orange in size and color; also, the fruit of this tree.

Osage River A river in eastern Kansas and west central Missouri, flowing 500 miles east to the Missouri.

O·sa·ka (ō·sä·kä) A port on SW Honshu island, on **Osaka Bay,** an arm of the Inland Sea.

Os·born (oz′bərn), **Henry Fairfield,** 1857–1935, U.S. paleontologist.

Os·can (os′kən) *n.* **1** One of an ancient people who inhabited SW Italy. **2** The language of these people, belonging to the Osco-Umbrian branch of the Italic languages: also called *Samnite.* —*adj.* Of or pertaining to the Oscans or their language. [< L *Osci* people of Campania]

Os·car (os′kər) *n.* One of the small gold statuettes awarded annually (since 1928) by the Academy of Motion Picture Arts and Sciences for outstanding performances, productions, photography, etc., in motion pictures. [Said to be from the remark of an Academy secretary that the statuette resembled her uncle *Oscar*]

Os·car (os′kər, *Fr.* ôs·kȧr′; *Ger., Sp.* ôs′kär; *Norw.* os′kär; *Russian, Sw.* ôs′kär) A masculine personal name. Also *Sw.* **Os·kar** (ôs′kär). [< Gmc., divine spear]

—**Oscar II,** 1829–1907, king of Sweden 1872–1907, and of Norway 1872–1905.

Os·ce·o·la (os′ē·ō′lə), 1804–38, Seminole chief.

os·cil·late (os′ə·lāt) *v.i.* **·lat·ed, ·lat·ing 1** To swing back and forth; vibrate, as a pendulum. **2** To vary undecidedly; waver; fluctuate. **3** *Physics* To produce oscillations. See synonyms under FLUCTUATE, SHAKE. [< L *oscillatus,* pp. of *oscillare* swing < *oscillum* a swing]

os·cil·la·tion (os′ə·lā′shən) *n.* **1** The act or state of oscillating. **2** *Physics* **a** A single swing of an oscillating body between two extremes. **b** A continual fluctuation between extreme values of quantity or force, as in a high-frequency electric current, the maximum value of which constantly diminishes with a speed dependent upon the damping effect present. —**os′cil·la·to′ry** (-lə·tôr′ē, -tō′rē) *adj.*

os·cil·la·tor (os′ə·lā′tər) *n.* **1** One who or that which oscillates. **2** Any oscillating machine. **3** *Electronics* A device for producing electromagnetic oscillations of a specified frequency.

os·cil·lo·gram (ə·sil′ə·gram) *n.* A record made by an oscillograph. [< *oscillo-* < L *oscillare* oscillate + -GRAM]

os·cil·lo·graph (ə·sil′ə·graf, -gräf) *n.* A device for making a visible representation of the oscillations of an alternating current, transmitted in the form of reflected light rays to a screen for observation, or to a moving photographic film for purposes of record.

os·cil·lo·scope (ə·sil′ə·skōp) *n.* A cathode-ray oscillograph of low voltage for recording wave forms on a fluorescent screen: used in radio and in sound-ranging devices.

os·cine[1] (os′in -īn) *n.* Any passerine bird of the suborder *Oscines,* having the most highly developed vocal ability among birds, as thrushes, sparrows, etc.: commonly called *singing birds.* —*adj.* Of or pertaining to the *Oscines.* [< NL < L *oscen, oscinis* a singing bird < *ob-* towards + *canere* sing]

os·cine[2] (os′ēn, -in) *n. Chem.* A decomposition product of scopolamine. [< G *oscin,* short for *hyoscin* hyoscine]

os·ci·tan·cy (os′ə·tən·sē) *n.* **1** The act of yawning or gaping. **2** Unusual drowsiness; dulness. Also **os′ci·tance.** [< L *oscitans, -antis,* ppr. of *oscitare* gape, yawn < *os* a mouth + *citare* move] —**os′ci·tant** *adj.*

os·ci·tate (os′ə·tāt) *v.i. Archaic* To yawn. [< L *oscitatus,* pp. of *oscitare.* See OSCITANCY.]

Os·co-Um·bri·an (os′kō·um′brē·ən) *n.* A branch of the Italic subfamily of Indo-European languages, comprising the ancient Oscan and Umbrian.

os·cu·lant (os′kyə·lənt) *adj. Biol.* **1** Intermediate in character between two groups of organisms; intergrading: an *osculant* genus or family. **2** Closely adherent. [< L *osculans, -antis,* ppr. of *osculari.* See OSCULATE.]

os·cu·lar (os′kyə·lər) *adj.* **1** Of or pertaining to the mouth. **2** *Zool.* Of or pertaining to an osculum. [< L *osculum.* See OSCULATE.]

os·cu·late (os′kyə·lāt) *v.t. & v.i.* **·lat·ed, ·lat·ing 1** To kiss. **2** To bring or come into close contact or union. **3** *Geom.* To touch so as to have three or more points in common, as two curves. **4** *Biol.* To have (characteristics) in common, as two genera or families. [< L *osculatus,* pp. of *osculari* kiss < *osculum* a little mouth, a kiss, dim. of *os* mouth]

os·cu·la·tion (os′kyə·lā′shən) *n.* **1** The act of kissing; also, a kiss. **2** *Math.* A point on a curve where two branches have a common tangent but do not reverse direction. —**os′cu·la·to′ry** (-lə·tôr′ē, -tō′rē) *adj.*

os·cu·lum (os′kyə·ləm) *n. pl.* **·la** (-lə) *Zool.* One of the comparatively large apertures in a sponge by which water with waste products is expelled. Also **os′cule** (-kyōōl). [< L, dim. of *os* a mouth]

ose (ōs) See OS[3].

-ose[1] *suffix of adjectives* **1** Full of or abounding in (what is indicated by the main element): *verbose.* **2** Like; resembling (the main element): *grandiose.* Compare -OUS. [< L *-osus*]

-ose[2] *suffix Chem.* **1** A carbohydrate: *glucose, cellulose.* **2** A derivative of a protein: *proteose.* [< (GLUC)OSE]

Ö·sel (œ′zəl) The Swedish name for the SAARE ISLANDS.

O-shaped (ō′shāpt′) *adj.* Having the round or oval shape of the letter O.

o·sier (ō′zhər) *n.* **1** Any various species of willow (genus *Salix*), producing long, flexible shoots used in wickerwork, especially the European **velvet osier** *(Salix viminalis).* **2** One of the shoots of an osier. **3** A similar plant of some other genus or family, or its osierlike shoots, as the squawbush. —*adj.* Consisting of twigs of willow, etc. [< OF, prob. < Med. L *ausaria, osaria* a bed of willows]

O·si·jek (ô′sē·yek) A city in NE Croatia, Yugoslavia.

os in·nom·i·na·tum (os i·nom′ə·nā′təm) *Anat.* The innominate bone. [< NL]

O·si·ris (o·sī′ris) In Egyptian mythology, the god of the underworld and lord of the dead, husband of his sister Isis.

-osis *suffix of nouns* **1** The condition, process, or state of: *metamorphosis.* **2** *Med.* **a** A diseased or abnormal condition of: *melanosis.* **b** A formation of: *sclerosis.* [< L < Gk. *-ōsis*]

-osity *suffix of nouns* Forming nouns corresponding to adjectives in *-ose*: *verbosity, grandiosity.* [< F *-osité* < L *-ositas;* or directly < L]

Os·ler (ōs′lər, ōz′-), **Sir William,** 1849–1919, Canadian physician.

Os·lo (os′lō, oz′-; *Norw.* ōōs′lōō) The capital of Norway, on **Oslo Fiord,** an arm of the Skagerrak extending 80 miles inland: formerly *Christiania.*

Os·man (oz′mən, os′-; *Turkish* os·män′), 1259–1326, founder of the Ottoman Empire. Also *Othman.*

Os·man·li (oz·man′lē, os-) *n.* **1** An Ottoman Turk; one of the western branch of the Turkish peoples. **2** The language of the Ottoman Turks; Turkish. [< Turkish *Osmānli* of Osman < *Osmān* Osman < Arabic *'Othmān*]

Os·me·ña (ōs·mā′nyä), **Sergio,** 1878–1961, president of the Philippines 1944–46.

os·mes·the·sia (os′məs·thē′zhə, -zhē·ə) *n. Physiol.* A high susceptibility to odors. [< NL < Gk. *osmē* scent + *aisthēsis* perception]

os·mic (oz′mik, os′-) *adj. Chem.* Of, pertaining to, or containing osmium, especially in its higher valence.

osmic acid anhydride A toxic yellowish, crystalline tetroxide of osmium, OsO_4, having a pungent odor, used as a selective biological stain and as a catalyst.

os·mi·dro·sis (os′mə·drō′sis, oz′-) *n. Pathol.* A condition in which the perspiration has an abnormally strong odor. [< Gk. *osmē* an odor + *drosos* dew, moisture]

os·mi·ous (oz′mē·əs, os′-) *adj. Chem.* Of, pertaining to, or containing osmium, especially in its lower valence.

os·mi·rid·i·um (os′mə·rid′ē·əm, oz′-) *n.* A varying isomorphous mixture of iridium and osmium, found native in flattened, metallic, tin-white, malleable grains, and used for pointing gold pens: also called *iridosmium.*

os·mi·um (oz′mē·əm, os′-) *n.* A hard, brittle, extremely dense metallic element (symbol Os, atomic number 76) often found associated with platinum. See PERIODIC TABLE. [< Gk. *osmē* odor, from the sharp odor of one of its oxides]

osmium tetroxide Osmic acid anhydride.

Os·mond (oz′mənd) A masculine personal name. Also **Os′mund.** [< Gmc., protection of God]

os·mo·pho·bi·a (os′mə·fō′bē·ə, oz′-) *n. Psychiatry* A morbid fear of odors. [< Gk. *osmē* an odor + -PHOBIA]

os·mose (oz′mōs, os′-) *v.t. & v.i.* **·mosed, ·mos·ing** To subject to or to undergo the process of osmosis. [< *osmose, n.,* var. of OSMOSIS]

os·mo·sis (oz·mō′sis, os-) *n.* **1** The diffusion of two miscible solutions through a semipermeable membrane in such a manner as to equalize their concentration: it is one of the essential processes of living matter, especially in its cellular forms: also called *diosmosis.* Also **os′mose.** Compare ENDOSMOSIS, EXOSMOSIS. **2** *Colloq.* A process resembling diffusion and marked especially by the absence of directed effort: Living in Paris, he learned French by *osmosis.* [Earlier *osmose* < *-osmose* (as in *endosmose, exosmose*) < Gk. *ōsmos* a thrust, push] —**os·mot·ic** (oz·mot′ik, os-) *adj.* —**os·mot′i·cal·ly** *adv.*

os·mund (os′mənd, oz′-) *n.* Any of a genus *(Osmunda)* of showy ferns having pinnate fronds growing upright from a large crown, especially the royal fern *(O. regalis).* [< AF *osmunde* < Med. L *osmunda;* ult. origin unknown]

Os·na·brück (oz′nə·brōōk, *Ger.* ôs′nä·brük) A city in Lower Saxony, West Germany.

os·na·burg (oz′nə·bûrg) *n.* A tough, unbleached cotton cloth, often part waste, used for upholstery, for grain and cement sacks, and as a material for camouflage. [from *Osnaburg,* var. of OSNABRÜCK]

os·phre·sis (os·frē′sis) *n. Physiol.* The sense of smell. Also **os·phre′sia** (-frē′zhə). [< NL < Gk. *osphrēsis* < *osphrainesthai* smell] —**os·phret′·ic** (-fret′ik) *adj.*

os·prey (os′prē) *n.* A fish-eating hawk *(Pandion haliaëtus),* brown above and white below, that preys upon fish. [Appar. < L *ossifraga* < *os, ossis* a bone + *frangere* break]

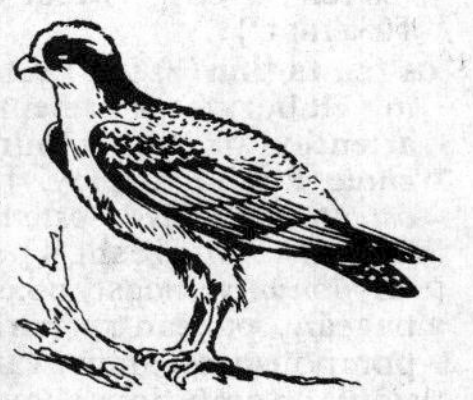

OSPREY
(From 22 to 24 inches in over-all length)

Os·sa (os′ə) A mountain in eastern Thessaly, Greece; 6,490 feet; in Greek mythology, the Titans attempted to scale Olympus by piling Pelion on Ossa.

os·sa·ture (os′ə·chər) *n. Anat.* The disposition and arrangement of the bones of the body. Compare MUSCULATURE. [< F, skeleton < L *os, ossis* a bone]

os·se·in (os′ē·in) *n. Biochem.* The soft protein substance of the bone that remains after the removal of mineral matter: also *ostein.* [< L *osse(us)* bony + -IN]

os·se·ous (os′ē·əs) *adj.* Pertaining to, of the nature of, or containing bones. [< L *osseus* bony < *os, ossis* a bone] —**os′se·ous·ly** *adv.*

Os·se·tia (o·sē′shə) A region in the central Caucasus mountains of the U.S.S.R., divided into the *North Ossetian S.S.R.* and the *South Ossetian Autonomous Region.*

Os·sian (osh′ən, os′ē·ən) A legendary Irish hero and bard of the third century, subject of a cycle of poems written by James MacPherson, published 1760–63, purporting to be translations from the original Ossian. —**Os·si·an·ic** (os′ē·an′ik) *adj.*

os·si·cle (os′i·kəl) *n. Anat.* **1** A small bone. **2** One of a chain of three small bones in the tympanic cavity of the ear. **3** One of various small, hard, nodular structures. [< L *ossiculum,* dim. of *os, ossis* a bone] —**os·sic·u·lar** (o·sik′yə·lər) *adj.*

os·sif·er·ous (o·sif′ər·əs) *adj.* Yielding or containing bones. [< L *os, ossis* bone + -FEROUS]

os·si·frage (os′ə·frij) *n.* **1** The osprey. **2** The

lammergeier. [< L *ossifraga.* See OSPREY.]

os·si·fy (os′ə·fī) *v.t. & v.i.* **·fied, ·fy·ing 1** To convert or be converted into bones. **2** To make or become set, conventional, etc. [< L *os, ossis* a bone + -FY] —**os·sif·ic** (o·sif′ik) *adj.* —**os′si·fi·ca′tion** *n.*

Os·si·ning (os′ə·ning) A village on the Hudson River in SE New York: formerly *Sing Sing.*

Os·so·li (ôs′sō·lē), **Marchioness** See FULLER, MARGARET.

os·su·ar·y (os′o͞o·er′ē, osh′-) *n. pl.* **·ar·ies** A place for holding the bones of the dead; charnel house; grave mound. [< LL *ossuarium* < L *ossuarius* of, for bones < *os, ossis* a bone]

Os·ta·de (ôs′tä·də), **Adriaen van,** 1610–85, Dutch painter.

os·te·al (os′tē·əl) *adj.* Of, pertaining to, or like bone; bony. [< Gk. *osteon* a bone]

os·te·in (os′tē·in) See OSSEIN.

os·te·i·tis (os′tē·ī′tis) *n. Pathol.* Inflammation of a bone. [< OSTE(O)- + -ITIS]

Os·tend (os′tend, os·tend′) A port of NW Belgium, on the North Sea. *French* **Os·tende** (ô·stäṅd′), *Flemish* **Oost·en·de** (ōst·en′də).

os·ten·si·ble (os·ten′sə·bəl) *adj.* Offered as real or having the character represented; seeming; professed or pretended. [< F < L *ostensus,* pp. of *ostendere* show < *ob-* against + *tendere* stretch] —**os·ten′si·bly** *adv.*

Synonyms : apparent, assigned, avowed, colorable, displayed, exhibited, expressed, plausible, professed, shown, specious. A man's *apparent* purpose or motive is what appears on the surface, with or without his own intent; his *ostensible* motive or purpose is that which is *assigned, avowed, displayed* by him; the word often implying that the *ostensible* may be only the pretended, a *specious* cover for a purpose or motive of a different sort. Compare synonyms for APPARENT. *Antonyms* : actual, genuine, real, true, veritable.

os·ten·sive (os·ten′siv) *adj.* Exhibiting; showing. —**os·ten′sive·ly** *adv.*

os·ten·so·ri·um (os′tən·sôr′ē·əm, -sō′rē-) *n. pl.* **·ri·a** (-rē·ə) A monstrance. Also **os·ten·so·ry** (os·ten′sər·ē). [< Med. L < L *ostensus.* See OSTENSIBLE.]

os·ten·ta·tion (os′tən·tā′shən) *n.* **1** The act of making elaborate or pretentious display to attract attention or elicit admiration or wonder. **2** *Archaic* Public display. [< OF *ostentacion* < L *ostentatio, -onis* < *ostentatus,* pp. of *ostentare,* freq. of *ostendere* show]

Synonyms : boast, boasting, display, flourish, pageant, pageantry, parade, pomp, pomposity, pompousness, show, vaunt, vaunting. *Ostentation* is an ambitious showing forth of whatever is thought adapted to win admiration or praise; *ostentation* may be without words; as, the *ostentation* of wealth in luxuriously equipped cars; when in words, *ostentation* is rather in manner than in direct statement; as, the *ostentation* of learning. *Boasting* is in direct statement, and is louder and more vulgar than *ostentation.* There may be great *display* or *show* with little substance; *ostentation* suggests something substantial to be shown. *Pomp* is some material demonstration of wealth and power, as in grand and stately ceremonial, etc., considered as worthy of the person or occasion in whose behalf it is manifested; *pomp* is the noble side of that which as *ostentation* is considered arrogant and vain. *Pageant* and *pageantry* are inferior to *pomp,* denoting spectacular *display* designed to impress the public mind. See PRIDE. *Antonyms:* diffidence, modesty, quietness, reserve, retirement, shrinking, timidity.

os·ten·ta·tious (os′tən·tā′shəs) *adj.* Elaborate or showy in order to attract attention; purposefully conspicuous. —**os′ten·ta′tious·ly** *adv.* **os′ten·ta′tious·ness** *n.*

osteo- *combining form* Bone; pertaining to bone or the bones: *osteoblast.* Also, before vowels, **oste-.** [< Gk. *osteon* a bone]

os·te·o·blast (os′tē·ə·blast′) *n.* A bone-forming cell.

os·te·oc·la·sis (os′tē·ok′lə·sis) *n.* **1** *Surg.* The operation of breaking a bone to correct a deformity or of rebreaking to remedy a bad setting. **2** The gradual absorption of bony tissue by osteoclasts. [< NL < Gk. *osteon* a bone + *klasis* a fracture < *klaein* break]

os·te·o·clast (os′tē·ə·klast′) *n.* **1** *Surg.* An instrument for effecting osteoclasis. **2** *Anat.* A large multinucleate cell found in the marrow of bones and concerned in the absorption of bony tissue during the formation of canals, cavities, etc. [< G *osteoklast* < Gk. *osteon* a bone + *klastos* broken < *klaein* break] —**os′te·o·clas′tic** *adj.*

os·te·oid (os′tē·oid) *adj.* Resembling bone; bony.

os·te·ol·o·gy (os′tē·ol′ə·jē) *n.* The science that treats of the bones of the skeleton and of the properties of osseous tissue. —**os′te·o·log′i·cal** (-ə·loj′i·kəl) *adj.* —**os′te·o·log′i·cal·ly** *adv.* —**os′te·ol′o·gist** *n.*

os·te·o·ma (os′tē·ō′mə) *n. pl.* **·ma·ta** (-mə·tə) *Pathol.* A tumor consisting of bony substance; a morbid outgrowth from bone or from cartilage. [< OSTE(O)- + -OMA]

os·te·o·ma·la·ci·a (os′tē·ō′mə·lā′shē·ə) *n. Pathol.* Softening of the bones, with progressive osseous deformity and exhaustion: caused by calcium deficiency. [< NL < Gk. *osteon* a bone + *malakia* softness]

os·te·o·my·e·li·tis (os′tē·ō·mī′ə·lī′tis) *n. Pathol.* Inflammation of the bone marrow. [< OSTEO- + MYEL(O)- + -ITIS]

os·te·op·a·thy (os′tē·op′ə·thē) *n.* A system of healing based on a theory that most diseases are caused by structural abnormalities of the body that may best be corrected by manipulation of the affected parts. [< OSTEO- + -PATHY] —**os′te·o·path′, os′te·op′a·thist** *n.* —**os′te·o·path′ic** (-ə·path′ik) *adj.*

os·te·o·phyte (os′tē·ə·fīt′) *n. Pathol.* A bony excrescence. —**os′te·o·phyt′ic** (-fit′ik) *adj.*

os·te·o·plas·ty (os′tē·ə·plas′tē) *n. Surg.* **1** An operation to remedy loss of bone. **2** The restoration to its place of a bone temporarily removed. —**os′te·o·plas′tic** *adj.*

os·te·o·po·ro·sis (os′tē·ō·pə·rō′sis) *n. Pathol.* A disease marked by loss of calcium from the bones, causing them to weaken.

os·te·o·scle·ro·sis (os′tē·ō·sklə·rō′sis) *n. Pathol.* A morbid condition marked by a hardening and increased density of bone. —**os′te·o·scle·rot′ic** (-sklə·rot′ik) *adj.*

os·te·o·sis (os′tē·ō′sis) *n. Pathol.* The abnormal formation of bony tissue. [< OSTE(O)- + -OSIS]

os·te·o·tome (os′tē·ə·tōm′) *n. Surg.* An instrument for dividing or cutting bone.

os·te·ot·o·my (os′tē·ot′ə·mē) *n. Surg.* The operation of dividing a bone, especially beneath the integuments, as to remedy deformity. —**os′te·ot′o·mist** *n.*

Ös·ter·reich (œs′tə·rīkh) The German name for AUSTRIA.

Os·ti·a (os′tē·ə, *Ital.* ô′styä) An ancient city and port of Rome at the mouth of the river Tiber.

os·ti·ar·y (os′tē·er′ē) *n. pl.* **·ar·ies 1** In the Roman Catholic Church, a cleric belonging to the lowest of the minor orders. **2** A doorkeeper. Also **os′ti·ar′i·us** (-âr′ē·əs). [< L *ostiarius* doorkeeper < *ostium* a door]

os·ti·na·to (ôs′tē·nä′tō) *n. Music* A melodic phrase persistently reiterated in the same voice and pitch. [< Ital. *(basso) ostinato,* lit., obstinate (bass)]

os·ti·ole (os′tē·ōl) *n.* **1** A small opening. **2** *Zool.* Any one of the small inhalant orifices of a sponge. [< L *ostiolum,* dim. of *ostium* a door] —**os′ti·o′lar** *adj.*

os·tler (os′lər) See HOSTLER.

ost·mark (ôst′märk′) See MARK[2] (def. 1).

os·to·my (os′tə·mē) *n. pl.* **·mies** A surgical operation, as a colostomy or an ileostomy, which involves the creation of an artificial opening in the abdominal wall for the discharge of waste matter. [See -STOMY]

os·to·sis (os·tō′sis) *n.* Ossification.

Ost·preus·sen (ôst′proi′sən) The German name for EAST PRUSSIA.

os·tra·cism (os′trə·siz′əm) *n.* **1** Exclusion, as from society or common privileges, by general consent. **2** In ancient Greece, banishment by popular vote. [< Gk. *ostrakismos* < *ostrakizein* OSTRACIZE]

os·tra·cize (os′trə·sīz) *v.t.* **·cized, ·ciz·ing 1** To shut out or exclude by ostracism. **2** In ancient Greece, to exile by ostracism. Also *Brit.* **os′tra·cise.** See synonyms under BANISH. [< Gk. *ostrakizein* < *ostrakon* a potsherd, shell, voting tablet]

Os·tra·va (ôs′trä·vä) See MORAVSKÁ OSTRAVA.

os·tre·o·dy·na·mom·e·ter (os′trē·ō·dī′nə·mom′ə·tər) *n.* An instrument for detecting the movements of an oyster in its shell without disturbing its normal activities: used especially in relation to water pollution. [< Gk. *ostreon* an oyster + DYNAMOMETER]

os·trich (ôs′trich, os′-) *n.* **1** A large, two-toed bird (genus *Struthio*) of Africa and Arabia, with aborted wings. Its long, powerful legs give it great speed. The plumage of the male is black, with white plumes at the ends of the wings and tail, much esteemed for ornamental purposes. **2** A rhea. [< OF *obstruce, ostruche* < LL *avistruthius* < L *avis* a bird + LL *struthio* an ostrich < Gk. *strouthiōn* < *strouthos* a sparrow, an ostrich]

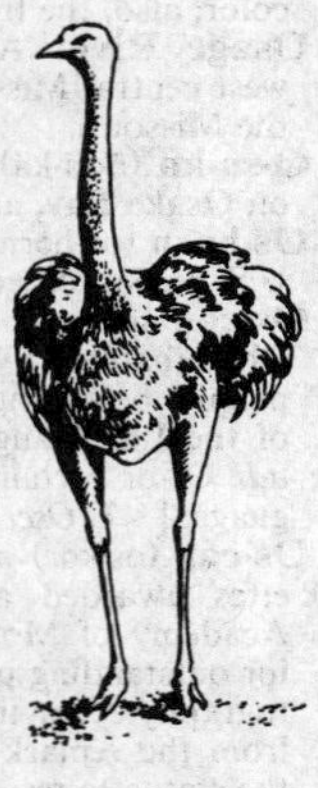

OSTRICH (The adult male about 8 feet tall)

Os·tro·goth (os′trə·goth) *n.* A member of the eastern branch of the Goths, who established a kingdom in Italy from 493 to 555. See VISIGOTH. [< LL *Ostrogothus* < *ostro-* eastward (prob. < OHG *oster*) + *Gothus* a Goth] —**Os′tro·goth′ic** *adj.*

Ost·wald (ôst′vält), **Wilhelm,** 1853–1932, German chemist.

Os·ty·ak (os′tē·ak) *n.* **1** One of a Finno-Ugric people inhabiting western Siberia and the Ural Mountains. **2** The Ugric language of these people. Also **Os′ti·ak.**

Os·we·go (os·wē′gō) A port of entry on Lake Ontario in central New York.

Oswego tea *n.* A species of mint *(Monarda didyma)* with a showy head of bright-red flowers, growing in wet places in the eastern, United States: also called *bee balm.*

Oś·wie·cim (ôsh·vyaṅ′chim) See AUSCHWITZ.

ot- Var. of OTO-.

O·ta·hei·te (ō′tə·hē′tē, -hā′-) A former name for TAHITI.

o·tal·gi·a (ō·tal′jē·ə) *n. Pathol.* Neuralgia of the ear; earache. Also **o·tal′gy.** [< NL < Gk. *ōtalgia* < *ous, ōtos* an ear + *algos* a pain] —**o·tal′gic** *adj.*

O·ta·ru (ō·tä·ro͞o) A port on SW Hokkaido island, Japan.

o·ta·ry (ō′tər·ē) *n. pl.* **·ries** or **·ry** An eared seal. [< NL *Otaria,* genus name < Gk. *ōtaros* large-eared < *ous, ōtos* an ear] —**o·tar·i·an** (ō·târ′ē·ən) *adj.*

O tem·po·ra! O mo·res! (ō tem′pər·ə ō môr′ēz, mō′rēz) *Latin* O the times! O the manners!

O·thel·lo (ō·thel′ō, ə-) In Shakespeare's tragedy of the same name, a Moor of Venice who smothers his wife, Desdemona, in a jealous rage inspired by the treachery of Iago, and who later kills himself after learning of her innocence.

oth·er (uth′ər) *adj.* **1** Different from the one specified; not the same. **2** Being over and above; additional. **3** Second: noting the remaining one of two persons or things. **4** Opposite; contrary: the *other* side. **5** Alternate: every *other* day. —**the other day (night,** etc.**)** A day (night, etc.) not long ago; recently. —*pron.* **1** A different person or thing. **2** The second of two; the opposite one. —*adv.* Otherwise: with *than.* [OE *ōther*] —**oth′er·ness** *n.*

oth·er·guess (uth′ər·ges′) *Obs. adj.* Of another sort; other. —*adv.* In a different manner.

oth·er·where (uth′ər·hwâr′) *adv. Archaic* or *Dial.* In some other place; elsewhere.

oth·er·while (uth′ər·hwīl′) *adv. Archaic* At another time. Also **oth′er·whiles′.**

oth·er·wise (uth′ər·wīz′) *adv.* **1** In a different manner or by other means. **2** In other circumstances or conditions. **3** In all other respects: an *otherwise* sensible writer. —*adj.* Different: How could such notions be *otherwise* than useless?

other world The unseen world; the life after death; the future state.

oth·er·world·ly (uth′ər·wûrld′lē) *adj.* **1** Of or characteristic of an ideal world, especially heaven. **2** Concerned with the hereafter to the neglect of the present. —**oth′er·world′li·ness** *n.*

O·thin (ō′thin) See ODIN.

Oth·man (oth′mən, *Arabic* o͞oth·män′) See OSMAN.

O·tho (ō′thō, *Du., Ger., Sw.* ō′tō) Dutch, Swedish, and German form of OTTO.

o·tic (ō'tik, ot'ik) *adj.* Pertaining to or situated near the ear. [<Gk. *ōtikos* < *ous, ōtos* ear]

-otic *suffix of adjectives* **1** *Med.* Of, related to, or affected by: corresponding to nouns in *-osis: psychotic, sclerotic.* **2** Causing or producing: *narcotic.* [<Gk. *-ōtikos,* suffix of adjectives]

o·ti·ose (ō'shē·ōs, -tē-) *adj.* **1** Being at rest or ease; having nothing to do. **2** Characterized by indolence or easy negligence. **3** Futile; useless. [<L *otiosus* < *otium* leisure] — **o'ti·ose'ly** *adv.* — **o'ti·os'i·ty** (-os'ə·tē) *n.*

O·tis (ō'tis), **James,** 1725–83, American patriot and orator.

o·ti·tis (ō·tī'tis) *n. Pathol.* Inflammation of the mucous membrane of the ear. [<OT(O)- + -ITIS]

oto- *combining form* Ear; pertaining to the ear: *otoscope.* Also, before vowels, *ot-.* [<Gk. *ous, ōtos* the ear]

o·to·co·ni·a (ō'tə·kō'nē·ə) *n. Anat.* A dustlike substance consisting of minute crystalline otoliths forming part of the contents of the statocyst: also called *ear dust.* [<NL <F *otoconic* <Gk. *ous, ōtos* an ear + *konis* sand, dust]

o·to·cyst (ō'tə·sist) *n. Anat.* **1** An auditory vesicle, as in many invertebrates. **2** The similar vesicle contained in the embryo of a vertebrate.

O·toe (ō'tō) *n.* One of a Siouan tribe of North American Indians living in southeastern Nebraska.

o·to·lar·yn·gol·o·gy (ō'tō·lar'ing·gol'ə·jē) *n.* The branch of medicine which treats of the ear and throat. — **o'to·lar'yn·gol'o·gist** *n.*

o·to·lith (ō'tə·lith) *n. Anat.* **1** One of the concretions of calcium carbonate and calcium phosphate found in the internal ear of vertebrates and in the auditory organ of many invertebrates. **2** An ear bone. [<OTO- + -LITH]

o·tol·o·gy (ō·tol'ə·jē) *n.* The science of the ear and its diseases. — **o·to·log·i·cal** (ō'tə·loj'i·kəl) *adj.* — **o·tol'o·gist** *n.*

O·to·nio (ô·tô'nyō) Spanish form of OTTO.

o·to·rhi·no·lar·yn·gol·o·gy (ō'tō·rī'nō·lar'ing·gol'ə·jē) *n.* The branch of medicine dealing with the ear, nose, and larynx in health and disease. [<OTO- + RHINO- + LARYNGO- + -LOGY] — **o'to·rhi'no·lar'yn·gol'o·gist** *n.*

o·to·scope (ō'tə·skōp) *n. Med.* An instrument for viewing or examining the interior of the ear; especially, an ear speculum.

O·tran·to (ō·trän'tō) A port of SE Italy on the **Strait of Otranto,** a strait between the Adriatic and Ionian seas (43 miles wide).

ot·tar (ot'ər) See ATTAR.

ot·ta·va (ōt·tä'vä) *n. Ital.* An octave.

ottava ri·ma (rē'mä) In English prosody, a stanza of eight-, ten-, or eleven-syllable iambic lines with the rime scheme *ababbcc:* used by Byron in *Don Juan.* [<Ital., octave rime]

Ot·ta·via (ōt·tä'vyä) Italian form of OCTAVIA.

Ot·ta·vio (ōt·tä'vyō) Italian form of OCTAVIUS. Also **Ot·ta·via·no** (ōt'tä·vyä'nō).

Ot·ta·wa (ot'ə·wə) *n.* One of a tribe of North American Indians of Algonquian stock, originally inhabiting the region around Georgian Bay, Lake Huron, Ontario, later migrating to the region around Lake Superior and Lake Michigan. [<dial. F *otaua, otawa* <Algonquian (Cree) *ataweu* a trader]

Ot·ta·wa (ot'ə·wə) The capital of Canada in SE Ontario on the **Ottawa River,** which flows 696 miles SE through Ontario and Quebec to the St. Lawrence.

ot·ter (ot'ər) *n.* **1** A weasel-like, web-footed carnivore (genus *Lutra*) inhabiting streams and lakes, and feeding upon fish. The common otter (*L. canadensis*) is about two feet long, exclusive of the flattened, oarlike tail, and furnishes a valuable, dark-brown fur. **2** The sea otter. [OE *oter.* Akin to WATER.]

OTTER

Ot·ter·burn (ot'ər·bûrn) A village in Northumberland, England; scene of a Scots defeat of the English, 1388. See CHEVY CHASE.

otter hound A breed of hound used in England for hunting otters: strongly built, with a close black-and tan coat, a large broad head, and floppy ears.

otter shrew An insectivorous, aquatic animal (family *Potamogalidae*) of central and western Africa.

Ot·to (ot'ō; *Dan., Du.* ot'ō; *Ger.* ôt'ō; *Sw.* ô'tōō) A masculine personal name. Also *Ital.* **Ot·to·ne** (ōt·tō'nā). [<Gmc., rich]
— **Otto I,** 912–973, king of Germany 936–973; Holy Roman Emperor 962–973. Called "Otto the Great."

ot·to·man (ot'ə·mən) *n.* **1** An upholstered, backless and armless seat or sofa. **2** An upholstered footrest. **3** A heavy corded silk or rayon fabric used for coats and trimmings. [<F *ottomane,* orig. fem. of *Ottoman* OTTOMAN]

Ot·to·man (ot'ə·mən) *n. pl.* **·mans** A Turk. — *adj.* Pertaining to the Turks. [<F <Ital. *Ottomano* <Med. L *Ottomanus* <Arabic *'Uthmāni, 'Othmāni* of Osman <*'Othmān* Osman]

Ottoman Empire A former empire (1300–1919) of the Turks in Asia Minor, NE Africa, and SE Europe; capital, Constantinople: also *Turkish Empire.*

OTTOMAN EMPIRE 1683-1913

Ot·way (ot'wā), **Thomas,** 1652–85, English dramatist.

oua·ba·in (wä·bä'in) *n. Chem.* A white, lustrous, extremely poisonous, crystalline glycoside, $C_{29}H_{44}O_{12}$, derived from two South African trees (*Strophanthus glaber* and *Acokanthera ouabaio*): used in medicine as a cardiac stimulant. It is a constituent of Zulu arrow poison. [<F *ouabaio,* a South African tree (<Somali native name) + -IN]

Ouach·i·ta River (wosh'ə·tô, wôsh'-) A river in SW Arkansas and NE Louisiana, flowing 605 miles SE to the Red River: also *Washita.*

Oua·daï (wä·dī') The French name for WADAI.

Oua·ga·dou·gou (wä'gä·dōō'gōō) The capital of the Republic of the Upper Volta.

oua·na·niche (wä'nə·nēsh', *Fr.* wä·nä·nēsh') *n.* A small Canadian salmon (*Salmo salar ouananiche*), identified with the Atlantic salmon of Maine. [<dial. F (Canadian) <Algonquian (Cree) *wananish*]

ou·bli·ette (ōō'blē·et') *n.* A secret dungeon with an entrance only through the top. [<OF <*oublier* forget]

ouch¹ (ouch) *interj.* An exclamation indicating sudden pain.

ouch² (ouch) *n.* **1** The setting of a jewel. **2** An ornament, as a clasp or brooch, of gold. — *v.t.* To ornament with or as with ouches. [<AF *nouche* <LL *nusca* <OHG *nuscka, nuscha* a buckle, clasp, appar. ult. <Celtic; in ME *a nouche* became *an ouche*]

Ou·de·naar·de (ou'də·när'də) A town on the Scheldt in eastern Flanders, Belgium; scene of an English victory over the French, 1708. *French* **Aude·narde** (ōd·närd').

Oude Rijn (oud rīn) See RHINE.

Oudh (oud) An historic region of east central Uttar Pradesh, northern India; 24,071 square miles.

Ou·di·not (ōō·dē·nō'), **Nicolas,** 1767–1847, Duc de Reggio, French general and marshal of France.

Oues·sant (dwe·sän', Île d' The French name for USHANT.

ought¹ (ôt) *v.* A defective verb now used only as an auxiliary followed by the infinitive with *to,* or elliptically with the infinitive understood, to express: **1** Obligation or moral duty: *He ought to keep his promises.* **2** Advisability or expedience: *You ought to be careful.* **3** Probability or expectation: *He ought to be here tomorrow.* ◆ A past is formed by placing the following verb in the perfect infinitive, as in *He ought to have been there.* ◆ Homophone: *aught.* [OE *āhte,* past tense of *āgan* owe, possess]

Synonym: should. Ought is the stronger word, holding most closely to the sense of moral obligation, or sometimes of imperative logical necessity; should may have the sense of moral obligation or may apply merely to propriety or expediency, as in the proverb, "The liar should have a good memory"; that is, he will need it. Ought is sometimes used as indicating what the mind deems to be logical in view of all the conditions; as, These goods ought to go into that space; should in such connections would be correct, but less emphatic. Compare DUTY.

ought² (ôt) *n.* Aught; anything. [Var. of AUGHT]

oui (wē) *interj. French* Yes.

Oui·da (wē'də) Pen name of *Louise de la Ramée,* 1839–1908, English novelist.

Oui·ja (wē'jə) *n.* A device consisting of a board inscribed with the alphabet and other characters and a planchette, the pointer of which is thought to spell out mediumistic communications: a trade name. Also **oui'ja.**

oui·sti·ti (wis'ti·tē) *n.* The common marmoset (genus *Callithrix* or *Hapale*) of South America, with tufted ears and a long, banded tail. [<F; name coined by Buffon, imit. of the animal's cry]

ounce¹ (ouns) *n.* **1** A unit of weight; one sixteenth of a pound avoirdupois, or 28.349 grams; one twelfth of a pound troy, or 31.1 grams. Abbr. *oz.* **2** A fluid ounce. **3** A small quantity. — **fluid ounce** **1** *U.S.* One sixteenth of a pint; 29.5737 cubic centimeters; 480 minims. **2** *Brit.* 28.413 cubic centimeters; 480 minims. [<OF *unce* <L *uncia* twelfth part (of a pound or foot), orig. a unit. Doublet of INCH.]

ounce² (ouns) *n.* **1** A feline carnivorous mammal (*Panthera uncia*) of central Asia, about the size of a leopard, having long fur and a long, thick tail; the snow leopard. **2** Some similar American cat, as the jaguar. [<OF *l'once,* var. of *lonce* the lynx <L *lyncea* < *lynx, lyncis* LYNX]

ounce metal An alloy of copper with five percent each of tin, zinc, and lead: formerly made by adding one ounce of each minor metal to one pound of copper.

ouphe (ōōf) *n. Archaic* A goblin or elf. [Var. of OAF]

our (our) *pronominal adj.* Belonging or pertaining to us: the possessive case of the pronoun *we* employed attributively. [OE *ūre,* earlier *ūser,* genitive of US]

–our See -OR.

ou·rang (ōō·rang') *n.* The orang-utan. [Var. of ORANG]

ou·ra·nog·ra·phy (ōōr'ə·nog'rə·fē) See URANOGRAPHY.

Ou·ra·nos (ōōr'ə·nos) See URANUS (def. 1).

ou·ra·ri (ōō·rä'rē) *n.* Curare. [Var. of WOORALI <Tupian]

Ourcq (ōōrk) A river in northern France, flowing 50 miles SW to the Marne; scene of a battle of World War I, 1918.

ou·re·bi (ōō'rə·bē) See ORIBI.

Our Lady The Virgin Mary.

Our Lord Jesus Christ.

ouro- See URO-.

ours (ourz) *pron.* **1** Belonging or pertaining to us: *That dog is ours:* the possessive case of *we* used predicatively. **2** The things or persons belonging or pertaining to us: *their country and ours.* — **of ours** Belonging or relating to us; our: the double possessive. [ME *ures* < *ure* OUR]

our·self (our·self') *pron.* Myself: only in formal or regal style.

our·selves (our·selvz') *pron. pl.* We or us.

-ous *suffix of adjectives* **1** Full of; having: *studious, glorious.* **2** *Chem.* Having a lower valence than that indicated by the suffix *-ic: nitrous.* [<OF <L *-osus*]

Ouse (ōōz) **1** A river in North Riding, Yorkshire, England, flowing 61 miles SE to the Humber. **2** A river in Northamptonshire and Lincolnshire, England, flowing 156 miles NE to the Wash: also **Greater Ouse.**

ou·sel (ōō′zəl) See OUZEL.

oust (oust) *v.t.* To force from possession or occupancy; turn out; eject. See BANISH. [<AF *ouster* take away, ? <L *obstare* obstruct < *ob-* against + *stare* stand]

oust·er (ous′tər) *n. Law* The act of putting one out of possession or occupancy; dispossession.

out (out) *adv.* **1** Away from the inside or center: to go *out*; to branch *out*. **2** Away from a specified or usual place: to set *out* from Paris. **3** From a receptacle or source: to pour *out* wine. **4** So as to free of undesired parts or refuse: to thresh *out* grain; to sweep *out* a room. **5** From among others: to pick *out* a dress. **6** Into the charge or care of another or others: to hire *out* laborers; to deal *out* cards. **7** So as to project or be extended: to stretch *out*. **8** Into extinction or inactivity: The flame went *out*; The excitement died *out*. **9** To a result or conclusion: to fight it *out*; to find *out*. **10** Completely; fully: tired *out*. **11** Into existence or outward manifestation: An epidemic broke *out*; The sun came *out*. **12** Into blossom or leaf. **13** Into public notice or circulation: to bring *out* a new edition. **14** Aloud: to call *out*. **15** On strike. **16** Into disagreement; at odds: to be put *out* over trifles. **17** *Colloq.* Into unconsciousness: to pass *out*. **18** In baseball, cricket, etc., so as to be retired from active or leading play: to strike *out*. — *adj.* **1** External; exterior; outer. **2** Away from one's home, place of work, or other place regarded as a base: to be *out* on maneuvers. **3** Away at a distance: to be *out* in California. **4** Exposed or bare, as by rents in the clothing: *out* at the knees. **5** Visible; manifest: The stars are *out*. **6** Made public; disclosed: The truth is *out*. **7** In blossom or leaf. **8** Removed; displaced: The stain is *out*. **9** Mistaken; in error: *out* in one's calculations. **10** Extinguished; exhausted: The fire is *out*. **11** Finished; at an end: before the week is *out*. **12** At odds; in disagreement. **13** At a financial loss; in default: to be *out* five dollars. **14** Not in effective operation: The machine is *out*. **15** *Colloq.* Unconscious: He's *out*. **16** In baseball, cricket, etc., no longer in active or leading play. — *prep.* **1** From within; forth from: *out* the door. **2** Outside; on the outside of: the view *out* this window. — *n.* **1** Something that is out. **2** An escape; a way to dodge responsibility or involvement: He had an *out*. **3** A person not in office or position of power; specifically, in the plural, the party not in power. **4** In baseball, retirement of a batter or base runner. **5** In tennis, a return of the ball, which, untouched by the opponent, falls outside the court. **6** *Printing* Matter in the copy omitted from the composed type. — *v.t.* To drive out; expel. — *v.i.* To come or go out; be revealed: Murder will *out*. — *interj.* Go out! away! begone! [OE *ūt*]

out- *combining form* **1** Living or situated outside; external; away from the center; detached: *outlying, outpatient*. **2** Going forth; issuing; outward: *outbound, outstretch*. **3** Used to denote the time, place, or result of the action expressed by the root verb: *outcome, outcry*. **4** Excessive; surpassing; more; beyond. Dissyllabic nouns with this prefix are pronounced with an almost even stress on each syllable, the first slightly more emphatic. In dissyllabic verbs the stress is usually strongly upon the second element; but when their participles are used as adjectives or nouns, the stress becomes even or, for emphasis, shifts to the first syllable.

Out- is widely used in sense 4 to form compounds, as in the following list:

outact	**outbeg**	**outbluster**
outambush	**outbeggar**	**outboast**
outargue	**outbellow**	**outbrag**
outbabble	**outblaze**	**outbrazen**
outbake	**outbleat**	**outbribe**
outbalance	**outbless**	**outbuild**
outbanter	**outbloom**	**outbully**
outbargain	**outblossom**	**outburn**
outbark	**outbluff**	**outcaper**
outbawl	**outblunder**	**outcavil**
outbeam	**outblush**	**outcharm**

outchatter	**outmatch**	**outsprint**
outcheat	**outpaint**	**outstare**
outchide	**outpass**	**outstate**
outclimb	**outperform**	**outstay**
outcomplete	**outpity**	**outstrain**
outcompliment	**outplan**	**outstride**
outcrawl	**outplod**	**outstrive**
outcrow	**outpoison**	**outstudy**
outcurse	**outpopulate**	**outstunt**
outdance	**outpractice**	**outsuffer**
outdare	**outpraise**	**outsulk**
outdazzle	**outpray**	**outswagger**
outdodge	**outpreach**	**outswear**
outdrink	**outpreen**	**outswindle**
outeat	**outprice**	**outtalk**
outecho	**outproduce**	**outtask**
outfable	**outpromise**	**outthieve**
outfast	**outpush**	**outthreaten**
outfawn	**outqueen**	**outthrob**
outfeast	**outquestion**	**outthwack**
outfight	**outquibble**	**outtower**
outflatter	**outquote**	**outtrade**
outfool	**outrace**	**outtravel**
outfrown	**outrank**	**outtrick**
outgabble	**outrave**	**outtrot**
outgain	**outreason**	**outtrump**
outgallop	**outredden**	**outtyrannize**
outgamble	**outring**	**outvalue**
outglare	**outrival**	**outvaunt**
outglitter	**outroar**	**outvenom**
outglow	**outrun**	**outvociferate**
outgnaw	**outsail**	**outvoice**
outgrin	**outsatisfy**	**outvote**
outguess	**outsavor**	**outwait**
outhasten	**outscold**	**outwalk**
outhowl	**outscorn**	**outwallop**
outhumor	**outscream**	**outwar**
outhyperbolize	**outshame**	**outwarble**
outinvent	**outshout**	**outwaste**
outjazz	**outshriek**	**outwatch**
outjinx	**outsin**	**outweary**
outjockey	**outsing**	**outweep**
outjourney	**outsit**	**outwhirl**
outleap	**outskirmish**	**outwile**
outlighten	**outslander**	**outwill**
outlinger	**outsleep**	**outwish**
outlove	**outsmile**	**outwrangle**
outluster	**outsnore**	**outwrestle**
out-maneuver	**outsoar**	**outwriggle**
outmarch	**outsophisticate**	**outyelp**
outmaster	**outsparkle**	**outyield**

out-and-out (out′ənd·out′) *adj.* Thoroughgoing; unqualified; genuine. — *adv.* Unqualifiedly; genuinely.

out·back (out′bak′) *n. Austral.* Unsettled inland country; the bush.

out·bid (out·bid′) *v.t.* **·bid, ·bid·den** or **·bid, ·bid·ding** To bid more than; offer a higher price than.

out·board (out′bôrd′, -bōrd′) *Naut. adj.* Situated on the outside of a vessel, as a motor for temporary attachment to the stern of a small boat. — *adv.* Away from the center.

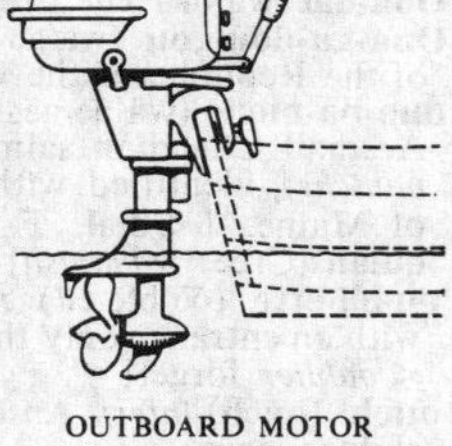

OUTBOARD MOTOR
Showing method of attachment.

out·bound (out′bound′) *adj.* Outward bound.

out·brave (out·brāv′) *v.t.* **·braved, ·brav·ing 1** To surpass in bravery. **2** To stand in defiance of. **3** To excel or surpass in splendor.

out·break (out′brāk′) *n.* A sudden and violent breaking forth: said of passion or of disease affecting large numbers of people at once. See synonyms under TUMULT. — *v.i.* (out′·brāk′) **·broke, ·brok·en, ·break·ing** To burst out; break forth.

out·breed (out′brēd′) *v.t.* **·bred, ·breed·ing** *Biol.* To breed or mate (individuals) belonging to stocks or families not closely related: opposed to *inbreed*. — **out′breed′ing** *n.*

out·build·ing (out′bil′ding) *n.* A smaller building appurtenant to a main building and generally separate from it; specifically, a chicken house, woodshed, smokehouse, etc.

out·burst (out′bûrst′) *n.* A bursting out; a violent manifestation, especially of passion.

out·cast (out′kast′, -käst′) *n.* **1** One who is cast out from home or country; one rejected and despised. **2** *Scot.* A quarrel; disagreement. — *adj.* Rejected as unworthy or useless; cast out; forlorn.

out·caste (out′kast′, -käst′) *n.* In India, a person who has forfeited his caste; a pariah.

out·class (out·klas′, -kläs′) *v.t.* To exceed decisively in skill, quality, or powers.

out·come (out′kum′) *n.* The consequence or visible result. See synonyms under CONSEQUENCE, END, EVENT, PRODUCT.

out·crop (out′krop′) *n. Geol.* **1** The exposure at or above the surface of the ground of any stratum, vein, etc. **2** The rock so exposed. — *v.i.* (out·krop′) **·cropped, ·crop·ping 1** To crop up or out. **2** To appear above the ground, as rocks.

out·cross (out·krôs′, -kros′) *Biol. v.t.* To mate (individuals) of the same breed but of different strains. — *n.* The act of so mating, or its result. — **out′cross′ing** *n.*

out·cry (out′krī′) *n. pl.* **·cries 1** A vehement or loud cry, as of distress, alarm, or opposition. **2** A public auction. See synonyms under NOISE. — *v.t.* (out·krī′) **·cried, ·cry·ing** To surpass in noise or crying; cry down.

out·curve (out′kûrv′) *n.* **1** In baseball, a pitched ball that curves away from the batter: opposed to *incurve*. **2** A small projection in a coastline.

out·date (out·dāt′) *v.t.* **·dat·ed, ·dat·ing** To make obsolete or out of date.

out·dat·ed (out·dā′tid) *adj.* Made obsolete; antiquated; old-fashioned.

out·dis·tance (out·dis′təns) *v.t.* **·tanced, ·tanc·ing 1** To outrun; outstrip. **2** To surpass completely; outdo.

out·do (out·dōō′) *v.t.* **·did, ·done, ·do·ing** To exceed in performance; surpass; excel. See synonyms under SURPASS. — **out·do′er** *n.*

out·done (out·dun′) *adj. U.S. Colloq.* Tired; exasperated; also, puzzled.

out·door (out′dôr′, -dōr′) *adj.* Being or done in the open air; belonging or occurring outside the house: *outdoor* sports. Also *out-of-door*.

out·doors (out·dôrz′, -dōrz′) *adv.* Outside of the doors; out of the house; in the open air. — *n.* The world beyond the house; the open air. Also *out-of-doors*. — **all outdoors** *Colloq.* The whole world.

out·en (out′n) *prep. Dial.* Out of.

out·er (ou′tər) *adj.* **1** Being on the exterior side; external. **2** Farther from a center or from something regarded as the inside. — *n.* **1** In rifle practice, the part of a target outside the rings. **2** A shot that strikes this part. Compare INNER. — **out′er·most′** *adj.* & *adv.*

Outer Hebrides See HEBRIDES.

Outer Mongolia See MONGOLIA.

outer space The space beyond the extreme limits of the earth's atmosphere; interplanetary and interstellar space.

out·face (out·fās′) *v.t.* **·faced, ·fac·ing 1** To face or stare down. **2** To defy or confront fearlessly or impudently.

out·fall (out′fôl′) *n.* **1** The place where a river, culvert, or conduit discharges; mouth. **2** The discharged matter.

out·field (out′fēld′) *n.* **1** In baseball, cricket, etc., the players who take their positions in the outer part of the field, or the field occupied by them; specifically, in baseball, right, left, and center field, or all the field beyond the bases. **2** *Scot.* Arable land continually cropped without being manured. **3** A field not situated near a house. **4** A bordering region or domain. — **out′field′er** *n.*

out·fit (out′fit′) *n.* **1** A fitting out or equipment. **2** The expenses occasioned by and incidental to a journey. **3** All the garments and incidentals of a person's costume. **4** The tools or equipment for any particular occupation, calling, or trade; a kit: a painter's *outfit*. **5** Mental acquirements suitable to any intellectual purpose. **6** Any expedition or party, with its proper equipment; hence, any industry, or any group of persons unified in a common undertaking; specifically, the cowboys, horses, wagons, etc., working on a certain ranch. — *v.t.* & *v.i.* **·fit·ted, ·fit·ting** To provide with or acquire an outfit. — **out′fit′ter** *n.*

out·flank (out·flangk′) *v.t.* To get around and in back of the flank of (an opposing force or army); turn the flank of; flank.

out·flow (out′flō′) *n.* **1** That which flows out, or the process of flowing out. **2** An outlet.

out·foot (out·fōōt′) *v.t.* **1** To exceed or surpass, as in running or dancing. **2** *Naut.* To sail faster than; outsail.

out·fox (out·foks′) v.t. U. S. Colloq. To outwit.

out·gen·er·al (out·jen′ər·əl) v.t. **·aled** or **·alled**, **·al·ing** or **·al·ling** To surpass in generalship; out-maneuver.

out·go (out·gō′) v.t. **·went**, **·gone**, **·go·ing** To go farther than; exceed or outstrip. — n. (out′·gō′) pl. **·goes** 1 That which goes out; cost or outlay: opposed to income. 2 An outgoing. 3 An exit. See synonyms under EXPENSE. — **out′go′er** n.

out·go·ing (out′gō′ing) adj. 1 Going out; leaving. 2 Friendly; sympathetic. — n. 1 The act of going out; departure. 2 That which goes out. 3 Usually pl. An expenditure; outlay.

out–group (out′grōop′) n. Sociol. Persons not included in an in–group.

out·grow (out·grō′) v.t. **·grew**, **·grown**, **·grow·ing** 1 To surpass in growth. 2 To grow too large for. 3 To lose or get rid of in the course of time or growth: to outgrow a habit.

out·growth (out′grōth′) n. That which grows out of something else; an excrescence. See synonyms under CONSEQUENCE.

out·guard (out′gärd′) n. An outlying guard or post; an advanced picket.

out·gush (out′gush′) n. A gushing out.

out·haul (out′hôl′) n. Naut. A rope for extending a sail along a spar.

out–Her·od (out·her′əd) v.t. 1 To outdo (Herod as depicted in the old mystery plays): usually, to **out–Herod Herod**. 2 To surpass (anyone) in cruelty or excess.

out·house (out′hous′) n. An outbuilding; specifically, a privy.

out·ing (ou′ting) n. 1 The act of going out; a holiday excursion; short pleasure trip; airing. 2 The distance out at sea: the farthest outing. — adj. Of, pertaining to, or suitable for an outing, as various garments and fabrics.

outing flannel A soft, lightweight cotton fabric, usually napped on both sides: used chiefly for sleeping garments.

out·land (out′land′) n. Land lying beyond the limits of occupation or cultivation. [OE ūtland] — **out′land′er** n.

out·land·ish (out·lan′dish) adj. 1 Of strange or barbarous aspect or action. 2 Situated in an unfamiliar spot; remote. 3 Not native. Also **out′land**. See synonyms under RUSTIC. [OE ūtlandisc] — **out·land′ish·ly** adv. — **out·land′ish·ness** n.

out·last (out·last′, ·läst′) v.t. To last longer than.

out·law (out′lô′) n. 1 A person deprived of the benefit of the law, as for having committed a crime. 2 One who habitually breaks or defies the law; a freebooter; a person having a price on his head. 3 A vicious horse. — v.t. 1 To declare an outlaw; proscribe. 2 To prohibit; ban. 3 To deprive of legal force or protection, as contracts or debts. [OE ūtlaga <ON ūtlagi]

out·law·ry (out′lô′rē) n. pl. **·ries** The state, fact, or process of outlawing or being outlawed.

out·lay (out·lā′) v.t. **·laid**, **·lay·ing** To expend (money). — n. (out′lā′) A laying out or disbursing; hence, that which is disbursed; expenditure. See synonyms under EXPENSE, PRICE.

out·ler (ōot′lər) n. Scot. An animal not housed during the night or during winter; hence, a person out of work.

out·let (out′let′) n. 1 A passage or vent for escape or discharge; an egress; specifically, in commerce, a market for the sale of any commodity. 2 The act of letting out. 3 Electr. That point in a wiring system at which the current is taken to supply fixtures, lamps, motors, etc.

out·li·er (out′lī′ər) n. 1 One whose residence is not in the same place as his office or business. 2 One who or that which is beyond or excluded from the main body. 3 A person who camps or lies out in the forest, prairie, or other deserted place. 4 Geol. An exposed mass of rock surrounded by older rock strata which have been worn away: opposed to inlier.

out·line (out′lin′) n. 1 A preliminary sketch showing the principal features of a thing; general plan. 2 The bordering line that serves to define a figure; hence, a sketch made of such lines without shading; also, the art of making such sketches. See synonyms under SKETCH. — v.t. **·lined**, **·lin·ing** 1 To draw the outline of; sketch. 2 To describe in general terms; give the main points of.

out·live (out·liv′) v.t. **·lived**, **·liv·ing** 1 To live longer than (another). 2 To live through; survive.

out·look (out′lōok′) n. 1 The expanse in view; hence, the condition or prospect of a thing. 2 Distance of view; hence, foresight. 3 Vigilance. 4 A place where watch is kept. 5 The watch; sentinel.

out·ly·ing (out′lī′ing) adj. 1 Situated apart from the main body. 2 Outside the boundary.

out–man (out·man′) v.t. **–manned**, **–man·ning** 1 To surpass in number of men. 2 To excel in manliness.

out·mo·ded (out·mō′did) adj. Out of fashion; not in current style.

out·most (out′mōst′) adj. Outermost.

out·ness (out′nis) n. 1 The quality or condition of being outside; externality. 2 The quality of being interested in external things.

out of 1 From or beyond the inside of; from among. 2 Beyond the limits, reach, scope, or proper position of; not in or included in: out of sight. 3 Without: out of breath. 4 Influenced, inspired, or caused by: out of pity; out of respect for him.

out–of–bounds (out′əv·boundz′) adv. Outside the playing area of a ball field. — adj. 1 Being out–of–bounds. 2 Beyond normal or proper limits, as of taste or behavior; uncalled–for.

out of commission Completely out of order; not working; laid aside.

out–of–date (out′əv·dāt′) adj. Old–fashioned.

out–of–door (out′əv·dôr′, ·dōr′) See OUTDOOR.

out–of–doors (out′əv·dôrz′, ·dōrz′) See OUT-DOORS.

out of sorts 1 Indisposed or unwell. 2 Dissatisfied or unhappy.

out–of–the–way (out′əv·thə·wā′) adj. 1 Remotely situated; difficult to reach; secluded. 2 Different from what is common; out of the common range; unusual; singular; eccentric.

out of the woods Clear of doubts and difficulties; safe after peril or hazard.

out page Printing The first page of a complete signature when folded.

out parish A parish situated in the country or somewhat distant from a city parish.

out part An outer or remote part.

out·pa·tient (out′pā′shənt) n. A patient, not an inmate, treated at a hospital or dispensary.

out·play (out·plā′) v.t. To play better than; defeat.

out·point (out·point′) v.t. 1 To score more points than. 2 Naut. To sail closer to the wind than.

out·post (out′pōst′) n. 1 A detachment of troops stationed at a distance from the main body as a guard against surprise. 2 The station occupied by them.

out·pour (out·pôr′, -pōr′) v.t. & v.i. To pour out. — n. (out′pôr′, -pōr′) A free outflow; outpouring. — **out′pour′er** n. — **out′pour′ing** n.

out·pull (out·pōol′) v.t. To pull more strongly than.

out·put (out′pōot′) n. 1 The quantity put out or produced in a specified time; amount or rate of production, collective or individual, as from a mine or mines, or from a furnace or a country. 2 That which is excreted from the body by the lungs, skin, or kidneys. 3 The electric power of a dynamo; also, the energy or power given by a machine. See synonyms under PRODUCT.

out·rage (out′rāj′) n. 1 An act of shocking violence or cruelty; a gross infringement of morality or decency; a gross insult. 2 Something that violates the feelings or the proprieties. 3 Obs. Violent rage; a dangerous display of passion. — v.t. **·raged**, **·rag·ing** 1 To commit outrage upon; wrong or abuse grossly; violate; offend. 2 To rape. See synonyms for VIOLATE. [<OF ultrage, ult. <L ultra beyond; infl. in meaning by RAGE]

Synonyms (noun): abuse, affront, indecency, indignity, injury, insult, offense, violence. An outrage combines insult and injury. See INJURY, OFFENSE, VIOLENCE. Compare synonyms for AFFRONT.

out·ra·geous (out·rā′jəs) adj. 1 Of the nature of an outrage; heinous; atrocious. 2 Heedless of authority or decency. 3 Exceeding bounds.

See synonyms under FLAGRANT, INFAMOUS, VIOLENT. — **out·ra′geous·ly** adv. — **out·ra′geous·ness** n.

ou·trance (ōo·träns′) n. French The utmost extremity; the bitter end.

out·range (out·rānj′) v.t. **·ranged**, **·rang·ing** 1 To surpass in range; have a greater range than. 2 To go beyond the range of.

ou·tré (ōo·trā′) adj. French Deviating from conventional usage; strikingly odd; exaggerated.

out·reach (out·rēch′) v.t. 1 To reach or go beyond; surpass. 2 To reach out; extend. — v.i. 3 To reach out. — n. (out′rēch′) The act of reaching out.

ou·tre–mer (ōo′trə·mer′, Fr. ōo·tr′·mâr′) n. The region beyond the sea; foreign lands. — adv. Beyond the sea. [<F <outre beyond (<L ultra) + mer the sea <L mare]

out·ride (out·rīd′) v.t. **·rode**, **·rid·den**, **·rid·ing** To ride faster, farther, or better than.

out·rid·er (out′rī′dər) n. 1 A mounted servant who rides in advance of a carriage. 2 One who rides along the edge of a herd of cattle to prevent stampeding or straying. 3 One who rides out or forth.

out·rig·ger (out′rig′ər) n. 1 A part built or arranged to project beyond a natural outline, as of a vessel or machine. 2 A projecting contrivance terminating in a boatlike float, braced to the side of a canoe to prevent capsizing. 3 Naut. a A spar for extending a sail or rope farther than the beam of the vessel would otherwise permit. b A boom swung out from a vessel, to which to secure boats. 4 A bracket projecting from the side of a narrow rowboat or shell, and provided with a rowlock for an oar or scull. 5 A boat or shell equipped with such a bracket. 6 Aeron. A projecting contrivance to support various components of an airplane: also called tail boom.

out·right (out′rīt′) adj. 1 Free from reserve or restraint; positive; downright. 2 Complete; entire. 3 Going straight on. — adv. (out′rīt′) 1 Without reservation or limitation; entirely; utterly; openly. 2 Without delay.

out·root (out·rōot′, -rōot′) v.t. To root out; eradicate.

out·run·ner (out′run′ər) n. 1 An attendant who runs before or beside a carriage. 2 The leading dog in a dog team.

out·sell (out·sel′) v.t. **·sold**, **·sell·ing** 1 To sell more readily or for a higher price than. 2 To sell more goods than.

out·sen·try (out′sen′trē) n. pl. **·tries** An outer sentry.

out·sert (out′sûrt′) n. Printing A folded sheet placed around a folded section of printed matter: opposed to insert.

out·set (out′set′) n. A first entrance on any business, journey, or the like; a setting out; beginning; start; opening. Also **out′set′ting**. See synonyms under BEGINNING.

out·shine (out·shīn′) v. **·shone**, **·shin·ing** v.t. 1 To shine brighter than. 2 To surpass, as in wit or finery. — v.i. 3 To shine forth. — **out·shin′er** n.

out·shoot (out·shōot′) v. **·shot**, **·shoot·ing** v.t. 1 To excel in shooting. 2 To shoot out or beyond; project. — v.i. 3 To shoot out; project. — n. (out′shōot′) 1 A projection; branch; bud, as of a plant. 2 A rushing forth, as of water. 3 In baseball, an outcurve.

out·shop (out′shop′) v.t. **–shopped**, **–shop·ping** In railroading, to turn out (equipment) from a repair shop or factory.

out·side (out′sīd′) n. 1 The external part of a thing; the side or part that forms or adjoins the surface. 2 The part or side that is seen; hence, superficial appearance. 3 The space beyond a bounding line or surface; outer region: opposed to inside. — at the outside At the farthest, longest, or most, as in an estimate. — adj. 1 Pertaining to, located on, or restricted to the outside; exterior. 2 Originating or situated beyond designated limits; foreign. 3 Reaching the limit; extreme: an outside estimate. 4 Slight; inconsequential: There is only an outside possibility. — adv. 1 On or to the outside; externally. 2 Beyond the outside limits of. 3 In the open air; outdoors. — prep. 1 On or to the exterior of: outside the park; outside the box. 2 Beyond the limit of: Don't tell it outside

the club. 3 *Colloq.* Except: No one knows *outside* yourself.

outside of 1 *U.S. Colloq.* Except; besides: No one came *outside of* me. 2 Outside.

out·sid·er (out'sī'dər) *n.* 1 One who is outside; an intruder. 2 A race horse whose chance of winning is slight.

outside roll *Aeron.* A roll executed while flying in a negative angle–of–range, which begins and ends with the airplane on its back.

out sister A member of a cloistered order of nuns who attends to the business of the order, or convent, with the outside world.

out·size (out'sīz') *n.* A size, as of clothing, footwear, etc., that is larger than the regular sizes.

out·skirt (out'skûrt') *n. Often pl.* A place on the skirts or border; outer verge.

out·smart (out·smärt') *v.t. U.S. Colloq.* To outwit; fool.

out·sole (out'sōl') *n.* The outside or lower sole of a boot or shoe: distinguished from *insole.* See illustration under SHOE.

out·span (out·span') *v.t. & v.i.* ·spanned, ·spanning In South Africa, to unharness or unyoke (animals). —*n.* The act or the place of outspanning. [<Afrikaans *uitspannen* <*uit·* + *spannen* stretch]

out·speak (out·spēk') *v.* ·spoke, ·spo·ken, ·speak·ing *v.t.* 1 To outdo in speaking. 2 To say openly or boldly. —*v.i.* 3 To speak out. —**out·speak'er** *n.*

out·spent (out·spent') *adj.* Completely spent or wearied; tired out.

out·spo·ken (out'spō'kən) *adj.* 1 Bold or free of speech; frank. 2 Spoken boldly or frankly. —**out'spo'ken·ly** *adv.* —**out'spo'ken·ness** *n.*

out·spread (out·spred') *v.t. & v.i.* ·spread, ·spread·ing To spread out; extend.

out·stand (out·stand') *v.* ·stood, ·stand·ing *v.i.* 1 To stand out; project. 2 *Naut.* To put to sea; sail. —*v.t.* 3 *Archaic* To stay or last beyond. 4 *Dial.* To withstand. —**out·stand'er** *n.*

out·stand·ing (out·stan'ding) *adj.* 1 Standing prominently forth; salient; conspicuous; preeminent. 2 Still standing, as a debt unpaid or not due.

out·stretch (out·strech') *v.t.* 1 To stretch out; expand; extend. 2 To extend beyond. —**out·stretched'** *adj.*

out·strip (out·strip') *v.t.* stripped, ·strip·ping 1 To leave behind; outrun, as in a race. 2 To excel; surpass. See synonyms under LEAD¹, SURPASS.

out·stroke (out'strōk') *n.* An outward stroke, as the thrust of an engine's piston toward the crankshaft. Compare INSTROKE.

out·take (out'tāk') *n. Motion Pictures.* Something taken out, esp. filmed scenes deleted during the editing process.

out·tell (out·tel') *v.t.* ·told, ·tell·ing To declare; say openly.

out·turn (out'tûrn') *n.* 1 Output; product. 2 In commerce, the quantity, condition, or quality of goods actually turned out and delivered.

out·ward (out'wərd) *adj.* 1 Of or pertaining to the exterior of an object; outer; external; outside: *outward* show. 2 Tending to the outside; directed outward: an *outward* course. 3 Derived or added from without; not inherent; extraneous; extrinsic: *outward* grace. 4 Relating to the physical or bodily as opposed to the mental aspect; external: His *outward* attitude belies his inward feeling. 5 Of or pertaining to the world or the outer man; not spiritual; carnal; corporeal. —*adv.* 1 To or in the direction of the outside; away from an inner place. 2 On the surface; superficially. 3 Away from port or home. Also **out'wards.** —*n.* External form; outside appearance. [OE

ūtweard] —**out'ward·ly** *adv.* —**out'ward·ness** *n.*

out·wash (out'wäsh', -wôsh') *n.* Detritus and waste materials carried away by the water of melting glaciers.

out·wear (out·wâr') *v.t.* ·wore, ·worn, ·wear·ing 1 To wear or stand use better than; outlast. 2 To wear out, as by constant use. 3 To exhaust; use up. 4 To outlive; outgrow.

out·weigh (out·wā') *v.t.* 1 To weigh more than. 2 To exceed in importance, value, etc.

out·wit (out·wit') *v.t.* ·wit·ted, ·wit·ting To defeat by superior ingenuity or cunning; overreach. See synonyms under BAFFLE, DECEIVE.

out·work¹ (out·wûrk') *v.t.* ·worked or ·wrought, ·work·ing 1 To work faster or better than; excel in working. 2 To work out; complete.

out·work² (out'wûrk') *n. Mil.* Any outer defense, as beyond the ditch of a fort. See synonyms under RAMPART.

out·worn (out·wôrn') Past participle of OUTWEAR.

out·wrought (out·rôt') Alternative past tense and past participle of OUTWORK.

ou·zel (ōō'zəl) *n.* 1 One of various European thrushes, as the blackbird *(Turdus merula),* the ring ouzel *(T. torquatus).* 2 The related dipper or **water ouzel** *(Cinclus aquaticus).* Also spelled *ousel.* [OE *ōsle*]

ou·zo (ōō'zō) *n.* An unsweetened Greek liqueur flavored with anise.

o·va (ō'və) Plural of OVUM.

o·val (ō'vəl) *adj.* 1 Having the figure of the plane longitudinal section of an egg, usually rounded at one end and tapering at the other. 2 Ellipsoidal. —*n.* A figure or body of such form or outline. [<NL *ovalis* <L *ovum* egg] —**o'val·ly** *adv.* —**o'val·ness** *n.*

o·var·i·ot·o·my (ō·vâr'ē·ot'ə·mē) *n. Surg.* The excision of either or both ovaries, or of an ovarian tumor: also called *oophorectomy.* [OVARY + -TOMY]

o·va·ri·tis (ō'və·rī'tis) *n. Pathol.* Inflammation of the ovary. [<OVARY + -ITIS]

o·va·ry (ō'və·rē) *n. pl.* ·ries 1 *Biol.* The genital gland of female animals in which are produced the essential reproductive elements or ova. In the higher vertebrates there are two. 2 *Bot.* In angiospermous plants, that portion of the pistil or gynoecium in which the ovules are contained. [<NL *ovarium* <L *ovum* an egg] —**o·var'i·an, o·var'i·al** *adj.*

o·vate (ō'vāt) *adj. Bot.* Egg–shaped: said of leaves. [<L *ovatus* <*ovum* egg] —**o'vate·ly** *adv.*

o·va·tion (ō·vā'shən) *n.* 1 A spontaneous acclamation of popularity; enthusiastic reception of a popular personage. 2 In ancient Rome, a secondary triumphal honor. [<L *ovatio, -onis* a rejoicing <*ovare* rejoice, exult] —**o·va'tion·al** *adj.*

ov·en (uv'ən) *n.* 1 An enclosed chamber in which substances are heated or cooked: used also for baking, annealing, etc., as in a kiln or assaying furnace. 2 A furnace. [OE *ofen*]

ov·en·bird (uv'ən·bûrd') *n.* 1 A bird that builds a domed nest, as a South American passerine bird (genus *Furnarius*), whose nests are oven–shaped structures of clay. 2 The American golden–crowned thrush *(Seiurus aurocapillus):* also called *teacher bird.*

o·ver (ō'vər) *prep.* 1 In or to a place or position above; higher than: the sky *over* our heads. 2 So as to pass or extend across; from one end or side of to the other: the plane flying *over* the lake; walking *over* the bridge. 3 On the other side of: lying *over* the ocean. 4 Upon the surface or exterior of: Oil was smeared *over* the axle. 5 Here and there upon or within; throughout all parts of: trav-

eling *over* land and sea. 6 So as to rise above, cover, or submerge: The mud is now *over* my boots. 7 So as to close or cover: a cloth tied *over* the mouth of the jar. 8 During the continuance of; through: a diary kept *over* the years. 9 Up to the end of and beyond: Stay with us *over* Christmas. 10 More than; in excess of, as in amount, degree, number, extent, etc.: *over* a million dollars in assets. 11 In preference to: chosen *over* all other contenders. 12 In higher rank, authority, power, etc., than: They want a strong man *over* them. 13 Upon, as an effect: His influence *over* her is profound. 14 Concerning; with regard to: time wasted *over* trifles. 15 While engaged in or partaking of: falling asleep *over* Shakespeare; a bargain made *over* a bottle of wine. —**over all** From one end or aspect to the other. —**over and above** In addition to; besides. —*adv.* 1 Above; on high. 2 So as to close, cover, or be covered: The pond froze *over.* 3 To pass above from one of two sides or places to the other; across an intervening space, brim, or edge. 4 At or on the other side; at a distance in a specified direction or place: *over* in Europe; They're playing music *over* there. 5 From one side, opinion, or purpose to another: to be won *over* to a point of view. 6 From one person, condition, or custody to another: to make property *over* to someone. 7 From beginning to end; all through; completely: I'll think the matter *over.* 8 With the upper surface downwards; from an upright position, especially so as to invert, reverse, or transpose: to turn one's hand *over;* to topple *over.* 9 With repetition; again: He added his figures *over.* 10 So as to overflow: The cup ran *over.* 11 So as to constitute a surplus; in excess; beyond: enough to have some left *over.* 12 Beyond a stated time; until later: Plan to stay *over.* —**all over** With Finished. —**over again** Once more; afresh. —**over against** Opposite to; as contrasted with; in front of. —**over and over** Repeatedly. —**over there** *Colloq.* In Europe: a phrase popularized in the United States during World War I. —*adj.* 1 Finished; complete. 2 On the other side; having got across. 3 Outer; superior; upper. 4 In excess or addition; extra. —*n.* 1 Something remaining or in addition. 2 In cricket: a The succession of four to six balls bowled during a turn at one end of the wicket. b The part of the game in which this occurs. 3 *Mil.* A shot hitting or exploding beyond the target. —*v.t. & v.i.* To go or pass over. [OE *ofer*]

over– *combining form* 1 Above; on top of; superior: *overlord.* 2 Passing above; going beyond the top or limit of: *overarch, overflow.* 3 Moving or causing to move downward, as from above: *overthrow, overturn.* 4 Excessively; excessive; too much.

Over– is widely used in def. 4 to form compounds, as in the list beginning at the foot of the page.

o·ver·act (ō'vər·akt') *v.t. & v.i.* To act with exaggeration.

o·ver·age (ō'vər·ij) *n.* In commerce, an amount of money or goods in excess of that which is listed as being on hand.

o·ver·age (ō'vər·āj') *adj.* Past the age of usefulness; too old to be of service: *over–age* guns.

o·ver–all (ō'vər·ôl') *adj.* 1 From one extremity to the other: said of dimensions measured. 2 Including or covering everything.

o·ver·alls (ō'vər·ôlz') *n. pl.* 1 Loose, coarse trousers, often with suspenders and a piece extending over the breast, worn over the clothing as protection from soiling. 2 *Brit.* Waterproof leggings.

overabound	overargue	overbig	overbrown	overcaution	overcold	overconscious
overabstemious	overassert	overbitter	overbrush	overcautious	overcolor	overconsciousness
overabundance	overassertion	overblame	overbrutal	overcautiously	overcommend	overconservatism
overabundant	overassertive	overblithe	overbulky	overcentralization	overcompetitive	overconservative
overaccentuate	overassess	overboastful	overburdensome	overcharitable	overcomplacency	overconsiderate
overaccumulation	overassessment	overbold	overbusy	overcheap	overcomplacent	overconsideration
overactive	overassumption	overbookish	overbuy	overcherish	overcomplete	overconsume
overactivity	overattached	overborrow	overcapacity	overchildish	overcomplex	overconsumption
overadvance	overattentive	overbravely	overcaptious	overchill	overcompliant	overcontented
overambitious	overbake	overbred	overcaptiousness	overcivil	overconcentration	overcontribute
overanalyze	overbanked	overbreed	overcareful	overcivilized	overconcern	overcook
overanxiety	overbarren	overbright	overcareless	overclean	overcondense	overcool
overanxious	overbashful	overbrilliant	overcaring	overclever	overconfidence	overcoolly
overapprehensive	overbelief	overbroaden	overcarry	overclose	overconfident	overcopious
overapt	overbet	overbroil	overcasual	overcloseness	overconscientious	overcorrect

o·ver·arch (ō′vər·ärch′) v.t. & v.i. To form an arch over (something).

o·ver·awe (ō′vər·ô′) v.t. ·awed, ·aw·ing To subdue or restrain by awe. See synonyms under ABASH.

o·ver·bal·ance (ō′vər·bal′əns) v. ·anced, ·anc·ing v.t. 1 To exceed in weight, importance, etc. 2 To cause to lose balance. — v.i. 3 To lose one's balance. — n. Excess of weight or value.

o·ver·bear (ō′vər·bâr′) v. ·bore, ·borne, ·bear·ing v.t. 1 To crush or bear down by physical weight or force. 2 To prevail over; domineer. — v.i. 3 To bear too much fruit; be too fruitful. See synonyms under SUBDUE.

o·ver·bear·ing (ō′vər·bâr′ing) adj. 1 Arrogant; dictatorial. 2 Overwhelming; crushing. See synonyms under ARBITRARY, DOGMATIC, IMPERIOUS. — o′ver·bear′ing·ly adv. — o′ver·bear′ing·ness n.

o·ver·bid (ō′vər·bid′) v.t. & v.i. ·bid, ·bid·den or ·bid, ·bid·ding 1 To outbid (someone). 2 To bid more than the fair value of (something).

o·ver·bite (ō′vər·bīt′) n. Dent. Projection of the upper incisor teeth in front of the lower in attempted occlusion.

o·ver·blow (ō′vər·blō′) v.t. ·blew, ·blown, ·blow·ing 1 To blow down, over, or away. 2 To cover by blowing, as with snow or sand.

o·ver·blown (ō′vər·blōn′) adj. Too productive of flowers; also, past flowering; past full bloom.

o·ver·board (ō′vər·bôrd′, -bōrd′) adv. Over the side of or out of a boat or ship.

o·ver·borne (ō′vər·bôrn′, -bōrn′) Past participle of OVERBEAR.

o·ver·build (ō′vər·bild′) v.t. ·built, ·build·ing 1 To build over: to overbuild a ravine. 2 To erect more buildings within (an area) than are needed. 3 To build, as a house, on too elaborate a scale.

o·ver·bur·den (ō′vər·bûr′dən) v.t. To load with too much weight.

o·ver·by (ō′vər·bī′) adv. Scot. & Brit. Dial. Nearby; a little way on; across the way.

o·ver·cap·i·tal·ize (ō′vər·kap′i·tal·īz′) v.t. ·ized, ·iz·ing 1 To invest capital in to an extent not warranted by actual prospects. 2 To affix an unjustifiable or unlawful value to the nominal capital of (a corporation). 3 To estimate the value of (a property, company, etc.) too highly. — o′ver·cap′i·tal·i·za′tion n.

o·ver·cast (ō′vər·kast′, -käst′, ō′vər·kast′, -käst′) v. ·cast, ·cast·ing v.t. 1 To overcloud; darken. 2 To sew, as the edge of a fabric, with long wrapping stitches so as to prevent raveling. — adj. 1 Clouded, as the sky. 2 Sewn with a blanket stitch. — n. Meteorol. A cloud or clouds covering more than nine tenths of the sky.

o·ver·charge (ō′vər·chärj′) v.t. ·charged, ·charg·ing 1 To charge (someone) too high a price. 2 To load or fill to excess; overburden. 3 To exaggerate. — n. An excessive charge.

o·ver·check (ō′vər·chek′) n. A checkrein passing over a horse's head between the ears to draw the bit upward.

o·ver·clothes (ō′vər·klōz′, -klōthz′) n. pl. Outer garments.

o·ver·cloud (ō′vər·kloud′) v.t. To cover with clouds; darken or make gloomy.

o·ver·coat (ō′vər·kōt′) n. An extra outdoor coat worn over a suit; a greatcoat; topcoat.

o·ver·come (ō′vər·kum′) v.t. 1 To get the better of in any conflict or struggle; defeat; conquer. 2 To prevail over or surmount, as difficulties, obstacles, etc. 3 To affect

violently so as to render helpless, as by emotion, sickness, etc. — v.i. 4 To gain mastery; win. See synonyms under BEAT, CONQUER, REPRESS, SUBDUE. [OE ofercuman] — o′ver·com′er n.

o·ver·com·pen·sate (ō′vər·kom′pən·sāt) v. ·sat·ed, ·sat·ing v.i. 1 To make too great a compensation, as in balancing the arms of a scales. 2 Psychol. & Psychoanal. To engage in overcompensation. — v.t. 3 To make too great a compensation for.

o·ver·com·pen·sa·tion (ō′vər·kom′pən·sā′shən) n. 1 Psychol. More than the necessary or normal adjustments in a given situation. 2 Psychoanal. The cultivation of attitudes and forms of behavior designed to compensate in an exaggerated manner for the fact or feeling of inferiority. — o′ver·com·pen′sa·to·ry (-kəm·pen′sə·tôr′ē, -tō′rē) adj.

o·ver·con·trol (ō′vər·kən·trōl′) v.t. & v.i. ·trolled, ·trol·ling Aeron. To move the controls of (an aircraft) so as to compensate excessively for a previously performed, incorrect movement.

o·ver·crop (ō′vər·krop′) v.i. ·cropped, ·crop·ping Agric. To exhaust by continuous cropping, as land.

o·ver·de·ter·mined (ō′vər·di·tûr′mind) adj. Psychoanal. Having several factors contributory to a given condition or state of mind: an overdetermined neurosis. — o′ver·de·ter′mi·na′tion (-tûr′mə·nā′shən) n.

o·ver·de·vel·op (ō′vər·di·vel′əp) v.t. 1 To develop excessively. 2 Phot. To develop (a plate or film) to too great a degree. — o′ver·de·vel′op·ment n.

o·ver·do (ō′vər·dōō′) v. ·did, ·done, ·do·ing v.t. 1 To do excessively; carry too far; exaggerate. 2 To overtax the strength of; exhaust: usually used passively or reflexively. 3 To cook too much, as meat. 4 Poetic To surpass; outdo. — v.i. 5 To do too much. [OE oferdōn]

o·ver·dose (ō′vər·dōs′) v.t. ·dosed, ·dos·ing To dose to excess. — n. (ō′vər·dōs′) An excessive dose.

o·ver·draft (ō′vər·draft′, -dräft′) n. 1 The act of overdrawing an account, as at a bank. 2 The amount by which a check or draft exceeds the sum against which it is drawn. 3 A current of air passing over, not through, the ignited fuel in a furnace. Also o′ver·draught′ (-draft′, -dräft′).

o·ver·draw (ō′vər·drô′) v.t. ·drew, ·drawn, ·draw·ing 1 To draw against (an account) beyond one's credit. 2 To draw or strain excessively, as a bow. 3 To exaggerate a representation of. — n. (ō′vər·drô′) The act of overdrawing; an overdraft.

o·ver·drive (ō′vər·drīv′) v.t. ·drove, ·driv·en, ·driv·ing 1 To push too hard or too far; overwork. 2 To drive too hard. — n. (ō′vər·drīv′) Mech. A gearing device which turns a drive shaft at a speed greater than that of the engine, thus decreasing power output: opposed to underdrive.

o·ver·due (ō′vər·dōō′, -dyōō′) adj. 1 Remaining unpaid after becoming due. 2 Past due: an overdue plane or train.

o·ver·dye (ō′vər·dī′) v.t. ·dyed, ·dye·ing 1 To dye with too much color. 2 To dye with a second color.

o·ver·ex·pose (ō′vər·ik·spōz′) v.t. ·posed, ·pos·ing 1 To expose excessively. 2 Phot. To expose (a film or plate) too long. — o′ver·ex·po′sure (-spō′zhər) n.

o·ver·fall (ō′vər·fôl′) n. 1 A rapid sea current formed by the peculiarities of the bottom, or by winds, tide, etc.; a race. 2 A sud-

den drop in the bottom of the sea. 3 A catch basin for overflow, as from a canal.

o·ver·flow (ō′vər·flō′) v. ·flowed, ·flown, ·flow·ing v.i. 1 To flow or run over the brim or bank, as water, rivers, etc. 2 To be filled beyond capacity; spill over. 3 To superabound. — v.t. 4 To flow over the brim or bank of. 5 To flow or spread over; cover. 6 To fill beyond capacity; cause to overflow. See synonyms under INUNDATE. — n. (ō′vər·flō′) 1 The act of overflowing. 2 That which flows over. 3 A flood. 4 A surplus. 5 A passage or outlet for liquid. [OE oferflōwan]

o·ver·flow·ing (ō′vər·flō′ing) adj. Running over the brim or edge; copious; abundant. — n. Overflow; copiousness.

o·ver·gar·ment (ō′vər·gär′mənt) n. An outer garment.

o·ver·glaze (ō′vər·glāz′) v.t. ·glazed, ·glaz·ing To glaze over; apply an overglaze to. — n. A decoration or second glaze applied to pottery.

o·ver·grow (ō′vər·grō′) v. ·grew, ·grown, ·grow·ing v.t. 1 To grow over; cover with growth. 2 To grow too big for; outgrow. — v.i. 3 To grow or increase excessively; grow too large. — o′ver·grown′ adj.

o·ver·growth (ō′vər·grōth′) n. 1 Luxuriant or excessive growth. 2 A growth upon or over something.

o·ver·hand (ō′vər·hand′) adj. 1 In baseball, delivering the ball, or delivered, as the ball, with the hand well above the level of the elbow or shoulder. 2 Made by carrying the thread over and over, as a seam. 3 With the hand above the object which it holds, seizes, or throws. 4 Striking downward. — adv. In an overhand manner. — v.t. In sewing, to overcast. — n. 1 An overhand stroke or delivery in baseball or tennis; also, a ball so served or delivered. 2 The act or method of such delivery or stroke. 3 A kind of knot. See illustration under KNOT.

o·ver·hand·ed (ō′vər·han′did) adj. Overhand (def. 1).

o·ver·hang (ō′vər·hang′) v. ·hung, ·hang·ing v.t. 1 To hang or project over (something); jut over. 2 To impend over; threaten. 3 To adorn with hangings. — v.i. 4 To hang or jut over something. — n. 1 An overhanging portion of a structure, as of a roof, the bow of a ship, etc.; also, the amount or degree of such projection. 2 Aeron. a One half the distance in span of any two main supporting surfaces of an airplane: when the upper surface is the greater, it is called **positive overhang**. b The distance from the outer strut attachment to the edge of a wing.

o·ver·haul (ō′vər·hôl′) v.t. 1 To examine carefully, as for needed repairs; turn over or take apart for this purpose. 2 To catch up with; gain on. 3 Naut. a To slacken (a rope) by hauling in the opposite direction. b To prepare (a tackle) for use by separating the blocks. See synonyms under EXAMINE. — n. (ō′vər·hôl′) 1 A thorough inspection or examination. 2 Examination and complete repair. Also o′ver·haul′ing.

o·ver·head (ō′vər·hed′) adj. 1 Placed or working above or aloft: an overhead railway; working from above; working downward: an overhead valve. 2 Chosen by random sampling; average: an overhead sample. 3 Situated or working overhead; also, passing over the head. 4 Denoting such general expenditure in a financial or industrial enterprise as cannot be attributed to any one department or product, excluding cost of materials, labor, and

overcorrupt	overcured	overdelicate	overdilute	overeasy	overenthusiastic	overexpenditure
overcostly	overcurious	overdelicately	overdiscipline	overeat	overesteem	overexpress
overcount	overcuriousness	overdemand	overdiscourage	overeducate	overestimate	overexuberant
overcourteous	overdaintiness	overdemocratic	overdistant	overelaborate	overestimation	overfacile
overcovetous	overdainty	overdepress	overdiversification	overelaboration	overexcelling	overfaithful
overcoy	overdance	overdepressive	overdiversify	overelate	overexcitable	overfamiliar
overcram	overdare	overdesirous	overdogmatic	overelegant	overexcite	overfanciful
overcredit	overdazzle	overdestructive	overdominate	overembellish	overexcitement	overfast
overcredulous	overdear	overdestructiveness	overdoubt	overemotional	overexercise	overfastidious
overcriticize	overdecorate	overdevoted	overdramatic	overemphasis	overexert	overfastidiousness
overcull	overdecorative	overdevotion	overdrink	overemphasize	overexertion	overfasting
overcultivate	overdeepen	overdiffuse	overdry	overemphatic	overexpand	overfat
overcultivation	overdeeply	overdignified	overeager	overenjoy	overexpansion	overfatigue
overcunning	overdeliberate	overdiligence	overearnest	overenrich	overexpect	overfatten
overcunningly	overdeliberation	overdiligent	overeasily	overenter	overexpectant	overfavor

selling; fixed charges; in transportation, bond interest and other expenses previous to operating expenses, taxes, etc. — *n.* **1** General expenditure applicable to all departments of a business, as light, heat, taxes, etc. **2** *Naut.* Ceiling of a cabin or hold. — *adv.* (ō′vər·hed′) **1** Above one's head; aloft. **2** So as to be submerged; over one's head.

overhead valve *Mech.* A valve that is located in the upper part of the combustion chamber of an engine, above the piston face. See VALVE-IN-HEAD ENGINE.

o·ver·hear (ō′vər·hir′) *v.t.* **·heard, ·hear·ing** To hear (something said or someone speaking) without the knowledge or intention of the speaker. — **o′ver·hear′er** *n.*

o·ver·hours (ō′vər·ourz′) *n. pl.* **1** Time outside and in addition to the assigned or usual number of hours; overtime. **2** Unduly long hours of employment.

O·ver·ijs·sel (ō′vər·ī′səl) A province of eastern Netherlands; 1,255 square miles; capital, Zwolle. Also **O′ver·ys′sel.**

o·ver·is·sue (ō′vər·ish′ōō, -yōō) *v.t.* **·sued, ·su·ing** To issue in excess of a legal or authorized amount, or in excess of ability to meet the demands thus created: to *overissue* stock, notes, or bonds. — *n.* (ō′vər·ish′ōō, -yōō) An excessive or unauthorized issue.

o·ver·joy (ō′vər·joi′) *v.t.* To delight or please greatly. See synonyms under RAVISH.

o·ver·kill (ō′vər·kil′) *n.* **1** The surplus of nuclear weapons beyond the number considered necessary to demolish all key enemy targets. **2** *Colloq.* Any action regarded as being more extreme than the circumstances warrant: Slashing the budget in half was a clear case of *overkill.*

o·ver·lade (ō′vər·lād′) *v.t.* **·lad·ed, ·lad·ed** or **·lad·en, ·lad·ing** To overload: now used chiefly in the past participle.

o·ver·lain (ō′vər·lān′) Past participle of OVERLIE.

o·ver·land (ō′vər·land′) *adj.* Journeying or accomplished by or principally by land. — *adv.* Across, over, or via land. — *n.* An overland stage or train.

overland stage A stagecoach used on any overland route.

o·ver·lap (ō′vər·lap′) *v.t.* & *v.i.* **·lapped, ·lap·ping** To lie or extend partly over or upon (another or one another); lap over. — *n.* (ō′vər·lap′) **1** The state, condition, or extent of overlapping; also, the part that overlaps. **2** *Geol.* The extension of younger rock strata beyond the limits of the older underlying strata.

o·ver·lay (ō′vər·lā′) *n.* **1** *Printing* A piece of paper placed on the tympan of a press to make the impression heavier at the corresponding part of the form, or to compensate for a depression in the form. **2** Anything that overlies, covers, or partly covers something. **3** Ornamental work overlaid on wood, as with veneers, etc. **4** A sheet of transparent material carrying information of a special or confidential nature to supplement the details of the map on which it is laid. **5** *Scot.* A cravat. — *v.t.* (ō′vər·lā′) **·laid, ·lay·ing 1** To spread something over, as with a decorative pattern or layer. **2** To lay or place over or upon something else. **3** *Printing* To put an overlay upon. **4** To overburden; weigh down.

o·ver·leaf (ō′vər·lēf′) *adv.* & *adj.* On the reverse side of a leaf (of paper).

o·ver·leap (ō′vər·lēp′) *v.t.* **1** To leap over or across. **2** To omit; overlook. **3** To leap farther than; outleap. — **to overleap oneself** To miss one's purpose by going too far. [OE *oferhlēapan*]

o·ver·learn·ing (ō′vər·lûr′ning) *n.* *Psychol.* A degree of learning beyond what is necessary for immediate or adequate use in prescribed situations.

o·ver·lie (ō′vər·lī′) *v.t.* **·lay, ·lain, ·ly·ing 1** To lie over or upon. **2** To suffocate by lying upon, as a baby.

o·ver·live (ō′vər·liv′) *v.* **·lived, ·liv·ing** *v.t.* To live longer than; survive. — *v.i.* To survive; live too long. [OE *oferlibban*]

o·ver·load (ō′vər·lōd′) *v.t.* To load excessively; overburden. — *n.* (ō′vər·lōd′) **1** An excessive burden. **2** *Electr.* A circuit-breaker.

o·ver·look (ō′vər·lo͝ok′) *v.t.* **1** To fail to see or notice; miss. **2** To disregard purposely or indulgently; ignore. **3** To look over or see from a higher place. **4** To afford a view of: The castle *overlooks* the harbor. **5** To supervise; oversee. **6** To examine or inspect. **7** To look upon or bewitch with the evil eye. See synonyms under PARDON. — *n.* (ō′vər·lo͝ok′) **1** The act of looking over, as from a height; an inspection; survey. **2** Oversight; neglect. **3** The jack bean: so called because believed by West Indian Negroes to serve as a watchman.

o·ver·lord (ō′vər·lôrd′) *n.* **1** In Saxon times, a superior lord or chief who outranked and held authority over other lords. **2** Hence, one who holds supremacy over another. — **o′ver·lord′ship** *n.*

o·ver·loup (ō′vər·lo͞op′) *n.* *Scot.* A leap over; hence, a trespass.

o·ver·ly (ō′vər·lē) *adv.* To an excessive degree; too much; too.

o·ver·man[1] (ō′vər·mən) *n.* *pl.* **·men** (-mən) **1** An overseer. **2** An umpire. **3** (ō′vər·man′) A superman.

o·ver·man[2] (ō′vər·man′) *v.t.* **·manned, ·man·ning** To provide with more men than necessary: The ship was *overmanned.*

o·ver·mas·ter (ō′vər·mas′tər, -mäs′-) *v.t.* To overcome; overpower. — **o′ver·mas′ter·ing** *n.* & *adj.*

o·ver·match (ō′vər·mach′) *v.t.* To be more than a match for; surpass. — *n.* (ō′vər·mach′) **1** One who or that which is superior in strength, skill, etc. **2** A contest in which one party overmatches the other.

o·ver·ma·ture (ō′vər·mə·cho͝or′) *adj.* Denoting the state of a forest in which, as a result of age, the growth of the trees has almost entirely ceased and degeneration has started.

o·ver·much (ō′vər·much′) *adj.* Exceeding what is necessary or proper; too much. — *adv.* In too great a degree. — *n.* An excess; too much.

o·ver·night (ō′vər·nīt′) *adj.* **1** Of or belonging to or done during the previous evening; lasting all night: an *overnight* visit. **2** For use in nighttime travel or for short visits: an *overnight* bag. — *adv.* **1** During or through the night. **2** On the previous evening. — *n.* (ō′vər·nīt′) The previous evening.

o·ver·pass (ō′vər·pas′, -päs′) *v.t.* **1** To pass across, over, or through; cross. **2** To surpass or exceed. **3** To overlook; disregard. **4** To transgress. — *n.* (ō′vər·pas′, -päs′) An elevated section of highway crossing other lines of travel.

o·ver·pay (ō′vər·pā′) *v.t.* **·paid, ·pay·ing 1** To pay more than (a sum due). **2** To pay (someone) too much. **3** To reward too highly. — **o′ver·pay′ment** *n.*

o·ver·per·suade (ō′vər·pər·swād′) *v.t.* **·suad·ed, ·suad·ing** To persuade (someone) to an action or view, especially against his judgment or inclination. — **o′ver·per·sua′sion** *n.*

o·ver·play (ō′vər·plā′) *v.t.* **1** To play or act (a part or role) to excess; overdo; exaggerate. **2** To outplay; surpass. **3** In golf, to send (the ball) beyond the putting green.

o·ver·plus (ō′vər·plus′) *n.* That which remains after a certain part has been used or set aside; surplus; excess. See synonyms under EXCESS. [Partial trans. of OF *surplus* < *sur-* over + *plus* more]

o·ver·pop·u·late (ō′vər·pop′yə·lāt) *v.t.* **·lat·ed, ·lat·ing** To cause to have too high a population. — **o′ver·pop·u·la′tion** *n.*

o·ver·pow·er (ō′vər·pou′ər) *v.t.* **1** To gain supremacy over; subdue. **2** To render wholly helpless or ineffective; overcome. **3** To supply with more power than necessary. See synonyms under CONQUER, REPRESS, SUBDUE. — **o′ver·pow′er·ing** *adj.* — **o′ver·pow′er·ing·ly** *adv.*

o·ver·pres·sure (ō′vər·presh′ər) *n.* Atmospheric pressure greater than normal.

o·ver·print (ō′vər·print′) *v.t.* To print additional material of another color on (sheets already printed). — *n.* (ō′vər·print′) **1** Anything printed over another impression. **2** Any word, symbol, etc., printed on a stamp which changes its value or use.

o·ver·prize (ō′vər·prīz′) *v.t.* **·prized, ·priz·ing** To value too highly.

o·ver·pro·duce (ō′vər·prə·do͞os′, -dyo͞os′) *v.t.* **·duced, ·duc·ing** To produce too much of or so as to exceed demand.

o·ver·pro·duc·tion (ō′vər·prə·duk′shən) *n.* Production in excess of demand.

o·ver·proof (ō′vər·pro͞of′) *adj.* Containing a larger proportion of alcohol than proof spirit; said of alcoholic liquors.

o·ver·pro·por·tion (ō′vər·prə·pôr′shən, -pōr′-) *v.t.* To make or depict in excess of true proportions. — **o′ver·pro·por′tion·ate** *adj.*

o·ver·rate (ō′vər·rāt′) *v.t.* **·rat·ed, ·rat·ing** To rate or value too highly; overestimate.

o·ver·reach (ō′vər·rēch′) *v.t.* **1** To reach over or beyond. **2** To spread over; cover. **3** To defeat (oneself), as by trying too hard or being too clever. **4** To miss by stretching or reaching too far. **5** To get the advantage of; outwit; cheat. — *v.i.* **6** To reach too far. **7** To cheat. **8** To hit a toe of the hind foot against the heel of the forefoot: said of horses, etc. See synonyms under DECEIVE. — **o′ver·reach′er** *n.* — **o′ver·reach′ing** *n.*

o·ver·re·act (ō′vər·rē·akt′) *v.i.* To react to a person, situation, etc., in an excessively emotional or uncontrolled manner. — **o′ver·re·ac′tion** *n.*

o·ver·ride (ō′vər·rīd′) *v.t.* **·rode, ·rid·den, ·rid·ing 1** To ride over or across. **2** To trample down; suppress. **3** To disregard summarily, as if trampling down; supersede; prevail over. **4** To ride (a horse) to exhaustion. **5** *Surg.* To slide over (the corresponding fragment), as one end of a fractured bone. — *n.* A commission paid a sales manager based on the sales of his staff. [OE *oferrīdan*]

o·ver·rid·ing (ō′vər·rī′ding) *adj.* Chief; primary; principal: an *overriding* concern.

o·ver·rule (ō′vər·ro͞ol′) *v.t.* **·ruled, ·rul·ing 1** To decide against or nullify by superior authority; set aside; invalidate. **2** To disallow the arguments of (someone). **3** To have control over; rule. **4** To influence, as to another opinion or course of action; prevail over.

o·ver·run (ō′vər·run′) *v.* **·ran, ·run, ·run·ning** *v.t.* **1** To spread or swarm over, especially harmfully, as vermin or invaders do; ravage; invade; infest. **2** To run or flow over; overflow. **3** To spread rapidly across or throughout: said of fads, ideas, etc. **4** To run beyond; pass the limit of. **5** *Printing* **a** To shift (words, lines of type, etc.) from one line, page, or column to another. **b** To rearrange (matter) in this way. **6** *Archaic* To run faster than; outrun. — *v.i.* **7** To run over; overflow. **8** To pass the usual or desired limit. — *n.* (ō′vər·run′) An instance of overrunning; the amount or extent of overrunning.

o·ver·seas (ō′vər·sēz′) *adv.* Beyond the sea;

overfear	**overfrank**	**overgenerous**	**overgreediness**	**overhelpful**	**overidealistic**	**overinflate**
overfearful	**overfraught**	**overgenial**	**overgreedy**	**overhigh**	**overidle**	**overinflation**
overfeatured	**overfree**	**overgentle**	**overgrieve**	**overhold**	**overillustrate**	**overinfluential**
overfed	**overfreedom**	**overgifted**	**overhandle**	**overholy**	**overimaginative**	**overinsistent**
overfeminine	**overfreely**	**overglad**	**overhappy**	**overhomely**	**overimitate**	**overinsolent**
overfierce	**overfrequency**	**overgloomy**	**overharass**	**overhonest**	**overimitative**	**overinstruct**
overflatten	**overfrequent**	**overglorious**	**overharden**	**overhonor**	**overimpress**	**overinsure**
overflourish	**overfrighten**	**overgoad**	**overhardy**	**overhope**	**overimpressible**	**overintellectual**
overfluent	**overfruitful**	**overgodly**	**overharsh**	**overhot**	**overinclination**	**overintense**
overfond	**overfull**	**overgracious**	**overhasty**	**overhotly**	**overinclined**	**overinterest**
overfondle	**overfullness**	**overgrasping**	**overhate**	**overhuman**	**overindividualistic**	**overinventoried**
overfondness	**overfunctioning**	**overgrateful**	**overhaughty**	**overhumanize**	**overindulge**	**overinvest**
overfoolish	**overfurnish**	**overgratify**	**overheartily**	**overhurriedly**	**overindulgence**	**overirrigate**
overfoul	**overgamble**	**overgraze**	**overhearty**	**overhysterical**	**overindulgent**	**overirrigation**
overfrail	**overgeneralize**	**overgreasy**	**overheavy**	**overidealism**	**overindustrialize**	**overjealous**

abroad. — *adj.* Coming from or for use beyond the sea; foreign. Also **o′ver·sea′.**

overseas cap A narrow, boat-shaped, visorless cap worn as part of the military uniform: also called *field cap.*

o·ver·see (ō′vər·sē′) *v.t.* **·saw**, **·seen**, **·see·ing** 1 To direct as supervisor; superintend. 2 To survey; watch. 3 To examine; peruse. [OE *ofersēon*]

o·ver·se·er (ō′vər·sē′ər) *n.* 1 A person who oversees; especially, one who superintends laborers at their work. 2 A parish officer who administrates relief funds: also **overseer of the poor.** See synonyms under MASTER, SUPERINTENDENT.

o·ver·sell (ō′vər·sel′) *v.t.* **·sold**, **·sell·ing** 1 To sell to excess. 2 To sell more of (a stock, etc.) than one can deliver or provide a margin for.

o·ver·set (ō′vər·set′) *v.* **·set**, **·set·ting** *v.t.* 1 To overcome or disorder mentally or physically; disconcert. 2 *Printing* **a** To set too much (type or copy) in a given space. **b** To set too much type in. 3 *Rare* To cause to overturn; capsize. — *v.i.* 4 To overturn; fall over; spill. — *n.* (ō′vər·set′) 1 A turning over; upset. 2 *Printing* Excess of composed type.

o·ver·sew (ō′vər·sō′, ō′vər·sō′) *v.t.* **·sewed**, **·sewed** or **·sewn**, **·sew·ing** To sew overhand, especially with close stitches.

o·ver·shade (ō′vər·shād′) *v.t.* **·shad·ed**, **·shad·ing** To overshadow.

o·ver·shad·ow (ō′vər·shad′ō) *v.t.* 1 To render unimportant or insignificant by comparison; loom above; dominate. 2 To throw a shadow over; dim; obscure. [OE *ofersceadwian*]

o·ver·shine (ō′vər·shīn′) *v.t.* **·shone**, **·shin·ing** 1 To shine over or upon; illumine. 2 To excel in some respect. [OE *oferscīnan*]

o·ver·shoe (ō′vər·shoo′) *n.* A shoe, usually of rubber, worn for protection over another.

o·ver·shoot (ō′vər·shoot′) *v.* **·shot**, **·shoot·ing** *v.t.* 1 To shoot or go over or beyond. 2 To go beyond; exceed, as a limit. 3 To drive or force (something) beyond the proper limit. — *v.i.* 4 To shoot or go over or beyond the mark. 5 To go too far.

o·ver·shot (ō′vər·shot′) *adj.* 1 Surpassed in any way. 2 Projecting, as the upper jaw beyond the lower jaw. 3 Driven by water flowing over from above: an *overshot* wheel.

overshot wheel A water wheel with buckets that are filled by water from a race over the top, the weight and impetus of the water turning the wheel.

o·ver·sight (ō′vər·sīt′) *n.* 1 An error due to inattention; an inadvertent mistake or omission. 2 Watchful supervision; superintendence.

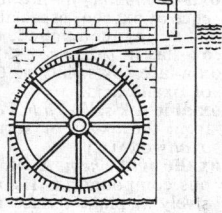

OVERSHOT WHEEL

Synonyms: care, charge, command, control, direction, inspection, management, superintendence, supervision, surveillance, watch, watchfulness. *Oversight* strictly implies constant personal presence; *superintendence* requires only so much of presence or communication as to know that the superintendent's wishes are carried out; the superintendent of a railroad will personally oversee very few of its operations; the railroad company has supreme *direction* of all its affairs without super-

intendence or *oversight.* But a person may look over a matter in order to survey it carefully in its entirety, or he may look over it with no attention to the thing itself because his gaze and thought are concentrated on something beyond; *oversight* has thus two contrasted senses, in the latter sense denoting inadvertent error or omission, and in the former denoting watchful *supervision. Control* is chiefly used with reference to restraint or the power of restraint. *Surveillance* signifies watching with something of suspicion. See CARE, ERROR, NEGLECT.

o·ver·signed (ō′vər·sīnd′) *n.* The person whose name appears at the head of an article, document, report, etc.: distinguished from *undersigned.*

o·ver·size (ō′vər·sīz′) *adj.* Of a larger size than necessary or larger than normal. — *n.* An exceptionally large size. — **o′ver·sized′** *adj.*

o·ver·skirt (ō′vər·skûrt′) *n.* A skirt or drapery worn over the skirt of a dress.

o·ver·sleep (ō′vər·slēp′) *v.* **·slept**, **·sleep·ing** *v.i.* To sleep too long. — *v.t.* To sleep beyond (a specified time).

o·ver·soul (ō′vər·sōl′) *n.* The spiritual being or element of the universe individualized in or uniting together and influencing human souls; the absolute unity, in which subject and object, knower and known, are one: a concept in Emerson's transcendentalist philosophy.

o·ver·spend (ō′vər·spend′) *v.* **·spent**, **·spend·ing** 1 To spend more than; exceed. 2 *Archaic* To use up; exhaust. — *v.i.* 3 To spend more than one can afford.

o·ver·spread (ō′vər·spred′) *v.t.* **·spread**, **·spread·ing** To spread or extend over; cover completely. [OE *ofersprǣdan*]

o·ver·square (ō′vər·skwâr′) *adj. Mech.* Having the cylinder bore greater than the piston stroke: said of engines.

o·ver·state (ō′vər·stāt′) *v.t.* **·stat·ed**, **·stat·ing** To state in too strong terms; exaggerate. — **o′ver·state′ment** *n.*

o·ver·stay (ō′vər·stā′) *v.t.* To stay beyond the limits or duration of.

o·ver·step (ō′vər·step′) *v.t.* **·stepped**, **·step·ping** To step over or go beyond; exceed (some limit or restriction). [OE *ofersteppan*]

o·ver·strung (ō′vər·strung′) *adj.* 1 Strung too tensely; too sensitive. 2 *Music* Having two sets of strings crossing obliquely, as the lower-bass strings in a piano.

o·ver·stuffed (ō′vər·stuft′) *adj.* Excessively stuffed; expecially, as furniture, completely covered with deep upholstery; heavily upholstered.

o·ver·sup·ply (ō′vər·sə·plī′) *n. pl.* **·plies** An excessive supply. — *v.t.* (ō′vər·sə·plī′) **·plied**, **·ply·ing** To supply in excess.

o·vert (ō′vûrt, ō·vûrt′) *adj.* 1 Open to view; outwardly manifest. 2 *Law* Done with criminal intent. [<OF, pp. of *ovrir* open] — **o′vert·ly** *adv.*

Synonyms: see EVIDENT, MANIFEST, NOTORIOUS, OPEN. *Antonyms:* contemplated, hidden, intended, meditated, secret.

o·ver·take (ō′vər·tāk′) *v.t.* **·took**, **·tak·en**, **·tak·ing** 1 To catch up with. 2 To come upon suddenly. See synonyms under CATCH.

o·ver-the-count·er (ō′vər·th ə·koun′tər) *adj.* Not sold on the floor of a stock exchange: said of stocks, bonds, etc.

o·ver·throw (ō′vər·thrō′) *v.t.* **·threw**, **·thrown**, **·throw·ing** 1 To throw over or down; upset. 2 To bring down or remove from power by force; defeat; ruin. See synonyms under

ABOLISH, CONQUER, DEMOLISH, EXTERMINATE, RUIN, SUBVERT. — *n.* (ō′vər·thrō′) 1 The act of overthrowing; destruction; demolition. 2 A throwing of a ball over and beyond the player at whom it is aimed.

o·ver·thrust (ō′vər·thrust′) *adj. Geol.* Characterized by or belonging to earlier and originally lower rock strata, which by faulting are pushed over later and originally higher strata. Compare FAULT, THRUST.

o·ver·time (ō′vər·tīm′) *v.t.* **·timed**, **·tim·ing** *Phot.* To expose too long, as a plate or film. — *n.* (ō′vər·tīm′) Time used in working beyond the specified hours. — *adj.* During or for extra working time: *overtime* pay. — *adv.* Beyond the stipulated time.

o·ver·tone (ō′vər·tōn′) *n.* 1 *Music* A harmonic: so called because it is heard with and above the fundamental tone produced by a musical instrument. 2 The color of the light reflected by a painted surface. 3 The associations, connotations, implications, etc., of language, thoughts, etc. [<G *oberton*]

o·ver·top (ō′vər·top′) *v.t.* **·topped**, **·top·ping** 1 To rise above the top of; tower over. 2 To surpass; excel.

o·ver·topped (ō′vər·topt′) *adj.* Having the crown shaded from above by other contiguous trees: said of a tree.

o·ver·trade (ō′vər·trād′) *v.i.* **·trad·ed**, **·trad·ing** To trade beyond one's capital or the requirements of the market.

o·ver·trick (ō′vər·trik′) *n.* In card games, a trick more than game or than the number bid.

o·ver·trump (ō′vər·trump′) *v.t.* In card games, to trump (a player or a trump played) with a higher trump.

o·ver·ture (ō′vər·chər) *n.* 1 *Music* **a** An instrumental prelude, as to an opera or other large work. **b** An orchestral piece of varying form, usually illustrating a dramatic or graphic theme. 2 A proposal intended to lead to further negotiations by expressing willingness to make terms; also, the proposal submitted. See synonyms under PROPOSAL. — *v.t.* **·tured**, **·tur·ing** 1 To offer as an overture or proposal. 2 To introduce with or as an overture. [<OF <*ouvert.* See OVERT.]

o·ver·turn (ō′vər·tûrn′) *v.t.* 1 To turn or throw over; capsize; upset. 2 To destroy the power of; overthrow; defeat; ruin. — *v.i.* 3 To turn over; capsize; upset. See synonyms under DEMOLISH, SUBVERT. — *n.* (ō′vər·tûrn′) 1 The act of overturning or the state of being overturned; an upset; overthrow. 2 A subversion or destruction. 3 Turnover (def. 5).

o·ver·view (ō′vər·vyoo′) *n.* A broad survey or review of a subject, activity, etc.

o·ver·volt·age (ō′vər·vōl′tij) *n.* 1 *Electr.* Excess voltage in a circuit. 2 *Chem.* The minimum potential at which a particular electrolytic reaction will take place at an appreciable rate on an electrode.

o·ver·watch (ō′vər·woch′, -wôch′) *v.t.* 1 To watch over. 2 To weary with watching.

o·ver·wear (ō′vər·wâr′) *v.t.* **·wore**, **·worn**, **·wear·ing** 1 To wear out. 2 To outgrow.

o·ver·wea·ry (ō′vər·wir′ē) *adj.* Overtired; exhausted. — *v.t.* **·ried**, **·ry·ing** To tire to excess.

o·ver·weath·er (ō′vər·weth′ər) *adj. Aeron.* Denoting flight conditions or activities which are not affected by storm, overcast, or other meteorological phenomena.

o·ver·ween·ing (ō′vər·wē′ning) *adj.* Characterized by presumptuous pride or conceit; arrogant; excessive; exaggerated. — *n.* Overconfidence; presumption. [OE *oferwenan*

overjocular	overlawful	overlogical	overmeasure	overmortgage	overnumerous	overparticular
overjoyful	overlax	overloud	overmeek	overmournful	overobedient	overpassionate
overjoyous	overlaxness	overlove	overmellow	overmultiply	overobese	overpatient
overjudicious	overlearnedness	overloyal	overmelt	overnarrow	overoblige	overpatriotic
overjust	overlet	overluscious	overmerciful	overnear	overobsequious	overpensive
overkeen	overlewd	overlustiness	overmerrily	overneat	overobsequiousness	overpert
overkind	overliberal	overlusty	overmerry	overneglect	overoffensive	overpessimistic
overknowing	overliberality	overluxuriant	overmighty	overnegligence	overofficious	overpiteous
overlabor	overlighted	overluxurious	overmild	overnegligent	overoften	overplain
overlade	overlinger	overmagnify	overminutely	overnervous	overoptimistic	overplausible
overlarge	overliterary	overmany	overminuteness	overnervousness	overornamented	overplease
overlate	overliveliness	overmasterful	overmix	overnew	overpainful	overplentiful
overlaudatory	overlively	overmasterfulness	overmodest	overnimble	overpamper	overplenty
overlaunch	overload	overmature	overmoist	overnotable	overpartial	overplump
overlavish	overlofty	overmeanness	overmoisten	overnourish	overpartiality	overpointed

< *ofer-* over + *wēnan* think] — **o′ver·ween′ing·ly** *adv.*

o·ver·weigh (ō′vər·wā′) *v.t.* 1 To outweigh; overbalance. 2 To overburden; oppress.

o·ver·weight (ō′vər·wāt′) *n.* 1 Excess of weight, as beyond the legal or customary amount: to give *overweight.* 2 Greater weight; preponderance; also, more than normal weight. — *adj.* Being more than the usual or permitted weight. — *v.t.* (ō′vər·wāt′) To weigh down; overburden.

o·ver·whelm (ō′vər·hwelm′) *v.t.* 1 To bury or submerge completely, as with a wave or flood. 2 To overcome or defeat by or as by irresistible force or numbers; crush; render helpless. 3 *Obs.* To overthrow. See synonyms under BURY[1], HIDE[1], INUNDATE, INVOLVE, SUBDUE.

o·ver·whelm·ing (ō′vər·hwel′ming) *adj.* Crushing by reason of force, weight, or numbers; irresistible. — **o′ver·whelm′ing·ly** *adv.*

o·ver·wind (ō′vər·wīnd′) *v.t.* **·wound, ·wind·ing** 1 To wind too far or too tightly, as a watch. 2 *Electr.* To wind (the magnet of a motor) in order to produce a maximum magnetism with a smaller current than is normally required.

o·ver·word (ō′vər·wûrd′) *n.* A word repeated; also, the burden of a song; refrain. See OWERWORD.

o·ver·work (ō′vər·wûrk′) *v.* **·worked** or **·wrought, ·work·ing** *v.t.* 1 To cause to work too hard; exhaust with work or use. 2 To work on or elaborate excessively: to *overwork* an argument. 3 To work up or excite excessively. — *v.i.* 4 To work too hard; do too much work. — *n.* (ō′vər·wûrk′) 1 Work done in overtime, or in excess of the stipulated amount. 2 Excessive work.

o·ver·write (ō′vər·rīt′) *v.t.* & *v.i.* **·wrote, ·writ·ten, ·writ·ing** 1 To write over other writing. 2 To write in too elaborate or labored a style. 3 To write too much about (a subject) or at too great length.

o·ver·wrought (ō′vər·rôt′) *adj.* 1 Worked up or excited excessively; overstrained: *overwrought* feelings. 2 Worked all over, as with embroidery. 3 Worked too hard. 4 Too elaborate; overdone. [< OVERWORK]

ovi– *combining form* Egg; of or pertaining to eggs: *oviparous.* Also **ovo–.** [< L *ovum* an egg]

o·vi·bos (ō′və·bos) *n.* The musk ox. [< NL < L *ovis* sheep + *bos* cow]

Ov·id (ov′id), 43 B.C.–A.D. 17, Roman poet: full name *Publius Ovidius Naso.* — **O·vid·i·an** (ō·vid′ē·ən) *adj.*

o·vi·duct (ō′vi·dukt) *n. Anat.* The passage by which the ova are conveyed from the ovary to the uterus, as the Fallopian tube.

O·vie·do (ō·vyā′thō) A city of NW Spain.

o·vif·er·ous (ō·vif′ər·əs) *adj.* Bearing or holding eggs. [< OVI- + -FEROUS]

o·vi·form (ō′vi·fôrm) *adj.* Having the form of an egg or ovum.

o·vine (ō′vīn, ō′vin) *adj.* Of or pertaining to a sheep; sheeplike. — *n.* An ovine animal. [< L *ovinus* < *ovis* sheep]

o·vip·a·ra (ō·vip′ər·ə) *n. pl.* Animals that lay eggs. [< NL < L *oviparus* laying eggs < *ovum* egg + *-parus* < *parere* bring forth]

o·vip·a·rous (ō·vip′ər·əs) *adj. Biol.* Producing eggs or ova that mature and are hatched outside the body: contrasted with *ovoviviparous*: opposed to *viviparous.* — **o·vip′a·rous·ly** *adv.* — **o·vip′a·rous·ness** *n.*

o·vi·pos·it (ō′vi·poz′it) *v.i.* 1 *Biol.* To lay eggs. 2 *Entomol.* To deposit eggs by means of an ovipositor. [< OVI- + L *positus,* pp. of *ponere* place] — **o·vi·po·si·tion** (ō′vi·pə·zish′ən) *n.*

o·vi·pos·i·tor (ō′vi·poz′ə·tər) *n. Entomol.* The tubular organ at the extremity of the abdomen in many insects, by which the eggs are deposited: sometimes modified as a sting, as in bees and wasps.

o·vi·sac (ō′vi·sak) *n. Anat.* The closed capsule in which ova are developed within the ovary; a Graafian vesicle. [< OVI- + SAC]

o·vo·glob·u·lin (ō′və·glob′yə·lin) *n. Biochem.* A globulin from egg yolk.

o·void (ō′void) *adj.* Egg-shaped: also **o·voi′dal.** — *n.* An egg-shaped body.

o·vo·lo (ō′və·lō) *n. pl.* **·li** (-lē) *Archit.* A convex molding: usually, a quarter of a circle or ellipse. [< Ital., dim. of *ovo* egg < L *ovum*]

o·vo·tes·tis (ō′və·tes′tis) *n. Zool.* The bisexual reproductive gland of certain gastropods, as the snail. [< *ovo-,* var. of OVI- + TESTIS]

o·vo·vi·vip·a·rous (ō′vō·vī·vip′ər·əs) *adj. Zool.* Producing eggs that are incubated and hatched within the parent's body, as some reptiles and fishes. [< OVO- + VIVIPAROUS] — **o′vo·vi·vip′a·rous·ly** *adv.* — **o′vo·vi·vip′a·rous·ness** *n.*

o·vu·late (ō′vyə·lāt) *v.i.* **·lat·ed, ·lat·ing** To produce ova; discharge ova from an ovary. [< NL *ovulum,* dim. of L *ovum* an egg]

o·vu·la·tion (ō′vyə·lā′shən) *n. Biol.* The formation and discharge of ova; the period when this occurs.

o·vule (ō′vyōōl) *n.* 1 *Bot.* The rudimentary seed of a plant; the body within the ovary which, upon fertilization, becomes the seed. 2 A small ovum. [< F, dim. of L *ovum* an egg] — **o′vu·lar, o·vu·lar·y** (ō′vyə·ler′ē) *adj.*

o·vum (ō′vəm) *n. pl.* **o·va** (ō′və) 1 *Biol.* **a** A cell formed in the ovary; an egg. **b** An ovule. 2 *Archit.* An egg-shaped ornament. [< L]

owe (ō) *v.* **owed** (*Obs.* **ought**), **ow·ing** *v.t.* 1 To be indebted to the amount of; be obligated to pay or repay. 2 To be obligated to render or offer: to *owe* an apology. 3 To have or possess by virtue of gift, labor, etc.: with *to*: He *owes* his success to his own efforts. 4 To cherish (a certain feeling) toward another: to *owe* a grudge. 5 *Obs.* To own; have. — *v.i.* 6 To be in debt. [OE *āgan*]

Ow·en (ō′in) A masculine personal name. [< Welsh, young warrior]

Owen, Robert, 1771–1858, Welsh social reformer. — **Wilfred,** 1893–1918, English poet.

Owen Falls A waterfall (65 feet high) in the Victoria Nile in SE Uganda; site of a dam 2,725 feet long, 85 feet high, built in 1949.

Ow·ens River (ō′inz) A river in eastern California, flowing 120 miles SE and supplying water to the city of Los Angeles.

Owen Stanley Range A mountain range in SE New Guinea; highest peak, 13,240 feet.

ow·er·word (ou′ər·wûrd′) *n. Scot.* The burden of a song; refrain.

ow·ing (ō′ing) *adj.* Due; yet to be paid: six dollars *owing.*

owing to Attributable to; on account of; in consequence of.

owl (oul) *n.* 1 A predatory nocturnal bird of the order *Strigiformes,* having large eyes and head, short, sharply hooked bill, long powerful claws, and a circular facial disk of radiating feathers. Of the North American owls, prominent species are the circumpolar **snowy owl** (genus *Nyctea*), the **great horned owl,** the **barred owl** *(Syrnium varium),* the **great gray owl** (genus *Scotiaptex*), **screech owl** (genus *Otus*), and the **long-eared** and **short-eared owls** (genus *Asio*). 2 One of a breed of domestic pigeons having an owl-like head and a prominent frill. 3 A person with nocturnal habits. 4 A person of solemn appearance, etc. [OE *ūle*]

owl·et (ou′lit) *n.* 1 A small owl: the European owlet *(Athene noctua),* or a similar Oriental species *(A. brama)* of India. 2 A young owl.

owl·ish (ou′lish) *adj.* 1 Like an owl; grave. 2 Nocturnally active. 3 *Brit. Dial.* Stupid. — **owl′ish·ly** *adv.* — **owl′ish·ness** *n.*

owl's-clo·ver (oulz′klō′vər) *n.* Any of a genus *(Orthocarpus)* of herbs of the figwort family of western North and South America, especially a California species *(O. purpurascens)* with crimson or purple flowers.

own (ōn) *adj.* 1 Belonging to oneself; peculiar; particular; individual: following the possessive (usually a possessive pronoun) as an intensive to express ownership, interest, or individual peculiarity with emphasis, or to indicate the exclusion of others: my *own* horse; his *own* idea; It is my *own*: in this sense often with ellipsis of the noun. 2 Being of the nearest degree: *own* cousin. — **to come into one's own** 1 To obtain possession of one's property. 2 To receive one's reward; come into one's rightful position. — **to hold one's own** 1 To maintain one's place or position. 2 To keep up with one's work, or remain undefeated. — **on one's own** Entirely dependent on one's self for support or success. — *v.t.* 1 To have or hold as one's own; have as a belonging; possess. 2 To admit or acknowledge. — *v.i.* 3 To confess. See synonyms under ACKNOWLEDGE, AVOW, CONFESS, HAVE. [OE *āgen,* orig. pp. of *āgan* owe, possess] — **own′a·ble** *adj.*

own·er (ō′nər) *n.* One who has the legal title or right to or has possession of a thing. See synonyms under MASTER. — **own′er·less** *adj.*

own·er·ship (ō′nər·ship) *n.* The state of being an owner; proprietorship; also, legal title. ◆ Collateral adjective: *allodial.* See synonyms under PROPERTY.

owre-hip (our′hip) *n. Scot.* A way of striking a blow with a hammer swung from the hip.

owse (ouz) *n. Scot.* Ox.

O·wy·hee River (ō·wī′hē) A river in SE Oregon, flowing 300 miles north to the Snake River.

ox (oks) *n. pl.* **ox·en** (ok′sən) 1 An adult castrated male of a domestic bovine quadruped. 2 A bovine quadruped, as a buffalo, bison, or yak; specifically, the common domesticated *Bos taurus,* or the zebu or Indian ox *(Bos indicus).* ◆ Collateral adjective: *bovine.* [OE *oxa*]

oxa– *combining form Chem.* Denoting the presence of oxygen, especially as replacing carbon in a ring compound. Also, before vowels, **ox–,** as in *oxazine.* [< OXYGEN]

ox·a·late (ok′sə·lāt) *n. Chem.* A salt or ester of oxalic acid.

ox·al·ic (ok·sal′ik) *adj.* Pertaining to or derived from the oxalis or sorrel. [< F *oxalique* < L *oxalis* OXALIS]

oxalic acid *Chem.* A white, crystalline, poisonous compound, $C_2H_2O_4 \cdot 2H_2O$, found extensively in plant tissues as oxalates, and made artificially in various ways, as by decomposing sugar with nitric acid: used in bleaching and in dyeing, and for removing ink stains from paper, linen, etc.

ox·a·lis (ok′sə·lis) *n.* A plant of a large, widely distributed genus *(Oxalis)* of mostly stemless herbs of the wood-sorrel family, with purple, rose, or white flowers; wood sorrel. [< L < Gk. < *oxys* sharp, acid]

ox·a·lu·ri·a (ok′sə·lōōr′ē·ə) *n. Pathol.* Excess of calcium oxalate in the urine. [< OXAL(ATE) + -URIA]

ox·a·lyl (ok′sə·lil) *n. Chem.* The bivalent OCCO radical: *Oxalyl* chloride, $C_2O_2Cl_2$, is a colorless, fuming, poisonous liquid obtained from oxalic acid.

ox·blood (oks′blud′) *n.* A monochrome glaze

overpolemical
overpolish
overponderous
overpopular
overpopulous
overpositive
overpowerful
overpraise
overprecise
overpreciseness
overpreoccupation
overpress
overpresumptuous
overprocrastination
overproductive
overproficient
overprolific
overprominent
overprompt
overpromptness
overprosperous
overprotect
overprotract
overproud
overprovide
overprovision
overprovocation
overprovoke
overpublic
overpublicity
overpunish
overpunishment
overquick
overquiet
overquietness
overrapturize
overrash
overrational
overrationalize
overreadiness
overready
overrealism
overrealistic
overrefinement
overreflection
overreflective
overrelax
overreliant
overreligious
overrepresent
overreserved
overresolute
overrestrain
overretention
overreward
overrich
overrife
overrighteous
overrighteousness
overrigid
overrigorous
overripe
overroast
overrough
overrude
oversad
oversalt
oversalty
oversanguine
oversaturate
oversaturation
oversaucy
overscare
overscented
overscrub
overscrupulous
overseason
overseasoned
oversecure
oversensible
oversensitive
oversententious
oversentimental
overserious
overservile
oversettled
oversevere
overseverely
overseverity
oversharp
overshort
overshorten
overshrink
oversick
oversilent
oversimple
oversimplicity
oversimplification
oversimplify
overskeptical
overslander
overslow
oversmall
oversmooth
oversoak

of Chinese porcelain, in various tones of brilliant, deep, warm red; also, any of the tones of this glaze: also called *sang de boeuf*.

ox·bow (oks′bō′) *n.* **1** A bent piece of wood in an ox yoke, that forms a collar for the ox. **2** A bend in a river shaped like this.

Ox·en·stiern (ok′sən·stirn), **Count Axel**, 1583–1654, Swedish statesman. Also **Ox·en·stier·na** (ok′sən·stir′nä).

ox·eye (oks′ī′) *n.* **1** Any of several plants of various genera of the composite family, especially any species of *Buphthalmum*, with large yellow heads. **2** The oxeye daisy. **3** One of various birds, as the least sandpiper. **4** An oval dormer window.

ox·eyed (oks′īd′) *adj.* Having large, calm eyes like those of an ox.

oxeye daisy An erect perennial weed (*Chrysanthemum leucanthemum*) with oblong leaves and solitary white flowers with yellow centers.

Ox·ford (oks′fərd) **1** A county of south central England; 749 square miles. Also **Ox′ford·shire** (-shir). **2** Its county town, on the Thames; site of **Oxford University**, established in the 12th century.

oxford gray 1 A very dark gray. **2** A woolen fabric of this color.

Oxford Group movement See BUCHMANISM.

Oxford movement See TRACTARIANISM.

Oxford shoe A low, laced shoe tied at the instep. Also **Oxford tie**.

Oxford unit That quantity of penicillin which, when dissolved in 50 cubic centimeters of meat extract, will completely inhibit growth in a test strain of *Staphylococcus aureus*. Also called *Florey unit*.

ox·heart (oks′härt) *n.* A variety of sweet cherry.

ox·i·dase (ok′si·dās) *n. Biochem.* One of many oxidizing ferments found widely distributed in plant and animal tissues. [<OXID(E) + -ASE] — **ox′i·da′sic** *adj.*

ox·i·date (ok′sə·dāt) *v.t. & v.i.* **·dat·ed, ·dat·ing** To oxidize.

ox·i·da·tion (ok′sə·dā′shən) *n. Chem.* **1** The act of uniting or of causing a substance to unite with oxygen. **2** The state of being so united. **3** Any changes in an element or a compound that result in addition to it of a negative radical or a relative decrease of the positive constituent. **4** The process by which the atoms of an element lose electrons: opposed to *reduction*. —**ox′i·da′tive** *adj.*

ox·ide (ok′sīd, -sid) *n. Chem.* Any binary compound of oxygen either with an element or with an organic radical, as iron rust. Also **ox·id** (ok′sid). [<F <*ox(ygène)* oxygen + (*ac)ide* acid]

ox·i·dize (ok′sə·dīz) *v.* **·dized, ·diz·ing** *v.t. Chem.* **1** To unite with oxygen; cause the oxidation of; rust. **2** To add an electronegative element or radical to, or to decrease by an electropositive element or radical. **3** To remove electrons from (an element or compound). **4** To change (an element) to a higher valence: to *oxidize* ferrous iron to ferric iron. —*v.i.* **5** *Chem.* To become oxidized. Also *Brit.* **ox′i·dise**. —**ox′i·diz′a·ble** *adj.*

ox·i·diz·er (ok′sə·dī′zər) *n.* That which oxidizes. or produces oxidation, as an oxygen compound that frees its oxygen easily.

ox·ime (ok′sēm, -sim) *n. Chem.* One of a series of compounds containing the group C·NOH, formed by the action of hydroxylamine on aldehydes, ketones, and ketonic compounds. Also **ox·im** (ok′sim). [<OX(YGEN) + IM(IDE)]

ox·lip (oks′lip) *n.* **1** A species of primrose (*Primula elatior*), closely resembling the cowslip. **2** A hybrid primrose.

Ox·o·ni·an (ok·sō′nē·ən) *adj.* Of or pertaining to Oxford, England, or to its university. —*n.* A student or graduate of Oxford University. [<LL *Oxonia* Oxford]

ox·o·ni·um compound (ok·sō′nē·əm) *Chem.* Any of a class of organic compounds containing a basic oxygen atom combined with a mineral acid.

ox·peck·er (oks′pek′ər) *n.* An African bird of the starling family (genus *Buphagus*) that devours the parasites on oxen, etc.

ox·tail (oks′tāl′) *n.* The tail of an ox, especially when skinned for use in soup.

ox·ter (ok′stər) *n. Brit. Dial. & Scot.* The armpit.

ox·tongue (oks′tung′) *n.* Any of various plants having rough, tongue-shaped leaves, as the bugloss.

Ox·us River (ok′səs) The ancient name for the AMU DARYA.

oxy-¹ *combining form* **1** Sharp; pointed; keen: *oxytone*. **2** Acid: *oxygen*. [<Gk. *oxys* sharp]

oxy-² *combining form Chem.* **1** Oxygen, or of or containing oxygen, or one of its compounds: *oxyphyte*. **2** An oxidation product of: *oxysulfide*. **3** Containing the hydroxyl group: *oxyacid*. [<OXYGEN]

ox·y·a·cet·y·lene (ok′sē·ə·set′ə·lēn) *adj.* Designating or pertaining to a mixture of acetylene and oxygen, used to obtain high temperatures, as in welding and blowpipe analysis.

ox·y·ac·id (ok′sē·as′id) *n. Chem.* **1** An acid containing oxygen: contrasted with *hydracid*. **2** A hydroxy acid.

ox·y·cal·ci·um (ok′si·kal′sē·əm) *adj.* Pertaining to or produced by oxygen and calcium; especially, designating the action of the oxy-hydrogen flame on lime, as in the calcium light.

ox·y·ceph·a·ly (ok′si·sef′ə·lē) *n.* The condition of having the skull conical in the upper frontal region. Also **ox′y·ce·pha′li·a** (-sə·fā′lē·ə). [<OXY-¹ + Gk. *kephalos* head] —**ox′y·ce·phal′ic** (-sə·fal′ik), **ox′y·ceph′a·lous** (-ləs) —**ox′y·ceph′a·lism** *n.*

ox·y·gen (ok′sə·jin) *n.* A colorless, tasteless, odorless gaseous element (symbol O, atomic number 8), occurring free in the atmosphere and combined in numerous compounds (of which water is the most familiar), comprising 21 percent by volume of the atmosphere and about 49 percent by weight of the lithosphere, the agent in combustion and an element essential to the formation and functioning of all forms of life. See PERIODIC TABLE. [<F *oxygène* <*oxy-* OXY-¹ + *-gène* -GEN; so called because formerly considered essential to all acids]

oxygen acid An oxyacid.

ox·y·gen·ate (ok′sə·jən·āt′) *v.t.* **·at·ed, ·at·ing** To treat, combine, or impregnate with oxygen; oxidize. —**ox′y·gen·a′tion** *n.*

ox·y·gen·ic (ok′sə·jen′ik) *adj.* Of, pertaining to, resembling, or containing oxygen. Also **ox·y·gen·ous** (ok·sij′ə·nəs).

ox·y·gen·ize (ok′sə·jən·īz′) *v.t.* **·ized, ·iz·ing** To oxidize; oxygenate.

oxygen mask A device worn over the nose and mouth to aid breathing, as at high altitudes, by conveying oxygen from a container to the user.

oxygen point *Physics* The boiling point of liquid oxygen at standard atmospheric pressure, −182.97° C.: one of the fixed points of the international temperature scale.

oxygen tent A tentlike chamber placed over a patient's head and shoulders and supplied with oxygen for the purpose of facilitating his respiration.

ox·y·he·mo·glo·bin (ok′si·hē′mə·glō′bin) *n. Biochem.* A combination of oxygen and hemoglobin, formed in the red blood corpuscles of the pulmonary capillaries.

ox·y·hy·dro·gen (ok′si·hī′drə·jən) *adj.* Of, pertaining to, or using a mixture of oxygen and hydrogen, especially for the production of very high temperatures. —*n.* A mixture of oxygen and hydrogen.

oxyhydrogen blowpipe A blowpipe in which jets of oxygen and hydrogen are combined in order to obtain very high temperatures: used in welding.

ox·y·mel (ok′sə·mel) *n.* A mixture of honey and vinegar boiled to a sirup. [<L *oxymel* <Gk. *oxymeli* <*oxys* acid + *meli* honey]

ox·y·mo·ron (ok′si·môr′on, -mō′ron) *n. pl.* **·mo·ra** (-môr′ə, -mō′rə) A figure of speech consisting of that form of antithesis in which, for emphasis or in an epigram, contradictory terms are brought sharply together, as in the phrase; "O heavy lightness, serious vanity!" [<Gk. *oxymōron*, neut. of *oxymōros* <*oxys* keen + *mōros* foolish]

ox·yn·tic (ok·sin′tik) *adj. Physiol.* Acid-secreting: said especially of certain cells of the stomach. [<Gk. *oxynein* sharpen]

ox yoke A yoke consisting of a heavy piece of wood which lies over the necks of the oxen and from which depend two oxbows.

ox·y·phyte (ok′si·fīt) *n. Bot.* A plant adapted to soil which lacks oxygen.

OX YOKE
With 2 oxbows.

Ox·y·rhyn·cus (ok′sə·ring′kəs) An excavation site of Upper Egypt near the Nile. Also **Ox′y·rhyn′chus**.

ox·y·salt (ok′si·sôlt) *n. Chem.* A salt of an acidic oxide.

ox·y·sul·fide (ok′si·sul′fīd) *n. Chem.* A compound of a sulfide with an oxide in which part of the sulfur has been replaced by oxygen. Also **ox′y·sul′phide**.

ox·y·toc·ic (ok′si·tos′ik, -tō′sik) *adj. Med.* Bringing on or hastening parturition. —*n.* A medicine efficacious in hastening parturition. [<OXY-¹ + Gk. *tokos* birth]

ox·y·to·cin (ok′si·tō′sin) *n.* **1** *Med.* Any drug which stimulates movements of the uterus, as ergotine. **2** *Physiol.* A hormone of the posterior lobe of the pituitary gland, believed to facilitate uterine contractions during childbirth.

ox·y·tone (ok′si·tōn) *adj.* **1** Having the acute accent on the last syllable. **2** Causing a preceding word to take an acute accent. —*n.* A word thus accented. [<Gk. *oxytonos* <*oxys* sharp + *tonos* pitch] —**ox′y·ton′i·cal** (-ton′i·kəl) *adj.*

oy (oi) *n. Scot.* A grandchild. Also **oye**.

o·yer (ō′yər, oi′ər) *n. Law* **1** A hearing or trial of causes; an assize; formerly, in pleading, a petition by a party to an action, praying that he might hear read to him a deed held by the opposite party; in modern practice, the production of such a document, or a copy thereof, by the party holding it. **2** Oyer and terminer: a contracted form. [<AF *oyer* <OF *oir*, *oyr*, ult. <L *audire* hear]

oyer and ter·min·er (tûr′mə·nər) **1** *Brit.* A court composed of two or more judges of assize held at least twice a year in each county. **2** *U.S.* A court of higher criminal jurisdiction. [<F, to hear and determine]

o·yez (ō′yes, ō′yez) *interj.* Hear! hear ye! an introductory word to call attention to a proclamation, as by a court crier: usually thrice

---

oversoft	overstretch	oversuspiciously	overtenderness	overtrim	overvigorous
oversoftness	overstrict	oversweet	overtense	overtrust	overviolent
oversolemn	overstrident	oversystematic	overtension	overtrustful	overwarm
oversolicitous	overstriving	oversystematize	overthick	overtruthful	overwarmed
oversoon	overstrong	overtalkative	overthin	overunionized	overwary
oversoothing	overstudious	overtalkativeness	overthoughtful	overurbanization	overwealthy
oversophisticated	overstudiousness	overtame	overthrifty	overurge	overwet
oversophistication	oversteadfast	overtart	overthrong	over-use	overwilling
overspacious	oversteadfastness	overtask	overthrust	overvaluable	overwily
oversparingly	oversteady	overtaxation	overtight	overvaluation	overwise
overspecialization	overstiff	oversufficient	overtimid	overvariety	overworry
overspecialize	overstimulate	oversuperstitious	overtimorous	overvehement	overworship
overspeculate	overstimulation	oversure	overtinseled	overventilate	overyoung
overspeculation	overstir	oversusceptible	overtire	overventuresome	overyouthful
overspeculative	overstout	oversuspicious	overtrain	overventurous	overzealous
	overstress				

---

add,āce,câre,pälm; end,ēven; it,īce; odd,ōpen,ôrder; tŏŏk,pōōl; up,bûrn; ə = a in *above*, e in *sicken*, i in *clarity*, o in *melon*, u in *focus*; yōō = u in *fuse*, oi,oil; ou,pout; ch,check; g,go; ng,ring; th,thin; ŧh,this; zh,vision. Foreign sounds å,œ,ü,kh,ṅ; and ◆: see page xx. <from; + plus; ? possibly.

repeated. Also **o'yes.** [< OF *oyez*, imperative of *oir*. See OYER.]

oys·ter (ois'tər) *n.* **1** Any of various marine mollusks of the family Ostreidae having a rough, unequal bivalve shell closed by a single adductor muscle and attached to stones, shells, etc., on the bottom, including species cultivated for food. **2** The morsel of dark meat found in the hollow of the bone on both sides of a fowl. **3** Some delicacy; titbit; prize. **4** *Slang* A very uncommunicative person. —*v.i.* To gather or cultivate oysters. [< OF *oistre* < L *ostrea* < Gk. *ostreon*]

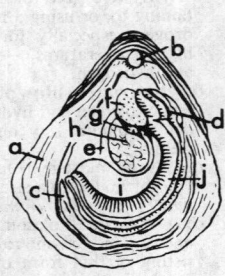

OYSTER
a. Shell.   *f.* Liver.
b. Hinge.   *g.* Heart.
c. Mantle.   *h.* Adductor.
d. Palpi.   *i.* Stomach.
e. Anus.   *j.* Gills.

oyster bed A place where oysters breed or are grown.

oyster catcher A shore bird of the genus *Haematopus*; especially, the American *H. palliatus*, about 20 inches long, having black-and-white plumage and red feet and bill. It feeds mainly upon small mollusks caught between tide marks.

oyster crab A smooth-bodied crab (*Pinnotheres ostreum*) living symbiotically in the mantle of the oyster.

oyster cracker A small biscuit or hard, salted cracker served with oysters.

oys·ter·ing (ois'tər·ing) *n.* The gathering or farming of oysters.

oys·ter·man (ois'tər·mən) *n. pl.* **·men** (-mən) **1** A man who dredges for, raises, or sells oysters. **2** A vessel engaged in the oyster trade.

oyster plant 1 Salsify. **2** The sea lungwort.

oyster planting The placing of small oysters on submerged artificial beds for propagation.

oy·ster·root (ois'tər·rōōt', -rŏot') *n.* Salsify.

oyster seed See SEED OYSTER.

oyster white Any of several very light gray tints: also called *off-white.*

O·zark Mountains (ō'zärk) The hilly uplands in SW Missouri, NW Arkansas, and NE Oklahoma; highest point, 2,500 feet. Also **Ozark Plateau.**

O·zarks (ō'zärks), **Lake of the** An artificial lake in the Osage River, central Missouri; 130 miles long.

Ozark State Nickname of MISSOURI.

o·ze·na (ō·zē'nə) *n. Pathol.* An evil-smelling ulceration of the nasal cavities. Also **o·zae'na.** [< L *ozaena* < Gk. *ozaina* < *ozein* smell] —**o·ze'nic, o·zae'nic** *adj.*

o·zo·ce·rite (ō·zō'kə·rīt, -sə-, ō'zō-sir'it) *n.* A waxy, translucent mixture of natural paraffins, or hydrocarbons. It is colorless to white when pure, but otherwise often leek-green, yellowish, brownish-yellow, or brown. It is used extensively as a purified paraffin. [< Gk. *ozein* smell + *keros* wax]

o·zo·na·tion (ō'zō·nā'shən) *n.* The act or process of producing or treating with ozone.

o·zone (ō'zōn) *n.* A blue gas with a pungent odor like that of chlorine, formed variously, as by the passage of electricity through the air, and regarded as an allotropic form of oxygen containing three atoms in the molecule (O_3). It is unstable and is a powerful oxidizing agent, being much more active than ordinary oxygen: employed for bleaching oils, waxes, ivory, flour, and starch, and for sterilizing drinking water. [< F < Gk. *ozein* smell] —**o·zon·ic** (ō·zon'ik, ō·zō'nik), **o·zo·nous** (ō'zə·nəs) *adj.*

ozone paper A filter paper coated with a mixture of starch and potassium iodide, which turns blue when exposed to the action of ozone.

ozonic ether A solution in ether of hydrogen peroxide and alcohol.

o·zo·nide (ō'zō·nīd) *n. Chem.* Any of a group of unstable, sometimes violently explosive, organic compounds containing ozone held in a double bond.

o·zo·nize (ō'zō·nīz) *v.t.* **·nized, ·niz·ing 1** To treat or charge with ozone. **2** To convert (oxygen) into ozone.

o·zo·niz·er (ō'zō·nī'zər) *n.* An apparatus for generating ozone.

o·zon·o·sphere (ō·zon'ə·sfir) *n.* A narrow layer in the stratosphere at a height of about 20 miles and containing an unusual concentration of ozone formed by the action of ultraviolet solar radiation on oxygen. Also called **ozone layer.** [< *ozono-* (< OZONE) + (STRATO)SPHERE]

P

p, P (pē) *n. pl.* **p's, P's,** or **ps, Ps, pees** (pēz) **1** The 16th letter of the English alphabet: from Phoenician *pe*, Greek *pi*, Roman *P*. **2** The sound of the letter *p*, the voiceless bilabial stop. See ALPHABET. —*symbol* **1** *Chem.* Phosphorus (P). **2** *Genetics* The parental generation: followed by a subscript numeral, as P_1, P_2, to indicate the first, second, etc., parental generation. — **to mind one's P's and Q's** To be careful of one's behavior.

pa (pä) *n. Colloq.* Papa.

Pa *Chem.* Protoactinium (symbol Pa).

Paan (pän) A town on the Yangtze, placed in the Tibetan Autonomous District in 1950: formerly *Batang*: also *Baan.*

Paar·de·berg (pär'də·bûrg, -berkh) A village of western Orange Free State, Union of South Africa; scene of a British victory in the Boer War, 1900.

Paa·si·ki·vi (pä'si·kē·vē), **Juhoo Kusti,** 1870–1956, president of Finland 1946–56.

Pa·bia·ni·ce (pä'byä·nē'tse) A city in central Poland SW of Łódź.

Pa·blo (pär'blō) Spanish form of PAUL.

pab·u·lum (pab'yə·ləm) *n.* Any substance affording nourishment; aliment. See synonyms under FOOD. [< L *pabulum* fodder < *pascere* feed] —**pab'u·lar** *adj.*

pac (pak) *n.* A leather moccasin having a wide sole that turns up and is sewed to the upper; also, a heavy half-boot or legged moccasin of felt or leather worn by lumbermen in the winter. [< N. Am. Ind.]

pa·ca (pä'kə, pak'ə) *n.* A large seminocturnal rodent (genus *Cuniculus*) of Central and South America, brownish with white spots. [< Pg. or Sp. < Tupian]

pace¹ (pās) *n.* **1** A step in walking; also, the progress made in one such movement. **2** A conventional measure of length approximating the average length of stride in walking: usually 3 feet, but sometimes 3.3 feet, making 5 paces to the rod. The **Roman pace** was measured from the point where the heel of one foot left the ground to the point where it descended in the next stride, and was 5 Roman feet, equal to about 58.1 inches, a thousand such double strides making a mile. Such a double step is now called a **geometrical pace,** reckoned at 5 feet. The U.S. Army **regulation pace** is 30 inches, quick time; 36 inches, double time. **3** The manner or speed of movement in going on the legs; gait; carriage and action, especially of a horse. **4** Rate of speed, as in movement or work: often applied to a fast or ruinous life: the *pace* that kills; also, the speed with which a baseball pitcher delivers the ball. **5** A gait of a horse, etc., in which both feet on the same side are lifted and moved forward at once. —**to put (one) through his paces** To test the abilities, speed, etc., of. —*v.* **paced, pac·ing** *v.t.* **1** To walk back and forth across: to *pace* the floor. **2** To measure by paces. **3** To set or make the pace for. **4** To train to a certain gait or pace. —*v.i.* **5** To walk with slow or regular steps. **6** To move at a pace (def. 5). [< F *pas* < L *passus* step < *pandere* stretch. Doublet of PASS *n.*]

pa·ce² (pā'sē) *adv. & prep.* With the permission (of): used to express courteous disagreement. [< L, ablative of *pax, pacis* peace, pardon]

paced (pāst) *adj.* **1** Having a particular pace: used in compounds: slow-*paced.* **2** Measured in paces or by pacing. **3** Done behind or with the help of a pacemaker.

pace·mak·er (pās'mā'kər) *n.* **1** One who makes or sets the pace for another in a race. **2** *Med.* Any of various devices, chiefly electrical, used to regulate the heartbeat and prevent heartblock. —**pace'mak'ing** *n. & adj*

pac·er (pā'sər) *n.* **1** A pacing horse: usually, five-gaited. **2** One who paces, or measures by paces. **3** A pacemaker.

pa·cha (pə·shä', pash'ə), **pa·cha·lic** (pə·shä'·lik) See PASHA, PASHALIK.

pa·chi·si (pə·chē'zē, pä-) *n.* **1** A game of East Indian origin resembling backgammon. **2** Parcheesi. [< Hind. *pach(ch)īsī*, lit., of twenty-five (the highest throw)]

Pach·mann (päkh'män), **Vladimir de,** 1848–1933, Russian pianist.

pach·ou·li (pach'ōō·lē, pə·chōō'lē) See PATCHOULI.

Pa·chu·ca (pä·chōō'kä) The capital of Hidalgo state, Mexico.

pachy- *combining form* Thick; massive: *pachyderm.* [< Gk. *pachys* thick]

pach·y·ceph·a·ly (pak'i·sef'ə·lē) *n.* Exceptional thickness of the skull. Also **path'y·ce·pha'li·a** (-sə·fā'lē·ə). [< PACHY- + Gk. *kephalē* head] —**pach'y·ce·phal'ic** (-sə·fal'ik), **pach'y·ceph'a·lous** *adj.*

pach·y·derm (pak'ə·dûrm) *n.* **1** Any of certain thick-skinned, non-ruminant ungulates; especially, an elephant, hippopotamus, or rhinoceros: formerly included in the obsolete order *Pachydermata,* which embraced also the horse, pig, tapir, etc. **2** A stolid, thick-skinned, insensitive person. [< F *pachyderme* < Gk. *pachydermos* < *pachys* thick + *derma* skin] —**pach'y·der'ma·tous, pach'y·der'mous** *adj.*

pach·y·me·ni·a (pak'ə·mē'nē·ə) *n. Pathol.* Any thickening of the skin or of a membrane. [< NL < Gk. *pachys* thick + *hymēn* a membrane] —**pach'y·men'ic** (-men'ik) *adj.*

pach·y·rhi·zid (pak'ə·rī'zid) *n.* A yellowish-green, poisonous glycoside, $C_{30}H_{18}O_9(OCH_3)_2$, extracted from the seeds of a tropical leguminous vine (*Pachyrhizus angulatus*). [< PACHY- + Gk. *rhiza* root]

pach·y·san·dra (pak'ə·san'drə) *n.* A hardy, evergreen, spurgelike plant (*Pachysandra terminalis*) of the box family, much cultivated for ground cover in shady spots: also called *shade grass.* [< NL, with thick stamens < Gk. *pachys* thick + *anēr, andros* man, a male]

pa·cif·ic (pə·sif'ik) *adj.* Pertaining to the making of peace; inclined or leading to peace or conciliation; peaceable; calm. Also **pa·cif'i·cal.** [< F *pacifique* < L *pacificus* peacemaking < *pax, pacis* peace + *facere* make] —**pa·cif'i·cal·ly** *adv.*

Synonyms: calm, conciliating, conciliatory, gentle, meek, mild, peaceable, peaceful, placid, quiet, smooth, still, tranquil, unruffled, waveless. *Antonyms:* belligerent, contentious, controversial, enraged, exasperated, exasperating, fighting, furious, harsh, hateful, hostile, irritated, irritating, provoked, provoking, quarrelsome, tumultuous, turbulent, warlike.

Pa·cif·ic (pə·sif'ik) *adj.* Pertaining to the Pacific Ocean.

pa·cif·i·cate (pə·sif'ə·kāt) *v.t.* **·cat·ed, ·cat·ing** To pacify. [< L *pacificatus,* pp. of *pacificare* make peace, pacify < *pax, pacis* peace + *facere* make] —**pac·i·fi·ca·tion** (pas'ə·fə·kā'·

shən) *n.* — **pa·cif'i·ca'tor** *n.* — **pa·cif'i·ca·to'ry** (-kə·tôr'ē, -tō'rē) *adj.*

Pacific Islands A United Nations Trust Territory (1947) administered by the United States, comprising the Marshall Islands, Marianas (except Guam), and the Caroline Islands; 680 square miles; headquarters, Agana on Guam; permanent capital, Truk.

pa·ci·fi·co (pä·sē'fē·kō) *n.* A peaceable person; a neutral; specifically, a native of Cuba or the Philippines who did not oppose the Spaniards. [<Sp. <L *pacificus*. See PACIFIC.]

Pacific Ocean An ocean between the American continents and Asia and Australia, extending from the Arctic to the Antarctic Ocean; 70,000,000 square miles: divided by the equator into the **North Pacific Ocean** and the **South Pacific Ocean.**

Pacific slope That region of North America west of the Continental Divide.

Pacific Standard Time See STANDARD TIME. Abbr. *P.S.T.*

pac·i·fi·er (pas'ə·fī'ər) *n.* 1 One who or that which pacifies; a peacemaker. 2 A rubber nipple attached to a round guard, used to quiet a fretful baby. 3 A rubber ring used to relieve the teething discomfort of a baby.

pac·i·fist (pas'ə·fist) *n.* One who opposes military ideals, war, or military preparedness, and proposes that all international disputes be settled by arbitration. — **pac'i·fism** *n.* — **pac'i·fis'tic** *adj.*

pac·i·fy (pas'ə·fī) *v.t.* **·fied, ·fy·ing** 1 To bring peace to; end war or strife in. 2 To allay the anger or agitation of; appease; calm. See synonyms under ALLAY, TEMPER, TRANQUILIZE. [<F *pacifier* <L *pacificare* <*pacificus*. See PACIFIC.]

Pa·cin·i·an body (pə·sin'ē·ən) *Anat.* One of the flattened, oval end organs of nerves, found especially in the hands, feet, and mesentery: after **Filippo Pa·ci·ni** (pä·chē'nē), 1812–1883, Italian anatomist. Also **Pacinian corpuscle.**

pack[1] (pak) *n.* 1 A bundle or large package, especially one to be carried on the back of a man or animal; a collection of anything; heap. 2 A full set of like or associated things usually handled collectively, as cards. 3 A number of dogs or wolves that hunt together; hence, any gang or band, especially one existing for criminal purposes. 4 A large area of floating broken ice: also **ice pack.** 5 Face pack. 6 A wrapping of sheets or blankets about a patient, used in certain water–cure treatments: a wet *pack,* cold *pack,* etc. 7 *Obs.* A lewd or low person: usually with *naughty.* 8 A parachute, fully assembled and folded for use. 9 The quantity of something, as vegetables or other foods, put in containers for preservation at one time or in a season. See synonyms under FLOCK, LOAD. — *v.t.* 1 To make a pack or bundle of. 2 To place compactly in a trunk, box, etc., for storing or carrying. 3 To fill compactly, as for storing or carrying: to *pack* a suitcase. 4 To put up for preservation or sale: to *pack* fruit. 5 To compress tightly; crowd together. 6 To fill completely or to overflowing; cram. 7 To cover, fill, or surround so as to prevent leakage, damage, etc.: to *pack* a piston rod. 8 To load with a pack; burden. 9 To carry or transport on the back or on pack animals. 10 To carry or wear habitually: to *pack* a gun. 11 To send or dispatch summarily: with *off* or *away.* 12 To treat with a pack (def. 6). 13 *Slang* To be able to inflict: He *packs* a wallop. — *v.i.* 14 To place one's clothes and belongings in trunks, boxes, etc., for storing or carrying. 15 To allow of being stowed or packed. 16 To crowd together; form a pack or packs. 17 To settle in a hard, firm mass. 18 To leave in haste: often with *off* or *away.* See synonyms under JAM. — **to send packing** To send away or dismiss summarily. [ME *pakke,* appar. <LG *pak*]

pack[2] (pak) *v.t.* To arrange, select, or manipulate to one's own advantage: to *pack* a jury. [? Var. of PACT]

pack[3] (pak) *adj. Scot.* Intimate: usually in the phrase *pack an' thick.* — **pack'ly** *adv.* — **pack'ness** *n.*

pack·age (pak'ij) *n.* 1 The act or process of packing; also, that which is packed, as for transportation; something wrapped up or

bound together; a packet or parcel. 2 A box, case, crate, or other receptacle in which goods are packed. 3 A combination of items considered as a unit: a salary increase and fringe benefits all in one *package.* — *v.t.* **·aged, ·ag·ing** To bind or tie into a package or bundle. [<PACK[1] + -AGE]

package store *U.S.* A store that sells liquor by the bottle only, for consumption elsewhere.

pack animal An animal, as a horse or mule, used to carry packs or burdens.

pack·er (pak'ər) *n.* 1 One who packs; specifically, one who makes a business of packing goods for transportation or preservation. 2 One who cures and packs wholesale provisions: a pork–*packer.* 3 One who transports goods on pack animals. 4 Any of certain machines or devices for packing commodities.

pack·et (pak'it) *n.* 1 A small package; parcel. 2 A steamship for conveying mails, passengers, and freight at stated times; especially, one plying up and down a coast or on a canal: also **packet boat.** — *v.t.* To make into a packet. [<AF *pacquet,* dim. of PACK[1]]

pack·ing (pak'ing) *n.* 1 The act or operation of filling an empty space, putting up for transportation, etc. 2 The canning or putting up of meat, fish, fruit, etc., for market, home consumption, etc. 3 The substance used in adjusting or protecting the article packed. 4 A greasy or other material for closing a joint. 5 A fibrous or porous substance for holding oil by absorption and assisting in the lubrication of a journal, etc. 6 A device for making a leakproof fit, as between a piston head and its cylinder.

packing box 1 A stout box in which goods are packed: also **packing case.** 2 A stuffing box.

packing effect *Physics* The crowding together of the component particles of the atomic nucleus resulting from the mass defect.

packing fraction *Physics* A measure of the binding force of the nucleus of an atom; the difference between the isotopic weight of an atom and the mass number, divided by the mass number, the quotient usually being multiplied by 10,000.

packing plant *U.S.* A factory where meats and meat products are processed and packed. Also *U.S.* **packing house.**

packing press A press used in baling cotton, hay, or the like.

pack·man (pak'mən) *n. pl.* **·men** (-mən) A peddler.

pack rat A common North American rat (genus *Neotoma*) which feeds chiefly on seeds, nuts, fruit, and green vegetation: so called from its habit of carrying off provisions: also called **wood rat** and **mountain rat.**

pack·sack (pak'sak') *n.* A canvas or leather traveling sack for blankets, etc.: usually carried across the shoulders.

pack·sad·dle (pak'sad'l) *n.* A saddle for a pack animal, to which the packs are fastened so as to balance evenly.

pack·thread (pak'thred') *n.* Strong thread or twine used for doing up packages.

pack·wax (pak'waks') See PAXWAX.

pact (pakt) *n.* An agreement; compact. [<OF *pact* <L *pactum* agreement <*pactus,* pp. of *paciscere* agree]

Pac·to·lus (pak·tō'ləs) A river of ancient Lydia; the gold washed from its sands was a traditional source of Croesus' gold.

pad[1] (pad) *n.* 1 A cushion; also, any stuffed, cushionlike thing serving to protect from jarring, friction, etc. 2 A launching pad. 3 A soft saddle. 4 A number of sheets of paper packed and gummed together at the edge; a tablet. 5 A large floating leaf of an aquatic plant: a lily *pad.* 6 A soft cushionlike enlargement of skin on the under surface of the toes of many animals. 7 The foot of a fox, otter, etc. 8 The footprint of an animal. 9 A pulvillus. 10 *Slang* A room or apartment; lodgings. — *v.t.* **pad·ded, pad·ding** 1 To stuff, line, or protect with pads or padding. 2 To lengthen (speech or writing) by inserting unnecessary matter. 3 To expand (an expense account) by recording non–existent expenditures. [Origin unknown]

pad[2] (pad) *v.i.* **pad·ded, pad·ding** 1 To travel by walking; tramp; trudge. 2 To move with

soft, almost noiseless footsteps. — *n.* A dull, padded sound, as of a footstep. [Related to PAD[3] (path). Cf. LG *padden* tread.]

pad[3] (pad) *n.* 1 An easy–paced road horse: also **pad horse.** 2 A footpad; a highwayman. 3 *Brit. Dial.* A path; road. [<LG *pad* path]

Pa·dang (pä·däng') An Indonesian port on the western coast of Sumatra.

Pa·dauk wood (pə·dôk') Amboina wood: also *Padouk wood.*

pad·ding (pad'ing) *n.* 1 The act of stuffing or forming a pad. 2 That of which a pad is made. 3 Matter used in writing to fill space.

Pad·ding·ton (pad'ing·tən) A metropolitan borough of NW London.

pad·dle (pad'l) *n.* 1 A broad–bladed implement resembling a short oar, used without a rowlock in propelling a canoe or small boat. 2 The distance covered during one trip in a canoe over a given time. 3 A paddle board. 4 A straight iron tool for stirring ore in a furnace. 5 A bat or pallet, as used in tempering clay. 6 A scoop for stirring and mixing, as used in glassmaking. 7 A paddle–shaped implement for inflicting bodily punishment. 8 A limb or appendage of service in swimming; a flipper. 9 The snout of the paddlefish. 10 The act of paddling. 11 A flat instrument with which clothes are beaten while being washed in a stream. — *v.* **·dled, ·dling** *v.i.* 1 To move a canoe, etc., on or through water by means of a paddle; ply a paddle. 2 To row gently or lightly. 3 To swim with short, downward strokes, as ducks do. 4 To play in water with the hands or feet; dabble; wade. — *v.t.* 5 To propel by means of a paddle or paddles. 6 To convey by paddling. 7 To beat with a paddle; spank. 8 To stir. — **to paddle one's own canoe** To be independent; get along without help. [ME *padell* small spade, prob. var. of *patel* shallow pan <L *patella*] — **pad'dler** *n.*

paddle board One of the broad, paddlelike boards set on the circumference of a paddle wheel or water wheel.

paddle boat A boat propelled by paddle wheels.

paddle box The housing or box over a paddle wheel: usually with semicircular upper outline.

pad·dle·fish (pad'l·fish') *n. pl.* **·fish** or **·fish·es** A large fish (*Polyodon spathula*) of the sturgeon family, having a scaleless body with inferior mouth and spatuliform snout, found in the Mississippi Valley streams.

paddle wheel A wheel having projecting floats or boards for propelling a vessel.

pad·dling (pad'ling) *n.* 1 The act of propelling by paddle. 2 A beating or spanking.

pad·dock[1] (pad'ək) *n.* 1 A pasture lot or enclosure for exercising horses, adjoining a stable. 2 A grassed enclosure at a racecourse where horses are walked about and saddled before a race. 3 In Australia, any enclosed piece of land, whether tilled or untilled. — *v.t.* To confine, as horses, in a paddock. [Alter. of dial. E *parrock,* OE *pearruc* enclosure. Akin to PARK.]

PADDLE WHEEL
As seen on a
Mississippi River
stern–wheeled steamboat.

pad·dock[2] (pad'ək) *n. Scot.* A toad or frog.

pad·dy[1] (pad'ē) *n. pl.* **·dies** The ruddy duck. Also *paddywhack.* [from PADDY, proper name]

pad·dy[2] (pad'ē) *n. pl.* **·dies** Rice in the husk, whether gathered or growing. [<Malay *pādī* rice in the straw]

Pad·dy (pad'ē) *n. Slang* An Irishman: a nickname for PATRICK. [See PATRICK]

paddy wagon *U.S. Slang* A patrol wagon.

pad·dy·whack (pad'ē·hwak') *n.* 1 *Brit. Dial.* A fit or rage of temper. 2 *Brit. Dial.* A beating or thrashing. 3 *U.S.* The ruddy duck. [<PADDY + WHACK]

Pa·de·rew·ski (pä·də·ref'skē). **Ignace Jan,**

1860–1941, Polish pianist, composer, and statesman; first premier of the Polish Republic 1919.

pa·di·shah (pä′di·shä) *n.* **1** Lord protector; chief ruler: a title of the shah of Iran. **2** Formerly, the title of the sultan of Turkey. **3** Formerly, the title of the British sovereign as emperor of India. Also **pad·shah** (päd′shä). [< Persian *Pādshāh* < *pati* master + *shāh* king]

pad·le (päd′l) *n. Scot.* A garden hoe.

pad·lock (pad′lok′) *n.* A detachable lock, designed to hang on the object fastened, having a shackle attached at one end, and devised so as to fasten through a staple. — *v.t.* To fasten with or as with a padlock. [ME *padlocke,* ? < *pad* a basket + LOCK[1]]

Pad·raic (pôth′rig) Irish form of PATRICK. Also **Pad′raig.**

pa·dre (pä′drā) *n.* **1** Father: a title used in Italy, Spain, and Spanish America in addressing or speaking of priests, and in India for all clergymen. **2** An army or navy chaplain. [< Ital., Sp., and Pg. < L *pater, patris* father]

pa·dro·ne (pä·drō′nā) *n. pl.* **·nes** (-nās) or **·ni** (-nē) **1** Master: an appellation of an Italian house proprietor or employer of labor. **2** The master of a small vessel in the Mediterranean trade. [< Ital. < L *patronus* PATRON] — **pa·dro′nism** *n.*

Pad·u·a (paj′ōō·ə, pad′yōō·ə) A city in NE Italy west of Venice. *Italian* **Pa·do·va** (pä′dō·vä).

pad·u·a·soy (paj′ōō·ə·soi′) *n.* A strong, rich silk fabric, originally made at Padua; also, an article made of it. [Prob. alter. of F *pou-de-soie* a silk fabric; infl. in form by *Padua say* serge from Padua]

Pa·dus (pā′dəs) The ancient name for the Po.

pae·an (pē′ən) *n.* **1** A choral ode; originally, a song of praise honoring Apollo. **2** Hence, any song of joy or exultation. Also spelled *pean.* [< L < Gk. *paian* a hymn addressed to Paian, the god Apollo]

paed–, paedo– See PEDO–.

paed·e·rast (ped′ər·ast), etc. See PEDERAST, etc.

pae·do·gen·e·sis (pē′dō·jen′ə·sis) *n.* The reproduction of young in the larval stage, as in the axolotl and certain dipterous insects.

pa·el·la (pī·ä′lə, pī·el′ə, *Sp.* pī·ä′yə, pī·ä′lyə) *n.* A Spanish dish of rice flavored with saffron, to which is added shellfish, chicken and other meats, and vegetables. [< Catalan, lit., casserole–like pot]

pae·on (pē′on) *n.* In Greek and Latin prosody, a foot of four syllables, one long and three short in any order. [< L < Gk. *paiōn* < *Paiōn* Apollo; because used in hymns to Apollo]

Paes·tum (pes′təm) An ancient Greek city in southern Italy; on the site of modern *Pesto.* Also **Pæs′tum.**

pa·gan (pā′gən) *n.* **1** One who is neither a Christian, a Jew, nor a Moslem; a heathen. **2** In early Christian use, an idol–worshiper; a non–Christian. **3** An irreligious person. — *adj.* Pertaining to pagans; heathenish; idolatrous. [< LL *paganus* heathen < L, orig., a rural villager < *pagus* the country] — **pa′gan·dom** *n.* — **pa′gan·ish** *adj.* — **pa′gan·ism** *n.*

Pa·ga·ni·ni (pä′gä·nē′nē), **Niccolò,** 1782–1840, Italian violinist and composer.

pa·gan·ize (pā′gən·īz) *v.t.* & *v.i.* **·ized, ·iz·ing** To make or become pagan.

page[1] (pāj) *n.* **1** A male servant or attendant; specifically, in chivalry, a lad or young man in training for knighthood, or a youth of gentle parentage attending a royal or princely personage. **2** A boy whose duty it is to attend upon legislators while in session. **3** A boy in livery, employed in a hotel, club, theater, or private house to perform light duties. — *v.t.* **paged, pag·ing 1** To seek or summon (a person) by calling his name, as a hotel page does. **2** To wait on as a page. [< OF < Ital. *paggio* < Med. L *pagius,* ? < Gk. *paidion,* dim. of *pais, paidos* child]

page[2] (pāj) *n.* **1** One side of a leaf of a book, letter, manuscript, etc.; also, the type for printing on one side: abbreviated p., *pl.* pp. **2** Hence, any source or record of knowledge. — *v.t.* **paged, pag·ing** To mark the pages of with numbers. [< F < L *pagina* leaf of a book, written page < *pag-,* stem of *pangere* fasten] — **pag′ing** *n.*

Page (pāj), **Thomas Nelson,** 1853–1922, U.S. novelist. — **Walter Hines,** 1855–1918, U.S. diplomat and publisher.

pag·eant (paj′ənt) *n.* **1** A community outdoor celebration presenting scenes from local history and tradition. **2** An imposing exhibition or spectacular parade devised for a public ceremony or celebration. **3** A theatrical spectacle; hence, unsubstantial display. **4** Hangings having scenic enrichment. **5** Originally, a traveling car or float having a stage for presenting mystery plays; hence, any pompous or showy object or decoration designed for public parades. See synonyms under OSTENTATION, SPECTACLE. [< Med. L *pagina* a framework, ? < L *pegma* < Gk. *pēgma* a framework, scaffold < *pēgnynai* fasten]

pag·eant·ry (paj′ən·trē) *n. pl.* **·ries** Pageants collectively; ceremonial splendor or display; pomp; showy quality. See synonyms under OSTENTATION.

Pag·et (paj′it), **Sir James,** 1814–99, English surgeon and pathologist.

pag·i·nal (paj′ə·nəl) *adj.* Consisting of, or pertaining to, the pages of a book; also, page for page. [< LL *paginalis* < L *pagina* leaf of a book, page]

pag·i·nate (paj′ə·nāt) *v.t.* **·nat·ed, ·nat·ing** To number the pages of (a book) consecutively. [< L *pagina* page + -ATE[1]]

pag·i·na·tion (paj′ə·nā′shən) *n.* **1** The numbering of the pages, as of a book. **2** The system of figures and marks used in paging.

pa·go·da (pə·gō′də) *n.* In the countries of the Far East, a sacred tower or temple, usually pyramidal and profusely adorned. Also **pag·od** (pag′əd, pə·god′). [< Pg. *pagode,* prob. < Persian *butkadah* idol–temple < *but* idol + *kadah* house, ? ult. < Skt. *bhagavati* divine]

Pa·go Pa·go (päng′ō päng′ō) The only port of call in American Samoa, on Tutuila island: also *Pango Pango.* Also **Pa′go·pa′go.**

pa·go·plex·i·a (pā′gō·plek′sē·ə) *n. Pathol.* **1** Frostbite. **2** Chilblain. [< NL < Gk. *pagos* frost + *plēxis* stroke < *plēssein* strike]

Pa·gu·ri·dae (pə·gyŏŏr′ə·dē) *n. pl.* A family of crustaceans containing the hermit crabs. [< NL < L *pagurus* a kind of crab < Gk. *pagouros* < *pagos* a fixed thing (< *pēgnynai* fasten) + *oura* a tail] — **pa·gu′ri·an** (-ē·ən), **pa·gu·rid** (pə·gyŏŏr′id, pag′yə·rid) *adj.* & *n.*

pah (pä, pa) *interj.* Bah! faugh! an exclamation of contemptuous disgust.

Pa·hang (pä·häng′) The largest State of Malaya, in the central part; 13,873 square miles; capital, Kuala Lipis.

pah·la·vi (pä′lə·vē) *n.* A gold coin of Iran, equivalent to 100 rials, adopted in 1927. [< Persian, after Rhiza Khan *Pahlavi,* shah of Persia]

Pah·la·vi (pä′lə·vē) *n.* A literary form of Middle Persian, in use from the third to the seventh century: preserved in the Zoroastrian sacred writings, transliterated in Semitic characters: also spelled *Pehlevi.* [< Persian *Pahlavī* Parthian < OPersian *Parthava* Parthia]

pa·ho·e·ho·e (pä·hō′ə·hō′ə) *n.* A variety of lava having a smooth, ropy, or corded appearance. [< Hawaiian, lit., smooth, polished]

Pai (pī) A river in Hopeh province, China, flowing 300 miles SE to the Gulf of Chihli: Chinese *Pei Ho.*

paid (pād) Past tense and past participle of PAY.

pai·deu·tics (pī·dōō′tiks, -dyōō′-) *n.* The theory or the art of instruction; pedagogy. [< Gk. *paideutikos* of teaching < *paideuein* teach < *pais, paidos* a child]

pai·dle (pād′l) *v.t.* & *v.i. Scot.* To paddle.

pai·dol·o·gy (pī·dol′ə·jē) *n.* Pedology. [< Gk. *pais, paidos* a child + -LOGY]

paik (pāk) *n. Scot.* A blow; a beating. — *v.t.* To beat or strike.

pail (pāl) *n.* **1** A cylindrical vessel for carrying liquids, etc., properly having a bail as a handle. **2** The amount carried in this vessel. ◆ Homophone: *pale.* [OE *paegel* a gill, wine measure; infl. by OF *paelle* frying pan, liquid measure < L *patella* a small pan] — **pail′ful′** *n.*

pail·lasse (pal·yas′, pal′yas) *n.* A mattress of straw, excelsior, or the like: also spelled *palliasse.* [< F < *paille* straw < L *palea* chaff]

pail·lette (pal·yet′) *n.* **1** A bit of metal or colored foil, used in enamel painting. **2** A spangle; one of a hanging bunch of spangles. [< F, dim. of *paille* straw] — **pail·let′ted** *adj.*

pain (pān) *n.* **1** The sensation or feeling resulting from or accompanying some injury, derangement, overstrain, or obstruction of the physical powers; any distressing or afflicting emotion, or such emotions in general; grief: opposite of *pleasure.* **2** *pl.* Care, trouble, effort, or exertion expended on anything: used often as singular: with much *pains.* **3** *pl.* The pangs of childbirth. — **on** (or **upon** or **under**) **pain of** With the penalty of (some specified punishment). — **to take pains** To be careful; to make an effort. — *v.t.* To cause pain to; hurt or grieve; disquiet. — *v.i.* To cause pain. See synonyms under HURT, PIQUE. ◆ Homophone: *pane.* [< OF *peine* < L *poena* < Gk. *poinē* a penalty]

Synonyms (noun): ache, affliction, agony, anguish, discomfort, distress, misery, pang, paroxysm, suffering, throe, torment, torture, trouble, twinge, uneasiness, woe, wretchedness. *Pain* is the most general term of this group, including all the others; *pain* is a disturbing sensation from which nature revolts, resulting from some injurious external interference (as from a wound, a bruise, a harsh word, etc.), or from some lack of what one needs, craves, or cherishes (as, the *pain* of hunger or bereavement), or from some abnormal action of bodily or mental functions (as, the *pains* of disease, envy, or discontent). *Ache* is lingering *pain,* more or less severe; *pang,* a *pain* short, sharp, intense, and perhaps repeated. We speak of the *pangs* of hunger or of remorse. *Throe* is a violent *pain. Paroxysm* applies to the alternately recurring and receding *pain,* which comes as though in waves; the *paroxysm* is the rising of the wave. *Torment* and *torture* are intense and terrible *sufferings.* Compare ADVERSITY, AFFLICTION, AGONY, INJURY, SUFFERING. *Antonyms:* comfort, delight, ease, enjoyment, peace, rapture, relief, solace.

painch (pānch) *n. Scot.* Paunch.

Paine (pān), **Robert Treat,** 1731–1814, American jurist; signer, for Massachusetts, of the Declaration of Independence. — **Thomas,** 1737–1809, American patriot, author, and political philosopher born in England.

pained (pānd) *adj.* **1** Hurt (physically or mentally); distressed. **2** Showing pain: a *pained* expression.

pain·ful (pān′fəl) *adj.* **1** Giving or attended with pain; distressing. **2** Requiring labor, effort, or care; arduous. **3** Affected with pain: said of the body or of some part of it. **4** *Archaic* Painstaking; laborious. See synonyms under TROUBLESOME. — **pain′ful·ly** *adv.* — **pain′ful·ness** *n.*

pain–kill·er (pān′kil′ər) *n. U.S. Colloq.* A medicine that relieves pain.

pain·less (pān′lis) *adj.* Free from pain; causing no pain. — **pain′less·ly** *adv.* — **pain′less·ness** *n.*

pains·tak·ing (pānz′tā′king) *adj.* Taking pains; careful; assiduous. — *n.* Diligent and careful endeavor. — **pains′tak′ing·ly** *adv.*

paint (pānt) *n.* **1** A color or pigment, either dry or mixed with oil, water, etc. **2** A cosmetic, as rouge. **3** A film, layer, or coat of pigment applied to the surface of an object. — *v.t.* **1 a** To make a representation of in paints or colors. **b** To make, as a picture, by applying paints or colors. **2** To describe or depict vividly, as in words or thoughts. **3** To cover or coat with or as with paint. **4** To decorate with or as with paints: The setting sun *paints* the clouds red. **5** To apply cosmetics to. **6** To apply (medicine, etc.) with or as with a swab. — *v.i.* **7** To cover or coat something with paint. **8** To practice the art of painting; paint pictures. **9** To apply cosmetics to the face, etc. [< OF *peint,* pp. of *peindre* < L *pingere* paint]

paint·brush (pānt′brush′) *n.* The painted cup.

paint brush A brush for applying paint.

paint·ed (pān′tid) *adj.* **1** Covered or coated with paint. **2** Depicted in colors; existing merely in semblance. **3** Marked with bright or varied colors.

painted beauty A brightly colored butterfly *(Vanessa virginiensis)* having dusky orange wings with two eyelike spots on the under side of each.

painted bunting A brilliantly colored finch *(Passerina ciris)* widely distributed in the southern United States. Also **painted finch.**

painted cup Any of several showy North American flowers *(genus Castilleja)* of the figwort family, especially the Wyoming painted cup *(C. linariaefolia)* with vivid scarlet bracts and calyxes and yellow corollas: the State flower of Wyoming. Also called *Indian paintbrush.*

Painted Desert A large arid area in northern

Arizona, extending SE along the Little Colorado River.

painted goose The emperor goose.

painted lady The thistle butterfly.

paint·er[1] (pān′tər) n. 1 One whose occupation is painting; specifically, one who covers surfaces with a preservative or decorative coat of paint. 2 An artist who portrays scenes or objects in colors.

paint·er[2] (pān′tər) n. Naut. A rope with which to fasten a boat by its bow. [Prob. <OF *pentoir* a rope for hanging things <L *pendere* hang]

paint·er[3] (pān′tər) n. U.S. Dial. The puma, or cougar. [Var. of PANTHER.]

Paint·er (pān′tər), **Theophilus Shickel,** born 1889, U.S. zoologist.

painters' colic Pathol. A form of lead poisoning characterized by sharp abdominal pains, slow pulse, and increased arterial tension.

paint horse In the western United States, a pied or spotted horse; a pinto.

paint·ing (pān′ting) n. 1 The act, art, or employment of laying on paints with a brush. 2 The art of representing objects on a surface by means of pigments. 3 A picture.

paint·y (pān′tē) adj. **paint·i·er, paint·i·est** 1 Of, belonging to, or covered with paint. 2 Heavily daubed with paint: said of a painting.

pair (pâr) v.t. 1 To bring together or arrange in a pair or pairs; match; couple; mate. — v.i. 2 To come together as a couple or pair. 3 To marry or mate. — **to pair off** 1 To separate into couples. 2 To arrange by pairs. — n. 1 In general, two persons or things of a kind, joined, related, correspondent, or associated; a couple; brace. 2 A single thing having two like or correspondent parts dependent on each other: a *pair* of scissors: in this sense, always linked with a singular verb when one object is counted. 3 A married couple; two animals mated. 4 In legislative bodies, two opposed members who agree to abstain from voting, and so offset each other. 5 A set of like or equal things making a whole: now restricted in use. 6 In some games of cards, two cards of the same denomination: a *pair* of queens. 7 Mech. A combination of two elements forming a unit in the mutual production or constraint of motion, as a piston and cylinder, a screw and nut, etc. 8 A racing shell for two oarsmen. ◆ Current usage calls for *pair* in the plural after a numeral of two or more, as, four *pairs* of shoes, though colloquially the singular is often used, as, four *pair* of shoes. ◆ Homophones: *pare, pear.* [<F *paire* <L *paria,* neut. plural of *par* equal]

pair-oar (pâr′ôr′, -ōr′) n. A boat in which two men sitting one behind the other pull one oar each.

pair production Physics The instantaneous conversion of a photon into an electron and positron by its passage through a strong electric field.

pairt (pârt) Scot. See PART.

pair-trick (pâr′trik′) n. Scot. Partridge.

pais (pā) n. The country; the people; especially, the people from whom a jury is selected: also spelled *pays.* [<OF, the country]

Pais·ley (pāz′lē) adj. Made of or resembling a certain patterned woolen fabric made in Paisley, a suburb of Glasgow, Scotland. — n. 1 The Paisley fabric. 2 A Paisley shawl: designed to imitate a Kashmir shawl.

Pai·ute (pī-yōōt′) n. One of a tribe of North American Indians of Shoshonean stock, living in SW Utah. Also spelled *Piute.*

TYPE OF PAISLEY DESIGN

pa·ja·mas (pə-jä′məz, -jam′əz) n. pl. 1 Loose trousers of silk or cotton, worn by both men and women in the Orient. 2 Similar trousers with coats to match, used as nightwear. Also, Brit., *pyjamas.* [<Hind. *pājāmā* <Persian *pāi* a leg + *jāmah* a garment] — **pajama** adj.

Pa·kis·tan (pak′ə·stan, pä′ki·stän′) **Islamic Republic of** An independent republic in southern Asia remaining within the Commonwealth of Nations; 311,406 square miles; capital, Islamabad. — **Pa′ki·sta′ni** adj. & n.

pak·tong (pak′tong) n. A Chinese alloy of zinc, nickel, and copper. [<dial. Chinese (Cantonese) <Chinese *peh t'ung* < *peh* white + *t'ung* copper]

pal (pal) n. Colloq. A mate; chum; confederate. [<Romany *pal* brother, mate, ult. <Skt. *bharātr.* Akin to BROTHER.]

Pal (päl) Hungarian form of PAUL.

pa·la·bra (pä·lä′brä) n. Spanish A word; speech.

pal·ace (pal′is) n. 1 A royal residence, or the official residence of some high dignitary, as of a bishop. 2 Any splendid residence or stately building. 3 A large building or room used as a place of public entertainment: an oyster *palace.* See synonyms under HOUSE. [<OF *palais* <L *palatium,* orig., the Palatine Hill at Rome, on which stood the palace of the Caesars]

Pa·la·cio Val·dés (pä·lä′thyō väl·thäs′), **Armando,** 1853–1938, Spanish novelist.

pal·a·din (pal′ə·din) n. Any of the twelve peers of Charlemagne; hence, a paragon of knighthood. [<F, <L *palatinus* of the palace < *palatium.* See PALACE.]

palae-, palaeo- See words beginning PALE-, PALEO-.

Pal·a·me·des (pal′ə·mē′dēz) In Greek legend, one of the Greek warriors in the Trojan War.

pal·an·quin (pal′ən·kēn′) n. A type of covered litter used as a means of conveyance in the Orient, borne by poles on the shoulders of two or more men. Also **pal′an·keen′.** [<Pg. *palanquim* <Javanese *pělangki* <Skt. *palyanka,* var. of *paryanka* bed]

pal·at·a·ble (pal′it·ə·bəl) adj. 1 Agreeable to the taste or palate; savory. 2 Agreeable to the mind; acceptable: a loss of business that was hardly *palatable* but at least bearable. — **pal′· at·a·bil′i·ty** n. — **pal′at·a·ble·ness** n. — **pal′at·a·bly** adv.

pal·a·tal (pal′ə·təl) adj. 1 Pertaining to the palate. 2 Phonet. **a** Produced by placing the front (not the tip) of the tongue near or against the hard palate, as *y* in English *yoke, ch* in German *ich.* **b** Produced with the blade of the tongue near the hard palate, as *ch* in *child, j* in *joy.* — n. Anat. 1 A bone of the palate. 2 Phonet. A palatal sound. [<F <L *palatum* palate]

pal·a·tal·ize (pal′ə·təl·īz′) v.t. & v.i. **·ized, ·iz·ing** Phonet. To change to a palatal sound, as (s) to (sh) in *censure,* (t) to (ch) in *nature.* — **pal′· a·tal·i·za′tion** n.

pal·ate (pal′it) n. 1 Anat. The roof of the mouth. The **hard** (or **bony) palate,** or anterior part, has a bony skeleton; the **soft palate,** or posterior division, is composed of muscular tissue and mucous membrane. 2 The sense of taste; relish: so used originally from the false notion that the palate is the organ of taste: a discriminating *palate.* 3 Intellectual taste; mental relish. ◆ Homophones: *palet, palette, pallet, pallette.* [<OF *palat* <L *palatum* palate]

pa·la·tial (pə·lā′shəl) adj. Of, like, or befitting a palace; magnificent. [<L *palatium* PALACE + -AL] — **pa·la′tial·ly** adv.

pal·at·i·nate (pə·lat′ə·nāt, -nit) n. 1 A political division ruled over by a prince possessing certain prerogatives of royalty within his own domain. 2 The office of a count palatine or of an elector palatine.

Pa·lat·i·nate (pə·lat′ə·nāt, -nit) n. A native or resident of the Palatinate.

Palatinate, the A region west of the Rhine, formerly a state of the German Empire, administered (1837–1945) by Bavaria; incorporated (1945) into the Rhineland–Palatinate: also *Rhine Palatinate. German Pfalz* (pfälts).

pal·a·tine[1] (pal′ə·tīn, -tin) adj. 1 Of or pertaining to the palate. — n. Anat. Either of the two bones forming the hard palate. [<F *palatin* <L *palatum* palate]

pal·a·tine[2] (pal′ə·tīn, -tin) adj. 1 Pertaining to a royal palace or its officials. 2 Possessing royal prerogatives; exercising or endowed with regal rights within a certain domain: a count or county *palatine.* — n. 1 A high judicial functionary in medieval France and Germany; hence, by the delegation of powers, a lord exercising sovereign power over a province; a vassal enjoying the exercise of royal privileges over his territory. See COUNT PALATINE. 2 The ruler of a palatinate or county palatine. 3 A fur tippet worn by women over the shoulders. — **the Palatine** or **the Palatine Hill** The central hill of the seven on which ancient Rome was built. [<F *palatin* <L *palatinus* < *palatium.* See PALACE.]

Pal·a·tine (pal′ə·tīn, -tin) adj. Of or pertaining to the Palatinate. — n. An inhabitant of the Palatinate.

Pa·lau Islands (pä·lou′) An island group in the western Caroline Islands; 188 square miles: also *Pelew Islands.*

pa·la·ver (pə·lav′ər) n. 1 Empty talk, especially that intended to flatter or deceive. 2 A profuse parley; hence, public discussion or conference: a term originated by the Portuguese explorers of Africa. — v.t. To flatter; cajole. — v.i. To talk idly and at length. See synonyms under BABBLE. [<Pg. *palavra* word, speech <LL *parabola* a story, word <L, comparison. Doublet of PARABLE, PARABOLA, PAROLE.] — **pa·lav′er·er** n. — **pa·lav′er·ing** adj. & n.

Pa·la·wan (pä·lä′wän) An island in the SW Philippines; 4,550 square miles.

pa·lay (pä·lī′) n. A natural rubber extracted by the natives of Madagascar from wild plants of the genus *Cryptostegia:* also spelled *pulay.* [<Tamil]

pale[1] (pāl) n. 1 Originally, a pointed stick of wood for driving into the ground; a stake; a paling; a fence picket. 2 A fence enclosing a piece of ground; hence, any boundary or limit. 3 That which is enclosed within bounds, literally or figuratively: the social *pale.* 4 Her. An ordinary consisting of a vertical band through the middle of the shield, occupying one third of its width. — **English pale 1** The varying portion of Irish territory which the Anglo–Normans conquered and governed for several centuries after their invasion of Ireland in the 12th century: also **the Pale.** 2 Formerly, the territory of Calais in France. — v.t. **paled, pal·ing** To enclose with pales; fence in. ◆ Homophone: *pail.* [<OF *pal* <L *palus* a stake]

pale[2] (pāl) adj. 1 Of a whitish or ashen appearance; pallid; wan. 2 Of a very light shade of any color; lacking in brightness or intensity of color. — v.t. & v.i. To make or turn pale; blanch. ◆ Homophone: *pail.* [<OF *palle* <L *pallidus.* Doublet of PALLID.] — **pale′ly** adv. — **pale′ness** n. — **pal′ish** adj.

Synonyms (adj.): ashy, bloodless, cadaverous, colorless, ghastly, marble, pallid, wan, white. See GHASTLY. *Antonyms:* blushing, flaming, florid, flushed, purple, red, roseate, rosy, rubicund, ruddy.

pa·le·a (pā′lē·ə) n. pl. **·le·ae** (-li·ē) Bot. 1 A chafflike bract. 2 One of the chaffy inner scales subtending a flower in the grass spikelet. [<NL <L, chaff] — **pa′le·a′ceous** (-ā′shəs) adj.

Pa·le·arc·tic (pā′lē·ärk′tik) adj. Designating a zoogeographical realm which embraces Europe, North Africa, and Asia north of the tropic of Cancer: also spelled *Palaearctic.*

pa·le·eth·nol·o·gy (pā′lē·eth·nol′ə·jē) n. Ethnology dealing with prehistoric man: also spelled *palaeethnology.* — **pa′le·eth′no·log′ic** (-eth′nə·loj′ik) or **·i·cal** adj. — **pa′le·eth·nol′o·gist** n.

pale·face (pāl′fās′) n. A white person: a term allegedly originated by North American Indians.

Pa·lem·bang (pä′lem·bäng′) The largest city of Sumatra, in the SE part.

Pa·len·que (pä·leng′kā) A village in NE Chiapas state, Mexico, on the site of extensive Mayan ruins.

paleo- combining form 1 Ancient; old: *paleography.* 2 Primitive: *paleolithic.* Also, before vowels, **pale-.** Also *palaeo-.* [<Gk. *palaios* old, ancient]

pa·le·o·bi·o·chem·is·try (pā′lē·ō·bī′ō·kem′is·trē) n. The study of the chemical composition of extinct plant and animal organisms as shown by their fossil remains.

pa·le·o·bot·a·ny (pā'lē·ō·bot'ə·nē) *n.* The study of fossil plants. —**pa'le·o·bo·tan'ic** (-bə·tan'·ik) or **·i·cal** *adj.* —**pa'le·o·bot'a·nist** *n.*

Pa·le·o·cene (pā'lē·ə·sēn') *n. Geol.* The oldest epoch of the Cenozoic era, preceding the Eocene.

pa·le·o·e·col·o·gy (pā'lē·ō·ē·kol'ə·jē) *n.* The study of the environment of plant and animal organisms living in past geologic periods. —**pa'le·o·ec'o·log'i·cal** (-ek'ə·loj'i·kəl) *adj.*

Pa·le·o·gene (pā'lē·ə·jēn') *n. Geol.* The Eogene.

pa·le·o·ge·og·ra·phy (pā'lē·ō·jē·og'rə·fē) *n.* The study and description of earth features in past geologic periods. —**pa'le·o·ge'o·graph'ic** (-jē'ə·graf'ik) *adj.*

pa·le·og·ra·phy (pā'lē·og'rə·fē) *n.* **1** An ancient mode of writing; ancient writings collectively. **2** The science of describing or deciphering ancient writings. —**pa·le·o·graph** (pā'lē·ə·graf', -gräf') *n.* —**pa'le·og'ra·pher** *n.* —**pa'le·o·graph'ic** or **·i·cal** *adj.*

pa·le·o·hy·drol·o·gy (pā'lē·ō·hī·drol'ə·jē) *n.* The study of ancient systems of irrigation, water supply, and the like. —**pa'le·o·hy'dro·log'ic** (-hī'drə·loj'ik) *adj.* —**pa'le·o·hy·drol'o·gist** *n.*

pa·le·o·lith (pā'lē·ō·lith') *n.* A chipped stone object or implement of the Paleolithic period of human culture.

Pa·le·o·lith·ic (pā'lē·ō·lith'ik) *adj. Anthropol.* Of, pertaining to, or associated with a period of human culture contemporaneous with the Pleistocene epoch and followed by the Mesolithic period. It is characterized by stone implements of increasing technical refinement; cave paintings, many in vivid color; sculptured forms and bas-reliefs. Also called *Old Stone Age.* The principal stages, reading from the earliest, are as follows:

LOWER PALEOLITHIC:
  Abbevillian
  Clactonian
  Acheulean
  Levalloisian
MIDDLE PALEOLITHIC:
  Mousterian

UPPER PALEOLITHIC:
  Chatelperronian
  Aurignacian
  Gravettian
  Solutrean
  Magdalenian

paleolithic man *Anthropol.* Any type of human being belonging to the Paleolithic period, such as the Neanderthal or Cro-Magnon men.

pa·le·ol·o·gy (pā'lē·ol'ə·jē) *n.* The study of antiquity or antiquities; archeology: also spelled *palaeology.* [< PALEO- + -LOGY] —**pa'le·o·log'i·cal** (-ə·loj'i·kəl) *adj.* —**pa'le·ol'o·gist** *n.*

pa·le·on·tog·ra·phy (pā'lē·on·tog'rə·fē) *n.* The description of fossils; descriptive paleontology: also spelled *palaeontography.* [< PALEO- + Gk. *ōn, ontos* being, ppr. of *einai* be + -GRAPHY] —**pa'le·on'to·graph'ic** (-on'tə·graf'ik) *adj.*

pa·le·on·tol·o·gy (pā'lē·on·tol'ə·jē) *n.* The science that treats of the ancient life of the globe or of fossil organisms, either plants or animals: also spelled *palaeontology.* —**pa'le·on'to·log'ic** (-on'tə·loj'ik) or **·i·cal** *adj.* —**pa'le·on·tol'o·gist** *n.*

pa·le·o·pa·thol·o·gy (pā'lē·ō·pə·thol'ə·jē) *n.* The study of pathological conditions in fossil or extinct organisms.

pa·le·o·ped·ol·o·gy (pā'lē·ō·pə·dol'ə·jē) *n.* The study of ancient or fossil soils.

pa·le·o·pho·bi·a (pā'lē·ō·fō'bē·ə) *n.* An immoderate hostility toward or fear of the past, considered as a trend in contemporary culture and as a possible factor in the origin and development of certain types of mental disorder. —**pa'le·o·pho'bic** *adj.*

pa·le·o·psy·chol·o·gy (pā'lē·ō·sī·kol'ə·jē) *n.* The investigation of mental phenomena traceable to or persisting from an earlier stage in evolution.

pa·le·o·tem·per·a·ture (pā'lē·ō·tem'pər·ə·chər, -prə·chər) *n.* The condition of heat and cold prevailing on the earth and in the oceans in past geologic eras: a determinative factor in the study of extinct forms of life.

Pa·le·o·zo·ic (pā'lē·ō·zō'ik) *adj. Geol.* Of or pertaining to the era following the Pre-Cambrian and below the Mesozoic. —*n.* The Paleozoic era or group. Also spelled *Palaeozoic.* [< PALEO- + Gk. *zōē* life]

pa·le·o·zo·ol·o·gy (pā'lē·ō·zō·ol'ə·jē) *n.* The branch of paleontology that treats of fossil animals. —**pa'le·o·zo'o·log'i·cal** (-zō'ə·loj'i·kəl) *adj.*

Pa·ler·mo (pä·ler'mō) The capital of Sicily, a port on the NW coast: ancient *Panormus.*

Pal·es·tine (pal'is·tīn) **1** In Biblical times, a territory on the eastern coast of the Mediterranean, the country of the Jews: Old Testament *Canaan:* also *Holy Land.* **2** Parts of this territory, not including Syria or Jordan, placed (1920) under British mandate by the League of Nations: 10,434 square miles; capital, Jerusalem: divided (1947) by the United Nations into independent Arab and Jewish states. See ISRAEL, JORDAN. —**Pal'es·tin'i·an** (-tin'ē·ən), **Pal'es·tin'e·an** *adj. & n.*

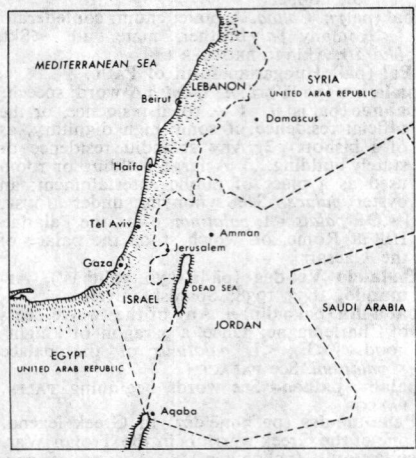

pa·les·tra (pə·les'trə) *n. pl.* **·trae** (-trē) **1** In ancient Greece, a school of athletics; also, the wrestling court in a public gymnasium; hence, any school for youth. **2** A gymnasium. Also spelled *palaestra.* [< L *palaestra* < Gk. *palaistra* < *palaiein* wrestle] —**pa·les'tral**, **pa·les'tri·an** *adj.*

Pa·les·tri·na (pä'les·trē'nä), **Giovanni Pierluigi da**, 1526?–94, Italian composer.

pal·et (pal'it) *n.* A palea. ◆ Homophones: *palate, palette, pallet, pallette.* [< L *palea* chaff + -ET]

pal·e·tot (pal'ə·tō, pal'tō) *n.* A loose overcoat or outer garment. [< F < OF *palletoc,* ? < *palle* cloak + *toque* hood, cap]

pal·ette (pal'it) *n.* **1** A thin tablet, with a hole for the thumb, upon which artists lay and mix their colors for painting. **2** An arrangement of colors placed on the tablet. ◆ Homophones: *palate, palet, pallet, pallette.* [< F, dim. of *pale* shovel < L *pala* spade]

palette knife A thin, flat knife with flexible blade, usually offset from the handle, for mixing and applying oil colors.

pal·frey (pôl'frē) *n.* A saddle horse, especially a woman's saddle horse. [< OF *palefrei* < LL *palafredus,* alter. of *paraveredus* < Gk. *para* beside, extra + LL *veredus* post horse]

Pal·grave (pôl'grāv), **Francis Turner,** 1824–1897, English poet and anthologist.

Pa·li (pä'lē) *n.* The sacred language of the early Buddhist writings, comprised of various Indic dialects: preserved in Ceylon and still surviving in the religious literature of Burma and Thailand. [< Skt. *pāli,* short for *pālibhāsā* language of the canonical texts < *pāli* line, canon + *bhāsā* language]

pal·i·kar (pal'i·kär) *n.* A Greek soldier in the struggle against Turkey for Grecian independence. [< Modern Gk. *palikari* lad < Gk. *pallax, pallakos* youth]

pal·i·mo·ny (pal'ə·mō·nē) *n. U.S. Slang.* Alimony expected by, or directed to be paid to, a person for having lived for a time with another, without legally being married.

pal·imp·sest (pal'imp·sest) *n.* A parchment, etc., written upon two or three times, the earlier writing having been wholly or partially erased to make room for the next. —*adj.* Rewritten or superinscribed. [< L *palimpsestus* < Gk. *palimpsēstos,* lit., scraped again < *palin* again + *pseein* rub]

pal·in·drome (pal'in·drōm) *n.* A word or words that read the same forward or backward, as "Madam, I'm Adam," or "radar." [< Gk. *palindromos* running back again < *palin* again + *dromos* a running]

pal·in·dro·mi·a (pal'in·drō'mē·ə) *n. Pathol.* The recurrence or worsening of a diseased condition;

a relapse. [< NL < Gk. *palin* again + *dromos* a running] —**pal'in·drom'ic** (-drom'·ik) *adj.*

pal·ing (pā'ling) *n.* **1** One of a series of upright pales forming a fence; also, such pales or pickets collectively. **2** A fence made of pales or pickets; hence, a limit or enclosure. **3** The act of erecting a fence with pales.

pal·in·gen·e·sis (pal'in·jen'ə·sis) *n.* **1** A new or second birth into a higher or better life or being; a regeneration; theory or belief that souls are continually reborn. **2** *Biol.* The development of an individual in which the ethnic or group history of its ancestors is repeated: opposed to *cenogenesis.* **3** *Entomol.* The metamorphosis of an insect. **4** *Obs.* The supposed generation of an animal from an organism on which it is parasitic or from decaying animal matter. [< NL < Gk. *palin* again + GENESIS] —**pal'in·ge·net'ic** (-jə·net'ik) *adj.*

pal·i·node (pal'i·nōd) *n.* **1** A poem retracting the matter of an earlier poem; metrical recantation. **2** Hence, any retraction or recantation. [< MF *palinod* < LL *palinodia* < Gk. *palinōidia* < *palin* again + *ōidē* a song]

Pal·i·nu·rus (pal'i·nyoor'əs) In Vergil's *Aeneid,* the helmsman of Aeneas, who fell asleep, fell overboard, and was drowned as the Trojans approached the western coast of Italy.

pal·i·sade (pal'ə·sād') *n.* **1** A fence or fortification made of strong timbers set in the ground. **2** *pl.* An extended cliff or precipice of rock, usually along the bank of a river. —*v.t.* **·sad·ed, ·sad·ing** To enclose or fortify with a palisade. [< MF *palissade* < *palisser* enclose with pales < L *palus* a stake]

Pal·i·sades (pal'ə·sādz'), **The** The ridge of cliffs extending about 25 miles along the western bank of the Hudson River in New York and New Jersey, included in **Palisades Interstate Park,** a chain of recreational areas, 47,070 acres.

pal·ish (pā'lish) *adj.* Somewhat pale; rather pale: *a palish countenance.*

Pa·lis·sy (pà·lē·sē'), **Bernard,** 1509?–89, French potter; creator of a type of highly colored ware decorated with reliefs of animals, fish, etc., known as **Palissy ware.**

Palk Strait (pôk) An inlet of the Bay of Bengal between India and the northern coast of Ceylon: 85 miles long.

pall¹ (pôl) *n.* **1** A covering, usually of black cloth, thrown over a coffin or over a tomb; figuratively, that which brings deep sorrow or fear; also, metaphorically, a dark, heavy covering: *a pall* of smoke. **2** *Eccl.* **a** A chalice cover, consisting of a square piece of cardboard faced on both sides with lawn or linen. **b** An altar cloth. **c** A prelate's pallium. —**heraldic pall** The Y-shaped bearing resembling a pallium. —*v.t.* To cover with or as with a pall. ◆ Homophone: *pawl.* [OE *paell* a cloak < L *pallium* a pallium]

HERALDIC PALL
From the arms of the See of Canterbury.

pall² (pôl) *v.i.* **1** To become insipid or uninteresting. **2** To have a dulling or displeasing effect: with *on.* —*v.t.* **3** To satiate; cloy; disgust. ◆ Homophone: *pawl.* [Appar. aphetic var. of APPAL]

Pal·la·di·an (pə·lā'dē·ən) *adj.* Belonging to or characteristic of the goddess Pallas or the Palladium; hence, characterized by wisdom or learning. [< L *Palladius* < Gk. *Palladios* of Pallas (Athena)]

Pal·la·di·an (pə·lā'dē·ən) *adj. Archit.* Pertaining to or in the Renaissance style of Andrea Palladio: a modification of the classic Roman style.

pal·lad·ic (pə·lad'ik) *adj. Chem.* Pertaining to or designating compounds containing tetravalent palladium.

Pal·la·di·o (päl·lä'dyō), **Andrea,** 1518–80, Italian architect.

pal·la·di·um¹ (pə·lā'dē·əm) *n. pl.* **·di·a** (-dē·ə) Any object considered essential to the safety of a community or organization; a safeguard. [< PALLADIUM]

pal·la·di·um² (pə·lā'dē·əm) *n.* A rare metallic element (symbol Pd, atomic number 46) resembling platinum and in the spongy state capable of absorbing hydrogen in large quantities. See PERIODIC TABLE. [< NL, after *Pallas,* an

Pal·la·di·um (pə·lā′dē·əm) In Greek and Roman legend, a statue of Pallas Athena in Troy on the preservation of which the city depended for safety. [<L <Gk. *palladion*, neut. of *palladios* of Pallas (Athena)]

pal·la·dous (pə·lā′dəs) *adj. Chem.* Of, pertaining to, or containing palladium, especially in its lower valence.

pal·lah (păl′ə) See IMPALA.

Pal·las (păl′əs) 1 In Greek mythology, a name of Pallas Athena, the goddess of wisdom: often **Pallas Athena.** 2 The second largest asteroid.

pall·bear·er (pôl′bâr′ər) *n.* One who attends a coffin at a funeral. [<PALL[1] + BEARER]

pal·les·the·sia (păl′is·thē′zhə, -zhē·ə) *n. Physiol.* Sensitiveness to vibration, as of the skin or a bony prominence to a vibrating tuning fork. [<Gk. *pallein* quiver + ESTHESIA] — **pal′les·thet′ic** (-thĕt′ik) *adj.*

pal·let[1] (păl′it) *n.* 1 *Mech.* A click or pawl used to convert a reciprocating into a rotary motion, or the reverse, as in a feed motion; also, the lip or point of a pawl. 2 A paddle for mixing and shaping clay for crucibles, etc. 3 A tool used in gilding the backs of books or for taking up gold leaf. 4 A movable platform for the storage or transportation of goods. 5 A painter's palette. ◆ Homophones: *palate, palet, palette, pallette.* [<F *palette.* See PALETTE.]

pal·let[2] (păl′it) *n.* 1 A small, mean bed or mattress, usually of straw. 2 A blanket laid on the floor for a bed. ◆ Homophones: *palate, palet, palette, pallette.* [<OF *paillet* < *paille* straw <L *palea* chaff]

pal·let·ize (păl′it·īz) *v.t.* **·ized, ·iz·ing** To load or store (goods) on pallets. See PALLET[1] (def. 4). [<PALLET[1] (def. 4) + -IZE]

pal·lette (păl′it) *n.* One of the plates in a suit of armor protecting the armpits. ◆ Homophones: *palate, palet, palette, pallet.* [<F *palette.* See PALETTE.]

pal·liasse (păl·yas′, păl′yas) See PAILLASSE.

pal·li·ate (păl′ē·āt) *v.t.* **·at·ed, ·at·ing** 1 To cause (a crime, fault, etc.) to appear less serious or offensive; extenuate. 2 To relieve the symptoms or effects of without curing, as a disease; alleviate; mitigate. [<LL *palliatus,* pp. of *palliare* cloak < *pallium* a cloak] — **pal′li·a′tion** *n.* — **pal′li·a′tor** *n.*

Synonyms: cloak, conceal, cover, excuse, extenuate, hide, mitigate, screen, veil. *Cloak,* from the French, and *palliate,* from the Latin, are the same in original signification, but have diverged in meaning; to *cloak* a sin is to attempt to *hide* it from discovery; to *palliate* it is to attempt to hide some part of its blameworthiness. Either to *palliate* or to *extenuate* is to admit the fault; but *extenuate* seeks especially to lessen the culpability involved; hence we speak of *extenuating* circumstances, since circumstances, while they cannot change the inherent wrong of an act, may yet lessen the blameworthiness of him who does it. In reference to diseases, to *palliate* is to diminish their violence, or partly to relieve the sufferer. See ALLAY, ALLEVIATE, HIDE. *Antonyms:* see synonyms for AGGRAVATE.

pal·li·a·tive (păl′ē·ā′tiv) *adj.* Having a tendency to palliate. — *n.* That which serves to palliate. — **pal′li·a′tive·ly** *adv.*

pal·lid (păl′id) *adj.* Of a pale or wan appearance; feeble in color. See synonyms under PALE[2]. [<L *pallidus* < *pallere* be pale. Doublet of PALE[2].] — **pal′lid·ly** *adv.* — **pal′lid·ness** *n.*

pal·li·um (păl′ē·əm) *n. pl.* **·li·a** (-ē·ə) 1 A himation, the distinctive ancient Greek mantle, later adopted by the Romans as a Hellenism. 2 A vestment of the pope, archbishops, and metropolitans in the Roman Catholic Church, and of patriarchs in the Eastern Church; a pall. The Roman pallium is a yokelike band of white wool, with pendants on the breast and back, and is adorned with crosses. 3 *Zool.* The mantle of a brachiopod, mollusk, or bird. 4 *Anat.* The brain mantle or cerebral cortex, which is developed from the anterior vesicle, including the central white substance and the cortical gray. [<L]

pall-mall (pel′mel′) *n.* 1 A game formerly played in England and France by driving a wooden ball along an alley and through a raised iron ring by means of a mallet. 2 The mallet used in this game. 3 An alley or long space for playing the game. It gave its name to one of the streets of London, **Pall Mall** (pel′ mel′, pal′ mal′), noted for its numerous clubs. [<MF *pallemaille* <Ital. *pallamaglio* < *palla* a ball + *maglio* a mallet <L *malleus* a hammer]

pal·lor (păl′ər) *n.* The state of being pale or pallid; paleness. [<L < *pallere* be pale]

palm[1] (päm) *n.* 1 The hollow inner surface of the hand between the wrist and the base of the fingers. ◆ Collateral adjective: *thenar.* 2 The breadth (3 or 4 inches) or the length (about 8 1/2 inches) of the hand used as a linear measure. 3 That which covers the palm, as part of a glove or mitten. 4 The flattened, palmate portion of an antler, as of a moose. 5 The flat expanding end of any armlike projection; specifically, the blade of an oar. 6 A shield attached to the palm of the hand, used by sailmakers in pushing a needle through heavy canvas. — **to grease the palm** To hide (cards, dice, etc.) in or about the hand, as in sleight of hand. 2 To handle or touch with the palm. — **to palm off** To pass off or impose fraudulently. [<F *paume* <OF *paulme* <L *palma* a hand; refashioned after L]

palm[2] (päm) *n.* 1 Any of a large and varied family (*Palmaceae*) of tropical trees or shrubs usually having an unbranched columnar trunk topped by a crown of large palmate or pinnate leaves. 2 A leaf or branch of the palm, used as a symbol of victory or joy. 3 Hence, supremacy; triumph; the reward or symbol of victory or preeminence. [OE *palm* <L *palma* a palm tree, orig., a hand; so called because its leaves are hand-shaped] — **pal·ma·ceous** (pal·mā′shəs) *adj.*

Pal·ma (päl′mä) 1 A port on Majorca, capital of the Balearic Islands. Also **Palma de Mallor·ca** (thä mä·lyôr′kä, mä·yôr′kä). 2 An island in the NW Canary group, 280 square miles: also **La Pal′ma.**

pal·ma-Chris·ti (päl′mä·kris′tē) *n.* The castor-oil plant.

pal·mar (păl′mər) *adj.* Pertaining to, like, or situated near or in the palm. [<L *palmaris* < *palma* a hand]

Pal·mas (päl′mäs), **Las** 1 One of two Spanish provinces in the Canary Islands; 1,583 square miles. Its capital. Also **Las Palmas de Gran Ca·na·ri·a** (thä grän kä·nä′rē·ä).

pal·mate (păl′māt) *adj.* 1 Resembling an open hand. 2 Broad and flat, with fingerlike projections, as the antlers of the moose, or some corals. 3 *Bot.* Having lobes (usually five) that diverge from the apex of the petiole, as a leaf. 4 *Zool.* Webbed, as a bird's foot. Also **pal′mat·ed.** [<L *palmatus,* pp. of *palmare* mark with, the palm of the hand < *palma* a hand] — **pal′mate·ly** *adv.*

pal·ma·tion (pal·mā′shən) *n.* 1 The state or quality of being palmate. 2 Any division of a palmate structure.

Palm Beach (päm) A resort town in SE Florida.

Palm Beach cloth A lightweight summer fabric of cotton warp and mohair filling: a trade name.

palm civet A long-tailed arboreal civet (family *Viverridae*) of Asia and Africa, especially the common *Paradoxurus hermaphroditus* of India.

palm·er (pä′mər) *n.* A medieval pilgrim who had visited Palestine and brought back a palm branch. [<AF <Med. L *palmarius* <L *palma* palm tree + *-arius* -ARY]

Palm·er (pä′mər), **Daniel David,** 1845–1913, U.S. founder of chiropractic. — **George Herbert,** 1842–1933, U.S. scholar and educator.

Palmer Archipelago An island group off the NW coast of Palmer Peninsula: also *Antarctic Archipelago.*

Palmer Peninsula A region of Antarctica, extending 800 miles toward South America; claimed (as *Graham Land*) by Great Britain as part of the Falkland Islands; 63–70° S., 53–68° W.

Palm·er·ston (pä′mər·stən), **Viscount,** 1784–1865, Henry John Temple, British statesman.

Palm·er·ston (pä′mər·stən) 1 One of the Cook Islands; one square mile: also *Avaran.* 2 The former name for DARWIN, Australia.

Palmerston North A city in southern North Island, New Zealand.

palm·er·worm (pä′mər·wûrm′) *n.* The caterpillar of a tineid moth, especially the *Dichomeris ligulella* which skeletonizes apple leaves.

pal·mette (pal·met′) *n.* A conventional carved or painted ornament in ancient art, resembling the palm leaf. [<F, dim. of *palme* a palm tree]

pal·met·to (pal·met′ō) *n. pl.* **·tos** or **·toes** Any one of various fan palms, especially the cabbage palm of the southern United States. [<Sp. *palmito,* dim. of *palma* a palm tree <L; ending infl. by Ital. *-etto,* dim. suffix]

Palmetto State Nickname of SOUTH CAROLINA.

palmi- *combining form* Palm. [<L *palma* palm]

pal·mi·ped (păl′mi·ped) *adj.* Web-footed, as a swimming bird. — *n.* A swimming bird. [<L *palmipes, palmipedis* < *palma* palm + *pes, pedis* foot]

palm·ist (pä′mist) *n.* One who practices palmistry.

palm·is·try (pä′mis·trē) *n.* The art of reading the past life or future of a person by the lines and marks in the palm of the hand. [ME *palmestrie* < *palme* palm + *-estrie,* prob. <OF *maistrie* mastery <L *magister* master]

pal·mi·tate (păl′mə·tāt) *n. Chem.* A salt or ester of palmitic acid. [<PALMITIC + -ATE[3]]

pal·mit·ic (pal·mit′ik) *adj.* Of, pertaining to, or derived from the palm, or especially, from palm oil. [<F *palmitique* <L *palma* a palm tree]

palmitic acid *Biochem.* A crystalline fatty acid, $C_{15}H_{31}CO_2H$, contained in numerous animal and vegetable fats and fixed oils, principally as glycerides: used in making candles and soaps.

pal·mi·tin (păl′mə·tin) *n. Chem.* A colorless crystalline compound, glyceryl palmitate, $(C_{15}H_{31}COO)_3C_3H_5$, contained in those natural fats that yield palmitic acid on saponification, and especially in palm oil: also called *tripalmitin.* [<F *palmitine*]

pal·mi·toyl (păl′mə·toil) *n. Chem.* The univalent radical, $CH_3(CH_2)_{14}CO$, from palmitic acid. [<PALMIT(IC ACID) + -(O)YL]

palm oil 1 A yellow or reddish fat or butter obtained from the fruit of several varieties of palm, especially the African oil palm (*Elaeis guineensis*): used in the manufacture of soap, candles, and for coloring and scenting ointments. 2 *Slang* Money given as a bribe or tip.

palm sugar Sugar made from palm sap.

Palm Sunday The Sunday before Easter, being the last Sunday in Lent and the first day in Holy Week: so called in commemoration of Christ's triumphal entry into Jerusalem, when palm branches were strewn before him. *John* xii 13.

palm·y (pä′mē) *adj.* **palm·i·er, palm·i·est** 1 Marked by prosperity; flourishing. 2 Abounding in or resembling palms.

pal·my·ra (pal·mī′rə) *n.* An East Indian palm (*Borassus flabellifer*) with a cylindrical stem 50 to 100 feet in height bearing a crown of large fan-shaped leaves. [<Pg. *palmeira* a palm tree <L *palma;* infl. by Gk. *Palmyra* PALMYRA]

Pal·my·ra (pal·mī′rə) 1 An ancient, ruined city in central Syria, NE of Damascus. 2 A northern atoll of the Line Islands, comprising part of the Territory of Hawaii; one square mile.

pal·nut (pôl′nut′, păl′-) *n. Mech.* A thin steel nut having a shallow, concave bottom face which by deformation under stress causes the nut to exert a binding grip on the bolt. [Origin unknown]

Pa·lo Al·to (pä′lō äl′tō) A battlefield of the Mexican War (1846) in southern Texas near Brownsville.

Pal·o·mar (păl′ə·mär), **Mount** A mountain of southern California, NW of San Diego; 6,126 feet; site of **Mount Palomar Observatory,** having the world's largest reflecting telescope.

pal·o·mi·no (păl′ə·mē′nō) *n. pl.* **·nos** A golden-brown or yellow horse. [<Am. Sp., orig. a

dove-colored horse <Sp. *palomillo,* dim. of *paloma* a dove <LL *palumbus* <L *palumbes* a ring dove]

pa·loo·ka (pə·lo͞o′kə) *n. U.S. Slang* An inferior or bungling athlete; a lout; lummox. [? <Sp. *peluca,* a term of reproof, lit., a wig]

Pa·los (pä′lōs) A village, formerly a port, in SW Spain, where Columbus embarked in 1492. Also **Palos de la Fron·te·ra** (thä lä frōn·tā′rä).

Pa·louse River (pə·lo͞os′) A river in northern Idaho and SE Washington, flowing 140 miles west to the Snake River.

palp (palp) *n.* A palpus. [<F *palpe* <L *palpus.* See PALPUS.]

pal·pa·ble (pal′pə·bəl) *adj.* **1** That may be touched or felt. **2** Readily perceived; obvious. **3** That may be perceived by touch, or by any of the other senses. See synonyms under EVIDENT, MANIFEST. [<LL *palpabilis* <L *palpare* touch] — **pal′pa·bil′i·ty, pal′pa·ble·ness** *n.* — **pal′pa·bly** *adv.*

pal·pate (pal′pāt) *v.t.* **·pat·ed, ·pat·ing** To feel or examine by touch, especially for medical diagnosis. — *adj.* Having a palpus or sense organ. [<L *palpatus,* pp. of *palpare* touch]

pal·pa·tion (pal·pā′shən) *n. Med.* The process of examining or exploring the body by means of touch; a digital exploration.

pal·pe·bra (pal′pi·brə) *n. pl.* **·brae** (-brē) An eyelid. [<NL <L, an eyelid] — **pal′pe·bral** *adj.*

pal·pi·tate (pal′pə·tāt) *v.i.* **·tat·ed, ·tat·ing** **1** To quiver; tremble. **2** *Med.* To beat more rapidly than normal; flutter: said especially of the heart. [<L *palpitatus,* pp. of *palpitare* tremble, freq. of *palpare* touch]

pal·pi·ta·tion (pal′pə·tā′shən) *n.* Rapid and irregular pulsation.

pal·pus (pal′pəs) *n. pl.* **·pi** (-pī) *Zool.* A feeler; especially, one of the jointed sense organs attached to the mouth parts of arthropods: also called *palp.* [<NL <L *palpus* a feeler <*palpare* touch]

pals·grave (pôlz′grāv, palz′-) *n.* In German history, one having charge of a royal or the imperial court or household; also, one of an order of nobility; one of the hereditary rulers of the Palatinate. [<MDu. *paltsgrave* <*palts* a palace (ult. <L *palatium*) + *grave* count] — **pals′gra·vine** (-grə·vēn) *n. fem.*

pal·sy (pôl′zē) *n.* **1** Paralysis. **2** Any impairment or loss of sensation or of ability to control movement. — *v.t.* **·sied, ·sy·ing** To paralyze. [<OF *paralisie* <L *paralysis.* Doublet of PARALYSIS.] — **pal′sied** *adj.*

pal·ter (pôl′tər) *v.i.* **1** To speak or act insincerely; equivocate; lie. **2** To treat something lightly; trifle. **3** To haggle or quibble. [Cf. dial. E *palt* a piece of coarse or dirty cloth] — **pal′ter·er** *n.*

pal·try (pôl′trē) *adj.* **·tri·er, ·tri·est** Having little or no worth or value; trifling; trivial; contemptible; petty. See synonyms under BASE, CHILDISH, INSIGNIFICANT, LITTLE, PITIFUL. [<dial. E, rags, rubbish <*palt* a piece of coarse or dirty cloth] — **pal′tri·ly** *adv.* — **pal′·tri·ness** *n.*

pa·lu·dal (pə·lo͞od′l) *adj.* Pertaining to a marsh; swampy. [<L *palus, paludis* marsh]

pal·u·dism (pal′yə·diz′əm) *n. Pathol.* The morbid condition observed in those who live among marshes; malaria.

pal·y[1] (pā′lē) *adj.* Lacking brilliance; pale; pallid.

pal·y[2] (pā′lē) *adj. Her.* Divided palewise, the number of such divisions (always even) being specified. [<OF *palé* a row of stakes <*pal* PALE[1]]

pal·y·nol·o·gy (pal′ə·nol′ə·jē) *n.* The scientific study of pollen and other spores, their dispersal and application; pollen analysis. [<Gk. *palynein* strew <*pallein* brandish + -LOGY]

pam (pam) *n.* **1** In the game of loo, the knave of clubs. **2** A game resembling napoleon, wherein the highest trump is the knave of clubs. [<Short for F *pamphile* knave of clubs <Gk. *Pamphilos,* a personal name; lit., beloved of all]

Pa·mir (pä·mir′) An elevated region of central Asia, chiefly in the Tadzik S.S.R., central Asia; a range of the Pamir-Alai, with high plains lying at 11,000 to 13,000 feet, and rising to Stalin Peak, 24,590 feet, the highest in the U. S. S. R.; known as "the roof of the world." Also **The Pamirs.**

Pa·mir-A·lai (pä·mir′a·lī′) A principal mountain system of Central Asia, in the U. S. S. R., China, and Afghanistan.

Pam·li·co Sound (pam′li·kō) A body of water between eastern North Carolina and its offshore islands; 80 miles long; greatest width, 25 miles.

Pam·pa (päm′pä), **La** See LA PAMPA.

pam·pas (pam′pəz, *Sp.* päm′päs) *n. pl.* The great open treeless plains south of the Amazon river, extending from the Atlantic to the Andes. [<Sp. *pampa* <Quechua, plain]

pam·pas grass (pam′pəs) A tall, ornamental, reedlike grass *(Cortaderia selloana)* native to South America, having very large, thick, silvery panicles.

pam·pe·an (pam′pē·ən, pam·pē′ən) *adj.* Of or pertaining to the pampas or to their native inhabitants. — *n.* An Indian of the pampas; a pampero.

pam·per (pam′pər) *v.t.* **1** To treat too indulgently; gratify the whims or wishes of; coddle. **2** *Obs.* To feed with rich food; glut. [Appar. freq. of obs. *pamp* cram] — **pam′per·er** *n.*

Synonyms: caress, coddle, glut, indulge, pet, spoil. See CARESS, INDULGE. *Antonyms*: deny, discipline, harden, inure, starve, stint.

pam·pe·ro (päm·pā′rō) *n. pl.* **·ros** **1** A strong, cold, dry, southwest wind of the Argentine pampas, generally advancing with a well-marked and very black cloud front. **2** An Indian of the pampas. [<Sp. <Quechua *pampa* plain + Sp. *-ero* -ARY[1]]

pam·phlet (pam′flit) *n.* **1** A printed work stitched or pasted, but not permanently bound. **2** A brief treatise or essay, printed and published without a binding, and usually on a subject of current interest. [<OF *Pamphilet,* popular title of a 12th c. Latin love poem, *Pamphilus, seu de Amore*]

pam·phlet·eer (pam′flə·tir′) *n.* One who writes pamphlets: sometimes a term of contempt. — *v.i.* To write and issue pamphlets.

Pam·phyl·i·a (pam·fil′ē·ə) An ancient country and Roman province in southern Asia Minor. *Acts* ii 10.

Pam·plo·na (päm·plō′nä) A city of northern Spain; capital of Navarre. Also **Pam·pe·lu·na** (päm′pā·lo͞o′nä).

Pa·mun·key River (pə·mung′kē) A river in eastern Virginia, flowing 90 miles SE to the York River; scene of Civil War battles, 1864.

pan[1] (pan) *n.* **1** A wide, shallow vessel, usually metallic or earthen, for domestic use, as in holding liquids or in cooking. **2** A vessel, either open or closed, for boiling and evaporating. **3** A natural or artificial depression in the earth for evaporating brine. **4** A circular sheet-iron dish with sloping sides, in which gold is separated. **5** The powder cavity of a flintlock. **6** The skull; brainpan. **7** Any natural depression in the earth containing water or mud. **8** Hardpan. **9** Either of the two receptacles on a pair of scales or a balance. — *v.* **panned, pan·ning** *v.t.* **1** To separate (gold) by washing gold-bearing earth in a pan. **2** To wash (earth, gravel, etc.) for this purpose. **3** To cook and serve in a pan. **4** *Colloq.* To criticize severely. **5** *Colloq.* To obtain; secure. — *v.i.* **6** To search for gold by washing earth, gravel, etc., in a pan. **7** To yield gold, as earth. — **to pan out** *U.S.* To result or turn out; transpire. [OE *panne,* ? <LL *panna* <L *patina* a pan or dish <*patere* stand open]

pan[2] (pan) *n.* **1** The leaf of the climbing pepper *(Piper betle)* used with the nuts of the betel palm as a masticatory in the East Indies. **2** The masticatory obtained from this leaf. [<Hind. *pān* a betel leaf <Skt. *parna* a feather, a leaf]

pan[3] (pan) *v.t.* **panned, pan·ning** To move (a motion-picture or television camera) across a scene in order to secure a panoramic effect. [<PANORAMA]

Pan (pan) In Greek mythology, a horned, goat-footed god of forests, flocks, and shepherds: identified with the Roman *Faunus.*

pan- *combining form* **1** All; every; the whole: *panchromatic.* **2** Comprising, including, or applying to all: usually capitalized when preceding proper nouns or adjectives, as in:

Pan-African	**Pan-Asian**	**Pan-Slav**
Pan-Arab	**Pan-Islam**	**Pan-Slavic**
Pan-Arabian	**Pan-Islamic**	**Pan-Slavonic**
Pan-Asia	**Pan-Russian**	**Pan-Syrian**

pan·a·ce·a (pan′ə·sē′ə) *n.* **1** A remedy for all diseases; a cure-all. **2** An herb credited with remarkable healing virtues; formerly, allheal. [<L <Gk. *panakeia* a universal remedy <*panakēs* all-healing <*pan,* neut. of *pas* all + *akos, akeos* cure] — **pan′a·ce′an** *adj.*

pa·nache (pə·nash′, -näsh′) *n.* A plume or bunch of feathers, especially as an ornament on a helmet. [<F <Ital. *pennacchio* <*penna* a feather <L]

PANACHE

pa·na·da (pə·nä′də, -nā′-) *n.* A dish made of crackers or bread soaked with boiling water, sweetened and eaten with milk, or flavored with wine, etc. [<Sp. <Ital. *pane* bread <L *panis*]

Pan·a·ma (pan′ə·mä, -mô; *Sp.* pä′nä·mä′) **1** A republic on the Isthmus of Panama; 28,575 square miles (excluding Canal Zone). **2** Its capital, near the Pacific terminus of the Panama Canal.

Panama, Isthmus of An isthmus connecting North and South America and separating the Atlantic and Pacific; 30 miles wide at its narrowest point: formerly *Isthmus of Darien.*

Panama Canal A ship canal across the Isthmus of Panama, extending about 40 miles from Colón on the SE Atlantic (Caribbean) to Panama on the Pacific; completed (1914) by the United States on the leased territory of Canal Zone.

Panama Canal Zone See CANAL ZONE.

Panama fever **1** Yellow fever. **2** Malaria.

Panama hat A hat woven from the young leaves of the jipijapa tree of Central and South America.

Pan·a·ma·ni·an (pan′ə·mā′nē·ən, -mä′-) *adj.* Of or pertaining to the Isthmus of Panama or its inhabitants: also **Pa·nam·ic** (pə·nam′ik). — *n.* A native or naturalized inhabitant of Panama. Also **Pan·a·man** (pan′ə·män′).

Pan American Including or pertaining to the whole of America, both North and South, or to all Americans. Also **Pan′-A·mer′i·can.**

Pan American Conference Any one of various conferences of delegates from the republics of North and South America.

Pan American Highway A projected system of roads, totaling 15,714 miles, to link the nations of the western hemisphere.

Pan-A·mer·i·can·ism (pan′ə·mer′ə·kən·iz′əm) *n.* The advocacy of a political union or alliance, or of closer political and economic cooperation, among the republics of the western hemisphere; also, the life of the American peoples as represented in republican forms of government and tending toward such a union.

Pan American Union A bureau (formerly the *International Bureau of the American Republics*) established in Washington, D.C., in 1890, by the 21 American republics to promote mutual peace, commerce, and friendship.

Pan·a·mint Mountains (pan′ə·mint) A range in SE California; highest point, 11,045 feet.

Pan-An·gli·can (pan′ang′gli·kən) *adj.* Pertaining to or including all branches or members of the Anglican church.

pan·a·tel·a (pan′ə·tel′ə) See PANETELA.

Pan·ath·e·nae·a (pan·ath′ə·nē′ə) *n. pl.* Ancient Athenian festivals celebrated yearly in midsummer, with special magnificence (the **greater Panathenaea**) every fifth year: held in honor of Athena, founded by Pisistratus, and said to commemorate the union of Attica under Theseus. The **lesser Panathenaea,** held in the other four years, were founded by Erechtheus. [<Gk. *Panathēnaia (hiera)* (festival of) Athena <*pan,* neut. of *pas* all + *Athēnē* Athena] — **Pan·ath′e·nae′an, Pan·ath′e·na′ic** (-nā′ik) *adj.*

pan·at·ro·phy (pan·at′rə·fē) *n. Pathol.* Atrophy involving many or all parts of the body.

Pa·nay (pä·nī′) An island of the central Philippines; 4,446 square miles; chief town, Iloilo.

pan-broil (pan′broil′) *v.t.* & *v.i.* To cook (meat) in a heavy frying pan placed over direct heat, using little or no fat.

pan·cake (pan′kāk′) *n.* **1** A thin battercake

fried in a pan or baked on a griddle: also **pan cake.** **2** *Aeron.* An abrupt or violent landing effected by an airplane which levels off and settles rapidly on a steep flight path. — *v.i.* **·caked, ·cak·ing** To level off and decelerate an airplane so that it drops to the ground with little forward movement.

pan·chro·mat·ic (pan′krō·mat′ik) *adj. Phot.* Sensitive to all the colors of the spectrum in proportion to their respective visual luminosities: said of an emulsion, film, or plate. — **pan·chro′ma·tism** (-krō′mə·tiz′əm) *n.*

pan·cra·ti·um (pan·krā′shē·əm) *n. pl.* **·ti·a** (-shē·ə) An ancient Greek contest of athletes, including both boxing and wrestling. [<L <Gk. *pan*, neut. of *pas* all + *kratos* strength] — **pan·crat′ic** (-krat′ik) *adj.*

pan·cre·as (pan′krē·əs, pang′-) *n. Anat.* A gland connecting with the alimentary canal; in vertebrates, a large racemose gland behind the peritoneum, between the lower part of the stomach and the vertebræ of the loins, and emptying into the duodenum by one or more small ducts; the sweetbread. [<NL <Gk. *pankreas* sweetbread <*pan*, neut. of *pas* all + *kreas* flesh] — **pan′cre·at′ic** (-at′ik) *adj.*

pancreatic juice *Biochem.* A colorless fluid, containing certain enzymes, secreted by the pancreas and forming an important factor in digestion by emulsifying fats.

pan·cre·a·tin (pan′krē·ə·tin, pang′-) *n.* **1** *Biochem.* One of the active ferments of the pancreatic juice, or a mixture of them. **2** A commercial digestant extract of the pancreas of the ox or hog. [<Gk. *pankreas, -atos* pancreas + -IN]

pan·da (pan′də) *n. pl.* **·das** or **·da** **1** A small raccoonlike carnivore *(Ailurus fulgens)* of the southeastern Himalayas, with long reddish-brown fur and ringed tail; the red bearcat. **2** The great or giant panda *(Ailuropoda melanoleuca)* found only in Kansu and Szechwan provinces in NW China, a mammal of bearlike appearance, with black-and-white coat and rings around the eyes: also *giant panda.* [Prob. <Nepalese]

GIANT PANDA
(About the size of a large bear)

Pan·da·nus (pan·dā′nəs) *n.* A genus of trees and shrubs of southeastern Asia (family *Pandanaceae*), characterized by stiltlike aerial roots and the spiral arrangement of their long gracefully recurved leaves; a screwpine. [<NL <Malay *pandan* conspicuous] — **pan·da·na·ceous** (pan′də·nā′shəs) *adj.*

Pan·da·rus (pan′də·rəs) In the *Iliad*, son of Lycaon and leader of the Lycians in the Trojan War; in medieval legend, Chaucer's *Troilus and Criseyde*, and Shakespeare's *Troilus and Cressida*, a go-between who procures Cressida for Troilus. Also **Pan·dar** (pan′dər).

Pan·de·an (pan·dē′ən) *adj.* Pertaining to the god Pan.

Pandean pipes A primitive wind instrument made of graduated reeds; a panpipe.

pan·dect (pan′dekt) *n.* **1** An encyclopedic treatise; a complete digest of some department of knowledge. **2** Any complete system of law. [<F *pandecte* <L *pandecta* <Gk. *pandektēs* an all-receiver <*pan*, neut. of *pas* all + *dechesthai* take]

Pan·dects (pan′dekts) *n. pl.* A compilation or digest from the decisions of Roman jurists, made by direction of the Emperor Justinian about A.D. 533: also called *The Digest.* See CORPUS JURIS CIVILIS.

pan·dem·ic (pan·dem′ik) *adj.* **1** Pertaining to or affecting all the people. **2** *Med.* Widely epidemic. — *n.* A pandemic disease. [<Gk. *pandēmos* pertaining to all the people <*pan*, neut. of *pas* all + *dēmos* people]

pan·de·mo·ni·um (pan′də·mō′nē·əm) *n.* **1** The abode of all demons; the infernal regions; as used by Milton, **Pandemonium,** the palace of Satan in Hell. **2** Hence, any place or gathering remarkable for disorder and uproar. **3** A fiendish or riotous uproar. Also **pan′dae·mo′ni·um.** [<NL <Gk. *pan*, neut. of *pas* all + *daimōn* an evil spirit]

pan·der (pan′dər) *n.* **1** A go-between in sexual intrigues; a procurer; pimp. **2** One who ministers to the passions or base desires of others. Also **pan′der·er.** — *v.i.* To act as a pander. — *v.t.* To act as a pander for. [after *Pandarus*, with ref. to his role in medieval legend] — **pan′der·age, pan′der·ism** *n.* — **pan′der·ess** *n. fem.*

Pan·do·ra (pan·dôr′ə, -dō′rə) In Greek mythology, the first mortal woman, sent to earth by the gods as punishment for the theft of fire by Prometheus. She brought with her a box **(Pandora's box)** containing all human ills. When in curiosity she opened the lid, the ills escaped into the world, leaving only Hope, which had been at the bottom of the box. See EPIMETHEUS. [<Gk., all-gifted]

pan·dore (pan′dôr, -dōr) *n.* A bandore. Also **pan·do′ra, pan·du·ra** (pan·dŏŏr′ə, -dyŏŏr′ə). [<F *pandore* <L *pandura.* See BANDORE.]

pan·dour (pan′dŏŏr) *n.* **1** A member of a force of Croatian foot soldiers, noted for their brutality: organized locally in 1741, and later incorporated in the Austrian army. **2** Any inhuman or marauding soldier. Also **pan′door.** [<F *pandour* <Serbo-Croatian *pandūr* constable, ult. <Med. L *banderius* follower of a banner]

pan·dow·dy (pan·dou′dē) *n. pl.* **·dies** A deep-dish pie or pudding made of baked sliced apples. Also **apple pandowdy.** [Cf. obs. dial. E (Somerset) *pandoulde* a custard]

pan·du·rate (pan′dyə·rāt) *adj. Bot.* Fiddle-shaped, as certain leaves. Also **pan·du·ri·form** (pan·dŏŏr′ə·fôrm, -dyŏŏr′-). [<L *pandura* a lute + -ATE[1]]

pan·dy (pan′dē) *n. pl.* **·dies** *Scot. & Dial.* A stroke on the palm of the hand with a cane or strap, as a punishment. — *v.t.* **·died, ·dy·ing** To punish thus. [<L *pande (palmam)* extend (your hand), imperative of *pandere* extend]

pane[1] (pān) *n.* **1** A piece or compartment, particularly if flat and rectangular. **2** A piece of window glass filling one opening in a frame. **3** A flat surface, as on an object having several sides: the *pane* of a tower, nut, or brilliant-cut diamond. **4** A panel, or space between timbers; also, a bay. ◆ Homophone: *pain.* [<OF *pan(e)* <L *pannus* a piece of cloth]

pane[2] (pān) *n.* The peen of a hammer. ◆ Homophone: *pain.* [Cf. F *panne* peen of a hammer]

pan·e·gyr·ic (pan′ə·jir′ik) *n.* A formal public eulogy, either written or spoken; encomium; laudation in general. See synonyms under EULOGY, PRAISE. — *adj.* Elaborately eulogistic or laudatory: also **pan′e·gyr′i·cal.** [<F *panégyrique* <L *panegyricus* <Gk. *panēgyrikos* of an assembly <*panēgyris* an assembly <*pan*, neut. of *pas* all + *agyris*, Aeolic form of *agora* gathering] — **pan′e·gyr′i·cal·ly** *adv.* — **pan′e·gyr′ist** *n.*

pan·e·gy·rize (pan′ə·jə·rīz′) *v.* **·rized, ·riz·ing** *v.t.* To deliver or write a panegyric upon; eulogize. — *v.i.* To make panegyrics.

pan·el (pan′əl) *n.* **1** A rectangular piece set in or as in a frame, as in a door, or sunken below it, as a window pane; hence, any such piece, even if raised above the general plane. **2** A bordered member to which the effect of framing is given by moldings or by working away material from the solid plane. **3** One or more pieces of a different fabric and color inserted lengthwise in the skirt of a woman's dress. **4** A tablet of wood, used as the surface for an oil painting; also, the picture on such a tablet. **5** A picture very long for its width, in a simple frame, or with no frame at all. **6** A size of photograph longer than it is wide, usually about 8 1/2 × 4 inches. **7** A face on a hewn stone. **8** A section of a book cover having a framed effect; also, a subdivision of the back of a bound book, between two bands. **9** *Law* The official list of persons summoned for jury duty; the body of persons composing a jury. **10** *Aeron.* **a** One of the construction units forming the wing surface of an airplane. **b** The unit of fabric of which the outer covering of a balloon or the canopy of a parachute is made. **11** An upright board of insulating material sustaining the controlling devices of an electric circuit. **12** An array of dials, gages, and instruments for the operation of an aircraft, automobile, or other complex apparatus. **13** A small group of persons assembled for judging, discussion, etc. — *v.t.* **·eled** or **·elled, ·el·ing** or **·el·ling** **1** To fit, furnish, or adorn with panels. **2** To divide into panels. **3** *Scot. Law* To indict. [<OF *panel* a piece of cloth <Med. L *panellus*, dim. of L *pannus* a cloth]

panel fence A kind of worm fence made in sections.

pan·el·ing (pan′əl·ing) *n.* **1** Work in panels; panels collectively. **2** The introduction or use of panelworking. Also **pan′el·ling.**

pan·el·ist (pan′əl·ist) *n.* A person serving on a panel of judges or debaters.

panel truck *U.S.* A small, light, enclosed truck, as for delivery of supplies.

pan·el·work (pan′əl·wûrk′) *n.* **1** Wainscoting; any work using or introducing panels. **2** Panelworking.

pan·el·work·ing (pan′əl·wûrk′ing) *n. Mining* A method of working a colliery by dividing it into large rooms separated by very wide masses of coal.

pa·nem et cir·cen·ses (pä′nəm et sər·sen′sēz) *Latin* Bread and circuses; food and amusements.

pan·e·tel·a (pan′ə·tel′ə) *n.* A long, slender, cylindrical-shaped cigar: also spelled *panatela.* Also **pan′e·tel′la.** [<Sp.]

pan fish Any little fish that can be fried whole.

pan-fry (pan′frī′) *v.t.* **-fried, -fry·ing** To fry in a frying pan.

pang[1] (pang) *n.* A sudden and poignant pain; keen transient agony; hence, a throe of mental anguish. See synonyms under AGONY, PAIN. [? Alter. of ME *prange* a prong, point]

pang[2] (pang) *Scot. v.t.* To cram; squeeze. — *adj.* Crammed full.

pan·ga·my (pang′gə·mē) *n. Biol.* Indiscriminate or random mating. — **pan·gam·ic** (pan·gam′ik), **pan′ga·mous** *adj.* — **pan′ga·mous·ly** *adv.*

pan·gen·e·sis (pan·jen′ə·sis) *n. Biol.* The theory, advanced by Charles Darwin, that all the cells of an organism throw off very minute gemmules, **pangens,** which circulate through the body and develop buds or germ cells which have the power of reproduction and contain the units of heredity which they transmit from parent to offspring. — **pan′ge·net′ic** (-jə·net′ik) *adj.*

Pan-Ger·man·ism (pan′jûr′mən·iz′əm) *n.* Originally, the theory of, or organized effort toward, political union of all Teutonic peoples; later, the German doctrine of world domination by aggression and ideology. — **Pan′-Ger′man** *adj.* & *n.* — **Pan′-Ger·man′ic** (-jər·man′ik) *adj.* — **Pan′-Ger′man·ist** *n.*

Pan·gim (puṅ·zhēṅ′) See NOVA GOA.

pan·go·lin (pang·gō′lin) *n.* A heavily armored, typically long-tailed edentate mammal (genus *Manis*) of Asia and Africa; the scaly ant-eater. [<Malay *peng-goling* a roller <*gōling* roll, in ref. to its power of rolling itself up]

Pang·o Pang·o (päng′ō päng′ō) See PAGO PAGO.

pan·han·dle[1] (pan′han′dəl) *v.i.* **·dled, ·dling** *U.S. Colloq.* To beg, especially on the street. [Back formation from PANHANDLER a beggar <PAN[1] (used to receive alms) + HANDLE, *v.*] — **pan′han′dler** *n.*

pan·han·dle[2] (pan′han′dəl) *n.* **1** A narrow strip of land attached to a larger region: from its resemblance to the handle of a pan. **2** *Usually cap.* A region of this shape in either Texas or West Virginia.

Panhandle State Nickname of WEST VIRGINIA.

Pan-Hel·le·nism (pan′hel′ə·niz′əm) *n.* The aspiration for the political union of all Greeks, or the effort to accomplish such union; also, that which pertains to universal Greek interests and ideas. — **Pan′-Hel·len′ic** (-he·len′ik) *adj.* — **Pan′-Hel′le·nist** *n.*

pan·ic (pan′ik) *adj.* **1** Of the nature of or resulting from sudden and infectious terror. **2** Of or pertaining to the Greek god Pan as the cause of fear: *panic* flight. — *n.* **1** A sudden, unreasonable, overpowering fear, especially when affecting a large number simultaneously. **2** Sudden and overpowering alarm or distrust in financial or commercial circles, precipitating mercantile and banking failures. See synonyms under ALARM, FEAR,

FRIGHT. — v. ·icked, ·ick·ing v.t. 1 To affect with panic. 2 U.S. Slang To move to great applause or laughter: He panicked his audience. — v.i. 3 To become affected with panic. [<MF panique <Gk. panikos of or for the god Pan, who was believed to cause sudden or groundless fear] —pan'ick·y adj.

pan ice Loose fragments of ice detached from ice floes and drifting along the seacoast.

panic grass A North American grass (Panicum capillare) used for forage: also called witch-grass. [<L panicum a kind of millet <panis bread + GRASS]

pan·i·cle (pan'i·kəl) n. Bot. A loose compound flower cluster, produced by irregular branching. [<L panicula, dim. of panus a swelling, an ear of millet] —pan'i·cled adj.

pan·ic-strick·en (pan'ik·strik'ən) adj. Overcome by panic. Also **pan'ic-struck'**.

pa·nic·u·late (pə·nik'yə·lāt, -lit) adj. Arranged or borne in panicles; panicled. Also **pa·nic'u·lat·ed**. — **pa·nic'u·late·ly** adv.

Pan·ja·bi (pun·jä'bē) See PUNJABI.

pan·jan·drum (pan·jan'drəm) n. An imaginary character of exaggerated importance or great pretensions; hence, a pompous personage in a small place. [Coined by Samuel Foote, English dramatist and actor, in 1755]

Pan·jim (puń·zhēn') See NOVA GOA.

Panj·nad (punj'näd) The combined waters of five rivers of the Punjab, West Pakistan, flowing 50 miles SW to the Indus.

Pank·hurst (pangk'hûrst), **Emmeline**, 1858–1928, née Goulden, English suffragist.

pan·mix·i·a (pan·mik'sē·ə) n. Indiscriminate interbreeding; unrestricted mating in a mixed population. [<NL <Gk. pan, neut. of pas all + mixis a mixture]

Pan·mun·jom (pän·mŏn·jom) A village in southern Korea south of Kaesong; site of truce talks, 1951.

panne satin (pan) Silk or rayon satin with an unusually high luster because of a special finish. [<F panne, a type of soft cloth + SATIN]

panne velvet Silk or rayon velvet with a flat-tened pile, lustrous and lightweight.

pan·nier (pan'yər) n. 1 One of a pair of baskets adapted to be slung on both sides of a beast of burden. 2 A basket for carrying a load on the back. 3 A light framework for extending a woman's dress at the hips; also, a skirt or overskirt extended at the hips. [<MF <L panarium bread basket <panis bread]

pan·ni·kin (pan'ə·kin) n. A small saucepan or tin cup. [Dim. of PAN¹]

Pan·no·ni·a (pə·nō'nē·ə) An ancient Roman province south and west of the Danube in modern Hungary and Yugoslavia.

pa·no·cha (pə·nō'chə) n. 1 A coarse Mexican sugar. 2 A kind of candy made from brown sugar, milk, and usually containing chopped nuts: also spelled penuche, penuchi. Also **pa·no'che**. [<Am. Sp. <L panucula, panicula. See PANICLE.]

pan·o·ply (pan'ə·plē) n. pl. ·plies 1 The complete equipment of a warrior. 2 Hence, any complete covering that protects or magnificently arrays. [<Gk. panoplia full armor < pan, neut. of pas all + hopla arms] —pan'o·plied adj.

pan·op·tic (pan·op'tik) adj. Inclusive of all that is visible in one view. Also **pan·op'ti·cal**.

pan·o·ram·a (pan'ə·ram'ə, -rä'mə) n. 1 A series of pictures representing a continuous scene, arranged to unroll and pass before the spectator. 2 A complete view in every direction; also, a complete or comprehensive view of a subject or of constantly passing events. 3 A cyclorama. [<PAN- + Gk. horama sight <horaein see] —pan'o·ram'ic adj. —pan'o·ram'i·cal·ly adv.

panoramic sight A sight constructed on the periscope principle, intended for use by marksmen.

Pan·or·mus (pə·nôr'məs) The ancient name for PALERMO.

pan·pipes (pan'pīps') n. pl. A wind instrument formed of short hollow tubes (originally reeds) fastened together in proper order to produce a scale.

pan·psy·chism (pan·sī'kiz·əm) n. The doctrine that the universe as a whole, and every physical part of it also, has a psychic aspect. [< PAN- + Gk. psychē soul, breath] —pan·psy'·chic adj. —pan·psy'chist n.

pan·so·phism (pan'sə·fiz'əm) n. Profession to

universal wisdom. —**pan'so·phist** n.

pan·so·phy (pan'sə·fē) n. Complete or comprehensive knowledge; a system embracing all human knowledge. [<PAN- + Gk. sophia wisdom] —**pan·soph·ic** (pan·sof'ik), **pan·soph'i·cal** adj.

pan·sy (pan'zē) n. pl. ·sies 1 A species of garden violet (Viola tricolor hortensis) having blossoms of a variety of colors of great beauty. 2 A bright, deep-purple color, the color of some pansies. 3 Slang An effeminate or homosexual man. [<MF pensée thought, orig. pp. of penser think]

pant (pant) v.i. 1 To breathe rapidly or spasmodically; gasp for breath. 2 To emit smoke, steam, etc., in loud puffs. 3 To gasp with desire; yearn: with for or after. 4 To beat or pulsate rapidly; throb, as the heart. — v.t. 5 To breathe out or utter gaspingly. See synonyms under PUFF. — n. A short or labored breath; a gasp; also, a quick or violent heaving, as of the breast; a throb, as of the heart. [Appar. <OF pantoisier gasp, ult. <L phantasia a nightmare] —**pant'er** n.

pant— Var. of PANTO-.

Pan·ta·gru·el (pan·tag'rŏo·el, pan'tə·grŏo'əl; Fr. pän·tá·grü·el') In François Rabelais' satirical romance Gargantua and Pantagruel, the giant son of Gargantua, characterized by his broad, somewhat cynical good humor. —**Pan·ta·gru·el·i·an** (pan'tə·grŏo·el'ē·ən) adj.

Pan·ta·gru·el·ism (pan'tə·grŏo'əl·iz'əm, pan·tag'rŏo·el·iz'əm) n. The theories and practices of Pantagruel; good-natured cynicism. —**Pan'·ta·gru'el·ist** n.

pan·ta·lets (pan'tə·lets') n. pl. Long ruffled drawers, formerly worn by women and children. Also **pan'ta·lettes'**. [Dim. of PANTALOON]

pan·ta·loon (pan'tə·lŏon') n. 1 In pantomimes, an absurd old man on whom the clown plays tricks. 2 pl. Trousers; formerly, a tight-fitting garment for the legs. [<F pantalon <Ital. pantalone a clown <Pantalone, nickname for a Venetian, after Pantaleone, a popular Venetian saint]

Pan·ta·loon (pan'tə·lŏon') In early Italian comedies, an old dotard wearing a certain kind of tight-fitting trousers.

Pan·tar (pän'tär) One of the Lesser Sunda Islands in the Alor group; 281 square miles.

pan·tech·ni·con (pan·tek'ni·kon) n. Brit. 1 Obs. A place for the exhibition and sale of manufactured articles. 2 A van for moving furniture. [<PAN- + Gk. technikon, neut. of technikos belonging to the arts <technē art, craft]

Pan·tel·le·ri·a (pän'tel·le·rē'ä) An Italian island off the SW coast of Sicily; 32 square miles: ancient Cossyra.

Pan-Teu·ton·ism (pan'tŏot'n·iz'əm, -tyŏot'n-) n. The doctrine advocating a political union, or a union of interests, of all Teutonic peoples. —**Pan'-Teu·ton'ic** (-tŏo·ton'ik, -tyŏo-) adj.

pan·the·ism (pan'thē·iz'əm) n. 1 The form of monism that identifies mind and matter, the finite and the infinite, making them manifestations of one universal or absolute being; the doctrine which holds that the self-existent and self-developing universe, conceived as a whole, is God. 2 The worship of all gods. —**pan'the·ist** n. —**pan'the·is'tic, pan'the·is'ti·cal** adj. —**pan'the·is'ti·cal·ly** adv.

pan·the·on (pan'thē·on) n. 1 All the gods of a people, collectively. 2 A mausoleum or temple resembling the Roman Pantheon, and commemorating the great. [<L pantheon < Gk. pantheion a temple consecrated to all the gods <pan, neut. of pas all + theos a god]

Pan·the·on (pan'thē·on) A circular temple at Rome, dedicated to all the gods: built by Agrippa, rebuilt by Hadrian: after A.D. 609, a Christian church (Santa Maria della Rotunda).

pan·ther (pan'thər) n. 1 A leopard, especially the black leopard of southern Asia. 2 Some other large feline carnivore, as the North American puma or cougar; also, a jaguar. [< OF pantere <L panthera <Gk. panthēr] —**pan'ther·ess** n. fem.

pant·ies (pan'tēz) n. pl. A woman's or child's underpants. Also **pant'ie**.

pan·tile (pan'tīl') n. A tile displaying a curved cross-section, making laps on each side with adjacent tiles of reverse form.

panto— combining form All; every: pantoscope.

Also, before vowels, pant-. [<Gk. pantos, genitive of pas all]

pan·to·base (pan'tə·bās) adj. Aeron. Designating an aircraft capable of landing on or taking off from any kind of terrain, as mud, ice, snow, water, etc.

pan·tof·fle (pan'tə·fəl, pan·tof'əl, -tŏo'fəl) n. A slipper. Also **pan'to·fle**. [<MF pantoufle < Ital. pantufola, pantofola, ? <Med. Gk. pantophellos cork shoe, lit. whole cork <Gk. pas, pantos all + phellos cork]

pan·to·graph (pan'·tə·graf, -gräf) n. 1 An instrument for copying a drawing, diagram, or map, either on the same scale or with reduction or enlargement. 2 Electr. A trolley whose current-collecting member is borne on a jointed, quadrilateral frame. —**pan'to·graph'ic** or ·i·cal adj. —**pan·tog·ra·phy** (pan·tog'rə·fē) n.

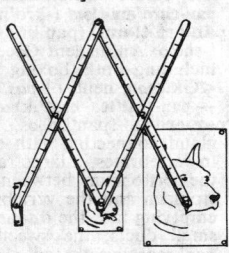

PANTOGRAPH (def. 1)

pan·tol·o·gy (pan·tol'ə·jē) n. A system comprehending all departments of human knowledge. —**pan·tol'o·gist** n.

pan·to·mime (pan'tə·mīm) n. 1 A series of actions, as gestures and postures, used to express ideas or convey information. 2 Any play in which the actors express their meaning by action without dialog. 3 An ancient, classical play or part of a play in which the actor used gestures or movement only, while the chorus sang. 4 Brit. A play relating some popular story accompanied with burlesque, gorgeous scenery, and music: a Christmastide production. — v.t. & v.i. ·mimed, ·mim·ing To act or express in pantomime. [<F <L pantomimus a pantomimist <Gk. pantomimos an imitator of all <pan, neut. of pas all + mimos an imitator] —**pan'to·mim'ic** (-mim'ik) or ·i·cal adj. —**pan'to·mi'mist** (-mī'mist) n.

pan·to·scope (pan'tə·skōp) n. Phot. A very wide-angled lens.

pan·to·then·ic (pan'tə·then'ik) adj. Biochem. Designating an acid, $C_9H_{17}NO_5$, of the vitamin B complex, widely distributed in many plant and animal tissues. It is obtained as a pale-yellow, viscous oil forming a calcium salt, and is also made synthetically. [<Gk. pantothen from every side]

pan·toum (pän·tŏom') n. A verse form of Malay origin, consisting of a series of quatrains in which the second and fourth lines of each quatrain recur as the first and third of the next, and in which the second and fourth lines of the final quatrain repeat the first and third lines of the first. Also **pan·tun'** (-tŏon'). [<F <Malay pantun]

pan·try (pan'trē) n. pl. ·tries A room or closet in which to keep provisions, dishes, table linen, etc. [<AF panetrie, OF paneterie bread room <Med. L. panetaria <panetarius baker <L panis bread]

pants (pants) n. pl. Trousers; drawers. [Short for PANTALOONS]

pant·suit (pant'sŏot') n. A woman's two-piece garment consisting of a jacket and matching pants. Also **pants suit**.

pan·ty·hose (pan'tē·hōz') n. pl. A woman's undergarment that combines panties and stockings.

pan·ty·waist (pan'tē·wāst') n. 1 A child's waist with buttons on which to fasten short pants. 2 Slang An effeminate young man.

Pá·nu·co (pä'nŏo·kō) A river in NE central Mexico, flowing 100 miles NE to the Gulf of Mexico.

pa·nung (pä'nung) n. A long, broad strip of cloth worn by Siamese men and women as a loincloth or skirt. [<Siamese <phā cloth + niñ one]

Pan·urge (pan·ûrj') In Rabelais' Pantagruel, the boon companion of the hero.

Pan·za (pan'zə, Sp. pän'thä), **Sancho** See SANCHO PANZA.

pan·zer (pan'zər, Ger. pän'tsər) adj. Armored; also, using armored tanks or mechanized troops: a panzer attack. [<G]

Pan·zer (pän'tsər) n. German Armor-plating; literally, coat of mail.

Panzer division *Mil.* An armored division; especially, a division of tanks.

Pão de A·cú·car (poun thi ə·sōō′kər) The Portuguese name for SUGAR LOAF MOUNTAIN.

Pa·o·li (pä′ō·lē), **Pasquale, di**, 1725–1807, Corsican patriot.

Pa·o·lo (pä′ō·lō) Italian form of PAUL.

Pa·o·lo (pä′ō·lō) See under FRANCESCA DA RIMINI.

Pao·ting (bou′ting′) The capital of Hopeh province, China.

pap[1] (pap) *n.* 1 A teat; nipple. 2 A hill or other object having a conical shape. [ME *pappe,* appar. <Scand. Cf. dial. Sw. *papp.*]

pap[2] (pap) *n.* 1 Any soft food for babes. 2 *Slang* The fees, favors, and privileges of public office. [ME *pappe,* ? <MLG]

pa·pa[1] (pä′pə, pə·pä′) *n.* Father. [<F <L <Gk. *papas,* a child's word]

pa·pa[2] (pä′pä) *n.* 1 The bishop of Rome; the pope. 2 In the Greek Church, the patriarch of Alexandria; also, a parish priest. [<Med. L Gk. *papas* father. Doublet of POPE.]

pa·pa·cy (pä′pə·sē) *n. pl.* **·cies** 1 The dignity, office, or jurisdiction of the pope of Rome. 2 The succession of popes and the administration of affairs in the Roman Catholic Church. 3 The tenure of office of the pope. [<Med. L *papatia* <*papa.* See PAPA[2].]

Pa·pa·cy (pä′pə·sē) *n.* The Roman Catholic system of church government.

pa·pa·in (pə·pā′in, ·pä′in) *n. Biochem.* A vegetable enzyme, resembling the trypsin of the pancreatic juice, contained in the milk of the papaya: used in medicine as a digestive.

pa·pal (pä′pəl) *adj.* 1 Pertaining to the papacy or the pope. 2 Assuming supreme authority. 3 Pertaining to the Roman Catholic Church. [<OF <Med. L *papalis* belonging to the pope <*papa.* See PAPA[2].]

papal delegate A representative of the pope in a country in which a papal nuncio is not in residence: also called *internuncio.*

Papal States See STATES OF THE CHURCH.

Pa·pav·er·a·ce·ae (pə·pav′ə·rā′si·ē) *n. pl. Bot.* A family of widely distributed herbs and shrubs with polypetalous, typically showy flowers and a milky juice yielding several important narcotic alkaloids; the poppy family. [<NL <L *papaver* poppy + *-aceus* of the nature of] — **pa·pav·er·a′ceous** (-rā′shəs) *adj.*

pa·pav·er·ine (pə·pav′ə·rēn, ·ər·in, pə·pā′və·) *n. Chem.* A white, odorless, tasteless, crystalline alkaloid, $C_{20}H_{21}O_4N$, obtained from opium: used in medicine chiefly as the hydrochloride. [<L *papaver* poppy + -INE[2]]

pa·pav·er·ous (pə·pav′ər·əs) *adj.* Having the properties of the poppy.

pa·paw (pə·pô′, pô′pô) *n.* 1 A small, deciduous, North American tree (*Asimina triloba,* family *Annonaceae*) bearing edible fruit. 2 The fruit. Also spelled *pawpaw.* [<Sp. *papayo* <Cariban]

pa·pa·ya (pä·pä′yä, pə·pä′yə) *n.* 1 The yellow, melonlike fruit of a tropical American evergreen tree (*Carica papaya*), valued for its nutritious and palatable qualities. The fruit may be eaten raw, cooked, or pickled. 2 The tree. [<Sp. <Cariban]

Pa·pe·e·te (pä′pā·ā′tā, pə·pē′tē) A port on Tahiti, capital of the Society Islands and of French Oceania.

PAPAYA
(The tree from 15 to 25 feet in height)

Pa·pen (pä′pən), **Franz von**, 1879–1969, German diplomat.

pa·per (pä′pər) *n.* 1 A substance made from fibrous cellulose material, as rags, wood, or bark, treated with various chemicals and formed into thin sheets or strips for writing, printing, wrapping and a wide variety of other uses in industry and the arts. 2 A sheet or a web of such material. 3 A printed or written instrument or document. 4 A printed journal; newspaper. 5 A written discourse; essay. 6 Written or printed pledges or promises to pay which are negotia-

ble, as bills of exchange, notes, etc.: called **commercial paper.** 7 A package containing in a paper wrapping a limited amount or number: a *paper* of pins. 8 Wallpaper, paperhangings. 9 *Slang* A marked playing card. 10 *pl.* Small strips of paper on which the hair is twisted to be curled: also **curl papers.** 11 *pl.* A ship's papers, as invoices, etc. See SHIP'S PAPERS. 12 *pl.* Personal documents or identification, etc. 13 Something having a similar appearance to paper, as papyrus or papier-mâché. 14 Collectively, free orders of admission to a place of amusement; also, an audience so admitted. —**first papers** Papers declaring intention of becoming a citizen of the United States: filed by an applicant for naturalization as the first step in the process. —**second papers** Popular name for a certificate of naturalization. —*v.t.* 1 To put paper on; cover with wallpaper. 2 To fold or enclose in paper. 3 To write or describe on paper. 4 To issue free tickets of admission to (a place of amusement): to *paper* the house. —*adj.* 1 Made of paper. 2 Enrolled, described, or stated on paper; existing only on paper. [<AF *papir,* OF *papier* <L *papyrus.* Doublet of PAPYRUS.] —**pa′per·y** *adj.*

pa·per·back (pä′pər·bak′) *adj.* Having a paper cover or binding. —*n.* A book so bound.

paper birch Any of a species of birch (*Betula papyrifera*) having chalk-white outer bark that peels off in large tough sheets used formerly by North American Indians to make canoes.

pa·per·bound (pä′pər·bound′) *adj.* Paperback.

paper boy One who delivers newspapers.

pa·per·er (pä′pər·ər) *n.* One who applies paper; a paperhanger.

paper gold Special Drawing Rights (which see).

pa·per·hang·ing (pä′pər·hang′ing) *n.* 1 The act or process of covering walls, etc., with paper. 2 *pl.* Wallpaper. —**pa′per·hang′er** *n.*

pa·per·knife (pä′pər·nīf′) *n. pl.* **·knives** (-nīvz′) A blade of bone or other hard substance, for cutting folded leaves, creasing paper, etc.

paper money 1 Currency consisting of paper on which certain fixed values are printed, as bank-notes, government notes, etc. 2 Negotiable commercial papers, as promissory notes, bills of exchange, etc.

paper nautilus A pelagic cephalopod mollusk (genus *Argonauta*), related to and resembling the octopus in having eight tentacles but in the female secreting a delicate, papery shell. Also called *argonaut.*

paper profit A potential profit, as in the stock market, that can be realized only by the sale of an appreciated holding.

paper tiger Something that seems mighty or threatening but is actually ineffectual and not to be taken seriously.

paper wasp Any of various wasps, as the hornets, yellow jackets, and certain other social wasps, that build nests of a material resembling paper.

pa·per·weight (pä′pər·wāt′) *n.* A small, heavy object, often ornamental, used to keep loose papers in place by its weight.

pa·per·work (pä′pər·wûrk′) *n.* Work involving the preparation or handling of reports, letters, correction of papers, etc.

pap·e·te·rie (pap′ə·trē, *Fr.* páp·trē′) *n.* A box or case containing writing materials. [<F <*papetier* a papermaker, ult. <*papier* paper]

Paph·la·go·ni·a (paf′lə·gō′nē·ə) An ancient country and Roman province in northern Asia Minor on the Black Sea.

Pa·phos (pä′fos) An ancient city in SW Cyprus, considered sacred to Aphrodite. —**Pa′phi·an** (-fē·ən) *adj. & n.*

pa·pier-mâ·ché (pä′pər·mə·shā′, *Fr.* pá·pyá′·mä·shā′) *n.* A tough plastic material made from paper pulp containing an admixture of size, paste, oil, resin, etc., or from sheets of paper glued and pressed together. [<F *papier* PAPER + *mâché,* pp. of *mâcher* chew <L *masticare*]

pa·pil·i·o·na·ceous (pə·pil′ē·ō·nā′shəs) *adj. Bot.* Butterfly-shaped, as the corolla of the sweet pea and other leguminous plants. [<NL *papilionaceus* <L *papilio, -onis* butterfly]

Pa·pil·i·on·i·dae (pə·pil′ē·on′i·dē) *n. pl.* A family of butterflies, including mostly large species with a tail-like lobe on each hind wing; the

swallowtail butterflies. [<NL <L *papilio, -onis* butterfly] —**pa·pil′i·on′id** *adj. & n.*

pa·pil·la (pə·pil′ə) *n. pl.* **·lae** (-ē) 1 *Anat.* a The nipple of the mammary glands. b Any small nipplelike process of connective tissue, as on the tongue or the epidermal layer of the skin, or at the root of a developing tooth, hair, feather, etc. 2 *Bot.* A small, elongate, nipple-shaped protuberance on a flower or leaf. [<L *papula* a swelling, pimple] —**pap·il·lar·y** (pap′ə·ler′ē) *adj.*

pap·il·lo·ma (pap′ə·lō′mə) *n. pl.* **·ma·ta** (-mə·tə) *Pathol.* A morbid growth on the skin, consisting of small tumors composed of and covered by the normal skin, as corns, warts, or mucous tubercles. [<PAPILLA]

pap·il·lon (pap′ə·lon) *n.* A breed of toy spaniel descended from the European 16th century dwarf spaniel, having large fringed ears resembling the wings of a butterfly, a plumy tail, and a thick, solidly colored coat. [<F, butterfly <L *papilio, -onis*]

pap·il·lose (pap′ə·lōs) *adj.* Papillary; also, pimply; warty. Also **pap·il·lous.** [<NL *papillosus* <L *papilla*] —**pap′il·los′i·ty** (-los′ə·tē) *n.*

pap·il·lote (pap′ə·lōt) *n. French* 1 A small strip of paper used in curling the hair. 2 A small paper encircling the end of the bone of a chop or cutlet when served.

pa·pist (pä′pist) *n.* An adherent of the papacy; a Roman Catholic: usually an opprobrious use. [<F *papiste* <Med. L *papa.* See PAPA[2].]

pa·pis·try (pä′pis·trē) *n.* Roman Catholicism: used disparagingly.

pa·poose (pa·pōos′) *n.* North American Indian infant. Also **pap·poose′.** [<Algonquian (Narraganset) *papoos* child]

Pap·pen·heim (päp′ən·hīm), **Count Gottfried zu,** 1594–1632, German general.

pap·pus (pap′əs) *n. pl.* **pap·pi** (pap′ī) *Bot.* The peculiar limb on the calyx of a floret of the composite family, consisting either of a downy tuft of hairs, as in thistles, or of teeth, scales, bristles, or awns. [<NL <Gk. *pappos* grandfather] — **pap′pose** (-ōs), **pap′pous** (-əs) *adj.*

pap·py[1] (pap′ē) *adj.* **·pi·er, ·pi·est** Resembling pap; pulpy; soft.

pap·py[2] (pap′ē) *n. pl.* **·pies** Papa; father. [Dim. of PAPA[1]]

pa·pri·ka (pa·prē′kə, pap′rə·kə) *n.* A condiment made from the ripe fruit of a mild variety of red pepper (*Capsicum frutescens*). Also **pa·pri′ca.** [<G <Magyar, red pepper <Gk. *peperi* pepper]

Pap smear A method of early detection of cervical cancer, consisting of removal of cervical cell samples, which are stained and examined. Also **Pap test.** [after George *Papanicolaou,* 1883–1962, U.S. scientist]

Pap·u·a (pap′yōō·ə, pä′pōō·ä′) New Guinea.

Pap·u·a (pap′yōō·ə, pä′pōō·ä′), **Territory of** An Australian territory in SE New Guinea; with its dependencies in adjacent islands, 90,540 square miles; capital, Port Moresby: formerly *British New Guinea*: became part of the Territory of Papua and New Guinea 1949.

Papua and New Guinea, Territory of A United Nations Trust Territory administered by Australia and comprising the formerly separate Territory of Papua and Territory of New Guinea; established 1949; 183,600 square miles; capital, Port Moresby.

Pap·u·an (pap′yōō·ən, pä′pōō·ən) *adj.* Of or pertaining to the Island of Papua or New Guinea, or to the Papuan peoples. —*n.* One of any of the dark peoples inhabiting the Melanesian Archipelago from Fiji westward to the Aru Islands, including New Guinea or Papua.

pap·u·la (pap′yə·lə) *n. pl.* **·lae** (-lē) *Pathol.* An isolated pimple. Also **pap′ule** (-yōōl). [<L, a pimple]

pap·y·ra·ceous (pap′ə·rā′shəs) *adj.* Made of papyrus; papery.

pa·py·rus (pə·pī′rəs) *n. pl.* **·ri** (-rī) 1 The writing paper of the ancient Egyptians, made from the papyrus plant. 2 A manuscript written on this material. 3 A perennial rushlike plant of the sedge family (*Cyperus papyrus*) having stems 6 to 10 feet high. [<L <Gk. *papyros.* Doublet of PAPER.]

par (pär) *n.* 1 Equality of value; equivalence;

parity; specifically, equality between nominal and actual value. Shares of stock are said to be **at** (or **up to**) **par** when exchangeable at face value in money, **above par** when the market price is greater, and **below par** when less than the nominal value. **2** An accepted standard with which to compare variations. **3** In golf, the number of strokes allotted to a round or hole on the basis of faultless play. **—mint par** The reduction of the monetary unit of one country to expression in terms of that of another: also **par of exchange. —on a par** On a level. [<L, equal]

par- *prefix* Per-: used in a few words from French: *pardoner.* [<F <L *per-* <*per* through]

pa·ra (pä·rä′, pä′rä) *n.* **1** A Turkish copper coin. **2** A small coin of Yugoslavia. [<Turkish *pārah* <Persian, a piece]

Pa·rá (pä·rä′) **1** An estuary of the Amazon; 200 miles long; 40 miles wide at its mouth. **2** A state in NE Brazil; 469,778 square miles; capital, Belém. **3** A former name for BELÉM.

para-[1] *prefix* **1** Beside; near by; along with: *paradigm.* **2** Beyond; aside from; amiss: *paradox.* **3** *Chem.* **a** An isomeric or polymeric modification of: *paraldehyde.* **b** A modification of or a compound similar to (not necessarily isomeric or polymeric): *paramorphine.* **c** A benzene derivative in which the substituted atoms or radicals occupy the positions 1, 4: *paradichlorobenzene*: abbr. *p-*. Compare META-, ORTHO-. See BENZENE RING. **4** *Med.* **a** A diseased or abnormal condition: *paranoia.* **b** Accessory to: *parasympathetic.* **c** Similar to but not identical with a true condition or form: *paratyphoid.* Also, before vowels and *h,* usually **par-**. [<Gk. <*para* beside]

para-[2] *combining form* Shelter or protection against: *parasol.* [<Ital. *parare* defend]

par·a-a·mi·no·ben·zo·ic acid (par′ə·ə·mē′·nō·ben·zō′ik, -am′ə·nō-) A yellowish crystalline compound, $C_7H_7O_2N$, forming part of the vitamin B complex and essential for growth in many organisms.

Par·a·bell·um (par′ə·bel′əm) *n.* The European name for the Luger pistol. [<G *(Pistole) Parabellum* (pistol) for war <Gk. *para* for + L *bellum* war]

par·a·bal·loon (par′ə·bə·lōōn′) *n.* A radar antenna in the form of an inflated sphere of Fiberglas partly coated with a thin metal layer forming the reflector. [<PARA-[2] + BALLOON]

par·a·bi·o·sis (par′ə·bī·ō′sis) *n.* **1** *Biol.* A fusion of two individuals, congenital or by surgery, resulting in mutual physiological intimacy, as in Siamese twins. **2** *Physiol.* A temporary suppression of the irritability and conductivity of a nerve. **—par′a·bi·ot′ic** (-ot′·ik) *adj.*

par·a·blast (par′ə·blast) *n. Biol.* The yolk of a meroblastic egg. **—par′a·blas′tic** *adj.*

par·a·ble (par′ə·bəl) *n.* A comparison; simile; specifically, a short narrative making a moral or religious point by comparison with natural or homely things: the New Testament *parables.* See synonyms under ALLEGORY. [<OF *parabole* <LL *parabola* allegory, speech <L, comparison <Gk. *parabolē* a placing side by side, a comparison <*para-* beside + *ballein* throw. Doublet of PALAVER, PARABOLA, PAROLE.]

pa·rab·o·la (pə·rab′ə·lə) *n Math.* The locus of a point moving in a plane so that its distances from a fixed point (focus) and a fixed straight line (directrix) are equal; the curve formed by the edges of a plane when cutting through a right circular cone at an angle parallel to one of its sides. [<Med. L <Gk. *parabolē.* Doublet of PALAVER, PARABLE, PAROLE.]

pa·rab·o·le (pə·rab′ə·lē) *n.* A rhetorical comparison; a formal simile. [<Gk. *parabolē.* See PARABLE.]

par·a·bol·ic (par′ə·bol′ik) *adj.* **1** Pertaining to a parable. **2** Pertaining to or having the form of a parabola. Also **par′a·bol′i·cal.** [<LL *parabolicus* <LGk. *parabolikos* figurative <*parabolē.* See PARABLE.] **—par′a·bol′i·cal·ly** *adv.*

parabolic spiral *Math.* The polar curve traced by a point moving so that the square of its distance from the pole is proportional to its polar angle: also called *Fermat's spiral.*

pa·rab·o·lize (pə·rab′ə·līz) *v.t.* **·lized, ·liz·ing 1** To relate in parable form. **2** *Math.* To give the form of a parabola to.

pa·rab·o·loid (pə·rab′ə·loid) *n. Math.* A surface or solid generated by the rotation of a parabola about its axis. **—pa·rab′o·loi′dal** *adj.*

par·a·ca·se·in (par′ə·kā′sē·in, -sēn) *n. Biochem.* A form of casein produced by the action of rennin.

Pa·ra·cel Islands (pä′rä′sel′) A Chinese island group SE of Hainan in the South China Sea.

Par·a·cel·sus (par′ə·sel′səs) Pseudonym of Theophrastus von Hohenheim, 1493–1541, Swiss physician and alchemist. **—Par′·a·cel′si·an** *adj.*

par·a·cen·es·the·sia (par′ə·sen′is·thē′zhə, -zhē·ə) *n. Psychiatry* Any perversion or abnormality of the general sense of well-being, as an obsession or mania.

par·a·cen·tric (par′ə·sen′trik) *adj.* Directed to or from the center: said of motion. Also **par′·a·cen′tri·cal.**

par·a·chor (par′ə·kôr) *n. Chem.* A constant expressing the relationship between the surface tension and density of a given substance or compound. [<PARA-[1] + Gk. *chōros* space]

par·a·chor·dal (par′ə·kôr′dəl) *adj. Anat.* Situated beside the notochord: said of the paired cartilaginous plates at the base of the developing cranium.

par·a·chro·ma·tism (par′ə·krō′mə·tiz′əm) *n. Pathol.* Abnormal perception of colors; color blindness. **—par′a·chro·mat′ic** (-krō·mat′ik) *adj.*

par·a·chute (par′ə·shōōt) *n.* **1** A large, expanding, umbrella-shaped apparatus for retarding the speed of a body descending through the air, especially from an airplane. **2** *Zool.* A lateral extension of the skin in flying squirrels, etc., enabling them to glide through the air. **—pilot parachute** *Aeron.* A small parachute whose release serves to open the canopy of the main parachute quickly and with minimum danger of jamming or tearing. *—v.* **·chut·ed, ·chut·ing** *v.t.* To land (troops, materiel, etc.) by means of parachutes. *—v.i.* To descend by parachute. [<F <*para* PARA-[2] + *chute* fall]

parachute fabric A plain-woven, very firm fabric used for making parachutes: made of silk or nylon if for humans, of rayon if for cargo, bombs, etc.

parachute flare A flare attached to a parachute and released from an aircraft to illuminate the terrain.

parachute troop See PARATROOP.

par·a·chut·ist (par′ə·shōō′tist) *n.* A person, specifically a soldier, trained and equipped to drop by parachute.

par·a·clete (par′ə·klēt) *n.* One called to the aid of another, especially in legal process; an advocate; hence, **Paraclete,** the Holy Spirit as the helper or comforter. [<OF *paraclet* <LL *paracletus* <LGk. *paraklētos* a comforter, advocate <*parakalein* call to one's aid <*para-* to + *kalein* call]

par·ac·me (par·ak′mē) *n.* **1** *Biol.* The stage of degeneration following maturity. **2** *Pathol.* The period of decline or remission, as of a disease. [<Gk. *parakmē* <*para-* beyond + *akmē* the highest point]

par·a·cy·mene (par′ə·sī′mēn) *n.* A common form of cymene.

pa·rade (pə·rād′) *n.* **1** A marshaling and maneuvering of troops for display or official inspection; a review. **2** A ceremonious procession. **3** A ground where military reviews are held. **4** A promenade or public walk. **5** A setting forth or arrangement of persons or things for display. **6** Pompous show; ostentation. See synonyms under OSTENTATION, SPECTACLE. *—v.* **·rad·ed, ·rad·ing** *v.t.* **1** To walk or march through or about: to *parade* the streets. **2** To display or show off ostentatiously; flaunt. **3** To cause to assemble for military parade or review. *—v.i.* **4** To march formally or with display. **5** To walk in public for the purpose of showing oneself. **6** To assemble in military order for inspection or review. See synonyms under FLAUNT. [<MF <Sp. *parada* a stopping place, exercise ground <LL *parare* adorn, prepare <L] **—pa·rad′er** *n.*

parade rest A formal ceremonial position of rest, exactly prescribed with or without rifle, in which soldiers stand without moving or speaking, as distinguished from the informal positions of *rest* and *at ease.*

par·a·di·chlo·ro·ben·zene (par′ə·dī·klôr′ō·ben′·zēn, -klō′rō-) *n. Chem.* A white, volatile, crystalline compound, $C_6H_4Cl_2$, widely used as an insecticide.

par·a·digm (par′ə·dim, -dīm) *n.* **1** *Gram.* An ordered list or table of all the inflected forms of a word or class of words, as of a particular declension, conjugation, etc. **2** Any pattern or example. [<LL *paradigma* <Gk. *paradeigma* a pattern <*para-* beside + *deiknynai* show] **—par′a·dig·mat′ic** (-dig·mat′ik) *adj.*

par·a·dise (par′ə·dīs) *n.* **1** The intermediate place or state where the souls of the saved await the resurrection. **2** Heaven, the ultimate abode of righteous souls; also, the abode of the deceased faithful of Islam. **3** Any region or state of surpassing delight. **4** In the Near East, a park or pleasure ground. [<F *paradis* <L *paradisus* <Gk. *paradeisos* park <OPersian *pairidaēza* an enclosure, park <*pairi* around + *daēza* wall]. **—par′a·di·sa′ic** (-di·sā′ik) or **·i·cal, par′a·dis′i·ac** (-dis′ē·ak) or **par·a·di·si·a·cal** (par′ə·di·sī′ə·kəl) *adj.*

Par·a·dise (par′ə·dīs) The garden of Eden.

Paradise Lost and **Paradise Regained** Epic poems by John Milton depicting the fall and redemption of man.

par·a·dos (par′ə·dos) *n.* An embankment, as behind a trench, for protection against gunfire from the rear. [<F <*para-* PARA-[2] + *dos* back]

par·a·dox (par′ə·doks) *n.* **1** A statement, doctrine, or expression seemingly absurd or contradictory to common notions or to what would naturally be believed, but in fact really true. **2** A statement essentially absurd and false. See synonyms under RIDDLE[2]. [<F *paradoxe* <L *paradoxum* <Gk. *paradoxos, -on* incredible <*para-* contrary to + *doxa* opinion <*dokeein* think] **—par′a·dox′·ical** *adj.* **—par′a·dox′i·cal′i·ty** (-kal′ə·tē), **par′a·dox′i·cal·ness** *n.* **—par′a·dox′i·cal·ly** *adv.*

par·a·drop (par′ə·drop) *n.* The dropping of supplies, equipment, and the like by parachute, especially over terrain not adapted to landings by aircraft. [<PARA(CHUTE) + DROP]

par·aes·the·sia (par′is·thē′zhə, -zhē·ə), etc. See PARESTHESIA, etc.

par·af·fin (par′ə·fin) *n. Chem.* **1** A translucent, waxy, solid mixture of hydrocarbons, indifferent to most chemical reagents: it is a constituent of peat, soft coal, and shale, but is derived principally from the distillation of petroleum. **2** Any saturated aliphatic hydrocarbon of the methane series having the formula C_nH_{2n+2}. *—v.t.* To treat or impregnate with paraffin. Also **par′af·fine** (-fin, -fēn). [<G <L *parum* too little + *affinis* related to; so named because it has little affinity for other bodies]

paraffin series Methane series.

paraffin wax Solid paraffin.

par·a·form (par′ə·fôrm) *n. Chem.* A white crystalline powder, $(CH_2O)_3$, obtained by concentrating formaldehyde solutions: used as a disinfectant. Also **par′a·for·mal′de·hyde** (-fôr·mal′də·hīd).

par·a·frag bomb (par′ə·frag) A demolition bomb designed to be dropped by parachute.

par·a·gen·e·sis (par′ə·jen′ə·sis) *n. Mineral.* The formation of minerals in contact in such manner as to affect the development of the individual crystals. Also **par′a·ge·ne′si·a** (-jə·nē′sē·ə). **—par′a·ge·net′ic** (-jə·net′ik) *adj.*

par·a·go·ge (par′ə·gō′jē) *n.* The addition of an inorganic sound or syllable at the end of a word without a change in meaning, as in *amongs-t, whils-t,* etc. [<L <Gk. *paragōgē* <*para-* beyond + *agōgē* a leading <*agein* lead] **—par′·a·gog′ic** (-goj′ik) *adj.*

par·a·gon (par′ə·gon) *n.* **1** A model of excellence. **2** *Printing* A size of type: about 3½ lines to the inch: 20-point. **3** A round pearl of exceptional size. *—v.t. Archaic* or *Poetic* **1** To match; equal. **2** To compare with. **4** To hold up as a paragon. [<OF <Ital. *paragone* a touchstone, prob. <Gk. *parakonaein* sharpen one thing against another <*para-* beside + *akonē* whetstone]

pa·rag·o·nite (pə·rag′ə·nīt) *n.* A scaly, pearly, variously colored, translucent mica containing sodium instead of potassium, and found massive. [<Gk. *paragōn,* ppr. of *paragein* lead astray + -ITE[1]]

par·a·graph (par′ə·graf, -gräf) *n.* **1** A short passage in a written or printed discourse, begun on a new and usually indented line. **2** A short article, complete and unified; especially, in a newspaper, a short article, item, or comment. **3** A mark (¶) used to indicate where

a paragraph is to be begun, or as a reference mark. —*v.t.* **1** To arrange in or into paragraphs. **2** To comment on or express in a paragraph. [<OF *paragraphe* <LL *paragraphus* <Gk. *paragraphos,* orig. a short line in a text marking a break in sense <*para-* beside + *graphein* write] **—par′a·graph′er, par′a·graph′ist** *n.* **—par′·a·graph′ic, par′a·graph′i·cal** *adj.*

par·a·graph·i·a (par′ə·graf′ē·ə) *n. Psychiatry* A symptom of mental disorder in which the patient writes wrong letters or words. [<NL <Gk. *para-* beside + *graphein* write]

Par·a·guay (par′ə·gwā, -gwī; *Sp.* pä·rä·gwī) A republic in south central South America; 157,047 square miles; capital, Asunción. — **Par′a·guay′an** *adj.* & *n.*

Paraguay A river in south central South America, flowing 1,300 miles south to the Paraná.

par·a·he·li·ot·ro·pism (par′ə·hē′lē·ot′rə·piz′əm) *n. Bot.* A manifestation of irritability in motile leaves when exposed to bright sunlight, whereby they assume such a position that their surfaces are parallel to the direction of the incident rays; diurnal sleep of leaves. **—par′a·he′li·o·trop′ic** (-ə·trop′ik) *adj.*

par·a·hy·dro·gen (par′ə·hī′drə·jən) *n. Chem.* A form of hydrogen which has been stabilized by treating orthohydrogen with hydrous ferric oxide acting as a catalyst: an important liquid fuel for rockets and missiles. [<PARA-[1] (def. 1) + HYDROGEN]

par·a·hyp·no·sis (par′ə·hip·nō′sis) *n. Psychiatry* Abnormal sleep, suggesting the effects of but not necessarily due to hypnosis, as in somnambulism. **—par′a·hyp·not′ic** (-not′ik) *adj.*

Pa·ra·í·ba (pä′rä·ē′bä) **1** A state of NE Brazil; 21,831 square miles; capital, João Pessoa. **2 Paraíba do Sul** (thōō sōōl′) The chief river of Rio de Janeiro state, SE Brazil, rising in SE São Paulo state and flowing about 600 miles SW and NE to the Atlantic, near Campos. **3 Paraíba do Norte** (thōō nôr′ti) A river of Paraíba state, NE Brazil, rising on the Pernambuco state border, and flowing about 180 miles NE to the Atlantic, near João Pessoa.

par·a·in·flu·en·za (par′ə·in·flōō·en′zə) *n.* An influenzalike respiratory disease caused by any of several viruses.

par·a·jour·nal·ism (par′ə·jûr′nə·liz·əm) *n.* A kind of writing for newspapers and other periodicals that departs from the style and standards of ordinary journalism.

par·a·keet (par′ə·kēt) *n.* **1** Any of certain small parrots, having a long, wedge-shaped tail, as the crimson rosella of Australia *(Platycercus elegans).* **2** The Carolina parakeet *(Conuropsis carolinensis)* of the southern United States: now extinct. [<OF *paroquet,* ? <Ital. *parrochetto,* dim. of *parroco* parson]

par·a·ki·ne·sia (par′ə·ki·nē′zhə, -zhē·ə) *n. Pathol.* Clumsy and unnatural movements, caused by impairment of motor functions. Also **par′a·ki·ne′sis** (-nē′sis). [<NL <Gk. *para-* beside + *kinēsis* movement] **—par′a·ki·net′ic** (-net′ik) *adj.*

par·al·de·hyde (pə·ral′də·hīd) *n. Chem.* A colorless, transparent liquid, $C_6H_{12}O_3$, derived by the action of sulfuric acid on acetaldehyde: used as a hypnotic.

par·a·le·gal (par′ə·lē′gəl) *adj.* Pertaining to the law at a subprofessional level. —*n.* A legal paraprofessional.

par·a·leip·sis (par′ə·līp′sis) *n.* In rhetoric, a pretended suppression of what is really said; a feigned omission, as in "not to mention his insufferable conceit"; apophasis. Also **par′a·lep′sis** (-lep′sis), **par′a·lip′sis** (-lip′sis). [<Gk., an omission <*paraleipein* <*para-* beside + *leipein* leave]

par·al·lax (par′ə·laks) *n.* **1** Such difference in the apparent position of an object, specifically a star or other heavenly body, as would appear if it were viewed from two points. It is **diurnal** or **geocentric parallax** when due to the change of place of the observer caused by the earth's rotation; **annual** or **heliocentric parallax** when the observer's change of place is due to the earth's motion around the sun. **2** Any apparent displacement of an object due to an observer's position. [<MF *parallaxe* <Gk. *parallaxis* a change <*parallassein* alter <*para-* beside + *allassein* change] **—par′al·lac′tic** (-lak′tik) or **·ti·cal** *adj.* **—par′·al·lac′ti·cal·ly** *adv.*

par·al·lel (par′ə·lel) *adj.* **1** Not meeting or intersecting, however far extended: said of straight lines or planes. **2** In projective geometry, meeting at infinity. **3** Having lines or surfaces lying in the same or about the same direction. **4** Having a like course; conforming in action. **5** Essentially alike; similar. **6** *Music* Separated by the same interval: *parallel* fifths. **7** Having sides parallel to one another. **8** *Electr.* Connected between like terminals, as a group of cells, condensers, etc. —*n.* **1** A line extending in the same direction and being equidistant at all points from another line. **2** Essential likeness. **3** A comparison tracing similarity, as between persons. **4** A counterpart. **5** Any person or thing ranked as equal to another; a match. **6** A trench dug parallel to the outline of a fortification. **7** A degree of latitude. —*v.t.* **·leled** or **·lelled, ·lel·ing** or **·lel·ling 1** To place in parallel; make parallel. **2** To be, go, or extend parallel to. **3** To furnish with a parallel or equal; find a parallel to. **4** To be a parallel to; correspond to. **5** To compare; liken. See synonyms under COMPARE. [<MF *parallele* <L *parallelus* <Gk. *parallēlos* <*para-* beside + *allēlos* one another]

parallel bars Two horizontal crossbars, parallel to each other and supported a few feet from the ground by upright posts: used for gymnastic exercises.

par·al·lel·e·pi·ped (par′ə·lel′ə·pī′ped,-pip′id) *n.* A prism with six faces, each of which is a parallelogram. Also **par′al·lel′o·pi′ped, par′al·lel′e·pip′e·don, par′al·lel′o·pip′e·don** (-pip′ə·don, -pī′·pə-). [<Gk. *parallēlepipedon* <*parallēlos* parallel + *epipedon* a plane surface <*epi-* upon + *pedon* ground]

par·al·lel·ism (par′ə·lel·iz′əm) *n.* **1** Parallel position. **2** Essential likeness; similarity; analogy. **3** Correspondence or similarity of construction in successive passages or clauses, especially in Hebrew poetry. **4** *Philos.* The opinion that the relation between physical and mental processes is one of concomitant or parallel variation, and not of cause and effect. **—psychophysical parallelism** *Philos.* The theory that related mental and physical events, although occurring simultaneously, are separate and distinct phenomena: opposed to *interactionism.*

parallel motion *Mech.* Motion of a machine element, as a piston, reproduced by a linkwork system and recorded as a straight line parallel to the original motion.

par·al·lel·o·gram (par′ə·lel′ə·gram) *n.* **1** *Geom.* A four-sided plane figure whose opposite sides are parallel and equal, including the *square, rectangle, rhombus,* and *rhomboid.* **2** Any area or object having such form. [<F *parallélogramme* <L *parallelogrammum* <Gk. *parallēlogrammon,* orig. adj., bounded by parallel lines <*parallēlos* parallel + *grammē* a line]

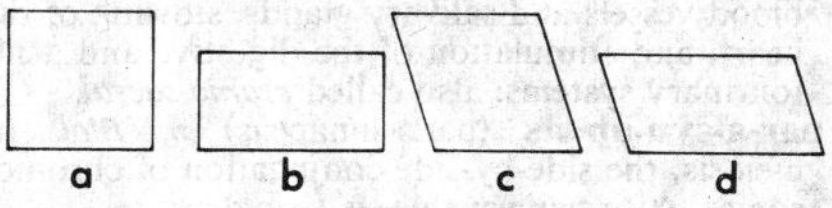

PARALLELOGRAMS
a. Square. *b.* Rectangle. *c.* Rhombus. *d.* Rhomboid.

pa·ral·o·gism (pə·ral′ə·jiz′əm) *n.* A fallacy in reasoning. See synonyms under SOPHISTRY. [<F *paralogisme* <LL *paralogismus* <Gk. *paralogismos* <*paralogizesthai* reason falsely, ult. <*para* beside + *logos* a word, reason] **—par·a·log·ic** (par′ə·loj′ik) or **·i·cal** *adj.*

pa·ral·y·sis (pə·ral′ə·sis) *n.* **1** *Pathol* Partial or complete loss of the power of voluntary motion and sometimes of the power of perceiving sensations; palsy. **2** Loss of power in general. [<L <Gk. <*paralyein* disable <*para-* beside + *lyein* loosen, untie. Doublet of PALSY.]

pa·ral·y·sis a·gi·tans (pə·ral′ə·sis aj′ə·tanz) *Latin* Shaking palsy.

par·a·lyt·ic (par′ə·lit′ik) *adj.* **1** Pertaining to or affected with paralysis. **2** Subject to paralysis. —*n.* A person subject to or suffering from paralysis. [<OF *paralytique* <L *paralyticus* <Gk. *paralytikos* <*paralyein.* See PARALYSIS.]

par·a·lyze (par′ə·līz) *v.t.* **·lyzed, ·lyz·ing 1** To bring about paralysis in; make paralytic. **2** To render powerless, ineffective, or inactive. See synonyms under WEAKEN. [Appar. <F *paralyser*] **—par′a·lyz′er** *n.*

par·a·mag·net·ic (par′ə·mag·net′ik) *adj. Physics* **1** Capable of being attracted by a magnet, as iron. **2** Having a magnetic permeability greater than that of a vacuum: distinguished from *diamagnetic.* **—par′a·mag′net** (-mag′nit) *n.* — **par′a·mag′net·ism** *n.*

Par·a·mar·i·bo (par′ə·mar′i·bō) A port, capital of Surinam.

par·a·mat·ta (par′ə·mat′ə) *n.* A kind of light, twilled, dress goods with cotton warp and filling of combed merino wool: also spelled *parramatta.* [from *Parramatta,* a city in N. So. Wales, Australia]

par·a·me·cin (par′ə·mē′sin) *n.* A powerful protein transmitted by inheritance within certain strains of paramecium and usually lethal to other strains of this organism.

par·a·me·ci·um (par′ə·mē′shē·əm, -sē·əm) *n. pl.* **·ci·a** (-shē·ə, -sē·ə) A ciliate infusorian (genus *Paramecium*) having a flattened elongate body, and feeding by a primitive oral groove, as *P. caudatum,* found in stagnant water. [<NL <Gk. *paramēkēs* oblong, oval]

par·a·med·ic (par′ə·med′ik) *n.* One trained to assist a physician.

par·a·med·i·cal (par′ə·med′ə·kəl) *adj.* Designating or pertaining to medical personnel trained to assist physicians, as by conducting routine tests, or to attend patients. **—par′a·med′i·cal·ly** *adv.*

pa·ram·e·ter (pə·ram′ə·tər) *n.* **1** *Math.* Any given constant or element whose values characterize one or more of the variables entering into a system of expressions, functions, etc.: A road gradient is a *parameter* of the performance of an automobile. **2** A fixed limit or guideline. [<NL *parametrum* <Gk. *para-* beside + *metron* a measure] **—par·a·met·ric** (par′ə·met′rik) *adj.*

par·a·mil·i·tar·y (par′ə·mil′ə·ter′ē) *adj.* Having a military structure although not officially military; capable of becoming, replacing, or supplementing a military force: said of certain political movements, police forces, etc.

par·am·ne·sia (par′am·nē′zhə, -zhē·ə) *n. Psychiatry* **1** Distortion and falsification of memory. **2** A condition in which the meaning or use of words cannot be remembered.

par·a·mor·phine (par′ə·môr′fēn) *n.* Thebaine.

par·a·mor·phism (par′ə·môr′fiz·əm) *n. Mineral.* The alteration of one mineral to another having the same chemical composition but other molecular structure and physical properties [<PARA-[1] + Gk. *morphē* a form + -ISM] **—par′a·mor′phic, par′a·mor′phous** *adj.*

par·a·mount (par′ə·mount) *adj.* **1** Having the highest title. **2** Superior to all others; supremely controlling. —*n.* A supreme lord; highest ruler. [<AF *paramont* above <OF *par* by (<L *per*) + *à mont* up, above <L *ad montem* to the hill] **—par′a·mount·ly** *adv.* **—par′a·mount·cy** *n.*

Synonyms (adj.): chief, eminent, foremost, preeminent, principal, superior, supreme.

par·a·mour (par′ə·mōōr) *n.* A lover, especially one who unlawfully takes the place of a husband or wife. [<OF *par amour* with love <*par* by, with (<L *per* through) + *amour* love <L *amor*]

Pa·ra·ná (pä′rä·nä′) **1** A state of southern Brazil; 77,717 square miles; capital, Curitiba. **2** An important river of SW Brazil and NE Argentina, forming the eastern and southern boundaries of Paraguay and flowing 2,050 miles south to the Rio de la Plata: above the confluence of the Paraguay, called the **Al·to Paraná** (äl′tō). **3** A city in eastern Argentina on the Paraná.

Pa·ra·na·í·ba (pä′rä·nä·ē′bä) A river of east central Brazil, flowing 500 miles SW to the Paraná. Formerly **Pa′ra·na·hi′ba.**

par·a·neph·ric (par′ə·nef′rik) *adj. Anat.* Found in the tissue beside the kidneys.

par·a·neph′ros (par′ə·nef′ros) *n. Anat.* A capsule of the suprarenal gland. [<NL <Gk. *para-* beside + *nephros* a kidney]

pa·rang (pä′räng) *n.* A short, heavy sheath knife with a straight edge, used especially by the Dyaks of Borneo for chopping and as a weapon. [<Malay *pārang*]

par·a·noi·a (par′ə·noi′ə) *n. Psychiatry* A chronic, often progressive, mental disorder or psychosis, characterized by monomania, systematized delusions of persecution, and sometimes hallucinations. Also **par′a·noe′a** (-nē′ə). [<NL <Gk., madness <*paranoos* distraught <*para-* beside + *noos, nous* mind]

par·a·noi·ac (par′ə·noi′ak) *adj.* Relating to or affected by paranoia. —*n.* One affected by paranoia. Also **par′a·no′ic** (-nō′ik), **par′a·noe′ac** (-nē′ak).

par·a·noid (par′ə·noid) *adj.* Resembling or suggestive of paranoia. —*n.* A person affected by paranoia.

par·a·no·sis (par′ə·nō′sis) *n. Psychoanal.* The primary advantage obtained by a patient from subjective exploitation of his illness. Compare EPINOSIS. [<NL <Gk. *para-* beside + *nosos* sickness] —**par′a·no′sic** *adj.*

par·a·nymph (par′ə·nimf) *n.* In ancient Greece, a groomsman or bridesmaid; specifically, the best man who went with a bridegroom to fetch home the bride, or the maiden who conducted the bride to the groom. [<L *paranymphus* <Gk. *paranymphos* best man or bridesmaid <*para-* near, beside + *nymphē* bride]

par·a·pet (par′ə·pit, -pet) *n.* **1** A low wall about the edge of a roof, terrace, bridge, fortification, etc. **2** A breastwork. See synonyms under BARRIER. [<F <Ital. *parapetto* <*para-* PARA-[2] + *petto* breast <L *pectus* breast] —**par′a·pet·ed** *adj.*

par·aph (par′əf) *n.* A flourish made with the pen at the end of a signature, often as a protection against forgery; a rubric. —*v.t.* To affix a paraph to; sign, especially with initials; initial. [<OF *paraphe* <Med. L *paraphus*, var. of L *paragraphus.* See PARAGRAPH.]

par·a·pher·na·li·a (par′ə·fər·nā′lē·ə, -nāl′yə, -fə) *n. pl.* **1** Trappings or accessories of equipment or adornment; furnishings, especially for ceremonious occasions; the parts of any outfit, apparatus, or equipment. **2** *Law* Formerly, the personal articles reserved to a wife over and above her dower. [<Med. L *paraphernalia (bona)* a wife's own (goods) <L *parapherna* <Gk. <*para-* beside + *phernē* dower <*pherein* carry]

par·a·phone (par′ə·fōn) *n.* Near rime. [<PARA-[1] + Gk. *phōnē* sound]

par·a·phrase (par′ə·frāz) *n.* A restatement of meaning of a passage, work, etc. —*v.t.* & *v.i.* **·phrased, ·phras·ing** To express in or make a paraphrase. [<F <L *paraphrasis* < Gk. <*paraphrazein* tell the same thing in other words <*para-* beside + *phrazein* tell]—**par′a·phras′er, par′a·phrast** (-frast) *n.*—**par′a·phras′tic** *adj.* —**par′a·phras′ti·cal·ly** *adv.*

pa·raph·y·sis (pə·raf′ə·sis) *n. pl.* **·ses** (-sēz) *Bot.* A sterile unicellular or pluricellular filament or narrow plate accompanying sexual or sporogenous organs found in certain mosses and other cryptogams. [<NL <Gk. *para-* beside, subsidiary + *physis* growth]

par·aple·gi·a (par′ə·plē′jē·ə) *n. Pathol.* Paralysis of the lower half of the body, due to disease or injury of the spinal cord. Also **par′a·ple′gy** (-plē′jē). [<NL <Gk. *paraplēgia, paraplēxia* a stroke on one side <*paraplēssein* strike at the side <*para-* beside + *plēssein* strike] —**par·a·ple·gic** (par′ə·plē′jik, plej′ik) *adj.* & *n.*

par·a·prax·is (par′ə·prak′sis) *n. Psychoanal.* Any faulty action, blunder, or lapse, as a slip of the tongue, failure of memory, etc. [<NL <Gk. *paraprassein* <*para-* beside + *prassein* do]

par·a·pro·fes·sion·al (par′ə·prə·fesh′ə·nal) One who assists professionals, as teachers or physicians, by performing tasks not requiring professional skills.

par·a·psy·chol·o·gy (par′ə·sī·kol′ə·jē) *n.* The investigation of extrasensory perception and the sporadic phenomena supposedly associated with it, such as telepathy, clairvoyance, telekinesis, prevision, dreams that prove prophetic, experiences of déjà vu, and poltergeist activity; metapsychics.

par·a·psy·cho·sis (par′ə·sī·kō′sis) *n. Psychiatry* A psychosis characterized by abnormal or unnatural thinking.

par·a·quat (par′ə·kwot) *n.* A toxic organic compound used as a herbicide. [<PARA-[1] + QUAT(ERNARY), part of the formula]

par·a·qui·none (par′ə·kwi·nōn′) *n.* Quinone.

Pa·rá rubber (pä·rä′) Rubber obtained from the tropical American rubber tree *(Hevea brasiliensis).* [<Pará, Brazil]

par·a·sang (par′ə·sang) *n.* An ancient Persian measure of length, varying from 2 to 4 miles. [<L *parasanga* <Gk. *parasangēs* <O Persian]

par·a·sceve (par′ə·sēv, par′ə·sē′vē) *n.* **1** The day before the Jewish Sabbath, on which preparation is made for the Sabbath; also, what is then prepared. **2** In the Roman Catholic Church, Good Friday. [<L, day of preparation, day before the Sabbath <Gk. *paraskeuē* preparation <*para-* beside, against +*skeuē* equipment]

par·a·se·le·ne (par′ə·si·lē′nē) *n. pl.* **·nae** (-nē) *Meteorol.* A luminous spot appearing on a lunar halo; a mock moon. [<NL <Gk. *para-* beside, subsidiary + *selēnē* moon]

par·a·shah (par′ə·shä) *n. pl.* **·shoth** (-shōth) One of the fifty-four sections or lessons into which the Pentateuch is divided for weekly readings throughout the annual cycle, or one of the smaller sections read on festivals. [<Hebrew *pārāshāh* a division <*pārash* divide]

par·a·site (par′ə·sīt) *n.* **1** *Biol.* An animal or a plant that lives on or in another organism at whose expense it obtains nourishment and shelter. **2** An obsequious sycophant who lives at another's expense. **3** In ancient Greece and Rome, one who secured a welcome at the tables of the rich by means of fawning and flattery. [<L *parasitus* <Gk. *parasitos,* lit., one who eats at another's table <*para-* beside + *sitos* food] —**par′a·sit′ic** (-sit′ik) or **·i·cal** *adj.* —**par′a·sit′i·cal·ly** *adv.*

parasite drag *Aeron.* That portion of the drag of an aircraft exclusive of the drag of the wings: also called *head resistance.*

par·a·sit·i·cide (par′ə·sit′ə·sīd) *n.* Any agent that destroys parasites. —*adj.* Efficacious for destroying parasites: also **par′a·sit′i·ci′dal.**

par·a·sit·ism (par′ə·sī′tiz·əm) *n.* **1** The condition or conduct of a fawner or sycophant. **2** The state or condition of being parasitic. **3** *Biol.* Destructive symbiosis. **4** *Med.* Disease, especially of the skin, caused by parasites.

par·a·si·tol·o·gy (par′ə·sī·tol′ə·jə) *n.* The scientific study of parasites and parasitism. —**par′a·si′to·log′i·cal** (-sī′tə·loj′i·kəl) *adj.* —**par′a·si·tol′o·gist** *n.*

par·a·sol (par′ə·sôl, -sol) *n.* A small, light sunshade carried by women. [<MF <Ital. *parasole* <*para-* PARA-[2] + *sole* sun]

par·a·sphe·noid (par′ə·sfē′noid) *n. Anat.* A bone forming the floor of the cranium in some vertebrates.

par·a·sym·pa·thet·ic (par′ə·sim′pə·thet′ik) *adj. Anat.* Designating that part of the autonomic nervous system originating in the cranial and sacral regions of the spinal cord. Its functions include constriction of the pupil, dilation of the blood vessels and salivary glands, slowing of the heart, and stimulation of the digestive and genitourinary systems: also called *cranio-sacral.*

par·a·syn·ap·sis (par′ə·si·nap′sis) *n. Biol.* In meiosis, the side-by-side conjugation of chromosomes. Also **par′a·syn′de·sis** (-sin′də·sis).

par·a·syn·the·sis (par′ə·sin′thə·sis) *n. Gram.* The principle or process of forming words by both combination and derivation; especially, the creation of a derivative word by compounding with a particle, as in *downfallen.* —**par′a·syn·thet′ic** (-sin·thet′ik) *adj.*

par·a·syph·i·lis (par′ə·sif′ə·lis) *n. Pathol.* A morbid sequela of syphilis, but not itself syphilitic. —**par′a·syph′i·lit′ic** (-sif′ə·lit′ik) *adj.*

par·a·tax·ic (par′ə·tak′sik) *adj. Psychol.* Pertaining to or characterized by behavior in which one or more individuals seek adjustment to a group situation in terms of private meanings or images projected upon other people or surroundings. [<PARA-[1] + Gk. *taxis* order]

par·a·tax·is (par′ə·tak′sis) *n. Gram.* Independent arrangement of clauses, phrases, etc., without connectives, as in "I die, I faint, I fail." Opposed to *hypotaxis.* [<Gk., lit., a placing side by side <*paratassein* place side by side <*para-* beside + *tassein* arrange] —**par′·a·tac′tic**(-tak′tik) or **·ti·cal** *adj.* —**par′·a·tac′ti·cal·ly** *adv.*

par·a·thi·on (par′ə·thī′on, -ən) *n.* An extremely poisonous synthetic organic compound, used as an agricultural insecticide. [<PARA-[1] + Gk. *theion* sulfur]

par·a·thy·roid (par′ə·thī′roid) *adj. Anat.* **1** Lying near the thyroid gland. **2** Pertaining to or designating one of several (usually four) small, bean-shaped glands found typically in pairs on the inner side near the back of each lobe of the thyroid.

par·a·troop (par′ə·trōōp) *n.* A military offensive force, with equipment, trained to land in hostile territory from an airplane by parachutes: also called *parachute troop.* [<PARA(CHUTE) + TROOP] —**par′a·troop′er** *n.*

par·a·ty·phoid (par′ə·tī′foid) *Pathol. adj.* Resembling typhoid fever but not responding to the tests for that disease. —*n.* Paratyphoid fever.

par·a·u·nit (par′ə·yōō′nit) *n.* A unit of paratroops. [<PARA(CHUTE) + UNIT]

par·a·vane (par′ə·vān) *n.* **1** A torpedo-shaped underwater device equipped with sharp projecting teeth for cutting the moorings of sunken mines. **2** A similar device loaded with high explosives for use against submarines. [<*para-*[1] + VANE]

par·boil (pär′boil′) *v.t.* **1** To boil partially. **2** To make uncomfortable with heat. [<OF *parboillir* <LL *parabullire* boil thoroughly <*per-* through + *bullire* bubble]

par·buck·le (pär′buk′əl) *n.* **1** A purchase made by looping a rope in the middle to aid in rolling casks, etc., up or down an incline, or in furling a sail by rolling the yards. **2** A sling made by passing both ends of a rope through its bight. —*v.t.* **·led, ·ling** To hoist or lower by means of a parbuckle. [Earlier *parbunkle*; origin unknown]

Par·cae (pär′sē) *n. pl.* In Roman mythology, the three Fates: also *Destinies.* Also **Par′cæ.**

par·cel (pär′səl) *n.* **1** Anything wrapped up; a package; bundle. **2** An integral part. **3** A group or lot composed of an indefinite number or quantity (of people or animals). **4** A distinct portion of land. **5** A separated part of anything; an indefinite number. —*v.t.* **·celed** or **·celled, ·cel·ing** or **·cel·ling 1** To divide or distribute in parts or shares: usually with *out.* **2** To make up into a parcel or parcels. **3** *Naut.* To wrap or cover with canvas strips, as a rope. —*adj.* & *adv.* Half or part; partly; partially. [<F *parcelle* <L *particula,* dim. of *pars, partis* part]

parcel post A postal service for the carriage and delivery of parcels not exceeding a specified size and weight: begun in the United States January 1, 1913. Also **parcels post.**

par·ce·nar·y (pär′sə·ner′ē) See COPARCENARY.

par·ce·ner (pär′sə·nər) *n. Law* A coparcener; coheir. [<AF *parcener,* OF *parçonier* <Med. L *partionarius* <L *partitionarius* <*partitio, -onis* share. See PARTITION]

parch (pärch) *v.t.* **1** To make extremely dry; shrivel with heat. **2** To dry (corn, peas, etc.) by exposing to great heat; roast slightly. **3** To dry up or shrivel with cold. —*v.i.* **4** To become extremely dry; shrivel with heat. [ME *parchen, perchen,*? ult. <L *persiccare* <*per-* thoroughly + *siccare* dry]

Par·chee·si (pär·chē′zē) *n.* A board game derived from pachisi: a trade name. Also **par·che′si, par·chi′si.**

parch·ment (pärch′mənt) *n.* **1** The skin of sheep, goats, and other animals prepared and polished with pumice stone for writing. **2** An imitation parchment made by treating paper with sulfuric acid and water: also called **vegetable parchment. 3** A formal writing on parchment. **4** A college graduation diploma. **5** A light-tan or cream color, the color of parchment. [<OF *parchemin* <LL *Pergamena (charta)* (paper) of Pergamum <Gk. *Pergamon* the city of Pergamum; because it was used there instead of papyrus]

pard[1] (pärd) *n. Archaic* A leopard; panther. [<OF *parde* <L *pardus* <Gk. *pardos* <*pardalis,* ? <Persian *pars* a panther]

pard[2] (pärd) *n. Slang* A partner; mate; chum. [Short for PARDNER]

par·di (pär·dē′) *adv.* & *interj. Archaic* By God; verily: formerly a form of profanity: also spelled *perdie, perdy.* Also **par·dee′, par·die′, par·dy′.** [<OF *par dé* by God <L *per* by + *deus* God]

pard·ner (pärd′nər) n. U.S. Dial. Chum; friend. [Alter. of PARTNER]

par·don (pär′dən) v.t. 1 To remit the penalty of (a crime, insult, etc.). 2 To release from punishment; forgive for an offense. 3 To grant courteous allowance for or to: Pardon my French. —n. 1 The act of pardoning; remission of penalty incurred. 2 A waiving, by sovereign prerogative, of the execution of the penal sanctions of the violated law: distinguished from justification. 3 Courteous forbearance; acquittal of blame: used in making polite excuses. 4 Law Remission of guilt; also, an official warrant declaring the act of pardon. 5 An indulgence. [< OF pardun < pardonner < LL perdonare grant < per- through + donare give] —par′don·a·ble adj. —par′don·a·bly adv.

Synonyms (verb): absolve, acquit, condone, exculpate, excuse, forgive, overlook, release, remit. Forgive has reference to feelings, pardon to consequences; hence, the executive may pardon, but has nothing to do officially with forgiving. To pardon is the act of a superior, implying the right to punish; to forgive is the privilege of the humblest person who has been wronged or offended. In law, to remit the whole penalty is equivalent to pardoning the offender; but a part of a penalty may be remitted and the remainder inflicted, as where the penalty includes both fine and imprisonment. To condone is to put aside a recognized offense by some act which restores the offender to forfeited right or privilege, and is the act of a private individual, without legal formalities. To excuse is to overlook some slight offense, error, or breach of etiquette; pardon is often used by courtesy in nearly the same sense. Compare ABSOLVE, MERCY. Antonyms: castigate, chasten, chastise, condemn, convict, correct, doom, punish, recompense, scourge, sentence, visit.

Synonyms (noun): absolution, acquittal, amnesty, forbearance, forgiveness, mercy, oblivion, remission. Acquittal is a release from a charge, after trial, as not guilty. Pardon is a removal of penalty from one who has been adjudged guilty. Acquittal is the adjudging one to be not guilty, as by the decision of a court, commonly of a jury; pardon is the act of the executive. An innocent man may demand acquittal, and need not plead for pardon. Oblivion signifies overlooking and virtually forgetting an offense, so that the offender stands before the law in all respects as if it had never been committed. Amnesty conveys the same idea. Pardon affects individuals; amnesty and oblivion are said of great numbers. Pardon is oftenest applied to the ordinary administration of law; amnesty or oblivion, to national and military affairs. An amnesty is issued after war, insurrection, or rebellion. Absolution is a religious word (compare synonyms for ABSOLVE). Remission is a discharge from penalty; as, the remission of a fine. Antonyms: penalty, punishment, retaliation, retribution, vengeance.

par·don·er (pär′dən·ər) n. 1 One who pardons. 2 In the Middle Ages, a layman commissioned to collect offerings for which indulgences were promised.

par·don·nez-moi (pär·dôn′ā·mwà′) French Pardon me.

pare (pâr) v.t. pared, par·ing 1 To cut off the covering layer or part of. 2 To cut away or trim away (a covering layer or part): often with off or away. 3 To reduce or diminish, especially gradually or little by little. ◆ Homophone: pair, pear. [< F parer prepare, trim < L parare] —par′er n. —par′ing adj. & n.

Pa·ré (pá·rā′), Ambroise, 1510?–90, French surgeon; father of modern surgery.

pa·re·cious (pə·rē′shəs), etc. See PAROECIOUS, etc.

par·e·gor·ic (par′ə·gôr′ik, -gor′ik) n. 1 A medicine that assuages pain. 2 A camphorated tincture of opium. [< LL paregoricus < Gk. parēgorikos, parēgoros soothing < para- beside + -agoros speaking < agora assembly, market place]

pa·rei·ra bra·va (pə·râr′ə brä′və, brä′və) A drug obtained from the roots of a tropical American plant of the moonseed family (Chondrodendron tomentosum): used in treating chronic disorders of the urinary passages. [< Brazilian Pg., a wild vine]

pa·ren·chy·ma (pə·reng′ki·mə) n. Biol. 1 The soft cellular substance of glandular and other organs. 2 The proper substance of an organ, excluding the connective tissue and the like. 3 Bot. The thin-walled, soft cell tissue of higher plants, as found in stem pith and in the pulp of fruits. Also **pa·ren′chyme** (-kīm). [< NL < Gk., lit., something poured in beside < para- beside + enchyma infusion] —**par·en·chym·a·tous** (par′eng·kim′ə·təs) adj.

par·ent (pâr′ənt) n. 1 A father or a mother. 2 Any organism that generates another; a producer. 3 Cause; occasion. [< OF < L parens, -entis parent, ancestor, orig. ppr. of parere beget]

par·ent·age (pâr′ən·tij) n. 1 The relation of parent to child, of producer to the produced. 2 Relation of cause to effect. 3 Descent or derivation from parents; extraction; lineage; origin. 4 Derivation from any source. 5 Parenthood.

pa·ren·tal (pə·ren′təl) adj. 1 Pertaining to or characteristic of a parent. 2 Genetics Pertaining to or designating that generation from whose crossbreeding hybrids are produced. —**pa·ren′tal·ly** adv.

Par·en·ta·li·a (par′ən·tā′lē·ə) n. pl. Latin In ancient Rome, an annual feast in commemoration of the dead and veneration of ancestors.

par·en·ter·al (par·en′tər·əl) adj. Med. Pertaining to or designating a mode of assimilation other than through the alimentary canal, as intravenous or subcutaneous. [< Gk. para- beside + enteron intestine]

pa·ren·the·sis (pə·ren′thə·sis) n. pl. ·ses (-sēz) 1 Gram. A word, phrase, or clause inserted in a sentence that is grammatically complete without it, separated usually by commas, dashes, or upright curves. 2 Either or both of the upright curves ( ) so used. 3 Hence, any intervening episode or incident; interval. [< Med. L < Gk. < parentithenai put in beside < para- beside + en- in + tithenai place]

pa·ren·the·size (pə·ren′thə·sīz) v.t. ·sized, ·siz·ing 1 To insert as a parenthesis. 2 To insert parentheses in. 3 To place within parentheses (def. 2).

par·en·thet·i·cal (par′ən·thet′i·kəl) adj. 1 Pertaining to a parenthesis. 2 Abounding in parentheses. 3 Thrown in; episodical. Also **par′en·thet′ic.** —**par′en·thet′i·cal·ly** adv.

par·ent·hood (pâr′ənt·hood) n. The condition or relation of a parent.

par·ent·ing (pâr′ən·ting) n. The act or process of functioning as parents; the act or process of raising children.

Par·ent-Teach·er Association (pâr′ənt·tē′chər) U.S. Any of several local organizations composed of parents and public-school teachers, seeking mutual cooperation in the guidance of school children.

pa·re·sis (pə·rē′sis, par′ə·sis) n. Pathol. Partial paralysis affecting muscular motion but not sensation. —**general paresis** General paralysis accompanied by dementia, caused by syphilitic degeneration of the brain. [< NL < Gk., a letting go < parienai let go < para- beside + hienai let go]

par·es·the·sia (par′is·thē′zhə, -zhē·ə) n. Pathol. Abnormal or perverted sense of touch; a sensation of itching, tingling, or prickling of the skin: also spelled paraesthesia. Also **par′es·the′sis.** —**par′es·thet′ic** (-thet′ik) adj.

pa·ret·ic (pə·ret′ik, -rē′tik) adj. Pertaining to or afflicted with paresis. —n. One who suffers from paresis. —**pa·ret′i·cal·ly** adv.

Pa·re·to (pä·rā′tō), Vilfredo, 1848–1923, Italian economist and sociologist.

pa·re·u (pä′rä·oo) n. A rectangular, figured cotton cloth worn as a skirt or loincloth by the natives of southern Pacific islands. [< Tahitian]

pa·reve (pär′ə·və) adj. Not made with milk or meat. [< Yiddish]

par ex·cel·lence (pär ek′sə·läns, Fr. pár ek·se·läns′) Of the highest excellence; beyond comparison; preeminently. [< F, by way of excellence]

par ex·em·ple (pár eg·zän′pl′) French For example; for instance.

par·fait (pär·fā′) n. A frozen dessert or confection made with eggs, sugar, whipped cream, and fruit or other flavoring. [< F, lit., perfect < L perfectus. See PERFECT.]

par·fleche (pär·flesh′) n. 1 Rawhide, usually of buffalo skin, which has been freed of hair and dried on a stretcher. 2 An article, as a shield, made from such a hide. Also **par·flesh′.** [< dial. F (Canadian) < F par- PARA-² + flèche an arrow]

par·get (pär′jit) n. 1 Gypsum. 2 Plaster suitable for lining chimneys. 3 Pargeting. —v.t. ·get·ed, ·get·ted, ·get·ing or ·get·ting To cover or adorn with parget or pargeting. [Appar. < OF pargeter, parjeter throw over a surface < par- all over + jeter throw < L per- thoroughly + jactare, freq. of jacere throw]

par·get·ing (pär′jit·ing) n. 1 Plastering; specifically, ornamental stuccowork or plasterwork in relief. 2 Parget (def. 2).

par·he·lic circle (pär·hē′lik, -hel′ik) A band of light or halo, passing through the sun and parallel to the horizon: it is an effect of solar reflection from the vertical faces of ice crystals in the atmosphere. Also **parhelic ring.**

par·he·li·on (pär·hē′lē·ən) n. pl. ·li·a (-lē·ə) One of two bright solar images appearing on the parhelic circle on either side of the sun; a mock sun or sundog. Also **par·he′li·um.** [< L parelion < Gk. parēlion < para- beside + hēlios sun] —**par·he′lic, par·he·li·a·cal** (pär′hi·lī′ə·kəl) adj.

pari- combining form Equal: parisyllabic. [< L par, paris equal]

Pa·ri·a (pär′yä), Gulf of An inlet of the Caribbean between Trinidad and the coast of Venezuela; enclosed on the north by Paria Peninsula, a promontory of NE Venezuela extending 75 miles east.

pa·ri·ah (pə·rī′ə, par′ē·ə) n. 1 One of low caste (but not lowest or outcast) people of southern India and Burma, employed as servants. 2 A person of low caste or no caste. 3 A social outcast. [< Tamil paraiyar, pl. of paraiyon, lit., (hereditary) drummer < parai a large festival drum]

Par·i·an (pâr′ē·ən) adj. 1 Of, from, or pertaining to Paros or the white marble mined there. 2 Resembling the marble of Paros. —n. 1 A native or inhabitant of Paros. 2 Ware of Parian marble: also **Parian biscuit.**

Pa·ri·cu·tín (pä′rē·koo·tēn′) A volcano in Michoacán state, Mexico; 8,200 feet; first erupted February, 1943.

pa·ri·es (pâr′i·ēz) n. pl. **pa·ri·e·tes** (pə·rī′ə·tēz) Usually pl. Biol. The wall of any cavity in the body, as of any organ. [< L, a wall]

pa·ri·e·tal (pə·rī′ə·təl) adj. 1 Biol. Of, pertaining to, or forming the walls of any cavity in the body. 2 Of or pertaining to a wall. 3 Pertaining to the care of or residence within walls or precincts, as of a college. 4 Bot. Pertaining to or borne on a wall: said especially of the placentae or ovules borne on the wall of the ovary of a plant. —n. 1 A parietal bone. 2 pl. U.S. the rules that govern dormitory visitation for members of the opposite sex.

parietal bone Anat. Either of two bones between the occipital and frontal bones that form a part of the top and sides of the cranium.

parietal lobe Anat. That portion of the hemispheres of the brain that lies between the central sulcus and the occipital lobe.

pa·ri·e·tes (pə·rī′ə·tēz) Plural of PARIES.

pa·ril·lin (pə·ril′in) n. Biochem. A white crystalline saponin of variable composition, contained in sarsaparilla root, and to which the drug owes its medicinal qualities: often called smilacin. Also **pa·ril′lic acid** (pə·ril′ik). [< Sp. parrilla, dim. of parra a vine + -IN]

pari-mu·tu·el (par′i·myoo′choo·əl) n. 1 A system of betting at races in which those who have bet on the winners share in the total amount wagered: also **parimutuel.** 2 A machine for recording bets under this system; a totalisator. [< F, a stake or mutual wager]

par·ing (pâr′ing) n. 1 The act of cutting off the surface or edge of. 2 The part pared off.

pa·ri pas·su (pâr′ī pas′oo, pär′ē) Latin With equal pace; of the same speed.

par·i·pin·nate (par′i·pin′āt) adj. Bot. Equally or abruptly pinnate: said of leaves.

par·is (par′is) *n.* The herb-Paris. [<L *pars, paris* equal; infl. by PARIS]

Par·is (par′is) In Greek mythology, a son of Priam and Hecuba who carried off Helen, wife of Menelaus, thus causing the Trojan War. See APPLE OF DISCORD.

Par·is (par′is, *Fr.* pà·re′) A port on the Seine, 111 miles from its mouth, and capital of France: ancient *Lutetia.*

Pa·ris (pä·res′), **Gaston,** 1839–1903, French philologist.

Paris Basin The chief depression of north and north central France, at the center of which is Paris.

Paris blue Prussian blue.

Paris green A poisonous compound prepared from copper acetate and arsenic trioxide, used largely as an insecticide and pigment.

par·ish (par′ish) *n.* **1** *Eccl.* In the Anglican, Roman Catholic, and some other churches, a district, usually part of a diocese, with its own church, and in charge of a priest or other clergyman. **2** *U.S.* **a** A religious congregation, comprising all those who worship at the same church. **b** The district in which they live. **3** *Brit.* A political subdivision of a county, often corresponding to an ecclesiastical parish. **4** In Louisiana, a civil district corresponding to a county. **5** The people of a parish, in any of the above senses. ◆ Collateral adjective: *parochial.* [<OF *paroche, paroisse* <LL *parochia* <Gk. *paroikia,* orig. a neighborhood, later a diocese <*para-* beside + *oikeein* dwell] —**pa·rish′ion·al** *adj.*

pa·rish·ion·er (pə·rish′ən·ər) *n.* A member of a parish.

Pa·ri·sian (pə·rizh′ən, -riz′e·ən) *adj.* Of or pertaining to the city of Paris. —*n.* A native or resident of Paris.

par·i·syl·lab·ic (par′i·si·lab′ik) *adj.* Having the same number of syllables. Also **par′i·syl·lab′i·cal.**

par·i·tor (par′ə·tər) *n. Obs.* An officer of an ecclesiastical court who issues summonses. [Aphetic var. of APPARITOR]

par·i·ty[1] (par′ə·tē) *n.* **1** Equality, as of condition or rank; like state or degree; equivalent position; equal value. **2** The equivalence in legal weight and quality of the legal tender of one class of money to another. **3** Par (def. 1). **4** Equality between the currency or prices of commodities of two countries or cities. **5** Perfect analogy; close resemblance. **6** *U.S.* A level for farm prices which gives to the farmer the same purchasing power that he averaged during each year of a chosen base period, originally the five years of farm prosperity prior to World War I. **7** *Physics* That property of a wave whereby its function is symmetrically unchanged by inversion in a coordinate system **(even parity),** or changed only in sign **(odd parity).** See synonyms under ANALOGY, SYMMETRY. [<L *paritas* equality <*pars* equal]

par·i·ty[2] (par′ə·tē) *n. Med.* Fitness or ability to bear offspring. [<L *parere* bear + -ITY]

par·i·vin·cu·lar (par′ə·ving′kyə·lər) *adj. Zool.* Designating a bivalve that has an elongated semicylindrical ligament. [<PARI- + VINCULUM]

park (pärk) *n.* **1** In English law, a tract of enclosed land stocked with wild beasts of the chase, and held through royal grant or by immemorial prescription. **2** A tract of land for public use in or near a city, usually laid out with walks, drives, and recreation grounds. **3** An open square or plaza in a city, usually containing shade trees and seats. **4** A large area of country containing natural curiosities reserved by the government for public enjoyment: a national *park.* **5** A plateaulike valley between mountain ranges: used most frequently in Colorado and Wyoming. **6** *Mil.* An enclosure where guns, trucks, wagons, animals, etc., are placed for safety; also, the objects thus enclosed: an artillery *park*; also, a complete train of cannon, including equipment, ammunition, gunners, etc., for an army in the field. —*v.t.* **1** To place or leave (an automobile, etc.) standing for a time, as on the street. **2** *U.S. Colloq.* To place; set: *Park* your hat on the table. **3** To assemble or mass together: to *park* artillery. **4** To enclose in or as in a park. —*v.i.* **5** To park an automobile, etc. [<OF *parc* a game preserve, ult. <Gmc. Akin to PADDOCK.]

Park (pärk), **Mungo,** 1771–1806, Scottish African explorer.

par·ka (pär′kə) *n.* **1** An outer garment of undressed skins worn by Eskimos. **2** A similar woolen garment, sometimes fur-lined, with attached hood: worn for skiing and other winter sports. Also **par′kee** (-ke). [<Aleut]

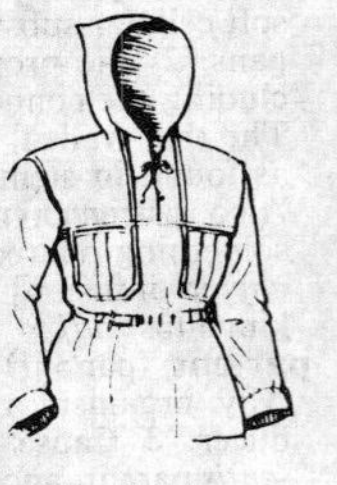

HOODED PARKA

Park Avenue A residential street running north and south in Manhattan borough of New York City: regarded as a symbol of wealth and fashion.

Par·ker (pär′kər), **Dorothy,** 1893–1968, *née* Rothschild. U.S. writer. —**Sir (Horatio) Gilbert,** 1862–1932, Canadian author and dramatist. —**Theodore,** 1810–60, U.S. minister, and New England abolitionist leader.

park·ing (pär′king) *n.* **1** Parks collectively, or ground resembling a park, as a strip of sward in a street. **2** The act of leaving a vehicle in a public place.

Par·kin·son's disease (pär′kin·sənz) *Pathol.* A chronic, progressive nervous disease characterized by muscle tremor when at rest, stiffness, and a rigid facial expression. Also **par′kin·son·ism** (-iz′əm). [after James *Parkinson,* 1755–1824, Eng. physician]

park·land (pärk′land′) *n. Often pl.* **1** Land used or designated for use as a park: federal *parklands*; urban *parkland.* **2** Grassland with trees, suitable for use as a park.

Park·man (pärk′mən), **Francis,** 1823–93, U.S. historian.

Park Range A part of the Rocky Mountains in west Colorado; highest peak, 14,284 feet.

park·way (pärk′wā′) *n.* A wide thoroughfare adorned with turf and trees.

par·lance (pär′ləns) *n.* **1** Manner of speech; language; phrase: common *parlance,* legal *parlance.* **2** *Archaic* Talk; conversation. [<OF <*parler* speak <LL *parabolare* <*parabola.* See PARABLE.]

par·lan·do (pär·län′dō) *adj. & adv. Music* Declamatory in style; in recitative. Also **par·lan′·te** (-tā). [<Ital. ppr. of *parlare* speak <LL *parabolare* <*parabola.* See PARABLE.]

Par·la·to·ri·a (pär′lə·tôr′ē·ə, -tō′rē·ə) *n.* A genus of scale insects (family *Coccidae*), including many species injurious to fruits, especially the date-palm scale *(P. blanchardi).* [<NL, after Felipe *Parlatore,* 1816–77, Italian physician and botanist]

par·lay (pär·lā′, pär′lē) *v.t. & v.i.* To place (an original bet and its winnings) on a later race, contest, etc. —*n.* Such a bet. [Alter. of earlier *paroli* <F <Ital., a grand cast at dice <*paro* equal <L *par*]

par·ley (pär′lē) *n.* **1** An oral conference, as with an enemy; a discussion of terms. **2** Mutual discourse. See synonyms under CONVERSATION. —*v.i.* To hold a conference, especially with an enemy. Also *Obs.* **parle** (pärl). [<F *parlée,* fem. pp. of *parler* speak <LL *parabolare* <*parabola.* See PARABLE.]

par·lia·ment (pär′lə·mənt) *n.* A meeting or assembly for consultation and deliberation; a legislative body; a national legislature, especially when composed of various estates. Also *Obs.* **par′le·ment.** [<OF *parlement* speaking <*parler* speak <LL *parabolare* <*parabola.* See PARABLE.]

Par·lia·ment (pär′lə·mənt) *n.* **1** The supreme legislature of Great Britain and Northern Ireland, composed of the three estates of the realm—the Lords Spiritual, the Lords Temporal, and the Commons—together with, in a strict legal sense, the sovereign. **2** The legislature in any of Great Britain's self-governing colonies or dominions. **3** In France, before the French Revolution, one of several tribunals of justice. **4** The legislative assembly of Scotland until 1707, or that of Ireland until 1800. —**Long Parliament** The British Parliament which first assembled in 1640 and finally dissolved by its own consent in 1660: after the enforced expulsion *(Pride's Purge)* of some of its members in 1648, it was known as the **Rump Parliament.**

par·lia·men·tar·i·an·ism (pär′lə·men·târ′ē·ən·iz′əm) *n.* The system of government, developed in England, in which the tenure of the cabinet is dependent on the will of the majority in the lower house: also called **parliamentary system.**

par·lia·men·ta·ry (pär′lə·men′tər·e) *adj.* **1** Pertaining to, characterized by, or enacted by a parliament. **2** According to the rules of Parliament; admissible in a deliberative assembly. —**par′lia·men·tar′i·an** *adj. & n.*

parliamentary law See under LAW.

par·lor (pär′lər) *n.* **1** A room for reception of callers or entertainment of guests; drawing-room. **2** A room in an inn, hotel, etc., for private conversation, appointments, etc. **3** *U.S.* Formerly, a smartly furnished room for the performance of personal or professional services: a tonsorial *parlor:* a genteelism. Also *Brit.* **par′lour.** [<AF *parlur,* OF *parleor* < Med. L *parlatorium* <*parlare* <LL *parabolare* speak <*parabola.* See PARABLE.]

parlor car A railway car fitted with luxurious chairs, and run as a day coach; a drawing-room car.

par·lous (pär′ləs) *Archaic adj.* **1** Dangerous or exciting; perilous. **2** Shrewd; venturesome; waggish; mischievous. —*adv.* Exceedingly; very. [Var. of PERILOUS] —**par′lous·ly** *adv.*

Par·ma (pär′mä) **1** A province and former duchy of north central Italy. **2** Its capital, a city near the Apennines.

Par·men·i·des (pär·men′ə·dez) Greek philosopher of the fifth century B.C.

Par·me·san (pär′me·zan′) *adj.* Of or pertaining to Parma. Also **Par·mese** (pär·mes′). [<F < Ital. *parmigiano* belonging to Parma]

Parmesan cheese A hard, dry cheese, originally made in Parma: usually grated and served on soups, spaghetti, etc.

par·mi·gia·na (pär′mə·jä′nə) *adj.* Cooked with Parmesan cheese.

Par·na·i·ba (pär′nä·e′bä) A river in NE Brazil, flowing 750 miles NE to the Atlantic. Also **Par′na·hy′ba.**

Par·nas·si·an (pär·nas′e·ən) *adj.* **1** Belonging or relating to Parnassus or the Parnassians. **2** Of or pertaining to poetry. —*n.* A representative or member of a school of poetry founded in France during the last half of the 19th century, which emphasized the technical aspect of the art of poetry: so called from the title of its first collection of poems, *Le Parnasse contemporain* (1866). [<L *Parnas(s)ius*] —**Par·nas′si·an·ism** *n.*

Par·nas·sus (pär·nas′əs) **1** A mountain north of the Gulf of Corinth in central Greece; 8,062 feet: formerly *Liákoura*: anciently regarded as sacred to Apollo and the Muses. *Greek* **Par·nas′sos.** **2** A domain of poetry or of literature. **3** A collection of poems or literary works.

Par·nell (pär·nel′), **Charles Stewart,** 1846–91, Irish statesman.

pa·ro·chi·al (pə·ro′kē·əl) *adj.* **1** Pertaining to, supported by, or confined to a parish. **2** Hence, narrow; provincial; restricted in scope: *parochial* ideas. [<OF <LL *parochialis* < *parochia.* See PARISH.]

pa·ro·chi·al·ism (pə·rō′ke·əl·iz′əm) *n.* **1** Government or control by a vestry or parochial board. **2** Narrow of view; provincialism.

parochial school See under SCHOOL.

par·o·dy (par′ə·dē) *n. pl.* **·dies** **1** A literary composition imitating and ridiculing some serious work; a comical imitation, especially of a poem; a travesty. **2** Any burlesque imitation of something serious. **3** A poor imitation. See synonyms under CARICATURE. —*v.t.* **·died, ·dy·ing** To make a parody of; travesty. [<Gk. *parōidia* a burlesque poem or song <*para-* beside + *ōidē* a song, poem] —**pa·rod·ic** (pə·rod′ik) or **·i·cal** *adj.* —**par′o·dist** *n.*

pa·roe·cious (pə·rē′shəs) *adj. Bot.* Having the male and female sexual organs of plants developed side by side or in the same inflorescence, as in many bryophytes: also spelled *parecious.* Also **pa·roi′cous.** [<Gk. *paroikos* dwelling side by side <*paroikeein* <*para-* beside + *oikeein* dwell] —**pa·roe′cious·ly** *adv.* —**pa·roe′cious·ness** *n.* —**pa·roe′cism** (-siz·əm) *n.*

pa·rol (pə·rōl′) *Law n.* **1** Something spoken or said; specifically, in the legal phrase **by parol,** by word of mouth. **2** The pleadings filed in an action. —*adj.* **1** Given or expressed by word of mouth; oral. **2** Written but not under seal. Also **pa·role′.** [<AF, var. of OF *parole* <L *parabola* word. See PARABLE.]

pa·role (pə·rōl′) *n.* **1** A pledge of honor by a prisoner of war that he will not seek to escape or will not serve against his captors until exchanged; also, the condition of being under parole. **2** The release of a prisoner from jail prior to the expiration of his term on his own recognizance. **3** The watchword used only by officers of the guard and of the day: distinguished from *countersign.* **4** *Law* Parol. **5** Word of honor. — *v.t.* **·roled, ·rol·ing** To release (a prisoner) on parole. [<F *parole (d'honneur)* word (of honor) <OF <L *parabola.* Doublet of PALAVER, PARABLE, PARABOLA.]

pa·role d'hon·neur (pà·rôl′ dô·nœr′) *French* Word of honor.

par·o·no·ma·si·a (par′ə·nō·mā′zhē·ə, -zē·ə) *n.* Any use for effect of words similar in sound, but differing in meaning; a play on words, especially one in which the similarity of sound is the prominent characteristic. Compare PUN. [<L <Gk. <*paronomazein* alter slightly in meaning <*para-* beside + *onoma* name] — **par′o·no·ma′si·al, par′o·no·mas′tic** (-mas′tik) or **·ti·cal** *adj.* — **par′o·no·mas′ti·cal·ly** *adv.*

par·o·nym (par′ə·nim) *n.* A word having the same root as another; a cognate word. [<Gk. *parōnymon,* orig. neut. of *parōnymos* derivative <*para-* beside + *onyma,* Aeolic var. of *onoma* name] — **pa·ron·y·mous** (pə·ron′ə·məs), **par′o·nym′ic** (-nim′ik) *adj.*

par·o·quet (par′ə·ket) See PARAKEET.

par·o·ral (par·ôr′əl, -ō′rəl) *adj.* Adjacent to the mouth or oral region.

Pa·ros (pä′ros) An island of the central Cyclades, Greece; 77 square miles.

pa·rot·ic (pə·rot′ik, -rō′tik) *adj.* Situated near the ear: the *parotic* region. [<NL *paroticus* <Gk. *para-* beside + *otikos* of the ear <*ous, ōtos* ear]

pa·rot·id (pə·rot′id) *Anat. adj.* **1** Situated near the ear. **2** Designating one of the paired salivary glands in front of and below the external ear in mammals. — *n.* A salivary gland below the ear. [<F *parotide* <L *parotis, -idis* <Gk. *parōtis, -idos* a tumor near the ear <*para-* beside + *ous, ōtos* ear]

par·o·ti·tis (par′ə·tī′tis) *n. Pathol.* Inflammation and swelling of the parotid gland; mumps. Also **par′o·ti·di′tis** (-ti·dī′tis). — **par′o·tit′ic** (-tit′ik) *adj.*

pa·ro·toid (pə·rō′toid) *Biol. adj.* **1** Resembling a parotid gland. **2** Designating a cutaneous gland situated behind the eye and above the tympanum in anurous amphibians. — *n.* A parotoid gland.

-parous *suffix* Giving birth to; bearing; producing: *oviparous.* [<L *-parus* <*parere* beget]

par·ox·ysm (par′ək·siz′əm) *n.* **1** *Pathol.* A periodic attack of disease; a fit. **2** Sudden and violent excitement or emotion, as of anger. **3** A convulsion of any kind. See synonyms under AGONY, PAIN. [<MF *paroxysme* <Med. L *paroxysmus* irritation <Gk. *paroxysmos* <*paroxynein* goad <*para-* beside, beyond + *oxynein* goad <*oxys* sharp]

par·ox·ys·mal (par′ək·siz′məl) *adj.* **1** Relating to, of the nature of, accompanied or characterized by a paroxysm. **2** Resulting from convulsive action of natural forces, as a volcanic eruption, flood, etc. Also **par′ox·ys′mic.** — **par′ox·ys′mal·ly** *adv.*

par·ox·y·tone (par·ok′sə·tōn) *adj.* Having the acute accent on the penultimate syllable. — *n.* A word thus accented, as *ly′kos.* [<NL *paroxytonus* <Gk. *paroxytonos* <*para-* beside, past + *oxytonos* OXYTONE]

par·quet (pär·kā′, -ket′) *n.* **1** The main-floor space behind the orchestra of a theater; sometimes, the whole lower floor. **2** Parquetry. — *v.t.* **·queted** (-kād′, -ket′id), **·quet·ing** (-kā′·ing, -ket′ing) To make of or ornament with parquetry. Also **par·quette** (pär·ket′). [<F <OF *parchet* a small compartment, dim. of *parc.* See PARK.]

parquet circle The section of theater seats at the rear of the parquet and under the balcony.

par·quet·ry (pär′kit·rē) *n.* Wooden mosaic, used especially for floor surfaces. [<F *parqueterie*]

par·quine (pär′kēn) *n. Chem.* A yellowish, bitter, crystalline alkaloid, $C_{21}H_{39}O_8N$, extracted from the bark of certain solanaceous plants, especially *Cestrum parqui*: similar in action to strychnine and atropine. [<NL *parqui,* name of a species + -INE[2]]

parr (pär) *n.* A young salmon before its first migration seaward. [? <dial. E (Scottish)]

Parr (pär), **Catherine,** 1513–48, sixth and last wife of Henry VIII of England.

par·ra·keet (par′ə·kēt), **par·ra·kee·to** (-tō) See PARAKEET.

par·ra·mat·ta (par′ə·mat′ə) See PARAMATTA.

Par·ran (par′ən), **Thomas,** born 1892, U.S. physician.

par·rel (par′əl) *n.* **1** A chimneypiece or the ornaments of a chimneypiece collectively. **2** *Naut.* A sliding hoop, rope, or chain by which a yard is attached to a mast. Also **par′·ral.** [ME *parail,* aphetic var. of *aparail* equipment. See APPAREL.]

par·ri·cide (par′ə·sīd) *n.* **1** The murder of a parent, or of an ancestor. **2** One who has committed such a crime. [<F <L *paricidium* a killing of a relative, and *paricida* a killer of a relative] — **par′ri·ci′dal** *adj.* — **par′ri·ci′dal·ly** *adv.*

Par·ring·ton (par′ing·tən), **Vernon Louis,** 1871–1929, U. S. literary historian.

Par·rish (par′ish), **Maxfield,** 1870–1966, U.S. artist.

Par·ris Island (par′is) One of the Sea Islands, NE of Savannah, Georgia; site of a United States Marine Corps training camp.

par·ritch (par′ich) *n. Scot.* Porridge of oatmeal. Also **par′ridge** (-ij).

par·ro·quet (par′ə·ket) See PARAKEET.

par·rot (par′ət) *n.* **1** Any of certain birds of warm regions of the order *Psittaciformes,* having a hooked bill, paired toes, and usually brilliant plumage, including the macaws, parakeets, cockatoos, lories, and related genera. Some parrots are noted for their ability to simulate human laughter and speech. ◆ Collateral adjective: *psittacine.* **2** A person who repeats or imitates without understanding. — *v.t.* To repeat or imitate by rote or without understanding. [? <F *perrot,* var. of *Pierrot,* dim. of *Pierre* Peter, a personal name] — **par′rot·er** *n.*

parrot fever Psittacosis.

parrot fish 1 Any of many small fishes of the family *Scaridae,* inhabiting warm seas: so called from their vivid coloring and beaklike jaws. **2** A labroid fish of the genus *Labrichthys,* especially the parrot perch *(L. psittacula)* of Australasia.

par·ry (par′ē) *v.* **·ried, ·ry·ing** *v.t.* **1** To ward off, as a thrust in fencing. **2** To avoid or evade. — *v.i.* **3** To make a parry. — *n. pl.* **·ries 1** A defensive movement, as in fencing. **2** An evasion or diversion in a contest of wits. [Prob. <F *parez,* imperative of *parer* ward off <Ital. *parare* defend <L, prepare]

Par·ry (par′ē), **Sir William Edward,** 1790–1855, English Arctic explorer.

Par·ry Islands (par′ē) An arctic archipelago in west central Franklin district, Northwest Territories, including Melville, Bathurst, and numerous smaller islands.

parse (pärs) *v.t.* **parsed, pars·ing 1** To describe (a sentence) grammatically by giving the form, function, etc., of each of its components. **2** To describe (a word) as to its part of speech, form, and relation to the other elements in a sentence. [Prob. <L *pars, partis* part] — **pars′er** *n.*

par·sec (pär′sek) *n. Astron.* A unit of length used in expressing the distance of stars. One parsec is almost exactly 206,265 times the mean distance of the earth from the sun, or 19.2 trillion miles, or 3.26 light years. A star is at a distance of one parsec from the earth if its annual parallax amounts to one second of arc (1″). [<PAR(ALLAX) + SEC(OND)[1] (def. 2)]

Par·see (pär′sē, pär·sē′) *n.* A Zoroastrian; especially, an adherent of the old Persian religion whose ancestors fled to India about the eighth century on account of Mohammedan persecution. Also **Par′si.** [<Persian *Pārsī* a Persian <*Pārs* Persia] — **Par′see·ism, Par′si·ism, Par′sism** *n.*

Par·si·fal (pär′si·fäl, -fəl) An opera by Richard Wagner based on the *Parzifal* of Wolfram von Eschenbach. See PERCEVAL.

par·si·mo·ni·ous (pär′sə·mō′nē·əs) *adj.* Niggardly; penurious. See synonyms under AVARICIOUS, SCANTY. — **par′si·mo′ni·ous·ly** *adv.* — **par′si·mo′ni·ous·ness** *n.*

par·si·mo·ny (pär′sə·mō′nē) *n.* Undue sparingness in the expenditure of money; stinginess. See synonyms under FRUGALITY. [<L *parsimonia* <*parcere* spare]

pars·ley (pärs′lē) *n.* A cultivated umbelliferous herb *(Petroselinum latifolium* or *crispum)* with aromatic, finely divided leaves and greenish-yellow flowers, used as a garnish and for flavoring soups. [Fusion of OF *peresil* and OE *petersilige,* both <LL *petrosilium,* alter. of L *petroselinum* <Gk. *petroselinon* <*petra* rock + *selinon* parsley]

pars·nip (pärs′nip) *n.* A European herb *(Pastinaca sativa)* of the parsley family, with a large, sweetish, edible root, widely cultivated as a vegetable and as fodder. The root of the wild plant is acrid and poisonous. [Alter. of ME *passenep,* ? <OF *pasnaie* <L *pastinaca* <*pastinare* dig up; infl. in form by OE *nǣp* turnip <L *napus*]

par·son (pär′sən) *n.* **1** The clergyman of a parish or congregation; a minister. **2** Specifically, a beneficed clergyman of the Anglican Church, having full charge of a parish; a rector. [<OF *persone* <Med. L *persona* a rector. Doublet of PERSON.] — **par·son·i·cal** (pär·son′i·kəl), **par·son′ic** *adj.*

par·son·age (pär′sən·ij) *n.* **1** A clergyman's dwelling, especially a free official residence provided for a pastor; in England, a rectory. **2** *Scot.* A tax paid for the maintenance of a parson. **3** The benefice of a parson.

Par·sons (pär′sənz), **Sir Charles Algernon,** 1854–1931, English engineer; invented the steam turbine. — **William Barclay,** 1859–1932, U. S. engineer; designed and built the subway system of New York, 1894–1904.

par·son's-nose (pär′sənz·nōz′) *n. Colloq.* The rump of a fowl: also called *pope's-nose.*

part (pärt) *n.* **1** A certain portion or amount of anything; a piece; segment; fraction. **2** *Math.* One of certain fractional portions or components of a thing; an aliquot division; a submultiple: a fifth *part.* **3** An essential portion of a body or an organism; a member. **4** *Usually pl.* A portion of territory; region; quarter: in foreign *parts.* **5** So much as is allotted or belongs to one; an individual share, as of duty, business, or performance: If he'll do his *part,* we'll win. **6** The role or lines assigned to an actor in a play; occasionally, a role played in actual life. **7** A side, cause, or party opposed to another. **8** *Usually pl.* A component or quality of mind or character; talent; intellectual gift or faculty: That man is a person of *parts.* **9** The melody intended for a single voice or instrument in a concerted piece; also, the written or printed copy for the performer's use. **10** A section of a book, poem, or play; also, a portion of a literary work issued at intervals, at a fixed price. **11** A parting or division of the hair. — **for my part** As far as I am concerned. — **in good** (or **ill**) **part** With a good (or a bad) grace. — **in part** Partly. — **part and parcel** An essential part: an emphatic phrase. — **principal part** One of the inflected forms of a verb from which all other inflected forms may be derived. In English, the principal parts of a verb are the infinitive *(go, walk),* the past tense *(went, walked),* and the past participle *(gone, walked).* In this dictionary, the past, past participle, and present participle are shown *(gave, given, giving)*; in cases where the past tense and past participle are identical, only the one is shown *(behaved, behaving).* — **to take part** To participate; share or cooperate: usually with *in.* — **to take someone's part** To support someone in a contest or disagreement; side with someone. — *v.t.* **1** To divide or break (something) into parts. **2** To sever or discontinue (a relationship or connection): to *part* company. **3** To separate by being or coming between; keep or move apart: The referee *parted* the two men. **4** To comb (the hair) so as to leave a dividing line on the sides or elsewhere on the scalp. **5** To separate (mingled substances) chemically or mechanically: to *part* gold and silver. **6** *Archaic* To divide into shares or portions. **7** *Obs.* To depart from; leave. — *v.i.* **8** To become divided or broken into parts; come

apart; divide. 9 To go away from each other; cease associating; separate. 10 To depart; leave. — **to part from** To separate from; leave. — **to part with** 1 To give up; relinquish. 2 To part from. — *adv.* In some degree; to some extent; partly. [<OF <L *pars, partis* part]

Synonyms (noun): atom, component, constituent, division, element, fraction, fragment, ingredient, member, particle, piece, portion, section, segment, share, subdivision. *Part* is the general word, including all the others. A *fragment* is the result of breaking, rending, or disruption of some kind, while a *piece* may be smoothly or evenly separated and have completeness in itself. *Division* and *fraction* are always regarded as in connection with the total; *divisions* may be equal or unequal; a *fraction* is one of several equal *parts* into which the whole is supposed to be divided. A *portion* is a *part* viewed with reference to some one who is to receive it or some special purpose to which it is to be applied; a *share* is a *part* to which one has or may acquire a right in connection with others; a *particle* is an exceedingly small *part*. A *component, constituent, ingredient,* or *element* is a *part* of some compound or mixture; an *element* is necessary to the existence, as a *component* or *constituent* is necessary to the completeness of that which it helps to compose; an *ingredient* may be foreign or accidental. A *subdivision* is a *division* of a *division*. We speak of a *segment* of a circle. Compare BRANCH, PARTICLE, PIECE, PORTION. *Antonyms*: see synonyms for AGGREGATE.

par·take (pär·tāk′) *v.* **·took, ·tak·en, ·tak·ing** *v.i.* 1 To take part or have a share; participate: with *in*. 2 To receive or take a portion or share: with *of*. 3 To have something of the quality or character; bear a trace: with *of*: replies *partaking* of insolence. — *v.t.* 4 To take or have a part in; share. [Back formation < *partaker*, var. of *part-taker*, trans. of L *particeps* < *pars, partis* a part + *capere* take] — **par·tak′er** *n.*

par·tan (pär′tan) *n. Scot.* A crab.

part·ed (pär′tid) *adj.* 1 Situated or placed apart; separated; cloven. 2 *Bot.* Cut almost but not quite to the base, as certain leaves. 3 Having or divided into parts. 4 *Archaic* Departed; dead.

par·terre (pär·târ′) *n.* 1 A flower garden having beds arranged in a pattern. 2 A level plot or space. 3 The part of a theater on the main floor under the balcony and behind the parquet. [<MF < *par terre* on (the) ground <L *per* through, all over + *terra* land]

par·the·no·gen·e·sis (pär′thə·nō·jen′ə·sis) *n.* 1 *Biol.* Reproduction by means of unfertilized eggs, as in many rotifers and polyzoans. 2 *Entomol.* Production of a new individual from a virgin female without intervention of a male, as in plant lice and some hymenopters. 3 *Bot.* Reproduction from unfertilized seeds or spores, as in many algae and fungi. Also **par′the·nog′e·ny** (-noj′ə·nē). [<Gk. *parthenos* virgin + GENESIS] — **par′the·no·ge·net′ic** (-jə·net′ik), **par′the·no·gen′ic** *adj.* — **par′the·no·ge·net′i·cal·ly** *adv.*

Par·the·non (pär′thə·non) The Doric temple of Athena Parthenos on the Acropolis at Athens, now largely in ruins; built under the supervision of Phidias during the administration of Pericles, and dedicated 438 B.C.

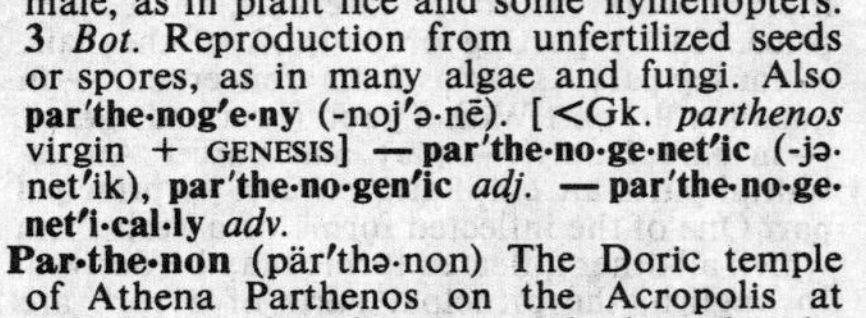

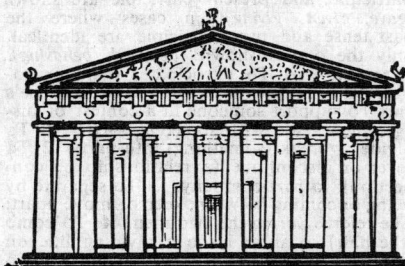

THE PARTHENON
Temple of Athena, on the Acropolis at Athens, representative of classical Greek architectural style.

Par·the·no·pae·us (pär′thə·nō·pē′əs) See SEVEN AGAINST THEBES. Also **Par′the·no·pæ′us.**

Par·then·o·pe (pär·then′ə·pē) 1 In Greek legend, one of the sirens, who, unable to charm Odysseus by her singing, cast herself into the sea. 2 The Greek name for NAPLES. [<Gk. *parthenos* virgin + *ōps* face]

Par·the·nos (pär′thə·nos) *n.* A virgin; epithet of several Greek goddesses, especially of Athena. [<Gk.]

Par·thi·a (pär′thē·ə) An ancient kingdom occupying what is now NE Iran.

Par·thi·an (pär′thē·ən) *n.* An inhabitant of Parthia. — *adj.* Of or pertaining to Parthia or the Parthians. — **Parthian shot** Any aggressive remark or action made in leaving or fleeing, after the manner of Parthian cavalry who shot at their enemies while retreating or pretending to retreat.

par·tial (pär′shəl) *adj.* 1 Pertaining to, constituting, or involving a part only. 2 Favoring one side; prejudiced; biased. 3 Having a special liking: usually with *to*. [<OF *parcial* <LL *partialis* <L *pars, partis* a part] — **par′tial·ly** *adv.*

partial fraction See under FRACTION.

par·ti·al·i·ty (pär′shē·al′ə·tē) *n.* 1 The state of being partial. 2 Unfairness; bias. 3 A particular fondness; predilection. Also **par′tial·ness** (-shəl·nis). See synonyms under RELISH.

partial tone *Music* A harmonic. — **upper partial tone** An overtone or harmonic; one of the accessory tones generated by the fundamental.

part·i·ble (pär′tə·bəl) *adj.* Divisible. — **part′i·bil′i·ty** *n.*

par·tic·i·pant (pär·tis′ə·pənt) *adj.* Sharing; taking part in. — *n.* One who participates; a sharer.

par·tic·i·pate (pär·tis′ə·pāt) *v.* **·pat·ed, ·pat·ing** *v.i.* 1 To take part or have a share in common with others; partake: with *in*. — *v.t.* 2 *Rare* To partake of. [<L *participatus*, pp. of *participare* < *particeps, -cipis* a partaker < *pars, partis* a part + *capere* take] — **par·tic′i·pa′tion** *n.* — **par·tic′i·pa′tor** *n.*

par·tic·i·pa·to·ry (pär′tis′ə·pə·tôr′ē, -tō′rē) *adj.* Based on or involving participation, especially active, voluntary participation in a political system.

par·ti·cip·i·al (pär′tə·sip′ē·əl) *Gram. adj.* Having the nature, form, or use of a participle; characterized by, consisting of, or based on a participle: a *participial* adjective, a *participial* meaning. — *n.* A word derived from a verb, essentially a noun or adjective, but having the syntactical use of the verb, as a gerund, gerundive, supine, or infinitive. — **par′ti·cip′i·al·ly** *adv.*

par·ti·ci·ple (pär′tə·sip′əl) *n. Gram.* A verbal derivative that may function as both a verb and an adjective. The **present participle** ends in *-ing* and the **past participle** commonly in *-d, -ed, -en, -n,* or *-t*. — **dangling participle** A participle that modifies the wrong substantive, as in "*Opening* the door, the *room* looked large" instead of "*Opening* the door, *I* saw that the room looked large." [<OF, var. of *participe* <L *participium* a sharing, partaking < *participare*. See PARTICIPATE.]

par·ti·cle (pär′ti·kəl) *n.* 1 A minute part, piece, or portion of matter. 2 Any very small amount or slight degree: without a *particle* of truth. 3 *Physics* One of the elementary components of an atom, as an electron, proton, neutron, meson, etc. 4 *Gram.* **a** A short, uninflected part of speech, as a preposition, an interjection, an article, and especially a conjunction. **b** A prefix or suffix. **c** A small part of a sentence or composition, as a clause. 5 In the Roman Catholic Church, the small Host used for lay communicants; also, a fragment of a consecrated Host. [<L *particula*, dim. of *pars, partis* a part]

Synonyms: atom, element, grain, iota, jot, mite, moleculé, scintilla, scrap, shred, tittle, whit. A *particle* is a very small part of any material substance; as, a *particle* of sand or dust; it is a general term, not accurately determinate in meaning. *Atom* etymologically signifies that which cannot be cut or divided, and was formerly considered the smallest conceivable *particle* of matter, regarded as absolutely homogeneous and as having but one set of properties. A *molecule* is made up of *atoms*, and is regarded as separable into its constituent parts. *Element* in chemistry denotes, without reference to quantity, a substance regarded as simple, that is, one incapable of being resolved into simpler substances without losing its specific physico-chemical properties; the *element* gold may be represented by an ingot or by a *particle* of gold dust. In popular language, an *element* is any essential constituent; the ancients believed that the universe was made up of the four *elements*, earth, air, fire, and water; a storm is spoken of as a manifestation of the fury of the *elements*. Compare synonyms for PART. *Antonyms*: aggregate, entirety, mass, quantity, sum, total, whole.

par·ti-col·ored (pär′tē·kul′ərd) *adj.* Having various colors; variegated; also, diversified. Also *party-colored*. [<F *parti*, pp. of *partir* divide + COLORED]

par·tic·u·lar (pər·tik′yə·lər) *adj.* 1 Specifying or comprising a part; separate: a *particular* act. 2 Peculiar or pertaining to a specified person, thing, time, or place; not common or general; private; specific: my *particular* hobby. 3 Specially noteworthy: of *particular* importance. 4 Comprising all details or circumstances; circumstantial: a *particular* description. 5 Marked by, requiring, or giving minute attention; exact in performance or requirement; precise; also, nice in taste; fastidious: *particular* in dress. 6 *Law* Separate or separable; being apart from others; special; limited; specific. 7 *Logic* Including some, not all, of a class: opposed to *subalternant* or *universal*: "Some trees are oaks" is a *particular* proposition. — *n.* 1 A separate matter or item, as of a class or number. 2 An individual instance; a single or separate case; a given fact that may be brought under or be the ground of a generalization. [<OF *particulier* <L *particularis* concerning a part < *particula*. See PARTICLE.]

Synonyms (adj.): accurate, appropriate, characteristic, circumstantial, definite, detailed, distinct, distinctive, especial, exact, individual, peculiar, separate, single, special. See MINUTE[2], PRECISE, SQUEAMISH.

par·tic·u·lar·ism (pər·tik′yə·lə·riz′əm) *n.* 1 Exclusive attachment to the interests of one's particular state, party, people, or religion. 2 Care or regard for particulars; attention to details. 3 The theological doctrine of the election of particular individuals to grace and salvation; particular election. — **par·tic′u·lar·ist** *n.* — **par·tic′u·lar·is′tic** *adj.*

par·tic·u·lar·i·ty (pər·tik′yə·lar′ə·tē) *n. pl.* **·ties** 1 The state, character, or quality of being particular; exactitude in description; circumstantiality; strict or careful attention to detail; fastidiousness. 2 Something that is particular; a circumstance or detail; also, a characteristic; peculiarity.

par·tic·u·lar·ize (pər·tik′yə·lə·rīz′) *v.* **·ized, ·iz·ing** *v.t.* To speak of or treat individually or in detail. — *v.i.* To give particulars; be specific. — **par·tic′u·lar·i·za′tion** *n.* — **par·tic′u·lar·iz′er** *n.*

par·tic·u·lar·ly (pər·tik′yə·lər·lē) *adv.* 1 With specific reference; distinctly: a fact *particularly* mentioned. 2 In an unusually great degree; in an especial manner: *particularly* difficult. 3 Part by part; in detail. 4 Severally; personally.

par·tic·u·late (pər·tik′yə·lāt) *adj.* 1 Of, pertaining to, having, or characterized by particles. 2 *Genetics* Designating the inheritance of specific characters from either or both of the parents. [<Med. L *particulatus*, pp. of *particulare* divide into particles < *particula*. See PARTICLE.]

par·tim (pär′tim) *adv. Latin* Partly: said of taxonomic synonyms that in part include the same things.

part·ing (pär′ting) *adj.* 1 Of or pertaining to a parting or going away, often in death. 2 Departing; declining. 3 Capable of being parted. 4 Separating; severing; dividing. — *n.* 1 The act of separating, or the state of being separated; division. 2 A leave-taking; a departure; especially, a final separation. 3 *Metall.* The separation of metals in an alloy; specifically, the separation of gold and silver by acid in assaying. 4 A place, line, or surface of separation or division. 5 Something that parts or separates.

parting strip A strip or piece of thin wood or metal separating contiguous parts.

par·ti pris (pȧr·tē′ prē′) *French* An opinion formed beforehand; prejudice.

par·ti·san (pär′tə·zən) *adj.* 1 Relating to or unreasonably devoted to a party or faction. 2 Pertaining to or carried on by partisans or irregular troops. — *n.* 1 An adherent and upholder of an individual or of a party or cause; especially, a blind or fanatical adherent or devotee. 2 A member of a body of detached or irregular troops; a guerilla. See synonyms under ADHERENT. Also **par′·ti·zan**. [<F <Ital. *partigiano, partisano* < *parte* a part <L *pars, partis*] — **par′ti·san·ship** *n.*

par·tite (pär′tīt) *adj.* 1 Divided into or composed of parts: used in composition: *bipartite, tripartite*. 2 *Bot.* Cleft nearly to the base, as a leaf. [<L *partitus*, pp. of *partire* divide]

par·ti·tion (pär·tish′ən) *n.* 1 Division; separation. 2 A dividing line or boundary. 3 A wall or other barrier dividing one part or apartment from another. 4 An internal wall separating cells or cavities. 5 *Law* The division of property, especially of lands, among co-owners, either by agreement or by judicial decree; also, the dividing of lands held by tenants in common into separate parcels, so that they may be held in severalty. 6 *Math.* The representation of a positive whole number as the sum of whole numbers in all possible ways; also, any one of such ways. 7 *Logic* **a** The form of analysis that systematically unfolds the properties or attributes of a concept. **b** The process of explanation that exhibits the theme by means of its attributes. 8 A compartment; apartment; department; division. — *v.t.* 1 To divide into parts, segments, etc. 2 To separate by a partition: with *off*. 3 To divide, as property, into shares or portions; apportion. [<OF *particion* <L *partitio, -onis* < *partire* divide] — **par·ti′tion·er** *n.*

par·ti·tion·ment (pär·tish′ən·mənt) *n.* 1 The act of partitioning, as property. 2 A compartment; partition.

par·ti·tive (pär′tə·tiv) *adj.* 1 Separating into integral parts or into distinct divisions. 2 *Gram.* Denoting a part as distinct from the whole. Example: *Of them* is the *partitive* genitive in the sentences "Many of them were there" and "They couldn't do it for the life of them." — *n. Gram.* A partitive word or case. [<F *partitif* <L *partitivus* < *partitus*, pp. of *partire* divide] — **par′ti·tive·ly** *adv.*

part·let (pärt′lit) *n.* A garment, frequently ruffled, covering the throat and bust, worn, especially by women, in the 16th century. [Var. of obs. *patlet* <OF *patelette* band of stuff, dim. of *pat* paw, flap]

part·ly (pärt′lē) *adv.* In some part; in some degree; partially.

part music Music with two or more melodies written in harmony and sung or played by two or more performers: said especially of vocal music.

part·ner (pärt′nər) *n.* 1 One who takes part or is associated with another or others; a sharer. 2 One of two or more persons associated by contract for the carrying on of a commercial, manufacturing, or other undertaking with their joint capital, labor, or skill. 3 One of two persons united in some enterprise, as marriage, a dance, or a game. 4 *pl. Naut.* Framing pieces surrounding a mast to strengthen and relieve the deck from strain. See synonyms under ACCESSORY, ASSOCIATE. — **secret** or **sleeping partner** One who is inactive and unknown in the business. — **silent partner** Strictly, one who is inactive, though he may be known to be a partner. The terms *silent partner* and *dormant partner* are often interchanged. — *v.t.* 1 To make a partner or partners. 2 To be or act as the partner of. [Var. of PARCENER; infl. by PART]

part·ner·ship (pärt′nər·ship) *n.* 1 The state of being a partner or partners; joint interests or ownership; also, the group of persons so associated. 2 *Law* An association founded on a contract between two or more persons to combine their money, effects, labor, or skill, or any or all of them, in lawful commerce or business, and to share the profit and bear the loss in certain proportions; a co-partnership. 3 Fellowship (def. 6). See synonyms under ALLIANCE, ASSOCIATION.

part of speech One of the eight traditional classes of words in English; namely: noun, pronoun, verb, adjective, adverb, conjunction, preposition, and interjection.

par·took (pär·tŏŏk′) Past tense of PARTAKE.

part owner One of two or more persons who own a thing in common, but not as partners; especially, one of the joint owners of a ship.

par·tridge (pär′trij) *n.* 1 Any of certain small, plump-bodied, Old World, gallinaceous game birds of genera *Perdix, Alectoris* (synonym *Caccabis*), etc. 2 Any of certain other similar birds, often so called, as the ruffed grouse of the northern United States and the bobwhite of the South. Compare QUAIL[1]. 3 A tinamou of the South American pampas. [<OF *perdriz*, var. of *perdiz* <L *perdix, -icis* <Gk. *perdix, -ikos* a partridge]

PARTRIDGE
(The ruffed grouse; 16 to 18 inches in length)

par·tridge·ber·ry (pär′trij·ber′ē) *n. pl.* **·ries** 1 A small, trailing evergreen herb (*Mitchella repens*) of the madder family, with dark-green leaves, fragrant white flowers, and a scarlet double berry; also, the berry. 2 The wintergreen or its berry.

partridge hawk The goshawk: also called *dove hawk*.

part song A song composed of three or more parts; specifically, a secular choral piece without accompaniment.

part–time (pärt′tīm′) *adj.* For, during, or by part of the time: a *part-time* student.

part time A part of the time.

par·tu·ri·ent (pär·tyŏŏr′ē·ənt, -tŏŏr′-) *adj.* Bringing forth or about to bring forth young; pertaining to childbirth: used also figuratively of plans, ideas, etc. [<L *parturiens, -entis*, ppr. of *parturire* be in labor, desiderative of *parere* bring forth] — **par·tu′ri·en·cy** *n.*

par·tu·ri·fa·cient (pär·tyŏŏr′ə·fā′shənt, -tŏŏr′-) *Med. adj.* Promoting parturition. — *n.* A medicine promotive of parturition. [<L *parturire* be in labor + -FACIENT]

par·tu·ri·tion (pär′tyŏŏ·rish′ən, -chŏŏ-) *n.* The act of bringing forth young; delivery; childbirth. [<L *parturitio, -onis* < *parturire* be in labor]

par·ty (pär′tē) *n. pl.* **·ties** 1 A body of persons united for some common purpose, as political ascendency; a political organization; also, partisanship. 2 A social company or gathering: a tea *party*. 3 *Mil.* A small company or detachment of soldiers: a firing *party*. 4 *Law* One of the persons named on the record in an action either as plaintiff or defendant; a person interested, as in a contract, deed, suit, etc.: a *party* to a suit. 5 One concerned in or privy to a matter: He was a *party* to the affair. 6 *Colloq.* A person. 7 *Obs.* A cause or interest; side. See synonyms under SECT. — *adj.* 1 Of or pertaining to a political party: *party* platforms. 2 Divided into or consisting of parts, or of different parties; composite. 3 *Her.* Divided; parted: said of a shield. [<OF *partie*, orig., fem. pp. of *partir* divide <L *partire* <*pars, partis* a part]

par·ty–col·ored (pär′tē·kul′ərd) See PARTI–COLORED.

party line 1 A telephone line or circuit serving two or more subscribers: also **party wire**. 2 A boundary line between the properties of two or more owners. 3 A belief or principle of a political party regarded as an essential conviction of every loyal member.

party wall A wall erected on a line between adjoining properties, and used in common.

pa·rure (pə·rŏŏr′, *Fr.* pà·rür′) *n.* A set of ornaments, especially of trimmings for a costume or of jewels to be worn together. Also **pa·ru′ra** (-rŏŏr′ə). [<F *parure* <L *paratura* preparation < *parare* make ready]

par·ve·nu (pär′və·nōō, -nyŏŏ) *n.* One who has suddenly attained wealth or position beyond his birth or worth, as by accident of fortune; an upstart. — *adj.* 1 Being a parvenu. 2 Like or characteristic of a parvenu. [<F, orig., pp. of *parvenir* arrive <L *pervenire*]

par·vis (pär′vis) *n.* 1 An enclosed or raised area in front of a church. 2 A portico or colonnade before a church. [<F <L *paradisum* paradise; later, the court in front of St. Peter's, Rome]

par·vo·line (pär′və·lēn, -lin) *n. Chem.* An oily liquid, $C_9H_{13}N$, obtained either as a ptomaine in decaying flesh or as a product of the destructive distillation of certain shales and coals. Also **par′vo·lin** (-lin). [<L *parvus* small + (QUIN)OLINE; so named because of its low volatility]

Par·zi·val (pär′tsi·fäl) See PERCEVAL.

pas (pä) *n.* 1 A step. 2 A dance. 3 Right of going before; precedence. [<F, a step]

Pas·a·de·na (pas′ə·dē′nə) A city in SW California.

Pa·sar·ga·dae (pə·sär′gə·dē) A ruined city of ancient Persia in south central Iran; capital of Cyrus the Great. Also **Pa·sar′ga·dæ**.

Pa·say (pä′sī) A city in Luzon on Manila Bay, Philippines.

Pas·cal (pas·kal′, pas′kəl; *Fr.* pàs·kàl′), **Blaise**, 1623–62, French mathematician and philosopher.

pasch (pask) *n.* The feast of the Passover; also, Easter. Also **pas·cha** (pas′kə). [<OF *pasche* <L *pascha* <Gk. <Aramaic *paskhā* <Hebrew *pesakh* a passing over, the Passover < *pāsakh* pass over]

pas·chal (pas′kəl) *adj.* Pertaining to the Jewish Passover or to Easter: *paschal* sacrifice. — *n.* 1 A paschal candle or candlestick. 2 The celebration of the Passover; also, the paschal lamb; the paschal supper. [<OF *pascal* <LL *paschalis* <L *pascha* PASCH]

paschal flower The pasqueflower.

paschal lamb The lamb eaten at the feast of the Passover.

Paschal Lamb Jesus Christ.

pas·cu·al (pas′kyŏŏ·əl) *adj. Ecol.* Of or pertaining to plants growing in pastures and grassy commons. [<OF <Med. L *pascualis* <L *pascuum* a pasture < *pascere* feed]

Pas–de–Ca·lais (pä·də·kà·le′) 1 A department of northernmost France, on the English Channel and the Strait of Dover; 2,607 square miles; capital, Arras. 2 The French name for the STRAIT OF DOVER.

pas de deux (pä də dœ′) *French* A dance or ballet figure for two persons.

pas du tout (pä dü tōō′) *French* Not at all.

pash[1] (pash) *Obs.* or *Dial. v.t.* To strike violently; dash to pieces. — *n.* A crushing blow. [ME *passchen*; prob. imit.]

pash[2] (pash) *n. Scot.* The head. [Prob. <PASH[1], with ref. to blows on the head]

pa·sha (pə·shä′, pash′ə, pä′shə) *n.* A Turkish honorary title placed after the name, formerly given to generals, governors of provinces, etc.: also spelled **pacha**. [<Turkish *pāshā* < *bāsh* head]

pa·sha·lik (pə·shä′lik) *n.* The province or jurisdiction of a pasha: also spelled *pachalic*. Also **pa·sha′lic**. [<Turkish *pāshālik*]

Pash·to (push′tō) See PUSHTU.

Pa·siph·a·e (pə·sif′i·ē) In Greek mythology, the wife of Minos and by him mother of Phaedra and Ariadne, and of the Minotaur by a white bull sent to Minos by Poseidon.

pasque·flow·er (pask′flou′ər) *n.* Any of several plants (genus *Anemone*) with showy white, red, or purple flowers, blooming about Easter; especially, the daneflower or campana (*A. pulsatilla*) of the Old World, or *A. ludoviciana*, the State flower of South Dakota. Also **pasch′·flow′er**. [Earlier *passeflower* <F *passefleur* < *passer* excel + *fleur* flower; infl. in form by F *pasque* Easter]

pas·quil (pas′kwil) *n.* A pasquinade. [<Med. L *pasquillus* <Ital. *pasquillo*, dim. of *pasquino*. See PASQUIN.]

pas·quin (pas′kwin) *n.* 1 A pasquinade. 2 A pasquinader. [<Ital. *pasquino*, orig., a disinterred statue at Rome on which satirical verses were pasted]

pas·quin·ade (pas′kwin·ād′) *n.* An abusive or coarse personal satire posted in a public place; a malicious squib. — *v.t.* **·ad·ed, ·ad·ing** To attack or ridicule in pasquinades; lampoon. — **pas′quin·ad′er** *n.*

pass (pas, päs) *v.* **passed** (*Rare* **past**), **passed** or **past, pass·ing** *v.t.* **1** To go by or move past and leave behind. **2** To go across, around, over, or through. **3** To permit to go unnoticed or unmentioned. **4** To undergo; experience: to *pass* a bad night. **5** To undergo successfully, as a test; meet the requirements of. **6** To go beyond or exceed; surpass: It *passes* comprehension. **7** To cause to go or move: to *pass* one's eyes over a book; to *pass* a rope through a pulley. **8** To cause to go or move past: to *pass* troops in review. **9** To cause or allow to advance or proceed: They *passed* him through their ranks. **10** To cause or allow to elapse; spend: to *pass* the night at an inn. **11** To give approval to; sanction; allow. **12** To enact, as a law. **13** To be approved by: The bill *passed* the senate. **14** To omit paying (a dividend). **15** To cause to go from person to person; put in circulation; transmit: *Pass* the word. **16** To utter or pronounce, especially judicially, as judgment or sentence. **17** To excrete (waste). **18** To pledge, as one's word. **19** To perform a pass (*n.* def. 5) on or over. **20** In sports, to transfer (the ball, etc.) to another player on the same side. **21** *Law* To transfer or assign ownership of to another by will, deed, etc. — *v.i.* **22** To go or proceed; move. **23** To have course or direction; extend: The road *passed* under a bridge. **24** To go away; depart. **25** To come to an end; disappear. **26** To elapse or go by; be spent: The day *passed* slowly. **27** To die. **28** To go by; move past in or as in review. **29** To go from person to person; obtain currency; circulate. **30** To be mutually given and received, as greetings or recriminations. **31** To go or change from one condition, circumstance, etc., to another; alter: to *pass* from hot to cold. **32** To take place; happen; occur. **33** To be allowed or tolerated; go unheeded or unpunished. **34** To undergo a test, examination, etc., successfully; meet the requirements. **35** To be approved, ratified, enacted, etc. **36** To obtain or force passage; make a way: They shall not *pass*! **37** To be excreted or voided. **38** *Law* **a** To give or pronounce judgment, sentence, etc.: with *on* or *upon*. **b** To sit in inquest: with *on* or *upon*. **c** To adjudicate: with *between*. **d** To be transferred or assigned to another by will, deed, etc. **39** In sports, to transfer the ball, etc., to another player on the same side. **40** In fencing, to make a pass or thrust; lunge. **41** In card games, to decline to make a play, bid, etc. **— to pass away** **1** To come to an end; disappear. **2** To die. **3** To allow (time) to elapse. **— to pass for** To be accepted as, usually incorrectly. **— to pass off** **1** To come to an end; disappear. **2** To give out or circulate as genuine; palm off. **3** To be emitted, as a vapor. **— to pass out** **1** To distribute. **2** *Colloq.* To faint. **— to pass over** To fail to notice or consider. **— to pass up** *Colloq.* To reject or fail to take advantage of, as an offer or opportunity. — *n.* **1** A way or opening that affords a passage; a place through which one can pass; a gap in a mountain range through which a road may be or has been made; a defile; waterway. **2** Permission or a permit to pass; a ticket; passport: a *pass* through an army's lines. **3** A state of affairs; crisis. **4** The successful undergoing of an examination, test, or inspection; in a university, a degree gained without honors. **5** A movement of a hand, wand, or the like, as in mesmeric manipulation; transference of objects in sleight-of-hand tricks, magic, etc. **6** A movement made in attempting to stab or strike; a thrust; lunge; also, figuratively, a verbal thrust; a witty sally. **7** In football, hockey, lacrosse, etc., the action of passing the ball between players, in the course of the game. **8** In court tennis, a ball so served that it strikes the penthouse or the floor of the court between the main wall and the pass line. **9** In baseball, a base on balls. **10** *Mil.* Authority in writing given a soldier to be absent from duty or station for a specified period. **— forward pass** In football, the throwing or passing of the ball toward the opponent's goal. **— lateral pass** In football, a pass which does not travel towards either goal. **— to bring to pass** To cause to be fulfilled, accomplished, or realized. **— to come to pass** To happen; come about; be realized. **— to make a pass at** **1** To attempt to hit. **2** *Slang* To attempt to caress. [<OF *passer* <L *passus* a step; *n.*, doublet of PACE]

pass·a·ble (pas′ə·bəl, päs′-) *adj.* **1** Capable of being passed in any sense; capable of being penetrated or traversed. **2** Fairly good or acceptable; not open to great objection; moderate; mediocre; tolerable. **3** Fit for general circulation. **— pass′a·bly** *adv.*

pas·sade (pə·sād′) *n.* **1** *Obs.* A forward thrust in fencing; a pass made by advancing the body: also **pas·sa·do** (pə·sä′dō). **2** In horsemanship, a moving of a horse back and forth over the same ground. [<F <Ital. *passata* or Provençal *passada* <LL *passare* pass <L *passus* a step]

pas·sage[1] (pas′ij) *n.* **1** The act of passing; a passing by, through, or over; transition from one state or condition to another. **2** A journey by conveyance, as by a vessel; a voyage: a stormy *passage*. **3** Hence, conveyance on a journey; right of transportation, especially on a ship; also, money paid for conveyance. **4** A way or channel by which a person or thing may pass; a way through or over. **5** Any corridor, hall, or gallery affording communication between apartments in a building: also called *passageway*. **6** Liberty or power of passing; free entrance, exit, or transit. **7** A separate portion of a discourse, treatise, or writing; a clause, verse, paragraph, or similar division. **8** The course of a legislative measure through the various stages of debate and action; especially, its enactment by the final vote or approval by the supreme authority. **9** A part of a train of events; a series of incidents; episode. **10** A navigable route; especially, a channel connecting large bodies of water. **11** A personal encounter; a fight or a dispute: a *passage* with swords. **12** Migration, especially of birds; a migratory flight. **13** An evacuation of the bowels. **14** *Music* **a** A portion of a musical composition. **b** A run or series of short notes. **15** *Obs.* Departure; hence, death. See synonyms under CAREER, MOTION, ROAD, WAY. — *v.i.* **·saged, ·sag·ing** **1** To make a journey. **2** To fence physically or verbally. [<OF <*passer*. See PASS.]

pas·sage[2] (pas′ij) *v.* **·saged, ·sag·ing** *v.t.* In equitation, to cause (a horse) to sidle or walk sidewise. — *v.i.* In equitation: **a** To move sidewise; sidle. **b** To cause a horse to move sidewise. — *n.* A sidewise movement made by a horse in which diagonal pairs of feet are raised alternately. [<F *passager*, alter. of *passéger* <Ital. *passeggiare* walk <L *passus* a step]

pas·sage·way (pas′ij·wā′) *n.* A way affording passage; especially, a way made or kept open for walking, between rooms, localities, etc., as a hall or corridor, gangway, lane, etc.

Pas·sa·ic (pə·sā′ik) A city in NE New Jersey on the **Passaic River,** a river flowing 80 miles south and east past Newark to Newark Bay.

Pas·sa·ma·quod·dy Bay (pas′ə·mə·kwod′ē) An inlet of the Bay of Fundy between SE Maine and SW New Brunswick.

pas·sant (pas′ənt) *adj. Her.* Walking and looking toward the dexter, with the dexter fore paw raised: said of a beast. [<F, ppr. of *passer.* See PASS.]

pass·book (pas′bŏŏk′, päs′-) *n.* **1** A bankbook. **2** A book given by a merchant to a customer, showing all items bought on credit.

pas·sé (pa·sā′, pas′ā; *Fr.* pȧ·sā′) *adj.* Past the prime; faded; also, out-of-date; old-fashioned. [<F, orig., pp. of *passer.* See PASS.] **— pas·sée′** *adj. fem.*

passed (past, päst) *adj.* **1** Having passed an examination for promotion. **2** Unpaid, as dividends.

passed ball In baseball, a pitched ball that the batsman fails to hit, which passes by the catcher and enables a runner to advance a base.

passe·garde (pas′gärd′, päs′-) *n.* In medieval armor, a projecting piece or ridge on the shoulder to turn the point of a lance. [Earlier *passguard*, appar. <PASS + GUARD: refashioned after the French]

pas·sel (pas′əl) *n. Dial.* A parcel (def. 3).

passe·men·terie (pas·men′trē, *Fr.* päs·män·trē′) *n.* Trimming for dresses, as beaded lace, tinsel, etc. [<MF <*passement* lace <*passer* PASS]

pas·sen·ger (pas′ən·jər) *n.* **1** A person who travels in a conveyance. **2** *Rare* A traveler; passer-by: a foot *passenger.* [<OF *passager* (with intrusive *-n*), orig. passing <*passage.* See PASSAGE.]

passenger pigeon The wild pigeon of North America (*Ectopistes migratorius*): now extinct.

passe par·tout (pas pär·tōō′, Fr. päs pȧr·tōō′) **1** A light picture frame consisting of a glass and a pasteboard back put together with strips of decorative tape pasted around the edge; also, the pasteboard mat of a picture. **2** Strips of gummed paper; tape. **3** A master key. [<F, orig. a key <*passe,* imperative of *passer* PASS + *partout* everywhere]

passe·pied (päs′pyā′) *n. Music* **1** A quick, lively French dance of the 17th century. **2** The music for this dance, sometimes used as the movement of a suite. [<MF, lit., pass the foot <*passe,* imperative of *passer* PASS + *pied* foot <L *pes, pedis*]

pas·ser-by (pas′ər·bī′, päs′-) *n. pl.* **pas·sers-by** A person who passes by.

Pas·ser·i·for·mes (pas′ər·i·fôr′mēz) *n. pl.* An order of birds, including all singing birds, and more than half of the living birds of various sizes ranging from crows and jays to sparrows and titmice. [<NL <L *passer, -eris* a sparrow + *forma* form]

pas·ser·ine (pas′ər·ēn, -in) *adj.* **1** Pertaining to the *Passeriformes.* **2** Resembling or characteristic of a sparrow. — *n.* One of the *Passeriformes.* [<L *passer* sparrow + -INE[1]]

Pas·se·ro (päs′sā·rō), **Cape** The NE tip of an islet in the Ionian Sea off SE Sicily.

pas seul (pä sœl′) *French* A dance or ballet figure by a single person.

Pass·field (pas′fēld), **Baron** See under WEBB.

pas·si·ble (pas′ə·bəl) *adj.* Capable of feeling or of suffering. [<F <LL *passibilis* <L *passus,* pp. of *patiri* suffer] **— pas′si·bil′i·ty, pas′si·ble·ness** *n.*

pas·si·flo·ra·ceous (pas′i·flō·rā′shəs) *adj.* Of or pertaining to a family (*Passifloraceae*) of climbing vines and erect herbs abundant in tropical America, including the passionflower. [<NL *passiflora,* genus of the passionflower <L *flos passionis* flower of the Passion]

pas·sim (pas′im) *adv. Latin* Here and there; in various passages: a reference.

pass·ing (pas′ing, päs′-) *adj.* **1** Going by or away. **2** Transitory; fleeting. **3** Happening or occurring; current. **4** Done, said, found, used, or given in or as in passing; cursory. **5** Indicating fulfilment of requirements for advancement; satisfactory: a *passing* grade. **6** *Obs.* Surpassing. See synonyms under TRANSIENT. — *n.* **1** A going by or away; hence, dying. **2** An act of passing or passage. **3** A means of passing, as a ford. **— in passing** Incidentally; in the course of discussion. — *adv.* In a surpassing degree or manner; exceedingly.

passing bell A bell tolled to announce a person's death.

passing note A note or tone foreign to the harmony: used in passing from one chord to another.

pas·sion (pash′ən) *n.* **1** Intense or overpowering emotion. **2** An eager outreaching of mind toward some special object, as art, travel, etc.; fervid devotion. **3** Ardent affection for one of the opposite sex; love; also, the object of such feeling. **4** A fit of intense and furious anger; rage. **5** Any transport of excited feeling; violent agitation. **6** A strong impulse tending to physical indulgence. **7** *pl.* Inordinate appetites; sexual desires. **8** The state or condition of being acted upon; subjecting to external force, as opposed to acting or doing: the philosophical sense. **9** The endurance of some painful infliction; suffering. **10** *Obs.* Some painful disease. See synonyms under ANGER, APPETITE, ENTHUSIASM, FEELING, LOVE, VIOLENCE, WARMTH. [<OF *passiun* <L *passio, -onis* suffering <*passus,* pp. of *patiri* suffer]

Pas·sion (pash′ən) *n.* **1** The sufferings of Christ, especially in the agony of the garden and on the cross; also, their representation in art. **2** That part of the Gospels which relates the Passion and death of Christ.

pas·sion·al (pash′ən·əl) *adj.* Of, pertaining to, or characterized by passion, especially amorous: *passional* poetry. — *n.* A book descriptive of the sufferings of saints and martyrs.

pas·sion·ate (pash′ən·it) *adj.* **1** Capable of or inclined to strong passion; susceptible of vehement emotion; excitable. **2** Easily moved

to anger; quick-tempered. **3** Expressing or displaying some passion; characterized by passion; intense; ardent. **4** Of a strong, ardent quality or excessive degree: said of feeling. See synonyms under ARDENT, HOT, IMPETUOUS, VIOLENT. [<Med. L *passionatus,* ult. <L *passio, -onis.* See PASSION.] **—pas′sion·ate·ly** *adv.* **—pas′·sion·ate·ness** *n.*

pas·sion·flow·er (pash′ən·flou′ər) *n.* Any of various climbing vines or shrubs (genus *Passiflora*) of tropical America, with showy flowers and sometimes edible berries: so called from the fancied resemblance of certain parts of the flower to the instruments of the crucifixion. [Trans. of Med. L *flos passionis*]

passion fruit The berries of the passionflower.

pas·sion·less (pash′ən·lis) *adj.* Unimpassioned; calm.

Passion play A mystery or drama representing the Passion of Christ.

Passion Sunday *Eccl.* The second Sunday before Easter.

Passion Week *Eccl.* **1** The week that begins with Passion Sunday. **2** Formerly, Holy Week.

pas·si·vate (pas′ə·vāt) *v.t.* **·vat·ed, ·vat·ing** *Chem.* To remove minute impurities from the surface of (stainless iron or steel) by submerging in a pickling solution, for the purpose of preventing rust. [<PASSIVE (def. 4) + -ATE[1]]

pas·sive (pas′iv) *adj.* **1** Acted upon or receiving impressions from external agents or causes; being the object rather than the subject of action; moved by or as by external force or influence. **2** In a state of rest or quiescence; not vitally or mentally active; unresponsive. **3** Unresisting; submissive; *passive* obedience. **4** *Chem.* Characterized by a disinclination to enter into combination; inactive; inert. **5** *Gram.* Designating a voice of the verb which indicates that the subject is being acted upon, as, *was killed* is in the passive voice in *Caesar was killed by Brutus*: opposed to *active.* **6** Not bearing interest: said of bonds which yield the holder a profit or benefit, while no rate percent is named; having reference to a debt which, by agreement, is non-interest-bearing; of the nature of a liability. **7** *Med.* Designating certain abnormal conditions marked by relaxation of blood vessels and tissues, indicating impaired vitality and reaction. **8** Not provided with, or not making use of, motive power. *—n. Gram.* **1** The passive voice. **2** A verb or construction in this voice. [<L *passivus* <*passus,* pp. of *pati* suffer] **—pas′sive·ly** *adv.* **—pas′sive·ness** *n.*

passive euthanasia Euthanasia (def. 3).

passive immunity Resistance to a disease acquired by a susceptible subject through the transfer of exogenous antibodies contained in the serum of an animal with active immunity.

passive resistance Opposition to constituted authority that does not offer open violence, but resorts instead to voluntary fasting, refusal to obey laws, etc.

pas·siv·i·ty (pa·siv′ə·tē) *n.* **1** Passiveness. **2** The suspension or abeyance of the rational functions and the reduction of the physical functions to the lowest possible degree. **3** Resistance to oxidation and chemical reagents, as iron which has been immersed in strong nitric acid.

pass·key (pas′kē′, päs′-) *n.* **1** A latch key or night key. **2** A skeleton key; master key.

pass·o·ver (pas′ō′vər, päs′-) *n.* The sacrifice offered at the paschal feast; the paschal lamb.

Pass·o·ver (pas′ō′vər, päs′-) *n.* **1** A Jewish feast commemorating the night when the Lord, smiting the first-born of the Egyptians, "passed over" the houses of the children of Israel. *Ex.* xii. **2** By extension, the entire festival of seven days following the paschal supper; the feast of unleavened bread.

pass·port (pas′pôrt′, -pōrt′, päs′-) *n.* **1** An official warrant certifying the citizenship of the bearer and affording protection to him when traveling abroad; a safe conduct. **2** A permit to travel or convey goods through a foreign country. **3** A documentary permission for a ship to proceed on a voyage. **4** A means or authority to pass; that which empowers one to arrive at anything: a *passport* to success. **5** That which gives the privilege or right to enter into some sphere of action. See NAVICERT. [<F *passeport* <*passer* pass + *port* harbor]

pas·sus (pas′əs) *n. pl.* **·sus** or **·sus·es** A part or canto, as of a poem. [<Med. L <L, a stop <*pandere* stretch]

pass·word (pas′wûrd′, päs′-) *n.* A word identifying one as entitled to pass; a watchword.

Pas·sy (pȧ·sē′), **Paul Édouard,** 1859–1940, French phoneticist; chief originator of the International Phonetic Alphabet.

past (past, päst) *adj.* **1** Belonging to time gone by; hence, accomplished or ended. **2** In the usage of some societies, having completed a full term and been succeeded by another person: a *Past* Master in Masonry. **3** *Gram.* Denoting a tense or construction which refers to time or action belonging to the past. *—n.* **1** Time gone by; an antecedent period; former days collectively. **2** One's antecedents or record, especially if disreputable or kept secret. **3** *Gram.* **a** The past tense. **b** A verb or construction in this tense. *—adv.* In such manner as to go by and beyond. *—prep.* **1** Beyond in time; at a later period than; after: It is now *past* noon. **2** Beyond in place or position; farther than: walking *past* the house. **3** Beyond the reach, scope, power, or influence of: The matter is *past* hope. **4** Beyond in amount or degree: He couldn't count *past* ten. [Orig. pp. of PASS].

pas·ta (päs′tə) *n.* Any of several noodlelike pastes or doughs containing semolina, as spaghetti, macaroni, etc. [<Ital. <LL, dough]

paste[1] (pāst) *n.* **1** An adhesive mixture, usually of flour and water: used for joining or affixing paper articles and the like, and in bookbinding, etc. **2** A mixture of flour and water, often with other materials, for culinary purposes; dough. **3** Any doughy or moist plastic substance; anything of the consistency of paste, as for consumption or application: usually with a qualifying word: fish *paste*; almond *paste.* **4** A vitreous composition for making imitation gems. **5** A confection made of fruit juices, sugar, gum, etc. **6** A mixture of clay for making stoneware or porcelain. *—v.t.* **past·ed, past·ing 1** To stick or fasten with paste or the like. **2** To cover by applying pasted material. *—adj.* Made of paste; artificial. [<OF <LL *pasta* <Gk. *pastē* barley porridge]

paste[2] (pāst) *Slang v.t.* **past·ed, past·ing** To strike, as with the fist; beat. *—n.* A hard blow. [<BASTE[3]]

paste·board (pāst′bôrd′, -bōrd′) *n.* **1** Paper pulp compressed, or paper pasted together and rolled into a stiff sheet. **2** A board on which dough for pastry is rolled. **3** *Colloq.* A visiting card; also, a playing card; playing cards generally. *—adj.* Made of or resembling pasteboard; hence, thin and flimsy.

pas·tel[1] (pas·tel′, pas′tel) *n.* **1** A picture drawn with colored crayons. **2** The art of drawing such pictures. **3** A hard crayon made of pipe clay and a pigment, mixed with gum water. **4** A sketchy poetic study in prose. *—adj.* **1** Of or pertaining to a pastel. **2** Having a delicate, soft, or grayish tint. [<MF <Ital. *pastello* PASTEL[2]] **—pas′·tel·ist** or **pas′tel·list** *n.*

pas·tel[2] (pas′tel) *n.* Woad, either as a dye or as a plant. [<MF <Ital. *pastello,* dim. of *pasta* <LL. See PASTE[1].]

past·er (pās′tər) *n.* **1** One who pastes. **2** A strip of gummed paper, to cover a portion of a circular, a ballot, or the like; a sticker.

pas·tern (pas′tərn) *n.* **1** That part of a horse's foot that is between the fetlock and the coffin joint. **2** A hobble for a horse's foot. [<OF *pasturon* <*pasture* a tether for a grazing animal]

pastern bone Either the proximal or first phalanx, **great pastern bone,** or the median or second phalanx, **small pastern bone,** of a horse's foot.

pastern joint The joint between the pastern bones.

Pas·teur (päs·tœr′), **Louis,** 1822–95, French chemist and bacteriologist.

Pas·teu·rel·la (pas′tə·rel′ə) *n.* A genus of Gram-negative, rod-shaped, aerobic bacteria parasitic in animals and man: *P. pestis* is the plague bacillus, and *P. tularensis* is the cause of tularemia. [<NL, after Louis *Pasteur*]

pas·teur·ism (pas′tə·riz′əm) *n. Med.* A method of progressive inoculation developed by Pasteur for the prevention or cure of certain diseases, as hydrophobia.

pas·teur·i·za·tion (pas′tər·ə·zā′shən, -chər-) *n.* A process of arresting or preventing fermentation in liquids, as beer, milk, wine, etc., by heating to a temperature of 60° to 70° C., so as to destroy the vitality of the ferment. Also *Brit.* **pas′teur·i·sa′tion.**

pas·teur·ize (pas′tə·rīz, -chə·rīz) *v.t.* **·ized, ·iz·ing 1** To treat (milk, beer, etc.) by pasteurization. **2** To treat by pasteurism. Also *Brit.* **pas′teur·ise.**

pas·teur·iz·er (pas′tə·rī′zər, -chə-) *n.* **1** One who pasteurizes. **2** An apparatus for pasteurizing liquids.

pas·tic·cio (päs·tē′chō) *n.* A work of art, music, or literature made up of fragments from various sources, as from other works, connected so as to form a complete work; medley. [<Ital., a paste <Med. L *pasticium* <LL *pasta.* See PASTE[1].]

pas·tiche (pas·tēsh′, päs-) *n.* A pasticcio, especially one imitating or satirizing the style of other works of art or artists. [<F <Ital. *pasticcio* PASTICCIO]

pas·tille (pas·tēl′, -til′) *n.* **1** A compound of aromatic substances with niter for fumigating. **2** A troche; lozenge. **3** A flavored confection. **4** A small paper disk coated with a chemical that changes color on exposure to X-rays: used to determine X-ray dosages. **5** Pastel[1] (def. 3). Also **pas·til** (pas′til). [<MF <L *pastillus* a little loaf, a lozenge, ? dim. of *pasta* PASTE[1]]

pas·time (pas′tīm′, päs′-) *n.* Something that serves to make time pass agreeably; recreation; sport. See synonyms under ENTERTAINMENT, SPORT. [<PASS, *v.* + TIME; trans. of F *passetemps*]

past·i·ness (pās′tē·nis) *n.* The appearance, feeling, or consistency of paste.

past master 1 One who has held the office of master in certain social and benevolent organizations. **2** One who has thorough experience in something; an adept.

Pas·to (päs′tō) A city in SW Colombia at the foot of the active **Pasto Volcano** (also *Galeras*) 13,996 feet.

pas·tor (pas′tər, -päs′-) *n.* **1** A Christian minister who has a church or congregation under his official charge. **2** *Obs.* A shepherd. [<AF *pastour,* OF *pastur* <L *pastor, -oris* a shepherd, lit., a feeder <*pascere* feed]

pas·tor·age (pas′tər·ij, päs′-) See PASTORATE.

pas·tor·al (pas′tər·əl, päs′-) *adj.* **1** Pertaining to the life of shepherds and rustics; rural in spirit or sentiments: a *pastoral* poem. **2** Pertaining to a pastor and his work. See synonyms under RUSTIC. *—n.* **1** A poem dealing with rural matters; a bucolic; an idyl. **2** A picture illustrating rural scenes. **3** *Eccl.* A letter from a pastor to his flock. **4** A simple melody in 6/8 time in a rustic style; also, a complete symphony portraying a series of pastoral scenes. **5** A book or treatise on the cure of souls. **6** *pl.* The pastoral epistles. **7** A crozier or pastoral staff. [<L *pastoralis* <*pastor.* See PASTOR.] **—pas′tor·al·ism** *n.*

pas·to·ra·le (pas′tə·rä′lē, päs′-, pas′tə·ral′) *n.* A cantata or operetta on a rustic theme; also, a piece of instrumental music simple and idyllic in character.

pastoral epistles In the New Testament, the three epistles addressed to Timothy and Titus, and ascribed to St. Paul: so called because they deal with Christian pastorship.

pas·tor·al·ist (pas′tər·əl·ist) *n.* **1** *Austral.* One who raises livestock on grazing land. **2** A writer or painter of pastorals.

pastoral staff *Eccl.* A staff, usually curved like a shepherd's crook, borne as an emblem of authority by or before a bishop, abbot, etc.

pas·tor·ate (pas′tər·it, päs′-) *n.* **1** The office or jurisdiction of a pastor. **2** The duration of a pastoral charge. **3** Pastors collectively.

pas·to·ri·um (pas·tôr′ē·əm, -tō′rē·əm, päs-) *n.* A parsonage.

pas·tor·ship (pas′tər·ship, päs′-) *n.* The place, dignity, or work of a pastor.

past participle See under PARTICIPLE.

past perfect *Gram.* The verb tense indicating

an action completed prior to the occurrence of some other past action or before some specified past time. Example: He *had finished* before the bell rang, or, He *had finished* by last Friday. Also called *pluperfect.*

pas·tra·mi (pə·strä′mē) *n.* Smoked beef, heavily seasoned and usually cut from the shoulder. [<Yiddish <Magyar]

pas·try (pās′trē) *n. pl.* **·tries** Articles of food made with a crust of shortened dough, as pies. [Appar. <PAST(E)[1] + -RY]

pas·tur·age (pas′chər·ij, päs′-) *n.* **1** Grass and herbage for cattle. **2** Ground used or suitable for grazing. **3** The business or right of grazing cattle. [<OF <*pasturer* feed <*pasture.* See PASTURE.]

pas·ture (pas′chər, päs′-) *n.* **1** Ground for the grazing of domestic animals. **2** Grass or herbage that cattle or other grazing domestic animals eat. —*v.t.* **·tured, ·tur·ing 1** To lead to or put in a pasture to graze. **2** To graze on (grass, land, etc.). **3** To provide pasturage for (cattle, etc.): said of land. [<OF <L *pastura,* lit., feeding <*pastus,* pp. of *pascere* feed] —**pas′tur·a·ble** *adj.* —**pas′tur·er** *n.*

past·y[1] (pās′tē) *adj.* **past·i·er, past·i·est** Like paste.

past·y[2] (pās′tē, *Brit.* pas′tē, päs′tē) *n. pl.* **past·ies** A pie, as of meat, enclosed and baked in a crust of pastry. [<OF *pastée* <LL *pasta.* See PASTE[1].]

pat[1] (pat) *v.* **pat·ted, pat·ting** *v.t.* **1** To touch or tap lightly with something flat, especially with the hand in caressing, soothing, etc. **2** To shape or mold by a pat or pats. **3** To strike or tap with lightly sounding steps, as in running. —*v.i.* **4** To tap or strike gently. **5** To run or walk with light steps. —*n.* **1** A light, caressing stroke; a gentle tap. **2** The sound of patting or pattering. **3** A small, molded mass, as of butter. —*adj.* **1** Exactly suitable in time or place; fitting; apt. **2** Formulated in a customary way without much thought; too neat; facile: a *pat* response to a complex question. **3** Satisfactory; needing no change: a *pat* hand in a card game. —*adv.* **1** Firm; steadfast: to stand *pat.* **2** In a fit or convenient manner; aptly; also, perfectly; unforgettably: to know one's lesson *pat.* [ME *patte;* prob. imit.] —**pat′ness** *n.* —**pat′ter** *n.*

pat[2] (pat) *n. Scot.* A pot.

pa·ta·gi·um (pə·tā′jē·əm) *n. pl.* **·gi·a** (-jē·ə) **1** *Zool.* The wing membrane of a bat; also, a parachute, as of a flying squirrel, and the membranous expansion of a bird's wing. **2** *Entomol.* One of two scalelike appendages on the front dorsal part of the thorax of some moths. [<NL <L, gold edging of a tunic <Gk. *patageion*]

Pat·a·go·ni·a (pat′ə·gō′nē·ə) A region at the southern extremity of South America; now divided between Chile and the Argentine; the name is, however, usually applied only to the Argentine portion; 300,000 square miles. —**Pat′a·go′ni·an** *adj.* & *n.*

pat·a·mar (pat′ə·mär) *n.* A coasting vessel with upward-arched keel rake used from Bombay to Ceylon: also spelled *pattemar.* [<Pg. <Malayalam *pattamāri*]

Pa·tan (pä′tən) A city in central Nepal.

Pa·tap·sco River (pə·tap′skō) A river in central Maryland, flowing 65 miles SE to Chesapeake Bay.

patch (pach) *n.* **1** A small piece of material, especially of cloth, used to repair a garment, etc. **2** Something resembling a patch, as a piece of courtplaster or the like, applied to the skin to hide a blemish or to set off the complexion; a beauty spot. **3** A small piece of ground; also, the plants growing on it: a *patch* of corn; a small area in a larger expanse. **4** A piece of cloth or other material worn over an injured eye. **5** Any small part of a surface not agreeing with the general character or appearance of the whole. **6** A shred or scrap. —*v.t.* **1** To put a patch or patches on. **2** To repair, make whole, or put together, especially hurriedly or crudely: often with *up* or *together.* **3** To make of patches, as a quilt. [ME *pacehe;* origin uncertain] —**patch′a·ble** *adj.* —**patch′er** *n.*

patch·head (pach′hed′) *n.* The surf scoter. Also **patchhead coot.**

patch·ou·li (pach′ŏŏ·lē, pə·chŏŏ′lē) *n.* **1** An East Indian herb (*Pogostemon heyneamus* or *patchouly*) of the mint family. **2** A perfume obtained from it. Also spelled *pachouli.* Also **patch′ou·ly.** [<F <Tamil *paccilai* <*paccu* green + *ilai* a leaf]

patch test *Med.* A test for allergy in which an area of unbroken skin is covered by a small patch of linen or blotting paper impregnated with the suspected substance: upon removal of the patch the skin reaction is noted.

patch·work (pach′wûrk′) *n.* **1** A fabric made of patches of cloth, as for quilts, etc. **2** Work made up of heterogeneous materials; work done hastily or carelessly; a jumble.

patch·y (pach′ē) *adj.* **patch·i·er, patch·i·est 1** Abounding in patches; resembling patchwork; hence, lacking in proper effect; incongruous: a *patchy* architectural design. **2** Peevish; irritable. —**patch′i·ly** *adv.* —**patch′i·ness** *n.*

pate (pāt) *n.* The top of the head, especially a human head; often, the head in reference to brains; intellect: usually derogatory. [ME; origin uncertain]

pâte (pät) *n. French* Paste; specifically, porcelain paste.

pâ·té (pä·tā′) *n.* A little pie or pasty; a patty. [<F <OF *pasté* <LL *pasta.* See PASTE[1].]

pâté de foie gras (də fwà grä′) *French* A paste of fat goose liver.

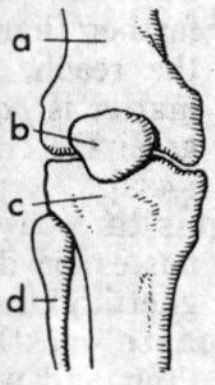

PATELLA
a. Femur.
b. Patella.
c. Tibia.
d. Fibula.

pa·tel·la (pə·tel′ə) *n. pl.* **·lae** (-ē) **1** *Anat.* The flat, movable, oval bone in front of the knee joint; kneecap. **2** A small pan or dish. [<L, dim. of *patina* a pan, dish <*patere* lie open] —**pa·tel′lar** *adj.* —**pa·tel·late** (pə·tel′āt, -it) *adj.*

pa·tel·li·form (pə·tel′i·fôrm) *adj.* **1** Having the form of a patella or kneepan, or of a flattened cone. **2** Having the shape of a limpet shell. [<NL *patelliformis* <L *patella* a patella + *forma* form]

pat·en (pat′n) *n.* **1** A plate; especially, a plate for the eucharistic bread, or one held beneath the chin of the person receiving it. **2** A thin, metallic plate. [<OF *patène* <L *patena, patina* a pan <*patere* lie open]

pa·ten·cy (pāt′n·sē) *n.* **1** The condition of being patent or evident. **2** The state of being open, spread, enlarged, or without obstruction.

pat·ent (pat′nt) *n.* **1** A government protection to an inventor, securing to him for a specific time the exclusive right of manufacturing, exploiting, using, and selling an invention; the right granted. **2** Hence, any official document securing a right. **3** A government grant or franchise of land; also, land so granted; the official certificate of such a grant. **4** That which is protected by a patent or its distinctive marks or features. —*v.t.* **1** To obtain a patent on (an invention). **2** *Rare* To grant a patent for or to. —**pa·tent** (pāt′nt *for defs. 1, 4, 5;* pat′nt *for defs. 2, 3, 6*) *adj.* **1** Manifest or apparent to everybody. **2** Protected or conferred by letters patent. **3** Open for general inspection or use: letters *patent.* **4** Expanded; spreading widely, as leaves from the stem of a plant. **5** Open; unobstructed, as an intestine. **6** Designating grades of flour, usually those of superior quality. See synonyms under EVIDENT, MANIFEST, NOTORIOUS, OPEN. ◆ In British English, pāt′nt is the usual pronunciation, except in *Patent Office* and *letters patent.* [<F <L *patens, -entis,* ppr. of *patere* lie open] —**pat′ent·a·bil′i·ty** *n.* —**pat′ent·a·ble** *adj.*

pat·en·tee (pat′n·tē′) *n.* One who holds a patent.

pat·ent leather (pat′nt) Leather finished with a glossy, black, varnishlike coat; lacquered leather.

patent log *Naut.* A torpedo-shaped device with projecting rotary fins: when trailed on a braided line from the stern of a vessel it records the distance traveled by means of an attached mechanism. Also called *screw log, taffrail log.*

pa·tent·ly (pāt′nt·lē, pat′nt-) *adv.* Manifestly.

Patent Office A bureau of the U. S. Department of Commerce where applications for patents are examined and patents are issued.

pat·en·tor (pat′n·tər) *n.* One who grants a patent, as of land: correlative of *patentee.*

patent right 1 An exclusive right conferred by a government grant. **2** The exclusive privilege, for a limited time, to the use and control of an invention and its manufacture.

pa·ter (pā′tər) *n.* Father. [<L]

Pa·ter (pā′tər), **Walter Horatio,** 1839-94, English essayist and critic.

pat·er·a (pat′ər·ə) *n. pl.* **·er·ae** (-ər·ē) **1** A shallow, platelike vessel of earthenware, silver, etc., used by the Romans in pouring libations. **2** In architecture and cabinetwork, a small, dishlike ornament, often in bas-relief. [<L <*patere* lie open] —**pat′er·i·form′** *adj.*

pa·ter·fa·mil·i·as (pā′tər·fə·mil′ē·əs) *n.* **1** The father of a family or master of a house. **2** In Roman law, an independent person; the head of a family. [<L <*pater* father + *familias,* archaic genitive of *familia* family, household]

pa·ter·nal (pə·tûr′nəl) *adj.* **1** Pertaining to a father; fatherly. **2** Derived from, related through, or connected with one's father; hereditary. [<LL *paternalis* <L *paternus* fatherly <*pater* a father] —**pa·ter′nal·ly** *adv.*

pa·ter·nal·ism (pə·tûr′nəl·iz′əm) *n.* The care or control of a country, community, group of employees, etc., in a manner suggestive of a father looking after his children. —**pa·ter′·nal·is′tic** *adj.* —**pa·ter′nal·is′ti·cal·ly** *adv.*

pa·ter·ni·ty (pə·tûr′nə·tē) *n.* **1** The condition of being a father. **2** Parentage on the male side; descent from a father. **3** Origin in general; authorship. [<OF *paternité* <L *paternitas, -tatis* <*paternus.* See PATERNAL.]

Pa·ter·nò (pä′ter·nō′) A town in eastern Sicily on the site of ancient Hybla.

pa·ter·nos·ter (pā′tər·nos′tər) *n.* **1** The Lord's Prayer: the prayer taught to his disciples by Jesus. *Matt.* vi 9-13. Also **Pater Noster. 2** A recitation of this prayer. **3** A bead of the rosary, indicating that a paternoster is to be recited. **4** Any formula repeated in a low voice. [<L *pater noster* our father, the opening words of the prayer in Latin]

pa·ter pa·tri·ae (pā′tər pā′tri·ē) *Latin* Father of his country.

Pat·er·son (pat′ər·sən) A city on the Passaic River in NE New Jersey.

path (path, päth) *n. pl.* **paths** (pathz, päthz, paths, päths) **1** A walk or way, as one beaten by the foot, used by men or animals. **2** Any road, track, or course. **3** Hence, course or way of life or action. See synonyms under ROAD, WAY. [OE *pæth*]

Pa·than (pə·tän′, pət·hän′) *n.* An Afghan; specifically, one of a people of Afghanistan of Indo-Iranian stock and Moslem religion, who settled in India and on its NW frontier. [<Hind. *Paṭhān* <Afghan *Pĕṣtana,* pl. of *Pĕṣtūn* an Afghan]

pa·thet·ic (pə·thet′ik) *adj.* Of the nature of or expressing sadness, pity, tenderness, etc.; arousing compassion. Also **pa·thet′i·cal.** See synonyms under PITIFUL. [<LL *patheticus* <Gk. *pathētikos* sensitive <*path-,* stem of *paschein* suffer] —**pa·thet′i·cal·ly** *adv.* —**pa·thet′i·cal·ness** *n.*

path·find·er (path′fīn′dər, päth′-) *n.* **1** One skilled in leading or finding a way; especially, one who opens new trails into unknown regions; an explorer; also, one who opens new fields, as in science, philosophy, art. **2** An aircraft carrying flares to light targets in enemy territory for raiding bombers.

-pathia See -PATHY.

path·less (path′lis, päth′-) *adj.* Trackless; untrodden: the *pathless* forest —**path′less·ness** *n.*

patho- *combining form* Suffering; disease: *pathogenesis.* Also, before vowels, **path-.** [<Gk. *pathos* suffering]

path·o·gen (path′ə·jən) *n.* Any disease-producing bacterium or micro-organism. Also **path′o·gene** (-jēn).

path·o·gen·e·sis (path′ə·jen′ə·sis) *n. Med.* The production or development of any morbid or diseased condition: also called *nosogenesis.* Also **pa·thog·e·ny** (pə·thoj′ə·nē).

path·o·gen·ic (path′ə·jen′ik) *adj. Med.* Productive of or pertaining to the production of disease. Also **path′o·ge·net′ic** (-jə·net′ik).

path·o·log·i·cal (path′ə·loj′i·kəl) *adj.* **1** Pertaining to pathology. **2** Related to, involving, concerned with, or caused by disease. Also **path′o·log′ic.** —**path′o·log′i·cal·ly** *adv.*

pa·thol·o·gist (pə·thol′ə·jist) *n.* One skilled in pathology.

pa·thol·ogy (pə·thol′ə·jē) *n. pl.* **·gies 1** The branch of medical science that treats of morbid conditions, their causes, nature, etc. **2** The sum of the morbid conditions, processes, and results in the course of a disease. [<PATHO- + -LOGY]

path·o·mi·me·sis (path′ō·mi·mē′sis, -mī·mē′-)

n. Psychiatry The simulation of a disease or of its symptoms, found in hysteria. Also **path'o·mim'i·cry** (-mim'i·krē). — **path'o·mi·met'ic** (-mi·met'ik, -mī·met'-) *adj.*

path·o·mor·phism (path'ə·môr'fiz·əm) *n. Pathol.* Any abnormality of bodily structure and appearance: said of extreme physical types. [<PATHO- + -MORPH(O)- + -ISM] — **path'o·mor'phic** *adj.*

path·o·pho·bi·a (path'ə·fō'bē·ə) *n.* A morbid fear of disease or of being sick. — **path'o·pho'bic** *adj.*

pa·thos (pā'thos) *n.* 1 The quality, attribute, or element, in events, speech, or art, that rouses emotion or passion, especially the tender emotions, as compassion or sympathy; also, tender or sorrowful feeling. 2 In art, the quality of the contingent and evanescent phenomena of life, as the facts of personality, individuality, human passion, or emotion, that the artist's conception embodies or concretely expresses: opposed to the quality of the ideal or *ethos.* 3 *Obs.* Suffering. See synonyms under FEELING. [<Gk., suffering < *path-*, stem of *paschein* suffer]

path·way (path'wā', päth'-) *n.* A path; a footway.

-pathy *combining form* 1 Suffering; affection: *sympathy.* 2 *Med.* Disease, or the treatment of disease: *psychopathy.* Also spelled *-pathia.* [<Gk. *-patheia* < *pathos* suffering]

Pat·i·a·la (put'ē·ä'lə) 1 A former princely state now included in Punjab State, India. 2 Its former capital, also formerly capital of Patiala and East Punjab States Union.

Patiala and East Punjab States Union A former constituent state of NW India, consisting of several detached areas surrounded by or bordering on Punjab State; became part of Punjab State, November 1, 1956; 10,099 square miles; capital, Patiala: also *Pepsu.*

pa·tience (pā'shəns) *n.* 1 The quality or habit of enduring without complaint. 2 The exercise of sustained endurance and perseverance. 3 Forbearance toward the faults or infirmities of others. 4 Tranquil waiting or expectation. 5 Ability to await events without perturbation. 6 Any solitaire card game. 7 *Obs.* Permission or sufferance. [<OF *pacience* <L *patientia* < *patiens.* See PATIENT.]

Synonyms: calmness, composure, endurance, forbearance, fortitude, leniency, long-suffering, resignation, submission, sufferance. *Endurance* hardens itself against suffering, and may be merely stubborn; by modifiers it may be made to have a passive force, as when we speak of "passive *endurance*"; *fortitude* is *endurance* animated by courage; *patience* is not so hard as *endurance* nor so self-effacing as *submission. Submission* is ordinarily and *resignation* always applied to matters of great moment, while *patience* may apply to slight worries and annoyances. *Patience* may also have an active force denoting uncomplaining steadiness in doing, as in tilling the soil. Compare INDUSTRY, SUBMISSION. *Antonyms*: see synonyms for ANGER, IMPATIENCE.

pa·tient (pā'shənt) *adj.* 1 Possessing quiet, uncomplaining endurance under distress or annoyance; long-suffering. 2 Tolerant, tender, and forbearing. 3 Capable of tranquilly awaiting events. 4 Capable of bearing: with *of*: *patient* of hunger. 5 Persevering. — *n.* 1 A person undergoing treatment for disease or injury. 2 Anything passively affected; the object of external impressions or actions: opposed to *agent.* See synonyms under CHARITABLE, PASSIVE. [<OF *pacient* <L *patiens, -entis,* ppr. of *patiri* suffer] — **pa'tient·ly** *adv.*

pat·i·na[1] (pat'ə·nə) *n. pl.* **·nae** (-nē) An earthenware or metal bowl or basin used as a domestic utensil by the Romans; a patella. [<L < *patere* be open]

pat·i·na[2] (pat'ə·nə) *n.* 1 A green rust or aerugo that covers ancient bronzes, copper coins, medals, etc. 2 An aspect of the surface of stone implements, giving evidence of antiquity. 3 Any surface of antique appearance. Also **pa·tine** (pə·tēn'). [<Ital. <F *patine,* prob. <L *patina* a plate; with ref. to the tarnish on a copper dish]

Pa·ti·ño (pä·tē'nyō), **Simón,** 1868?–1947, Bolivian industrialist and diplomat.

pa·ti·o (pä'tē·ō, pat'ē·ō; *Sp.* pä'tyō) *n. pl.* **·ti·os** 1 The open inner court of a Spanish or Spanish-American dwelling. 2 *U.S.* The enclosed outdoor terrace of a ranch-type dwelling. [<Sp., prob. <L *patere* lie open]

pa·tis·se·rie (pə·tis'ər·ē, *Fr.* pä·tēs·rē') *n.* A pastry shop; also, one in which light luncheons are served. [<F *pâtisserie* < *pâtissier* a pastry cook <Med. L *pasticerius* < *pasticium* a pastry <LL *pasta.* See PASTE[1].]

Pat·more (pat'môr, -mōr), **Coventry Kersey Dighton,** 1823–96, English poet.

Pat·mos (pat'mos, -môs, pät'-) An Aegean island in the northern Dodecanese off the western coast of Turkey: place of St. John's exile. *Rev.* i 9. *Italian* **Pat·mo** (pät'mō).

Pat·na (put'nə) A city on the Ganges, capital of Bihar State, India.

pat·ois (pat'wä, *French* pȧ·twȧ') *n. pl.* **pat·ois** (pat'wäz, *French* pȧ·twȧ') A dialect, especially one that is provincial or illiterate. See synonyms under LANGUAGE. [<OF, a village, later, rustic speech <Med. L *patriensis* a native <L *patria* native land]

pa·to·la (pə·tō'lə) *n.* An East Indian silk fabric, used especially for native wedding garments. [<Skt. *paṭola*]

Pa·tos (pä'to͞os), **Lagoa dos** A tidal lagoon in SE Río Grande do Sul, Brazil; 3,917 square miles; 150 miles long.

Pa·tras (pə·träs', pat'rəs) A port in northern Peloponnesus, Greece, on the **Gulf of Patras** (ancient *Gulf of Calydon*), an inlet of the Ionian Sea west of the Gulf of Corinth. *Greek* **Pa·trai** (pä'tre).

patri- *combining form* Father: *patricide.* [<L *pater, -tris* father]

pa·tri·arch (pā'trē·ärk) *n.* 1 The leader of a family or tribe who rules by paternal right. 2 One of the earliest fathers of the human race, from Adam to Noah: in full: **antediluvian patriarch.** 3 One of the fathers of the Hebrew race, Abraham, Isaac, or Jacob. 4 One of the twelve sons of Jacob considered as the progenitors of the tribes of Israel. 5 A venerable man; especially the founder of a religion, order, etc. 6 In later Jewish history, the title of the president of the Sanhedrin in Syria and Babylon. 7 *Eccl.* **a** In the primitive Christian church, any of the bishops of Antioch, Alexandria, Rome, Constantinople, or Jerusalem. **b** In the Roman Catholic Church, a prelate inferior only to the pope and the cardinals, appointed as head of one of the ancient eastern patriarchates or of some modern Uniat churches. **c** In the Greek Orthodox Church, any of the bishops of Constantinople, Alexandria, Antioch, or Jerusalem, sometimes also a prelate of other cities. The bishop of Constantinople, the highest ranking dignitary in the Greek Church, is titled the **ecumenical patriarch.** **d** The title of the heads of other Eastern churches, as the Coptic, Armenian, Jacobite, or Nestorian churches. 8 In the Mormon Church, one of the superior order of priests, with special authority and jurisdiction in bestowing blessings. [<OF *patriarche* <L *patriarcha* <Gk. *patriarchēs* head of a family < *patria* family, clan + *archein* rule]

pa·tri·ar·chal (pā'trē·är'kəl) *adj.* 1 Of or pertaining to a patriarch; governed by a patriarch: a *patriarchal* see. 2 Of the nature of a patriarchy. 3 Of or belonging to the patriarchs. 4 Having the nature or character of a patriarch; venerable. — **pa'tri·ar'chal·ly** *adv.*

pa·tri·ar·chate (pā'trē·är'kit) *n.* 1 The office, dominion, or residence of a patriarch. 2 A patriarchal system of government.

pa·tri·ar·chy (pā'trē·är'kē) *n. pl.* **·chies** 1 A patriarchate. 2 A system of government in which the father or the male heir of his choice rules.

Pa·tri·cia (pə·trish'ə) A feminine personal name. [<L. See PATRICK.]

pa·tri·cian (pə·trish'ən) *adj.* 1 Pertaining to the aristocracy. 2 Noble or aristocratic. 3 Of or pertaining to the Roman aristocracy; also, relating to patricians of the Italian republics, German free cities, etc. — *n.* 1 An aristocrat; specifically, a member of the hereditary aristocracy that, for the first four centuries of her history, monopolized the government and priesthood of Rome. 2 Any one of the upper classes. 3 An honorary title bestowed by the later Roman emperors. 4 In medieval history, one of the upper class in the Italian republics, German free cities, etc. [<OF *patricien* <L *patricius* belonging to the senatorial class < *pater, -tris* a senator, lit., a father] — **pa·tri'·cian·ly** *adv.*

pa·tri·ci·ate (pə·trish'ē·it, -āt) *n.* 1 The patricians as a class; the nobility. 2 The rank, dignity, or term of office of a patrician.

pat·ri·cide (pat'rə·sīd) *n.* 1 The killing of a father. 2 One who slays a father; a parricide. — **pat'ri·ci'dal** *adj.*

pat·rick (pat'rik) *n. Scot.* A partridge.

Pat·rick (pat'rik) A masculine personal name. Also *Fr.* **Pa·trice** (pȧ·trēs'), **Pa·tri·ci·o** (*Pg.* pə·trē'sē·o͞o, *Sp.* pä·trē'thyō), **Pa·tri·ci·us** (*Du.* pä·trē'sē·o͞os, *Lat.* pə·trish'əs), *Ital.* **Pa·tri·zi·o** (pä·trē'tsē·ō), *Greek* **Pa·tri·zi·us** (pä·trē'tsē·əs). [<L, patrician]

— **Patrick, Saint,** 389?–461?, apostle to and patron saint of Ireland.

pat·ri·cli·nous (pat'rə·klī'nəs) *adj.* Showing hereditary characteristics inclining toward the paternal side: opposed to *matriclinous.* Also **pat'ro·cli'nous.** [<PATRI- + Gk. *klinein* lean]

pat·ri·lin·e·al (pat'rə·lin'ē·əl) *adj.* Derived from or descending through the male line. Compare MATRILINEAL.

pat·ri·lo·cal (pat'rə·lō'kəl) *adj. Anthropol.* Describing that form of residence in clan societies in which a married couple lives in the husband's community. Compare MATRILOCAL. [<PATRI- + L *locus* a place]

pat·ri·mo·ny (pat'rə·mō'nē) *n. pl.* **·nies** 1 An inheritance from a father or an ancestor; also, any inheritance. 2 An endowment, as of a church. [<OF *patrimoine* <L *patrimonium* < *pater, -tris* a father] — **pat'ri·mo'ni·al** *adj.* — **pat'ri·mo'ni·al·ly** *adv.*

pa·tri·ot (pā'trē·ət, -ot) *n.* One who loves his country and zealously guards its welfare; especially, a defender of popular liberty. [<F *patriote* <LL *patriota* a fellow countryman <Gk. *patriōtēs,* < *patris* fatherland]

pa·tri·ot·ic (pā'trē·ot'ik) *adj.* Characterized by patriotism; intended for the public good. — **pa'tri·ot'i·cal·ly** *adv.*

pa·tri·ot·ism (pā'trē·ə·tiz'əm) *n.* Devotion to one's country.

Patriots' Day The day of the battle of Lexington, April 19, 1775: its anniversary is observed as a legal holiday in Maine and Massachusetts.

pa·tris·tic (pə·tris'tik) *adj.* Of or pertaining to the fathers of the Christian church or to their writings. Also **pa·tris'ti·cal.** [<L *pater, -tris* father + -IST + -IC] — **pa·tris'ti·cal·ly** *adv.*

Pa·tro·clus (pə·trō'kləs) In the *Iliad,* a Greek soldier and friend of Achilles in the Trojan War: wearing Achilles' armor, he was mistaken for him and killed by Hector.

pa·trol (pə·trōl') *v.t. & v.i.* **·trolled, ·trol·ling** To walk or go through or around (an area, town, etc.) for the purpose of guarding or inspecting. — *n.* 1 One or more soldiers, policemen, etc., patrolling a district. 2 A reconnaissance or safety group sent out from a security detachment or by the main body in air, ground, or naval warfare. 3 The act of patrolling. 4 A division of a troop of Boy Scouts. [<MF *patrouille* a night watch < *patrouiller,* alter. of *patouiller,* orig. paddle in mud, ? ult. < *patte* a paw, foot] — **pa·trol'·ler** *n.*

patrol boat A small, ruggedly built boat for patrolling harbors and coastal waters.

patrol bomber A large navy bombing plane adapted for long-range patrol activities.

patrol car A squad car.

pa·trol·man (pə·trōl'mən) *n. pl.* **·men** (-mən) One who patrols; specifically, a policeman assigned to a beat.

patrol torpedo boat A small, rugged, highly maneuverable vessel, lightly armed and equipped with torpedoes for rapid action against enemy shipping: also called *PT boat.*

patrol wagon A police wagon or truck for the conveyance of prisoners, etc.

pa·tron (pā'trən) *n.* 1 One who protects, fosters, countenances, or supports some person or thing; a protector or benefactor. 2 A regular customer. 3 A saint regarded as the

peculiar protector of some special person, country, cause, etc.; a tutelary saint; also, the canonized founder of a religious order. **4** In Greek and Roman religion, a tutelary deity; protector of some city, cause, occupation, etc. **5** One in the position of father, guardian, or helper, as one who sponsors a concert or charitable entertainment, one who champions a cause. **6** In ancient Rome, a master who freed his slave and sustained toward him a legal relation analogous to that of father. [<OF *patrun* <L *patronus* protector < *pater, -tris* father] **—pa'tron·al** *adj.*

pa·tron·age (pā'trən·ij, pat'rən-) *n.* **1** Special countenance; guardianship. **2** An uncalled-for distribution of favors, or an overly condescending manner. **3** The right to control the distribution of offices, etc., in the public service; also, the offices, etc., so distributed. **4** The financial support given by customers to commercial enterprises; the customers themselves, as a group.

pa·tron·ess (pā'trən·is, pat'rən-) *n.* A female patron; a matron who promotes and assists in the management of a social event.

pa·tron·ize (pā'trən·īz, pat'rən-) *v.t.* **·ized, ·iz·ing 1** To act as a patron toward; give support or protection to. **2** To treat in a condescending manner. **3** To trade with as a regular customer; frequent. **—pa'tron·iz'er** *n.* **—pa'·tron·iz'ing·ly** *adv.*

pat·ro·nym·ic (pat'rə·nim'ik) *adj.* Formed after one's father's name. **—***n.* **1** A name derived from an ancestor; a family name. **2** A name formed by the addition of a prefix or suffix to a proper name: Fitzhugh, son of Hugh; Johnson, son of John. Also **pat'ro·nym** *n.* [<Gk. *patronymos* (< *patēr, -tros* father + *onyma, onoma* name) + -IC] **—pat'·ro·nym'i·cal·ly** *adv.*

pa·troon (pə·trōōn') *n.* **1** Formerly, a holder of entailed estates, chiefly in New York and New Jersey, with manorial rights, under old Dutch law. **2** *Obs.* The master of a vessel; also, the steersman. [<Du. <F *patron* <L *patronus.* See PATRON.]

pat·te·mar (pat'ə·mär) See PATAMAR.

pat·ten (pat'n) *n.* A shoe having a thick, wooden sole; a clog. [<OF *patin,* prob. < *patte* a paw, foot]

pat·ter[1] (pat'ər) *v.i.* **1** To make a succession of light, sharp sounds. **2** To move with light, quick steps. **—***v.t.* **3** To cause to patter. **—***n.* Pattering, or the sound of pattering. [Freq. of PAT[1]]

pat·ter[2] (pat'ər) *v.t.* & *v.i.* To speak or say glibly or rapidly; mumble or recite (prayers, etc.) mechanically or indistinctly. **—***n.* **1** Glib and rapid talk, as used by comedians, etc. **2** Patois or dialect; any professional jargon. **3** Rapid speech set to music. [Short for PATERNOSTER; from the rapid repetition of the prayer] **—pat'ter·er** *n.*

pat·tern (pat'ərn) *n.* **1** An original or model proposed for or worthy of imitation: Ancient Athens was a *pattern* of democracy. **2** Anything shaped or designed to serve as a model or guide in making something else: a *pattern* for a coat. **3** Any decorative design or figure, or such design worked on something: a vase with a geometrical *pattern.* **4** Arrangement of natural or accidental markings: the *pattern* of a butterfly's wings. **5** The stylistic composition or design of a work of art: the *pattern* of Hardy's novels. **6** A complex of integrated parts functioning as a whole: the behavior *pattern* of a five-year-old; *patterns* of American culture. **7** In gunnery, the distribution of shot or shots about a target. **8** A representative example; sample or instance: a book of *patterns.* **9** *U.S.* Material in sufficient quantity to make a garment, especially a dress. **10** *Obs.* Something made after a model or prototype; a copy. See synonyms under EXAMPLE, IDEA, IDEAL, MODEL, SIGN. **—***v.t.* **1** To make after a model or pattern: with *on, upon,* or *after.* **2** To decorate or furnish with a pattern. [Alter. of PATRON]

pattern bombing The covering of an entire target area, according to a definite plan, by bombs dropped simultaneously by a formation of aircraft.

Pat·ter·son (pat'ər·sən), **Robert Porter,** 1891–1952, U.S. lawyer and statesman.

Pat·ti (pät'tē), **Adelina,** 1843–1919, Baroness Cederstrom, Italian soprano born in Madrid.

pat·tle (pat'l) *n. Scot.* A plow staff.

Pat·ton (pat'n), **George Smith,** 1885–1945, U.S. Army officer in World War II.

pat·tu (put'ōō) *n.* An East Indian homespun wool or tweed, used for shawls, etc. [<Hind. *pattu*]

pat·ty (pat'ē) *n.* *pl.* **·ties** A small pie. [Alter. of F *pâté.* See PÂTÉ.]

patty shell A small puff-paste shell in which to serve creamed meat, fish, vegetables, or fruit.

pat·u·lous (pach'ōō·ləs) *adj.* **1** Spreading; gaping. **2** *Bot.* Spreading slightly, as a calyx. **3** Having a wide aperture. [<L *patulus* standing open < *patere* lie open] **—pat'u·lous·ly** *adv.* **—pat'u·lous·ness** *n.*

Pau (pō) A city of SW France.

pau·cis ver·bis (pô'sis vûr'bis) *Latin* In few words.

pau·ci·ty (pô'sə·tē) *n.* Smallness of number or quantity; fewness; also, scarcity; insufficiency. [<L *paucitas, -tatis* <*paucus* few]

paugh·ty (pôkh'tē) *adj. Scot.* Haughty; insolent.

Pau·ker (pou'kər), **Ana,** 1894?–1960, *née* Rabinsohn, Rumanian Communist leader.

Paul (pôl; *Fr.* pôl, *Dan., Ger., Sw.* poul) **1** A masculine personal name. Also *Lat.* **Pau·li·nus** (pô·lī'nəs), *Pg.* **Pau·lo** (pou'lōō), *Lat.* **Pau·lus** (pô'ləs). **2** Appellation of five popes. [<L, small]

—Paul The apostle to the Gentiles, a Hebrew who, before his conversion, was called *Saul of Tarsus*; author of various New Testament books; died about A.D. 67. Also *Paul the Apostle, Saint Paul.*

—Paul I, 1754–1801, emperor of Russia 1798–1801; assassinated.

—Paul I, born 1901, king of Greece 1947–.

—Paul III, 1468–1549, pope 1534–49; real name Alessandro Farnese; excommunicated Henry VIII; approved Jesuit order.

—Paul VI, born 1897, pope 1963–; real name Giovanni Battista Montini.

Paul and Virginia An idyllic romance by Bernardin de St. Pierre; also, the juvenile lovers around whom the story centers.

Paul Bunyan The famous hero lumberjack of American folklore, of superhuman size and strength and credited with amazing feats.

Paul·ding (pôl'ding), **James Kirk,** 1778–1860, U.S. author.

paul·dron (pôl'drən) *n.* A detachable piece of plate armor to protect the shoulder. [Aphetic var. of OF *espauleron* < *espaule* shoulder; with intrusive *-d*]

Pau·li (pou'lē), **Wolfgang,** 1900–1958, U.S. physicist born in Austria.

pau·lin (pô'lin) *n.* A sheet of heavy canvas, usually waterproof. [Short for TARPAULIN]

Paul·ine (pô'lēn, -lin) *adj.* **1** Relating to the apostle Paul, his teachings, or writings. **2** Characterized by the assumed trend of Paul in his theological thinking. **—Paul'in·ism** *n.* **—Paul'in·ist** *n.*

Pau·line (pô·lēn'; *Fr.* pō·lēn', *Ger.* pou·lē'nə) A feminine personal name. Also **Pau·li·na** (pô·lī'nə; *Pg., Sp.* pou·lē'nä). [<L, of Paul]

Paul·ing (pô'ling), **Linus Carl,** born 1901, U.S. chemist.

Pau·li·nus (pô·lī'nəs), **Saint,** died 644, a Roman missionary to England in 601; archbishop of York.

Paul·ist (pô'list) *n.* A member of the Congregation of the Missionary Priests of St. Paul the Apostle, founded in New York in 1858.

pau·low·ni·a (pô·lō'nē·ə) *n.* Any of a genus *(Paulownia)* of Chinese trees of the figwort family, with heart-shaped leaves and panicles of handsome, fragrant, purple flowers. [<NL, after Anna *Paulovna,* daughter of Czar Paul I]

Paul Pry **1** A comedy by John Poole; also, the inquisitive title character. **2** An inquisitive person.

Pau·lus (pou'lōōs), **Friedrich von,** 1890–1957 German field marshal.

Pa·u·mo·tu Archipelago (pä'ōō·mō'tōō) A former name for TUAMOTU ARCHIPELAGO.

paunch (pônch) *n.* **1** The abdomen; the belly; also, a potbelly. **2** The first stomach of a ruminant. [<AF *panche* <L *pantex, -ticis* belly, bowels] **—paunch'y** *adj.* **—paunch'i·ness** *n.*

pau·per (pô'pər) *n.* One dependent on charity; a destitute person who receives, or is entitled to receive, public charity; any very poor person. [<Med. L *(in forma) pauperis* (in the character) of a poor man < *pauper* poor; orig. a legal phrase. Doublet of POOR.]

pau·pered (pô'pərd) *adj.* Made a pauper.

pau·per·ism (pô'pə·riz'əm) *n.* **1** Poverty. **2** Paupers collectively. See synonyms under POVERTY.

pau·per·ize (pô'pər·īz) *v.t.* **·ized, ·iz·ing** To make a pauper of.

pauper's oath An oath that one is destitute and incapable of supporting oneself: sometimes required when making a plea for public assistance.

pau·ro·me·tab·o·lous (pô'rō·mə·tab'ə·ləs) *adj. Entomol.* Having a gradual or incomplete metamorphosis, as in the grasshopper and certain other insects. Also **pau'ro·met'a·bol'ic** (-met'ə·bol'ik). [<Gk. *pauros* small + *metabolos* changing]

Pau·sa·ni·as (pô·sā'nē·əs) Greek traveler and geographer of the second century A.D.

pause (pôz) *v.i.* **paused, paus·ing 1** To cease action or utterance temporarily; stop; hesitate; delay. **2** To dwell or linger: with *on* or *upon*: to *pause* on a word. See synonyms under CEASE, STAND. [<*n.*] **—***n.* **1** A ceasing of action; an intermission; rest; stop. **2** A holding back because of doubt or irresolution; suspense; hesitation. **3** A momentary cessation in speaking or music for the sake of meaning or expression. **4** A character or sign indicating such cessation, as most marks of punctuation, a break, or a paragraph, or, in music, a hold or a rest. **5** A calculated interval of silence in a meter, or the place at which the voice naturally pauses in reading a verse. See CAESURA. See synonyms under RESPITE, REST[1]. [<MF <L *pausa* a stop <Gk. *pausis* < *pauein* stop] **—paus'er** *n.*

pav·an (pav'ən) *n.* **1** A slow, stately dance of the 16th and 17th centuries. **2** The music for this dance. Also **pav·ane** (pav'ən, *Fr.* pà·vàn'). [<MF *pavane* <Sp. *pavana,* prob. < *pavo* a peacock <L *pavo, -onis*]

pave (pāv) *v.t.* **paved, pav·ing** To cover or surface with asphalt, gravel, concrete, macadam, etc., as a road. **—to pave the way (for)** To make preparation (for); lead up to. [<F *paver* <L *pavire* ram down]

pa·vé (pä·vā') *n.* **1** A street pavement. **2** The close setting of jewels in which no metal shows. [<F, orig. pp. of *paver.* See PAVE.]

Pa·vel (pä'vyel) Polish and Russian form of PAUL.

pave·ment (pāv'mənt) *n.* **1** A hard, solid, surface covering or flooring for a road or footway, usually resting immediately on the ground. **2** A paved road or footway. **3** The material with which a surface is paved. [<OF <L *pavimentum* a rammed floor < *pavire* ram down]

pav·er (pā'vər) *n.* **1** One who lays pavement. **2** A paver's rammer.

Pa·vi·a (pä·vē'ä) A city in northern Italy on the Ticino; scene of a victory of Charles V over Francis I of France, 1525.

pa·vil·ion (pə·vil'yən) *n.* **1** A movable or open structure for temporary shelter or dwelling; a large tent; summerhouse. **2** A related or connected part of a principal building, especially such a structure appropriated to amusement: the dancing *pavilion.* **3** A canopy. **4** The external ear. **5** The sloping surface of a brilliant-cut gem between the girdle and the culet. **6** A detached building for patients, as at a hospital. **—***v.t.* **1** To provide with a pavilion or pavilions. **2** To shelter by a pavilion. [<OF *pavillon* <L *papilio, -onis* a butterfly, tent]

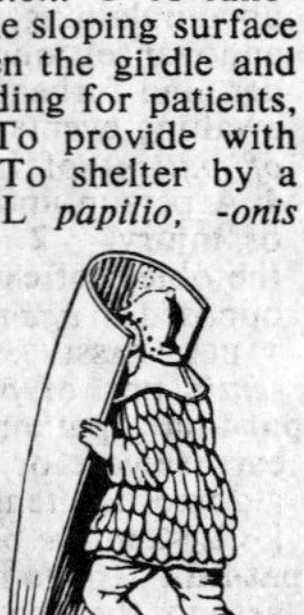

PAVISER

pav·ing (pā'ving) *n.* **1** The laying of a pavement. **2** A pavement; also, the material used for pavement.

pav·ior (pāv'yər) *n.* A pavement layer. Also, *esp. Brit.* **pav'iour.** [Alter. of PAVER]

pav·is (pav'is) *n.* A large, medieval shield protecting the whole body of the soldier bearing it. [<OF *pavais,* appar. <Ital. *Pavia* Pavia, where these shields were made]

pav·is·er (pav'is·ər) *n.* A soldier bearing a pavis.

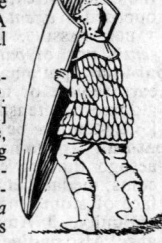

Pav·lov (päv'lôf), **Ivan Petrovich,** 1849–1936, Russian physiologist.

Pav·lo·va (päv·lō'və), **Anna,** 1885–1931, Russian ballet dancer.

Pa·vo (pā'vō) A southern constellation, the

Peacock; its principal star, also called Peacock, is used by navigators. See CONSTELLATION. [< L, a peacock]

pav·o·nine (pav′ə-nīn, -nin) *adj.* **1** Resembling or characteristic of the peacock. **2** Iridescent like the tail of a peacock. [< L *pavoninus* like a peacock < *pavo, -onis* a peacock]

pa·vor noc·tur·nus (pā′vər nok·tûr′nəs) *Latin* Night terrors.

paw (pô) *n.* **1** The foot of an animal having nails or claws. **2** A clumsy human hand. —*v.t. & v.i.* **1** To strike or scrape with the feet or paws: to *paw* the air; to *paw* at the ground. **2** *Colloq.* To handle rudely or clumsily; maul. [< OF *powe*, prob. < Gmc.] —**paw′er** *n.*

pawk·y (pô′kē) *adj. Scot.* **pawk·i·er**, **pawk·i·est** Cunning; sly; humorous. —**pawk′i·ly** *adv.* —**pawk′i·ness** *n.*

pawl (pôl) *n. Mech.* A hinged or pivoted member shaped to engage with ratchet teeth, either to drive a ratchet wheel or to stop its reverse motion; a click or detent. ◆ Homophone: *pall.* [? < Welsh, a pole, prob. ult. < L *palus* a stake]

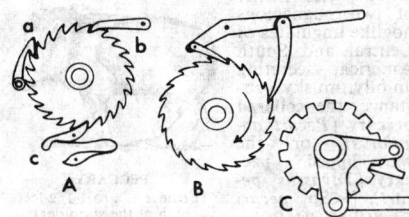

PAWLS
A. Types of pawls: *a.* Hook; *b.* Straight gravity; *c.* Spring.
B. Double pawl.
C. Reversible double pawl.

pawn[1] (pôn) *n* **1** A chessman of lowest rank, that moves on file but captures diagonally. **2** Hence, any insignificant person used at another's will. [< AF *poun*, OF *paon*, var. of *peon, pedon* a foot soldier < LL *pedo, -onis* < L *pes, pedis* a foot. Doublet of PEON.]

pawn[2] (pôn) *n.* **1** Something pledged as security for a loan; especially, personal property pledged to secure a loan. **2** The condition of being held as a pledge for money loaned. **3** The act of pawning. —*v.t.* **1** To give (personal property) as security for a loan. **2** To risk or stake; pledge: to *pawn* one's life. [< OF *pan*, prob. < L *pannus* a cloth; infl. in meaning by MDu. *pand* a pledge < Gmc.] —**pawn′a·ble** *adj.* —**pawn′age** *n.*

pawn·brok·er (pôn′brō′kər) *n.* One engaged in the business of lending money on pledged personal property. —**pawn′brok′ing** *n.*

pawn·ee (pô·nē′) *n. Law* One with whom goods have been left in pawn; a pawnbroker.

Paw·nee (pô·nē′) *n.* A member of one of four tribes of North American Indians of Caddoan linguistic stock, formerly inhabiting the region between the Arkansas River and the Platte River, Nebraska: now living in Oklahoma.

pawn·er (pô′nər) *n.* One who pawns personal property. Also **pawn′or.**

pawn·shop (pôn′shop′) *n.* The place of business of a pawnbroker.

pawn ticket A certificate given by a pawnbroker for goods pawned.

paw·paw (pô′pô) See PAPAW.

Paw·tuck·et (pô·tuk′it) A city in NE Rhode Island.

Pax (paks) In Roman mythology, the goddess of peace: identified with the Greek *Irene.*

pax vo·bis·cum (paks vō·bis′kəm) *Latin* Peace be with you.

pax·wax (paks′waks) *n.* A strong fibrous band extending from the dorsal vertebrae to the occiput, and supporting the head in many mammals, as horses: also spelled *packwax.* [Alter. of dial. *fax-wax* < OE *feax* hair + *weaxan* grow]

pay[1] (pā) *v.* **paid**, **pay·ing** *v.t.* **1** To give to (someone) what is due for a debt, purchase, etc.; recompense; remunerate. **2** To give (money, etc.) for a purchase, service rendered, etc. **3** To provide or hand over the amount of; discharge, as a

debt, bill, etc. **4** To yield as return or recompense. **5** To afford profit or benefit to: It wouldn't *pay* me to do it. **6** To defray, as expenses. **7** To requite, as for an insult. **8** To render or give, as a compliment, attention, etc. **9** To make, as a call or visit. —*v.i.* **10** To make recompense or payment. **11** To afford compensation or profit; be worthwhile: It *pays* to be honest. —**to pay back** To repay. —**to pay off 1** To pay the entire amount of (a debt, mortgage, etc.). **2** to pay the wages of and discharge. **3** To gain revenge upon or for. **4** *Colloq.* To afford full return; be fully effective. **5** *Naut.* To turn or cause to turn to leeward. —**to pay out 1** To disburse or expend. **2** *Naut.* To let out by slackening, as a rope or cable. —**to pay up** To make full payment of. —*n.* **1** That which is given as a recompense or to discharge a debt; compensation; wages. **2** The act of paying or the state of being paid. **3** Whatever compensates for labor or loss; an equivalent. **4** Requital; reward; also, punishment; retaliation. **5** A person considered from the point of view of his ability to pay or his promptness or slowness in paying. **6** A worthwhile yield of metal in a vein or ore. **7** Retribution. See synonyms under SALARY. —*adj.* **1** Of or pertaining to payments, persons who pay, or services paid for: *pay* day, *pay* students, a *pay* library, etc. **2** Yielding enough metal to be worth mining: *pay* dirt, *pay* quartz, etc. [< OF *payer* pay, appease < L *pacare* appease < *pax, pacis* peace] —**pay′er** *n.*

pay[2] (pā) *v.t.* **paid** or **payed**, **pay·ing** To coat with pitch or other waterproof composition, as the seams of a vessel, etc. [< AF *peier* < L *picare* < *pix, picis* pitch]

pay·a·ble (pā′ə-bəl) *adj.* **1** Due and unpaid. **2** Capable of being discharged by payment; that can or will be paid. **3** Likely to be profitable; specifically, likely to yield a surplus, as a mine. —**pay′a·bly** *adv.*

pay-as-you-go (pā′əz-yōō-gō′) *adj.* Of or pertaining to a policy of meeting expenses as they occur or become due, instead of deferring payment.

pay dirt Soil containing enough metal, especially gold, to be profitable to mine.

pay·ee (pā·ē′) *n.* A person to whom money has been or is to be paid.

pay·load (pā′lōd′) *n.* **1** That part of a cargo producing revenue. **2** The explosive material in the warhead of a guided missile. **3** The persons, instruments, etc., carried in a spacecraft that are directly related to the objective of the flight rather than to the operation of the craft.

pay·mas·ter (pā′mas′tər, -mäs′-) *n.* One who has charge of the paying of employees.

pay·ment (pā′mənt) *n.* **1** The act of paying. **2** Pay; requital; recompense. **3** Punishment. See synonyms under SALARY.

Payne (pān), **John Howard**, 1791–1852, U.S. dramatist and song writer.

pay-off (pā′ôf′, -of′) *n.* **1** Payment; specifically, the time or act of payment of wages to employees; also, the time or act of paying an employee in full and discharging him. **2** *Colloq.* Any settlement; the end; reward or punishment. **3** *Colloq.* The climax of an incident or narrative. **4** *U.S. Slang* A bribe.

pay·o·la (pā·ō′lə) *n. U.S. Slang* A secret payment for favors, as for publicizing a commercial product.

pay-roll (pā′rōl′) *n.* A list of those entitled to receive pay, with the amounts due them; also, the total sum of money needed to make the payments. Also **pay roll.**

pays (pās) See PAIS.

Paz (päz, *Sp.* päs), **La** See LA PAZ.

Pb *Chem.* Lead (symbol Pb). [< L *plumbum*]

PCB Polychlorinated biphenyl.

Pd *Chem.* Palladium (symbol Pd).

pe (pā) *n.* The seventeenth Hebrew letter. See ALPHABET.

pea (pē) *n. pl.* **peas** or **pease 1** A climbing annual leguminous herb (*Pisum sativum*) having pinnate leaves. **2** Its edible seed. **3** The seed of any one of various other plants of the same family, as the chickpea or cowpea. [< PEASE, incorrectly taken as a plural]

peace (pēs) *n.* **1** A state of quiet or tranquillity; freedom from disturbance or agitation; calm;

repose. **2** Specifically, absence or cessation of war. **3** General order and tranquillity; freedom from riot or violence. **4** A state of reconciliation after strife or enmity; peaceable or friendly relations; agreement; concord. **5** Freedom from mental agitation or anxiety. **6** Spiritual content. See synonyms under REST. —**to hold** (or **keep**) **one's peace** To be silent. —*v.i. Obs. except as an imperative.* To be or become quiet or silent. ◆ Homophone: *piece.* [< OF *pais* < L *pax, pacis*]

Peace may appear as a combining form in hyphenes or solidemes, or as the first element in two-word phrases; as in:

peace-breaker	peace-minded
peace-bringer	peacemonger
peace conference	peace movement
peace congress	peace offer
peace-giving	peace party
peace-keeper	peace plan
peace-lover	peace-seeker
peace-loving	peacetime

peace·a·ble (pē′sə-bəl) *adj.* **1** Inclined to peace. **2** Peaceful; tranquil. —**peace′a·ble·ness** *n.* —**peace′a·bly** *adv.*

Peace Corps A U.S. government organization, established in 1961, that trains and sends volunteers to live in and aid underdeveloped countries by teaching farming, building, etc.

peace·ful (pēs′fəl) *adj.* **1** Exempt from war, riot, or commotion; undisturbed. **2** Averse to strife. **3** Inclined to or used in peace. See synonyms under CALM, PACIFIC. —**peace′ful·ly** *adv.* —**peace′ful·ness** *n.*

peace·mak·er (pēs′mā′kər) *n.* One who effects, or seeks to effect, a reconciliation between unfriendly parties. —**peace′mak′ing** *n. & adj.*

peace·nik (pēs′nik) *n. Colloq.* A person who demonstrates against war or a particular war: a derogatory term. [< PEACE + Yiddish -*nik* (< Russ.), suffix meaning "a person"]

peace offering An offering made for the sake of peace or reconciliation.

peace officer Any conservator of the peace, especially a justice of the peace, sheriff, constable, or policeman.

peace pipe The calumet.

Peace River (pēs) A river in western Canada, flowing 1,050 miles NE to the Slave River.

peach[1] (pēch) *n.* **1** The fruit of the peach tree (*Prunus persica*), a fleshy, juicy, edible drupe. **2** The tree, widely cultivated in many varieties. **3** The orange-yellow color of the fruit. **4** *Slang* Any person or thing particularly beautiful, pleasing, or excellent. [< OF *peche, pesche* < LL *persica* < L *Persicum* (*malum*) Persian (apple) < Gk. *persikos*]

peach[2] (pēch) *v.i. Slang* To inform against an accomplice; turn informer. —*v.t. Obs.* To impeach; inform against. [Aphetic var. of APPEACH]

peach·bloom (pēch′blōōm′) *n.* **1** A monochrome glaze in Chinese porcelain in various tones of pinkish-red: also **peach′blow′** (-blō′). **2** A kind of ware thus glazed or tinted. **3** A delicate pink color.

peach·y (pē′chē) *adj.* **peach·i·er**, **peach·i·est 1** Resembling a peach, especially in color or downiness. **2** *Slang* Delightfully pleasant. —**peach′i·ness** *n.*

pea-coat (pē′kōt′) *n.* A peajacket. [< PEA(JACKET) + COAT]

pea·cock (pē′kok) *n.* The male of a gallinaceous crested bird (genus *Pavo*), which has the tail coverts enormously elongated, erectile, and marked with ocelli or eyelike spots, and the neck and breast of an iridescent greenish-blue. ◆ Collateral adjective: *pavonine.* —*v.i.* To strut vainly; make a display. [OE *pēa, pāwa* a peacock (< L *pavo*) + COCK[1]]

Pea·cock (pē′kok) A

PEACOCK
(Body length about 30 to 36 inches; tail up to 6 feet)

star of 2.12 magnitude in the constellation Pavo. See STAR.

Pea·cock (pē′kok), **Thomas Love,** 1785–1866, English novelist.

peacock blue A vivid greenish blue, the color of the blue in a peacock's feathers.

peacock copper Bornite.

pea·cock·ish (pē′kok·ish) *adj.* Vain; pretentious. Also **pea′cock·y.**

peacock moth A large moth *(Saturnia pyri)* of southern Europe and western Asia.

pea·fowl (pē′foul) *n.* A peacock or peahen. [< obs. *pea,* OE *pēa* a peacock + FOWL]

peag (pēg) *n.* Wampum. [<Algonquian (Massachuset) *piak,* pl. of *pi* a strung bead of shell money]

pea green Any of several shades of light yellowish green.

pea·hen (pē′hen) *n.* A female peafowl. [OE *pēa* a peacock + *henne* a hen]

pea·jack·et (pē′jak·it) *n.* A short coat of thick woolen cloth, worn by seamen. [Prob. <obs. *pee* a coat of coarse wool <MDu. *pie* + JACKET]

peak[1] (pēk) *n.* **1** A projecting point or edge; an end terminating in a point; summit: the *peak* of a roof. **2** A mountain with pointed summit; a conspicuous or precipitous mountain. **3** The highest point in a pattern of change or development: at the *peak* of his career. **4** *Naut.* **a** The after upper corner of a fore-and-aft sail. **b** The upper end of a gaff. **c** The sharply narrowed part of the hull or hold of a vessel at the bow or stern, called respectively the *forepeak* and *afterpeak.* **5** A point formed on the forehead by the growth or cut of the hair: a widow's *peak.* See synonyms under SUMMIT. — *v.i.* **1** To reach a peak; climax: His campaign *peaked* two weeks before the election. — *v.t.* **2** *Naut.* To raise to or almost to a vertical position, as a gaff. ◆ Homophones: *peek, pique.* [OE *pīc;* def. 2 infl. by Sp. *pico* a beak, peak; *v.* infl. by *peak* vertically, aphetic var. of *apeak* <F *à pic* to a peak]

peak[2] (pēk) *v.i.* To become sickly, weak, or dispirited. ◆ Homophones: *peek, pique.* [Origin unknown]

peak·ed (pē′kid, pēkt) *adj.* Having a thin or sickly appearance. [<PEAK[2]]

peak load *Electr.* The maximum power load consumed or produced by a generating unit or group of units during a specified time.

peal (pēl) *n.* **1** A prolonged, sonorous sound, as of a bell, trumpet, or thunder. **2** A set of large bells attuned to the major scale. **3** The change rung on a chime, usually a scale or part of a scale. — *v.t.* & *v.i.* To sound with a peal or peals; ring out; resound. See synonyms under ROAR. ◆ Homophone: *peel.* [ME *pele,* aphetic var. of *apele* <OF *apeler.* See APPEAL.]

Peale (pēl) Name of a family of American artists, especially, **Charles Willson,** 1741–1827, who painted many portraits of George Washington; his brother **James,** 1749–1831, and his son **Rembrandt,** 1778–1860.

pe·an[1] (pē′ən) See PAEAN.

pean[2] (pēn) See PEEN.

pea·nut (pē′nut′) *n.* **1** The nutlike seed or seed pod of an annual herbaceous vine *(Arachis hypogaea)* of the pea family, ripening underground from the pistillate flowers, which bury themselves after fertilization. **2** The plant. **3** A small or insignificant person.

peanut brittle A hard candy containing roasted peanuts.

peanut butter A spread resembling butter in consistency, made from ground, roasted peanuts.

peanut oil Oil from the seeds of the peanut.

pear (pâr) *n.* **1** The juicy, edible, fleshy fruit of a tree *(Pyrus communis)* of the rose family, cultivated in many varieties. **2** The tree. ◆ Homophones: *pair, pare.* [OE *pere* <LL *pera, pira* <L *pira,* orig. pl. of *pirum* a pear]

pearl (pûrl) *n.* **1** A lustrous, calcareous concretion deposited in layers around a central nucleus in the shells of various mollusks, and largely used as a gem. **2** Something like or likened to such a jewel in form, luster, value, etc. **3** Nacre or mother-of-pearl; also, the color of nacre, or **pearl blue. 4** The color of a pearl, a delicate gray: also **pearl gray. 5** *Printing* A size of type, smaller than agate, 5 points. — *adj.* **1** Pertaining to, consisting of, set with, or made of pearl or mother-of-pearl: a *pearl* button; a *pearl* ring. **2** Shaped like a pearl: *pearl* barley. — *v.i.* **1** To seek or fish for pearls. **2** To form beads like pearls. — *v.t.* **3** To adorn or set with or as with pearls. **4** To color or shape like pearls. **5** To make into small round grains, as barley. ◆ Homophone: *purl.* [<OF *perle* <Med. L *perla;* ult. origin unknown]

Pearl (pûrl), **Raymond,** 1879–1940, U. S. biologist.

pearl ash Crude potassium carbonate.

pearl barley Barley reduced to a round shotlike form by pearling: used in soups. Also **pearled barley.**

pearl·er (pûr′lər) *n.* **1** A diver for or trader in pearls. **2** A boat engaged in pearling.

pearl·es·cent (pûr·les′ənt) *adj.* Having a pearly luster, as certain facial cosmetics; iridescent. [<PEARL + -ESCENT]

Pearl Harbor An inlet on the southern coast of Oahu, near Honolulu, Hawaii; site of a U. S. naval base, attacked by Japanese, December 7, 1941.

pearl·ing (pûr′ling) *n.* **1** The process of removing the outer coat of grain, as in making pearl barley. **2** The business of fishing for pearls.

pearl·ite (pûr′līt) *n.* Perlite.

pearl millet The East Indian millet, a tall cereal grass *(Pennisetum glaucum)* having edible seeds: used as a forage grass.

Pearl River A river in central Mississippi, flowing 480 miles SW to the Gulf of Mexico and forming part of the boundary between Mississippi and Louisiana. See CANTON RIVER.

pearl·y (pûr′lē) *adj.* **pearl·i·er, pearl·i·est** Adorned with, yielding, or resembling pearls; margaric.

pear·main (pâr′mān) *n.* A variety of apple. [<OF *permain, parmain,* lit., of Parma, Italy]

Pearse (pirs), **Padraic,** 1879–1916, Irish educator and patriot; executed.

Pear·son (pir′sən), **Karl,** 1857–1936, English scientist. — **Lester Bowles,** 1897–1972, Canadian statesman; prime minister 1963–68.

peart (pirt, pûrt) *adj. Dial.* In good health and spirits; active; lively. [Var. of PERT] — **peart′ly** *adv.*

Pea·ry (pir′ē), **Robert Edwin,** 1856–1920, U.S. Arctic explorer; first to reach the North Pole, April 6, 1909.

Peary Land A region of northern Greenland along the Arctic Ocean, the world's northernmost land region.

peas·ant (pez′ənt) *n.* **1** In Europe, a small farmer; a farm laborer; any rustic workman. **2** *Obs.* A rascal; base character; scamp. [<AF *paisant* <OF *païs* country <L *pagensis (ager)* (territory) of a canton <*pagus* a district]

peas·ant·ry (pez′ən·trē) *n.* **1** The peasant class; a body of peasants. **2** Rusticity.

peas·cod (pēz′kod) *n.* A pea pod. Also **pease′·cod.** [<PEAS(E) + COD[2]]

pease (pēz) *n. pl.* Peas collectively. [OE *pise* <LL *pisa* <L, orig. pl. of *pisum* <Gk. *pison* <*pisos* pulse, pease]

pea-shoot·er (pē′shōō′tər) *n.* A toy blowgun through which small pellets, as dried peas, are blown.

peat[1] (pēt) *n.* **1** A substance consisting of partially carbonized vegetable material, chiefly mosses, found usually in bogs. **2** A block of this substance, pressed and dried for fuel. [<Med. L *peta* a piece of peat, ? <*petia* a fragment]

peat[2] (pēt) *n. Obs.* **1** A pet; a favorite woman or girl. **2** A favorite; a minion. [Cf. MDu. *pete* a goddaughter]

peat bog A marsh with an accumulation of peat.

peat·man (pēt′mən) See PETEMAN.

peat moss 1 A moss that enters largely into the composition of peat. **2** *Brit.* A peat bog.

peat·y (pē′tē) *adj.* **peat·i·er, peat·i·est** Resembling or containing peat.

pea·vy (pē′vē) *n. pl.* **·vies** An iron-pointed lever fitted with a movable hook and used for handling logs. Also **pea′vey.** [after Joseph *Peavey,* its inventor]

peb·ble (peb′əl) *n.* **1** A small, rounded fragment of rock, its form being due to attrition of water, ice, etc. **2** Quartz crystal; also, a lens made of it. **3** Leather that has been pebbled. **4** Pebbleware. — *v.t.* **·bled, ·bling 1** To impart a rough grain to (leather). **2** To pave, cover, or pelt with pebbles. [OE *pabol(stān)* a pebble(stone)] — **peb′bly** *adj.*

peb·ble·stone (peb′əl·stōn′) *n.* **1** A pebble. **2** A material consisting of a mass of pebbles. [See PEBBLE]

peb·ble·ware (peb′əl·wâr′) *n.* A ware having different-colored clays in the paste.

pe·can (pi·kan′, -kän′, pē′kan) *n.* **1** A large hickory *(Carya illinoensis)* of the central and southern United States, with olive-shaped, thin-shelled nuts. **2** The nut borne by this tree, containing a sweet, oily kernel. [Earlier *paccan* <Algonquian (Cree) *pakan*]

pec·ca·ble (pek′ə·bəl) *adj.* Capable of sinning. [<OF <Med. L *peccabilis* <L *peccare* sin] — **pec′ca·bil′i·ty** *n.*

pec·ca·dil·lo (pek′ə·dil′ō) *n. pl.* **·los** or **·loes** A slight or trifling sin; a fault. See synonyms under FOIBLE. [<Sp. *pecadillo,* dim. of *pecado* a sin <L *peccatum,* orig. pp. of *peccare* sin]

pec·cant (pek′ənt) *adj.* **1** Guilty of sin; sinful; offending. **2** Corrupt and offensive; diseased. **3** Violating some rule or principle. [<L *peccans, -antis,* ppr. of *peccare* sin] — **pec′can·cy** *n.* — **pec′cant·ly** *adv.*

pec·ca·ry (pek′ər·ē) *n. pl.* **·ries** Either of two pugnacious hoglike ungulates of Central and South America, secreting an oily, musky substance, the **collared peccary** *(Pecari angulatus),* or the **white-lipped peccary** *(Tayassus pecari).* [<Sp. *pecari* <Cariban *pakira*]

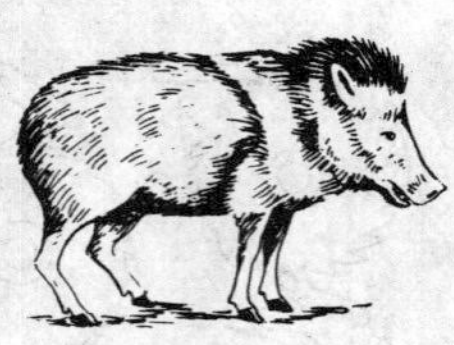

PECCARY
(From 1 1/4 to 1 1/2 feet high at the shoulder)

pec·ca·vi (pe·kā′vī, -kä′vē) *n. Latin* A confession of guilt; literally, I have sinned.

pech (pekh) *v.i. Scot. & Brit. Dial.* To pant; puff. — **pech′in** *n.*

pech·an (pekh′an) *n. Scot.* The gullet; stomach.

Pe·chen·ga (pə·cheng′gə) A port of Russian S.F.S.R. on the Barents Sea, near the Norwegian border. *Finnish* **Pet·sa·mo** (pet′sə·mō).

Pe·cho·ra (pə·chôr′ə) A river of NE European U.S.S.R., flowing 1,110 miles north from the Urals to the Barents Sea.

peck[1] (pek) *v.t.* **1** To strike with the beak, as a bird does, or with something pointed. **2** To make by striking thus: to *peck* a hole in a wall. **3** To pick up, as food, with the beak. — *v.i.* **4** To make strokes with the beak or with something pointed. — *n.* **1** A quick, sharp blow, as with a beak or something pointed. **2** A mark, dent, or hole made by such a blow. [Var. of PICK] — **peck′er** *n.*

peck[2] (pek) *n.* **1** A measure of capacity: the fourth of a bushel, 8 quarts, or 8.8 liters. See DRY MEASURE. **2** A vessel for measuring a peck. **3** *Slang* A great quantity. [<OF *pek,* a measure of oats for horses]

peck·er·wood (pek′ər·wo͝od′) *n. U.S. Dial.* **1** A woodpecker. **2** A poor white.

peck-or·der (pek′ôr′dər) *n.* A hierarchy of social privilege and status among the members of a flock of chickens, established by the enforced right of the more aggressive hens or cocks to peck at, harass, and dominate all those lower in the scale.

Peck·sniff (pek′snif), **Seth** An unctuous, canting hypocrite in Dickens' *Martin Chuzzlewit.*

Peck·sniff·i·an (pek·snif′ē·ən) *adj.* Suggestive of Seth Pecksniff; hypocritical; insincere.

Pe·cos Bill (pā′kōs) A legendary cowboy of the American West, who was raised by coyotes and performed many fantastic feats, such as digging the Rio Grande.

Pe·cos River (pā′kəs, -kōs) The principal tributary of the Rio Grande, flowing 926 miles from north central New Mexico to western Texas.

Pécs (pāch) A city of SW Hungary: German *Fünfkirchen.*

pec·tase (pek′tās) *n. Biochem.* An enzyme obtained from fruits which combines with pectin to yield pectic acid. [<PECT(IN) + (DIAST)ASE]

pec·tate (pek′tāt) *n. Chem.* A salt or ester of pectic acid. [<PECT(IC) + -ATE[3]]

pec·ten (pek′tən) *n. pl.* **·ti·nes** (-tə·nēz) *Zool.* **1** A comb, or comblike part or process; specifically, in birds and reptiles, a vascular pigmented membrane of the eyeball. **2** A scallop. **3** *Anat.* The pubic bone. [<L, a comb, a scallop <*pectere* comb, dress the

hair] — **pec′ti·nate, pec′ti·nat′ed** *adj.* — **pec′ti·na′tion** *n.*

pec·tic (pek′tik) *adj.* Of, pertaining to, or derived from pectin. [<Gk. *pēktikos* < *pēktos* congealed < *pēgnynai* make solid]

pectic acid *Chem.* Any of a group of compounds derived from pectin by the hydrolysis of methyl ester.

pec·tin (pek′tin) *n. Biochem.* Any of a class of compounds of high molecular weight contained in the cell walls of various fruits and vegetables, as apples, lemons, or carrots: it is the basis of fruit jellies. [<PECT(IC) + -IN]

pec·tize (pek′tīz) *v.t.* & *v.i.* **·tized, ·tiz·ing** To coagulate. [<Gk. *pēktos* congealed + -IZE]

pec·to·ral (pek′tər·əl) *adj.* **1** Of or pertaining to the breast or thorax. **2** As if proceeding from the breast or inner consciousness; more especially, of an emotional character: *pectoral* theology. **3** Adapted to, efficacious in, or designed for relieving or curing diseases of the lungs or chest. — *n.* **1** An ornament worn on the breast; especially, the **pectoral cross** worn on the breast by bishops, abbots, etc. **2** A pectoral organ, fin, or muscle. **3** Any medicine for ailments of the chest. [<L *pectoralis* < *pectus, -oris* the breast]

pectoral arch or **girdle** *Anat.* **1** The arch formed by the collar bone and shoulder blade in man. **2** That part of the skeleton with which the forelimbs of a vertebrate animal are articulated.

pectoral fin *Zool.* One of the anterior paired fins of fishes, homologous with the anterior limb of higher vertebrates.

pectoral sandpiper An American sandpiper (*Pisobia melanotos*), occasional in Europe, having a buff-gray breast with dusky streaks: also called *grass snipe*.

pec·u·late (pek′yə·lāt) *v.t.* & *v.i.* **·lat·ed, ·lat·ing** To steal or appropriate wrongfully (funds, especially public funds) entrusted to one's care; embezzle. [<L *peculatus*, pp. of *peculari* embezzle < *peculium*. See PECULIUM.] — **pec′u·la′tion** *n.* — **pec′u·la′tor** *n.*

pe·cul·iar (pi·kyōōl′yər) *adj.* **1** Having a character exclusively its own; unlike anything else or anything of the same class or kind; specific; particular. **2** Singular; odd; strange. **3** Select or special; separate; distinguished. **4** Belonging particularly or exclusively to one. — *n.* **1** A person or thing that is peculiar; formerly, any private possession. **2** A member of the sect known as the Peculiar People. See synonyms under EXTRAORDINARY, ODD, PARTICULAR, QUEER, RARE[1]. [<MF *peculier* <L *peculiaris* < *peculium*. See PECULIUM.] — **pe·cul′iar·ly** *adv.*

pe·cu·li·ar·i·ty (pi·kyōō′lē·ar′ə·tē) *n. pl.* **·ties** **1** A characteristic. **2** The quality of being peculiar. See synonyms under CHARACTERISTIC.

Peculiar People **1** A denomination of Christians, founded in England in 1838, who hold that sinless perfection is immediately obtainable by those willing to seek and accept it. **2** In the Scripture, the Jews, as being God's chosen people and separated from the rest of mankind. *Deut.* xxvi 18.

pe·cu·li·um (pi·kyōō′lē·əm) *n.* In Roman law, property that a slave, a wife, or a child was permitted to hold as his own. [<L, private property, orig. one's cattle < *pecus* cattle, money]

pe·cu·ni·ar·y (pi·kyōō′nē·er′ē) *adj.* **1** Consisting of or relating to money; monetary. **2** Having a monetary penalty; entailing a fine. See synonyms under FINANCIAL. [<L *pecuniarius* < *pecunia* money < *pecus* cattle]

ped–[1] Var. of PEDI–.

ped–[2] Var. of PEDO–.

–ped Var. of –PEDE.

ped·a·gog (ped′ə·gog, -gôg) *n.* **1** A schoolmaster; especially, a pedantic, narrow-minded teacher. **2** In ancient Greece and Rome, a slave who attended children to school. Also **ped′a·gogue.** [<OF *pedagoge* <L *paedagogus* <Gk. *paidagōgos* < *pais, paidos* a child + *agōgos* a leader < *agein* lead]

ped·a·gog·ic (ped′ə·goj′ik, -gō′jik) *adj.* **1** Pertaining to the science or art of teaching. **2** Of or belonging to a pedagog; affected with a conceit of learning. Also **ped′a·gog′i·cal.** — **ped′a·gog′i·cal·ly** *adv.*

ped·a·gog·ics (ped′ə·goj′iks) *n. pl.* (*construed as singular*) The science and art of teaching; pedagogy.

ped·a·gog·ism (ped′ə·gog′iz·əm, -gôg′-) *n.* The nature, character, or business of teachers or a teacher. Also **ped′a·gogu′ism.**

ped·a·go·gy (ped′ə·gō′jē, -goj′ē) *n.* The science or profession of teaching; also, the theory or the teaching of how to teach.

ped·al (ped′l) *adj.* **1** Of or pertaining to a foot, feet, or a footlike part. **2** Of or pertaining to a pedal. — *n. Mech.* A lever operated by the foot, differing from a treadle in that it is usually applied only to musical instruments, cycles, sewing machines, and light machinery. — *v.t.* & *v.i.* **·aled** or **·alled, ·al·ing** or **·al·ling** To move or operate by working pedals; use the pedals (of). ◆ Homophone: *peddle.* [<L *pedalis* < *pes, pedis* the foot]

pedal curve *Math.* The curve traced by the foot of a perpendicular drawn from a fixed point to a variable tangent to a given curve: the curve so traced is called the pedal of the curve with respect to the point.

ped·al·fer (ped·al′fər) *n.* A type of soil characterized by a downward shifting of alumina and iron oxide, with an absence of carbonate of lime accumulations. Compare PEDOCAL. [<Gk. *ped(on)* ground + AL(UMINA) + L *fer(rum)* iron]

ped·a·lier (ped′ə·lir′) *n.* A pedal keyboard for a pianoforte. [<F *pédalier* < *pédale* <L *pedalis*. See PEDAL.]

pedal point *Music* A tonic or dominant note sustained (usually in the bass) while the other parts proceed with varying harmonies. Also **pedal note.**

ped·ant (ped′ənt) *n.* **1** A scholar who makes needless and inopportune display of his learning, or who insists upon the importance of trifling points of scholarship. **2** *Obs.* A schoolmaster; teacher. [<F *pédant* <Ital. *pedante*, prob. <Med. L *paedagogans, -antis*, ppr. of *paedagogare* teach <L *paedagogus*. See PEDAGOG.] — **pe·dan·tic** (pi·dan′tik) *adj.* — **pe·dan′ti·cal·ly** *adv.*

ped·ant·ry (ped′ən·trē) *n. pl.* **·ries** **1** Ostentatious display of knowledge. **2** Undue and slavish adherence to forms or rules.

ped·ate (ped′āt) *adj.* **1** Resembling or having the functions of a foot; having feet. **2** *Bot.* Palmately divided or parted, the lateral divisions being subdivided: said especially of leaves. [<L *pedatus* having feet < *pes, pedis* a foot] — **ped′ate·ly** *adv.*

pedati– *combining form Bot.* Pedately: *pedatifid.* [<L *pedatus* having feet < *pes, pedis* foot]

pe·dat·i·fid (pi·dat′ə·fid, -dā′tə-) *adj. Bot.* Having the subdivisions of a simple leaf, which is pedately nerved, extending half-way to the base.

pe·dat·i·sect (pi·dat′ə·sekt, -dā′tə-) *adj. Bot.* Pedate and cleft almost to the midrib: said of leaves. Also **pe·dat′i·sect′ed** (-sek′tid).

ped·dle (ped′l) *v.* **·dled, ·dling** *v.i.* **1** To travel about selling small wares. **2** To occupy oneself with trifles; piddle. — *v.t.* **3** To carry about and sell in small quantities. **4** To sell or dispense in small quantities. ◆ Homophone: *pedal.* [Appar. back formation <ME *ped(d)ler(e)* a peddler; infl. by PIDDLE]

ped·dler (ped′lər) *n.* One who peddles; a hawker: also spelled *pedlar, pedler.* [ME *pedlere*, ? alter. of *pedder* a peddler < *ped* a basket] — **ped′dler·y** *n.*

ped·dling (ped′ling) *adj.* Small; trifling; piddling.

–pede *combining form* Footed: *centipede.* Also spelled *-ped*, as in *quadruped.* [<L *pes, pedis* foot]

Pe·der (pā′thər) Danish form of PETER.

ped·er·ast (ped′ə·rast, pē′də-) *n.* One addicted to pederasty: also spelled *paederast.*

ped·er·as·ty (ped′ə·ras′tē, pē′də-) *n.* Sodomy, especially as practiced between men and boys. [<NL *paederastia* <Gk. *paiderastia* < *paiderastēs* a lover of boys < *pais, paidos* a boy + *erastēs* a lover < *eraein* love] — **ped′er·as′tic** *adj.* — **ped′er·as′ti·cal·ly** *adv.*

pe·des (pē′dēz) *Latin* Plural of PES.

ped·es·tal (ped′is·təl) *n.* **1** A base or support for a column, statue, or vase. **2** Hence, any foundation, base, or support, either material or immaterial. — **to put on a pedestal** To hold in high estimation; to put in the position of an idol or hero. [<MF *pédesta*; <Ital. *piedestallo* < *pie di stallo* < *piè*, pried foot (<L *pes, pedis*) + *di* of (<L *de*) + *stallo* a stall, standing place <OHG *stal*]

pedestal table A table whose top is supported by a central column.

pe·des·tri·an (pə·des′trē·ən) *adj.* **1** Moving on foot; walking; pertaining to walking. **2** Pertaining to common people; plebeian. **3** Hence, commonplace, prosaic, or dull, as prose or mechanical verse. — *n.* One who journeys or moves from place to place on foot; a walker. [<L *pedester, -tris* on foot < *pes, pedis* a foot] — **pe·des′tri·an·ism** *n.*

pedi–[1] *combining form* Foot; related to the foot or feet: *pedicure.* Also, before vowels, *ped–.* [<L *pes, pedis* foot]

pedi–[2] *combining form* Pedo–. [<Gk. *pais, paidos* a child]

pe·di·a·tri·cian (pē′dē·ə·trish′ən, ped′ē-) *n.* A physician specializing in pediatrics. Also **pe′di·at′rist.**

pe·di·at·rics (pē′dē·at′riks, ped′ē-) *n.* That branch of medicine dealing with the diseases and hygienic care of children: also spelled *paediatrics.* [<Gk. *pais, paidos* a child + -IATRICS] — **pe′di·at′ric** *adj.*

ped·i·cab (ped′i·kab′) *n.* A three-wheeled vehicle operated by pedaling and having an attached seat for a passenger, available for public hire in some Asian countries. [< PEDI-[1] + CAB[1]]

ped·i·cel (ped′ə·səl) *n.* **1** *Bot.* **a** The stalk supporting a single flower in an inflorescence composed of flowers arranged upon a common peduncle. **b** A small or delicate support of various special organs, as of a sporangium in ferns or a capsule in mosses. **2** *Entomol.* A stalk or supporting part, as the second segment of the antenna of an insect, between the scape and the funicle. **3** *Zool.* An ambulacral sucker in an echinoderm. [<NL *pedicellus*, dim. of L *pediculus*, dim. of *pes, pedis* a foot] — **ped′i·cel′lar** (-sel′ər) *adj.*

ped·i·cel·late (ped′ə·sə·lit, -lāt′) *adj.* Borne on or having a pedicel.

pe·dic·u·lar (pə·dik′yə·lər) *adj.* Of, pertaining to, or infested with lice. [<L *pedicularis* < *pediculus*, dim. of *pedis* a louse]

pe·dic·u·late (pə·dik′yə·lit, -lāt) *adj.* Pertaining or belonging to an order (*Pediculati*) of teleost fishes having a spinous dorsal fin with the front ray adapted as a lure, and including the broad, soft-bodied angler fish. [<L *pediculus* footstalk + -ATE[1]]

ped·i·cure (ped′i·kyŏŏr) *n.* **1** The care of the feet; the surgical treatment of corns, bunions, etc. **2** A chiropodist. **3** The cosmetic treatment of the feet and toenails. — *v.t.* **·cured, ·cur·ing** To treat (the feet) for corns, bunions, etc. [<L *pes, pedis* a foot + *cura* care] — **ped′i·cur′ist** *n.*

ped·i·form (ped′i·fôrm) *adj.* Resembling a foot in shape.

ped·i·gree (ped′ə·grē) *n.* **1** A line of ancestors; lineage. **2** A list or table of descent and relationship; a genealogical register, especially of an animal of pure breed. [<MF *pié de grue* a crane's foot; from a three line mark denoting succession in pedigrees]

ped·i·greed (ped′ə·grēd) *adj.* Having a pedigree; of notable ancestry.

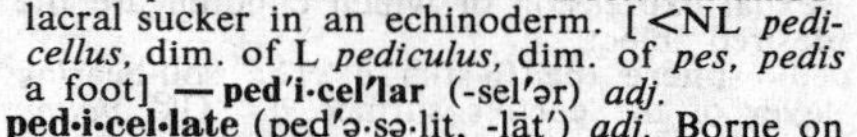

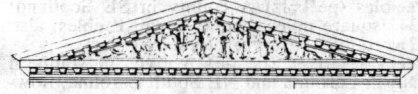

PEDIMENT
Pediment of the U. S. Supreme Court, Washington, D.C.

ped·i·ment (ped′ə·mənt) *n. Archit.* **1** A broad triangular part above a portico or door. **2** Any similar piece with a long base surmounting a door, screen, bookcase, etc. [Earlier *periment*, prob. alter. of PYRAMID; infl. in form by *pes, pedis* a foot] — **ped′i·men′tal** (-men′təl) *adj.*

ped·i·palp (ped′i·palp) *n. Zool.* **1** One of the second pair of appendages at the sides of the mouth in arachnids, terminally pincerlike, as in scorpions; long and leglike, as in solpugids;

or leglike with the terminal joint serving to convey the semen in copulation, as in male spiders. 2 One of the *Pedipalpi*. **—ped′i·pal′pous** *adj.*

Ped·i·pal·pi (ped′i·pal′pī) *n. pl.* An order of arachnids with segmented abdomen; whip scorpions. [<NL <L *pes, pedis* foot + *palpus* feeler]

ped·lar (ped′lər), **ped·ler,** etc. See PEDDLER.

pedo- *combining form* Child; children; offspring: also, before vowels, *ped-*, as in *pedagogy.* Also spelled *paedo-*. [<Gk. *pais, paidos* a child]

pe·do·bap·tism (pē′dō·bap′tiz·əm) *n.* Infant baptism, and the system that sustains it. **—pe′do·bap′tist** *n.*

ped·o·cal (ped′ō·kal) *n.* A type of soil characterized by an accumulation of carbonates of calcium or of calcium and magnesium. Compare PEDALFER. [<Gk. *pedon* ground + CAL(CIUM)]

pe·do·gen·e·sis (pē′dō·jen′ə·sis) *n. Entomol.* Reproduction in the sexually immature or larval stage, as in certain insects.

pe·dol·o·gy[1] (pi·dol′ə·jē) *n.* The scientific study of the development and behavior of children. [<PEDO- + -LOGY] **—ped·o·log·i·cal** (*ped′ə·loj′i·kəl) adj.* **—ped′o·log′i·cal·ly** *adv.* **—pe·dol′o·gist** *n.*

pe·dol·o·gy[2] (pi·dol′ə·jē) *n.* The science that treats of the origin, nature, and properties of soils, especially in their more fundamental aspects. [<Gk. *pedon* ground + -LOGY] **—pe·dol′o·gist** *n.*

pe·dom·e·ter (pi·dom′ə·tər) *n.* An instrument that measures distance traveled by recording the number of steps taken by the person who carries it. [<F *pédomètre* <L *pes, pedis* foot + Gk. *metron* measure]

pe·do·phil·ia (pē·də·fil′ē·ə) *n.* A perversion of sexual expression of which children are the desired object.

ped·o·sphere (ped′ə·sfir) *n.* The soil-bearing layer of the earth's surface. [< Gk. *pedon* ground + -SPHERE]

ped·re·gal (ped′rə·gäl′) *n.* In Mexico and SW United States, a rough, rocky tract of land, especially in a volcanic region; a lava field. [<Sp. <*piedra* a stone]

pe·dro (pē′drō) *n. pl.* **·dros** 1 The five of trumps in the card game of cinch. 2 A game of pitch in which the five of trumps counts five. [<Sp. *Pedro* Peter]

Pe·dro (pā′thrō) Portuguese and Spanish form of PETER.

ped·ule (pej′ŏŏl) *n.* A leg covering of flexible leather, flannel, or other material, worn in ancient and medieval times. [<L, neut. of *pedulis* of or for the feet <*pes, pedis* a foot]

pe·dun·cle (pi·dung′kəl) *n.* 1 *Bot.* The general stalk or support of an inflorescence. 2 *Anat.* A stalk or stem, as for the attachment of an organ or organism: the *peduncles* of the brain. [<NL *pedunculus* a footstalk, dim. of *pes, pedis* a foot] **—pe·dun′cled, pe·dun′cu·lar** *adj.*

pe·dun·cu·late (pi·dung′kyə·lit, -lāt) *adj.* Borne on or having a peduncle. Also **pe·dun′cu·lat′ed.**

pee·been (pē′bēn) *n.* A large hardwood evergreen tree *(Syncarpia hilli)* of the myrtle family, native to Australia: also called *turpentine tree.*

Pee·bles (pē′bəlz) A county in SE Scotland; 347 square miles; county town, Peebles: also *Tweeddale.* Also **Pee′bles·shire** (-shir).

Pee Dee River (pē dē) A river in southern North Carolina and NE South Carolina, flowing 233 miles SE to Winyah Bay.

peek (pēk) *v.i.* To look furtively, slyly, or quickly; peep. *—n.* A peep, glance. ◆Homophones: *peak, pique.* [ME *piken.?* var. of *kiken* peer; infl. by PEEP[2]]

peek-a-boo (pē′kə·bōō′) *n.* A children's game in which one hides (one's face) and calls out "peek-a-boo!" or "Bo-peep!"

peel[1] (pēl) *n.* The natural coating of certain kinds of fruit, as oranges and lemons; skin; rind. *—v.t.* 1 To strip off the bark, skin, etc., of. 2 To strip off; remove. *— v.i.* 3 To lose bark, skin, etc. 4 To come off: said of bark, skin, etc. 5 *Slang* To undress. **—to keep one's eye peeled** *Colloq.* To keep watch; be alert. **—to peel off** *Aeron.* To veer off from a flight formation so as to dive or prepare for a landing. ◆Homophone: *peal.* [Var. of earlier *pill* a skin, covering; infl. by F *peler* strip of skin]

peel[2] (pēl) *n.* 1 A broad, thin, long-handled, shovel-like implement used by bakers in moving bread, etc., about an oven. 2 The blade or broad part of an oar. ◆Homophone: *peal.* [<OF *pele* <L *pala* a spade]

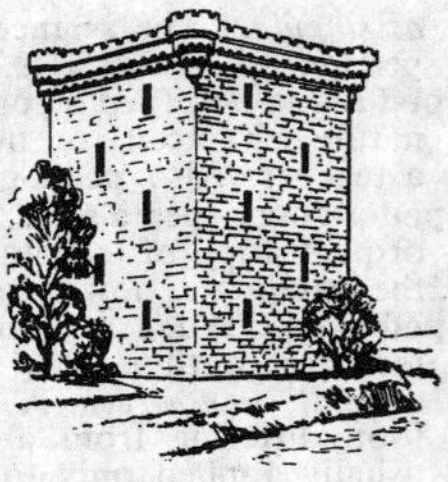

PEEL
Vaulted lower story often used as a stable; living quarters above.

peel[3] (pēl) *n.* 1 A square stronghold or tower of the 16th century, especially on the borders of Scotland and England: also **peel′-house′** (-hous′). 2 *Obs.* A stake; stockade; palisade. ◆Homophone: peal. [<AF *pel* <L *palus* a stake]

Peel (pēl) A port and resort on the west coast of the Isle of Man; site of an ancient castle.

Peel (pēl), **Sir Robert,** 1788–1850, English statesman; introduced police reforms.

Peele (pēl), **George,** 1558?–97?, English playwright and poet.

peel·ing (pē′ling) *n.* Something peeled off; a strip of rind, bark, skin, or outer layer.

Peel River (pēl) A river in Northwest Territories, Canada, flowing 365 miles north to the Mackenzie River.

peel·er (pē′lər) *n. Brit. Slang* A policeman. [after Sir Robert *Peel*]

peen (pēn) *n.* The end of a hammer head opposite the face: usually shaped for indenting, riveting, chipping, etc., as when straight, pointed, conical, hemispherical, or wedge-shaped: ball-*peen*, cross- *peen*, etc. See illustration under HAMMER. *—v.t.* To beat, bend, or shape with the peen. Also spelled *pane, pean, pein.* [Appar. var. of PANE[2], ? infl. by Scand. Cf. Norw. *paenn* the sharp end of a hammer.]

peenge (pēnj) *v.i. Scot. Brit. Dial.* To complain.

peep[1] (pēp) *v.i.* 1 To utter the small, sharp cry of a young bird or chick; chirp; cheep. 2 To speak in a weak, small voice. *— n.* 1 The cry of a chick or small bird, or of a young frog; chirp. 2 A small sandpiper; especially, the least sandpiper; sandpeep. [ME *pepen,* var. of *pipen* PIPE]

peep[2] (pēp) *v.i.* 1 To look through a small hole, from concealment, etc.; look furtively or quickly; peek. 2 To begin to appear; be just visible. *—v.t.* 3 *Rare* To cause to stick out slightly. *—n.* 1 A furtive look; a glimpse or glance. 2 An aperture or crevice through which one may look; peephole. 3 The earliest appearance: the *peep of day. [ME pepen.?* Akin to ME *piken* PEEK.]

peep[3] (pēp) *n. Slang* A jeep; also, sometimes, a larger command car. [Alter. of JEEP]

peep·er[1] (pē′pər) *n.* An animal that peeps or makes a chirping sound, especially a very young chick or any of several tree frogs.

peep·er[2] (pē′pər) *n.* 1 One who peeps or peeks; a spying person. 2 *Slang* An eye.

peep·hole (pēp′hōl′) *n.* An aperture, as a hole or crack, through which one may peep; also, a small window in a door.

peep·ing-tom (pē′ping·tom′) *n.* An overly inquisitive or pruriently prying person, especially one who peeps in at windows.

Peeping Tom of Coventry In British legend, a curious tailor who peeped at Lady Godiva during her ride through Coventry and was struck blind.

peep·show (pēp′shō′) *n.* An exhibition of pictures or other objects viewed through a small orifice fitted with a magnifying lens.

peep sight *Mil.* An adjustable plate on the breech of a gun or cannon, having in its center a small orifice through which an aim can be taken with great accuracy by centering the front sight therein.

pee·pul (pē′pəl) See PIPAL.

peer[1] (pir) *v.i.* 1 To look narrowly or searchingly, as in an effort to see clearly. 2 To come partially into view: The sun *peers* over the horizon. 3 *Poetic* To appear. ◆Homophone: *pier.* [Cf. obs. *pear, pere,* aphetic var. of APPEAR]

peer[2] (pir) *n.* 1 An equal, as in natural gifts or in social rank. 2 An equal before the law. 3 A noble; especially, a member of a hereditary legislative body. In the United Kingdom, a duke, marquis, earl, viscount, or baron; also an archbishop or a bishop having a seat in the House of Lords. Until 1922 peers were of three classes: **Peers of the United Kingdom,** all of whom sit in the House of Lords, **Peers of Scotland,** and **Peers of Ireland.** 4 *Obs.* A companion; mate; associate; also, rival. See synonyms under ASSOCIATE. **—House of Peers** *Brit.* The House of Lords. ◆Homophone: *pier.* [<OF *per* <L *par* equal]

peer[3] (pir) *n.* Scot. 1 A pear. 2 A peg top. ◆Homophone: *pier.*

peer·age (pir′ij) *n.* 1 In England, the office or rank of a peer of the realm, or nobleman. 2 Peers collectively; the nobility. 3 A book containing a genealogical list of the nobility.

peer·ess (pir′is) *n.* A woman who holds a title of nobility, either in her own right or by marriage with a peer.

peer·less (pir′lis) *adj.* Of unequaled excellence. **—peer′less·ly** *adv.* **—peer′less·ness** *n.*

peer of the blood royal A member of the royal family who is entitled to sit as a member of the House of Lords.

peer of the realm One of the lords of Parliament.

peer·y (pir′ē) *n. pl.* **perr·ies** *Scot.* A child's top spun with a string. Also **peer′ie.**

pees·weep (pēz′wēp′) *n. Scot.* The pewit or apwing.

peet·weet (pēt′wēt) *n.* The spotted sandpiper. [Imit.]

peeve (pēv) *v.t.* **peeved, peev·ing** *Colloq.* To make peevish. *—n. Colloq.* A complaint; grievance. [Back formation <PEEVISH]

peeved (pēvd) *adj.* Vexed; discontented; disagreeable.

pee·vish (pē′vish) *adj.* 1 Irritable or querulous; fretful; cross. 2 Showing or marked by petulant discontent and vexation. See synonyms under FRETFUL. [ME *pevische;* origin unknown] **—pee′vish·ly** *adv.* **—pee′vish·ness** *n.*

pee·wee (pē′wē) *n.* 1 The pewee. 2 *Colloq.* Anything or anyone especially small or diminutive. *—adj.* Tiny; insignificant. [Prob. <Algonquian (Massachuset) *pewe* little]

peg (peg) *n.* 1 A wooden pin used for fastening articles together or for holding fast the end of a string and adjusting its tension in a musical instrument. 2 A projecting wooden pin upon which something may be fastened or hung, or which may serve to mark a boundary. 3 Hence, a reason or excuse for an action: a *peg* to hang an argument upon. 4 A degree or step, as in rank or estimation. 5 *Brit.* A drink of brandy and soda or of whisky and soda. 6 *Colloq.* A leg, often one of wood. **—to take (one) down a peg** To lower the self-esteem of (a person), as by humiliating. *—v.* **pegged, peg·ging** *v.t.* 1 To drive or force a peg into; fasten with pegs. 2 To mark or designate with pegs. 3 To strike or pierce with a peg or sharp instrument. 4 *Colloq.* To throw: to *peg* stones. *—v.i.* 5 To work or strive hard and perseveringly: usually with *away.* 6 In croquet, to hit a peg. 7 In cribbage, etc., to mark the score with pegs. [ME *pegge* <LG; cf. MDu. *pegge*]

Peg (peg), **Peg·gy** (peg′ē) Diminutive of MARGARET.

Peg·a·sus (peg′ə·səs) 1 In Greek mythology, a winged horse, sprung from the blood of Medusa, a blow of whose hoof caused the fountain of poetic inspiration, Hippocrene, to spring from Mount Helicon; hence, poetic inspiration. See BELLEROPHON. 2 *Astron.* A northern constellation. See CONSTELLATION. [<L <Gk. *Pēgasos,* after *pēgai* the springs of Ocean, where Medusa was killed]

peg leg *Colloq.* 1 An artificial leg of rodlike or tapering shape. 2 A person with such a leg.

peg·ma·tite (peg′mə·tīt) *n.* A very coarse-grained granitic rock composed chiefly of orthoclase, quartz, and mica (usually muscovite); graphic granite: often occurs in veins or dikes. [<Gk. *pēgma, -atos* a solid mass + -ITE[1]] **—peg′ma·tit′ic** (-tit′ik) *adj.*

peg-top (peg′top′) *adj.* Having the shape of a peg top: applied especially to trousers wide at the hip and narrow at the ankle.

peg top A child's wooden spinning top, pear-shaped and having a sharp metal peg.

Pe·gu (pe·gōō′) An administrative division of Lower Burma east of the Irrawaddy; 20,223 square miles; capital, Rangoon.

Pe·gu·an (pe·gōō′ən) *n.* Mon.

Peh·le·vi (pā′lə·vē) See PAHLAVI.

pei·gnoir (pān·wär′, pān′wär) n. A loose dressing robe worn by women; a bathrobe; a negligée. [<F <peigner comb <L pectinare < pecten a comb]

Pei Ho (bā′ hō′) The Chinese name for the PAI.

pein (pēn) See PEEN.

pei·no·ther·a·py (pī′nō·ther′ə·pē) n. Med. The treatment of disease by severe fasting and starvation; the hunger cure. [<Gk. peina hunger + THERAPY]

Pei·ping (bā′ping′) A former name for PEKING.

Pei·pus (pī′pəs) A lake on the boundary between Estonia and the U.S.S.R.; 1,356 square miles: Russian Chudskoe. Estonian Peip·si (pāp′sē).

Pei·rai·evs (pē′rē·efs′) The Greek name for PIRAEUS.

Peirce (pûrs), **Charles Sanders**, 1839–1914, U.S. mathematician and logician; founder of philosophical pragmatism.

Peirse (pirs), **Sir Richard Edmund**, born 1892, British air marshal.

Peix·ot·to (pā·shō′tō), **Ernest Clifford**, 1869–1940, U.S. painter and illustrator.

pe·jo·ra·tion (pē′jə·rā′shən, pej′ə-) n. 1 A worsening; deterioration. 2 Ling. A degeneration or lowering in the meaning of a word, as in silly (formerly "blessed"): opposed to melioration.

pe·jo·ra·tive (pē′jə·rā′tiv, pej′ə-, pi·jôr′ə·tiv, -jor′-) adj. Giving a deteriorating effect or meaning, as to the sense of a word. — n. A word expressing depreciation. [<L pejoratus, pp. of pejorare make worse <pejor worse] — pe′jo·ra′tive·ly adv.

Pe·ka·long·an (pə·kä′long′än) An Indonesian port on the north central coast of Java.

pek·an (pek′ən) n. A North American carnivore; the fisher. [<dial. F (Canadian) <Algonquian pékané]

pe·kin (pē′kin′) n. A silk fabric, usually figured or striped. [<F pékin <Pékin Peking, China]

Pe·king (pē′king′, Chinese bā′ping′) A city in northern Hopeh province, the capital of the People's Republic of China; from 1928 to 1949 known as Peiping.

Pe·king·ese (pē′king·ēz′) n. pl. ·ese 1 A native or inhabitant of Peking. 2 The dialect spoken in Peking. 3 (pē′kə·nēz′) A Pekingese dog. — adj. Of or pertaining to Peking. Also Pe′kin·ese′.

Pekingese dog A variety of the Chinese (or Pekingese) pug, with long silky hair, especially upon the ears, diminutive snub nose, and short legs.

Peking lacquer Chinese carved lacquer.

Peking man Paleontol. Sinanthropus.

PEKINGESE DOG
(From 7 to 10 inches high at the shoulder)

pe·koe (pē′kō, Brit. pek′ō) n. A superior kind of black tea, made from the downy tips of the young buds of the tea plant. [<dial. Chinese (Amoy) pek-ho <pek white + ho down]

pel·age (pel′ij) n. The coat or covering of a mammal, as of fur, wool, etc. [<MF <OF peil, pel hair <L pilus]

pe·la·gi·an (pə·lā′jē·ən) adj. Pelagic. — n. A deep-sea animal. [<L pelagius of the sea <Gk. pelagios <pelagos the sea]

Pe·la·gi·an·ism (pə·lā′jē·ən·iz′əm) n. Theol. The body of doctrines held by the followers of Pelagius, who denied original sin, confined grace to forgiveness, and affirmed that man's unaided will is capable of spiritual good. — Pe·la′gi·an n. & adj.

pe·lag·ic (pə·laj′ik) adj. 1 Of, pertaining to, or inhabiting the sea far from land; oceanic. 2 Living on or near the surface of the ocean. 3 Conducted or operating on the open sea: pelagic sealing or sealers. [<L pelagicus <Gk. pelagikos <pelagos the sea]

Pe·la·gie Islands (pə·lä′jē) A Sicilian island group in the Mediterranean between Tunis and Malta; 10 square miles.

Pe·la·gi·us (pə·lā′jē·əs), 360?–420, British monk. See PELAGIANISM.

pel·ar·gon·ic acid Chem. A colorless compound, CH₃(CH₂)₇·COOH, liquid at ordinary temperatures, obtained as an ester from oil of pelargonium: also called nonanoic acid.

pel·ar·go·ni·um (pel′är·gō′nē·əm) n. Any of a large genus (Pelargonium) of strong-scented, ornamental evergreen herbs or shrubs, generally known in cultivation as geraniums, having entire lobed or dissected leaves, and handsome, variously colored flowers. [<NL <Gk. pelargos a stork <pelos blackish + argos shining] — pel·ar·gon′ic (-gon′ik) adj.

Pe·las·gi (pə·laz′jī) n. pl. A primitive, seafaring people who inhabited the coasts of Greece, Asia Minor, Crete, Thrace, etc.: mentioned by ancient Greek writers as the pre-Greek inhabitants of the eastern Mediterranean region. Also Pe·las′gi·ans. — Pe·las′gi·an adj. & n. — Pe·las′gic adj.

Pe·le (pā′lā) In Polynesian mythology, the goddess of volcanoes.

Pe·lée (pə·lā′), **Mont** A volcano in northern Martinique; 4,429 feet; last eruption, 1902.

pel·er·ine (pel′ə·rēn′) n. A waist-length cape worn by women. [<F pèlerine, fem. of pèlerin. See PILGRIM.]

Pe·le's hair (pā′lāz) Volcanic glass drawn out into long, fine threads by ejected driblets of fused lava; capillary volcanic glass. [after PELE]

Pe·leus (pēl′yōōs, pē′lē·əs) In Greek legend, a king of the Myrmidons and father of Achilles.

Pe·lew Islands (pē·lōō′) See PALAU ISLANDS.

pelf (pelf) n. Money; wealth: often implying ill-gotten gains. See synonyms under WEALTH. [<AF peufe, OF pelfre spoil; ult. origin uncertain]

Pe·li·as (pē′lē·əs, pel′ē·əs) In Greek mythology, a son of Poseidon and king of Iolcus; who sent his nephew Jason to get the Golden Fleece: after Jason's return, Medea caused Pelias' death by persuading his daughters to cut their father into little pieces and stew him as a means of restoring his youth.

pel·i·can (pel′i·kən) n. A large, gregarious, fish-eating, web-footed bird (genus Pelecanus) of warm regions, having a distensible membranous pouch on the lower jaw for the temporary storage of fish. [OE pellican <LL pelicanus, pelecanus <Gk. pelekan, ? <pelekys an ax; in ref. to its bill]

Pelican State Nickname of LOUISIANA.

Pel·i·des (pel′ə·dēz) Patronymic of Achilles. See PELEUS.

Pe·li·on (pē′lē·on) A mountain range on the coast of SE Thessaly; highest peak, 5,252 feet. See OSSA.

pe·lisse (pə·lēs′) n. A long outer garment or cloak: originally one of fur or lined with fur. [<F <Med. L pellicia <L, a garment of skins or fur <pellis skin]

pe·lite (pē′līt) n. A sedimentary rock composed of clay, quartz particles, or rock flour: also called argillite. [<Gk. pēlos clay + -ITE¹] — pe·lit·ic (pi·lit′ik) adj.

Pel·la (pel′ə) A city of ancient Greece; birthplace of Alexander the Great and capital of Macedonia.

pel·la·gra (pə·lā′grə, -lag′rə) n. Pathol. A disease characterized by gastric disturbance, skin eruptions, and nervous derangement: endemic in many parts of the world, and known to be caused by nutritional deficiencies. [<NL prob. <Ital. pelle agra rough skin; ? infl. by Gk. -agra <agra a seizure, as in podagra gout, lit., a seizure in the feet] — pel·la′grous adj.

pel·la·grin (pə·lā′grin, -lag′rin) n. A sufferer from pellagra.

Pel·le·as (pel′ē·əs), **Sir** In Arthurian legend, one of the Knights of the Round Table.

pel·let (pel′it) n. 1 A small round ball or imitation projectile, as of wax, paper, bread, etc. 2 A small shot. 3 A very small pill. 4 A slingstone; also, a bullet; cannonball. — v.t. 1 To make into pellets. 2 To strike with pellets. [<OF pelote a ball <Med. L pelota, pilota <L pila]

pel·le·tier·ine (pel′ə·tir′in, -ēn) n. Chem. A sirupy liquid alkaloid, C₈H₁₅ON, from the roots of the pomegranate tree: its salts are powerful anthelminthics. [after Bertrand Pelletier, 1761–1797, French chemist]

pel·li·cle (pel′i·kəl) n. A thin skin, film, or layer. [<L pellicula, dim. of pellis skin] — pel·lic·u·lar (pə·lik′yə·lər) adj.

pel·li·to·ry (pel′ə·tôr′ē, -tō′rē) n. pl. ·ries Any of various diffuse or tufted weedlike herbs of the nettle family (genus Parietaria); especially, the European wall pellitory (P. officinalis), which grows on old walls. [Alter. of earlier paretarie <AF paritarie <L (herba) parietaria wall (plant) <parietarius of a wall <paries, -etis a wall]

pellitory of Spain A perennial herb (Anacyclus pyrethrum) of the composite family, with procumbent stems, dissected leaves, and white flowers: cultivated for its pungent roots, and used in medicine.

pell–mell (pel′mel′) adv. 1 In a confused or promiscuous way or manner; indiscriminately; higgledy-piggledy. 2 With a headlong rush. — adj. Devoid of order or method. — n. A confused crowd or mixture; a medley; disorder. Also pell′mell′. [<F pêle-mêle <OF pesle-mesle, varied reduplication <mesler mix]

pel·lo·tine (pel′ə·tēn, -tin) n. Chem. A white crystalline alkaloid, C₁₃H₁₉O₃N, from the mescal cactus: used as a sedative. [< pellotte, var. of PEYOTE, + -INE²]

pel·lu·cid (pə·lōō′sid) adj. 1 Permitting to a certain extent the passage of light; translucent; limpid. 2 Transparent; clear; understandable: a pellucid style. See synonyms under CLEAR, TRANSPARENT. [<L pellucidus <perlucere <per- through + lucere shine] — pel·lu′cid·ly adv. — pel·lu′cid·ness, pel·lu·cid·i·ty (pel′ōō·sid′ə·tē) n.

Pel·ly River (pel′ē) A river in south central Yukon, Canada, flowing 330 miles NW to a confluence with the Lewes River, forming the Yukon River.

pe·lon (pē′lōn) adj. Hairless: said of animals. [<Am. Sp. <Sp. pelón bald]

pelon dog The Mexican hairless dog.

pel·o·phyte (pel′ō·fīt) n. A plant subsisting in clayey soil. [<Gk. pēlos clay + -PHYTE]

Pe·lop·i·das (pə·lop′i·dəs), died 364 B.C., Theban general.

Pel·o·pon·ne·sian (pel′ə·pə·nē′shən, -zhən) adj. Of or pertaining to the Peloponnesus. — n. A native or inhabitant of the Peloponnesus.

Peloponnesian War See table under WAR.

Pel·o·pon·ne·sus (pel′ə·pə·nē′səs) The southern peninsula of Greece between the Ionian and Aegean seas; 8,400 square miles: formerly Morea. Also Pel′o·pon·nese′. Greek Pel′o·pon·ne′sos.

Pe·lops (pē′lops) In Greek mythology, the son of Tantalus who was restored to life by Demeter after his father had killed him and served his flesh to the gods.

pe·lo·ri·a (pə·lôr′ē·ə, -lō′rē·ə) n. Bot. Reversion of an irregular flower form, by abnormal development of complementary irregularities or by the loss of the irregular parts. Also pel·o·rism (pel′ə·riz′əm). [<NL <Gk. pelōros monstrous <pelōr a monster] — pe·lo′ri·ate, pe·lor·ic (pə·lôr′ik, -lor′-) adj.

pe·lo·rus (pə·lôr′əs, -lō′rəs) n. 1 Aeron. A circular plate having its movable rim graduated in degrees: used to determine the actual or relative bearings of objects. 2 Nav. An instrument for correcting errors in the compass by stellar observations. [after Pelorus, said to have been Hannibal's pilot]

pe·lo·ta (pe·lō′tə) n. A game similar to handball, popular among Basques, Spaniards, and Spanish Americans: it is played in a court with a hard rubber ball and a long wickerwork gauntlet (cesta) attached to the player's wrist. See JAI ALAI. [<Sp., lit., a ball, aug. of pella <L pila]

Pe·lo·tas (pə·lō′təs) A port in southern Río Grande do Sul state, Brazil.

pelt¹ (pelt) n. 1 An undressed fur skin; raw hide; also, a garment made of skin. 2 Slang The human skin. [Prob. back formation <AF pelterie. See PELTRY.]

pelt² (pelt) v.t. 1 To strike repeatedly with or as with missiles or blows. 2 To throw or hurl

---

WHITE PELICAN
(From 4 to 5 feet high according to species)

(missiles). 3 To assail with words. — *v.i.* 4 To beat or descend with violence. 5 To move rapidly; hurry. — *n.* 1 A blow, as one given by something thrown. 2 A steady or swift pace: especially in the expression **full pelt.** [ME *pelten,* ? var. of *pulten* thrust <L *pultare,* freq. of *pellere* beat, drive] — **pelt′er** *n.*

pel·ta (pel′tə) *n.* In ancient Greece, a light, leather-covered shield. [<Gk. *peltē* a shield]

pel·tast (pel′tast) *n.* In ancient Greece, a soldier who bore a pelta; a lightly armed soldier. [<L *peltasta* <Gk. *peltastēs* < *peltē* a shield]

pel·tate (pel′tāt) *adj.* 1 Shield-shaped. 2 *Bot.* Attached to the stalk at or near the center of the lower surface, as a leaf. Also **pel′tat·ed.** See SCUTATE. [<L *peltatus* armed with a shield <Gk. *peltē* a shield] — **pel′tate·ly** *adv.*

pelt·ry (pel′trē) *n. pl.* **·ries** 1 Pelts collectively. 2 A pelt. 3 A place for keeping or storing pelts. [<AF *pelterie* <OF *peletier* a furrier < *pel* a skin <L *pellis*]

pel·vic (pel′vik) *adj.* Of or pertaining to the pelvis.

pelvic arch *Anat.* That part of the skeleton in vertebrates to which the hind limbs (in man, the lower limbs) are attached. Also **pelvic girdle.**

pel·vim·e·ter (pel·vim′ə·tər) *n. Med.* An instrument used in pelvimetry. [<PELVI(S) + -METER]

pel·vim·e·try (pel·vim′ə·trē) *n. Med.* The measurement of the size and capacity of the pelvis, especially by X-rays prior to childbirth. — **pel·vi·met·ric** (pel′vi·met′rik) *adj.*

pel·vi·ra·di·og·ra·phy (pel′vi·rā′dē·og′rə·fē) *n. Med.* X-ray examination of the pelvis. [<PELVI(S) + RADIOGRAPHY]

pel·vis (pel′vis) *n. pl.* **·ves** (-vēz) 1 A basin or basinlike structure. 2 *Anat.* **a** The part of the skeleton that forms a bony girdle joining the lower or hind limbs to the body: composed, in man, of two hip bones and the sacrum. **b** The hollow interior portion of the kidney, into which the uriniferous tubules empty: formed by the expanded part of the ureter. [<NL <L, a basin]

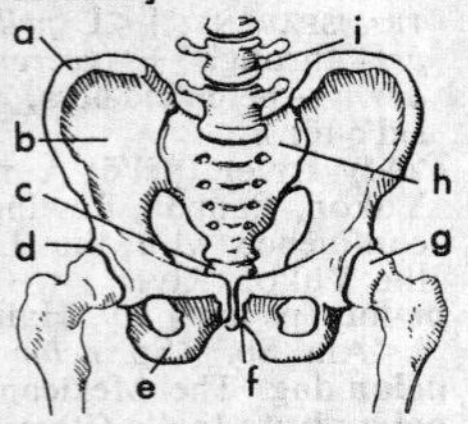

HUMAN PELVIS
a. Crest of ilium.
b. Ilium.
c. Coccyx.
d. Socket of thigh bone.
e. Ischium.
f. Pubic symphysis.
g. Head of femur.
h. Sacrum.
i. Lumbar vertebrae.

Pem·ba (pem′bə) An island in the Indian Ocean off the NE coast of Tanganyika, in Tanzania; 380 square miles.

Pem·broke (pem′brŏŏk) 1 A maritime county of SW Wales; 614 square miles: also **Pem′broke·shire** (-shir). 2 Its county town.

pem·mi·can (pem′ə·kən) *n.* 1 Lean venison cut into strips, dried, pounded into paste with fat and a few berries, and pressed into cakes. 2 A similar concentrated and nutritious food made from beef and dried fruits: used by Arctic explorers, etc. Also **pem′i·can.** [< Algonquian (Cree) *pimekan* < *pime* fat]

pem·phi·gus (pem′fə·gəs, pem·fī′-) *n. Pathol.* A skin disease characterized by watery vesicles successively formed on various parts of the body; water blebs; bladdery fever. Also **pem′phix** (-fiks). [<NL <Gk. *pemphix, -igos* a breath, a pustule]

pen[1] (pen) *n.* 1 An instrument for writing with a fluid ink: formerly made of a quill, now usually of metal and fitted to a holder; by extension, pen and holder together. 2 Quality of penmanship or of composition. 3 A writer; also, the profession of writing. 4 *Bot.* The midrib of a leaf. 5 *Zool.* The internal shell of a cuttlefish. 6 *Ornithol.* A feather; quill; also, in the plural, wings. — *v.t.* **penned, pen·ning** To write with a pen; indite. [<OF *penne* a pen, a feather <LL *penna* <L, a feather] — **pen′ner** *n.*

pen[2] (pen) *n.* 1 A small enclosure, as for pigs; also, the animals contained in a pen collectively. 2 Any small place of confinement, as in a police court. 3 *Slang* A penitentiary. — *v.t.* **penned** or **pent, pen·ning** To enclose in or as in a pen; confine. [OE *penn*]

pen[3] (pen) *n.* A female swan. [Origin unknown]

pe·nal (pē′nəl) *adj.* 1 Pertaining to punishment or its means or place. 2 Liable, or rendering liable, to punishment. 3 Enacting or prescribing punishment. [<OF *penal* <L *penalis, poenalis* < *poena* a penalty <Gk. *poinē* a fine]

penal code See under CODE.

pe·nal·ize (pē′nəl·īz, pen′əl-) *v.t.* **·ized, ·iz·ing** 1 To subject to a penalty, as for a violation. 2 To declare, as an action, subject to a penalty. Also *Brit.* **pe′nal·ise.** — **pe′nal·i·za′tion** *n.*

pen·al·ty (pen′əl·tē) *n. pl.* **·ties** 1 The consequences, as suffering, detriment, etc., that follow the transgression of laws. 2 Judicial punishment for crime or violation of the law. 3 *Law* **a** A sum of money fixed by a statute as a fine or mulct for a violation of its provisions. **b** A sum of money paid and stipulated to be forfeited in case of the non-performance of the conditions of a contract. 4 A handicap imposed for a violation of rules or regulations of a game. [<Med. L *poenalitas, -tatis* <L *poenalis* PENAL]

pen·ance (pen′əns) *n.* 1 *Eccl.* A sacramental rite involving contrition, confession to a priest, the acceptance of penalties, and absolution. 2 A feeling of sorrow for sin or fault, evinced by some outward act; repentance. 3 A penalty, suffering, mortification, or act of piety, imposed or voluntarily undertaken as an atonement or outward sign of repentance for sin. 4 The performance of a penitential act or acts. — **to do penance** To perform an act or acts of penance; to repent of one's sins. — *v.t.* **pen·anced, pen·anc·ing** To impose a penance upon. [<OF <L *paenitentia.* Doublet of PENITENCE.]

pe·nang (pē·nang′) *n.* A heavy cotton fabric resembling percale. [? from *Penang*]

Pe·nang (pē′nang′), **Settlement of** A State of Malaya in the NW part, formerly under British protection; 400 square miles; capital, George Town; comprising **Penang Island** (formerly *Prince of Wales Island*); 110 square miles; and Province Wellesley on the mainland; 290 square miles.

Pe·na·tes (pə·nā′tēz) In the ancient Roman religion, the household gods: associated with the *Lares.* [<L, prob. akin to *penus* the inmost part of the temple of Vesta]

pence (pens) Plural of PENNY.

pen·cel (pen′səl) *n.* A small pennon or streamer; a pennoncel: also spelled *pensil, pensile.* ◆ Homophone: *pencil.* [<AF, alter. of *penoncel.* See PENNONCEL.]

pen·chant (pen′chənt, *Fr.* päṅ·shäṅ′) *n.* A strong leaning or inclination in favor of something. [<F, orig. ppr. of *pencher* incline, ult. <L *pendere* hang]

pen·cil (pen′səl) *n.* 1 A long, pointed strip of graphite, colored chalk, slate, etc., often encased in wood: used for writing or drawing. 2 A small, finely pointed paint brush: also **hair pencil.** 3 A set of rays diverging from or converging upon a given point. 4 Skill, as in drawing or painting; the painter's art. 5 A small stick of any substance having caustic or styptic properties. 6 An eyebrow pencil. — *v.t.* **·ciled** or **·cilled, ·cil·ing** or **·cil·ling** To mark, write, or draw with or as with a pencil. ◆ Homophone: *pencel.* [<OF *pincel* <L *penicillum* a paint brush, double dim. of *penis* a tail; infl. by *pen*[1]] — **pen′cil·er** or **pen′cil·ler** *n.*

pen·ciled (pen′səld) *adj.* 1 Marked with fine lines, with or as if with a finely pointed pencil. 2 Having pencils, or lines or rays. Also **pen′cilled.**

pend (pend) *v.i.* 1 To await or be in process of adjustment or settlement. 2 *Dial.* To hang; depend. [<MF *pendre* hang <L *pendere*]

pen·dant (pen′dənt) *n.* 1 Anything that hangs or depends from something else, either for ornament or for use. 2 Something attached to another thing as an ending; an appendix. 3 A parallel; one of a pair. 4 *Archit.* A hanging ornament, as a long boss or knot, particularly in late Perpendicular work, on ceilings, roofs, etc. 5 The stem of a watchcase and the ring by which it is attached to a chain. 6 A suspended chandelier; also, an electrical fitting hanging from a ceiling, lamp, chandelier, etc., by which to switch on and off a light. Also spelled *pendent.* — *adj.* Pendent. [<OF, orig. ppr. of *pendre.* See PEND.]

pen·dent (pen′dənt) *adj.* 1 Hanging loosely; drooping downward; suspended. 2 Projecting or overhanging. 3 Undetermined; pending; incomplete. Also spelled *pendant.* — *n.* Pendant. [Var. of PENDANT, refashioned after L] — **pen′dent·ly** *adv.*

pen·den·te li·te (pen·den′tē lī′tē) *Latin* Pending or during suit.

pen·den·tive (pen·den′tiv) *n. Archit.* 1 The vaulting that serves to connect an angle of a square area enclosed by four arches with a dome that rests upon the arches. 2 The principle or system of such vaulting and use of the dome. [<MF *pendentif* <L *pendens, -entis,* ppr. of *pendere* hang]

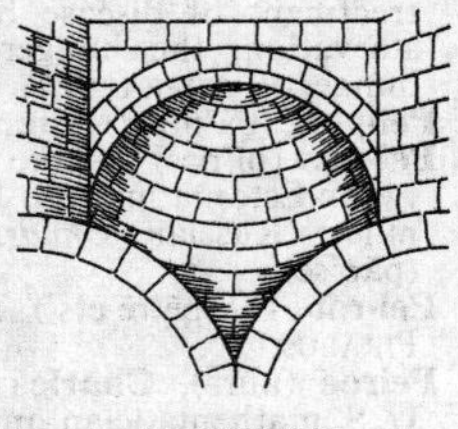

PENDENTIVE

pend·ing (pen′ding) *adj.* 1 Remaining unfinished or undecided. 2 Imminent; impending. — *prep.* 1 During the continuance of. 2 Awaiting; until: The court adjourned *pending* the jury's verdict.

pen·drag·on (pen·drag′ən) *n.* A supreme head, ruler, or chief: in early Britain, a title conferred in times of danger. [<Welsh, a chief leader in war < *pen* head + *dragon* a war chief <L *draco, -onis,* orig. a dragon (used as a military standard)] — **pen·drag′on·ish** *adj.* — **pen·drag′on·ship** *n.*

pen·du·lous (pen′jŏŏ·ləs) *adj.* Hanging, especially so as to swing. [<L *pendulus* hanging < *pendere* hang] — **pen′du·lous·ly** *adv.* — **pen′du·lous·ness** *n.*

pen·du·lum (pen′jŏŏ·ləm, -də-) *n.* 1 A body suspended from a fixed point, and free to swing to and fro. 2 Such a device, consisting of rod and bob, and serving, by oscillation under the forces of gravity plus momentum, to regulate the rate of running of a clock. [<NL <L, neut. of *pendulus.* See PENDULOUS.]

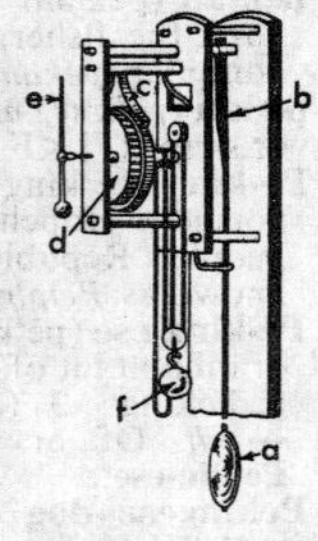

PENDULUM
a. Bob (adjustable on rod)
b. Rod.
c. Pallets.
d. Escape wheel.
e. Second hand.
f. Weight.

Pe·nel·o·pe (pə·nel′ə·pē) A feminine personal name. Also *Fr.* **Pé·né·lope** (pā·nā·lōp′). [<Gk., a weaver] — **Penelope** In the *Odyssey,* the faithful wife of Odysseus, who, during her husband's absence after the fall of Troy, kept her many suitors in check under pretext of having to complete a shroud she was weaving for Laertes, her father-in-law: the moment of her choice among them was indefinitely postponed, since every night she unraveled all the work she had done during the previous day. See TELEGONUS.

pe·ne·plain (pē′nə·plān′, pē′nə·plān′) *n. Geol.* A region of faint or low relief, the penultimate result of long-continued action of denudation on a once larger land mass, whose ultimate result is a base-leveled plain. Also **pe′ne·plane′.** [<L *paene* almost + PLAIN]

pen·e·tra·li·a (pen′ə·trā′lē·ə) *n. pl.* 1 The inmost parts of anything, but especially of a house or temple; a sanctuary; shrine. 2 Secret things. [<L, orig. neut. pl. of *penetralis* innermost < *penetrare.* See PENETRATE.]

pen·e·trance (pen′ə·trəns) *n. Genetics* A measure of the frequency with which a given gene will show its effects, expressed as a percentage of the total number of cases observed. [<L *penetrans, -antis,* ppr. of *penetrare.* See PENETRATE.]

pen·e·trate (pen′ə·trāt) *v.* **·trat·ed, ·trat·ing** *v.t.* 1 To force a way into or through; pierce; enter. 2 To spread or diffuse itself throughout; permeate. 3 To perceive the meaning of; understand. 4 To affect or move profoundly. — *v.i.* 5 To enter or pass through something. 6 To have effect on the mind or emotions. See synonyms under PIERCE. [<L *penetratus* < *penetrare* put within < *penitus* inside] — **pen′e·tra·ble** (-trə·bəl) *adj.* — **pen′e·tra·bil′i·ty** *n.* — **pen′e·trant** *adj.* & *n.*

pen·e·trat·ing (pen′ə·trā′ting) *adj.* Tending or having power to penetrate; acute; discerning.

See synonyms under ACUTE, ASTUTE, KNOWING, SHARP. —**pen′e·trat′ing·ly** *adv.* —**pen′e·trat′ing·ness** *n.*

pen·e·tra·tion (pen′ə·trā′shən) *n.* **1** The act or power of penetrating physically. **2** Ability to penetrate mentally; acuteness; sagacity. **3** The depth to which a bullet or other projectile sinks in a target. See synonyms under ENTRANCE[1].

pen·e·tra·tive (pen′ə·trā′tiv) *adj.* Tending or having power to penetrate, physically or mentally; insinuating and pervasive; pungent: a *penetrative* odor; acute; discerning: *penetrative* wisdom. See synonyms under ASTUTE. —**pen′e·tra′tive·ly** *adv.* —**pen′e·tra′tive·ness** *n.*

pen·e·trom·e·ter (pen′ə·trom′ə·tər) *n.* **1** An instrument for indicating the quality and measuring the strength of X-rays. **2** A device for testing the hardness of relatively plastic substances under given conditions. [<L *penetrare* PENETRATE + -METER]

Pe·ne·us (pē·nē′əs) The chief river of Thessaly, Greece, flowing 135 miles SE to the Aegean: formerly *Salambria. Greek* **Pi·nei′os.**

Peng·hu Islands (pung′hōō′) An island group in Formosa Strait, comprising a district of the Chinese province of Taiwan; 49 square miles: formerly *Pescadores.*

pen·gö (pen′gœ′) *n. pl.* **·gö** or **·gös** A former monetary unit of Hungary; a coin equivalent to 100 filler.

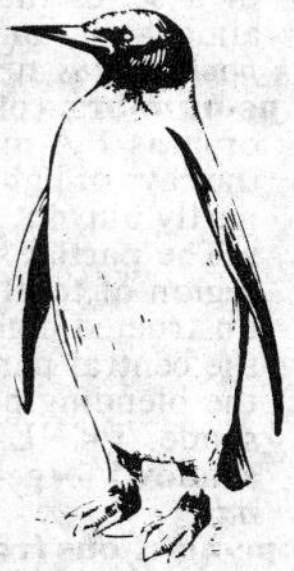

EMPEROR PENGUIN
(From 3 to 3 1/2 feet tall: the largest of the flightless, swimming birds)

pen·guin (pen′gwin, peng′-) *n.* **1** A web-footed, flightless, aquatic bird (genus *Spheniscus*) of the southern hemisphere, with flipperlike wings, short legs, and plantigrade feet. **2** Originally, the great auk. **3** *Aeron.* An airplane with an engine of low motive power, so as to be incapable of flight: used in the early training of aviators. [Cf. F *pingouin, penguyn* the great auk]

pen·hold·er (pen′hōl′dər) *n.* A handle with a device for inserting a metallic pen; also, a rack for pens.

pen·i·cil·late (pen′ə·sil′it, -āt) *adj.* **1** Pencil-shaped. **2** *Biol.* Bordered or tufted with fine hairs resembling a hair pencil. Also **pen′i·cil′li·form.** [<L *penicillus* a pencil + -ATE[1]] —**pen′i·cil′late·ly** *adv.* —**pen′i·cil·la′tion** (-si·lā′shən) *n.*

pen·i·cil·lin (pen′ə·sil′in) *n.* A powerful antibacterial substance found in the mold fungus *Penicillium*: prepared in several forms for the treatment of a wide variety of infective conditions. [<PENICILL(IUM) + -IN]

pen·i·cil·li·um (pen′ə·sil′ē·əm) *n. pl.* **·li·a** (-ē·ə) Any member of a genus *(Penicillium)* of ascomycetous fungi characterized by feltlike masses of tubular hyphae, and growing on decaying fruits, ripening cheese, etc. *P. notatum* is the principal source of penicillin. [<NL <L *penicillus* a pencil; so called because of resemblance of its tufts to small paint brushes]

pe·nin·su·la (pə·nin′sə·lə, -syə-) *n.* A piece of land almost surrounded by water, and connected with the mainland by an isthmus. [<L *paeninsula* <*paene* almost + *insula* an island] —**pe·nin′su·lar** *adj.*

Peninsula, the 1 The Iberian Peninsula, comprising Spain and Portugal. **2** The region between the James and York rivers in SE Virginia; scene of several battles of the Civil War, 1862.

pe·nin·su·lar·i·ty (pə·nin′sə·lar′ə·tē, -syə-) *n.* The state or quality of being a peninsula; hence, narrowness of views; provincialism; bigotry. Compare INSULARITY.

Peninsula State A nickname for FLORIDA.

pe·nis (pē′nis) *n. pl.* **·nes** (-nēz) The male copulatory organ. [<L, orig. a tail] —**pe′ni·al** (-nē·əl), **pe′nile** (-nil, -nīl) *adj.*

pen·i·tence (pen′ə·təns) *n.* The state of being penitent; sorrow for sin, with desire to amend and atone; contrition. See synonyms under CONTRITION. [<OF *penitence* <L *paenitentia* <*paenitens,* ppr. of *paenitare* repent. Doublet of PENANCE.]

pen·i·tent (pen′ə·tənt) *adj.* Affected by a sense of one's own guilt, and resolved on amendment; repentant; contrite. —*n.* **1** One who is penitent. **2** One who confesses his sins to a priest and submits himself to the penance prescribed. —**pen′i·tent·ly** *adv.*

pen·i·ten·tial (pen′ə·ten′shəl) *adj.* **1** Pertaining to or expressing penitence. **2** Pertaining to penance or punishment. —*n.* **1** *Eccl.* A book of rules relating to penance and the reconciliation of penitents. **2** A penitent. —**pen′i·ten′tial·ly** *adv.*

pen·i·ten·tia·ry (pen′ə·ten′shər·ē) *n. pl.* **·ries 1** A prison, especially one operated by a state or government as a place of confinement and correction for those convicted of serious crimes. **2** One who prescribes or superintends penances; also, something that has to do with penances; specifically, in the Roman Catholic Church, an office, having at its head a cardinal (called the **Grand Penitentiary**), for deciding questions of conscience, absolution, special dispensation, etc. —*adj.* **1** Pertaining to penance. **2** Relating to or used for the punishment and discipline of criminals. **3** Rendering the offender liable to imprisonment in a penitentiary. [<Med. L *poenitentiarius* <L *poenitentia* PENITENCE]

Pen·ki (bun′chē′) A city in west central Liaotung province, Manchuria.

pen·knife (pen′nīf′) *n. pl.* **·knives** (-nīvz′) A small pocket knife: formerly used for making or sharpening quill pens.

pen·man (pen′mən) *n. pl.* **·men** (-mən) **1** A person considered with regard to his handwriting; also, a teacher of penmanship, or one skilled in penmanship. **2** A writer.

pen·man·ship (pen′mən·ship) *n.* **1** The art of writing. **2** Handwriting; calligraphy.

Penn (pen), **William,** 1644–1718, English Quaker; founder of Pennsylvania.

pen·na (pen′ə) *n. pl.* **·nae** (-ē) *Ornithol.* A feather; plume; especially, a quill feather of wing or tail. [<NL <L, a feather] —**pen·na·ceous** (pə·nā′shəs) *adj.*

pen name An author's assumed name; pseudonym; nom de plume.

pen·nant (pen′ənt) *n.* **1** A long, narrow flag displayed on a commissioned naval vessel; also, a triangular flag flown as a signal. **2** A small flag peculiar in shape, color or design, flown during a public function. **3** A flag awarded to the winners in some sports leagues; also, the championship thus symbolized. **4** *Music* The hook distinguishing notes shorter than quarter notes. [<PENNON; infl. by PENDANT]

pen·nate (pen′āt) *adj.* Having wings or feathers: usually in composition: *longipennate.* Also **pen′nat·ed.** [<L *pennatus* winged <*penna* a feather]

Pen·nell (pen′əl), **Joseph,** 1857–1926, U.S. etcher and illustrator.

pen·ni·less (pen′i·lis) *adj.* Being without even a penny; poverty-stricken.

Pen·nine Alps (pen′in, -in) A SW division of the Alps on the Swiss-Italian border; highest peak, 15,203 feet.

Pen·nine Chain (pen′in, -īn) A long hill range, called "the backbone of England," extending south from the Cheviot Hills on the Scottish border to Derbyshire and Staffordshire; highest point, 2,930 feet.

pen·non (pen′ən) *n.* **1** A small, pointed or swallow-tailed flag, borne by medieval knights on their lances and displaying a personal device. **1** A wing. **3** A banner or flag of any sort. [<OF *penon* a streamer, feather of an arrow <L *penna* a feather]

pen·non·cel (pen′ən·sel) *n.* A small, narrow pennon: also spelled *penoncel.* Also **pen′non·celle.** [<OF *penoncel,* dim. of *penon.* See PENNON.]

Penn·syl·va·ni·a (pen′səl·vā′nē·ə, -vān′yə) An eastern State of the United States; 45,333 square miles; capital, Harrisburg; entered the Union Dec. 12, 1787; one of the thirteen original States; nickname, *Keystone State* or *Quaker State*: abbr. PA Official name: *Commonwealth of Pennsylvania.*

Pennsylvania Avenue A principal street of Washington, D.C., which runs in part from the Capitol to the White House.

Penn·syl·va·ni·a-Dutch (pen′səl·vā′nē·ə·duch′, -vān′yə-) *adj.* **1** Pertaining to the Pennsylvania Dutch. **2** Denoting a style of furniture, pottery, etc., made by these people, characterized by carved or gaily colored decorations of flowers, fruits, etc.

Pennsylvania Dutch 1 Descendants of immigrants from the Palatinate, SW Germany, and Switzerland who settled in Pennsylvania in the 17th and 18th centuries. **2** The language spoken by these people: a High German dialect with an admixture of English. Also **Pennsylvania German.**

Penn·syl·va·ni·an (pen′səl·vā′nē·ən, -vān′yən) *adj.* **1** Belonging to or relating to the State of Pennsylvania. **2** *Geol.* Belonging to or denoting a Paleozoic period between the Mississippian and the Permian periods of the Carboniferous. —*n.* **1** A native or inhabitant of Pennsylvania. **2** *Geol.* The Pennsylvanian period or system.

pen·ny (pen′ē) *n. pl.* **pen·nies** or *Brit.* **pence** (pens) **1** In the United States and Canada, a cent. **2** A coin of Great Britain, Ireland, and various members of the Commonwealth of Nations, equivalent to 1/12 shilling. **3** In the United Kingdom, a coin equal in value to 1/100 pound: also *new penny.* **4** Money in general. [OE *penning, penig, pending*]

-penny *combining form* Costing (a specified number of) pennies: formerly designating the cost of nails per hundred, but now denoting their length, beginning at 1 inch for twopenny nails and increasing by quarter-inches up to tenpenny, thereafter irregularly. [<PENNY]

pen·ny-a-line (pen′ē·ə·līn′) *adj.* Cheap; inferior: said of writing.

pen·ny-a-lin·er (pen′ē·ə·lī′nər) *n.* A literary drudge; a hack writer.

penny ante A poker game in which the ante is limited to one cent.

penny dreadful *Brit. Colloq.* A cheap book or magazine containing popular, usually sensational fiction.

pen·ny·roy·al (pen′ē·roi′əl) *n.* **1** A low, erect, branching, strong-scented American herb *(Hedeoma pulegioides)* of the mint family, yielding the oil of pennyroyal used in medicine. **2** A species of European mint *(Mentha pulegium)* resembling the American pennyroyal in taste, odor, and uses. [Alter. of earlier *pulyole ryale* <AF *puliol real* <L *pulegium* fleabane + *regale* royal]

pen·ny·weight (pen′ē·wāt′) *n.* The twentieth part of an ounce in troy weight, or 1.55 grams.

penny wheep *Scot.* Small beer or ale. Also **penny whip.**

pen·ny-wise (pen′ē·wīz′) *adj.* Unduly economical in small matters: usually in the phrase **penny-wise and pound-foolish,** economical in small matters, but wasteful in large ones. —**pen′ny-wis′dom** (-wiz′dəm) *n.*

pen·ny·wort (pen′ē·wûrt′) *n.* Anyone of various plants with round or peltate leaves, as the several species of *Hydrocotyle,* of the parsley family, the navelwort, and the American gentian *(Obolaria virginica),* with funnel-shaped, white, pink, or purple flowers.

pen·ny·worth (pen′ē·wûrth′) *n.* **1** As much as can be bought for a penny. **2** The amount given or received for money paid; a bargain. **3** A small amount; trifle.

Pe·nob·scot (pə·nob′skot) *n.* One of a tribe of North American Indians of the Algonquian confederacy of 1749.

Penobscot River A river in central Maine, flowing 350 miles south to **Penobscot Bay,** an inlet of the Atlantic Ocean.

pe·nol·o·gy (pē·nol′ə·jē) *n.* The science that treats of the punishment and prevention of crime and of the management of prisons and reformatories: also spelled *poenology.* [<L *poena* a penalty + -LOGY] —**pe·no·log·i·cal** (pē′nə·loj′i·kəl) *adj.* —**pe·nol′o·gist** *n.*

pen·on·cel (pen′ən·sel) See PENNONCEL.

pen·point (pen′point′) *n.* The point of a pen; especially, the metal nib for insertion into a holder.

Pen·rhyn (pen′rin) An atoll of the Manihiki group in the South Pacific; 4,000 acres: also *Tongareva.*

Pen·sa·co·la (pen′sə·kō′lə) A port on **Pensacola Bay,** an arm of the Gulf of Mexico in NW Florida; site of a U.S. naval and air base.

pen·se·mon (pen·sē′mən) See PENSTEMON.

pen·sil (pen′sil), **pen·sile** (pen′sil) See PENCEL.

pen·sile (pen′sil) *adj.* **1** Pendent and swaying; pendulous; suspended. **2** Hanging loosely: a *pensile* nest. **3** Constructing pensile nests: said of birds. [<L *pensilis* hanging down < *pensus,* pp. of *pendere* hang] — **pen′·sile·ness, pen·sil′i·ty** *n.*

pen·sion[1] (pen′shən) *n.* **1** A periodical allowance to an individual or his representative on account of some meritorious work or service; especially, an allowance made by a government to a veteran soldier or to his widow or children. **2** *Obs.* A payment; specifically, a payment made to one not a servant to retain his good will, or to a man of science or letters to enable him to carry on his work. See synonyms under SUBSIDY. — *v.t.* **1** To grant a pension to. **2** To dismiss with a pension: with *off.* [<OF <L *pensio, -onis* payment < *pensus,* pp. of *pendere* weigh, pay] — **pen′sion·a·ble** *adj.*

pen·sion[2] (pen′shən, *Fr.* päṅ·syôṅ′) *n. French* A boarding school; also, a boarding house.

pen·sion·ar·y (pen′shən·er′ē) *adj.* **1** Living by means of a pension; pensioned. **2** Consisting of a pension: a *pensionary* provision. — *n. pl.* **·ar·ies 1** A pensioner. **2** A hireling: often used in a contemptuous sense.

pen·sion·er (pen′shən·ər) *n.* **1** One who receives a pension; hence, one who is dependent on the bounty of another. **2** In Cambridge University, England, and Dublin University, Ireland, a student who pays his own expenses: at Oxford University, England, called *commoner.* **3** A boarder, as in a convent or school. **4** *Archaic* One of the gentlemen-at-arms comprising the royal bodyguard within the palace: instituted by Henry VIII. **5** *Obs.* A paid soldier; a mercenary.

pen·sive (pen′siv) *adj.* **1** Engaged in or addicted to serious or quiet reflection; thoughtful with a touch of sadness. **2** Expressive of, suggesting, or causing sad thoughtfulness. [<OF *pensif, pensive* < *penser* think] — **pen′sive·ly** *adv.* — **pen′sive·ness** *n.*

pen·ste·mon (pen·stē′mən) *n.* Any member of a North American genus (*Penstemon*) of perennial or shrubby plants of the figwort family, with opposite leaves and variously colored flowers; the beard tongues: also spelled *pensemon, pentstemon.* [Var. of NL *pentstemon* <Gk. *pente* five + *stēmōn* thread, stamen; so called from the rudimentary fifth stamen of this genus]

pen·stock (pen′stok′) *n.* **1** A conduit from a millrace to a water-wheel gate. **2** A sluice or floodgate, controlling the discharge of water, as from a pond, or of sewage. **3** A fire hydrant. **4** A penholder.

pent (pent) *adj.* Penned up or in; closely confined. [Pp. of *pend,* obs. var. of PEN², *v.*]

penta- *combining form* Five: *pentahedron.* Also, before vowels, **pent-.** [<Gk. *pente* five]

pen·ta·cle (pen′tə·kəl) *n.* **1** A figure composed of five straight lines, making a star that includes a pentagon. **2** In magic, a circle containing certain mystical figures and symbols; a pentagram: also spelled *penticle.* Also **pen·tal·pha** (pen·tal′fə). [<Med. L *pentaculum,* ult. <Gk. *pente* five]

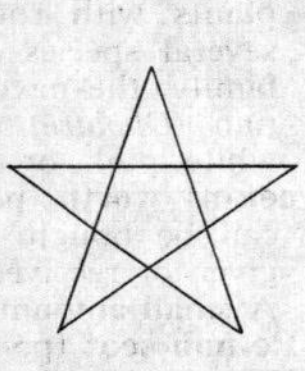

PENTACLE

pen·tad (pen′tad) *n.* **1** The number five; a group of five things. **2** A period of five years. **3** *Chem.* An atom, radical, or element with a combining power of five. — *adj.* Having a combining power of five. [<Gk. *pentas, -ados* a group of five < *pente* five]

pen·ta·dac·tyl (pen′tə·dak′til) *n.* An animal having five fingers or toes. — *adj.* Having five fingers or toes. [<L *pentadactylus* <Gk. *pentadactylos* < *pente* five + *dactylos* a finger] — **pen′ta·dac′ty·lous** *adj.*

pen·ta·gon (pen′tə·gon) *n.* A figure with five angles and five sides. [<L *pentagonum* <Gk. *pentagōnon* < *pente* five + *gonia* an angle] — **pen·tag·o·nal** (pen·tag′ə·nəl) *adj.* — **pen·tag′o·nal·ly** *adv.*

Pentagon, the A five-sided building in Arlington, Virginia, housing the Department of Defense and other military and naval installations and government offices.

pen·ta·gram (pen′tə·gram) *n.* A figure having five points or lobes; specifically, a pentacle. [<Gk. *pentagrammon,* neut. of *pentagrammos* having five lines < *pente* five + *grammē* a line]

pen·ta·he·dron (pen′tə·hē′drən) *n. pl.* **·dra** (-drə) A solid bounded by five plane faces. — **pen′ta·he′dral** *adj.*

pen·tam·er·ous (pen·tam′ər·əs) *adj.* **1** Composed of or having five similar parts. **2** *Bot.* Five-parted, as a corolla. Also **pen·tam′er·al.**

pen·tam·e·ter (pen·tam′ə·tər) *n.* **1** A line of verse of five metrical feet; especially, English iambic pentameter. **2** Verse comprised of pentameters; heroic verse. **3** In classical prosody, the second line of an elegiac distich: a hexameter with third and sixth feet lacking one long syllable. [<L <Gk. *pentametros* (a verse) of five measures < *pente* five + *metron* a measure]

pen·tane (pen′tān) *n. Chem.* Any one of three isomeric, volatile, liquid hydrocarbons of the alkane series, C_5H_{12}, two of which are contained in petroleum and similar compounds. They differ from one another in behavior with reagents.

pentane lamp A lamp burning pentane under standardized conditions, and used in photometric work: also called *Harcourt lamp.*

Pen·tap·o·lis (pen·tap′ə·lis) A name for any of several groups of five ancient cities in Italy, North Africa, and Asia Minor; the most important was that of the chief cities of Cyrenaica: Apollonia, Arsinoë, Berenice, Cyrene, and Ptolemaïs.

pen·tar·chy (pen′tär·kē) *n. pl.* **·chies 1** A government administered by five joint rulers; also, a group of five such rulers. **2** An association of five kingdoms, each ruled separately. [<Gk. *pentarchia* < *pente* five + *archein* rule] — **pen·tar′chi·cal** *adj.*

pen·ta·stich (pen′tə·stik) *n.* A stanza of five lines, or a poem containing five lines. [<NL *pentastichus* <Gk. *pentastichos* of five lines < *pente* five + *stichos* a row, line]

pen·ta·style (pen′tə·stīl) *Archit. adj.* Having five columns in front. — *n.* A pentastyle portico or other edifice. [<PENTA- + Gk. *stylos* a pillar]

Pen·ta·teuch (pen′tə·to͞ok, -tyo͞ok) *n.* The first five books of the Bible taken collectively. [<LL *pentateuchus* <Gk. *pentateuchos* (*biblos*) (the book) of five books < *pente* five + *teuchos* a book, orig. an implement, vessel] — **Pen′ta·teuch′al** *adj.*

pen·tath·lon (pen·tath′lən) *n.* **1** In ancient Greece, an athletic contest of five events — leaping, running, wrestling, throwing the discus, and hurling the spear (earlier, boxing) — that occurred all on the same day between the same contestants. **2** In the modern Olympic games, a contest comprising a 200-meter running race, a 1,500-meter running race, throwing the discus, throwing the javelin, and a running broad jump. [<Gk. < *pente* five + *athlon* a contest] — **pen·tath′lete** (-lēt) *n.* — **pen·tath′lic** *adj.*

pen·ta·va·lent (pen′tə·vā′lənt, pen·tav′ə-) *adj. Chem.* Having a valence of five. Also *quinquevalent.* [<PENTA- + L *valens, -entis,* ppr. of *valere* be strong, have power]

Pen·te·cost (pen′tə·kôst, -kost) *n.* **1** A Jewish festival occurring fifty days after the Passover; Shabuoth. **2** The feast of Whitsunday, commemorating the descent of the Holy Ghost upon the apostles on the Jewish Pentecost. *Acts* ii. [<LL *pentecoste* <Gk. *pentēkostē* (*hēmera*) the fiftieth (day) < *pentēkonta* fifty] — **pen′te·cos′tal** *adj.*

Pen·tel·i·kon (pen·tel′i·kon) A mountain NW of Athens, Greece; 3,640 feet. Also **Pen·del′·i·kon** (-del′i·kon), *Latin* **Pen·tel′i·cus** (-tel′i·kəs).

Pen·the·si·le·a (pen′thə·si·lē′ə) In Greek legend, a queen of the Amazons who aided the Trojans against the Greeks and was killed by Achilles.

pent·house (pent′hous′) *n.* **1** An apartment or dwelling on the roof of a building. **2** A shed or roof with a single slope affixed to the wall of another building. **3** A small building, generally one-storied, adjoined to the wall of another building; an annex. **4** A canopy or awning projecting above a doorway or window. [Alter. of *pentice,* ME *pentis,* aphetic form of OF *apentis, apendis* <LL *appendicium,* lit., an appendage <L *appendere* APPEND]

pen·ti·cle (pen′ti·kəl) See PENTACLE (def. 2).

pen·tom·ic (pen·tom′ik) *adj.* Referring to a U. S. Army division designed primarily for use in nuclear warfare, having as its basic elements five self-contained battle groups of high mobility, supported by atomic weapons. [<Gk. *pente* five + (AT)OMIC]

pen·to·san (pen′tə·san) *n. Biochem.* One of a group of polysaccharides, found in foods and plant juices, which yield pentoses on hydrolysis. [<PENTOS(E) + -AN]

pen·tose (pen′tōs) *n. Biochem.* Any of an unfermentable class of simple sugars derived from woods, gums, fruits, and some animal tissues, and having five carbon atoms in the molecule. [<Gk. *pent*(*e*) five + -OSE²]

pent·ste·mon (pent·stē′mən) See PENSTEMON.

pent-up (pent′up′) *adj.* Confined; repressed: *pent-up* emotions.

pe·nu·che (pə·no͞o′chē), **pe·nu·chi** See PANOCHA.

pe·nuch·le (pē′nuk·əl), **pe·nuck·le** See PINOCHLE.

pe·nult (pē′nult, pi·nult′) *n.* The syllable next to the last in a word. Also **pe·nul·ti·ma** (pi·nul′tə·mə). [Short for *penultima* <L *paenultima* (*syllaba*) next to the last (syllable) < *paene* almost + *ultimus* last]

pe·nul·ti·mate (pi·nul′tə·mit) *adj.* **1** Being the last but one. **2** Of or belonging to the last syllable but one. — *n.* A syllable or member of a series that is last but one. [<L *paene* almost + ULTIMATE, on analogy with L *paenultimus* next to the last]

pe·num·bra (pi·num′brə) *n. pl.* **·brae** (-brē) or **·bras 1** A margin of a shadow within which the rays of light from an illuminating body are partly but not wholly intercepted. **2** *Astron.* **a** The partial shadow between the umbra, or region of total eclipse, and the region of unobstructed light. **b** The dark fringe around the central part of a sunspot. **3** In painting, the blending point, or line between light and shade. [<NL <L *paene* almost + *umbra* a shadow] — **pe·num′bral, pe·num′brous** (-brəs) *adj.*

pe·nu·ri·ous (pə·no͝or′ē·əs, -nyo͝or′-) *adj.* **1** Excessively sparing or saving in the use of money; parsimonious. **2** Affording or yielding little; scanty. See synonyms under AVARICIOUS. — **pe·nu′ri·ous·ly** *adv.* — **pe·nu′ri·ous·ness** *n.*

pen·u·ry (pen′yə·rē) *n.* Extreme poverty or want. See synonyms under POVERTY. [<OF *penurie* <L *penuria, paenuria* want]

Pe·nu·ti·an (pə·no͞o′tē·ən, -shən) *n.* A postulated family of northwestern North American Indian languages, including the Chinook and Shahaptian linguistic stocks.

Pen·za (pen′zä) A city in south central European Russian S.F.S.R.

Pen·zance (pen·zans′) A port and municipal borough in Cornwall, England; the westernmost town in England.

pe·on (pē′ən) *n.* **1** In Latin America: **a** A laborer; servant. **b** Formerly, a debtor kept in virtual servitude until he had worked out his debt. **2** In India: **a** A foot soldier. **b** A messenger, attendant, or orderly. **c** A native police officer or constable. [<Sp. *peón* <LL *pedo, -onis* a foot soldier. Doublet of PAWN¹.]

pe·on·age (pē′ən·ij) *n.* The condition of a peon, or the system of employing this form of labor. Also **pe′on·ism.**

pe·o·ny (pē′ə·nē) *n. pl.* **·nies 1** A plant of the crowfoot family (genus *Paeonia*) having large, handsome, crimson, rose, or white flowers. **2** Its flower. [Fusion of OE *peonie* and AF *pione,* both from L *paeonia* <Gk. *paiōnia* < *Paion* Paeon, the physician of the gods]

peo·ple (pē′pəl) *n. pl.* **·ple** or (*for def.* **1**) **·ples 1** The aggregate of human beings living under the same government, speaking the same language, or being of the same blood: a general term, used when the technical terms *race, tribe, nation,* or *language* would be misleading: the *people* of England. **2** Ethnologically, a body of human beings belonging to the same linguistic stock and having the same culture. **3** The whole body of persons composing a state or nation, or that part of the population invested with political rights; the enfranchised: the *people* of the state. **4** Persons collectively: taking a verb in the plural: *people* say; also, bodies of persons classified according to their collective occupation or interest: literary *people.* **5** The commonalty, as distinguished from the titled, the rich, or the learned; the populace: with *the.* **6** Those who are connected with one as subjects, attendants, kinfolk, etc.; formerly, all the Negro

slaves belonging to one family. 7 Animals collectively: the ant *people.* 8 Human beings; also, a collection oı company. — **chosen people** The Israelites. — **good people** In Ireland, fairies: also **little people.** — *v.t.* **·pled, ·pling** To fill with inhabitants; populate. [<AF *people, poeple* <L *populus* the populace] — **peo′pler** *n.*

Synonyms (noun): commonwealth, community, folk, nation, population, race, state, tribe. A *community* is the aggregate of persons inhabiting any territory in common and having common interests; a *commonwealth* is such a body of persons having a common government, especially a republican government; as, the *commonwealth* of Massachusetts. A *community* may be very small; a *commonwealth* is ordinarily of considerable extent. A *people* is the aggregate of any public *community*, either in distinction from their rulers or as including them; a *race* is a division of mankind in the line of origin and ancestry; the *people* of the United States includes members of almost every *race.* The term *people* is used ethnologically to mean *folk* having the same linguistic and cultural origins, the same customs, traditions, and beliefs, and usually the same geographic distribution: as distinguished from political affiliations or physical origins. The *population* of a country is simply the aggregate of persons residing within its borders, without reference to *race*, organization, or allegiance; unnaturalized residents form part of the *population*, but not of the *nation*, possessing none of the rights and being subject to none of the duties of citizens. In American usage *state* signifies one *commonwealth* of the federal union known as the United *States. Tribe* is now almost wholly applied to primitive *peoples* with primitive political organization; as, the Indian *tribes*; nomadic *tribes.* Compare MOB, STATE.

People's party A political organization formed in the United States in 1891, its platform being increase in currency, free coinage of silver, public control of railways, an income tax, and limitation of ownership of land: also called *Populist party.*

Pe·o·ri·a (pē·ôr′ē·ə, -ō′rē·ə) A city in NW central Illinois.

pep (pep) *Slang n.* Vim; energy; sprightliness; activity; punch; snap; vigor; ginger. — *v.t.* **pepped, pep·ping** To inspire with energy or pep: usually with *up.* [Short for PEPPER] — **pep′pi·ness** *n.* — **pep′py** *adj.*

Pe·phre·do (pə·frē′dō) See GRAEAE.

Pep·in the Short (pep′in), 714?–768, king of the Franks, 751–768; father of Charlemagne. Also *Pippin.*

pep·los (pep′ləs) *n.* In ancient Greece, an elaborate shawl or upper garment worn by women: also *peplum.* Also **pep′lus.** [<Gk.]

pep·lum (pep′ləm) *n. pl.* **·la** (-lə) 1 A short over-skirt, ruffle, or flounce attached to a blouse or coat at the waist, and extending down over the hips. 2 A peplos. [<L <Gk. *peplos* a peplos]

pe·po (pē′pō) *n. pl.* **·pos** The fleshy fruit of the gourd family, with hardened rind and numerous enclosed seeds, as the squash, cucumber, pumpkin, melon, etc. Also **pe·pon·i·da** (pi·pon′ə·də), **pe·po·ni·um** (pi·pō′nē·əm). [<L, a pumpkin <Gk. *pepōn (sikyos)* a ripe (gourd)]

pep·per (pep′ər) *n.* 1 A pungent aromatic condiment consisting of the dried immature berries of the pepper plant, entire or powdered. It is usually black, but when the outer coating of the seeds is removed, the product is **white pepper.** 2 Any plant yielding pepper; especially, a tropical climbing shrub *(Piper nigrum)* of the pepper family *(Piperaceae)*, native to India, now widely distributed. 3 Any plant of the genus *Capsicum*, or its product, entire or powdered: red *pepper* or Cayenne *pepper.* 4 *Colloq.* Spiciness; pungency; raciness. — *v.t.* 1 To sprinkle or season with pepper. 2 To sprinkle like pepper. 3 To shower, as with missiles; spatter; pelt. — *v.i.* 4 To discharge missiles at something. [OE *pipor*, ult. <L *piper* <Gk. *peperi* < an Oriental source. Cf. Skt. *pippali* a peppercorn.]

pep·per-and-salt (pep′ər·ən·sôlt′) *adj.* Mixed white and black, so closely intermingled as to present a finely speckled grayish appearance: said of cloth. — *n.* A pepper-and-salt cloth.

pep·per·box (pep′ər·boks′) *n.* 1 A cylindrical container with a perforated lid for sprinkling pepper. 2 A quick-tempered person.

pep·per·corn (pep′ər·kôrn′) *n.* 1 A berry of the pepper plant. 2 Anything trifling.

pep·per·grass (pep′ər·gras′, -gräs′) *n.* Any cress of the genus *Lepidium*, especially *L. sativum*, a garden salad, and *L. virginicum*, the wild peppergrass or tonguegrass. Also **pep′per·weed′** (-wēd′). — **California peppergrass** A herbaceous annual *(Brassica japonica)* sometimes used in salads.

pep·per·idge (pep′ər·ij) *n.* The tupelo, sourgum, or blackgum tree. [Var. of dial. E *pip(p)eridge* a barberry tree <Med. L *berberis*]

pep·per·mint (pep′ər·mint′) *n.* 1 A pungent aromatic herb *(Mentha piperita)*, used in medicine and confectionery. 2 An oil or other preparation from peppermint. 3 A confection, usually disk-shaped, flavored with peppermint.

pep·per·pot (pep′ər·pot′) *n.* 1 A pepperbox. 2 A West Indian stew of meat or fish with okra, chilis, and other vegetables, flavored with cassareep, Cayenne pepper, and the like. 3 In Pennsylvania, a soup of tripe and dough balls highly seasoned with pepper.

pep·per·root (pep′ər·rōōt′, -rŏŏt′) *n.* Crinkleroot.

pepper tree 1 A Tasmanian and Australian shrub *(Drimys aromatica)* with small, greenish-yellow flowers and globular berries sometimes used as a substitute for pepper. 2 The Peruvian mastic *(Schinus molle)*, whose seeds are used as a spice known as mollé and whose fruit yields an intoxicating beverage.

pep·per·wort (pep′ər·wûrt′) *n.* 1 Any plant of the pepper family. 2 Peppergrass.

pep·per·y (pep′ər·ē) *adj.* 1 Pertaining to or like pepper; pungent. 2 Quick-tempered; hasty; stinging. See synonyms under HOT.

pep pill *Slang* Any of various pills or tablets acting to stimulate the central nervous system.

pep·sin (pep′sin) *n.* 1 *Biochem.* A proteolytic enzyme secreted by the gastric juices of the stomach. 2 A medicinal preparation obtained from the stomachs of various animals, as the pig and the calf, used to aid digestion. 3 A similar enzyme found in the cells of certain plants. Also **pep′sine.** [<G <Gk. *pepsis* digestion < *peptein* digest]

pep·sin·ate (pep′sin·āt) *v.t.* **·at·ed, ·at·ing** To treat, make up, or prepare with pepsin.

pep·sin·o·gen (pep·sin′ə·jən) *n. Biochem.* The inactive form of pepsin, found in the stomach mucosa and converted into pepsin in a slightly acid solution.

Pep·su (pep′sōō) An acronym for PATIALA AND EAST PUNJAB STATES UNION. Also **PEPSU.**

pep talk *Colloq.* A brief talk meant to inspire confidence, spark enthusiasm, etc.

pep·tic (pep′tik) *adj.* 1 Of, pertaining to, or promotive of digestion. 2 Of, pertaining to, or producing pepsin. 3 Able to digest: opposed to *dyspeptic.* — *n.* An agent that promotes digestion. [<Gk. *peptikos* able to digest < *peptein* digest]

pep·tide (pep′tīd, -tid) *n. Biochem.* Any combination of amino acids in which the carboxyl group of one is joined with the amino group of another. [<PEPT(ONE) + -IDE]

pep·tize (pep′tīz) *v.t.* **·tized, ·tiz·ing** *Chem.* To bring about or increase the colloidal dispersion of (a substance); especially, to convert (a sol) into a gel.

pep·tone (pep′tōn) *n. Biochem.* Any of the soluble protein compounds into which the albuminous substances contained in food are converted when acted upon by pepsin, by acids and alkalis, by putrefaction, etc. [<G *pepton* <Gk., neut. of *peptos* digested, cooked < *peptein* digest] — **pep·ton·ic** (pep·ton′ik) *adj.*

pep·to·nize (pep′tə·nīz) *v.t.* **·nized, ·niz·ing** 1 To change into peptones. 2 To subject, as food, to the action of a peptone or other proteolytic enzyme. 3 To subject to partial predigestion. — **pep′to·ni·za′tion** *n.*

Pepys (pēps, peps, pep′is), **Samuel,** 1633–1703, English diarist. — **Pepys′i·an** *adj.*

Pe·quot (pē′kwot) *n.* One of a tribe of North American Indians of Algonquian stock, formerly inhabiting southern New England. Also **Pe′quod** (-kwod).

per (pûr) *prep.* 1 By; by means of; through: used in commercial and business English: *per* bearer. 2 To or for each: ten cents *per* yard. 3 By the; every: especially in Latin phrases: *per diem.* [<L, through, by]

per- *prefix* 1 Through; throughout: *pervade, perennial.* 2 Thoroughly; completely: *perturb.* 3 Away: *pervert, peremptory.* 4 Very: *perfervid.* 5 *Chem.* **a** Denoting the higher degree of valence in two similar compounds: *barium peroxide* as distinguished from *barium monoxide.* **b** Indicating a relatively large amount of the compound or radical named: *perchloric acid*, contrasted with *chloric acid.* ◆ The prefix occurs in other forms in *pardon, paramour, pellucid*, etc. [<L *per* through, by means of; in some words <OF or F]

Pe·ra (pā′rä) A suburb of Istanbul; formerly the foreign quarter.

per·ac·id (pûr′as′id) *n. Chem.* Any of a class of acids containing more than the normal proportion of oxygen, as perboric, or persulfuric acids.

per·a·cid·i·ty (pûr′a·sid′ə·tē) *n.* Excessive acidity, as of the stomach.

per·ad·ven·ture (pûr′əd·ven′chər) *adv.* Perchance; it may be; perhaps; not improbably: often preceded by *if* or *unless.* — *n.* Possibility of failure, miscarriage, or error; doubt; question. [<OF *par aventure* by chance; infl. in form by L *adventura* chance]

Pe·rae·a (pə·rē′ə) In ancient geography, a region east of the Jordan, corresponding to Gilead, and sometimes including Bashan.

Pe·rak (pā′rak, *Malay* pe′rä) A State of Malaya on the Strait of Malacca; 7,980 square miles; capital, Ipoh.

per·am·bu·late (pə·ram′byə·lāt) *v.* **·lat·ed, ·lat·ing** *v.t.* 1 To walk through or over; traverse. 2 To walk through or around so as to inspect, survey, etc. — *v.i.* 3 To walk about; stroll. [<L *perambulatus*, pp. of *perambulare* < *per-* through + *ambulare* walk]

per·am·bu·la·tion (pə·ram′byə·lā′shən) *n.* 1 The act of perambulating; specifically, an annual survey of boundaries. 2 The district or jurisdiction within which one perambulates or surveys.

per·am·bu·la·tor (pə·ram′byə·lā′tər) *n.* 1 One who perambulates. 2 A rolling chair. 3 A baby carriage. 4 A surveyor's measuring wheel, constructed on the principle of the odometer. — **per·am′bu·la·to′ry** *adj.*

per an·num (pûr an′əm) *Latin* By the year.

per·bo·rate (pər·bôr′āt, -bō′rāt) *n. Chem.* A salt of perboric acid, as sodium *perborate.*

per·bo·ric (pər·bôr′ik, -bō′rik) *adj. Chem.* Denoting an acid, HBO_3, known only from salts formed by the action of hydrogen peroxide on borates.

per·cale (pər·kāl′, -kal′) *n.* A closely woven cotton fabric without gloss, in solid colors or prints. [<F, prob. <Persian *pergālah* a rag]

per·ca·line (pûr′kə·lēn′) *n.* A glossy cotton cloth, usually dyed in a solid color: used chiefly as lining. [<F, dim. of *percale* PERCALE]

per cap·i·ta (pûr kap′ə·tə) *Latin* For each person; literally, by heads.

per·ceive (pər·sēv′) *v.t.* & *v.i.* **·ceived, ·ceiv·ing** 1 To become aware of (something) through the senses; see, hear, feel, taste, or smell. 2 To come to understand; apprehend with the mind. [<AF *perceivre*, OF *perçoivre* <L *percipere* seize, perceive < *per-* thoroughly + *capere* take] — **per·ceiv′a·ble** *adj.* — **per·ceiv′a·bly** *adv.* — **per·ceiv′er** *n.*

Synonyms: apprehend, comprehend, conceive, know, understand. We *perceive*, primarily, what is presented through the senses. We *apprehend* what is presented to the mind, whether through the senses or by any other means. That which we *apprehend* we catch, as with the hand; that which we *conceive* we are able to analyze and recompose in our mind; that which we *comprehend* we, as it were, grasp around, take together, seize, embrace wholly within the mind. Compare APPREHEND, KNOW, KNOWLEDGE, LEARN. *Antonyms*: ignore, lose, misapprehend, misconceive, miss, overlook.

per·cent (pər·sent′) *n.* **1** Number of parts in or to every hundred, often specified: fifty *percent* of the people. **2** Amount or quantity commensurate with the number of units in proportion to one hundred: ten *percent* of fifty is five: (symbol, %). **3** *pl.* Securities bearing a certain percentage of interest. Also **per cent., per cent** [Short for L *per centum* by the hundred]

per·cent·age (pər·sen′tij) *n.* **1** Rate per hundred, or proportion in a hundred parts. **2** A proportion of what is under consideration; a part considered in its quantitative relation to the whole. **3** In commerce, the allowance, commission, duty, or interest on a hundred. **4** *Colloq.* Advantage; profit.

per·cen·tile (pər·sen′tīl, -til) *n. Stat.* Any of 100 points measured within the range of a plotted variable, each of which denotes that percentage of the total cases lying below it in value: thus, 1, 2, 3, etc., percent of the cases are in the first, second, third, etc., percentile. Also called *centile.* — *adj.* **1** Of or pertaining to a percentile. **2** Having to do with percentage.

per·cept (pûr′sept) *n. Psychol.* **1** The object of knowledge as mentally presented in sense perception. **2** Immediate knowledge derived from perceiving. [<L *perceptum* (a thing) perceived, orig. neut. pp. of *percipere* PERCEIVE, on analogy with *concept*]

per·cep·ti·ble (pər·sep′tə·bəl) *adj.* That may be seen or apprehended; perceivable; cognizable; evident. See synonyms under EVIDENT. — **per·cep′ti·bil′i·ty, per·cep′ti·ble·ness** *n.* — **per·cep′ti·bly** *adv.*

per·cep·tion (pər·sep′shən) *n.* **1** The act, power, process, or product of perceiving; knowledge through the senses of the existence and properties of matter and the external world. **2** Cognition of fact or truth in general by the activity of thinking: moral *perception*; apprehension; knowledge. **3** *Psychol.* **a** The faculty or power of acquiring immediate and fundamental knowledge through the senses: often called *sense perception.* **b** The process of acquiring such knowledge. **c** The mental product so obtained, often called the *percept.* **4** Any insight or intuitive judgment that implies unusual discernment of fact or truth. **5** *Law* The taking into possession, as of crops or profits. See synonyms under KNOWLEDGE, SENSATION, UNDERSTANDING. [<OF <L *perceptio, -onis* a receiving <*percipere* PERCEIVE] — **per·cep′tion·al** *adj.*

per·cep·tive (pər·sep′tiv) *adj.* **1** Perceiving, or having the power of perception. **2** Pertaining to perception; perceptional. — **per·cep′tive·ly** *adv.* — **per·cep·tiv·i·ty** (pûr′sep·tiv′ə·tē), **per·cep′tive·ness** *n.*

per·cep·tu·al (pər·sep′choo͞·əl) *adj.* Pertaining to or involving the power or act of perceiving. — **per·cep′tu·al·ly** *adv.*

Per·ce·val (pûr′sə·vəl) A knight of Arthur's Round Table, type of high chivalry and purity, who together with Galahad achieved the Grail. Also spelled *Percival, Percivale.*

perch[1] (pûrch) *n.* **1** A staff, pole, or slat, variously used, especially as a roost for poultry, etc.; any place on which birds alight or rest; hence, any elevated seat or situation. **2** A measure: one rod (16.5 feet), or, in surveying, a square rod; also, in stonework, a variable measure, usually about 25 cubic feet. **3** A bracket or corbel; a console. **4** A frame on which cloth is examined for imperfections. **5** A pole set to mark a shallow place in navigable water. **6** A pole connecting the fore gear and hind gear of a spring carriage; a reach. — *v.i.* **1** To alight or sit on or as on a perch; roost. — *v.t.* **2** To set on or as on a perch. **3** To examine (cloth) on a perch. [<OF *perche* <L *pertica* a pole]

perch[2] (pûrch) *n.* **1** A small, spiny-finned, predaceous, fresh-water fish (genus *Perca*); especially, the common **European perch** *(P. fluviatilis),* and the American **yellow perch** *(P. flavescens).* **2** One of various other similar or related fishes, including many marine forms. [<OF *perche* <L *perca* <Gk. *perkē,* ? <*perknos* dark-colored]

per·chance (pər·chans′, -chäns′) *adv.* **1** In a possible case; peradventure; perhaps. **2** *Obs.* By chance. [<AF *par chance* by chance <*par* (<L *per* through) + *chance* CHANCE]

Perche (persh) A region of NW France, mostly in western Maine and southern Normandy.

perch·er (pûr′chər) *n.* **1** One who or that which perches. **2** A perching or insessorial bird. **3** A person who perches or examines cloth.

Per·che·ron (pûr′chə·ron, -shə-) *adj.* Belonging or originating in Perche: said of a breed of large, usually dapple-gray or black draft horses. The name *Norman* or *Percheron-Norman* is erroneously applied to this breed. — *n.* A horse of the Percheron breed. [<F, from Perche]

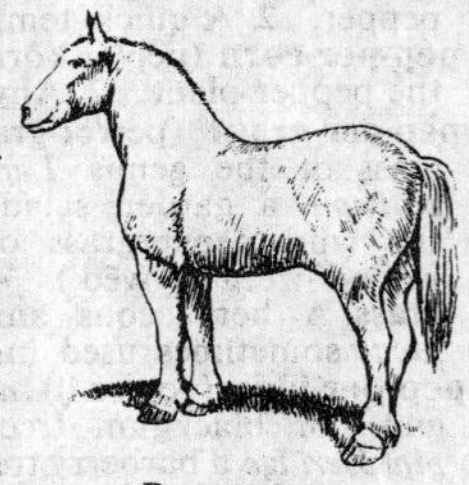
PERCHERON
(16–17 hands high at the withers)

per·chlo·rate (pər·klôr′āt, -klō′rāt) *n. Chem.* A salt of perchloric acid.

per·chlo·ric (pər·klôr′ik, -klō′rik) *adj. Chem.* Pertaining to or designating a colorless, liquid, unstable acid, $HClO_4$, formed when potassium perchlorate is distilled with sulfuric acid.

per·chlo·ride (pər·klôr′īd, -klō′rīd) *n. Chem.* A chloride having a larger proportion of chlorine than any other chloride of the same series: iron *perchloride,* $FeCl_3$. Also **per·chlo′rid** (-klôr′id, -klō′rid).

per·chlo·ron (pər·klôr′on, -klō′ron) *n. Chem.* Calcium hypochlorite, $Ca(ClO)_2 \cdot 4H_2O$, a bleaching agent with a high chlorine content.

per·cip·i·ent (pər·sip′ē·ənt) *adj.* **1** Having the power of perception. **2** Perceiving rapidly or keenly. — *n.* One who or that which perceives. [<L *percipiens, -entis,* ppr. of *percipere* PERCEIVE] — **per·cip′i·ence** or **·en·cy** *n.*

Per·ci·val, Per·ci·vale (pûr′sə·vəl) See PERCEVAL.

per·coid (pûr′koid) *adj.* Of or pertaining to an order *(Percomorphi)* of spiny-finned teleost fishes, including the fresh-water perches, the sunfishes, mackerels, tunas, blennies, and many others; perchlike. — *n.* One of the *Percomorphi.* Also **per·coi′de·an.** [<L *perca* PERCH[2] + -OID]

per·co·late (pûr′kə·lāt) *v.t.* & *v.i.* **·lat·ed, ·lat·ing** To pass or cause to pass through fine interstices; filter; strain; permeate. — *n.* **1** That which has percolated; a filtered liquid. **2** A liquid containing the soluble portion of a drug through which it has passed. [<L *percolatus,* pp. of *percolare* <*per-* through + *colare* strain <*colum* a strainer] — **per′co·la′tion** *n.*

per·co·la·tor (pûr′kə·lā′tər) *n.* **1** One who or that which percolates, as a filter. **2** A filtering coffee pot.

per con·tra (pûr kon′trə) *Latin* On the contrary.

per·cur·rent (pər·kûr′ənt) *adj. Bot.* Extending from one end to another or from base to apex, as the veins of certain leaves. [<L *percurrens, -entis,* ppr. of *percurrere* <*per-* through + *currere* run]

per·cuss (pər·kus′) *v.t.* **1** To strike or tap quickly or forcibly. **2** *Med.* To test or treat by percussion. [<L *percussus,* pp. of *percutere* strike <*per-* through + *quatere* shake] — **per·cus′sor** *n.*

per·cus·sion (pər·kush′ən) *n.* **1** The sharp striking of one body against another; sudden collision, especially such as causes a shock or sound. **2** The act of striking the percussion cap in a firearm. **3** The shock or vibration produced by collision; the impression of sound upon the ear. **4** *Med.* A light, quick tapping of the finger tips upon the back, chest, or abdomen, for determining, by the resonance, the condition of the organ beneath. **5** Those musical instruments, collectively, whose tone is produced by striking or hitting, as the timpani, glockenspiel, piano, etc. — *adj.* Pertaining to or operating by percussion; percussive: *percussion* cap, *percussion* lock. — **per·cus′sive** (-kus′iv) *adj.* — **per·cus′sive·ly** *adv.* — **per·cus′sive·ness** *n.*

percussion cap A percussion primer.

percussion figure *Mineral.* The figure assumed by the various cracks in a crystal or mineral made by the impact of a dull point against it: also called *strike figure.*

percussion fuze A fuze within a projectile or bomb that causes explosion by impact.

percussion instruments Musical instruments played by striking, as cymbals, drums, piano, etc.

percussion lock The hammer of a firearm.

percussion primer A small cap of thin metal, containing mercury fulminate, or other detonator, used in ammunition to explode the propelling charge.

Per·cy (pûr′sē) A masculine personal name. [<*Percy,* an English surname]

Per·cy (pûr′sē), **Sir Henry,** 1364–1403, English soldier; in Shakespeare's *Richard II* and *Henry IV*: known as *Hotspur.* — **Thomas,** 1729–1811, English antiquary; editor of *Reliques of Ancient English Poetry.*

Per·di·do (per·thē′thō), **Monte** A peak in the central Pyrenees of NE Spain near the French border; 10,997 feet. *French* **Mont Per·du** (môn per·dü′).

per·die, per·dy (pər·dē′) See PARDI.

per di·em (pər dē′əm, dī′əm) **1** By the day. **2** An allowance (of money) for expenses each day. [<L]

per·di·tion (pər·dish′ən) *n.* **1** *Theol.* Future misery or eternal death as the condition of the wicked; hell. **2** *Obs.* Utter destruction or ruin. **3** *Obs.* Lessening; diminution. See synonyms under RUIN. [<OF *perdiciun* <L *perditio, -onis* <*perdere* destroy, lose <*per-* through, away + *dare* give]

per·du (pər·doo͞′) *adj.* Hidden; concealed. — *n. Obs.* A soldier on a perilous assignment. Also **per·due′.** [<F *perdue,* orig. pp. fem. of *perdre* lose <L *perdere.* See PERDITION.]

per·du·ra·ble (pər·do͝or′ə·bəl, -dyo͝or′-) *adj.* Very durable; lasting. [<OF <LL *perdurabilis* <L *perdurare* <*per-* through + *durare* endure <*durus* hard] — **per·du·ra·bil·i·ty** (pûr′do͝or·ə·bil′ə·tē, -dyo͝or-) *n.* — **per·du′ra·bly** *adv.*

père (pâr) *n. French* Father: used after a surname to distinguish father from son: Dumas *père.*

per·e·gri·nate (per′ə·gri·nāt′) *v.* **·nat·ed, ·nat·ing** *v.i.* To travel from place to place. — *v.t.* To travel through or along. — *adj. Obs.* Of foreign birth or manners; traveled; foreign. [<L *peregrinatus,* pp. of *peregrinari* travel abroad <*peregrinus.* See PEREGRINE.] — **per′e·gri·na′tion** *n.* — **per′e·gri·na′tor** *n.*

per·e·grine (per′ə·grin) *adj.* **1** Coming from foreign regions. **2** Foreign. **3** Upon a pilgrimage; on one's travels. — *n.* The peregrine falcon. Also **per′e·grin.** [<L *peregrinus* foreign <*pereger* traveling <*per-* through + *ager, agri* a field, land]

peregrine falcon A widely distributed falcon *(Falco peregrinus)* generally blackish-blue above and whitish below, streaked with black in the typical form, and with black cheek patches: formerly much used in falconry on account of its courage and speed; the duck hawk. See FALCON.

pe·rei·ra bark (pə·rā′rə) The bark of a tropical American tree *(Geissospermum vellosii),* valued for its medicinal properties. [<NL *pereira,* former genus name, after J. *Pereira,* 1804–53, English medical professor]

pe·rei·rine (pə·rā′rēn, -rin) *n. Chem.* An amorphous alkaloid, $C_{20}H_{26}N_2O$, contained in pereira bark, and used in medicine as an antipyretic tonic. [<PEREIR(A BARK) + -INE[2]]

per·emp·to·ry (pə·remp′tər·ē, per′əmp·tôr′ē, -tō′rē) *adj.* **1** Not admitting of debate or appeal; decisive; absolute. **2** Positive in judgment or opinion; dogmatic. **3** Intolerant of opposition; dictatorial. **4** *Law* Precluding or putting an end to debate or discussion; final; positively fixed: a *peremptory* challenge. See synonyms under ARBITRARY. [<AF *peremptorie* <L *peremptorius* destructive <*peremptor* a destroyer <*perimere* destroy <*per-* entirely + *emere* buy, take] — **per·emp′to·ri·ly** *adv.* — **per·emp′to·ri·ness** *n.*

per·en·ni·al (pə·ren′ē·əl) *adj.* **1** Continuing or enduring through the year or through many years. **2** Hence, unfailing; unceasing: *perennial* courage. **3** Growing continually; surviving more than one year. **4** *Bot.* Lasting more than two years. See synonyms under ETERNAL, PERPETUAL. — *n.* A plant that grows for three or more years, usually blossoming and fructifying annually. [<L *perennis* <*per-* through + *annus* a year] — **per·en′ni·al·ly** *adv.*

Pé·rez Gal·dós (pā′rāth gäl·thōs′), **Benito,** 1843–1920, Spanish novelist and dramatist.

per·fect (pûr′fikt) *adj.* **1** Having all the qualities, excellences, or elements that are requisite

to its nature or kind; without defect or lack; consummated; supremely excellent; complete. **2** Thoroughly versed or informed; completely skilled: a *perfect* soldier. **3** Closely correspondent; accurately reproducing: a *perfect* replica. **4** Thoroughly effectual; meeting the requirements of the occasion: a *perfect* antidote; a *perfect* answer. **5** *Colloq.* Excessive in degree; very great: She has a *perfect* horror of spiders. **6** *Bot.* Having the essential organs, stamens, and pistils: said of flowers. **7** *Gram.* Denoting the tense of the verb expressing completed action in the past. Some grammarians note in English a *present perfect, past perfect* (or *pluperfect*), and a *future perfect* tense, a *conditional perfect,* and a *perfect infinitive* and *participle.* **8** *Music* **a** Of a character not altered by inversion: said of interval: a *perfect* fifth or octave. **b** Complete: a *perfect* cadence. **9** *Obs.* Assured; positive. — *n. Gram.* The perfect tense, or a verb in this tense. — *v.t.* (pər·fekt′) **1** To bring to perfection; complete; finish. **2** To make thoroughly skilled or accomplished: to *perfect* oneself in an art. [<OF *parfit* <L *perfectus,* pp. of *perficere* accomplish <*per-* thoroughly + *facere* do, make] — **per·fect′er** *n.* — **per·fect′i·bil′i·ty** *n.* — **per·fect′i·ble** *adj.* — **per′·fect·ly** *adv.*

Synonyms (adj.): absolute, accurate, blameless, complete, completed, consummate, correct, entire, faultless, finished, holy, ideal, immaculate, infallible, sinless, spotless, stainless, unblemished, undefiled. That is *perfect* to which nothing can be added and from which nothing can be taken without impairing its excellence, symmetry, or worth; as, a *perfect* flower; a copy of a document is *perfect* when it is *accurate* in every particular; a vase may be called *perfect* when *entire* and *unblemished,* even if not artistically *faultless*; the best judges never pronounce a work of art *perfect,* because they see always *ideal* possibilities not yet attained; even the *ideal* is not *perfect,* by reason of the imperfection of the human mind; a human character faultlessly *holy* would be morally *perfect* but finite. That which is *absolute* is free from admixture (as *absolute* alcohol) and from imperfection or limitation. See CORRECT, IMPLICIT, INNOCENT, PURE, RADICAL, RIPE. *Antonyms*: bad, blemished, corrupt, corrupted, defaced, defective, deficient, deformed, fallible, faulty, imperfect, incomplete, inferior, insufficient, marred, meager, perverted, poor, ruined, short, spoiled, worthless.

per·fec·tion (pər·fek′shən) *n.* **1** The state or condition of being perfect; supreme excellence; also, an embodiment of this: also **per′fect·ness.** **2** A particular quality that is supreme. **3** The highest degree of a thing: the *perfection* of rudeness. **4** The act or process of perfecting; the fact of having been perfected.

per·fec·tion·ism (pər·fek′shən·iz′əm) *n. Philos.* The theory that moral perfection may be attained, or has been attained, by men: variously held and taught by different sects and schools. Also **per·fect′ism.**

per·fec·tion·ist (pər·fek′shən·ist) *n.* **1** One who demands an exceedingly high degree of excellence in the performance, behavior, etc., of himself or in that of others. **2** One who adheres to the theory of perfectionism.

per·fec·tive (pər·fek′tiv) *adj.* **1** Tending to make perfect. **2** *Gram.* Denoting an aspect of the verb expressing the completion of an action: opposed to *imperfective.* — **per·fec′·tive·ly** *adv.* — **per·fec′tive·ness** *n.*

perfect number See under NUMBER.

per·fec·to (pər·fek′tō) *n.* A cigar shaped to taper at either end, and of medium size. [< Sp., perfect <L *perfectus.* See PERFECT.]

perfect pitch Absolute pitch (def. 2).

per·fer·vid (pər·fûr′vid) *adj.* Very or excessively fervid; glowing; intensely zealous. [<NL *perfervidus* <L *per-* thoroughly + *fervidus* FERVID]

per·fid·i·ous (pər·fid′ē·əs) *adj.* **1** Characterized by or guilty of perfidy; treacherous. **2** Involving a breach of faith; contrary to loyalty and truth. [<L *perfidiosus* <*perfidia* PERFIDY] — **per·fid′i·ous·ly** *adv.* — **per·fid′i·ous·ness** *n.*

Synonyms: deceitful, disloyal, double-faced, faithless, false, forsworn, perjured, traitorous, treacherous, two-faced, unfaithful, untrue, untrustworthy. *Antonyms*: faithful, honest, incorruptible, staunch, steadfast, true, trustworthy, trusty.

per·fi·dy (pûr′fə·dē) *n. pl.* **·dies** The act of violating faith or allegiance; treachery; faithlessness. [<MF *perfidie* <L *perfidia* treachery <*per-* through, away + *fides* faith]

per·fo·li·ate (pər·fō′lē·it, -āt) *adj. Bot.* Growing so that the stem passes, or seems to pass, through it: said of a leaf. The condition is brought about by the union of the basal lobes of a clasping leaf. [<NL *perfoliatus* <L *per-* through + *folium* a leaf] — **per·fo′li·a′tion** *n.*

per·fo·rate (pûr′fə·rāt) *v.t.* **·rat·ed, ·rat·ing** **1** To make a hole or holes through, by or as by stamping or drilling. **2** To pierce with holes in rows or patterns, as sheets of stamps, etc. See synonyms under PIERCE. — *adj.* (-rit) Perforated. [<L *perforatus,* pp. of *perforare* <*per-* through + *forare* bore] — **per′fo·ra·ble** *adj.* — **per′fo·ra′tive, per′fo·ra·to′ry** *adj.* — **per′fo·ra′tor** *n.*

per·fo·rat·ed (pûr′fə·rā′tid) *adj.* Pierced with a hole or holes, especially in lines or patterns, as sheets of stamps to facilitate tearing.

per·fo·ra·tion (pûr′fə·rā′shən) *n.* **1** A perforating or state of being perforated. **2** A hole or series of holes drilled in or stamped through something, especially in lines or patterns.

per·force (pər·fôrs′, -fōrs′) *adv.* By force; by or of necessity; necessarily. [<OF *par force* < *par* through, by (<L *per-*) + *force* FORCE]

per·form (pər·fôrm′) *v.t.* **1** To carry out in action; execute; do: to *perform* an operation. **2** To act in accord with the requirements or obligations of; fulfil; discharge, as a duty or command. **3** To act (a part) or give a performance of (a play, piece of music, etc.). — *v.i.* **4** To carry through to completion an action, undertaking, etc. **5** To give an exhibition or performance, as of a role in a play, singing, etc.: The actress will *perform* tomorrow. See synonyms under ACCOMPLISH, EFFECT, EXECUTE, MAKE, TRANSACT. [<AF *parfourmer,* OF *parfournir* accomplish entirely <*par-* thoroughly (<L *per-*) + *fournir* accomplish; infl. in form by OF *former* form] — **per·form′·a·ble** *adj.*

per·form·ance (pər·fôr′məns) *n.* **1** The act of performing; also, the thing done; execution; completion; action; achievement. **2** A representation before spectators; an exhibition of feats; any entertainment: two *performances* daily. See synonyms under ACT, EXERCISE, OPERATION, PRODUCTION, WORK.

per·form·er (pər·fôr′mər) *n.* **1** One who performs or acts; one who carries a part upon the stage or in any performance, as an actor, musician, or acrobat. **2** One who carries out his promise or does his duty. See synonyms under AGENT.

per·frig·er·a·tion (pər·frij′ə·rā′shən) *n.* Frostbite. [<L *perfrigeratus,* pp. of *perfrigerare* <*per-* thoroughly + *frigerare* cool <*frigus* cold]

per·fume (pûr′fyo͞om, pər·fyo͞om′) *n.* **1** A pleasant odor, as from flowers; fragrance. **2** A fragrant substance, usually a volatile liquid, prepared to emit a pleasant odor; scent. See synonyms under SMELL. — *v.t.* (pər·fyo͞om′) **·fumed, ·fum·ing** To fill or impregnate with a fragrant odor; scent. [<F *parfum* <Ital. *perfumare,* lit., impregnate with smoke <*per-* through (<L) + *fumare* smoke <*fumus* smoke]

per·fum·er (pər·fyo͞o′mər) *n.* **1** One who makes or deals in perfumes. **2** One who or that which perfumes.

per·fum·er·y (pər·fyo͞o′mər·ē) *n. pl.* **·er·ies** **1** Perfumes in general, or a specific perfume. **2** A place where perfumes are manufactured.

per·func·to·ry (pər·fungk′tər·ē) *adj.* Done merely for the sake of getting through; mechanical and without interest; half-hearted; negligent; superficial; careless. [<LL *perfunctorius* negligent <*perfunctor* one who performs an act <*perfungi* get through with <*per-* through + *fungi* perform] — **per·func′·to·ri·ly** *adv.* — **per·func′to·ri·ness** *n.*

per·fuse (pər·fyo͞oz′) *v.t.* **·fused, ·fus·ing** **1** To overspread, suffuse, or sprinkle with a liquid, color, etc.; permeate. **2** To spread, as a liquid, over or through something; diffuse. [<L *perfusus,* pp. of *perfundere* <*per-* through, all over + *fundere* pour out] — **per·fu′sion** (-zhən) *n.* — **per·fu′sive** (-siv) *adj.*

Per·ga·mum (pûr′gə·məm) **1** An ancient kingdom of western Asia Minor, later a Roman province. **2** Its capital, a Greek city on the site of modern Bergama. Also **Per′ga·mon, Per′ga·mos** (-məs), **Per′ga·mus.**

per·go·la (pûr′gə·lə) *n.* An arbor; specifically, an arbor or trellisework of a structural nature, covered with vegetation or flowers; a covered walk. [< Ital., an arbor <L *pergula* a projecting roof, arbor < *pergere* go forward <L *per-* through + *regere* keep straight]

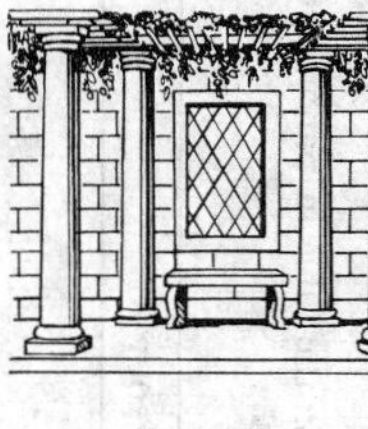
PERGOLA

Per·go·le·si (per′gō·lā′zē), **Giovanni Battista,** 1710–36, Italian composer.

per·haps (pər·haps′) *adv.* It may be; possibly. [<PER + *happes, haps,* pl. of HAP[1]]

pe·ri (pir′ē) *n.* In Persian mythology, a fairy or elf descended from the disobedient angels, doing penance until readmitted into paradise. [<Persian *pari, peri* a demon, fairy]

peri– *prefix* **1** Around; encircling; all about: *periphery.* **2** Situated near; close; adjoining: *perihelion.* [<Gk. <*peri* around]

Per·i·an·der (per′ē·an′dər), died 585 B.C., tyrant of Corinth, 625–585 B.C.; one of the seven wise men of Greece.

per·i·anth (per′ē·anth) *n. Bot.* The combined calyx and corolla of a flower when so alike as to be indistinguishable: sometimes called *perigonium.* [Appar. <F *périanthe* <NL *perianthium* <Gk. *peri-* around + *anthos* a flower] — **per′i·an′the·ous** *adj.*

per·i·apt (per′ē·apt) *n. Obs.* A charm to protect the wearer from disease or misfortune; an amulet. [<MF *périapte* <Gk. *periapton* < *peri-* around + *aptos* fastened <*aptein* fasten]

per·i·as·tron (per′ē·as′tron) *n. Astron.* That point in the orbit of either member of a double star when the stars are closest to each other: opposed to *apastron.* [<NL <Gk. *peri-* around + *astron* a star]

per·i·blem (per′ə·blem) *n. Bot.* A sheath of meristematic tissue surrounding the plerome of a plant and giving rise to the primary cortex tissue. [<G <Gk. *periblēma* a covering <*periballein* put on, around <*peri-* around + *ballein* throw]

per·i·blep·sis (per′ə·blep′sis) *n.* The wild, intense, staring expression of a delirious or insane person. [<NL <Gk. *peri-* around + *blepsis* an act of sight <*blepein* look]

per·i·car·di·al (per′ə·kär′dē·əl) *adj.* Of or pertaining to the pericardium. Also **per′i·car′·di·ac** or **·di·an.**

per·i·car·di·ec·to·my (per′ə·kär′dē·ek′tə·mē) *n. Surg.* Removal of the pericardium. [<*pericardi-* (<PERICARDIUM) + -ECTOMY]

per·i·car·di·ot·o·my (per′ə·kär′dē·ot′ə·mē) *n. Surg.* Incision of the pericardium.

per·i·car·di·tis (per′ə·kär·dī′tis) *n. Pathol.* Inflammation of the pericardium.

per·i·car·di·um (per′ə·kär′dē·əm) *n. pl.* **·di·a** (-dē·ə) *Anat.* A membranous bag that surrounds and protects the heart. [<NL <Gk. *pericardion* (the membrane) around the heart <*peri-* around + *kardia* heart]

per·i·carp (per′ə·kärp) *n. Bot.* The wall of the ripened ovary of a flower, constituting the germ of the fruit. [<NL *pericarpium* <Gk. *pericarpion* a husk <*peri-* around + *karpos* a fruit] — **per′i·car′pi·al** *adj.*

per·i·chon·dri·um (per′ə·kon′drē·əm) *n. pl.* **·dri·a** (-drē·ə) *Anat.* The vascular membrane that envelops the surface of a cartilage between the joints. [<NL <Gk. *peri-* around + *chondros* a cartilage] — **per′i·chon′dri·al** *adj.*

Per·i·cle·an (per′ə·klē′ən) *adj.* Pertaining to, characteristic of, or named after Pericles, or the period of his supremacy, the age when Greek art, literature, philosophy, and statesmanship are considered to have been at their height.

add,āce,câre,pälm; end,ēven; it,īce; odd,ōpen,ôrder; to͝ok,po͞ol; up,bûrn; ə = a in *above,* e in *sicken,* i in *clarity,* o in *melon,* u in *focus*; yo͞o = u in *fuse*; oi,oil; ou,pout; ch,check; g,go; ng,ring; th,thin; th,this; zh,vision. Foreign sounds à,œ,ü,kh,ṅ; and ◆: see page xx. < from; + plus; ? possibly.

PERIODIC TABLE OF ELEMENTS

The atomic number will be found in the upper left corner of each box; the atomic weight (1961), based on carbon 12.01115, in the lower right (numbers in the table in parentheses are mass numbers of the most stable isotopes); and the symbol in the lower left.

PERIOD	GROUP 1	GROUP 2	GROUP 3	GROUP 4	GROUP 5	GROUP 6	GROUP 7	GROUP 8			GROUP 0
1	1 Hydrogen H 1.00797										2 Helium He 4.0026
2	3 Lithium Li 6.939	4 Beryllium Be 9.0122	5 Boron B 10.811	6 Carbon C 12.01115	7 Nitrogen N 14.0067	8 Oxygen O 15.9994	9 Fluorine F 18.9994				10 Neon Ne 20.183
3	11 Sodium Na 22.9898	12 Magnesium Mg 24.312	13 Aluminum Al 26.9815	14 Silicon Si 28.086	15 Phosphorus P 30.9738	16 Sulfur S 32.064	17 Chlorine Cl 35.453				18 Argon Ar 39.948
4A	19 Potassium K 39.102	20 Calcium Ca 40.08	21 Scandium Sc 44.956	22 Titanium Ti 47.90	23 Vanadium V 50.942	24 Chromium Cr 51.996	25 Manganese Mn 54.938	26 Iron Fe 55.847	27 Cobalt Co 58.9332	28 Nickel Ni 58.71	
4B	29 Copper Cu 63.54	30 Zinc Zn 65.37	31 Gallium Ga 69.72	32 Germanium Ge 72.59	33 Arsenic As 74.9216	34 Selenium Se 78.96	35 Bromine Br 79.909				36 Krypton Kr 83.80
5A	37 Rubidium Rb 85.47	38 Strontium Sr 87.62	39 Yttrium Y 88.905	40 Zirconium Zr 91.22	41 Niobium Nb 92.906	42 Molybdenum Mo 95.94	43 Technetium Tc (99)	44 Ruthenium Ru 101.07	45 Rhodium Rh 102.905	46 Palladium Pd 106.40	
5B	47 Silver Ag 107.87	48 Cadmium Cd 112.40	49 Indium In 114.82	50 Tin Sn 118.69	51 Antimony Sb 121.75	52 Tellurium Te 127.60	53 Iodine I 126.9044				54 Xenon Xe 131.30
6A	55 Cesium Cs 132.905	56 Barium Ba 137.34	57–71 LANTHANIDE SERIES	72 Hafnium Hf 178.49	73 Tantalum Ta 180.948	74 Tungsten W 183.85	75 Rhenium Re 186.20	76 Osmium Os 190.20	77 Iridium Ir 192.2	78 Platinum Pt 195.09	
6B	79 Gold Au 196.967	80 Mercury Hg 200.59	81 Thallium Tl 204.37	82 Lead Pb 207.19	83 Bismuth Bi 208.98	84 Polonium Po 210.00	85 Astatine At (210)				86 Radon Rn 222.00
7	87 Francium Fr (223)	88 Radium Ra 226.05	89–103 ACTINIDE SERIES								
LANTHANIDE SERIES	57 Lanthanum La 138.91	58 Cerium Ce 140.12	59 Praseodymium Pr 140.907	60 Neodymium Nd 144.24	61 Promethium Pm (147)	62 Samarium Sm 150.35	63 Europium Eu 151.96	64 Gadolinium Gd 157.25	65 Terbium Tb 158.924	66 Dysprosium Dy 162.50	67 Holmium Ho 164.93
	68 Erbium Er 167.26	69 Thulium Tm 168.934	70 Ytterbium Yb 173.04	71 Lutetium Lu 174.97							
ACTINIDE SERIES	89 Actinium Ac 227.0	90 Thorium Th 232.038	91 Protactinium Pa 231	92 Uranium U 238.03	93 Neptunium Np (237)	94 Plutonium Pu (242)	95 Americium Am (243)	96 Curium Cm (247)	97 Berkelium Bk (249)	98 Californium Cf (251)	99 Einsteinium Es (254)
	100 Fermium Fm (253)	101 Mendelevium Md (256)	102 Nobelium No (253)	103 Lawrencium Lw (257?)							

Per·i·cles (per′ə·klēz), died 429 B.C., Athenian statesman and general.
— **Pericles, Prince of Tyre** Hero of Shakespeare's play of that name.

per·i·cline (per′ə·klīn) *n.* One of the varieties of albite found in the Swiss Alps in the form of white twinned crystals. [<Gk. *periklinēs* sloping all around <*peri-* around + *klinein* lean; with ref. to the large inclination between the terminal and lateral faces of the crystals]

per·i·cra·ni·um (per′ə·krā′nē·əm) *n. pl.* **·ni·a** (-nē·ə) *Anat.* The periosteum of the external surface of the cranium. [<NL <Gk. *perikranion* <*perikranios* (*chitōn*) (the membrane) under the skin of the skull <*peri-* around + *kranion* skull] — **per′i·cra′ni·al** *adj.*

per·i·cy·cle (per′ə·sī′kəl) *n. Bot.* The outer portion of the central or fibrovascular cylinder in plants, capable of active growth. [<Gk. *perikyklos* all around, spherical <*perikykloein* <*peri-* around + *kykloein* encircle] — **per′i·cy′clic** *adj.*

per·i·den·tal (per′ə·den′təl) *adj.* Periodontal.

per·i·derm (per′ə·dûrm) *n. Bot.* The outer bark; the tissue produced by the cork cambium layer in plants. — **per′i·der′mal** or **·der′mic** *adj.*

pe·rid·i·um (pə·rid′ē·əm) *n. pl.* **·i·a** (-ē·ə) *Bot.* The outer coat or coats of an angiocarpous fungus, forming a complete investment of the fructification, as in puffballs. [<NL <Gk. *pēridion,* dim. of *pēra* a leather bag] — **pe·rid′i·al** *adj.*

per·i·dot (per′ə·dot) *n.* A yellowish-green gem variety of olivine. [<F *péridot* <OF *peritot;* ult. origin uncertain] — **per′i·dot′ic** *adj.*

per·i·do·tite (per′ə·dō′tīt) *n.* A granular igneous rock composed essentially of olivine or chrysolite. [<PERIDOT + -ITE[1]]

per·i·gee (per′ə·jē) *n. Astron.* The point in the orbit of the moon or of an artificial satellite where it is nearest the earth; opposed to *apogee.* [<MF *périgee* <Med. L *perigaeum* <Gk. *perigeion,* orig. neut. of *perigeios* close around the earth <*peri-* around + *gē* earth] — **per′i·ge′al, per′i·ge′an** *adj.*

per·i·gon (per′ə·gon) *n. Geom.* An angle equal to two straight angles or 360 degrees.

per·i·go·ni·um (per′ə·gō′nē·əm) *n. pl.* **·ni·a** (-nē·ə) The perianth. [<NL <Gk. *peri-* around + *gonos* offspring, a seed]

Pé·ri·gord (pā·rē·gôr′) A former division of Guienne, SW France.

Per·i·gor·di·an (per′ə·gôr′dē·ən) *adj. Anthropol.* Pertaining to either of two extensions of the Aurignacian culture stage: the Lower Perigordian (Chatelperronian) and the Upper Perigordian (Gravettian). [from *Périgord*]

Pé·ri·gueux (pā·rē·gœ′) A city of SW France, former capital of Périgord.

pe·rig·y·nous (pə·rij′ə·nəs) *adj. Bot.* Situated around the ovary: said of parts of a flower, as the stamens, in which the ovary is nearly or quite free and surrounded by a cup formed by the torus or by the adnation of two or more of the floral organs, upon which the other parts seem to be inserted. [<NL *perigynus* <Gk. *peri-* around + *gynē* female] — **pe·rig′y·ny** *n.*

per·i·he·li·on (per′ə·hē′lē·ən) *n. pl.* **·li·a** (-lē·ə) *Astron.* The point in the orbit of a planet or comet where it is nearest the sun: opposed to *aphelion.* [<NL *perihelium* <Gk. *peri-* close about + *hēlios* the sun; refashioned after Greek]

per·il (per′əl) *n.* Exposure to the chance of injury, loss, or destruction; danger; jeopardy; risk. See synonyms under DANGER, HAZARD. — *v.t.* **·iled** or **·illed, ·il·ing** or **·il·ling** To expose to danger; imperil. [<OF *péril* <L *periculum* trial, danger]

per·il·ous (per′əl·əs) *adj.* Full of, involving, or attended with peril; hazardous. See synonyms under PRECARIOUS. — **per′il·ous·ly** *adv.* — **per′il·ous·ness** *n.*

Pe·rim (pə·rim′) An island dependency of Aden Colony in the strait Bab el Mandeb; 5 square miles. *Arabic* **Ba·rim** (bä·rim′).

pe·rim·e·ter (pə·rim′ə·tər) *n.* **1** The bounding line of any figure of two dimensions. **2** The sum of the sides of a plane figure. **3** An instrument for testing the scope of the field of vision. [<L *perimetros* <Gk. <*peri-* around + *metron* a measure] — **per·i·met·ric** (per′ə·met′rik) or **·ri·cal** *adj.* — **per′i·met′ri·cal·ly** *adv.*

pe·rim·e·try (pə·rim′ə·trē) *n.* Measurement of the scope of vision by use of a perimeter.

per·i·morph (per′ə·môrf) *n.* A mineral that encloses another. Compare ENDOMORPH. [<PERI- + Gk. *morphē* a form] — **per′i·mor′phic** or **·phous** *adj.* — **per′i·mor′phism** *n.*

per·i·ne·phri·tis (per′ə·nə·frī′tis) *n. Pathol.* Inflammation of the cellular and fibrous tissues around the kidney. [<NL <Gk. *peri-* around + *nephros* a kidney + -ITIS] — **per′i·ne·phrit′ic** (-frit′ik) *adj.*

per·i·neph·ri·um (per′ə·nef′rē·əm) *n. Anat.* The capsule of adipose tissue that invests the kidney. [<NL <Gk. *peri-* around + *nephros* a kidney] — **per′i·neph′ral** or **·ri·al** or **·ric** *adj.*

per·i·ne·um (per′ə·nē′əm) *n. pl.* **·ne·a** (-nē′ə) *Anat.* **1** The region of the body at the lower end of the trunk, between the genital organs and the rectum. **2** The entire region at the outlet of the pelvis, comprising the anus and the internal genitals. Also **per′i·nae′um.** [<LL <Gk. *perinaion, perineos*] — **per′i·ne′al** *adj.*

per·i·neu·ri·tis (per′ə·nōō·rī′tis, -nyōō-) *n. Pathol.* Inflammation of the perineurium.

per·i·neu·ri·um (per′ə·nōōr′ē·əm, -nyōōr′-) *n. pl.* **·ri·a** (-ē·ə) *Anat.* The connective tissue investing one of the bundles of fibers composing a nerve. [<NL <Gk. *peri-* around + *neuron* a nerve] — **per′i·neu′ri·al** *adj.*

per in·ter·im (pər in′tər·im) *Latin* In the meantime.

pe·ri·od (pir′ē·əd) *n.* **1** A definite portion of time marked and defined by some recurring event or phenomenon. **2** A lapse of time; a series of years; an age; era; also, a stage of life. **3** The concluding limit of any sequence of years, events, acts, or phenomena; termination. **4** The present day or time: with *the.* **5** *Astron.* The time of revolution of a heavenly body about its primary. **6** *Med.* A special phase or epoch distinguishable in the course of a disease: the *period* of augmentation; also, the menses. **7** A dot (.) placed on the line: used as a mark of rhetorical punctuation after every complete declarative sentence, after most abbreviations, as LL.D., pp., after titles, headings, and sideheads, and often after Roman numerals. The same mark serves also as a decimal point. **8** A sentence in which completion of the sense is suspended till the close. **9** *Geol.* One of the divisions of geologic time, intermediate between the shorter *epoch* and the longer *era*: the Cretaceous *period.* **10** *Music* A group of measures arranged in two or more phrases and comprising a complete musical statement. **11** *Math.* **a** The interval between the equal recurring values of a dependent variable. **b** Any one of similar groups into which a number is divided, as when a root is to be extracted: in numeration or in recurring decimals. **c** The length of the smallest subinterval in the graph of the function of a real variable. **12** *Physics* The time that elapses between two successive similar phases of a vibration. **13** The completion or end of a cycle, event, or series of events. **14** *Obs.* A particular occasion or moment. See synonyms under END, TIME. [<OF *periode* <L *periodus* <Gk. *periodos* a going around, a rounded surface <*peri-* around + *hodos* a way]

per·i·o·date (pə·rī′ə·dāt) *n. Chem.* A salt of periodic acid. [<PERIOD(IC ACID) + -ATE[3]]

period furniture Furniture in a style characteristic of any given period.

pe·ri·od·ic (pir′ē·od′ik) *adj.* **1** Pertaining to or of the nature of a period; characterized by periods; recurring after a definite interval; cyclic. **2** *Gram.* Belonging to a sentence that is grammatically complete. **3** In rhetoric, pertaining to or expressed in complete sentences: pertaining especially to a style in which several clauses hang upon one principal statement or sentence; hence, rhetorically elaborate. See also PERIODIC SENTENCE. **4** *Math.* **a** Of or pertaining to curves with ordinates repeated at equal distances along the abscissa. **b** Of or pertaining to the function of a real variable such that a graph of the function is identical within each subinterval.

per·i·od·ic acid (pûr′ī·od′ik) *Chem.* A compound, $HIO_4 \cdot 2H_2O$, containing iodine combined with oxygen at its highest valence. [<PER- (def. 5) + IODIC]

pe·ri·od·i·cal (pir′ē·od′i·kəl) *adj.* **1** Pertaining to publications, as magazines, etc., that appear at fixed intervals of more than one day; also, published at regular intervals. **2** Periodic (def. 1). — *n.* A publication, usually a weekly, monthly, or quarterly magazine, appearing at regular intervals. — **pe′ri·od′i·cal·ly** *adv.*

pe·ri·o·dic·i·ty (pir′ē·ə·dis′ə·tē) *n.* The quality of being periodic or of recurring at definite intervals of time, as in sunspots, an electric current, or the symptoms of a disease.

periodic law *Chem.* The statement that the physicochemical properties of the elements are functionally related to their atomic numbers and recur periodically when the elements are arranged in the order of these numbers.

periodic sentence A sentence that is not grammatically complete until the end; specifically, one of several rhetorical clauses so constructed as to suspend completion of both sense and structure until the close.

periodic spiral *Chem.* A complex graphic diagram of the elements arranged in a series of curves so as to illustrate the various relationships of properties, chemical behavior, etc., as expressed in the periodic law.

periodic system *Chem.* A classification of the elements in accordance with the relationships formulated by the periodic law.

periodic table *Chem.* A table in which the elements are arranged in physicochemical groups as determined, formerly by their atomic weights, now by atomic numbers. See opposite page.

per·i·o·dide (pə·rī′ə·dīd) *n. Chem.* An iodide having a larger proportion of iodine than any other iodide of the same series. Also **per·i′o·did** (-did).

per·i·o·don·tal (per′ē·ə·don′təl) *adj. Anat.* Occurring or situated around a tooth: the *periodontal* membrane lining the cement of a tooth: also called *peridental.* [<PERI- + -ODONT(O)- + -AL]

per·i·o·ma·ni·a (per′ē·ə·mā′nē·ə, -mān′yə) *n.* Dromomania. [<Gk. *peraioein* carry across, pass over + MANIA]

per·i·os·te·um (per′ē·os′tē·əm) *n. Anat.* A tough, fibrous, two-layered vascular membrane that surrounds and nourishes the bones. [<NL <L *periosteon* <Gk., neut. of *periosteos* around the bones <*peri-* around + *osteon* a bone] — **per′i·os′te·al, per′i·os′te·ous** *adj.*

per·i·os·ti·tis (per′ē·əs·tī′tis) *n. Pathol.* Inflammation of the periosteum. [<PERIOST(EUM) + -ITIS] — **per′i·os·tit′ic** (-tit′ik) *adj.*

per·i·o·tic (per′ē·ō′tik, -ot′ik) *Anat. adj.* Surrounding the inner ear; specifically, relating to the bony structure or capsule enclosing the labyrinth. — *n.* A periotic bone.

per·i·pa·tet·ic (per′i·pə·tet′ik) *adj.* **1** Walking about; moving from place to place. **2** Rambling, as of speech. — *n.* One given to walking about. [<OF *peripatetique* <L *peripateticus* <Gk. *peripatētikos* given to walking about <*peripatētēs* one who walks about <*peri-* around + *pateein* walk]

Per·i·pa·tet·ic (per′i·pə·tet′ik) *adj.* Pertaining to the philosophy of Aristotle, who lectured to his disciples while walking in the Lyceum at Athens. — *n.* A disciple of Aristotle; an adherent of his teachings.

pe·riph·er·al (pə·rif′ər·əl) *adj.* **1** Of or pertaining to a periphery. **2** Distant from the center; hence, distal; external. Also **per′i·pher′ic** or **·i·cal** (per′ə·fer′i·kəl). — **pe·riph′er·al·ly** *adv.*

pe·riph·er·y (pə·rif′ər·ē) *n. pl.* **·er·ies** **1** The outer surface. **2** The surface of the body. **3** Circumference. **4** *Geom.* The sum of the sides of any polygon. **5** A surrounding region, country, or area. [<OF *periferie* <LL *peripheria* <Gk. *periphereia* circumference <*peripherēs* moving around <*peri-* around + *pherein* carry]

per·i·phrase (per′i·frāz′) *n.* Periphrasis.

pe·riph·ra·sis (pə·rif′rə·sis) *n. pl.* **·ses** (-sēz) Circumlocution, or an instance of it. See synonyms under CIRCUMLOCUTION. [<L <Gk. <*periphrazein* <*peri-* around + *phrazein* speak]

per·i·phras·tic (per′ə·fras′tik) *adj.* **1** Of the nature of or involving periphrasis; employing

indirect words; circumlocutory. 2 *Gram.* Denoting a construction in which a phrase is substituted for an inflected form of similar function, as, *the hat of John* for *John's hat.* Also **per′i·phras′ti·cal.** — **per′i·phras′ti·cal·ly** *adv.*

periphrastic conjugation A conjugation formed by simple verbs with the aid of auxiliaries, instead of by inflection of the verb itself, as, *he did run* for *he ran.*

periphrastic genitive A genitive case formed not by inflection, but by a preposition, as in English by *of.*

per·i·plo·cin (per′ə·plō′sin) *n.* A powerful glycoside, $C_{30}H_{49}O_{12}$, extracted from the bark of the silk vine in the form of a yellow, bitter, amorphous powder: it resembles digitalis in action and is sometimes used in the treatment of certain heart conditions. [<NL *Periploca (graeca)* silk vine [<Gk. *periplokē* a twining (< *peri-* around + *plekein* twine) + -IN]

pe·rip·ter·al (pə·rip′tər·əl) *Archit. adj.* Having a detached row of columns extending around the cella: said especially of a temple. — *n.* A peripteral temple; peristyle: also **pe·rip′·ter, pe·rip′ter·os** (-tər·os). [<MF *périptère* <Med. L *peripteron* <Gk., neut. of *peripteros* winged about < *peri-* around + *pteron* a wing]

pe·rique (pə·rēk′) *n.* A dark, strongly flavored tobacco grown in Louisiana. [<Creole, prob. alter. of slang E *prick* a phallus; so called when made into a carotte]

per·i·sarc (per′ə·särk) *n. Zool.* The chitinous excretion by which the soft parts of a hydroid colony are invested. [<PERI- + Gk. *sarx, sarkos* flesh] — **per′i·sar′cal, per′i·sar′cous** *adj.*

per·i·scope (per′ə·skōp) *n.* 1 An instrument consisting of a revolving prism capable of reflecting light rays down a vertical tube: used to guide submarine boats or to watch an enemy from a trench. 2 A special variety of photographic objective; a periscopic or wide-angled lens. — **per′i·scop′ic** or **·i·cal** (-skop′i·kəl) *adj.*

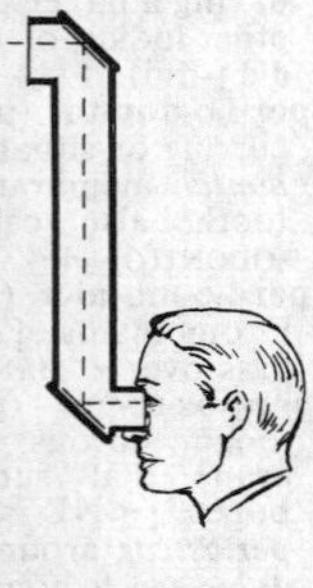

PERISCOPE
Showing the principle of reflection.

per·ish (per′ish) *v.i.* 1 To suffer a violent or untimely death. 2 To be destroyed; pass from existence. See synonyms under DIE. [<OF *periss-*, stem of *perir* <L *perire* < *per-* away + *ire* go]

per·ish·a·ble (per′ish·ə·bəl) *adj.* Liable to perish; mortal; liable to speedy decay, as fruit in transportation. — **per′ish·a·ble·ness, per′ish·a·bil′i·ty** *n.* — **per′·ish·a·bly** *adv.*

per·ish·a·bles (per′ish·ə·bəlz) *n. pl.* Goods liable to speedy decay: used chiefly of foods in transit.

per·i·sperm (per′ə·spûrm) *n. Bot.* Tissue surrounding the embryo sac in an ovule, in which nutrient material is stored. [<F *périsperme* <NL *perispermum* <Gk. *peri-* around + *sperma* seed] — **per′i·sper′mic** *adj.*

per·i·sphere (per′ə·sfir) *n. Physics* That portion of space within which the magnetic, electrical, or gravitational fields of an object produce observable effects.

per·i·spom·e·non (per′ə·spom′ə·non) *Gram. adj.* In Greek, having the circumflex accent on the final syllable. — *n.* A perispomenon word. [<Gk. *perispōmenon,* neut. ppr. passive of *perispaein* mark with the circumflex < *peri-* around + *spaein* draw]

pe·ris·so·dac·tyl (pə·ris′ō·dak′til) *adj.* 1 Odd-toed. 2 Of or pertaining to an order of ungulates *(Perissodactyla)* with an odd number of digits and an enlarged cecum, including horses, tapirs, rhinoceroses, etc. — *n.* An ungulate mammal belonging to this order. Also **pe·ris′so·dac′tyle.** [<NL <Gk. *perissos* odd, uneven + *dactylos* finger, toe] — **pe·ris′·so·dac·tyl′ic, ·dac′ty·lous** *adj.* — **pe·ris′so·dac′·ty·lism** *n.*

per·i·stal·sis (per′ə·stôl′sis, -stal′-) *n. pl.* **·ses** (-sēz) *Physiol.* A contractile muscular movement of any hollow organ of the body, as of the alimentary canal and intestines, whereby the contents are gradually propelled toward the point of expulsion. Compare SYSTALTIC. [<NL <Gk. *peristaltikos* < *peristellein* surround < *peri-* around + *stellein* place] — **per′i·stal′tic** *adj.*

pe·ris·ta·sis (pə·ris′tə·sis) *n. Biol.* The total environment of an individual organism, including all its vital processes. [<NL <Gk., an environment < *peri-* around + *stasis* a standing < *histanai* stand]

per·i·stome (per′ə·stōm) *n.* 1 *Bot.* The fringe of delicate teeth, generally some multiple of four, around the mouth of the capsule of mosses. 2 *Zool.* The parts that surround the mouth; specifically, the lip or margin of the mouth of a univalve; the space between the mouth and the tentacles of a sea anemone. 3 *Entomol.* The oval margin of the face or border of the mouth in a dipterous insect. Also **pe·ris·to·ma** (pə·ris′tə·mə), **per′i·sto′·mi·um.** [<NL *peristoma* <Gk. *peri-* around + *stoma* a mouth]

per·i·style (per′ə·stīl) *n. Archit.* 1 A system of columns about a building or an internal court. 2 An area or space so enclosed. [<MF *péristyle* <L *peristylum* <Gk. *peristylon,* neut. of *peristylos* surrounded by a colonnade < *peri-* around + *stylos* a pillar] — **per′i·sty′lar** *adj.*

per·i·the·ci·um (per′ə·thē′shē·əm, -sē·əm) *n. pl.* **·ci·a** (-shē·ə, -sē·ə) *Bot.* A closed or narrow-mouthed receptacle containing the fructification in certain fungi, especially the powdery mildews. [<NL <Gk. *peri-* around + *thēkē* a case] — **per′i·the′ci·al** *adj.*

per·i·to·ne·um (per′ə·tə·nē′əm) *n. pl.* **·ne·a** (-nē′ə) *Anat.* A serous membrane that lines the abdominal cavity in mammals and is reflected as a more or less complete investment over the viscera. In the higher vertebrates the peritoneum forms a completely closed sac, except in females, where the Fallopian tubes open into the cavity. Also **per′i·to·nae′um.** [<LL *peritonaeum* <Gk. *peritonaion* < *peritonos* stretched round < *peri-* around + *teinein* stretch] — **per′i·to·ne′al** or **·nae′al** *adj.*

per·i·to·ni·tis (per′ə·tə·nī′tis) *n. Pathol.* Acute inflammation of the peritoneum. [< *periton-* (<PERITONEUM) + -ITIS]

pe·rit·ri·cha (pə·rit′rə·kə) *n. pl.* Bacteria having flagella all around the body. [<NL <Gk. *peri-* around + *thrix, trichos* hair] — **pe·rit′·ri·chous** *adj.*

per·i·vis·cer·al (per′i·vis′ər·əl) *adj. Anat.* Situated about the viscera: the *perivisceral* cavity.

per·i·wig (per′ə·wig) *n.* A wig; peruke. [Earlier *perwyke,* alter. of *perruck* <MF *perruque* PERUKE]

per·i·win·kle[1] (per′ə·wing′kəl) *n.* 1 A small marine snail of the genus *Littorina,* especially the edible **European periwinkle** *(L. littorea),* now common on the east coast of the United States, or the **American periwinkle** *(L. palliata).* 2 Any of various other small univalves. [OE *pinewinclan, winewinclan,* pl., ? <L *pinna* a mussel (<Gk.) + OE *wincla* a shellfish; ? infl. in form by PERIWINKLE[2]]

per·i·win·kle[2] (per′ə·wing′kəl) *n.* A plant of the genus *Vinca* (family *Apocynaceae*); especially, either of two European trailing shrubs, *V. minor* and *V. major,* with shining, evergreen, opposite leaves, and blue, or sometimes white, flowers. They are commonly called *myrtle* or *creeping myrtle* in the United States. [OE *peruince* <L *pervinca* < *vinca pervinca,* prob. < *pervincire* < *per-* thoroughly + *vincire* bind]

periwinkle blue A medium mauve blue, the color of a periwinkle flower.

per·jure (pûr′jər) *v.t.* **·jured, ·jur·ing** 1 To make (oneself) guilty of perjury. 2 To find guilty of or involved in perjury: usually in the passive: if they are *perjured.* [<OF *parjurer* <L *perjurare* < *per-* through, badly + *jurare* swear] — **per′jur·er** *n.*

per·jured (pûr′jərd) *adj.* Guilty of perjury; having sworn falsely; forsworn: a *perjured* witness. — **per′jured·ly** *adv.*

per·ju·ry (pûr′jə·rē) *n. pl.* **·ries** *Law* The wilful and voluntary giving of false testimony or the withholding of material facts or evidence, in regard to a matter or thing material to the issue or point of inquiry in a legal document or while under oath lawfully administered in a judicial proceeding.

perk[1] (pûrk) *v.i.* 1 To recover one's spirits or vigor: with *up.* 2 To carry oneself or lift one's head jauntily. — *v.t.* 3 To raise quickly or smartly, as the ears: often with *up.* 4 To make (oneself) trim and smart in appearance: often with *up* or *out.* — *adj.* Holding up the head smartly or jauntily; pert: also **perk′y.** [ME *perken,* ? <AF *perquer* pérch, roost] — **perk′i·ly** *adv.* — **perk′i·ness** *n.*

perk[2] (pûrk) *v.i. Colloq.* To percolate. [Short for PERCOLATE]

Per·kin (pûr′kin), **Sir William Henry,** 1838–1907, English chemist; founder of aniline dye industry, 1856.

Per·kins (pûr′kinz), **Frances,** 1882–1965, U.S. social worker and administrator; secretary of labor 1933–45.

Per·lis (pûr′lis) A State of Malaya, on the Strait of Malacca; 310 square miles; capital, Kangar.

per·lite (pûr′līt) *n.* An acid, igneous, glassy rock of the composition of obsidian, but divided into small spherical bodies by the stress developed by its contraction on cooling: also spelled *pearlite.* [<F < *perle* a pearl] — **per·lit′ic** (-lit′ik) *adj.*

Perm (pûrm) A city on the Kama in western Asiatic Russian S.F.S.R.: formerly *Molotov.*

per·ma·frost (pûr′mə·frôst, -frost) *n.* That part of the earth's surface in arctic regions which is permanently frozen. [<PERMA(NENT) + FROST]

Perm·al·loy (pûr′mə·loi) *n.* Any of a group of iron and nickel alloys with small quantities of other metals, characterized by high magnetic permeability: a trade name. [<PERM(EABLE) + ALLOY]

per·ma·nence (pûr′mə·nəns) *n.* The state of being permanent; durability; fixity. [<Med. L *permanentia* <L *permanens.* See PERMANENT.]

per·ma·nen·cy (pûr′mə·nən·sē) *n. pl.* **·cies** 1 Permanence. 2 Something permanent.

per·ma·nent (pûr′mə·nənt) *adj.* Continuing in the same state or without essential change; durable; fixed; stable: opposed to *temporary.* — *n.* A permanent wave. [<L *permanens, -entis* < *permanere* stay to the end < *per-* through + *manere* remain] — **per′ma·nent·ly** *adv.*

Synonyms (adj.): abiding, changeless, constant, durable, enduring, fixed, immutable, invariable, lasting, perpetual, persistent, stable, steadfast, unchangeable, unchanging. *Durable* is said almost wholly of material substances that resist wear; *lasting* is said of either material or immaterial things. *Permanent* is a word of wider meaning; a thing is *permanent* which is not liable to change; as, a *permanent* color. Buildings upon a farm are called *permanent* improvements. *Enduring* is applied to that which resists both time and change; as, *enduring* fame. See PERPETUAL. *Antonyms*: see synonyms for TRANSIENT.

Permanent Court of Arbitration See under COURT.

Permanent Court of International Justice See under COURT.

permanent set *Physics* A deformation of a rigid body or material that persists after the stress has been removed.

permanent wave An artificial wave mechanically or chemically produced on growing hair and lasting several months.

per·man·ga·nate (pər·mang′gə·nāt) *n. Chem.* A dark-purple salt of permanganic acid.

per·man·gan·ic (pûr′man·gan′ik) *adj. Chem.* Of, pertaining to, or designating an acid, $HMnO_4$, which is a powerful oxidizing agent in aqueous solutions.

per·me·a·bil·i·ty (pûr′mē·ə·bil′ə·tē) *n.* 1 The quality or condition of being permeable. 2 *Physics* The property of being easily traversed by magnetic lines of force; susceptibility to magnetization. 3 *Aeron.* The measure of the rate of diffusion of a gas per unit area of a balloon fabric under standard conditions: generally given in liters per square meter per 24 hours.

per·me·a·ble (pûr′mē·ə·bəl) *adj.* 1 Allowing passage, especially of fluids. 2 Designating a type of protective clothing treated to resist penetration by vapors and gases, but not by liquids. [<L *permeabilis* < *permeare* PERMEATE] — **per′me·a·bly** *adv.*

per·me·ance (pûr′mē·əns) *n. Electr.* Permeation; the reciprocal of the reluctance of a magnetic circuit.

per·me·ate (pûr′mē·āt) *v.* **·at·ed, ·at·ing** *v.t.* 1 To spread thoroughly through; pervade. 2 To pass through the pores or interstices of. — *v.i.* 3 To spread itself. [<L *permeatus,* pp. of *permeare* < *per-* through + *meare* pass] — **per′me·ant** *adj.* — **per′me·a′tion** *n.* — **per′·me·a′tive** *adj.*

per men·sem (pûr men′səm) *Latin* By the month.

Per·mi·an (pûr′mē·ən) *Geol. n.* The latest period of the Paleozoic era, following the Pennsylvanian and succeeded by the Triassic; also, the Permian rock system. — *adj.* Relating to this period. [after *Perm*, a former E. Russian province]

per mill (pûr mil′) In, into, or by the thousand. Also **per mil.** [<L *per* by + *mille* thousand]

per·mil·lage (pər·mil′ij) *n.* Proportion or rate per thousand; the number of thousandth parts.

per·mis·si·ble (pər·mis′ə·bəl) *adj.* That can be permitted; allowable. — **per·mis′si·bil′i·ty** *n.* — **per·mis′si·bly** *adv.*

per·mis·sion (pər·mish′ən) *n.* The act of permitting or allowing; license granted; formal authorization; consent. [<L *permissio, -onis* < *permissus,* pp. of *permittere* PERMIT]
Synonyms: allowance, authority, authorization, consent, leave, liberty, license, permit. *Authority* is rightful power conferred and limited by law; in a more general sense, *authority* is applied to any conceded power of control. *Permission* justifies another in acting without interference or censure, and usually implies some degree of approval. A *permit* is a special authorization, generally given in writing. A *license* is *permission* granted rather than *authority* conferred; the sheriff has *authority* (not *permission* or *license*) to make an arrest. *Consent* is *permission* by the concurrence of wills in two or more persons, a mutual approval or acceptance of something proposed. Compare synonyms for ALLOW. *Antonyms*: denial, hindrance, objection, opposition, prevention, prohibition, refusal, resistance.

per·mis·sive (pər·mis′iv) *adj.* 1 That permits; granting permission. 2 Permitted; optional. 3 Tolerant; lenient; indulgent: *permissive* parents. — **per·mis′sive·ly** *adv.* — **per·mis′sive·ness** *n.*

per·mis·so·ry (pər·mis′ər·ē) *adj.* 1 Pertaining to or of the nature of permission. 2 *Law* Arising from or founded on permission; authorized; licensed.

per·mit (pər·mit′) *v.* **·mit·ted, ·mit·ting** *v.t.* 1 To allow the doing of; consent to. 2 To give (someone) leave or consent; authorize. 3 To afford opportunity for: His answer *permits* no misinterpretation. — *v.i.* 4 To afford possibility or opportunity. — *n.* (pûr′mit) Permission or warrant; especially, a written authorization to do something. [<L *permittere* < *per-* through < *mittere* send, let go] — **per·mit′ter** *n.*
Synonyms (verb): allow, authorize, empower, let, license, suffer, tolerate. See ALLOW, ENDURE. Compare synonyms for PERMISSION. *Antonyms*: disallow, forbid, prohibit, refuse.

per·mit·tiv·i·ty (pûr′mə·tiv′ə·tē) *n. Electr.* Specific inductive capacity of a dielectric.

per·mut·a·ble (pər·myōō′tə·bəl) *adj.* Capable of being changed or of undergoing change or interchange.

per·mu·ta·tion (pûr′myōō·tā′shən) *n.* 1 The act of permuting; change; transformation. 2 *Math.* **a** Change in the order of sequence of elements or objects in a series; especially, the making of all possible changes of sequence, as *abc, acb, bac, bca,* etc. **b** Any one of the arrangements thus made: distinguished from *combination.* [<OF *permutacion* <L *permutatio, -onis* < *permutatus,* pp. of *permutare.* See PERMUTE.]

per·mute (pər·myōōt′) *v.t.* **·mut·ed, ·mut·ing** To subject to permutation, especially, to change the order of. [<L *permutare* < *per-* thoroughly + *mutare* change]

Per·nam·bu·co (pûr′nəm·byōō′kō, *Pg.* per′·nəm·bōō′kōō) 1 A state in NE Brazil on the Atlantic; 37,458 square miles; capital, Recife. 2 Recife.

per·ni·cious (pər·nish′əs) *adj.* 1 Having the power of destroying or injuring; tending to kill or hurt; very injurious; deadly. 2 Malicious; wicked. [<OF *pernicieux* <L *perniciosus* < *pernicies* destruction < *per-* thoroughly + *nex, necis* death] — **per·ni′cious·ly** *adv.* — **per·ni′cious·ness** *n.*
Synonyms: bad, baneful, deadly, destructive, evil, harmful, hurtful, injurious, mischievous, noxious, perverting, ruinous. *Pernicious* is stronger than *injurious*; that which is *injurious* is capable of doing harm; that which is *pernicious* is likely to be *destructive.* See BAD, INIMICAL, NOISOME. *Antonyms*: advantageous, beneficial, favorable, good, healthful, helpful, profitable, salutary, serviceable, wholesome.

pernicious anemia *Pathol.* A morbid condition characterized by a diminution in the number of red blood corpuscles, abnormalities in the composition of the blood, and progressive disturbances in the muscular, nervous, and gastrointestinal systems.

per·nick·e·ty (pər·nik′ə·tē) See PERSNICKETY.

Pe·rón (pā·rōn′), **Juan Domingo,** 1895–1974, Argentine president 1946–55; 1973–74.

per·o·ne·al (per′ə·nē′əl) *adj. Anat.* Of, pertaining to, or near, the fibula. [<NL *peronaeus* < *perone* the fibula <Gk. *peronē,* orig. a pin < *peirein* pierce]

Pe·ron·ist (pə·rōn′ist) *n.* A follower of Juan Perón or of his policies. Also **Pe·ron·is·ta** (per′ə·nēs′tə). — **Pe·ron′ism** *n.*

per·o·rate (per′ə·rāt) *v.i.* **·rat·ed, ·rat·ing** 1 To speak at length; harangue. 2 To sum up or conclude a speech.

per·o·ra·tion (per′ə·rā′shən) *n.* The concluding portion of an oration; the recapitulation and summing up of an argument. [<L *peroratio, -onis* < *peroratus,* pp. of *perorare* speak to the end < *per-* through + *orare* speak]

per·ox·i·dase (pə·rok′sə·dās) *n. Biochem.* Any of a class of enzymes which, in the presence of hydrogen peroxide, accelerate the oxidation of various compounds. [<PEROXID(E) + -ASE]

per·ox·ide (pə·rok′sīd) *n. Chem.* 1 An oxide having a larger proportion of oxygen than any other oxide of the same series: distinguished from *protoxide.* 2 Hydrogen peroxide. Also **per·ox′id** (-sid). — *v.t.* **·id·ed, ·id·ing** To treat with peroxide; bleach, as hair, with peroxide.

per·pend[1] (pər·pend′) *v.t.* & *v.i. Obs.* To ponder; consider. [<L *perpendere* < *per-* thoroughly + *pendere* weigh]

per·pend[2] (pûr′pənd) *n.* In masonry, a stone header extending through a wall so that one end appears on each side of it. Also **perpend stone, per′pent** (-pənt). [Var. of *parpen* <OF *parpain,* ? < *par-* through (<L *per-*) + *pan (de mur)* a side (of a wall); infl. in form by PEND]

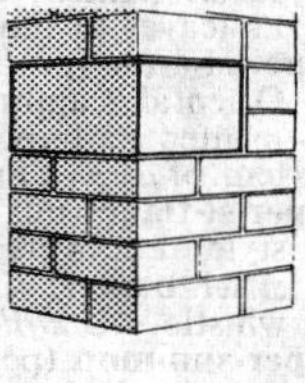
PERPEND

per·pen·dic·u·lar (pûr′pən·dik′yə·lər) *adj.* 1 Being at right angles to the plane of the horizon; upright or vertical. 2 *Math.* Meeting a given line or plane at right angles. See synonyms under RIGHT. — *n.* 1 A perpendicular line. 2 An appliance or instrument used to indicate the vertical line from any point; a plumb rule. 3 A line at right angles to another line or to a plane. 4 A vertical line or vertical face; loosely, any steep incline or face. 5 Perpendicular position. 6 Moral uprightness. [<OF *perpendiculer* <L *perpendicularis* < *perpendiculum* a plumb line < *per-* thoroughly + *pendere* hang] — **per′·pen·dic′u·lar′i·ty** (-lar′ə·tē) *n.* — **per′pen·dic′u·lar·ly** *adv.*

Perpendicular architecture A late style of Gothic architecture in England from the end of the 14th century through the 16th century: characterized by accentuation of vertical lines in its tracery.

per·pe·trate (pûr′pə·trāt) *v.t.* **·trat·ed, ·trat·ing** To do, perform, or commit (a crime, etc.). [<L *perpetratus,* pp. of *perpetrare* carry through < *per-* through + *patrare* effect] — **per′pe·tra′tion** *n.* — **per′pe·tra′tor** *n.*

per·pet·u·al (pər·pech′ōō·əl) *adj.* 1 Continuing unlimited in time. 2 Incessant; ceaseless. 3 *Bot.* Being in bloom during all or nearly all the year, as certain hybrid flowers. — *n.* Any perennial plant; also, any of certain perpetual hybrid roses. [<OF *perpetuel* <L *perpetualis* < *perpetuus* < *per-* through + *petere* seek] — **per·pet′u·al·ly** *adv.* — **per·pet′u·al·ness** *n.*
Synonyms (adj.): ceaseless, constant, continual, continuous, endless, enduring, eternal, incessant, interminable, lasting, perennial, permanent, sempiternal, unceasing, unending, unfailing, unintermitted, uninterrupted. See CONTINUAL, ETERNAL, PERMANENT. *Antonyms*: see synonyms for TRANSIENT.

perpetual calendar See under CALENDAR.

perpetual motion See under MOTION.

per·pet·u·ate (pər·pech′ōō·āt) *v.t.* **·at·ed, ·at·ing** To make perpetual or enduring. [<L *perpetuatus,* pp. of *perpetuare* perpetuate < *perpetuus* PERPETUAL] — **per·pet′u·a′tion** *n.* — **per·pet′u·a′tor** *n.*

per·pe·tu·i·ty (pûr′pə·tōō′ə·tē, -tyōō′-) *n. pl.* **·ties** 1 The quality or state of being perpetual. 2 Something that has perpetual existence or worth. 3 Unending or unlimited time. 4 *Law* A limitation rendering property inalienable; also, the property so limited. 5 In annuities, a perpetual annuity, or the number of years' purchase to be given for it; the number of years in which the simple interest of a sum becomes equal to the principal. [<OF *perpetuité* <L *perpetuitas* < *perpetuus* PERPETUAL]

Per·pi·gnan (per·pē·nyän′) A city of southern France near the Spanish border and the Mediterranean.

per·plex (pər·pleks′) *v.t.* 1 To cause to hesitate, as from doubt; confuse, as with difficult problems; puzzle. 2 To make complicated, intricate, or confusing. [Back formation from PERPLEXED]
Synonyms: bewilder, bother, complicate, confound, confuse, distract, embarrass, entangle, harass, involve, mystify, pose, puzzle, trouble. *Antonyms*: clarify, disentangle, elucidate, explain, simplify.

per·plexed (pər·plekst′) *adj.* 1 Confused; embarrassed. 2 Of a complicated character; involved. [Appar. alter. of obs. *perplex,* adj., intricate <L *perplexus* involved < *per-* thoroughly + *plexus,* pp. of *plectere* plait] — **per·plex′ed·ly** *adv.* — **per·plex′ed·ness** (-plek′sid·nis) *n.*

per·plex·ing (pər·plek′sing) *adj.* Confusing; puzzling; embarrassing; intricate. — **per·plex′·ing·ly** *adv.*

per·plex·i·ty (pər·plek′sə·tē) *n. pl.* **·ties** 1 Mental difficulty owing to doubt, confusion, etc. 2 That which perplexes; also, an instance of bewilderment. 3 The quality of being intricate or complicated; entanglement.
Synonyms: amazement, astonishment, bewilderment, confusion, distraction, disturbance, doubt, embarrassment. *Perplexity* is the drawing of the thoughts or faculties by turns in different directions or toward contrasted or contradictory conclusions; *confusion* is a state in which the mental faculties are thrown into chaos, so that the clear and distinct action of perception, memory, reason, and will, is lost; *bewilderment* is akin to *confusion,* but is less overwhelming, and more readily recovered from. *Perplexity* has not the unsettling of the faculties implied in *confusion,* nor the overwhelming of the faculties implied in *amazement* or *astonishment.* With an excitable person, *bewilderment* may deepen into *confusion* that will make him unable to think clearly or even to see or hear distinctly. *Amazement* results from the sudden and unimagined occurrence of great good or evil or the sudden awakening of the mind to unthought-of truth. *Astonishment* often produces *bewilderment,* which the word was formerly understood to imply. See AMAZEMENT, ANXIETY, CARE, DOUBT.

per·qui·site (pûr′kwə·zit) *n.* Any incidental profit from service beyond salary or wages; hence, any privilege or benefit claimed as due. [<Med. L *perquisitum* an acquisition <L, a thing diligently sought, orig. pp. neut. of *perquirere* < *per-* thoroughly + *quaerere* seek]

Per·rault (pe·rō′), **Charles,** 1628–1703, French author and compiler of fairy tales.

Per·rin (pe·raṅ′), **Jean,** 1870–1942, French physicist.

per·ron (per′ən, *Fr.* pe·rôn′) *n. Archit.* A flight of external steps and a platform before the entrance door of a building. [<OF <L *petra* stone]

per·ry (per′ē) *n.* A fermented drink made from the expressed juice of pears. [<OF *peré* <LL *pera.* See PEAR.]

Perry (per′ē), **Bliss,** 1860–1954, U.S. author and critic. — **Matthew Calbraith,** 1794–1858,

U.S. commodore; opened Japan to commerce in 1852. **— Oliver Hazard,** 1785–1819, U.S. naval commander; defeated British on Lake Erie, Sept. 10, 1813; brother of the preceding. **— Ralph Barton,** 1876–1956, U. S. philosopher and educator.

per·salt (pûr′sôlt′) *n. Chem.* A salt formed by combination of a negative radical or ion with a metal at a high, or its highest, state of oxidation.

per sal·tum (pər sôl′təm) *Latin* By a leap; without intermediate degrees.

perse (pûrs) *adj.* Grayish–blue. **—** *n.* A grayish blue. [<OF *pers* <LL *persus*]

per se (pûr sē′, sā′) *Latin* By itself, himself, or herself; intrinsically; in or of its own nature, without reference to its relations.

per·se·cute (pûr′sə·kyōōt) *v.t.* **·cut·ed, ·cut·ing** **1** To harass with cruel or oppressive treatment, especially because of race, religion, or opinions. **2** To annoy or harass persistently. [<OF *persecuter* <L *persecutus*, pp. of *persequi* pursue <*per-* thoroughly + *sequi* follow] **— per′se·cu′tive** *adj.* **— per′se·cu′tor** *n.*

Synonyms: afflict, distress, harass, harry, molest, oppress, torment, worry. See ABUSE. *Antonyms*: advance, advocate, aid, assist, befriend, cherish, countenance, encourage, favor, help, indulge, support, sustain, tolerate.

per·se·cu·tion (pûr′sə·kyōō′shən) *n.* **1** The act or process of persecuting; cruel oppression. **2** Any period characterized by systematic oppression, infliction of torture, death, or the like, on account of religious belief. **— per′se·cu′tion·al, per·se·cu·to·ry** (pûr′sə·kyōō′tər·ē) *adj.*

Per·se·ids (pûr′sē·idz) *n. pl. Astron.* The meteors belonging to the group that has its radiant point in the constellation Perseus, which appear about August 12 of each year. Also **Per·se·i·des** (pər·sē′ə·dēz). [<NL *Perseis*, pl. *Perseides* <Gk. *Perseïs*, pl. *Perseïdes*, a daughter of Perseus]

Per·seph·o·ne (pər·sef′ə·nē) In Greek mythology, the daughter of Zeus and Demeter, abducted by Pluto and made queen of the kingdom of the dead, but allowed to return to the earth for a third of each year: identified with the Roman *Proserpine*.

Per·sep·o·lis (pər·sep′ə·lis) An ancient, ruined capital of Persia NE of Shiraz in SW central Iran.

Per·seus (pûr′syōōs, -sē·əs) **1** In Greek mythology, the son of Zeus and Danae, slayer of Medusa and savior and husband of Andromeda. **2** In the Apocrypha, the last king of Macedonia; died about 164 B.C. I *Mac.* viii 5. **3** A northern constellation. See CONSTELLATION. [<L <Gk.]

per·se·ver·ance (pûr′sə·vir′əns) *n.* **1** The act or habit of persevering; persistence. **2** *Theol.* In Calvinism, the continuance in grace and certain salvation of those whom God effectually calls, accepts in Christ, and sanctifies by his spirit. [<OF *perseverance* <L *perseverantia* steadfastness <*perseverans, -antis*, pp. of *perseverare* PERSEVERE]

Synonyms: constancy, indefatigableness, persistence, persistency, resolution, steadiness, steadfastness, tenacity. See INDUSTRY. *Antonyms*: caprice, fickleness, fitfulness, inconstancy, irresolution, levity, unsteadiness, vacillation, volatility.

per·sev·er·a·tion (pər·sev′ə·rā′shən) *n. Psychol.* **1** The continual repetition of an activity or mental state. **2** The spontaneous recurrence in the mind of the same idea, phrase, tune, mental image, etc., irrespective of associative factors.

per·se·vere (pûr′sə·vir′) *v.i.* **·vered, ·ver·ing** To persist in any purpose or enterprise; continue striving in spite of difficulties, etc. [<OF *perseverer* <L *perseverare* <*perseverus* very strict <*per-* thoroughly + *severus* strict]

Synonyms: continue, endure, persist. *Persevere* is almost uniformly employed in the good and high sense of holding to a worthy course against all difficulty, danger, hindrance, or opposition; *persist* is often used of an annoying or perverse adherence to a demand or purpose that might well be abandoned. See INSIST, PERSIST. Compare OBSTINATE. *Antonyms*: see synonyms for CEASE.

per·se·ver·ing (pûr′sə·vir′ing) *adj.* Persistent of purpose. **— per′se·ver′ing·ly** *adv.*

Per·shing (pûr′shing), **John Joseph,** 1860–1948, U. S. general; commander in chief of the American Expeditionary Force of World War I.

Per·sia (pûr′zhə, -shə) The former name for IRAN. See PERSIAN EMPIRE.

Per·sian (pûr′zhən, -shən) *adj.* Of or pertaining to ancient Persia or modern Iran, its people, its language, or its architecture. **—** *n.* **1** A native or inhabitant of Persia or Iran. **2** The Iranian language of the Persians: historically divided into **Old Persian**, recorded in the cuneiform inscriptions of Darius I and his successors, and closely related to the language of the Avesta; **Middle Persian,** chiefly represented by Pahlavi, a literary language written in a Semitic alphabet, used in the sacred writings of the Zoroastrian religion from the third to the seventh century; and **Modern Persian,** containing many Arabic loan words and written in Arabic script. **3** A fine silk used formerly for linings. **4** *pl.* Persian blinds. [<OF *persien*, ult. <L *Persia* Persia <Gk. *Persis* <OPersian *Pārsa*]

Persian blinds Outside window shutters of thin, movable slats fastened in a frame.

Persian carpet A hand–woven Oriental carpet with connected design, the warp and filling of silk, wool, or cotton, and the pile of wool.

Persian Empire An empire of SW Asia, extending from the Indus to the Mediterranean: founded by Cyrus the Great (sixth century B.C.) and destroyed by Alexander the Great (331 B.C.).

Persian Gulf An arm of the Arabian Sea between Iran and Arabia; 90,000 square miles.

Persian lamb The young of certain sheep of central Asia, especially of the karakul; also, its skin, used as a fur; astrakan. See KARAKUL.

Persian wheel A noria.

per·si·car·y (pûr′sə·ker′ē) *n. pl.* **·car·ies** The knotweed; especially, the lady's–thumb (*Polygonum persicano*). [<NL *persicaria* <L *persicum (malum)* a peach; from the likeness of its leaves to those of the peach tree]

per·si·enne (pûr′zē·en′, *Fr.* per·syen′) *n.* **1** An Oriental cambric or muslin with colored printed pattern. **2** *pl.* Persian blinds. [<F, fem. of *persien* PERSIAN]

per·si·flage (pûr′sə·fläzh′) *n.* A light, flippant style of conversation or writing. [<F <*persifler* banter <L *per-* through + F *siffler* whistle <L *sifilare*]

per·sim·mon (pər·sim′ən) *n.* **1** The orange–red or yellow, plumlike fruit of an American tree of the ebony family (genus *Diospyros*), very astringent in taste until exposed to frost. **2** The tree, its hard blackish wood, or its tonic and astringent bark. [<Algonquian. Cf. Cree *pasiminan* dried fruit.]

Per·sis (pûr′sis) The ancient name for FARS.

per·sist (pər·sist′, -zist′) *v.i.* **1** To continue firmly in some course, state, etc., especially despite opposition or difficulties. **2** To be insistent, as in repeating a statement. **3** To continue to exist; endure. [<L *persistere* <*per-* thoroughly + *sistere* stand]

Synonyms: continue, endure, insist, last, persevere, remain, stay. As applied to duration, *last* is applied chiefly to things, *endure* to either persons or things. That *remains* or *stays* which is simply let alone; that which *endures* or *persists* does so against opposing forces. A man *insists* upon his demand, *persists* in his refusal. See under INSIST, PERSEVERE. *Antonyms*: see synonyms for CEASE.

per·sis·tence (pər·sis′təns, -zis′-) *n.* **1** The act of persisting in any course or enterprise; the quality of being persistent; perseverance; fixed adherence to a resolve, course of conduct, etc. **2** The continuance of an effect longer than the cause that first produced it. Also **per·sis′ten·cy.** See synonyms under INDUSTRY, PERSEVERANCE.

per·sis·tent (pər·sis′tənt, -zis′-) *adj.* **1** Firm and persevering in a course or resolve. **2** Enduring; permanent; continuous. **3** *Bot.* Not falling away; remaining for a long time or after the neighboring parts have reached maturity, as the calyx or petals in certain flowers. **4** *Zool.* Retained throughout life, as the gills of fishes and some amphibians. Compare DECIDUOUS. See synonyms under INDEFATIGABLE, INFLEXIBLE, OBSTINATE, PERMANENT. [<L *persistens, -entis*, ppr. of *persistere*. See PERSIST.] **— per·sis′tent·ly** *adv.*

Per·si·us (pûr′shē·əs, -shəs), A.D. 34–62, Roman satirist.

per·snick·e·ty (pər·snik′ə·tē) *adj. Colloq.* **1** Unduly fastidious; fussy; overprecise. **2** Demanding minute care or pains. Also *pernickety.* [<dial. E, ? alter. of PARTICULAR] **— per·snick′e·ti·ness** *n.*

per·son (pûr′sən) *n.* **1** A human being as including body and mind; an individual. **2** The body of a human being or its characteristic appearance and condition. **3** *Law* Any human being, corporation, or body politic having legal rights and duties. **4** *Theol.* One of the three individualities in the triune God; hypostasis. **5** *Gram.* **a** A modification of the pronoun and verb that distinguishes the speaker (**first person**), the person or thing spoken to (**second person**), and the person or thing spoken of (**third person**). **b** Any of the forms or inflections indicating this, as *I* or *we, you, he, she, it*. **6** An individual. **7** Superciliously, a common individual. **8** A part acted on the stage. **— in person** Present in the flesh; present and acting for oneself. [<F *personne* <L *persona* mask for actors. Doublet of PARSON.]

per·so·na (pər·sō′nə) *n. pl.* **·nae** (-nē) **1** Literally, person; specifically, a character in a drama, novel, etc.: dramatis *personae.* **2** In Jung's analytic psychology, the conscious artificial or masked personality complex developed by an individual, in contrast to his innate personality characteristics, for purposes of concealment, defense, deception, or adaptation to his environment. [<L, a person, orig. a mask]

per·son·a·ble (pûr′sən·ə·bəl) *adj.* Attractive in person; of good appearance. **— per′son·a·bly** *adv.*

per·son·age (pûr′sən·ij) *n.* **1** A man or woman of importance or rank. **2** An assumed character; an impersonation. **3** A character in fiction, history, etc.; a character in a play. [<OF <L *persona* a person]

per·so·na gra·ta (pər·sō′nə grä′tə, grā′tə) *Latin* An acceptable person.

per·son·al (pûr′sən·əl) *adj.* **1** Pertaining to or characteristic of a particular person; not general or public: a purely *personal* matter. **2** Belonging or relating to or constituting a person or persons, as distinguished from things; characteristic of human beings or free agents. **3** Performed by or done to the person directly concerned; done in person: a *personal* service. **4** Affecting or relating to one individually: *personal* habits. **5** Of or pertaining to the body or appearance: *personal* beauty. **6** Directly characterizing an individual; hence, concerning one's character or conduct, often in the sense of disparaging. **7** *Law* Appertaining to the person; movable: *personal* effects. **8** *Gram.* Denoting or indicating the person: *personal* pronouns. **—** *n.* **1** *Law* A movable article of property; chattel. **2** A paragraph or advertisement of personal reference or application. [<OF <LL *personalis* <L *persona* a person]

personal effects Goods, articles, and items of property having a more or less intimate relation to the person of the possessor.

personal equation **1** In precision observations and measurements, any deviation from a correct or standard value caused by variations in the technical skill or personal qualities of the observer. **2** Any individual characteristic which influences attitudes, judgments, or the full use of the reasoning powers in any situation.

per·son·al·i·ty (pûr′sən·al′ə·tē) *n. pl.* **·ties** **1** That which constitutes a person; also, that which distinguishes and characterizes a person; personal existence. **2** Anything said of a person, especially if disparaging: usually in the plural: offensive *personalities.* **3** A person, especially one of exceptional qualities. **— double** or **multiple personality** *Psychiatry* A condition in which two or more relatively distinct sets of experiences and behavior patterns reveal themselves alternately in the same individual. See synonyms under CHARACTER. [<OF *personalité* <Med. L *personalitas, -tatis* <LL *personalis* of a person]

per·son·al·ize (pûr′sən·əl·īz′) *v.t.* **·ized, ·iz·ing** **1** To make personal. **2** To personify.

per·son·al·ly (pûr′sən·əl·ē) *adv.* **1** In proper person; not through an agent. **2** With reference to one's own personality. **3** In a personal manner.

personal pronoun See under PRONOUN.

personal property Property that may attend the person of the owner; movables.

per·son·al·ty (pûr′sən·əl·tē) *n. pl.* **·ties** Personal property. [<AF *personaltie* <Med. L *personalitas.* See PERSONALITY.]

per·so·na non gra·ta (pər·sō′nə non grä′tə, grā′tə) *Latin* A person not acceptable.

per·son·ate (pûr′sən·āt) *v.t.* **·at·ed, ·at·ing** 1 To act the part of, as a character in a play. 2 To personify, as in poetry, art, etc. 3 *Law* To impersonate with intent to deceive. See synonyms under IMITATE. —*adj.* 1 *Bot.* Masklike; masked: said specifically of a gamopetalous, two-lipped corolla in which the mouth of the tube is closed by an inflated projection of the throat. 2 Impersonated; feigned. [<L *personatus* masked <*persona* a mask] —**per′son·a′tion** *n.* —**per′son·a′tive** *adj.* —**per′son·a′tor** *n.*

per·son·i·fi·ca·tion (pər·son′ə·fə·kā′shən) *n.* 1 The figurative endowment of inanimate objects or qualities with personality or human attributes. 2 Striking or typical exemplification of a quality or attribute in one's person; embodiment: She was the *personification* of joy. 3 The emblematic representation of an abstract quality or idea by a human figure. 4 Impersonation.

per·son·i·fy (pər·son′ə·fī) *v.t.* **·fied, ·fy·ing** 1 To think of or represent as having life or human qualities. 2 To represent (an abstraction or inanimate object) as a person; symbolize. 3 To be the embodiment of; typify: He *personifies* honor. [<F *personnifier* <L *persona* a mask, person + *facere* make] —**per·son′i·fi′er** *n.*

per·son·nel (pûr′sə·nel′) *n.* 1 Persons collectively. 2 The persons employed in a business or in military service. 3 The collective characteristics of such a body of persons. —*adj.* Of or pertaining to personnel; directing personnel. [<F <OF *personal* PERSONAL]

per·spec·tive (pər·spek′tiv) *n.* 1 The art or theory of representing, by a drawing made on a flat or curved surface, solid objects or surfaces conceived of as not lying in that surface; delineation of objects as they appear to the eye. 2 The art of conveying the impression of depth and distance; representation of scenes as they appear to the eye, by means of correct drawing, shading, etc. 3 The effect of distance upon the appearance of objects, by means of which the eye judges spatial relations. 4 The relative importance of facts or matters from any special point of view; also, their presentation with just regard to their proportional importance. 5 A distant view; vista; prospect: also figuratively. 6 A picture giving the illusion of a scene of nature. —**aerial perspective** The art of indicating the relative distances of objects by gradations of tone and color. —**linear perspective** The art or method of producing an appearance of distance by means of converging lines. —*adj.* Pertaining to the art of perspective; also, drawn in perspective. [<Med. L *perspectiva (ars)* optical (art) <LL *perspectivus* optical <L *perspectus,* pp. of *perspicere* <*per-* through + *specere* look] —**per·spec′tive·ly** *adv.*

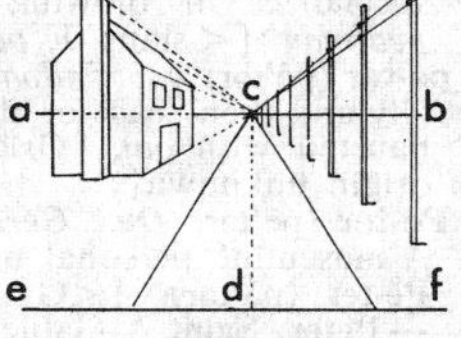

PERSPECTIVE
ab. Horizon.
c. Vanishing point (point of sight).
dc. Line of sight.
ef. Ground line.

per·spi·ca·cious (pûr′spə·kā′shəs) *adj.* 1 Keenly discerning or understanding. 2 Quick-eyed; sharp-sighted. See synonyms under ACUTE, ASTUTE, SAGACIOUS. [<L *perspicax, -acis* sharp-sighted <*perspicere.* See PERSPECTIVE.] —**per′spi·ca′cious·ly** *adv.* —**per′spi·ca′cious·ness** *n.*

per·spi·cac·i·ty (pûr′spə·kas′ə·tē) *n.* Keenness in mental penetration or discernment. See synonyms under ACUMEN.

per·spi·cu·i·ty (pûr′spə·kyōō′ə·tē) *n.* Clearness of expression or style; lucidity.
Synonyms: clearness, distinctness, explicitness, intelligibility, lucidity, plainness. *Antonyms*: ambiguity, cloudiness, confusion, incomprehensibility, indistinctness, intricacy, obscurity, unintelligibility, vagueness.

per·spic·u·ous (pər·spik′yōō·əs) *adj.* Having the quality of perspicuity; clear; lucid. See synonyms under CLEAR, PLAIN. [<L *perspicuus* clear, transparent <*perspicere.* See PERSPECTIVE.] —**per·spic′u·ous·ly** *adv.* —**per·spic′u·ous·ness** *n.*

per·spi·ra·tion (pûr′spə·rā′shən) *n.* 1 The exuding of the saline fluid secreted by the sweat glands of the skin. 2 The saline fluid excreted; sweat. —**per·spir·a·to·ry** (pər·spī′rə·tôr′ē, -tō′rē) *adj.*

per·spire (pər·spīr′) *v.* **·spired, ·spir·ing** *v.i.* To give off perspiration through the pores of the skin; sweat. —*v.t.* To give off through pores; exude. [<L *perspirare* breathe, blow constantly <*per-* through + *spirare* breathe] —**per·spir′a·ble** *adj.*

per·suade (pər·swād′) *v.t.* **·suad·ed, ·suad·ing** 1 To move (a person, etc.) to do something by arguments, inducements, pleas, etc. 2 To induce to a belief; convince. [<L *persuadere* <*per-* thoroughly + *suadere* advise] —**per·suad′a·ble** *adj.* —**per·suad′er** *n.*
Synonyms: allure, coax, convince, dispose, entice, impel, incite, incline, induce, influence, lead, move, urge, win. Of these words *convince* alone has no direct reference to moving the will, denoting an effect upon the understanding only; one may be *convinced* of truth that has no manifest connection with duty or action, as of a mathematical proposition. To *persuade* is to bring the will of another to a desired decision by some influence exerted upon it short of compulsion; one may be *convinced* that the earth is round; he may be *persuaded* to travel around it; but persuasion is so largely dependent upon conviction that it is commonly held to be the orator's work first to *convince* in order that he may *persuade.* *Coax* is a slighter word than *persuade,* seeking the same end by shallower methods, largely by appeal to personal feeling, with or without success; as, a child *coaxes* a parent to buy him a toy. One may be *induced* by means not properly included in persuasion, as by bribery or intimidation; he is *won* over chiefly by personal influence. See ACTUATE, BEND, CONVINCE, INFLUENCE. *Antonyms*: deter, discourage, dissuade, hinder, repel, restrain.

per·sua·si·ble (pər·swā′sə·bəl) *adj.* Open to persuasion; persuadable. —**per·sua′si·bil′i·ty, per·sua′si·ble·ness** *n.*

per·sua·sion (pər·swā′zhən) *n.* 1 The act of persuading or of using persuasive methods. 2 The state of being persuaded; settled opinion; conviction. 3 A settled belief; accepted creed; hence, a party, sect, or denomination. 4 *Colloq.* Sort; kind: the male *persuasion.* See synonyms under COUNSEL. [<L *persuasio, -onis* <*persuasus,* pp. of *persuadere* PERSUADE]

per·sua·sive (pər·swā′siv) *adj.* Having power or tendency to persuade. —*n.* That which persuades or tends to persuade. —**per·sua′sive·ly** *adv.* —**per·sua′sive·ness** *n.*

per·sul·fate (pər·sul′fāt) *n. Chem.* A salt of persulfuric acid. Also **per·sul′phate.**

per·sul·fu·ric (pûr′sul·fyŏŏr′ik) *adj. Chem.* Designating an acid, $H_2S_2O_8$, formed by the electrolysis of concentrated sulfuric acid. Also **per′sul·phu′ric.**

pert (pûrt) *adj.* 1 Disrespectfully forward or free; saucy. 2 *Dial.* Of fine appearance; comely; sprightly. See synonyms under IMPUDENT. [Aphetic var. of APERT] —**pert′ly** *adv.* —**pert′ness** *n.*

per·tain (pər·tān′) *v.i.* 1 To have reference; relate. 2 To belong as an adjunct, function, quality, etc.: the house and lands that *pertain* thereto. 3 To be fitting or appropriate: the joys that *pertain* to youth. [<OF *partenir* <L *pertinere* extend <*per-* through + *tenere* hold]
Synonyms: appertain, belong, concern, regard, relate.

pertaining to Having to do with or characteristic of; belonging or relating to.

Perth (pûrth) 1 An eastern midland county of Scotland; 2,493 square miles; county town, Perth. Also **Perth′shire** (-shir). 2 The capital of Western Australia, near the SW coast.

per·ti·na·cious (pûr′tə·nā′shəs) *adj.* 1 Tenacious of purpose; stubbornly adhering to a pursuit or opinion; also, perversely or doggedly persistent. 2 Continuing without abatement; incessant. See synonyms under INFLEXIBLE, OBSTINATE, URGENT. [<L *pertinax, -acis* <*per-* thoroughly, very + *tenax, -acis* tenacious] —**per′ti·na′cious·ly** *adv.*

per·ti·nac·i·ty (pûr′tə·nas′ə·tē) *n.* 1 Persistent tenacity of purpose; unyielding adherence. 2 Dogged perseverance; obstinacy.

per·ti·nent (pûr′tə·nənt) *adj.* Related to or properly bearing upon the matter in hand; relevant. See synonyms under APPROPRIATE. [<OF *partenant,* ppr. of *partenir* PERTAIN; refashioned after L *pertinens, -entis*] —**per′ti·nence, per′ti·nen·cy** *n.* —**per′ti·nent·ly** *adv.*

per·turb (pər·tûrb′) *v.t.* To disquiet or disturb greatly; alarm; agitate. [<OF *perturber* <L *perturbare* <*per-* thoroughly + *turbare* disturb <*turba* turmoil] —**per·turb′a·ble** *adj.*

per·tur·ba·tion (pûr′tər·bā′shən) *n.* 1 The state of being perturbed, or the act of perturbing. 2 *Astron.* Deviation in the motion of a heavenly body, caused by the attraction of some other body than that round which it moves. 3 A cause of disquiet or disturbance. Also **per·turb·ance** (pər·tûr′bəns). [<OF *perturbacion* <L *perturbatio, -onis* <*perturbare* PERTURB]

per·tus·sis (pər·tus′is) *n.* 1 *Pathol.* Whooping cough. 2 Any violent convulsive or spasmodic cough. [<NL <L *per-* thoroughly, very great + *tussis* a cough] —**per·tus′sal** *adj.*

Pe·ru (pə·rōō′, *Sp.* pā·rōō′) A republic in western South America on the Pacific; 533,916 square miles; capital, Lima.

Pe·ru·gia (pā·rōō′jä) A city in central Italy.

Pe·ru·gia (pā·rōō′jä), **Lake of** See TRASIMENO.

Pe·ru·gi·no (pā′rōō·jē′nō), 1446–1523, Italian painter; real name *Pietro Vannucci.*

pe·ruke (pə·rōōk′) *n.* A periwig. [<MF *perruque* <Ital. *perruca,* ? ult. <L *pilus* hair]

per·ul·ti·mate (pər·ul′tə·mit) *adj.* Designating a magnitude or condition that cannot be exceeded: a *perultimate* yield of crops. [<PER- (def. 2) + ULTIMATE]

pe·ruse (pə·rōōz′) *v.t.* **·rused, ·rus·ing** 1 To read carefully or attentively. 2 To read. 3 To examine; scrutinize. [<PER- + USE, *v.*] —**pe·rus′a·ble** *adj.* —**pe·ru′sal** *n.* —**pe·rus′er** *n.*

Pe·ru·vi·an (pə·rōō′vē·ən) *adj.* Of or pertaining to Peru or the Peruvians. —*n.* 1 A native or inhabitant of Peru. 2 An Indian of any of the Quechuan tribes of the ancient Inca empire.

Peruvian bark Jesuits' bark.

Pe·ruz·zi (pā·rōō′tsē), **Baldassare,** 1481–1536, Italian architect and painter.

per·vade (pər·vād′) *v.t.* **·vad·ed, ·vad·ing** To pass or spread through every part of; be diffused throughout; permeate. [<L *pervadere* <*per-* through + *vadere* go] —**per·va′sion** (-zhən) *n.*

per·va·sive (pər·vā′siv) *adj.* Thoroughly penetrating or permeating. [<L *pervasus,* pp. of *pervadere* PERVADE] —**per·va′sive·ly** *adv.* —**per·va′sive·ness** *n.*

per·verse (pər·vûrs′) *adj.* 1 Wrong or erring; different or varying from the correct or normal; also, unreasonable. 2 Thwarting or refractory. 3 Disposed to vex; petulant. [<OF *pervers* <L *perversus* turned the wrong way, orig. pp. of *pervertere.* See PERVERT.] —**per·verse′ly** *adv.* —**per·verse′ness** *n.* —**per·ver′sive** *adj.*
Synonyms: contrary, factious, fractious, froward, intractable, obstinate, petulant, stubborn, ungovernable, untoward, wayward, wilful. *Perverse* signifies wilfully wrong or erring, unreasonably set against right, reason, or authority. The *stubborn* or *obstinate* person will not do what another desires or requires; the *perverse* person will do anything contrary to what is desired or required of him. The *petulant* person frets, but may comply; the *perverse* individual may be smooth or silent, but is wilfully *intractable.* *Wayward* refers to a *perverse* disregard of morality and duty; *froward* is now almost obsolete; *untoward* is rarely heard except in certain phrases; as, *untoward* circumstances. Compare OBSTINATE. *Antonyms*: accommodating, amenable, complaisant, compliant, genial, governable, kind, obliging.

per·ver·sion (pər·vûr′zhən, -shən) *n.* **1** The act of perverting, or the state of being perverted. **2** *Pathol.* A deviation from the normal in structure or function. **3** *Psychiatry* Deviation from the normal in sexual desires or activities.

per·ver·si·ty (pər·vûr′sə·tē) *n. pl.* **·ties 1** The state or quality of being perverse. **2** Perverse nature or behavior. **3** An instance of perverseness.

per·vert (pər·vûrt′) *v.t.* **1** To turn to an improper use or purpose; misapply. **2** To distort the meaning of; misconstrue. **3** To turn from approved opinions or conduct; lead astray; corrupt. — *n.* (pûr′vûrt) **1** An apostate; renegade: opposed to *convert.* **2** *Psychiatry* One affected with or addicted to sexual perversion. [<F *pervertir* <L *pervertere* turn around, over < *per-* away + *vertere* turn] — **per·vert′er** *n.* — **per·vert′i·bil′i·ty** *n.* — **per·vert′i·ble** *adj.* — **per·vert′i·bly** *adv.*

Synonyms (verb): corrupt, distort, falsify, garble, misquote, misrepresent, misstate, stretch, twist. See ABUSE. *Antonyms*: correct, quote, rectify, restore.

per·vert·ed (pər·vûr′tid) *adj.* **1** Turned from the right purpose; misused. **2** Wilfully sinful; wicked; vicious. — **per·vert′ed·ly** *adv.*

per·vi·ous (pûr′vē·əs) *adj.* Capable of being penetrated; permeable. [<L *pervius* having a way through < *per-* through + *via* way] — **per′vi·ous·ly** *adv.* — **per′vi·ous·ness** *n.*

pes (pēz) *n. pl.* **pe·des** (pē′dēz) *Zool.* **1** The distal segment of the hind limb of a vertebrate, composed of tarsus, metatarsus, and phalanges. **2** A footlike organ, appearance, or part. **3** In prosody, the name for each of the first two quatrains of a sonnet. [<L, a foot]

Pe·sach (pā′säkh) *n.* The feast of the Passover. Also **Pe′sah.** See JEWISH HOLIDAYS. [<Hebrew *pesakh,* lit., a passing over < *pāsakh* pass over]

pe·sade (pə·säd′, -zäd′, -zäd′) *n.* The act or position of a saddle horse in rearing. [<F, alter. of *posade* <Ital. *posata* a pause < *posare* pause <L *pausare* halt < *pausa* a stop]

Pe·sa·ro (pā′zä·rō) A port on the Adriatic in The Marches, central Italy.

Pes·ca·do·res (pes′kä·dō′räs) A former name for the PENGHU ISLANDS.

Pes·ca·ra (päs·kä′rä) A port on the Adriatic in south central Italy.

pe·se·ta (pə·sā′tə, *Sp.* pā·sā′tä) *n.* A Spanish monetary unit; a silver coin equivalent to 100 centesimos. [<Sp., dim. of *pesa* a weight]

Pe·sha·war (pə·shä′wər, pā′shä·vər) **1** A commissioners' division of northern West Pakistan, near Afghanistan; 27,563 square miles. **2** The chief city of this division, anciently, a Greco-Buddhist cultural center; capital of North-West Frontier Province, British India, 1901–47; capital of North-West Frontier Province, West Pakistan, 1947–55.

Pe·shi·to (pə·shē′tō) *n.* The oldest Syriac version of the Bible. Also **Pe·schi′to, Pe·shit′ta** (-shē′tä), **Pe·shit·to.** [<Syriac *p'shī(t)to,* lit. plain, simple]

pes·ky (pes′kē) *adj.* **·ki·er, ·ki·est** *Colloq.* **1** Annoying; troublesome; plaguy. **2** Darned; damned: a euphemism. [< dial. E, prob. alter. of *pesty* <PEST] — **pes′ki·ly** *adv.*

pe·so (pā′sō) *n. pl.* **·sos 1** A monetary unit of Cuba, the Philippines, Mexico, and certain other Latin-American countries, equal to 100 centavos. **2** An old Spanish coin equal to 8 reales; the Spanish dollar or piece-of-eight. [<Sp., orig. a weight <L *pensum,* orig. pp. neut. of *pendere* weigh]

pes·sa·ry (pes′ə·rē) *n. pl.* **·ries** *Med.* **1** An instrument used to remedy a uterine displacement. **2** A medicated suppository for use in the vagina. **3** A contraceptive device worn over or in the uterine cervix. [<Med. L *pessarium* <L *pessum* <Gk. *pessos* an oval stone]

pes·si·mism (pes′ə·miz′əm) *n.* **1** A disposition to take a gloomy view of affairs: opposed to *optimism.* **2** Cynicism. **3** A theory of cosmology that regards the cosmos, or the world and life, or some main constituent thereof, as essentially evil, or (in its extreme form) as the worst possible world. [<L *pessimus* worst + -ISM, on analogy with *optimism*] — **pes′si·mist** *n.* — **pes′si·mis′tic** or **·ti·cal** *adj.* — **pes′si·mis′ti·cal·ly** *adv.*

pest (pest) *n.* **1** A pernicious or vexatious person or thing, especially a destructive or injurious insect. **2** A virulent epidemic; pestilence. [<MF *peste* <L *pestis* a plague]

Pes·ta·loz·zi (pes′tä·lôt′tsē), **Johann Heinrich,** 1746–1827, Swiss educational reformer who held that development was the chief end of education. — **Pes′ta·loz′zi·an** *adj. & n.*

pes·ter (pes′tər) *v.t.* To harass with petty and persistent annoyances; bother; plague. [Aphetic var. of obs. *impester* entangle <OF *empestrer, empasturer,* orig. hobble a grazing horse < *em-* (<L *in-* in) + LL *pastorium* foot shackles <L *pastus,* pp. of *pascere* feed] — **pes′ter·er** *n.*

pest·hole (pest′hōl′) *n.* A breeding place for pestilence.

pest·house (pest′hous′) *n.* A public hospital where patients suffering from infectious or pestilential diseases are treated and kept isolated.

pes·ti·cide (pes′tə·sīd) *n.* A chemical or other substance effective in the destruction of such plant and animal pests as fungi, bacteria, insects, and the like. — **pes′ti·ci′dal** *adj.*

pes·tif·er·ous (pes·tif′ər·əs) *adj.* **1** Carrying pestilence. **2** Threatening or bringing danger or evil. **3** *Colloq.* Annoying; disagreeable. See synonyms under NOISOME. [<L *pestiferus* bringing plague < *pestis* a plague + *ferre* bear] — **pes·tif′er·ous·ly** *adv.* — **pes·tif′er·ous·ness** *n.*

pes·ti·lence (pes′tə·ləns) *n.* **1** Any wide-spread and fatal infectious or contagious malady. **2** Figuratively, a noxious or malign doctrine, influence, etc.

pes·ti·lent (pes′tə·lənt) *adj.* **1** Tending to produce malignant zymotic disease; pestilential. **2** Having a malign influence or effect. **3** Making trouble; causing irritation; vexatious. [<L *pestilens, -entis* < *pestis* a plague] — **pes′ti·lent·ly** *adv.*

pes·ti·len·tial (pes′tə·len′shəl) *adj.* **1** Having the nature of or breeding pestilence. **2** Morally harmful or pernicious; baneful. See synonyms under NOISOME.

pes·tle (pes′əl) *n.* **1** An implement used for braying, bruising, or mixing substances, as in a mortar. **2** A vertical moving bar employed in pounding, as in a stamp mill, etc. — *v.t. & v.i.* **·tled, ·tling** To pound, grind, or mix with or as with a pestle. [<OF *pestel* <L *pistillum* < *pistus,* pp. of *pinsere* pound]

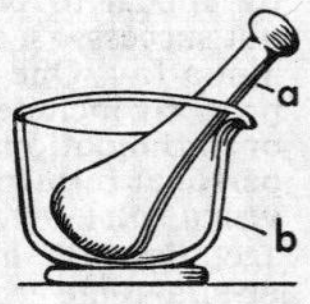

PESTLE
a. Pestle.
b. Mortar.

Pe·sto (pā′stō) A village on the site of ancient PAESTUM.

Pest·szent·er·zsé·bet (pesht′sent·er′zhā·bet) A city in north central Hungary SE of Budapest.

pet[1] (pet) *n.* **1** A tame, fondled animal. **2** Any loved and cherished creature; also, a favorite: teacher's *pet.* — *adj.* **1** Being a pet; indulged and fondled: a *pet* cat. **2** Regarded as a favorite; cherished: my *pet* hobby. — *v.* **pet·ted, pet·ting** — *v.t.* **1** *Rare* To treat as a pet; indulge. **2** To stroke or caress. — *v.i.* **3** *U.S. Slang* To make love by kissing and caressing. See synonyms under PAMPER, CARESS. [< dial. E (Scottish), ? back formation <PETTY, in affectionate use]

pet[2] (pet) *n.* A fit of pique or ill temper; peevish mood. [< obs. *to take the pet* take offence, sulk; origin uncertain]

Pé·tain (pā·tan′), **Henri Philippe,** 1856–1951, French marshal; chief of state 1940–44; convicted of treason 1945.

pet·al (pet′l) *n. Bot.* One of the leaves or subordinate parts of a corolla. [<NL *petalum* <L, a metal plate <Gk. *petalon* a thin plate, leaf, orig. neut. of *petalos* outspread < *petannynai* expand] — **pet′aled** or **pet′alled** *adj.*

-petal *combining form* Seeking: *centripetal.* [<L *petere* seek]

pet·a·lif·er·ous (pet′ə·lif′ər·əs) *adj.* Bearing petals. [<PETAL + -(I)FEROUS]

pet·a·line (pet′ə·lin, -līn) *adj.* Of, pertaining to, or like a petal.

pet·al·ism (pet′l·iz′əm) *n.* A form of ostracism in use among the Greeks of ancient Syracuse, who wrote on olive leaves their votes to banish for five years a citizen obnoxious to his fellow citizens. [<Gk. *petalismos* < *petalon* a leaf]

pet·a·lo·dy (pet′ə·lō′dē) *n. Bot.* A metamorphosis of other organs, as sepals or stamens, into petals, as in cultivated roses and double flowers. [<Gk. *petalōdēs* leaflike < *petalon* a leaf + *eidos* a form] — **pet′a·lod′ic** (-lod′ik) *adj.*

pet·al·oid (pet′l·oid) *adj.* Like or consisting of petals.

pet·al·ous (pet′l·əs) *adj.* Petaled; provided with petals.

pe·tard (pi·tärd′) *n.* **1** An explosive device formerly used for making breaches, etc., as in walls. **2** A small paper bomb used in pyrotechnics to imitate the sound of musketry. [<MF *pétard* < *péter* break wind <OF *pet* a fart <L *peditum,* orig. pp. neut. of *pedere* break wind]

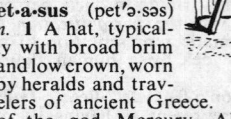

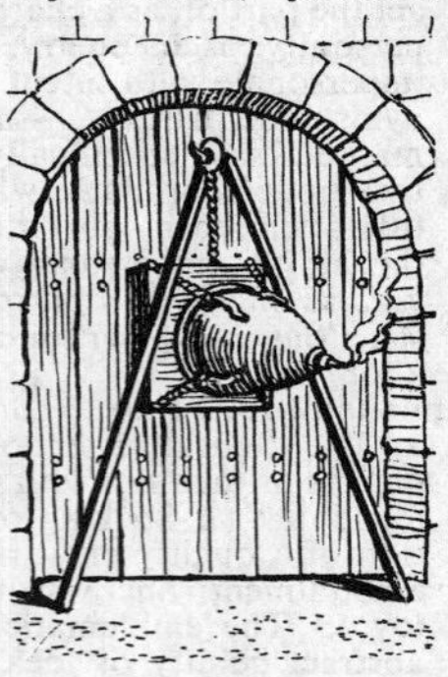
PETARD

pet·a·sus (pet′ə·səs) *n.* **1** A hat, typically with broad brim and low crown, worn by heralds and travelers of ancient Greece. **2** The winged hat of the god Mercury. Also **pet′a·sos.** [<L <Gk. *petasos* < *petannynai* spread out]

pet·cock (pet′kok′) *n. Mech.* A small cock, as at the end of a steam cylinder or on a pipe or pump, for testing or draining. [? < obs. *pet* a fart + COCK[1] a valve]

Pete (pēt) Diminutive of PETER.

pe·te·chi·a (pə·tē′kē·ə) *n. pl.* **·chi·ae** (-ki·ē) *Pathol.* One of a number of small purplish spots on the skin, which appear in certain severe fevers. [<NL <Ital. *petecchia* a freckle; ult. origin unknown] — **pe·te′chi·al** *adj.*

pete·man (pēt′mən) *n. Slang* A criminal who specializes in blowing safes: also spelled *peatman.* [< slang E *pete(r)* a safe + MAN]

pe·ter (pē′tər) *v.i. Colloq.* To diminish gradually and then cease or disappear; become exhausted: with *out.* [Orig. U.S. mining slang; origin unknown]

Pe·ter (pē′tər; *Du., Ger., Norw., Sw.* pā′tər) A masculine personal name. Also *Hungarian* **Pé·ter** (pā′tər). [<Gk., a stone]

— **Peter, Saint** A Galilean fisherman, one of the Twelve Apostles, reputed author of two epistles of the New Testament; also called "Simon Peter."

— **Peter I,** 1672–1725, czar of Russia 1682–1725, known as **Peter the Great.**

— **Peter II,** 1923–1970, king of Yugoslavia 1934–45.

— **Peter the Hermit,** 1050?–1115?, French monk; preacher of the First Crusade.

Pe·ter·bor·ough (pē′tər·bûr′ō, -bər·ə) A city in NE Northamptonshire, England.

Peterborough, Soke of See SOKE OF PETERBOROUGH.

Pe·ter·kin (pē′tər·kin) Diminutive of PETER.

Pe·ter·mann Peak (pā′tər·män) A mountain in eastern Greenland; 9,645 feet.

Peter Pan 1 In J. M. Barrie's play, *Peter Pan* (1904), the little boy "who never grew up." **2** A statue, in Kensington Gardens, London, symbolizing perpetual youth; hence, any fully grown person of youthful or childish enthusiasm.

Pe·ters (pā′tərs), **Karl,** 1856–1918, German explorer and colonial statesman in Africa.

Pe·ters·burg (pē′tərz·bûrg) A port on the Appomattox River in SE Virginia; scene of Civil War battles, 1864, 1865.

pe·ter·sham (pē′tər·shəm) *n.* **1** A heavy, rough, tufted woolen cloth. **2** Formerly, a heavy greatcoat of such cloth. [after Viscount *Petersham,* who introduced it]

Peter's pence 1 Voluntary contributions raised by Roman Catholics for the pope since 1860. **2** The tax of a penny for every house, once paid by the English to support the English hospice in Rome; also, a like tribute paid by them and other peoples to aid the pope: so called because collected on St. Peter's Day: also called *hearth money.* Also **Peter pence.**

pet·i·ole (pet′ē·ōl) *n.* **1** *Bot.* The footstalk of a leaf. **2** *Zool.* A stalk or peduncle. [<L *petiolus* a stem, fruitstalk, orig. dim. of *pes, pedis* a foot] — **pet′i·o′lar** *adj.* — **pet′i·o·late′, pet′i·o·lat′ed** *adj.*

pet·it (pet′ē) *adj.* Small; lesser; minor; trivial: used in legal phrases: *petit* larceny: also spelled *petty*. [< OF, small, ? < Celtic *pit* something pointed, thin]

Pe·tit (pə·tē′), **Alexis Thérèse,** 1791–1820, French physicist. See DULONG AND PETIT'S LAW.

pe·tite (pə·tēt′) *adj. fem.* Diminutive; little. [< F, fem. of *petit*. See PETIT.]

Petite Terre (pə·tē târ′) An island group comprising a dependency of Guadeloupe; 1.2 square miles.

pe·ti·tion (pə·tish′ən) *n.* 1 A request, supplication, or prayer; a solemn or formal supplication. 2 A formal request, written or printed, addressed to a person in authority and asking for some grant or benefit, the redress of a grievance, etc. 3 *Law* A formal application in writing made to a court, requesting judicial action concerning some matter therein set forth. 4 That which is requested or supplicated. —*v.t.* 1 To make a petition to; entreat. 2 To ask for. —*v.i.* 3 To make a petition. See synonyms under ASK, PRAY. [< OF *peticiun* < L *petitio, -onis* < *petere* seek; refashioned after L] —**pe·ti′tion·ar′y** *adj.* —**pe·ti′tion·er** *n.*

Synonyms (noun): appeal, application, craving, entreaty, pleading, prayer, request, supplication. See PRAYER. *Antonyms:* command, demand, denial, exaction, refusal, requirement.

pe·ti·ti·o prin·cip·i·i (pə·tish′ē·ō prin·sip′ē·ī) *Logic* Begging the question; assuming in the premise that which is to be proved. [< L]

petit juror A member of a petit jury: also spelled *petty juror.*

petit jury See under JURY.

petit larceny The theft of property of less than such amount as may be fixed by statute: the distinction between petit and grand larceny has been almost wholly abolished: also spelled *petty larceny.* See LARCENY.

pe·tit mal (pə·tē′ mäl′) *Pathol.* A form of epileptic seizure characterized by a momentary loss of memory or consciousness and a brief interval of helplessness. See GRAND MAL.

pet·i·to·ry (pet′ə·tôr′e, -tō′re) *adj.* Soliciting or solicited by petition. [< LL *petitorius* < L *petitor* a candidate < *petere* seek]

pet·it point (pet′ē) A fine needle-tapestry stitch: also called *tent stitch.*

pe·tits fours (pet′ē fôrz′, fōrz′; *Fr.* pə·tē′ foor′) Small cakes, often elaborately iced. [< F, lit., little ovens]

pet·nap·ping (pet′nap′ing) *n.* The act of stealing a pet or pets, esp. for commercial gain.

Pe·tra (pē′trə) A ruined ancient city of SW Jordan.

Pe·trarch (pē′trärk), **Francesco,** 1304–74, Italian scholar and poet.

Pe·trar·chan sonnet (pi·trär′kən) See under SONNET.

pet·rel (pet′rəl) *n.* A long-winged, black-and-white sea bird (order *Procellariiformes*); Mother Carey's chicken. [Earlier *pitteral,* ? a dim. of PETER; from its seeming to walk on the water like St. *Peter. Matt.* xiv 29]

PETREL
(Body from 7 to 16 inches long; the storm petrel, Mother Carey's chicken, 5 to 6 inches)

pe·tres·cent (pi·tres′ənt) *adj.* Petrifying or tending to petrify. [< L *petra* a rock + -ESCENT]

Pe·tri dish (pē′tre) A shallow, thin glass dish having a loose cover, used esp. to grow bacterial cultures. [after Julius *Petri,* 1852–1921, a German bacteriologist]

pet·ri·fac·tion (pet′rə·fak′shən) *n.* 1 Partial or entire replacement of the material of an organism by mineral matter: also **pe·tres′cence, pe·tres′cen·cy.** 2 Anything petrified. Also **pet′ri·fi·ca′tion** (on analogy with *satisfaction, stupefaction,* etc.) —**pet′ri·fac′tive** *adj.*

Petrified Forest National Monument A region of eastern Arizona containing petrified flora; 133 square miles; established 1906.

pet·ri·fy (pet′rə·fī) *v.* **·fied, ·fy·ing** *v.t.* 1 To convert (organic material) into a substance of stony character. 2 To make fixed and unyielding; deaden; harden. 3 To daze or paralyze with fear, surprise, etc. —*v.i.* 4 To become stone or a

stony substance. [< MF *pétrifier* < L *petra* a rock + *facere* make] —**pe·trif·ic** (pə·trif′ik) *adj.*

petro- combining form Rock; stone: *petroglyph.* Also, before vowels, **petr-.** [< Gk. *petra* a rock and *petros* a stone]

pet·ro·chem·is·try (pet′rō·kem′is·tre) *n.* The chemistry of petroleum and its derivatives, especially the natural and synthetic hydrocarbons. —**pet′ro·chem′i·cal** *adj. & n.*

pet·ro·dol·lars (pet′rō·dol′ərz) *n. pl.* Surplus dollars accumulated by oil-producing countries from oil sales, and usually invested in industrial countries.

pet·ro·glyph (pet′rə·glif) *n.* A primitive figure or legend cut in rock. [< F *pétroglyphe* < Gk. *petra* a rock + *glyphē.* See GLYPH.] —**pet′ro·glyph′ic** *adj.*

Pet·ro·grad (pet′rə·grad, *Russian* pe·trô·grät′) A former name for LENINGRAD.

pet·ro·graph (pet′rə·graf, -gräf) *n.* A prehistoric carving or inscription on a rock.

pe·trog·ra·phy (pə·trog′rə·fe) *n.* The systematic description and classification of rocks. —**pe·trog′ra·pher** *n.* —**pet·ro·graph·ic** (pet′rə·graf′ik) or **·i·cal** *adj.* —**pet′ro·graph′i·cal·ly** *adv.*

pet·rol (pet′rəl) *n.* 1 *Brit.* Gasoline. 2 *Obs.* Petroleum. [< OF *petrole* < Med. L *petroleum* PETROLEUM]

PETROGRAPH
From Australia.

pet·ro·la·tum (pet′rə·lā′təm) *n.* A fatty semisolid mixture of the paraffin hydrocarbons, obtained from petroleum, used in preparing ointments, and internally: often called *mineral jelly.* [< NL < PETROLEUM]

pe·tro·le·um (pə·trō′le·əm) *n.* An oily, liquid mixture of numerous hydrocarbons, chiefly of the paraffin series, found in many widely scattered subterranean deposits, and extensively used for heat and light. A number of very important substances are obtained by the fractional distillation of petroleum, such as petroleum ether, gasoline, naphtha, benzine, kerosene, paraffin, etc. [< Med. L < *petra* a rock (< Gk.) + *oleum* oil]

pe·trol·ic (pə·trol′ik) *adj.* Of or pertaining to petroleum.

pe·trol·o·gy (pə·trol′ə·je) *n.* The science of the origin, structure, constitution, and characteristics of rocks: a branch of geology. —**pet·ro·log·ic** (pet′rə·loj′ik) or **·i·cal** *adj.* —**pet′ro·log′cal·ly** *adv.* —**pe·trol′o·gist** *n.*

pet·ro·nel (pet′rə·nəl) *n.* A 15th century firearm about the size of a large horse pistol, fired with the stock resting against the breast. [< MF *petrinal,* dial. var. of *poitrinal,* adj., pectoral < *poitrin* the chest, ult. < L *pectus*]

Pe·tro·ni·us (pə·trō′ne·ə), **Gaius,** died A.D. 66?, Roman author, called "Arbiter of Elegance."

Pet·ro·pav·lovsk (pet′rō·päv·lôfsk′, *Russian* pe′tro·päv′ləfsk) A city in Kazakh S.S.R., on the shim.

Pe·tró·po·lis (pə·trô′poo·lēs) A city in Rio de Janeiro state, Brazil.

pet·rous (pet′rəs, pē′trəs) *adj.* 1 Hard, like stone. 2 *Anat.* Pertaining to or situated near the hard portion of the temporal bone. Also **pe·tro·sal** (pə·trō′səl) [< L *petrosus* rocky < L *petra* rock < Gk.]

Pe·tro·vitch (pe′trô·vich), **George** See KARAGEORGE.

Pet·ro·za·vodsk (pet′rə·zä·vôtsk′) A city on Lake Onega, capital of Karelo-Finnish S.S.R. *Finnish* **Pe·tro·skoi** (pe′trô·skoi).

Pe·trus (*Lat.* pē′trəs, *Du., Sw.* pā′trəs) See PETER. Also *Greek* **Pe·tros** (pā′tros).

pet·ti·coat (pet′ē·kōt) *n.* 1 A skirt or loose garment depending from the waist; especially, a

woman's underskirt. 2 One who wears a petticoat; hence, a woman. 3 An electric insulator shaped like an inverted cup, for use on high-tension wires. —*adj.* Of, pertaining to or influenced by, women: *petticoat* politics. [Earlier *petty coat* < PETTY + COAT]

pet·ti·fog (pet′ē·fog, -fôg) *v.i.* **fogged, ·fog·ging** To be a pettifogger. [Appar. back formation < PETTIFOGGER]

pet·ti·fog·ger (pet′ē·fog′ər, -fôg′ər) *n.* An inferior lawyer, especially one chiefly employed on mean or petty cases, or resorting to small or tricky methods. [Earlier *petty fogger* < PETTY + obs. *fogger* a trickster for gain, prob. < FUGGER] —**pet′ti·fog·ger·y** *n.*

pet·tish (pet′ish) *adj.* Capriciously ill-tempered; testy. See synonyms under FRETFUL. [Prob. < PET[2] + -ISH] —**pet′tish·ly** *adv.*

pet·ti·toes (pet′ē·tōz) *n. pl.* The aborted toes at the back of a pig's foot. [Earlier sense "giblets" < F *petit oie* goose giblets, lit., a little goose; later mistakenly understood as *petty toes*]

pet·tle (pet′l) *n. Scot.* A plowstaff. Also **pet′tul.**

pet·to (pet′ō) *n.* The breast. —**cardinal in petto** A cardinal appointed, but not yet formally announced. —**in petto** Within one's own breast; to oneself. [< Ital., the breast < L *pectus*]

pet·ty (pet′ē) *adj.* **·ti·er, ·ti·est** 1 Having little worth, importance, position, or rank; trifling; inferior: also spelled *petit.* 2 Having little scope or generosity; narrow-minded. 3 Mean; spiteful. See synonyms under CHILDISH, INSIGNIFICANT, LITTLE, SMALL. —*n.* A small amount of money advanced from a week's wages. [< F *petit* small. See PETIT.] —**pet′ti·ly** *adv.* —**pet′ti·ness** *n.*

petty cash Money used for the purchase of small items.

petty jury, petty larceny, etc. See PETIT JURY, etc.

petty officer In the navies of the United States and Great Britain, an enlisted man comparable in rank with a non-commissioned officer of the army.

pet·u·lance (pech′oo·ləns) *n.* 1 Fretfulness; peevishness; temporary ill-humor. 2 *Obs.* Insolence; pertness. Also **pet′u·lan·cy.** See synonyms under IMPATIENCE.

pet·u·lant (pech′oo·lənt) *adj.* 1 Displaying or characterized by capricious fretfulness; peevish. 2 *Obs.* Saucily rude; insolent; wanton; pert. See synonyms under FRETFUL, PERVERSE. [< OF *petulant* < L *petulans, -antis* forward, ult. < *petere* seek, assail] —**pet′u·lant·ly** *adv.*

pe·tu·ni·a (pə·tōō′ne·ə, -tyōō′-) *n.* A plant of a tropical American genus (*Petunia*) of herbs of the nightshade family with funnel-shaped, fragrant flowers, in various shades of red, purple, and white. [< NL < obs. E *petun* tobacco < F < Guarani *petün;* so called because of its close relation to tobacco]

pe·tun·tze (pe·toon′tse, *Chinese* bǐ′dun′dzu′) A variety of feldspar that is mixed with kaolin, and used by the Chinese in the manufacture of porcelain. Also **pe·tun′tse.** [< Chinese *pai-tun-tze* < *pai* white + *tun* stone]

peu à peu (pœ à pœ′) *French* Little by little.

peu de chose (pœ də shōz′) *French* A small matter; a trifle.

pew (pyōō) *n.* A bench for seating people in church, frequently with a kneeling rack attached; formerly, a boxlike quadrangle, usually raised on a low platform, with seats on three sides for a family. [ME *puwe,* appar. < OF *puye* a parapet < L *podia,* pl. of *podium* a height, a balcony < Gk. *podion* a base, dim. of *pous, podos* a foot]

pew·age (pyōō′ij) *n.* Rent paid for a pew or pews, or income derived from the rental of pews.

pe·wee (pē′wē) *n.* 1 A small olive-green flycatcher, especially the eastern wood pewee (*Myiochanes virens*) of North America; the pewee flycatcher. 2 The phoebe. Also spelled *peewee.* [Imit.]

pe·wit (pē′wit, pyōō′it) *n.* 1 A pewee. 2 The lapwing. 3 The black-headed gull (*Larus ridibundus*). 4 The spotted sandpiper. [Imit.]

pew·ter (pyōō′tər) *n.* 1 An alloy, usually of tin and lead, formerly much used for tableware. 2 Pewter vessels collectively. —*adj.* Made of pewter. [< OF *peutre, pialtre,* prob. < Ital. *peltro;* ult. origin unknown]

pew·ter·er (pyōō′tər·ər) *n.* A smith who works in pewter.

Pey·e·ri·an (pī·ir′ē·ən) *adj. Anat.* Pertaining to or designating certain glands (called **Peyer's patches**) in the lower part of the small intestine. [after **J. K.** *Peyer,* 1653–1712, Swiss anatomist]

pe·yo·te (pā·ō′tē, *Sp.* pā·yō′tā) *n.* A powerful intoxicant and narcotic drug obtained from the dried upper part of the mescal cactus found in Mexico and Texas. Also **pe·yo′tl** (-yōt′l). [< Am. Sp., the mescal cactus < Nahuatl *peyotl,* lit., a caterpillar; so called because of the down at its center]

pfen·nig (pfen′ikh) *n. pl.* **·nigs** or **pfen·ni·ge** (pfen′i·ge) A small bronze coin of Germany, equivalent to 1/100 of a mark: formerly called *reichspfennig.* [< G, a penny]

Pforz·heim (pfôrts′hīm) A city in Baden-Württemberg, West Germany.

pH *Chem.* Denoting the negative logarithm of the hydrogen-ion concentration, in grams per liter, of a solution: used in expressing relative acidity and alkalinity. Thus, the pH of pure water is 7, indicating a concentration of 10^{-7}, or 0.0000001 gram per liter, usually regarded as neutral. Decreasing acidity means decreasing hydrogen-ion concentration, or a rise in the absolute value of pH. [< P(OTENTIAL OF) H(YDROGEN)]

Phae·a·cia (fē·ā′shə) In Homeric legend, an island visited by Ulysses after the fall of Troy the home of Nausicaa. Also **Phæ·a′cia. —Phae·a′cian** *adj.* & *n.*

Phae·dra (fē′drə) In Greek mythology, a daughter of Minos and Pasiphaë, and wife of Theseus: she fell in love with her stepson Hippolytus and killed herself because he spurned her, indirectly causing his death. Also **Phæ′dra.**

Phae·drus (fē′drəs) Roman fabulist of the first century A.D.; 97 of his stories are extant.

phae·no·gam (fē′nə·gam) *n.* A phanerogam. [< NL *Phaenogama (Vegetabilia)* flowering (plants) < Gk. *phainein* show + *gamos* marriage]

phae·o·phy·ce·an (fē′ə·fī′sē·ən, -fish′ən) *n.* One of a family *(Phaeophyceae)* of brown algae. —*adj.* Of or pertaining to the *Phaeophyceae.* [< NL < Gk. *phaios* dusky + *phykos* seaweed]

Pha·e·thon (fā′ə·thon) In Greek mythology, the son of Helios, who borrowed his father's chariot of the sun, and would have set heaven and earth on fire by his careless driving if Zeus had not slain him with a thunderbolt.

pha·e·ton (fā′ə·tən, *esp. Brit.* fā′tən) *n.* **1** A light four-wheeled boxless carriage, having one or two seats, open at the sides, and sometimes having a top. **2** An open two-seated automobile. [< F < *phaéton* < L *Phaethon* Phaethon]

AMERICAN TWO-SPRING PHAETON (*def. 1*)

-phage *combining form* One who or that which eats or consumes: *bacteriophage.* [< Gk. *phagein* eat]

phag·e·de·na (faj′ə·dē′nə) *n. Pathol.* **1** An eating, sloughing ulcer; hospital gangrene. **2** Leishmaniasis of the skin. **3** Ravenous hunger; bulimia. Also **phag′e·dae′na.** [< L *phagedaena* an eating ulcer < Gk. *phagedaina* < *phagein* eat] — **phag′a·den′ic** (-den′ik) *adj.*

phago- *combining form* Eating: *phagocyte.* Also, before vowels, **phag-.** [< Gk. *phagein* eat]

phag·o·cyte (fag′ə·sīt) *n.* A leucocyte that engulfs and digests bacteria and other foreign material in the blood and tissues of the body. — **phag′o·cyt′ic** (-sit′ik) *adj.*

phagocytic index A number expressing the average number of bacteria ingested by a single leucocyte under specified conditions.

phag·o·cy·to·sis (fag′ə·sī·tō′sis) *n.* The destruction and absorption of bacteria of micro-organisms by phagocytes.

pha·gol·y·sis (fə·gol′ə·sis) *n.* The dissolution or destruction of phagocytes. Also **phag·o·cy·tol·y·sis** (fag′ə·sī·tol′ə·sis). **—phag′o·lyt′ic** (-lit′ik) *adj.*

phag·o·ma·ni·a (fag′ə·mā′nē·ə, -mān′yə) *n.* A morbid or uncontrollable desire to eat.

-phagous *combining form* Consuming; tending to eat: *anthropophagous.* [< Gk. *phagein* eat]

-phagy *combining form* The consumption or eating of: *geophagy.* Also **-phagia.** [< Gk. *-phagia* < *phagein* eat]

pha·i·no·pep·la (fā·ī′nō·pep′lə, fā′ə-) *n.* A small flycatcher of the western United States *(Phainopepla nitens)* with a slender crest and, in the male, conspicuous white wing patches. [< NL < Gk. *phainein* show + *peplos* a peplos]

phal·ange (fal′ənj, fə·lanj′) *n.* A phalanx of the fingers or toes. See illustration under FOOT. [< F < L *phalanx, phalangis* a line of battle]

pha·lan·ge·al (fə·lan′jē·əl) *adj.* Of, pertaining to, or resembling the phalanges. Also **pha·lan′gal** (-gəl), **pha·lan′ge·an.**

pha·lan·ger (fə·lan′jər) *n.* Any one of a family *(Phalangeridae)* of small marsupials of Australia and New Guinea, having long tails, often prehensile: also called *possum.* [< NL < *phalanges,* pl. of *phalanx* phalanx (def. 3); in ref. to the peculiarly constructed phalanges of its hind feet]

pha·lan·ges (fə·lan′jēz) Plural of PHALANX.

phal·an·ster·y (fal′ən·ster′ē) *n. pl.* **·ster·ies 1** The building inhabited by a community of Fourierites; also, such a community. **2** Any group or community of individuals. [< F *phalanstère* < *phalan(x)* a phalanx (< L) + *(mona)stère* < LL *monasterium* a monastery] **—phal′an·ste′ri·an** (-stir′ē·ən) *adj.* & *n.* **—phal′an·ste′ri·an·ism** *n.*

pha·lanx (fā′langks, *esp. Brit.* fal′angks) *n. pl.* **pha·lan·ges** (fə·lan′jēz) or **pha·lanx·es 1** In ancient Greece, a marching order of heavy infantry, with close ranks and files, joined shields, and spears overlapping. **2** Any massed or compact body or corps, such as a group of Fourierites. **3** *Anat.* One of the bones articulating with the joints of the fingers or toes. See synonyms under ARMY. [< L *phalanx, phalangis* < Gk. *phalanx, phalangos* a line of battle]

phal·a·rope (fal′ə·rōp) *n.* A migratory swimming bird (family *Phalaropodidae*), breeding in northern regions, resembling the sandpiper, but having the body depressed, the toes bordered by lateral webs, and the plumage close underneath. [< F < NL *Phalaropus,* the genus name < Gk. *phalaris* coot + *pous* foot]

phal·lin (fal′in) *n.* The characteristic hemolytic poison of the deathcup fungus. [< NL *phall(oides),* species name of the deathcup (< L *phallus* a phallus) + -IN]

phal·lism (fal′iz·əm) *n.* Worship of the generative power in nature as symbolized by the phallus; phallic worship, as in the Dionysiac festivals of ancient Greece. Also **phal′li·cism.** [< PHALL(US) + -ISM] **—phal′list, phal′li·cist** *n.*

phal·lus (fal′əs) *n. pl.* **·li** (-ī) **1** A figure of the male generative organ, used in many systems of religion, especially in the Orient, as a symbol of the generative power of nature. **2** The generative organ of the male or the clitoris of the female. **3** *Psychoanal.* The sexually immature penis. [< L < Gk. *phallos* penis] **—phal′lic** or **phal′li·cal** *adj.*

Pha·nar (fä·när′) A section of Istanbul, formerly the residence of privileged Greek families known as **Pha·nari·ots** (fə·nar′ē·ōts): also *Fanar.*

-phane *combining form* That which resembles or is similar to (a specified substance or material): *cellophane.* [< Gk. *-phanēs* < *phainein* appear]

pha·ner·ic (fə·ner′ik) *adj. Geol.* Clearly visible to the naked eye, as the textures of certain igneous rocks. Also **phan·ic** (fan′ik).

phanero- *combining form* Visible: *phanerophyte.* Also, before vowels, **phaner-.** [< Gk. *phaneros* visible < *phainein* appear]

phan·er·o·crys·tal·line (fan′ər·ō·kris′tə·lin, -līn) *adj. Mineral.* Obviously crystalline: opposed to *cryptocrystalline.*

phan·er·o·gam (fan′ər·ə·gam′) *n. Bot.* A flowering, seed-producing plant: also called *phaenogam.* Compare CRYPTOGAM. [< F *phanérogame* < Gk. *phaneros* visible (< *phainein* show) + *gamos* marriage] **—phan′er·o·gam′ic, phan·er·og·a·mous** (fan′ə·rog′ə·məs) *adj.*

Phan·er·o·ga·mi·a (fan′ər·ə·gā′mē·ə) *n. pl.* One of the two primary divisions into which Linnaeus divided all plants, embracing those with flowers having stamens and pistils; flowering plants: distinguished from *Cryptogamia,* or flowerless plants. [< NL < Gk. *phaneros* visible + *gamos* marriage]

phan·er·o·phyte (fan′ər·ə·fīt′) *n. Bot.* A plant having aerial buds.

phan·tasm (fan′taz·əm), etc. See FANTASM, etc.

phan·tas·ma·go·ri·a (fan·taz′mə·gôr′ē·ə, -gō′·rē·ə) See FANTASMAGORIA.

phan·tom (fan′təm) *n.* **1** Something that exists only in appearance. **2** An apparition; specter; illusion. **3** The visible representative of an abstract state or incorporeal person. —*adj.* Illusive; ghostlike: a *phantom* ship. Also spelled *fantom.* [< OF *fantosme* < L *phantasma* < Gk., an appearance < *phantazein* make visible < *phantos* visible < *phainein* show. Doublet of FANTASM.]

phantom section In mechanical drawing, cross-hatching superimposed on an external view of an object, assembly, or structure to show interior construction and details, often eliminating the need for an additional drawing or view.

phantom word A spurious word that exists only through the error of a lexicographer, writer, or printer, as one resulting from a false etymology or wrong attribution of meaning. Also called *ghost word.*

-phany *combining form* Appearance; manifestation: *epiphany, theophany.* [< Gk. *-phaneia* < *phainein* appear]

Phar·a·mond (far′ə·mənd) A legendary king of the Franks during the fifth century.

Phar·aoh (fâr′ō, fā′rō, far′ē·ō) *n.* Any one of the monarchs of ancient Egypt. [OE *Pharaon* < LL *Pharao, -onis* < Gk. *Pharaō* < Hebrew *Par'ōh* < Egyptian *pr-'ōh* the great house] **—Phar′a·on′ic** (-ē·on′ik) or **·i·cal** *adj.*

Pharaoh's serpent A stick or pellet of mercuric thiocyanate which, when ignited, glows and swells up, developing a long strip of ash which curls out like a serpent.

phar·i·sa·ic (far′ə·sā′ik) *adj.* **1** Pertaining to the Pharisees. **2** Observing the form, but neglecting the spirit, of religion; self-righteous; hypocritical. Also **phar′i·sa′i·cal.** [< LL *pharisaïcus* < Gk. *pharisaïkos* < *pharisaios* PHARISEE] **—phar′i·sa′i·cal·ly** *adv.* **—phar′i·sa′i·cal·ness** *n.*

phar·i·sa·ism (far′ə·sā·iz′əm) *n.* The principles and practices of the Pharisees; hence, formality, self-righteousness, censoriousness, or hypocrisy. Also **phar′i·see·ism** (-sē·iz′əm).

Phar·i·see (far′ə·sē) *n.* **1** One of an ancient, exclusive Jewish sect that paid excessive regard to tradition and ceremonies, and in so doing led its members, by their sense of superior sanctity, to separate themselves from the other Jews. **2** Hence, a formal, sanctimonious, hypocritical person. [OE *fariseus,* infl. by OF *pharise,* both < L *pharisaeus.* < Gk. *pharisaios* < Aramaic *perīshayā,* pl. of *perīsh* < Hebrew *pārūsh* separated < *parash* cleave]

phar·ma·ceu·tic (fär′mə·sōō′tik) *adj.* Pertaining to, using, or relating to pharmacy or the pharmacopoeia: also **phar·ma·cal** (fär′mə·kəl). —*n.* A drug. Also **phar′ma·ceu′ti·cal.** [< L *pharmaceuticus* < Gk. *pharmakeutikos* of drugs < *pharmakeutēs* druggist < *pharmakeuein* give drugs < *pharmakon* a drug] **—phar′ma·ceu′ti·cal·ly** *adv.* **—phar′ma·ceu′tist** *n.*

phar·ma·ceu·tics (fär′mə·sōō′tiks) *n.* The science of pharmacy.

phar·ma·cist (fär′mə·sist) *n.* A qualified druggist; pharmaceutist.

pharmaco- *combining form* A drug; of or pertaining to drugs: *pharmacology.* Also, before vowels, **pharmac-.** [< Gk. *pharmakon* a drug]

phar·ma·co·dy·nam·ics (fär′mə·kō·dī·nam′iks) *n.* The experimental science of the action and effects of drugs.

phar·ma·cog·no·sy (fär′mə·kog′nə·sē) *n.* The knowledge of drugs, especially their origin, structure, and chemical constitution. [< NL *pharmacognosia* < Gk. *pharmakon* a drug + *gnōsis* a knowing, knowledge] **—phar′ma·cog′·no·sist** *n.*

phar·ma·col·o·gy (fär′mə·kol′ə·jē) *n.* The science of the action of medicines, their nature, preparation, administration, and effects: includes materia medica and therapeutics.— **phar′ma·co·log′ic** (-kə·loj′ik) or **·i·cal** *adj.* **—phar′ma·co·log′i·cal·ly** *adv.* **—phar′ma·col′o·gist** *n.*

phar·ma·co·ma·ni·a (fär′mə·kō·mā′nē·ə, -mān′·yə) *n.* A morbid craving for drugs.

phar·ma·co·poe·ia (fär′mə·kə·pē′ə) *n.* **1** A book, usually published by authority, containing standard formulas and methods for the

preparation of medicines, drugs, and other remedial substances. 2 A collection of drugs. [<NL <Gk. *pharmakopoiïa* art of making drugs <*pharmakon* a drug + *poieein* make] — **phar′ma·co·poe′ial** *adj.* —**phar′ma·co·poe′ist** *n.*

phar·ma·cy (fär′mə·sē) *n. pl.* **·cies** 1 The art or business of compounding, preserving, and identifying drugs, and of compounding and dispensing medicines. 2 A drugstore. [<OF *farmacie* <LL *pharmacia* <Gk. *pharmakeia* <*pharmakeus* a druggist <*pharmakon* a drug]

pha·ros (fâr′os, fā′rôs, fā′-) *n.* A lighthouse; beacon. [<L <Gk. <*Pharos* Pharos]

Pha·ros (fâr′os, fā′rôs, fā′-) A peninsula of Alexandria, Egypt; formerly an island, the site of an ancient lighthouse.

Phar·sa·la (fär′sä·lä) A city of southern Thessaly, Greece; chief town of the ancient district of **Phar·sa·li·a** (fär·sā′lē·ə) and scene of Caesar's victory over Pompey, 48 B.C.: also *Farsala.* Ancient **Phar·sa·lus** (fär·sā′ləs).

pha·ryn·ge·al (fə·rin′jē·əl, far′in·jē′əl) *adj.* Of or pertaining to the pharynx. Also **pha·ryn′gal** (-gəl). [<NL *pharyngeus* <*pharynx, -yngis* PHARYNX]

phar·yn·gi·tis (far′in·jī′tis) *n. Pathol.* Inflammation of the pharynx. [<NL <*pharynx, -yngis* pharynx]

pharyngo- *combining form* The throat; related to the throat: *pharyngoscope.* Also, before vowels, **pharyng-.** [<Gk. *pharynx* throat]

phar·yn·gol·o·gy (far′ing·gol′ə·jē) *n.* The science of the pharynx and its diseases.

pha·ryn·go·scope (fə·ring′gə·skōp) *n.* An apparatus for examining the pharynx. —**phar·yn·gos·co·py** (far′ing·gos′kə·pē) *n.*

phar·yn·got·o·my (far′ing·got′ə·mē) *n. Surg.* Incision into the pharynx.

phar·ynx (far′ingks) *n. pl.* **pha·ryn·ges** (fə·rin′jēz) or **phar·ynx·es** *Anat.* The part of the alimentary canal between the palate and the esophagus, serving as a passage for air and food. [<NL *pharynx, -yngis* <Gk. *pharynx, -yngos* throat]

phase (fāz) *n.* 1 The view that anything presents to the eye; any one of varying distinctive manifestations of an object. 2 *Astron.* One of the appearances or forms presented periodically by the moon and planets. 3 *Physics* **a** In an oscillatory motion, the position and character of a wave at any instant: often measured as an angle, the whole period being regarded as a circle, or 360°. **b** The instant when the maximum, zero, or other relative value is attained by any cyclical system, as sound or light waves, an alternating electric current, etc. **c** Any of the homogeneous forms of a given substance that may occur alone, or exist independently as a component of a larger heterogeneous system, as ice in water, water vapor in fog, etc. 4 *Biol.* **a** One of the distinct stages in the reduction or division process of a cell. **b** Any characteristic or decisive stage in the growth, development, or life pattern of an organism. —**to phase out** To terminate work on, production of, etc., step by step and according to plan. Also **pha·sis** (fā′sis). ◆ Homophone: *faze.* [<NL *phasis* <Gk., an appearance <*phainein* make appear] —**pha·sic** (fā′zik) *adj.*

phase meter An instrument for measuring the difference in phase between two alternating oscillations of the same frequency.

phase modulation *Electronics* Modulation of a carrier wave by varying its phase in accordance with the amplitude or pitch of the transmitted signal.

phase rule *Physics* A mathematical generalization of the equilibrium relations between two or more phases of a material system, according to which the degrees of freedom possible to a given heterogeneous system equal the number of components in the system, less the number of phases, plus 2.

-phasia *combining form Med.* Defect or malfunction of speech: *dysphasia.* Also **-phasy.** [<Gk. *-phasia* <*phanai* speak]

pha·sine (fā′sēn, -sin) *n. Biochem.* A poisonous substance isolated as a white amorphous powder from soya and certain other beans: it acts as a strong agglutinating agent on the red blood cells of man and other animals. Also **pha′sin** (-sin). [<NL *Phas(eolus),* a genus of beans (<L, a kidney bean, dim. of *phaseolus* <Gk. *phasēlos,* a kind of bean) + -INE[2]]

phat (fat) See FAT *adj.* (def. 4).

pheas·ant (fez′ənt) *n.* 1 A long-tailed gallinaceous bird of *Phasianus* or related genus, noted for the gorgeous plumage of the male: native to Asia, but long semidomesticated elsewhere and bred in game preserves. 2 One of various other birds, as the ruffed grouse. [<AF *fesant* <L *Phasianus* <Gk. *Phasianos (ornis)* the Phasian (bird) <*Phasis* the Phasis, a river in the Caucasus, where it was first found]

RING–NECKED PHEASANT
(From 31 to 36 inches long over-all)

pheasant eye 1 A low, hardy European annual *(Adonis annua)* having crimson or scarlet flowers with dark centers: cultivated in the United States. 2 The garden pink.

Phe·be (fē′bē) See PHOEBE.

Phei·dip·pi·des (fī·dip′ə·dēz) Greek runner sent from Athens to Sparta to secure help against the Persians, 490 B.C.: sometimes confused with the runner, whose name is not preserved, who carried news of victory at Marathon to Athens. Also *Phidippides.*

phel·lo·derm (fel′ə·dûrm) *n. Bot.* A layer of green parenchymatous tissue sometimes developed on the inner side of a layer of cork. [<Gk. *phellos* cork + *derma* skin] —**phel′lo·der′mal** *adj.*

phel·lo·gen (fel′ə·jən) *n. Bot.* The active meristematic tissue out of which cork is developed. [<Gk. *phellos* cork + -GEN] —**phel′lo·ge·net′ic** (-jə·net′ik), **phel′lo·gen′ic** *adj.*

Phelps (felps), **William Lyon,** 1865–1943, U.S. educator and critic.

phen- Var. of PHENO-.

phe·na·caine (fē′nə·kān) *n.* A white, odorless, crystalline substance, $C_{18}H_{25}O_3N_2Cl$, used as a quick-acting local anesthetic. [<PHEN- + A(CETO)- + (CO)CAINE]

phe·nac·e·tin (fə·nas′ə·tin) *n.* Acetophenetidin.

phen·a·cite (fen′ə·sīt) *n.* A brittle, vitreous, colorless, transparent to subtranslucent beryllium silicate, Be_2SiO_4, sometimes used as a gemstone. [<Gk. *phenax, -akos* a cheat + -ITE[1]; so called because mistaken for quartz]

phen·a·kis·to·scope (fen′ə·kis′tə·skōp) *n.* A disk bearing a series of representations of an object in successive phases of motion, revolved before a mirror to give the illusion of continuous motion. Compare ZOETROPE. [<Gk. *phenakistēs* a cheat + -SCOPE]

phe·nan·threne (fə·nan′thrēn) *n. Chem.* A crystalline isomer, $C_{14}H_{10}$, of anthracene; a coal-tar product used in the synthesis of drugs and dyes. [<PHEN(YL) + ANTHR(AC)ENE]

phen·a·zine (fen′ə·zēn, -zin) *n. Chem.* A yellowish basic compound, $C_{12}H_8N_2$, on which many dyestuffs are based. Also **phen′a·zin** (-zin). [<PHEN(YL) + AZ(O)- + -INE[2]]

phe·net·i·dine (fə·net′ə·dēn, -din) *n. Chem.* Any one of three isomeric liquid derivatives, $C_8H_{11}ON$, of phenetole, especially the *para* form, which is the base of acetophenetidin. Also **phe·net′i·din** (-din). [<PHEN(OL) + ET(HYL) + (AM)ID(O)- + -INE[2]]

phen·e·tole (fen′ə·tōl, -tol) *n. Chem.* An aromatic liquid compound, $C_6H_5OC_2H_5$, the ethyl ether of phenol. Also **phen′e·tol.** [<PHEN(YL) + ET(HYL) + -OLE]

phen·ic acid (fen′ik) See PHENOL.

Phe·ni·cia (fə·nē′shə, -nish′ə), **Phe·ni·cian,** etc. See PHOENICIA, etc.

phe·nix (fē′niks) See PHOENIX.

pheno- *combining form Chem.* Related to benzene; a derivative of benzene: *phenobarbital.* Also, before vowels, *phen-.* [<PHENYL]

phe·no·bar·bi·tal (fē′nō·bär′bə·tal, -tôl) *n.* A barbiturate, $C_{12}H_{12}N_2O_3$, having a long-lasting effect as a sedative, anticonvulsant, and hypnotic. Also **phe′no·bar′bi·tone** (-tōn). [<PHENO- + BARBITAL]

phe·no·cryst (fē′nō·krist) *n. Geol.* A mineral constituent of a rock, occuring in well-defined crystals embedded in a fine-grained groundmass. [<F *phénocryste* <Gk. *phainein* show + *krystallos* a crystal] —**phe′no·crys′tic** *adj.*

phe·nol (fē′nōl, -nol) *n. Chem.* 1 Any one of a series of aromatic hydroxyl derivatives of benzene or its homologs. 2 A white crystalline compound, $C_6H_5 \cdot OH$, with a burning taste and characteristic odor, derived from coal-tar oil by distillation and used as a disinfectant: popularly called *carbolic acid,* formerly *phenic acid.* Phenol is a powerful caustic poison. [<Gk. *phainoshining* (<*phainein* show) + -OL[1]; so called because derived from coal tar, a by-product of illuminating gas]

phe·no·late (fē′nə·lāt) *n. Chem.* A salt of phenol.

phe·nol·ic (fi·nol′ik, -nō′lik) *adj. Chem.* Of, pertaining to, derived from, or containing phenol: *phenolic* resins, a large and important class of synthetic plastics made from an aldehyde-phenol base.

phe·nol·o·gy (fi·nol′ə·jē) *n.* The study of the periodic phenomena of plant life and animal behavior in relation to seasonal changes, climatic and other ecological factors. [Contraction of PHENOMENOLOGY, with a restricted application] —**phe·no·log·ic** (fē′nə·loj′ik) or **·i·cal** *adj.* —**phe′no·log′i·cal·ly** *adv.* —**phe·nol′o·gist** *n.*

phe·nol·phthal·ein (fē′nōl·thal′ēn, fē′nolf·thal′·ē·in) *n.* A whitish or yellowish-white crystalline compound, $C_{20}H_{14}O_4$, obtained by treating phenol with phthalic anhydride. Because its brilliant red alkaline solutions are readily decolorized by acid, it is valuable as an indicator in acid-base titrations: used also in medicine as a laxative.

phe·nom·e·na (fi·nom′ə·nə) Plural of PHENOMENON: erroneously used as a singular.

phe·nom·e·nal (fi·nom′ə·nəl) *adj.* 1 Pertaining to phenomena. 2 Extraordinary or marvelous. —**phe·nom′e·nal·ly** *adv.*

phe·nom·e·nal·ism (fi·nom′ə·nəl·iz′əm) *n.* The metaphysical opinion that no realities of which the human mind can have knowledge underlie phenomena. Compare POSITIVISM. —**phe·nom′e·nal·ist** *n.* —**phe·nom′e·nal·is′tic** *adj.* —**phe·nom′e·nal·is′ti·cal·ly** *adv.*

phe·nom·e·nol·o·gy (fi·nom′ə·nol′ə·jē) *n.* 1 The scientific investigation or description of phenomena. 2 *Philos.* The general doctrine of phenomena, as distinguished from ontology. [<PHENOMENO(N) + -LOGY] —**phe·nom′e·no·log′i·cal** (-nə·loj′i·kəl) *adj.* —**phe·nom′e·no·log′i·cal·ly** *adv.*

phe·nom·e·non (fi·nom′ə·non) *n. pl.* **·na** (-nə) 1 Something visible or directly observable, as an appearance, action, change, or occurrence of any kind, as distinguished from the force by which, or the law in accordance with which, it may be produced. 2 Any unusual occurrence; an inexplicable fact; marvel; prodigy. 3 Any fact, appearance, or occurrence in consciousness; that which is apprehended by the senses, in contrast with or in opposition to that which really exists, or to things in themselves: contrasted with *noumenon.* 4 A symptom of disease. [<LL *phaenomenon* <Gk. *phainomenon* an appearance, orig. ppr. passive neut. of *phainein* show]

phe·no·thi·a·zine (fē′nō·thī′ə·zēn, -zin) *n. Chem.* A light-yellow crystalline compound, $C_{12}H_9NS$, prepared by combining diphenylamine and sulfur in the presence of iodine: used as an insecticide and as a remedy against livestock parasites.

phe·no·type (fē′nə·tīp) *n. Biol.* A type or strain of organisms distinguishable from others by some visibly manifested group of characters, as contrasted with genetic constitution. Compare GENOTYPE. [<F *phéno-* (<Gk. *phaino-* <*phainein* show, appear) + -TYPE] —**phe′no·typ′ic** (-tip′ik) or **·i·cal** *adj.* —**phe′no·typ′i·cal·ly** *adv.*

phen·yl (fen′əl, fē′nəl) *n. Chem.* The univalent radical C_6H_5, regarded as the basis of numerous aromatic derivatives. [<obs. *phene* benzene + -YL]

phen·yl·al·a·nine (fen′əl·al′ə·nēn, fē′nəl-; -nin) *n. Biochem.* An essential amino acid, $C_9H_{11}NO_2$. [<PHENYL + ALANINE]

phen·yl·a·mine (fen′əl·ə·mēn′, -am′in, fē′nəl-) *n.* Aniline.

phen·yl·ene (fen′əl·ēn, fē′nəl-) *n. Chem.* A

bivalent radical, C_6H_4, contained in certain benzene derivatives.

phen·yl·ke·to·nu·ri·a (fen′əl·kēt′n·yŏŏr′ē·ə, fē′nəl-) *n. Pathol.* A rare, inherited metabolic disorder that can cause permanent mental impairment if untreated within a few weeks after birth: also called *PKU.* [<PHENYL + KETON(E) + -URIA]

phew (fyōō, fōō) *interj.* An exclamation of disgust or surprise.

phi (fī, fē) *n. Greek* The twenty-first letter in the Greek alphabet (Φ, φ): corresponding to English *ph* and *f.* As a numeral it denotes 500.

phi·al (fī′əl) See VIAL.

Phi Be·ta Kap·pa (fī bā′tə kap′ə, bē′tə) An American honorary society founded in 1776 with membership based on conditions of high academic standing.

Phid·i·as (fid′ē·əs), 500?–432? B.C., Greek sculptor and architect; designed the Parthenon. — **Phid′i·an** *adj.*

Phi·dip·pi·des (fī·dip′ə·dēz) See PHEIDIPPIDES.

Phil (fil) Diminutive of PHILIP.

phil- Var. of PHILO-.

-phil Var. of -PHILE.

phil·a·beg, phil·i·beg (fil′ə·beg) See FILIBEG.

Phil·a·del·phi·a (fil′ə·del′fē·ə) **1** A city on the Delaware River in SE Pennsylvania. **2** An ancient city of Lydia, Asia Minor. — **Phil′a·del′phi·an** *adj. & n.*

Philadelphia Chippendale Fine, usually richly carved mahogany furniture in the Chippendale style, made in Philadelphia in the 18th century.

Philadelphia lawyer An unusually sharp lawyer, especially one adept in phrasing legal technicalities: originally a tribute to the high caliber of the Philadelphia bar, now implying over-shrewd trickery.

Phi·lae (fī′lē) An island in the Nile river, near Aswan, Upper Egypt; submerged half the year by the backwater from the Aswan Dam; site of the temples of Isis and Hathor. Also **Phi′læ.**

phi·lan·der (fi·lan′dər) *v.i.* To make love without serious intentions: said of a man. [<*n.*] — *n.* A male flirt or suitor: also **phi·lan′der·er.** [<Gk. *philandros* <*phileein* love + *anēr, andros* man; from its use as a proper name for a lover in drama] — **phi·lan′der·ing** *n.*

Phi·lan·der (fi·lan′dər) A masculine personal name. [<Gk., loving man or mankind]

phi·lan·thro·pize (fi·lan′thrə·pīz) *v.* **·pized, ·piz·ing** *v.t.* To deal with philanthropically. — *v.i.* To act as a philanthropist.

phi·lan·thro·py (fi·lan′thrə·pē) *n. pl.* **·pies** Disposition or effort to promote the happiness or social elevation of mankind; desire, effort, or beneficence, as by making donations, intended to mitigate social evils and increase social comfort; comprehensive benevolence, but often specific in its objects; literally, love of man. See synonyms under BENEVOLENCE. [<LL *philanthropia* <Gk. *philanthrōpia* < *phileein* love + *anthropos* man] — **phil·an·throp·ic** (fil′ən·throp′ik) or **·i·cal** *adj.* — **phil′an·throp′i·cal·ly** *adv.* — **phi·lan′thro·pist** *n.*

phi·lat·e·ly (fi·lat′ə·lē) *n.* The study and collection of postage stamps, stamped envelopes, wrappers, etc.; stamp collecting. [<F *philatélie* <Gk. *philos* loving + *ateleia* exemption from tax; with ref. to prepaid postage] — **phil·a·tel·ic** (fil′ə·tel′ik) or **·i·cal** *adj.* — **phil′a·tel′i·cal·ly** *adv.* — **phi·lat′e·list** *n.*

-phile *combining form* One who supports or is fond of; one devoted to: *bibliophile.* [<Gk. *-philos* loving <*phileein* love]

Phi·le·mon (fi·lē′mən) A masculine personal name. Also *Fr.* **Phi·lé·mon** (fē·lā·môn′). [<Gk., loving thought]

— **Philemon** In Greek mythology, the husband of Baucis.

— **Philemon** A Greek of Colossae, converted to Christianity by Paul; also, the epistle addressed by Paul to him, forming one of the books of the New Testament.

phil·har·mon·ic (fil′här·mon′ik, -ər·mon′-) *adj.* Fond of harmony or music; often, **Philharmonic,** used in the names of musical societies. [<F *philharmonique* <Ital. *filarmonico* <Gk. *philos* loving + *harmonikos* HARMONIC]

Phil·hel·lene (fil·hel′ēn) *n.* **1** One who loves Greece or the Greeks. **2** A sympathizer with the modern Greeks in their effort (1821–29) to throw off the Turkish yoke and revive the Greek nation. Also **Phil·hel′le·nist.** [<Gk. *philellēn* loving Greeks <*phileein* love + *Hellēn* a Greek] — **Phil·hel·len·ic** (fil′he·len′ik) *adj.* — **Phil·hel′le·nism** *n.*

-philia *combining form* **1** A tendency toward: *hemophilia.* **2** A morbid affection or fondness for: *necrophilia.* Also spelled *-phily.* [<Gk. *-philia* <*phileein* love]

Phil·ip (fil′ip) A masculine personal name. Also *Ger.* **Phi·lipp** (fē′lip), *Fr.* **Phi·lippe** (fē·lēp′), **Phi·lip·pus** (*Du.* fē·lip′əs, *Lat.* fi·lip′əs). [<Gk., a lover of horses]

— **Philip** One of the seven deacons of the early Christian church. *Acts* viii 5.

— **Philip, King,** died 1676, American Indian chief; made war on New England colonists, **King Philip's War,** 1675–76: Indian name *Metacomet.*

— **Philip, Prince,** born 1921, consort of Queen Elizabeth II of Great Britain; third duke of Edinburgh (1947).

— **Philip, Saint** One of the Twelve Apostles.

— **Philip II,** 382–336 B.C., king of Macedon 359–336; conqueror of Thessaly and Greece; father of Alexander the Great.

— **Philip II,** 1165–1223, king of France 1180–1223; went on Third Crusade; took English provinces in France from King John: called "Philip Augustus."

— **Philip II,** 1527–98, king of Spain 1556–98; sent the Armada against England.

— **Philip IV,** 1268–1314, king of France 1285–1314; supported Clement V at Avignon: called "Philip the Fair."

— **Philip V,** 1683–1746, king of Spain 1700–1746; founder of Bourbon line in Spain.

— **Philip the Bold,** 1342–1404, duke of Burgundy; conquered Flanders.

— **Philip the Good,** 1396–1467, duke of Burgundy; acquired the Netherlands.

Phi·lip·pa (fi·lip′ə) A feminine personal name; feminine of PHILIP. Also *Fr.* **Phi·lip·pine** (fē·lē·pēn′), *Ger.* **Phi·lip·pi·ne** (fē′lē·pē′nə).

Phi·lippe·ville (fil′ip·vil, *Fr.* fē·lēp·vēl′) A port of NE Algeria on the Mediterranean.

Phi·lip·pi (fi·lip′ī) An ancient town in northern Macedonia, Greece; scene of the defeat of Brutus and Cassius by Octavius and Anthony, 42 B.C., and of St. Paul's first preaching in Europe. *Acts* xvi 12. — **Phi·lip′pi·an** *adj. & n.*

Phi·lip·pi·ans (fi·lip′ē·ənz) In the New Testament, an epistle of St. Paul addressed to Christians at Philippi.

phi·lip·pic (fi·lip′ik) *n.* An impassioned speech characterized by invective: from **the Philippics,** a series of twelve speeches in which Demosthenes denounced Philip of Macedon. [<L *Philippicus* <Gk. *Philippikos* of Philip]

Phil·ip·pine Islands (fil′ə·pēn) An archipelago of 7,083 islands SE of China and NE of Borneo; 114,830 square miles; ceded by Spain to the United States, 1898, for $20,000,000; a commonwealth since 1935; seized by Japan, 1942–44, in World War II; since 1946 the **Republic of the Philippines;** capital, Quezon City. Also **Phil′ip·pines.** A native of the Philippines is known as a *Filipino.* — **Phil′ip·pine** *adj.*

Philippine Scouts The regiments of U.S. troops formerly maintained in the Philippines, consisting of native enlisted personnel and American officers.

Philippine Sea A part of the western Pacific between the Philippines and the Marianas.

Phil·ip·pop·o·lis (fil′i·pop′ə·ləs) An ancient name for PLOVDIV.

Phi·lis·ti·a (fi·lis′tē·ə) An ancient region on the Mediterranean, SW Palestine. *Ps.* lx 8.

Phi·lis·tine (fi·lis′tin, -tēn, -tīn, fil′əs-) *n.* **1** One of a warlike race of ancient Philistia. *I Sam.* xvii 23. **2** An ignorant, narrow-minded person, devoid of culture and indifferent to art. [<F *Philistin* <LL *Philistinus,* pl. *Philistini* <Gk. *Philistinoi, Palaistinoi* <Hebrew *p'lishtim*]

Phi·lis·tin·ism (fi·lis′tin·iz′əm) *n.* Blind conventionalism; lack of culture, taste, etc.

Phil·lips (fil′ips), **Stephen,** 1868–1915, English poet and dramatist. — **Wendell,** 1811–84, U.S. orator and abolitionist.

Phil·lips screw (fil′ips) A screw having a head (called a **Phillips head**) with crossing grooves for use with a special screwdriver. [after *Phillips* Screws, a trademark]

Phil·lis (fil′is) See PHYLLIS.

philo- *combining form* Loving; fond of: *philomath.* Also, before vowels, *phil-.* [<Gk. *philos* loving <*phileein* love]

Phil·oc·te·tes (fil′ək·tē′tēz) In Greek legend, a Greek hero, heir to the bow and poisoned arrows of Hercules, who killed Paris with one of them in the tenth year of the siege of Troy.

phil·o·den·dron (fil′ə·den′drən) *n.* Any of a genus (*Philodendron*) of tropical American climbing plants, with thick, glossy, evergreen leaves: cultivated as an ornamental house plant. [<NL <Gk., neut. of *philodendros* fond of trees <*philos* fond + *dendron* a tree]

phi·log·y·ny (fi·loj′ə·nē) *n.* Fondness for or devotion to women: opposed to *misogyny.* [<Gk. *philogynia* <*philos* fond + *gynē* a woman] — **phi·log′y·nist** *n.* — **phi·log′y·nous** *adj.*

Phi·lo Ju·dae·us (fī′lō jōō·dē′əs) Jewish Platonist philosopher of the first century.

phi·lol·o·gy (fi·lol′ə·jē) *n.* **1** The scientific study of written records (chiefly literary works of art), in order to set up accurate texts and determine their meaning, often in terms of linguistic and cultural history. **2** Linguistics. **3** In popular use, etymology. **4** Formerly, literary scholarship, especially classical scholarship. [<F *philologie* <L *philologia* <Gk. <*philologos* fond of argument, words <*philos* fond + *logos* a word] — **phil·o·log·ic** (fil′ə·loj′·ik) or **·i·cal** *adj.* — **phil′o·log′i·cal·ly** *adv.* — **phi·lol′o·gist, phi·lol′o·ger, phil′o·log** or **·logue** (-lôg, -log) *n.*

phil·o·math (fil′ə·math) *n.* One who loves learning; a scholar. [<Gk. *philomathēs* fond of learning <*philos* fond + *math-,* root of *manthanein* learn] — **phil′o·math′ic** or **·i·cal** *adj.* — **phi·lom·a·thy** (fi·lom′ə·thē) *n.*

phil·o·mel (fil′ə·mel) *n.* In poetic usage, the nightingale. Also **phil′o·me′la.** [<F *philomèle* <L *philomela* <Gk. *philomēla,* ? <*philos* fond of + *melos* a song]

Phil·o·me·la (fil′ə·mē′lə) In Greek mythology, a princess of Athens who was raped by her brother-in-law Tereus, who then tore out her tongue; when, in revenge, she and her sister Procne killed his son Itys, the gods changed Tereus into a hoopoe, Procne into a swallow, and Philomela into a nightingale.

phi·lom·e·try (fi·lom′ə·trē) *n.* The study and collecting of postal meter impressions on mail matter: a branch of philately. [<PHILO- + (*postal*) *meter,* on analogy with PHILATELY] — **phi·lom′e·trist** *n.* — **phil·o·met·ric** (fil′ə·met′rik) *adj.*

phil·o·pe·na (fil′ə·pē′nə) *n.* **1** A game in which anyone finding a nut with twin kernels shares it with another person. The one who first says *philopena* when next they meet receives a forfeit from the other. **2** The twin kernels shared. **3** The gift made as a forfeit. Often spelled *fillipeen.* Also **phil′lip·pine, phil′li·peen′er.** [Appar. <Du. *phillipine,* alter. of G *vielliebchen* very dear <*viel* much + *liebchen,* dim. of *liebe* love]

Phil·o·poe·men (fil′ə·pē′mən), 252?–183 B.C., Greek patriot; advocate of unity among Greek city-states; called "Last of the Greeks."

phil·o·pro·gen·i·tive (fil′ə·prō·jen′ə·tiv) *adj.* **1** Fond of offspring or of children in general. **2** Prolific. [<PHILO- + L *progenitus,* pp. of *progignere* beget] — **phil′o·pro·gen′i·tive·ly** *adv.* — **phil′o·pro·gen′i·tive·ness** *n.*

phi·los·o·pher (fi·los′ə·fər) *n.* **1** A student of or specialist in philosophy. **2** The creator of a system of philosophy. **3** A man of practical wisdom; one who schools himself to calmness and patience under all circumstances, as originally enjoined by the Stoic philosophy. [<AF *philosophre,* var. of OF *filosofe* <L *philosophus* <Gk. *philosophos* a lover of wisdom <*philos* loving + *sophos* wise]

philosopher's stone An imaginary stone or substance having the property of transmuting the baser metals into gold: sought by the alchemists.

phil·o·soph·i·cal (fil′ə·sof′i·kəl) *adj.* **1** Pertaining to or founded on the principles of philosophy. **2** Proper to or characteristic of a philosopher. **3** Self-restrained and serene; rational; thoughtful; calm. **4** *Archaic* Pertaining to or used in the study of natural philosophy or physics. Also **phil′o·soph′ic.** — **phil′o·soph′i·cal·ly** *adv.*

phi·los·o·phism (fi·los′ə·fiz′əm) *n.* Unsound or pretended philosophy; sophistry.

phi·los·o·phist (fi·los′ə·fist) *n.* One who affects philosophy; a would-be philosopher.

phi·los·o·phis·tic (fi·los′ə·fis′tik) *adj.* Of the nature of philosophism; characteristic of a philosophist. Also **phi·los′o·phis′ti·cal.**

phi·los·o·phize (fi·los′ə·fīz) *v.i.* **·phized, ·phiz-ing** To speculate like a philosopher; seek ultimate causes and principles; moralize. — **phi·los′o·phiz′er** *n.*

phi·los·o·phy (fi·los′ə·fē) *n. pl.* **·phies 1** The love of wisdom as leading to the search for it; hence, knowledge of general principles—elements, powers, or causes and laws—as explaining facts and existences. **2** The general laws that furnish the rational explanation of anything: the *philosophy* of banking. **3** The calm judgment and equable temper resulting from study of causes and laws; practical wisdom; fortitude, as in enduring reverses and suffering. **4** Reasoned science; a scientific system; as (formerly), natural *philosophy*, now natural science. **5** A philosophical system or treatise. **6** The sciences as formerly studied in the universities. [<OF *filosofie, philosophie* <L *philosophia* <Gk. < *philosophos.* See PHILOSOPHER.]

philosophy of the Academy Platonism: so called because Plato taught in the Academy, near Athens: also **intuitional philosophy.**

philosophy of the garden Epicureanism: so called because Epicurus taught in a garden at Athens.

philosophy of the Lyceum Aristotelianism: so called because Aristotle taught it in the Lyceum at Athens: also **empirical philosophy.**

philosophy of the Porch Stoicism: so called because Zeno taught in the porch of the Poecile in Athens.

-philous *combining form* Loving; fond of: *anemophilous.* [<Gk. *-philos.* See -PHILE.]

phil·ter (fil′tər) *n.* A charmed draft supposed to have power to excite sexual love; a love potion; hence, any magic potion. — *v.t.* To charm with a philter. Also **phil′tre.** ◆ Homophone: *filter.* [<MF *philtre* <L *philtrum* <Gk. *philtron* a love potion < *phileein* love]

-phily Var. of -PHILIA.

phi·mo·sis (fi·mō′sis) *n. Pathol.* The abnormal constriction of the opening of the prepuce, preventing the uncovering of the glans penis. [<NL <Gk. *phimōsis* a muzzling < *phimos* a muzzle] — **phi·mot′ic** (-mot′ik) *adj.*

Phin·e·as (fin′ē·əs) A masculine personal name. Also **Phin′e·has** (-həs), *Fr.* **Phi·né·as** (fē·nā·à′). [Prob. <Egyptian; mouth of brass]

Phi·neus (fi·nyōōs′, fī-, fin′ē·əs) In Greek mythology, a Thracian king who for some offense against the gods was punished by having the Harpies defile or snatch away his food.

Phin·ti·as (fin′tē·əs) Pythias.

Phips (fips), **Sir William,** 1651–95, first royal governor of Massachusetts. Also **Phipps.**

phiz (fiz) *n. Slang* Visage; face. [Short for *phiznomy,* obs. var. of PHYSIOGNOMY]

phle·bi·tis (fli·bī′tis) *n. Pathol.* Inflammation of the inner membrane of a vein. [<NL <Gk. *phleps, phlebos* a vein + *-itis* -ITIS] — **phle·bit′ic** (-bit′ik) *adj.*

phlebo- *combining form* Venous: *phlebotomy.* Also, before vowels, **phleb-.** [<Gk. *phleps, phlebos* a vein]

phleb·o·scle·ro·sis (fleb′ō·skli·rō′sis) *n. Pathol.* Thickening and hardening of the walls of the veins. [<PHLEBO- + Gk. *sklērōsis* a hardening < *sklēros* hard] — **phleb′o·scle·rot′ic** (-rot′ik) *adj.*

phle·bot·o·mize (fli·bot′ə·mīz) *v.t.* **·mized, ·miz-ing** To treat by phlebotomy.

phle·bot·o·my (fli·bot′ə·mē) *n. Surg.* The practice of opening a vein for letting blood as a remedial measure; bloodletting. [<OF *flebothomie* <L *phlebotomia* <Gk., the opening of a vein < *phleps, phlebos* a vein + *temnein* cut] — **phleb·o·tom·ic** (fleb′ə·tom′ik) or **·i·cal** *adj.* — **phle·bot′o·mist** *n.*

Phleg·e·thon (fleg′ə·thon, flej′-) In Greek mythology, the river of fire, one of the five rivers surrounding Hades. [<Gk., lit., blazing]

phlegm (flem) *n.* **1** *Physiol.* A viscid, stringy mucus secreted in the air passages or in the stomach, especially when produced as a morbid discharge. **2** Apathy; indifference; cold, undemonstrative temper; self-possession. **3** *Obs.* One of the four natural humors (the cold and moist) in ancient physiology. See synonyms under APATHY. [<OF *fleume, flemme* <L *phlegma* the clammy humor of the body <Gk., inflammation < *phlegein* blaze; refashioned after Gk.]

phleg·ma·si·a do·lens (fleg·mā′zhē·ə dō′lənz) *Pathol.* Milk leg. [<L < *phlegmasia* an inflammation + *dolens, -entis* painful, ppr. of *dolere* feel pain]

phleg·mat·ic (fleg·mat′ik) *adj.* Sluggish; indifferent; not easily moved or excited. Also **phleg·mat′i·cal.** [<OF *fleumatique* <L *phlegmaticus* <Gk. *phlegmatikos < phlegma, -matos.* See PHLEGM.] — **phleg·mat′i·cal·ly** *adv.*

phlegm·y (flem′ē) *adj.* **1** Relating to, resembling, or containing phlegm. **2** Phlegmatic in temperament.

phlo·em (flō′em) *n. Bot.* The complex plant tissue composed of sieve tubes with associated cells, and forming part of the vascular system serving for the conduction of the sap; the bast; leptome. Compare XYLEM. [<G <Gk. *phloos* bark]

phlo·gis·tic (flō·jis′tik) *adj.* **1** Pertaining to phlogiston or to the theory of its existence. **2** Inflammatory; inflamed. [<Gk. *phlogistos* inflammable. See PHLOGISTON.]

phlo·gis·ton (flō·jis′tən) *n.* The fiery principle formerly assumed to be a necessary constituent of all combustible bodies, and to be given up by them in burning. [<NL <Gk., neut. of *phlogistos* inflammable < *phlogizein* set on fire < *phlox, phlogos* a flame < *phlegein* burn]

phlog·o·pite (flog′ə·pīt) *n.* A yellowish-brown to brownish-red monoclinic magnesium mica. [<G *phlogopit* <Gk. *phlogōpos* fiery; so called from its appearance]

phlo·go·sis (flō·gō′sis) *n. Pathol.* **1** Inflammation. **2** Erysipelas. [<NL <Gk. *phlogōsis* an inflammation < *phlox, phlogos* a flame] — **phlo·gosed′** (-gōzd′, -gōst′), **phlo·got′ic** (-got′ik) *adj.*

phlor·i·zin (flôr′ə·zin, flor′-, flə·rī′-) *n. Chem.* A bitter crystalline glycoside, $C_{21}H_{24}O_{10}$, contained in the root bark of the apple, pear, plum, and cherry tree: used in medicine as a tonic. Also **phlo·rid·zin** (flə·rid′zin). [<Gk. *phloos* bark + *rhiza* a root + -IN]

phlox (floks) *n.* Any plant or flower of a North American genus (*Phlox*) of herbs of the *Polemoniaceae* family, with opposite leaves and clusters of showy flowers in various shades of red, purple, white, or variegated. [<NL <L, a kind of flower <Gk. *phlox* a wallflower, lit., a flame < *phlegein* flame]

PERENNIAL PHLOX
(Plant from 2 to 6 feet tall)

phlyc·te·na (flik·tē′nə) *n. pl.* **·nae** (-nē) *Pathol.* A small blister containing watery or serous fluid. Also **phlyc·tae′na.** [<NL <Gk. *phlyktaina* a blister < *phlyein* swell]

Phnôm·penh (pə·nôm′pen′) See PNOM-PENH.

-phobe *combining form* One who fears or has an aversion to: *Anglophobe.* [<Gk. *-phobos* fearing < *phobeesthai* fear]

pho·bi·a (fō′bē·ə) *n.* **1** A morbid, compulsive, and persistent fear of any specified type of object, stimulus, or situation. **2** Any strong aversion or dislike. [<L <Gk. *phobos* fear] — **pho′bic** (-bik) *adj.*

-phobia *combining form Psychiatry* Aversion to; morbid fear or dislike of. [<Gk. *phobos* fear]

In the following list each entry denotes a morbid fear or dislike of the thing or situation indicated by the translation of the first part of the word:

acrophobia	heights
agoraphobia	open spaces
ailurophobia	cats
algophobia	pain
androphobia	men
astraphobia	thunder and lightning
autophobia	being alone; self
bathophobia	depth
claustrophobia	closed space
cynophobia	dogs (rabies)
demophobia	crowds
dromophobia	crossing streets
genophobia	sex
gynophobia	women
haptephobia	being touched
hemophobia	blood
hydrophobia	water
hypnophobia	falling asleep
musophobia	mice
mysophobia	contamination
neophobia	the new
nyctophobia	night, darkness
ophidiophobia	snakes
photophobia	light
sitophobia	eating; food
taphephobia	being buried alive
thanatophobia	death
toxicophobia	poison
xenophobia	strangers, foreigners
zoophobia	animals

pho·ca (fō′kə) *n. pl.* **·cae** (-sē) One of a genus (*Phoca*) of seals (family *Phocidae*), including the typical earless seals of temperate waters. [<NL <L <Gk. *phōkē* a seal] — **pho′cine** (-sīn, -sin) *adj.* — **pho′coid** (-koid) *adj. & n.*

Pho·cis (fō′sis) A region of central Greece on the north shore of the Gulf of Corinth.

pho·co·me·li·a (fō′kō·mē′lē·ə, -lyə) *n. Pathol.* A congenital deformity in which one or both hands or feet are attached to the trunk by single, very short bones, giving them a flipper-like appearance. [<Gk. *phōkē* seal + -(o)melia* condition of the limbs <NL <Gk. *melos* limb]

phoe·be (fē′bē) *n.* An American flycatcher (*Sayornis phoebe*) with grayish-brown plumage and slightly crested head: common throughout the eastern United States. Also **phoebe bird.** [Imit. of its cry; infl. in form by PHOEBE]

Phoe·be (fē′bē) **1** A feminine personal name. **2** In Greek mythology, a Titaness, mother of Leto. **3** A name for Artemis as goddess of the moon. **4** *Poetic* The moon. **5** Saturn's ninth satellite. Also spelled *Phebe.* Also **Phœ′be.** [<Gk., bright]

Phoe·bus (fē′bəs) **1** In Greek mythology, Apollo as god of the sun. **2** *Poetic* The sun. Also **Phœ′bus.**

Phoe·ni·cia (fə·nē′shə, -nish′ə) An ancient country of western Asia at the eastern end of the Mediterranean in modern Syria and Lebanon, comprising a group of city-states that flourished around 1200 B.C.: also *Phenicia.*

Phoe·ni·cian (fə·nē′shən, -nish′ən) *adj.* Of or pertaining to ancient Phoenicia, its people, or its language. — *n.* **1** One of the people of ancient Phoenicia or any of its colonies, as Carthage: ethnically belonging to the Canaanite branch of the Semitic peoples. **2** The Northwest Semitic language of these people. Also spelled *Phenician.*

phoe·nix (fē′niks) *n.* **1** In Egyptian mythology, a legendary bird of great beauty, unique of its kind, which was supposed to live for 500 or 600 years in the Arabian Desert and then consume itself by fire, rising again from its ashes young and beautiful to live through another cycle: a symbol of immortality. **2** A person of matchless beauty or excellence; a paragon. Also spelled *phenix.* [OE *fenix* <Med.L *phenix* <L *phoenix* <Gk. *phoinix* the phoenix]

PHOENIX
Described by Herodotus as golden-winged with eagle-like red body.

Phoe·nix (fē′niks) *Astron.* A southern constellation. See CONSTELLATION.

Phoe·nix (fē′niks) The capital of Arizona.

Phoenix Islands A group of eight islands, comprising a district of the Gilbert and Ellice Islands colony of Great Britain: the islands of Canton and Enderbury are administered jointly with the United States; total, 11 square miles; headquarters on Canton.

phon (fon) *n. Physics* The unit of loudness level of a sound, numerically equal to the sound-pressure level in decibels, relative to a pressure of 0.0002 microbar, of a simple tone of 1,000 cycles per second which is judged by the listener as equal in loudness. [<Gk. *phōnē* a voice]

phon- Var. of PHONO-.

pho·nate (fō′nāt) *v.t.* **·nat·ed, ·nat·ing** To make

articulate sounds. [<Gk. *phōnē* + -ATE¹] **— pho·na′tion** *n.*

pho·nau·to·graph (fō·nô′tə·graf, -gräf) *n.* **1** An apparatus designed to record the vibrations of sounds. It was the forerunner of Edison's phonograph. **2** A writing or tracing produced by the mechanical use of sound vibrations. Also **pho·nau′to·gram.** [<Gk. *phōnē* sound + *autos* self + -GRAPH] **— pho·nau′to·graph′ic** or **·i·cal** *adj.* **— pho·nau′to·graph′i·cal·ly** *adv.*

phone¹ (fōn) *n.* & *v. Colloq.* Telephone. [Short for TELEPHONE]

phone² (fōn) *n.* A sound used in human speech. [<Gk. *phōnē* a sound]

-phone *combining form* Voice; sound: used in names of musical instruments and other sound-transmitting devices: *saxophone, microphone.* [<Gk. *phōnē* voice]

pho·neme (fō′nēm) *n.* A class of acoustically similar sounds in a language, usually written with the same phonetic symbol, which differ non-relevantly as conditioned by environment; the smallest unit in the sound system of a language, functioning to distinguish one morpheme from another. The contrasting phonemes /t/ and /p/ distinguish the words *tin* and *pin,* whereas the varying pronunciations of *t* in *tip, stop* and *pit* are not recognized by speakers of English and are considered members of the one phoneme /t/. See ALLOPHONE. [<F *phonème* a sound <Gk. *phōnēma* < *phōnē* a voice, sound]

pho·ne·mic (fə·nē′mik) *adj.* **1** Of or referring to phonemes: the *phonemic* pattern of a language. **2** Involving distinctive speech sounds: a *phonemic* difference. **— pho·ne′mi·cal·ly** *adv.*

pho·ne·mics (fə·nē′miks) *n.* The study of the phonemic system of a language.

pho·nen·do·scope (fə·nen′də·skōp) *n. Med.* An amplifying stethoscope. [<PHON- + END(O)- + -SCOPE]

pho·net·ic (fə·net′ik) *adj.* **1** Of or pertaining to phonetics, or to speech sounds and their production. **2** Representing articulate sounds or speech; specifically, designating the representation of each speech sound by a distinct character, or by a distinctive spelling or mark: *phonetic* alphabet, *phonetic* spelling. Also **pho·net′i·cal.** [<Gk. *phōnētikos* < *phōnē* sound] **— pho·net′i·cal·ly** *adv.*

pho·ne·ti·cian (fō′nə·tish′ən) *n.* An authority on phonetics. Also **pho·net·i·cist** (fə·net′ə·sist), **pho′ne·tist.**

phonetic law A description of a pattern of sound-changes occurring under given conditions in a language or group of languages, as Grimm's law.

pho·net·ics (fə·net′iks) *n.* **1** The branch of linguistics which deals with the analysis, description, and classification of the sounds of speech, including **articulatory phonetics,** the study of the physiological processes involved in speech production, by means of which the sounds of a language are recorded and described, and **acoustic phonetics,** the study of the physical attributes of speech sounds by the use of laboratory instruments. **2** The system of sounds of a language: the *phonetics* of American English.

pho·ney (fō′nē) See PHONY.

-phonia See -PHONY.

phon·ic (fon′ik, fō′nik) *adj.* **1** Pertaining to or of the nature of sound. **2** Caused or accompanied by sound-articulation.

phon·ics (fon′iks, fō′niks) *n. pl. (construed as singular)* **1** The phonetic rudiments used in teaching reading and pronunciation. **2** Acoustics.

phono- *combining form* Sound; speech; voice: *phonograph.* Also, before vowels, *phon-.* [<Gk. *phōnē* a voice]

pho·no·chem·is·try (fō′nō·kem′is·trē) *n.* The study of chemical reactions as induced or affected by sound waves. **— pho′no·chem′i·cal** *adj.*

pho·no·deik (fō′nə·dēk) *n.* An instrument for making sound waves visible by converting them into light waves reflected from a vibrating mirror. [<PHONO- + Gk. *deiknynai* show]

pho·no·gram (fō′nə·gram) *n.* **1** The tracing produced by a phonograph, from which articulate sounds are reproduced; a phonograph record. **2** A graphic character symbolizing an articulate sound, word, syllable, etc. **3** A telephone message taken down on paper and delivered, like a telegram. **— pho′no·gram′ic** or **·gram′mic** *adj.* **— pho′no·gram′i·cal·ly** or **·gram′mi·cal·ly** *adv.*

pho·no·graph (fō′nə·graf, -gräf) *n.* An apparatus for recording and reproducing sounds, as speech, music, etc.

pho·no·graph·ic (fō′nə·graf′ik) *adj.* **1** Pertaining to or produced by a phonograph. **2** Pertaining to or written in phonography. **3** Relating to the representation of articulate sound. **— pho′no·graph′i·cal·ly** *adv.*

pho·nog·ra·phy (fə·nog′rə·fē) *n.* **1** The art or science of writing by sound; especially, the art of representing words according to a system of sound elements that reduces their graphic reproduction to the simplest form: a style of shorthand which owes its principal development to Isaac Pitman, of Bath, England, upon whose alphabet the majority of the existing stenographic systems are based. **2** The art of representing articulate sounds by marks or letters. **3** The art of making or using phonographs; the mechanical recording and reproduction of sounds or speech. **— pho·nog′ra·pher, pho·nog′ra·phist** *n.*

pho·no·lite (fō′nə·līt) *n.* A grayish-green compact igneous rock composed essentially of orthoclase, nephelite, and augite; clinkstone. **— pho′no·lit′ic** (-lit′ik) *adj.*

pho·nol·o·gy (fə·nol′ə·jē) *n.* **1** The study of the sound system of a language. **2** The historical study of the sound-changes that have taken place in a language. **3** The phonetic or phonemic pattern of a language. **— pho·no·log·ic** (fō′nə·loj′ik) or **·i·cal** *adj.* **— pho′no·log′i·cal·ly** *adv.* **— pho·nol′o·gist** *n.*

pho·no·ma·ni·a (fō′nə·mā′nē·ə, -mān′yə) *n.* Homicidal mania. [<Gk. *phonos* murder + -MANIA]

pho·nom·e·ter (fə·nom′ə·tər) *n.* An instrument for measuring the intensity of sounds or the frequency of sound vibrations. **— pho·nom′e·try** *n.*

pho·no·scope (fō′nə·skōp) *n.* An instrument for observing, testing, or exhibiting the properties of musical strings or other sounding bodies.

pho·no·type (fō′nə·tīp) *n.* **1** A writing or printing alphabet having a distinct character for each simple sound of speech. **2** A production written or printed in such characters. **— pho′no·typ′ic** (-tip′ik) or **·i·cal** *adj.* **— pho′no·typ′i·cal·ly** *adv.*

pho·no·typ·y (fō′nə·tī′pē) *n.* The art or practice of representing every elementary sound of articulate speech by a mark or letter of its own; phonetic transcription. **— pho′no·typ′ist** *n.*

pho·ny (fō′ne) *U.S. Slang adj.* **·ni·er, ·ni·est** Fake; false; spurious; counterfeit. **—** *n.* **1** Something fake or not genuine. **2** One who impersonates another; an impostor. Also spelled *phoney.* [< slang E *fawney* a gilt brass ring used in a fraud <Irish *fain(n)e* a ring]

-phony *combining form* A (specified) type of sound or sounds: *cacophony.* Also *-phonia,* as in *aphonia.* [<Gk. *phōnē* sound, voice]

Phor·cus (fôr′kəs) In Greek mythology, the leader of the Tritons and father of the Graeae.

-phore *combining form* A bearer or producer of: *semaphore.* [<Gk. *-phoros* < *pherein* bear]

pho·re·sis (fə·rē′sis) *n. Chem.* The passage of ions through a membrane by the action of an electric current. [<NL <Gk. *phorēsis* a being borne < *phoreein,* freq. of *pherein* bear]

phor·e·sy (fôr′ə·sē, for′-) *n. Biol.* An interrelationship between small and large organisms by which the smaller, by attachment to the bodies of the larger, are transported or dispersed, as mites on the bodies of certain insects. [<Gk. *phorēsis.* See PHORESIS.]

-phorous *combining form* Bearing or producing: found in adjectives corresponding to nouns in *-phore.* [See -PHORE]

phos·gene (fos′jēn) *n. Chem.* Carbonyl chloride, $COCl_2$, a colorless, highly toxic gas with a suffocating odor: used in organic chemistry and as a chemical warfare agent. [<Gk. *phōs* light + *gen-,* root of *gignesthai* be born]

phos·ge·nite (fos′jə·nīt) *n.* A white, adamantine carbonate and chloride of lead, $Pb_2Cl_2CO_3$, crystallizing in the tetragonal system. [< PHOSGENE + -ITE¹]

phosph- Var. of PHOSPHO-.

phos·pha·tase (fos′fə·tās) *n. Biochem.* An enzyme found in various animal tissues, as the kidneys and intestines, which hydrolyzes phospholipids. [<PHOSPHAT(E) + -ASE]

phos·phate (fos′fāt) *n.* **1** *Chem.* A salt or ester of phosphoric acid. Phosphates, especially those of calcium, are necessary to the growth of plants, which absorb them in the form of soluble salts. **2** *Agric.* Any fertilizer valued for its phosphoric acid. **3** A beverage of carbonated water, variously flavored, containing small amounts of phosphoric acid. [<F]

phos·phat·ic (fos·fat′ik) *adj.* **1** Relating to the phosphates. **2** Containing some phosphate.

phos·pha·tide (fos′fə·tīd, -tid) *n.* A phospholipid. [<PHOSPHAT(E) + -IDE]

phos·pha·tize (fos′fə·tīz) *v.t.* **·tized, ·tiz·ing** **1** To treat with phosphates. **2** To reduce to a phosphate. **— phos′pha·ti·za′tion** *n.*

phos·pha·tu·ri·a (fos′fə·tŏŏr′ē·ə, -tyŏŏr′-) *n. Pathol.* Excess of phosphates in urine. [<NL < *phosphatum* phosphate + Gk. *ouron* urine] **— phos′pha·tu′ric** *adj.*

phos·phene (fos′fēn) *n. Physiol.* The spectrum or luminous image made by pressing the eyeball: due to mechanical excitement of the retina, and seen internally opposite the point of pressure. [<Gk. *phōs* light + *phainein* make appear]

phos·phide (fos′fīd, -fid) *n. Chem.* A binary compound of phosphorus with a more positive element: calcium *phosphide,* Ca_3P_2. Also **phos′phid** (-fid).

phos·phine (fos′fēn, -fin) *n. Chem.* **1** A colorless, gaseous, highly toxic hydride of phosphorus, PH_3, with an odor resembling that of putrid fish. **2** One of a class of compounds derived from phosphine by replacing the hydrogen with alkyl radicals. **3** An acridine dye. Also **phos′phin** (-fin).

phos·phite (fos′fīt) *n.* A salt of phosphorous acid.

phospho- *combining form* Phosphorus; of or containing phosphorus, or any of its compounds: *phospholipid.* Also, before vowels, *phosph-.* [<PHOSPHORUS]

phos·pho·cre·a·tine (fos′fō·krē′ə·tēn, -tin) *n. Biochem.* An organic compound, $C_4H_{10}O_5N_3$, present in muscle tissue, to which it supplies the energy for contraction. [<PHOSPHO(RIC ACID) + CREATINE]

phos·pho·lip·id (fos′fō·lip′id) *n. Biochem.* Any of a group of fatty substances widely distributed in plant and animal tissue, as cephalin and lecithin: they contain nitrogen and phosphoric acid. Also called *phosphatide.* [<PHOSPHO- + LIPID]

phos·pho·ni·um (fos·fō′nē·əm) *n. Chem.* The univalent radical PH_4 regarded as a base. It resembles the radical ammonium, and forms crystalline halides. [<PHOSPH(ORUS) + (AMM)ONIUM]

phos·pho·pro·te·in (fos′fō·prō′tē·in, -tēn) *n. Biochem.* Any of a class of conjugated proteins containing phosphoric acid combined with the hydroxy group of certain amino acids, as the casein of milk.

phos·phor (fos′fər) *n. Chem.* **1** Phosphorus. **2** Any of a class of substances that will emit light under the action of certain chemicals or radiations. **—** *adj.* Phosphorescent. [<L *phosphorus* PHOSPHORUS]

Phos·phor (fos′fər) *n.* The morning star, especially Venus, as the harbinger of day. Also **Phos′phore.** [<L *Phosphorus* the morning star <Gk. *phōsphoros.* See PHOSPHORUS.]

phosphor bronze An alloy of copper and tin containing small amounts of phosphorus, noted for its toughness, durability, and high tensile strength.

phos·phor·esce (fos′fə·res′) *v.i.* **·esced, ·esc·ing** To glow with a faint light unaccompanied by sensible heat. [? Back formation <PHOSPHORESCENT]

phos·phor·es·cence (fos′fə·res′əns) *n.* **1** The emission of light without sensible heat, or the light so emitted. **2** The property of continuing to shine in the dark after exposure to light, shown by many mineral substances: distinguished from *fluorescence.* **3** *Biol.* The property of producing a faint light, shown by infusorians, fireflies, etc.

phos·phor·es·cent (fos′fə·res′ənt) *adj.* Exhibiting phosphorescence. [<PHOSPHORUS + -ESCENT]

phos·phor·et·ed (fos′fə·ret′id) *adj. Chem.* Combined with phosphorus: *phosphoreted* hydrogen, PH_3. Also **phos′phor·et′ted, phos′phu·ret′ed** (-fyə·ret′id) or **·ret′ted.** [<NL *phosphoretum* a phosphide]

phos·phor·ic (fos·fôr′ik, -for′-) *adj.* 1 *Chem.* Pertaining to or derived from phosphorus, especially in its highest valence. 2 Phosphorescent.

phosphoric acid *Chem.* One of three oxyacids of phosphorus known respectively as *metaphosphoric acid* (HPO_3), *orthophosphoric acid* (H_3PO_4), and *pyrophosphoric acid* ($H_4P_2O_7$).

phos·phor·ism (fos′fə·riz′əm) *n. Pathol.* Chronic phosphorus poisoning.

phos·phor·ite (fos′fə·rīt) *n.* 1 A massive fibrous variety of apatite. 2 Phosphate rock in general.

phos·phor·o·scope (fos′fər·ə·skōp′) *n.* An apparatus for measuring the duration of phosphorescent light after the source is withdrawn.

phos·pho·rous (fos′fər·əs, fos·fôr′əs, -fō′rəs) *adj. Chem.* Of, pertaining to, resembling, containing, or derived from phosphorus, especially in its lower valence.

phosphorous acid *Chem.* A crystalline acid, H_3PO_3, with a garlic taste, obtained by the oxidation of phosphorus.

phos·pho·rus (fos′fər·əs) *n.* 1 A widely distributed nonmetallic element (symbol P, atomic number 15) existing in several allotropic forms, including red phosphorus and the more common white phosphorus, a yellowish, waxy, exceedingly poisonous solid that ignites spontaneously in air. See PERIODIC TABLE. 2 Any phosphorescent substance. [<NL <L *Phosphorus* the morning star <Gk. *phōsphoros (astēr),* lit., light-bringing <*phōs* a light + *phoros* bearing <*pherein* bear]

phot (fot, fōt) *n.* The cgs unit of illumination, equal to one lumen per square centimeter. [<Gk. *phōs, phōtos* a light]

pho·tic (fō′tik) *adj.* 1 Relating to light and the production of light. 2 Designating those underwater regions which are penetrated by sunlight: the *photic* zone.

Pho·ti·us (fō′shē·əs, -shəs), 816?–891?, a patriarch of Constantinople who refused to recognize papal jurisdiction and was therefore excommunicated.

pho·to (fō′tō) *n. pl.* **·tos** *Colloq.* A photograph. [Short for PHOTOGRAPH]

photo- *combining form* 1 Light; of, pertaining to, or produced by light: *photometer.* 2 Photograph; photographic: *photoengrave.* [<Gk. *phōs, phōtos* light]

pho·to·ac·tin·ic (fō′tō·ak·tin′ik) *adj.* Capable of emitting actinic radiation.

pho·to·ar·chive (fō′tō·är′kīv) *n.* A collection of photographs assembled and classified for purposes of study and research.

pho·to·bi·ot·ic (fō′tō·bī·ot′ik) *adj.* 1 Living in the light. 2 Requiring light for life or development.

pho·to·cell (fō′tō·sel′) *n.* A photoelectric cell.

pho·to·chem·is·try (fō′tō·kem′is·trē) *n.* The branch of chemistry dealing with chemical reactions produced or influenced by light. —**pho′to·chem′i·cal** *adj.*

pho·to·chro·mism (fō′tō·krō′miz′əm) *n. Physics* The property of changing color under irradiation by the light of a suitable wavelength, the change being reversible by exposure to light of a suitable different wavelength or, in some cases, simply by removal of the stimulating radiation. Also **pho′to·chro′ma·tism** (-krō′mə·tiz′əm). —**pho′to·chro′mic** *adj.*

pho·to·chro·mog·ra·phy (fō′tō·krō·mog′rə·fē) *n.* The art of reproducing on a printing press photographic images in several colors.

pho·to·chro·my (fō′tə·krō′mē) *n.* Color photography. [<PHOTO- (def. 2) + CHROM- + -Y[1]]

pho·to·chron·o·graph (fō′tō·kron′ə·graf, -gräf) *n.* 1 An instrument for taking pictures at minute, regular, timed intervals, of a body in motion. 2 A picture so taken. 3 A chronograph adapted for use in photographing a moving body, as a star in transit. —**pho′to·chro·nog′ra·phy** (-krə·nog′rə·fē) *n.*

pho·to·com·pos·er (fō′tō·kəm·pō′zər) *n.* Any machine or apparatus which composes printed matter by photographic means.

pho·to·com·po·si·tion (fō′tō·kom′pə·zish′ən) *n.* The composing of printed matter by photographic means.

pho·to·con·duc·tion (fō′tō·kən·duk′shən) *n. Physics* The property, possessed by many substances, of exhibiting increased electrical conductivity when subjected to light waves. —**pho′to·con·duc′tive** (-duk′tiv) *adj.*

pho·to·cop·y (fō′tō·kop′ē) *n. pl.* **·cop·ies** A photographic reproduction of printed or other graphic material. —*v.* **·cop·ied, ·cop·y·ing** *v.t.* 1 To make a photocopy of. —*v.i.* 2 To make a photocopy. —**pho′to·cop′i·er** *n.*

pho·to·cur·rent (fō′tō·kûr′ənt) *n.* An electric current produced by the action of light or by the photoelectric effect.

pho·to·dis·in·te·gra·tion (fō′tō·dis·in′tə·grā′·shən) *n. Physics* A breaking down by the action of radiant energy: said especially of the atomic nucleus.

pho·to·dra·ma (fō′tə·drä′mə, -dram′ə) *n.* A motion picture or photoplay. —**pho′to·dra·mat′ic** (-drə·mat′ik) *adj.*

pho·to·dy·nam·ic (fō′tō·dī·nam′ik, -di·nam′-) *adj.* Of, pertaining to, or operating by the energy of light.

pho·to·dy·nam·ics (fō′tō·dī·nam′iks, -di·nam′-) *n.* The study of the action and influence of light on plants and animals.

pho·to·e·lec·tric (fō′tō·i·lek′trik) *adj.* Of or pertaining to the electrical effects due to the action of light, as in the emission of electrons from gaseous, liquid, or solid bodies when subjected to radiation of suitable wavelength. Also **pho′to·e·lec′tri·cal.**

photoelectric cell A vacuum tube, one of whose electrodes gives off electrons under the action of light: incorporated in electrical circuits as a controlling, testing, and counting device: also called *phototube, electric eye,* or *photocell.*

pho·to·e·lec·tron (fō′tō·i·lek′tron) *n.* An electron emitted from a metal surface when exposed to suitable radiation.

pho·to·e·lec·tro·type (fō′tō·i·lek′trə·tīp) *n.* 1 An electrotype produced by a photomechanical process. 2 A picture printed from such a block.

pho·to·en·grave (fō′tō·in·grāv′) *v.t.* **·graved, ·grav·ing** To reproduce by photoengraving. —**pho′to·en·grav′er** *n.*

pho·to·en·grav·ing (fō′tō·in·grā′ving) *n.* 1 The act or process of producing by the aid of photography a relief block or plate for printing. 2 A plate or picture so produced.

photo finish The finish of a game or race, as in horse-racing, in which the two leads are so close as they cross the finish line that only a photograph can determine the winner.

pho·to·flash bulb (fō′tō·flash′) An electric bulb containing aluminum or magnesium which, on the passage of a current, ignites and gives an incandescent light of brief duration: used in photography.

pho·to·flood lamp (fō′tō·flud′) An electric lamp operating at excess voltage to give high illumination, as in taking photographs and motion pictures.

pho·to·gel·a·tin (fō′tō·jel′ə·tin) *adj.* Characterized by the use of gelatin: said of a photographic process.

pho·to·gen (fō′tō·jen) *n. Biol.* An organism that generates light; a phosphorescent plant or animal.

pho·to·gene (fō′tō·jēn) *n.* An afterimage.

pho·to·gen·ic (fō′tō·jen′ik) *adj.* 1 Of or pertaining to the action of light; generating or producing light. 2 Producing phosphorescence; phosphorescent, as fireflies. 3 Having certain characteristics and qualities, as coloration, form, etc., suitable for being photographed. [<PHOTO- + -GENIC; def. 3 coined from PHOTO(GRAPH), on analogy with *pathogenic, eugenic,* etc.] —**pho′to·gen′i·cal·ly** *adv.*

pho·to·ge·ol·o·gy (fō′tō·jē·ol′ə·jē) *n. Geol.* The study of geological formations and processes by means of aerial photographs taken on a uniform scale. —**pho′to·ge′o·log′i·cal** (-jē′ə·loj′i·kəl) *adj.*

pho·to·go·ni·om·e·ter (fō′tō·gō′nē·om′ə·tər) *n.* A device for studying the phenomena of crystal X-ray diffraction and X-ray spectra.

pho·to·gram·me·try (fō′tō·gram′ə·trē) *n.* The art and technique of making surveys or maps by means of photographs. [<*photogram,* var. of PHOTOGRAPH + -METRY]

pho·to·graph (fō′tə·graf, -gräf) *n.* A picture taken by photography. —*v.t.* 1 To take a photograph of. —*v.i.* 2 To practice photography. 3 To undergo photographing. See synonyms under PICTURE.

pho·tog·ra·pher (fə·tog′rə·fər) *n.* One who makes a business of or is expert in photography.

pho·to·graph·ic (fō′tə·graf′ik) *adj.* 1 Pertaining to, used in, or produced by photography. 2 Like a photograph; vividly depicted. Also **pho′to·graph′i·cal.** —**pho′to·graph′i·cal·ly** *adv.*

pho·tog·ra·phy (fə·tog′rə·fē) *n.* 1 The process of forming and fixing an image of an object or objects by the chemical action of light and other forms of radiant energy on photosensitive surfaces. 2 The art or business of producing and printing photographs.

pho·to·gra·vure (fō′tō·grə·vyŏŏr′, -gräv′yər) *n.* 1 The process of producing an intaglio plate for printing in which there are no sharp incised lines, but minute depressions, the deep parts producing the shadows, and the high parts showing white. 2 A picture produced from such a plate. [<F]

pho·to·he·li·o·graph (fō′tō·hē′lē·ə·graf′, -gräf′) *n.* A telescopic photographic instrument, variously constructed, for taking pictures of the sun, as during an eclipse.

pho·to·jour·nal·ism (fō′tō·jûr′nəl·iz′əm) *n.* A form of journalism in which a story or news item is recounted largely or entirely by means of photographs. —**pho′to·jour′nal·ist** *n.*

pho·to·ki·net·ic (fō′tō·ki·net′ik) *adj. Biol.* Capable of movement under the influence of light, as certain plants. —**pho′to·ki·ne′sis** (-ki·nē′sis) *n.*

pho·to·lith·o·graph (fō′tō·lith′ə·graf, -gräf) *v.t.* To reproduce by photolithography. —*n.* A picture produced by photolithography.

pho·to·li·thog·ra·phy (fō′tō·li·thog′rə·fē) *n.* The art or operation of producing on stone, largely by photographic means, a printing surface from which impressions may be taken by a lithographic process. —**pho′to·lith′o·graph′ic** (-lith′ə·graf′ik) *adj.*

pho·tol·y·sis (fō·tol′ə·sis) *n.* Chemical or biological decomposition due to the action of light. [<NL <Gk. *phōs, phōtos* a light + *lysis* a loosening <*lyein* loosen] —**pho·to·lyt·ic** (fō′tə·lit′ik) *adj.*

pho·to·map (fō′tō·map′) *n.* A map composed of one or more aerial photographs, laid off into a grid, contour lines, etc.

pho·to·me·chan·i·cal (fō′tō·mi·kan′i·kəl) *adj.* Pertaining to a process, illustration, plate, etc., produced by any one of a variety of methods, by which photography is brought to the aid of the etcher or engraver. —**pho′to·me·chan′i·cal·ly** *adv.*

pho·tom·e·ter (fō·tom′ə·tər) *n.* 1 Any instrument for measuring the intensity of light or comparing the intensity of two lights. 2 A device for determining the proper duration of exposure in photography.

pho·tom·e·try (fō·tom′ə·trē) *n.* 1 The art of measuring the intensity of light, especially by means of the photometer. 2 The branch of optics that treats of such measurement. —**pho·to·met·ric** (fō′tə·met′rik) *adj.* —**pho·tom′e·trist** *n.*

pho·to·mi·cro·graph (fō′tō·mī′krə·graf, -gräf) *n.* A photograph of a microscopic object taken through a microscope. Compare MICROPHOTOGRAPH.

pho·to·mi·crog·ra·phy (fō′tō·mī·krog′rə·fē) *n.* The art or process of making photographs of minute objects, as by a camera attached to a microscope.

pho·to·mon·tage (fō′tō·mon·täzh′, -môn-) *n.* The process of montage with photographs; also, a picture produced by this process.

pho·to·mu·ral (fō′tō·myŏŏr′əl) *n.* A photograph enlarged to a size suitable for wall decoration.

pho·ton (fō′ton) *n. Physics* A quantum of light or other electromagnetic radiation. [<PHOTO- + (ELECTR)ON] —**pho·ton′ic** *adj.*

Pho·ton (fō′ton) *n.* A keyboard-operated machine assembly for the composition of printed matter by means of high-speed photography and photoelectric action geared to a matrix disk bearing the required characters in a series of concentric fonts, thus eliminating the use of metal type: a trade name.

pho·to·neu·tron (fō′tō·nŏŏ′tron, -nyŏŏ′-) *n.*

Physics A neutron emitted in a photonuclear reaction.

pho·to·nu·cle·ar (fō'tō·nōō'klē·ər, -nyōō'-) *adj.* *Physics* Of, pertaining to, or designating a reaction initiated in an atomic nucleus by a photon.

pho·to·off·set (fō'tō·ôf'set, -of'-) *n.* Offset printing from a metal surface on which the text or design has been imprinted by photography.

pho·to·pe·ri·od (fō'tō·pir'ē·əd) *n.* The relative duration of illumination in a cycle of darkness and light, whether occurring naturally as night and day or imposed artificially. **pho·to·pe·ri·od·ic** (-pir'ē·od'ik), **·i·cal** *adj.*

pho·to·pe·ri·od·ism (fō'tō·pir'ē·ə·diz·əm) *n.* The response of an organism to variations in the duration of day and night or other cyclic illumination. Also **pho·to·pe·ri·od·i·ci·ty** (pir'ē·ə·dis'ə·tē).

pho·toph·i·lous (fō·tof'ə·ləs) *Biol. adj.* Light-loving; possessing positive phototaxis. —*n.* A photophilous organism.

pho·to·pho·bi·a (fō'tə·fō'bē·ə) *n.* **1** Aversion to or intolerance of light. **2** *Pathol.* Morbid sensitivity of the eye to light.

pho·to·pia (fō·tō'pē·ə) *n.* Vision under lighting conditions which permit color discrimination; daylight vision. [< NL < Gk. *phōs, phōtos* a light + *ōps, ōpos* an eye] **—pho·top·ic** (fō·top'ik) *adj.*

pho·to·play (fō'tō·plā') *n.* **1** The representation of a play in motion pictures. **2** A play arranged for a motion-picture performance.

pho·to·pro·ton (fō'tō·prō'ton) *n.* *Physics* A proton resulting from a photonuclear reaction.

pho·to·re·cep·tor (fō'tō·ri·sep'tər) *n.* *Physiol.* A nerve receptor sensitive to light stimuli.

pho·to·sen·si·tive (fō'tō·sen'sə·tiv) *adj.* Sensitive to light. **—pho'to·sen'si·tiv'i·ty** *n.*

pho·to·shock (fō'tō·shok') *n.* *Psychiatry* A method of treating certain forms of mental disorder by the application of controlled flashes of light used in connection with appropriate drugs.

pho·to·spec·tro·scope (fō'tō·spek'trə·skōp) *n.* A spectrograph.

pho·to·sphere (fō'tə·sfir) *n.* *Astron.* The visible shining surface of the sun, or, more rarely, of a fixed star. **—pho'to·spher'ic** (-sfer'ik) *adj.*

pho·to·sta·ble (fō'tə·stā'bəl) *adj.* Unaffected by or resistant to the influence of light.

pho·to·stat (fō'tə·stat) *v.t.* & *v.i.* **·stat·ed** or **·stat·ted, ·stat·ing** or **·stat·ting** To make a reproduction (of) with a Photostat. —*n.* A reproduction so produced. **—pho'to·stat'ic** *adj.*

Pho·to·stat (fō'tə·stat) *n.* A camera designed to reproduce documents, drawings, etc., directly, prints being made from the primary negative: a trade name.

pho·to·sur·vey (fō'tō·sûr'vā) *n.* A survey, as of industrial processes or social phenomena, illustrated and documented by photographs.

pho·to·syn·the·sis (fō'tō·sin'thə·sis) *n.* *Biol.* **1** The synthesis of chemical compounds by means of light and other forms of radiant energy. **2** The process by which plants form carbohydrates from carbon dioxide and water through the agency of sunlight acting upon chlorophyll. **—pho'to·syn·thet'ic** (-sin·thet'ik) *adj.* **—pho'to·syn·thet'i·cal·ly** *adv.*

pho·to·tax·is (fō'tō·tak'sis) *n.* *Biol.* The assumption by an organism of a definite position with reference to the direction of the incident ray of light, called **negative phototaxis** when the movement is away from the light, and **positive phototaxis** when the movement is toward the light. Also **pho'to·tax'y.** [< NL < Gk. *phōs, phōtos* a light + *taxis* an arrangement] **—pho'to·tac'tic** (-tak'tik) *adj.* **—pho'·to·tac'ti·cal·ly** *adv.*

pho·to·tel·e·graph (fō'tō·tel'ə·graf, -gräf) *v.t.* & *v.i.* To transmit by phototelegraphy. —*n.* Something so transmitted.

pho·to·te·leg·ra·phy (fō'tō·tə·leg'rə·fē) *n.* **1** The electrical transmission of messages, photographs, etc., by facsimile. **2** Telephotography. **—pho'to·tel'e·graph'ic** (-tel'ə·graf'ik) *adj.* **—pho'to·tel'e·graph'i·cal·ly** *adv.*

pho·to·tel·e·scope (fō'tō·tel'ə·skōp) *n.* A telescope provided with a photographic apparatus, photographing the heavenly bodies. **—pho'to·tel'e·scop'ic** (-tel'ə·skop'ik) *adj.*

pho·to·ther·a·py (fō'tō·ther'ə·pē) *n.* Treatment of diseases, especially diseases of the skin, by the application of light. Also **pho'to·ther'a·peu'tics** (-ther'ə·pyōō'tiks). **—pho'to·ther'a·peu'tic, pho'to·the·rap'ic** (-thə·rap'ik) *adj.*

pho·to·ther·mic (fō'tō·thûr'mik) *adj.* Denoting the thermic activity of the light rays.

pho·tot·o·nus (fō·tot'ə·nəs) *n.* *Biol.* **1** The influence of light upon the movement and the growth of plants. **2** The condition thus induced. **3** Increased irritability or motility induced by exposure to light. [< NL < Gk. *phōs, phōtos* a light + *tonos* tension. See TONE.] **—pho·to·ton·ic** (fō'tə·ton'ik) *adj.*

pho·to·to·pog·ra·phy (fō'tō·tə·pog'rə·fē) *n.* The art and technique of preparing topographic maps with the aid of photographs, as in the multiplex system or by data provided by aerial photographs. **—pho'to·top'o·graph'ic** (-top'ə·graf'ik) *adj.*

pho·to·tran·sis·tor (fō'tō·tran·zis'tər) *n.* A very small disk of germanium which produces a multiplied photocurrent by transistor action.

pho·to·trop·ic (fō'tə·trop'ik) *adj.* *Biol.* Turning toward the light; heliotropic. **—pho'to·trop'i·cal·ly** *adv.*

pho·tot·ro·pism (fō·tot'rə·piz'əm) *n.* *Biol.* The effect of light on the direction of growth of plant and animal organisms.

pho·tot·ro·py (fō·tot'rə·pē) *n.* **1** Phototropism. **2** The color alteration observed in some substances after exposure to light.

pho·to·tube (fō'tō·tōōb', -tyōōb') *n.* A photoelectric cell.

pho·to·type (fō'tə·tīp') *n.* **1** A relief plate made for printing by photography. **2** The process by which it is produced. **3** A picture printed from such a plate. **—pho'to·typ'ic** (-tip'ik) *adj.*

pho·to·ty·pog·ra·phy (fō'tō·ti·pog'rə·fē) *n.* Any photomechanical process of engraving in relief that may be reproduced in connection with type on a printing press. **—pho'to·ty'po·graph'ic** (-tī'pə·graf'ik) *adj.*

pho·to·typ·y (fō'tō·tī'pē) *n.* The production or use of phototypes.

pho·to·vol·ta·ic (fō'tō·vol·tā'ik) *adj.* Capable of producing an electromotive force under the action of light; photoelectric.

pho·to·zin·cog·ra·phy (fō'tō·zing·kog'rə·fē) *n.* Photoengraving which uses a sensitized zinc plate.

phrais·in (frā'zin) *adj.* *Scot.* Flattering.

phrase (frāz) *n.* **1** An expression, consisting usually of but a few words, denoting a single idea or forming a separate part of a sentence; specifically, a group of two or more associated words, not containing a subject and predicate: distinguished from *clause.* See synonym below. **2** A concise, sententious expression. **3** Characteristic mode of expression; peculiar habit of language; phraseology. **4** *Music* A fragment of a melody having well-determined motion and repose, but incomplete sense. —*v.t.* & *v.i.* **phrased, phras·ing** **1** To express or be expressed in words or phrases. **2** *Music* To execute or divide (notes) into phrases by accentuation. [< LL *phrasis* diction < Gk., speech < *phrazein* point out, tell] **—phras'al** *adj.*

Synonym (noun): clause. A *clause* is a short sentence forming a distinct part of a composition, or in more extended use a distinct and separable statement forming part of a legal or state document, as of a will, an indictment, etc.; a *phrase* is a group of words conveying a single idea, and forming a distinct part of a sentence. In grammar, a *clause* is a simple sentence which is combined with some other sentence or sentences, so as to form a complex or compound sentence. A simple sentence standing alone is not, in grammatical use, called a *clause,* but every *clause* of a complex or compound sentence is a simple sentence. Thus, the *clause* always contains a subject and predicate. A *phrase* does not contain a subject and predicate, but it may include as many words as a *clause.* See DICTION, TERM.

phra·se·o·gram (frā'zē·ə·gram') *n.* A symbol or combination of stenographic signs standing for a phrase. [< PHRASE + -(O)GRAM; on analogy with PHRASEOLOGY]

phra·se·o·graph (frā'zē·ə·graf', -gräf') *n.* A phrase having a symbol or phraseogram. **—phra'se·o·graph'ic** *adj.*

phra·se·ol·o·gist (frā'zē·ol'ə·jist) *n.* **1** One who pays much attention to phraseology; a maker of phrases. **2** One who collects phrases.

phra·se·ol·o·gy (frā'zē·ol'ə·jē) *n.* **1** The choice and arrangement of words and phrases in expressing ideas; diction; style. **2** A compilation or handbook of phrases. See synonyms under DICTION. [< NL *phraseologia,* irregularly formed < Gk. *phrasis, -eōs* speech + *logos* a word] **—phra'se·o·log'i·cal** (-ə·loj'·i·kəl) *adj.*

phras·ing (frā'zing) *n.* **1** The rendering of phrases. **2** *Music* Grouping and accentuation of the sounds in a melody. **3** Manner or form of verbal expression.

phra·try (frā'trē) *n. pl.* **·tries** **1** In ancient Athens, a clan or subdivision of a phyle. **2** Any similar tribal unit among primitive peoples, as a tribe composed of several totemic clans among North American Indians. [< Gk. *phratria* < *phratēr* clansman, brother] **—phra'tric** *adj.*

phre·at·ic (frē·at'ik) *adj.* Of or pertaining to underground waters, especially those at or below the water table and accessible through wells. [< Gk. *phrear, phreatos* well]

phre·net·ic (frə·net'ik) *adj.* **1** Of, pertaining to, or suffering from brain fever. **2** Excessively excited; frantic. Also **phre·net'i·cal.** —*n.* A madman. Also spelled *frenetic.* [< OF *frenetike* < L *phreneticus* < L Gk. *phrenētikos,* var. of Gk. *phrenitikos* afflicted with delirium < *phrenitis* PHRENITIS] **—phre·net'i·cal·ly** *adv.*

phren·ic (fren'ik) *adj.* **1** Of or pertaining to the mind. **2** *Anat.* Of or pertaining to the diaphragm; diaphragmatic: the *phrenic* nerve. [< NL *phrenicus* < Gk. *phrēn, phrenos* diaphragm, mind]

phre·ni·tis (fri·nī'tis) *n.* *Pathol.* **1** Brain fever. **2** Wild delirium; frenzy. **3** Inflammation of the diaphragm. [< LL < Gk., delirium < *phrēn, phrenos* diaphragm, mind]

phreno- *combining form* **1** Mind; brain: *phrenotropic.* **2** Diaphragm; of or related to the diaphragm. Also, before vowels, **phren-.** [< Gk. *phrēn, phrenos* the diaphragm (thought to be the seat of intellect)]

phre·nol·o·gy (fri·nol'ə·jē) *n.* The doctrine that the conformation of the human skull, its shape and protuberances, indicate the position and degree of development of separate parts of the brain which control the various mental faculties and characteristics; loosely, character analysis by interpreting cranial formations. [< Gk. *phrēn, phrenos* mind + -LOGY] **—phren·o·log·ic** (fren'ə·loj'ik) or **·i·cal** *adj.* **—phren'o·log'i·cal·ly** *adv.* **—phre·nol'o·gist** *n.*

phren·o·sin (fren'ə·sin) *n.* *Biochem.* A cerebroside found in brain substance and isolated as a yellowish-white powder, $C_{48}H_{93}O_9N$: also called *cerebrin.* [< Gk. *phrēn, phrenos* mind, on analogy with *myosin*]

phren·o·trop·ic (fren'ə·trop'ik) *adj.* *Med.* Acting upon, influencing, or affecting the mind, as certain drugs.

Phrix·us (frik'səs) In Greek legend, son of Athamas and Nephele who, with his sister Helle, escaped his stepmother on a ram with golden fleece: only Phrixus arrived safely in Colchis, where he sacrificed the ram. See GOLDEN FLEECE.

Phryg·i·a (frij'ē·ə) An ancient country in Asia Minor divided into **Greater Phrygia,** the central part, and **Lesser Phrygia,** the NW section. *Acts* xvi 6.

Phryg·i·an (frij'ē·ən) *adj.* Of or pertaining to Phrygia or to its people. —*n.* **1** One of a prehistoric European people who migrated to Phrygia via Thrace and settled there. **2** The Indo-European language of this people, known from a few inscriptions.

Phrygian cap An ancient headdress. See LIBERTY CAP.

Phry·ne (frī'nē) A beautiful Athenian courtesan of the fourth century B.C.; supposedly the model for sculptures by Praxiteles.

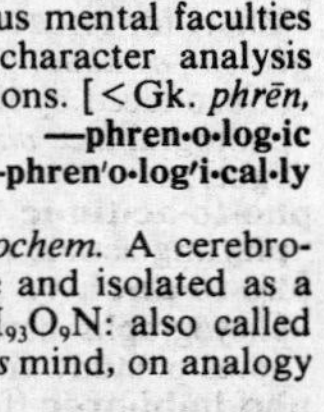
PHRYGIAN CAP

phthal·e·in (thal'ē·in, -ēn, fthal'-) *n.* *Chem.* Any one of a series of organic compounds formed, with elimination of water, by the combination of a phenol with phthalic acid or its anhydride. Some compounds of phthalein are coloring matters. Also **phthal'e·ine.** [< PHTHAL(IC) + *-ein,* var. of -IN]

phthal·ic (thal'ik, fthal'-) *adj.* *Chem.* Of, pertaining to, or derived from naphthalene. [Short for NAPHTHALIC]

phthalic acid *Chem.* Any of three isomeric forms of an acid consisting of a benzene ring with two carboxyl groups, $C_6H_4(CO_2H)_2$, especially the ortho form, which is used as an intermediate in the manufacture of dyes, medicines, and other products.

phthal·in (thal′in, fthal′-) *n. Chem.* Any of several colorless crystalline compounds obtained by reducing phthalein. Also **phthal′ine.** [< PHTHAL(EIN) + -IN]

phthal·o·cy·a·nin (thal′ō·sī′ə·nin, fthal′-) *n. Chem.* Any of a group of organic dyestuffs related to porphyrin and yielding blue and green pigments. [< *phthalo-* (< PHTHALIC) + CYANIN]

phthi·ri·a·sis (thi·rī′ə·sis, fthi-) *n.* Pediculosis; lousiness. [< L < Gk. *phtheiriasis* < *phtheiriaein* be lousy < *phtheir* a louse]

phthis·ic (tiz′ik) *n.* **1** *Pathol.* A wasting disease of the lungs. **2** Asthma; difficulty of breathing. [< OF *tisike* < L *phthisicus* < Gk. *phthisikos* consumptive < *phthisis* PHTHISIS]

phthis·i·cal (tiz′i·kəl) *adj.* **1** Relative to or having disease of the lungs; consumptive. **2** Asthmatic; wheezy. Also **phthis′·ick·y.**

phthis·i·o·pho·bi·a (tiz′ē·ə·fō′bē·ə) *n.* Morbid dread of phthisis. [< NL < Gk. *phthisis* phthisis + *phobeein* fear]

phthi·sis (thī′sis, fthī′-) *n. Pathol.* **1** Pulmonary consumption; tuberculosis of the lungs; less frequently, tuberculosis of some other part. **2** Progressive emaciation; any continuous destruction of tissue. [< L < Gk., a wasting away < *phthiein* decay]

-phyceae *combining form Bot.* Seaweed: used in the names of various classes of algae: *Rhodophyceae.* [< Gk. *phykos* seaweed]

phyco- *combining form* Seaweed; of or related to seaweed. [< Gk. *phykos* seaweed]

phy·co·e·ryth·rin (fī′kō·ə·rith′rin) *n. Biochem.* The accessory pigment associated with chlorophyll in red algae. [< PHYCO- + Gk. *erythros* red + -IN]

phy·col·o·gy (fī·kol′ə·jē) *n.* The branch of botany dealing with seaweeds or algae.

Phy·co·my·ce·tes (fī′kō·mī·sē′tēz) *n. pl.* A class of fungi, both saprophytic and parasitic, resembling algae, but destitute of chlorophyll, including the water molds and downy mildews. [< NL < Gk. *phykos* seaweed + *mykēs, -ētos* a mushroom] **—phy′co·my·ce′·tous** *adj.*

phy·co·phae·in (fī′kō·fē′in) *n.* Fucoxanthin. [< PHYCO- + Gk. *phaios* dusky + -IN]

Phyfe (fīf), **Duncan,** 1768?–1854, American cabinetmaker, noted for the excellence and beauty of his furniture; born in Scotland.

phy·lac·ter·y (fi·lak′tər·ē) *n. pl.* **·ter·ies 1** A charm or amulet worn on the person; specifically, among the Jews, a strip or strips of cowhide parchment inscribed with passages of Scripture (*Ex.* xiii 8–10, 11–16; *Deut.* vi 4–9, xi 13–22) and enclosed in a black calfskin case, having thongs for binding it on the forehead or around the left arm in memory of the early Israelitish history and of the duty to observe the law, or sometimes to serve as an amulet: also **phyl·ac·te·ri·um** (fil′ak·tir′ē·əm). **2** An inscribed scroll represented in medieval art as held in the hands, or issuing from the mouths, of angels. **3** A reminder. [< LL *phylacterium* < Gk. *phylaktērion* a safeguard < *phylaktēr* a guard < *phylassein* guard]

phy·le (fī′lē) *n. pl.* **·lae** (-lē) In ancient Athens, a political subdivision. [< Gk. *phylē* a tribe]

phy·let·ic (fī·let′ik) *adj.* **1** Pertaining to a phyle or clan. **2** Of or pertaining to a phylum. Also **phy·lic** (fī′lik). [< Gk. *phyletikos* < *phyletēs* a tribesman < *phylē* a tribe] **—phy·let′·i·cal·ly** *adv.*

Phyl·lis (fil′is) A feminine personal name. [< Gk., green leaf]

—Phyllis In Greek mythology, a maiden who, believing herself deserted by her betrothed, hanged herself and was changed to an almond tree.

—Phyllis A country girl in Vergil's *Eclogues*; hence, a poetic name for a rustic maiden: often written *Phillis.*

phyl·lite (fil′īt) *n.* A lustrous schistose rock containing small particles of mica. [< Gk. *phyllon* a leaf + -ITE[1]]

phyl·li·um (fil′ē·əm) *n.* Any of a genus *(Phyllium)* of green, flattened, leaflike insects (family *Phasmatidae*); a leaf insect. [< NL < Gk. *phyllion,* dim. of *phyllon* a leaf]

phyllo- *combining form* Leaf; pertaining to a leaf: *phyllotaxis.* Also, before vowels, **phyll-.** [< Gk. *phyllon* a leaf]

phyl·lo·clade (fil′ə·klād) *n. Bot.* A flattened branch or stem performing the functions of a leaf in certain plants, as the cacti. Also **phyl′lo·clad** (-klad). [< NL *phyllocladium* < Gk. *phyllon* a leaf + *klados* a branch]

phyl·lode (fil′ōd) *n. pl.* **phyl·lo·di·a** (fi·lō′dē·ə) *Bot.* A petiole that develops into a flattened expansion, thus taking the place, structure, and function of a leaf. [< F < NL *phyllodium* < Gk. *phyllōdēs* leaflike < *phyllon* a leaf + *eidos* form] **—phyl·lo′di·al** *adj.*

phyl·lo·dy (fil′ə·dē) *n.* Frondescence.

phyl·loid (fil′oid) *adj.* Resembling a leaf; foliaceous. [< NL *phylloides* < Gk. *phyllon* a leaf + *eidos* form]

phyl·lome (fil′ōm) *n. Bot.* The leaf or its equivalent; foliage: one of the four members that make up a perfect plant. [< NL *phylloma* < Gk. *phyllōma* foliage, leaves < *phyllon* a leaf] **—phyl·lom·ic** (fi·lom′ik) *adj.*

phyl·lo·phore (fil′ə·fôr, -fōr) *n. Bot.* The budding summit of a stem, especially a palm stem on which leaves are developed. [< Gk. *phyllophoros* bearing leaves < *phyllon* a leaf + *pherein* bear] **—phyl·loph·o·rous** (fi·lof′ər·əs) *adj.*

phyl·lo·pod (fil′ə·pod) *adj.* **1** Having leaflike feet. **2** Of or pertaining to the *Phyllopoda.* —*n.* One of the *Phyllopoda.*

Phyl·lop·o·da (fi·lop′ə·də) *n. pl.* A division of crustaceans (subclass *Entomostraca*), with the body elongated, a shell or bivalve carapace, and at least four pairs of flattened, leaflike swimming feet which also function as gills, as the freshwater fairy shrimp. [< NL < Gk. *phyllon* a leaf + *pous, podos* a foot] **—phyl·lop′o·dan** *n. & adj.*

phyl·lo·qui·none (fil′ə·kwī′nōn) *n.* Vitamin K_1.

phyl·lo·tax·is (fil′ə·tak′sis) *n. Bot.* **1** The arrangement of leaves upon a stem. **2** The laws governing this arrangement. Also **phyl′lo·tax′y.** [< NL < Gk. *phyllon* a leaf + *taxis* arrangement < *tassein* arrange] **—phyl′lo·tac′tic** (-tak′tik) *adj.*

-phyllous *combining form* Having (a specified kind or number of) leaves: *monophyllous.* [< Gk. *phyllon* a leaf]

phyl·lox·e·ra (fil′ək·sir′ə, fi·lok′sər·ə) *n.* A minute aphis or plant louse (family *Phylloxeridae*), especially the grape phylloxera *(Dactylosphaera vitifoliae),* which is very destructive to grape vines. For illustration see INSECTS (injurious). [< NL < Gk. *phyllon* a leaf + *xēros* dry]

phylo- *combining form* Tribe; race; species: *phylogeny.* Also, before vowels, **phyl-.** [< Gk. *phylē, phylon* a tribe]

phy·log·e·ny (fī·loj′ə·nē) *n. Biol.* The history of the evolution of a species or group; tribal or racial history. Compare ONTOGENY. Also **phy·lo·gen·e·sis** (fī′lə·jen′ə·sis). [< G *phylogenie* < Gk. *phylon* a race + *-geneia* birth, origin < *gen-,* root of *gignesthai* be born] **—phy′lo·ge·net′ic** (-jə·net′ik), **phy′lo·gen′ic** *adj.* **—phy′lo·ge·net′i·cal·ly** *adv.*

phy·lum (fī′ləm) *n. pl.* **·la** (-lə) *Biol.* A great division of animals or plants ranking next below a kingdom and above a class, of which the members are believed to have a common evolutionary ancestor. [< NL < Gk. *phylon* a race < *phyein* produce]

-phyre *combining form Geol.* In petrography, a porphyritic rock: *granophyre.* [< F *porphyre* porphyry]

physi- Var. of PHYSIO-.

phys·ic (fiz′ik) *n.* **1** Medicine in general. **2** A cathartic; a purge. **3** *Archaic* The art or practice of medicine; the medical profession. **4** *Obs.* Physics. —*v.t* **phys·icked, phys·ick·ing 1** To treat with medicine or, especially, a cathartic; purge. **2** To cure or relieve. [< OF *fisique* < L *physica* < Gk. *physikē (epistēmē)* (the knowledge) of nature < *physis* nature < *phyein* produce]

phys·i·cal (fiz′i·kəl) *adj.* **1** Relating to the material universe or to the physical sciences. **2** Pertaining to material things, as opposed to *mental, moral,* or *spiritual*; especially, relating to the human body apart from the mind or spirit; material; corporeal. **3** Of or pertaining to the phenomena treated of in physics. **4** Accessible to the senses; external: *physical* characteristics of a mineral; *physical* changes. [< Med. L *physicalis* < L *physica.* See PHYSIC.] **—phys′i·cal·ly** *adv.*

Synonyms: bodily, corporal, corporeal, material, natural, sensible, tangible, visible. Whatever is composed of or pertains to matter may be termed *material*: *physical* applies to *material* things considered as parts of a system or organic whole; hence, we speak of *material* substances, *physical* forces. *Bodily, corporal,* and *corporeal* apply primarily to the human body; *bodily* and *corporal* both denote pertaining or relating to the body; *corporeal* signifies of the nature of or like the body; *corporal* is now almost wholly restricted to signify applied to or inflicted upon the body; we speak of *bodily* sufferings, *bodily* presence, *corporal* punishment, the *corporeal* frame. See NATURAL (def. 8). *Antonyms*: hyperphysical, immaterial, intangible, intellectual, invisible, mental, moral, spiritual, unreal, unsubstantial.

physical anthropology 1 The study of the physical characteristics of man during the course of his evolution from the primate stock, and of the genetic relations between ethnic groups. **2** Anthropometry.

physical chemistry The branch of chemistry that deals with the physical properties of substances, especially in their quantitative relations to energy transformations and chemical change.

physical education Training and development of the human body by means of athletics and other exercises; also, education in hygiene.

physical geography Geography dealing with the natural features of the earth, as vegetation, land forms, drainage, ocean currents, climate, etc.

physical sciences The sciences that treat of the structure, properties, and energy relations of matter apart from the phenomena of life, as physics, astronomy, chemistry, geology, mineralogy, meteorology, etc.

physical therapy The science of treating disability, injury, and disease by external physical means, such as electricity, heat, light, massage, exercise, etc.: also called *physiotherapy.*

phy·si·cian (fi·zish′ən) *n.* **1** One legally authorized to practice medicine; a doctor. **2** One engaged in the general practice of medicine as distinguished from a surgeon. **3** Any healer.

phys·i·cist (fiz′ə·sist) *n.* A student of or specialist in physics.

phys·i·co·chem·i·cal (fiz′i·kō·kem′i·kəl) *adj.* **1** Of or pertaining to the physical and chemical properties of matter. **2** Pertaining to physical chemistry. [< *physico-* (< PHYSICAL) + CHEMICAL]

phys·ics (fiz′iks) *n.* The science that treats of matter and energy and of the laws governing their reciprocal interplay under conditions susceptible to precise observation, experimental control, and exact measurement. Physics generally includes the subjects of mechanics, heat, light and sound, electricity and magnetism, and radiation, but not the phenomena peculiar to living matter or to chemical change.

physio- *combining form* Nature; related to natural functions or phenomena: *physiology.* Also, before vowels, *physi-.* [< Gk. *physis* nature]

phys·i·oc·ra·cy (fiz′ē·ok′rə·sē) *n.* The doctrine of François Quesnay, who taught that society should be governed by a natural order inherent in itself, that land and its unmanufactured products are the only true wealth, the precious metals being a false standard, that the proper source of state revenue is direct taxation of land; and maintained the right of freedom of trade, person, opinion, and property. [< F *physiocratie*] **—phys′i·o·crat′** (-ə·krat′) *n.* **—phys′i·o·crat′ic** *adj.*

phys·i·og·no·my (fiz′ē·og′nə·mē, *esp. Brit.* fiz′ē·on′ə·mē) *n. pl.* **·mies 1** The face or features as revealing character or disposition.

add,āce,câre,pälm; end,ēven; it,īce; odd,ōpen,ôrder; to͝ok,po͞ol; up,bûrn; ə = a in *above,* e in *sicken,* i in *clarity,* o in *melon,* u in *focus*; yo͞o = u in *fuse,* oi,oil; ou,pout; ch,check; g,go; ng,ring; th,thin; th,this; zh,vision. Foreign sounds á,œ,ü,kh,ṅ; and ◆: see page xx. < from; + plus; ? possibly.

2 The outward look of a thing. 3 The art of reading character by the lineaments of the face or form of the body. [<OF *fiznomie* <Med. L *phisnomia* <Gk. *physiognōmonia* the judging of a man's nature (by his features) < *physis* nature + *gnōmōn, -onos* a judge] **— phys'i·og·nom'ic** (-og·nom'ik) or **·i·cal** *adj.* **— phys'i·og·nom'i·cal·ly** *adv.* **— phys'i·og'no·mist** *n.*

phys·i·og·ra·phy (fiz'ē·og'rə·fē) *n.* 1 A description of nature. 2 The study of the development of the features of the earth's surface; physical geography. [<PHYSIO- + -GRAPHY] **— phys'i·og'ra·pher** *n.* **— phys'i·o·graph'ic** (-ə·graf'ik) or **·i·cal** *adj.* **— phys'i·o·graph'i·cal·ly** *adv.*

phys·i·o·log·i·cal (fiz'ē·ə·loj'i·kəl) *adj.* Pertaining to the functions of living organisms. Also **phys'i·o·log'ic. — phys'i·o·log'i·cal·ly** *adv.*

phys·i·ol·o·gy (fiz'ē·ol'ə·jē) *n.* 1 The branch of biology that treats of the vital phenomena manifested by animals or plants; the science of organic functions, as distinguished from *anatomy* and *morphology.* 2 The aggregate of organic processes: the *physiology* of the frog. [<F *physiologie* <L *physiologia* <Gk., natural philosophy < *physiologos* a speaker on nature < *physis* nature + *logos* a word] **— phys'i·ol'o·gist** *n.*

phys·i·o·ther·a·py (fiz'ē·ō·ther'ə·pē) See PHYSICAL THERAPY.

phy·sique (fi·zēk') *n.* The physical structure, organization, or appearance of a person. [<F, orig. adj., physical <L *physicus* <Gk. *physikos* natural < *physis.* See PHYSIC.]

phy·so·clis·tous (fī'sō·klis'təs) *adj. Zool.* Having no connection between the air bladder and the digestive tract, as in most teleost fishes. [<NL *Physoclisti,* a genus of fishes <Gk. *physa* a bladder + *kleistos* closed < *kleiein* close]

phy·so·stig·mine (fī'sō·stig'mēn, -min) *n. Chem.* A white, tasteless, toxic alkaloid, $C_{15}H_{21}N_3O_2$, derived from the Calabar bean; used as a miotic: also called *eserine.* [<NL *Physostigma,* genus of the Calabar bean (<Gk. *physa* a bladder + *stigma* a mark) + -INE[2]]

phy·sos·to·mous (fī·sos'tə·məs) *adj. Zool.* Having the air bladder united by a duct with the intestinal canal, as in certain teleost fishes. Also **phy·so·stom·a·tous** (fī'sō·stom'ə·təs). [<NL *physostomus* <Gk. *physa* a bladder + *stoma* a mouth]

-phyte *combining form* A (specified) kind of plant; a plant having a (specified) habitat: *thallophyte, hydrophyte.* [<Gk. *phyton* a plant]

phy·tin (fī'tin) *n. Biochem.* A calcium-magnesium salt isolated as a white, odorless powder from the seeds of various plants, as sunflowers, hemp, peas, etc.

phyto- *combining form* Plant; of or related to vegetation: *phytogenesis.* Also, before vowels, **phyt-.** [<Gk. *phyton* a plant]

phy·to·ben·thon (fī'tō·ben'thon) *n. Bot.* Plant organisms growing at the bottom of seas, lakes, and other large bodies of water. Compare GEOBENTHOS. [<PHYTO- + Gk. *benthos* the depth of the sea]

phy·to·gen·e·sis (fī'tō·jen'ə·sis) *n.* The science of the generation, origin, and development of plants. Also **phy·tog·e·ny** (fī·toj'ə·nē). **— phy'to·ge·net'ic** (-jə·net'ik) or **·i·cal** *adj.* **— phy'to·ge·net'i·cal·ly** *adv.*

phy·to·gen·ic (fī'tō·jen'ik) *adj.* 1 Phytogenetic. 2 Of plant origin, as coal and some other biogenic formations. Also **phy·tog·e·nous** (fī·toj'ə·nəs).

phy·to·ge·og·ra·phy (fī'tō·jē·og'rə·fē) *n.* That department of geography which deals with the distribution of plants; plant geography: also called *geobotany.*

phy·tog·ra·phy (fī·tog'rə·fē) *n.* Descriptive botany. [<NL *phytographia* <Gk. *phyton* a plant + *graphein* write]

phy·toid (fī'toid) *adj.* Plantlike.

phy·tol·o·gy (fī·tol'ə·jē) *n.* Botany. [<NL *phytologia* <Gk. *phyton* a plant + *logos* a word, study] **— phy·to·log·ic** (fī'tə·loj'ik) or **·i·cal** *adj.*

phy·to·pa·thol·o·gy (fī'tō·pə·thol'ə·jē) *n.* 1 The study of the diseases of plants and their control. 2 The pathology of diseases which are caused by fungi, bacteria, and other plant organisms.

phy·toph·a·gous (fī·tof'ə·gəs) *adj. Biol.* Feeding on plants; herbivorous. [<PHYTO- + -PHAGOUS]

phy·to·plank·ton (fī'tō·plangk'tən) *n.* Free-floating aquatic plants.

phy·tos·te·rol (fī·tos'tə·rōl, -rol) *n. Biochem.* Any of various sterols found in and isolated from plant organisms, as ergosterol, sitosterol, etc. [<PHYTO- + -STEROL]

phy·to·tron (fī'tə·tron) *n.* A large-scale field laboratory for the study of plant growth under artificially produced climatic conditions ranging from the tropical to the arctic. [< PHYTO- + Gk. *-tron,* instrumental suffix]

pi[1] (pī) *n.* 1 The sixteenth letter in the Greek alphabet (Π, π): corresponding to English *p.* As a numeral it denotes 80. 2 This letter used to designate the ratio of the circumference of a circle to its diameter, 3.14159 + ; also, this ratio. [Def. 2 <Gk. *p(eriphereia)* periphery]

pi[2] (pī) *n. Printing* Type that has been thrown into disorder; hence, any jumble or disorder. **—** *v.t.* **pied, pie·ing** To jumble or disorder, as type. Also spelled *pie.* [Var. of PIE[1]]

Pia·cen·za (pyä·chen'tsä) A city on the Po in northern Italy: ancient *Placentia.*

pi·ac·u·lar (pī·ak'yə·lər) *adj.* 1 Expiatory; having power to atone. 2 Requiring expiation; criminal. [<L *piacularis* < *piaculum* an expiation < *piare* appease]

piaffe (pyaf) *v.i.* **piaffed, piaf·fing** To perform or move by performing the piaffer. [<F *piaffer* paw the ground, lit., strut; ult. origin uncertain]

piaf·fer (pyaf'ər) *n.* In equitation, a movement in which the horse lifts one forefoot and the opposite hind foot in unison and slowly places them forward, backward, or to the side. [<F *piaffer.* See PIAFFE.]

pi·a ma·ter (pī'ə mā'tər) *Anat.* The delicate inner vascular membrane that invests the brain and spinal cord: it is overlaid by the arachnoid and dura mater. [<Med. L, trans. of Arabic *umm raqīqah* a tender mother]

pi·an·ism (pē·an'iz·əm, pē'ə·niz'əm) *n.* 1 Arrangement of music for the pianoforte. 2 Performance on the piano; the technique of piano playing.

pi·a·nis·si·mo (pē'ə·nis'i·mō, *Ital.* pyä·nēs'sē·mō) *adj. & adv. Music* Very soft or softly; a musical direction: abbr. *pp.* or *ppp.* **—** *n.* A musical movement played very softly. [<Ital. <L *planissimus,* superl. of *planus.* See PIANO[2].]

pi·an·ist (pē·an'ist, pē'ə·nist) *n.* One who plays on the piano; specifically, an expert or a professional performer.

pi·an·o[1] (pē·an'ō) *n. pl.* **·an·os** A stringed musical instrument having felt-covered hammers, operated from a manual keyboard, which strike upon steel wires to produce the tones; a pianoforte. **— concert grand piano** The largest size of grand piano, used for concert performances. **— grand piano** A horizontal, harp-shaped piano, having three or more strings to each note, and action without springs. **— square piano** A piano having a horizontal rectangular case and horizontally strung wires. **— upright piano** A piano in which the case is upright, with the strings vertical and overstrung to save space. [< Ital., short for *pianoforte* PIANOFORTE]

pi·a·no[2] (pē·ä'nō, *Ital.* pyä'nō) *adv.* With slight force; softly: a direction to a singer or player of a musical instrument: abbr. *p.* **—** *adj.* Performed or to be performed with slight force; soft: a *piano* passage. **—** *n.* A passage of music rendered softly and lightly. [<Ital. <L *planus* flat, soft (of sound)]

pi·an·o·for·te (pē·an'ə·fôr'tē, -fôr'-, -fôrt', -fōrt') *n.* A piano. [<Ital. < *piano e forte* soft and strong]

Pi·a·no·la (pē'ə·nō'lə) *n.* A small, portable, cabinetlike, piano-playing mechanism: a trade name.

Pi·a·rist (pī'ə·rist) *n.* One of a Roman Catholic monastic order the members of which are known as Regular Clerks of the Scuole Pie, an institute of instruction, founded in Rome about 1600. [<NL *(patres scholarum) piarum* (fathers of the) religious (schools) <L *pius* dutiful, pious]

pi·as·sa·va (pē'ə·sä'və) *n.* 1 A coarse, stiff fiber obtained from the leafstalks of two Brazilian palms, *Attalea funifera* and *Leopoldinia piassaba*: used for making ropes, brooms, brushes, etc. 2 Either of these palms. Also **pi'a·sa'ba** (-bə), **pi'as·sa'ba, pi'a·sa'va.** [<Pg. *piassava, piassaba* <Tupian *piaçába*]

pi·as·ter (pē·as'tər) *n.* 1 A Turkish and Egyptian coin and monetary unit. 2 The Spanish peso or dollar. Also **pi·as'tre.** [<F *piastre* <Ital. *piastra,* lit., a plate of metal, short for *piastra d'argento* a plate of silver, ult. <L *emplastrum* PLASTER]

Pi·au·í (pē'ou·ē') 1 A river in NE Brazil, flowing 250 miles north to the Canindé river. 2 A state in NE Brazil; 97,150 square miles; capital, Teresina. Formerly **Pi'au·hy'.**

Pia·ve (pyä'vä) A river in NE Italy, flowing 137 miles SE to the Adriatic; scene of World War I battles, 1917–18.

pi·az·za (pē·az'ə, *Ital.* pē·at'tsä) *n.* 1 A veranda or porch. 2 In Europe, especially in Italy, a plaza. 3 A covered outer walk or gallery. [<Ital., a square, market place, ult. <L *platea* a broad street <Gk. *plateia (hodos).* Doublet of PLACE, PLAZA.]

pi·bal (pī'bal) *n. Meteorol.* An observation on conditions in the atmosphere as reported by or from a pilot balloon. [<PI(LOT) + BAL(LOON)]

pi·broch (pē'brokh) *n.* A martial air played on the bagpipe. [< dial. E (Scottish) <Scottish Gaelic *piobaireachd* playing the bagpipe < *piobair* a piper < *piob* a pipe <PIPE]

pi·ca[1] (pī'kə) *n.* A size of type; 12-point; 1/6 inch; also, a standard unit of measurement, as for leads or pages. See POINT SYSTEM. **— small pica** A size of type; about six and a half lines to the inch; 11-point. **— two-line** or **double pica** Type having a depth of body of two lines of pica; 24-point. ◆ Homophone: *pika.* [<Med. L, a pie[4]; ? because used in printing pies]

pi·ca[2] (pī'kə) *n. Pathol.* A morbid appetite for unusual or unfit food, as clay, chalk, ashes, etc., showing itself especially in hysteria, pregnancy, and chlorosis. ◆ Homophone: *pika.* [<L *pica* a magpie, ? trans. of Gk. *kissa, kitta* a magpie, a craving for strange food; with ref. to the bird's omnivorousness] **— pi'cal** *adj.*

pi·ca·cho (pē·kä'chō) *n. pl.* **·chos** *SW U.S.* An isolated peak of a hill or butte. [<Am. Sp. <Sp. *pico* a peak]

pic·a·dor (pik'ə·dôr, *Sp.* pē'kä·thōr') *n.* 1 In bullfighting, a horseman armed with a lance, whose function is to enrage the bull. 2 A clever debater; one with ready wit. [<Sp., lit., a pricker < *picar* prick, pierce < *prica.* Akin to PIKE[1].]

Pi·card (pē·kär'), **Jean,** 1620–82, French astronomer.

Pic·ar·dy (pik'ər·dē) A region and former province of northern France. **— Pic'ard** *adj. & n.*

pic·a·resque (pik'ə·resk') *adj.* Pertaining to picaroons or rogues: specifically applied to the **picaresque novel,** a form having a slight plot consisting of episodes loosely connected by the hero, a rogue; originated in Spain in the 17th century, popular in France and England in the 18th century, and still used occasionally. [<Sp. *picaresco* roguish < *pícaro* a rogue; ult. origin uncertain]

pic·a·roon[1] (pik'ə·rōōn') *n.* 1 One who lives by cheating or robbery: a wrecker or pirate; rogue; adventurer. 2 A pirate vessel. [<Sp. *picaron,* aug. of *pícaro* a rogue]

pic·a·roon[2] (pik'ə·rōōn') *n.* A piked pole used by log drivers: also spelled *pickaroon.* [? <MF *piqueron* a spur, dim. of *pique* a pike[1]]

Pi·cas·so (pē·kä'sō), **Pablo,** 1881–1973, Spanish painter and sculptor active in France.

pic·a·yune (pik'i·yōōn') *adj. U.S.* Little; worthless; mean. **—** *n.* 1 A former small Spanish-American coin; a half-real. 2 *U.S.* A person or thing of trifling value. [<F *picaillon* an old Piedmontese coin, a farthing <Provençal *picaioun, picalhoun,* dim. of *picalo* money] **— pic'a·yun'ish** *adj.*

Pic·ca·dil·ly (pik'ə·dil'ē) A famous thoroughfare of western London, running from Piccadilly Circus to Hyde Park Corner.

pic·ca·lil·li (pik'ə·lil'ē) *n.* A highly seasoned relish of chopped vegetables. [? <PICKLE[1]]

Pic·card (pē·kär'), **Auguste,** 1884–1962, and his twin brother **Jean Felix,** 1884–1963, Swiss physicists and aeronauts.

pic·co·lo (pik'ə·lō) *n. pl.* **·los** 1 A small flute with tones an octave higher than those of the ordinary flute. 2 An organ stop of similar tone. [<Ital., small] **— pic'co·lo'ist** *n.*

pice (pīs) *n.* A copper coin of British India;

1/4 anna. [<Hind. *paisā,* ? <*pāi, paī* a quarter <Skt. *pad, padi*]

pic·e·ous (pis′ē·əs, pī′sē-) *adj.* **1** Relating to or resembling pitch; inflammable. **2** Pitch-black. [<L *piceus* <*pix, picis* pitch]

Piche·gru (pēsh·grü′), **Charles,** 1761–1804, French Revolutionary general.

pich·i·ci·a·go (pich′ə·sē·ä′gō, -ā′gō) *n. pl.* **·gos** A small burrowing armadillo *(Chlamydophorus truncatus)* of South America. [<Am. Sp. *pichiciego* <Guarani *pichey* the little armadillo + Sp. *ciego* blind <L *caecus*]

pich·u·rim (pich′ə·rim) *n.* One of the aromatic cotyledons of the seed of a South American tree (genus *Ocotea* or *Nectandra)* of the laurel family, resembling in taste and smell both sassafras and nutmeg: used medicinally and for flavoring. Also **pichurim bean.** [<Tupian]

pick[1] (pik) *v.t.* **1** To choose; select; cull, as from a group or number. **2** To detach; pluck, as with the fingers or beak: to *pick* a flower. **3** To gather or harvest: to *pick* cotton. **4** To prepare by removing the feathers, hulls, leaves, etc.: to *pick* a chicken. **5** To remove extraneous matter from (the teeth, etc.) with the fingers, a pointed instrument, etc. **6** To pull apart, as rags. **7** To break up, penetrate, or indent with or as with a pointed instrument. **8** To form or make in this manner: to *pick* a hole. **9** To seek or point out too critically: to *pick* flaws. **10** To seek or bring on purposely; provoke: to *pick* a quarrel. **11** To remove the contents of by stealth: to *pick* a pocket or purse. **12** To open (a lock) by means other than the key, as by a piece of wire or metal. **13 a** To pluck (the strings) of a musical instrument. **b** To play: to *pick* a banjo. —*v.i.* **14** To work with a pick. **15** To eat daintily or without appetite; nibble. **16** To make careful selection: to *pick* and choose. **17** To pilfer: to *pick* and steal. See synonyms under CHOOSE. —**to pick at 1** To touch or toy with. **2** To eat without appetite. **3** *U.S. Colloq.* To nag at. —**to pick off 1** To remove by picking. **2** To shoot with careful and deliberate aim. —**to pick on** *Colloq.* To single out for attention, duty, etc.; tease; annoy. —**to pick one's way** (or **steps**) To advance by careful selection of one's course or actions. —**to pick out 1** To choose or select. **2** To distinguish (something) from its surroundings. **3** To produce the notes of (a tune) singly or slowly, as by ear. —**to pick over** To examine carefully or one by one. —**to pick to pieces 1** To pull apart. **2** To destroy the arguments or claims of by critical or carping analysis. —**to pick up 1** To take up, as with the hand. **2** To take up or receive into a group, vehicle, etc.: We *picked up* more passengers in Hoboken. **3** To get or acquire casually or by chance. **4** To gain speed; accelerate. **5** To recover spirits, health, etc.; improve. **6** To be able to perceive or receive, as a distant radio station. **7** *Colloq.* To make the acquaintance of, casually or informally. —*n.* **1** Right of selection; choice; hence, the best. **2** The quantity of certain crops that are picked by hand. **3** A blow, as with a spear. **4** The act of picking. See synonyms under ALTERNATIVE. [ME *piken, pikken,* OE *pican, picián* (assumed), infinitive of OE *picung* pricking, infl. by OF *piquer* pierce. Akin to PIKE[1].]

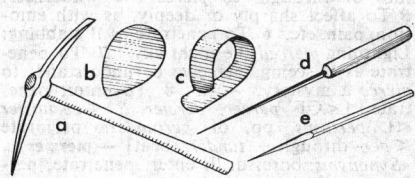

TYPES OF PICKS
a. Pickax. *c.* Guitar thumb pick.
b. Mandolin pick. *d.* Ice pick.
e. Quill toothpick.

pick[2] (pik) *n.* **1** A double-headed, pointed metal tool mounted on a strong wooden handle, as a pickax: used for breaking ground, etc. **2** Any of various implements for picking, as an ice pick, toothpick, or a picklock. **3** A plectrum, as for a stringed instrument. [Appar. var. of PIKE[1]]

pick[3] (pik) *n.* **1** In weaving, the blow that drives a loom shuttle. **2** A thread: the number of picks to the inch determines the relative value of cotton cloth or muslin. [<dial. E *pick, v.,* var. of PITCH[2] throw]

pick-a-back (pik′ə·bak′) *adv.* On the back or shoulders: also spelled *piggy-back.* [Earlier *a pickback, a pickpack.* Cf. dial. E *pick* throw, toss.]

pick·a·dil (pik′ə·dil) *n.* A standing collar, usually with a scalloped edge, as worn in the 17th century. Also **pick′a·dill.** [Var. of *piccadil* <MF *piccadilles* pieces fastened on edge of a doublet's collar <dim. of Sp. *picado,* pp. of *picar* prick]

pick·a·nin·ny (pik′ə·nin′ē) *n. pl.* **·nies** A little child; specifically, a Negro child: a condescending or contemptuous term. Also **pic′·ca·nin′ny.** [Alter. of Sp. *pequenino,* dim. of *pequeño* little, small]

pick·a·roon (pik′ə·ro͞on′) See PICAROON.

pick·ax (pik′aks′) *n.* A pick or mattock with one arm of the head edged like a chisel and the other pointed; also, one with both arms pointed. Also **pick′axe′.** [Alter. of ME *pikoys* <OF *picois,* ? <*pic* a pike[1]; infl. in form by *ax*]

pick·ed[1] (pik′id, pikt) *adj.* **1** Having spines or prickles. **2** Sharp-pointed, as a stick. [<PICK[2], *n.*]

picked[2] (pikt) *adj.* **1** Carefully selected; chosen for a purpose. **2** Cleaned by picking out refuse, stalks, etc., as cotton. **3** Caused intentionally or sought out, as a quarrel. See synonyms under CHOICE. [Orig. pp. of PICK[4], *v.*]

picked-o·ver (pikt′ō′vər) *adj.* **1** Handled; left after the best have been removed. **2** Left after the undesirable ones have been removed, as berries.

Pick·ens (pik′inz), **Andrew,** 1739–1817, American Revolutionary general.

pick·er[1] (pik′ər) *n.* **1** One who or that which picks. **2** A machine for loosening up fibrous material. **3** A tool like a graver used by electrotypers. [<PICK[1]]

pick·er[2] (pik′ər) *n.* In a loom, the part that strikes the shuttle. [<dial. E *pick, v.* See PICK[3].]

pick·er·el (pik′ər·əl) *n.* **1** A North American fresh-water fish (family *Esocidae*); a pike; especially, one of the smaller species. *Esox reticulatus* is the common pond pickerel of the eastern United States. **2** A young pike. [Dim. of PIKE[1], ? <AF]

pickerel frog A frog *(Rana palustris)* of the eastern United States: also called *marsh frog.*

pick·er·el·weed (pik′ər·əl·wēd′) *n.* A perennial aquatic herb *(Pontederia cordata),* growing in the shallows of lakes of the United States and Canada, or other species of the same genus.

Pick·er·ing (pik′ər·ing), **Timothy,** 1745–1829, American Revolutionary general. —**William Henry,** 1858–1938, U.S. astronomer.

pick·et (pik′it) *n.* **1** A pointed stick, tent peg, bar, fence paling, or stake. **2** *Mil.* A soldier or detachment of soldiers posted to guard a camp, army, etc. **3** A person stationed by a labor organization outside a place affected by a strike. —*v.t.* **1** To fence or fortify with pickets or pointed stakes. **2** *Mil.* **a** To guard by means of a picket. **b** To post as a picket. **3** To station pickets outside of. **4** To tie to a picket, as a horse. —*v.i.* **5** To act as a picket (def. 3). [<F *piquet* a pointed stake <*piquer* pierce] —**pick′et·er** *n.*

picket fence A fence made of upright pickets.

picket pin A long iron pin or wooden stake driven into the ground and having a swivel loop at the upper end: used for tethering horses.

Pick·ett (pik′it), **George Edward,** 1825–75, American Confederate general.

Pick·ford (pik′fərd), **Mary,** born 1893, U.S. motion-picture actress born in Canada: real name *Gladys Smith.*

pick glass A magnifying glass for determining the thread count of fabrics.

pick·ing (pik′ing) *n.* **1** The act of picking; also, that which is or may be picked. **2** *pl.* That which is left to be picked up or gleaned: scanty *pickings.* **3** Pilfering, or that which is pilfered. **4** *Usually pl.* That which is taken by questionable means; spoils.

pick·le[1] (pik′əl) *n.* **1** A preserving, flavoring liquid, as brine or vinegar, sometimes spiced, for meat, fish, vegetables, etc. **2** One of certain objects preserved or flavored in pickle, as a cucumber or onion. **3** Diluted acid used in cleaning metal castings, etc. **4** *Colloq.* An embarrassing condition or position. **5** *Colloq.* A mischievous child. —*v.t.* **·led, ·ling 1** To preserve with brine or vinegar. **2** To immerse in diluted acid, as castings, for cleansing. [Appar. <MDu. *pekel, peeckel;* ult. origin uncertain]

pick·le[2] (pik′əl) *n. Scot.* A grain of corn; a small quantity.

pickled finish A finish having the effect of a cloudy white patina over light-toned wood: originally produced on old painted furniture by removing the plaster base of the paint with vinegar, or exposing a surface which had been bleached with lime.

pick·lock (pik′lok′) *n.* **1** A special implement, as a bent wire, for opening a lock; a false key. **2** A burglar.

pick·maw (pik′mô′) *n. Dial.* The laughing gull. [Prob. <dial. E *pick* PITCH[2] + obs. E *maw* a gull[1]]

pick-me-up (pik′mē′up′) *n. Colloq.* A drink, especially an alcoholic drink, taken to renew one's energy or spirits.

pick·pock·et (pik′pok′it) *n.* One who steals from pockets.

pick·thank (pik′thangk′) *n. Archaic & Dial.* A flatterer; sycophant. [Earlier *pick a thank(s)*]

pick·up (pik′up′) *n.* **1** Acceleration, as in the speed of an automobile, engine, etc. **2** The electromagnetic vibrating device holding the needle in a phonograph or similar sound-reproducing apparatus. **3** *Telecom.* **a** In radio, the location of microphones in relation to program elements. **b** The system for broadcasting material gathered outside the studio. **c** In television, the scanning of an image by the electron beam. **d** The scanning apparatus. **4** *Colloq.* Gain; improvement; renewal of prosperity, etc. **5** *Slang* A stranger with whom a casual acquaintance is made, usually in a public place and for the purposes of lovemaking. **6** A small, usually open, truck for light loads.

Pick·wick (pik′wik), **Mr. (Samuel)** In Dickens's *Pickwick Papers,* the president of the Pickwick Club, a stout, good-hearted man, fond of travel, and distinguished for blundering simplicity.

Pick·wick·i·an (pik·wik′ē·ən) *adj.* Relating to or characteristic of Mr. Pickwick.

Pickwickian sense A technical or esoteric sense; not the common sense: usually said of a word or a phrase.

pic·nic (pik′nik) *n.* **1** An outdoor party, usually held in the countryside, during which a meal is eaten. **2** *Slang* An easy or pleasant time or experience. —*v.i.* **·nicked, ·nick·ing** To have or attend a picnic. Also **pick′nick.** [<F *pique-nique,* ? reduplication of *piquer* pick, peck] —**pic′nick·er** *n.*

Pi·co (pē′kō) An active volcano on **Pico Island** (167 square miles) in the central Azores; 7,613 feet.

Pico de Aneto See ANETO, PICO DE.

Pi·co del·la Mi·ran·do·la (pē′kō del′lä mē·rän′dō·lä), **Count Giovanni,** 1463–94, Italian humanist scholar.

pic·o·line (pik′ə·lēn, -lin) *n. Chem.* Any of three isomeric liquid compounds, C_6H_7N, contained in coal tar, naphtha, bone oil, etc., and homologous with pyridine. Also **pic′o·lin** (-lin). [<L *pix, picis,* PITCH[1] + -OL[2] + -INE[2]]

pi·cot (pē′kō) *n.* A small thread loop on ornamental edging, sometimes having knots or stitches added. —*v.t.* & *v.i.* To sew with this edging. [<F, dim. of OF *pic* a point]

pic·o·tee (pik′ə·tē′) *n.* A variety of carnation, having white or light-colored petals edged with scarlet or other strong color. [<F *picotée,* pp. fem. of *picoter* mark with pricks or dots <*picot* PICOT]

picot stitch A loop stitch.

pic·quet (pi·kā′, -ket′) See PIQUET.

pic·rate (pik′rāt) *n. Chem.* One of the salts

or esters of picric acid, exploding when heated or struck.

pic·ric (pik′rik) *adj.* Of, pertaining to, or having an exceedingly bitter taste. [<Gk. *pikros* bitter]

picric acid *Chem.* A yellow crystalline compound, $C_6H_2(NO_2)_3OH$, obtained variously, as by the action of nitric acid on phenol: used in dyeing and as an ingredient in certain explosives.

pic·rite (pik′rīt) *n.* An olivine–augite peridotite containing some magnetite or ilmenite, biotite, and brown hornblende. [<Gk. *pikros* bitter + -ITE[1]]

picro– *combining form* Bitter: *picrol.* Also, before vowels, **picr–.** [<Gk. *pikros* bitter]

pic·rol (pik′rōl, -rol) *n. Chem.* A colorless, bitter, crystalline compound, $C_6H_3O_5I_2SK$, used in medicine. [<PICR(O)- + -OL[2]]

pic·ro·tox·in (pik′rə·tok′sin) *n. Chem.* A bitter, odorless, crystalline compound, $C_{30}H_{34}O_{13}$, contained in and forming the poisonous principle of the seeds of the fishberry: it resembles strychnine in action. **—pic′ro·tox′ic** *adj.*

Pict (pikt) *n.* One of an ancient people of uncertain origin who inhabited Britain and the Scottish Highlands, and waged war on the Romans: conquered in 846 by the Scots. [<LL *Picti,* ? <L *pictus,* pp. of *pingere* paint; with ref. to their being painted or tattooed]

Pict·ish (pik′tish) *n.* The language of the Picts, of undetermined relationship. **—** *adj.* Of or pertaining to the Picts.

pic·to·graph (pik′tə·graf, -gräf) *n.* A picture representing an idea: the earliest form of record. [<*picto-* pictorial (<L *pictus,* pp. of *pingere* paint) + -GRAPH] **—pic′to·graph′ic** *adj.* **—pic′to·graph′i·cal·ly** *adv.* **—pic·tog·ra·phy** (pik·tog′rə·fē) *n.*

Pic·tor (pik′tər) A southern constellation. [<L, lit., a painter <*pictus,* pp. of *pingere* paint]

pic·to·ri·al (pik·tôr′ē·əl, -tō′rē-) *adj.* **1** Pertaining to or concerned with pictures. **2** Representing in or as if in pictures; graphic. **3** Containing or illustrated by pictures. **—** *n.* An illustrated publication. See synonyms under GRAPHIC. [<LL *pictorius* <L *pictor.* See PICTOR.] **—pic·to′ri·al·ly** *adv.*

pic·ture (pik′chər) *n.* **1** A surface representation of an object or scene, as by a painting, drawing, engraving, or photograph; also, a mental image. **2** A vivid or graphic verbal delineation. **3** A striking resemblance to another person, object, or general idea: She is the *picture* of her mother; the very *picture* of despair. **4** A tableau vivant: also called **living picture. 5** A visual image or scene produced by the working of physical laws or their use, as in the lens. **6** A motion picture. **—to be in the picture** To belong to the group or the occasion; also, to be successful. **—** *v.t.* **·tured, ·tur·ing 1** To give visible representation to; draw, paint, etc. **2** To describe graphically; depict verbally. **3** To form a mental image of. [<L *pictura* <*pictus,* pp. of *pingere* paint]

Synonyms (noun): cartoon, copy, delineation, drawing, engraving, image, likeness, miniature, painting, photograph, print, representation, resemblance, semblance, similitude, sketch. See IMAGE, SKETCH.

picture gallery A room or hall for the exhibition of pictures; also, the pictures exhibited.

picture hat A woman's hat with a very wide brim which frames the face: often trimmed with plumes, as hats seen in certain famous paintings, especially those of Gainsborough.

Pic·ture·phone (pik′chər·fōn′) *n.* A telephone equipped with a television screen: a trade name.

picture ratio In television, the ratio of the length of the received image to the width.

pic·tur·esque (pik′chə·resk′) *adj.* **1** Having pictorial quality; like or suitable for a picture; especially, having a striking, irregular beauty, quaintness, or charm. **2** Abounding in striking or original expression or imagery; figurative; richly graphic. See synonyms under BEAUTIFUL, GRAPHIC, ROMANTIC. [<F *pittoresque* <Ital. *pittoresco* <*pittore* a painter <L *pictor.* See PICTOR.] **—pic′tur·esque′ly** *adv.* **—pic′tur·esque′ness** *n.*

picture window A large window, usually in a living room, designed to give a wide view of the outside.

picture writing 1 The use of pictures or pictorial symbols in writing. **2** A writing so made.

pic·tur·ize (pik′chə·rīz) *v.t.* **·ized, ·iz·ing** To make a picture or motion picture of; present pictorially. **—pic′tur·i·za′tion** *n.*

pic·ul (pik′ul) *n.* A varying commercial weight, usually about 100 catties, or 133 1/3 pounds: used in China, Thailand, and other countries of Asia. [<Malay *pikul* a man's load]

pid·dle (pid′l) *v.* **·dled, ·ding** *v.t.* **1** To trifle; dawdle: usually with *away.* **—** *v.i.* **2** To trifle; dawdle. **3** To urinate. [Origin unknown]

pid·dling (pid′ling) *adj.* Unimportant; trivial.

pid·dock (pid′ək) *n.* A bivalve mollusk (genus *Pholas*) with an elongated shell, which burrows in clay and sand. [Cf. OE *puduc* wart]

pidg·in (pij′ən) *n.* A mixed language, such as bêche–de–mer, combining the vocabulary and grammar of dissimilar languages and providing a simplified, mutually intelligible form of communication for use in commerce: distinguished from a *creolized language* in that it is used only as an additional, auxiliary language. [<Pidgin English, alter. of BUSINESS]

Pidgin English A jargon composed of English and local native elements, used as the language of commerce between natives and foreigners in areas of China, Melanesia, Northern Australia, and West Africa.

pie[1] (pī) *n.* **1** A baked food consisting of one or two layers or crusts of pastry with a filling of fruit, vegetables, or meat. **2** Pi[2]. **3** *Slang* Anything very good or very easy. **4** *Slang* Political graft. **—to have** (or **put**) **one's finger in the pie** To have a share in an activity or project; hence, to meddle. [ME *pie, pye,* ? <PIE[2]; with ref. to the variety of objects collected by magpies and of foods baked in pies]

pie[2] (pī) *n.* A magpie, or a related bird. [<OF <L *pica* a magpie]

pie[3] (pī) *n.* A former coin of India of smallest value, worth a third of a pice. [<Hind. *pā′ī* <Skt. *pad, padi* a fourth]

pie[4] (pī) *n.* **1** In the pre–Reformation English church, a book of rules and directions for services on days when two or more feasts concur. **2** An index; a register. Also spelled *pye.* [<LL *pica* <L, a magpie; ? because its pages resembled the bird's black–and–white plumage]

pie·bald (pī′bôld′) *adj.* Having spots, especially of white and black. **—** *n.* A spotted or mottled animal, especially a horse. [<PIE[2] + BALD; because like a magpie's plumage]

piece (pēs) *n.* **1** A small portion considered as forming or having formed a distinct part of a whole. **2** A portion or quantity existing as an individual entity or mass: a *piece* of paper; a *piece* of music. **3** An object considered as forming one of a class or group: a *piece* of furniture, luggage, etc. **4** A definite quantity or length in which an article is manufactured or sold. **5** An instance; specimen; example: a *piece* of luck. **6** A firearm. **7** A coin: a fifty–cent *piece.* **8** A literary composition. **9** A drama; play. **10** A picture. **11** A musical composition. **12** *Dial.* A short time, space, or distance: to walk a *piece.* **13** *Archaic* or *Dial.* A person; individual. **14** Any of the figures used in the game of chess; technically, any man but the pawns. **15** One of the disks or counters used in checkers, backgammon, etc. **—a piece of one's mind** Criticism or censure frankly expressed. **—in one piece** Unharmed; intact. **—of a piece 1** Of the same kind, sort, or class. **2** Of one piece; undivided. **—to go to pieces 1** To fall apart. **2** To lose moral or emotional self–control. **—to speak one's piece** To voice one's opinions. **—** *adj.* Of, made of, or by the piece. **—** *v.t.* **pieced, piec·ing 1** To add or attach a piece or pieces to, as for enlargement. **2** To unite or reunite the pieces of, as in mending. **3** To unite (parts or fragments) into a whole. **4** To find meaning or coherence in by linking elements: often with *together:* to *piece* together a sequence of events from the testimony of eyewitnesses. ◆ Homophone: *peace.* [<OF *pece* <LL *pettia* (assumed), prob. ult. <Celtic. Cf. Welsh *peth* little.]

pièce de résistance (pyes də rā·zē·stäns′) *pl.* **pièces de résistance** (pyes) *French* The principal or most important work in a collection, as of art, poems, etc.; also, the most substantial dish of a dinner.

piece goods Dry–goods; fabrics, usually sold by the piece, as shirtings and sheetings.

piece·meal (pēs′mēl′) *adj.* Made up of pieces. **—** *adv.* **1** Piece by piece; gradually. **2** In pieces. [ME *pece-mele* <*pece* PIECE + *-mele,* OE *-maelum* <*mael* a measure; partial trans. of OE *styccemaelum* in pieces]

piec·er (pē′sər) *n.* One who or that which pieces; especially, one who ties broken threads in a spinning mill.

piece·work (pēs′wûrk′) *n.* Work done, or paid for, by the piece or quantity. **—piece′work′er** *n.*

pie chart *Stat.* A graph in the form of a circle each of whose sectors is proportional in area and subtended angle to a component part of an entire series.

piec·ing (pē′sing) *n.* Pieces of cloth, especially those collected and saved to be sewed together, as for a quilt.

Pieck (pēk), **Wilhelm,** 1876–1960, German politician; president of the German Democratic Republic (East Germany) 1949–1960.

pie–crust table (pī′krust′) A small table having a top, usually round, with a raised scalloped edge.

pied (pīd) *adj.* Spotted; piebald; mottled. [<PIE[2]]

pied–à–terre (pyā·dȧ·târ′) *n. French* Temporary lodging; literally, foot on the ground.

pied·mont (pēd′mont) *adj.* At the foot of a mountain or mountain range: a *piedmont* plain. [<*Piedmont,* Italy <L *Pedimontium* <*pes, pedis* a foot + *mons, montis* a mountain]

Pied·mont (pēd′mont) **1** A region of northern and NW Italy; 9,817 square miles; capital, Turin. *Italian* **Pie·mon·te** (pyā·mōn′tā). **2** A region of the eastern U.S. extending from New Jersey to Alabama east of the Appalachian Mountains; approximately 80,000 square miles. **—Pied′mont·ese′** (-ēz′, -ēs′) *adj.* & *n.*

Pied Piper of Hamelin In medieval legend, a piper who rid the town of Hamelin of its rats by leading them with his music into the river: when not rewarded as promised, he led the town's children to a hill into which they disappeared.

PIER
Steamship pier and dock.

pie–eyed (pī′īd′) *adj. Slang* Drunk.

pie plant The garden rhubarb.

pier (pir) *n.* **1** A plain, detached mass of masonry, usually serving as a support: the *pier* of a bridge. **2** An upright projecting portion of a wall. **3** A mole or jetty, or projecting wharf. **4** A solid portion of a wall between window openings, etc. ◆ Homophone: *peer.* [ME *per* <Med. L *pera,* ? ult. <Gk. *petra* rock]

pierce (pirs) *v.* **pierced, pierc·ing** *v.t.* **1** To pass into or through; penetrate, in the manner of a pointed object, weapon, etc.; puncture; stab. **2** To make an opening or hole in, into, or through: Many windows *pierced* the old walls. **3** To make or cut (an opening or hole) in or through something. **4** To force a way into or through: to *pierce* the wilderness. **5** To affect sharply or deeply, as with emotion, pain, etc. **6** To penetrate as if stabbing: Lightning *pierced* the night sky. **7** To penetrate as if seeing; perceive or understand: to *pierce* a mystery. **—** *v.i.* **8** To enter; penetrate. [<OF *percer, percier,* ? <*pertuisier* <L *pertusus,* pp. of *pertundere* perforate <*per-* through + *tundere* beat] **—pierc′er** *n.*

Synonyms: bore, drill, enter, penetrate, perforate, puncture, stab, transfix.

Pierce (pirs), **Franklin,** 1804–69, president of the United States 1853–57.

pierc·ing (pir′sing) *adj.* Penetrating by or as if by a sharp–pointed instrument; cutting; keen; poignant; shrill, as a look or cry. See synonyms under ACUTE, BLEAK, SHARP. **—** *n.* Penetration. **—pierc′ing·ly** *adv.* **—pierc′ing·ness** *n.*

pier glass A large, high mirror intended to stand against a pier and thus fill the space between two openings in the wall.

Pi·e·ri·a (pī·ir′ē·ə) A coastal region of ancient Macedon, at the base of Mount Olympus:

legendary birthplace of the nine Muses. — **Pi·e'ri·an** *adj.*

Pierian Spring A spring in Pieria, supposed to give poetic inspiration to those who drank from it.

Pi·er·i·des (pī·er'ə·dēz) 1 In Greek mythology, the nine Muses. 2 The nine daughters of Pierus, who were vanquished by the Muses in a musical contest and changed into magpies.

pi·er·i·dine (pī·er'ə·dīn, -din) *adj.* Of or pertaining to a family (*Pieridae*) of butterflies, including species of predominantly white or yellow color. [<NL *Pierdinae*, subfamily name <*Pieris*, genus name <Gk., a Muse]

Pie·ro del·la Fran·ces·ca (pyä' rō del'lä frän·ches'kä), 1418?–92, Italian painter. Also **Piero de·i Fran·ces·chi** (dā'ē frän·ches'kē).

Pierre (pyâr) French form of PETER. Also *Du.* **Pie·ter** (pē'tər), *Ital.* **Pie·tro** (pyā'trō).

Pierre (pir) The capital of South Dakota, on the Missouri River.

Pier·rot (pye·rō') *n.* Originally, a stock character of French pantomimes, usually taking the part of valet, wearing white pantaloons and loose white jacket with big buttons; now, **pierrot**, a white-faced buffoon dressed in Pierrot costume. [<F, dim. of *Pierre* Peter]

Piers Plow·man (pirz plou'mən) The chief character in the 14th century allegorical poem, *Vision of Piers Plowman*, ascribed to William Langland.

pier table A low table occupying the space between two wall openings, usually combined with a pier glass.

Pi·er·us (pī'ər·əs) In Greek mythology, a king of Thrace, father of the nine Pierides.

pi·et (pī'ət) *n.* 1 The magpie. 2 *Scot.* The water ouzel. [ME *piot*, dim. of PIE²]

Pie·tà (pyä·tä') *n.* In painting, sculpture, etc., a representation of Mary mourning over the body of Christ in her lap. [<Ital., lit., piety <L *pietas, -tatis* PIETY]

pi·et·ed (pī'it·id) *adj. Scot.* Piebald.

Pie·ter·mar·itz·burg (pē'tər·mär'its·bōōrk) The shared capital (with Umlundi) of Kwa Zulu/ Natal province, Republic of South Africa: also *Maritzburg.*

pi·e·tism (pī'ə·tiz'əm) *n.* 1 Piety or godliness; devotion, as distinguished from insistence on religious creeds or forms. 2 Affected or exaggerated piety. — **pi'e·tist** *n.* — **pi·e·tis'tic** *adj.*

Pi·e·tism (pī'ə·tiz'əm) *n.* A movement in the Lutheran Church in Germany during the later 17th century, advocating a revival of the devotional ideal. — **Pi'e·tist** *n.* — **Pi·e·tis'tic** *adj.*

pi·e·ty (pī'ə·tē) *n.* 1 Reverence toward God or the gods; religious devoutness. 2 Religiousness in general. 3 Filial honor and obedience as due to parents, superiors, or country. See synonyms under RELIGION. [<OF *piete* <L *pietas, -tatis* dutifulness <*pius* dutiful. Doublet of PITY]

piezo- *combining form* Pressure; related to or produced by pressure: *piezometer*. [<Gk. *piezein* press]

pi·e·zo·chem·is·try (pī·ē'zō·kem'is·trē) *n.* The study of chemical reactions under the influence of high pressures.

pi·e·zo·e·lec·tric·i·ty (pī·ē'zō·i·lek'tris'ə·tē, -ē'· lek-) *n.* Electricity of electric phenomena resulting from pressure upon certain bodies, especially crystals. — **pi·e'zo·e·lec'tric** or **·tri·cal** *adj.*

pi·e·zom·e·ter (pī'ə·zom'ə·tər) *n.* 1 An instrument for determining pressure; specifically, an apparatus for measuring the compressibility of liquids. 2 An attachment for a sounding line that denotes by the compression of air in a tube the depth of water to which the appliance descends. 3 A similar instrument used in ascertaining the sensitiveness of the skin to pressure. — **pi'e·zo·met'ric** (-zō·met'·rik) or **·ri·cal** *adj.* — **pi'e·zom'e·try** *n.*

pif·fle (pif'əl) *Colloq. v.i.* **·fled, ·fling** To talk nonsensically; babble. — *n.* Nonsense. [? OE *pyffan* puff + LE]

pig (pig) *n.* 1 A hog or hoglike animal, especially when small or young; also, its flesh (pork). ◆Collateral adjective: *porcine.* 2 An oblong mass of metal, especially iron or lead, just run from the smelter and cast in a rough mold, usually in sand; also, the mold or trough. 3 Pig iron or iron pigs in general. 4 *Colloq.* A person regarded as like a pig, especially one who is filthy, gluttonous, or grasping. 5 *Scot.* An earthen article or vessel. 6 *Colloq.* A railroad locomotive: also called *hog.* — *v.i.* **pigged, pig·ging** 1 To bring forth pigs. 2 To act or live like pigs: with *it.* [ME *pigge*, ? OE *picga*, as in *pic(g)bred* food for hogs]

pig bed The bed of sand into which iron is run in casting pigs.

pig·boat (pig'bōt') *n. Colloq.* A submarine.

pig·eon (pij'ən) *n.* 1 Any of a widely distributed family (*Columbidae*) of birds, of arboreal and terrestrial habit, as the rock pigeon (*Columba livia*); a dove. 2 *Slang* One easily swindled. [<OF *pijon* <LL *pipio, -onis* a young chirping bird <L *pipire* chirp]

pigeon breast *Pathol.* A deformity in which the chest is flattened from side to side and the breast bone pressed forward and outward. — **pig'eon-breast'ed** *adj.*

pigeon hawk The American merlin.

pig·eon-heart·ed (pij'ən·här'tid) *adj.* Timid; fearful.

pig·eon·hole (pij'ən·hōl') *n.* 1 A hole for pigeons to nest in, especially in a compartmented pigeon house. 2 A small compartment, as in a desk, for filing papers. — *v.t.* **·holed, ·hol·ing** 1 To place in a pigeonhole; file. 2 To file away and ignore. 3 To place in categories; classify mentally.

pig·eon-liv·ered (pij'ən·liv'ərd) *adj.* Very mild or weak-spirited; meek.

pig·eon-toed (pij'ən·tōd') *adj.* Having the toes turned inward; toeing in.

pig·eon·wing (pij'ən·wing') *n.* 1 A fancy dance step. 2 A figure in skating, outlining the shape of a pigeon's spread wing.

pig·fish (pig'fish') *n. pl.* **·fish** or **·fish·es** 1 A salt-water fish that makes a grunting noise; especially, a grunt, as the sailor's-choice (*Orthopristis chrysopterus*), common off the South Atlantic coast of the United States. 2 A sculpin. 3 A sea robin.

pig·ger·y (pig'ər·ē) *n. pl.* **·ger·ies** A place for keeping or raising pigs.

pig·gin (pig'in) *n.* A small wooden vessel having one stave projecting above the rim for a handle; also, a pitcher. [? Dim. of dial. E *pig* a crock]

pig·gish (pig'ish) *adj.* Like a pig; greedy; dirty; selfish. — **pig'gish·ly** *adv.* — **pig'gish·ness** *n.*

pig·gy (pig'ē) *n.* A little pig. Also **pig'gie.**

pig·gy-back (pig'ē·bak') *adv.* Pick-a-back.

pig·gy-back·ing (pig'ē·bak'ing) *n. U.S.* Transshipment of loaded truck bodies on railway flat cars.

pig·head·ed (pig'hed'id) *adj.* Stupidly obstinate. — **pig'·head'ed·ly** *adv.* — **pig'·head'ed·ness** *n.*

pig iron Crude iron poured from a blast furnance into variously shaped molds or pigs of sand or the like.

pig·ment (pig'mənt) *n.* 1 Any of a class of finely powdered, insoluble coloring matters suitable for making paints, enamels, oil colors, etc. 2 Any substance that imparts color to animal or vegetable tissues, as chlorophyll. 3 Any substance used for coloring. [<L *pigmentum* < *pingere* paint. Doublet of PIMENTO.]

pig·men·tar·y (pig'mən·ter'ē) *adj.* Producing, secreting, or containing pigment, as a cell.

pig·men·ta·tion (pig'mən·tā'shən) *n.* 1 Coloration. 2 *Biol.* Deposition of pigment by cells.

pigment cell *Biol.* A cell secreting or containing pigment, as an epithelial cell of the iris or a connective-tissue cell; a chromatophore.

pig·my (pig'mē) *adj.* Diminutive; dwarfish: also **pig·me'an.** — *n. pl.* **·mies** A dwarf. Also spelled **pygmy.** [<L *pygmaeus* <Gk. *pygmaios* dwarfish, a dwarf <*pygmē*, the length from elbow to knuckles]

Pig·my (pig'mē) See PYGMY.

pig·nus (pig'nəs) *n. pl.* **·no·ra** (-nər·ə) *Law* A contract of pawn of personal property; also, personal property pawned. [<L, a pledge, a pawn]

pig·nut (pig'nut') *n.* 1 The fruit of a species of hickory (*Carya glabra*) common in the United States. 2 The tree. 3 St. Anthony's nut. 4 The Old World earthnut.

pig·pen (pig'pen') *n.* A pen or sty where pigs are kept.

pig·skin (pig'skin') *n.* 1 The skin of a pig. 2 Something made of this skin, as a saddle or football.

pig-stick·ing (pig'stik'ing) *n.* The hunting of wild boars with spears.

pig·sty (pig'stī') *n. pl.* **·sties** A sty or pen for pigs.

pig·tail (pig'tāl') *n.* 1 The tail of a pig. 2 *Colloq.* A cue or plait or hair; also, one who wears a cue. 3 A twist of tobacco. — **pig'tailed'** *adj.*

pig·weed (pig'wēd') *n.* 1 Any of several American goosefoots; especially, the white pigweed (*Chenopodium album*). 2 The common purslane. 3 One of several amaranths, as the redroot (*Amaranthus retroflexus*).

pi·ka (pī'kə) *n.* A small mammal (family *Ochotonidae*) mostly of North America and Asia; a tailless hare. *Ochotona princeps* is the little chief hare or cony of the Rocky Mountains. ◆ Homophone: *pica.* [<Tungusic *peeka*]

pike¹ (pīk) *n.* A long pole having a metal spearhead, used by foot soldiers in medieval warfare. — *v.t.* **piked, pik·ing** To run through or kill with a pike. [<MF *pique* <*piquer* pierce <OF *pic* PIKE⁵]

PIKE HEADS

pike² (pīk) *n.* 1 A slender, long-snouted, voracious, spingy-finned food fish (family *Esocidae*), widely distributed in fresh waters of Europe, Asia, and America. 2 Some other fish resembling it, as the garpike. [Appar. short for *pikefish* <PIKE⁵ + FISH ; with ref. to its pointed snout]

pike³ (pīk) *n.* 1 A turnpike road. 2 A tollbar. — *v.i. Slang* **piked, pik·ing** To go in haste. [Short for TURNPIKE]

pike⁴ (pīk) *n.* A mountain peak or pointed hill. [? <ON *pik* a pointed mountain. Akin to OE *piic* PIKE⁵.]

pike⁵ (pīk) *n.* A spike or sharp point, as the central spike in a buckler. [OE *piic, pic*, prob. <OF, ? <L *picus* a woodpecker]

Pike (pīk), Zebulon Montgomery, 1779–1813, U.S. soldier and explorer.

piked (pīkt, pī'kid) *adj.* Having a pike; pointed. [<PIKE⁵]

pike·man (pīk'mən) *n. pl.* **·men** (-mən) One of a body of soldiers armed with pikes, as in the 16th and 17th centuries. [<PIKE¹ + MAN]

pike perch A pikelike percoid fish, as the walleyed pike or sauger.

pik·er (pī'kər) *n. U.S. Slang* 1 One who bets or speculates in a small, niggardly way. 2 One who does anything in a small, niggardly way. [Appar. from *Pike* County, Missouri, whose inhabitants were considered lazy, poor, suspicious, etc.]

Pike's Peak A mountain in central Colorado; 14,110 feet.

pike·staff (pīk'staf', -stäf') *n. pl.* **·staves** (-stāvz') 1 A piked staff, formerly carried by pilgrims, travelers, etc. 2 The wooden handle of a pike. [<PIKE⁵ + STAFF¹]

pi·lar (pī'lər) *adj.* Of, pertaining to, or covered with hair. [<NL *pilaris* <L *pilus* hair]

pi·las·ter (pi·las'tər) *n. Archit.* A rectangular column, with capital and base, engaged in a wall. [<F *pilastre* <Ital. *pilastro* <L *pila* a column]

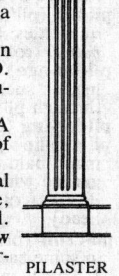

PILASTER

Pi·late (pī'lept), Pontius A Roman official; procurator of Judea A.D. 26–36?; delivered Jesus to be crucified.

Pi·la·tus (pē·lä'tōōs), Mount A peak 7 miles SW of the Lake of Lucerne, Switzerland; 6,998 feet.

pi·lau (pi·lou', -lô') *n.* An Oriental dish of boiled rice, raisins, spice, and some kind of meat or fowl. Also **pi·laf** (pi·läf'), **pi·laff', pi·law** (pi·lô'). [< Turkish *pilāw* <Persian *pilāw*]

pil·chard (pil'chərd) *n.* 1 A herringlike food fish (*Sardinia pilchardus*) of European Atlantic and Mediterranean waters,

the sardine. 2 The California sardine. Also *Obs.* **pil′cher, pil′cherd.** [Earlier *pilcher,* ? <Scand. Cf. Norw. *pilk* an artificial bait.]

Pil·co·ma·yo (pēl′kō·mä′yō) A river in south central South America, flowing 700 miles to the Paraguay, and forming part of the boundary between Argentina and Paraguay.

pile[1] (pīl) *n.* 1 A quantity of anything gathered or thrown together in one place; a heap. 2 *Electr.* Any of various devices for generating an electric current by means of superimposed plates of different metals in contact with a suitable liquid: a galvanic *pile,* voltaic *pile.* 3 A funeral pyre. 4 A large accumulation or number of something. 5 A massive building or group of buildings. 6 A pyramid. 7 A great quantity, especially of money; a fortune. 8 *Physics* A reactor. — **to make one's pile** To amass a fortune. — *v.* **piled, pil·ing** *v.t.* 1 To make a heap or pile of: often with *up.* 2 To cover or burden with a pile or piles: to *pile* a plate with food. — *v.i.* 3 To form a heap or pile. 4 To proceed or go in a confused mass: with *in, on, off, out,* etc. See synonyms under HEAP. — **to pile up** 1 To accumulate. 2 *Colloq.* To reduce or become reduced to a pile or wreck. [<OF <L *pila* a pillar, pier]

pile[2] (pīl) *n.* 1 A heavy timber pointed at one end, forced into the earth to form a foundation; a spile. 2 An arrowhead. 3 Formerly, a pointed stake. 4 *Obs.* A javelin. — *v.t.* **piled, pil·ing** 1 To drive piles into, as for a foundation. 2 To furnish or strengthen with piles. [OE *pil* a dart, pointed stake <L *pilum* a heavy javelin]

pile[3] (pīl) *n.* 1 Hair collectively; fur. 2 The manner in which hair is laid or set. 3 A fiber, as of cotton. 4 The cut or uncut loops which make the surface of certain fabrics, as velvets, plushes, corduroys, etc. [<L *pilus* hair] — **piled** *adj.*

CROSS–SECTION OF PILE WEAVE

pi·le·at·ed (pī′lē·ā′tid, pil′ē-) *adj.* 1 *Bot.* Provided with a pileus or cap. 2 *Ornithol.* Having the feathers of the pileum elongated or conspicuous; crested: the *pileated* woodpecker. Also **pi′le·ate.** [<L *pileatus* capped < *pileus* a felt cap]

pile driver A machine for driving piles. In the ordinary forms, a heavy weight, raised by a small hoisting engine and sliding between upright guides, falls on the head of the pile by the force of gravity: also **pile engine.**

pi·le·ous (pī′lē·əs) See PILOSE.

piles (pīlz) *n. pl.* Hemorrhoids. [<LL *pilae,* pl. of *pila* a ball]

pi·le·um (pī′lē·əm, pil′ē-) *n. pl.* **·le·a** (-lē·ə) *Ornithol.* The top of the head of a bird, from the base of the bill to the nape and above the eyes. [<L, var. of *pileus* a felt cap]

pi·le·us (pī′lē·əs, pil′ē-) *n. pl.* **·le·i** (-lē·ī) 1 *Bot.* The cap or expanded umbrella-shaped portion of a mushroom. See illustration under MUSHROOM. 2 In ancient Rome, a brimless round felt cap. [<L, a felt cap]

pile·wort (pīl′wûrt′) *n.* 1 An Old World crowfoot (*Ranunculus ficaria*), producing tuberous roots and yellow flowers. 2 An American species of fireweed (*Erechtites hieracifolia*). 3 The princess feather. [Trans. of Med. L *ficaria* <L *ficus* a fig, piles; with ref. to its reputed ability to cure hemorrhoids]

pil·fer (pil′fər) *v.t.* & *v.i.* To steal in small quantities. See synonyms under STEAL. [<OF *pelfrer* rob < *pelfre* plunder] — **pil′fer·er** *n.*

pil·fer·age (pil′fər·ij) *n.* 1 The act of pilfering, or such acts collectively. 2 Goods lost through pilfering.

pil·fer·ing (pil′fər·ing) *n.* Petty thieving.

pil·gar·lic (pil·gär′lik) *n.* 1 *Obs.* A person made bald by disease. 2 *Dial.* A person regarded with mock pity or contempt. [<PILL[2] + GARLIC; from the appearance of a bald head]

pil·grim (pil′grim) *n.* 1 One who journeys to some sacred place from religious motives. 2 Any wanderer or wayfarer. [ME *pelegrim* <OF *pelegrin* (assumed) <L *peregrinus.* See PEREGRINE.]

Pil·grim (pil′grim) *n.* One of the English Puritans who founded Plymouth Colony in 1620.

pil·grim·age (pil′grə·mij) *n.* 1 A long journey, especially one made to a shrine or sacred place. 2 Man's life as a journey through the world. See synonyms under JOURNEY. [<OF *pelrimage, pelerinage* < *peleriner* go as a pilgrim < *pelerin,* var. of *pelegrin* PILGRIM]

Pilgrim Fathers The founders of Plymouth Colony, Massachusetts, in 1620.

Pilgrim's Progress A religous allegory in two parts (1678 and 1684) by John Bunyan, depicting the life journey of Christian from the City of Destruction to the Celestial City.

pi·li (pē·lē′) *n.* 1 An edible nut of a Philippine tree (*Canarium ovatum*), considered a delicacy after roasting. 2 The tree. [<Tagalog]

pili– *combining form* Hair; related to the hair. [<L *pilus* a hair]

pil·ing (pī′ling) *n.* 1 Piles collectively. 2 A structure formed of piles. 3 The act or process of driving piles. [<PILE[2]]

pill[1] (pil) *n.* 1 A medicinal substance put up in a pellet, convenient for swallowing whole. 2 Hence, a disagreeable necessity. 3 *Slang* A person difficult to bear with; a bore. 4 *Colloq.* A baseball or a golf ball. — **the pill** or **the Pill** Any of various oral contraceptive drugs in tablet form, taken by women. — *v.t.* 1 To form into pills. 2 To dose with pills. 3 *Slang* To blackball. [Prob. <MDu. *pille* <L *pilula,* dim. of *pila* a ball]

pill[2] (pil) *v.t.* & *v.i. Obs.* 1 To pillage. 2 To peel off; scale. 3 To make or become bald. [OE *pylian,* prob. <L *pilare* make hairless, plunder; infl. by OF *piller* plunder and OF *peler* peel]

pil·lage (pil′ij) *n.* 1 The act of pillaging; open robbery, as in war. 2 Spoil; booty. See synonyms under PLUNDER. — *v.* **·laged, ·lag·ing** *v.t.* 1 To strip of money or property by open violence, especially in war; loot. 2 To take as loot. — *v.i.* 3 To take plunder. See synonyms under STEAL. [<OF < *piller* plunder <LL *pillare,* var. of L *pilare* plunder] — **pil′·lag·er** *n.*

pil·lar (pil′ər) *n.* 1 A firm, upright, separate support; column or shaft. 2 Something resembling a column in form or use. 3 One who or that which strongly supports a work or cause. — **from pillar to post** From one thing to another; from one predicament to another; hither and thither. — *v.t.* To adorn or support with or as with pillars. [<OF *piler* <LL *pilare* <L *pila* a pillar]

pillar box *Brit.* A box, supported by a pillar or post in the street, in which letters, etc., may be placed to be collected by a postman. Also **pillar post.**

Pillars of Hercules Two promontories on opposite sides of the eastern entrance to the Strait of Gibraltar: identified with *Gibraltar* and *Jebel Musa.*

pill·box (pil′boks′) *n.* 1 A small box for pills. 2 A small, round, concrete emplacement for a machine–gun, antitank gun, etc.

pill bug A small isopod crustacean (family *Armadillidiidae*), found under logs, etc.: so called because they roll into tiny pills when disturbed.

pil·lion (pil′yən) *n.* A pad on a horse's back, behind the saddle, on which a second person may ride: formerly used by women. [Appar. <Scottish Gaelic *pillean,* dim. of *pell* a cushion <L *pellis* a skin]

pil·li·winks (pil′ē·wingks) *n.* An old instrument of torture; thumbscrew: also called *pinnywinkle.* [ME *pyrwykes*; origin unknown]

pil·lo·ry (pil′ər·ē) *n. pl.* **·ries** Formerly, a framework in which an offender was fastened by the neck and wrists and exposed to public scorn. — *v.t.* **·ried, ·ry·ing** 1 To set in the pillory. 2 To hold up to public scorn or ridicule. [<OF *pellori, pilori,* appar. < dial. OF (Gascon) *espilori* <Provençal *espitlori,* ? < Catalan *espitlera* a little window, peephole]

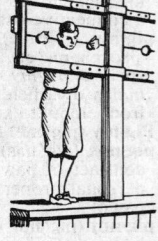

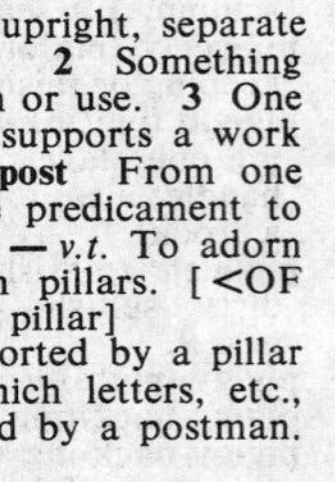
PILLORY

pil·low (pil′ō) *n.* 1 A case of cloth stuffed with some yielding material, or inflated with air, used as a support for the head, as in sleeping. 2 Any body rest. 3 One of various supporting blocks or devices, as a journal bearing. — *v.t.* 1 To rest on or as on a pillow. 2 To act as a pillow for. — *v.i.* 3 To recline as on a pillow. [OE *pyle, pylu,* ult. <L *pulvinus* a cushion] — **pil′·low·y** *adj.*

pillow block *Mech.* A block or other device resting on firm foundations and designed to support a journal or shaft; a bearing.

pillow case A covering drawn over a pillow. Also **pillow slip.**

pillow lace Bobbin lace.

pillow sham A decorative covering or spread to be laid over a bed pillow.

pi·lo·car·pine (pī′lō·kär′pēn, -pin, pil′ō-) *n. Chem.* A colorless to yellow, poisonous, liquid or crystalline alkaloid, $C_{11}H_{16}N_2O_2$, contained in jaborandi: its salts are used in medicine. Also **pi′lo·car′pin** (-pin). [<NL *Pilocarpus,* genus of the jaborandi + -INE[2]]

pi·lose (pī′lōs) *adj.* Covered with hair, especially with fine and soft hair; hairy: also spelled *pileous, pilous.* [<L *pilosus* < *pilus* hair] — **pi·los·i·ty** (pī·los′ə·tē) *n.*

pi·lot (pī′lət) *n.* 1 A helmsman; specifically, one duly qualified by training and licensed by law to conduct vessels in and out of port. 2 Any guide. 3 One who controls the operation of an airplane, dirigible, or other aircraft. 4 The cowcatcher of a locomotive. — *v.t.* 1 To act as the pilot of; steer. 2 To guide or conduct through difficulties, intricate dealings, etc. 3 To serve as pilot on, over, or upon. [<MF *pillotte, pilot* <Ital. *pilota,* ? < *pedota,* ult. <Gk. *pēda* a rudder, orig. pl. of *pēdon* an oar]

pi·lot·age (pī′lət·ij) *n.* 1 The act of piloting a vessel or aircraft. 2 The fee for such service.

pilot balloon A small balloon sent up before dispatching a large one, to show the direction and velocity of the wind.

pilot bread Ship biscuit. Also **pilot biscuit.**

pilot cell A selected cell of a storage battery whose voltage, temperature, etc., are considered to indicate the condition of the whole battery.

pilot engine A locomotive preceding and piloting a train.

pilot fish 1 An oceanic fish (*Naucrates ductor*), often seen in warm latitudes in company with sharks; the banded pilot. 2 A whitefish of North American waters (*Prosopium quadrilaterale*).

pilot house An enclosed structure, usually in the forward part of a vessel, containing the steering wheel and compass.

pi·lot·ing (pī′lət·ing) *n.* 1 The occupation of a pilot. 2 The branch of navigation that has to do with steering vessels in and out of ports or along coasts, or finding a ship's position by knowledge of landmarks, buoys, etc.

pilot lamp A small electric light used to indicate whether the power in a given circuit, motor, control unit, etc., is on or off.

pi·lot·less plane (pī′lət·lis) An aircraft designed and equipped to operate without a pilot.

pilot light A minute jet of gas kept burning beside an ordinary burner, for igniting the latter as soon as the gas is turned on. Also **pilot burner.**

pilot parachute See under PARACHUTE.

pilot plant An experimental assembly of various units of machinery and other equipment for the purpose of testing the value of new production methods.

pilot snake 1 The copperhead. 2 A black snake (*Elaphe obsoleta*) of the eastern United States.

pilot whale The blackfish.

pi·lous (pī′ləs) See PILOSE.

Pil·sen (pil′zən) A city of western Bohemia, Czechoslovakia: Czech *Plzeň.*

Pil·sud·ski (pēl·sōōt′skē), **Joseph,** 1867–1935, Polish general; first president of Poland 1918–1921.

Pilt·down (pilt′doun) A locality of eastern Sussex, England.

Piltdown man Eoanthropus.

pil·ule (pil′yōōl) *n.* A little pill; pellet. [<L *pilula.* See PILL[1].] — **pil′u·lar** *adj.*

Pi·man (pē′mən) *n.* A branch of the Uto-Aztecan linguistic family of North American Indians of southern Arizona and northern Mexico. — *adj.* Of or pertaining to this linguistic branch.

pim·e·lo·sis (pim′ə·lō′sis) *n. Pathol.* Conversion into fat; fatty degeneration; obesity. [<Gk. *pimelē* fat + -OSIS] — **pim′e·lot′ic** (-lot′ik) *adj.*

pi·men·to (pi-men'tō) *n. pl.* **·tos 1** The dried, unripe, aromatic berries of the West Indian allspice; also, the spice made from these berries, or the tree producing them. **2** The Spanish paprika or the sweet pepper from which it is made; pimiento. [<Sp. *pimienta* pepper <Med. L *pigmentum* a spiced drink, spice <L, a paint, juice of plants. Doublet of PIGMENT.]

pimento cheese Cheese made from processed Neufchâtel curds, cream cheese, or cheddar with pimientos added.

pi·mes·on (pī'mes'on, -mē'son) *n. Physics* A short-lived, highly unstable, radioactive particle produced by the impact of fast-moving protons on atomic nuclei. It has a mass about 275 times that of the electron, may be either positive or negative in charge, and decays spontaneously into mu-mesons and neutrinos.

pi·mien·to (pi-myen'tō) *n. pl.* **·tos** The sweet pepper, of which the fruit is used as a relish and for stuffing olives. [<Sp. <*pimienta*. See PIMENTO.]

pim·o·la (pi-mō'lə) *n.* An olive which has been stuffed with a sweet red pepper. [<PIM(IENTO) + OL(IVE) + -*a*]

pimp (pimp) *n.* A pander. — *v.i.* To act as a pimp. [Prob. <F *pimpant* seductive, ppr. of *pimper* dress elegantly; ult. origin uncertain]

pim·per·nel (pim'pər·nel) *n.* A plant of the primrose family (genus *Anagallis*) usually with red flowers, as the common **scarlet pimpernel** (*A. arvensis*). [<OF *pimprenele, piprenelle* <Med. L *pipinella*, ? <a dim. of L *bipennis* two–winged <*bi-* two + *penna* a feather]

pimp·ing (pim'ping) *adj. Colloq.* Puny; mean; sickly. [<dial. E. Akin to Du. *pimpel* a weak man.]

pim·ple (pim'pəl) *n.* **1** A minute swelling or small elevation of the skin, with an inflamed base. **2** Any small protuberance. [ME *pimplis* pimples. Cf. OE *piplígende* afflicted with herpes.] — **pim'pled, pim'ply** *adj.*

pin (pin) *n.* **1** A short stiff piece of wire, with a sharp point and a round, usually flattened head, used in fastening together parts of clothing, sheets of paper, etc. **2** An ornamental device mounted on a pin or having a pin as a clasp: often serving to fasten parts of the dress in addition to its use as a decoration: frequently a badge. **3** A peg or bar of metal or

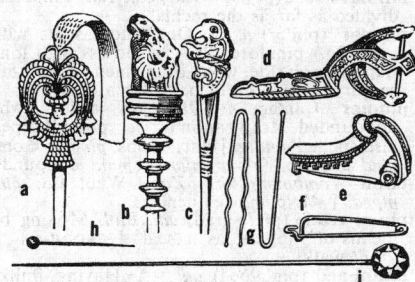

PINS OF VARIOUS TYPES

a. Greek.	*f.* Safety pin.
b. Roman.	*g.* Hairpins.
c. Early French.	*h.* Round–headed.
d. Russian.	*i.* Hatpin.
e. Scandinavian.	

wood used for a fastening or support, as the thole of a boat, the bolt of a door, a peg serving to stop a hole or to fasten two beams together, or to keep a wheel from slipping from an axle, or one of the pegs to which the strings of a musical instrument are fastened. **4** Anything like a pin, as a hairpin or clothespin. **5** *Usually pl.* A wooden club turned in long, oval, or cylindrical shape, set up as a mark or target in various bowling or ball–throwing games; a skittle. **6** *pl. Colloq.* Legs. **7** A belaying–pin; a rolling pin; a thole pin. **8** The merest trifle. **9** The cylindrical part of a key forward of the stem that enters the lock. **10** *Obs.* A peg showing the center of a target. — *v.t.* **pinned, pin·ning 1** To fasten with a pin or pins. **2** To transfix with a pin, spear, etc. **3** To seize and hold firmly: to *pin* an opponent against a wall. **4** To force (someone) to make a definite statement, abide by a promise, etc.:

usually with *down*. [OE *pinn* a peg, ? ult. <L *pinna* a point, pinnacle]

pi·ña (pē'nyä) *n.* **1** The pineapple. **2** A sweet drink prepared from the pineapple. Also **pi'na** (-nä). [<Sp., a pineapple, orig., a pine cone <L *pinea*. See PINEAL.]

Pi·na·ce·ae (pī-nā'si-ē) *n. pl.* A family of widely distributed coniferous trees and shrubs having needlelike leaves and bearing hard, woody cones, as the pine, cedar, redwood, larch, hemlock, etc.; the pine family. [<NL <L *pinus* a pine] — **pi·na'ceous** (-shəs) *adj.*

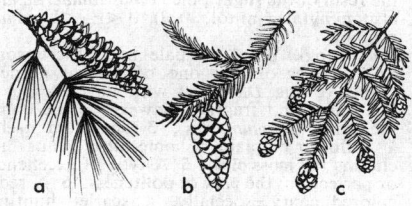

PINACEAE
a. White pine. *b.* Red spruce. *c.* Hemlock.

piña cloth A material for scarfs, handkerchiefs, etc., made from the fibers of the pineapple leaf. It is soft, transparent, and pale yellow.

pin·a·fore (pin'ə-fôr, -fōr) *n.* A sleeveless apron, especially for protecting the front of a child's dress. [<PIN + AFORE]

pi·nang (pi-nang') *n.* The betel palm, or its fruit. [<Malay, an areca, a betel nut]

Pi·nar del Rí·o (pē-när' ŧħel rē'ō) A province in western Cuba; 5,211 square miles; capital, Pinar del Río.

pi·nas·ter (pī-nas'tər, pi-) *n.* An Old World pine (*Pinus pinaster*) common in the Mediterranean region. [<L, a wild pine <*pinus* a pine]

pin·ball (pin'bôl') *n.* A game in which a ball, spring–propelled to the top of an inclined board, contacts in its descent any of various numbered pins, holes, etc., the contacts so made comprising the player's score.

pince-nez (pans'nā', pins'-, *Fr.* paṅs·nā') *n.* Eyeglasses held upon the nose by a spring. [<F, lit., pinch–nose <*pincer* pinch + *nez* nose]

pin·cers (pin'sərz) *n. pl. (sometimes construed as singular)* **1** An instrument having two handles and a pair of jaws working on a pivot, used for holding objects. **2** *Zool.* A nipperlike organ, as the chela of a lobster. Also spelled *pinchers*. [ME *pinsours*, appar. <AF *pincer*, OF *pincier* pinch]

pinch (pinch) *v.t.* **1** To squeeze between two hard edges, or surfaces, a finger and thumb, etc. **2** To bind or compress painfully: This collar *pinches* my neck. **3** To affect with pain or distress: The cold *pinched* his fingers. **4** To contract or make thin, as from cold or hunger. **5** To reduce in means; distress, as for lack of money; straiten. **6** To move by means of a pinchbar. **7** *Slang* To capture or arrest. **8** *Slang* To steal. **9** *Naut.* To sail (a vessel) close–hauled. — *v.i.* **10** To squeeze; hurt. **11** To be careful with money; be stingy. **12** *Mining* Of veins, to become narrow; also, to disappear: with *out*. — **to pinch pennies** To be economical or stingy. — *n.* **1** The act of pinching. **2** Painful pressure of any kind. **3** A case of emergency. **4** So much of a loose substance as can be taken between the finger and thumb. **5** A narrow or tapering section on a vein of rock or fissure of earth. **6** A pinchbar. **7** *Slang* A theft. **8** *Slang* An arrest or raid. [<AF *pincher*, OF *pincier*, prob. <Gmc.] — **pinch'er** *n.*

pinch·bar (pinch'bär') *n.* A crowbar with a short projection and a heel or fulcrum at the end so that it may be used to pry forward heavy objects.

pinch·beck (pinch'bek) *n.* **1** An alloy of copper, zinc, and tin, forming a cheap imitation of gold. **2** Anything spurious or pretentious. — *adj.* Made of pinchbeck; spurious. [after Christopher *Pinchbeck*, 1670?–1732, English inventor]

pinch·bug (pinch'bug') *n.* A stag beetle.

pinch effect *Physics* The constriction produced in a plasma jet or vaporized electrical conductor when forced through a narrow orifice by the combined action of magnetohydrodynamic and thermal forces applied in the generating chamber.

pinch·ers (pin'chərz) See PINCERS.

pinch–hit (pinch'hit') *v.i.* **–hit, –hit·ting 1** In baseball, to go to bat in place of a regular player, as when a hit is needed. **2** *Colloq.* To substitute for another in an emergency. [<PINCH an emergency + HIT]

pinch hitter One who pinch–hits.

Pin·chot (pin'shō), **Gifford**, 1865–1946, U. S. conservationist and politician.

Pinck·ney (pingk'nē), **Charles Cotesworth,** 1746–1825, American soldier and patriot.

pin·cush·ion (pin'ko͝osh'ən) *n.* A small cushion into which pins are stuck when they are not being used.

Pin·dar (pin'dər), 522?–443 B.C., Greek lyric poet.

Pin·dar·ic (pin-dar'ik) *adj.* Of or pertaining to Pindar. — *n.* A Pindaric ode; any ode written in the complex style of Pindar.

pin·der (pin'dər) See PINNER².

pind·ling (pind'ling) *adj.* **1** Dwindling; delicate; sickly. **2** Trifling. **3** *Dial.* Peevish. [Var. of PIDDLING]

Pin·dus (pin'dəs) The mountain range of northern Greece, between Epirus and Thessaly; highest point, 8,650 feet.

pine¹ (pīn) *n.* **1** A cone-bearing tree (genus *Pinus*) having needle–shaped evergreen leaves growing in clusters; especially, the American **white pine** (*P. strobus*), the long-leaved southern **Georgia** or **yellow pine** (*P. palustris*), the **loblolly** or **oldfield pine** (*P. taeda*), the **red pine** (*P. resinosa*) of the eastern United States, and a **nut pine** (*P. cembroides*) of the Pacific States. **2** The wood of any pine tree. **3** *Colloq.* The pineapple. [Fusion of OE *pīn* and OF *pin*, both <L *pinus* a pine tree]

pine² (pīn) *v.* **pined, pin·ing** *v.i.* **1** To grow thin or weak with longing, grief, etc. **2** To have great desire or longing: with *for*. — *v.t.* **3** *Archaic* To grieve for. [OE *pīnian* torment, ult. <L *poena* a punishment]

pin·e·al (pin'ē-əl) *adj.* **1** Shaped like a pine cone: the *pineal* body. **2** Pertaining to the pineal body. [<F *pinéal* <L *pinea* a pine cone <*pinus* a pine tree]

pineal body *Anat.* A small, reddish-gray, vascular, conical body of rudimentary glandular structure found behind the third ventricle of the brain, embraced by its two peduncles, but not a part of the brain, and having no known function. Also **pineal gland.**

pineal eye *Biol.* The pineal body which in certain reptiles emerges as an eyelike structure.

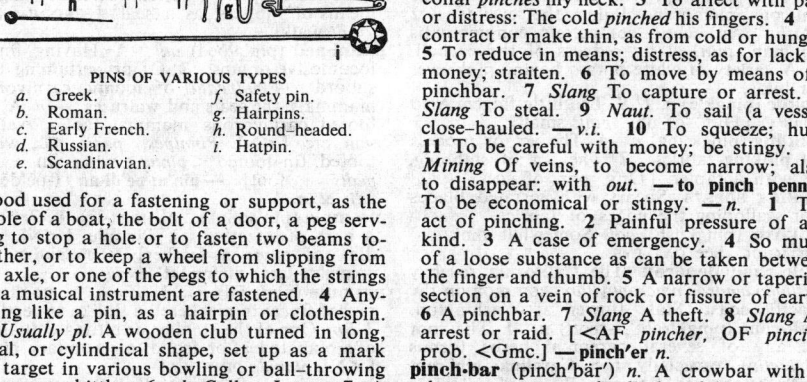

PINEAPPLE
Fruit in crown of plant.

pine·ap·ple (pīn'ap'əl) *n.* **1** A tropical American plant (*Ananas comosus*) having spiny, recurved leaves and a cone–shaped fruit consisting of the inflorescence clustering densely around a fleshy axis tipped with a rosette of spiked leaves. **2** The edible fruit of this plant. **3** *Slang* A bomb. **4** In decoration, an ornament frequently in the form of a finial resembling either a pineapple or a pine cone: used especially on furniture. [OE *pīnæppel* a pine cone <*pīn* a pine + *æppel* an apple; so called because the fruit resembles a pine cone]

pine cone The cone-shaped fruit of the pine tree. The pine cone and tassel compose the floral emblem of Maine.

pine·drops (pīn'drops') *n.* **1** Beechdrops. **2** A stout brownish–purple saprophytic plant (*Pterospora andromedea*) with terminal clusters of nodding white flowers.

pine grosbeak A north American finch (*Pinicola enucleator*) having a slate-gray plumage which in the male is tinged with red.

Pine·hurst (pīn'hûrst) A winter resort in central North Carolina.

---

add,āce,câre,pälm; end,ēven; it,īce; odd,ōpen,ôrder; to͝ok,po͞ol; up,bûrn; ə = a in *above*, e in *sicken*, i in *clarity*, o in *melon*, u in *focus*; yo͞o = u in *fuse*; oi,oil; ou,pout; ch,check; g,go; ng,ring; th,thin; ŧħ,this; zh,vision. Foreign sounds ä,œ,ü,kh,ṅ; and ◆: see page xx. < from; + plus; ? possibly.

pine knot 1 A knot in pine wood. 2 Any person or thing as tough as a pine knot.

Pi·nel (pē·nel′), **Philippe,** 1745–1826, French physician.

pine mouse The little reddish-brown vole *(Pitymys pinetorum)* of the pine barrens of the eastern United States.

pi·nene (pī′nēn) *n. Chem.* Either of two isomeric terpenes, $C_{10}H_{16}$, the principal constituent of turpentine, and an ingredient of many essential oils, such as oil of juniper, eucalyptus, etc. [<PIN(E)[1] + -ENE]

pine needle The needle-shaped leaf of the pine tree.

Pi·ner·o (pi·nâr′ō, -nir′ō), **Sir Arthur Wing,** 1855–1934, English dramatist.

pin·er·y (pī′nər·ē) *n. pl.* **·er·ies** 1 A hothouse for growing pineapples. 2 A pine forest, especially one where lumbering is carried on. 3 A large collection of pine trees.

Pines, Isle of See ISLE OF PINES.

pine·sap (pīn′sap′) *n.* A low, fragrant plant *(Hypopitys latisquama),* whitish or reddish, parasitic on roots or living on dead vegetable material: native of the north temperate zone. [<PINE[1] + SAP[2]]

pine siskin A finch *(Spinus pinus)* of North America having streaked plumage. Also **pine finch.**

pine squirrel The American red squirrel *(Sciurus hudsonicus).*

pine tar A dark, viscous tar obtained by the destructive distillation of the wood of pine trees: used in the treatment of skin ailments.

pine-tree shilling (pīn′trē′) A famous silver coin of Massachusetts from 1652 to about 1684, stamped with the image of a tree resembling a pine tree.

Pine-Tree State Nickname of MAINE.

pi·ne·tum (pi·nē′təm) *n. pl.* **·ta** (-tə) A plantation of pine trees. [<L, a pine grove <*pinus* a pine tree]

pine warbler A small, olive-green warbler *(Dendroica pinus* or *D. vigosi)* common in the pine forests of the eastern United States.

pine·y (pī′nē) See PINY.

Pine·y (pī′nē) *n. U.S.* A poor white living in a pine woods area of New Jersey or the South. Also **Pin′er.**

pin feather *Ornithol.* 1 A rudimentary feather. 2 A feather just beginning to grow through the skin.

pin·fish (pin′fish′) *n. pl.* **·fish** or **·fish·es** A sparoid fish *(Lagodon rhomboides)* common on the Atlantic coast of the southern United States.

pin·fold (pin′fōld′) *n.* A pound for stray animals; especially, a cattle pound. —*v.t.* To shut in a pinfold; confine. [OE *pundfald.* See POUND[2], FOLD[2]; infl. in form by *pyndan* enclose.]

ping (ping) *n.* 1 The sound made by a bullet striking an object. 2 The sound made by a bullet as it cuts the air. —*v.i.* To make this sound. [Imit.]

Ping (ping) A river in northern Thailand, flowing 300 miles south to the Chao Phraya.

Ping-pong (ping′pong′, -pông′) *n.* The game of table tennis: a trade name.

pin·grass (pin′gras′, -gräs′) *n.* Alfileria.

pin·guid (ping′gwid) *adj.* Containing or resembling oil or fat; unctuous. [<L *pinguis* fat] —**pin·guid′i·ty** *n.*

Ping·yu·an (ping′yü·än′) A former province of north central China, constituted, 1949; repartitioned among other provinces, 1952; 20,072 square miles; former capital, Sinsiang.

pin·head (pin′hed′) *n.* 1 A small minnow. 2 *Slang* A brainless or stupid person; a fool.

pin head 1 The head of a pin. 2 Any small object. —**pin-head·ed** (pin′hed′id) *adj.*

pin·hole (pin′hōl′) *n.* A minute puncture made by or as by a pin.

pinhole camera A camera of simple design and construction, usually home-made, consisting of a box having a small aperture functioning as a lens at one end, the image being projected on the film at the other end.

pin·ion[1] (pin′yən) *n.* 1 The wing of a bird. 2 A feather; a quill. 3 The outer segment of a bird's wing, bearing the flight feathers. 4 The anterior border of the wing of an insect. —*v.t.* 1 To cut off one pinion or bind the wings of (a bird) so as to prevent flight. 2 To cut or bind (the wings) of a bird. 3 To bind or hold the arms of (someone) so as to render helpless. 4 To shackle; confine. [<OF *pignon* a streamer, a feather <L *penna, pinna* a feather] —**pin′ioned** *adj.*

pin·ion[2] (pin′yən) *n. Mech.* A toothed wheel (or sometimes, in watches, a ribbed wire) driving or driven by a larger cogwheel. [<F *pignon,* orig. a battlement <OF *pinun* <L *pinna,* orig. a pinnacle]

pin·ite[1] (pin′īt, pī′nīt) *n.* A hydrous potassium-aluminum silicate. [<G *pinit* <*Pin(i),* a mine in Saxony + *-it* -ITE[1]]

pi·nite[2] (pī′nīt) *n. Chem.* A white, very sweet, crystalline substance, $C_6H_6(OH)_5 \cdot OCH_3$, from the resin of the sugar pine *(Pinus lambertiana)*: also **pi′ni·tol** (-ni·tôl, -tol). [<F <L *pinus* a pine]

pink[1] (pingk) *n.* 1 A pale hue of crimson. 2 A flower of any one of several garden plants (genus *Dianthus*) with narrow grass-like leaves and fragrant flowers, as the common pink *(D. plumarius).* 3 The plant itself. 4 A flower or plant of some other genus, including the **moss pink.** 5 A type of excellence or perfection: the *pink* of politeness. 6 A red-colored coat; especially, a scarlet hunting coat; also, one who wears such a coat. 7 *Often cap.* A person who holds somewhat radical economic and political opinions. —**in the pink** *Colloq.* In the best possible condition or degree. —*adj.* 1 Having the color called pink; pale rose. 2 Fashionably dainty. [? Short for obs. *pink eye* a small eye (<obs. *pink* small + EYE), trans. of F *oeillet* a pink (flower), orig. dim. of *oeil* an eye]

pink[2] (pingk) *v.t.* 1 To prick or stab with a pointed weapon. 2 To decorate, as cloth or leather, with a pattern of holes. 3 To cut or finish the edges of (cloth) with a notched pattern, as to prevent raveling or for decoration. 4 *Brit.* To adorn; deck. [ME *pynken,* prob. a nasalized form of *pikken* PICK[1]]

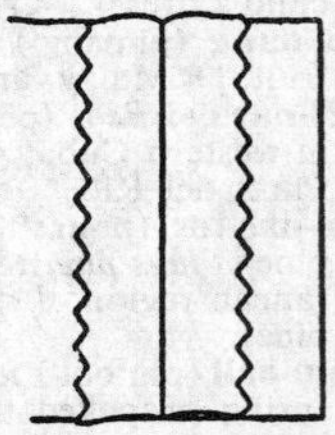

PINKED SEAM
(*v.t. def.* 3)

pink[3] (pingk) *n. Naut.* 1 A sailing vessel with a narrow stern, originally flat-bottomed with bulging sides. 2 A small sailing vessel with a narrow stern, used for fishing and coasting: also called *pink-stern*: also **pink′ie, pink′y.** [<MDu. *pincke* a small sea-going ship; ult. origin unknown]

pink[4] (pingk) *v.i. Brit. Dial.* To draw in; fade. [Cf. Du. *pinken* blink, glimmer]

Pink·er·ton (pingk′ər·tən), **Allan,** 1819–84, U. S. private detective born in Scotland.

pink·eye (pingk′ī′) *n.* 1 A febrile contagious keratitis of sheep, with inflammation of the mucous membrane lining the eyelids. 2 *Pathol.* An acute, contagious conjunctivitis in man, marked by redness of the eyeball. 3 A variety of white potato having pink eyes or buds.

pink·ie (pingk′ē) *n. U.S.* The little finger. Also **pink′y.** [Dim. of obs. *pink* small]

pink·ing (pingk′ing) *n.* 1 The act or process of pinking fabrics. 2 The act of stabbing, as with a rapier. [Orig. ppr. of PINK[2]]

pinking shears Shears with serrated blades for scalloping the edges of fabrics.

pink·ish (pingk′ish) *adj.* Somewhat pink.

pin knot See CAT-EYE.

pink rhododendron The California rosebay *(Rhododendron macrophyllum)* common on the Pacific coast: State flower of Washington.

pink·root (pingk′rōōt′, -rŏŏt′) *n.* 1 The root of any of several perennial herbs (genus *Spigelia*), especially the **Carolina pinkroot** with bright red flowers *(S. marilandica),* a well-known anthelminthic: also called *wormroot.* 2 A plant yielding this root.

Pink·ster (pingk′stər) *n.* Whitsuntide: formerly observed as a day of revelry in New York. [<Du. *pinkster,* ult. <Gothic *paintekuste* <Gk. *pentēkostē* PENTECOST]

pinkster flower An American shrub (*Azalea nudiflora* or *Rhododendron nudiflorum*) with showy, flesh-colored to dark-red flowers, blooming at Whitsuntide: also spelled *pinxter flower.* Also called *wild honeysuckle.*

pink-stern (pingk′stûrn′) See PINK[3] (def. 2).

pink tea *U.S. Colloq.* 1 A women's social gathering or tea, at which the decorations or refreshments are exceptionally dainty. 2 Any innocuous occasion.

pink·y (pingk′ē) *adj.* Small and blinking: said of eyes. [Prob. <obs. *pink* small]

pin money An allowance for incidentals; formerly, an allowance made by a husband to his wife for her personal expenses.

pin·na (pin′ə) *n. pl.* **pin·nae** (pin′ē) 1 *Bot.* A single leaflet of a pinnate leaf. 2 *Anat.* The auricle of the ear. 3 *Zool.* A wing, fin, or the like. [<NL <L *pinna, penna* a feather] —**pin′·nal** *adj.*

pin·nace (pin′is) *n. Naut.* 1 A six- or eight-oared boat, carried by men-of-war; any ship's boat. 2 Formerly, a small schooner-rigged vessel used as a tender, scout, etc. [<OF *pinasse* <Ital. *pinaccia,* prob. <L *pinus* a pine]

pin·na·cle (pin′ə·kəl) *n.* 1 A small turret or tall ornament, as on a parapet. 2 Anything resembling a pinnacle; a high or topmost point, as a mountain peak; summit. —*v.t.* **·cled, ·cling** 1 To place on or as on a pinnacle. 2 To furnish with a pinnacle; crown. See synonyms under SUMMIT. [<OF *pinacle* <LL *pinnaculum,* dim. of L *pinna* a wing, a pinnacle]

pin·nate (pin′āt, -it) *adj.* 1 *Bot.* Having the shape or arrangement of a feather: said of compound leaves or leaflets arranged on each side of a common axis: when terminated by a single leaf, *odd-pinnate*; when lacking a terminal leaf, *abruptly pinnate.* 2 Having winglike parts or appendages. Also **pin′nat·ed.** [<L *pinnatus* feathered <*pinna* a feather, wing] —**pin′nate·ly** *adv.* —**pin·na′tion** *n.*

pinnati- *combining form* 1 *Bot.* Feathered; resembling a feather: *pinnatifid.* 2 *Zool.* Pinni-. [<L *pinnatus* feathered <*pinna* feather]

pin·nat·i·fid (pi·nat′ə·fid) *adj. Bot.* Cleft in a pinnate manner, with the incisions half-way down or more and the lobes or sinuses narrow.

pin·nat·i·lo·bate (pi·nat′ə·lō′bāt) *adj. Bot.* Pinnately lobed.

pin·nat·i·par·tite (pi·nat′ə·pär′tīt) *adj. Bot.* Pinnately parted.

pin·nat·i·ped (pi·nat′ə·ped) *adj. Ornithol.* Having lobed membranes to the toes, as certain birds.

pin·nat·i·sect (pi·nat′ə·sekt) *adj. Bot.* Pinnately divided as far as the rachis.

pin·ner[1] (pin′ər) *n.* 1 One who fastens with pins. 2 A pinafore. 3 A headdress with long flaps at each side, worn by women in the 18th century; also, a cloth band for a dress.

pin·ner[2] (pin′ər) *n. Obs.* An officer who impounded stray animals; a poundkeeper: also spelled *pinder.* [Var. of obs. *pinder* <obs. *pind* enclose, OE *pyndan* <*pund* a pound[2]]

pinni- *combining form Zool.* Web; fin: *pinniped.* [<L *pinna* feather]

pin·ni·grade (pin′ə·grād) *adj. Biol.* Moving by means of flippers, as a seal. [<PINNI- + L *gradi* walk]

pin·ni·ped (pin′ə·ped) *adj.* 1 Having finlike locomotive organs. 2 Of or pertaining to a suborder *(Pinnipedia)* of aquatic carnivorous mammals, the seals and walruses. —*n.* A fin-footed carnivorous mammal, as a walrus, seal, etc. [<NL *Pinnipes, -pedis* <L, wing-footed, fin-footed <*pinna* a wing, fin + *pes, pedis* a foot] —**pin′ni·pe′di·an** (-pē′dē·ən) *adj.* & *n.*

pin·nu·la (pin′yə·lə) *n. pl.* **·lae** (-lē) 1 *Ornithol.* A barb of a feather. 2 Pinnule. [<NL <L, dim. of *pinna* a feather] —**pin′nu·lar** *adj.* —**pin′nu·late, pin′nu·lat′ed** *adj.*

pin·nule (pin′yōōl) *n.* 1 *Zool.* A small, detached fin, as in mackerel; a finlike appendage. 2 *Bot.* One of the smaller or ultimate divisions of a pinnate leaf or frond; a secondary pinna. [<NL *pinnula* PINNULA]

pin·ny·win·kle (pin′ē·wing′kəl) See PILLIWINKS.

pin oak An oak tree *(Quercus palustris)* common in the eastern United States, forming a conical head with long pendulous branches, the leaves of which turn a bright scarlet in autumn.

pi·noch·le (pē′nuk·əl, -nok-) *n.* A card game resembling bezique played with a double pack of 48 cards, ranking as follows: ace, ten, king, queen, jack, and nine: also spelled *penuchle, penuckle.* Also **pi′noc·le.** —**check pinochle** A four-handed, partnership card game, based on bridge and pinochle, with a double-scoring

pi·no·le (pi·nō'lā) *n. SW U.S.* A meal ground from corn, mesquite beans, or other plant seeds, and roasted. [< Am. Sp. < Nahuatl *pinolli*]

pi·ñon (pin'yən, pēn'yōn; *Sp.* pē·nyōn') *n.* 1 The edible seed of any of various pines of the Pacific coast of the United States; especially, the New Mexican piñon (*Pinus cembroides*). 2 The tree: also spelled *pinyon*. [< Sp., a pine nut < L *pinea* a pine cone < *pinus* a pine]

pin·point (pin'point') *n.* 1 The point of a pin. 2 Something extremely small. —*v.t.* To locate or define precisely: to *pinpoint* a target, argument, etc.

pins and needles A tingling or prickling sensation in some part of the body, as the fingers or toes; paresthesia. —**on pins and needles** Uneasy; nervous.

pin·scher (pin'shər) *n.* One of a breed of large, short-haired dogs, originally bred in Germany, usually black, brown, or gray-blue, with rust markings: usually called **Doberman pinscher**, after its first breeder. [< G, a terrier]

DOBERMAN PINSCHER
(From 26 to 28 inches high at the shoulder)

Pinsk (pinsk) A city in the SW Pripet Marshes of western Belorussian S.S.R.

pin·son (pin'sən) *n.* A thin, light shoe or slipper. [? < OF *pinçon* toe-piece of a horseshoe, dim. of *pince* toe of a hoof]

pint (pīnt) *n.* 1 A dry and liquid measure of capacity equal to half a quart (liquids only) four gills or 0.832 British pint. 2 *Scot.* A measure equivalent to three English pints. [< OF *pinte*, prob. < MDu.; ult. origin uncertain]

pin·ta (pin'tə, *Sp.* pēn'tä) *n. Pathol.* A tropical skin disease caused by a treponeme and characterized by patches of discoloration: also called *carate*. [< Sp., lit., a colored spot < LL *pincta* < L *picta*, orig. pp. fem. of *pingere* paint]

Pin·ta (pin'tə, *Sp.* pēn'tä) *n.* One of the three ships of Columbus on his initial voyage to America.

pin·ta·do (pin·tä'dō) *n. pl.* **·dos** A large, spotted fish (*Scomberomorus maculatus*) of the mackerel family, found in tropical Atlantic waters of North and South America; the Spanish mackerel. [< Pg., lit., painted, pp. of *pintar* paint, ult. < L *pingere* paint]

pin·tail (pin'tāl') *n.* 1 A duck (*Dafila acuta*) of the northern hemisphere, the male of which has a long, sharp tail. 2 A sharp-tailed grouse (*Pediaecetes phasianellus*) of northern North America. 3 The ruddy duck.

pin·ta·no (pin·tä'nō) *n. pl.* **·nos** or **·no** A tropical fish (genus *Abudefduf*) having a green body marked with dark bands: found in the neighborhood of coral reefs. Also called *cow pilot*. [Prob. < Sp. *pinta*. See PINTA.]

pin·tle (pin'təl) *n.* A pin upon which anything pivots, as one of the metal braces or hooks upon which a rudder swings, the pin of a hinge of a gunlock, etc. [OE *pintel* penis. Akin to PIN.]

pin·to (pin'tō) *adj. SW U.S.* Piebald; pied, as an animal. —*n. pl.* **·tos** 1 A pied animal: said especially of a horse, or Western pony. 2 A kind of spotted bean (*Phaseolus vulgaris*) of the southwestern United States: also **pinto bean**. [< Am. Sp. < Sp., lit., painted, ult. < L *pingere* paint]

Pintsch gas (pinch) A fuel and illuminating gas made by the destructive distillation of oil. [after Richard *Pintsch*, 1840–1919, German inventor]

Pin·tu·ric·chio (pēn'tŏŏ·rēk'kyō) 1454–1513, Italian painter; original name *Bernardino di Betti.*

pin-up (pin'up') *U.S. Colloq. n.* That which is affixed to a board or wall for scrutiny or perusal; specifically, a clipping or photograph, usually of an attractive young woman. —*adj.* Designating a photograph, clipping, or drawing used in this manner, or a person who models such a picture: She's my *pin-up* girl.

pin·weed (pin'wēd') *n.* Any one of various perennial herbs (genus *Lechea*), with very small greenish or purplish flowers.

pin·wheel (pin'hwēl') *n.* 1 A firework that revolves when ignited, forming a wheel of fire. 2 A wheel with pins set in its face in place of cogs on the periphery. 3 A child's toy resembling a windmill, made of colored paper, revolving on a pin attached to a stick.

pin·worm (pin'wûrm') *n.* A nematode worm (*Enterobius vermicularis*) parasitic in the lower intestines and rectum of man, especially of children.

pinx·it (pingk'sit) *Latin* He (or she) painted (it).

pinx·ter flower (pingk'stər) See PINKSTER FLOWER.

pin·y (pī'nē) *adj.* Pertaining to, suggestive of, or covered with pines: also spelled *piney*.

Pin·yin (pin'yin') *n.* The official Chinese system of transliterating Chinese into Roman alphabet characters. [< Chinese]

pin·yon (pin'yən) See PIÑON.

pinyon jay A small, short-tailed, uncrested corvine bird (*Cyanocephalus cyanocephalus*) of the Rocky Mountain region having a dark plumage and a long, sharp bill.

Pin·zón (pēn·thōn'), **Martín Alonzo,** 1441–1493, Spanish navigator; commanded the *Pinta* of Columbus' fleet. —**Vicente Yáñez,** 1460–1524, commanded the *Nina*; discovered Brazil; brother of the preceding.

pi·on (pī'on) *n.* A pi-meson. [< PI + (MES)ON]

pi·o·neer (pī'ə·nir') *n.* 1 One of the first explorers, settlers, or colonists of a new country or region. 2 One of the first investigators or developers in a new field of research, enterprise, etc. 3 *Mil.* An engineer who goes before the main body building roads, bridges, etc. See synonyms under HERALD. —*v.t.* 1 To prepare (a way, etc.). 2 To prepare the way for. 3 To be a pioneer of. —*v.i.* 4 To act as a pioneer. [< F *pionnier* < OF *paonier*, orig. a foot soldier < *peon*, dim.]

Pio·tr·ków (pyô'tər·kŏŏf') A city in central Poland SE of Łódź. *Russian* **Pe·tro·kov** (pet'rə·kôv, Russian pye'tro·kôf').

pi·ous (pī'əs) *adj.* 1 Actuated by reverence for a Supreme Being; religious; godly. 2 Marked by a reverential spirit. 3 Practiced in the name of religion. 4 *Obs.* Exhibiting filial respect and affection; filial. See synonyms under GOOD, MORAL. [< L *pius* dutiful, devout] —**pi'ous·ly** *adv.* —**pi'ous·ness** *n.*

pip¹ (pip) *n.* 1 The seed of an apple, orange, etc. 2 *Slang* An admirable person or thing. [Short for PIPPIN]

pip² (pip) *n.* 1 A spot, as on a playing card, domino, or die. 2 Any of the small buds of the lily-of-the-valley. 3 Any dormant rootstock of several flowering plants, as anemones and peonies. 4 One of the diamond-shaped sections on the rind of a pineapple. 5 A sharp sound or luminous signal produced mechanically or electronically, as in radar. [< earlier *peep*; origin unknown]

pip³ (pip) *v.* **pipped, pip·ping** *v.t.* To break through (the shell), as a chick in the egg. —*v.i.* To peep; chirp. [Prob. var. of PEEP¹]

pip⁴ (pip) *n.* 1 A contagious disease of fowls in which mucus forms in the throat or a scale on the tongue. 2 *Slang* A mild human ailment: used humorously; also, a grouch; an ill temper. [< MDu. *pippe* < LL *pipita* < L *pituita* mucus, the pip]

pip·age (pī'pij) *n.* 1 Pipes collectively; a system of pipes. 2 The carriage of oil, gas, water, etc., through pipes.

pi·pal (pē'pəl) *n.* The sacred fig tree of India (*Ficus religiosa*): also spelled *peepul*. [< Hind. *pipal* < Skt. *pippala*]

pipe (pīp) *n.* 1 An apparatus, usually a small bowl with a hollow stem, for smoking tobacco, opium, or other narcotic. 2 Enough tobacco to fill the bowl of a pipe. 3 A long conducting passage of wood, metal, tiling, etc., for conveying a fluid. 4 A single tube or long, hollow case: when part of a line of piping, often called a *piece of pipe.* 5 Any hollow or tubular part in an animal or plant body. 6 *Music* a A tubular wind instrument, such as the flageolet. b *pl.* The bagpipe. 7 The voice; also, a bird's note or call. 8 A large cask for wine; also, a liquid measure of half a tun. 9 *Metall.* A conical cavity in the head of a steel ingot, made by an escape of gas while the metal was cooling. 10 *Slang* An easy college course. 11 A boatswain's whistle. 12 *Mining* An elongated, usually vertical or highly inclined body of mineral or rich ore: also called a *chimney.* —*v.* **piped, pip·ing** *v.i.* 1 To play on a pipe. 2 To make a shrill sound. 3 *Naut.* To signal the crew by means of a boatswain's pipe. 4 *Metall.* To form conical cavities in hardening, as ingots. —*v.t.* 5 To convey by or as by means of pipes. 6 To provide with pipes. 7 To play, as a tune, on a pipe. 8 To utter shrilly or in a high key. 9 *Naut.* To call to order by means of a boatswain's pipe. 10 To lead, entice, or bring by piping. 11 To trim, as a dress, with piping. —**to pipe down** *Slang* To become silent; stop talking or making noise. —**to pipe up** 1 To start playing or singing: *Pipe up* the band! 2 To speak out, especially in a shrill voice. [OE *pipe*, ult. < L *pipare* cheep. Doublet of FIFE.]

pipe-clay (pīp'klā') *v.t.* To whiten with pipe clay.

pipe clay A white clay used for pottery, especially pipes, and, formerly, for whitening military accouterments: also called *terra alba.*

pipe dream Any wish, plan, or groundless hope; a daydream.

pipe·fish (pīp'fish') *n. pl.* **·fish** or **·fish·es** 1 One of a family (*Syngnathidae*) of slender marine and fresh-water fishes having a straight, tubelike snout and bodies enclosed in a series of bony rings. 2 A sea horse.

pipe·fit·ter (pīp'fit'ər) *n.* One who joins pipes together; a plumber.

pipe·fit·ting (pīp'fit'ing) *n.* 1 A piece of pipe used to connect two or more pipes together. 2 The work of a pipefitter.

pipe·line (pīp'līn') *n.* 1 A line of pipe, as for the transmission of water, oil, etc. 2 A channel for the transmission of information, usually private or secret. —*v.t.* 1 To convey by pipeline. 2 To furnish with a pipeline.

pipe of peace The calumet.

pipe organ An organ having pipes: distinguished from a *reed organ.*

pip·er (pī'pər) *n.* 1 One who lays pipes. 2 One who plays upon a pipe, especially a bagpipe.

Pi·per·a·ce·ae (pī'pə·rā'si·ē, pip'ə-) *n. pl.* A family of tropical aromatic herbs and shrubs, including the common pepper plant of Asia and South America. [< NL < L *piper* pepper] —**pi·per·a'ceous** (-rā'shəs) *adj.*

pi·per·a·zine (pi·per'ə·zēn) *n. Chem.* A crystalline substance, $C_4H_{10}N_2$, formed by the action of aniline on ethylene bromide: used in the treatment of rheumatism and gout. [< PIPER(INE) + AZ- + -INE²]

pi·per·i·dine (pi·per'ə·dēn) *n. Chem.* A colorless liquid alkaloid, $C_5H_{11}N$, with a strong odor and caustic taste, contained in piperine and made synthetically. [< L *piper* pepper + -ID(E) + -INE²]

pip·er·ine (pip'ər·ēn, -in) *n. Chem.* A colorless crystalline alkaloid, $C_{17}H_{19}NO_3$, contained in pepper and made synthetically: used in medicine as an antipyretic. [< L *piper* pepper + -INE²]

pip·er·o·nal (pip'ər·ə·nal') *n. Chem.* A white crystalline aldehyde, $C_8H_6O_3$, derived from benzene: used in making perfumes. [< G < *piper(in)* piperine]

pipe stem 1 The stem of a tobacco pipe. 2 *pl.* Thin skinny legs. —**pipe·stem** (pīp'stem') *adj.*

pipe·stone (pīp'stōn') *n.* An indurated red clay much valued by the American Indians for making tobacco pipes.

pi·pette (pi·pet', pī-) *n.* 1 A small tube, often graduated, for removing small portions of a fluid. 2 A funnel-like can used in applying liquid decoration. Also **pi·pet'.** [< F, dim. of *pipe* pipe]

pip·ing (pī'ping) *adj.* 1 Playing on the pipe. 2 Hissing or sizzling: *piping* hot. 3 Having a shrill sound. 4 Characterized by peaceful rather than martial music. —*n.* 1 The act of one who pipes. 2 The music of pipes; hence, a wailing or whistling sound. 3 A system of

pipes, as for drainage. 4 A narrow strip of cloth folded on the bias, used for trimming dresses. 5 A cordlike decoration of icing on a cake.

pip·it (pip′it) *n.* 1 One of various larklike singing birds (genus *Anthus*) widely distributed in North America; especially, the common American pipit *(A. spindetta)*; a titlark. 2 The Missouri skylark *(A. spraguei)*: also called *Sprague's pipit.* [Prob. imit.]

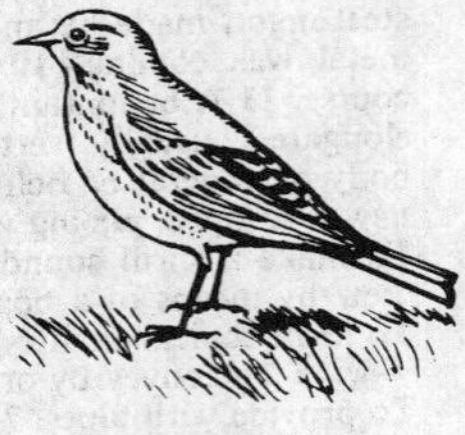

AMERICAN PIPIT
(About 6 inches long)

pip·kin (pip′kin) *n.* 1 A small earthenware jar. 2 A piggin. [? Dim. of PIPE]

pip·pin (pip′in) *n.* 1 An apple of many varieties. 2 A seed; pip. 3 *Slang* An admirable person or thing. [<OF *pepin* seed of a fruit; origin uncertain]

Pip·pin (pip′in) Pepin the Short.

pip·sis·se·wa (pip·sis′ə·wə) *n.* A low-growing evergreen (genus *Chimaphila*) of the heath family, with white or pink flowers and thick leaves, used in medicine as an astringent and diuretic. [<Algonquian. Cf. Cree *pipisisikweu,* lit., it breaks it (gallstone) into pieces.]

pip–squeak (pip′skwēk′) *n.* 1 A petty and contemptible person or thing. 2 A small, insignificant person. [Orig. imit. name for a small German high-velocity shell employed in World War I]

pip·y (pī′pē) *adj.* **pip·i·er, pip·i·est** 1 Pipelike; tubular; containing pipes. 2 Piping; thin and shrill, or reedlike, in sound.

pi·quant (pē′kənt) *adj.* 1 Having an agreeably pungent or tart taste. 2 Interesting; tart; racy; also, charmingly lively. 3 *Obs.* Stinging; sharp. [<F, orig. ppr. of *piquer* sting] **— pi′quan·cy** *n.* **— pi′quant·ly** *adv.*

pique[1] (pēk) *n.* A feeling of irritation or resentment. *— v.t.* **piqued, pi·quing** 1 To excite resentment in. 2 To stimulate or arouse; provoke. 3 To pride (oneself): with *on* or *upon.* ◆ Homophones: *peak, peek.* [<MF <*piquer* sting, prick]

Synonyms (noun): displeasure, grudge, irritation, offense, resentment, umbrage. *Pique* signifies primarily a prick or a sting, as of a nettle; the word denotes a sudden feeling of mingled pain and anger, usually transient, arising from some neglect or *offense,* real or imaginary. *Umbrage* is a deeper and more persistent *displeasure* at being overshadowed or subjected to any treatment that one deems unworthy of oneself. *Resentment* rests on more solid grounds, and is deep and persistent. See ANGER. *Antonyms*: approval, complacency, contentment, delight, gratification, pleasure, satisfaction.

Synonyms (verb): affront, annoy, chafe, displease, fret, goad, irritate, nettle, offend, pain, provoke, rouse, stimulate, sting, stir, urge, vex, wound. See ANGER.

pique[2] (pēk) *n.* In piquet, the scoring of 30 points in one hand before the other side scores at all. *— v.t.* To win a pique from. ◆ Homophones: *peak, peek.* [<F *pic* a mountain peak]

pi·qué (pē·kā′) *n.* A fabric of cotton, rayon, or silk, with raised cord or welts, called wales, running lengthwise in the fabric. [<F, lit., quilted, orig. pp. of *piquer* prick, backstitch]

pi·quet (pē·ket′, *Fr.* pē·ke′) *n.* A two-handed game of cards in which the cards below the seven are excluded: also spelled *picquet.* [<F, ? dim. of *pique* a spade in cards]

pi·ra·cy (pī′rə·sē) *n. pl.* **·cies** 1 Robbery on the high seas. 2 The unauthorized publication, reproduction, or use of another's invention, idea, or literary creation. [<Med. L *piratia* <Gk. *peirateia* <*peiratēs* a pirate]

Pi·rae·us (pī·rē′əs) A town in SE Greece, 5 miles SW of Athens and its ancient port; the leading port and industrial city of Greece: Greek *Peiraievs.*

pi·ra·gua (pi·rä′gwə) *n.* 1 A dug-out canoe. 2 A flat-bottomed boat with two masts: used in the Caribbean Sea. Also called *pirogue.* [<Sp. <Cariban, a dug-out]

Pi·ran·del·lo (pē′rän·del′lō), **Luigi,** 1867–1936, Italian dramatist and novelist.

pi·ra·nha (pi·rä′nyə) *n.* A caribe. Also **pi·ra′ya** (-rä′yä). [<Pg. (Brazilian) <Tupian, toothed fish <*piro* a fish + *sainha* a tooth]

pi·rate (pī′rit) *n.* 1 A rover and robber on the high seas. 2 A vessel engaged in piracy. 3 A person who appropriates without right the work of another. See synonyms under ROBBER. *— v.t. & v.i.* **·rat·ed, ·rat·ing** 1 To practice or commit piracy (upon). 2 To publish or appropriate (the work, ideas, etc., of another) wrongfully or illegally; plagiarize. [<L *pirata* <Gk. *peiratēs* <*peiraein* attack] **— pi·rat·ic** (pī·rat′ik) or **·i·cal** *adj.* **— pi·rat′i·cal·ly** *adv.*

Pi·rith·o·us (pī·rith′ō·əs) In Greek mythology, a king of the Lapithae who, with his friend Theseus, attempted to carry off Persephone from Hades; he was punished by Pluto by being bound to a rock. See LAPITHAE.

Pir·ma·sens (pir′mä·zens) A city in Rhineland-Palatinate, West Germany.

pirn (pûrn) *n. Scot.* 1 A small spindle. 2 Yarn on a shuttle. 3 A spinning-wheel bobbin. 4 A fishing-rod reel.

pi·rogue (pi·rōg′) *n.* A piragua. [<F <Cariban *piragua*]

pir·ou·ette (pir′ōō·et′) *n.* A rapid whirling upon the toes in dancing. *— v.i.* **·et·ted, ·et·ting** To make a pirouette. [<F, lit., a spinning top, prob. <dial. F *piroue* a top; ult. origin uncertain]

Pi·sa (pē′zə, *Ital.* pē′sä) A city on the Arno river in north central Italy; celebrated for its Leaning Tower. **— Pi′san** *adj. & n.*

pis al·ler (pē zà·lā′) *French* The last shift; last resource; literally, to go worse.

Pi·sa·no (pē·sä′nō), **Andrea,** 1270–1348?, Italian goldsmith, sculptor, and architect. **— Giovanni,** 1245?–1320?, Italian sculptor and architect. **— Nicola,** 1225?–78?, Italian sculptor; father of the preceding.

pis·ca·ry (pis′kər·ē) *n. pl.* **·ries** 1 *Law* The right of fishing in waters that belong to another: now usually in the phrase **common of piscary.** 2 A fishing place; fishery. [<Med. L *piscaria* fishing rights, orig. neut. pl. of L *piscarius* of fishing <*piscis* a fish]

pis·ca·tol·o·gy (pis′kə·tol′ə·jē) *n.* The science of fishing. [<L *piscatus,* pp. of *piscari* fish + -LOGY]

pis·ca·tor (pis·kā′tər) *n.* An angler; fisherman. [<L]

pis·ca·to·ri·al (pis′kə·tôr′ē·əl, -tō′rē-) *adj.* 1 Pertaining to fishes or fishing. 2 Engaged in fishing. Also **pis′ca·to′ry.** [<L *piscatorius* <*piscator* a fisherman <*piscatus,* pp. of *piscari* fish] **— pis′ca·to′ri·al·ly** *adv.*

Pis·ces (pis′ēz, pī′sēz) *n. pl.* 1 A class of vertebrates: the true fishes. 2 The twelfth sign of the zodiac. See ZODIAC. 3 *Astron.* A zodiacal constellation south of Pegasus and Andromeda; the Fish or Fishes. See CONSTELLATION. [<L, pl. of *piscis* a fish]

Pisces Aus·tri·nus (ô·strī′nəs) *Astron.* A zodiacal constellation. See CONSTELLATION.

pisci- *combining form* Fish; of or related to fish: *piscivorous.* Also, before vowels, **pisc-.** [<L *piscis* a fish]

pis·ci·cul·ture (pis′i·kul′chər) *n.* The hatching and rearing of fish. **— pis′ci·cul′tur·al** *adj.* **— pis′ci·cul′tur·ist** *n.*

pis·ci·na (pi·sī′nə, -sē′-) *n. pl.* **·nae** (-nē) *Eccl.* A stone basin with a drain in which the priest washes the chalice after administering communion. [<Med. L <L, lit., a fish pond, basin <*piscis* fish] **— pis·ci·nal** (pis′ə·nəl) *adj.*

pis·cine (pis′īn, -in) *adj.* Of, pertaining to, or resembling a fish or fishes. [<L *piscis* a fish + -INE[1]]

pis·civ·o·rous (pi·siv′ər·əs) *adj.* Feeding or subsisting on fish.

Pis·gah (piz′gə), **Mount** A mountain in Jordan, NE of the Dead Sea: in the Old Testament, the peak from which Moses beheld the Promised Land; highest peak, Mount Nebo.

pish (pish) *interj.* An exclamation of contempt. *— v.t. & v.i.* To use this exclamation (to).

Pi·sid·i·a (pi·sid′ē·ə) An ancient country, later a Roman province, of south central Asia Minor. **— Pi·sid′i·an** *adj.*

pi·si·form (pī′sə·fôrm) *adj.* 1 Shaped like a pea. 2 *Anat.* Pertaining to a pea-shaped bone on the inner or ulnar side of the carpus. [<NL *pisiformis* <L *pisum* a pea + *forma* form]

Pi·sis·tra·tus (pī·sis′trə·təs, pi-), 600?–527 B.C., Athenian tyrant and statesman.

pis·mire (pis′mīr) *n.* An ant. [ME *pissemyre* <*pisse* urine + *myre, mire* an ant; with ref. to urinous smell of an anthill]

pis·mo clam (piz′mō) A clam *(Tivela stultorum)* of the southwestern coast of North America. [from *Pismo* beach, California]

pi·so·lite (pī′sə·līt) *n.* A coarse concretionary limestone, composed of globules with a distinct pisiform structure. [<NL *pisolithus* <Gk. *pisos* a pea + *lithos* a stone] **— pi′so·lit′ic** (-lit′ik) *adj.*

piss (pis) *n.* Urine. [<*v.*] *— v.i.* To urinate. *— v.t.* To discharge as or with the urine. [<OF *pissier*; prob. orig. imit.]

Pis·sar·ro (pē·sà·rō′), **Camille,** 1831?–1903, French painter.

pis·ta·chi·o (pis·tä′shē·ō, -tash′ē·ō) *n. pl.* **·chi·os** 1 The edible nut of a small tree (genus *Pistacia*) of western Asia and the Levant. 2 The tree. 3 The flavor produced by, or a delicacy flavored with the pistachio nut. 4 A delicate shade of green, the color of the pistachio nut. Also **pis·tache′** (-täsh′). [<Ital. *pistacchio* <L *pistacium* <Gk. *pistakion* <*pistakē* a pistachio tree, prob. <OPersian *pistah* a pistachio nut]

pis·ta·reen (pis′tə·rēn′) *n.* An old Spanish coin formerly worth about 20 cents: used in the West Indies and United States in the 18th century. [Appar. alter. of Sp. *peseta* a peseta]

pis·til (pis′til) *n. Bot.* The seed-bearing organ of flowering plants, composed of the ovary, with its contained ovules, and the stigma, usually with a style. [<F <L *pistillum* a pestle]

pis·til·late (pis′tə·lit, -lāt) *adj. Bot.* 1 Having a pistil. 2 Having pistils and no stamens. Also **pis′til·lar′y** (-ler′ē).

Pis·to·ia (pēs·tō′yä) A city in north central Italy; where pistols are said to have been first manufactured.

pis·tol (pis′təl) *n.* A small firearm having a stock to fit the hand, and a short barrel: now either the revolver or automatic type fired from one hand. *— v.t.* **·toled** or **·tolled, ·tol·ing** or **·tol·ling** To shoot with a pistol. [<F *pistole* <Ital. *pistola,* prob. ult. <PISTOIA]

Pis·tol (pis′təl) In Shakespeare's *Merry Wives of Windsor* and *Henry IV,* a despicable follower of Falstaff.

pis·tole (pis·tōl′) *n.* An obsolete gold coin of varying value, formerly current in Europe. [<F, short for MF *pistolet* a pistol. Earlier called an *écu,* lit., a shield; the name was changed in humorous allusion to the coin's debasement in value.]

pis·to·leer (pis′tə·lir′) *n.* One who fires a pistol; formerly, a soldier carrying a pistol. Also **pis′to·lier′.**

pis·tol-whip (pis′təl·hwip′) *v.t.* **-whipped** or **-whipt, -whip·ping** To strike or beat with the barrel of a pistol.

pis·ton (pis′tən) *n.* 1 *Mech.* A disk fitted to slide in a cylinder, as in a steam engine, and connected with a rod for receiving the pressure of or exerting pressure upon a fluid in the cylinder. 2 A valve in a wind instrument for altering the pitch of tones. [<F <Ital. *pistone* a piston, var. of *pestone* a large pestle <*pestare* pound <LL *pistare,* freq. of L *pinsere* pound]

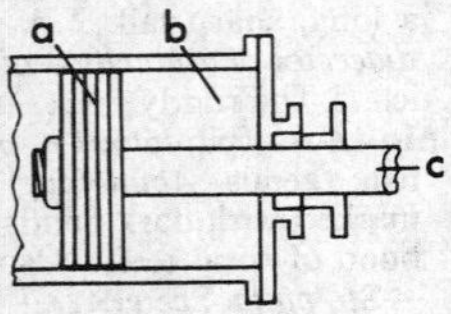

STEAM-ENGINE PISTON
a. Piston. *b.* Cylinder.
c. Piston rod.

piston ring *Mech.* An adjustable ring, usually of cast iron, fitted within a groove on the piston body and designed to prevent leakage of the fluid by expansion against the cylinder wall.

piston rod *Mech.* A rod attached to a piston at one end and to a cross-head or crankpin at the other: used to impart motion.

pit[1] (pit) *n.* 1 A natural or artificial cavity in the ground, especially when relatively wide and deep. 2 A pitfall for snaring animals; snare. 3 An abyss so deep that one cannot return from it, as the grave. 4 Hell. 5 Great distress or trouble. 6 The main floor of the auditorium of a theater, especially, in Great Britain, that portion under the first balcony; also, that part of the audience occupying this portion of the theater. Compare ORCHESTRA, PARQUET. 7 An enclosed space in which

animals trained for combat are pitted against each other. **8** Any natural cavity or depression in the body: the *armpit,* the *pit* of the stomach. **9** An indention like that made by a smallpox pustule; any slight depression or excavation. **10** A thin spot in the cell walls of some plants. **11** That part of the floor of an exchange where a special line of trading is done: the wheat *pit.* **12** A mining excavation, or the shaft of a mine. —*v.* **pit·ted, pit·ting** *v.t.* **1** To mark with dents, pits, or hollows. **2** To put, bury, or store in a pit. **3** To match as antagonists; set in opposition. —*v.i.* **4** To become marked with pits. [OE *pytt* <L *puteus* a well]

pit[2] (pit) *n.* The kernel of certain fruits, as the plum. —*v.t.* **pit·ted, pit·ting** To remove pits from, as fruits. [<Du. <MDu. *pitte* kernel, pith. Akin to PITH.]

pi·ta (pē′tə) *n.* **1** The fiber of the century plant and other allied species of *Agave*: used for making paper, cordage, etc. **2** The plant yielding the fiber. **3** The fiber obtained from several kinds of yucca. [<Sp. <Quechua, a fine thread made from vegetable fiber]

pit–a–pat (pit′ə·pat′) *v.i.* **–pat·ted, –pat·ting** To move or sound with a succession of light, quick steps or pulsations. —*n.* A tapping or succession of taps, steps, or similar sounds. —*adv.* With a rapid succession of light steps, beats or taps; flutteringly. Also spelled *pitty–pat.* [Imit.]

Pit·cairn Island (pit′kârn) A British colony in the South Pacific, settled in 1790 by mutineers of the British ship *Bounty*; 2 square miles; with dependencies 18.5 square miles.

pitch[1] (pich) *n.* **1** A thick, viscous, dark substance obtained by boiling down tar from the residues of distilled turpentine, etc. used in coating seams. **2** Any of a class of hydrocarbon residues obtained from the refining of fats, oils, and greases: linseed *pitch,* cottonseed *pitch,* etc. **3** The resinous sap of pines. **4** Bitumen or asphaltum, especially when unrefined. —*v.t.* To smear, cover, or treat with or as with pitch. [OE *pic*<L *pix, picis* pitch]

pitch[2] (pich) *v.t.* **1** To erect or set up (a tent, camp, etc.). **2** To throw or hurl; toss; fling. **3** To set the level, angle, degree, etc., of. **4** To put in a definite place or position. **5** To set in order; arrange: obsolete except in *pitched battle.* **6** In baseball, to deliver (the ball) to the batter. **7** *Music* To set the pitch or key of. **8** In card games, to determine or announce (the trump suit) by leading a card of that suit. —*v.i.* **9** To fall or plunge forward or headlong. **10** To lurch. **11** To rise and fall alternately at the bow and stern, as a ship: to *pitch* and roll. **12** To incline downward; slope. **13** To encamp; settle. **14** To decide, especially at random: with *on* or *upon.* **15** In baseball, to deliver the ball to the batter; act as pitcher. —**to pitch in** *Colloq.* To start vigorously. —**to pitch into** To attack; assail. —*n.* **1** Point or degree of elevation or depression; especially, the extreme top or bottom point; hence, the ultimate reach. **2** The degree of descent of a declivity; also, a descent, slope, or inclination to the horizon. **3** In building, the inclination of a roof. **4** *Aeron.* **a** An angular displacement about an axis parallel to the lateral axis of an aircraft. **b** The distance an aircraft advances along its flight path for one revolution of the propeller. **5** *Mech.* **a** The amount of advance of a screw thread in a single turn. **b** The distance between two corresponding points on the teeth of a gearwheel. **6** *Physics* The dominant frequency of a sound wave perceived by the ear, ranging from a low tone of about 20 cycles per second to a maximum high approaching 30,000 cycles. **7** *Music* The acuteness or gravity of all the tones of a given instrument with reference to some standard. The pitch of an instrument is expressed by the vibrations per second of some one of its notes, generally middle C, treble C, or the A between them. The high pitch, known as **concert pitch,** has about 450 vibrations for middle A. In 1859 acommission of French musicians and scientists determined the pitch of A′ as 435 (true C″ 522, equal temperament C″ 517) which is known as **French, international,** or **low pitch.** The present standard or **philharmonic pitch** has 440 vibrations for middle A. **8** In games, the act of pitching; a throw; specifically, in baseball, the delivery of the ball by the pitcher; also, the place of pitching or the distance pitched. **9** *Geol.* The inclination or dip of a rock stratum or vein of ore. **10** The act of dipping or plunging downward; the pitching of a ship: correlative of *scend.* **11** A game of cards; seven–up. **12** A location or station for a vender, on a sidewalk, etc. **13** A short, steep stretch of a mountain climb. **14** An attempt to sell or persuade: to make a *pitch.* —**auction pitch** A variety of the game of pitch in which the privilege of pitching is sold at auction by the player entitled to it. —**full pitch** In cricket, bowled to hit the wicket before touching the ground. [ME *picchen*; origin uncertain]

pitch–and–toss (pich′ən·tôs′, -tos′) *n. Brit.* A game played by pitching pennies at a line.

pitch–black (pich′blak′) *adj.* Intensely black; as dark as pitch.

pitch·blende (pich′blend′) *n.* A black or brown uranium oxide with a luster resembling that of pitch: the chief source of uranium and radium. See URANINITE. [<G *pechblende* <*pech* pitch[1] +*blende* blende]

pitch–dark (pich′därk′) *adj.* Very dark; as black as pitch.

pitch·er[1] (pich′ər) *n.* One who pitches; specifically, in baseball, the player who delivers the ball to the batter. [<PITCH[2]]

pitch·er[2] (pich′ər) *n.* **1** A vessel with a spout and a handle, used for holding liquids to be poured out. **2** A peculiar form of leaf suggestive of a pitcher. [<OF *pichier, picher* <LL *bicarium* a jug <Gk. *bikos* a wine jar]

pitch·er·plant (pich′·ər·plant′, -plänt′) *n.* A plant having leaves arranged in the form of pitchers, urns, or goblets which often function as insect traps; especially, the common American pitcher plant (genus *Sarracenia*).

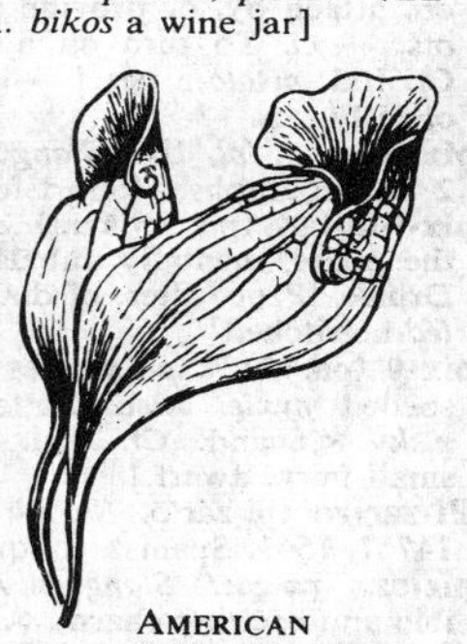

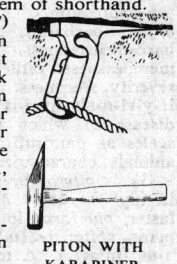

AMERICAN PITCHERPLANT
(From 6 inches to 4 feet tall according to variety)

pitch·fork (pich′·fôrk′) *n.* **1** A large fork with which to handle hay, straw, etc. **2** A tuning fork. —*v.t.* To lift and throw with or as with a pitchfork. [<PITCH[2] + FORK]

pitch·man (pich′mən) *n. pl.* **·men** (-mən) *Slang* One who sells small articles from a temporary stand, as at a fair, etc.; a sidewalk vender.

pitch·out (pich′out′) *n.* **1** In baseball, a pitch deliberately wide of the strike zone so that the catcher has a better chance to throw out a runner trying to steal a base. **2** In football, a lateral pass, usu. from the quarterback to a running back.

pitch pine Any of several American pines that yield pitch; especially, *Pinus rigida* and the longleaf Georgia pine *(P. palustris).*

pitch ratio *Aeron.* The ratio of the pitch of an aircraft propeller to its diameter.

pitch·stone (pich′stōn′) *n.* An acid volcanic glass having a resinous luster and containing more water than obsidian. [Trans. of G *pechstein* <*pech* pitch[1] + *stein* stone]

pitch·y (pich′ē) *adj.* **pitch·i·er, pitch·i·est** **1** Resembling pitch; pitchlike; intensely dark. **2** Full of or daubed with pitch. —**pitch′i·ly** *adv.* —**pitch′i·ness** *n.*

pit·e·ous (pit′ē·əs) *adj.* **1** Exciting pity, sorrow, or sympathy. **2** *Archaic* Affected with or feeling pity. See synonyms under PITIFUL. [<OF *pitos, piteus,* ult. <L *pietas, -tatis.* See PIETY.] —**pit′e·ous·ly** *adv.* —**pit′e·ous·ness** *n.*

pit·fall (pit′fôl′) *n.* A pit contrived for entrapping wild beast or men; hence, any hidden danger. [ME *pitfalle, putfal* <PIT[1]+ *falle, fal* <OE *fealle* a trap]

pith (pith) *n.* **1** *Bot.* The cylinder of soft, spongy tissue in the center of the stems and branches of certain plants. **2** *Ornithol.* The spongy substance of the interior of the shaft of a feather. **3** The marrow of bones or of the spinal cord. **4** Concentrated force; vigor; substance; hence, the essential part; quintessence; gist. —*v.t.* **1** To destroy the central nervous system or spinal cord of, as a frog, by passing a wire through the vertebral column. **2** To remove the pith from, as a plant stem. **3** To kill (cattle) by severing the spinal cord. [OE *pitha.* Akin to PIT[2].]

pith·e·can·thrope (pith′ə·kan′thrōp) *n. Paleontol.* A member of the genus *Pithecanthropus.*

Pith·e·can·thro·pus (pith′ə·kan′thrə·pəs, -kan·thrō′pəs) *n. pl.* **·pi** (-pī) *n. Paleontol.* The type genus of two small–brained Pleistocene primates transitional between ape and man: *P. erectus,* represented by a fossil cranium, femur, and other fragments discovered near Trinil, central Java, in 1891; and *P. robustus,* based upon skeletal remains found in the same area about 1938. Also called *Java man, Trinil man.* [<NL <Gk. *pithēkos* an ape + *anthrōpos* a man] —**pith′e·can′thro·pine** (-pēn, -pin) *adj.*

pith·less (pith′lis) *adj.* Having no pith; lacking force.

pith·y (pith′ē) *adj.* **pith·i·er, pith·i·est** **1** Consisting of pith; like pith. **2** Forcible; effective. See synonyms under TERSE. —**pith′i·ly** *adv.* —**pith′i·ness** *n.*

pit·i·a·ble (pit′ē·ə·bəl) *adj.* **1** Arousing or meriting pity or compassion; pathetic. **2** Insignificant; contemptible. See synonyms under PITIFUL. [<OF *piteable* <*piteer, pitier* pity <*pitie* PITY] —**pit′i·a·ble·ness** *n.* —**pit′i·a·bly** *adj.*

pit·i·ful (pit′i·fəl) *adj.* **1** Calling forth pity or compassion; miserable; wretched. **2** Calling forth a feeling of contempt, because of littleness, meanness, or the like; contemptible. **3** *Archaic* Full of pity; compassionate. —**pit′i·ful·ly** *adv.* —**pit′i·ful·ness** *n.*

Synonyms: abject, base, contemptible, despicable, lamentable, miserable, mournful, moving, paltry, pathetic, piteous, pitiable, sorrowful, touching, woeful, wretched. *Pitiful* originally signified full of pity; as, "the Lord is very *pitiful* and of tender mercy"; but this usage is now archaic, and the meaning in question is appropriated by such words as merciful and compassionate. *Pitiful* and *pitiable* now refer to what may be deserving of pity, *pitiful* being used chiefly for that which is merely an object of thought, *pitiable* for that which is brought directly before the senses; as, a *pitiful* story; a *pitiable* condition. Since pity, however, always implies weakness or inferiority in that which is pitied, *pitiful* and *pitiable* are often used, by an easy transition, for what might awaken pity, but does awaken contempt; as, a *pitiful* excuse; He presented a *pitiable* appearance. *Piteous* is now rarely used in its earlier sense of feeling pity, but in its derived sense applies to what really excites the emotion; as, a *piteous* cry. See MERCIFUL. Compare HUMANE, MERCY, PITY. *Antonyms*: august, beneficent, commanding, dignified, exalted, glorious, grand, great, lofty, mighty, noble, superb.

pit·i·less (pit′i·lis) *adj.* Having no pity or mercy; ruthless. See synonyms under IMPLACABLE. —**pit′i·less·ly** *adv.* —**pit′i·less·ness** *n.*

pit·man (pit′mən) *n.* **1** *pl.* **·men** (-mən) One who works in a pit, as in sawing, mining, etc.; especially, in mining, the man who has charge of the underground machinery. **2** *pl.* **·mans** (-mənz) A rod that connects a rotary with a reciprocating part; a connecting rod.

Pit·man (pit′mən), **Sir Isaac,** 1813–97, English educator; inventor of a system of shorthand.

pi·ton (pi·ton′, *Fr.* pē·tôn′) *n.* An iron spike, with an eye or ring in one end, that can be driven into a crack in rock or ice: used in mountaineering as a hold or support for hand or foot, or fork arabiner and rope. See KARABINER. [<F, ? <Sp., a little horn; ult. origin unknown]

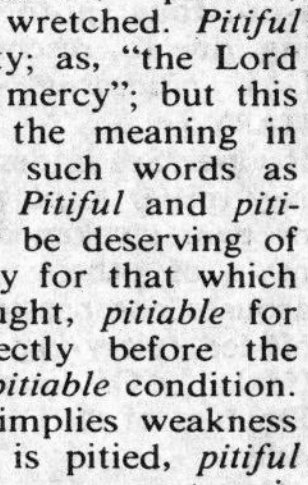

PITON WITH KARABINER AND PITON HAMMER

piton hammer A short–handled hammer for driving in pitons.

Pi·tot tube (pē·tō′) **1** A device for measuring the velocity of a fluid flow, consisting of a narrow

bent tube with its opening against the current and its upper portion above the surface of the fluid. **2** Any similar device for measuring pressure or pressure differences. [after Henri *Pitot*, 1695–1771, French hydraulic engineer]

pit saw A two-handled saw for cutting logs over the mouth of a pit, one man standing in the pit.

Pitt (pit), **William,** 1708–78, first Earl of Chatham, English statesman. —**William,** 1759–1806, English prime minister 1784–1801, 1804–1806; son of the preceding: called "William Pitt the Younger."

pit·tance (pit′əns) *n.* **1** A small allowance of money. **2** Any meager income or remuneration. [<OF *pitance*, orig. a monk's food allotment, pity <Med. L *pietantia* <L *pietas, -tatis.* See PIETY.]

pit·ter–pat·ter (pit′ər·pat′ər) *n.* A rapid series of light sounds or taps. [Varied reduplication of PATTER[1]]

Pitts·burgh (pits′bûrg) A city at the confluence of the Allegheny, Monongahela, and Ohio rivers in SW Pennsylvania.

Pittsburg Landing A village in SW Tennessee; scene of the Civil War battle of Shiloh, 1862.

pit·ty–pat (pit′ē·pat′) See PIT–A–PAT.

pi·tu·i·tar·y (pi·to͞o′ə·ter′ē, -tyo͞o′-) *adj.* **1** Secreting mucus; mucous. **2** Of or pertaining to the pituitary gland. —*n. pl.* **·tar·ies 1** The pituitary gland. **2** Any of various preparations made from extracts of the anterior or posterior lobe of the pituitary gland. [<L *pituitarius* pertaining to mucus <*pituita* phlegm <*sputus*, pp. of *spuere* spit]

pituitary gland *Anat.* A small, rounded body at the base of the brain in vertebrates, consisting of an anterior and a posterior lobe, which secretes hormones having a wide range of effects upon the growth, metabolism, and other functions of the body; the hypophysis cerebri. Also **pituitary body.**

pi·tu·i·tous (pi·to͞o′ə·təs, -tyo͞o′-) *adj.* Containing, due to, resembling, or discharging mucus. [<L *pituitosus* <*pituita* phlegm. See PITUITARY.]

pit viper See under VIPER.

pit·y (pit′ē) *n. pl.* **pit·ies 1** The feeling of grief or pain awakened by the misfortunes or sorrows of others; compassion. **2** That which arouses compassion; misfortune. —*v.t. & v.i.* **pit·ied, pit·y·ing** To feel compassion or pity (for). [<OF *pitet, pitié* <LL *pietas, -tatis.* Doublet of PIETY.] —**pit′i·er** *n.* —**pit′y·ing·ly** *adv.*

Synonyms (noun): commiseration, compassion, condolence, mercy, sympathy, tenderness. *Pity* is a feeling of grief or pain aroused by the weakness, misfortunes, or distresses of others, joined with a desire to help or relieve. *Sympathy* (feeling or suffering with) implies some degree of equality, kindred, or union; *pity* is for what is weak or unfortunate; hence *pity* is often resented where *sympathy* would be welcomed. We have *sympathy* with one in joy or grief, in pleasure or pain, *pity* only for those in suffering or need. *Pity* may be only in the mind, but *mercy* does something for those who are its objects. *Compassion*, like *pity*, is exercised only with respect to the suffering or unfortunate, but combines with the tenderness of *pity* the dignity of *sympathy* and the active quality of *mercy*. *Commiseration* is as tender as *compassion*, but more remote and hopeless; we have *commiseration* for sufferers whom we cannot reach or cannot relieve. *Condolence* is the expression of *sympathy.* See MERCY. *Antonyms*: barbarity, brutality, cruelty, ferocity, hard–heartedness, harshness, inhumanity, mercilessness, pitilessness, rigor, ruthlessness, severity, sternness, truculence.

pit·y·ri·a·sis (pit′i·rī′ə·sis) *n.* **1** *Pathol.* A skin disease in which the epidermis sheds thin scales as dandruff. **2** A disease of domestic animals characterized by dry scales. [<NL <Gk. <*pityron* bran, scale]

più (pyo͞o) *adv. Music* More: *più* allegro, faster; *più* forte, louder; *più* lento, slower; *più* piano, softer. [<Ital. *più* <L *plus*]

Pi·us (pī′əs) **1** A masculine personal name. **2** Appellation of 12 popes. [<L, dutiful, devout]

—**Pius II,** 1405–64, real name Aeneas Silvius Piccolomini, pope 1458–64; diplomat, humanist, and historian.

—**Pius IV,** 1499–1565, real name Giovanni Angelo Medici, pope 1559–65; issued the *Tridentine Creed.*

—**Pius V,** 1504–72, real name Michele Ghislieri, pope 1566–72; promoted the Counter Reformation.

—**Pius VII,** 1742–1823, real name Luigi Barnaba Chiaramonti, pope 1800–23; crowned Napoleon I as emperor of France, was later imprisoned by him at Fontainebleau.

—**Pius IX,** 1792–1878, real name Giovanni Maria Mastai–Ferretti, pope 1846–78; lost temporal power to Victor Emmanuel, 1870.

—**Pius X,** 1835–1914, real name Giuseppi Melchiore Sarto, pope 1903–14; canonized in 1954.

—**Pius XI,** 1857–1939, real name Achille Ratti, pope 1922–39; signed treaty with Mussolini establishing Vatican City as a sovereign state and regulating the position of the Roman Catholic Church in Italy.

—**Pius XII,** 1876–1958, real name Eugenio Pacelli, pope 1939–58.

Pi·ute (pī·o͞ot′) See PAIUTE.

piv·ot (piv′ət) *n.* **1** *Mech.* Something, typically a pin or a short shaft, upon which a related part turns, oscillates, or rotates: often a short cylindrical bearing, fixed on only one end, for carrying or rotating a swinging part. **2** Something on which an important matter hinges or turns; a turning point. **3** *Mil.* In wheeling troops, the soldier, officer, or point upon which the line turns. —*v.t.* To place on, attach by, or provide with a pivot or pivots. —*v.i.* To turn on a pivot; swing. [<F. Cf. Ital. *pivolo* a peg.] —**piv′ot·al** *adj.* —**piv′·ot·al·ly** *adv.*

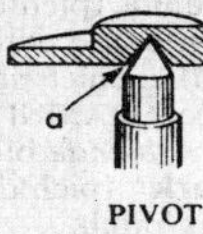

PIVOT
a. Bearing point.

pix (piks) *n. pl. U.S. Slang* **1** Motion pictures. **2** Photographs. [Short for PICTURES]

pix·i·lat·ed (pik′sə·lā′tid) *adj.* **1** Affected by the pixies; mentally unbalanced; fey. **2** *Slang* Drunk. [Prob. alter. of dial. E (Cornish) *pixy–led* bewitched]

pix·y (pik′sē) *n. pl.* **pix·ies** A fairy or elf: also spelled *pyxie.* Also **pix′ie.** [<dial. E *pixey, pisky* <Scand. Cf. dial. Sw. *pysk, pyske* a small fairy, dwarf.]

Pi·zar·ro (pi·zär′ō, *Sp.* pē·thär′rō), **Francisco,** 1475?–1541, Spanish conqueror of Peru.

piz·azz (pə·zaz′) *Slang. n.* A quality of irresistible and exciting charm. Also, **piz·zazz.**

piz·za (pēt′sə, *Ital.* pēt′tsä) *n.* An Italian food comprising a doughy crust overlaid with a mixture of cheese, tomatoes, spices, etc., and baked. [<Ital., ? <dial. Ital. *picca* a pie]

piz·ze·ri·a (pēt′sə·rē′ə) *n.* A place where pizzas are prepared, sold, and eaten. [<Ital. <*pizza* a pizza]

piz·zi·ca·to (pit′sə·kä′tō, *Ital.* pēt′tsē·kä′tō) *Music adj.* Plucked: a direction to the performer that the notes for a bowed instrument are to be played with the fingers. —*n. pl.* **·ti** (-tē) A musical movement or phrase played by plucking the strings. [<Ital., orig. pp. of *pizzicare* pluck, pinch <*pizzare* <*picciare* peck <*picco* a beak]

pla·ca·ble (plā′kə·bəl, plak′ə-) *adj.* Appeasable; yielding; forgiving. [<OF <L *placabilis* < *placare* appease] —**pla′ca·bil′i·ty, pla′ca·ble·ness** *n.* —**pla′ca·bly** *adv.*

plac·ard (plak′ärd) *n.* **1** A printed or written paper publicly displayed, as a proclamation or poster. **2** A tag or plate bearing the owner's name.

—**pla·card** (plə·kärd′, plak′ärd) *v.t.* **1** To announce by means of placards. **2** To post placards on or in. **3** To display as a placard. [<OF *plackart* <*plaquier* plaster, lay flat < M Flemish *placken* bedaub, plaster]

pla·cate (plā′kāt, plak′āt) *v.t.* **·cat·ed, ·cat·ing** To appease the anger of; pacify. [<L *placatus*, pp. of *placare* appease] —**pla′cat·er** *n.*

pla·ca·to·ry (plā′kə·tôr′ē, -tō′rē, plak′ə-) *adj.* Tending or intended to placate or appease. Also **pla′ca·tive.**

place (plās) *n.* **1** A particular point or portion of space, especially that part of space occupied by or belonging to a thing under consideration; a definite locality or location. **2** An occupied situation or building; space regarded as abode or quarters; an estate, town, military post, etc. **3** An open space or square in a city; also, a court or street. **4** Position in relative order; hence, station in life; degree; rank. **5** An office, appointment, or employment; also, rank, position, or station. **6** Room for occupation; hence, reception; welcome; lodgment; seat. **7** Room; stead; hence, precedence: One thing gives *place* to another. **8** A particular passage, as in a book; a text; a topic. **9** The second position among the first three competitors in a horse race. **10** The position of a figure in relation to the other figures of a given arithmetical series or group. —**in place 1** In its natural position; also, in a suitable place, situation, job, etc. **2** In situ. —**in place of** In substitution or exchange for; instead of. —**out of place** Removed from or not situated in the natural or appropriate place, order, or relation; unsuitable; inappropriate; ill–timed. —**to go places** *Slang* To rise to success. —**to take place** To happen; occur. —*v.* **placed, plac·ing** *v.t.* **1** To put in a particular place or position. **2** To put or arrange in a particular relation or sequence. **3** To find a place, situation, home, etc., for. **4** To appoint to a post or office. **5** To identify; classify: Historians *place* him in the time of Nero. **6** To arrange for the satisfaction, handling, or disposition of: to *place* an order for a garbage truck. **7** To bestow or entrust: I *place* my life in your hands. **8** To invest, as funds. **9** To emphasize or resonate tones of (the voice) consciously, as in singing or speaking. —*v.i.* **10** In racing, to finish among the first three contestants; especially, to finish second. See synonyms under PUT, SET. ◆ Homophone: *plaice.* [<OF, ult. <L *platea* a wide street <Gk. *plateia (hodos)* <*platys* wide. Doublet of PIAZZA, PLAZA.]

Synonyms (noun): locality, location, part, position, post, room, site, situation, space, spot, station. See SCENE.

pla·ce·bo (plə·sē′bō) *n. pl.* **·bos** or **·boes 1** In the Roman Catholic Church, the opening antiphon of the vespers for the dead. **2** *Med.* Any harmless substance given to humor a patient or as a test in controlled experiments on the effects of drugs. **3** Anything said to flatter or please. [<L *placebo* I shall please < *placere* please]

place kick In football, a kick for a goal in which the ball is placed on the ground for kicking.

place mat A mat on which a table setting is placed.

place·ment (plās′mənt) *n.* **1** The act of placing or the state of being placed. **2** In football, the putting of the ball in position for a place kick from the field; also, the kick itself.

place name The name of a geographical place.

pla·cen·ta (plə·sen′tə) *n. pl.* **·tas** or **·tae** (-tē) **1** *Anat.* In higher mammals, the vascular, spongy organ of interlocking fetal and maternal tissue by which the fetus is nourished in the uterus. **2** *Bot.* The part of the ovary that supports the ovules. [<NL *placenta (uterina)* (uterine) cake <L, a cake <Gk. *plakoeis, -oentos* a flat cake <*plax, plakos* a flat plate] —**pla·cen′tal, plac·en·tar·y** (plas′ən·ter′ē, plə·sen′tər·ē) *adj.*

pla·cen·tate (plə·sen′tāt) *adj.* Having a placenta.

plac·en·ta·tion (plas′ən·tā′shən) *n.* **1** *Biol.* **a** The process of fetal attachment to the uterus. **b** The type of placenta or manner of its construction. **2** *Bot.* The way in which the seeds are arranged in the pericarp of a plant, or the manner in which the placentas are attached.

Pla·cen·tia (plə·sen′shə) Ancient name for PIACENZA.

Pla·cen·tia Bay (plə·sen′shə) An inlet of the Atlantic extending NE 100 miles into SE Newfoundland.

plac·er[1] (plā′sər) *n.* One who or that which places.

plac·er[2] (plas′ər) *n. Mining* **1** An alluvial or glacial deposit of sand, gravel, etc., containing gold or other mineral in particles large enough to be obtained by washing. **2** Any place where deposits are washed for valuable minerals. [<Am. Sp. *placer* a deposit <Sp. *plaza* a place, ult. <L *platea.* See PLACE.]

placer digging The act of obtaining minerals from deposits by washing.

pla·cet (plā′sit) *n. Latin* **1** Literally, it pleases; permission given by authority; sanction. **2** A vote of assent, as by a council: expressed by saying the word *placet.*

pla·ce·ta (plä·thā′tä) *n. Spanish* A small garden

adjoining a building. Also **pla·ci·ta** (-thē′tä).

plac·id (plas′id) *adj.* Having a smooth, unruffled surface, as a sheet of still water; unruffled; calm. See synonyms under CALM, PACIFIC. [<L *placidus* pleasing <*placere* please] — **pla·cid·i·ty** (plə·sid′ə·tē), **plac′id·ness** *n.* — **plac′id·ly** *adv.*

plack (plak) *n.* A small copper coin, formerly current in Scotland. [Prob. <Flemish *placke,* a small coin of Brabant and Flanders <*plak* a flat disk. Doublet of PLAQUE.]

plack·et (plak′it) *n.* **1** The opening or slit in the upper part of a petticoat or skirt: also **placket hole.** **2** A pocket in a woman's skirt. [? Var. of *placat,* var. of *placard,* in obs. sense of "a breastplate, top of a skirt"]

plac·oid (plak′oid) *adj.* Platelike, as the hard, spiny scales resembling teeth found on sharks and rays. — *n.* A fish having platelike scales; an elasmobranch. [<Gk. *plax, plakos* a flat plate + -OID]

pla·fond (plȧ·fôṅ′) *n. Archit.* **1** A flat or arched ceiling, decorated with painting or carving. **2** The under side of a projecting member (cornice, soffit, balcony, etc.); the under face of an architrave between columns, or of a staircase. **3** A painting on a ceiling. [<F <MF *platfond* <*plat* flat + *fond* bottom <L *fundus*]

pla·gal (plā′gəl) *adj. Music* Designating a cadence in which the tonic chord is preceded by the major or minor chord of the subdominant. [<Med. L *plagalis* <*plaga* a plagal mode <Med. Gk. *plagios (ēchos)* <Gk., oblique <*plagos* a side]

pla·gia·rism (plā′jə·riz′əm, -jē·ə-) *n.* The act of plagiarizing, or something plagiarized. — **pla′gia·rist** *n.* — **pla′gia·ris′tic** *adj.*

pla·gia·rize (plā′jə·riz, -jē·ə-) *v.* **·rized, ·riz·ing** *v.t.* **1** To appropriate and pass off as one's own (the writings, ideas, etc., of another). **2** To appropriate and use passages, ideas, etc., from. — *v.i.* **3** To commit plagiarism. Also *Brit.* **pla′gia·rise.** — **pla′gia·riz′er** *n.*

pla·gia·ry (plā′jər·ē, -jē·ər·ē) *n.* **1** Plagiarism, the act or its result. **2** A plagiarist. [<L *plagiarius* a kidnapper, a plagiarist <L *plagium* a kidnapping <Gk. *plagios* oblique, treacherous]

plagio- *combining form* Oblique; slanting: *plagiotropism.* Also, before vowels, **plagi-.** [<Gk. *plagios* slanting]

pla·gi·o·clase (plā′jē·ə·klās′) *n.* Feldspar consisting chiefly of the silicates of sodium, calcium, and aluminum, and crystallizing in the triclinic system. [<PLAGIO- + Gk. *klasis* a cleavage] — **pla·gi·o·clas′tic** (-klas′tik) *adj.*

pla·gi·ot·ro·pism (plā′jē·ot′rə·piz′əm) *n. Bot.* Oblique geotropism, under the influence of which certain plant organs grow at an angle from the vertical. — **pla·gi·o·trop·ic** (plā′jē·ə·trop′ik), **pla′gi·ot′ro·pous** *adj.*

plague (plāg) *n.* **1** Anything troublesome or harassing, producing mental distress; affliction. **2** A pestilence or epidemic disease of man or animals, occurring in many forms and usually intensely malignant and contagious: bubonic *plague,* pulmonary *plague.* **3** Any great natural evil or calamity. **4** *Colloq.* Nuisance; bother. See synonyms under ABOMINATION. — *v.t.* **plagued, pla·guing 1** To harass or torment; vex; annoy. **2** To afflict with plague or disaster. [<OF *plage, plague* <LL *plaga* a pestilence <L, a stroke, prob. <dial. Gk. (Doric) *plaga* a stroke <*plag-,* root of *plēssein* strike]

pla·guy (plā′gē) *Colloq. adj.* Characterized by vexation or annoyance; troublesome. — *adv.* Vexatiously; intolerably. — **pla′gui·ly** *adv.*

plaice (plās) *n.* **1** A European flounder (*Pleuronectes platessa*). **2** One of various American flatfishes, as the summer flounder (*Paralichthys dentatus*). ◆ Homophone: *place.* [<OF *plaïz* <LL *platessa,* prob. <Gk. *platys* broad]

plaid (plad) *adj.* Having a tartan pattern; checkered. — *n.* An oblong woolen scarf of tartan or checkered pattern, worn in the Scottish Highlands as a cloak fastened over one shoulder; also, any fabric of this pattern. [<Scottish Gaelic *plaide* a blanket <*peallaid* a sheepskin <*peall* <L *pellis* a skin] — **plaid′ed** *adj.*

plain[1] (plān) *adj.* **1** Having no noticeable elevation or depression; flat; smooth. **2** Presenting few difficulties; easy. **3** Clear; understandable: *plain* English; also, straightforward; guileless. **4** Lowly in condition or station; unlearned. **5** Having no conspicuous ornamentation; unadorned; unvariegated; in the case of cloths, not figured or twilled. **6** Homely. **7** Not rich, as food. — *n.* An expanse of level, treeless land; a prairie. ◆ Homophone: *plane.* [<OF <L *planus* flat; *n.,* doublet of PLAN] — **plain′ly** *adv.* — **plain′·ness** *n.*

Synonyms (adj.): clear, distinct, explicit, intelligible, perspicuous, straightforward, transparent, unadorned, unambiguous, unequivocal. That is *clear* which offers no impediment to vision—is not dim, dark, or obscure. *Transparent* refers to the medium through which a substance is seen, *clear* to the substance itself, without reference to anything to be seen through it; we speak of a stream as *clear* when we think of the water itself; we speak of it as *transparent* with reference to the ease with which we see objects at the bottom. *Plain* is level to the thought, so that one goes straight on without difficulty or hindrance; as, *plain* language; a *plain* statement; a *clear* explanation. *Perspicuous* is often equivalent to *plain,* but *plain* never wholly loses the meaning of *unadorned,* so that we can say the style is *perspicuous* even if highly ornate, when we could not call it at once ornate and *plain.* See APPARENT, BLANK, CLEAR, EVIDENT, EXPLICIT, HORIZONTAL, LEVEL, MANIFEST, NOTORIOUS, RUSTIC, SMOOTH. *Antonyms*: see synonyms for EQUIVOCAL, OBSCURE.

plain[2] (plān) *v.i.* **1** *Dial.* To complain. **2** *Obs.* To mourn. ◆ Homophone: *plane.* [<OF *plaign-,* stem of *plaindre* <L *plangere* beat the breast, lament]

plain-clothes man (plān′klōz′, -klōthz′) A member of a police force not in uniform; specifically, a detective.

plain-deal·ing (plān′dē′ling) *adj.* Dealing frankly and sincerely. — *n.* Frankness; straightforwardness.

plain·dress (plān′dres′) *n.* A radiotelegraph message carrying the address either in plain text or in a cipher different from that used for the message. Compare CODRESS. [<PLAIN + (AD)DRESS]

plain-laid (plān′lād′) *adj.* Consisting of strands twisted together in the ordinary way: a *plain-laid* rope.

Plains Indian A member of any of the tribes of American Indians formerly inhabiting the Great Plains of North America, belonging variously to the Algonquian, Athapascan, Caddoan, Kiowan, Siouan, and Uto-Aztecan linguistic stocks, but having in common the nomadic culture of the plains and dependence on the buffalo: also called *Buffalo Indian.*

plains·man (plānz′mən) *n. pl.* **·men** (-mən) A dweller on the plains.

Plains of Abraham See ABRAHAM, PLAINS OF.

plain people *U.S.* The Amish, Mennonites, and Dunkers: so called from their plain dress.

plain song The old ecclesiastical chant, having simple melody, not governed by strict rules of time, but by accentuation of the words. Also **plain chant.** [Trans. of Med. L *cantus planus*]

plain-spo·ken (plān′spō′kən) *adj.* Plainly or frankly uttered: a *plain-spoken* promise; also, habitually frank.

plain·stanes (plān′stānz′) *n. Scot.* A pavement; flagstones, as opposed to cobbles. Also **plain′·stones′** (-stōnz′).

plaint (plānt) *n.* **1** Audible utterance of sorrow or grief; lamentation; a complaint. **2** In English law, a writ setting forth a grievance and asking redress. [<OF *plainte* <Med. L *plancta* <L, pp. fem. of *plangere* lament]

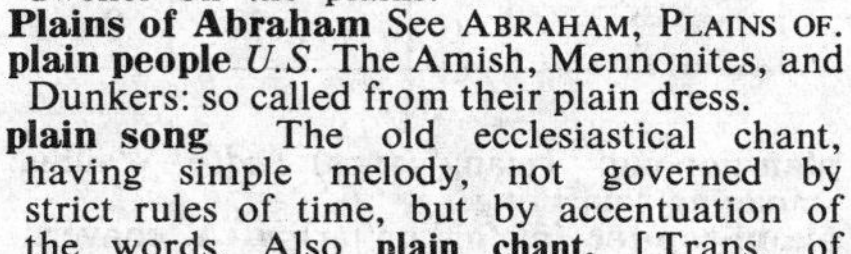

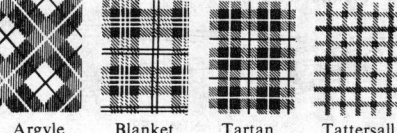

Argyle Blanket Tartan Tattersall

PLAIDS

plain text In cryptography, the original text of a message to be converted into or reconverted from a code or cipher cryptogram: also called *clear text.*

plain·tiff (plān′tif) *n.* The party that begins an action at law; the complaining party in an action. [<OF *plaintif, plaintive* plaintive <L *planctus.* See PLAINT.]

plain·tive (plān′tiv) *adj.* Expressing a subdued sadness; mournful. [<OF, fem. of *plaintif*] — **plain′tive·ly** *adv.* — **plain′tive·ness** *n.*

plait (plāt, *Brit.* plat) *v.t.* **1** To braid. **2** To pleat. **3** To make by pleating or braiding. — *n.* **1** A braid, especially of hair. **2** A pleat. [<OF *pleit* <L *plicitum* a folded thing, orig. pp. neut. of *plicare* fold]

plan (plan) *n.* **1** An arrangement of means or steps for the attainment of some object; a scheme; method; design. **2** A drawing showing the proportion and relation of parts, as of a building; any outline sketch; draft. **3** A mode of action. **4** One of a number of hypothetical planes perpendicular to the line of vision in which the size of the pictured object is increased or diminished proportionately to the distance from the eye at which they are interposed. See PERSPECTIVE. See synonyms under DESIGN, IDEA, PROJECT, PURPOSE, SKETCH. — *v.* **planned, plan·ning** *v.t.* **1** To form a scheme or method for doing, achieving, etc. **2** To make a plan of, as a building; design. **3** To have as an intention or purpose. — *v.i.* **4** To make plans. [<OF, a plane (surface), a ground plan <Ital. *plano* <L *planus* flat. Doublet of PLAIN[1], *n.*] — **plan′·ner** *n.*

Synonyms (verb): concoct, contrive, design, devise, invent, plot, project, propose, purpose, scheme, sketch. Compare BREW, PROPOSE.

pla·nar (plā′nər) *adj.* Of or pertaining to a plane; lying in one plane; flat. [<L *planaris* <*planum* a plane <*planus* flat]

pla·nar·i·an (plə·nâr′ē·ən) *n. Zool.* Any turbellarian, chiefly aquatic flatworm, usually dark-colored, having a body covered with cilia: a few species dwell in moist places upon land, and others are parasitic in or upon holothurians. [<NL *Planaria,* genus name of the flatworm <L, fem. of *planarius* flat <*planus*]

planch (planch, plänch) *n.* A plank; board. Also **planche.** [<OF *planche* <LL *planca*]

planch·et (plan′chit) *n.* A piece of metal ready to receive an impression. [Dim. of PLANCH, in sense "a flat plate of metal"]

plan·chette (plan·chet′, -shet′) *n.* **1** A small board, usually resting on a vertical pencil and two casters; believed by some to spell out messages, as on a ouija board, when the fingers are rested lightly upon it, independently of the volition of the persons touching it: used in the investigation of psychic phenomena. [<F, dim. of *planche* a plank]

Planck (plängk), **Max,** 1858–1947, German physicist; developed the quantum theory.

Planck's constant *Physics* The quantum of action (symbol *h*); a universal constant having the value of approximately 6.624×10^{-27} erg second. For any specified radiation, the magnitude of the energy emitted is given by the product *hν,* where *ν* is the frequency of the radiation in cycles per second.

Plan·çon (plän·sôṅ′), **Pol,** 1854–1914, French bass singer.

plane[1] (plān) *n.* **1** *Geom.* A surface such that a straight line joining any two of its points lies wholly within the surface. **2** Hence, any flat or uncurved surface. **3** A grade of development; stage; level, as of thought, knowledge, rank, etc. **4** *Aeron.* A supporting surface of an airplane: often used in combination: *monoplane.* **5** An airplane. — *adj.* **1** Lying in a plane; level; flat. **2** Having a flat surface; dealing only with flat surfaces: *plane* geometry. See synonyms under HORIZONTAL, LEVEL, SMOOTH. ◆ Homophone: *plain.* [Var. of PLAIN[2], *n.*; refashioned after L *planus* flat]

plane[2] (plān) *n.* **1** A tool used for smoothing boards or other surfaces of wood. **2** A trowel-like tool for striking off clay that projects above the mold. — *v.* **planed, plan·ing** *v.t.* **1** To make smooth or even with or as with a plane. **2** To remove with or as with a plane. — *v.i.* **3** To use a plane. **4** To do the work of a plane. ◆ Homophone: *plain.* [<MF *plane* <OF *plain* <LL *plana* a plane <*planare* plane <L *planus* flat]

plane[3] (plān) *n.* A plane tree. ✦ Homophone: *plain*. [<OF *plane* < *plasne* <L *platanus* <Gk. *platanos* < *platys* broad; because of its broad leaves]

plane[4] (plān) *v.i.* **planed, plan·ing** 1 To rise partly out of the water, as a power boat when driven at high speed. 2 To glide; soar. 3 To travel by airplane. ✦ Homophone: *plain*. [<F *planer* < *plan* a plane <L *planus* flat]

plan·er (plā′nər) *n.* 1 A machine for planing wood or metal. 2 A smooth wooden block used for leveling a form of type, etc. 3 One who or that which planes. [<PLANE[2]]

planer tree A small tree (*Planera aquatica*) allied to and resembling the elms, but with nut-like wingless fruit and small ovate leaves, growing in wet places in the southern United States; the water elm. [after J.J. *Planer*, 1743–1789, German botanist]

plane sailing *Nav.* A system for ascertaining a vessel's position on the supposition that the earth's surface is plane, not spherical.

plane–sheer (plān′shir′) See PLANK–SHEER.

plan·et (plan′it) *n.* 1 *Astron.* One of the non-self-luminous bodies of the solar system revolving around the sun as their center of motion. Those within the Earth's orbit, Mercury and Venus, are called **inferior planets;** those beyond it, the **superior planets,** are Mars, the asteroids or planetoids (known collectively as **minor planets**), Jupiter, Saturn, Uranus, Neptune, and Pluto. 2 In ancient astronomy, one of the seven heavenly bodies (the Sun, Moon, Mercury, Venus, Mars, Jupiter, and Saturn) that have an apparent motion among the fixed stars. 3 One of these bodies considered in relation to its supposed influence on human beings and their affairs. [<OF *planete* <LL *planeta* <Gk. *(asteres) planētai* wandering (stars) < *planaesthai* wander]

at the same time rotating axially. 5 In astrology, under the influence or domination of some of the planets. [<LL *planetarius* an astrologer < *planeta* PLANET]

plan·e·tes·i·mal (plan′ə·tes′ə·məl) *Astron. adj.* Of or pertaining to the small, solid, planetary bodies of space. — *n.* Any of such bodies resembling a meteorite in composition and revolving around a larger mass as a planet revolves around the sun. [<PLANET + (IN-FINIT)ESIMAL]

planetesimal hypothesis *Astron.* The hypothesis that the solar system developed from large masses of planetesimals which, by the crossing of orbits, gravity, and electric attraction, coalesced gradually.

plan·et·fall (plan′it·fôl′) *n.* The descent of a rocket or artificial satellite to the surface of a planet.

plan·e·toid (plan′ə·toid) *n.* An asteroid. — **plan′e·toi′dal** *adj.*

plan·e·tol·o·gy (plan′ə·tol′ə·jē) *n.* The science that treats of the history, composition, and structure of the planets and other natural bodies, as comets, asteroids, etc., in orbit around the sun.

plane tree Any tree of the genus *Platanus* characterized by broad, lobed leaves and spreading growth, as the sycamore or buttonwood. [See PLANE[3]]

plan·et–struck (plan′it–struk′) *adj.* Affected by the influence of planets; blasted; moon-struck. Also **plan′et–strick′en** (–strik′ən).

planet wheel One of the smaller wheels in an epicyclic train.

plan·gent (plan′jənt) *adj.* Dashing noisily; resounding; reverberating, as the sound of bells; plaintive, as certain qualities of the voice. [<L *plangens, -entis,* ppr. of *plangere* mourn] — **plan′gen·cy** *n.* — **plan′gent·ly** *adv.*

TABLE OF MAJOR PLANETS

NAME	Symbol	Distance from sun: millions of miles	Mean diameter: miles	Period of sidereal revolution	Period of rotation	No. of satellites	Mass: Earth considered as 1.	Escape velocity: in miles per second.
Mercury	☿	36	3,000	88 days	88 days?	0	0.0543	2
Venus	♀	67	7,600	225 "	20–30 d.	0	0.8136	6.3
Earth	♁	93	7,918	365.25 d.	23 h. 56 m.	1	1.0000	6.95
Mars	♂	142	4,200	687 days	24 h. 37 m.	2	0.1069	3.1
Jupiter	♃	483	87,000	12 years	9 h. 50 m.	12	318.35	37.
Saturn	♄	886	72,000	29.5 "	10 h. 14 m	9	95.3	22.
Uranus	♅	1780	29,600	84 "	10 h. 45 m.	5	14.58	13.
Neptune	♆	2790	27,700	165 "	15 h. 48 m.	2	17.26	15.
Pluto	♇	3670	4,000	248 "	?	0	.1?	?

plane·ta·ble (plān′tā′bəl) *n.* A surveying instrument used in mapping in the field. [<PLANE[1] + TABLE]

plan·e·tar·i·um (plan′ə·târ′ē·əm) *n. pl.* **·tar·i·ums** or **·tar·i·a** 1 An apparatus for exhibiting the features of the heavens as they exist at any time and for any place on earth, consisting of a suitably mounted projector installed in a room having a circular dome. 2 An apparatus or model representing the planetary system. [<NL *planetarius* PLANETARY]

plan·e·tar·y (plan′ə·ter′ē) *adj.* 1 Of or pertaining to a planet or the planets: the *planetary* bodies. 2 Mundane; terrestrial. 3 Having the character anciently ascribed to the planets; wandering; erratic: a *planetary* career. 4 *Mech.* Pertaining to or noting a type of gearing in which one or more small wheels mesh with the toothed circumference of a larger wheel, around which they revolve,

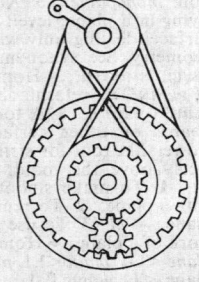

PLANETARY GEARING

plan·gor·ous (plang′gər·əs) *adj.* Wailing; moaning; lamenting.

pla·ni·cop·ter (pla′ni·kop′tər) *n.* A convertiplane.

pla·ni·form (plā′nə·fôrm, plan′ə-) *adj.* Having the surfaces nearly flat.

plan·i·gale (plan′i·gāl) *n.* A tiny insectivorous marsupial (*Planigali ingrami*) of Australia, the smallest of the marsupials.

pla·nim·e·ter (plə·nim′ə·tər) *n.* An instrument for measuring the area of any plane surface, however irregular, by moving a pointer around its boundary and reading the indications of a scale. [<F *planimètre* < *plani-* + *-mètre* -METER] — **pla·ni·met·ric** (plā′nə·met′rik, plan′ə-) or **·ri·cal** *adj.* — **pla·nim′e·try** *n.*

PLANIMETER

plan·ish (plan′ish) *v.t.* To condense, smooth, toughen, or polish, as metal, by hammering, rolling, etc. [<MF *planiss-,* stem of *planir* flatten < *plan* flat <L *planus* flat]

plan·i·sphere (plan′ə·sfir) *n.* A plane projection of the sphere; especially, a polar pro-

jection of the heavens on a chart, which shows the stars visible at a given place and time. [<OF *planisphère* <Med. L *planisphaerium* <L *planus* flat + *sphaera* a sphere]

plank (plangk) *n.* 1 A broad piece of sawed timber, thicker than a board. 2 Timber when sawed into planks. 3 Anything that sustains or upholds; a support. 4 One of the principles of a political platform. — **to walk the plank** To walk off a plank projecting from the side of a ship: a method once used by pirates for executing prisoners. — *v.t.* 1 To cover, furnish, or lay with planks. 2 To broil or bake and serve on a plank, as fish. 3 *Colloq.* To put down emphatically or forcibly. 4 *Colloq.* To pay: with *out, down,* etc. [<AF *planke* <LL *planca* a board, slab, prob. <Gk. *plax, plakos* flat]

plank·ing (plangk′ing) *n.* 1 The act of laying planks; also, anything made of planks. 2 Planks collectively.

plank–sheer (plangk′shir′) *n. Naut.* A timber extending around a vessel's deck, covering and fastening the timberheads: also called *plane–sheer.* [Var. of *planesheer,* alter. of *plancher* <OF *planchier* planking, floor < *planche* PLANCH]

plank·ton (plangk′tən) *n. Biol.* The floating, weakly swimming or drifting plant or animal organic life of the sea, as distinguished from the coastal or the bottom forms: used also of analogous life forms in fresh-water lakes. Compare BENTHOS. [<G <Gk., neut. of *planktos* drifting, wandering < *plazesthai* wander] — **plank·ton·ic** (plangk·ton′ik) *adj.*

plano–[1] *combining form* Roaming; wandering: *planoblast.* Also, before vowels, **plan–.** [<Gk. *planos* wandering]

plano–[2] *combining form* Flat; level; plane: *plano–convex:* also, before vowels, **plan–.** Also **plani–.** [<L *planus* flat]

plan·o·blast (plan′ə·blast) *n. Zool.* The free-swimming or medusa form of a hydroid. [<PLANO-[1] + Gk. *blastos* a sprout]

pla·no–con·cave (plā′nō·kon′kāv) *adj.* Flat or plane on one side and concave on the other. See illustration under LENS. [<PLANO-[2] + CONCAVE]

pla·no–con·vex (plā′nō·kon′veks) *adj.* Flat or plane on one side and convex on the other. See illustration under LENS. [<PLANO-[2] + CONVEX]

pla·nom·e·ter (plə·nom′ə·tər) *n.* A device for gaging a plane surface. [<PLANO-[2] + -METER] — **pla·nom′e·try** *n.*

plant (plant, plänt) *n.* 1 A living organism belonging to the vegetable, as distinguished from the animal kingdom, having typically rigid cell walls, promoting an indefinite growth of tissue, and characterized by growth from the synthesis of simple, usually inorganic food materials from soil, water, and air or, in some cases, from other organisms. 2 Loosely, one of the smaller forms of vegetable life, in distinction from shrubs and trees. 3 A set of machines, tools, apparatus, etc., necessary to conduct a manufacturing enterprise or other business: a chemical *plant:* often including the buildings and grounds, or, in case of a railroad, the rolling stock, but not including the material or product; hence, the permanent appliances needed for any institution, as a post office, a college, etc. 4 A sapling; a slip or cutting from a tree or bush. 5 *Slang* A trick; dodge; imposition; swindle. 6 A person placed in a theater audience to encourage applause, speak lines, or contribute to the action of a play. 7 An apparently trivial passage early in a story or play that later becomes important in shaping the outcome of the action. — *v.t.* 1 To set in the ground for growing. 2 To furnish with plants or seed: to *plant* a field. 3 To set or place firmly; put in position. 4 To found; establish. 5 To introduce into the mind; implant, as an idea or principle. 6 To introduce into a country, as a breed of animal. 7 To deposit (fish or spawn) in a body of water. 8 To stock, as a river. 9 To bed (oysters). 10 *Slang* To deliver, as a blow. 11 *Slang* To place or station for purposes of deception, observation, etc.: to *plant* evidence. 12 *Slang* To hide; bury. [OE *plante* <L *planta* a sprout, something planted] *Synonyms (verb):* seed, set, sow. We *set* or *set out* slips, cuttings, young trees, etc., but we may also be said to *plant* them; we *plant*

corn, potatoes, etc., which we put in definite places, as in hills; we *sow* wheat or other small grains and seeds which are scattered in the process. Land is *seeded* to grass. See SET. *Antonyms*: eradicate, extirpate, uproot.

Plan·tag·e·net (plan·taj′i·net) A patronymic of the English sovereigns from Henry II (1154) to the accession of the House of Tudor (1485): from the sprig of broom (in Medieval Latin, *planta genista*) worn by Geoffrey of Anjou, founder of the line. See table under ENGLAND.

plan·tain[1] (plan′tin) *n.* An annual or perennial herb (genus *Plantago*) widely distributed in temperate regions; especially, the **common** or **greater plantain** *(P. major)* with large, ovate, or oval, ribbed leaves. [<OF <L *plantago, -ginis* <*planta* sole of the foot; with ref. to its broad, flat leaves]

plan·tain[2] (plan′tin) *n.* A tropical perennial herb *(Musa paradisiaca)*; also, its edible, bananalike fruit [Earlier *plantan* <Sp. *plátano, plántano* <Cariban *balatanna*; infl. in form by PLANTAIN[1]]

plan·tar (plan′tər) *adj.* Pertaining to the sole of the foot. See illustration under FOOT. [<L *plantaris* <*planta* sole of the foot]

plant association *Ecol.* A group of plants (including several species) in a certain area, needing similar nourishment and growing conditions, and taking on a similar aspect.

plan·ta·tion (plan·tā′shən) *n.* **1** Any place that is planted; especially, a farm or estate of many acres in the southern United States planted in cotton, tobacco, rice, or sugarcane, and formerly worked by slave labor. **2** A colony. **3** An oyster bed or oyster farm. **4** A grove cultivated to provide a certain product. **5** The act of planting. [<L *plantatio, -onis* a planting <*plantare* plant]

plant·er (plan′tər) *n.* **1** One who plants. **2** An early settler or colonizer. **3** An owner of a plantation. **4** An agricultural implement for dropping seed in soil. **5** A decorative container in which shrubs and flowers are planted, especially outdoors.

plan·ti·grade (plan′tə·grād) *adj.* Walking on the whole sole of the foot, as men, bears, etc. —*n.* A plantigrade animal. Compare DIGITIGRADE. [<F <NL *plantigradus* <L *planta* the sole of the foot + *gradi* walk]

plant louse **1** A small insect (family *Aphididae*) which infests plants and sucks the juices from leaves and stalks; an aphid. See illustration under INSECTS (injurious). **2** A similar leaping insect (family *Psyllidae*).

plan·u·la (plan′yə·lə) *n. pl.* **·lae** (-lē) *Zool.* The free-moving, ciliated embryo of certain coelenterates, as the hydroids. [<NL <L, dim. of *planus* flat] **—plan′u·lar, plan′u·late** (-lit, -lāt) *adj.*

plaque (plak) *n.* **1** A plate, disk, or slab of metal, porcelain, ivory, etc., artistically ornamented, as for wall decoration. **2** A brooch. **3** A deposit of bacteria-bearing mucus on teeth, often leading to decay. [<F <MDu. *placke* flat disk, tablet. Doublet of PLACK.]

plash[1] (plash) *n.* A slight splash. —*v.t.* & *v.i.* To splash lightly, as water. [Prob. imit.] **—plash′y** *adj.*

plash[2] (plash) *n.* A small pool. [OE *plæsc* a pool]

plash[3] (plash) *v.t.* **1** To bend down and interweave, as twigs or branches, so as to form a hedge or arbor. **2** To form or trim (a hedge) in this manner. [<OF *plaissier* <L *plectere* weave] **—plash′er** *n.*

-plasia *combining form* Growth; development; formative action: *heteroplasia*: also spelled *-plasy.* Also **-plasis.** [<Gk. *plasis* a molding <*plassein* make, form]

-plasm *combining form Biol.* The viscous material of an animal or vegetable cell: *protoplasm.* [<Gk. *plasma* figure, form <*plassein* mold, make]

plas·ma (plaz′mə) *n.* **1** The liquid portion of nutritive animal fluids, as blood, lymph, or intercellular fluid. **2** The clear, fluid portion of blood, freed from blood cells and used for transfusions. **3** The viscous material of a cell; protoplasm. **4** A green, translucent variety of chalcedony, used among the Romans as a gem. **5** *Physics* That region in a gas-discharge tube which is rendered nearly neutral by the presence of approximately equal numbers of positive ions and electrons. [<LL, a molded thing <Gk. *plasma* <*plassein* mold, form] **—plas·mat·ic** (plaz·mat′ik), **plas′mic** *adj.*

plasma engine A reaction engine producing a small but sustained thrust by emission of a plasma jet. Compare ION ENGINE.

plasma gun *Physics* A magnetohydrodynamic apparatus for the generation of plasma and its forcible expulsion as a plasma jet.

plasma jet *Physics* A beam of plasma ejected from a specially constructed generator which utilizes the pinch effect in forming a brilliantly luminous jet of extremely high energy and temperature.

plasmo- *combining form* Plasma; of or pertaining to plasma: *plasmolysis.* Also, before vowels, **plasm-.** [See -PLASM]

Plas·mo·chin (plaz′mə·kin) *n.* Proprietary name of a white to pale-yellow, tasteless powder, $C_{19}H_{20}N_3O$, synthesized from quinoline, used as an antimalarial drug.

plas·mo·di·um (plaz·mō′dē·əm) *n. pl.* **·di·a** (-dē·ə) **1** A mobile, naked, slimy mass of protoplasm resulting from the fusion of ameboid organisms, typical of the slime molds. **2** A malaria parasite. [<NL <Gk. *plasma* + *eidos* form]

Plas·mo·di·um (plaz·mō′dē·əm) *n.* A genus of protozoan blood parasites (class *Sporozoa*) which includes the causative agents of malaria in man and animals, especially *P. vivax, P. malariae,* and *P. falciparum.*

plas·moid (plaz′moid) *n. Physics* A small particle of plasma ejected from a plasma gun and capable of reacting as a unit under the influence of a wide range of magnetic, electrical, and thermal forces.

plas·mol·y·sis (plaz·mol′ə·sis) *n. Biol.* The process of withdrawing water from the protoplasm of a cell, resulting in shrinkage of the cell body.

plas·mo·lyze (plaz′mə·līz) *v.t.* & *v.i.* **·lyzed, ·lyz·ing** To subject to or undergo plasmolysis.

plas·mo·some (plaz′mə·sōm) *n. Biol.* A nucleolus. [<PLASMO- + Gk. *sōma* a body]

Plas·sey (plas′ē) A village north of Calcutta in West Bengal, India; scene of Clive's victory over the nawab of Bengal, 1757.

-plast *combining form* An organized living particle or cell: *protoplast.* [<Gk. *plastos* formed <*plassein* form]

plas·te·in (plas′tē·in, -tēn) *n. Biochem.* Any of a class of proteins formed in the presence of pepsin during digestion. [<G *plastein* <Gk. *plastos* formed]

plas·ter (plas′tər, pläs′-) *n.* **1** A composition of lime, sand, and water for coating walls and partitions. **2** Calcined gypsum for making sculptor's casts, etc.; plaster of Paris. **3** A viscid substance spread on linen, silk, etc., and applied to some part of the body: used for healing purposes. —*v.t.* **1** To cover or overlay with or as with plaster. **2** To apply a plaster to, as a boil or part of the body. **3** To apply like plaster or a plaster: to *plaster* posters on a fence. **4** To cause to adhere or lay flat like plaster. **5** *Slang* To strike with great force or effect. [OE <LL *plastrum* <L *emplastrum* <Gk. *emplastron, emplaston* <*en-* on + *plassein* daub, mold; defs. 1, 2, and 4 reborrowed in ME from cognate OF *plastre*] **—plas′ter·er** *n.* **—plas′ter·ing** *n.*

plas·ter·board (plas′tər·bôrd′, pläs′-, -bōrd′) *n.* A board made of a slab of gypsum mixed with fibers or of plaster between sheets of fibrous paper, used as wallboard or as backing for a plaster finish on walls.

plaster cast **1** A cast or model of a person or object made by molding plaster of Paris. **2** *Surg.* An application of gauze stiffened with plaster of Paris, applied to an injured or broken part of the body to prevent movement, allow knitting of bones, etc.

plas·tered (plas′tərd, pläs′-) *adj. Slang* Drunk; intoxicated.

plaster of Paris Calcined gypsum: mixed with water it sets readily and is useful in making molds, casts, bandages, etc.

plas·tic (plas′tik) *adj.* **1** Giving form or fashion to matter. **2** Capable of being molded; pliable. **3** Pertaining to modeling or molding; sculptural. **4** Made of plastic. **5** *Surg.* Efficacious or instrumental in recreating or remodeling injured or destroyed protoplasm; also, capable of being thus renewed. **6** *Slang* Not genuine; sham: *plastic* moral values. —*n.* **1** Anything moldable; specifically, any material, natural or synthetic, which may be fabricated into a variety of shapes, usually by the application of heat and pressure. **2** *Chem.* One of a class of organic compounds synthesized from hydrocarbons, proteins, cellulose, or resins, capable of being molded, extruded, cast, or otherwise fabricated into various shapes: usually in the plural, **plas′tics.** [<L *plasticus* <Gk. *plastikos* moldable <*plastos* formed <*plassein* form, mold] **—plas′ti·cal·ly** *adv.*

-plastic *combining form* Growing; developing; forming: *cytoplastic.* [<Gk. *plastikos* plastic]

Plas·ti·cine (plas′tə·sēn) *n.* A claylike substance with an oil base, used for modeling: a trade name.

plas·tic·i·ty (plas·tis′ə·tē) *n.* **1** Plastic quality. **2** *Physics* The ability of certain bodies to exhibit a continous change of shape under suitable distorting forces. **3** Capacity for mental or spiritual molding.

plas·ti·cize (plas′tə·sīz) *v.t.* & *v.i.* **·cized, ·ciz·ing** To make or become plastic.

plas·ti·ciz·er (plas′tə·sī′zər) *n.* **1** That which functions to make a substance plastic. **2** *Chem.* Any of a class of substances adapted to preserve the softness and flexibility of materials to which they are added.

plastic surgery Surgery that deals with the restoration or healing of lost, wounded, or deformed parts of the body; anaplasty.

plas·tid (plas′tid) *n. Biol.* **1** An elementary organism, as a cell. **2** Any permanent organ of the cell situated in the cytoplasm. [<G *plastiden,* pl. <Gk. *plastides,* fem. pl. of *plastēs* a molder <*plastos.* See PLASTIC.]

plas·ti·sol (plas′tə·sôl, -sol) *n.* A suspension of finely divided resin particles in a plasticizer: useful in the application of plastic coatings to surfaces. [<PLASTI(C) + SOL[4]]

plas·to·mer (plas′tə·mər) *n. Chem.* Any of a group of polymerized, thermosetting plastics, as Celluloid or the acrylic resins. [<PLAST(IC) + (POLY)MER]

plas·tom·e·ter (plas·tom′ə·tər) *n.* An instrument for measuring the plasticity of a substance. [<*plasto-* (<PLASTICITY) + -METER]

plas·tron (plas′trən) *n.* **1** An ornamental addition to the front of a woman's dress, reaching from the throat to the waist. **2** A leather shield worn on the breast by fencers. **3** *Zool.* The under or ventral part of the shell or armor of a turtle or tortoise: also **plas′trum. 4** The starched bosom of a man's shirt. **5** An iron breastplate worn under a coat of mail. [<F, orig. a breastplate <Ital. *piastrone,* aug. of *piastra* a breastplate] **— plas′tral** *adj.*

-plasty *combining form Med.* An operation in plastic surgery involving: **a** A (specified) part of the body: *osteoplasty.* **b** Tissue from a (specified) source: *zooplasty.* **c** A (specified) process or formation: *neoplasty.* [<Gk. *-plastia* formation <*plastos.* See -PLAST.]

-plasy See -PLASIA.

plat[1] (plat) *v.t.* **plat·ted, plat·ting** To plait or braid. —*n.* A plait. [ME *platten,* var. of *playten* <OF *pleit* PLAIT]

plat[2] (plat) *n.* **1** A small piece of ground; a plot. **2** A plotted map, chart, or plan. —*v.t.* To make a plot or plan of. [Var. of PLOT; infl. in form by obs. *plat* a flat thing or area <OF. See PLATE.]

plat- Var. of PLATY-.

Pla·ta (plä′tä), **La** See LA PLATA.

Pla·ta (plä′tä), **Río de la** The estuary of the Paraná and Uruguay rivers, extending 170 miles SE between Uruguay and Argentina to the Atlantic where it is 140 miles wide; scene of a British naval engagement with Germany in World War II, 1939. Also **River Plate.**

Pla·tae·a (plə·tē′ə) An ancient city NW of Athens, Greece; scene of a Spartan and Athenian victory over the Persians, 479 B.C. Also **Pla·tae′ae** (-tē′ē). **—Pla·tae′an** *adj.*

plat·an (plat′ən) *n.* The plane tree. Also **plat′·ane** (-ən). [<L *platanus* PLANE[3]]

plate (plāt) *n.* **1** A flat, extended, rigid body of metal or any material of slight but even thickness. **2** Metal in sheets. **3** A shallow vessel, formerly often of wood or pewter, now usually of crockery, in which food is served or from which it is eaten at table. **4** Articles of household service, as goblets, tea sets, etc., made originally of precious metals, but now largely of base metal coated with precious metals. **5** A portion of food served at table; a dish; a plateful; also, a whole course served on one plate. **6** A cup or other article of silver or gold offered as a prize in a race or other contest. **7** A piece of flat metal bearing a design or inscription, either for use in that form, as in a door plate or coffin plate, or intended for reproduction by stamping, printing, or otherwise, as in a bookplate; also, an impression from a plate of the latter kind. **8** An electrotype or stereotype. **9** A horizontal timber laid on a wall to receive a framework. **10** *Dent.* A piece of metal, vulcanite, or plastic, fitted to the mouth and holding one or more artificial teeth. **11** Plate armor. **12** A thin part of the brisket of beef. **13** *Phot.* A sensitized sheet of glass, metal, or the like, for taking photographs. **14** In baseball, the home base, a flat, pentagonal figure, 12 inches in diameter and usually of hard white rubber level with the surface of the diamond. **15** *Biol.* A lamina; a lamella. **16** *Geol.* One of the vast discrete sections into which the earth's crust is divided, that float on the underlying magma. **17** A dish like a table plate used in taking up collections, as in churches; also, a collection. **18** A hinge. See illustration under HINGE. **19** The principal anode in a vacuum tube. **20** *Obs.* A piece of silver money. —*v.t.* **plat·ed, plat·ing 1** To coat with a thin layer of gold, silver, etc. **2** To cover or sheathe with metal plates for protection. **3** In papermaking, to give a high gloss to (paper) by pressure between metal plates. **4** *Printing* To make an electrotype or stereotype from. [<OF, a plate of metal, orig. fem. of *plat* flat <LL *plattus,* prob. <Gk. *platys* broad, flat]

plate armor *Mil.* **1** Defensive armor of strong metallic plates for protecting ships or fortifications against artillery. **2** Formerly, defensive armor for the person made of overlapping plates, in distinction from chain or mail. See ARMOR.

pla·teau (pla·tō′, *esp. Brit.* plat′ō) *n. pl.* **·teaus** or **·teaux** (-tōz′) **1** An extensive stretch of elevated and comparatively level land; tableland; mesa. **2** A broad, low stand for table decorations; also, a decorative plaque. **3** *Psychol.* A relatively level portion in the curve indicating a subject's rate of learning; also, the condition it typifies. **4** *Mil.* A device for making a rough preliminary setting on certain gun sights. [<F <OF *platel* a flat piece of metal or wood, orig. dim. of *plat.* See PLATE.]

plat·ed (plā′tid) *adj.* **1** Provided with plates of metal, as for defense. **2** Coated with a layer of silver, tin, etc. **3** Having one kind of yarn on the face and another on the back: said of certain fabrics.

plate·ful (plāt′fo͝ol′) *n. pl.* **·fuls** The quantity that fills a plate.

plate glass See under GLASS.

plate hinge A hinge with one long, narrow plate as the movable unit. See illustration under HINGE.

plate·let (plāt′lit) *n.* **1** A small, platelike object. **2** *Physiol.* One of the small, disk-shaped bodies found in blood and thought to aid in the process of clotting. [Dim. of PLATE]

plat·en (plat′n) *n. Mech.* **1** The part of a printing press, typewriter, or the like, on which the paper is supported to receive the impression. **2** In a machine tool, the adjustable table that carries the work. [<OF *platine* a flat piece, metal plate <*plat.* See PLATE.]

plat·er (plā′tər) *n.* **1** One who plates articles with a layer of gold, silver, etc. **2** One who makes or works upon metallic plates. **3** An inferior race horse.

plate rail A shelflike molding around a room, for holding ornamental plates or bric-a-brac.

plat·form (plat′fôrm) *n.* **1** Any floor or flat surface raised above the adjacent level, as a stage for public speaking, a raised walk upon which passengers alight from railroad cars. **2** A projecting stage at the end of a car or similar vehicle. **3** A formal scheme of principles put forth by a religious, political, or other body; also, the document stating the principles of a political party. **4** The business of public speaking. [<MF *plateforme* <*plate* flat + *forme* form]

platform car A flat car.

platform scale A scale for weighing heavy objects, having a platform on which the load may stand.

pla·tie (plā′tē) *n. Scot.* A small plate.

pla·til·la (plə·til′ə) *n.* A kind of white linen fabric, originally of Silesian manufacture. [<Sp., appar. orig. dim. of *plata* silver]

pla·ti·na (plat′ə·nə, plə·tē′nə) *n.* **1** Platinum. **2** A white, brittle alloy of zinc and copper. [<NL <Sp., platinum, orig. dim. of *plata* silver]

plat·i·nate (plat′ə·nāt) *n. Chem.* A salt of platinic acid. [<PLATIN(IC) + -ATE[3]]

plat·ing (plā′ting) *n.* **1** A layer of metal of varying thickness: silver *plating.* **2** A sheathing of metal plates, or plate armor for protection. **3** The act or process of sheathing or coating something with plates or metal.

pla·tin·ic (plə·tin′ik) *adj. Chem.* Of, pertaining to, or containing platinum, especially in its higher valence. [<PLATIN(UM) + -IC]

plat·i·nif·er·ous (plat′ə·nif′ər·əs) *adj.* Containing or yielding platinum. [<PLATIN(UM) + -(I)FEROUS]

plat·in·i·rid·i·um (plat′in·i·rid′ē·əm) *n.* A whitish to gray native alloy of iridium, platinum, and other allied metals. [<PLATIN(UM) + IRIDIUM]

plat·i·nize (plat′ə·nīz) *v.t.* **·nized, ·niz·ing** To coat or combine with platinum, especially by electroplating.

platino– *combining form* Platinum; of, related to, or containing platinum: *platinocyanic.* Also, before vowels, **platin–.** [<PLATINUM]

plat·i·no·cy·an·ic (plat′ə·nō·sī·an′ik) *adj. Chem.* Of, pertaining to, or derived from compounds containing platinum and cyanogen.

plat·i·no·cy·a·nide (plat′ə·nō·sī′ə·nīd, -nid) *n. Chem.* A cyanide of platinum and some other element or radical. Also **plat′i·no·cy′a·nid** (-nid).

plat·i·noid (plat′ə·noid) *adj.* Like platinum. —*n.* **1** An alloy of German silver and 1 or 2 percent of tungsten, used in the manufacture of resistance coils and other electrical appliances. **2** A platinum metal.

plat·i·no·type (plat′ə·nō·tīp′) *n. Phot.* **1** A process in which the positive is obtained by a deposit of finely precipitated platinum in combination with iron salts. **2** A positive print obtained by the foregoing process.

plat·i·nous (plat′ə·nəs) *adj. Chem.* Of, pertaining to, or containing platinum, especially in its lower valence. [<PLATIN(UM) + -OUS]

plat·i·num (plat′ə·nəm) *n.* **1** A whitish, steel-gray, malleable and ductile metallic element (symbol Pt), usually found native, and also in combination. It is very infusible and resistant to most acids, has a high electrical resistance, and is widely used as a catalyst, for jewelry, and in dental work. See ELEMENT. **2** A color resembling that of platinum, but having a slightly bluish tone. [<NL, alter. of Sp. *platina* PLATINA]

platinum blond A very light, almost white, blond.

plat·i·tude (plat′ə·to͞od, -tyo͞od) *n.* **1** A flat, dull, or common place statement; an obvious truism. **2** Dulness; triteness. [<F, flatness <*plat* flat]

plat·i·tu·di·nize (plat′ə·to͞o′də·nīz, -tyo͞o′-) *v.i.* **·nized, ·niz·ing** To utter platitudes.

plat·i·tu·di·nous (plat′ə·to͞o′də·nəs, -tyo͞o′-) *adj.* **1** Of the nature of platitude; insipid; flat. **2** Abounding in or given to platitudes.

Pla·to (plā′tō), 427?–347? B.C., Greek philosopher.

Pla·ton·ic (plə·ton′ik) *adj.* Of, pertaining to, or characteristic of Plato or of Platonism; academic; theoretical. Also **Pla·ton′i·cal.** —**Pla·ton′i·cal·ly** *adv.*

Platonic love Love which is purely spiritual, or devoid of sensual feeling.

Platonic year See PRECESSION OF THE NOXES.

Pla·to·nism (plā′tə·niz′əm) *n.* **1** The philosophy of Plato; specifically, the doctrine that objects are copies or images of eternal ideas, that these ideas are the ultimate metaphysical realities and therefore the object of true knowledge. **2** A tenet or maxim of the Platonic philosophy. **3** The doctrine or practice of Platonic love. —**Pla′to·nist** *n.*

Pla·to·nize (plā′tə·nīz) *v.* **·nized, ·niz·ing** *v.t.* To make Platonic; idealize. —*v.i.* To conform to Platonism in views or utterance.

pla·toon (plə·to͞on′) *n.* **1** A subdivision of a company, troop, or other military unit, commanded by a lieutenant. **2** A company of people; set. **3** In football, a group of players assigned to play either defense or offense and put into or taken from the game as a unit. [<F *peloton* ball, group of men, dim. of *pelote* a ball]

Platt·deutsch (plät′doich′) *n.* The Low German vernacular of the north of Germany.

Plat·ten·see (plät′ən·zā) The German name for BALATON, LAKE.

plat·ter (plat′ər) *n.* **1** An oblong shallow dish for serving meat or fish. **2** *Colloq.* A phonograph record. [<AF *plater* <*plat* dish]

Platte River (plat) A river in Nebraska formed by the confluence of the North Platte and the South Platte and flowing 310 miles east to the Missouri River.

plat·ting (plat′ing) *n.* **1** The process of weaving by hand. **2** Any fabric made by coarse weaving, as a straw hat.

Platt National Park A federal park in southern Oklahoma containing mineral springs; 912 acres.

Platts·burg (plats′bûrg) A city in NE New York, on Lake Champlain; scene of an American naval victory over the British (1814) in the War of 1812.

platy– *combining form* Flat: *platyrrhine.* Also, before vowels, *plat–.* [<Gk. *platys* flat]

plat·y·hel·minth (plat′ē·hel′minth) *n. Zool.* Any of a phylum *(Platyhelminthes)* of soft-bodied, bilaterally symmetrical, flattened or cylindrical worms, including many parasitic tapeworms. [<PLATY- + Gk. *helmins* worm]

plat·y·pus (plat′ə·pəs) *n. pl.* **·pus·es** A burrowing egg-laying and aquatic monotrematous mammal *(Ornithorhynchus anatinus)* of Australia, with a ducklike bill and webbed forepaws; duckbill. [<PLATY- + Gk. *pous* foot]

PLATYPUS
(Body about 18 inches in length)

plat·yr·rhine (plat′ə·rīn, -rin) *adj.* **1** Having a broad nose, with widely separated nostrils. **2** *Zool.* Designating a group of monkeys (the *Platyrrhini*) inhabiting the New World. —*n.* A broad-nosed person or monkey. Also **plat′·yr·rhin′i·an** (-rin′ē·ən). [<PLATY- + Gk. *rhis, rhinos* nose]

plau·dit (plô′dit) *n.* An expression of applause, praise bestowed. See synonyms under APPLAUSE. [Short for L *plaudite,* 2nd pl. imperative of *plaudere* applaud]

Plau·en (plou′ən) A city in the former state of Saxony, south central East Germany. Also **Plauen im Vogt·land** (im fōkht′länt).

plau·si·ble (plô′zə·bəl) *adj.* **1** Seeming likely to be true, but open to doubt; specious. **2** Superficially trustworthy; endeavoring or calculated to gain trust or confidence: a *plausible* speaker. **3** *Colloq.* Apparently believable; credible. See synonyms under OSTENSIBLE. [<L *plausibilis* deserving applause] —**plau′si·bil′i·ty, plau′si·ble·ness** *n.* —**plau′si·bly** *adv.*

plau·sive (plô′siv) *adj.* **1** Manifesting praise; applauding. **2** *Obs.* Plausible.

Plau·tus (plô′təs), **Titus Maccius,** 254?–184 B.C., Roman comic dramatist.

play (plā) *v.i.* **1** To engage in sport or diversion; amuse oneself; frolic; gambol. **2** To take part in a game of skill or chance; gamble. **3** To act in a way which is not to be taken seriously. **4** To act or behave in a specified manner: to *play* false. **5** To deal carelessly; behave lightly or insincerely: with *with.* **6** To make love sportively. **7** To move quickly or irregularly as if frolicking: lights *playing* along a wall. **8** To discharge or be discharged freely or continuously: a fountain *playing* in the square. **9** To perform on a musical instrument. **10** To give forth musical sounds;

sound: The bugles are *playing.* **11** To be performed or exhibited: *Hamlet* is *playing* tonight. **12** To act on or as on a stage; perform. **13** To move freely or loosely, especially within limits, as part of a mechanism. — *v.t.* **14** To engage in (a game, etc.). **15** To pretend to be; imitate in play: to *play* cowboys and Indians. **16** To perform sportively or wantonly: to *play* a trick. **17** To oppose in a game or contest. **18** To move or employ (a piece, card, etc.) in a game. **19** To employ (someone) in a game as a player. **20** To cause; bring about: to *play* hob. **21** To perform upon (a musical instrument). **22** To perform or produce, as a piece of music, a play, etc. **23** To act the part of on or as on the stage; assume the character of: to *play* the fool. **24** To perform or act in: to *play* Chicago. **25** To cause to move quickly or irregularly: to *play* lights over a surface. **26** To put into or maintain in action; wield; ply. **27** In angling, to let (a hooked fish) tire itself by maintaining pressure on the line. **28** **a** To bet. **b** To bet on. **— to play at** **1** To take part in. **2** To pretend to be doing; do half-heartedly. **— to play down** To treat as being of little importance; minimize. **— to play into the hands of** To act to the advantage of (a rival or opponent). **— to play it cool** *Slang* To act unconcerned or nonchalant. **— to play off** **1** To oppose against one another. **2** To decide (a tie) by playing one more game. **— to play on** **1** To take unscrupulous advantage of (another's hopes, emotions, etc.) for one's own advantage. **2** To continue: The band *played on.* **— to play out** **1** To come to an end; be exhausted. **2** To continue to the end; finish. **— to play the game** To behave in a fair manner. **— to play up** *Colloq.* To emphasize. **— to play up to** *Colloq.* To try to win the favor of by flattery, etc. — *n.* **1** Action without special aim or for amusement: opposed to *work.* **2** Exercise or action for recreation or diversion; sport; jest; fun; competitive trial of skill for amusement. **3** Gambling. **4** Manner of contending in a game; also, a move in a game: rough *play,* a fine *play,* sword *play.* **5** A dramatic composition; also, a dramatic representation; especially, a public theatrical exhibition. **6** Action without specified or special hindrance; freedom of movement. **7** Manner of acting toward others; dealing. **8** Active operation. **9** Light, quick, fitful movement. **10** Length of stroke, as of a piston. **— to make a play for** *Colloq.* To attempt to ingratiate oneself with. [OE *plegan*] **— play'a·ble** *adj.*

pla·ya (plä'yä) *n.* A plain with a hard clayey surface intermittently covered by a shallow lake. [<Sp.]

play·back (plā'bak') *n.* The reproduction of sound or pictures or both from a disc, tape, or film recording.

play·bill (plā'bil') *n.* A bill or program advertising or giving the cast of a play.

play·book (plā'bŏŏk') *n.* **1** A book containing the script of a play. **2** A book of plays.

play·boy (plā'boi') *n.* **1** *Colloq.* An irresponsible pleasure–seeker. **2** One who assumes a role for his own advantage or glory; a pretender: from the central character in J. M. Synge's *The Playboy of the Western World.*

play–by–play (plā'bī·plā') *adj.* Dealing with each play consecutively: a *play–by–play* report.

played out **1** Performed until finished. **2** Used up; exhausted: originally employed by gamblers.

play·er (plā'ər) *n.* **1** One who takes part in a game; also, one who specializes in a game: a tennis *player.* **2** One who performs on the dramatic stage; an actor. **3** A performer on a musical instrument. **4** One who works without a purpose or makes idle pretensions; also, an idler; a trifler. **5** A gambler. **6** An automatic device for playing a musical instrument; specifically, a mechanical device for playing a piano: also **player piano.**

play·fel·low (plā'fel'ō) *n.* An associate in games; a playmate.

play·ful (plā'fəl) *adj.* Frolicsome; merry; jocose. See synonyms under WANTON. **— play'ful·ly** *adv.* **— play'ful·ness** *n.*

play·go·er (plā'gō'ər) *n.* A frequenter of the theater.

play·ground (plā'ground') *n.* A ground used for playing games; space set aside for recreation.

play·house (plā'hous') *n.* **1** A theater. **2** A small house for children to play in.

playing card One of a pack of cards used in playing various games, the pack usually consisting of 52 cards divided into four suits (spades, hearts, diamonds, clubs) of 13 cards each.

play·mate (plā'māt') *n.* A companion in sports, games, or recreation; especially, a child's companion in play.

play–off (plā'ôf', -of') *n.* In sports, a decisive game or contest, especially after a tie.

play·thing (plā'thing') *n.* A thing to play with; a toy.

play·time (plā'tīm') *n.* Time allowed for or given up to play or amusement.

play upon words Words used with double meaning; a pun.

play·wright (plā'rīt') *n.* A writer of plays.

pla·za (plä'zə, plaz'ə; *Sp.* plä'thä) *n.* An open square or market place, especially in a Spanish or Spanish–American town. [<Sp. <L *platea.* Doublet of PIAZZA, PLACE.]

plea (plē) *n.* **1** An act of pleading, or that which is pleaded; an appeal; entreaty; prayer: a *plea* for aid. **2** An excuse; pretext or justification: necessity, the tyrant's *plea.* **3** *Law* **a** An allegation made by either party in a cause; a pleading. **b** In common–law practice, a defendant's answer of fact to the plaintiff's declaration, known in the United States as the *answer.* **c** In equity, a special answer, showing a reason why the writ should be dismissed, delayed, or barred. **d** A suit or action: usually in the plural. See synonyms under APOLOGY. **— Common Pleas** The Court of Common Pleas. See under COURT. **— special plea** A plea to prevent action which, while admitting the plaintiff's allegations, avoids them by setting up new matter. [<OF *plait* <L *placitum* opinion, orig. pp. of *placere* seem right, please]

plea–bar·gain·ing (plē'bär'gən·ing) *n.* A process in which a defendant in a law case arranges, as with a district attorney, to plead guilty to a lesser charge in order to avoid standing trial for a more serious one and the risk of severer punishment.

pleach (plēch) *v.t.* To plait (vines or twigs) together, as in forming a hedge or arbor; interweave. [<AF *plechier,* OF *plaissier* <L *plectere* weave]

pleached (plēcht) *adj.* Interwoven; covered with interwoven branches.

plead (plēd) *v.* **plead·ed** (*Colloq.* or *Dial.* **pled**), **plead·ing** *v.i.* **1** To make earnest entreaty; implore; beg. **2** *Law* **a** To advocate a case in court. **b** To file a pleading. — *v.t.* **3** To allege as an excuse or defense: to *plead* insanity. **4** *Law* To discuss or maintain (a case) by argument. [<OF *plaider* <*plait.* See PLEA.] **— plead'a·ble** *adj.* **— plead'er** *n.*

Synonyms: advocate, argue, ask, beg, beseech, entreat, implore, press, solicit, urge. To *plead* for one is to employ argument or persuasion, or both, in his behalf, with earnestness or importunity. One *argues* a case solely on rational grounds with fair consideration of both sides; he *advocates* one side for the purpose of carrying it, and under the influence of motives that may range all the way from cold self–interest to the highest and noblest impulses; he *pleads* a cause, or *pleads for* a person, with still more intense feeling. *Beseech, entreat,* and *implore* imply impassioned earnestness, with direct and tender appeal to personal considerations. *Press* and *urge* imply determined or perhaps authoritative insistence. *Solicit* is a weak word denoting merely an attempt to secure one's consent or cooperation.

plead·ing (plē'ding) *n.* **1** The act of making a plea or argument in behalf of someone or something; specifically, the oral advocacy of a cause in court. **2** *Law* The art, science, or system of preparing the formal written statements of the parties to an action, leading to the joinder of issue; also, any one of such statements: collectively called the *pleadings* in a case. See synonyms under PETITION. **— plead'ing·ly** *adv.*

pleas·ance (plez'əns) *n.* **1** A secluded garden; pleasure ground. **2** *Archaic* The feeling of being pleased; that which pleases. Also **pleas'·aunce.** [<OF *plaisance* <*plaisant.* See PLEASANT.]

pleas·ant (plez'ənt) *adj.* **1** Giving or promoting pleasure; pleasing: agreeable. **2** Conducive to merriment; gay. [<F *plaisant* <L *placens,* ppr. of *placere* please] **— pleas'ant·ly** *adv.* **— pleas'ant·ness** *n.*

Synonyms: agreeable, attractive, good–natured, kind, kindly, obliging, pleasing, pleasurable. That is *pleasing* from which pleasure is received, or may readily be received, without reference to any action or intent in that which confers it; as, a *pleasing* picture; a *pleasing* landscape. Whatever has active qualities adapted to give pleasure is *pleasant*; as, a *pleasant* breeze; a *pleasant* (not a *pleasing*) day. As applied to persons, *pleasant* always refers to a disposition ready and desirous to please, and in this sense is near akin to *kind,* but *kind* refers to act or intent, while *pleasant* stops with the disposition. *Pleasant* keeps always something of the sense of actually giving pleasure, and thus surpasses the meaning of *good–natured*; there are *good–natured* people who by reason of rudeness and ill–breeding are not *pleasant* companions. A *pleasing* face has good features, complexion, expression, etc.; a *pleasant* face indicates a *kind* heart and an *obliging* disposition, as well as *kindly* feelings in actual exercise. See AGREEABLE, AMIABLE, ATTRACTIVE, COMFORTABLE, DELIGHTFUL, GOOD, VIVACIOUS. *Antonyms*: arrogant, austere, crabbed, disagreeable, displeasing, dreary, forbidding, gloomy, glum, grim, harsh, hateful, ill–humored, ill–natured, offensive, repellent, repulsive, unkind, unpleasant.

Pleasant Island A former name for NAURU.

pleas·an·try (plez'ən·trē) *n. pl.* **·tries** **1** The spirit of playful and jocose companionship; playfulness. **2** A playful, amusing, or good–natured remark, jest, or trick. See synonyms under SPORT, WIT[1].

please (plēz) *v.* **pleased, pleas·ing** *v.t.* **1** To give pleasure to; be agreeable to; gratify. **2** To be the wish or will of: May it *please* you. — *v.i.* **3** To give satisfaction or pleasure. **4** To have the will or preference; wish: Go when you *please.* See synonyms under ENTERTAIN, INDULGE, REJOICE. [<OF *plaisir* <L *placere* please]

pleas·ing (plē'zing) *adj.* Affording pleasure or satisfaction. See synonyms under AGREEABLE, AMIABLE, LOVELY, PLEASANT. **— pleas'·ing·ly** *adv.* **— pleas'ing·ness** *n.*

pleas·ur·a·ble (plezh'ər·ə·bəl) *adj.* Affording gratification; pleasant. See synonyms under DELIGHTFUL, PLEASANT. **— pleas'ur·a·ble·ness** *n.* **— pleas'ur·a·bly** *adv.*

pleas·ure (plezh'ər) *n.* **1** An agreeable sensation or emotion; gratification; enjoyment. **2** Sensual or mental gratification. **3** Amusement in general; diversion. **4** One's preference; choice. See synonyms under COMFORT, ENTERTAINMENT, HAPPINESS, SPORT. — *v.* **·ured, ·ur·ing** *v.t.* To give or afford pleasure to; please; gratify. — *v.i.* To take pleasure; delight. [<OF *plaisir.* See PLEASE.]

pleasure principle *Psychoanal.* The concentration of the ego on securing a maximum gratification of instincts with a minimum of pain and effort. Compare REALITY PRINCIPLE.

pleat (plēt) *n.* A fold of cloth doubled on itself and pressed or sewn in place. — *v.t.* To make a pleat or pleats in. Also *plait.* [Var. of PLAIT]

pleat·er (plē'tər) *n.* **1** One who pleats. **2** A sewing–machine attachment for pleating; a ruffler.

pleb (pleb) *n.* **1** A plebeian. **2** A plebe.

plebe (plēb) *n.* **1** *U.S.* A member of the lowest class in the academies at West Point and Annapolis. **2** *Obs.* Plebs. [Short for PLEBEIAN]

ple·be·ian (pli·bē'ən) *adj.* Pertaining to the common people, originally to the common people of ancient Rome; hence, common. — *n.* One of the common people. [<L *plebeius* <*plebs* the common people] **— ple·be'·ian·ism** *n.* **— ple·be'ian·ly** *adv.* **— ple·be'ian·ness** *n.*

pleb·i·scite (pleb'ə·sīt, -sit) *n.* An expression of the popular will by means of a vote by the

whole people, usually resorted to in important changes, as those dealing with the constitution, sovereignty, [<F *plébiscite* <L *plebiscitum* <*plebs* people + *scitum* decree < *scire* know] —**ple·bis·ci·tar·y** (plə·bis′ə·ter′ē) *adj.*

plebs (plebz) *n.* **1** The lower order of the ancient Roman people. **2** The populace. [<L, common people]

ple·cop·ter·an (plə·kop′tər·ən) *n.* Any of an order *(Plecoptera)* of soft-bodied, flattened insects of which the nymphs are aquatic: the adults usually have a pair of long caudal appendages, and two pairs of wings folding flat over the abdomen; a stone fly. [<Gk. *plekein* twine + *pteron* wing]

plec·tog·nath (plek′tog·nath) *n.* Any of an order of suborder *(Plectognathi)* of teleost fishes having spiny bodies, generally inedible and often poisonous flesh, and including a large number of odd forms, as the triggerfishes, swellfishes, globefishes, etc. —*adj.* Of or pertaining to the *Plectognathi.* [<Gk. *plektos* twisted + *gnathos* jaw]

plec·trum (plek′trəm) *n. pl.* **·tra** (-trə) A small implement with which the player on a lyre, zither, etc., picks or strikes the strings to set them in vibration. Also **plec′tron** (-tron). [<L <Gk. *plēktron* spur <*plēssein* strike]

pled (pled) *Dial.* or *Colloq.* Past tense and past participle of PLEAD.

pledge (plej) *v.t.* **pledged, pledg·ing 1** To give or deposit as security for a loan, etc.; pawn. **2** To bind by or as by a pledge. **3** To promise solemnly, as assistance. **4** To offer (one's word, life, etc.) as a guaranty or forfeit. **5** To drink a toast to. **6** To promise to join (a fraternity). **7** To accept (someone) as a pledge (def. 5). [<*n.*] —*n.* **1** A guaranty for the performance of an act, contract, or duty. **2** A formal promise to do or not to do something; especially, a vow to abstain from intoxicating liquors. **3** The drinking of a health or to good cheer. **4** A pawn of personal property; also, the property delivered. **5** One who has promised to join a fraternity but who has not yet been formally inducted. [<OF *plege* security, prob. <Gmc.]

pledg·ee (plej·ē′) *n.* The person to whom anything is pledged.

pledg·er (plej′ər) *n.* One who gives a pledge.

pledg·or (plej′ər) *n. Law* A pledger. Also **pledge′or.**

pledg·et (plej′it) *n.* **1** A little plug. **2** A compressed wad of lint, cotton, etc., as for a wound. **3** An oakum string used in calking. [Origin unknown]

–plegia *combining form Med.* A (specified) kind of paralysis, or paralytic condition: *hemiplegia.* Also **–plegy.** [<Gk. *plēgē* a stroke]

Plei·ad (plē′əd, plī′ad) *n. pl.* **Plei·a·des** (plē′ə·dēz, plī′-) **1** One of the Pleiades. **2** One of any cluster of brilliant persons, usually seven.

Plei·a·des (plē′ə·dēz, plī′-) **1** In Greek mythology, the seven daughters of Atlas (Maia, Electra, Taygeta, Alcyone, Celaeno, Sterope, and Merope), who were set by Zeus among the stars: also called *Atlantides.* **2** *Astron.* A loose cluster of many hundred stars in the constellation Taurus, six of which are visible to ordinary sight and represent the daughters of Atlas, of whom the seventh, Merope, is known as the **Lost Pleiad.**

plein–air (plān′âr′) *adj.* Characterizing the work of a school of French impressionist painters concerned with the representation of objects seen under brilliant sunlight, and other outdoor effects. [<F, open-air] —**plein–air·ism** (plān′âr′iz·əm) *n.* —**plein′–air′ist** *n.*

Plei·o·cene (plī′ə·sēn) See PLIOCENE.

plei·o·syl·lab·ic (plī′ə·si·lab′ik) *adj.* Having more than one syllable; especially, having two or three syllables. See POLYSYLLABLE. [<Gk. *pleiōn* more + *syllabē* syllable]

Pleis·to·cene (plīs′tə·sēn) *Geol. n.* **1** The epoch following the Pliocene; the first of the two epochs of the Quaternary period, characterized by ice sheets over much of the northern hemisphere; the glacial epoch of northern Asia, Europe, and North America. **2** The rock series of this period. —*adj.* Pertaining to this epoch or to its rock series. [<Gk. *pleistos* most + *kainos* new]

ple·na·ry (plē′nə·rē, plen′ə-) *adj.* **1** Full in all respects or requisites; entire; absolute; also, complete, as embracing all the parts or members: *plenary* authority. **2** Having full powers: *plenary* jurisdiction. **3** Fully or completely attended; consisting of the full number of members: said of an assembly. [<L *plenus* full] —**ple′na·ri·ly** *adv.* —**ple′na·ri·ness** *n.*

plenary indulgence In the Roman Catholic Church, the remission of all temporal penalties incurred by sin.

ple·nip·o·tent (plə·nip′ə·tənt) *adj.* Possessing full power or authority.

plen·i·po·ten·ti·ar·y (plen′i·pə·ten′shē·er′ē, -shə·rē) *adj.* Possessing or conferring full powers. —*n. pl.* **·ar·ies 1** A person fully empowered, especially an ambassador, minister, or envoy, invested with full powers by a government. **2** Specifically, a diplomatic representative of the second class ranking next below an ambassador, accredited by the sovereign or head of one state to that of another: full title *envoy extraordinary and minister plenipotentiary.* [<L *plenus* full + *potens* powerful]

plen·ish (plen′ish) *v.t. Scot. & Brit. Dial.* To fill or stock; replenish.

ple·nism (plē′niz·əm) *n.* The doctrine that space is a plenum. —**ple′nist** *n.*

plen·i·tude (plen′ə·tōōd, -tyōōd) *n.* The state of being full, complete, or abounding; also, that which fills to repletion. [<L *plenitudo* < *plenus* full]

plen·te·ous (plen′tē·əs) *adj.* **1** Characterized by plenty; amply sufficient. **2** Yielding an abundance. See synonyms under AMPLE, PLENTIFUL. [<OF *plentieus, plentivous* <*plenté* PLENTY] —**plen′te·ous·ly** *adv.* —**plen′te·ous·ness** *n.*

plen·ti·ful (plen′ti·fəl) *adj.* **1** Existing in great quantity; abundant. **2** Yielding or containing plenty; affording ample supply. —**plen′ti·ful·ly** *adv.* —**plen′ti·ful·ness** *n.*

Synonyms: abounding, abundant, adequate, affluent, ample, bounteous, bountiful, complete, copious, enough, exuberant, full, generous, large, lavish, liberal, luxuriant, overflowing, plenteous, profuse, replete, rich, sufficient, teeming. *Plentiful* is used of supplies, as of food, water, etc. We may say a *copious* rain; but *copious* can also be applied to thought, language, etc., where *plentiful* cannot well be used. *Affluent* and *liberal* both apply to riches, resources; *liberal,* with especial reference to giving or expending. *Affluent,* referring especially to riches, may be used of thought, feeling, etc. Neither *affluent, copious,* nor *plentiful* can be used of time or space; a field is sometimes called *plentiful,* with reference to its productiveness. *Complete* expresses not excess or overplus, and yet not mere sufficiency, but harmony, proportion, fitness to a design, or ideal. *Ample* and *abundant* may be applied to any subject and mean more than *enough. Lavish* and *profuse* imply a decided excess. We rejoice in *abundant* resources, and honor *generous* hospitality; *lavish* or *profuse* expenditure suggests extravagance and wastefulness. *Luxuriant* is used especially of that which is *abundant* in growth; as, a *luxuriant* crop. Compare ADEQUATE, AMPLE, ENOUGH. *Antonyms*: deficient, drained, exhausted, impoverished, inadequate, insufficient, mean, miserly, narrow, niggardly, poor, scanty, scarce, scrimped, short, small, sparing, stingy, straitened.

plen·ty (plen′tē) *n.* **1** The state of being abundantly sufficient, or of having an abundance, particularly of necessaries and comforts: to live in peace and *plenty.* **2** As much as can be required; an abundance or sufficiency: now generally without the article: *plenty* of water; I have *plenty.* See synonyms under COMFORT, WEALTH. —*adj.* Existing in abundance; plentiful. —*adj. Colloq.* In a sufficient degree: The house is *plenty* large enough. [<OF *plenté* < L *plenitas, -tatis* <*plenus* full]

ple·num (plē′nəm) *n. pl.* **·nums** or **·na** (-nə) **1** Fullness of matter in space; that state of things in which space is considered as fully occupied by matter, especially by absolutely continuous matter. **2** Space so considered: opposed to *vacuum.* **3** Any condition of fullness or plethora, or that which produces it. **4** An enclosed body of gas under greater than normal pressure. **5** A completely attended meeting, as of an association or legislative body. **6** Fullness. —*adj.* Pertaining to or utilizing fullness (of air, etc.) [<L <*plenus* full]

ple·och·ro·ism (plē·ok′rō·iz′əm) *n. Mineral.* The property exhibited by double-refracting colored crystals of showing different colors when the transmitted light is viewed along different axes. [<Gk. *pleōn* more + *chroos* color + -ISM] —**ple·o·chro·ic** (plē′ə·krō′ik) *adj.*

ple·o·mor·phism (plē′ə·môr′fiz·əm) *n.* **1** *Mineral.* The ability of a substance to crystallize in two or more distinct fundamental forms, embracing *dimorphism* and *trimorphism.* **2** *Biol.* The occurrence of several independent stages in the life cycle of an organism or plant. Also **ple′o·mor′phy.** [<Gk. *pleōn* more + *morphē* form] —**ple′o·mor′phic, ple′o·mor′phous** *adj.*

ple·o·nasm (plē′ə·naz′əm) *n.* **1** The use of needless words; redundancy; tautology or any instance of it; a redundant word or phrase. **2** A superabundance of parts, as in an organism. [<Gk. *pleonasmos* <*pleōn* more] —**ple′o·nas′tic** (-nas′tik) *adj.* —**ple′o·nas′ti·cal·ly** *adv.*

ple·o·nex·i·a (plē′ə·nek′sē·ə) *n.* **1** *Pathol.* A tendency of the hemoglobin of the blood to retain oxygen, yielding less than normal amounts to the tissues of the body. **2** *Psychiatry* A morbid greediness. [<NL <Gk., greediness] —**ple′o·nec′tic** (-nek′tik) *adj.*

ple·o·pod (plē′ə·pod) *n. Zool.* An abdominal limb of a crustacean; a swimmeret. [<Gk. *pleein* swim + *pous, podos* foot]

ple·rome (plē′rōm) *n. Bot.* That part of the actively growing tissue of the apex of the stem and root out of which the stele arises. Also **ple′rom** (-rəm) [<Gk. *plērēs* full]

ple·si·o·saur (plē′sē·ə·sôr) *n. Paleontol.* Any of an extinct genus *(Plesiosaurus)* of fish-eating marine reptiles which flourished in the Jurassic period, having a small head, long neck, and limbs modified into swimming paddles. Also **ple′si·o·sau′rus.** [<Gk. *plēsios* near + *sauros* lizard]

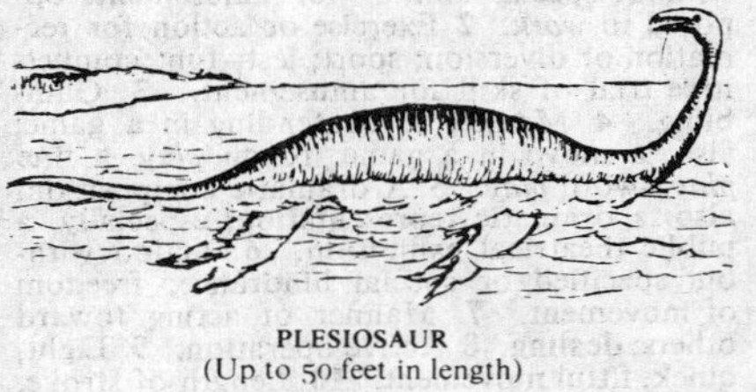

PLESIOSAUR
(Up to 50 feet in length)

ples·sor (ples′ər) *n.* Plexor.

pleth·o·ra (pleth′ər·ə) *n.* **1** A state of excessive fullness; superabundance; excess. **2** *Bot.* An excess of juices. **3** *Pathol.* Superabundance of blood in the whole system or in an organ or part. [<Med. L <Gk. *plēthōrē* fullness <*plēthein* be full]

ple·thor·ic (ple·thôr′ik, -thor′-, pleth′ə·rik) *adj.* **1** Affected or characterized by plethora. **2** Excessively full; overloaded; turgid; inflated. See synonyms under CORPULENT. —**ple·thor′i·cal·ly** *adv.*

ple·thys·mo·graph (ple·thiz′mə·graf, -gräf, -this′-) *n.* An instrument for recording variations in size of parts of the body, especially as caused by the circulation of the blood. [<Gk. *plēthysmos* enlargement (<*plēthyein* increase) + -GRAPH]

pleu·ra (ploor′ə) *n. pl.* **pleu·rae** (ploor′ē) *Anat.* The serous membrane that infolds the lungs and is reflected upon the walls of the thorax and upon the diaphragm. [<Gk. *pleura* side] —**pleu′ral** *adj.*

pleu·ri·sy (ploor′ə·sē) *n. Pathol.* Inflammation of the pleura, commmonly attended with fever, pain in the chest, difficult breathing, exudation, etc. [<OF *pleurisie* <L *pleurisis* < Gk. *pleuritis* <*pleura* side] —**pleu·rit·ic** (ploo·rit′ik) *adj.*

pleurisy root 1 Butterfly weed. **2** Its root, formerly used in treating pleurisy.

pleuro– *combining form* **1** Of or pertaining to the side: *pleurodont.* **2** *Med.* Of, related to, or affecting the pleura: *pleurotomy.* Also, before vowels, **pleur–.** [<Gk. *pleura* side and *pleuron* rib]

pleu·ro·dont (ploor′ə·dont) *Zool. adj.* Having teeth attached to the inner side of the alveolar ridge of the jaw, as in an iguanoid lizard. —*n.* A lizard with pleurodont denition. [< PLEUR(O)- + -ODONT]

pleu·ron (ploŏr'on) *n. pl.* **pleu·ra** (ploŏr'ə) 1 *Entomol.* The lateral wall of a thoracic segment in insects. 2 *Zool.* In crustaceans, the lateral process of an abdominal segment. [< NL < Gk., a rib]

pleu·ro·pneu·mo·ni·a (ploŏr'ō-noo-mō'nē-ə, -mōn'yə, -nyoō-), *n. Pathol.* Pleurisy combined with pneumonia.

pleu·rot·o·my (ploŏr-ot'ə-mē) *n. Surg.* The operation of making an incision into the pleural cavity, for drawing off effused liquids.

pleus·ton (ploōs'ton) *n. Bot.* That type of vegetation which consists of large aquatic plants floating on the water. [< NL < Gk. *pleus-*, stem of *pleein* swim]

Plev·en (plev'ən) A city in northern Bulgaria; surrendered by the Turks after a siege, 1877. Also **Plev·na** (plev'nä).

plex·i·form (plek'sə-fôrm) *adj.* Having the form of a plexus; complicated.

Plex·i·glas (plek'si-glas, gläs) *n.* A thermoplastic acrylic resin used in the fabrication of transparent objects, as windows for airplane gun turrets, gages, etc.: a trade name.

plex·im·e·ter (plek-sim'ə-tər) *n.* A plate to be placed against the body to receive the blows in percussion. [< Gk. *plēxis* a stroke + -METER] — **plex·i·met·ric** (plek'si-met'rik) *adj.* — **plex·im'e·try** *n.*

plex·or (plek'sər) *n. Med.* An instrument used like a hammer in percussion of the chest: also called *plessor.* [< Gk. *plēssein* strike, on analogy with *flexor*]

plex·us (plek'səs) *n. pl.* **·us·es** or **·us** 1 A network or interlacement; a complication of structures, such as nerves. [< L, braid]

pli·a·ble (plī'ə-bəl) *adj.* 1 Easily bent or twisted; flexible. 2 Easily persuaded or controlled. See synonyms under DOCILE, SUPPLE. — **pli'a·bil'i·ty**, **pli'a·ble·ness** *n.* — **pli'a·bly** *adv.*

pli·an·cy (plī'ən-sē) *n.* The state or quality of being pliant; pliability: opposed to *rigidity.*

pli·ant (plī'ənt) *adj.* 1 Capable of being bent or twisted with ease; supple; lithe. 2 Easily yielding to influence; tractable. [< OF, ppr. of *plier.* See PLY.] — **pli'ant·ly** *adv.*

pli·ca (plī'kə) *n. pl.* **·cae** (-sē) 1 A fold of membrane, skin, or the like, as between the fingers. 2 *Zool.* A ridge, as on the outer wall of the body whorl in a shell, or on the wing covers of some beetles. 3 *Pathol.* A disease affecting the hair, causing it to become matted and agglutinated. [< Med. < L *plicare* fold]

pli·cate (plī'kāt) *adj.* Plaited; folded in plaits like a fan, as a leaf. Also **pli'cat·ed.** — **pli'cate·ness** *n.* — **pli'cate·ly** *adv.*

pli·ca·tion (plī-kā'shən) *n.* A folding, or that which is folded; a fold. Also **plic·a·ture** (plik'ə-choŏr).

pli·er (plī'ər) *n.* 1 One who or that which plies. 2 *pl.* Small pincers for bending, holding, or cutting.

plight[1] (plīt) *n.* A condition, state, or case: usually distressed or complicated. [< OF *ploit,* var. of *pleit.* See PLAIT.]

plight[2] (plīt) *n.* A solemn engagement; betrothal; a pledge subject to forfeiture. — *v.t.* 1 To pledge (one's word, faith, etc.). 2 To promise, as in marriage; betroth: She is *plighted* to a judge. — **to plight one's troth** 1 To pledge one's solemn word. 2 To promise oneself in marriage. [OE *pliht* peril] — **plight'er** *n.*

Plim·soll (plim'səl), **Samuel,** 1824–98, English statesman; secured Parliamentary reforms, 1876, against overloading of ships.

Plimsoll line A mark painted on the outside of a British vessel's hull to show how deeply she may be loaded; load line. Also called **Plimsoll mark.** [after Samuel *Plimsoll*]

VARIOUS TYPES
OF PLIERS
a. Round-nose.
b. Flat-nose, showing wire running through.
c. Flat-nose, with wire-cutting attachment.
d. Gas fitter's.

plinth (plinth) *n. Archit.* 1 The slab, block, or stone on which a column, pedestal, or statue rests. 2 A thin course, as of slabs, usually projecting: also **plinth course.** [< L *plinthus* < Gk. *plinthos* a brick]

Plin·y (plin'ē) Anglicized name of two Roman authors; **Pliny the Elder,** 23–79, Gaius Plinius Secundus, naturalist, and his nephew, **Pliny the Younger,** 62–113, Galus Plinius Caecilius Secundus, statesman.

Pli·o·cene (plī'ə-sēn) *Geol. adj.* Of or pertaining to the latest epoch of the Tertiary period, following the Miocene and succeeded by the Pleistocene. — *n.* The Pliocene epoch or rock series. Also *Pleiocene.* [< Gk. *pleiōn* more + *kainos* new] — **Pli'o·cen'ic** (-sen'ik) *adj.*

Pli·o·film (plī'ə-film) *n.* A flexible, transparent rubber sheeting, used for raincoats, umbrellas, etc.: a trade name.

plod (plod) *v.* **plod·ded, plod·ding** *v.t.* 1 To walk heavily or laboriously; trudge. 2 To work in a steady, laborious manner; drudge. — *v.t.* 3 To walk along heavily or laboriously. — *n.* 1 A tiring walk; tramp; act or duration of plodding. 2 The sound of a heavy step, as of a horse. [Imit.] — **plod'ding** *adj.* — **plod'ding·ly** *adv.*

plod·der (plod'ər) *n.* One who plods; a drudge; also, a slow but perserving person.

Plo·es·ti (plō-yesh'tē) A city of south central Rumania; chief center of the Rumanian petroleum industry. Also **Plo·esh'ti.**

–ploid *combining form Biol.* In cytology and genetics, having a (specified) number of chromosomes: *diploid.* Corresponding nouns end in **–ploidy.** [< Gk. *-ploos,* as in *diploos* twofold]

plonk (plonk) *n. Austral. Slang* Cheap wine.

plop (plop) *v.t. & v.i.* **plopped, plop·ping** To drop with a sound like that of a pebble striking the water without making a splash. — *n.* The act or sound of plopping. — *adv.* Suddenly with the sound of plop: They fell *plop* into the river. [Imit.]

plo·sion (plō'zhən) *n. Phonet.* The sudden release of breath after closure of the oral passage in the articulation of a stop consonant, as after the *p* in *pat:* also *explosion.* [< EXPLOSION]

plo·sive (plō'siv) *Phonet. adj.* Designating a speech sound produced by a total blockage of the breath stream followed by an explosive release, as (p) and (t) before vowels. — *n.* A consonant so produced; a stop. Also *explosive.*

plot (plot) *n.* 1 A piece or patch of ground set apart; also called *plat.* 2 A chart or diagram, as of a building, for showing certain data; also, a surveyor's map. 3 A secret plan to accomplish some questionable purpose; conspiracy. 4 The series of incidents forming the plan of action of a story, play, or poem. — *v.* **plot·ted, plot·ting** *v.t.* 1 To make a map, chart, or plan of, as a ship's course, a building, etc. 2 To plan for secretly: to *plot* an enemy's ruin. 3 To arrange the plot of (a novel, etc.) 4 *Math.* **a** To represent graphically the position of (a measured value) by a point located with reference to its coordinates on plotting paper. **b** To draw (a curve) through a series of such points. — *v.i.* 5 To form a plot; conspire. [OE]

Plo·ti·nus (plō-tī'nəs), 205?–270?, Roman philosopher born in Egypt.

plot·ter (plot'ər) *n.* 1 One who plots or contrives; a conspirator. 2 A maker of a plot or map. 3 A contrivance, as for plotting coordinates.

plotting paper Paper which has been ruled into small squares for plotting curves, and making diagrams.

plot·ty (plot'ē) *n. Scot.* A hot, spiced beverage.

plough (plou) See PLOW.

Plov·div (plôv'dēf) The second largest city of Bulgaria, in the south central part: ancient *Philippopolis.*

plov·er (pluv'ər, plō'vər) *n.* 1 A shore bird (family *Charadriidae*), especially of *Charadrius* or related genus, with long, pointed wings and a short tail, especially the **American golden plover** (*Pluvialis dominica*). 2 Any of certain related shore birds, as the ruddy turnstone and the **upland plover** (*Bartramia longicauda*). [< AF, ult. < L *pluvia* rain]

plow (plou) *n.* 1 An implement (usually drawn by horses, or oxen, or by mechanical power) for cutting, turning over, stirring, or breaking up the soil. 2 Any implement that operates like a plow: often in combination: a *snowplow;* also, any one of various furrowing or grooving tools. 3 Figuratively, agriculture. — *v.t.* 1 To turn up the surface of (land) with a plow. 2 To make or form (a furrow, ridge, etc.) by means of a plow. 3 To furrow or score the surface of: Shot *plowed* the field. 4 To dig out or remove with a plow: with *up* or *out.* 5 To move out or cut through (water): to *plow* the waves. 6 To pluck (def. 7). — *v.i.* 7 To turn up soil with a plow. 8 To undergo plowing in a specified way, as land. 9 To move or proceed as a plow does: usually with *through* or *into.* 10 To advance laboriously; plod. — **to plow under** *U.S.* To put from sight by or as by plowing in such a way as to cover with soil; obliterate. Also spelled *plough.* [OE *ploh*] — **plow'a·ble** *adj.* — **plow'er** *n.*

Plow The group of seven stars commonly called *Charles's Wain* or *the Dipper,* sometimes also *Ursa Major.* Also **Plough.**

plow beam The horizontal projecting part of a plow frame, whose front end is attached to the swingletree. See illustration under SWINGLETREE.

plow·boy (plou'boi') *n.* A boy who drives or guides a team in plowing; hence, a young rustic. Also **plough'boy.**

plow·man (plou'mən) *n. pl.* **·men** (-mən) One who plows; a cultivator; hence, a rustic. Also **plough'man.**

plow·share (plou'shâr') *n.* The blade of a plow. Also **plough'share'.**

plow·staff (plou'staf', -stäf') *n.* The handle of a plow. Also **plough'staff.**

ploy[1] (ploi) *v.i. Mil.* To diminish front; maneuver from line into column: opposite of *deploy.* [< DEPLOY] — **poly'ment** *n.*

ploy[2] (ploi) *n. Scot.* Sport; merrymaking.

pluck (pluk) *v.t.* 1 To pull out or off; pick: to *pluck* a flower. 2 To pull with force; snatch or drag: with *off, away,* etc. 3 To pull out the feathers, hair, etc., of: to *pluck* a chicken. 4 To give a twitch or pull to, as a sleeve. 5 To cause the strings of (a musical instrument) to sound by such action. 6 To rob; swindle. 7 *Brit. Slang* To reject (a candidate) for failure to pass an examination. — *v.i.* 8 To give a sudden pull; tug: with *at.* — **to pluck up** To rouse or summon (one's courage). — *n.* 1 Confidence and spirit in the face of difficulty or danger; courage. 2 The heart, liver, windpipe, and lungs of an animal. 3 A sudden pull; twitch. 4 The act of plucking or state of being plucked; also, the person plucked. See synonyms under COURAGE. [OE *pluccian*] — **pluck'er** *n.*

pluck·y (pluk'ē) *adj.* **pluck·i·er, pluck·i·est** Brave and spirited; courageous. — **pluck'i·ly** *adv.* — **pluck'i·ness** *n.*

plug (plug) *n.* 1 Anything, as a piece of wood or a cork, used to stop a hole; a wedge or peg driven into anything. 2 A spark plug. 3 *Electr.* A device containing conducting material, as projecting prongs, for inserting in an outlet, etc., so as to complete a circuit or make contact. 4 A flat cake of pressed or twisted tobacco. 5 Any worn-out or useless thing, particularly a horse past its prime: often with *old.* 6 *U.S. Slang* A man's high silk hat; also **plug hat.** 7 *Slang* Mention of a product, song, etc., as on a radio or television program, to give it publicity; an advertisement. 8 *Geol.* The hard core of igneous rock which fills the neck of a volcano. 9 The discharge outlet from a water main: also called *hydrant.* 10 *Mech.* The cylindrical part of a cylinder lock which contains the keyhole and is turned by the key. 11 In angling, a type of lure, usually cylindrical and with several hooks attached, similar to a spoon. — *v.* **plugged, plug·ging** *v.t.* 1 To stop or close, as a hole, by inserting a plug: often with *up.* 2 To insert as a plug. 3 *Slang* To shoot a bullet into. 4 *U.S. Slang* To advertise frequently or insistently; publicize. — *v.i.* 5 *Colloq.* To work doggedly; persevere. — **to plug in** To insert the plug of (a lamp, etc.) in an electrical outlet. [< MDu. *plugge*] — **plug'ger** *n.*

plug-ug·ly (plug′ug′lē) *n. pl.* **·lies** *U.S. Slang* A city ruffian; gangster; a street rowdy.

plum (plum) *n.* **1** The edible drupaceous fruit of any one of various trees of the genus *Prunus,* especially *P. domestica,* the **European** or **garden plum. 2** The tree. **3** The plumlike fruit of any one of various other trees having an edible drupe; also, the tree bearing such fruit. **4** A raisin, especially as used in cooking: *plum* pudding. **5** The best part of anything; a choice piece or portion; a desirable post or appointment. **6** *Brit. Slang* A sum of £100,000 sterling; a handsome fortune, or the possessor of it. **7** Any of various shades of dull reddish purple or purplish red. **8** A sugarplum; anything resembling a plum, as in shape or flavor. ◆ Homophone: *plumb.* [OE *plume* <LL *pruna.* Doublet of PRUNE[1].]

plum·age (plo͞o′mij) *n.* **1** The feathers that cover a bird, collectively. **2** Gaudy costume; adornment. [<F < *plume* plume]

plu·mate (plo͞o′māt) *adj.* Resembling plumage or feathers. [<L *plumatus* feathered]

plumb (plum) *n.* **1** A lead weight on the end of a line used by masons, carpenters, etc., to find the exact perpendicular; a plumb bob; a plummet. **2** A plummet or nautical sounding lead; a sinker on a fishing line, etc. **— off** (or **out of**) **plumb** Not exactly vertical; not in alinement. *— adj.* **1** True, accurate, and upright; vertical or perpendicular; hence, figuratively, upright in principle. **2** *Colloq.* Sheer; complete: also **plum.** *— adv.* **1** In a line perpendicular to the plane of the horizon; vertically. **2** *Colloq.* With exactness; correctly; exactly; completely; entirely: also **plum.** *— v.t.* **1** To test the perpendicularity of with a plumb. **2** To make vertical; straighten: usually with *up.* **3** To test the depth of; sound. **4** To reach the lowest level or extent of; fathom: to *plumb* the depths of despair. **5** To seal with lead. ◆ Homophone: *plum.* [<F *plomb* <L *plumbum* lead]

plumb– Var. of PLUMBO–.

plum·ba·go (plum·bā′gō) *n. pl.* **·gos 1** Graphite: used for pencils, crucibles, lubricating, and in electroplating to coat non-conducting surfaces, as gutta-percha. **2** A drawing made with a lead-pointed instrument. **3** Any of a genus *(Plumbago)* of hardy, shrubby plants cultivated for their showy blue, white, or purplish flowers: also called *leadwort.* [<L *plumbum* lead] **— plum·bag′i·nous** (-baj′ə·nəs) *adj.*

plumb bob The weight used at the end of a plumb line.

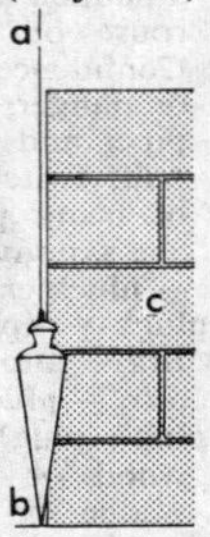

PLUMB BOB
a. Plumb line.
b. Bob.
c. Wall.

plum·be·ous (plum′bē·əs) *adj.* **1** Resembling lead; heavy. **2** Lead-colored. [<L *plumbeus* < *plumbum* lead]

plumbeous vireo A blue-headed vireo *(Vireo solitarius plumbeus),* of northern Nevada to Mexico.

plumb·er (plum′ər) *n.* One who makes a business of plumbing.

plumb·er's friend (plum′ərz) A plunger (def. 3).

plumb·er·y (plum′ər·ē) *n. pl.* **·er·ies 1** The business of plumbing. **2** A plumber's place of business. **3** Leadwork.

plum·bic (plum′bik) *adj. Chem.* Of or pertaining to lead, especially in its higher valence.

plum·bif·er·ous (plum·bif′ər·əs) *adj.* Containing or yielding lead.

plumb·ing (plum′ing) *n.* **1** The art or trade of putting into buildings the tanks, pipes, etc., for water, gas, and sewage. **2** The pipe system of a building. **3** The act of sounding for depth, etc., with a plumb line.

plum·bism (plum′biz·əm) *n. Pathol.* Chronic lead poisoning.

plumb line 1 A cord by which a weight is suspended to test the perpendicularity or depth of something. **2** A plumb bob and its cord together. **3** A sounding line.

plumbo– *combining form* Lead; of or containing lead. Also, before vowels, *plumb–,* as in *plumbiferous.* [<L *plumbum* lead]

plum·bous (plum′bəs) *adj. Chem.* Of, pertaining to, or containing lead, especially in its lower valence.

plumb rule A narrow rule furnished with a plumb line or a cross level, with which masons and carpenters test the verticality of their work.

plum·bum (plum′bəm) *n.* Lead: so called in pharmacy and old chemistry. [<L]

plum duff A suet and flour pudding with raisins, currants, etc., boiled in a cloth bag.

plume (plo͞om) *n.* **1** A feather, especially when long and ornamental. **2** A large feather or tuft of feathers worn as an ornament, especially on a helmet; a panache. **3** *Her.* Three feathers, unless more are specified. **4** A featherlike form or part; the plumose appendage of a seed. **5** Plumage. **6** A decoration of honor; a prize. *— v.t.* **plumed, plum·ing 1** To adorn, dress, or furnish with or as with plumes. **2** To smooth or dress (itself or its feathers); preen. **3** To congratulate or pride (oneself): with *on* or *upon.* [<F <L *pluma* small soft feather]

PLUME *(def. 3)*
Prince of Wales.

plumed partridge The mountain quail *(Oreortyx picta)* of the western United States.

plume·let (plo͞om′lit) *n.* **1** A plumule. **2** A little plume.

plu·mi·ped (plo͞o′mə·ped) *adj.* Having feathered feet. *— n.* A plumiped bird, as an owl. Also **plu′mi·pede** (-pēd). [<L *pluma* feather + -PED]

plum·met (plum′it) *n.* **1** A piece of lead or heavy substance, attachable to a line for making soundings, adjusting walls to the vertical, etc.; a plumb bob; hence, a standard of truth or rectitude. **2** A plumb rule. **3** A weight; especially an oppressive weight. *— v.i.* To drop straight down; plunge. [<OF *plommet,* dim. of *plom* lead]

plum·my (plum′ē) *adj.* **·mi·er, ·mi·est 1** Full of plums. **2** *Colloq.* Full of desirable things; profitable.

plu·mose (plo͞o′mōs) *adj.* **1** Bearing feathers or plumes. **2** Having fine processes on opposite sides, like the vane of a feather. **3** Resembling plumes. [<L *plumosus* < *pluma* feather] **— plu′mose·ly** *adv.* **— plu·mos·i·ty** (plo͞o·mos′ə·tē) *n.*

plump[1] (plump) *adj.* Swelled out or enlarged to the full; somewhat fat. See synonyms under ROUND[1]. *— v.t.* & *v.i.* To make or become plump: often with *up* or *out.* *— n. Archaic* A closely united group; a cluster or clump. [<MDu. *plomp*] **— plump′ly** *adv.* **— plump′·ness** *n.*

plump[2] (plump) *v.i.* **1** To fall suddenly or heavily; drop with full impact. **2** To give one's complete support: with *for.* *— v.t.* **3** To drop or throw down heavily or all at once. **4** To utter bluntly or abruptly: often with *out.* *— n.* The act of plumping or falling; the sound made by the impact of a falling object. *— adj.* Containing no reservation or qualification; blunt; downright. *— adv.* **1** With a sudden impact or fall into or as into water; in a sudden or forcible manner; also, unexpectedly. **2** Directly; without hesitation, circumlocution, or qualification; bluntly. [< MDu. *plompen*] **— plump′ly** *adv.*

plump·er[1] (plum′pər) *n.* **1** A heavy fall or drop. **2** Votes cast all for one candidate instead of for several; also, a person so voting. **3** *Brit. Slang* An unqualified lie.

plump·er[2] (plum′pər) *n.* A disk or padding placed in the mouth, as by persons who have lost their teeth, to distend the cheek and give it an appearance of plumpness.

plum pudding A boiled pudding made with flour, raisins, suet, currants, spices, etc.

plu·mule (plo͞o′myo͞ol) *n.* **1** *Ornithol.* A feather having the barbs soft and free; a downy feather. **2** *Bot.* The rudimentary or first bud of a plant embryo; the first bud of a germinating plant above the cotyledons. [<L *plumula,* dim. of *pluma* feather]

plum·y (plo͞o′mē) *adj.* **plum·i·er, plum·i·est 1** Covered with feathers. **2** Adorned with plumes.

plun·der (plun′dər) *v.t.* **1** To rob of goods or property by open violence, as in war; pillage; loot. **2** To despoil by robbery or fraud. **3** To take as plunder. *— v.i.* **4** To take plunder; steal. See synonyms under STEAL. *— n.* **1** That which is taken by plundering; booty. **2** The act of plundering or robbing. **3** *U.S. Colloq.* Personal belongings or goods, etc. **4** Political booty. [<G *plündern*] **— plun′der·er** *n.*

Synonyms (noun): booty, pillage, prey, rapine, robbery, spoil.

plun·der·age (plun′dər·ij) *n.* Pillage.

plunge (plunj) *v.* **plunged, plung·ing** *v.t.* **1** To thrust or force suddenly into a fluid, penetrable substance, hole, etc. **2** To force into some condition or state: to *plunge* a nation into debt. *— v.i.* **3** To dive, jump, or fall into a fluid, chasm, etc. **4** To move suddenly or with a rush: to *plunge* through a door. **5** To move violently forward and downward, as a horse or ship. **6** To descend abruptly or steeply, as a road or cliff. **7** *Colloq.* To gamble or speculate heavily and recklessly. See synonyms under IMMERSE. *— n.* **1** The act of plunging; a leap; dive. **2** A sudden and violent motion, as of a breaking wave. **3** A place, tank, or pool for diving or swimming. **4** An extravagant or reckless bet or speculation. [<OF *plunjer,* ult. <L *plumbum* lead]

plung·er (plun′jər) *n.* **1** One who or that which plunges; a heavy or reckless speculator. **2** *Mech.* Any appliance having or adapted for a plunging motion, as the piston of a pump. **3** A cuplike device made of rubber and attached to a stick, used to clean out clogged drains, etc.: also called *plumber's friend.*

plunk (plungk) *Colloq. v.t.* **1** To pluck, as a banjo or its strings; strum. **2** To place or throw heavily and suddenly: with *down.* *— v.i.* **3** To emit a twanging sound. **4** To fall heavily or suddenly; plump. *— n.* **1** A heavy blow, or its sound. **2** *Slang* A dollar. [Imit.]

plu·per·fect (plo͞o·pûr′fikt) See PAST PERFECT.

plu·ral (plo͝or′əl) *adj.* **1** Containing, consisting of or designating more than one. **2** *Gram.* Denoting more than one (in languages that have dual number, such as Sanskrit and Greek, more than two): opposed to *singular.* *— n.* *Gram.* The plural number, or a word in this number. [<L *pluralis* < *plus* more] **— plu′·ral·ly** *adv.*

◆ English nouns regularly form their plurals by adding *s* or *es* to the singular; most nouns ending in *f* change the *f* to *v* and add *es*; as wol*f,* wol*ves*; hal*f,* hal*ves.* Nouns ending in *y* change it to *ies* if it is preceded by a consonant: bod*y,* bod*ies*; or merely add an *s* if it is preceded by a vowel; as donke*y,* donke*ys.* Some nouns of Old English origin have an irregular plural in *en,* as, child, childr*en*; or by a vowel change; as, mouse, *mice*; goose, *geese*; man, *men*; tooth, *teeth.* A few nouns retain the singular form unchanged in the plural; as, *deer, hose, moose, series, sheep, species, vermin.* Some such nouns, especially the names of animals, have also an alternative plural regularly formed: as, fish, *fish* or *fishes. Fish* is the usual collective plural; *fishes* is used to indicate more than one genus, variety, species, etc. Many words of foreign derivation retain the plural form peculiar to the languages from which they are severally derived; as, addendum, *addenda*; antithesis, *antitheses*; crisis, *crises*; datum, *data,* etc. Many nouns of this class have also a plural of the regular English form; as, appendix, *appendixes* or *appendices*; beau, *beaus* or *beaux*; cherub, *cherubs* or *cherubim*; focus, *focuses* or *foci*; index, *indexes* or *indices,* etc. Compounds commonly form the plural regularly by adding *s* or *es* to the complete word; as, armful, *armfuls*; cut-throat, *cut-throats*; football, *footballs*; teaspoonful, *teaspoonfuls.* If the last element of the compound forms its plural irregularly, the same form usually appears in the plural of the compound; as, footman, *footmen.* Nouns that end in *-man,* but are not compounds, form the plural regularly by adding *s,* as Mussulman, *Mussulmans.* Hyphenated compounds in which the principal word forms the first element change that element to form the plural; as, father-in-law, *fathers-in-law.*

plu·ral·ism (plo͝or′əl·iz′əm) *n.* **1** The condition of being plural. **2** *Eccl.* The holding of more than one office, or, in the Anglican church, of more than one ecclesiastical living, at one time. **3** *Philos.* The doctrine that there is a plurality of ultimate substances, as spirit and matter: opposed to *monism.* **4** The existence within a society of diverse groups, as in religion, race, or ethnic origin, which contribute to the cultural matrix of the society while retaining their distinctive characters; also, a doctrine advocating this. **— plu′ral·is′tic** *adj.*

plu·ral·ist (plo͝or′əl·ist) *n.* **1** One who holds more than one ecclesiastical benefice at the same time. **2** Anyone who holds a plurality

of offices. 3 One who believes in or advocates pluralism.

plu·ral·i·ty (plōō·ral′ə·tē) *n. pl.* **·ties** 1 The state of being plural. 2 The larger portion or greater number; majority. 3 In U.S. politics, the greatest of more than two numbers, whether it is or is not a majority of the whole; also, the excess of the highest number of votes cast for any one candidate over the next highest number. 4 *Eccl.* Pluralism; also, one of the livings held by a pluralist. 5 Polygamy.

plu·ral·ize (plōō′əl·īz) *v.t.* **·ized, ·iz·ing** 1 To make plural. 2 To express in the plural.

pluri- *combining form* More; many; several: *pluriaxial.* [<L *plus, pluris* more]

plu·ri·ax·i·al (plōō′ē·ak′sē·əl) *adj.* 1 Having more than one axis. 2 *Bot.* Denoting plants whose flowers grow on secondary shoots.

plus (plus) *prep.* 1 Added to or to be added to: Three *plus* two equals five: opposed to *minus.* 2 Increased by: salary *plus* commission. *—adj.* 1 Being or indicating more than nothing; above zero; positive. 2 Electrified positively. 3 *Colloq.* Possessing (something) in addition: used predicatively: He was *plus* a new hat. 4 Extra; supplemental: *plus* value. 5 *Colloq.* Denoting a value higher than ordinary in a specified grade: B *plus.* 6 *Bot.* Designating a form of sexual differentiation in certain plants: the *plus* strain of heterothallic fungi. *—n. pl.* **plus·es** 1 The plus sign. 2 An addition; an extra quantity. 3 A positive quantity. 4 *Colloq.* Something considered advantageous or desirable: a definite *plus* for the business. *—adv. Electr.* Positively. [<L, more]

plus-fours (plus′fôrz′, -fōrz′) *n.* Knickerbockers, cut very full and bagging below the knees. [Orig. tailor's cant; because they were four inches longer than ordinary knickerbockers]

plush (plush) *n.* A pile fabric of silk, rayon, or mohair having a deeper pile than velvet. *—adj.* 1 Of or made of plush. 2 *Slang* Luxurious. [<F *pluche, peluche* <L *pilus* hair] **—plush′y** *adj.*

plus sign The symbol (+) signifying addition or a positive quantity: opposed to *minus sign.*

Plu·tarch (plōō′tärk), A.D. 46?–120?, Greek moralist and biographer.

plu·tar·chy (plōō′tär·kē) *n. pl.* **·chies** Government by the rich. [<Gk. *ploutos* wealth + *archein* rule]

Plu·to (plōō′tō) 1 In Greek and Roman mythology, the god of the infernal regions and spouse of Persephone: identified with the Greek *Hades* and the Roman *Dis.* 2 *Astron.* The ninth planet of the solar system in order of distance from the sun, invisible to the naked eye: discovered 1930. See PLANET. [<L <Gk. *Ploutōn*]

plu·toc·ra·cy (plōō·tok′rə·sē) *n. pl.* **·cies** 1 A class in a community that controls the government by its wealth; the wealthy classes. 2 Plutarchy. [<Gk. *ploutokratia* <*ploutos* wealth + *kratein* rule]

plu·to·crat (plōō′tə·krat) *n.* One who has or exercises power by virtue of his wealth; one of a plutocracy. **—plu′to·crat′ic** or **·i·cal** *adj.* **—plu′to·crat′i·cal·ly** *adv.*

plu·to·ma·ni·a (plōō′tə·mā′nē·ə, -mān′yə) *n.* An excessive desire for great wealth. [<Gk. *ploutos* wealth + -MANIA]

Plu·to·ni·an (plōō·tō′nē·ən) *adj.* 1 Pertaining to Pluto and the lower world; hence, subterranean. 2 *Geol.* Of or pertaining to the Plutonic theory of rock formation. Also **Plu·ton′ic** (-ton′ik). [<L *Plutonius* <Gk. *Ploutonios* like Pluto]

plu·ton·ic (plōō·ton′ik) *adj. Geol.* Deeply subterranean in original position; crystallized, probably from a fused condition: said of igneous rocks: distinguished from *volcanic.* [<L *Pluto, -onis*]

Plutonic theory *Geol.* The doctrine that the principal phenomena of rock structure are chiefly due to igneous agency: distinguished from *Neptunian theory.*

plu·to·ni·um (plōō·tō′nē·əm) *n.* A toxic, radioactive metallic element (symbol Pu, atomic number 94) occurring in minute traces in uranium ores and produced in quantity in nuclear reactors by irradiation of uranium. See PERIODIC TABLE. [<NL <*Pluto* (the planet)]

Plu·tus (plōō′təs) In Greek mythology, the god of riches, blinded by Zeus so that his gifts should be distributed without discrimination.

plu·vi·al (plōō′vē·əl) *adj.* 1 Pertaining to rain; rainy. 2 Arising from the action of rain. [<L *pluvialis* <*pluvia* rain]

pluvio- *combining form* Rain; pertaining to rain: *pluviometer.* Also, before vowels, **pluvi-.** [<L *pluvia* rain]

plu·vi·om·e·ter (plōō′vē·om′ə·tər) *n.* An instrument for measuring the depth of rainfall. [<PLUVIO- + -METER] **—plu′vi·o·met′ric** (-ə·met′rik) or **·ri·cal** *adj.* **—plu′vi·o·met′ri·cal·ly** *adv.* **—plu′vi·om′e·try** *n.*

Plu·vi·ôse (plōō′vē·ōs, *Fr.* plü·vyôs′) See under CALENDAR (Republican).

plu·vi·ous (plōō′vē·əs) *adj.* Pertaining to rain; rainy. Also **plu′vi·ose** (-ōs). [<L *pluviosus*]

Plu·vi·us (plōō′vē·əs) *n.* In Roman mythology, an epithet of Jupiter as god of the rain.

ply[1] (plī) *v.* **plied, ply·ing** *v.t.* To bend; mold; shape. *—v.i. Obs.* To bend or yield. *—n. pl.* **plies** 1 A web, layer, fold, or thickness, as in a carpet, cloth, etc. 2 A strand, turn, or twist of rope, yarn, thread, etc.: used in combination to mean (a certain) number of folds, twists, or strands: three-*ply* yarn. 3 A bent or bias; inclination to one side, as of the mind. [<F *plier* <L *plicare*]

ply[2] (plī) *v.* **plied, ply·ing** *v.t.* 1 To use in working, fighting, etc.; wield; employ. 2 To work at; be engaged in: He *plies* the trade of shoemaker. 3 To subject to repeated action, as by offering unwanted gifts, asking questions insistently, etc.: to *ply* a person with drink; to *ply* one with requests. 4 To strike or assail persistently: He *plied* the donkey with a whip. 5 To traverse regularly: ferryboats that *ply* the river. *—v.i.* 6 To make regular trips; sail: usually with *between.* 7 To work steadily; do one's or its work. 8 *Poetic* To proceed; steer. 9 *Naut.* To beat; tack. [Aphetic var. of APPLY]

ply·er (plī′ər) *n.* 1 A plier. 2 *pl.* A balance of crossed timbers used in raising and lowering a drawbridge.

Plym·outh (plim′əth) 1 A city of eastern Massachusetts; first settlement *(Plymouth Colony)* in New England; site of Plymouth Rock. 2 A port on **Plymouth Sound,** an inlet of the English Channel between Cornwall and Devon in SW England.

Plymouth Colony The colony on the shore of Massachusetts Bay founded by the Pilgrim Fathers who sailed from Plymouth, England, in 1620.

Plymouth Rock 1 The rock at Plymouth, Massachusetts, on which the Pilgrim Fathers are said to have stepped when landing from the *Mayflower* in 1620. 2 One of a breed of domestic fowls of large size, with small single comb and buff, white, black, or gray barred plumage.

ply·wood (plī′wŏŏd′) *n.* Laminated wood consisting of an odd number of sheets or plies tightly glued together, the grains of adjoining layers usually being at right angles to each other: widely used as a structural and building material.

Pl·zeň (pul′zen′y′) The Czech name for PILSEN.

Pm *Chem.* Promethium (symbol Pm).

pne·o·ste·no·sis (nē′ō·stə·nō′sis) *n. Pathol.* A condition marked by any obstruction of air entering or leaving the respiratory tract. [<Gk. *pneein* breathe + STENOSIS]

pneu·ma (nōō′mə, nyōō′-) *n.* The breath of life; the soul or spirit. [<Gk.]

pneu·mat·ic (nōō·mat′ik, nyōō-) *adj.* 1 Pertaining to the science of pneumatics. 2 Describing machines or devices that make use of compressed air: a *pneumatic* engine. 3 Pertaining to or containing air or gas, especially compressed air: a *pneumatic* tire. Also **pneu·mat′i·cal.** *—n.* A pneumatic tire. [<L *pneumaticus* <Gk. *pneumatikos* <*pneuma* breath <*pneein* breathe] **pneu·mat′i·cal·ly** *adv.*

pneu·ma·tics (nōō·mat′iks, nyōō-) *n.* The branch of physics that treats of the mechanical properties of air and other gases, such as their pressure, elasticity, and density, and also of pneumatic mechanisms.

pneumato- *combining form* 1 Air: *pneumatophore.* 2 Breath; breathing: *pneumatometer.* 3 Spirit; spirits: *pneumatology.* Also, before vowels, **pneumat-.** [<Gk. *pneuma, pneumatos* air, spirit, breath]

pneu·ma·tog·ra·phy (nōō′mə·tog′rə·fē, nyōō′-) *n.* Spirit writing. [<PNEUMATO- + -GRAPHY]

pneu·ma·tol·o·gy (nōō′mə·tol′ə·jē, nyōō′-) *n.* 1 The doctrine of the nature and operation of spirit, or a treatise on that science; the science of spiritual beings or existence. 2 The science of the beliefs of men touching a world of spirits. 3 The science dealing with the physiology of air or gases. 4 *Obs.* Pneumatics. **—pneu′ma·to·log′ic** (-tə·loj′ik) or **·i·cal** *adj.* **—pneu′ma·tol′o·gist** *n.*

pneu·ma·tol·y·sis (nōō′mə·tol′ə·sis, nyōō′-) *n. Geol.* The process of forming minerals during the later stages in the consolidation of molten rock-magmas under the influence of the gases which are then present.

pneu·ma·to·lyt·ic (nōō′mə·tō·lit′ik, nyōō′-) *adj.* Of, pertaining to, formed by, or characteristic of pneumatolysis.

pneu·ma·tom·e·ter (nōō′mə·tom′ə·tər, nyōō′-) *n.* An instrument for measuring the volume of air exhaled or inhaled at one breath; a spirometer. **—pneu′ma·tom′e·try** *n.*

pneu·ma·to·phore (nōō′mə·tə·fôr′, -fōr′, nyōō′-) *n.* 1 *Zool.* The air-containing sac of a siphonophore. 2 *Bot.* A root structure found on certain tropical swamp trees: it contains lenticels and is supposed to act as a respiratory organ. **—pneu′ma·toph′o·rous** (-tof′ər·əs) *adj.*

pneu·ma·to·ther·a·py (nōō′mə·tō·ther′ə·pē, nyōō′-) *n. Med.* The treatment of disease by rarefied or condensed air; also, the use of gases for the relief of pain, asphyxiation, etc.

pneu·mec·to·my (nōō·mek′tə·mē, nyōō-) *n. Surg.* The operation of removing lung tissue or a part of the lung. [<PNEUM(O)- + -ECTOMY]

pneumo- *combining form* Lung; related to the lungs; respiratory: *pneumobacillus:* also *pneumono-.* Also, before vowels, **pneum-.** [<Gk. *pneumon, pneumonos* a lung]

pneu·mo·ba·cil·lus (nōō′mō·bə·sil′əs, nyōō′-) *n. pl.* **·cil·li** (-sil′ī) A bacillus *(Klebsiella pneumoniae)* found in infections of the respiratory tract.

pneu·mo·coc·cus (nōō′mə·kok′əs, nyōō′-) *n. pl.* **·coc·ci** (-kok′sī) Any of a group of bacteria that cause a common type of pneumonia and some other diseases. **—pneu′mo·coc′cal, pneu′mo·coc′cous, pneu′mo·coc′cic** (kok′sik) adj.

pneu·mo·con·i·o·sis (nōō′mō·kon′ē·ō′sis, nyōō′-) *n. Pathol.* Any of various lung disorders resulting from the inhalation of dust or other minute particles. Also **pneu′mo·no·con′i·o′sis** (nōō′mə·nō-, nyōō′-). [<PNEUMO- + Gk. *konia* dust + -OSIS]

pneu·mo·dy·nam·ics (nōō′mō·dī·nam′iks, nyōō′-) *n.* The dynamics of gases; pneumatics.

pneu·mo·ec·ta·sis (nōō′mō·ek′tə·sis, nyōō′-) *n. Pathol.* Emphysema of the lungs. [<PNEUMO- + Gk. *ektasis* extension, swelling <*ekteinein* stretch out <*ek-* out + *teinein* stretch]

pneu·mo·e·de·ma (nōō′mō·i·dē′mə, nyōō′-) *n. Pathol.* An abnormal accumulation of fluid in the intercellular cavities of the lungs. [<PNEUMO- + EDEMA]

pneu·mo·gas·tric (nōō′mō·gas′trik, nyōō′-) *adj.* 1 Of or pertaining to the lungs and the stomach. 2 Of or pertaining to the vagus. *—n.* The vagus.

pneu·mo·graph (nōō′mə·graf, -gräf, nyōō′-) *n.* An instrument which records movements of the chest in breathing.

pneu·mo·nec·to·my (nōō′mō·nek′tə·mē, nyōō′-) *n. Surg.* The total removal of a lung. [<PNEUMON(O)- + -ECTOMY]

pneu·mon·ia (nōō·mōn′yə, nyōō-) *n. Pathol.* An infectious disease characterized by inflammation of the lung tissue. The two principal types are *bronchopneumonia,* involving the bronchi and parenchyma of the lungs; and *lobar* or *croupous pneumonia,* affecting one or more lobes of the lungs. [<NL <Gk. *pneumonia* <*pneumōn* lung <*pneein* breathe]

pneu·mon·ic (nōō·mon′ik, nyōō-) *adj.* 1 Affected with pneumonia; pertaining to pneumonia. 2 Pulmonary. [<NL *pneumonicus* <Gk. *pneumonikos*]

pneumono- *combining form* Pneumo-.

pneu·mo·tho·rax (nōō′mō·thôr′aks, -thō′raks,

nyōō′-) *n.* An accumulation of air or gas within the pleural cavity: sometimes artificially induced to collapse the lung in tuberculosis.

Pnom-Penh (nom′pen′, pnōōm·pen′y′) A city on the Mekong, capital of Cambodia; also *Phnompenh.* Also **Pnom Penh.**

Pnyx (niks) The place in ancient Athens where the people met to deliberate and vote upon public affairs.

Po (pō) The largest river in Italy, flowing 405 miles from the Alps to the Adriatic: ancient *Padus.*

Po *Chem.* Polonium (symbol Po).

po·a·ceous (pō·ā′shəs) *adj. Bot.* Of or pertaining to a large, widely distributed family *(Poaceae)* of annual or perennial herbs, the grasses. The inflorescence is spicate, racemose, or paniculate, with very small flowers, generally perfect or staminate. The fruit is a seedlike grain (*caryopsis*), having a starchy endosperm. The grasses producing food grains are known as cereals. Formerly called *Gramineae* or *Graminaceae.* [<Gk. *poa* grass + -ACEOUS]

poach[1] (pōch) *v.t.* To cook (eggs without their shells, fish, etc.) in boiling water, milk, or other liquid until coated. [<OF *pochier* put in a pocket <*poche* pocket; from the "pocketed" position of the egg yolk]

poach[2] (pōch) *v.i.* **1** To trespass on another's property, etc., especially for the purpose of taking game or fish. **2** To take game or fish unlawfully. **3** To become soft and muddy by being trampled: said of land. **4** To sink into mud or soft earth while walking. —*v.t.* **5** To trespass on, as for taking game or fish. **6** To take (game or fish) unlawfully. **7** To make muddy or tear up (land, etc.) by trampling. **8** To reduce to a uniform consistency by mixing with water, as clay. [<OF *pochier* thrust one's fingers into <LG *poken* poke] **—poach′·er** *n.*

poach·y (pō′chē) *adj.* Easily trodden into holes by cattle; soft and miry. [<POACH[2] (def. 3)] **—poach′i·ness** *n.*

Po·ca·hon·tas (pō′kə·hon′təs), 1595?–1617, American Indian princess; daughter of Powhatan, a Virginian chief; she reputedly saved the life of Captain John Smith.

po·chard (pō′chərd, -kərd) *n.* A sea duck (genus *Aythya)* having the head and neck reddish, found in America, Europe, and South Africa. *A. ferina* is the **common pochard** of the Old World; *A. americana,* the **American pochard** or redhead. [Origin uncertain]

pock[1] (pok) *n.* **1** A pustule in an eruptive disease, as in smallpox; a pockmark. **2** *Obs.* Smallpox. [OE *poc*]

pock[2] (pok) *n. Scot.* A bag; pouch: also *poke.*

pock·et (pok′it) *n.* **1** A small bag or pouch; especially, a pouch attached to a garment, as for carrying money. **2** Hence, money; pecuniary means or interests. **3** A cavity, opening, or receptacle. **4** *Mining* A cavity containing gold or other ore; also, an accumulation of alluvial gold in one spot. **5** One of the pouches in a billiard or pool table, into which the balls are driven. **6** A bin for holding grain, coal, etc., for storage. **7** A glen among mountains. **8** In horse-racing, a position in which a horse is behind the leading horse or horses, and is kept from going past by others at the side. **9** An air pocket. **—in one's pocket 1** On terms of intimacy as close to one as one's pocket. **2** Under one's influence or control. —*adj.* **1** Diminutive, as if pocketable. **2** Pertaining to, for, or carried in a pocket: *pocket* lining, *pocket* knife. —*v.t.* **1** To put into or confine in a pocket. **2** To appropriate as one's own, especially dishonestly, as profits or funds. **3** To enclose as if in a pocket. **4** To accept or endure without open resentment or reply, as an insult. **5** To conceal or suppress: *Pocket* your pride. **6** To retain without signing. See POCKET VETO. **7** In billiards, etc., to drive (a ball) into a pocket. [<AF *pokette, poquette,* dim. of OF *poque, poche* bag, pouch] **—pock′et·a·ble** *adj.* **—pock′et·er** *n.*

pock·et·book (pok′it·bŏŏk′) *n.* **1** A small book or case for carrying money and papers in the pocket; wallet. **2** A woman's purse or handbag. **3** A notebook or other book for the pocket. **4** Money or pecuniary resources.

pocket borough In England before the Reform Bill of 1832, a Parliamentary borough owned or controlled by a single individual or family; hence, any constituency controlled by a boss.

pocket edition An edition or copy of a book small enough to be carried in the pocket.

pock·et·ful (pok′it·fŏŏl′) *n. pl.* **·fuls** As much as a pocket will hold.

pocket knife A knife, having one or more blades which fold into the handle, for carrying in the pocket; a penknife.

pocket money Money for occasional expenses; spending money.

pocket veto *U.S.* The act of a chief executive who, where the legislative session will end within the period allowed for returning a measure with his signature or veto, simply retains ("pockets") it until the session adjourns and thus achieves an indirect veto.

pock·et·y (pok′it·ē) *adj.* **1** Characterized by pockets: said of a lode or a placer. **2** Characterized by air pockets.

pock·mark (pok′märk′) *n.* A pit or scar left on the skin by smallpox or similar diseases. **—pock′marked′** *adj.*

pock·y (pok′ē) *adj.* **pock·i·er, pock·i·est 1** Pertaining to, resembling, or affected with smallpox; pockmarked. **2** Syphilitic.

po·co (pō′kō) *adv. Music* Slightly; a little. [<Ital.]

po·co a po·co (pō′kō ä pō′kō) *Music* Little by little; gradually. [<Ital.]

po·co·cu·ran·te (pō′kō·kōō·ran′tē, *Ital.* pō′kō·kōō·rän′tā) *adj.* Indifferent; not caring. —*n.* An indifferent person. [<Ital. *poco curante* caring (but) little <*poco* (<L *paucus)* little + *curante,* ppr. of *curare* care <L] **—po′co·cu·ran′te·ism** or **·ran′tism** *n.*

po·co·sin (pō′kə·sin) *n.* A marsh in an upland region in the southwestern United States. [<Lenape *pakwesen*]

pod[1] (pod) *n.* **1** A seed vessel or capsule of a plant; a legume. **2** Any dry and many-seeded dehiscent fruit. —*v.i.* **pod·ded, pod·ding 1** To fill out like a pod. **2** To produce pods. [Origin uncertain]

pod[2] (pod) *n.* A flock or collection of animals, especially of seals, whales, or walruses. [Origin unknown]

pod[3] (pod) *n. Mech.* **1** The lengthwise groove in certain augers, bits, and gimlets. **2** An auger so grooved. [Origin unknown]

-pod *combining form* **1** One who or that which has (a specified number or kind of) feet: *arthropod.* **2** A (specified kind of) foot: *pleopod.* Also **-pode.** [<Gk. *pous, podos* a foot]

-poda *combining form Zool.* Plural of -POD: used in names of phyla, orders, classes, etc.: *Arthropoda.* [<NL <Gk. *pous, podos* a foot]

po·dag·ra (pō·dag′rə, pod′ə·grə) *n. Pathol.* Gout in the foot. [<L <Gk. <*pous, podos* foot + *agra* seizure] **—po·dag′ral, po·dag′ric** *adj.*

pod·dy (pod′ē) *Austral. n.* A handfed calf, lamb, or foal. —*v.i.* **·died, ·dy·ing** To rear by hand feeding.

po·des·ta (pō·des′tə, *Ital.* pō′des·tä′) *n.* **1** A chief magistrate in the medieval Italian republics. **2** One of the governors of the Lombard cities appointed by Frederick I. **3** A subordinate municipal judge in Fascist Italy. [<Ital. *podestà* <L *potestas* power]

podg·y (poj′ē) *adj.* **podg·i·er, podg·i·est** Dumpy and fat. [Var. of PUDGY] **—podg′i·ness** *n.*

po·di·a·try (pə·dī′ə·trē, pō-) *n.* The study and treatment of diseases of the feet. [<Gk. *pous, podos* foot + -IATRY] **—po·di′a·trist** *n.*

po·dis·mos (pō·dis′məs) *n.* In ancient Greece, a dance performed in full battle dress, simulating pursuit and victory. [<Gk.]

po·di·um (pō′dē·əm) *n. pl.* **·di·a** (-dē·ə) **1** *Archit.* **a** A solid basement or pedestal supporting a structure, as a Roman temple. **b** The parapet surrounding the arena of an ancient amphitheater or circus, and hence also the platform or path behind or above it. **2** A dais, platform, or stage; especially, the platform for the conductor of an orchestra. **3** *Zool.* A foot, or any footlike structure. [<L <Gk. *podion,* dim. of *pous, podos* foot]

-podium *combining form* A footlike part: *pseudopodium.*

Po·do·li·a (pō·dō′lē·ə) A region of SW Ukrainian S.S.R.

Po·dolsk (pō·dôlsk′) A city 23 miles south of Moscow in Russian S.F.S.R.

pod·o·phyl·lin (pod′ə·fil′in) *n.* A bitter, resinous substance obtained from the dried root of *Podophyllum,* the May apple, used in medicine as a purgative. [<NL *Podophyllum,* generic name of the May apple <Gk. *pous, podos* foot + *phyllon* leaf]

-podous *combining form* -footed: used in adjectives corresponding to nouns in *-pod* and *-poda*: *arthropodous.* [<-POD + -OUS]

Po·dunk (pō′dungk) *n.* One of a tribe of North American Indians of Algonquian stock, formerly inhabiting parts of Connecticut and Massachusetts.

Po·dunk (pō′dungk) *n.* Any small town regarded as typically dull and non-progressive. [? from *Podunk,* Massachusetts <N. Am. Ind.]

po·du·rid (pō·dŏŏr′id, -dyŏŏr′-) *n.* Any of a widely distributed family *(Poduridae)* of primitive insects which includes the springtails. [<NL *Podura* <Gk. *pous, podos* foot + *oura* tail; from their ability to leap by sudden extensions of their infolded tails]

pod·zol (pod′zol) *adj.* Of, pertaining to, or designating a major soil type of northern regions developed principally under forest conditions and characterized by a strongly acid, infertile humus underlying a thin mat of leaves and decayed vegetation. Also **pod·zol′ic.** —*n.* Podzol soil. Also **pod′sol** (-sol). [<Russian, ashlike, salty <*sol′* salt]

pod·zol·i·za·tion (pod′zol·ə·zā′shən, -ī·zā′-) *n.* The process or processes by which a soil develops podzol characteristics.

Poe (pō), **Edgar Allan,** 1809–49, U.S. poet, critic, and short story writer.

po·e·chore (pō′ə·kôr, -kōr) *n. Ecol.* The semi-arid regions of the steppes. [<Gk. *poa* grass + *chōra* region] **—po′e·chor′ic** (-kôr′ik, -kor′·ik) *adj.*

po·em (pō′əm) *n.* **1** A composition in verse, either in meter or in free verse, characterized by the imaginative treatment of experience and a heightened use of language more intensive than ordinary speech. **2** Any composition in verse. **3** Any composition characterized by intensity and beauty of language or thought: a prose *poem.* **4** Any experience which produces an effect upon the mind similar or likened to that of a poem: a *poem* in stone. See synonyms under POETRY, SONG. [<F *poème* <L *poema* <Gk. *poiēma,* lit., anything made <*poieein* make]

poe·nol·o·gy (pē·nol′ə·jē) See PENOLOGY.

po·e·sy (pō′ə·sē, -zē) *n. pl.* **·sies 1** *Poetic* Poetry taken collectively. **2** *Poetic* The art or faculty of writing poetry. **3** *Obs.* A poem. **4** *Obs.* A motto or conceit, as one engraved on jewelry. See synonyms under POETRY, SONG. [<OF *poesie* <L *poesia* <Gk. *poiēsis* <*poieein*]

po·et (pō′it) *n.* **1** One who writes poems. **2** One especially endowed with imagination, the power of rhythmical expression, and the creative faculty or power of artistic construction. [<OF *poete* <L *poeta* <Gk. *poiētēs* <*poieein* make] **—po′et·ess** *n. fem.*

po·et·as·ter (pō′it·as′tər) *n.* An inferior poet; a mere rimer or writer of mediocre verse. [<NL]

po·et·ic (pō·et′ik) *adj.* **1** Pertaining to poetry; having the nature or quality of or expressed in poetry: a *poetic* theme. **2** Pertaining to, befitting, or characteristic of a poet: *poetic* fire. **3** Fit to be described in poetry; of a nature to evoke poetic expression: a *poetic* incident or scene. **4** Having or showing the sensibility, feelings, faculty, etc., of a poet. **5** Celebrated or recounted in poetry or verse. Also **po·et′i·cal.** —*n.* Poetics. [<F *poétique* <L *poeticus* <Gk. *poiētikos*]

poetic justice The distribution of rewards to the good and punishment to the evil as often represented in literature; ideal justice.

poetic license The departure from the rules of diction, pronunciation, or from what is generally regarded as fact, for the sake of rime, meter, or an over-all enhancement of effect.

po·et·ics (pō·et′iks) *n. pl. (construed as singular)* **1** The principles and nature of poetry or, by extension, of any art: the *poetics* of music. **2** A treatise on poetry. Also *poetic.*

po·et·ize (pō′it·īz) *v.* **·ized, ·iz·ing** *v.i.* **1** To write poetry. —*v.t.* **2** To turn into or describe by means of poetry; express in poetic form. **3** To make poetic. **—po′et·iz′er** *n.*

poet laureate *pl.* **poets laureate 1** The poet officially invested with the title of laureate by the crown of England, an officer of the

royal household receiving a salary and formerly expected to write for public occasions. **2** In former times, a poet publicly crowned with laurel in recognition of his merits, usually by a sovereign. **3** A poet acclaimed as the most eminent in a locality.

po·et·ry (pō′it·rē) *n.* **1** The writing of poems; the art by which the poet projects feeling and experience onto an imaginative plane, in rhythmical words, to stir the imagination and the emotions. **2** The quality or effect of a poem manifested in any work of literature. **3** That which resembles poetry: Dancing is the *poetry* of motion. **4** A work or works metrically composed; verse or poems collectively; also, metrical composition in general: a book of *poetry.* [<OF *poetrie* <LL *poetria* <L *poeta* poet]

Synonyms: meter, numbers, poem, poesy, rime, song, verse. In ordinary usage, *poetry* is both imaginative and metrical. *Poetry* often exists without *rime*; it may exist without regular *meter,* as in free verse; substitution may be made for *meter,* as in the Hebrew parallelism; *poetry* may be expressed in a way beautiful, lyrically comic, or sharply satiric, but it must involve, besides the artistic form, the exercise of the fancy or imagination to heighten, intensify, and integrate feeling or experience. Failing this, there may be *verse, rime,* and *meter,* but not *poetry.* In a very wide sense *poetry* may be anything rhythmical; as, the *poetry* of motion. There is much in literature that is beautiful and sublime in thought and artistic in construction, which is yet not *poetry,* in the strict sense, because quite devoid of the rhythmical element, and the patterned arrangement and economy of words; the dividing line between poetry and "the other music of prose" is hard to draw. Compare METER^{2}, SONG. *Antonym*: prose.

pog·a·mog·gan (pog′ə·mog′ən) *n.* A war club consisting of a stone or antler secured to the end of a wooden handle, used as a weapon and as a ceremonial symbol by the Plains Indians and also by the Algonquians around the Great Lakes. [<Algonquian]

Po·ga·ny (pō·gä′nē, *Hungarian* pō′gän·y′), **Willy,** 1882–1955, U. S. illustrator, mural painter, and designer, born in Hungary.

po·gey bait (pō′gē) *U. S. Slang* Any confection, as candy bars, etc.

po·go·ni·a (pə·gō′nē·ə, -gōn′yə) *n.* One of a genus *(Pogonia)* of widely distributed terrestrial orchids, especially an American species, *P. ophioglossoides,* having fragrant, rose-pink flowers. [<NL <Gk. *pōgōn* a beard]

pog·o·nip (pog′ə·nip) *n. Meteorol.* A cold fog containing particles of ice, characteristic of the Sierra Nevada mountains and valleys; a frost fog. [<Shoshonean (Paiute)]

po·go stick (pō′gō) A stiltlike toy, with a spring at the base and fitted with two projections for the feet, on which a person may stand and propel himself in a series of hops.

po·grom (pō′grəm, pō·grom′) *n.* An officially instigated local massacre, especially one directed against the Jews. [<Russian, destruction]

po·gy (pō′gē, pog′ē) *n. pl.* **·gies** or **·gy** The menhaden. [<N. Am. Ind. *pauhagen*]

poh (pô) *interj.* Pshaw! bah! an expletive signifying disgust or contempt. [Imit.]

Po·hai (bō′hī′), **Strait of** See CHIHLI, STRAIT OF.

Po·hang (pō·häng) A town in southern Korea on the Sea of Japan. *Japanese* **Ho·ko** (hō·kō).

poi (poi, pō′ē) *n.* A native Hawaiian food made from the ground root of the taro. [<Hawaiian]

-poietic *combining form* Making; producing; creating: *hemapoietic.* [<Gk. *poiētikos* forming <*poieein* make]

poign·ant (poin′yənt, poi′nənt) *adj.* **1** Severely painful or acute to the spirit; keenly piercing; bitter; severe: *poignant* grief; a *poignant* retort. **2** Sharp or stimulating to the taste; pungent; biting. See synonyms under VIOLENT. [<OF, ppr. of *poindre* prick <L *pungere*] —**poign′·an·cy** *n.* —**poign′ant·ly** *adv.*

poi·ki·lo·ther·mal (poi′kə·lō·thûr′məl) *adj. Zool.* Variable in body temperature, as cold-blooded animals: distinguished from *homothermal.* [<Gk. *poikilos* variegated + THERMAL]

poi·lu (pwȧ·lü′) *French adj.* Hairy; bearded. —*n.* A French soldier; originally, an experienced French soldier of World War I.

Poin·ca·ré (pwaṅ·kȧ·rā′), **Jules Henri,** 1854–1912, French mathematician and author. —**Raymond,** 1860–1934, French statesman.

poin·ci·a·na (poin′sē·ā′nə, -an′ə) *n.* **1** One of a small genus of tropical trees or shrubs *(Poinciana,* family *Leguminosae),* especially the flower-fence. **2** The royal poinciana *(Delonix regia),* a tropical tree with bright orange and scarlet flowers and large flat pods. [<NL, after M. de *Poinci,* a 17th century governor of the West Indies]

poind (poind) *v.t. Scot.* **1 a** To seize and sell (the property of a debtor) to satisfy a debt. **b** To distrain the property of. **2** To impound.

poin·set·ti·a (poin·set′ē·ə) *n.* Any of a genus *(Euphorbia)* of American plants of the spurge family, with large showy bracts and inconspicuous flowers, especially an ornamental evergreen hothouse shrub *(E. pulcherrima)* from Mexico, with richly colored, red, leaflike bracts. [after J. R. *Poinsett,* 1779–1851, U. S. statesman]

POINSETTIA
Flower in bracts.

point (point) *n.* **1** The sharp end of a thing, particularly of anything that tapers so as to be very small and keen at the extremity: the *point* of a needle or a thorn. **2** *pl.* The extremities of a horse. **3** An object, as a tool or instrument, having a sharp or tapering end, as a needle, etching tool, etc. **4** A tapering tract of land extending into water; a promontory; cape: *Point* Judith. **5** A prominent feature or peculiarity; typical attribute; salient quality; essential physical characteristic: the *points* of a thoroughbred horse. **6** That to which effort is directed, on which attention is fixed, or to which especial importance is attached; the precise subject of discussion; aim; gist; purport: the *point* of a story. **7** A particular place, location, or position. **8** A position considered as one of a series; a unit of fluctuation, as of count in a game: to gain a *point.* **9** A precise grade, limit, or degree attained or determined, especially in temperature. **10** A particular juncture in the course of events. **11** Any single item or particular; detail. **12** A vital step or division of an argument or discourse; a proposition; head: to note every *point*; to contest *point* by *point.* **13** In schools and colleges, a unit of credit equal to a certain number of hours of academic work. **14** An indivisible portion of time; a particular moment. **15** The moment when something is about or likely to be done or to take place; verge: on the *point* of starting; at the *point* of death. **16** Point lace. **17** A cord or strap by which a thing is fastened, as a rope for reefing sails. **18** In 16th and 17th century costume, a ribbon or string with an aglet on one end, used to fasten together two pieces of clothing. **19** A mark made by or as by the end of a pointed instrument or tool; a prick; puncture; dot. **20** Any mark of punctuation; especially, among printers, a period; stop; end. **21** *Ling.* A vowel point as used in Hebrew. **22** *Music* A dot or other mark to designate time, or formerly tone; also, a short tune or strain; also, such tune when played on an instrument as a signal. **23** A decimal point. **24** Point system (def. 5). **25** The attitude of a pointer or setter when it finds game: The dog came to a *point.* **26** In fencing, a thrust; also, in dancing, the act of pointing the foot downward. **27** A trifle; punctilio: a mere *point.* **28** In cricket, a fielder stationed the nearest to the right of the wicket and slightly in advance of it; also, the position thus occupied. **29** *pl.* In baseball, the positions occupied by the pitcher and catcher. **30** The leading group of an advanced guard. **31** One of the 32 divisions of the compass. See POINT OF THE COMPASS. **32** That which is conceived to have position, but not parts or dimensions, as the extremity of a line. **33** A unit of variation in price of shares, stocks, etc., in the stock market; also, a rumor on which speculation is made; a tip. **34** A fixed place from which position and distance are reckoned. **35** A spot or place which is regarded as having position only, without extent, as a locality. **36** The tail of an animal: used in the phrase *heads and points.* **37** *Electr.* Any of a set of contacts determining the direction of current flow in a circuit. See synonyms under CIRCUMSTANCE, END, TOPIC. —**at** (or **on, upon**) **the point of** On the verge of. —**beside the point** Irrelevant. —**in point** Pertinent. —**in point of** In the matter of; as regards. —**to make a point of** To treat as vital or essential. —**to see the point** To understand the purpose of a course of action; get the important meaning of a story, joke, etc. —**to stretch a point** To make an exception. —**to the point** Relevant. —*v.t.* **1** To direct or aim, as a finger or weapon. **2** To indicate; direct attention to: often with *out*: to *point* the way; to *point* out errors. **3** To give force or point to, as a meaning or remark: often with *up.* **4** To shape or sharpen to a point. **5** To punctuate, as writing. **6** To mark or separate with points, as decimal fractions: with *off.* **7** In hunting, to indicate the presence or location of (game) by standing rigid and directing the muzzle toward it: said of dogs. **8** In masonry, to fill and finish the joints of (brickwork) with mortar. **9** *Ling.* To mark with a vowel point. —*v.i.* **10** To call attention or indicate direction by or as by extending the finger: usually with *at* or *to.* **11** To direct the mind: Everything *points* to your being wrong. **12** To be directed; have a specified direction; tend; face: with *to* or *toward.* **13** To point game: said of hunting dogs. **14** *Med.* To come to a head, as an abscess. **15** *Naut.* To sail close to the wind. See synonyms under ALLUDE. [Fusion of OF *pointe* a sharp point (<Med. L *puncta* <L *punctus*) + OF *point* prick, dot, moment <L *punctum,* neut. of *punctus,* pp. of *pungere* prick]

point alphabet The alphabet of the point system for the blind.

Point Bar·row (bar′ō) See BARROW, POINT.

point-blank (point′blangk′) *adj.* **1** Aimed directly at the mark; in gunnery, fired horizontally without allowing for dropping. **2** Hence, direct; plain: a *pointblank* question. —*n.* A shot with direct aim. —*adv.* In a horizontal line; hence, directly; without circumlocution.

point d'ap·pui (pwaṅ dȧ·pwē′) *French* Point of support; base.

Point de Galle (pwaṅ də gäl) A former name for GALLE.

point d'es·prit (pwaṅ des·prē′) *French* **1** Net or tulle with dots. **2** Lace with the small oval or square dots first used in Normandy lace.

point-de·vice (point′di·vīs′) *adj.* Scrupulously neat; precise; finical. —*adv.* Precisely; exactly. Also **point′-de·vise′.** [ME *(at point) devis,* i.e., (at an) exact (point) <OF *devis* exact]

Pointe-à-Pi·tre (pwaṅ·tȧ·pē′tr′) A city on Grande-Terre, principal port and commercial center of Guadeloupe.

point·ed (poin′tid) *adj.* **1** Having a point. **2** Piquant; pungent; epigrammatic; to the point. **3** Aimed at a particular person; emphasized; conspicuous. See synonyms under ACUTE, SHARP. —**point′ed·ly** *adv.* —**point′ed·ness** *n.*

pointed arch A narrow, pointed arch used in medieval architecture in Europe, characteristic of the Gothic style: also called *Gothic arch.*

pointed architecture The European architecture of the Middle Ages characterized by its consistent use of the pointed arch, with details to correspond.

Pointe-Noire (pwaṅt·nwȧr′) The capital of Middle Congo since 1950.

point·er (poin′tər) *n.* **1** One who or that which points. **2** A hand or index finger, as on a clock or scale. **3** A long tapering rod used in class rooms to point out things on wall maps, charts, diagrams, etc. **4** One of a breed of dogs trained to scent and point out game. **5** A useful bit of information; hint. **6** *Nav.*

One whose business is to bring the gun or turret to its proper elevation. Compare TRAINER. **7** The cowboy who rides at the head of the herd in a cattle drive.

Point·ers (poin′terz) *n. pl. Astron.* Two stars, Alpha and Beta in the constellation Ursa Major, whose connecting line points nearly to the North Star: called *Dubhe* and *Merak.*

pointes (points) *n. pl.* In ballet, dancing on tiptoe. [<F]

Point Four The fourth point in President Truman's Inaugural Address, January 20, 1949, in which he recommended "a bold new program for making the benefits of our scientific advances and industrial progress available for the improvement and growth of underdeveloped areas."

poin·til·lism (pwan′tə·liz′əm) *n.* A French neo-impressionist method of producing effects of light by placing small spots of varying hues on a surface in close proximity, the eye blending them together. [<F *pointillisme* <*pointiller* mark with dots] —**point′til·list** *n.*

point·ing (poin′ting) *n.* **1** The act of sharpening or bringing to a point. **2** *Punctuation.* See under PUNCTUATION. **3** In sculpture, the making of a plaster or clay model with points or marks at intervals and the transferring of these points to the surface of a stone block as an aid in reproducing the model accurately. **4** *Archit.* **a** The process of treating joints in masonry, slating, or tiling, by filling interstices, smoothing out, etc., to finish or repair and to weatherproof. **b** The removal of the thin top layer of mortar between courses of brick and masonry, to replace it with a more moisture-resistant compound. **5** In milling, the rubbing off of the points of grain.

Point Judith A promontory and lighthouse at the western entrance of Narragansett Bay, Rhode Island.

point lace Needlepoint (def. 2). —**point-laced** (point′lāst′) *adj.*

point·less (point′lis) *adj.* Without a point; dull; also, having no significance: a *pointless* remark. See synonyms under BLUNT, FLAT¹. —**point′less·ly** *adv.* —**point′less·ness** *n.*

point of honor Something that vitally affects one's honor.

point of order In parliamentary language, a question of procedure under the rules.

point of the compass One of the 32 equidistant directions or division points marked on the card of the mariners' compass, or a corresponding point in the horizon, or a vertical plane passing through the horizon and one of such points. See COMPASSCARD.

point of view The relative position from which one sees an object, a proposition, or the like. Compare STANDPOINT.

point system 1 *Printing* A standard system of sizes for type bodies, 996 points of which are equal to 35 centimeters, one point being .0138 inch (or approximately 1/72 inch), as adopted by the Typefounders' Association of the United States. **2** Any system of raised letters for the blind, as braille, in which the alphabet is formed of groups of raised dots or points. **3** An academic system of allowing students to progress according to points or credits earned in individual subjects. **4** Any method of rating based on the accumulation of points.

point target A particular structure, object, or installation selected for direct gunfire or bombing. Compare AREATARGET.

poise¹ (poiz) *v.* **poised, pois·ing** *v.t.* **1** To bring into or hold in balance; maintain in equilibrium. **2** To hold; support, as in readiness. **3** *Rare* To weigh. —*v.i.* **4** To be balanced or suspended; hover. —*n.* **1** The state or quality of being balanced; equilibrium; equipoise; also, indecision; suspense. **2** Equanimity; repose; dignity, as in bearing or carriage. **3** A balance weight or counterpoise. **4** Any position that indicates suspended motion. [<OF *il poise, peise,* 3rd person sing. of *peser* <L *pensare,* intens. of *pendere* weigh] —**pois′er** *n.*

poise² (poiz) *n. pl.* **poise** The unit of viscosity in the cgs system, equal to 1 dyne-second per square centimeter. [after Jean Marie *Poiseuille,* 1797?–1869, French physiologist]

poi·son (poi′zən) *n.* **1** Any substance which, introduced into an organism in relatively small amounts, acts chemically upon the tissues to produce serious injury or death. **2** *Physics* Any substance or material which, by

absorbing neutrons, prevents fission in an atomic reactor. **3** Anything that tends to taint or destroy character or to mislead, corrupt, or pervert. —*v.t.* **1** To administer poison to; kill or injure with poison. **2** To put poison into or on. **3** To affect wrongfully; corrupt; pervert: to *poison* one's mind. —*adj.* Killing; venomous; corrupting. [<OF <L *potio, -onis* a drink, poisonous draft. Doublet of POTION.] —**poi′son·er** *n.*

poison dogwood, poison elder Poison sumac.

poison gas Any of a class of toxic chemical agents, usually a liquid under high vapor pressure, employed in warfare for the purpose of disabling or killing enemy personnel.

poison hemlock See under HEMLOCK.

poison ivy A climbing shrub (*Toxicodendron radicans* or *Rhus toxicodendron*), a species of sumac with three broadly ovate, variously notched, sinuate or cut-lobed leaflets and whitish berries: poisonous to many persons by touch.

poison oak 1 A species of poison sumac, especially *Toxicodendron quercifolium.* **2** A species of poison ivy (*T. rydlergii*) common in the western United States.

poi·son·ous (poi′zən·əs) *adj.* **1** Containing or being a poison. **2** Having the effect of a poison; toxic; vitiating. See synonyms under NOISOME. —**poi′son·ous·ly** *adv.* —**poi′son·ous·ness** *n.*

poison sumac 1 A handsome shrub or small tree (*Toxicodendron vernix* or *Rhus vernix*), growing in swamps in the United States and Canada. It has smooth, entire leaflets, and loose panicles of smooth greenish-yellow drupes. The whole plant is poisonous to taste or touch. **2** Poison ivy.

Poi·tiers (pwä·tyā′) A city of west central France; formerly, capital of Poitou.

Poi·tou (pwä·tōō′) A region and former province of west central France.

poi·trel (poi′trəl) *n.* The armor formerly used to protect the breast of a war horse. [<OF *poitral* <L *pectorale* breastplate < *pectus* breast]

poke¹ (pōk) *v.* **poked, pok·ing** *v.t.* **1** To push or prod, as with the elbow; jab: to *poke* a person in the ribs. **2** To make by or as by thrusting: to *poke* a hole. **3** To thrust or push in, out, through, from, etc.: to *poke* one's head from a window. **4** To stir (a fire, etc.) by prodding: often with *up.* —*v.i.* **5** To make thrusts, as with a stick or weapon: often with *at.* **6** To intrude or meddle. **7** To go or look curiously; pry. **8** To appear or show: logs *poking* above the surface. **9** To proceed slowly; dawdle; putter. —**to poke one's nose into** To meddle in. —**to poke fun at** To ridicule, especially slily. —*n.* **1** A push; prod. **2** A yokelike collar with long projections to prevent animals from passing through fences. **3** One who moves sluggishly; a dawdler. **4** *Colloq.* A punch. [ME *poken.* Cf. LG, Du. *poken* push.]

poke² (pōk) *n.* **1** A pocket, or small bag. See POCK². [<OF <Gmc. Cf. ON *poki* and MDu. *poke.*]

poke³ (pōk) *n.* The pokeweed. [<earlier *pocan* <Algonquian (Virginian) *pakon* weed used for staining <*pak* blood. Akin to PUCCOON.]

poke⁴ (pōk) *n.* A large bonnet with projecting front. Also **poke bonnet.**

poke·ber·ry (pōk′ber′ē) *n. pl.* **·ries 1** A berry of the pokeweed. **2** The plant.

pok·er¹ (pō′kər) *n.* **1** One who or that which pokes. **2** An iron rod for poking a fire.

pok·er² (pō′kər) *n.* Any of several games of cards in which the players bet on the value of the cards, usually five, dealt to them, and he whose hand contains the group of highest value wins the entire sum wagered, provided he has not dropped out of the betting. The groups usually recognized, in the ascending order of value, are the *pair, two pairs, three of a kind, straight, flush, full hand* or *house, four of a kind, straight flush, royal flush.* [Origin uncertain. Cf. G *pochspiel,* lit., bragging game <*pochen* brag.]

pok·er·face (pō′kər·fās′) *n.* A face that reveals nothing: so called from the controlled and inscrutable faces of professional poker-players.

pok·er·ish (pō′kər·ish) *adj.* **1** Stiff or unbending, as a poker. **2** Ghastly; unearthly. —**pok′er·ish·ly** *adv.*

poke·weed (pōk′wēd′) *n.* A stout perennial herb of the United States (*Phytolacca americana*), having dark-purple berries and a root

used in medicine: often called *inkberry.* Also **poke′root′** (-rōōt′, -rŏŏt′). [See POKE³]

pok·ing (pō′king) *adj.* **1** Drudging; servile; mean. **2** Projecting.

pok·y (pō′kē) *adj.* **pok·i·er, pok·i·est 1** Lacking life or spirit; dull; slow. **2** Shabby. **3** Cramped; stuffy. Also **poke′y.**

Po·la (pō′lä) The Italian name for PULA.

po·lac·ca (pō·lak′ə) *n.* A two- or three-masted Mediterranean vessel. Also **po·la·cre** (pō·lä′·kər). [< Ital.]

Po·lack (pō′lok, -lak) *n. Slang* A Pole; especially, an immigrant from Poland: a contemptuous term. —*adj.* Polish. [<Polish *polak*]

Po·land (pō′lənd) A republic of north central Europe; 120,359 square miles; capital, Warsaw: Polish *Polska.*

Poland China An American mixed breed of large pigs, similar to Berkshires.

Po·land·er (pō′lən·dər) *n.* A Pole.

po·lar (pō′lər) *adj.* **1** Pertaining to the poles of a sphere, as of the earth. **2** Coming from or found near the North or South Pole. **3** Pertaining to the poles of a magnet or other center of attraction or repulsion. **4** Exhibiting ionization. **5** Having or proceeding from a point of radiation. **6** Attracting; guiding. **7** *Math.* **a** Of or pertaining to a coordinate system of representing equations graphically whereby a point is located by its linear distance from the pole and by the angle subtended by a line from the point to the pole and the polar axis. **b** Of or pertaining to a curve or an equation traced or traceable by means of such coordinates. [<Med. L *polaris* <*polus* pole]

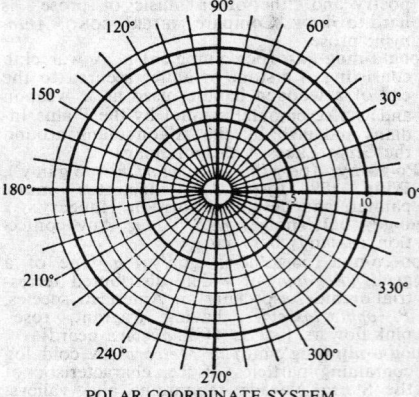

POLAR COORDINATE SYSTEM
The polar axis is the horizontal axis.

polar angle *Math.* In a polar coordinate system, the angle subtended between the polar axis and a line drawn from a point to the pole.

polar axis *Math.* A fixed line directed from the pole in the polar coordinate system from which angles are measured in a counterclockwise direction.

polar bear A large, amphibious, white bear of arctic regions (*Thalarctus maritimus*).

polar body *Biol.* One of the two spherical bodies that separate from the ovum at the time of its maturation.

polar circles The Arctic and Antarctic circles.

polar compound *Chem.* Any of a class of compounds which will conduct an electric current when either fused or in solution, as most inorganic acids, bases, and salts.

polar distance Codeclination.

polar front *Meteorol.* The line or surface of discontinuity separating an air mass originating in polar regions from one of tropical origin.

po·lar·im·e·ter (pō′lə·rim′ə·tər) *n.* **1** An instrument for measuring the rotation of the plane of polarization or the proportion or polarized light in a beam. **2** A form of polariscope. [<L *polaris* polar + -METER]

Po·lar·is (pō·lar′is) **1** The polestar or North Star: Alpha in the constellation Ursa Minor. See under STAR. **2** An intermediate range ballistic missile of the U.S. Navy designed to be launched from a submerged submarine. [<L]

po·lar·i·scope (pō·lar′ə·skōp) *n.* An optical instrument for exhibiting or measuring the polarization of light. [<L *polaris* polar + -SCOPE]

po·lar·i·ty (pō·lar′ə·tē) *n.* 1 The quality of having opposite poles. 2 *Physics* That quality of a body by which it exhibits certain properties related to a line of direction through its mass, the properties at one end of this line being of opposite or contrasting nature to the properties at the other end, as in a magnet. 3 The quality of being attracted to one pole and repelled from the other.

po·lar·i·za·tion (pō′lər·ə·zā′shən, -ī·zā′-) *n.* 1 The act of polarizing, or state of being polarized; bestowal or gaining of polarity. 2 *Physics* A condition of radiant energy, most noticeable in light, in which its vibrations assume a definite form or direction when subjected to special influences. Light may be polarized by reflection, at an angle which differs for different substances, or by transmission, as through most crystals or solutions. If light thus treated be examined by subjecting it to such reflection or transmission a second time, it is found that in certain positions of the reflector or crystal it will pass most easily, while in the positions at right angles to these it will be totally quenched, and in intermediate positions it will pass partially. The plane of polarization is altered or rotated by the passage of light through suitable media; this is called **rotary polarization,** which takes two directions, right–handed and left–handed. 3 *Electr.* A change in the potential of the electrode of a cell due to the accumulation upon it of dissociation products liberated by the current. — **angle of polarization** or **polarizing angle** That angle of reflection from a plane surface at which light is polarized. — **plane of polarization** The plane in which the light vibrations occur when polarized.

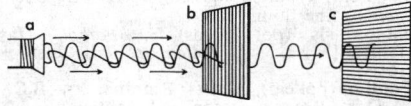

POLARIZATION
Of the light emitted at *a,* only the part whose electric oscillations are parallel to the axis of polarizing medium *b* can pass through it. This is blocked at polarizing medium *c,* whose axis is at right angles to that of *b.*

po·lar·ize (pō′lə·rīz) *v.t.* **·ized, ·iz·ing** 1 To develop polarization in; give polarity to. 2 To give a special meaning or direction to. Also *Brit.* **po′lar·ise.** — **po′lar·iz′a·ble** *adj.* — **po′lar·iz′er** *n.*

polar lights The aurora borealis or the aurora australis.

Po·lar·oid (pō′lə·roid) *n.* A material composed of a sheet of specially prepared plastic between layers of glass and having the property of polarizing and thus reducing the intensity of the light passing through it: a trade name.

Polar Regions The areas within the Arctic and Antarctic circles.

polar star The polestar.

pol·der (pōl′dər) *n.* A tract of marshy land, lower than the sea, which has been diked and reclaimed to cultivation. Also **pol′der·land′.** [<Du.]

pole[1] (pōl) *n.* 1 Either of the extremities of an axis or sphere. 2 One of two points where the axis of rotation, as of the earth, meets the surface. 3 Either of the Polar Regions of the earth; also, either of the two extremities of the earth's axis, called the North *Pole* and the South *Pole.* See CELESTIAL POLE. 4 *Physics* One of the two points at which opposite physical qualities are concentrated; especially, a point (usually one of two) of maximum intensity of electric or magnetic force. 5 The polestar. 6 *Biol.* The differentiated extremities of an ovum or other cell. 7 *Physiol.*

The point of a nerve cell where a process has its origin. 8 *Math.* In polar coordinate and spherical coordinate systems, that point where all radius vectors equal zero. ◆ Homophone: poll. [<L *polus* <Gk. *polos* pivot, pole < *pelein* be in motion]

pole[2] (pōl) *n.* 1 A long slender piece of wood or metal, commonly tapering and more or less rounded; a Maypole, beanpole, the mast of a vessel, etc. 2 The tongue of a vehicle. 3 In linear and surface measure, a perch or rod. 4 A fishing rod. — *v.* **poled, pol·ing** *v.t.* 1 To propel, push, or strike with a pole. 2 To support on poles, as growing beans. — *v.i.* 3 To push a boat, raft, etc., with a pole. ◆ Homophone: poll. [OE *pal* <L *palus* stake]

Pole (pōl) *n.* A native or inhabitant of Poland.

Pole (pōl), **Reginald,** 1500–58, English statesman; archbishop of Canterbury.

pole–ax (pōl′aks′) *n.* A medieval weapon consisting of an ax, or a combined ax and pick, set on a long pole; a battle–ax. — *v.t.* To strike or fell with a pole–ax. Also **pole′–axe′.** [ME *pollax* < *pol* poll[1] + AX]

pole bean Any variety of climbing bean supported by poles.

pole·cat (pōl′kat′) *n.* 1 One of certain European carnivores (genus *Mustela*) of the weasel family, noted for a fetid odor when irritated or alarmed. 2 *U.S.* A skunk. [<F *poule* pullet + CAT; from its predacity]

pole fence A fence made of horizontal unsplit poles.

pole horse A horse hitched beside the pole, as distinguished from a leader.

pole jump See POLE VAULT.

pole line A line of telephone or telegraph poles.

po·lem·ic (pō·lem′ik) *adj.* Pertaining to controversy; disputatious. Also **po·lem′i·cal.** — *n.* 1 A controversy; also, the speeches, papers, etc., comprising this. 2 One who engages in controversy. [<Gk. *polemikos* warlike < *polemos* war]

po·lem·i·cist (pō·lem′ə·sist) *n.* One skilled or engaged in polemics. Also **pol·e·mist** (pol′ə·mist).

po·lem·ics (pō·lem′iks) *n.* The art or practice of disputation; especially, the use of aggressive argument to refute errors of doctrine.

pol·e·mo·ni·a·ceous (pol′ə·mō′nē·ā′shəs) *adj. Bot.* Designating or belonging to a family (*Polemoniaceae*) of herbs (rarely shrubs or small trees) including many ornamental garden species; the phlox family. [<Gk. *polemōnion* kind of plant]

pol·er (pō′lər) *n.* 1 The draft animal harnessed nearest the pole of a cart or wagon; a wheeler. 2 One who poles a boat.

pole·star (pōl′stär′) *n.* 1 *Astron.* The North Star; Polaris; Alpha in Ursa Minor. 2 That which governs, guides, or directs; an attracting or controlling principle.

pole–vault (pōl′vôlt′) *v.i.* To perform a pole vault. — **pole′–vault′er** *n.*

pole vault A vault or jump with a long pole, usually over a light horizontal bar: an athletic field event.

po·lice (pə·lēs′) *n.* 1 A body of civil officers, especially in a city, organized under authority to maintain order and enforce law; constabu-

lary. 2 The whole system of internal regulation of a state, or the local government of a city or town; that department of government that maintains and enforces law and order, and prevents, detects, or deals with crime. 3 The cleansing or keeping clean of a camp or garrison; also, the soldiers detailed for the duties of policing in camp. — *v.t.* **·liced, ·lic·ing** 1 To protect, regulate, or maintain order in (a city, country, etc.) with or as with police. 2 *U.S.* To make clean or orderly, as a military camp. [<F <LL *politia* governmental administration <Gk. *politeia* polity < *politēs* citizen < *polis* city]

police court A municipal court where minor criminal cases are tried. Its jurisdiction corresponds with that of a justice of the peace.

police dog See GERMAN SHEPHERD DOG.

po·lice·man (pə·lēs′mən) *n. pl.* **·men** (-mən) A member of a police force.

police power The broad authority of a state to limit private rights to the extent necessary to promote the peace, good order, morals, health, and safety of the general community.

police state A country whose citizens are rigidly supervised by a national police, often working secretly.

police station The headquarters of a community police force, to which arrested persons are taken and from which policemen operate.

po·lice·wom·an (pə·lēs′wŏŏm′ən) *n. pl.* **·wom·en** (-wim′in) A woman member of a police force.

pol·i·clin·ic (pol′i·klin′ik) *n.* The dispensary of a hospital, or that part of it in which outpatients are treated. Compare POLYCLINIC. [<G *poliklinik* <Gk. *polis* city + G *klinik* clinic]

pol·i·cy[1] (pol′ə·sē) *n. pl.* **·cies** 1 Prudence or sagacity in the conduct of affairs. 2 A course or plan of action, especially of administrative action. 3 Any system of management based on self–interest as opposed to equity; finesse in general; artifice. 4 *Obs.* Political science; government. See synonyms under POLITY. [<OF *policie* <L *politia* <Gk. *politeia.* See POLICE.]

pol·i·cy[2] (pol′ə·sē) *n. pl.* **·cies** 1 A written contract of insurance. 2 A gambling game in which certain numbers (12 or 13) are drawn from a possible 78, bets being made as to what combinations will appear; also, any variation of this game. [<F *police* <Ital. *polizza,* aphetic alter. of Med. L *apodixa, apodissa* receipt <Gk. *apodeixis* proof < *apodeiknynai* make known]

pol·i·cy·hol·der (pol′ə·sē·hōl′dər) *n.* One who holds a policy of insurance.

policy racket Numbers pool.

Po·lil·lo Islands (pō·lē′yō) A Philippine island group off the eastern coast of central Luzon; approximately 295 square miles.

po·li·o (pō′lē·ō) *n. Colloq.* Poliomyelitis.

polio– *combining form Med.* Of or pertaining to the gray matter of the brain, or the spinal cord: *polioencephalitis.* [<Gk. *polios* gray]

pol·i·o·en·ceph·a·li·tis (pol′ē·ō·en·sef′ə·lī′tis) *n. Pathol.* Inflammation of the gray matter of the brain. Also **pol′i·en·ceph′a·li′tis.** [< POLIO– + ENCEPHALITIS]

po·li·o·my·e·li·tis (pol′ē·ō·mī′ə·lī′tis, pō′lē-) *n.*

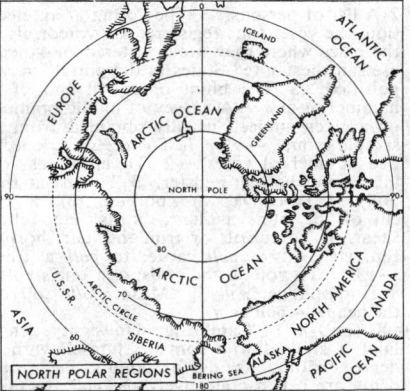

NORTH POLAR REGIONS

SOUTH POLAR REGIONS

Pathol. An acute, communicable disease caused by infection with a virus, occurring especially in children, and characterized by inflammation of the gray matter of the spinal cord, followed by paralysis and atrophy of various muscle groups: also called *infantile paralysis.* [<NL <POLIO- + Gk. *myelos* marrow + -ITIS]

pol·ish (pol′ish) *n.* **1** Smoothness or glossiness of surface; finish. **2** A substance used to produce a bright, smooth, or glossy surface; a varnish. **3** Refinement of manner or style. **4** The process of polishing. — *v.t.* **1** To make smooth or lustrous, as by rubbing. **2** To make complete; finish; perfect. **3** To free from crudeness; make refined or elegant: to *polish* the mind. — *v.i.* **4** To take a gloss; shine. **5** To become elegant or refined. — **to polish off 1** To do or finish completely or quickly. **2** To dispose of; overwhelm. — **to polish up** To make better; improve. [<OF *poliss-,* stem of *polir* <L *polire* make smooth] — **pol′ish·er** *n.*

Po·lish (pō′lish) *adj.* Pertaining to Poland, its inhabitants, or their language. — *n.* The West Slavic language of the Poles.

Polish Corridor A strip of land in NW Poland, extending to the Baltic between Germany and East Prussia 1919–1939; part of Germany prior to 1919, and from 1939 to 1945; now a part of Poland.

pol·ished (pol′isht) *adj.* **1** Made smooth by polishing. **2** Naturally smooth and glossy. **3** Refined and polite. See synonyms under FINE[1], POLITE, SMOOTH.

Po·lit·bu·ro (po·lit′byŏŏr′ō) *n.* The leading policy-forming committee of the Communist party in the U. S. S. R. until 1952, when it was replaced by the Presidium. [<Russian *polit- (icheskoe) buro*]

po·lite (pə·līt′) *adj.* **1** Exhibiting in manner or speech a considerate regard for others; courteous; also, cultivated: *polite* society. **2** Finished and elegant in style. [<L *politus,* pp. of *polire* polish] — **po·lite′ly** *adv.* — **po·lite′ness** *n.*

Synonyms: accomplished, civil, complaisant, courteous, courtly, cultivated, cultured, elegant, genteel, gracious, obliging, polished, urbane, well-behaved, well-bred, well-mannered. A man may be *civil* with no consideration for others, simply because self-respect forbids him to be rude; but one who is *polite* has at least some care for the opinions of others, and if *polite* in the highest and truest sense, he cares for the comfort and happiness of others in the smallest matters. *Civil* is a colder and more distant word than *polite; courteous* is fuller and richer, dealing often with greater matters, and is used only in the good sense. *Courtly* suggests that which befits a royal court, and is used of external grace and stateliness without reference to the prompting feeling. *Genteel* refers to an external elegance, which may be showy and superficial, and the word is thus inferior to *polite* or *courteous. Urbane* refers to a politeness that is genial and successful in giving others a sense of ease and cheer. *Polished* refers to external elegancies of speech and manner without reference to spirit or purpose; as, a *polished* gentleman or a *polished* scoundrel; *cultured* refers to a real and high development of mind and soul, of which the external manifestation is the smallest part. *Complaisant* denotes a disposition to please or favor. *Antonyms:* awkward, bluff, blunt, boorish, brusk, clownish, coarse, discourteous, ill-behaved, ill-bred, ill-mannered, impertinent, impolite, impudent, insolent, insulting, raw, rude, rustic, uncivil, uncouth, unpolished, untaught, untutored.

po·li·tesse (pô·lē·tes′) *n. French* Politeness; civility.

pol·i·tic (pol′ə·tik) *adj.* **1** Sagacious and wary in planning; artful; crafty; shrewd, especially in statesmanship. **2** Wisely adapted to an end; specious. **3** *Rare* Pertaining to public polity, or to the state or its government; political. See BODY POLITIC. [<OF *politique* <L *politicus* <Gk. *politikos* civic <*politēs* citizen] — **pol′i·tic·ly** *adv.*

Synonyms: artful, crafty, cunning, diplomatic, discreet, judicious, prudent, sagacious, shrewd, wary, wily, wise.

po·lit·i·cal (pə·lit′i·kəl) *adj.* **1** Pertaining to public policy; concerned in the administra-

tion of government: a *political* system: distinguished from *civil.* **2** Belonging to the science of government; treating of polity or politics: *political* principles. **3** Having an organized system of government; administering a polity. **4** Pertaining to or connected with a party or parties controlling or seeking to control government in a state: *political* methods. [<L *politicus*] — **po·lit′i·cal·ly** *adv.*

political economist A person skilled in political economy.

political economy Economics.

political science The science of the form and principles of civil government, and the extent and manner of its intervention in public and private affairs; politics.

pol·i·ti·cian (pol′ə·tish′ən) *n.* **1** One engaged in politics, especially professionally. **2** *U.S.* One who engages in politics for personal or partisan aims rather than for reasons of principle; also, a political schemer or opportunist. **3** *Brit.* One skilled in the science of government or politics; a statesman. **4** The white-eyed vireo: so called because it feathers its nest with bits of newspaper or whatever comes easily. [<F *politicien*]

po·lit·i·cize (pə·lit′ə·sīz) *v.t.* ·**cized,** ·**ciz·ing 1** To make politically active or aware. **2** To make into a political issue. Also **po·lit′i·cal·ize′** (-kəl·īz′). — **po·lit′i·ci·za′tion** *n.*

pol·i·tick·ing (pol′ə·tik·ing) *n.* Involvement in politics. — **pol′i·tick·er** *n.*

po·lit·i·co (pə·lit′i·kō) *n. pl.* ·**cos** A politician. [<Sp. *político*]

pol·i·tics (pol′ə·tiks) *n.* **1** The science of civil government. **2** Political affairs in a party sense; party intrigues, etc. **3** One's political sentiments: construed as plural. — **to play politics** To speak or act for political reasons; hence, to scheme for an advantage.

pol·i·ty (pol′ə·tē) *n. pl.* ·**ties 1** The form or method of government of a nation, state, church, etc. **2** Any community living under some definite form of government. [<OF *politie,* var. of *policie.* See POLICY[1].]

Synonym: policy. *Polity* is the permanent system of government of a state, a church, or a society; *policy* is the method of management with reference to the attainment of certain ends; the national *polity* of the United States is republican; each administration has a *policy* of its own. *Policy* is often used as equivalent to expediency; as, Many think honesty to be good *policy. Polity* in ecclesiastical use serves a valuable purpose in distinguishing that which relates to administration and government from that which relates to faith and doctrine. See LEGISLATION.

Polk (pōk), **James Knox,** 1795–1849, president of the United States 1845–49.

pol·ka (pōl′kə, pō′-) *n.* **1** A round dance of Bohemian origin in common time, with three steps to every second measure. **2** Music for such a dance: a lively Bohemian or Polish tune in 2/4 time. — *v.i.* ·**kaed,** ·**ka·ing** To dance the polka. [<F <Czech *pulka* half (step)]

polka dot 1 One of a series of spots of various sizes and spacing on a textile fabric. **2** A pattern made up of such spots.

poll[1] (pōl) *n.* **1** The head; hence, a person; also, the top or back of the head; crown. **2** A list of persons. **3** The voting at an election; the votes thus registered or voted; also, the place where they are registered or voted: used in the United States in the plural. **4** A poll tax. **5** The blunt or round end of a hammer or ax. **6** A survey of public opinion on a given subject, usually obtained from a sample group. — *v.t.* **1** To receive (a specified number of votes). **2** To enrol, as for taxation or voting; register. **3** To cast at the polls. **4** To canvass in a poll (def. 6). **5** To cut off or trim, as hair, horns, etc.; clip; shear. **6** To cut off or trim the hair, horns, top, etc., of: to *poll* cattle; to *poll* a tree. — *v.i.* **7** To vote at the polls; cast one's vote. ◆ Homophone: pole. [<MDu. *polle* top of the head] — **poll′er** *n.*

poll[2] (pol) *n.* In Cambridge University, England, a student who contents himself with a degree, without trying for honors. Such students are called collectively *the poll.* [<Gk. *(hoi) polloi* (the) many]

Poll (pol) *n.* A parrot. Also **Poll parrot, Pol′ly.**

pol·lack (pol′ək) *n.* A gadoid food fish (genera

Pollachius and *Theragra*), resembling the true cod, but with the lower jaw projecting and barbel obsolete. *P. pollachius* is the common **European pollack,** *P. virens,* the **green pollack** or coalfish of the North Atlantic, and *T. chalcogramma,* of the North Pacific. Also spelled *pollock.* [Origin uncertain]

pol·lard (pol′ərd) *n.* **1** A tree shorn of its top so that it puts out a dense head of slender shoots. **2** An animal that has lost its horns. — *v.t.* To convert into a pollard. [<POLL[1]]

polled (pōld) *adj.* **1** Shorn of the head or top. **2** Shorn of the hair; bald.

poll·ee (pōl·ē′) *n.* A person whose opinion is polled.

pol·len (pol′ən) *n.* The fine yellowish powder formed within the anther of the flowering plant; the fecundating element in seed plants. [<L, fine flour]

pollen count A measure of the relative concentration of pollen grains in the atmosphere at a given locality and date: usually expressed in the number of grains of a specified variety of pollen per cubic yard.

poll evil An ulcerous abscess on a horse's poll, usually resulting from a bruise.

pol·lex (pol′eks) *n. pl.* **pol·li·ces** (pol′ə·sēz) The first or radial digit of the hand or forelimb of a vertebrate; the thumb. [<L] — **pol′li·cal** *adj.*

pol·li·ce ver·so (pol′ə·sē vûr′sō) *Latin* With thumbs reversed or extended downward: used among the Romans to denote that a defeated gladiator be killed. (The exact signals of mercy and punishment are matters of dispute.)

pol·li·nate (pol′ə·nāt) *v.t.* ·**nat·ed,** ·**nat·ing** To supply or convey pollen to. Also **pol′len·ate.**

pol·li·na·tion (pol′ə·nā′shən) *n.* The transfer of pollen from anthers to stigmas. Also **pol′len·a′tion.**

pol·li·nif·er·ous (pol′ə·nif′ər·əs) *adj.* **1** Producing pollen. **2** Bearing or carrying pollen. Also **pol′len·if·er·ous.**

pol·lin·i·um (pə·lin′ē·əm) *n. pl.* ·**i·a** (-ē·ə) A mass or body of pollen grains more or less coherent; a pollen mass. [<NL <L *pollen, pollinis* fine flour]

pol·li·no·sis (pol′ə·nō′sis) *n. Pathol.* Hay fever. [<NL <L *pollen, pollinis* dust + -OSIS]

Pol·li·o (pol′ē·ō), **Gaius Asinius,** 75 B.C.–A.D. 5, Roman orator and politician.

pol·li·wog (pol′ē·wog) *n.* A tadpole. Also **pol′ly·wog.** [ME *polwygle.* Cf. POLL[1], WIGGLE.]

pol·lock (pol′ək) See POLLACK.

Pol·lock (pol′ək), **Channing,** 1880–1946, U.S. dramatist, novelist, and lecturer. — **Sir Frederick,** 1845–1937, English jurist. — **Jackson,** 1912–1956, U.S. painter.

poll·ster (pōl′stər) *n.* One who takes public opinion polls. Also **poll′ist.**

poll tax A tax on a person, as distinguished from that on property, especially as a prerequisite for voting.

pol·lut·ant (pə·lōō′tənt) *n.* **1** That which pollutes. **2** Any of various noxious chemicals and refuse materials which impair the purity of water, soil, or the atmosphere.

pol·lute (pə·lōōt′) *v.t.* ·**lut·ed,** ·**lut·ing** To make unclean or impure; dirty; corrupt; profane. [<L *pollutus,* pp. of *polluere* make unclean] — **pol·lut′ed** *adj.* — **pol·lut′ed·ly** *adv.* — **pol·lut′ed·ness** *n.* — **pol·lut′er** *n.* — **pol·lu′tion** *n.*

Synonyms: abuse, contaminate, corrupt, debauch, defile, degrade, deprave, dishonor, infect, ravish, soil, stain, taint, violate, vitiate. See CORRUPT, DEFILE[1], VIOLATE. *Antonyms:* clarify, clean, cleanse, clear, filter, fine, purge, purify, redeem, refine, renew, restore.

Pol·lux (pol′əks) See CASTOR AND POLLUX.

Pol·ly (pol′ē) **1** Mary; a familiar nickname used instead of *Molly.* **2** A parrot.

Pol·ly·an·na (pol′ē·an′ə) *n.* A person who always finds good in everything: so called from the heroine of stories by Eleanor H. Porter, 1868–1920.

po·lo (pō′lō) *n.* **1** A game played on horseback, usually with a light wooden ball and long-handled mallets. **2** A similar game played on ice or roller skates. [Cf. Tibetan *pulu* ball] — **po′lo·ist** *n.*

Po·lo (pō′lō), **Marco,** 1254?–1324?, Venetian traveler and author.

polo coat A tailored coat of camel's hair or material imitating camel's hair.

pol·o·naise (pol′ə·nāz′, pō′lə-) *n.* **1** A garment

for women, consisting of a waist and an overskirt in one piece. **2** A stately marchlike Polish dance, or the music for it. **3** A kind of antique Oriental carpet with a silk pile. [< F]

po·lo·ni·um (pə·lō′nē·əm) *n.* An intensely radioactive metallic element (symbol Po, atomic number 84) occurring in traces in uranium ores and produced synthetically by neutron bombardment of bismuth and other metals. See PERIODIC TABLE. [< NL < Med. L *Polonia*, Poland]

Po·lo·ni·us (pə·lō′nē·əs) In Shakespeare's *Hamlet*, the chamberlain to the king and father of Ophelia and Laertes.

Pol·ska (pōl′skä) The Polish name for POLAND.

Pol·ta·va (pol·tä′və) A city of NE Ukrainian S.S.R.; scene of Peter the Great's victory over the Swedes under Charles XII, 1709.

pol·ter·geist (pōl′tər·gīst) *n.* A ghost or spirit reputed to make its presence known by any kind of clatter, as knockings and the noises of moving objects. [< G < *poltern* make a noise + *geist* spirit]

pol·troon (pol·trōōn′) *n.* **1** A mean-spirited coward; dastard. **2** A lazy idler; sluggard. —*adj.* Cowardly; contemptible. [< F *poltron* < Ital. *poltrone* cowardly, sluggish < *poltro* bed] —**pol·troon′er·y** *n.*

poly- *combining form* **1** Many; several; much: *polygamy, polygon.* **2** Excessive; abnormal: *polydactylism.* [< Gk. *polys* much, many]

pol·y·am·ide (pol′ē·am′īd) *n. Chem.* A polymer derived from compounds containing amine and carboxyl groups: used in the making of various synthetic fibers.

pol·y·an·dry (pol′ē·an′drē) *n.* **1** The civil condition of having more than one husband. **2** A social order than includes a plurality of husbands. **3** *Bot.* Having 20 or more stamens. [< POLY- + Gk. *anēr, andros* a man] —**pol′y·an′drous** *adj.*

pol·y·an·thus (pol′ē·an′thəs) *n.* **1** A variety of primrose (*Primula polyantha*), with many-flowered umbels. **2** A widely distributed, fragrant-flowered narcissus (*Narcissus tazetta*). [< POLY- + Gk. *anthos* flower]

pol·y·ar·chy (pol′ē·är′kē) *n. pl.* **·chies** Government by several persons of whatever class. —**pol′y·ar′chic** or **·chi·cal** *adj.*

pol·y·a·tom·ic (pol′ē·ə·tom′ik) *adj. Chem.* **1** Having more than one atom in the molecule. **2** Containing or capable of combining with several replaceable atoms.

po·ly·ba·sic (pol′ē·bā′sik) *adj. Chem.* Containing two or more atoms of hydrogen replaceable by a base or basic radicals: said of certain acids.

pol·y·ba·site (pol′ē·bā′sīt) *n.* A metallic, iron-black ore of silver crystallizing in the monoclinic system. [< G *polybasit*]

Po·lyb·i·us (pə·lib′ē·əs), 205?–120? B.C., Greek historian.

pol·y·brid (pol′i·brid) *n. Bot.* A hybrid plant derived from the crossing of two particular genera, species, or varieties. [< POLY- + (HY)BRID]

Pol·y·carp (pol′i·kärp), Saint, 69?–155?, bishop of Smyrna; martyred.

pol·y·car·pel·lar·y (pol′i·kär′pə·ler′ē) *adj. Bot.* Made up of many carpels.

pol·y·car·pous (pol′i·kär′pəs) *adj. Bot.* **1** Having the fruit composed of two or more distinct carpels. **2** Fruiting many times. Also **pol′y·car′pic.**

pol·y·cen·trism (pol′i·sen′triz·əm) *n.* The existence of several centers of power within an organization or political system, especially in the Communist world. —**pol′y·cen′trist** *n. & adj.*

pol·y·chae·tous (pol′i·kē′təs) *adj. Zool.* **1** Having several setae. **2** Of or pertaining to a class (*Polychaeta*) of annelids, including most marine worms. Also **pol′y·chae′tal, pol′y·chae′tan.** [< POLY- + Gk. *chaitē* hair] —**pol′y·chaete** *adj. & n.*

pol·y·cha·si·um (pol′i·kā′zē·əm, -zhē·əm) *n. pl.* **·si·a** (-zē·ə, -zhē·ə) *Bot.* A form of cymose inflorescence in which, below each flower, more than two secondary branches are given off from the main axis. [< NL < POLY- + Gk. *chasis* division]

pol·y·chrome (pol′i·krōm) *adj.* Done in several or many colors. —*n.* An association of several colors, as in decoration.

pol·y·chro·mic (pol′i·krō′mik) *adj.* Exhibiting many colors or changes of color. Also **pol′y·chro·mat′ic** (-krō·mat′ik) **pol′y·chro′mous.**

pol·y·chro·my (pol′i·krō′mē) *n.* The art of decorating or executing in several or many colors, as in ancient statuary and architecture.

pol·y·clin·ic (pol′i·klin′ik) *n.* **1** An institution furnishing clinical instruction in all kinds of diseases. **2** A general hospital in which many diseases are treated. Compare POLICLINIC.

Pol·y·cli·tus (pol′i·klī′təs) A Greek sculptor of the fifth century B.C. Also **Pol′y·cle′tus** (-klē′təs). —**Pol′y·cli′tan** or **·cle′tan** *adj.*

pol·y·con·ic (pol′i·kon′ik) *adj.* Of, relating to, or based on many cones.

polyconic projection A type of map projection in which the parallels of latitude are arcs of circles which are not concentric and the meridians, except the central one, are curved lines.

Po·lyc·ra·tes (pə·lik′rə·tēz), died 522 B.C., tyrant of Samos; crucified.

pol·y·cy·the·mi·a (pol′ē·sī·thē′mē·ə) *n.* The presence of an abnormally large number of erythrocytes in the bloodstream. [< POLY- + CYT- + -EMIA]

POLYCONIC PROJECTION

pol·y·dac·tyl (pol′i·dak′til) *adj.* Having an abnormally large number of fingers or toes; many-fingered or many-toed: also **pol′y·dac′ty·lous.** —*n.* A polydactyl animal. —**pol′y·dac′tyl·ism** *n.*

pol·y·dem·ic (pol′i·dem′ik) *adj. Ecol.* Occurring or dwelling in two or more regions: said of plants and animals. [< POLY- + Gk. *dēmos* region]

Pol·y·deu·ces (pol′i·dōō′sēz, -dyōō′-) Pollux. See CASTOR AND POLLUX.

pol·y·em·bry·o·ny (pol′ē·em′brē·ō′nē, -brē·ə-nē) *n.* **1** *Bot.* The production of two or more viable embryos in a seed. **2** *Zool.* The production of two or more offspring from a single fertilized ovum, as identical twins in man.

pol·y·er·gic (pol′ē·ûr′jik) *adj.* Capable of accomplishing many tasks; energetically versatile. [< POLY- + Gk. *ergon* work]

pol·y·es·ter fiber (pol′ē·es′tər) *Chem.* A synthetic fiber of high tensile strength made by the esterification of ethylene glycol and other organic compounds.

pol·y·eth·y·lene (pol′ē·eth′ə·lēn) *n. Chem.* A tough, flexible thermoplastic resin, C_2H_4, made by the polymerization of ethylene: used in the making of moistureproof plastics having high electrical resistance.

pol·yg·a·la (pə·lig′ə·lə) *n.* **1** Any of a large genus (*Polygala*) of herbs and shrubs, natives of temperate and subtropical regions, and distinguished by simple, entire leaves, sometimes dotted, and showy magenta, purple, or white flowers; especially, the North American fringed polygala (*P. paucifolia*). **2** The milkwort. [< POLY- + Gk. *gala* milk]

pol·yg·a·mous (pə·lig′ə·məs) *adj.* **1** Of, pertaining to, or characterized by polygamy. **2** Mating with more than one of the opposite sex. **3** *Bot.* Bearing male, female, and bisexual or hermaphrodite flowers on the same plant. [< POLY- + -GAMOUS] —**pol·yg′a·mous·ly** *adv.*

pol·yg·a·my (pə·lig′ə·mē) *n.* **1** The condition of having more than one wife or husband at the same time. **2** The state of having more than one mate. Compare MONOGAMY. —**pol·yg′a·mist** *n.*

pol·y·gen·e·sis (pol′i·jen′ə·sis) *n. Biol.* The doctrine that organisms originate from cells of different kinds. Compare MONOGENESIS. —**pol′y·ge·net′ic** (-jə·net′ik), **pol′y·gen′ic** *adj.*

pol·y·glot (pol′i·glot) *adj.* **1** Expressed in several tongues. **2** Speaking several languages. —*n.* **1** A book giving versions of the same text, as of the Scriptures, in several languages. **2** One who speaks or writes several languages. [< Gk. *polyglōttos*]

pol·y·gon (pol′i·gon) *n. Geom.* A closed, usually plane, figure bounded by straight lines or arcs, especially more than four; a figure having many sides and angles. [< LL *polygonum* < Gk. *polygōnon*]

pol·y·go·na·ceous (pol′i·gə·nā′shəs) *adj. Bot.* Designating a family (*Polygonaceae*) of apetalous, widely distributed herbs, vines, shrubs, and trees; the buckwheat family, including the sorrels. [< POLYGONUM]

po·lyg·o·nal (pə·lig′ə·nəl) *adj.* Constituting or having the form of a polygon; having many angles: a *polygonal* figure. Also **po·lyg′o·nous.** —**po·lyg′o·nal·ly** *adv.*

polygonal number See under NUMBER.

po·lyg·o·num (pə·lig′ə·nəm) *n.* Any of a large and widely distributed genus (*Polygonum*) of annual or perennial herbs. The common smartweed, the prince's-feather, and the bistort are among the best-known species. Also **po·lyg′o·ny.** [< NL < L *polygonos* < Gk. *polygonon* knotgrass < *poly-* many + *gony* knee; from its many joints]

pol·y·graph (pol′i·graf, -gräf) *n.* **1** A device for reproducing a drawing or writing many times; a copy pad. **2** A mechanism for multiplying a drawing or writing. **3** A versatile or prolific author. **4** A collection of different treatises or books. **5** *Med.* A device for recording variations in the heartbeat and in respiratory movements: used as a lie detector. Compare PSYCHOGALVANOMETER. [< Gk. *polygraphos*] —**pol′y·graph′ic** or **·i·cal** *adj.*

po·lyg·ra·phy (pə·lig′rə·fē) *n.* **1** The use of a polygraph. **2** The art of writing in or of interpreting various ciphers.

po·lyg·y·nous (pə·lij′ə·nəs) *adj.* **1** Of, pertaining to, or practicing polygyny. **2** *Bot.* Having many styles.

po·lyg·y·ny (pə·lij′ə·nē) *n.* The marriage, mating, or cohabitation of one male with more than one female. [< POLY- + Gk. *gynē* woman]

pol·y·he·dral (pol′i·hē′drəl) *adj.* Of or pertaining to a polyhedron.

polyhedral angle *Geom.* The angle formed by three or more planes passing through a point; an angle at a vertex of a solid.

pol·y·he·dron (pol′i·hē′drən) *n. pl.* **·dra** (-drə) or **·drons** *Geom.* A solid bounded by plane faces, especially by more than four. [< NL < Gk. *polyedros* many-sided < *polys* many + *hedra* side]

POLYHEDRAL ANGLE
Lateral angles *bac, bad,* etc., form angle at vertex *a.*

Pol·y·hym·ni·a (pol′i·him′nē·ə) The Muse of sacred song. Also **Po·lym·ni·a** (pə·lim′nē·ə).

pol·y·math (pol′ə·math) *n.* One who is learned in many different fields or disciplines. [< POLY- + Gk. *mathanein* learn] —**pol′y·math′ic** *adj.*

pol·y·mer (pol′i·mər) *n. Chem.* Any of two or more polymeric compounds. **2** Any compound formed by polymerization, especially one of higher molecular weight than the parent substance. [< POLY- + Gk. *meros* part]

pol·y·mer·ic (pol′i·mer′ik) *adj. Chem.* **1** Of, pertaining to, or manifesting polymerism. **2** Having the same chemical composition but different molecular weights and different properties, as acetylene and benzene.

po·lym·er·ism (pə·lim′ə·riz′əm, pol′i·mə-) *n. Chem.* The property possessed by several compounds of having identical percentage composition but different molecular weights.

po·lym·er·i·za·tion (pə·lim′ər·ə·zā′shən, pol′i·mər·ə-) *n. Chem.* The process of changing the molecular arrangement of a compound so as to form new compounds having the same percentage composition as the original, but of different (usually greater) molecular weight and different properties. The method may be *linear,* by the successive addition of small structural units to form a chain; *cyclic,* by the formation of rings; or *cross-linked,* by a three-dimensional fusion of either linear or cyclic elements.

po·lym·er·ize (pə·lim′ə·rīz, pol′i·mə·rīz′) *v.t. & v.i.* **·ized, ·iz·ing** To subject to or undergo polymerization. Also *Brit.* **po·lym′er·ise.**

po·lym·er·ous (pə·lim′ər·əs) *adj.* **1** *Biol.* Consisting of many parts. **2** *Bot.* Having many parts or members in each whorl or series.

pol·y·morph (pol′i·môrf) *n.* A substance or organism that exhibits polymorphism. [< Gk. *polymorphos* < *poly-* many + *morphē* form]

pol·y·morph·ism (pol′i·môr′fiz·əm) *n.* **1** *Zool.* The property of assuming or passing through several forms, as an animal exhibiting seasonal changes in coloration. **2** *Mineral.* The occurrence in a mineral of two or more distinct crystal forms of identical chemical composition.

pol·y·mor·phous–per·verse (pol′i·môr′fəs·pər·vûrs′) *adj. Psychoanal.* Designating the generalized sexual potentialities of an individual, especially of a young child.

Pol·y·ne·sia (pol′i·nē′zhə, -shə) The islands of Oceania in the central and SE Pacific, extending east of Melanesia and Micronesia from the Hawaiian Islands to New Zealand; total, about 10,000 square miles.

Pol·y·ne·sian (pol′i·nē′zhən, -shən) *n.* **1** One of the native brown-skinned people of Polynesia: believed to be either of Malay stock originally stemming from a Caucasian strain of Asia, or of mixed Melanesian, Malay, and Caucasian stock. **2** A subfamily of the Austronesian family of languages spoken by these people. — *adj.* Of or pertaining to Polynesia, its people, or their languages.

pol·y·neu·ri·tis (pol′i·nŏŏ·rī′tis, -nyŏŏ-) *n. Pathol.* Simultaneous inflammation of many peripheral nerves.

pol·y·neu·rop·a·thy (pol′i·nŏŏ·rop′ə·thē, -nyŏŏ-) *n. Pathol.* Any morbid condition which affects several nerves at once, as alcoholism or vitamin deficiency. [<POLY- + NEURO- + -PATHY] — **pol′y·neu′ro·path′ic** (-nŏŏr′ə·path′·ik, -nyŏŏr′-) *adj.*

Pol·y·ni·ces (pol′i·nī′sēz) In Greek legend, a son of Oedipus and Jocasta. See SEVEN AGAINST THEBES.

pol·y·no·mi·al (pol′i·nō′mē·əl) *adj.* Of, pertaining to, or consisting of many names or terms. — *n.* **1**. *Math.* An expression, as in algebra, containing two or more terms. **2** *Biol.* A scientific name consisting of more than two terms. [<POLY- + (BI)NOMIAL]

pol·y·nu·cle·ar (pol′i·nŏŏ′klē·ər, -nyŏŏ′-) *adj.* Having many nuclei. Also **pol′y·nu′cle·ate** (-klē·it).

pol·y·ose (pol′ē·ōs) *n.* Polysaccharide. [<POLY- + -OSE[2]]

pol·yp (pol′ip) *n.* **1** *Zool.* **a** A many-tentacled, sessile aquatic coelenterate having a radially symmetrical body typically cylindrical or cup-shaped, as a sea anemone or coral. **b** A single unit of a colonial organism. **2** *Pathol.* A polypus. [<MF *polype* <L *polypus* a cuttlefish, a polypus <Gk. *polypous* <*poly-* many + *pous* a foot]

pol·y·par·y (pol′i·per′ē) *n. pl.* **·par·ies** *Zool.* The solid calcareous or chitinous stock of a colony of polyps, especially of coral. Also called *polypidom.* [<NL *polyparium* <L *polypus* a polypus]

pol·y·pep·tide (pol′i·pep′tīd) *n. Chem.* A compound formed by the union of two or more amino acids.

pol·y·pet·al·ous (pol′i·pet′əl·əs) *adj. Bot.* Having the petals free and distinct. [<NL *polypetalus* <Gk. *poly-* many + *petalon* a leaf, a petal]

pol·y·pha·gi·a (pol′i·fā′jē·ə) *n.* **1** Excessive craving for food; voracity. **2** *Zool.* The practice of eating many kinds of food. [<NL <Gk. <*polyphagos* eating to excess <*poly-* much + *phagein* eat] — **pol′y·pha′gi·an** *n.* & *adj.*

pol·y·phag·ic (pol′i·faj′ik) *adj.* Eating many things; subsisting on various kinds of food. Also **po·lyph·a·gous** (pə·lif′ə·gəs).

pol·y·phase (pol′i·fāz) *adj. Electr.* Having or producing several phases, as an alternating current.

pol·y·phe·mus (pol′i·fē′məs) *n.* **1** An animal, or sometimes a person, having but one eye. **2** A large American silkworm moth *(Telea polyphemus)* having a conspicuous ocellus on each hind wing. [<NL <L, POLYPHEMUS]

Pol·y·phe·mus (pol′i·fē′məs) In Homer's *Odyssey,* the Cyclops who imprisoned Odysseus and his companions in a cave, from which they escaped after blinding him in his sleep. [<L <Gk. *Polyphēmos,* a Cyclops, lit., many-voiced <*poly-* many + *phēmē* a voice]

pol·y·phon·ic (pol′i·fon′ik) *adj.* **1** *Phonet.* Representing more than one sound or combination of sounds, as some written characters. **2** Consisting of many sounds or voices. **3** *Music* **a** Designating or involving the simultaneous and harmonious combination of two or more independent parts or melodies. **b** Denoting an instrument, as a piano, by which two or more sounds may be produced simultaneously. Also **po·lyph·o·nous** (pə·lif′ə·nəs). [<Gk. *polyphōnos* having many tones <*poly-* many + *phōnē* a voice, sound]

polyphonic prose A poem set down on the page as prose: closer to the rhythms of prose than to those of verse and employing such devices as rime, assonance, and alliteration to produce poetic effects.

po·lyph·o·ny (pə·lif′ə·nē, pol′i·fō′nē) *n.* **1** Multiplicity of sounds, as in an echo. **2** *Phonet.* The representation by one written character or sign of more than one sound. **3** Counterpoint. [<Gk. *polyphōnia* a variety of tones or speech <*polyphōnos.* See POLYPHONIC.]

pol·y·phy·le·sis (pol′i·fī·lē′sis) *n. Biol.* The separate and distinct origin of a species of plants or animals from more than one line of descent. Also **pol·y·phy·ly** (pol′i·fī′lē). [<NL <Gk. *polyphylos* of many tribes <*poly-* many + *phylē* a clan] — **pol′y·phy·let′ic** (-let′ik) *adj.*

po·lyp·i·dom (pə·lip′ə·dəm) *n.* A polypary. [<L *polypus* a polypus + *domus* house <Gk. *domos*]

pol·y·ploid (pol′i·ploid) *adj. Genetics* Having more than two basic chromosome sets in the body cells. — *n.* A polyploid cell. [<POLY- + -PLOID]

pol·y·pod (pol′i·pod) *adj.* **1** Having many feet. **2** *Zool.* Pertaining to many-footed organisms. — *n.* A myriapod. [<POLY- + -POD]

pol·y·po·dy (pol′i·pō′dē) *n. pl.* **·dies** **1** Any one of a genus *(Polypodium)* of widely distributed ferns, typically epiphytic, and having naked sori. **2** The possession of many legs or abdominal attachments. [<NL <L <Gk. *polypodion* a kind of fern, dim. of *polypous, -podos* many-footed; so called from its many root branches]

pol·y·pous (pol′i·pəs) *adj.* **1** Having many feet or roots. **2** Pertaining to or resembling a polyp. **3** *Pathol.* Pertaining to, afflicted with, or resembling polypi.

pol·yp·tych (pol′ip·tik) *n.* An altarpiece or panel having more than three folds or leaves. [<Gk. *polyptychos* having many folds <*poly-* many + *ptyx, ptychos* a fold]

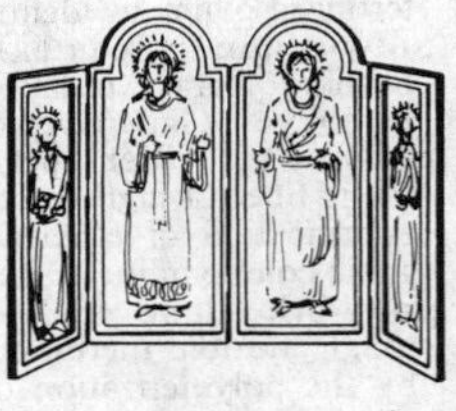

POLYPTYCH

pol·y·pus (pol′i·pəs) *n. pl.* **·pi** (-pī) *Pathol.* **1** A smooth growth of hypertrophied mucus found in mucous membrane, as in the nasal passages, bladder, rectum, etc. **2** A tumor. [<NL <L, a polypus]

pol·y·sac·cha·rid (pol′i·sak′ə·rid, -rid) *n. Chem.* Any of a class of carbohydrates of high molecular weight, formed by the union of three or more monosaccharide molecules: they include starch, dextrin, inulin, cellulose, mucilage, and glycogen. Also **pol′y·sac′cha·rose** (-rōs).

pol·y·sep·al·ous (pol′i·sep′əl·əs) *adj. Bot.* Having sepals free and unconnected.

pol·y·sperm (pol′i·spûrm) *n. Bot.* A tree bearing a many-seeded fruit. [<Gk. *polyspermos* abounding in seed <*poly-* many + *sperma* a seed]

pol·y·sper·my (pol′i·spûr′mē) *n. Bot.* The condition of having numerous seeds in the fruit. Also **pol′y·sper′mi·a.** [<Gk. *polyspermia* <*polyspermos.* See POLYSPERM.] — **pol′y·sper′·mal** or **·sper′mic** or **·sper′mous** *adj.*

pol·y·ste·lic (pol′i·stē′lik) *adj. Bot.* Consisting of more than one stele or internal vascular cylinder. [<POLY- + STELE[2]]

pol·y·sty·rene (pol′i·stī′rēn) *n. Chem.* A thermoplastic polymer of styrene, C_8H_8; a clear, colorless, water-resistant resin: much used in the making of plastics, housewares, light fixtures, electrical components, surface coatings, etc. [<POLY(MER) + STYRENE]

pol·y·sul·fide (pol′i·sul′fīd, -fid) *n. Chem.* A binary compound containing more than one atom of sulfur in the molecule.

pol·y·syl·la·ble (pol′i·sil′ə·bəl) *n.* A word of several syllables, especially of more than three. [<Med. L *(vox) polysyllaba* (a) many-syllabled (word), fem. of *polysyllabus* polysyllabic <Gk. *polysyllabos* <*poly-* many + *syllabē* a syllable] — **pol′y·syl·lab′ic** (-si·lab′·ik) or **·i·cal** *adj.* — **pol′y·syl′la·bism** *n.*

pol·y·syn·de·ton (pol′i·sin′də·ton) *n.* Repetition of connectives or conjunctions for rhetorical effect, as, "east and west and south and north": distinguished from *asyndeton.* [<NL <Gk. *poly-* much + *syndetos* bound together <*syndeein* <*syn-* together + *deein* bind]

pol·y·syn·thet·ic (pol′i·sin·thet′ik) *adj. Ling.* Describing a language, such as Eskimo, or certain of the American Indian languages, in which the subject, object, verb, etc., of a sentence are combined into a single word and have no existence as separate elements. [<Gk. *polysynthetos* much compounded <*poly-* much + *syntithenai* <*syn-* together + *tithenai* put]

pol·y·tech·nic (pol′i·tek′nik) *adj.* Embracing many arts: also **pol′y·tech′ni·cal.** — *n.* A school of applied science and the industrial arts. [<F *polytechnique* <Gk. *polytechnos* skilled in many arts <*poly-* many + *technē* an art]

pol·y·the·ism (pol′i·thē·iz′əm) *n.* The belief in and worship of more gods than one. [<F *polythéisme* <Gk. *polytheos* of many gods <*poly-* many + *theos* a god] — **pol′y·the′ist** *n.* — **pol′y·the·is′tic** or **·is′ti·cal** *adj.*

Pol·y·thene (pol′ə·thēn) *n.* Polyethylene: a trade name. [Contraction of POLYETHYLENE]

pol·y·troph·ic (pol′i·trof′ik, -trō′fik) *adj.* Obtaining nourishment from several sources, as certain pathogenic bacteria. [<Gk. *polytrophos* highly nourished <*poly-* much + *trephein* feed]

pol·y·typ·ic (pol′i·tip′ik) *adj.* Existing in many types or forms. Also **pol′y·typ′i·cal.** [<POLY- + Gk. *typikos* <*typos* a type]

pol·y·un·sat·u·rat·ed (pol′ē·un′sach′ə·rā′tid) *adj. Chem.* Pertaining to or designating an aliphatic compound having many pairs of adjacent carbon atoms linked by two or more pairs of shared valence electrons: used especially of edible oils and fats.

pol·y·u·re·thane (pol′ē·yŏŏr′ə·thān′) *n. Chem.* Any of a group of synthetic, nitrogen-containing polymers with diverse properties, widely used in the manufacture of rigid or flexible solid foams for insulation and upholstery, resins for waterproofing, etc.

pol·y·u·ri·a (pol′i·yŏŏr′ē·ə) *n. Pathol.* Excessive urination. [<NL <Gk. *poly-* much + *ouron* urine] — **pol′y·u′ric** *adj.*

pol·y·va·lent (pol′i·vā′lənt) *adj.* **1** *Bacteriol.* Designating a type of vaccine containing antigens derived from two or more different strains of micro-organisms. **2** *Chem.* Multivalent. — **pol′y·va′lence** *n.*

pol·y·vi·nyl (pol′i·vī′nil) *adj. Chem.* Designating any of a group of polymerized vinyl derivatives extensively used in the production of high-quality resins: *polyvinyl* acetate.

Po·lyx·e·na (pə·lik′sə·nə) In Greek legend, a daughter of Priam, betrothed to Achilles and after his death sacrificed to appease his shade by Neoptolemus.

pol·y·zo·ar·i·um (pol′i·zō·âr′ē·əm) *n. pl.* **·ar·i·a** (-âr′ē·ə) *Zool.* The entire colony of a compound bryozoan, or its supporting skeleton. [<NL <*polyzoa* a bryozoan <Gk. *poly-* many + *zōion* an animal]

pol·y·zo·ic (pol′i·zō′ik) *adj. Zool.* **1** Of or pertaining to the *Bryozoa.* **2** Denoting a spore which produces many sporozoites. [<NL *polyzoa.* See POLYZOARIUM.]

pom·ace (pum′is) *n.* **1** The substance of apples or like fruit crushed by grinding. **2** Fish scrap. **3** The cake left after the expression of oil from castor beans. [<Med. L *pomacium* cider <L *pomum* an apple]

pomace fly A fruit fly.

po·ma·ceous (pō·mā′shəs) *adj.* **1** Relating to or made of apples. **2** Of or pertaining to a pome, or to trees of the rose family that produce pomes. [<NL *pomaceus* <L *pomum* an apple]

po·made (pō·mād′, -mäd′) *n.* A perfumed dressing for the hair or an ointment for the scalp. — *v.t.* **·mad·ed, ·mad·ing** To anoint with pomade. [<MF *pommade* <Ital. *pomata* <*pomo* an apple, fruit <L *pomum*]

po·man·der (pō′man·dər, pō·man′dər) *n.* A perfume ball, or perfumed powder, formerly worn as an amulet; also, a box for carrying such perfume. [Earlier *pomamber* <OF *pomme*

d'ambre apple of amber <*pomme* an apple (<L *pomum*) + *ambre* amber]

pome (pōm) *n. Bot.* A fleshy, many-celled fruit with a core, as an apple, quince, pear, or the like. [<OF, an apple <L *pomum*, orig. a fruit]

pome·gran·ate (pom′gran·it, pum′-, pəm·gran′·it) *n.* **1** The fruit of a tropical Asian and African tree (*Punica granatum*), about the size of an orange and having a hard rind and subacid red pulp with many seeds. **2** The tree. [<OF *pome grenate* <*pome* an apple (<L *pomum*) + *grenate* <LL *granata* <L *granatum*, orig. neut. of *granatus* very seedy <*granum* a grain, a seed]

pom·e·lo (pom′ə·lō) *n. pl.* **·los** A small variety of the shaddock; grapefruit. [Prob. <POME; infl. in form by Du. *pompelmoes* a pompelmous]

Pom·e·ra·ni·a (pom′ə·rā′nē·ə) A region of north central Europe along the Baltic, extending from Stralsund to the Vistula and including a former Prussian province with its capital at Stettin and the former Free City of Danzig; now a part of Poland except for a small area in NE East Germany: German *Pommern.*

Pom·e·ra·ni·an (pom′ə·rā′nē·ən) *adj.* Relating to Pomerania or its inhabitants. —*n.* **1** A native or inhabitant of Pomerania. **2** A small dog with pointed ears and muzzle, a bushy tail turned over the back, and long, straight, silky coat varying in color: believed to have originated in Pomerania.

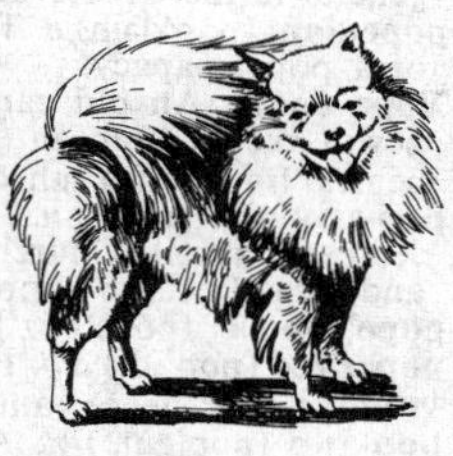

POMERANIAN
(From 7 to 10 inches high; weight, 3 to 7 pounds)

Pom·er·el·ia (pom′ə·rēl′yə) A region of northern Poland on the Baltic and the Gulf of Danzig. *German* **Pom·mer·el·len** (pôm′ə·rel′·ən), *Polish* **Po·mo·rze** (pô·mô′zhe).

po·mi·cul·ture (pō′mi·kul′chər) *n.* Fruit culture. [<*pomi-* (<L *pomum* an apple, fruit) + CULTURE]

po·mif·er·ous (pō·mif′ər·əs) *adj.* Pome-bearing. [<L *pomifer* <*pomum* an apple, fruit + *ferre* bear]

pom·mel (pum′əl, pom′-) *v.t.* **·meled** or **·melled, ·mel·ing** or **·mel·ling** To beat with or as if with the pommel of a sword or with the fists. See synonyms under BEAT. —*n.* **1** A knob at the front of a saddle or on the hilt of a sword. **2** The butt of a firearm. Also spelled *pummel.* [<OF *pomel* a rounded knob, dim. of *pome.* See POME.]

Pom·mern (pôm′ərn) The German name for POMERANIA.

po·mol·o·gy (pō·mol′ə·jē) *n.* The science of fruits and the art of fruit culture. [<NL *pomologia* <L *pomum* an apple, fruit + *-logia* -LOGY] —**po·mo·log·i·cal** (pō′mə·loj′i·kəl) *adj.* —**po′mo·log′i·cal·ly** *adv.* —**po·mol′o·gist** *n.*

Po·mo·na (pə·mō′nə) In Roman mythology, the goddess of fruit and fruit trees.

Po·mo·na Island (pə·mō′nə) Largest of the Orkney Islands, Scotland; about 189 square miles: also *Mainland.*

pomp (pomp) *n.* **1** Magnificent or ostentatious display, especially in costume, equipage, etc. **2** *Obs.* A grand procession; pageant. See synonyms under OSTENTATION. [<OF *pompe* <L *pompa* <Gk. *pompē* a sending, pomp <*pempein* send]

pom·pa·dour (pom′pə·dôr, -dŏŏr, -dōr) *n.* **1** A style of arranging the hair by brushing it up from the forehead in a manner reminiscent of an 18th century style. **2** A style of bodice with low, square neck. —*adj.* Characterizing anything made fashionable by the Marquise de Pompadour: *pompadour* silk. [after Marquise de *Pompadour*]

Pom·pa·dour (pôn·pà·dōōr′), **Marquise de,** 1721–64, Jeanne Antoinette Poisson, mistress of Louis XV of France.

pom·pa·no (pom′pə·nō) *n. pl.* **·nos** **1** A highly prized carangoid food fish (genus *Trachinotus*) of warm seas, especially *T. carolinus,* found off the coasts of the South Atlantic States. **2** A food fish of the American Pacific coast (*Rhombus simillimus*). [<Sp. *pámpano*]

Pom·pe·ii (pom·pā′ē) An ancient city of southern Italy SE of Naples; destroyed by an eruption of Vesuvius, A.D. 79. —**Pom·pe·ian** (pom·pā′ən, -pē′ən) *adj.* & *n.*

pom·pel·mous (pom′pəl·mōōs) *n.* An East Indian variety of shaddock. [<Du. *pompelmoes,* ? <Du. *pompoen* a pumpkin + older Malay *limoes* a shaddock <Pg., pl. of *limão* a lemon, citron]

Pom·pey (pom′pē) Anglicized name of Gnaeus Pompeius Magnus, 106–48 B.C., Roman general, statesman, and triumvir; rival of Julius Caesar: known as *Pompey the Great.*

pom·pho·ly·he·mi·a (pom′fə·li·hē′mē·ə) *n. Pathol.* An abnormal accumulation of gas bubbles in the blood, as in caisson disease. [<NL <Gk. *pompholyx* a bubble (<*pomphos* a blister) + *haima* blood]

pom-pom (pom′pom′) *n.* A rapid-fire, automatic cannon used especially as an anti-aircraft weapon. [From the sound made by the charge when fired]

pom·pon (pom′pon, *Fr.* pôn·pôn′) *n.* **1** In millinery, a tuft or ball, as of feathers or ribbon. **2** The colored ball of wool on the front of a shako, or on top of a sailor's cap. **3** A variety of chrysanthemum or dahlia having a small, compact, globe-shaped flower head. [<F <MF *pomper* exhibit pomp <OF *pompe* pomp]

pom·pous (pom′pəs) *adj.* **1** Marked by assumed stateliness; overbearing; ostentatious. **2** Magnificent; marked by ceremonious or impressive display. —**pom·pos·i·ty** (pom·pos′ə·tē), **pom′pous·ness** *n.* —**pom′pous·ly** *adv.*

Po·na·pe (pō′nə·pā) One of the most important of the eastern Caroline Islands; 129 square miles: formerly *Ascension.*

Pon·ce (pôn′sā) A port in southern Puerto Rico.

Ponce de Le·ón (pons′ də lē′ən, *Sp.* pôn′·thā thā lā·ôn′), **Juan,** 1460–1521, Spanish discoverer of Florida.

pon·cho (pon′chō) *n. pl.* **·chos** **1** A South American cloak like a blanket with a hole in the middle for the head. **2** A similar garment, waterproofed or rubberized, and used as a raincoat. [<Sp. <Araucan *poncho, pontho*]

pond (pond) *n.* A body of still water, smaller than a lake. [ME *ponde,* var. of POUND²]

pon·der (pon′dər) *v.t.* To weigh in the mind; consider carefully. —*v.i.* To meditate; reflect. See synonyms under CONSIDER, DELIBERATE, EXAMINE, MUSE. [<OF *ponderer* <L *ponderare* <*pondus, ponderis* a weight] —**pon′der·a·ble** *adj.* —**pon′der·a·bil′i·ty** *n.* —**pon′der·er** *n.*

pon·der·ous (pon′dər·əs) *adj.* **1** Having great weight; also, huge; bulky. **2** Heavy to the extent of dulness; lumbering; labored. See synonyms under HEAVY. [<OF *pondereux* <L *ponderosus* <*pondus, ponderis* a weight] —**pon′der·os′i·ty** (-də·ros′ə·tē), **pon′der·ous·ness** *n.* —**pon′der·ous·ly** *adv.*

Pon·di·cher·ry (pon′di·cher′ē, -sher′ē) A former French settlement in SE Madras, India; a free city 1947–54; incorporated into India, November 1, 1954; 112 square miles. *French* **Pon·di·ché·ry** (pôn·dē·shā·rē′).

pond·lil·y (pond′lil′ē) *n. pl.* **·lil·ies** The water-lily.

Pon·do·land (pon′dō·land′) A district of eastern Cape of Good Hope Province, Union of South Africa; 4,000 square miles.

pond scum Any of a group of free-floating, fresh-water, green algae (*Spirogyra* and related genera).

pond·weed (pond′wēd′) *n.* Any of various submersed or partially floating perennial aquatic plants (genus *Potamogeton*) common in the Old and the New World.

pone¹ (pōn) *n.* **1** Bread made of cornmeal, sometimes with milk and eggs: also *corn pone.* **2** A small cake or patty of cornbread. [<Algonquian (Virginian), bread <*äpân* something baked]

pone² (pōn) *n.* In card games, the player at the dealer's right. [<L, imperative sing. of *ponere* place]

po·nent (pō′nənt) *adj.* Affirmative; constructive; positing: term used in logic. [<L *ponens, -entis,* ppr. of *ponere* place]

pon·gee (pon·jē′) *n.* A thin, natural, unbleached silk with a knotty, rough weave, originally made in China from the product of wild silkworms. [? Alter of dial. Chinese *pen chi* home loom <Chinese *pun ki*]

pon·iard (pon′yərd) *n.* A small dagger, especially one with a slender triangular or square blade. —*v.t.* To stab with a poniard. [<MF *poignard* <*poing* a fist <L *pugnus*]

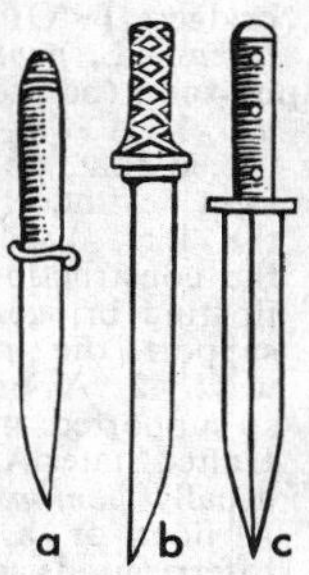

PONIARDS
a. Knife.
b. Japanese.
c. Senegalese.

pons (ponz) *n. pl.* **pon·tes** (pon′tēz) *Latin* A bridge: in Latin phrases.

pons as·i·no·rum (ponz as′·i·nôr′əm, -nō′rəm) *Latin* Asses' bridge.

pons Va·ro·li·i (ponz və·rō′·lē·ī) *Anat.* The organ containing the commissural fibers which connect the cerebrum, cerebellum, and medulla oblongata. Also **pons.** [<NL, bridge of Varoli; after Costanzo *Varoli,* 1542–75, Italian anatomist]

Pon·selle (pon·sel′), **Rosa,** born 1897, U.S. soprano.

Pon·ta Del·ga·da (pon′tə del·gä′də) **1** Easternmost of the three districts of the Azores; 326 square miles. **2** Its capital, a port and chief city of the Azores, on São Miguel.

Pont·char·train (pon′chər·trān), **Lake** A shallow lake in SE Louisiana, joining with the Mississippi at New Orleans by a canal; about 40 by 25 miles.

Pon·te·fract (pom′frit, pum′-, pon′ti·frakt) A municipal borough of West Riding, Yorkshire; site of an 11th century castle where Richard II died. Also **Pom·fret** (pom′frit).

Pon·te·ve·dra (pōn′tā·vā′thrä) An Atlantic province of NW Spain; 1,427 square miles; capital, Pontevedra.

Pon·ti·ac (pon′tē·ak), died 1769, Ottawa Indian chief who made war on the British.

Pon·ti·ac (pon′tē·ak) An industrial city in SE Michigan, 24 miles NW of Detroit.

pon·ti·a·nak (pon′tē·ä′näk) *n.* **1** A grayish-white gum resin obtained from the jelutong tree of Borneo: used as a friction compound on belting, etc. **2** A variety of copal from various species of dammar pine (genus *Agathis*): used in varnishes. [after *Pontianak*]

Pon·ti·a·nak (pon′tē·ä′näk) An Indonesian port on the west coast of Borneo.

Pon·tic (pon′tik) *adj.* Of or pertaining to the Black Sea or adjacent regions. [<L *Ponticus* <Gk. *Pontikos* <*Pontos* the Black Sea, Pontus <*pontos* open sea]

pon·ti·fex (pon′tə·feks) *n. pl.* **pon·tif·i·ces** (pon·tif′ə·sēz) A member of the highest priestly college of ancient Rome, the Pontifical College, which had supreme jurisdiction in religious matters. [<L *pontifex, -ficis* <Osco-Umbrian *puntis* a sacrificial offering + L *facere* make; infl. in form by L *pons, pontis* a bridge]

pon·tiff (pon′tif) *n.* **1** The pope; also, any bishop. **2** A pontifex of ancient Rome. [<F *pontife* <L *pontifex* a pontifex] —**pon·tif′ic** *adj.*

pon·tif·i·cal (pon·tif′i·kəl) *adj.* **1** Of, pertaining to or appropriate for a pontiff. **2** Having the pomp or dogmatism sometimes ascribed to a pontiff; hence, haughty; pompous; dogmatic. [<L *pontificalis* <*pontifex* a pontifex]

pon·tif·i·cate (pon·tif′ə·kit, -kāt) *n.* **1** The office of a pontiff. **2** A pope's term of office. —*v.i.* (-kāt) **·cat·ed, ·cat·ing** **1** To perform the offices of a pontiff. **2** To act or speak pompously or dogmatically.

pon·til (pon′til) *n.* An iron rod used in glass-making to shape hot glass; a punty. [<F, appar. <Ital. *pontello, puntello,* dim. of *punto* a point <L *punctus*]

pontil mark The slight excrescence or scar left on a finished glass article after detaching it from the pontil: also spelled *punty mark.*

pon·tine (pon′tīn) *adj.* Of or pertaining to a bridge or bridges. [<L *pons, pontis* a bridge + -INE¹]

Pon·tine Marshes (pon′tin, -tīn) A plain SE of Rome in west central Italy; about 300 square miles; formerly a swamp.

Pon·tius (pon′shəs, -tē·əs) See PILATE.
pon·ton (pon′tən) *n.* A pontoon. [<OF. See PONTOON.]
pon·to·nier (pon′tə·nir′) *n.* **1** A soldier in charge of pontoons. **2** A builder of pontoon bridges. [<OF *pontonnier* <Med. L *pontonarius* <L, *ponto, -onis* a pontoon]
pon·toon (pon·tōōn′) *n.* **1** A flat-bottomed boat, an airtight cylinder, or the like, used in the construction of floating bridges, to support the roadway. **2** A bridge so supported: in the United States Army, usually *ponton.* **3** A float or a raft to ferry goods across water. **4** A float on the landing gear of a hydroplane. [<OF *ponton* <L *ponto, pontonis* < *pons, pontis* a bridge]

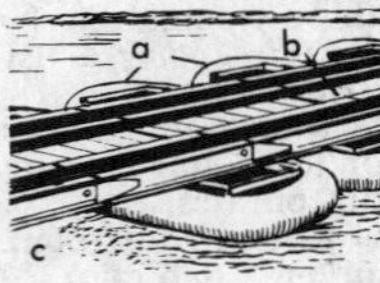

PONTOON BRIDGE
a. Pontoons.
b. Locking bridge sections.
c. Shore.

pontoon bridge A bridge supported on pontoons: distinguished from *fixed bridge.* Also **ponton bridge.**
Pon·top·pi·dan (pôn·tôp′i·dän), **Henrik,** 1857–1943, Danish novelist.
Pon·tus (pon′təs) An ancient country, later a Roman province, on the Black Sea in NE Asia Minor.
po·ny (pō′nē) *n. pl.* **·nies 1** A very small horse, especially one of a small breed; specifically, an Indian pony. **2** Anything small of its kind; specifically, a pony engine. **3** *U. S. Slang* A translation used in the preparation of foreign language lessons; a crib; trot. **4** In British racing slang, the sum of 25 pounds. **5** *Colloq.* A very small glass, for spirits, beer, etc. — *v.t.* & *v.i.* **·nied, ·ny·ing** *U. S. Slang* **1** To translate (lessons) with the aid of a pony or trot. **2** To pay (money) that is due: with *up.* [Var. of dial. E (Scottish) *powney,* prob. <OF *poulenet,* dim. of *poulain* a foal, colt <LL *pullanus* <L *pullus* a young animal]
pony engine *U. S.* A small locomotive for use in railroad yards.
pony express In 1860–61, a postal system by which mail was relayed from Missouri to California by riders mounted on swift ponies; also, the rider. See HORSE-POST.
po·ny·tail (pō′nē·tāl′) *n.* **1** A style of arranging long hair by gathering it tightly at the back of the head and letting it hang down like a pony's tail. **2** Hair so worn.
poo (pōō) *v.t. Scot.* To pull.
pooch (pōōch) *n. Slang* A dog, especially a small mongrel. [? < dial. E and obs. *pooch,* var. of POUCH; ? with ref. to appetite]
pood (pōōd) *n.* A Russian weight equivalent to 36.1 pounds avoirdupois. [<Russian *pud* < LG *pund* ult. <L *pondo* a pound]
poo·dle (pōōd′l) *n.* One of a breed of dogs of high intelligence, with long, curly, usually white or black hair. [<G *pudel* <LG, short for *pudelhund* < *pudeln* splash in water; with ref. to its being a water dog]
pooh (pōō) *interj.* Bah! foh!: an exclamation of disdain: also spelled *poh.*
Pooh-Bah (pōō′bä′) *n. Colloq.* One who fills many offices inefficiently: from a character in Gilbert and Sullivan's *The Mikado.*
pooh-pooh (pōō′pōō′) *v.t.* To reject or speak of disdainfully. — **pooh′-pooh′er** *n.*
pook (pŏŏk) *v.t. Scot.* To pluck; pick.
pool[1] (pōōl) *n.* **1** A small body, usually of fresh water, as a spring. **2** A deep place in a stream. **3** Any small, isolated body of liquid: a *pool* of blood; a puddle. [OE *pōl*]
pool[2] (pōōl) *n.* **1** A collective stake in a gambling game. **2** A combination, generally formed to overcome the effects of excessive competition, whereby companies or corporations agree to fix rates or prices and divide the collective profits pro rata; also, any combination formed for a speculative operation, as in stocks or the like, or the common fund raised for that purpose. **3** Any of various games played on a six-pocket billiard table, in which the object is to drive balls numbered from 1 to 15 into the pockets. **4** A combining of efforts or resources, as for a purpose or the benefit of the contributors. — *v.t.* To combine in a mutual fund or pool, as to satisfy a mutual need, finance an enterprise, etc. — *v.i.* To form a pool. [<F *poule* a stake, orig. a hen <L *pulla;* infl. in form by POOL[1]]
Poole (pōōl) A municipal borough of SE Dorset, England, on the English Channel.
pool·room (pōōl′rōōm′, -rŏŏm′) *n.* A place equipped for playing pool, billiards, etc.
pool table A billiard table with six pockets, one at each corner and one in the middle of each long side.
pool train *Canadian* A train operated by more than one railroad. Also **pooled train.**
poon (pōōn) *n.* Any of various East Indian trees (genus *Calophyllum*): also spelled *puna.* [<Singhalese *pūna*]
Poo·na (pōō′nə) A city of central Bombay State, India.
poop[1] (pōōp) *Naut. n.* **1** A short deck built over the after part of the spar deck of a vessel of war; hence, generally, the stern of a vessel: also **poop deck. 2** A cabin covered by the poop deck: also **poop cabin.** — *v.t.* **1** To break over the stern or poop of: said of a wave. **2** To take (a wave) over the stern. [<OF *pupe, pope* <Ital. *poppa* <L *puppis*]
poop[2] (pōōp) *U.S. Slang v.t.* To bring to exhaustion; weary: usually used passively: He was *pooped* by the long climb. — *v.i.* To stop; cease or withdraw. [Origin uncertain]
Po·o·pó (pō′ō·pō′), **Lake** A lake in west central Bolivia; 12,106 feet above sea level; 60 miles long, 20 to 30 miles wide; about 8 feet deep.
poo·quaw (pōō′kwä) *n.* A quahaug. [<Algonquian *poquau hock* a tightly closed shell]
poor (pŏŏr) *adj.* **1** Lacking means of comfortable subsistence; indigent; needy. **2** Lacking in good qualities, or the qualities that render a thing valuable; specifically, lacking in abundance or quality; scanty: a *poor* crop; of inferior workmanship or quality: a *poor* watch; deficient in vigor; feeble: *poor* health; lean; thin; feeble from ill feeding: That animal is *poor*; lacking in fertility; sterile: *poor* soil. **3** Wanting in strength or spirit; cowardly. **4** Devoid of elegance or refinements; uncomfortable: *poor* surroundings. **5** Deserving of pity; unhappy; wretched: the *poor* dog. **6** Devoid of merit; unsatisfactory: a very *poor* speaker. See synonyms under BAD[1], BASE[2], HUMBLE, MEAGER, SCANTY. [<OF *povre* <L *pauper.* Doublet of PAUPER.] — **poor′ness** *n.*
Poor Clare A member of a religious order founded in 1212 by St. Clare of Assisi and following a rule prescribed by St. Francis of Assisi; a Franciscan nun.
poor farm A farm where paupers are cared for at public expense.
poor·house (pŏŏr′hous′) *n.* A public establishment maintained as a dwelling for paupers.
poor·ly (pŏŏr′lē) *adv.* **1** With poor results. **2** Imperfectly; badly. **3** In the manner of the poor. **4** In a spiritless manner. — *adj. Colloq.* Poor in health; somewhat ailing.
poor-mouth (pŏŏr′mouth′) *v.i. Colloq.* To exaggerate one's financial difficulties. — **poor mouth**
Poor Richard Richard Saunders, the imaginary author of wise precepts in almanacs issued by Benjamin Franklin from 1732 to 1757.
poor-spir·it·ed (pŏŏr′spir′it·id) *adj.* Having little spirit or courage; cowardly. See synonyms under BASE[2]. — **poor′-spir′it·ed·ness** *n.*
poor white In the southern United States, one of a class of poverty-stricken white farmers or laborers, contemptuously called **poor white trash.**
pop[1] (pop) *v.* **popped, pop·ping** *v.i.* **1** To make a sharp, explosive sound. **2** To burst open or explode with such a sound. **3** To move or go suddenly or quickly: with *in, out,* etc. **4** To protrude; bulge: His eyes *popped.* **5** In baseball, to bat the ball into the air so that an opposing player can catch it, thus retiring the batter: with *up* or *out.* — *v.t.* **6** To cause to burst or explode, as corn by heating. **7** To thrust or put suddenly: with *in, out,* etc.: He *popped* his head out of the window. **8** To fire (a gun, etc.). **9** To shoot; also, to hit. **10** In baseball, to bat (the ball) into the air. **11** *Slang* To take (habit-forming or harmful drugs) by mouth or injection: to *pop* pills. — **to pop the question** *Colloq.* To make a proposal of marriage. — *n.* **1** A sharp explosive noise; a small report: the *pop* of a pistol. **2** The shot of a firearm. **3** A flavored soft drink containing carbon dioxide. **4** A shot, as in basketball. — *adv.* Like, or with the sound of, a pop; suddenly. [Imit.]
pop[2] (pop) *n. Slang* Papa. [Short for *poppa,* var. of PAPA]
pop[3] (pop) *adj. Colloq.* **1** Of or pertaining to a pervasive mass culture, especially that of young people. **2** Of or characteristic of the music favored by this group. **3** Of or suggesting pop art. [Short for POPULAR]
pop art *U. S.* A style of painting the subjects and manner of which resemble those of comic strips and advertising posters.
pop·corn (pop′kôrn′) *n.* A variety of maize, the kernels of which explode when heated, forming large white balls; also, the corn after popping.
pope (pōp) *n.* **1** *Often cap.* The bishop of Rome, the visible head of the Roman Catholic Church, accounted by that church the vicar of Christ and successor of St. Peter. He is elected by the college of cardinals, usually from their own number. **2** Any person having, or thought to have, similar great authority. **3** In the Greek Church, a parish priest. [OE *papa* <LL <LGk. *papas* a bishop, father <Gk. *pappas* father]
Pope (pōp), **Alexander,** 1688–1744, English poet and satirist. — **John,** 1822–92, U.S. general in the Civil War.
pope·dom (pōp′dəm) *n.* The office or dominion of a pope; papacy.
Pope Joan An old card game, a variety of newmarket. [after an alleged female pope, central figure of a 9th c. legend]
pop·er·y (pō′pər·ē) *n.* The religion of the Roman Catholic Church with all its doctrines and practices: an opprobrious term.
pope's-nose (pōps′nōz′) See PARSON'S-NOSE.
pop-eyed (pop′īd′) *adj.* Having bulging or protruding eyes; hence, amazed.
pop·gun (pop′gun′) *n.* A tube with a piston that expels a pellet with a pop.
pop·in·jay (pop′in·jā) *n.* **1** A coxcomb. **2** The figure of a bird, formerly used as a mark in archery, and later for firearms. **3** *Archaic* A parrot. [<OF *papegai* <Med. Gk. *papagas* a parrot <Arabic *babhagā*; infl. in form by AF *gai,* OF *geai* a jay]
pop·ish (pō′pish) *adj.* Pertaining to popes or popery: used opprobriously. — **pop′ish·ly** *adv.* — **pop′ish·ness** *n.*
pop·lar (pop′lər) *n.* **1** Any of a genus *(Populus)* of dioecious trees and bushes of the willow family, widely distributed in the northern hemisphere; especially, the **white** or **silver poplar** *(P. alba)* or the **Lombardy poplar** *(P. nigra).* **2** The wood of any of these trees. **3** Any one of several trees in some way resembling a poplar: the **Queensland poplar** *(Homalanthus populifolius)* of tropical Australia, and the **western, white,** or **yellow poplar** of the United States, more properly called *tuliptree.* [<OF *poplier* <L *populus*]
pop·lin (pop′lin) *n.* A durable plain-weave silk, cotton, rayon, or wool fabric, having cross ribs made of warp threads finer than the woof or filling threads: used for dresses, upholstery, etc. [<F *popeline, papeline* <Ital. *papalina* papal; with ref. to Avignon, a papal residence where the fabric was originally made]
pop·lit·e·al (pop·lit′ē·əl, pop′li·tē′əl) *adj.* Of or pertaining to the back part of the leg behind the knee. Also **pop·li·tae·al** (pop′li·tē′əl), **pop·lit′ic.** [<NL *(musculus) popliteus* popliteal (muscle) <L *poples, poplitis* ham]
Po·po·cat·e·pet·l (pō′pə·kat′ə·pet′l, pō·pō′·kä·tā′pet′l) A dormant volcano in central Mexico 45 miles SE of Mexico City in Puebla state; crater 250 feet deep, 2,000 feet across, and over a mile in circumference; 17,887 feet high.
pop·o·ver (pop′ō′vər) *n.* A very light egg muffin: so named from its rising over the dish in which it is baked.
Pop·pae·a Sa·bi·na (po·pē′ə sə·bī′nə), died A.D. 65?, wife of Nero.
pop·per (pop′ər) *n.* **1** Anything that pops or makes an explosive noise, as a popgun, firecracker, etc. **2** A container or device for popping corn.
pop·pet (pop′it) *n.* **1** *Mech.* A poppet head or a poppet valve. **2** A dainty little person; darling: a pet name. **3** One of several small bits of wood on a boat's gunwale to support the rowlocks. [Earlier form of PUPPET]
poppet head A pulley frame over a mine shaft, bearing the hoisting gear.
poppet valve *Mech.* A disk valve mounted on a stem and having a reciprocating motion in

the direction of the longitudinal axis of the stem.
pop·pied (pop′ēd) *adj.* **1** Abounding in or adorned with poppies. **2** Caused by or as by the poppy; causing sleep: a *poppied* drink. **3** Drowsy as with opium.
pop·ple[1] (pop′əl) *v.i.* **·pled, ·pling** To have a heaving motion; ripple; bubble, as agitated water. — *n.* Rippling or bubbling water; bubbling, or its sound. [Prob. imit.]
pop·ple[2] (pop′əl) *n. Dial.* Poplar. [<L *populus*]
pop·py (pop′ē) *n. pl.* **·pies 1** Any plant of the genus *Papaver,* typical of a widely distributed family *(Papaveraceae)* having lobed or toothed leaves and vivid red, violet, orange, or white flowers; especially, the **opium poppy** *(P. somniferum),* the **oriental poppy** *(P. orientale),* the **Iceland poppy** *(P. nudicaule),* the **mission poppy** *(P. californicum),* etc. ◆ Collateral adjective: *papaverous.* **2** The medicinal extract from such a plant. **3** The bright scarlet color of certain poppy blossoms: also **poppy red.** See CALIFORNIA POPPY. [OE *popæg, papoeg* <L *papaver*]
pop·py·cock (pop′ē·kok) *n. Colloq.* Pretentious talk; humbug; nonsense. [<colloq. Du. *pappekak,* lit., soft dung]
pop·py·head (pop′ē·hed′) *n.* A small, carved wooden finial, particularly at the end of a church pew.
Pop·si·cle (pop′sik·əl) *n.* A slab of frozen colored and flavored water at the end of two flat sticks: a trade name. Also **pop′si·cle.**
pop·u·lace (pop′yə·lis) *n.* The body of the common people; the masses. See synonyms under MOB[1]. [<MF <Ital. *popolaccio, popolazzo* <L *populus*]
pop·u·lar (pop′yə·lər) *adj.* **1** Pertaining to the people at large: *popular* demonstrations or government. **2** Widely approved or admired: a *popular* officer. **3** Suitable for the common people; easily comprehended: *popular* lectures. **4** Prevalent among the people: *popular* errors. **5** Suited to the means of the people: *popular* prices. **6** Of folk origin: the *popular* ballad. **7** Used by the people; current; colloquial: said also of many words on the borderline between slang and reputable usage. **8** Plebeian; vulgar; common. See synonyms under COMMON, GENERAL. [<L *popularis* < *populus* the people] — **pop′u·lar·ly** *adv.*
popular etymology A folk etymology.
pop·u·lar·i·ty (pop′yə·lar′ə·tē) *n.* The condition of being popular, especially of possessing the confidence and favor of the people or of a set of people.
pop·u·lar·ize (pop′yə·lə·rīz′) *v.t.* **·ized, ·iz·ing** To make popular. Also *Brit.* **pop′u·lar·ise′.** — **pop′u·lar·i·za′tion** *n.* — **pop′u·lar·iz′er** *n.*
pop·u·late (pop′yə·lāt) *v.t.* **·lat·ed, ·lat·ing 1** To furnish with inhabitants; people. **2** To inhabit. [<Med. L *populatus,* pp. of *populare* <L *populus* the people]
pop·u·la·tion (pop′yə·lā′shən) *n.* **1** The whole number of people in a place or given area; also, any specific portion of that number: the foreign *population* of New York. **2** The act or process of populating or furnishing with inhabitants; the multiplying of inhabitants. **3** *Biol.* The total number of individual organisms being studied by statistical or biometric methods. See synonyms under PEOPLE. [<LL *populatio, -onis* <L *populus* the people]
Pop·u·list (pop′yə·list) *adj.* Of or pertaining to the Populist or People's party. — *n.* A member of the People's party. [<L *populus* the people] — **Pop′u·lism** *n.* — **Pop′u·lis′tic** *adj.*
Populist party See PEOPLE'S PARTY.
pop·u·lous (pop′yə·ləs) *adj.* Containing many inhabitants; thickly settled. [<L *populosus* < *populus* the people] — **pop′u·lous·ly** *adv.* — **pop′u·lous·ness** *n.*
por·bea·gle (pôr′bē·gəl) *n.* A large voracious shark *(Lamna nasus)* of northern waters, sometimes 10 feet long. [<dial. E (Cornish); ult. origin unknown]
porce·lain (pôrs′lin, pōrs′-, pôr′sə-, pōr′-) *n.* A white, hard, translucent ceramic ware, usually glazed, existing in many varieties, according to its composition and method of manufacture; china; chinaware. It is made from pure clay to which a little of the more fusible feldspar is added. [<OF *porcelaine* <Ital. *porcellana,* orig. a cowry] — **por·ce·la·ne·ous** (pôr′sə·lā′nē·əs, pōr′-) or **por′cel·la′ne·ous** *adj.*
porch (pôrch, pōrch) *n.* **1** A covered structure forming an entrance to a building, outside and with a separate roof, or as a recess in the interior as a kind of vestibule; a veranda. **2** An ancient covered walk or portico. Compare LOGGIA. — **the Porch** The Stoic school of philosophy in ancient Athens, named from the Stoa Poecile, or Painted Porch. See STOIC. [<OF *porche* <L *porticus* a colonnade < *porta* a gate. Doublet of PORTICO.]
por·cine (pôr′sīn, -sin) *adj.* Pertaining to, like, or characteristic of swine. [<F, fem. of *porcin* <L *porcinus* < *porcus* a hog]
por·cu·pine (pôr′kyə·pīn) *n.* A large, hystricomorphic rodent, having coarse hair thickly interspersed with erectile quill-like spines used for defense. *Hystrix cristata* is the common porcupine of the Mediterranean region; *Erethizon dorsatum* is the common Canada porcupine of eastern North America: also called *hedgehog.* [<OF *porc espin,* lit., a spiny hog < *porc* a hog (<L *porcus*) + *espin* a thorn <L *spina*]

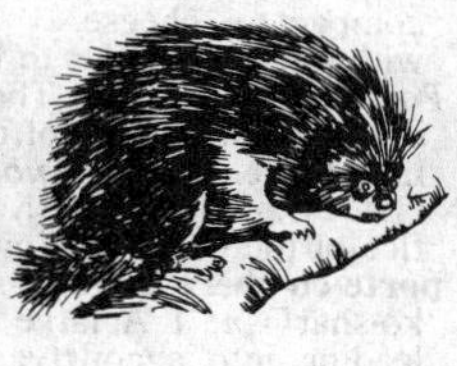
CANADA PORCUPINE
(From 30 to 35 inches long in body length)

porcupine ant-eater An echidna.
porcupine fish A globefish.
porcupine grass A tall grass *(Stipa spartea)* of the western United States, yielding good forage and hay, but having long, stiff, sharp awns which twist through the wool into the flesh of sheep.
Porcupine River A river in northern Yukon and NE Alaska, flowing 525 miles north to the Yukon River.
pore[1] (pôr, pōr) *v.i.* **pored, por·ing 1** To gaze steadily or intently. **2** To study or read with care and application: with *over*: to *pore* over one's accounts. **3** To meditate; ponder. [ME *pouren*; origin unknown]
pore[2] (pôr, pōr) *n.* **1** A small orifice or opening, especially a minute perforation in a membrane or tissue, as in the skin. **2** A minute interstice between the molecules of a body. **3** Any inlet or means of absorption or communication. [<OF *pore, porre* <L *porus* < Gk. *poros*]
por·gy (pôr′gē) *n. pl.* **·gies 1** A sparoid, perchlike, salt-water food fish *(Pagrus pagrus)* of the Mediterranean and North Atlantic: often called **red porgy. 2** Any of various other fishes, as the scup, sailor's-choice, or pinfish. [? Var. of PARGO; infl. by *pogy*]
po·rif·er·ous (pō·rif′ər·əs, pō-) *adj.* **1** Bearing or having pores. **2** Of or pertaining to a phylum *(Porifera)* of primitive, aquatic, chiefly marine animals, having bodies perforated by pores which lead to an internal cavity, and living attached to rocks, shells, and other supports; the sponges. [<NL *porifer* <L *porus* a pore + *ferre* bear]
po·rism (pôr′iz·əm, pō′riz-) *n. Math.* One of an ancient class of geometrical propositions intermediate between theorems and problems that asserted a relation between variables or affirmed the possibility of finding conditions under which a problem would become indeterminate. [<L *porisma* a corollary, a problem <Gk. < *porizein* carry, deduce < *poros* a way, a voyage]
pork (pôrk, pōrk) *n.* **1** The flesh of swine used as food. **2** A swine or swine collectively. **3** *U.S. Slang* Government money, distinctions, favors, etc., obtained by a representative for his constituency: a form of political patronage. [<OF *porc* <L *porcus* a hog]
pork barrel 1 A barrel in which pork is pickled and kept. **2** *U.S. Slang* A Federal appropriation for some local enterprise that will favorably impress a representative's constituents.
pork·er (pôr′kər, pōr′-) *n.* A pig or hog, especially regarded as a source of pork.
pork·pie (pôrk′pī, pōrk′-) *n.* **1** A thick-crusted pie with pork filling. **2** A man's hat with a low, flat crown.
pork·wood (pôrk′wŏŏd′, pōrk′-) *n.* **1** The brown, coarse-grained wood of a small tree *(Torrubia longifolia)* with small flowers in cymes, found in southeastern Florida and tropical America. **2** The tree.
pork·y (pôr′kē, pōr′-) *adj.* **pork·i·er, pork·i·est 1** Of or like pork. **2** Obese; fat.
porn (pôrn) *Slang adj.* Pornographic. — *n.* Pornography. Also **por·no** (pôr′nō).
por·no·graph·ic (pôr·nə·graf′ik) *adj.* Of or having the nature of pornography. — **por′no·graph′i·cal·ly** *adv.*
por·nog·ra·phy (pôr·nog′rə·fē) *n.* **1** Depictions of sexual acts or behavior, as in writing, photographs, motion pictures, etc., to stimulate erotic feelings. **2** The material containing such descriptions. [<Gk. *pornographos* writing of harlots < *pornē* a harlot + *graphein* write] — **por·nog′ra·pher** *n.*
po·ros·co·py (pô·ros′kə·pē, pō-) *n.* The study of the character and arrangement of the sweat pores, especially as shown on fingerprints: used in identification. [< *poro-* (<Gk. *poros* a pore) + -SCOPY] — **po·ro·scop·ic** (pôr′ə·skop′ik, pō′rə-) or **·i·cal** *adj.*
po·ros·i·ty (pô·ros′ə·tē, pō-) *n.* **1** The property of being porous; porousness. **2** A porous part or structure. [<Med. L *porositas, -tatis* < *porosus* <L *porus* a pore]
po·rous (pôr′əs, pō′rəs) *adj.* Having pores. — **po′rous·ly** *adv.* — **po′rous·ness** *n.*
por·phy·rin (pôr′fə·rin) *n. Biochem.* Any of a class of organic pigments derived from the breakdown of hemoglobin and chlorophyll, and consisting of four pyrrole nuclei. [Short for *(hemato)porphyrin* <HEMATO- + Gk. *porphyra* the purple whelk and its dye + -IN]
por·phy·rit·ic (pôr′fə·rit′ik) *adj.* **1** Pertaining or relating to porphyry. **2** *Mineral.* Containing well-defined, relatively large crystals in a fine-grained, glassy base or groundmass. Also **por′phy·rit′i·cal.** [<Med. L *porphyriticus* <L *porphyrites* porphyry <Gk. *porphyritēs (lithos),* lit., (a) purplelike (stone) < *porphyros* purple]
Por·phy·ro·gen·i·tus (pôr′fə·rō·jen′i·təs) See CONSTANTINE VII.
por·phy·roid (pôr′fə·roid) *n.* A greenish, grayish, or reddish crystalline and perfectly schistose rock, containing porphyritic crystals.
por·phy·ry (pôr′fə·rē) *n. pl.* **·ries** An igneous rock that has a groundmass enclosing crystals of feldspar or quartz. [<OF *porfire* <Med. L *porphyreus* <Gk. *porphyros* purple < *porphyra* the purple whelk and its dye]
Por·phy·ry (pôr′fə·rē) Anglicized name of Malchus Porphyrius, 233–304?, Neo-Platonic philosopher of Syrian origin; a disciple of Plotinus; opposed Christianity.
por·poise (pôr′pəs) *n. pl.* **·poises** or **·poise 1** A gregarious cetacean, of the genus *Phocaena,* without a distinct beak; especially, *P. phocaena* of the North Atlantic and Pacific, from 5 to 6 feet long, blackish above and white below. **2** Any small cetacean; popularly, the common dolphin or the bottlenose. [<OF *porpeis, porpois,* lit., hog fish <L *porcus* a hog + *piscis* a fish]

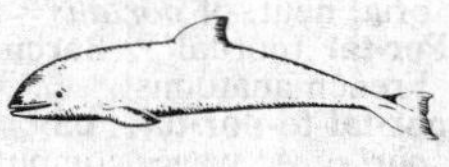
COMMON PORPOISE
(Smaller than the 7 to 8 foot common dolphin)

por·ridge (pôr′ij, por′-) *n.* **1** A soft food made by boiling meal or flour in water or milk until it becomes thick. **2** A broth or stew of vegetables, sometimes containing meat. [Alter. of POTTAGE; infl. in form by OF *poree* vegetable soup]
por·rin·ger (pôr′in·jər, por′-) *n.* A small, shallow dish, having straight sides and sometimes ears. [Earlier *pottanger* <MF *potager* a soup bowl; infl. in form by PORRIDGE]
Por·se·na (pôr′sə·nə), **Lars** A semilegendary Etruscan king of the sixth century B.C. who marched against Rome to restore the Tarquins. Also **Por·sen·na** (pôr·sen′ə).
port[1] (pôrt, pōrt) *n.* **1** A harbor or haven; hence, a place of customary entry and exit for vessels, as for commerce. **2** *Law* Any place designated as a point at which persons or merchandise may enter or pass out of a country, under specified supervision: also *port of entry.*

add, āce, câre, pälm; end, ēven; it, īce; odd, ōpen, ôrder; tŏŏk, pōōl; up, bûrn; ə = a in *above,* e in *sicken,* i in *clarity,* o in *melon,* u in *focus*; yōō = u in *fuse*; oi, oil; ou, pout; ch, check; g, go; ng, ring; th, thin; th, this; zh, vision. Foreign sounds à, œ, ü, kh, ṅ; and ◆: see page xx. < from; + plus; ? possibly.

[Fusion of OE and OF, both <L *portus* a harbor]

port^{2} (pôrt, pōrt) *n.* **1** An opening in the side of a ship, as for a gun, light and air, or for the passage of cargo. **2** A gate, portal, door, or other entrance. **3** An orifice for the passage of a motive fluid, as air, gas, etc.: a steam *port;* exhaust *port.* [Prob. fusion of OE and OF, both <L *porta* a gate, door]

port^{3} (pôrt, pōrt) *n.* **1** The way in which one bears or carries himself; mien; external manner: a majestic *port.* **2** The position of a rifle when ported. See synonyms under AIR^{1}. **high port** *Mil.* The position in which a soldier carries his rifle, diagonally across his body, while running or jumping. —*v.t.* **1** *Mil.* To carry, as a rifle, saber, or other weapon, diagonally across the body and sloping to the left shoulder. **2** To carry. [<OF *porte* < *porter* carry <L *portare*]

port^{4} (pôrt, pōrt) *Naut. n.* The left side of a vessel as one looks from stern to bow: formerly called *larboard*: opposed to *starboard.* —*v.t.* To put or turn to the port or larboard side: to *port* the helm. —*adj.* Left; larboard: *port* side. [Prob. <PORT^{1}]

port^{5} (pôrt, pōrt) *n.* A sweet variety of wine, usually of a dark-red color. [Short for *Oporto wine,* from *Oporto,* Portugal; so called because orig. shipped from there]

port·a·ble (pôr′tə·bəl, pōr′-) *adj.* **1** That can be readily carried or moved. **2** *Obs.* Endurable; supportable. [<LL *portabilis* <L *portare* carry] **—port′a·ble·ness, port′a·bil′i·ty** *n.* **—port′a·bly** *adv.*

port·age (pôr′tij, pōr′-) *n.* **1** The act of transporting, especially canoes, boats, and goods, from one navigable water to another. **2** The route over which such transportation is made, or that which is transported. **3** The charge for transportation. [<F <OF <Med. L *portaticum* <L *portare* carry]

Por·ta (pôr′tä), **Giacomo della,** 1541–1604, Italian architect and sculptor. **—Giambattista della,** 1538?–1577, Italian physicist.

por·tal (pôr′təl, pōr′-) *n.* **1** A passage for gaining entrance; door; gate; especially, one that is grand and imposing. **2** The architectural composition that includes the entrances and porches of a large church or similar building. **3** Any opening or entrance resembling or suggesting the portal of an edifice: often in the plural. See synonyms under ENTRANCE^{1}. —*adj.* **1** Pertaining to or entering at a port or gate. **2** *Anat.* Pertaining to or arranged like the **portal vein,** which conveys blood from the intestines and other abdominal viscera to the liver, there subdividing into capillaries. [<OF, a gate <Med. L *portale* a city gate, a porch, orig. neut. of *portalis* <L *porta* a gate]

Por·tal (pôr·täl′), **Baron Antoine,** 1742–1832, French anatomist.

por·tal-to-por·tal pay (pôr′tə l·tə·pôr′təl, pōr′-) A wage computed on the full time spent on mine or factory property from arrival to departure, not on actual working time.

por·ta·men·to (pôr′tə·men′tō, pōr′-; *Ital.* pôr′tä·men′tō) *n. pl.* **·ti** (-tē) *Music* **1** A slur or glide from one note to another, sounding all the intervening tones. **2** Loosely, a legato passage or effect. [<Ital., lit., a carrying <*portare* carry <L]

port·ance (pôr′təns, pōr′-) *n. Archaic* Personal carriage; deportment; mien. [< MF, a carrying, support <*porter* carry <L *portare*]

Port A·pra (ä′prä) See APRA HARBOR.

port arms *Mil.* **1** A command to carry a rifle, saber, or other weapon at the port. **2** The position of the weapon when so carried. [< PORT^{3}, *v.* + ARMS]

Port Arthur A city of southern Manchuria at the tip of Liaotung Peninsula; site of a major naval base, operated jointly by the Soviet Union and the Chinese People's Republic after 1945: Chinese *Lüshun,* Japanese *Ryojun.*

por·ta·tive (pôr′tə·tiv, pōr′-) *adj.* **1** Of or pertaining to carrying; capable of carrying. **2** Portable. [< OF, fem. of *portatif,* lit., portable <L *portatus,* pp. of *portare* carry]

Port-au-Prince (pôrt′ō·prins′, pōrt′-; *Fr.* pôr·tō·prañs′) A port, capital of Haiti.

port authority Any official body having charge of the coordination of all rail and water traffic of a port.

Port Blair The capital of the Andaman andNicobar Islands, a port on SE South Andaman Island.

Port Castries See CASTRIES.

port·cul·lis (pôrt·kul′is, pōrt-) *n.* A grating made of strong bars of wood or iron that can be let down suddenly to close the portal of a fortified place. [<OF *porte coleïce* < *porte* a gate (<L *porta*) + fem. of *coleis* sliding <L *colare* strain, filter]

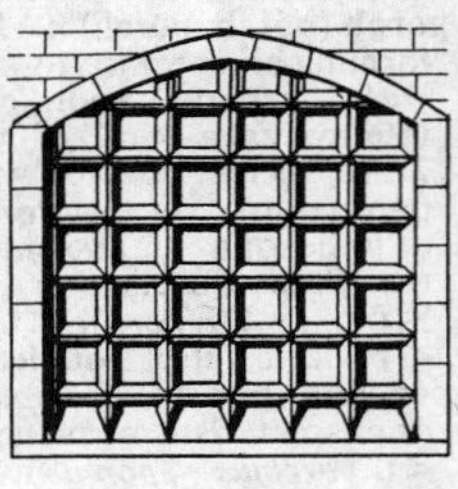

MEDIEVAL PORTCULLIS

Port du Sa·lut (pôrt də sə·lōōt′, sə·lōō′) A creamy, compact cheese with a flavor similar to that of Gouda.

Porte (pôrt, pōrt) *n.* The former Turkish government: with *the*: officially called **the Sublime Porte.** [<F *(la Sublime) Porte* (the High) Gate, trans. of Turkish *Babi Ali,* the chief office of the Ottoman Empire]

porte-co·chère (pôrt′kō·shâr′, pōrt′-; *Fr.* pôrt·kô·shâr′) *n.* **1** A large gateway for vehicles, leading into a courtyard. **2** A porch at the door of a building for sheltering persons entering or leaving carriages. [<F <*porte* a gate (<L *porta*) + *cochère,* fem. adj. < *coche* a coach]

por·tée (pôr·tē′, -tā′, pōr-) *adj.* Towed, carried, or transported by vehicles: said of artillery, cavalry units, etc. Also **por·té′** (-tē′, -tā′). [<F, pp. fem. of *porter* carry <L *portare*]

Port Elizabeth A port of Eastern Cape Province, Republic of South Africa.

porte-mon·naie (pôrt′mun′ē, pōrt′-; *Fr.* pôrt·mô·ne′) *n. French* A pocketbook for money; especially, a small purse with clasps.

por·tend (pôr·tend′, pōr-) *v.t.* **1** To warn of as an omen; presage; forebode. **2** *Obs.* To mean; signify. See synonyms under AUGUR. [<OF *portendre* stretch forth <L *portendere,* var. of *protendere* <*pro-* forth + *tendere* stretch]

Por·te·ño (pôr·tā′nyō) *n.* A native or inhabitant of Buenos Aires.

por·tent (pôr′tent, pōr′-) *n.* **1** Anything that portends what is to happen, especially a momentous or calamitous event. **2** The quality of portending; ominous significance. **3** A prodigy; marvel. [<L *portentum* <*portendere.* See PORTEND.]

por·ten·tous (pôr·ten′təs, pōr-) *adj.* **1** Full of portents of ill; ominous. **2** Of strange and ill-boding character, as if supernatural; monstrous; prodigious. See synonyms under AWFUL, FRIGHTFUL. **—por·ten′ tous·ly** *adv.* **—por·ten′tous·ness** *n.*

por·ter^{1} (pôr′tər, pōr′-) *n.* **1** One who carries things; especially, a man who carries travelers' luggage, etc., for hire, as in a hotel or at a railroad station. **2** *U.S.* An attendant in a Pullman car. [<OF *porteour* <L *portator* <*portatus,* pp. of *portare* carry]

por·ter^{2} (pôr′tər, pōr′-) *n.* **1** A keeper of a door or gate. **2** One who waits at a door to carry messages. [<AF, OF *portier* <LL *portarius* <L *porta* a gate, a door]

por·ter^{3} (pôr′tər, pōr′-) *n.* A dark-brown, heavy, English malt liquor resembling ale. [Short for *porter's beer* <PORTER^{1}; so called because formerly drunk chiefly by porters]

Por·ter (pôr′tər, pōr′-), **Cole,** born 1893, U.S. composer and lyricist. **— David,** 1780–1843, U.S. commodore. **—David Dixon,** 1813–91, U.S. admiral; son of David Porter. **—Jane,** 1776–1850, English novelist. **—Noah,** 1811–1892, U.S. educator and editor. **—William Sydney** See O. HENRY.

por·ter·age (pôr′tər·ij, pōr′-) *n.* **1** The business of a porter. **2** The cost of carriage by a porter.

por·ter·house (pôr′tər·hous′, pōr′-) *n.* **1** A place where porter, ale, etc., are retailed. **2** A restaurant; chophouse. **3** A choice cut of beefsteak including a part of the tenderloin, usually next to the sirloin: also **porterhouse steak.** [<PORTER^{3} + HOUSE]

port·fo·li·o (pôrt·fō′lē·ō, pōrt-) *n. pl.* **·li·os** **1** A portable case for holding drawings, writing materials, documents, etc. **2** The position or office of a minister of state or member of a government. **3** A list of investments.[Earlier *porto folio* <Ital. *portafoglio* <*portare* carry (< L) + *foglio* a leaf <L *folium*]

port·hole (pôrt′hōl′, pō rt′-) *n.* **1** A small opening in a ship's side. **2** Hence, an embrasure; loophole for shooting through. **3** The entrance to a port in an engine. See PORT^{2}.

Port Hudson A village on the east bank of the Mississippi in Louisiana; scene of a Union victory in the Civil War, 1863.

Port Huron A city on the St. Clair River and Lake Huron, SE Michigan.

Por·tia (pôr′shə, -shē·ə, pōr′-) The heroine of Shakespeare's *The Merchant of Venice.* She acts the part of a lawyer and defeats Shylock's claim for a pound of Antonio's flesh.

por·ti·co (pôr′ti·kō, pōr′-) *n. pl.* **·coes** or **·cos** An open space or ambulatory with roof upheld by columns; a porch. [<Ital. <L *porticus.* Doublet of PORCH.] **—por′ti·coed** *adj.*

por·tière (pôr·tyâr′, pōr-; *Fr.* pôr·tyâr′) *n.* A curtain for a doorway, used either instead of a door or as an ornament. Also **por·tiere′.** [<F <*porte* a door <L *porta*]

por·tion (pôr′shən, pōr′-) *n.* **1** A part of a whole, whether separated from it or not. **2** An allotment; share; especially, the quantity of any kind of food usually served to one person. **3** The part of an estate coming to an heir. **4** A dowry (def. 1). **5** One's fortune or destiny. —*v.t.* **1** To divide into shares for distribution; parcel: often with *out.* **2** To give a dowry to; dower. **3** To assign; allot. [< OF *porcion* <L *portio, -onis*] **— por′tion·a·ble** *adj.* **—por′tion·less** *adj.*

Synonyms (noun) : part, proportion. When any whole is divided into *parts,* any *part* that is allotted to some person, subject, or purpose is called a *portion,* whether or not the division may be by some fixed rule or relation. But when we speak of a *part* as a *proportion,* we think of the whole as divided according to some rule or scale, so that the different *parts* bear a contemplated and intended relation or ratio to one another; thus, the *portion* allotted to a child by will may not be fair *proportion* of the estate. See PART.

por·tion·er (pôr′shən·ər, pōr′-) *n.* One who divides in shares or holds a share or shares.

Port Jackson An inlet on the southern shore of New South Wales, Australia, forming the harbor of Sydney.

Port Jin·nah (jin′ə) A port of SW East Bengal, East Pakistan: also *Chalna Anchorage.*

Port·land (pôrt′lənd, pōrt′-) **1** A port on Casco Bay, SW Maine. **2** A port of entry on the Willamette River, NW Oregon.

Portland Bight See OLDHARBOR BAY.

Portland cement See under CEMENT.

Portland Race A dangerous, swift current off the coast of Dorset, SW England.

Port Lou·is (lōō′is, lōō′ē) A port, capital of Mauritius.

port·ly (pôrt′lē, pōrt′-) *adj.* **·li·er, ·li·est** **1** Somewhat corpulent; stout. **2** Of a stately appearance and carriage; impressive, especially on account of size. See synonyms under CORPULENT. [<PORT^{3} + -LY] **—port′li·ness** *n.*

Port-Ly·au·tey (pôrt′lē·ō·tā′, *Fr.*pôr·lyō·tā′) A river port of NW French Morocco ten miles from the Atlantic: formerly *Kénitra.*

Port Ma·hón (mə·hōn′, *Sp.* mä·ōn′) A former name for MAHÓN.

port·man·teau (pôrt·man′tō, pōrt-) *n. pl.* **·teaus** or **·teaux** (-tōz) **1** Originally, a case for carrying clothing, etc., behind a saddle. **2** An oblong leather suitcase, hinged at the back, and fitted with catches, straps, and a lock, and with handles by which it can be carried. [<MF <*porter* carry (<L *portare*) + *manteau* a coat <OF *mantel* a mantle]

portmanteau word A word arbitrarily formed of two distinct words, as *chortle,* from *chuckle* and *snort; cyclotron,* from *cycle electron;* a telescope word; a blend. [Coined by Lewis Carroll]

Port Mores·by (môrz′bē, mōrz′-) A port on the SE coast of New Guinea; administrative center of the Territory of Papua and New Guinea.

Pôr·to (pôr′tōō) The Portuguese name for OPORTO.

Pôr·to A·le·gre (pôr′tōōä·le′grə) A port of southern Brazil, capital of Rio Grande do Sul state.

Por·to Bel·lo (pôr′tō bel′ō) A port NE of

Colón on the Caribbean coast of Panama. Also **Por·to·be·lo** (pôr'tō·bā'lō).

port of call A port where vessels put in for supplies, repairs, discharge or taking on of cargo, etc.

port of entry A place, whether on the coast or inland, designated as a point at which persons or merchandise may enter or pass out of a country under the supervision of customs and other proper authorities.

Port–of–Spain (pôrt'əv·spān', pôrt'-) A port of NW Trinidad, capital of Trinidad and Tobago colony. Also **Port of Spain**.

Por·to–No·vo (pôr'tō·nō'vō, pôr'-) A port in western Africa, capital of Benin.

Porto No·vo (nō'vō) A port in SE Madras State, India.

Porto Ri·co (rē'kō) The former official name of **Puerto Rico**.

Porto San·to (sän'tō) Northernmost island of Madeira; 16 square miles.

Pôr·to Vê·lho (pôr'tŏŏ ve'lyŏŏ) Capital of Guaporé territory, western Brazil.

Port Philip Bay A bay on the southern coast of Victoria, Australia, forming the harbor of Melbourne.

por·trait (pôr'trit, pôr'-, -trāt) n. 1 A likeness of an individual, especially of the face, produced by an artist in oils, water color, etc., or by photography. 2 Hence, a vivid description of something or someone having existence. [<MF, orig. pp. of *portraire* <OF *pourtraire* PORTRAY]

por·trait·ist (pôr'trā·tist, pôr'-) n. One who makes portraits; a portrait painter or photographer.

por·trai·ture (pôr'tri·chər, pôr'-) n. 1 A representation of an object. 2 The act or art of portraying; especially, the art or practice of making portraits. 3 Portraits or pictures collectively. [<OF <*pourtrait*, pp. of *pourtraire* PORTRAY]

por·tray (pôr·trā', pōr-) v.t. 1 To represent by drawing, painting, etc.; delineate. 2 To describe in words; depict verbally. 3 To represent, as in a play; act. See synonyms under IMITATE. [<OF *pourtraire* <Med. L *protrahere* <L, draw forth <*pro-* forth + *trahere* draw] — **por·tray'a·ble** adj. — **por·tray'er** n.

por·tray·al (pôr·trā'əl, pōr-) n. 1 The act of portraying by any method of depiction or delineation: the *portrayal* of a character on the stage. 2 The making of a likeness of persons, places, or things; picturing. 3 A portrait.

por·tress (pôr'tris, pōr'-) n. A woman porter or doorkeeper. Also **por'ter·ess**.

Port–Roy·al (pôrt'roi'əl, pōrt'-; *Fr.* pôr·rwä·yäl') A Cistercian abbey SW of Paris, France; noted as a Jansenist center in the 17th century; suppressed, 1709. Also **Port–Royal–des–Champs** (-dä·shän').

Port Royal 1 A town and naval station in Jamaica, British West Indies; destroyed by earthquake, 1692. 2 A town in southern South Carolina on **Port Royal Island**, one of the Sea Islands. 3 The former name for Annapolis Royal.

Port Sa·id (sä·ēd') A port on the Mediterranean end of the Suez Canal, Egypt.

Ports·mouth (pôrts'məth, pōrts'-) 1 A port and the chief naval station of Great Britain, in Hampshire, England. 2 A port and naval station in New Hampshire; site of the signing of the **Treaty of Portsmouth**, ending the Russo–Japanese war, Sept. 5, 1905. 3 A port in SE Virginia, site of a U.S. naval base.

Por·tu·gal (pôr'chə·gəl, pōr'-; *Pg.* pôr'tŏŏ·gäl') A republic of SW Europe in the western Iberian Peninsula; 34,222 square miles, including the Azores and Madeira islands, 35,419 square miles; capital Lisbon: ancient *Lusitania*.

Por·tu·guese (pôr'chə·gēz', -gēs', pôr'-) adj. Pertaining to Portugal, its inhabitants, or their language. — n. 1 A native or inhabitant of Portugal. 2 The people of Portugal collectively: with *the*. 3 The Romance language of Portugal and Brazil. [<Pg. *Portuguez* <*Portugal* <*Portucal* <Med. L *Portus Cale* Oporto]

Portuguese East Africa A former name of MOZAMBIQUE.

Portuguese Guin·ea (gin'ē) A Portuguese overseas province on the coast of western Africa; 13,944 square miles; capital, Bissau.

Portuguese India A former Portuguese overseas province on the west coast of India, comprising the territories of Goa, Damão, and Diu; annexed by India in 1961.

Portuguese man–of–war A pelagic siphonophore (genus *Physalia*) of warm seas, having long, stinging tentacles hanging down from a bladderlike float: also *man–of–war*.

Portuguese Timor See TIMOR.

Portuguese West Africa See ANGOLA.

por·tu·lac·a (pôr'chə·lak'ə, pōr'-) n. Any plant of a genus (*Portulaca*) of low, fleshy herbs of the purslane family, with scattered leaves, ephemeral flowers which open only in sunshine, and a globular pod. [<L, purslane] — **por'tu·la·ca'ceous** (-lə·kā'shəs) adj.

po·sa·da (pō·sä'thä) n. *Spanish* An inn.

pose¹ (pōz) n. 1 The position of the whole or part of the body, especially such a position assumed for or represented by an artist, photographer, etc.: the *pose* of the head. 2 Hence, a mental attitude; attitudinizing for effect. See synonyms under ATTITUDE. — v. **posed, pos·ing** v.i. 1 To assume or hold an attitude or position, as for a portrait. 2 To affect poses; attitudinize. 3 To represent oneself: to *pose* as an expert. — v.t. 4 To cause to assume an attitude or position, as an artist's model. 5 To state or propound; put forward, as a theory or problem. [<F <*poser* put down, rest; fusion of L *pausare* lie down and *pos-*, stem of *ponere* lay down, put]

pose² (pōz) v.t. **posed, pos·ing** 1 To puzzle or confuse by asking a difficult question. 2 *Obs.* To question closely. [Aphetic var. of obs. *appose*, var. of OPPOSE]

Po·sei·don (pō·sī'dən) In Greek mythology, brother of Zeus and husband of Amphitrite, god of the sea and of horses: identified with the Roman Neptune. — **Po·sei·do'ni·an** (-dō'nē·ən) adj.

Po·sen (pō'zən) The German name for POZNAŃ.

pos·er¹ (pō'zər) n. One who poses; one who strikes affected attitudes. [<POSE¹, v.]

pos·er² (pō'zər) n. A question or problem that baffles. [<POSE², v.]

po·seur (pō·zœr') n. One who assumes or affects a particular attitude to make an impression on others. [<F <*poser* POSE¹, v.]

posh (posh) adj. *Slang* Very luxurious or elegant. [Origin unknown] — **posh'ly** adv. — **posh'ness** n.

po·sied (pō'zēd) adj. 1 Inscribed with a posy, as a ring. 2 With many posies or bunches of flowers.

pos·it (poz'it) v.t. To lay down or assume as a fact; affirm; postulate. Compare INFER. — n. That which is posited. [<L *positus*, pp. of *ponere* place]

po·si·tion (pə·zish'ən) n. 1 The manner in which a thing is placed; also, the place of its location. 2 Disposition of the parts of the body, especially with reference to therapeutic, surgical, or obstetric procedures; posture. 3 Relative social standing; high rank: Wealth commands *position*. 4 Employment or job: He lost his *position*. 5 The act of positing a principle or proposition, or the proposition posited; also, ground of argument; hence, the attitude assumed with reference to a subject; point of view: my *position* on the labor question. 6 *Music* The arrangement of the notes of a chord, as in voice parts. 7 In ancient prosody, the situation of a short vowel before two consonants or their equivalent, causing prolonged utterance: In "texunt," the vowels are long by *position*. See synonyms under ATTITUDE, CIRCUMSTANCE, PLACE. — v.t. To place in a particular or appropriate position. [<OF <L *positio*, *-onis* <*positus*, pp. of *ponere* place] — **po·si'tion·al** adj.

position light *Aeron.* Any of several variously colored lights used on an aircraft to indicate its position and path of motion.

position paper A report from a person or group setting forth a set of principles, a description of policy, or recommendations for action on a specific issue.

pos·i·tive (poz'ə·tiv) adj. 1 That is or may be directly affirmed; real; actual; existing: opposed to *negative*. 2 Inherent in a thing by and of itself, regardless of its relations to other things; absolute: opposed to *relative*. 3 Openly and plainly expressed; explicit; express; emphatic: opposed to *implied* or *inferred*: a *positive* denial. 4 Imperative: opposed to *discretionary*. 5 Dependent on authority, agreement, or convention: opposed to *natural*: *positive* law. 6 Not admitting of doubt or denial; incontestable: *positive* proof. 7 Free from doubt or hesitation; confident; certain; also, overconfident; dictatorial. 8 *Philos.* Pertaining to positivism (def. 2). 9 Noting one of two opposite directions, qualities, properties, etc., which is taken as primary, or as indicating increase or progression. 10 *Math.* Greater than zero; plus: said of quantities. 11 *Electr.* Having a relatively high potential: the *positive* electrode of a cell; specifically, designating the kind of electricity exhibited by a glass object when rubbed with silk. 12 *Physics* Having a deficiency of electrons: said of atoms which yield electrons. 13 *Biol.* Noting the response of an organism toward a stimulus: a *positive* tropism. 14 *Bacteriol.* Noting the presence of a specified condition or organism: a *positive* bacterial culture. 15 *Mech.* Operated by mechanical power, not by springs or gravity; operated or communicating power through intermediate inelastic parts that are under exact control. 16 Noting the north-seeking pole of a magnet and the corresponding (south) pole of the earth. 17 *Phot.* Having the lights and shades in their natural relation, as in a photograph. 18 *Gram.* Denoting the simple, uncompared degree of the adjective or adverb. See synonyms under DOGMATIC, RADICAL, SURE. — n. 1 That which is capable of being directly and certainly affirmed. 2 *Philos.* That which is cognizable by the senses. 3 *Phot.* A picture giving the lights and shades as in nature; a print from a negative. 4 *Gram.* The positive degree of an adjective or adverb; also, a word in this degree, as *good*, *glad*. 5 *Electr.* A positive plate, pole, etc. See synonyms under CERTAINTY. [<OF, fem. of *positif* <L *positivus* <*positus*. See POSITION.] — **pos'i·tive·ly** adv. — **pos'i·tive·ness** n.

positive rays *Physics* Canal rays.

pos·i·tiv·ism (poz'ə·tiv·iz'əm) n. 1 A way of thinking that regards nothing as ascertained or ascertainable beyond the facts of physical science or of sense. 2 A system of philosophy elaborated by Auguste Comte, holding that man can have no knowledge of anything but actual phenomena and facts and their interrelations, rejecting all speculation concerning ultimate origins or causes. Compare HUMANITARIANISM. 3 Certitude, or the claim of certitude, in knowledge. — **pos'i·tiv·ist** n. — **pos'i·tiv·is'tic** adj.

pos·i·tron (poz'ə·tron) n. *Physics* A positively charged particle of an atom, with a mass equal to that of the electron. [<POSI(TIVE) + (ELEC)TRON]

pos·i·tron·i·um (poz'ə·trō'nē·əm) n. *Physics* An unstable, short–lived atomic entity consisting of a positron and an electron subject to mutual annihilation, with conversion of mass into energy. [<NL <POSITRON + -*ium*, suffix of names of elements]

po·sol·o·gy (pō·sol'ə·jē) n. The branch of medicine that treats of the dosages of drugs. [<F *posologie* <Gk. *posos* how much + *logos* word, study] — **pos·o·log·ic** (pos'ə·loj'ik) or **·i·cal** adj.

pos·se (pos'ē) n. 1 A posse comitatus. 2 A force of men; squad. 3 *Law* Possibility: chiefly in the phrase *in posse* (capable of being): distinguished from *in esse*. [<Med. L, power, armed force <L, be able]

pos·se com·i·ta·tus (pos'ē kom'ə·tā'təs) The body of men that a sheriff or other peace officer calls or may call to his assistance in the discharge of his official duty, as to quell a riot or make an arrest. [<Med. L, power of the county <*posse* a posse + *comitatus* a county <*comes*, -*itis* a count]

pos·sess (pə·zes') v.t. 1 To have as property; own. 2 To have as a quality, attribute, etc.: to *possess* a conscience. 3 To enter and exert control over; dominate: often used passively: He was *possessed* by a devil; The idea *possessed* him. 4 To maintain control over

(oneself, one's mind, etc.): *Possess* yourself in patience. **5** To put in possession, as of property, news, etc.: with *of.* **6** To have knowledge of, as a language. **7** To imbue or impress, as with an idea: with *with.* **8** *Obs.* To seize; gain. See synonyms under HAVE, OCCUPY. [<OF *possessier* <L *possessus,* pp. of *possidere* possess] — **pos·ses′sor** *n.*

pos·sessed (pə·zest′) *adj.* **1** Having; owning: *possessed* of a ready tongue. **2** Calm; cool: to be *possessed* in time of danger. **3** Controlled by or as if by evil spirits; beyond self-control; frenzied. — **like all possessed** *U.S. Colloq.* As if driven by the devil; frenziedly.

pos·ses·sion (pə·zesh′ən) *n.* **1** The act or state of possessing. **2** A thing possessed or owned. **3** *pl.* Property; wealth. **4** The state of being possessed, as by evil spirits. **5** Self-possession. See synonyms under OCCUPATION, PROPERTY, WEALTH. Compare POSSESS.

pos·ses·sive (pə·zes′iv) *adj.* **1** Pertaining to or expressive of possession. **2** *Gram.* Designating a case of the noun or pronoun that denotes possession, origin, or the like. In English, this is formed in nouns by adding *'s* to the singular and to irregular plurals: *John's* book; *men's* souls; the *boss's* office; and a simple apostrophe to the regular plural and sometimes to singulars and proper names ending in a sibilant: *boys'* shoes; *Dickens'* (or *Dickens's*) writings; *James'* (or *James's*) brother. See also -'s[1]. Pronouns in the possessive case have special forms, as *my, mine, his, her, hers, its, our, ours, your, yours, their, theirs, whose.* By some grammarians possessive nouns and pronouns are called *possessive adjectives.* — *n. Gram.* **1** The possessive case. **2** A possessive form or construction. — **double possessive** A redundant possessive. Example: a book *of Mike's.*

pos·ses·sive·ness (pə·zes′iv·nis) *n.* Strong or excessive concern with one's own possessions.

pos·ses·so·ry (pə·zes′ər·ē) *adj.* **1** Pertaining to or having possession. **2** *Law* Proceeding from or depending upon possession.

pos·set (pos′it) *n.* A drink of hot milk curdled with liquor, sweetened and spiced. [ME *poshote, possot;* origin unknown]

pos·si·bil·i·ty (pos′ə·bil′ə·tē) *n. pl.* **·ties** **1** The fact or state of being possible. **2** A possible thing. See synonyms under ACCIDENT, EVENT.

pos·si·ble (pos′ə·bəl) *adj.* **1** That may be or may become true: opposed to *actual:* said of a thing, an event, or a statement. **2** That may be true in some contingency; imaginably true: sometimes used to denote extreme improbability: opposed to *certain, necessary, impossible.* [<OF <L *possibilis* <*posse* be able <*potis* able + *esse* be] — **pos′si·bly** *adv.*

pos·sum (pos′əm) *n.* **1** *Colloq.* An opossum. **2** *Austral.* A phalanger. — **to play possum** To pretend; deceive; feign ignorance or inattention; dissemble: from the fact that the opossum feigns death when threatened. [Short for OPOSSUM]

possum glider *Austral.* A flying phalanger.

pos·sum·haw (pos′əm·hô′) *n.* The bearberry. [<POSSUM + HAW[2]]

post[1] (pōst) *n.* **1** An upright piece of timber or other material used as a support, a point of attachment, etc., as in a building. **2** A central projection in a lock for receiving the tube of a key. **3** A line or post serving to mark the starting or finishing point of a racecourse. — *v.t.* **1** To put up (a poster, etc.) in some public place. **2** To fasten posters upon; placard. **3** To announce by or as by a poster: to *post* a reward. **4** To denounce thus: to *post* one as a coward. **5** To publish the name of on a list. **6** To publish the name of (a ship) as lost or overdue. See synonyms under SET. [OE <L *postis* a door post]

post[2] (pōst) *n.* **1** Any fixed place or station, occupied or for occupation; especially, a place occupied by a detachment of troops; also, the garrison of such a station; the limits of a sentry's beat; the beat or position to which a policeman is assigned. **2** *U.S.* A local unit of a veterans' organization. **3** An office or employment; a position, as of trust or emolument; situation; especially, a public office. **4** A trading post or settlement. **5** *Brit.* One of the two bugle calls known respectively as **first post** and **last post.** The latter corresponds to *taps* in the army of the United States. See synonyms under PLACE. — *v.t.* **1** To assign to a particular position or post; station, as a sentry. **2** To appoint to a military or naval command. [<MF *poste* a post, a station < Ital. *posto* <LL *postum,* contraction of L *positum,* pp. neut. of *ponere* place]

post[3] (pōst) *n.* **1** **a** A rider or courier who travels over a fixed route or between stations on such a route carrying letters, dispatches, etc. **b** Any of the series of stations furnishing relays of men and horses on such a route. **2** An established system, especially a government system, for transporting the mails; also, the aggregate of mail matter transported from one place to another at one time; the mail; by extension, a post office: Has the *post* come in? Put your letter in the *post.* **3** A size of writing paper, 16 by 20 inches: so called because it bore a postman's horn for watermark. — *v.t.* **1** *Brit.* To place in a mailbox or post office; mail. **2** To inform: He *posted* us on the latest news. **3** In bookkeeping: **a** To transfer (items or accounts) to the ledger. **b** To make the proper entries in (a ledger). — *v.i.* **4** To travel with post horses. **5** To travel with speed; hasten. **6** In horseback riding, to rise from the saddle in rhythm with a horse's gait when trotting. — *adv.* By post horses; hence, rapidly. [<MF *poste* <Ital. *posta,* orig. a station <LL, contraction of L *posita,* pp. fem. of *ponere* place]

post- *prefix* **1** After in time or order; following: *postdate, postwar.* **2** Chiefly in scientific terms, after in position; behind: *postorbital.* [<L *post-* <*post* behind, after]

Post (pōst), **Emily,** 1873–1960, *née* Price, U. S. columnist and writer on social etiquette.

post·age (pōs′tij) *n.* **1** The charge levied on mail matter. **2** The act of going by post. [< POST[3] (def. 2) + -AGE]

postage stamp A small, printed label issued and sold by a government to be affixed to letters, parcels, etc., in payment of postage.

pos·tal (pōs′təl) *adj.* Pertaining to the mails or to mail service. — *n.* A postal card.

postal card A card, issued officially, for carrying a written or printed message through the mails under government stamp: also *postal.* Compare POSTCARD.

postal currency An emergency stamp money, used during the Civil War in the United States (1862–65). Also **postage currency.**

Postal Union An aggregation of countries, organized in 1874, agreeing to deliver foreign mail: officially designated *Universal Postal Union.*

post-bel·lum (pōst′bel′əm) *adj.* Coming or occurring after the war, especially the Civil War. [<L, after the war <*post* after + *bellum* a war]

post box A mailbox.

post·ca·non·i·cal (pōst′kə·non′i·kəl) *adj.* Occurring later than the writing of the Scripture canon.

post captain **1** Formerly, in the British Navy, a captain of three years' standing. **2** Formerly, in the U.S. Navy, a senior captain.

post·card (pōst′kärd′) *n.* **1** A postal card. **2** An unofficial card of any regulation size transmissible under postal regulations through the mails on prepayment of the same postage as a postal card.

post-chaise (pōst′shāz′) *n.* A traveling carriage.

post·clas·si·cal (pōst′klas′i·kəl) *adj.* Being or occurring between the Greek and Latin classical and the medieval writers. Also **post′·clas′sic.**

post·com·mun·ion (pōst′kə·myōōn′yən) *adj.* Coming after communion: a *postcommunion* prayer. — *n.* The part of the Eucharist which follows the distribution of the elements.

post·date (pōst′dāt′) *v.t.* **·dat·ed, ·dat·ing** **1** To assign or affix a date later than the actual date to (a check, document, etc.). **2** To follow in time.

post·di·lu·vi·al (pōst′di·lōō′vē·əl) *adj.* Coming after the deluge.

post·di·lu·vi·an (pōst′di·lōō′vē·ən) *n.* One living after the deluge. — *adj.* Postdiluvial.

post·ed (pōs′tid) *adj.* Possessed of the latest information or news: Keep me *posted.* [< POST[3], *v.* (def. 2)]

pos·teen (pos·tēn′) *n.* An Indian garment made of sheepskin with the fleece left on: also *postin.* [<Persian *pōstīn* of leather <*pōst* a skin]

post·er[1] (pōs′tər) *n.* **1** A placard or bill used for advertising, public information, etc., to be posted on a wall or other surface. **2** A billposter. [<*post*[1], *v.*]

post·er[2] (pōs′tər) *n.* **1** One who travels post. **2** A post horse. [<POST[3], *v.*]

poste res·tante (pōst res·tänt′, *Fr.* pôst res·tänt′) *French* The department of a post office that has charge of mail matter to be held until called for.

pos·te·ri·or (pos·tir′ē·ər) *adj.* **1** Situated behind or toward the hinder part: opposed to *anterior.* **2** Coming after another in a series; especially, subsequent in point of time; later: in this sense opposed to *prior.* **3** *Bot.* Situated or growing on the side next the parent axis: the *posterior* side of an axillary flower. **4** *Zool.* In the direction of the tail; caudal. **5** *Anat.* Dorsal. — *n. Often pl.* The buttocks. [<L *posterior,* comp. of *posterus* following <*post* after]

pos·te·ri·or·i·ty (pos·tir′ē·ôr′ə·tē, -or′ə-) *n.* The state of being posterior or later in point of time: opposed to *priority.*

pos·te·ri·or·ly (pos·tir′ē·ər·lē) *adv.* **1** Subsequently. **2** Behind.

pos·ter·i·ty (pos·ter′ə·tē) *n.* **1** The stock that proceeds from a progenitor; a person's descendants; also, succeeding generations, taken collectively: the *posterity* of Adam. **2** Posteriority. [<OF *posterite* <L *posteritas* <*posterus.* See POSTERIOR.]

pos·tern (pōs′tərn, pos′-) *n.* **1** A back gate or door; a private entrance, especially a small gate beside a large one in a fortified place. **2** A covered passage closed by a gate and leading from a bastion to the ditch. — *adj.* Situated at the back; private: a *postern* gate. [<OF *posterne, posterle* <L *posterus.* See POSTERIOR.]

Post Exchange An establishment for the sale of merchandise and services to military personnel: abbr. *PX.*

post·ex·il·i·an (pōst′eg·zil′ē·ən) *adj.* Pertaining to that period of Jewish history subsequent to the Babylonian exile (605 to 536 B.C.). Also **post′ex·il′ic.**

post·fix (pōst′fiks′) *v.t.* To add at the end of a word, as a letter, syllable, etc.: opposed to *prefix.* — *n.* (pōst′fiks′) That which is so added; a suffix. [<POST- + (AF)FIX]

post·gla·cial (pōst′glā′shəl) *Geol. adj.* Later than the glacial epoch; specifically, formed since the disappearance of the Pleistocene continental glaciers. — *n.* A sedimentary deposit resulting from the retreat of a continental glacier.

post·grad·u·ate (pōst′graj′ōō·it, -āt) *adj.* Of or pertaining to studies pursued after receiving a first degree; graduate. — *n.* One who pursues or has completed a postgraduate course.

post·haste (pōst′hāst′) *adj.* Done with speed; instant. — *n.* Great haste or speed like that of the post. — *adv.* With utmost speed; hurriedly. [Appar. <*Haste, post, haste,* an old direction written on letters]

post horse A horse kept at a post-house for postriders or for hire to travelers.

post-house (pōst′hous′) *n.* A house where post horses were kept for relay; also, formerly, a post office.

post·hu·mous (pos′chōō·məs) *adj.* **1** Born after the father's death: said of a child. **2** Published after the author's death, as a book. **3** Arising or continuing after a person's death: a *posthumous* reputation. [<LL *posthumus* <L *postumus* latest, last, superl. of *posterus.* See POSTERIOR.] — **post′hu·mous·ly** *adv.*

pos·tiche (pôs·tēsh′) *adj.* **1** Added after the completion of the work: said especially of a superadded and inappropriate architectural ornament. **2** Spurious; artificial. — *n.* **1** Pretense; sham. **2** An imitation; artificial substitute. Also **pos·tique′** (-tēk′). [<F <Ital. *posticcio* counterfeit <LL *appositicius* <L *appositus.* See APPOSITE.]

pos·ti·cous (pos·tī′kəs) *adj. Bot.* Hinder; posterior. [<L *posticus* <*post* after]

pos·til (pos′til) *n.* A marginal note; especially, one written on the margin of the Scriptures; also, a series of Scriptural comments. [<OF *postille* <Med. L *postilla* a gloss on the gospel, ? <L *post illa (verba textus)* after those (words of the text) <*post* after + *illa* those]

pos·til·ion (pōs·til′yən, pos-) *n.* A rider of one of the near horses of a team drawing a vehicle, with or without a coachman. Also **pos·til′lion.** [<MF *postillon* <Ital. *postiglione* <*posta* a post, station]

post·im·pres·sion·ism (pōst′im·presh′ən·iz′əm) *n.* The methods, theories, or practice of a group of painters of the late 19th century who emphasized the subjective prerogatives of the artist as opposed to the literal or idealistic representation of academic painting and the supposed objectivity of impressionism. Cézanne, Van Gogh, and Gauguin are considered its chief exponents. **—post′im·pres′sion·ist** *n.* & *adj.* **—post′im·pres′sion·is′·tic** *adj.*

pos·tin (pos·tēn′, -tin′) See POSTEEN.

post·li·min·i·um (pōst′li·min′ē·əm) *n.* In international law, a right (*Latin* **jus postliminii**), derived from Roman law, whereby persons or things taken in war by the enemy are restored to their former civil condition or previous ownership upon their coming again under the power of the nation to which they belonged. Also **post·lim·i·ny** (pōst·lim′ə·nē). [< L < *post* after, behind + *limen, liminis* a threshold]

post·lude (pōst′lo͞od) *n.* An organ voluntary concluding a church service. See PRELUDE. [< POST- + (PRE)LUDE]

post·man (pōst′mən) *n. pl.* **·men** (-mən) A letter-carrier; mail-carrier; formerly, a courier. **post′wo′man** *n. fem.*

post·mark (pōst′märk′) *n.* The stamp of a post office on mail matter handled there, sometimes also serving to cancel stamps, and giving the name of the office and the day (in larger cities also the hour) of mailing or arrival. *—v.t.* To stamp with a postmark.

post·mas·ter (pōst′mas′tər, -mäs′-) *n.* **1** An official having charge of a post office. **2** One who provides horses for posting. **—post′mis′tress** (-mis′tris) *n. fem.*

postmaster general *pl.* **postmasters general** The executive head of the postal service of a government.

post·me·rid·i·an (pōst′mə·rid′ē·ən) *adj.* Pertaining to the afternoon. Also **post′me·rid′i·o·nal.** [< L *postmeridianus* < *post-* after + *meridianus* MERIDIAN]

post me·rid·i·em (pōst mə·rid′ē·əm) After midday: abbr. *p.m.* or *P.M.* [< L]

post·mil·len·ni·al (pōst′mi·len′ē·əl) *adj.* Of or pertaining to a period after the millennium. Also **post′mil·len′ni·an.**

post·mil·len·ni·al·ism (pōst′mi·len′ē·əl·iz′əm) *n. Theol.* The tenet that Christ's second coming will follow the millennium: opposed to *premillennialism.* Also **post·mil·le·nar·i·an·ism** (pōst·mil′ə·nâr′ē·ən·iz′əm). **—post′mil·len′ni·al·ist** *n.*

post-mor·tem (pōst·môr′təm) *n.* Expert examination of a human body after death for pathological or judicial purposes; an autopsy. [< L, after death < *post* after + *mors, mortis* death]

post mor·tem (môr′təm) *Latin* After death.

post·na·tal (pōst·nāt′l) *adj.* Occurring after birth.

post note A promissory note issued by a bank and payable at a fixed time after its date.

post·nup·tial (pōst·nup′chəl) *adj.* Happening or occurring after marriage; made after marriage: a *postnuptial* settlement.

post-o·bit (pōst·ō′bit) *adj.* Made or done after death; taking effect after death: also **post′-o·bit′u·ar′y** (-ō·bich′o͞o·er′ē). *—n.* A bond given to secure payment by the obligor of a sum of money on the death of a designated person, generally one from whose estate he has expectations: also **post-obit bond.** [Contraction of POST OBITUM]

post ob·i·tum (ob′i·təm) *Latin* After death.

post office 1 That branch of the civil service of a government charged with carrying and delivering the mails. **2** An office for the receipt, transmission, and delivery of mails, and for the transaction of business connected with the same. **3** Any town or place having a post office. **4** A kissing game. **—post-of·fice** (pōst′ôf′is, -of′-*adj.*

Post Office Department An executive department of the U.S. government since 1872 (originally established in 1789), headed by the Postmaster General, which maintains and operates the postal system.

post·op·er·a·tive (pōst·op′ər·ə·tiv, -ə·rā′-) *adj. Surg.* Occurring after an operation.

post·or·bi·tal (pōst·ôr′bi·təl) *adj. Anat.* Situated behind the orbit or socket of the eye. *—n.* **1** A bone of some reptiles at the posterior part of the orbit. **2** A scale behind the orbit, as in snakes.

post·paid (pōst′pād′) *adj.* Having postage prepaid.

post·par·tum (pōst′pär′təm) *adj. Med.* After childbirth: a *postpartum* fever. [< POST- + L *partus* childbirth < *parere* bear]

post·pone (pōst·pōn′) *v.t.* **·poned, ·pon·ing 1** To put off to a future time; defer; delay. **2** To subordinate. [< L *postponere* < *post-* after + *ponere* put] **—post·pon′a·ble** *adj.* **—post·pone′ment** *n.* **—post·pon′er** *n.*

Synonyms: adjourn, defer, delay, procrastinate. *Adjourn* signifies literally to put off to another day, and, hence, to any future time. A deliberative assembly may *adjourn* to another day or to another hour of the same day, and resume business, where it left off, as if there had been no interval; or it may *adjourn* to a definite later date or, when no day can be fixed, to meet at the call of the president or other officer. In common usage, to *adjourn* a matter is to hold it in abeyance until it may be more conveniently or suitably attended to; in such use *defer* and *postpone* are close synonyms of *adjourn; defer* is simply to lay or put aside temporarily; to *postpone* is strictly to lay or put aside until after something else occurs, or is done, known, obtained, or the like; but *postpone* is often used without such limitation. *Adjourn, defer,* and *postpone* all imply definite expectation of later consideration or action; *delay* is much less definite, while *procrastinate* is hopelessly vague. One who *procrastinates* gives no assurance that he will ever act. Compare HINDER, PROCRASTINATE. *Antonyms*: act, complete, consummate, dispatch, do, expedite, hasten, hurry, quicken.

post·po·si·tion (pōst′pə·zish′ən) *n.* **1** The act of placing after or state of being placed behind. **2** *Gram.* A word placed after another word, as an enclitic; especially, a suffixed element which functions as a preposition, as *-de* in Greek *oikade* homeward. [< L *postpositus,* pp. of *postponere.* See POSTPONE.]

post position The place, in relation to the inner rail, occupied by a horse at the start of a race.

post·pos·i·tive (pōst·poz′ə·tiv) *Gram. adj.* Appended to something; suffixed; enclitic. *—n.* An appended word; a postposition. [< L *postpositus.* See POSTPOSITION.]

post·pran·di·al (pōst·pran′dē·əl) *adj.* After-dinner.

post·rid·er (pōst′rī′dər) *n.* A person who journeys by relays of horses.

post road A road built and maintained for the transportation of mail, formerly having post-houses at specified distances.

post·script (pōst′skript′) *n.* **1** A supplemental addition to a written or printed document. **2** Something added to a letter after the writer's signature: abbr. *P.S.* [< L *postscriptum,* pp. of *postscribere* write after]

post terminal A point or port of destination to which goods are transshipped after being delivered by an oceanic carrier: usually applied to additional rates for extra haulage.

post town 1 A town furnishing relays of post horses. **2** A town containing a post office.

pos·tu·lant (pos′chə·lənt) *n.* **1** One who or that which presents a request. **2** *Eccl.* An applicant for admission into a religious order or the sacred ministry. Compare NOVICE. [< F < L *postulans, -antis,* ppr. of *postulare* demand] **—pos′tu·lant·ship** *n.*

pos·tu·late (pos′chə·lit) *n.* **1** A position claimed or basis of argument laid down as well known or too plain to require proof; a self-evident truth. **2** *Geom.* A self-evident statement regarding the possibility of a geometrical construction: distinguished from *axiom.* **3** A condition precedent that must be assumed to explain or account for a thing: Peace is a *postulate* of prosperity. **4** A hypothesis; an unproved assumption. *—v.t.* (pos′chə·lāt) **·lat·ed, ·lat·ing 1** To claim; demand; require. **2** To set forth as self-evident or already known: to *postulate* the existence of matter. **3** To assume the truth or reality of, especially as a basis for discussion: His theory *postulates* the validity of an older theory. See synonyms under ASSUME. [< L *postulatus,* pp. of *postulare* demand] **—pos′tu·la′tor** *n.*

pos·tu·la·tion (pos′chə·lā′shən) *n.* **1** The act of postulating or supposing something as not needing proof; the assumption of a thing as a fact or truth. **2** *Eccl.* The election or presentation of a person to an office notwithstanding some disqualification.

pos·tu·la·tum (pos′chə·lā′təm) *n. pl.* **·ta** (-tə) A postulate. [< L]

pos·ture (pos′chər) *n.* **1** The visible disposition, either natural or assumed, of the several parts of a material thing, and especially of a living thing, with reference to each other; attitude; pose; in art, the position of a figure with regard to its members. **2** Situation as connected with or resulting from a relation of parts; state: the *posture* of national affairs. **3** Mental or spiritual attitude or condition. See synonyms under ATTITUDE. — *v.t.* & *v.i.* **·tured, ·tur·ing** To place in or assume a posture; pose. [< F < L *positura* < *positus,* pp. of *ponere* place] **—pos′tur·al** *adj.* **—pos′tur·er, pos′tur·ist** *n.*

pos·tur·ize (pos′chə·rīz) *v.t.* & *v.i.* **·ized, ·iz·ing** To posture.

post·war (pōst′wôr′) *adj.* After a war.

po·sy (pō′zē) *n. pl.* **·sies 1** A bunch of flowers, or a single flower; a bouquet; nosegay. **2** Generally, a brief inscription or motto, originally one in verse; especially, one inscribed on a ring or other trinket. [Contraction of POESY]

pot (pot) *n.* **1** A round earthen, metal, or glass vessel for culinary and other domestic purposes. **2** A metal drinking cup; mug. **3** The contents of a pot; hence, liquor; drink. **4** The amount of stakes wagered or played for; the pool, as in poker. **5** *Colloq.* A large sum of money. **6** A chimney pot. **7** *Scot.* A deep pit. **8** In fishing, the circular part of a net; also, a basketlike trap for catching lobsters, eels, fish, etc. **9** *Colloq.* A pot shot. **10** *Slang* A potbelly. **11** *Slang* Marihuana. *—v.* **pot·ted, pot·ting** *v.t.* **1** To put into a pot. **2** To preserve, as meat, in pots or jars. **3** To cook in a pot; stew. **4** To shoot (game) for food rather than for sport. **5** To shoot with a pot shot. **6** *Colloq.* To secure, capture, or win; bag. *—v.i.* **7** To take a pot shot. [OE *pott*]

po·ta·ble (pō′tə·bəl) *adj.* Suitable for drinking: said of water. *—n.* Something drinkable; a drink. [< F < L *potabilis* < *potare* drink]

po·tage (pō·täzh′) *n. French* Any thick soup.

pot·ash (pot′ash′) *n.* **1** Potassium hydroxide: also called *caustic potash* or *potassa.* **2** The crude potassium carbonate obtained by leaching the ashes of plants: when purified it is called *pearl ash.* **3** The oxide of potassium, K_2O. **4** Potash water. Also, in pharmaceutical use, **po·tass** (pə·tas′). [Earlier *potashes,* pl., after Du. *potasschen*; from being prepared in iron pots]

potash feldspar Orthoclase.

potash water An artificial mineral water containing potassium bicarbonate and charged with carbon dioxide. Also **potassic water.**

po·tas·sa (pə·tas′ə) *n.* Potassium hydroxide.

po·tas·si·um (pə·tas′ē·əm) *n.* A soft, silvery, very light element (symbol K, atomic number 19) of the alkali group, an essential element in living systems and in nature containing traces of a long-lived radioactive isotope. See PERIODIC TABLE. [< NL < POTASSA] **—po·tas′sic** *adj.*

potassium arsenite *Chem.* A white, hygroscopic, very poisonous mixture of potassium, arsenic, hydrogen, and oxygen, used mostly in solution, as in Fowler's mixture.

potassium carbonate *Chem.* A white, strongly alkaline compound, K_2CO_3, prepared from wood ashes and also from potassium sulfate obtained from salt beds: used in the manufacture of soft soap and glass. Also called *potash.*

potassium chlorate *Chem.* A colorless crystalline salt, $KClO_3$, used in the manufacture of matches, explosives, etc.

potassium chloride *Chem.* A colorless crystalline salt, KCl, occurring naturally in large mineral deposits in Germany, and also in certain giant kelps of the Pacific Coast; sylvite.

potassium cyanide *Chem.* An intensely poisonous, white, crystalline compound, KCN, used in photography, in electrometallurgy, and as a reagent.
potassium dichromate *Chem.* A reddish crystalline salt, $K_2Cr_2O_7$, used in the arts as an oxidizing agent and in making sensitive coatings for photographs.
potassium hydroxide *Chem.* A whitish deliquescent solid, KOH, yielding a strong caustic solution: used in saltmaking, electroplating, as a chemical reagent, etc. Also called *potash.*
potassium nitrate Niter.
potassium permanganate *Chem.* A purple-red crystalline salt, $KMnO_4$, used as an oxidizing agent in antiseptics and deodorizing substances.
potassium sulfate *Chem.* A salt, K_2SO_4, used in the manufacture of glass and alum, and in the crude state as a component of fertilizers: derived from kainite.
po·ta·tion (pō·tā′shən) *n.* **1** The act of drinking; a drink. **2** A drinking bout. [<OF <L *potatio, -onis* < *potatus,* pp. of *potare* drink]
po·ta·to (pə·tā′tō) *n. pl.* **·toes** **1** One of the edible, farinaceous tubers of a plant *(Solanum tuberosum)* of the nightshade family. **2** The plant. **3** The sweet potato. [<Sp. *patata* < Arawakan (Taino) *batata* sweet potato]
potato beetle **1** The Colorado beetle *(Leptinotarsa decemlineata),* yellowish, with ten longitudinal black stripes on the wing covers. Both the adult and the larva feed on the leaves of the potato, tomato, and similar plants, and are among the world's greatest agricultural pests: also **potato bug.** For illustration see also INSECTS (injurious). **2** Any of several beetles feeding on the foliage of the potato, especially *Lema trilineata,* with three longitudinal black stripes on the wing covers.

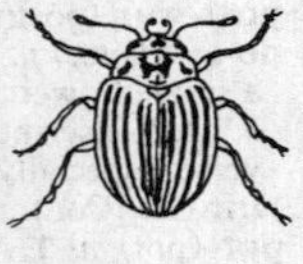
POTATO BEETLE
First described in 1824; widespread by 1874. (About 3/8 inch long; 1/4 inch wide)

potato chip A very thin slice of potato fried crisp and salted.
potato rot A disease of the potato caused by a mildew (genus *Phytophthora).*
po·ta·to·ry (pō′tə·tôr′ē, -tō′rē) *adj.* Pertaining to potation; given or addicted to drinking: a *potatory* club. [<L *potatorius* < *potator* drinker < *potare* drink]
potato stone A quartz geode resembling a potato.
pot-au-feu (pô·tō·fœ′) *n. French* A variety of beef stew.
Pot·a·wat·o·mi (pot′ə·wot′ə·mē) *n.* One of a tribe of North American Indians of Algonquian stock, formerly inhabiting the western shores of Lake Michigan.
pot·bel·ly (pot′bel′ē) *n. pl.* **·lies** A protuberant belly. **— pot′bel′lied** *adj.*
pot·boil·er (pot′boi′lər) *n. Colloq.* A literary or artistic work produced simply to obtain the means of subsistence. **— pot′boil′ing** *n.*
pot·boy (pot′boi′) *n.* In a public house, a boy or young man who cleans the pots, serves customers, etc.
pot cheese Cottage cheese.
pot companion A boon companion; fellow toper.
po·teen (pō·tēn′) *n.* In Ireland, illicitly manufactured whisky: also spelled *potheen, potteen.* [<Irish *poitín,* dim. of *poite* pot]
Po·tem·kin (pō·tem′kin, *Russian* pô·tyôm′kin), **Prince Grigory Alexandrovich,** 1739–91, Russian field marshal and favorite of Catherine the Great.
po·ten·cy (pōt′n·sē) *n. pl.* **·cies** **1** The quality of being potent; inherent ability; mental, moral, or physical power. **2** The power of effecting particular results: the *potency* of a drug or liquor. **3** In homeopathy, the efficacy of a drug as increased by dilution or attenuation; also, the degree to which such attenuation has been carried. **4** Power arising from external circumstances; authority: the *potency* of the prime minister; hence, power to move or influence. **5** Capacity to respond to certain influences; latent power. Also **po′tence.** [<L *potentia*]
po·tent (pōt′nt) *adj.* **1** Physically powerful; able to accomplish material results; efficacious: a *potent* drug. **2** Morally powerful; of a character to influence; convincing: a *potent* argument. **3** Having great authority: a *potent* prince. **4** Sexually competent; able to procreate. See synonyms under POWERFUL. [<L *potens, -entis,* ppr. of *posse* be able, have power < *potis* able + *esse* be] **— po′tent·ly** *adv.* **— po′tent·ness** *n.*
po·ten·tate (pōt′n·tāt) *n.* One having great power or sway; a sovereign. [<LL *potentatus*]
po·ten·tial (pə·ten′shəl) *adj.* **1** Possible but not actual. **2** Having capacity for existence, but not yet existing. **3** *Physics* Existing by virtue of position: said of energy: distinguished from *kinetic.* **4** *Gram.* Indicating possibility or power. See POTENTIAL MOOD. **5** Having force or power. **—** *n.* **1** Anything that may be possible; a possible development. **2** *Gram.* The potential mood. **3** *Physics* A condition at a point in space, due to local attraction or repulsion, such that a mass, electric charge, etc., at that point becomes capable of doing work. **4** *Electr.* The ratio of the potential energy possessed by an electrically charged body because of its position in an electric field to the charge carried by the body. [<LL *potentialis*] **— po·ten′tial·ly** *adv.*
potential energy Energy stored in any of numerous forms, as chemical energy in coal, mechanical energy in a coiled spring, etc.
po·ten·ti·al·i·ty (pə·ten′shē·al′ə·tē) *n. pl.* **·ties** **1** Inherent capacity for development or accomplishment; capability; power; efficiency. **2** Potential quality or being; possibility. [< Med. L *potentialitas, -tatis*]
potential mood *Gram.* The verb phrase made up by means of the auxiliaries *may, can, could, must, should,* or *would,* with an infinitive, and expressing power, liberty, or possibility: I *could* go; it *may* be.
po·ten·til·la (pō′tən·til′ə) *n.* Any plant of a large genus *(Potentilla)* of herbs or, rarely, of shrubs of the rose family, the cinquefoils or five-fingers, having compound leaves and solitary or cymose flowers with a many-bracted calyx. Many are in cultivation for their profuse, showy flowers. [<NL <L *potens, -entis,* ppr. of *posse* be able + *-illa,* dim. suffix]
po·ten·ti·om·e·ter (pə·ten′shē·om′ə·tər) *n.* An apparatus for measuring electromotive force or difference of potential. [<L *potenti(a)* potency + -METER]
po·tent·ize (pōt′n·tīz) *v.t.* **·ized, ·iz·ing** In homeopathy, to render potent, as drugs, by attenuation. **— po′tent·iz′er** *n.*
pot·head (pot′hed′) *n. U.S. Slang* A person who habitually smokes marihuana.
poth·e·car·y (poth′ə·ker′ē) *n. Scot. & Brit. Dial.* Apothecary.
po·theen (pō·thēn′) See POTEEN.
poth·er (poth′ər) *n.* Excitement mingled with confusion; bustle; fuss. **—** *v.t. & v.i.* To worry; bother. [Origin uncertain]
pot herb Any plant, especially greens, cooked by boiling, or used to flavor boiled foods.
pot·hold·er (pot′hōl′dər) *n.* A padded cloth or mitten used for handling hot cooking pots and pans.
pot·hole (pot′hōl′) *n.* **1** A pot-shaped cavity in a rock, as that worn by loose stone gyrated in an eddy. **2** A deep hole, as in a road.
pot·hook (pot′hŏŏk′) *n.* **1** A curved or hooked piece of iron for lifting or hanging pots. **2** A curved mark or elementary stroke used in teaching penmanship; also, a scrawl, or, popularly, any curved stroke in stenography.
pot·house (pot′hous′) *n.* An alehouse; saloon.
pot·hunt·er (pot′hun′tər) *n.* **1** One who kills game for food rather than for sport: usually a contemptuous use. **2** One who engages in a competition simply to win the prizes offered. **— pot′hunt′ing** *adj. & n.*
po·tiche (pô·tēsh′) *n.* A vase having an elongated round body, a cylindrical neck, and a detached cover. [<F]
Pot·i·dae·a (pot′ə·dē′ə) An ancient Macedonian city on the Chalcidice peninsula, near the Aegean Sea. Also **Pot′i·dæ′a.**
po·tion (pō′shən) *n.* A draft, as a large dose of liquid medicine: often used of a magic or poisonous draft. [<F <L *potio, -onis* < *potare* drink. Doublet of POISON.]
Pot·i·phar (pot′i·fär, -fər) An officer of Pharaoh, who bought Joseph as a slave. *Gen.* xxxix 1.
pot·latch (pot′lach) *n.* **1** Among American Indians of the northern Pacific coast: **a** A gift. **b** *Often cap.* A winter festival. **2** A ceremonial feast in which gifts are exchanged and property destroyed in a competitive show of wealth. Also **pot′lach, pot′lache.** [< Chinook *patshatl* gift]
pot·lead (pot′led′) *n.* Graphite, especially as used on the bottoms of racing vessels to reduce friction.
pot-lead (pot′led′) *v.t.* To coat with potlead.
pot liquor The liquid left in a pot after cooking greens and meat (usually pork or bacon) together.
pot luck Whatever may chance to be in the pot; hence, a meal or food not prepared for guests: usually in the phrase **to take pot luck.**
pot marigold The calendula.
pot metal **1** Cast iron suitable for making pots. **2** A copper-and-lead alloy formerly used for large pots. **3** A kind of glass colored throughout while still in a molten state.
Po·to·mac River (pə·tō′mək) A river forming the boundaries between Maryland, West Virginia, and Virginia, and flowing 287 miles from the Allegheny Mountains near Cumberland, Md., to Chesapeake Bay about 70 miles SE of Washington, D.C.
po·to·ma·ni·a (pō′tə·mā′nē·ə, -mān′yə) *n.* Delirium tremens; dipsomania. [<Gk. *potos* drunk + -MANIA]
po·tom·e·ter (pō·tom′ə·tər) *n.* An instrument for measuring the amount of moisture absorbed by a plant, as determined by the amount lost in transpiration. [<Gk. *poton* drink + -METER]
Po·to·sí (pō′tō·sē′) A city of south central Bolivia; 13,255 feet above sea level.
pot·pie (pot′pī′) *n.* A pie, baked in a deep dish, containing meat and vegetables and having only a top crust; also, meat stewed with dumplings.
pot·pour·ri (pot·pŏŏr′ē, *Fr.* pō·pōō·rē′) *n.* **1** A ragout of meats and vegetables; a stew. **2** A mixture of dried sweet-smelling flower petals used to perfume a room; also, a small covered jar for containing such a mixture. **3** A collection of various things; miscellany. [<F, lit., rotten pot. See OLLA PODRIDA.]
pot roast Meat braised and cooked in a pot until tender, often with vegetables.
Pots·dam (pots′dam, *Ger.* pôts′däm) A city in East Germany, capital of the former state of Brandenburg; scene of a United Nations conference, July–August, 1945.
pot·sherd (pot′shûrd) *n.* A bit of broken crockery. Also **pot′shard** (-shärd). [<POT + SHARD]
pot shot **1** A shot fired to kill, without regard to the rules of sports. **2** A shot fired, as from ambush, at a person or animal within easy range. **3** A random shot.
pot·stone (pot′stōn′) *n.* Steatite.
pott (pot) *n.* A size of paper, varying in size according to use, but generally about 15 1/2 × 12 1/2 inches. [Var. of POT; so named from having once borne the watermark of a pot]
pot·tage (pot′ij) *n.* **1** A thick broth or stew. **2** A porridge. [<F *potage* < *pot* pot]
pot·ted (pot′id) *adj.* **1** Placed or kept in a pot. **2** Cooked or preserved in a pot. **3** *Slang* Drunk.
pot·teen (pō·tēn′) See POTEEN.
pot·ter[1] (pot′ər) *v.t. & v.i., n. Brit.* Putter.
pot·ter[2] (pot′ər) *n.* **1** One who makes earthenware or porcelain. **2** One who pots meats, vegetables, etc. [OE *potere*]
Pot·ter (pot′ər), **Paul,** 1625–54, Dutch painter.
potter's field A piece of ground appropriated as a burial ground for the destitute and the unknown. *Matt.* xxvii 7.
potter's flint Finely pulverized quartz mixed with porcelain to impart strength and rigidity and to reduce shrinkage: used also in enamel mixtures.
potter's wheel A horizontal rotating disk used by potters for holding and manipulating prepared clay.
potter wasp A digger wasp (genus *Eumenes)* which constructs vaselike cells of mud as a nest, especially the North

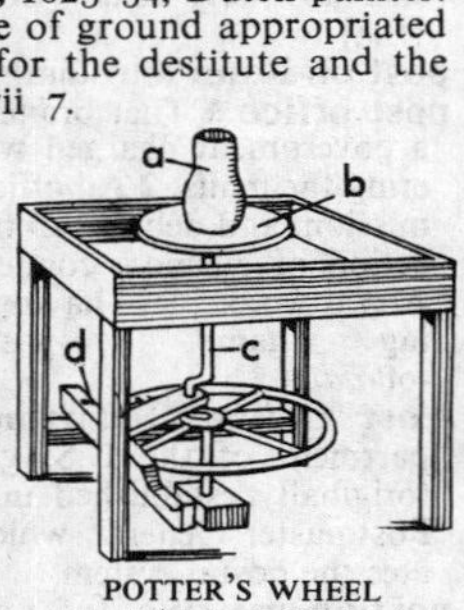

POTTER'S WHEEL
a. Molding clay.
b. Rotating wheel.
c. Shaft.
d. Treadle.

American potter wasp, *E. fraterna.* For illustration see INSECTS (beneficial).

pot·ter·y (pot'ər·ē) *n. pl.* **·ter·ies** 1 A factory where potters' ware is made. 2 The manufacture of earthenware or porcelain. 3 Clay ware molded and hardened. ◆ Collateral adjective: *fictile.* [< F *poterie* < *potier* a potter < *pot* a pot]

pot·ting (pot'ing) *n.* 1 The preserving of articles of food in pots for future use. 2 The placing of buds, bulbs, or plants in pots.

pot·tin·ger (pot'in·jər) *n.* 1 *Obs.* A maker of pottage; a cook. 2 *Scot. & Brit. Dial.* A porridge dish. [See PORRINGER]

pot·tle (pot'l) *n.* 1 A drinking vessel, pot, or tankard holding about half a gallon. 2 An old liquid measure of half a gallon. 3 A small vessel or basket for holding fruit. [< OF *potel,* dim. of *pot* pot]

pot·to (pot'ō) *n. pl.* **·tos** A small, nocturnal, arboreal primate *(Perodicticus potto)* of African forests, having a stumpy tail and feet and hands adapted for grasping. See KINKAJOU. [< West African native name]

Pott's disease *Pathol.* Caries or tuberculosis of the vertebrae, causing angular curvature of the spine: first described scientifically by Percival Pott, 1714–88, English surgeon.

pot·ty (pot'ē) *adj. Brit. Colloq.* 1 Insignificant. 2 Slightly drunk; hence, a little silly. [Prob. < POT, in the phrase *go to pot* deteriorate]

pot-val·iant (pot'val'yənt) *adj.* Courageous from drink. —**pot'-val'ian·cy, pot'-val'ian·try, pot'-val'or** (-val'ər) *n.*

pot-wal·lo·per (pot'wol'ə·pər, pot'wol'-) *n.* 1 *Slang* One employed to clean or wash pots, etc.; a scullion. 2 *Brit.* Formerly, by the requirements of some boroughs before 1832, a parliamentary voter who was a householder (not a tenant), having his own fireplace as a qualification for suffrage. [< POT + WALLOP (def. 5)]

pouch (pouch) *n.* 1 A small bag or sack, or something serving a similar purpose, as a pocket or a purse. 2 *Zool.* A saclike part for temporarily containing food, as in gophers and pelicans; also, a marsupium. 3 *Bot.* Any pouchlike cavity, as the silique of the mustard plant. 4 A leather receptacle for carrying small-arms ammunition; also, a wooden cartridge box. 5 An inner mailbag. —*v.t.* 1 To put in or as in a pouch; pocket. 2 To fashion or arrange in pouchlike form. 3 To swallow. —*v.i.* 4 To take on a pouchlike shape; form a pouchlike cavity. [< OF *poche,* var. of *poke, poque* bag] —**pouch'y** *adj.*

pouched (poucht) *adj.* Having pouches or sacs; characterized by pouches.

pouched rat 1 A rodent with cheek pouches; especially, a pocket gopher. 2 A kangaroo rat. 3 Any of certain ratlike rodents of Africa having large cheek pouches (genera *Cricetomys* and *Saccostomus*).

pouf (pōōf) *n.* 1 A hair arrangement in high rolled puffs, popular in the 18th century. 2 Any puffed part of a dress. 3 An upholstered tabouret for one or more persons. [< F, a puff]

Pough·keep·sie (pə·kip'sē) A city on the Hudson River in SE New York.

pou·laine (pōō·lān') *n.* 1 The long pointed toe of a medieval shoe. 2 A shoe with such a toe. [< OF *(soulier à la) poulaine* (shoe in the) Polish (fashion)]

pou·lard[1] (pōō·lärd') *n.* A pullet having the ovaries removed to produce abnormal growth and fattening and superior quality; hence, a fat pullet. Compare CAPON. [< F *poularde* < *poule* pullet]

pou·lard[2] (pōō·lärd') *n.* A variety of spring or winter wheat closely related to durum, having broad leaves, thick culms, and hard, starchy kernels. Also **poulard wheat.** [< POULARD[1]; so named because suitable only for stock feed]

Poul·sen (poul'sən), **Valdemar,** 1869–1942, Danish electrical engineer and inventor.

poult (pōlt) *n.* A young turkey, chicken, etc. [Contraction of ME *pulet* pullet]

poul·ter (pōl'tər) *n. Obs.* A poulterer. [< OF *pouletier* < *poulet* pullet]

poul·ter·er (pōl'tər·ər) *n.* A dealer in poultry. [< POULTER + -ER[2]]

poulter's measure A verse form consisting of alternating lines of twelve and fourteen syllables: so called from the poulterer's custom of sometimes giving fourteen eggs to the dozen.

poul·tice (pōl'tis) *n.* A mollifying remedy of a moist, mealy nature, applied to inflamed surfaces. —*v.t.* **·ticed, ·tic·ing** To cover or treat with a poultice. [< L *pultes,* pl. of *puls* porridge]

poul·try (pōl'trē) *n.* Domestic fowls, generally or collectively, as hens, ducks, etc. [< OF *pouleterie* < *poulet* fowl]

pounce[1] (pouns) *v.i.* **pounced, pounc·ing** To swoop or spring in or as in seizing prey: with *on, upon,* or *at.*—*n.* 1 A talon or claw. 2 The act of pouncing; a sudden leap, swoop, spring, or seizure. [Origin uncertain] —**pounc'er** *n.*

pounce[2] (pouns) *v.t.* 1 To perforate with holes in decorative patterns; scallop; pink. 2 To emboss (metalwork) with a design hammered on the reverse side. [< OF *poinçonner, ponchonner* < *poinçon, poinchon* a puncheon]

pounce[3] (pouns) *n.* 1 A powder formerly used to absorb excess of ink, as on a manuscript. 2 A finely pulverized substance used in transferring designs. —*v.t.* **pounced, pounc·ing** To sprinkle, smooth, or rub with pounce. [< F *ponce* < L *pumex, pumicis* pumice]

pounce box 1 A box with perforated lid formerly used for dusting out pounce as a perfume; a perfume box. 2 A box formerly used for dusting powder or sand on freshly written paper. Also **poun·cet** (poun'sit) **box.**

pound[1] (pound) *n.* 1 A variable unit of weight (symbol lb.): the avoirdupois pound is 16 ounces, 7,000 grains, or 453.59 grams; the troy pound, 12 ounces, 5,760 grains, or 373.24 grams. 2 An English money of account, equal to 20 shillings; specifically, a pound sterling (symbol £). See SOVEREIGN. [OE *pūnd* < L *pondus* weight]

pound[2] (pound) *n.* 1 A place, enclosed by authority, in which stray or trespassing cattle and distrained cattle or goods are left till redeemed; also, a similar enclosure for stray dogs. 2 An enclosed shelter for cattle or sheep. 3 A trap for wild animals. 4 An area or place in which to catch or stow fish; a poundnet. —*v.t.* To confine in or as in a pound; impound; restrain. [OE *pund(fald)* pinfold] —**pound'keep'er** (-kē'pər) *n.*

pound[3] (pound) *v.t.* 1 To strike heavily and repeatedly, as with a hammer; beat. 2 To reduce to a pulp or powder by beating; pulverize; triturate. 3 To teach or impress by constant repetition: to *pound* facts into someone's head. 4 To walk heavily or heavily: to *pound* a beat. —*v.i.* 5 To strike heavy, repeated blows: with *on, at,* etc. 6 To move or proceed heavily or vigorously. 7 To rise and fall heavily, as a ship in rough water. 8 To throb heavily or resoundingly: Her heart was *pounding* from fear and excitement. —*n.* 1 A heavy blow; thump; thud. 2 The act of pounding. See synonyms under BEAT. [OE *punian*] —**pound'er** *n.*

Pound (pound), **Sir Dudley,** 1877–1943, English admiral in World War II. —**Ezra Loomis,** 1885–1972, U.S. poet. —**Louise,** 1872–1958, U.S. linguist. —**Roscoe,** 1870–1964, U.S. jurist; brother of Louise.

pound·age[1] (poun'dij) *n.* 1 A rate on the pound sterling. 2 Formerly, in England, a subsidy to the crown on each pound of merchandise exported or imported.

pound·age[2] (poun'dij) *n.* 1 The charges for the redemption of impounded cattle. 2 The act of impounding cattle.

pound·al (poun'dəl) *n. Physics* The unit of force in the foot-pound-second system, which, acting on the mass of a pound, imparts to it an acceleration of one foot per second per second.

pound cake A rich cake having ingredients equal in weight, as a pound each of flour, butter, and sugar, with eggs added.

pound·er (poun'dər) *n.* 1 Anything weighing a pound: The trout's a *pounder.* 2 A person or thing weighing, having, or having a certain relation to, a given number of pounds: used only in compounds: The baby is an eight-*pounder.*

pound-fool·ish (pound'fōōl'ish) *adj.* 1 Extrava-

gant with large sums, but watching small sums closely: penny-wise and *pound-foolish.* 2 Having little capacity for business.

pound-net (pound'net') *n.* A weir or arrangement of nets supported upon stakes to form a trap for fish.

pound party *U.S.* A social gathering to which each guest brings a pound of something, usually food, to be given to an individual or a charitable cause.

pour (pôr, pōr) *v.t.* 1 To cause to flow in a continuous stream, as water, sand, etc. 2 To send forth, emit, or utter profusely or continuously: The radio *poured* forth music. —*v.i.* 3 To flow in a continuous stream; gush. 4 To rain heavily. 5 To move in great numbers; swarm: The northern hordes *poured* over Italy. 6 To serve as a hostess at a social tea. —*n.* A pouring, flow, or downfall. [Origin unknown] —**pour'er** *n.*

pour·boire (pōōr·bwàr') *n. French* A gratuitous gift of money as a tip; literally, for drink.

pour le mé·rite (pōōr lə mā·rēt') *French* For merit.

pour·par·ler (pōōr·pàr·lā') *n. French* A preliminary or informal conference or consultation.

pour·point (poor'point', *Fr.* pōōr·pwàn') *n.* A quilted cloth doublet worn in the 14th and 15th centuries. [< F, prob. orig. pp. of *pourpoindre* perforate]

pour point 1 *Physics* The lowest temperature at which a liquid, especially a fuel oil, will flow under prescribed conditions. 2 *Metall.* The temperature at which molten metal is cast.

pousse-ca·fé (pōōs·kà·fā') *n. French* A drink, commonly a mixture of cordials and brandy in successive layers, served after the coffee at dinner.

pous·sette (pōō·set') *n.* A dance figure in which a couple or couples swing round and round while holding hands. —*v.i.* **·set·ted, ·set·ting** To perform a poussette. [< F, dim. of *pousse* a push < *pousser* push]

pous·sie (pōō'sē) *n. Scot.* Pussy; also, a hare.

Pous·sin (pōō·san'), **Nicolas,** 1594–1665, French painter.

pou sto (pōō' stō', pou') A place to stand on; hence, a foundation for operations in any line of endeavor. [< Gk. *pou stō* where I may stand: from the alleged saying of Archimedes on his discovery of the lever, "Give me a place where I may stand and I will move the earth."]

pout[1] (pout) *v.i.* 1 To thrust out the lips, especially in ill humor. 2 To be sullen; sulk. 3 To swell out; protrude. —*v.t.* 4 To thrust out (the lips, etc.). 5 To utter with a pout. —*n.* A pushing out of the lips as in pouting; hence, a fit of ill humor. [Cf. Sw. *puta* be swollen]

pout[2] (pout) *n.* 1 One of various fresh-water catfishes having a pouting appearance. 2 The eelpout. [< *(æle)pūte* eelpout]

pout·er[1] (pou'tər) *n.* 1 One who or that which pouts. 2 A breed of pigeon having the habit of puffing out the crop.

pout·er[2] (pou'tər) *v.t. & v.i. Scot.* To poke; stir.

pou·ther (pōō'thər) *v. & n. Scot.* Powder. Also spelled *powther.*

pou·try (pōō'trē) *n. Scot.* Poultry.

pov·er·ty (pov'ər·tē) *n.* 1 The state of being poor or without competent subsistence; need; penury. 2 The condition that relates to the absence or scarcity of requisite substance or elements. 3 A lack or meagerness of supply; dearth. [< OF *poverté* < L *paupertas* < *pauper* poor]

Synonyms: beggary, destitution, distress, indigence, mendicancy, need, pauperism, penury, privation, want. *Poverty* denotes a condition below that of easy, comfortable living; *privation* denotes a condition of painful lack of what is useful or desirable; *indigence* is lack of ordinary means of subsistence; *destitution* is lack of the comforts, and even of the necessaries of life; *penury* is cramping *poverty; pauperism* is such *destitution* as throws one upon public charity for support; *beggary* and *mendicancy* denote *poverty* that appeals for indiscriminate private charity.

poverty grass Any of certain grasses, especially *Aristida divaricata,* having little or no

nutriment and found growing in old fields too poor for cultivation.

pov·er·ty-strick·en (pov′ər·tē·strik′ən) *adj.* Suffering from poverty; destitute.

pow (pou) *n. Scot.* The poll; head.

pow·der (pou′dər) *n.* **1** A finely ground or comminuted mass of free particles formed from a solid substance in the dry state; dust. **2** A pulverized cosmetic preparation for toilet use. **3** A medicine in the form of powder. **4** An explosive dry powder, as gunpowder. —*v.t.* **1** To reduce to powder; pulverize. **2** To sprinkle or cover with or as with powder. **3** To sprinkle with small objects or ornaments. —*v.i.* **4** To be reduced to powder. **5** To use powder as a cosmetic. [< OF *poudre* < L *pulvis, pulveris* dust] —**pow′der·er** *n.*

powder blue 1 Pulverized smalt having a deep-blue color: used as laundry bluing. **2** Its deep-blue color. **3** A valuable porcelain glaze. **4** The color of this glaze, a soft medium blue.

powder flask A metallic or other flask for carrying gunpowder.

powder horn The hollow horn of an ox or cow, formerly fitted with a cover and used by hunters or soldiers for holding gunpowder.

powder metallurgy The science and technique of manufacturing objects from finely powdered metals and alloys.

powder puff A soft pad used to apply powder to the skin.

Powder River 1 A river in NE Oregon, flowing 110 miles NE to the Snake River. **2** A river in Wyoming and Montana, flowing 486 miles north to the Yellowstone River.

powder room 1 A women's rest-room. **2** A small room or bathroom decorated daintily for use as a woman's dressing-room.

pow·der·y (pou′dər·ē) *adj.* **1** Consisting of or like fine powder or dust. **2** Covered with or as with powder; mealy; dusty. **3** Capable of being easily powdered or crumbled; friable.

Pow·ell (pou′əl), **Lewis F., Jr.,** born 1907, U.S. jurist, associate Supreme Court justice 1972–.

pow·er (pou′ər) *n.* **1** Ability to act; potency; specifically, the property of a substance or being that is manifested in effort or action, and by virtue of which that substance or being produces change, moral or physical. **2** Potential capacity. **3** Strength or force actually put forth. **4** The right, ability, or capacity to exercise control; legal authority, capacity, or competency, particularly, authority to do some act in relation to lands, as to create estates therein or charges thereon; also, a legal instrument or document conferring it. See POWER OF APPOINTMENT. **5** Any agent that exercises power, as in control or dominion; a military or naval force; an important and influential sovereign nation. **6** Great or telling force or effect. **7** *Colloq.* A great number or quantity. **8** Religious frenzy, especially as exemplified in exhortation: believed to be by possession of the Holy Spirit. **9** Any form of energy available for doing work; specifically, energy developed by mechanical or electrical means. **10** *Physics* The time rate at which energy is transferred, or converted into work. **11** *Math.* **a** The product of a number multiplied by itself a given number of times. **b** An exponent. **12** *Optics* Magnifying capacity, as of a lens. **13** *pl.* The sixth of the nine grades or orders of angels. —*v.t.* **1** To provide with means of propulsion. **2** *Colloq.* To force or push in the act of overcoming resistance: *powered* his way through for a touchdown. —*v.i.* **3** *Colloq.* To move forcefully: to *power* through mud. [< OF *poeir,* ult. < L *posse* be able]

Synonyms: ability, capacity, efficacy, efficiency, energy, force, might, potency, puissance, strength. *Power* is the most general term of this group of words, including every quality, property, or faculty by which any change, effect, or result is, or may be, produced, as, the *power* of the legislature to enact laws, or of the executive to enforce them; the *power* of an acid to corrode a metal; the *power* of a polished surface to reflect light. *Ability* is nearly coextensive with *power,* but does not reach its positiveness and vigor, *ability* often implying latent, as distinguished from active, *power. Power* and *ability* include *capacity,* which is *power* to receive; but *ability* is often distinguished from *capacity,* as *power* that may be manifested in doing, as *capacity* is in receiving. *Efficacy* is *power* to produce effects; *efficiency* is effectual agency, competent *power. Energy* is *power* both actual and potential; *force* is *power* enough to overcome resistance. *Puissance* is a poetic or literary synonym. See ABILITY, CAUSE, GENIUS, WEIGHT.

power- *combining form* Powered by a motor or by electricity: *power drill, power mower.*

power boat A motorboat.

power dive *Aeron.* A descent in which the engine increases the acceleration due to gravity.

power drill A motor-operated drill.

pow·er·ful (pou′ər·fəl) *adj.* **1** Possessing great force; very efficient; strong. **2** Having great intensity or energy. **3** Exercising great authority, or manifesting high qualities; mighty. **4** Having great effect on the mind; convincing. —*adv. Colloq.* Very; exceedingly. —**pow′er·ful·ly** *adv.*

Synonyms (adj.): able, cogent, commanding, controlling, effective, effectual, efficacious, efficient, forceful, influential, mighty, potent, puissant, robust, strong, sturdy, vigorous.

pow·er·house (pou′ər·hous′) *n.* **1** *Electr.* A station where electricity is generated. **2** *Slang* A person or thing of great might or force.

pow·er·less (pou′ər·lis) *adj.* **1** Destitute of power; unable to accomplish an effect; impotent. **2** Without authority. —**pow′er·less·ly** *adv.* —**pow′er·less·ness** *n.*

power loading *Aeron.* The gross weight of an aircraft divided by its rated engine power.

power of appointment *Law* Authority conferred, as by power of attorney, deed, or will, to appoint or designate a person or persons to make disposition of an estate or interest in the property of another.

power of attorney *Law* **1** The authority or power to act conferred upon an agent. **2** The instrument or document by which that power or authority is conferred or guaranteed. See under ATTORNEY.

power pack A compact assemblage of electrical units to provide requisite steady power, as in radio communication from an airplane.

power plant Any source of power, together with its housing, installations and accessory equipment: the *power plant* of an airplane.

power politics The use or threatened use of force to exact international concessions.

power train Drive train.

Pow·ha·tan (pou′hə·tan′) *n.* **1** A confederacy of Algonquian Indian tribes of Virginia (1607–1705) comprising about thirty tribes. **2** One of a tribe of North American Indians of Algonquian stock, formerly inhabiting a part of eastern Virginia.

pow·ney (pou′nē) *n. Scot.* A pony.

pow·ter (pou′tər) *n.* The pouter pigeon.

pow·ther (po͞o′thər) See POUTHER.

pow·wow (pou′wou′) *U.S. n.* **1** A North American Indian medicine man, priest, or magician. **2** The ceremony of a medicine man involving a dance, feast, or other demonstration, to cure the sick or effect success in hunting, war, etc. **3** Hence, magic; witchcraft. **4** An Indian council. **5** *Colloq.* Any meeting for conference. —*v.i.* To hold a deliberative council. [< Algonquian (Massachuset) *pauwaw,* lit., he dreams]

Pow·ys (pō′is) Name of three English authors, brothers: **John Cowper,** 1872–1963; **Llewelyn,** 1884–1939; **Theodore Francis,** 1875–1953.

pox (poks) *n.* **1** Any disease characterized by eruptions of a purulent nature: chicken *pox.* **2** Syphilis [Var. of *pocks,* pl. of POCK]

Po·yang (pō′yäng′) A lake in northern Kiangsi province, eastern China; about 1,070 square miles at low water, 3,600 square miles when flooded in summer by waters of the Yangtze.

poy·ou (poi′o͞o) *n.* The six-banded armadillo *(Dasypus sexcinctus)* of Argentina and Brazil. [< Guarani *(tatu) -po-yu* (armadillo) with a yellow band < *po* band + *yu* yellow]

Poz·nań (pôz′nän·y′) A city of western Poland: German *Posen.*

Po·zsony (pô′zhôn′y′) The Hungarian name for BRATISLAVA.

poz·zuo·la·na (pot′swə·lä′nə, *Ital.* pōt′tswô·lä′nä) *n.* A volcanic ash, first collected at Pozzuoli, used in making hydraulic cement: also made artificially. Also **poz′zo·la′na** (pot′sə-). [< Ital., from *Pozzuoli*] —**poz′zuo·lan′ic** (-lan′ik) *adj.*

Poz·zuo·li (pōt·tswô′lē) A town on the site of an ancient city SW of Naples, Italy. Ancient **Pu·te·o·li** (pyo͞o·tē′ə·lī).

P-P factor *Biochem.* The pellagra-preventive factor of the vitamin B complex; nicotinic acid.

Pr *Chem.* Praseodymium (symbol Pr).

praam (präm) *n.* A Baltic flat-bottomed barge, Also spelled *pram.* [< Du. < Slavic. Cf. Polish *pram* boat.]

prac·tic (prak′tik) *adj. Obs.* Practical.

prac·ti·ca·ble (prak′tə·kə·bəl) *adj.* **1** That can be put into practice; feasible. **2** That can be used for an intended purpose; usable. —**prac′ti·ca·bil′i·ty, prac′ti·ca·ble·ness** *n.* —**prac′ti·ca·bly** *adv.*

prac·ti·cal (prak′ti·kəl) *adj.* **1** Pertaining to or governed by actual use and experience or action, as contrasted with ideals and speculations. **2** Trained by or derived from practice or experience. **3** Having reference to useful ends to be attained; applicable to use. **4** Manifested in practice. **5** Being such to all intents and purposes; virtual. [< obs. *practic* < obs. F *practique* < LL *practicus* < Gk. *praktikos* fit for doing < *prassein* do] —**prac′ti·cal′i·ty** (-kal′ə·tē), **prac′ti·cal·ness** *n.*

Practical Christianity New Thought.

practical joke A joke involving action instead of wit or words; a prank or trick.

prac·ti·cal·ly (prak′tik·lē) *adv.* **1** In a practical manner. **2** To all intents and purposes; in fact or effect; virtually.

practical nurse A nurse with practical experience in the care of the sick, but who is not a registered nurse.

prac·tice (prak′tis) *v.* **·ticed, ·tic·ing** *v.t.* **1** To make use of habitually or often: to *practice* economy. **2** To apply in action; make a practice of: *Practice* what you preach. **3** To work at or pursue as a profession: to *practice* law. **4** To do or perform repeatedly in order to acquire skill or training; rehearse. **5** To instruct, as pupils, by repeated exercise or lessons. —*v.i.* **6** To repeat or rehearse something in order to acquire skill or proficiency: to *practice* for a concert. **7** To work at or pursue a profession: He *practiced* for twenty years. **8** *Rare* To conspire; scheme. —*n.* **1** Any customary action or proceeding regarded as individual; habit. **2** An established custom or usage. **3** The act or process of executing or accomplishing; doing or performance: distinguished from *theory.* **4** The regular prosecution of a business pursuit requiring education; professional business. **5** Frequent and repeated exercise in any matter. **6** *pl.* Stratagems or schemes for bad purposes; tricks. **7** A rule or method in arithmetic to facilitate multiplying quantities in different denominations. **8** The rules governing legal proceedings. Also **prac′tise.** [< OF *practiser* < *practiquer* < Med. L *practicare* < LL *practicus.* See PRACTICAL.] —**prac′tic·er** *n.*

◆ In Britain, *practice* is almost invariably the spelling used for the noun, *practise* for the verb. In the U.S., the noun form is more commonly *practice,* although *practise* is also used; both spellings are widely used as verbs.

Synonyms (noun): drill, exercise. *Exercise* is action with a view to employing, maintaining, or increasing power, or merely for enjoyment; *practice* is systematic *exercise* with a view to the acquirement of facility and skill; a person takes a walk for *exercise,* or takes time for *practice* on the piano. *Practice* is also used of putting into action and effect what one has learned or holds as a theory; as, the *practice* of law or medicine. Educationally, *practice* is the voluntary and persistent attempt to make skill a *habit;* as, *practice* in penmanship. *Drill* is systematic, rigorous, and commonly enforced *practice* under a teacher or commander. See CUSTOM, EXERCISE, HABIT, MANNER.

prac·ticed (prak′tist) *adj.* **1** Expert by practice; skilled by use or habit; experienced. **2** Acquired by practice. Also **prac′tised.**

prac·ti·tion·er (prak·tish′ən·ər) *n.* **1** One who practices an art or profession. **2** A Christian Science healer. [< earlier *practician* < OF *practicien,* ult. < L *practica* practice]

prae- See PRE-.

prae·ci·pe (pres′i·pē, prē′si-) See PRECIPE.

prae·di·al (prē′dē·əl), **prae·fect** (prē′fekt), etc. See PREDIAL, PREFECT, etc.

prae·mu·ni·re (prē′myo͞o·nī′rē) *n.* In English law, the offense of introducing an alien power within the realm; specifically, the offense of maintaining the papal power in England. [< Med. L *praemunire (facias)* (see that you)

warn, a legal phrase; from a confusion of L *praemunire* protect with *praemonere* warn]

prae·no·men (prē·nō′mən) *n. pl.* **·nom·i·na** (-nom′ə·nə) The name prefixed to an ancient Roman family name to mark the individual, corresponding to the modern Christian name: also spelled *prenomen.* [< PRAE- + L *nomen* name]

prae·pos·tor (prē·pos′tər) *n.* A prepositor: also spelled *prepostor.* Also **prae·pos′i·tor.** [< Med. L *praepositor* one who puts another in charge < L *praepositus,* pp. of *praeponere.* See PREPOSITION.]

praeter- See PRETER-.

prae·tex·ta (prē·teks′tə) *n. pl.* **·tae** (-tē) An ordinary white toga with a purple border or stripe, worn by free-born Roman boys until they assumed the toga virilis at 14–16 years, and by girls until they were married. It was also the distinctive mark of the Roman curule magistrates, censors, state priests (when performing their functions), and emperors. [< L, lit., woven before, fringed, fem. of *praetextus,* pp. of *praetexere*]

prae·tor (prē′tər), **prae·to·ri·al** (prē·tôr′ē·əl, -tō′rē-), **prae·to·ri·an** (prē·tôr′ē·ən, -tō′rē-), etc. See PRETOR, etc.

Pra·ga (prä′gä) A suburb of Warsaw, Poland, on the east bank of the Vistula.

prag·mat·ic (prag·mat′ik) *adj.* **1** Pertaining to the accomplishment of duty or of business; specifically, relating to the civil affairs of a sovereign state. **2** Pertaining to or occupied with the scientific evolution of causes and effects; philosophical: said especially of history: the *pragmatic* method. **3** Pragmatical; practical. **4** Of or pertaining to the philosophy of pragmatism. [< L *pragmaticus* active or skilled in practical affairs < Gk. *pragmatikos* < *pragma, pragmatos* a thing done, an affair < *prassein* do, perform]

prag·mat·i·cal (prag·mat′i·kəl) *adj.* **1** Inclined to be officious or meddlesome; self-important; busy. **2** Relating to or engrossed with everyday business; practical; hence, commonplace. — **prag·mat′i·cal·ly** *adv.* —**prag·mat′i·cal·ness** *n.*

prag·mat·i·cism (prag·mat′ə·siz′əm) *n. Philos.* The pragmatism of C. S. Peirce, renamed by him to distinguish it from the teachings of William James and others, and referring to his philosophy that concepts are predictions of facts to be found and consequences to result should specified action be taken.

pragmatic sanction An imperial or royal edict or decree operating as a fundamental law. The most famous of these edicts was that of Charles VI of Austria in 1724, which admitted heirs in the female line to the Austrian succession.

prag·ma·tism (prag′mə·tiz′əm) *n. Philos.* The doctrine that thought or ideas have value only in terms of their practical consequences, and that results are the sole test of the validity or truth of one's beliefs. —**prag′ma·tist** *n.*

Prague (präg) The capital of Czechoslovakia, on the Vltava, in central Bohemia. *German* **Prag** (präkh), *Czech* **Pra·ha** (prä′hä).

pra·hu (prä·hōō′) *n.* A proa. [< Malay *práu*]

Prai·ri·al (pre·rē·äl′) See under CALENDAR (Republican).

prai·rie (prâr′ē) *n.* A level or rolling tract of treeless land covered with coarse grass and generally of rich soil, especially as in parts of the western United States. [< F, a large meadow < Med. L *prataria* < L *pratum* meadow]

prairie chicken See under GROUSE. Also **prairie hen.**

prairie cock The cock of the plains.

prairie dog A burrowing rodent (genus *Cynomys*) of the plains of North America; specifically, *C. ludovicianus,* which lives in large communities and is very destructive to vegetation. Also **prairie squirrel.**

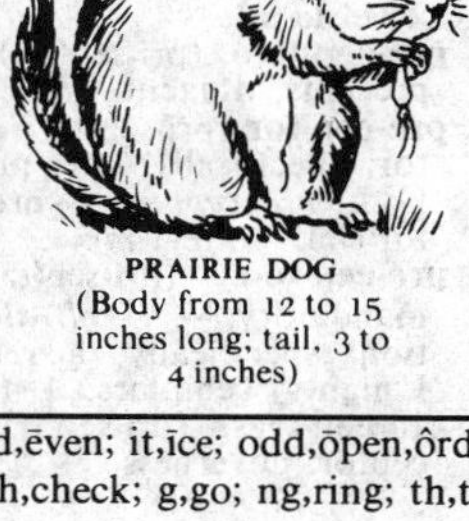

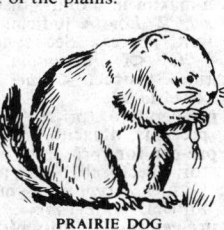

PRAIRIE DOG
(Body from 12 to 15 inches long; tail, 3 to 4 inches)

prairie owl **1** The burrowing owl. **2** The short-eared owl.

Prairie Provinces The provinces of Manitoba, Saskatchewan, and Alberta, in western Canada.

prairie schooner A covered wagon.

prairie state One of the States of the prairie regions of the Western and Middle Western United States.

Prairie State Nickname of ILLINOIS.

prairie wolf A coyote: distinguished from *timber wolf.*

praise (prāz) *v.t.* **praised, prais·ing 1** To express approval and commendation of; applaud; eulogize. **2** To express adoration of; glorify (God, etc.). —*n.* **1** Commendation expressed, as of a person for his virtues, or concerning meritorious actions; utterance of approval; honor given; also, applause. **2** Thanksgiving for blessings conferred; laudation to God; worship expressed in song. **3** The object, ground, reason, or subject of praise. ◆ Homophone: *prase.* [< OF *preisier* < LL *pretiare* prize < L *pretium* price. See PRICE.] —**prais′er** *n.*

Synonyms (verb): adore, applaud, approve, bless, celebrate, commend, eulogize, extol, flatter, glorify, honor, laud, magnify, worship. See PUFF. *Antonyms*: see synonyms for ASPERSE, BLAME.

Synonyms (noun): acclaim, acclamation, adulation, applause, approbation, approval, commendation, compliment, encomium, eulogy, flattery, laudation, panegyric, plaudit, sycophancy. *Praise* is the hearty approval of an individual, or of a multitude considered individually, and is expressed by spoken or written words; *applause,* the spontaneous outburst of many at once. *Applause* is expressed by stamping of feet, clapping of hands, waving of handkerchiefs, etc., as well as by the voice; *acclamation* is the spontaneous and hearty approval of many at once, and strictly by the voice alone. One is chosen moderator by *acclamation* when he receives a practically unanimous viva voce vote; he could not be nominated by *applause. Acclaim* is the more poetic term for *acclamation*; as, a nation's *acclaim. Plaudit* is a shout of *applause,* and is commonly used in the plural; as, the *plaudits* of a throng. *Applause* is also used in the general sense of *praise. Approbation* is a milder and more qualified word than *praise*; *praise* is always uttered, *approbation* may be silent. The industry and intelligence of a clerk win his employer's *approbation*; his decision in a special instance receives his *approval. Praise* is always understood as genuine and sincere, unless the contrary is expressly stated; *compliment* is a light form of *praise* that may or may not be sincere; *flattery* is often insincere. Compare APPLAUSE, EULOGY. *Antonyms*: abuse, animadversion, blame, censure, condemnation, contempt, denunciation, disapprobation, disapproval, disparagement, obloquy, reproach, reproof, repudiation, scorn, slander, vilification, vituperation.

praise·wor·thy (prāz′wûr′thē) *adj.* Worthy of praise; commendable. —**praise′wor′thi·ly** *adv.* — **praise′wor′thi·ness** *n.*

Pra·ja·dhi·pok (prä·jä′di·pôk), 1893–1941, king of Siam 1925–35; abdicated.

Pra·krit (prä′krit) *n.* The popular dialects or any one of the vernaculars of northern and central India, arising from or connected with Sanskrit, and forming a link between Sanskrit and the modern Indic languages. [< Skt. *prakṛtā* natural, common, lit., created before < *pra-* before + *kṛ* do. Cf. SANSKRIT.]

pra·line (prä′lēn, prā′-) *n.* A crisp confection made of pecans or other nuts browned in boiling sugar. [< F, after Marshal Duplessis-*Praslin,* 1598–1675, whose cook invented it]

prall·tril·ler (präl′tril·ər) *n. Music* An inverted mordent. [< G, lit., elastic trill]

pram[1] (pram) *n. Brit. Colloq.* A baby carriage. [Short for PERAMBULATOR]

pram[2] (präm) See PRAAM.

prance (prans, präns) *v.* **pranced, pranc·ing** *v.i.* **1** To move proudly with high steps, as a spirited horse; spring from the hind legs. **2** To ride gaily, proudly, or insolently, as on a prancing horse. **3** To move in an arrogant or elated manner; swagger. **4** To gambol; caper. —*v.i.* **5** To cause to prance. —*n.* The act of prancing; a high step; a caper. [ME *prauncen,* ? < Scand. Cf. dial. Dan. *pranse* walk proudly.] —**pranc′er** *n.*

pran·di·al (pran′dē·əl) *adj.* Of or pertaining to a meal, especially a dinner. [< L *prandium* breakfast or lunch]

prank[1] (prangk) *v.t.* To decorate gaudily; deck with showy ornaments. —*v.i.* To make an ostentatious show. [Cf. Du. *pronken,* G *prunken* make a show of]

prank[2] (prangk) *n.* A mischievous or frolicsome act. See synonyms under FROLIC, SPORT. —*v.i.* To play pranks or tricks. [Origin uncertain] —**prank′ish** *adj.*

pranked (prangkt) *adj.* Decorated; dressed up: often with *out* or *up.*

prase (prāz) *n.* An olive-green, translucent quartz, usually cryptocrystalline. ◆ Homophone: *praise.* [< F < L *prasius* light green < Gk. *prason* leek; with ref. to its color]

pra·se·o·dym·i·um (prā′zē·ō·dim′ē·əm, prā′sē-) *n.* A soft, silvery, ductile metallic element (symbol Pr, atomic number 59) of the lanthanide series. See PERIODIC TABLE. [< NL < Gk. *prasios* light green + (DI)DYMIUM]

prate (prāt) *v.* **prat·ed, prat·ing** *v.i.* To talk idly and at length; chatter. —*v.t.* To utter idly or emptily. See synonyms under BABBLE. —*n.* Idle talk; prattle. [< Cf. MDu. & MLG *praten* chatter, ON *prata* talk] —**prat′er** *n.* —**prat′ing·ly** *adv.*

prat·fall (prat′fôl′) *n. Slang* A fall on the buttocks.

prat·in·cole (prat′ing·kōl, prā′tin-) *n.* Any one of a genus *(Glareola)* of Old World shore birds having long, pointed wings and deeply forked tail. [< L *pratum* meadow + *incola* inhabitant]

pra·tique (pra·tēk′, prat′ik; *Fr.* prà·tēk′) *n.* Intercourse or correspondence; especially, privilege granted to the master of a vessel to land passengers after compliance with sanitary inspection or quarantine. [< F]

prat·tle (prat′l) *v.* **·tled, ·tling** *v.i.* To talk foolishly or like a child; prate. —*v.t.* To utter in a foolish or childish way: to *prattle* secrets. See synonyms under BABBLE. —*n.* **1** Childish speech; babble. **2** Idle or foolish talk. [Freq. of PRATE] —**prat′tler** *n.*

Prav·dinsk (präv′dēnsk) **1** A town on the Volga in Russian S.F.S.R. **2** A city in the former German province of East Prussia, now in Russian S.F.S.R.: formerly *Friedland.*

prawn (prôn) *n.* An edible shrimplike decapod (suborder *Natantia*) occurring in a variety of genera and species, especially numerous in tropical and temperate waters, principally marine. [ME *prane*; origin unknown]

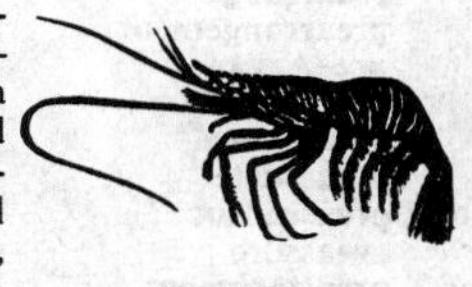

PRAWN
(Up to 6 inches in length)

prax·is (prak′sis) *n.* Exercise or discipline for a specific purpose; practical application of rules as distinguished from theory. [< NL < Gk. < *prassein* accomplish, do]

Prax·it·e·les (prak·sit′ə·lēz) Greek sculptor of the fourth century B.C.

pray (prā) *v.i.* **1** To address prayers to a deity, idol, etc.; say prayers. **2** To make entreaty; beg. —*v.t.* **3** To address by means of prayers; say prayers to. **4** To ask (someone) earnestly; entreat. **5** To ask for by prayers or entreaty. **6** To effect by prayer. ◆ Homophone: *prey.* [< OF *preier* < LL *precare* < L *precari* ask, pray < *prex, precis* prayer]

Synonyms: ask, beg, beseech, bid, conjure, entreat, implore, importune, invoke, petition, request, supplicate. See ASK.

prayer (prâr) *n.* **1** The act of offering reverent petitions, especially to God. **2** The act of beseeching earnestly; entreaty. **3** *Often pl.* A religious service of which prayer is the most prominent part: evening *prayers.* **4** Communion with God and recognition of His presence, as in praise, thanksgiving, intercession, etc. **5** A form of words appropriate to prayer. **6** A memorial or petition. **7** *Law* The request in a bill in equity for the specific relief sought by the complainant; also, the part of the bill

in which the request is made. — **common prayer** The prescribed form of public worship of the Anglican Church as contained in the *Book of Common Prayer*. [<OF *preiere* < Med.L *precaria* <L *precarius* obtained by prayer < *precari*. See PRAY.]
Synonyms: adoration, devotion, invocation, litany, orison, petition, request, suit, supplication. See PETITION.

prayer book A book of ritual prescribed for conducting divine service.

prayer·ful (prâr′fəl) *adj.* Inclined or given to prayer; devotional. — **prayer′ful·ly** *adv.* — **prayer′ful·ness** *n.*

prayer wheel A wheel, cylinder, or vertical drum containing written prayers, which is revolved to make the prayers efficacious: used by the Buddhists of Tibet. Also **praying wheel.**

praying mantis The mantis.

pre- *prefix* **1** Before in time or order; prior to; preceding; as in:

preaccusation	preconfiguration
preacquaint	preconfirm
preacquaintance	preconnection
preacquire	preconnubial
preact	preconsent
preaction	preconsideration
preadapt	preconsign
preadaptation	preconstitute
preadjust	preconstruction
preadjustment	preconsult
preadministration	preconsultation
preadmit	preconsume
preadmonish	precontract
preadmonition	precontrive
preadvertise	preconviction
preadvertiser	pre-cool
preadvise	precorrupt
preadviser	precounsel
preaestival	pre-Darwinian
preallege	predecision
preannounce	prededication
preannouncement	predeliberation
preannouncer	predemand
preantiquity	predescribe
preapperception	predesign
preappoint	predeterminable
preappointment	predevised
preapproval	predirect
prearm	prediscipline
prearrange	prediscovery
prearrangement	preelect
pre-Aryan	preelection
preassemble	preembodiment
preassigned	preembody
preassume	preemploy
preassurance	preenact
preassure	preengage
preattachment	preengagement
preattune	pre-epic
preavowal	preestablish
prebaptize	preestablishment
prebasal	preexamination
prebasilar	preexamine
preboding	preexist
preboil	preexistence
prebranchial	preexistent
pre-British	preexpose
prebronchial	preform
prebuccal	preglacial
precalculable	preheat
precalculate	preheater
precalculation	preinhabitation
precancerous	preinstruct
pre-Carboniferous	preintimation
pre-Centennial	preknowledge
precerebellar	prepaid
pre-Christian	pre-Paleozoic
pre-Christianize	pre-Reformation
precited	pre-Renaissance
preclassical	prerequire
precogitate	prerevolutionary
precogitation	pre-Roman
precognition	preselect
precognizable	preshadow
precognizant	pre-Shakespearian
precollection	preshow
pre-Columbian	presuccess
precompose	pre-Tertiary
precomputation	pretribal
precompute	pretypify
preconcession	preunite
preconclusion	pre-Victorian
precondemn	prewarm
precondemnation	prewarn

2 Before in position; anterior: chiefly in scientific terms; as in:

preabdomen	precardiac	prerectal
preanal	precerebral	prerenal
preaortic	precostal	preretinal
preauricular	prepatellar	prevertebral

3 Preliminary to; preparing for; as in:

precollege	prelegal	premedical
preflight	prelexical	pre-military

[<L *prae-* < *prae* before]

preach (prēch) *v.i.* **1** To deliver a sermon, as on a religious topic or a text of Scripture. **2** To give advice or instruction, especially persistently and intrusively. — *v.t.* **3** To advocate or recommend urgently: to *preach* temperance. **4** To proclaim; expound upon: to *preach* the gospel. **5** To deliver (a sermon, etc.). [<OF *prechier* <L *praedicare* proclaim < *prae-* before + *dicare* make known]

preach·er (prē′chər) *n.* One who preaches; specifically, a clergyman. [<OF *prechor*]

preach·i·fy (prē′chə·fī) *v.i.* **·fied**, **·fy·ing** *Colloq.* To preach or discourse tediously. — **preach′i·fi·ca′tion** *n.*

preach·ing (prē′ching) *n.* **1** The act or practice of delivering sermons. **2** The style of a preacher. **3** The doctrine preached.

Preaching Friars See DOMINICAN.

preach·ment (prēch′mənt) *n.* A preaching or moral lecture; especially, a wearisome exhortation. [<OF *prechement*]

preach·y (prē′chē) *adj.* **preach·i·er**, **preach·i·est** Given to or resembling preachments; marked by sanctimony or cant: not a complimentary term.

pre·ad·am·ite (prē·ad′əm·īt) *adj.* Existing before Adam; relating to the preadamites. Also **pre·a·dam·ic** (prē·ə·dam′ik), **pre·ad′am·it′ic** (-it′ik). — *n.* **1** One who or that which existed before Adam or before man. **2** One holding that there were men on the earth before Adam.

pre·ag·o·nal (prē·ag′ə·nəl) *adj.* Immediately preceding the death agony. [<PRE- + AGON(Y) + -AL¹]

pre·am·ble (prē′am·bəl) *n.* **1** A statement introductory to and explanatory of what follows; the introductory portion of a writing or speech: used chiefly of formal resolutions. **2** *Law* An introductory clause in a constitution, contract, or other instrument. [<F *préamble* <Med.L *praeambulum*, orig. neut. of L *praeambulus* walking before <L *praeambulare* precede < *prae-* before + *ambulare* walk] — **pre·am′bu·lar′y** *adj.*

pre·ax·i·al (prē·ak′sē·əl) *adj.* *Biol.* Situated on that side of the axis of a limb or body that is in front.

preb·end (preb′ənd) *n.* **1** A stipend allotted to an ecclesiastic from the revenues of a cathedral or conventual church in consideration of his officiating and serving therein; also, the land or tithe yielding the stipend, the tenure of which is a benefice. **2** A prebendary. [<OF *prebende* <Med.L *praebenda*, lit., things to be furnished, neut. pl. of L *praebendus*, gerundive of *praebere* supply < *prae-* in front of, before + *habere* have] — **preb′en·dal** *adj.*

preb·en·dar·y (preb′ən·der′ē) *n.* *pl.* **·dar·ies** A person, as a canon, who receives a stated income from the revenues of a cathedral. [<Med.L *prebendarius*]

Preb·le (preb′əl), **Edward**, 1761–1807, U.S. naval officer; captain of the *Constitution*.

Pre-Cam·bri·an (prē·kam′brē·ən) *adj.* *Geol.* Of or pertaining to all geological time and rock formations preceding the Cambrian. — *n.* Pre-Cambrian rocks.

pre·can·cel (prē·kan′səl) *v.t.* **·celed** or **·celled**, **·cel·ing** or **·cel·ling** To cancel (stamps) before use on mail. — *n.* A stamp so canceled.

pre·car·i·ous (pri·kâr′ē·əs) *adj.* **1** Subject to continued risk; that may be taken away at another's pleasure or by accident; uncertain. **2** Subject to or leading to danger; hazardous. **3** Not firmly established; untrustworthy; without foundation. [<L *precarius*. See PRAYER.] — **pre·car′i·ous·ly** *adv.* — **pre·car′i·ous·ness** *n.*
Synonyms: doubtful, dubious, equivocal, hazardous, insecure, perilous, risky, unassured, uncertain, unsettled, unstable, unsteady. *Uncertain* is applied to things about which human knowledge cannot certainly determine or that

human power cannot certainly control; *precarious* originally meant dependent on the will or pleasure of another; now it also means dependent on chance or hazard; one holds office by a *precarious* tenure, or land by a *precarious* title; the strong man's hold on life is *uncertain*, the invalid's is *precarious. Antonyms:* assured, certain, firm, immutable, incontestable, settled, stable, steady, strong, sure, undoubted, unquestionable.

pre-cast (prē′kast′, -käst′) *adj.* Receiving a finished shape before being put to final use: *pre-cast* concrete blocks.

prec·a·tive (prek′ə·tiv) *adj.* Expressing entreaty; supplicatory. Also **prec′a·to·ry.** [<L *precativus*]

pre·cau·tion (pri·kô′shən) *n.* **1** Prudent forethought, as against danger, etc. **2** A provision made for some emergency. See synonyms under CARE. [<F *précaution* <LL *praecautio, -onis* <L *praecautus*, pp. of *praecavere* guard against beforehand < *prae-* before + *cavere* take care]

pre·cau·tion·ar·y (pri·kô′shən·er′ē) *adj.* **1** Of or pertaining to precaution. **2** Expressing, advising, or using precaution. Also **pre·cau′tion·al.**

pre·cau·tious (pri·kô′shəs) *adj.* Exercising care; precautional. — **pre·cau′tious·ly** *adv.* — **pre·cau′tious·ness** *n.*

pre·cede (pri·sēd′) *v.* **·ced·ed**, **·ced·ing** *v.t.* **1** To go before in order, place, rank, time, etc. **2** To preface; introduce. — *v.i.* **3** To have or take precedence. [<F *précéder* <L *praecedere* go before < *prae-* before + *cedere* go]
Synonyms: head, herald, lead. See LEAD¹. *Antonyms:* see synonyms for FOLLOW.

pre·ce·dence (pri·sēd′ns, pres′ə·dəns) *n.* The act or right of preceding, or the state of being precedent; priority in place, time, or rank. Also **pre·ce′den·cy.**
Synonyms: antecedence, ascendency, lead, leadership, preeminence, preference, priority, superiority, supremacy. *Antonyms:* inferiority, subjection, subjugation, subordination.

prec·e·dent (pres′ə·dənt) *n.* **1** Previous usage or established mode of procedure. **2** An antecedent. **3** A judicial decision taken as furnishing a rule for subsequent decisions. — **pre·ce·dent** (pri·sēd′nt) *adj.* Former; previous; preceding. [<F *précédent* <L *praecedens, -entis*, ppr. of *praecedere*. See PRECEDE.]
Synonyms (noun): antecedent, case, example, instance, pattern, warrant. A *precedent* is an authoritative *case, example*, or *instance.* Cases decided by irregular or unauthorized tribunals are not *precedents* for the regular administration of law. See ANTECEDENT, CAUSE, EXAMPLE.

prec·e·den·tial (pres′ə·den′shəl) *adj.* Of the nature of a precedent; preliminary; having social priority.

pre·ced·ing (pri·sē′ding) *adj.* Going before, as in time, place, or rank; earlier; foregoing; immediately antecedent: The citation was on the *preceding* page.

pre·cent (pri·sent′) *v.i.* To act as precentor. [Back formation <PRECENTOR]

pre·cen·tor (pri·sen′tər) *n.* The leader of the musical part of a church service. [<LL *praecentor* <L *praecinere* sing before < *prae-* before + *canere* sing] — **pre·cen·to·ri·al** (prē′sen·tôr′ē·əl, -tō′rē-) *adj.* — **pre·cen′tor·ship** *n.*

pre·cept (prē′sept) *n.* **1** A prescribed rule of conduct or action; instruction or direction regarding a given course or action; especially, a maxim in morals: distinguished from *counsel.* **2** *Law* A judicial command in writing; writ; process. See synonyms under ADAGE. [<OF <L *praeceptum*, pp. of *praecipere* give rules, instruct < *prae-* before + *capere* receive, take]

pre·cep·tive (pri·sep′tiv) *adj.* Consisting of precepts; didactic.

pre·cep·tor (pri·sep′tər) *n.* A teacher; instructor; specifically, the principal of a school. [<L *praeceptor*] — **pre·cep·to·ri·al** (prē′sep·tôr′ē·əl, -tō′rē-) *adj.*

pre·cep·to·ry (pri·sep′tər·ē) *adj.* Preceptive; mandatory. — *n.* *pl.* **·ries** A place of instruction; specifically, a religious house of the Knights Templars. [<Med.L *praeceptoria*]

pre·cep·tress (pri·sep′tris) *n.* A woman preceptor; governess.

pre·ces·sion (pri·sesh′ən) *n.* The act of preceding or coming in advance of time or of other persons or things. [<LL *praecessio, -onis* < *praecessus,* pp. of *praecedere.* See PRECEDE.]

pre·ces·sion·al (pri·sesh′ən·əl) *adj.* Pertaining to or of the nature of precession.

precession of the equinoxes *Astron.* A slow rotary motion of the equinoctial points on the ecliptic from east to west, causing the time between successive equinoxes to be appreciably shorter than it would otherwise be: caused by the combined attractive forces of the moon, sun, and planets upon the equatorial protuberance of the earth and completing a full cycle in about 26,000 years, a period known as the *Platonic* or *great year.*

pre·cinct (prē′singkt) *n.* **1** A place definitely marked off by fixed lines; also, the boundary of a designated place. **2** A minor territorial or jurisdictional district. **3** An election district of a town, township, county, etc. **4** A police subdivision of a city or town, or its police station. **5** *Brit.* The immediate neighborhood of a church or temple. **6** *pl.* Neighborhood; environs. [<LL *praecinctum* boundary, orig. neut. of *praecinctus,* pp. of *praecingere* gird about < *prae-* before + *cingere* gird]

pre·ci·os·i·ty (presh′ē·os′ə·tē) *n.* Extreme fastidiousness or affected refinement, as in speech, style, or taste. [<OF *preciosité* <L *pretiositas* < *pretiosus.* See PRECIOUS.]

pre·cious (presh′əs) *adj.* **1** Highly priced or prized, as for rarity, or for intrinsic, exchangeable, or other value; valuable. **2** Beloved; dear. **3** Good-for-nothing; undeserving: used ironically. **4** *Colloq.* Very considerable; surpassing: a *precious* scoundrel. **5** Overnice; fastidious: a *precious* writer. See synonyms under CHOICE, EXCELLENT, GOOD, RARE[1]. [<OF *precios* <L *pretiosus* < *pretium* price] **— pre′cious·ly** *adv.* **— pre′cious·ness** *n.*

precious garnet Pyrope.

prec·i·pe (pres′i·pē, prē′si-) *n. Law* **1** A written order directing the issuance of a specified writ. **2** *Brit.* Formerly, a writ commanding a defendant, in the alternative, to do some particular thing, or to show cause for not doing it. Also spelled *praecipe.* [<L *praecipe,* lit., admonish, imperative of *praecipere* admonish, instruct. See PRECEPT.]

prec·i·pice (pres′i·pis) *n.* **1** A high, steep place; the brink of a cliff. **2** A perilous situation. [<F *précipice* <L *praecipitium* < *praeceps* headlong < *prae-* before + *caput* head]

pre·cip·i·ta·ble (pri·sip′ə·tə·bəl) *adj.* Capable or susceptible of being precipitated: a *precipitable* salt.

pre·cip·i·tance (pri·sip′ə·təns) *n.* **1** The quality of being precipitant; rashness. **2** An instance of this. Also **pre·cip′i·tan·cy.**

pre·cip·i·tant (pri·sip′ə·tənt) *adj.* **1** Rushing or falling headlong; moving onward quickly and heedlessly: *precipitant* speed. **2** Rash in thought or action; overhasty; impulsive; precipitate; sudden; abrupt. **—** *n. Chem.* Any substance, as a reagent, that when added or applied to a solution results in the formation of a precipitate. [<L *praecipitans, -antis,* ppr. of *praecipitare.* See PRECIPITATE.] **— pre·cip′i·tant·ly** *adv.*

pre·cip·i·tate (pri·sip′ə·tāt, -tit) *adj.* **1** Rushing down headlong; moving or moved speedily or hurriedly. **2** Wanting due deliberation; hasty; rash. **3** Done prematurely; hurried; undeliberated. **4** Sudden and brief, as a disease. See synonyms under IMPETUOUS. **—** *v.* (pri·sip′ə·tāt) **·tat·ed, ·tat·ing** *v.t.* **1** To bring about before expected or needed; hasten the occurrence of: to *precipitate* a quarrel. **2** To throw headlong; hurl from or as from a height. **3** *Meteorol.* To cause (vapor, etc.) to condense and fall as dew, rain, etc. **4** *Chem.* To separate (a constituent) in solid form, as from a solution. **—** *v.i.* **5** *Meteorol.* To fall as condensed vapor. **6** *Chem.* To separate and settle, as a substance held in solution. **7** To fall headlong; rush. **—** *n.* (pri·sip′ə·tāt, -tit) *Physics* A deposit of solid matter formed in a solution by the action of chemical reagents or by certain physical forces, as low temperature. [<L *praecipitatus,* pp. of *praecipitare* < *praeceps.* See PRECIPICE.] **— pre·cip′i·tate·ly** *adv.* **— pre·cip′i·tate·ness** *n.* **— pre·cip′i·ta′tive** *adj.* **— pre·cip′i·ta′tor** *n.*

pre·cip·i·ta·tion (pri·sip′ə·tā′shən) *n.* **1** The act of casting down; the state of being thrown downward. **2** Headlong or rash haste or hurry; precipitancy; hastening; acceleration. **3** A falling, flowing, or rushing down with violence or rapidity. **4** *Chem.* The process of rendering insoluble and so separating any of the constituents of a solution, as by reagents; also, the precipitate. **5** *Meteorol.* The deposition of moisture from the atmosphere upon the general surface of the earth. **6** Materialization, as of spirits. [<F *précipitation*]

pre·cip·i·tin (pri·sip′ə·tin) *n. Biochem.* An antibody produced in the blood serum by inoculation with foreign protein and capable of providing immunity against specific bacteria; coagulin. [<PRECIPIT(ATE) + -IN]

pre·cip·i·tin·o·gen (pri·sip′ə·tin′ə·jen) *n. Biochem.* The antigen which reacts with the blood to form precipitin. [<PRECIPITIN + -(O)GEN]

pre·cip·i·tous (pri·sip′ə·təs) *adj.* **1** As steep as or consisting of a precipice; very steep. **2** Headlong and downward in motion. **3** Headlong in disposition; precipitate; hasty. See synonyms under STEEP[1]. [<MF *précipiteux*] **— pre·cip′i·tous·ly** *adv.* **— pre·cip′i·tous·ness** *n.*

pré·cis (prā·sē′, prā′sē) *n. pl.* **·cis** (-sēz′, -sēz) A concise, brief summary of the ideas and point of view of a book, article, or document. [<F]

pre·cise (pri·sīs′) *adj.* **1** Sharply or clearly determined; strictly accurate; exact. **2** No more and no less than. **3** Noting or confined to a certain thing; particular; identical. **4** Scrupulously observant of rule; punctilious. [<F *précis* <L *praecisus,* pp. of *praecidere* cut off short < *prae-* before + *caedere* cut] **— pre·cise′ly** *adv.* **— pre·cise′ness** *n.*

Synonyms: accurate, careful, correct, definite, distinct, exact, explicit, faultless, flawless, minute, nice, particular, perfect, rigid, right, scrupulous, strict. *Accurate, correct, definite, exact, precise, nice,* all denote absolute conformity to some standard or truth. *Accurate* indicates conformity secured by *scrupulous* care. An *accurate* measurement or account can be verified and found true in all particulars. *Careful* carries less sharp certainty. *Exact* indicates that which is worked out to the utmost limit of requirement in every respect; *precise* refers to a like conformity or to an excessive *exactness. Exact* and *precise* are often interchangeable; but *precise* has often an invidious meaning, denoting excessive care of petty details; we speak of the martinet as insufferably *precise,* not insufferably *exact. Correct* applies to a required or enforced correspondence with a standard. This is especially seen in the use of the verb; the printer *corrects* the proof. That is *correct* which is free from fault or mistake. *Nice* denotes a very fine and discriminating exactness, and refers to intellectual distinctions oftener than to material measurements. Compare CORRECT, MINUTE[2]. *Antonyms*: careless, doubtful, erroneous, false, faulty, inaccurate, inexact, loose, mistaken, misty, nebulous, untrue, vague, wrong.

pre·ci·sian (pri·sizh′ən) *n.* One who adheres punctiliously to rules and forms: a term especially applied in a religious sense to the Puritans.

pre·ci·sion (pri·sizh′ən) *n.* The quality of being precise; accuracy of limitation, definition, or adjustment. [<F *précision* <L *praecisio, -onis*] **— pre·ci′sion·ist** *n.*

pre·clin·i·cal (prē·klin′i·kəl) *adj.* **1** *Med.* In the period of disease before the appearance of symptoms sufficient for diagnosis. **2** Pertaining to medical studies which precede practical study of patients.

pre·clude (pri·klōōd′) *v.t.* **·clud·ed, ·clud·ing** **1** To render impossible or ineffectual by antecedent action; prevent. **2** To shut out; exclude. [<L *praecludere* < *prae-* before + *cludere* shut] **— pre·clu′sion** (-klōō′zhən) *n.* **— pre·clu′sive** (-klōō′siv) *adj.* **— pre·clu′sive·ly** *adv.*

Synonyms: obviate, prevent. To *obviate* is to *prevent* by interception and making unnecessary; to *preclude,* to close or shut in advance, is to *prevent* by anticipation or by logical necessity; walls and bars *precluded* the possibility of escape; a supposition is *precluded*; a necessity or difficulty is *obviated.* Compare PROHIBIT, SHUT.

pre·co·cial (pri·kō′shəl) *adj. Ornithol.* Of or pertaining to birds whose young are able to run about as soon as they are hatched. [See PRECOCIOUS]

pre·co·cious (pri·kō′shəs) *adj.* **1** Developing before the natural season. **2** Unusually forward or advanced, especially mentally. **3** *Bot.* Flowering or ripening early, as certain plants. [<OF *precoce* <L *praecox, praecocis* < *praecoquere* cook or ripen beforehand < *prae-* before + *coquere* cook] **— pre·co′cious·ly** *adv.* **— pre·co′cious·ness, pre·coc′i·ty** (-kos′ə·tē) *n.*

pre·con·ceive (prē′kən·sēv′) *v.t.* **·ceived, ·ceiv·ing** To conceive in advance; form an idea or opinion of beforehand.

pre·con·cep·tion (prē′kən·sep′shən) *n.* **1** An idea or opinion formed or conceived in advance. **2** A prejudice or misconception; bias. **— pre′con·cep′tion·al** *adj.*

pre·con·cert (prē′kən·sûrt′) *v.t.* To arrange in advance, as by agreement. **—** *n.* (prē·kon′sûrt) Previous arrangement.

pre·co·nize (prē′kə·nīz) *v.t.* **·nized, ·niz·ing** **1** To announce the appointment of (a new bishop) in public consistory: said of the pope. **2** To proclaim or extol publicly. [<LL *praeconizare* proclaim <L *praeco, praeconis* crier, herald]

pre·con·scious (prē·kon′shəs) *n. Psychoanal.* That area of the psyche containing mental processes of which the individual is unaware at any given time but which are more or less readily available to consciousness: formerly called *foreconscious.*

pre·crit·i·cal (prē·krit′i·kəl) *adj. Med.* Preceding the crisis (of a disease).

pre·cur·sive (pri·kûr′siv) *adj.* Going before as a precursor or harbinger; premonitory; preliminary. Also **pre·cur′so·ry** (-sər·ē).

pre·cur·sor (pri·kûr′sər) *n.* One who or that which precedes and gives intimation of a coming event. See synonyms under HERALD. [<L *praecursor* < *praecursus,* pp. of *praecurrere* run before < *prae-* before + *currere* run]

pre·da·cious (pri·dā′shəs) *adj.* Predatory. Also **pre·da′ceous.** [<L *praeda* prey] **— pre·da′cious·ness, pre·dac′i·ty** (-das′ə·tē) *n.*

pre·date (prē·dāt′) *v.t.* **·dat·ed, ·dat·ing** **1** To date before the actual time. **2** To precede in time.

pred·a·to·ry (pred′ə·tôr′ē, -tō′rē) *adj.* **1** Characterized by or undertaken for plundering. **2** Addicted to pillaging. **3** Constituted for living by preying upon others, as a beast or bird; raptorial. [<L *predatorius* < *praeda* prey] **— pred′a·to′ri·ly** *adv.* **— pred′a·to′ri·ness** *n.*

pre·de·cease (prē′di·sēs′) *v.t.* **·ceased, ·ceas·ing** To die before: She *predeceased* her husband by five years.

pred·e·ces·sor (pred′ə·ses′ər) *n.* **1** One who goes or has gone before another in point of time, as an early settler, a previous incumbent of an office, etc. **2** An ancestor. [<OF *predecesseur* <LL *praedecessor* < *prae-* before + *decessor* retiring official < *decessus* pp. of *decedere* go away. See DECEASE.]

pre·des·ig·nate (prē·dez′ig·nāt) *v.t.* **·nat·ed, ·nat·ing** **1** To designate beforehand. **2** *Logic* To begin (a proposition) with a designation of quantity, as *some, many,* etc. **— pre·des′ig·na′tion** *n.*

pre·des·ti·nar·i·an (prē·des′tə·nâr′ē·ən) *adj.* **1** Pertaining to predestination. **2** Holding the doctrine of predestination. **—** *n.* A believer in theological predestination; also, a fatalist. **— pre·des′ti·nar′i·an·ism** *n.*

pre·des·ti·nate (prē·des′tə·nit, -nāt) *adj.* **1** Designed for some special fate. **2** Foreordained by divine decree, as to salvation. **—** *n.* One who is predestined, as to salvation. **—** *v.t.* (-nāt) **·nat·ed, ·nat·ing** **1** To destine or decree beforehand; foreordain. **2** *Theol.* To foreordain by divine decree or purpose. [<L *praedestinatus,* pp. of *praedestinare* < *prae-* before + *destinare* destine]

pre·des·ti·na·tion (prē·des′tə·nā′shən) *n.* **1** The act of predestinating, or the state of being predestinated; destiny; fate. **2** *Theol.* The foreordination of all things by God, including

the future bliss or sorrow of men. See CALVINISM. [<LL *predestinatio, -onis*]
pre·des·tine (prē·des′tin) *v.t.* **·tined, ·tin·ing** To predestinate.
pre·de·ter·mi·nate (prē′di·tûr′mə·nit, -nāt) *adj.* Decided or decreed beforehand.
pre·de·ter·mine (prē′di·tûr′min) *v.t.* **·mined, ·min·ing** 1 To determine beforehand; decide in advance. 2 To foreordain. 3 To imbue with an antecedent tendency. — **pre′de·ter′mi·na′tion** *n.*
pre·di·al (prē′dē·əl) *adj.* Of, pertaining to, or attached to the land. Also spelled *praedial.* [<OF <Med. L *praedialis* <L *praedium*]
pred·i·ca·ble (pred′i·kə·bəl) *adj.* That may be predicated or affirmed. — *n.* 1 Anything ascribable. 2 *Logic* A property or attribute affirmable of a class. [<F *prédicable* <L *praedicabilis* <*praedicare.* See PREACH.] — **pred′i·ca·bil′i·ty, pred′i·ca·ble·ness** *n.*
pre·dic·a·ment (pri·dik′ə·mənt) *n.* 1 A trying, embarrassing, puzzling, or amusing situation or plight. 2 A specific state, position, or situation. 3 *Logic* A class or kind distinguished by definite marks; a category. [<LL *praedicamentum* that which is predicated < *praedicare.* See PREACH.]
pred·i·cate (pred′i·kāt) *v.* **·cat·ed, ·cat·ing** *v.t.* 1 To declare; affirm; proclaim. 2 To state or affirm concerning the subject of a proposition. 3 To affirm as a quality or attribute of something. 4 To imply or connote. 5 *U.S.* To found or base (an argument, proposition, etc.): with *on* or *upon.* — *v.i.* 6 To make a statement or affirmation. See synonyms under AFFIRM. — *adj.* (-kit) 1 Predicated. 2 *Gram.* Belonging, relating to, or of the nature of a predicate: a *predicate* adjective. — *n.* (-kit) 1 *Gram.* The word or words in a sentence that express what is affirmed or denied of a subject, as, in the sentence, "Life is short," "is short" is the *predicate.* 2 A quality or property inherent in or asserted to belong to a thing. 3 *Logic* In a proposition, that which is stated about a subject. [<L *praedicatus,* pp. of *praedicare* make known] — **pred′i·ca′tive** *adj.* — **pred′i·ca′tive·ly** *adv.*
predicate adjective *Gram.* An adjective which describes the subject of a copulative verb, as, He is *sad*; The water turned *green,* etc.
predicate noun *Gram.* A noun which designates or identifies the subject of a copulative verb, as, He was *king*; The water became *ice.*
pred·i·ca·tion (pred′i·kā′shən) *n.* 1 The act of publicly setting forth or proclaiming. 2 The act of predicating or asserting. 3 *Logic* The assertation of something of or concerning a subject; assertion. 4 Something predicated; a predicate. [<L *praedicatio, -onis*] — **pred′i·ca′tion·al** *adj.*
pred·i·ca·to·ry (pred′i·kə·tôr′ē, -tō′rē) *adj.* 1 Of or pertaining to a preacher or preaching. 2 Proclaimed. [<LL *praedicatorius*]
pre·dict (pri·dikt′) *v.t.* 1 To make known beforehand; prophesy; foretell. 2 To assert on the basis of theory, data, or experience but in advance of proof: Einstein *predicted* that space was curved; The computer *predicted* the winning candidate based on a sample poll of voters. — *v.i.* 3 To make a prediction. See synonyms under AUGUR, PROPHESY. [<L *praedictus,* pp. of *praedicere* speak beforehand < *prae-* before + *dicere* say] — **pre·dict′a·ble** *adj.* — **pre·dict′a·bly** *adv.*
pre·dic·tion (pri·dik′shən) *n.* 1 The act of predicting. 2 The thing predicted; forecast: an accurate *prediction.* [<L *praedictio, -onis*] — **pre·dic′tive** *adj.* — **pre·dic′tive·ly** *adv.*
pre·dic·tor (pri·dik′tər) *n.* 1 One who or that which predicts. 2 *Mil.* A mechanism used in connection with anti-aircraft guns for automatically determining the position, speed, and course of approaching aircraft.
pre·di·gest (prē′di·jest′, -dī-) *v.t.* To treat (food) by a process of partial digestion before introduction into the stomach; peptonize. — **pre′di·ges′tion** *n.*
pre·di·lec·tion (prē′də·lek′shən, pred′ə-) *n.* A favorable prepossession or predisposition; partiality; preference: with *for.* See synonyms under FANCY, INCLINATION, RELISH. [<F *prédilection* <Med. L *praedilectio, -onis* < *praedilectus,* pp. of *praedilegere* prefer <L *prae-* before + *diligere* love, choose]
pre·dis·pose (prē′dis·pōz′) *v.t.* **·posed, ·pos·ing** 1 To give a tendency or inclination to; make susceptible or liable: Exhaustion *predisposes* one to sickness. 2 To dispose beforehand. 3 To dispose of beforehand; bequeath. — **pre·dis·po·si·tion** (prē′dis·pə·zish′ən) *n.*
pre·dom·i·nance (pri·dom′ə·nəns) *n.* 1 The state or quality of being predominant. 2 Superiority; ascendance; preponderance. Also **pre·dom′i·nan·cy.**
pre·dom·i·nant (pri·dom′ə·nənt) *adj.* Superior in power, influence, effectiveness, number, or degree; prevailing over others. [<F *prédominant*] — **pre·dom′i·nant·ly** *adv.*
Synonyms: ascendent, chief, commanding, controlling, dominant, prevailing, prevalent, regnant, sovereign, superior, supreme. *Antonyms*: accessory, complementary, contributory, inferior, subordinate, subsidiary, unimportant.
pre·dom·i·nate (pri·dom′ə·nāt) *v.i.* **·nat·ed, ·nat·ing** 1 To have governing influence or control; be in control: often with *over.* 2 To be superior to all others, as in power, height, number, etc.; prevail; preponderate. [<Med. L *predominatus*] — **pre·dom′i·nat′ing·ly** *adv.* — **pre·dom′i·na′tion** *n.*
pree (prē) *v.t. Scot.* To test, especially by tasting; also, to kiss.
preef (prēf) *n. Scot.* Proof.
pre·em·i·nent (prē·em′ə·nənt) *adj.* 1 Supremely eminent; distinguished above all others; transcendent; supreme. 2 Extraordinary in degree; outstanding; conspicuous; superlative. See synonyms under PARAMOUNT. [<L *praeëminens, -entis,* ppr. of *praeëminere* be prominent < *prae-* before + *eminere* stand out, project] — **pre·em·i·nent·ly** *adv.* — **pre·em′i·nence** *n.*
pre·empt (prē·empt′) *v.t.* 1 To acquire or appropriate beforehand. 2 To secure by preemption; occupy (public land) so as to acquire by preemption. [Back formation < PREEMPTION] — **pre·emp′tor** *n.* — **pre·emp′to·ry** (-tər·ē) *adj.*
pre·emp·tion (prē·emp′shən) *n.* 1 The right or act of purchasing before others. 2 Public land obtained by exercising this right. [< Med. L *praeëmptio, -onis* <L *prae-* before + *emptus,* pp. of *emere* buy]
pre·emp·tive (prē·emp′tiv) *adj.* Pertaining to or capable of preemption.
preemptive bid In auction or contract bridge, a bid of a high number of tricks in order to shut out probable bids of an opponent.
preen[1] (prēn) *v.t.* 1 To trim and dress with the beak, as birds their feathers. 2 To dress or adorn (oneself) carefully; primp; prink. — *v.i.* 3 To primp; prink. [Prob. var. of PRUNE[3]]
preen[2] (prēn) *n. Scot.* A pin; a brooch. — *v.t.* To sew; pin.
pre·ex·il·i·an (prē′eg·zil′ē·ən) *adj.* In Jewish history, pertaining to or denoting a period prior to the Babylonian exile (sixth century B.C.). Also **pre′ex·il′ic.**
pre·fab (prē′fab′) *n.* A prefabricated structure or part: also used attributively.
pre·fab·ri·cate (prē·fab′rə·kāt) *v.t.* **·cat·ed, ·cat·ing** 1 To fabricate or build beforehand. 2 To manufacture in standard sections that can be rapidly assembled. — **pre·fab′ri·ca′tion** *n.*
pref·ace (pref′is) *n.* 1 A brief explanation or address to the reader at the beginning of a book or other publication. 2 Any introductory speech, writing, etc. — *v.t.* **·aced, ·ac·ing** 1 To introduce or furnish with a preface. 2 To serve as a preface for. [<OF <L *praefatio* < *praefatus,* pp. of *praefari* utter beforehand, premise < *prae-* before + *fari* speak]
Pref·ace (pref′is) *n. Eccl.* 1 The prayer of thanksgiving, ending with the Sanctus, which introduces the canon of the mass. 2 The corresponding section in other eucharistic liturgies.
pref·a·to·ry (pref′ə·tôr′ē, -tō′rē) *adj.* Of the nature of a preface; introductory. Also **pref′a·to′ri·al.** — **pref′a·to′ri·ly** *adv.*
pre·fect (prē′fekt) *n.* 1 In ancient Rome, any of various civil and military officials, as certain magistrates, governors, and commanders. 2 Any magistrate, chief official, etc.; specifically, in France, the chief administrator of a department, or the head of the Paris police. 3 In Roman Catholic schools, the dean. 4 *Brit.* A senior pupil charged with maintaining order and discipline among other pupils. Also spelled *praefect.* [<OF <L *praefectus,* orig. pp. of *praeficere* set over <L *prae-* before + *facere* make, do]
pre·fec·ture (prē′fek·chər) *n.* 1 The office, jurisdiction, or province of a prefect. 2 The official building for his use. [<L *praefectura*] — **pre·fec′tur·al** *adj.*
pre·fer (pri·fûr′) *v.t.* **·ferred, ·fer·ring** 1 To hold in higher regard or esteem; like better. 2 To give priority to, as one creditor or form of securities over others. 3 To advance or promote, as in status or rank. 4 To offer, as a suit or charge, for consideration or decision. See synonyms under CHOOSE, PROMOTE. [<F *préferer* <L *praeferre* carry, set in front < *prae-* before + *ferre* bear] — **pre·fer′rer** *n.*
pref·er·a·ble (pref′ər·ə·bəl) *adj.* To be preferred; more desirable; worthy of choice. — **pref′er·a·ble·ness, pref′er·a·bil′i·ty** *n.* — **pref′er·a·bly** *adv.*
pref·er·ence (pref′ər·əns) *n.* 1 The act of preferring; estimation or choice of one thing or person over another; also, the privilege of making such choice. 2 The state of being preferred. 3 That which is preferred; an object of favor or choice. 4 A priority of payment given by an insolvent debtor to one or to a certain class of his creditors over others; also, priority of payment by operation of law. 5 Promotion; preferment. 6 The granting of special advantage over others to one country or group of countries in international trade. See synonyms under ALTERNATIVE, PRECEDENCE. [<F *préférence* <L *praeferentia,* orig. neut. pl. of *praeferens, -entis,* ppr. of *praeferre.* See PREFER.]
pref·er·en·tial (pref′ə·ren′shəl) *adj.* 1 Indicating or arising from preference or partiality. 2 Possessing or giving priority or preference, as in tariffs or railroad charges. — **pref′er·en′tial·ism** *n.* — **pref′er·en′tial·ly** *adv.*
preferential shop A shop that gives precedence to union members when hiring employees, usually by agreement with a union.
preferential voting A form of voting in which an order of choice of candidates may be signified by a voter on his ballot.
pre·fer·ment (pri·fûr′mənt) *n.* 1 The act of preferring. 2 The state of being preferred. 3 The act of promoting or appointing to higher office; advancement; promotion. 4 A superior post or dignity: said especially of ecclesiastical rank.
pre·ferred (pri·fûrd′) *adj.* 1 Having the first claim: *preferred* bonds or stock. 2 Having gained promotion. 3 Chosen by preference.
pre·fig·ur·a·tion (prē·fig′yə·rā′shən) *n.* 1 Antecedent representation by types, figures, etc. 2 A prototype. — **pre·fig·ur·a·tive** (prē·fig′yər·ə·tiv) *adj.* — **pre·fig′ur·a·tive·ly** *adv.* — **pre·fig′ur·a·tive·ness** *n.*
pre·fig·ure (prē·fig′yər) *v.t.* **·ured, ·ur·ing** 1 To represent in advance; serve as an indication or suggestion of; foreshadow. 2 To imagine or picture to oneself beforehand. [<LL *praefigurare*]
pre·fix (prē′fiks) *n.* 1 *Gram.* A non-separable syllable, or syllables, affixed to the beginning of a word to modify or alter the meaning, as *pre-* in prefix, *be-* in behead, *dis-* in disagree, *re-* in renew, *post-* in postwar, *un-* in unhorse, etc. 2 Something placed before, as a title before a noun. Compare SUFFIX. — *v.t.* (prē·fiks′) 1 To put or attach before or at the beginning; add as a prefix: opposed to *postfix.* 2 *Obs.* To arrange or settle beforehand. [< OF *prefixer* <L *praefixus,* pp. of *praefigere* < *prae-* before + *figere* fix] — **pre′fix·al** *adj.* — **pre′fix·al·ly** *adv.* — **pre·fix·ion** (prē·fik′shən) *n.*
pre·flight training (prē′flīt) *Aeron.* Preliminary ground instruction in aviation.
pre·flo·ra·tion (prē′flə·rā′shən) *n. Bot.* The disposition of flowers within the flower bud; estivation. [<PRE- + L *flos, floris* flower + -ATION]
pre·fo·li·a·tion (prē·fō′lē·ā′shən) *n. Bot.* The disposition of leaves within a bud; vernation.
pre·for·ma·tion (prē′fôr·mā′shən) *n.* 1 The act of preforming; the state of being formed in advance. 2 *Biol.* An early theory of generation according to which an organism exists fully preformed in the germ, developing only by increase in size. Compare EPIGENESIS.
Pre·gel (prā′gəl) A river in the former German province of East Prussia, now in Russian

S.F.S.R., flowing 78 miles west to the Vistula Lagoon below Kaliningrad.

Pre·gl (prā′gəl), **Fritz,** 1869–1930, Austrian chemist.

preg·na·ble (preg′nə·bəl) *adj.* Weak enough to be conquered; likely to yield when attacked, as a fort. [<OF *prenable* <*prendre* take <L *prehendere* seize] — **preg′na·bil′i·ty** *n.*

preg·nan·cy (preg′nən·sē) *n.* **1** The state of being with young or with child. **2** *Obs.* Quickness of intelligence.

preg·nan·di·ol (preg·nan′dē·ôl, -ol) *n. Biochem.* A complex organic compound of the sterol group, found in the urine of pregnant women and chemically related to progesterone. [< *pregnane,* a sterol from the urine of pregnant women + *diol,* a glycol]

preg·nant (preg′nənt) *adj.* **1** Carrying a growing fetus in the uterus; with child; impregnated; gestating. **2** Carrying great weight or significance; full of meaning or contents; leading to important results. **3** Fruitful; prolific; teeming with ideas; imaginative; inventive. **4** In rhetoric and logic, implying more than is expressed. [<L *praegnans, -antis,* ult. < *prae-* before + *gnasci* be born] — **preg′nant·ly** *adv.*

pre·hen·si·ble (pri·hen′sə·bəl) *adj.* Capable of being apprehended or grasped. [<L *prehensus,* pp. of *prehendere* seize]

pre·hen·sile◆ (pri·hen′sil) *adj.* Adapted for grasping or holding; formed to grasp or coil around and cling to objects, as the tail of a monkey. [<F *préhensile*] — **pre·hen·sil·i·ty** (prē′hen·sil′ə·tē) *n.*

pre·hen·sion (pri·hen′shən) *n.* The act of grasping, physically or mentally. [<L *prehensio, -onis*]

pre·his·tor·ic (prē′his·tôr′ik, -tor′-) *adj.* Of or belonging to a period before that covered by written history. Also **pre′his·tor′i·cal.** — **pre′his·tor′i·cal·ly** *adv.*

pre·his·to·ry (prē·his′tə·rē) *n.* The history of the development of mankind based on archeological and ethnological findings; the period of history preceding written records.

prehn·ite (pren′it) *n.* A light-green, gray, or white hydrous silicate of calcium and aluminum: similar in composition and occurrence to zeolite. [after Col. van *Prehn,* 18th century Dutch colonist]

pre·ig·ni·tion (prē′ig·nish′ən) *n.* Ignition of the charge in the cylinder of an internal-combustion engine previous to the completion of the compression stroke, often the result of faulty ignition timing.

pre·judge (prē·juj′) *v.t.* **·judged, ·judg·ing** To judge before or without proper inquiry; pass judgment on hastily or beforehand. [<F *préjuger* <*praejudicare* <*prae-* before + *judicare* judge] — **pre·judg′er** *n.* — **pre·judg′ment,** *Brit.* **pre·judge′ment** *n.*

prej·u·dice (prej′o͝o·dis) *n.* **1** A judgment or opinion, favorable or unfavorable, formed beforehand or without due examination; a mental decision based on other grounds than reason or justice; especially, a premature or adversely biased opinion. **2** Detriment arising from a hasty and unfair judgment; injury; harm. — **in** (or **to**) **the prejudice of** To the injury or detriment of. — **without prejudice** *Law* Without detriment to any right that previously existed: usually applied to the dismissal of a bill in equity without consideration of the merits; or to the reservation, express or implied, of all rights in favor of one who offers to compromise a claim or litigation, in case his offer is rejected. — *v.t.* **·diced, ·dic·ing 1** To affect or influence with a prejudice; bias. **2** To affect injuriously or detrimentally; damage; impair. [<OF <L *praejudicium* <*prae-* before + *judicium* judgment]

Synonyms (noun): bias, preconception, predilection, prepossession, unfairness. A *prejudice* or *prepossession* is grounded often on feeling, fancy, associations, etc. A *prepossession* is always favorable, a *prejudice* usually unfavorable, unless the contrary is expressly stated. See INJURY. *Antonyms*: certainty, conclusion, conviction, demonstration, evidence, reason, reasoning.

prej·u·di·cial (prej′o͝o·dish′əl) *adj.* Having power or tendency to prejudice or injure; injurious; detrimental. — **prej′u·di′cial·ly** *adv.*

prel·a·cy (prel′ə·sē) *n. pl.* **·cies 1** The system of church government by prelates: often a hostile term for episcopacy. **2** The dignity or function of a prelate. **3** Prelates collectively. [<AF *prelacie* <Med. L *praelatia* <*praelatus.* See PRELATE.]

prel·ate (prel′it) *n.* One of a higher order of clergy, as a bishop or abbot. [<OF *prelat* <L *praelatus,* pp. to *praeferre* set over. See PREFER.] — **prel′ate·ship** *n.* — **pre·lat·ic** (pri·lat′ik) or **·i·cal** *adj.*

prel·a·tism (prel′ə·tiz′əm) *n.* **1** Prelacy; episcopacy. **2** Prelatic partisanship.

prel·a·tist (prel′ə·tist) *n.* One who supports the prelacy; an advocate of High Church government: sometimes used contemptuously.

prel·a·ture (prel′ə·chər) *n.* Prelacy (defs. 2 and 3).

pre·lect (pri·lekt′) *v.i.* To lecture; discourse. [<L *praelectus,* pp. of *praelegere* read before <*prae-* before + *legere* read] — **pre·lec′tion** *n.* — **pre·lec′tor** *n.*

pre·li·ba·tion (prē′li·bā′shən) *n.* **1** A preliminary offering. **2** A tasting beforehand or by anticipation; anticipation. [<LL *praelibatio, -onis* <*prae-* before + *libatio* a libation]

pre·lim·i·nar·y (pri·lim′ə·ner′ē) *adj.* Antecedent or introductory to the main discourse, proceedings, or business; prefatory; preparatory. — *n. pl.* **·ries 1** An initiatory step; a preparatory act. **2** A preliminary examination. See synonyms under ANTECEDENT. [<PRE- + L *liminaris* pertaining to a threshold < *limen, liminis* threshold] — **pre·lim′i·nar′i·ly** *adv.*

pre·lit·er·ate (prē·lit′ər·it) *adj.* Without written records; prehistoric: said especially of the earliest human cultures.

prel·ude (prel′yo͞od, prē′lo͞od) *n.* **1** *Music* **a** An independent instrumental composition of moderate length, in a free style suggesting improvisation. **b** An opening piece at the start of a church service; a voluntary. **c** The overture of an opera. **d** An opening strain or movement at the beginning of a musical composition, usually introducing the theme of the whole work. **2** Any introductory or opening performance or event, or that which foreshadows a coming event. — *v.* **·ud·ed, ·ud·ing** *v.t.* **1** To introduce with a prelude. **2** To serve as a prelude to. — *v.i.* **3** To serve as a prelude. **4** To provide or play a prelude. [<F *prélude* <Med. L *praeludium* <L *praeludere* play before <*prae-* before + *ludere* play] — **pre·lud·er** (pri·lo͞o′dər, prel′yə·dər) *n.* — **pre·lu·di·al** (pri·lo͞o′dē·əl) *adj.*

pre·lu·sion (pri·lo͞o′zhən) *n.* That which serves as a prelude. [<L *praelusio, -onis* <*praelusus,* pp. of *praeludere.* See PRELUDE.]

pre·lu·sive (pri·lo͞o′siv) *adj.* Having the character of a prelude; indicating beforehand. Also **pre·lu′so·ry** (-sər·ē). [<L *praelusus.* See PRELUSION.] — **pre·lu′sive·ly, pre·lu′so·ri·ly** *adv.*

pre·ma·ture (prē′mə·cho͝or′, -to͝or′, -tyo͝or′) *adj.* Existing, happening, matured or developed before the natural period; done before the proper time; untimely. [<L *praematurus* <*prae-* before + *maturus* ripe, seasonable] — **pre′ma·ture′ly** *adv.* — **pre′ma·tu′ri·ty, pre′ma·ture′ness** *n.*

pre·max·il·la (prē′mak·sil′ə) *n. pl.* **·max·il·lae** (-mak·sil′ē) *Anat.* One of the two bones set between the maxillae in front of the vertebrate jaw. [<NL] — **pre·max·il·lar·y** (prē·mak′sə·ler′ē) *adj.*

pre·med·i·tate (prē·med′ə·tāt) *v.t.* & *v.i.* **·tat·ed, ·tat·ing** To plan or consider beforehand. [<L *praemeditatus,* pp. of *praemeditari* think over <*prae-* before + *meditari.* See MEDITATE.] — **pre·med′i·tat′ed·ly** *adv.* — **pre·med′i·ta′tive** *adj.* — **pre·med′i·ta′tor** *n.*

pre·med·i·ta·tion (prē·med′ə·tā′shən) *n.* The considering and planning of a subsequent act; deliberate intention and plan to do a certain thing, especially to commit a crime.

pre·mi·er (prē′mē·ər, *esp. Brit.* prem′yər) *adj.* **1** First in rank or position; principal: the *premier* place, *premier* officer. **2** First in order of occurrence; earliest; specifically, first in order of creation; senior: the *premier* duke of England. — *n.* (prē′mē·ər, pri·mir′; *Brit.* prem′yər) The head of government; the prime minister of England, France, etc. [<F <L *primarius* <L *primus* first] — **pre′mi·er·ship′** *n.*

pre·mière (pri·mir′, *Fr.* prə·myâr′) *adj.* First. — *n.* **1** The leading lady in a theatrical company. **2** The first public presentation of a play, etc. [<F]

pre·mil·le·nar·i·an (prē′mil·ə·nâr′ē·ən) *adj.* Existing or occurring before the millennium: also **pre′mil·len′ni·al** (-mi·len′ē·əl). — *n.* One who believes in premillennialism: also **pre′mil·len′ni·al·ist.**

pre·mil·len·ni·al·ism (prē′mi·len′ē·əl·iz′əm) *n.* The doctrine that the millennium is to be introduced by the personal return of Christ: opposed to *postmillennialism.*

prem·ise (prem′is) *n.* **1** A proposition laid down, proved, supposed, or assumed, that serves as a ground for argument or for a conclusion; a judgment leading to another judgment as a conclusion. **2** *Logic* Either of the two propositions in a syllogism from which, their truth being granted, the conclusion necessarily follows. **3** *pl. Law* **a** Foregoing statements; facts previously stated. **b** That part in a deed that sets forth the date, names of parties, the land or thing conveyed or granted, the consideration, and all other matters down to the phrase "to have and to hold." **4** *pl.* A distinct portion of real estate; land or lands; land with its appurtenances, as buildings: He lingered about the *premises.* Also **prem′iss.** — **major premise** *Logic* The premise in which the predicate of the conclusion of a syllogism, called the **major term,** is contained; the first proposition of a syllogism. — **minor premise** *Logic* The premise in which the subject of the conclusion of a syllogism, called the **minor term,** is contained; the second proposition of a syllogism.

— **pre·mise** (pri·mīz′, prem′is) *v.* **·mised, ·mis·ing** *v.t.* **1** To stay or state beforehand, as by way of introduction or explanation. **2** To state or assume as a premise or basis of argument. **3** *Obs.* To send in advance. — *v.i.* **4** To make a premise. [<OF *premisse* <Med. L *praemissa,* orig. fem. of L *praemissus,* pp. of *praemittere* send before <*prae-* before + *mittere* send]

pre·mi·um (prē′mē·əm) *n.* **1** A reward or prize for a superior performance or production in competition. **2** A price paid for a loan; a sum offered or given to secure a loan, either a sum in addition to interest, a bonus, or the interest itself. **3** The rate or price at which stocks, shares, or money are valued in excess of their nominal or par value: bank shares at a *premium* of five percent. **4** The amount paid for insurance, as admission fees, annual dues, periodical payments, etc., according to the kind of insurance secured. **5** Any object offered free to those who purchase goods to a certain value, as a set of books given free as an inducement to subscribe to a magazine. **6** A fee for instruction in a trade or a profession. See synonyms under SUBSIDY. — **at a premium** Above par; hence, valuable and in demand. [<L *praemium,* ult. <*prae-* before + *emere* buy]

pre·mo·lar (prē·mō′lər) *n. Anat.* One of the teeth situated before the molars and behind the canines. Compare BICUSPID. — *adj.* Situated in front of or appearing before the molar teeth.

pre·mon·ish (pri·mon′ish) *v.t.* To admonish in advance; forewarn. [<PRE- + MONISH]

pre·mo·ni·tion (prē′mə·nish′ən, prem′ə-) *n.* **1** An actual warning of something yet to occur. **2** A presentiment not based on information received; an instinctive foreboding. [<OF *premonicion* <LL *praemonitio, -onis* <*praemonitus,* pp. of *praemonere* premonish <*prae-* before + *monere* warn] — **pre·mon·i·to·ry** (pri·mon′ə·tôr′ē, -tō′rē) *adj.* — **pre·mon′i·to′ri·ly** *adv.*

pre·morse (pri·môrs′) *adj. Biol.* Terminating abruptly, as if bitten or broken off: a *premorse* root. [<L *praemorsus,* pp. of *praemordere* bite off <*prae-* before + *mordere* bite]

pre·mun·dane (prē·mun′dān) *adj.* Antemundane.

pre·name (prē′nām′) *n.* A forename; Christian name. [Trans. of L *praenomen*]

pre·na·tal (prē·nāt′l) *adj.* Before birth: *prenatal* care or health. — **pre·na′tal·ly** *adv.*

pre·no·men (prē·nō′mən) See PRAENOMEN.

pre·nom·i·nate (prē·nom′ə·nāt) *Obs. v.t.* To mention or name beforehand. —*adj.* Named beforehand.

prent (prent) *v. & n. Scot.* Print.

pren·tice (pren′tis) *n.* An apprentice. Also **'pren′tice.** [Aphetic var. of APPRENTICE]

pre·oc·cu·pa·tion (prē·ok′yə·pā′shən) *n.* **1** The act of occupying before others, or the state of being or having a prior occupant: also **pre·oc′cu·pan·cy. 2** The state of being preoccupied, as in mind, attention, or inclination; prepossession. **3** Something that preoccupies. [<L *praeoccupatio, -onis*] —**pre·oc′cu·pant** *n.*

pre·oc·cu·pied (prē·ok′yə·pīd) *adj.* **1** Engrossed in thought or business; abstracted. **2** Previously occupied. **3** Already in use, as a scientific name. See synonyms under ABSTRACTED.

pre·oc·cu·py (prē·ok′yə·pī) *v.t.* **·pied, ·py·ing 1** To engage fully; engross, as the mind. **2** To occupy or take possession of in advance of another or others. See synonyms under OCCUPY. [<L *praeoccupare*]

pre·or·dain (prē′ôr·dān′) *v.t.* To foreordain. —**pre·or·di·na·tion** (prē′ôr·də·nā′shən) *n.*

prep (prep) *adj. Colloq.* Preparatory: a *prep* school, student, etc.

pre·pack·age (pre·pak′ij) *v.t.* **-aged, -ag·ing** To package foods and other items into specific weights or portions before selling them.

prep·a·ra·tion (prep′ə·rā′shən) *n.* **1** The act, process, or operation of preparing. **2** An act or proceeding designed to bring about some event; a precaution; provision: *preparations* for war or for a journey. **3** The fact or state of being prepared; readiness. **4** Something made or prepared, as a compound, composition, etc.: medicinal or chemical *preparations.* **5** Preliminary study; training, as for college or business. **6** *Music* The previous introduction, as an integral part of a chord, of a note which is then continued into a following dissonance; also, the note so treated. **7** *Eccl.* Devotional exercises introducing an office, as that of the Eucharist. [<OF <L *praeparatio, -onis*]

pre·par·a·tive (pri·par′ə·tiv) *adj.* Serving or tending to prepare. —*n.* **1** That which is preparatory. **2** An act of preparation. —**pre·par′a·tive·ly** *adv.*

pre·par·a·tor (pri·par′ə·tər) *n.* One who prepares subjects for scientific purposes, as specimens for dissection or objects for preservation in collections. [<LL *praeparator*]

pre·par·a·to·ry (pri·par′ə·tôr′ē, -tō′rē) *adj.* **1** Serving as a preparation. **2** Occupied in preparation: a *preparatory* scholar. —*adv.* As a preparation: *Preparatory* to writing, I will consider this: also **pre·par′a·to′ri·ly.**

preparatory school A school in which students are prepared for admission to a college or university.

pre·pare (pri·pâr′) *v.* **·pared, ·par·ing** *v.t.* **1** To make ready, fit, or qualified; put in readiness. **2** To provide with what is needed; outfit; equip: to *prepare* an expedition. **3** To bring to a state of completeness, as a meal, lesson, or prescription. **4** *Music* To introduce by a preliminary note or notes. —*v.i.* **5** To make preparations; get ready. [<F *préparer* <L *praeparare* <*prae-* before +*parare* make ready] —**pre·par·ed·ly** (pri·pâr′id·lē) *adv.* —**pre·par′er** *n.*

pre·par·ed·ness (pri·pâr′id·nis, -pârd′-) *n.* Readiness; especially, a condition of military readiness for war.

pre·pay (prē·pā′) *v.t.* **·paid, ·pay·ing** To pay or pay for in advance. —**pre·pay′ment** *n.*

pre·pense (pri·pens′) *adj.* Premeditated; considered beforehand: chiefly in the phrase malice *prepense.* [<OF *purpensé,* pp. of *purpenser* < *pur-* (<L *pro-*) ahead +*penser* think <L *pensare*] —**pre·pense′ly** *adv.*

pre·pon·der·ance (pri·pon′dər·əns) *n.* Superiority in weight, influence, force, quantity, etc. Also **pre·pon′der·an·cy.**

pre·pon·der·ant (pri·pon′dər·ənt) *adj.* Having such superior force, weight, importance, efficacy, quantity, or number as to overbalance something else or all other things of a class; predominant. —**pre·pon′der·ant·ly** *adv.*

pre·pon·der·ate (pri·pon′də·rāt) *v.i.* **·at·ed, ·at·ing 1** To be of greater weight. **2** To incline downward or descend, as the scale of a balance. **3** To be of greater power, importance, quantity, etc.; predominate; prevail. [<L *praeponderatus,* pp. of *praeponderare* <*prae-*before +*ponderare* weigh <*pondus, ponderis* weight] —**pre·pon′der·a′tion** *n.*

prep·o·si·tion (prep′ə·zish′ən) *n. Gram.* **1** In some languages, a word functioning to indicate the relation of a substantive (the object of the preposition) to another substantive, a verb, or an adjective: one of the eight traditional parts of speech. Some English prepositions are *by, for, from, in, to, with.* A preposition is usually placed before its object (whence its name), and together they constitute a prepositional phrase which serves as an adjectival or an adverbial modifier: He sat *beside* the fire; sick *at* heart; a man *of* honor. There is a close relationship between certain prepositions and adverbs, and the same word may have either function, depending on the context: We saw it *through* (adverb); It sailed out *through* the window (preposition). **2** Any word or construction that functions in a similar manner: He telephoned *in reference to* (equals *about*) your letter. —**inseparable preposition** A preposition so closely connected with a verb as to have all the force of a compound: to *laugh at.* —**participal preposition** A participle used without direct connection with a subject, so that it has the force of a preposition: They spoke to him *concerning* that affair. —**postpositive preposition** A preposition in postposition; also, a suffix added to a noun and serving as a preposition: Hope soars heaven*ward.* [<L *praepositio, -onis* <*praepositus,* pp. of *praeponere* place before <*prae-* before +*ponere* place]

prep·o·si·tion·al (prep′ə·zish′ən·əl) *adj.* Pertaining to, formed with, or having the character or force of prepositions. —**prep′o·si′tion·al·ly** *adv.*

pre·pos·i·tive (prē·poz′ə·tiv) *adj.* **1** Prefixed. **2** *Gram.* Placed before the word governed or qualified. —*n. Gram.* A prepositive word or particle. [<L *praepositivus* <*praepositus.* See PREPOSITION.]

pre·pos·i·tor (prē·poz′ə·tər) *n. Brit.* A pupil or student in a school or college who directs or oversees others; monitor. [Alter. of L *praepositus.* See PREPOSITION.] —**pre·pos·i·to·ri·al** (prē·poz′ətôr′ē·əl, -tō′rē-) *adj.*

pre·pos·sess (prē′pə·zes′) *v.t.* **1** To preoccupy to the exclusion of other ideas, beliefs, etc.; prejudice; bias. **2** To impress or influence beforehand or at once, especially favorably. **3** *Rare* To take possession of in advance of others, as land.

pre·pos·sess·ing (prē′pə·zes′ing) *adj.* Inspiring a favorable opinion from the beginning. —**pre′pos·sess′ing·ly** *adv.*

pre·pos·ses·sion (prē′pə·zesh′ən) *n.* **1** The state of being prepossessed; a previous impression of a particular person or thing; a preconceived liking; bias. **2** Prior possession. See synonyms under INCLINATION, PREJUDICE.

pre·pos·ter·ous (pri·pos′tər·əs) *adj.* Contrary to nature, reason, or common sense; strikingly or utterly absurd or impracticable. See synonyms under ABSURD, EXTRAORDINARY, RIDICULOUS. [<L *praeposterus* the last first, inverted <*prae-* before +*posterus* last] —**pre·pos′ter·ous·ly** *adv.* —**pre·pos′ter·ous·ness** *n.*

pre·pos·tor (prē·pos′tər) *n.* A prepositor. [Alter. of PREPOSITOR]

pre·po·ten·cy (pri·pō′tən·sē) *n.* **1** The quality of superior potency; preponderance of influence of efficiency. **2** *Biol.* The pronounced capacity of one parent, strain, or breed to transmit its own characteristics to the offspring. Also **pre·po′tence.** [<PREPOTENT]

pre·po·tent (pri·pō′tənt) *adj.* **1** Endowed with prevailing potency; predominant. **2** Having potential power or efficacy; possessing power to shape or influence what comes after. **3** Pertaining to or exhibiting prepotency. Also **pre·po·ten·tial** (prē′pə·ten′shəl). [<L *praepotens, -entis* very powerful] —**pre·po′tent·ly** *adv.*

pre·puce (prē′pyōōs) *n. Anat.* The loose skin that covers the glans of the penis; the foreskin. [<F *prépuce* <L *praeputium*] —**pre·pu·tial** (pri·pyōō′shəl) *adj.*

Pre-Raph·a·el·ite (prē·raf′ē·ə·līt, -rā′fē-) *n.* **1** A follower or adherent of the Pre-Raphaelite Brotherhood, a society of artists, formed in England, 1847–49, by D. G. Rossetti, W. Holman-Hunt, John Millais, and others, stressing the truth to nature and delicacy of poetic sentiment that supposedly characterized Italian art before the time of Raphael. **2** Any modern artist with similar or related aims. **3** Any Italian painter before the time of Raphael. —*adj.* **1** Before the time of Raphael. **2** Of or pertaining to the Pre-Raphaelite Brotherhood or its followers. —**Pre-Raph′a·el·it′ism** *n.*

pre·req·ui·site (prē·rek′wə·zit) *adj.* Required as an antecedent condition; necessary to something that follows. —*n.* A necessary antecedent condition.

pre·rog·a·tive (pri·rog′ə·tiv) *n.* **1** An indefeasible and unquestionable right belonging to a person or body of persons by virtue of position or relation, and exercised without control or accountability; specifically, a hereditary or official right: the royal *prerogative.* **2** Hence, any characteristic and generally recognized privilege peculiar to a person or class: It is a woman's *prerogative* to change her mind. **3** Precedence; preeminence. See synonyms under RIGHT. —*adj.* Of or pertaining to a prerogative; possessing or held by prerogative. [<OF <L *praerogativa* right of voting first <*praerogatus,* pp. of *praerogare* ask before another <*prae-* before +*rogare* ask]

prerogative court 1 *Brit.* Formerly, a court having jurisdiction of testamentary matters, as an archbishop's court in which were involved effects up to five pounds in each of two or more dioceses of the archiepiscopal province. **2** *U.S.* A court held in New Jersey by the chancellor sitting as ordinary in probate matters, and for the determination of appeals from the Orphan's Court.

pre·sa (prā′sä) *n. Music* A sign :S:, +, or ✻ in fugues or canons, where the voices are successively to take up the theme. [<Ital., lit., a taking, orig. fem. of *preso,* pp. of *prendere* take <L *prehendere*]

pres·age (pres′ij) *n.* **1** An indication of something to come; prophetic token; portent; omen. **2** A prophetic impression; presentiment; foreboding. **3** Prophetic meaning or import; prediction; foresight. See synonyms under SIGN.
— **pre·sage** (pri·sāj′) *v.* **·saged, ·sag·ing** *v.t.* **1** To give presage or portent of; betoken; foreshadow. **2** To have a presentiment of. **3** To predict; foretell. —*v.i.* **4** To make a prediction; prophesy. See synonyms under AUGUR. [<F *présage* <L *presagium* omen <*praesagire* perceive beforehand <*prae-* before +*sagire* be aware of. Akin to SAGACIOUS] —**pre·sage′ment** *n.* —**pre·sag′er** *n.*

pres·by·cu·sis (prez′bi·kyōō′sis, pres′-) *n. Pathol.* Impairment of hearing due to advancing years or old age. Also **pres·by·a·cu·sis** (prez′bē·ə·kyōō′sis, pres′-). [<NL <Gk. *presbys* old +*akousis* hearing]

pres·by·o·phre·ni·a (prez′bē·ə·frē′nē·ə, pres′-) *n. Psychiatry* Failure of mental powers due to old age, characterized by confabulation and loss of memory. [<NL <Gk. *presbys* old +*phrēn* mind] —**pres′by·o·phren′ic** (-fren′ik) *adj.*

pres·by·o·pi·a (prez′bē·ō′pē·ə, pres′-) *n. Pathol.* Long-sightedness, especially that incident to old age and due to rigidity of the crystalline lens, which renders accommodation difficult for near objects. [<NL <Gk. *presbys* old +-OPIA] —**pres′by·op′ic** (-op′ik) *adj.*

pres·by·ter (prez′bə·tər, pres′-) *n.* **1** In the early church, one of the elders of a church. **2** *Eccl.* **a** In hierarchical churches, a priest. **b** In Presbyterian churches, an ordained clergyman (a **teaching elder**); also, a layman who is a member of the governing body of a congregation (a **ruling elder**). [<LL <Gk. *presbyteros* an elder. Doublet of PRIEST.]

pres·byt·er·ate (prez·bit′ər·it, -ə·rāt, pres-) *n.* **1** The office or dignity of a presbyter or elder. **2** The order or the body of presbyters.

pres·by·te·ri·al (prez′bə·tir′ē·əl, pres′-) *adj.* Pertaining to a presbytery or a presbyter. Also **pres·byt′er·al.** —**pres·byt′er·al·ly** *adv.*

Pres·by·te·ri·an (prez′bə·tir′ē·ən, pres′-) *n.* **1** One who believes in the government of the church by presbyters. **2** A member of any of various Protestant churches, mostly Calvinist in doctrine, and holding to the government of the church by presbyters. —*adj.* Of or pertaining to the Presbyterian Church, its form of government, or its doctrines. [<LL *presbyterium* presbytery +-IAN] —**Pres′by·te′ri·an·ism** *n.*

pres·by·ter·y (prez′bə·ter′ē, pres′-) *n. pl.* **·ter·ies** 1 In the Presbyterian Church, a court having the ecclesiastical and spiritual rule and oversight of a given district; the district so represented; also, presbyters collectively. 2 The system of church government by presbyters: distinguished from the *Independent* system and *prelacy.* 3 That part of a church set apart for the clergy. 4 In the Roman Catholic Church, the residence of the priest. [<OF *presbiterie* <LL *presbyterium* assembly of elders <Gk. *presbyterion* <*presbyteros* elder]

pre·school (prē·skōōl′) *adj.* For or designating a child past infancy but under school age.

pre·sci·ence (prē′shē·əns, presh′ē-) *n.* Knowledge of events before they take place. See synonyms under WISDOM. [<OF <L *praescientia,* orig. neut. pl. of *praesciens, -entis,* ppr. of *praescire* know beforehand <*prae-* before + *scire* know]

pre·sci·ent (prē′shē·ənt, presh′ē-) *adj.* Having prescience; foreknowing; also, far-seeing. [<F <L *presciens, -entis.* See PRESCIENCE.] **—pre′sci·ent·ly** *adv.*

pre·scind (pri·sind′) *v.t.* 1 To set apart in thought; consider separately. 2 To cut off; remove. *—v.i.* 3 To withdraw the attention: with *from.* [<L *praescindere* cut off in front <*prae-* before + *scindere* cut]

Pres·cott (pres′kət), **William,** 1726–95, American officer; commanded at Bunker Hill in the Revolutionary War. **—William Hickling,** 1796–1859, U.S. historian.

pre·scribe (pri·skrīb′) *v.* **·scribed, ·scrib·ing** *v.t.* 1 To set down as a direction or rule to be followed; ordain; enjoin. 2 *Med.* To order the use of (a medicine, treatment, etc.) as a remedy. 3 *Law* To render invalid by lapse of time. *—v.i.* 4 To lay down laws or rules; give directions. 5 *Law* a To assert a title to something on the basis of prescription: with *for* or *to.* b To become invalid or unenforceable by lapse of time. See synonyms under DICTATE, SET. [<L *praescribere* write beforehand <*prae-* before + *scribere* write] **—pre·scrib′er** *n.*

pre·script (prē′skript) *n.* A prescription or direction, as a rule of conduct. *—adj.* (pri·skript′, prē′skript) Prescribed as a rule or model; laid down. [<L *praescriptus,* pp. of *praescribere.* See PRESCRIBE.]

pre·scrip·ti·ble (pri·skrip′tə·bəl) *adj.* Derived from or acquirable by prescription; depending on prescriptive right. **—pre·scrip′ti·bil′i·ty** *n.*

pre·scrip·tion (pri·skrip′shən) *n.* 1 The act of prescribing, directing, or dictating. 2 That which is prescribed or appointed, as a rule or precept; a prescript. 3 *Med.* a A physician's formula for compounding and administering a medicine. b The remedy so prescribed. c A formula issued by a licensed oculist or optometrist giving directions for the grinding of eyeglass lenses. 4 *Law* A title to property, or a mode of acquiring title to property, founded on uninterrupted possession; a mode of losing a right or title by failure to assert it within a given time; the period after which a neglected right or title cannot be asserted; also, the period, if any, after which prosecution for a crime is barred. 5 Old or continued custom, particularly when considered authoritative. 6 A claim based on long usage. [<L *praescriptio, -onis*]

pre·scrip·tive (pri·skrip′tiv) *adj.* 1 Making strict requirements or rules: *prescriptive* grammar. 2 Sanctioned by custom or long use: a *prescriptive* right to grumble. 3 *Law* Acquired by immemorial use; based on prescription: a *prescriptive* title. [<LL *praescriptivus*] **—pre·scrip′tive·ly** *adv.*

pres·ence (prez′əns) *n.* 1 The state or fact of being present; opposed to *absence.* 2 Situation face to face; close approach or vicinity within view or access. 3 Something invisible but near and sensible, as a spiritual being. 4 Personal appearance; bearing. 5 Personal qualities collectively; self; personality: used also absolutely of a sovereign. 6 *Obs.* A distinguished assembly, as before a prince or exalted personage. 7 Formerly, the room or apartment in which a high dignitary or ruler received assemblies: also **presence chamber.** [<OF <L *praesentia,* orig. neut. pl of *praesens, -entis,* ppr. of *praeesse.* See PRESENT.]

presence of mind Full command of one's faculties; coolness, alertness, and readiness of resource in a situation of sudden danger, embarrassment, etc.

pres·ent[1] (prez′ənt) *adj.* 1 Being in a place or company referred to or contemplated; being at hand: opposed to *absent.* 2 Now going on; current; not past or future. 3 Actually in mind. 4 Immediately impending or actually coming on; not delayed; instant. 5 *Gram.* Relating to or signifying what is going on at the time being: the *present* tense, *present* participle. 6 Ready at hand; prompt in emergency: a *present* wit, a *present* aid. See synonyms under IMMEDIATE. *—n.* 1 Present time; now; the time being. 2 *Gram.* The present tense; also, a verbal form denoting it. 3 A present matter or affair; a question under consideration. 4 *pl. Law* Present writings: term for the document in which the word occurs: Know all men by these *presents.* **—at present** Now. **—for the present** For the time being. [<OF <L *praesens, -entis* being in front of or at hand, ppr. of *praeesse* <*prae-* before + *esse* be]

pre·sent[2] (pri·zent′) *v.t.* 1 To bring into the presence or acquaintance of another; introduce, especially to a superior: The ambassador was *presented* to the king. 2 To exhibit to view or notice; display. 3 To suggest to the mind: This *presents* a problem. 4 To put forward for consideration or action; submit, as a petition. 5 To make a gift or presentation of or to, usually formally. 6 *Archaic* To represent on the stage; act. 7 *Law* a To offer, as a charge, for judicial action or inquiry. b To bring a charge or indictment against.
—pres·ent (prez′ənt) *n.* That which is presented or given; a gift; donation. [<OF *presenter* <L *praesentare* set before <*praesens, -entis* present. See PRESENT[1].] **—pre·sent′er** *n.*

pre·sent·a·ble (pri·zen′tə·bəl) *adj.* 1 Fit to be presented; in suitable condition or attire for company. 2 Capable of being offered, exhibited, or bestowed. **—pre·sent′a·bil′i·ty, pre·sent′·a·ble·ness** *n.* **—pre·sent′a·bly** *adv.*

present arms A command requiring a soldier to salute by holding his gun or other weapon vertically, in front of and close to his body. Correct position for the gun is muzzle up and trigger facing forward.

pres·en·ta·tion (prez′ən·tā′shən, prē′zən-) *n.* 1 The act of presenting or proffering for acceptance, approval, etc.; especially, the formal offering of a complimentary gift. 2 *Rare* That which is bestowed; a present. 3 The act of introducing or bringing to notice; formal introduction, especially to a superior: *presentation* at court. 4 *Eccl.* The nomination of a clergyman to a living; also, the right of such nomination. 5 The manner of bringing into view, as a play, thought, or case; way of putting; exhibition; representation; also, that which is represented. 6 The fact or process of being present in consciousness; also, the object of consciousness, without added reference. 7 *Med.* The position of the fetus at birth: designated by the part that is first presented to the touch at the mouth of the womb: breech *presentation,* etc. 8 The condition of being placed in a certain position or direction, with regard to something else, or to an observer. 9 Presentment; the offering of a negotiable instrument for payment. [<OF *presentacion* <L *praesentatio, -onis*]

pres·en·ta·tion·al (prez′ən·tā′shən·əl, prē′zən-) *adj.* Relating to or composed of presentations.

pres·en·ta·tion·al·ism (prez′ən·tā′shən·əl·iz′·əm, prē′zən-) *n. Philos.* The doctrine that man has an immediate perception of all the elemental forms of entity, as space, time, substance, and power; natural realism. Also **pres·en·ta′tion·ism. —pres′en·ta′tion·ist** *adj. & n.*

pre·sen·ta·tive (pri·zen′tə·tiv) *adv.* 1 Having to do with the mental awareness or knowledge of an activity, power, or object: distinguished from *representative:* a *presentative* judgment. 2 Having the right to present to a benefice; also, admitting of the presentation of a clergyman. **—pre·sen′ta·tive·ness** *n.*

pres·ent-day (prez′ənt·dā′) *adj.* Of the present time; current.

pres·en·tee (prez′ən·tē′) *n.* 1 One who is presented, as to a benefice or at court. 2 The recipient of a gift.

pre·sen·ti·ment (pri·zen′tə·mənt) *n.* A prophetic sense of something to come; a foreboding. See synonyms under ANTICIPATION. [<MF <L *praesentire* perceive beforehand <*prae-* before + *sentire* feel]

pre·sen·tive (pri·zen′tiv) *adj.* Conveying or embodying (as nouns, adjectives, and most verbs) a distinct and complete conception, whether of an object, act, or quality: distinguished from *symbolic.* *—n.* A presentive word. **—pre·sen′tive·ly** *adv.* **—pre·sen′tive·ness** *n.*

pres·ent·ly (prez′ənt·lē) *adv.* 1 After a little time; shortly. 2 *Archaic & Dial.* At once; immediately. See synonyms under IMMEDIATELY. ◆ *Presently* in the sense "at once" has not been in use in literary English since the 17th century, though it has persisted in dialectal use in both England and the United States.

pre·sent·ment (pri·zent′mənt) *n.* 1 The act of presenting; also, the state or manner of being presented; presentation. 2 That which is represented or exhibited; a representation or picture; semblance. 3 *Law* A report made by a grand jury, concerning some wrongdoing, and presented to the court; also, the finding and setting forth of charges in an indictment by a grand jury; an indictment. 4 The presentation of a negotiable instrument for payment. 5 *Philos.* The mental images of a perception or idea.

present participle See under PARTICIPLE.

present perfect *Gram.* The verb tense expressing an action completed by the present time: By now he *has finished* the task.

present tense The tense marking present time: I *go, do go, am going.*

pre·ser·va·tive (pri·zûr′və·tiv) *adj.* Serving or tending to preserve. *—n.* That which serves or tends to preserve; a substance that preserves; a safeguard. [<F *préservatif, -ive* <Med. L *praeservativus*]

pre·serve (pri·zûrv′) *v.* **·served, ·serv·ing** *v.t.* 1 To keep in safety; protect from destruction, loss, death, or detriment; guard: May the gods *preserve* you. 2 To keep intact or unimpaired; maintain: to *preserve* appearances. 3 To prepare (food) for future consumption, as by boiling with sugar or salting. 4 To keep from decomposition or change, as by chemical treatment: to *preserve* a specimen in alcohol. 5 To keep for one's private hunting or fishing: to *preserve* foxes; to *preserve* a wood. *—v.i.* 6 To make preserves, as of fruit. 7 To maintain a game preserve. *—n.* 1 *Usually pl.* Fruit which has been cooked, usually with sugar, to prevent its fermenting. 2 Something preserved or which preserves. 3 A place set apart for one's own private use, or in which game or fish are protected for purposes of sport. [<OF *preserver* <LL *praeservare* <L *prae-* before + *servare* keep] **—pre·serv′a·bil′i·ty** *n.* **—pre·serv′a·ble** *adj.* **—pres·er·va·tion** (prez′ər·vā′shən) *n.* **—pre·serv′er** *n.*

Synonyms (verb): conserve, defend, guard, keep, maintain, protect, save, secure, sustain, uphold. See KEEP, RETAIN. *Antonyms*: abandon, lavish, lose, neglect, scatter, spend, spoil, waste.

pre-shrunk (prē′shrungk′) *adj.* Shrunk during manufacture to minimize later shrinkage: *preshrunk* cotton.

pre·side (pri·zīd′) *v.i.* **·sid·ed, ·sid·ing** 1 To sit in authority, as over a meeting; be in charge of an assembly, government, etc.; act as chairman or president. 2 To exercise direction or control. [<F *présider* <L *praesidere* sit in front of, protect, guard <*prae-* before + *sedere* sit] **—pre·sid′er** *n.*

pres·i·den·cy (prez′ə·dən·sē) *n. pl.* **·cies** 1 The office, function, or term of office of a president. 2 *Often cap.* The office of president of the United States. 3 *Often cap.* Formerly, any of the three original provinces of British India: Bengal, Madras, and Bombay. 4 *Brit.* An administrative subdivision. 5 In the Mormon Church, a local administrative council of three men; also, the highest governing body of the church **(First Presidency),** consisting of the president and his two counselors. [<Med. L *praesidentia*]

pres·i·dent (prez′ə·dənt) *n.* **1** One who is chosen to preside over an organized body; specifically, the chief executive of a republic. **2** The chairman of the meetings and chief executive officer of a department of the government, a corporation, society, etc. **3** The chief officer of a college or university. **4** The chairman of a meeting conducted under parliamentary rules. [<F *président* <L *praesidens, -entis,* ppr. of *praesidere.* See PRESIDE.] — **pres·i·den·tial** (prez′ə·den′shəl) *adj.*

THE PRESIDENTS OF THE UNITED STATES

Number—Name
Birthplace—Inaugurated: *Year* *Age*

1 George Washington		
Westmoreland Co., Va.	1789	57
2 John Adams		
Quincy, Mass.	1797	61
3 Thomas Jefferson		
Shadwell, Va.	1801	57
4 James Madison		
Port Conway, Va.	1809	57
5 James Monroe		
Westmoreland Co., Va.	1817	58
6 John Quincy Adams		
Quincy, Mass.	1825	57
7 Andrew Jackson		
Union Co., N.C.	1829	61
8 Martin Van Buren		
Kinderhook, N.Y.	1837	54
9 William H. Harrison		
Berkeley, Va.	1841	68
10 John Tyler		
Greenway, Va.	1841	51
11 James K. Polk		
Little Sugar Creek, N.C.	1845	49
12 Zachary Taylor		
Orange Co., Va	1849	64
13 Millard Fillmore		
Summerhill, N.Y.	1850	50
14 Franklin Pierce		
Hillsboro, N.H.	1853	48
15 James Buchanan		
Cove Gap, Pa.	1857	65
16 Abraham Lincoln		
Hardin Co., Ky.	1861	52
17 Andrew Johnson		
Raleigh, N.C.	1865	56
18 Ulysses S. Grant		
Point Pleasant, O.	1869	46
19 Rutherford B. Hayes		
Delaware, O.	1877	54
20 James A. Garfield		
Cuyahoga Co., O.	1881	49
21 Chester A. Arthur		
Fairfield, Vt.	1881	50
22 Grover Cleveland		
Caldwell, N.J.	1885	47
23 Benjamin Harrison		
North Bend, O.	1889	55
24 Grover Cleveland		
Caldwell, N.J.	1893	55
25 William McKinley		
Niles, O.	1897	54
26 Theodore Roosevelt		
New York, N.Y.	1901	42
27 William H. Taft		
Cincinnati, O.	1909	51
28 Woodrow Wilson		
Staunton, Va.	1913	56
29 Warren G. Harding		
Corsica, O.	1921	55
30 Calvin Coolidge		
Plymouth, Vt.	1923	51
31 Herbert C. Hoover		
West Branch, Ia.	1929	55
32 Franklin D. Roosevelt		
Hyde Park, N.Y.	1933	51
33 Harry S Truman		
Lamar, Mo.	1945	60
34 Dwight D. Eisenhower		
Denison, Tex.	1953	62
35 John F. Kennedy		
Brookline, Mass.	1961	43
36 Lyndon B. Johnson		
Gillespie County, Tex.	1963	55
37 Richard M. Nixon		
Yorba Linda, Calif.	1969	56
38 Gerald R. Ford		
Omaha, Nebr.	1974	61
39 Jimmy Carter		
Plains, Ga.	1977	55
40 Ronald W. Reagan		
Tampico, Ill.	1981	69
41 George H. Walker Bush		
Milton, Massachusetts	1989	64
42 William Jefferson Clinton		
Hope, Arkansas	1993	46

pre·sid·i·al (pri·sid′ē·əl) *adj.* Of or having a garrison or a garrisoned post. [<F *présidial* <LL *praesidium* a garrison, fort]

pre·sid·i·o (pri·sid′ē·ō) *n. pl.* **·sid·i·os** **1** A garrisoned post; fort; fortified settlement. **2** A Spanish penal settlement in a foreign country. **—the Presidio** A U.S. military reservation in San Francisco. [<Am. Sp.]

pre·sid·i·um (pri·sid′ē·əm) *n.* Any of several executive committees in the U.S.S.R. that served as the permanent organ of a larger governmental body. [<L *praesidium*]

Pre·sid·i·um (pri·sid′ē·əm) *n.* **1** A governmental body of the Soviet Union that exercised the powers of the Supreme Soviet between plenary sessions. **2** The supreme policy-making committee of the Communist party of the Soviet Union, headed by the party secretary. See POLITBURO.

pre·sig·ni·fy (prē·sig′nə ·fī) *v.t.* **·fied, ·fy·ing** To signify in advance; presage.

press¹ (pres) *v.t.* **1** To act upon by weight or pressure: to *press* a button. **2** To compress so as to extract the juice: to *press* grapes. **3** To extract by pressure, as juice. **4** To exert pressure upon so as to smooth, shape, make compact, etc. **5** To smooth or shape by heat and pressure, as clothes; iron. **6** To embrace closely; hug. **7** To force or impel; drive. **8** To distress or harass; place in difficulty: I am *pressed* for time. **9** To urge persistently; importune; entreat: They *pressed* me for an answer. **10** To advocate persistently; insist on; emphasize. **11** To put forward insistently: to *press* a gift on a friend. **12** To urge onward; hasten. **13** *Obs.* To crowd. —*v.i.* **14** To exert pressure; bear heavily. **15** To advance forcibly or with speed: *Press* on! **16** To press clothes, etc. **17** To crowd; cram. **18** To be urgent or importunate. See synonyms under IMPRESS¹, JAM, PLEAD, PUSH. —*n.* **1** A dense throng. **2** The act of crowding together or of straining forward. **3** Hurry or pressure of affairs; urgency: the *press* of business. **4** A movable upright closet or case in which clothes, books, etc., are kept: a linen *press.* **5** An apparatus or machine by which pressure is applied, as for making wine, compressing bulky substances for packing, etc.; a printing press. **6** Newspapers or periodical literature collectively, or the body of persons collectively, as editors, reporters, etc., engaged upon such publications; also, printed literature in the abstract. **7** The art, process, or business of printing. **8** The place of business in which a printing press is set up and where printing is carried on: the Clarendon *Press* ; to go to *press.* **9** Criticism, comments, news, etc., in newspapers and periodicals. See synonyms under THRONG. [<OF *presser* <L *pressare,* freq. of *premere* (pp. *pressus*) press]

PRESS
Cider, wine, and fruit press.

press² (pres) *v.t.* **1** To force into military or naval service; impress. **2** To put to use in a manner not intended or desired. —*n.* A commission to impress men into the public service; also, the impressment of men. [<obs. *prest* engage for military service by payment of earnest money <OF *prester* lend <L *praestare* guarantee, furnish money for <*prae-* before + *stare* stand; influenced in form and meaning by *press¹*]

press agent A person employed to advance the interests of his client by advertisements and other notices; a publicity agent for any person or business. — **press·a·gen·try** (pres′ā′jən·trē) *n.*

press·board (pres′bôrd′, -bōrd′) *n.* **1** A wooden board placed between sheets in a standing press. **2** An ironing board. — **imitation pressboard** Millboard. **—electrical pressboard** Fullerboard.

Press·burg (pres′bŏŏrkh) The German name for BRATISLAVA.

press conference An interview granted by a celebrity, government official, etc., to a number of journalists at the same time.

press·er (pres′ər) *n.* **1** One who or that which presses. **2** *Mech.* Any machine or apparatus exerting pressure, as by a spring; a presser foot. **3** One who cleans and presses clothes. **4** One who operates a press: a cotton *presser.*

presser foot A footpiece in a sewing machine to hold the fabric down to the feed plate.

press·gang (pres′gang′) *n.* A detachment of men detailed to press men into naval or military service. Also **press gang.**

press·ing (pres′ing) *adj.* **1** Demanding immediate attention; urgent; important. **2** Importunate. **—press′ing·ly** *adv.*

press·man¹ (pres′mən) *n. pl.* **·men** (-mən) **1** A man who has charge of a press, as a printing press. **2** A man who presses clothes. **3** *Brit.* A member of the press; journalist.

press·man² (pres′mən) *n. pl.* **·men** (-mən) *Obs.* A member of a pressgang.

press·mark (pres′märk′) *n.* **1** A mark in a book to point out its particular place in a book press or bookcase of a library. **2** A mark, as a number or letter on the margin of a newspaper, showing on which press it was printed.

press money The king's shilling. See under SHILLING.

press of canvas or **sail** *Naut.* The maximum spread of sail that can be carried with safety under wind pressure.

press·or (pres′ər) *adj. Physiol.* Increasing the functional activities of an organ: a *pressor* nerve, the stimulating of which raises the arterial blood pressure: opposed to *depressor.* [< PRESS¹]

press·pahn (pres′pän) *n.* Fullerboard. [<G]

press proof 1 The last proof taken before printing. **2** A proof taken on a press.

press release A bulletin, prepared by a press agent, public relations department, or other official representative, announcing an event, development in a business, newsworthy decision, etc.

press·room (pres′rŏŏm′, -rōōm′) *n.* A room containing the presses of a printing concern.

pres·sure (presh′ər) *n.* **1** The act of pressing, or the state of being pressed. **2** *Physics* Any force which acts against an opposing force; a thrust, stress, or strain between opposed masses, uniformly distributed over the surfaces in contact: steam *pressure* ; the *pressure* of gas in a confined space. **3** An impelling or constraining moral force; compulsory motive: bringing *pressure* to bear. **4** Exigent demand on one's time or strength; urgency: the *pressure* of business. **5** The oppressive influence or depressing effect of something hard to bear; weight, as of grief or trouble; onerousness: *pressure* of taxation; *pressure* of calamity. **6** A printed character; stamp; an impression. **—fluid pressure** Pressure of a fluid or resembling that of a fluid, being invariable and uniform in all directions. —*v.t.* **·sured, ·sur·ing** *Colloq.* To compel, as by forceful persuasion or influence: He was *pressured* to accept the job. [<OF <L *pressura* <*pressus,* pp. of *premere* press]

pressure cabin *Aeron.* An enclosed compartment in an airplane, supplied with air maintained at or near sea-level pressure to provide sufficient oxygen for crew and passengers at high altitudes.

pressure cooker An airtight receptacle for the cooking of food at high temperature under pressure; an autoclave.

pressure gage An instrument for measuring the pressure of a gas or liquid, and for indicating it by a pointer on a graduated dial; a manometer. Also **pressure gauge.**

pressure gradient *Meteorol.* The decrease in barometric pressure per unit of horizontal distance along the course in which the pressure decreases most rapidly.

pressure group An organized minority group which seeks, through propaganda and lobbying, to influence legislators and public opinion in behalf of its own special interests, or to defeat restrictive legislation.

pres·sur·ize (presh′ə·rīz) *v.t.* **·ized, ·iz·ing 1** To subject to high pressure. **2** *Aeron.* To maintain normal atmospheric pressure in (the cabin or cockpit of an airplane) at high altitudes. — **pres′sur·i·za′tion** *n.*

press·work (pres′wûrk′) *n.* **1** The operating, adjustment, or management of a printing press. **2** The work done by the press. **3** Cabinetwork made up of cross veneers glued together and pressed while hot.

prest[1] (prest) *adj. Obs.* Ready; prepared at hand; daring; also, tidy; neat. [<OF <L *praesto,* dative of *praestus* ready, at hand]

prest[2] (prest) *n.* **1** An advance or loan; also, ready money. **2** Press money; also **prest money.** [<OF <*prester* lend <L *praestare.* See PRESS.]

Pres·teigne (pres·tēn′) The county town of Radnorshire, Wales.

pres·ti·dig·i·ta·tion (pres′tē·ij′ə·tā′shən) *n.* The practice of sleight of hand; jugglery; legerdemain. [<F <*preste* (<Ital. *presto* <LL *praestus*) nimble + L *digitus* finger] — **pres′ti·dig′i·ta′tor** *n.*

pres·tige (pres·tēzh′, pres′tij) *n.* Authority or importance based on past achievements or reputation; ascendency based on recognition of power; renown. [<F <L *praestigium* illusion, juggler's trick, spell <*praestringere* bind fast < *prae-* before + *stringere* bind]

pres·ti·gious (pres·tij′əs, -tē′jəs) *adj.* Having or bestowing prestige. —**pres·ti′gious·ly** *adv.* —**pres·ti′gious·ness** *n.*

pres·tis·si·mo (pres·tis′i·mō, *Ital.* pres·tēs′sē·mō) *adj. adv. Music* As fast as possible; in very quick time. [<Ital., superlative of *presto.* See PRESTO.]

pres·to (pres′tō) *adv. Adj.* **1** *Music* In fast time. **2** At once; speedily. —*n. Music* A movement, passage, or phrase performed in fast tempo. [<Ital. <L *praesto.* See PREST.]

Pres·ton (pres′tən) A county borough and river port in central Lancashire, England.

Pres·tone (pres′tōn) *n.* Ethylene glycol, used as an anti-freeze mixture: a trade name.

Pres·ton·pans (pres′tən·panz′) A burgh in East Lothian, Scotland, east of Edinburgh on the Firth of Forth; scene of a Scottish victory over the English, 1745.

pre·stressed concrete (prē′strest′) Concrete cast over taut steel cables, etc., to increase its tensile strength.

pre·sum·able (pri·zōō′mə·bəl) *adj.* That may be assumed or presumed; reasonable. See synonyms under APPARENT, LIKELY, PROBABLE. —**pre·sum′a·bly** *adv.*

pre·sume (pri·zōōm′) *v.* **·sumed, ·sum·ing** *v.t.* **1** To take upon oneself without warrant or permission; dare; venture; usually with the infinitive: Do you *presume* to address me? **2** To take for granted; assume to be true until disproved: I *presume* you are right. **3** To indicate the probability of; seem to prove: The receipt for this month *presumes* preceding payments. — *v.i.* **4** To act or proceed presumptuously or overconfidently. **5** To make excessive demands; rely too heavily: with *on* or *upon:* He *presumes* on my good nature. See synonyms under ASSUME. [<OF *presumer* <L *praesumere* take first <*prae* - before + *sumere* take] —**pre·sum·ed·ly** (pri·zōō′mid·lē) *adv.* —**pre·sum′er** *n.*

pre·sump·tion (pri·zump′shən) *n.* **1** Blind or overweening confidence or self-assertion. **2** A passing beyond the ordinary bounds of good breeding, respect, or reverence; offensively forward or arrogant conduct or expression; effrontery. **3** The act of forming a judgment on probable grounds, awaiting further evidence; also, the judgment so formed, or a ground or reason for it. **4** That which may be logically or legally assumed to be true until disproved: the *presumption* of guilt. **5** *Law* The inference of a fact on proof of circumstances that usually or necessarily attend such a fact. See synonyms under ARROGANCE, ASSURANCE, IMPUDENCE, PROBABILITY, TEMERITY. [<OF *presomption* <L *praesumtio, -onis* < *praesumptus,* pp. of *praesumere.* See PRESUME.]

pre·sump·tive (pri·zump′tiv) *adj.* Creating or resting upon a presumption; affording reasonable grounds for belief. [<F *présomptif*] —**pre·sump′tive·ly** *adv.*

presumptive heir See HEIR PRESUMPTIVE.

pre·sump·tu·ous (pri·zump′chōō·əs) *adj.* **1** Unduly confident or bold; audacious; arrogant; insolent. **2** Exhibiting, characterized by, or founded on presumption; presuming unduly, as upon success or the forebearance of others; foolhardy. [<OF *presumptuoux* <LL *praesumptiosus*] —**pre·sump′tu·ous·ly** *adv.* —**pre·sump′tu·ous·ness** *n.*

pre·sup·pose (prē′sə·pōz′) *v.t.* **·posed, ·pos·ing** **1** To imply or involve as a necessary antecedent condition. **2** To take for granted; assume to start with. [<F *présupposer*] —**pre·sup·po·si·tion** (prē′sup·ə·zish′ən) *n.*

pre·tend (pri·tend′) *v.t.* **1** To assume or display a false appearance of; feign: to *pretend* friendship for an enemy. **2** To claim or assert falsely: He *pretended* that there was gold on his property. **3** To feign in play; make believe. —*v.i.* **4** To make believe, as in play or for the purpose of deception: She is only *pretending* when she says that. **5** To put forward a claim: with *to.* [<OF *pretendre* <L *praetendere* spread out before <*prae-* before + *tendere* spread out]

Synonyms: affect, assume, counterfeit, feign, profess, sham, simulate. See ASSUME, MASK.

pre·tend·ed (pri·ten′did) *adj.* Alleged; asserted; professed. —**pre·tend′ed·ly** *adv.*

pre·tend·er (pri·ten′dər) *n.* **1** One who advances a claim or title; a claimant; specifically, a claimant of a throne who is an heir of a deposed dynasty. **2** In English history, the son and grandson of James II, the former being known in literature as the **Pretender** or the **Old Pretender,** and the latter as the **Young Pretender.** **3** A hyprocrite. See synonyms under HYPOCRITE.

pre·tense (pri·tens′, prē′tens) *n.* **1** That which is pretended; a pretext; a ruse or wile. **2** The act or state of pretending, or of being a pretender or claimant; specifically, a false assumption of a character or condition; hence, affectation; ostentation. **3** Any act of simulation. **4** A right or title asserted. **5** An intention, aim, or effort. Also *Brit.* **pre·tence′.** [<AF *pretensse* <Med. L *praetensus,* alter. of L *praetentus,* pp. of *praetendere.* See PRETEND.]

Synonyms: affection, air, assumption, cloak, color, disguise, dissimulation, excuse, mask, pretension, pretext, ruse, seeming, semblance, show, simulation. A *pretense,* in the unfavorable and usual sense, is something advanced or displayed for the purpose of concealing the reality. A person makes a *pretense* of something for the credit or advantage to be gained by it; he makes what is allowed or approved a *pretext* for doing what would be opposed or condemned; a tricky schoolboy makes a *pretense* of doing an errand which he does not do, or he makes the actual doing of an errand a *pretext* for playing truant. A *ruse* is something employed to blind or deceive so as to mask an ulterior design, and enable a person to gain some end that he would not be allowed to approach directly. A *pretension* is a claim that is or may be contested; the word is now commonly used in an unfavorable sense. See DISGUISE, HYPOCRISY. *Antonyms*: actuality, candor, fact, guilelessness, honesty, ingenuousness, openness, reality, simplicity, sincerity, truth.

pre·ten·sion (pri·ten′shən) *n.* **1** A claim put forward, whether true or false. **2** Affectation; display. **3** A bold or presumptuous assertion. See synonyms under PRETENSE.

pre·ten·tious (pri·ten′shəs) *adj.* Characterized by pretension; making an ambitious outward show; ostentatious. [<F *prétentieux*] —**pre·ten′tious·ly** *adv.* —**pre·ten′tious·ness** *n.*

preter- *prefix* Beyond; past; more than: *preternatural.* [<L *praeter* beyond < *prae* before]

pret·er·hu·man (prē′tər·hyōō′mən) *adj.* Beyond what is human.

pret·er·it (pret′ər·it) *adj.* **1** *Gram.* Signifying past time or completed past action. **2** *Rare* Belonging to the past; bygone. —*n. Gram.* The tense that expresses absolute past time; the past tense. Also **pret′er·ite.** [<OF *preterit* <L *praeteritus* past, pp. of *praeterire* go past < *praeter* - beyond + *ire* go]

pret·er·i·tion (pret′ə·rish′ən) *n.* **1** The act of passing over or omitting. **2** The omission or passing by of a natural heir without mention by a testator in his will. **3** In the doctrine of predestination, the passing-by of the nonelect. [<LL *praeteritio, -onis* <L *praeteritus.* See PRETERIT.]

pre·ter·i·tive (pri·ter′ə·tiv) *adj. Gram.* **1** Used to indicate past actions or states: said of tenses of verbs. **2** Employed only in a past tense or past tenses: said of certain verbs.

pre·ter·mit (prē′tər·mit′) *v.t.* **·mit·ted, ·mit·ting** **1** To fail or cease to do; neglect; omit. **2** To let pass without noticing; overlook; disregard. [<L *praetermittere* let go by <*praeter* - beyond + *mittere* send] —**pre′ter·mis′sion** (-mish′ən) *n.*

pre·ter·nat·u·ral (prē′tər·nach′ər·əl) *adj.* Diverging from or exceeding the common order of nature; inexplicable in terms of the known facts and laws of science, but not outside the universal natural order: distinguished from *supernatural.* See synonyms under SUPERNATURAL. —**pre′ter·nat′u·ral·ism***n.* —**pre′ter·nat′·u·ral·ly** *adv.*

pre·text (prē′tekst) *n.* **1** A fictitious reason or motive advanced to conceal a real one. **2** A specious excuse or explanation. See synonyms under PRETENSE. [<F *pré texte* <L *praetextus.* See PRAETEXTA.]

pre·tor (prē′tər) *n.* An ancient Roman city magistrate having charge of the administration of justice; also spelled *praetor.* [<L *praetor* <*praeire* go before. See PRETERITE.] —**pre·to·ri·al** (pri·tôr′ē·əl, -tō′rē-) *adj.* —**pre′tor·ship** *n.*

Pre·to·ri·a (pri·tôr′ē·ə, -tō′rē·ə) Capital of Gauteng province and administrative capital of the Republic of South Africa.

pre·to·ri·an (pri·tôr′ē·ən, -tō′rē-) *adj,* Of or pertaining to a pretor; pretorial. —*n.* A pretor or ex-pretor. Also spelled *praetorian.*

Pre·to·ri·an (pri·t;pgr′ē·ən, -tō′rē-) *adj.* Denoting the imperial bodyguard of the Ceasars. —*n.* A soldier of the imperial bodyguard of the Caesars. Also spelled *Praetorian.*

Pretorian Guard **1** The bodyguard of the Roman emperors, organized by Augustus to take the place of the old *cohors praetoria,* or bodyguard of the general, and disbanded by Constantine the Great. **2** A member of the Pretorian Guard.

Pre·to·ri·us (prə·tōō′rē ·ōōs), **Andries Wilhelmus,** 1799–1853, and his son **Marthinus,** 1819–1901, South African Dutch colonizers.

pret·ti·fy (prit′i·fī) *v.t.***·fied, ·fy·ing** To make pretty; embellish overmuch. [<PRETTY + -FY]

pret·ty (prit′ē) *adj.***·ti·er, ·ti·est** **1** Characterized by delicacy, gracefulness, or proportion rather than by striking beauty; pleasing; attractive. **2** Decent; good; sufficient: often used ironically as a term of depreciation: A *pretty* mess you've made of it! **3** *Colloq.* Considerable; rather large in size or degree. **4** Sweet; precious: a diminutive of endearment: *pretty* girl. **5** Characterized by effeminacy; affected; foppish. **6** *Scot.* Bold; vigorous; athletic. **7** *Obs.* Strong; able; cunning. See synonyms under BEAUTIFUL. —*adv.* **1** Moderately; somewhat; to a fair extent: He looked *pretty* well. **2** Very; quite: He's grown *pretty* fast. **3** *Dial.* Prettily; finely. —**sitting pretty** *Colloq.* In good circumstances. —*n.* A pretty thing or person. [OE *prættig* tricky, cunning] —**pret′ti·ly** *adv.* —**pret′ti·ness** *n.*

pret·zel (pret′səl) *n.* A glazed salted biscuit baked in the form of a loose knot. [<G *brezel*]

Preus·sen (proi′sən) The German name for PRUSSIA.

pre·vail (pri·vāl′) *v.i.* **1** To gain mastery; be victorious; triumph: with *over* or *against.* **2** To be effective or efficacious; succeed. **3** To use persuasion or influence successfully: with *on, upon,* or *with.* **4** To be or become a predominant feature or quality; be prevalent. **5** To have general or wide-spread use or acceptance; be in force. See synonyms under SUCCEED. [<OF *prevaloir* <L *prevalere* <*prae*- before + *valere* be strong]

pre·vail·ing (pri·vā′ling) *adj.* **1** Current; prevalent. **2** Having effective power or influence; efficacious. See synonyms under PREDOMINANT, USUAL. — **pre·vail′ing·ly** *adv.* —**pre·vail′ing·ness** *n.*

prev·a·lent (prev′ə·lənt) *adj.* **1** Predominant. **2** Of wide extent or frequent occurrence; common. **3** Efficacious; effective. See synonyms under GENERAL, PREDOMINANT, USUAL. [<L *praevalens, -entis,* ppr. of *praevalere* PREVAIL] —**prev′a·lence***n.* —**prev′a·lent·ly** *adv.*

pre·var·i·cate (pri·var′ə·kāt) *v.i.***·cat·ed, ·cat·ing** To speak or act in a deceptive, ambiguous, or evasive manner; quibble; lie. [<L *praevaricatus,* pp. of *praevaricare,* lit., walk crookedly <*prae* - before + *varicare* straddle <*varicus* straddling <*varus* crooked] —**pre·var′i·ca′·tor** *n.*

pre·var·i·ca·tion (pri·var′ə·kā′shən) *n.* **1** The act of prevaricating. **2** Misleading or equivocal statement. **3** A trick. See synonyms under DECEPTION, SOPHISTRY.

pré·ve·nance (prā·və·näns′) *n. French* Prevenience.

pre·ven·ience (pri·vēn′yəns) *n.* The act or state of going before; anticipation.

pre·ven·ient (pri·vēn′yənt) *adj.* **1** Preceding or preventing. **2** Anticipatory; expectant. [<L *praeveniens, -entis,* ppr. of *praevenire.* See PREVENT.]

pre·vent (pri·vent′) *v.t.* **1** To keep from happening, as by previous measures or preparations; preclude; thwart. **2** To keep from doing something; forestall; hinder. **3** *Obs.* To anticipate; precede. [<L *praeventus;* pp. of *praevenire* precede, come before, anticipate < *prae-* before + *venire* come] **— pre·vent′a·ble** or **pre·vent′i·ble** *adj.* **— pre·vent′a·bil′i·ty** or **pre·vent′i·bil′i·ty** *n.* **— pre·vent′er** *n.*

Synonyms: anticipate, forestall. The original sense of *prevent,* to go or come before, act in advance of, now practically obsolete, was still in good use when the authorized version of the Bible was made, as appears in such passages as "Thou *preventest* him with the blessings of goodness" (that is, by sending the blessings before the desire is formulated or expressed), *Ps.* xxi 3. *Anticipate* is now the only single word usable in this sense; to *forestall* is to take or act in advance in one's own behalf and to the prejudice or hindrance of another. But to *anticipate* is very frequently used in the favorable sense; as, his thoughtful kindness *anticipated* my wish (that is, met the wish before it was expressed); or one *anticipates* a payment (by making it before the time). For the present use of *prevent,* see synonyms for HINDER[1], PRECLUDE, PROHIBIT.

pre·ven·tion (pri·ven′shən) *n.* **1** The act of preventing. **2** A hindrance; obstruction. **3** A preventive.

pre·ven·tive (pri·ven′tiv) *adj.* Intended or serving to ward off harm, diseases, etc.: *preventive* medicine. **—** *n.* That which prevents or hinders, as a medicine to ward off disease; a precautionary measure. Also **pre·vent·a·tive** (pri·ven′tə·tiv). **— pre·ven′tive·ly** *adv.* **— pre·ven′tive·ness** *n.*

pre·verb (prē′vûrb′) *n.* A verbal prefix, as *be-* in *behave.*

pre·ver·nal (pri·vûr′nəl) *adj.* **1** Prior to spring. **2** *Bot.* Flowering in the early spring, as certain trees and plants.

pre·view (prē′vyo͞o′) *n.* **1** An advance showing, as of a motion picture, a fashion show, etc., to invited guests before it is presented publicly. **2** In motion pictures, the showing of scenes or parts of scenes to advertise a coming picture.

pre·vi·ous (prē′vē·əs) *adj.* **1** Being or taking place before something else in time or order; antecedent; prior to. **2** *Colloq.* Acting, occurring, or speaking too soon; premature. [<L *praevius* going before < *prae-* before + *via* way, road] **— pre′vi·ous·ly** *adv.* **— pre′vi·ous·ness** *n.*

Synonyms: antecedent, anterior, earlier, foregoing, former, precedent, preceding, preliminary, prior. *Antecedent* may denote simple priority in time, implying no direct connection between that which goes before and that which follows; as, the striking of one clock may be always *antecedent* to the striking of another with no causal connection between them. *Antecedent* and *previous* may refer to that which goes or happens at any distance in advance, *preceding* is limited to that which is immediately or next before; an *antecedent* event may have happened at any time before; the *preceding* transaction is the one completed just before the one with which it is compared; a *previous* statement or chapter may be in any part of the book that has gone before; the *preceding* statement or chapter comes next before without an interval. *Foregoing* is used only of that which is spoken or written; as, the *foregoing* statements. *Anterior,* while it can be used of time, is coming to be employed chiefly with reference to place; as, the *anterior* lobes of the brain. *Prior* bears exclusive reference to time, and commonly where that which is first in time is first also in right; as, a *prior* demand. *Former* is used of time, or of position in written or printed matter, not of space in general. We say *former* times, a *former* chapter, etc. *Former* has a close relation, or sharp contrast, with something following; the *former* always implies the latter, even when not fully expressed. Compare ANTECEDENT. *Antonyms*: after, concluding, consequent, following, hind, hinder, hindmost, later, latter, posterior, subsequent, succeeding.

Previous Examination See LITTLE GO.

previous question In parliamentary practice, a motion to avoid or secure a vote at once. In the British Parliament, the motion is put to prevent a speedy vote on a measure. In the United States House of Representatives it is used to end debate and secure an immediate vote. Compare CLOSURE.

previous to **1** Antecedent to; being before. **2** Before: *previous* being loosely used for *previously.*

pre·vise (prē·vīz′) *v.t.* **·vised, ·vis·ing** **1** To see beforehand; foresee. **2** To notify beforehand; forewarn. [<L *praevisus,* pp. of *praevidere* foresee < *prae-* before + *videre* see]

pre·vi·sion (prē·vizh′ən) *n.* **1** The act or power of foreseeing; prescience; foresight. **2** A prophetic or anticipatory vision. See synonyms under ANTICIPATION. [<F *prévision*]

pre·vo·ca·tion·al (prē′vō·kā′shən·əl) *adj.* Of or pertaining to the training given or requisite in schools of a lower grade than the vocational schools.

Pré·vost (prā·vō′), **Marcel,** 1862–1941, French novelist.

Pré·vost d'Ex·iles (prā·vō′ deg·zēl′), **Antoine François,** 1679–1763, French novelist: known as *Abbé Prévost.*

pre·vue (prē′vyo͞o′) *n.* A preview. [<F *prévue,* fem. pp. of *prévoir* foresee]

pre·war (prē′wôr′) *adj.* Of or pertaining to a condition, arrangement, time, etc., before a war.

prex·y (prek′sē) *n. Slang* A college president. Also **prex.**

prey (prā) *n.* **1** Any animal seized by another for food. **2** Booty; plunder; pillage. **3** Anything made the victim of that which is hostile or evil. **4** The act of preying; depredation; robbery. See synonyms under PLUNDER. **—** *v.i.* **1** To seek or take prey for food: Cats *prey* on birds. **2** To take booty; plunder. **3** To make a victim of someone, as by cheating. **4** To exert a wearing or harmful influence: His losses *preyed* on his mind. ◆ Homophone: *pray.* [<OF *preie* <L *praeda* booty] **— prey′er** *n.*

Pri·am (prī′əm) In Greek legend, the son of Laomedon, husband of Hecuba, and father of fifty sons including Hector and Paris; he was the last king of Troy and was killed during its capture at the end of the Trojan War.

Pri·a·pe·an (prī′ə·pē′ən) *adj.* Of or pertaining to Priapus; phallic.

pri·a·pus (prī·ā′pəs) *n.* A phallus. [<PRIAPUS]

Pri·a·pus (prī·ā′pəs) In Greek and Roman mythology, the god of male procreative power, son of Dionysos and Aphrodite. [<L <Gk. *Priapos*]

Prib·i·lof Islands (prib′i·lof) A group of four Alaskan islands in the SE Bering Sea; major breeding ground of the Alaska fur seal.

price (prīs) *n.* **1** An equivalent given or asked in exchange; valuation; cost (to the buyer). **2** Anything given or done to obtain something: Death is the *price* of glory. **3** The quality of possessing value; worth; especially, high value. **4** A bribe or anything used for a bribe. **5** A reward for the capture or death of. **— beyond price** **1** So valuable that no adequate price can be set; priceless. **2** Unbribable. **— market price** The price that something will bring in the open market. **— to set a price on one's head** To offer a reward for the capture of a person, dead or alive. **—** *v.t.* **priced, pric·ing** **1** To ask the price of. **2** To set a price on; value; appraise. [<OF *pris* <L *pretium.* Related to PRAISE.]

Synonyms (noun): charge, cost, expenditure, expense, outlay, value, worth. The *cost* of a thing is all that has been expended upon it, whether in discovery, production, refinement, decoration, transportation, or otherwise, to bring it to its present condition in the hands of its present possessor; the *price* of a thing is what the seller asks for it. *Price* always implies that an article is for sale; what a man will not sell he declines to put a *price* on. *Value* is the estimated equivalent for an article, whether the article is for sale or not; the market *value* is what something would bring if it were for sale in the open market; the intrinsic *value* is the inherent *worth* of the article considered by itself alone; the market *value* of an old and rare volume may be very great, while its intrinsic *value* may be practically nothing. *Value* has always more reference to others' estimation (literally, what the thing will avail with others) than *worth,* which regards the thing in and by itself; thus, intrinsic *value* is a weaker expression than intrinsic *worth. Charge* has especial reference to services, *expense* to outlays; as, the *charges* of a lawyer or physician; traveling *expenses,* etc.

Price may appear as a combining form in hyphemes or solidemes, or as the first element in two-word phrases:

price adjustment	**price–making**
price administration	**price–manipulation**
price boom	**price notice**
price–control	**price reduction**
price cut	**price–ruling**
price–fixer	**price–stabilizer**
price freeze	**price–stabilizing**
price history	**price–support**
price–level	**price–supporting**
price–maintenance	**price tag**

price cutting The act of reducing the price of an article to one below the figure at which it is usually advertised or sold.

price–fix·ing (prīs′fik′sing) *n.* **1** The establishment and maintenance of a scale of prices agreed upon within specified groups of producers or distributors. **2** The establishing by government action of maximum or minimum or fixed prices for certain goods and services. **3** The fixing by a manufacturer or producer of the price at which retailers must sell his product. **—** *adj.* Of or pertaining to price–fixing.

price·less (prīs′lis) *adj.* **1** Beyond price or valuation; invaluable. **2** *Colloq.* Wonderfully amusing or absurd.

price·list (prīs′list′) *n.* A catalog of goods in which the prices are named.

prick (prik) *v.t.* **1** To pierce slightly, as with a sharp point; puncture. **2** To affect with sharp mental pain; sting; spur. **3** To mark, outline, or indicate by or as by punctures. **4** *Obs.* To urge on with or as with a spur; goad. **5** In farriery: **a** To drive a nail into the quick of (a horse's hoof), causing lameness. **b** To nick (a horse's tail). **6** To transplant, as young plants, preparatory to later planting. **—** *v.i.* **7** To have or cause a stinging or piercing sensation. **8** *Archaic* To ride at full speed; go at a gallop. **— to prick up one's (or its) ears** **1** To raise the ears erect. **2** To listen attentively. **—** *n.* **1** The act of pricking; the state or sensation of being pricked. **2** A mental sting or spur: the *prick* of conscience. **3** That which pricks; a slender, sharp–pointed thing, as a thorn or pointed weapon. **4** A mark made by a sharp, pointed instrument; puncture; dot. **5** The footprint of an animal, as a rabbit or deer. **6** *Archaic* A goad or spur. [OE *prica* sharp point] **— prick′er** *n.*

prick·et (prik′it) *n.* **1** A buck of the second year. **2** A sharp point upon which to stick a candle; hence, a candlestick. [Dim. of PRICK]

prick·ing (prik′ing) *n.* **1** The act of puncturing with a sharp point, or the resulting sensation. **2** The laming of a horse by improper shoeing. **3** The nicking of a horse's tail.

pricking wheel A toothed wheel mounted on a handle, used by saddlers to mark equidistant places for stitch holes, or by dressmakers in copying patterns. Also **prick wheel.**

prick·le (prik′əl) *n.* **1** A small, sharp point, as on the bark of a plant. **2** A prickling or stinging sensation. **—** *v.* **·led, ·ling** *v.t.* **1** To prick; pierce. **2** To cause a prickling or stinging sensation in. **—** *v.i.* **3** To have a prickling or stinging sensation; tingle. [OE *pricel*]

prick·ly (prik′lē) *adj.* **1** Furnished with prickles. **2** Stinging, as if from a prick or sting: a *prickly* sensation.

prickly ash A prickly shrub or tree (*Zanthoxylum americanum*) of the rue family, with pungent and aromatic bark.

prickly heat *Pathol.* A summer rash of bright red pimples, with heat, itching, and pricking as if by needles; miliaria.

prickly pear 1 A flat-stemmed cactus (genus *Opuntia*) bearing a pear-shaped and often prickly fruit. 2 The fruit itself.

prickly poppy A weedlike annual (*Argemone mexicana*) of the poppy family, with prickly stem and leaves, showy yellow flowers, and yellow juice.

prick punch A pointed steel punch for marking reference points on metal.

prick-song (prik′sông′, -sŏng′) *n. Archaic* 1 Music pricked down or written. 2 Counterpoint.

pride (prīd) *n.* 1 An undue sense of one's superiority; inordinate self-esteem; arrogance or superciliousness; conceit. 2 A proper sense of personal dignity and worth; honorable self-respect. 3 That of which one is justly proud; a cause of exultation. 4 The acme of excellence. 5 Consciousness of youth or power; high spirits; mettle. 6 *Obs.* Sexual desire. 7 *Archaic* Ostentatious splendor; display. 8 A group or company: said only of lions. — *v.t.* **prid·ed, prid·ing** To take pride in (oneself) for something: with *on* or *upon.* [OE *prȳte < prūt* proud]

Synonyms (noun): conceit, ostentation, self-complacency, self-conceit, self-esteem, self-exaltation, self-respect, vainglory, vanity. *Conceit* and *vanity* are associated with weakness, *pride* with strength. *Conceit* may be founded upon nothing; *pride* is founded upon something that one is, or has, or has done; *vanity,* too, is commonly founded on something real, but far slighter than would afford foundation for *pride. Vanity* is eager for admiration and praise and seeks them; *pride* could never solicit admiration or praise. *Conceit* is stronger than *self-conceit. Self-conceit* is ridiculous; *conceit* is offensive. *Self-respect* is a thoroughly worthy feeling; *self-esteem* is a more generous estimate of one's own character and abilities than the rest of the world is ready to allow. *Vainglory* is more pompous and boastful than *vanity.* Compare synonyms for ARROGANCE, EGOTISM, OSTENTATION, RESERVE. *Antonyms:* humility, lowliness, meekness, modesty, self-abasement.

Pride (prīd), **Thomas,** died 1658, English general; one of the judges who condemned Charles I.

pride-ful (prīd′fəl) *adj.* Full of pride; haughty; disdainful.

pride of China The azedarach tree.

Pride's Purge The expulsion of Royalist and Presbyterian members from the House of Commons in 1648, conducted by Thomas Pride.

Prid·win (prid′win) King Arthur's shield.

prie-dieu (prē-dyœ′) *n.* A small desk arranged to support a book or books and with a footpiece on which to kneel; a praying desk. [<F, pray God]

PRIE-DIEU

pri·er (prī′ər) *n.* One who pries.

priest (prēst) *n.* 1 One especially consecrated to the service of a divinity, and serving as mediator between the divinity and his worshipers in sacrifice, worship, prayer, teaching, etc. 2 In the Anglican, Greek, and Roman Catholic churches, a clergyman in the second order of the ministry, ranking next below a bishop, and having authority to administer the sacraments. 3 Any ordained clergyman or pastor; an official minister of any religious system: distinguished from *layman.* 4 In the early Christian church, an elder or presbyter. 5 One who performs functions or duties similar to those of a priest. — **parish priest** The priest in charge of a parish; specifically, in the Roman Catholic Church, a priest exercising personal jurisdiction in a parish, all members of which are obliged to apply to him for the ministrations of the church: distinguished from *rector* and *curate.* [OE *prēost,* ult. < *presbyter.* Doublet of PRESBYTER.]

priest-craft (prēst′kraft′, -kräft′) *n.* 1 Priestly arts and wiles: an invidious term. 2 The knowledge and skill of priests.

priest·ess (prēs′tis) *n.* A woman or girl who exercises priestly functions or who performs sacred rites.

priest-hood (prēst′hŏŏd) *n.* 1 The priestly office or character. 2 The priestly order; priests collectively. [OE *prēosthad*]

Priest·ley (prēst′lē), **J(ohn) B(oynton)** born 1894, English author. — **Joseph,** 1733–1804, English philosopher and chemist; discoverer of oxygen.

priest·ly (prēst′lē) *adj.* 1 Of or pertaining to a priest or the priesthood; sacerdotal. 2 Suitable to or befitting a priest. — **priest′li·ness** *n.*

priest–rid·den (prēst′rid′n) *adj.* Completely under the influence or domination of priests.

prig[1] (prig) *n.* A formal and narrow-minded person who assumes superior virtue, wisdom, or learning; pedant. [Origin unknown]

prig[2] (prig) *v.* **prigged, prig·ging** *v.t. Brit. Slang* To steal. — *v.i. Scot & Brit. Dial.* To bargain; haggle.

prig·gish (prig′ish) *adj.* Like a prig; conceited. — **prig′gish·ly** *adv.* — **prig′gish·ness** *n.*

prig·gism (prig′iz·əm) *n.* The characteristics or manners of a prig.

prill (pril) *n.* 1 A small metal particle formed in assay work. 2 A spherical pellet about the size of buckshot. — *v.t.* To convert into prills for some purpose or use. [? <Cornish]

prim (prim) *adj.* Minutely or affectedly precise and formal; stiffly proper and neat. See synonyms under NEAT[1]. — *v.* **primmed, prim·ming** *v.i.* To fix the face or mouth in a precise or prim expression; be prim. — *v.t.* To fix in a precise or prim manner. [Prob. <OF *prim* first, prime, fine, delicate <L *primus* first] — **prim′ly** *adv.* — **prim′ness** *n.*

Pri·ma·cord (prī′mə·kôrd) *n.* A flexible tube of fabric or lead, filled with high explosive and used as a primer or bursting charge: a trade name.

pri·ma·cy (prī′mə·sē) *n. pl.* **·cies** 1 The state of being first, as in rank or excellence. 2 The office or province of a primate; archbishopric: also **pri′mate·ship** (-mit·ship). [<OF *primacie* <Med. L *primatia* <LL *primas, primatis* one of the first. See PRIMATE.]

pri·ma don·na (prē′mə don′ə) 1 A leading female singer, as in an opera company. 2 *Colloq.* A temperamental or vain person. [<Ital., lit., first lady]

pri·ma fa·ci·e (prī′mə fā′shi·ē, fā′shē) *Latin* At first view; so far as it first appears.

prima-facie evidence Evidence which, if unexplained or uncontradicted, would establish the fact alleged.

pri·mage (prī′mij) *n.* An allowance in addition to wages, formerly paid by a shipper to the master of a vessel, now paid to the owner of the vessel as an addition to freight charges, for care in loading or unloading goods in port. [<PRIME + -AGE; after Med. L *primagium*]

pri·mal (prī′məl) *adj.* 1 Being at the beginning or foundation; first; original. 2 Most important; chief. See synonyms under PRIMEVAL. [<Med. L *primalis*]

primal cut Any one of the cuts into which a side of beef may be divided for sale at wholesale. These cuts are: hindquarter, trimmed full loin, round sirloin, short loin, flank, flank steak, kidney, hanging tender, forequarter, cross-cut chuck, triangle, arm chuck, rib, short plate, brisket, fore shank, back, regular chuck.

pri·ma·quine (prī′mə·kwīn) *n.* An antimalarial drug synthesized from chemicals derived from corn and coal tar. [<PRIM(E) + A(MINO)-QUIN(OLIN)E]

pri·ma·ri·ly (prī′mer·ə·lē, -mər·ə·lē, *emphatic* prī·mâr′ə·lē) *adv.* In the first place; originally; essentially.

pri·ma·ry (prī′mer·ē, -mər·ē) *adj.* 1 First in time or origin; primitive; original. 2 First in a series or sequence. 3 First in degree, rank, or importance; chief. 4 Constituting the fundamental or original elements of which a whole is comprised; basic; elemental: the *primary* forces of life. 5 Of the first stage of development; elementary; lowest: *primary* school. 6 *Ornithol.* Of or pertaining to the principal flight feathers of a bird's wing. 7 *Geol.* Paleozoic. 8 *Electr.* Of, pertaining to, or noting an inducing current or its circuit: a *primary* coil. 9 *Chem.* **a** Having some characteristic in the first degree, as an initial replacement, substitution, etc. **b** In organic compounds, denoting a radical in which a carbon atom is directly joined to only one other carbon atom. **c** Denoting a compound containing such a radical. — *n. pl.* **·ries** 1 That which is first in rank, dignity, or importance, as a primary planet in distinction from a satellite. 2 A primary meeting or balloting of the voters belonging to one political party in an election district to nominate candidates. 3 *Ornithol.* One of the large flight feathers of the pinion or hand bones of a bird's wings. See synonyms under FIRST, PRIMEVAL. — **direct primary election** A primary election in which candidates for office are nominated directly by the voters and not by a convention or by a body of delegates. [<L *primarius* < *primus* first]

primary cell *Electr.* A cell which cannot be efficiently recharged after use owing to an irreversible electrochemical reaction.

primary colors See under COLOR.

pri·mate (prī′mit, -māt) *n.* 1 The prelate highest in rank in a nation or province. 2 Any of an order (*Primates*) of mammals, including the tarsiers, lemurs, marmosets, monkeys, apes, and man. [<OF *primat* <LL *primas, primatis* of the first <L *primus*] — **pri·ma·tial** (prī·mā′shəl) *adj.*

pri·ma·tol·o·gy (prī′mə·tol′ə·jē) *n.* The branch of zoology which treats of the origin, structure, evolution, and development of primates. — **pri′ma·tol′o·gist** *n.*

pri·ma·ve·ra (prē′mä·vā′rä) *n.* A tropical American tree (*Cybistax donnell-smithi*) of the bignonia family, yielding a creamy-white or yellowish wood resembling satinwood: erroneously called *white mahogany.* [<Sp., lit., spring <L *prima vera,* pl. of *primum ver* earliest spring]

prime[1] (prīm) *adj.* 1 First in rank, dignity, or importance; chief. 2 First in value or excellence; of excellent quality; first-rate. 3 First in time or order; original; primitive; primeval. 4 *Math.* Divisible by no whole number except itself and unity: said of a number. Two or more numbers are said to be *prime* to each other when they have no common factor but unity. 5 Having or pertaining to the strength and vigor of fresh maturity; blooming. 6 Original; not derived; first: opposed to *secondary.* 7 Marked with the sign (′). See synonyms under EXCELLENT, PRIMEVAL. — *n.* 1 The period of fresh, full vigor, beauty, and power succeeding youth and preceding age; formerly, youth. 2 The period of full perfection in anything. 3 The beginning of anything, as of the day; dawn; spring. 4 The best of anything; a prime grade. 5 A prime number. 6 A mark or accent (′) written above and to the right of a letter or figure; also, an inch, a minute, etc., as indicated by that sign, used in indicating and measuring degrees. 7 *Music* The tonic; the interval of unison; also, a note in unison with another. — *v.* **primed, prim·ing** *v.t.* 1 To prepare; make ready for some purpose. 2 To put a primer into (a gun, mine, etc.) preparatory to firing. 3 To pour water into (a pump) so as to displace air and promote suction. 4 To cover (a surface) with sizing, a first coat of paint, etc. 5 To supply beforehand with facts, information, etc.: to *prime* a witness. — *v.i.* 6 To carry water along with the steam into the cylinder: said of a steam boiler or engine. 7 To make something ready, as for firing, pumping, etc. [<OF <L *primus*] — **prime′ly** *adv.* — **prime′ness** *n.*

prime[2] (prīm) *n.* 1 The first canonical hour succeeding lauds; first of the day hours. 2 The office recited at this time. [OE *prim* <LL *prima (hora)* first (hour)]

prime conductor *Electr.* The conductor of a frictional machine which collects and retains the positive electricity.

prime cost The direct cost of obtaining or producing something; the cost of labor and material, exclusive of capital and management expenses.

prime meridian A meridian from which longitude is reckoned: now, generally, the one that passes through Greenwich, England, but formerly that of the local capital, as, in the United States, Washington, D.C.: in France, Paris; etc.

prime minister The chief of the cabinet or ministry; in Great Britain, the principal minister of the sovereign. Compare PREMIER.

prime ministry The office of a prime minister.

prime mover **1** An original or chief force in an undertaking. **2** That which is regarded as an original or natural source of the energy required to perform work or develop power, as muscular force, wind, the motion of water, etc. **3** An object or machine used to convert natural forces to productive power, as a turbine, water wheel, windmill, or the like. **4** In Aristotelian philosophy, the first cause of all movement, which does not itself move.

prime number See under NUMBER.

prim·er[1] (prim′ər) *n.* **1** An elementary textbook; especially, a beginning reading book. **2** Originally, a small prayer book or the like. **3** *Printing* Either of two sizes of type, **great primer** (18-point) and **long primer** (10-point). [<Med. L *primarius*]

prim·er[2] (prī′mər) *n.* **1** Any device, as a cap, tube, etc., used to detonate the main charge of a gun, mine, etc. **2** One who or that which primes.

prim·er[3] (prim′ər, prī′mər) *adj. Obs.* First; original; primary. [<OF <L *primarius* < *primus* prime]

pri·me·ro (pri·mâr′ō) *n.* An old gambling card game. [<Sp.]

pri·me·val (prī·mē′vəl) *adj.* Belonging to the first ages; primitive in time; primary. [<L *primaevus* youthful < *primus* first + *aevum* age] — **pri·me′val·ly** *adv.*

Synonyms: aboriginal, ancient, autochthonic, immemorial, indigenous, native, old, original, primal, primary, prime, primitive, primordial, pristine. *Aboriginal* signifies pertaining to the earliest known inhabitants of a country in the widest sense, including not merely human beings, but animals and plants. *Primeval* signifies strictly belonging to the first ages, earliest in time, but often only the earliest of which man knows or conceives. *Prime* and *primary* may signify either first in time, or first in importance; *primary* has also the sense of elementary or preparatory; we speak of a *prime* minister, a *primary* school. *Primal* is chiefly poetic, in the sense of *prime*; as, the *primal* curse. *Primordial* is first in an order of existence or development; as, a *primordial* leaf. *Primitive* frequently signifies having the original characteristics of that which it represents, as well as standing first in time; as, the *primitive* church, or early characteristics without remoteness in time. *Primeval* simplicity is the simplicity of the earliest ages; *primitive* simplicity may be found in retired villages now. *Pristine* is used almost exclusively in a good sense of that which is *original* and perhaps *ancient*; as, *pristine* purity, innocence, vigor. *Immemorial* refers solely to time, independently of quality, denoting, in legal phrase, that "whereof the memory of man runneth not to the contrary." Compare synonyms for ANCIENT, FIRST, OLD. *Antonyms*: adventitious, exotic, foreign, fresh, late, modern, new, novel, recent.

pri·mi·ge·ni·al (prī′mə·jē′nē·əl) *adj.* Being the first or first-born; primal; primitive; original. [<L *primigenius* first, original]

pri·mine (prī′min) *n. Bot.* The outermost and last-developed integument of an ovule; also, the inner integument as being formed first. Compare SECUNDINE. [<L *primus* first]

prim·ing (prī′ming) *n.* **1** That with which anything is primed. **2** A combustible composition used to ignite an explosive charge. **3** The ground or first layer of paint laid on a surface that is to be painted.

pri·mip·a·ra (prī·mip′ər·ə) *n. pl.* **·a·rae** (-ər·ē) A woman pregnant for the first time or one who has borne just one child. [<L < *primus* first + *parere* give birth to] — **pri·mi·par·i·ty** (prī′mi·par′ə·tē) *n.* — **pri·mip′a·rous** *adj.*

prim·i·tive (prim′ə·tiv) *adj.* **1** Pertaining to the beginning or origin; first; earliest; primary. **2** Resembling the manners or style of long ago; old-fashioned; simple; plain. **3** *Geol.* Of, belonging to, or characterized by the earliest geological period: said especially of the crystalline, unstratified, and massive rocks, the oldest known. **4** *Anthropol.* Of or pertaining to the beginning or earliest anthropological forms or civilizations: *primitive* man, *primitive* weapons. **5** *Biol.* **a** Being or occurring at an early stage of development or growth; first-formed; rudimentary. **b** Not much changed by evolution: a *primitive* species. **6** *Ling.* Standing in original relation, as a word from which a derivative is made; radical: opposed to *derived.* **7** *Theol.* Adhering to strictly traditional interpretation of doctrine and Scripture: the *primitive* church. — *n.* **1** *Ling.* A primary or radical word; also, a word from which another is derived. **2** *Math.* A form in algebra or geometry from which another is derived. **3** An artist, or a work of art, belonging to a very early period of art, or to the earliest phase of an art development or movement; also, a work of any period resembling or imitating such art, or an artist producing it: often characterized by simplicity or a childlike quality. See synonyms under FIRST, PRIMEVAL, RADICAL. [<L *primitivus* < *primus* first] — **prim′i·tive·ly** *adv.* — **prim′i·tive·ness, prim′i·tiv′i·ty** *n.*

Primitive Baptist A member of a branch of the Baptist church (separate since 1835) holding to Calvinistic and antimission doctrines: also called *Hardshell Baptist.*

prim·i·tiv·ism (prim′ə·tiv·iz′əm) *n.* Belief in or adherence to primitive forms and customs.

pri·mo·gen·i·tor (prī′mə·jen′ə·tər) *n.* An earliest ancestor; a forefather. [<Med. L <L *primus* first + *genitor* a father]

pri·mo·gen·i·ture (prī′mə·jen′ə·chər) *n.* **1** The state of being the first-born child of the same parents. **2** The right of the eldest son to inherit the property, title, etc., of a parent, to the exclusion of all other children. See ULTIMOGENITURE. [<Med. L *primogenitura* <L *primus* first + *genitura* birth < *genitus,* pp. of *gignere* beget]

prim′·o·mo (prē·mô′mō) *Italian* First man; leading actor or singer.

pri·mor·di·al (prī·môr′dē·əl) *adj.* **1** First in order or time; original; elemental. **2** *Biol.* First in order of appearance in the growth or development of an organism. — *n.* An elementary principle. See synonyms under FIRST, PRIMEVAL, TRANSCENDENTAL. [<LL *primordialis* < *primordius* original < *primordium* beginning < *primus* first + *ordiri* begin a web] — **pri·mor′di·al·ly** *adv.*

pri·mor·di·al·ism (prī·môr′dē·əl·iz′əm) *n.* The survival or persistence of primitive arts and customs.

primp (primp) *v.t.* & *v.i.* To prink; dress up, especially with superfluous attention to detail. [Akin to PRIM]

prim·rose (prim′rōz) *n.* **1** An early-blossoming perennial herb (genus *Primula*) with tufted basal leaves and variously colored flowers. **2** The flower. **3** The evening primrose. **4** A pale-yellow color, named for the common English primrose: a term indiscriminately applied to various yellow pigments. — *adj.* **1** Pertaining to a primrose; of primrose color. **2** Flowery; gay. [Alter. of ME *primerole* <OF <Med. L *primula,* fem. dim. of L *primus* first; infl. by *rose*]

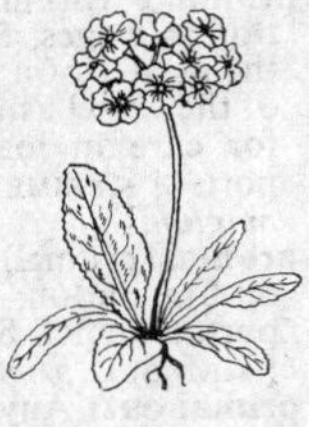

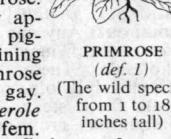

PRIMROSE
(def. 1)
(The wild species from 1 to 18 inches tall)

primrose path The life of worldly or sensual pleasures.

prim·sie (prim′zē) *adj. Scot.* Demure; prim.

prim·u·la·ceous (prim′yə·lā′shəs) *adj. Bot.* Designating or belonging to a family (*Primulaceae*) of herbs widely distributed in the northern hemisphere, including the pimpernel, cyclamen, and loosestrife. [<NL <Med. L *primula* a primrose]

pri·mum mo·bi·le (prī′məm mō′bi·lē) **1** A prime mover. **2** *Astron.* In the Ptolemaic cosmology, the tenth and outermost of the concentric spheres of the universe, regarded as causing all the other spheres to repeat its own revolution around the earth once in 24 hours. [<L, first moving thing]

pri·mus in·ter pa·res (prī′məs in′tər pâr′ēz) *Latin* First among equals.

prince (prins) *n.* **1** A non-reigning male member of a royal family. **2** A male monarch or sovereign. **3** *Brit.* The son of a sovereign or of a son of the sovereign. **4** One of a high order of nobility. **5** The ruler of a small state; head of a principality. **6** A chief or leader, or one of the highest rank of the class to which he belongs: a merchant *prince.* See synonyms under MASTER. [<OF <L *princeps* first, principal < *primus* first + stem of *capere* take]

Prince Albert A long, double-breasted frock coat.

Prince Albert National Park A park in central Saskatchewan, Canada; 1,496 square miles; established 1927.

prince consort The husband of a reigning female sovereign.

Prince Edward Island An island in the Gulf of St. Lawrence off eastern New Brunswick, comprising a maritime province of Canada; 2,184 square miles; capital, Charlottetown.

Prince Island The English name for PRINCIPE. See SÃO TOMÉ E PRINCIPE.

prince·kin (prins′kin) *n.* A little or inferior prince.

prince·ling (prins′ling) *n.* **1** A young prince. **2** A subordinate prince. Also **prince′let** (-lit).

prince·ly (prins′lē) *adj.* **·li·er, ·li·est** **1** Like or characteristic of a prince; liberal; generous. **2** Belonging to, ruled by, or suitable for a prince. **3** Having the rank of a prince. See synonyms under KINGLY. — *adv.* In a princely manner. — **prince′li·ness** *n.*

Prince of Darkness Satan.

Prince of Peace Jesus Christ.

Prince of Wales The eldest son or male heir apparent of the British sovereign: he is born Duke of Cornwall, and becomes Prince of Wales only by creation.

Prince of Wales, Cape The westernmost point of the American continent, at the tip of Seward Peninsula, Alaska, on the Bering Strait 100 miles NW of Nome.

Prince of Wales Island **1** A former name for PENANG ISLAND. **2** An island in the Arctic Ocean, in south central Franklin district of Northwest Territories, Canada; 13,736 square miles; the north magnetic pole was located on it in 1948. **3** The largest island of the Alexander Archipelago, SE Alaska, in the North Pacific west of Ketchikan; 2,231 square miles; 135 miles long, 45 miles wide.

Prince of Wales plumes In furniture and decoration, a motif of three ostrich feathers tied with a bowknot.

Prince Rupert A port in western British Columbia, Canada.

prin·ce's-feath·er (prin′siz-feth′ər) *n.* A tall, hardy plant (*Polygonum orientale*) with plume-like inflorescences and dark-crimson flowers, growing wild in eastern North America.

prin·cess (prin′sis) *n.* **1** A non-reigning female member of a royal family. **2** The consort of a prince. **3** A female sovereign. **4** *Brit.* The daughter of a sovereign or of a son of the sovereign. [<F *princesse*]

prin·cesse (prin·ses′, prin′sis) *adj.* Designating a woman's close-fitting garment cut in a single piece from shoulder to flared hem. Also **prin′cess.** [<F, princess]

princess feather A tall, graceful plant (*Amaranthus hybridus hypochondriacus*) with many-branched panicles of showy flowers.

princess royal The eldest daughter of a sovereign.

Prince·ton (prins′tən) A borough of central New Jersey; scene of an American victory in the Revolutionary War (1777) and seat of Princeton University, founded 1746.

Prince William Sound An inlet of the Gulf of Alaska in southern Alaska; 100 miles across.

prin·ci·pal (prin′sə·pəl) *adj.* First in rank, character, or importance; chief. See synonyms under FIRST, PARAMOUNT. — *n.* **1** One who takes a leading part; one concerned directly and not as an auxiliary; one who is a leader or chief in some action. **2** *Law* **a** The actor in a crime, or one present aiding and abetting. **b** The employer of one who acts as an agent. **c** One primarily liable for whom another has become surety. **d** The most important thing, or part of a given property, to which other things or parts are incidental. **e** The capital or body of an estate. **3** One who is at the head of some body; a chief; one in authority; a presiding officer, as of a society. **4** The head teacher or master in a public or private school. **5** The chief executive of some colleges

and universities in Great Britain. **6** Property or capital, as opposed to interest or income. **7** A rafter extending to the ridge pole; a principal rafter. **8** *Music* **a** The chief metal organ stop, an octave higher in pitch than the other diapasons. **b** The subject of a fugue: distinguished from *answer.* See synonyms under CHIEF, MASTER. ◆ Homophone: *principle.* [< F < L *principalis* < *princeps* chief] **—prin′ci·pal·ly** *adv.* **—prin′ci·pal·ship′** *n.*

prin·ci·pal·i·ty (prin′sə·pal′ə·tē) *n. pl.* **·ties 1** The territory of a reigning prince, or one that gives to a prince a title of courtesy. **2** *pl.* Powers or powerful influences, as celestial or demoniacal powers; in the celestial hierarchy of Dionysius, the seventh of the nine emanations from the Divine. **3** *Obs.* Sovereignty.

principal part See under PART.

Prin·ci·pe (prin′si·pē, *Pg.* prēn′sē·pə) See under SÃO TOMÉ E PRINCIPE.

prin·cip·i·um (prin·sip′ē·əm) *n. pl.* **·cip·i·a** (-sip′ē·ə) **1** Beginning; origin; first principle. **2** *pl.* Fundamentals. [< L]

prin·ci·ple (prin′sə·pəl) *n.* **1** A general truth or law, basic to other truths: the *principle* of self-government. **2** A settled law or rule of personal conduct: He followed the *principle* of the Golden Rule. **3** That which is inherent in anything, determining its nature; essential character; essence. **4** A source or cause from which a thing proceeds; fundamental cause. **5** An established mode of action or operation in natural phenomena: the *principle* of Archimedes. **6** *Chem.* An essential constituent of a compound or substance that gives character to it. **7** Moral standards collectively. See synonyms under DOCTRINE, LAW[1], REASON. ◆ Homophone: *principal.* [< L *principium* a beginning]

prin·cock (prin′kok) *n. Obs.* A coxcomb. Also **prin′cox** (-koks). [Prob. < PRIM + COCK[1]]

prink (pringk) To dress or (oneself) for show. —*v.i.* To dress oneself showily or fussily. [Prob. alter. of PRANK[1] under infl. of PREEN] **—prink′er** *n.*

print (print) *n.* **1** An impression with ink from type, plates, etc.; printed characters collectively; printed matter. **2** Anything printed from an engraved plate or lithographic stone; a proof; a printed picture or design. **3** A newspaper, pamphlet, or the like. **4** An impression or mark made upon or sunk into a substance by pressure; imprint. **5** A reproduction from such an impression. **6** Any fabric stamped with a design by means of dyes used on engraved rollers, wood blocks, or screens. **7** Any tool or device bearing a pattern or design, or that upon which it is impressed. **8** *Phot.* A positive picture made from a negative. **9** Newsprint. **—in print 1** Printed; also, for sale in printed form: opposed to *out of print.* **2** *Obs.* In an exact or formal manner. **—India print** Muslin printed, specifically hand blocked, with the native patterns and glowing colors of India. **—out of print** No longer on sale, the edition being exhausted. See synonyms under MARK[1], PICTURE. —*v.t.* **1** To mark, as with inked type, a stamp, die, etc. **2** To stamp or impress (a mark, seal, etc.) on or into a surface. **3** To fix as if by impressing: The scene is *printed* on my memory. **4** To produce (a book, newspaper, etc.) by the application of inked type, plates, etc., to paper or similar material. **5** To cause to be put in print; publish: The newspaper *printed* the story. **6** To write in letters similar to those used in print: Please *print* your name and address. **7** *Phot.* To produce (a positive picture) by transmitting light through a negative onto a sensitized surface. —*v.i.* **8** To be a printer. **9** To take or give an impression in printing. **10** To form letters similar to printed ones. **—to print out** To deliver (information) automatically in printed form, as a computer. See synonyms under IMPRESS[1]. [< OF *preinte, priente,* fem. of pp. of *preindre* < L *premere* press] **—print′a·ble** *adj.*

printed circuit A circuit in various electronic devices, the paths and connections for which are printed or otherwise deposited on an insulating surface.

print·er (prin′tər) *n.* **1** One engaged in the trade of typographical printing; one who sets type or runs a printing press; specifically, a compositor. **2** One who owns a printing establishment and employs printers. **3** One who prints, stamps, impresses, or transfers copies of anything as a business.

printer's devil A printer's apprentice. See under DEVIL.

print·er·y (prin′tər·ē) *n. pl.* **·er·ies 1** A place where cotton goods, as calico, are printed. **2** A printing office.

print·ing (prin′ting) *n.* **1** The making and issuing of matter for reading by means of type and the printing press. **2** Presswork. **3** The act of reproducing a design upon a surface by any process. **4** That which is printed.

printing press A mechanism for printing from an inked surface as of type, plates, woodblocks etc., operating by pressure, either against a flat bed, as in the platen press, or against a series of revolving cylinders, as in the rotary press.

print·less (print′lis) *adj.* Making, bearing, or retaining no print or impression.

print·out (print′out′) *n.* Material printed automatically, as by a computer.

pri·or (prī′ər) *adj.* Preceding in time, order, or importance. See synonyms under ANTECEDENT, ANTERIOR. **—prior to** Before: The theater closed *prior to* our arrival. —*n.* **1** A monastic officer next in rank below an abbot. **2** Formerly, an Italian magistrate. [< L, earlier, superior] **—pri′or·ate** (-it), **pri′or·ship** *n.*

Pri·or (prī′ər), **Matthew,** 1664–1721, English poet and diplomat.

pri·or·ess (prī′ər·is) *n.* A woman holding a position corresponding to that of a prior; a nun next in rank below an abbess.

pri·or·i·tize (prī·ôr′ə·tīz) *v.t.* **·tized, ·tiz·ing** *Colloq.* To arrange in order of priority: to *prioritize* one's goals.

pri·or·i·ty (prī·ôr′ə·tē, -or′-) *n. pl.* **·ties 1** Antecedence; precedence: opposed to *posteriority.* **2** A first right established on emergency or need: Defense plants have *priority* on steel in time of war. **3** A certificate giving this right to a manufacturer or contractor; hence, a restriction on the use of a commodity or service.

pri·or·y (prī′ər·ē) *n. pl.* **·or·ies** A monastic house presided over by a prior or prioress. See synonyms under CLOISTER. [< OF *priorie*]

Pri·pet (prē′pet) A river in NE Ukrainian S.S.R. and southern Belorussian S.S.R., flowing about 500 miles east through the **Pripet Marshes,** a swampy region of 33,500 square miles, to the Dnieper, 50 miles north of Kiev. *Russian* **Pri·pyat** (pryē′pyət·y′), *Polish* **Pry·peć** (prē′pech).

Pris·cil·la (pri·sil′ə; *Du.* pri·sil′ä, *Ital.* prē·sil′lä) A feminine personal name. Also *Fr.* **Pris·cille** (prē·sēl′). [< L, somewhat ancient] **—Priscilla** In Longfellow's poem *The Courtship of Miles Standish,* the Puritan maiden, Priscilla Mullens, courted by John Alden as proxy for Standish. Later she married Alden.

Pris·cil·li·an (pri·sil′ē·ən, -sil′yən), died 385, bishop of Ávila, Spain; burned at the stake for sorcery. **—Pris·cil′li·an·ist, Pris·cil′li·an·ite′** *n.*

prise (prīz) *n.* & *v.t.* Prize[2]; lever.

prism (priz′əm) *n.* **1** *Geom.* A solid whose bases or ends are any similar equal and parallel plane figures, and whose lateral faces are parallelograms. **2** *Optics* An instrument consisting of such a solid, usually having triangular ends and made of glass or other translucent substance, its refracting surfaces making an angle with each other. **3** Any

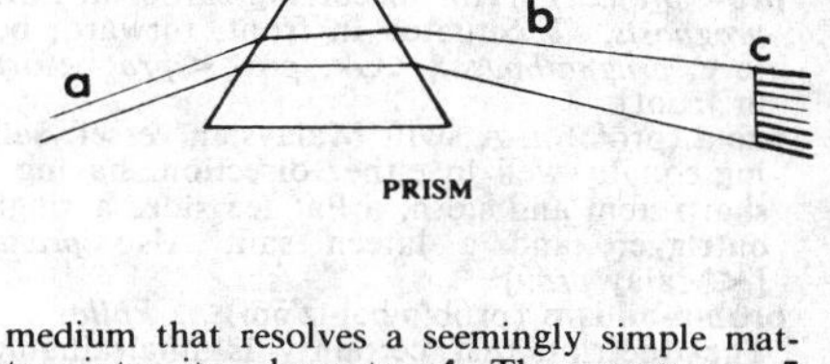

PRISM

medium that resolves a seemingly simple matter into its elements. **4** The spectrum. **5** *Mineral.* A crystal form consisting of three or more intersecting planes whose intersections are parallel and vertical. **—Nicol prism** A prism of calcite (Iceland spar) so cut that light emerging from it is polarized in a definite plane: used in polarizing microscopes, etc. [< LL *prisma* < Gk., something sawed < *prizein* saw]

pris·mat·ic (priz·mat′ik) *adj.* **1** Refracted or formed by a prism. **2** Resembling the spectrum; exhibiting rainbow tints. **3** Pertaining to or shaped like a prism. **4** Orthorhombic. Also **pris·mat′i·cal.** [< Gk. *prisma, prismatos*] **—pris·mat′i·cal·ly** *adv.*

pris·moid (priz′moid) *n.* A body resembling a prism in form. **—pris·moi·dal** (priz·moid′l) *adj.*

pris·on (priz′ən) *n.* A place of confinement; specifically, a public building for the safekeeping of persons in legal custody; a penitentiary. —*v.t.* To imprison. [< F *prisoun* < L *praehensio, -onis* seizure < *praehensus,* pp. of *praehendere*]

pris·on-breach (priz′ən·brēch′) *n.* The escape of a prisoner, against the will of his custodian, from the place where he is held in lawful custody. Also **pris′on-break′ing** (-brā′king).

pris·on·er (priz′ən·ər, -nər) *n.* **1** One who is confined in a prison or whose liberty is forcibly restrained; one held in custody; a captive; specifically, in law, a person confined in a prison by virtue of an order of arrest or of a legal commital. **2** A person confined to a place or position through some cause over which he has not control: A sick man is a *prisoner* to his bed. [< OF *prisonier*]

prisoner of war A combatant or person in arms taken by the enemy either by capture or surrender during war.

prisoner's base A game played in various forms and popular in England as early as the 14th century. Opposing players occupy opposite bases, the object being to touch a player of the opposite side while he is away from his base, when he either joins his captor's side or is confined at another goal called a prison.

prison fever Malignant typhus: so called from its former prevalence in prisons: also called *ship fever.*

pris·sy (pris′ē) *adj.* **·si·er, ·si·est** Effeminate; over precise; prim. —*n.* A person who acts, dresses, or speaks very meticulously. [Blend of PRIM or PRECISE + SISSY]

Priš·ti·na (prēsh′ti·na) A city of south central Yugoslavia, capital of an autonomous region included in Serbia as its SW part; a 12th century capital of Serbia; included in Albania 1941–44.

pris·tine (pris′tēn, -tin; *Brit.* pris′tīn) *adj.* Of or pertaining to the earliest state or time; primitive; untouched. See synonyms under FIRST. [< L *pristinus* primitive]

prith·ee (prith′ē) *interj. Archaic* I pray thee.

pri·va·cy (prī′və·sē) *n. pl.* **·cies 1** The condition of being private; seclusion; retirement. **2** A matter that is or should be private. **3** The state of being secret; avoidance of display or publicity; secrecy. **4** A place of seclusion; retreat. See synonyms under RETIREMENT, SECLUSION, SOLITUDE.

Pri·vat·do·zent (prē·vät′dō·tsent′) *n. German* A lecturer or tutor recognized by a university but unsalaried and dependent on his student fees. Also **Pri·vat′do·cent′.**

pri·vate (prī′vit) *adj.* **1** Removed from public view; retired; secluded; confidential; secret: a *private* parlor, a *private* agreement. **2** Personal or unofficial, as opposed to public; hence, without rank: a *private* citizen, *private* property, a *private* soldier. **3** Not common or general; special: a *private* interpretation. **4** *Obs.* Privy. See synonyms under SECRET. —*n.* **1** A soldier in the ranks. See table under GRADE. **2** *pl.* The private parts; genitals. **3** Privacy. **—in private** In secret; privately. See synonyms under SECRET. [< L *privatus* apart from the state, orig. pp. of *privare* set apart < *privus* single, one's own. Doublet of PRIVY.] **—pri′vate·ly** *adv.* **—pri′vate·ness** *n.*

private enterprise 1 Business owned and operated by private individuals, as opposed to government-owned operations. **2** An economic system based upon private ownership and operation of business. Also called *free enterprise.*

pri·va·teer (prī′və·tir′) *n.* **1** A vessel owned and officered by private persons, but carrying

on maritime war under letters of marque. **2** The commander or one of the crew of a privateer: also **pri·va·teers·man.** —*v.i.* To cruise in or as a privateer. — **pri·va·teer·ing** *n.*
private first class A soldier ranking next above a private and below a corporal. See table under GRADE.
private nurse A nurse in exclusive attendance on one patient, whether in a hospital or at home.
private school See under SCHOOL.
pri·va·tion (prī·vā′shən) *n.* **1** The state of lacking something necessary or desirable; especially, want of the common comforts of life. **2** Deprivation. **3** *Logic* The absence from an object of what ordinarily or naturally belongs to objects of that kind. **4** *Eccl.* Suspension or degradation from office, as of a priest. See synonyms under LOSS, POVERTY, WANT. [<OF <L *privatio, -onis* <*privare.* See PRIVATE.]
priv·a·tive (priv′ə·tiv) *adj.* **1** Causing privation, want, or destitution; depriving. **2** *Gram.* Altering a word so as to express a negative instead of a positive meaning; also, denoting negation: *privative* particles (such prefixes and suffixes as *a-, an-, in-, -less*). **3** *Logic* Noting or denoting negation or privation. — *n.* **1** That which has its only reality in the absence of something; a negative conception. **2** *Gram.* A prefix indicating negation; an adjective indicating the absence of that which is ordinarily or naturally inherent. [<L *privativus.*] — **priv′a·tive·ly** *adv.* — **priv′a·tive·ness** *n.*
priv·et (priv′it) *n.* **1** An ornamental, bushy European shrub (*Ligustrum vulgare*) with white flowers and black berries, used for hedges: naturalized in the United States. **2** Any other plants of the same genus. **3** The swamp privet, an oleaceous tree (*Forestiera acuminata*) of the southern United States. [Earlier *primet*; prob. infl. by *private* because of its screening effect]
priv·i·lege (priv′ə·lij) *n.* **1** A special or peculiar benefit, favor, or advantage; a right or immunity enjoyed only under special conditions; a prerogative, franchise, or permission: the *privileges* of the rich. **2** A special right or power conferred on or possessed by one or more individuals, in derogation of the general right; also, the law or grant conferring it. **3** An exemption, by virtue of one's office or station, from burdens or liabilities to which others are subject: the *privilege* of a member of Congress. **4** A fundamental or specially important legal or political right: the *privilege* of voting. **5** A form of contract used by speculators, but not recognized by the exchanges, giving the holder the privilege of putting (tendering to) or calling for, or either (in which latter case the privilege is called a *straddle*), a certain number of shares of a certain stock, or a specified quantity, as of grain or provisions, under specified conditions as to time and price. Compare OPTION. **6** An advantage. See synonyms under RIGHT. — *v.t.* **·leged, ·leg·ing** **1** To grant a privilege to. **2** To exempt or free: with *from.* [<OF <L *privilegium* a piece of special legislation < *privus* one's own + *lex, legis* law]
priv·i·leged (priv′ə·lijd) *adj.* Having or invested with a privilege; enjoying a peculiar right or immunity.
priv·i·ly (priv′ə·lē) *adv.* Privately; secretly.
priv·i·ty (priv′ə·tē) *n.* *pl.* **·ties** **1** Knowledge shared with another or others regarding a private matter: usually implying consent or concurrence. **2** *Law* **a** A mutual or successive relationship to the same rights of property. **b** A participation in interest. **c** A relation to another founded on common knowledge. **3** *Obs.* Privacy; secrecy; a secret. [<OF *privité* <L *privus* one's own]
priv·y (priv′ē) *adj.* **1** Participating with another or others in the knowledge of a secret transaction: with *to*: *privy* to the plot. **2** *Archaic* Removed from publicity; clandestine; secret: a *privy* meeting. **3** Designed for individual or private use; personal: a *privy* purse, *privy* chamber. — *n. pl.* **priv·ies** **1** One who is concerned with another in a matter affecting the interests of both: *privies* in contract, *privies* in estate. **2** A small room or outhouse for evacuation and disposal of feces. See WATERCLOSET. [<F *privé* <L *privatus.* Doublet of PRIVATE.]
Privy Council In Great Britain, the sover-

eign's ordinary council. Since the duties of government were assumed by the cabinet, the political importance of the Privy Council has largely disappeared.
privy council 1 A body similar to the Privy Council in some British colonies and dominions. **2** A term used by British writers for an analogous body in other countries.
privy councilor 1 A member of a privy council. Also **privy councillor** or **counsellor.**
privy seal In Great Britain, the seal used by the king on papers which later pass under the great seal: also affixed to such documents as do not demand the great seal.
prix fixe (prē fēks′) *French* Table d'hôte: literally, fixed price.
prize[1] (prīz) *n.* **1** That which is offered or won as an honor and reward for superiority or success, as in a contest; an award. **2** Anything to be striven for; a desirable acquisition; also, anything offered or won in a scheme of chance. — *adj.* **1** Offered or awarded as a prize: a *prize* medal. **2** Having drawn a prize; entitled to a prize. **3** Highly valued or esteemed. — *v.t.* **prized, priz·ing 1** To value highly; regard as very valuable. **2** To estimate the value of; appraise. See synonyms under APPRECIATE, ESTEEM. [Var. of PRICE]
prize[2] (prīz) *n.* **1** In international law, property, as a vessel and cargo, captured by a belligerent at sea in conformity with the laws of war. **2** The act of capturing; also, the person or thing captured. **3** A lever or pry; also, the hold or purchase of a lever: also spelled *prise.* — *v.t.* **prized, priz·ing 1** To seize as a prize, as a ship. **2** To raise or force with a lever; pry: also spelled *prise.* [<F *prise* something taken, booty, orig. fem. of pp. of *prendre* take <L *praehendere* seize]
prize court A court sitting for the adjudication of prize causes. In the United States the federal courts have exclusive jurisdiction as prize courts.
prize crew A crew put on board a captured vessel by the captor, to navigate and carry her into port.
prize fight A fight between pugilists for a wager or prize, generally limited to a specified number of rounds. — **prize fighter** — **prize fighting**
prize money The proceeds of the sale of a maritime prize, distributable among the officers and crew of the vessel making the capture: abolished in the United States in 1899.
priz·er (prī′zər) *n.* **1** An appraiser. **2** *Archaic* A contestant for a prize, as in athletics.
prize ring A roped enclosure, 16 or 24 feet square, within which pugilists fight; also, with the definite article, professional pugilism.
pro[1] (prō) *n. pl.* **pros 1** An argument or vote in favor of something: in the phrase *pros and cons.* **2** One who votes for or favors a proposal: usually in the plural. — *adv.* In behalf of; in favor of; for: to argue *pro* and *con.* [<L *pro* for]
pro[2] (prō) *n. pl.* **pros** *Colloq.* **1** A professional athlete. **2** An expert in any field.
pro-[1] *prefix* **1** Forward; to or toward the front from a position behind; forth: *produce*, to lead forth; *project*, to throw forth. **2** Forth from its place; away: *profugate*, to flee away. **3** To the front of; forward and down: *prolapse*, to slip forward and down. **4** Forward in time or direction: *proceed*, to go forward. **5** In front of: *prohibit*, to hold in front of. **6** In behalf of: *prolocutor.* **7** In place of; substituted for: *procathedral, proconsul.* **8** In favor of: *pro-Russian.* [<L *pro-* < *pro* before, forward, for]
pro-[2] *prefix* **1** Prior; occurring earlier in time: *prognosis.* **2** Situated in front; forward; before: *prognathous.* [<Gk. *pro-* < *pro* before, in front]
pro·a (prō′ə) *n.* A swift Malaysian vessel, sailing equally well in either direction, having a sharp stem and stern, a flat lee side, a single outrigger, and a lateen sail. Also *prahu.* [<Malay *prāu*]
prob·a·bil·ism (prob′ə·bəl·iz′əm) *n. Philos.* **1** The doctrine that certainty is unattainable, but that belief and action must be governed by probability. **2** The doctrine that, as long as the existence, interpretation, or application of a law remains truly doubtful, one may follow his own inclination, on the ground that a doubtful law cannot impose a certain obliga-

tion. [<L *probabilis*] — **prob′a·bil·ist** *n.* — **prob′a·bil·is′tic** *adj.*
prob·a·bil·i·ty (prob′ə·bil′ə·tē) *n. pl.* **·ties 1** The state or quality of being probable; likelihood; also, a probable event or statement. **2** *Stat.* The ratio of the chances favoring an event to the total number of chances for and against it. [<F *probabilité* <L *probabilitas, -tatis* < *probabilis.* See PROBABLE.]
Synonyms: chance, credibility, likelihood, likeliness, presumption, verisimilitude. *Antonyms:* doubt, dubiousness, impossibility, improbability, inconceivability, inconceivableness, unlikelihood.
prob·a·ble (prob′ə·bəl) *adj.* **1** Having more evidence than the contrary, but not proof; likely to be true or to happen, but leaving room for doubt. **2** That renders something worthy of belief, but falls short of demonstration: *probable* evidence. [<OF <L *probabilis* < *probare* prove, test]
Synonyms: credible, likely, presumable, reasonable. See APPARENT, LIKELY. *Antonyms:* doubtful, dubious, improbable, incredible, questionable, unlikely.
probable cause A state of facts to warrant the belief that an accused person committed the crime charged.
prob·a·bly (prob′ə·blē) *adv.* In all probability; so far as the evidence shows; presumably.
pro·bands (prō′bandz) *n. Genetics* The original cases constituting the starting point of studies of a specific tainted family. [<L *probandus* to be proved, gerundive of *probare*]
pro·bang (prō′bang) *n. Med.* A slender, flexible rod, tipped with sponge, ball, button, or other attachment, especially used for the insertion of remedies into, or the removal of an obstruction from, the esophagus or larynx; also, a larger form for the relief of choking cattle. [Earlier *provang,* ? blend of obs. *provet* a probe + *fang* catch; infl. in form by *probe*]
pro·bate (prō′bāt) *adj.* **1** Of or pertaining to a probate court. **2** Pertaining to making proof: *probate* proceedings. — *n.* **1** Formal, legal proof, as of a will. **2** The right or jurisdiction of proving wills. Compare PROBATE COURT under COURT. — *v.t.* **·bat·ed, ·bat·ing** To secure probate of, as a will. [<L *probatus,* pp. of *probare* prove]
pro·ba·tion (prō·bā′shən) *n.* **1** A proceeding designed to test character, qualifications, etc., as of candidates for holy orders; examination; trial; novitiate. **2** In criminal administration, a method of allowing a person convicted of a minor offense to go at large under suspension of sentence, but usually under the supervision of a probation officer. **3** The period throughout which a trial or examination extends. **4** The act of proving; also, proof. [<L *probatio, -onis*] — **pro·ba′tion·al, pro·ba′tion·ar′y** *adj.*
pro·ba·tion·er (prō·bā′shən·ər) *n.* **1** One on probation or trial; a novice. **2** A candidate for membership in a church. **3** A convicted criminal or delinquent allowed to be at large but under the supervision of the convicting court and its probation officer.
probation officer A person delegated by the magistrate of a municipal criminal court to supervise an offender on suspended sentence.
pro·ba·tive (prō′bə·tiv) *adj.* **1** Serving to prove or test. **2** Pertaining to probation; proving. Also **pro·ba·to·ry** (prō′bə·tôr′ē, -tō′rē). [<L *probativus*]
probe (prōb) *v.* **probed, prob·ing** *v.t.* **1** To explore with a probe. **2** To investigate or examine thoroughly. — *v.i.* **3** To penetrate; search. — *n.* **1** *Med.* An instrument for exploring cavities, the course of wounds, etc. **2** That which proves or tests. **3** *U.S.* An examination; a searching investigation or inquiry, especially into crime. **4** A space probe. [<L *probare* < *probus* good, proper. Doublet of PROVE.] — **prob′er** *n.*
pro·bi·ty (prō′bə·tē, prob′ə-) *n.* Virtue or integrity tested and confirmed; strict honesty. See synonyms under VIRTUE. [<F *probité* <L *probitas* < *probus* good, honest]
prob·lem (prob′ləm) *n.* **1** A perplexing question demanding settlement, especially when difficult or uncertain of solution; also, any puzzling circumstance or person. **2** *Math.* A proposition in which some operation or construction is required, as to bisect an angle; anything proposed to be worked out. See synonyms under RIDDLE[2]. — *adj.* **1** Presenting

and dealing with a problem, especially a moral, sociological, or emotional problem: *problem* drama. 2 Being a problem, especially in point of behavior, maladjustment, etc.: a *problem* child. [<L *problema* <Gk. *problēma* something thrown forward (for discussion) < *pro-* forward + *ballein* throw]

prob·lem·at·ic (prob'ləm·at'ik) *adj.* Constituting or involving a problem; questionable; contingent. Also **prob'lem·at'i·cal.** [<Gk. *problēmatikos*] — **prob'lem·at'i·cal·ly** *adv.*

pro bo·no pub·li·co (prō bō'nō pub'li·kō) *Latin* For the public good; for the benefit of the public.

pro·bos·cid·i·an (prō'bə·sid'ē·ən) *n.* Any of an order (*Proboscidea*) of ungulates with columnar legs and a snout bearing a proboscis, consisting of the elephants and certain extinct related mammals, as the mammoth, mastodon, etc. — *adj.* 1 Pertaining or belonging to the *Proboscidea.* 2 Of, having, or pertaining to a proboscis.

pro·bos·cis (prō·bos'is) *n.* *pl.* **·bos·cis·es** or **·bos·ci·des** (-bos'ə·dēz) 1 *Zool.* A long flexible snout, as in the tapir; specifically, the trunk of an elephant. 2 *Entomol.* One of various tubular structures protruding or capable of being protruded from the front of the head of certain insects, as the combined mouth parts adapted for sucking in bees, or in certain dipterous insects, as the mosquito, the sheath and needlelike organs for piercing. 3 A human nose, especially when unusually large or prominent: a humorous use. [<L <Gk. *proboskis* < *pro-* before + *boskein* feed]

pro·caine (prō·kān', prō'kān) *n.* A white crystalline compound, $C_{13}H_{20}O_2N_2$, used in its hydrochloride form as a local anesthetic. [<PRO-¹ + (CO)CAINE]

pro·cam·bi·um (prō·kam'bē·əm) *n. Bot.* The nascent tissue giving rise to the vascular bundle of plants. [<NL <PRO-¹ + CAMBIUM] — **pro·cam'bi·al** *adj.*

pro·carp (prō'kärp) *n. Bot.* A one– or several–celled female sexual organ in certain algae, which on fertilization becomes a sporocarp. [<PRO-¹ + -CARP]

pro·ca·the·dral (prō'kə·thē'drəl) *n.* A church or edifice used temporarily as a cathedral.

pro·ce·den·do (prō'sə·den'dō) *n.* *pl.* **·dos** *Law* A writ issued by a superior court to an inferior, remitting a cause that had been brought up on insufficient grounds, and commanding the inferior court to proceed to its determination. [<L, oblique case of *procedendum,* gerundive of *procedere* proceed]

pro·ce·dure (prə·sē'jər) *n.* 1 A manner of proceeding or acting; also, an act or a special course of action. 2 The methods or forms of conducting a business, collectively. 3 *Law* The methods of conducting judicial proceedings as distinguished from the legal definition and recognition of rights. 4 A course of action; a proceeding. 5 The manner of carrying on parliamentary affairs. See synonyms under OPERATION. [<F *procédure*] — **pro·ce'du·ral** *adj.*

pro·ceed (prə·sēd') *v.i.* 1 To go on or forward, especially after a stop or interruption. 2 To begin and carry on an action or process: He *proceeded* to strike her about the head. 3 To issue or come, as from some cause, source, or origin: with *from.* 4 *Law* To institute and carry on legal proceedings. [<OF *proceder* <L *procedere* go forward < *pro-* forward + *cedere* go] — **pro·ceed'er** *n.*

pro·ceed·ing (prə·sē'ding) *n.* 1 An act or course of action; a transaction or procedure: an outrageous *proceeding.* 2 The action of issuing forth; emanation. 3 *pl.* The records or minutes of the meetings of a society, etc. 4 *Law* **a** Any action instituted in a court: a judicial *proceeding.* **b** Any of the various steps taken in a cause by either party: a *proceeding* by writ of error. See synonyms under ACT, TRANSACTION.

pro·ceeds (prō'sēdz) *n. pl.* The useful or material results of an action or course; also, that which accrues therefrom; the amount derived from the disposal of goods, work, or the use of capital; return; yield. See synonyms under HARVEST, PRODUCT, PROFIT.

proc·e·leus·mat·ic (pros'ə·lo͞os·mat'ik) *adj.* 1 In prosody, composed of four short syllables, or pertaining to feet so composed. 2 Animating or inciting, as a song. — *n.* A metrical foot of four short syllables. [<Gk. *prokeleusmatikos* < *prokeleusma* incitement < *prokeleuein* incite < *pro-* before + *keleuein* rouse]

pro·ce·phal·ic (prō'sə·fal'ik) *adj. Anat.* Of or pertaining to the anterior part of the head: a *procephalic* lobe of an invertebrate.

proc·ess (pros'es, *esp. Brit.* prō'ses) *n.* 1 A course or method of operations in the production of something: a metallurgical *process.* 2 A forward movement; progressive or continuous proceeding; passage; advance; course. 3 Any judicial writ or order issued at the commencement or during the progress of an action, as summons, citation, subpoena, or execution; especially, a writ issued to bring a defendant into court; also, the whole course of proceedings in a cause, civil or criminal, from beginning to end. 4 *Biol.* An accessory outgrowth or prominence of an organism. 5 *Physiol.* The fibrous prolongation from the body of the nerve cell (neuron) that carries the outgoing nervous impulse. 6 In patent law, a means of effecting a result otherwise than by mechanism, as by chemical action. 7 *Phot.* Any of the modern methods of producing relief printing surfaces by photography and mechanical or chemical means. — *adj.* 1 Produced by a special method: *process* butter; *process* cheese. 2 Pertaining to, for, or made by, a mechanical or chemical photographic process: a *process* illustration. — *v.t.* 1 To treat or prepare by a special method. 2 *Law* **a** To issue or serve a process on. **b** To proceed against. [<L *processus* progress, orig. pp. of *procedere.* See PROCEED.]

processing tax A tax imposed by the government on the processing of various farm products.

pro·ces·sion (prə·sesh'ən) *n.* 1 An array, as of persons or vehicles, arranged in succession and moving in a formal manner; a parade: a funeral *procession*; also, any continuous course: the *procession* of the stars. 2 The act of proceeding or issuing forth: the *procession* of the Holy Ghost from the Father. 3 A litany or hymn sung by persons moving in orderly array; a processional. — *v.i.* To march in procession. [<OF]

Synonyms: cavalcade, column, cortège, train. *Antonyms*: herd, mob, rabble, rout.

pro·ces·sion·al (prə·sesh'ən·əl) *adj.* Of or pertaining to or moving in a procession. — *n.* 1 A book containing the services in a religious procession. 2 A hymn sung during a religious procession. — **pro·ces'sion·al·ly** *adv.*

process printing Color printing from halftone plates each of which carries one of the primary colors, red, yellow, and blue, with sometimes a fourth plate for black.

process server A person, as a deputy sheriff, who serves summonses or processes.

pro·cès–ver·bal (prô·se'ver·bȧl') *n.* *pl.* **·baux** (-bō') In French law, a detailed statement in writing made by an official relating to the commission of a crime within his jurisdiction; hence, any official report. [<F, lit., verbal process]

pro·chein (prō'shen) *adj. Law* Nearest in time, relation, or degree. Also **pro·chain** (prō'shān, *Fr.* prô·shaṅ'). [<F *prochain* <L *proximus* next]

pro·claim (prō·klām') *v.t.* 1 To announce or make known publicly or officially; declare. 2 To make plain; manifest: His manner *proclaimed* his innocence. 3 To outlaw, prohibit, or restrict by proclamation. See synonyms under ANNOUNCE, AVOW, PUBLISH. [<OF *proclamer* <L *proclamare* < *pro-* before + *clamare* call] — **pro·claim'er** *n.*

proc·la·ma·tion (prok'lə·mā'shən) *n.* 1 The act of proclaiming. 2 That which is proclaimed; a public authoritative announcement. [<OF *proclamacion*]

pro·clit·ic (prō·klit'ik) *adj.* Attached to or dependent on a following word: said of monosyllables attached so closely as to have no separate accent. Compare ENCLITIC, ATONIC. — *n.* A proclitic word. [<NL *procliticus* <Gk. *proklinein* lean forward; formed on analogy of ENCLITIC]

pro·cliv·i·ty (prō·kliv'ə·tē) *n.* *pl.* **·ties** Natural disposition or tendency; propensity: usually with *to*: a *proclivity* to grumble. See synonyms under APPETITE, DESIRE, INCLINATION. [<L *proclivitas* < *proclivus* downward < *pro-* before + *clivus* slope]

Proc·ne (prok'nē) In Greek mythology, an Athenian princess whom the gods transformed into a swallow after she killed her son. Compare PHILOMELA.

pro·con·sul (prō·kon'səl) *n.* 1 In ancient Rome, an official, usually an ex–consul, who exercised consular authority over a province or an army. 2 A governor of a dependency, especially a British one; a viceroy. [<L] — **pro·con'su·lar** (-sə·lər) *adj.* — **pro·con'su·late** (-sə·lit), **pro·con'sul·ship** *n.*

Pro·con·sul (prō·kon'səl) *n. Paleontol.* An extinct ape related to Dryopithecus. [<NL]

Pro·co·pi·us (prō·kō'pē·əs), 500?–565?, Byzantine historian.

pro·cras·ti·nate (prō·kras'tə·nāt) *v.* **·nat·ed, ·nat·ing** *v.i.* To put off taking action until a future time; be dilatory. — *v.t.* To defer or postpone. [<L *procrastinatus,* pp. of *procrastinare* < *pro-* forward + *crastinus* pertaining to the morrow < *cras* tomorrow] — **pro·cras'ti·na'tor** *n.*

Synonyms: adjourn, defer, delay, postpone. See POSTPONE. *Antonyms*: accelerate, dispatch, drive, expedite, hasten, hurry, press, quicken, urge.

pro·cras·ti·na·tion (prō·kras'tə·nā'shən) *n.* The act, tendency, or habit of procrastinating; dilatoriness; delay.

pro·cre·ant (prō'krē·ənt) *adj.* Effecting, conducive to, or connected with procreation or reproduction; generating; fruitful. [<L *procreans, -antis*]

pro·cre·ate (prō'krē·āt) *v.t.* **·at·ed, ·at·ing** 1 To engender or beget (offspring). 2 To originate; produce. See synonyms under PROPAGATE. [<L *procreatus,* pp. of *procreare* < *pro-* before + *creare* create] — **pro'cre·a'tion** *n.* — **pro'cre·a'tor** *n.*

pro·cre·a·tive (prō'krē·ā'tiv) *adj.* Possessed of generative power; reproductive; pertaining to procreation.

Pro·crus·te·an (prō·krus'tē·ən) *adj.* 1 Pertaining to or characteristic of Procrustes. 2 Hence, ruthlessly or violently forcing to conform.

Pro·crus·tes (prō·krus'tēz) In Greek mythology, an Attic giant, killed by Theseus, who tied travelers to an iron bed and amputated or stretched their limbs until they fitted it. [<L <Gk. *Prokroustēs* < *prokrouein* stretch out < *pro-* thoroughly + *krouein* beat]

pro·cryp·tic (prō·krip'tik) *adj. Biol.* 1 Having protective or imitative coloration: said of certain animals, insects, etc. 2 Having the power to adapt coloration to environment, as chameleons. [<PRO-¹ + CRYPTIC]

procto– *combining form Med.* Related to or affecting the rectum or anus: *proctology.* Also, before vowels, **proct–.** [<Gk. *proktos* the anus]

proc·tol·o·gy (prok·tol'ə·jē) *n.* The branch of medicine which treats of the anatomy, physiology, and diseases of the rectum. [< PROCTO- + -LOGY] — **proc·to·log·i·cal** (prok'·tə·loj'i·kəl) *adj.* — **proc·tol'o·gist** *n.*

proc·to·plas·ty (prok'tə·plas'tē) *n.* Plastic surgery of the rectum and anus. [<PROCTO- + -PLASTY]

proc·tor (prok'tər) *n.* 1 An agent acting for another; attorney; proxy; specifically, a practitioner in an admiralty, ecclesiastical, or probate court. 2 A university or college official charged with maintaining order, supervising examinations, etc. — *v.t.* & *v.i.* To supervise (an examination). [ME *proketour, procutour,* contraction of L *procurator* PROCURATOR] — **proc·to·ri·al** (prok·tôr'ē·əl, -tō'rē-) *adj.* — **proc'tor·ship** *n.*

proc·to·scope (prok'tə·skōp) *n.* A surgical instrument for examining the interior of the rectum. — **proc·tos·co·py** (prok·tos'kə·pē) *n.*

Proc·u·lus (prok'yə·ləs), 412?–485, Greek Neo–Platonist and religious commentator. Also **Pro·clos** (prō'kləs, prok'ləs).

pro·cum·bent (prō·kum'bənt) *adj.* 1 *Bot.* Lying on the ground; trailing: said of certain vines and trailing plants. 2 Leaning forward

or lying down or on the face; prone; prostrate. [<L *procumbens, -entis,* ppr. of *procumbere* lean forward <*pro-* forward + *cubare* lie down]

pro·cur·a·ble (prō·kyŏŏr′ə·bəl) *adj.* That can be procured.

proc·u·ra·cy (prok′yər·ə·sē) *n. pl.* **·cies** The management of another's affairs; the office or service of a procurator or proctor.

pro·cur·ance (prō·kyŏŏr′əns) *n.* The process of procuring. Also **pro·cur′al.**

proc·u·ra·tion (prok′yə·rā′shən) *n.* **1** The act of procuring. **2** *Law* **a** The function of an attorney; an agency; a proxy. **b** A power of attorney. [<F <L *procuratio, -onis*] **—proc′u·ra·to′ry** (-rə·tôr′ē, -tō′rē) *adj.*

proc·u·ra·tor (prok′yə·rā′tər) *n.* **1** A person authorized and employed to act for and manage the affairs of another. **2** In ancient Rome, one who had charge of the imperial revenues; an imperial collector, especially in a province; a provincial administrator; a viceroy. **3** The public magistrate of some Italian cities. [<L <*procurare.* See PROCURE.] **—proc′u·ra·to′ri·al** (-rə·tôr′ē·əl, -tō′rē-) *adj.* **—proc′u·ra′tor·ship** *n.*

pro·cure (prō·kyŏŏr′) *v.* **·cured, ·cur·ing** *v.t.* **1** To obtain by some effort or means; acquire. **2** To bring about; cause. **3** To obtain (women) for the gratification of the lust of others. *—v.i.* **4** To be a procurer or procuress. See synonyms under GAIN, GET, OBTAIN, PROVIDE, PURCHASE. [<F <L *procurare* look after <*pro-* on behalf of + *curare* attend to <*cura* care]

pro·cure·ment (prō·kyŏŏr′mənt) *n.* **1** The act of procuring; obtainment; attainment. **2** The act of effecting or causing to be effected.

pro·cur·er (prō·kyŏŏr′ər) *n.* One who procures for another, as to gratify lust; a pander. [<AF *procurour* <L *procurator*] **—pro·cur′ess** *n. fem.*

Pro·cy·on (prō′sē·on) *n.* The most conspicuous star in the constellation Canis Minor; magnitude, 0.5. See STAR. [<L <Gk. *Prokyōn* <*pro-* before + *kyōn* dog]

prod (prod) *v.t.* **prod·ded, prod·ding 1** To punch or poke with or as with a pointed instrument. **2** To arouse mentally; urge; goad. *—n.* **1** Any pointed instrument used for prodding; a goad. **2** A thrust or punch with or as with a prod; a poke. **3** Hence, a reminder. [Origin unknown] **—prod′der** *n.*

prod·i·gal (prod′ə·gəl) *adj.* **1** Addicted to wasteful expenditure, as of money, time, or strength; extravagant. **2** Yielding in profusion; bountiful. **3** Lavish; profuse. *—n.* One who is wasteful or profligate; a spendthrift. See synonyms under IMPROVIDENT. [<OF <Med. L *prodigalis* <L *prodigus* wasteful <*prodigere* drive forth, get rid of <*pro-* forward + *agere* drive] **—prod′i·gal·ly** *adv.*

prod·i·gal·i·ty (prod′ə·gal′ə·tē) *n. pl.* **·ties** Extravagance; wastefulness; lavishness; also, bounteousness. See synonyms under EXCESS. [<OF *prodigalité*]

pro·di·gious (prə·dij′əs) *adj.* **1** Enormous or extraordinary in size, quantity, or degree; vast; excessive. **2** Marvelous; amazing. **3** *Obs.* Of the nature of a prodigy. See synonyms under IMMENSE. [<L *prodigiosus*] **—pro·dig′ious·ly** *adv.* **—pro·dig′ous·ness** *n.*

prod·i·gy (prod′ə·jē) *n. pl.* **·gies 1** Something so extraordinary as to excite wonder and admiration. **2** A person or thing of remarkable qualities or powers: an infant *prodigy.* **3** Something out of the ordinary course of nature; a monstrosity. **4** *Archaic* A portent. [<L *prodigium*]

Synonyms: marvel, monster, miracle, portent, wonder.

pro·drome (prō′drōm) *n. Pathol.* A sign of approaching disease; a premonitory symptom. [<F <L *prodromus* <Gk. *prodromos* forerunner <*pro-* before + *dromos* a running] **—prod·ro·mal** (prod′rə·məl) *adj.*

pro·duce (prə·dōōs′, -dyōōs′) *v.* **·duced, ·duc·ing** *v.t.* **1** To bring forth or bear; yield, as young or a natural product. **2** To bring forth by mental effort; compose, write, etc.: to *produce* a book. **3** To bring about; cause to happen or be: His words *produced* a violent reaction. **4** To bring to view; exhibit; show: to *produce* evidence. **5** To manufacture; make. **6** To bring to performance before the public, as a play. **7** To extend or lengthen, as a line. **8** *Econ.* To create (anything with exchangeable value). *—v.i.* **9** To yield or generate an appropriate product or result.
—prod·uce (prod′ōōs, -yōōs, prō′dōōs, -dyōōs) *n.* That which is produced; a product; specifically, farm products collectively. See synonyms under HARVEST, PRODUCT, WEALTH. [<L *producere* lead forward <*pro-* forward + *ducere* lead] **—pro·duc′i·ble** *adj.*

Synonyms (verb): bear, breed, cause, create, effect, engender, furnish, generate, make, manufacture, occasion, originate, propagate, yield. See ALLEGE, EFFECT, PROVIDE.

pro·duc·er (prə·dōō′sər, -dyōō′-) *n.* **1** One who produces. **2** One who cultivates or makes things for sale and use in distinction from the user or consumer. **3** That which produces or generates. **4** An apparatus for manufacturing producer gas.

producer gas A gaseous fuel with a high content of carbon monoxide and hydrogen, obtained by forcing air or steam through burning coke. Also called *air gas.*

producers' goods *Econ.* Goods having indirect use, as tools or raw materials used in making other goods: opposed to *consumers' goods.*

prod·uct (prod′əkt, -ukt) *n.* **1** Anything produced or obtained as a result of some operation or work, as by generation, growth, labor, study, or skill. **2** *Math.* The result obtained by multiplication. **3** *Chem.* Any substance resulting from chemical change. Compare EDUCT. [<L *productus,* pp. of *producere.* See PRODUCE.]

Synonyms: crop, effect, fruit, harvest, outcome, output, proceeds, produce, production, result, return, yield. See HARVEST, WORK.

pro·duc·tile (prə·duk′til) *adj.* Capable of being extended or drawn out. [<PRO-[1] + DUCTILE]

pro·duc·tion (prə·duk′shən) *n.* **1** The act or process of producing. **2** In political economy, a producing for use, involving the creating or increasing of economic wealth: in contradistinction to *consumption* (by use). **3** That which is produced or made; any tangible result of industrial, artistic, or literary labor. [<F <L *productio, -onis* a prolongation]

Synonyms: composition, performance, work. See PRODUCT, WORK.

pro·duc·tive (prə·duk′tiv) *adj.* **1** Producing or tending to produce; fertile; creative, as of artistic things. **2** Producing or tending to produce profits or increase in quantity, quality, or value: *productive* labor. **3** Causing; resulting in: with *of.* See synonyms under FERTILE, PROFITABLE. [<Med. L *productivus* <LL, fit for production] **—pro·duc′tive·ly** *adv.* **—pro·duc·tiv·i·ty** (prō′duk·tiv′ə·tē), **pro·duc′tive·ness** *n.*

pro·em (prō′əm) *n.* An introductory statement; preface; prelude. [<OF *proeme* <L *prooemium* <Gk. *prooimion* an overture <*pro-* before + *oimē* way of a song, lay] **—pro·e·mi·al** (prō·ē′mē·əl) *adj.*

pro et con (prō′ et kon′) *Latin* For and against.

prof·a·na·tion (prof′ə·nā′shən) *n.* **1** The act of profaning; abuse or dishonoring of sacred things; desecration. **2** Abusive or improper treatment of anything; misuse. [<F <LL *profanatio, -onis*]

pro·fane (prə·fān′) *v.t.* **·faned, ·fan·ing 1** To treat (something sacred) with irreverence or abuse; desecrate; pollute. **2** To put to an unworthy or degrading use; debase. See synonyms under VIOLATE. *—adj.* **1** Manifesting irreverence, disrespect, or undue familiarity toward the Deity or sacred things; blasphemous. **2** Secular: opposed to *sacred.* **3** Not initiated into the inner mysteries; hence, vulgar; common. [<F *profaner* <L *profanare* <*profanus* before or outside the temple, hence, unsacred <*pro-* before + *fanum* temple] **—pro·fan·a·to·ry** (prə·fan′ə·tôr′ē, -tō′rē) *adj.* **—pro·fane′ly** *adv.* **—pro·fan′er** *n.*

Synonyms (adj.): blasphemous, godless, impious, irreligious, sacrilegious, secular, temporal, unconsecrated, ungodly, unhallowed, unholy, unsanctified, wicked, worldly. *Antonyms*: consecrated, devout, godly, holy, pious, religious, reverent, sacred, piritual.

pro·fan·i·ty (prə·fan′ə·tē) *n. pl.* **·ties 1** The state of being profane. **2** Profane speech or action. Also **pro·fane′ness** (-fān′nis). See synonyms under OATH.

pro·fa·num vul·gus (prō·fā′nəm vul′gəs) *Latin* The common herd.

pro·fert (prō′fərt) *n. Law* The formal allegation in a pleading or on the record that the pleader produces in court an instrument on which an action or defense is founded. [<L, he brings forward]

pro·fess (prə·fes′) *v.t.* **1** To declare openly; avow; affirm. **2** To assert, usually insincerely; make a pretense of: to *profess* remorse. **3** To declare or affirm faith in: to *profess* Taoism. **4** To claim skill or learning in; have as one's profession: to *profess* the law. **5** To receive into a religious order. *—v.i.* **6** To make open declaration; avow; offer public affirmation. **7** To take the vows of a religious order. See synonyms under ACKNOWLEDGE, AVOW, PRETEND. [<OF *professe,* fem. of *profes* bound by a vow <L *professus,* pp. of *profiteri* avow, confess <*pro-* before + *fateri* confess]

pro·fess·ed·ly (prə·fes′id·lē) *adv.* **1** By open profession; avowedly. **2** Pretendedly.

pro·fes·sion (prə·fesh′ən) *n.* **1** An occupation that properly involves a liberal education or its equivalent, and mental rather than manual labor; especially, one of **the three learned professions,** law, medicine, or theology. **2** Hence, any calling or occupation other than commercial, manual, etc., involving special attainments or discipline, as editing, music, teaching, etc.; also, the collective body of those following such vocation. **3** The act of professing or declaring; declaration; avowal: *professions* of good will. **4** That which is avowed or professed; a declaration; a faith; also, a pretense: His *professions* are not trustworthy. See synonyms under BUSINESS. [<F]

pro·fes·sion·al (prə·fesh′ən·əl) *adj.* **1** Connected with, preparing for, engaged in, appropriate, or conforming to a profession: *professional* courtesy, a *professional* soldier, a *professional* job. **2** Of or pertaining to a special occupation, often for gain: opposed to *amateur*: a *professional* ball game or player. *—n.* **1** One who pursues as a business some vocation or occupation. **2** A person who engages for money to compete in sports: opposed to *amateur.* **3** One skilled in a profession. **—pro·fes′sion·al·ly** *adv.*

pro·fes·sion·al·ism (prə·fesh′ən·əl·iz′əm) *n.* **1** The methods, manner, or spirit of a profession; also, its practitioners. **2** The practice of some profession as a business: opposed to *amateurism.*

pro·fes·sor (prə·fes′ər) *n.* **1** A teacher of the highest grade in a university or college, or in an institution where professional or technical studies are pursued; usually, an officer holding a chair in some particular branch of higher instruction. **2** One who professes skill and offers instruction in some sport or art: a *professor* of gymnastics. **3** One who makes open declaration of his opinions or sentiments; specifically, one who avows a religious faith. [<L, a public teacher <*professus.* See PROFESS.]

pro·fes·sor·ate (prə·fes′ər·it) *n.* The position of a professor.

pro·fes·so·ri·al (prō′fə·sôr′ē·əl, -sō′rē-, prof′ə-) *adj.* Of or pertaining to a professor; pedagogic; academic. **—pro′fes·so′ri·al·ly** *adv.*

pro·fes·so·ri·ate (prō′fə·sôr′ē·it, -sō′rē, prof′ə-) *n.* Professors collectively, as in a college; professorship.

pro·fes·sor·ship (prə·fes′ər·ship) *n.* The office and duties of a professor; the state of being a professor.

prof·fer (prof′ər) *v.t.* To offer for acceptance. *—n.* The act of proffering, or that which is proffered; a tender; offer. [<AF *proffrir,* OF *poroffrir* <*por-* (<L *pro-*) in behalf of + L *offerre.* See OFFER.] **—prof′fer·er** *n.*

pro·fi·cien·cy (prə·fish′ən·sē) *n. pl.* **·cies** An advanced state of attainment in some knowledge, art, or skill; expertise.

pro·fi·cient (prə·fish′ənt) *adj.* Thoroughly versed, as in an art or science; skilled; expert. *—n.* An expert in any branch of skill or knowledge; an adept. See synonyms under SKILFUL. [<L *proficiens, -entis,* ppr. of *proficere* make progress, go forward <*pro-* forward + *facere* do] **—pro·fi′cient·ly** *adv.*

pro·file (prō′fīl, *esp. Brit.* prō′fēl) *n.* **1** An outline, or contour; a drawing in outline. **2** *Archit.* The outline of a perpendicular section of a building, fort, etc., or the contour of an architectural member, as a base or cornice. **3** A drawing showing the outline of a human face or figure as seen from the side. **4** A short biographical sketch vividly

presenting the most striking characteristics of a personality. 5 Degree of exposure to public attention; public image: The army generals who seized control maintained a very low *profile.* 6 A vertical section of soil extending from the surface through all its levels to the underlying parent material. —*v.t.* **·filed, ·fil·ing** 1 To draw a profile of; outline. 2 To write a profile of. [<Ital. *profilo, proffilo* outline <*proffilare* draw in outline <L *pro-* forward + *filum* thread, line]

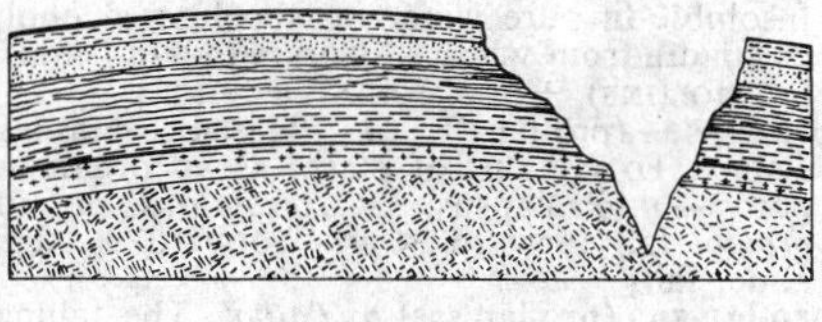

PROFILE OF GRAND CANYON AND KAIBAB PLATEAU

profile drag *Aeron.* The difference between the total wing drag of an airplane and the induced drag.

prof·it (prof′it) *n.* 1 Any accession of good—physical, mental, or moral—from labor or exertion; benefit; return. 2 *Often pl.* Excess of returns over outlay or expenditure: a business yielding fair *profits.* 3 The return from the employment of capital after deducting the amount paid for raw material and for wages, real or estimated rent, interest, insurance, etc. 4 That part of the amount received for goods which exceeds the sum originally paid for them with or without all secondary expenses involved. 5 The income of invested property without counting its increased value by any actual rise in the market. 6 In invested capital, the ratio of the increment to the actual amount of capital for a given year. —**gross profit** The profit apparent on the face of a transaction or business; the excess of receipts from sales over expenditures for purchase: opposed to **net profit,** the surplus remaining after all necessary deductions, as for interest, transportation, bad debts, etc. —*v.i.* 1 To be of advantage or benefit. 2 To derive gain or benefit. —*v.t.* 3 To be of profit or advantage to. ◆ Homophone: *prophet.* [<OF <L *profectus,* pp. of *proficere* go forward. See PROFICIENT.]

Synonyms (noun): advantage, avail, benefit, emolument, expediency, gain, good, improvement, proceeds, receipts, return, returns, service, utility, value. The *returns* or *receipts* include all that is received from any outlay or investment; the *profit* is the excess (if any) of the *receipts* over the outlay; hence, in government, morals, etc., the *profit* is what is really good, helpful, useful, valuable. *Utility* is chiefly used in the sense of some immediate or personal and generally some material *good. Advantage* is that which gives one a vantage ground, either for coping with competitors or with difficulties, needs, or demands; as, to have the *advantage* of a good education; it is frequently used of what one has beyond another or secures at the expense of another; as, to have the *advantage* in argument, or to take *advantage* in a bargain. *Gain* is what one secures beyond what he previously possessed. *Benefit* is anything that does one good. *Emolument* is *profit, return,* or *value* accruing through official position. *Expediency* has respect to *profit* or *advantage,* real or supposed, considered apart from or perhaps in opposition to right, in actions having a moral character. See UTILITY. *Antonyms*: damage, detriment, disadvantage, harm, hurt, injury, loss, ruin, waste.

prof·it·a·ble (prof′it·ə·bəl) *adj.* Bringing profit or gain; remunerative; advantageous. —**prof′·it·a·ble·ness** *n.* —**prof′it·a·bly** *adv.*

Synonyms: advantageous, beneficial, desirable, expedient, gainful, lucrative, productive, remunerative, useful. See EXPEDIENT, GOOD, USEFUL. Compare synonyms for PROFIT. *Antonyms*: detrimental, disadvantageous, disastrous, fruitless, harmful, hurtful, undesirable, unproductive, unprofitable, worthless.

profit and loss In bookkeeping, an account in the ledger in which profits are entered on the creditor side and losses on the debtor side. —**prof′it-and-loss′** (prof′it·ənd·lôs′, -los′) *adj.*

prof·i·teer (prof′ə·tir′) *v.i.* To seek or obtain excessive profits. —*n.* One who is given to making excessive profits, especially to the detriment of others. —**prof′i·teer′ing** *n.*

prof·it·less (prof′it·lis) *adj.* Resulting in no gain or benefit; unprofitable.

prof·it–shar·ing (prof′it·shâr′ing) *n.* A system of remuneration by which workmen are given a percentage, according to wages, of the net profits of a business. —*adj.* Of or related to profit–sharing.

prof·li·ga·cy (prof′lə·gə·sē) *n.* 1 Corruptness of morals; viciousness of character or conduct. 2 Great extravagance; wastefulness; overabundance. Also **prof′li·gate·ness** (-gitnis, -gāt′nis).

prof·li·gate (prof′lə·git, -gāt) *adj.* 1 Lost or insensible to principle, virtue, or decency; abandoned to vice. 2 Recklessly extravagant; in great profusion. —*n.* 1 A depraved or dissolute person. 2 A reckless spendthrift. See synonyms under IMMORAL. [<L *profligatus,* pp. of *profligare* strike to the ground, destroy <*pro-* forward + *fligere* dash] —**prof′li·gate·ly** *adv.*

prof·lu·ent (prof′lo͞o·ənt) *adj.* Fluent. [<L *profluens, -entis,* ppr. of *profluere* flow along <*pro-* before + *fluere* flow] —**prof′lu·ence** *n.*

pro for·ma (prō fôr′mə) *Latin* As a matter of form.

pro·found (prə·found′) *adj.* 1 Intellectually deep; thorough; exhaustive: *profound* learning. 2 Reaching to, arising from, or affecting the depth of one's nature or of any matter: *profound* respect. 3 Situated far below the surface; deep; unfathomable. 4 Bent low: said of a bow. —*n.* 1 A fathomless depth; an abyss. 2 The ocean; the deep. See synonyms under OBSCURE, WISE. [<OF *profond* <L *profundus* <*pro-* very + *fundus* deep] —**pro·found′ly** *adv.* —**pro·found′ness** *n.*

pro·fun·di·ty (prə·fun′də·tē) *n. pl.* **·ties** 1 The state or quality of being profound, in any sense; depth. 2 A deep place or thing. 3 A profound or abstruse statement, theory, or the like. See synonyms under WISDOM. [<OF *profundité* <LL *profunditas*]

pro·fuse (prə·fyo͞os′) *adj.* 1 Giving or given forth lavishly; liberal; extravagant; prodigal. 2 Copious; overflowing: *profuse* vegetation. [<L *profusus,* pp. of *profundere* pour forth <*pro-* forward + *fundere* pour] —**pro·fuse′ly** *adv.* —**pro·fuse′ness** *n.*

pro·fu·sion (prə·fyo͞o′zhən) *n.* 1 A lavish supply or condition; plenty: a *profusion* of ornaments. 2 The act of pouring forth or supplying in great abundance; prodigality: *profusion* in giving. See synonyms under EXCESS. [<F]

pro·gen·i·tor (prō·jen′ə·tər) *n.* A forefather or parent. [<L <*progenitus,* pp. of *progignere* beget <*pro-* forth + *gignere* beget] —**pro·gen′i·tor·ship′** *n.*

prog·e·ny (proj′ə·nē) *n. pl.* **·nies** Offspring. [<L *progenies* <*progignere.* See PROGENITOR.]

pro·ge·ri·a (prō·jir′ē·ə) *n. Pathol.* Retarded development with premature senility. [<NL <PRO-[1] + Gk. *gēras* old age]

pro·ges·ta·tion·al (prō′jes·tā′shən·əl) *adj. Med.* 1 Promoting gestation. 2 Designating those substances and processes which are active in the menstrual cycle or during pregnancy.

pro·ges·ter·one (prō·jes′tə·rōn) *n. Biochem.* A hormone from the corpus luteum: isolated as a white, crystalline compound, $C_{21}H_{30}O_2$, and also made synthetically. It is active in preparing the uterus for reception of the fertilized ovum. [<PRO-[1] + GE(STATION) + STER(OL) + -ONE]

pro·ges·tin (prō·jes′tin) *n. Biochem.* 1 Any substance which promotes the gestational activity of the corpus luteum and uterus after fertilization of the ovum. 2 Progesterone.

pro·glot·tid (prō·glot′id) *n. pl.* **·glot·ti·des** (-glot′ə·dēz) *Zool.* One of the segments or joints of a tapeworm, in which the reproductive organs develop. Also **pro·glot′tis.** [<NL *proglottis, proglottidis* <Gk. *proglossis* tip of the tongue; from its shape] —**pro·glot′tic** *adj.*

prog·na·thous (prog′nə·thəs, prog·nā′-) *adj.* Having projecting jaws: opposed to *opisthognathous.* Also **prog·nath·ic** (prog·nath′ik). [<PRO-[2] + -GNATHOUS] —**prog·na·thism** (prog′nə·thiz′əm), **prog·na·thy** (prog′nə·thē) *n.*

prog·no·sis (prog·nō′sis) *n. pl.* **·ses** (-sēz) 1 *Med.* A prediction or conclusion in regard to the course and termination of a disease. 2 Any prediction or forecast; foreknowledge. [<NL <Gk. *prognōsis* <*pro-* before + *gignōskein* know]

prog·nos·tic (prog·nos′tik) *adj.* Relating to prognosis. —*n.* 1 A sign of some future occurrence; an omen. 2 *Med.* A symptom indicative of the course of a disease. [<Med. L *prognosticum* omen <Gk. *prognōstikon* <*prognōsis.* See PROGNOSIS.]

prog·nos·ti·cate (prog·nos′tə·kāt) *v.t.* **·cat·ed, ·cat·ing** 1 To foretell (future events, etc.) by present indications. 2 To indicate beforehand; foreshadow. See synonyms under AUGUR, PROPHESY. [<Med. L *prognosticatus,* pp. of *prognosticare* <L *prognosticum.* See PROGNOSTIC.] —**prog·nos′ti·ca′tor** *n.*

prog·nos·ti·ca·tion (prog·nos′tə·kā′shən) *n.* 1 The act of prognosticating; prediction. 2 That which foretokens.

pro·gram (prō′gram, -grəm) *n.* 1 A list giving in order the items, turns, selections, etc., making up an entertainment; also, the selections, etc., collectively. 2 Any prearranged plan or course of proceedings; a prospectus. 3 *Electronics* A sequence of instructions set up on the control panels of an electronic computer as guides in the performance of a desired operation or group of operations. 4 A preface, or prefatory statement. 5 *Obs.* A public proclamation; official edict or decree. Also *Brit.* **pro′gramme.** —*v.t.* **·gramed** or **·grammed, ·gram·ing** or **·gram·ming** 1 To arrange in an appropriate sequence the separate items of (a program, set of instructions, etc.). 2 To schedule (an act, performer, etc.) for a program. 3 To furnish a program for (a computer). 4 To feed (information, instructions, etc.) into a computer. [<F *programme* <LL *programma* public announcement <Gk. <*prographein* write in public <*pro-* before + *graphein* write] —**pro′gram·er** or **pro′gram·mer** *n.* —**pro·gram·mat·ic** (prō′grə·mat′ik) *adj.*

programed instruction Instruction in which the learner responds to a prearranged series of questions, items, or statements, using various printed texts, audio-visual means, or a teaching machine. Also **programmed instruction.**

program music Descriptive music; music intended to suggest moods, scenes, or incidents: distinguished from *absolute music.*

Pro·gre·so (prō·grā′sō) A port of entry in Yucatán state, SE Mexico.

prog·ress (prog′res, *esp. Brit.* prō′gres) *n.* 1 A moving forward in space; movement forward nearer a goal. 2 Advancement toward maturity or completion; gradual development, as of mankind or civilization; improvement. 3 A journey of state, as of a monarch.

—**pro·gress** (prə·gres′) *v.i.* 1 To move forward or onward. 2 To advance toward completion or fuller development. [<OF *progres* <L *progressus,* pp. of *progredi* go forward <*pro-* forward + *gradi* walk]

Synonyms (noun): advance, advancement, attainment, development, growth, improvement, increase, proficiency, progression. *Attainment, development,* and *proficiency* are more absolute than the other words of the group, denoting some point of advantage or of comparative perfection reached by forward or onward movement; we speak of *attainments* in scholarship, *proficiency* in music or languages, the *development* of new powers or organs; *proficiency* includes the idea of skill. *Advance* denotes a forward movement or the point gained by forward movement; *progress* (Latin *progredior,* walk forward) is steady and constant forward movement, admitting of pause, but not of retreat. Compare ATTAIN. *Antonyms*: check, decline, delay, retreat, recession, retrogression, stay, stop, stoppage.

pro·gres·sion (prə·gresh′ən) *n.* 1 The act of progressing; advancement. 2 *Math.* A sequence of numbers or quantities each of which is derived from the preceding by a constant law. See ARITHMETIC PROGRESSION, GEOMETRIC PROGRESSION, SERIES (def. 2). 3 *Music*

a An advance from one tone or chord to another. **b** A sequence or succession of tones or chords. **4** Course or lapse of time; passage. See synonyms under PROGRESS. [<L *progressio, -onis*] **— pro·gres′sion·al** *adj.* **— pro·gres′sion·ism** *n.*

pro·gres·sion·ist (prə·gresh′ən·ist) *n.* **1** One who believes that society is progressing toward perfection. **2** An evolutionist.

prog·ress·ist (prog′res·ist, prō′gres-) *n.* **1** A progressionist. **2** A member of any party devoted to some scheme of progress.

pro·gres·sive (prə·gres′iv) *adj.* **1** Moving forward; advancing: *progressive* movement; also, moving forward gradually or step by step. **2** Aiming at or characterized by progress. **3** Spreading from one part to others; increasing: said of a disease: *progressive* paralysis. **4** Striving for or favoring progress or reform, especially social, political, educational or religious: a *progressive* party, *progressive* schools. **5** *Gram.* Designating an aspect of the verb which expresses the action as being in progress at some time in the past, present, or future: formed with any tense of the auxiliary *be* and the present participle; as, He *is speaking*; he *had been speaking*; he *was to have been speaking*; he *will be speaking*. See synonyms under GRADUAL. **—** *n.* **1** One who believes in progress or progressive methods; especially, one who favors or promotes reforms or changes, as in politics or religion; a radical: opposed to *conservative* or *reactionary*. **2** *Gram.* A progressive verb form. **— pro·gres′sive·ly** *adv.* **— pro·gres′sive·ness** *n.* **— pro·gres′siv·ism** *n.* **— pro·gres′siv·ist** *n.*

Progressive party **1** A political party formed under the leadership of Theodore Roosevelt in 1912, which sought political and labor reforms and social security legislation. **2** A political party seeking labor and agricultural reforms, formed in 1924 under the leadership of Robert M. LaFollette. **3** A political party formed in 1948, which nominated Henry A. Wallace for president on a platform advocating full employment and a modification of the then current U.S. foreign policy, particularly in respect to the U.S.S.R.

pro·hib·it (prō·hib′it) *v.t.* **1** To forbid, especially by authority or law; interdict. **2** To prevent or hinder. [<L *prohibitus,* pp. of *prohibere* < *pro-* before + *habere* have] **— pro·hib′it·er** *n.*

Synonyms: debar, disallow, forbid, hinder, inhibit, interdict, preclude, prevent. *Debar* is said of persons, *disallow* of acts; one is *debarred* from anything when shut off by authority or necessity; an act is *disallowed* by the authority that might have allowed it. *Forbid* is less formal and more personal, *prohibit* more official and judicial, with the implication of readiness to use force; a parent *forbids* a child to take part in some game or to associate with certain companions; the opium trade is now *prohibited* by the leading nations of the world. Many things are *prohibited* by law which cannot be wholly *prevented,* as gambling and prostitution; on the other hand, things may be *prevented* which are not *prohibited,* as the services of religion, the payment of bets or military conquest. Compare ABOLISH, HINDER, PREVENT, SHUT. *Antonyms*: allow, authorize, command, direct, empower, enjoin, let, license, order, permit, require, sanction, suffer, tolerate, vouchsafe, warrant.

pro·hi·bi·tion (prō′ə·bish′ən) *n.* **1** The act of prohibiting, preventing, or stopping; also, a decree or order forbidding anything; an interdiction. **2** The forbidding of the manufacture, transportation, and sale of alcoholic liquors as beverages: instituted in the United States effective January 16, 1920. See synonyms under BARRIER, ORDER. [<L *prohibitio, -onis*]

Prohibition Amendment The Eighteenth Amendment to the Constitution of the United States, ratified January 1919, prohibiting the manufacture, sale, or transportation of intoxicating liquors for beverage purposes: repealed in 1933. Compare VOLSTEAD ACT.

Pro·hi·bi·tion·ist (prō′ə·bish′ən·ist) *n.* **1** One who believes in prohibition. **2** One who favors the prohibition by law of the manufacture and sale of alcoholic liquors as beverages.

Prohibition party A political party advocating the prohibition by law of the manufacture and sale of alcoholic liquors as beverages.

pro·hib·i·tive (prō·hib′ə·tiv) *adj.* Prohibiting or tending to prohibit. Also **pro·hib′i·to′ry** (-tôr′ē, -tō′rē). **— pro·hib′i·tive·ly** *adv.*

proj·ect (proj′ekt) *n.* **1** Something proposed or mapped out in the mind, as a course of action; a plan. **2** In schools, a problem involving the theory of the subject matter, given to a student or group of students to be worked out in practice.

— pro·ject (prə·jekt′) *v.t.* **1** To cause to extend forward or out. **2** To throw forth or forward, as missiles. **3** To visualize as an external reality: to *project* an image of one's destiny. **4** To cause (an image, shadow, etc.) to fall on a surface. **5** To propose or plan. **6** *Math.* **a** To make a projection of (a solid, etc.) on a plane. **b** To reproduce (a figure) by drawing lines from a vertex through every point (of the figure) to the corresponding point of the reproduction. **—** *v.i.* **7** To extend forward or out; protrude. See synonyms under PLAN, THROW. [<L *projectus,* pp. of *projicere* throw out, cause to protrude < *pro-* before + *jacere* throw]

Synonyms (noun): contrivance, design, device, invention, plan, purpose, scheme.

pro·jec·tile (prə·jek′təl) *adj.* **1** Projecting, or impelling forward. **2** Capable of being or intended to be projected or shot forth. **3** Protrusile. **—** *n.* **1** A body projected or thrown forth by force. **2** *Mil.* A missile for discharge from a gun or cannon. [<F]

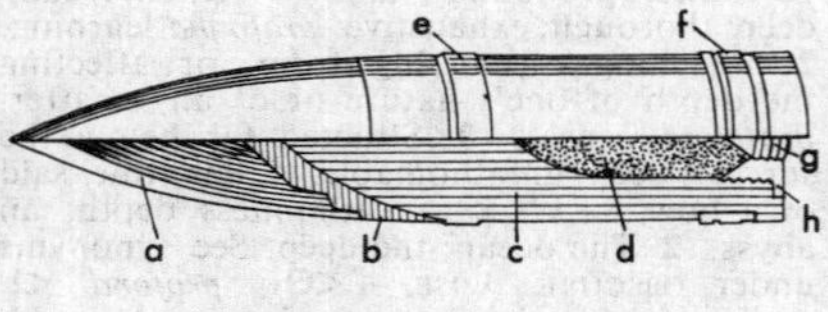

ARMOR–PIERCING PROJECTILE

a. Windshield.	*e.* Bourrelet.
b. Armor–piercing cap.	*f.* Copper rotating band.
c. Body.	*g.* Fuze.
d. Bursting charge.	*h.* Plug.

pro·jec·tion (prə·jek′shən) *n.* **1** The act of projecting; a jutting, throwing, or shooting out or forth. **2** That which projects; a prominence; projecting part or subject. **3** A scheme; project. **4** A system of lines drawn on a given fixed plane, as in a map, which represents, point for point, a corresponding system of imaginary lines on a given terrestrial or celestial datum surface: when used in delineating part of the earth's surface, called a *map projection.* **5** *Psychol.* The process or result of externalizing or objectifying a perception or mental image: compare INTROJECTION. **6** The exhibiting of motion pictures or lantern slides upon a screen. [<F <L *projectio, -onis*] **— pro·jec′tion·al** *adj.*

pro·jec·tion·ist (prə·jek′shən·ist) *n.* **1** One who projects. **2** The operator of motion–picture and sound–reproducing equipment.

projection printing *Phot.* The process of enlarging a photograph by projecting the original negative onto sensitized paper by appropriate adjustment of light source and lens.

projection test *Psychol.* Any of various tests for the determination of personality traits and concealed motivations, as by theatrical performances, the completion of sentences or designs, the interpretation of ink blots, and the like.

pro·jec·tive (prə·jek′tiv) *adj.* **1** Pertaining to, treating of, or derived by projection: *projective* geometry, a *projective* figure. **2** *Geom.* Such as may be derived from one another by projection, as two plane figures. **— pro·jec′tive·ly** *adv.*

projective geometry A branch of geometry which investigates the properties of figures by means of projections in two or three dimensions, including the study of corresponding forms of various dimensions.

pro·jec·tor (prə·jek′tər) *n.* **1** One who devises projects; a schemer; a promoter. **2** That which projects something. **3** A mirror or combination of lenses for projecting a beam of light. **4** An apparatus for throwing illuminated images or motion pictures upon a screen. **5** A device for throwing grenades, bombs, etc.

pro·jet (prô·zhe′) *n. French* A plan or outline; specifically, a draft of a proposed treaty or law.

Pro·kof·iev (prô·kôf′yəf), **Sergei,** 1891–1953, Russian composer. Also **Pro·kof′ieff.**

Pro·ko·pyevsk (prô·kô′pyifsk) A city in the Kuznetsk Basin of Russian S.F.S.R.

pro·lac·tin (prō·lak′tin) *n. Biochem.* A hormone from the anterior lobe of the pituitary gland, believed to be active in initiating lactation. [<PRO-[1] + LACT- + -IN]

pro·la·mine (prō′lə·mēn, -min) *n. Biochem.* Any of a group of simple proteins that are insoluble in pure water or absolute alcohol, as gliadin from wheat. Also **pro′la·min** (-min). [<PROL(INE) + AM(MONIA) + -INE[2]]

pro·lapse (prō·laps′) *v.i.* **·lapsed, ·laps·ing** *Pathol.* To fall out of place, as an organ or part. **—** *n.* Prolapsus. [<L *prolapsus,* pp. of *prolabi* fall forward < *pro-* forward + *labi* glide, fall]

pro·lap·sus (prō·lap′səs) *n. Pathol.* The falling down of an organ, as the womb, from its normal position. [<L]

pro·late (prō′lāt) *adj.* **1** Extended lengthwise. **2** Lengthened toward the poles, as a spheroid generated by the revolution of an ellipse around its long axis: opposed to *oblate.* [<L *prolatus,* pp. to *proferre* extend, carry forward < *pro-* forward + *ferre* carry]

pro·leg (prō′leg) *n. Entomol.* One of the abdominal legs of insect larvae, as of caterpillars. [<PRO-[1] + LEG]

pro·le·gom·e·non (prō′lə·gom′ə·non) *n. pl.* **·na** (-nə) *Often pl.* An introductory remark or remarks; a preface. [<Gk., neut. passive ppr. of *prolegein* say beforehand < *pro-* before + *legein* say] **— pro′le·gom′e·nous** *adj.*

pro·lep·sis (prō·lep′sis) *n. pl.* **·ses** (-sēz) **1** Anticipation. **2** A rhetorical figure consisting in the anticipation, and answering or nullifying beforehand, of objections or opposing arguments. **3** The use of an adjective or a noun as an objective predicate in anticipation of the result of the verbal action: to shoot a person *dead.* **4** An error by which a date earlier than the true date is assigned to an event. [<L <Gk. *prolēpsis* anticipation < *prolambanein* take beforehand < *pro-* before + *lambanein* seize, take] **— pro·lep′tic** (-tik) or **·ti·cal** *adj.*

pro·le·tar·i·an (prō′lə·târ′ē·ən) *adj.* **1** Formerly, of or pertaining to the lower classes of society. **2** Of or pertaining to proletarians or the proletariat. **—** *n.* **1** Formerly, a person of the lowest or poorest class. **2** A laborer; a wageworker. [<L *proletarius* < *proles* offspring; so called because, being propertyless, they served the state only by having children] **— pro′le·tar′i·an·ism** *n.*

pro·le·tar·i·at (prō′lə·târ′ē·ət) *n.* **1** Formerly, the indigent classes collectively of a community; the lower classes. **2** Wageworkers collectively, regarded as the creators of wealth; workingmen. **3** *Bot.* Self–pollinated plants having a small or limited reserve of food materials. [<F *prolétariat.* See PROLETARIAN.]

pro·le·tar·y (prō′lə·ter′ē) *n. pl.* **·tar·ies** In ancient Rome, one of the lowest or poorest class, regarded as contributing to the state nothing but offspring. [See PROLETARIAN]

pro·let·cult (prō·let′kŏŏlt) *n.* A group formed in Russia at the time of the 1917 revolution, originally to develop a proletarian culture as an educational instrument; later transformed into a literary movement. [< Russian *Prolet(arskaya) Kult(ura)* proletarian culture]

pro·li·cide (prō′lə·sīd) *n.* The crime of killing one's own child, before or after birth; infanticide. [<L *proles* offspring + -CIDE]

pro·lif·er·ate (prō·lif′ə·rāt) *v.t.* & *v.i.* **·at·ed, ·at·ing** To produce, reproduce, or grow, especially with rapidity, as cells in tissue formation. [<PROLIFER(OUS) + -ATE[1]] **— pro·lif′er·a′tion** *n.* **— pro·lif′er·a′tive** *adj.*

pro·lif·er·ous (prō·lif′ər·əs) *adj.* **1** Producing offspring freely. **2** Producing branchlets; as a coral. **3** *Bot.* Having an excessive development of parts; developing buds, branches, and flowers from unusual places; bearing progeny in the way of offshoots, buds, etc. [<Med. L *prolifer* <L *proles, prolis* offspring + *ferre* bear]

pro·lif·ic (prō·lif′ik) *adj.* **1** Producing abundantly, as offspring or fruit; fertile. **2** Producing results abundantly; creative: a *prolific* writer. See synonyms under FERTILE. [<F

prolifique <Med. L *prolificus* <L *proles, prolis* offspring + stem of *facere* make] **—pro·lif′i·ca·cy** (-i·kə·sē), **pro·lif′ic·ness** *n.* **—pro·lif′i·cal·ly** *adv.*

pro·line (prō′lēn, -lin) *n. Biochem.* An amino acid, $C_5H_9O_2N$, found in proteins. [Contraction of *pyrroline* <PYRROLE + -INE[2]]

pro·lix (prō′liks, prō·liks′) *adj.* **1** Unduly long and verbose, as an address. **2** Indulging in long and wordy discourse; tedious: a *prolix* orator. [<F *prolixe* <L *prolixus* extended <*pro-* before + stem of *liquere* flow] **—pro·lix·i·ty** (prō·lik′sə·tē), **pro′lix·ness** *n.* **—pro′lix·ly** *adv.*

pro·loc·u·tor (prō·lok′yə·tər) *n.* **1** One who speaks for another; a spokesman or advocate. **2** The presiding officer of a convocation; specifically, the speaker or chairman of the lower house of convocation in the Church of England. [<L <*prolocutus,* pp. of *proloqui* declare, speak for <*pro-* in behalf of + *loqui* talk]

Pro·loc·u·tor (prō·lok′yə·tər) *n. Brit.* In the House of Lords, the lord chancellor. [See PROLOCUTOR]

pro·log (prō′lôg, -log) *n.* A prefatory statement to a poem, discourse, or performance; specifically, an introduction, often in verse, spoken or sung by an actor before a play or opera; hence, any anticipatory act or event. *—v.t.* To introduce with a prolog or preface. Also **pro′logue.** [<OF *prologue* <L *prologus* <Gk. *prologos* <*pro-* before + *logos* discourse]

pro·log·ize (prō′lôg·iz, -log-) *v.i.* **·ized, ·iz·ing** To make or utter a prolog. Also **pro′logu·ize. —pro′log·iz′er** or **pro′logu·iz′er** *n.*

pro·long (prə·lông′, -long′) *v.t.* To extend in time or space; continue; lengthen. See synonyms under INCREASE, PROTRACT. Also **pro·lon′gate** (-lông′gāt, -long′-). [<OF *prolonguer* <L *prolongare* <*pro-* forth + *longus* long] **—pro·long′er** *n.* **—pro·long′ment** *n.*

pro·lon·ga·tion (prō′lông·gā′shən, -long-) *n.* **1** The act of prolonging. **2** That by which anything is increased; an extension. [<F]

pro·longe (prō·lonj′, *Fr.* prô·lôṅzh′) *n. Mil.* A rope having a hook at one end and a toggle at the other: used for drawing a gun carriage. [<F <*prolonger* <OF *prolonguer.* See PROLONG.]

pro·lu·sion (prō·lo͞o′zhən) *n.* **1** That which is introductory to the principal effort or performance; a preliminary attempt; a prolog; prelude. **2** An essay written as a test of the writer's powers, or as preliminary to a more elaborate treatise. [<L *prolusio, -onis* prelude <*prolusus,* pp. of *proludere* play beforehand <*pro-* before + *ludere* play]

prom (prom) *n. U.S. Colloq.* A formal college or school dance or ball: short for *promenade.*

prom·e·nade (prom′ə·nād′, -näd′) *n.* **1** A walk for amusement or exercise, or as part of a formal or social entertainment. **2** A ceremonious parade on horseback or in a vehicle. **3** A place for promenading. **4** A concert or ball opened with a formal march; also, the march. *—v.* **·nad·ed, ·nad·ing** *v.i.* **1** To take a promenade. *—v.t.* **2** To take a promenade through or along. **3** To take or exhibit on or as on a promenade; parade. [<F <*promener* take for a walk <L *prominare* drive forward <*pro-* before + *minare* drive (cattle)] **—prom′e·nad′er** *n.*

promenade deck The deck above the shelter deck in merchant vessels.

Pro·me·the·an (prə·mē′thē·ən) *adj.* **1** Of, pertaining to, or like Prometheus. **2** Creative or life-bringing.

Pro·me·theus (prə·mē′thē·əs) In Greek mythology, a Titan who stole fire from heaven for mankind and as a punishment was chained to a rock, where an eagle daily devoured his liver, which was made whole again at night: he was released by Hercules.

pro·me·thi·um (prə·mē′thē·əm) *n* A radioactive, synthetic metallic element (symbol Pm, atomic number 61) of the lanthanide series, having several isotopes, of which the most stable has a half-life of 17.7 years. See PERIODIC TABLE. [<NL <PROMETHEUS]

prom·i·nence (prom′ə·nəns) *n.* **1** The state of being prominent; conspicuousness; fame. **2** That which is prominent; a protuberance. **3** *Astron.* One of the great tongues of flame shooting out from the sun's surface, seen during total eclipses: also **solar prominence.** Also **prom′i·nen·cy.**

prom·i·nent (prom′ə·nənt) *adj.* **1** Jutting out; projecting; protuberant. **2** Conspicuous in position, character, or importance. **3** Eminent. See synonyms under EMINENT, IMPORTANT. [<L *prominens, -entis,* ppr. of *prominere* project] **—prom′i·nent·ly** *adv.*

pro·mis·cu·i·ty (prō′mis·kyo͞o′ə·tē, prom′is-) *n.* **1** Condition or state of being promiscuous; indiscriminate or confused mixture. **2** Promiscuous sexual union.

pro·mis·cu·ous (prə·mis′kyo͞o·əs) *adj.* **1** Composed of individuals or things confusedly mingled. **2** Unrestricted in distribution or application; exercised or shared without discrimination. **3** Indiscriminate; not fastidious, especially in sexual relations. **4** *Colloq.* Lacking plan or purpose; casual; irregular. [<L *promiscuus* mixed <*pro-* thoroughly + stem of *miscere* mix] **—pro·mis′cu·ous·ly** *adv.* **—pro·mis′cu·ous·ness** *n.*

prom·ise (prom′is) *n.* **1** An assurance given by one person to another that the former will or will not do a specified act. **2** Reasonable ground for hope or expectation, especially of future excellence or satisfaction: a youth of great *promise.* **3** Something promised; the fulfilment or obtainment of that which is promised. See synonyms under CONTRACT. *—v.* **·ised, ·is·ing** *v.t.* **1** To engage or pledge by a promise: used with the infinitive or a clause: He *promised* that he would do it. **2** To make a promise of (something) to someone. **3** To give reason for expecting: The sky *promised* rain. **4** *Colloq.* To assure (someone). *—v.i.* **5** To make a promise. **6** To give reason for expectation: often with *well* or *fair.* [<F *promesse* <L *promissum,* pp. of *promittere* send forward <*pro-* forth + *mittere* send] **—prom′is·er** *n.*

Promised Land See LAND OF PROMISE.

prom·is·ee (prom′is·ē′) *n. Law* One to whom a promise is made.

prom·is·ing (prom′is·ing) *adj.* Giving promise of good results or development. See synonyms under AUSPICIOUS. **—prom′is·ing·ly** *adv.*

prom·is·or (prom′is·ôr) *n. Law* One who makes a promise.

prom·is·so·ry (prom′ə·sôr′ē, -sō′rē) *adj.* **1** Containing or of the nature of a promise; expressing an engagement to pay: a *promissory* note. **2** Indicating what is to be required or to take place after the signing of an insurance contract. Compare WARRANTY. [<Med. L *promissorius*]

promissory note A written promise by one person to pay another unconditionally a certain sum of money at a specified time: also called *note of hand.*

prom·on·to·ry (prom′ən·tôr′ē, -tō′rē) *n. pl.* **·ries** **1** A high point of land extending into the sea; headland. **2** *Anat.* A rounded projection or part. [<LL *promontorium* <L *promunturium,* ? <*prominere.* See PROMINENT.]

Promontory Point A peninsula extending 20 miles south into Great Salt Lake, NW Utah.

pro·mote (prə·mōt′) *v.t.* **·mot·ed, ·mot·ing** **1** To contribute to the progress, development, or growth of; further; encourage. **2** To advance to a higher position, grade, or honor. **3** To work in behalf of; advocate actively: to *promote* social reforms. **4** In education, to advance (a pupil) to the next higher school grade. [<L *promotus,* pp. of *promovere* move forward <*pro-* forward + *movere* move]

Synonyms: advance, aid, assist, elevate, encourage, exalt, excite, foment, forward, foster, further, help, prefer, raise. We *promote* a person by *advancing, elevating,* or *exalting* him to a higher position or dignity. A person *promotes* a scheme or an enterprise which others have projected or begun, and which he *encourages, forwards, furthers,* especially when he acts as the agent of the prime movers of the enterprise. One who *excites* a quarrel originates it; to *promote* a quarrel is strictly to *foment* it, the one who *promotes* keeping himself in the background. See ABET, ENCOURAGE, QUICKEN, SERVE. *Antonyms*: see synonyms for ABASE, ALLAY.

pro·mot·er (prə·mō′tər) *n.* **1** One who or that which promotes. **2** One who assists (by securing capital, etc.) in promoting a financial or commercial enterprise, or who makes this his regular business. **3** *Chem.* A substance used to increase the action of a catalyst. See synonyms under AGENT, AUXILIARY.

pro·mo·tion (prə·mō′shən) *n.* **1** Advancement or preferment in honor, dignity, rank or grade. **2** Furtherance; encouragement. **3** The act of promoting. **4** The state of being promoted. **—pro·mo′tion·al** *adj.*

pro·mo·tive (prə·mō′tiv) *adj.* Tending to promote.

prompt (prompt) *v.t.* **1** To incite to action; instigate. **2** To suggest or inspire (an act, thought, etc.). **3** To remind of what has been forgotten or of what comes next; give a cue to. *—v.i.* **4** To give help or suggestions. See synonyms under ACTUATE, ENCOURAGE, INFLUENCE, STIR[1]. *—adj.* **1** Acting, or ready to act, at the moment; quick to respond or decide; punctual. **2** Done or rendered with readiness or alacrity; taking place at the appointed time. See synonyms under ACTIVE, ALERT, NIMBLE. *—n.* **1** A term of credit allowed for the payment of a debt as stated in a prompt-note. **2** An act of prompting; also, the information imparted by prompting; a reminder. [<OF <L *promptus* brought forth, hence, at hand, pp. of *promere* <*pro-* forth + *emere* take] **—prompt′ly adv. —prompt′ness** *n.*

prompt·book (prompt′bo͝ok′) *n.* An annotated script of a play used by a prompter or director.

prompt·er (promp′tər) **1** In a theater, one who follows the lines and prompts the actors. **2** One who or that which prompts.

promp·ti·tude (promp′tə·to͞od, -tyo͞od) *n.* The quality, habit, or fact of being prompt; promptness. [<F]

prompt-note (prompt′nōt′) *n.* In commerce, a note or memorandum delivered to a purchaser of merchandise as a reminder, and containing a statement of the sum due, day of payment, etc.

pro·mul·gate (prō·mul′gāt, prom′əl·gāt) *v.t.* **·gat·ed, ·gat·ing** To make known or announce officially and formally; put into effect by public proclamation, as a law or dogma. See synonyms under ANNOUNCE, PUBLISH, SPREAD. [<L *promulgatus,* pp. of *promulgare* make known, prob. alter. of *provulgare* <*pro-* forth + *vulgus* the people] **—pro·mul·ga·tion** (prō′mul·gā′shən, prom′əl-) *n.* **—pro·mul·ga·tor** (prō·mul′gā·tər, prom′əl-) *n.*

pro·mulge (prō·mulj′) *v.t.* **·mulged, ·mulg·ing** *Archaic* To promulgate. [<L *promulgare*]

pro·my·ce·li·um (prō′mī·sē′lē·əm) *n. pl.* **·li·a** (-lē·ə) *Bot.* A short-jointed filament, developed on the germination of certain smut or rust spores, and which gives rise to sporidia. **—pro′my·ce′li·al** *adj.*

pro·na·os (prō·nā′os) *n.* In ancient Greece, a portico or vestibule of a temple. [<Gk. <*pro-* before + *naos* temple]

pro·nate (prō′nāt) *v.t.* **·nat·ed, ·nat·ing** To place in a position of pronation. [<L *pronatus,* pp. of *pronare* bow <*pronus* prone]

pro·na·tion (prō·nā′shən) *n. Physiol.* **1** The act or movement of turning the palm of the hand, or the corresponding surface of the forelimb, downward or backward. **2** The position of a limb so turned: opposed to *supination.*

pro·na·tor (prō·nā′tər) *n. pl.* **pro·na·to·res** (prō′nə·tôr′ēz, -tō′rēz) *Anat.* A muscle of the forearm by which pronation is effected.

prone (prōn) *adj.* **1** Lying flat, especially with the face, front, or palm downward; prostrate: opposed to *supine.* **2** Leaning forward or downward; also, moving or sloping sharply downward. **3** Mentally inclined or predisposed: with *to.* See synonyms under ADDICTED, SUBJECT. [<L *pronus* prostrate <*pro-* before] **—prone′ly** *adv.* **—prone′ness** *n.*

pro·neph·ros (prō·nef′ros) *n. Anat.* The primordial kidney, the anterior of three similar tubular organs found in connection with the genitourinary apparatus of typical vertebrates. [<NL <Gk. *pro-* before + *nephros* kidney] **—pro·neph′ric** *adj.*

prong (prông, prong) *n.* **1** A pointed end of an instrument; a tine of a fork. **2** Any pointed

and projecting part, as the end of an antler, etc. — *v.t.* To prick or stab with or as with a prong. [Cf. LG *prange* a pointed stick, Du. *prangen* pinch.]

prong·buck (prông′buk, prong′-) *n.* The male of the pronghorn.

prong·horn (prông′hôrn′, prong′-) *n. pl.* **·horns** or **·horn** A ruminant (*Antilocapra americana*) of western North America, having deciduous branched horns; the Rocky Mountain antelope: not a true antelope.

PRONGHORN
(About 3 feet high at the shoulder)

pro·nom·i·nal (prō·nom′ə-nəl) *adj.* Of, pertaining to, like, or having the nature of a pronoun. [<LL *pronominalis* <L *pronomen.* See PRONOUN.] — **pro·nom′i·nal·ly** *adv.*

pronominal adjective The possessive case of a personal pronoun used attributively: *my, your, his, her, its, our, their, whose,* and, poetically, *mine* and *thine.*

pro·noun (prō′noun) *n.* A word used as a substitute for a noun, as *he, she, that.* [<OF *pronom* <L *pronomen* <*pro-* in place of + *nomen* name, noun]
— **adjective pronoun** Any pronoun used like an adjective; as, *that* boy, *this* house, *which* man. Any demonstrative pronoun, any indefinite pronoun (except *none*), and any interrogative and relative pronoun (except *who*) may be used as an adjective pronoun.
— **demonstrative pronoun** A pronoun that directly points out its antecedents.

	Singular	Plural
	this	these
	that	those

The same forms are used for all genders, persons, and cases.
— **indefinite pronoun** A pronoun that represents an object indefinitely or generally. The principal indefinite pronouns are *another, any, both, each, either, neither, none, one, other, some, such. None* and *any* are both singular and plural.
— **interrogative pronoun** A pronoun that is used to ask a question.

	Subjective	Possessive	Objective
Singular	who	whose	whom
and	which	whose, of which	which
Plural	what	of what	what

Of what occurs in such sentences as *Of what are you speaking? What* are you speaking *of?*
— **personal pronoun** A pronoun that shows by its form the person speaking, the person spoken to, or the person or thing spoken of.

	Singular	*Subjective*	*Possessive*	*Objective*
1st person	I	my *or* mine	me
2nd person	you	your *or* yours	you
	(thou)	(thy *or* thine)	(thee)
3rd person			
masculine	he	his	him
feminine	she	her *or* hers	her
neuter	it	its	it
Plural:			
1st person	we	our *or* ours	us
2nd person	you (ye)	your *or* yours	you
3rd person	they	their *or* theirs	them

— **reflexive pronoun** A pronoun formed by adding *-self* or *-selves* to the oblique cases of the personal pronoun. They serve as an intensive: I, *myself,* was there; or a reference back to a personal pronoun where the same person is both subject and object: He hit *himself.*

	Singular	*Plural*
1st person	myself	ourselves
2nd person	yourself	yourselves
3rd person	himself, her-self, itself	themselves

— **relative pronoun** A pronoun that relates to an antecedent and introduces a qualifying clause: We found a boatman *who* ferried us.

	Subjective	Possessive	Objective
	who	whose	whom
	which	of which	which
	what	of what	what
	that		that

Sometimes *as* and *but* are regarded as relative pronouns: Such men *as* survived the accident;

There is not a man *but* remembers that day.
◆ The relative pronouns *who* (with its inflected forms *whose* and *whom*), *which,* and *what,* are identical in form with the interrogative pronouns but they undergo shifts of meaning in interrogative use, often being indefinite and general in reference: *What* (if anything or of all possible things) is he talking about? But: He is talking about *what* (specifically) he knows best. These pronouns, when used to introduce an indirect question, are by nature both relative and interrogative: They asked *what* he wanted; *whom* he preferred as a colleague; *which* party he belonged to. Similarly, *that* is not only a demonstrative but a relative pronoun and it makes a specific and limiting reference in either use.

pro·nounce (prə·nouns′) *v.* **·nounced, ·nounc·ing** *v.t.* **1** To utter or deliver officially or solemnly; proclaim. **2** To assert; declare, especially as one's judgment: The judge *pronounced* her insane. **3** To give utterance to; articulate (words, etc.). **4** To articulate in a prescribed manner. **5** To indicate the sound of (a word) by phonetic symbols. — *v.i.* **6** To make a pronouncement or assertion. **7** To articulate words; speak. See synonyms under ASSERT, SPEAK. [<OF *pronuncier* <LL *pronunciare* <L *pronuntiare* proclaim <*pro-* forth + *nuntiare* announce] — **pro·nounce′a·ble** *adj.* — **pro·nounc′er** *n.*

pro·nounced (prə·nounst′) *adj.* Of marked character; decided.

pro·nounce·ment (prə·nouns′mənt) *n.* The act of pronouncing; a formal declaration or announcement.

pro·nounc·ing (prə·noun′sing) *adj.* Pertaining to or serving as a guide in pronunciation.

pron·to (pron′tō) *adv. U.S. Slang* Quickly; promptly; instantly. [<Sp. <L *promptus.* See PROMPT.]

pro·nu·cle·us (prō·nōō′klē-əs, -nyōō′-) *n. pl.* **·cle·i** (-klē-ī) *Biol.* The nucleus of either the spermatozoon or ovum, the union of which forms the nucleus of the fertilized ovum. [<NL <Gk. *pro-* before + L *nucleus* a kernel]

pro·nu·mer·al (prō·nōō′mər-əl, -nyōō′-) *n. Math.* A letter or symbol that stands for a number, as x, y, and z in the equation $3x + 2y - z = 13$.

pro·nun·ci·a·men·to (prə·nun′sē-ə·men′tō, -shē-ə-) *n. pl.* **·tos** A public announcement; proclamation; manifesto. [<Sp. *pronunciamiento,*

tion. [<L *pronunciatio, -onis* <*pronuntiatus,* pp. of *pronuntiare.* See PRONOUNCE.]

proof (prōōf) *n.* **1** The act or process of proving, in any sense; specifically, the establishment of a fact by evidence or a truth by other truths. **2** A trial of strength, truth, fact, or excellence, etc.; a test. **3** Evidence and argument sufficient to induce belief. **4** *Law* Anything that serves to convince the mind of the truth or falsity of a fact or proposition, including facts and admissions of parties, which are properly called *evidence,* and presumptions either of fact or of law, and citations of law. **5** The state or quality of having successfully undergone a proof or test; impenetrability; also, impenetrable armor. **6** The standard of strength of alcoholic liquors: see PROOF SPIRIT. **7** *Printing* A printed trial sheet showing the contents or condition of matter in type or of a plate, or the like, either with or without marked corrections. **8** In engraving and etching, a trial impression taken from an engraved plate, stone, or block; also, a perfect impression from such a plate, etc., when finished, and usually before the title or inscription has been added. **9** *Phot.* A trial print from a negative. **10** *Math.* A process to check a computation by using its result; also, a demonstration. **11** Anything proved true; experience. **12** In philately, an experimental printing of a stamp. — *adj.* **1** Employed in or connected with proving or correcting. **2** Capable of resisting successfully; firm; impenetrable: with *against: proof* against bribes. **3** Of standard alcoholic strength, as liquors. [<OF *prueve* <LL *proba* < *probare* PROVE]
— Synonyms (*noun*): attestation, certification, confirmation, demonstration, essay, evidence, fact, ordeal, test, testimony, trial. See CERTAINTY, DEMONSTRATION, TESTIMONY. *Antonyms:* assertion, conjecture, disproof, failure, fallacy, fancy, hypothesis, imagination, likelihood, possibility, presumption, probability, refutation.

-proof *combining form* **1** Impervious to; able to withstand; not damaged by: *waterproof, bombproof.* **2** Protected against: *mothproof, stormproof.* **3** As strong as: *armorproof.* **4** Resisting; showing no effects of: *joyproof, panicproof.* Adjectives formed with *-proof* may also be used as verbs. [<PROOF, *adj.*]

proof·read (prōōf′rēd′) *v.t. & v.i.* **·read** (-red′) **·read·ing** (-rē′ding) To read and correct (printers' proofs).

PROOFREADER'S MARKS

Symbols in the column headed MARGIN are used only in the outer margins of the proof: the symbols used within the body of the text are given in the TEXT column.

MARGIN		TEXT	MARGIN		TEXT
l.c.	Set in lower-case type	circled or /	×	Broken letter: examine	circled
Cap.	Set in capitals	underscored	*tr.*	Transpose matter marked	⌐⌐
s.c.	Set in small capitals	underscored	*eq. #*	Equalize spacing	∨∨∨ ∧∧∧
C+s.c.	Set in caps and small caps		⌐	Move to left to point marked	⌐
l.f.	Set in lightface type	circled	⌐	Move to right to point marked	⌐
b.f.	Set in boldface type	underscored	⌐⌐	Raise to point marked	⌐⌐
Rom.	Set in roman type	circled	⌐⌐	Lower to point marked	⌐⌐
Ital.	Set in italic type	underscored	⌣	Push down space	/
⊙	Insert period	∧	⊃	Close up	⊃
???	Insert colon; semicolon	∧ ∧	⁋	Begin new paragraph	⌐⌐
⌃	Insert comma	∧	*No ⁋*	Run matter on, not a paragraph	∼
⌄	Insert apostrophe	∧	⹀	Aline type	
/?/	Insert interrogation mark	∧	*Stet.*	Retain words crossed out	.....
/!/	Insert exclamation mark	∧	𝔖	Take out and close up	⌐
/=/	Insert hyphen	∧	‖	Line up matter	‖
⹂	Insert quotation marks	∧∧	*Out*	Omission here; see copy	∧
⌄	Insert superior figure or letter	∧	⌐	Move this to left	
⌃	Insert inferior figure or letter	∧	⌐	Move this to right	
⊣ᴍ⊢	Insert one em–dash	∧	*Qu. ?*	Query: is this right?	∧
𝔖	Take out (delete matter marked)	/	*Sp.*	Spell out	circled
w.f.	Wrong font	circled or /	#	Insert space	∧

---

lit., a pronouncement <L *pronuntiare.* See PRONOUNCE.]

pro·nun·ci·a·tion (prə·nun′sē-ā′shən) *n.* The act or manner of pronouncing words; articula-

proof·read·er (prōōf′rē′dər) *n.* One whose business is to read and mark the errors in printers' proofs. — **proof′read′ing** *n.*

proof spirit An alcoholic liquor that contains

a standard amount of alcohol: in the United States, half its volume of alcohol, with a specific gravity of 0.7939 at 60° F., which is rated *100-proof.*

prop[1] (prop) *v.t.* **propped, prop·ping** 1 To support or keep from falling by or as by means of a prop. 2 To lean or place: usually with *against.* 3 To support; sustain. —*n.* That which sustains an incumbent weight; a buttress; stay. [<MDu. *proppe* a vine prop, a support]
Synonyms: bolster, brace, buttress, shore, stay, support, sustain. See SUPPORT.

prop[2] (prop) *n. Colloq.* On a theater stage, any adjunct except the scenery or the costumes of the actors; a property. [Short for PROPERTY]

prop[3] (prop) *n. Colloq.* A propeller.

pro·pae·deu·tic (prō'pə·dōō'tik, -dyōō'-) *adj.* Pertaining to or of the nature of preliminary instruction; relating to or introductory to an art or science: also **pro'pae·deu'ti·cal.** —*n.* A preparatory or introductory subject or course. [<Gk. *propaideuein* teach beforehand <*pro-* before + *paideuein* teach <*pais, paidos* a child]

pro·pae·deu·tics (prō'pə·dōō'tiks, -dyōō'-) *n.* The body of principles or rules introductory to an art or science.

prop·a·ga·ble (prop'ə·gə·bəl) *adj.* That can be propagated; capable of being disseminated or spread abroad, as principles, etc. [<L *propagare* PROPAGATE + -ABLE]

prop·a·gan·da (prop'ə·gan'də) *n.* 1 Any institution or scheme for propagating a doctrine, or system. 2 Effort directed systematically toward the gaining of public support for an opinion or course of action. 3 The tenets, views, etc., put forward by propaganda. [<PROPAGANDA]

Prop·a·gan·da (prop'ə·gan'də) *n.* A society of cardinals, the overseers of foreign missions; also, the College for the Propagation of the Faith, founded by Pope Urban VIII, in 1627, for the education of missionary priests; Sacred Congregation *de Propaganda Fide.* Also **College of Propaganda.** [<Ital. <NL *(congregatio de) propaganda (fide)* (the congregation for) propagating (the faith) <L, gerund of *propagare.* See PROPAGATE.]

prop·a·gan·dism (prop'ə·gan'diz·əm) *n.* The art, practice, or system of using propaganda. —**prop'a·gan'dist** *n.*

prop·a·gan·dize (prop'ə·gan'dīz) *v.* **·dized, ·diz·ing** *v.t.* 1 To subject to propaganda. 2 To spread by means of propaganda. —*v.i.* 3 To carry on or spread propaganda.

prop·a·gate (prop'ə·gāt) *v.* **·gat·ed, ·gat·ing** *v.t.* 1 To cause (animals, plants, etc.) to multiply by natural reproduction; breed. 2 To reproduce (itself). 3 To spread abroad or from person to person; diffuse; disseminate. 4 To transmit through a medium; extend the action of: to *propagate* heat. 5 *Obs.* To increase. —*v.i.* 6 To multiply by natural reproduction; have offspring; breed. [<L *propagatus,* pp. of *propagare* slip or layer a plant, multiply <*propago* a slip for transplanting <*pro-* forth + *pag-,* root of *pangere* fasten] —**prop'a·ga'tive** *adj.* —**prop'a·ga'tor** *n.*
Synonyms: beget, breed, engender, generate, increase, multiply, originate, procreate. See PRODUCE, SPREAD. *Antonyms*: annihilate, destroy, eradicate, exterminate, extirpate.

prop·a·ga·tion (prop'ə·gā'shən) *n.* 1 The act of propagating; reproduction. 2 Dissemination; diffusion.

prop·a·gule (prop'ə·gyōōl) *n. Bot.* A bud, shoot, or other plant part which vegetatively propagates the species. Also **pro·pag·u·lum** (prō·pag'yə·ləm). [<NL *propagulum,* dim. of L *propago.* See PROPAGATE.]

pro·pane (prō'pān) *n. Chem.* A gaseous hydrocarbon of the methane series, C_3H_8, obtained from petroleum and also made synthetically. [<PROP(YL) + (METH)ANE]

pro·par·ox·y·tone (prō'pə·rok'sə·tōn) *adj.* Having an acute accent on the antepenult. —*n.* A word with an acute accent on the antepenult. [<Gk. *proparoxytonos* <*pro-* before + *paroxytonos* paroxytone]

pro pa·tri·a (prō pā'trē·ə) *Latin* For one's country.

pro·pel (prə·pel') *v.t.* **·pelled, ·pel·ling** To cause to move forward or ahead; drive or urge forward. See synonyms under DRIVE, PUSH, SEND. [<L *propellere* drive before one <*pro-* forward + *pellere* drive]

pro·pel·lant (prə·pel'ənt) *n.* 1 That which propels. 2 *Mil.* An explosive which, upon ignition, propels a projectile from a gun. 3 A solid or liquid fuel which serves to propel a rocket, guided missile, or the like.

pro·pel·lent (prə·pel'ənt) *adj.* Propelling; able to propel. [<L *propellens, -entis,* ppr. of *propellere.* See PROPEL.]

pro·pel·ler (prə·pel'ər) *n.* 1 One who or that which propels. 2 Any device for propelling a craft through water or air; especially, one having blades mounted at an angle on a power-driven shaft and producing a thrust by their rotary action on the fluid.

pro·pend (prō·pend') *v.i. Obs.* To be disposed in favor; tend. [<L *propendere* hang forward, be inclined or favorable <*pro-* forward + *pendere* hang]

pro·pene (prō'pēn) *n.* Propylene. [<PROP(YL) + -ENE]

pro·pe·no·ic acid (prō'pə·nō'ik) See under ACRYLIC. [<PROPEN(E) + (BENZ)OIC]

pro·pense (prō·pens') *adj. Obs.* Having a propensity; prone. [<L *propensus,* pp. of *propendere.* See PROPEND.] —**pro·pense'ly** *adv.*

pro·pen·si·ty (prə·pen'sə·tē) *n. pl.* **·ties** 1 Natural disposition to or for; tendency. 2 *Obs.* A liking for; partiality. See synonyms under APPETITE, DESIRE, INCLINATION. [<L *propensus.* See PROPENSE.]

prop·er (prop'ər) *adj.* 1 Having special adaptation or fitness; specially suited; applicable; appropriate. 2 Conforming to a standard; becoming; seemly; correct. 3 Naturally belonging to a person or thing; particular; peculiar. 4 Understood in the most correct sense; strictly so called: commonly following the noun modified. 5 *Gram.* Belonging to an individual person, family, place, or the like: a *proper* noun: opposed to *common.* 6 *Archaic* Belonging to or affecting oneself; own. 7 *Her.* Represented in the natural color. 8 *Eccl.* Appointed for special use: the *proper* psalms for Christmas. 9 *Archaic* Of becoming form or appearance. 10 *Archaic* Good; excellent; pleasant. 11 *Obs.* Respectable; worthy; honest. See synonyms under APPROPRIATE, BECOMING, CONVENIENT, CORRECT, GOOD, MODEST. —*n.* A collection of prayers; specifically, that portion of the breviary or missal containing the prayers and collects suitable to special occasions. [<OF *propre* <L *proprius* one's own] —**prop'er·ness** *n.*

proper fraction See under FRACTION.

prop·er·ly (prop'ər·lē) *adv.* In a proper manner; suitably; rightly.

proper noun See under NOUN.

prop·er·tied (prop'ər·tēd) *adj.* Owning property.

Pro·per·tius (prō·pûr'shəs), **Sextus,** 50?–14? B.C., Roman poet.

prop·er·ty (prop'ər·tē) *n. pl.* **·ties** 1 Any object of value that a person may lawfully acquire and hold; anything that may be owned; stocks, land, etc.; any possession. 2 Ownership or dominion; the legal right to the possession, use, enjoyment, and disposal of a thing; a valuable legal right or interest in or to particular things. 3 Whatever belongs or pertains to any object, as a distinguishing quality or characteristic; a peculiarity. 4 In the theater, any portable article, except scenery, which is not personally owned by the actors, but which is used by them in the performance, as flowers, books, dishes, etc. 5 A characteristic attribute of a body or substance under stated conditions, especially in relation to the senses, as color, odor, hardness, density, etc. 6 Any typical mode of action or behavior observed in natural phenomena: a *property* of radiation. [<OF *proprieté* <L *proprietas, -tatis* <*proprius* one's own. Doublet of PROPRIETY.]
Synonyms: chattels, estate, goods, means, money, ownership, possessions, resources, right, wealth. See ATTRIBUTE, CHARACTERISTIC, MONEY, WEALTH.

pro·phase (prō'fāz) *n. Biol.* One of the preparatory changes in the mitosis of the cell, during which the chromatin of the nucleus is formed into longitudinally split chromosomes. [<PRO-[2] before + PHASE]

proph·e·cy (prof'ə·sē) *n. pl.* **·cies** 1 A prediction made under divine influence and direction; loosely, any prediction. 2 Discourse delivered by a prophet under divine inspiration: the common Biblical sense. 3 A book of prophecies. 4 *Obs.* Public interpretation of Scripture; preaching. [<OF *profecie* <LL *prophetia* <Gk. *prophēteia* <*prophētēs* <*pro-* before + *phanai* speak]

proph·e·sy (prof'ə·sī) *v.* **·sied, ·sy·ing** *v.t.* 1 To utter or foretell with or as with divine inspiration. 2 To predict (a future event). 3 To point out beforehand. —*v.i.* 4 To speak by divine influence, or as a medium between God and man. 5 To foretell the future; make predictions. 6 To explain or teach religious subjects; preach. [<OF *prophecier* <*profecie* PROPHECY] —**proph'e·si'er** *n.*
Synonyms: augur, divine, foretell, predict, prognosticate. *Prophesy* differs from *predict* by assuming a claim to supernatural or divine inspiration. To *prognosticate* is to *predict* from observed signs, indications, or conditions. To *prophesy* in the Scriptural sense is to utter religious truth under divine inspiration, not necessarily to *foretell* future events, but to warn, exhort, comfort, etc. See AUGUR. *Antonyms*: chronicle, recall, recite, recollect, record, remember.

proph·et (prof'it) *n.* 1 One who delivers divine messages or interprets the divine will. 2 One who foretells the future; especially, an inspired predictor. 3 A religious leader. 4 An interpreter or spokesman for any cause. 5 A mantis. —**the Prophet** According to Islam, Mohammed. —**the Prophets** The Old Testament books written by the prophets. ◆ Homophone: *profit.* [<Gk. *prophētēs* <*pro-* before + *phanai* speak] —**proph'et·ess** *n. fem.* — —**proph'et·hood** (-hŏŏd) *n.*

pro·phet·ic (prə·fet'ik) *adj.* 1 Of or pertaining to a prophet or prophecy; vatic. 2 Pertaining to or involving prediction or presentiment; predictive. Also **pro·phet'i·cal.** —**pro·phet'i·cal·ly** *adv.* —**pro·phet'i·cal·ness** *n.*

pro·phy·lac·tic (prō'fə·lak'tik, prof'ə-) *adj.* Operating to ward off something, especially disease; preventive. —*n.* A prophylactic medicine or appliance. [<Gk. *prophylaktikos* <*prophylassein* be on guard <*pro-* before + *phylassein* guard]

pro·phy·lax·is (prō'fə·lak'sis, prof'ə-) *n.* Preventive treatment for disease. [<NL <Gk. *pro-* before + *phylaxis* a guarding]

pro·pine (prō·pīn') *Scot. v.t.* To offer, as a gift; propose. —*n.* An offering; pledge.

pro·pin·qui·ty (prō·ping'kwə·tē) *n.* 1 Nearness in place or time. 2 Kinship. See synonyms under APPROXIMATION. [<OF *propinquité* <L *propinquitas, -tatis* <*propinquus* near]

pro·pi·o·nate (prō'pē·ə·nāt') *n. Chem.* An organic compound containing the radical CH_3-CH_2COO. [<PRO(TO)- + Gk. *piōn* fat + -ATE[3]]

pro·pi·on·ic (prō'pē·on'ik, -ō'nik) *adj. Chem.* Designating a colorless, liquid acid, $C_3H_6O_2$, occurring in nature, as in beet root molasses, and also produced variously by synthesis. It is the first member in the series of fatty acids.

pro·pi·theque (prō'pə·thēk') *n.* Sifaka. [<F <NL *Propithecus* <Gk. *pro-* before + *pithēkos* an ape]

pro·pi·ti·ate (prō·pish'ē·āt) *v.t.* **·at·ed, ·at·ing** To cause to be favorably disposed; appease; conciliate. [<L *propitiatus,* pp. of *propitiare* render favorable, appease <*propitius* PROPITIOUS] —**pro·pi·ti·a·ble** (prō·pish'ē·ə·bəl) *adj.* —**pro·pi'ti·at'ing·ly** *adv.* —**pro·pi'ti·a'tive** *adj.* —**pro·pi'ti·a'tor** *n.*

pro·pi·ti·a·tion (prō·pish'ē·ā'shən) *n.* 1 The act of propitiating. 2 That which propitiates.
Synonyms: atonement, expiation, reconciliation, satisfaction. *Atonement* (at-one-ment), originally denoting *reconciliation,* or the bringing into agreement of those who have been estranged, is now chiefly used, as in theology, in the sense of some offering, sacrifice, or suffering sufficient to win forgiveness or make up for an offense. *Expiation* is the enduring of the full penalty of a wrong or crime. *Propitiation* is an offering, action, or sacrifice that makes the governing power propitious toward the offender. *Satisfaction*

denotes the rendering a full legal equivalent for the wrong done. *Propitiation* appeases the lawgiver; *satisfaction* meets the requirements of the law. *Antonyms*: alienation, condemnation, estrangement, offense, penalty, punishment, reprobation.

pro·pi·ti·a·to·ry (prō·pish′ē·ə·tôr′ē, -tō′rē) *adj.* Pertaining to or causing propitiation. —*n. pl.* **·ries 1** A propitiation. **2** In Jewish antiquity, the mercy seat regarded as symbolizing the merciful presence of Jehovah.

pro·pi·tious (prō·pish′əs) *adj.* **1** Kindly disposed; gracious. **2** Attended by favorable circumstances; auspicious. [<OF *propicius* <L *propitius* favorable, prob. <*pro-* before, forward + *petere* seek] —**pro·pi′tious·ly** *adv.* —**pro·pi′tious·ness** *n.*

Synonyms: auspicious, benign, benignant, clement, favorable, friendly, gracious, kind, kindly, merciful. That which is *auspicious* is of *favorable* omen; that which is *propitious* is of favoring influence or tendency; as, an *auspicious* morning; a *propitious* breeze. *Propitious* applies to persons, implying *kind* disposition and *favorable* inclinations, especially toward the suppliant; *auspicious* is not used of persons. See AUSPICIOUS. *Antonyms*: adverse, antagonistic, ill–disposed, inauspicious, repellent, unfavorable, unfriendly, unpropitious.

prop·jet (prop′jet′) *n.* Turboprop.

prop·o·lis (prop′ə·lis) *n.* A resinous, adhesive substance elaborated by bees to serve as a cementing material. [<L <Gk. <*pro-* before + *polis* a city]

pro·pone (prə·pōn′) *v.t.* **·poned, ·pon·ing** *Scot.* To propose or propound; put forward.

pro·po·nent (prə·pō′nənt) *n.* **1** One who makes a proposal or puts forward a proposition; one who propounds a thing. **2** *Law* One who presents a will for probate. **3** One who advocates or supports a cause or doctrine. [<L *proponens, -entis,* ppr. of *proponere* set forth <*pro-* forth + *ponere* put]

Pro·pon·tis (prə·pon′tis) The ancient name for the SEA OF MARMARA.

pro·por·tion (prə·pôr′shən, -pōr′-) *n.* **1** Relative magnitude, number, or degree, as existing between parts, a part and a whole, or different things. **2** Fitness and harmony; symmetry. **3** A proportionate or proper share; any share or part. **4** An equality or identity between ratios. **5** *Math.* That rule by which, when three numbers are given, a fourth can be found having the same ratio to the third as the second has to the first: also called *the rule of three,* three of the four terms being always given. **6** *pl.* Size; dimensions: a picture of large *proportions.* See synonyms under ANALOGY, PORTION, SYMMETRY. —*v.t.* **1** To adjust properly as to relative magnitude, amount, or degree: to *proportion* one's expenses to one's means. **2** To form with a harmonious relation of parts. [<OF *proporcion* <L *proportio, -onis* <*pro* before + *portio, -onis* a share] —**pro·por′tion·a·ble** *adj.* —**pro·por′tion·a·bly** *adv.* —**pro·por′tion·er** *n.*

pro·por·tion·al (prə·pôr′shən·əl, -pōr′-) *adj.* **1** Of, pertaining to, or being in proportion. **2** *Math.* **a** Constituting the terms of a proportion: said of four quantities: The numbers 2, 3, and 8, 12 are *proportional.* **b** Varying so that corresponding values form a proportion. —*n.* Any quantity or number in proportion to another or others. —**pro·por′tion·al·ly** *adv.* —**pro·por′tion·al′i·ty** (-al′ə·tē) *n.*

proportional representation A system of election by which political parties secure legislative representation in a government in proportion to voting strength.

pro·por·tion·ate (prə·pôr′shən·it, -pōr′-) *adj.* Being in due proportion; proportional. —*v.t.* (-āt) **·at·ed, ·at·ing** To make proportionate. —**pro·por′tion·ate·ly** *adv.* —**pro·por′tion·ate·ness** *n.*

pro·por·tion·ment (prə·pôr′shən·mənt, -pōr′-) *n.* The act of placing or putting things in proportion; arrangement; distribution.

pro·po·sal (prə·pō′zəl) *n.* **1** An offer proposing something to be accepted or adopted. **2** An offer of marriage. **3** Something proposed, as a scheme or plan.

Synonyms: bid, offer, overture, proposition. An *offer* or *proposal* puts something before one for acceptance or rejection, *proposal* being the more formal word; a *proposition* sets forth truth (or what is claimed to be truth) in formal statement. The *proposition* is for consideration, the *proposal* for action; as, a *proposition* in geometry, a *proposal* of marriage; but *proposition* is often used nearly in the sense of *proposal* when it is a matter for deliberation; as, a *proposition* for the surrender of a fort. A *bid* is commercial and often verbal; as, a *bid* at an auction. An *overture* opens negotiation or conference, and the word is especially used of some movement toward reconciliation; as, *overtures* of peace. See synonyms under DESIGN. *Antonyms*: acceptance, decision, denial, refusal, rejection, repulse.

pro·pose (prə·pōz′) *v.* **·posed, ·pos·ing** *v.t.* **1** To put forward for acceptance or consideration. **2** To nominate, as for admission or appointment. **3** To intend; purpose. **4** To suggest the drinking of (a toast or health). —*v.i.* **5** To form or announce a plan or design. **6** To make an offer, as of marriage. [<OF *proposer* <*pro-* forth (<L) + *poser.* See POSE[1].] —**pro·pos′er** *n.*

Synonym: purpose. In its most frequent use, *propose* differs from *purpose* in that what we *purpose* lies in our own mind as a decisive act of will, a determination; what we *propose* is offered or stated to others. In this use of the word, what we *propose* is open to deliberation, as what we *purpose* is not. In another use of the word one *proposes* something to or by himself which may or may not be stated to others. In this latter sense *propose* is nearly identical with *purpose.* See PLAN, PURPOSE.

prop·o·si·tion (prop′ə·zish′ən) *n.* **1** A scheme or proposal offered for consideration or acceptance. **2** *U.S. Colloq.* Any matter or person to be dealt with: a tough *proposition.* **3** *Colloq.* An indecent or immodest proposal. **4** A subject or statement presented for discussion. **5** *Logic* A statement in which something (the *subject*) is affirmed or denied in terms of something else (the *predicate*), the two being related usually by a copula. In the propositions, *Grass is green* and *Grass is not red,* grass in each case is the subject and green and red are the predicates respectively. **6** *Math.* A statement of a truth to be demonstrated (a *theorem*) or of an operation to be performed (a *problem*). See synonyms under PROPOSAL. —*v.t. Colloq.* To make an improper suggestion to. [<OF <L *propositio, -onis* a setting forth <*propositus,* pp. of *proponere.* See PROPONENT.] —**prop′o·si′tion·al** *adj.* —**prop′o·si′tion·al·ly** *adv.*

pro·pos·i·tus (prō·poz′i·təs) *n. pl.* **·ti** (-tī) *Law* The person from whom a line of descent is reckoned. [<L. See PROPOSITION.]

pro·pound (prō·pound′) *v.t.* To put forward for consideration, solution, etc. See synonyms under AFFIRM, ANNOUNCE. [Earlier *propone* <L *proponere* set forth. See PROPONENT.] —**pro·pound′er** *n.*

pro·pre·tor (prō·prē′tər) *n.* In ancient Rome, an officer, especially a governor of a province, having the authority of a pretor without pretorian rank. Also **pro·prae′tor.** [<L *propraetor* <*pro praetore* (one acting) for the pretor < *pro-* for + *praetor* a pretor]

pro·pri·e·tar·y (prə·prī′ə·ter′ē) *adj.* **1** Pertaining to a proprietor; subject to exclusive ownership. **2** Designating an article, as a therapeutic device or medicine, protected as to name, composition, or process of manufacture by copyright, patent, secrecy, or other means. —*n. pl.* **·tar·ies 1** A proprietor or proprietors collectively. **2** Proprietorship. [<LL *proprietarius* <*proprietas* PROPERTY]

proprietary colony A colony organized under a royal grant of territory with full administrative powers to a private person or persons. Maryland, Pennsylvania, and Delaware remained proprietary colonies until the Revolution.

pro·pri·e·tor (prə·prī′ə·tər) *n.* A person having the exclusive title to anything. —**pro·pri′e·tor·ship′** *n.* —**pro·pri′e·tress** *n. fem.*

pro·pri·e·ty (prə·prī′ə·tē) *n. pl.* **·ties 1** The character or quality of being proper; especially, accordance with recognized usage, custom, or principles; becomingness; fitness; correctness. **2** *Obs.* An exclusive right of possession; also, a possession or property owned. —**the proprieties** The methods or standards of good society. [<OF *proprieté.* Doublet of PROPERTY.]

pro·pri·o·cep·tor (prō′prē·ə·sep′tər) *n. Physiol.* One of the sensory receptors situated within the body which are responsive to internal stimuli, as the muscles, joints, and tendons. [<NL <L *proprius* one's own + (RE)CEPTOR] —**pro′pri·o·cep′tive** *adj.*

prop root *Bot.* The supporting root of a plant, growing into the soil from above ground, as in corn.

prop·to·sis (prop·tō′sis) *n. Med.* A forward displacement; bulging, as of the eyeball. [< LL <Gk. *proptōsis* a falling forward < *propiptein* fall forwards <*pro-* forward + *piptein* fall]

pro·pul·sion (prə·pul′shən) *n.* **1** The act or operation of propelling. **2** An impulse given or received. [<F <L *propulsus,* pp. of *propellere* PROPEL] —**pro·pul′sive** (-siv) *adj.*

pro·pyl (prō′pil) *n. Chem.* The univalent radical, C_3H_7, derived from propane. [<PROP(IONIC) + -YL]

prop·y·lae·um (prop′ə·lē′əm) *n. pl.* **·lae·a** (-lē′ə) *Usually pl.* A structure forming an imposing entrance or gateway before an ancient temple; more widely, a porch or vestibule. [<L <Gk. *propylaion* <*pro-* before +*pylē* a gate]

pro·pyl·ene (prō′pə·lēn) *n. Chem.* A gaseous hydrocarbon, C_3H_6, obtained from propane and as a by–product in petroleum refining. Also called *propene.* [<PROPYL +-ENE]

prop·y·lite (prop′ə·līt) *n.* A variety of andesite which has been altered by the action of hot water. [<Gk. *propylon* PROPYLON + -ITE[1]; so called because thought of as opening the Tertiary epoch]

prop·y·lon (prop′ə·lon) *n. pl.* **·la** (-lə) A monumental gateway placed before the principal entrance of an important building of ancient Egypt, as a temple. [<L <Gk. <*pro-* before + *pylē* a gate]

pro ra·ta (prō rā′tə, rat′ə, rä′tə) In proportion: The loss was shared *pro rata.* [<L *pro rata (parte)* according to the calculated (share)]

pro·rate (prō·rāt′, prō′rāt′) *v.t.* & *v.i.* **·rat·ed, ·rat·ing** To distribute or divide proportionately. [<PRO RATA] —**pro·rat′a·ble** *adj.* —**pro·ra′tion** *n.*

prore (prôr) *n. Obs.* A prow. [<MF <L *prora* a prow]

pro·ro·ga·tion (prō′rə·gā′shən) *n.* **1** The act of proroguing, as a session of the British Parliament. **2** The act of prolonging or extending in time; also, continuance; prolongation. [< OF *prorogacion* <L *prorogatio, -onis* < *prorogatus,* pp. of *progrogare* PROROGUE]

pro·rogue (prō·rōg′) *v.t.* **·rogued, ·ro·guing 1** To discontinue a session of (an assembly, especially the British Parliament). **2** *Obs.* To put off or postpone. **3** *Obs.* To protract or prolong. [<MF *proroguer* <L *prorogare* prolong <*pro-* forth + *rogare* ask]

pro·sa·ic (prō·zā′ik) *adj.* **1** Lacking in those qualities that impart animation or interest; unimaginative; commonplace; dull. **2** Pertaining to or having the form of prose. Also **pro·sa′i·cal.** [<LL*prosaicus* <L *prosa* prose] —**pro·sa′ic·ness** *n.*

pro·sa·ism (prō′zā·iz′əm) *n.* A prosaic expression, phrase or style. [<F *prosaïsme* <L *prosa* prose]

pro·sce·ni·um (prō·sē′nē·əm) *n. pl.* **·ni·a** (-nē·ə) **1** In a modern theater or similar building, that part of the stage between the curtain or drop scene and the orchestra, sometimes including the curtain and its arch. **2** In the ancient theater, the wall that formed a background for the actors. [<L <Gk. *proskēnion* <*pro-* before + *skēnē* a stage, orig. a tent]

pro·sciut·to (prō·shōō′tō) *n.* A spicy, cured ham. [<Ital.]

pro·scribe (prō·skrīb′) *v.t.* **·scribed, ·scrib·ing 1** To denounce or condemn; prohibit; interdict. **2** To outlaw or banish. **3** In ancient Rome, to publish the name of (one condemned or exiled). [<L *proscribere* <*pro-* before + *scribere* write] —**pro·scrib′er** *n.*

pro·scrip·tion (prō·skrip′shən) *n.* The act of proscribing. or state of being proscribed; interdiction; ostracism; outlawry. [<L *proscriptio, -onis* <*proscriptus,* pp. of *proscribere* PROSCRIBE] —**pro·scrip′tive** *adj.* —**pro·scrip′tive·ly** *adv.* —**pro·scrip′tive·ness** *n.*

prose (prōz) *n.* **1** Speech or writing without metrical structure: opposed to *verse* or *poetry.* **2** Common place or tedious discourse. **3** *Eccl.* A hymn of irregular meter sometimes sung

in the eucharistic liturgy after the gradual; a sequence. **4** A proser. —*adj.* Pertaining to prose; not poetic; hence, tedious. —*v.t.* & *v.i.* **prosed, pros·ing** To write or speak in prose. [< OF < L *prosa (oratio)* straightforward (discourse) < *prorsus* < *pro-* forward + *versus,* pp. of *vertere* turn]

pro·se·cre·tin (prō′si·krē′tin) *n. Biochem.* The inactive form of secretin converted into the active form by stomach acids. [< PRO-² before + SECRETIN]

pro·sect (prō·sekt′) *v.t.* To dissect for purposes of anatomical demonstration and instruction. [Back formation < *prosector* an anatomist < LL < L *prosectus,* pp. of *prosecare* cut up < *pro-* before + *secare* cut] —**pro·sec′tion** (-sek′shən) *n.* —**pro·sec′tor** *n.*

pros·e·cute (pros′ə·kyo͞ot) *v.* **·cut·ed, ·cut·ing** *v.t.* **1** To go on with so as to complete; pursue to the end: to *prosecute* an inquiry. **2** To carry on or engage in, as a trade or profession. **3** *Law* **a** To bring suit against for redress of wrong or punishment of crime. **b** To seek to enforce or obtain, as a claim or right, by legal process. —*v.i.* **4** To begin and carry on a legal proceeding. See synonyms under PUSH. [< L *prosecutus,* pp. of *prosequi* pursue < *pro-* before + *sequi* follow]

prosecuting attorney The attorney empowered to act in behalf of the government, whether state, county, or national, in prosecuting for penal offenses.

pros·e·cu·tion (pros′ə·kyo͞o′shən) *n.* **1** The act or process of prosecuting. **2** *Law* **a** The instituting and carrying forward of a judicial proceeding to obtain some right or to redress and punish some wrong. **b** The institution and continuance of a criminal proceeding. **c** The party instituting and conducting it.

pros·e·cu·tor (pros′ə·kyo͞o′tər) *n.* **1** One who prosecutes, in any sense. **2** *Law* **a** One who institutes and carries on a suit, especially a criminal suit. **b** A prosecuting attorney.

pros·e·lyte (pros′ə·līt) *n.* One brought over to any opinion, belief, sect, or party, especially from one religious belief to another. See synonyms under CONVERT. —*v.* **·lyt·ed, ·lyt·ing** *v.i.* To make proselytes. —*v.t.* To make a convert of. [< LL *proselytus* < Gk. *prosēlytos* a convert to Judaism, orig. a newcomer < *prosēlyth-,* stem of *proserchesthai* approach]

pros·e·lyt·ism (pros′ə·lit′iz·əm, -li·tiz′əm) *n.* The making of converts to a religion, sect, or party, or the state of being thus converted. —**pros′e·lyt·ist** *n.*

pros·e·lyt·ize (pros′ə·lit·īz′) *v.t.* & *v.i.* **·ized, ·iz·ing** To proselyte. Also *Brit.* **pros′e·lyt·ise′.**

pros·en·ceph·a·lon (pros′en·sef′ə·lon) *n. Anat.* The forebrain. [< NL < Gk. *pros-* near, before + *encephalon* the brain. See ENCEPHALON.] —**pros′en·ce·phal′ic** (-sə·fal′ik) *adj.*

pros·en·chy·ma (pros·eng′ki·mə) *n. Bot.* Plant tissue composed of elongated, pointed, typically thick-walled cells, as distinguished from the parenchyma. [< NL < Gk. *pros-* toward, near + *enchyma* an infusion. See ENCHYMA.] —**pros·en·chym·a·tous** (pros′eng·kim′ə·təs) *adj.*

prose poem A prose work which resembles poetry either in style, structure, or emotional content.

pros·er (prō′zər) *n.* A dull or tedious writer or talker; a bore.

Pros·er·pine (pros′ər·pīn, prō·sûr′·pə·nē) In Roman mythology, the daughter of Ceres and wife of Pluto: identified with the Greek *Persephone.* Also **Pro·ser·pi·na** (prō·sûr′pə·nə).

pro·sim·i·an (prō·sim′ē·ən) *adj. Zool.* Designating any member of a suborder or group *(Prosimii)* of widely distributed early primates, as lemurs, indris, lorises, and tarsiers, characterized by small size, primitive brain development, and extensive adaptive radiation. —*n.* Any primate of this group. [< NL < Gk. *pro-* before + L *simia* an ape]

pro·sit (prō′sit) *Latin* Literally, may it benefit (you): a toast used in drinking health.

pro·slav·er·y (prō·slā′vər·ē, -slāv′rē) *adj.* In United States history, advocating Negro slavery or the policy of non-interference with it. —*n.* The advocacy of slavery.

pros·o·dem·ic (pros′ə·dem′ik) *adj. Med.* Transmitted from one person to another: said of diseases which spread by contact with affected individuals. [< *proso-* forward (< Gk. *prosō*) + (EPI)DEMIC]

pros·o·dist (pros′ə·dist) *n.* One versed in prosody.

pros·o·dy (pros′ə·dē) *n.* The science of poetical forms, including quantity and accent of syllables, meter, and versification and metrical composition. [< L *prosodia* the accent of a syllable < Gk. *prosōidia* a song sung to music < *pros-* to + *ōidē* a song] —**pro·sod·ic** (prō·sod′ik) or **·i·cal, pro·so·di·ac** (prō·sō′·dē·ak). **pro·so·di·al** (prō·sō′·dē·əl) *adj.*

pro·so·po·pe·ia (prō·sō′pə·pē′ə) *n.* **1** A rhetorical figure in which the speaker impersonates another. **2** Personification. Also **pro·so′po·poe′ia.** [< L < Gk. *prosōpopoiia* < *prosōpon* a face, person + *poieein* make]

pros·pect (pros′pekt) *n.* **1** A future probability based on present indications. **2** A scene spread out before one's eyes; an extended view. **3** The direction in which anything faces; an exposure; outlook. **4** A prospective buyer. **5** The act of observing; sight; survey. **6** *Mining* **a** An indication of the presence of mineral ore. **b** A place having promising signs of the presence of mineral ore. **c** The sample or specimen of mineral obtained by washing a small portion of ore or dirt. **7** A consideration of the future; foresight. See synonyms under SCENE. —*v.t.* & *v.i.* To explore (a region) for gold, oil, etc. [< L *prospectus* a look-out, view < *prospicere* look forward < *pro-* forward + *specere* look]

pro·spec·tive (prə·spek′tiv) *adj.* **1** Being still in the future; anticipated; expected. **2** Looking toward or concerned with the future; anticipatory. —**pro·spec′tive·ly** *adv.*

pros·pec·tor (pros′pek·tər) *n.* One who searches or examines a region for mineral deposits or precious stones.

pro·spec·tus (prə·spek′təs) *n.* **1** A paper containing information of a proposed literary, commercial, or industrial undertaking. **2** A summary; outline. [< L. See PROSPECT.]

pros·per (pros′pər) *v.i.* To be prosperous; thrive; flourish. —*v.t.* To render prosperous: God *prospers* the Republic. [< OF *prosperer* < L *prosperare* cause to succeed or prosper < *prosper, prosperus* prosperous]

pros·per·i·ty (pros··r′ə·tē) *n.* The state of being prosperous; attainment of the object desired; material well-being; success.

Pros·per·o (pros′pər·ō) In Shakespeare's *Tempest,* the banished Duke of Milan.

pros·per·ous (pros′pər·əs) *adj.* **1** Successful; flourishing. **2** Favoring or tending to success; auspicious. **3** Promising; favorable. [< MF *prospereus* < OF *prospere* < L *prosper, prosperus* favorable] —**pros′per·ous·ly** *adv.* —**pros′·per·ous·ness** *n.*

pros·ta·glan·din (pros′tə·glan′din) *n.* Any of a class of hormonelike compounds composed of fatty acids, occurring in tissues throughout the body and affecting circulation, neural activity, female reproduction, and other functions. [< PROSTA(TE) + GLAND + -IN]

pros·tate (pros′tāt) *adj.* **1** *Anat.* Designating a partly muscular gland at the base of the bladder around the urethra in male mammals. **2** Standing in front. —*n.* The prostate gland. [< Med. L *prostata* < Gk. *prostatēs* one who stands before < *proïstania* < *pro-* before + *histanai* set] —**pro·stat·ic** (prō·stat′ik) *adj.*

pros·ta·tec·to·my (pros′tə·tek′tə·mē) *n. Surg.* Excision of the prostate gland.

prostato- *combining form Med.* The prostate gland; of or related to the prostate: *prostatotomy.* Also, before vowels, **prostat-.** [< Gk. *prostatēs.* See PROSTATE.]

pros·the·sis (pros′thə·sis) *n.* **1** The addition of a letter or syllable to a word, especially at the beginning, as *yclept, bewail:* also spelled *prothesis.* **2** *Surg.* The fitting of artificial parts to the body, as a glass eye, a false tooth, etc. **3** Replacement or substitution of parts. [< L < Gk., addition < *prostithenai* add < *pros-* toward, besides + *tithenai* place, put] —**pros·thet·ic** (pros·thet′ik) *adj.*

pros·thet·ics (pros·thet′iks) *n.* The branch of surgery or dentistry which specializes in artificial parts and organs. [< Gk. *prosthetikos* additional < *prosthetos* added, put on < *prostithenai.* See PROSTHESIS.] —**pros·the·tist** (pros′thə·tist) *n.*

pros·tho·don·ti·a (pros′thə·don′shē·ə, -shə) *n.* Dental prosthetics. [< NL < Gk. *prosthesis* addition + *odous, odontos* tooth]

pros·tho·don·tist (pros′thə·don′tist) *n.* A dentist who specializes in dental prosthetics.

pros·ti·tute (pros′tə·to͞ot) *n.* **1** A woman who practices prostitution; a harlot; whore. **2** Any base hireling; a corrupt person. —*v.t.* **·tut·ed, ·tut·ing 1** To apply to base or unworthy purposes: to *prostitute* one's talent. **2** To offer (oneself or another) for lewd purposes, especially for hire. See synonyms under ABUSE. —*adj.* **1** Openly devoted to lewdness or promiscuity, as a woman. **2** Surrendered to base purposes. [< L *prostitutus,* pp. of *prostituere* expose publicly, prostitute < *pro-* before + *statuere* cause to stand] —**pros′ti·tu′tor** *n.*

pros·ti·tu·tion (pros′tə·to͞o′shən, -tyo͞o′-) *n.* **1** The act or business of prostituting; the offering, by a woman, of her body for purposes of intercourse with men for hire. **2** The act of hiring or devoting to base purposes, as one's honor, talents, resources, etc.

pros·trate (pros′trāt) *adj.* **1** Lying prone, or with the face to the ground; hence, figuratively, brought low in mind or spirit. **2** Lying at the mercy of another; defenseless. **3** *Bot.* Trailing along the ground; procumbent. —*v.t.* **·trat·ed, ·trat·ing 1** To bow or cast (oneself) down, as in adoration or pleading. **2** To throw flat; lay on the ground. **3** To overthrow or overcome; reduce to weakness or helplessness. [< L *prostratus,* pp. of *prosternere* lay flat < *pro-* before + *sternere* stretch out] —**pros′tra·tor** *n.*

pros·tra·tion (pros·trā′shən) *n.* **1** The act of prostrating in any sense. **2** Exhaustion of body or mind; great dejection or depression.

pro·style (prō′stīl) *adj. Archit.* Having a range of detached columns in front, but no columns on the sides or back of the building; also, constituting such a portico: a *prostyle* temple. [< L *prostylus* < Gk. *prostylos* < *pro-* before + *stylos* a pillar]

pros·y (prō′zē) *adj.* **pros·i·er, pros·i·est 1** Like mere prose; prosaic. **2** Dull; tedious; commonplace. —**pros′i·ly** *adv.* —**pros′i·ness** *n.*

prot- Var. of PROTO-.

pro·tac·tin·i·um (prō′tak·tin′ē·əm) *n.* A toxic, radioactive metallic alement (symbol Pa, atomic number 91) occurring in minute amounts in uranium ores, where it decays to form actinium. See PERIODIC TABLE. [< PROT- + ACTINIUM]

pro·tag·o·nist (prō·tag′ə·nist) *n.* The actor who played the chief part in a Greek drama; hence, a leader in any enterprise or contest. [< Gk. *prōtagōnistēs* < *prōtos* first + *agōnistēs* a contestant, an actor]

Pro·tag·o·ras (prō·tag′ər·əs), 481?–411 B.C., Greek philosopher.

pro·ta·mine (prō′tə·mēn, -min) *n. Biochem.* One of a class of strongly basic simple proteins, uncoagulable by heat, soluble in ammonia, and yielding a few amino acids when hydrolyzed. Also **pro′ta·min** (-min). [< PROT- + -AMINE]

pro·ta·no·pi·a (prō′tə·nō′pē·ə) *n. Pathol.* Color blindness marked by inability to distinguish between red and green; red blindness. [< NL < Gk. *prōtos* first + *an-* not + *ōps, ōpos* an eye] —**pro·ta·nope** (prō′tə·nōp) *n.*

prot·a·sis (prot′ə·sis) *n.* **1** In a conditional sentence, the clause (usually introductory) that contains the condition or antecedent: distinguished from *apodosis.* **2** The introductory or subordinate clause in a sentence not conditional. **3** In classical drama, the introductory part of a play. [< LL < Gk., a hypothesis < *pro-* before + *teinein* stretch]

pro·te·an (prō′tē·ən, prō·tē′an) *adj.* Readily assuming different forms or various aspects; changeable. —*n. Biochem.* Any of a group of derived proteins which are the first product of protein hydrolysis. [< PROTEUS]

pro·te·ase (prō′tē·ās) *n. Biochem.* An enzyme that digests proteins. [< PROTE(OLYSIS) + -ASE]

pro·tect (prə·tekt′) *v.t.* **1** To shield or defend from attack, harm, or injury; guard; defend. **2** *Econ.* To assist (domestic industry) by means of protective tariffs. **3** In commerce, to provide funds to guarantee payment of (a draft, etc.). See synonyms under CHERISH,

KEEP, PRESERVE, SHELTER. [< L *protectus,* pp. of *protegere* protect < *pro-* before + *tegere* cover] —**pro·tect′ing** *adj.* —**pro·tect′ing·ly** *adv.*

pro·tec·tant (prə·tek′tənt) *n.* That which protects from or guards against damage, disease, or injury; especially, a germicide, insecticide, fungicide, or the like.

pro·tect·ed (prə·tek′tid) *adj.* Shielded from harm; cared for; guarded.

pro·tec·tion (prə·tek′shən) *n.* **1** The act of protecting; a protected condition; that which protects. **2** Specifically, a system aiming to protect the industries of a country by governmental action, as by imposing duties. See PROTECTIVE TARIFF. **3** A safe-conduct; passport. **4** *U.S. Slang* Security purchased under threat of violence from racketeers; also, the money so paid. See synonyms under DEFENSE, REFUGE, SHELTER.

pro·tec·tion·ism (prə·tek′shən·iz′əm) *n.* The economic doctrine or system of protection. —**pro·tec′tion·ist** *n.*

pro·tec·tive (prə·tek′tiv) *adj.* **1** Affording or suitable for protection; sheltering; defensive; specifically, in political economy, insuring or intended to insure protection to home industries: a *protective* tariff. **2** Providing or alleging to provide protection: *protective* custody. —*n.* Something that protects; specifically, an aseptic covering for a wound. —**pro·tec′tive·ly** *adv.* —**pro·tec′tive·ness** *n.*

protective coloration *Biol.* Any coloration of a plant or animal that makes it almost indistinguishable from its natural or habitual environment, and thus safe from detection by its enemies.

protective tariff *Econ.* A tariff that is intended to insure protection of domestic industries against foreign competition: opposed to *free trade.*

pro·tec·tor (prə·tek′tər) *n.* **1** One who protects; a defender. **2** In English history, one appointed as a regent of the kingdom during minority or incapacity of the sovereign. Also **pro·tect′er.** —**pro·tec′tress** *n. fem.*

Pro·tec·tor (prə·tek′tər) *n.* The official title of the chief ruler during the Commonwealth: in full, **Lord Protector.** The title was borne by Oliver Cromwell, 1653–58, and by Richard Cromwell, 1658–59.

pro·tec·tor·ate (prə·tek′tər·it) *n.* **1** A relation of protection and partial control by a strong nation over a weaker power. **2** A country or region under the protection of another. **3** The office, or period of office, of a protector of a kingdom. Also **pro·tec′tor·ship.**

Pro·tec·tor·ate (prə·tek′tər·it) *n.* The English government during the time of the Cromwells, 1653–59.

pro·tec·to·ry (prə·tek′tər·ē) *n. pl.* **·to·ries** An institution for the care and education of homeless or destitute children.

pro·tect·o·scope (prə·tek′tə·skōp) *n. Mil.* A device resembling the periscope, to permit tank gunners to observe around their protective shields without exposing themselves to gunfire. [< PROTECT + -(O)SCOPE]

pro·té·gé (prō′tə·zhā), *Fr.* prô·tā·zhā′) *n.* One specially cared for by another who is older or more powerful. [< F pp. of *protéger* < L *protegere* PROTECT] —**pro′té·gée** *n. fem.*

pro·te·in (prō′tē·in, -tēn) *n. Biochem.* Any of a class of highly complex nitrogenous organic compounds occurring naturally in all living matter, and forming an essential part of animal food requirements. They are composed principally of amino acids in varying combinations, and are usually classified as: *simple* (hydrolyzed only by enzymes or acids into alpha-amino acids or their derivatives); *conjugated* (simple proteins combined with non-proteins in a form other than a salt); *derived* (obtained by the action of heat, enzymes, or reagents upon naturally occurring proteins). Also **pro′te·id** (-id). [< G < Gk. *prōteios* chief < *prōtos* first; so called because the chief constituent of living matter]

pro tem·po·re (prō tem′pə·rē) *Latin* For the time being; temporary: abbr. *pro tem.*

pro·tend (prō·tend′) *v.i. Psychol.* To exhibit protensity. [< L *protendere* stretch forth < *pro-* forth + *tendere* stretch]

pro·ten·si·ty (prō·ten′sə·tē) *n. Psychol.* The temporal attribute of a sensation or other mental phenomenon: the psychic analog of duration. [< L *protensus,* pp. of *protendere.* See PROTEND.] —**pro·ten′sive** *adj.*

pro·te·ol·y·sis (prō′tē·ol′ə·sis) *n. Biochem.* The change or splitting up of proteins into simpler products during digestion. [< NL < *proteo-* (< PROTEIN) + Gk. *lysis* a loosening < *lyein* loosen] —**pro′te·o·lyt′ic** (-ə·lit′ik) *adj.*

pro·te·ose (prō′tē·ōs) *n. Biochem.* Any of a group of derived proteins formed naturally in the process of digestion and produced artificially, as by treating the corresponding proteins with dilute mineral acids. [< PROTE(IN) + -OSE^{2}]

Prot·er·o·zo·ic (prot′ər·ə·zō′ik) *Geol. adj.* Pertaining to or designating the geological era following the Archeozoic and succeeded by the Paleozoic. —*n.* The Proterozoic *era.* [< *protero-* (< Gk. *proteros* former) + Gk. *zōikos* < *zōē* life]

Pro·tes·i·la·us (prō·tes′ə·lā′əs) In the *Iliad,* the husband of Laodamia and first of the Greeks killed at Troy.

pro·test (prō′test) *n.* **1** The act of protesting; a solemn or formal objection or declaration. **2** A public expression of dissent, especially if organized. **3** A formal notarial certificate attesting the fact that a note or bill of exchange has been presented for acceptance or payment and that it has been refused. **4** In maritime law, a written declaration by the master of a vessel stating that an injury to the vessel or the cargo was not owing to the neglect or misconduct of the master. **5** A formal statement in writing made by a person called upon by public authority to pay a sum of money, as an import duty or a tax, in which he declares that he does not concede the legality of the claim. —*adj.* Of or relating to public protest: *protest* demonstrations. —*v.* (prə·test′) *v.t.* **1** To assert earnestly or positively; state formally, especially against opposition or doubt. **2** To make a protest against; object to: I *protested* his actions. **3** To declare formally that payment of (a promissory note, etc.) has been duly submitted and refused. —*v.i.* **4** To make solemn affirmation. **5** To make a protest; object. See synonyms under AFFIRM, ASSERT, AVOW. [< OF *protester* < L *protestari* < *pro-* forth + *testari* affirm, give evidence < *testis* a witness] —**pro·test′er** *n.*

prot·es·tant (prot′is·tənt, prə·tes′-) *n.* One who makes a protest. [< MF < L *protestans, -antis,* ppr. of *protestari* PROTEST]

Prot·es·tant (prot′is·tənt) *n.* **1** A member of one of those bodies of Christians that adhere to Protestantism, as opposed to Roman Catholicism: a use opposed by some Anglicans. **2** In the 17th century, a Lutheran or Anglican. **3** Originally, one of those German princes who, at the second Council of Spires, April 19, 1529, protested against the decree of the majority representing the Roman Catholic states which involved a virtual submission to the authority of the Roman Catholic Church. —*adj.* Pertaining to Protestants or Protestantism.

Protestant Episcopal Church A religious body in the United States which is descended from the Church of England, but has been organized as a separate and independent body since 1789.

Prot·es·tant·ism (prot′is·tənt·iz′əm) *n.* **1** The principles and common system of doctrines taught by Luther, and by the evangelical churches since. Its positive and formal principle is that nothing that is not taught in the Holy Scriptures, the authoritative rule of faith and practice in the church, enters as an essential element into the Christian system. **2** The ecclesiastical system founded upon this faith; also, Protestants, collectively. **3** The state of being a Protestant.

prot·es·ta·tion (prot′is·tā′shən) *n.* **1** The act of protesting; also, that which is protested. **2** A formal declaration of dissent. **3** Any solemn or urgent avowal.

Pro·test·er (prə·tes′tər) *n.* A Scotsman who protested against the union of the Presbyterians and the Royalists in 1650. Also **Pro·tes′tor.**

pro·test·ing·ly (prə·tes′ting·lē) *adv.* In such a manner as to protest.

Pro·te·us (prō′tē·əs, -tyōōs) In Greek mythology, a sea god who had the power of assuming different forms. —**Pro′te·an** *adj.*

pro·tha·la·mi·on (prō′thə·lā′mē·on, -ən) *n. pl.* **·mi·a** (-mē·ə) A song celebrating a marriage; a nuptial song. Also **pro′tha·la′mi·um** (-me·əm). [< NL < Gk. *pro-* before + *thalamos* a bridal chamber; coined by Spenser on analogy with *epithalamion*]

pro·thal·li·um (prō·thal′ē·əm) *n. pl.* **·li·a** (-ē·ə) *Bot.* The first or false thallus formed on the germination of the asexually produced spores in pteridophytes; a delicate, evanescent cellular structure bearing the sexual organs. Also **pro·thal′lus.** [< NL < Gk. *pro-* before + *thallion,* dim. of *thallos* a shoot] —**pro·thal′li·al** *adj.* —**pro·thal′line** (-thal′īn, -in) *adj.*

proth·e·sis (proth′ə·sis) *n.* **1** Prosthesis (def. 1). **2** In the Greek Orthodox Church, a service by which the elements are prepared for consecration in the Eucharist. [< LL < Gk., a placing before, or in public < *protithenai* set before < *pro-* before + *tithenai* place] —**pro·thet·ic** (prō·thet′ik) *adj.* —**pro·thet′i·cal·ly** *adv.*

pro·thon·o·tar·y (prō·thon′ə·ter′ē, prō′thə·nō′·tər·ē) *n. pl.* **·tar·ies** **1** A chief clerk; specifically, in the Roman Catholic Church, one of the seven (formerly twelve) ecclesiastics at Rome who keep the registry of important pontifical proceedings, or one having the title and some of the associated privileges. **2** In some States of the United States, a probate officer. Also spelled *protonotary.* [< LL *protonotarius* < LGk. *prōtonotarios* < Gk. *prōtos* first + L *notarius.* See NOTARY.] —**pro·thon′o·tar′i·al** (-târ′ē·əl) *adj.*

prothonotary warbler A North American warbler *(Protonotaria citrea)* the male of which is noted for the brilliant yellow to orange coloring of its head and under parts, with bluish-gray wings and tail.

pro·tho·rax (prō·thôr′aks, -thō′raks) *n. pl.* **·rax·es** or **·tho·ra·ces** (-thôr′ə·sēz, -thō′rə-) *Entomol.* The anterior segment of the thorax of an insect. [< NL < Gk. *pro-* in front + *thorax* thorax] —**pro·tho·rac·ic** (prō′thô·ras′·ik, -thō-) *adj.*

pro·throm·bin (prō·throm′bin) *n. Biochem.* The inactive precursor of thrombin: it is converted into thrombin by the action of calcium and thromboplastin, and is essential to the process of blood-clotting; also called *thrombogen.* [< NL < Gk. *pro-* before + *thrombos* a clot]

pro·tist (prō′tist) *n. Biol.* **1** Any unicellular organism, whether animal or plant. **2** Formerly, any member of a large division *(Protista)* including all single-celled organisms. [< NL < Gk. *prōtista,* neut. pl. of *prōtistos* the very first, superl. of *prōtos* first] —**pro·tis′tan** *adj.* & *n.* —**pro·tis′tic** *adj.*

pro·ti·um (prō′tē·əm) *n. Chem.* The hydrogen isotope of atomic mass 1 (symbol H^1): sometimes so called in distinction from deuterium and tritium. [< NL < Gk. *prōtos* first. CF. PROTO- (def. 3).]

proto- *combining form* **1** First in rank or time; chief; typical: *protomartyr.* **2** Primitive; original: *prototype.* **3** *Chem.* **a** Designating the first or lowest member of a series; having the least amount (of an element or radical): *protoxide.* **b** Denoting the parent form or source of: *protoactinium.* Also, before vowels, *prot-.* [< Gk. *prōto-* < *prōtos* first]

Pro·to·coc·cus (prō′tə·kok′əs) *n.* The typical genus of a family *(Chlorophyceae)* of green algae, growing on damp walls, rocks, and trunks of trees. [< PROTO- + COCCUS]

pro·to·col (prō′tə·kol) *n.* **1** The preliminary draft of an official document, as a treaty; specifically, the preliminary draft or report of the negotiations and conclusions arrived at by a diplomatic conference, having the force of a treaty when ratified. **2** The rules of diplomatic and state etiquette and ceremony. —*v.i.* To write or form protocols. [< OF *prothocole* < Med. L *protocollum* < LGk. *prōtokollon* the first glued sheet of a papyrus roll < *prōtos* first + *kolla* glue]

pro·to·derm (prō′tə·dûrm) *n.* Dermatogen.

pro·to·gene (prō′tə·jēn) *n.* The hypothetical prototype of the gene, assumed to have been formed from complex carbon compounds at the time when life evolved from inorganic matter.

pro·to·gram (prō′tə·gram) *n.* An acronym.

Pro·to·hip·pus (prō′tō·hip′əs) *n. Paleontol.* A genus of extinct, three-toed horses of the Miocene period. [< NL < Gk. *prōtos* first + *hippos* a horse]

pro·to·hu·man (prō′tō·hyōō′mən) *adj.* **1** Anterior to or more primitive than man. **2** *Paleontol.* Of, pertaining to, or describing any of several hominoid primates regarded

as being at an earlier stage of development than *Homo sapiens.* —*n.* Any primate antedating modern man in evolutionary characteristics. Principal types are:

Africanthropus	Meganthropus
Australopithecus	Oreopithecus
Dryopithecus	Pithecanthropus
Gigantopithecus	Sinanthropus

pro·to·lith·ic (prō′tō·lith′ik) *adj.* Pertaining to the earliest period of the stone age; eolithic.

pro·to·mar·tyr (prō′tō·mär′tər) *n.* The first martyr or victim in any cause. [<OF *prothomartir* <Med. L *protomartyr* <Gk. *prōtomartyr* <*prōtos* first + *martyr* a witness]

pro·to·mor·phic (prō′tō·môr′fik) *adj. Biol.* Of or pertaining to, or having the most primitive or elementary form or structure. **—pro′·to·morph** *n.*

pro·ton (prō′ton) *n. Physics* **1** The positively charged nucleus of the atom of the light isotope of hydrogen (symbol, H^1), constituting its principal mass. **2** One of the elementary particles in the nucleus of an atom, having a unitary positive charge and a mass of approximately 1.672 $\times$ 10^{-24} gram. The atomic number of an element is equivalent to the number of protons in its nucleus. [<NL <Gk. *prōton,* neut. of *prōtos* first]

pro·to·ne·ma (prō′tə·nē′mə) *n. pl.* **·ne·ma·ta** (-nē′mə·tə) *Bot.* An early stage in the development of the prothallium of ferns; a green confervoid or filamentous structure developed from the spore in mosses, on which the leafy plant arises as a lateral or terminal shoot. Also **pro′to·neme** (-nēm). [<NL <Gk. *prōtos* first + *nēma* a thread]

pro·ton·o·tar·y (prō·ton′ə·ter′ē, prō′tə·nō′tər·ē) See PROTHONOTARY.

pro·ton-pro·ton reaction (prō′ton·prō′ton) A thermonuclear chain reaction which is assumed to provide stellar energy by means of the fusion of 4 protons to make a helium nucleus, with a residue of 2 protons returned to the cycle. Compare CARBON CYCLE.

proton synchrotron *Physics* A bevatron.

pro·to·path·ic (prō′tə·path′ik) *adj. Physiol.* Pertaining to or designating primary sensibility, responsive only to gross, typically painful stimuli: distinguished from *epicritic.* [<PROTO- + -PATHIC]

pro·to·phyte (prō′tə·fīt) *n. Bot.* **1** Any single-celled plant. **2** A member of a former division *(Protophyta)* embracing only the lowest and simplest plants. [<NL <Gk. *prōtos* first + *phyton* a plant]

pro·to·plasm (prō′tə·plaz′əm) *n. Biol.* **1** The physicochemical basis of living matter, a viscid, grayish, translucent, colloidal substance of granular structure and complex composition that forms the essential part of plant and animal cells. **2** The cytoplasm of the cell, as distinguished from the nuclear material. [<G *protoplasma* <Gk. *prōtos* first + *plasma.* See PLASMA.] **—pro′to·plas′mic** or **·plas′mal** or **·plas·mat′ic** *adj.*

pro·to·plast (prō′tə·plast) *n. Biol.* **1** That which is first formed; the original or primordial cell. **2** The parent pair or one of the parent pair of the first-formed individuals of a species. **3** The protoplasmic contents of a cell. **4** A plastid. [<F *protoplaste* <LL *protoplastus* <Gk. *protoplastos* formed first <*prōtos* first + *plastos* formed <*plassein* form] **—pro′to·plas′tic** *adj.*

pro·to·ste·le (prō′tə·stē′lē, -stēl) *n. Bot.* The dense central cylinder of roots and young stems, and, in various pteridophytes, the axes. [<PROTO- + STELE[2]] **—pro′to·ste′lic** *adj.*

Pro·to·the·ri·a (prō′tə·thir′ē·ə) *n. pl.* A subclass of primitive, egg-laying mammals; the monotremes, as the duckbill. [<NL <Gk. *prōtos* first + *thēria,* pl. of *thērion,* dim. of *thēr* a beast]

pro·to·troph·ic (prō′tə·trof′ik, -trō′fik) *adj. Biol.* Capable of assimilating only simple inorganic substances: said of the earliest forms of life.

pro·to·type (prō′tə·tīp) *n.* **1** *Biol.* A primitive or ancestral organism; an archetype: opposed to *ectype.* **2** A first or original model on which subsequent forms are to be based. **3** An accepted standard to which all others must conform. See synonyms under EXAMPLE, IDEAL, MODEL. [<MF <NL *prototypon* <Gk. *prōtotypon,* orig. neut. sing. of *prōtotypos* original <*prōtos* first + *typos* a model] **—pro′to·typ′al** (-tī′pəl), **pro′to·typ′ic** (-tip′ik), **pro′to·typ′i·cal** *adj.*

pro·tox·ide (prō·tok′sīd, -sid) *n. Chem.* An oxide containing the lowest proportion of oxygen for a given series: contrasted with *peroxide:* iron *protoxide* (ferrous oxide). Also **pro·tox′id** (-sid). [<PROT- + OXIDE]

pro·to·zo·an (prō′tə·zō′ən) *n.* Any of a large, diverse, and universal phylum of eucaryotic microorganisms, including free-living unicellular and colonial forms, often having complicated life cycles and parasitizing various animals. Also **pro′to·zo′on** *pl.* **·zo′a.** [<NL <Gk. *prōtos* first + *zōia,* pl. of *zōion* an animal] **—pro′to·zo′an, pro′to·zo′ic** *adj.*

pro·to·zo·ol·o·gy (prō′tō·zō·ol′ə·jē) *n.* The branch of biology concerned with protozoans. **—pro′to·zo′o·log′i·cal** (-zō′ə·loj′i·kəl) *adj.* **—pro′to·zo·ol′o·gist** *n.*

pro·tract (prō·trakt′) *v.t.* **1** To extend in time; prolong. **2** In surveying, to draw or map by means of a scale and protractor; plot. **3** *Zool.* To protrude or extend: opposed to *retract.* [<L *protractus,* pp. of *protrahere* extend <*pro-* forward + *trahere* draw] **—pro·trac′tive** *adj.*

Synonyms: continue, delay, elongate, extend, lengthen, prolong. To *protract* is to cause to occupy a longer time than is usual, expected, or desirable. We *protract* a negotiation which we are slow to conclude; *delay* may be used either of the beginning or of any stage in the proceedings; we may *delay* a person as well as an action, but *protract* is not used of persons. *Elongate* is used only of material objects or extension in space; *protract* is rarely, except in mathematics, used of concrete objects or extension in space; we *elongate* a line, *protract* a discussion. *Protract* has usually an unfavorable sense; *continue* is neutral, applying equally to the desirable or the undesirable. Compare HINDER. *Antonyms:* abbreviate, abridge, conclude, contract, curtail, hasten, hurry, limit, reduce, shorten.

pro·tract·ed (prō·trak′tid) *adj.* Unduly or unusually extended or prolonged.

protracted meeting A series of religious, usually revival, meetings, held morning, afternoon, and evening, and sometimes continued for several days.

pro·tract·er (prō·trak′tər) *n.* **1** One who or that which protracts. **2** A protractor.

pro·trac·tile (prō·trak′til) *adj.* Capable of being protracted or protruded; protrusile.

pro·trac·tion (prō·trak′shən) *n.* **1** The act of drawing out or lengthening in time; the act of delaying the termination of anything. **2** In prosody, the irregular lengthening of a syllable ordinarily short. **3** The making of a surveyor's plot on paper.

pro·trac·tor (prō·trak′tər) *n.* **1** An instrument for measuring and laying off angles. **2** A tailor's adjustable pattern. **3** *Anat.* A muscle that extends a limb or moves it forward. **4** *Surg.* An instrument for extracting foreign bodies from a wound.

pro·trude (prō·trōōd′) *v.t.* & *v.i.* **·trud·ed, ·trud·ing** To push or thrust out; project outward. [<L *protrudere* <*pro-* forward + *trudere* thrust]

pro·tru·sile (prō·trōō′sil) *adj.* Adapted to being thrust out, often rapidly, as the tongue of an ant-eater. Also **pro·tru′si·ble.** [<L *protrusus,* pp. of *protrudere* PROTRUDE + -ILE]

pro·tru·sion (prō·trōō′zhən) *n.* **1** The act of protruding, or the state of being protruded. **2** The part or object protruded. [<F <L *protrusus.* See PROTRUSILE.]

pro·tru·sive (prō·trōō′siv) *adj.* **1** Tending to protrude; protruding. **2** Pushing or driving forward. **—pro·tru′sive·ly** *adv.* **—pro·tru′sive·ness** *n.*

pro·tu·ber·ance (prō·tōō′bər·əns, -tyōō′-) *n.* **1** Something that protrudes; a knob; prominence. **2** The state of being protuberant. Also **pro·tu′ber·an·cy, pro·tu′ber·a′tion.**

pro·tu·ber·ant (prō·tōō′bər·ənt, -tyōō′-) *adj.* Swelling out beyond the surrounding surface; bulging [LL *protuberans, -antis,* ppr. of *protuberare* bulge out <L *pro-* forth + *tuber* a swelling] **—pro·tu′ber·ant·ly** *adv.*

pro·tu·ber·ate (prō·tōō′bə·rāt, -tyōō′-) *v.i.* **·at·ed, ·at·ing** To be protuberant; bulge out. [<LL *protuberatus,* pp. of *protuberare.* See PROTUBERANT.]

pro·tyle (prō′tīl, -til) *n.* The hypothetical primitive material of the universe; a substance of which all existing elements have been supposed to be modifications. Also **pro′tyl** (-til). [<Gk. *prōtos* first + *hylē* timber, matter]

proud (proud) *adj.* **1** Actuated by, possessing, or manifesting pride; arrogant; haughty; also, self-respecting. **2** Sensible of honor and personal elation: generally followed by *of* or by a verb in the infinitive. **3** High-mettled, as a horse; spirited. **4** Proceeding from or inspired by pride. **5** Being a cause of honorable pride, as a distinction or achievement. **6** *Obs.* Bold; fearless; daring. See synonyms under HAUGHTY, HIGH. [OE *prūt, prūd* <OF *prud, prod,* prob. ult. <L *prodesse* be of value] **—proud′ly** *adv.*

proud flesh *Pathol.* A granulated growth resembling flesh in a wound or sore. [So called because of its swelling up]

Prou·dhon (prōō·dôn′), **Pierre Joseph,** 1809–1865, French socialist, philosophical anarchist, and writer on politics and economics.

Proust (prōōst), **Joseph Louis,** 1754–1826, French chemist. **—Marcel,** 1871–1922, French novelist.

proust·ite (prōōs′tīt) *n.* An adamantine ruby-red sulfide of silver and arsenic, crystallizing in the rhombohedral system. [<F, after J. L. *Proust,* its discoverer]

Prout's hypothesis (prouts) *Chem.* A hypothesis that all atomic weights are simple multiples of the atomic weight of hydrogen. [after William *Prout,* 1785–1850, English chemist]

prove (prōōv) *v.* **proved, proved** or **prov·en, prov·ing** *v.t.* **1** To show to be true or genuine, as by evidence or argument. **2** To determine the quality or genuineness of; test: to *prove* a gun. **3** To establish the authenticity or validity of, as a will. **4** *Math.* To verify the accuracy of (a calculation or demonstration) by an independent process. **5** *Printing* To take a proof of or from. **6** *Archaic* To learn by experience; undergo. —*v.i.* **7** To be shown to be by the result or outcome; turn out to be: His hopes *proved* vain. **8** *Archaic* To make trial. See synonyms under CONFIRM. [OF *prouver* <L *probare* test, try. Doublet of PROBE.] **—prov′a·ble** *adj.* **—prov′er** *n.*

pro·vec·tion (prō·vek′shən) *n. Ling.* A transfer of the final consonant of one word to the beginning of the next word, as in *a newt,* the old form of which was *an ewt.* [<LL *provectio, -onis* <*provectus,* pp. of *provehere* advance <*pro-* forward + *vehere* carry]

prov·en (prōō′vən) Alternative past participle of PROVE: the less common form. —*adj.* Proved; established; verified.

prov·e·nance (prov′ə·nəns) *n.* Provenience; origin. [<F <*provenant,* ppr. of *provenir* come forth <L *provenire* <*pro-* forth + *venire* come]

Pro·ven·çal (prō′vən·säl′, *Fr.* prō·väṅ·sȧl′) *n.* **1** A native or resident of Provence, France. **2** The Romance language of Provence: developed from *langue d'oc,* and used especially in the 12th and 13th centuries in the lyric literature of the troubadours. —*adj.* Of or pertaining to Provence, its inhabitants, or their language. [<MF, of Provence <L *provincialis* <*(nostra) provincia* (our) province, i.e., Provence]

Pro·vence (prô·väṅs′) A region and former province of SE France.

prov·en·der (prov′ən·dər) *n.* Food for cattle; especially, dry food, as hay; rarely, provisions generally. See synonyms under FOOD. —*v.t.* To provide with food, as cattle. [<OF *provendre, provende* an allowance of food <L *praebenda.* See PREBEND.]

pro·ve·ni·ence (prō·vē′nē·əns, -vēn′yəns) *n.* The origin or source of a thing: used especially in the fine arts and archeology. [<L *proveniens, -entis,* ppr. of *provenire.* See PROVENANCE.]

prov·erb (prov′ərb) *n.* **1** A pithy saying, especially one condensing the wisdom of experience; adage; saw; maxim. **2** An enigmatical saying: to speak in a *proverb.* **3** Something

add,āce,câre,pälm; end,ēven; it,īce; odd,ōpen,ôrder; tŏŏk,pōōl; up,bûrn; ə = a in *above,* e in *sicken,* i in *clarity,* o in *melon,* u in *focus* ; yōō = u in *fuse,* oi,oil; ou,pout; ch,check; g,go; ng,ring; th,thin; th,this; zh,vision. Foreign sounds ȧ,œ,ü,kh,ṅ; and ◆: see page xx. <from; + plus; ? possibly.

proverbial; a typical example; byword. [<OF *proverbe* <L *proverbium* < *pro-* before + *verbum* a word]

Synonyms: adage, aphorism, apothegm, axiom, byword, dictum, maxim, motto, precept, saw, saying, truism. The *proverb* or *adage* gives homely truth in condensed, practical form; the latter especially gains authority by long usage. An *aphorism* is a summary statement of a general truth. An *apothegm* is a sententious statement. A *dictum* is a statement of some person or school, on whom it depends for authority. A *saying* is impersonal, current among the people. A *saw* is a *saying* that is old, but somewhat worn and tiresome. *Precept* is a command or a rule for behavior; a *motto* or *maxim* is a brief statement of cherished truth, the *maxim* being more uniformly and directly practical. A *byword* is a *saying* used reproachfully or contemptuously. Compare ADAGE, AXIOM.

pro·ver·bi·al (prə·vûr′bē·əl) *adj.* **1** Of the nature of, pertaining to, or like a proverb: *proverbial* brevity. **2** Supplying the subject for a proverb; being the object of general remark, especially as a typical case; well-known; notorious. — **pro·ver′bi·al·ly** *adv.*

Prov·erbs (prov′ərbz) An Old Testament didactic poetical book of moral sayings and instructions.

pro·vide (prə·vīd′) *v.* **·vid·ed**, **·vid·ing** *v.t.* **1** To supply or furnish. **2** To afford; yield. **3** To prepare, make ready, or procure beforehand. **4** To set down as a condition; stipulate. — *v.i.* **5** To take measures in advance: with *for* or *against*. **6** To furnish means of subsistence: usually with *for*. **7** To make a stipulation. [<L *providere* foresee < *pro-* before + *videre* see. Doublet of PURVEY.]

Synonyms: arrange, cater, furnish, prepare, procure, produce, supply. *Antonyms:* alienate, divert, lose, misemploy, mismanage, neglect, overlook, scatter, squander, waste.

pro·vid·ed (prə·vī′did) *conj.* On condition: with *that* expressed or understood: He will get the loan *provided* he offers good security. See synonyms under BUT. [Orig. pp. of PROVIDE]

prov·i·dence (prov′ə·dəns) *n.* **1** The care exercised by the Supreme Being over the universe. **2** An event or circumstances ascribable to divine interposition. **3** The exercise of foresight and care for the future; prudent economy. See synonyms under FRUGALITY, PRUDENCE. [<OF <L *providentia* < *providens*, *-entis*, ppr. of *providere*. See PROVIDE.]

Prov·i·dence (prov′ə·dəns) God; the Deity.

Prov·i·dence (prov′ə·dəns) The capital of Rhode Island, a port of entry on Narragansett Bay.

Providence Plantations Original name of the colony established by Roger Williams (1636) in Rhode Island.

prov·i·dent (prov′ə·dənt) *adj.* Exercising foresight; economical; anticipating and making ready for future wants or emergencies. See synonyms under THOUGHTFUL. — **prov′i·dent·ly** *adv.*

prov·i·den·tial (prov′ə·den′shəl) *adj.* Resulting from or exhibiting the action of God's providence. — **prov′i·den′tial·ly** *adv.*

pro·vid·er (prə·vī′dər) *n.* One whose income supports a family: He's a good *provider.*

pro·vid·ing (prə·vī′ding) *conj.* Provided; in case that.

prov·ince (prov′ins) *n.* **1** A considerable country incorporated with a kingdom or empire and subject to the central administration without having itself any voice in that administration. **2** Any large administrative division of a country with a permanent local government: the *provinces* of the Roman Empire, the *Provinces* of the Dominion of Canada or of the Union of South Africa, the United *Provinces* of Agra and Oudh. The word is often loosely used in the plural to denote those regions that lie at a distance from the capital; specifically, in Great Britain, the whole country except London. **3** A comprehensive department or sphere of knowledge or activity: the *province* of chemistry. **4** A definite sphere of action, especially one authoritatively assigned or properly belonging to a person: The *province* of the judge is to apply the laws. **5** *Ecol.* A zoogeographical area less than a region, having its own special flora, fauna, and types of mankind.

[<OF <L *provincia* an official duty or charge, a province]

Province Welles·ley (welz′lē) See PENANG, SETTLEMENT OF.

pro·vin·cial (prə·vin′shəl) *adj.* **1** Pertaining to or characteristic of a province. **2** Confined to a province; rustic; hence, local, as a word or idiom; also, narrow; uncultured; illiberal: said of people. — *n.* A native or inhabitant of a province; one who is provincial, in any sense. — **pro·vin′ci·al·i·ty** (-shē·al′ə·tē) *n.* — **pro·vin′cial·ly** *adv.*

pro·vin·cial·ism (prə·vin′shəl·iz′əm) *n.* The quality of being provincial; a provincial custom or peculiarity, especially of speech.

proving ground A site used for testing new weapons, equipment, scientific theories, etc.

pro·vi·sion (prə·vizh′ən) *n.* **1** Measures taken or means made ready in advance; the act of taking such measures. **2** *pl.* Food or a supply of food; victuals. **3** Something provided or prepared, as against future need. **4** A stipulation or requirement; the part of an agreement, instrument, etc., referring to one specific thing. **5** Appointment to a see or benefice not yet vacant, including designation, institution, and installation; especially, such appointment when made by the pope, before a vacancy, so as to set aside nomination by the ordinary patron. **6** *pl.* Medieval English statutes by which certain important matters were provided for: the *provisions* of Oxford. See synonyms under NUTRIMENT, STOCK. — *v.t.* To provide with food or provisions. [<OF <L *provisio, -onis* a foreseeing < *provisus*, pp. of *providere*. See PROVIDE.] — **pro·vi′sion·er** *n.*

pro·vi·sion·al (prə·vizh′ən·əl) *adj.* Provided for a present service or temporary necessity: a *provisional* army; adopted tentatively or for lack of something better. — **pro·vi′sion·al·ly** *adv.*

provisional government A temporary government established to provide for a present situation or emergency, to be superseded later by a permanent government.

pro·vi·sion·ar·y (prə·vizh′ən·er′ē) *adj.* **1** Providing or intended to provide for some future occasion or want; provident; also, containing the statement of a provision. **2** Provisional.

pro·vi·so (prə·vī′zō) *n.* *pl.* **·sos** or **·soes** A conditional stipulation; a clause, as in a contract or statute, limiting, modifying, or rendering conditional its operation. [<Med. L *proviso (quod)* it being provided (that), ablative neut. sing. pp. of L *providere*. See PROVIDE.]

pro·vi·so·ry (prə·vī′zər·ē) *adj.* **1** Containing or made dependent on a proviso; conditional. **2** Provisional. — **pro·vi′so·ri·ly** *adv.*

pro·vi·ta·min (prō·vī′tə·min) *n.* *Biochem.* Any of various substances believed to promote the formation of vitamins, as carotene (**provitamin A**) or ergosterol. [< *pro-* undeveloped (<L, before) + VITAMIN]

prov·o·ca·tion (prov′ə·kā′shən) *n.* **1** The act of provoking. **2** An incitement to action; stimulus; something that stirs to anger. [<OF <L *provocatio, -onis* < *provocatus*, pp. of *provocare* PROVOKE]

pro·voc·a·tive (prə·vok′ə·tiv) *adj.* Serving to provoke; stimulating. — *n.* That which provokes or tends to provoke. — **pro·voc′a·tive·ly** *adv.* — **pro·voc′a·tive·ness** *n.*

pro·voke (prə·vōk′) *v.t.* **·voked**, **·vok·ing** **1** To stir to anger or resentment; irritate; vex. **2** To arouse or stimulate to some action. **3** To stir up or bring about: to *provoke* a quarrel. **4** To induce or cause; elicit: to *provoke* a smile. **5** *Obs.* To call forth; summon. [<OF *provoker* <L *provocare* challenge < *pro-* forth + *vocare* call] — **pro·vok′ing** *adj.* — **pro·vok′ing·ly** *adv.* — **pro·vok′ing·ness** *n.*

prov·ost (prov′əst) *n.* **1** A person having charge or authority over others. **2** The chief magistrate of a Scottish city, corresponding to the English mayor: in Edinburgh, Dundee, Glasgow, and Aberdeen called **Lord Provost**. **3** In some English and American colleges, the head of the faculty. **4** The head of a collegiate chapter or a cathedral; a dean. **5** (prō′vō) Provost marshal. [Fusion of OE *profost*, *prafost* and AF, OF *provost*, both <LL *propositus* <L *praepositus* a prefect, orig. pp. of *praeponere* < *prae-* before + *ponere* place] — **prov′ost·ship** *n.*

pro·vost court (prō′vō) A summary military court for trying those (especially civilians in a theater of war) charged with minor offenses committed within areas controlled by the army. They are usually guided by the rules of evidence. Their jurisdiction is concurrent with that of courts martial. The military commission is resorted to in like situations for graver offenses such as espionage.

pro·vost guard (prō′vō) A company of soldiers detailed for police duty under the provost marshal.

pro·vost marshal (prō′vō) A military or naval officer exercising police functions.

pro·vost sergeant (prō′vō) A non-commissioned officer who supervises the work and duties of the military police.

prow¹ (prou) *n.* **1** The fore part of a vessel's hull or of an airship; the bow. **2** Any pointed projection. **3** *Poetic* A ship. [<MF *prove* <Provençal *proa* <L *prora* <Gk. *prōira*]

prow² (prou) *adj.* *Archaic* Brave; valiant: a *prow* knight. [<OF *prou* brave <LL *prode*, back formation <L *prodesse* be of use < *pro-*, *prod-* for + *esse* be]

prow·ess (prou′is) *n.* **1** Strength, skill, and courage in battle. **2** A daring and valiant deed. [<OF *prouesse, proece* < *prou* PROW²]

Synonyms: bravery, courage, gallantry, heroism, intrepidity, strength, valor. *Bravery, courage, heroism,* and *intrepidity* may be silent, spiritual, or passive; they may be exhibited by a martyr at the stake. *Courage* is a nobler word than *bravery,* involving more of the deep, spiritual, and enduring elements of character; it applies to matters to which *valor* and *prowess* cannot, as submission to a surgical operation, or the facing of censure or detraction for conscience' sake. *Prowess* and *valor* imply both daring and doing. *Valor* meets odds or perils with courageous action, doing its utmost to conquer at any risk or cost; *prowess* has power and ability adapted to the need; dauntless *valor* is often vain against superior *prowess.* Compare synonyms for BRAVE, COURAGE, FORTITUDE. *Antonyms:* cowardice, cowardliness, effeminacy, fear, timidity.

prowl (proul) *v.t.* & *v.i.* To roam about stealthily, as in search of prey or plunder. — *n.* A roaming about for prey. [ME *prollen* search; ult. origin uncertain] — **prowl′er** *n.*

prowl car *U.S.* A police patrol car.

prox·i·mal (prok′sə·məl) *adj.* **1** *Anat.* Relatively nearer the central portion of the body or point of origin: opposed to *distal.* **2** Proximate. — **prox′i·mal·ly** *adv.*

prox·i·mate (prok′sə·mit) *adj.* Being in immediate relation with something else; next. See synonyms under IMMEDIATE. [<LL *proximatus,* pp. of *proximare* come near <L *proximus* nearest, superl. of *prope* near] — **prox′i·mate·ly** *adv.*

prox·im·i·ty (prok·sim′ə·tē) *n.* The state or fact of being near or next; nearness. [<MF *proximité* <L *proximitas, -tatis* < *proximus.* See PROXIMATE.]

proximity fuze A complete miniature radio set placed in the nose of a projectile or bomb, capable of detonating the charge by simple proximity to the target: also called *VT fuze.*

prox·i·mo (prok′sə·mō) *adv.* In or of the next or coming month: opposed to *ultimo.* Abbr. *prox.* [<L *proximo (mense)* in the next (month), ablative of *proximus.* See PROXIMATE.]

prox·y (prok′sē) *n.* *pl.* **prox·ies** A person empowered by another to act for him, the office or right so to act, or the instrument conferring it. [Contraction of PROCURACY]

prude (prōōd) *n.* A person who makes an affected display of modesty and propriety, especially in matters relating to sex. [<F, prob. back formation < *prudefemme* an excellent woman <OF *prou, prode* honest, upright + *feme* a woman]

pru·dence (prōōd′ns) *n.* The quality of being prudent; sagacity; economy; discretion.

Synonyms: care, carefulness, caution, circumspection, consideration, discretion, forecast, foresight, forethought, frugality, judgment, judiciousness, providence, wisdom. *Care* may respect only the present; *prudence* and *providence* look far ahead and sacrifice the present to the future, *prudence* watching, saving, guarding, *providence* planning, doing, preparing, and perhaps expending largely to meet the future demand. *Frugality* is in many cases

one form of *prudence*. *Foresight* merely sees the future, and may even lead to the recklessness and desperation to which *prudence* and *providence* are strongly opposed. *Forethought* is thinking of the future, a *consideration* of what might arise. See CARE, FRUGALITY, WISDOM. *Antonyms*: folly, heedlessness, improvidence, imprudence, indiscretion, rashness, recklessness, thoughtlessness.

pru·dent (prōō'dnt) *adj.* 1 Habitually careful to avoid errors and in following the most politic and profitable course; cautious; worldly-wise. 2 Exercising sound judgment; sagacious; judicious. 3 Characterized by practical wisdom or discretion; not extravagant. 4 Decorously discreet: a *prudent* maiden. [< OF < L *prudens, -entis* knowing, skilled, contraction of *providens*. See PROVIDENCE.] —**pru'dent·ly** *adv.*

Synonyms: careful, cautious, circumspect, considerate, discreet, economical, frugal, judicious, politic, provident, sagacious, thoughtful, thrifty, wary, wise. See POLITIC. Compare synonyms for PRUDENCE. *Antonyms*: audacious, daring, desperate, foolhardy, foolish, imprudent, indiscreet, rash, reckless, spendthrift, thoughtless, unwary.

pru·den·tial (prōō·den'shəl) *adj.* 1 Proceeding from or marked by prudence. 2 Exercising prudence and wisdom officially. —**pru·den'tial·ly** *adv.*

prud·er·y (prōō'dər·ē) *n. pl.* **·er·ies** Primness; extreme priggishness; also, prudish action or language.

prud·ish (prōō'dish) *adj.* Showing prudery; prim. —**prud'ish·ly** *adv.* —**prud'ish·ness** *n.*

pru·i·nose (prōō'i·nōs) *adj. Biol.* Having the surface characterized by a secretion or outgrowth so as to appear frosted; powdery, as the bloom on a cabbage leaf, or the floury appearance of some cicadas and beetles. [< L *pruinosus* frosty < *pruina* hoarfrost]

prune[1] (prōōn) *n.* 1 The dried fruit of any of several varieties of plum. 2 Any of various plums that may be dried without spoiling. 3 *Slang* A stupid or uninteresting person. [< OF < LL *pruna* < L *prunum* < Gk. *proumnon, prounon* a plum. Doublet of PLUM.]

prune[2] (prōōn) *v.t. & v.i.* **pruned, prun·ing** 1 To trim or cut superfluous branches or parts (from) so as to improve growth, appearance, etc. 2 To cut off (superfluous branches or parts). See Synonyms under ABBREVIATE. [< OF *prooïgnier, proignier,* ? < *provaignier* cut < *provain* a slip < L *propago*; prob. infl. in form by *rooignier* cut off, ult. < L *rotundus* round] —**prun'er** *n.*

prune[3] (prōōn) *v.t. & v.i.* **pruned, prun·ing** *Archaic* To dress up; preen. [< OF *poroindre* anoint < *por-* (< L *pro* before) + *oindre* anoint < L *ungere*]

pru·nel·la (prōō·nel'ə) *n.* 1 A strong woolen cloth used for the uppers of shoes. 2 A similar twilled heavy dress fabric. 3 *pl.* Shoes made partly of prunella. Also **pru·nel'lo** (-nel'ō). [< F *prunelle* a sloe, dim. of *prune* plum, prune; prob. from its dark color]

pru·nelle (prōō·nel') *n.* 1 A small yellow prune, usually packed with the stone and skin removed. 2 A plum-flavored liqueur. [< F, dim. of *prune*. See PRUNE[1].]

pru·nif·er·ous (prōō·nif'ər·əs) *adj.* Plum-bearing. [< *pruni-* plum (< L *prunum*) + -FEROUS]

pru·ri·ent (prōōr'ē·ənt) *adj.* 1 Impure in thought and desire; lewd. 2 Having lustful cravings or desires. 3 Longing; desirous. [< L *pruriens, -entis,* ppr. of *prurire* itch, long for] —**pru'ri·ence, pru'ri·en·cy** *n.* —**pru'ri·ent·ly** *adv.*

pru·ri·go (prōō·rī'gō) *n. Pathol.* A chronic inflammatory skin disease marked by eruption and severe itching. [< L, an itching, lasciviousness < *prurire* itch] —**pru·rig'i·nous** (-rij'ə·nəs) *adj.*

pru·ri·tus (prōō·rī'təs) *n. Pathol.* Itching. [< L < *prurire* itch] —**pru·rit'ic** (-rit'ik) *adj.*

pruritus hi·e·ma·lis (hī'ə·mā'lis) Frost itch.

Pru·sa (prōō'sä) An ancient name for BRUSA.

Prus·sia (prush'ə) A former state, the largest and most important, of northern Germany; 113,410 square miles; capital, Berlin; formally dissolved, Feb. 1947; territory divided between East and West Germany, Poland, and Russian S.F.S.R.: German *Preussen.*

Prus·sian (prush'ən) *adj.* 1 Of or pertaining to Prussia, its inhabitants, or their language. 2 Characteristic of the Junkers of Prussia; militaristic; overbearing. —*n.* 1 A native or naturalized inhabitant of Prussia. 2 The old language of Prussia, belonging to the Baltic branch of the Balto-Slavic subfamily of Indo-European languages: extinct since the 17th century, and often called *Borussian*: also **Old Prussian.**

Prussian blue 1 *Chem.* Any one of a group of cyanogen compounds formed from ferrous sulfate and potassium ferrocyanide: formerly much used in dyeing. 2 A deep, strong, blue pigment with a coppery sheen, obtained from these compounds: used in oil painting but impermanent on alkali surfaces, as fresco: also called *Paris blue* (formerly called *Berlin blue*). Heat changes it to **Prussian brown.** [So called because discovered accidentally in Berlin, 1704, by H. de Diesbach, a colormaker]

Prus·sian·ism (prush'ən·iz'əm) *n.* The practices or policies of the Prussian ruling class during its leadership of Germany, characterized by militarism and *esprit de corps.*

prus·si·ate (prush'ē·āt, prus'-) *n. Chem.* 1 A salt of prussic acid; also, a cyanide. 2 A ferrocyanide or a ferricyanide.

prus·sic (prus'ik) *Chem. adj.* Hydrocyanic. —*n.* Prussic acid. [< F *prussique* < *Prusse* Prussia + *-ique* -IC; so called because derived from *Prussian blue*]

prussic acid Hydrocyanic acid.

Prut (prōōt) A river forming the boundary between SW U.S.S.R. and Rumania and flowing 530 miles from the Carpathians in SW Ukrainian S.S.R. to the Danube. Formerly **Pruth.**

pry[1] (prī) *v.i.* **pried, pry·ing** To look or peer carefully, curiously, or slyly; snoop. —*n. pl.* **pries** 1 A sly and searching inspection. 2 One who pries; an inquisitive, prying person. [ME *prien*; ult. origin unknown] **pry'ing** *adj. & n.* —**pry'ing·ly** *adv.*

pry[2] (prī) *v.t.* **pried, pry·ing** 1 To raise, move, or open by means of a lever; prize. 2 To obtain by effort. —*n.* A lever, as a bar, stick, or beam; also, leverage. [Back formation < PRIZE[2], *v.,* mistaken as a 3rd person sing.]

pry·er (prī'ər) PRIER.

Prynne (prin), **William,** 1600–69, English Presbyterian lawyer, pamphleteer, and statesman.

Prze·myśl (pshe'mish·əl) A city in SE Poland near the Ukrainian S.S.R. border; scene of several battles in World War I, 1915.

psalm (säm) *n.* A sacred song or lyric, especially one of those contained in the Old Testament Book of Psalms; a hymn. See synonyms under SONG. —*v.t.* To celebrate or praise in psalms; hymn. [Fusion of OE *sealm, psalm* and OF *salme, psaume,* both < LL *psalmus* < Gk. *psalmos* a song sung to the harp, lit., a twanging < *psallein* twitch]

psalm·ist (sä'mist) *n.* 1 A maker or composer of psalms. 2 In the early Christian church, one of the minor clergy who led the singing; a precentor. —**the Psalmist** King David, as the traditional author of many of the Scriptural psalms.

psalm·o·dy (sä'mə·dē, sal'-) *n. pl.* **·dies** 1 The use of psalms in divine worship; psalm-singing. 2 A collection of psalms. [< LL *psalmodia* < Gk. *psalmōidia* singing to the harp < *psalmōidos* a psalmist < *psalmos* a psalm + *ōidē* a song] —**psalm'o·dist** *n.*

Psalms (sämz) A lyrical book of the Old Testament, containing 150 hymns, many ascribed to David. Also **Book of Psalms.**

psal·ter (sôl'tər) *n.* 1 The psalms appointed to be read or sung at any given service. 2 In the Roman Catholic Church, a rosary of 150 beads, equaling the number of the Psalms. [OE *psaltere, saltere* < L *psalterium* a psaltery] —**psal·te·ri·an** (sôl·tir'ē·ən, sal-) *adj.*

Psal·ter (sôl'tər) *n.* 1 The Book of Psalms; specifically, the version of Psalms in the Book of Common Prayer. 2 The Latin version of Psalms used in the Roman Catholic breviary. Also **Psal'ter·y.**

psal·te·ri·um (sôl·tir'ē·əm, sal-) *n. pl.* **·te·ri·a** (-tir'ē·ə) The manyplies, or third stomach of a ruminant. [< L, a psaltery; so called because its many folds make it resemble the instrument] —**psal·te'ri·al** *adj.*

psal·ter·y (sôl'tər·ē) *n. pl.* **·ter·ies** An ancient stringed musical instrument, similar to a dulcimer but played by plucking with the fingers or a plectrum. [< OF *sautere, psalterie* < L *psalterium* < Gk. *psaltērion* < *psallein* twitch, twang]

PSALTERY
Twelfth century.

psam·mite (sam'īt) *n.* Fine-grained sandstone. [< F < Gk. *psammos* sand + -ITE[1]]

psam·mit·ic (sa·mit'ik) *adj. Geol.* 1 Composed of material in the form of rounded grains of sand: contrasted with *gritty.* 2 Specifically, having the texture of fine sand: said of detrital deposits or fragmental rocks: contrasted with *psephitic.*

psel·lism (sel'iz·əm) *n.* Imperfect articulation; stammering. [< Gk. *psellismos* stammering < *psellizein* stammer]

pse·phite (sē'fīt) *n.* A conglomeration of small pebbles; fragmental rock. [< Gk. *psēphos* a pebble + -ITE[1]]

pse·phit·ic (sē·fit'ik) *adj. Geol.* Having the texture of coarse sand: said of detrital deposits or fragmental rocks: contrasted with *psammitic.*

pse·phol·o·gy (sef·ol'ə·jē) *n.* The study and statistical analysis of the elective process and its results. [< Gk. *psēphos* pebble used in voting, the vote itself + -LOGY; coined by R. B. McCallum of Oxford University in 1952] —**pseph·ol'o·gist** *n.*

pseu·dax·is (sōō·dak'sis) *n.* A sympodium. [< PSEUD(O)- + AXIS]

pseu·de·pig·ra·pha (sōō'də·pig'rə·fə) *n. pl.* Spurious writing; especially, spurious religious writings, falsely ascribed to Scriptural characters or times and not considered as canonical by any branch of the Christian church. [< Gk., neut. pl. of *pseudepigraphos* with a false title < *pseudēs* false + *epigraphein* See EPIGRAPH.] —**pseu·dep·i·graph·ic** (sōō'dep·i·graf'ik) or **·i·cal, pseu'de·pig'ra·phous** *adj.*

pseu·do (sōō'dō) *adj.* Pretended; sham.

pseudo- *combining form* 1 False; pretended: *pseudonym.* 2 Counterfeit; not genuine: *pseudepigrapha.* 3 Closely resembling; serving or functioning as: *pseudopodium.* 4 Illusory; apparent: *pseudoaquatic.* 5 Abnormal; erratic: *pseudocarp.* Also, before vowels, **pseud-.** [< Gk. < *pseudēs* false]

pseu·do·a·quat·ic (sōō'dō·ə·kwat'ik, -kwot'-) *adj.* Not really aquatic, but native to or found — in wet places.

pseu·do·bulb (sōō'dō·bulb') *n. Bot.* A swollen, bulblike internode at the base of the stem in many orchids.

pseu·do·carp (sōō'dō·kärp) *n. Bot.* A false fruit; an often conspicuous portion of a fructification which consists of other parts besides the pericarp and seeds, as the apple, checkerberry, and mulberry. Also called *accessory fruit.* [< PSEUDO- + -CARP] **pseu'do·car'pous** *adj.*

pseu·do·clas·sic (sōō'dō·klas'ik) *adj.* Emulating classic style; pretending to be classic; wrongly classed as classic.

pseu·do·Is·i·dore (sōō'dō·iz'ə·dôr, -dōr) The unknown author or compiler of the "False Decretals." See DECRETALS. —**pseu·do·Is·i·do'ri·an** *adj.*

pseu·do·morph (sōō'dō·môrf) *n.* 1 An irregular or false form. 2 *Mineral.* A mineral having the external crystalline form of another mineral. [< PSEUDO- + -MORPH] **pseu'do·mor'phic** *adj.* **pseu'do·mor'phism** *n.* —**pseu'do·mor'phous** *adj.*

pseu·do·nym (sōō'də·nim) *n.* A fictitious name; pen name. [< F < Gk. *pseudonymos,* orig. neut. of *pseudonymos* having a false name < *pseudēs* false + *onoma, onyma* a name] **pseu·don·y·mous** (sōō·don'ə·məs) *adj.* —**pseu·don'y·mous·ly** *adv.* **pseu·don'y·mous·ness, pseu'do·nym'i·ty** *n.*

pseu·do·pod (sōō'də·pod) *n.* 1 A pseudopodium. 2 An organism with pseudopodia;

a rhizopod. —**pseu·dop·o·dal** (sōō·dop′ə·dəl) *adj.*

pseu·do·po·di·um (sōō′də·pō′dē·əm) *n. pl.* **·di·a** (-dē·ə) **1** *Zool.* A process formed by the temporary extension of the protoplasm of a cell or of a unicellular animal, serving for taking in food, for locomotion, etc. **2** *Bot.* A false pedicel in certain mosses. Also **pseu′do·pode** (-pōd). [< NL < Gk. *pseudēs* false + *podion.* See PODIUM.]

pshaw (shô) *interj. & n.* An exclamation of annoyance, disapproval, disgust, or impatience. —*v.t. & v.i.* To exclaim *pshaw* at (a person or thing).

psi[1] (sī, psī, psē) *n.* The twenty-third letter in the Greek alphabet (Ψ, ψ): equivalent to English *ps.*

psi[2] (sī) *n.* Pounds per square inch: a unit of pressure.

psi·lo·cy·bin (sī′lə·sī′bin) *n.* A hallucinogenic drug derived from a Mexican mushroom, used in Indian religious rites. [< *Psilocybe (mexicana),* the mushroom from which it is obtained + -IN]

Psi·lo·ri·ti (psē′lô·rē′tē) See IDA.

Psit·ta·ci·for·mes (sit′ə·si·fôr′mēz) *n. pl.* An order of climbing, arboreal birds, including the parrots, macaws, and cockatoos. [< NL < Gk. *psittakos* a parrot + L *forma* form]

psit·ta·cine (sit′ə·sīn, -sin) *adj.* Of or pertaining to parrots. [< L *psittacinus* < *psittacus* a parrot < Gk. *psittakos*]

psit·ta·co·sis (sit′ə·kō′sis) *n.* An acute, infectious, wasting disease of parrots and related birds, caused by a filtrable virus: transmitted to man, it causes fever and nausea, with complications resembling influenza and typhoid fever: also called *parrot fever.* [< NL < Gk. *psittakos* a parrot + *-osis*-OSIS]

Pskov (pskôf) A city of NW European Russian S.F.S.R. near the border of the Estonian S.S.R. on the southern end of **Lake Pskov.**

pso·as (sō′əs) *n. Anat.* Either of two muscles of the interior of the pelvis, arising from the spine and constituting the loins. [< NL < Gk., acc. pl. of *psoa* the muscle of the loins]

Pso·cop·ter·a (sō·kop′tər·ə) See CORRODENTIA.

pso·ra (sôr′ə, sō′rə) *n. Pathol.* **1** Scabies. **2** Psoriasis. [< L < Gk. *psōra* an itch] —**pso′ric** *adj. & n.*

pso·ra·le·a (sə·rā′lē·ə) *n.* A scented herb or shrub (genus *Psoralea*) of the bean family, especially the common breadroot. [< NL < Gk. *psōraleos* scabby]

pso·ri·a·sis (sə·rī′ə·sis) *n. Pathol.* A non-contagious, inflammatory skin disease, chronic or acute, characterized by reddish patches and white scales. [< NL < Gk. *psōriaein* have an itch < *psōra* an itch] —**pso·ri·at·ic** (sôr′ē·at′ik, sō′rē-) *adj.*

psych (sīk) *v.t. Slang* **1** To make mentally ready, as by inducing alertness or tension; key up: often with *up.* **2** To cause to lose self-assurance, especially in order to place at a competitive disadvantage; demoralize: often with *out*: to *psych* rivals. **3** To manipulate by the use of psychology; especially, to outwit: often with *out*: *psyched* him into giving me a loan. **4** To understand: with *out*: couldn't *psych* it out. Also **psyche.**

psych- See PSYCHO-.

psy·chal·gi·a (sī·kal′jē·ə) *n. Psychiatry* Mental suffering; morbid depression: distinguished from *somatalgia.* [< NL < Gk. *psychē* mind + *algos* a pain, an affliction]

psy·chas·the·ni·a (sī′kas·thē′nē·ə) *n. Psychiatry* A morbid mental state characterized by mental fatigue, obsessive anxiety, phobias, tics, etc. [< NL < Gk. *psychē* mind + *astheneia* debility, weakness] —**psy′chas·then′ic** (-then′ik) *adj. & n.*

psy·che (sī′kē) *n.* **1** The human soul; the mind; the intelligence. **2** *Psychoanal.* The aggregate of all the psychic components constituting a human individual, sometimes considered as an entity functioning apart from or independently of the body. **3** A knot of hair coiled at the back of the head by women in imitation of an ancient Greek style of hairdressing: also **Psyche knot.** [< Gk. *psychē* < *psychein* breathe, blow]

Psy·che (sī′kē) In Greek and Roman mythology, a maiden beloved by Eros, who, after many tribulations caused by the jealousy of Venus, is united with her lover and accorded a place among the gods as a personification of the soul.

psy·che·de·li·a (sī′kə·dē′lē·ə, -dēl′yə) *n.* Psychedelic drugs and accessories, or things associated with them.

psy·che·del·ic (sī′kə·del′ik) *adj.* Causing or having to do with an abnormal stimulation of consciousness or perception: *psychedelic* drugs; a *psychedelic* experience. [< Gk. *psychē* + *del(os)* manifest + -IC]

psy·chi·a·trist (sī·kī′ə·trist) *n.* A medical doctor specializing in the practice of psychiatry.

psy·chi·a·try (sī·kī′ə·trē) *n.* The branch of medicine that treats disorders of the mind or psyche, especially psychoses, but also neuroses. [< PSYCH- + -IATRY] —**psy·chi·at·ric** (sī′kē·at′rik) or **·ri·cal** *adj.*

psy·chic (sī′kik) *adj.* **1** Pertaining to the mind or soul; mental, as distinguished from physical and physiological. **2** *Psychol.* Pertaining to or designating those mental phenomena which are, or appear to be, independent of normal sensory stimuli and which cannot be fully explained in terms of the known data of experimental science, as clairvoyance, telepathy, and extrasensory perception. Compare PARAPSYCHOLOGY. **3** Caused by, proceeding from, associated with, or attributed to a non-material or occult agency. **4** Sensitive to mental or occult phenomena. Also **psy′chi·cal.** —*n.* **1** A person sensitive to mental or extrasensory phenomena; especially, a spiritualistic medium. **2** The field of extrasensory phenomena: with *the.* [< Gk. *psychikos* < *psychē* soul] —**psy′chi·cal·ly** *adv.*

psy·cho (sī′kō) *n. pl.* **·chos** *Slang* A mentally disturbed person; a neurotic or psychopath. —*adj.* **1** Psychologically disturbed. **2** Psychological or psychiatric. [< PSYCHO(NEUROTIC)]

psycho- *combining form* Mind; soul; spirit: *psychosomatic.* Also, before vowels, *psych-.* [< Gk. *psychē* spirit, soul]

psy·cho·ac·tive (sī′kō·ak′tiv) *adj.* Having a specific effect on mental activities: *psychoactive* drugs.

psy·cho·a·nal·y·sis (sī′kō·ə·nal′ə·sis) *n.* **1** The doctrine that mental life and all forms of behavior may be interpreted in terms of reciprocally acting forces largely governed by the dynamic interplay of conflicting drives and processes originating in the unconscious. **2** A system of psychotherapy originated and developed by Freud which seeks to alleviate mental and nervous disorders by the technical analysis of controlling factors persistently repressed in, and manifested through, the unconscious. —**psy′cho·an′a·lyt′ic** (-an′ə·lit′ik) or **·i·cal** *adj.* —**psy′cho·an′a·lyt′i·cal·ly** *adv.*

psy·cho·an·a·lyst (sī′kō·an′ə·list) *n.* One who practices psychoanalysis.

psy·cho·an·a·lyze (sī′kō·an′ə·līz) *v.t.* **·lyzed, ·lyz·ing** To treat by psychoanalysis. Also *Brit.* **psy′cho·an′a·lyse.**

psy·cho·bi·ol·o·gy (sī′kō·bī·ol′ə·jē) *n.* **1** The study of the mind and of mental processes in relation to anatomy, physiology, and the nervous system, with special reference to the influence of the environment. **2** Psychology in its biological aspects. Also called *biopsychology.* —**psy′cho·bi′o·log′i·cal** (-bī′ə·loj′i·kəl) *adj.* —**psy′cho·bi·ol′o·gist** *n.*

psy·cho·dra·ma (sī′kō·drä′mə, -dram′ə) *n.* A form of psychotherapy in which the patient acts out situations involving his problems. —**psy′cho·dra·mat′ic** *adj.*

psy·cho·dy·nam·ics (sī′kō·dī·nam′iks) *n.* The study of mental processes in action. —**psy′cho·dy·nam′ic** *adj.*

psy·cho·gen·e·sis (sī′kō·jen′ə·sis) *n.* **1** The development of the individual soul; the science of the origin of psychic life. **2** Genesis or specific change due to vitality of the organism, as opposed to external influences. Also **psy·chog·e·ny** (sī·koj′ə·nē). —**psy′cho·ge·net′ic** (-jə·net′ik) *adj.* —**psy′cho·ge·net′i·cal·ly** *adv.*

psy·cho·gen·ic (sī′kō·jen′ik) *adj.* Having mental origin, or being affected by mental actions and states.

psy·chog·no·sis (sī′kog·nō′sis) *n.* The close study and diagnosis of mental states. [< PSYCHO- + -GNOSIS] —**psy′chog·nos′tic** (-nos′·tik) *adj.*

psy·cho·graph (sī′kə·graf, -gräf) *n.* **1** A chart graphically representing the personality traits of an individual: also **psy′cho·gram** (-gram). **2** A description of the personality traits of an individual, especially in literary form. —**psy′cho·graph′ic** *adj.*

psy·chog·ra·phy (sī·kog′rə·fē) *n.* **1** Involuntary or unconscious writing, as by a medium. **2** The making of a psychograph.

psy·cho·his·to·ry (sī′kō·his′tə·rē, -his′trē) *n.* History or a work of history in which major emphasis is given the psychological states or dispositions of important participants as contributing causes of certain actions, decisions, or developments. —**psy′cho·his·tor′i·an** (-his′tôr′ē·ən, -tō′rē-) *n.* —**psy′cho·his′tor′i·cal** *adj.* —**psy′cho·his′tor′i·cal·ly** *adv.*

psy·cho·ki·ne·sis (sī′kō·ki·nē′sis) *n.* The alleged power of controlling the chance behavior of physical objects, as cards, dice, etc., by the direct influence upon them of emotional states, strong desire, or other psychic factors.

psy·cho·log·i·cal (sī′kə·loj′i·kəl) *adj.* **1** Of or pertaining to psychology. **2** Of or in the mind. **3** Suitable for affecting the mind: the *psychological* moment. Also **psy′cho·log′ic.** —**psy′cho·log′i·cal·ly** *adv.*

psy·chol·o·gism (sī·kol′ə·jiz′əm) *n.* Idealistic philosophy as opposed to sensationalism. Compare ONTOLOGISM.

psy·chol·o·gist (sī·kol′ə·jist) *n.* A student of or a specialist in psychology.

psy·chol·o·gize (sī·kol′ə·jīz) *v.i.* **·gized, ·giz·ing** **1** To study psychology. **2** To theorize psychologically.

psy·chol·o·gy (sī·kol′ə·jē) *n.* **1** The science of the human mind in any of its aspects, operations, powers, or functions. **2** The systematic investigation of mental phenomena, especially those associated with consciousness, behavior, and the problems of adjustment to the environment. **3** The aggregate of the emotions, traits, and behavior patterns regarded as characteristic of an individual or type: the *psychology* of a fanatic. [< NL *psychologia* < Gk. *psychē* soul + -LOGY]

psy·chom·e·try (sī·kom′ə·trē) *n.* **1** The science of the measurement of psychophysical processes, especially of their accuracy or duration in time; mental testing: also **psy·cho·met·rics** (sī·kō·met′riks). **2** Divination by physical contact or proximity of the properties of things touched or approached. —**psy·chom′e·trist** *n.*

psy·cho·mo·tor (sī′kō·mō′tər) *adj. Physiol.* Of or pertaining to muscular movements resulting from or caused by compulsive mental processes.

psy·cho·neu·ro·sis (sī′kō·nōō·rō′sis, -nyōō-) *n. pl.* **·ses** (-sēz) *Psychiatry* A nervous disorder originating in distrubed psychic or mental functions, usually without or independent of organic symptoms: characterized by anxiety, phobias, compulsions, obsessions, etc. —**psy′cho·neu·rot′ic** (-rot′ik) *adj. & n.*

psy·cho·path (sī′kō·path) *n.* One subject to or afflicted by mental instability.

psy·cho·path·ic (sī′kō·path′ik) *n.* A psychopath. —*adj.* Of or marked by psychopathy.

psy·cho·pa·thol·o·gy (sī′kō·pə·thol′ə·jē) *n.* The pathology of the mind. —**psy′cho·path′o·log′i·cal** (-path′ə·loj′i·kəl) *adj.* —**psy′cho·pa·thol′o·gist** *n.*

psy·chop·a·thy (sī·kop′ə·thē) *n.* **1** Mental disorder, especially as apart from disease of the brain, and typified by emotional immaturity and instability, moral deficiency, and perversions. **2** Psychotherapy.

psy·cho·phar·ma·col·o·gy (sī′kō·fär′mə·kol′ə·jē) *n.* The branch of pharmacology which investigates the properties and uses of drugs acting primarily on the nervous system and serving to modify human behavior.

psy·cho·phys·ics (sī′kō·fiz′iks) *n.* The science of the relations between mental and physical phenomena. —**psy′cho·phys′i·cal** *adj.* —**psy′cho·phys′i·cist** *n.*

psy·cho·phys·i·ol·o·gy (sī′kō·fiz′ē·ol′ə·jē) *n.* The physiology of mental processes.

psy·cho·sex·u·al (sī′kō·sek′shōō·əl) *adj.* Of or pertaining to the psychological aspects of sexuality or sexual development. —**psy′cho·sex′u·al′i·ty** (-sek′shōō·al′ə·tē) *n.* —**psy′cho·sex′u·al·ly** *adv.*

psy·cho·sis (sī·kō′sis) *n. pl.* **·ses** (-sēz) *Psychiatry* A mental disorder, severe in character, often involving disorganization of the total personality, with or without organic disease. ◆Homophone: *sycosis.* [< NL < Gk. *psychōsis* a giving of life < *psychoein* animate < *psychē* a soul]

psy·cho·so·mat·ic (sī′kō·sō·mat′ik) *adj.* **1** Of

or pertaining to the interrelationships of mind and body, with especial reference to disease. **2** Designating a branch of medicine which investigates the reciprocal influences of body and mind in the cause, prevention, treatment, and cure of disease.

psy·cho·sur·ger·y (sī′kō·sûr′jər·ē) *n.* Brain surgery performed to treat a mental disorder or alter behavior. **—psy′cho·sur′geon** (-sûr′jən) *n.* **—psy′cho·sur′gi·cal** *adj.*

psy·cho·tech·ni·cian (sī′kō·tek·nish′ən) *n.* One skilled in psychotechnics.

psy·cho·tech·nics (sī′kō·tek′niks) *n.* The direct application of psychological principles and methods to practical ends, especially in the management of large industrial and business enterprises. **—psy′cho·tech′ni·cal** *adj.*

psy·cho·ther·a·py (sī′kō·ther′ə·pē) *n.* The treatment of nervous and mental disorders, especially by psychological methods, as hypnosis, re-education, psychonanalysis, etc. Also **psy′cho·ther′a·peu′tics** (-ther′ə·pyōō′tiks). **—psy′chother′a·peu′tic** *adj.* **—psy′cho·ther′a·pist** *n.*

psy·chot·ic (sī·kot′ik) *n.* One suffering from a psychosis. *—adj.* Of or characterized by a psychosis.

psy·chot·o·mi·met·ic (sī·kot′ō·mə·met′ik) *adj.* Pertaining to or productive of psychotic behavior: *psychotomimetic drugs.* **—psy·chot′o·mi·met′i·cal·ly** *adv.*

psy·cho·trop·ic (sī′kō·trop′ik) *adj.* Acting on or affecting the mind, as certain drugs. *—n.* A psychotropic drug. [< PSYCHO- + -TROPIC]

psychro- *combining form* Cold: *psychrophobia.* [< Gk. *psychros* cold]

psy·chrom·e·ter (sī·krom′ə·tər) *n.* An instrument for measuring the vapor tension and relative humidity of the air, consisting of two thermometers, the bulb of one being kept moist. [< PSYCHRO- + -METER]

psy·chro·ther·a·py (sī′krō·ther′ə·pē) *n.* Medical treatment by the use of cold.

psyl·li·um (sil′ē·əm) *n.* **1** A plantain of Asia Minor *(Plantago psyllium).* **2** Its small, reddish-brown seeds, resembling flaxseed in medicinal properties, used as a mild laxative. [< L < Gk. *psyllion* < *psylla* a flea; so called because supposed to destroy fleas]

Pt *Chem.* Platinum (symbol Pt).

Ptah (ptä, ptäkh) In ancient Egyptian religion, the chief divinity of ancient Memphis, the creator of gods and men.

ptar·mi·gan (tär′mə·gən) *n. pl.* **·gans** or **·gan** A grouse (genus *Lagopus*) of the northern hemisphere, with the winter plumage chiefly pure white, and with feathered toes. [< Scottish Gaelic *tarmachan;* excrescent *p* prob. due to false analogy with Gk. *pteron* wing]

PT boat A patrol torpedo boat.

pter·i·dol·o·gy (ter′i·dol′ə·jē) *n.* The department of botany that treats of ferns. [< Gk. *pteris, pteridos* a fern + -LOGY] **—pter′i·do·log′i·cal** (-dō·loj′i·kəl) *adj.* **—pter′i·dol′o·gist** *n.*

pter·i·do·phyte (ter′i·dō·fīt′) *n.* Any of a phylum *(Pteridophyta)* of flowerless plants comprising the ferns, clubmosses, and their allies. [< NL < Gk. *pteris, pteridos* a fern + *phyton* a plant] **—pter′i·do·phyt′ic** (-fit′ik), **pter′i·doph′y·tous** (-dof′ə·təs) *adj.*

ptero- *combining form* Wing; feather; plume; resembling wings: *pterodactyl.* Also, before vowels, **pter-.** [< Gk. *pteron* wing]

pter·o·dac·tyl (ter′ə·dak′til) *n. Paleontol.* **1** Any of a genus *(Pterodactylus)* of extinct flying reptiles which flourished in the Jurassic period, characterized by a large, birdlike skull, long jaws, and flying membrane somewhat like that of a bat. **2** A pterosaurian. [< NL < Gk. *pteron* a wing + *daktylos* a finger]

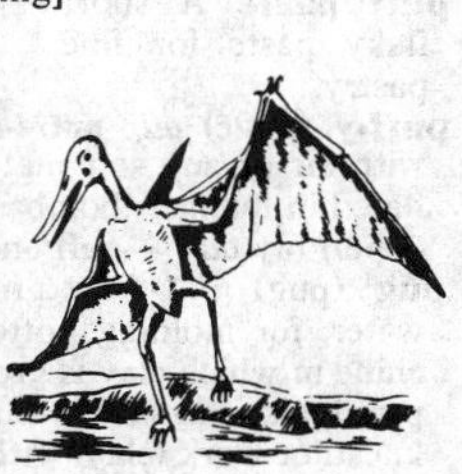

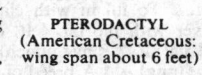

PTERODACTYL
(American Cretaceous: wing span about 6 feet)

pter·o·pod (ter′ə·pod) *n.* One of a subclass or order *(Pteropoda)* of gastropods with the middle region of the foot expanded into winglike lobes or fins; a sea butterfly. *—adj.* **1** Having the foot expanded into swimming lobes. **2** Of or pertaining to the *Pteropoda:* also **pte·rop·o·dan** (tə·rop′ə·dən). [< NL < Gk. *pteron* a wing + *pous, podos* a foot]

pter·o·sau·ri·an (ter′ə·sôr′ē·ən) *n. Paleontol.* One of an extinct order *(Pterosauria)* of flying reptiles, including pterodactyls, of the Mesozoic, with external digits long and developed to support a flying membrane. Also **pter′o·saur.** *—adj.* Of or pertaining to the *Pterosauria.* [< NL < Gk. *pteron* a wing + *sauros* a lizard]

pter·y·goid (ter′ə·goid) *adj.* **1** Having the form of a wing; winglike. **2** *Anat.* Pertaining to, or situated near the winglike processes of the sphenoid. Also **pter′y·goi′dal, pter′y·goi′de·an.** *—n. Anat.* A pterygoid bone, plate, process, or muscle. [< Gk. *pteryx, pterygos* a wing + -OID]

ptis·an (tiz′ən) *n.* **1** A slightly medicinal decoction or tea of herbs: also spelled *tisane.* **2** The juice of grapes drained off without pressure. **3** A decoction of barley water. [< OF *ptisane, tisane* < L *ptisana* barley groats, a drink made from them < Gk. *ptisanē* peeled barley < *ptissein* peel]

Ptol·e·ma·ic (tol′ə·mā′ik) *adj.* Of or pertaining to Ptolemy, the astronomer, or to the Ptolemies, the Egyptian kings.

Ptolemaic system The ancient astronomical system of Ptolemy, which assumed that the earth was the central body around which the sun, planets, and celestial bodies revolved: this system was accepted till replaced in the 16th century by the Copernican system.

Ptol·e·ma·is (tol′ə·mā′is) The New Testament name for ACRE.

Ptol·e·ma·ist (tol′ə·mā′ist) *n.* A believer in or adherent of the Ptolemaic system.

Ptol·e·my (tol′ə·mē) Second century A.D. astronomer, mathematician, and geographer of Alexandria: full name *Claudius Ptolomaeus.*

Ptol·e·my (tol′ə·mē) Name of 14 kings of Egypt, of whom the most noted are:
—Ptolemy I, 367?–283? B.C., king 323–285; a general of Alexander the Great; founded the dynasty: called "Soter."
—Ptolemy II, 309–246 B.C., king 285–46; patron of literature and the arts: called "Philadelphus."
—Ptolemy III, 282?–221 B.C., king 246–21; conquered much of the Seleucid dominions; built many temples: called "Euergetes."

pto·maine (tō′mān, tō·mān′) *n. Biochem.* Any of a class of basic organic chemical compounds derived from decomposing or putrefying animal or vegetable protein. They bear some resemblance to the alkaloids, and some of them are poisonous. Also **pto′main.** [< Ital. *ptomaina* < Gk. *ptōma* a corpse]

ptomaine poisoning Poisoning due to bacteria or bacterial toxins in food: an inexact term.

pto·sis (tō′sis) *n. Pathol.* The permanent drooping of the upper eyelid, due to paralysis of the lifting muscle of the lid. [< NL < Gk. *ptōsis* a falling < *piptein* fall] **—pto·tic** (tō′tik) *adj.*

pty·a·lin (tī′ə·lin) *n. Biochem.* An amylase contained in the saliva of man and other mammals; the enzyme of saliva which converts starch into dextrin and maltose. [< Gk. *ptyalon* saliva + -IN]

pty·a·lism (tī′ə·liz′əm) *n.* Abnormal flow of saliva. [< Gk. *ptyalon* saliva + -ISM]

Pu *Chem.* Plutonium (symbol Pu).

pub (pub) *n. Brit. Slang* A public house; an inn; tavern. [Short for *public house*]

pu·ber·ty (pyōō′bər·tē) *n.* The period in life at which a person of either sex becomes functionally capable of reproduction: in civil law, usually the age of 14 years in males and 12 in females. [< OF *puberte* < L *pubertas* < *pubes, puberis* an adult]

pu·bes (pyōō′bēz) *n.* **1** *Anat.* The part of the lower central hypogastric region covered with hair in the adult; the pubic region. **2** The hair that appears on the body at puberty; specifically, the hair on the pubic region. **3** *Biol.* Pubescence. [< L, pubic hair, groin]

pu·bes·cence (pyōō·bes′əns) *n.* **1** The state or quality of being pubescent (def. 1). **2** *Biol.* A covering or growth of soft, fine hairs or down, especially that upon certain plants.

pu·bes·cent (pyōō·bes′ənt) *adj.* **1** Arriving or having arrived at puberty. **2** *Biol.* Covered with hairs, especially fine, soft, short hairs; hairy or downy, as leaves etc. [< MF < L *pubescens, -entis,* ppr. of *pubescere* become downy, attain puberty < *pubes.* See PUBES.]

pu·bic (pyōō′bik) *adj.* Of or pertaining to the region in the lower part of the abdomen.

pu·bis (pyōō′bis) *n. pl.* **·bes** (bēz) *Anat.* Either of the two bones which join with a third to form an arch on either ventral side of the pelvis. [< NL, short for L *os pubis* pubic bone < *pubes.* See PUBES.]

pub·lic (pub′lik) *adj.* **1** Of, pertaining to, or affecting the people at large or the community: distinguished from *private* or *personal.* **2** Open to all; maintained by or for the public: *public* parks; participated in by the people: a *public* demonstration. **3** For the use of the public; specifically, for hire: a *public* cab, hall, etc. **4** Done or made in public or without concealment; well-known; open; notorious: a *public* scandal. **5** Occupying an official or professional position; acting before or for the community: a *public* speaker. See synonyms under COMMON, GENERAL. *—n.* The people collectively, or in general, of a particular locality or nation; also, all those persons who may be grouped together for any given purpose: the church-going *public.* [< OF < L *publicus,* alter. of *poplicus* (through infl. of *pubes* an adult) < *poplus, populus* people]

pub·lic-ad·dress system (pub′lik·ə·dres′) A complete assembly of sound-reproducing apparatus for broadcasting messages, etc., in public places.

pub·li·can (pub′lə·kən) *n.* **1** In England, the keeper of a public house. **2** In ancient Rome, one who farmed or collected the public revenues. [< OF *publicain* < L *publicanus* a tax farmer, tax gatherer < *publicum* public revenue, orig. neut. of *publicus* PUBLIC]

pub·li·ca·tion (pub′lə·kā′shən) *n.* **1** The act of publishing or offering to public notice; notification to people at large orally or by writing or print; promulgation; proclamation. **2** In the law of libel and slander, the communication of a defamation to a third person. **3** That which is published; any printed work placed on sale or otherwise distributed or offered for distribution. See PUBLISH. [< OF *publicacion* < L *publicatio, -onis* < *publicatus,* pp. of *publicare* PUBLISH]

public debt The national debt.

public domain Lands owned by a state or national government; public lands. **—in the public domain** Available for unrestricted use: said of material on which copyright or patent right has expired.

public enemy **1** Any government with which a nation is at open war. **2** A person, especially a criminal, regarded as a menance to the public.

Public Health Service *U.S.* A Federal agency under the Surgeon General, which, as a constituent organization of the Department of Health, Education, and Welfare, is responsible for protecting and improving the health of the nation.

public house **1** An inn, tavern, or hotel. **2** In England, a place licensed to sell intoxicating liquors; a saloon.

pub·li·cist (pub′lə·sist) *n.* **1** A writer on international law or on topics of public interest. **2** A public-relations man or publicity agent. [< F *publiciste*]

pub·lic·i·ty (pub·lis′ə·tē) *n.* **1** The state of being public, or the act or fact of making or becoming public; exposure; notoriety: opposed to *secrecy.* **2** Advertising; advance information, or personal news intended to promote the interests of individuals, institutions, causes, etc., especially that appearing in print. **3** The attention or interest of the public gained by any method.

pub·li·cize (pub′lə·sīz) *v.t.* **·cized, ·ciz·ing** To give publicity to; advertise.

public library **1** A library maintained for the use of the public. **2** The building in which it is contained.

pub·lic·ly (pub′lik·lē) *adv.* **1** In an open or public manner; openly. **2** In the name or with the consent and concurrence of the public.

pub·lic·ness (pub′lik·nis) *n.* **1** The state or quality of being public or of belonging to the public. **2** Publicity.

add,āce,câre,pälm; end,ēven; it,īce; odd,ōpen,ôrder; tŏŏk,pōōl; up,bûrn; ə = a in *above,* e in *sicken,* i in *clarity,* o in *melon,* u in *focus* ; yōō = u in *fuse,* oi,oil; ou,pout; ch,check; g,go; ng,ring; th,thin; th,this; zh,vision. Foreign sounds á,œ,ü,kh,ṅ; and ◆: see page xx. < from; + plus; ? possibly.

public opinion The prevailing ideas, beliefs, and aims of the people, collectively: in politics, considered as a massed power or entity.
public relations 1 The activities and techniques utilized by public and private organizations and enterprises to establish favorable attitudes and responses in their behalf on the part of the general public or of special groups: included are analysis of attitudes, appraisal of procedures and policies, recommendations for internal change, and effective presentation of the organization's purposes and objectives. 2 The public conduct of the affairs of an organization with regard to its reputation and standing and to public opinion. 3 The relationship between the general public and an institution of any kind.
public school See under SCHOOL.
public servant A government official.
public service 1 Official employment under the government, especially in the civil departments. 2 The radio or television broadcasting of announcements of civic interest.
pub·lic-ser·vice corporation (pub′lik·sûr′vis) Any corporation operating a public utility, as a railroad, gas, electric, or water company.
public spirit Active, enlightened interest in and concern for matters that affect the welfare of the community. **—pub·lic-spir·it·ed** (pub′lik·spir′·it·id) *adj.*
public utility A business organization or industry which performs some public service, as the supplying of water or electric power, and is subject to particular governmental regulations; a public-service corporation.
public works Permanent architectural or engineering works or improvements built with public money, as post offices, museums, canals, harbors, parks, playgrounds, roads, bridges, etc.
pub·lish (pub′lish) *v.t.* 1 To make known or announce publicly; promulgate; proclaim. 2 To print and issue (a book, magazine, map, etc.) to the public. 3 *Law* To communicate (a defamation) to a third person. 4 To print and issue the work of: to *publish* Hemingway. —*v.i.* 5 To engage in the business of publishing books, magazines, newspapers, etc. 6 To have one's work printed and issued. [<OF *publier, puplier* <L *publicare* make public <*publicus* PUBLIC] —**pub′lish·a·ble** *adj.*
Synonyms: advertise, announce, blazon, bruit, communicate, declare, disclose, divulge, impart, proclaim, promulgate, reveal, spread, tell. See ANNOUNCE, SPREAD. *Antonyms*: conceal, cover, hide, hush, suppress, withhold.
pub·lish·er (pub′lish·ər) *n.* One who publishes; especially, one who makes a business of publishing books or periodicals.
Puc·ci·ni (po͞ot·chē′nē), **Giacomo,** 1858–1924, Italian operatic composer.
puc·coon (pə·ko͞on′) *n.* 1 Any of several North American herbs of the genus *Lithospermum*, having red roots and sessile leaves, especially a species *(L. canescens)* with orange-yellow flowers and roots that yield a red dye. Also called *alkanet.* 2 A red pigment or dye obtained from these plants. 3 The bloodroot. [<Algonquian (Virginian) *puccoon, pakon* <*pak* blood]
puce (pyo͞os) *adj.* Of a dark-brown or purplish-brown. [<F, flea color, a flea <L *pulex, -icis* a flea]
pu·celle (pyo͞o·sel′, *Fr.* pü·sel′) *n.* A virgin; maid: obsolete except in the phrase **La Pucelle,** Joan of Arc, the Maid of Orleans. [<OF *pucele, pulcella* <LL *pulicella* a young girl; ult. origin uncertain]
puck[1] (puk) *n.* 1 An evil sprite or hobgoblin. 2 In English folklore, **Puck,** a mischievous elf or goblin: also called *Robin Goodfellow*; specifically, in Shakespeare's *A Midsummer Night's Dream,* a mischievous fairy servant of Oberon. [OE *pūca* a goblin] **—puck′ish** *adj.* **—puck′ish·ly** *adv.*
puck[2] (puk) *n.* The hard rubber disk used in playing hockey. [<dial. E, strike. Akin to POKE[1].]
puck·a (puk′ə) *adj. Anglo-Indian* Made of good materials; substantial; hence, genuine; superior: also spelled *pukka.* [<Hind. *pakkā* substantial, lit., cooked, ripe]
puck·er (puk′ər) *v.t.* & *v.i.* To gather or draw up into small folds or wrinkles. —*n.* 1 A wrinkle, or group of wrinkles. 2 *Colloq.* Agitation; perplexity; confusion. [Appar. freq. of POKE[2]] —**puck′er·y** *adj.*
pud·ding (po͝od′ing) *n.* 1 A sweetened and flavored dessert of soft food, usually farinaceous. 2 A skin or gut filled with seasoned minced meat, blood, or the like, and usually boiled or broiled. [ME *poding,* orig. sausage, black pudding, prob. <OF *bodin, boudin*]
pud·dle (pud′l) *n.* 1 A small pool of dirty water. 2 Puddling (def. 2). —*v.t.* **·dled, ·dling** 1 *Metall.* To convert (molten pig iron) into wrought iron by melting and stirring in the presence of oxidizing substances. 2 To mix (clay, etc.) with water so as to obtain a watertight paste. 3 To line, as canal banks, with such a mixture. 4 To make muddy; stir up. [ME *podel,* appar. dim. of OE *pudd* a ditch] **—pud′dly** *adj.*
pud·dle·ball (pud′l·bôl′) *n.* A ball of heated iron fresh from the puddling furnace.
pud·dle·bar (pud′l·bär′) *n.* A bar into which a puddleball is rolled or hammered.
pud·dler (pud′lər) *n.* 1 One who puddles. 2 A device for stirring fused metal. 3 A puddling furnace.
pud·dling (pud′ling) *n.* 1 *Metall.* The operation or business of making wrought iron from pig iron in a puddling furnace. 2 Puddled clay for lining the banks of canals, etc.; puddle. 3 The operation of lining a canal with such clay.
puddling furnace A reverberatory furnace for puddling pig iron.
pu·den·cy (pyo͞o′dən·sē) *n.* Shame; modesty; also, prudishness. [<LL *pudentia* <L *pudens, -entis,* ppr. of *pudere* be ashamed]
pu·den·dum (pyo͞o·den′dəm) *n. pl.* **·da** (-də) 1 The vulva. 2 *pl.* The external genitals of either sex. [<L, neut. of *pudendus* (something) to be ashamed of, gerundive of *pudere* be ashamed] —**pu′dic, pu·den′dal** *adj.*
pudg·y (puj′ē) *adj.* **pudg·i·er, pudg·i·est** Short and thick; fat. [? <dial. E (Scottish) <*pud* belly] —**pudg′i·ly** *adv.* **—pudg′i·ness** *n.*
Pue·bla (pwā′blä) A state in SE Mexico; 13,124 square miles; capital, Puebla.
pueb·lo (pweb′lō *for def. 1,* pwā′blō *for defs. 2 and 3*) *n. pl.* **·los** 1 A communal adobe or stone building or group of buildings of the Indians of the SW United States. 2 A town or village of Indians or Spanish Americans, as in Mexico. 3 In the Philippines, a municipality: originally the civilian quarter of a Spanish community. [<Sp., a town, people <L *populus*]

HOPI INDIAN PUEBLO

Pueb·lo (pweb′lō) *n.* A member of one of the Indian tribes of Mexico and the SW United States, representing several linguistic stocks, as Zuñi, Uto-Aztecan, ect., but having in common the pueblo culture.
pu·er·ile (pyo͞o′ər·il, *Brit.* pyo͞o′ə·rīl) *adj.* Pertaining to or characteristic of childhood; juvenile; hence, immature; weak; silly: a *puerile* suggestion. See synonyms under CHILDISH, YOUTHFUL. [<MF *puéril* <L *puerilis* <*puer, pueri* a boy] —**pu′er·ile·ly** *adv.* **—pu′er·ile·ness** *n.*
pu·er·il·ism (pyo͞o′ər·il·iz′əm) *n.* Childishness, especially as indicative of mental disorder.
pu·er·il·i·ty (pyo͞o′ə·ril′ə·tē) *n. pl.* **·ties** 1 Puerile state; childishness. 2 A childish act or expression.
pu·er·per·al (pyo͞o·ûr′pər·əl) *adj. Med.* Pertaining to, resulting from, or following childbirth: *puerperal* fever. [<L *puerperus* parturient <*puer* a boy + *parere* bring forth]
Puer·to A·ya·cu·cho (pwer′tō ä′yä·ko͞o′chō) Capital of Amazonas territory, on the Orinoco in southern Venezuela.
Puerto Bar·rios (bär′ryōs) A port of eastern Guatemala.
Puerto Ca·bel·lo (kä·bā′yō) A port on the Caribbean in northern Venezuela.
Puerto Li·món (lē·mōn′) See LIMÓN.
Puerto Me·xi·co (mā′hē·kō) A former name of COATZACOALCOS.
Puerto Montt (mōnt) A port of south central Chile.
Puerto Ri·co (rē′kō) The easternmost island of the Greater Antilles, ceded to the United States by Spain in 1898; since 1952 a commonwealth; 3,423 square miles; capital, San Juan: former official name, *Porto Rico.* Abbr. PR **—Puer′to-Ri′can** *adj.* & *n.*
puff (puf) *n.* 1 A breath emitted suddenly and with force; a sudden emission, as of air, smoke, or steam; a whiff. 2 A light, air-filled piece of pastry: a cream *puff.* 3 A light ball, tuft, wad, or pad for dusting powder on the hair or skin; a powder puff. 4 A loose roll of hair in a coiffure, or a light cushion over which it is rolled. 5 A quilted bed coverlet, usually filled with cotton, wool, or down; a comforter. 6 In dressmaking, a part of a fabric so gathered as to produce a loose, fluffy distention. 7 A public expression of fulsome praise, as in a newspaper or advertisement. 8 A puffball. —*v.i.* 1 To blow in puffs, as the wind. 2 To breathe hard, as after violent exertion. 3 To emit smoke, steam, etc., in puffs. 4 To smoke a cigar, etc., with puffs. 5 To move, act, or exert oneself while emitting puffs: with *away, up,* etc. 6 To swell as with air or pride; dilate: often with *up* or *out.* —*v.t.* 7 To send forth or emit with short puffs or breaths. 8 To move, impel, or stir up with or in puffs. 9 To smoke, as a pipe or cigar, with puffs. 10 To swell or distend: He *puffed* his cheeks with pride. 11 To praise fulsomely; advertise in a puff (def. 7). 12 To arrange (the hair) in a puff. [ME *puf* <*puffen, pyffan*]
Synonyms (verb): blow, compliment, flatter, inflate, pant, praise, swell. Compare SWELL. *Antonyms*: belittle, contract, disparage, shrink, shrivel.
puff adder 1 A large, sluggish, venomous African viper *(Bitis arietans),* with variously colored chevron-and-crescent markings and a habit of violently puffing out its breath. 2 The American hognose snake.
puff·ball (puf′bôl′) *n.* A globular fungus (genus *Lycoperdon*) that puffs out its dustlike spores when broken open. Some species are edible.
puff·er (puf′ər) *n.* 1 One who puffs. 2 A plectognath fish that inflates its body with air; a globefish. 3 The little harbor porpoise *(Phocaena phocaena)* of the North Atlantic and Pacific oceans.
puff·er·y (puf′ər·ē) *n.* **·er·ies** 1 The act or practice of puffing. 2 Fulsome public praise or commendation.
puf·fin (puf′in) *n.* 1 A sea bird allied to the auk and murre (family *Alcidae*), with deep compressed bill and thick naked skin at the corner of the mouth; especially, the common puffin *(Fratercula arctica)* of the North Atlantic; the Labrador auk. 2 The Pacific coast sea parrot *(Lunda cirrhata).* [Prob. <PUFF; with ref. to its puffed-out beak or the plumpness of its young]

PUFFIN
(Body from 12 to 15 inches long)

puff paste A short flaky paste for fine pastry.
puff·y (puf′ē) *adj.* **puff·i·er, puff·i·est** 1 Swollen with air or any soft matter; soft; bloated. 2 Inflated in manner; bombastic. 3 Blowing in puffs. **—puff′i·ly** *adv.* **—puff′i·ness** *n.*
pug[1] (pug) *n.* 1 Clay ground and worked with water, for molding pottery or bricks. 2 A machine in which clay is ground and mixed or tempered: also **pug mill.** —*v.t.* **pugged, pug·ging** 1 To knead or work (clay) with water, as in brickmaking. 2 To fill in with clay, etc. 3 To fill in or cover with mortar, felt, etc., to deaden sound. [<dial. E, ? <*pug* punch]
pug[2] (pug) *n.* 1 A breed of dog characterized by a short, square body, upturned nose, curled tail, and short, smooth coat. 2 A pug nose. [Prob. alter. of PUCK]
pug[3] (pug) *n. Anglo-Indian* An animal's footprint; trail. —*v.t.* **pugged, pug·ging** To track,

as game, by pugs; trail. [<Hind. *pag* a foot]

pug[1] (pug) *n. Slang* A professional pugilist. [Short for PUGILIST]

Pu·get Sound (pyōo'jit) An inlet of the Pacific in NW Washington, extending 100 miles south from Juan del Fuca Strait to Olympia.

pugh (pyōo, pōo) *interj.* An exclamation of contempt or disgust.

pu·gi·lism (pyōo'jə·liz'əm) *n.* The art or practice of boxing or fighting with the fists, as in the prize ring. [<L *pugil* a boxer]

pu·gi·list (pyōo'jə·list) *n.* One who fights with his fists; a boxer; specifically, a prize fighter. —**pu'gi·lis'tic** *adj.*

pug·na·cious (pug·nā'shəs) *adj.* Disposed or inclined to fight; quarrelsome. [<L *pugnax, -acis* < *pugnare* fight < *pugnus* a fist] —**pug·na'cious·ly** *adv.*

pug·nac·i·ty (pug·nas'ə·tē) *n.* The quality of being pugnacious; quarrelsome disposition; combativeness. Also **pug·na'cious·ness** (-nā'shəs·nis).

pug nose A thick, short nose, tilted upward at the end. [<PUG[2] + NOSE] —**pug-nosed** (pug'nōzd') *adj.*

pug·ree (pug'rē) *n. Anglo-Indian* A light scarf wound round a hat to keep off the sun; also, a turban worn by natives of India. Also **pug'gree, pug'gry.** [<Hind. *pagri* a turban]

puir (pür) *adj. Scot.* Poor.

puis·ne (pyōo'nē) *adj. Law* Junior as to rank; younger; inferior: a *puisne* judge. —*n.* One who is of inferior rank or younger; a junior associate. ♦ Homophone: *puny.* [<OF *puisne* < *puis* afterwards (<L *postea* < *post* after) + *ne* born <L *natus*]

puis·sance (pyōo'ə·səns, pyōo·is'əns, pwis'əns) *n.* The power to accomplish or achieve, especially against resistance; potency. [<OF]

puis·sant (pyōo'ə·sənt, pyōo·is'ənt, pwis'ənt) *adj.* Powerful; mighty. See synonyms under POWERFUL. [<OF <L *posse* be able] —**pu'is·sant·ly** *adv.*

puke (pyōok) *v.t. & v.i.* **puked, puk·ing** To vomit or cause to vomit. —*n.* Vomit, or the act of vomiting. [Cf. LG *spucken* spew, spit <L *spuere*]

puk·ka (puk'ə) See PUCKA.

Pu·la (pōo'lä) A port of NW Croatia, Yugoslavia; formerly in Italy: Italian *Pola.*

Pu·las·ki (pōo·las'kē, pə-; *Polish* pōo·läs'kē), **Count Casimir,** 1748?–79, Polish soldier and American Revolutionary general; killed at Savannah.

pu·lay (pōo·lī') See PALAY.

pul·chri·tude (pul'krə·tōod, -tyōod) *n.* Beauty; grace; physical charm. [<L *pulchritudo, -inis* < *pulcher* beautiful]

pul·chri·tu·di·nous (pul'krə·tōo'də·nəs, -tyōo'-) *adj.* Beautiful; lovely; especially, having physical beauty.

pule (pyōol) *v.i.* **puled, pul·ing** To cry plaintively, as a child; whimper; whine. [Cf. F *piauler* <MF *pioler* chirp] —**pul'er** *n.*

pu·lex (pyōo'leks) *n.* **1** One of a genus (*Pulex*) of fleas, including the human flea (*P. irritans*). **2** Any flea. [<L, a flea]

pu·li (pōo'lē) *n. pl.* **pu·lik** (pōo'lik) A breed of working dog, of medium height, white, gray, or black in color, with a long, wavy coat: used in Hungary for sheepherding. [Hungarian]

pu·li·cene (pyōo'lə·sēn) *adj.* Of, pertaining to, or abounding with fleas. [<L *pulex, -icis* a flea]

pul·ing (pyōo'ling) *n.* A plaintive cry; whining. —*adj.* Whimpering; whining. —**pul'ing·ly** *adv.*

Pul·itz·er (pyōo'lit·sər, pōol'it-), **Joseph,** 1847–1911, U.S. journalist and publisher, born in Hungary.

Pulitzer Prize One of several annual awards for outstanding work in American journalism and literature: established by Joseph Pulitzer.

pul·kha (pool'kä) *n.* A canoe-shaped traveling sledge, drawn by one reindeer: used in Lapland. [<Lapp *pulkke*]

pull (pool) *v.t.* **1** To apply force to so as to cause motion toward or after the person or thing exerting force; drag; tug. **2** To draw or remove from a natural or fixed place: to *pull* a tooth or plug. **3** To give a pull or tug to. **4** To pluck, as a fowl. **5** To draw asunder; tear; rend: with *to pieces, apart,* etc. **6** To

strain so as to cause injury: to *pull* a ligament. **7** In sports, to strike (the ball) so as to cause it to curve obliquely from the direction in which the striker faces. **8** *Slang* To put into effect; carry out: often with *off:* to *pull* off a prank. **9** *Slang* To make a raid on; arrest. **10** *Slang* To draw out so as to use: to *pull* a knife. **11** *Printing* To make or obtain by impression from type: to *pull* a proof. **12** In boxing, to deliver (a punch, etc.) with less than one's full strength. **13** In horse-racing, to rein in or otherwise restrain (a horse) so as to prevent its winning. **14** In rowing: **a** To operate (an oar) by drawing toward one. **b** To propel or transport by rowing. **c** To be propelled by: The gig *pulls* four oars. —*v.i.* **15** To use force in hauling, dragging, moving, etc. **16** To move: with *out, in, away, ahead,* etc. **17** To drink deeply: to *pull* at a bottle. **18** To inhale deeply: to *pull* at a cigar. **19** To row. See synonyms under DRAW. —**to pull for 1** To strive in behalf of. **2** *Colloq.* To declare one's allegiance to. —**to pull oneself together** To regain one's composure. —**to pull out** *Aeron.* To return to level flight after a dive, as an airplane. —**to pull through 1** Succeed. **2** To survive. —**to pull up** To come to a halt. —**to pull up with** To advance to a position even with. —*n.* **1** The act of pulling; the exertion of force to draw something toward one. **2** Something that is pulled; specifically, the handle of a doorbell, drawer, cabinet, or the like. **3** An impression made by pulling the lever of a hand press. **4** A long swallow, or a deep puff, as on a pipe or cigar. **5** Exercise in rowing: a *pull* on the river. **6** The exertion expended in climbing a mountain; hence, any steady, continuous effort. **7** *Slang* A means of influencing those in power: political *pull;* influence to one's advantage. **8** Attraction: These ads have *pull.* **9** The action of restraining a horse by pulling on the reins; specifically, in horse-racing, the dishonest checking of a horse so that he may be defeated. **10** In sports, the act of pulling the ball. [OE *pullian* pluck] —**pull'er** *n.*

pull·back (pool'bak') *n.* The act of pulling back; a withdrawal, as of troops.

pull-doo (pool'dōo) *n.* The coot. [<F *poule d'eau* a water hen]

pul·let (pool'it) *n.* A young hen, or one not fully grown. [<OF *polete, poulet,* dim. of *poule* a hen <L *pullus* a chicken, young animal]

pul·ley (pool'ē) *n.* **1** A wheel grooved to receive a rope, and usually mounted in a block, used to increase the mechanical advantage of an applied force and to transmit or change the direction of power by means of a flexible belt or rope; a sheave. **2** A block with its pulleys or tackle. **3** *Mech.* A flat or flanged wheel driving, carrying, or being driven by a flat belt, used in a system for transmitting power. [<OF *polie* <Med. L *poleia,* prob. ult <Gk. *polos* a pivot, axis]

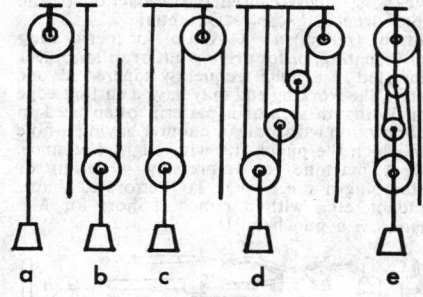

PULLEYS
a. Single fixed.   c. Fixed and runner.
b. Single runner.   d. First system.
          e. Second system.

Pull·man (pool'mən) *n.* A sleeping-car or chair car on a passenger train: a trade name. Also **Pullman car.** [after George M. *Pullman,* 1831–97, U. S. inventor]

pull-out (pool'out') *n.* **1** A withdrawal or removal, as of troops. **2** Something to be pulled out, as an oversize leaf folded into a magazine. **3** *Aeron.* The maneuver of an airplane in passing from a dive to horizontal flight.

pull–o·ver (pool'ō'vər) *adj.* Donned by being drawn over the head. —*n.* A garment so donned, as a sweater or shirt.

pull toy A toy designed to be pulled by a string, often producing a noise as it moves.

pul·lu·late (pul'yə·lāt) *v.i.* **·lat·ed, ·lat·ing 1** To germinate; bud. **2** To breed in abundance; swarm; teem. [<L *pullulatus,* pp. of *pullulare* sprout < *pullulus,* dim. of *pullus* a young animal] —**pul'lu·la'tion** *n.* —**pul'lu·la'tive** *adj.* —**pul'lu·la'tive·ly** *adv.*

pul·mom·e·ter (pul·mom'ə·tər) *n.* An instrument for determining lung capacity by measuring the quantity of air in a single respiration; a spirometer. [<L *pulma* lung + -METER] —**pul·mom'e·try** *n.*

pul·mo·nar·y (pul'mə·ner'ē) *adj.* **1** Pertaining to or affecting the lungs. **2** Having lunglike organs. [<L *pulmonarius* < *pulmo, -onis* lung]

pulmonary artery *Anat.* An artery which conveys (venous) blood from the right ventricle of the heart to the lungs. In man it divides into the right and left pulmonary arteries, leading respectively to the right and left lungs.

pulmonary vein *Anat.* One of four veins which return arterial blood from the lungs to the left side of the heart.

pul·mo·nate (pul'mə·nāt, -nit) *adj.* **1** Having lunglike organs. **2** Of or pertaining to an order of gastropods (*Pulmonata*), including most land snails, slugs, and fresh-water snails, which have lunglike organs. —*n.* One of the Pulmonata. [<NL *pulmonatus* <L *pulmo, -onis* lung]

pul·mon·ic (pul·mon'ik) *adj.* **1** Pertaining to or affecting the lungs; pulmonary. **2** Pertaining to pneumonia. —*n.* **1** A medicine for lung disease. **2** One affected by lung disease. [<MF *pulmonique* <L *pulmo, -onis* lung]

Pul·mo·tor (pul'mō'tər, pool'-) *n.* An apparatus for producing artificial respiration by forcing oxygen into the lungs: a trade name. [<L *pul(mo)* lung + MOTOR]

pulp (pulp) *n.* **1** A moist, soft, slightly cohering mass of matter, usually organic, as chyme, or the soft, succulent part of fruit. **2** A mixture of wood fibers or rags, reduced to a pulpy consistency, and forming the basis from which paper is made. **3** *pl.* Magazines printed on rough, unglazed, wood-pulp paper, and usually having contents of a cheap, sensational nature: distinguished from *slicks.* **4** Powdered ore mixed with water; slime. **5** A pulplike organ or part. **6** *Dent.* The soft tissue of vessels and nerves that fills the central cavity of a tooth. —*v.t.* **1** To reduce to pulp. **2** To remove the pulp or envelope from. —*v.i.* **3** To be or become of a pulpy consistency. [<MF *pulpe* <L *pulpa* flesh, pulp of fruit, pith] —**pulp'less** *adj.*

pulp·ous (pul'pəs) *adj.* Resembling pulp; pulpy.

pul·pit (pool'pit) *n.* **1** An elevated stand or desk for a preacher in a church. **2** The office or work of preaching; hence, the clergy as a class. **3** An elevated platform usually boxed in and variously used: the harpooner's *pulpit* on a whaling vessel. —*adj.* Of or pertaining to the pulpit: *pulpit* oratory. [<L *pulpitum* a scaffold, stage, platform]

pulp·wood (pulp'wood') *n.* The soft wood of certain trees, as the spruce, used in the manufacture of paper.

pulp·y (pul'pē) *adj.* **pulp·i·er, pulp·i·est 1** Consisting of or resembling pulp. **2** Of a soft, juicy consistency; succulent. —**pulp'i·ly** *adv.* —**pulp'i·ness** *n.*

pul·que (pul'kē, pool'-; *Sp.* pool'kä) *n.* A fermented drink made from various species of agave, especially from the juice of the maguey. [<Sp., prob. <Nahuatl]

pul·sar (pul'sär) *n.* An astronomical object that emits radio waves in pulses whose repetition rate is extremely uniform. [< *puls(ating)* + (st)ar]

pul·sate (pul'sāt) *v.i.* **·sat·ed, ·sat·ing 1** To move or throb with rhythmical impulses, as the pulse or heart. **2** To vibrate; quiver. [<L *pulsatus,* pp. of *pulsare,* freq. of *pellere* (pp. *pulsus*) beat]

pul·sa·tile (pul'sə·til) *adj.* **1** Pulsatory. **2** That must be struck in order to produce sound; specifically, in music, percussive.

pul·sa·til·la (pul'sə·til'ə) *n.* The dried herb of

the pasqueflower, used as a sedative and alterative; also, the plant itself. [<Med. L, dim. of L *pulsata,* pp. fem. of *pulsare* beat, strike; with ref. to the beating of the flower by the wind]

pul·sa·tion (pul·sā′shən) *n.* **1** A throbbing or vibrating. **2** A single throb or heartbeat.

pul·sa·tive (pul′sə·tiv) *adj.* Pulsating; throbbing; pulsatile. **— pul′sa·tive·ly** *adv.*

pul·sa·tor (pul·sā′tər) *n.* A machine which operates by pulsation, as a pneumatic rock drill operated by puffs of air.

pul·sa·to·ry (pul′sə·tôr′ē, -tō′rē) *adj.* Of or pertaining to pulsation; having rhythmical movement; throbbing; beating; pulsatile.

pulse[1] (puls) *n.* **1** *Physiol.* The rhythmic beating of the arteries due to the successive contractions of the heart, especially as felt in pressing upon the radial artery at the wrist. ◆ Collateral adjectives: *sphygmic, sphygmoid.* **2** Any throbbing characterized by a short, quick, regular stroke or motion; pulsation. **3** *Telecom.* A brief surge of electrical or electromagnetic energy, usually transmitted as a signal in communication. **4** Any movement, drift, or tendency indicative of general opinion, feeling, or sentiment. **—** *v.i.* **pulsed, puls·ing** To manifest a pulse; pulsate; throb. [< OF *pous* <L *pulsus (venarum)* the beating (of the veins), orig. pp. of *pellere* beat] **— pulse′less** *adj.*

pulse[2] (puls) *n.* Leguminous plants collectively, as peas, beans, etc., or their edible seeds. [< OF *pols* <L *puls* pottage of meal or pulse]

pulse·jet (puls′jet′) *adj. Aeron.* Designating a type of jet engine equipped in front with movable vanes which intermittently take in air to develop power in rapid bursts rather than continuously. Also **pul′so·jet′.**

pulse repeater *Electronics* A transponder.

pul·sim·e·ter (pul·sim′ə·tər) *n.* An instrument for indicating and registering the frequency, force, and variations of the pulse; a sphygmograph. [< *pulsi-* (<PULSE[1]) + -METER]

pul·som·e·ter (pul·som′ə·tər) *n.* **1** A device for pumping liquids by steam pressure, operating without pistons and consisting of two pear-shaped chambers connected by valves; a vacuum pump. **2** A pulsimeter.

Pul·tusk (pōō·ōō·tōōsk′) A town in east central Poland, north of Warsaw.

pul·ver·a·ble (pul′vər·ə·bəl) *adj.* Pulverizable.

pul·ver·a·ceous (pul′və·rā′shəs) *adj.* Having a powdery surface; pulverulent. [<L *pulvis, pulveris* a powder + -ACEOUS]

pul·ver·ize (pul′və·rīz) *v.* **·ized, ·iz·ing** *v.t.* **1** To reduce to powder or dust, as by grinding or crushing. **2** To demolish; annihilate. **—** *v.i.* **3** To become reduced to powder or dust. Also *Brit.* **pul′ver·ise.** [<MF *pulveriser* <LL *pulverizare* <L *pulvis, pulveris* a powder, dust] **— pul′ver·iz′a·ble** *adj.* **— pul′ver·i·za′tion** *n.* **— pul′ver·iz′er** *n.*

pul·ver·u·lent (pul·ver′yə·lənt) *adj.* **1** Consisting of, reducible or reduced to, fine powder or dust. **2** Dusty; powdery. [<L *pulverulentus* dusty < *pulvis, pulveris* a powder, dust] **— pul·ver′u·lence** *n.*

pul·vil·lus (pul·vil′əs) *n. pl.* **·vil·li** (-vil′ī) *Entomol.* One of a pair of adhesive pads between the claws of an insect's foot, as the paired cushions of a fly's foot. [<L, contraction of *pulvinulus,* dim. of *pulvinus* a cushion]

pul·vi·nate (pul′və·nāt) *adj.* **1** Cushion- or pillow-shaped. **2** Having a pulvinus. **3** Swelling out like a pillow: said of a convex frieze. Also **pul′vi·nat′ed.** [<L *pulvinatus* < *pulvinus* a cushion] **— pul′vi·nar** *adj.*

pul·vi·nus (pul·vī′nəs) *n. pl.* **·ni** (-nī) *Bot.* The enlargement or swelling at the base of the leaves and leaflets of many leguminous and other plants, through which the sensitive movements are rendered possible. [<L, a cushion]

pu·ma (pyōō′mə) *n.* An American carnivore *(Felis cougar)* ranging from Canada to Patagonia, of a reddish-tawny color, about 4 feet in length, exclusive of the tail; the cougar: also called *mountain lion.* [<Sp. <Quechua]

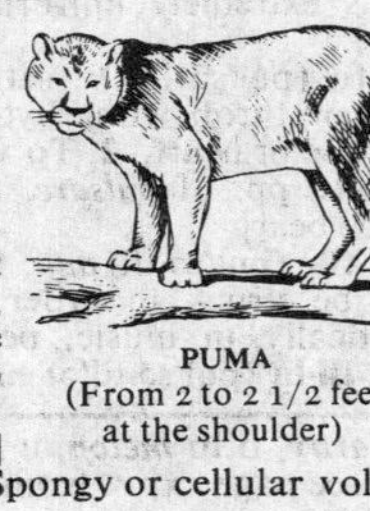

PUMA
(From 2 to 2 1/2 feet at the shoulder)

pum·ice (pum′is) *n.* Spongy or cellular volcanic lava, used as an abrasive and polishing material, especially when powdered: also **pumice stone.** **—** *v.t.* **·iced, ·ic·ing** To smooth, polish, or clean with pumice. [<OF *pomis, pumis* <L *pumex, pumicis*] **— pu·mi·ceous** (pyōō·mish′əs) *adj.*

pum·mel (pum′əl) See POMMEL.

pump[1] (pump) *n.* A mechanical device for raising, circulating, exhausting, or compressing a liquid or gas by drawing or pressing it through apertures and pipes. **—** *v.t.* **1** To raise with a pump, as water or other liquid. **2** To remove the water, etc., from. **3** To inflate with air by means of a pump. **4** To propel, discharge, force, etc., from or as if from a pump: The heart *pumps* blood. **5** To cause to operate in the manner of a pump or pump handle. **6** To question or obtain information from persistently or subtly: to *pump* a witness. **7** To obtain (information) in such a manner. **—** *v.i.* **8** To work a pump; raise water or other liquid with a pump. **9** To move up and down like a pump or pump handle. [<MDu. *pompe,* prob. <Sp. *bomba;* prob. ult. imit.] **— pump′er** *n.*

pump[2] (pump) *n.* A low-cut slipper without a fastening, having either a high or a low heel. [? <F *pompe* pomp]

pum·per·nick·el (pum′pər·nik′əl) *n.* A coarse, dark, sour bread made from unsifted rye. [<G, Westphalian rye bread, orig. a lout, a peasant]

pump gun A repeating shotgun operated by a sliding handle.

pump·kin (pump′kin, pung′-) *n.* **1** A large trailing vine *(Cucurbita pepo)* with heart-shaped leaves. **2** Its large, round, edible, yellow fruit. **3** In Europe, the winter squash *(C. maxima)* or any of its varieties. [Earlier *pompion* <MF *pompon, popon* <L *pepo, peponis* <Gk. *pepōn* a melon, lit., ripe, cooked by the sun]

pump·kin·seed (pump′kin·sēd′, pung′-) *n.* **1** The seed of a pumpkin. **2** A small freshwater sunfish, especially the common North American sunfish (*Lepomis gibbosus*). **3** The butterfish.

pump-prim·ing (pump′prī′ming) *n.* **1** Any device or method for priming a pump, usually the application of a little water to wet the valve. **2** Government spending for the purpose of stimulating business.

pun (pun) *n.* The witty use of two words having the same or similar sounds but different meanings, or of two different, more or less incongruous meanings of the same word. **—** *v.* **punned, pun·ning** *v.i.* **1** To make a pun or puns. **—** *v.t.* **2** To treat as a pun. **3** To affect in a specified manner by puns. [? <Ital. *puntiglio* a fine point, a verbal quibble. See PUNCTILIO.] **— pun′ning·ly** *adv.*

pu·na[1] (pōō′nä) See POON.

pu·na[2] (pōō′nä) *n.* **1** A cold, arid region at high altitudes, as in the Andes. **2** Mountain sickness; illness caused by rarefaction of the air; soroche. [<Sp. <Quechua]

punch[1] (punch) *n.* **1** A tool for perforating or indenting, or for driving out or in an object inserted in a hole: frequently tapered at one end. The working end may have a cutting edge enclosing an area or a pattern: often used in connection with a die or counter having a hole in which the punch fits with slight clearance. **2** A machine for impressing a design or stamping a die. **—** *v.t.* To perforate, shape, indent, etc., with a punch. [Short for ME *punchon* a puncheon[1]]

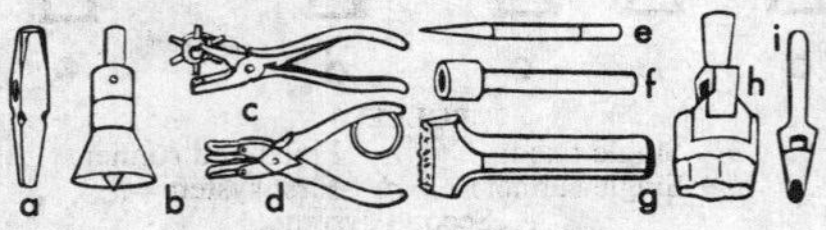

PUNCHES

a. Blacksmith's square. *b.* Center. *c.* Revolving belt. *d.* Ticket. *e, g.* Stamping. *f, h, i.* Cutting.

punch[2] (punch) *v.t.* **1** To strike sharply, especially with the fist. **2** To poke with a stick; prod. **3** *Western U.S.* To drive (cattle). **—** *n.* **1** A swift blow with the fist; also, a thrust or nudge. **2** *Slang* Hence, vitality; effectiveness; force; directness: an editorial with *punch.* [Prob. var. of POUNCE[2]]

punch[3] (punch) *n.* A beverage having wine or spirits, milk, tea, or fruit juices as a basic ingredient, sweetened, sometimes spiced, and diluted with water. [<Hind. *pānch* <Skt. *pañchan* five; from the five original ingredients: arrack, tea, sugar, water, and lemon]

Punch (punch) The quarrelsome, grotesque hero of a comic puppet show, **Punch and Judy.** **— pleased as Punch** Extremely pleased; highly gratified. [Short for PUNCHINELLO]

Punch (punch) An English illustrated humorous weekly journal, founded in 1841.

punch card In data processing, a card having a well-defined arrangement of positions by means of which information can be stored by the presence or absence of punched holes. Also **punched card** (puncht).

punch-drunk (punch′drungk′) *adj.* **1** Suffering from the effects of repeated blows so as to be groggy, slow in movement, etc.: said usually of prize fighters. **2** Confused; dazed. Also *Slang* **punch·y** (punch′ē).

pun·cheon[1] (pun′chən) *n.* **1** An upright supporting timber. **2** A punch or perforating tool, especially one for chipping stone or for stamping figures. **3** A broad, heavy piece of roughly dressed timber, having one flat, hewed side. [<OF *poinçon, poinchon* a punch, ult. <L *punctus,* pp. of *pungere* prick]

pun·cheon[2] (pun′chən) *n.* **1** A liquor cask of variable capacity, from 72 to 120 gallons. **2** A liquor measure of varying amount: mostly of wine, 84 gallons. [<OF *ponçon, poinchon;* ult. same as PUNCHEON[1]]

punch·er (pun′chər) *n.* **1** One who or that which punches. **2** A cowboy; cowpuncher.

Pun·chi·nel·lo (pun′chə·nel′ō) *n. pl.* **·los** or **·loes** **1** A character in an Italian burlesque or puppet show, the original of the English Punch. **2** Hence, **punchinello,** any comic or grotesque character; buffoon. [Earlier *polichinello* < dial. Ital. (Neapolitan) *Polcenella*]

punching bag An inflated or stuffed ball, usually suspended, that is punched with the fists for exercise.

punch press A machine equipped with dies for cutting or forming metal.

punc·tate (pungk′tāt) *adj.* **1** Covered or studded with dots, points, or minute depressions. **2** Pointed. Also **punc′tat·ed.** [<NL *punctatus* <L *punctum* a point] **— punc·ta′tion** *n.*

punc·til·i·o (pungk·til′ē·ō) *n. pl.* **·til·i·os** **1** A nice point of etiquette. **2** Preciseness in the observance of etiquette or ceremony. [<Sp. *puntillo* <Ital. *puntiglio,* dim. of *punto* a point <L *punctum*]

punc·til·i·ous (pungk·til′ē·əs) *adj.* **1** Very nice or exact in the observance of forms of etiquette, etc. **2** Of or pertaining to precise etiquette. [<F *pointelleux* < *pointille* <Ital. *puntiglio* small point] **— punc·til′i·ous·ly** *adv.* **— punc·til′i·ous·ness** *n.*

punc·tu·al (pungk′chōō·əl) *adj.* **1** Exact as to appointed time; acting or arriving promptly; prompt. **2** Done or made precisely at an appointed time. **3** Punctilious; exact. **4** Consisting of or confined to a point as related to space. [<Med. L *punctualis* <L *punctus* a pricking, a point] **— punc′tu·al·ly** *adv.*

punc·tu·al·i·ty (pungk′chōō·al′ə·tē) *n. pl.* **·ties** The quality, characteristic, or habit of being punctual, in any sense.

punc·tu·ate (pungk′chōō·āt) *v.* **·at·ed, ·at·ing** *v.t.* **1** To divide or mark with punctuation. **2** To interrupt at intervals. **3** To emphasize. **—** *v.i.* **4** To use punctuation. [<Med. L *punctuatus,* pp. of *punctuare* <L *punctus* a point] **— punc′tu·a′tor** *n.*

punc·tu·a·tion (pungk′chōō·ā′shən) *n.* The use of points or marks in written or printed matter, to indicate the separation of the words into sentences, clauses, and phrases, and to aid in the better comprehension of the meaning and grammatical relation of the words; also, the marks so used. See also under PRINTING. **— punc′tu·a′tive** *adj.* The chief punctuation points are:

period	.	parentheses	()
colon	:	brackets	[]
semicolon	;	dash (em-dash)	—
comma	,	(en-dash)	–
interrogation point (question mark)	?	hyphen	-
exclamation point	!	quotation marks	“ ”
		virgule (virgil)	/

punc·ture (pungk′chər) *v.* **·tured, ·tur·ing** *v.t.* **1** To pierce with a sharp point. **2** To make

by pricking, as a hole. **3** To cause to collapse: to *puncture* a reputation. — *v.i.* **4** To be pierced or punctured. See synonyms under PIERCE. — *n.* **1** A small hole, as in a pneumatic tire, made by piercing with something sharp-pointed. **2** A minute depression; pit. **3** The act of puncturing. [<LL *punctura* a prick, puncture <L *punctus,* pp. of *pungere* prick] — **punc'tur·a·ble** *adj.*

punc·ture·vine (pungk'chər·vīn') *n.* A low-growing weed *(Tribulus terrestris)* of the caltrop family, having sharp divergent spines which often damage automobile tires: common in the western United States.

pun·dit (pun'dit) *n.* A learned Brahman, especially one versed in Sanskrit lore and in the science, laws, and religion of the Hindus; hence, any learned man. [<Hind. *paṇḍit* <Skt. *paṇḍita,* lit., learned, skilled]

pung (pung) *n. U.S. Dial.* A low box sled for one horse. [Short for *tom pung,* prob. alter. of TOBOGGAN]

pun·gent (pun'jənt) *adj.* **1** Having or causing sharp pricking, stinging, piercing, or acrid effects upon the senses. **2** Affecting the mind or feelings, as by sharp points, so as to cause pain; piercing; sharp. **3** Caustic; keen; racy: *pungent* sarcasm. **4** Terminating in a hard sharp point, as a pine needle. See synonyms under BITTER, HOT, RACY. [<L *pungens, -entis,* ppr. of *pungere* prick] — **pun'gence** or **pun'gen·cy** *n.* — **pun'gent·ly** *adv.*

Pu·nic (pyōō'nik) *adj.* Of or pertaining to ancient Carthage or the Carthaginians, who were regarded by the Romans as treacherous; hence, faithless; untrustworthy. — *n.* The Northwest Semitic language of the Carthaginians, a dialect of Phoenician. [<L *punicus* <*poenicus* <*Poenus* a Carthaginian, a Phoenician <Gk. *Phoinix, -ikos*]

Punic Wars See table under WAR.

pun·ish (pun'ish) *v.t.* **1** To subject (a person) to pain, confinement, or other penalty for a crime or fault. **2** To subject the perpetrator of (an offense) to a penalty: to *punish* forgery. **3** To use roughly; injure; hurt. **4** To make heavy inroads upon; deplete, as a stock of food. See synonyms under AVENGE, CHASTEN, REQUITE. [<OF *puniss-,* stem of *punir* <L *punire* punish <*poenire* <*poena* a punishment, penalty, fine] — **pun'ish·er** *n.*

pun·ish·a·ble (pun'ish·ə·bəl) *adj.* Deserving of or liable to punishment: said of offenders or offenses. — **pun'ish·a·bil'i·ty** *n.*

pun·ish·ment (pun'ish·mənt) *n.* **1** Penalty imposed, as for transgression of law. ◆ Collateral adjective: *penal.* **2** Any ill suffered in consequence of wrongdoing. **3** The act of punishing. **4** *Colloq.* Rough handling, as in a pugilistic encounter, a naval engagement, etc.

pu·ni·tive (pyōō'nə·tiv) *adj.* **1** Pertaining to or inflicting punishment. **2** *Law* Of a character to punish or vindicate. Also **pu'ni·to'ry** (-tôr'ē, -tō'rē). [<Med. L *punitivus* <L *punitus,* pp. of *punire* PUNISH] — **pu'ni·tive·ly** *adv.* — **pu'ni·tive·ness** *n.*

Pun·jab (pun'jäb, pun·jäb') **1** A region of NW India and West Pakistan; 148,610 square miles. **2** A former province of British India in this region, divided in 1947 between Punjab State, India, and West Pakistan; 99,089 square miles; former capital, Lahore. **3** A State of India in this region; 47,456 square miles; capital, Chandigarh. **4** A former province of West Pakistan in this region, a part of West Pakistan province since October, 1955; 63,134 square miles; former capital, Lahore.

Punjab Hill States A former political agency in NW India, under British rule, consisting of 22 princely states which came to be part of India: one in Uttar Pradesh, two in Punjab, and the rest in Himachal Pradesh; from 1936 to 1947–48 included in Punjab States; 11,375 square miles; headquarters, Simla.

Pun·ja·bi (pun·jä'bē) *n.* **1** A native of the Punjab. **2** The Sanskritic language of the Punjab, belonging to the Indic branch of the Indo-Iranian languages: also spelled *Panjabi.*

Punjab States A former political agency in NW India, under British rule, consisting of 14 princely states (of which two were included in West Pakistan, three in Himachal Pradesh, India, and the rest in Punjab, India) and also, after 1936, the Punjab Hill States; 38,146 square miles; headquarters, Lahore.

punk[1] (pungk) *n.* **1** Wood decayed through the action of some fungus, and useful as tinder; touchwood. **2** An artificial preparation that will smolder without flame. [<Algonquian (Lenape) *punk, ponk* fine ashes]

punk[2] (pungk) *n.* **1** *U.S. Slang* Rubbish; nonsense; anything worthless. **2** *U.S. Slang* A petty hoodlum. **3** *Obs.* A prostitute. — *adj. U.S. Slang* Worthless; useless. [Origin uncertain]

pun·ka (pung'kə) *n.* A fan; especially, a rectangular strip of cloth, etc., swung from the ceiling and moved by a servant or by machinery. Also **pun'kah.** [<Hind. *pankhā* a fan <Skt. *pakshaka* <*paksha* a wing]

pun·ky (pung'kē) *n. pl.* **·kies** A minute, annoying, bloodsucking gnat or midge (genus *Culicoides*): also called *sand fly.* Also **pun'key, pun'kie.** [<Du. *punki* <Algonquian (Lenape) *punk, ponk,* orig. fine ashes]

pun·ster (pun'stər) *n.* One who puns; one addicted to punning. Also **pun'ner.**

punt[1] (punt) *n.* A flat-bottomed, square-ended boat, usually with a seat in the middle and a well or seat at one or each end, for use in shallow waters, and propelled with a pole. — *v.t.* **1** To propel (a boat) by pushing with a pole against the bottom of a shallow stream, lake, etc. **2** To convey in a punt. — *v.i.* **3** To go or hunt in a punt. [OE <L *ponto, -onis* a punt, a pontoon <*pons, pontis* a bridge] — **punt'er** *n.*

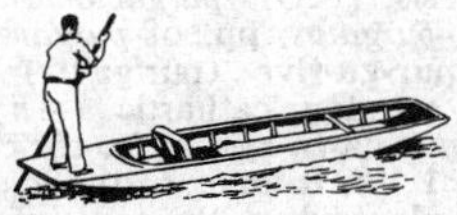

PUNT

punt[2] (punt) *v.i.* To gamble or bet, especially against a bank, as at faro, roulette, or baccarat. [<F *ponter* <*ponte* a point <L *punctum*] — **punt'er** *n.*

punt[3] (punt) *n.* In football, a kick made by dropping the ball from the hands and kicking it before it strikes the ground. — *v.t.* In football, to propel (the ball) with a punt. — *v.i.* In football, to make a punt. [Prob. var. of BUNT] — **punt'er** *n.*

Pun·ta A·re·nas (pōōn'tä ä·rā'näs) A port of southern Chile, on the Strait of Magellan.

pun·til·la (pun·til'ə) *n.* Lacework, lace edging, or lace design with points. [<Sp., dim. of *punto* a point <L *punctum*]

pun·to (pun'tō) *n.* A hit or thrust in fencing. [<Ital., a point <L *punctum*]

pun·ty (pun'tē) See PONTIL.

pu·ny (pyōō'nē) *adj.* **·ni·er, ·ni·est** **1** Weak and insignificant; of small and feeble development or importance; petty. **2** *Obs.* Puisne; born later; younger. See synonyms under SMALL. ◆ Homophone: *puisne.* [<OF *puisne.* See PUISNE.] — **pu'ni·ly** *adv.* — **pu'ni·ness** *n.*

pup (pup) *n.* **1** A puppy (def. 1). **2** A young seal. — *v.i.* **pupped, pup·ping** To bring forth pups. [Short for PUPPY]

pu·pa (pyōō'pə) *n. pl.* **·pae** (-pē) **1** *Entomol.* The quiescent stage in the development of an insect that undergoes a complete metamorphosis, following the larval and preceding the adult stage; also, an insect in such a stage. **2** *Zool.* A similar developmental state in some echinoderms, as holothurians. [<NL <L, a girl, doll, puppet] — **pu'pal** *adj.*

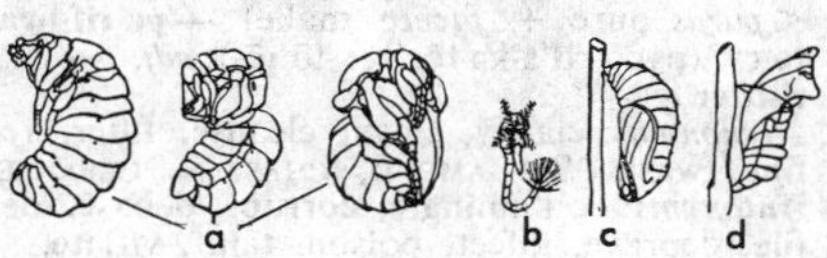

PUPAE

a. Three pupal stages of a bumblebee.
b. Aquatic pupa of a gnat.
c. Suspended pupa of a butterfly.
d. Girdled pupa of a butterfly.

pu·pate (pyōō'pāt) *v.i.* **·pat·ed, ·pat·ing** To enter upon or undergo the pupal condition. — **pu·pa'tion** *n.*

pu·pil[1] (pyōō'pəl) *n.* **1** A person of either sex or of any age under the care of a teacher; scholar; learner. **2** In civil law, a minor who is under the age of puberty and has a guardian. See synonyms under SCHOLAR. [<OF *pupille,* orig. an orphan, ward <L *pupillus,* dim. of *pupus* a boy and *pupilla,* dim. of *pupa* a girl]

pu·pil[2] (pyōō'pəl) *n. Anat.* The contractile opening in the iris of the eye, through which light reaches the retina. [<L *pupilla* a figure reflected in the eye, the pupil of the eye, dim. of *pupa.* See PUPA.]

pu·pil·age (pyōō'pəl·ij) *n.* The state or period of being a pupil. Also **pu'pil·lage.**

pu·pi·lar·i·ty (pyōō'pə·lar'ə·tē) *n.* In Scots law, the interval between birth and the age of 14 in males and 12 in females. Also **pu'pil·lar'i·ty.** [<OF *pupillarité* <L *pupillaris* pertaining to an orphan <*pupillus, pupilla.* See PUPIL[1].]

pu·pi·lar·y (pyōō'pə·ler'ē) *adj.* Of or pertaining to a pupil or a ward. Also **pu'pil·lar'y.**

Pu·pin (pyōō·pēn', *Hungarian* pōō·pēn'), **Michael Idvorsky,** 1858–1935, U. S. physicist and inventor born in Hungary.

pu·pip·a·rous (pyōō·pip'ər·əs) *adj.* Of or pertaining to a division *(Pupipara)* of dipterous insects in which the young are born ready to pupate, as bat ticks, sheep ticks, etc. [<NL <PUPA + L *parere* bring forth]

pup·pet (pup'it) *n.* **1** A small figure of a human being, that by means of strings or wires is made to perform mock drama; a marionette. **2** A person slavishly subject to the will of another; a tool. **3** A doll. — *adj.* **1** Of or pertaining to puppets or mummery. **2** Performing the will of an unseen power; not autonomous: a *puppet* state or government. [<OF *poupette* <L *pupa* a girl, doll, puppet]

pup·pet·eer (pup'i·tir') *n.* A person who manipulates puppets.

pup·pet·ry (pup'it·rē) *n.* The performances of puppets or the manipulation of puppets; mummery.

puppet show A mock drama, with puppets for the actors.

pup·py (pup'ē) *n. pl.* **·pies** **1** The young of a canine mammal, as of a dog; a pup. **2** A conceited and forward young man; a silly fop. [<OF *poupee, popee* <L *pupa* a girl, doll] — **pup'py·ish** *adj.*

puppy love Adolescent love; sentimental, temporary infatuation.

pup tent A shelter tent.

pur (pûr) See PURR.

Pu·ra·cé (pōō'rä·sā') An active volcano in SW Colombia; 15,420 feet; last major eruption, 1869.

Pu·ra·na (pōō·rä'nə) *n.* Any of a number of Hindu scriptures in the form of verse dialogs, coming next in order after the Vedas, dealing mainly with theogony and cosmogony, especially with the god Vishnu and his incarnations. There are 18 Puranas and 18 Upa Puranas or subordinate works. [<Skt. *purāna,* lit., ancient <*purā* of old]

pur·blind (pûr'blīnd') *adj.* **1** Afflicted with dimness of vision; near-sighted. **2** Having little or no insight or understanding. **3** *Obs.* Totally blind. [ME *pur blind* <*pur* (<OF, plain) + *blind* blind] — **pur'blind'ly** *adv.* — **pur'blind'ness** *n.*

Pur·cell (pûr'səl), **Henry,** 1658?–95, English composer.

Pur·chas (pûr'chəs), **Samuel,** 1575?–1626, English author and compiler.

pur·chas·a·ble (pûr'chəs·ə·bəl) *adj.* That can be purchased; hence, venal; corrupt. — **pur'chas·a·bil'i·ty** *n.*

pur·chase (pûr'chəs) *v.t.* **·chased, ·chas·ing** **1** To acquire by paying money or its equivalent; buy. **2** To obtain by exertion, sacrifice, flattery, etc. **3** *Law* To acquire (property) by means other than descent or inheritance. **4** To move, hoist, or hold by a mechanical purchase. — *n.* **1** The act of purchasing; acquisition by giving an equivalent in money or other exchange, or by exertion, risk, etc. **2** That which is purchased; especially, that which is bought with money. **3** A mechanical hold or grip. **4** A device that gives a mechanical advantage, as a tackle or lever. **5** Leverage. **6** Any means of increasing influence or advantage. **7** *Law* The act of acquiring property by payment of a price or value; hence, any lawful mode of acquiring property other than by inheritance or descent or by the mere operation of law. **8** Value; worth, especially as measured by the annual income, expressed

in terms of years to indicate the period at the end of which the income received from a property will have covered the price paid for it: to buy at ten years' *purchase.* **9** A small territorial division in New Hampshire, originally made when the land was sold in lots to individuals by the State. **10** *Obs.* A seeking; also, attempt; endeavor. [<AF *purchacer,* OF *porchacier* seek for < *pur-, por-* for (<L *pro-*) + *chacier* CHASE] — **pur′chas·er** *n.*

Synonyms (verb): acquire, buy, get, obtain, procure, secure. *Buy* and *purchase* are close synonyms, in numerous cases freely interchangeable, but with the difference usually found between words of Anglo-Saxon and French or Latin origin. The Anglo-Saxon *buy* is used for all the concerns of common life, the French *purchase* is often restricted to transactions of more dignity; yet *buy* is commonly more emphatic, and also appeals more strongly to the feelings. One may either *buy* or *purchase* fame, favor, honor, pleasure, etc., but we speak of victory or freedom as dearly *bought. Antonyms*: barter, exchange, sell.

pur·dah (pûr′də) *n. Anglo-Indian* **1** A curtain or screen, especially one used to seclude women; also, the state of seclusion so secured. **2** The material of which a curtain is made. [<Urdu *pardah* <Persian]

pure (pyŏŏr) *adj.* **1** Free from mixture or contact with that which weakens, impairs, or pollutes; containing no foreign or vitiating material. **2** Free from adulteration; clear; clean; hence, genuine; stainless: *pure* food, *pure* motives. **3** Free from moral defilement; innocent; chaste; unsullied; also, free from coarseness; refined: a *pure* life, *pure* language. **4** Free from foreign or imported elements: said especially of language and works of art. **5** *Music* Mathematically correct as to intervals; free from harsh quality in tone; also, correct in form or style; finished. **6** *Philos.* Considered apart from its attributes or from concrete experience; abstract; also, a priori. **7** *Phonet.* Having a single, unvarying tone or sound: said of vowels. **8** Theoretical; concerned with fundamental research, as distinguished from practical application: said of sciences. **9** *Genetics* Breeding true with respect to one or more characters; homozygous. **10** Nothing but; real; sheer: *pure* mischief, *pure* luck. [<OF *pur* <L *purus* clean, pure] — **pure′ness** *n.*

Synonyms: absolute, chaste, classic, classical, clean, clear, continent, fair, genuine, guileless, guiltless, holy, immaculate, incorrupt, innocent, mere, perfect, real, sheer, simple, spotless, stainless, true, unadulterated, unblemished, uncorrupted, undefiled, unmingled, unmixed, unpolluted, unspotted, unstained, unsullied, untainted, untarnished, upright, virtuous. Material substances are called *pure* in the strict sense when free from foreign admixture of any kind; as, *pure* oxygen; the word is often used to signify free from any defiling or objectionable admixture (the original sense); we speak of water as *pure* when it is bright, clear, and refreshing, even if it contains mineral salts in solution; in the medical and chemical sense, only distilled water *(aqua distillata)* is *pure.* In moral and religious use *pure* denotes positive excellence of a high order; one is *innocent* who knows nothing of evil and has experienced no touch of temptation; one is *pure* who, with knowledge of evil and exposure to temptation, keeps heart and soul *unstained. Virtuous* refers primarily to right action, *pure* to right feeling; as, "Blessed are the *pure* in heart: for they shall see God." *Matt.* v 8. See FINE[1], INNOCENT, MODEST, VIRTUOUS. *Antonyms*: adulterated, defiled, dirty, filthy, gross, impure, indecent, indelicate, lewd, mixed, obscene, polluted, stained, sullied, tainted, tarnished, unchaste, unclean; see also synonyms for FOUL, IMMODEST.

pure·blood (pyŏŏr′blud) *n.* **1** An individual descended from a long line of ancestors of the same ethnic or racial stock: said especially of American Indians. **2** A purebred animal. — **pure′-blood′ed** *adj.*

pure·bred (pyŏŏr′bred′) *adj.* Bred from stock having had no admixture for many generations: said especially of livestock. — *n.* (pyŏŏr′-bred′) A purebred animal.

pure culture *Bacteriol.* A culture or medium for the isolation and cultivation of microorganisms of a particular kind, as those of anthrax, diphtheria, etc.

pu·rée (pyŏŏ·rā′, pyŏŏr′ā; *Fr.* pü·rā′) *n.* A thick pulp, usually of vegetables, boiled and strained. — *v.t.* **·réed, ·rée·ing** To put (cooked or soft food) through a sieve, blender, etc.: to *purée* vegetables. [<F <OF, pp. fem. of *purer* strain <L *purare* purify < *purus* pure]

pure line *Genetics* A strain of plants or animals which through self-fertilization, continued inbreeding, or other means, exhibit a high degree of stability in one or more genetic characteristics.

pure·ly (pyŏŏr′lē) *adv.* **1** So as to be free from admixture, taint, or any harmful substance. **2** Chastely; innocently. **3** Merely.

pur·fle (pûr′fəl) *v.t.* **·fled, ·fling** To decorate, as with a wrought or flowered border; border. — *n.* A richly ornamented border: also **pur′·fling.** [<OF *porfiler, pourfiler* < *por-, pour-* for (<L *pro-*) + *fil* a thread <L *filum*]

pur·ga·tion (pûr·gā′shən) *n.* A purging; catharsis. [<OF *purgacion* <L *purgatio, -onis* < *purgatus,* pp. of *purgare* PURGE]

pur·ga·tive (pûr′gə·tiv) *adj.* Efficacious in purging; cathartic. — *n.* A cathartic.

pur·ga·to·ry (pûr′gə·tôr′ē, -tō′rē) *n. pl.* **·ries** **1** In Roman Catholic theology, a state or place where the souls of those who have died penitent are made fit for paradise by expiating venial sins and undergoing any punishment remaining for previously forgiven sins. **2** Any place or state of temporary banishment, suffering, or punishment. [<AF *purgatorie,* OF *purgatoire* <Med. L *purgatorium* <L *purgatorius* cleansing < *purgare* PURGE] — **pur′ga·to′ri·al** *adj.*

purge (pûrj) *v.* **purged, purg·ing** *v.t.* **1** To cleanse of what is impure or extraneous; purify. **2** To remove (impurities, etc.) in cleansing: with *away, off,* or *out.* **3** To rid (a group, nation, etc.) of elements regarded as undesirable or inimical, especially by killing. **4** To remove or kill (a person or persons) in such a manner. **5** To cleanse or rid of sin, fault, or defilement. **6** *Med.* **a** To cause evacuation of (the bowels, etc.). **b** To induce evacuation of the bowels of. **7** *Law* To clear of accusation, suspicion, or guilt. — *v.i.* **8** To become clean or pure. **9** *Med.* To have or induce evacuation. — *n.* **1** The act or operation of purging, in any sense. **2** That which purges; specifically, a medicine causing active evacuation of the bowels; a cathartic; also, its administration or operation. [<OF *purgier* <L *purgare* cleanse < *purigare* < *purus* pure] — **purg′er** *n.* — **purg′ing** *n.*

Pu·ri (pŏŏ′rē) A port and Hindu pilgrimage center on the Bay of Bengal in SW Orissa, India: also *Jaganath.*

pu·ri·fi·ca·tion (pyŏŏr′ə·fə·kā′shən) *n.* **1** The act or operation of purifying: said of things physical or spiritual. **2** The act or observance of formal cleansing from ceremonial defilement. ◆ Collateral adjective: *lustral.*

pu·ri·fy (pyŏŏr′ə·fī) *v.* **·fied, ·fy·ing** *v.t.* **1** To make pure or clean; rid of extraneous or noxious matter. **2** To free from sin or defilement. **3** To free of foreign or debasing elements, as a language. — *v.i.* **4** To become pure or clean. [<OF *purifier* <L *purificare* < *purus* pure + *facere* make] — **pu·rif·i·ca·to·ry** (pyŏŏ·rif′ə·kə·tôr′ē, -tō′rē-) *adj.* — **pu′·ri·fi′er** *n.*

Synonyms: clarify, clean, cleanse, filter, refine, wash. See AMEND, CHASTEN, CLEANSE. *Antonyms*: contaminate, corrupt, debase, defile, deprave, infect, poison, taint, vitiate.

Pu·rim (pŏŏr′im, pyŏŏr′im; *Hebrew* pŏŏ·rēm′) A Jewish festival commemorating the defeat of Haman's plot to massacre the Jews (*Esth.* ix 26), observed about the first of March. [<Hebrew *pūrīm,* pl. of *pūr* a lot]

pu·rine (pyŏŏr′ēn, -in) *n. Biochem.* A white, crystalline compound, $C_5H_4N_4$, which is closely related to uric acid in structure. Also **pu·rin** (pyŏŏr′in). [<G *purin* <L *purus* pure + NL *uricum* uric acid + *-in* -INE[2]]

purine group *Biochem.* An important group of organic compounds widely distributed in nature and related to purine, as caffeine, xanthine, uric acid, etc.

pur·ism (pyŏŏr′iz·əm) *n.* Extreme strictness in regard to the use of words, or an instance of it. — **pur′ist** *n.* — **pu·ris′tic** *adj.*

Pu·ri·tan (pyŏŏr′ə·tən) *n.* **1** One of a group or party of English Protestants (1599) who advocated simpler forms of creed and ritual in the established church, freedom of conscience and worship, and condemned all laxity of morals. Many of them emigrated to the American colonies in the 17th century, especially to the Massachusetts Bay colony. **2** One who is scrupulously strict, or censorious and exacting in his religious life: often not capitalized. — *adj.* Of or pertaining to the Puritans or their beliefs or customs. [<LL *puritas* purity <L *purus* pure + -AN; orig. used by opponents to suggest a resemblance to the *Cathari* (lit., purists)] — **Pu′ri·tan′ic** *adj.*

pu·ri·tan·i·cal (pyŏŏr′ə·tan′i·kəl) *adj.* Governed by the Puritan code; rigidly scrupulous in religious observance and morals; strict. — **pu′·ri·tan′i·cal·ly** *adv.* — **pu′ri·tan′i·cal·ness** *n.*

Pu·ri·tan·ism (pyŏŏr′ə·tən·iz′əm) *n.* **1** The spirit, doctrines, and practices of the Puritans. **2** Religious and moral scrupulousness and austerity. **3** The New England character and spirit.

pu·ri·ty (pyŏŏr′ə·tē) *n.* **1** The character or state of being pure, in any sense, as freedom from dirt or foreign or adulterating matter; cleanness; moral cleanness; innocence; freedom from sinister or improper design; absence of admixture. **2** Saturation: said of a color. **3** The use of no foreign words, phrases, or idioms; use of words with only the precise form, connection, and meaning assigned to them by good usage. See synonyms under INNOCENCE, VIRTUE.

Pur·kin·je (pŏŏr′kin·ye), **Johannes Evangelista,** 1787–1869, Czech physiologist.

Purkinje cell *Physiol.* One of the large, flask-shaped ganglion cells interposed as a single layer between the two layers of gray matter in the cerebellar cortex of the brain. [after J. E. *Purkinje*]

purl[1] (pûrl) *v.i.* **1** To whirl; turn. **2** To flow with a bubbling sound; ripple. **3** To move in eddies. — *n.* **1** A circling movement of water; an eddy. **2** A gentle, continued murmur, as of a rippling stream. ◆ Homophone: *pearl.* [Cf. Norw. *purla* gush out, bubble up]

purl[2] (pûrl) *v.t.* **1** To purfle. **2** In knitting, to make (a stitch) backward. **3** To edge with lace, embroidery, etc. — *v.i.* **4** To do edging with lace, etc. [< *n.*] — *n.* **1** An edge of lace, embroidery, etc.; in lacework, a spiral of gold or silver wire. **2** In knitting, the inversion of the knit stitch giving a horizontal rib effect. ◆ Homophone: *pearl.* [Earlier *pyrle,* orig. twisted gold or silver thread < *pyrl* twist; ult. origin unknown]

pur·lieu (pûr′lōō) *n.* **1** *pl.* The outlying districts or outskirts of any place. **2** A place in which one is free to come and go; a haunt. **3** Formerly, ground unlawfully taken for a royal forest, but afterward disafforested and restored to its rightful owners. [<AF *puralee* <OF < *puraler* go through < *pur-* through (<L *per-*) + *aler* go; infl. in form by MF *lieu* a place]

pur·lin (pûr′lin) *n.* One of several horizontal timbers supporting rafters. Also **pur′line** (-lin). [ME *purlyn,* prob. <OF]

pur·loin (pûr·loin′) *v.t.* & *v.i.* To steal; filch. See synonyms under ABSTRACT, STEAL. [<AF *purloignier,* OF *porloignier* remove, put far off < *pur-, por-* for (<L *pro-*) + *loing, loin* far <L *longe*] — **pur·loin′er** *n.*

pur·ple (pûr′pəl) *n.* **1** A color of mingled red and blue, between crimson and violet; in ancient times, the color obtained from the murex, properly a crimson. **2** Cloth or a garment of this color, worn formerly by sovereigns, especially the emperors of Rome; hence, royal power or dignity; preeminence in rank or wealth. **3** The office of a cardinal: from the official red hat and robes; also, the episcopal dignity: from its purple insignia. — *v.t.* & *v.i.* **·pled, ·pling** To make or become purple. — *adj.* **1** Of the color of purple. **2** Hence, imperial; regal. **3** Conspicuously brilliant or ornate: said of language. [Alter. of ME *purpre,* OE *purpure,* the color purple <L *purpura,* orig. the shellfish yielding Tyrian purple dye, the dye, or cloth dyed with it <Gk. *porphyra*]

purple finch The rose-breasted American finch *(Carpodacus purpureus).*

pur·ple-fringed orchid (pûr′pəl-frinjd′) A terrestrial orchid of North America (genus

Habenaria) with fragrant, purple, lilac, or, rarely, white flowers.

Purple Heart A decoration of honor of the **Order of the Purple Heart** in the form of a purple enameled heart surrounded by a gold-colored border and bearing the head of George Washington in gold-colored relief: established by George Washington in 1782, revived 1932: awarded to members of the armed forces or to citizens of the United States honorably wounded in action, or as a result of enemy action.

PURPLE HEART

purple loosestrife A tall, perennial, European plant (*Lythrum salicaria*) of moist habitats, having long spikes of magenta flowers, naturalized in North America and often choking out native vegetation.

purple medic or **medick** Alfalfa.

purple of Cassius A rich and powerful pigment obtained from a mixture of stannic, stannous, and gold chlorides: used chiefly in miniature painting and enamel painting.

purple osier Red osier.

pur·plish (pûr′plish) *adj.* Somewhat purple.

pur·port (pər·pôrt′, -pōrt′, pûr′pôrt, -pōrt) *v.t.* **1** To have or bear as its meaning; signify; imply. **2** To claim or profess (to be), especially falsely. See synonyms under IMPORT. —*n.* (pûr′pôrt, -pōrt) **1** That which is conveyed or suggested to the mind as the meaning or intention; import; significance. **2** The substance of a statement, etc., given in other than the exact words. See synonyms under PURPOSE. [< AF, OF *purporter* extend < *pur-* forth (< L *pro-*) + *porter* carry < L *portare*] —**pur·port′ed·ly** *adv.*

pur·pose (pûr′pəs) *v.t. & v.i.* ·**posed**, ·**pos·ing** To have the intention of doing or accomplishing (something); intend; aim; design. —*n.* **1** The idea or ideal kept before the mind as an end of effort or action; plan; design; aim. **2** The particular thing to be effected or attained; practical advantage or result; consequence; use: words to little *purpose*. **3** Settled resolution; determination; constancy. **4** Purport; intent, as of spoken or written language. **5** A proposition; proposal; question at issue. —**on purpose** With previous design; intentionally. [< OF *porposer*, var of *proposer*. See PROPOSE.]

Synonyms (noun): aim, design, determination, drift, end, intent, intention, meaning, motive, object, plan, project, purport, resolution, resolve, view. Compare AIM, CAUSE, DESIGN, END, IDEA, PLAN, PROJECT, REASON, SERVICE. *Antonyms:* See synonyms for ACT.

Synonyms (verb): design, determine, intend, mean, propose, resolve. See PROPOSE.

pur·pose·ful (pûr′pəs·fəl) *adj.* Having, or marked by, purpose; intentional; important; significant. —**pur′pose·ful·ly** *adv.* —**pur′pose·ful·ness** *n.*

pur·pose·less (pûr′pəs·lis) *adj.* Having no definite design or use; aimless. See synonyms under FAINT. —**pur′pose·less·ly** *adv.*

pur·pose·ly (pûr′pəs·lē) *adv.* For a purpose; intentionally; deliberately; on purpose.

pur·po·sive (pûr′pə·siv) *adj.* **1** Pertaining to, having, or indicating purpose. **2** Functional. —**pur′po·sive·ly** *adv.* —**pur′po·sive·ness** *n.*

pur·pu·ra (pûr′pyŏŏ·rə) *n. Pathol.* A disease characterized by especially livid spots on the skin caused by extravasated blood. [< L. See PURPLE.]

pur·pure (pûr′pyŏŏr) *n.* Purple: one of the colors or tinctures used in heraldic description. [OE]

pur·pu·ric (pûr·pyŏŏr′ik) *adj.* **1** Of or pertaining to a purple tint. **2** Relating to or resembling purpura.

pur·pu·rin (pûr′pyŏŏ·rin) *n. Chem.* A red crystalline compound, $C_{14}H_8O_5$, contained in madder, largely used in dyeing: also prepared synthetically. Also **pur′pu·rine** (-rin). [< L *purpura* purple + -IN]

purr (pûr) *n.* An intermittent murmuring sound, such as a cat makes when pleased. —*v.i.* To

make such a sound. —*v.t.* To express by or as by purring. Also spelled *pur.* [Imit.]

purse (pûrs) *n.* **1** A small bag or pouch of leather or the like, often having the mouth drawn together with a drawstring; especially, one for carrying money on the person. **2** Available resources or means; a treasury: the public *purse.* **3** A sum of money offered as a prize or tendered as a gift, as for a contest or charitable collection. —*v.t.* **pursed, purs·ing 1** To contract into wrinkles or folds like the mouth of a purse; pucker: to *purse* the lips. **2** *Rare* To place in a purse. [OE *purs* < LL *bursa* < Gk. *byrsa* a skin, a hide]

purse-pride (pûrs′prid′) *n.* Arrogance due to the possession of wealth. —**purse′proud′** (-proud′) *adj.*

purs·er (pûr′sər) *n.* An officer having charge of the accounts, etc., of a vessel; formerly, a naval paymaster. —**purs′er·ship** *n.*

purs·lane (pûrs′lin, -lān) *n.* A procumbent fleshy annual plant (*Portulaca oleracea*) of gardens and waste places, with reddish-green stem and leaves and small yellow flowers: used in Europe as a salad, but regarded as a weed in the United States. Also spelled *pussley.* [< OF *porcelaine* < L *porcilaca* < *portulaca*]

PURSLANE

pur·su·ance (pər·sōō′əns) *n.* The act of pursuing; a following after or following out; prosecution: usually in the phrase *in pursuance of.*

pur·su·ant (pər·sōō′ənt) *adj.* Done in accordance with or by reason of something; conformable. —*adv.* In accordance; conformably: usually with *to:* also **pur·su′ant·ly.**

pur·sue (pər·sōō′) *v.* ·**sued**, ·**su·ing** *v.t.* **1** To follow in an attempt to overtake or capture; chase. **2** To seek or attain or gain: to *pursue* fame. **3** To advance along the course of; keep to the direction or provisions of, as a path, plan, or system. **4** To apply one's energies to or have as one's profession or chief interest: to *pursue* one's studies. **5** To follow persistently; harass; worry. —*v.i.* **6** To follow. **7** To continue. See synonyms under FOLLOW. [< AF *pursuer*, OF *porsievre* < LL *prosequere* < L *prosequi* < *pro-* forth + *sequi* follow] —**pur·su′a·ble** *adj.* —**pur·su′er** *n.*

pur·suit (pər·sōōt′) *n.* **1** The act of pursuing; a chase. **2** That which is followed as a continued employment; a business; vocation. See synonyms under HUNT. [< AF *purseute*, OF *porsieute*, *poursuite* < *porsievre* PURSUE]

pursuit plane *Mil.* A powerful, speedy, highly maneuverable airplane, heavily armed, but with short range, designed to intercept, pursue, and attack enemy aircraft: also called *fighter plane.*

pur·sui·vant (pûr′swi·vənt) *n.* **1** An attendant upon a herald; an officer of the third and lowest rank in the College of Heralds, performing similar duties to a herald. **2** *Obs.* A follower; especially, a military attendant of the king. [< OF *porsivant*, ppr. of *porsievre* pursue]

purs·y (pûr′sē) *adj.* **purs·i·er, purs·i·est** Short-breathed; asthmatic; hence, fat. See synonyms under CORPULENT. [Earlier *pursive* < AF *pursif,* OF *polsif* < *polser* pant, gasp] —**purs′i·ness** *n.*

pur·te·nance (pûr′tə·nəns) *n. Obs.* Appurtenance; specifically, the inwards of an animal. [< AF *purtinaunt,* OF *partenant.* See PERTINENT.]

pu·ru·lent (pyŏŏr′ə·lənt, -yə·lənt) *adj.* Consisting of or secreting pus; suppurating. [< L *purulentus* < *pus, puris* pus] —**pu′ru·lence** or **·len·cy** *n.* —**pu′ru·lent·ly** *adv.*

Pu·rus (pŏŏ·rōōs′) A river in SE Peru and western Brazil, flowing 2,100 miles NE to the Amazon.

pur·vey (pər·vā′) *v.t. & v.i.* To furnish or provide (provisions, etc.). [< AF *purveier,* OF *porveier* < L *providere.* Doublet of PROVIDE.]

pur·vey·ance (pər·vā′əns) *n.* **1** The act of purveying. **2** That which is purveyed or supplied; provisions. **3** A former prerogative of royalty, abolished in 1660, enabling a monarch to buy goods at an appraised value, and also to enforce personal service.

pur·vey·or (pər·vā′ər) *n.* **1** One who furnishes supplies for living, especially for the table; a ca-

terer. **2** Formerly, an officer who, by exaction or otherwise, made provision for the king's household.

pur·view (pûr′vyōō) *n.* **1** Extent, sphere, or scope of anything, as of official authority. **2** Range of view, experience, or understanding; outlook. **3** *Law* The body or the scope or limit of a statute. [< AF *purveu* provided, OF *porveu,* pp. of *porveier* PURVEY; orig. in AF legal phrases *purveu est* it is provided and *purveu que* provided that]

pus (pus) *n. Med.* A secretion from inflamed tissues, as in healing wounds, usually viscid or creamy, and consisting of modified leucocytes and other cells in a liquid plasma: the result of suppuration. [< L. Akin to PUTRID.]

Pu·san (pōō·sän) A port on Korea Strait in SE Korea: Japanese *Fusan.*

Pu·sey (pyōō′zē), **Edward Bouverie**, 1800–82, English theologian.

Pu·sey·ism (pyōō′zē·iz′əm) *n.* Tractarianism. [after E. B. *Pusey*] —**Pu′sey·ite** *n.*

push (pŏŏsh) *v.t.* **1** To exert force upon or against (an object) for the purpose of moving. **2** To force (one's way), as through a crowd, jungle, etc. **3** To press forward, prosecute, or develop with vigor and persistence: to *push* trade with South America. **4** To urge, advocate, or promote vigorously and persistently: to *push* a new product. **5** To bear hard upon; distress; harass: **1** am *pushed* for time. **6** *Slang* To sell (narcotic drugs) illegally. —*v.i.* **7** To exert steady pressure against something so as to move it. **8** To move or advance vigorously or persistently. **9** To exert great effort. **10** To project; extend; reach: The island *pushed* out far into the sea. —*n.* **1** A propelling or thrusting pressure; repulsion as opposed to attraction or pull; a shove. **2** *Colloq.* An extremity; exigency: at a *push* for money. **3** Determined activity; energy. **4** Anything pushed to cause action; a pushbutton. **5** *Slang* The crowd; a number of friends or associates: He fooled the whole *push;* also, an influential clique. **6** *Austral. Slang* A body of larrikins. [< OF *pousser, polser* < L *pulsare.* See PULSATE.]

push·ball (pŏŏsh′bôl′) *n.* A game, played with a ball 6 feet in diameter and weighing 48 pounds, in which each of two sides tries to push the ball across the opponent's goal.

push·but·ton (pŏŏsh′but′n) *n.* A button or knob which, on being pushed, opens or closes a circuit in an electric system, thereby turning on or off a light, ringing a bell, etc.

push·cart (pŏŏsh′kärt′) *n.* A two- or four-wheeled cart pushed by hand: used by fruit venders, peddlers, hawkers, etc.

push·er (pŏŏsh′ər) *n.* **1** One who or that which pushes; especially, an active, energetic person. **2** *Aeron.* An airplane with the propeller in the rear of the wings. **3** *U.S. Slang* One who sells illegally, especially one who sells narcotics to addicts.

push·ing (pŏŏsh′ing) *adj.* **1** Possessing business enterprise and energy. **2** Possessing aggressiveness; impertinent. —**push′ing·ly** *adv.*

Push·kin (pŏŏsh′kin) A city south of Leningrad in Russian S.F.S.R.: formerly *Tsarskoe Selo.*

Push·kin (pŏŏsh′kin), **Alexander Sergeyevich,** 1799–1837, Russian poet.

push·o·ver (pŏŏsh′ō′vər) *v. Slang* A susceptible person; an easy mark; also, anything done or that can be done with little or no effort.

push·pin (pŏŏsh′pin′) *n.* A sharp pin with a large head, inserted by thumb pressure into a bulletin board, drawing board, etc., for mounting and holding in place papers, drawings, etc.

Push·tu (push′tōō) *n.* The Iranian language of the dominant peoples of Afghanistan; Afghan: also spelled *Pashto.* Also **Push′to** (-tō).

pu·sil·la·nim·i·ty (pyōō′sə·lə·nim′ə·tē) *n.* Faintheartedness; indecision; cowardice. Also **pu·sil·lan′i·mous·ness.**

pu·sil·lan·i·mous (pyōō′sə·lan′ə·məs) *adj.* **1** Lacking strength of mind, courage, or spirit; mean-spirited; cowardly. **2** Characterized by weakness of purpose or lack of courage.

[<LL *pusillanimis* <L *pusillus* very little + *animus* mind] —**pu′sil·lan′i·mous·ly** *adv.*
Synonyms: cowardly, dastardly, faint-hearted, feeble, mean-spirited, recreant, spiritless, timid, timorous, weak. *Antonyms*: see synonyms for BRAVE.

puss[1] (po͝os) *n.* **1** A cat. **2** A child or young woman: a term of affection. [Cf. Du. *poes,* LG *puus,* a name for a cat]

puss[2] (po͝os) *n. Slang* The mouth; face. [<Irish *pus* mouth, lips]

puss·ley (pus′lē) *n.* Purslane. Also **puss′ly.** [Alter. of PURSLANE]

puss moth A common European moth *(Cerura vinula)* with grayish wings and two rows of black spots on the abdomen.

pus·sy[1] (po͝os′ē) *n. pl.* **·sies 1** Puss; a cat: a diminutive. **2** A fuzzy catkin, as of a willow, a birch, etc. [Dim. of PUSS[1]]

pus·sy[2] (pus′ē) *adj.* Full of pus.

pus·sy·foot (po͝os′ē·fo͝ot′) *v.i.* **1** To move softly and stealthily, as a cat does. **2** To act or proceed without committing oneself or revealing one's intentions.

pus·sy willow (po͝os′ē) **1** A small American willow *(Salix discolor)* with silky catkins in early spring: also called *glaucous willow.* **2** One of various other willows bearing catkins in early spring.

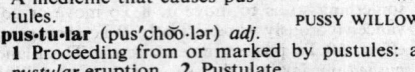

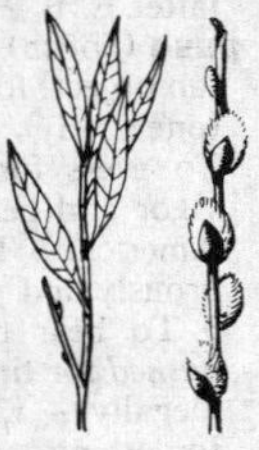
PUSSY WILLOW

pus·tu·lant (pus′cho͞o·lənt) *adj.* Causing pustules. —*n.* A medicine that causes pustules.

pus·tu·lar (pus′cho͞o·lər) *adj.* **1** Proceeding from or marked by pustules: a *pustular* eruption. **2** Pustulate.

pus·tu·late (pus′cho͞o·lāt) *v.t. & v.i.* **·lat·ed, ·lat·ing** To form into or become pustules. —*adj.* (-lāt, -lit) Covered with pustules or pustule-like elevations. [<L *pustulatus,* pp. of *pustulare* blister < *pustula* a pustule]

pus·tu·la·tion (pus′cho͞o·lā′shən) *n.* **1** The formation of pustules; a pustular eruption. **2** A pustule.

pus·tule (pus′cho͞ol) *n.* **1** *Pathol.* A small, circumscribed elevation of the skin with an inflamed base containing pus. **2** Any elevation resembling a pimple or a blister. [<L *pustula*]

put (po͝ot) *v.* **put, put·ting** *v.t.* **1** To bring into or set in a specified or implied place or position; lay: *Put* the book on the table. **2** To bring into a specified state, condition, or relation: to *put* a prisoner to death. **3** To apply; bring to bear: *Put* your back into it! **4** To impose: to *put* a tariff on bicycles. **5** To ascribe or attribute, as the wrong interpretation on a remark. **6** To place according to one's estimation: I *put* the time at five o'clock. **7** To throw with a pushing motion of the arm: to *put* the shot. **8** To incite; prompt: Who *put* him up to it? **9** To bring forward for debate, answer, consideration, etc.: to *put* a question. **10** To subject: Let's *put* it to a vote. **11** To express in words; state: That's *putting* it mildly. **12** To risk; bet: I'll *put* six dollars on that horse. —*v.i.* **13** To go; proceed: to *put* to sea. —**to put about** *Naut.* To change to the opposite tack; change direction. —**to put aside** (or **away** or **by**) **1** To place in reserve; save. **2** To thrust aside; discard. —**to put down 1** To repress; crush. **2** To degrade; demote. **3** To write. —**to put forth 1** To extend, as the arm or hand. **2** To grow, as shoots or buds. **3** To exert. **4** To set out; leave port. —**to put forward** To advance; urge, as a claim. —**to put in 1** *Naut.* To enter a harbor or place of shelter. **2** To interpolate; interpose. **3** *Colloq.* To devote; expend, as time. **4** To advance (a claim, etc.). **5** To submit, as an application. —**to put off 1** To delay; postpone. **2** To discard. **3** To make uneasy or uncomfortable; disconcert. —**to put on 1** To don. **2** To bring into action; turn on. **3** To simulate; pretend. **4** To give a representation of; stage. —**to put out 1** To extinguish. **2** To expel; eject. **3** To disconcert; embarrass. **4** To inconvenience. **5** To put forth. **6** In baseball, to retire (a batter or base runner). —**to put over 1** To place in command or charge. **2** *Colloq.* To accomplish successfully. —**to put one** (or **something**) **over on** *Colloq.* To deceive or dupe. —**to put through 1** To bring to successful completion. **2** To cause to perform. —**to put up 1** To erect; build. **2** To preserve or can. **3** To wager. **4** To provide (money, capital, etc.). **5** To sheathe, as a weapon. —**to put upon** To deceive; cheat. —**to put up with** To endure; tolerate. —*n.* **1** The act of putting, as a cast or throw. **2** A contract by which one person, in consideration of money paid to another, acquires the privilege of selling or delivering to the latter within a certain time some article named, as wheat or cotton, or shares at a stipulated price: opposed to *call.* —*adj. Colloq.* Fixed; settled as fixed: My hat won't stay *put.* [Fusion of OE *putian* place, *potian* thrust, and *pӯtan* push, prob. all <Scand. Cf. Dan. *putte.*]
Synonyms (verb): deposit, lay, place, set. *Put* is the most general term for bringing an object to some point or within some space, however exactly or loosely; we may *put* a horse in a pasture, or *put* a bullet in a rifle or into an enemy. *Place* denotes more careful movement and more exact location; as, to *place* a crown on one's head, or a garrison in a city. To *lay* is to *place* in a horizontal or recumbent position; to *set* is to *place* or adjust in a certain place or position; we *lay* a cloth, and *set* a dish upon a table. To *deposit* is to *put* in a place of security for future use; as, to *deposit* money in a bank; the original sense, to *lay* down is also common; as, the stream *deposits* sediment; insects *deposit* eggs. Compare SET.

pu·ta·men (pyo͞o·tā′min) *n. pl.* **·tam·i·na** (-tam′·ə·nə) *Bot.* The hard bony stone of certain fruits, as the cherry. [<L, waste, a husk < *putare* cleanse, prune] —**pu·tam′i·nous** *adj.*

put and take A game of chance in which the players add to or take from a pool.

pu·ta·tive (pyo͞o′tə·tiv) *adj.* Supposed; reported; reputed. [<MF *putatif* <LL *putativus* <L *putatus,* pp. of *putare* think] —**pu′ta·tive·ly** *adv.*

put-down (po͝ot′doun′) *n. Slang* Something that humbles or deflates, as a cutting remark, a snub, or the like.

Put-in-Bay (po͝ot′in·bā′) A harbor on South Bass Island in Lake Erie near the Canadian border in northern Ohio; site of Perry's defeat of the British in a naval battle (1813) in the War of 1812.

put·log (po͝ot′lôg, -log, put′-) *n.* A crosspiece in a scaffolding, its inner end resting in a hole in the wall and its outer on a ledger. [Earlier *putlock* <*put,* pp. of PUT[1]]

Put·nam (put′nəm), **Israel,** 1718–90, American Revolutionary general.

put-off (po͝ot′ôf′, -of′) *n.* An evasion; excuse.

put-on (po͝ot′on′) *n. Slang* A hoax; deception.

put-out (po͝ot′out′) *n.* The act of causing an out, as of batter or base runner in baseball.

put-put (put′put′) *n. Slang* A gasoline engine; especially, one used in propelling a small boat. [Imit.]

pu·tre·fac·tion (pyo͞o′trə·fak′shən) *n.* **1** The progressive chemical decomposition of organic matter, as by the agency of anaerobic bacteria, with the production of evil-smelling compounds. **2** The state of being putrefied. **3** Putrescent or putrefied matter. [<OF <L *putrefactio, -onis* < *putrefacere* PUTREFY]

pu·tre·fac·tive (pyo͞o′trə·fak′tiv) *adj.* **1** Of or pertaining to putrefaction. **2** Producing putrefaction.

pu·tre·fy (pyo͞o′trə·fī) *v.t. & v.i.* **·fied, ·fy·ing 1** To decay or cause to decay with fetid odor; rot; decompose. **2** To make or become gangrenous. [<L *putrefacere* <*putrere* decay (< *puter* rotten) + *facere* make] —**pu′tre·fi′er** *n.*
Synonyms: corrupt, decay, decompose, rot. See CORRUPT, DECAY. *Antonyms*: disinfect, embalm, freshen, preserve, purify, vitalize.

pu·tres·cence (pyo͞o·tres′əns) *n.* **1** The state of undergoing putrefaction. **2** Something that is putrescent.

pu·tres·cent (pyo͞o·tres′ənt) *adj.* **1** Becoming putrid; undergoing putrefaction. **2** Pertaining to putrefaction. [<L *putrescens, -entis,* ppr. of *putrescere* grow rotten, inceptive of *putrere.* See PUTREFY.]

pu·tres·ci·ble (pyo͞o·tres′ə·bəl) *adj.* Liable to putrefy. —*n.* A substance that decomposes at a certain temperature in contact with air and moisture: generally containing nitrogen. —**pu·tres′ci·bil′i·ty** *n.*

pu·tres·cine (pyo͞o·tres′ēn, -in) *n. Biochem.* A colorless, ill-smelling ptomaine, $C_4H_{12}N_2$, resulting from the bacterial decomposition of animal tissues.

pu·trid (pyo͞o′trid) *adj.* **1** Being in a state of putrefaction; decomposed or decomposing; rotten: *putrid* meat. **2** Indicating or produced by putrefaction: a *putrid* smell. **3** Rotten; corrupt. See synonyms under BAD[1], ROTTEN. [<L *putridus* < *putrere.* See PUTREFY.] —**pu·trid′i·ty** *n.* —**pu′trid·ness** *n.*

Putsch (po͝och) *n.* An outbreak or rebellion; an attempted coup d'état. [<G <dial. G (Swiss), lit., a push, blow]

putt (put) *n.* In golf, a light stroke made on a putting green to place the ball in or near the hole. [< *v.*] —*v.t. & v.i.* To strike (the ball) with such a stroke. [Var. of PUT[1]]

put·tee (put′ē, pu·tē′) *n.* A strip of cloth wound spirally about the leg from knee to ankle, as used by soldiers, sportsmen, etc.; also, a leather gaiter strapped around the leg. Also **put′ty.** [<Hind. *paṭṭī* a bandage <Skt. *paṭṭa* a strip of cloth]

put·ter[1] (put′ər) *n.* **1** One who putts: He is a poor *putter.* **2** An upright, stiff-shafted golf club used on the putting green. [<PUTT]

put·ter[2] (put′ər) *v.i.* To act, work, or proceed in a dawdling or ineffective manner; trifle. —*v.t.* To waste or spend (time, etc.) in dawdling or puttering. [Var. of POTTER[1]]

put·ti·er (put′ē·ər) *n.* One who putties; a glazier. [<PUTTY]

put·ting (po͝ot′ing) *n.* The action of the verb *to put,* as *putting* the shot.

put·ting green (put′ing) In golf, the smooth ground within twenty yards of the hole; also, a place set aside for putting practice. [<PUTT]

put·ty (put′ē) *n.* **1** Whiting mixed with linseed oil to the consistency of dough: used for filling holes or cracks in wood surfaces, securing panes of glass in the sash, making relief ornaments, etc. **2** Fine lime mortar for filling cracks, finishing, etc. —**iron putty** Ferric oxide mixed with boiled linseed oil: used in making pipe-joint connections. —**red-lead putty** Red and white lead mixed with boiled linseed oil, used mainly for cementing pipe joints. —*v.t.* **·tied, ·ty·ing** To fill, stop, fasten, etc., with putty. [<OF *potee* calcined tin, lit., a potful < *pot* a pot]

putty knife A knife with a spatulalike blade, used by glaziers in puttying window glass, etc.

putty powder Tin oxide, or tin and lead oxide, used for polishing glass, metals, etc.

put·ty·root (put′ē·ro͞ot′, -ro͝ot′) *n.* An American orchid *(Aplectrum hyemale)* with a scape bearing a loose raceme of brownish flowers produced yearly. [So called from a sticky substance found in its bulbs]

Pu·tu·ma·yo (po͞o′to͞o·mä′yō) A river in Ecuador, Colombia, and Peru, flowing about 1,000 miles SE to the Amazon, forming the greater part of the boundary between Colombia and Peru: called *Içá* in its lower courses in Brazil.

put-up (po͝ot′up′) *adj. Colloq.* Prearranged or contrived in an artful manner: a *put-up* job.

Pu·vis de Cha·vannes (pü·vē′ də shá·vàn′), **Pierre,** 1824–98, French painter.

puy (pwē) *n.* A conical hill of volcanic origin. [<F <OF *pui, poi* a hill <L *podium* a height]

Puy-de-Dôme (pwē·də·dōm′) An extinct volcano of the Massif Central in central France; site of an observatory and a ruined temple of Mercury; 4,806 feet.

Pu-yi (po͞o′yē′), **Henry,** 1906–1967, last Manchu emperor of China 1908–12; abdicated; puppet emperor of Manchukuo 1934–45, under name *Kang Te*; abdicated.

puz·zle (puz′əl) *v.* **·zled, ·zling** *v.t.* **1** To confuse or perplex; mystify. **2** To solve by investigation and study, as something perplexing: with *out.* —*v.i.* **3** To be perplexed or confused. See synonyms under PERPLEX. —**to puzzle over** To attempt to understand or solve. —*n.* **1** A thing difficult to understand or explain; perplexing problem; an enigma or problem. **2** Something, as a toy, purposely arranged so as to require time, patience, and ingenuity to solve its intricacies. **3** The state of being puzzled; a quandary; perplexity. See synonyms under RIDDLE[2]. —**cross-word puzzle** A pattern of white and black spaces, of which the white spaces are to be filled with letters that form words, vertically, horizontally, or diagonally, to agree with accompanying definitions. [Related to ME *poselet* confused; ult. origin unknown]

puz·zle·ment (puz′əl·mənt) *n.* State of being nonplused; perplexity.

puz·zler (puz′lər) *n.* One who or that which puzzles; a knotty question.

PX A military post exchange or general store. [<P(OST) (E)X(CHANGE)]

py- Var. of PYO-.

Pya·ti·gorsk (pyä′ti·gôrsk′) A city in the northern Caucasus, Russian S.F.S.R.

pyc·nid·i·um (pik·nid′ē-əm) *n.* *pl.* **·nid·i·a** (-nid′ē-ə) *Bot.* A spore–bearing receptacle found in certain fungi. [<NL <Gk. *pyknos* thick + *-idion*, dim. suffix] — **pyc·nid′i·al** *adj.*

pyc·nom·e·ter (pik·nom′ə·tər) *n.* A specific-gravity bottle or flask. [<Gk. *pyknos* dense, thick + -METER]

pyc·no·spore (pik′nə·spôr, -spōr) *n.* *Bot.* A conidium developed within a pycnidium. [Contraction of *pycnidiospore* <PYCNIDIUM + SPORE]

Pyd·na (pid′nə) An ancient city in south central Macedonia, Greece; scene of the final Roman victory over Macedonia, 168 B.C.

pye (pī) See PIE⁴.

py·e·li·tis (pī′ə·lī′tis) *n.* *Pathol.* Inflammation of the pelvis and calices of the kidneys. [<NL <Gk. *pyelos* the pelvis, orig. a trough + *-itis* -ITIS] — **py′e·lit′ic** (-lit′ik) *adj.*

py·e·lo·gram (pī′ə·lō·gram′) *n.* A picture taken by pyelography. [<*pyelo-* <Gk. *pyelos* a trough, pelvis + -GRAM]

py·e·log·ra·phy (pī′ə·log′rə·fē) *n.* The technique of making X–rays of the ureter and the kidney by the use of a radiopaque dye. [<*pyelo-* <Gk. *pyelos* a trough, pelvis + -GRAPHY] — **py′e·lo·graph′ic** (-lō·graf′ik) *adj.*

py·e·mi·a (pī·ē′mē·ə) *n.* *Pathol.* A poisonous infection of the blood, due to the absorption of vitiated pus or pyogenic micro–organisms into the circulation: it causes suppuration marked by multiple abscesses, phlebitis, high fever, etc. Also **py·ae′mi·a**. [<NL <Gk. *pyon* pus + *haima* blood] — **py·e′mic** *adj.*

py·et (pī′it) *n.* *Scot.* The magpie.

py·gid·i·um (pī·jid′ē·əm) *n.* *pl.* **·gid·i·a** (-jid′ē·ə) *Entomol.* The terminal or posterior segment, as of an insect; a caudal shield. [< NL <Gk. *pygidion*, dim. of *pygē* rump] — **py·gid′i·al** *adj.*

Pyg·ma·li·on (pig·mā′lē·ən, -māl′yən) In Greek mythology, a sculptor of Cyprus, who fell in love with his statue, Galatea, which Aphrodite later brought to life.

pyg·my (pig′mē) See PIGMY.

Pyg·my (pig′mē) *n.* *pl.* **·mies** **1** A member of a Negroid people of equatorial Africa, ranging in height from four to five feet. **2** Any of the Negrito peoples of the Philippines, Andaman Islands, and Malaya. **3** In the *Iliad*, one of a race of dwarfs. [<L *pygmaeus*. See PIGMY.]

py·ic (pī′ik) *adj.* Of or pertaining to pus; purulent. [<PY- + -IC]

py·in (pī′in) *n.* *Biochem.* A protein compound contained in pus. [<PY- + -IN]

py·ja·mas (pə·jä′məz, -jam′əz) See PAJAMAS.

pyke (pīk) *v.t.* *Scot.* To pick.

pyk·nic (pik′nik) *adj.* Characterized by plump contours and a broad, stocky build; fat; squat. — *n.* A person of this physical type. [<Gk. *pyknos* thick, compact]

pyk·no·phra·si·a (pik′nə·frā′zhē·ə, -zhə) *n.* *Pathol.* A thickening of speech. [<NL <Gk. *pyknos* thick + *phrasis* speech]

Pyl·a·des (pil′ə·dēz) In Greek legend, a nephew of Agamemnon and friend of Orestes, whose sister Electra he married.

pyle (pīl) *n.* *Scot.* A grain.

Pyle (pīl) , **Howard**, 1853–1911, U.S. illustrator, painter, and writer.

py·lon (pī′lon) *n.* **1** *Archit.* A monumental structure constituting an entrance to an Egyptian temple or other large edifice, consisting of a central gateway, flanked on each side by a truncated pyramidal tower. **2** A stake marking the course in an airdrome or turning point in an aerial race. **3** One of the tall, mastlike metal structures from whose summits high–tension wires are carried across open country. **4** *Surg.* An artificial leg, usually temporary. [<Gk. *pylōn* a gateway <*pylē* a gate]

py·lo·rec·to·my (pī′lə·rek′tə·mē) *n.* *Surg.* Excision of the pylorus. [<PYLOR(US) + -ECTOMY]

py·lo·rus (pī·lôr′əs, -lō′rəs, pi-) *n.* *pl.* **·ri** (-rī) *Anat.* The opening between the stomach and the duodenum, surrounded by circular muscle fibers; also, the adjoining portion of the stomach. [<LL <Gk. *pylōros* a gatekeeper < *pylē* a gate + *ouros* a watcher] — **py·lor′ic** (-lôr′ik, -lor′ik) *adj.*

Py·los (pī′los) **1** A port of SW Peloponnesus, Greece, at the southern entrance to **Pylos Bay**. **2** An ancient city, 4 miles NW of modern Pylos; said to be the seat of Nestor. Medieval *Navarino*: also *Pilos*. Latin **Py·lus** (pī′ləs).

Pym (pim) , **John**, 1584–1643, English statesman and orator.

pyo- *combining form* Pus; of or related to pus: *pyorrhea*. Also, before vowels, *py-*. [<Gk. *pyon* pus]

py·o·gen·e·sis (pī′ō·jen′ə·sis) *n.* **1** *Pathol.* The formation or secretion of pus; suppuration. **2** The doctrine or theory of the origin, source, and process of the generation of pus. — **py′o·gen′ic** *adj.*

py·oid (pī′oid) *adj.* Resembling pus; purulent. [<PY- + -OID]

Pyong·yang (pyông·yäng) A city in northern Korea, capital of the Democratic People's Republic of Korea: *Japanese* **Hei·jo** (hā·jō).

py·or·rhe·a (pī′ə·rē′ə) *n.* *Pathol.* A discharge of pus with a continuous flow; especially, **pyorrhea al·ve·o·la·ris** (al·vē′ō·lā′ris), a loosening of the teeth accompanied by progressive inflammation of their lining membrane; Riggs's disease. Also **py′or·rhoe·a**. [<NL <Gk. *pys, pyos* pus + *rheein* flow] — **py′or·rhe′al** *adj.*

py·o·sis (pī·ō′sis) *n.* Suppuration. [<NL <Gk. *pyōsis* <*pys, pyos* pus]

pyr- Var. of PYRO-.

py·ra·can·tha (pī′rə·kan′thə, pir′ə-) *n.* The firethorn. [<L <Gk. *pyrakantha* < *pyr, pyros* fire + *akantha, -ēs* a thorn]

py·ral·i·did (pi·ral′ə·did) *adj.* Of or pertaining to a family (*Pyralididae*) of small or medium–sized moths of slender build and broad hind wings, including many groups sometimes classified as separate families. — *n.* A moth belonging to this family. Also **pyr·a·lid** (pir′ə·lid). [<NL <L *pyralis, -idis* a winged insect supposed to live in fire <Gk. < *pyr, pyros* a fire] — **pyr·al′i·dan** *adj.* & *n.*

pyr·a·mid (pir′ə·mid) *n.* **1** *Archit.* A solid structure of masonry with a square base and triangular sides meeting in an apex. Such structures were used as tombs or temples. The pyramids of Egypt, raised over the sepulchral chambers of kings, are the best examples. The most interesting group is at Giza, near Cairo. The pyramids of Mexico

THE PYRAMIDS AT GIZA

served as temples. The largest is the pyramid near Cholula on the Pueblo plateau, in central Mexico. **2** Something in pyramidal form. **3** *Geom.* A solid consisting of a polygonal base and triangular sides, the apices of the triangles coming together at the vertex. **4** *Mineral.* A crystal form consisting of three or more similar planes having a common point of intersection. **5** *Physiol.* One of various pyramidal or conical structures found in animal organisms. **6** *Anat.* A small bony projection in the cavity of the tympanum. **7** Any tree trained in pyramidal form. **8** The operations involved in pyramiding. — *v.t.* & *v.i.* **1** To arrange or form in the shape of a pyramid. **2** To buy or sell (stock) with paper profits shown by the change in price of stock already purchased or sold, without any additional deposit of money being made, and to continue

so buying or selling on each movement in price. [<F *pyramide* <L *pyramis, -idis* <Gk. *pyramis, -idos*, prob. <Egyptian *pi–mar* a pyramid]

py·ram·i·dal (pi·ram′ə·dəl) *adj.* Of or shaped like a pyramid. Also **pyr·a·mid·ic** (pir′ə·mid′ik), **pyr·a·mid′i·cal.** — **py·ram′i·dal·ly** *adv.*

py·ram·i·da·lis (pi·ram′i·dā′lis) *n.* *pl.* **·les** (-lēz) *Anat.* Any one of several conical or triangular muscles; especially, the flat triangular muscle arising from the pubis and inserted into the linea alba. [<NL <LL, pyramidal; with ref. to its shape]

Pyr·a·mus and This·be (pir′ə·məs, thiz′bē) In classical legend, two Babylonian lovers: believing Thisbe slain by a lion, Pyramus killed himself, and Thisbe, finding his body, took her own life.

py·ran (pī′ran, pī·ran′) *n.* *Chem.* Either of two isomeric cyclic compounds, C_5H_6O, each having in its ring 5 carbon atoms: the parent forms of certain carbohydrates, alkaloids, and other physiologically active compounds. [< PYRONE]

py·ra·nom·e·ter (pī′rə·nom′ə·tər) *n.* An instrument for measuring sky radiation or radiation from the earth, especially at night. [< PYR- + ANO- + -METER]

py·rar·gy·rite (pī·rär′jə·rīt) *n.* A metallic, black sulfide of antimony and silver, Ag_3SbS_3, crystallizing in the rhombohedral system. [<PYR- + Gk. *argyros* silver + -ITE¹]

pyre (pīr) *n.* **1** A heap of combustibles arranged for burning a dead body. **2** Any pile or heap of combustible material. [<L *pyra* a hearth, funeral pile <Gk. < *pyr* a fire]

py·rene (pī′rēn) *n.* *Chem.* A tetracyclic hydrocarbon, $C_{16}H_{10}$, contained in that portion of coal–tar oil boiling above 360° C. [<PYR- + -ENE]

py·rene² (pī′rēn) *n.* *Bot.* The stone of a drupe; also, any nutlet; putamen. [<NL *pyrena* <Gk. *pyrēn* fruit stone]

Py·rene (pī′rēn) *n.* Carbon tetrachloride, prepared for use as a chemical fire extinguisher: a trade name.

Pyr·e·nees (pir′ə·nēz) A mountain chain between France and Spain, extending about 270 miles from the Bay of Biscay to the Mediterranean; highest point, Pico de Aneto, 11,168 feet. — **Pyr′e·ne′an** *adj.*

py·re·noid (pī·rē′noid) *adj.* Having the form of a fruit stone. — *n.* **1** *Bot.* A small, colorless mass of protein substance of a crystalline form, appearing in the chloroplasts of green algae. **2** *Zool.* A transparent body in the chromatophores of certain protozoa. [<Gk. *pyrēnoeidēs* < *pyrēn* a fruit stone + *eidos* a form, shape] — **py·re·no·de·an** (pī′ri·nō′dē·ən) *adj.*

Pyr·e·no·my·ce·tes (pī·rē′nō·mī·sē′tēz) *n. pl.* A large class of fungi characterized by the forcible expulsion of ascospores from the perithecium, including many parasitic species, as ergot. [<NL <Gk. *pyrēn* a fruit stone + *mykēs, mykētis* a mushroom]

py·reth·rum (pī·reth′rəm, -rē′thrəm) *n.* **1** The dried and powdered roots of the pellitory used in medicine as a sialogog and rubefacient. **2** The powdered flowers of a chrysanthemum (*Chrysanthemum cinerariaefolium*), used medically as an ointment, and as an insecticide. [<L, feverfew <Gk. *pyrethron* < *pyr* fire]

py·ret·ic (pī·ret′ik) *adj.* **1** Affected with or relating to fever; febrile. **2** Remedial in fevers. — *n.* A febrifuge. [<NL *pyreticus* <Gk. *pyretos* a fever < *pyr* fire]

py·re·tol·o·gy (pir′ə·tol′ə·jē, pī′rə-) *n.* The department of medical science that treats of fevers. [<Gk. *pyretos* a fever + -LOGY] — **pyr′e·tol′o·gist** *n.*

py·re·to·ther·a·py (pir′ə·tō·ther′ə·pē, pī′rə-) *n.* Medical treatment by the artificial induction of fever by electricity, bacterial infection, etc.; fever therapy. [<Gk. *pyretos* (a fever) + THERAPY]

Py·rex (pī′reks) *n.* A type of heat–resisting glass having a high silica content, with additions of soda, aluminum, and boron: a trade name.

py·rex·i·a (pī·rek′sē·ə) *n.* *Pathol.* An abnormal elevation of bodily temperature; fever. [<NL <Gk. *pyrexis* < *pyressein* be feverish

< *pyretos.* See PYRETIC.] — **py·rex′i·al** *adj.* — **py·rex′ic** *adj.*

pyr·ge·om·e·ter (pīr′jē·om′ə·tər, pir′-) *n.* A pyranometer. [< PYR- + GEO- + -METER]

pyr·he·li·om·e·ter (pīr·hē′lē·om′ə·tər, ′pir-) *n. Astron.* An instrument for measuring the quantity and rate of solar radiation by its thermal effects on a silvered disk or other sensitive surface. [< PYR- + HELIO- + -METER]

Pyr·i·ben·za·mine (pir′ə·ben′zə·mēn, -min) *n.* Proprietary name of an antihistamine drug, $C_{16}H_{21}N_3HC$, used in the treatment of certain allergies.

pyr·i·dine (pir′ə·dēn, -din) *n. Chem.* A colorless, liquid, nitrogenous compound, C_5H_5N, with a pungent, noxious odor, obtained by the distillation of coal tar and bone oil and also made synthetically: used in organic syntheses, as a disinfectant, antiseptic, alcohol denaturant, and asthma remedy. [< PYR(ROLE) + -ID(E) + -INE[2]] — **py·rid·ic** (pī·rid′ik) *adj.*

pyr·i·dox·ine (pir′ə·dok′sēn, -sin) *n. Biochem.* A factor of the vitamin B complex known to prevent dermatitis in rats, vitamin B_6, a water-soluble compound, $C_8H_{10}NO_3$, occurring in cereal grains, vegetable oils, legumes, yeast, meats, and fish: also made synthetically. [PYRID(INE) + OX(Y)-[2] + -INE[2]]

pyr·i·form (pir′ə·fôrm) *adj.* Pear-shaped. [< NL *pyriformis* <Med. L *pyrum* a pear (<L *pirum*) + L *forma* form]

py·rim·i·dine (pī·rim′ə·dēn, -din, pir′ə·mə·dēn′, -din′) *n. Chem.* An organic compound, $C_4H_4N_2$, resulting from the acid hydrolysis of a nucleic acid; a constituent of thiamine. Also **py·rim′i·din** (-din). [<G *pyrimidin* < *pyridin* pyridine]

py·rite (pī′rīt) *n. pl.* **py·ri·tes** (pī·rī′tēz) A metallic, pale brass-yellow, opaque, isometric iron disulfide, FeS_2; fool's gold; iron pyrites. [<L *pyrites* <Gk. *pyritēs* flint < *pyritēs (lithos)* fire (stone) < *pyr* fire] — **py·rit′ic** (-rit′ik) or **·i·cal** *adj.*

py·ri·tes (pī·rī′tēz) *n. pl.* The common name for various metallic sulfides: copper *pyrites.* Compare CHALCOPYRITE, PYRITE.

py·ro (pī′rō) *n.* Pyrogallol: so called in photography. [Short for PYROGALLOL]

pyro– *combining form* **1** Fire; heat: *pyromania.* **2** *Chem.* Denoting actual or hypothetical derivation by the action of heat; specifically, in certain inorganic acids, indicating derivation from two molecules of an ordinary acid by the elimination of one molecule of water: $2H_3AsO_4$ (arsenic acid) — H_2O = $H_4As_2O_7$ (*pyroarsenic* acid). **3** *Geol.* Resulting from the action of fire or heat: *pyrolusite.* Also, before vowels, *pyr–.* [<Gk. *pyr, pyros* fire]

py·ro·cat·e·chol (pī′rə·kat′ə·kōl, -chōl, -kol, pir′ə-) *n. Chem.* A white crystalline phenol compound, $C_6H_6O_2$, contained in various barks, originally obtained when catechin was subjected to dry distillation: used in photography as a developer and in medicine. Also **py′ro·cat′e·chin** (-kin, -chin). [<PYRO- + CATECH(U) + (PHEN)OL]

py·ro·cel·lu·lose (pī′rə·sel′yə·lōs) *n.* A form of guncotton used as a propellant in smokeless powder. Also **py′ro·cot′ton** (-kot′n).

Py·ro·ce·ram (pī′rō·sə·ram′) *n.* A strongly heat-resistant, crystalline ceramic material formed from glass and characterized by extreme hardness, great tensile strength, and high dielectric properties: a trade name.

py·ro·chem·i·cal (pī′rə·kem′i·kəl) *adj.* Pertaining to chemical changes induced or effected by high temperature.

py·ro·clas·tic (pī′rə·klas′tik) *adj. Geol.* Formed from or consisting of the fragmentary or comminuted ejecta of volcanic or igneous eruptions: said of rocks or their composition. [<PYRO- + CLASTIC]

py·ro·con·duc·tiv·i·ty (pī′rə·kon′duk·tiv′ə·tē) *n.* Conductivity of an electric current dependent upon or improved by the application of heat. — **py′ro·con·duc′tive** (-kən·duk′tiv) *adj.*

py·ro·crys·tal·line (pī′rə·kris′tə·lin, -līn, pir′ə-) *adj.* Crystallized from materials in a state of fusion: *pyrocrystalline* masses.

py·ro·e·lec·tric (pī′rō·i·lek′trik, pir′ō-) *adj.* **1** Of or pertaining to pyroelectricity. **2** Manifesting pyroelectricity; developing poles when heated. —*n.* A substance that becomes polar when heated.

py·ro·e·lec·tric·i·ty (pī′rō·i·lek′tris′ə·tē, -ē′lek-, pir′ō-) *n.* **1** Electrification or electric polarity developed in certain minerals by a change in temperature. **2** The branch of science treating of this phenomenon.

py·ro·gal·late (pī′rə·gal′āt, pir′ə-) *n.* A salt of pyrogallol.

py·ro·gal·lic (pī′rə·gal′ik, pir′ə-) *adj. Chem.* **1** Of, pertaining to, or derived by heat from gallic acid. **2** Pertaining to or designating pyrogallol.

py·ro·gal·lol (pī′rə·gal′ōl, -ol, -gə·lōl′, pir′ə-) *n. Chem.* A white, crystalline, poisonous compound, $C_6H_3(OH)_3$, obtained by heating gallic acid: used to reduce silver and mercury salts to a metallic state, as a photographic developer, as a dye, and in certain medical preparations. Also **pyrogallic acid.** [<PYRO- + GALL(IC) + (PHEN)OL]

py·ro·gen·ic (pī′rə·jen′ik, pir′ə-) *adj.* **1** Causing or produced by heat. **2** Caused by or inducing fever. **3** Igneous. Also **py·rog·e·nous** (pī·roj′ə·nəs, pi-).

py·rog·nos·tics (pī′rog·nos′tiks, pir′əg-) *n. pl.* The characteristics of a mineral as shown by heat of varying intensity produced with a blowpipe. [<PYRO- + Gk. *gnostikos* knowing]

py·rog·ra·phy (pī·rog′rə·fē, pi-) *n.* The art or process of producing a design, as on wood or leather, by a red-hot point or fine flame. — **py·ro·graph** (pī′rə·graf, -gräf, pir′ə-) *n.* — **py·rog′ra·pher** *n.* — **py′ro·graph′ic** *adj.*

py·ro·gra·vure (pī′rō·grə·vyŏŏr′, pir′ō-) *n.* **1** The art or process of producing a design on wood by pyrography. **2** A picture thus made.

py·ro·lig·ne·ous (pī′rə·lig′nē·əs, pir′ə-) *adj.* Pertaining to that which is derived from wood by heat, specifically by dry distillation. [<PYRO- + LIGNEOUS]

pyroligneous acid Crude acetic acid as derived from wood by distillation; wood vinegar.

py·rol·o·gy (pī·rol′ə·jē, pi-) *n.* **1** The scientific examination of materials by heat; blowpipe analysis. **2** The branch of physics that treats of heat. [<PYRO- + -LOGY] — **py·ro·log·i·cal** (pī′rə·loj′i·kəl, pir′ə·loj′i·kəl) *adj.*

py·ro·lu·site (pī′rə·lōō′sīt, pī·rol′yə·sīt) *n.* A soft, metallic, iron-black or steel-gray manganese dioxide, MnO_2, of great value in the arts, and used in the manufacture of oxygen, chlorine, etc. [<G *pyrolusit* <Gk. *pyr, pyros* a fire + *lousis* a washing (< *louein* wash) + G *-it* -ITE[1]]

py·rol·y·sis (pī·rol′ə·sis) *n. Chem.* Decomposition by the application of or as a result of heat. [<NL <Gk. *pyr, pyros* a fire + *lysis* a loosing < *lyein* loosen] — **py·ro·lit·ic** (pī′rə·lit′ik, pir′ə-) *adj.*

py·ro·mag·net·ic (pī′rō·mag·net′ik, pir′ō-) *adj.* Of, pertaining to, or produced by the changes in magnetic intensity caused by change of temperature.

py·ro·man·cy (pī′rə·man′sē, pir′ə-) *n.* Divination by fire. [<PYRO- + -MANCY]

py·ro·ma·ni·a (pī′rə·mā′nē·ə, -mān′yə, pir′ə-) *n.* A morbid propensity to set things on fire. — **py·ro·ma′ni·ac** (-ak) *adj.* & *n.* – **py·ro·ma·ni·a·cal** (pī′rō·mə·nī′ə·kəl, pir′ō-) *adj.*

py·ro·man·tic (pī′rə·man′tik, pir′ə-) *adj.* Of or pertaining to pyromancy. —*n.* One who professes to divine by means of fire.

py·rom·e·ter (pī·rom′ə·tər) *n.* An instrument for measuring high degrees of heat, as caused by electrical resistance, degree of incandescence, expansion, radiation, etc. — **py·ro·met·ric** (pī′rə·met′rik, pir′ə-) or **·ri·cal** *adj.* — **py·rom′e·try** *n.*

py·ro·mor·phite (pī′rə·môr′fīt, pir′ə-) *n.* A resinous, variously colored phosphate and chloride of lead, found in masses or crystals; green lead ore. [<G *pyromorphit* <Gk. *pyr, pyros* a fire + *morphos* form]

py·rone (pī′rōn, pī·rōn′) *n. Chem.* A cyclic compound, $C_5H_4O_2$, existing in two isomeric forms: it yields yellow dyestuffs. [<G *pyron*]

py·rope (pī′rōp) *n.* A variety of deep-red garnet: also called *precious garnet.* [<OF *pirope* <L *pyropus* gold-bronze <Gk. *pyrōpos,* lit., fiery-eyed < *pyr, pyros* a fire + *ōps, ōpos* eye, face]

py·ro·phor·ic (pī′rə·fôr′ik, -for′ik) *adj.* **1** Fire-bearing; spontaneously combustible. **2** Designating materials which are easily and quickly inflammable, as finely divided metals on exposure to air. [<Gk. *pyrophoros* < *pyr, pyros* a fire + *pherein* carry] — **py′ro·phore** (-fôr, -fōr) *n.*

py·ro·phos·phate (pī′rə·fos′fāt, pir′ə-) *n.* A salt of pyrophosphoric acid.

py·ro·phos·phor·ic acid (pī′rō·fos·fôr′ik, -for′ik, pir′ō-) *Chem.* An acid, $H_4P_2O_7$, obtained by heating orthophosphoric acid to about 255° C.

py·ro·pho·tom·e·ter (pī′rō·fō·tom′ə·tər, pir′ō-) *n.* A pyrometer used to determine high temperatures by means of the luminosity of a substance.

py·ro·phyl·lite (pī′rə·fil′īt, pir′ə-) *n.* A compact, soft, variously colored, hydrous aluminum silicate, $HAlSi_2O_6$, used in making slate pencils. [<PYRO- + PHYLL(O)- + -ITE[1]]

py·ro·sis (pī·rō′sis) *n. Pathol.* Heartburn; acid dyspepsia, accompanied by a burning sensation and belching of an acrid fluid. [<NL <Gk. *pyrōsis* a burning < *pyroein* burn < *pyr* fire]

py·ro·stat (pī′rə·stat, pir′ə-) *n.* A thermostat; specifically, one for the higher temperatures. [<PYRO- + -STAT]

py·ro·sul·fate (pī′rə·sul′fāt, pir′ə-) *n.* A salt of pyrosulfuric acid; a disulfate.

py·ro·sul·fu·ric acid (pī′rō·sul·fyŏŏr′ik, pir′ō-) *Chem.* A brown, fuming liquid, $H_2SO_4SO_3$, obtained by adding liquid sulfuric oxide to strong sulfuric acid: also called *disulfuric acid.*

py·ro·tech·nic (pī′rə·tek′nik, pir′ə-) *adj.* Pertaining to fireworks or their manufacture. Also **py′ro·tech′ni·cal.**

py·ro·tech·nics (pī′rə·tek′niks, pir′ə-) *n.* **1** The art of making or using fireworks: also **py′ro·tech′ny.** **2** A display of fireworks. **3** An ostentatious display, as of oratory. [Earlier *pyrotechny* <F *pyrotechnie* <Gk. *pyr, pyros* fire + *technē* an art; infl. in form by *pyrotechnic*] — **py′ro·tech′nist** *n.*

py·rot·ic (pī·rot′ik, pi-) *adj.* Caustic. —*n.* A caustic substance or remedy. [<NL *pyroticus* <Gk. *pyrōtikos* < *pyroein* burn < *pyr* fire]

py·ro·tox·in (pī′rə·tok′sin, pir′ə-) *n. Biochem.* Any one of a number of toxic substances found in the body as a result of bacterial action and inducing a rise of bodily temperature, or symptoms of fever.

py·rox·ene (pī′rok·sēn) *n.* **1** A monoclinic mineral, usually in short, prismatic crystals, composed principally of calcium and magnesium: next to feldspar, the most frequent component of igneous rocks. **2** Any member of the pyroxene group, as diopside and augite: they are essentially metasilicates. [<F *pyroxène* <Gk. *pyr, pyros* fire + *xenos* a stranger; because at first considered alien to igneous rocks] — **py·rox·en·ic** (pī′rok·sen′ik) *adj.*

py·rox·e·nite (pī·rok′sə·nīt) *n.* A granitoid igneous rock composed mostly of pyroxene, but without olivine. [<PYROXENE + -ITE[1]]

py·rox·y·lin (pī·rok′sə·lin) *n. Chem.* A cellulose nitrate mixture soluble in ether, alcohol, and organic solvents, less explosive than guncotton, and widely used in making Celluloid, lacquers, adhesives, etc. Also **py·rox′y·line** (-lēn, -lin). [<F *pyroxyline* <Gk. *pyr, pyros* fire + *xylon* wood + -INE[2]]

Pyr·rha (pir′ə) In Greek mythology, the daughter of Epimetheus and wife of Deucalion.

pyr·rhic[1] (pir′ik) *n.* A foot in ancient prosody composed of two short syllables. —*adj.* Of, pertaining to, or composed of pyrrhics. [<L *(pes) pyrrhicius* a pyrrhic (foot) <Gk. *(pous) pyrrichios* warlike, martial]

pyr·rhic[2] (pir′ik) *adj.* In Greek antiquity, pertaining to a martial dance in which the movements necessary to assail and avoid an enemy were imitated. —*n.* The pyrrhic dance. [<L *pyrrhicius* <Gk. *pyrrhichios* < *pyrrhichē* a war-dance <*Pyrrhichos* Pyrrhichus, a Greek said to have invented it]

Pyrrhic victory A victory gained at a ruinous loss, such as that of Pyrrhus over the Romans at Heracles Asculum, 279 B.C. [after *Pyrrhus*]

Pyr·rho·nism (pir′ə·niz′əm) *n.* A system of philosophy taught by Pyrrho of Elis, 365?–275? B.C., founder of the first and inspirer of subsequent skeptical schools of Greek philosophy; skepticism. [<L *Pyrrhoneus* pertaining to Pyrrho <Gk. *Pyrrhōn* Pyrrho]

pyr·rho·tite (pir′ə·tīt) *n.* A metallic, bronze-colored, magnetic iron sulfide, FeS; magnetic pyrites. Also **pyr′rho·lite** (-līt), **pyr′rho·tine** (-tīn). [<Gk. *pyrrhotēs* redness (< *pyrrhos* flame-colored < *pyr* a fire) + -ITE[1]]

pyr·rhu·lox·i·a (pir′ə·lok′sē·ə) *n.* A grosbeak of the western United States *(Pyrrhuloxia*

sinuata) with a slender, gray-and-red body and parrotlike bill. [< NL < *Pyrrhula*, a genus of Fringillidae (dim. < Gk. *pyrrhos* fiery < *pyr* fire) + *Loxia*, genus of the cross-bills < Gk. *loxos* oblique]

PYTHAGOREAN THEOREM

Sum of squares ABDE and BCGF equals square ACHK ($a^2 + b^2 = c^2$)

Pyr·rhus(pir'əs), 318?-272 B.C., king of Epirus; aided Tarentum against the Romans.

Pyr·rhus(pir'əs) In Greek legend, Neoptolemus.

pyr·role(pi·rōl', pir'ōl) *n. Chem.* A colorless, poisonous, weakly basic, liquid compound, C_4H_4NH, having an odor of chloroform, obtained from bone oil, coal tar, and by synthesis, and occurring in many natural substances, as chlorophyll and hemoglobin. Also **pyr·rol'**. [< G *pyrrol* (< Gk. *pyrros* reddish < *pyr* fire) + -ol·OLE[1]]

pyr·rol·i·dine(pi·rol'ə-dēn, -din) *n. Chem.* A colorless nitrogenous compound, C_4H_9N, with a mild ammonia odor, found in tobacco and carrot leaves. [< PYRROL(E) + -ID(E) + -INE[2]]

py·ru·vic acid(pī-rōō'vik, pi-) *Chem.* A colorless to pale-yellow ketone compound, $C_3H_4O_3$, obtained by the distillation of a mixture of racemic acid and potassium bisulfate. [< PYR- + L *uva* grape + -IC]

Py·thag·o·ras(pi-thag'ər-əs) Greek philosopher of the sixth century B.C. — **Py·thag'o·re'an** *adj.* & *n.*

Py·thag·o·re·an·ism(pi-thag'ə-rē'ən·iz'əm) *n.* The mystical philosophy taught by Pythagoras, its central idea being that number is the essence of all things and the metaphysical principle of ra-

tional order in the universe. The leading theological doctrine was metempsychosis. [< L *Pythagoreus* < Gk. *Pythagoreios* < *Pythagoras* Pythagoras]

Pythagorean numbers See under NUMBER.

Pythagorean theorem *Math.* The theorem that the sum of the squares of the legs of a right triangle is equal to the square of the hypotenuse.

Pyth·i·a(pith'ē-ə) In ancient Greece, the priestess of the Pythian Apollo at Delphi, who was believed to be inspired by the god when seated on a tripod over the rock sacred to him, and to utter his oracles. — **Pyth'ic** *adj.*

Pyth·i·ad(pith'ē-ad) *n.* The period from one celebration of the ancient Greek Pythian games to another. [< Gk. *Pythias, -ados* < (*hiera*) *Pythia* the Pythian (games), neut. pl. of *Pythios* Pythian]

Pyth·i·an(pith'ē-ən) *adj.* 1 Relating to Delphi, to Apollo's temple here, its oracle, or priestess. 2 Relating to the Pythian games. — *n.* 1 A native or inhabitant of Delphi; specifically, the priestess of Apollo. 2 An epithet of the Delphic Apollo. [< L *Pythius* < Gk. *Pythios* < *Pytho*, older name for Delphi]

Pythian games Games held every four years in ancient Greece, of which musical contests were a feature.

Pyth·i·as (pith'e-əs) See DA-MON AND PYTHIAS. Also *Phintias*

py·tho·gen·e·sis(pī'thō-jen'ə-sis, pith'ō-) *n.* Generation from or because of filth. [< Gk. *pythein* rot + GENE-SIS] — **py'tho·gen'ic, py'·tho·ge·net'ic** (-jə·net'ik) *adj.*

pythogenic fever *Pathol.* 1 Typhoid fever. 2 Any fever due to filth. Also **pythogenetic fever.**

py·thon(pī'thon, -thən) *n.* 1 A large, non-venomous ser-

PYTHON
(From 3 to 32 feet in length)

pent (genus *Python*) that crushes its prey in its folds. 2 Any non-venomous serpent related to the boas. 3 A soothsayer or soothsaying spirit: from the tradition that the Python delivered oracles at Delphi; also, a ventriloquist. [< L < Gk. *Pythōn* Python < *Pytho*. See PYTHIAN.]

Py·thon(pī'thon, -thən) In Greek mythology, a monstrous serpent which haunted the caves of Parnassus and was killed by Apollo near Delphi.

Py·tho·ness(pī'thə-nis, pith'ə-) *n.* 1 The priestess of the Delphic oracle. 2 Any woman supposed to be possessed of the spirit of prophecy; a witch. [< OF *phitonise* < Med. L *phitonissa* < LL *pythonissa* < Gk. *Pytho* a familiar spirit, orig. Delphi]

py·thon·ic(pīthon'ik, pi-) *adj.* 1 Of, pertaining to, or resembling pythons or a python. 2 Inspired; prophetic.

py·u·ri·a(pī-yōōr'ē-ə) *n. Pathol.* The presence of pus in the urine. [< NL < Gk. *pyon* pus + *ouron* urine]

pyx(piks) *n.* 1 A vessel or casket, usually of precious metal, in which the Host is preserved. 2 A receptacle for coins selected for trial at the British mint: short for **pyx chest.** [< L *pyxis* a box < Gk. < *pyxos* a box tree. Doublet of BOX.]

pyx·ie[1](pik'sē) See PIXY.

pyx·ie[2](pik'sē) *n.* A creeping shrub (*Pyxidanthera barbulata*) with numerous solitary white or rose-colored flowers: it is the flowering moss or pixie of the pine barrens of New Jersey and North Carolina. [Prob. short for NL *Pyxidanthera*, the genus name < Gk. *pyxos* the box tree + *antheros* flowery]

pyx·is(pik'sis) *n. pl.* **pyx·i·des** (pik'sə-dēz) 1 A box or pyx; especially, an ancient form of ornamental jewel case or toilet box. 2 An emollient ointment. 3 *Bot.* A capsule or seed vessel with transverse dehiscence, the upper portion separating as a lid, as in the common purslane: also **pyx·id·i·um** (pik·sid'ē-əm). [< L. See PYX.]

Q

q, Q(kyōō) *n. pl.* **q's Q's** or **qs, Qs, ques** (kyōōz) 1 The 17th letter of the English alphabet, from Phoenician *Q'oph* and Greek *koppa*, which was present in five eastern Greek alphabets, obsolete in the late alphabets of Elis and Athens, but survived in the Chalcidian and Boeotian, whence it passed into the Italian, to Roman *Q.* 2 The sound of the letter *q.* In English *q* is always followed by *u* and is pronounced *kw*, as in quack, queen, quest, quote, conquest, equal, etc. In some words borrowed from French, however, it retains its French pronunciation of *k*, as in appliqué, conquer, coquette, pique, piquant, toque. Final *-que* is always pronounced as *k*, as in antique, oblique, physique, unique, etc. See ALPHABET.

Qair·wan(kīr·wän') See KAIROUAN.

Qan·da·har(kän'dä·här') See KANDAHAR.

Qaz·vin(käz·vēn') See KAZVIN.

Qa·tar(kä'tär) An independent Arab sheikdom, containing the whole **Qatar Peninsula** on the Persian Gulf coast of the Arabian Peninsula; about 8,000 miles; capital, Doha.

Qat·ta·ra Depression(kä·tä'rä) A desert basin in the Libyan Desert of northern Egypt; 7,500 square miles. Also **Qat·ta'rah.**

Q-boat(kyōō'bōt') *n.* A merchant vessel having masked guns: used in World War I as a decoy for submarines. Also **Q'-ship'.**

Qe·na(kā'nə) A city on the east bank of the Nile, Upper Egypt. Also **Qi·na** (kē'nə).

Qishm(kish'əm) The largest island in the Persian Gulf, at the entrance of the Strait of Hormuz, southern Iran; 70 by 7 to 20 miles.

Qi·shon(kī'shon, kish'on) A river in NW Israel, flowing 45 miles NW to the Bay of Acre.

qua(kwā, kwä) *adv.* In the capacity of; by virtue of being; in so far as. [< L, ablative sing. fem. of *qui* who]

Quaa·lude(kwā'lüd') *n.* Methaqualone: a trade name.

quack[1](kwak) *v.i.* To utter a harsh, croaking cry, as a duck. — *n.* The sound made by a duck, or a similar croaking noise. [Imit.]

quack[2](kwak) *n.* 1 A pretender to medical knowledge or skill. 2 A charlatan. — *adj.* Of or pertaining to quacks or quackery; ignorantly or falsely pretending to cure. — *v.i.* To play the quack. [Short for QUACKSALVER] — **quack'ish** *adj.* —**quack'ish·ly** *adv.*

Synonyms (noun): charlatan, empiric, humbug, impostor, mountebank. Antonyms: adept, expert, master.

quack·er·y(kwak'ər·ē) *n. pl.* **·er·ies** Ignorant or fraudulent practice.

quack·grass(kwak'gras', -gräs') *n.* Couchgrass.

quack·sal·ver(kwak'sal'vər) *n.* A quack. [< MDu. < *quacken* quack[1] + *salf* a salve]

quad[1](kwod) *n. Colloq.* A quadrangle of a college or prison. [Short for QUADRANGLE]

quad[2] (kwod) *n. Printing* A quadrat. [Short for QUADRAT]

quad[3](kwod) See QUOD.

quad[4](kwod) *adj.* Quadraphonic.

quad·ra·ge·nar·i·an(kwod'rə·jə·nâr'ē·ən) *adj.* Forty years old or relating to this age. — *n.* A person forty years old. [< L *quadragenarius* < *quadrageni* forty each < *quadraginta* forty]

Quad·ra·ges·i·ma(kwod'rə·jes'ə·mə) *n. Obs.* The forty fast days before Easter; Lent. [< L, fortieth]

quad·ra·ges·i·mal(kwod'rə·jes'ə·məl) *adj.* 1 Of or pertaining to the number forty, especially to the forty days of Lent. 2 Used during or appropriate to Lent; Lenten.

Quadragesima Sunday The first Sunday in Lent.

quad·ran·gle(kwod'rang·gəl) *n.* 1 *Geom.* A plane figure having four sides and four angles. 2 A court, square or oblong, as within a public building. 3 A tract of land as represented by the United States Geological Survey on one of its atlas sheets. [< L *quadrangulum* < *quattuor* four + *angulus* angle] — **quad·ran'gu·lar** *adj.*

quad·rant(kwod'rənt) *n.* 1 The quarter of a circle, or of its circumference. 2 An instrument having a graduated arc of 90°, with a movable radius for measuring angles on it; especially, a nautical instrument for measuring the altitude of the sun. 3 *Geom.* In a Cartesian coordinate system, any of the four sections formed by the intersection of the axes: beginning with the upper right-hand quadrant where the ordinate and abscissa are positive, they are called the **first, second, third,** and **fourth quadrants,** in counterclockwise order. See illustration on page 1030. 4 A device or machine-part having the shape of, or suggest-

ing the quadrant of a circle. [< L *quadrans, -antis* a fourth part < *quattuor* four] —**quad·ran·tal** (kwod·ran′təl) *adj.*

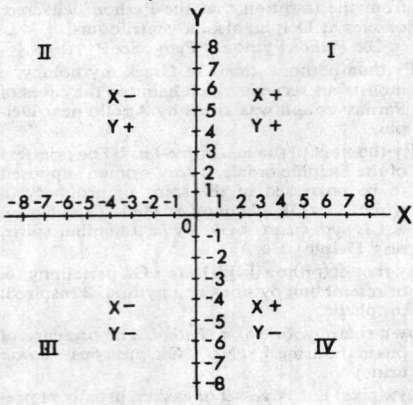

CARTESIAN QUADRANT

quad·ra·phon·ic (kwod′rə·fon′ik) *adj.* Of, pertaining to, or employing a system of sound reproduction that uses four transmission channels and loudspeakers.

quad·rat (kwod′rət) *n.* **1** *Printing* A piece of type metal lower than the letters, used for spacing: abbreviated *quad.* **2** *Ecol.* A square area of varying size laid down in a plant association or formation to estimate the number of plants enclosed, or to determine the character of successional changes. [SEE QUADRATE]

quad·rate (kwod′rāt, -rit) *n.* **1** *Zool.* A bone of cartilaginous element suspending the lower jaw in certain vertebrates below the mammals. **2** In astrology, an aspect of two heavenly bodies in which they are distant from each other 90°. **3** A cubical or square object, or an object resembling a cube. —*adj.* **1** Square; four-sided, as a muscle. **2** Distant from each other 90°: said of two heavenly bodies. **3** Of or pertaining to the quadrate bone or cartilage. —*v.* (-rāt) **·rat·ed, ·rat·ing** *v.i.* To correspond or agree: with *with.* —*v.t.* To cause to conform; bring in accordance with. [< L *quadratus,* pp. of *quadrare* square < *quattuor* four]

quad·rat·ic (kwod·rat′ik) *adj.* **1** Pertaining to or resembling a square. **2** Relating to a quadratic equation. —*n.* *Math.* **1** An equation of the second degree. It is a **pure, simple,** or **incomplete quadratic** when it contains only the second power of the variable, as $ax^2+c = 0$; a **complete** or **adfected quadratic** when it contains also the first power, as $ax^2 + bx + c = 0$. **2** A formula, $x = \dfrac{-b \pm \sqrt{b^2 - 4ac}}{2a}$, for computing the roots of the standard quadratic equation, $ax^2 + bx + c = 0$. **3** *pl.* The part of algebra that treats of quadratic equations.

quad·ra·ture (kwod′rə·chər) *n.* **1** The act or process of squaring. **2** The finding in square measure of the area of any surface, especially one bounded by a curve. **3** *Astron.* **a** The relative position of two heavenly bodies that are 90° apart as viewed from the center of a third body. **b** Either intersection of an orbit with a line whose ends terminate in the curve drawn perpendicular to the major axis through the focus.

quad·ren·ni·al (kwod·ren′ē·əl) *adj.* **1** Occurring once in four years. **2** Comprising four years. —**quad·ren′ni·al·ly** *adv.*

quad·ren·ni·um (kwod·ren′ē·əm) *n. pl.* **·ren·ni·a** (-ren′ē-ə) A space or period of four years. Also **quad·ri·en·ni·um** (kwod′rē·en′ē·əm). [< L]

quadri- *combining form* Four: *quadrinomial.* Also, before vowels, **quadr-:** also *quadru-.* [< L *quattuor* four]

quad·ric (kwod′rik) *adj. Math.* Of the second degree: applied especially where there are more than two variables. —*n.* A quantic of the second degree. [< L *quadra* square]

quadric curve *Math.* A curve with an algebraic Cartesian equation of the second degree.

quad·ri·cen·ten·ni·al (kwod′ri·sen·ten′ē·əl) *n.* A four-hundredth anniversary. —*adj.* Of or pertaining to such an anniversary.

quad·ri·ceps (kwod′rə·seps) *n. Anat.* The extensor of the leg. [< QUADRI- + L *caput* head] —**quad·ri·cip′i·tal** (-sip′ə·təl) *adj.*

quad·ri·fid (kwod′rə·fid) *adj. Bot.* Four-cleft; divided into four segments, as a flower petal.

quad·ri·ga (kwod·rī′gə) *n. pl.* **·gae** (-jē) In ancient Rome, a two-wheeled chariot to which four horses were harnessed abreast. [< L < *quattuor* four + *jugum* yoke]

quad·ri·lat·er·al (kwod′rə·lat′ər·əl) *adj.* Formed or bounded by four lines; four-sided. —*n.* **1** *Geom.* **a** A figure bounded by four straight lines terminated at four angles. **b** A figure formed of four infinite straight lines, having six intersections. **2** A space or area defended by four enclosing fortresses. [< L *quadrilaterus* < *quattuor* four + *latus, lateris* side]

QUADRILATERAL
abdc. Quadrilateral.
ad., bc. Diagonals.
ebfc. Quadrilateral.
a., b.., c.., d., f. Vertices.
ai., bh., ei. Diagonals.
g., hh.., i. Centers.

quad·ri·lin·gual (kwod′rə·ling′gwəl) *adj.* **1** Consisting of, or knowing, four languages. **2** Written in four languages.

qua·drille[1] (kwə·dril′) *n.* **1** A square dance for four couples and having five figures. **2** Music for such a dance. [< F < Sp. *cuadrilla* little square < L *quadrum* < *quattuor* four]

qua·drille[2] (kwə·dril′) *n.* A card game for four persons, played with a deck of 40 cards and popular in the 18th century. [< F < Sp. *cuartillo* < *cuarto* fourth < L *quartus*]

quadrille paper See GRAPH PAPER.

quad·ril·lion (kwod·ril′yən) *n.* **1** In the French and United States system of numeration, a thousand trillions, or 1 followed by 15 ciphers. **2** In the English system, a million trillions, or 1 followed by 24 ciphers. [< F < *quatre* four + (*m*)*illion*]

quad·ri·no·mi·al (kwod′rə·nō′mē·əl) *n. Math.* An algebraic expression having four terms.

quad·ri·par·tite (kwod′rə·pär′tīt) *adj.* **1** Consisting of or embracing four parts. **2** Having four parties, as an agreement or contract. [< L *quadripartitus* < *quattuor* four + *partitus* divided] —**quad′ri·par·ti′tion** (-tish′ən) *n.*

quad·ri·ple·gi·a (kwod′rə·plē′jē·ə) *n. Pathol.* Paralysis of the arms and legs. —**quad·ri·ple·gic** (kwod′rə·plē′jik, -plej′ik) *adj.*

quad·ri·syl·la·ble (kwod′rə·sil′ə·bəl) *n.* A word of four syllables. —**quad′ri·syl·lab′ic** (-si·lab′ik) *adj.*

quad·ri·va·lent (kwod′rə·vā′lənt) *adj. Chem.* Having a valence of four, as carbon; tetravalent. [< QUADRI- + L *valens, -entis,* ppr. of *valere* be worth] —**quad′ri·va′lence** or **·len·cy** *n.*

quad·riv·i·al (kwod·riv′ē·əl) *adj.* **1** Having four radiating ways. **2** Leading to or going in four directions: *quadrivial* streets. [< L *quadrivius* < *quattuor* four + *via* way]

quad·riv·i·um (kwod·riv′ē·əm) *n. pl.* **·i·a** (-ē-ə) In the Pythagorean system, the four sciences, geometry, astronomy, arithmetic, and music, making up with the trivium the seven liberal arts. Compare TRIVIUM. [< L, a place where four roads meet]

quad·ro·min·i·um (kwod′rə·min′ē·əm) *n.* A multiple residence containing four condominiums.

quad·roon (kwod·rōōn′) *n.* A person having one-fourth Negro and three-fourths white blood. [< Sp. *cuarteron* < *cuarto* fourth]

quadru- Var. of QUADRI-.

quad·ru·ma·nous (kwod·rōō′mə·nəs) *adj.* **1** Four-handed; having four feet resembling hands. **2** Of or pertaining to a former order (*Quadrumana*) of mammals now classed with man under the primates. [< QUADRU- + L *manus* hand]

quad·ru·ped (kwod′rōō·ped) *n.* An animal having four feet; especially, a four-footed mammal. —*adj.* Having four feet. [< L *quadrupes, -pedis* < *quattuor* four + *pes* foot] —**quad·ru·pe·dal** (kwod·rōō′pə·dəl, kwod·rōō·ped′l) *adj.*

quad·ru·ple (kwod·rōō′pəl, kwod′rōō·pəl) *adj.* Consisting of four; having four parts or members; fourfold; also, taken by fours. —*n.* A number or sum four times as great as another. —*v.t.* & *v.i.* **·pled, ·pling** To multiply by four; make or become four times larger.

—*adv.* Fourfold. [< L *quadruplus*]

quad·ru·plet (kwod′rōō·plit, kwod·rōō′-) *n.* **1** A compound or combination of four things or objects. **2** One of four offspring born of the same mother at one birth.

quadruple time *Music* Measure or time having four beats; four-two, four-four, or four-eight time.

quad·ru·plex (kwod′rōō·pleks, kwod·rōō′-) *adj.* **1** Fourfold. **2** Pertaining to or designating a telegraph system such that four messages, two in each direction, may be sent simultaneously over one wire. —*n.* A sending instrument used in quadruplex telegraphy. [< L < *quattuor* four + stem of *plicare* fold]

quad·ru·pli·cate (kwod·rōō′plə·kit, -kāt) *adj.* **1** Fourfold. **2** Raised to the fourth power. —*v.t.* (-kāt) **·cat·ed, ·cat·ing** To multiply by four; quadruple. —*n.* One of four like things. —**quad·ru′pli·ca′tion** —**quad·ru′pli·cate·ly** *adv.*

quae·re (kwē′rē) *n.* Literally, seek; inquire: an annotation inserted, as in law reports. [< L. See QUERY.]

quaes·tor (kwes′tər, kwēs′-) *n.* Any of a number of public officials in ancient Rome; originally, one of two magistrates who inquired into and punished capital crimes; later, one who took charge of the public treasury and expenditure: also spelled *questor.* [< L < *quaerere* seek, inquire] —**quaes·to·ri·al** (kwes·tôr′ē·əl, -tō′rē-, kwēs-) *adj.* —**quaes′tor·ship** *n.*

quaff (kwaf, kwof, kwôf) *v.t.* & *v.i.* To drink, especially copiously or with relish. —*n.* A drink; swallow. [< earlier *quaft,* ? blend of QUENCH and DRAUGHT] —**quaff′er** *n.*

quag (kwag, kwog) *n.* A quagmire. [< obs. *quag, v.,* blend of QUAKE and SAG]

quag·ga (kwag′ə) *n.* A South African equine mammal (*Equus quagga*) intermediate between the ass and the zebra and resembling the latter: now extinct. **2** A zebra: an erroneous use. [< native Hottentot name]

QUAGGA
(About 11 hands high at the withers)

quag·gy (kwag′ē, kwog′ē) *adj.* Yielding to or quaking under the foot, as soft, wet earth; boggy.

quag·mire (kwag′mīr′, kwog′-) *n.* **1** Marshy ground that gives way under the foot; bog. **2** A difficult situation. [< QUAG + MIRE] —**quag′mired,** **quag′mir·y** *adj.*

qua·haug (kwô′hôg, -hog, kwə·hôg′, -hog′) *n.* The round, thick-shelled clam (*Venus mercenaria*) of the Atlantic coast of North America. The young are called cherrystone clams. Also **qua·hog:** sometimes spelled *cohog, quohog.* [< Algonquian (Narraganset) *poquauhock*]

Quai d'Or·say (kā dôr·sā′) **1** A quay on the left bank of the Seine in Paris, toward which the French Foreign Office faces. **2** The French Foreign Office.

quaigh (kwākh) *n. Scot.* A small cup or drinking vessel. Also **quaich.**

quail[1] (kwāl) *n.* **1** An Old World migratory game bird (*Coturnix coturnix*) similar to the partridge, having a very short tail. **2** Any of various small American game birds related to the partridge (family *Perdicidae*), especially the bobwhite and the California quail (*Lophortyx californica*). See BOBWHITE. **3** *Obs.* A prostitute. [< OF *quaille,* prob. < Gmc.]

quail[2] (kwāl) *v.i.* To shrink with fear; lose heart or courage. [ME *quailen;* origin uncertain]

quaint (kwānt) *adj.* **1** Combining an antique appearance with a pleasing oddity, fancifulness, or whimsicalness. **2** Hence, pleasingly odd or old-fashioned; fanciful. **3** *Obs.* Curiously wrought; hence, ornamental. **4** *Obs.* Crafty. See synonyms under ANTIQUE, ODD, QUEER. [< OF *cointe* < L *cognitus* known] —**quaint′ly** *adv.* —**quaint′ness** *n.*

quake (kwāk) *v.i.* **quaked, quak·ing 1** To shake, as with violent emotion or cold; quiver. **2** To shake or tremble, as earth during an earthquake. —*n.* A shaking, tremulous motion, quickly repeated; a shaking or shuddering. [OE *cwacian* shake]

Synonyms (verb): quaver, quiver, shake, shiver, shudder, tremble, vibrate, waver. See SHAKE.

Quak·er (kwā′kər) *n.* A member of the Society of Friends: originally a term of derision, and still not used within the society. See SOCIETY OF FRIENDS. [<QUAKE, *v.*; with ref. to their founder's admonition to them to tremble at the word of the Lord] — **Quak′er·ess** *n. fem.* — **Quak′er·ish** *adj.* — **Quak′er·ish·ly** *adv.*

quaker buttons The dried, ripe seeds of nux vomica.

Quaker City A nickname of PHILADELPHIA.

Quaker gun A dummy gun, as one made of wood: from the Friends' doctrine of non-resistance.

Quak·er·ism (kwā′kə·riz′əm) *n.* The beliefs or practices of the Quakers.

quaker ladies Bluets.

Quak·er·ly (kwā′kər·lē) *adj.* Like the Quakers. — *adv.* After the manner of the Quakers.

Quaker meeting 1 Any meeting of the Society of Friends for worship, in which, following their usage, they remain silent until the Spirit moves some member to speak or pray aloud. 2 Any silent gathering.

Quaker State Nickname of PENNSYLVANIA.

quak·y (kwā′kē) *adj.* **quak·i·er**, **quak·i·est** Shaky; tremulous. — **quak′i·ly** *adv.* — **quak′i·ness** *n.*

qual·i·fi·ca·tion (kwol′ə·fə·kā′shən) *n.* 1 The act of qualifying, or the state of being qualified. 2 That which fits a person or thing for something. 3 A restriction; mitigation. See synonyms under ABILITY.

qual·i·fied (kwol′ə·fīd) *adj.* 1 Competent or fit, as for public office. 2 Restricted or modified in some way. See synonyms under COMPETENT. — **qual′i·fied·ly** *adv.*

qual·i·fy (kwol′ə·fī) *v.* **·fied**, **·fy·ing** *v.t.* 1 To make fit or capable, as for an office, occupation, or privilege. 2 To make legally capable, as by the administration of an oath. 3 To limit or restrict, as by conditions or exceptions. 4 To attribute a quality to; describe; characterize or name. 5 To make less strong or extreme; soften; moderate. 6 To change the strength or flavor of. 7 *Gram.* To modify. — *v.i.* 8 To be or become qualified or fit; meet the requirements, as for entering a race. See synonyms under CHANGE. [<MF *qualifier* <Med. L *qualificare* <L *qualis* of such a kind + *facere* make] — **qual′i·fi′a·ble** *adj.* — **qual′i·fi′er** *n.*

qual·i·ta·tive (kwol′ə·tā′tiv) *adj.* Of or pertaining to quality: distinguished from *quantitative*. [<LL *qualitativus* <L *qualitas* quality] — **qual′i·ta·tive·ly** *adv.*

qualitative analysis *Chem.* The process of finding how many and what elements or ingredients are present in a substance or compound.

qual·i·ty (kwol′ə·tē) *n. pl.* **·ties** 1 That which makes a being or thing such as it is; a distinguishing element or characteristic. 2 The characteristics of anything regarded as determining its value, place, worth, rank, position, etc., or the condition of a thing as so determined; character; kind; when unqualified, peculiar excellence. 3 A moral trait or characteristic. 4 Degree of excellence; relative goodness; grade: high *quality* of fabric. 5 Capability of producing specific effects. 6 Particular character or part; capacity; function. 7 *Archaic* Social rank; persons of rank, collectively. 8 *Music* That which distinguishes sounds of the same pitch and intensity from different sources, as from different instruments; timbre. 9 *Logic* The character of a proposition or judgment as asserting or denying. 10 *Philos.* An essential property or attribute. 11 *Phonet.* The character of a vowel sound as determined by the resonance of the oral cavity. See synonyms under ATTRIBUTE, CHARACTERISTIC. — *adj.* Characterized by high quality: a *quality* product. [<L *qualitas, -tatis* < *qualis* of such a kind]

qualm (kwäm, kwôm) *n.* 1 A feeling of sickness. 2 A twinge of conscience; moral scruple. 3 A sensation of fear or misgiving. [OE *cwealm* death]

qualm·ish (kwä′mish, kwô′-) *adj.* 1 Feeling or affected with qualms. 2 Likely to produce qualms. See synonyms under SQUEAMISH. Also **qualm′y**. — **qualm′ish·ly** *adv.* — **qualm′ish·ness** *n.*

quam·ash (kwom′ash, kwə·mash′) *n.* Camas.

quan·da·ry (kwon′dər·ē, -drē) *n. pl.* **·da·ries** A state of hesitation or perplexity; predicament. [Origin uncertain]

quand même (kän mem′) *French* Notwithstanding; even though; nevertheless.

quan·dong (kwon′dong) *n.* 1 A small Australian tree of the sandalwood family (*Fusanus acuminatus*). 2 Its edible drupaceous fruit, used as a preserve. Also **quan′dang**. [< native Australian name]

quant (kwant, kwont) *n. Brit.* A punting pole with a flange at the end to prevent its sinking in the mud. — *v.t. & v.i.* To propel or be propelled with a quant. [? <L *contus* a boat pole]

quan·ta (kwon′tə) Plural of QUANTUM.

quan·tic (kwon′tik) *n. Math.* A rational homogeneous function of two or more variables, usually containing only positive integers.

Quan·ti·co (kwon′ti·kō) A town on the Potomac in northern Virginia; site of a United States Marine Corps base.

quan·ti·fy (kwon′tə·fī) *v.t.* **·fied**, **·fy·ing** 1 To determine the quantity of. 2 *Logic* To express the quantity of explicitly, as by using *all*, *some*, or *none*. [<Med. L *quantificare* <L *quantus* how great + *facere* make] — **quan′ti·fi·ca′tion** *n.* — **quan′ti·fi′er** *n.*

quan·tim·e·ter (kwon·tim′ə·tər) *n. Med.* A dosimeter.

quan·ti·ta·tive (kwon′tə·tā′tiv) *adj.* 1 Of or pertaining to quantity. 2 Having to do with quantities only: distinguished from *qualitative*. [<LL *quantitativus* <L *quantitas* quantity] — **quan′ti·ta·tive·ly** *adv.* — **quan′ti·ta·tive·ness** *n.*

quantitative analysis *Chem.* The process of finding the amount or percentage of each element or ingredient present, as in a compound.

quan·ti·ty (kwon′tə·tē) *n. pl.* **·ties** 1 The condition of being much. 2 That property of a thing which admits of exact measurement and numerical statement. 3 An object regarded as possessing a certain determinable magnitude, as of length, size, mass, volume, or number. 4 *Electr.* The strength of a current, as opposed to intensity or potential. 5 In prosody, the relative period of time, regarded as short or long, required to pronounce a syllable. 6 *Music* The duration of a musical note. 7 A specified, or indefinite, number of persons or things. 8 *Logic* The extent of a general term or proposition as applying to the whole or to a part of a class. Considered with reference to quantity, propositions are *universal*, as "all men are mortal," and *particular*, as "some men are honest," while with reference to conceptions quantity relates either to their extension, or to their intension or comprehension. 9 Considerable bulk or amount. [<OF *quantité* <L *quantitas, -tatis* < *quantus* how much, how large]

quan·tize (kwon′tīz) *v.t.* **·tized**, **·tiz·ing** *Physics* To express (an energy relationship) in terms of quanta or in accordance with the quantum theory. — **quan′ti·za′tion** *n.*

quan·tum (kwon′təm) *n. pl.* **·ta** (-tə) 1 An object that has quantity or is concrete. 2 A certain amount; also, a prescribed or a sufficient quantity. 3 *Physics* A fundamental unit of energy or action as provided for in the quantum theory. [<L, neuter of *quantus* how much]

quantum liquid *Physics* Helium in the superfluid condition: so called because it confirms the quantum theory that even at temperature of absolute zero molecular motion does not completely cease.

quantum number *Physics* A number indicating any of the energy levels possible in an atom under specified conditions.

quantum state Energy level.

quantum theory *Physics* The theory that energy is not a smoothly flowing continuum but is manifested by the emission from radiating bodies of discrete particles or *quanta*, the values of which are expressed as the product of Planck's constant, *h*, and the frequency, *v*, of the given radiation.

Qua·paw (kwä′pô) *n.* One of a tribe of North American Indians of Siouan stock, formerly living in Arkansas, now in Oklahoma: also called *Arkansas*.

quar·an·tine (kwôr′ən·tēn, kwor′-) *n.* 1 The enforced isolation for a fixed period of persons, ships, or goods arriving from places infected with contagious disease, or of any persons who have been exposed to such infection. 2 A place designated for the enforcement of such interdiction. 3 The enforced isolation of any person or place infected with contagious disease; loosely, any enforced isolation. 4 A period of forty days. — *v.t.* **·tined**, **·tin·ing** To subject to or retain in quarantine; isolate by or as by quarantine. [<Ital. *quarantina* <L *quadraginta* forty]

quark (kwärk) *n. Physics* Any of a group of three types of hypothetical fundamental particles proposed as the entities of which all other strongly interacting particles are composed. [Coined by Murray Gell-Mann, born 1929, U.S. physicist, appar. after use by James Joyce in *Finnegans Wake*]

Quarles (kwôrlz, kworlz), **Francis**, 1592–1644, English poet.

Quar·ne·ro (kwär·ne′rō), **Gulf of** See VELIKI KVARNER.

quar·rel[1] (kwôr′əl, kwor′-) *n.* 1 An unfriendly, angry, or violent dispute. 2 A falling out or contention; breach of amity: a lover's *quarrel*. 3 The cause for dispute. — *v.i.* **·reled** or **·relled**, **·rel·ing** or **·rel·ling** 1 To engage in a quarrel; dispute; contend; fight: to *quarrel* about money. 2 To break off a mutual friendship; fall out; disagree. 3 To find fault; cavil. [<F *querelle* <L *querela* complaint] — **quar′rel·er** or **quar′rel·ler** *n.*

Synonyms (noun): affray, altercation, bickering, brawl, breach, broil, contention, contest, controversy, disagreement, discussion, dispute, dissension, feud, fracas, fray, fuss, jangle, jar, misunderstanding, quarreling, rupture, scene, squabble, strife, wrangle. A *quarrel* is in word or act, or both, and is often slight and transient, as we speak of childish *quarrels*; but *quarrel* may denote the cause or ground of *contention* or *strife*, and so be deep and enduring. *Contention* and *strife* may be in word or deed; *contest* ordinarily involves some form of action. *Controversy* is commonly in words; *strife* extends from verbal controversy to the *contests* of armies. See ALTERCATION, FEUD[1]. *Antonyms:* accord, amity, acquiescence, concord, harmony, peace, reconciliation.

quar·rel[2] (kwôr′əl, kwor′-) *n.* 1 A dart or arrow with a four-edged head, formerly used with a crossbow. 2 A graver, stonemason's chisel, glazier's diamond, or other tool having a several-edged point. [<OF <LL *quadrellus*, dim. of L *quadrum* a square < *quattuor* four]

quar·rel·some (kwôr′əl·səm, kwor′-) *adj.* Inclined to quarrel; contentious. — **quar′rel·some·ly** *adv.* — **quar′rel·some·ness** *n.*

quar·ri·er (kwôr′ē·ər, kwor′-) *n.* A workman in a stone quarry.

quar·ry[1] (kwôr′ē, kwor′ē) *n. pl.* **·ries** 1 A beast or bird hunted, seized, or killed, as in the chase; game; prey: now chiefly poetical. 2 Anything hunted, slaughtered, or eagerly pursued. 3 *Obs.* A heap of slaughtered game. [<OF *cuirée* <L *corium* hide]

quar·ry[2] (kwôr′ē, kwor′ē) *n. pl.* **·ries** An excavation from which stone is taken by cutting, blasting, or the like. — *v.t.* **·ried**, **·ry·ing** 1 To cut, dig, or take from or as from a quarry. 2 To establish a quarry in. [<Med. L *quareia, quareria* <LL *quadraria* place for squaring stone < *quadrare*. See QUADRATE.]

quar·ry[3] (kwôr′ē, kwor′ē) *n. pl.* **·ries** 1 A square or lozenge. 2 A small square or lozenge-shaped pane of glass, tile, etc. 3 In archery, a quarrel. [<OF *quarré* <L *quadratus*. See QUADRATE.]

quart[1] (kwôrt) *n.* 1 A measure of capacity; the fourth part of a gallon, or two pints. In the United States, the dry quart is equal to 1.10 liters and the liquid quart is equal to 0.946 liter. 2 A vessel of such capacity. [<F *quarte* <L *quartus* fourth]

quart[2] (kärt) *n.* 1 In fencing, a quarte. 2 In piquet, a sequence of four cards of the same suit: called **quart major** if they are the highest four. [<F *quarte*. See QUART[1].]

quar·tan (kwôr′tən) *adj.* Pertaining to the fourth in a series; especially, occurring every fourth day. — *n. Pathol.* A malarial fever caused by the parasite *Plasmodium malariae*, in which the paroxysms recur every fourth

day, or 72 hours, reckoning inclusively. [<F *quartaine* <L *quartanus* < *quartus* fourth]

quarte (kärt, *Fr.* kȧrt) *n.* In fencing, a thrust or parry: the fourth regular position: also spelled *carte.* [<F]

quar·ter (kwôr′tər) *n.* **1** One of four equal parts into which anything is or may be divided; a fourth part; specifically, the fourth of a hundredweight; eight bushels; a fourth of a ton (of grain); the fourth of a yard, or a span; a fourth of a pound; a fourth of a mile; fifteen minutes or the fourth of an hour, or the moment with which it begins or ends. **2** A fourth of a year or three months; hence, a term of school. **3** A limb of a quadruped with the adjacent parts; also, a haunch of venison. **4** In the United States and Canada, a coin of the value of 25 cents. **5** *Astron.* Either of two phases of the moon: the first quarter, between the new and full moon; or the last quarter, between the full moon and the new. **6** *Music* A quarter note. **7** *Nav.* One of the four principal points of the compass or divisions of the horizon; also, a point or direction of the compass. **8** The place, origin, or source from which anything comes. **9** A particular division or district; a locality. **10** *Usually pl.* Proper or assigned station, position, or place, as of officers and crew on a warship. **11** *pl.* A place of lodging or residence, especially temporary shelter; specifically, a group of cabins provided for the Negroes on a Southern plantation. **12** A region embracing one fourth, or about one fourth, of a space; one of four corresponding localities or parts. **13** The side of a horse's hoof, just in front of the heel; also that part of a boot or shoe from the middle of the heel to the line of the ankle bone. **14** *Naut.* **a** The upper part of a vessel's side from the after part of the main chains to the stern. **b** That part of a yard outside the slings. **15** *Her.* Any of four equal divisions into which a shield is divided, or an ordinary occupying such a division. **16** Mercy shown to a vanquished foeman by sparing his life; clemency. **17** One of the four periods into which a game, as football, is divided. **— at close quarters** Close by; at close range. **—** *adj.* **1** Being one of four equal parts. **2** Having one fourth of a standard value. **—** *v.t.* **1** To divide into four equal parts. **2** To divide into a number of parts or pieces. **3** To cut the body of (an executed person) into four parts: He was hanged, drawn, and *quartered.* **4** To range from one side to the other of (a field, etc.) while advancing: The dogs *quartered* the field. **5** To furnish with quarters or shelter; lodge, station, or billet. **6** *Her.* **a** To divide (a shield) into quarters by vertical and horizontal lines. **b** To bear or arrange (different coats of arms) quarterly upon a shield or escutcheon. **7** *Mech.* To mark or place at intervals of a quarter, especially of a quarter of a circle. **—** *v.i.* **8** To be stationed or lodged. **9** To range from side to side of an area, as dogs in hunting. **10** *Naut.* To blow on a ship's quarter: said of the wind. [<OF <L *quartarius* < *quartus* fourth]

quar·ter·age (kwôr′tər·ij) *n.* **1** A quarterly allowance or payment. **2** Board and lodging; quarters, especially for troops, a work gang, etc.; also, the cost of lodging or shelter.

quar·ter·back (kwôr′tər·bak′) *n.* In American football, one of the backfield, who often calls the signals.

quar·ter–crack (kwôr′tər·krak′) *n.* A crack on the inner quarter of a horse's forehoof. Compare SANDCRACK.

quar·ter–day (kwôr′tər·dā′) *n.* One fourth of a day.

quarter day Any of the days of the year when quarterly payments are due. Quarter days for the U.S. government are the first days of January, April, July, and October; for England, Lady Day (March 25), Midsummer Day (June 24), Michaelmas (September 29), and Christmas (December 25).

quar·ter–deck (kwôr′tər·dek′) *n. Naut.* The rear part of a ship's upper deck, reserved for officers.

quar·tered (kwôr′tərd) *adj.* **1** Divided into four quarters. **2** *Her.* Divided into quarterings. **3** Quarter–sawed: *quartered* oak. **4** Lodged; stationed; also, having quarters.

quar·ter·fi·nal (kwôr′tər·fī′nəl) *n.* A competition immediately preceding the semifinal in sporting events; also, one of four competitions in a tournament, the winners of which play in the two semifinals. **—** *adj.* Next to the semifinal. **— quar′ter·fi′nal·ist** *n.*

quar·ter·foil (kwôr′tər·foil′) See QUATREFOIL.

Quarter horse A breed of horse descendent from the thoroughbred stallion *Janus* imported from England in 1756: first known as a racing breed, now widely popular as a ranch horse and cow pony. [From the quarter–of–a–mile path over which it was raced by the early settlers of Virginia]

quar·ter–hour (kwôr′tər·our′) *n.* Fifteen minutes. **— quar′ter–hour′ly** *adj.*

quar·ter·ing (kwôr′·tər·ing) *adj.* **1** *Naut.* **a** Blowing against or being on the quarter. **b** Blowing from any point between beam and stern: a *quartering* wind. **c** Sailing so as to have the wind on the quarter. **2** Set or being at right angles. **—** *n.* **1** A dividing or marking off into quarters. **2** *Her.* **a** The grouping of two or more coats of arms in compartments on one shield, to indicate family alliances, etc. **b** Any of the coats which are quartered on the shield, or the quarter containing it. **3** Quarters, or the assigning of quarters, as for soldiers.

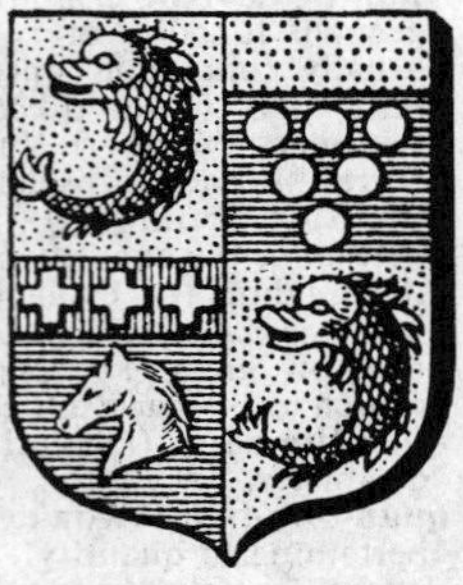

QUARTERING

quar·ter·ly (kwôr′tər·lē) *adj.* **1** Containing or being a fourth part. **2** Occurring at intervals of three months. **—** *n. pl.* **·lies** A publication issued once every three months. **—** *adv.* **1** Once in a quarter of a year. **2** In or by quarters.

quar·ter·mas·ter (kwôr′tər·mas′tər, -mäs′-) *n.* **1** *Usually cap.* The officer on an Army post who is responsible for carrying out the functions required of the Quartermaster Corps. **2** On shipboard, a petty officer who assists the navigator.

Quartermaster Corps A branch of the U.S. Army which is responsible for the supply of food, fuel, clothing, and other equipment.

Quartermaster General In the U.S. Army, the major general who is at the head of the Quartermaster Corps.

quar·tern (kwôr′tərn) *n.* **1** A fourth part of certain measures or weights, as of a peck or pound; a gill. **2** A four–pound loaf of bread. [<OF *quarteron* < *quarte* a fourth part <L *quartus* fourth]

quar·ter·ni·on (kwôr·tûr′nē·ən) *n. Printing* A gathering of four sheets, each folded into pages, usually four to a sheet, to make a section of a book, pamphlet, etc.

quarter note *Music* A note having one fourth the value of a semibreve. See illustration under NOTE.

quar·ter–phase (kwôr′tər·fāz′) *adj. Electr.* Diphase.

quar·ter–sawed (kwôr′tər·sôd′) *adj.* Sawed lengthwise into quarters, as a log, or sawed from quartered timber.

quar·ter–sec·tion (kwôr′tər·sek′shən) *n.* A tract of land half a mile square, containing one fourth of a square mile; 160 acres.

quar·ter–ses·sions (kwôr′tər·sesh′ənz) *n.* A court held quarterly. In England and Scotland it tries many indictable offenses, hears appeals from the petty sessions, and exercises a minor civil jurisdiction.

quar·ter·staff (kwôr′tər·staf′, -stäf′) *n. pl.* **·staves** (-stāvz′) A stout, iron–tipped staff about 6 1/2 feet long, formerly used in England as a weapon; also, the use of, or exercise with, the quarterstaff.

quar·ter·tone (kwôr′tər·tōn′) *n.* **1** In photo-engraving, a coarse zinc halftone plate having 65 lines or less to the inch. **2** *Music* Half of a semitone: **quarter tone.**

quar·tet (kwôr·tet′) *n.* **1** A composition for four voices or instruments. **2** The set of four persons who render such compositions. **3** A stanza of four lines. **4** Any group or set of four things of a kind. Also **quar·tette′.** [< Ital. *quartetto* < *quarto* fourth]

quar·tic (kwôr′tik) *Math. adj.* Denoting a quantic function of the fourth degree. **—** *n.* Such a function.

quar·tile (kwôr′tīl, -til) *n.* **1** In astrology, a quadrate. **2** *Stat.* That portion of a frequency distribution which comprises an exact fourth of the total observed cases. **—** *adj.* Of or pertaining to a quartile. [<LL *quartilis* <L *quartus* fourth]

quar·to (kwôr′tō) *adj.* Having four leaves or eight pages to the sheet: a *quarto* book. **—** *n. pl.* **·tos** A book or pamphlet whose pages are of the size of the fourth of a sheet: often written *4to* or *4°*. [<L *(in) quarto* (in) fourth]

quartz (kwôrts) *n.* Silicon dioxide, SiO_2, a hard, vitreous, widely distributed mineral occurring in many varieties, sometimes massive, as jasper and chalcedony: sometimes in colorless and transparent or diversely colored forms crystallizing in the hexagonal system. [<G *quarz*]

quartz crystal A thin section of pure quartz, accurately ground so as to vibrate at the required frequency in radio transmission; a piezoelectric oscillator. Also **quartz plate.**

quartz·if·er·ous (kwôrt·sif′ər·əs) *adj.* Consisting of or containing quartz.

quartz·ite (kwôrt′sīt) *n.* A massive or schistose metamorphic rock formed by the induration of sandstone through the deposition of secondary quartz about each grain.

quartz lamp A mercury–vapor lamp enclosed in a quartz tube, which transmits ultraviolet wavelengths.

qua·sar (kwā′zär, -sär) *n. Astron.* Any of a class of very distant, celestial objects that are strong radio sources, have unusual light spectra, show large red shifts, and have a vast, unexplained energy output. [<QUAS(I) + (STELL)AR]

quash[1] (kwosh) *v.t. Law* To make void or set aside, as an indictment; annul. See synonyms under ANNUL, CANCEL. [<OF *quasser* <LL *cassare* < *cassus* empty]

quash[2] (kwosh) *v.t.* To put down or suppress forcibly or summarily. [<OF *quasser* <L *quassare,* freq. of *quatere* shake]

quasi– *prefix* **1** (With nouns) Resembling; not genuine, as in:

quasi–accident	**quasi–injury**
quasi–adult	**quasi–insight**
quasi–approval	**quasi–integrity**
quasi–artist	**quasi–invasion**
quasi–attack	**quasi–kindred**
quasi–authority	**quasi–lament**
quasi–bargain	**quasi–luxury**
quasi–blunder	**quasi–market**
quasi–certificate	**quasi–method**
quasi–characteristic	**quasi–miracle**
quasi–comprehension	**quasi–neutrality**
quasi–conquest	**quasi–owner**
quasi–conservative	**quasi–pleasure**
quasi–consultation	**quasi–poem**
quasi–dependence	**quasi–protection**
quasi–despair	**quasi–purity**
quasi–development	**quasi–reality**
quasi–difference	**quasi–recreation**
quasi–distress	**quasi–refusal**
quasi–endorsement	**quasi–remedy**
quasi–escape	**quasi–repair**
quasi–faith	**quasi–scholar**
quasi–farmer	**quasi–tradition**
quasi–friend	**quasi–triumph**
quasi–guarantee	**quasi–victory**
quasi–handicap	**quasi–worship**
quasi–illness	**quasi–zeal**

2 (With adjectives) Nearly; almost, as in:

quasi–absolute	**quasi–grateful**
quasi–amiable	**quasi–hereditary**
quasi–beneficial	**quasi–human**
quasi–classic	**quasi–humorous**
quasi–colloquial	**quasi–important**
quasi–comic	**quasi–infinite**
quasi–complex	**quasi–internal**
quasi–conservative	**quasi–jocose**
quasi–continuous	**quasi–medical**
quasi–converted	**quasi–natural**
quasi–devoted	**quasi–normal**
quasi–eligible	**quasi–official**
quasi–equal	**quasi–practical**
quasi–evil	**quasi–private**
quasi–exempt	**quasi–probable**
quasi–explicit	**quasi–righteous**
quasi–financial	**quasi–similar**
quasi–forgotten	**quasi–spiritual**
quasi–formidable	**quasi–stylish**
quasi–genteel	**quasi–sufficient**

quasi–tangible   quasi–valid
quasi–theatrical   quasi–vital
quasi–typical   quasi–willing

3 *Law* Superficially resembling but intrinsically different, as in:

quasi–corporation   quasi–entail
quasi–delict   quasi–legislative
quasi–deposit   quasi–partner

[<L, as if]

qua·si–con·tract (kwä′sī·kon′trakt, -zī-, kwä′-sē-) *n.* An obligation to do something, enforceable by a contract remedy, but imposed by operation of law regardless of the consent of the defendant.

qua·si–ju·di·cial (kwä′sī·jōō·dish′əl, -zī-, kwä′-sē-) *adj.* Exercising functions of a judicial nature as a guide for official action, as a committee investigating facts and drawing conclusions from them.

quas·qui·cen·ten·ni·al (kwäs′kwi·sen·ten′ē·əl) *adj.* Of or pertaining to a century and a quarter. — *n.* A 125th anniversary, or its celebration. [coined <L *quadrans que* plus a fourth + CENTENNIAL, for Delavan, Illinois (1962).]

quas·si·a (kwosh′ē·ə, kwosh′ə) *n.* 1 The wood of either of two tropical American trees (*Picrasma excelsa* or *Quassia amara*). 2 The bitter principle of this wood, used in medicine as a tonic and anthelmintic. 3 The tree itself. [<NL, after Graman *Quassi,* a Surinam Negro who discovered its use in 1730]

quas·sin (kwos′in, kwas′-) *n. Chem.* A white, crystalline, intensely bitter amaroid, $C_{22}H_{30}O_6$, contained in quassia wood.

quatch·grass (kwoch′gras′, -gräs′) *n.* Couchgrass.

qua·ter·na·ry (kwə·tûr′nə·rē) *adj.* 1 Consisting of four things. 2 Fourth in order. — *n. pl.* **·ries** 1 The number four; a group of four things. 2 *Math.* A quantic function having four variables. [<L *quaternarius* < *quaterni* by fours]

Qua·ter·na·ry (kwə·tûr′nə·rē) *adj. Geol.* Of, pertaining to, or designating a geological period and system of the Cenozoic era, following the Tertiary and still continuing. — *n.* The Quaternary system or period.

qua·ter·ni·on (kwə·tûr′nē·ən) *n.* 1 A set, system, or file of four. 2 *Math.* **a** An operator or factor that changes one vector into another: so called because expressible as the sum of four quantities. **b** The form of the calculus of vectors based on and making use of the quaternion operator. [<LL *quaternio, -onis* < *quattuor* four]

Quath·lam·ba (kwät·läm′bä) See DRAKENSBERG.

quat·rain (kwot′rān) *n.* A stanza of four lines. [<F < *quatre* four]

qua·tre (kä′tər, *Fr.* kà′tr′) *n. French* 1 Anything, as a card or a domino, marked with four spots or pips. 2 The number four; four.

Qua·tre–Bras (kä′tr′·brä′) A village in Belgium, SE of Brussels; scene of an English victory by Wellington over French forces under Marshal Ney in the Waterloo campaign of the Napoleonic Wars, 1815.

quat·re·foil (kat′ər·foil, kat′rə-) *n.* 1 *Bot.* A leaf or flower with four leaflets or petals. 2 *Archit.* An ornament with four foils or lobes. Sometimes spelled *quarterfoil.* [<OF *quatre* four + *foil* leaf]

quat·tro·cen·to (kwät′trō·chen′tō) *n.* The 15th century as connected with the revival of art and literature (especially in Italy). — *adj.* Of or pertaining to the quattrocento. [<Ital., four hundred < *quattro* four + *cento* hundred]

qua·ver (kwā′vər) *v.i.* 1 To tremble or shake: said usually of the voice. 2 To produce trills or quavers in singing or in playing a musical instrument. — *v.t.* 3 To utter or sing in a tremulous voice. See synonyms under QUAKE, SHAKE. — *n.* 1 A quavering or tremulous motion. 2 A shake or trill, as in singing. 3 An eighth note. [Freq. of

QUATREFOILS

obs. *quave,* ME *cwafian* tremble] — **qua′ver·y** *adj.*

quay (kē) *n.* A wharf or artificial landing place where vessels unload. ◆ Homophone: *key.* [<F]

quay·age (kē′ij) *n.* 1 Wharfage; quay dues. 2 Space for quays; quays collectively.

quean (kwēn) *n.* 1 A brazen or ill-behaved woman; harlot; prostitute. 2 *Scot.* A young or unmarried woman; a girl. [OE *cwene* prostitute]

quea·sy (kwē′zē) *adj.* **·si·er, ·si·est** 1 Sick at the stomach. 2 Nauseating; also, caused by nausea. 3 Easily nauseated; hence, fastidious; squeamish. 4 Requiring to be carefully treated; delicate; ticklish. 5 Uncertain; hazardous. [Cf. Norw. *kveis* nausea] — **quea′si·ly** *adv.* — **quea′si·ness** *n.*

Que·bec (kwi·bek′) 1 A province in eastern Canada; 523,860 square miles: formerly *Lower Canada:* abbr. *Que.* or *P.Q.* 2 Its capital, a port on the St. Lawrence River; captured from the French under Montcalm by Wolfe, Sept. 13, 1759.

que·bra·cho (kā·brä′chō) *n. pl.* **·chos** 1 Any of several tropical American trees producing a medicinal bark, especially the **white quebracho** (*Aspidosperma quebracho–blanco*), a Chilean tree whose bark is used as a febrifuge and for diseases of the respiratory organs; also, **red quebracho** (*Schinopsis lorentzii*), a tree whose heartwood is rich in tannin. 2 The wood or bark of any of these trees. [<Sp., var. of *quiebrahacha,* lit., ax–breaker < *quebrar* break + *hacha* ax]

Quech·ua (kech′wä) *n.* 1 One of a tribe of South American Indians which dominated the Inca empire prior to the Spanish conquest. 2 The language of the Quechuas, still spoken as a mother tongue in parts of Peru and Ecuador: also called *Incan.* Also spelled *Kechua.*

Quech·uan (kech′wən) *adj.* Of or pertaining to the Quechua or their language. — *n.* Quechua. Also spelled *Kechuan.*

queen (kwēn) *n.* 1 The wife of a king. 2 A female sovereign or monarch. 3 A woman preeminent in a given sphere. 4 The most powerful piece in chess, capable of moving any number of squares in a straight line. 5 A playing card bearing a conventional picture of a queen in her robes. 6 *Entomol.* The single fully developed female in a colony of social insects, as bees, ants, etc.: distinguished from workers, soldiers, and unproductive females. — *v.t.* 1 To make a queen of. 2 In chess, to make a queen of (a pawn) by moving it to the eighth row. — *v.i.* 3 To reign as or play the part of a queen: usually with *it.* [OE *cwēn* woman, queen]

Queen Anne's lace The wild carrot (*Daucus carota*), having filmy white flowers in umbels.

Queen Anne style 1 *Archit.* A style prevalent in England in the early 18th century, or a style similar to it used in the United States in the latter part of the 19th century, characterized by the use of red brickwork on which relief ornaments are carved, and by plain, unpretentious design. 2 A type of furniture characterized by much upholstery and marquetry.

Queen Anne's War See WAR OF THE SPANISH SUCCESSION in table under WAR.

Queen Charlotte Sound A bay of the Pacific in British Columbia between Vancouver Island and **Queen Charlotte Islands,** an archipelago (3,970 square miles) of western British Columbia; narrowing to **Queen Charlotte Strait,** 60 miles long and 16 miles wide, the northern end of the channel separating Vancouver Island from the mainland.

queen consort The wife of a reigning king, who does not share his sovereignty.

queen dowager The widow of a king who has reigned in his own right.

queen·ly (kwēn′lē) *adj. & adv.* Like a queen; stately; reginal. See synonyms under IMPERIAL. — **queen′li·ness** *n.*

Queen Mary Coast Part of Antarctica on the Indian Ocean, west of Wilkes Land.

Queen Maud Land Part of Antarctica south of Africa, claimed by Norway, 1939; made a dependency of Norway, 1949.

Queen Maud Mountains A range extending

south of the Ross Shelf Ice, Antarctica; rising over 13,000 feet.

queen mother A queen dowager who is mother of a reigning sovereign.

queen of the meadows An Old World meadowsweet (*Filipendula ulmaria*), naturalized in the United States.

queen of the prairie A tall perennial herb (*Filipendula rubra*) common to American meadows and prairies.

queen olive A large variety of Spanish olive.

queen–post (kwēn′pōst′) *n.* One of two upright suspending or sustaining posts or compression members in a truss.

queen regent 1 A queen who rules in behalf of another. 2 A queen who rules in her own right: also **queen regnant.**

Queens (kwenz) The easternmost borough of New York City, located on Long Island; 108 square miles.

Queen's Bench See under COURT.

Queens·ber·ry Rules (kwenz′ber·ē) See MARQUIS OF QUEENSBERRY RULES.

queen's counsel See KING'S COUNSEL.

queen's–de·light (kwenz′di·līt′) *n.* A smooth, erect perennial (*Stillingia sylvatica*) of the spurge family, with alternate leaves and a medicinal root.

queen's English See KING'S ENGLISH under ENGLISH.

queen's evidence See STATE'S EVIDENCE.

Queens·land (kwenz′lənd) The second largest state of the Commonwealth of Australia, in the NE part; 670,500 square miles; capital, Brisbane.

queen's metal An alloy of tin, antimony, bismuth, and lead, used for ornamental purposes.

queen snake A water snake (*Natrix lebris*) of the central and eastern United States.

Queens·town (kwenz′toun) A former name for COBH.

queen's ware Fine, glazed, cream-colored English earthenware; specifically, cream-colored Wedgwood: named for Queen Charlotte by Josiah Wedgwood, 1761.

queer (kwir) *adj.* 1 Being out of the usual course of events in minor respects; singular; odd. 2 Of questionable character; open to suspicion; mysterious. 3 *Slang* Counterfeit. — *n. Slang* 1 Counterfeit money. 2 A homosexual, especially a male homosexual: a contemptuous term. — *v.t. U.S. Slang* To jeopardize or spoil. [<G *quer* oblique] — **queer′ly** *adv.* — **queer′ness** *n.*

Synonyms (adj.): anomalous, bizarre, crotchety, curious, droll, eccentric, erratic, fantastic, funny, grotesque, laughable, ludicrous, mysterious, odd, peculiar, quaint, ridiculous, singular, strange, unique, unusual, whimsical. *Odd* is unmated, as an *odd* shoe, and so uneven, as an *odd* number. *Singular* is alone of its kind; as, the *singular* number. What is *singular* is odd, but what is *odd* may not be *singular,* as, a drawerful of *odd* gloves. A *strange* thing is something either unnatural or extraordinary. A *singular* coincidence is one the happening of which is unusual; a *strange* coincidence is one the cause of which is hard to explain. That which is *peculiar* belongs especially to a person as his own; in its ordinary use there is the implication that the thing *peculiar* to one is not common to the majority. *Eccentric* is off center, and so off or aside from the ordinary and normal course; as, genius is commonly *eccentric. Eccentric* is a higher and more respectful word than *odd* or *queer. Erratic* signifies wandering, a stronger and more censorious term than *eccentric. Queer* is aside from the common in a way that is comical or perhaps slightly *ridiculous* or *mysterious. Quaint* denotes that which is pleasingly *odd* and fanciful, often with something of the antique; as, the *quaint* architecture of medieval towns. That which is *funny* is calculated to provoke laughter; that which is *droll* is more quietly amusing. That which is *grotesque* in the material sense is irregular or misshapen in form or outline or ill-proportioned so as to be somewhat *ridiculous;* the French *bizarre* is practically equivalent to *grotesque.* See ODD. *Antonyms:* common, customary, familiar, natural, normal, ordinary, regular, usual.

quell (kwel) *v.t.* 1 To put down or suppress

by force; extinguish. **2** To quiet; allay, as pain. [OE *cwellan* kill] —**quell′er** *n.*

Quel·part (kwel′pärt) A former name for CHEJU.

quel·que chose (kel′kə shōz′) *French* A trifle; something.

quench (kwench) *v.t.* **1** To put out or extinguish, as a fire. **2** To put an end to; cause to cease. **3** To slake or satisfy (thirst). **4** To suppress or repress, as emotions. **5** To cool, as heated iron or steel, by thrusting into water or other liquid. [ME *cwenken*] —**quench′a·ble** *adj.* —**quench′er** *n.*

quench·less (kwench′lis) *adj.* Incapable of being quenched; insatiable; irrepressible. —**quench′less·ly** *adv.* —**quench′less·ness** *n.*

que·nelle (kə·nel′) *n. French* A ball of savory paste made of minced meat, as chicken, veal, or fish, with bread crumbs and egg, usually poached.

Quen·tin (kwen′tin) A masculine personal name. [<L, fifth]

quer·ce·tin (kwûr′sə·tin) *n. Biochem.* A yellow crystalline compound, $C_{15}H_{10}O_7 \cdot H_2O$, found in the bark of the American oak and in the rind of certain fruits: used as a base for dyestuffs. [Prob. <L *quercus* oak + -IN] —**quer·cet·ic** (kwər·set′ik, -sē′tik) *adj.*

quer·cine (kwûr′sin, -sīn) *adj.* Of or pertaining to oaks. [<LL *quercinus* <L *quercus* oak]

quer·cit·rin (kwûr′sit′rin) *n. Biochem.* A yellow crystalline glycoside, $C_{21}H_{20}O_{11} \cdot 2H_2O$, contained in quercitron bark. Also **quer′cit′rine.**

quer·cit·ron (kwûr′sit·ron) *n.* **1** The crushed and powdered inner bark of the American black oak (*Quercus velutina*), used in dyeing and tanning. **2** The yellow dye made therefrom. **3** The dyer's oak (*Q. coccinea*). [<L *quercus* oak + CITRON]

Quer·cus (kwûr′kəs) *n.* A genus of hardwood trees and shrubs of the beech family, widely distributed in north temperate regions; the oaks. [<NL <L, an oak]

Que·ré·ta·ro (kā·rā′tä·rō) A state in central Mexico; 4,432 square miles; capital, Querétaro.

que·ri·da (kā·rē′dä) *n. fem. SW U.S.* A beloved; a darling. [<Sp.]

que·rist (kwir′ist) *n.* An inquirer; questioner.

querl (kwûrl) *v.t.* & *n. U.S. Dial.* Curl; twist: also spelled *quirl.* [? <G]

quern (kwûrn) *n.* **1** An old form of hand mill for grinding grain. **2** A small hand mill for grinding spices. [OE *cweorn*]

quer·u·lous (kwer′ə·ləs, -yə·ləs) *adj.* **1** Disposed to complain or be fretful; faultfinding. **2** Indicating or expressing a complaining or whining disposition. **3** Quarrelsome. [<LL *querulosus* <L *querulus* <*queri* complain] —**quer′u·lous·ly** *adv.* —**quer′u·lous·ness** *n.*

que·ry (kwir′ē) *v.* **·ried, ·ry·ing** *v.t.* **1** To inquire into; ask about. **2** To ask questions of; interrogate. **3** To express doubt concerning the correctness or truth of, especially, as in printing, by marking with a query. —*v.i.* **4** To have or express doubt; question. See synonyms under INQUIRE, QUESTION. [<*n.*] —*n. pl.* **·ries 1** An inquiry, or a memorandum of an inquiry, to be answered; a question. **2** A doubt; interrogation: often indicated, as in printing, by the interrogation point (?). See synonyms under INQUIRY, QUESTION. [<L *quaere,* imperative sing. of *quaerere* ask]

Ques·nay (ke·nā′), **François,** 1694–1774, French physician and economist.

quest (kwest) *n.* **1** The act of seeking; a looking for something; a search, as an adventure or expedition in medieval romance; also, the person or persons making the search. **2** *Rare* An inquest. —*v.i.* **1** To go on a quest. **2** To make a search. **3** To search for game; also, to bay on the trail of game: said of hunting dogs. —*v.t.* **4** To search for; seek. [<OF *queste* <L *quaesitus,* pp. of *quaerere* ask, seek] —**quest′er** *n.*

ques·tion (kwes′chən) *n.* **1** An interrogative sentence calling for an answer; an inquiry. **2** A subject of inquiry or debate; a matter to be decided; a point at issue; problem. **3** A subject of dispute; a controversy; difference: A *question* rose about it. **4** A proposition under discussion in a deliberative assembly. **5** Objection raised or entertained; doubt: a statement accepted without *question.* **6** Interrogation; the act of asking or inquiring. —*v.t.* **1** To put a question or questions to; interrogate. **2** To be uncertain of; doubt. **3** To make objection to; challenge; dispute. —*v.i.* **4** To ask a question or questions. [<AF *questiun* <L *quaestio, -onis* <*quaerere* ask] —**ques′tion·er** *n.*

Synonyms (noun): doubt, inquiry, inquisition, interrogation, interrogatory, investigation, query. An *inquiry* seeks information for the benefit of the inquirer; a *question* may do the same, or may have the intent to perplex, confuse, or entrap the one of whom it is asked; one makes *inquiry* as to his way; we speak of idle or frivolous *questions* rather than of idle or frivolous *inquiries.* A *query* is a *question* more or less vaguely formulated and indefinite in purpose, often amounting to no more than a suspense of judgment. An *interrogation* or *interrogatory* is a formal *inquiry. Interrogatory* has a special legal use, denoting an *inquiry* in writing by order of a court, to be answered under oath. An *investigation* is an elaborate search for truth or fact, not only by *questions,* but by every other means of procuring information; an *inquisition* is an *investigation* which is either unwarranted, unduly minute, or in some other way offensive. See DOUBT, INQUIRY, TOPIC.

Synonyms (verb): ask, challenge, dispute, doubt, inquire, interrogate, investigate, query, quiz. To *ask* is to seek information, favor, or aid; *inquire, question, interrogate,* respect only the obtaining of information. To *interrogate* is to *examine* formally or officially, commonly by a series of questions. One may *inquire* casually and indifferently; he *questions* intently and resolutely. *Question* also has nearly the meaning of *challenge*; as, "I *question* that statement." See INQUIRE.

ques·tion·a·ble (kwes′chən·ə·bəl) *adj.* **1** Liable to be called in question; debatable; open to question or to suspicions; dubious; suspicious: *questionable* motives. **2** Of doubtful meaning; difficult to decide. **3** *Obs.* Capable of being questioned or inquired of. See synonyms under EQUIVOCAL. —**ques′tion·a·ble·ness, ques′tion·a·bil′i·ty** *n.* —**ques′tion·a·bly** *adv.*

ques·tion·ar·y (kwes′chən·er′ē) *adj.* Of the nature of an examination; interrogatory. —*n. pl.* **·ar·ies** A questionnaire.

ques·tion·less (kwes′chən·lis) *adj.* Unquestionable; indubitable; also, unquestioning. —**ques′tion·less·ly** *adv.*

question mark 1 An interrogation point (?). **2** Something open to question; an unknown.

ques·tion·naire (kwes′chə·nâr′) *n.* A written or printed form comprising a series of questions submitted to a number of persons in order to obtain data for a survey or report. [<F]

ques·tor (kwes′tər) See QUAESTOR.

Quet·ta (kwet′ə) **1** A commissioners' division of west central West Pakistan, near the border of Afghanistan; 35,027 square miles. **2** The leading city of this division, formerly capital of the former province of Baluchistan, included, October, 1955, in the province of West Pakistan.

quet·zal (ket·säl′) *n. pl.* **·zal·es** (-sä′lās) **1** A trogon (*Pharomacrus mocinno*) of brilliant plumage, the national symbol of Guatemala, and anciently regarded as a deity by the Mayas, whose chiefs alone were permitted to wear its plumes. **2** A silver coin, the monetary unit of Guatemala. Also **que·zal** (kā·säl′). [<Sp. <Nahuatl]

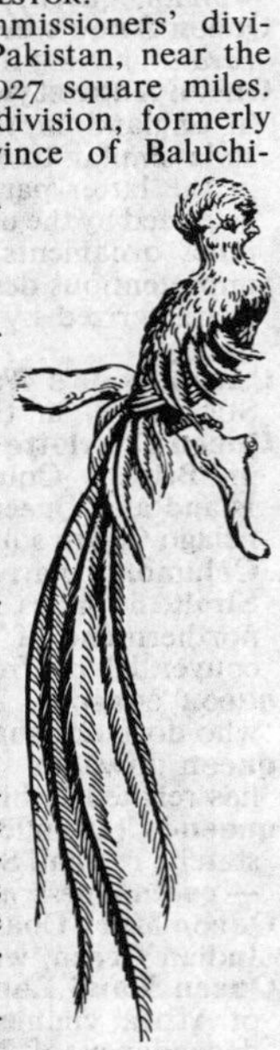

QUETZAL
(About 4 feet long including tail)

Quet·zal·co·a·tl (ket·säl′kō·at′l) A traditional god and heroic figure of the Aztecs.

queue (kyoo) *n.* **1** A pendent braid of hair on the back of the head; a pigtail. **2** A line of persons or vehicles waiting in the order of their arrival. —*v.i.* **queued, queu·ing** *Brit.* To form such a line: usually with *up.* Also spelled *cue.* [<F <OF *coe, coue* <L *cauda* a tail]

que vou·lez-vous (kə vōō·lā·vōō′) *French* What do you want? What can you expect?: an expression of indifference or cynicism.

Que·zal·te·nan·go (kā·säl′tā·näng′gō) The second largest city of Guatemala, in the SW part of the western highlands.

Que·zon (kā′zon, *Sp.* kā′sôn, -thôn), **Manuel Luis,** 1878–1944, Filipino statesman; first president of the Philippines, 1935–1944. Also **Que·zon y Mo·li·na** (kā′sôn ē mō·lē′nä).

Que·zon City (kā′sôn, -thôn) The capital (since 1948) of the Philippines, in southern Luzon, NE of Manila.

quib·ble (kwib′əl) *n.* **1** An evasion of a point or question; an equivocation. **2** *Rare* A pun. —*v.i.* **·bled, ·bling** To use quibbles; evade the truth or the point in question. [<obs. *quib* <L *quibus,* ablative pl. of *qui* who, which; with ref. to its use in legal documents] —**quib′bler** *n.*

Qui·be·ron (kēb·rôn′) A town at the southern end of **Quiberon Peninsula,** which projects seven miles into the Bay of Biscay from Brittany, France, nearly enclosing **Quiberon Bay.**

quiche (kēsh) *n.* Any of various non–dessert, custardlike pies, having meat, cheese, vegetables, etc., as principal ingredients. [<F]

Qui·ché (kē·chā′) *n.* **1** An Indian of a tribe of Mayan linguistic stock inhabiting Guatemala. **2** The Mayan language of this tribe.

quick (kwik) *adj.* **1** Done or occurring in a short time; expeditious; brisk; rapid; swift; speedy. **2** Characterized by rapidity or readiness of movement or action; nimble; prompt. **3** Sharp; steep, as a curve. **4** Alert; sensitive; perceptive: a *quick* ear; *quick* wit. **5** Responding readily to impressions; excitable; hasty. **6** Having life; living: opposed to *dead*: an archaic use. **7** Pregnant; with child. **8** Burning briskly; fiery. **9** Shifting; moving: said of soil or sand. **10** Refreshing; bracing. See synonyms under ACTIVE, ALIVE, CLEVER, IMPETUOUS, NIMBLE, SWIFT[1], VIVID. —*n.* **1** That which has life; those who are alive: chiefly in the phrase **the quick and the dead. 2** The living flesh; any vital or tender part; especially, the tender flesh under a nail; hence, the feelings: cut to the *quick.* **3** A hedge plant; quickset. —*adv.* Quickly; rapidly. [OE *cwic* alive]

quick assets Assets which are readily convertible into cash; liquid assets.

quick bread Any bread, biscuits, etc., whose leavening agent makes immediate baking possible.

quick–break (kwik′brāk′) *n. Electr.* A current switch equipped with a spring or other device to permit rapid contact–opening independent of the operator.

quick·en (kwik′ən) *v.t.* **1** To cause to move more rapidly; hasten or accelerate. **2** To make alive or quick; give or restore life to. **3** To excite or arouse; stimulate: to *quicken* the appetite. —*v.i.* **4** To move or act more quickly; become more rapid. **5** To come or return to life; revive. **6** To reach the stage of pregnancy at which the motions of the fetus first become perceptible: said of the mother. **7** To begin to manifest signs of life: said of the fetus. —**quick′en·er** *n.*

Synonyms: accelerate, advance, dispatch, drive, expedite, facilitate, further, hasten, hurry, promote, speed, urge. To *quicken* is to increase speed, move or cause to move more rapidly, as through more space or with a greater number of motions in the same time. To *accelerate* is to increase the speed of action or of motion. A motion whose speed increases upon itself is said to be *accelerated,* as the motion of a falling body, which becomes swifter with every second of time. To *accelerate* any work is to *hasten* it toward a finish. To *dispatch* is to do and be done with, to get a thing off one's hands. To *dispatch* an enemy is to kill him outright and quickly; to *dispatch* a messenger is to send him in haste; to *dispatch* a business is to bring it quickly to an end. To *promote* a cause is in any way to bring it forward, *advance* it in power, prominence, etc. To *speed* is really to secure swiftness; to *hasten* is to attempt it, whether successfully or unsuccessfully. *Hurry* always indicates something of confusion. To *facilitate* is to *quicken* by making easy; to *expedite* is to *quicken* by removing hindrances. *Antonyms*: check, clog, delay, drag, hinder, impede, obstruct, retard.

quick fire The firing of quick successive shots:

faster than *rapid fire,* and used chiefly against moving or bobbing targets. **—quick–fire** (kwik′fīr′) *adj.*

quick–fir·ing (kwik′fīr′ing) *adj.* Able to fire shots rapidly and continuously.

quick–freeze (kwik′frēz′) *v.t.* **–froze, –fro·zen, –freez·ing** To subject (food) to rapid refrigeration for storing at or below freezing temperatures. **—quick′–fro′zen** *adj.*

quick·grass (kwik′gras′, -gräs′) *n.* Couchgrass.

quick·ie (kwik′ē) *n. U.S. Slang* Anything done hastily, as by short cuts or makeshift methods.

quick·lime (kwik′līm′) *n.* Unslaked lime. See LIME[1].

quick·ly (kwik′lē) *adv.* In a quick manner; rapidly; soon.

quick march A march in quick time; quickstep.

quick·match (kwik′mach′) *n.* A cord impregnated with black powder and used as a fast-burning fuse for flares, fireworks, etc.

quick·ness (kwik′nis) *n.* **1** The state or quality of being quick; speed; celerity; liveliness; readiness. **2** Acuteness of perception or sensibility; sharpness; keenness.

quick·sand (kwik′sand′) *n.* A bed of sand so water–soaked as readily to engulf any person or animal that attempts to move or rest upon it.

quick·set (kwik′set′) *n.* **1** A hedge plant, especially hawthorn. **2** A hedge made of it. **—***adj.* Composed of quickset.

quick·sil·ver (kwik′sil′vər) *n.* **1** Metallic mercury: widely used in metallurgy, industry, and the arts. All of its compounds are poisonous. **2** An amalgam of tin, used for the backs of mirrors. [Trans. of L *argentum vivum*]

quick·step (kwik′step′) *n.* A march or dance written in a rapid tempo; also, a quick march.

quick–tem·pered (kwik′tem′pərd) *adj.* Easily angered.

quick time A marching step of 120 paces a minute, each pace of 30 inches: used in military drills and ceremonies.

quick·wa·ter (kwik′wô′tər, -wot′ər) *n.* A stream or that part of a stream having a decided current.

quick–wit·ted (kwik′wit′id) *adj.* Having a ready wit or quick discernment; keen; alert. See synonyms under CLEVER, SAGACIOUS. **—quick′–wit′ted·ly** *adv.* **—quick′–wit′ted·ness** *n.*

qui·cun·que vult (kwī·kung′kwē vult) *Latin* Whosoever will. See ATHANASIAN CREED.

quid[1] (kwid) *n.* **1** A small portion of chewing tobacco. **2** A cud, as of a cow. [Var. of CUD]

quid[2] (kwid) *n. Brit. Slang* In England, a pound sterling, or a sovereign. [Origin uncertain]

Quid·de (kvid′ə), **Ludwig,** 1858–1941, German historian and pacifist.

quid·di·ty (kwid′ə·tē) *n. pl.* **·ties 1** The essence of a thing. **2** A subtle or trifling distinction or objection; cavil. [<LL *quidditas, -tatis* <L *quid* which, what]

quid·nunc (kwid′nungk′) *n.* One who seeks or affects to know all that is going on; an inquisitive busybody. [<L *quid nunc* what now]

quid pro quo (kwid′ prō kwō′) *Latin* **1** Something for something; an equivalent in return. **2** Formerly, one medicine used in place of another; hence, a substitution.

quién sa·be (kyen sä′vā) *Spanish* Literally, "who knows?": used to mean, in reply to a question, "I do not know," or "I do not care to say."

qui·es·cent (kwī·es′ənt, kwē-) *adj.* **1** Being in a state of repose or inaction; quiet; still. **2** Resting free from anxiety, emotion, or agitation. **3** *Phonet.* In Semitic languages, having no sound; silent. See synonyms under PASSIVE. [<L *quiescens, -entis,* ppr. of *quiescere* be quiet] **—qui·es′cence** *n.* **—qui·es′cent·ly** *adv.*

qui·et (kwī′ət) *adj.* **1** Being in a state of repose; still; calm; motionless. **2** Free from turmoil, strife, or alarm; tranquil; peaceful. **3** Silent. **4** Gentle or mild of disposition. **5** Undisturbed by din or bustle; retired; secluded: a *quiet* nook. **6** Restful to the eye; soft in hue; hence, not showy or obtrusive, as dress. See synonyms under CALM, PACIFIC, SEDATE, SOBER. **—***n.* The condition or quality of being free from motion, disturbance, noise, etc.; peace; calm. See synonyms under REST[1]. **—***v.t.* & *v.i.* To make or become quiet: often with *down.* See synonyms under ALLAY, REPRESS, SETTLE, TRANQUILIZE. **—***adv.* In a quiet or peaceful manner. [<OF *quiete* <L *quietus* <*quies* rest, repose. Doublet of COY.] **—qui′et·ly** *adv.* **—qui′et·ness** *n.*

qui·et·en (kwī′ə·tən) *v.t.* & *v.i. Brit. or Dial.* To make or become quiet: often with *down.*

qui·et·ism (kwī′ə·tiz′əm) *n.* **1** The doctrine that spiritual exaltation is attained by self-abnegation and passive religious contemplation; especially, mystic meditation or introspection, as cultivated by certain devotees in the 17th century. **2** A state of quiet; quietude.

qui·et·ist (kwī′ə·tist) *n.* **1** An advocate or practicer of quietism. **2** One who seeks or enjoys quiet.

qui·e·tude (kwī′ə·to͞od, -tyo͞od) *n.* A state or condition of calm or tranquillity; repose; rest.

qui·e·tus (kwī·ē′təs) *n.* **1** A silencing or suppressing; death; repose. **2** A final discharge or quittance; a settlement. **3** A killing blow. [<L *quietus est* he is quiet]

quill[1] (kwil) *n.* **1** *Ornithol.* One of the large, strong flight feathers or tail feathers of a bird. **2** A pen made from a feather; hence, any pen. **3** The hollow, horny stem of a feather; a calamus. **4** Such a stem used for a receptacle or measure, as for a drug, or as a plectrum for playing a stringed instrument. **5** *Zool.* One of the large, sharp spines of a porcupine or hedgehog. **6** A piece of cane or reed used as a musical pipe. **7** A slow–burning fuse made formerly of the quill of a feather filled with powder. **8** A piece of bark rolled into cylindrical form: a cinnamon *quill.* **9** A quill toothpick. **10** *Mech.* A hollow shaft, with or without openings, designed to revolve on a solid shaft when the clutches are engaged. **11** In weaving, a spindle or bobbin; pirn. **12** A fluted, rounded ridge, or cylindrical fold, as in a ruff or ruffle. **—***v.t.* **1** To make or iron (a garment or fabric) with rounded plaits or ridges. **2** To wind (thread or yarn) on a quill or quills. **—***v.i.* **3** To wind thread or yarn on a quill or quills. [Cf. LG *quiele* a quill of a feather]

quil·lai (ki·lī′) *n.* A large Chilean evergreen tree, the soapbark tree, whose alkaline inner bark (**quillai bark**) is used as medicine and as a substitute for soap: also spelled *cullay.* [<Sp. <Araucanian]

quill·back (kwil′bak′) *n.* A carplike fish (*Carpiodes velifer*) common in the Mississippi Valley.

quill·driv·er (kwil′drī′vər) *n. Colloq.* **1** One who writes; a literary hack. **2** Formerly, a clerk; copyist.

Quil·ler–Couch (kwil′ər·ko͞och′), **Sir Arthur Thomas,** 1863–1944, English author and editor.

quil·let (kwil′it) *n. Obs.* A quibble; subtlety; nice distinction. [?Alter. of L *quidlibet* what you please <*quid* what + *libet* it pleases]

quill·pig (kwil′pig′) *n. U.S. Colloq.* A porcupine.

quill·wort (kwil′wûrt′) *n.* A small plant (genus *Isoetes*), found in marshes, pond edges, etc., consisting of a cormlike stem sending up a tuft of quill–like leaves.

Quil·mes (kēl′mās) A city on the Río de la Plata SE of Buenos Aires, Argentina.

quilt (kwilt) *n.* **1** A bedcover made by stitching together firmly two layers of cloth or patchwork with some soft and warm substance (as wool or cotton) between them. **2** Any bedcover, especially if thick. **3** A quilted skirt or other quilted article. **4** *Obs.* A mattress. **—***v.t.* **1** To stitch together (two pieces of material) with a soft substance between. **2** To stitch in ornamental patterns or crossing lines. **3** To sew up or secure between two layers. **4** To pad or line with something soft. **—***v.i.* **5** To make a quilt or quilted work. [<OF *cuilte* <L *culcita*]

quilt·ing (kwil′ting) *n.* **1** The act or process of making a quilt, or of stitching as in making a quilt. **2** Material for quiltwork. **3** A quilting bee or party.

quilting bee A social gathering of the women of a community for working on a quilt or quilts. Also **quilting frolic, quilting party.**

quin·a·crine (kwin′ə·krēn) *n.* Atabrine.

qui·na·ry (kwī′nər·ē) *adj.* Consisting of or containing five parts or elements; arranged by fives, or in sets or groups of five. **—***n. pl.* **·ries** A number, body, group, or system of five; something composed of five like parts. [<L *quinarius* <*quini* five each]

qui·nate (kwī′nāt, kwin′āt) *adj.* **1** Arranged in five. **2** *Bot.* Having five similar parts together, as the five leaflets of the Virginia creeper. [<L *quini* five each <*quinque* five]

quince (kwins) *n.* **1** The hard, acid, applelike, yellowish fruit, used for preserves, of a small deciduous Asian tree (*Cydonia oblonga*) of the rose family. **2** The tree. [Orig. pl. of obs. *coyn* <OF *cooin* <L *cotoneum,* var. of (*malum*) *cydonium* (apple) of Cydonia <Gk. *Kydōnia,* a town in Crete]

quin·cun·cial (kwin·kun′shəl) *adj.* **1** Arranged in the form of a quincunx. **2** *Bot.* Arranged in a set of five, as leaves. Also **quin·cunx′ial** (-kungk′shəl). **—quin·cun′cial·ly** *adv.*

quin·cunx (kwin′kungks) *n.* **1** An arrangement of five things, as trees, in a square having one in each corner and one in the center. **2** A disposition of such squares repeated indefinitely. **3** A quincuncial arrangement, as of flower parts. [<L *quincunx* five twelfths <*quinque* five + *uncia* twelfth part]

Quin·cy (kwin′sē), **Josiah,** 1744–75, American statesman and Revolutionary leader.

Quin·cy (kwin′sē) A city in eastern Massachusetts south of Boston.

quin·dec·a·gon (kwin·dek′ə·gon) *n. Geom.* A figure, especially a plane figure, with fifteen sides and fifteen angles. [<L *quindecim* fifteen + Gk. *gōnia* angle]

quin·de·cen·ni·al (kwin′di·sen′ē·əl) *n.* A fifteenth anniversary. **—***adj.* Of or pertaining to the fifteenth anniversary. [<L *quindecim* fifteen + *annus* year]

quin·dec·i·mal (kwin·des′ə·məl) *adj.* Fifteen. [<L *quindecim* fifteen]

quin·ic (kwin′ik) *adj.* Of, pertaining to, or derived from quinine.

quinic acid *Chem.* A white crystalline compound, $C_7H_{12}O_6$, contained in cinchona bark, coffee beans, etc.

quin·i·dine (kwin′ə·dēn, -din) *n. Chem.* A white crystalline alkaloid, $C_{20}H_{24}N_2O_2$, isomeric with quinine, contained in certain cinchona barks. It is used in medicine to regulate the heartbeat, and its sulfate is officinal.

qui·nine (kwī′nīn, *esp. Brit.* kwi·nēn′) *n. Chem.* A white, amorphous or slightly crystalline, very bitter alkaloid, $C_{20}H_{24}N_2O_2$, contained in cinchona barks. Its salts, as the hydrochlorate, sulfate, and others, are largely used in medicine on account of their tonic and antipyretic qualities, especially in malarial affections of all kinds. Also **quin·in** (kwin′in). [<earlier *quina* (<Sp. <Quechua *kina* bark) + -INE[2]]

quin·nat (kwin′at) *n.* A salmon (*Oncorhynchus tschawytscha*) of the coasts of the North Pacific: also called *Chinook salmon.* [<Chinook *ikwána*]

quin·oid (kwin′oid) *adj.* Having a quinone nucleus.

qui·noi·dine (kwi·noi′dēn, -din) *n. Chem.* A brown, resinous, amorphous compound, consisting chiefly of uncrystallizable products of cinchona bark: a cheap substitute for real quinine. Also **qui·noi′din** (-din).

quin·o·line (kwin′ə·lēn, -lin) *n. Chem.* **1** A colorless liquid compound, C_9H_7N, with a tarry odor, obtained variously, as by distilling quinine, cinchonine, or by the destructive distillation of coal and bones. **2** Any of a class of quinoline derivatives, among which are many dyes and medicinal compounds. Also **quin′o·lin** (-lin).

qui·none (kwi·nōn′, kwin′ōn) *n. Chem.* Either of two isomeric compounds obtained from benzene and its homologs; especially, a golden-yellow crystalline compound, $C_6H_4O_2$, with pungent odor, formed variously, as by the oxidation of quinic acid, aniline, etc.: also called *paraquinone.*

qui·non·i·mine (kwi·non′ə·mēn, -min) *n. Chem.* A crystalline organic compound, C_6H_5NO, derived from a quinone through replacement of an oxygen atom by an imine. See INDOPHENOL.

quin·o·noid (kwin′ə·noid) *adj.* Resembling or like quinone.

quin·ox·a·line (kwin·ok′sə·lēn, -lin) *n. Chem.*

A fully basic, white, crystalline compound, $C_8H_6N_2$, used in organic synthesis.

quin·qua·ge·nar·i·an (kwin′kwə·jə·nâr′ē·ən) *adj.* Being fifty years old; relating to this age. — *n.* A person fifty years old.

quin·qua·gen·a·ry (kwin′kwə·jen′ər·ē) *adj.* **1** Consisting of or containing fifty. **2** Denoting a group or set of fifty. [<L *quinquagenarius* < *quinquageni* fifty each]

quin·qua·ges·i·ma (kwin′kwə·jes′ə·mə) *adj.* Fiftieth. — *n.* A period of fifty days. [<L *quinquagesima (dies)* fiftieth (day)]

quin·qua·ges·i·mal (kwin′kwə·jes′ə·məl) *adj.* Of, pertaining to, comprising, or containing fifty.

Quinquagesima Sunday The fiftieth day before Easter; the Sunday before Lent; Shrove Sunday.

quinque– *combining form* Five: *quinquefoliate.* Also, before vowels, **quinqu–.** [<L *quinque* five]

quin·que·fo·li·ate (kwin′kwə·fō′lē·it, -āt) *adj. Bot.* Five-leaved. Also **quin′que·fo′li·o·late′** (-fō′lē·ə·lāt′). [<QUINQUE- + L *foliatus* < *folium* leaf]

quin·quen·ni·al (kwin·kwen′ē·əl) *adj.* Occurring every five years, or once in five years; also, lasting five years. — *n.* **1** A fifth anniversary or its celebration. **2** A quinquennium. [<L *quinque* five + *annus* year]

quin·quen·ni·um (kwin·kwen′ē·əm) *n.* A period of five years. [<L]

quin·que·va·lent (kwin′kwə·vā′lənt) *adj. Chem.* Having a valence or combining value of five; pentavalent. See VALENCE. — **quin′que·va′·lence** *n.*

quin·sy (kwin′zē) *n. Pathol.* Inflammation of the tonsils and the adjoining tissues, especially when suppurative. [<Med. L *quinancia* <Gk. *kynanchē* a dog's collar < *kyōn* dog + *anchein* choke]

quint (kwint) *n.* **1** A fifth. **2** A set of five. **3** The E string of a violin. **4** *Colloq.* A quintuplet. **5** In piquet, a sequence of five of the same suit: if of the five highest cards, called a **quint major.** **6** An organ stop giving tones a fifth above those of the keys that are pressed. [<L *quintus* < *quinque* five]

quin·tain (kwin′tin) *n. Obs.* An object set up to be tilted at; also, the place for the sport. [OF *quintaine* <L *quintana* street in a camp < *quintus* fifth]

quin·tal (kwin′təl) *n.* A measure of weight, a hundredweight; in the metric system, 100 kilograms: also called *metric centner.* See METRIC SYSTEM. [<OF <Arabic *qinṭar*]

quin·tan (kwin′tən) *adj.* Recurring on every fifth day, reckoning inclusively: a *quintan* fever. — *n.* A quintan fever. [<L *quintanus* < *quintus* fifth]

Quin·ta·na Ro·o (kēn·tä′nä rō′ō) A territory in the eastern part of the Yucatán peninsula, Mexico; 19,625 square miles; capital, Chetumal.

Quin·te·ro (kēn·tā′rō), **Alvarez** See ALVAREZ QUINTERO.

quin·tes·sence (kwin·tes′əns) *n.* **1** An extract from anything, containing in concentrated form its most essential principle. **2** The purest and most essential part, manifestation, or embodiment of anything. **3** *Philos.* In the doctrine of the Pythagoreans, the fifth or celestial essence, ether, above the four elements of earth, air, fire, and water. [<F <L *quinta essentia* fifth essence] — **quin′tes·sen′tial** *adj.*

quin·tet (kwin·tet′) *n.* **1** A musical composition arranged for five voices or instruments; also, the five persons performing it. **2** Any group of five; anything arranged for a set of five performers, as in a game. Also **quin·tette′.** [<Ital. *quintetto* < *quinto* fifth]

quin·tic (kwin′tik) *Math. adj.* Denoting a quantic function of the fifth degree. — *n.* Such a function.

quin·tile (kwin′til) *n.* **1** In astrology, the aspect of planets separated by 72°, or the fifth part of the zodiac. **2** *Stat.* **a** That part of a frequency distribution containing one fifth of the total observations or cases. **b** The point marking such a part. [<L *quintus* fifth, on analogy with *quartile*]

Quin·til·i·an (kwin·til′ē·ən, -til′yən), A.D. 35?–95?, Roman rhetorician: full name *Marcus Fabius Quintilianus.*

quin·til·lion (kwin·til′yən) *n.* In the French system of numeration, almost universally followed in the United States, 1 followed by 18 ciphers; in the English system, 1 followed by 30 ciphers. [<L *quintus* fifth + MILLION] — **quin·til′lionth** (-yənth) *adj.* & *n.*

quin·tin (kwin′tin) *n. Rare* A fine linen fabric. Also **quin′tain** (-tin). [from *Quintin,* a town in Brittany]

quin·tu·ple (kwin′tōō·pəl, -tyōō-, kwin·tōō′pəl, -tyōō′-) *v.t.* & *v.i.* **·pled, ·pling** To multiply by five; make or become five times as large. [< *adj.*] — *adj.* **1** Consisting of five united or of five parts. **2** Multiplied by five. — *n.* A number or a sum five times as great as another. [<F <L *quintuplex* < *quintus* fifth + *plic-,* stem of *plicare* fold]

quin·tu·plet (kwin′tōō·plit, -tyōō-, kwin·tōō′·plit, -tyōō′-) *n.* **1** Five things of a kind used or occurring together. **2** One of five born of the same mother at one birth.

quin·tu·pli·cate (kwin·tōō′plə·kit, -tyōō′-) *adj.* **1** Fivefold. **2** Raised to the fifth power. — *v.t.* & *v.i.* (-kāt) **·cat·ed, ·cat·ing** To multiply by five; quintuple. — *n.* (-kit) One of five identical things. [<L *quintuplex, -icis* + -ATE[1]] — **quin·tu′pli·cate·ly** *adv.* — **quin·tu′·pli·ca′tion** *n.*

quip (kwip) *n.* **1** A sarcastic or sharp jest, remark, or retort; gibe; also, a clever or witty sally without sarcasm. **2** A quibble. **3** An odd, fantastic action or object. — *v.i.* **quipped, quip·ping** To make a witty remark; jest. [Earlier *quippy* <L *quippe* indeed] — **quip′pish** *adj.*

quip·ster (kwip′stər) *n.* One who makes quips.

qui·pu (kē′pōō, kwip′·ōō) *n.* An aboriginal Peruvian device for recording and conveying information, consisting of a series of varicolored and knotted strings tied at one end to a thicker cord. The order, color, and knots of the strings were used like elements of a written language. Also **quip′pu.** [<Quechua *quipu* knot]

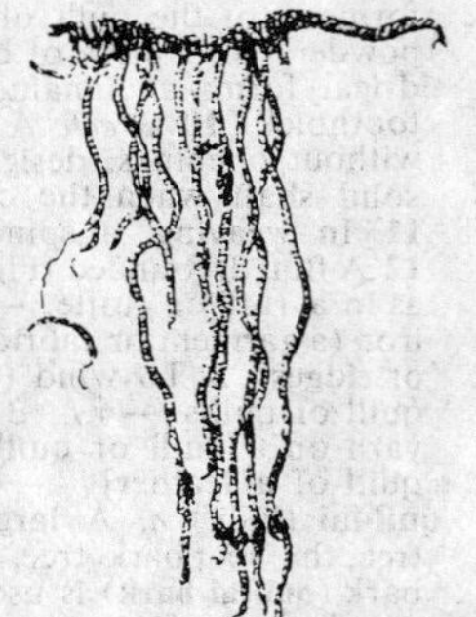

PERUVIAN QUIPU

quire[1] (kwīr) *n.* **1** The twentieth part of a ream of paper; 24 (or 25) sheets. **2** A set of all the sheets necessary to make a book; hence, a book. — *v.t.* **quired, quir·ing** To fold or separate into quires. ◆ Homophone: *choir.* [<OF *quaire* <L *quaterni* by fours]

quire[2] (kwīr) See CHOIR.

Quir·i·nal (kwir′ə·nəl) **1** One of the seven hills on which Rome stands, containing the **Quirinal palace,** formerly a papal residence; after 1870 the official residence of the kings of Italy. **2** Figuratively, the monarchical regime of Italy, as distinguished from the *Vatican,* or papal government. — *adj.* Pertaining to or situated on the Quirinal.

Qui·ri·no (kē·rē′nō), **Elpidio,** 1890–1956, president of the Philippines 1948–54.

Qui·ri·nus (kwi·rī′nəs) An ancient Italic god of war: ultimately identified with the deified *Romulus.*

Qui·ri·tes (kwi·rī′tēz) *n. pl.* The citizens of ancient Rome in their civil as distinguished from their military or political capacity. [<L]

quirk (kwûrk) *n.* **1** A short or sharp turn; twist. **2** A quaint turn of the fancy; bright retort; hence, a personal peculiarity; caprice. **3** An artful turn for evasion or subterfuge; quibble. **4** A sudden curve or flourish, especially in drawing or writing. **5** *Archit.* **a** A small groove in, beside, or between moldings or beads. **b** A molding or bead having a groove on one or both edges. See synonyms under WHIM. [Origin uncertain]

quirk·y (kwûrk′ē) *adj.* **quirk·i·er, quirk·i·est** Peculiar, unpredictable, and idiosyncratic: a *quirky* individual. — **quirk′i·ly** *adv.* — **quirk′·i·ness** *n.*

quirl (kwûrl) See QUERL.

quirt (kwûrt) *n.* A short-handled riding whip with a braided rawhide lash. — *v.t.* To strike with a quirt. [<Mexican Sp. *cuarta*]

quish (kwish) See CUISH.

quis·ling (kwiz′ling) *n.* One who betrays his country to the enemy and is then given political power by the conquerors. [after Vidkun *Quisling,* 1887–1945, Norwegian Nazi party leader and traitor] — **quis′ling·ism** *n.*

quit (kwit) *v.* **quit** or **quit·ted, quit·ting** *v.t.* **1** To cease or desist from; discontinue. **2** To give up; renounce; relinquish. **3** To go away from; leave. **4** To let go of (something held). **5** *Archaic* To acquit (oneself). — *v.i.* **6** To stop; cease; discontinue. **7** To leave; depart. **8** *Colloq.* To resign from a position, etc. See synonyms under ABANDON, CEASE, END, REQUITE. — *adj.* Released, relieved, or absolved from something, as a duty, obligation, encumbrance, or debt; clear; free; rid. — *n.* The act of quitting. — **to be quits** To be even (with another). — **to cry quits** To declare to be even, or that neither has the advantage; declare (oneself) willing to stop competing. [<OF *quiter* <LL *quietare* set free <L *quies* rest, repose]

quitch·grass (kwich′gras′, -gräs′) *n.* Couchgrass. Also **quitch.**

quit·claim (kwit′klām′) *n. Law* A full release and acquittance given by one to another in regard to a certain demand, suit, or right of action: also **quit′claim′ance.** — *v.t.* To relinquish or give up claim or title to; release from a claim. [<QUIT + CLAIM]

quitclaim deed A conveyance, in the nature of a release, of all the maker's interest in the land in question, but not professing that the title is valid, nor containing any warranty or covenants for title.

quite (kwīt) *adv.* **1** To the fullest extent; without limitation or reservation; fully; totally: *quite* dead. **2** *Colloq.* To a great or considerable extent; noticeably; very: *quite* ill. [ME; var. of QUIT, *adj.*]

Qui·to (kē′tō) The capital of Ecuador; 9,343 feet above sea level in the Andes of north central Ecuador.

quit–quit (kwit′kwit′) *n.* The honey creeper.

quit–rent (kwit′rent′) *n.* A fixed rent formerly paid by a freeholder, whereby he was released from feudal services.

quit·tance (kwit′ns) *n.* **1** Discharge or release, as from a debt or obligation; acquittance. **2** Something given or tendered by way of requital; repayment. [<F < *quiter* QUIT]

quit·ter[1] (kwit′ər) *n.* One who quits needlessly; a shirker; slacker; coward.

quit·ter[2] (kwit′ər) *n.* **1** A fistulous sore on the hoof of a horse or any solid-hoofed animal: also **quit′ter·bone′** (-bōn′), **quit′tor.** **2** Purulent matter. [? <OF *quiture* a cooking]

qui va là? (kē vá lá′) *French* Who goes there?: a watchword.

quiv·er[1] (kwiv′ər) *v.i.* To shake with a slight, tremulous motion; vibrate; tremble. See synonyms under QUAKE, SHAKE. — *n.* The act or fact of quivering; a trembling or shaking. [Prob. related to QUAVER]

quiv·er[2] (kwiv′ər) *n.* A portable case or sheath for arrows; also, its contents. [<AF *quiveir,* OF *coivre* <Gmc.]

quiv·er[3] (kwiv′ər) *adj. Obs.* Brisk; active; nimble. [OE *cwifer-,* found in *cwiferlice* zealously]

Qui·vi·ra (kē·vē′rä) A land in the central United States, sought and found by Coronado in 1541: often identified with Kansas.

qui vive? (kē vēv′) *French* Literally, who lives?: as used by French sentinels, "Who goes there?" — **to be on the qui vive** To be on the look-out; be wide-awake.

quix·ot·ic (kwik·sot′ik) *adj.* Pertaining to or like Don Quixote, the hero of a Spanish romance ridiculing knight-errantry; hence, ridiculously chivalrous or romantic; having high but impractical sentiments, aims, etc.; extravagant; visionary. See synonyms under IMAGINARY. — **quix·ot′i·cal·ly** *adv.* — **quix·ot·ism** (kwik′sə·tiz′əm) *n.*

quiz (kwiz) *n. pl.* **quiz·zes** **1** The act of questioning; specifically, an oral or written examination of a class or individual. **2** Something or someone odd or ridiculous; an eccentric. **3** A hoax; practical joke. — *v.t.* **quizzed, quiz·zing** **1** To examine by asking questions; question. **2** *Brit.* To make fun of; ridicule. See synonyms under QUESTION. [Origin unknown] — **quiz′zer** *n.*

quiz program A television or radio program in which selected contestants or a panel of experts try to answer questions presented by the master of ceremonies.

quiz·zi·cal (kwiz′i·kəl) *adj.* **1** Addicted to quizzing or chaffing; bantering. **2** Queer; odd. — **quiz′zi·cal·ly** *adv.*

quizzing glass A monocle or single eyeglass.

Qum (kŏŏm) A city in north central Iran. Also **Qom** (kōm).

quo' (kwō) v. Scot. Quoth.

quod (kwod) n. Brit. Slang A prison. Also spelled *quad.*

quod e·rat de·mon·stran·dum (kwod er′at dem′ən·stran′dəm) Latin Which was to be demonstrated: abbreviated Q.E.D.

quod·li·bet (kwod′li·bet) n. **1** A debatable or nice point; subtlety; especially, a scholarly dissertation on such a subject. **2** Music A fantasia or medley, usually humorous. [< L, anything at all] —**quod·li·bet·ic** (kwod′li·bet′ik) or **·i·cal** adj.

quod vi·de (kwod vī′dē) Latin Which see: usually abbreviated to *q.v.* and used in parentheses after a word by way of reference.

quo·hog (kwō′hôg, -hog, kwə·hôg′, -hog′) n. A quahaug.

quoin (koin, kwoin) n. **1** A large square ashlar or stone at the angle of a wall. **2** An external angle of a building. **3** A vertical, angular, ornamental projection from a wall face. **4** A wedge-shaped stone of an arch. **5** A block cut obliquely at the bottom to support a vertical column or pilaster on an inclined plane. **6** An internal angle, as of a room; a corner. **7** A wedge, or wedgelike piece. **8** Printing A wedge, or pair of wedges, by which to lock up type in a chase or galley. —v.t. To fasten or provide with a quoin or quoins. [Var. of COIN]

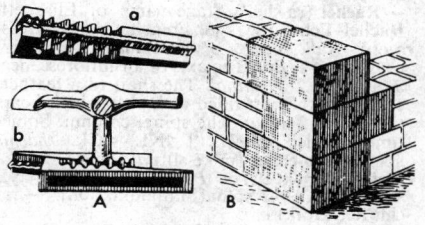

QUOINS

A. Printer's metal quoins.
  a. Single quoin.
  b. Pair of quoins ready for locking with key.
B. Quoins of dressed stone.

quoit (kwoit, esp. Brit. koit) n. **1** A disk of iron or other material with a round hole in the center to be thrown over a stake: used in the game of quoits. **2** pl. A game played by throwing these disks at a short stake. —v.t. To pitch as a quoit. [ME *coyte;* origin unknown]

quo ju·re (kwō jŏŏr′ē) Latin By what right? By what law?

quoll (kwol) n. Any of several carnivorous marsupials of Australia, as the **northern quoll** (*Satanellus hallucatus*).

quo·mo·do (kwō·mō′dō) Latin adv. In what manner? How? —n. The means: manner.

quon·dam (kwon′dəm) adj. Having been formerly; former. [< L]

Quon·set hut
(kwon′sit) A portable structure resembling the Nissen hut, designed for use by the U.S. armed services: a trade name. [from *Quonset,* a town in Rhode Island where first made]

QUONSET HUT

quo·rum (kwôr′əm, kwō′rəm) n. **1** Such a number of members of any deliberative or corporate body as is necessary for the legal transaction of business: commonly, a majority. **2** Formerly, in England, certain designated justices of the peace without the presence of some one of whom the others could not act: now applied loosely to all justices. **3** A select or chosen body. [< L, of whom < qui who]

quo·ta (kwō′tə) n. A proportional part or share required for making up a certain number or quantity; proportionate contribution. [< Med. L quota (pars) how great (a part) < L quotus how great]

quot·a·ble (kwō′tə·bəl) adj. Suitable for quotation. —**quot′a·bil′i·ty** n.

quo·ta·tion (kwō·tā′shən) n. **1** The act of quoting. **2** The words quoted or cited; a passage from a book or writing, cited or adduced. **3** A price quoted or current, as of securities, etc. [< Med. L quotatio, -onis < quotare. See QUOTE.] —**quo·ta′tion·al** adj. —**quo·ta′tion·al·ly** adv. —**quo·ta′tion·ist** n.

quotation mark One of the marks placed at the beginning and end of a quoted word or passage. In English usage, one or two inverted commas (',") mark the beginning of a quotation, and, correspondingly, one or two apostrophes (',") the close, the single marks usually being used to set off a quotation within a quotation.

quote (kwōt) v. **quot·ed, quot·ing** v.t. **1** To repeat or reproduce the words of. **2** To repeat or cite (a rule, author, etc.), as for authority or illustration. **3** In commerce: **a** To state (a price). **b** To give the current or market price of. **4** Printing To enclose within quotation marks. —v.i. **5** To make a quotation, as from a book. —n. A quotation; also, a quotation mark. [< Med. L quotare distinguish by number (of how many)] —**quot′a·ble** adj. —**quot′er** n. —**quote′·wor′thy** (-wûr′thē) adj. —**quot′ing·ly** adv.

Synonyms (verb): cite, excerpt, extract, paraphrase, plagiarize, recite, repeat. To *quote* is to give an author's words, either exactly, as in direct quotation, or in substance, as in indirect quotation; to *cite* is, etymologically, to call up a passage, as a witness is summoned. In *citing* a passage its exact location by chapter, page, or otherwise must be given, so that it can be promptly called into evidence; in *quoting,* the location may or may not be given, but the words or substance of the passage must be given. To *paraphrase* is to state an author's thought more freely than in indirect quotation, keeping the substance of his thought and his order of statement, but changing the language and style, and perhaps expanding by explanation, inference, etc. To *plagiarize* is to *quote* without credit, appropriating another's words or thought as one's own. To *recite* or *repeat* is usually to *quote* orally, but *recite* is applied in legal phrase to a particular statement of facts which is not a quotation.

quoth (kwōth) v.t. Said or spoke; uttered: the imperfect tense of the obsolete verb *queth,* used only in the first and third persons, the nominative always following the verb, as *quoth* he. [OE *cwœth,* pt. of *cwethan* say]

quo·tha (kwō′thə) interj. Archaic Indeed! forsooth!: usually in slight contempt. [< *quoth he*]

quo·tid·i·an (kwō·tid′ē·ən) adj. Recurring or occurring every day. —n. A fever whose paroxysms return every day. [< L *quotidianus* daily]

quo·tient (kwō′shənt) n. Math. The result obtained by division; a number indicating how many times one number or quantity is contained in another. [< L *quotiens* how often < *quot* how many]

quo war·ran·to (kwō wô·ran′tō, wo-) Latin Literally, by what warrant; a judicial writ commanding a person to show by what authority he exercises an office or franchise never granted or forfeited by some fault. In England, and generally in the United States, this writ has given way to **an information in the nature of a quo warranto,** criminal in form, but in substance civil.

R

r, R (är) n. pl. **r's, R's** or **rs, Rs, ars** (ärz) **1** The 18th letter of the English alphabet: from Phoenician *resh,* Greek *rho,* Roman R. **2** The sound of the letter r. See ALPHABET. —*symbol* **1** Chem. An organic radical. **2** Math. Ratio. **3** Electr. Resistance. —**the three R's** Reading, writing, and arithmetic (regarded humorously as spelled *reading, 'riting,* and *'rithmetic*); hence, the essential elements of a primary education.

Ra (rä) The supreme Egyptian deity, the sun-god, usually represented as a hawk-headed man crowned with the solar disk and uraeus: also spelled *Re.* [< Egyptian *Rā* the sun]

Ra Chem. Radium (symbol Ra).

ra·ban·na (rə·ban′ə) n. A textile fabric of raffia, made in Madagascar and used for

RA

draperies, curtains, and the like. [< Malagasy *rebana*]

Ra·bat (rä·bät′) A port on the Atlantic, capital of Morocco.

ra·ba·to (rə·bā′tō, -bä′-) See REBATO.

Ra·baul (rə·boul′, rä′boul) The chief city of New Britain; fomerly the administrative center of the Territory of New Guinea.

Rab·bath Am·mon (rab′əth am′ən) The Old Testament name for AMMAN.

rab·bet (rab′it) n. **1** A recess or groove in or near the edge of one piece of wood or other material to receive the edge of another piece. **2** A joint so made. **3** A rabbet plane. —v. **·bet·ed, ·bet·ing** v.t. **1** To cut a rectangular groove in. **2** To unite in a rabbet. —v.i. **3** To be jointed by a rabbet. Also spelled *rebate.* ◆ Homophone: *rabbit.* [< OF *rabat < rabattre* beat down. See REBATE.]

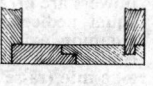

RABBET JOINTS

rabbet joint A joint between two edges, as of timbers, each of which is partly cut away so that their faces are flush.

rabbet plane A plane for cutting a rectangular groove, as in or near the edge of a plank.

rab·bi (rab′ī) n. pl. **·bis** Master, teacher: a Jewish title for those distinguished for learning, authoritative teachers of the Law, and appointed spiritual heads of a community. Also **rab′bin** (-in). [OE < L < Gk. *rhabbi* < Hebrew *rabbī* my master < *rab* great, master + *-i* my (prominal suffix)]

rab·bin·ate (rab′in·āt) n. **1** The office or term of office of a rabbi. **2** Rabbis collectively. [< Med. L *rabbinus* rabbi]

Rab·bin·ic (rə·bin′ik) n. The language or dialect of the rabbis; especially, the Hebrew language as used in Biblical and Talmudic exegesis by Jewish scholars of the late ancient and early medieval periods.

rab·bin·i·cal (rə·bin′i·kəl) adj. Pertaining to the rabbis or to their opinions, languages, or writings. Also **rab·bin′ic.** —**rab·bin′i·cal·ly** adv.

rab·bin·ism (rab′in·iz′əm) n. **1** The teachings or doctrines of the rabbis. **2** A rabbinical phrase, expression, or idiom.

rab·bin·ist (rab′in·ist) n. One among the Jews who adhered to the Talmud and the

traditions of the rabbis, in opposition to those who rejected the traditions. Also **rab′bin·ite** (-īt). [<Med. L *rabbinus*] **— rab′bin·is′tic, rab′bin·is′ti·cal, rab′bin·it′ic** (-it′ik) *adj.* **— rab′bin·is′ti·cal·ly** *adv.*

rab·bit (rab′it) *n.* **1** Any of various small burrowing rodents (family *Leporidae*), resembling but smaller than the hare, as the common American cottontail *(Sylvilagus floridanus)*. **2** A hare. **3** The pelt of a rabbit or hare. **4** Welsh rabbit. *— v.i.* To hunt rabbits. ◆ Homophone: *rabbet*. [ME *rabette*. Akin to Walloon *robbett*, Flemish *robbe*.] **— rab′bit·er** *n.*

rabbit fever Tularemia.

rab·bit–foot (rab′it·fo͝ot′) *n.* **1** A common clover *(Trifolium arvense)* having soft, hairy flower heads supposed to resemble rabbits' paws: also **rabbit's–foot clover. 2** The left hind foot of a rabbit carried as a good–luck charm.

rabbit hawk The red–tailed hawk *(Buteo borealis)*.

rabbit hutch A coop in which domestic rabbits are bred.

rabbit punch In boxing, a short chopping blow at the base of the skull or back of the neck.

rab·bit·ry (rab′it·rē) *n. pl.* **·ries** A place where rabbits are kept; also, a group of rabbit hutches.

rab·ble[1] (rab′əl) *n.* A rude crowd; mob. **— the rabble** The populace; hoi polloi: used contemptuously. *— adj.* Of or pertaining to, suited to, or characteristic of a rabble; noisy; disorderly. *— v.t.* **·bled, ·bling** To mob. [? <RABBLE[3]]

rab·ble[2] (rab′əl) *n. Metall.* An iron implement, usually bent at one end, for stirring or skimming melted iron in puddling: also **rab′bler.** *— v.t.* **·bled, ·bling** To stir or skim with a rabble. [<F *râble* <L *rutabulum* poker]

rab·ble[3] (rab′əl) *v.t. & v.i.* **·bled, ·bling** *Scot. & Brit. Dial.* To speak or utter in an incoherent or disconnected manner; gabble. [Cf. Du. *rabbelen* speak indistinctly]

rab·ble·ment (rab′əl·mənt) *n.* **1** An uproar; disturbance. **2** A rabble; crowd.

rab·ble–rous·er (rab′əl·rou′zər) *n.* One who tries to incite mobs by arousing prejudices and passions; a demagog.

rab·bo·ni (ra·bō′nē) *n.* My great master: a term of address. [<Hebrew, aug. of RABBI]

rab·do·man·cy (rab′də·man′sē) See RHABDOMANCY.

Rab·e·lais (rab′ə·lā, *Fr.* rȧ·ble′), **François,** 1494?–1553, French humorist and satirist.

Rab·e·lai·si·an (rab′ə·lā′zē·ən, -zhən) *adj.* Characteristic of or like Rabelais or his works, especially with regard to his boisterous, coarse humor and his extravagance of satire and caricature. *— n.* A student or imitator of Rabelais. **— Rab′e·lai′si·an·ism, Rab′e·la′ism** *n.*

Ra·bi (rä′bē), **Isadore Isaac,** born 1898, U. S. physicist born in Austria.

Ra·bi·a (rə·bē′ə) *n.* Either of two Mohammedan months. See under CALENDAR (Mohammedan). [<Arabic *Rabī*, lit., spring]

rab·id (rab′id) *adj.* **1** Affected with, arising from, or pertaining to rabies; mad. **2** Unreasonably zealous; fanatical; violent. **3** Furious; raging. Also **rab′ic.** [<L *rabidus* < *rabere* be mad. Akin to RAGE.] **— rab′id·ly** *adv.* **— rab′id·ness** *n.*

ra·bies (rā′bēz, -bi·ēz) *n.* An acute infectious disease of animals, especially of dogs, caused by a virus and affecting the central nervous system; hydrophobia: readily transmissible to man by the bite of an affected animal. [<L < *rabere* rave] **— ra′bi·et′ic** (-et′ik) *adj.*

ra·ca (rā′kə, rə·kä′) *adj.* Worthless; contemptible. *Matt.* v 22. [<LL <Gk. *rhakē* <Aramaic *rēqā*]

rac·coon (ra·ko͞on′) *n.* **1** An American nocturnal plantigrade carnivore (genus *Procyon*): the common North American raccoon *(P. lotor)* is grayish–brown, with a black cheek patch, and black–and–white–ringed bushy tail. **2** The fur of this animal. Also spelled *racoon*. [Alter. of Algonquian *arakunem* hand–scratcher]

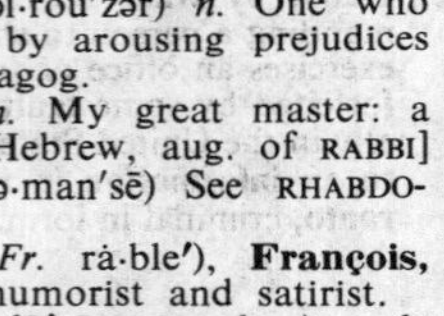

RACCOON
(Body from 20 to 30 inches long; tail, 10 to 12 inches)

raccoon dog A wild dog *(Nyctereutes procyonoides)* of Japan and northeastern Asia, with long, loose fur, short ears, and a long bushy tail.

race[1] (rās) *n.* **1** One of the major subdivisions of mankind, regarded as having a common origin and exhibiting a relatively constant set of physical traits. On the basis of the more commonly used criteria such as stature, the cephalic index, the nasal index, prognathism, skull capacity, texture of the hair, degree of pilosity, color of the skin, and hair and eye color, mankind has been divided into primary stocks or races, each of which is regarded as including a varying number of ethnic groups. According to some, the primary stocks are: the Caucasoid, the Mongoloid, and the Negroid. A number of races, such as the Australian and Polynesian, are of doubtful classification. **2** Any group of people or any grouping of peoples having, or assumed to have, common characteristics. **3** A nation: the German *race*. **4** A genealogical or family stock; clan: the *race* of MacGregor. **5** Pedigree; lineage: a noble *race*. **6** Any class of beings having characteristics uniting them, or differentiating them from others: the *race* of lawyers. **7** *Biol.* A group of plants or animals, having characteristics clearly differentiating it from other groups within the same species, which breeds true except for minor variations; a variety: a *race* of wheat. **8** A stock, breed, or strain of domestic animals or plants. **9** A quality or aggregate of qualities by which origin is determined; especially, the characteristic flavor or taste of wine. See synonyms under AFFINITY, KIN, PEOPLE, SORT. [<F <Ital. *razza* <L *(gene)ratio* lineage, breed]

race[2] (rās) *n.* **1** A contest to determine the relative speed of the contestants. **2** Any contest. **3** Movement or progression; swift movement. **4** Duration of life; course; career. **5** A swift current of water or its channel. **6** A swift current or heavy sea resulting from the meeting of two tides: the Portland *Race*. **7** A sluice or channel by which to conduct water to or from a waterwheel or around a dam. See HEADRACE, MILLRACE, TAILRACE. **8** Any groove or channel along which some part of a machine slides or is guided. **9** Slipstream. *— v.* **raced, rac·ing** *v.i.* **1** To take part in a contest of speed. **2** To move at great or top speed. **3** To move at an accelerated or too great speed, usually because of decreased resistance: said of machinery. *— v.t.* **4** To contend against in a race. **5** To cause to take part in a race. **6** To cause to move at an accelerated or too great speed: to *race* an engine. [<ON *rās*. Akin to OE *rǣs* a rushing.]

race[3] (rās) *n.* A root; specifically, a root of ginger. [<OF *rais* <L *radix* root]

Race (rās), **Cape** The southeasternmost point of Newfoundland.

race–a·bout (rās′ə·bout′) *n. Naut.* A sloop–rigged racing boat having a short bowsprit. Compare KNOCK–ABOUT.

race·course (rās′kôrs′, -kōrs′) *n.* The track over which a horse race, dog race, or the like is run. Also *racetrack*.

race horse A horse bred and trained for contests of speed; a racer.

race knife A tool having a very narrow U–shaped blade, used for tracing or outlining on metal or glass or for scribing on wood.

ra·ceme (rā·sēm′, rə-) *n. Bot.* A centripetal or indeterminate flower cluster in which the flowers are arranged singly on distinct, nearly equal pedicels at intervals on an elongated common axis. [<L *racemus* cluster] **— rac·e·mif·er·ous** (ras′ə·mif′ər·əs) *adj.*

ra·ce·mic (rā·sē′mik, -sem′ik, rə-) *adj.* **1** *Bot.* Of, pertaining to, or contained in racemes or in grapes. **2** *Chem.* Indicating or relating to any chemical compound that is optically inactive. Also **rac·e·moid** (ras′ə·moid).

racemic acid *Chem.* A white, crystalline, optically inactive compound, $C_4H_6O_6$, contained with tartartic acid in certain grapes and extracts from tartar: it is separable into dextrorotatory and levorotatory forms.

rac·e·mism (ras′ə·miz′əm, rā·sē′miz·əm) *n. Chem.* The quality or condition of being racemic.

rac·e·mize (ras′ə·mīz, rā·sē′mīz) *v.t.* **·mized, ·miz·ing** *Chem.* To change (an optically active compound) into an optically inactive compound. **— rac′e·mi·za′tion** *n.*

rac·e·mose (ras′ə·mōs) *adj.* Arranged in or as in clusters or racemes: a *racemose* gland. Also **rac′e·mous.** [<L *racemosus*] **— rac′e·mose·ly** *adv.*

race psychology A division of psychology which investigates human traits and behavior in relation to racial factors, actual or assumed.

rac·er (rā′sər) *n.* **1** One who races, or one who contends in a race. **2** Anything having unusually rapid speed, as a race horse, steamer, or yacht; also, an automobile designed for racing. **3** A turntable on which a heavy gun is turned to left or right. **4** One of various colubrine snakes, as the blacksnake.

race riot A violent conflict between groups in the same community, based on differences of color, creed, etc.

race suicide The slow reduction in numbers of a people through voluntary failure on the part of individuals to maintain the birth rate at or above the level of the death rate.

race·track (rās′trak′) *n.* A racecourse.

race·way (rās′wā′) *n.* **1** A channel for conducting water. **2** A tube for protecting wires, as in a subway. **3** *U.S.* A racecourse for trotting horses.

Ra·chel (rā′chəl; *Fr.* rȧ·shel′, *Pg.* rä·kel′, *Sw.* rä′kel) A feminine personal name. Also *Ital.* **Ra·che·le** (rä·kā′lā). [<Hebrew, ewe] **— Rachel** The wife of Jacob; mother of Joseph and Benjamin. *Gen.* xxix 6.
— Rachel (rȧ·shel′) Stage name of Elisabeth Rachel–Félix, 1821–58, French tragic actress.

ra·chis (rā′kis) *n. pl.* **ra·chi·des** (rā′kə·dēz) or **·chis·es 1** *Bot.* The axis of an inflorescence; a raceme. **2** *Ornithol.* The shaft of a feather, especially the part filled with pith, which bears the barbs. **3** *Anat.* The spinal column. Sometimes spelled *rhachis*. [<NL <Gk. *rhachis* spine] **— ra·chi·al** (rā′kē·əl) *adj.*

ra·chi·tis (rə·kī′tis) *n. Pathol.* Rickets. [<NL <Gk. *rhachitis* spinal inflammation] **— ra·chit′ic** (-kit′ik) *adj.*

Rach·ma·ni·nov (räkh·mä′ni·nôf), **Sergei Vassilievich,** 1873–1943, Russian pianist and composer. Also **Rach·ma′ni·noff.**

ra·cial (rā′shəl) *adj.* Pertaining to or characteristic of a race, races, or descent. **— ra′cial·ly** *adv.*

ra·cial·ism (rā′shəl·iz′əm) *n.* **1** The doctrine of the preponderant influence of actual or assumed racial factors in the origin, development, and rank of various human societies; race prejudice. **2** Racism. **— ra′cial·ist** *n.*

Ra·ci·bórz (rä·chē′bo͞osh) See RATIBOR.

Ra·cine (rə·sēn′) A city on Lake Michigan in SE Wisconsin.

Ra·cine (rȧ·sēn′), **Jean,** 1639–99, French dramatist.

ra·cism (rā′siz·əm) *n.* An excessive and irrational belief in or advocacy of the superiority of a given group, people, or nation, on racial grounds alone; race hatred. **— ra′cist** *n.*

rack[1] (rak) *n.* **1** An open grating, framework, or the like, in or on which articles may be placed, as a frame to hold dishes, a tier or row of pigeonholes, or a framework to hold fodder for horses, cattle, or sheep. **2** A triangular frame for arranging the balls on a billiard table. **3** A device in an airplane for carrying bombs: also **bomb rack. 4** *Mech.* A bar or the like having teeth that engage with those of a gearwheel, pinion, or worm gear. **5** A machine for stretching or making tense; especially, an intrument of torture which stretches the limbs of victims. **6** Torture or punishment as by the rack; hence, intense mental or physical suffering. **7** A wrenching or straining, as from a storm. *— v.t.* **1** To place or arrange in or on a rack. **2** To torture on the rack. **3** To cause suffering to; torment. **4** To strain, as with the effort of thinking: to *rack* one's brains. **5** To raise (rents) excessively: see RACK–RENT. ◆ Homophone: *wrack*. [ME *rekke*, prob. <MDu. *rec, recke* < *recken* stretch] **— rack′er** *n.*

rack[2] (rak) *n.* The single–foot. *— v.i.* To proceed or move with this gait. ◆ Homophone: *wrack*. [? Var. of ROCK[2]]

rack[3] (rak) *n.* **1** Thin, flying, or broken clouds. **2** Any floating vapor. *— v.i.* To move rapidly; send, as clouds before the wind. Also spelled *wrack*. [<Scand. Cf. ON *rek* drifting wreckage, *reka* drive, drift.]

rack⁴ (rak) *n.* Wrack; wreck; demolition: obsolete except in the phrase "to go to rack and ruin." [*Var. of* WRACK²]

rack⁵ *v.t.* To draw off from the lees, as liquor. ◆ Homophone: *wrack.* [<Provençal *arracar* < *raca* refuse of grapes]

rack and pinion *Mech.* A machine movement in which a toothed rack and a pinion mesh together for converting rotary motion into reciprocating motion or vice versa.

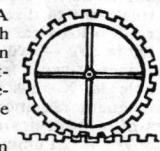

RACK AND PINION

rack·et¹ (rak′it) *n.* **1** An implement for striking a ball, as in the game of tennis. It is a nearly elliptical hoop of bent wood, usually strung with catgut, and has a handle. **2** A large wooden sole or shoe to support the weight of a man or horse on swampy ground. **3** A snowshoe. **4** A ratchet: a misnomer. **5** An organ stop. **6** *sing. & pl.* A game resembling court tennis, played in a court with four walls. Often spelled *racquet.* [<F *raquette* < Arabic *rāha* palm of the hand]

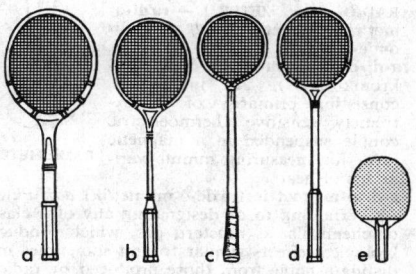

TYPES OF RACKETS
a. Tennis.   *c, d.* Squash.
b. Badminton.   *e.* Table tennis.

rack·et² (rak′it) *n.* **1** A clattering, vociferous, or confused noise; fuss; commotion. **2** *Colloq.* **a** A scheme for getting money or other benefits by fraud, intimidation, or other illegitimate means. **b** Any business or occupation: the retailing *racket.* **3** Social activity or excitement. — *v.i.* **1** To make a loud, clattering noise. **2** To indulge in noisy sport or diversion; carouse. [? Metathetic var. of dial. *rattick* make a din, clatter]

rack·et·eer (rak′ə·tir′) *n.* **1** One who extorts money from, or seeks to gain control over, a person or organization by intimidation, fraud, violence, or other criminal means; one engaged in a racket. **2** Formerly, a bootlegger or rum-runner. — **rack′et·eer′ing** *n.*

rack·et·y (rak′it·ē) *adj.* Making a racket; noisy.

Rack·ham (rak′əm), **Arthur,** 1867–1939, English artist and illustrator.

rack railway An inclined railway having a rack or toothed rail (**rack rail**) placed between the regular rails, in the cogs of which open pinions on the driving axle of the locomotive engage: also called *cogway.*

rack–rent (rak′rent′) *n.* An exorbitant rent (equal or nearly equal to the full annual value of the property). — *v.t.* To exact rack–rent from or for. [<RACK¹ (stretch) +RENT¹]

rack·work (rak′wûrk′) *n.* A mechanism with a rack, or rack and pinion, as the leading characteristic.

ra·con (rā′kon) *n.* A device for the immediate identification of friendly or hostile aircraft by means of radar signals automatically transmitted in code: adapted also as an aid in navigation. [<RA(DAR) (BEA)CON]

rac·on·teur (rak′on·tûr′, *Fr.* rȧ·kôn·tœr′) *n.* A skilled story teller. [<F *raconter* recount] —**ra′con·teuse′** (-tœz′, -tœz′) *Fr.* -tœz′) *n. fem.*

ra·coon (ra·kōōn′) See RACCOON.

rac·quet (rak′it) See RACKET¹.

rac·quet·ball (rak′it·bôl′) *n.* **1** An indoor walled–court game played with a hollow rubber ball and a short–handled racquet. **2** The ball used in this game, somewhat larger and softer than a handball.

rac·y (rā′sē) *adj.* **rac·i·er, rac·i·est** **1** Having a spirited or pungent interest; spicy; piquant: a *racy* style. **2** Having a characteristic flavor assumed to be indicative of origin, as wine; rich, fresh, or fragrant. **3** Suggestive; slightly immodest: a *racy* story. [<RACE¹] —**rac′i·ly** *adv.* —**rac′i·ness** *n.*

Synonyms: flavorous, forcible, high–flavored, lively, piquant, pungent, rich, spicy, spirited. *Racy* applies (def. 2) to the pleasing flavor characteristic of certain wines. *Pungent* denotes something sharply stimulating to the organs of taste or smell, as vinegar, ammonia; *piquant* denotes a quality similar in kind to *pungent* but less in degree, alluring and agreeable; *pungent* spices may be deftly compounded in a *piquant* sauce. *Antonyms:* dull, flat, flavorless, insipid, tasteless, vapid.

rad (rad) *n. Physics* A unit of absorbed nuclear radiation equivalent to 100 ergs of absorbed energy per gram of absorbing material. Compare REM, REP. [<R(ADIATION) + A(BSORBED) + D(OSE)]

ra·dar (rā′där) *n. Electronics* A locating device which instantaneously detects the presence and indicates the position of aircraft, ships, etc., by measuring the interval between the emission and return of high–frequency radio waves effective under varied conditions. [< RA(DIO) D(ETECTING) A(ND) R(ANGING)]

ra·dar·scope (rā′där·skōp) *n. Electronics* The oscilloscope of a radar set.

Rad·cliffe (rad′klif), **Ann,** 1764–1823, *née* Ward, English novelist.

rad·dle¹ (rad′l) See REDDLE, RUDDLE.

rad·dle² (rad′l) *v.t.* **·dled, ·dling** To intertwine or weave together. [<obs. *raddle* a wattle < AF *reidele,* OF *reddale* stout stick]

ra·deau (rȧ·dō′) *n. French* A raft; float.

Ra·dek (rä′dek), **Karl,** 1885–1959, U.S.S.R. revolutionist and journalist.

Ra·detz·ky (rä·dets′kē), **Count Joseph Wenzel,** 1766–1858, Austrian field marshal.

Rad·ford (rad′fərd), **Arthur William,** born 1896, U.S. admiral; chairman, joint chiefs of staff 1953–57.

ra·di·ac (rā′dē·ak) *n. Physics* A Geiger counter. [<RA(DIOACTIVITY) D(ETECTION), I(DENTIFICATION), A(ND) C(OMPUTATION)]

ra·di·al (rā′dē·əl) *adj.* **1** Pertaining to, consisting of, or resembling a ray or radius. **2** Extending from a center in the manner of rays. **3** Of or pertaining to the radius or a radiating part. **4** Developing uniformly on all sides. — *n.* **1** A radiating part. **2** A radial tire. —**ra′di·al·ly** *adv.*

radial engine A multicylinder internal–combustion engine having its cylinders arranged like the spokes in a wheel.

radial tire A pneumatic tire constructed with plies of fabric that are laid at right angles to the circumference of the tread and extend to the beads, sometimes reinforced with other plies, as of steel, laid at right angles to the radial plies under the tread. Also **ra·di·al–ply tire** (rā′dē·əl·plī′).

ra·di·an (rā′dē·ən) *n. Math.* **1** An arc equal in length to the radius of the circle of which it is a part. **2** The angle subtended by such an arc: 2π radians $= 360°$, π radians $= 180°$ or 1 radian $= (180/\pi)°$ or $57°\ 17'\ 44.80625'' +$. [<RADIUS]

ra·di·ance (rā′dē·əns) *n.* The quality or state of being radiant; brilliant or sparkling luster; lightness; effulgence. Also **ra′di·an·cy, ra′di·ant·ness.**

ra·di·ant (rā′dē·ənt) *adj.* **1** Emitting rays of light or heat. **2** Beaming with light or brightness, kindness, or love: a *radiant* smile. **3** Resembling rays; consisting of or transmitted by radiations: *radiant* heat. See synonyms under BRIGHT. — *n.* **1** A straight line proceeding from and conceived as revolving around a given point. **2** *Astron.* That point in the heavens from the direction of which, during a meteoric shower, the meteors seem to shoot. **3** The luminous point from which light proceeds or is made to radiate. **4** That which radiates. [< L *radians, -antis,* ppr. of *radiare* emit rays < *radius* ray] —**ra′di·ant·ly** *adv.*

radiant energy *Physics* **1** The energy associated with and transmitted by waves emanating from some specified source, as of light, heat, or sound. **2** The energy of radium, atomic disintegration, X–rays, electromagnetic radiation, or the like.

ra·di·ate (rā′dē·āt) *v.* **·at·ed, ·at·ing** *v.i.* **1** To emit rays or radiation; be radiant. **2** To issue forth in rays, as light from the sun. **3** To spread out from a center, as the spokes of a wheel. — *v.t.* **4** To send out or emit in rays. **5** To cause to spread as if from a center; diffuse; disseminate. — *adj.* (-dē·it) **1** Divided or separated into rays; having rays; radiating. **2** *Bot.* Bearing rays or ray flowers. **3** *Zool.* Characterized by radial symmetry, as echinoderms and coelenterates. **4** Adorned with rays, as a head on a coin; radiated. — *n.* (-dē·it) **1** An organism having radial symmetry. **2** A ray or raylike projection. [<L *radiatus,* pp. of *radiare* emit rays. See RADIANT.] —**ra′di·a·tive** *adj.*

ra·di·a·tion (rā′dē·ā′shən) *n.* **1** The act of radiating or the state of being radiated. **2** *Physics* **a** The emission and propagation of radiant energy or of alpha or beta rays. **b** The energy so propagated. **c** The stages of emission, absorption, and transmission involved in such propagation: distinguished from *conduction.* **3** *Biol.* Adaptive radiation.

radiation pressure *Physics* The force exerted upon an exposed surface by radiant energy, as from light or electromagnetic waves.

radiation sickness *Pathol.* A morbid condition due to the body's absorption of excess radiation and marked by fatigue, nausea, vomiting, internal hemorrhage, and progressive tissue breakdown.

ra·di·a·tor (rā′dē·ā′tər) *n.* **1** That which radiates. **2** A chamber, coil, or flat hollow vessel, through which is passed steam or hot water for warming a building or apartment. **3** In engines, a nest of tubes for cooling water flowing through them. —**ra′di·a·to·ry** (-ə·tôr′ē, -tō′rē) *adj.*

rad·i·cal (rad′i·kəl) *adj.* **1** Of, proceeding from, or pertaining to the root or foundation; essential; fundamental; inherent; basic. **2** Thoroughgoing; unsparing; extreme: a *radical* operation; *radical* measures. **3** *Math.* Pertaining to the root or roots of a number. **4** In philology, belonging or referring to a root or a root syllable; underived. **5** *Bot.* Springing from or belonging or relating to the root: *radical* leaves. **6** *Chem.* Pertaining to a radical. **7** Of or pertaining to political radicals. — *n.* **1** One who carries his theories or convictions to their furthest application; an extremist. **2** In politics, one who advocates wide–spread governmental changes and reforms at the earliest opportunity. **3** The primitive or underived part of a word; a primitive word or syllable; a root; radicle. **4** *Math.* **a** A quantity of which the root is to be extracted or used in calculation; a radical expression. **b** The radical sign. **5** *Chem.* A fundamental constituent or part of a compound; specifically, a group of atoms which acts as a unit in a compound and may either pass unchanged through a series of reactions or be replaced as though it were a single atom. ◆ Homophone: *radicle.* [<LL *radicalis* having roots <L *radix, radicis* root] —**rad′i·cal·ness** *n.*

Synonyms (adj.): basic, complete, constitutional, entire, essential, extreme, fundamental, ingrained, inherent, innate, native, natural, organic, original, perfect, positive, primary, primitive, thorough, thoroughgoing, total. The widely divergent senses in which the word *radical* is used, by which it can be at sometime interchanged with any word in the above list, are all formed upon the one primary sense of that which is connected with the root (Latin *radix*). A *radical* difference is one that springs from the root, and is thus *constitutional, essential, fundamental, organic, original;* a *radical* change is one that does not stop at the surface, but reaches down to the very root, and is *entire, thorough, total;* since the majority find superficial treatment of any matter the easiest and most comfortable, *radical* measures, which strike at the root of evil or need, are apt to be looked upon as *extreme.* See NATURAL. *Antonyms:* compromising, conciliatory, conservative, half–way, inadequate, incomplete, moderate, palliative, partial, superficial.

radical expression *Math.* A surd, or an algebraic expression involving a surd.

rad·i·cal·ism (rad′i·kəl·iz′əm) *n.* **1** The state of being radical. **2** Advocacy of thoroughgoing or extreme measures.

rad·i·cal·ize (rad′i·kə·līz′) *v.t.* **·ized, ·iz·ing** To make radical, especially in politics. —**rad·i·cal·i·za·tion** (rad′i·kə·lə·zā′shən), **rad′i·cal·iz′·er** *n.*

rad·i·cal·ly (rad′ik·lē) *adv.* **1** Completely; thoroughly; fundamentally. **2** With reference to root or origin; originally; primitively.

radical sign *Math.* The symbol √ placed before a quantity to indicate that its root is to be taken: a modification of the letter *r* (Latin *radix* root). A number written above it (called its *index*) shows what root is to be taken; thus $\sqrt[4]{a}$ stands for the fourth root of *a*; when used without a superior number, the symbol means square root of.

rad·i·cand (rad′i·kand′) *n. Math.* The quantity under the radical sign: $x + 1$ is the *radicand* of $\sqrt{x + 1}$. [<RADIC(AL) + *-and,* as in *multiplicand*]

rad·i·cel (rad′i·sel) *n.* A rootlet. [<NL *radicella,* dim. of L *radix, radicis* root]

rad·i·cle (rad′i·kəl) *n.* **1** *Bot.* **a** The embryonic root below the cotyledon of a plant. **b** A diminutive root or rootlet. **2** *Anat.* A rootlike part, as the stem of an embryo, the initial fiber of a nerve, the beginning of a vein, etc. **3** *Chem.* A radical. ◆ Homophone: *radical.* [< L *radicula,* dim. of *radix, radicis* root]

ra·di·i (rā′dē·ī) Plural of RADIUS.

ra·di·o (rā′dē·ō) *n. pl.* **·os 1** The science, art, and process of communicating by means of radiant energy transmitted directly through space in waves. **2** The wireless transmission of radio waves within assigned frequencies and their reception by devices adapted for reconverting the frequencies into their corresponding original signals. **3** A radio program or broadcast; also, the combined operations for its production. **4** A radio receiving set and its accessories. **5** A radio message or radiogram. **6** The exploitation and development of radio as a commercial enterprise; the radio business and industry. —*adj.* **1** Of, pertaining to, designating, employing, or produced by radiant energy, especially in the form of electromagnetic waves: a *radio* beam. **2** Wireless. —*v.t. & v.i.* To transmit (a message, etc.) or communicate with (someone) by radiotelegraphy or radiotelephony. [<RADIO(TELEGRAPHY)]

radio– *combining form* **1** *Anat.* Radial; pertaining to the radius: *radiodigital,* of the fingers on the radial edge of the hand. **2** Radio; produced by or related to radio: *radiogram.* **3** *Chem.* Radioactive; of, produced by, or causing radioactivity: *radioscope, radiothorium.* **4** *Med.* Radiant energy; using radiant energy: *radiotherapy.* [<L *radius* a ray]

ra·di·o·ac·tive (rā′dē·ō·ak′tiv) *adj.* Pertaining to, exhibiting, caused by, or characteristic of radioactivity: a *radioactive* isotope.

radioactive series *Physics* The sequence of products formed in the disintegration of a heavy radioactive element. The disintegration of any member of the series produces each of the following members in turn. The three naturally occurring series are those of uranium, thorium, and actinium, each terminating with a stable isotope of lead.

ra·di·o·ac·tiv·i·ty (rā′dē·ō·ak·tiv′ə·tē) *n. Physics* **1** The propagation of radiant energy. **2** The spontaneous nuclear disintegration of certain elements and isotopes, with the emission of alpha particles, electrons, positrons, or electromagnetic radiation. **3** A particular form of such disintegration: gamma *radioactivity.*

radio astronomy That branch of astronomy and astrophysics which studies celestial phenomena by the interception and analysis of radio waves emitted by stars and other objects in interstellar space.

ra·di·o·au·tog·ra·phy (rā′dē·ō·ô·tog′rə·fē) *n.* Autoradiography. [<RADIO- + AUTOGRAPH + -Y]

ra·di·o·au·to·gram (rā′dē·ō·ô′tə·gram) *n.* Autoradiograph. Also **ra′di·o·au′to·graph** (-graf, -gräf).

radio beacon A stationary radio transmitter which sends out characteristic signals for the guidance of ships and aircraft.

radio beam 1 A steady flow of radio signals concentrated along a given course or direction. **2** The narrow zone marked out for the guidance of aircraft by the overlapping of recurrent signals transmitted from ground radio stations on either side of an assigned flight course.

ra·di·o·broad·cast (rā′dē·ō·brôd′kast′, -käst′) *v.t. & v.i.* **·cast** or **·cast·ed, ·cast·ing** To broadcast by radio. —*n.* Broadcast (def. 1). —**ra′di·o·broad′cast′er** *n.*

ra·di·o·car·bon (rā′dē·ō·kär′bən) *n. Physics* The radioactive isotope of carbon of mass 14, with a half–life of about 5,700 years: it is much used in the dating of fossils, artifacts, and certain kinds of geological formations. Also called *carbon 14.*

ra·di·o·car·di·o·gram (rā′dē·ō·kär′dē·ə·gram) *n.* The record made in radiocardiography.

ra·di·o·car·di·og·ra·phy (rā′dē·ō·kär′dē·og′rə·fē) *n. Med.* A method for studying the blood flow through the heart by recording the passage of injected radioisotopes with the aid of a specially constructed Geiger counter.

ra·di·o·chem·is·try (rā′dē·ō·kem′is·trē) *n.* That branch of chemistry dealing with the properties and reactions of radioactive substances, as radium and thorium.

radio circuit A radio system consisting of two stations in direct communication with each other.

radio compass *Aeron.* A direction–finder serving to determine the position of a radio transmitting station.

radio conductor Any material or apparatus that indicates, by some alteration of its conductivity, the presence and strength of electric waves, such as the coherer of a wireless telegraph.

ra·di·o·dat·ing (rā′dē·ō·dā′ting) *n.* The technique of dating objects by measuring their radioactivity.

ra·di·ode (rā′dē·ōd) *n.* **1** A radium container, built to prevent any dangerous leakage of radioactivity. **2** *Med.* An apparatus used in some forms of radiotherapy. [<RADIO- + -ODE[1]]

ra·di·o·dust (rā′dē·ō·dust′) *n.* Radioactive dust particles precipitated from the atmosphere, especially in the fall–out from an atomic or thermonuclear bomb.

ra·di·o·el·e·ment (rā′dē·ō·el′ə·mənt) *n. Physics* **1** An element exhibiting radioactivity. **2** Any of the disintegration products of such elements, as radon, thoron, etc., which are themselves radioactive.

radio fix The position of an aircraft, ship, or radio transmitter, as determined with reference to radio signals from two or more stations, or by similar means.

radio frequency Any wave frequency, or set of frequencies, adapted for the transmission of radio signals. The range is roughly from the upper limit of normal audibility to the lower limit of heat and light waves, or upwards from about 10 kilocycles per second.

ra·di·o–ge·net·ics (rā′dē·ō·jə·net′iks) *n.* The study of genetics in relation to the effects of radioactivity upon the processes of inheritance and the nature of hereditary changes. —**ra′di·o–ge·net′ic** *adj.*

ra·di·o·ge·nic (rā′dē·ō·jē′nik, -jen′ik) *adj.* Resulting from or developed by radioactivity.

ra·di·o·gram (rā′dē·ō·gram′) *n.* **1** A message sent by wireless telegraphy. **2** A radiographic negative or print.

ra·di·o·graph (rā′dē·ō·graf′, -gräf′) *n.* A negative or picture made by means of radioactivity; an X–ray photograph. —*v.t.* To make a radiograph of. —**ra′di·og′ra·pher** (-og′rə·fər) *n.* —**ra′di·o·graph′ic** or **·ic** *adj.* —**ra′di·og′ra·phy** *n.*

ra·di·o·im·mu·no·as·say (rā′dē·ō·im′yə·nō·ə·sā′, -im·yōō′-) *n.* A method of assaying the amount or other characteristics of a substance by labeling it with a radioactive chemical and combining it with an antibody to induce an immunological reaction.

ra·di·o·i·so·tope (rā′dē·ō·ī′sə·tōp) *n. Physics* A radioactive isotope, usually one produced artificially from a normally stable element: extensively used in biological and physical research and used in medicine for diagnostic and therapeutic purposes.

ra·di·o·lar·i·an (rā′dē·ō·lâr′ē·ən) *n.* Any member of an order *(Radiolaria,* class *Sarcodina)* of marine protozoans having typically a siliceous skeleton enclosing a perforated membrane. —*adj.* Of or pertaining to the *Radiolaria* [<NL *Radiolaria,* name of the order <*radiolus,* dim. of L *radius* ray]

ra·di·o·lo·ca·tion (rā′dē·ō·lō·kā′shən) *n.* Radar.

ra·di·ol·o·gy (rā′dē·ol′ə·jē) *n.* That branch of science that relates to radiant energy and its applications, especially in the diagnosis and treatment of disease. [<RADIO- + -LOGY] —**ra·di·o·log·i·cal** (rā′dē·ə·loj′i·kəl) or **ra′di·o·log′ic** *adj.* —**ra′di·ol′o·gist** *n.*

ra·di·o·lu·cent (rā′dē·ō·lōō′sənt) *adj.* Permeable to X–rays and other forms of electromagnetic radiation. See RADIOPAQUE.

ra·di·o·lu·mi·nes·cence (rā′dē·ō·lōō′mə·nes′·əns) *n.* Luminescence produced by, or resulting from, any form of radiant energy, as X–rays, radioactivity, etc. —**ra′di·o·lu′mi·nes′·cent** *adj.*

ra·di·o·ma·te·ri·al (rā′dē·ō·mə·tir′ē·əl) *n.* Any material that is, or has been made, radioactive.

ra·di·om·e·ter (rā′dē·om′ə·tər) *n.* An instrument for detecting and measuring radiant energy by converting it into mechanical energy, as by the rotation of blackened disks suspended in a vacuum and exposed to sunlight. [< RADIO- + METER[1]] —**ra′di·o·met′ric** (-ō·met′rik) *adj.* —**ra′di·om′e·try** *n.*

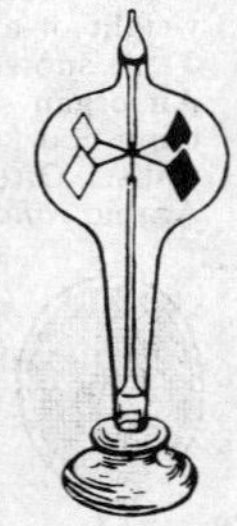
RADIOMETER

ra·di·o·mi·crom·e·ter (rā′dē·ō·mī·krom′ə·tər) *n.* An instrument, consisting primarily of an extremely sensitive thermoelectric couple suspended in a magnetic field, for measuring minute variations of heat.

ra·di·o·mi·met·ic (rā′dē·ō·mi·met′ik) *adj. Physics* Pertaining to or designating any of a class of chemicals, as mustard gas, which produce biological effects similar to and sometimes indistinguishable from those produced by radioactive substances.

ra·di·o·nu·clide (rā′dē·ō·nōō′klīd, -nyōō′-) *n. Physics* A radioactive nuclide.

ra·di·o·paque (rā′dē·ō·pāk′) *adj.* Impermeable to X–rays or other forms of electromagnetic radiation. [<RADIO + OPAQUE]

ra·di·o·phone (rā′dē·ō·fōn′) *n.* **1** Any device for the production or transmission of sound by radiant energy. **2** A radiotelephone. —**ra′di·o·phon′ic** (-fon′ik) *adj.* —**ra′di·oph′o·ny** (-of′ə·nē) *n.*

ra·di·o·pho·tog·ra·phy (rā′dē·ō·fə·tog′rə·fē) *n.* The transmission of a photograph by radio in such a way that each spot on the picture is reproduced by an electric impulse. —**ra′di·o·pho′to·graph** (-fō′tə·graf, -gräf) *n.*

ra·di·o·prax·is (rā′dē·ō·prak′sis) *n.* Radiotherapy.

ra·di·o·scope (rā′dē·ō·skōp′) *n.* An apparatus for detecting radioactivity or X–rays.

ra·di·os·co·py (rā′dē·os′kə·pē) *n.* Examination of opaque bodies with the aid of X–rays or some other form of radiant energy. [<RADIO- + -SCOPY] —**ra′di·o·scop′ic** (-skop′ik) or **·i·cal** *adj.*

ra·di·o·sen·si·tive (rā′dē·ō·sen′sə·tiv) *adj.* **1** Sensitive to X–rays and ultraviolet rays. **2** *Med.* Reducible or destructible by X–rays. as certain tumors.

radio shielding *Aeron.* Metallic covering on the electric wiring and ignition apparatus of an aircraft, intermittently grounded to the frame in order to eliminate disturbances in radio communication.

ra·di·o·sonde (rā′dē·ō·sond′) *n. Meteorol.* A device, attached to a small balloon sent aloft, which measures the pressure, temperature, and humidity of the upper air and radios the data to the ground. Also **ra′di·o·me′te·or·o·graph′** (-mē′tē·ər·ə·graf′, -gräf′). [<RADIO- + F *sonde* sounding]

radio spectrum The full range of frequencies pertaining to and associated with radiant energy; specifically, those frequencies employed in radio and television.

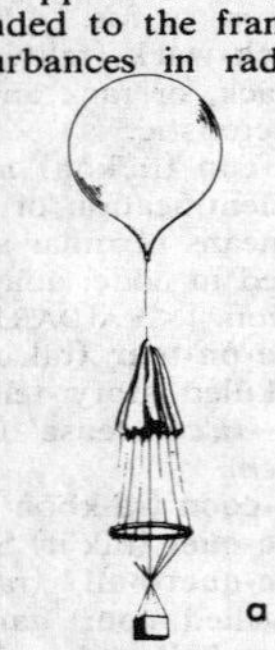

RADIOSONDE
a. Instrument box.

radio star Any of a large number of stars which may be identified and studied by means of the characteristic electromagnetic impulses which they emit.

radio station An installation of all the equipment and apparatus necessary for effective radio communication.

ra·di·o·stron·tium (rā′dē·ō·stron′shəm, -tē·əm) *n.* Any of the synthetic radioactive isotopes of strontium, especially the most stable of them, strontium 90.

ra·di·o·tel·e·gram (rā′dē·ō·tel′ə·gram) *n.* A message sent by radiotelegraphy.

ra·di·o·te·leg·ra·phy (rā′dē·ō·tə·leg′rə·fē) *n.* Telegraphic communication by means of radio waves. —**ra′di·o·tel′e·graph′ic** (-tel′ə·graf′ik) *adj.* —**ra′di·o·tel′e·graph** (-graf, -gräf) *n.*

ra·di·o·tel·e·phone (rā′dē·ō·tel′ə·fōn) *n.* A telephone set that, without the agency of connecting wires, transmits a verbal message to a similar set by means of radio waves. —**ra′di·o·tel′e·phon′ic** (-tel′ə·fon′ik) *adj.* —**ra′di·o·te·leph′o·ny** (-tə·lef′ə·nē) *n.*

radio telescope A sensitive astronomical instrument designed on the principle of a radio receiver, but adapted to intercept and amplify electromagnetic waves in the megacycle range emanating from interstellar space.

ra·di·o·ther·a·py (rā′dē·ō·ther′ə·pe) *n.* The treatment of disease with electromagnetic radiation or with radioactive substances. Also called *actinotherapy.*

ra·di·o·tho·ri·um (rā′dē·ō·thôr′ē·əm, -thō′rē·əm) *n.* A radioactive product of the thorium series, with a half-life of 1.9 years.

ra·di·o·tox·ic (rā′dē·ō·tok′sik) *adj. Med.* Of or pertaining to the toxic effect of radioactive materials, especially radioisotopes. —**ra′di·o·tox·ic′i·ty** (-tok·sis′ə·tē) *n.*

radio transcription An electrically recorded radio program, speech, musical selection, or the like, intended for subsequent broadcasting.

radio tube A vacuum tube for radio.

radio wave Any of a class of electromagnetic waves propagated at frequencies intermediate between those of audible sound and infrared.

rad·ish (rad′ish) *n.* **1** A tall, branching herb *(Raphanus sativus)* of the mustard family. **2** Its pungent, edible root, commonly eaten raw. [< F *radis* < Ital. *radice* < L *radix, radicis* root. Doublet of RADIX.]

ra·di·um (rā′dē·əm) *n.* A luminescent, intensely radioactive metallic element (symbol Ra, atomic number 88) chemically related to barium, occurring in small amounts in uranium ores, emitting alpha and beta particles and gamma rays, and having 16 known isotopes, the most abundant of which has a half-life of 1620 years. See PERIODIC TABLE. [< NL < L *radius* ray]

radium F Polonium of mass 210.

radium therapy The treatment of skin diseases and of cancer by means of radium.

ra·di·us (rā′dē·əs) *n. pl.* **·di·i** (-dē·ī) **1** A straight line from the center of a circle or sphere to its periphery. **2** *Anat.* The thicker and shorter bone of the forearm, on the same side as the thumb. **3** *Bot.* A ray floret of a composite flower; also, a branch of an umbel. **4** *Zool.* **a** In radiolarians and similar organisms, the imaginary line or plane dividing the body into two theoretically equal parts. **b** A ray or radiating part, as, the barb of a feather. **c** A lateral part of a cirriped shell when overlapping others. **5** *Entomol.* One of the main longitudinal veins of an insect's wings. **6** In a sextant, quadrant, etc., a pivoted arm, mounted so as to move radially, as on a graduated arc or circle. **7** *Mech.* A wheel spoke; a rod or bar which with others extends from a common point. **8** A circular area or boundary measured by the length of its radius. **9** Sphere, scope, or limit, as of activity. **10** A fixed limit of travel beyond which higher fares are charged. [< L, orig., rod, spoke of a wheel, hence radius, ray of light. Doublet of RAY]

radius vector *pl.* **radius vectors** or **ra·di·i vec·to·res** (rā′dē·ī vek·tôr′ēz, -tō′rēz) **1** *Math.* **a** The distance from a fixed origin to any point of a curve. **b** The distance from a point to the pole in the polar coordinate or spherical coordinate system. **2** *Astron.* A line from a center of attraction to a body describing an orbit about it.

ra·dix (rā′diks) *n. pl.* **rad·i·ces** (rad′ə·sēz, rā′də-) or **ra·dix·es 1** *Rare* The origin or source. **2** *Math.* A number or symbol used as the basis of a scale of enumeration: 10 is the *radix* of the common system of logarithms. **3** *Bot.* The root of a plant. **4** An original word from which others are derived; radical; root; etymon. [< L, root. Doublet of RADISH.]

Rad·nor·shire (rad′nər·shir) A county of eastern Wales; 471 square miles; county town, Presteigne. Also **Rad′nor.**

Ra·dom (rä′dôm) A city in east central Poland.

ra·dome (rā′dōm) *n. Electronics* A protective housing, radiolucent to radar waves, for the antenna and other equipment of a radar assembly. [< RA(DAR) + DOME]

ra·don (rā′don) *n.* A heavy, radioactive, chemically inert gaseous element (symbol Rn, atomic number 86) having isotopes which are decay products in the several natural radioactive series. See PERIODIC TABLE. [< RAD(IUM) + -ON, as in *neon*]

rad·waste (rad′wāst′) *n.* Radioactive waste.

rad·u·la (raj′o͞o·lə) *n. pl.* **·lae** (-lē) *Zool.* A rasplike organ, the odontophore or lingual ribbon of a mollusk. [< L, scraper < *radere* scrape]—**rad′u·lar** *adj.*

Rae·burn (rā′bərn), **Sir Henry,** 1756–1823, Scottish painter.

Rae·der (rā′dər), **Erich,** 1876–1960, German admiral in World War II.

Ra·fa·el (rä′fä·el′) Spanish form of RAPHAEL. Also *Ital.* **Raf·fa·e·le** (räf′fä·ā′lā) or **Raf·fa·el·lo** (räf′fä·el′lō).

raff (raf) *n.* **1** The rabble; riff-raff. **2** *Scot. & Brit. Dial.* A disorderly collection. [< RIFF-RAFF]

raf·fer·ty rules (raf′ər·tē) *Austral.* No rules at all; rough-and-ready.

raf·fi·a (raf′ē·ə) *n.* **1** A cultivated palm *(Raphia pedunculata)* of Madagascar, the leafstalks of which furnish fiber for making hats, mats, baskets, etc. **2** Its fiber. Also spelled *raphia.* [< Malagasy *rafia*]

raf·fi·nose (raf′ə·nōs) *n. Chem.* A colorless crystalline carbohydrate, $C_{18}H_{32}O_{16}$, having a mildly sweetish taste, found in cottonseed and in the molasses of the sugar beet: it hydrolyzes into fructose, galactose, and glucose. [< F *raffiner* refine + -OSE[2]]

raff·ish (raf′ish) *adj.* **1** Tawdry; gaudy; flashy. **2** Disreputable. [< RAFF + -ISH[1]]

raf·fle [1] (raf′əl) *n.* A form of lottery in which a number of people buy chances on an object. —*v.* **·fled, ·fling** *v.t.* To dispose of by a raffle: often with *off.* —*v.i.* To take part in a raffle. [< OF *rafle* a clean sweep at dice < *rafler* snatch, prob. < Gmc.]—**raf′fler** *n.*

raf·fle [2] (raf′əl) *n.* A jumble of rubbish; tangle: a nautical term. [Prob. < RAFF]

raf·fle·si·a (ra·flē′zhē·ə, -zē·ə) *n.* Any plant of the genus *Rafflesia* (family *Rafflesiaceae*), parasitic on the stems of the Malayan grape, and having huge, stemless, malodorous flowers and no leaves. [<NL, after Sir T. S. *Raffles,* 1781–1826, British governor in Sumatra, who discovered it]—**raf·fle′si·a′ceous** (-zē·ā′shəs) *adj.*

raft [1] (raft, räft) *n.* A float of logs, planks, etc., fastened together for transportation by water. —*v.t.* **1** To transport on a raft. **2** To form into a raft. —*v.i.* **3** To travel by, be employed on, or manage a raft. [< ON *raptr* log]

raft [2] (raft, räft) *n. Colloq.* A large number or an indiscriminate collection of any kind. [< RAFF]

raft·er (raf′tər, räf′-) *n.* A timber or beam giving form, slope, and support to a roof. [OE *ræfter*]

rafts·man (rafts′mən, räfts′-) *n. pl.* **·men** (-mən) One who manages or works on a raft.

rag [1] (rag) *v.t.* **ragged, rag·ging** *Slang* **1** To tease or irritate. **2** To scold. **3** *Brit.* To play a practical joke on. **4** *Brit.* To wreck; make a mess of. —*n. Brit.* A ragging. [? < ON *ragna* curse, swear]

rag [2] (rag) *n.* **1** A torn piece of cloth; a fragment or semblance of anything. **2** *pl.* Cotton or linen textile remnants used in the making of rag paper. **3** *pl.* Tattered or shabby clothing; hence, any clothing: a jocular use. **4** A cloth of any kind, or something resembling one or characterized as such: used humorously or in disparagement. **5** In citrus fruits, the axis and carpellary walls. —**glad rags** *Slang* One's best clothes. —**to chew the rag** *Slang* To talk or argue at great length. [< ON *rögg* tuft or strip of fur]

rag [3] (rag) *n.* **1** A roofing slate rough on one side, and measuring 2 × 3 feet. **2** *Brit.* Any hard rock of cellular or coarsely granular texture. [Origin uncertain]

rag [4] (rag) *v.t.* **ragged, rag·ging** To compose or play in ragtime. —*n.* Ragtime.

rag·a·muf·fin (rag′ə·muf′in) *n.* Anyone, especially a boy, wearing very ragged clothes; a vagabond. [after *Ragamoffyn,* demon in a 15th century mystery play < RAG[2] + fanciful ending]

rag-bag (rag′bag′) *n.* A bag in which rags or scraps of unused cloth are kept.

rag carpet A carpet made from rags woven together by hand.

rag doll A cloth doll stuffed with rags.

rage (rāj) *n.* **1** Violent anger; wrath; fury. **2** Any great violence or intensity, as of a fever or a storm. **3** Extreme eagerness or emotion; ardent desire; great enthusiasm. **4** Any object eagerly sought after; a fad; fashion: Crossword puzzles are all the *rage.* See synonyms under ANGER, VIOLENCE—*v.i.* **raged, rag·ing 1** To speak, act, or move with unrestrained anger; feel or show violent anger. **2** To act or proceed with great violence: The storm *raged* for three days. **3** To spread or prevail uncontrolled, as an epidemic. [< OF < LL *rabia* < L *rabies* madness]—**rag′ing** *adj.* —**rag′ing·ly** *adv.*

rag·ged (rag′id) *adj.* **1** Rent or worn into rags; frayed: a *ragged* coat. **2** Wearing worn, frayed, or shabby garments; ill-dressed. **3** Of rough, broken or uneven character or aspect; harsh; dissonant: *ragged* rocks, *ragged* sounds. **4** Naturally of a rough or shaggy appearance (the original meaning): a *ragged* horse or sheep. See synonyms under ROUGH. —**rag′ged·ly** *adv.* —**rag′ged·ness** *n.*

ragged edge *Colloq.* The extreme or precarious edge; the verge: the *ragged edge* of starvation; *ragged edge* of insanity. —**on the ragged edge** Dangerously near to losing one's self-control, sanity, etc.

ragged lady Fennelflower.

ragged robin A slender perennial European herb *(Lychnis floscuculi)* having red or pink flowers in panicles; the cuckoo flower.

rag·i (rag′ē, rä′gē) *n.* A cereal grass *(Eleusine coracona)* of the East Indies. Also **rag′ee, rag′·gy.** [< Hind. *rāgī*]

rag·lan (rag′lən) *n.* An overcoat or topcoat, the sleeves of which extend in one piece up to the collar. —*adj.* Denoting a garment with such sleeves. [after Lord Fitzroy *Raglan*]

Rag·lan (rag′lən), **Lord Fitzroy,** 1788–1855, English field marshal.

rag·man (rag′man′, -mən) *n. pl.* **·men** (-men′, -mən) One who buys and sells old rags and other waste; a ragpicker.

Rag·na·rök (räg′nä·rœk) In Norse mythology, the twilight of the gods, and the doomsday of the world, preceding its regeneration. Also **Rag′na·rok** (-rok). [< ON < *ragna* of the gods (genitive pl. of *regin*) + *rök* judgment]

ra·gout (ra·go͞o′) *n.* A highly seasoned dish of meat and vegetables stewed; hence, something spicy or piquant. —*v.t.* **ra·gouted** (-go͞od′), **ra·gout·ing** (-go͞o′ing) To make into a ragout. [< F < *ragouter* revive the appetite < *re-* anew + *-à* (< L *ad*) to + *goût* (< L *gustus*) taste]

rag·pick·er (rag′pik′ər) *n.* One who picks up rags and other junk for a livelihood.

rag rug A rug made of rags.

rag·stone (rag′stōn′) *n.* **1** Rag; a rough, sandy, fossiliferous limestone: also **ragg. 2** Stone quarried in thin slabs, as for pavements. Also **ragg′ stone′.**

rag-tag (rag′tag′) *n.* Ragged people; the rabble. Also **rag-tag and bobtail.**

rag·time (rag′tīm′) *n.* **1** A kind of American dance music, developed from about 1890 to 1920, achieving its effects by highly syncopated rhythm in fast time. **2** The rhythm of this dance. [< *ragged time*]

Ra·gu·el (rə·gyo͞o′el) One of the seven archangels of Hebrew and Christian legend.

Ra·gu·sa (rä·go͞o′sä) **1** Italian name for DU-BROVNIK. **2** A city in SE Sicily.

rag·weed (rag′wēd′) *n.* **1** A coarse, very common, annual or perennial herb (genus *Ambrosia*), especially the common ragweed *(A. artemisifolia),* which induces hay fever, and the **great ragweed** *(A. trifida),* a tall species

with stout hairy stem 5 to 15 feet high: also called *hogweed.* 2 *Brit.* The ragwort.

rag·wort (rag′wûrt′) *n.* Any one of several herbs of the genus *Senecio,* as the European ragwort *(S. jacoboea),* a tall, smooth, cottony plant, with bright-yellow flowers.

rah (rä) *interj.* Hurrah! a cheer used chiefly in college yells. [<HURRAH]

Ra·hab (rā′hab) A harlot of Jericho who sheltered two Israelite spies. *Josh.* ii 1.

Ra·hab (rä′hab) In the Old Testament, a symbolical name for Egypt. *Isaiah* li 9.

Ra·hel (rä′həl) German form of RACHEL.

ra·ia (rä′yə, rī′ə) See RAYAH.

Ra·ia·te·a (rä′yä·tā′ä) The largest of the Society Islands in the Leeward group; 92 square miles.

rai·ble (rā′bəl) *v.t. & v.i. Scot.* To gabble.

raid (rād) *n.* **1** A hostile or predatory incursion by a rapidly moving body of troops or an armed vessel; a foray. **2** An attack by military aircraft: an air raid. **3** Any sudden invasion, capture, or irruption, as by the police. **4** An attempt to lower stock prices. See synonyms under INVASION —*v.t.* To make a raid on. —*v.i.* To participate in a raid. [Scottish var. of ROAD] —**raid′er** *n.*

raiding party A body of troops assigned to make a sudden raid in enemy territory.

rail[1] (rāl) *n.* **1** A bar, usually of wood or iron, resting on supports, as in a fence, at the side of a stairway, or capping the bulwarks of a ship; a horizontal wooden piece between panels, joining the stiles; also, a railing. **2** One of a series of parallel bars, of iron or steel, resting upon cross-ties, forming a support and guide for wheels, as of a railway. **3** A railway track considered as a means of transportation: to ship by *rail.* —**to go by rail** To travel by train. —**to ride (someone) on a rail** To put (a person) astride a rail and carry around or beyond the limits of a community, as a punishment. —*v.t.* To furnish or shut in with rails; fence. [<OF *reille* <L *regula.* Doublet of RULE.]

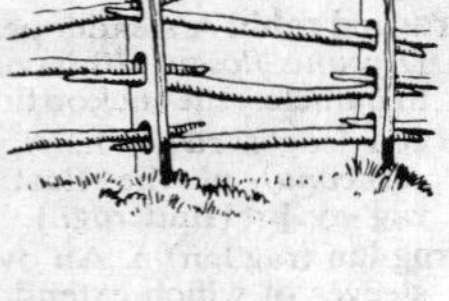

RAIL FENCE

rail[2] (rāl) *n.* **1** Any of numerous marsh-haunting, wading birds (family *Rallidae,* subfamily *Rallinae*) having very short wings, moderately long legs and toes, a short turned-up tail, long compressed bill, and soft, dun-colored plumage; specifically, in North America, the **king rail** *(Rallus elegans),* the **clapper rail** or mud hen *(R. longirostris),* and the sora or **Carolina rail.** They are esteemed as game birds. ◆ Collateral adjective: *ralline.* **2** Any of various other birds of northern Europe, as the corn crake. Also **rail′bird′.** [<OF *raale, ralle,* prob. ult. <L *radere* scratch]

rail[3] (rāl) *v.i.* To use scornful, insolent, or abusive language: with *at* or *against.* —*v.t.* To drive or force by railing. [<F *railler* <Pg. *ralhar* chatter, prob. <L *ragere* shriek. Doublet of RALLY[2].] —**rail′er** *n.*

rail·head (rāl′hed′) *n.* **1** On an incompleted railroad, the farthest point to which rails have been laid. **2** That point on a railroad from which a military unit draws its supplies, ammunition, etc.

rail·ing (rā′ling) *n.* **1** A series of rails; a balustrade. **2** Rails, or material from which rails are made.

rail·ler·y (rā′lər·ē) *n. pl.* **·ler·ies** Merry jesting or teasing; a merry jest or bantering speech. [<F *raillerie* jesting]

rail·road (rāl′rōd′) *n.* **1** A graded road, having metal rails supported by ties or sleepers, for the passage of rolling stock drawn by locomotives. **2** The system of tracks, stations, rolling stock, etc., used in transportation by rail. **3** The corporation or persons owning or operating such a system. —*v.t.* **1** To transport by railroad. **2** *U.S. Colloq.* To rush or force with great speed or without deliberation: to *railroad* a bill through Congress. **3** *U.S. Slang* To cause to be imprisoned on false charges or without fair trial. —*v.i.* **4** To work on a railroad.

rail·road·er (rāl′rō′dər) *n.* One who works on a railroad.

rail·road·ing (rāl′rō′ding) *n.* The construction, operation, or business of a railroad.

rail-split·ter (rāl′split′ər) *n.* One who splits logs into fence rails. —**the Rail-Splitter** Abraham Lincoln.

rail·way (rāl′wā′) *n.* **1** A railroad: the common British term. **2** A trackway or set of rails, as in a warehouse or factory, for convenience in handling heavy articles, etc.: a parcel *railway* in a store.

railway post office Formerly, a government post office in a railroad car, sometimes occupying a whole car.

rai·ment (rā′mənt) *n. Archaic* Wearing apparel; clothing; garb. See synonyms under DRESS. [Aphetic var. of *arrayment* <ARRAY + -MENT]

Rai·mon·do (rī·mōn′dō) Italian form of RAYMOND. Also *Sp.* **Rai·mun·do** (rī·mo͞on′dō).

rain (rān) *n.* **1** The condensed vapor of the atmosphere falling in drops. ◆ Collateral adjective: *hyetal.* **2** The fall of such drops. **3** A fall or shower of anything in the manner of rain, or the substance poured down: a *rain* of bombs. **4** A rainstorm; shower; in the plural, the rainy season in a tropical country; also, a rainy region of the Atlantic Ocean. —*v.i.* **1** To fall from the clouds in drops of water: usually with *it* as the subject. **2** To fall like rain, as tears. **3** To send or pour down rain: said of clouds, God, etc. —*v.t.* **4** To send down like rain; shower. ◆ Homophones: *reign, rein.* [OE *regn*]

rain·band (rān′band′) *n. Astron.* A dark band in the solar spectrum, caused by the presence of water vapor in the atmosphere.

rain·bow (rān′bō′) *n.* **1** An arch of light formed opposite the sun during or after the close of a shower, exhibiting the colors of the spectrum, and caused by refraction, reflection, and dispersion of light in drops of water falling through the air. **2** Hence, any brilliant display of color. [OE *regnboga*]

Rainbow Bridge National Monument A region in southern Utah, site of a natural bridge; 160 acres; established, 1910.

rainbow cactus A cactus *(Echinocereus rigidissimus)* of the SW United States having red and white spines and red flowers.

rain·bow-chas·er (rān′bō′chā′sər) *n.* One who seeks the legendary pot of gold at the foot of the rainbow; a visionary.

rainbow trout See under TROUT.

rain check The stub of a ticket to an outdoor event, as a baseball game, entitling the holder to free admission at a future date if for any reason the event is called off: used figuratively of any postponed invitation.

rain·coat (rān′kōt′) *n.* A cloak or coat intended to be worn in rainy weather.

rain crow The yellow-billed or the black-billed cuckoo (genus *Coccyzus*), so called from the belief among farmers that its cry is a sign of rain.

rain·drop (rān′drop′) *n.* A drop of rain.

rain·fall (rān′fôl′) *n.* **1** A fall of rain. **2** *Meteorol.* The amount of water precipitated in a given region over a stated time, as rain, hail, snow, or the like: measured in inches.

rain gage An instrument for measuring rainfall at a given place or during a given time; a pluviometer. Also **rain gauge.**

Rai·nier (rā·nir′, rā′nir), **Mount** An extinct volcano in the Cascade Range, SW Washington; 14,408 feet; in Mount Rainier National Park.

rain-mak·er (rān′mā′kər) *n.* One reputedly able to cause rain; specifically, among certain American Indians, one who brings rain by incantation.

rain·out (rān′out′) *n.* **1** *Physics* Precipitation of radioactive water droplets from cloud masses resulting from an underwater nuclear explosion. **2** A baseball game postponed because of rain. **3** Postponement of an outdoor event, esp. a baseball game.

rain·proof (rān′pro͞of′) *adj.* Impervious to or shedding rain: said of garments. —*n. Brit.* A raincoat.

rain shadow *Meteorol.* An area of relatively small average rainfall on the leeward side of mountain barriers which serve to break the prevailing rain-bearing winds.

rain·spout (rān′spout′) *n.* A waterspout (def. 2).

rain·storm (rān′stôrm′) *n.* A storm accompanied by rain.

rain water Water that falls or has fallen directly from the clouds in the form of rain.

rain·wear (rān′wâr′) *n.* Clothing for rainy weather, esp. raincoats, rubbers, galoshes, ponchos, etc.

rain·y (rā′nē) *adj.* **rain·i·er, rain·i·est** Characterized by, abounding in, or bringing rain. —**rain′i·ly** *adv.* —**rain′i·ness** *n.*

rainy day A time of need; hard times.

Rain·y Lake (rā′nē) A lake in northern Minnesota and SW Ontario; 50 miles long; 350 square miles.

raise (rāz) *v.* **raised, rais·ing** *v.t.* **1** To cause to move upward or to a higher level; lift; elevate. **2** To place erect; set up. **3** To construct or build; erect. **4** To make greater in amount, size, or value: to *raise* the price of corn. **5** To advance or elevate in rank, estimation, etc. **6** To increase the strength, intensity, or degree of. **7** To breed; grow: to *raise* chickens or tomatoes. **8** *U.S.* To rear (children, a family, etc.). **9** To give utterance to; cause to be heard: to *raise* a hue and cry. **10** To cause; occasion, as a smile or laugh. **11** To stir to action or emotion; arouse. **12** To waken; animate or reanimate: to *raise* the dead. **13** To gather together; obtain or collect, as an army, capital, etc. **14** To bring up for consideration, as a question. **15** To cause to swell or become lighter; leaven. **16** To put an end to, as a siege. **17** In poker, to bet more than. **18** *Naut.* To cause to appear above the horizon, as land or a ship, by approaching nearer. **19** *Scot.* To madden; enrage. —*v.i.* **20** *Colloq.* To cough up phlegm. **21** *Dial.* To rise or arise. **22** In poker, to make a raise. —**to raise Cain** (or **the devil, the dickens, a rumpus,** etc.) *Colloq.* To make a great disturbance; stir up confusion. —**to raise steam** To get or produce steam, as in a boiler, for the purpose of starting up a steam engine. —*n.* **1** The act of raising, in any sense; specifically, an increase, as of wages or a bet. **2** *Brit. Dial.* Something raised; an ascent; mound. ◆ Homophone: *raze.* [<ON *reisa* lift, set up. Akin to OE *rǣran* rear.] ◆ In British usage, *rise* is used for an increase in wages. —**rais′er** *n.*

Synonyms (verb): aggrandize, elevate, erect, exalt, lift, rear, uplift. See HEIGHTEN, INCREASE, PROMOTE. *Antonyms*: degrade, depress, humble, lower, reduce, sink.

raised (rāzd) *adj.* **1** Elevated in low relief. **2** Made with yeast or leaven.

rai·sin (rā′zən) *n.* A grape of a special sort dried in the sun or in an oven, and used for a dessert or in cookery. [<OF <L *racemus* bunch of grapes]

rais·ing (rā′zing) *n.* **1** The act or process of causing to rise, in any sense. **2** A gathering of persons for the purpose of erecting the frame of a building: also **raising bee.**

Rai·sin River (rā′zən) A river in SE Michigan, flowing 115 miles SE to Lake Erie.

rai·son d'ê·tre (re·zôṅ′ de′tr′) *French* Literally, a reason for being; a reason or excuse for existing.

rai·son·né (re·zô·nā′) *adj. French* Arranged analytically or systematically; logical: a catalog *raisonné.*

Rai·su·li (ra·so͞o′lē), **Ahmed ibn-Muhammed,** 1875?–1925, Berber brigand in Morocco.

raj (räj) *n.* In India, sovereignty; rule. [<Hind. *rāj*]

ra·ja (rä′jə) *n.* A Hindu prince or chief of a tribal state in India; also, a Malay or Javanese ruler: often a mere title of distinction. Also **ra′jah.** [<Hind. *rājā* <Skt. *rājan* king]

Ra·ja·go·pa·la·cha·ria (rä′jə·gō·pä′lä·chä′ryə) **Chakravarti,** 1879–1972, governor general of India 1948–50.

Raj·ab (ruj′əb) See under CALENDAR (Mohammedan). [<Arabic]

Ra·ja·sthan (rä′jə·stän) A constituent State of NW India, formed by the merger of most of the Rajputana States (1948–50) and the former state of Ajmer (1956); 132,077 square miles; capital, Jaipur. Also **Ra′ja·stan.**

Raj·kot (räj′kōt) The capital city of the former state of Saurashtra, western India, in NW Bombay State after 1956.

Raj·put (räj′po͝ot) *n.* One of a powerful and warlike Hinducaste, said to be a branch of the Kshatriyas, which gives its name to Rajputana. Also **Raj′poot.** [<Hind. *rājpūt* prince <Skt. *rājaputra* <*rājan* a king, ruler + *putra* son]

Raj·pu·ta·na (räj′po͝o·tä′nə) A region in NW India, land of the Rajput princes; 134,959

square miles; roughly equivalent to the constituent State of Rajasthan.

Rajputana States The former princely states in Rajputana, merged 1948–50, to form Rajasthan, except for four included in Bombay State; 132,559 square miles.

rake[1] (rāk) *n.* A toothed implement for drawing together loose material, or making a surface loose. —*v.* **raked, rak·ing** *v.t.* **1** To scrape or gather together with or as with a rake. **2** To smooth, clean, or prepare with a rake: to *rake* a lawn. **3** To gather by diligent effort; scrape together. **4** To search or examine carefully. **5** To direct heavy gunfire along the length of, as a ship or column of troops; enfilade. —*v.i.* **6** To use a rake. **7** To scrape or pass roughly or violently; with *across, over,* etc. **8** To make a search. —**to rake in** *Colloq.* To earn or acquire (money, etc.) in large quantities. [OE *raca*] —**rak'er** *n.*

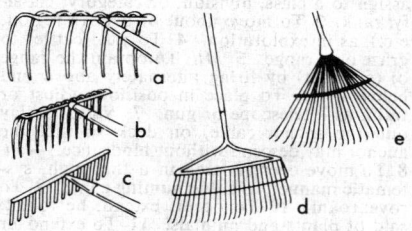

TYPES OF RAKES
a. Refuse. *b.* Clam. *c.* Garden.
d. Steel lawn. *e.* Broom lawn.

rake[2] (rāk) *v.* **raked, rak·ing** *v.i.* To lean from the perpendicular, as a ship's masts. —*v.t.* To cause to lean; incline. —*n.* Inclination from the perpendicular or horizontal, as of the sustaining surfaces of an airplane, or the edge of a cutting tool. [Origin uncertain. Cf. G *ragen* project.] —**raked** *adj.*

rake[3] (rāk) *n.* A dissolute, lewd person; debauchee. —*v.i.* **raked, rak·ing** To play the rake; live a lewd, dissolute life; with *it.* [Short for RAKEHELL]

rake[4] (rāk) *v.i.* **raked, rak·ing 1** To hunt with the nose to the ground, thus following or track rather than by wind: said of hunting dogs. **2** To fly after game: said of hawks; also, to fly wide of the game. [OE *racian* go forward, proceed]

rake·hell (rāk'hel') *adj. Archaic* Recklessly abandoned and dissolute: also **rake'hell'y.** —*n.* A rake; a profligate debauchee. [ME *rakel* rash, wild; refashioned after RAKE[1] + HELL. Cf. ON *reikal* reckless.]

rake–off (rāk'ôf', -of') *n. U.S. Slang* A share, as of profits; commission; rebate, usually illegitimate.

rak·i (rak'ē, rä'kē) *n. Turkish* An aromatic liquor flavored with mastic; mastic brandy; also, a coarse liquor made from grain spirit. Compare ARRACK. Also **rak'ee.** [< Turkish *rāqi* < Arabic *'araq.* Akin to ARRACK.]

rak·ish[1] (rā'kish) *adj.* **1** *Naut.* Having the masts unusually inclined: usually connoting a suggestion of speed. **2** Dashing; jaunty. [< RAKE[2]; def. 2 infl. by *rakish*[2]] —**rak'ish·ly** *adv.* —**rak'ish·ness** *n.*

rak·ish[2] (rā'kish) *adj.* Like or behaving like a rake; dissolute; profligate. —**rak'ish·ly** *adv.* —**rak'ish·ness** *n.*

Rá·kó·czy March (rä'kō·tsē) A national patriotic song of Hungary. [after Francis *Rákóczy,* 1676–1735, Hungarian patriot]

râle (räl) *n. Pathol.* A sound additional to that of normal respiration, heard on auscultation of the chest and indicative of the presence, nature, or stage of a disease. [< F, rattle]

Ra·leigh (rô'lē) The capital of North Carolina.

Ra·leigh (rô'lē), **Sir Walter,** 1552–1618, English courtier, colonizer of Roanoke, soldier, and author; beheaded. Also spelled **Ra'legh.**

Ra·lik Chain (rä'lik) The western group of the Marshall Islands, including Kwajalein, Eniwetok, Bikini, Rongelap, Rongerik and others.

ral·len·tan·do (ral'ən·tan'dō, *Ital.* räl'len·tän'dō) *adv. Music* Gradually slower. [< Ital. ppr. of *rallentare* slow down < *lento* slow < L *lentus*]

ral·li·form (ral'ə·fôrm) *adj.* Pertaining to or like the rails. See RAIL[2]. [< NL *rallus* (< OF *ralle* rail[2]) + -FORM]

ral·line (ral'in, -in) *adj.* Of, pertaining, or belonging to the rail subfamily of birds (*Rallinae*). [< NL *rallus* rail[2]]

ral·ly[1] (ral'ē) *n. pl.* **·lies 1** An assembling or reassembling, as of scattered troops. **2** A rapid recovery of a normal condition after exhaustion or depression: a *rally* from sickness, a *rally* in stocks. **3** A mass meeting to arouse enthusiasm. **4** In tennis, the interchange of several strokes before one side wins the point. —*v.* **·lied, ·ly·ing** *v.t.* **1** To bring together and restore to effective discipline: to *rally* fleeing troops. **2** To summon up or revive: to *rally* one's spirits. **3** To bring together for common action. —*v.i.* **4** To return to effective discipline or action: The enemy *rallied.* **5** To unite for common action. **6** To make a partial or complete return to a normal condition. **7** In tennis, to engage in a rally. See synonyms under ENCOURAGE. [< F *rallier* < *re-* again + *allier* join. See ALLY.] —**ral'li·er** *n.*

ral·ly[2] (ral'ē) *v.t. & v.i.* To attack with raillery; joke; tease; banter. See synonyms under RIDICULE. [< F *railler* rail. Doublet of RAIL[3].] —**ral'li·er** *n.*

Ralph (ralf, *Brit.* rāf) A masculine personal name. Also *Lat.* **Ra·dul·phus** (ra·dul'fəs). [< Gmc. house wolf]

ram (ram) *n.* **1** A male sheep. **2** An instrument or device for driving, forcing, or crushing by heavy blows or thrusts; specifically, a battering-ram, the striking weight of a pile driver or steamhammer, or the plunger of a force pump. **3** Formerly, a projection or beak on the bow of a warship, for crushing or cutting into an opposing vessel; also, a warship constructed with such a beak. **4** An instrument for raising water by pressure of condensed air; a hydraulic ram. —*v.t.* **rammed, ram·ming 1** To strike with or as with a ram; dash against. **2** To drive or force down or into something. **3** To cram; stuff. [OE] —**ram'mer** *n.*

Ram (ram) *Astron.* The zodiacal constellation Aries.

Ra·ma (rä'mə) In Hindu mythology, the name of three heroes, especially that of Ramachandra.

Ra·ma·chan·dra (rä'mə·chun'drə) The hero of the *Ramayana,* called the seventh avatar of Vishnu.

Ram·a·dan (ram'ə·dän') *n.* The Mohammedan ninth month, the time of the annual fast of thirty days; also, the fast. See under CALENDAR (Mohammedan). Also **Ram'a·dhan', Ram'a·zan'** (-zän'). [< Arabic *ramaḍān,* lit., the hot month]

Ra·ma·krish·na (rä'mä·krish'nə), 1834–86, religious name of Gadadhar Chatterji, a Hindu mystic and religious teacher, regarded as a divine incarnation by his disciples.

Ra·man (rä'mən), **Sir Chandrasekhara Venkata,** 1888–1970, Indian physicist.

Raman effect (rä'mən) *Physics* The scattering of monochromatic light by a medium, in frequencies both equal to and other than the frequency of the incident light, because of a gain or loss in quanta during transmission. [after Sir Chandrasekhara Venkata *Raman*]

Ra·ma·pi·the·cus (rä'mə·pith'ə·kəs) *n.* a manlike primate, originally discovered in the Siwalik Range of NW India. [< RAMA + Gk *pithēkos* ape]

Ra·ma·ya·na (rä·mä'yə·nə) A Hindu epic poem in seven books, of about 400 B.C. Compare MAHABHARATA. [< Skt. *Rāmāyana* < *Rāma* Rama + *-ayana* relating to]

ram·ble (ram'bəl) *v.i.* **·bled, ·bling 1** To walk about freely and aimlessly; roam. **2** To write or talk aimlessly or without sequence of ideas. **3** To proceed with turns and twists; meander. —*n.* **1** The act of rambling; an aimless movement with change of direction; a leisurely stroll. **2** A meandering path; maze. [Origin unknown]

Synonyms (verb): range, roam, rove, stray, stroll, wander. See WANDER.

ram·bler (ram'blər) *n.* **1** One who or that which rambles. **2** Any of several varieties of roses, as the crimson rambler (*Rosa bar-*

bierana), with climbing stems and huge clusters of small or medium-sized flowers.

Rambler, The A semiweekly publication, 1750–52, published and written for the most part by Dr. Samuel Johnson.

ram·bling (ram'bling) *adj.* Showing absence of plan or system; aimless; wandering. —**ram'bling·ly** *adv.*

Ram·bouil·let (ram'boo·lā, *Fr.* rän·boo·ye') *n.* A variety of merino sheep bred in France for meat and wool. [from *Rambouillet,* a town in northern France]

ram·bunc·tious (ram·bungk'shəs) *adj. U.S. Colloq.* Rude and boisterous; rough and uncontrollable. [Prob. < RAM + alter. of BUMPTIOUS]

ram·bu·tan (ram·boo'tən) *n.* **1** The spiny, bright–red, pleasantly acid fruit of an East Indian and Malaysian tree (*Nephelium lappaceum*). **2** The tree that bears it. [< Malay < *rambut* hair]

Ra·mée (rə·mā'), **Louise de la** See OUIDA.

ram·e·kin (ram'ə·kin) *n.* **1** A seasoned dish of bread crumbs baked with eggs and cheese. **2** A dish in which ramekins are baked. **3** Any dish used both for baking and serving. Also **ram'e·quin.** [< F *ramequin*]

ra·men·tum (rə·men'təm) *n. pl.* **·ta** (-tə) **1** A part of something scraped off; a minute part. **2** *Bot.* A thin, membranous, chaffy scale, formed on the surface of leaves, the stems of ferns, etc.: an outgrowth from the epidermis. [< L, scraping < *radere* scrape] —**ram·en·ta·ceous** (ram'ən·tā'shəs) *adj.*

Ram·e·ses (ram'ə·sez) Name of 12 Egyptian monarchs: also spelled *Ramses.* —**Rameses II,** 1292–25 B.C., built many temples; sometimes said to be the pharaoh who oppressed the Israelites.

ra·met (rā'mit) *n. Bot.* Any individual member of a clon. [< L *ramus* branch]

Ram·gan·ga (räm·gung'gə) A river in northern Uttar Pradesh, India, flowing about 350 miles SW and SE to the Ganges.

ram·ie (ram'ē) *n.* **1** A shrubby Chinese and East Indian perennial (*Boehmeria nivea*) of the nettle family, with numerous rodlike stems and large heart-shaped leaves. **2** The fine, glossy bast fiber yielded by its stem, used for cordage and certain coarse textile fabrics. Also **ram'ee.** [< Malay *rami*]

ram·i·fi·ca·tion (ram'ə·fə·kā'shən) *n.* **1** The act or process of ramifying. **2** *Bot.* The arrangement of branches or parts, as on a plant; also, one of the parts. **3** An offshoot or subdivision.

ram·i·form (ram'ə·fôrm) *adj.* **1** Branch-shaped. **2** Branched. [< L *ramus* branch + -FORM]

ram·i·fy (ram'ə·fi) *v.t. & v.i.* **·fied, ·fy·ing** To divide or spread out into or as to branches; branch out. [< F *ramifier* < Med. L *ramificare* < L *ramus* branch + *facere* make]

ram·il·lie (ram'ə·lē) *n.* A type of wig with a plaited tail, worn in 18th century England: named in honor of the British victory at Ramillies. Also **ram'i·lie, ram'i·lies, ram'il·lies.**

Ram·il·lies (ram'ə·lēz, *Fr.* rä·me·ye') A village in central Belgium; scene of Marlborough's victory over French forces, 1706. Also **Ra·mil-Ois–Of·fus** (rä·me·yēō·fü').

ram·mish (ram'ish) *adj.* **1** Like a ram; strong-scented. **2** Lustful. Also **ram'my.** —**ram'mish·ness** *n.*

ram·jet (ram'jet') *n.* A type of jet engine which provides continuous jet propulsion on the principle of the athodyd.

Ra·món (rä·mōn') Spanish form of RAYMOND.

Ra·món y Ca·jal (rä·mōn' ē kä·häl'), **Santiago,** 1852–1934, Spanish histologist.

ra·mose (rā'mōs, rə·mōs') *adj.* **1** Branching. **2** Consisting of or having branches. [< L *ramosus* < *ramus* branch]

ra·mous (rā'məs) *adj.* **1** Of, pertaining to, or like branches. **2** Ramose. [See RAMOSE]

ramp[1] (ramp) *n.* **1** An inclined passageway or roadway, as between floors or different levels of a building. **2** In building, a concave part at the top or cap of a railing, wall, or coping. [< F *rampe* < *ramper* climb]

ramp[2] (ramp) *v.i.* **1** To rear up on the hind legs and stretch out the forepaws. **2** *Her.* To be in a rampant or threatening position.

3 To act in a violent or threatening manner; storm; rampage. — *n.* The act of ramping. [<OF *ramper* climb]

ram·page (ram′pāj) *n.* Boisterous agitation or excitement; a dashing about with anger or violence. — *v.i.* (ram·pāj′) **·paged, ·pag·ing 1** To rush or act violently. **2** To storm; rage. [Prob. <RAMP[2]] — **ram·pag′er** *n.*

ram·pa·geous (ram·pā′jəs) *adj.* Violent; boisterous. — **ram·pa′geous·ly** *adv.* — **ram·pa′geous·ness** *n.*

ram·pan·cy (ram′pən·sē) *n.* The condition or quality of being rampant.

ram·pant (ram′pənt) *adj.* **1** Exceeding all bounds; unrestrained; wild. **2** Widespread; unchecked, as an erroneous belief or superstition. **3** Standing on the hind legs; rearing; leaping: said of a quadruped. **4** *Her.* Standing on the sinister hind leg, with both forelegs elevated, the dexter above the sinister, and the head in profile: said of a beast of prey. **5** *Archit.* Springing from points on an inclined plane. [<OF, ppr. of *ramper* climb] — **ram′pant·ly** *adv.*

RAMPANT

ram·part (ram′pärt, -pərt) *n.* **1** The embankment surrounding a fort, on which the parapet is raised: sometimes including the parapet. **2** A bulwark or defense. — *v.t.* To supply with or as with ramparts; fortify. [<F *rempart* < *remparer* fortify < *re-* again + *emparer* prepare <L *ante* before + *parare* prepare]

Synonyms (noun): barbican, barricade, barrier, breastwork, bulwark, defense, embankment, fence, fortification, guard, mole, mound, outwork, security, wall.

ram·pike (ram′pīk′) *n. Canadian* The bleached skeleton of a tree killed by fire: also *ranpike.* Also **ram′pole′** (-pōl′).

ram·pi·on (ram′pē·ən) *n.* **1** A European perennial *(Campanula rapunculus)* cultivated in gardens for its root, which is eaten as a salad. **2** One of various similar plants, as the horned rampion (genus *Phyteuma*), bearing spikes of blue flowers. [<Ital. *ra(m)ponzolo* <L *rapum* turnip]

Ram·pur (räm′po͝or) A former princely state in north central India, included (1949) in Uttar Pradesh State; 894 square miles; also, a city, its capital.

ram·rod (ram′rod′) *n.* **1** A rod used to drive home the charge of a muzzleloading gun or pistol. **2** A similar rod used for cleaning the barrel of a rifle, etc.

Ram·say (ram′zē), **Allan,** 1686–1758, Scottish poet. — **James Andrew** See DALHOUSIE, MARQUIS OF. — **Sir William,** 1852–1916, Scottish chemist. — **Sir William Mitchell,** 1851–1939, Scottish classicist and geologist.

Ram·ses (ram′sēz) See RAMESES.

Rams·gate (ramz′gāt, *Brit.* -git) A port on the North Sea in eastern Kent, England; a seaside resort.

ram·shack·le (ram′shak′əl) *adj.* About to go to pieces from age and neglect; shaky; unsteady. [Origin uncertain]

ram·son (ram′zən, -sən) *n.* **1** A species of garlic *(Allium ursinum)*; broad-leaved garlic. **2** Its root, used for salads. [OE *hrameson,* pl. of *hramsa*]

ram-stam (ram′stam′, räm′stäm′) *Brit. Dial. & Scot. adj.* Rash; thoughtless; precipitate. — *n.* **1** A hasty and venturesome person. **2** Recklessness. — *adv.* With rashness; heedlessly.

ram·til (ram′til) *n.* An annual herb *(Guizotia abyssinica)* cultivated in Abyssinia and India for its oil-producing seeds, **ramtil seeds.** Also called *Niger seed.* [<Hind.]

ram·u·lose (ram′yə·lōs) *adj. Bot.* Bearing many small branches. [<L *ramulosus* < *ramulus,* dim. of *ramus* branch]

ra·mus (rā′məs) *n. pl.* **·mi** (-mī) **1** A branch. **2** *Biol.* One division of a forked structure, as the branch of a nerve, etc. [<L, branch]

ran (ran) Past tense of RUN.

Ran (rän) In Norse mythology, the wife of Ægir and goddess of the sea.

Ra·na (rä′nä) *n.* Prince: formerly the title of a ruling chief in various parts of India. [< Hind.]

ra·nar·i·um (rə·nâr′ē·əm) *n. pl.* **·nar·i·a** (-nâr′ē·ə) A place where frogs are raised or kept. [<L *rana* frog]

rance (rans) *n.* A fine hard stone, dull red in color, with blue and white markings; Belgian marble. [<F]

ranch (ranch) *n.* **1** An establishment for rearing or grazing cattle, sheep, horses, etc., in large herds. **2** The buildings, personnel, and lands connected with it. **3** A large farm: a fruit *ranch.* Also **ranche.** — *v.i.* To manage or work on a ranch. [<Sp. *rancho* mess]

ranch·er (ran′chər) *n.* **1** The owner of a ranch. **2** One who works on a ranch; a cowboy.

ran·che·ro (ran·châr′ō) *n. pl.* **·ros** *SW U.S.* A rancher. [<Sp.]

ranch·ing (ran′ching) *n.* **1** The operation of a ranch. **2** Work on a ranch.

ranch·man (ranch′mən) *n. pl.* **·men** (-mən) **1** A herdsman on a ranch. **2** The owner of a ranch; a rancher.

ran·cho (ran′chō, rän′-) *n. pl.* **·chos** *SW U.S.* **1** A hut or group of huts, in which ranchmen lodge. **2** A stock farm; ranch. [<Sp.]

ran·cid (ran′sid) *adj.* Having the peculiar tainted smell of oily substances that have begun to spoil owing to oxidation or hydrolysis; rank; sour. Compare SWEET. [<L *rancidus* < *rancere* be rancid]

ran·cid·i·ty (ran·sid′ə·tē) *n.* **1** The quality or state of being rancid. **2** A rancid smell or taste. Also **ran′cid·ness.**

ran·cor (rang′kər) *n.* Bitter and vindictive enmity; malice; spitefulness. Also *Brit.* **ran′cour.** See synonyms under ENMITY, HATRED. [<OF <L < *rancere* be rank] — **ran′cor·ous** *adj.* — **ran′cor·ous·ly** *adv.* — **ran′cor·ous·ness** *n.*

rand[1] (rand) *n.* **1** In shoe manufacturing, a strip of leather at the heel of a shoe to which the lifts are attached. **2** *Brit. Dial. & Scot.* A river border overgrown with reeds, or the unplowed border round a field; margin; strip. [OE, border, edge]

rand[2] (rand, ränd) *n.* The standard monetary unit of South Africa, worth in 1964 about $1.40. [< THE RAND]

Rand (rand), **The** See WITWATERSRAND.

ran·dan (ran′dan, ran·dan′) *n.* **1** A boat rowed by three persons, the one amidships having two oars and the others one each. **2** This style of rowing. [Origin uncertain]

ran·dem (ran′dəm) *adv.* With three horses harnessed one in front of the other. — *n.* A team or vehicle driven randem. Also **ran′dem-tan′dem.** [<RANDOM, on analogy with *tandem*]

RANDEM

Ran·dolph (ran′dolf), **A(sa) Philip,** born 1889, U.S. labor leader. — **John,** 1773–1833, U. S. statesman: known as *Randolph of Roanoke.* — **Peyton,** 1723?–75, American patriot; first president, Continental Congress, 1774–75.

ran·dom (ran′dəm) *n.* **1** Want of definite aim or intention. **2** Something done, made, or chosen without method or purpose. **3** *Printing* A sloping board for holding galleys of type matter intended for making up forms. — **at random** Without definite purpose or aim; haphazardly. — *adj.* **1** Done or chosen without definite aim or deliberate purpose; chance; casual. **2** In statistics, erratic. [<OF *randon* force, violence < *randonner, rander* move rapidly, gallop] — **ran′dom·ly** *adv.*

random sample *Stat.* A limited group of individuals, cases, or observations, so assembled from the total array as to be truly representative of its characteristics, properties, trends, and the like. Also **random selection.**

ran·dy (ran′dē) *Scot. adj.* **1** Disorderly; riotous; also, coarse. **2** Lewd; lustful. — *n.* **1** An impudent beggar. **2** A boisterous, coarse, or loose woman; also, a virago.

ra·nee (rä′nē) See RANI.

rang (rang) Past tense of RING[2].

range (rānj) *n.* **1** The area over which anything moves, operates, or is distributed. **2** *U.S.* An extensive tract of land over which cattle, sheep, etc., roam and graze. **3** *U.S.* Pasturage; grazing ground. **4** *Bot. & Zool.* The geographical area throughout which a specific plant or animal exists. **5** The extent or scope of something: the whole *range* of politics. **6** The extent to which any power can be made effective: *range* of vision; *range* of influence. **7** The extent of variation of anything: the temperature *range.* **8** The extent of possible variation in pitch: said of musical instruments or the voice. **9** A line, row, or series, as of mountains. **10** *U.S.* A row of townships, each six miles square, numbered east or west from a base meridian. **11** *Rare* Rank; order. **12** The horizontal distance between a gun and its target. **13** The horizontal distance covered by a projectile. **14** A place for shooting at a mark: a rifle *range.* **15** In archery, the number of ends shot at each given distance: compare ROUND. **16** A large cooking stove for conducting several cooking operations at one time. **17** *Stat.* The inclusive difference between the extreme values in any series of variable data: a *range* of 20 from a value of 0 to a value of 19. — *adj.* Of or pertaining to a range. — *v.* **ranged, rang·ing** *v.t.* **1** To place or arrange in definite order, as in rows or lines. **2** To assign to a class, division, or category; classify; rank. **3** To move about or over (a region, etc.), as in exploration. **4** To put (cattle) to graze on a range. **5** *Mil.* To obtain the range of (a target) by firing alternately above and below it. **6** To place in position; adjust or train, as a telescope or gun. **7** *Naut.* To lay out (the anchor cable) on deck so that the anchor may descend without hindrance. — *v.i.* **8** To move over an area in a thorough, systematic manner, as a dog hunting game. **9** To rove; roam. **10** To occur; extend; be found: said of plants and animals. **11** To extend or proceed: The shot *ranged* to the right. **12** To exhibit variation within specified limits: weights *ranging* from 20 to 50 pounds. **13** To lie in the same direction, line, etc. **14** *Mil.* To be capable of achieving a specified range (def. 12): That old cannon *ranged* about one mile. See synonyms under RAMBLE, WANDER. [<OF < *ranger, rengier* arrange < *renc* row <Gmc. Doublet of RANK[1].]

range finder An instrument with which to determine the distance of an object or target from a given point, as from a gun.

Range·ley Lakes (rānj′lē) A chain of lakes in western Maine.

rang·er (rān′jər) *n.* **1** One who or that which ranges; a rover. **2** One of an armed band, usually mounted, designed to protect large tracts of country. **3** One of a herd of cattle that feeds on a range. **4** *Brit.* A government official in charge of a royal forest or park: formerly a gamekeeper. **5** *U.S.* A warden employed in patrolling forest tracts. — **rang′er·ship** *n.*

Rang·er (rān′jər) *n.* One of a select group of U. S. soldiers who were trained for raiding action on enemy territory: the equivalent of the English *Commando.*

range rake A T-shaped instrument for obtaining quick angular measurements in correcting deviations in the range of a gun.

Ran·gi·ro·a (rän′gi·rō′ä) Largest of the Tuamotu islands, consisting of 20 islets around a lagoon 45 miles long and 15 miles wide.

Rang·i·tik·ei (räng′gi·tik′ē) A river in southern North Island, New Zealand, flowing 115 miles SW to Cook Strait.

Ran·goon The capital of Myanmar, a port city on the **Yangon River,** a marine estuary formed at Rangoon by the junction of two inland rivers, flowing 25 miles SE to the Andaman Sea. Also **Yangon.**

rang·y (rān′jē) *adj.* **rang·i·er, rang·i·est 1** Disposed to roam, or adapted for roving, as cattle. **2** Having long legs adapted to a long, limber gait. **3** Having long thin arms and legs: said of a person. **4** Affording wide range; roomy. **5** Resembling a mountain range.

ra·ni (rä′nē) *n.* **1** The wife of a raja or prince. **2** A reigning Hindu queen or princess. Also spelled *ranee.* [<Hind.]

Ran·jit Singh (run′jēt siṅ′hə), 1780–1839, maharajah of the Punjab; founded Sikh empire. Also *Runjeet Singh.*

rank[1] (rangk) *n.* **1** A series of objects ranged in a line or row; a range. **2** Degree of official standing, especially in the army and navy. See table under GRADE. **3** A line of soldiers drawn up side by side in close order: distinguished from *file.* **4** *pl.* An army; also, the mass of soldiery; the order of private soldiers: The colonel rose from the *ranks.* **5** A row of eight squares on a chessboard extending from the left of the player to the

right. 6 Relative position in a scale of dignity or of life; degree; grade: the *rank* of baronet; the *rank* of a plant or animal organism. 7 High degree or position; especially, the state of being a member of a titled nobility: a lady of *rank*. 8 Degree of worth or excellence; relative status. See synonyms under CLASS, SORT. — *v.t.* 1 To place or arrange in a rank or ranks. 2 To place in a class, order, etc.; assign to a position or classification. 3 To take precedence of; outrank: Sergeants *rank* corporals. — *v.i.* 4 To hold a specified place or rank: His poetry *ranks* with the best. 5 To have the highest rank or grade. [<OF *ranc. renc* <Gmc. Doublet of RANGE.]

rank[2] (rangk) *adj.* 1 Very vigorous and flourishing in growth as from fertilization or moisture. 2 Strong and disagreeable to the taste or smell. 3 Excessive or immoderate, in unfavorable sense: *rank* injustice. 4 Producing a luxuriant growth; fertile. 5 *Law* Inequitable; excessive. 6 Strong or deep: said of a cut or the adjustment of the tool making a cut. 7 *Obs.* In heat; lustful. [OE *ranc* strong] — **rank'ly** *adv.* — **rank'ness** *n.*

rank and file 1 The common soldiers of an army, including all from the corporals downward. 2 Those who form the bulk of any organization, as distinct from officers or leaders.

Ran·ke (räng'kə), **Leopold von,** 1795–1886, German historian.

rank·er (rangk'ər) *n.* 1 One who has served in the ranks. 2 A commissioned officer who has risen from the ranks.

rank·ing (rangk'ing) *adj.* Superior in rank; taking precedence (over others in the grade): a *ranking* senator, officer, etc.

ran·kle (rang'kəl) *v.* **·kled, ·kling** *v.i.* 1 To cause continued resentment, sense of injury, etc.: The defeat *rankles* in his breast. 2 To become irritated or inflamed; fester. — *v.t.* 3 To irritate; embitter. [<OF *rancler,* alter. of *draoncler* fester <Med. L *dracunculus,* dim. of *draco* dragon]

Ran·noch (ran'əkh), **Loch** A lake in NW Perth, central Scotland; 9 miles by 1 mile.

ran·oid (ran'oid) *adj. Zool.* Of, pertaining, or belonging to a family *(Ranidae)* of frogs, especially as distinguished from the toads. [<L *rana* a frog + -OID]

ran·pike (ran'pīk') *n.* A rampike.

ran·sack (ran'sak) *v.t.* 1 To search through every part of. 2 To search throughout for plunder; pillage. See synonyms under EXAMINE. [<ON *rannsaka* search a house < *rann* house + *sækja* seek] — **ran'sack·er** *n.*

ran·som (ran'səm) *v.t.* 1 To secure the release of (a person, property, etc.) for a required price, as from captivity or detention. 2 To set free on payment of ransom. 3 To redeem from sin or its consequences. See synonyms under DELIVER. — *n.* 1 The consideration paid for the release of a person or property captured or detained. 2 Release purchased, as from captivity. [<OF *rançon, raençon* <L *redemptio, -onis* redemption < *redimere* redeem. Doublet of REDEMPTION.] — **ran'som·er** *n.* — **ran'som·less** *adj.*

Ran·som (ran'səm), **John Crowe,** U.S. poet, 1888–1974.

rant (rant) *v.i.* 1 To speak in loud, violent, or extravagant language; declaim vehemently; rave. 2 *Scot.* & *Brit. Dial.* To frolic noisily; be uproariously jolly. — *v.t.* 3 To exclaim or utter in a ranting manner. — *n.* 1 Declamatory and bombastic talk. 2 *Scot.* & *Brit. Dial.* Wild gaiety; a boisterous revel. [<MDu. *ranten* rave] — **rant'ing** *adj.* — **rant'ing·ly** *adv.*

rant·er (ran'tər) *n.* One who rants; a noisy, boisterous speaker or declaimer: applied opprobriously to various religious speakers.

ra·nun·cu·la·ceous (rə·nung'kyə·lā'shəs) *adj. Bot.* Belonging or pertaining to a family *(Ranunculaceae)* of plants, the crowfoot or buttercup family, including larkspur, aconite, peony, and hellebore.

ra·nun·cu·lus (rə·nung'kyə·ləs) *n. pl.* **·lus·es** or **·li** (-lī) Any of a genus *(Ranunculus)* of herbaceous annuals or perennials, the buttercups or crowfoots, typical of the family *Ranunculaceae.* [<L *ranunculus,* a medicinal plant, orig. dim. of *rana* frog]

Ra·oul (rà·o͞ol') French form of RALPH.

rap[1] (rap) *v.* **rapped, rap·ping** *v.t.* 1 To strike sharply and quickly; hit. 2 To utter in a sharp manner: with *out:* to *rap* out an oath. 3 *Slang* To criticize severely. — *v.i.* 4 To strike sharp, quick blows. 5 *Slang* To have a frank discussion; talk. — *n.* 1 A sharp blow. 2 A sound caused by or as by knocking; specifically, such a sound ascribed to the agency of spirits. 3 *Slang* A reprimand; blame; also, consequences: to take the *rap.* 4 *Slang* A prison sentence. 5 *Slang* A severe criticism. 6 *Slang* A talk; discussion. See synonyms under BLOW[2]. — *adj. Slang* Marked by frank discussion: a *rap* session. [Imit. Cf. Dan. *rap,* Sw. *rapp.*] — **rap'per** *n.*

rap[2] (rap) *v.t.* **rapt** or **rapped, rap·ping 1** *Obs.* To snatch. 2 *Archaic* To seize or transport as with ecstasy; carry away: now current only in the past participle *rapt* (sometimes erroneously spelled *wrapt*). [Back formation <RAPT]

rap[3] (rap) *n.* A counterfeit coin used as a halfpenny in Ireland in the 18th century; hence, anything worthless: I don't care a *rap.* [Origin uncertain. Cf. G. *rappe,* a small coin.]

rap[4] (rap) *n.* A skein of yarn containing 120 yards. [Origin unknown]

ra·pa·cious (rə·pā'shəs) *adj.* 1 Given to plunder or rapine. 2 Extortionate; grasping. 3 Predaceous; subsisting on prey seized alive: said of hawks, etc. [<L *rapax, -acis* < *rapere* seize] — **ra·pa'cious·ly** *adv.*

ra·pac·i·ty (rə·pas'ə·tē) *n.* The quality or character of being rapacious. Also **ra·pa'cious·ness.** [<L *rapacitas, -tatis*]

Ra·pal·lo (rä·päl'lō) A port in NW Italy, at the head of the **Gulf of Rapallo,** an inlet on the Gulf of Genoa.

Ra·pa Nu·i (rä'pä no͞o'ē) The native name for EASTER ISLAND.

rape[1] (rāp) *v.* **raped, rap·ing** *v.t.* 1 To commit rape upon; ravish. 2 To plunder or sack (a city, etc.). 3 *Archaic* To carry off by force. — *v.i.* 4 To commit rape. See synonyms under VIOLATE. — *n.* 1 The act of a man who has sexual intercourse with a woman against her will or (called **statutory rape**) with a girl below the age of consent. 2 Any unlawful sexual intercourse or sexual connection by force or threat: homosexual *rape* in prison. 3 The plundering or sacking of a city, etc. 4 Any gross violation, assault, or abuse: the *rape* of our natural resources. [<AF <L *rapere* seize]

rape[2] (rāp) *n.* An Old World annual *(Brassica napus)* grown as a forage crop for sheep and hogs, and having seeds which yield rape oil. [<L *rapum* turnip]

rape[3] (rāp) *n.* 1 *pl.* In winemaking, refuse stalks and skins of grapes. 2 A filter used in vinegarmaking. [<F *râpe* <Med. L *raspa* < *raspare* grate <Gmc. Cf. OHG *raspon.*]

rape oil A yellowish to brown oil obtained from rapeseed: used as a lubricant and in the manufacture of rubber substitutes, soft soaps, etc. Also called *colza oil.*

rape·seed (rāp'sēd') *n.* 1 The seed of the rape. 2 The plant.

Raph·a·el (raf'ē·əl, rā'fē-; *Fr.* rà·fà·el', *Du.* rä'fel, *Ger.* rä'fä·el) A masculine personal name. [<Hebrew, God hath healed]
— **Raphael** One of the seven archangels of Christian legend.
— **Raphael,** 1483–1520, Italian painter: full name Raffaello Sanzio.

Raph·a·el·esque (raf'ē·əl·esk') *adj.* Characteristic of, or in the style of Raphael.

ra·phe (rā'fē) *n. pl.* **·phae** (-fē) 1 *Anat.* A seamlike appearance often seen in organs, especially at the median line of the body. 2 *Bot.* The fibrovascular cord that connects the hilum of plant ovules with the chalaza. 3 A line or rib connecting the nodules on a diatom valve. Also spelled *rhaphe.* [<NL <Gk. *rhaphē* seam < *rhaptein* stitch together]

ra·phi·a (rā'fē·ə) See RAFFIA.

ra·phide (rā'fid) *n. pl.* **raph·i·des** (raf'ə·dēz) *Bot.* A needle-shaped crystal of oxalate of lime found in many plant cells. Also **ra'phis.** [<Gk. *rhaphis, rhaphidos* needle]

rap·id (rap'id) *adj.* 1 Having great speed. 2 Bearing the marks of or characterized by rapidity. 3 Done or completed in a short time; advancing speedily to a termination: *rapid* growth. See synonyms under SWIFT[1]. — *n. Usually pl.* A descent in a river less abrupt than a waterfall. [<L *rapidus* < *rapere* seize, rush] — **rap'id·ly** *adv.* — **rap'id·ness** *n.*

Rap·i·dan River (rap'ə·dan') A river of northern Virginia, flowing 90 miles east to the Rappahannock; scene of severe fighting in the Civil War.

rap·id-fire (rap'id·fīr') *adj.* 1 Firing shots rapidly. 2 Characterized by speed: *rapid-fire* repartee. Also **rap'id-fir'ing.**

rapid fire A rate of gunfire lower than that of quick fire.

ra·pid·i·ty (rə·pid'ə·te) *n.* The quality or state of being rapid; swiftness.

rapid transit The local transportation of passengers by means faster than surface vehicles; specifically, elevated or subway passenger transportation.

ra·pi·er (rā'pē·ər, rāp'yər) *n.* 1 In the 16th and 17th centuries, a long, straight, two-edged sword with a large cup hilt, used in dueling, chiefly for thrusting. 2 The French small sword of the 18th century, a shorter straight sword without cutting edge and therefore used for thrusting only. [<F *rapière,* prob. < *raspière* poker, rasper; appar. first used derisively]

RAPIER

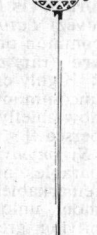

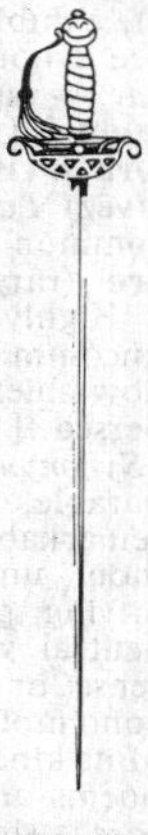

rap·ine (rap'in) *n.* The taking of property by force, as in war; spoliation; pillage. See synonyms under PLUNDER. [<F <L *rapina* < *rapere* seize. Doublet of RAVEN[2], *n.,* RAVINE.]

rap·ist (rā'pist) *n.* One who commits rape.

rap·loch (rap'ləkh) *Scot.* & *Brit. Dial. adj.* Unkempt; coarse. — *n.* Coarse homespun cloth made of inferior undyed wool.

Rap·pa·han·nock (rap'ə·han'ək) A river in northern Virginia, flowing 212 miles SE to Chesapeake Bay.

rap·pa·ree (rap'ə·rē') *n.* 1 An Irish guerrilla of the 17th century. 2 A freebooter or bandit. [<Irish *rapaire* short pike]

rap·pee (ra·pē') *n.* A dark, coarse, strong-flavored snuff. [<F *(tabac) râpé* grated (tobacco), pp. of *râper* scrape]

rap·pel (ra·pel') *v.i.* **·pelled, ·pel·ling** In mountaineering, to descend from a precipitous height by letting oneself down on a rope. — *n.* Descent by means of a rope. [<F]

rap·per (rap'ər) *n.* 1 One who raps. 2 A spiritualist medium. 3 A knocker, as on a door or at the mouth of a mining shaft.

rap·port (ra·pôrt', -pōrt'; *Fr.* rà·pôr') *n.* Harmony of relation; accordance; sympathetic relation: commonly with *in.* — **en rapport** *French* In close accord. [<F < *rapporter* refer, bring back < *re-* again + *apporter* bring <L *apportare* < *ad-* to + *portare* bring]

rap·proche·ment (rà·prôsh·män') *n. French* The act of coming or of being brought together; a state of harmony or reconciliation; restoration of cordial relations, as between nations.

rap·scal·lion (rap·skal'yən) *n.* A rogue; scamp; rascal. [<earlier *rascallion* <RASCAL + fanciful ending]

rapt (rapt) *adj.* 1 Carried away with lofty emotion; enraptured; transported. 2 Engrossed; intent; deeply engaged. Sometimes erroneously spelled *wrapt.* [<L *raptus,* pp. of *rapere* seize]

Rap·ti (räp'tē) A river in Nepal and northern India, flowing 400 miles SE to the Gogra river in Uttar Pradesh State.

rap·to·ri·al (rap·tôr'ē·əl, -tō'rē-) *adj.* 1 Seizing and devouring living prey; predatory. 2 *Ornithol.* Having talons adapted for seizing and holding prey: said especially of hawks, vultures, eagles, owls, and other carnivorous birds. [<L *raptor* snatcher < *raptus,* pp. of *rapere* seize]

rap·ture (rap'chər) *n.* 1 The state of being rapt or transported; ecstatic joy; ecstasy. 2 The act of transferring a person from one place to another: Elijah's *rapture* to heaven. 3 An act or expression of excessive delight. 4 *Obs.* A snatching away; violent seizure. — *v.t.* **·tured, ·tur·ing** To enrapture. [<RAPT]

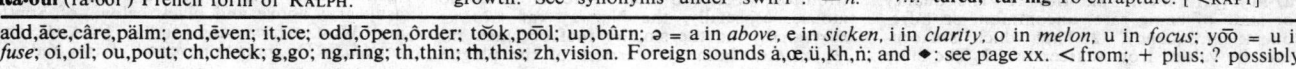

Synonyms (noun): bliss, delight, ecstasy, exultation, happiness, joy, rejoicing, transport, triumph. *Rejoicing* is *happiness* or *joy* that finds utterance in word, song, festivity, etc. *Delight* is vivid, overflowing *happiness* of a somewhat transient kind; *ecstasy* is a state of extreme or extravagant *delight*; *rapture* is closely allied to *ecstasy*, but is more serene, exalted, and enduring. *Transport* is the condition of one carried away out of himself by some powerful passion or emotion, whether joyous or the reverse. *Triumph* is such *joy* as results from victory, success, achievement. See ENTHUSIASM, HAPPINESS. *Antonyms*: agony, apathy, dejection, despair, distress, ennui, horror, misery, pain, tedium, torture, woe, wretchedness.

rap·tur·ous (rap′chər·əs) *adj.* Being in a state of, exhibiting, or characterized by rapture. See synonyms under HAPPY. **— rap′tur·ous·ly** *adv.* **— rap′tur·ous·ness** *n.*

Ra·quel (rä·kel′) Spanish form of RACHEL.

ra·ra a·vis (râr′ə ā′vis) *pl.* **ra·rae aves** (râr′ē ā′vēz) *Latin* Literally, a rare bird; any uncommon or peculiar person or thing.

rare[1] (râr) *adj.* **1** Of infrequent occurrence. **2** Highly esteemed because of infrequency or uncommonness; valuable; choice. **3** Rarefied: now chiefly of the atmosphere. **4** *Obs.* Dispersed. [<F <L *rarus* rare]

Synonyms: curious, extraordinary, incomparable, infrequent, odd, peculiar, precious, remarkable, scarce, singular, strange, uncommon, unique, unusual. *Extraordinary*, signifying greatly beyond the ordinary, is a neutral word, capable of a high and good sense or of an invidious, opprobrious, or contemptuous signification. *Unique* is alone of its kind; *rare* is *infrequent* of its kind; great poems are *rare*. To say of a thing that it is *rare* is simply to affirm that it is now seldom found, whether previously common or not; as, a *rare* old book; a *rare* word; to call a thing *scarce* implies that it was at some time more plentiful, as when we say money is *scarce*. A particular coin may be *rare*; *scarce* applies to demand and use, and almost always to concrete things; to speak of virtue, genius, or heroism as *scarce* would be somewhat ludicrous. See CHOICE, EXTRAORDINARY, OBSOLETE, ODD. *Antonyms*: see synonyms for COMMON.

rare[2] (râr) *adj.* Not thoroughly cooked: applied to roasted or broiled meat retaining its redness and juices: in England commonly termed *underdone*. [OE *hrēre* lightly boiled]

rare·bit (râr′bit) *n.* Welsh rabbit. [Alter. of (WELSH) RABBIT]

rare earth *Chem.* Any of the metallic oxides of the rare-earth elements.

rare-earth elements (râr′ûrth′) *Chem.* A group of metallic elements comprising the lanthanide series. Also **rare-earth metals.**

rar·ee show (râr′ē) **1** A show carried or contained in a box; a peepshow. **2** A cheap street show or any street show or spectacle. [Alter. of *rare show*; after the mispronunciation characteristic of the Savoyard promoters of these shows]

rar·e·fac·tion (râr′ə·fak′shən) *n.* The process or act of making rare or less dense. Also **rar′e·fi·ca′tion.** [<L *rarefactus*, pp. of *rarefacere*] **— rar′e·fac′tive** *adj.*

rar·e·fy (râr′ə·fī) *v.* **·fied, ·fy·ing** *v.t.* **1** To make rare, thin, less solid, or less dense; expand by dispersion of the particles. **2** To refine or purify. **—** *v.i.* **3** To become rare, thin, or less solid. **4** To become more pure. [<F *raréfier* <L *rarefacere* <*rarus* rare + *facere* make] **— rar′e·fi′a·ble** *adj.*

rare·ly (râr′lē) *adv.* **1** Not often; infrequently. **2** With unusual excellence or effect; finely: The breeze blows *rarely*. **3** Exceptionally; extremely; in an unusual degree: She dressed in raiment *rarely* rich.

rare·ness (râr′nis) *n.* The condition or quality of being rare in any sense.

rare·ripe (râr′rīp′) *adj.* Ripening early. **—** *n.* A fruit that ripens early: applied especially to many varieties of peaches, and to a variety of onion. [OE *hrathe* early, soon + RIPE]

Rar·i·tan River (rar′ə·tən) A river of NE New Jersey, flowing 25 miles south to **Raritan Bay,** a western arm of Lower New York Bay.

rar·i·ty (râr′ə·tē) *n.* *pl.* **·ties** **1** The quality or state of being rare, uncommon, or infrequent; infrequency. **2** That which is exceptionally valued from scarceness. **3** The state of being rare, thin, or tenuous; tenuity: opposed to *density*. [<L *raritas, -tatis*]

Ra·ro·ton·ga (rä′rō·tông′gə) The largest and southwesternmost of the Cook Islands, capital of the group; 26 square miles.

ras (räs) *n.* In Ethiopia, a prince. [<Arabic *ra's* the head]

ras·cal (ras′kəl) *n.* **1** An unprincipled fellow; a rogue; knave: sometimes used playfully. **2** *Obs.* One of the common herd; a man of low birth or station. **—** *adj.* Pertaining to the rabble; contemptible; base; mean. [<OF *rascaille* <*rasque* filth, shavings, ult. <L *radere* shave, scrape]

ras·cal·i·ty (ras·kal′ə·tē) *n.* *pl.* **·ties** **1** The quality of being rascally. **2** A rascally act.

ras·cal·ly (ras′kəl·ē) *adj.* Worthy of a rascal; knavish; base. See synonyms under BAD[1]. **—** *adv.* After the manner of a rascal.

Ras Da·shan (räs dä·shän′) The highest peak in Ethiopia; 15,157 feet.

rase (rāz) *v.t.* **rased, ras·ing** To raze. [Var. of RAZE]

rash[1] (rash) *adj.* **1** Acting without due caution or regard of consequences; reckless; precipitate. **2** Exhibiting recklessness or precipitancy. **3** *Obs.* Quick; speedy. See synonyms under IMPETUOUS, IMPRUDENT. [ME *rasch*. Akin to Du. & G *rasch* quick.] **— rash′ly** *adv.* **— rash′ness** *n.*

rash[2] (rash) *n.* A superficial eruption of the skin, often localized. [? <F *rache* <OF *rasque*. See RASCAL.]

rash[3] (rash) *n.* *Scot.* A rush; bulrush.

rash·er[1] (rash′ər) *n.* A thin slice of meat: used especially of bacon. [Prob. < obs. *rash* cut, slash]

rash·er[2] (rash′ər) *n.* A vermilion-colored California rockfish (*Sebastodes miniatus*). [<Sp. *rascacio*, kind of fish]

Rask (räsk), **Rasmus Christian,** 1787–1832, Danish philologist and writer.

Ras·kol·nik (räs·kôl′nik) *n.* *pl.* **·ni·ki** (-nē·kē) or **·niks** A Russian dissenter; a member of one of the sects that split off from the Orthodox Church in the 17th century. [<Russian *raskolenik* dissenter < *raskole* schism]

Ras·mus·sen (räs′mŏŏs·ən), **Knud Johan Victor,** 1879–1933, Danish Arctic explorer.

ra·son (rā′son) *n.* *Meteorol.* A method of obtaining and recording weather information at high altitudes by combining a radiosonde with automatic signal-recording devices and radio direction-finders. [<RA(DIO)SON(DE)]

ra·so·ri·al (rə·sôr′ē·əl, -sō′rē-) *adj.* In the habit of scratching the ground for food, as domestic fowl and other gallinaceous birds. [<NL *Rasores*, lit., scratchers <L *rasum*, pp. of *radere* scrape]

rasp (rasp, räsp) *n.* **1** A filelike tool having coarse pyramidal projections for abrasion. **2** A machine containing a large cylindrical grater. **3** The act or sound of rasping. **—** *v.t.* **1** To scrape with or as with a rasp. **2** To scrape or rub roughly. **3** To affect unpleasantly; irritate. **4** To utter in a rough voice. **—** *v.i.* **5** To grate; scrape [<OF *raspe* < *rasper* scrape, prob. <Gmc.] **— rasp′er** *n.*

rasp·ber·ry (raz′ber′ē, -bər·ē, räz′-) *n.* *pl.* **·ries** **1** The round fruit of certain brambles (genus *Rubus*) of the rose family, composed of drupes clustered around a fleshy receptacle. **2** The plant yielding this fruit. **3** *Slang* A vulgar sound indicating contempt and produced by vibrating the tongue between the lips [< earlier *rasp* raspberry (? <OF *(vin) raspé* thin wine < *râpe* RAPE[3]) + BERRY]

rasped (raspt, räspt) *adj.* Rough or roughened, with or as with a coarse file: said of uncut book edges.

rasp·ing (ras′ping, räs′-) *adj.* Making a harsh sound; hence, irritating.

Ras·pu·tin (ras·pyŏŏ′tin, *Russian* räs·pŏŏ′tin), **Grigori,** 1871–1916, Russian monk, favorite of Czar Nicholas II and his wife; assassinated: real name Novikh.

rasp·y (ras′pē, räs′-) *adj.* **rasp·i·er, rasp·i·est** **1** Inclined to rasp; rough; grating. **2** Irritable.

Ras·se·las (ras′ə·ləs) The hero of a philosophical romance of this name by Samuel Johnson.

ra·sure (rā′zhər) *n.* Erasure.

rat (rat) *n.* **1** A destructive and injurious rodent (family *Muridae*) of world-wide distribution, larger and more aggressive than the mouse; especially, the **Norway rat** (*Rattus norvegicus*) and the smaller **roof** or **black rat** (*R. rattus*): both are carriers of the plague bacillus transmitted by the rat flea. **2** Some other mammal like or likened to the rat. **3** *Slang* A cowardly or selfish person who deserts or betrays his associates. **4** A slender cushion of curled hair or the like, worn by women, with the natural hair rolled over it. **—** *v.i.* **rat·ted, rat·ting** **1** To hunt rats. **2** *Slang* To desert one's party, companions, etc., especially for one's own safety or advantage. **3** *Slang* To inform; act the betrayer. [OE *ræt*]

rat·a·ble (rā′tə·bəl) *adj.* **1** *Brit.* Subject to assessment; legally liable to taxation. **2** Estimated proportionally; pro rata: a *ratable* distribution. **3** That may be rated or valued. Also **rate′a·ble. — rat′a·bil′i·ty, rat′a·ble·ness** *n.* **— rat′a·bly** *adv.*

rat·a·fi·a (rat′ə·fē′ə) *n.* **1** A cordial flavored with fruits. **2** A flavoring essence based on the essential oil of bitter almonds. **3** A sweet biscuit. Also **rat′a·fee′** (-fē′). [<F]

Ra·tak (rä′täk) The eastern chain of the Marshall Islands.

ra·tal (rāt′l) *n.* An amount on which rates are assessed. [<RATE + -AL[1]]

ra·tan (ra·tan′) See RATTAN.

rat·a·ny (rat′ə·nē) See RHATANY.

rat·a·plan (rat′ə·plan′) *n.* A rapidly repeated sound, as of the beating of a drum. **—** *v.t.* & *v.i.* **·planned, ·plan·ning** To sound a rataplan (on). [<F; imit. of drumming]

rat·a·tat·tat (rat′ə·tat′tat′) *n.* A quick, sharp rapping sound, as a knock at a door. [Imit.]

rat·bag (rat′bag′) *n.* *Austral. Slang* An eccentric person: a derogatory term.

rat·bag·ger·y (rat′bag′ər·ē) *n.* *Austral. Slang* Eccentric behavior.

rat·bite fever (rat′bīt′) *Pathol.* An infectious disease caused by the bite of a rat infested with certain bacteria: characterized by local ulcerations, rash, severe muscular pains, and relapsing fever. Also **ratbite disease.**

ratch[1] (rach) *n.* **1** A ratchet or ratchet wheel. **2** A spot on a horse's face. [Short for RATCHET]

ratch[2] (rach) *v.i.* *Naut.* To sail by the wind on any tack. [Back formation < obs. *raught*, pp. of REACH, on analogy with *caught, catch*]

ratch·et (rach′it) *n.* **1** A mechanism consisting of a notched wheel, the teeth of which engage with a pawl, permitting motion of the wheel in one direction only. **2** The pawl or the wheel thus used. Also **ratchet wheel.** [<F *rochet* spool <Ital. *rochetto* bobbin, dim. of *rocca* distaff <Gmc. Cf. OHG *roccho* spindle.]

rate[1] (rāt) *n.* **1** The measure of a thing by its relation to a standard; proportional or comparative amount or degree: a high *rate* of interest. **2** Degree of value; price: railway *rates*; also, the unit cost of a commodity or service: the *rate* for electricity, gas, water, and the like. **3** Comparative rank or class; condition. **4** The amount of variation of a timepiece; gain or loss in seconds. **5** A ratio for the assessment of property taxes: a *rate* of 40 mills per thousand dollars. **6** *Brit.* A local tax on property. **7** The proportion which a given fact or event bears to the total of relevant cases involved: a death *rate*, marriage *rate*. **8** A fixed allowance or amount. **9** *Obs.* Degree; estimation. See synonyms under TAX. **— at any rate** In any case; under any circumstances; anyhow. **— differential rate** The lower of two rates given usually by two competing railroad lines to one of two places in the same territory in order to make profits even: in England called **preferential rate. —** *v.* **rat·ed, rat·ing** *v.t.* **1** To estimate the value or worth of; appraise. **2** To place in a certain rank or grade. **3** To fix the amount of tax or liability on. **4** To consider; regard: He is *rated* as a great statesman. **5** To fix the rate for the transportation of (goods), as by rail, water, or air. **—** *v.i.* **6** To have rank, rating, or value. See synonyms under CALCULATE. [<OF <L *rata (pars)* reckoned (part), fem. of *ratus*, pp. of *reri* reckon]

rate[2] (rāt) *v.t* & *v.i.* **rat·ed, rat·ing** To reprove with vehemence; rail at; scold. [Origin uncertain. Cf. OF *rater* scold and Sw. *rata* find fault.]

ra·tel (rā′təl, rä′-) *n.* A nocturnal carnivore (genus *Mellivora*) resembling the badger, ashy-gray above and black below, of South and West Africa and India. [<Afrikaans *rateldas* <Du. *raat* honeycomb + *das* badger]

rate·pay·er (rāt′pā′ər) *n. Brit.* One who pays local property taxes or rates.
rat·er[1] (rā′tər) *n.* One who or that which rates or estimates.
rat·er[2] (rā′tər) *n.* One who scolds or berates.
rat–foot dots In Chinese painting, a method of representing pine boughs or branches by brush strokes that resemble the print of a rat's foot: four or five slightly curved strokes radiating from a white center dot.
rath (rath) *adj. Obs.* 1 Unusually early; vehement. 2 Swift; quick; soon. 3 Relating to the forenoon, or to the early part of a period of time. Also **rathe** (rāth). [OE *hrathe* early]
Rat·haus (rät′hous′) *n. German* A government or municipal building; a town hall.
rathe (rāth) *adv. Obs.* Early; betimes; promptly. [OE *hrathe* soon]
Ra·the·nau (rä′tə·nou), **Walther,** 1867–1922, German statesman and industrialist.
rath·er (rath′ər, rä′thər) *adv.* 1 With preference for one of two things or courses; more willingly. 2 With more reason; more wisely; more strictly or accurately. 3 Somewhat; in a greater or less degree; to a certain extent. 4 Very much; exceedingly. 5 *Obs.* Sooner; earlier; more quickly. [OE *hrathor* sooner, compar. of *hrathe* soon; quick]
rath·er·est (rath′ər·ist, rä′thər-) *adv. Brit. Dial.* Most especially; most of all.
raths·kel·ler (rath′skel·ər, räts′kel·ər) *n.* 1 In Germany, the cellar of a city hall, often used as a beer hall or restaurant. 2 Any beer hall or restaurant patterned after the German type, but not necessarily located below the street level. [<G < *rat* town hall + *keller* cellar]
Ra·ti·bor (rä′tē·bôr) A port on the Oder in southern Poland: Polish *Racibórz.*
rat·i·fi·ca·tion (rat′ə·fə·kā′shən) *n.* The act of ratifying, or the state of being ratified.
rat·i·fy (rat′ə·fī) *v.t.* **·fied, ·fy·ing** To give sanction to, especially official or authoritative sanction; make valid by approving, especially the work of an agent or representative; confirm. [<F *ratifier* <Med. L *ratificare* <L *ratus* fixed, reckoned + *facere* make] **—rat′i·fi′er** *n.*
Synonyms: accept, approve, confirm, corroborate, endorse, establish, justify, sanction, seal, settle, substantiate, validate. See ASSENT, CONFIRM, JUSTIFY. *Antonyms*: abolish, abrogate, annul, cancel, deny, disavow, disown, extinguish, nullify, repeal, rescind, revoke.
rat·ing[1] (rā′ting) *n.* 1 Classification according to a standard; grade; rank. 2 The classification of a vessel. 3 An evaluation of the financial standing of a business firm or an individual. 4 The designation of the operating capacity of a piece of machinery, as expressed in horsepower, kilowatts, etc. 5 Any specialist grade held by an enlisted man or officer: the *rating* of a pilot, gunner, parachutist, etc., in the U.S. Army, or of boatswain's mate in the Navy. 6 *Brit.* An enlisted man in the Royal Navy. See synonyms under TAX.
rat·ing[2] (rā′ting) *n.* A harsh rebuke; scolding. [<RATE[2]]
ra·tio (rā′shō, -shē·ō) *n. pl.* **·tios** 1 Relation of degree, number, etc.; relative amount; proportion; rate: There has always been a *ratio* between demand and supply. 2 The relation between two numbers or two magnitudes of the same kind; especially, the quotient of one magnitude divided by the other, or the factor that, multiplied into one, will produce the other. 3 Formerly, the relation expressed by subtracting one quantity from the other; the difference. 4 *Obs.* A portion; ration. [<L. Doublet of RATION, REASON.]
ra·ti·oc·i·nant (rash′ē·os′ə·nənt) *adj.* Reasoning, as contrasted with *ratiocinate.* [See RATIOCINATE]
ra·ti·oc·i·nate (rash′ē·os′ə·nāt) *v.i.* **·nat·ed, ·nat·ing** To make a deduction from premises; reason. —*adj.* Reasoned about. [<L *ratiocinatus,* pp. of *ratiocinari* calculate, deliberate < *ratio* reckoning. See REASON.] **—ra′ti·oc′i·na′tor** *n.*
ra·ti·oc·i·na·tion (rash′ē·os′ə·nā′shən) *n.* The deduction of conclusions from premises; reasoning. See synonyms under REASONING. [<L *ratiocinatio, -onis*]
ra·ti·oc·i·na·tive (rash′ē·os′ə·nā′tiv) *adj.* 1 Of or pertaining to the act or process of reasoning. 2 Given to ratiocination; argumentative. [<L *ratiocinativus*]
ra·tio·ing (rā′shō·ing) *n.* The reduction or enlargement of a series of aerial photographs so that all are on one scale for use in a mosaic map. [<RATIO + -ING]
ra·tion (rash′ən, rā′shən) *n.* 1 A portion; share. 2 A fixed allowance or portion of food, etc., allotted in time of scarcity. — **emergency ration** Portions of canned beef, hardtack, milk chocolate, etc., for use in the field by soldiers. —*v.t.* 1 To provide with rations; issue rations to, as an army. 2 To give out or allot in rations, as gasoline, rubber, butter, etc. [<F <L *ratio, -onis.* Doublet of RATIO, REASON.] **—ra′tion·ing** *n.*
ra·tion·al (rash′ən·əl) *adj.* 1 Possessing the faculty of reasoning. 2 Conformable to reason; judicious; sensible. 3 Pertaining to reason; attained by reasoning. 4 Pertaining to rationalism. 5 *Math.* **a** Pertaining to a rational number. **b** Denoting an algebraic expression containing variables within radicals, as $\sqrt{x^2 - y^2}$, $\sqrt{4x - 1}$. Compare IRRATIONAL. 6 In Greek and Latin prosody, denoting the measurement of metrical units; capable of being measured in metrical units. —*n.* That which is rational. [<L *rationalis* < *ratio, -onis*] **—ra′tion·al·ly** *adv.* **—ra′tion·al·ness** *n.*
Synonym (adj.): reasonable. A *rational* mind is one that is capable of the ordinary and normal processes of thought; a *reasonable* mood is one at the time susceptible to the influence of reasons. A *rational* man is capable of using his reasoning powers; a *reasonable* man has them habitually in exercise. *Rational* is opposed to *insane, reasonable* to *fanatical, misguided, obstinate, unreasonable, visionary.* See SAGACIOUS, SANE[1], WISE[1].
ra·tion·ale (rash′ən·al′, -ä′lē, -ā′lē) *n.* 1 A rational exposition of principles. 2 The logical basis of a fact; the reason or reasons collectively. [<L, neut. of *rationalis*]
ra·tion·al·ism (rash′ən·əl·iz′əm) *n.* 1 The formation of opinions by relying upon reason alone, independently of authority or of revelation: opposed to *supernaturalism.* 2 *Philos.* **a** The theory of a priori ideas, that truth and knowledge are attainable through reason rather than through experience: opposed to *empiricism.* **b** The theory that reason itself is a source of knowledge independent of sense perception: opposed to *sensationalism.* — **ra′tion·al·ist** *n.* **—ra′tion·al·is′tic** or **·ti·cal** *adj.* **—ra′tion·al·is′ti·cal·ly** *adv.*
ra·tion·al·i·ty (rash′ən·al′ə·tē) *n. pl.* **·ties** 1 Sanity; reasonableness; naturalness. 2 The cause or reason; rationale. [<LL *rationalitas*]
ra·tion·al·i·za·tion (rash′ən·əl·ə·zā′shən, -ī·zā′·shən) *n.* 1 The act or process of rationalizing. 2 *Psychol.* The process of devising acceptable reasons for desires, emotions, acts, beliefs, or opinions which cannot be creditably justified to oneself or to others in terms of their actual motives. 3 *Brit.* The act of bringing an industry into accord with up–to–date methods of organization and operation.
ra·tion·al·ize (rash′ən·əl·īz′) *v.* **·ized, ·iz·ing** *v.t.* 1 *Psychol.* To explain (one's behavior) on grounds ostensibly rational but not in accord with the actual or unconscious motives. 2 To explain or treat from a rationalistic point of view. 3 To make rational or reasonable; render conformable to reason. 4 *Math.* To remove the radicals containing variables from (an expression or equation); also, to alter the radicals so as to change (the expression) into more workable form: thus, if $\sqrt{x^2 + 2x} = 3$, then, by squaring, $x^2 + 2x = 9$, and $x^2 + 2x - 9 = 0$. —*v.i.* 5 To think in a rational or rationalistic manner. 6 *Psychol.* To rationalize one's behavior. **—ra′tion·al·iz′er** *n.*
rational number See under NUMBER.
Rat·is·bon (rat′is·bon, -iz-) An English name for REGENSBURG.
Rat Islands (rat) A group in the Aleutian Islands, extending 110 miles west of the Andreanof Islands.
rat·ite (rat′īt) *adj.* Designating a division of flightless birds *(Ratitae),* including ostriches, cassowaries, kiwis, emus, etc., which have aborted wings and a breastbone without a keel. —*n.* One of the *Ratitae.* [<L *ratis* raft]
rat kangaroo Any of several tiny kangaroos, as the **rufous rat kangaroo** *(Aepyprymnus rufescens).*
rat·line (rat′lin) *n. Naut.* 1 One of the small ropes fastened across the shrouds of a ship, used as the rounds of a ladder for going aloft or descending. 2 The material so used. See SHROUD[2]. Also **rat′lin** (-lin), **rat′·ling** (-ling). [Origin unknown]

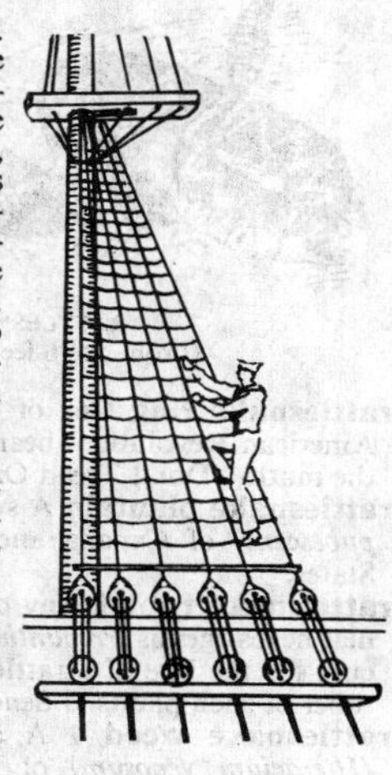
RATLINES

ra·toon (ra·to͞on′) *n.* 1 A new shoot from the root of a cropped plant, as from a sugarcane. 2 One of the heart leaves in a tobacco plant. —*v.i.* To sprout from a root planted the previous year. [<Sp. *retoño* <Hind. *ratun*]
rat race *Slang* A frantic, usually fruitless, struggle; a wearisome hustle or strife.
rats·bane (rats′bān′) *n.* Rat poison.
rat–tail (rat′tāl′) *adj.* Resembling a rat's tail in form. Also **rat′–tailed′.**
rat·tan (ra·tan′) *n.* 1 The long, tough, flexible stem of a palm (genera *Calamus* and *Daemonorops*) growing in East India, Africa, and Australia. 2 The palm itself. 3 A cane or switch of rattan. Also spelled *ratan.* [<Malay *rotan*]
rat·teen (ra·tēn′) *n. Obs.* A thick woolen twilled cloth. [<F *ratine*]
rat·ten[1] (rat′n) *v.t. Brit. Slang* To persecute or harass (an employer or employee) because of refusal to join or obey a trade union. [<RATTEN[2]] **—rat′ten·er** *n.* **—rat′ten·ing** *n.*
rat·ten[2] (rat′n) *n. Scot. & Brit. Dial.* A rat.
rat·ter (rat′ər) *n.* 1 A dog or cat that catches rats. 2 *Slang* A deserter or traitor.
rat·tish (rat′ish) *adj.* Belonging to or resembling a rat.
rat·tle[1] (rat′l) *v.* **·tled, ·tling** *v.i.* 1 To make a series of sharp noises in rapid succession, as by striking together: dead limbs *rattling* in the wind. 2 To move or act with such noises. 3 To talk rapidly and foolishly; chatter. —*v.t.* 4 To cause to rattle: to *rattle* pennies in a tin cup. 5 To utter or perform rapidly or noisily. 6 *Colloq.* To confuse; disconcert: Her reaction *rattled* me. See synonyms under SHAKE. —*n.* 1 A series of short, sharp sounds in rapid succession, as from the collision of small, hard objects. 2 A plaything, implement, etc., adapted to produce a rattling noise: a watchman's *rattle.* 3 The series of jointed horny rings in the tail of a rattlesnake, or one of these; also, the noise produced by the vibration of this organ. 4 Rapid and noisy talk; chatter. 5 One who talks fast and foolishly. 6 A râle; the death rattle, caused by the passage of air through mucus. See synonyms under NOISE. [Imit.]
rat·tle[2] (rat′l) *v.t.* **·tled, ·tling** *Naut.* To fit with ratlines: used in the phrase **to rattle down the rigging.** [<RATLINE]
rat·tle·box (rat′l·boks′) *n.* 1 A toy or the like having a chamber to contain something, as a ball, that will rattle. 2 A low hairy North American annual (genus *Crotalaria*) having seeds which rattle in the inflated pod. 3 The bladder campion.
rat·tle·brain (rat′l·brān′) *n.* A talkative, flighty person; foolish chatterer. Also **rat′tle·head′** (-hed′), **rat′tle·pate′** (-pāt′). **—rat′tle–brained′** *adj.*
rat·tler (rat′lər) *n.* 1 One who or that which rattles. 2 A rattlesnake.
rat·tle·snake (rat′l·snāk′) *n.* Any of various venomous, thick–bodied American snakes (genera *Crotalus* and *Sistrurus,* family *Viperidae*) with a tail ending in a series of

add,āce,câre,pälm; end,ēven; it,īce; odd,ōpen,ôrder; to͝ok,po͞ol; up,bûrn; ə = a in *above,* e in *sicken,* i in *clarity,* o in *melon,* u in *focus;* yo͞o = u in *fuse;* oi,oil; ou,pout; ch,check; g,go; ng,ring; th,thin; t͟h,this; zh,vision. Foreign sounds à,œ,ü,kh,ṅ; and ◆: see page xx. < from; + plus; ? possibly.

horny, loosely connected, modified joints, which clash together with a rattling noise when the tail is vibrated.

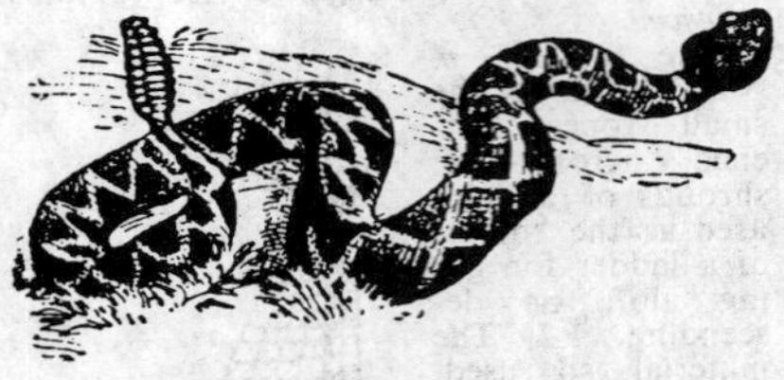

RATTLESNAKE
(From 2 to 8 feet in length)

rattlesnake flag One of the early flags of the American Revolution, bearing a rattlesnake and the motto "Don't Tread On Me."

rattlesnake plantain A small orchid *(Goodyera pubescens)* of Canada and the eastern United States.

rattlesnake root 1 Any of several erect perennial herbs (genus *Prenanthes)* considered to be a cure for the bite of a rattlesnake. 2 The root or tuber of such plants. 3 Senega.

rattlesnake weed 1 A species of hawkweed *(Hieracium venosum)* of the northern United States. 2 Rattlebox. 3 Button snakeroot (genus *Eryngium).*

rat·tle·trap (rat′l·trap′) *n.* 1 Any rickety, clattering, or worn-out vehicle or article. 2 *Slang* A loquacious or gossipy person. *—adj.* Shaky; dilapidated.

rat·tling (rat′ling) *adj.* 1 Making a clatter. 2 Garrulous; sprightly. 3 *Colloq.* Very; extraordinary; good. *—adv. Colloq.* Extraordinarily; very: a *rattling* good time.

rat·tly (rat′lē) *adj.* 1 Inclined to rattle. 2 Clattering.

rat·ton (rat′n) *n. Scot. & Brit. Dial.* A small rat.

rat·trap (rat′trap′) *n.* 1 A trap for catching rats. 2 A situation from which escape is impossible; any hopeless or fatal predicament.

rat·ty (rat′ē) *adj.* **·ti·er, ·ti·est** 1 Ratlike, or abounding in rats. 2 *Slang* Disreputable; shabby.

rau·cle (rô′kəl) *adj. Scot.* Rough; harsh; strong; fearless.

rau·cous (rô′kəs) *adj.* Rough in sound; hoarse; harsh. [<L *raucus*] **—rau′cit·y** (-sə·tē), **rau′·cous·ness** *n.* **—rau′cous·ly** *adv.*

raunch·y (rôn′chē, rän′-) *adj. Slang* **raunch·i·er, raunch·i·est** 1 Sloppy; inept; slovenly. 2 Sexually vulgar; lewd; a *raunchy* joke. 3 Lustful. [? Alter. of Scot. *randy* disorderly, lewd; ult. origin unknown] **—raunch′i·ly** *adv.* **—rauch′i·ness** *n.*

Rau·wol·fi·a (rô·wol′fē·ə, -wŏŏl′-) *n.* A genus of tropical trees or shrubs of the dogbane family, several of which contain alkaloids having valuable medicinal properties; especially, *R. serpentina,* an Indian species from which the alkaloid reserpine was first isolated. [after Leonard *Rauwolf,* 17th century German botanist]

rav·age (rav′ij) *v.* **·aged, ·ag·ing** *v.t* To lay waste, as by pillaging or burning; despoil; ruin. *—v.i.* To wreak havoc; be destructive. *—n.* Violent and destructive action, or its result; ruin; desolation. [<F <*ravir.* See RAVISH.] **—rav′ag·er** *n.*

rave[1] (rāv) *v.* **raved, rav·ing** *v.i.* 1 To speak wildly or incoherently. 2 To speak with extravagant enthusiasm. 3 To make a wild, roaring sound; rage: The wind *raved* through the trees. *—v.t.* 4 To utter wildly or incoherently. *—n.* 1 The act or state of raving; a frenzy. 2 *Colloq.* A highly favorable critical comment: The play drew *raves. —adj. Colloq.* Extravagantly enthusiastic: *rave* reviews. [<OF *raver, rever* <L *rabere* rage]

rave[2] (rāv) *n.* 1 A vertical sidepiece in a wagon body, or in a hand car or sleigh. 2 The wooden or iron piece that fastens the beam to the runners of a logging sled. [Origin unknown]

rav·el (rav′əl) *v.* **·eled** or **·elled, ·el·ing** or **·el·ling** *v.t.* 1 To separate the threads or fibers of; unravel. 2 To make clear or plain; explain: often with *out.* 3 *Archaic* To tangle; confuse. *—v.i.* 4 To become separated thread from thread or fiber from fiber; unravel; fray. 5 *Archaic* To become tangled or confused. *—n.* 1 A broken or rejected thread. 2 A raveling. [? <MDu. *ravelen* tangle] **—rav′el·er** or **rav′el·ler** *n.*

Ra·vel (rȧ·vel′), **Maurice Joseph,** 1875–1937, French composer.

rave·lin (rav′lin) *n. Mil.* An outwork with two faces forming a salient angle at the front. [<F <Ital. *ravellino.* Origin uncertain.]

rav·el·ing (rav′əl·ing) *n.* 1 A thread or threads raveled from a fabric. 2 The act of raveling. 3 The process of being raveled. Also **rav′el·ling.**

rav·el·ment (rav′əl·mənt) *n.* A ravel, or the act of raveling; confusion.

ra·ven[1] (rā′vən) *n.* A large, omnivorous, crowlike bird *(Corvus corax)* of North America, Europe, and Asia, having lustrous black plumage, with the feathers of the throat elongated and lanceolate. *—adj.* Black and shining, like the plumage of a raven. [OE *hrœfn*]

rav·en[2] (rav′ən) *v.t.* 1 To devour hungrily or greedily. 2 To take by force; ravage. *—v.i.* 3 To search for or take prey or plunder. 4 To eat voraciously; be ravenous. *—n.* The act of plundering; spoliation; pillage. [<OF *raviner* <*ravine* rapine <L *rapina; n.* doublet of RAPINE, RAVINE] **—rav′en·er** *n.*

Ra·ven (rā′vən) The southern constellation, Corvus. See CONSTELLATION.

Rav·e·na·la (rav′i·nā′lə) *n.* A genus of palmlike trees of the banana family, having a fan-shaped group of elongated flat leaves arranged around the trunk, especially the traveler's tree *(R. madagascariensis).* [<Malagasy]

rav·en·ing (rav′ən·ing) *adj.* 1 Seeking eagerly for prey; rapacious. 2 Mad; rabid. *—n.* 1 Propensity for prey or booty; rapacity. 2 The prey seized. [ppr. of RAVEN[2]] **—rav′en·ing·ly** *adv.*

Ra·ven·na (rä·ven′nä) A city in north central Italy, 6 miles west of the Adriatic, formerly on it; capital of the Western Roman Empire 402–476.

rav·en·ous (rav′ən·əs) *adj.* 1 Violently voracious or hungry. 2 Extremely eager for gratification. See synonyms under GREEDY. [<OF *ravinos.* See RAVEN[2].] **—rav′en·ous·ly** *adv.* **—rav′en·ous·ness** *n.*

Ra·vi (rä′vē) A river in NW India and West Pakistan, flowing SW 474 miles from northern Punjab State, India to the Chenab river above Multan, West Pakistan: ancient *Hydraotes.*

rav·in (rav′in) *n.* 1 The act of plundering or ravaging. 2 That which is obtained by violence or robbery. *—v.t. & v.i.* To raven. [<OF *ravine.* See RAPINE.]

ra·vine (rə·vēn′) *n.* 1 A deep gorge or gully, especially one worn by a stream or flow of water. 2 A long, narrow cleft between heights. See synonyms under VALLEY. [<F. Doublet of RAVEN[2], *n.,* RAPINE.]

rav·ing (rā′ving) *adj.* 1 Furious; delirious; frenzied. 2 *Colloq.* Excessive; extraordinary: a *raving* beauty. *—n.* Furious, incoherent, or irrational utterance. See synonyms under FRENZY. Compare INSANITY.

ra·vi·o·li (rä·vyō′lē, rä′vē·ō′lē, rav′ē-) *n. pl.* Balls of forcemeat, encased in little envelopes of dough and boiled in broth or water: commonly construed in the singular. [<Ital., dim. pl. of dial. *rava* <L *rapa* turnip, beet]

rav·ish (rav′ish) *v.t.* 1 To fill with strong emotion, especially delight; enrapture. 2 To commit a rape upon. 3 To carry off (a woman) by force. 4 To seize and carry off by violence. [<OF *ravis-s-,* stem of *ravir* carry off <L *rapere* seize. Related to RAPE, RAPTURE.] **—rav′ish·er** *n.* **—rav′ish·ing·ly** *adv.*

Synonyms: captivate, charm, delight, enchant, enrapture, entrance, overjoy, transport. See ABUSE, CHARM[1], POLLUTE, REJOICE.

rav·ish·ing (rav′ish·ing) *adj.* Filling with transports of delight; enchanting.

rav·ish·ment (rav′ish·mənt) *n.* The act of ravishing or the state of being ravished; especially, ecstasy; delight. [<OF *ravissement*]

raw (rô) *adj.* 1 Not changed or prepared by cooking; in its natural state; uncooked. 2 Not covered with whole skin; abraded. 3 Bleak; chilling: a *raw* wind. 4 In a natural state; crude; unprepared, as wool, drugs, etc.; also, untempered or without tone, as colors; unrefined; unfinished. 5 Newly done; fresh: *raw* paint, *raw* work. 6 Inexperienced; undisciplined: a *raw* recruit. 7 Unrefined; crude; off-color: a *raw* joke. 8 Unexposed: said of photographic film. *—n.* 1 A sore or abraded spot; a sensitive point. 2 The state of being raw, untamed, or unspoiled: nature in the *raw.* [OE *hrēaw*] **—raw′ly** *adv.* **—raw′ness** *n.*

Ra·wal·pin·di (räʹwəl·pin′dē, rôl·pin′dē) A city in the northern Punjab region of Pakistan, near the border of Jammu and Kashmir state.

raw-boned (rô′bōnd) *adj.* Having large bones and little flesh; bony; gaunt.

Raw·bones (rô′bōnz′) Death.

raw deal *Slang* Harsh or unfair treatment in a transaction.

raw fibers Textile fibers in their natural state, as silk in the gum or cotton as it comes from the bale.

raw·hide (rô′hīd′) *n.* 1 A hide dressed without tanning. 2 A whip made of such hide.

raw·ish (rô′ish) *adj.* Somewhat raw.

Raw·lin·son (rô′lin·sən), **George,** 1812–1902, English Orientalist and historian. **—Sir Henry,** 1810–95, English soldier and Assyriologist; brother of the preceding.

raw material Unprocessed material (animal, vegetable, or mineral) needed and used in manufacturing, as contrasted with finished products.

raw milk Unpasteurized milk.

rax (raks) *v.t. & v.i. Scot.* To stretch out; reach.

ray[1] (rā) *n.* 1 A narrow beam of light or other line of propagation of any form of radiant energy; line of radiating force; radiation. 2 A manifestation of intellectual light. 3 One of several lines radiating from an object. 4 *Geom.* A straight line emerging from a center and unlimited in one direction only. 5 A streak or line; a straight row. 6 *Zool.* **a** One of the rods supporting the membrane of a fish's fin. **b** One of the radiating parts of a radiate animal, as a starfish. 7 *Bot.* **a** A raylike flower. **b** One of the pedicels or flower stalks of an umbel. 8 *Physics* A stream of particles spontaneously emitted by a radioactive substance. 9 A trace or minute particle: Not a *ray* of life was present. *—v.i.* 1 To emit rays; shine. 2 To issue forth as rays; radiate. *—v.t.* 3 To send forth as rays. 4 To mark with rays or radiating lines. 5 To irradiate. 6 To treat with or expose to X-rays, etc. [<OF *rai* <L *radius.* Doublet of RADIUS.]

ray[2] (rā) *n.* Any of a large order (Batoidea) of elasmobranch fishes having the eyes on the top and the mouth and gill slits on the underside of a usually flat body, with the pectoral fins forming a winglike extension on either side, and usually having a slender, whiplike tail, as the mantas, skates, stingrays, etc. [<F *raie* <L *raia*]

Ray (rā), **Cape** A promontory at the SW extremity of Newfoundland at the entrance to the Gulf of Saint Lawrence.

ra·yah (rä′yə, rī′ə) *n.* A non-Moslem inhabitant of Turkey: sometimes spelled *raia.* Also **ra′ya.** [<Arabic *ra'iyah* flock, herd]

ray flower *Bot.* Any of the flat, straplike florets of a composite flower head. Also **ray floret.**

ray·grass (rā′gras′, -gräs′) *n.* Ryegrass.

Ray·leigh (rā′lē), **Lord,** 1842–1919, John William Strutt, third baron, English physicist.

ray·less (rā′lis) *adj.* 1 Having no light rays. 2 Extremely dark. 3 Having no rays, as certain composite plants. **—ray′less·ly** *adv.* **—ray′less·ness** *n.*

Ray·mond (rā′mənd, *Fr.* rā·môn′) A masculine personal name. Also **Ray′mund.** Also *Lat.* **Ray·mun·dus** (rā·mun′dəs). [<Gmc., wise protection]

ray·on (rā′on) *n.* A lustrous synthetic fiber variously made by chemical means from cellulose or with cellulose as a base, the viscous material being forced through fine spinnerets to produce filaments suitable for textiles and fabrics. [<F, ray; from its sheen]

raze (rāz) *v.t.* **razed, raz·ing** 1 To level to the ground; tear down; demolish. 2 *Rare* To scrape or shave off. 3 *Obs.* To wound slightly; graze. See synonyms under DEMOLISH. Also spelled *rase.* ◆ Homophone: *raise.* [<F *raser* <L *rasum,* pp. of *radere* scrape]

ra·zee (rā·zē′) *v.t.* To make lower by cutting down, as a ship of war by removing the upper deck or decks; reduce; abridge. *—n.* A vessel that has been reduced by cutting away the upper deck or decks. [<F *rasé,* pp. of *raser* shave, raze]

ra·zor (rā′zər) *n.* A sharp cutting implement

used for shaving off the beard or hair. —**safety razor** A razor provided with a guard or guards or the blade to prevent accidental gashing of the skin. [< OF *rasor* < *raser* scrape]

ra·zor·back (rā′zər·bak′) n. 1 A rorqual. 2 A lean-bodied, half-wild hog with long legs, common in the southeastern United States. 3 A hill with a sharp narrow ridge. —**ra′zor·backed′** *adj.*

ra·zor-billed   **auk** (rā′zər·bild′) A small auk (*Alca torda*) of the North Atlantic, having a compressed and deeply furrowed bill. Also **ra′zor·bill′**.

razor clam A clam (genus *Ensis*) having a long, narrow, slightly curved shell resembling a razor. Also **ra′zor-shell′·clam.**

razor grinder One who sharpens or grinds razors or razor blades.

RAZOR–BILLED AUK
(About 16 inches in length)

razor strop A strip, of specially prepared leather, canvas, or other material, upon which the blade of a razor is stroked to give it a fine edge.

razz (raz) n. *Slang* Raspberry (def. 3). —*v.t.* To heckle; deride. [< RASPBERRY]

raz·zi·a (raz′ē·ə) n. A foray or armed expedition, as for plunder or conquest. [< F < Arabic *ghāzīah* < *ghasw* war, battle]

raz·zle-daz·zle (raz′əl·daz′əl) n. *U.S. Slang* Anything bewildering and exciting; dazzling activity or performance [Varied reduplication of DAZZLE]

razz·ma·tazz (raz′mə·taz′) n. *U.S. Slang* 1 Razzle-dazzle. 2 Skill.

Rb *Chem.* Rubidium (symbol Rb).

re¹ (rā) n. *Music* The second note of any major scale in solmization. [< L *re(sonare)* resound. See GAMUT.]

re² (rē) prep. Concerning; about; in the matter of: used in business letters: *re* your letter of the 6th instant. [< L, ablative of *res* thing]

Re¹ (rā) See RA.

Re² *Chem.* Rhenium (symbol Re).

re- *prefix* 1 Back: *reduce* to lead back, *remit* to send back. 2 Again; anew; again and again: *regenerate*. *Re-* in this second sense is freely used in Modern English, as in the list of words below. It is hyphenated, in certain cases, to prevent confusion with a similarly spelled word having a different meaning (*re-treat* to treat again, *retreat* to go back), to prevent mispronunciation (*re-ar-gue*, *re-urge*), and also in the coining of new words. Also, before vowels, sometimes *red-*, as in *redeem*. [< L *re-*, *red-* back, again]

reach (rēch) *v.t.* 1 To stretch out or forth, as the hand or foot. 2 To present by means of or as by means of the outstretched hand; deliver; hand over. 3 To extend as far as; touch or grasp, as with the hand: Can you *reach* the top shelf? 4 To arrive at or come to by motion or progress; attain: When do we *reach* Miami? 5 To achieve communication with; gain access to. 6 To amount to; total. 7 To strike or hit, as with a blow or missile. —*v.i.* 8 To stretch the hand, foot, etc., out or forth. 9 To attempt to touch or grasp something: He *reached* for his wallet. 10 To have extent in space, time, amount, or influence: The ladder *reached* to the ceiling. 11 *Naut.* To sail on a tack with the wind on or forward of the beam. —*n.* 1 The act or power of reaching; also, the distance one is able to reach, as with the hand, an instrument, or missile, or by thought,

influence, etc.; scope; range. 2 A point, position, or result attained or attainable. 3 An unbroken stretch, as of a stream; a vista or expanse. 4 A pole or bar connecting the rear axle, truck, or runners of a vehicle with some part at the forward end. 5 *Naut.* The sailing, or the distance sailed, by a vessel on one tack. [OE *ræcan*. Akin to G *reichen* reach]

Synonyms (verb) : attain, gain, hit, land, make, strike, touch. To *reach*, in the sense here considered, is to come to by motion or progress. *Attain* is now oftenest used of abstract relations; as, to *attain* success. To *gain* is to *reach* or *attain* a thing eagerly sought; the wearied swimmer *reaches* or *gains* the shore. See ARRIVE, GET, MAKE¹, STRETCH.

reach·less (rēch′lis) *adj.* That cannot be reached; unattainable; lofty.

reach-me-down (rēch′mē·doun′) *Slang adj.* Ready-made, as a garment; also, second-hand.

re·act (rē·akt′) *v.i.* 1 To act in response, as to a stimulus. 2 To act in a manner contrary to some preceding act; come into or tend toward a former state or an opposite state. 3 *Physics* To exert an opposite and equal force on an acting or impinging body: said of the body acted upon. 4 *Chem.* To exert mutual action, as substances undergoing chemical change. Compare RE-ACT.

re·act (rē·akt′) *v.t.* To act again.

re·ac·tance (rē·ak′təns) n. *Electr.* In an alternating-current circuit, that component of the impedance that does not oppose the current, but tends to cause a difference of phase between it and the electromotive force: measured in ohms.

re·ac·tion (rē·ak′shən) n. 1 Reverse or return action; tendency toward a former or reversed state of things; especially, a trend toward an earlier social, political, or economic policy or condition. 2 *Physiol.* Contrary action or reversed effects following a stimulus; a reflex action. 3 *Psychol.* The partial or total response made to any kind or degree of stimulation. 4 *Physics* In the second law of motion, the equal and opposite force exerted on an agent by the body acted upon. 5 *Chem.* The mutual action of substances subjected to chemical change, or some distinctive result of such action. 6 *Biol.* The effect upon any organism or any of its parts made by the introduction of any foreign substance for diagnostic or therapeutic purposes, or for testing, immunizing, etc. —**re·ac′tive** *adj.*

re·ac·tion·ar·y (rē·ak′shən·er′ē) *adj.* Of, relating to, favoring, or characterized by reaction. —*n.* pl. ·**ar·ies** One who favors political or social reaction; a conservative. Also **re·ac′tion·ist.**

reaction engine An engine which obtains thrust by the expulsion of the hot gases of combustion to the rear; a jet engine.

reaction formation *Psychoanal.* The conscious development of character traits, attitudes, and forms of behavior in contrast with and opposition to original trends of the ego, for which they serve as deceptive and relatively unstable concealment. Compare SUBLIMATION.

reaction time *Physiol.* 1 The time required for a response to a sensory stimulus. 2 The time required for an electric current to act on a muscle.

re·ac·ti·vate (rē·ak′tə·vāt) *v.t.* ·**vat·ed, ·vat·ing** To make active or effective again. —**re·ac′ti·va′tion** n.

re·ac·tive (rē·ak′tiv) *adj.* 1 Reacting, tending to react, or resulting from reaction. 2 Responsive to a stimulus.

reactive factor *Electr.* In a circuit, the ratio of the reactive volt-amperes to the total volt-amperes.

reactive volt-ampere *Electr.* That component of the volt-amperes in an alternating-current circuit not representing the work done in watts. Also **reactive power.** See VAR.

re·ac·tor (rē·ak′tər) n. 1 One who or that which reacts. 2 *Electr.* A device for introducing reactance into a circuit, as for starting motors, con-

trolling current, and the like. 3 *Biol.* An animal or person giving a positive reaction to a specified bacteriological or medical test. 4 *Physics* Any of variously designed assemblies for the initiation and control of nuclear fission, consisting essentially of reserves of fissionable material used as fuel, moderators to check the rate of nuclear reactions, reflectors, and auxiliary structures, equipment, shielding, etc.: also called *pile.*

read (rēd) *v.* **read** (red), **read·ing** (rē′ding) *v.t.* 1 To apprehend the meaning of (a book, writing, etc.) by perceiving the form and relation of the printed or written characters. 2 To utter aloud (something printed or written). 3 To understand the significance of as if by reading: to *read* the sky. 4 To apprehend the meaning of something printed or written in (a foreign language). 5 To make a study of; also, to obtain knowledge of: to *read* law. 6 To discover the true nature of (a person, character, etc.) by observation or scrutiny. 7 To interpret (something read) in a specified manner. 8 To take as the meaning of something read. 9 To have or exhibit as the wording: The passage *reads* "principal," not "principle." 10 To indicate or register: The meter *reads* zero. 11 To bring in to a specified condition by reading: I *read* her to sleep. —*v.i.* 12 To apprehend the characters of a book, musical score, etc. 13 To utter aloud the words or contents of a book, etc. 14 To gain information by reading: with *of* or *about.* 15 To learn by means of books; study. 16 To have a specified wording: The contract *reads* as follows. 17 To admit of being read in a specified manner. 18 To give a public reading or recital. —**to read between the lines** To perceive or infer what is not expressed or obvious, as a hidden or true meaning, implication, or motive. —**to read into** To discern (implicit meanings or implications) in a statement or position: Don't *read* anything *into* my decision not to run for office. —**to read out** To expel from a religious body, political party, etc., by proclamation or concerted action. —**to read up (or up on)** To learn by reading. —*adj.* (red) Informed by books or reading; acquainted with books or literature: well *read.* —*n.* (rēd) *Colloq.* A reading; a period spent in reading. [OE *rǣdan* advise, read]

read·a·ble (rē′də·bəl) *adj.* 1 Legible. 2 Easy and pleasant to read. —**read·a·bil′i·ty, read′a·ble·ness** *n.* —**read′a·bly** *adv.*

Reade (rēd), **Charles,** 1814–84, English novelist.

read·er (rē′dər) n. 1 One who reads; specifically, a professional reciter or elocutionist. 2 One who reads and criticizes manuscripts offered to publishers. 3 A proofreader. 4 A layman authorized to read the lesson in church services. 5 A textbook containing matter for exercises in reading. 6 *Brit.* A university or college lecturer.

read·er·ship (rē′dər·ship) n. The estimated number of people who read a particular author, publication, or kind of reading material.

read·i·ly (red′ə·lē) *adv.* 1 In a ready manner; promptly; easily. 2 Willingly.

read·i·ness (red′i·nis) n. 1 The quality or state of being ready. 2 The quality of being quick or prompt; facility; aptitude. 3 A disposition for prompt compliance; willingness.

read·ing (rē′ding) n. 1 The act, practice or art of reading, in any sense of the verb; a public recital; the act of reading formally to a legislative body a bill, etc., proposed for adoption. 2 Literary research; study; scholarship. 3 Matter which is read or is designed to be read. 4 The indication of a graduated instrument, as a thermometer. 5 The form in which any passage or word appears in any copy of a work. 6 An interpretation, as of a riddle, or of any latent and hidden meaning; delineation; rendering. See synonyms under EDUCATION. —*adj.* Pertaining to or suitable for reading.

Read·ing (red′ing) 1 A county borough and

---

reabsorb	readdress	readvance	reallege	reanimation	reappear	reapportion
reabsorption	readjourn	reafforest	re-alliance	reannex	reappearance	reapportionment
reaccess	readjournment	reafforestation	re-ally	reannexation	reapply	re-argue
reaccommodate	readopt	reagree	realphabet	reanoint	reappoint	re-argument
reaccuse	readorn	re-alinement	reamputate	reapparel	reappointment	reascend

---

add, āce, câre, pälm; end, ēven; it, īce; odd, ōpen, ôrder; tŏŏk, pŏŏl; up, bûrn; ə = a in *above*, e in *sicken*, i in *clarity*, o in *melon*, u in *focus*; yōō = u in *fuse*; oi, oil; ou, pout; ch, check; g, go; ng, ring; th, thin; ŧħ, this; zh, vision. Foreign sounds à, œ, ü, kh, ṅ; and ◆: see page xx. < from; + plus; ? possibly.

county town of Berkshire, England. 2 A city on the Schuylkill River in SE Pennsylvania.

reading desk A desk adapted to hold books, manuscripts, etc., for a speaker or reader, as in church services.

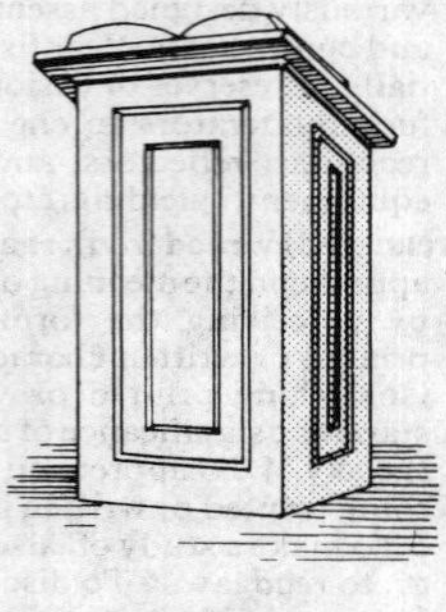
READING DESK

reading room A room provided with periodicals, books, etc., in which the public, or certain classes of readers, may read.

re·ad·just (rē′ə·just′) *v.t.* & *v.i.* To adjust again or anew; rearrange. **—re′ad·just′er** *n.*

re·ad·just·ment (rē′ə·just′mənt) *n.* **1** The act or process of readjusting, or the state of being readjusted. **2** The reorganization of a company or corporation, usually voluntary.

re·ad·mit (rē′əd·mit′) *v.t.* **·mit·ted, ·mit·ting** To admit again; allow to enter again. **—re′ad·mis′sion, re′ad·mit′tance** *n.*

read·out (rēd′out′) *n.* The information displayed from computer memory in readable form, or transcribed therefrom.

read·y (red′ē) *adj.* **read·i·er, read·i·est 1** Prepared for use or action. **2** Prepared in mind; willing. **3** Likely or liable: with *to*: *ready* to sink. **4** Quick to act, follow, occur, or appear; prompt. **5** At hand; immediately available; convenient; handy. **6** Designating the standard position in which a rifle is held just before aiming. **7** Quick to understand; alert; quick; facile: a *ready* wit. **8** *Obs.* Here; present: used in answering a roll call. See synonyms under ACTIVE, ALERT, GOOD, RIPE[1]. —*n.* **1** In the manual of arms, the position in which a rifle is held before aiming, the left hand at the balance, the right hand at the small of the stock. **2** *Slang* Cash: with *the*. —*v.t.* **read·ied, read·y·ing** To make ready; prepare. [OE *rǣde, gerǣde*]

read·y-made (red′ē·mād′) *adj.* **1** Not made to order; prepared or kept on hand for general demand: said especially of clothing. **2** Prepared beforehand; not impromptu. **3** Prepared by someone else. **4** Borrowed; lacking in originality; inferior.

ready money Money in hand; cash.

read·y-to-wear (red′ē·tə·wâr′) *adj.* Ready-made: said of clothing.

read·y-wit·ted (red′ē·wit′id) *adj.* Quick to apprehend or learn; alert.

re·af·firm (rē′ə·fûrm′) *v.t.* To affirm again, as for emphasis. **—re′af·firm′ance, re·af·fir·ma·tion** (rē′af·ər·mā′shən) *n.*

Rea·gan (rā′gən), **Ronald,** 1911–, 40th president of the United States 1981–

re·a·gent (rē·ā′jənt) *n.* **1** One who or that which reacts; a source of reflex action. **2** *Chem.* Any substance used to ascertain the nature or composition of another by means of their mutual chemical action. **3** *Psychol.* The subject of an experiment; particularly, one who or that which reacts to a stimulus. [<RE- + AGENT]

re·al[1] (rē′əl, rēl) *adj.* **1** Having existence or actuality as a thing or state; not imaginary: a *real* event. **2** Being in accordance with appearance or claim; genuine; not artificial or counterfeit. **3** Representing the true or actual, as opposed to the apparent or ostensible: the *real* reason. **4** Unaffected; unpretentious: a *real* person. **5** *Philos.* Having actual existence, and not merely possible, apparent, or imaginary. **6** *Law* **a** Of, pertaining to, or consisting of land and tenements: *real* property, as contrasted with personal property. **b** Pertaining to things, as distinguished from persons. —*n.* That which is real; a real thing. —*adv.* *Colloq.* Very; extremely: to be *real* glad. [<OF <Med. L *realis* <L *res* thing] **—re′al·ness** *n.*

re·al[2] (rē′əl, *Sp.* rā·äl′) *n.* **1** *pl.* **re·als** or **re·a·les** (rā·ä′lās) A small silver coin of several Spanish countries, including Mexico, and formerly current in the United States, where it was called a *bit,* and had the value of 12½ cents. **2** *pl.* **reis** (rās) A former Portuguese and Brazilian coin; one thousandth of a milreis. [<Sp., lit., royal <L *regalis*]

real estate Land, including whatever is made part of or attached to it by man or nature, as trees, houses, etc. Also **real property.**

re·al·gar (rē·al′gər) *n.* A resinous, orange-red arsenic sulfide, As_2S_2, formerly extensively used as a pigment and still employed in pyrotechnics. [<OF <Med. L <Arabic *rahj al-ghār* powder of the cave. Cf. Sp. *rejalgar.*]

re·al·i·a (rē·ā′lē·ə) *n. pl.* Real or actual objects used in teaching.

real image See under IMAGE.

re·al·ism (rē′əl·iz′əm) *n.* **1** In literature and art, the principle of depicting persons and scenes as they exist, without any attempt at idealization. **2** The tendency to be concerned solely with reality, as opposed to ideals; specifically, the tendency to think and act in the light of actuality, disregarding idealistic motives. **3** *Philos.* **a** The doctrine that universals (abstract concepts) have objective existence and are more real than things: opposed to *nominalism.* Compare CONCEPTUALISM. **b** The doctrine that things have reality apart from the conscious perception of them: opposed to *idealism.* **—re′al·is′tic** *adj.* **—re′al·is′ti·cal·ly** *adv.*

re·al·ist (rē′əl·ist) *n.* **1** An adherent of the doctrine of realism in any of its forms, as applied in literature, art, or philosophy. **2** One who is devoted to what is real rather than imaginary or ideal.

re·al·i·ty (rē·al′ə·tē) *n. pl.* **·ties 1** The fact, state, condition, or quality of being real or genuine. **2** That which is real; an actual person, thing, situation, or event; in the aggregate, the sum of real things; also, the substance that lies back of form and external appearances. **3** That which exists, as contrasted with what is fictitious; that which is objective, not merely an idea. **4** *Philos.* The absolute; that which is self-existent; the ultimate, as contrasted with phenomena or the apparent. See synonyms under VERACITY. [<Med. L *realitas, -tatis* <*realis* real]

reality principle *Psychoanal.* The adjustment of the ego to meet the requirements of the external world. Compare PLEASURE PRINCIPLE.

re·al·i·za·tion (rē′əl·i·zā′shən) *n.* **1** The act of realizing. **2** The state of being realized. **3** A product or instance of realizing. **4** The conversion into fact or action (of plans, ambitions, fears, etc.).

re·al·ize (rē′əl·īz) *v.* **·ized, ·iz·ing** *v.t.* **1** To understand or appreciate fully. **2** To make real or concrete. **3** To cause to appear real. **4** To obtain as a profit or return. **5** To obtain money in return for: He *realized* his holdings for a profit. **6** To bring as a profit or return: said of property. —*v.i.* **7** To sell property for cash. See synonyms under ACCOMPLISH, EFFECT, GAIN[1], KNOW. **—re′al·iz′a·ble** *adj.* **—re′al·iz′er** *n.*

re·al·iz·ing (rē′əl·īz′ing) *adj.* **1** Conceiving of as real; comprehending. **2** Able to visualize vividly. **3** Converting (hopes, plans, etc.) into fact, or (assets) into money.

re·al·ly (rē′ə·lē, rē′lē) *adv.* In reality; in point of fact; as a matter of fact; actually; indeed: also used without precise meaning, for emphasis.

realm (relm) *n.* **1** A kingdom. **2** The domain or jurisdiction of any power or influence: the *realm* of imagination. **3** A primary division of the globe with reference to its fauna; a zoogeographical area larger than a region; also, as used by some authors, a division equivalent to a region. [<OF *realme* <L *regalis* royal. See REGAL.]

real number See under NUMBER.

Re·al·po·li·tik (rā·äl′pō·li·tēk′) *n. German* Literally, practical or realistic politics: a term often used cynically to mean the attainment of political ends by the use or threatened use of armed force.

Re·al·schu·le (rā·äl′shōō′lə) *n. pl.* **·len** (-lən) *German* A modern non-classical German secondary school preparing students for commercial or technical occupations that do not require a university education.

Re·al·tor (rē′əl·tər, -tôr) *n.* A person engaged in the real estate business, as a broker, appraiser, manager, etc., who is a member of the National Association of Realtors: a trade name.

re·al·ty (rē′əl·tē) *n. pl.* **·ties** *Law* Real estate or real property in any form. [<REAL[1] (def. 6) + -TY[1]]

real wages Wages evaluated in terms of purchasing power, as contrasted with *nominal wages,* evaluated in money.

ream[1] (rēm) *n.* **1** Twenty quires of paper; properly, 480 sheets (a **short ream**), but often 500 sheets (a **long ream**) or, in a **printer's** or **perfect ream,** 516 sheets. **2** *pl. Colloq.* A prodigious amount of printed, written, or spoken material: *reams* of footnotes. [<OF *reyme* <Sp. *resma* <Arabic *rizmah* packet <*raxama* pack together]

ream[2] (rēm) *v.t.* **1** To increase the size of (a hole). **2** To enlarge or taper (a hole) with a rotating cutter or reamer. **3** To turn or roll over the edge of: to *ream* a cartridge shell. **4** To get rid of (a defect) by reaming. [OE *rēman* enlarge, make room. Akin to ROOM.]

ream[3] (rēm) *n. Scot.* & *Brit. Dial.* Cream; froth; foam. —*v.t. Scot.* To skim, as cream.

ream·er (rē′mər) n. **1** One who or that which reams. **2** A finishing tool with a rotating cutting edge for reaming: sometimes spelled *rimmer.* **3** A device with a ridged cone for extracting juice from citrus fruits.

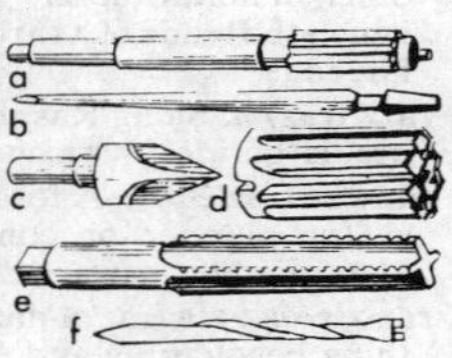

REAMERS
a. Adjustable.
b. Square.
c. Center.
d. Rose–shell.
e. Roughening taper.
f. Root reamer.

re·an·i·mate (rē·an′ə·māt) *v.t.* **·mat·ed, ·mat·ing 1** To bring back to life; resuscitate. **2** To revive; encourage. **—re′an·i·ma′tion** *n.*

reap (rēp) *v.t.* **1** To cut and gather (grain); harvest or gather (a fruit or product) with a scythe, reaper, or the like. **2** To cut the growth from or gather the fruit of, as a field. **3** To obtain as the result of action or effort; receive as a return or result. —*v.i.* **4** To harvest grain, etc. **5** To receive a return or result. See synonyms under GAIN[1] [OE *repan*] **—reap′a·ble** *adj.* **—reap′ing** *n.*

reap·er (rē′pər) *n.* **1** One who reaps. **2** A machine for harvesting standing grain; a reaping machine.

reaper and binder A reaping machine having a device that binds the grain as it cuts it.

reaping machine A machine for harvesting standing grain. It usually consists of a reciprocating cutter resembling that of a mowing machine, a platform or table on which the cut grain falls, and a dropper which is dropped to deposit the bundles of grain. In addition, it often has a reel for bending the grain toward the cutter, or a raking mechanism for pressingthe grain down on the table and sweeping it off in bundles, and a binding mechanism. Also called *harvester.*

rear[1] (rir) *n.* **1** The hinder or hindmost part. **2** A place or position at the back of or behind any person or thing. **3** That division of a military force which is last or farthest from the front: opposed to *van.* —*adj.* Being in the rear; last; hindmost. [Aphetic form of ARREAR]

rear[2] (rir) *v.t.* **1** To place upright; raise; elevate. **2** To build; erect. **3** To care for and bring to maturity. **4** To breed or grow. —*v.i.* **5** To rise upon its hind legs, as a horse. **6** To rise high; tower: The mountain *rears* above the forest. See synonyms under RAISE. [OE *rǣran* set upright, causative of *rīsan* rise. Akin to ON *reisa* raise.] **—rear′er** *n.*

rear admiral See under ADMIRAL.

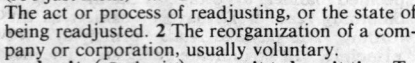

reascension	**reassertion**	**reassume**	**reattempt**	**rebind**	**rebury**	**rechange**
reascent	**reassign**	**reattach**	**reavow**	**rebloom**	**recarriage**	**recharge**
reassemblage	**reassimilate**	**reattachment**	**reawake**	**reblossom**	**recarry**	**recharter**
reassemble	**reassimilation**	**reattain**	**rebaptism**	**reboil**	**recelebrate**	**rechoose**
reassert	**reassociate**	**reattainment**	**rebaptize**	**rebuild**	**recelebration**	**rechristen**

rear–end (rir'end') *n.* In automobiles, the after part of the drive train, consisting of the differential gears and rear axles with their housings and the driving wheels. — *adj.* Of or pertaining to the rear–end of an automobile.

rear guard A body of troops to protect the rear of an army. [<AF *reregard,* OF *rereguarde.* Doublet of REARWARD².]

rear–horse (rir'hôrs') *n.* A mantis. [From its habit of rearing when touched]

rear·arm (rē-ärm') *v.t. & v.i.* 1 To arm again. 2 To arm with more modern weapons. — **re·ar'ma·ment** *n.*

rear·most (rir'mōst') *adj.* Coming or stationed last.

rear·mouse (rir'mous') See REREMOUSE.

rear·range (rē'ə·rānj') *v.t. & v.i.* **·ranged, ·rang·ing** To arrange again or in some new way. — **re'ar·range'ment** *n.*

rear sight The sight of a gun which is nearest the breech.

rear–view mirror (rir'vyōō') In motor vehicles, a mirror so placed in front of the driver that he can see the reflection of the road and vehicles behind. Also **rear'–vi'sion mirror.**

rear·ward¹ (rir'wərd) *adj.* Coming last or toward the rear; hindward. — *adv.* Toward or at the rear; backward. Also **rear'wards.** — *n.* Hindward position; the rear; end.

rear·ward² (rir'wôrd') *n. Obs.* A rear guard. [<AF *rereward.* Doublet of REAR GUARD.]

rea·son (rē'zən) *n.* 1 That which is thought or alleged as the basis or ground for any opinion, determination, or action; something adduced or adapted to influence the mind in determining or acting; proof; argument; motive; principle. 2 That which explains or accounts for any fact, act, proceeding, or event; loosely, an efficient or final cause, or a condition. 3 The entire mental or rational nature of man, as distinguished from the intelligence of the brute; the mind; in a more limited sense, the purely intellectual faculties. 4 Specifically, the normal exercise of the rational faculties. 5 That which is in conformity to general opinion; common sense: *The anarchist was brought to reason.* 6 A logical ground for thinking; an antecedent; also, the premise or premises of an argument, generally the minor premise. 7 That which is right or befitting; just procedure; a reasonable act or proposition. 8 Intuition. — *v.i.* 1 To think logically; obtain inferences or conclusions from known or presumed facts. 2 To talk or argue logically. — *v.t.* 3 To think out carefully and logically; analyze: with *out.* 4 To influence by means of reason; persuade or dissuade. 5 To argue; debate. See synonyms under ARGUE, DISPUTE. [<OF *raison* <L *ratio, -onis* <*ratus,* pp. of *reri* reckon. Doublet of RATION, RATIO.]
Synonyms (noun): account, aim, argument, cause, consideration, design, end, ground, motive, object, principle, purpose. While the *cause* of any event, act, or fact, as commonly understood, is the power that makes it to be, the *reason* of or for it is the explanation given by the human mind; but *reason* is often used as equivalent to *cause,* especially in the sense of *final cause.* In the statement of any reasoning, the *argument* may be an entire syllogism, or the premises considered together apart from the conclusion, or in logical strictness the middle term only by which the particular conclusion is connected with the general statement. But when the reasoning is not in strict logical form, the middle term following the conclusion is called the *reason;* thus in the statement "All tyrants deserve death; Caesar was a tyrant; therefore Caesar deserved death," "Caesar was a tyrant" would in the strictest sense be called the *argument;* but if we say "Caesar deserved death because he was a tyrant," the latter clause would be termed the *reason.* See CAUSE, INTELLECT, MIND, REASONING, UNDERSTANDING, WISDOM. Compare BECAUSE.

rea·son·a·ble (rē'zən·ə·bəl) *adj.* 1 Conformable to reason; sensible. 2 Having the faculty of reason; rational. 3 Governed by reason in acting or thinking. 4 Moderate, as in price; fair. See synonyms under JUST, LIKELY, PROBABLE, RATIONAL, WISE¹. [<OF *raisonable;* after L *rationabilis*] — **rea'son·a·bil'i·ty, rea'son·a·ble·ness** *n.* — **rea'son·a·bly** *adv.*

rea·soned (rē'zənd) *adj.* Founded upon or characterized by reason; premeditated or studied.

rea·son·er (rē'zən·ər) *n.* One who reasons or argues.

rea·son·ing (rē'zən·ing) *n.* The act or process of the mind by which from propositions known or assumed new propositions are reached; argumentation; also, the reasons, proofs, or arguments employed in such process.
Synonyms: argument, argumentation, debate, ratiocination. *Argumentation* and *debate* always suppose two parties alleging reasons for and against a proposition. *Reasoning* may be the act of one alone, as it is simply the orderly setting forth of reasons, whether for the instruction of inquirers, the confuting of opponents, or the clear establishment of truth for oneself. *Reasoning* may be either deductive or inductive. *Argument* or *argumentation* was formerly used of deductive *reasoning* only. With the rise of the inductive philosophy these words have come to be applied to inductive processes also; but while *reasoning* may be informal or even unconscious, *argument* and *argumentation* strictly imply logical form. Compare INTELLECT, REASON.

rea·son·less (rē'zən·lis) *adj.* Devoid of the faculty of reason; also, not conformable to reason.

re·as·sur·ance (rē'ə·shŏŏr'əns) *n.* 1 The act of reassuring; repeated assurance. 2 Restored confidence. 3 Reinsurance.

re·as·sure (rē'ə·shŏŏr') *v.t.* **·sured, ·sur·ing** 1 To restore to courage or confidence. 2 To assure again. 3 To reinsure. See synonyms under ENCOURAGE. — **re'as·sur'ing** *adj.* — **re'as·sur'ing·ly** *adv.*

Re·au·mur (rā'ə·myŏŏr', rā'ə·myŏŏr'; *Fr.* rā·ō·mür') *adj.* Relating to or designating the thermometric scale devised by de Réaumur, in which the zero point corresponds to the temperature of melting ice, and 80° to the temperature of boiling water. Also **Ré'au·mur'.** Abbr. *R.*

Ré·au·mur (rā'ə·myŏŏr', rā'ə·myŏŏr'; *Fr.* rā·ō·mür'), **René Antoine de,** 1683–1757, French physicist and naturalist.

reave (rēv) *v.t.* **reaved** or **reft, reav·ing** *Obs.* 1 To carry off as spoil or booty; rape; rob; plunder. 2 To deprive of something; bereave. 3 To tear up or apart; unravel; pull down; strip. [OE *rēafian* rob]

re·bate¹ (rē'bāt, ri·bāt') *v.t.* **·bat·ed, ·bat·ing** 1 To allow as a deduction. 2 To make a deduction from. 3 *Obs.* To blunt, as a sharp edge. — *n.* A deduction from a gross amount; discount: also **re·bate'ment.** [<OF *rabattre* beat down <*re-* again + *abattre.* See ABATE.] — **re'bat·er** *n.*

re·bate² (rē'bāt, rab'it) See RABBET.

re·ba·to (re·bä'tō) *n. pl.* **·tos** A collar turned down and falling over the shoulders: worn by both sexes in the 15th and 16th centuries. Also spelled *rabato.* [<MF *rabat* < *rabattre* beat down. See REBATE.]

re·bec (rē'bek) *n.* The earliest form of the violin. Also **re'beck.** [<F alter. of OF *rebebe* <Arabic *rabāb*]

Re·bec·ca (ri·bek'ə, *Ital.* rā·bek'kä) A feminine

MEDIEVAL
THREE–STRING
REBEC

personal name. Also *Fr.* **Ré·bec·ca** (rā·be·kä'), *Sp.* **Re·be·ca** (rā·bā'kä), *Ger.* **Re·bek·ka** (rā·bek'ə). [<Hebrew, ensnarer]
— **Rebecca** Wife of Isaac; mother of Esau and Jacob. *Gen.* xxiv 15.

re·bel (ri·bel') *v.i.* **·belled, ·bel·ling** 1 To rise in armed resistance against the established government or ruler of one's land. 2 To resist any authority or established usage. 3 To react with violent aversion: usually with *at.*
— **reb·el** (reb'əl) *n.* One who rebels; specifically, one who espoused the American Revolution, or the cause of the South during the Civil War. — *adj.* Rebellious; refractory. [<OF *rebeller* <L *rebellare* make war again <*re-* again + *bellare* make war <*bellum* war. Doublet of REVEL.]

reb·el·dom (reb'əl·dəm) *n.* 1 The domain of rebels; specifically, the Confederate States during the Civil War; also, rebels collectively. 2 Rebellious behavior.

re·bel·lion (ri·bel'yən) *n.* 1 The act of rebelling. 2 Organized resistance to a government or to any lawful authority. See synonyms under REVOLUTION. — **the Rebellion** The American Civil War. [<OF <L *rebellio, -onis*]

re·bel·lious (ri·bel'yəs) *adj.* 1 Being in a state of rebellion; insubordinate. 2 Of or pertaining to a rebel or rebellion. 3 Resisting control; refractory: *rebellious curls.* — **re·bel'lious·ly** *adv.* — **re·bel'lious·ness** *n.*
Synonyms: contumacious, disobedient, insubordinate, intractable, mutinous, refractory, seditious, uncontrollable, ungovernable, unmanageable. *Ungovernable* applies to that which successfully defies authority and power; *unmanageable* to that which resists the utmost exercise of skill or of skill and power combined; *rebellious* to that which is defiant of authority, whether successfully or unsuccessfully; *seditious* to that which partakes of or tends to excite a *rebellious* spirit, *seditious* suggesting more of covert plan, scheming, or conspiracy, *rebellious* more of overt act or open violence. While the *unmanageable* or *ungovernable* defies control, the *rebellious* or *seditious* may be forced to submission. *Insubordinate* applies to the disposition to resist and resent control as such; *mutinous,* to open defiance of authority, especially in the army, navy, or merchant marine. A *contumacious* act or spirit is contemptuous as well as defiant. See RESTIVE, TURBULENT. Compare OBSTINATE, REVOLUTION. *Antonyms:* compliant, controllable, deferential, docile, dutiful, manageable, obedient, submissive, subservient, tractable, yielding.

re·bill (rē·bil') *v.t.* To render another bill to; bill again.

re·birth (rē·bûrth', rē'bûrth') *n.* 1 A new birth. 2 A revival or renaissance.

reb·o·ant (reb'ō·ənt) *adj.* Bellowing back; resounding loudly. [<L *reboans, -antis,* ppr. of *reboare* resound <*re-* again + *boare* bellow. Ult. imit.]

re·born (rē·bôrn') *adj.* Born again; having undergone emotional or mental regeneration; renascent.

re·bound (ri·bound') *v.i.* To bound back; recoil. — *v.t.* To cause to rebound. — *n.* (rē'bound', ri·bound') 1 Recoil; elasticity. 2 Something which rebounds or resounds; an echo. 3 Reaction of feeling or emotion after a disappointment: *to fall in love on the rebound.* [<F *rebondir* <*re-* back + *bondir* bound]

re·bo·zo (rā·bō'sō) *n. Spanish* A long scarf of cotton or silk, often embroidered, worn wrapped about the head and shoulders, and sometimes over the face, by women in Spain and Spanish America.

re·broad·cast (rē·brôd'kast', -käst') *v.t.* **·cast** or **·cast·ed, ·cast·ing** 1 To broadcast (the same program) more than once from the same station. 2 To broadcast (a program received from another station). — *n.* A program so transmitted.

re·buff (ri·buf') *v.t.* 1 To reject or refuse abruptly or rudely. 2 To drive or beat back; repel; repulse. — *n.* 1 A sudden repulse; curt

reclasp	recolonize	recommission	recondense	reconquest	reconstitute	recopy
reclose	recolor	recommittal	reconduct	reconsecrate	reconstitution	recross
reclothe	recombine	recompact	reconjoin	reconsecration	reconvene	recrucify
recoin	recomfort	reconceive	reconjoin	reconsolidate	reconversion	recrystallization
recoinage	recommence	recondensation	reconquer	reconsolidation	reconvert	recrystallize

add, āce, câre, pälm; end, ēven; it, īce; odd, ōpen, ôrder; tŏŏk, pōōl; up, bûrn; ə = a in *above,* e in *sicken,* i in *clarity,* o in *melon,* u in *focus;* yōō = u in *fuse;* oi, oil; ou, pout; ch, check; g, go; ng, ring; th, thin; t̶h, this; zh, vision. Foreign sounds á, œ, ü, kh, ṅ; and ◆: see page xx. < from; + plus; ? possibly.

denial. 2 A sudden check; defeat. 3 A beating back. [<MF *rebuffer* <Ital. *ribuffare*, metathetic alter. of *baruffare* <OHG *biroufan* scuffle]
re-buff (rē-buf′) *v.t.* To buff again.
re·buke (ri·byōōk′) *v.t.* **·buked, ·buk·ing** 1 To reprove sharply; reprimand. 2 *Obs.* To check or restrain by a command. See synonyms under ADMONISH, BLAME, REPROVE. — *n.* A strong and authoritative expression of disapproval. See synonyms under ANIMADVERSION, REPROOF. [<AF *rebuker*, OF *rebuchier* < *re-* back + *bucher* beat] — **re·buk′a·ble** *adj.*
re·buk·er (ri·byōō′kər) *n.* One who rebukes.
re·bus (rē′bəs) *n.* A puzzle representing a word, phrase, or sentence by letters, numerals, pictures, etc., often with pictures of objects whose names have the same sounds as the words represented. [<L, ablative pl. of *res* thing]
re·but (ri·but′) *v.t.* **·but·ted, ·but·ting** 1 *Law* To overthrow by contrary evidence; contradict by countervailing proof; disprove; refute. 2 *Obs.* To push or drive back. [<OF *rebouter* push back < *re-* back + *bouter, boter*. See BUTT[1].]
re·but·ta·ble (ri·but′ə·bəl) *adj.* Capable of being rebutted.
re·but·tal (ri·but′l) *n.* The act of rebutting; refutation.
re·but·ter (ri·but′ər) *n.* 1 One who or that which rebuts. 2 In common-law pleading, a defendant's answer to the plaintiff's surrejoinder.
re·cal·ci·trant (ri·kal′sə·trənt) *adj.* Not complying; obstinate; rebellious; refractory. — *n.* One who is recalcitrant. [<L *recalcitrans, -antis*, ppr. of *recalcitrare* kick back < *re-* back + *calcitrare* kick < *calx, calcis* heel] — **re·cal′ci·trance, re·cal′ci·tran·cy** *n.*
re·cal·ci·trate (ri·kal′sə·trāt) *v.i.* **·trat·ed, ·trat·ing** To refuse compliance or submission; be recalcitrant. [<L *recalcitratus*, pp. of *recalcitrare*. See RECALCITRANT.] — **re·cal′ci·tra′tion** *n.*
re·ca·lesce (rē′kə·les′) *v.i.* **·lesced, ·lesc·ing** To grow hot again; specifically, in physics, to exhibit recalescence. [<L *recalescere* < *re-* again + *calescere* grow warm, inceptive of *calere* be warm]
re·ca·les·cence (rē′kə·les′əns) *n.* 1 A glowing again. 2 *Physics* A phenomenon peculiar to heated iron or steel of glowing more brightly when certain temperatures are reached in the process of gradual cooling from a state of high incandescence. [<L *recalescens*, ppr. of *recalescere*. See RECALESCE.] — **re′ca·les′cent** *adj.*
re·call (ri·kôl′) *v.t.* 1 To call back; order or summon to return. 2 To summon back in awareness or attention. 3 To recollect; remember. 4 To take back; revoke; countermand. 5 *Poetic* To revive; restore. See synonyms under REMEMBER, RENOUNCE. — *n.* (ri·kôl′, rē′kôl′) 1 A calling back or to mind. 2 A signal to call back soldiers, etc., as by a bugle call, the display of a flag, etc. 3 Revocation, as of an order. 4 In certain States, a system whereby public officials may be removed from office by popular vote.
Ré·ca·mier (rā·kà·myā′), **Jeanne Françoise Julie Adélaïde**, 1777–1849, *née* Bernard, French social leader and patroness of literature: commonly known as *Madame Récamier*.
re·cant (ri·kant′) *v.t.* To withdraw formally one's belief in (something previously believed or maintained). — *v.i.* To disavow an opinion or belief previously held. [<L *recantare* < *re-* again + *cantare* sing, freq. of *canere* sing] — **re·can·ta·tion** (rē′kan·tā′shən) *n.* — **re·cant′er** *n.*

Synonyms: abandon, abjure, deny, disavow, discard, disclaim, disown, forswear, recall, renounce, repudiate, retract, revoke. To *recant* is to *deny* formally and publicly some opinion or statement, especially in religion, that one has held or advocated. *Abjure* is etymologically the exact equivalent of the Saxon *forswear*, signifying to put away formally and under oath, as an error, heresy, or evil practice, or a condemned and detested person. A man *recants* his belief, *abjures* or *renounces* his allegiance, *repudiates* another's claim, *renounces* his own, *retracts* a false statement. A person may *deny, disavow, disclaim, disown* what has been truly or falsely imputed to him or supposed to be his. He may *deny* his signature, *disavow* the act of his agent, *disown* his child; he may *repudiate* either a just claim or a base suggestion. Compare ABANDON, RENOUNCE.

re·cap (rē′kap′, rē·kap′) *v.t.* **·capped, ·cap·ping** To reprocess (an automobile tire) by vulcanizing new rubber onto the surface which comes into contact with the road. — *n.* (rē′kap′) A tire which has been so treated. Also *retread*. [RE- + CAP]
re·cap·i·tal·ize (rē·kap′ə·təl·īz′) *v.t.* **·ized, ·iz·ing** To capitalize again or differently. — **re·cap′i·tal·i·za′tion** *n.*
re·ca·pit·u·late (rē′kə·pich′ōō·lāt) *v.t.* & *v.i.* **·lat·ed, ·lat·ing** To review briefly; sum up. [<LL *recapitulare* < *re-* again + *capitulare*. See CAPITULATE.]
re·ca·pit·u·la·tion (rē′kə·pich′ōō·lā′shən) *n.* 1 The act of recapitulating; a summing up. 2 *Biol.* The process in which a developing embryo reproduces many of the typical forms of the organisms that precede it in the line of evolution. [<L *recapitulatio, -onis*]
re·ca·pit·u·la·to·ry (rē′kə·pich′ōō·lə·tôr′ē, -tō′rē) *adj.* Containing or of the nature of recapitulation. Also **re′ca·pit′u·la′tive** (-lā′tiv).
re·cap·tion (rē·kap′shən) *n.* *Law* 1 The rearrest of one who has escaped custody. 2 The retaking by peaceable means of one's goods, wife, child, or chattel from one who wrongfully detains them. [<RE- + CAPTION (def. 5)]
re·cap·ture (rē·kap′chər) *v.t.* **·tured, ·tur·ing** 1 To capture again; obtain by recapture. 2 To recall; remember. — *n.* 1 The act of retaking; especially, in war, the forcible recovery of booty or goods. 2 A prize retaken; anything recaptured. 3 The taking by the public of the earnings of a public service corporation over and above a stated profit.
re·cast (rē·kast′, -käst′) *v.t.* **·cast, ·cast·ing** 1 To form anew; cast again. 2 To fashion anew by changing style, arrangement, etc., as a discourse. 3 To calculate anew. — *n.* (rē′kast′, -käst′) Something which has been recast.
re·cede (ri·sēd′) *v.i.* **·ced·ed, ·ced·ing** 1 To move back; withdraw, as flood waters. 2 To withdraw, as from an assertion, position, agreement, etc. 3 To slope backward: a *receding* forehead. 4 To become more distant; incline away. [<L *recedere* < *re-* back + *cedere* go]
re-cede (rē·sēd′) *v.t.* **-ced·ed, -ced·ing** To cede back; grant or yield to a former owner. [<RE- + CEDE]
re·ceipt (ri·sēt′) *n.* 1 The act or state of receiving anything: to be in *receipt* of good news. 2 That which is received: usually in the plural: cash *receipts*. 3 A written acknowledgment of the payment of money, of the delivery of goods, etc. 4 A recipe. — *v.t.* 1 To give a receipt for the payment of. 2 To write acknowledgment of payment on, as a bill. — *v.i.* 3 To give a receipt, as for money paid. [<OF *recete* <L *recepta*, fem. of *receptus*, pp. of *recipere* RECEIVE; refashioned after Latin]
re·ceipt·or (ri·sē′tər) *n.* *Law* One who gives a receipt; specifically, one who gives a receipt for goods that have been attached.
re·ceiv·a·ble (ri·sē′və·bəl) *adj.* 1 Capable of being received; fit to be received, as legal tender. 2 Maturing for payment: said of a bill.
re·ceiv·a·bles (ri·sē′və·bəlz) *n. pl.* Outstanding accounts listed among the assets of a business.
re·ceive (ri·sēv′) *v.* **·ceived, ·ceiv·ing** *v.t.* 1 To take into one's hand or possession (something given, offered, delivered, etc.); acquire; accept. 2 To gain knowledge or information of: He *received* the news at breakfast. 3 To take from another by hearing or listening: The king *received* his oath of fealty. 4 To bear; support: These columns *receive* the weight of the building. 5 To experience; meet with: to *receive* abuse. 6 To undergo; suffer: He *received* a wound in his arm. 7 To intercept or encounter the force of (a blow, etc.). 8 To contain; hold. 9 To allow entrance to; admit to one's presence; greet. 10 To perceive mentally; understand. 11 To accept as true, proven, authoritative, etc. — *v.i.* 12 To be a recipient; get, obtain, or acquire something from some other person or source. 13 To welcome visitors or callers. 14 To partake of the Eucharist. 15 *Telecom.* To convert incoming radio waves into intelligible sounds or shapes, as a radio or television receiving set. See synonyms under ACCOMMODATE, GET, OBTAIN. [<OF *receivre* <L *recipere* < *re-* back + *capere* take]
re·ceived (ri·sēvd′) *adj.* *Chiefly Brit.* Accepted by established opinion or authority; standard: *received* ways of thinking.
Received Standard The form of educated English identified with that spoken at the English public schools and the universities of Oxford and Cambridge.
re·ceiv·er (rī·sē′vər) *n.* 1 One who receives; a recipient. 2 An official assigned to receive money due. 3 *Law* A person appointed by a court to take into his custody, control, and management the property or funds of another pending judicial action concerning them. 4 One who buys or receives stolen or embezzled goods, knowing them to be stolen. 5 Something which receives; a receptacle. 6 A vessel considered as a receptacle for a gas or fluid, as a jar for receiving and condensing a fluid that has been distilled. 7 A bolthead. 8 *Telecom.* An instrument in an electric circuit serving to receive and reproduce signals transmitted from another part of the circuit: a telephone *receiver*. 9 A radio or television receiving set.
re·ceiv·er·ship (ri·sē′vər·ship) *n.* 1 The office and functions pertaining to a receiver under appointment of a court. 2 *Law* The state of being in the hands of a receiver.
receiving set An apparatus for the reception of radio or television signals.
receiving ship A vessel stationed in a harbor to receive and provide for naval recruits, or for men awaiting transfer to new assignments.
re·cense (ri·sens′) *v.t.* **·censed, ·cens·ing** *Obs.* To revise or review, as a book; make a recension of. [<L *recensere*. See RECENSION.]
re·cen·sion (ri·sen′shən) *n.* 1 A critical revision of the text of a book; also, the edition so revised. 2 A review; critique. [<L *recensio, -onis* enumeration < *recensere* examine, survey < *re-* thoroughly + *censere* estimate, value]
re·cent (rē′sənt) *adj.* Pertaining to, or formed, developed, or created in time not long past; modern; fresh; new. See synonyms under FRESH, MODERN, NEW. [<OF <L *recens, -entis*] — **re′cent·ly** *adv.* — **re′cen·cy, re′cent·ness** *n.*
Re·cent (rē′sənt) *adj.* *Geol.* Pertaining to or designating the present or Holocene geological epoch, succeeding the Pleistocene.
re·cept (rē′sept) *n.* *Psychol.* A mental image of an external object, formed by the repetition of the same percept, with reinforcing of common characteristics. [<L *receptum*, neut. pp. of *recipere* receive; on analogy with *concept*]
re·cep·ta·cle (ri·sep′tə·kəl) *n.* 1 Anything that serves to contain or hold other things. 2 *Bot.* The base to which the parts of the flower, fruit, or seeds are fixed. 3 An outlet (def. 3). [<OF <L *receptaculum* < *receptare*, freq. of *recipere* RECEIVE]
re·cep·tion (ri·sep′shən) *n.* 1 The act of receiving, or the state of being received; receipt. 2 A formal social entertainment of guests: a wedding *reception*; also, the manner of receiving a person or persons: a warm *reception*. 3 Mental acceptance, as of a proposition. 4 In radio and television, the act or process of receiving or, especially, the quality of reproduction achieved: This radio gives very poor *reception*. [<OF <L *receptio, -onis* < *receptus*, pp. of *recipere* RECEIVE]
reception center A central receiving point; specifically, the point at which newly inducted military personnel are received and examined, and from which they are sent to their assigned units.
re·cep·tion·ist (ri·sep′shən·ist) *n.* A person employed to receive callers, provide information, and the like, at the entrance to an office.
reception room 1 A room for callers in a private house. 2 A waiting room in a hospital, or adjoining a doctor's, dentist's, or

recultivate
recultivation
redecorate
rededicate
rededication
redeliberate
redemonstrate
redeposit
redescend
redescent
redescribe
redetermine
redigest
rediminish
rediscover
rediscovery
redispose
redissolution
redissolve
redistil
redistrainer
redistribute
redistribution
redivide
redo
redraw
redrawer
redrive
re-echo
re-edify
reelaborate
reelect
reelection
re-elevate
reembark

lawyer's office. 3 A large room for a formal reception.

re·cep·tive (ri·sep′tiv) *adj.* Able or inclined to receive, as truths or impressions; able to take in or hold. [<OF *receptif* <Med. L *receptivus* <L *recipere* RECEIVE] —**re·cep′tive·ly** *adv.* —**re·cep·tiv·i·ty** (rē′sep·tiv′ə·tē), **re·cep′tive·ness** *n.*

re·cep·tor (ri·sep′tər) *n.* 1 *Bacteriol.* A combination of atoms in a cell that, by combining with extraneous substances, as drugs or toxins, may be thrown off from the cell and circulate in the blood, thus conferring immunity. 2 *Physiol.* The terminal structure, or free nerve ending, which is specialized to receive various forms of external and internal stimuli, transmitting them to the brain nerve centers: also called *sense organ.* Compare EFFECTOR. [<L, receiver]

re·cess (ri·ses′, rē′ses; *for def. 2, usually* rē′ses) *n.* 1 A depression or indentation in any otherwise continuous line, especially in a wall; niche; alcove. 2 A time of cessation from employment or occupation: The school took a *recess.* 3 *Usually pl.* A quiet and secluded spot; withdrawn or inner place: the *recesses* of the mind. 4 *Anat.* & *Bot.* A depression or cavity. —*v.* (ri·ses′) *v.t.* 1 To place in or as in a recess. 2 To make a recess in, as a wall. 3 To interrupt for a recess: to *recess* a court. —*v.i.* 4 To take a recess. [<L *recessus,* pp. of *recedere.* See RECEDE¹.]

re·ces·sion (ri·sesh′ən) *n.* 1 The act of receding; a withdrawal. 2 The procession of the clergy, choir, etc., as they leave the chancel after a church service. 3 An economic setback in commercial and industrial activity; especially, one occurring as a downward turn during a period of generally rising prosperity; a slight depression. [<L *recessio, -onis* < *recedere.* See RECEDE¹.]

re–ces·sion (rē·sesh′ən) *n.* The act of ceding again; a giving back.

re·ces·sion·al (ri·sesh′ən·əl) *adj.* Of or pertaining to recession. —*n.* A hymn sung as the choir or clergy leave the chancel after service: also **recessional hymn.**

re·ces·sive (ri·ses′iv) *adj.* 1 Having a tendency to recede or go back; receding. 2 Failing to come into expression. 3 *Genetics* Designating that one of a pair of contrasted allelomorphic characters which is suppressed in a hybrid offspring when both are present: opposed to *dominant.* —*n. Genetics* 1 A hybrid which carries and transmits a character suppressed by the corresponding dominant character. 2 The suppressed character. —**re·ces′sive·ly** *adv.*

Rech·a·bite (rek′ə·bīt) *n.* 1 One of a Jewish family descended from Jonadab, son of Rechab, who abstained from wine and the planting of vineyards. *Jer.* xxxv 3. 2 Hence, a total abstainer from intoxicants; a teetotaler. 3 A member of a society of teetotalers called the Independent Order of Rechabites, founded in England in 1835 and in the United States in 1842. —**Rech′a·bit′ism** *n.*

ré·chauf·fé (rā·shō·fā′) *n. French* 1 Food warmed over. 2 Reworked or "warmed over" literary work; rehash.

re·cheat (ri·chēt′) *n. Archaic* A strain sounded on a huntsman's horn to recall the hounds from a wrong course or at the end of the hunt; also, the act of sounding this signal. —*v.i. Obs.* To sound the recheat. [<OF *rachater* rally, reassemble]

re·cher·ché (rə·sher·shā′) *adj. French* 1 Much sought after; hence, choice; rare. 2 Far-fetched.

re·cid·i·vist (rə·sid′ə·vist) *n.* 1 Anyone who relapses into a former state or condition. 2 A confirmed criminal; in the United States, one committed to prison for a second term. [<F *récidiviste* <L *recidivus* relapsing < *recidere* < *re-* back + *cadere* fall] —**re·cid′i·vism, rec·i·div·i·ty** (res′ə·div′ə·tē) *n.* —**re·cid′i·vis′tic** *adj.*

re·cid·i·vous (rə·sid′ə·vəs) *adj.* Liable to backslide.

Re·ci·fe (re·sē′fə) A port of NE Brazil; capital of Pernambuco state: also *Pernambuco.*

rec·i·pe (res′ə·pē) *n.* 1 A formula or list of ingredients of a mixture, giving the exact proportions together with proper directions for compounding, cooking, etc. 2 A medical prescription: so called from its opening word: usually abbreviated to ℞. 3 A method prescribed for attaining a desired result. [<L, take, imperative of *recipere.* See RECEIVE.]

re·cip·i·ence (ri·sip′ē·əns) *n.* 1 The process or act of receiving. 2 Receptivity. Also **re·cip′i·en·cy.**

re·cip·i·ent (ri·sip′ē·ənt) *adj.* Receiving or ready to receive; receptive. —*n.* One who or that which receives; one who accepts a gift or favor. [<L *recipiens, -entis,* ppr. of *recipere* RECEIVE]

re·cip·ro·cal (ri·sip′rə·kəl) *adj.* 1 Done or given by each of two to the other; mutual. 2 Mutually interchangeable. 3 Alternating; moving to and fro. 4 So related, as two concepts, that if the first determines the second, then the second determines the first. 5 Expressive of mutual relationship or action: used in connection with certain pronouns and verbs or their meaning. 6 *Math.* Of or pertaining to a fraction the numerator and denominator of which have been reversed. —*n.* 1 That which is reciprocal. 2 *Math.* The quotient obtained by dividing unity by a number or expression, as $\frac{1}{x}$ is the reciprocal of *x.* In a fraction, this reverses the numerator and denominator, as $\frac{3}{2}$ is the reciprocal of $\frac{2}{3}$. See synonyms under MUTUAL. [<L *reciprocus*] —**re·cip′ro·cal′i·ty** (-kal′ə·tē), **re·cip′ro·cal·ness** *n.* —**re·cip′ro·cal·ly** *adv.*

reciprocal pronouns *Gram.* Pronouns or pronominal phrases denoting reciprocal action or relation, as *each other, one another.*

re·cip·ro·cate (ri·sip′rə·kāt) *v.* **·cat·ed, ·cat·ing** *v.t.* 1 To cause to move backward and forward alternately. 2 To give and receive mutually, as favors or gifts; interchange. 3 To give, feel, do, etc., in return; requite, as an emotion. —*v.i.* 4 To move backward and forward. 5 To make a return in kind. 6 To give and receive favors, gifts, etc., mutually. 7 To correspond; be equivalent. See synonyms under REQUITE. [<L *reciprocatus,* pp. of *reciprocare* move to and fro < *reciprocus* returning] —**re·cip′ro·ca′tive** *adj.* —**re·cip′ro·ca′tor** *n.*

reciprocating engine An engine having a piston or pistons which move to and fro: distinguished from *rotary engine.*

re·cip·ro·ca·tion (ri·sip′rə·kā′shən) *n.* The act of reciprocating; a mutual giving and returning; alternation; alternate motion. See synonyms under INTERCOURSE. [<L *reciprocatio, -onis* < *reciprocus* returning]

re·cip·ro·ca·to·ry (ri·sip′rə·kə·tôr′ē, -tō′rē) *adj.* Alternating in direction or movement; reciprocating: opposed to *rotary.*

rec·i·proc·i·ty (res′ə·pros′ə·tē) *n.* 1 Reciprocal obligation, action, or relation. 2 That trade relation or policy between two countries by which each makes concessions favoring the importation of the products of the other. See synonyms under INTERCOURSE. [<F *réciprocité*]

re·ci·sion (ri·sizh′ən) *n.* 1 The act of rescinding. 2 The act of pruning. [<OF <L *recisio, -onis* < *recisum,* pp. of *recidere* cut off < *re-* back + *caedere* cut]

re·cit·al (ri·sīt′l) *n.* 1 A telling over in detail, or that which is thus told; a narration. 2 A public delivery of something previously memorized. 3 A musical program performed by one person, or consisting of works by one person. 4 A detailed statement. See synonyms under HISTORY, REPORT, STORY¹.

rec·i·ta·tion (res′ə·tā′shən) *n.* 1 The act of repeating from memory; the reciting of a lesson, or the meeting of a class for that purpose. 2 That which is allotted for recital or actually recited. [<L *recitatio, -onis* < *recitare.* See RECITE.]

rec·i·ta·tive¹ (res′ə·tā′tiv, ri·sī′tə·tiv) *adj.* Of the nature of a recital as of facts or details; narrative.

rec·i·ta·tive² (res′ə·tə·tēv′, rə·sit′ə·tiv) *n. Music* Language uttered as in ordinary speech, but in musical tones; that style of singing or a vocal passage so rendered. Also *Italian* **re·ci·ta·ti·vo** (rā′chē·tä·tē′vō). —*adj.* Having the character of a recitative. [<Ital. *recitativo,* ult. <L *recitare*]

re·cite (ri·sīt′) *v.* **·cit·ed, ·cit·ing** *v.t.* 1 To declaim or say from memory, especially formally, as a lesson in class. 2 To tell in particular detail; relate. 3 To enumerate. —*v.i.* 4 To declaim or speak something from memory. 5 To repeat or be examined in a lesson or part of a lesson in class. See synonyms under RELATE. [<F *réciter* <L *recitare* < *re-* again + *citare.* See CITE.] —**re·cit′er** *n.*

re–cite (rē·sīt′) *v.t.* & *v.i.* **–cit·ed, –cit·ing** To cite again. [<RE- + CITE]

reck (rek) *v.t.* & *v.i. Obs.* 1 To have a care or thought (for); heed; mind. 2 To be of concern or interest (to): It *recks* me not. ◆ Homophone: *wreck.* [OE *rēccan*]

reck·less (rek′lis) *adj.* 1 Foolishly heedless of danger; rash. 2 Indifferent; neglectful. See synonyms under IMPROVIDENT, IMPRUDENT, WANTON. [OE *recceléas*] —**reck′less·ly** *adv.* —**reck′less·ness** *n.*

Reck·ling·hau·sen (rek′ling·hou′zən) A city in the Ruhr in NW North Rhine–Westphalia, West Germany.

reck·on (rek′ən) *v.t.* 1 To count; compute; calculate. 2 To look upon as being; regard: They *reckon* him a fool. 3 *Dial.* To suppose or guess; expect. —*v.i.* 4 To make computation; count up. 5 To rely or depend: with *on* or *upon*: to *reckon* on help. See synonyms under CALCULATE. —**to reckon for** To pay for; receive the penalty of. —**to reckon with** 1 To settle accounts with. 2 To take into consideration; bear in mind; consider. —**to reckon without one's host** To reckon a bill without consulting the landlord; hence, to neglect important facts in reaching a conclusion. [OE *recenian* explain. Akin to G *rechnen* count.]

reck·on·er (rek′ən·ər) *n.* 1 One who reckons. 2 A book or device for aiding one to compute: often called **ready reckoner.**

reck·on·ing (rek′ən·ing) *n.* 1 The act of counting; computation; a settlement of accounts. 2 Account; score; bill, as at a hotel. 3 *Naut.* The calculation of a ship's position, especially when made only by log and compass; dead reckoning. 4 An accounting to God.

re·claim (ri·klām′) *v.t.* 1 To bring (swamp, desert, etc.) into a condition to support cultivation or life, as by draining or irrigating. 2 To obtain (a substance) from used or waste products: to *reclaim* rubber. 3 To cause to return from wrong or sinful ways of life; reform. 4 *Obs.* To tame, as a hawk. —*n.* 1 The act of reclaiming or state of being reclaimed; also, that which is reclaimed. 2 A fresh claim. [<OF *reclamer* call back <L *reclamare* < *re-* against + *clamare* cry out] —**re·claim′a·ble** *adj.* —**re·claim′er, re·claim′ant** *n.*

Synonyms (verb): amend, convert, correct, recover, redeem, reform, renew, rescue, restore, subdue, tame. *Antonyms*: corrupt, degrade, deprave, destroy, seduce, vitiate.

re–claim (rē·klām′) *v.t.* To claim again.

rec·la·ma·tion (rek′lə·mā′shən) *n.* 1 The act or process of reclaiming, in any sense. 2 Restoration, as to ownership, cultivation, usefulness, or a moral life. —**Bureau of Reclamation** A branch of the U. S. Department of the Interior which constructs and operates Federal water-power plants and irrigation projects. [<F *réclamation* <L *reclamatio, -onis* a cry of disapproval < *reclamare.* See RECLAIM.]

ré·clame (rā·klàm′) *n. French* 1 Publicity. 2 A striving after publicity.

re·cline (ri·klīn′) *v.* **·clined, ·clin·ing** *v.i.* To assume a recumbent position; lie down or back. —*v.t.* To cause to assume a recumbent position; lay down or back. See synonyms under

reembarkation	**re–emit**	**reencouragement**	**reenjoy**	**reenslave**	**reerect**	**reexamine**
reembody	**reenact**	**reendow**	**reenjoyment**	**reenslavement**	**reestablish**	**reexhibit**
reembrace	**reenaction**	**reengage**	**reenkindle**	**reenstamp**	**reestablishment**	**reexpel**
reemerge	**reenactment**	**reengagement**	**reenlist**	**reenthrone**	**re–evaluate**	**reexperience**
reemergence	**reencourage**	**reengrave**	**reenlistment**	**reenthronement**	**reexamination**	**reexport**

add,āce,câre,pälm; end,ēven; it,īce; odd,ōpen,ôrder; to͝ok,po͞ol; up,bûrn; ə = a in *above,* e in *sicken,* i in *clarity,* o in *melon,* u in *focus;* yo͞o = u in *fuse;* oi,oil; ou,pout; ch,check; g,go; ng,ring; th,thin; th,this; zh,vision. Foreign sounds à,œ,ü,kh,ṅ; and ◆: see page xx. < from; + plus; ? possibly.

LEAN[1], REST[1]. [<L *reclinare* <*re-* back + *clinare* lean] —**rec·li·na·tion** (rek′lə·nā′shən) *n.* —**re·clin′er** *n.*

rec·luse (rek′lo͞os, ri·klo͞os′) *n.* **1** One who lives in retirement or seclusion. **2** One who retires from intercourse with the world, as a religious devotee; specifically, one who lives shut up in a cell and practices exceptional austerities. —**re·cluse** (ri·klo͞os′) *adj.* Secluded or retired from the world; solitary. [<OF *reclus* <LL *reclusus,* pp. of L *recludere* shut off <*re-* again + *claudere* close] —**re·clu′sive** *adj.*

re·clu·sion (ri·klo͞o′zhən) *n.* **1** The state of being a recluse; retirement from the world. **2** Rigorous immurement as practiced by certain ascetics in the Middle Ages. **3** Imprisonment; especially, solitary confinement.

re·clu·sive (ri·klo͞o′siv) *adj.* Affording or living in seclusion; recluse.

rec·og·ni·tion (rek′əg·nish′ən) *n.* **1** The act of recognizing; the process of memory that identifies an object, person, etc., as already known or experienced. **2** Acknowledgment of a fact or claim. **3** Friendly notice; salutation; attention: *recognition* of a speaker by the chair. **4** Acknowledgment and acceptance on the part of one government of the independence and validity of another. See synonyms under KNOWLEDGE. [<L *recognitio, -onis* <*recognitus,* pp. of *recognoscere.* See RECOGNIZANCE.] —**re·cog·ni·to·ry** (ri·kog′nə·tôr′ē, -tō′rē), **re·cog′ni·tive** *adj.*

re·cog·ni·zance (ri·kog′nə·zəns, -kon′ə-) *n.* **1** *Law* **a** An acknowledgment or obligation of record, with condition to do some particular act, as to appear and answer, or to keep the peace. **b** A sum of money deposited as surety for fulfilment of such act or obligation, and forfeited by its non-performance. **2** *Obs.* A badge or token to aid in recognition. [<OF *recognoissance* <*reconoissant,* ppr. of *reconoistre* <L *recognoscere* call to mind <*re-* again + *cognoscere* know. See COGNITION.] —**re·cog′ni·zant** *adj.*

rec·og·nize (rek′əg·nīz) *v.t.* **·nized, ·niz·ing 1** To know again; perceive as identical with someone or something previously known. **2** To identify or know, as by previous experience or knowledge: I *recognize* poor poetry when I see it. **3** To perceive as true; realize: to *recognize* the facts in a case. **4** To acknowledge the independence and validity of, as a newly constituted government. **5** To indicate appreciation or approval of: to *recognize* merit. **6** To approve formally; regard as valid or genuine: to *recognize* a claim. **7** To give (someone) permission to speak, as in a legislative body. **8** To admit the acquaintance of; greet. **9** *Law* To bind by a recognizance. See synonyms under ACKNOWLEDGE, CONFESS, DISCERN. [Back formation <RECOGNIZANCE] —**rec′og·niz′a·ble** *adj.* —**rec′og·niz′a·bly** *adv.* —**rec′og·niz′er** *n.*

re·cog·ni·zee (ri·kog′nə·zē′, -kon′ə-) *n. Law* One in whose favor a recognizance is made.

re·cog·ni·zor (ri·kog′nə·zər, -kon′ə-) *n. Law* One who enters into a recognizance.

re·coil (ri·koil′) *v.i.* **1** To start back, as in fear or loathing; shrink: He *recoiled* at the sight. **2** To spring back, as from force of discharge or force of impact. **3** To return to the source; react: with *on* or *upon*: Crime *recoils* upon its perpetrator. **4** To move or draw back; retreat. —*n.* (rē′koil′) **1** A backward movement or impulse, as of a gun at the moment of firing; rebound; also, a shrinking. **2** The condition existing as the result of a recoil. [<OF *reculer* <L *re-* again + *culus* buttocks] —**re·coil′er** *n.*

re·coil-op·er·at·ed (rē′koil·op′ə·rā′tid) *adj.* Operated or working by the energy generated in recoil, as certain automatic weapons.

rec·ol·lect (rek′ə·lekt′) *v.t.* To call back to the mind; revive in the memory; remember. —*v.i.* To have a recollection of something. See synonyms under REMEMBER. [<L *recollectus,* pp. of *recolligere* gather together again <*re-* again + *colligere.* See COLLECT.]

re-col·lect (rē′kə·lekt′) *v.t.* **1** to collect again, as things scattered. **2** To collect or compose (one's thoughts or nerves); compose or recover (oneself). [<RE- + COLLECT]

rec·ol·lect·ed (rek′ə·lek′tid) *adj.* Recalled to mind; remembered.

re-col·lect·ed (rē′kə·lek′tid) *adj.* Calm; composed; collected.

rec·ol·lec·tion (rek′ə·lek′shən) *n.* **1** The act or power of recollecting or remembering; remembrance. **2** Something remembered; a reminiscence; a memory. See synonyms under MEMORY. —**rec′ol·lec′tive** *adj.* —**rec′ol·lec′tive·ly** *adv.*

re-col·lec·tion (rē′kə·lek′shən) *n.* The act of re-collecting, or the state of being re-collected.

re·com·bi·na·tion (rē′kom·bə·nā′shən) *n. Genetics* **1** A cross-over. **2** An offspring exhibiting characters caused by such a rearrangement.

rec·om·mend (rek′ə·mend′) *v.t.* **1** To commend with favorable representations; praise as desirable, worthy, etc. **2** To make attractive or acceptable: His sagacity *recommends* him. **3** To advise; urge. **4** To give in charge; commend. [<Med. L *recommendare* <*re-* again + *commendare.* See COMMEND.] —**rec′om·mend′er** *n.*

rec·om·men·da·tion (rek′ə·men·dā′shən) *n.* **1** The act of recommending, or that which recommends. **2** A note commending a person to confidence or favor. See synonyms under COUNSEL.

rec·om·mend·a·to·ry (rek′ə·men′də·tôr′ē, -tō′rē) *adj.* **1** Serving to recommend. **2** Advisory but not imperative, as applied to certain official appointments.

re·com·mit (rē′kə·mit′) *v.t.* **·mit·ted, ·mit·ting 1** To commit again. **2** To refer back to a committee, as a bill.

rec·om·pense (rek′əm·pens) *v.t.* **·pensed, ·pens·ing 1** To give compensation to; pay or repay; reward; requite. **2** To give compensation for; make up for, as a loss. See synonyms under PAY[1], REQUITE. —*n.* An equivalent for anything given, done, or suffered; payment or repayment; compensation; reward. [<OF *recompenser* <LL *recompensare* <L *re-* again + *compensare.* See COMPENSATE.]

Synonyms (noun): amends, compensation, indemnification, indemnity, remuneration, repayment, requital, retribution, reward, satisfaction. See RESTITUTION, SALARY.

re·com·pose (rē′kəm·pōz′) *v.t.* **·posed, ·pos·ing 1** To restore the composure of; tranquilize. **2** To compose or form anew; rearrange; reconstitute; recombine. —**re·com·po·si·tion** (rē′kom·pə·zish′ən) *n.*

re·con·cen·tra·do (rā·kōn′sen·trä′dō) *n. pl.* **·dos** In Cuba and the Philippine Islands, during and before the Spanish-American War, a dweller in the country who was forced by decree of the Spanish authorities to move within the city limits. [<Sp., pp. of *reconcentrar* move to the center again; so called because the authorities had previously ordered the country population to move within a certain radius of the town]

re·con·cen·trate (rē·kon′sən·trāt) *v.t.* **·at·ed, ·at·ing** To concentrate again; specifically, to treat as reconcentrados. —**re·con′cen·tra′tion** *n.*

rec·on·cil·a·ble (rek′ən·sī′lə·bəl) *adj.* **1** Capable of being reconciled or of renewing friendship. **2** Capable of being adjusted or harmonized. —**rec′on·cil′a·bil′i·ty, rec′on·cil′a·ble·ness** *n.* —**rec′on·cil′a·bly** *adv.*

rec·on·cile (rek′ən·sīl) *v.t.* **·ciled, ·cil·ing 1** To bring back to friendship after estrangement; also, to make friendly; win the good will of. **2** To settle or adjust, as a quarrel. **3** To bring to acquiescence, content, or submission: to *reconcile* one to his lot. **4** To make or show to be consistent or congruous; harmonize: often with *to* or *with*: Can he *reconcile* his statement with his conduct? See synonyms under ACCOMMODATE. [<OF *reconciler* <L *reconciliare* <*re-* again + *conciliare* unite. See CONCILIATE.] —**rec′on·cile′ment** *n.* —**rec′on·cil′er** *n.*

rec·on·cil·i·a·tion (rek′ən·sil′ē·ā′shən) *n.* **1** The act of reconciling, or the state of being reconciled; atonement. **2** The effecting or showing of agreement between things; explanation of differences. See synonyms under PROPITIATION. —**rec′on·cil′i·a·to′ry** (-sil′ē·ə·tôr′ē, -tō′rē) *adj.*

rec·on·dite (rek′ən·dīt, ri·kon′dīt) *adj.* **1** Remote from ordinary or easy perception; abstruse; secret. **2** Dealing in abstruse matters; profound. **3** Hidden; not readily observed. See synonyms under MYSTERIOUS, SECRET. [<L *reconditus,* pp. of *recondere* put away, hide <*re-* back + *condere* construct, hide] —**rec′on·dite′ly** *adv.* —**rec′on·dite′ness** *n.*

re·con·di·tion (rē′kən·di′shən) *v.t.* To put into good or working condition, as by making repairs; overhaul.

re·con·nais·sance (ri·kon′ə·səns, -säns) *n.* **1** A reconnoitering; a preliminary examination or survey, as of the territory and resources of a country. **2** The act of obtaining information of military value, especially regarding the position, strength, and movement of enemy forces. Also **re·con′nois·sance.** [<F]

re·con·noi·ter (rē′kə·noi′tər, rek′ə-) *v.t.* To examine by the eye; survey, as for military, engineering, or geological purposes. —*v.i.* To make a reconnaissance. Also **re′con·noi′tre.** [<OF *reconoistre.* See RECOGNIZANCE.] —**re′con·noi′ter·er, re′con·noi′trer** *n.*

re·con·sid·er (rē′kən·sid′ər) *v.t.* **1** To consider again, especially with a view to a reversal of previous action. **2** In parliamentary usage, to bring before the house for renewed action (a matter previously decided). —*v.i.* **3** To reconsider a matter or decision. —**re′con·sid′er·a′tion** *n.*

re·con·sign (rē′kən·sīn′) *v.t.* To consign again; specifically, to consign (goods) to a different place or person while still in transit. —**re′·con·sign′ment** *n.*

re·con·sti·tute (rē·kon′stə·to͞ot, -tyo͞ot) *v.t.* **·tut·ed, ·tut·ing** To constitute again; make over: to *reconstitute* dehydrated fruits by adding water. —**re·con′sti·tu′tion** *n.*

re·con·struct (rē′kən·strukt′) *v.t.* To construct again; rebuild.

re·con·struct·ed (rē′kən·struk′tid) *adj.* Rebuilt or made anew: said especially of gems artificially made: a *reconstructed* ruby.

re·con·struc·tion (rē′kən·struk′shən) *n.* **1** The act of reconstructing, or the state of being reconstructed; specifically, the restoration of the seceded States as members of the Union under the **Reconstruction Acts** of March 2 and 23, 1867. **2** The repair of mutilated limbs, as of soldiers, by means of mechanical appliances. —**re′con·struc′tive** *adj.*

Reconstruction Finance Corporation A former (1932–54) branch of the Federal Loan Agency of the U.S. Department of the Interior, authorized to extend financial assistance to agriculture, industry, and commerce.

Reconstruction period *U.S.* The period following the Civil War during which the seceded Southern States were reorganized in accordance with the Congressional program.

re·con·vey (rē′kən·vā′) *v.t.* To convey back to an original owner or place. —**re′con·vey′ance** *n.*

rec·ord (rek′ərd) *n.* **1** An account in written or other permanent form serving as a memorial or authentic evidence of a fact or event. **2** Something on which such an account is made, as a document or monument. **3** Information on facts or events, preserved and handed down: the heaviest rainfall on *record.* **4** The known career or performance of a person, animal, organization, etc., regarded as a series of things done or achieved: a good *record* in politics. **5** The best listed achievement, as in a competitive sport: to beat the world *record.* **6** *Law* **a** A written account of an act, statement, or transaction made by an officer acting under authority of law, and intended as permanent evidence thereon. **b** An official written account of a judicial or legislative proceeding, including the judgments or enactments and an official copy of all related documents. **7** A cylinder, disk, roll, or other article perforated, indented, or otherwise prepared so as to reproduce sounds. —**off the record 1** Unofficial or unofficially. **2** Not for quotation or publication, or not from a source to be identified. —*adj.* Surpassing any previously recorded achievement or performance of its kind: a *record* vote. —**re·cord** (ri·kôrd′) *v.t.* **1** To write down or otherwise inscribe, as for preserving an

reexportation	**refertilize**	**refluctuation**	**refortify**	**regerminate**	**regreet**	**rehybridize**
reexpulsion	**reflorescence**	**refold**	**refreeze**	**regermination**	**rehandle**	**rehypothecate**
reface	**reflourish**	**reforge**	**refurbish**	**regild**	**rehearing**	**reillume**
refashion	**reflow**	**reforger**	**refurnish**	**regraft**	**reheel**	**reimplant**
refasten	**reflower**	**refortification**	**regather**	**regrant**	**rehire**	**reimport**

authentic account, evidence, etc. **2** To indicate; register, especially in permanent form, as a cardiograph does. **3** To make a phonograph record of. —*v.i.* **4** To record something. [<OF <*recorder* <L *recordari* call to mind <*re-* again + *cor, cordis* heart, mind]

Synonyms (noun): account, archives, catalog, chronicle, document, enrolment, entry, enumeration, history, inscription, instrument, inventory, memorandum, memorial, muniment, register, roll, scroll. *Record* is a word of wide signification, applying to any writing, mark, or trace that serves as a *memorial* giving enduring attestation of an event or fact; an extended *account, chronicle,* or *history* is a *record*; so, too, may be a brief *inventory* or *memorandum.* A *memorial* is any object, whether a writing, a monument, or other permanent thing that is designed or adapted to keep something in remembrance. A *register* is a formal or official written *record,* especially a series of entries made for preservation or reference; as, a *register* of births and deaths. *Archives,* in the sense here considered, are *documents* or *records,* often legal *records,* preserved in a public or official depository; the word *archives* is also applied to the place where such *documents* are regularly deposited and preserved. *Muniments* are *records* that enable one to defend his title. See CHARACTER, HISTORY, REPORT, STORY[1].

re·cord·er (ri·kôr′dər) *n.* **1** One who records. **2** A magistrate having criminal jurisdiction in a city or borough. **3** A registering apparatus. **4** A fipple flute, having eight holes and any one of four ranges: treble, alto, tenor, or bass. **5** A tape recorder or wire recorder. —**re·cord′er·ship** *n.*

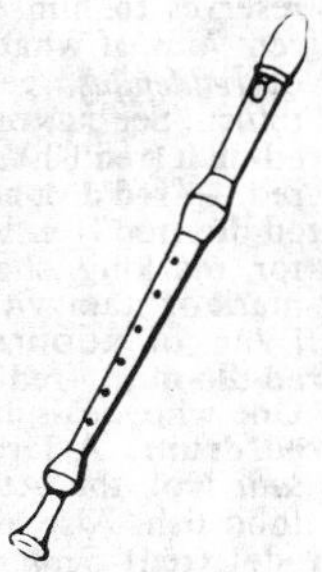

TREBLE RECORDER

re·count (ri·kount′) *v.t.* **1** To relate the particulars of; narrate in detail. **2** To enumerate; recite. See synonyms under RELATE. [<AF, OF *reconter* relate]

re–count (rē·kount′) *v.t.* To count again. —*n.* (rē′kount′, rē·kount′) A repetition of a count; specifically, a second count of votes cast.

re·count·al (ri·koun′təl) *n.* A thing told, or the act of telling; a detailed narration. Also **re·count′ment.**

re·coup (ri·ko͞op′) *v.t.* **1** To recover or obtain an equivalent for; make up, as a loss. **2** To reimburse for a loss; indemnify. **3** *Law* To keep back (something due) in order to make good a counterclaim. —*n.* The act or process of recouping. [<F *recouper* <*re-* again + *couper* cut. See COUP.] —**re·coup′a·ble** *adj.* —**re·coup′ment** *n.*

re·course (rē′kôrs, -kōrs, ri·kôrs′, -kōrs′) *n.* **1** Resort to or application for help or security in trouble. **2** *Law* The right to exact payment from a party secondarily liable, where the first party liable has failed to pay. **3** A source of help or supply; the person or thing resorted to. **4** *Obs.* Admission; entrance. —**without recourse** A restricted or qualified endorsement of a promissory note or transfer thereof, which signifies that the endorser merely transfers the title to the instrument, but disclaims liability for non–payment. —**to have recourse to** To go to for advice or help. [<OF *recours* <L *recursus* a running back <*recurrere.* See RECUR.]

re·cov·er (ri·kuv′ər) *v.t.* **1** To obtain again after losing; regain, as property, self–control, health, etc. **2** To make up for; retrieve, as a loss. **3** To restore (oneself) to natural balance, health, etc. **4** In sports, to regain (one's normal position of guard, balance, etc.). **5** To reclaim, as land. **6** *Law* **a** To gain in judicial proceedings: to *recover* judgment. **b** To gain or regain by legal process. —*v.i.* **7** To regain health, composure, etc. **8** *Law* To succeed in a lawsuit. **9** In sports, to regain one's balance or position of guard. [<OF *recovrer* <L *recuperare.* See RECUPERATE.] —**re·cov′er·a·ble** *adj.* —**re·cov′er·er** *n.*

Synonyms: cure, heal, reanimate, recruit, recuperate, regain, repossess, restore, resume, retrieve. See RECLAIM. *Antonyms*: die, fail, lapse, sink.

re–cov·er (rē·kuv′ər) *v.t.* To cover again. —**re–cov′er·er** *n.*

re·cov·er·y (ri·kuv′ər·ē) *n. pl.* **·er·ies** **1** The act of recovering. **2** The state of being or having recovered. **3** Restoration from sickness or from any undesirable or abnormal condition. **4** In boating, the forward movement of an oarsman, after having finished one stroke, to take the next. **5** In fencing and sparring, the act of regaining a defensive position after attack. **6** The extraction of valuable substances and materials from original sources, by–products, waste, etc. **7** The retrieval of a flying object, as a balloon, space vehicle, meteorite, etc., after it has fallen to earth. [<AF *recoverie*]

recovery room A room in a hospital for the treatment of patients recovering immediately after an operation or childbirth.

rec·re·ant (rek′rē·ənt) *adj.* **1** Unfaithful to a cause or pledge; apostate; false. **2** Crying for mercy, as in the old trial by combat; hence, craven; cowardly. See synonyms under PUSILLANIMOUS. —*n.* A cowardly or faithless person; also, a deserter; an apostate. [<OF, ppr. of *recreire* surrender allegiance <Med. L *recredere* <L *re-* back + *credere* believe] —**rec′re·an·cy, rec′re·ance** *n.* —**rec′re·ant·ly** *adv.*

rec·re·ate (rek′rē·āt) *v.* **·at·ed, ·at·ing** *v.t.* To impart fresh vigor to; refresh, especially after toil, by some form of relaxation or entertainment. —*v.i.* To take recreation. See synonyms under ENTERTAIN, RELAX. [<L *recreatus,* pp. of *recreare* create anew <*re-* again + *creare* create] —**rec′re·a′tive** *adj.*

re–cre·ate (rē′krē·āt′) *v.t.* **·at·ed, ·at·ing** To create anew. —**re′–cre·a′tion** *n.*

rec·re·a·tion (rek′rē·ā′shən) *n.* **1** Refreshment of body or mind, but generally of both; diversion; amusement. **2** Any pleasurable exercise or occupation. See synonyms under ENTERTAINMENT, REST[1], SPORT. —**rec′re·a′tion·al** *adj.*

rec·re·ment (rek′rə·mənt) *n.* **1** *Physiol.* A secretion reabsorbed by the body after having performed its function, as gastric juice, saliva, etc. **2** Waste material; dross; scoria; spume. [<F *récrément* <L *recrementum* dross <*re-* back + *cretum,* pp. of *cernere* sift] —**rec′re·men′tal** (-men′təl) *adj.* —**rec′re·men·ti′tial** (-men·tish′əl), **rec′re·men·ti′tious** *adj.*

re·crim·i·nate (ri·krim′ə·nāt) *v.* **·nat·ed, ·nat·ing** *v.t.* To accuse in return. —*v.i.* To repel one accusation by making another in return. [<Med. L *recriminatus,* pp. of *recriminare* < L *re-* again + *criminare.* See CRIMINATE.] —**re·crim′i·na′tive, re·crim·i·na·to·ry** (ri·krim′ə·nə·tôr′ē, -tō′rē) *adj.* —**re·crim′i·na′tor** *n.*

re·crim·i·na·tion (ri·krim′ə·nā′shən) *n.* **1** The act of recriminating. **2** An accusation made in return; a countercharge.

re·cru·desce (rē′kro͞o·des′) *v.i.* **·desced, ·desc·ing** To break out or become active again. [<L *recrudescere* <*re-* again + *crudescere* become harsh, break out <*crudus* raw, harsh]

re·cru·des·cence (rē′kro͞o·des′əns) *n.* **1** A breaking out afresh, as of a disease or wound. **2** A reappearance; return. [<L *recrudescens, -entis* ppr. of *recrudescere.* See RECRUDESCE.] —**re′cru·des′cent** *adj.*

re·cruit (ri·kro͞ot′) *v.t.* **1** To enlist (men) for military or naval service. **2** To muster; raise, as an army, by enlistment. **3** To supply with recruits. **4** To regain or revive (lost health, strength, etc.). **5** *Rare* To replenish. —*v.i.* **6** To enlist new men for military or naval service. **7** To regain lost health or strength. **8** To gain or raise new supplies of anything lost or needed. —*n.* **1** A newly enlisted soldier, sailor, or marine; loosely, any new adherent of a cause, organization, or the like. **2** *Obs.* A new supply of something necessary or useful. [<F *recruter* <*recrute* a recruit <*recrû* grown again, pp. of *recroître* <L *re-* again + *crescere* grow, increase] —**re·cruit′er** *n.* —**re·cruit′ment** *n.*

Synonyms (verb): enlist, reinforce, repair, replenish. See RECOVER. *Antonyms*: decimate, disperse, lose, reduce, scatter.

rec·tal (rek′təl) *adj. Anat.* Relating to, involving, or in the region of the rectum.

rec·tan·gle (rek′tang′gəl) *n.* A right–angled parallelogram. [<F <LL *rectiangulum* <L *rectus* straight + *angulus* angle]

rec·tan·gu·lar (rek·tang′gyə·lər) *adj.* **1** Having one or more right angles. **2** Resembling a rectangle in shape or appearance. —**rec·tan′gu·lar′i·ty** (-lar′ə·tē) *n.* —**rec·tan′gu·lar·ly** *adv.*

rectangular coordinate system See CARTESIAN COORDINATE SYSTEM.

rectangular hyperbola *Math.* A hyperbola with axes of equal length and perpendicular asymptotes.

recti– *combining form* Straight: *rectilinear.* Also, before vowels, **rect–.** [<L *rectus* right]

rec·ti·fi·ca·tion (rek′tə·fə·kā′shən) *n.* **1** The act or process of rectifying. **2** A setting right of what is wrong. **3** Refining by fractional or renewed distillation. [<F]

rec·ti·fi·er (rek′tə·fī′ər) *n.* **1** On who or that which rectifies. **2** *Electr.* A device used to convert an alternating current into a direct or unidirectional current. **3** A refiner or compounder of spirituous liquors.

rec·ti·fy (rek′tə·fī) *v.t.* **·fied, ·fy·ing** **1** To make right; correct; amend. **2** *Chem.* To refine, as a liquid, by repeated distillations until a desired degree of purity is obtained. **3** *Electr.* To change (an alternating current) into a direct current by reversing the direction of alternate impulses. **4** *Math.* To determine the length of (a curve or arc). **5** To allow for errors or inaccuracies in, as a compass reading. **6** To adjust for accurate calculations: to *rectify* a globe. See synonyms under AMEND. [< OF *rectifier* <LL *rectificare* <L *rectus* right + *facere* make] —**rec′ti·fi′a·ble** *adj.*

rec·ti·graph (rek′tə·graf, -gräf) *n. Optics* A separable part which may be inserted into the tube of an optical instrument in order to reinvert an inverted image. [<RECTI- + -GRAPH] —**rec′ti·graph′ic** *adj.*

rec·ti·lin·e·ar (rek′tə·lin′ē·ər) *adj.* Pertaining to, consisting of, moving in, or bounded by a right line or lines; straight. Also **rec′ti·lin′e·al.** —**rec′ti·lin′e·ar·ly** *adv.*

rec·ti·tude (rek′tə·to͞od, -tyo͞od) *n.* **1** Upright in principles and conduct. **2** Freedom from error; correctness of judgment, method, or application; accuracy. **3** *Obs.* Straightness. See synonyms under JUSTICE, VIRTUE. [<F <LL *rectitudo* <L *rectus* right]

rec·to (rek′tō) *n. pl.* **·tos** A right–hand page, as of a book: opposed to *verso* (or *reverso*). [< L *recto (folio)* on the right (page)]

recto– *combining form* Rectal; pertaining to the rectum: *rectocele,* hernia of the rectum. Also, before vowels, **rect–.** [See RECTUM]

rec·tor (rek′tər) *n.* **1** In the Church of England, a priest who has full charge of a parish, and receives the parochial tithes: distinguished from *vicar.* **2** In the Protestant Episcopal Church, a priest in charge of a parish. **3** In the Roman Catholic Church: **a** A priest in charge of a congregation or church, especially one not having parochial status: distinguished from *parish priest.* **b** The head of a seminary or religious house. **4** In certain universities, colleges, and schools, the head or chief officer. [<L *rectus,* pp. of *regere* rule] —**rec′tor·ate** (-it) *n.* —**rec·to·ri·al** (rek·tôr′ē·əl, -tō′rē-) *adj.*

rec·to·ry (rek′tər·ē) *n. pl.* **·ries** **1** A rector's dwelling. **2** In England, a parish domain with its buildings, revenue, etc.

reimportation	**reimpress**	**reincrease**	**reinflame**	**reinoculation**	**reinspection**	**reinter**
reimportune	**reimprison**	**reincur**	**reinform**	**reinscribe**	**reinspire**	**reinterment**
reimpose	**reinaugurate**	**reinduce**	**reinfuse**	**reinsert**	**reinstruct**	**reinterrogate**
reimposition	**reincite**	**reinfect**	**reingratiate**	**reinsertion**	**reintegrate**	**reintrench**
reimpregnate	**reincorporate**	**reinfection**	**reinhabit**	**reinspect**	**reintegration**	**reintroduce**

rec·tum (rek′təm) *n. pl.* **·ta** (-tə) *Anat.* The terminal portion of the large intestine, extending from the sigmoid bend of the colon to the anus. [<NL *rectum (intestinum)* straight (intestine)]

rec·tus (rek′təs) *n. pl.* **·ti** (-tī) *Anat.* A straight muscle, as of the eye, the abdomen, the femur, etc. [<NL <L, straight]

rec·u·ba·tion (rek′yə·bā′shən) *n. Obs.* A lying down; specifically, in Roman antiquity, a reclining at table. [<L *recubare* recline]

Re·cu·let (rə·kü·le′) The highest peak of the Jura mountains, in eastern France.

re·cum·ben·cy (ri·kum′bən·sē) *n. pl.* **·cies** 1 The state of being recumbent. 2 The act of reclining. 3 A recumbent attitude. Also **re·cum′bence.**

re·cum·bent (ri·kum′bənt) *adj.* 1 Lying down, wholly or partly; reclining; leaning. 2 *Biol.* Tending to rest upon a surface from which they extend: said of certain structures. [<L *recumbens, -entis*, ppr. of *recumbere* < *re-* back + *cumbere* lie, nasalized var. of *cubare* lie down] — **re·cum′bent·ly** *adv.*

re·cu·per·ate (ri·kōō′pə·rāt, -kyōō′-) *v.* **·at·ed, ·at·ing** *v.i.* 1 To regain health or strength. 2 To recover from loss, as of money. — *v.t.* 3 To obtain again after loss; recover. 4 To restore to vigor and health. See synonyms under RECOVER. [<L *recuperatus*, pp. of *recuperare*]

re·cu·per·a·tion (ri·kōō′pə·rā′shən, -kyōō′-) *n.* The recovery of lost power or excellence, especially of health or strength.

re·cu·per·a·tive (ri·kōō′pə·rā′tiv, -pər·ə·tiv, -kyōō′-) *adj.* Tending, assisting, or pertaining to recovery; restorative. Also **re·cu′per·a·to′ry** (-pər·ə·tôr′ē, -tō′rē).

re·cu·per·a·tor (ri·kōō′pə·rā′tər, -kyōō′-) *n.* 1 One who or that which recuperates. 2 A mechanism, operated by springs or compressed air, for restoring a gun to firing position after the recoil. 3 *Chem.* An apparatus for the recovery of heat from hot gases.

re·cur (ri·kûr′) *v.i.* **·curred, ·cur·ring** 1 To happen again or repeatedly, especially at regular intervals: a paroxysm that *recurs.* 2 To come back or return; especially, to return to the mind or in recollection. 3 *Rare* To turn for aid; have recourse. [<L *recurrere* < *re-* back + *currere* run]

re·cur·rence (ri·kûr′əns) *n.* The act or fact of recurring; recourse. Also **re·cur′ren·cy.**

re·cur·rent (ri·kûr′ənt) *adj.* 1 Happening or appearing again or repeatedly; recurring. 2 Running back: said of arteries and nerves. See synonyms under FREQUENT. [<L *recurrens, -entis*, ppr. of *recurrere.* See RECUR.] — **re·cur′rent·ly** *adv.*

recurrent fever Relapsing fever.

recurring decimal A circulating decimal.

re·cur·vant (ri·kûr′vənt) *adj. Her.* Coiled with the head raised to strike: said of a serpent. [<L *recurvans, -antis*, ppr. of *recurvare* bend back]

re·cur·vate (ri·kûr′vit, -vāt) *adj.* Bent back. [<L *recurvatus*, pp. of *recurvare.* See RECURVE.] — **re·cur′va·ture** (-və·chər) *n.*

re·curve (ri·kûrv′) *v.t. & v.i.* **·curved, ·curv·ing** To curve or bend back or down. [<L *recurvare* < *re-* back + *curvus* curved] — **re·cur·va·tion** (rē′kûr·vā′shən) *n.*

rec·u·sant (rek′yə·zənt, ri·kyōō′zənt) *adj.* Persistently refusing to conform; specifically, in English history, refusing to attend services of the Anglican Church. — *n.* One of a recusant character, position, or party; a non-conformist. [<L *recusans, -antis*, ppr. of *recusare.* See RECUSE.] — **rec′u·san·cy** *n.*

rec·u·sa·tion (rek′yə·zā′shən) *n. Law* An exception by which a defendant challenges the judge on grounds of interest or prejudice as to his right to sit. [<L *recusatio, -onis* < *recusatus*, pp. of *recusare* < *re-* against + *causa* cause, case]

re·cy·cle (rē·sī′kəl) *v.t.* **·cy·cled, ·cy·cling** To reclaim (waste materials, as newsprint, bottles, etc.) by using in the manufacture of new products. — **re·cy′cla·ble** *adj.*

red[1] (red) *adj.* **red·der, red·dest** 1 Of a bright color resembling blood; of the same hue as that color of the spectrum farthest from the violet; also, of a hue approximating red: *red* gold. 2 Ultra-radical in politics; especially, communistic. 3 Pertaining to the pole of a magnet which points to the north. Compare BLUE. — *n.* 1 One of the primary colors, occurring at the opposite end of the spectrum from violet; the color of fresh human blood. 2 Any pigment or dye having or giving this color. 3 An ultra-radical in political views, especially a communist. 4 A red object considered with special reference to its color: the *red* (color) in roulette, the *red* (ball) in billiards. — **in the red** *Colloq.* Operating at a loss; owing money: from the practice of making entries in the debit column of an account book in red ink. — **to see red** To be very angry. [OE *rēad*] — **red′ly** *adv.* — **red′ness** *n.*

red[2] (red) See REDD.

Red (red) *n.* 1 A member of the Communist party of Russia; hence, often, any Russian. 2 A member of the Communist party of any country. 3 Any person who supports or approves of the aims of the Communist party. 4 An ultra-radical; anarchist. [<RED; from the color of their flags and banners]

re·dact (ri·dakt′) *v.t.* 1 To prepare, as for publication; edit; revise. 2 To draw up or frame, as a message or edict. [<L *redactus*, pp. of *redigere* reduce to order < *re-* back + *agere* drive] — **re·dac′tor** *n.*

re·dac·tion (ri·dak′shən) *n.* 1 The act of reducing or shaping, as literary matter, into proper form and condition for publication; editing. 2 Literary matter so edited or revised. [<F *rédaction* <LL *redactio, -onis* < *redactus.* See REDACT.]

red algae See RHODOPHYCEAE.

re·dan (ri·dan′) *n.* A fortification with two parapets meeting at a salient angle. See also illustration under BASTION. [<F *redan* <OF *redent* < *re-* back + *dent* tooth; from its appearance]

Red Army The army of the U.S.S.R.: now officially the Soviet Army.

red astrachan A large roundish variety of apple, yellow with red stripes or slashes.

red·bay (red′bā′) *n.* A tree of the laurel family *(Persea borbonia)* of eastern North America, yielding a bluish-black fruit sometimes called alligator pear.

red·bird (red′bûrd′) *n.* 1 The cardinal bird. 2 The scarlet tanager.

red-blood·ed (red′blud′id) *adj.* Having vitality and vigor; hence, manly.

Red Book *Brit.* 1 A book containing a list of all persons in state offices. 2 An official list of the peerage; specifically, a *Royal Kalendar* or *Complete . . . Annual Register* published from 1767 to 1893; also, a similar later publication.

red·breast (red′brest′) *n.* 1 A bird having a red breast, as the American or European robin. 2 The long-eared sunfish *(Lepomis auritus)* of the Atlantic coast of the United States: also **red-breasted bream.** 3 An American sandpiper, the knot *(Calidris canutus rufus)*: also **red-breasted sandpiper.**

red·bud (red′bud′) *n.* The Judas tree.

red·bug (red′bug′) *n.* 1 Any of several red insects; especially, the chigger of the southern United States. 2 The cotton stainer *(Dysdercus suturellus)*, that stains growing cotton an indelible red.

red·cap (red′kap′) *n.* 1 *U.S.* A railroad porter: so called from his red-colored cap. 2 The European goldfinch.

red cedar 1 An American juniper tree (genus *Juniperus*) of the cypress family, having a fine-grained, durable wood of a bright- or dark-red color resembling cedar; especially, the **eastern** *(J. virginiana)* and the **western** *(J. scopulorum)* **red cedar.** 2 The giant arborvitae *(Thuja plicata)* of the western United States, having a light, brittle but durable heartwood: known in the lumber trade and popularly as **western red cedar.** 3 The wood of any of these trees.

red cent A United States copper one-cent piece. — **not worth a red cent** *U.S. Colloq.* Worthless.

red·coat (red′kōt′) *n.* 1 A person wearing a red coat. 2 A British soldier of the period when a red coat was part of the uniform worn by the British Army, during the American Revolution and the War of 1812.

red corpuscle An erythrocyte.

red cross 1 The cross of St. George, the emblem of the English. 2 A Greek cross, red on a white ground.

Red Cross Convention See GENEVA CONVENTION.

Red Cross Society A society for the succor of the sick and wounded in war, formed in accordance with the international convention signed at Geneva in 1864, the members wearing a red Geneva cross as a badge of neutrality. These societies are now national organizations, as the **American Red Cross,** and continue their beneficent activities in times of peace, as in fighting disease, etc.

redd (red) *v.t. Dial.* 1 To put in order, as a room; make ready: usually with *up.* 2 To make clear or empty. 3 To adjust, as a quarrel. Also spelled *red.* [OE *hreddan* rescue] — **redd′er** *n.*

red deer 1 The common European and Asian stag *(Cervus elaphus).* 2 The common Virginia white-tailed deer in its rufous summer coat.

red·den (red′n) *v.t.* To make red. — *v.i.* To grow red; flush.

red·den·dum (ri·den′dəm) *n. pl.* **·da** (-də) *Law* A clause in a deed whereby the grantor reserves to himself some new thing, such as rent, out of what he has granted. [<L, neut. of *reddendus*, gerundive of *reddere* give in return. See RENDER.]

red·dish (red′ish) *adj.* Mixed with or somewhat red. — **red′dish·ness** *n.*

red·dle (red′l) *n.* Red ocher or red chalk, used for marking sheep. — *v.t.* **·dled, ·dling** To mark or stain with reddle. Also spelled *raddle.* [Var. of RUDDLE]

red·dle·man (red′l·mən) *n. pl.* **·men** (-mən) One who deals in reddle.

red drum A large drumfish *(Sciaenops ocellatus)* of the Atlantic coast, esteemed as a food fish. Also **red drumfish.**

rede[1] (rēd) *Scot.* or *Obs. v.t.* 1 To advise; counsel. 2 To explain; interpret. — *n.* 1 Advice; counsel. 2 A plan or scheme; decision. 3 A story or narrative; also, interpretation.

rede[2] (rēd) *adj. Scot.* 1 Fierce; impetuous. 2 Drunk.

re·deem (ri·dēm′) *v.t.* 1 To regain possession of by paying a price; specifically, to recover, as mortgaged property. 2 To pay off; receive back and satisfy, as a promissory note. 3 To set free; rescue; ransom. 4 *Theol.* To rescue from sin and its penalties. 5 To fulfil, as an oath or promise. 6 To make amends for; compensate for: The play was *redeemed* by its acting. See synonyms under DELIVER, RECLAIM. [<F *rédimer* <L *redimere* < *re-* back + *emere* buy] — **re·deem′a·ble** *adj.*

re·deem·er (ri·dē′mər) *n.* One who redeems. — **The Redeemer** Jesus Christ.

re-de·fec·tor (rē′di·fek′tər) *n.* One who returns to his native country after having previously fled because of real or imagined injustice.

re·de·liv·er (rē′di·liv′ər) *v.t.* 1 To deliver again, as a message or a speech. 2 To give back; return; restore. — **re′de·liv′er·ance, re′de·liv′er·y** *n.*

re·de·mand (rē′di·mand′, -mänd′) *v.t.* 1 To demand again. 2 To demand or ask the return of.

re·demp·ti·ble (ri·demp′tə·bəl) *adj.* Redeemable. [<L *redemptus* + -IBLE]

re·demp·tion (ri·demp′shən) *n.* 1 The act of redeeming, or the state of being redeemed. 2 The recovery of what is mortgaged or pledged. 3 The payment of a debt or obligation; specifically, the paying of the value of its notes, warrants, etc., by a government. 4 *Theol.* Salvation from sin through the atonement of Christ. [<OF <L *redemptio, -onis* < *redemptus*, pp. of *redimere* redeem. Doublet of RANSOM.]

re·demp·tion·er (ri·demp′shən·ər) *n.* One who redeems himself, as an emigrant by service in payment of passage money.

reintroduction	**reinvigorate**	**rejolt**	**relet**	**reload**	**remake**	**remerge**
reinundate	**reinvigoration**	**rejudge**	**reliquidate**	**reloan**	**remast**	**remigrate**
reinvent	**reinvite**	**rekindle**	**reliquidation**	**relocate**	**remasticate**	**remigration**
reinvestigate	**reinvolve**	**relade**	**relisten**	**relocation**	**remeasure**	**remix**
reinvestment	**rejoint**	**reland**	**relive**	**relodge**	**remelt**	**remodification**

re·demp·tive (ri·demp′tiv) *adj.* Serving to redeem, or connected with redemption. Also **re·demp·to·ry** (-tər·ē). [<L *redemptus,* pp. of *redimere.* See REDEEM.]
Re·demp·tor·ist (ri·demp′tər·ist) *n.* A member of a religious order, the Congregation of the Most Holy Redeemer, founded in 1732 by St. Alphonso de Liguori.
re·des·ig·nate (rē·dez′ig·nāt) *v.t.* **·nat·ed, ·nat·ing** To designate again.
re·de·vel·op (rē′di·vel′əp) *v.t.* **1** To develop again. **2** *Phot.* To intensify with chemicals and put through a second developing process. —*v.i.* **3** To develop again. —**re′de·vel′op·er** *n.* —**re′de·vel′op·ment** *n.*
red eye 1 *U.S. Colloq.* The danger signal in a railroad semaphore system. **2** *U.S. Slang* Poor-quality whisky. **3** The American rock bass. **4** The red-eyed vireo. **5** The rudd.
red–eyed vireo (red′īd′) See under VIREO.
red–fig·ured (red′fig′yərd) *adj.* Having red figures or markings; specifically, denoting an ancient Greek ceramic ware in which a black glaze was painted over the surface so as to leave the design in the red of the body: a style developed early in the fifth century B.C.
red·fin (red′fin′) *n. pl.* **·fins** or **·fin** One of various cyprinoid fishes, especially the common shiner or red dace *(Notropis cornutus)* of eastern North America.
red fir 1 Any of several varieties of fir, as the **California red fir** *(Abies magnifica),* the largest of the genus. **2** The wood of any of these trees. **3** Douglas fir.
red fire A mixture of easily combustible ingredients, especially strontium salts, that burns with a red light.
red fox The common American fox. See under FOX.
red grouper A grouper *(Epinephelus morio)* of the southern Atlantic and Gulf coasts.
red gum Strophulus.
red–hand·ed (red′han′did) *adj.* **1** Having hands red with blood, as a murderer caught in the act; hence, having just committed any crime. **2** Caught in the act of doing some particular thing: not always in a bad sense. —**red′–hand′ed·ly** *adv.* —**red′–hand′ed·ness** *n.*
red·head (red′hed′) *n.* **1** A person with red hair. **2** An American duck *(Aythya americana)*; the pochard. **3** The red-headed woodpecker.
red–head·ed woodpecker (red′hed′id) See under WOODPECKER.
red heat 1 The state of being red-hot. **2** The temperature at which a metal is red-hot.
red herring 1 Herring dried and smoked to a reddish brown color. **2** An irrelevant topic introduced in order to divert attention from the main point under discussion: from the use of a red herring to distract a hunting dog from the scent being followed (used to train hounds to ignore such distractions).
red hind A serranoid fish *(Epinephelus maculosus)* of the West Indies and southward: one of the groupers. See CABRILLA.
red–hot (red′hot′) *adj.* **1** Heated to redness. **2** New, as if just from the fire. **3** Heated; excited: *red–hot* argument. **4** Extreme.
red Indian 1 A North American Indian: also **Red Indian. 2** The painted cup.
red·in·gote (red′ing·gōt) *n.* An outer coat with long full skirts. [<F *rédingote,* alter. of E *riding coat*]
red·in·te·grate (ri·din′tə·grāt) *v.t.* **·grat·ed, ·grat·ing** To restore to a perfect state; make complete; renew. —*adj.* Restored to a whole or perfect state; renewed. [<L *redintegratus,* pp. of *redintegrare* <*red-,* var. of *re-* again + *integrare.* See INTEGRATE.]
re·din·te·gra·tion (ri·din′tə·grā′shən) *n.* **1** The act or process of restoration to a whole or sound state. **2** *Psychol.* The act or tendency of the mind to complete again a complex mental state previously experienced, upon the renewal of any part of it.
re·di·rect[1] (rē′di·rekt′) *v.t.* To direct again or anew: to *redirect* a letter. —**re′di·rec′tion** *n.*
re·di·rect[2] (rē·di·rekt′) *adj. Law* Designating the examination of a witness, after cross-examination, by the party who first examined him.
re·dis·count (rē·dis′kount) *n.* **1** A second (or any subsequent) discount on a sum. **2** *Usually pl.* Commercial paper which has been rediscounted. —*v.t.* To discount again.
re·dis·trict (rē·dis′trikt) *v.t.* To district again; especially, to redraw the boundaries of the election districts of.
red·i·vi·vus (red′ə·vī′vəs) *adj.* Come or brought into existence again; revived; restored. [<LL <*redivivus* renewed]
Red Jacket, 1751–1830, a chief of the Senecas, ally of the United States in the War of 1812: real name *Sagoyewatha.*
red lead (led) A lead preparation having a fine red color, used chiefly as a pigment; minium.
red–lead ore (red′led′) Crocoite.
red–let·ter (red′let′ər) *adj.* Happy, fortunate, or memorable: from the use on calendars of red letters to indicate holidays.
red light 1 A traffic signal light meaning stop: opposed to *green light.* **2** Any similar light used to warn of danger or an emergency.
red–light district (red′līt′) That part of a city or town in which brothels, sometimes marked by a red light, are numerous.
red·line (red′līn′) *v.t.* **·lined, ·lin·ing.** *U.S.* **1** To cross out with, or as with, a red line; cancel. **2** To discriminate against economically, esp. by refusing to grant mortgages or by charging unreasonably high mortgage.
red lobelia The cardinal flower.
red man An American Indian.
red maple The swamp maple.
Red·mond (red′mənd), **John Edward,** 1851–1918, Irish statesman.
red·neck (red′nek′) *n. U.S.* In the rural South, a poor, uneducated, white person, especially one having violently anti-Negro sentiments: a disparaging term. Also **red′-neck′.**
red oak 1 One of several oaks having a dense, cross-grained wood, as the northern red oak *(Quercus borealis).* **2** The wood of these oaks.
red ocher Ocher.
red·o·lent (red′ə·lənt) *adj.* Full of or diffusing a pleasant fragrance; odorous: often figuratively: *redolent* of the past. [<OF <L *redolens, -entis,* ppr. of *redolere* emit a smell <*red-* thoroughly + *olere* smell] —**red′o·lence, red′o·len·cy** *n.* —**red′o·lent·ly** *adv.*
Re·don (rə·dôn′), **Odilon,** 1840–1916, French painter.
Re·don·da (rə·don′də) See ANTIGUA.
red osier 1 A willow *(Salix purpurea)* whose red-tinted twigs are used in making baskets: also called *purple osier.* **2** The red-osier dogwood *(Cornus stolonifera),* with dark-reddish branches and bluish or white fruit.
re·dou·ble (rē·dub′əl) *v.t. & v.i.* **·led, ·ling 1** To make or become double. **2** To increase greatly. **3** To echo or re-echo. **4** To fold or turn back. **5** In bridge, to double (an opponent's double).
re·doubt (ri·dout′) *n.* **1** An enclosed fortification, especially a temporary one of any form, employed to defend a pass, a hilltop, etc. **2** An earthwork or simple fortification placed within the main rampart line of a permanent fortification. [<F *redoute* <Ital. *ridotto* < Med. L *reductus,* lit., a refuge, orig. pp. of *reducere* lead back]
re·doubt·a·ble (ri·dou′tə·bəl) *adj.* **1** Inspiring fear; formidable. **2** Deserving respect or deference. Also **re·doubt′ed.** See synonyms under FORMIDABLE. [<F *redoubtable* <*redouter* fear, dread <L *re-* thoroughly + *dubitare* doubt] —**re·doubt′a·ble·ness** *n.* —**re·doubt′a·bly** *adv.*
re·dound (ri·dound′) *v.i.* **1** To have an effect, as by reaction, to the credit, discredit, advantage, etc., of the original agent; return; react; accrue. **2** *Obs.* To surge or flow back. **3** *Obs.* To overflow. —*n.* A return by way of consequence; result; requital. [<F *redonder* < L *redundare* overflow <*red-* back + *undare* surge <*unda* wave]
red·o·wa (red′ə·wə, -və) *n.* Either of two Bohemian dances, one in 3/4 time, resembling a mazurka, the other in 2/4 time. [<F <Czech *rejdovák* <*rejdovati* steer, whirl, carouse]
red pepper See PEPPER (def. 3).
red·poll (red′pōl′) *n.* A small finch (genus *Acanthis*) of northern regions, having a reddish crown.
Red Poll One of an English breed of hornless, reddish dairy cattle.
re·draft (rē′draft′, -dräft′) *n.* **1** A second draft or copy. **2** A bill of exchange drawn by the holder of a protested bill on the drawer or endorsers for the reimbursement of the amount of the original bill with costs and charges.
re·dress (ri·dres′) *v.t.* **1** To set right, as a wrong, by compensation or by punishment of the wrongdoer; make reparation for. **2** To make reparation to; compensate: to *redress* the victims of injustice. **3** To remedy; correct. **4** To adjust, as balances. —*n.* (rē′dres, ri·dres′) **1** Satisfaction for wrong done; reparation; amends. **2** A restoration; reformation; correction. [<F *redresser* straighten <*re-* again (<L) +*dresser.* See DRESS.] —**re·dress′·er** or **re·dres′sor** *n.*
re–dress (rē·dres′) *v.t. & v.i.* To dress again.
Red River 1 A river in Texas, Arkansas, and Louisiana, flowing 1,018 miles east to the Mississippi. **2** A river in the United States and Canada, flowing 545 miles north from NW Minnesota through Manitoba to Lake Winnipeg: also **Red River of the North. 3** The longest river of Northern Vietnam, flowing 730 miles SE from Yünnan province, China, to the Gulf of Tonkin: Annamese *Song Coi. Chinese* **Yü·an Chiang** (yü·än′ jyäng′) or **Hung Ho** (ho͝ong′ hu′).
red·root (red′ro͞ot′, -ro͝ot′) *n.* **1** An herb *(Lachnanthes tinctoria)* with sword-shaped, fleshy leaves and fibrous red root, found in swamps along the Atlantic coast of the United States. **2** Any of certain other American plants, as bloodroot, alkanet, bittersweet, etc.
Red Sea An elongated sea between Egypt and Arabia; 1,450 miles long; 170,000 square miles; joined to the Mediterranean by the Suez Canal and connected with the Indian Ocean by the Gulf of Aden.
red·sear (red′sir′) *v.i. Metall.* To break or crack when red-hot, as iron when hammered.
red·shank (red′shangk′) *n.* **1** A Scottish Highlander: so called in allusion to the national costume of Scotland, which leaves the legs bare. **2** A common Old World shore bird *(Totanus totanus)*; a tattler.
red shift *Physics* Displacement toward the red end of the spectrum of light from a nebula, star, or other luminous celestial body: caused by an apparent increase in the wavelength of the emitted light. See DOPPLER EFFECT.
red·shirt (red′shûrt′) *n.* A member of Garibaldi's brigade in the struggle for Italian independence.
red–short (red′shôrt′) *adj. Metall.* Weak or brittle while red-hot, as iron or steel. [<Sw. *rödskört* <*röd* red + *skör* brittle] —**red′–short′ness** *n.*
red·skin (red′skin′) *n.* A North American Indian. —*adj.* Pertaining to or characteristic of the North American Indians.
red squirrel The chickaree.
red·start (red′stärt′) *n.* **1** A small singing bird (genus *Phoenicura*) allied to the warblers; especially, the common **Old World redstart** *(P. phoenicura),* dark-gray, with a black throat, white forehead, and rust-red breast, sides, and tail: also called *brantail.* **2** A small fly-catching warbler (genus *Setophaga*), especially *S. ruticilla,* with bright orange-red patches, common in eastern North America. [<RED[1] + START[2]]
red–tailed buzzard (red′tāld′) See under BUZZARD.
red tape Rigid official procedure involving delay or inaction: from the tying of public

remodify	**renerve**	**reobtain**	**reordain**	**repack**	**reperuse**	**replume**
remold	**renominate**	**reobtainable**	**reorder**	**repaint**	**rephrase**	**replunge**
remolten	**renomination**	**reoccupation**	**reordination**	**repass**	**replant**	**repolarization**
rename	**renumber**	**reoccupy**	**reossify**	**repassage**	**replantation**	**repolish**
renavigate	**renumerate**	**reoppose**	**repacify**	**reperusal**	**repledge**	**repopulate**

add,āce,câre,pälm; end,ēven; it,īce; odd,ōpen,ôrder; to͝ok,po͞ol; up,bûrn; ə = a in *above,* e in *sicken,* i in *clarity,* o in *melon,* u in *focus;* yo͞o = u in *fuse;* oi,oil; ou,pout; ch,check; g,go; ng,ring; th,thin; th,this; zh,vision. Foreign sounds à,œ,ü,kh,ṅ; and ◆: see page xx. <from; + plus; ? possibly.

documents with red tape. —**red-tape** (red′tāp′) adj. —**red′-tap′ism** n.

red tide The episodic appearance of a reddish discoloration in coastal waters due to the proliferation of certain minute, toxic protozoans.

red-top (red′top′) n. Any of certain grasses valuable for hay and pasturage; specifically, herd's-grass (Agrostis alba). [From the reddish panicle of some varieties]

re-duce (ri-dōōs′, -dyōōs′) v. -**duced**, -**duc-ing** v.t. **1** To make less in size, amount, number, intensity, etc.; diminish. **2** To bring from a higher to a lower condition; lower; degrade. **3** To bring to submission; subdue; conquer. **4** To bring to a specified condition or state: with to: to reduce rock to powder; to reduce a person to desperation. **5** To thin (paint, etc.) with oil or turpentine. **6** Math. To change (an expression) to a more elementary form. **7** Surg. To restore (displaced parts) to normal position. **8** Chem. **a** To decrease the positive valence of (an element) by the addition of electrons. **b** To deprive wholly or partially of oxygen; deoxidize. **9** Phot. To diminish the density of (a photographic negative). — v.i. **10** To become less in any way. **11** To decrease one's weight, as by dieting. [< L reducere < re- back + ducere lead] —**re-duc′i-bil′i-ty** n. —**re-duc′i-ble** adj. —**re-duc′i-bly** adv.
Synonyms: compress, concentrate, condense, consolidate, contract, diminish, solidify, thicken. See ABASE, ABATE, ABBREVIATE, ALLAY, ALLEVIATE, CONQUER, IMPAIR, RELAX, RETRENCH, SCRIMP, SUBDUE, WEAKEN.

re-duc-er (ri-dōōs′ər, -dyōō′-) n. **1** One who or that which reduces. **2** Phot. A chemical solution for reducing the density of negatives.

reducing agent Chem. A substance used to effect a chemical reduction; more specifically, any element which gives up a valence electron to another.

reducing glass A concave lens of considerable diameter used to produce a minified view of drawings, to see how they will appear when they are reduced in size.

reducing valve A valve for maintaining uniform reduced pressure of a fluid, as steam or gas, above or below the valve.

re-duc-tase (ri-duk′tās) n. Biochem. Any of a class of enzymes which promote the reduction of compounds to simpler forms. [< REDUCT(ION) + -ASE]

re-duc-ti-o ad ab-sur-dum (ri-duk′shē-ō ad ab-sûr′dəm) Latin Literally, reduction to an absurdity; disposal of a proposition by showing that its logical conclusion is absurd; also, proof of a proposition by showing its contradiction to be absurd.

re-duc-tion (ri-duk′shən) n. **1** The act or process of reducing, or its results. **2** Biol. The halving of the total number of chromosomes during meiotic cell division. **3** Chem. **a** The process of depriving a compound of oxygen. **b** The process of decreasing the positive valence of an element by the addition of electrons: distinguished from oxidation. **4** Math. **a** One of those formulas by means of which trigonometric functions of angles greater than 90° can be reduced to functions of angles less than 90°. **b** The process of expressing a fraction in decimal terms. See synonyms under ABBREVIATION. [< F réduction < L reductio, -onis < reductus, pp. of reducere. See REDUCE.] —**re-duc′tion-al** adj. —**re-duc′tive** adj.

re-dun-dance (ri-dun′dəns) n. **1** The condition or quality of being redundant. **2** That which is redundant. **3** Excess; surplus. See synonyms under CIRCUMLOCUTION, EXCESS.

re-dun-dan-cy (ri-dun′dən-sē) n. pl. -**cies** **1** Redundance. **2** In information theory, deliberate repetition in a message, in whatever medium expressed, in order to lessen the possibility of error.

re-dun-dant (ri-dun′dənt) adj. **1** Being more than is required; constituting an excess. **2** Unnecessarily verbose; tautological. [< L redundans, -antis, ppr. of redundare. See REDOUND.] —**re-dun′dant-ly** adv.

re-du-pli-cate (ri-dōō′plə-kāt, -dyōō′-) v. -**cat**-

ed, -**cat-ing** v.t. **1** To repeat again and again; redouble; iterate. **2** Ling. To affix a reduplication to. —v.i. **3** To undergo reduplication. —adj. (-kit) **1** Repeated again and again; duplicated; doubled. **2** Bot. Valvate with the margins reflexed. [< L reduplicatus, pp. of reduplicare < re-again + duplicare. See DUPLICATE.]

re-du-pli-ca-tion (ri-dōō′plə-kā′shən, -dyōō′-) n. **1** The act of reduplicating, or the state of being reduplicated; a redoubling. **2** A rhetorical figure in which the ending of a sentence, line, or clause is repeated and emphasized at the beginning of the next. **3** Ling. **a** The repetition of an initial element or elements in a word; especially, in the verbs of some Indo-European languages, repetition of some part of the root, usually with vowel modification, serving as a mark of the perfect, as in Greek bebeka I have walked, Latin dedidi I have given. **b** The doubling of all or part of a word, often with vowel or consonant change, as in fiddle-faddle, razzle-dazzle. **c** The sound or syllable thus repeated.

re-du-pli-ca-tive (ri-dōō′plə-kā′tiv, -dyōō′-) adj. **1** Tending to reduplicate. **2** Of or formed by reduplication. **3** Bot. Reduplicate.

red-vein maple (red′vān′) The flowering maple.

red-ware (red′wâr′) n. A large brown seaweed (Laminaria digitata) of the New England coast, sometimes used for food.

red-wat (red′wot′) adj. Scot. Made wet by something red, as blood.

red-wing (red′wing′) n. **1** An American blackbird (Agelaius phoeniceus) with bright scarlet patches on the wings of the male: commonly **red-winged blackbird**. **2** An Old World red-winged thrush (Turdus musicus), bright reddish-orange on the sides of the throat and the under-wing coverts.

red-wood (red′wŏŏd′) n. **1** An immense California tree (Sequoia sempervirens, family Taxodiaceae). See SEQUOIA. **2** Its durable reddish wood. **3** Any one of various other trees yielding a reddish wood, or the wood itself, which yields a red dye.

red-wud (red′wŭd′) adj. Scot. Raging mad; furious; insane.

red-yel-low (red′yel′ō) n. One of the range of colors situated between the red and yellow portions of the visible spectrum, sharing the hue of each but identical with neither.

ree [1] (rē) adj. Scot. Wild; tipsy; delirious.

ree [2] (rē) See REEVE [3].

reed (rēd) n. **1** The slender, frequently jointed stem of certain tall grasses growing in wet places, or the grasses themselves. **2** A thin, elastic plate of reed, wood, or metal nearly closing an opening, as in a pipe: used in reed organs, the reed pipes of pipe organs, and instruments of the bassoon and clarinet order, to produce a musical tone either by itself or when reinforced by the vibration of air in a pipe. **3** A musical pipe made of the hollow stem of a plant; a shepherd's pipe. **4** Archit. A semicylindrical ornamental molding or bead. **5** That part of a loom that drives the filling against the woven fabric, consisting of two horizontal parallel bars near together and connected by numerous thin parallel slips. See illustration under LOOM. **6** An arrow. **7** An ancient Hebrew measure of length; six cubits. —v.t. **1** To fashion into or decorate with reeds. **2** To thatch with reeds. [OE hrēod]

Reed (rēd), **John**, 1887–1920, U.S. journalist and poet. —**Sampson**, 1800–80, U.S. Swedenborgian. —**Walter**, 1851–1902, U.S. army surgeon; demonstrated the transmission of yellow fever by mosquitos.

reed-bird (rēd′bûrd′) n. The bobolink: so called chiefly in the southern United States.

reed-buck (rēd′buk′) n. An antelope (Redunca arundineum) of southern Africa that frequents reedy places; the reitbok.

REDWOOD
(From 200
to 240 feet
high)

reed bunting The European black-headed bunting (genus Emberiza), with a white collar, common in marshy places.

reed-ing (rē′ding) n. **1** Beading or semicylindrical moldings collectively. **2** Ornamentation by such moldings. **3** A molding of this kind: the reverse of fluting. **4** The knurling on the edge of a coin, as distinguished from milling.

reed-ling (rēd′ling) n. The European bearded titmouse (Panurus biarmicus), common in reedy places. The male has a black tuft of feathers on each side of the chin.

reed-mace (rēd′mās′) n. A cat-tail; any plant of the genus Typha, especially T. latifolia and T. angustifolia.

reed organ A keyboard musical instrument sounding by means of free reeds.

reed pipe An organ pipe having a reed whose vibrations set in motion the air column: distinguished from flue pipe.

reed-stop (rēd′stop′) n. An organ stop controlling a set of reed pipes.

re-ed-u-cate (rē-ej′ŏŏ-kāt) v.t. -**cat-ed**, -**cat-ing** **1** To educate again. **2** To rehabilitate, as a criminal, by education. —**re′ed-u-ca′tion** n.

reed warbler A bird (genus Acrocephalus) with moderately rounded tail, found in most parts of the Old World.

reed-y (rē′dē) adj. **reed-i-er**, **reed-i-est** **1** Full of reeds. **2** Like a reed. **3** Having a thin, sharp tone, like a reed instrument. —**reed′i-ness** n.

reef [1] (rēf) n. **1** A ridge of sand or rocks, or especially of coral, at or near the surface of the water. **2** A lode, vein, or ledge. **3** A shoal. [< ON rif rib, reef] —**reef′y** adj.

reef [2] (rēf) Naut. n. **1** The part of a sail that is folded and secured or untied and let out in regulating its size on the mast. **2** The tuck taken in a sail when reefed. —v.t. **1** To reduce (a sail) by folding a part and tying it round, and usually fastening it to, a yard or boom. **2** To shorten or lower, as a topmast by taking part of it in. [ME riff, prob. < ON rif rib]

reef-band (rēf′band′) n. Naut. A strip of canvas used to give additional strength to sails along the lines where the reef-points are attached.

reef-er [1] (rē′fər) n. **1** One who reefs. **2** A short double-breasted coat or jacket of heavy material.

reef-er [2] (rē′fər) n. U.S. Slang A marihuana cigarette. [? from its resemblance to the reef of a sail]

reef knot A square knot. See illustration under KNOT.

reef-point (rēf′point′) n. Naut. One of a series of short lines attached by their centers to the eyelets of a reef-band, and used to fasten the sail in reefing.

reek (rēk) v.i. **1** To give off smoke, vapor, etc. **2** To give off a strong, offensive smell. **3** To be pervaded with anything offensive. **4** To expose to smoke or its action. **5** To give off; emit. —n. Scot. Smoke; vapor; steam. ◆Homophone: wreak. [OE rēc] —**reek′er** n.

reek-y (rē′kē) adj. **reek-i-er**, **reek-i-est** Having been smoked; smoky; soiled by or emitting smoke. Also **reek′ie**.

reel [1] (rēl) n. **1** A rotatory device or frame for winding rope, cord, photographic film, or other flexible substance. **2** In cinematography, the film wound on one reel: used as a unit of length, usually from 1,000 to 2,000 feet. **3** A wooden spool for wire, thread, etc. **4** Material, such as thread, paper, and the like, when wound on a reel. —v.t. **1** To wind on a reel or bobbin, as a line. **2** To draw in by reeling a line: with in: to reel a fish in. **3** To say, do, etc., easily and fluently: with off. [OE hrēol] —**reel′a-ble** adj. —**reel′er** n.

reel [2] (rēl) v.i. **1** To stagger, sway, or lurch, as when giddy or drunk. **2** To whirl round and round. **3** To have a sensation of giddiness or whirling: My head reels. **4** To waver or fall back, as attacking troops. —v.t. **5** To cause to reel. See synonyms under SHAKE. —n. **1** A

repopulation	re-prove	requicken	rerestitution	reseek	resettle	resolder
repour	reprune	reread	rerise	reseize	resettlement	re-solve
re-press	repurchase	re-record	resail	reseizure	reshape	resow
repromulgate	repurge	re-refer	resale	resend	resharpen	restipulate
repromulgation	repurify	rereign	resalute	re-serve	resmooth	restipulation

staggering motion; giddiness. 2 A lively Scottish dance, or its music; also, the Virginia reel. [<REEL[1]] — **reel′er** *n.*

re·em·pha·size (rē·em′fə·sīz) *v.t.* **·sized, ·siz·ing** To stress or emphasize again.

re·en·force (rē′en·fôrs′, -fōrs′), **re·en·force·ment** (rē′en·fôrs′mənt, -fōrs′-), etc. See REINFORCE, etc.

re·en·ter (rē·en′tər) *v.t.* & *v.i.* To enter again. — **re·en′trance** *n.*

re·en·ter·ing (rē·en′tər·ing) *adj.* 1 Entering again. 2 Extending inward, as an angle.

reentering angle An angle which is turned inward, as in a figure or structure.

re·en·trant (rē·en′trənt) *adj.* Reentering; extending inward. — *n.* 1 One who or that which reenters. 2 A reentering angle, as in a fortification wall.

re·en·try (rē·en′trē) *n.* 1 The act of entering again. 2 *Law* The act of resuming possession of lands or tenements. 3 In whist and bridge, a card by which a player gains or can gain the lead. 4 *Aerospace* The return into the atmosphere of an object launched into space from the earth.

reest[1] (rēst) *v.t.* & *v.i.* *Scot.* & *Brit. Dial.* To check; balk. — **reest′y** *adj.*

reest[2] (rēst) *v.t.* & *v.i.* *Scot.* To dry or cure, as by smoking.

reeve[1] (rēv) *v.t.* **reeved** or **rove** (*for pp. also* **rov·en**), **reev·ing** *Naut.* 1 To pass, as a rope or rod, through a hole, block, or aperture. 2 To fasten in such manner. 3 To pass a rope, etc., through (a block or pulley). [<Du. *reven* reef a sail]

reeve[2] (rēv) *n.* In medieval England, a high administrative officer formerly holding authority over landed areas; bailiff; overseer; steward. [OE *gerēfa* steward]

reeve[3] (rēv) *n.* The female of the ruff: also called *ree.* [Origin unknown]

re·ex·change (rē′iks·chānj′) *v.t.* **·changed, ·chang·ing** To exchange again. — *n.* 1 A second or renewed exchange. 2 The sum that the holder of a bill of exchange may demand of the drawer or indorser as indemnity for the loss incurred by its dishonor in a foreign country, where it was payable.

re·fect (ri·fekt′) *v.t.* *Obs.* To refresh after weariness or hunger; restore; repair. [<L *refectus* refreshed. See REFECTION.]

re·fec·tion (ri·fek′shən) *n.* 1 Refreshment by food; a light meal. 2 In civil law, repair of property. 3 *Med.* Spontaneous recovery, as from an ailment or the effects of a vitamin deficiency. [<OF <L *refectio, -onis* <*refectus,* pp. of *reficere* remake, refresh <*re-* again + *facere* make] — **re·fec′tion·er** *n.* — **re·fec′tive** *adj.*

re·fec·to·ry (ri·fek′tər·ē) *n.* *pl.* **·ries** A room for eating; usually, in a religious house or college, a hall set apart for meals. [<Med. L *refectorium* <L *refectus.* See REFECTION.]

re·fer (ri·fûr′) *v.* **·ferred, ·fer·ring** *v.t.* 1 To direct or send for information or other purpose: I *refer* you to another department. 2 To hand over or submit for consideration, settlement, etc.: They *referred* the bill to a special committee. 3 To attribute the cause or source of; assign; relate: He *refers* his success to unceasing application. 4 To assign or attribute to a group, class, period, etc. — *v.i.* 5 To make reference; allude. 6 To turn, as for information, help, or authority; have recourse: to *refer* to the dictionary. See synonyms under ALLUDE, ATTRIBUTE. [<OF *referer* <L *referre* <*re-* back + *ferre* bear, carry] — **ref·er·a·ble** (ref′ər·ə·bəl), **re·fer′ra·ble** or **re·fer′ri·ble** *adj.* — **re·fer′rer** *n.*

ref·e·ree (ref′ə·rē′) *n.* 1 A person to whom a thing is referred. 2 In certain games, as football, an official who has general control of the game. 3 *Law* A person to whom a case is sent by order of court for investigation and report; an arbitrator. See synonyms under JUDGE. — *v.t.* & *v.i.* To judge as a referee.

ref·er·ence (ref′ər·əns, ref′rəns) *n.* 1 The act of referring. 2 An incidental allusion or direction of the attention: *reference* to a recent event. 3 A note or other indication in a book, referring to some other book or passage: compare CROSS-REFERENCE. 4 One who or that which is or may be referred to. 5 The state of being referred or related: used in the phrases *with* or *in reference to.* 6 *Law* The act or process of submitting a matter to a referee; also, the proceedings of and before a referee. 7 The person or persons to whom one seeking employment may refer for recommendation; also, a written statement or testimonial, as of character or dependability. — **ref′er·enc·er** *n.*

ref·er·end (ref′ə·rend) *n.* The instrument, vehicle, or means by which an act of reference is made. [<REFERENDUM]

ref·er·en·dum (ref′ə·ren′dəm) *n.* *pl.* **·dums** or **·da** (-də) 1 The submission, by a diplomatic representative to his government, of a proposition not covered by his original instructions. 2 The submission of a proposed public measure or law, which has been passed upon by a legislature or convention, to a vote of the people for ratification or rejection. [<L, gerund of *referre.* See REFER.]

ref·er·ent (ref′ər·ənt) *n.* The particular object, concept, class, event, or the like to which reference is made in any verbal statement or its symbolic equivalent. [<L *referens, -entis,* ppr. of *referre.* See REFER.]

re·fer·ral (ri·fûr′əl) *n.* 1 The act of referring, or the condition of being referred. 2 One who has been referred.

re·fill (rē·fil′) *v.t.* To fill again. — *n.* (rē′fil′) Any commodity packaged to fit and fill a container originally containing that commodity: a *refill* for a lipstick case.

re·fine (ri·fīn′) *v.* **·fined, ·fin·ing** *v.t.* 1 To make fine or pure; free from impurities or extraneous matter. 2 To make polished or cultured; free from coarseness or vulgarity. — *v.i.* 3 To become fine or pure. 4 To become more polished or cultured. 5 To make fine distinctions; use subtlety. See synonyms under CHASTEN, PURIFY. — **re·fin′er** *n.*

re·fined (ri·fīnd′) *adj.* 1 Characterized by refinement or polish. 2 Free from impurity; purified; clarified. 3 Exceedingly precise or exact; subtle: *refined* tortures. See synonyms under FINE.

re·fine·ment (ri·fīn′mənt) *n.* 1 Fineness of thought, taste, language, etc.; freedom from coarseness or vulgarity; delicacy; culture. 2 The act, effect, or process of refining; purification. 3 A nice distinction; subtlety; also, fastidiousness. [<REFINE]

Synonyms: civilization, cultivation, culture. *Civilization* applies to nations, denoting the sum of those civil, social, economic, and political attainments by which a community is removed from barbarism; a people may be civilized while still far from *refinement* or *culture,* but *civilization* is susceptible of various degrees and of continued progress. *Refinement* applies either to nations or individuals, denoting the removal of what is coarse and rude, and a corresponding attainment of what is delicate, elegant, and beautiful. *Culture* in the fullest sense, as distinct from *cultivation,* denotes that degree of *refinement* and development which results from continued *cultivation* through successive generations; a man's faculties may be brought to a high degree of *cultivation* in some specialty, while he himself remains uncultured even to the extent of coarseness and rudeness. See HUMANITY. *Antonyms*: barbarism, boorishness, brutality, clownishness, coarseness, grossness, rudeness, rusticity, vulgarity.

re·fin·er·y (ri·fī′nər·ē) *n.* *pl.* **·er·ies** A place where some crude material, as sugar or petroleum, is purified.

re·fit (rē·fit′) *v.t.* & *v.i.* **·fit·ted, ·fit·ting** To make or be made fit or ready again; return to serviceable condition, as by making repairs, replacing equipment, etc. — *n.* The repair of damages or wear, as of a ship.

re·flate (rē·flāt′) *v.t.* **·flat·ed, ·flat·ing** To inflate again. [<RE- + (IN)FLATE]

re·flect (ri·flekt′) *v.t.* 1 To turn or throw back, as rays of light, heat, or sound. 2 To give back an image of; mirror. 3 To cause to rebound or return; cast: He *reflects* credit on his teacher. 4 *Obs.* To bend or fold back. — *v.i.* 5 To send back rays, as of light or heat. 6 To return in rays: The light *reflects* into my eyes. 7 To give back an image; also, to be mirrored. 8 To think carefully; ponder. 9 To bring blame, discredit, etc.: with *on* or *upon.* See synonyms under CONSIDER, DELIBERATE, MUSE. [<OF *reflecter* <L *reflectere* <*re-* back + *flectere* bend]

re·flec·tance (ri·flek′təns) *n.* *Physics* The ratio of the radiant or luminous flux reflected from a given surface to the total light falling upon it.

reflecting telescope See under TELESCOPE.

re·flec·tion (ri·flek′shən) *n.* 1 The act of reflecting, or the state of being reflected. 2 *Physics* The throwing off or back (from a surface) of impinging light, heat, sound, or any form of radiant energy. 3 The result of reflecting; reflected rays or an image thrown by reflection. 4 Consideration of or meditation upon past knowledge or experience; thought: *Reflection* increases wisdom; also, its result: a wise *reflection.* 5 The casting of blame; censure. 6 *Anat.* The folding of a part upon itself; a fold, as in a membrane. 7 Reflex action, as of the nerves. Also spelled *reflexion.* [<OF *reflexion* <L *reflexio, -onis*] — **re·flec′tion·al** or **re·flex′ion·al** *adj.*

Synonyms: cogitation, consideration, contemplation, deliberation, meditation, musing, rumination, study, thinking, thought. See ANIMADVERSION, THOUGHT[1]. *Antonyms*: carelessness, heedlessness, imprudence, inconsiderateness, negligence, thoughtlessness.

re·flec·tive (ri·flek′tiv) *adj.* 1 Given to reflection or thought; meditative: a *reflective* person. 2 Used in or capable of consideration or reflection. 3 Having the quality of throwing back light, heat, sound, etc. — **re·flec′tive·ly** *adv.* — **re·flec′tive·ness** *n.*

re·flec·tiv·i·ty (rē′flek·tiv′ə·tē) *n.* 1 The state or quality of being reflective. 2 *Physics* That portion of light or other forms of radiant energy which is reflected by a surface exposed to uniform radiation.

re·flec·tor (ri·flek′tər) *n.* 1 That which reflects. 2 A polished surface, of glass or metal (usually concave), for reflecting light, heat, or sound, and also pictures or slides in a particular direction. 3 A telescope which transmits an image from a reflecting surface to the eyepiece. 4 *Physics* A substance placed around the core of a nuclear reactor for the purpose of reducing neutron leakage and maintaining the level of the chain reaction: sometimes called a *tamper.* 5 *Telecom.* The rear portion of an antenna, serving to increase its directional characteristics.

re·flet (rə·fle′) *n.* 1 Iridescence of surface; especially, the metallic glaze on pottery. 2 Pottery having metallic or iridescent luster. [<F, reflection]

re·flex (rē′fleks) *adj.* 1 Turned or thrown backward; reflected, as light. 2 *Physiol.* Of, pertaining to, or produced by a reflex. 3 Turned back upon itself or in the direction whence it came: *reflex* motion. 4 Bent back; reflexed. 5 *Telecom.* Designating a radio receiving circuit in which a single vacuum tube serves for the simultaneous amplification of two different frequencies. — *n.* 1 Reflection, or an image produced by reflection, as from a mirror or like surface. 2 An image or copy; also, an adaptation from another language or dialect, as of a word. 3 Light reflected from an illuminated surface to a shady one. 4 *Physiol.* An involuntary movement or action produced by the transmission of an afferent impulse to a nerve center and its reflection thence as an efferent impulse, as in winking when the eye is threatened: also **reflex action.** — *v.t.* (ri·fleks′) To bend back; turn back or reflect. [<L *reflexus* reflected, pp. of *reflectere.* See REFLECT.]

restrengthen	**resubjection**	**resurprise**	**retrim**	**re–utter**	**revegetate**	**revindication**
restrike	**resummon**	**resurvey**	**re–urge**	**revaluation**	**revictual**	**reweigh**
restrive	**resummons**	**retraverse**	**re–use**	**revalue**	**revictualment**	**rewin**
resubject	**resupply**	**retrial**	**re–utilize**	**revarnish**	**revindicate**	**rework**

add,āce,câre,pälm; end, ēven; it,īce; odd,ōpen,ôrder; tŏŏk,pōōl; up,bûrn; ə = a in *above,* e in *sicken,* i in *clarity,* o in *melon,* u in *focus*; yōō = u in *fuse*; oi,oil; ou,pout; ch,check; g,go; ng,ring; th,thin; th,this; zh,vision. Foreign sounds à,œ,ü,kh,ṅ; and ◆: see page xx. < from; + plus; ? possibly.

reflex angle See under ANGLE.
reflex arc *Physiol.* The entire path covered by a nerve impulse from the point of origin in the receptors to the nerve center, and thence outwards to the effectors.
re·flex·ive (ri·flek′siv) *adj.* **1** Reflex. **2** *Gram.* Reflected upon or referring to itself or its subject: in the sentence "He dresses himself," "dresses" is a *reflexive* verb, "himself" is a *reflexive* pronoun. — *n.* A reflexive verb or pronoun. — **re·flex′ive·ly** *adv.* — **re·flex′ive·ness, re·flex·iv·i·ty** (rē′flek·siv′ə·tē) *n.*
re·flight (rē′flīt′) *n. Aeron.* A subsequent flight made over a given area to obtain supplementary photographs or to obtain other necessary details of information.
ref·lu·ent (ref′lo͞o·ənt) *adj.* Flowing back; ebbing, as the tide. [<L *refluens, -entis,* ppr. of *refluere* flow back < *re-* back + *fluere* flow] — **ref′lu·ence, ref′lu·en·cy** *n.*
re·flux (rē′fluks′) *n.* A flowing back; ebb; return: the flux and *reflux* of fortune. [<L *refluxus,* pp. of *refluere.* See REFLUENT.]
re·for·est (rē·fôr′ist, -for′-) *v.t.* & *v.i.* To replant (an area) with trees. — **re′for·es·ta′tion** *n.*
re·form (ri·fôrm′) *v.t.* **1** To make better by removing abuses, altering, etc.; restore to a better condition: to *reform* a corrupt city government; to *reform* inefficient business procedures. **2** To make better morally; persuade or educate from a sinful to a moral life: to *reform* a prostitute. **3** To put an end to; stop (an abuse, malpractice, etc.). — *v.i.* **4** To give up sin or error; become better. See synonyms under AMEND, RECLAIM. — *n.* An act or result of reformation; change for the better, especially in administration; correction of evils or abuses; abandonment of vicious habits. [<OF *reformer* <L *reformare* < *re-* again + *formare* form] — **re·form′a·tive** *adj.* — **re·form′er, re·form′ist** *n.*
Reform Judaism Judaism as practiced by those who emphasize the historical continuity of the Jewish community and the ethical and prophetic content of the Scriptures and the oral laws, and reject or modify much of the traditional ritual. Compare CONSERVATIVE JUDAISM, ORTHODOX JUDAISM.
re-form (rē·fôrm′) *v.t.* & *v.i.* To form again. [<RE- + FORM] — **re′-for·ma′tion** *n.*
ref·or·ma·tion (ref′ər·mā′shən) *n.* **1** The act of reforming. **2** The state of being reformed. **3** Moral or religious restoration or revival.
Ref·or·ma·tion (ref′ər·mā′shən) *n.* The religious revolution of the 16th century in Europe which began as a movement to reform Catholicism and ended with the establishment of Protestantism in many parts of northern and western Europe.
re·form·a·to·ry (ri·fôr′mə·tôr′ē, -tō′rē) *adj.* Having a tendency or aiming to produce reformation. — *n. pl.* **·ries** An institution for the reformation and instruction of juvenile offenders.
Reform Bill The electoral reform bill passed by the British Parliament in 1832 for the correction and extension of the suffrage.
re·formed (ri·fôrmd′) *adj.* Restored to a better state; corrected or amended; delivered from vicious habits.
Re·formed (ri·fôrmd′) *adj.* Designating those Protestant churches which separated from the Lutherans in the 16th century on questions of doctrine; specifically, those churches which follow the teachings of Calvin and Zwingli. See CALVINISM, ZWINGLIAN.
reform school A reformatory.
re·fract (ri·frakt′) *v.t.* **1** To deflect (a ray) by refraction. **2** *Optics* To determine the degree of refraction of (an eye or lens). [<L *refractus,* pp. of *refringere* turn aside < *re-* back + *frangere* break]
refracting telescope See under TELESCOPE.
re·frac·tion (ri·frak′shən) *n. Physics* The change of direction of a ray, as of light or heat, in oblique passage from one medium to another of different density, or in traversing a medium whose density is not uniform.

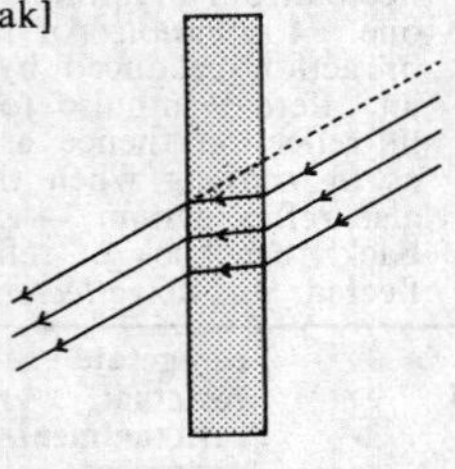
LIGHT REFRACTION

— **double refraction** The property possessed by certain types of crystals of breaking up a beam of light into two differently refracted and polarized rays. — **re·frac′tive** *adj.* — **re·frac′tive·ness, re·frac·tiv·i·ty** (rē′frak·tiv′ə·tē) *n.* — **re·frac′tor** *n.*
re·frac·tom·e·ter (rē′frak·tom′ə·tər) *n.* Any instrument for measuring indices of refraction. [<REFRACT + -(O)METER]
re·frac·to·ry (ri·frak′tər·ē) *adj.* **1** Not amenable to control; disobedient; unmanageable; obstinate. **2** Resisting ordinary methods of reduction: said of an ore. See synonyms under OBSTINATE, REBELLIOUS, RESTIVE, TURBULENT. — *n. pl.* **·ries** **1** A refractory or obstinate person or thing. **2** Any of various materials highly resistant to the action of great heat, as fireclay, graphite, magnesite, etc. [<L *refractarius*] — **re·frac′to·ri·ly** *adv.* — **re·frac′to·ri·ness** *n.*
ref·ra·ga·ble (ref′rə·gə·bəl) *adj.* Capable of being refuted. [<Med. L *refragabilis* <L *refragari* oppose]
re·frain[1] (ri·frān′) *v.i.* To keep oneself back; abstain from action; forbear. — *v.t.* To restrain; curb. [<OF *refrener* <L *refrenare* curb < *re-* back + *frenum* a bridle] — **re·frain′er** *n.*
Synonyms: abstain, forbear, restrain. See CEASE, KEEP. *Antonyms*: begin, continue, persevere, persist.
re·frain[2] (ri·frān′) *n.* **1** A phrase or strain repeated at intervals, generally regular, in a poem or a song; the burden. It generally recurs at the end of a stanza or strophe, and is common in old ballads and in Provençal poetry. **2** Any saying that is repeated over and over. [<OF < *refraindre* check, repeat <L *refringere* break off. See REFRACT.]
re·fran·gi·ble (ri·fran′jə·bəl) *adj.* Capable of being refracted, as light. [<RE- + L *frangere* break + -IBLE] — **re·fran′gi·bil′i·ty, re·fran′gi·ble·ness** *n.*
re·fresh (ri·fresh′) *v.t.* **1** To make (a person) fresh or vigorous again, as by food or rest; reinvigorate; revive. **2** To make fresh, clean, cool, etc. **3** To stimulate, as the memory. **4** To renew or replenish with or as with new supplies. — *v.i.* **5** To become fresh again; revive. **6** To take refreshment. **7** To lay in provisions. [<OF *refreschier* < *re-* again (<L) + *fres* fresh. See FRESH.]
re·fresh·er (ri·fresh′ər) *n.* **1** One who or that which refreshes. **2** A refresher course. — *adj.* Designating something that reacquaints one with the material of subjects previously studied and forgotten: a *refresher* course.
re·fresh·ing (ri·fresh′ing) *adj.* Serving to refresh: often used sarcastically: *refreshing* impudence. See synonyms under DELIGHTFUL. — **re·fresh′ing·ly** *adv.*
re·fresh·ment (ri·fresh′mənt) *n.* **1** The act of refreshing, or the state of being refreshed; restoration of vigor or liveliness. **2** That which refreshes, as food or drink. **3** *pl.* Food, or food and drink, served as a light meal.
re·frig·er·ant (ri·frij′ər·ənt) *adj.* Cooling or freezing; allaying heat or fever. — *n.* **1** Any medicine or material, as ice, which reduces abnormal heat of the body. **2** A substance used for obtaining and maintaining a low temperature, as carbon dioxide, ammonia, or methyl chloride; a freezing mixture; a freezing agent. [<L *refrigerans, -antis,* ppr. of *refrigerare.* See REFRIGERATE.]
re·frig·er·ate (ri·frij′ə·rāt) *v.t.* **·at·ed, ·at·ing** **1** To keep or cause to become cold; cool. **2** To freeze or chill (foodstuffs) for preservative purposes. [<L *refrigeratus,* pp. of *refrigerare* < *re-* thoroughly + *frigerare* cool < *frigus, frigoris* cold] — **re·frig′er·a′tion** *n.* — **re·frig′er·a′tive** *adj.* & *n.*
re·frig·er·a·tor (ri·frij′ə·rā′tər) *n.* **1** That which makes or keeps cold. **2** A box, cabinet, room, railroad car, etc., equipped with apparatus for preserving the freshness of perishable foods, etc., by means of ice or other refrigerant.
re·frig·er·a·to·ry (ri·frij′ər·ə·tôr′ē, -tō′rē) *adj.* Reducing heat. — *n. pl.* **·ries** That which cools or refrigerates. [<L *refrigeratorius*]
re·frin·gen·cy (ri·frin′jən·sē) *n.* Power to refract. Also **re·frin′gence.** [< obs. *refringe* <L *refringere.* See REFRACT.] — **re·frin′gent** *adj.*
reft (reft) Past tense and past participle of REAVE.
re·fu·el (rē·fyo͞o′əl, -fyo͞ol′) *v.* **·eled** or **·elled, ·el·ing** or **·el·ling** *v.t.* To replenish with fuel. — *v.i.* To take on a fresh supply of fuel.
ref·uge (ref′yo͞oj) *n.* **1** Shelter or protection, as from danger or distress. **2** One who or that which shelters or protects. **3** A safe place; asylum. **4** *Brit.* A raised or enclosed safety area for the use of pedestrians at busy street crossings. — *v.t.* & *v.i. Obs.* To give or take refuge. [<OF <L *refugium* < *refugere* retreat < *re-* back + *fugere* flee]
Synonyms (noun): asylum, cover, covert, harbor, hiding-place, protection, retreat, sanctuary, stronghold. See SHELTER.
ref·u·gee (ref′yo͝o·jē′) *n.* **1** One who flees to a refuge. **2** One who flees from invasion, persecution, or political danger. [<F *réfugié,* pp. of *réfugier* <L *refugere.* See REFUGE.]
re·ful·gence (ri·ful′jəns) *n.* Splendor; brilliant radiance. Also **re·ful′gen·cy.**
re·ful·gent (ri·ful′jənt) *adj.* Shining with a bright light; brilliant; splendid. See synonyms under BRIGHT. [<L *refulgens, -entis,* ppr. of *refulgere* reflect light < *re-* back + *fulgere* shine] — **re·ful′gent·ly** *adv.*
re·fund (ri·fund′) *v.t.* **1** To give or pay back (money, etc.). **2** *Obs.* To pour back. — *v.i.* **3** To make repayment. — *n.* (rē′fund) A repayment; refunding; also, the amount repaid. [<L *refundere* pour back < *re-* back + *fundere* pour out, discharge] — **re·fund′er** *n.* — **re·fund′ment** *n.*
re–fund (rē·fund′) *v.t.* To fund anew; replace (an old loan) by issuing new securities.
re·fus·al (ri·fyo͞o′zəl) *n.* **1** The act of refusing; denial of what is asked. **2** The privilege of accepting or rejecting; an option.
re·fuse[1] (ri·fyo͞oz′) *v.* **·fused, ·fus·ing** *v.t.* **1** To decline to do, permit, take, or yield. **2** *Mil.* To turn back (the wing of a line of troops), so that it stands at an angle with the main body. **3** To decline to jump over: said of a horse at a ditch, hedge, etc. **4** *Obs.* To disown; renounce; resign. — *v.i.* **5** To decline to do, permit, take, or yield something. [<OF *refuser* <L *refusus,* pp. of *refundere.* See REFUND.] — **re·fus′er** *n.*
ref·use[2] (ref′yo͞os) *adj.* Rejected as worthless. — *n.* Anything worthless; rubbish. See synonyms under WASTE. [<OF *refus,* pp. of *refuser.* See REFUSE[1].]
re–fuse (rē·fyo͞oz′) *v.t.* & *v.i.* **–fused, –fus·ing** To fuse again.
re–fu·sion (rē·fyo͞o′zhən) *n. Med.* The temporary withdrawing of blood from circulation, as for exposing it to air or other treatment. Compare TRANSFUSION.
ref·u·ta·tion (ref′yo͝o·tā′shən) *n.* The act of refuting or proving the falsity or error in a statement, proposition, or argument; evidence applied to overthrow an erroneous statement or position. Also **re·fu·tal** (ri·fyo͞ot′l). [<L *refutatio, -onis* < *refutare* stop, repel]
re·fute (ri·fyo͞ot′) *v.t.* **·fut·ed, ·fut·ing** **1** To prove the incorrectness or falsity of (a statement). **2** To prove (a person) to be in error; confute. [<L *refutare*] — **re·fut′a·bil′i·ty** *n.* — **re·fut′a·ble** *adj.* — **re·fut′a·bly** *adv.* — **re·fut′er** *n.*
Synonyms: confound, confute, disprove. To *refute* and to *confute* are to answer so as to admit of no reply. *Refute* applies either to arguments and opinions or to accusations; *confute* is not applied to accusations and charges, but to overwhelming arguments or opinions that confound; a person is *confuted* when his arguments are *refuted.*
re·gain (ri·gān′) *v.t.* **1** To get possession of again, as something lost; gain anew. **2** To reach again; get back to: He *regained* the street. See synonyms under RECOVER. [<MF *regaigner*] — **re·gain′er** *n.*
re·gal (rē′gəl) *adj.* Belonging to or fit for a king; royal; also, stately. See synonyms under IMPERIAL, KINGLY. [<OF <L *regalis* < *rex, regis* king. Doublet of ROYAL.] — **re′gal·ly** *adv.*
re·gale (ri·gāl′) *v.* **·galed, ·gal·ing** *v.t.* **1** To give unusual pleasure to; delight: He *regaled* us with stories. **2** To entertain royally or sumptuously; feast. — *v.i.* **3** To feast. — *n. Obs.* **1** A sumptuous feast. **2** Refreshment. **3** A choice dish. [<F *régaler*; ult. origin uncertain] — **re·gale′ment** *n.*
re·ga·li·a (ri·gā′lē·ə, -gāl′yə) *n. pl.* **1** The insignia and emblems of royalty, as the crown, scepter, verge, vestments, etc. **2** The distinctive symbols, insignia, etc., of any society, order, or rank; hence, fine clothes; fancy trappings. **3** In old English law, royal rights; the six prerogatives of sovereignty: the powers of judicature, life and death, war and peace,

taxation, minting money, and taking masterless goods, as waifs, strays, etc. [<L, neut. pl. of *regalis* kingly <*rex, regis* king]

re·gal·i·ty (ri·gal′ə·tē) *n. pl.* **·ties 1** Sovereign jurisdiction; royalty. **2** A territorial jurisdiction conferred by the crown on a subject. **3** A country subject to royal authority; a kingdom. [<OF *regalité*]

Re·gan (rē′gən) In Shakespeare's *King Lear,* the second daughter of Lear. See LEAR.

re·gard (ri·gärd′) *v.t.* **1** To look at or observe closely or attentively. **2** To look on or think of in a certain or specified manner; consider: I *regard* him as a friend. **3** To take into account; consider. **4** To have relation or pertinence to; concern. **5** *Obs.* To care for. —*v.i.* **6** To pay attention. **7** To gaze or look. See synonyms under ESTEEM, LOOK, PERTAIN. —*n.* **1** Observant attention or notice; heed; consideration. **2** Common estimation or repute, especially good repute: a man of *regard.* **3** Reference; relation. **4** A look or aspect; view. **5** *Usually pl.* Respect; affection: My kindest *regards* to your family. **6** Motive. [<OF *regarder* look at <*re-* again + *garder* guard, heed. Doublet of REWARD.]

Synonyms (noun): esteem, favor, respect. *Regard* is more personal and less distant than *esteem,* and adds a special kindliness; *respect* is a more distant word than *esteem. Respect* may be wholly on one side, while *regard* is more often mutual; *respect* in the fullest sense is given to what is lofty, worthy, and honorable, or to a person of such qualities; we may pay an external *respect* to one of lofty station, regardless of personal qualities, showing *respect* for the office. See ATTACHMENT, ESTEEM, FAVOR, FRIENDSHIP, LOVE. *Antonyms*: abhorrence, antipathy, aversion, contempt, dislike, hatred, loathing, repugnance.

re·gard·ant (ri·gär′dənt) *adj. Her.* Looking backward. Compare GARDANT. [<F, ppr. of *regarder* look at]

re·gard·ful (ri·gärd′fəl) *adj.* **1** Having or showing regard; heedful. **2** Respectful. —**re·gard′ful·ly** *adv.* —**re·gard′ful·ness** *n.*

re·gard·ing (ri·gär′ding) *prep.* In reference to; with regard to.

re·gard·less (ri·gärd′lis) *adj.* Having no regard or consideration; heedless; negligent. See synonyms under INATTENTIVE. —*adv. Colloq.* In spite of everything.

re·gat·ta (ri·gat′ə, -gä′tə) *n.* A boat race, or a series of such races. [<Ital. <*regatar* strive]

re·ge·late (rē′jə·lāt) *v.i.* **·lat·ed, ·lat·ing** To unite by regelation. [<RE- + L *gelatus,* pp. of *gelare* freeze]

re·ge·la·tion (rē′jə·lā′shən) *n.* The refreezing of melting ice by reducing the pressure to which it is subjected, thus raising the freezing point.

re·gen·cy (rē′jən·sē) *n. pl.* **·cies 1** The government or office of a regent or body of regents; vicarious government. **2** The period during which a regent or body of regents governs. **3** A body of regents. **4** The district under the rule of a regent. Also **re′gent·ship.** —**the Regency 1** In English history, the years 1811–20. **2** In French history, the years 1715–1723.

re·gen·er·a·cy (ri·jen′ər·ə·sē) *n.* The state of being regenerate.

re·gen·er·ate (ri·jen′ə·rāt) *v.* **·at·ed, ·at·ing** *v.t.* **1** To cause complete moral and spiritual reformation or regeneration in. **2** To produce or form anew; re-create; reproduce. **3** To make use of (heat or other energy that might otherwise be wasted) by means of various devices. **4** *Biol.* To grow or form by regeneration. **5** *Electronics* To raise the amplification of (a vacuum tube) by transferring to the input circuit some of the power of the output circuit. —*v.i.* **6** To form anew; be reproduced. **7** To become spiritually regenerate. **8** To effect regeneration. —*adj.* (ri·jen′ər·it) **1** Having new life; restored. **2** Spiritually renewed; regenerated. [<L *regeneratus,* pp. of *regenerare* generate again <*re-* again +*generare.* See GENERATE.]

re·gen·er·a·tion (ri·jen′ə·rā′shən) *n.* **1** The act of regenerating, or the state of being regenerated. **2** The impartation of spiritual life by divine grace. **3** *Biol.* **a** The reproduction of a lost part or organ, as in lizards. **b** The renewal or reproduction of cells, tissues, etc., in the ordinary vital processes: the *regeneration* of the ectodermic layers. **4** The process by which, in various devices, heat or other forms of energy are saved and re-utilized. **5** *Electronics* The amplification of radiosignal strength by returning part of the output of a vacuum tube to the grid: an effect of feedback. [<OF] —**re·gen·er·a·tive** (ri·jen′ə·rā′tiv, -ər·ə·tiv) *adj.* —**re·gen′er·a′tive·ly** *adv.*

re·gen·er·a·tor (ri·jen′ə·rā′tər) *n.* **1** One who or that which regenerates. **2** A device in a furnace, gas burner, or similar apparatus, by which the waste heat of escaping gases is used to heat the gas and air just entering. **3** A furnace containing such a device.

Re·gens·burg (rā′gənz·bŏŏrkh) A city of eastern Bavaria, West Germany, a port on the Danube at its northernmost point: English *Ratisbon.*

re·gent (rē′jənt) *n.* **1** One who rules in the name and place of the sovereign. **2** Any ruler or governor; one who governs. **3** resident master who takes part in the government of a university or college. **4** One of various officers having charge of the higher education, as of a state. —*adj.* **1** Exercising authority in another's place. **2** Governing; ruling. [<OF <L *regens, -entis,* ppr. of *regere* rule]

reg·gae (reg′ā) *n.* A simple, lively, rhythmic kind of rock 'n' roll music, of West Indian origin. [< a native West Indian name]

reg·i·cide (rej′ə·sīd) *n.* **1** The killing of a king or sovereign. **2** The killer of a king or sovereign. [<L *rex, regis* king + -CIDE] —**reg′i·ci′dal** *adj.*

Re·gil·lus (ri·jil′əs) In ancient geography, a small lake near Rome; scene of the victory of the Romans over the Latins in 496 B.C.

re·gime (ri·zhēm′) *n.* **1** System of government or administration. **2** Prevalent mode in social matters; social system. **3** Regimen (def. 1). Also **ré·gime** (rā·zhēm′). [<F *régime* <L *regimen.* Doublet of REGIMEN.]

reg·i·men (rej′ə·mən) *n.* **1** A systematized course of living, as to food, clothing, etc. **2** Government; control. **3** *Gram.* The influence of one word in determining the form of another connected with it; grammatical government. See synonyms under FOOD. [<L *regimen* <*regere* rule. Doublet of REGIME.]

reg·i·ment (rej′ə·mənt) *n.* **1** A body of soldiers constituting the unit of infantry, cavalry, artillery, etc., commanded by a colonel. **2** *Obs.* Government over a people or country. —*v.t.* **1** To form into a regiment or regiments; organize. **2** To assign to a regiment. **3** To form into well-defined or specific units or groups; systematize. **4** To make uniform at the expense of individual differences: Certain types of education *regiment* children. [<OF <LL *regimentum* <L *regere* rule] —**reg′i·men′tal** *adj.*

reg·i·men·tals (rej′ə·men′təlz) *n. pl.* Military uniform; the uniform worn by the men and officers of a regiment.

reg·i·men·ta·tion (rej′ə·men·tā′shən)*n.* **1** The act of regimenting; formation into or as into a regiment. **2** Organization into disciplined, uniform groups.

Re·gin (rā′gin) In Norse mythology, a dwarf, foster father of Sigurd, by whom he was slain. Also **Re′ginn.** See FAFNIR, SIGURD.

re·gi·na (ri·jī′nə) *n. Latin* Queen.

Re·gi·na (ri·jī′nə) The capital of Saskatchewan province, Canada.

re·gi·nal (ri·jī′nəl) *adj.* Pertaining to a queen; queenly; also, supporting or favoring a queen. [<Med. L *reginalis*]

re·gion (rē′jən) *n.* **1** A portion of territory or space; a country or district; also, realm; specifically, one of the strata into which the air or the sea is divided by imaginary boundaries. **2** A zoogeographical division of the earth's surface: the Australian *region.* **3** A portion of the body, arbitrarily circumscribed for anatomical and medical purposes: the abdominal *region.* See synonyms under LAND. [<AF *regiun,* OF *regium* <L *regio, -onis* <*regere* rule]

re·gion·al (rē′jən·əl) *adj.* **1** Of or pertaining to a particular region; sectional; local: *regional* planning. **2** Of or pertaining to an entire region or section, especially a geographic one: *regional* features. —**re′gion·al·ly** *adv.*

re·gion·al·ism (rē′jə·nə·liz′əm) *n.* **1** An emotional loyalty or strong feeling for a particular region. **2** An emphasis on regional flavor in art and literature. **3** A specific habit, custom, or way of speaking of a certain region.

ré·gis·seur (rā·zhē·sœr′) *n. French* Director; manager.

reg·is·ter (rej′is·tər) *n.* **1** An official record, the book containing it, or an entry therein; roll; list; schedule; a registry. **2** A registrar. **3** That which registers; a registering apparatus, as for recording velocity, pressure, etc. **4** A device for regulating the admission of heated air to a room. **5** A machine or apparatus which automatically records cash intake; a cash register. **6** *Music* **a** The range or compass of a voice or musical instrument. **b** A class or series of tones of a particular quality or belonging to a particular portion of the compass of a voice or of some instruments. The normal and natural register of the voice is the chest, or thick, register; a middle and an upper register are also recognized, the latter being also termed a head, or thin, register. **7** *Phot.* Relation of position between the sensitive plate or film and the focusing screen. **8** *Printing* **a** Exact correspondence of the lines and margins on the opposite sides of a printed sheet. **b** Correct relation of the colors in color printing. See synonyms under HISTORY, RECORD. —*v.t.* **1** To enter in or as in a register; enrol; specifically, to record formally, as a document, securities, etc. **2** To indicate on a scale. **3** To express or indicate: His face *registered* his disapproval. **4** To effect the exact correspondence of (parts), as the two sides of a printed sheet, the separate plates or films of a color print, etc. **5** To cause (mail) to be recorded, on payment of a fee, when deposited with the postal system, so as to insure delivery. —*v.i.* **6** To enter one's name in a register, poll, etc. **7** To have effect; make an impression. **8** *Printing* To be in register. See synonyms under ENROL. [<OF *registre* < Med. L *registrum* <L *regesta* records, neut. pl of *regestus,* pp. of *regerere* record <*re-* back + *gerere* carry] —**reg·is·tra·ble** (rej′is·trə·bəl) *adj.*

reg·is·tered (rej′is·tərd) *adj.* **1** Recorded, as a birth, a voter, an animal's pedigree, etc. **2** Having a required or official certificate, as a nurse.

registered mail First-class mail, specially entered and recorded at a higher fee, to insure safe delivery.

registered nurse A graduate nurse licensed to practice by the appropriate State authority and entitled to add R.N. after her name.

reg·is·trant (rej′is·trənt) *n.* One who registers, as a voter; especially, one who registers a trademark or patent. [<F]

reg·is·trar (rej′is·trär, rej′is·trär′) *n.* The authorized keeper of a register or of records; especially, a college or university officer who records the enrolment of students, their grades, etc. [<Med. L *registrarius*]

reg·is·tra·tion (rej′is·trā′shən) *n.* **1** The act of entering in a registry; also, an entry in a registry. **2** The registering of voters; also, the number of voters registered. **3** Enrolment in a school, college, or university. **4** The combination of stops used in playing a composition on the organ. [<Med. L *registratio, -onis*]

reg·is·try (rej′is·trē) *n. pl.* **·tries 1** Registration. **2** A register, or the place where it is kept. **3** The condition of being registered: a certificate of *registry.*

re·gi·us (rē′jē·əs) *adj. Latin* Royal: a designation of certain English university professorships founded by the crown, or of their incumbents, and also of certain Scottish professors appointed by the crown.

reg·let (reg′lit) *n.* **1** A flat, narrow molding. **2** *Printing* A thin wooden strip used for making space between lines of type, as in posters; also, the strips collectively or the material of which they are made. [<OF, dim. of *regle* < L *regula.* See RULE.]

reg·ma (reg′mə) *n.* *pl.* **·ma·ta** (-mə·tə) *Bot.* A capsular fruit made up of two or more carpels, each of which dehisces at maturity. [<NL <Gk. *rhēgma* fracture < *rhēgnynai* break]

reg·nal (reg′nəl) *adj.* Of or pertaining to a reign, a king, or a kingdom. [<LL *regnalis* <L *regnum* reign]

reg·nant (reg′nənt) *adj.* Reigning in one's own right; hence, dominant. [<L *regnans, -antis,* ppr. of *regnare* < *regnum* reign]

reg·nant pop·u·li (reg′nənt pop′yōō·lī) *Latin* The people rule: motto of Arkansas.

Re·gnauld (rə·nyō′) French form of REGINALD. Also **Re·gnault′.**

Ré·gnier (rā·nyā′), **Henri de,** 1864–1936, French author.

re·gorge (ri·gôrj′) *v.* **·gorged, ·gorg·ing** *v.t.* To vomit up; disgorge. — *v.i.* To gush or flow back. [<F *regorger* <*re-* again + *gorger* gorge < *gorge* throat <L *gurges* whirlpool. Related to REGURGITATE.]

re·grade (ri·grād′) *v.t.* **·grad·ed, ·grad·ing** To grade again.

re·grate (ri·grāt′) *v.t.* **·grat·ed, ·grat·ing** **1** To buy up, as provisions, for the purpose of selling at a higher price in or near the same market. **2** To retail, as provisions. [<OF *regrater*; ult. origin uncertain]

re·gress (rē′gres) *n.* **1** Passage back; return; also, the power or right of passing back or returning. **2** Retrogression. — *v.i.* (ri·gres′) **1** To go back; move backward; return. **2** *Astron.* To move in a direction opposite to that of the general motion of the heavenly bodies, as the moon's nodes. **3** *Stat.* To return to the mean value of a series of observations. [<L *regressus,* pp. of *regredi* go back < *re-* back + *gradi* walk] — **re·gres′sor** *n.*

re·gres·sion (ri·gresh′ən) *n.* **1** The act of moving back or returning. **2** *Astron.* Motion in a direction opposite to that of the general motion of the heavenly bodies. **3** *Psychoanal.* A retreat of the libido to earlier levels of development or to infantile tendencies belonging to a period preceding the obstacles which prevented their normal fulfilment. **4** *Stat.* The return to a mean or average value. **5** *Med.* The subsidence of a disease or of its symptoms.

re·gres·sive (ri·gres′iv) *adj.* **1** Passing back; returning. **2** Retroactive. **3** Retrogressive. — **re·gres′sive·ly** *adv.*

re·gret (ri·gret′) *v.t.* **·gret·ted, ·gret·ting** **1** To look back upon with a feeling of distress or loss. **2** To feel sorrow or grief concerning. See synonyms under MOURN. — *n.* **1** Distress of mind in recalling some past event; a wish that something had or had not happened. **2** Remorseful sorrow; compunction. **3** An expression of sorrow or disappointment. **4** *pl.* A polite declination in response to an invitation. See synonyms under GRIEF, REPENTANCE. [<OF *regreter*; ult. origin uncertain] **re·gret′ter** *n.*

re·gret·ful (ri·gret′fəl) *adj.* Feeling, expressive of, or full of regret. — **re·gret′ful·ly** *adv.* — **re·gret′ful·ness** *n.*

re·gret·ta·ble (ri·gret′ə·bəl) *adj.* Causing or demanding regret; unfortunate; deplorable. — **re·gret′ta·bly** *adv.*

reg·u·la (reg′yə·lə) *n.* *pl.* **·lae** (-lē) *Archit.* A fillet, especially one of a series in a Doric architrave, placed under the taenia and bearing six guttae on the under side. [<L, ruler < *regere* rule, lead straight]

reg·u·lar (reg′yə·lər) *adj.* **1** Made according to rule; symmetrical; normal. **2** Acting according to rule; recurring without fail; methodical; orderly: *regular* habits. **3** Constituted, appointed, or conducted in the proper manner; duly authorized: a *regular* meeting, a *regular* practitioner. **4** *Gram.* Undergoing the inflection that is normal or most common to the class of words to which it belongs; following the rule; not exceptional. **5** *Bot.* Having all the parts or organs of the same kind uniform in structure or shape and size: said mainly of flowers. **6** *Zool.* Conforming to an established type; exhibiting radial or bilateral symmetry. **7** *Music* Following strict and classical rules of composition: a *regular* movement. **8** *Eccl.* Bound by a religious rule; pertaining or belonging to a religious order: the *regular* clergy. **9** *Mil.* Belonging to the standing army; permanent. **10** In politics, adhering loyally to a party organization or platform; also, nominated by the official party organization: said of a candidate. **11** *Geom.* Having equal sides and angles. **12** Controlled or governed by one law or operation throughout: a *regular* equation. **13** *Colloq.* Thorough; unmitigated; absolute. **14** *Slang* Fine; good: a *regular* guy. **15** *U.S.* Designating that component of a branch of the armed services which consists of persons in continuous service on active duty in both peace and war: the **Regular Army, Regular Navy, Regular Air Force.** See synonyms under CONTINUAL, GRADUAL, HABITUAL, NORMAL, SOBER, USUAL. — *n.* **1** A soldier belonging to a standing army as opposed to a volunteer, draftee, or member of a reserve unit. **2** *Colloq.* One regularly employed or engaged; also, a habitual customer. **3** *Eccl.* A member of a religious or monastic order. **4** A person loyal to a certain political party. [<L *regularis* < *regula* rule] — **reg′u·lar·ness** *n.*

reg·u·lar·i·ty (reg′yə·lar′ə·tē) *n.* *pl.* **·ties** The state, quality, or character of being regular: *regularity* of form or in occurrence. See synonyms under SYMMETRY, SYSTEM.

reg·u·lar·ize (reg′yə·lə·rīz′) *v.t.* **·ized, ·iz·ing** To make regular. — **reg′u·lar·i·za′tion** *n.*

reg·u·lar·ly (reg′yə·lər·lē) *adv.* In a regular manner; according to the usual method or order.

reg·u·late (reg′yə·lāt) *v.t.* **·lat·ed, ·lat·ing** **1** To direct, manage, or control according to certain rules, principles, etc. **2** To adjust according to a standard, degree, etc.: to *regulate* currency. **3** To adjust to accurate operation: to *regulate* a watch. **4** To put in order; set right. [<LL *regulatus,* pp. of *regulare* rule <L *regula* a rule < *regere* rule, lead straight] — **reg′u·la′tive** *adj.*

Synonyms: adjust, arrange, conduct, direct, dispose, govern, guide, manage, methodize, order, rule, systematize. See SET, SETTLE. *Antonyms*: confuse, derange, disorder, displace, distract, disturb, unsettle.

reg·u·la·tion (reg′yə·lā′shən) *n.* **1** The act of regulating, or the state of being regulated. **2** A rule prescribed for conduct: army *regulations*: also used adjectively. See synonyms under LAW[1], RULE.

reg·u·la·tor (reg′yə·lā′tər) *n.* **1** One who or that which regulates. **2** A clock used as a standard; also, an index arm for regulating the rate of a watch. **3** *Mech.* A contrivance for governing or equalizing motion or flow; the governor of a steam engine; a damper or other device for regulating a draft; a throttle valve. **4** A register (def. 4). **5** A thermostat. **6** *Electr.* A device for keeping at constant strength the current produced by a dynamo. — **reg′u·la′tor·ship** *n.*

Reg·u·la·tor (reg′yə·lā′tər) *n.* **1** A member of any of several bands or committees organized in North Carolina (1768–71) to resist official extortion, and in South Carolina (1767–69) to exterminate horse thieves. **2** One belonging to a volunteer band or committee, which, in the absence of lawful authority, took it upon itself to preserve order and punish crime, but which often deteriorated into lawless bands of violent men.

reg·u·la·to·ry (reg′yə·lə·tôr′ē, -tō′rē) *adj.* Tending or serving to regulate: *regulatory* measures. Also **reg′u·la′tive.**

reg·u·lus (reg′yə·ləs) *n.* *pl.* **·li** (-lī) *Metall.* **1** The metallic mass that sinks to the bottom of the vessel in which slag is being treated. **2** An intermediate product obtained in smelting ores of copper, lead, silver, and nickel. [<L, lit., kinglet, dim of *rex, regis* king] — **reg′u·line** (-lin, -līn) *adj.*

Reg·u·lus (reg′yə·ləs) A white star, Alpha in the constellation Leo; magnitude, 1.34: sometimes called *Cor Leonis.* [<L]

Reg·u·lus (reg′yə·ləs), **Marcus Attilius** Roman general; put to death by the Carthaginians about 250 B.C.

re·gur·gi·tate (ri·gûr′jə·tāt) *v.* **·tat·ed, ·tat·ing** *v.i.* To rush, pour, or surge back; vomit. — *v.t.* To cause to surge back, as partially digested food; vomit. [<LL *regurgitatus,* pp. of *regurgitare* < *re-* back + *gurgitare* flood, engulf < L *gurges, gurgites* whirlpool] — **re·gur′gi·tant** *adj.*

re·gur·gi·ta·tion (ri·gûr′jə·tā′shən) *n.* **1** The act of rushing back or reswallowing. **2** *Physiol.* The backward rush of blood into the heart, due to defective valves.

re·ha·bil·i·tate (rē′hə·bil′ə·tāt) *v.t.* **·tat·ed, ·tat·ing** **1** To restore to a former state, capacity, privilege, rank, etc.; reinstate. **2** To make one capable of becoming a useful member of society again: to *rehabilitate* a crippled soldier. [<Med. L *rehabilitatus,* pp. of *rehabilitare* < *re-* back + *habilitare.* See HABILITATE.] — **re′ha·bil′i·ta′tion** *n.*

re·hash (rē·hash′) *v.t.* To work into a new form; go over again. — *n.* (rē′hash′) Something hashed over, or made or served up from something used before, as old matter issued under a new name.

re·hears·al (ri·hûr′səl) *n.* **1** The act of rehearsing, as a play. **2** The act of reciting or telling over again.

re·hearse (ri·hûrs′) *v.* **·hearsed, ·hears·ing** *v.t.* **1** To perform privately in preparation for public performance, as a play or song. **2** To cause to perform or recite by way of preparation; instruct by rehearsal. **3** To say over again; repeat aloud; recite. **4** To give an account of; relate. **5** To enumerate. — *v.i.* **6** To rehearse a play, song, dance, etc. See synonyms under RELATE. [<OF *reherser* harrow over, repeat < *re-* again + *herser* harrow < *herse.* See HEARSE.] — **re·hears′er** *n.*

re·heat (rē·hēt′) *v.t.* To heat again or anew. — **re·heat′er** *n.*

Rehn·quist (ren′kwist), **William H.,** born 1924, U.S. jurist, associate Supreme Court justice 1972–.

Re·ho·bo·am (rē′ō·bō′əm) Son and successor of Solomon; king of Judah after the revolt of the ten tribes. II *Chron.* ix 31.

rei (rā) Erroneous English form for Portuguese *real.* See MILREIS, REAL[2].

Reich (rīkh) Germany or its government. — **First Reich** The Holy Roman Empire from its establishment in the ninth century to its collapse in 1806. — **Second Reich** The German Empire, 1871–1919, or the Weimar Republic, 1919–1933, or both German governments in the period 1871–1933. — **Third Reich** The Nazi state under Adolf Hitler, 1933–45. [<G, realm]

Reich (rīkh), **Wilhelm,** 1897–1957, U. S. psychotherapist and natural scientist, born in Germany.

Reich·en·berg (rīkh′ən·berkh) The German name for LIBEREC.

Reichs·bank (rīkhs′bängk) *n.* The state or national bank of Germany, founded in 1876. [<G]

Reichs·land (rīkhs′länt) **1** From 1806 to 1871, all German crown lands. **2** From 1871 to 1918, Alsace-Lorraine.

reichs·mark (rīkhs′märk) See MARK[2] (def. 1). [<G]

reichs·pfen·nig (rīkhs′pfen′ikh) See PFENNIG. [<G]

Reichs·rat (rīkhs′rät) *n.* **1** The former parliament of the Austrian Empire, excluding Hungary. **2** The Council of the Reich under the Weimar Republic. Also **Reichs′rath.** [<G, lit., council of the empire]

Reichs·tag (rīkhs′täkh) *n.* The former legislative assembly of Germany. [<G, lit., day of the empire. Cf. DIET for analogous development.]

Reid (rēd), **Whitelaw,** 1837–1912, U. S. journalist and diplomat.

reif (rēf) *n. Scot.* Robbery; plunder.

re·i·fy (rē′ə·fī) *v.t.* **·fied, ·fy·ing** To make real or concrete; materialize: to *reify* an idea. [<L *res, rei* thing + -FY] — **re′i·fi·ca′tion** *n.* — **re′i·fi′er** *n.*

reign (rān) *n.* **1** The possession or exercise of supreme political power; sovereignty; dominion. **2** The time or duration of a sovereign's rule. — *v.i.* **1** To hold and exercise sovereign power; be the head of a monarchy. **2** To hold sway; be predominant; prevail: Winter *reigns.* See synonyms under GOVERN. ◆ Homophones: *rain, rein.* [<F *règne* <L *regnum* rule]

Reign of Terror The period of the French Revolution from May, 1793, to August, 1794, during which Louis XVI, Marie Antoinette, and thousands of other persons were guillotined, and confiscation, violence, and terror reigned under the revolutionary leaders.

re·im·burse (rē′im·bûrs′) *v.t.* **·bursed, ·burs·ing** **1** To pay back (a person) an equivalent for what has been spent or lost; recompense; indemnify. **2** To pay back; refund. [< RE- + obs. *imburse* <LL *imbursare* <L *in-* in

+ *bursa* purse] — **re′im·burse′ment** *n.* — **re′im·burs′er** *n.*

re·im·plan·ta·tion (rē′im·plan·tā′shən) *n. Surg.* The act of restoring in place a bone, or part of a bone, removed in an operation.

re·im·pres·sion (rē′im·presh′ən) *n.* **1** A new or second impression of anything. **2** A reprint of a book without editorial change.

Reims (rēmz, *Fr.* rañs) A city in NE France; its cathedral, former coronation place of the French kings, was greatly damaged by German bombardment in 1870 and 1914: also *Rheims.*

rein (rān) *n.* **1** *Usually pl.* A strap attached to the bit to control a horse or other draft animal. **2** Any means of restraint or control; government. — *v.t.* **1** To guide, check, or halt with or as with reins. **2** To furnish with reins. — *v.i.* **3** To check or halt a horse by means of reins: with *in* or *up.* **4** To obey the reins. See synonyms under REPRESS. ◆ Homophones: *rain, reign.* [<AF *redne,* OF *resne* <L *retinere.* See RETAIN.]

Rei·nach (re·nȧk′), **Salomon,** 1858–1932, French archeologist.

re·in·car·nate (rē′in·kär′nāt) *v.t.* **·nat·ed, ·nat·ing** To cause to undergo reincarnation.

re·in·car·na·tion (rē′in·kär·nā′shən) *n.* A rebirth of the soul in successive bodies; specifically, in Vedic religions, the becoming of an avatar again: one of the series in the transmigrations of souls. — **re′in·car·na′tion·ist** *n.*

rein·deer (rān′dir′) *n. pl.* **·deer** A deer (genus *Rangifer*) of northern regions, having branched antlers in both sexes: long domesticated for its milk, hide, and flesh, and used as a draft and pack animal. [<ON *hreindȳri* < *hreinn* reindeer + *dȳr* deer]

Reindeer Lake A lake in northern Saskatchewan and Manitoba provinces, Canada; 2,444 square miles.

reindeer moss A gray, branched lichen *(Cladonia rangiferina)* found as far as the extreme limits of arctic vegetation, and furnishing food for reindeer and sometimes man.

re in·fec·ta (rē in·fek′tə) *Latin* The business being unfinished.

re·in·force (rē′in·fôrs′, -fōrs′) *v.t.* **·forced, ·forc·ing 1** To give new force or strength to. **2** To increase the military or naval strength of by providing with more troops or ships. **3** To add some strengthening part or material to; thicken; strengthen; support. See synonyms under RECRUIT. — *n.* That which strengthens or reinforces, as the part of a cannon near the breech that is cast thicker than the rest. Also spelled *reenforce.* [<RE- + *inforce,* var. of ENFORCE]

reinforced concrete Concrete containing metal bars, rods, or netting disposed through the mass in such a way as to increase its tensile strength and durability; ferroconcrete.

re·in·force·ment (rē′in·fôrs′mənt, -fōrs′-) *n.* **1** The act of reinforcing. **2** Increase of force; a fresh body of troops or additional vessels: often in the plural. See synonyms under INCREASE. Also spelled *reenforcement.*

Rein·hardt (rīn′härt), **Max,** 1873–1943, Austrian theatrical director and producer active in Germany and the United States.

Rein·hold (rīn′hōld; *Dan.* rīn′hōlth, *Ger.* rīn′·hōlt, *Sw.* rīn′hōld) See REGINALD. Also *Ger.* **Rei·nald** (rī′nält), *Du.* **Rei·nold** (rī′nōlt).

reins (rānz) *n. pl. Archaic* **1** The kidneys. **2** The region near the kidneys. **3** The affections and passions, formerly thought to have their seat in the loins. [<OF <L *renes,* pl. of *ren*]

re·in·stall (rē′in·stôl′) *v.t.* To install again. — **re·in·stal·la·tion** (rē′in·stə·lā′shən) *n.* — **re′in·stal′ment** or **re′in·stall′ment** *n.*

re·in·state (rē′in·stāt′) *v.t.* **·stat·ed, ·stat·ing** To restore to a former state, position, etc. — **re′in·state′ment** *n.*

re·in·sure (rē′in·shŏŏr′) *v.t.* **·sured, ·sur·ing 1** To protect (the risk on a policy already issued) by obtaining insurance from a second insurer: said of a first insurer. **2** To insure anew. — **re′in·sur′ance** *n.* — **re′in·sur′er** *n.*

re·in·vest (rē′in·vest′) *v.t.* To invest (money) again; especially, to invest earnings from previous investments. — **re′in·vest′ment** *n.*

Rein·wald (rīn′vält) A German form of REGINALD.

reis (rēs) Plural of REAL[2] (def. 2). See MILREIS.

reise (rēs) *n. Scot.* A twig; brush; brushwood.

re·is·sue (rē·ish′ōō) *n.* **1** A second or subsequent issue, as of a publication changed only in form or price. **2** A second printing of postage stamps from the same plates. — *v.t.* **·sued, ·su·ing** To issue again.

reit·bok (rēt′bok) *n.* The reedbuck. [<Du. *rietbok*]

re·it·er·ate (rē·it′ə·rāt) *v.t.* **·at·ed, ·at·ing** To say or do again and again; repeat. [<L *reiteratus,* pp. of *reiterare* < *re-* again + *iterare.* See ITERATE.] — **re·it′er·a′tion** *n.*

re·it·er·a·tive (rē·it′ə·rā′tiv) *adj.* Characterized by reiteration. — *n.* **1** A word or syllable repeated, usually with some slight change, so as to make a reduplicated word; also, the word so formed, as *tittle–tattle.* **2** A word expressing repeated action. — **re·it′er·a′tive·ly** *adv.*

Ré·jane (rā·zhän′), **Gabrielle Charlotte,** 1857–1920, French actress and comedienne: real name *Réju.*

re·ject (ri·jekt′) *v.t.* **1** To refuse to accept, recognize, believe, etc. **2** To refuse to grant; deny, as a petition. **3** To refuse (a person) recognition, acceptance, etc. **4** To expel, as from the mouth; vomit. **5** To cast away as worthless; discard. — *n.* (rē′jekt) A person or thing that has been discarded or rejected. [<L *rejectus,* pp. of *reicere* fling back < *re-* back + *jacere* throw] — **re·ject′er** or **re·jec′·tor** *n.*

re·jec·ta·men·ta (ri·jek′tə·men′tə) *n. pl.* Things thrown away; especially, things rejected from a living organism; excrement. [<NL <L *rejectare,* freq. of *reicere* fling back]

re·jec·tion (ri·jek′shən) *n.* **1** The act of rejecting. **2** That which is rejected.

re·joice (ri·jois′) *v.* **·joiced, ·joic·ing** *v.i.* To feel joyful; be glad. — *v.t.* To fill with joy; gladden. [<OF *rejoiss-, resjoiss-,* stem of *resjoir* enjoy < *re-* again (<L) + *esjoir* <L *ex-* thoroughly + *gaudere* be joyous < *gaudium* joy] — **re·joic′er** *n.*

Synonyms: cheer, delight, enjoy, enrapture, exhilarate, exult, gladden, gratify, joy, please, ravish, triumph. Compare HAPPINESS, HAPPY. *Antonyms*: afflict, agonize, bewail, grieve, lament, mourn, pain, regret, sadden, sorrow.

re·joic·ing (ri·joi′sing) *adj.* Pertaining to or characterized by joyfulness. See synonyms under HAPPY. — *n.* The feeling or expression of joy. See synonyms under HAPPINESS, LAUGHTER, RAPTURE.

re·join[1] (ri·join′) *v.t.* **1** To say in reply; answer. — *v.i.* **2** To answer. **3** *Law* To make answer to the plaintiff's replication. [<F *rejoindre* < *re-* again (<L) + *joindre.* See JOIN.]

re·join[2] (rē·join′) *v.t.* **1** To come again into company with. **2** To join together again; reunite. — *v.i.* **3** To come together again. [<RE- + JOIN]

re·join·der (ri·join′dər) *n.* **1** An answer to a reply; also, any reply or retort. **2** *Law* The answer filed by a defendant to a plaintiff's replication. See synonyms under ANSWER. [< F *rejoindre* answer, reply]

re·ju·ve·nate (ri·jōō′və·nāt) *v.t.* **·nat·ed, ·nat·ing 1** To make young; give new vigor or youthfulness to. **2** *Geog.* To restore (a mature or old river) to its youthful condition by the development of lakes, as by obstruction through mountain growth or elevation. Also **re·ju′ve·nize.** [<RE- again + L *juvenis* young + -ATE[1]] — **re·ju′ve·na′tion** *n.*

re·ju·ve·nes·cence (ri·jōō′və·nes′əns) *n.* **1** A renewal of youth; the state of being or growing young again. **2** *Biol.* The transformation of the entire protoplasm of a vegetative cell into a primordial cell, which subsequently invests itself with a new cell wall, and forms the starting point of the life of a new individual. [<L *rejuvenescens,* ppr. of *rejuvenescere* renew youth < *re-* again + *juvenescere* grow young < *juvenis* young] — **re·ju′ve·nes′cent** *adj.*

re·lapse (ri·laps′) *v.i.* **·lapsed, ·laps·ing 1** To lapse back, as into disease after partial recovery. **2** To return to bad habits or sin; backslide. — *n.* (*also* rē′laps) A relapsing; lapse into a former evil state. [<L *relapsus,* pp. of *relabi* slide back < *re-* back + *labi* slide] — **re·laps′er** *n.*

relapsing fever *Pathol.* An acute infectious disease occurring in several forms and due to certain spirochetes transmitted by lice and ticks. It is characterized by febrile paroxysms recurring every five or seven days. Also called *recurrent fever.*

re·late (ri·lāt′) *v.* **·lat·ed, ·lat·ing** *v.t.* **1** To tell the events or the particulars of; narrate. **2** To bring into connection or relation. — *v.i.* **3** To have relation: with *to.* **4** To have reference: with *to.* [<F *relater* <L *relatus,* pp. to *referre.* See REFER.] — **re·lat′er** *n.*

Synonyms: describe, detail, narrate, recite, recount, rehearse, report, state, tell. See PERTAIN. *Antonyms*: deny, hide, suppress, withhold.

re·lat·ed (ri·lā′tid) *adj.* **1** Standing in relation; connected. **2** Of common ancestry; connected by blood or marriage; akin. **3** Narrated. **4** Belonging to the same harmonic or melodic series. — **re·lat′ed·ness** *n.*

re·la·tion (ri·lā′shən) *n.* **1** The fact or condition of being related or connected, or that by which things are connected, either objectively or in the mind; interdependence; connection. **2** The act of relating or narrating; also, that which is related or told. **3** Connection by blood or marriage; kinship. **4** A person connected by blood or marriage; a kinsman: now mostly supplanted by *relative.* **5** *Law* **a** The statement of the grounds of a complaint or grievance by a relator. **b** The reaching back and taking effect of an act or judicial decree at a date anterior to its actual occurrence: Assignment in bankruptcy operates by *relation* back to the date of filing the petition. **6** Reference; regard; allusion: chiefly in the phrase, **in relation to. 7** The position of one person with respect to another: the *relation* of ruler to subject. **8** *pl.* Conditions in general which bring an individual in touch with his fellows; also, the various ways in which one country may come into contact with another politically and commercially. See synonyms under ANALOGY, KINDRED, KINSMAN, REPORT, STORY[1]. [<F <L *relatio, -onis* < *relatus,* pp. to *referre.* See REFER.]

re·la·tion·al (ri·lā′shən·əl) *adj.* **1** Pertaining to or expressing relation: said especially of certain parts of speech. **2** Having relation or kinship.

re·la·tion·ship (ri·lā′shən·ship) *n.* The state of being related; connection. See synonyms under AFFINITY, KIN.

rel·a·tive (rel′ə·tiv) *adj.* **1** Having connection; pertinent: an inquiry *relative* to one's health. **2** Resulting from or depending upon relation; comparative: a *relative* truth. **3** Intelligible only in relation to each other: the *relative* terms "father" and "son." **4** Referring to, relating to, or qualifying an antecedent term: a *relative* pronoun. **5** Having the same key signature, as major and minor keys and scales. — *n.* **1** One who is related; a kinsman. **2** A relative word or term; especially, a relative pronoun. See synonyms under KINDRED, KINSMAN. [<F *relatif* <LL *relativus* <L *relatus*] — **rel′a·tive·ly** *adv.* — **rel′a·tive·ness** *n.*

relative pronoun See under PRONOUN.

rel·a·tiv·ism (rel′ə·tiv·iz′əm) *n. Philos.* The theory that truths are relative and may vary according to the individual, the group, the place, or the time. — **rel′a·tiv·ist** *n.* — **rel′a·tiv·is′tic** *adj.*

rel·a·tiv·i·ty (rel′ə·tiv′ə·tē) *n.* **1** The quality or condition of being relative; relativeness. **2** *Philos.* Existence only as an object of, or in relation to, a thinking mind; phenomenality: sometimes called the doctrine of the relativity of existence. **3** A condition of dependence or of close relation, as of the solar system on the sun. **4** *Physics* The principle of the interdependence of matter, energy, space, and time, as mathematically formulated by A. Einstein. The **special theory of relativity** states that the velocity of light is independent of the motion of its source and that motion itself is a meaningless concept except as between two physical systems or material bodies moving relatively to each other. The **general theory of relativity** extends these principles to the law of gravitation and the motions of the heavenly bodies.

relativity of knowledge *Philos.* The theory that knowledge of what things really are is

impossible, since knowledge itself is dependent upon the mind's purely subjective forms of relating its objects.

re·la·tor (ri·lā'tər) *n.* **1** One who relates; a relater. **2** *Law* One who institutes a special proceeding by relation or by information: the *relator* in the writ of quo warranto. [<L]

re·lax (ri·laks') *v.t.* **1** To make lax or loose; make less tight or firm. **2** To make less stringent or severe, as discipline. **3** To abate; slacken, as efforts. **4** To relieve from strain or effort: to *relax* the eyes. —*v.i.* **5** To become lax or loose; loosen. **6** To become less stringent or severe. **7** To rest; engage in relaxation. **8** To unbend; become less formal. [< L *relaxare* <*re-* again + *laxare* loosen < *laxus* loose. Doublet of RELEASE.] —**re·lax'·a·ble** *adj.* —**re·lax'er** *n.*

Synonyms: abate, divert, ease, loose, loosen, mitigate, recreate, reduce, relieve, remit, slacken, unbend. Compare WEAKEN. *Antonyms*: bind, confine, contract, strain, stretch, tighten.

re·lax·a·tion (rē'lak·sā'shən) *n.* **1** The act of relaxing, or the state of being relaxed. **2** Indulgence in diversion, or the diversion indulged in; entertainment. [<L *relaxatio, -onis*] —**re·lax·a·tive** (ri·lak'sə·tiv) *adj. & n.*

re·lay (rē'lā, ri·lā') *n.* **1** A fresh set, as of men, horses, or dogs, to replace or relieve a tired set. **2** A supply of anything kept in store for anticipated use or need. **3** A relay race, or one of its laps or legs. **4** *Electr.* A device which utilizes variations in the condition or strength of a current in a circuit to effect the operation of similar devices in the same or another circuit: a telegraph *relay.* —*v.t.* **1** To send onward by or as by relays. **2** To provide with relays. **3** *Electr.* To operate or retransmit by means of a relay. [<F *relais* <Ital. *rilascio* <*rilasciare, rilassare* leave behind, release <L *relaxare* loosen again. See RELAX.]

re–lay (rē·lā') *v.t.* **–laid, –lay·ing** To lay again.

relay race A race between two or more teams of runners, each of whom runs a set part of the course and is relieved by a teammate.

re·lease (ri·lēs') *v.t.* **·leased, ·leas·ing 1** To set free; liberate; deliver from worry, pain, obligation, etc. **2** To free from something that holds, binds, etc. **3** To permit the circulation, sale, performance, etc., of, as a motion picture, phonograph record, or news item. —*n.* **1** The act of releasing or setting free, or the state of being released; liberation from restraint of any kind. **2** A deliverance or final relief, as from anything grievous or oppressive. **3** A discharge from responsibility or penalty, as from a debt. **4** *Law* An instrument of conveyance by which one of two persons having a mutual interest in lands surrenders and relinquishes all his interest and estate to the other; quitclaim. **5** A motion picture, phonograph record, news item, or the like ready for distribution or circulation. **6** Exhaust of motive fluid in a steam engine; also, the point at which such exhaust begins. **7** *Mech.* Any catch or device to hold and release a mechanism, weights, etc. [<OF *relaisser* let free <L *relaxare.* Doublet of RELAX.] —**re·leas'er** *n.*

Synonyms (verb): deliver, discharge, disengage, emancipate, exempt, extricate, free, liberate, loose, unbind, unfasten, unloose, untie. See ABSOLVE.

released time Time made available by public schools for religious education or other legally authorized instruction outside of school.

rel·e·gate (rel'ə·gāt) *v.t.* **·gat·ed, ·gat·ing 1** To send off or consign, as to an obscure position or place. **2** To assign, as to a particular class or sphere. **3** To refer (a matter) to someone for decision. **4** To banish; exile. See synonyms under COMMIT. [<L *relegatus,* pp. of *relegare* send away <*re-* away, back + *legare* send] —**rel'e·ga'tion** *n.*

re·lent (ri·lent') *v.i.* To soften in temper; become more gentle or compassionate. —*v.t.* *Obs.* To cause to relent. [<OF *ralentir* <L *relentescere* grow soft <*re-* again + *lentus* soft]

re·lent·less (ri·lent'lis) *adj.* **1** Indifferent to the pain of others; not relenting; pitiless. **2** Unremitting; continuous. See synonyms under AUSTERE, IMPLACABLE. —**re·lent'less·ly** *adv.* —**re·lent'less·ness** *n.*

rel·e·vant (rel'ə·vənt) *adj.* **1** Fitting or suiting given requirements; pertinent; applicable: commonly with *to.* **2** *Ling.* Designating those features of a phoneme which function to distinguish it from other phonemes in a language, as place of articulation in English consonants. [<Med. L *relevans, -antis,* ppr. of *relevare* bear upon <L, raise up. See RELIEVE.] —**rel'·e·vance, rel'e·van·cy** *n.* —**rel'e·vant·ly** *adv.*

re·li·a·ble (ri·lī'ə·bəl) *adj.* **1** That may be relied upon; worthy of confidence; trustworthy. **2** *Stat.* Exhibiting a reasonable consistency in results obtained, as in a group of repeated tests: distinguished from *valid.* [<RELY + -ABLE] —**re·li'a·bil'i·ty, re·li'a·ble·ness** *n.* —**re·li'a·bly** *adv.*

Synonyms: trustworthy, trusty. *Trusty* and *trustworthy* refer to inherent qualities of a high order, *trustworthy* being especially applied to persons, and denoting moral integrity and truthfulness; we speak of a *trusty* sword, a *trustworthy* man. *Reliable* is inferior in meaning, denoting merely the possession of such qualities as are needed for safe reliance; as, a *reliable* pledge, *reliable* information. A man is said to be *reliable* with reference not only to moral qualities, but to judgment, knowledge, skill, habit, or perhaps pecuniary ability. A *reliable* messenger is one who may be depended on to do his errand correctly and promptly; a *trusty* or *trustworthy* messenger is one who may be admitted to knowledge of the views and purposes of those who employ him.

re·li·ance (ri·lī'əns) *n.* **1** The act of relying or the condition of being reliant; confidence; trust; pendence. **2** That upon which one relies; a ground of confidence. See synonyms under BELIEF, FAITH. [<RELY + -ANCE]

re·li·ant (ri·lī'ənt) *adj.* Confident; manifesting reliance, especially upon oneself. [<RELY + -ANT] —**re·li'ant·ly** *adv.*

rel·ic (rel'ik) *n.* **1** Some remaining portion or fragment of that which has vanished or is destroyed: a *relic* of barbarism. **2** Something cherished in memory of one deceased; an object of sacred reverence or of affection; a keepsake or memento. **3** The body or part of the body of a saint, or an object connected with a saint or his tomb; a sacred memento. **4** *pl. Obs.* A corpse; remains. Also spelled *relique.* [<F *relique* <L *reliquiae* remains, leavings <*relinquere* leave. See RELINQUISH.]

rel·ict (rel'ikt) *n.* **1** A widow; rarely, a widower. **2** *Biol.* A plant or animal species persisting in a given area as a survival from an earlier period or type. —*adj.* (ri·likt') *Geol.* Left by gradual erosion; residual. [<L *relicta* widow, fem. of *relictus,* pp. of *relinquere* leave behind. See RELINQUISH.]

re·lief (ri·lēf') *n.* **1** The act of relieving, or the state of being relieved; removal in whole or in part of any evil, hardship, or trial; alleviation; comfort. **2** That which relieves. **3** Charitable aid, given in the form of money or food to the needy. **4** The release, as of a sentinel or guard, from his post or duty, and the substitution of some other person or persons; also, the person or persons so substituted. **5** In architecture and sculpture, the projection of a figure, ornament, etc., from a surface; also, any such figure: opposed to *round.* Sculptural relief is of three principal kinds: *alto–relievo, bas–relief,* and *mezzo–relievo.* Extremely low relief is called *stiacciato.* **6** In painting, the apparent projection of forms and masses from the plane or ground of a picture given by the arrangement of the lines, colors, or gradations of color; hence, sharpness of outline caused by contrast. **7** In feudal law, a tribute of a fee paid to the lord by the vassal–heir of a deceased tenant for the right of assuming the lapsed tenancy. **8** *Geog.* **a** The unevenness of land surface, as caused by mountains, hills, etc. **b** The parts of a map which portray the configuration of the district represented; contour lines. —**on relief** Receiving money, food, clothing, etc., from a local or other government because of need. [< OF <*relever.* See RELIEVE.]

re·li·er (ri·lī'ər) *n.* One who or that which relies. See RELY.

re·lieve (ri·lēv') *v.t.* **·lieved, ·liev·ing 1** To free wholly or partly from pain, embarrassment, etc. **2** To lessen or alleviate, as pain or anxiety. **3** To give aid or assistance to: to *relieve* a besieged city. **4** To free from obligation, injustice, etc. **5** To release from duty, as a sentinel, by providing or serving as a substitute. **6** To make less monotonous, harsh, or unpleasant; vary. **7** To bring into relief or prominence; display by contrast. See synonyms under ALLAY, ALLEVIATE, RELAX. [< OF *relever* give assistance to, succor <L *relevare* lift up <*re-* again + *levare* lift, raise < *levis* light] —**re·liev'a·ble** *adj.* —**re·liev'er** *n.*

re·lie·vo (ri·lē'vō) *n. pl.* **·vos** Relief (defs. 5 and 6). [<Ital. <*rilevare* emphasize, elevate <L *relevare.* See RELIEVE.]

re·li·gieuse (rə·lē·zhyœz') *n. pl.* **·gieuses** (-zhyœz') *French* A nun.

re·li·gieux (rə·lē·zhyœ') *n. pl.* **·gieux** (-zhyœ') *French* A man under monastic vows; a monk.

re·lig·ion (ri·lij'ən) *n.* **1** A belief binding the spiritual nature of man to a supernatural being, as involving a feeling of dependence and responsibility, together with the feelings and practices which naturally flow from such a belief. **2** Any system of faith and worship: the Christian *religion.* **3** An essential part or a practical test of the spiritual life. See *James* i 27. **4** An object of conscientious devotion or scrupulous care: His work is a *religion* to him. **5** *Obs.* Religious practice or belief. [< OF <L *religio, -onis*]

Synonyms: devotion, faith, godliness, holiness, pietism, piety, worship. *Piety* is primarily filial duty, and hence, in its purest sense, a loving obedience and service to God as the heavenly Father; *pietism* often denotes a mystical, sometimes an affected *piety; religion* is the reverent acknowledgment of a divine being. *Religion* includes *worship* whether it be external and formal, or the reverence of the human spirit for the divine, seeking outward expression. *Devotion,* which in its fullest sense is self–consecration, is often used to denote an act of *worship,* especially prayer or adoration; as, He is engaged his *devotions. Godliness* is a character and spirit like that of God. *Holiness* is the highest sinless perfection of any spirit, whether divine or human, and often used for purity or for consecration. *Faith,* strictly a firm reliance on the truth of religious doctrines, is often used as a comprehensive word for a whole system of *religion* considered as the object of *faith*; as, the Christian *faith,* the Buddhist *faith. Antonyms*: atheism, blasphemy, godlessness, impiety, infidelity, irreligion, profanity, sacrilege, unbelief, ungodliness.

re·lig·ion·ism (ri·lij'ən·iz'əm) *n.* The practice of or adherence to religion: used derogatorily to imply affectation and insincerity. —**re·lig'ion·ist** *n.*

re·lig·i·os·i·ty (ri·lij'ē·os'ə·tē) *n.* Religiousness; also, pious sentimentality. [<LL *religiositas, -tatis*]

re·lig·ious (ri·lij'əs) *adj.* **1** Feeling and manifesting religion; devout; pious. **2** Of or pertaining to religion; teaching or setting forth religion: a *religious* teacher. **3** Having thorough and genuine fidelity; strict in performance; conscientious: a *religious* loyalty. **4** Belonging to the monastic life; bound by monastic vows; following or devoted to a life of religion and devotion. —*n. pl.* **·ious** A person or people devoted to a life of piety and devotion; a monk or nun. [<OF *religious* <L *religiosus*] —**re·lig'ious·ly** *adv.* —**re·lig'ious·ness** *n.*

re·lin·quish (ri·ling'kwish) *v.t.* **1** To give up; abandon; surrender. **2** To cease to demand; renounce: to *relinquish* a claim. **3** To let go (a hold or something held). See synonyms under ABANDON, SURRENDER. [<OF *relinquiss-,* stem of *relinquir* <L *relinquere* < *re-* back, from + *linquere* leave] —**re·lin'·quish·er** *n.* —**re·lin'quish·ment** *n.*

rel·i·quar·y (rel'ə·kwer'ē) *n. pl.* **·quar·ies** A casket, coffer, shrine, or other repository for relics. [<F *reliquaire* <L *reliquiae* remains. See RELIC.]

rel·ique (rel'ik, ri·lēk') See RELIC.

re·liq·ui·ae (ri·lik'wi·ē) *n. pl. Latin* Fossil organisms; relics; organic remains.

rel·ish (rel'ish) *n.* **1** Appetite; appreciation; liking: a *relish* for excitement. **2** The flavor, especially when agreeable, in food and drink; figuratively, the quality in anything that lends spice or zest: Danger gives *relish* to adventure. **3** A slight savory dish served to stimulate appetite; also, something taken with food to lend it flavor or zest; a condiment. **4** An admixture or a small but important characteristic; flavoring: no *relish* of nature in his

poetry. — *v.t.* 1 To like the taste or savor of; enjoy: to *relish* a dinner or a joke. 2 To give pleasant flavor to. — *v.i.* 3 To have an agreeable flavor; afford gratification. See synonyms under LIKE. [ME *reles* <OF *reles,* var. of *relais* remainder < *relaisser* leave behind. See RELEASE.] — **rel'ish·a·ble** *adj.*

Synonyms (noun): appetite, appreciation, fondness, gusto, inclination, partiality, predilection, taste, zest. See APPETITE, SAVOR. *Antonyms*: antipathy, aversion, disgust, dislike, distaste, loathing, repugnance.

re·lo·cate (rē·lō'kāt) *v.t.* & *v.i.* **·cat·ed, ·cat·ing** To locate again or anew.

re·lu·cent (ri·lōō'sənt) *adj.* Shining back; reflecting light; gleaming. [<L *relucens, -entis,* ppr. of *relucere* < *re-* back + *lucere* shine. See LUCENT.]

re·luct (ri·lukt') *v.i.* 1 To show reluctance; hesitate. 2 To rebel; make opposition. [<L *reluctari.* See RELUCTANT.]

re·luc·tance (ri·luk'təns) *n.* 1 The state of being reluctant; unwillingness. 2 *Electr.* Capacity for opposing magnetic induction: the reciprocal of *permeance.* 3 *Obs.* Resistance; opposition. Also **re·luc'tan·cy.** [<RELUCTANT]

re·luc·tant (ri·luk'tənt) *adj.* 1 Disinclined to yield to some requirement; unwilling. 2 Marked by unwillingness or rendered unwillingly. 3 *Obs.* Struggling; offering opposition. [<L *reluctans, -antis,* ppr. of *reluctari* fight back < *re-* back + *luctari* fight] — **re·luc'·tant·ly** *adv.*

Synonyms: averse, backward, disinclined, indisposed, loath, opposed, slow, unwilling. *Reluctant* signifies struggling against what one is urged or impelled to do, or is actually doing; *averse* signifies turned away as with dislike or repugnance; *loath* signifies having a repugnance, disgust, or loathing for, but the adjective *loath* is not so strong as the verb *loathe.* A man may be *slow* or *backward* in entering upon that to which he is by no means *averse.* A man is *loath* to believe evil of his friend, *reluctant* to speak of it, absolutely *unwilling* to use it to his injury. A legislator may be *opposed* to a certain measure, while not *averse* to what it aims to accomplish. Compare ANTIPATHY. *Antonyms*: desirous, disposed, eager, favorable, inclined, willing.

rel·uc·tiv·i·ty (rel'ək·tiv'ə·tē) *n. Electr.* The specific electrical reluctance, or the resistance to magnetization of a given substance per unit of length or cross-section: the reciprocal of *permeability.*

re·lume (ri·lōōm') *v.t.* **·lumed, ·lum·ing** 1 To light again; rekindle. 2 To illuminate again. Also **re·lu·mine** (ri·lōō'min). [<RE- + (IL)LUME]

re·ly (ri·lī') *v.i.* **·lied, ·ly·ing** To place trust or confidence: with *on* or *upon.* See synonyms under LEAN[1]. [<OF *relier* bind (together), adhere to <L *religare* < *re-* again + *ligare* bind]

rem (rem) *n. Physics* That dose of absorbed ionizing radiation which has the same biological effect as one roentgen of high-voltage X-ray radiation. [<R(OENTGEN) + E(QUIVALENT) + M(AN)]

REM (rem) *n.* See REM SLEEP. [Acronym formed from *rapid eye movement*]

Re·ma·gen (rā'mä·gən) A town on the Rhine in northern Rhineland-Palatinate, West Germany.

re·main (ri·mān') *v.i.* 1 To stay or be left behind after the removal, departure, or destruction of other persons or things. 2 To continue in one place, condition, or character: He *remained* in office. 3 To be left as something to be done, dealt with, etc.: It *remains* to be proved. 4 To endure or last; abide. See synonyms under ABIDE, PERSIST, STAND. [<OF *remaindre* <L *remanere* < *re-* back + *manere* stay, remain]

re·main·der (ri·mān'dər) *n.* 1 That which remains; something left after a subtraction, expenditure, or passing over of a part; a residue; remnant. 2 *Math.* **a** That which is left after the subtraction of one quantity from another. **b** In division, the excess of the dividend over the product of the divisor by the integral part of the quotient. 3 *Law* An estate in expectancy, but not in actual possession and enjoyment; that remnant or residue of interest which, on the creation of a particular prior estate, is by the same instrument limited to another to be enjoyed on the termination of that estate. 4 In philately, an obsolete issue of stamps, demonetized by the government and sold at a large discount, generally to dealers. 5 A copy or part of an edition of a book remaining with a publisher after sales have ceased. — *adj.* Left over; remaining. — *v.t.* To sell as a remainder (def. 5). [<AF <OF *remaindre* REMAIN]

re·mains (ri·mānz') *n. pl.* 1 That which is left after a part has been removed or destroyed; remnants. 2 The body of a deceased person; a corpse. 3 Writings of an author published after his death. 4 Survivals of the past, as fossils, monuments, etc.: the *remains* of ancient Troy. See synonyms under BODY.

re·make (rē·māk') *v.t.* **·made, ·mak·ing** To make again or in a different form: to *remake* a silent film. — *n.* (rē'māk) Something that is remade, especially a motion picture.

re·man (rē·man') *v.t.* **·manned, ·man·ning** 1 To furnish with a fresh complement of men. 2 To instil courage or manliness into.

re·mand (ri·mand', -mänd') *v.t.* 1 To order or send back: to *remand* a soldier to his post. 2 *Law* **a** To recommit to custody, as an accused person after a preliminary examination. **b** To send back to a lower court, as a case improperly brought before the court so ordering. — *n.* 1 Recommittal, as of an accused person to custody; also, the recommitted person. 2 A judicial order of recommittal. [<OF *remander* <LL *remandare* <L *re-* back + *mandare* order] — **re·mand'ment** *n.*

rem·a·nence (rem'ə·nəns) *n.* 1 The state or quality of remaining; permanence; also, the remainder. 2 *Electr.* That part of magnetic induction remaining in a material after the removal of an applied magnetomotive force. [<L *remanens, -entis,* ppr. of *remanere* remain] — **rem'a·nent** *adj.*

re·mark (ri·märk') *n.* 1 A comment or saying, oral or written; a casual observation; also, conversational speech in general: I enjoyed his *remarks.* 2 The act of observing or noticing; observation; notice. 3 Remarque. — *v.t.* 1 To say or write by way of comment. 2 To take particular notice of. 3 *Obs.* To mark; distinguish. — *v.i.* 4 To make remarks: with *on* or *upon.* [<F *remarque* observation < *remarquer* notice < *re-* again + *marquer* mark. See MARK.] — **re·mark'er** *n.*

Synonyms (noun): annotation, comment, note, observation, utterance. A *comment* is an explanatory or critical *remark,* as upon some passage in a literary work or some act or speech in common life. A *note* is something to call attention, hence a brief written statement; in correspondence, a *note* is briefer than a letter. *Annotations* are especially brief *notes,* commonly marginal, and closely following the text. *Comments, observations,* or *remarks* may be oral or written, *comments* being oftenest written, and *remarks* oftenest oral. An *observation* is properly the result of fixed attention and reflection; a *remark* may be the suggestion of the instant.

re·mark·a·ble (ri·mär'kə·bəl) *adj.* Worthy of special notice; hence, extraordinary; unusual; conspicuous; distinguished. See synonyms under EMINENT, RARE, EXTRAORDINARY. — **re·mark'a·ble·ness** *n.* — **re·mark'a·bly** *adv.*

re·marque (ri·märk') *n.* 1 A small engraved picture or other distinguishing mark on an engraved plate, appearing on the engraved surface or in the margin, to indicate a stage in its progress before completion. 2 A print bearing such a mark. [<F]

Re·marque (rə·märk'), **Erich Maria,** 1897–1970, U.S. novelist born in Germany: real name *Erich Paul Kramer.*

re·mar·ry (rē·mar'ē) *v.t.* & *v.i.* **·ried, ·ry·ing** To marry again. — **re·mar'riage** (-mar'ij) *n.*

Rem·brandt (rem'brant, *Du.* rem'bränt), 1606–1669, Dutch painter and etcher: full name *Rembrandt Harmenszoon van Rijn* or *van Ryn.*

re·me·di·a·ble (ri·mē'dē·ə·bəl) *adj.* Capable of being cured or remedied. [<F *remédiable*] — **re·me'di·a·bly** *adv.*

re·me·di·al (ri·mē'dē·əl) *adj.* Of the nature of or adapted to be used as a remedy. [<L *remedialis*] — **re·me'di·al·ly** *adv.*

rem·e·di·less (rem'ə·dē·lis) *adj.* Without remedy; incurable; irreparable.

rem·e·dy (rem'ə·dē) *v.t.* **·died, ·dy·ing** 1 To cure or heal, as by medicinal treatment. 2 To make right; repair; correct. 3 To overcome or remove (an evil or defect). — *n. pl.* **·dies** 1 That which cures or affords relief to bodily disease or ailment; a medicine; also, remedial treatment. 2 A means of counteracting or removing evil; relief. 3 *Law* A legal mode for enforcing a right or redressing or preventing a wrong. 4 Tolerance (def. 5). [<AF <L *remedium* < *re-* thoroughly + *mederi* heal, restore]

re·mem·ber (ri·mem'bər) *v.t.* 1 To bring back or present again to the mind or memory; recall; recollect. 2 To keep in mind carefully, as for a purpose. 3 To bear in mind with affection, respect, awe, etc. 4 To bear in mind as worthy of a reward, gift, etc.: She *remembered* me in her will. 5 To reward; tip: *Remember* the steward. 6 *Obs.* To remind. — *v.i.* 7 To have or use one's memory. — **to remember (one) to** To inform a person of the regard of: *Remember* me *to* your wife. [<OF *remembrer* <LL *rememorari* <L *re-* again + *memorare* bring to mind < *memor* mindful] — **re·mem'ber·er** *n.*

Synonyms: recall, recollect, retain. Compare synonyms for MEMORY. *Antonyms*: forget, overlook.

re·mem·brance (ri·mem'brəns) *n.* 1 The act or power of remembering; the state of being remembered; memory. 2 The period within which one can remember. 3 That which is remembered; a reminiscence. 4 A memento; keepsake; also, a token or message of friendship: often in the plural. 5 Mindful regard. See synonyms under MEMORY.

re·mem·branc·er (ri·mem'brən·sər) *n.* 1 One who or that which causes one to remember; a reminder. 2 One of the recording officers of the Exchequer in England, as the **King's** or **Queen's remembrancer,** responsible for collecting debts due to the sovereign: since 1873, an officer of the Supreme Court.

re·mex (rē'meks) *n. pl.* **rem·i·ges** (rem'ə·jēz) *Ornithol.* One of the large quill feathers of a bird's wing: usually in the plural. [<L, oarsman < *remus* oar] — **re·mig·i·al** (ri·mij'ē·əl) *adj.*

re·mind (ri·mīnd') *v.t.* To bring to (someone's) mind; cause to remember. See synonyms under ADMONISH. [<RE- + MIND] — **re·mind'er** *n.*

re·mind·ful (ri·mīnd'fəl) *adj.* 1 Tending to remind; serving as a reminder: said of things. 2 Mindful: said of persons.

Rem·ing·ton (rem'ing·tən), **Frederic,** 1861–1909, U. S. painter and sculptor. — **Philo,** 1816–89, U. S. inventor and gunsmith.

rem·i·nisce (rem'ə·nis') *v.i.* **·nisced, ·nisc·ing** To recall incidents or events of the past; indulge in reminiscences. [Back formation < REMINISCENT]

rem·i·nis·cence (rem'ə·nis'əns) *n.* 1 The recalling to mind of past incidents and events; also, the narration of past experiences. 2 The act or power of reproducing past cognitions in consciousness. 3 An expression, fact, or feature serving as a reminder of something else. See synonyms under MEMORY. [<F]

rem·i·nis·cent (rem'ə·nis'ənt) *adj.* 1 Of the nature of or possessing reminiscence; also, recalling or dwelling upon the past; remembering. 2 Inducing a reminiscence of a person or thing; suggestive. [<L *reminiscens, -entis,* ppr. of *reminisci* recollect < *re-* again + *memini* remember] — **rem'i·nis'cent·ly** *adv.*

re·mise (ri·mīz') *Law v.t.* **·mised, ·mis·ing** To give; surrender; release; relinquish: used in conveyancing. — *n.* The act of remising. [<F, fem. of *remis,* pp. of *remettre* <L *remittere* send back. See REMIT.]

re·miss (ri·mis') *adj.* Slack or careless in matters requiring attention; dilatory; negligent; hence, lacking in earnestness or energy. See synonyms under INATTENTIVE. [<L *remissus,* pp. of *remittere* send back, slacken. See REMIT.] — **re·miss'ness** *n.*

re·mis·si·ble (ri·mis'ə·bəl) *adj.* Capable of being remitted or pardoned, as sins. [<F *rémissible*] — **re·mis'si·bil'i·ty** *n.*

re·mis·sion (ri·mish'ən) *n.* 1 The act of remitting, or the state of being remitted; specifically, discharge from penalty; pardon; deliverance, as from a debt or obligation.

2 Abatement, as of a fine erroneously imposed. 3 Relaxation, as from work or study. 4 Temporary abatement of a disease or of pain. 5 The act of sending a remittance. [<OF <L *remissio, -onis*]

re·mit (ri·mit′) *v.* **·mit·ted, ·mit·ting** *v.t.* 1 To send, as money in payment for goods; transmit. 2 To refrain from exacting or inflicting, as a penalty. 3 To pardon; forgive, as a sin or crime. 4 To abate; relax, as vigilance. 5 To restore; replace. 6 To put off; postpone. 7 To refer or submit for judgment, settlement, etc., as to one in authority. 8 *Law* To refer (a legal proceeding) to a lower court for further consideration. 9 *Rare* To send back, as to prison. 10 *Obs.* To resign; renounce. 11 *Obs.* To free; release. —*v.i.* 12 To send money, as in payment. 13 To diminish; abate. —*n.* The act of remitting; specifically, the sending of a legal cause from one tribunal to another. [<L *remittere* send back < *re-* back + *mittere* send] —**re·mit′ta·ble** *adj.* —**re·mit′ter** or **re·mit′tor** *n.*

re·mit·tal (ri·mit′l) *n.* Remission.

re·mit·tance (ri·mit′ns) *n.* The act of transmitting money or credit; also, that which is remitted, as money.

remittance man A ne'er-do-well living outside his home country on money transmitted at regular intervals by friends or relatives: originally applied to British persons living in the colonies or in the western United States.

re·mit·tent (ri·mit′nt) *adj.* 1 Having remissions. 2 Having partial, irregular, or temporary diminutions of energy or action: a *remittent* fever or geyser. —*n.* A remittent fever. [<L *remittens, -entis,* ppr. of *remittere.* See REMIT.]

remittent fever *Pathol.* A form of malaria in which the fever fluctuates daily but does not entirely disappear.

rem·nant (rem′nənt) *n.* 1 That which remains of anything; specifically, the piece of cloth, silk, etc., left over after the last cutting. 2 A remaining trace or survival of anything, suggestive of former condition, use, or belief. 3 A small piece or quantity. 4 A small remaining number of people. See synonyms under TRACE[1]. —*adj.* Remaining. [<OF *remenant,* ppr. of *remaindre.* See REMAIN.]

re·mod·el (rē·mod′l) *v.t.* **·eled** or **·elled, ·el·ing** or **·el·ling** 1 To model again. 2 To make over or anew.

re·mon·e·tize (ri·mon′ə·tīz) *v.t.* **·tized, ·tiz·ing** To reinstate, especially silver, as lawful money. [<RE- again + L *moneta* money + -IZE] —**re·mon′e·ti·za′tion** *n.*

re·mon·strance (ri·mon′strəns) *n.* 1 The act of remonstrating; protest; expostulation. 2 Expostulatory counsel or reproof. [<OF]

Re·mon·strance (ri·mon′strəns) *n.* The document formulating the five points of Arminian dissent from strict Calvinism, presented to the states of Holland and Friesland in 1610 and condemned by the synod of Dort in 1619. —**the Grand Remonstrance** A document presented by Parliament to King Charles I of England, Nov. 22, 1641, protesting against his misgovernment. —**Re·mon′strant** *n.*

re·mon·strant (ri·mon′strənt) *adj.* Having the character or tendency of a remonstrance; expostulatory. —*n.* One who presents or signs a remonstrance. [<Med. L *remonstrans, -antis,* ppr. of *remonstrare.* See REMONSTRATE.]

re·mon·strate (ri·mon′strāt) *v.* **·strat·ed, ·strat·ing** *v.t.* 1 To say or plead in protest or opposition. 2 *Obs.* To point out; demonstrate. —*v.i.* 3 To urge strong reasons against any course or action; protest; object. [<Med. L *remonstratus,* pp. of *remonstrare* demonstrate <L *re-* again + *monstrare* show] —**re·mon·stra·tion** (rē′mon·strā′shən, rem′ən-) *n.* —**re·mon′stra·tive** (-strə·tiv) *adj.* —**re·mon′stra·tor** (strā·tər) *n.*

re·mon·ta (rā·mōn′tä) *n.* *SW U.S.* A group of saddle horses. [<Sp.]

re·mon·tant (ri·mon′tənt) *adj. Bot.* Ascending again: said of roses that bloom more than once in a season. —*n.* A remontant rose. [<F, ppr. of *remonter.* See REMOUNT.]

rem·on·toir (rem′ən·twär′, *Fr.* rə·môn·twär′) *n. Mech.* An apparatus that utilizes force from the train of a clock to give new impulse to the escape wheel at certain intervals, usually once in 30 seconds. [<F]

rem·o·ra (rem′ər·ə) *n.* 1 Any of a genus (*Remora*) of fish (family *Echeneididae*) having on its head an oval suctorial disk by means of which it attaches itself to sharks, other fishes, or floating objects, being thus carried great distances. 2 Any delay or impediment. [<L, hindrance < *re-* back + *mora* delay]

re·morse (ri·môrs′) *n.* 1 The keen or hopeless anguish caused by a sense of guilt; compunction; distressing self-reproach. 2 *Obs.* Compassion; pity. See synonyms under REPENTANCE. [<OF *remors* <LL *remorsus* a biting back <L *remordere* keep biting < *re-* again + *mordere* bite] —**re·morse′ful** *adj.* —**re·morse′ful·ly** *adv.* —**re·morse′ful·ness** *n.*

re·morse·less (ri·môrs′lis) *adj.* Having no compassion; pitiless; cruel. —**re·morse′less·ly** *adv.* —**re·morse′less·ness** *n.*

re·mote (ri·mōt′) *adj.* 1 Located far from a specified place or some place regarded as a point of reference: *remote* regions. 2 Removed far from present time; distant in time: the *remote* future. 3 Having slight relation or connection; separated; foreign; distant in relation: a *remote* cause, *remote* kinship. 4 Not obvious; inconsiderable; slight: a *remote* likeness or analogy. 5 Abstracted; absent-minded; hence, aloof. —*n.* A television or radio broadcast made from a mobile camera or microphone operated at a distance from the station, and sent to the transmitter by cable or through relay towers. See synonyms under ALIEN. [<L *remotus,* pp. of *removere* remove < *re-* again + *movere* move] —**re·mote′ly** *adv.* —**re·mote′ness** *n.*

remote control Control from a distance, as of a machine, apparatus, aircraft, guided missile, etc., by electrical or radio circuits.

re·mo·tion (ri·mō′shən) *n.* 1 The act of removing; removal. 2 *Obs.* Departure. [<OF]

ré·mou·lade (rā′mə·läd′, *Fr.* rā·mōō·läd′) *n.* A sharp sauce made of hard-boiled egg yolks, oil, vinegar, and seasoning. [<F <Ital. *remolata,* lit., vigorously stirred]

re·mount (rē·mount′) *v.t.* & *v.i.* To mount again or anew. —*n.* (rē′mount′) 1 A new setting or framing. 2 A fresh riding horse. [<OF *remonter*]

re·mov·a·ble (ri·mōō′və·bəl) *adj.* Capable of being removed; movable; also, capable of being displaced, dismissed, or obliterated: *removable* walls, officials, or stains. —**re·mov′a·bil′i·ty** *n.* —**re·mov′a·bly** *adv.*

re·mov·al (ri·mōō′vəl) *n.* 1 The act of removing or the state of being removed. 2 Dismissal, as from office. 3 Changing of place, especially of habitation.

re·move (ri·mōōv′) *v.* **·moved, ·mov·ing** *v.t.* 1 To take or move away or from one place to another. 2 To take off; doff, as a hat. 3 To get rid of; do away with: to *remove* abuses. 4 To kill; assassinate. 5 To displace or dismiss, as from office. 6 To take out; extract: with *from.* —*v.i.* 7 To change one's place of residence or business; move. 8 *Poetic* To go away; depart. See synonyms under ABOLISH, ABSTRACT, ALLEVIATE, CANCEL, CARRY, CONVEY, DISPLACE, EXTERMINATE, SEPARATE. —*n.* 1 A removal; a move; the act of removing, as one's business or belongings. 2 The space moved over in changing an object from one position to another; hence, a degree of difference; step; interval: He is only one *remove* from a fool. 3 *Brit.* A dish or course at dinner removed to give place to another. 4 *Obs.* A period of absence. [<OF *remouvoir* <L *removere* < *re-* again + *movere* move] —**re·mov′er** *n.*

re·moved (ri·mōōvd′) *adj.* 1 Separated, as by intervening space, time, or relationship, or by difference in kind: a cousin twice *removed.* 2 Taken away; transferred.

Rem·scheid (rem′shīt) An industrial city in North Rhine-Westphalia, West Germany.

Rem·sen (rem′sən), **Ira,** 1846–1927, U.S. chemist and educator.

REM sleep A recurrent stage of normal sleep characterized by distinctive patterns of brain waves, rapid movement of the eyes under closed lids, and dreaming: also called *paradoxical sleep.*

re·mu·da (rā·mōō′dä) *n.* *SW U.S.* The extra mounts or saddle horses of each cowboy herded together, usually a herd of 90 to 100 geldings for an outfit of eight to ten men: called a *saddle band* in the Northwest. [<Sp., lit., exchange < *remudar* replace]

re·mu·ner·ate (ri·myōō′nə·rāt) *v.t.* **·at·ed, ·at·ing** To make just or adequate return to or for; compensate; pay or pay for; reward. See synonyms under PAY, REQUITE. [<L *remuneratus,* pp. of *remunerari* < *re-* again + *munus, muneris* gift] —**re·mu′ner·a·bil′i·ty** *n.* —**re·mu′ner·a·ble** *adj.*

re·mu·ner·a·tion (ri·myōō′nə·rā′shən) *n.* 1 The act or fact of remunerating. 2 That which remunerates; pay; compensation; recompense. See synonyms under RECOMPENSE, RESTITUTION, SALARY.

re·mu·ner·a·tive (ri·myōō′nə·rā′tiv, -nər·ə·tiv) *adj.* 1 Profitable; lucrative. 2 Serving to pay or remunerate: *remunerative* justice. —**re·mu′ner·a′tive·ly** *adv.* —**re·mu′ner·a′tive·ness** *n.*

Re·mus (rē′məs) In Roman mythology, the twin brother of Romulus, by whom he was killed.

Remus (rē′məs), **Uncle** See UNCLE REMUS.

ren- Var. of RENI-.

ren·ais·sance (ren′ə·säns′, -zäns′, ri·nā′səns; *Fr.* rə·ne·säṅs′) *n.* A new birth; resurrection; renascence. [<F < *renaître* be reborn < *re-* again + L *natus,* pp. of *nasci* be born]

Ren·ais·sance (ren′ə·säns′, -zäns′, ri·nā′səns; *Fr.* rə·ne·säṅs′) *n.* 1 The revival of letters and art in Europe, marking the transition from medieval to modern history: it began in Italy in the 14th century and gradually spread to other countries. 2 The period of this revival, from the 14th to the 16th century; also, the style of art, literature, etc., marked by a classical influence, that was developed in and characteristic of this period. Also *Renascence.* —*adj.* Of or characteristic of the Renaissance.

Renaissance architecture A style of building and decoration that followed the medieval, originating in Italy in the 15th century, and based on the classic Roman style.

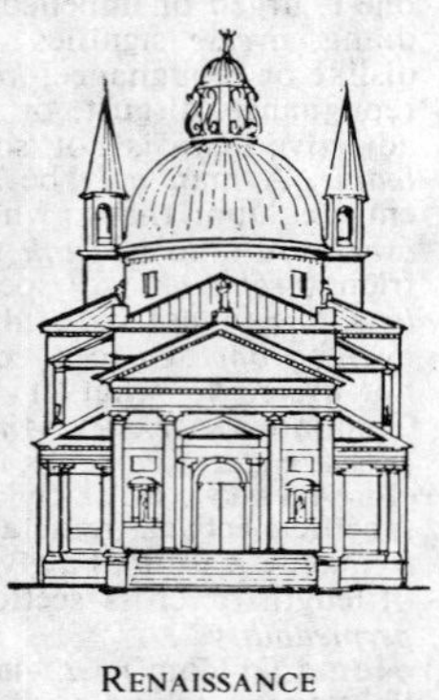

RENAISSANCE ARCHITECTURE
Church of the Redentore, Venice, 1578–80.

re·nal (rē′nəl) *adj. Med.* Of, pertaining to, affecting, or situated near the kidneys. [<F *rénal* <L *renalis* < *renes* kidneys]

renal capsule or **gland** The suprarenal gland.

Re·nan (rə·näṅ′), **Joseph Ernest,** 1823–1892, French historian, philologist, and critic.

Ren·ard (ren′ərd) See REYNARD.

re·nas·cence (ri·nas′·əns) *n.* Rebirth; new birth or life; a renaissance; a revival. [<L *renascens, -entis,* ppr. of *renasci* < *re-* again + *nasci* be born] —**re·nas′cent** *adj.*

Re·nas·cence (ri·nas′əns) *n.* The Renaissance.

Re·naud (rə·nō′) French form of REGINALD.

ren·con·tre (ren·kon′tər, *Fr.* räṅ·kôṅ′tr′) *n.* *French* A rencounter.

ren·coun·ter (ren·koun′tər) *n.* 1 *Obs.* A sudden hostile collision, as with an enemy. 2 An unexpected encounter, as of travelers. 3 A contest or debate. —*v.t.* & *v.i. Obs.* To meet unexpectedly or by surprise. [<F *rencontrer.* See RE- and ENCOUNTER.]

rend (rend) *v.* **rent** or **rend·ed, rend·ing** *v.t.* 1 To tear apart forcibly; split; break. 2 To pull or remove forcibly: with *away, from, off,* etc. 3 To pass through (the air) violently and noisily. 4 To distress (the heart, etc.), as with grief or despair. —*v.i.* 5 To split; part. [OE *rendan* tear, cut down] —**rend′er** *n.*

Synonyms: break, burst, cleave, lacerate, mangle, rip, rive, rupture, sever, slit, sunder, tear. *Rend* and *tear* are applied usually to the sundering of textile substances, *tear* being the milder, *rend* the stronger word. To *rip,* as applied to articles made by sewing or stitching, is to divide along the line of a seam by cutting or breaking the stitches. *Rive* is a woodworkers' word for parting wood in the way of the grain without a clean cut, as by splitting. To *lacerate* is to *tear* roughly the flesh or animal tissue, as by the teeth of a wild beast. *Mangle* is a stronger word than *lacerate*; *lacerate* is more superficial, *mangle* more complete. To *burst* or *rupture* is to tear or rend by force from within, *burst* denoting the greater violence; as, to *burst* a gun; to

rupture a blood vessel. Compare BREAK. *Antonyms*: heal, join, mend, reunite, secure, stitch, unite, weld.

ren·der (ren′dər) *v.t.* **1** To give, present, or submit for action, approval, payment, etc. **2** To provide or furnish; give: to *render* aid to the poor. **3** To give as due: to *render* obedience. **4** To perform; do: to *render* great service. **5** To give or state formally: to *render* judgment. **6** To give by way of requital or retribution: to *render* double for one's sins. **7** To represent or depict, as in music or painting. **8** To cause to be or become: to *render* a ship seaworthy. **9** To express in another language; translate. **10** To melt and clarify, as lard. **11** To give back; return: often with *back*. **12** To surrender; give up: to *render* a fortress. See synonyms under INTERPRET. —*n.* **1** A payment, specifically of rent, made to a superior. **2** A coat of plaster applied without intervening lathing. [<F *rendre* <L *reddere* give back < *re-* back + *dare* give] —**ren′der·a·ble** *adj.* —**ren′der·er** *n.*

ren·dez·vous (rän′dā·vōō, -də-; *Fr.* rän·de·vōō′) *n. pl.* **·vous** (-vōōz, *Fr.* -vōō′) **1** An appointed place of meeting. **2** A meeting or an appointment to meet. **3** A base for naval ships or for military units. **4** *Obs.* A resort; refuge. —*v.t.* & *v.i.* **·voused** (-vōōd), **·vous·ing** (-vōō′ing) To assemble or cause to assemble at a certain place or time. [<F *rendez-vous*, lit., betake yourself < *se rendre* betake oneself]

ren·di·tion (ren·dish′ən) *n.* **1** A translation; the interpretation of a text. **2** Artistic, dramatic, or musical interpretation; also, the performance or execution of a dramatic or musical composition. **3** A surrendering, especially of a person. **4** The act of rendering, or the amount rendered. [< obs. F < *rendre* render]

Ren·do·va (ren·dō′və) An island in the New Georgia group of the Solomon Islands; of volcanic origin; 75 square miles.

Re·né (rə·nā′, *Fr.* rə·nā′) A masculine personal name. [<F, reborn] —**Re·née** (rə·nā′) *fem.*

ren·e·gade (ren′ə·gād) *n.* **1** An apostate. **2** A traitor; deserter. Also **ren′e·ga′do** (-gā′dō). —*adj.* Traitorous. [<Sp. *renegado*, pp. of *renegar* deny <Med. L *renegare* <L *re-* again and again + *negare* deny]

re·nege (ri·nig′, -neg′, -nēg′) *v.i.* **·neged, ·neg·ing 1** In card games, to fail to follow suit when able to do so. See REVOKE. **2** *Colloq.* To fail to fulfil a promise. **3** *Obs.* To renounce; deny. Also **re·nig′**. [<Med. L *renegare*. See RENEGADE.] —**re·neg′er** *n.*

re·new (ri·nōō′, -nyōō′) *v.t.* **1** To make new or as if new again; restore to a former or sound condition. **2** To begin again; resume: to *renew* an argument. **3** To repeat: to *renew* an oath of loyalty. **4** To acquire again; regain (vigor, strength, etc.). **5** To cause to continue in effect; extend: to *renew* a subscription. **6** To revive; reestablish. **7** To replenish or replace, as provisions. —*v.i.* **8** To become new again. **9** To begin or commence again. See synonyms under RECLAIM. [<RE- again + NEW] —**re·new′a·ble** *adj.*

re·new·al (ri·nōō′əl -nyōō′-) *n.* The act of renewing, or the state of being renewed.

re·newed (ri·nōōd′, -nyōōd′) *adj.* Made new; restored; revived; repeated. See synonyms under FRESH. —**re·new·ed·ly** (ri·nōō′id·lē, -nyōō′-) *adv.*

Renewed Church of the United Brethren See MORAVIAN.

Ren·frew (ren′frōō) A county in SW Scotland; 240 square miles; county town, Renfrew. Also **Ren′frew·shire** (-shir).

Re·ni (rā′nē), **Guido**, 1575–1642, Italian painter.

reni- *combining form* Kidney; of or related to the kidneys: *reniform*: also, before vowels, *ren-*. Also **reno-**. [<L *ren, renis* a kidney]

ren·i·form (ren′ə·fôrm, rē′nə-) *adj.* Kidney-shaped. [<RENI- + -FORM]

ren·in (ren′in) *n. Biochem.* A protein substance secreted by an ischemic kidney or blood vessel and supposed to be responsible for a rise in blood pressure. [<L *ren* kidney]

re·ni·tent (ri·nī′tənt, ren′ə·tənt) *adj.* Offering resistance to any influence or force; continuously reluctant; recalcitrant; specifically, presenting elastic resistance to pressure. [<L *renitens, -entis*, ppr. of *reniti* resist < *re-* back + *niti* struggle] —**re·ni′tence, re·ni′ten·cy** *n.*

Rennes (ren) A city in NW central France; the intellectual center of Brittany.

ren·net (ren′it) *n.* **1** The dried stomach of certain young hoofed animals, especially the mucous membrane lining the fourth stomach of a suckling calf or sheep, which is capable of curdling milk. **2** Anything used to curdle milk. **3** An aqueous or vinous infusion of animal rennet. **4** Rennin. [Alter. of ME *rennels* <OE *rinnan* run together, coagulate]

ren·nin (ren′in) *n. Biochem.* An enzyme present in rennet; the milk-curdling ferment: also called *chymosin*. [<RENN(ET) + -IN]

Re·no (rē′nō) A city in western Nevada.

Re·noir (rə·nwär′), **Pierre Auguste**, 1841–1919, French Impressionist painter.

re·nounce (ri·nouns′) *v.* **·nounced, ·nounc·ing** *v.t.* **1** To give up, especially by formal statement. **2** To disown; repudiate. **3** In card games, to indicate inability to follow (a suit led) by playing a card of another suit. —*v.i.* **4** In card games, to renounce the suit led. [<F *renoncer* <L *renuntiare* protest against, announce < *re-* back, against + *nuntiare* report < *nuntius* messenger] —**re·nounce′ment** *n.* —**re·nounc′er** *n.*

Synonyms: abandon, abjure, deny, disavow, discard, disclaim, disown, forswear, recall, recant, refuse, reject, repudiate, retract, revoke. *Abjure, discard, forswear, recall, recant, renounce, retract,* and *revoke,* like *abandon,* imply some previous connection. *Renounce* is to declare against and give up formally and definitively; as, to *renounce* the pomps and vanities of the world. *Retract* is to take back something that one has said as not true or as what one is not ready to maintain; as, to *retract* a charge or accusation; one *recants* his own opinions or beliefs. *Repudiate* is to put away with emphatic and determined repulsion; as, to *repudiate* a debt. To *deny* is to affirm to be not true or not binding; as, to *deny* a statement or relationship; or to refuse to grant, as a request or petition. To *discard* is to cast away as useless or worthless; thus, one *discards* a worn garment. *Revoke,* etymologically the equivalent of the English *recall,* is to take back something given or granted; as, to *revoke* a command, a will, or a grant; *recall* may be used in the exact sense of *revoke,* but is often applied to persons, as *revoke* is not; we *recall* a messenger and *revoke* an order. Compare ABANDON, ABDICATE, ABJURE, RECANT. *Antonyms*: acknowledge, advocate, assert, avow, cherish, claim, defend, hold, maintain, own, proclaim, retain, uphold, vindicate.

ren·o·vate (ren′ə·vāt) *v.t.* **·vat·ed, ·vat·ing 1** To make as good as new; repair. **2** To renew; refresh; reinvigorate. —*adj.* Renovated. [<L *renovatus*, pp. of *renovare* < *re-* again + *novare* make new < *novus* new] —**ren′o·va′tion** *n.* —**ren′o·va′tor** *n.*

re·nown (ri·noun′) *n.* **1** Exalted reputation; celebrity; the state of being widely known for great achievements or merits; fame. **2** *Obs.* Rumor; report. See synonyms under FAME. —*v.t. Obs.* To spread the fame of; render famous. [<OF *renon* < *renomer* name again, make famous <L *re-* again + *nominare* name < *nomen* a name]

re·nowned (ri·nound′) *adj.* Having renown; famous. See synonyms under ILLUSTRIOUS.

rens·se·laer·ite (ren′sə·lə·rīt′, ren′sə·lâr′īt) *n.* A light-colored variety of talc of such waxlike consistency that it may be worked on a lathe. [after Stephen Van *Rensselaer*, 1764–1839, U. S. soldier and politician]

rent[1] (rent) *n.* **1** Compensation made in any form by a tenant to a landlord or owner for the use of land, buildings, etc.; especially, such compensation paid in money at regular or specified intervals. **2** Similar payment for the use of any property, movable or fixed. **3** *Econ.* **a** Income derived by the owner from the use of his land or property. **b** The return afforded by cultivated land in excess of the costs, as of labor or materials. **c** That which is yielded by land in excess of the yield of the poorest land cultivated under equal conditions: also called **economic rent.** **d** Hence, a return derived from a similar advantage, as in a monopoly of natural resources. **4** *Obs.* **a** Landed or other property affording revenue. **b** Income or revenue. —**for rent** Available for use or occupancy by the paying of rent. —*v.t.* **1** To obtain the temporary possession and use of for a compensation, usually made at fixed intervals. **2** To grant the temporary possession and use of for a rent. —*v.i.* **3** To be let for rent. [<OF *rente* <LL *rendita*, L *reddita* what is given back or paid, fem. of pp. of *reddere*. See RENDER.] —**rent′a·ble** *adj.*

rent[2] (rent) Alternative past tense and past participle of REND. —*n.* **1** A hole or slit made by rending or tearing; tear; rip; fissure. **2** A schism; violent separation; split. See synonyms under BREACH, HOLE. [<REND]

rent·al (ren′təl) *n.* **1** The revenue derived from rented property. **2** A schedule of rents. —*adj.* Of or pertaining to rent. [<AF]

rente (räṅt) *n. French* **1** *pl.* The bonds and other securities representing the government indebtedness of France; also, the sums paid as interest on this indebtedness: also **rentes sur l'État** (räṅt sür lā·tà′). **2** Income or revenue in general; annuity.

rent·er (ren′tər) *n.* One who rents; specifically, one who rents an estate or tenement; a tenant.

ren·tier (räṅ·tyā′) *n. French* One who owns, or derives a fixed income from, invested capital or lands.

re·nun·ci·a·tion (ri·nun′sē·ā′shən, -shē-) *n.* **1** The act of renouncing or disclaiming; repudiation. **2** A declaration, statement, or formula in which something is renounced. [<L *renunciatio, -onis* a proclamation] —**re·nun′ci·a′tive** *adj.* —**re·nun·ci·a·to·ry** (ri·nun′sē·ə·tôr′ē, -tō′·rē-, -shē-) *adj.*

re·o·pen (rē·ō′pən) *v.t.* & *v.i.* **1** To open again. **2** To begin again; resume.

re·or·gan·i·za·tion (rē′ôr·gən·ə·zā′shən, -ī·zā′-) *n.* **1** The act of reorganizing, or the condition of being reorganized. **2** The legal reconstruction of a corporation, usually after or to avert a failure.

re·or·gan·ize (rē·ôr′gən·īz) *v.t.* & *v.i.* **·ized, ·iz·ing** To organize anew. —**re·or′gan·iz′er** *n.*

re·o·ri·ent (rē·ôr′ē·ənt, -ō′rē-) *adj. Rare* Rising again. [See ORIENT]

rep[1] (rep) *n.* A silk, cotton, rayon, or wool fabric having a distinctive crosswise rib: also spelled *repp*. [<F *reps* <E *ribs*]

rep[2] (rep) *n. Slang* Reputation.

rep[3] (rep) *n. Slang* A representative.

rep[4] (rep) *n. Physics* **1** A unit of absorbed nuclear radiation equivalent to the release of from 83 to 97 ergs per gram of absorbing material. **2** The rad. [<R(OENTGEN) + E(QUIVALENT) + P(HYSICAL)]

re·pair[1] (ri·pâr′) *v.t.* **1** To restore to sound or good condition after damage, injury, decay, etc.; mend. **2** To make amends for (an injury); remedy. **3** To make up, as a loss; compensate for. See synonyms under AMEND, RECRUIT. —*n.* **1** Restoration, as after decay, waste, injury, etc.; reparation. **2** Condition after use or after repairing: in good *repair*. [<OF *reparer* <L *reparare* < *re-* again + *parare* prepare, make ready] —**re·pair′er** *n.*

re·pair[2] (ri·pâr′) *v.i.* **1** To betake oneself; go: to *repair* to the garden. **2** To return. —*n.* **1** The act of repairing, or the place to which one repairs; a haunt. **2** *Scot.* A concourse of people to a certain spot. [<OF *repairer* <LL *repatriare* < *re-* again + *patria* native land]

re·pair·man (ri·pâr′man′, -mən) *n. pl.* **·men** (-men′, -mən) A man whose work is to make repairs.

re·pand (ri·pand′) *adj. Bot.* Having a wavy or uneven outline: said of leaves. [<L *repandus* bent back < *re-* back + *pandus*, pp. of *pandare* bend]

rep·a·ra·ble (rep′ər·ə·bəl) *adj.* Capable of repair or reparation. Also **re·pair·a·ble** (ri·pâr′·ə·bəl). [<F *réparable* <L *reparabilis*] —**rep′·a·ra·bil′i·ty** *n.* —**rep′a·ra·bly** *adv.*

rep·a·ra·tion (rep′ə·rā′shən) *n.* **1** The act of making amends; atonement; amends; indemnity; also, that which is done by way of amends or satisfaction. **2** The act of repairing or the state of being repaired. **3** *pl.* Repairs; specifically, indemnities paid by defeated countries for acts of war. See synonyms under RESTITUTION. [<L *reparatio*,

-onis a renewal] — **re·par·a·tive** (ri·par′ə·tiv) *adj.*

rep·ar·tee (rep′är·tē′, -ər-) *n.* **1** Conversation marked by quick and witty replies. **2** Skill or quickness in such conversation. **3** A witty or quick reply; a sharp rejoinder. See synonyms under ANSWER. [<F *repartie,* pp. of *repartir* depart again, reply < *re-* again + *partir* depart]

re·par·ti·tion (rē′pär·tish′ən) *n.* **1** Distribution; allotment. **2** Redistribution.

re·past (ri·past′, -päst′) *n.* **1** Food taken at a meal; hence, a meal. **2** Food in general; also, mealtime. [<OF *repas* <Med. L *repastum,* orig. pp. of LL *repascere* feed again <L *re-* again + *pascere* feed]

re·pa·ten·cy (ri·pāt′n·sē, -pat′n-) *n.* The reopening of a part or vessel that had been closed. [<RE- + L *patentia,* neut. pl. of *patens, patentis,* ppr. of *patere* be open]

re·pa·tri·ate (rē·pā′trē·āt) *v.t.* & *v.i.* **·at·ed, ·at·ing** To send back or return to his own country, as a soldier interned in a neutral territory; restore to citizenship. — *n.* (rē·pā′trē·it) A person who has been repatriated. [<LL *repatriatus,* pp. of *repatriare* <L *re-* again + *patria* native land] — **re·pa′tri·a′tion** *n.*

re·pay (ri·pā′) *v.* **·paid, ·pay·ing** *v.t.* **1** To pay back; refund. **2** To pay back or refund something to. **3** To make compensation or retaliation for; give a reward or inflict a penalty for. — *v.i.* **4** To make repayment or requital. See synonyms under REQUITE. [<OF *repaier*] — **re·pay′a·ble** *adj.* — **re·pay′ment** *n.*

re·peal (ri·pēl′) *v.t.* **1** To rescind, as a law; revoke. **2** *Obs.* To summon back, as from exile. See synonyms under ABOLISH, ANNUL, CANCEL. — *n.* **1** The act of repealing; revocation; rescission. **2** *Obs.* Recall, as from exile. [<OF *rapeler* recall < *re-* again + *appeler.* See APPEAL.] — **re·peal′a·ble** *adj.* — **re·peal′·er** *n.*

re·peat (ri·pēt′) *v.t.* **1** To say again; reiterate: to *repeat* a question. **2** To recite from memory. **3** To say (what another has just said). **4** To tell, as a secret, to another. **5** To do, make, or experience again. — *v.i.* **6** *U.S.* To vote more than once at the same election: an offense punishable by law. — *n.* **1** The act of repeating; a repetition. **2** *Music* **a** A sign consisting of dots placed in the spaces at the left hand of a bar, to indicate that the preceding passage is to be repeated. **b** A repeated passage, song, refrain, etc. **3** Anything repeated, as a new supply of goods, or a renewed order for such supply. [<OF *repeter* <L *repetere* do or say again < *re-* again + *petere* seek]

re·peat·ed (ri·pē′tid) *adj.* Occurring or spoken again and again; reiterated. See synonyms under FREQUENT. — **re·peat′ed·ly** *adv.*

re·peat·er (ri·pē′tər) *n.* **1** One who or that which repeats. **2** A timepiece, especially a watch, which will strike again the hour last struck when a spring is pressed. **3** A repeating firearm. **4** An instrument for automatically retransmitting electromagnetic signals: a telegraph *repeater.* **5** *U.S.* One who votes, or attempts to vote, more than once at the same election. **6** One who has been repeatedly imprisoned for criminal offenses.

repeating decimal *Math.* **1** A decimal fraction in which one figure is repeated indefinitely. **2** A circulating decimal.

repeating firearm A gun, rifle, or pistol arranged to deliver several shots without reloading.

re·pêch·age (rə·pesh·äzh′) *n. French* Consolation race; a second heat to afford another chance to those running second best in preliminary heats.

re·pel (ri·pel′) *v.* **·pelled, ·pel·ling** *v.t.* **1** To force or drive back; repulse. **2** To reject; refuse, as a suggestion. **3** To cause to feel distaste or aversion: His manner *repels* me. **4** To refuse to mix with or adhere to: Mercury *repels* iron. **5** To push or keep away, especially with invisible force: Like magnetic poles *repel* each other: opposed to *attract.* — *v.i.* **6** To act so as to drive something back or away. **7** To cause distaste or aversion. [<L *repellere* < *re-* back + *pellere* drive] — **re·pel′ler** *n.*

Synonyms: check, oppose, repulse, resist. *Repulse* is stronger and more conclusive than *repel*; one may be *repelled* by the very aspect of the person whose favor he seeks, but is not *repulsed* except by a direct refusal of his suit. See DRIVE. *Antonyms*: accept, admit, encourage, entertain, favor, grant, welcome.

re·pel·lent (ri·pel′ənt) *adj.* **1** Serving, tending, or having power to repel. **2** Waterproof. **3** Repugnant. — *n.* **1** A waterproof cloth. **2** A remedial application that tends to repel fluids from a swollen part. **3** A chemical compound intended to be distasteful to insects and other vermin and to keep them at a distance. — **re·pel′len·cy, re·pel′lence** *n.*

re·pent[1] (ri·pent′) *v.i.* **1** To feel remorse or regret, as for something done or undone; be contrite. **2** To change one's mind concerning past action because of disappointment, failure, etc.: with *of*: He *repented* of his generosity to the old man. **3** *Theol.* To feel such sorrow for one's sins as to reform. — *v.t.* **4** To feel remorse or regret for (an action, sin, etc.). **5** To change one's mind concerning (a past action): He *repented* his decision. [<OF *repentir* <L *re-* again + *poenitere* cause to repent < *poena* punishment] — **re·pent′er** *n.*

re·pent[2] (rē′pənt) *adj.* **1** *Bot.* Lying flat and rooting, as certain plants; procumbent. **2** *Zool.* Reptant. [<L *repens, repentis,* ppr. of *repere* creep]

re·pen·tance (ri·pen′təns) *n.* A turning with sorrow from a past course or action; loosely, regret or contrition; also, the condition of being penitent.

Synonyms: compunction, contrition, penitence, regret, remorse, sorrow. *Regret* is *sorrow* for any painful or annoying matter. One is moved with *penitence* for wrongdoing. To speak of *regret* for a fault of our own marks it as slighter than one for which we should express *penitence. Repentance* is *sorrow* for sin with self-condemnation, and complete turning from the sin. *Compunction* is a momentary sting of conscience, in view either of a past or of a contemplated act. *Contrition* is a subduing *sorrow* for sin, as against the divine holiness and love. *Remorse* is, as its derivation indicates, a biting or gnawing back of guilt upon the heart. *Antonyms*: approval, comfort, complacency, content, hardness, impenitence, obduracy, obstinacy, recusancy, stubbornness.

re·pen·tant (ri·pen′tənt) *adj.* Showing, experiencing, or characterized by repentance. [<OF] — **re·pen′tant·ly** *adv.*

re·peo·ple (rē·pē′pəl) *v.t.* **·pled, ·pling** **1** To people anew. **2** To provide again with animals; restock.

re·per·cus·sion (rē′pər·kush′ən) *n.* **1** The act of driving or throwing back, or the state of being driven back; repulse; also, echo; reverberation. **2** A stroke or blow given in return; recoil after impact; hence, the indirect result of something; aftereffect: the *repercussions* of the peace treaty. **3** *Med.* The motion produced on a fetus by the process of ballottement. [<L *repercussio, -onis* < *repercussus,* pp. of *repercutere* rebound < *re-* again + *percutere* strike. See PERCUSS.]

re·per·cus·sive (rē′pər·kus′iv) *adj.* Causing, of the nature of, or produced by repercussion; reverberated.

rep·er·toire (rep′ər·twär, -twôr) *n.* A list of songs, plays, operas, or the like, that a person or company is prepared to perform; also, such pieces collectively. [<F <LL *repertorium.* See REPERTORY.]

rep·er·to·ry (rep′ər·tôr′ē, -tō′rē) *n. pl.* **·ries** **1** A place where things are gathered together, or the things so gathered; a repository; collection. **2** Repertoire. [<LL *repertorium* inventory <L < *repertus,* pp. of *reperire* find, discover < *re-* again + *parire* produce]

repertory company A theatrical group having a repertoire of productions, each typically running for a few weeks, and usually having some acting personnel continuing from one production to the next. Also **repertory theater.**

rep·e·tend (rep′ə·tend, rep′ə·tend′) *n.* **1** *Math.* That part of a circulating decimal which is repeated indefinitely. **2** Something repeated or to be repeated. [<L *repentendus* to be repeated, gerundive of *repetere.* See REPEAT.]

rep·e·ti·tion (rep′ə·tish′ən) *n.* **1** The act of repeating; the doing, making, or saying of something again; recital from memory. **2** *Music* The singing or playing of the same note, chord, or passage over again. **3** That which is repeated; a copy. [<F *répétition*]

rep·e·ti·tious (rep′ə·tish′əs) *adj.* Characterized by or containing useless or tedious repetition. — **rep′e·ti′tious·ly** *adv.* — **rep′e·ti′tious·ness** *n.*

re·pet·i·tive (ri·pet′ə·tiv) *adj.* Marked by repetition; recurrent. — **re·pet′i·tive·ly** *adv.*

re·pine (ri·pīn′) *v.i.* **·pined, ·pin·ing** To be discontented or fretful; complain; murmur. See synonyms under COMPLAIN. [<RE- + PINE[2]] — **re·pin′er** *n.* — **re·pin′ing** *n.*

re·place (ri·plās′) *v.t.* **·placed, ·plac·ing** **1** To put back in place. **2** To take or fill the place of; supersede. **3** To refund; repay. — **re·place′a·ble** *adj.* — **re·plac′er** *n.*

re·place·ment (ri·plās′mənt) *n.* **1** The act of replacing; also, that which takes the place of anything discarded or worn out. **2** *Mineral.* The formation of a new crystal face which obliterates an edge or angle. **3** A soldier available for assignment to fill a vacancy or a quota. **4** The act of putting a thing back in place. **5** *Chem.* A substitution. **6** A substitute.

re·play (rē·plā′) *v.t.* **1** To play again. **2** To show a replay of. — *n.* (rē′plā′) **1** The act of playing again. **2** The playing of a television tape, often in slow motion and usually immediately following the live occurrence of the action shown. **3** The action shown in such a replay.

re·plead·er (ri·plē′dər) *n. Law* **1** An order of court directing the parties to file new pleadings in order to present a better issue for trial. **2** The right of pleading again. [<RE- + obs. *pleader* a pleading in court]

re·plen·ish (ri·plen′ish) *v.t.* **1** To fill again, as something that has been wholly or partially emptied. **2** To bring back to fullness or completeness, as diminished supplies. **3** To repeople. [<OF *repleniss-,* stem of *replenir* < *re-* again + L *plenus* full] — **re·plen′ish·er** *n.* — **re·plen′ish·ment** *n.*

re·plete (ri·plēt′) *adj.* **1** Full to the uttermost. **2** Gorged with food or drink; sated. **3** Abundantly supplied or stocked; abounding. [<OF *replet* <L *repletus,* pp. of *replere* fill again < *re-* again + *plere* fill] — **re·ple′tion** *n.*

re·plev·in (ri·plev′in) *Law n.* **1** An action to regain possession of personal property unlawfully retained, on giving security to try the title and respond to the judgment; recovery of property by such action. **2** The judicial writ or process by which such proceedings are instituted. — *v.t.* To replevy. [<AF *replevine* <OF *replevir* warrant, pledge < *re-* back + *plevir* pledge <Gmc.]

re·plev·y (ri·plev′ē) *Law v.t.* **·plev·ied, ·plev·y·ing** **1** To recover possession of (chattels) by proceedings in replevin. **2** To admit to bail or give bail for. — *n.* Replevin. [<OF *replevir.* See REPLEVIN.] — **re·plev′i·a·ble, re·plev′is·a·ble** *adj.*

rep·li·ca (rep′lə·kə) *n.* **1** A duplicate, as of a picture, executed by the original artist. **2** Any close copy or reproduction. See synonyms under DUPLICATE, MODEL. [<Ital. <L *replicare* reply, answer to. See REPLY.]

rep·li·cate (rep′lə·kit) *adj.* Folded backward, as the upper part of a leaf on the lower, or the wing of an insect. Also **rep′li·cat′ed** (-kā′·tid). — *v.t.* (-kāt) **·cat·ed, ·cat·ing** **1** To fold over. **2** To make a replica of. **3** To answer; reply. [<L *replicatus,* pp. of *replicare* answer. See REPLY.]

rep·li·ca·tion (rep′lə·kā′shən) *n.* **1** A reply. **2** *Law* A plaintiff's reply to a defendant's plea or answer. **3** A repetition or copy. **4** A methodical or systematic doubling over of a surface. [<OF] — **rep′li·ca′tive** *adj.*

re·ply (ri·plī′) *v.* **·plied, ·ply·ing** *v.i.* **1** To give an answer, orally or in writing. **2** To respond by some act, gesture, etc.: He *replied* with a blow. **3** To echo. **4** *Law* To file a pleading in answer to the statement of the defense. — *v.t.* **5** To say in answer: often with a clause as object: She *replied* that she would do it. — *n. pl.* **·plies** Something said, written, or done by way of answer; a response; rejoinder. See synonyms under ANSWER. [<OF *replier* bend back <L *replicare* fold back, answer to, make a reply < *re-* back + *plicare* fold] — **re·pli′er** *n.*

ré·pon·dez s'il vous plaît (rā·pôn·dā′ sēl vōō ple′) *French* Reply, if you please: used on formal invitations: abbr. *R.S.V.P.*

re·port (ri·pôrt′, -pōrt′) *v.t.* **1** To make or give an account of, especially formally: to *report* the minutes of a meeting, or an event for a newspaper. **2** To relate, as information obtained by investigation: Please *report* your

findings. 3 To bear back or repeat to another, as an answer. 4 To complain about, especially to a superior: I'll *report* you to the manager. 5 To state the result of consideration concerning: The committee *reported* the bill. —*v.i.* 6 To make a report. 7 To act as a reporter. 8 To present oneself, as for duty. See synonyms under ANNOUNCE. —*n.* 1 That which is reported; an announcement, statement, or account; the formal statement of the result of an investigation: a medical *report.* 2 Common talk; rumor; hence, fame, reputation, or character: good *report; reports* grossly untrue. 3 A record with more or less detail of the transactions of a deliberative body. 4 An account of any occurrence prepared for publication through the press. 5 *Law Usually pl.* A published narration (usually official) of a case or series of cases judicially considered: the Supreme Court *reports.* 6 An explosive sound: the *report* of a gun. [<OF *reporter* carry back <L *reportare* <*re-* back +*portare* carry]—**re·port'a·ble** *adj.*

Synonyms (noun): account, description, narration, narrative, recital, record, rehearsal, relation, rumor, statement, story, tale. *Account,* primarily a commercial summary, carries a similar meaning in the derived sense; an *account* of an occurrence is circumstantial, adequate, complete, and unembellished; we speak of a clear, a full, or a partial *account;* a glowing *account* is still supposed to be circumstantially as well as substantially correct. A *statement* is definite, confined to essentials and properly to matters within the personal knowledge of the one who states them. A *narrative* is a somewhat extended and embellished *account* of events in order of time, ordinarily with a view to please or entertain. A *description* gives especial scope to the pictorial element. A *report* is supposed or intended to bring back the past, and may be concise and formal or highly descriptive and dramatic. Compare ALLEGORY, ANECDOTE, HISTORY, NEWS, RECORD.

report card *U.S.* A periodic statement of a pupil's scholastic record, which is presented to the parents or guardian.

re·port·ed·ly (ri·pôr'tid·lē, -pōr'-) *adv.* According to report.

re·port·er (ri·pôr'tər, -pōr'-) *n.* 1 A bearer of news; specifically, one employed by a newspaper to gather and report news for publication. 2 One who edits reports of important cases in court for official publication. [<OF *reporteur*]—**rep·or·to·ri·al** (rep'ər·tôr'ē·əl, -tō'rē-) *adj.*

re·pose[1] (ri·pōz') *n.* 1 The act of taking rest, or the state of being at rest; especially, rest in a recumbent posture. 2 Freedom from excitement or anxiety; composure; hence, ease of manner; graceful and dignified calmness. 3 That which conduces to rest or calm. See synonyms under REST. —*v.* **·posed, ·pos·ing** *v.t.* 1 To lay or place in a position of rest: to *repose* oneself on a bed. —*v.i.* 2 To lie at rest. 3 To rely; depend: with *on, upon,* or *in.* See synonyms under REST. [<F *reposer* <LL *repausare* <*re-* again +*pausare* pause]—**re·pos'al** *n.* —**re·pos'er** *n.*

re·pose[2] (ri·pōz') *v.t.* **·posed, ·pos·ing** 1 To place, as confidence or hope: with *in.* 2 *Rare* To deposit. [<L *repositus,* pp. of *reponere* put back, on analogy with *depose, oppose,* etc.]—**re·pos'al** *n.*

re·pose·ful (ri·pōz'fəl) *adj.* Full of repose; restful.

re·pos·it (ri·poz'it) *v.t.* To put in some secure and proper place; deposit. [<L *repositus.* See REPOSE.]—**re·po·si·tion** (rē'pə·zish'ən, rep'ə-) *n.*

re·pos·i·to·ry (ri·poz'ə·tôr'ē, -tō'rē) *n. pl.* **·ries** 1 A place in which goods are or may be stored; a depository. 2 A person to whom a secret is entrusted. 3 A building used as a place of exhibition and sale. 4 A burial vault. 5 A sepulcher (def. 2). [<L *repositorium* <*repositus.* See REPOSE.]

re·pos·sess (rē'pə·zes') *v.t.* 1 To have possession of again; regain possession of. 2 To give back possession or ownership to. 3 *Scot.* To reinstate: with *in.* See synonyms under RECOVER. —**re'pos·ses'sion** (-zesh'ən) *n.*

re·pous·sé (rə·pōō·sā') *adj.* Formed in relief, as a design in metal, or adorned with such designs. [<F, lit., thrust back <L *repulsus.* See REPULSE.]

repp (rep) See REP[1].

Rep·plier (rep'lir), **Agnes,** 1855–1950, U.S. essayist.

rep·re·hend (rep'ri·hend') *v.t.* To criticize sharply; find fault with; blame. See synonyms under BLAME, REPROVE. [<L *reprehendere* <*re-* back +*prehendere* hold]

rep·re·hen·si·ble (rep'ri·hen'sə·bəl) *adj.* Deserving blame or censure. —**rep're·hen'si·bil'i·ty, rep're·hen'si·ble·ness** *n.* —**rep're·hen'si·bly** *adv.*

rep·re·hen·sion (rep'ri·hen'shən) *n.* A finding fault; expression of blame; rebuke. See synonyms under ANIMADVERSION, REPROOF. —**rep're·hen'sive** *adj.* —**rep're·hen'sive·ly** *adv.*

rep·re·sent (rep'ri·zent') *v.t.* 1 To serve as the symbol, expression, or designation of; symbolize: The letters of the alphabet *represent* the sounds of speech. 2 To express or symbolize in this manner: to *represent* royal power with a scepter. 3 To set forth a likeness or image of; depict; portray, as in painting or sculpture. 4 a To produce on the stage, as an opera. b To act the part of; impersonate, as a character in a play. 5 To serve as or be the delegate, agent, etc., of: He *represents* the State of Maine. 6 To describe as being of a specified character or condition: They *represented* him as a genius. 7 To set forth in words; state; explain: He *represented* the circumstances of his case. 8 To bring before the mind; present clearly. 9 To serve as an example, specimen, type, etc., of; typify: His use of words *represents* an outmoded school of writing. See synonyms under IMITATE. [<OF *representer* <L *repraesentare* <*re-* again +*praesentare.* See PRESENT[2].]—**rep're·sent'a·ble** *adj.* —**rep're·sent'a·bil'i·ty** *n.*

re-present (rē'pri·zent') *v.t.* To present again. —**re'pre'sen·ta'tion** *n.*

rep·re·sen·ta·tion (rep'ri·zen·tā'shən) *n.* 1 The act of representing, or the state of being represented. 2 That which represents a likeness; model; picture; statue; statement; description; also, a dramatic performance. 3 The right of acting authoritatively for others, especially in a legislative body; also, the system of electing delegates to act for a constituency. 4 Representatives collectively. 5 The stage or process of mental conservation that consists in the presenting to itself by the mind of objects previously known. 6 *Law* The authorized acting for or in the stead of another in regard to that other's affairs. 7 A setting forth by statement or account; specifically, an argument against some object or proposal. See synonyms under IMAGE, MODEL, PICTURE. [<OF]

rep·re·sen·ta·tive (rep'ri·zen'tə·tiv) *adj.* 1 Typifying or typical of a group or class. 2 Acting, having the power or authority to act, or qualified to act, as an agent. 3 Made up of representatives. 4 Based on or pertaining to the political principle of representation. 5 Presenting, portraying, or representing, or capable of so doing. 6 Having to do with cognition of a memory image: distinguished from *presentative.* —*n.* 1 One who or that which is fit to stand as a type; a typical instance. 2 One who is a qualified agent of any kind. 3 A member of a deliberative or legislative body chosen by vote of the people; specifically, in the United States, a member of the lower house of Congress or of a State legislature. See synonyms under DELEGATE. —**rep're·sen'ta·tive·ly** *adv.* —**rep'·re·sen'ta·tive·ness** *n.*

re·press (ri·pres') *v.t.* 1 To keep under restraint or control; curb. 2 To put down; quell, as a rebellion. 3 *Psychoanal.* To effect the repression of, as fears, impulses, etc. [<L *repressus,* pp. of *reprimere* <*re-* back +*premere* press]—**re·press'er** or **re·pres'sor** *n.* —**re·press'i·ble** *adj.*

Synonyms: bridle, chasten, check, crush, curb, overcome, overpower, quiet, rein, restrain, stay, still, subdue, suppress. See LIMIT, RESTRAIN, SUBDUE. *Antonyms*: agitate, animate, arouse, awaken, encourage, excite, incite, inspirit, instigate, kindle, provoke, rouse, stimulate.

re·pressed (ri·prest') *adj.* Suppressed.

re·pres·sion (ri·presh'ən) *n.* 1 The act of repressing, or the condition of being repressed. 2 That which holds in check; a restraint. 3 *Psychoanal.* The exclusion from consciousness of painful, unpleasant, or unacceptable psychic material, as memories, desires, and impulses, which are thus compelled to manifest themselves through the unconcious.

re·pres·sive (ri·pres'iv) *adj.* 1 Tending to repress. 2 Capable of repressing. —**re·pres'sive·ly** *adv.* —**re·pres'sive·ness** *n.*

re·prieve (ri·prēv') *v.t.* **·prieved, ·priev·ing** 1 To suspend temporarily the execution of a sentence upon. 2 To relieve for a tme from suffering, danger, or trouble. 3 To postpone or delay, as a danger. —*n.* 1 The temporary suspension of a sentence, or the instrument officially ordering such a suspension. 2 Temporary relief or cessation of pain or ill; respite. See synonyms under RESPITE. [<earlier *repry* <F *repris,* pp. of *reprendre* take back; infl. in form by ME *repreven* <OF *reprover* reprove]

rep·ri·mand (rep'rə·mand, -mänd) *v.t.* To reprove sharply or formally. See synonyms under ADMONISH, REPROVE. —*n.* Severe reproof or formal censure, public or private. See synonyms under REPROOF. [<F *réprimande* reproof <L *reprimenda,* fem. of *reprimendus* to be repressed, gerundive of *reprimere.* See REPRESS.]

re·print (rē'print') *n.* An edition of a printed work that is a verbatim copy of the original; specifically, a copy of matter already printed, as in another country. —*v.t.* (rē·print') To print a new edition or copy of; print anew or again. —**re·print'er** *n.*

re·pri·sal (ri·prī'zəl) *n.* 1 Forcible seizure of anything from an enemy by way of retaliation or indemnity. 2 Anything taken from an enemy as indemnification or in retaliation; also, any act or infliction by way of retaliation; specifically, the infliction of suffering or death on a prisoner of war in retaliation for acts of inhumanity inflicted by him. 3 Any act of retaliation. 4 *Obs.* A prize seized or gained. [<OF *reprisaille* <*repris,* pp. of *reprendre* take back <L *reprehendere.* See REPREHEND.]

re·prise (ri·prīz' *for def. 1;* rə·prēz', -prīz' *for def. 2*) *n.* 1 *pl. Brit. Law* Deductions and payments (as for annuities) out of lands: a manor's yearly value over and above *reprises.* 2 *Music* A repeated phrase; specifically, the repetition of or return to the subject after an intermediate movement. [<OF fem. of *repris.* See REPRISAL.]

re·pro (rē'prō) *n. pl.* **·pros** A very sharp, clear proof printed on glossy paper, to be photographed for making a printing plate. [<REPRO(DUCTION PROOF)]

re·proach (ri·prōch') *v.t.* 1 To charge with or blame for something wrong; rebuke; censure; upbraid. 2 To bring discredit and disgrace upon; to disgrace. See synonyms under ABUSE, BLAME, REPROVE, REVILE.—*n.* 1 The act of reproaching, or the words of one who reproaches; censure; reproof; rebuke. 2 A cause of blame or disgrace; hence, disgrace or discredit. See synonyms under BLEMISH, REPROOF, SCANDAL. [<F *reprocher.* Origin uncertain.]—**re·proach'a·ble** *adj.* —**re·proach'a·ble·ness** *n.* —**re·proach'a·bly** *adv.* —**re·proach'er** *n.*

re·proach·ful (ri·prōch'fəl) *adj.* 1 Containing or full of reproach; expressing reproach. 2 *Obs.* Reproachable. —**re·proach'ful·ly** *adv.* —**re·proach'ful·ness** *n.*

rep·ro·bate (rep'rə·bāt) *adj.* 1 Abandoned in sin; lost to all sense of duty; utterly depraved; profligate. 2 Abandoned to punishment; condemned. 3 *Obs.* Not enduring proof or trial; inferior or base. —*n.* One lost to all sense of duty or decency; one abandoned to depravity or doom. —*v.t.* **·bat·ed, ·bat·ing** 1 To disapprove of heartily; condemn. 2 *Theol.* To abandon, condemn, or foreordain to damnation. See synonyms under BLAME, CONDEMN. [<LL *reprobatus,* pp. of *reprobare.* See REPROVE.]

rep·ro·ba·tion (rep'rə·bā'shən) *n.* 1 The act of reprobating, or the condition of being reprobated; censure. 2 *Theol.* Rejection or condemnation by God's purpose. See synonyms under OATH.

rep·ro·ba·tive (rep′rə·bā′tiv) *adj.* Of, pertaining to, or expressing reprobation. **—rep′ro·ba′·tive·ly** *adv.*

re·proc·ess (rē·pros′es) *v.t.* To process again.

reprocessed wool Wool fibers previously woven or knitted but never used by a consumer, unraveled and spun and rewoven into fabric.

re·pro·duce (rē′prə·do͞os′, -dyo͞os′) *v.* **·duced, ·duc·ing** *v.t.* **1** To make a copy, image, or reproduction of. **2** *Biol.* **a** To give rise to (offspring) by sexual or asexual generation. **b** To replace (a lost part or organ) by regeneration. **3** To cause the reproduction of (plant life, etc.). **4** To produce again; bring forward or exhibit anew. **5** To bring into existence again; recreate; revive. **6** To recall to the mind; visualize again; re-create mentally. *—v.i.* **7** To produce offspring. **8** To undergo copying, reproduction, etc. **—re′pro·duc′i·ble** *adj.*

re·pro·duc·er (rē′prə·do͞o′sər, -dyo͞o′-) *n.* **1** One who or that which reproduces. **2** A diaphragm used for the reproduction of sounds in a phonograph, etc.

re·pro·duc·tion (rē′prə·duk′shən) *n.* **1** The act or power of reproducing. **2** *Biol.* The process by which an animal or plant gives rise to another of its kind; generation. **3** *Psychol.* The process of the memory by which objects that have previously been known are brought back into consciousness. **4** That which is reproduced, as a revival in drama or a copy in art. See synonyms under DUPLICATE.

re·pro·duc·tive (rē′prə·duk′tiv) *adj.* Pertaining to, employed in, or tending to reproduction. — re′pro·duc′tive·ly *adv.* **—re′pro·duc′tive·ness** *n.*

re·pro·gram (rē·prō′gram, -grəm) *v.t.* **-gramed** or **-grammed, -gram·ing** or **-gram·ming** To program (a computer) again.

re·prog·ra·phy (rē·prog′rə·fē) *n.* The reproduction of graphic material, esp. by electronic devices. [< REPRO(DUCTION) + -GRAPHY]

re·proof (ri·pro͞of′) *n.* **1** The act of reproving; rebuke; blame; censure. **2** *Obs.* Ignominy; reproach. Also **re·prov·al** (ri·pro͞o′vəl). [< OF *reprove* < *reprover.* See REPROVE.]

Synonyms: admonition, animadversion, blame, censure, check, chiding, comment, condemnation, criticism, denunciation, disapproval, objurgation, rebuke, reflection, reprehension, reprimand, reproach, reproval, upbraiding. *Blame, censure,* and *disapproval* may either be felt or uttered; *comment, criticism, rebuke, reflection, reprehension,* and *reproof* are always expressed. The same is true of *admonition* and *animadversion. Comment* and *criticism* may be favorable as well as censorious; they imply no superiority or authority on the part of him who utters them; nor do *reflection* or *reprehension,* which are simply turning the mind back upon what is disapproved. *Reprehension* is supposed to be calm and just, and with good intent; *reflection* is often from mere ill feeling, and is likely to be more personal and less impartial than *reprehension. Rebuke,* literally a stopping of the mouth, is administered to a forward or hasty person; *reproof* is administered to one intentionally or deliberately wrong; both words imply authority in the reprover, and direct expression of *disapproval* to the face of the person *rebuked* or *reproved. Reprimand* is official *censure* formally administered by a superior to one under his command. *Rebuke* may be given at the outset, or in the midst of an action; *reflection, reprehension, reproof,* always follow the act; *admonition* is anticipatory, and meant to be preventive. *Check* is allied to *rebuke,* and given before or during action; *chiding* is nearer to *reproof,* but with more personal bitterness and less authority. Compare CONDEMN, REPROVE. *Antonyms*: applause, approbation, approval, commendation, encomium, eulogy, panegyric, praise.

re·prove (ri·pro͞ov′) *v.t.* **·proved, ·prov·ing 1** To censure, as for a fault; rebuke. **2** To express disapproval of (an act). **3** *Obs.* To convince; convict. [< OF *reprover* < LL *reprobare* < *re-* again + *probare* test < *probus* upright] **—re·prov′a·ble** *adj.* **—re·prov′er** *n.* **—re·prov′ing·ly** *adv.*

Synonyms: admonish, blame, censure, chasten, check, chide, condemn, rebuke, reprehend, reprimand, reproach, upbraid. To *censure* is to pronounce an adverse judgment that may or may not be expressed to the person *censured*; to *rebuke* is to *reprove* sharply, and often abruptly; to *blame* is a familiar word signifying to pass *censure* upon, make answerable, as for a fault. To *reproach* is to *censure* openly and vehemently, and with intense personal feeling as of grief or anger; as, to *reproach* one for ingratitude; *reproach* knows no distinction of rank or character; a subject may *reproach* a king or a criminal a judge. Compare REPROOF. See ADMONISH, BLAME, CONDEMN. *Antonyms*: see synonyms for PRAISE.

rep·tant (rep′tənt) *adj. Zool.* Creeping; crawling: also *repent.* [< L *reptans, -antis,* ppr. of *reptare,* intens. of *repere* creep]

rep·tile (rep′til, -tīl) *n.* **1** A cold-blooded, air-breathing vertebrate, especially one with scales, as a lizard, snake, or crocodile; a reptilian; any member of the class *Reptilia.* **2** A groveling, abject person; one morally base or odious. *—adj.* **1** Crawling on the belly; creeping; reptant. **2** Groveling morally; sly and base; treacherous; venomous. **3** Of, pertaining to, or resembling a reptile. [< LL, neut. sing. of *reptilis* crawling < *reptus,* pp. of *repere* creep]

rep·til·i·an (rep·til′ē·ən) *adj.* **1** Of or pertaining to a class *(Reptilia)* of cold-blooded, air-breathing vertebrates, the reptiles, having fully ossified skeletons and bodies usually covered with horny plates or scales. In addition to the limbless snakes, the class includes crocodiles, alligators, lizards, and turtles. **2** Malicious; base; mean. — *n.* One of the *Reptilia*; any reptile.

re·pub·lic (ri·pub′lik) *n.* **1** A state in which the sovereignty resides in the people or a certain portion of the people, and the legislative and administrative powers are lodged in officers elected by and representing the people; a representative democracy: applied to almost every form of government except kingdoms, empires, and dictatorships. **2** A community of persons working freely in or devoted to the same cause; the *republic* of letters. **—The Republic 1** The United States. **2** Plato's dialog on government. [< F *république* < L *respublica* commonwealth < *res* thing + *publica,* fem. of *publicus* public]

re·pub·li·can (ri·pub′li·kən) *adj.* Pertaining to, of the nature of, or suitable for a republic; agreeable to the nature of a republic; also, of or pertaining to any party supporting republican government. *—n.* One who advocates or upholds a republican form of government or belongs to a party upholding republican government; one who believes in equality and liberty.

Re·pub·li·can (ri·pub′li·kən) *adj.* Pertaining to or belonging to the Republican party of the United States, or to any political group which calls itself by this name: the *Republican* parties of Spain or France. *—n.* A member of the Republican party. **—black Republican** Formerly, a member of the Republican party: derisively so called in allusion to their opposition to Negro slavery.

Republican calendar See under CALENDAR.

re·pub·li·can·ism (ri·pub′li·kən·iz′əm) *n.* **1** The theory or principles of republican government. **2** A liking for republican principles.

Re·pub·li·can·ism (ri·pub′li·kən·iz′əm) *n.* The policy and principles of the Republican party of the United States.

re·pub·li·can·ize (ri·pub′li·kən·īz′) *v.t.* **·ized, ·iz·ing** To make republican in spirit or character. **—re·pub′li·can·i·za′tion** *n.*

Republican party 1 One of the two major political parties of the United States, founded in 1854 in opposition to the extension of slavery. **2** The political party founded by Thomas Jefferson in 1792: full name, *Democratic-Republican party.* One of its several factions became, in 1828, the present Democratic party. **3** One of various political parties of foreign countries, devoted to the overthrow of monarchy or the establishment or extension of democratic ideals.

re·pub·li·ca·tion (rē′pub·lə·kā′shən) *n.* The act of republishing, or that which is republished.

re·pub·lish (rē·pub′lish) *v.t.* **1** To publish again. **2** *Law* To revive, as a canceled will, by executing anew. **—re·pub′lish·er** *n.*

re·pu·di·ate (ri·pyo͞o′dē·āt) *v.t.* **·at·ed, ·at·ing 1** To refuse to accept as valid, true, or authorized; reject; condemn. **2** To refuse to acknowledge or pay. **3** To cast off; disown, as a son. **4** *Obs.* To divorce; put away (a wife). See synonyms under ABANDON, RECANT, RENOUNCE. [< L *repudiatus,* pp. of *repudiare* divorce < *repudium* divorce, separation, ? < *re-* back + *pudere* feel shame] **—re·pu′di·a′tive** *adj.* **—re·pu′di·a′tor** *n.*

re·pu·di·a·tion (ri·pyo͞o′dē·ā′shən) *n.* **1** The act of repudiating. **2** The state of being repudiated. **3** The rejection of the whole or a part of a contract, debt, or obligation, as by a government.

re·pug·nance (ri·pug′nəns) *n.* **1** A feeling of aversion and resistance. **2** *Logic* The relation of contradictories; inconsistency. **3** *Obs.* Opposition. Also **re·pug′nan·cy.** See synonyms under ANTIPATHY, HATRED.

re·pug·nant (ri·pug′nənt) *adj.* **1** Offensive to taste or feeling; exciting aversion or repulsion. **2** Being inconsistent or opposed; antagonistic. **3** *Law* Contrary to or in conflict with something else in the same or in another document or statute. **4** Hostile; rebellious; resisting. See synonyms under INCONGRUOUS, INIMICAL. [< OF < L *repugnans, -antis,* ppr. of *repugnare.* See REPUGN.]

re·pulse (ri·puls′) *v.t.* **·pulsed, ·puls·ing 1** To drive back; repel, as an attacking force. **2** To repel by coldness, discourtesy, etc.; reject; rebuff. See synonyms under DRIVE, REPEL. *—n.* **1** The act of repulsing, or the state of being repulsed. **2** Rejection; refusal. [< L *repulsus,* pp. of *repellere.* See REPEL.] **—re·puls′er** *n.*

re·pul·sion (ri·pul′shən) *n.* **1** The act of repelling or repulsing, or the state of being repelled or repulsed. **2** Aversion; repugnance. **3** *Physics* The mutual action of two bodies which tends to drive them apart: opposed to *attraction.*

re·pul·sive (ri·pul′siv) *adj.* **1** Exciting such feelings, as of dislike, disgust, or horror, that one is repelled; grossly offensive; causing aversion. **2** Such as to forbid approach or familiarity; forbidding. **3** Acting by repulsion: *repulsive* forces. — **re·pul′sive·ly** *adv.* **—re·pul′sive·ness** *n.*

rep·u·ta·ble (rep′yə·tə·bəl) *adj.* **1** Having a good reputation; estimable; honorable. **2** Consistent with honorable standing; complying with the usage of the best writers and speakers. — **rep′u·ta·bil′i·ty** *n.* **—rep′u·ta·bly** *adv.*

rep·u·ta·tion (rep′yə·tā′shən) *n.* **1** The general estimation in which a person or thing is held by others, especially by a community; repute, either good or bad. **2** The state of being in high regard or esteem; good repute: to ruin one's *reputation.* **3** A particular credit or character ascribed to a person or thing: usually with *for*: a *reputation* for honesty. See synonyms under CHARACTER, FAME. [< L *reputatio, -onis* < *reputatus,* pp. of *reputare* be reputed. See REPUTE.]

re·pute (ri·pyo͞ot′) *v.t.* **·put·ed, ·put·ing** To regard or consider to be as specified; esteem: usually in the passive: They are *reputed* to be an intelligent people. *—n.* **1** Reputation, good or bad. **2** Public opinion; general report. [< L *reputare* reckon, be reputed < *re-* again + *putare* think, count]

re·put·ed (ri·pyo͞o′tid) *adj.* Generally thought or supposed; having a specified reputation. — **re·put′ed·ly** *adv.*

re·quest (ri·kwest′) *v.t.* **1** To express a desire for, especially politely; ask for; solicit. **2** To address a request to; ask: to *request* a person to do one a favor. See synonyms under ASK, DEMAND, PRAY. *—n.* **1** The act of requesting; entreaty; petition. **2** That which is asked for. **3** The state of being so esteemed as to be in demand; demand: in *request.* See synonyms under PETITION, PRAYER. *—adj.* Having been asked for; in response to a request: a *request* program. [< OF *requeste* < Med. L *requisita,* orig. fem. of L *requisitus,* pp. of *requirere* seek, again. See REQUIRE.]

re·qui·em (rē′kwē·əm, rek′wē-) *n.* **1** Any musical hymn, composition, or service for the dead. **2** *Often cap. Eccl.* In the Roman Catholic Church, a solemn mass sung for the repose of the souls of the dead, the **Requiem mass. 3** *Often cap.* A musical setting for such a mass; also a similar piece of music using different words. [< L *Requiem (aeternam dona eis, Domine)* rest (eternal give unto them, O Lord), the opening words of the introit of this mass]

req·ui·es·cat (rek′wē·es′kat) *n.* A prayer for the repose of a departed soul: the first word of the Latin petition **requiescat in pa·ce** (in pā′sē), may he rest in peace. Abbr. *R.I.P.* [<L]

re·quire (ri·kwīr′) *v.* **·quired, ·quir·ing** *v.t.* **1** To have need of; find necessary. **2** To demand authoritatively; insist upon: to *require* absolute silence. **3** To command; order: He *requires* us to be punctual. —*v.i.* **4** To make demand or request. See synonyms under ASK, DEMAND, DICTATE, MAKE. [<L *requirere* seek again, be in want of < *re-* again + *quaerere* ask, seek] —**re·quir′a·ble** *adj.* —**re·quir′er** *n.*

re·quire·ment (ri·kwīr′mənt) *n.* **1** That which is required; a requisite. **2** The act of requiring, or that which requires; a demand. See synonyms under NECESSITY, ORDER.

req·ui·site (rek′wə·zit) *adj.* Required by the nature of things or by circumstances; indispensable. See synonyms under NECESSARY. —*n.* That which cannot be dispensed with; a necessity; requirement. See synonyms under NECESSITY. [<L *requisitus*, pp. of *requirere*. See REQUEST.] —**req′ui·site·ly** *adv.* —**req′ui·site·ness** *n.*

req·ui·si·tion (rek′wə·zish′ən) *n.* **1** A formal request, summons, or demand, as by a government. **2** A necessity or requirement. **3** The state of being required. **4** A demand for the surrender of a fugitive from justice made by the governing official of one state or country upon another. —*v.t.* To make a requisition for or upon; demand or take upon requisition. [<L *requisitio*, *-onis* < *requisitus*, pp. of *requirere*. See REQUIRE.]

re·qui·tal (ri·kwīt′l) *n.* **1** The act of requiting. **2** That which requites; adequate return for good or ill; in the favorable sense, reward or compensation; in the unfavorable sense, retaliation. See synonyms under RECOMPENSE, REVENGE. [<REQUITE]

re·quite (ri·kwīt′) *v.t.* **·quit·ed, ·quit·ing** **1** To make equivalent return for, as kindness, service, or injury; make up for. **2** To make return to; compensate or repay in kind: Does she *requite* me for my love? **3** To give or do in return. [<RE- + *quite*, obs. var. of QUIT] —**re·quit′a·ble** *adj.* —**re·quit′er** *n.*

Synonyms: avenge, compensate, pay, punish, quit, reciprocate, recompense, remunerate, repay, retaliate, return, revenge, reward, satisfy. *Requite* is often used in the more general sense of *recompense* or *repay*, but always with the suggestion, at least, of the original idea of full equivalent. To *repay* or to *retaliate*, to *punish* or to *reward*, may be to make some return very inadequate to the benefit or injury received or the right or wrong done; but to *requite* is to make such return as to *quit* oneself of all obligation of favor or hostility, of punishment or reward. See PAY. *Antonyms*: absolve, acquit, excuse, forget, forgive, neglect, overlook, pardon, slight.

re–ra·di·a·tion (rē′rā′dē·ā′shən) *n.* **1** *Telecom.* The emission of one or more radio frequencies from the antenna of a radio receiver through improper oscillation of the tubes, with resulting confusion of signals. **2** *Physics* Secondary emission.

rere·dos (rir′dos) *n.* **1** An ornamental screen behind an altar. **2** The back of an open fire hearth; a fireback. **3** In old armor, a backplate. [<AF *areredos* <OF *arere* at the back (<L *ad* to + *retro* behind) + *dos* back <L *dorsum*]

rere·mouse (rir′mous) *n.* *pl.* **·mice** (-mīs) *Brit. Dial.* A bat: also spelled *rearmouse*. [OE *hreremūs*]

re·run (rē′run′) *n.* **1** A running over again or a second time. **2** The presenting of a motion picture after its original presentation. —*v.t.* (rē·run′) **·ran, ·run·ning** To run again.

Re·sa·ca (ri·sä′kə) A town of NW Georgia; scene of a Civil War battle, 1864.

Re·sa·ca de la Pal·ma (rā·sä′kä dā lä päl′mä) A locality in southern Texas north of Brownsville; scene of an American victory over the Mexicans, 1846.

res ad·ju·di·ca·ta (rēz a·jōō′də·kā′tə) See RES JUDICATA.

re·scind (ri·sind′) *v.t.* To make void, as an act; abrogate; repeal: to *rescind* a resolution. See synonyms under ANNUL, CANCEL. [<L *rescindere* < *re-* back + *scindere* cut] —**re·scind′a·ble** *adj.* —**re·scind′er** *n.*

re·scis·si·ble (ri·sis′ə·bəl) *adj.* Capable of being rescinded.

re·scis·sion (ri·sizh′ən) *n.* The act of rescinding or abrogating.

re·scis·so·ry (ri·sis′ər·ē, -siz′-) *adj.* Having power to rescind; rescinding; revoking. [<LL *rescissorius* <L *rescissus*, pp. of *rescindere*. See RESCIND.]

re·script (rē′skript) *n.* **1** In ancient Rome, an imperial decree, consisting of the emperor's answer to questions on matters of state or law. **2** Any decree, edict, order, or formal announcement, especially one made by a monarch or ruler. **3** A formal, written reply by the pope to a petition or question of morality or canon law submitted to him. **4** A facsimile; counterpart; something written over again. [<L *rescriptum* edict, orig. neut. pp. of *rescribere* write back (in reply) < *re-* again + *scribere* write]

res·cue (res′kyōō) *v.t.* **·cued, ·cu·ing** **1** To save or free from danger, captivity, evil, etc.; deliver. **2** *Law* To take or remove forcibly from the custody of the law. See synonyms under DELIVER, RECLAIM. —*n.* The act of rescuing; deliverance. [<OF *rescourre* <Med. L *rescutere* <L *re-* again + *excutere* shake off < *ex-* off, out + *quatere* shake. Related to QUASH.] —**res′cu·a·ble** *adj.* —**res′cu·er** *n.*

rescue grass A high bromegrass (*Bromus catharticus*), cultivated for hay. [Origin uncertain; perhaps confused with FESCUE]

re·search (ri·sûrch′, rē′sûrch) *n.* **1** Diligent, protracted investigation; studious inquiry. **2** A systematic investigation of some phenomenon or series of phenomena by the experimental method. See synonyms under INQUIRY. —*v.i.* To make research; investigate. [<F *recherche*] —**re·search′er** *n.*

re–search (rē·sûrch′) *v.t.* & *v.i.* To search again or anew.

re·seat (rē·sēt′) *v.t.* **1** To seat again. **2** To put a new seat or seats in or on.

ré·seau (rā·zō′) *n.* *pl.* **·seaux** (-zō′) **1** In textile work, a laceground composed of regular meshes; netground. **2** *Astron.* The small lines forming squares cut upon a glass plate: used in mapping out the heavens by photography. **3** A network. **4** *Meteorol.* A group of weather stations operating in the same territory or under common direction. **5** *Phot.* A sensitive filter screen for use in making color films. [<F, dim. of OF *roix* net <L *rete*]

re·sect (ri·sekt′) *v.t.* *Surg.* To cut or pare off: distinguished from *excise*. [<L *resectus*, pp. of *resecare* < *re-* back + *secare* cut, amputate]

re·sec·tion (ri·sek′shən) *n.* **1** A cutting or paring off. **2** *Surg.* The operation of cutting out part of a bone, organ, etc. **3** The determination of a position with reference to points of known location, whether on the ground or on a map or chart. [<L *resectio*, *-onis*]

re·se·da (ri·sē′də) *n.* **1** An herb of the mignonette family (genus *Reseda*). **2** A light or grayish green. [<L, prob. < *resedare* assuage; because once thought to be a sedative]

res·e·da·ceous (res′ə·dā′shəs) *adj.* *Bot.* Designating a family (*Resedaceae*) of annual or perennial herbs with alternate simple leaves and terminal spikes of small unsymmetrical flowers; the mignonette family. [<RESEDA + -ACEOUS]

re·sell (rē·sel′) *v.t.* **·sold, ·sell·ing** To sell anew or again. —**re·sell′er** *n.*

re·sem·blance (ri·zem′bləns) *n.* **1** The quality of similarity in nature, form, etc.; relative identity; likeness. **2** That which resembles; a semblance or likeness of a person or thing. **3** *Obs.* A characteristic quality or attribute. **4** *Obs.* Probability or likelihood. See synonyms under ANALOGY, APPROXIMATION, PICTURE. [<AF]

re·sem·ble (ri·zem′bəl) *v.t.* **·bled, ·bling** **1** To be similar to in appearance, quality, or character. **2** *Obs.* To compare; liken. See synonyms under IMITATE. [<OF *resembler* < *re-* again and again + *sembler* seem <L *simulare*. See SIMULATE.] —**re·sem′bler** *n.*

re·sent (ri·zent′) *v.t.* To feel or show resentment at; be indignant at, as an injury or insult. [<F *ressentir* feel the effects < *re-* again + *sentir* feel <L *sentire*]

re·sent·ful (ri·zent′fəl) *adj.* Disposed to resent; full of or characterized by resentment. See synonyms under MALICIOUS. —**re·sent′ful·ly** *adv.* —**re·sent′ful·ness** *n.*

re·sent·ment (ri·zent′mənt) *n.* Anger and ill will in view of real or fancied wrong or injury. See synonyms under ANGER, HATRED, OFFENSE, PIQUE.

re·ser·pine (ri·sûr′pēn, -pin, res′ər-) *n.* An ataractic drug prepared from alkaloids found in certain species of *Rauwolfia*, especially *R. serpentina*.

res·er·va·tion (rez′ər·vā′shən) *n.* **1** The act of reserving. **2** That which is reserved, kept back, or withheld. **3** The unexpressed qualification of a statement, promise, etc., that would, if uttered, so affect or alter its meaning for the person addressed as to vitiate its truth: also **mental reservation.** **4** Hence, any limitation. **5** A tract of government land reserved for the use and occupancy of an Indian tribe or for some other special purpose, as the preservation of forests, wild birds, etc. See synonyms under RESERVE. [<OF <LL *reservatio*, *-onis*]

re·serve (ri·zûrv′) *v.t.* **·served, ·serv·ing** **1** To hold back or set aside for special or future use; store up. **2** To keep as one's own; retain: He *reserves* that privilege for himself. **3** To arrange for ahead of time; have set aside for one's use: I *reserved* two tickets on the train. **4** To set aside (a portion of the consecrated elements of the Eucharist) for communion of the sick. See synonyms under RETAIN. —*n.* **1** That which is reserved; something stored up for future use, as in a reservoir; something set apart for a particular purpose; specifically, a reservation of land. **2** In banking, the amount of funds reserved from investment, in order promptly to meet regular or emergent demands. **3** The act of reserving; reservation. **4** The state of being reserved; silence as to one's feelings, opinions, or affairs; reticence; also, absence of exaggeration. **5** A fighting force held back from action to meet possible emergencies or demands. **6** That component of the armed forces of a nation composed of civilians trained for military service or assignment and subject to call to active duty in emergencies or under particular circumstances; specifically, *U.S.*, the **Army Reserve, Air Force Reserve, Naval Reserve, Marine Corps Reserve,** and **Coast Guard Reserve.** —*adj.* Held in reserve; constituting a reserve: a *reserve* supply of money. [<OF *reserver* <L *reservare* keep back < *re-* back + *servare* keep] —**re·serv′a·ble** *adj.* —**re·serv′er** *n.*

Synonyms (noun): backwardness, coldness, constraint, coyness, haughtiness, limitation, modesty, pride, reservation, reservedness, restraint, reticence, shyness, taciturnity. *Reserve* is the holding oneself aloof from others, or holding back one's feelings from expression, or one's affairs from communication to others; it may spring from *coldness* or *pride*, but is not identical with either and may arise from timidity or policy. See MODESTY.

reserve bank A member of the Federal Reserve System.

reserve clause In professional sports, the stipulation in a contract that commits a player to work for a particular team until released or traded by the employer or until retirement.

re·served (ri·zûrvd′) *adj.* **1** Showing or characterized by reserve of manner; distant; undemonstrative. **2** Retained; kept back. See synonyms under HAUGHTY, TACITURN. —**re·serv·ed·ly** (ri·zûr′vid·lē) *adv.* —**re·serv′ed·ness** *n.*

re·serv·ist (ri·zûr′vist) *n.* A member of the military reserve.

res·er·voir (rez′ər·vwôr, -vwär, -vôr) *n.* **1** A receptacle where some material, especially of a liquid or gas, may be kept in store. **2** A basin, either natural or artificial, for collecting and containing a supply of water, as for use in a city or for water power. **3** An attachment to a stove, machine, or instrument, for containing a fluid to be used in its operation: the *reservoir* of a lamp. **4** An

extra supply; a store of anything. [<F *réservoir*]

re·set (rē·set′) *v.t.* **·set, ·set·ting** To set again. — *n.* (rē′set′) The act of resetting, or that which is reset; specifically, a resetting of type. — **re·set′ter** *n.*

res ges·ta (rēz jes′tə) *pl.* **res ges·tae** (jes′tē) *Latin* **1** Anything done; a transaction. **2** *Usually pl.* All the essential circumstances attending a transaction.

resh (resh) *n.* The twentieth Hebrew letter. See ALPHABET. [<Hebrew *rēsh*, lit., the head]

re·ship (rē·ship′) *v.* **·shipped, ·ship·ping** *v.t.* **1** To ship again. **2** To transfer (oneself) to another vessel. — *v.i.* **3** To go on a vessel again. **4** To sign for another voyage as a crew member or a passenger.

re·ship·ment (rē·ship′mənt) *n.* **1** The act of reshipping. **2** The thing reshipped.

Resht (resht) A city in northern Iran, near the Caspian Sea.

re·side (ri·zīd′) *v.i.* **·sid·ed, ·sid·ing** **1** To dwell for a considerable time; make one's home; live. **2** To exist as an attribute or quality: with *in.* **3** To be vested: with *in.* See synonyms under ABIDE. [<F *résider* <L *residere* sit back, abide < *re-* back + *sedere* sit] — **re·sid′er** *n.*

res·i·dence (rez′ə·dəns) *n.* **1** The place or the house where one resides. **2** The act of residing. **3** Inherence in a thing, as of an attribute in a subject. **4** The fact of being officially present; the statutory presence of an incumbent in a benefice, as a bishop in his diocese: especially in the phrase **in residence:** the canon *in residence.* **5** The seat or place of power or government. **6** The length of time one resides in a place. See synonyms under HOME, HOUSE. [<OF <LL *residentia*]

res·i·den·cy (rez′ə·dən·sē) *n. pl.* **·cies** **1** Residence. **2** In the East Indies, the official abode of the representative of the governor general, as at a native court. **3** Formerly, a government division of the Dutch East Indies.

res·i·dent (rez′ə·dənt) *n.* **1** One who resides or dwells in a place. **2** A diplomatic representative residing at a foreign court or seat of government; specifically, a **minister resident,** a diplomatic agent of the third rank, accredited by the sovereign or head of one country to the sovereign or head of another country; also, an agent in a protectorate. — *adj.* **1** Having a residence; residing. **2** Abiding in a place in connection with one's official work: a *resident* physician. **3** Inherent: Pungency is *resident* in pepper. **4** Not migratory: said of certain birds. [<OF]

res·i·den·tial (rez′ə·den′shəl) *adj.* **1** Pertaining to, fitted for, or resulting from residence; having residence. **2** Used by residents.

res·i·den·ti·ar·y (rez′ə·den′shē·er′ē, -shər·ē) *adj.* **1** Having or maintaining a residence, especially an official residence. **2** Pertaining to residence. — *n. pl.* **·ar·ies** A resident.

re·sid·u·al (ri·zij′o͞o·əl) *adj.* **1** Pertaining to or having the nature of a residue or remainder. **2** Left over as a residue. — *n.* **1** That which is left over from a total mass, magnitude, or quantity which has been acted upon in any specified way; a remainder or remnant. **2** *Stat.* **a** The difference between observed results and those obtained by computation according to formula. **b** The difference between the value of a given observation and the mean of a series to which it belongs. **3** *Often pl.* A payment made to a performer for each rerun of taped or filmed television material in which he or she has appeared. — **re·sid′u·al·ly** *adv.*

re·sid·u·ar·y (ri·zij′o͞o·er′ē) *adj.* Of or pertaining to a residuum or remainder; residual.

res·i·due (rez′ə·do͞o, -dyo͞o) *n.* **1** A remainder or surplus after a part has been separated or otherwise treated. **2** *Chem.* **a** Insoluble matter left after filtration or separation from a liquid. **b** An atom or radical separated from a molecule of a substance. **c** A residuum. **3** *Law* That portion of an estate which remains after all charges, debts, and particular bequests have been satisfied. [<OF *residu* <L *residuum,* neut. of *residuus* remaining < *residere.* See RESIDE.]

re·sid·u·um (ri·zij′o͞o·əm) *n. pl.* **·u·a** (-o͞o·ə) **1** That which remains after any process of subtraction; a residue. **2** *Chem.* A residual product: the *residuum* from the distillation of coal tar. **3** Residue (def. 3). [<L]

re·sign (ri·zīn′) *v.t.* **1** To give up, as a position, office, or trust. **2** To relinquish (a privilege, claim, etc.). **3** To give over (oneself, one's mind, etc.), as to fate or domination. — *v.i.* **4** To resign a position, etc. See synonyms under ABANDON. [<OF *resigner* <L *resignare* sign back, transfer, cancel < *re-* back + *signare* sign] — **re·sign′er** *n.*

re–sign (rē·sīn′) *v.t.* To sign again.

res·ig·na·tion (rez′ig·nā′shən) *n.* **1** The act of resigning, as a position, office, or trust, or the formal document declaring such act. **2** The quality of being submissive; unresisting acquiescence. See synonyms under PATIENCE, SUBMISSION. [<F *résignation*]

re·signed (ri·zīnd′) *adj.* Characterized by resignation; submissive. — **re·sign·ed·ly,** (ri·zī′nid·lē) *adv.* — **re·sign′ed·ness** *n.*

re·sile (ri·zīl′) *v.i.* **·siled, ·sil·ing** **1** To spring back; recoil. **2** To resume original shape or position after being stretched or compressed. [<MF *resiler* <L *resilire* rebound < *re-* back + *salire* leap]

re·sil·ience (ri·zil′yəns) *n.* **1** The act or power of springing back to a former position or shape; elasticity. **2** *Physics* The quantity of work given back by a body that is compressed to a certain limit and then allowed freely to recover its former size or shape. Also **re·sil′·ien·cy.**

re·sil·ient (ri·zil′yənt) *adj.* **1** Springing back to a former shape or position. **2** Capable of recoiling from pressure or shock unchanged or undamaged. **3** Elastic; buoyant. [<L *resiliens, -entis,* ppr. of *resilire.* See RESILE.] — **re·sil′ient·ly** *adv.*

res·in (rez′in) *n.* **1** An amorphous organic substance exuded from plants, especially from fir or pine trees, yellowish or dark in color and usually translucent or transparent: it is soluble in alcohol and ether, and is a non-conductor of electricity. **2** Any of various substances made by chemical synthesis, especially those used in the making of plastics. **3** The resinous precipitate obtained from a vegetable tincture by treatment with water: used in pharmacy. **4** Rosin. — *v.t.* To apply resin to. [<OF *resine* <L *resina* <Gk. *rhētinē*] — **res·i·na·ceous** (rez′ə·nā′shəs) *adj.*

res·in·ate (rez′ən·āt) *v.t.* **·at·ed, ·at·ing** To infuse or impregnate with resin.

res·in·if·er·ous (rez′ən·if′ər·əs) *adj.* Producing resin.

res·in·og·ra·phy (rez′ən·og′rə·fē) *n.* The microscopic study of the etched or polished surfaces of synthetic resins in order to identify the pigments, fillers, or other substances composing them. — **res′in·og′ra·pher** *n.*

res·in·oid (rez′ən·oid) *adj.* Resembling resin. — *n.* **1** A substance either wholly or partially of a resinous nature. **2** Any of a class of thermosetting synthetic resins.

res·i·nous (rez′ə·nəs) *adj.* **1** Of the nature of resins, or containing more or less resin as an ingredient. **2** Obtained from resin: *resinous* electricity; electronegative.

res·in·y (rez′ən·ē) *adj.* Resinous.

re·sist (ri·zist′) *v.t.* **1** To strive against; act counter to for the purpose of stopping, preventing, defeating, etc. **2** To be proof against; withstand; defeat. **3** To refrain from: I can't *resist* teasing him. — *v.i.* **4** To offer opposition. See synonyms under DRIVE, HINDER, OPPOSE, REPEL. — *n.* Any substance used to prevent the action of another substance, as a coating applied to a surface to protect it from an acid. [<OF *resister* <L *resistere* cause to stand back < *re-* back + *sistere,* causative of *stare* stand] — **re·sist′er** *n.*

re·sis·tance (ri·zis′təns) *n.* **1** The act of resisting. **2** Any force tending to hinder motion. **3** *Electr.* **a** The opposition offered by a body to the passage through it of an electric current: expressed in ohms: the reciprocal of *conductance.* **b** Impedance. **4** *Psychol.* The force tending to prevent the return to consciousness of unpleasant incidents and experiences. **5** The underground and guerrilla movement opposing an occupying power. See synonyms under DEFENSE. [<F *résistance*]

re·sis·tant (ri·zis′tənt) *adj.* Offering or tending to produce resistance; resisting. — *n.* One who or that which resists. [<F *résistant*]

Re·sis·ten·cia (rā′sēs·ten′syä) The capital of Chaco province, northern Argentina.

re·sist·i·ble (ri·zis′tə·bəl) *adj.* Capable of being resisted. — **re·sist′i·bil′i·ty** *n.* — **re·sist′i·bly** *adv.*

re·sis·tive (ri·zis′tiv) *adj.* Having or exercising the power of resistance. — **re·sis′tive·ly** *adv.*

re·sis·tiv·i·ty (rē′zis·tiv′ə·tē) *n.* **1** The capacity to resist, or the degree of that capacity. **2** *Electr.* Specific resistance to the electric or magnetic force of a substance as tested in a cube measuring one centimeter: the reciprocal of *conductivity.*

re·sist·less (ri·zist′lis) *adj.* **1** Irresistible. **2** Offering no resistance; powerless. — **re·sist′·less·ly** *adv.* — **re·sist′less·ness** *n.*

re·sis·tor (ri·zis′tər) *n. Electr.* A device, as a coil of wire, for introducing resistance into an electrical circuit.

res ju·di·ca·ta (rēz jo͞o′də·kā′tə) *Latin* Literally, a matter decided; an issue or point of law that has been previously decided by a court of authoritative or competent jurisdiction and which when pleaded is conclusive of the matter in controversy. Also *res adjudicata.*

re·sole (rē·sōl′) *v.t.* **·soled, ·sol·ing** To sole again.

res·o·lu·ble (rez′ə·lo͝o·bəl, ri·zol′yə·bəl) *adj.* Capable of being resolved; soluble. [<LL *resolubilis*] — **res′o·lu·bil′i·ty, res′o·lu·ble·ness** *n.*

res·o·lute (rez′ə·lo͞ot) *adj.* Having a fixed purpose; determined; constant; steady; also, bold; unflinching. See synonyms under FIRM, INFLEXIBLE, OBSTINATE. [<L *resolutus,* pp. of *resolvere.* See RESOLVE.] — **res′o·lute·ly** *adv.* — **res′o·lute·ness** *n.*

res·o·lu·tion (rez′ə·lo͞o′shən) *n.* **1** The act of resolving or of reducing to a simpler form. **2** The state of being resolute; active fortitude; resoluteness. **3** The making of a resolve; also, the purpose or course resolved upon; a resolve; determination. **4** Chemical, mechanical, or mental analysis; separation of anything into component parts. **5** A proposition offered to or adopted by an assembly. **6** *Law* A judgment or decision of a court. **7** *Med.* The termination of an abnormal condition. **8** *Music* **a** The replacement of a dissonant tone or chord by a higher or lower one so that a consonance, or, sometimes, another dissonance occurs. **b** The tone or chord replacing the original dissonant tone or chord. See synonyms under COURAGE, DETERMINATION, FORTITUDE, PURPOSE, PERSEVERANCE, WILL. — **concurrent resolution** A resolution adopted by both of the houses of Congress and having the force of law without the signature of the President. — **joint resolution** A resolution which, when passed by both houses of Congress and approved by the President, has the force of law. [<L *resolutio, -onis* < *resolutus.* See RESOLUTE.] — **res′o·lu′tion·er, res′o·lu′·tion·ist** *n.*

re·solv·a·ble (ri·zol′və·bəl) *adj.* Capable of being resolved, analyzed, or solved. — **re·solv′a·bil′i·ty, re·solv′a·ble·ness** *n.*

re·solve (ri·zolv′) *v.* **·solved, ·solv·ing** *v.t.* **1** To decide; determine (to do something). **2** To cause to decide or determine. **3** To separate or break down into constituent parts; analyze. **4** To make clear; explain or solve, as a problem. **5** To explain away; remove (doubts, etc.). **6** To state or decide by vote, as in a legislative assembly. **7** To transform; convert: He *resolves* his anger into pride. **8** *Music* To change, as a chord, from dissonance to consonance; cause to undergo resolution. **9** *Chem.* To separate (a racemic compound) into its optically active components. **10** *Optics* To make distinguishable the structure or parts of. **11** *Med.* To cause to disperse or be absorbed without the formation of pus. **12** *Obs.* To melt; dissolve. **13** *Obs.* To inform. — *v.i.* **14** To make up one's mind; arrive at a decision: with *on* or *upon.* **15** To become separated into constituent parts. **16** *Music* To undergo resolution. — *n.* **1** Fixity of purpose; resolution. **2** A fixed determination; a resolution. **3** The action of a deliberative body expressing formally its intention or purpose. See synonyms under DETERMINATION, PURPOSE. [<L *resolvere* loosen again, relax < *re-* again + *solvere* loosen] — **re·solv′er** *n.*

re·solved (ri·zolvd′) *adj.* Fixed or set in purpose; determined; also, having formed a resolve. See synonyms under OBSTINATE. — **re·solv·ed·ly** (ri·zol′vid·lē) *adv.*

re·solv·ent (ri·zol′vənt) *adj.* Having the power to cause the dissolution or resolution of a thing into its elements; solvent. — *n.* **1** That

which has the power of resolving or dissolving; a solvent. 2 *Med.* A preparation which has the property of reducing or dispersing a swelling. [<L *resolvens, -entis,* ppr. of *resolvere.* See RESOLVE.]

res·o·nance (rez′ə·nəns) *n.* 1 The state or quality of being resonant; resonant sound. 2 *Physics* **a** The phenomenon exhibited by any vibratory system responding with large amplitude to a series of imposed vibrations of equal, or nearly equal, frequency. **b** That property of a molecule by virtue of which it assumes an electronic structure intermediate between two other theoretically possible structures. **c** The prolongation and amplification of sound by reverberation within a cavity. 3 *Electr.* The condition of an electric circuit in which maximum flow of current is obtained by impressing an electromotive force of given frequency. [<L *resonantia* echo]

res·o·nant (rez′ə·nənt) *adj.* 1 Sending back or having the quality of sending back or prolonging sound. 2 Resounding; specifically, having resonance. [<L *resonans, -antis,* ppr. of *resonare* resound, echo < *re-* back, again + *sonare* sound] —**res′o·nant·ly** *adv.*

res·o·nate (rez′ə·nāt) *v.i.* **·nat·ed, ·nat·ing** 1 To have or produce resonance. 2 To manifest sympathetic vibration, as a resonator. [<L *resonatus,* pp. of *resonare.* See RESONANT.]

res·o·na·tor (rez′ə·nā′tər) *n.* 1 That which resounds. 2 *Electronics* Any device used to exhibit or utilize the effects of resonance. 3 *Physics* A set or cluster of electrons which absorbs electromagnetic waves of certain frequencies. [<NL]

re·sorb (ri·sôrb′) *v.t.* To reabsorb. [<L *resorbere* drink in again, suck back < *re-* back, again + *sorbere* drink in, suck up] —**re·sorp·tion** (ri·sôrp′shən) *n.*

re·sor·cin·ol (ri·zôr′sin·ōl, -ol) *n. Chem.* A colorless crystalline compound, $C_6H_6O_2$, of peculiar odor and sweetish taste, used as an antiseptic and in the treatment of skin eruptions. Also **re·sor′cin.** [<RES(IN) + ORCINOL] —**re·sor′cin·al** *adj.*

re·sort (ri·zôrt′) *v.i.* 1 To go frequently or habitually; repair. 2 To have recourse; apply or betake oneself for relief or aid: with *to.* —*n.* 1 The act of frequenting a place. 2 A place resorted to or frequented to regain health, or for amusement or entertainment. 3 The use of something as a means; a recourse; refuge. [<OF *resortir* < *re-* again + *sortir* go out] —**re·sort′er** *n.*

re·sound (ri·zound′) *v.i.* 1 To be filled with sound; echo; reverberate. 2 To make a loud, prolonged, or echoing sound. 3 To ring; echo: said of sounds. 4 *Poetic* To be famed or extolled. —*v.t.* 5 To give back (a sound, etc.); re-echo. 6 *Poetic* To celebrate; extol. 7 *Rare* To utter or repeat loudly. See synonyms under ROAR. [<OF *resoner* <L *resonare.* See RESONANT.]

re-sound (rē·sound′) *v.t.* & *v.i.* To sound again.

re·source (ri·sôrs′, -sōrs′, rē′sôrs, -sōrs) *n.* 1 That which is resorted to for aid or support; resort. 2 *pl.* Available means or property; a supply that can be drawn on; any natural advantages or products: natural *resources.* 3 Capacity for finding or adapting means; power of achievement. 4 Fertility in expedients; resourcefulness; skill or ingenuity in meeting any situation. See synonyms under ALTERNATIVE, PROPERTY. [<OF *ressource* < *resourdre* rise again < *re-* (<L *re-*) back + *sourdre* <L *surgere* rise, surge]

re·source·ful (ri·sôrs′fəl, -sōrs′-) *adj.* 1 Fertile in resources or expedients. 2 Full of resources. —**re·source′ful·ly** *adv.* —**re·source′ful·ness** *n.*

re·spect (ri·spekt′) *v.t.* 1 To have deferential regard for; esteem. 2 To treat with propriety or consideration. 3 To regard as inviolable; avoid intruding upon. 4 To have relation or reference to; concern. See synonyms under ADMIRE, DEFER, VENERATE. —*n.* 1 A just regard for and appreciation of worth; honor and esteem: I have great *respect* for the man. 2 Demeanor or deportment indicating deference; courteous regard: to have *respect* for one's elders. 3 *pl.* Expressions of consideration or esteem; compliments: to pay one's *respects.* 4 Conformity to duty or obligation; compliance or observance: *respect* for the law. 5 The condition of being honored or respected: He is held in *respect* by his colleagues. 6 A specific aspect or feature; detail: In what *respect* is he wanting? 7 Reference or relation: usually with *to*: with *respect* to profits. 8 Undue inclination or bias of mind: to have *respect* of persons. 9 *Obs.* Consideration. [<L *respectare* < *respectus,* pp. of *respicere* look back, consider < *re-* again + *specere* look]

re·spect·a·bil·i·ty (ri·spek′tə·bil′ə·tē) *n. pl.* **·ties** 1 The characteristic or quality of being respectable; fair social standing; good repute. 2 The respectable people of a community, collectively. 3 *pl.* Certain conventions and other features of conduct presumed to be signs of gentility, social position, morality, etc. Also **re·spect′a·ble·ness.**

re·spect·a·ble (ri·spek′tə·bəl) *adj.* 1 Deserving of respect; being of good name or repute; also, respected. 2 Being of moderate excellence; fairly good; considerable in number, quantity, size, quality, etc.; average. 3 Having a good appearance; presentable. 4 Conventionally correct or socially acceptable in conduct; of decent character. —**re·spect′a·bly** *adv.*

re·spect·er (ri·spek′tər) *n.* One who respects, usually one who respects persons: often in the phrase **respecter of persons,** one who shows favoritism or is influenced in his opinions or actions by others.

re·spect·ful (ri·spekt′fəl) *adj.* Marked by or manifesting respect; deferential. —**re·spect′ful·ly** *adv.* —**re·spect′ful·ness** *n.*

re·spect·ing (ri·spek′ting) *prep.* In relation to; regarding.

re·spec·tive (ri·spek′tiv) *adj.* 1 Pertaining or relating severally to each of those under consideration; several; particular. 2 *Obs.* Characterized by partiality. 3 *Obs.* Attentive.

re·spec·tive·ly (ri·spek′tiv·lē) *adv.* As singly or severally considered; singly in the order designated: The first, second, and third seats belong to John, James, and William *respectively.*

re·spell (rē·spel′) *v.t.* To spell again, especially in a system whereby pronunciation is indicated. —**re·spell′ing** *n.*

Re·spi·ghi (rā·spē′gē), **Ottorino,** 1879–1936, Italian composer.

re·spir·a·ble (ri·spīr′ə·bəl, res′pər·ə·bəl) *adj.* 1 Capable of being respired or breathed; fit for respiration. 2 Able to breathe or respire. [<F]

res·pi·ra·tion (res′pə·rā′shən) *n.* 1 The act of inhaling air into the lungs and expelling it; breathing. 2 The process by which a plant or animal takes in oxygen from the air and gives off carbon dioxide and other products of oxidation in the tissues. [<L *respiratio, -onis*]

res·pi·ra·tor (res′pə·rā′tər) *n.* 1 A screen, as of fine gauze, worn over the mouth or nose, as a protection against dust, etc. 2 A device worn over the nose and mouth for the inhalation of medicated vapors, or to warm or sift the air for lung patients. 3 A gas mask. 4 An apparatus for artificial respiration, as a Pulmotor. [<L *respiratus,* pp. of *respirare.* See RESPIRE.]

respirator cabinet An iron lung.

re·spir·a·to·ry (ri·spīr′ə·tôr′ē, -tō′rē, res′pər·ə-) *adj.* Of, pertaining to, employed in, or caused by respiration.

re·spire (ri·spīr′) *v.* **·spired, ·spir·ing** *v.i.* 1 To inhale and exhale air; breathe. 2 To breathe again; recover vitality, hope, ambition, courage, etc. —*v.t.* 3 To inhale and exhale; breathe. 4 *Rare* To breathe or give forth; exhale. [<F *respirer* <L *respirare* < *re-* again + *spirare* breathe]

res·pite (res′pit) *n.* 1 Postponement; delay. 2 Temporary intermission of labor or effort; an interval of rest. 3 *Law* Temporary suspension of the execution of a sentence for a capital offense; reprieve. —*v.t.* **·pit·ed, ·pit·ing** 1 To relieve by a pause or rest. 2 To grant delay in the execution of (a penalty, sentence, etc.). 3 To put off or postpone. [<OF *respit* <Med. L *respectus* delay <L, consideration, regard < *respicere.* See RESPECT.]

Synonyms (noun): delay, forbearance, interval, pause, postponement, reprieve, rest, stay. *Antonyms*: accomplishment, completion, consummation, effect, execution, operation, performance.

re·splen·dence (ri·splen′dəns) *n.* The state or quality of being resplendent; brilliant luster; splendor. Also **re·splen′den·cy.**

re·splen·dent (ri·splen′dənt) *adj.* Shining with brilliant luster; vividly bright; splendid; gorgeous. See synonyms under BRIGHT. [<L *resplendens, -entis,* ppr. of *resplendere* glitter < *re-* again and again + *splendere* shine] —**re·splen′dent·ly** *adv.*

re·spond (ri·spond′) *v.i.* 1 To give an answer; reply. 2 To act in reply or return. 3 *Law* To be liable or answerable. —*v.t.* 4 To say in answer; reply. —*n. Archit.* A pilaster, semi column, or similar feature placed against a wall, to receive an arch. [<L *respondere* give back in return < *re-* back + *spondere* pledge, promise] —**re·spond′er** *n.*

re·spon·dence (ri·spon′dəns) *n.* 1 The character or condition of being respondent. 2 The act of responding. 3 Agreement. Also **re·spon′den·cy.**

re·spon·dent (ri·spon′dənt) *adj.* 1 Giving response, or given as a response; answering; responsive. 2 *Law* Occupying the position of defendant. 3 *Obs.* Correspondent. —*n.* 1 One who responds or answers. 2 *Law* The party called upon to answer an appeal or petition; a defendant; especially, the defendant in a suit in equity, admiralty, or divorce. [<L *respondens, -entis,* ppr. of *respondere.* See RESPOND.]

re·sponse (ri·spons′) *n.* 1 The act of responding, or that which is responded; words or acts evoked by the words or acts of another or others; an answer; reply. 2 *Eccl.* A portion of a liturgy or church service said or sung by the congregation or choir in reply to the officiating priest; also, an anthem sung or said during or after a reading. 3 *Biol.* The action of an organism or a part, or the cessation of action, resulting from a stimulus or influence; a reaction. [<OF <L *responsum,* neut. of pp. of *respondere.* See RESPOND.]

Synonyms: answer, rejoinder, repartee, reply, retort. A *rejoinder* is strictly an *answer* to a *reply,* while often used in the general sense of *answer,* but always with the implication of something more or less controversial or opposed, yet lacking the conclusiveness implied in *answer.* A *response* is accordant or harmonious, designed or adapted to carry on the thought of the words that called it forth, or to meet the wish of him who seeks it; as, The appeal for aid met a prompt and hearty *response. Repartee* is a prompt, witty, and commonly good-natured *answer* to some argument or attack; a *retort* may also be witty, but is severe and may be even savage in its intensity. See ANSWER.

re·spon·ser (ri·spon′sər) *n. Electronics* The receiving element connected with the transponder of an interrogator assembly. Also **re·spon′sor.**

re·spon·si·bil·i·ty (ri·spon′sə·bil′ə·tē) *n. pl.* **·ties** 1 The state of being responsible or accountable. 2 That for which one is answerable; a duty or trust. 3 Ability to meet obligations or to act without superior authority or guidance. See synonyms under DUTY. Also **re·spon′si·ble·ness.**

re·spon·si·ble (ri·spon′sə·bəl) *adj.* 1 Answerable legally or morally for the discharge of a duty, trust, or debt. 2 Having capacity to perceive the distinctions of right and wrong; having ethical discrimination. 3 Able to meet legitimate claims; having sufficient property or means for the payment of debts. 4 Involving accountability or obligation. 5 Denoting the status of a cabinet or ministry with respect to the legislative body to which it is answerable. [< obs. F *responsible* <L *responsus,* pp. of *respondere.* See RESPOND.] —**re·spon′si·bly** *adv.*

re·spon·sion (ri·spon′shən) *n.* 1 *Rare* A response; reply. 2 *pl.* At Oxford University, the first of the three examinations to be passed

by a candidate for a B.A. degree. [<L *responsio, -onis*]

re·spon·sive (ri·spon′siv) *adj.* **1** Inclined or ready to respond; being or reacting in accord, sympathy, or harmony; responding. **2** Constituting, or of the nature of, response or reply. **3** Characterized by or containing responses. **4** *Obs.* Correspondent. — **re·spon′sive·ly** *adv.* — **re·spon′sive·ness** *n.*

re·spon·so·ry (ri·spon′sər·ē) *adj. Obs.* Of or pertaining to response; containing answer; responsive. — *n. pl.* **·ries** *Eccl.* **1** A response sung between readings. **2** A response of the people or congregation to the officiating priest or clergyman. [<Med. L *responsorium*]

res pub·li·ca (rēz pub′li·kə) *pl.* **res pub·li·cae** (pub′li·sē) *Latin* **1** The commonwealth. **2** *pl.* Things that belong to the state.

rest[1] (rest) *v.i.* **1** To cease working, exerting oneself, etc., so as to refresh oneself. **2** To cease from effort or activity for a time. **3** To seek or obtain ease or refreshment by lying down, sleeping, etc. **4** To sleep. **5** To be at peace; be tranquil. **6** To lie in death; be dead. **7** To remain unchanged: And there the matter *rests.* **8** To be supported; stand, lean, lie, or sit: with *against, on,* or *upon.* **9** To be founded or based: with *on* or *upon.* **10** To rely; depend: with *on* or *upon*: Our hopes *rest* on you. **11** To be placed as a burden or responsibility: with *on* or *upon.* **12** To be or lie in a specified place: The blame *rests* with me. **13** To be directed; remain on something, as the gaze or eyes. **14** *Law* To cease presenting evidence in a case. **15** *Agric.* To lie fallow. — *v.t.* **16** To give rest to; refresh by rest. **17** To put, lay, lean, etc., as for support or rest. **18** To found; base. **19** To direct (the gaze, eyes, etc.). **20** *Law* To cease presenting evidence in (a case). — *n.* **1** The act or state of resting; cessation from labor, exertion, action, or motion of any kind; repose; quiet. **2** Freedom from disturbance or disquiet; peace; tranquillity. **3** Sleep; also, death. **4** That on which anything rests; a support; base; basis; foundation; specifically, in billiards and pool, a support for a cue; a bridge. **5** A place of repose or quiet; a stopping place; abode. **6** *Music* **a** A pause, or an interval of silence. **b** A character indicating such pause: an eighth *rest.* **7** In prosody, a pause in a verse; a caesura. **8** *Obs.* Restored or renewed strength. **9** *Mil.* A command given troops, allowing them to relax. ◆ Homophone: *wrest.* [OE *restan*] — **rest′er** *n.*

Synonyms: (*verb*): abide, acquiesce, cease, desist, halt, hold, lean, lie, pause, recline, repose, sleep, slumber, stand, stay, stop, unbend. See ABIDE, LEAN[1]. *Antonyms*: contend, fight, labor, strive, struggle, toil, wake, watch, work.

Synonyms (noun): calm, calmness, cessation, ease, pause, peace, peacefulness, quiescence, quiet, quietness, quietude, recreation, repose, sleep, slumber, stay, stillness, stop, tranquillity. *Ease* denotes freedom from cause of disturbance, whether external or internal. *Quiet* denotes freedom from agitation, or especially from annoying sounds. *Rest* is a *cessation* of activity, especially of wearying or painful activity. *Recreation* is some pleasing activity of certain organs or faculties that affords *rest* to other parts of our nature that have become weary. *Repose* is a laying down, primarily of the body, and figuratively, a relaxing freedom from toil or strain of mind. *Sleep* is the perfection of *repose,* the most complete *rest*; *slumber* is a light and ordinarily pleasant form of *sleep.* See REMAINDER, RESPITE. *Antonyms*: agitation, commotion, disquiet, disturbance, excitement, motion, movement, restlessness, stir, strain, toil, tumult, unrest, work.

rest[2] (rest) *n.* **1** That which remains or is left over; a remainder. **2** Those remaining or not enumerated; the others: in this sense a collective noun taking a plural verb. **3** A balance, as of resources. — *v.i.* **1** To be and remain; continue; stay: *Rest* content. **2** *Obs.* To be left: Nothing *rests* but hope. — *v.t.* **3** *Obs.* To cause to remain: God *rest* you well. ◆ Homophone: *wrest.* [<OF *reste* < *rester* remain <L *restare* stop, stand < *re-* again + *stare* stand]

rest[3] (rest) *n.* A support for a lance attached to medieval armor: an aphetic form of *arrest.* ◆ Homophone: *wrest.*

re·state (rē·stāt′) *v.t.* **·stat·ed, ·stat·ing** To state again or anew. — **re·state′ment** *n.*

res·tau·rant (res′tər·ənt, -tə·ränt) *n.* A place where refreshments or meals are provided; a public dining-room. [<F, lit., restoring, ppr. of *restaurer* <OF *restorer.* See RESTORE.]

res·tau·ra·teur (res′tər·ə·tûr′, *Fr.* res·tō·rȧ·tœr′) *n.* The proprietor or keeper of a restaurant. [<F]

rest–balk (rest′bôk′) *n. Agric.* An unplowed ridge between furrows.

rest cure A treatment, as of nervous disorders, prescribing seclusion and quiet, generous diet, massage, etc.

rest·ful (rest′fəl) *adj.* **1** Full of or giving rest; affording freedom from disturbance, work, or trouble. **2** Being at rest or in repose; quiet. — **rest′ful·ly** *adv.* — **rest′ful·ness** *n.*

rest·har·row (rest′har′ō) *n.* A low European undershrub (*Ononis hircina*) of the bean family, with pink and white flowers. [Aphetic form of ARREST + HARROW; from the resistance offered by its tough roots]

res·ti·form (res′tə·fôrm) *adj. Anat.* Ropelike; twisted, as the **restiform bodies,** ropelike bundles of nerve fibers of the medulla oblongata that pass upward to the cerebellum. [<L *restis* cord + -FORM]

rest·ing (res′ting) *adj.* **1** At rest; reposing; also, dead. **2** Dormant.

resting spore *Bot.* A spore that germinates only after a lapse of a number of weeks or months, or at the end of the winter season.

res·ti·tu·tion (res′tə·tōō′shən, -tyōō′-) *n.* **1** The act of restoring something that has been taken away or lost. **2** The act of making good or rendering an equivalent for injury or loss; indemnification. **3** Restoration to, return to, or recovery of a former position or condition. **4** *Physics* The property of elastic bodies by which they tend to recover their shape after compression. **5** Establishment of the true nature or position of objects distorted in an aerial photograph. [<OF <L *restitutio, -onis* < *restitutus,* pp. of *restituere* restore, set up again < *re-* again + *statuere* set up]

Synonyms: amends, compensation, indemnification, indemnity, recompense, remuneration, reparation, repayment, restoration, return. *Antonyms*: cheat, cheating, defrauding, embezzlement, extortion, fraud, plunder, robbery, stealing, theft.

res·tive (res′tiv) *adj.* **1** Impatient of control; unruly. **2** Restless; fidgety; also, stubborn; balky. [<F *restif* < *rester* remain, balk <L *restare.* See REST[2].] — **res′tive·ly** *adv.* — **res′tive·ness** *n.*

Synonyms: fidgety, fractious, fretful, frisky, impatient, intractable, mutinous, rebellious, refractory, restless, skittish, unruly, vicious. The disposition to offer active resistance to control by any means whatever is what is commonly indicated by *restive.* A horse may be made *restless* by flies or by martial music, but with no refractoriness; the *restive* animal impatiently resists or struggles to break from control, as by bolting, flinging his rider, or otherwise. With this the metaphorical use of the word agrees, which is always in the sense of such terms as *impatient, intractable, rebellious,* and the like; a people *restive* under despotism are not disposed to "rest" under it, but to resist it and fling it off. *Antonyms*: docile, gentle, manageable, obedient, peaceable, quiet, submissive, tractable, yielding.

rest·less (rest′lis) *adj.* **1** Having no rest; never quiet; unresting: the *restless* waves. **2** Unable or disinclined to rest. **3** Uneasy; constantly seeking change. **4** Discontented. **5** Devoid of or destructive to rest or repose; obtaining no rest or sleep; sleepless. See synonyms under ACTIVE. — **rest′less·ly** *adv.* — **rest′less·ness** *n.*

re·stock (rē·stok′) *v.t.* To stock again or anew.

res·to·ra·tion (res′tə·rā′shən) *n.* **1** The act of restoring a person or thing to a former place or condition. **2** The state of being restored; rehabilitation; renewal. **3** The bringing back of a building or work of art as nearly as may be to its original state; also, the restored building or object. **4** *Paleontol.* The reconstruction of the skeleton of a fossil animal. **5** *Theol.* The doctrine that all men will eventually be restored to a sinless state and divine favor. See UNIVERSALISM. — **the Restoration** **1** The return of Charles II to the English throne in 1660, after the overthrow of the Cromwellian Protectorate; also, the following period until 1685. **2** The return of the Bourbons to power in 1814 under Louis XVIII; also, the period following the return. **3** The return of the Jews to Palestine after the Babylonian captivity. [<OF *restauration* <LL *restauratio, -onis* <L *restauratus,* pp. of *restaurare.* See RESTORE.]

re·sto·ra·tive (ri·stôr′ə·tiv, -stō′rə-) *adj.* **1** Tending or able to restore. **2** Pertaining to restoration. — *n.* That which restores; specifically, something to restore consciousness after a fainting fit.

re·store (ri·stôr′, -stōr′) *v.t.* **·stored, ·stor·ing** **1** To bring into existence or effect again: to *restore* peace. **2** To bring back to a former or original condition, appearance, etc.: to *restore* a great painting. **3** To put back in a former place or position; reinstate, as a deposed monarch. **4** To bring back to health and vigor. **5** To give back (something lost or taken away); return. See synonyms under RECLAIM, RECOVER. [<OF *restorer* <L *restaurare* < *re-* again + *-staurare* make firm, as in *instaurare* repair] — **re·stor′er** *n.*

re–store (rē·stôr′, -stōr′) *v.t.* **–stored, –stor·ing** To store again or anew.

re·strain (ri·strān′) *v.t.* **1** To hold back from acting, proceeding, or advancing; keep in check; repress. **2** To deprive of freedom or liberty, as by placing in a prison or asylum. **3** To restrict or limit. [<OF *restraindre, restreindre* <L *restringere* < *re-* back + *stringere* draw tight] — **re·strain′a·ble** *adj.* — **re·strain′ed·ly** *adv.*

Synonyms: abridge, bridle, check, circumscribe, confine, constrain, curb, hinder, hold, keep, repress, restrict, suppress. *Constrain* is positive; *restrain* is negative; one is *constrained* to an action; he is *restrained* from an action. *Constrain* refers almost exclusively to moral force, *restrain* frequently to physical force, as when we speak of putting one under restraint. To *restrain* an action is to hold it partially or wholly in check, thus controlling it even in performance; to *restrict* an action is to fix a limit or boundary which it may not pass, but within which it is free. To *repress,* literally to press back, is to hold in check, and perhaps only temporarily, that which is still very active; it is a feebler word than *restrain*; to *suppress* is finally and effectually to put down; *suppress* is a much stronger word than *restrain*; as, to *suppress* a rebellion. See ARREST, BIND, GOVERN, KEEP, LIMIT, REFRAIN, REPRESS, TEMPER. *Antonyms*: aid, animate, arouse, emancipate, encourage, excite, free, impel, incite, release.

re·strain·er (ri·strā′nər) *n.* **1** One who or that which restrains. **2** *Phot.* A chemical agent used to retard the action of the developer.

re·straint (ri·strānt′) *n.* **1** The act of restraining. **2** The state of being restrained; abridgment of liberty; confinement. **3** That which restrains; a restriction. **4** Self–repression; constraint. See synonyms under BARRIER, RESERVE. [<OF *restrainte,* noun use of pp. of *restraindre.* See RESTRAIN.]

re·strict (ri·strikt′) *v.t.* To hold or keep within limits or bounds; confine. See synonyms under BIND, CIRCUMSCRIBE, LIMIT, RESTRAIN. [<L *restrictus,* pp. of *restringere.* See RESTRAIN.]

re·strict·ed (ri·strik′tid) *adj.* **1** Limited; confined. **2** Not for general consumption, use, or service: *restricted* traffic or supplies. **3** Denoting specified defense information the unauthorized publication or dissemination of which is prohibited by law. — **re·strict′ed·ly** *adv.*

re·stric·tion (ri·strik′shən) *n.* **1** The act of restricting, or the state of being restricted; limitation. **2** That which restricts; a restraint. **3** Reservation; self–repression. See synonyms under BARRIER.

re·stric·tive (ri·strik′tiv) *adj.* **1** Serving, tending, or operating to restrict. **2** *Gram. & Logic* Limiting in thought, expression, or application. — **re·stric′tive·ly** *adv.*

rest–room (rest′rōōm′, -rŏŏm′) *n.* A room in a public building, as a railroad station, theater, office building, etc., provided with means and conveniences for the rest and comfort of patrons or employees; also, a toilet in a public building.

re·sult (ri·zult′) *n.* **1** The outcome of an action, course, process, or agency; consequence;

effect; conclusion. 2 *Math.* A quantity or value ascertained by calculation. 3 The final determination of a deliberative assembly. See synonyms under CONSEQUENCE, END, EVENT, HARVEST, OPERATION, PRODUCT. — *v.i.* 1 To be a result or outcome; be a physical or logical consequent; follow: with *from.* 2 To have an issue; terminate; end: with *in.* [<Med.L *resultare* <L, spring back, freq. of *resilire* rebound. See RESILE.]

re·sul·tant (ri·zul′tənt) *adj.* Arising or following as a result. — *n.* 1 That which results; a consequence. 2 *Physics* A force, velocity, etc., resulting from the action of two or more quantities of the same kind. [<L *resultans, -antis,* ppr. of *resultare.* See RESULT.]

re·sume (ri·zōōm′) *v.* **·sumed, ·sum·ing** *v.t.* 1 To begin again; take up again after cessation or interruption. 2 To take or occupy again: *Resume* your places. 3 To take for oneself again: to *resume* a title. — *v.i.* 4 To continue after cessation or interruption. See synonyms under RECOVER. [<F *résumer* <L *resumere* take up again, take back < *re-* again + *sumere* take, seize] — **re·sum′a·ble** *adj.* — **re·sum′er** *n.*

res·u·mé (rez′ōō·mā′, rez′ōō·mā) *n.* A summary, as of one's employment record. [<F]

re·sump·tion (ri·zump′shən) *n.* The act of resuming. [<L *resumptio, -onis* < *resumptus,* pp. of *resumere.* See RESUME.]

re·su·pi·nate (ri·sōō′pə·nāt) *adj. Bot.* Having the appearance of being upside down; inverted; reversed: said of the flowers of orchids. [<L *resupinatus,* pp. of *resupinare* bend back < *resupinus.* See RESUPINE.] — **re·su′pi·na′tion** *n.*

re·su·pine (rē′sōō·pīn′) *adj.* Lying on the back; supine. [<L *resupinus* < *re-* again + *supinus* on the back]

re·sur·face (rē·sûr′fis) *v.t.* **·faced, ·fac·ing** To provide with a new surface.

re·sur·gam (ri·sûr′gam) *Latin* I shall rise again.

re·surge (ri·sûrj′) *v.i.* **·surged, ·surg·ing** 1 To rise again; be resurrected. 2 To surge or sweep back again, as the tide. [<L *resurgere* < *re-* again + *surgere* rise]

re·sur·gence (ri·sûr′jəns) *n.* A rising again.

re·sur·gent (ri·sûr′jənt) *adj.* 1 Rising again, as from the grave. 2 Surging back or again. [<L *resurgens, -entis,* ppr. of *resurgere*]

res·ur·rect (rez′ə·rekt′) *v.t.* 1 To bring back to life; raise from the dead. 2 To bring back into use or to notice. — *v.i.* 3 To rise again from the dead. [Back formation <RESURRECTION]

res·ur·rec·tion (rez′ə·rek′shən) *n.* 1 A rising again from the dead. 2 The state of those who have risen from the dead. 3 Any revival or renewal, as of a practice or custom, after disuse, decay, etc.; restoration; rebirth. 4 In Christian Science, spiritualization of thought; a new and higher idea of immortality, or spiritual existence; material belief yielding to spiritual understanding. — **the Resurrection** *Theol.* 1 The rising of Christ from the dead. 2 The rising again of all the dead at the day of final judgment. [<L *resurrectio, -onis* < *resurrectus,* pp. of *resurgere.* See RESURGE.] — **res′ur·rec′tion·al** *adj.*

res·ur·rec·tion·ar·y (rez′ə·rek′shən·er′ē) *adj.* 1 Of or pertaining to resurrection. 2 Of or pertaining to the exhuming of dead bodies.

res·ur·rec·tion·ist (rez′ə·rek′shən·ist) *n.* 1 One who steals bodies from the grave; a body-snatcher. 2 One who brings to light anything buried in obscurity. 3 A believer in the rising again of the dead. — **res′ur·rec′tion·ism** *n.*

resurrection plant The rose of Jericho.

re·sus·ci·tate (ri·sus′ə·tāt) *v.t.* & *v.i.* **·tat·ed, ·tat·ing** To bring or come back to life; revive from unconsciousness or apparent death. [<L *resuscitatus,* pp. of *resuscitare* < *re-* again + *suscitare* revive < *sub-* under + *citare* call, rouse. See CITE.] — **re·sus′ci·ta′tive** *adj.* — **re·sus′ci·ta′tor** *n.*

re·sus·ci·ta·tion (ri·sus′ə·tā′shən) *n.* The act of resuscitating, or the state of being resuscitated; revivification; reanimation.

Resz·ke (resh′ke), **Édouard de,** 1856–1917, Polish basso. — **Jean de,** 1853–1925, Polish tenor; brother of the preceding.

ret (ret) *v.t.* **ret·ted, ret·ting** To steep or soak, as flax, to facilitate the separation of the fibers: also *rot.* [ME *reten,* ? <MDu. *reten* soak]

re·ta·ble (ri·tā′bəl) *n.* 1 A shelf or ledge raised above the back of an altar to support ornaments, lights, etc. 2 A panel containing a picture or bas-relief of subjects from sacred history. [<F <OF *rere-table* <Med. L *retrotabulum* <L *retro-* behind + *tabula* plank]

re·tail (rē′tāl) *n.* The selling of goods in small quantities: opposed to *wholesale.* — *adj.* Of, pertaining to, or concerned in the sale of goods in small quantities or parcels. — *v.t.* 1 To sell in small quantities; sell directly to the ultimate consumer. 2 (ri·tāl′) To repeat, as gossip. — *v.i.* 3 To be sold at retail. [<OF, cutting < *retailler* cut up < *re-* again + *tailler* cut <LL *taliare* split]

re·tail·er (rē′tā·lər) *n.* One who sells in small quantities to the consumer.

re·tain (ri·tān′) *v.t.* 1 To keep or continue to keep in one's possession; hold. 2 To maintain in use, practice, etc.: to *retain* one's standards. 3 To keep in a fixed condition or place. 4 To keep in mind; remember. 5 To hire, as a servant; also, to engage (an attorney or other representative) by paying a retainer. [<OF *retenir* <L *retinere* < *re-* back + *tenere* hold]

Synonyms: detain, employ, engage, hire, hold, keep, maintain, preserve, reserve, secure, withhold. See KEEP, REMEMBER. *Antonyms*: abandon, cede, discard, discharge, dismiss, eject, relinquish, renounce, resign, surrender.

re·tain·er[1] (ri·tā′nər) *n.* 1 One retained in the service of a person of rank or position. 2 One who retains or keeps. 3 *Mech.* A device for holding the parts of ball or roller bearings in place.

re·tain·er[2] (ri·tā′nər) *n.* 1 The fee paid, or the agreement made, to employ an attorney to serve in a suit; a retaining fee. 2 A similar fee paid to anyone to retain his services. [<OF *retenir* hold back, in a noun use]

retaining wall A wall to prevent the material of an embankment or cut from sliding.

re·take (rē·tāk′) *v.t.* **·took, ·tak·en, ·tak·ing** 1 To take back; receive again. 2 To recapture. 3 To photograph again. — *n.* (rē′·tāk′) A motion-picture scene or sequence photographed again.

re·tal·i·ate (ri·tal′ē·āt) *v.* **·at·ed, ·at·ing** *v.i.* To return like for like; especially, to repay evil with evil. — *v.t.* To repay (an injury, wrong, etc.) in kind; revenge. See synonyms under AVENGE. [<L *retaliatus,* pp. of *retaliare* < *re-* back + *talio* punishment in kind < *talis* such] — **re·tal′i·a′tive** *adj.*

re·tal·i·a·tion (ri·tal′ē·ā′shən) *n.* The act of retaliating; reprisal; requital. See synonyms under REVENGE.

re·tal·i·a·to·ry (ri·tal′ē·ə·tôr′ē, -tō′rē) *adj.* Of, containing, or of the nature of retaliation.

re·tard (ri·tärd′) *v.t.* To cause to move or proceed slowly; hinder the advance or course of; impede; delay. — *v.i.* To be delayed. See synonyms under HINDER, OBSTRUCT. — *n.* Delay; retardation. [<F *retarder* <L *retardare* < *re-* back + *tardare* make slow < *tardus* slow] — **re·tard′a·tive** *adj.* — **re·tard′er** *n.*

re·tard·ant (ri·tär′dənt) *n.* Something that retards. — *adj.* Tending to hinder.

re·tar·date (ri·tär′dāt) *n.* A mentally retarded person.

re·tar·da·tion (rē′tär·dā′shən) *n.* 1 The act of retarding. 2 The state of being retarded. 3 A lessening of velocity, gain, or progress; a delaying. 4 The amount of delay or hindrance effected. 5 That which retards; a hindrance. 6 Slowness. 7 *Music* A gradual slackening of the time. [<L *retardatio, -onis*]

re·tard·ed (ri·tärd′id) *adj.* Abnormally slow in development, especially mentally.

retch (rech) *v.i.* To make an effort to vomit; strain; heave. ◆ Homophone: *wretch.* [OE *hrǣcan* bring up (blood or phlegm)]

re·te (rē′tē) *n. pl.* **·ti·a** (-shē·ə, -tē·ə) A plexiform arrangement, as of vessels or nerves; network. [<L, net]

re·tell (rē·tel′) *v.t.* **·told, ·tell·ing** To count or relate again.

re·tem (rē′təm) *n.* A desert shrub (genus *Retama*) of Arabia and Syria, with small white flowers: the Old Testament juniper. [<Arabic *ratam,* pl. of *ratamah*]

ret·ene (ret′ēn, rē′tēn) *n. Chem.* A colorless crystalline compound, $C_{18}H_{18}$, contained in resinous pine wood and fir wood, also in fossil pine stems found in beds of peat and lignite. [<Gk. *rhētinē* resin]

re·tent (ri·tent′) *n.* That which is retained. [<L *rententus,* pp. of *retinere.* See RETAIN.]

re·ten·tion (ri·ten′shən) *n.* 1 The act of retaining. 2 The ability to remember; memory. 3 The keeping up or maintenance, as of a custom, practice, opinion, or intention. 4 *Med.* A holding within the body of materials normally excreted, as urine, etc. [<OF <L *retentio, -onis*]

re·ten·tive (ri·ten′tiv) *adj.* Having the power or tendency to retain; retaining: a *retentive* memory.

re·ten·tive·ness (ri·ten′tiv·nis) *n.* 1 The capacity of holding or retaining. 2 *Psychol.* The preservative function of memory.

re·ten·tiv·i·ty (rē′ten·tiv′ə·tē) *n.* 1 Retentiveness. 2 *Physics* The capacity of a material to retain magnetism after the withdrawal of the magnetizing force.

re·think (rē·thingk′) *v.t.* **·thought** (-thôt), **·think·ing** To think about again, especially in order to reassess; reconsider.

Re·thondes (rə·tônd′) A village 5 miles east of Compiègne, eastern France; armistice to suspend hostilities of World War I signed here, Nov. 11, 1918; during World War II, armistice to suspend hostilities between Germany and France signed here, June 22, 1940.

re·ti·ar·i·us (rē′shē·âr′ē·əs) *n. pl.* **·ar·i·i** (-âr′ē·ī) One of a class of ancient Roman gladiators, armed with a net to enmesh their adversaries, and a trident and dagger to dispatch them. See illustration under GLADIATOR. [<L < *rete* net]

ret·i·cence (ret′ə·səns) *n.* The quality, act, or an instance of being reserved in speech; reserve; taciturnity. Also **ret′i·cen·cy.** See synonyms under RESERVE. [<L *reticentia,* orig. neut. pl. of *reticens.* See RETICENT.]

ret·i·cent (ret′ə·sənt) *adj.* Habitually silent or reserved in utterance. See synonyms under TACITURN. [<L *reticens, -entis,* ppr. of *reticere* remain silent < *re-* again + *tacere* be silent] — **ret′i·cent·ly** *adv.*

ret·i·cle (ret′i·kəl) *n. Optics* The network of fine threads or lines of reference in the focal plane of a telescope or other optical instrument, serving to determine the position of an observed object: also spelled *reticule.* [<L *reticulum.* Doublet of RETICULUM.]

re·tic·u·lar (ri·tik′yə·lər) *adj.* 1 Like a network; reticulate; intricate. 2 *Anat.* Of or pertaining to a reticulum. Also **re·tic′u·lar′y.** [<NL *reticularis* <L *reticulum.* See RETICULUM.]

re·tic·u·late (ri·tik′yə·lāt) *v.* **·lat·ed, ·lat·ing** *v.t.* 1 To make a network of. 2 To cover with or as with lines of network. — *v.i.* 3 To form a network. — *adj.* (-lit, -lāt) Having the form or appearance of a network; having lines or veins crossing, as in leaves: also **re·tic′u·lat′ed.** [<L *reticulatus* < *reticulum.* See RETICULUM.]

re·tic·u·la·tion (ri·tik′yə·lā′shən) *n.* Any formation that is reticulated; a network. [< RETICULATE]

ret·i·cule (ret′ə·kyōōl) *n.* 1 A small bag formerly used by women for carrying personal articles, sewing materials, etc. 2 *Optics* A reticle. [<F *réticule*]

re·tic·u·lum (ri·tik′yə·ləm) *n. pl.* **·la** (-lə) 1 *Anat.* A protoplasmic network of cells or cellular tissue. 2 *Zool.* The honeycomb bag or second stomach of a ruminant, with the lining membrane raised into folds forming hexagonal cells. [<L, dim. of *rete* net. Doublet of RETICLE.]

Re·tic·u·lum (ri·tik′yə·ləm) A southern constellation, the Net. See CONSTELLATION. [<NL]

re·ti·form (rē′tə·fôrm, ret′ə-) *adj.* Arranged like a network; reticulate. [<F *rétiforme* <L *rete* net + *forma* shape]

ret·i·na (ret′ə·nə, ret′nə) *n. pl.* **·nas** or **·nae** (-nē) *Anat.* The inner membrane at the back of the eyeball, containing the light-sensitive rods and cones which receive the optical image. See illustration under EYE. [<LL <L *rete* net] — **ret′i·nal** *adj.*

ret·in·ene (ret′ən·ēn) *n. Biochem.* The yellow

add, āce, câre, pälm; end, ēven; it, īce; odd, ōpen, ôrder; to͝ok, pōōl; up, bûrn; ə = a in *above,* e in *sicken,* i in *clarity,* o in *melon,* u in *focus;* yōō = u in *fuse;* oi, oil; ou, pout; ch, check; g, go; ng, ring; th, thin; th, this; zh, vision. Foreign sounds à, œ, ü, kh, ṅ; and ◆: see page xx. < from; + plus; ? possibly.

pigment found in visual yellow and associated also in the production of vitamin A. [< RETINA]

ret·i·nite (ret′ə·nīt) *n.* A hard, brittle, vitreous resin obtained from lignite. [< Gk. *rhētinē* + -ITE[1]]

ret·i·ni·tis (ret′ə·nī′tis) *n. Pathol.* Inflammation of the retina.

ret·i·nol (ret′ə·nōl, -nol) *n.* A yellowish fat-soluble alcohol, $C_{20}H_{29}OH$, vitamin A, a component of visual pigments and essential to the health of epithelial tissues, occurring in liver oils, green and yellow vegetables and dairy products, and produced synthetically. [< Gk. *rhētinē* resin + -OL[2]]

ret·i·nos·co·py (ret′ə·nos′kə·pē) *n.* Skiascopy. [< L *retino* (< RETINA) + -SCOPY] — **ret′i·no·scop′ic** (-nō·skop′ik) *adj.*

ret·i·nue (ret′ə·nōō, -nyōō) *n.* The body of retainers attending a person of rank; an escort; cortège. [< F *retenue,* fem. of *retenu,* pp. of *retenir.* See RETAIN.]

re·tire (ri·tīr′) *v.* **·tired, ·tir·ing** *v.i.* **1** To go away or withdraw, as for privacy, shelter, or rest. **2** To go to bed. **3** To withdraw oneself from business, public life, or active service. **4** To fall back; retreat, as troops under attack. **5** To move back; recede or appear to recede. —*v.t.* **6** To remove from active service, as an officer of the army or navy. **7** To pay off and withdraw from circulation: to *retire* bonds. **8** To withdraw (troops, etc.) from action. **9** In baseball, etc., to keep (a batter or runner) from reaching base or scoring by putting him out, or to remove (a side) from an opportunity of scoring. [< F *retirer* < *re-* back + *tirer* draw]

re·tired (ri·tīrd′) *adj.* **1** Withdrawn from public view; existing or passed in seclusion; solitary; secluded: a *retired* life. **2** Withdrawn from active service, business, office, or public life: a *retired* sea captain. **3** Due or received by a person withdrawn from active service: *retired* pay. See synonyms under SECRET.

retired list One of the lists of officers or enlisted men voluntarily or involuntarily retired from an active status in one of the armed services of the United States.

re·tir·ee (ri·tīr′ē′) *n.* A person who is retired.

re·tire·ment (ri·tīr′mənt) *n.* **1** The act of retiring, or the state of being retired; withdrawal; seclusion. **2** A secluded place.

Synonyms: loneliness, privacy, seclusion, solitude. In *retirement* one withdraws from association he has had with others; in *seclusion* one shuts himself off from the society of all except intimate friends or attendants; in *solitude* no other person is present. As private denotes what concerns ourselves individually, *privacy* denotes freedom from the presence or observation of those not concerned or whom we do not wish to have concerned in our affairs; *privacy* is more temporary than *seclusion*; we speak of a moment's *privacy.* There may be *loneliness* without *solitude,* as amid an unsympathizing crowd, and *solitude* without *loneliness,* as when one is glad to be alone. See SECLUSION, SOLITUDE. *Antonyms*: association, companionship, company, fellowship, society.

re·tir·ing (ri·tīr′ing) *adj.* **1** Shy; modest; reserved; unobtrusive. **2** Pertaining to retirement: a *retiring* pension. See synonyms under MODEST.

re·tort[1] (ri·tôrt′) *v.t.* **1** To direct (a word or deed) back upon the originator. **2** To reply to, as an accusation or argument, by a similar one. —*v.i.* **3** To make answer, especially sharply. —*n.* A retaliatory speech; a turning back of an accusation or insult upon the one who makes it; a keen rejoinder or caustic riposte; also, the act of making such reply: to be quick at *retort.* See synonyms under ANSWER. [< L *retortus,* pp. of *retorquere* < *re-* back + *torquere* twist] —**re·tort′er** *n.*

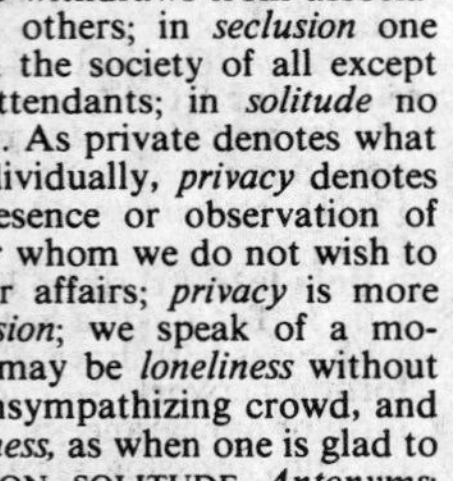

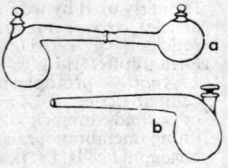

RETORTS
a. Retort with receiver.
b. Common retort.

re·tort[2] (ri·tôrt′) *n.* **1** *Chem.* A vessel with a bent tube, for the heating of substances, or for distillation. **2** *Metall.* A vessel in which ore may be heated for the removal of its metal content. [< L *retortus* bent back. See RETORT[1].]

re·tor·tion (ri·tôr′shən) *n.* **1** The act of retorting. **2** A bending, turning, or twisting back. **3** Retaliation; in international law, the infliction by one nation upon the subjects of another of the samee ill treatment that its own citizens have received from the latter government. Also **re·tor′sion.** [< Med. L *retortio, -onis*]

re·touch (rē·tuch′) *v.t.* **1** To add new touches to; modify; revise. **2** *Phot.* To change, or improve, as a print, by a hand process in which a hard, sharp pencil or fine brush is used. —*n.* (*also* rē′tuch′) An additional touch, as to a picture, model, or other work of art, previously regarded as finished. [< F *retoucher*] —**re·touch′er** *n.*

re·trace (ri·trās′) *v.t.* **·traced, ·trac·ing 1** To go back over; follow backward, as a path. **2** To trace the whole story of, from the beginning. **3** To go back over with the eyes or mind. [< F *retracer*] —**re·trace′a·ble** *adj.*

re-trace (rē·trās′) *v.t.* **-traced, -trac·ing** To trace again, as an engraving, drawing, or map.

re·tract (ri·trakt′) *v.t.* & *v.i.* **1** To take back (an assertion, accusation, admission, etc.); make a disavowal (of); recant. **2** To draw back or in, as the claws of a cat. See synonyms under RECANT, RENOUNCE. [< F *rétracter* < L *retractare* draw back < *re-* back + *tractare* draw violently, freq. of *trahere* draw] —**re·tract′a·ble** or **·i·ble** *adj.* — **re·trac·ta·tion** (rē′trak·tā′shən) *n.*

re·trac·tile (ri·trak′til) *adj. Zool.* Capable of being drawn back or in, as a cat's claws or the head of a tortoise. [< F *rétractile*] —**re·trac·til·i·ty** (rē′trak·til′ə·tē) *n.*

re·trac·tion (ri·trak′shən) *n.* **1** The act of retracting or drawing something back or in. **2** The state of being retracted. **3** The act of withdrawing or recalling something said or avowed; recantation; revocation.

re·trac·tive (ri·trak′tiv) *adj.* Having the power or tendency to retract; retracting.

re·trac·tor (ri·trak′tər) *n.* **1** One who or that which retracts. **2** *Surg.* An instrument used to hold apart the edges of a wound.

re·tral (rē′trəl) *adj.* Situated at the back; posterior. [< L *retro* backward + -AL[1]]

re·tread[1] (rē′tred′) *n.* A new outer covering of a pneumatic tire, to replace a worn or damaged one. —*v.t.* (rē·tred′) **·tread·ed, ·tread·ing** To fit or furnish (an automobile tire) with a new tread. Also *recap.*

re-tread[2] (rē·tred′) *v.t.* **-trod, -trod·den, -tread·ing** To tread again.

re·treat (ri·trēt′) *v.i.* **1** To go back or backward; withdraw; retire. **2** To curve or slope backward. —*v.t.* **3** In chess, to move (a piece) back. —*n.* **1** The act of retreating, as from contest or danger. **2** The retirement of a naval or land force from a position of danger or from an enemy; also, a signal for retreating, made by trumpet or drum. **3** In the army or navy, a signal, as by bugle, for the lowering of the flag at sunset. **4** Retirement; seclusion; solitude. **5** A place of retirement, quiet, or security; a refuge; shelter; haunt. **6** Religious retirement; also, the time spent in religious retirement. **7** An establishment for the mentally ill, for alcoholics, etc. See synonyms under REFUGE, SECLUSION, SHELTER. Compare RETIREMENT. [< F *retraite,* orig. fem. of pp. of *retraire* draw back < L *retrahere* < *re-* again + *trahere* draw]

re·trench (ri·trench′) *v.t.* **1** To cut down or reduce; curtail (expenditures). **2** To cut off or away; remove; omit. —*v.i.* **3** To make retrenchments; economize. [< MF *retrencher* < *re-* back + *trencher* cut. See TRENCH.]

Synonyms: abridge, clip, curtail, cut, decrease, diminish, economize, lessen, reduce. *Antonyms*: elongate, expand, extend, lavish, lengthen, prolong, protract, squander, waste.

re·trench·ment (ri·trench′mənt) *n.* **1** The act of retrenching. **2** Reduction, as of expenses, for the sake of economy. **3** An interior breastwork or rampart from which the enemy can be resisted should the outer line be taken.

ret·ri·bu·tion (ret′rə·byōō′shən) *n.* **1** The act of requiting; impartial infliction of punishment. **2** That which is done or given in requital. **3** A reward or (especially) a punishment. See synonyms under RECOMPENSE, REVENGE. [< OF < L *retributio, -onis* < *retributus,* pp. of *retribuere* pay back < *re-* back + *tribuere* pay]

re·trib·u·tive (ri·trib′yə·tiv) *adj.* Tending to reward or punish. Also **re·trib′u·to′ry** (-tôr′ē, -tō′rē).

re·triev·al (ri·trē′vəl) *n.* **1** The act of retrieving. **2** Restoration from loss, damage, or failure.

re·trieve (ri·trēv′) *v.* **·trieved, ·triev·ing** *v.t.* **1** To get back; regain. **2** To restore; revive, as flagging spirits. **3** To make up for; remedy the consequences of. **4** To call to mind; remember. **5** To find and bring in (wounded or dead game): said of dogs. —*v.i.* **6** To retrieve game. See synonyms under RECOVER. —*n.* The act of retrieving; retrieval; recovery. [ME *retreve* < OF *retroev-,* stressed stem of *retrouver* find again < *re-* again + *trouver* find] —**re·triev′a·bil′i·ty** *n.* — **re·triev′a·ble** *adj.* —**re·triev′a·bly** *adv.*

re·triev·er (ri·trē′vər) *n.* **1** A sporting dog variously bred and specifically trained to retrieve game. **2** A person who retrieves.

retro- *prefix* **1** Back; backward: *retroflex, retrograde.* **2** Chiefly in scientific terms, behind: *retrolental.* [< L *retro-* < *retro* back, backward]

ret·ro·act (ret′rō·akt′, rē′trō-) *v.i.* **1** To act reciprocally or in return; react. **2** *Law* To affect past acts, obligations, or penalties. [Back formation < RETROACTIVE] —**ret′ro·ac′tion** *n.*

ret·ro·ac·tive (ret′rō·ak′tiv, rē′trō-) *adj.* Having or designed to have a retrospective effect or reversed action; in effect also during a specified prior period. —**ret′ro·ac′tive·ly** *adv.* — **ret′ro·ac·tiv′i·ty** *n.*

retroactive law A law legalizing past proceedings; a retrospective law.

ret·ro·cede (ret′rō·sēd′) *v.* **·ced·ed, ·ced·ing** *v.t.* To cede, grant, or give back. —*v.i.* To go back; recede. [< L *retrocedere* < *retro-* back + *cedere* go]

ret·ro·ces·sion (ret′rō·sesh′ən) *n.* **1** The act of retroceding or giving back. **2** *Law* The conveyance of an estate to a former owner. [< LL *retrocessio, -onis*]

ret·ro·choir (ret′rə·kwīr) *n.* That part of a church interior which is east of or beyond the altar. [< RETRO- + CHOIR, modeled on Med. L *retrochorus*]

ret·ro·fit (ret′rō·fit′) *v.t.* **-fit·ted, -fit·ting** To furnish (something previously manufactured) with new parts, equipment, or materials.

ret·ro·flex (ret′rə·fleks) *adj.* **1** Bent or turned backward; reflexed. **2** *Phonet.* Cacuminal. Also **ret′ro·flexed.** [< LL *retroflexus,* pp. of *retroflectere* < L *retro-* back + *flectere* bend]

ret·ro·flex·ion (ret′rə·flek′shən) *n.* **1** A bending or being bent backward. **2** *Anat.* A position or condition of the uterus in which its body is bent back at an angle with the cervix. Also **ret′ro·flec′tion.**

ret·ro·grade (ret′rə·grād) *v.* **·grad·ed, ·grad·ing** *v.i.* **1** To move or appear to move backward; recede. **2** To grow worse; decline; degenerate. **3** *Astron.* To have a retrograde motion. —*v.t.* **4** To cause to move backward; reverse. —*adj.* **1** Going, moving, or tending backward; contrary; reversed. **2** Declining to or toward a worse state or character. **3** *Astron.* Apparently moving from east to west relatively to the fixed stars. **4** Reversed; inverted. **5** *Obs.* Opposed; contrary. —*n.* A retrograde movement; decline. [< L *retrogradus*] —**ret′ro·gra·da′tion** (-grā·dā′shən) *n.*

ret·ro·gress (ret′rə·gres) *v.i.* To go back to an earlier or worse condition. [< L *retrogressus,* pp. of *retrogradi* < *retro-* backward + *gradi* walk]

ret·ro·gres·sion (ret′rə·gresh′ən) *n.* **1** A retreat; degeneration; motion in a reverse direction. **2** A moving toward a lower plane. **3** *Biol.* Descent to or toward a less complex or less perfect structure.

ret·ro·gres·sive (ret′rə·gres′iv) *adj.* **1** Retrograde. **2** Deteriorating; degenerating. **3** *Biol.* Descending from a higher to a less complex organization.

ret·ro·len·tal fi·bro·pla·sia (ret′rō·len′təl fī′brō·plā′zhə, -zhē·ə) *Pathol.* The persistence or growth of embryonic vascular tissue behind the lens of the eye.

ret·ro·rock·et (ret′rō·rok′it) *n.* An auxiliary jet engine whose thrust acts to lessen

the velocity of fall of a rocket or spaceship to the surface of the earth or other celestial body.

re·trorse (ri·trôrs′) *adj.* Turned, bent, or directed backward. [< L *retrorsus,* contraction of *retroversus* < *retro-* backward + *versus,* pp. of *vertere* turn] —**re·trorse′ly** *adv.*

ret·ro·spect (ret′rə·spekt) *v.i. Rare* **1** To think about the past. **2** To look or refer back. —*v.t.* **3** *Rare* To consider or think about in retrospect. —*n.* A looking back on things past; view or contemplation of something past. See synonyms under MEMORY. [< L *retrospectus,* pp. of *retrospicere* reexamine, look back < *retro-* back + *specere* look]

ret·ro·spec·tion (ret′rə·spek′shən) *n.* A calling to remembrance; a looking back upon or recollection of the past.

ret·ro·spec·tive (ret′rə·spek′tiv) *adj.* **1** Looking back on the past; of, pertaining to, or referring to the past. **2** Retroactive: said of some legislation. **3** Characterized by retrospection. —**ret′ro·spec′tive·ly** *adv.*

re·trous·sage (rə·trōō·säzh′) *n.* In etching, a process of wiping a soft cloth across the ink-filled incisions of an etched plate before printing to produce an effect of softness or richness. [< F < *retrousser* turn up]

ret·rous·sé (ret′rōō·sā′, *Fr.* rə·trōō·sā′) *adj.* Turned up at the end: said of noses. [< F, pp. of *retrousser* turn up, tuck up < *re-* back + *trousser* fasten together]

ret·ro·ver·sion (ret′rə·vûr′zhən, -shən) *n.* **1** A tipping or bending backward. **2** The state of being turned backward. **3** The act of looking or turning back.

ret·ro·vert (ret′rə·vûrt) *v.t.* To turn back. [< LL *retrovertere* < L *retro-* back + *vertere* turn]

ret·ro·vi·rus (ret′rō·vī′rəs; ret ′rō·vī′rəs) *n.* Any of a family of viruses that contain RNA genetic material, and are responsible for AIDS, leukemia, etc.

re·turn (ri·tûrn′) *v.i.* **1** To come or go back, as to or toward a former place or condition. **2** To come back or revert in thought or speech. **3** To revert to a former owner. **4** To answer; respond. —*v.t.* **5** To bring, carry, send, or put back; restore; replace. **6** To give in return for something: to *return* ingratitude for kindness. **7** To repay or requite, especially with an equivalent: to *return* a compliment. **8** To yield or produce, as a profit or interest. **9** To send back; reflect, as light or sound. **10** To render (a verdict, etc.) **11** To submit, as a report or writ, to one in authority. **12** To report or announce officially. **13** To replace (a weapon, etc.) in its holder. **14** In card games, to lead (a suit previously led by one's partner). —*n.* **1** The act, process, state, or result of coming back or returning; also, that which is returned; resumption; restoration or replacement; repayment or requital; response; answer; retort; reappearance or recurrence. **2** That which accrues, as from investments, labor, or use; profit. **3** A coming back, reappearance, or recurrence, as of a periodical event or season. **4** A report, list, etc.; especially, a formal or official report, or, in the plural, a set of tabulated statistics: election *returns.* **5** *Archit.* **a** A continuation of a dripstone, hood molding, etc., to form a termination having a different direction from the main part. **b** A part or face of a building at an angle with the main part of the façade. **6** The sending back by a sheriff of a writ to the court from which it was issued; also, a sheriff's report on such writ. **7** *Law* A brief statement, usually endorsed on a writ by the officer to whom it was issued, of what has been done under it; also, the filing of the writ thus endorsed in the office of the clerk or the tribunal whence it was issued. **8** In card games, a returned lead. **9** Any volley, stroke, or thrust received from an opponent; specifically, in a game, the sending of an object, as a tennis ball, from one player to another from whom he has received it. See synonyms under HARVEST, INCREASE, PRODUCT, PROFIT, RESTITUTION. —*adj.* Of or pertaining to a return; given, taken, or done in return; returning: a *return* visit; a *return* ticket. [< OF *returner*]—**re·turn′er** *n.*

re-turn (rē·tûrn′) *v.t.* & *v.i.* To turn again; fold over or back.

re·turn·a·ble (ri·tûr′nə·bəl) *adj.* **1** Capable of being or suitable to be returned. **2** Due and required: said of a judicial writ in reference to the time when and the place where it is to be returned by the officer to whom it is directed.

re·tuse (ri·tōōs′, -tyōōs′) *adj. Bot.* Having a rounded end or apex in which there is a slight depression, indentation, or notch: said of leaves. [< L *retusus,* pp. of *retundere* beat back < *re-* back + *tundere*]

Retz (rets), **Cardinal de,**1614–79, Jean François Paul de Gondi, French ecclesiastic and author.

Reu·ben (rōō′bin) A masculine personal name. [< Hebrew, behold, a son]
— **Reuben** The eldest son of Jacob. *Gen.* xxix 32.

Reuch·lin (roikh′lēn, roikh·lēn′), **Johann,** 1455–1522, German humanist and Hebraist. — **Reuch·lin′i·an** *adj.* —**Reuch′lin·ism** *n.*

re·un·ion (rē·yōōn′yən) *n.* **1** The act of reuniting; renewed harmony. **2** A social gathering of persons who have been separated: a family *reunion.*

Ré·un·ion (rē·yōōn′yən, *Fr.* rā·ü·nyôn′) A French island of the Mascarene group, east of Madagascar; 970 square miles; capital, Saint-Denis: formerly *Bourbon Island.*

re·un·ion·ism (rē·yōōn′yən·iz′əm) *n.* The principle of renewed union as a policy; specifically, advocacy of reunion of the various Christian churches. —**re·un′ion·ist** *n.* —**re·un′ion·is′tic** *adj.*

re·u·nite (rē′yōō·nīt′) *v.t.* & *v.i.* **·nit·ed, ·nit·ing** To unite, cohere, or combine again after separation. —**re′u·nit′er** *n.*

Reu·ter·dahl (roi′tər·däl), **Henry,** 1871–1935, U.S. marine and naval painter born in Sweden.

Reu·ters (roi′tərz) *n.* A British organization for collecting news and distributing it to member newspapers. Also **Reuter's News Agency.** [after Baron Paul Julius von *Reuter,* 1816–99, English founder of the agency]

Reu·ther (rōō′thər), **Walter Philip,** 1907–1970, U.S. labor leader.

rev (rev) *n.* A revolution, as of a motor or machine part. —*v.t.* & *v.i.* **revved, rev·ving** To alter the speed of (a motor): with *up* or *down.*

Re·val (rā′väl) The German name for TALLINN.

re·vamp (rē·vamp′) *v.t.* **1** To vamp (a boot or shoe) anew. **2** To patch up; make over. —*n.* A thing which is revamped. [< RE- + VAMP]

re·veal (ri·vēl′) *v.t.* **1** To make known; disclose; divulge. **2** To make visible; expose to view; exhibit; show. See synonyms under ANNOUNCE, INFORM, PUBLISH. —*n. Archit.* The vertical side of an aperture or opening in a wall; especially, the portion of the side of a door or window between the line where the window frame or door frame stops and the outer edge of the opening. [< OF *reveler* < L *revelare* unveil < *re-* back + *velum* veil]—**re·veal′a·ble** *adj.* —**re·veal′er** *n.*

re·veal·ment (ri·vēl′mənt) *n.* A revelation; act of revealing; disclosure.

rev·eil·le (rev′i·lē) *n.* **1** A morning signal by drum or bugle, notifying soldiers or sailors to rise. **2** The hour at which this signal is sounded. [< F *reveillez-vous,* imperative of *se reveiller* wake up < *re-* (< L *re-*) again + L *vigilare* watch. See VIGIL.]

rev·el (rəv′əl) *v.i.* **·eled** or **·elled, ·el·ing** or **·el·ling** **1** To take delight; indulge freely: with *in:* He *revels* in his freedom. **2** To make merry; engage in boisterous festivities. —*n.* **1** Merrymaking; carousing; noisy festivity. **2** An occasion of boisterous festivity; a celebration. [< OF *reveler* make an uproar < L *rebellare.* Doublet of REBEL.]—**rev′el·er** or **rev′el·ler** *n.*

Synonyms (noun): carnival, carousal, carouse, feast, festivity, jollification, merrymaking, revelry, rout.

Re·vel (re′vel′y′) The Russian name for TALLINN.

rev·e·la·tion (rev′ə·lā′shən) *n.* **1** The act or process of revealing, or the state of being revealed. **2** That which is or has been revealed. **3** *Theol.* **a** The act of revealing or communicating divine truth, especially by divine agency or supernatural means. **b** That which has been so revealed, as concerning God in his relations to man. **c** That which is revealed inthe Bible itself. [< OF < LL *revelatio, -onis* < L *revelatus,* pp. of *revelare.* See REVEAL.]

Rev·e·la·tion (rev′ə·lā′shən) The Apocalypse, or Book of Revelation: in full, **The Revelation of Saint John the Divine;** the last book of the Bible.

rev·e·la·tion·ist (rev′ə·lā′shən·ist) *n.* One who holds that God has made a supernatural revelation of himself and his will.

rev·e·la·tor (rev′ə·lā′tər) *n.* A revealer. [< LL]

rev·el·ry (rev′əl·rē) *n. pl.* **·ries** Noisy or boisterous merriment.

rev·e·nant (rev′ə·nənt) *n.* **1** One who or that which returns. **2** A ghost; an apparition. [< F, ppr. of *revenir* come back < *re-* back + *venir* come]

re·venge (ri·venj′) *v.* **·venged, ·veng·ing** *v.t.* **1** To inflict punishment, injury, or loss in return for; to take vengeance for; avenge. **2** To take or seek vengeance in behalf of. —*v.i.* **3** *Obs.* To take vengeance. —*n.* **1** The act of returning injury for injury; the infliction of injury or punishment in the spirit of personal vindictiveness; retaliation. **2** A mode or means of avenging oneself or others. **3** The desire for vengeance. [< OF *revenger* < *re-* (< L *re-*) again + *venger* take vengeance < L *vindicare.* See VINDICATE.]—**re·veng′er** *n.*

Synonyms (noun): avenging, requital, retaliation, retribution, vengeance. *Retaliation* and *revenge* are personal and often bitter. *Retaliation* may be partial; *revenge* is meant to be complete and may be excessive. *Vengeance,* which once meant an indignant vindication of justice, now signifies the most furious and unsparing *revenge. Revenge* emphasizes more the personal injury in return for which it is inflicted. A *requital* is an even return, such as to quit one of obligation for what has been received, and may be good or bad. *Avenging* and *retribution* give a solemn sense of exact justice, *avenging* being more personal in its infliction, and *retribution* the impersonal visitation of the doom of righteous law. See HATRED. *Antonyms:* compassion, excuse, forgiveness, grace, mercy, pardon, pity.

re·venge·ful (ri·venj′fəl) *adj.* Vindictive; disposed to, or full of, revenge. —**re·venge′ful·ly** *adv.* —**re·venge′ful·ness** *n.*

rev·e·nons à nos mou·tons (rəv·nôn′zà nō mōō·tôn′) *French* Let us return to our sheep; that is, to our subject.

rev·e·nue (rev′ə·nyōō, -nōō) *n.* **1** Total current income of a government, except duties on imports: also **internal revenue. 2** Income from any form of property. **3** The department of government or civil service which collects the national funds: in the United States, the **Internal Revenue Service** of the Department of the Treasury. **4** A source of an item of income. [< F, fem. of *revenu,* pp. of *revenir* return]

revenue cutter An armed vessel in the government revenue service used to enforce customs regulations and prevent smuggling.

revenue sharing *U.S.* The distribution among state and municipal governments, based on their population, of a part of the revenue from Federal taxes.

re·ver·ber·ant (ri·vûr′bər·ənt) *adj.* Resounding. [< L *reverberans, -antis,* ppr. of *reverberare.* See REVERBERATE.]

re·ver·ber·ate (ri·vûr′bə·rāt) *v.* **·at·ed, ·at·ing** *v.i.* **1** To resound or re-echo. **2** To be reflected or repelled. **3** To bend back, as flames in a reverberatory furnace. **4** To rebound or recoil. —*v.t.* **5** To echo back (a sound); re-echo. **6** To reflect. **7** To cause to bend back, as flames in a reverberatory furnace; deflect. **8** To expose to heat in a reverberatory furnace. See synonyms under ROAR. [< L *reverberatus,* pp. of *reverberare* strike back, cause to rebound < *re-* back + *verberare* beat]

re·ver·ber·a·tion (ri·vûr′bə·rā′shən) *n.* **1** The act or process of reverberating. **2** That which constitutes reverberating. **3** The rebound or reflection or light, heat, or sound waves. —**re·ver′ber·a′tive** *adj.*

re·ver·ber·a·tor (ri·vûr′bə·rā′tər) *n.* **1** One who or that which causes reverberation. **2** A reflecting lamp, or a reverberatory furnace.

re·ver·ber·a·to·ry (ri·vûr′bər·ə·tôr′ē, -tō′rē)

adj. Producing or intended to produce reverberation; reverberative. — *n.* *pl.* **·ries** A reverberatory furnace.

reverberatory furnace A furnace having a vaulted ceiling that deflects the flame and heat toward the hearth or the upper surface of the substance to be treated.

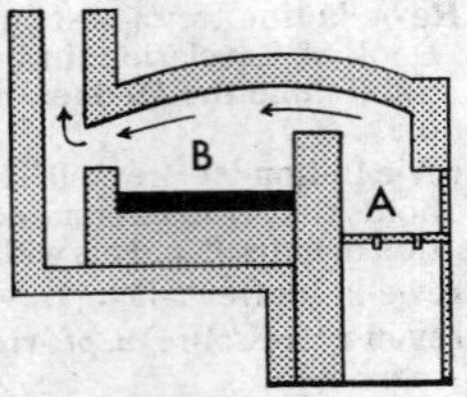

REVERBERATORY FURNACE
A. Flames and gases.
B. Bed of molten iron.

re·vere (ri·vir′) *v.t.* **·vered, ·ver·ing** To regard with veneration; reverence; venerate. See synonyms under ADMIRE, DEFER, VENERATE, WORSHIP. [<L *revereri* feel awe of < *re-* again and again + *vereri* fear] — **re·ver′er** *n.*

Re·vere (ri·vir′), **Paul,** 1735–1818, American silversmith, famous for his midnight ride from Charlestown to Lexington, Mass., the night of April 17–18, 1775, to warn the colonists of the approach of British troops.

rev·er·ence (rev′ər·əns) *n.* **1** A feeling of profound respect often mingled with awe and affection; veneration. **2** An act of respect; an obeisance. **3** The quality or character that commands respect. **4** A reverend person: used as a respectful appellation or title, especially applied to a clergyman. — *v.t.* **·enced, ·enc·ing** To regard with reverence. See synonyms under VENERATE. [<OF <L *reverentia*]
Synonyms (noun): adoration, awe, homage, honor, veneration, worship. See VENERATION. *Antonyms*: contumely, derision, dishonor, insult, irreverence, mockery, outrage, ridicule, scoff, scoffing.

rev·er·end (rev′ər·ənd) *adj.* **1** Worthy of reverence. **2** Being a clergyman; of or pertaining to the clergy or the clerical office. — *n. Colloq.* A clergyman; minister. [<L *reverendus,* gerundive of *revereri.* See REVERE.]

rev·er·ent (rev′ər·ənt) *adj.* **1** Impressed with or feeling reverence. **2** Expressing reverence. [<L *reverens, -entis*] — **rev′er·ent·ly** *adv.*

rev·er·en·tial (rev′ə·ren′shəl) *adj.* Proceeding from or expressing reverence. — **rev′er·en′tial·ly** *adv.*

rev·er·ie (rev′ər·ē) *n. pl.* **·er·ies** **1** Abstracted musing; dreaming. **2** A product of such musing in written or musical composition. Also **rev′er·y.** See synonyms under DREAM, THOUGHT. [<F *rêverie* < *rêver* dream, rave, ? <L *rabere* rage]

re·vers (rə·vir′, -vâr′) *n. pl.* **·vers** (-virz′, -vârz′) **1** A part of a garment folded over to show the inside, as the lapel of a coat. **2** Material used to cover such a part. [<OF. See REVERSE.]

re·ver·sal (ri·vûr′səl) *n.* **1** The act of reversing. **2** *Physics* The change of a dark to a bright spectral line, or vice versa. **3** *Law* An annulling or setting aside: the *reversal* of a decree.

re·verse (ri·vûrs′) *adj.* **1** Turned backward; contrary or opposite in direction, character, order, etc. **2** On the other side; backward; inverted. **3** Causing backward motion: the *reverse* gear of an automobile. — *n.* **1** That which is directly opposite or contrary: The *reverse* of what you say is true. **2** The back, rear, or secondary side or surface, as distinguished from the front or principal side. **3** A reversing; change to an opposite position, direction, or state; reversal: a *reverse* of a gun or gun carriage. **4** A change or alteration for the worse; a check or partial defeat; misfortune. **5** *Mech.* A reversing gear or movement. See synonyms under MISFORTUNE. — *v.* **·versed, ·vers·ing** *v.t.* **1** To turn upside down or inside out; invert or overturn. **2** To turn in an opposite direction. **3** To transpose; exchange. **4** To change into something different or opposite; alter: to *reverse* policy. **5** To set aside; annul: to *reverse* a decree. **6** *Mech.* To cause to have an opposite motion or effect: *Reverse* engines! — *v.i.* **7** To move or turn in the opposite direction, as in dancing. **8** To reverse its action: said of engines, etc. See synonyms under ABOLISH. [<OF *revers* <L *reversus,* pp. of *revertere.* See REVERT.] — **re·vers′er** *n.*

reverse fault *Geol.* A thrust fault.

re·verse·ly (ri·vûrs′lē) *adv.* In a reverse or contrary manner.

re·vers·i·ble (ri·vûr′sə·bəl) *adj.* **1** Capable of being reversed in direction or position. **2** Capable of going either forward or backward, as a chemical reaction or physiological process. **3** Capable of being used or worn inside out or backward: a *reversible* coat. **4** Having the finish on both sides, as a fabric. — *n.* A reversible coat. — **re·vers′i·bil′i·ty, re·vers′i·ble·ness** *n.* — **re·vers′i·bly** *adv.*

re·ver·sion (ri·vûr′zhən, -shən) *n.* **1** A return to or toward some former state or condition. **2** The act of reversing or the state of being reversed. **3** A return, as to a former practice or belief. **4** *Biol.* **a** The recurrence or reappearance in an individual of characteristics which had not been evident for two or more generations; atavism. **b** An example of such recurrence. **5** *Law* **a** The return of an estate to the grantor or his heirs after the expiration of the grant. **b** The estate so returning. **c** The right of succession to an estate. **6** *Obs.* Remainder. [<OF <L *reversio, -onis.* See REVERT.]

re·ver·sion·al (ri·vûr′zhən·əl, -shən-) *adj.* Reversionary.

re·ver·sion·ar·y (ri·vûr′zhən·er′ē, -shən-) *adj.* Of, pertaining to, characterized by, or involving reversion.

re·ver·sion·er (ri·vûr′zhən·ər, -shən-) *n. Law* One entitled to an estate in reversion.

re·ver·so (ri·vûr′sō) *n. pl.* **·sos** A left-hand page: opposed to *recto.* [<Ital. *riverso* reverse]

re·vert (ri·vûrt′) *v.i.* **1** To go or turn back to a former place, condition, attitude, topic, etc. **2** *Biol.* To return to or show characteristics of an earlier, primitive type. **3** *Law* To return to the former owner or to his heirs. — *n.* **1** One who is reconverted to a former faith. **2** That which reverts. [<OF *revertir* <L *revertere* turn back < *re-* back + *vertere* turn] — **re·vert′i·ble** *adj.* — **re·ver′tive** *adj.*

re·vest (rē·vest′) *v.t.* **1** To vest again, as with rank, authority, or ownership; reinvest. **2** To vest again, as office or powers. — *v.i.* **3** To take effect again, as a title reverting to a former owner. [<OF *revestir* <LL *revestire* reclothe <L *re-* again + *vestire* clothe < *vestis* a garment]

re·vet (ri·vet′) *v.t.* **·vet·ted, ·vet·ting** To face, as an embankment, with masonry. [<F *revêtir* clothe <L *revestire.* See REVEST.]

re·vet·ment (ri·vet′mənt) *n.* A facing, sheathing, or retaining wall, as of masonry, for protecting earthworks, river banks, etc. [<F *revêtement*]

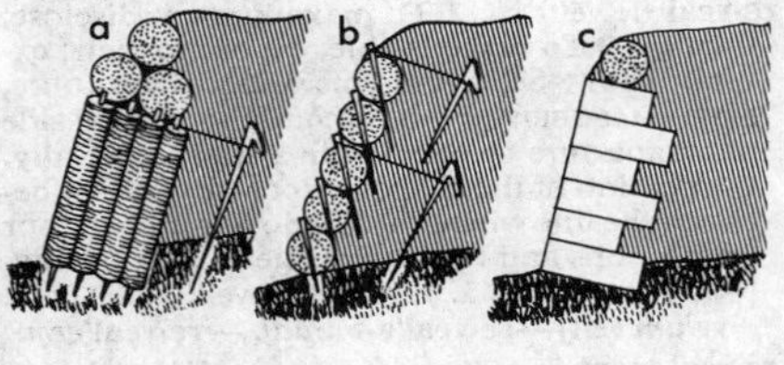

REVETMENTS
a. Built of gabions supporting fascines.
b. Built of fascines only.
c. Built of timbers or concrete.

re·view (ri·vyōō′) *v.t.* **1** To go over or examine again; look at or study again. **2** To look back upon, as in memory; think of retrospectively. **3** To go over, as a manuscript, so as to correct defects. **4** To make an inspection of, especially formally. **5** To write or make a critical review of, as a new book. **6** *Law* To examine (something done or adjudged by a lower court) so as to determine its legality or correctness. — *v.i.* **7** To write a review or reviews, as for a magazine. [<RE- + VIEW; modeled on F *revoir* look at again] — *n.* **1** A second, repeated, or new view, examination, consideration, or study of something; a retrospective survey. **2** A lesson studied or recited again. **3** Critical study or examination. **4** An article or essay containing a critical examination, discussion, or notice of some work; a criticism; critique. **5** A periodical devoted to essays in criticism and on general subjects. **6** A formal or official inspection or view, as of troops. **7** *Law* A judicial revision by a superior court of the order or decree of a subordinate court. **8** A revision, as of a work by its author; examination with a view to correction or improvement. [<MF *reveue* <pp. of *revoir* <L *revidere* < *re-* again + *videre* see]

re·view·al (ri·vyōō′əl) *n.* A review; the act of reviewing.

re·view·er (ri·vyōō′ər) *n.* A critic or examiner; an essayist in critical periodicals; a book reviewer.

re·vile (ri·vīl′) *v.* **·viled, ·vil·ing** *v.t.* To assail with abusive or contemptuous language; vilify; abuse. — *v.i.* To use abusive or contemptuous language. [<OF *reviler* treat as vile < *re-* + *vil* vile] — **re·vile′ment** *n.* — **re·vil′er** *n.* — **re·vil′ing·ly** *adv.*
Synonyms: abuse, asperse, calumniate, defame, malign, reproach, slander, traduce, upbraid, vilify. See ABUSE, ASPERSE. *Antonyms*: see synonyms for PRAISE.

Re·vil·la·gi·ge·do Island (ri·vil′ə·gi·gē′dō) An island in the Alexander Archipelago, SE Alaska; 1,120 square miles.

re·vis·al (ri·vī′zəl) *n.* Revision; the act of revising.

re·vise (ri·vīz′) *v.t.* **·vised, ·vis·ing** **1** To read or read over so as to correct errors, suggest or make changes, etc.: to *revise* a manuscript or the proofs of a book. **2** To change; alter: He has *revised* his opinions. — *n.* **1** The act or result of revising or reviewing; a revision. **2** A corrected proof after revision. [<F *reviser* <L *revisere* look back, see again < *re-* again + *visum,* pp. of *videre* see] — **re·vis′er** or **re·vi′sor** *n.*

Revised Version A translation of the Bible into English, made by two bodies, one of English and one of American scholars, in the years 1870–84.

re·vi·sion (ri·vizh′ən) *n.* The act or result of revising; a revised version or edition. — **re·vi′sion·al, re·vi′sion·ar′y** *adj.*

re·vi·sion·ism (ri·vizh′ən·iz′əm) *n.* The advocacy of revision.

re·vi·sion·ist (ri·vizh′ən·ist) *n.* **1** One who advocates revision. **2** A reviser.

re·vis·it (rē·viz′it) *v.t.* To visit again. — *n.* A return visit. — **re′vis·i·ta′tion** *n.*

re·vi·so·ry (ri·vī′zər·ē) *adj.* Effecting, or capable of effecting, revision; revising: *revisory* powers.

re·vi·tal·ize (rē·vī′təl·īz) *v.t.* **·ized, ·iz·ing** To restore vitality to; bring back to life; revive. — **re·vi′tal·i·za′tion** *n.*

re·vi·val (ri·vī′vəl) *n.* **1** The act of reviving, or the state of being revived; specifically, a recovery, as from depression. **2** A restoration or resuscitation after neglect, oblivion, or obscurity: the *revival* of letters. **3** A renewal of special interest in and attention to religious services and duties and the subject of personal salvation; a religious awakening. **4** A series of emotional and sensational evangelical meetings.

re·vi·val·ism (ri·vī′vəl·iz′əm) *n.* **1** The spirit and methods of religious revivals or revivalists, or that promote revivals. **2** A tendency to restore former conditions or principles.

re·vi·val·ist (ri·vī′vəl·ist) *n.* A preacher or leader in a religious revival movement.

revival of learning or **literature** See RENAISSANCE.

re·vive (ri·vīv′) *v.* **·vived, ·viv·ing** *v.t.* **1** To bring to life again after real or apparent death; restore to consciousness. **2** To give new vigor, health, etc., to. **3** To bring back into use or currency. **4** To make effective or operative again. **5** To renew in the mind or memory; refresh; reawaken. **6** To produce again, as an old play. — *v.i.* **7** To come back to life again; return to consciousness. **8** To assume new vigor, health, etc. **9** To come back into use or currency. **10** To become effective or operative again. [<F *revivre* <L *revivere* < *re-* again + *vivere* live] — **re·viv′er** *n.*

re·viv·i·fy (ri·viv′ə·fī) *v.t.* **·fied, ·fy·ing** To give new life or spirit to; revive. [<F *revivifier* <L *revivificare* < *re-* again + *vivificare* vivify < *vivus* alive + *facere* make] — **re·viv′i·fi·ca′tion** *n.*

rev·i·vis·cence (rev′ə·vis′əns) *n.* A renewal of life or of vital activities and vigor; a return to life; restoration; revival. Also **rev′i·vis′cen·cy.** [<L *reviviscens, -entis,* ppr. of *reviviscere* < *re-* again + *viviscere* come to life, freq. of *vivere* live] — **rev′i·vis′cent** *adj.*

rev·o·ca·ble (rev′ə·kə·bəl) *adj.* Capable of being revoked. [<F *révocable*] — **rev′o·ca·bil′i·ty** *n.* — **rev′o·ca·bly** *adv.*

rev·o·ca·tion (rev′ə·kā′shən) *n.* **1** The act of

revoking, or the state of being revoked; repeal; reversal. 2 *Law* The annulment or cancellation of an instrument, act, or promise by or in behalf of the party who made it. 3 *Obs.* A summoning back or recalling. [<OF *revocacion*] —**rev·o·ca·to·ry** (rev′ə·kə·tôr′ē, -tō′rē) *adj.*

re·voice (rē·vois′) *v.t.* **·voiced, ·voic·ing** 1 To restore or give the proper quality of tone to: to *revoice* an organ pipe. 2 To voice again or in return; echo.

re·voke (ri·vōk′) *v.* **·voked, ·vok·ing** *v.t.* 1 To annul or make void by recalling; cancel; rescind. 2 *Obs.* To call or summon back; recall. —*v.i.* 3 In card games, to fail to follow suit when possible and when required by the rules. See synonyms under ABOLISH, ANNUL, CANCEL, RECANT, RENOUNCE. —*n.* 1 An annulling or cancellation. 2 In card games, neglect to follow suit; a renege. [<OF *revoquer* <L *revocare* <*re-* back + *vocare* call] —**re·vok′er** *n.*

re·volt (ri·vōlt′) *n.* 1 A throwing off of allegiance and subjection; an uprising against authority; a rebellion or mutiny; insurrection. 2 An act of protest, refusal, revulsion, or disgust. See synonyms under REVOLUTION. —*v.i.* 1 To rise in rebellion against constituted authority; renounce allegiance; mutiny; rebel. 2 To turn away in disgust or abhorrence; be shocked or repelled: with *against, at,* or *from.* —*v.t.* 3 To cause to feel disgust or revulsion; repel. [<F *révolte* <*révolter* <Ital. *rivoltare* <L *revolutus,* pp. of *revolvere.* See REVOLVE.] —**re·volt′er** *n.*

re·volt·ing (ri·vōl′ting) *adj.* Abhorrent; loathsome; nauseating. —**re·volt′ing·ly** *adv.*

rev·o·lute (rev′ə·lo͞ot) *adj. Bot.* Rolled backward or downward from the margins upon the under surface, as certain leaves. [<L *revolutus.* See REVOLT.]

rev·o·lu·tion (rev′ə·lo͞o′shən) *n.* 1 The act or state of revolving. 2 A motion in a closed curve around a center, or a complete or apparent circuit made by a body in such a course: used generally in this sense in distinction from *rotation.* 3 Rotation about an axis; especially, a complete rotation so that every part of the moving body returns to the position from which it started. 4 *Mech.* Any winding or turning about an axis, as in a spiral or other bend, so as to come to a point corresponding to the starting point. 5 A group, round, or cycle of successive events or changes; a cycle; also, the period of space or time occupied by a cycle or by the accomplishment of a circuit. 6 The overthrow and replacement of a government or political system by those governed. 7 An extensive or drastic change in a condition, method, idea, etc.: a *revolution* in industry. [<OF *revolucion* <LL *revolutio, -onis* <L *revolutus,* pp. of *revolvere.* See REVOLVE.]

Synonyms: anarchy, confusion, disintegration, disorder, insubordination, insurrection, lawlessness, mutiny, rebellion, revolt, riot, sedition, tumult. The essential idea of *revolution,* in definition 6, is a change in the form of government or constitution, or a change of rulers, otherwise than as provided by existing laws of succession, election, etc.; while such change is apt to involve armed hostilities, these make no necessary part of a *revolution,* which may be accomplished without a battle. *Anarchy* refers to the condition of a state when government is superseded or destroyed by factions. A *revolt* is an uprising against existing authority without the comprehensive views of change in the form or administration of government that are involved in *revolution.* See CHANGE. Compare ANARCHY, REBELLION, REVOLT. *Antonyms*: authority, command, control, domination, dominion, empire, government, law, loyalty, obedience, order, rule, sovereignty, submission, supremacy.

—**American Revolution** The war for independence carried on by the thirteen American colonies against Great Britain, 1775–83. Also *Revolutionary War.* See table under WAR.

—**Chinese Revolution** The events in China during the years 1911–12, inspired by Sun Yat-sen, which overthrew the authority of the Dowager Empress and the Manchu Empire, and resulted in the establishment of a republic. —**English Revolution** The course of events in England in 1642–89 that brought about the execution of Charles I, the rise of the Commonwealth, the dethronement of James II, and the establishment of a constitutional government under William III and Mary: called in England **The Revolution,** sometimes with reference to the events of 1688.

—**French Revolution** The revolution which began in 1789, overthrew the French monarchy, and culminated in the Empire of Napoleon I.

—**Russian Revolution** The conflict (1917–22), beginning in a Petrograd uprising on March 12, 1917, that resulted in a provisional moderate government and the abdication of Nicholas II. On November 6 (October 24, Old Style), the Bolsheviks under Lenin overthrew this government (the *October Revolution*), and after resisting counter-revolution and libertarian revolution until December, 1922, united the soviet states in the Union of Soviet Socialist Republics under Communist (Bolshevik) control.

rev·o·lu·tion·ar·y (rev′ə·lo͞o′shən·er′ē) *adj.* 1 Pertaining to or of the nature of revolution, especially political; causing or tending to produce revolution. 2 Rotating; revolving. —*n. pl.* **·ar·ies** A revolutionist.

Revolutionary calendar See CALENDAR (Republican).

Revolutionary War See AMERICAN REVOLUTION under REVOLUTION.

rev·o·lu·tion·ist (rev′ə·lo͞o′shən·ist) *n.* One who takes part in a revolution.

rev·o·lu·tion·ize (rev′ə·lo͞o′shən·īz) *v.t.* **·ized, ·iz·ing** To effect a radical or entire change in the character, government, or affairs of: to *revolutionize* a country.

re·volve (ri·volv′) *v.* **·volved, ·volv·ing** *v.i.* 1 To move in an orbit about a center; move in a circle. 2 To rotate. 3 To move in cycles; recur periodically. —*v.t.* 4 To cause to move in a circle or orbit. 5 To cause to rotate. 6 To turn over mentally; consider; ponder. [<L *revolvere* <*re-* back + *volvere* roll, turn] —**re·volv′a·ble** *adj.* —**re·volv′ing** *adj.*

Synonyms: roll, rotate, turn. Any round body *rolls* which continuously touches with successive portions of its surface successive portions of another surface; a wagon wheel *rolls* along the ground. To *rotate* is said of a body that has a circular motion about its own center or axis; to *revolve* is said of a body that moves about a center outside of itself. A *revolving* body may also either *rotate* or *roll* at the same time; the earth *revolves* around the sun, and *rotates* on its own axis. Any object that is in contact with or connected with a *rolling* body is often said to *roll*; as, The car *rolls* smoothly along the track. Objects whose motion approximates or suggests a rotary motion along a supporting surface are also said to *roll*; as, Ocean waves *roll* in upon the shore. *Antonyms*: bind, chafe, grind, slide, slip, stick.

re·volv·er (ri·vol′vər) *n.* 1 One who or that which revolves. 2 A type of pistol with a revolving cylinder in the breech chambered to hold several cartridges so that it may be fired in succession without reloading.

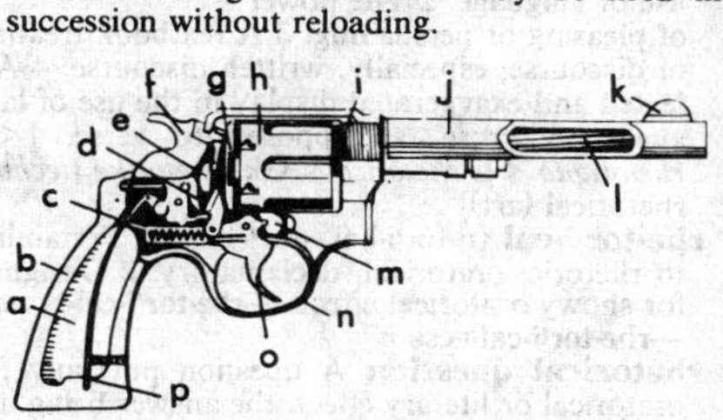

NOMENCLATURE OF THE REVOLVER

a. Stock.	*f.* Hammer.	*l.* Rifling.
b. Frame.	*g.* Extractor.	*m.* Cylinder stop.
c. Trigger spring.	*h.* Cylinder.	*n.* Trigger guard.
d. Sear.	*i.* Barrel pin.	*o.* Trigger.
e. Bolt.	*j.* Barrel.	*p.* Mainspring.
	k. Front sight.	

revolving door A door rotating like a turnstile about a central post and consisting of three or four adjustable leaves so encased in a doorway as to exclude drafts of air.

revolving fund A fund set up to finance loans or operations which yield returns that are placed in the fund for re-use.

revolving stage A circular stage divided in sections, each set for a different scene: by revolving the stage, scenes may be rapidly changed.

re·vue (ri·vyo͞o′) *n.* A kind of musical comedy, without plot or dramatic sequence, characterized by songs and dances, and by a series of skits which lampoon or burlesque contemporary people and events. [<F. See REVIEW.]

re·vul·sion (ri·vul′shən) *n.* 1 A sudden change of feeling, conduct, or conditions; a strong reaction of any kind. 2 The drawing back or away from something; violent withdrawal or recoil. 3 *Med.* A turning or diverting of any disease from one part of the body to another, as by counterirritation. [<OF <L *revulsio, -onis,* <*revulsus,* pp. of *revellere* pluck away <*re-* back + *vellere* pluck, pull] —**re·vul′sive** *adj.*

Re·wa (rē′wə) 1 A trading city in northern Madhya Pradesh State, India; capital of the former state of Vindhya Pradesh, 1948–56; before 1948, capital of the princely state of Rewa. 2 A former princely state of central India; 12,830 square miles.

re·ward (ri·wôrd′) *n.* 1 Something given or done in return; especially, a gift, prize, or recompense for merit, service, or achievement; also, punishment or retribution for evil. 2 Money offered for information, for the return of lost goods, the apprehension of criminals, etc. 3 Merited results; just deserts: He has gone to his *reward.* See synonyms under RECOMPENSE, SUBSIDY. —*v.t.* To give a reward to or for; requite; be a reward for; recompense. See synonyms under PAY, REQUITE. [<AF *rewarder,* OF *regarder* look at. Doublet of REGARD.] —**re·ward′er** *n.*

re·ward·ing (ri·wôrd′ing) *adj.* Yielding intangible rewards; worthwhile; satisfying.

re·wind (rē·wīnd′) *v.t.* **·wound, ·wind·ing** To wind or coil anew.

re·wire (rē·wīr′) *v.t.* **·wired, ·wir·ing** To wire again, as a house or a machine.

re·word (rē·wûrd′) *v.t.* 1 To say again in other words; express differently. 2 To utter or say again in the same words; repeat.

re·write (rē·rīt′) *v.t.* **·wrote, ·writ·ten, ·writ·ing** 1 To write over again. 2 In American journalism, to put into publishable form (a story submitted by a reporter). —*n.* (rē′rīt′) A news item sent in by a reporter and rewritten for publication.

Rex (reks) A masculine personal name. [<L, king]

Rey·kja·vik (rā′kyä·vēk′) The capital of Iceland, a port on the SW coast.

Rey·mont (rā′mônt), **Wladyslaw Stanislaw,** 1867–1925, Polish novelist.

Rey·nal·do (rā·näl′thō) Spanish form of REGINALD.

Reyn·ard (ren′ərd, rā′nərd) *n.* The fox, especially as the personification of cunning. [<MDu. <OF *Renard* <OHG *Reginhard,* name of the protagonist in *Reynard the Fox,* the medieval beast epic]

Rey·naud (rā·nō′), **Paul,** 1878–1966, French statesman; premier, 1940.

Reyn·old (ren′əld) See REGINALD.

Reyn·olds (ren′əldz), **Sir Joshua,** 1723–92, English painter.

Re·za·i·yeh (ri·zä′ē·yä′) See RIZAIYEH.

Rh *Chem.* Rhodium (symbol Rh).

rhab·do·man·cy (rab′də·man′sē) *n.* Divination; the discovery of springs, precious metals, etc., by means of a divining rod: also spelled *rabdomancy.* [<LL *rhabdomantia* <Gk. *rhabdomanteia* <*rhabdos* a rod + *manteia* divination] —**rhab′do·man′tist** *n.*

rha·chis (rā′kis) See RACHIS.

Rhad·a·man·thus (rad′ə·man′thəs) In Greek mythology, a son of Zeus and Europa who was noted for justice during his lifetime, and in the afterworld was made a judge, together with Minos and Aeacus. Also **Rhad′a·man′thys.** —**Rhad′a·man′thine** (-thin) *adj.*

Rhae·ti·a (rē′shē·ə) An ancient Roman province, including part of modern Tirol and the Grisons, and later extended to the Danube. Also **Rhæ′ti·a.** —**Rhae·tian** (rē′shən) *adj. & n.*

Rhaetian Alps A division of the central Alps

on the Italo-Swiss and Swiss-Austrian borders, within the boundaries of ancient Rhaetia; highest peak, 13,300 feet.

Rhae·tic (rē′tik) *adj.* **1** *Geol.* Of or pertaining to a group of rock strata representing the upper division of the Triassic system in England and western Europe. **2** Of or pertaining to the Rhaetian Alps. Also **Rhe′tic.** [< L *Rhaeticus*]

Rhae·to-Ro·man·ic (rē′tō-rō-man′ik) *adj.* Of or pertaining to the peoples of SE Switzerland, northern Italy, and Tirol, or to their Romance dialects known as Ladin, Romansch, and Friulian. —*n.* These dialects as a group.

-rhage, -rhagia, -rhagy See -RRHAGIA.

rham·na·ceous (ram-nā′shəs) *adj. Bot.* Of, pertaining to, or designating a family (*Rhamnaceae*) of spiny shrubs and small trees, the buckthorn family, having simple leaves and regular flowers in cymes. [< Gk. *rhamnos*, a kind of prickly shrub]

rha·phe (rā′fē) See RAPHE.

-raphy See -RRHAPHY.

rhap·so·dist (rap′sə-dist) *n.* **1** Among the ancient Greeks, a wandering minstrel who recited epic poems, either his own or another's; especially, one who declaimed the Homeric poems. **2** One who expresses himself with exaggeration of sentiment in speech or writing.

rhap·so·dize (rap′sə-dīz) *v.t. & v.i.* **-dized, -diz·ing** To express or recite rhapsodically.

rhap·so·dy (rap′sə-dē) *n. pl.* **-dies 1** A series of disconnected and often extravagant sentences, extracts, or utterances, gathered or composed under excitement; rapt or rapturous utterance. **2** In ancient Greece, an epic poem, or a part of such a poem, especially from the *Odyssey* or *Iliad*, recited by a rhapsodist; also, the recitation itself. **3** *Music* An instrumental composition of irregular form, often suggesting the qualities of improvisation. **4** A miscellaneous collection; a medley. [< F *rapsodie* < L *rhapsodia* < Gk. *rhapsōidia* < *rhapsōidos* rhapsodist < *rhaptein* stitch together + *ōidē* song] —**rhap·sod·ic** (rap·sod′ik) or **-i·cal** *adj.* —**rhap·sod′i·cal·ly** *adv.*

rhat·a·ny (rat′ə-nē) *n.* **1** Either of two perennial, shrubby South American plants of the pea family (genus *Krameria*), the **Peruvian rhatany** (*K. triandra*) or the **Brazilian rhatany** (*K. argentea*), whose dried roots are used in medicine. **2** The roots of these plants, or medicinal substances prepared from them. Also spelled *ratany*. [< NL < Sp. *ratania* < Quechua]

rhe·a (rē′ə) *n.* A ratite bird (genus *Rhea*) of the plains of South America, smaller than true ostriches, and having three toes: also called *ostrich*. [< NL]

Rhe·a (rē′ə) In Greek mythology, the daughter of Uranus and Gaea, wife of her brother Kronos, and mother of Zeus, Poseidon, Hades, Hera, Demeter, and Hestia: identified with the Phrygian *Cybele* and the Roman *Ops*: also called *Mother of the Gods.* See KRONOS.

-rhea See -RRHEA.

Rhea Sylvia In Roman legend, a vestal, the mother by Mars of Romulus and Remus.

Rhee (rē), **Syngman,** 1875–1965, Korean statesman; president 1948–1960.

Rheims (rēmz, *Fr.* rans) See REIMS.

rhe·in (rē′in) *n. Chem.* A yellow crystalline acid, $C_{15}H_8O_6$, obtained from senna leaves and Chinese rhubarb: sometimes used as a purgative. [< Gk. *rhēon* rhubarb + -IN]

Rhein (rīn) The German name for RHINE.

Rhein·fall (rīn′fäl) The German name for SCHAFFHAUSEN FALLS.

Rhein·gold (rīn′gōld, *Ger.* rīn′gōlt) **1** In Wagner's *Der Ring des Nibelungen*, the gold snatched from the Rhine by Alberich, from which he made the magical ring. **2** The title of the first of the tetralogy of music dramas by Wagner forming *Der Ring des Nibelungen*. Also spelled *Rhinegold*. [< G]

Rhein·land (rīn′länt) The German name for RHINELAND.

Rhein·pfalz (rīn′pfälts) The German name for RHINE PALATINATE.

rhe·mat·ic (ri-mat′ik) *adj.* **1** Relating to or derived from a verb. **2** Pertaining to the formation of words. [< Gk. *rhēma* word, verb]

Rhen·ish (ren′ish) *adj.* Pertaining to the river Rhine, or to the adjacent lands. —*n.* Rhine wine. [< L *Rhenus* Rhine]

Rhenish Hesse An administrative division of Rhineland-Palatinate, West Germany; 517 square miles.

Rhenish Prussia See RHINE PROVINCE.

rhe·ni·um (rē′nē-əm) *n.* A heavy, ductile, silvery-white element (symbol Re, atomic number 75) having a high melting point. See PERIODIC TABLE. [< NL < L *Rhenus* Rhine]

Rhe·nus (rē′nəs) Ancient name for the RHINE.

rheo- *combining form* Current or flow, as of water or electricity: *rheostat.* [< Gk. *rheos* a current]

rhe·o·base (rē′ə-bās) *n. Physiol.* The minimum voltage of an electric current required to stimulate a nerve or muscle. Compare CHRONAXY.

rhe·ol·o·gy (rē-ol′ə-jē) *n.* The study of the properties and behavior of flowing substances; the science of flow. [< RHEO- + -LOGY] —**rhe·ol′o·gist** *n.*

rhe·om·e·ter (rē-om′ə-tər) *n.* A device for indicating the force or velocity of blood circulation. [< RHEO- + -METER]

rhe·o·scope (rē′ə-skōp) *n.* A galvanoscope. —**rhe′o·scop′ic** (-skop′ik) *adj.*

rhe·o·stat (rē′ə-stat) *n. Electr.* A device for regulating current-strength of electricity, as by resistance coils. [< RHEO- + Gk. *statos* standing] —**rhe′o·stat′ic** *adj.*

rhe·o·tax·is (rē′ə-tak′sis) *n. Biol.* The response of an organism to the influence of a current, especially of water. —**rhe′o·tac′tic** (-tak′tik) *adj.*

rhe·ot·ro·pism (rē-ot′rə-piz′əm) *n. Biol.* A tendency in plant or animal organisms, when exposed to the influence of a current of water, to arrange themselves with their long axes either in the direction of or against the current. —**rhe·o·trop·ic** (rē′ə-trop′ik) *adj.*

rhe·sus (rē′səs) *n.* A macaque (*Macaca mulatta*) with a moderate tail, common throughout India. [< NL < Gk. *Rhēsos* Rhesus; arbitrarily assigned]

Rhe·sus (rē′səs) In the *Iliad*, a king of Thrace and ally of the Trojans, killed by Odysseus the night of his arrival before Troy.

Rhe·sus factor (rē′səs) See RH FACTOR.

rhe·tor (rē′tər) *n.* **1** Formerly, one who taught rhetoric. **2** An orator. [< L < Gk. *rhētōr*]

rhet·o·ric (ret′ə-rik) *n.* **1** The art of discourse; skill in the use of language. **2** The power of pleasing or persuading. **3** A textbook treating of discourse; especially, written discourse. **4** Affected and exaggerated display in the use of language. **5** Prose, as opposed to verse. [< F *rhétorique* < L *rhetorica* < Gk. *rhētorikē* (*technē*) rhetorical (art)]

rhe·tor·i·cal (ri-tôr′i-kəl, -tor′-) *adj.* **1** Pertaining to rhetoric; oratorical; declamatory. **2** Designed for showy oratorical effect. —**rhe·tor′i·cal·ly** *adv.* —**rhe·tor′i·cal·ness** *n.*

rhetorical question A question put only for oratorical or literary effect, the answer being implied in the question.

rhetorical stress The emphasis required by the meaning of a line or the lines in a poem: opposed to *metrical stress.*

rhet·o·ri·cian (ret′ə-rish′ən) *n.* **1** A master or teacher of rhetoric. **2** An orator; one who writes or speaks eloquently. [< F *rhétoricien*]

rheum (rōōm) *n.* **1** *Pathol.* Catarrhal discharge from the nose and eyes; hence, a cold. **2** *Med.* Any thin watery flux, as tears or saliva. [< OF *reume* < L *rheuma* < Gk. *rheuma* a flow < *rheein* flow] —**rheum′y** *adj.*

rheu·mat·ic (rōō·mat′ik) *adj.* Pertaining to, causing, or affected with rheumatism. —*n.*

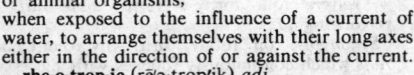

RHEOSTAT
a. Sliding contact.
b. Resistance coil.
c. Lug.

RHESUS
(From 12 to 18 inches long: tail, 6 to 8 inches)

1 One affected with or liable to rheumatism. **2** *pl. Colloq.* Rheumatic pains. [< OF *reumatique* < L *rheumaticus* < Gk. *rheumatikos* < *rheuma.* See RHEUM.]

rheumatic fever *Pathol.* A severe, probably infectious disease chiefly affecting children and young adults, characterized by painful inflammation around the joints, typically intermittent fever, and inflammation of the pericardium and valves of the heart.

rheu·ma·tism (rōō′mə-tiz′əm) *n. Pathol.* **1** A variable, shifting, painful inflammation and stiffness of the muscles, joints, or other structures. **2** Rheumatic fever. **3** Rheumatoid arthritis. [< L *rheumatismus* rheum < Gk. *rheumatismos* < *rheuma* rheum]

rheu·ma·toid (rōō′mə-toid) *adj. Pathol.* **1** Resembling rheumatism or rheumatic symptoms: *rheumatoid* arthritis. **2** Afflicted with rheumatism. Also **rheu′ma·toi′dal** (-toid′-). —**rheu′ma·toi′dal·ly** *adv.*

rheumatoid arthritis *Pathol.* A persisting inflammatory disease of the joints, marked by atrophy, rarefaction of the bones, and deformities.

Rheydt (rīt) A city in western North Rhine-Westphalia, West Germany; the twin city of München-Gladbach.

Rh factor *Biochem.* Any of a group of genetically transmitted agglutinogens present in the blood of most individuals (Rh positive) and which may cause hemolytic reactions under certain conditions, as during pregnancy or following transfusions with blood lacking this factor (Rh negative). Also called *Rhesus factor.*

rhig·o·lene (rig′ə-lēn) *n. Chem.* A colorless, volatile, inflammable liquid distillate of petroleum: used in medicine as a local freezing anesthetic for minor operations. [< Gk. *rhigos* frost + L *oleum* oil]

rhin- Var. of RHINO-.

rhi·nal (rī′nəl) *adj.* Of or pertaining to the nose; nasal. [< RHIN- + -AL]

Rhine (rīn) The principal river of west central Europe, flowing 810 miles north from SE Switzerland, through Germany and Netherlands, to the North Sea, forming part of the SW boundary of Germany, and dividing, in the Netherlands, into the *Waal*, the *Lek*, the *Oude Rijn*, and the *Ijssel*: ancient *Rhenus*, German *Rhein*, Dutch *Rijn*. French **Rhin** (ran).

Rhine (rīn), **Joseph Banks,** born 1895, U.S. psychologist.

Rhine·gold (rīn′gōld) The hoard of the Nibelungs, secreted in the Rhine. Compare RHEINGOLD.

Rhine·land (rīn′land′) **1** That part of Germany west of the Rhine. **2** The Rhine Province. German *Rheinland.*

Rhine·land-Pa·lat·i·nate (rīn′land′pə-lat′ə-nāt) A state of West Germany; 7,654 square miles; capital, Mainz. German **Rhein·land-Pfalz** (rīn′länt·pfälts′).

rhi·nen·ceph·a·lon (rī′nen-sef′ə-lon) *n. pl.* **-la** (-lə) *Anat.* That portion of the brain which forms the olfactory lobe, consisting of the olfactory tubercle, tract, and bulb, which give origin to the sense of smell. [< RHIN- + ENCEPHALON] —**rhi·nen·ce·phal·ic** (rī′nen-sə-fal′ik) *adj.*

Rhine Palatinate See PALATINATE, THE. German *Rheinpfalz.*

Rhine Province A former Prussian province in western Germany, included since 1945 in Rhineland-Palatinate; 9,451 square miles; former capital, Coblenz: also *Rhenish Prussia.*

rhine·stone (rīn′stōn′) *n.* A highly refractive, colorless glass or paste, used as an imitation gemstone. [Trans. of F *caillou du Rhin*; orig. made at Strasbourg]

Rhine wine Wine made from grapes grown in the neighborhood of the Rhine; specifically, the white, still wines of this region, noted for their delicate bouquet; hock.

rhi·ni·tis (rī-nī′tis) *n. Pathol.* Inflammation of the mucous membranes of the nose; nasal catarrh. [< RHIN- + -ITIS]

rhi·no (rī′nō) *n. pl.* **-nos** A rhinoceros.

rhino- *combining form* Nose; nasal: *rhinoplasty.* Also, before vowels, *rhin-.* [< Gk. *rhis, rhinos* nose]

rhi·noc·e·ros (rī-nos′ər-əs) *n. pl.* **-ros·es** or **-ros** A large, herbivorous, odd-toed mammal (family *Rhinocerotidae*) of Africa and Asia, with one or two keratin-fiber horns on the

snout, a very thick hide, and the upper lip protruded and prehensile. [< LL <Gk. *rhino-kerōs* <*rhis, rhinos* nose + *keras* horn]

RHINOCEROS
a. African: About 5 feet at the shoulder;
to 3000 pounds.
b. Indian: About 5½ feet at the shoulder;
to 4000 pounds.

rhi·nol·o·gy (rī·nol′ə·jē) *n.* The branch of medicine that relates to the nose and its diseases. [<RHINO- + -LOGY] —**rhi·nol′o·gist** *n.*

rhi·no·plas·ty (rī′nō·plas′tē) *n.* Plastic surgery of the nose. —**rhi′no·plas′tic** *adj.*

rhi·no·scope (rī′nə·skōp) *n.* An instrument for inspecting the nasal cavities.

rhi·nos·co·py (rī·nos′kə·pē) *n.* Inspection of the nasal passages.

rhizo- *combining form* Root; pertaining to a root or to roots: *rhizogenic.* Also, before vowels, **rhiz-**. [<Gk. *rhiza* a root]

rhi·zo·bi·um (rī·zō′bē ·əm) *n. pl.* **·bi·a** (-bē·ə) *Bacteriol.* One of a genus (*Rhizobium*) of rod-shaped, nitrogen-fixing bacteria causing nodules on the roots of leguminous plants. [<NL <RHIZO- + Gk. *bios* life]

rhi·zo·car·pous (rī′zō·kär′pəs) *adj. Bot.* Having annual stems and foliage growing from perennial roots: said of perennial plants. Also **rhi′zo·car′pic.**

rhi·zo·ceph·a·lous (rī′zō ·sef′ə·ləs) *adj. Zool.* Naming or pertaining to a suborder (*Rhizo-cephala*) of parasitic cirripeds, without antennae or feet, which attach themselves to crabs by a short peduncle from which rootlike processes branch out.

rhi·zo·gen·ic (rī′zō·jen′ik) *adj. Bot.* Root-producing: said of the layer of mother cells at the periphery of the central cylinder of a root that gives rise to rootlets. Also **rhi·zog·e·nous** (rī·zoj′ə·nəs).

rhi·zoid (rī′zoid) *adj.* Rootlike; similar to or resembling a root. —*n. Bot.* A delicate filiform or hairlike organ developed on all kinds of thalli, moss stems, etc.: the analog of the roots of flowering plants, serving for absorption and attachment. —**rhi·zoi·dal** (rī·zoid′l) *adj.*

rhi·zome (rī′zōm) *n. Bot.* A procumbent or subterranean rootlike stem, producing roots from its lower surface and leaves or shoots from its upper surface; a rootstock. Also **rhi·zo·ma** (rī·zō′mə). [<NL *rhizoma* < Gk. *rhizōma* mass of roots, ult. <*rhiza* root] —**rhi·zom·a·tous** (rī·zom′ə·təs, -zō′mə-) *adj.*

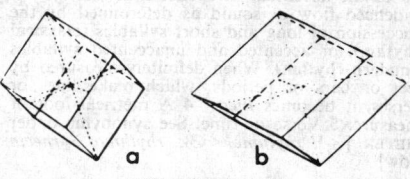

RHIZOME
The bearded iris

rhi·zo·morph (rī′zə·môrf) *n. Bot.* One of the rootlike parts of the mycelium, composed of many united hyphal strands, by which certain fungi attach themselves to and penetrate the higher plants.

rhi·zo·mor·phous (rī′zō·môr′fəs) *adj. Bot.* Branching after the manner of rootlets: said of mycelia.

rhi·zoph·a·gous (rī·zof′ə ·gəs) *adj.* Feeding on roots. [<RHIZO- + -PHAGOUS]

rhi·zo·pod (rī′zə·pod) *n.* Any member of a subclass (*Rhizopoda*) of protozoans with pseudopodia for locomotion and the ingestion of food. —**rhi·zop·o·dan** (rī·zop′ə·dən) *adj. & n.* —**rhi·zop′o·dous** *adj.*

rhi·zot·o·my (rī·zot′ə·mē) *n. Surg.* The division of the roots of the spinal nerves, for the relief of pain or spastic paralysis. [<RHIZO- + -TOMY]

rho (rō) *n.* The seventeenth letter and twelfth consonant of the Greek alphabet (P, ≥R/ρ); equivalent to the English *r* aspirated. As a numeral it denotes 100. [<Gk. *rhō*]

Rho·da (rō′də) A feminine personal name. [<Gk., rose] —**Rhoda** A damsel in the house of Mary, the mother of John. *Acts* xii 13.

rho·da·mine (rō′də·mēn, -min) *n. Chem.* Any of various red or pink dyestuffs obtained by condensing an amino derivative of phenol with phthalic anhydride. The solution shows green fluorescence. Also **rho′da·min** (-min). [<Gk. *rhodon* rose + AMINE]

Rhode Island (rōd) A southern New England State of the United States; 1,214 square miles; capital, Providence; entered the Union May 29, 1790, one of the original thirteen States: officially **The State of Rhode Island and Providence Plantations;** the smallest State in the Union; nickname *Little Rhody:* abbr. RI —**Rhode Islander**

Rhode Island Red An American breed of domestic fowls, reddish and black in color, having smooth yellow legs and a small single comb.

Rhodes (rōdz) **1** The largest island of the Dodecanese group; 545 square miles. **2** Its chief city, capital of the Dodecanese Islands. Italian *Rodi.* Greek **Ró·dhos** (rô′thôs). See COLOSSUS OF RHODES.

Rhodes (rōdz), **Cecil (John),** 1853–1902, British South African financier and statesman. —**Eugene Manlove,** 1869–1934, U.S. government scout, cowboy, and short-story writer. —**James Ford,** 1848–1927, U.S. industrialist and historian.

Rhodes, Knights of See HOSPITALER.

Rho·de·sia (rō·dē′zhə, -zhē·ə) **1** Formerly, a region of south central Africa divided by the Zambezi river into **Northern Rhodesia,** now ZAMBIA a British Prontectorate, and **Southern Rhodesia,** now ZIMBABWE a British Colony. **2** A British Colony in south central Africa consisting of the former Southern Rhodesia; unilaterally declared its independence in 1965; 150,333 sq. mi.; capital, Salisbury. —**Rho·de′sian** *adj. & n.*

Rhodesian man K(rō-dē′zhən) An African forerunner (*Homo rhodesiensis*) of Neanderthal man, represented by the massive upper jaw and cranium of a skull discovered in 1921 at Broken Hill, Rhodesia.

Rhodes scholarship Any of a number of scholarships, tenable at Oxford University, established by the will of Cecil John Rhodes and providing for the support of selected students from the British colonies, Germany, and the States and Territories of the United States.

Rho·di·an (rō′dē·ən) *adj.* Of or pertaining to the island of Rhodes or to the Knights of Rhodes. —*n.* A Knight of Rhodes; also, a native of that island.

rho·dic (rō′dik) *adj. Chem.* Of, pertaining to, or derived from rhodium: *rhodic* sulfate.

rho·di·um (rō′dē·əm) *n.* A silvery-white metallic element (symbol Rh, atomic number 45) sometimes occurring native and in ores associated with platinum, used in alloys. See PERIODIC TABLE. [<NL <Gk. *rhodon* rose; from the color of its salts]

rho·do·chro·site (rō′də·krō′sīt) *n.* A vitreous rose-red or variously colored rhombohedral manganese carbonate, MnCO₃. [<G *rhodoch-rosit* <Gk. *rhodochrōs* rose-colored <*rhodon* (rose + *chrōs* color]

rho·do·den·dron (rō′də·den′drən) *n.* Any of a genus (*Rhododendron*) of showy evergreen shrubs or small trees of the heath family, with profuse clusters of beautiful flowers, found growing wild in mountainous regions; especially, the **great rhododendron** (*R. macrophyllum*), the State flower of Washington, and the **rosebay rhododendron** (*R. maximum*), the State flower of West Virginia. [<L <Gk. *rhodon* rose + *dendron* tree]

rho·do·lite (rō′də·līt) *n.* A pale rose-colored garnet, used as a gem. [< Gke. *rhodon* rose + -LITE]

rho·do·nite (rō′də·nīt) *n.* A vitreous, red or pink manganese silicate, MnSiO₃, crystallizing in the triclinic system, and often used as an ornamental stone. [<Gk. *rhodon* rose]

Rhod·o·pe Mountains (rod′ə·pē) A mountain chain of the Balkan Peninsula, dividing Bulgaria from Thrace and Macedonia; highest peak, 9,591 feet.

rho·dop·sin (rō·dop′sin) *n. Biochem.* The rose-colored component of visual purple, breaking down into retinene on exposure to light. [<Gk. *irhodon* rose + *opsis* appearance]

rho·do·ra (rō·dôr′ə, -dō′rə) *n.* A handsome shrub (*Rhododendron canadense*), from 1 to 3 feet high, with terminal clusters of pale-purple flowers preceding the leaves. It is found in cool bogs, from Pennsylvania to Canada. [< L *rhodora* meadowsweet]

-rhoea See -RRHEA.

rhomb (rom, romb) *n.* A rhombus. [<F *rhombe.* See RHOMBUS.]

rhom·ben·ceph·a·lon (rom′ben·sef′ə·lon) *n. Anat.* The parts of the cerebrospinal axis that develop from the posterior cerebral vesicle; medulla oblongata and cerebellum taken together. [<NL]

rhom·bic (rom′bik) *adj.* **1** Pertaining to or having the shape of a rhombus. **2** Orthorhombic. Also **rhom′bi·cal.**

rhom·bo·he·dral (rom′bə·hē′drəl) *adj. Geom.* Pertaining to a rhombohedron.

rhombohedral system In the classification of some authors, the trigonal division of the hexagonal crystal system.

rhom·bo·he·dron (rom′bə·hē ′drən) *n. pl.* **·drons** or **·dra** (drə) *Geom.* A prismatic form included within six equal rhombic faces.

RHOMBOHEDRONS
a. Acute. *b.* Obtuse.

rhom·boid (rom′boid) *nw. Geom.* **1** A parallelogram having opposite sides and opposite angles equal but no right angle. **2** A solid bounded by such parallelograms. —*adj.* **1** Having the character or shape of a rhomboid. **2** Having a shape approaching that of a rhombus, as one of two muscles attached to the shoulder blades. [<F *rhomboïde*] —**rhom·boi·dal** (rom·boid′l) *adj.*

rhom·bus (rom′bəs) *n. pl.* **·bus·es** or **·bi** (-bī) *Geom.* **1** An equilateral parallelogram having the angles usually, but not necessarily, oblique; a square may be considered as a special case of the *rhombus.* **2** A rhombohedron. [<L <Gk. *rhombos* spinning top, rhomb]

rhon·chus (rong′kəs) *n. pl.* **·chi** (-kī) *Pathol.* A rattling or whistling sound in respiration, especially when it resembles snoring; a râle. [<L <Gk. *rhonchos*] — **rhon′chal, rhon′chi·al** *adj.*

Rhond·da (ron′də) An urban district and coalmining center of Glamorganshire, SE Wales: (also *Ystradyfodwg*).

Rhond·da (ron′də), **Viscount,** 1856–1918, David Alfred Thomas, British industrialist and administrator.

Rhône (rōn) A river in Switzerland and SE France, flowing 504 miles to the Mediterranean including 45 miles through Lake Geneva above Geneva; enters the Gulf of the Lion below Arles. Also **Rhone.**

rhu·barb (rōō′bärb) *n.* **1** A stout, coarse, perennial herb (genus *Rheum*) of the buckwheat family, having large leaves and small clusters of flowers on tall fleshy stalks; especially, the common rhubarb or pie plant (*R. rhaponticum*), whose acid leaf stalks are used in cooking. **2** The dried roots of the medicinal rhubarb (*R. officinale* and *R. palmatum*), used as a cathartic and bitter tonic. **2** *U.S. Slang* A heated argument; scuffle or quarrel. [<OF *reubarbe* <LL *rhabarbarum* <Gk. *Rha* Volga river, Volga plant, rhubarb + *barbaron* foreign; so called because orig. imported from Russia]

rhumb (rum, rumb) *n. Naut.* **1** One of the 32 points of the mariners' compass, separated by arcs of 11° 15′. **2** One of these arcs or divisions. [<OF *rumb*]

rhum·ba (rum′bə) See RUMBA.

rhumb line A line or course along the surface of a sphere crossing successive meridians at the same angle; a loxodromic curve.

Rhus (rus) *n.* A large genus of trees or shrubs

of the cashew family, including the true sumacs. Poison ivy and poison oak, also often included, are now placed in the genus *Toxicodendron*. [<NL <L <Gk. *rhous* sumac]

rhyme (rīm), **rhym·er** (rī′mər), **rhyme·ster** (rīm′stər), etc. See RIME, etc.

rhyn·cho·ce·pha·li·an (ring′kō·sə·fā′lē·ən) *adj.* Pertaining to or designating a nearly extinct order of lizardlike reptiles *(Rhynchocephalia)*, represented by only one genus *(Sphenodon)*, the tuatara of New Zealand. —*n.* One of the *Rhynchocephalia*. [<NL *Rhynchocephalia*, name of the order <Gk. *rhynchos* snout + *kephalē* head]

rhy·o·lite (rī′ə·līt) *n.* A highly acidic, variously colored volcanic rock. [<Gk. *rhyax* stream + -LITE]

rhythm (rith′əm) *n.* **1** Movement characterized by regular measured or harmonious recurrence of stress, beat, sound, accent, or motion: the *rhythm* of the pulse, the *rhythm* of moving oars. **2** The musical property dependent on the regular succession of accents or tone-impulses; accent-movement or accent-structure; also, a system or kind of accentuation as determined by the make-up of the accentual divisions. **3** In poetry, the cadenced flow of sound as determined by the succession of long and short syllables (**classical rhythm**), or accented and unaccented syllables (**modern rhythm**). When definitely measured by feet or bars or periods, which make lines or verses, it becomes *meter*. **4** A metrical foot or measure. **5** Verse or rime. See synonyms under METER. [<F *rhythme* <Gk. *rhythmos* <*rheein* flow]

CHARACTERISTIC DANCE RHYTHMS
a. Cracovienne. *b.* Polka. *c.* Mazurka.

rhythm and blues Rock-and-roll music with blues elements added.

rhythm method A method of birth control that involves not having intercourse during the female's period of ovulation.

rhyth·mic (rith′mik) *adj.* Relating to or characterized by rhythm: contrasted with *harmonic*. Also **rhyth′mi·cal.** —**rhyth′mi·cal·ly** *adv.*

rhyth·mics (rith′miks) *n.* The science of rhythm.

rhyth·mist (rith′mist) *n.* A master of rhythmical composition; also, one versed in rhythmics.

ri·al (rī′al) *n.* The monetary unit of Iran; a silver coin, twenty of which equal one pahlavi. [<OF *rial, real* royal]

ri·al·to (rē·al′tō) *n. pl.* **·tos** A market or place of exchange. [from *Rialto* <*Rivo Alto* ancient name of the island on which Venice was founded about 800 <Ital. *rivo* channel (<L *rivus* brook) + *alto* deep <L *altus*]

Ri·al·to (rē·al′tō, *Ital.* rē·äl′tō) **1** An island comprising the ancient business quarter of Venice. **2** A bridge over the Grand Canal connecting the old Rialto with the island of San Marco at Venice, Italy: short for **Ponte del Rialto. 3** In New York City, the theater district.

ri·ant (rī′ənt) *adj.* Laughing. [<F, laughing, ppr. of *rire* laugh] —**ri′ant·ly** *adv.*

ri·a·ta (rē·ä′tə) *n.* A lasso; lariat. [<Sp. *reata* <*reatar* tie again <L *re-* again + *aptare* fit]

Ri·au Archipelago (rē′ou) See RIOUW ARCHIPELAGO.

rib (rib) *n.* **1** *Anat.* One of the series of bony rods attached to the spine of most vertebrates, and nearly encircling the thoracic cavity. In man there are twelve ribs on each side, forming the walls of the thorax, of which the first seven (**true** or **sternal ribs**) are attached to the sternum, the last five (**false** or **asternal ribs**) being either attached by their edges to the rib above, as in the upper three, or free distally (**floating ribs**), as in the lower two. ◆ Collateral adjective: *costal*. **2** Something likened to the rib of animal; a ridge, strip, or band. **3** A curved side timber bending away from the keel in a boat or ship, or a curved timber or support in a vault. **4** A raised wale or stripe in cloth or knit goods, as stockings. **5** *Aeron.* An element in the construction of an airplane wing, usually extending fore and aft and crossing the wing spars, to hold the fabric of the wing in shape. **6** *Bot.* A vein or nerve of a leaf, especially the middle one; any ridge on a plant. **7** Cut of meat including one or more ribs. **8** A wife: in jocular allusion to *Gen.* ii 22. **9** *Slang* A practical joke. —*v.t.* **ribbed, rib·bing 1** To make with ridges: to *rib* a piece of knitting. **2** To strengthen or protect by or enclose within ribs. **3** *Slang* To make fun of; tease. [OE *ribb*]

rib·ald (rib′əld) *adj.* Pertaining to or indulging in coarse or offensive language or vulgar jokes; coarsely jocular. —*n.* One who uses coarse or abusive language. [<OF *ribauld* <Gmc. Cf. MHG *riben* copulate, MDu. *ribe* whore.]

rib·ald·ry (rib′əl·drē) *n.* Coarse or ribald language. [<OF *ribauderie*]

rib·and (rib′ənd) *n. Archaic* A decorative ribbon. [Earlier form of RIBBON]

rib·band (rib′band′, rib′ənd, -ən) *n. Naut.* A lengthwise strip following a vessel's curves and bolted to its ribs, to hold them in place until they receive the planking or plating. Also **rib′-band′**. [<RIB + BAND[1]]

Rib·ben·trop (rib′ən·trôp), **Joachim von,** 1893–1946, German Nazi diplomat; executed.

rib·bing (rib′ing) *n.* An arrangement or collection of ribs, as in ribbed cloth, etc.

rib·bon (rib′ən) *n.* **1** A narrow strip of fine fabric, usually silk or satin, having two selvages, and commonly less than eight inches wide, made in a variety of weaves: used as trimming. **2** Something shaped like or suggesting a ribbon, as a watch spring, or a painted stripe on the side of a vessel. **3** A narrow strip; a shred: torn to *ribbons*. **4** An ink-bearing strip of cloth in a typewriter. **5** A ribband. **6** *pl. Colloq.* Driving reins. **7 a** A colored strip of cloth worn to signify membership in an order, the award of a prize, etc. **b** A similar strip of cloth worn on the left breast of a military or naval uniform to indicate campaigns served in, medals won, etc. **8** A ticker tape. —*v.t.* To ornament with ribbons; also, to form or tear into ribbons. —*adj.* **1** Made of or like ribbon. **2** Having parallel bands or streaks, as certain minerals: *ribbon* jasper. **3** Of a standard to receive a prize in a competitive show: a *ribbon* hog. [<OF *riban*; origin unknown]

rib·bon·fish (rib′ən·fish′) *n. pl.* **·fish** or **·fish·es** A long marine fish with a compressed, ribbonlike body, as an oarfish or dealfish.

ribbon snake The American garter snake.

Ri·be·ra (rē·vā′rä), **José,** 1588–1656, Spanish painter: sometimes called "Lo Spagnoletto."

ri·bo·fla·vin (rī′bō·flā′vin) *n. Biochem.* A member of the vitamin B complex, vitamin B_2, an orange-yellow, crystalline compound, $C_{17}H_{20}N_4O_6$, found in milk, green leafy vegetables, egg yolk, and meats, and also made synthetically: formerly called *lactoflavin, vitamin G.* [<RIBO(SE) + FLAVIN]

ri·bo·nu·cle·ic acid (rī′bō·nōō·klē′ik, -nyōō-) *Biochem.* A nucleic acid that serves to promote the synthesis of cell proteins. Abbr. *RNA*.

ri·bose (rī′bōs) *n. Chem.* A sugar, $C_5H_{10}O_5$, derived from pentose and occurring in certain nucleic acids. [<RIB(ONIC ACID) + -OSE[2]]

ri·bo·some (rī′bə·sōm) *n. Biol.* One of a class of minute protein particles found in the cytoplasm of plant and animal cells, associated with ribonucleic acid in the transmission of genetic characteristics.

rib·wort (rib′wûrt′) *n.* The English plantain *(Plantago lanceolata)*, or a related species. See PLANTAIN.

-ric *combining form* Realm or jurisdiction of: *bishopric*. [OE *rīce* kingdom, realm]

Ri·car·do (*Ital.* rē·kär′dō, *Pg.* rē·kär′thōō, *Sp.* -thō) Italian, Portuguese, and Spanish form of RICHARD. Also *Ital.* **Ric·car·do** (rēk·kär′dō), *Lat.* **Ri·car·dus** (rē·kär′dəs).

Ri·car·do (ri·kär′dō), **David,** 1772–1823, English political economist. —**Ri·car′di·an** *adj.* & *n.*

Ric·cio (rēt′chō), **David** See RIZZIO.

rice (rīs) *n.* **1** An annual cereal grass *(Oryza sativa)*, widely cultivated on wet land in warm climates. **2** The edible grain or seeds of this plant. [<F *riz* <L *oryza* <Gk. *oryza*]

Rice (rīs), **Elmer,** 1892–1967, U.S. dramatist. —**Grantland,** 1888–1954, U.S. journalist.

rice·bird (rīs′bûrd′) *n.* **1** Any bird frequenting rice fields; especially, in the southern United States, the bobolink: also **rice bunting. 2** The Java sparrow.

rice·braid (rīs′brād′) *n.* Braid made to resemble rice grains strung together lengthwise.

rice paper 1 Paper made from rice straw. **2** A delicate vegetable paper made from the pith of a Chinese shrub, the **rice-paper plant** *(Tetrapanax papyriferus)*, pared into thin rolls and flattened into sheets.

ric·er (rī′sər) *n.* A kitchen utensil consisting of a perforated container through which potatoes and other vegetables are pressed, emerging in small particles resembling grains of rice.

rice weevil A small brown weevil *(Sitophilus* or *Calandra oryza)* destructive to growing rice and the stored grain. For illustration see INSECTS (injurious).

rich (rich) *adj.* **1** Having large possessions, as of money, goods, or lands; wealthy; opulent. **2** Composed of rare or precious materials; valuable; costly: *rich* fabrics. **3** Having in a high degree qualities pleasing to the senses; luscious to the taste: often implying an unwholesome excess of butter, fats, flavoring, etc. **4** Full, satisfying, and pleasing, as a tone, voice, color, or perfume. **5** Luxuriant; abundant: *rich* hair; *rich* crops. **6** Yielding abundant returns; fruitful. **7** Abundantly supplied: often with *in* or *with*. **8** Abounding in desirable qualities; of full strength, as blood. **9** *Colloq.* Exceedingly humorous; amusing or ridiculous: a *rich* joke. See synonyms under FERTILE, RACY. [OE *rīce*; infl. in form by OF *riche* <Gmc.] —**rich′ly** *adv.* —**rich′ness** *n.*

Rich·ard (rich′ərd; *Fr.* rē·shär′, *Ger.* rē′khärt) A masculine personal name. Also *Lat.* **Ri·char·dus** (rē·kär′dəs), *Du.* **Ri·chart** (rē′shärt). [<Gmc., strong ruler]

—**Richard I,** 1157–99, king of England 1189–1199; went on Third Crusade: called "Coeur de Lion" or "the Lion-Hearted."

—**Richard II,** 1367–1400, king of England 1377–99, deposed by Henry IV.

—**Richard III,** 1452–85, king of England 1483–85; usurped throne; killed at Bosworth.

Richard Roe See JOHN DOE.

Rich·ards (rich′ərdz), **Ivor Armstrong,** 1893-1979, English literary critic. —**Theodore William,** 1868–1928, U.S. chemist.

Rich·ard·son (rich′ərd·sən), **Henry Handel** Pseudonym of Henrietta Richardson, 1878?–1946, Australian novelist. —**Henry Hobson,** 1838–1886, U.S. architect. —**Owen Willans,** 1879–1959, English physicist. —**Samuel,** 1689?–1761, English novelist.

Ri·che·lieu (rē·shə·lyœ′), **Duc de,** 1585–1642, Armand Jean Duplessis, French cardinal and statesman; prime minister of Louis XIII.

Ri·che·lieu River (rē·shə·lyœ′, rish′ə·lōō) A river of southern Quebec, flowing 75 miles north from Lake Champlain to the Saint Lawrence.

rich·es (rich′iz) *n. pl.* [In Middle English, this was a singular noun and spelled *richess* or *richesse*; now, from its form, used in the plural] **1** Abundant possessions; wealth. **2** Hence, abundance of whatever is precious. See synonyms under WEALTH. [<F *richesse* <*riche* <Gmc.]

Ri·chet (rē·she′), **Charles Robert,** 1850–1935, French physiologist.

Rich·mond (rich′mənd) **1** The capital of Virginia, a port on the James River: capital of the Confederacy, 1861–65. **2** A borough on the Thames in northern Surrey, England. **3** A borough of New York City coextensive with Staten Island.

Rich·ter (rikh′tər), **Johann Paul Friedrich,** 1763–1825, German author and humorist: pseudonym *Jean Paul*.

Rich·ter scale (rik′tər) A logarithmic measure of the estimated energy released by earthquakes according to which 1 represents an imperceptible tremor and 10 a theoretical maximum about one thousand times greater than any recorded earthquake. [after Charles R. *Richter*, born 1900, U.S. seismologist]

Richt·ho·fen (rikht′hō·fən), **Baron Manfred von,** 1892–1918, German aviator in World War I; killed in action.

rich·weed (rich′wēd′) *n.* **1** An herb *(Pilea pumila)* of the nettle family growing in wet,

cool places: also called *clearweed.* 2 A strong-scented herb *(Collinsonia canadensis)* of the mint family: also called *horse balm.* 3 Ragweed. 4 White snakeroot.

ri·cin (rī′sin, ris′in) *n. Chem.* A very toxic protein isolated from the castor bean in the form of a white powder: it agglutinates red blood corpuscles. [<L *ricinus* castor bean]

ric·in·o·le·ic (ris′in·ō·lē′ik) *adj.* Of, pertaining to, or derived from the castor bean.

ricinoleic acid *Chem.* An unsaturated fatty acid, $C_{18}H_{34}O_3$, present in castor oil and hardening in a thick, yellow, crystalline or viscid mass.

ric·in·o·le·in (ris′in·ō′lē·in) *n. Chem.* The glycerol ester derivative of ricinoleic acid, preponderant in castor oil. [<L *ricinus* castor bean + *oleum* oil + -IN]

rick (rik) *n.* 1 A stack, as of hay, having the top rounded and thatched to protect the interior from rain. 2 A haycock in the field. —*v.t.* To pile in ricks. [OE *hrēac*]

Rick·en·back·er (rik′ən·bak′ər), **Edward Vernon,** 1890–1973, U.S. aviation executive; military aviator in World War I.

rick·ets (rik′its) *n. Pathol.* A disease of early childhood, chiefly due to a deficiency of calcium salts as provided by vitamin D, characterized by softening of the bones and consequent deformity; rachitis. [Origin uncertain]

rick·ett·si·a (rik·et′sē·ə) *n. pl.* **·si·ae** (-si·ē) Any of a genus *(Rickettsia)* of micro-organisms typically parasitic in the bodies of certain ticks and lice, but transmissible to other animals and to man; especially, *R. prowazeki,* the causative agent of typhus. [after Howard T. *Ricketts,* 1871–1910, U.S. pathologist]

rick·ett·si·al (rik·et′sē·əl) *adj.* Pertaining to or designating any of the various infective diseases caused by micro-organisms of *Rickettsia* or related genera, as typhus, Rocky Mountain spotted fever, or trench fever.

rick·et·y (rik′it·ē) *adj.* 1 Ready to fall; tottering. 2 Affected with rickets. **—rick′et·i·ly** *adv.* **—rick′et·i·ness** *n.*

rick·ey (rik′ē) *n.* A cooling drink of which spirits, lime juice, and carbonated water are the chief ingredients. [Origin uncertain]

rick·le (rik′əl) *n. Scot.* 1 A heap or bundle. 2 A small rick of grain or hay; a stook.

rick-rack (rik′rak′) *n.* Flat braid in zigzag form, made of cotton, rayon, silk, or wool; also, the openwork trimming made with this serpentine braid. [Reduplication of RACK[1]]

rick·shaw (rik′shô) *n.* A jinriksha. Also **rick′·sha.** [Short for JINRIKSHA]

ric·o·chet (rik′ə·shā′, -shet′) *v.i.* **·cheted** (-shād′) or **·chet·ted** (-shet′id), **·chet·ing** (-shā′ing) or **·chet·ting** (-shet′ing) To glance from a surface, as a projectile over the water; make a series of skips or bounds. —*n.* 1 A bounding, as of a projectile over a surface. 2 The method of firing by which a projectile is made to rebound. 3 A projectile so rebounding. [<OF]

ri·cot·ta (ri·kot′ə; *Ital.* rē·kôt′tä) *n.* An unripened cheese, Italian in origin and similar to cottage cheese but smoother. [<Ital. <L *recoquere* to cook again]

ric·tus (rik′təs) *n.* 1 The expanse of the open mouth; a gaping. 2 A fissure or cleft. [<L, open, gaping mouth < *ringi* open the mouth wide] **—ric′tal** *adj.*

rid[1] (rid) *v.t.* **rid** or **rid·ded, rid·ding** 1 To free, as from a burden or annoyance; clear: usually with *of*: to *rid* a house of vermin. 2 *Obs.* To rescue; deliver. 3 *Obs.* To drive away; expel; banish. —*adj.* Free; clear; quit: with *of*: We are well *rid* of him. [Fusion of OE *geryddan* clear (land) + ON *rythja* clear (land) of trees]

rid[2] (rid) Obsolete past tense and past participle of RIDE.

rid·a·ble (rī′də·bəl) *adj.* That may be ridden on, through, or over, as an animal or a road.

rid·dance (rid′ns) *n.* A ridding of something undesirable, or the state of being rid.

rid·den (rid′n) Past participle of RIDE.

rid·dle[1] (rid′l) *v.t.* **·dled, ·dling** 1 To perforate in numerous places, as with shot. 2 To sift through a coarse sieve. 3 To damage, injure, refute, etc., as if by perforating: to *riddle* a theory. [<*n.*] —*n.* 1 A coarse sieve, such as one used in a foundry or in washing for gold. 2 A board set with pins, used for straightening wire. [OE *hriddel* sieve] **—rid′·dler** *n.*

rid·dle[2] (rid′l) *n.* 1 A puzzling question or conundrum; anything ambiguous or puzzling. 2 Any mysterious object or person. —*v.* **·dled, ·dling** *v.t.* To solve; explain. —*v.i.* To utter or solve riddles; speak in riddles. [OE *rǣdels* <stem of *rǣdan* interpret, solve]

Synonyms (noun): conundrum, enigma, paradox, problem, puzzle. *Conundrum* signifies some question or statement in which some hidden and fanciful resemblance is involved, the answer often depending upon a pun; an *enigma* is a dark saying; a *paradox* is a true statement or fact that appears absurd or contradictory. The *riddle* is not so petty as the *conundrum;* it is an ambiguous or paradoxical statement with a hidden meaning to be guessed by the mental acuteness of the one to whom it is proposed; a *problem* may require simply study and scholarship, as a *problem* in mathematics; a *puzzle* may be in something other than a verbal statement, as a dissected map or any perplexing mechanical contrivance. Both *enigma* and *puzzle* may be applied to any matter difficult of answer or solution, *enigma* conveying an idea of greater dignity, *puzzle* applying to something more commonplace and mechanical. *Antonyms*: answer, axiom, explanation, proposition, solution.

ride (rīd) *v.* **rode** (*Obs.* **rid**), **rid·den** (*Obs.* **rid**), **rid·ing** *v.i.* 1 To sit on and be borne along by a horse or other animal, especially while guiding or controlling its motion. 2 To be borne along as if on horseback. 3 To travel or be carried on or in a vehicle or other conveyance. 4 To be supported in moving: The wheel *rides* on the shaft. 5 To move; be borne; float: The ship *rides* on the waves. 6 To support and carry a rider in a specified manner: This car *rides* easily. 7 To seem to float in space, as a star. 8 *Naut.* To lie at anchor, as a ship. 9 To overlap or overlie, as broken bones. 10 To work or move upward out of place: with *up*: His sleeve has *ridden* up. 11 *Slang* To continue unchanged: Let it *ride.* —*v.t.* 12 To sit on and control the motion of (a horse, bicycle, etc.). 13 To move or be borne or supported upon: The glider *rides* air currents. 14 To overlap or overlie. 15 To travel or traverse (an area, etc.) on horseback, in an automobile, etc. 16 To control imperiously or oppressively: usually in the past participle: a king-*ridden* people. 17 To accomplish by riding: to *ride* a race. 18 To cause to ride. 19 To place (someone) astride something and carry him, especially as a punishment: They *rode* him out of town on a rail. 20 *Naut.* To keep at anchor. 21 *Colloq.* To tease or harass by ridicule or petty criticisms; tyrannize. See synonyms under DRIVE. **—to ride out** To survive; endure successfully. —*n.* 1 An excursion by any means of conveyance, as on horseback, by car, etc. 2 A road intended for riding. **—to take for a ride** *Slang* 1 To remove (a person) to a place with the intent to murder. 2 To cheat; swindle. [OE *rīdan*]

rid·er (rī′dər) *n.* 1 One who or that which rides; a horseman; a bicyclist; specifically, one who breaks in horses. 2 Any device that rides upon or weighs down something else, actually or figuratively. 3 A separate piece of writing or print added to a document, record, or the like. 4 An addition or proposed addition to a legislative bill, adding to or modifying its original purport. 5 A metallic weight for use astride the graduated beam of a delicate balance. 6 The top rail of a rail fence.

rid·er·less (rī′dər·lis) *adj.* Without a rider, as a horse.

ridge (rij) *n.* 1 An elevation or protuberance long in proportion to its width and height and generally having sloping sides; a raised strip; especially, a lengthened elevation of land; a long hill, or range of hills. 2 That part of a roof where the rafters meet the ridge pole. 3 A slight elevation of earth in a garden or field thrown up by the plow, hoe, or other implement. 4 The back or backbone of an animal, especially of a whale. 5 *Meteorol.* A relatively narrow band of high pressure between two cyclone areas, as shown on a weather map. —*v.* **ridged, ridg·ing** *v.t.* 1 To mark with ridges. 2 To form into ridges. —*v.i.* 3 To form ridges. [OE *hrycg* spine, ridge]

ridge pole A horizontal timber at the ridge of a roof, to which the upper ends of the rafters are nailed. Also **ridge beam, ridge piece, ridge plate.**

Ridg·way (rij′wā), **Matthew Bunker,** born 1895, U.S. general; chief of staff 1953–55.

ridg·y (rij′ē) *adj.* Having ridges; raised in a ridge; ridged.

rid·i·cule (rid′ə·kyo͞ol) *n.* 1 Language calculated to make a person or thing the object of contemptuous humorous disparagement; also, looks or acts expressing amused contempt; derision; mockery. 2 An object of mocking merriment; butt. 3 *Obs.* Ridiculousness. —*v.t.* **·culed, ·cul·ing** To make fun of; hold up as a laughingstock; deride. [<OF <L *ridiculum* a jest, joke, orig. neut. of *ridiculus* comical <*ridere* laugh] **—rid′i·cul′er** *n.*

Synonym (noun) : derision. *Ridicule* may be merely sportive or thoughtless; *derision* is always hostile or malicious. See BANTER.

Synonyms (verb): banter, chaff, deride, flout, jeer, lampoon, mock, quiz, rally, satirize, scoff, scout, taunt. *Antonyms*: applaud, celebrate, compliment, eulogize, extol, honor, praise.

ri·dic·u·lous (ri·dik′yə·ləs) *adj.* Exciting or calculated to excite ridicule; absurdly comical; unworthy of consideration. [< L *ridiculus*] **—ri·dic′u·lous·ly** *adv.* **—ri·dic′u·lous·ness** *n.*

Synonyms: absurd, comical, droll, farcical, funny, grotesque, laughable, ludicrous, preposterous, risible, silly, trifling, trivial. See ABSURD, QUEER. *Antonyms*: clever, commendable, grave, imposing, judicious, majestic, sensible, venerable, wise.

rid·ing[1] (rī′ding) *n.* The act of one who rides; a ride. —*adj.* 1 To be ridden on or in; suitable for riding: a *riding* horse. 2 To be used while riding: *riding* boots. 3 For use while at anchor: a *riding* light.

rid·ing[2] (rī′ding) *n.* 1 One of the three administrative divisions of Yorkshire, England: North Riding, East Riding, and West Riding. 2 Any similar administrative division, as in Canada, New Zealand, etc. [OE *thrithing* the third part (of a county); the initial *th* having been lost through the influence of the final *t* or *th* of *East, West,* and *North.* Related to THIRD.]

riding habit Apparel worn by horseback riders, especially that designed for women, consisting usually of a jacket and breeches or jodhpurs.

riding horse A horse used for riding.

riding school An establishment where the art of riding on horseback is taught.

Rid·ley (rid′lē), **Nicholas,** 1500?–55, Anglican bishop, reformer, and martyr.

ri·dot·to (ri·dot′ō) *n. pl.* **·tos** A public musical and dancing entertainment much in vogue in England in the 18th century. [<Ital., a festival, redoubt. See REDOUBT.]

Rid·path (rid′path, -päth), **John Clark,** 1840–1900, U.S. historian.

Rie·mann (rē′män), **Georg Friedrich Bernhard,** 1826–66, German mathematician.

Ri·en·zi (rē·en′zē), **Cola di,** 1313–54, Italian popular orator and leader. Also **Ri·en′zo.**

Rie·sen·ge·bir·ge (rē′zən·gə·bir′gə) The highest range of the Sudetes, in Lower Silesia and northern Bohemia; highest point, 5,259 feet. *Czech* **Kr·ko·no·še** (kûr′kô·nô·she′), *Polish* **Kar·ko·no·sze** (kär′kô·nô′she).

Riet (ryet) A river in Orange Free State Province of the Republic of South Africa, flowing 250 miles NW to the Vaal.

Rif (rif) The mountain range of NW Africa, bordering the northern coast of Morocco; highest point, 8,060 feet. Also **Riff.**

ri·fa·ci·men·to (rē·fä′chē·men′tō) *n. pl.* **·ti** (-tē) *Italian* A remaking; recasting: said of literary or musical adaptations.

rife (rīf) *adj.* 1 Great in number or quantity; plentiful; abundant; prevalent; current. 2 Containing in abundance: followed by *with.* [OE *rīfe* abundant]

riff (rif) *n.* In jazz music, a melodic phrase or

motif, played repeatedly as background or used as the main theme. [Prob. back formation of RIFFLE]

Riff (rif) *n.* One of a Berber tribe inhabiting the mountainous region of northern Morocco. — **Rif′fi·an** *adj.* & *n.*

rif·fle¹ (rif′əl) *n.* **1** *U.S.* A shoal or rocky obstruction lying beneath the surface of a river or other stream. **2** A stretch of shallow, choppy water caused by such a shoal; a rapid. **3** A way of shuffling cards. — *v.t.* & *v.i.* **·fled, ·fling** **1** To cause or form a rapid. **2** To shuffle (cards) by bending up adjacent corners of two halves of the pack, and permitting the cards to slip together as they are released. **3** To thumb through (the pages of a book). [? Blend of RIPPLE and RUFFLE]

rif·fle² (rif′əl) *n. Mining* **1** A groove or indentation set in the bottom of an inclined trough or sluice, for arresting gold contained in sands or gravels. **2** A cross slat or cleat rising above the bottom of such a sluice and adapted for catching gold: also **riffle bar, riffle block.** [Cf. LG *riffel* furrow]

rif·fler (rif′lər) *n.* **1** A file with curved working surfaces at one or both ends and a smooth center serving as a handle: used in sculpture, woodcarving, diemaking, etc. **2** A workman in any of these fields who handles such a tool. [<RIFFLE²]

riff–raff (rif′raf′) *n.* **1** The populace; rabble. **2** Miscellaneous rubbish. [<OF *rif et raf* every bit]

ri·fle¹ (rī′fəl) *n.* **1** A firearm, of any size, having grooves, now always spiral, on the surface of the bore for imparting rotation to the projectile and increasing the accuracy of the weapon. **2** One of these grooves. **3** Such a weapon fired from the shoulder, as distinguished from pistols, a carbine, or artillery, and provided with a device for attaching a bayonet. **4** *pl.* A body of soldiers

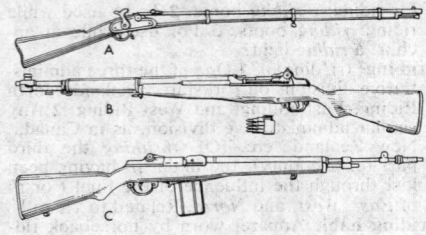

AMERICAN RIFLES
A. Springfield—Civil War.
B. Garand—World War II.
C. M–14, Automatic—1958.

equipped with rifles. **5** An emery–coated stick for whetting scythes. — **magazine rifle** A rifle with a chamber containing extra cartridges which are brought one by one into position for firing; a semi–automatic or repeating rifle. — *v.t.* **·fled, ·fling** To cut a spirally grooved bore in (a firearm, etc.). [Cf. G *reifeln* flute, LG *rifeln* furrow, F *rifler* scratch; *n.*, short for *rifled gun*]

ri·fle² (rī′fəl) *v.t.* **·fled, ·fling** **1** To search through and rob, as a safe. **2** To search and rob (a person). **3** To seize and take away by force. [<OF *rifler* scratch, plunder <Gmc.]

rifle grenade A grenade designed to be discharged from a rifle by means of a launching device.

ri·fle·man (rī′fəl·mən) *n. pl.* **·men** (-mən) One armed or skilled with the rifle.

rifle pit A trench, the earth from which is thrown up in front, as a protection for riflemen.

ri·fler (rī′flər) *n.* A robber.

rifle salute A salute in the position of right shoulder arms or order arms, with the left hand carried smartly to the rifle, palm down and fingers together.

ri·fling (rī′fling) *n.* **1** The operation of forming the grooves in a rifle. **2** The grooves of a rifle collectively: shallow or deep *rifling.* [<RIFLE¹]

rift¹ (rift) *n.* An opening made by riving or splitting; a cleft; fissure. — *v.t.* & *v.i.* To rive; burst open; split. [<Scand. Cf. Dan. *rift* cleft, ON *ript* < *ripta* break. Akin to RIVE.]

rift² (rift) *n.* **1** A shallow place in a stream; fording place. **2** The wash up the beach after

a wave has broken. [? Alter. of *riff*, obs. var. of REEF¹]

Rift Valley See GREAT RIFT VALLEY.

rig¹ (rig) *v.t.* **rigged, rig·ging 1** To fit out; equip. **2** *Naut.* **a** To fit, as a ship, with rigging. **b** To fit (sails, stays, etc.) to masts, yards, etc. **3** *Colloq.* To dress; clothe, especially in finery. **4** To make or construct hurriedly or by makeshifts: often with *up*: to *rig* up a door from old boards. — *n.* **1** *Naut.* The arrangement of sails, rigging, spars, etc., on a vessel. **2** *Colloq.* A style of dress; costume. **3** *U.S. Colloq.* A turnout for driving; a horse or horses and vehicle. **4** Gear, machinery, or equipment: an oil–well *rig.* **5** Fishing tackle. [<Scand. Cf. ON *rigga* wrap around, Norw. *rigga* bind.]

rig² (rig) *v.t.* **rigged, rig·ging** To control fraudulently; manipulate: to *rig* an election. — **to rig the market** To manipulate the exchange market by raising or lowering prices without regard to the value of the security or commodity traded in, in order to derive a profit. — *n.* **1** A practical joke; a trick; jest. **2** A tumult; frolic. [Origin uncertain]

rig³ (rig) *n. Scot. & Brit. Dial.* **1** A ridge or strip of ground. **2** The back of an animal. **3** A path; way. [Var. of RIDGE]

Ri·ga (rē′gə) The capital of Latvia, a port on the **Gulf of Riga,** an arm of the Baltic Sea between Estonia and Latvia.

rig·a·doon (rig′ə·dōōn′) *n.* **1** A gay, quick dance for two, originating probably in Provence. **2** The music for such a dance. [<F *rigodon* a dance]

Ri·gel (rī′jəl, -gəl) A star, Beta in the constellation of Orion; magnitude, 0.34. See STAR. [<Arabic *rijl* foot]

rig·ger (rig′ər) *n.* **1** One who rigs. **2** One who fits the rigging of ships. **3** One who assembles and alines the major parts of an aircraft.

rig·ging (rig′ing) *n.* **1** *Naut.* The entire cordage system of a vessel. **2** Tackle used in logging.

Riggs's disease (rig′ziz) Pyorrhea alveolaris. [after J. M. *Riggs,* 1810–85, U. S. dentist]

Ri·ghi (rē′gē) See RIGI.

right (rīt) *adj.* **1** Done in accordance with or conformable to moral law or to some standard of rightness; equitable; just; righteous. **2** Conformable to truth or fact; correct; true; accurate; not mistaken. **3** Conformable to a standard of propriety or to the conditions of the case; proper; fit; suitable. **4** Most desirable or preferable; also, fortunate. **5** Pertaining to that side of the body which is toward the south when one faces the sunrise: opposed to *left.* **6** Holding one direction, as a line; straight; direct. **7** Properly placed, disposed, or adjusted; well–regulated; orderly; correctly done. **8** Sound in mind or body; healthy; well. **9** *Geom.* Formed with reference to a line or plane perpendicular to another line or plane: a *right* angle. See ANGLE. **10** Designed to be worn outward or placed toward an observer in use: the *right* side of cloth. **11** *Law* Rightful; legal. **12** *Obs.* Real or genuine in character; not spurious. — *adv.* **1** In accordance with justice or moral principle. **2** According to the fact or truth; correctly. **3** In a straight line; directly. **4** Very: used dialectically or in some titles: a *right* good time, *Right* Reverend. **5** Suitably; properly. **6** Precisely; just; also, immediately. **7** Without delay or evasion. **8** Toward the right. **9** Completely or quite: The house burned *right* to the ground. — *n.* **1** That which is right; moral rightness: opposed to *wrong;* also, justice. **2** A just and proper claim or title to anything, or that which may be claimed on just, moral, legal, or customary grounds: often in the plural. **3** *Law* A claim or title to, or interest in, anything whatsoever that is enforceable by law. **4** The right hand, side, or direction. **5** Anything adapted for right–hand use or position. **6** *Often cap.* In politics, a conservative or reactionary position, or a party or group advocating such a position, so designated because of the views of the party occupying seats on the right side of the presiding officer in certain European legislative bodies: used with *the.* Compare LEFT. **7** The outside or front side of a thing: opposed to *reverse.* **8** In boxing, a blow delivered with the right hand. **9** A stockholder's privilege to purchase new stock in a corporation at a special price, usually at par. — **natural rights**

Rights with which mankind is supposedly endowed by nature, such as the right to life, liberty, security, and the pursuit of happiness. — *v.t.* **1** To restore to an upright or normal position. **2** To put in order; set right. **3** To make correct or in accord with facts. **4** To make reparation for; redress or avenge: to *right* a wrong. **5** To make reparation to (a person); do justice to. — *v.i.* **6** To regain an upright or normal position. — *interj.* I agree! I understand! — **right on** *Colloq.* An interjectory phrase expressing enthusiastic agreement or encouragement: also used adjectivally. ◆ Homophones: *rite, wright, write.* [OE *riht*] — **right′er** *n.*

Synonyms (adj.): correct, direct, equitable, fair, good, honest, just, lawful, perpendicular, rightful, straight, true, unswerving, upright. See CORRECT, INNOCENT, JUST, MORAL, PRECISE, VIRTUOUS. *Antonyms:* bad, evil, false, improper, incorrect, iniquitous, unjust, wrong.

Synonyms (noun): advantage, claim, exemption, franchise, immunity, liberty, license, prerogative, privilege. In the sense of that which one may rightly claim, a *right* may be either general or special, natural or artificial. "Life, liberty, and the pursuit of happiness" are the natural and inalienable *rights* of all men; *rights* of property, inheritance, etc., are individual and special, and often artificial, as the *right* of inheritance by primogeniture. A *privilege* is always special, exceptional, and artificial. It is something peculiar to one or some, as distinguished from others. A *privilege* may be of doing or avoiding; in the latter case it is an *exemption* or *immunity;* as, a *privilege* of hunting or fishing; *exemption* from military service; *immunity* from arrest. A *franchise* is a specific *right* or *privilege* granted by the government or established as such by governmental authority; as, the elective *franchise,* a railroad *franchise.* A *prerogative* is an official *right* or *privilege,* especially one inherent in the royal or sovereign power; in a wider sense it is an exclusive and peculiar *privilege* which one possesses by reason of being what he is; as reason is the *prerogative* of man; kings and nobles have often claimed *prerogatives* and *privileges* opposed to the inherent *rights* of the people. See DUTY, JUSTICE, PROPERTY.

right–a·bout (rīt′ə·bout′) *n.* **1** The opposite direction. **2** A turning in or to the opposite direction, physically or mentally.

right angle See under ANGLE.

right–an·gled (rīt′ang′gəld) *adj.* Forming or containing a right angle or angles.

right ascension *Astron.* The angular distance of a celestial body from the vernal equinox, measured eastward along the celestial equator in hours, minutes, and seconds from 0 hours to 24 hours.

right away At once; immediately.

right·eous (rī′chəs) *adj.* Conforming in disposition and conduct to a standard of right and justice; upright; virtuous; blameless; morally right; equitable; right–thinking. See synonyms under GOOD, INNOCENT, JUST, MORAL, VIRTUOUS. [OE *rihtwīs* < *riht* right + *wīs* wise] — **right′eous·ly** *adv.*

right·eous·ness (rī′chəs·nis) *n.* **1** The quality or character of being righteous; uprightness; rectitude. **2** A righteous act or quality. **3** Rightfulness; justice. See synonyms under DUTY, JUSTICE, VIRTUE.

right face In military drill, a 90–degree turn to the right, using the ball of the left foot and the heel of the right.

right·ful (rīt′fəl) *adj.* **1** Characterized by or conformed to a right or just claim according to established laws or usage; also, owned or held by just claim: *rightful* heritage. **2** Consonant with moral right or with justice and truth. **3** Proper. **4** Upright; just. See synonyms under JUST, RIGHT. [OE *rihtful*] — **right′ful·ly** *adv.* — **right′ful·ness** *n.*

right–hand (rīt′hand′) *adj.* **1** Of, pertaining to, or situated on the right side; dextral. **2** Chiefly depended on: my *right–hand* man.

right–hand·ed (rīt′han′did) *adj.* **1** Using the right hand habitually or more easily than the left. **2** Done with the right hand. **3** Turning or moving from left to right, as the hands of a clock. **4** Adapted for use by the right hand, as a tool. **5** In conchology, having the spirals rising from left to right. — **right′hand′ed·ness** *n.*

right–hand rope Plain–laid rope.

right·ism (rī′tiz·əm) *n.* The advocacy of conservative or reactionary policies. —**right′ist** *n.* & *adj.*

right·ly (rīt′lē) *adv.* 1 Correctly. 2 Honestly; uprightly. 3 Properly; aptly.

right-mind·ed (rīt′mīn′did) *adj.* Having approved feelings or opinions.

right·ness (rīt′nis) *n.* 1 The quality or condition of being right. 2 Moral rectitude. 3 Correctness. 4 Straightness. See synonyms under VIRTUE.

right·o (rīt′ō) *interj. Brit. Colloq.* An exclamation of satisfaction or assent.

right off Right away.

right of search In international law, the right of a belligerent vessel in time of war to verify the nationality of a vessel and to ascertain, if neutral, whether it carries contraband goods. Also **right of visit and search.**

right of way 1 *Law* The right, general or special, of a person to pass over the land of another; also, the path or piece of land over which passage is made. 2 The strip of land, acquired by easement, condemnation, or purchase, over which a railroad lays its tracks, or that land on which a public highway is built; also, the strip of land above which a high-tension power line is built. 3 The legal or customary precedence which allows one vehicle or vessel to cross in front of another.

right on *Informal* An interjectional phrase expressing enthusiastic agreement or encouragement; also used adjectivally: He was *right on* in that speech.

right shoulder arms The position in which the rifle is held at an angle of 45 degrees on the right shoulder, barrel uppermost.

right-to-work law *U.S.* Any law that guarantees a worker's right to a job, whether or not he or she joins a union.

right triangle A plane triangle containing one right angle.

right whale A whale, especially *Balaena mysticetus* of circumpolar seas, having a large head with long, narrow, highly elastic whalebone plates in its mouth, for straining food: it yields more oil than any other species. [Prob. orig. so called because advantageous to pursue]

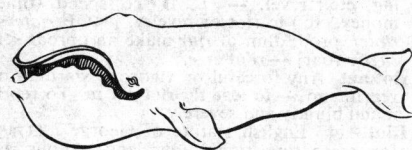

ATLANTIC, OR SOUTHERN, RIGHT WHALE
(From 50 to 60 feet in length;
the pigmy right whale to 20 feet)

right wing 1 A political party or group advocating moderate or conservative policies. 2 That part of any group advocating conservative policies. Also **Right Wing.** —**right′-wing′** *adj.* —**right′-wing′er** *n.*

rig·id (rij′id) *adj.* 1 Resisting change of form; stiff. 2 Rigorous; inflexible; severe. 3 Strict; exact, as reasoning. 4 *Aeron.* Designating a type of airship whose gas compartments are enclosed within a rigid structure. See synonyms under AUSTERE, HARD, INFLEXIBLE, PRECISE, SEVERE. [< L *rigidus* < *rigere* be stiff] —**rig′id·ly** *adv.* —**rig′id·ness** *n.*

ri·gid·i·ty (ri·jid′ə·tē) *n.* 1 The character of being rigid; inflexibility. 2 The property of bodies by which they resist a change in shape: opposed to *ductility.*

Rig·il Ken·tau·rus (rij′il ken·tôr′əs) A star of .06 magnitude in the constellation Centaurus. See STAR.

rig·ma·role (rig′mə·rōl) *n.* A succession of confused or nonsensical statements; incoherent talk or writing; nonsense. [Alter. of *ragman (roll)* document (with pendant seals), catalog, ME *rageman* document; origin unknown]

ri·go·let·to (rē′gō·let′ō) *n. Italian* A round dance.

rig·or (rig′ər) *n.* 1 The condition of being stiff or rigid. 2 Stiffness of opinion or temper; harshness. 3 Exactness without allowance or indulgence; in-

flexibility; strictness; severity. 4 **Inclemency,** as of the weather; hardship. 5 A severe, harsh, or cruel act. 6 *Med.* **a** A violent chill from cold or nervous shock. **b** The trembling observed in the chill preceding a fever. 7 *Biol.* A rigid state in an organism or in any of its parts, caused by adverse or unfavorable conditions. Also *Brit.* **rig′our.** [< L < *rigere* be stiff]

rig·or·ism (rig′ə·riz′əm) *n.* Stiffness in opinion or conduct; severity in style or living, etc.; strictness; austerity. Also *Brit.* **rig′our·ism.** —**rig′or·ist** *n.* —**rig′or·is′tic** *adj.*

rig·or mor·tis (rig′ər môr′tis, rī′gər) The rigidity that affects the body of an animal a few hours after death due to coagulation of the muscle protein myosin. [< L, stiffness of death]

rig·or·ous (rig′ər·əs) *adj.* 1 Marked by or acting with rigor; uncompromising; severe. 2 Logically accurate; exact; strict. 3 Inclement; severe; bitter; causing hardship: a *rigorous* climate. See synonyms under AUSTERE, SEVERE. [< OF *rigoureux*] —**rig′or·ous·ly** *adv.* —**rig′or·ous·ness** *n.*

Rigs·dag (rigz′däg) *n.* The two chambers that form the Danish parliament: the Landsting and Folketing. [< Dan. < *rige* kingdom + *dag* day. See REICHSTAG.]

rigs·da·ler (rigz′dä′lər), **rijks·daal·der** (rēks′däl′dər) See RIX-DOLLAR.

Rig-Ve·da (rig-vā′də, -vē′-) The oldest collection of hymns and verses in Hindu sacred literature; supposed date, 2000 B.C. See VEDA. [< Skt. *Rigveda* < *ric* praise, hymn + *veda* knowledge]

rig·wid·die (rig·wid′ē) *adj. Scot.* Bony; sapless; scrawny. Also **rig·wood′ie** (-wood′ē).

Riis (rēs), **Jacob August,** 1849–1914, U.S. journalist and sociologist born in Denmark.

Ri·je·ka (rē·ye′kä) A port of NW Croatia, Yugoslavia, on the Adriatic SW of Zagreb: 40 miles, across Istria, from Trieste: Italian *Fiume.*

Rijn (rīn) The Dutch name for the RHINE.

Rijs·wijk (rīs′wīk) The Dutch name for RYSWICK.

Riks·mål (rēks′mōl) *n.* One of the two official forms of Norwegian, based on literary Danish: also called *Dano-Norwegian.* Danish **Rigs·mål** (rēks′mōl). Compare LANDSMÅL. [< Norw., speech of the realm]

rile (rīl) *v.t. Colloq.* or *Dial.* 1 To vex; irritate. 2 To roil; make muddy. [Var. of ROIL]

ri·ley (rī′lē) *adj.* 1 Roiled; muddy. 2 Ill-tempered; also, irritated.

Ri·ley (rī′lē), **James Whitcomb,** 1849?–1916, U.S. poet.

ri·lie·vo (rē·lye′vō) *n.* Relief (defs. 5 and 6). [Ital.]

Ril·ke (ril′kə), **Rainer Maria,** 1875–1926, German poet born in Prague.

rill (ril) *n.* 1 A small stream; rivulet. 2 A long, narrow, and generally straight valley on the face of the moon: also **rille.** See synonyms under STREAM. [Cf. Du. *dil,* G *rille*]

rill·et (ril′it) *n.* A little rill (def. 1).

rim (rim) *n.* 1 The edge of an object, usually of a circular object; a margin; border. 2 The peripheral part of a wheel, connected to the hub by spokes. 3 On an automobile wheel, the detachable band over which the tire is fitted. 4 The frame of a pair of spectacles surrounding the lenses. See synonyms under BANK. —*v.t.* **rimmed,** **rim·ming** 1 To provide with a rim; border. 2 In sports, to roll around the edge of (the basket, cup, etc.) without falling in: The ball *rimmed* the cup. [OE *rima*]

Rim·baud (raɴ·bō′), **Arthur,** 1854–91, French poet.

rime¹ (rīm) *n.* [The spelling *rhyme,* introduced in the 17th century through association with *rhythm,* is etymologically unjustified.] 1 A correspondence of sounds in two or more words, especially at the ends of lines of poetry. See also NEAR RIME, INTERNAL RIME, TERMINAL RIME. 2 A verse, line, etc., corresponding in terminal sound with another. 3 A word corresponding in sound with another. 4 Poetry; verse; also, a tale in verse. See synonyms under POETRY. —*v.* **rimed, rim·ing** *v.i.* 1 To make rimes or verses; compose poetry. 2 To correspond in sound or in terminal sounds. —*v.t.* 3 To put or write in rime or verse. 4 To use as a rime. 5 To cause to correspond in sound. Also spelled *rhyme.* [Prob. fusion of OF *rime* < Gmc. + OE *rīm*

a number] —**rime′less** *adj.*

rime² (rīm) *n.* 1 Hoarfrost. 2 *Meterol.* A rough or feathery coating of ice deposited by fog on terrestrial objects. —*v.t.* & *v.i.* **rimed, rim·ing** To cover with or congeal into rime. [OE *hrīm* frost]

rim·er (rī′mər) *n.* One who makes riming verse, especially inferior verse: also spelled *rhymer.*

rime riche (rēm rēsh′) *French* In prosody, rime involving words identical in sound but of different meaning. Also **rich rime.**

rime royal A stanza of seven lines in iambic pentameter, rimed *ababbcc:* first used in Chaucer's *Complaint unto Pity.*

rime scheme The pattern of rimes in a stanza or poem, usually represented by letters: A standard *rime scheme* is abab.

rime·ster (rīm′stər) *n.* One who makes rimes; a mere versifier; a maker of inferior verses: also spelled *rhymester.*

Rim·i·ni (rim′i·nē, *Ital.* rē′mē·nē) A port in north central Italy on the Adriatic: ancient *Ariminum.*

ri·mose (rī′mōs, rī·mōs′) *adj.* Full of fissures or cracks; chinky. Also **ri′mous.** [< L *rimosus* < *rima* chink] —**ri′mose·ly** *adv.* —**ri·mos·i·ty** (rī·mos′ə·tē) *n.*

rim·ple (rim′pəl) *n.* A fold or wrinkle. —*v.t.* & *v.i.* **·pled, ·pling** To wrinkle; rumple. [OE *hrympel*]

Rim·sky-Kor·sa·kov (rim′skē·kôr′sə·kôf, *Russian* rēm′skē·kôr·sä·kôf′), **Nicholas Andreievich,** 1844–1908, Russian composer.

rim·y (rī′mē) *adj.* 1 White with rime. 2 Cold; frosty.

rin (rin) *v.t.* & *v.i. Scot.* 1 To run. 2 To melt.

Ri·nal·do (rē·näl′dō) Italian form of REGINALD.

rind¹ (rīnd) *n.* The skin or outer coat that may be peeled or taken off, as of flesh, fruit, or trees. [OE *rind* bark, crust]

rind² (rind, rīnd) See RYND.

rin·der·pest (rin′dər·pest) *n.* An infectious disease of cattle and sometimes of sheep, characterized by inflammation of the mucous membranes of the intestines; cattle plague: formerly known as *murrain.* [< G < *rinder* cattle + *pest* plague]

Rine·hart (rīn′härt), **Mary Roberts,** 1876–1958, U.S. fiction writer.

rin·for·zan·do (rēn′fôr·tsän′dō) *adj.* Reinforcing or increasing the power and emphasis: a musical direction. [< Ital., ppr. of *rinforzare* reinforce]

ring¹ (ring) *n.* 1 Any circular object having an opening of nearly its own diameter. 2 A circular band of precious metal, worn on a finger. 3 Any metal or wooden band used for holding or carrying something: a napkin *ring;* also, a hoop. 4 A group of persons or things in a circle. 5 A combination of persons, often for corrupt or mercenary cooperation, as in business or politics; a clique. 6 A place where the bark has been cut away around a branch or tree trunk. 7 One of a series of concentric layers of wood in an exogenous stem, formed by annual growth: also **annual ring.** 8 An area or arena, as that in which boxers fight; hence prize fighting in general; a circular racecourse or track, as of a circus or horse show. 9 The field of competition or rivalry: He tossed his hat into the *ring.* 10 Thearea set apart for bookmakers and other betters at a racetrack. 11 *Chem.* An arrangement of atoms in a closed chain: the benzene *ring.* 12 The space between two concentric circles. —*v.* **ringed, ring·ing** *v.t.* 1 To surround with a ring; encircle. 2 To form into a ring or rings. 3 To provide or decorate with a ring or rings. 4 To cut a ring of bark from (a branch or tree); girdle. 5 To put a ring in the nose of (a pig, bull, etc.). 6 To hem in (cattle, etc.) by riding in a circle around them. 7 In certain games, to cast a ring over (a peg or pin). —*v.i.* 8 To form a ring or rings. 9 To move or fly in rings or spirals; circle. ◆ Homophone: *wring.* [OE *hring*]

ring² (ring) *v.* **rang, rung, ring·ing** *v.i.* 1 To give forth a resonant, sonorous sound, as a bell when struck. 2 To sound loudly or be filled with sound or resonance; reverberate; resound. 3 To cause a bell or bells to sound, as in summoning a servant. 4 To have or

suggest a sound expressive of a specified quality: His story *rings* true. **5** To have a continued sensation of ringing or buzzing: My ears *ring*. — *v.t.* **6** To cause to ring, as a bell. **7** To produce, as a sound, by or as by ringing. **8** To announce or proclaim by ringing: to *ring* the hour. **9** To summon, escort, usher, etc., in this manner: with *in* or *out*: to *ring* out the old year. **10** To strike (coins, etc.) on something so as to test their quality by the sound produced. **11** To call on the telephone: often with *up*. — **to ring the changes** See under CHANGE. — *n.* **1** The sound produced by a bell or other vibrating, sonorous body; the act of sounding a bell; also, a telephone call. **2** Any reverberating sound, as of acclamation. **3** A sound that is characteristic or indicative: His words have the *ring* of truth. **4** A set, chime, or peal of bells. ◆ Homophone: *wring*. [OE *hringan*]

ring-billed (ring′bild′) *adj.* Having a ring of color around the beak: said of certain birds.

ring-billed gull The common gull (*Larus delawarensis*) having a black ring around the bill.

ring bolt A bolt having a ring through an eye in its head.

ring·bone (ring′bōn′) *n.* A bony enlargement or excrescence on the pastern bones of a horse, usually causing lameness.

ring dove **1** The cushat: also called *wood pigeon*. **2** One of several other pigeons related to the turtle dove (*Streptopelia risoria*) of southeastern Europe.

ringed (ringd) *adj.* **1** Having a wedding ring; hence, lawfully married. **2** Encircled by raised or depressed lines or bands, as the stems or roots of some plants. **3** Encircled by a ring or rings of color; composed of rings.

rin·gent (rin′jənt) *adj. Biol.* Gaping, as a two-lipped corolla in which the lips are widely separated, or as the valves of certain bivalves. [<L *ringens, -entis*, ppr. of *ringi* gape]

ring·er[1] (ring′ər) *n.* **1** One who or that which rings (a bell or chime). **2** *Slang* An athlete who illegally enters a contest by concealing facts which would disqualify him. **3** *Slang* A person who bears a marked resemblance to another: You are a *ringer* for Jones.

ring·er[2] (ring′ər) *n.* **1** One who or that which rings or encircles. **2** A quoit or horseshoe that falls around one of the posts.

ring·er[3] (ring′ər) *n. Austral.* **1** The fastest shearer in a crew; hence, a remarkably competent person. **2** A cattleman.

Ring·er's solution (ring′ərz) *Chem.* A physiologically balanced solution of the chlorides of sodium, potassium, and calcium, used to keep organs alive outside the body. [after Sidney *Ringer*, 1835–1910, English physiologist]

ring finger The third finger of the left hand, on which the marriage ring is worn.

ring·hals (ring′hals) *n.* The spitting snake. [<G, lit., ring-neck]

ring·head (ring′hed′) *n.* An instrument for stretching woolen cloth.

ring·lead·er (ring′lē′dər) *n.* A leader or organizer of any undertaking, especially of an unlawful undertaking like a riot.

ring·let (ring′lit) *n.* **1** A long, spiral lock of hair; a curl. **2** A small ring.

ring·mas·ter (ring′mas′tər, -mäs′-) *n.* One who has charge of a circus ring and of the performances in it.

ring·neck (ring′nek′) *n.* **1** The ring snake. **2** The ring plover. **3** The ring-necked duck.

ring-necked (ring′nekt′) *adj.* Having a ring of color around the neck: said of certain birds and animals.

ring-necked duck A North American duck (*Aythya collaris*), blackish with a chestnut collar about the neck: also called *marsh bluebill*. Also spelled *ringneck*.

Ring of the Ni·be·lung (nē′bə·lo͝ong) In German legend, the ring which Alberich made from the Rheingold. In his tetralogy of music dramas, *Das Rheingold, Die Walküre, Siegfried*, and *Die Götterdämmerung*, which collectively bear this title, Richard Wagner traces the story of the ring. Also *German* **Der Ring des Ni·be·lung·en** (der ring des nē′bə·lo͝ong′ən).

ring plover Any of certain small plovers (genus *Charadrius*) marked with a black breast-encircling band; especially *C. semipalmatus* and the smaller piping plover (*C. melodus*) of eastern North America; also, a European plover (*C. niaticula*); also *ringneck*.

ring·shake (ring′shāk′) *n.* A cupshake.

ring·side (ring′sīd′) *n.* The space or seats immediately surrounding a ring, as at a prize fight.

ring snake **1** A small, harmless, grayish-green snake of North America (*Diadophis punctatus*) having a bright yellow ring around the neck: also *ringneck*. **2** The hoop snake.

ring·ster (ring′stər) *n. U.S. Colloq.* A member of a political ring.

ring-streaked (ring′strēkt′) *adj.* Streaked with encircling rings, as an animal. Also *Archaic* **ring′straked′** (-strākt′).

ring-tailed (ring′tāld′) *adj. Slang* Very extraordinary or superior; stupendous.

ring-tailed roarer In U.S. folklore, a person of extraordinary size, strength, or athletic prowess; a bragging, swaggering fellow.

ring·time (ring′tīm′) *n. Obs.* The time of marriage or betrothal.

ring·worm (ring′wûrm′) *n. Pathol.* One of several contagious skin diseases affecting both man and domestic animals, caused by certain fungi, and marked by the localized appearance of discolored, scaly patches on the skin and by disorders of the scalp.

rink (ringk) *n.* **1** A smooth, artificial surface of ice, usually covered, used for ice-skating. **2** A smooth floor, similarly enclosed, used for roller-skating. **3** A building containing a surface smoothed and prepared for ice-skating or roller-skating. **4** An area on a field of ice marked off for the game of curling. **5** The part of a bowling green occupied by one side. **6** In bowling, quoits, and curling, the players on one side. [< dial. E (Scottish), prob. <OF *renc* row, rank]

rinse (rins) *v.t.* **rinsed, rins·ing** **1** To remove soap from by putting through clear water. **2** To wash lightly, as by dipping in water or by running water over or into. **3** To remove (dirt, etc.) by this process. See synonyms under CLEANSE. — *n.* The act of rinsing. [<OF *rincer, reïncer*, ? ult. <L *recens* recent, fresh] — **rins′er** *n.*

rins·ing (rin′sing) *n.* **1** A rinse. **2** The liquid in which anything is rinsed. **3** That which is removed by rinsing.

Ri·o Bran·co (rē′o͝o vraṅng′ko͝o) **1** Capital of Acre territory, western Brazil. **2** A federal territory of northern Brazil; 89,035 square miles; capital, Boa Vista. **3** A river in Río Branco territory, northern Brazil, flowing 350 miles south from the Uraricoera to the Río Negro.

Rí·o Bra·vo (rē′ō brä′vō) The Mexican name for the RIO GRANDE. Also **Río Bravo del Norte** (thel nôr′tā).

Ri·o da Dú·vi·da (rē′o͝o thə tho͞o′vē·thə) A former Portuguese name for the ROOSEVELT RIVER.

Ri·o de Ja·nei·ro (rē′ō də jə·nâr′ō, zhə·nâr′ō; *Pg.* rē′o͝o thə zhə·nā′ro͝o) The capital of Brazil (until the transfer of the federal capital, in April, 1960, to the new city of **Bra·si·li·a** (brə·zē′lē·ə), located in a federal district, on the central plateau of Goiás state, about 120 miles NE of Goiânia, the state capital), a port on Guanabara Bay or **Rio de Janeiro Bay:** also **Rio.** An inhabitant of the city is known as a *Carioca*. **2** A state in SE Brazil; 16,439 square miles; capital, Niterói.

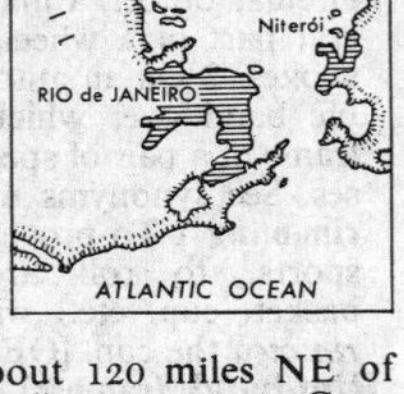

Rí·o de la Pla·ta (rē′ō thä lä plä′tä) See PLATA, RÍO DE LA.

Rí·o de O·ro (rē′ō thā ō′rō) **1** The undefined area of Spanish interest on the NW coast of Africa SW of Morocco. **2** A zone of Spanish Sahara; 73,362 square miles; capital, Villa Cisneros.

Rí·o Gal·le·gos (rē′ō gä·yā′gōs) The capital of Santa Cruz national territory, southern Argentina.

Ri·o Grande (rē′ō grand′) **1** A river flowing 1,800 miles from the Rocky Mountains in SW Colorado to the Gulf of Mexico and forming the boundary between Texas and Mexico: Mexican *Río Bravo*. **2** See RIO GRANDE DO SUL (def. 2).

Ri·o Gran·de do Nor·te (rē′o͝o graṅn′də tho͞o nôr′tə) A maritime state in NE Brazil; 20,482 square miles; capital, Natal.

Ri·o Gran·de do Sul (rē′o͝o graṅn′də tho͞o so͞ol′) **1** The southernmost state of Brazil; 109,037 square miles; capital, Pôrto Alegre. **2** A port in Rio Grande do Sul state: formerly *São Pedro de Rio Grande do Sul*: also *Rio Grande*.

Rio·ja (ryō′hä) See LA RIOJA.

Rí·o Mu·ni (rē′ō mo͞o′nē) The mainland district of Spanish Guinea, including the islands of Annobon, Corisco, and Great and Little Elobey; mainland area, 10,040 square miles; chief town, Bata: also *Continental Guinea*.

Rí·o Ne·gro (rē′ō nā′grō) **1** A river in the southern Argentine Republic, flowing 400 miles east and SE to the Atlantic. **2** A river in NW Brazil, flowing SE about 1,400 miles to the Amazon. **3** A national territory of south central Argentina; 78,363 square miles; capital, Viedma. **4** A river in central Uruguay, rising in southern Brazil, and flowing 500 miles SW to the Uruguay river.

Ri·on Strait (rē·ôn′) A strait of the Ionian Sea, joining the Gulf of Patras to the Gulf of Corinth: 1 mile wide: formerly *Strait of Lepanto*.

Rí·o Pie·dras (rē′ō pyā′thräs) A city of northern Puerto Rico, the second largest of the commonwealth.

Rí·o Roo·se·velt (rē′ō rō′zə·velt) A Spanish name for the ROOSEVELT RIVER.

ri·ot (rī′ət) *n.* **1** A disturbance consisting of wild and turbulent conduct of a large number of persons, as a mob; uproar; tumult. **2** *Law* Specifically, a tumultuous disturbance of the public peace by three or more assembled persons who, in the execution of some private object, do an act, lawful or unlawful, in a manner calculated to terrorize the people. **3** A state of confusion; a jumble: The garden was a *riot* of color. **4** Boisterous festivity; revelry. **5** *U.S. Slang* An uproariously amusing person, thing, or performance. See synonyms under REVOLUTION, TUMULT. — **to run riot** **1** To act or move wildly and without restraint. **2** To grow rankly, as vines. — *v.i.* **1** To take part in a riot or public disorder. **2** To live a life of unrestrained feasting, drinking, etc.; revel. — *v.t.* **3** To spend (time, money, etc.) in riot or revelry. [<OF *riote* < *rioter*, prob. dim. of *ruir* make an uproar <L *rugire* roar] — **ri′ot·er** *n.*

riot act Any forceful or vigorous warning or reprimand. — **to read the riot act to** To reprimand bluntly and severely.

Riot Act English statute of George I (1715) for preventing tumultuous and riotous assemblages.

Rí·o Té·o·do·ro (rē′ō tā′ō·thō′rō) A Spanish name for the ROOSEVELT RIVER.

riot gun A short-barreled shotgun for use on guard duty or against rioters.

ri·ot·ous (rī′ət·əs) *adj.* **1** Pertaining to riot; engaged in riot or tumultuous disorder; tumultuous. **2** Indulging in revelry; also, profligate: more *riotous* spending. See synonyms under NOISY, TURBULENT. — **ri′ot·ous·ly** *adv.* — **ri′ot·ous·ness** *n.*

Ri·ouw Archipelago (rē′ou) An Indonesian island group south of Singapore; 2,279 square miles; comprising, with other islands, a province of Indonesia; 12,503 square miles; capital, Tandjungpinang. Also *Riau Archipelago*.

rip[1] (rip) *v.* **ripped, rip·ping** *v.t.* **1** To tear or cut apart roughly or violently; slash. **2** To tear or cut from something else in a rough or violent manner: with *off, away, out*, etc. **3** To saw or split (wood) in the direction of the grain. — *v.i.* **4** To be torn or cut apart; split. **5** *Colloq.* To utter with vehemence: with *out*. **6** *Colloq.* To rush headlong. — **to rip into** *Colloq.* To attack violently, as with blows or words. — **to rip off** *Slang* **1** To steal or steal from. **2** To copy, imitate, or reproduce illegally or dishonestly. **3** To swindle; dupe; cheat. — **to rip out** To utter with vehemence. See synonyms under REND. — *n.* **1** A place torn or ripped open, especially along a seam; a tear. **2** A ripsaw. [ME *rippen*, prob. <LG. Cf. Frisian *rippe*, Flemish *rippen*.]

rip[2] (rip) *n.* **1** A ripple; a rapid in a river. **2** A riptide. [? <RIP[1]]

rip[3] (rip) *n. Colloq.* **1** A dissipated or worthless person. **2** A worn-out, worthless animal or object. [? Var. of *rep*, short for REPROBATE]

rip[4] (rip) *n. Scot.* A handful of unthreshed grain or of hay.

ri·par·i·an (ri·pâr′ē·ən, rī-) *adj.* **1** Pertaining to the bank of a river: *riparian* rights. **2** Growing naturally in the sides or banks of water-courses, ponds, etc. [<L *riparius* < *ripa* bank of a river]

ri·par·i·ous (ri·pâr′ē·əs, rī-) *adj.* Growing or living along the banks of streams, as an animal or a plant.

rip·cord (rip′kôrd′) *n. Aeron.* **1** The cord, together with the handle and fastening pins, which, when pulled, releases the canopy of a parachute from its pack. **2** A cord attached to the rip panel of a balloon, which, when pulled, frees the panel from the envelope.

ripe[1] (rīp) *adj.* **1** Grown to maturity and fit for food, as fruit or grain. **2** Brought by keeping and care to a condition for use, as wine. **3** Fully developed; matured. **4** In full readiness to do or try; prepared; ready: The men are *ripe* for mutiny. **5** Fit; opportune: The times are *ripe* for war. **6** Resembling ripe fruit; rosy; luscious. **7** *Surg.* Ready for an operation of removal or opening, as an appendix or an abscess. [OE *rīpe* ready for reaping] — **ripe′ly** *adv.* — **ripe′ness** *n.*

Synonyms: complete, consummate, finished, fit, mature, matured, mellow, perfect, perfected, ready, seasoned. *Antonyms*: budding, callow, crude, green, immature, imperfect, sour, undeveloped.

ripe[2] (rīp) *v.t.* **riped, rip·ing** *Scot. & Brit. Dial.* **1** To cleanse. **2** To examine thoroughly. **3** To search.

rip·en (rī′pən) *v.t. & v.i.* To make or become ripe; mature. — **rip′en·er** *n.*

Rip·ley (rip′lē), **William Zebina,** 1867–1941, U.S. economist.

rip–off (rip′of′, -ôf′) *n. Slang* **1** The act of ripping off; an act of stealing or cheating. **2** Anything dishonest, illegal, or exploitative.

Rip·on (rip′ən) A municipal borough of West Riding, Yorkshire, England.

Rip·on Falls (rip′ən) A waterfall in SE Uganda on the Victoria Nile just below Lake Victoria; about 16 feet high; 900 feet wide.

ri·poste (ri·pōst′) *n.* **1** A return thrust, as in fencing. **2** A quick, clever reply. — *v.i.* **1** To make a riposte. **2** To reply quickly. Also **ri·post′.** [<F *riposte* <Ital. *risposta*, properly fem. of pp. of *rispondere* <L *respondere.* See RESPOND.]

rip panel *Aeron.* A segment of the fabric in a balloon or nonrigid airship that may be ripped open quickly to permit emergency deflation.

rip·per (rip′ər) *n.* **1** One who or that which rips. **2** A tool for ripping, as a ripsaw. **3** A double–ripper. **4** *Brit. Slang* A thorough-going or efficient person or thing; something or someone very good.

rip·ping (rip′ing) *Brit. Slang adj.* Splendid; excellent. — *adv.* Very; extraordinarily: a *ripping* good time.

rip·ple[1] (rip′əl) *v.* **·pled, ·pling** *v.i.* **1** To become slightly agitated on the surface, as water running over a rough, pebbly surface or blown on by a light breeze; form small waves or undulations. **2** To flow with small waves or undulations on the surface. **3** To make a sound like water flowing in small waves. — *v.t.* **4** To cause to form ripples. — *n.* **1** One of the wavelets on the surface of water; a ruffle, or slight curling wave. **2** Any sound like that made by rippling. **3** Any appearance like a wavelet. See synonyms under WAVE. [Origin uncertain] — **rip′pler** *n.* — **rip′pling** *adj.* — **rip′·pling·ly** *adv.*

rip·ple[2] (rip′əl) *n.* A toothed tool, especially a comblike instrument for cleaning flax fiber or broomcorn. — *v.t.* **·pled, ·pling** To cleanse, as flax or hemp, by removing the seeds and capsules from the stalk. [<Gmc. Cf. Frisian *ripelje.*]

rip·plet (rip′lit) *n.* A small ripple.

rip·ply (rip′lē) *adj.* Marked by or sounding like ripples.

rip–rap (rip′rap′) *n.* **1** Broken stones loosely thrown together for a foundation, as in deep water or on a soft bottom, or for a sustaining wall, as along a river bank; also, the stones used, or the foundation so made. **2** *pl.* Artificial islands in Chesapeake Bay. — *v.t.* **–rapped, –rap·ping** To make a rip–rap in or upon; strengthen with rip–raps.

rip–roaring (rip′rôr′ing, -rōr′-) *adj. U.S. Slang* **1** Excellent; superior; exciting: a *rip–roaring* time. **2** Lively; full of vigor.

rip–roar·i·ous (rip·rôr′ē·əs, -rōr′-) *adj. U.S. Slang* Uproarious; boisterous; violent. — **rip–roar′i·ous·ly** *adv.*

rip·saw (rip′sô′) *n.* A coarse–toothed saw used for cutting wood in the direction of the grain.

rip·snort·er (rip′snôr′tər) *n.* **1** Any person or thing excessively noisy, violent, or striking. **2** A violent windstorm.

rip·tide (rip′tīd′) *n.* Water agitated and made dangerous for swimmers by conflicting tides or currents. Also called *rip, tiderip.*

Rip·u·ar·i·an (rip′yōō·âr′ē·ən) *adj.* Designating or pertaining to a branch of the Frankish people that dwelt on both sides of the Rhine, near Cologne, in the fourth century. — *n.* A Ripuarian Frank. [<L *ripuarius* < *ripa* bank]

Rip Van Win·kle (rip van wing′kəl) In Washington Irving's tale by that name in *The Sketch Book*, a Dutch villager, who, while out hunting in the Catskills, falls asleep for twenty years, and awakes to find his world changed and himself forgotten.

rise (rīz) *v.* **rose, ris·en, ris·ing** *v.i.* **1** To move upward; go from a lower to a higher position. **2** To slope gradually upward: The ground *rises* here. **3** To have height or elevation; extend upward: The city *rises* above the plain. **4** To gain elevation in rank, status, fortune, or reputation. **5** To swell up: Dough *rises.* **6** To become greater in force, intensity, height, etc. **7** To become greater in amount, value, etc. **8** To become erect after lying down, sitting, etc.; stand up. **9** To get out of bed. **10** To return to life. **11** To revolt; rebel: The people *rose* against the tyrant. **12** To adjourn: The House passed the bill before *rising.* **13** To appear above the horizon: said of heavenly bodies. **14** To come to the surface, as a fish after a lure. **15** To have origin; begin: The river *rises* in the mountains. **16** To become perceptible to the mind or senses: The scene *rose* in his mind. **17** To occur; happen. **18** To be able to cope with an emergency, danger, etc.: Will he *rise* to the occasion? — *v.t.* **19** To cause to rise. **20** *Naut.* To cause, as a ship, to appear above the horizon by drawing nearer to it. — **to rise above** To prove superior to; show oneself indifferent to. — *n.* **1** The act of rising; ascent. **2** Degree of ascent; elevation; also, an ascending course. **3** The act of beginning to be or appear, as from a source: the *rise* of a stream. **4** An elevated place; rising ground; a small hill. **5** The act of appearing above the horizon. **6** Increase or advance, as in price. **7** Advance, as in rank, prosperity, or importance; also, elevation morally, mentally, or spiritually. **8** The spring or height of an arch above the impost level. **9** The height of a stair step. **10** Ascent in the diatonic scale; also, increase in volume of tone; a swell. **11** The ascent of a fish to food or bait; also, the flying up of a game bird. **12** *Colloq.* An emotional reaction; a response or retort. **13** *Brit.* An increase in salary. See synonyms under BEGINNING. [OE *rīsan*]

Synonyms (verb): arise, ascend, flow, spring.

ris·en (riz′ən) Past participle of RISE.

ris·er (rī′zər) *n.* **1** One who rises or gets up, as from bed: He is an early *riser.* **2** The vertical part of a step or stair.

ris·i·bil·i·ty (riz′ə·bil′ə·tē) *n. pl.* **·ties** **1** A tendency to laughter. **2** *pl.* Impulses to laughter; appreciation of what seems ridiculous: also **ris′i·bles.**

ris·i·ble (riz′ə·bəl) *adj.* **1** Having the power of laughing. **2** Of a nature to excite laughter. **3** Pertaining to laughter. See synonyms under RIDICULOUS. [<F <LL *risibilis* <L *risus*, pp. of *ridere* laugh] — **ris′i·bly** *adv.*

ris·ing (rī′zing) *adj.* **1** Increasing in wealth, power, or distinction. **2** Ascending: the *rising* moon; also, sloping upward: a *rising* hill. **3** Advancing to adult years or to a state of vigor and activity; growing: the *rising* generation. — *n.* **1** The act of one who or that which rises. **2** That which rises above the surrounding surface; specifically, a tumor; wen. **3** An insurrection or revolt; an uprising. **4** Yeast or leaven used to make dough rise; also, the quantity of dough prepared at once. — *prep. Dial.* **1** Approaching; going on: He's six years old, *rising* seven. **2** More than; upwards of: a crop *rising* 5,000 bushels.

risk (risk) *n.* **1** A chance of encountering harm or loss; hazard; danger. **2** In insurance, hazard of loss, as of a ship or cargo, or of goods or other property; also, degree of exposure to loss or injury. **3** An obligation or contract of insurance on the part of the insurer: to take a *risk* on a cargo. **4** An applicant for an insurance policy considered with regard to the advisability of placing insurance upon him. See synonyms under DANGER, HAZARD. — *v.t.* **1** To expose to a chance of injury or loss; hazard. **2** To incur the risk of. [<F *risque* <Ital. *rischio* < *risicare* dare, ult. <Gk. *rhiza* cliff, root] — **risk′er** *n.*

risk·y (ris′kē) *adj.* **risk·i·er, risk·i·est** Attended with risk; hazardous; dangerous. See synonyms under PRECARIOUS.

Ri·sor·gi·men·to (rē·sôr′jē·men′tō) *n.* The movement for the liberation and unification of Italy in the 19th century. [<Ital., resurgence]

ri·sot·to (rē·sôt′tō) *n.* Rice cooked in broth and served with meat, cheese, and various condiments. [<Ital. < *riso* rice]

ris·qué (ris·kā′, *Fr.* rēs·kā′) *adj.* Bordering on or suggestive of impropriety; bold; daring; off–color: a *risqué* story or play. [<F]

Riss (ris) See GLACIAL EPOCH. [from *Riss*, name of a German stream]

ris·sole (ris′ōl, *Fr.* rē·sôl′) *n.* In cookery, a sausagelike roll consisting of minced meat or fish, enclosed in a thin puff paste and fried. [<F, <OF *ruissolle, rousole* <LL *russeola*, fem. of L *russeolus* reddish < *russus* red]

ris·so·lé (rē·sô·lā′) *adj. French* Browned by frying.

Rist (rēst), **Charles,** 1874–1955, French economist.

ri·sus (rī′səs) *n.* A grin or laugh, especially the **risus sar·do·ni·cus** (sär·don′i·kəs), the twisted, grinning expression caused by spasm of the facial muscles, as in tetanus. [<L, a grimace < *ridere* laugh]

ri·tar·dan·do (rē′tär·dän′dō) *adj. Music* Slackening the speed gradually; retarding. [<Ital., gerund of *ritardare* delay]

rite (rīt) *n.* **1** A solemn or religious ceremony performed in an established or prescribed manner, or the words or acts constituting or accompanying it. **2** Any formal practice or custom. See synonyms under FORM, SACRAMENT. ◆ Homophones: *right, wright, write.* [<L *ritus*]

rite de pas·sage (rēt də pa·säzh′) *pl.* **rites de pas·sage** (rēt) *Sociol.* A ritual event signifying a change in status in the course of life of an individual, as one marking puberty, marriage, the achievement of adult responsibility, or death. Also **rite of passage.** [<F]

Rit·ter (rit′ər) *n. German* A knight; one of the lowest of the noble orders in Austria and Germany.

rit·u·al (rich′ōō·əl) *n.* A prescribed form or method for the performance of a religious or solemn ceremony; any body of rites or ceremonies; also, a book setting forth such a system of rites or observances. See synonyms under FORM. — *adj.* Of, pertaining to, or consisting of a rite or rites. [<OF <L *ritualis* < *ritus* rite] — **rit′u·al·ly** *adv.*

rit·u·al·ism (rich′ōō·əl·iz′əm) *n.* **1** A system of conducting public worship according to prescribed or established forms. **2** Strenuous insistence upon ritual.

rit·u·al·ist (rich′ōō·əl·ist) *n.* One who practices or advocates ritualism. — *adj.* Ritualistic.

rit·u·al·is·tic (rich′ōō·əl·is′tik) *adj.* **1** Of or pertaining to ritual or ritualism. **2** Advocating ritualism. — **rit′u·al·is′ti·cal·ly** *adv.*

rit·u·al·ly (rich′ōō·əl·ē) *adv.* According to ritual or to a certain ritual.

ritz·y (rit′sē) *adj. U.S. Slang* Smart; elegant; classy. [after César *Ritz*, 1850–1918, Swiss hotelier who founded hotels bearing his name in London, Paris, and New York]

riv·age (riv′ij) *n. Archaic* A shore; coast; bank. [<OF < *rive* <L *ripa* shore]

ri·val (rī′vəl) *n.* **1** One who strives to equal

or excel another, or is in pursuit of the same object as another; a competitor. 2 One equaling or nearly equaling another, in any respect. 3 *Obs.* An associate, or companion in office. See synonyms under ENEMY. —*v.* **·valed** or **·valled**, **·val·ing** or **·val·ling** *v.t.* 1 To strive to equal or excel; compete with. 2 To be the equal of or a match for. —*v.i.* 3 *Archaic* To be a competitor. —*adj.* Standing in competition or emulation; having opposing claims to the same object; competing. [< F < L *rivalis*]

ri·val·ry (rī'vəl·rē) *n. pl.* **·ries** 1 The act of rivaling. 2 The state of being a rival or rivals; competition. See synonyms under AMBITION, COMPETITION, EMULATION.

rive (rīv) *v.* **rived**, **rived** or **riv·en**, **riv·ing** *v.t.* 1 To split asunder by force; cleave. 2 To break (the heart, etc.). —*v.i.* 3 To become split. See synonyms under BREAK, REND. [< ON *rifa* tear, rend] —**riv·er** (rī'vər) *n.*

rived (rīvd) Alternative past participle of RIVE. —*adj.* Split instead of sawed.

riv·en (riv'ən) Alternative past participle of RIVE. —*adj.* Rent, burst, or torn asunder; split; cleaved.

riv·er (riv'ər) *n.* 1 A large, natural stream of water, usually fed by converging tributaries along its course and discharging into a larger body of water, as into the ocean, a lake, or another stream. ◆ Collateral adjective: *fluvial.* 2 A large stream of any kind; copious flow. See synonyms under STREAM. —**to sell down the river** 1 Formerly, to sell (a Negro slave) into unsparing and rigorous servitude: from the severe conditions on the lower Mississippi cane and cotton plantations. 2 Hence, to betray the trust of; deceive. —**to send up the river** To send to the penitentiary: from the fact that Sing Sing is up the Hudson from New York. [< OF *rivière* < LL *riparia* < L *riparius.* See RIPARIAN.]

Ri·ve·ra (rē·vä'rä), **Diego**, 1886–1957, Mexican painter.

Ri·ve·ra y Or·ba·ne·ja (rē·vä'rä ē ôr'vä·nä'hä), **Miguel Primo de,** 1870–1930, Spanish general; chief of state 1923–30.

river basin *Geog.* An extensive area of land drained by a river and its branches.

river bottom Low-lying alluvial land along a river.

riv·er·head (riv'ər·hed') *n.* The source of a river.

river horse A hippopotamus.

riv·er·ine (riv'ə·rīn, -ə·rin) *adj.* Pertaining to or like a river; riparian.

River of Doubt A former name for the ROOSEVELT RIVER.

Riv·ers (riv'ərz), **William Halse,** 1864–1922, English physiologist and anthropologist.

riv·er·side (riv'ər·sīd') *n.* The space alongside of or adjacent to a river.

riv·er·weed (riv'ər·wēd') *n.* A small aquatic plant (*Podostemon ceratophyllum*) resembling a seaweed, found in the eastern and southern United States.

Rives (rēvz), **Amélie,** 1863–1945, Princess Troubetzkoy, U.S. novelist.

riv·et (riv'it) *n.* A short, soft metal bolt, having a head on one end, used to join objects, as metal plates, by passing the shank throughholes and forming a new head by flattening out the headless end. —*v.t.* 1 To fasten with or as with a rivet. 2 To batter the headless end of (a bolt, etc.) so as to make fast. 3 To fasten firmly. 4 To engross or attract (the eyes, attention, etc.). [< OF < *river* clench] —**riv·et·er** *n.*

Riv·i·er·a (riv·ē·âr'ə, *Ital.* rē·vyä'rä) The coastal strip between the southernmost Alpine ranges and the Mediterranean, extending from Hyères, France, about 230 miles to La Spezia, Italy.

ri·vière (rē·vyâr') *n. French.* A necklace of diamonds or other gems, usually in several strings.

riv·u·let (riv'yə·lit) *n.* A small stream or brook; streamlet. See synonyms under STREAM. [< Ital. *rivoletto,* dim. of *rivolo* < L *rivulus,* dim. of *rivus* brook]

rix·dol·lar (riks'dol'ər) *n.* 1 Any one of several small silver coins formerly current in the Scandinavian countries and the Netherlands: also called *rigsdaler, rijksdaalder.* 2 A former British silver coin of Ceylon, Cape Colony, etc. [< Du. *rijksdaler* dollar of the realm]

Ri·yadh (rē·yäd') The capital of Nejd and

(with Mecca) of Saudi Arabia. Also **Ri·yad'.**

Ri·za·i·yeh (rē·zā'ē·yä) 1 A city of NE Iran: also *Rezaiyeh.* 2 See URMIA.

Ri·zal (rē·säl'), **José,** 1861–96, Filipino patriot and author; shot for alleged conspiracy against Spain.

Rizal Day A holiday observed on December 30 in the Philippine Islands in memory of José Rizal.

Ri·za Shah Pah·la·vi (ri·zä' shä' pä'lə·vē), 1877–1944, shah of Iran 1925–41; abdicated.

riz·zer (riz'ər) *v.t. Scot.* To parch or dry in the sun. Also **riz'zar.**

Riz·zi·o (rit'tsyō), **David,** 1533?–66, Italian musician; secretary of Mary Queen of Scots; assassinated: also *Riccio.*

Rn *Chem.* Radon (symbol Rn).

ro (rō) *n. Archit.* In Japanese houses, a firepan set into the floor and used in connection with formal tea ceremonies.

Ro (rō) *n.* An artificial, international language based on the classification of ideas and dispensing with existing words and roots. [Coined by Rev. E. P. Foster of Ohio, who devised it in 1906]

roach[1] (rōch) *n.* 1 A European fresh-water fish (*Rutilus rutilus*) of the carp family, with a greenish back. 2 One of certain other related cyprinoid fishes, as the American fresh-water sunfish. [< OF *roche*]

roach[2] (rōch) *n.* A cockroach. [See COCKROACH]

roach[3] (rōch) *v.t.* To clip or trim, as the mane of an animal. [Origin unknown]

road (rōd) *n.* 1 An open way for public passage, especially from one city, town, or village to another; a highway: distinguished from a *street.* 2 Any way of advancing or progressing; any course followed in a journey; a path. 3 A roadstead: commonly in the plural: *Hampton Roads.* 4 *U.S.* A railroad. —**on the road.** 1 On tour: said of circuses, theatrical companies, etc. 2 Traveling, as a canvasser or salesman. 3 Living the life of a tramp or hobo. [OE *rād* a ride, a riding < *ridan* ride. Related to RIDE.]

Synonyms: course, highway, lane, passage, path, pathway, route, street, thoroughfare, track, turnpike, way. See WAY

road·a·gent (rōd'ā'jənt) *n.* A highway robber; highwayman, especially on stage routes of the western United States.

road·bed (rōd'bed') *n.* 1 The graded foundation of gravel, etc., on which the ties, rails, etc., of a railroad are laid. 2 The graded foundation or surface of a road.

road·block (rōd'blok') *n.* 1 An obstruction in a road. 2 Any arrangement of men and materials for blocking passage, as of enemy troops along a course of advance or retreat.

road hog An automobilist or other driver who keeps his vehicle in or near the middle of a road, making it difficult for other drivers to pass.

road·house (rōd'hous') *n.* A restaurant, dance hall, or similar establishment located at the side of the road in a rural area.

road metal Broken stone or the like, used for making or repairing roads.

road·run·ner (rōd'run'ər) *n.* A long-tailed ground cuckoo (genus *Geococcyx*), especially *G. californianus,* inhabiting open regions of southwestern North America, and running with great swiftness: also called *chaparral cock* or *hen.*

road·stead (rōd'sted) *n. Naut.* A sheltered place of anchorage offshore, but less sheltered than a harbor. [< ROAD + STEAD (def. 4)]

ROADRUNNER
(Length about 22 inches over all)

road·ster (rōd'stər) *n.* 1 A light, open automobile, usually single-seated and having a luggage compartment or a rumble seat in the rear. 2 A horse adapted for use on the road, as in light driving; also, a buggy or light carriage. 3 One who journeys a great deal on roads.

road test 1 A test of a person's ability to operate a motor vehicle, esp. as part of an official driving-licence examination. 2 A test of a motor

vehicle in actual driving situations on a road or highway.

road train *Austral.* A train of trailer trucks carrying livestock.

road·way (rōd'wā) *n.* A road; specifically, that part over which vehicles pass.

Ro·ald (rō'äl) A Norwegian masculine personal name. [< Norw., lit., famous power < Gmc.]

roam (rōm) *v.i.* To move about purposelessly from place to place; wander; rove. —*v.t.* To wander over; range: to *roam* the fields. See synonyms under RAMBLE, WANDER. —*n.* The act of roaming; a ramble. [ME *romen;* origin unknown] —**roam'er** *n.*

roan (rōn) *adj.* 1 Of a color consisting of bay, sorrel, or chestnut, thickly interspersed with gray or white, as a horse. 2 Made of roan leather. —*n.* 1 A roan color. 2 An animal of a roan color. 3 A soft sheepskin leather, tanned to a roan color and used in bookbinding: also **roan leather.** [< OF < Sp. *roano,* ? ult. < L < *ravus* grayish-yellow]

Ro·a·noke (rō'ə·nōk) A city in western Virginia.

Roanoke Island An island off the eastern coast of North Carolina north of Cape Hatteras; settlements attempted by Raleigh in 1585 and 1587 failed; 12 miles long, 3 miles wide. See CROATAN.

Roanoke River A river in Virginia and North Carolina, flowing 410 miles to the head of Albemarle Sound.

roar (rôr, rōr) *v.i.* 1 To utter a deep, prolonged cry, as of rage or distress. 2 To make a loud noise or din, as the sea or a cannon. 3 To laugh loudly. 4 To move, proceed, or act noisily. 5 To make a labored, rasping sound in breathing, as a horse. —*v.t.* 6 To utter or express by roaring: The crowd *roared* its disapproval. —*n.* 1 A full, deep, resonant cry, as of a beast; a similar cry of a human being, as in pain, grief, or anger. 2 Any loud, prolonged sound, as of wind or waves, or a confused mingling of sounds suggesting the cry of wild beasts. See synonyms under NOISE. [OE *rārian*]

Synonyms (verb): bawl, bellow, boom, bray, shout, shriek, yell. See CALL.

roar·er (rôr'ər, rōr'ər) *n.* 1 One who or that which roars. 2 An oil gusher.

roar·ing (rôr'ing, rōr'ing) *adj.* 1 Emitting or uttering roars; bellowing. 2 *Archaic* Characterized by riotous merriment; boisterous. 3 *Colloq.* Very prosperous or brisk: a *roaring* business. —*n.* 1 A loud, deep, continued sound, as of some animals, or of the waves. 2 A disease among horses, characterized by labored, rasping breathing.

roast (rōst) *v.t.* 1 To cook by subjecting to the action of heat, as in an oven. 2 Originally, to cook before an open fire, or by placing in hot ashes, embers, etc. 3 To heat excessively, or to an extreme degree. 4 To dry and parch under the action of heat: to *roast* coffee. 5 *Metall.* To heat (ores) with access of air, but without fusing, for the purpose of driving off or volatilizing impurities, or for oxidizing them. 6 *Colloq.* To banter or ridicule severely. —*v.i.* 7 To roast food in an oven, etc. 8 To be cooked or prepared by this method. 9 To be uncomfortably hot. —*n.* 1 Something roasted; a piece of meat that is adapted or prepared for roasting, or that is roasted. 2 The act of roasting. —*adj.* Roasted. [< OF *rostir* < OHG *rosten* < *rost* a gridiron, a roast]

roast·er (rōs'tər) *n.* 1 A person who roasts. 2 A pan for roasting. 3 Something suitable for roasting, especially a pig.

rob (rob) *v.* **robbed, rob·bing** *v.t.* 1 To seize and carry off the property of by unlawful violence or threat of violence; commit robbery upon. 2 To deprive (a person) of something belonging or due; defraud. 3 To plunder; rifle, as a house. 4 To steal. —*v.i.* 5 To commit robbery. See synonyms under STEAL. [< OF *rober* < OHG *roubon.* Akin to REAVE, ROBE.]

Rob (rob) Diminutive of ROBERT.

rob·a·lo (rob'ə·lō, rō'bə·) *n. pl.* **·los** or **·lo** Any of a family (*Centropomidae*) of perchlike fishes of tropical American seas, especially *Centropomus undecimalis,* a large and esteemed food fish; a sergeant fish. [< Sp. *róbalo* < Catalan *elobarro,* ult. < L *lupus* a wolf]

rob·and (rob'ənd) *n. Naut.* A piece of spun yarn for fastening the head of a sail to a spar: sometimes called *rope band.* Also **rob'bin.**

[Earlier *raband*, ult. <ON *rābenda* bend asail on a yard <*ra* a yard for a sail + *benda* bend, bind]

rob·ber (rob′ər) *n.* A plunderer, as a burglar or highwayman.

Synonyms: bandit, brigand, buccaneer, burglar, depredator, footpad, freebooter, highwayman, marauder, pillager, pirate, plunderer, thief. A *robber* seeks to obtain the property of others by force or intimidation; a *thief* by stealth and secrecy.

robber fly The assassin fly.

rob·ber·y (rob′ər·ē) *n. pl.* **·ber·ies** The act of robbing; the taking away of the property of another unlawfully, by force or fear. See synonyms under PLUNDER.

Rob·bia (rôb′byä), **del·la** (del′lä) A family of Italian sculptors and workers in glazed terra cotta; especially **Luca**, 1400–82; his nephew, **Andrea**, 1435–1525; and grandnephew, **Giovanni**, 1469–1529.

robe (rōb) *n.* **1** A long, loose, flowing garment, worn over other dress; a gown. **2** *pl.* Such a garment worn as a badge of office or rank. **3** Any kind of costume; dress; figuratively, anything that covers in the manner of a robe. **4** A blanket or covering, as for use in a carriage or automobile: lap *robe*. **5** The dressed skin of an animal, formerly especially of the American bison, used as a garment or blanket. **—v. robed, rob·ing** *v.t.* To put a robe upon; clothe; dress. **—v.i.** To put on robes. [<OF, orig. booty <OHG *roub* spoils, robbery. Akin to ROB.]

robe de chambre (rôb′ də shän′br′) *French* A dressing gown. Also **robe′–de–cham′bre.**

robe de nuit (rôb′ də nwē′) *French* A nightgown.

Rob·ert (rob′ərt; *Du., Ger., Sw.* rō′bert, *Fr.* rô·bâr′) A masculine personal name. Also *Ital., Pg., Sp.* **Ro·ber·to** (rō·ber′tō), *Lat.* **Ro·ber·tus** (rə·bûr′təs). [<Gmc., bright fame]

—Robert I, died 1035, duke of Normandy 1028–35; father of William the Conqueror: called "Robert the Devil."

—Robert II, 1054?–1134, duke of Normandy 1087–1134; son of William the Conqueror; invaded England, defeated by his brother Henry I.

—Robert the Bruce See BRUCE.

Ro·ber·ta (rə·bûr′tə) A feminine personal name. [Fem. of ROBERT]

Rob·erts (rob′ərts), **Frederick Sleigh,** 1832–1914, Earl Roberts of Kandahar, Pretoria, and Waterford, British field marshal: known as *Bobs.* **—Kenneth,** 1885–1957, U.S. novelist.

Rob·ert·son (rob′ərt·sən), **William,** 1721–93, Scottish historian. **—Sir William Robert,** 1860–1933, English field marshal; chief of British general staff 1915–18.

Ro·ber·val (rô·ber·val′), **Gilles Personne de,** 1602–75, French mathematician.

Robe·son (rōb′sən), **Paul,** 1898–1976, U.S.baritone.

Robes·pierre (rōbz′pir′, *Fr.* rô·bəs·pyâr′), **Maximilien François Marie Isidore de,** 1758–1794, French revolutionist; guillotined.

rob·in (rob′in) *n.* **1** A large North American thrush (*Turdus migratorius*) with black head and tail, grayish wings and sides, and reddish-brown breast and underparts. **2** A small European bird (*Erithacus rubecula*) of the thrush family, especially common in Great Britain, with the forehead, cheeks, and breast yellowish-red. [<OF *Robin*, dim. of ROBERT]

Rob·in (rob′in) Diminutive of ROBERT. [<OF]

Rob·in Good·fel·low (rob′in good′fel′ō) **1** In English folklore, a merry and mischievous sprite: originally identified with Puck, but later believed to work his mischief around houses. Compare PUCK. **2** Any fairy or elf.

Robin Hood A legendary medieval hero of England, bold, chivalrous, courteous, and generous, an outlaw of great skill in archery, who robbed the rich to relieve the poor, especially in Sherwood Forest in Nottinghamshire, England. Compare ALLAN–A–DALE, FRIAR TUCK.

robin redbreast The European or American robin.

rob·in's–egg blue (rob′inz·eg′) A light greenish blue; the color of the egg shell of the American robin.

Rob·in·son (rob′in·sən), **Edwin Arlington,** 1869–1935, U.S. poet. **—James Harvey,** 1863–1936, U.S. historian. **—Sir Robert,** born 1886, English biochemist.

Rob·in·son Cru·soe (rob′in·sən krōō′sō) In Defoe's *Robinson Crusoe* (1719), the hero, a sailor shipwrecked on a tropical island, where, by ingenious devices, he maintained himself until rescued. See FRIDAY; SELKIRK, ALEXANDER.

ro·ble (rō′blā) *n.* One of various trees of the oak family, especially the Californian white oak (*Quercus lobata*). [<Sp. <L *robur*, a hard variety of oak]

rob·o·rant (rob′ər·ənt) *adj.* Restoring strength; strengthening. **—n.** Any strengthening medicine; a tonic. [<L *roborans, -antis,* ppr. of *roborare* strengthen <*robur, -oris.* See ROBUST.]

ro·bot (rō′bət, rob′ət) *n.* **1** An automaton; a manufactured, mechanical person that performs all hard work. **2** One who works mechanically and heartlessly. [after a creation introduced by Karel Čapek, Bohemian playwright, in his *Rossum's Universal Robots (R. U. R.)* in 1921; ult. < Czech *robota* work, compulsory service <*robotiti* drudge]

robot bomb See under BOMB.

robot pilot An automatic pilot.

Rob Roy (rob roi) Nickname of Robert Macgregor, 1671?–1734, a Highland outlaw; hero and title of one of Scott's novels.

Rob·son (rob′sən), **Mount** The highest peak in the Canadian Rockies, in eastern British Columbia, near Alberta; 12,972 feet.

ro·bust (rō·bust′, rō′bust) *adj.* **1** Possessing or characterized by great strength or endurance; rugged; healthy. **2** Requiring strength. **3** Violent; rude. **4** Rich, as in flavor: a *robust* soup. See synonyms under FIRM, POWERFUL, STRONG. [<L *robustus* <*robur, roboris,* a hard variety of oak, strength] **—ro·bust′ly** *adv.* **—ro·bust′ness** *n.*

ro·bus·tious (rō·bus′chəs) *adj. Archaic* Of a robust character; also, rough: now often used humorously. **—ro·bus′tious·ly** *adv.* **—ro·bus′·tious·ness** *n.*

roc (rok) *n.* In Arabian and Persian legend, an enormous and powerful bird of prey. [<Arabic *rokh, rukhkh* <Persian *rukh*]

Ro·ca (rō′kä), **Cape** A cape near Lisbon in Portugal, westernmost point of continental Europe. *Portuguese* **Ca·bo da Ro·ca** (kä′vŏŏ thə rō′kə).

roc·am·bole (rok′əm·bōl) *n.* A European perennial (*Allium scorodoprasum*), allied to the leek, with bulbs or cloves resembling those of garlic. [<F <G *rokenbolle* rye bulb]

Ro·cham·beau (rō·shän·bō′), **Comte de,** 1725–1807, Jean Baptiste Donatien de Vimeure, French marshal; commanded French allies in the American Revolution.

Roch·dale (roch′dāl) A county borough in SE Lancashire, England, where, in 1844, the first cooperative stores were established.

Roche·fort (rôsh′fôr′) A port on the Charente in western France, 10 miles above the Bay of Biscay. Also **Roche·fort′–sur–mer′** (-sür·mâr′).

Ro·chelle (rô·shel′), **La** See LA ROCHELLE.

Ro·chelle powder (rō·shel′) Seidlitz powder.

Rochelle salt Potassium sodium tartrate, $KNaC_4H_4O_6·4H_2O$, a white crystalline salt used as a cathartic. [from LA ROCHELLE]

roches mou·ton·nées (rôsh′ mōō·tô·nā′, rôsh′) Rounded knobs of rock ground down and smoothed by glacial action: so called because smooth and rounded like a sheep's back: also called *sheepbacks.* [<F, sheep–shaped rocks]

Roch·es·ter (roch′es·tər, -is-) **1** A municipal borough of northern Kent, England. **2** A city of western New York, near Lake Ontario.

Roch·es·ter (roch′es·tər, -is-), **Earl of,** 1648?–1680, John Wilmot, English courtier and poet.

roch·et (roch′it) *n.* A ceremonial garment similar to a surplice, but with closer sleeves or without sleeves: worn by bishops and other high churchmen. [<OF, dim. of *roc* a cloak <Gmc. Cf. G *rock* coat.]

Ro·ci·nan·te (rō′thē·nän′tā) The raw-boned steed of Don Quixote; hence, any ill-looking riding horse: also spelled *Rosinante.* [<Sp. *rocín* nag]

rock¹ (rok) *n.* **1** Any large mass of stone or stony matter; a boulder; also, a stone small

enough to throw; stony fragments; a cliff. **2** A firm or immovable support; refuge; defense. **3** That on which one may be wrecked, as a reef; some source of ruin or injury. **4** *Geol.* The consolidated material forming the crust of the earth; any mass of mineral matter forming an essential part of the earth's crust. **5** The rockfish, or striped bass. **6** The rock dove. **7** A hard confection, of varied flavors. **8** Any of several very hard objects, as ice, rock candy, rock salt, etc.; also, a kind of cooky. **9** *U.S. Slang* A dollar; in the plural, money. **—on the rocks** *U.S. Slang* **1** Ruined; also, destitute; bankrupt. **2** Served with ice cubes but without soda or water: said of whisky or other spirituous beverage. **—adj.** Made or composed of rock; hard; stony: a *rock* wall. [<OF *roque, roke*; ult. origin uncertain]

rock² (rok) *v.i.* **1** To move backward and forward or from side to side; sway. **2** To sway, reel, or stagger, as from a blow; shake. **3** *Mining* To be washed in a cradle, as ores. **—v.t.** **4** To move backward and forward or from side to side, especially so as to soothe or put to sleep. **5** To cause to sway or reel: The earthquake *rocked* the houses. **6** *Mining* To wash (ores) in a cradle. **7** In mezzotint engraving, to prepare (a plate) by roughing its surface with a rocker (def. 8). See synonyms under SHAKE. **—n.** The act of rocking; a rocking motion. [OE *roccian*]

Rock, the Gibraltar.

rock·a·by (rok′ə·bī) *interj.* Go to sleep: from a nursery song intended to lull a child to slumber. **—n.** A lullaby. Also **rock′a·bye, rock′–a–bye.**

rock·a·hom·i·ny (rok′ə·hom′ə·nē) *n.* Indian corn parched and pounded; hominy. [<N. Am. Ind. (Algonquian) <*roc* corn + *oham* grind + termination *-min*]

rock–air (rok′âr′) *n.* A rocket launched from an aircraft, usually equipped with instruments for the investigation and recording of conditions in the upper atmosphere. Compare ROCKOON.

rock–and–roll (rok′ən·rōl′) *adj.* Describing a form of popular music, derived from hillbilly styles, achieving its effect by repetition of simple melodic elements, strongly marked rhythms, and exaggerated vocal mannerisms. **—n.** Rock–and–roll music. Also **rock 'n' roll.**

rock·a·way (rok′ə·wā) *n.* A four–wheeled, two–seated pleasure carriage with standing top. [from *Rockaway,* town in New Jersey]

rock bass A fresh–water food fish (*Ambloplites rupestris*) common in eastern North America.

rock bottom 1 The very bottom; the lowest possible level: Prices have hit *rock bottom.* **2** The basis or foundation of any issue. **—rock′–bot′tom** *adj.*

rock–bound (rok′bound′) *adj.* Encircled by or bordered with rocks.

rock candy Sugar candied in hard, clear crystals.

rock cork A variety of asbestos. Also called *rock leather.*

rock crystal Colorless transparent quartz.

rock dove The European wild pigeon (*Columba livia*), the parent of domestic varieties.

Rock·e·fel·ler (rok′ə·fel′ər) Name of a family of American capitalists and philanthropists, including **John Davison,** 1839–1937; his son, **John Davison, Jr.,** 1874–1960; and the latter's sons, **John Davison, III,** 1906–1978; **Nelson Aldrich,** 1908–1979, vice president of the United States (1974–77); **Laurance S.,** born 1910; **Winthrop,** born 1912, and **David,** born 1915.

rock·er¹ (rok′ər) *n.* **1** One who or that which rocks, in any sense. **2** One of the curved pieces on which a rocking chair or a cradle rocks. **3** A rocking chair. **4** A rock shaft. **5** A rocking–horse. **6** *Mining* A cradle. **7** An ice skate having a curved runner. **8** A small steel plate with a serrated edge for preparing a copper plate for a mezzotint.

rock·er² (rok′ər) *n.* The rock dove.

rocker arm *Mech.* An arm on a rock shaft, as in the valve mechanism of a steam engine.

rocker cam A cam on a rock shaft.

rocker shaft A rock shaft.

rock·er·y (rok′ər-ē) *n. pl.* **·er·ies 1** Rockwork. **2** A rock garden.

rock·et[1] (rok′it) *n.* **1** A firework, projectile, missile, or other device, usually cylindrical in form, that is propelled by the reaction of escaping gases produced during flight. **2** A vehicle operated by rocket propulsion and designed for space travel. — *v.i.* **1** To move like a rocket. **2** To fly straight up into the air, as a bird when alarmed. — *v.t.* **3** To propel by means of a rocket. [<Ital. *rocchetta* spool, dim. of *rocca* distaff <OHG *roccho*; from its resemblance to a distaff]

rock·et[2] (rok′it) *n.* **1** Any of several ornamental Old World herbs (genus *Hesperis*), especially the common garden **dame rocket** (*H. matronalis*), or damewort. **2** An annual (*Eruca sativa*) used in southern Europe as a salad. [<F *roquette*, ult. <L *eruca* colewort]

rocket bomb See under BOMB.

rock·et·eer (rok′ə-tir′) *n.* One who designs or launches rockets.

rocket gun A gun having the barrel open at both ends and used for the discharge of rocket projectiles. Compare BAZOOKA.

rocket launcher See under LAUNCHER.

rocket projector A device for aiming and discharging rockets.

rock·et·ry (rok′it-rē) *n.* The science, art, and technology of rocket flight, including all aspects from fundamental research to design, engineering, construction, and operation.

rock·et·sonde (rok′it-sond′) *n. Meteorol.* A radiosonde adapted for use on high-altitude rockets.

Rock fever Undulant fever. [from ROCK (OF GIBRALTAR)]

rock·fish (rok′fish′) *n. pl.* **·fish** or **·fish·es 1** A fish living about rocks. **2** Any of several food fishes (*Sebastodes* and related genera) of the west coast of North America. The black, orange, red, and spotted rockfish, as well as other species, are familiar in California markets. **3** One of various other fishes, as the striped bass, or the killifish.

rock flour Finely pulverized rock produced by the grinding action of glacier ice: also called *glacier meal.*

rock garden A garden with flowers and plants growing in rocky ground or among rocks arranged to imitate this.

rocking chair A chair having the legs set on rockers.

Rock·ing·ham (rok′ing-əm), **Marquis de,** 1730–1782, Charles Watson-Wentworth, English statesman.

rock·ing-horse (rok′ing-hôrs′) *n.* A toy horse mounted on rockers, large enough to be ridden by a child.

rocking stone A stone, often very large, so poised as to rock under little pressure.

rock leather Rock cork.

rock lobster The spiny lobster.

rock maple The sugar maple.

rock milk Agaric mineral.

Rock·ne (rok′nē), **Knute Kenneth,** 1888–1931, U.S. football coach born in Norway.

rock oil Petroleum.

rock·oon (rok-ōōn′) *n.* A small rocket equipped with various meteorological recording devices and attached to a balloon from which it is released at altitudes determined chiefly by its weight. Compare ROCKAIR. [<ROCK(ET) + (BALL)OON]

rock rabbit A hyrax.

rock·rose (rok′rōz′) *n.* One of several plants (genera *Cistus, Helianthemum,* and *Crocanthemum*) having flowers resembling the wild rose.

rock salt Halite.

rock shaft A shaft made to rock on its bearings; particularly, such a shaft for operating a slide valve in an engine: also called *rocker, rocker shaft.*

rock·weed (rok′wēd′) *n.* Any one of various coarse seaweeds (genera *Fucus* and *Sargassum*) growing on rocks.

rock wool Mineral wool.

rock·work (rok′wûrk′) *n.* **1** A mound or wall of stones set with mortar and arranged to imitate a rocky surface. **2** An artificial grotto.

rock·y[1] (rok′ē) *adj.* **rock·i·er, rock·i·est 1** Consisting of, abounding in, or resembling rocks. **2** Tough; unfeeling; hard; also, disreputable.

rock·y[2] (rok′ē) *adj.* **rock·i·er, rock·i·est** *Colloq.* Shaky or dizzy, as if rocking; unsteady in the head, as from past intoxication. — **rock′i·ness** *n.*

Rocky Mountain goat A conspicuous, typically white antelope (*Oreamnos americanus*) found in the mountains of NW North America.

Rocky Mountain National Park A mountainous region in northern Colorado; 395.5 square miles; established, 1915.

ROCKY MOUNTAIN
GOAT
(About 40 inches high at the shoulder)

Rocky Mountains The major mountain system of western North America, extending from the Arctic to Mexico; highest peak, Mount Elbert, 14,431 feet. Also **Rock′ies.**

Rocky Mountain sheep The bighorn.

Rocky Mountain spotted fever *Pathol.* An acute infectious rickettsial disease caused by a micro-organism (*Rickettsia rickettsii*) transmitted by the bite of certain ticks (genus *Dermacentor*): it is marked by fever, chills, headache, and diffuse pains, and is endemic in Rocky Mountain and Pacific coast States.

ro·co·co (rə-kō′kō) *n.* **1** A style of decoration and architecture, developed from the baroque and distinguished by profuse, elaborate, and often delicately executed ornament in imitation of rockwork, shells, foliage, and scrolls massed together: prevalent during the 17th and 18th centuries. **2** Anything regarded as florid, fantastic, or odd in literature. — *adj.* **1** Having, or built in, the style of rococo. **2** Overelaborate; florid. [<F, fanciful alter. of *rocaille* shellwork <*roc* rock]

rod (rod) *n.* **1** A shoot or twig of any woody plant; a straight, slim piece of wood or other material, used as an instrument of punishment, a badge of office, etc.; hence, with the definite article, discipline; correction. **2** A scepter; hence, dominion; power. **3** A bar, commonly of metal, forming part of a machine; a connecting rod. **4** A light pole used to suspend and manipulate a fishing line. **5** A measure of length, equal to 5.5 yards or 16.5 feet, or 5.02 meters; also, in England, a **cubic rod,** a unit of volume equal to 1,000 cubic feet. **6** A measuring rule. **7** One of the rodlike bodies of the retina sensitive to faint light. **8** A particular line of family descent. **9** *U.S. Slang* A pistol. **10** A lightning rod. **11** The drawbar of a freight train. — **to ride the rods** *U.S. Slang* To steal a ride by getting on the metal framework underneath a freight train. See synonyms under STICK. [OE *rod.* Related to ROOD.]

rode (rōd) Past tense of RIDE.

ro·dent (rōd′nt) *n.* A gnawing mammal (order *Rodentia*) having in each jaw two (rarely four) incisors, growing continually from persistent pulps, and no canine teeth, as a squirrel, beaver, or rat. — *adj.* **1** Gnawing. **2** Pertaining to the rodents. [<L *rodens, -entis,* ppr. of *rodere* gnaw] — **ro·den·tial** (rō-den′shəl) *adj.*

rodent ulcer *Pathol.* A malignant ulcer that progressively destroys soft tissues and bones, especially of the face. Also called *noli-me-tangere.*

ro·de·o (rō′dē-ō, rō-dā′ō) *n. pl.* **·de·os 1** The driving of cattle together to be branded, counted, inspected, etc.; a roundup. **2** An enclosure in a stock farm, in which cattle are collected to be counted and branded. **3** A public spectacle in which the more exciting features of a roundup are presented, as the riding of broncos, branding, lariat-throwing, etc. [<Sp. *<rodear* go around <*rueda* wheel <L *rota*]

Rod·er·ick (rod′ər-ik) A masculine personal name. Also **Rod′er·ic,** *Lat.* **Ro·der·i·cus** (rō′də-rī′kəs), *Ger.* **Ro·de·rich** (rō′də-rikh), *Fr.* **Ro·drigue** (rō-drēg′), *Ital., Sp.* **Ro·dri·go** (Ital.

rō·drē′gō, *Sp.* -thrē′-). [<Gmc., famous king] — **Roderick,** died 711, last king of the Visigoths.

Rod·gers (roj′ərz), **Richard,** born 1902, U.S. composer.

Ro·di (rō′dē) Italian name for RHODES.

Ro·din (rō-daṅ′), **Auguste,** 1840–1917, French sculptor.

rod·man (rod′mən) *n. pl.* **·men** (-mən) One who uses or carries a surveyor's leveling rod. Also **rods′man.**

Rod·ney (rod′nē), **George Brydges,** 1719?–1792, Baron Rodney, English admiral.

Ro·dó (rō-thō′), **José Enrique,** 1872–1917, Uruguayan essayist.

Ro·dol·fo (*Ital.* rō·dôl′fō, *Sp.* rō·thōl′fō) Italian and Spanish form of RUDOLPH. Also *Fr.* **Ro·dolphe** (rō·dôlf′), *Ital.* **Ro·dol·pho** (rō·dôl′fō), **Ro·dol·phus** (*Du.* rō·dol′fōōs, *Lat.* rō·dol′fəs).

rod·o·mon·tade (rod′ə·mon·tād′, -täd′) *n.* Vainglorious boasting; bluster. — *adj.* Bragging. — *v.i.* **·tad·ed, ·tad·ing** To boast; bluster; brag. [<F *rodomontade* <Rodomonte,* name of a boastful Saracen king in Ariosto's *Orlando Furioso*]

roe[1] (rō) *n.* **1** The spawn or eggs of female fish. **2** The milt of male fish. **3** The eggs of crustaceans. ◆ Homophone: *row.* [Var. of dial. *roan,* appar. <ON *hrogn*]

roe[2] (rō) *n.* **1** A small, graceful deer (genus *Capreolus*) of Europe and western Asia, with slender antlers rising vertically from the head. Also **roe deer. 2** Improperly, the doe of the red deer. ◆ Homophone: *row.* [OE *rā*]

Roeb·ling (rōb′ling), **John Augustus,** 1806–1869, U.S. engineer born in Germany; built the Niagara and Cincinnati suspension bridges. — **Washington Augustus,** 1837–1926, son of preceding; built Brooklyn Bridge, completed in 1883.

roe·buck (rō′buk′) *n.* A roe, especially the male.

Roe·mer (rœ′mər), **Olaus,** 1644–1710, Danish astronomer.

roent·gen (rent′gən, runt′-; *Ger.* rœnt′gən) *n.* The international unit of X-ray intensity; the quantity of radiation which, with full use of secondary electrons and without loss to the walls of the chamber, produces in 1 cubic centimeter of air at normal temperature and pressure 1 electrostatic unit of electricity of either sign: also spelled *röntgen.* [after Wilhelm Konrad *Roentgen*]

Roent·gen (rent′gən, runt′-; *Ger.* rœnt′gən), **Wilhelm Konrad,** 1845–1923, German physicist; discoverer of Roentgen rays, better known as X-rays.

roentgen equivalent man See REM.

roentgen equivalent physical See REP.

roent·gen·ize (rent′gən-īz, runt′-) *v.t.* **ized, ·iz·ing** To subject or expose to the action of X-rays. — **roent′gen·i·za′tion** *n.*

roentgeno- *combining form* X-rays; using, produced by, or producing X-rays: *roentgenogram.* Also, before vowels, **roentgen-.** [<ROENTGEN]

roent·gen·o·gram (rent′gən-ə-gram′, runt′-) *n.* An X-ray photograph, especially one taken for medical or therapeutic purposes; a skiagraph.

roent·gen·og·ra·phy (rent′gən-og′rə-fē, runt′-) *n. Med.* Photography by means of X-rays; radiography.

roent·gen·ol·o·gy (rent′gən-ol′ə-jē, runt′-) *n.* The science which treats of the properties, action, and effects of X-rays. — **roent′gen·ol′o·gist** *n.*

roent·gen·o·paque (rent′gən-ō-pāk′, runt′-) *adj.* Impervious to X-rays.

roent·gen·o·ther·a·py (rent′gən-ō-ther′ə-pē′, runt′-) *n. Med.* Treatment of disease by means of X-rays.

Roentgen rays X-rays.

Roer·ich (rœr′ikh), **Nicholas Konstantin,** 1874–1947, Russian painter.

ro·ga·tion (rō-gā′shən) *n.* **1** In ancient Rome, the submission of a proposed law by the executive (consul or tribune) to the people, requesting its adoption; also, a law submitted in this manner and accepted. **2** Litany; supplication. [<L *rogatio, -onis* <*rogatus,* pp. of *rogare* ask]

Rogation days *Eccl.* The three days immediately preceding Ascension Day, observed as days of special supplication by litanies, processions, etc.

ROCKET
a. Head.
b. Bursting-charge.
c. Composition.
d. Clay choke.
e. Fuse.
f. Gas exhaust.
g. Stick.

ro·ga·to·ry (rō′gə·tôr′ē, -tō′rē) *adj.* **1** Commissioned to gather information. **2** Officially requesting another court to ascertain and report certain facts: letters *rogatory.*

Rog·er (roj′ər) *interj.* **1** Message received: a code signal used in radiotelephone communication. **2** *U.S. Colloq.* All right; O.K. [from *Roger,* personal name]

Roger (roj′ər, *Fr.* rô·zhā′) A masculine personal name. Also *Lat.* **Ro·ger·us** (rō·jir′əs), *Ital.* **Ro·ge·ro** (rō·jā′rō), **Ro·ge·rio** (*Pg.* rō·zhā′ryo͞o, *Sp.* rō·hā′ryō). [<Gmc., spear of fame]

Rog·ers (roj′ərz), **Will,** 1879–1935, U. S. actor and humorist: full name *William Penn Adair Rogers.*

Ro·get (rô·zhā′), **Peter Mark,** 1779–1869, English physician and philologist; compiled *Roget's Thesaurus of English Words and Phrases,* 1852.

rogue (rōg) *n.* **1** A dishonest and unprincipled person; trickster; rascal. **2** One who is innocently mischievous or playful: sometimes said familiarly and endearingly. **3** An idle, sturdy beggar; a roving vagrant. **4** *Biol.* A variation from a standard. **5** A fierce and dangerous elephant separated from the herd: in this sense also used adjectively: a *rogue* elephant. **—** *v.* **rogued, ro·guing** *v.t.* **1** To practice roguery upon; defraud. **2** To eliminate (inferior individuals) from a plot of plants undergoing selection. **—** *v.i.* **3** To live or act like a rogue. [Origin uncertain]

Rogue River A river in SW Oregon, flowing 200 miles SW to the Pacific.

ro·guer·y (rō′gər·ē) *n. pl.* **·guer·ies** **1** Knavery, cheating, or dishonesty, or an instance of it. **2** Playful mischievousness.

rogues' gallery A collection of photographs of criminals taken to aid the police in their future identification.

rogues' march Music played in derision of a person when he is expelled or driven away in disgrace, as from a military body or community.

ro·guish (rō′gish) *adj.* **1** Playfully mischievous. **2** Knavish; dishonest. **— ro′guish·ly** *adv.* **— ro′guish·ness** *n.*

Ro·han (rô·äṅ′), **de** A feudal family of France; especially, its descendants, **Henri,** 1579–1638, duke and Huguenot leader; and **Louis René Édouard,** 1734–1803, grand almoner and cardinal.

Ro·hil·khand (rō′hil·kund′) A division of north central Uttar Pradesh State, India; 11,759 square miles; capital, Bareilly.

roil (roil) *v.t.* **1** To make muddy, as a liquid, by stirring up sediment. **2** To irritate or anger. Also spelled *rile.* [<F *rouiller* rust, make muddy <OF *rouil* mud, rust]

roil·y (roi′lē) *adj.* **1** Full of sediment; stirred up; turbid. **2** Irritated; vexed.

roist·er (rois′tər) *v.i.* **1** To act in a blustery manner; swagger. **2** To engage in revelry; riot. [<earlier *roister* loud bully <OF *ruistre* <L *rusticus.* See RUSTIC.] **— roist′er·er** *n.* **— roist′er·ing** *adj.*

rok·e·lay (rok′ə·lā) See ROQUELAURE.

Ro·kos·sov·sky (ro·kə·sôf′skē), **Konstantin,** born 1893?, U.S.S.R. marshal.

Ro·land (rō′lənd, *Dan.* rō′län, *Fr.* rô·läṅ′, *Ger.* rō′länt) A masculine personal name. Also *Du.* **Roe·land** (ro͞o′länt), *Ital., Sp.* **Ro·lan·do** (rō·län′dō), *Pg.* **Ro·lan·do** (rō·läṅ′do͞o), **Rol·dão** (rōl·douṅ′), *Lat.* **Ro·lan·dus** (rō·lan′dəs). [<Gmc., fame of the land]

— Roland Hero of the Anglo-Norman epic *Chanson de Roland* and of many other stories of the Charlemagne cycle. According to legend he was the nephew of Charlemagne, and a bulwark of Christianity against the Saracens, dying in battle at Roncesvalles in 788. He is known as *Orlando* in Italian romances concerning Charlemagne. **— a Roland for an Oliver** Action taken in retaliation, or by way of matching something said or done by another; a tit for tat: in allusion to an indecisive battle between Roland and Oliver, his companion-in-arms.

role (rōl) *n.* A part or character taken by an actor; any assumed character or function. Also **rôle.** ◆ Homophone: *roll.* [<F]

Rolfe (rolf), **John,** 1585–1622, English colonist in Virginia; husband of Pocahontas.

roll (rōl) *v.i.* **1** To move forward upon a surface by turning round and round, as the wheel of a vehicle. **2** To move or be moved on wheels: The cart *rolled* down the hill. **3** To rotate wholly or partially: Her eyes *rolled* with pleasure. **4** To assume the shape of a ball or cylinder by turning over and over upon itself. **5** To move or appear to move in undulations or swells, as waves or plains. **6** To sway or move from side to side, as a ship: to pitch and *roll.* **7** To walk with a swaying motion; swagger; also, to stagger. **8** To make a sound as of heavy, rolling wheels; rumble: Thunder *rolled* across the sky. **9** To become spread or flat because of pressure applied by a roller, etc.. The metal *rolls* easily. **10** To perform a periodic revolution, as the sun. **11** To move ahead; progress. **—** *v.t.* **12** To cause to move along a surface by turning round and round, as a ball, log, etc. **13** To move, push forward, etc., on wheels or rollers. **14** To impel or cause to move onward with a steady, surging motion: The ocean *rolls* its waves upon the shore. **15** To rotate, as the eyes. **16** To impart a swaying motion to. **17** To spread or make flat by means of a roller. **18** To wrap round and round upon itself. **19** To cause to assume the shape of a ball or cylinder by means of rotation and pressure: to *roll* a cigarette. **20** To wrap or envelop in or as in a covering. **21** To utter with a trilling sound: to *roll* one's r's. **22** To emit in a full and swelling manner, as musical sounds. **23** To beat a roll upon, as a drum. **24** To cast (dice) in the game of craps. **25** *Printing* To apply ink to (a form) by means of a roller or rollers. See synonyms under REVOLVE. **— to roll back** To cause (prices or wages) to return to a previous, lower level, as by government order. **— to roll in** **1** To arrive. **2** To gather. **3** *Colloq.* To luxuriate; wallow. **— to roll out** **1** To unroll. **2** *Colloq.* To leave. **3** To flatten by means of rollers. **— to roll up** **1** To assume or cause to assume the shape of a ball or cylinder by turning over and over upon itself. **2** To accumulate; amass: to *roll up* large profits. **—** *n.* **1** Anything rolled up in cylindrical form: a *roll* of parchment. **2** Hence, an official writing, especially a list of names or a register. **3** *U.S. Slang* A wad of paper money; also, money in general. **4** A long strip, as of ribbon or carpet, rolled upon itself or upon a core: sometimes of an agreed length used as a measure of quantity. **5** Any food rolled up in preparation for use, as bread by rolling up pieces of dough, meat for roasting, or a pudding or cake formed in a similar way: a jelly *roll.* **6** A roller; particularly, a cylinder in fixed bearings used as a roller. **7** A reverberation, as of thunder. **8** A trill. **9** The rapid beating of a drum to make its sound continuous. **10** A rolling gait or movement; also, motion from side to side, as of a ship in a seaway. **11** *Aeron.* A single turn of an airplane about its long axis without change in the direction of flight: also called **barrel roll;** when performed quickly, called a **snap roll.** **12** A strip of leather or other material fitted with pockets to hold tools or toilet articles, etc., around which it is rolled and fastened. See synonyms under RECORD. ◆ Homophone: *role.* [<OF *roller* <L *rotula* <*rota* wheel]

Rol·land (rô·läṅ′), **Romain,** 1868–1944, French novelist and dramatist.

roll·a·way (rōl′ə·wā′) *adj.* Mounted on rollers for easy movement into storage: a *rollaway* bed.

roll-back (rōl′bak′) *n.* A return, by government order, to a previous, lower price or wage level.

roll call **1** The act of calling over a roll or list of the names of a number of persons, as soldiers or workmen, to ascertain which are present. **2** The time of or signal for calling the roll.

roll·er (rō′lər) *n.* **1** One who or that which rolls anything. **2** Any cylindrical device that rolls. **3** The wheel of a caster or roller skate. **4** A rod for carrying a curtain, towel, map, or the like. **5** A heavy cylinder for rolling, smoothing, or crushing something: a steam *roller.* **6** *Printing* A cylindrical device, often of hard rubber, to spread the ink on a form before impressing on paper. **7** *Surg.* A long rolled bandage to be wrapped around a limb or the like. **8** One of a series of long, swelling waves which break on a coast, especially after a storm. **9** *Ornithol.* **a** An Old World bird of crowlike form with gaudy colors, remarkable for its irregular rolling or tumbling flight, especially the common roller (*Coracias garrula*) found in Europe. **b** A tumbler pigeon.

roller bearing A bearing employing steel rollers to lessen friction between the parts of a mechanism.

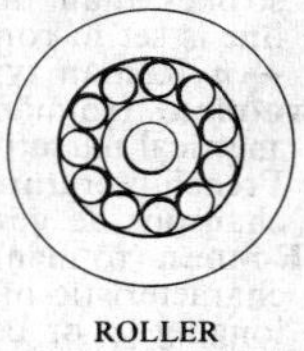

ROLLER BEARING

roller coaster A circular switchback railway with many steep inclines, over which small cars are run: common at amusement parks.

roller derby *U.S.* A race between two teams on roller skates: a player scores points for his team by overtaking opposing players after skating completely around the track within a given time limit.

roll·er-skate (rō′lər·skāt′) *v.i.* **-skat·ed, -skat·ing** To go on roller skates.

roller skate A skate having rollers or wheels instead of a runner.

roller towel An endless towel for use on a roller.

rol·lick (rol′ik) *v.i.* To move in a careless, frolicsome manner; act carelessly and jovially. [Blend of ROMP and FROLIC]

rol·lick·ing (rol′ik·ing) *adj.* **1** Moving in a careless or swaggering manner; jovial. **2** Expressive of a careless, frolicsome spirit: *rollicking* behavior. Also **rol′lick·some** (-səm), **rol′lick·y.**

roll·ing (rō′ling) *adj.* **1** Having a succession of sloping elevations and depressions; undulating: *rolling* prairies. **2** Turned back or down as if over a roll: a *rolling* collar. **3** Of or pertaining to rolling; used in rolling. **4** Moving on or as if on wheels; rotating. **5** Surging in puffs or billows, as smoke, clouds, etc. **6** Recurring; elapsing: said of time. **7** Swaying from side to side: a *rolling* gait. **—** *n.* The act of a person or thing that rolls, or of one who uses a rolling tool.

rolling barrage *Mil.* An artillery barrage in which the range is steadily increased so that the shells fall just ahead of advancing ground troops.

rolling hitch A hitch with one or more intermediate turns between the first and last hitch. See illustration under HITCH.

rolling kitchen *Mil.* A field kitchen equipped to move with troops.

rolling mill An establishment in which metal is rolled into sheets, bars, etc.

rolling pin A roller, usually of wood, with a handle at each end, for rolling out dough, etc.

rolling stock The wheeled transportation equipment of a railroad.

rolling stone **1** A stone worn smooth by friction and wear. **2** A person of restless, unsettled habits and occupation.

Rol·lo (rol′ō) A masculine personal name. [See RUDOLPH]

— Rollo, 860?–932?, Norwegian Viking leader; first duke of Normandy: also *Hrolf.*

roll-top (rōl′top′) *adj.* Having a cover which slides back out of the way: a *roll-top* desk.

roll·way (rōl′wā′) *n.* An inclined way, natural or artificial, down which logs may be rolled or shot; chute.

Röl·vaag (rœl′väg), **Ole Edvart,** 1876–1931, U. S. educator and novelist born in Norway.

ro·ly-po·ly (rō′lē·pō′lē) *adj.* Short and fat; pudgy; dumpy. **—** *n.* **1** *Brit.* A pudding made of a sheet of pastry dough spread with fruit, preserves, etc., rolled up and cooked. **2** A pudgy person. [Reduplication of ROLL]

Ro·ma·gna (rō·mä′nyä) A region and former province of the Papal States in north central Italy on the Adriatic.

Ro·ma·ic (rō·mā′ik) *adj.* Pertaining to or characteristic of the language or people of modern Greece. **—** *n.* Modern Greek, especially the popular spoken form. [<LL *Romaicus* <Gk. *Rhōmaikos* Roman <*Rhōmē* Rome]

ro·maine (rō·mān′) *n.* A variety of lettuce (*Lactuca sativa longifolia*) characterized by

long, crisp leaves. [<F, fem. of *romain* Roman]

Ro·mains (rô·maṅ'), **Jules** Pseudonym of Louis Farigoule, 1885–1972, French novelist.

ro·man[1] (rō'mən) *adj. Printing* Designating or pertaining to a common style of type or letter, characterized chiefly by serifs, perpendicularity, and the greater thickness of its upright strokes than of its horizontal strokes: This line is set in roman: distinguished from *italic.* — *n.* Roman type. Also **Ro'man.**

ro·man[2] (rō·mäṅ') *n. French* 1 A type of metrical narrative, especially common in Old French literature, developed from the ancient chansons de geste. 2 A romantic novel.

Ro·man (rō'mən) *adj.* 1 Of, pertaining to, or characteristic of Rome or its people. 2 Belonging to or connected with the Church of Rome or its head; Roman Catholic. 3 Somewhat aquiline: a *Roman* nose. — *n.* 1 A native, resident, or citizen of modern Rome or a citizen of ancient Rome. 2 A Roman Catholic. 3 *pl.* The Epistle to the Romans. — **Epistle to the Romans** One of the books of the New Testament; a letter from the apostle Paul to the Christians at Rome. [<OF *romain* <L *Romanus* < *Roma* Rome]

ro·man à clef (rō·mäṅ' à klē') *French* A novel in which actual persons and places appear under fictitious names; literally, a novel with a key.

Roman alphabet The Latin alphabet.

Roman architecture A style of architecture

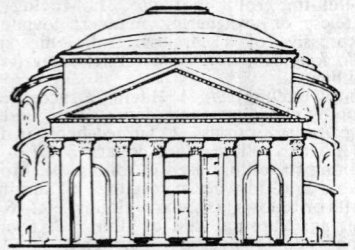

ROMAN ARCHITECTURE
Pantheon, Rome, A.D. 123

which is characterized by the size, massiveness, and boldness of its round arches and vaults, by the somewhat lavish adoption of Greek embellishments, and by excellent stonemasonry and brickmasonry of every kind.

Roman calendar See under CALENDAR.

Roman candle A firework consisting of a tube filled with a composition which discharges colored balls and sparks of fire.

Roman Catholic A member of the Roman Catholic Church.

Roman Catholic Church The church in communion with the pope, whom it recognizes as its supreme head on earth: an official designation. Also called the *Catholic Church.*

ro·mance (rō·mans', rō'mans) *n.* 1 Adventurous, heroic, or picturesque character or nature; strange and fascinating appeal: the *romance* of faraway places. 2 A disposition to delight in the mysterious or adventurous: a child of *romance.* 3 A love affair. 4 A long narrative from medieval legend, presenting chivalrous ideals and aristocratic society and usually involving heroes in strange adventures and affairs of love. 5 Any long fictitious narrative embodying scenes and events remote from common life and filled with extravagant adventures and often long digressions. 6 The class of literature consisting of romances (defs. 4 and 5). 7 An extravagant or fanciful falsehood. 8 *Music* A simple rhythmic melody, often sentimental, suggestive of a love song. See synonyms under DREAM, FICTION. — *v.* (rō·mans') **·manced**, **·manc·ing** *v.i.* 1 To tell romances. 2 To think or act in a romantic manner. 3 *Colloq.* To make love. — *v.t.* 4 *Colloq.* To make love to; woo. [<OF *romans* a story written in French <L *Romanice* in Roman style <*Romanicus* Roman]

Ro·mance (rō·mans') *adj.* Pertaining or belonging to one or more, or all, of the languages which have developed from the vulgar Latin speech, and which exist now as French, Italian, Spanish, Portuguese, Catalan, Provençal, Rhaeto-Romanic, and Rumanian. — *n.*

One, or all collectively, of the Romance languages.

ro·manc·er (rō·man'sər) *n.* 1 A writer of romances. 2 One who indulges in extravagant fictions or fancies.

Ro·man de la Rose (rō·mäṅ' də là rôz') An allegorical Old French verse romance, begun by Guillaume de Lorris about the middle of the 13th century, and completed in satirical tone by Jean de Meung toward the end of the century: source of Chaucer's *Romaunt of the Rose.*

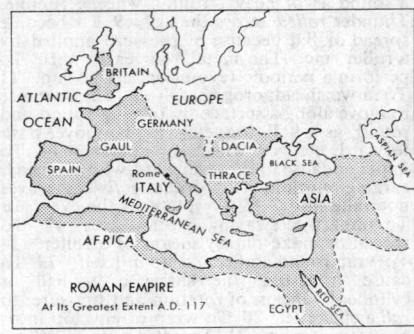

ROMAN EMPIRE
At Its Greatest Extent A.D. 117

Roman Empire The empire of ancient Rome, established by Augustus in 27 B.C. and continuing until the reign of Theodosius in A.D. 395, when it was divided into the Eastern Roman Empire and the Western Roman Empire.

ro·man·esque (rō'mən·esk') *adj.* Romantic; fabulous; fanciful. [<F <Ital. *romanesco* <Med. L *romaniscus* <L *romanus* Roman]

Ro·man·esque (rō'mən·esk') *adj.* 1 Pertaining to or designating the Romanesque style of architecture. 2 Pertaining to or characterized by the Romance languages, especially Provençal. — *n.* 1 Romanesque architecture. 2 The vernacular of Languedoc and other provinces in southern France.

Romanesque architecture The prevailing style, developed from Roman principles, of Western architecture from the 5th to the 12th centuries, embracing the Saxon, Norman, Lombard, etc., characterized by the round arch and general massiveness. It reached its

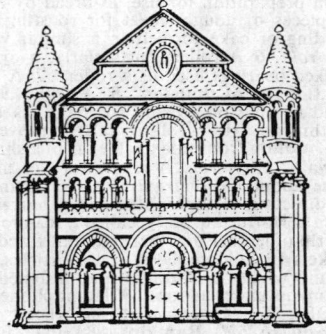

ROMANESQUE ARCHITECTURE
Notre Dame la Grande, Poitiers, France,
A.D. 11th Century.

best form in France in the 11th and 12th centuries.

Roman holiday 1 A day of gladiatorial and other contests in ancient Rome. 2 Enjoyment or profit whereby others suffer.

Ro·ma·ni·a (rō·mān'ya, Rumanian rô·mœ'nyä) The Rumanian name for RUMANIA.

Ro·man·ic (rō·man'ik) *adj.* Roman; also, Romance.

Ro·man·ism (rō'mən·iz'əm) *n.* The dogmas, forms, etc., of the Roman Catholic Church: a term used chiefly in disparagement. — **Ro'man·ist** *adj. & n.*

Ro·man·ize (rō'mən·īz) *v.t. & v.i.* **·ized**, **·iz·ing** 1 To make or become Roman or Roman Catholic. 2 To write or speak in a Latinized style. — **Ro'man·i·za'tion** *n.*

Roman mile See MILE.

Roman nose A nose that is somewhat aquiline.

Roman numerals The letters used by the

ancient Romans as symbols in arithmetical notation. See NUMERAL.

Ro·ma·nov (rō'mə·nôf, Russian rô·mä'nôf) A Russian dynasty, 1613–1917, founded by *Czar Michael*, 1596–1645. Also **Ro'ma·noff.**

Roman punch An ice consisting of the white of eggs beaten with rum and lemon juice.

Ro·mansch (rō·mansh', -mänsh') *n.* 1 A Rhaeto-Romanic dialect spoken in the Grisons canton, Switzerland. 2 The Rhaeto-Romanic dialects as a group. Also **Ro·mansh'.** [<L *Romanicus* <*Roma* Rome]

ro·man·tic (rō·man'tik) *adj.* 1 Characterized or influenced by romance or the extravagantly ideal; imaginative; marvelous; fanciful: a *romantic* tale. 2 Given to feelings or thoughts of romance; dreamy: a *romantic* girl. 3 Characterized by or conducive to love or amorousness. 4 Visionary; fantastic; impractical: a *romantic* scheme. 5 Strangely wild or picturesque: *romantic* scenery. 6 Of, pertaining to, or characteristic of a style of art and literature tending toward free expression of subjective feeling, impressive picturesqueness, imagination, sensuousness, etc.: opposed to *classic* or *classical.* 7 Of or pertaining to romanticism in art and literature in the 19th century. — *n.* 1 An adherent of romanticism; a romanticist. 2 A romantic person. 3 A romantic trait, idea, etc. [<F *romantique* < *romant, roman* romance, novel] — **ro·man'ti·cal·ly** *adv.*

Synonyms (*adj.*): airy, chimerical, dreamy, extravagant, fanciful, fantastic, fictitious, ideal, imaginative, picturesque, poetic, sentimental, visionary, wild. *Antonyms:* exact, historical, literal, precise, truthful, unadorned, unimaginative, unvarnished.

ro·man·ti·cism (rō·man'tə·siz'əm) *n.* 1 The quality or characteristic of being romantic. 2 In art, music, and literature, a romantic style as opposed to the classical. 3 In the late 18th century and the 19th, a social and esthetic movement, beginning as a reaction to neo-classicism, that sought to free the individual from unpleasant realities by appealing to his aspirations for wonder and mystery. It emphasized a love for strange beauty, for the past and the far-away, and for the wild, irregular, or grotesque in nature, and found creative expression in spontaneity, lyricism, reverie, sentimentalism, mysticism, and individualism. — **ro·man'ti·cist** *n.*

ro·man·ti·cize (rō·man'tə·sīz) *v.t.* **·cized**, **·cizing** To regard or interpret in a romantic manner.

Romantic Movement See ROMANTICISM (def. 3).

Rom·a·ny (rom'ə·nē) *adj.* Of or pertaining to the Gipsies or their language. — *n.* 1 A Gipsy. 2 The Indic language of the Gipsies, containing elements of the language of each country in which they live: also called *Gipsy.* Also **Rom'ma·ny.** [<Romany *romani* < *rom* man]

ro·maunt (rō·mänt', -mônt') *n.* A romance, usually in verse. [<OF *romant*, var. of *romans.* See ROMANCE.]

Rom·berg (rom'bûrg), **Sigmund,** 1887–1951, U. S. composer born in Hungary.

Rom·blon (rôm·blôn') A Philippine province, comprising a group of Visayan Islands including Romblon Island (32 square miles); 512 square miles; capital, Romblon.

Rome (rōm) 1 A city on the Tiber river, capital of Italy and the site of Vatican City, center of the Roman Catholic Church; formerly the capital of the Roman republic, the Roman Empire, and the States of the Church. *Italian* and *Latin* **Ro·ma** (rō'mä). 2 The Roman Catholic Church. 3 Roman Catholicism. 4 A city in central New York.

Ro·me·o (rō'mē·ō) In Shakespeare's tragedy *Romeo and Juliet,* the hero of the play, son of Montague, in love with Juliet, daughter of Capulet who is the enemy of the house of the Montagues.

Rom·ford (rum'fərd, rom'-) A municipal borough in SW Essex, England.

Rom·ish (rō'mish) *adj.* Pertaining to the Roman Catholic Church: an invidious usage.

Rom·mel (rum'əl, Ger. rôm'əl), **Erwin,** 1891–1944, German field marshal in World War II.

Rom·ney (rom'nē, rum'-), **George,** 1734–1802, English painter.

romp (romp) *v.i.* 1 To play boisterously. 2 To win easily. — *n.* 1 One, especially a girl, who

romps. **2** Noisy, exciting frolic or play. [Var. of RAMP[2]]

romp·er (rom′pər) *n.* **1** One who romps. **2** *pl.* A combination of waist and bloomers, as worn by young children at play.

romp·ing (rom′ping) *n.* Boisterous playing. —**romp′ing·ly** *adv.*

romp·ish (rom′pish) *adj.* Inclined toward boisterousness in play. —**romp′ish·ly** *adv.* —**romp′ish·ness** *n.*

Rom·u·lus (rom′yə·ləs) In Roman mythology, a son of Mars and founder of Rome, later deified as *Quirinus* : abandoned in the Tiber with his twin brother Remus, the infant Romulus was reared by a she-wolf, later killing his brother to become the first ruler of Rome.

Ron·ald (ron′əld, *Norw.* rō ·näl′) A masculine personal name. [See REGINALD]

Ron·ces·val·les (ron′sə·valz, *Sp.* rôn′thes·vä′lyäs) A village in the Pyrenees, northern Spain; nearby **Roncesvalles Pass** was the scene of Roland's death and the defeat of Charlemagne's rear guard, 778. *French* **Ronce·vaux** (rôns·vō′).

ron·deau (ron′dō, ron·dō′) *n.* A poem of French origin, consisting of thirteen lines with only two rimes: the opening words of the first line are added, as an unrimed refrain, after the eighth and thirteenth lines. [<F <*rondel* <*rond* round]

ron·del (ron′dəl, -del) *n.* A form of French verse consisting of 13 or 14 lines, in two stanzas of four and one of five or six lines, the first two lines being repeated, as a refrain, in the seventh and eighth lines, and again in the thirteenth and fourteenth. The names *rondeau* and *rondel* are often used interchangeably in English. [<F. See RONDEAU.]

ron·de·let (ron′də·let) *n.* A brief French verse form with a refrain, which generally consists of two or more words of the first line. [<OF, dim. of *rondel*. See RONDEAU.]

ron·do (ron′dō, ron·dō′) *n.* **1** *Music* A composition or movement having a main theme and several contrasting episodes, the former being repeated in its original key after each subordinate theme. **2** The musical setting of a rondeau. [<Ital., round]

Ron·dô·nia (rôn·dô′nyä) A federal territory of western Brazil; 1,381,877 square miles; capital, Porto Velho: formerly *Guaporé*.

ron·dure (ron′jər) *n.* Anything circular or spherical; a curve or swell. [<F *rondeur* roundness]

Rong·e·lap (rông′ə·läp) An atoll in the Ralik chain of the Marshall Islands; 35 miles long; 3 square miles. Also **Rong′e·lab.**

Rong·e·rik (rông′ə·rik) An atoll in the Ralik chain of the Marshall Islands; about 30 miles in circumference.

ron·ion (run′yən) *n. Obs.* A mangy or scabby animal or person. Also **ron′yon.** [<F *rogne* scab]

Røn·ne (rœn′ə) A Danish city, chief port of Bornholm island.

ron·quil (ron′kil) *n.* A deep-water fish (family *Bathymasteridae*) of the North Pacific. [<Sp. *ronquillo*, dim. of *ronco* hoarse <L *raucus* hoarse]

Ron·sard (rôn·sär′), **Pierre de,** 1524–85, French poet.

Rönt·gen (rent′gən, runt′-; *Ger.* rœnt′gən) See ROENTGEN.

rood (rood) *n.* **1** A cross or crucifix; specifically, a crucifix or a representation of the Crucifixion over the altar screen of a church. **2** A square land measure, **square rood**, equivalent to one fourth of a statute acre, or 40 square rods. **3** A linear measure varying locally between six and eight yards. ◆Homophone: *rude*. [OE *rōd* rod, measure of land, cross. Related to ROD.]

rood beam A beam over the entrance to a choir for supporting a cross or crucifix.

Roo·de·poort-Ma·rais·burg (rō′də·pôrt·mär′is·bûrg, -pōrt-, rōō′-) A town of Gauteng Province, Republic of South Africa.

rood screen An enriched screen, usually surmounted by a rood, separating the choir presbytery from the nave.

roof (roof, roof) *n.* **1** The exterior upper covering of a building. **2** Any top covering, as of a car or oven. **3** A house; home. **4** The most el-

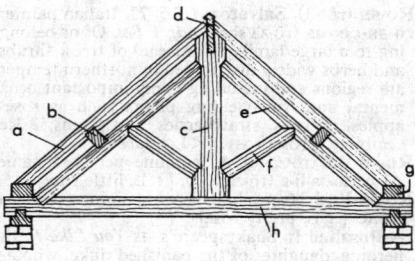

ROOF CONSTRUCTION—KINGPOST TYPE
a. Common rafters.   *e.* Principal rafters.
b. Purlin.   *f.* Struts.
c. Kingpost.   *g.* Pole plate.
d. Ridge pole.   *h.* Tie beams.

evated part of anything; top; summit. —*v.t.* To cover with or as with a roof. [OE *hrōf*]

roof·age (roo′fij, roof′ij) *n.* The material forming a roof; roofing.

roof·er (roo′fər, roof′ər) *n.* One who makes or repairs roofs.

roof garden A garden on the roof of a building; especially, a space on a roof used for public entertainments, restaurants, etc.

roof·ing (roo′fing, roof′ing) *n.* **1** Roofs collectively. **2** Material for roofs. **3** Shelter. **4** The act of covering with a roof.

roof·less (roof′lis, roof′-) *adj.* **1** Having no roof. **2** Destitute of shelter; homeless.

roof of the mouth The hard palate.

roof·tree (roof′trē, roof′-) *n.* **1** The ridge pole of a roof. **2** The roof. **3** A home or dwelling.

rook[1] (rook) *n.* **1** An Old World corvine bird with the feathers of the face lost in the adult state; especially, the common *Corvus frugilegus*, noted for its gregariousness. **2** A sharper; cheat; trickster. —*v.t. & v.i.* To cheat; defraud. [OE *hrōc*]

rook[2] (rook) *n.* One of a pair of castle-shaped chessmen which can move any number of unoccupied squares parallel to the sides of the board; a castle. [<OF *roc* <Persian *rukh*; orig. meaning unknown]

rook·er·y (rook′ər·ē) *n. pl.* **·er·ies 1** A colony or breeding place of rooks. **2** A breeding place of sea birds, seals, etc. **3** A rambling building; an old tenement densely populated.

rook·ie (rook′ē) *n. Slang* **1** A raw recruit in the army, police, or any other service. **2** A novice in professional baseball. [Prob. alter. of RECRUIT]

rook·y (rook′ē) *adj.* **1** Pertaining to rooks and their habits. **2** Gregarious. **3** Abounding in rooks.

room (room, room) *n.* **1** Extent of space considered with regard to its sufficiency for some implied or specified purpose; free or open space. **2** A space for occupancy or use enclosed on all sides, as in a building; an apartment; chamber. **3** Suitable or warrantable occasion; opportunity: *room* for doubt. See synonyms under PLACE. —*v.i.* To occupy a room; lodge. [OE *rūm* space]

room·er (room′mər, room′ər) *n.* A lodger; especially, one who rents a room and eats elsewhere.

room·ette (room·met′, room·et′) *n.* A compartment with a single bed in some railroad sleeping-cars.

room·ful (room′fool′, room′-) *n.* **1** As many or as much as a room will hold. **2** A number of persons present in a room considered collectively.

rooming house A house for roomers; lodging house.

room·mate (room′māt′, room′-) *n.* One who occupies a room with another or others.

room·y (roo′mē, room′ē) *adj.* **room·i·er, room·i·est** Having abundant room; spacious. —**room′i·ly** *adv.* —**room′i·ness** *n.*

roon[1] (roon) *adj. Scot.* Round.

roon[2] (roon) *n. Scot.* A shred; border; strip of cloth.

roop (roop) *n. Brit. Dial.* **1** An outcry; call. **2** Hoarseness. [OE *hrōp* clamor]

roor·back (roor′bak) *n. U.S.* A fictitious report circulated for political purposes. [after *Roorback,* purported author of a (non-existent) book of travel, which was cited as

authority for certain defamatory charges made against President Polk in the 1844 campaign]

roose (rooz, rœz) *v.t. Scot.* To praise. —*n.* Praise. —**roos′er** *n.*

Roo·se·velt (rō′zə·velt, rōz′velt, -vəlt), **(Anna) Eleanor,** 1884–1962, *née* Roosevelt, U.S. lecturer, writer, and diplomat; wife of F. D. Roosevelt. —**Franklin Delano,** 1882–1945, president of the United States 1933–45; reelected to fourth consecutive term 1944. — **Theodore,** 1858–1919, president of the United States 1901–09.

Roosevelt Dam A dam in the Salt River, central Arizona; 280 feet high; 1,125 feet long; completed 1911.

Roosevelt River A river in western Brazil, flowing 400 miles north to the Aripuaña; formerly *River of Doubt* (Portuguese *Río da Dúvida*): Spanish *Río Roosevelt, Río Teodoro.*

roost (roost) *n.* **1** A perch upon which fowls rest at night; also, any place where birds resort to spend the night. **2** Any temporary resting place. —*v.i.* **1** To sit or perch upon a roost. **2** To come to rest; settle. [OE *hrōst*]

roost·er (roos′tər) *n.* The male of the chicken; cock. [<ROOST + -ER[1]]

roost·it (roos′tit) *adj. Scot.* **1** Rusty. **2** Dry; parched.

root[1] (root, root) *n.* **1** The underground portion or descending axis of a plant, which absorbs moisture, obtains or stores nourishment, and provides support. It differs from the stem in that it branches irregularly and lacks joints or leaves. **2** Loosely, any underground growth, as a tuber or bulb. **3** One of certain other growths serving for attachment, support, etc., as in the ivy or mistletoe. **4** That from which anything derives origin, growth, or life and vigor: Money is the *root* of evil; Industry is the *root* of prosperity. **5** An antecedent; ancestor. **6** Some rootlike part of an organ or struture: the *root* of a tooth or nerve. **7** *Ling.* A morpheme serving as the common center or basic constituent element of a related group of words, as *know* in *unknown, knowledge, knowable,* and *knowingly.* A root to which affixes or other morphemes may be added directly is equivalent to a stem. **8** *Math.* A quantity that, taken a specified number of times as a factor, will give another quantity called its *power* : 2 is the fourth *root* of 16. The number of times the root is thus taken as a factor is called its *index,* and roots are named from the indices, the words **square root** and **cube root** being often used for *second* and *third* root. **9** A tone on which a chord is built up. —*v.i.* **1** To put forth roots and begin to grow; take root. **2** To be or become firmly fixed or established. —*v.t.* **3** To fix or implant by or as by roots. **4** To pull, dig, or tear up by or as by the roots; extirpate; eradicate: with *up* or *out.* [OE *rōt* <ON *rōt*]

root[2] (root, root) *v.t.* **1** To turn up or dig with the snout or nose, as swine. —*v.i.* **2** To turn up the earth with the snout. **3** To search for something; rummage. **4** To work hard; toil. [OE *wrōtan* root up <*wrōt* snout]

root[3] (root, root) *v.i. U.S. Colloq.* To cheer for or encourage a contestant: with *for* : He *rooted* for Harvard. [Prob. var. of ROUT[3]]

Root (root, root), **Elihu,** 1845– 1937, U.S. lawyer and statesman.

root beer A beverage made with yeast and the extracts of several roots.

root climber Any plant that climbs by means of adventitious roots developed from stems.

root·er[1] (roo′tər, root′ər) *n.* One who or that which takes root.

root·er[2] (roo′tər, root′ər) *n.* One who or that which roots, as a swine, or tears up as by rooting; a destroyer; eradicator.

root·er[3] (roo′tər, root′ər) *n. U.S. Colloq.* One who gives encouragement, as by applauding.

root hair *Bot.* Hairlike outgrowths of plant roots, having an absorbent and protective function.

root·less (root′lis, root′-) *adj.* Without roots.

root·let (root′lit, root′-) *n.* A small root.

root sheath The tough membrane covering the root portion of a hair. See illustration under HAIR.

root·stalk (root′stôk′, root′-) *n. Bot.* An underground rootlike stem; a rhizome.

root·stock (rōōt′stok′, rŏŏt′-) *n.* **1** A rhizome. **2** Original source; origin.

root·y (rōō′tē, rŏŏt′ē) *adj.* **root·i·er, root·i·est 1** Full of or consisting of roots. **2** Resembling roots. **—root′i·ness** *n.*

rope (rōp) *n.* **1** A construction of twisted fibers, as of hemp, cotton, flax, etc., so intertwined in several strands as to form a thick cord. **2** A collection of things plaited or united in a line. **3** A slimy or glutinous filament or thread. **4** A cord or halter used in hanging; hence, execution or death by strangling or hanging. **5** A lasso. **—to give (one) plenty of rope** To allow (a person) to pursue unchecked a course that will end in disaster. **—to know the ropes** To be familiar with all the conditions in any sphere of activity; hence, to be sophisticated in the ways of the world. *—v.* **roped, rop·ing** *v.t.* **1** To tie or fasten with or as with rope. **2** To enclose, border, or divide with a rope: usually with *off:* He *roped* off the arena. **3** To catch with a lasso. **4** *Colloq.* To deceive; take in: with *in.* *—v.i.* **5** To become drawn out or extended into a filament or thread. [OE *rāp*]

rope band Roband.

rope-dancer (rōp′dan′sər, -dän′-) *n.* One who performs on the tightrope. **—rope′-danc′ing** *n.*

rope ferry A set of ropes overhanging a stream or defile, over which supplies and equipment may be pulled by a towline.

rope ladder A ladder made of ropes or with rope sides and wooden or other rounds.

rop·er·y (rō′pər·ē) *n.* **1** A ropewalk. **2** *Archaic* Roguery.

rope's end 1 A short piece of rope used for flogging. **2** A hangman's noose.

rope·walk (rōp′wôk′) *n.* A long alley formerly used for the spinning of rope yarn: now in general superseded by some structure using improved machinery.

rope-walk·er (rōp′wô′kər) *n.* One who performs on the tightrope.

rop·y (rō′pē) *adj.* **rop·i·er, rop·i·est 1** That may be drawn into threads, as a glutinous substance; stringy. **2** Resembling ropes or cordage. **—rop′i·ly** *adv.* **—rop′i·ness** *n.*

roque (rōk) *n.* A form of croquet requiring more skill than the ordinary game. [Aphetic alter. of CROQUET]

Roque·fort (rōk′fərt, *Fr.* rôk·fôr′) A village in south central France. Also **Roquefort-sur-Soul·zon** (-sür·sōōl·zôn′).

Roquefort cheese A strong cheese with a blue mold *(Penicillium roqueforti)* made from ewe's and goat's milk at Roquefort, France.

roqu·e·laure (rok′ə·lôr, rok′lôr, -lōr) *n.* A form of short cloak worn by men in the 18th century: also spelled *rokelay.* [after Duc de *Roquelaure,* 1656–1738, French nobleman]

ro·quet (rō·kā′) *v.t. & v.i.* **·queted** (-kād′), **·quet·ing** (-kā′ing) In croquet, to strike (another player's ball). *—n.* The act of roqueting. [See ROQUE]

Ro·rai·ma (rō·rī′mä), **Mount** A peak at the junction of the Brazil-Venezuela-Guyana boundaries; 9,219 feet.

Ro·rer (rôr′ər, rō′rər), **Sarah Tyson,** 1849–1937, *née* Heston, U.S. home economist.

ror·qual (rôr′kwəl) *n.* Any of a genus *(Balaenoptera)* of whales of the Atlantic and Pacific oceans; especially, *B. physalis* of the North Atlantic: also called *finback, finback whale.* [< F < Norw. *röyrkval*]

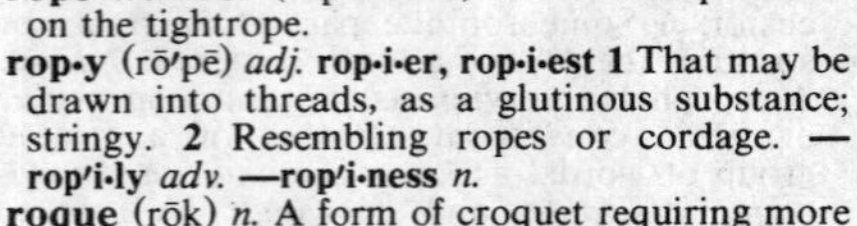

RORQUAL
(About 60 feet in length)

Ror·schach test (rôr′shäk, -shäkh, rōr′-) *Psychol.* A test in which personality characteristics are made accessible to analysis by the subject's interpretation of the nature and meaning of a series of standard inkblot patterns. [after Hermann *Rorschach,* 1884–1922, Swiss psychiatrist]

Ro·sa (rō′zə) A feminine personal name. See ROSE.

Ro·sa (rō′zä), **Monte** The highest mountain group of the Pennine Alps on the Swiss-Italian border; its highest peak, 15,216 feet, is the second highest in the Alps.

Ro·sa (rô′zä), **Salvator,** 1615–73, Italian painter.

ro·sa·ceous (rō·zā′shəs) *adj.* **1** *Bot.* Of or belonging to a large family (Rosaceae) of trees, shrubs, and herbs widely distributed in northern temperate regions and including many important ornamental and fruit-yielding plants such as roses, apples, cherries, strawberries, and plums. **2** Resembling a rose; rosy. [< L *rosaceus*]

Ro·sa·lie (rō′zə·lē) A feminine personal name. Also **Ro·sa·li·a** (rō·zā′lē·ə). [< L, little rose]

Ros·a·lind (roz′ə·lind) A feminine personal name. [< L, pretty rose]
—Rosalind In Shakespeare's *As You Like It,* the heroine, daughter of the banished duke, who assumes male attire.

Ros·a·mond (roz′ə·mənd) A feminine personal name. Also *Fr.* **Rose·monde** (rōz·mônd′), **Ro·sa·mun·da** (*Lat.* rō′zə·mun′də, *Sp.* rō′sä·mōōn′dä). [< L, rose of the world]

ro·san·i·line (rō·zan′ə·lin, -lēn) *n. Chem.* **1** A colorless, crystalline organic compound, $C_{20}H_{21}ON_3$, having basic properties, obtained from aniline by treatment with reagents, as arsenic acid, nitric acid, and stannic chloride. It forms reddish salts, used as dyestuffs. **2** Some salt of this base used as a dyestuff, as fuchsin or rosein. [< ROSE[1] + ANILINE]

Ro·sa·rio (rō·sä′ryō) A port on the Paraná in Santa Fé province, Argentina.

ro·sa·ry (rō′zə·rē) *n. pl.* **·ries 1** *Eccl.* **a** A series of prayers, consisting in its common form **(Dominican rosary)** of fifteen decades, each containing ten Aves preceded by a paternoster and followed by the Gloria Patri, and each related to a mystery or event in the life of Christ or the Virgin Mary which is contemplated during its recitation. **b** A string of beads for keeping count of the prayers thus recited. **2** A garden or bed of roses. **3** A chaplet or garland, as of roses. **4** A collection of literary selections. [< LL *rosarium* a rose garden < L *rosa* a rose]

Ros·cius (rosh′əs), **Gallus Quintus,** died 62? B.C., Roman comic actor. **—Ros′cian** *adj.*

Ros·coe (ros′kō), **Sir Henry Enfield,** 1833–1915, English chemist.

Ros·com·mon (ros·kom′ən) A county of eastern Connacht province, Ireland; 951 square miles; county town, Roscommon.

rose[1] (rōz) *n.* **1** A hardy, erect or climbing shrub (genus *Rosa*) grown in many varieties, with rodlike, prickly stems. In cultivation the stamens are transformed into petals and the flowers become double. It is the national flower of England and the State flower of New York, North Dakota, and Iowa. **2** The flower, having 5, or rarely 4, sepals. **3** Any one of various other plants or flowers having some real or fancied likeness to the true rose. **4** A light pinkish red, like the color of many roses. **5** An ornamental knot, as of ribbon or lace; a rosette. **6** A perforated cap, plate, or nozzle at the end of a pipe, for throwing water in a fine spray. **7** A compass rose. **8** A form in which gems, especially diamonds, are often cut, characterized by a flat base with a hemispherical upper surface covered with small facets; also, a diamond so cut. **9** Erysipelas. **—golden rose** A rose of wrought gold, blessed by the pope and presented, usually to a Roman Catholic sovereign, as a distinguished honor. **—under the rose** In secret. See SUB ROSA. *—v.t.* **rosed, ros·ing** To cause to blush; redden; flush. [OE < L *rosa* < Gk. *rhodon*]

rose[2] (rōz) Past tense of RISE.

Rose (rōz) A feminine personal name. Also **Ro·sa** (rō′zə; *Fr.* rō·zä′, *Ger.* rō′zä, *Ital.* rô′zä, *Sp.* rō′sä). [< L, rose]

rose acacia A locust tree *(Robinia hispida)* of the SE United States, bearing racemes of large rose or pale-purple flowers.

ro·se·ate (rō′zē·it, -āt) *adj.* **1** Of a rose color. **2** Rosy; rose-colored; hence, optimistic. [< L *roseus*] **—ro′se·ate·ly** *adv.*

roseate spoonbill A tropical American wading bird *(Ajaia ajaja)* having a bare head and throat and pink plumage.

rose·bay (rōz′bā′) *n.* **1** Any rhododendron, especially *Rhododendron maximum.* **2** The oleander. **3** The willow herb.

rose beetle 1 The goldsmith beetle. **2** The rose chafer.

Rose·ber·y (rōz′bər·ē), **Earl of,** 1847–1929, Archibald Philip Primrose, English statesman and author.

rose-breast·ed grosbeak (rōz′bres′tid) See under GROSBEAK.

rose·bud (rōz′bud′) *n.* **1** The bud of a rose. **2** A young girl; a debutante.

rose bush A rose-bearing shrub or vine.

rose campion 1 Any species of *Lychnis,* especially *L. coronaria.* **2** The corncockle.

rose chafer A hairy, fawn-colored beetle *(Macrodactylus subspinosus)* injurious to roses: also called *rose beetle.* Also **rose bug.** For illustration see INSECTS (injurious).

rose cold *Pathol.* A variety of hay fever, assumed to be caused by rose pollen. Also **rose fever.**

rose-col·ored (rōz′kul′ərd) *adj.* Pink or crimson, as a rose. **—to see through rose-colored glasses** To see things in an unduly favorable light; to look too much or only on the bright side. Compare COULEUR DE ROSE.

Rose·crans (rōz′kranz), **William Starke,** 1819–1898, U.S. general.

rose-cross (rōz′krôs′, -kros′) *n.* The symbol of the Rosicrucians, a rose and cross combined in some form.

rose·fish (rōz′fish′) *n. pl.* **·fish** or **·fish·es** An orange-red scorpaenoid food fish *(Sebastes marinus)* of the North Atlantic.

rose geranium A cultivated geranium *(Pelargonium capitatum)* with rose-scented leaves and dense clusters of rose-purple flowers, grown extensively in South Africa.

Rose Island Easternmost island in the American Samoa group.

rose mallow Any of various species of hibiscus, especially *Hibiscus moscheutos,* a tall, coarse marsh plant having large flowers with creamy petals and a musky odor. Also *mallow rose.*

rose·mar·y (rōz′mâr′ē) *n. pl.* **·mar·ies** An evergreen, fragrant shrub *(Rosmarinus officinalis)* of the mint family of southern Europe and western Asia, with usually blue flowers: cultivated for its stimulating and refreshing perfume, for an oil obtained from it, and for use in cookery. [Alter. of L *rosmarinus* < *ros* dew + *marinus* marine; infl. by *rose, Mary*]

rose moss A garden variety of portulaca *(Portulaca grandiflora).*

Ro·sen·wald (rō′zən·wôld), **Julius,** 1862–1932, U.S. businessman and philanthropist.

rose of Jericho A small annual *(Anastatica hierochuntica)* growing in desert places from Syria to Algeria, which rolls up when dry and expands again when moist: also called *resurrection plant, Jericho rose.*

rose of Sharon 1 In the Bible (Song of Sol. 2:1), an unknown flower, perhaps the autumn crocus or the narcissus. **2** A tall, hardy deciduous shrub or small tree *(Hibiscus syriacus)* of Asian origin, having large, usually roseate flowers. Also called *althea, hibiscus.* **3** A species *(Hypericum calycinum)* of shrubby plants having evergreen leaves and large yellow flowers.

ro·se·o·la (rō·zē′ə·lə) *n. Pathol.* A rose-colored rash appearing on the skin. Also **rose rash.** [< NL, dim. of L *roseus* rosy]

rose quartz A translucent to semitransparent variety of quartz, pink or rose in color and often asteriated: used for ornament, as a gemstone, etc.

Ro·set·ta (rō·zet′ə) **1** The western branch of the Nile in its delta, Lower Egypt. Ancient **Bol·bi·ti·ne** (bol′bə·tī′nē). **2** A town on the Rosetta.

Ro·set·ta stone (rō·zet′ə) A tablet of basalt containing an inscription in two forms of Egyptian hieroglyphics (demotic and hieratic) and in Greek, found near Rosetta, Egypt, in 1799. It supplied Champollion with the key to the ancient inscriptions of Egypt.

ro·sette (rō·zet′) *n.* **1** An ornament or badge having some resemblance to a rose; specifically, a painted or sculptured architectural ornament with parts circularly arranged. **2** A ribbon badge worn in the lapel buttonhole of civilian clothes to indicate possession of a certain military decoration. **3** A ribbon decoration shaped like a full-blown

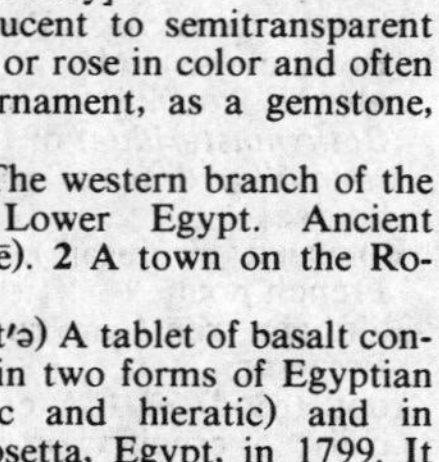

ROSETTE

or double rose and made of gathered or pleated silk, lace, etc. **4** A flowerlike cluster or combination of leaves, organs, parts, or markings, arranged in circles, as in certain plants. [<F, little rose]

rose·wa·ter (rōz′wô′tər, -wot′ər) n. A fragrant toilet and pharmaceutical water made variously by the distillation of rose petals or rose oil with water. — adj. **1** Made with or resembling rosewater. **2** Extremely or affectedly delicate or sentimental: *rosewater* philosophy.

rose window A circular window filled with tracery, called, when this takes the form of spokes, a *wheel window*.

rose·wood (rōz′wŏŏd′) n. **1** A hard, close-grained, dark-colored, fragrant wood yielded by different Brazilian trees of the genus *Dalbergia*, etc., especially that produced by *D. nigra*, the most highly prized for cabinet work. Some species are said to be rose-scented when fresh. **2** Any of various other woods in some way resembling the true rose-woods. **3** Any tree yielding such a wood.

Rosh Ha·sha·na (rosh hə·shä′nə, rōsh) The Jewish New Year, celebrated on Tisri 1st and 2nd (September–early October). Also **Rosh Ha·sho′nah** (-shō′-). [<Hebrew *rōsh* head of + *hash-shānāh* the year]

Ro·si·cru·cian (rō′zə·krōō′shən, roz′ə-) n. One who is a member of an international fraternity, said to have originated in Egypt, and devoted to the practical application of an occult philosophy to human relationship. See ILLUMINATI. — adj. Of or pertaining to this society, its members, or its doctrines. [<L *rosae crucis* roses of the cross; said to be the trans. of the name of Christian *Rosen-kranz*, 1387–1484, a German to whom the founding of this order has been attributed] — **Ro′si·cru′cian·ism** n.

ros·in (roz′in) n. **1** Resin. **2** The hard, amber-colored resin forming the residue after the distillation of oil of turpentine from crude turpentine; colophony. — v.t. To apply rosin to. [Var. of RESIN] — **ros′in·y** adj.

Ros·i·nan·te (roz′ə·nan′tē) See ROCINANTE.

rosin oil Retinol.

ros·in·weed (roz′in·wēd′) n. **1** A coarse perennial herb (genus *Silphium*) of the composite family, with copious resinous juice, growing in the central and western United States. **2** The compass plant.

ro·so·lio (rō·zō′lyō) n. A cordial made from raisins and brandy in the Mediterranean countries. [<Ital. <Med.L *ros solis* (<L *ros* dew + *solis* of the sun) sundew, from which it was once extracted]

Ross (rôs), **Betsy**, 1752–1836, American patriot; made first American flag, 1777. — **Sir James Clark**, 1800–62, English Arctic explorer; discovered the north magnetic pole in 1831. — **Sir John**, 1777–1856, Scottish Arctic explorer; uncle of the preceding. — **Sir Ronald**, 1857–1932, English physician; first investigator of malaria-bearing mosquitoes.

Ross and Crom·ar·ty (krom′ər·tē, krum′-) A maritime county of NW Scotland; 3,089 square miles; county town, Dingwall.

Ross Dependency An uninhabited, ice-covered region of the Antarctic Zone under the jurisdiction of New Zealand; 175,000 square miles.

Ros·set·ti (rō·set′ē, -zet′ē), **Christina Georgina**, 1830–94, English poet; sister of Dante Gabriel. — **Dante Gabriel**, 1828–82, English painter and poet.

Ros·si (rôs′sē), **Bruno**, born 1905, Italian physicist.

Ros·si·ni (rôs·sē′nē), **Gioacchino Antonio**, 1792–1868, Italian composer.

Ross Island 1 An island off the NE tip of Palmer Peninsula, Antarctica; 39 nautical miles long, 31 nautical miles wide. **2** A volcanic island in the western Ross Sea off Victoria Land, Antarctica, on which Mount Erebus is located; 43 nautical miles long, 45 nautical miles wide.

Ros·si·ya (ros·sē′yä) The Russian name for RUSSIA.

Ross Sea An inlet of the South Pacific in Antarctica south of New Zealand.

Ross Shelf Ice The extensive area of shelf ice in Antarctica, occupying the southern

---

part of the Ross Sea; about 400 miles wide on its seaward side. Also called **Ross Barrier**.

Ros·tand (rôs·tän′), **Edmond**, 1869?–1918, French dramatist and poet.

ros·tel·late (ros′tə·lāt, -lit) adj. Having a small beak or rostellum. [<NL *rostellatus*]

ros·tel·lum (ros·tel′əm) n. pl. **·tel·la** (-tel′ə) **1** Bot. A small, beaklike structure developed from the stigma of an orchid. **2** Zool. The hooked scolex of a tapeworm. [<L, dim. of *rostrum* beak]

ros·ter (ros′tər) n. **1** A list of officers and men enrolled for duty; also, a list of active military organizations. **2** Any list of names. [<Du. *rooster* list]

Ros·tock (ros′tok, Ger. rôs′tôk) **1** A port on the Baltic in Rostock district, northern East Germany. **2** A district of East Germany, formerly part of the former state of Mecklenburg; 2,722 square miles.

Ros·tov (ros′tof′) A city in southern Russian S.F.S.R., on the Don near its mouth on the Sea of Azov. Also **Ros·tov′-on-Don′** (-dôn′).

Ros·tov·tzeff (ro·stôf′tsəf), **Michael Ivanovich**, 1870–1952, U.S. historian and archeologist born in Russia.

ros·tral (ros′trəl) adj. **1** Of or pertaining to a rostrum. **2** Having a rostrum, or beaklike process; beaked: often used in combination, as in *curvirostral*, having a crossed or curved-down beak. Also **ros′trate** (-trāt). [<LL *rostralis*]

ros·trum (ros′trəm) n. pl. **·trums** or **·tra** (-trə) **1** A pulpit or platform. **2** pl. **ros·tra** The orators' platform in the Roman forum: embellished with the beaks of the Latin ships captured 338 B.C. **3** A beak or snout; a beaklike process or part. **4** One of various beaklike parts, as the beak or prow of an ancient war galley. [<L *rostrum* beak]

ROSTRUM *(def. 4)*

ros·y (rō′zē) adj. **ros·i·er, ros·i·est 1** Like a rose; rose-red; blooming; blushing. **2** Figuratively, bright, pleasing, or flattering. **3** Made of or ornamented with roses. **4** Auguring success; favorable: *rosy* predictions. **5** Optimistic. — **ros′i·ly** adv. — **ros′i·ness** n.

rot (rot) v. **rot·ted, rot·ting** v.i. **1** To undergo decomposition; decompose; decay. **2** To fall or pass by decaying: with *away, off*, etc. **3** To become morally rotten. — v.t. **4** To cause to decompose; decay. **5** To ret. See synonyms under DECAY, PUTREFY. — n. **1** That which is rotten, or the process of rotting. **2** A wasting disease, as of the lungs. **3** A parasitic disease affecting sheep and other domestic animals. **4** A form of decay in plants, caused by fungi and bacteria. **5** Colloq. Trashy and nonsensical opinions or expressions; twaddle; bosh. — interj. Nonsense; bosh. [OE *rotian*]

ro·ta (rō′tə) n. **1** A roll of names, giving order of duty; a roster. **2** A routine. **3** A wheel. [<L, wheel]

Ro·ta (rō′tə) n. In the Roman Catholic Church, an ecclesiastical court composed of ten prelates or auditors, subject only to papal authority, and serving as a court of final appeal: also known as *Sacra Romana Rota*.

Ro·ta (rō′tä) An island in the southern Marianas group; 33 square miles.

Ro·tar·i·an (rō·târ′ē·ən) n. A member of a Rotary Club. — adj. Of or pertaining to the organization of Rotary Clubs or to their members. — **Ro·tar′i·an·ism** n.

ro·ta·ry (rō′tər·ē) adj. **1** Turning around its axis, like a wheel, or so constructed as to turn thus. **2** Having some part that so turns: a *rotary* press. [<LL *rotarius* <*rota* wheel]

Rotary Club A club belonging to an international association of clubs, **Rotary International**, whose aim is to improve civic service, and whose motto is "Service."

rotary engine 1 An engine in which rotary motion is directly produced without reciprocating parts, as in a steam turbine: distin-

---

guished from *reciprocating engine*. **2** In internal-combustion engines, a radial engine revolving about a fixed crankshaft.

rotary harrow Agric. A harrow with many spikes set along the rim of a wheel which turns on a horizontal axis as it is pulled along the ground.

rotary motor See under MOTOR.

rotary plow Agric. A set of plowshares arranged on the rim of a rotating, power-driven shaft.

rotary press A printing press using curved type plates which revolve against the paper.

ro·tate (rō′tāt) v.t. & v.i. **·tat·ed, ·tat·ing 1** To turn or cause to turn on or as on its axis. **2** To alternate in a definite order or succession. See synonyms under REVOLVE. — adj. **1** Wheel-shaped; circular, as the corollas of certain flowers. **2** Forming a circle around a part, as spines or hairs. [<L *rotatus*, pp. of *rotare* turn <*rota*] — **ro′tat·a·ble** adj.

ro·tat·ed (rō′tā·tid) adj. **1** Turned around. **2** Rotate.

ro·ta·tion (rō·tā′shən) n. **1** The act or state of rotating; rotary motion. **2** Change by alternation; order of succession, variation, or sequence: *rotation* of crops or office. **3** The period represented by the age of a forest, or a part of a forest, at the time when it is cut, or intended to be cut. — **ro·ta′tion·al** adj.

ro·ta·tive (rō′tə·tiv) adj. Pertaining to or causing rotation; turning.

ro·ta·tor (rō′tā·tər) n. **1** One who or that which rotates or causes rotation. **2** pl. **ro·ta·to·res** (rō′tə·tôr′ēz, -tō′rēz) Anat. A muscle that rolls or rotates a part upon its axis. [<L]

Ro·ta·to·ri·a (rō′tə·tôr′ē·ə, -tō′rē·ə) See ROTIFER.

ro·ta·to·ry (rō′tə·tôr′ē, -tō′rē) adj. **1** Having, pertaining to, or producing rotation. **2** Following in succession. **3** Alternating or recurring.

rotche (roch) n. A bird, the dovekie. Also **rotch**. [Var. of *rotge* <Du. *rotje* petrel]

rote[1] (rōt) n. **1** Mechanical routine. **2** Repetition of words as a means of learning them, with slight attention to the sense. — **by rote** Mechanically; without intelligent attention: to learn *by rote*. [Var. of ROUTE]

rote[2] (rōt) n. Rare The roar of the surf. [Cf. ON *rōt* breaking of waves]

ro·te·none (rō′tə·nōn) n. Chem. A white crystalline substance, $C_{23}H_{22}O_6$, the effective principle in insecticides and fish poisons, obtained from the roots of various plants, especially an Amazonian tree (genus *Lonchocarpus*) and the Indian derris. [Origin unknown]

rot·gut whisky (rot′gut′) U.S. An inferior raw whisky. Also **rot′gut′**.

Roth·er·ham (roth′ər·əm) A county borough in the West Riding, southern Yorkshire, England.

Roth·schild (rôth′child, Ger. rōt′shilt) A family of European bankers, of whom the first, **Meyer Amschel**, 1743–1812, established a bank in Frankfort on the Main. His sons opened branches: **James**, 1792–1868, at Paris; **Karl**, 1788–1855, at Naples; **Nathan Meyer**, 1777–1836, at London; **Salomon**, 1774–1855, at Vienna.

ro·ti·fer (rō′tə·fər) n. One of a division (*Rotifera*) of many-celled, microscopic, aquatic organisms usually found in stagnant fresh water, having rings of cilia which in motion resemble revolving wheels; a wheel animalcule. Some authorities place the *Rotifera* in a separate class or phylum, *Rotatoria*. [<NL <L *rota* wheel + *ferre* bear] — **ro·tif·er·al** (rō·tif′ər·əl), **ro·tif′er·ous** adj.

ro·ti·form (rō′tə·fôrm) adj. Shaped like a wheel; rotate. [<L *rota* wheel + -FORM]

ro·tis·se·rie (rō·tis′ə·rē) n. **1** A restaurant where patrons select uncooked food and have it roasted and served. **2** A shop where food is roasted and sold. **3** A rotating device for roasting meat, etc. [<F <*rôtir* roast]

ro·tl (rot′l) n. pl. **ar·tal** (är′täl) A weight used in Moslem countries, varying in different localities between one and five pounds. [<Arabic *raṭl*]

ro·to·chute (rō′tə·shōōt′) n. Aeron. A long, dartlike, high-altitude parachute equipped with a propeller having rapidly rotating

---

blades for breaking the speed of descent [< L *rota* wheel + CHUTE]

ro·to·graph (rō′tə·graf, -gräf) *n.* One of a series of photographs printed from a developed roll of sensitized paper that bears the images. [< L *rota* wheel + -GRAPH]

ro·to·gra·vure (rō′tə·grə·vyoor′, -grāv′yər) *n.* **1** A picture engraved on a cylindrical printing surface and run through a rotary press that prints both sides of the paper at the same time. **2** The process of making such pictures. [< L *rota* wheel + GRAVURE]

ro·tor (rō′tər) *n.* **1** *Electr.* The portion of an alternating-current motor which revolves. **2** A revolving part of a machine, as the wheel or wheels of a turbine. Compare STATOR. **3** *Aeron.* The horizontally rotating unit of a helicopter. [Contraction of ROTATOR]

ro·tor·craft (rō′tər·kraft′) *n.* An aircraft, esp. a helicopter, supported while airborne by rotors.

rotor ship A vessel propelled by rotors operated by wind power but fitted with auxiliary power for propulsion when the wind fails.

ro·to·till (rō′tō·til′) *v.t.* To till by means of a powered rotary cultivating machine.

rot·ten (rot′n) *adj.* **1** Decomposed by natural process; putrid. **2** Unsound; liable to break. **3** Untrustworthy; treacherous; also, venal; corrupt. **4** Afflicted with the rot, as sheep. **5** *Colloq.* Worthless. [< ON *rotinn*] **—rot′ten·ly** *adv.* **—rot′ten·ness** *n.*

Synonyms: carious, corrupt, decayed, deceitful, decomposed, defective, fetid, offensive, putrefied, putrescent, putrid, tainted, treacherous, unsound. See BAD. *Antonyms*: complete, fresh, healthful, healthy, perfect, pure, sound, sweet, untainted, wholesome.

rotten borough **1** Any English borough prior to 1832 having few voters, yet entitled to send a member to Parliament. **2** Any election district or political unit no longer having sufficient population to justify the representation alloted to it.

rot·ter (rot′ər) *n. Slang* A scoundrel; a worthless scamp; any objectionable person.

rot·ten·stone (rot′n·stōn′) *n.* A soft, friable rock, consisting largely of siliceous particles, used for polishing: also called *tripoli.*

Rot·ter·dam (rot′ər·dam) The largest port of the Netherlands, in the western part.

rot·wei·ler (rot′wī′lər, -vī′-) *n.* A breed of strong, shorthaired, black or black and tan dogs.

Ro·tu·ma (rō·too͞′mə) An Island dependency of Fiji; 18 square miles.

ro·tund (rō·tund′) *adj.* **1** Rounded out; spherical; plump. **2** Full-toned, as a voice or utterance; in style, using sonorous words. **3** Complete; entire. **4** Circular, or nearly so; orbicular. See synonyms under ROUND. [< L *rotundus* < *rota* wheel. Doublet of ROUND.] **—ro·tund′ly** *adv.* **—ro·tund′ness** *n.*

ro·tun·da (rō·tun′də) *n.* A circular building or an interior hall, surmounted with a dome. [< Ital. *rotonda* < L *rotunda*, fem. of *rotundus.* See ROTUND.]

ro·tun·di·ty (rō·tun′də·tē) *n.* **1** The condition of being rotund; sphericity. **2** A protuberance.

ro·ture (rō·tür′) *n. French* **1** A plebeian condition or rank. **2** In French-Canadian law, a tenure of feudal lands by a constituted rent, without feudal duties and charges.

ro·tu·rier (rō·tü·ryā′) *n. French* **1** A person without rank; plebeian or peasant. **2** In French-Canadian law, one who holds lands by the tenure of roture.

Rou·ault (roo͞·ō′), **Georges,** 1871–1958, French painter.

rou·ble (roo͞′bəl) See RUBLE.

rouche (roo͞sh) See RUCHE.

rou·é (roo͞·ā′) *n.* A sensualist; debauchee. [< F, jaded, orig. pp. of *rouer* break on the wheel, beat severely < *roue* wheel < L *rota*; from the appearance of a debauchee]

Rou·en (roo͞·äṅ′) A city on the Seine in Normandy, northern France; noted for its cathedral; scene of the burning of Joan of Arc.

rouge (roo͞zh) *n.* **1** Any cosmetic used for coloring the cheeks or lips pink or red. **2** A ferric oxide used in polishing metals and glass. —*v.* **rouged, roug·ing** *v.t.* To color, as the face, with rouge. —*v.i.* To apply rouge. [< F, red < L *rubeus* ruby]

rouge et noir (roo͞zh′ e nwär′) A gambling game played with cards on a table having four diamond-shaped figures, two red and two black. See TRENTE-ET-QUARANTE. [< F, red and black]

Rou·get de l'Isle (roo͞·zhe′ də lēl′), **Claude Joseph,** 1760–1836, French poet; author and composer of the *Marseillaise.*

rough (ruf) *adj.* **1** Having an uneven surface; having small inequalities on the surface; not smooth or polished: *rough* stone. **2** Coarse in texture; shaggy; also, disordered or ragged; shabby: said of dress or appearance: a *rough* suit, a *rough* shock of hair. **3** Having the surface broken; uneven: a *rough* country. **4** Characterized by rude or violent action: *rough* sports. **5** *Naut.* Boisterous or tempestuous; stormy: a *rough* passage. **6** Characterized by harshness of spirit; brutal. **7** Lacking the finish and polish bestowed by art or culture; unpolished; crude. **8** Done or made hastily and without attention to details; approximate. **9** *Phonet.* Uttered with an aspiration; aspirated: a *rough* breathing. **10** Harsh to the ear; grating; inharmonious: *rough* sounds. —*n.* **1** A low, rude, and violent fellow; a ruffian; a rowdy. **2** A crude, incomplete, or unpolished object, material, or condition. **3** Any part of a golf course on which tall grass, bushes, etc., grow. **4** A spike for insertion in a horseshoe, to prevent slipping. —*v.t.* **1** To make rough; roughen. **2** To treat roughly; specifically, in football, to treat (a player) with needless and intentional violence. **3** To make, cut, or sketch roughly: with *in* or *out*: to *rough* in the details of a plan. —*v.i.* **4** To become rough. **5** To behave roughly. **—to rough it** To live under rough, hard, or impoverished conditions; also, to camp out or travel in a rough manner; rusticate. —*adv.* In a rude manner; roughly. ◆ Homophone: *ruff.* [OE *rūh*] **—rough′ly** *adv.* **—rough′ness** *n.*

Synonyms (adj.) coarse, craggy, harsh, jagged, ragged, rude, rugged, shaggy, uneven, unfinished, unhewn, unpolished. See AWKWARD, BLUFF. *Antonyms*: bland, even, glossy, level, plain, polished, sleek, smooth.

rough·age (ruf′ij) *n.* **1** Any coarse or tough substance. **2** Food material containing a high percentage of indigestible constituents, as cellulose.

rough-and-ready (ruf′ən·red′ē) *adj.* **1** Characterized by or acting with rude but effective promptness. **2** Unpolished but good enough.

rough-and-tum·ble (ruf′ən·tum′bəl) *adj.* **1** Disregarding all rules: said of a certain kind of fighting. **2** Scrambling; disorderly. —*n.* **1** A fight disregarding procedure according to rule, or in which anything goes; also, a scuffle. **2** Rough or adventurous existence.

rough breathing See under BREATHING.

rough-cast (ruf′kast′, -käst′) *v.t.* **-cast, -cast·ing** **1** To shape or prepare in a preliminary or incomplete form. **2** To roughen the surface of (pottery) before firing. **3** To coat, as a wall, with coarse plaster, and cover with thin mortar by dashing it on. —*n.* **1** Very coarse plaster for the outside of buildings. **2** A rude model; the form of a thing in its first rough stage. **—rough′-cast′er** *n.*

rough-draft (ruf′draft′, -dräft′) *v.t.* To make a rough or unfinished draft of; design or sketch hastily, as a plan or discourse.

rough-draw (ruf′drô′) *v.t.* **-drew, -drawn, -draw·ing** To sketch hastily or crudely.

rough-dry (ruf′drī′) *v.t.* **-dried, -dry·ing** To dry without ironing, as washed clothes.

rough·en (ruf′ən) *v.t.* & *v.i.* To make or become rough.

rough·er (ruf′ər) *n.* One who makes things in the rough.

rough-hew (ruf′hyoo͞′) *v.t.* **-hewed, -hewed** or **-hewn, -hew·ing** **1** To hew or shape roughly or irregularly or without smoothing. **2** To make crudely; rough-cast.

rough-house (ruf′hous′) *Slang n.* A noisy, boisterous or violent game or disturbance; rough play, especially within a room or house. —*v.* **-housed, -hous·ing** *v.i.* To make a disturbance; engage in horseplay or violence. —*v.t.* To handle or treat roughly but without hostile intent.

rough-leg·ged hawk (ruf′leg′id, -legd′) A large hawk *(Buteo lagopus sanctijohannis)* of Alaska and Canada, having the legs feathered all the way to the toes.

rough·neck (ruf′nek′) *n. U.S. Slang* A rowdy.

rough-rid·er (ruf′rī′dər) *n. U.S.* **1** One skilled in breaking broncos or performing dangerous feats in horsemanship. **2** A western cowboy.

Rough Riders The 1st U.S. Volunteer Cavalry in the Spanish-American War of 1898, mainly organized and subsequently commanded by Theodore Roosevelt.

rough-shod (ruf′shod′) *adj.* Shod with rough shoes to prevent slipping, as a horse. **—to ride rough-shod (over)** To act overbearingly; domineer without consideration.

rou·lade (roo͞·läd′) *n.* **1** In singing, a run of short notes on one syllable; also, a roll or flourish, as on a drum. **2** A slice of meat rolled around a filling and cooked. [< F < *rouler* roll]

rou·leau (roo͞·lō′) *n. pl.* **·leaux** (-lōz) or **·leaus** **1** A roll of coins in paper. **2** *Usually pl.* In millinery, a roll or fold of ribbon used for piping. [< F, dim. of *rôle* roll]

Rou·lers (roo͞·lâr′) A town in western Belgium south of Bruges; scene of several battles of World War I, 1914, 1917. *Flemish* **Roe·se·la·re** (roo͞′sə·lä′rə).

rou·lette (roo͞·let′) *n.* **1** A game played at a table divided into spaces numbered and colored red and black, and having in the center a rotating disk on which a ball is rolled until it drops into one of 37 correspondingly numbered and colored spaces, a player winning if he has staked his money on that space or its color or on a combination including it. **2** An engraver's disk of tempered steel, as for tracing points on a copperplate; also, a draftsman's wheel for making dotted lines. **3** In philately, a series of incisions, made in any of several shapes, without removal of paper. Compare PERFORATION. —*v.t.* **·let·ted, ·let·ting** To use or produce a roulette upon. [< F, dim. of *rouelle,* dim. of *roue* wheel < L *rota*]

Roum (roo͞m) See RUM.

Rou·ma·ni·a (roo͞·mā′nē·ə, -mān′yə), **Rou·ma·ni·an** (roo͞·mā′ne·ən, -mān′yən) See RUMANIA, etc.

Rou·me·li·a (roo͞·mē′lē·ə) See RUMELIA.

rounce (rouns) *n.* A game of cards with a full pack for two to nine persons, in which each player seeks to efface the score of 15 with which he starts, each trick taken subtracting one from it. [< Du. *rondse*]

round[1] (round) *adj.* **1** Having such a contour that a section in some direction will be circular or approximately so; circular, spherical, or cylindrical. **2** Having a curved contour or surface; not angular or flat; convex or concave. **3** Liberal; ample; large: a good *round* fee. **4** Easy and free, as in motion; brisk: a *round* pace. **5** Of full cadence; well-balanced; full-toned: a *round* sentence or tone. **6** Made without reserve; bold; outspoken: a *round* assertion. **7** Open; just; honorable. **8** Formed or moving in rotation or a circle: a *round* dance. **9** Returning to the point of departure, usually by the same means of transportation: a *round* trip. **10** Passing through the same or a like series of mutations: the *round* year. **11** Free from fractions; also, not exact in the small denominations; especially, evenly divisible by 10: *round* numbers. **12** Semicircular: a *round* arch; also, characterized by the round arch: the *round* style. **13** *Phonet.* Labialized; rounded. —*n.* **1** Something round, as a globe, ring, or cylinder, a rung of a ladder, a crossbar connecting the legs of a chair, a portion of the thigh of a beef, etc. **2** A circular course or range; circuit; beat: often in the plural; also, revolving motion or one revolution. **3** A series of recurrent movements; a routine; a completed succession or order: the daily *round* of life. **4** One of a series of concerted actions performed in succession by a number of persons: a *round* of toasts or applause. **5** One of the divisions of a boxing match; a bout. **6** In archery, the total number of arrows shot; the sum of all arrows in two or three ranges. **7** A short melody taken up at intervals by several voices; a rondo, roundel, or roundelay. **8** A firing by a company or squad in which each soldier fires once; volley. **9** A single charge of ammunition. **10** A round dance. **11** The state of being carved out on all sides: opposed to *relief.* **12** The state or condition of being circular; roundness. **13** A thick slice from a haunch: a *round* of beef. **—to go the rounds** **1** To take the usual walk of inspection. **2** To pass from mouth to mouth or person to person of a certain group. —*v.t.* **1** To make

round. **2** To bring to completion; perfect: usually with *off* or *out*. **3** To free of angularity; fill out to fullness of form. **4** *Phonet.* To utter (a vowel) with the lips in a rounded position; labialize. **5** To travel or go around; make a circuit of. **6** *Archaic* To encircle; surround. — *v.i.* **7** To become round. **8** To come to completeness or perfection. **9** To fill out; become plump. **10** To make a circuit; travel a circular course. **11** To turn around. — **to round off** *Math.* To reduce the number of decimal places to which a number is carried in a calculation: usually, a final figure less than 5 is eliminated and a final figure of 5 or greater increases the preceding figure to its next highest value, as, 2.1414, rounded off, becomes 2.141; 3.14159 becomes 3.1416. — **to round up 1** To collect (cattle, etc.) in a herd, as for driving to market. **2** *Colloq.* To gather together; assemble. — *adv.* **1** On all sides; in such a manner as to encircle: A crowd gathered *round*. **2** With a circular or rotating motion: The wheel turns *round*. **3** Through a circle or circuit; more or less completely from person to person or point to point: provisions enough to go *round*. **4** In circumference: a log 3 feet *round*. **5** From one view or position to another; hither and yon; to and fro. **6** In the vicinity: to hang *round*. See AROUND. — *prep.* **1** Enclosing; encircling: a belt *round* his waist. **2** On every side of, or from every side toward; surrounding. **3** Toward every side from; about: He peered *round* him. [< OF *roonde*, fem. of *roond* < L *rotundus*. Doublet of ROTUND.] — **round′ness** *n.*

Synonyms (adj.): circular, curved, curvilinear, cylindrical, globose, globular, orbed, orbicular, plump, rotund, spherical, spheroidal. See BLUNT. *Antonyms:* angular, conical, cubical, flat, polygonal, quadrangular, quadrilateral, rectangular, square, triangular.

Round may appear as a combining form in hyphemes or solidemes:

round–arched	round–hoofed
round–armed	round–horned
round–backed	round–leaved
round–barreled	round–limbed
round–bellied	round–lobed
round–billed	round–mouthed
round–bodied	round–nosed
round–boned	round–pointed
round–bottomed	round–ribbed
round–bowled	round–rooted
round–celled	round–sided
round–cornered	round–skirted
round–crested	round–spun
round–eared	round–stalked
round–edged	round–tailed
round–faced	round–toed
round–fenced	round–topped
round–footed	round–trussed
round–furrowed	round–visaged
round–handed	round–winged
round–headed	round–wombed

round[2] (round) *v.t.* & *v.i. Obs.* To whisper (to). [OE *rūnian*]
round–a·bout (round′ə·bout′) *adj.* **1** Circuitous; indirect. **2** Covering the whole field; ample. **3** Encircling. — *n.* **1** An outer garment reaching to the waist; a jacket. **2** *Brit.* A merry–go–round.
round–about chair A corner chair.
round clam A quahaug.
round dance 1 A country dance in which the dancers form a circle. **2** A dance with a revolving motion, as a waltz or polka, performed by two persons.
round·ed (roun′did) *adj.* **1** Round or spherical. **2** *Phonet.* Labialized.
roun·del (roun′dəl) *n.* **1** A roundelay. **2** In prosody, a modification of the rondeau, introduced by Swinburne, written in three stanzas of three lines each, with a refrain after the first and third. Compare RONDEL. **3** *Archit.* A semicircular recess, small round window, etc. [< OF *rondel* a roundelay]
roun·de·lay (roun′də·lā) *n.* **1** A simple melody. **2** A musical setting of a poem with a recurrent refrain. **3** A dance performed in a circle. [< OF *rondelet*, dim. of *rondel* < *rond* round]
round·er (roun′dər) *n.* **1** *U.S. Slang* A dissolute person who makes the rounds of public

resorts at night, or who is often arrested for misdemeanors. **2** A tool for rounding. **3** *pl.* An old English game of ball somewhat resembling baseball: construed as singular.
round·hand (round′hand′) *n.* A style of handwriting in which the tendency is to make all letters round, full, and distinct.
Round·head (round′hed′) *n.* A member of the Parliamentary party in England in the civil war of 1642–49: so called in contempt by the Royalists, from their close–cropped hair.
round·house (round′hous′) *n.* **1** A cabin on the after part of the quarter–deck of a vessel. **2** A round building with a turntable in the center for housing and switching locomotives. **3** *Obs.* A lockup. **4** A round trip in pinochle.
round·ing (roun′ding) *adj.* **1** Pertaining to or denoting something, as a tool, used in or for rounding. **2** Becoming round; also, somewhat round.
round·ish (roun′dish) *adj.* Somewhat round. — **round′ish·ness** *n.*
round·let (round′lit) *n.* A little circle. [< F *rondelet*]
round·ly (round′lē) *adv.* **1** In a round manner or form; circularly; spherically. **2** Severely; vigorously: to be *roundly* denounced. **3** Frankly; bluntly. **4** Thoroughly; completely.
round–nose (round′nōz′) *adj.* Designating a kind of pliers whose gripping surfaces meet in a round, tapering point. See illustration under PLIERS.
round ringing A method of change–ringing a set of chimes in sequence from the bell of the highest note to that of the lowest, and then repeating this sequence while the earlier overtones are still vibrating, thus producing an effect like a round.
round robin 1 A number of signatures, as to a petition, written in a circle so as to avoid giving prominence to any single name; also, a paper so signed. **2** The cigar fish. **3** A tournament, as in tennis or chess, in which each player meets every other player.
rounds (roundz) *n. pl.* The position of a set of chiming bells when struck in a descending scale from highest to lowest.
round–shoul·dered (round′shōl′dərd) *adj.* Having the back rounded or the shoulders stooping.
rounds·man (roundz′mən) *n. pl.* **·men** (-mən) A police officer having charge of a group of patrolmen.
round table Any meeting place for conference or discussion; also, any discussion group. — **round–ta·ble** (round′tā′bəl) *adj.*
Round Table The table of King Arthur, made exactly circular so as to avoid any question of precedence among his knights; also, collectively, King Arthur and the body of knights having places there.
round–the–clock (round′thə·klok′) *adj.* Through all twenty–four hours of the day.
round tower 1 Any cylindrical tower; especially, a slender, tapering tower of circular plan, with a conical cap. **2** In Ireland, a detached campanile built as a watchtower to guard church treasures, etc., against viking raids.
round trip 1 A trip to a place and back again; a return trip. **2** In pinochle, a meld of four kings and four queens: also called *roundhouse*. — **round′–trip′** *adj.*
round·up (round′up′) *n.* **1** The bringing together of cattle scattered over a range for inspection, branding, or selection for sale. **2** The cowboys, horses, etc., employed in this work. **3** *U.S. Colloq.* A bringing together of several persons: a *roundup* of pickpockets by the police.
round·worm (round′wûrm′) *n.* A nematode worm, especially one parasitic in the human intestines.
roup[1] (rōōp) *n.* An infectious respiratory and catarrhal disease affecting poultry. [Origin uncertain]
roup[2] (roup, rōōp) *Scot. n.* An auction. — *v.t.* To auction. [OE *hrōpan*]
roup·et (rōō′pit, rou′pit) *adj. Scot.* Roupy.
Rou·phi·a (rōō·fē′ə) The former name for the ALPHEUS RIVER.
roup·y (rōō′pē) *adj.* **1** Pertaining to, like, or affected with roup. **2** *Scot.* Hoarse.

rouse[1] (rouz) *v.* **roused, rous·ing** *v.t.* **1** To cause to awaken from slumber, repose, unconsciousness, etc. **2** To excite to vigorous thought or action; stir up. **3** To startle or drive (game) from cover. — *v.i.* **4** To awaken from sleep or unconsciousness. **5** To become active. **6** To start from cover: said of game. See synonyms under PIQUE, SPUR, STIR. — *n.* **1** The act of rousing; an awakening to or signal for action. **2** *Brit.* Reveille. [Origin unknown] — **rous′er** *n.*
rouse[2] (rouz) *n.* **1** *Archaic* A full draft of liquor; a bumper. **2** Noisy mirth; a drinking bout; carousal. [Aphetic form of CAROUSE]
rouse[3] (rouz) *v.t.* & *v.i.* **roused, rous·ing** *Naut.* To pull together and with vigor. [? < ROUSE[1]]
rouse·a·bout (rous′ə·bout) *n. Austral.* A handyman, especially one at a sheep or cattle station.
rouse·ment (rouz′mənt) *n.* A stirring up of interest or enthusiasm; especially, a widespread religious awakening or excitement.
rous·ing (rou′zing) *adj.* **1** Able to rouse or excite: a *rousing* speech. **2** Lively; active; vigorous: a *rousing* trade.
Rous·seau (rōō·sō′), **Henri**, 1844–1910, French painter: called "Le Douanier." — **Jean Jacques**, 1712–78, French philosopher and author. — **Pierre Étienne Théodore**, 1812–67, French painter.
Rous·sil·lon (rōō·sē·yôn′) A region and former province of southern France on the Spanish border; former capital, Perpignan.
roust (roust) *v.t.* & *v.i. Colloq.* To arouse and drive (a person or thing); stir up: usually with *out*. [Blend of ROUSE and ROUT]
roust·a·bout (rous′tə·bout′) *n.* **1** A laborer on river craft or on the waterfront; a deck hand. **2** One employed for casual work, especially, a transient laborer. **3** A man of all work on a cattle ranch or in a cow camp.
rout[1] (rout) *n.* **1** A disorderly and overwhelming defeat or flight. **2** A boisterous and disorderly assemblage; the rabble. **3** An entourage; a retinue. **4** *Law* A disturbance of the peace by three or more persons with riotous intent. **5** *Archaic* A large and festive evening social gathering. **6** *Archaic* Any assembly; a throng. See synonyms under REVEL. — *v.t.* To defeat disastrously; put to flight. See synonyms under CONQUER. [< OF *route* < L *rupta*, fem. of *ruptus*, pp. of *rumpere* break]
rout[2] (rout) *v.i.* **1** To root, as swine. **2** To search; rummage. — *v.t.* **3** To dig or turn up with the snout. **4** To disclose to view; turn up as if with the snout: with *out*. **5** To hollow, gouge, or scrape, as with a scoop. **6** To drive or force out. [Var. of ROOT[2]]
rout[3] (rout, rōōt) *v.i. Scot.* or *Obs.* To make a loud noise; snore. — *n. Obs.* **1** Snoring. **2** A roaring noise; uproar. [OE *hrūtan*]
route (rōōt, rout) *n.* **1** A course, road, or way taken in passing from one point to another by any person or moving object. **2** The specific course over which mail is sent; also, the territory covered by a newsboy. See synonyms under ROAD, WAY. — *v.t.* **rout·ed, rout·ing** To dispatch or send by a certain way, as passengers, goods, etc. [< OF < L *rupta (via)* broken (road), fem. of *ruptus*, pp. of *rumpere* break] — **rout′er** *n.*
route column Close marching order for troops.
route formation An open formation of military aircraft prior or subsequent to action.
route march A troop march with discipline reduced to permit singing, talking, etc. Also **route step.**
route of march In a military march order, the designation of the way to be taken and the location of headquarters for each evening.
rout·er (rou′tər) *n.* **1** One who scoops or routs. **2** A tool for routing. **3** A plane devised for working a molding around a circular sash. [< ROUT[2]]
routh (rōōth, routh) *Scot. adj.* Abundant. — *n.* Plenty; abundance. Also spelled *rowth*.
rou·tine (rōō·tēn′) *n.* **1** A detailed method of procedure, regularly followed; prescribed course of action: an official *routine*. **2** Habitual methods of action induced by circumstances. See synonyms under HABIT. — *adj.* Customary; habitual; everyday. [< F < *route* way, road]

---

add, āce, câre, pälm; end, ēven; it, īce; odd, ōpen, ôrder; tŏŏk, pōōl; up, bûrn; ə = a in *above*, e in *sicken*, i in *clarity*, o in *melon*, u in *focus*; yōō = u in *fuse*; oi, oil; ou, pout; ch, check; g, go; ng, ring; th, thin; ᵺ, this; zh, vision. Foreign sounds á, œ, ü, kh, ṅ; and ◆: see page xx. < from; + plus; ? possibly.

rou·tin·ism (rōō·tē′niz·əm) *n.* Adherence to routine or routine methods in general. **—rou·tin′ist** *n.*

roux (rōō) *n. French* Melted butter mixed with browned flour for thickening soups, gravies, etc.

rove[1] (rōv) *v.* **roved, rov·ing** *v.i.* To wander from place to place; go or move without any definite destination. *—v.t.* To roam over, through, or about. See synonyms under RAMBLE, WANDER. *—n.* The act of roving or roaming; a ramble. [< Du. *rooven* rob]

rove[2] (rōv) *v.t.* **roved, rov·ing 1** To join and elongate, as a number of slivers from a carding machine, by passing between one or more pairs of rollers. **2** To pass through an eye. **3** To draw into thread; ravel out. **4** To reduce the diameter of with a hooked, flat tool: to *rove* a grindstone. *—n.* **1** A slightly twisted wool, cotton, flax, jute, or silk sliver. **2** A metal ring or washer for use in clinching a nail in boatbuilding. [Origin uncertain]

rove[3] (rōv) Past participle of REEVE[1].

rove beetle Any of a family *(Staphylinidae)* of beetles having elongated bodies with very short elytra: most species are scavengers. For illustration see INSECTS (beneficial).

rov·er[1] (rō′vər) *n.* **1** One who roves; a wanderer. **2** A pirate, or pirate vessel. **3** A croquet ball that has been sent through all the arches and has only to strike the final stake to go out. [< MDu., a robber. Akin to ROBBER.]

rov·er[2] (rō′vər) *n.* In archery, any object, usually distant, chosen as a mark. Also **roving mark.** [Origin unknown]

Ro·vu·ma (rō·vōō′mə) The Portuguese name for the RUVUMA.

row[1] (rō) *n.* An arrangement or series of persons or things in a continued line; a rank; file; specifically, a line of houses on a street, or the street: Park *Row*; also, a line of plants, trees, etc., in a field or garden. **—a long row to hoe** A hard task or undertaking. **—at the end of one's row** Exhausted; also, having used up one's resources. *—v.t.* To arrange in a row: with *up.* ◆ Homophone: *roe.* [OE *rāw, rǣw* line]

row[2] (rō) *v.i.* **1** To use oars, sweeps, etc., in propelling a boat. *—v.t.* **2** To propel across the surface of the water with oars, as a boat. **3** To transport by rowing. **4** To be propelled by (a specific number of oars): said of boats. **5** To make use of (oars or rowers), especially in a race. **6** To row against in a race. *—n.* A trip in a rowboat; also, a turn at the oars, or the distance covered. ◆ Homophone: *roe.* [OE *rōwan*]

row[3] (rou) *n.* A noisy disturbance or quarrel; dispute; brawl; hence, any disturbance. *—v.t. & v.i.* To engage in a row or brawl. [Prob. back formation < ROUSE[2] (taken as a pl.)]

row[4] (rō) *Scot. n.* A roll, as of wool. *—v.t. & v.i.* To roll.

row·an (rō′ən, rou′-) *n.* **1** The European mountain ash *(Sorbus aucuparia).* **2** The related American mountain ash *(S. americana).* **3** The fruit of these trees. [< Scand. Cf. Norw. *raun, roun,* ON *reynir.*]

row·an·ber·ry (rō′ən·ber′ē) *n. pl.* **·ries** The fruit of the rowan.

row·boat (rō′bōt′) *n.* A boat propelled by oars.

row·dy (rou′dē) *n. pl.* **·dies** One inclined to create disturbances or engage in rows; a rough, quarrelsome person. *—adj.* **·di·er, ·di·est** Rough and loud; disorderly. [Origin uncertain] **—row′dy·ish** *adj.* **—row′dy·ism, row′di·ness** *n.*

Rowe (rō), **Nicholas,** 1674–1718, English poet and dramatist; poet laureate 1715.

row·el (rou′əl) *n.* **1** A spiked or toothed wheel, as on a spur. **2** The spur so furnished. **3** A hair or silk thread passed through a horse's skin, to facilitate the discharge of pus. *—v.t.* **·eled** or **·elled, ·el·ing** or **·el·ling 1** To prick with a rowel; spur. **2** To attach or apply a rowel to. [< OF *roele* < LL *rotella* little wheel < L *rota* wheel]

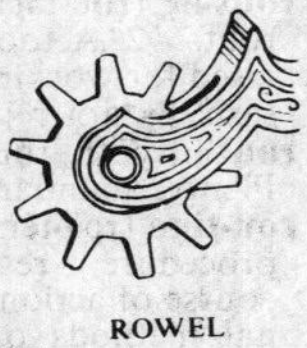

ROWEL ON SPUR

row·en (rou′ən) *n.* A second growth of grass or hay; aftermath. [< OF *regain*]

Row·lands (rō′ləndz), **John** See STANLEY, HENRY.

Row·land·son (rō′lənd·sən), **Thomas,** 1756–1827, English artist and caricaturist.

row·lock (rō′lok′) *n. Brit.* A device in which an oar plays and which serves as a point for applying its power to a boat: also called *oarlock.* [Alter. of OARLOCK: infl. by *row*[2]]

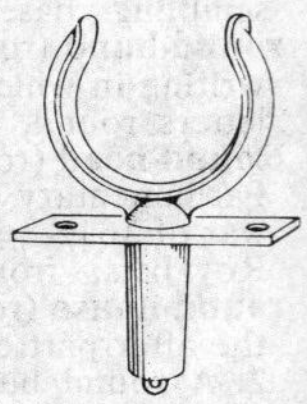

ROWLOCK

rowth (rōōth, routh) See ROUTH.

Rox·an·a (rok·san′ə) A feminine personal name. Also **Rox·y** (rok′sē), *Fr.* **Rox·ane** (rôk·sàn′). [< Persian, dawn of day]

—Roxane In Rostand's *Cyrano de Bergerac,* the heroine.

Ro·xas y A·cu·ña (rō′häs ē ä·kōō′nyä), **Manuel,** 1892–1948, Philippine statesman; president of the Philippines 1946–48.

Rox·burgh·shire (roks′bûr·ə·shir′) An inland county in southern Scotland; 666 square miles; capital, Jedburgh. Also **Rox′burgh** (-bûr·ə).

roy·al (roi′əl) *adj.* **1** Pertaining to a monarch; kingly. **2** Under the patronage or authority of a king, or connected with a monarchical form of government: the *Royal* Society; a *royal* governor. **3** Like a king; princely; regal. **4** Of superior quality or size: *royal* octavo. **5** Surpassingly pleasant or fine: We had a *royal* time. See synonyms under IMPERIAL, KINGLY. *—n.* **1** A size of paper, 19 × 24 for writing, 20 × 25 for printing. **2** *Naut.* A sail next above the topgallant, used in a light breeze. [< F < L *regalis* kingly < *rex* king. Doublet of REGAL.] **—roy′al·ly** *adv.*

Royal Academy A society established in 1768 by George III of England for the advancement of painting, sculpture, and design: in full, *Royal Academy of Arts.*

Royal Air Force The air force of Great Britain.

Royal Australian Air Force The air force of Australia.

Royal Australian Navy The navy of Australia.

royal blue 1 Originally, the color of smalt, or cobalt blue; also, Prussian blue. **2** A more modern, brilliant blue; a reddish blue.

Royal Canadian Air Force The air force of Canada.

royal fern An attractive, deep-rooted fern *(Osmunda regalis)* of Asia, Africa, and America, having branched stems with oval or elliptical leaflets.

royal flush See under FLUSH.

Royal Gorge A canyon of the Arkansas River in south central Colorado, extending 10 miles; over 1,000 feet deep.

roy·al·ism (roi′əl·iz′əm) *n.* Adherence to the principles or cause of royalty.

roy·al·ist (roi′əl·ist) *n.* A supporter of a royal dynasty. *—adj.* Supporting a royal house; pertaining to royalists: also **roy′al·is′tic.**

Roy·al·ist (roi′əl·ist) *n.* **1** In English history, a Cavalier or adherent of King Charles I, as against the Parliament, in the middle of the 17th century. **2** In French history, a supporter of the Bourbon or Orléans claims to the throne since 1793. **3** In the American Revolution, a supporter of the king; Loyalist; Tory.

roy·al·mast (roi′əl·mast′, -mäst′) *n. Naut.* The section of a mast next above the topgallant mast.

Royal Navy The naval forces of Great Britain.

royal purple 1 A very deep violet color verging toward blue. **2** Originally, a rich crimson.

Royal Society A society founded about 1660 in London and chartered in 1662, concerned with the advancement of science.

royal tine The tine of an antler projecting away from or above the bez tine: also called *trez tine.* For illustration see ANTLER.

royal touch The touch of a reigning monarch once believed to cure scrofula (king's evil).

roy·al·ty (roi′əl·tē) *n. pl.* **·ties 1** Royal rank, birth, or lineage; kingly nature or quality; kingliness; regal authority; sovereignty. **2** A royal personage; royal persons collectively. **3** A share of proceeds paid to a proprietor, author, or inventor, by those doing business under some right belonging to him. **4** A tax or seigniorage paid to the crown on the produce of royal mines, or on gold and silver coinage. **5** A royal possession or domain; hence, domain or province in general. [< OF *roialté*]

Royce (rois), **Josiah,** 1855–1916, U.S. philosopher and psychologist.

Ro·za·mond (rō′zə·mont) Dutch form of ROSAMOND.

-rrhagia *combining form Pathol.* A morbid or violent discharge or flow; an eruption: *metrorrhagia:* also spelled *-rhagia.* Also **-rrhage, rrhagy.** Corresponding adjectives are formed in **-rrhagic.** [< Gk. < *rrhag-,* root of *rhēgnynai* burst]

-rrhaphy *combining form* A sewing together; a suture: *neurorrhaphy,* the suturing of a nerve. Also spelled *-rhaphy.* [< Gk. *rrhaphē* a seam]

-rrhea *combining form Pathol.* An abnormal or excessive flow or discharge: *diarrhea*: also spelled *-rhea, -rhoea.* Also **-rrhoea.** [< Gk. *-rrhoia* < *rheein* flow]

Ru *Chem.* Ruthenium (symbol Ru).

Ru·an·da-U·run·di (rōō·än′dä·ōō·rōōn′dē) A former United Nations Trust Territory in central Africa, administered by Belgium, and once part of German East Africa. See BURUNDI, RWANDA.

rub (rub) *v.* **rubbed, rub·bing** *v.t.* **1** To move or pass over the surface of with pressure and friction. **2** To cause (something) to move or pass with friction; scrape; grate. **3** To cause to become frayed, worn, or sore from friction: This collar *rubs* my neck. **4** To clean, shine, burnish, etc., by means of pressure and friction, or by means of a substance applied thus. **5** To apply or spread with pressure and friction: to *rub* polish on a table. **6** To force by rubbing: with *in* or *into*: to *rub* oil into wood. **7** To remove or erase by friction: with *off* or *out.* *—v.i.* **8** To move along a surface with friction; scrape. **9** To exert pressure and friction. **10** To become frayed, worn, or sore from friction; chafe. **11** To undergo rubbing or removal by rubbing: with *off, out,* etc. **—to rub it in** *Slang* To harp on someone's errors, faults, etc. **—to rub out** *Slang* To kill. **—to rub the wrong way** *Slang* To irritate; annoy. See synonyms under WEAR. Compare FRICTION. *—n.* **1** A subjection to frictional pressure; rubbing: Give it a *rub.* **2** That which renders progress difficult; a hindrance or a doubt: There's the *rub.* **3** Something that rubs or is rough to the feelings; a sarcasm: a *rub* in debate. **4** A roughness or unevenness of surface, quality, or character. [ME *rubben,* prob. < LG. Cf. G *reiben.*]

rub-a-dub (rub′ə·dub′) *n.* The sound of a drum when beaten; hence, any clatter. [Imit.]

ru·bái·yát (rōō′bī·yät, -bē-) *n. pl.* **1** In Persian poetry, four-lined stanzas; quatrains. **2** Hence, **Rubáiyát,** a poem by Omar Khayyám and an English translation of it by Edward FitzGerald. [< Arabic *rubā'īyāt,* pl. of *rubā'īyah* quatrain, fem. of *rubā'ī* fourfold < *rubā* four]

Rub al Kha·li (rōōb′ äl khä′lē) The desert region of southern Arabia; 250,000 square miles; English *Empty Quarter*: also *Ar Rimal.*

ru·basse (rōō·bas′, -bäs′) *n.* A crystalline variety of quartz stained a ruby red by spangles of hematite. Also **ru·bace′.** [< F *rubace* < *rubi.* See RUBY.]

ru·ba·to (rōō·bä′tō) *adj. Music* Literally, robbed; noting the lengthening of one note at the expense of another. *—n. pl.* **·tos** A rubato modification. [< Ital.]

rub·ber[1] (rub′ər) *n.* **1** A tenacious, elastic material obtained by coagulating the milky latex of certain tropical plants, especially the tree *Hevea brasiliensis.* When purified, the crude rubber or caoutchouc is a white polymerized isoprene; it is insoluble in water or alcohol, and for commercial use is mixed with various vulcanizing agents, fillers, and pigments, then heated and molded into the desired form. **2** Anything used for rubbing, erasing, polishing, etc. **3** One who or that which rubs. **4** An article made of rubber, as an elastic band or an overshoe. *—adj.* Made of rubber. [< RUB] **—rub′ber·y** *adj.*

rub·ber[2] (rub′ər) *n.* In bridge, whist, and other card games, a series of two or three games played by the same partners against the same adversaries, terminated when one side has won two games; also, the odd game which breaks a tie between the players.

rub·ber·ize (rub′ər·īz) *v.t.* **·ized, ·iz·ing** To coat, impregnate, or cover, as silk, with a preparation of rubber.

rub·ber·neck (rub′ər·nek′) *n. U.S. Slang* One who cranes his neck in order to see something;

a sightseer; tourist. —*v.i.* To stretch or crane one's neck; gape.

rubber plant 1 Any of several plants yielding rubber. **2** An East Indian tree of the mulberry family (*Ficus elastica*) having large, glossy, leathery leaves: much cultivated as an ornamental house plant.

rub·ber-stamp (rub′ər·stamp′) *v.t.* **1** To endorse, initial, or approve with the mark made by a rubber stamping device. **2** *Colloq.* To pass or approve as a matter of course or routine.

rub·bish (rub′ish) *n.* Waste refuse, or broken matter; trash. [Origin unknown]

rub·bish·y (rub′ish·ē) *adj.* Worthless; without value.

rub·ble (rub′əl) *n.* **1** Rough, irregular pieces of broken stone. **2** The debris to which buildings of brick, stone, etc., have been reduced by a violent action, such as earthquake or bombing. **3** (*also* rōō′bəl) **a** In quarrying, the weathered or friable surface layer of rock. **b** Rough pieces of stone for use in construction, especially in residences. **4** Water-worn stones. **5** Rubblework. [Origin uncertain. Prob. related to RUBBISH.]

rub·ble·work (rub′əl·wûrk′) *n.* Masonry composed of irregular or broken stone, or fragments of stone mingled with cement or clay.

rub-down (rub′doun′) *n.* A massage.

rube (rōōb) *n. Slang* A countryman; farmer; rustic. [Abbreviation of REUBEN]

ru·be·fa·cient (rōō′bə·fā′shənt) *adj.* Causing redness, as of the skin. —*n.* A medicament for producing irritation of the skin. [< L *rubefaciens, -entis* < *rubefacere* redden < *rubeus* red + *facere* make] —**ru′be·fa′cience** *n.* —**ru′be·fac′tion** (-fak′shən) *n.*

ru·bel·la (rōō·bel′ə) *n. Pathol.* A contagious eruptive fever intermediate between scarlatina and measles: also called *German measles.* [< NL, neut. pl. of L *rubellus* reddish, dim. of *ruber* red]

ru·bel·lite (rōō′bə·līt) *n.* A red, usually transparent, tourmaline: used as a gem. [< L *rubellus.* See RUBELLA.]

Ru·bens (rōō′bənz, *Flemish* rü′bəns), **Peter Paul,** 1577–1646, Flemish painter.

ru·be·o·la (rōō′bē·ə·lə) *n. Pathol.* **1** Measles. **2** Rubella. [< NL, neut. pl. dim. of L *rubeus* red] —**ru·be′o·lar** *adj.*

Ru·ber·to (rōō·ber′tō) Italian and Spanish form of RUPERT.

ru·bes·cent (rōō·bes′ənt) *adj.* Becoming red; reddening. [< L *rubescens, -entis,* ppr. of *rubescere* grow red, inceptive of *rubere* < *rubeus* red] —**ru·bes′cence** *n.*

ru·bi·a·ceous (rōō′bē·ā′shəs) *adj. Bot.* Belonging or pertaining to a large, chiefly tropical family (*Rubiaceae*) of trees, shrubs, and herbs, the madder family of the order *Rubiales,* with simple opposite or whorled leaves and perfect, often dimorphous, flowers, including plants yielding coffee, quinine, and ipecac. [< L *rubia* madder]

Ru·bi·con (rōō′bi·kon) A river in north central Italy, flowing 15 miles NE to the Adriatic: modern *Fiumicino;* it formed the boundary separating Caesar's province of Gaul from Italy, and by crossing it under arms he committed himself to a civil war with the Roman government then controlled by Pompey; hence, **to cross the Rubicon,** to be committed definitely to some course of action; make an irrevocable move.

ru·bi·cund (rōō′bə·kənd) *adj.* Red, or inclined to redness; rosy. [< L *rubicundus* red] —**ru′bi·cun′di·ty** *n.*

ru·bid·i·um (rōō·bid′ē·əm) *n.* A silvery-white, very reactive alkali metal (symbol Rb, atomic number 37), abundant but difficult to prepare in pure form, and having two naturally occurring isotopes, one of which is radioactive with a very long half-life. [< NL < L *rubidus* red]

ru·big·i·nous (rōō·bij′ə·nəs) *adj.* Having a rusty or brownish-red color: *rubiginous* plants. Also **ru·big′i·nose** (-nōs). [< LL *rubiginosus* < L *rubigo, rubiginis* rust]

ru·bi·go (rōō·bī′gō, -bē′-) *n.* Red iron oxide, used as a polishing powder and pigment. [< L, rust]

Ru·bin·stein (rōō′bin·stīn), **Anton Gregor,** 1829–94, Russian pianist and composer.

—**Artur,** 1886–1982, U.S. pianist born in Poland.

ru·bi·ous (rōō′bē·əs) *adj.* Red; ruby-colored. [< RUBY]

ru·ble (rōō′bəl) *n.* The Russian monetary unit containing 100 kopecks, and equivalent to one tenth of a chervonets: also spelled *rouble.* [< Russian *rubl′*]

ru·bric (rōō′brik) *n.* **1** That exceptional part of an early manuscript or a book that appears in red, or in some distinctive type: once used to indicate initial letters, caption words, headings, etc. **2** The heading or title of a statute or of a section in a code of law, formerly written in red. **3** *Eccl.* A direction or rule printed in devotional or liturgical office, as in a prayer book, missal, or breviary; also, such rules collectively. **4** A division, group, or category. **5** The color red. **6** *Obs.* Red ochre or chalk; reddle. **7** Any direction or rule of conduct. **8** A distinguishing flourish or mark after a person's signature. —*adj.* **1** Red or reddish. **2** Written or printed in red. —*v.t.* **·bricked, ·brick·ing** *Rare* To rubricate. [< OF *rubrique* < L *rubrica* red earth < *ruber* red] —**ru′bri·cal** *adj.* —**ru′bri·cal·ly** *adv.*

ru·bri·cate (rōō′brə·kāt) *v.t.* **·cat·ed, ·cat·ing 1** To mark or tint with red; illuminate with red, as a book. **2** To furnish with a rubric or rubrics; arrange in permanent form. —*adj.* Marked, written, or printed in red. [< L *rubricatus,* pp. of *rubricare* redden < *rubrica.* See RUBRIC.] —**ru′bri·ca′tion** *n.* —**ru′bri·ca′tor** *n.*

ru·bri·cian (rōō·brish′ən) *n.* One versed in the knowledge of, or punctiliously adhering to, rubric or rubrics.

ru·by (rōō′bē) *n. pl.* **·bies 1** A red variety of corundum including specimens of great value as gemstones. **2** An ornament or a watchmaker's jewel fashioned of ruby. **3** A rich red color like that of a ruby. **4** Something like a ruby in color, as red wine or a carbuncle. **5** In England, a size of type (5½ points): equivalent to the American *agate.* —*adj.* Pertaining to or like a ruby; being of a rich crimson: *ruby* lips. —*v.t.* **·bied, ·by·ing** To redden; tint with the color of a ruby. [< OF *rubi* < L *rubeus* red]

ru·by-crowned kinglet (rōō′bē·kround′) See under KINGLET.

ru·by-throat (rōō′bē·thrōt′) *n.* The hummingbird (*Archilochus colubris*) of eastern North America, having in the male a gorget of brilliant metallic red. Also **ruby-throated hummingbird**

ru·cer·vine (rōō·sûr′vēn, -vin) *adj.* **1** Of or pertaining to a genus (*Rucervus*) of large deer native in southeastern Asia. **2** Denoting the antlers characteristic of this genus. For illustration see ANTLER. [< NL *Rucervus,* name of the genus < Malay *rusa* deer + L *cervinus* < *cervus* deer]

ruche (rōōsh) *n.* A quilted or ruffled strip of fine fabric, worn about the neck or wrists of a woman's costume: also spelled *rouche.* [< F, beehive < Med. L *rusca* tree bark, ? < Celtic]

ruch·ing (rōō′shing) *n.* Material for ruches; ruches collectively.

ruck[1] (ruk) *n.* The common herd or run; a crowd; also, trash; rubbish. [< Scand. Cf. Norw. *ruka* heap, crowd.]

ruck[2] (ruk) *v.t. & v.i.* **1** To wrinkle, rumple, crease, etc. **2** To annoy; ruffle: usually with *up.* —*n.* A wrinkle, crease, or ridge, as in cloth or paper; a wrinkled place. [< ON *hrukka* wrinkle]

ruck·sack (ruk′sak′, rŏŏk′-) *n.* A canvas knapsack. [< G, lit., back sack]

ruck·us (ruk′əs) *n. U.S. Slang* An uproar; commotion; rumpus. [Prob. blend of RUMPUS and RUCTION]

ruc·tion (ruk′shən) *n. Colloq.* A riotous outbreak; quarrel; uproar. [Prob. alter. of INSURRECTION]

ruc·tious (ruk′shəs) *adj. Slang* Difficult; quarrelsome. [< RUCTION]

rud·beck·i·a (rud·bek′ē·ə) *n.* Any of a genus (*Rudbeckia*) of North American herbs of the composite family, the coneflowers, with alternate simple or compound leaves and showy yellow heads; especially, the black-eyed Susan. [after Olaus *Rudbeck,* 1630–1702, Swedish botanist]

rudd (rud) *n.* A European fresh-water fish (*Scardinius erythrophthalmus*), olive-brown with red fins: also called *red eye.* [OE *rudu* red color]

rud·der (rud′ər) *n.* **1** *Naut.* A broad, flat device hinged vertically at the stern of a vessel to direct its course. **2** Anything that guides or directs a course. **3** *Aeron.* A hinged or pivoted surface, used to control the position of an aircraft about its vertical axis. [OE *rōthor* oar, scull] —**rud′der·less** *adj.*

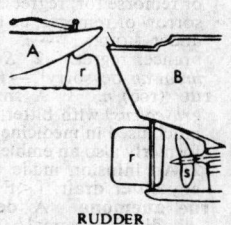

RUDDER
A. Sailboat   *B.* Motorboat.
r. Rudder
s. Screw.

rudder bar *Aeron.* A foot-operated rod by which the pilot controls the rudder of an airplane.

rudder fish Any of various fishes that follow vessels, as the pilot fish, etc.

rudder stock The vertical shaft to which the rudder of a ship or boat is attached, having at its upper portion a yoke (the **rudder cross-head**) or tiller by which it may be turned. Also **rudder post.**

rud·dle (rud′l) *n.* A variety of red ocherous iron ore; reddle. —*v.t.* **·dled, ·dling** To color or stain with red ocher. Also spelled *raddle.* [OE *rudu* red color]

rud·dle·man (rud′l·mən) *n. pl.* **·men** (-mən) A reddleman.

rud·dock (rud′ək) *n.* The European robin. [OE *rudduc* robin < *rudu* red color]

rud·dy (rud′ē) *adj.* **·di·er, ·di·est 1** Tinged with red. **2** Having a healthy glow; rosy: a *ruddy* complexion. See synonyms under FRESH. [OE *rudig*] —**rud′di·ly** *adv.* —**rud′di·ness** *n.*

ruddy duck A small North American duck (*Erismatura jamaicensis rubida*) having the tail feathers stiffened with narrow webs. The adult male is bright chestnut-reddish above. Also called *paddywhack.*

rude (rōōd) *adj.* **rud·er, rud·est 1** Rough or abrupt; severe or tempestuous; offensively blunt or uncivil; impudent. **2** Characterized by lack of polish or refinement; uncultivated; uncouth. **3** Unskilfully made or done; lacking in skill or training; crude; rough: *rude* workmanship. **4** Characterized by robust vigor; strong: *rude* health. **5** Barbarous; savage. **6** Humble; lowly; rustic. See synonyms under BARBAROUS, BLUFF, IMPUDENT, ROUGH, RUSTIC, VULGAR. ◆ Homophone: *rood.* [< OF < L *rudis* rough] —**rude′ly** *adv.*

rude·ness (rōōd′nis) *n.* **1** The state or quality of being rude. **2** A rude action. See synonyms under IMPUDENCE.

rudes·by (rōōdz′bē) *n. Archaic* An ill-bred boor.

Rü·di·ger (rü′di·ger) German form of ROGER.

ru·di·ment (rōō′də·mənt) *n.* **1** A first principle, step, stage, or condition. **2** That which is as yet undeveloped or only partially developed. **3** *Biol.* **a** Something in a first, embryonic, incomplete, or early stage that may develop by growth; a germ. **b** A part, organ, or other structure that has become aborted or stunted and will always be undeveloped; a vestige; vestigial part. [< F < L *rudimentum* first attempt < *rudis* rough]

ru·di·men·ta·ry (rōō′də·men′tər·ē) *adj.* **1** Pertaining to or of the nature of a rudiment: *rudimentary* knowledge. **2** Being or remaining in an imperfectly developed state; germinal; undeveloped; abortive. Also **ru′di·men′tal.** —**ru′di·men′ta·ri·ly** *adv.* —**ru′di·men′ta·ri·ness** *n.*

Ru·dolf (rōō′dolf; *Du.* rü′dolf, *Ger.* rōō′dŏlf, *Sw.* rōō′dôlf) A masculine personal name. Also **Ru′dolph.** [< Gmc., wolf of fame]

—**Rudolf I,** 1218–91, Holy Roman Emperor 1273–91; founded the Hapsburg dynasty.

—**Rudolf II,** 1552–1612, Holy Roman Emperor 1576–1612; persecuted Protestants.

—**Rudolf of Hapsburg,** 1858–89, crown prince of Austria; son of Francis Joseph; committed suicide.

Rudolf, Lake A lake in NW Kenya, extending into Ethiopia on the northwest; 3,500 square miles.

rue[1] (rōō) *v.* **rued, ru·ing** *v.t.* To feel sorrow or remorse for; regret extremely. — *v.i.* To feel sorrow or remorse; be regretful. See synonyms under MOURN. — *n.* 1 Sorrowful remembrance; regret. 2 *Scot.* Repentance. [OE *hrēowan* be sorry] — **ru'er** *n.*

rue[2] (rōō) *n.* 1 A small, bushy herb *(Ruta graveolens)* with bitter, acrid leaves, formerly much used in medicine for stimulating effects: formerly also an emblem of bitterness or grief. 2 An infusion made from this plant; hence, any bitter draft. [<F <L *ruta* <Gk. *rhytē*]

rue anemone A delicate little American woodland perennial *(Anemonella thalictroides)*, having white flowers in the spring.

Rue de la Paix (rü də lȧ pe') A street in Paris, France, famous for its fashionable shops.

rue·ful (rōō'fəl) *adj.* 1 Feeling or causing sorrow, regret, or pity; deplorable; sorrowful. 2 Expressing sorrow or pity. — **rue'ful·ly** *adv.* — **rue'ful·ness** *n.*

ru·fes·cent (rōō·fes'ənt) *adj.* Inclining to reddishness; somewhat reddish or rufous. [<L *rufescens, -entis,* ppr. of *rufescere* redden < *rufus* red] — **ru·fes'cence** *n.*

ruff[1] (ruf) *n.* 1 A pleated, round, heavily starched collar popular in the 16th century. 2 Ruffle[1] (def. 1). 3 A natural collar of projecting feathers or hair around the neck of a bird or mammal. 4 An Old World sandpiper *(Philomachus pugnax)* of which the male in the breeding season has an erectile frill of elongated feathers about the neck. The female is called a *reeve.* — *v.i.* To become ruffled; stand out like a ruff. ◆ Homophone: *rough.* [Short for RUFFLE[1]]

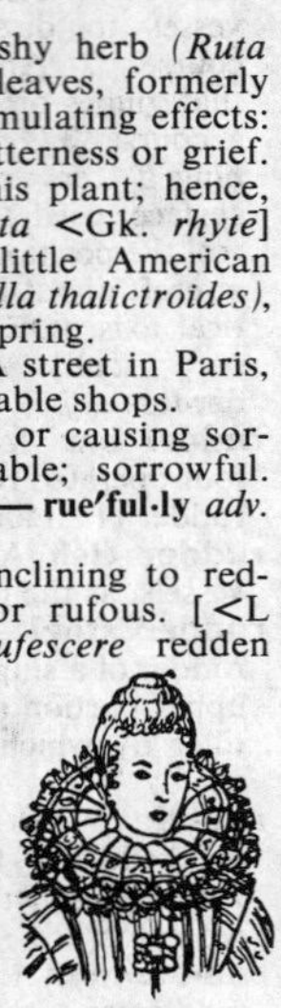

RUFF
17th century.

ruff[2] (ruf) *n.* 1 The playing of a trump upon another suit when one has no cards of that suit. 2 An old game, the predecessor of whist. — *v.t.* & *v.i.* To trump when unable to follow suit. ◆ Homophone: *rough.* [<OF *roffle, rouffle, ronfle,* aphetic alter. of *triomphe* triumph. Cf. Ital. *ronfa* a game at cards < *trionfo* triumph. Related to TRUMP[1].]

ruff[3] (ruf) *n.* A small perchlike fish *(Acerina cernua)* of European fresh waters. Also **ruffe.** ◆ Homophone: *rough.* [<ROUGH]

ruff[4] (ruf) See RUFFLE[3].

ruffed (ruft) *adj.* Having a ruff, ruffle, or frill; ruffled.

ruffed grouse A North American grouse *(Bonasa umbellus)*: called *partridge* in the northern and *pheasant* in the southern United States.

ruf·fi·an (ruf'ē·ən, ruf'yən) *n.* A lawless, brutal, cruel fellow; a rough; one ready for or given to riotous, cruel, or murderous deeds. — *adj.* Lawlessly or recklessly brutal or cruel. [<F *rufian* <Ital. *ruffiano* pimp, ? <OHG *ruf* dirty] — **ruf'fi·an·ism** *n.* — **ruf'·fi·an·ly** *adj.*

ruf·fle[1] (ruf'əl) *n.* 1 A pleated strip; frill, as for trim or ornament; also, anything resembling this: also *ruff.* 2 A temporary discomposure. 3 A ripple. — *v.* **·fled, ·fling** *v.t.* 1 To disturb or destroy the smoothness or regularity of: The wind *ruffles* the lake. 2 To draw into folds or ruffles; gather. 3 To furnish with ruffles. 4 To erect (the feathers) in a ruff, as a bird when frightened. 5 To disturb or irritate; upset. 6 a To riffle (the pages of a book). b To shuffle (cards). — *v.i.* 7 To be or become rumpled or disordered. 8 To become disturbed or irritated. [ME *ruffelen.* Cf. LG *ruffelen* rumple, ON *hrufla* scratch.]

ruf·fle[2] (ruf'əl) *n.* A low, continuous beat of a drum, not as loud as a roll: also *ruff.* — *v.t.* **·fled, ·fling** To beat a ruffle upon, as a drum. [< earlier *ruff*; imit.]

ruf·fle[3] (ruf'əl) *v.t.* **·fled, ·fling** To act in a rough or turbulent manner; swagger; bluster. [? Special use of RUFFLE[2]] — **ruf'fler** *n.*

ru·fous (rōō'fəs) *adj.* Dull-red; rust-colored. [<L *rufus* red]

Ru·fus (rōō'fəs) A masculine personal name. [<L, red]

rug[1] (rug) *n.* 1 A heavy textile fabric, made in one piece, to cover a portion of a floor. 2 A covering made from the skins of animals dressed with the hair or wool on. 3 A heavy coverlet or lap robe. [<Scand. Cf. Norw. *rugga* coarse coverlet, *skinrugga* skin rug, ON *rögg* long, rough fleece.]

rug[2] (rug) *v.t.* **rugged, rug·ging** *Scot.* & *Brit. Dial.* To tug or tear roughly.

ru·ga (rōō'gə) *n. pl.* **·gae** (-jē) A fold, wrinkle, or crease. [<L]

ru·gate (rōō'gāt, -git) *adj.* Covered with or having rugae; corrugated; wrinkled. [<L *rugatus,* pp. of *rugare* wrinkle < *ruga* a wrinkle]

Rug·bei·an (rug·bē'ən) *adj.* Of or pertaining to Rugby, England, or to the school there located. — *n.* A native or inhabitant of Rugby; a pupil at Rugby school.

Rug·by (rug'bē) A municipal borough of eastern Warwickshire, England; seat of a boys' school founded in 1567.

Rugby football A form of football played between two teams of fifteen men each, in which the ball is propelled toward the opponents' goal by kicking or carrying, but in which no player of the side in possession of the ball may be ahead of the ball while it is in play.

Rü·gen (rü'gən) The largest German island in the Baltic, NE of Stralsund; 358 square miles.

rug·ged (rug'id) *adj.* 1 Having a surface full of abrupt inequalities; broken into irregular points or crags; steep and rocky; rough; uneven. 2 Shaggy; unkempt; disordered; ragged. 3 Rough in temper, character, or action; harsh; stern. 4 Having strongly marked features; wrinkled; frowning; furrowed. 5 Lacking culture or refinement; rude. 6 Rough to the ear; grating . 7 Robust; sturdy. 8 Tempestuous; stormy. See synonyms under FIRM, ROUGH. [<Scand. Cf. Sw. *rugga* roughen. Prob. related to RUG[1].] — **rug'ged·ly** *adv.* — **rug'ged·ness** *n.*

Rug·gie·ro (rōōd·jā'rō) Italian form of ROGER.

ru·gose (rōō'gōs) *adj.* 1 Covered with or full of rugae or wrinkles; corrugate; rugate. 2 *Bot.* Having a rough or wrinkled surface, as some strongly veined leaves. Also **ru'gous.** [<L *rugosus* < *ruga* wrinkle] — **ru·gos·i·ty** (rōō·gos'ə·tē) *n.*

Ruhr (rōōr) 1 A river of western Germany, flowing 142 miles west to the Rhine. 2 The region south of which the Ruhr river flows, noted as an industrial and coal-mining district; about 2000 square miles; included in North Rhine-Westphalia, West Germany.

ru·in (rōō'in) *n.* 1 Total destruction of value or usefulness; in morals, the loss of character, chastity, or honor; seduction; corruption. 2 That which remains of something demolished, destroyed, or decayed: often in the plural. 3 A condition of desolation or degradation. 4 That which causes destruction, downfall, decay, or injury: Gambling was his *ruin.* 5 The act of falling down; collapse. — *v.t.* 1 To bring to ruin; destroy; demolish. 2 To bring to bankruptcy or poverty. 3 To deprive of chastity; seduce. — *v.i.* 4 To fall into ruin. See synonyms under ABUSE, DEMOLISH. [<OF *ruine* <L *ruina* < *ruere* fall] — **ru'in·a·ble** *adj.* — **ru'in·er** *n.*

Synonyms (noun): collapse, decay, defeat, desolation, destruction, discomfiture, downfall, fall, overthrow, perdition, subversion, undoing, wreck. See ADVERSITY, MISFORTUNE. *Antonyms*: conservation, preservation, prosperity, recovery, regeneration, reparation, success.

ru·in·ate (rōō'in·āt) *v.t.* **·at·ed, ·at·ing** *Rare* To ruin. — *adj.* Ruined. [<Med. L *ruinatus,* pp. of *ruinare* ruin < *ruina*]

ru·in·a·tion (rōō'in·ā'shən) *n.* 1 The act of ruining. 2 The state of being ruined. 3 Something that ruins.

ru·ined (rōō'ind) *adj.* 1 Destroyed; ravaged; in ruins. 2 Bankrupt.

ru·in·ous (rōō'in·əs) *adj.* 1 Causing or tending to ruin. 2 Falling to ruin; decayed; dilapidated; ruined. See synonyms under PERNICIOUS. [<OF *ruineux* <L *ruinosus*] — **ru'in·ous·ly** *adv.* — **ru'in·ous·ness** *n.*

Ruis·dael (rois'däl, *Du.* rœis'däl) See RUYSDAEL.

Ru·iz (rōō·ēth', -ēs') A Spanish masculine personal name.

rule (rōōl) *n.* 1 Controlling power, or its possession and exercise; government; dominion; authority. 2 A method or principle of action; common or regular course of procedure, or customary standard or form: I make early rising my *rule.* 3 An authoritative direction or enactment; a concise direction respecting the doing or method of doing something, as one of the regulations of a legislative or deliberative body for the government of its own proceedings, or a regulation to be observed in playing a given game. 4 A regulation for the conduct of religious services or for the government of life; specifically, the body of directions laid down by or for a religious order: the *rule* of St. Francis. 5 A prescribed form, method, or set of instructions for solving a given class of mathematical problems. 6 An established usage or law, fixing the form or use of words or the construction of sentences: a *rule* for forming the plural. 7 What belongs to the ordinary course of events or condition of things: In some communities illiteracy is the *rule.* 8 Regular or proper method; propriety, as of conduct; regularity. 9 *Law* A formal regulation prescribed by authority touching a certain matter: a *rule* of court; also, a judicial decision on some motion or special application: a *rule* to show cause. A **rule of court** is an order made by a court, and is either *general,* as for regulating the practice of the court, or *special,* as an order sending a case before a referee. 10 A straight-edged instrument for use in measuring, or as a guide in drawing lines; a ruler, usually marked in inches, feet, etc. 11 *Printing* A strip of type-high metal for handling type or for printing a rule or line. 12 A ruled line. — **as a rule** Ordinarily; usually. — *v.* **ruled, rul·ing** *v.t.* 1 To have authority or control over; govern. 2 To influence greatly; dominate: Greed has *ruled* his life. 3 To decide or determine judicially or authoritatively. 4 To restrain; keep in check: *Rule* your temper. 5 To mark with straight, parallel lines. 6 To make (such a line) with or as with a ruler. — *v.i.* 7 To have authority or control; be in command. 8 To maintain a standard of rates: Prices *ruled* high. 9 To form and express a decision: The judge *ruled* on that point. — **to rule out** 1 To dismiss from consideration: They *ruled out* a strike. 2 To preclude; prevent. See synonyms under GOVERN, REGULATE. [<OF *reule* <L *regula* ruler, rule < *regere* lead straight, direct. Doublet of RAIL[1].] — **rul'a·ble** *adj.*

Synonyms (noun): canon, formula, guide, maxim, method, order, regulation, standard. See HABIT, LAW, STICK, SYSTEM.

ruled surface *Math.* A surface capable of being generated by a straight line, as a hyperboloid of one sheet.

rule of three *Math.* A rule for finding any term of a proportion, the three others being given.

rule of thumb 1 Measurement by the thumb. 2 Roughly practical rather than scientifically accurate measure.

rul·er (rōō'lər) *n.* 1 One who rules or governs, as a sovereign. 2 A straight-edged strip for guiding a marking implement; a rule; a ruling machine. 3 One who rules lines, as with a ruling machine. See synonyms under CHIEF.

rul·ing (rōō'ling) *adj.* Exercising dominion; controlling; predominant. — *n.* 1 The act of one who rules or governs. 2 A decision, as of a judge or presiding officer. 3 The act of making ruled lines, or the lines so made.

rum[1] (rum) *n.* 1 An alcoholic liquor distilled from fermented molasses or cane juice. 2 Any alcoholic liquor. [Short for obs. *rumbullion* rum, alter. of *Rambouillet,* town in France]

rum[2] (rum) *adj. Brit. Slang* Queer; strange; peculiar. [? <Romany *rom* man]

Rum (rōōm) The Arabic name for the BYZANTINE EMPIRE: also *Roum.*

Ru·ma·ni·a (rōō·mā'nē·ə, -mān'yə), **People's Republic of** A state in SE Europe; 91,671 square miles; capital, Bucharest: also *Romania, Roumania*: Rumanian *România.*

Ru·ma·ni·an (rōō·mā'nē·ən, -mān'yən) *adj.* Of Rumania, its people, or their language. — *n.* 1 A native or inhabitant of Rumania. 2 The Romance language of the Rumanians. Also *Romanian, Roumanian.*

rum·ba (rum'bə, *Sp.* rōōm'bä) *n.* 1 A frenzied dance formerly performed by Cuban Negroes. 2 A modern dance based on this. Also spelled *rhumba.* [<Sp.]

rum·ble (rum'bəl) *v.* **·bled, ·bling** *v.i.* 1 To make a low, heavy, rolling sound, as thunder.

2 To move or proceed with such a sound. —*v.t.* 3 To cause to make a low, heavy, rolling sound. 4 To utter with such a sound. 5 To subject to the action of a tumbling box. —*n.* 1 A continuous low, heavy, rolling sound; a muffled roar. 2 A tumbling box: also **rum′bler.** 3 A seat or baggage compartment in the rear of a carriage. 4 A folding seat in the back of a coupé or roadster: in full, **rumble seat.** 5 *U.S. Slang* A fight involving a group, usually deliberately provoked. [ME *romblen* <MDu. *rommelen*] —**rum′bler** *n.* —**rum′bling·ly** *adv.*

Ru·me·li·a (ro͞o·mē′lē·ə) The possessions of the former Ottoman Empire in the Balkan Peninsula, including Macedonia, Thrace, and Albania: also *Roumelia.*

ru·men (ro͞o′men) *n. pl.* **ru·mi·na** (ro͞o′mə·nə) 1 The first stomach of a ruminant. 2 The cud of a ruminant. [<L, throat]

Rum·ford (rum′fərd), **Count,** 1753–1814, Benjamin Thompson, physicist, born in America, active in Germany, England, and France.

ru·mi·nant (ro͞o′mə·nənt) *n.* One of a division (*Ruminantia*) of even-toed ungulates, as a deer, antelope, sheep, goat, or cow, that has a stomach with four complete cavities: the rumen, the reticulum, the manyplies (omasum, psalterium), and the reed or abomasum, the food entering the first being returned to the mouth, rechewed and swallowed, and digested in the other compartments. —*adj.* 1 Chewing the cud. 2 Of or pertaining to the *Ruminantia.* 3 Meditative or contemplative; thoughtful; drowsily quiet. [<L *ruminans, -antis,* ppr. of *ruminare* ruminate < *rumen* gullet]

ru·mi·nate (ro͞o′mə·nāt) *v.t.* & *v.i.* **·nat·ed, ·nat·ing** 1 To chew (food previously swallowed and regurgitated) over again; chew (the cud). 2 To meditate or reflect (upon); ponder. See synonyms under MUSE. —*adj.* Perforated or mottled, as the albumen of a betelnut or nutmeg: also **ru′mi·nat′ed.** [<L *ruminatus,* pp. of *ruminare.* See RUMINANT.] —**ru′mi·nat′ing·ly** *adv.* —**ru′mi·na′tive** *adj.* —**ru′mi·na′tive·ly** *adv.* —**ru′mi·na′tor** *n.*

ru·mi·na·tion (ro͞o′mə·nā′shən) *n.* 1 The act, process, or characteristic of chewing the cud. 2 The act of ruminating mentally. 3 The regurgitation of imperfectly digested food. See synonyms under REFLECTION.

Ruml (rum′əl, ro͝om′əl), **Beardsley,** 1894–1960, U.S. businessman and financier.

rum·mage (rum′ij) *v.* **·maged, ·mag·ing** *v.t.* 1 To search through (a place, box, etc.) by turning over and disarranging the contents; ransack. 2 To find or bring out by searching: with *out* or *up.* —*v.i.* 3 To make a thorough search. —*n.* 1 Any act of rummaging; especially, disarranging things by searching thoroughly. 2 An upheaval or stirring up; bustle. 3 *Obs.* Room in a ship for stowing cargo; also, the arrangement or stowing of the cargo. 4 A rummage sale. [< obs. F *arrumage* place or act of stowage < *arrumer* stow away, ? < *rum* ship's hold <OE *rūm* room] —**rum′mag·er** *n.*

rummage sale 1 A sale of all sorts of second-hand objects gathered up from benevolent givers, to obtain money for some charitable object. 2 A sale of unclaimed articles, or a clearing-out sale prior to restocking.

rum·mer (rum′ər) *n.* A glass or cup for drinking; specifically, a tall stemless glass; also, its contents. [<Du. *roemer* < *roemen* praise; from its use in drinking toasts]

rum·my[1] (rum′ē) *n.* A card game in which each player in turn draws a card from the talon or the discard pile beside it, and discards another card, the object being to get rid of one's hand in sequences of three cards or more of the same suit. [Origin unknown]

rum·my[2] (rum′ē) *n. pl.* **·mies** *Slang* A drunkard. —*adj.* 1 Of or pertaining to rum: a *rummy* flavor. 2 Affected by rum; befuddled; drunk.

ru·mor (ro͞o′mər) *n.* 1 Popular report; common gossip; also, reputation. 2 A story circulating without known foundation or authority; an unverified report passing from person to person. 3 *Obs.* A confused sound; confusion; murmur. —*v.t.* To tell or spread as a rumor; report abroad. Also *Brit.* **ru′mour.** [<OF <L, noise]

rump (rump) *n.* 1 The hinder parts or buttocks. 2 The fag-end of anything; an inferior remnant. 3 A legislative group having only a remnant of its former membership and therefore lacking authority because unrepresentative. 4 The piece of beef between aitchbone and loin. [<Scand. Cf. Dan. *rumpl,* ON *rumpr.*]

Rum·pel·stilts·kin (rum′pəl·stilt′skin, *Ger.* ro͝om′pəl·shtilts′kin) In German folklore, a dwarf who saves the life of a girl who has married a king, by spinning for her the fabulous quantity of flax her mother has boasted that she can spin. In return for this, the dwarf demands her first child. When it is born the distressed mother begs to be released from her promise. The dwarf consents if she can guess his name within three days. She does so at the crucial moment and Rumpelstiltskin's power is broken. Also **Rum·pel·stiltz·chen** (ro͝om′pəl·shtilts′khən).

rum·ple (rum′pəl) *v.t.* & *v.i.* **·pled, ·pling** To form into creases or folds; wrinkle; ruffle. —*n.* 1 An irregular fold; a rumpled fabric. 2 The condition of being rumpled. [<MDu. *rumpelen*]

Rump Parliament See LONG PARLIAMENT under PARLIAMENT.

rum·pus (rum′pəs) *n. Colloq.* A row; wrangle; to-do. [Origin uncertain]

rumpus room A room for games, informal gatherings, etc.

rum-run·ner (rum′run′ər) *n.* One who illicitly transports or smuggles alcoholic liquors across a border; also, a vessel employed in illegal liquor traffic.

run (run) *v.* **ran, run, run·ning** *v.i.* 1 To move by rapid steps, faster than walking, in such a manner that both feet are off the ground for a portion of each step. 2 To move rapidly; go swiftly. 3 To flee; take flight. 4 To make a brief or rapid journey: We *ran* over to Staten Island last night. 5 To make regular trips; ply: This steamer *runs* between New York and Liverpool. 6 **a** To take part in a race. **b** To be a candidate or contestant: to *run* for dog-catcher. 7 To finish a race in a specified position: I *ran* a poor last. 8 To move or pass easily: The rope *runs* through the block. 9 To pass continuously and rapidly; elapse: The hours *run* by. 10 To proceed in direction or extent: This road *runs* north. 11 To move in or as in a stream; flow. 12 To become liquid and flow, as wax; also, to spread or mingle confusedly, as colors when wet. 13 To move or pass inadvertently: The ship *ran* aground. 14 To pass into a specified condition: to *run* to seed. 15 To come undone; unravel, as a fabric. 16 To give forth a discharge or flow; suppurate. 17 To leak. 18 To continue or proceed without restraint: The conversation *ran* on and on. 19 To be in operation; be operative; work: Will the engine *run*? 20 To continue in existence or effect; extend in time: Genius *runs* in her family. 21 To be reported or expressed: The story *runs* as follows. 22 To migrate, as salmon from the sea to spawn. 23 To occur or return to the mind: An idea *ran* through his head. 24 To occur with specified variation of size, quality, etc.: The corn is *running* small this year. 25 To be performed or repeated in continuous succession: The play *ran* for forty nights. 26 To make a rapid succession of demands for payment, as on a bank. 27 To continue unexpired or unpaid, as a debt; become payable. —*v.t.* 28 To run or proceed along, as a route or path. 29 To make one's way over, through, or past: to *run* rapids. 30 To perform or accomplish by or as by running: to *run* a race or an errand. 31 To compete against in or as in a race. 32 To enter (a horse) for a race. 33 To present and support as a candidate. 34 To hunt or chase, as game. 35 To bring to a specified condition by or as by running: to *run* oneself out of breath. 36 To drive or force: with *out of, off, into, through,* etc. 37 To cause (a vessel) to move rapidly or freely: They *ran* the ship into port. 38 To move (the eye, hand, etc.) quickly or lightly: He *ran* his hand over the table. 39 To cause to move, slide, etc., as into a specified position: to *run* up a flag. 40 To cause to go or ply: to *run* a train between New York and Washington. 41 To transport or convey in a vessel or vehicle. 42 To smuggle. 43 To cause to flow: to *run* water into a pot. 44 To give forth a flow of; emit: Her eyes *ran* tears. 45 To mold, as from melted metal; found. 46 To sew (cloth) in a continuous line, usually by taking a number of stitches with the needle at a time. 47 To maintain or control the motion or operation of. 48 To direct or control; manage; oversee. 49 To allow to continue or mount up, as a bill. 50 In games, to make (a number of points, strokes, etc.) successively. 51 To publish in a magazine or newspaper: to *run* an ad. 52 To mark, set down, or trace, as a boundary line. 53 To suffer from (a fever, etc.). —**to run across** To meet by chance. —**to run down** 1 To pursue and overtake, as a fugitive. 2 To strike down while moving. 3 To exhaust, damage, lessen in worth, vigor, etc., as by abuse or overwork. 4 To speak of disparagingly; decry. —**to run in** 1 To insert; include. 2 *Printing* To print without a paragraph or break. 3 *Slang* To arrest and place in confinement. —**to run into** 1 To meet by chance. 2 To collide with. —**to run off** 1 To produce on a typewriter, printing press, etc. 2 To decide (a tied race, game, etc.) by the outcome of another, subsequent race, game, etc. 3 To flee or escape; elope. —**to run out** To come to an end; be exhausted, as supplies. —**to run out of** To exhaust one's supply of. —**to run over** 1 To ride or drive over; run down. 2 To overflow. 3 To go over or examine hastily or quickly; rehearse. —**to run through** 1 To spend wastefully; squander. 2 To stab or pierce. 3 To run over (def. 3). —**to run up** To produce; make hurriedly, as on a sewing machine. —*n.* 1 The act, or an act, of running or going rapidly. 2 A running pace: to break into a *run.* 3 Flow; movement; sweep: the *run* of the tide. 4 A distance covered by running. 5 A journey or passage, especially between two points, made by a vessel, train, etc.: the *run* from New York to Albany. 6 A rapid journey or excursion, marked by a brief stay at the destination: to take a *run* into town. 7 A swift stream or brook. 8 A migration of fish, especially to up-river spawning grounds. 9 A grazing or feeding ground for animals or fowl; a range: a sheep *run.* 10 The regular trail or path of certain animals: an elephant *run.* 11 The bower of a bowerbird. 12 The privilege of free use or access: to have the *run* of the place. 13 A runway. 14 *Music* A rapid succession of tones; a roulade. 15 A series or succession. 16 A sequence of three or more playing cards in consecutive order. 17 A trend or tendency: the general *run* of the market. 18 The direction or course (of something): the *run* of the grain of wood. 19 A continuous length (of something): a *run* of pipe. 20 A continuous spell (of some condition): a *run* of luck. 21 A surge of demands made upon a bank or treasury to meet its obligations. 22 Any great sustained demand. 23 A period of continuous performance, occurrence, popularity, etc.: a play with a long *run.* 24 Class or type: the general *run* of readers. 25 A period of operation of a machine or device: an experimental *run.* 26 The output during such a period. 27 A period during which a liquid is allowed to run. 28 The amount of liquid allowed to flow at one time. 29 A measure of yarn (about 1,600 yards). 30 A narrow, lengthwise ravel, as in a sheer stocking. 31 An approach to a target made by a bombing plane. 32 In baseball, a complete circuit of the bases from home plate and back before three outs are made, thus scoring a point. 33 In cricket, an act in which both batsmen successfully run to opposite popping creases, thereby scoring a point. 34 A hunt, especially on horseback; a chase. 35 *Naut.* The after part of a ship's bottom where it narrows off from the floor timbers to the sternpost. 36 *Mining* A vein. 37 *Austral.* A sheep or cattle station. —**dry run** Any practice test; specifically, an approach to a target made by a bombing plane, without dropping bombs. —**in the long run** As the ultimate outcome of any train of

circumstances. **—on the run 1** Almost without pausing while doing something else; hastily: to eat *on the run.* **2** In full retreat. **3** While running. *—adj.* **1** Made liquid; melted. **2** Made by a process of melting and casting or molding: *run* metal; *run* butter. **3** Extracted or drained: *run* honey. **4** Smuggled; contraband: *run* liquor. [OE *rinnan* flow]

run·a·bout (run′ə·bout′) *n.* **1** A light, handy, open automobile for ready service. **2** A light, open wagon. **3** A small motorboat.

run·a·gate (run′ə·gāt) *n. Archaic* **1** A deserter; renegade. **2** A vagabond; homeless wanderer. [Alter. of RENEGADE; infl. by *run,* dial. *agate* on the way]

run·a·round (run′ə·round′) *n.* **1** *Slang* Artful deception; evasion. **2** Run-round. **3** *Printing* Type set narrower than the body of the text, as around illustrations.

run·a·way (run′ə·wā′) *adj.* **1** Escaping or escaped from restraint or control; fugitive. **2** Brought about by running away: a *runaway* marriage. **3** Easily won: said of a horse race; hence, decisive; one-sided. *—n.* **1** One who or that which runs away or flees; a fugitive or deserter; also, a horse of which the driver has lost control. **2** An act of running away: said especially of a horse.

run·back (run′bak′) *n.* A run in football made after receiving an opponent's kick or after intercepting a pass.

run·ci·ble spoon (run′sə·bəl) A fork having three broad tines, of which one has a sharp edge. [< RUNC(INATE) + -IBLE]

run·ci·nate (run′sə·nāt, -nit) *adj. Bot.* Saw-toothed, with the incisions or teeth inclined backward: said of leaves. [< L *runcinatus,* pp. of *runcinare* plane off < *runcina* plane, saw]

run·dle (run′dəl) *n.* **1** A rung, as of a ladder. **2** Something that rotates about an axis, as the drum of a capstan. [Var. of ROUNDEL]

rund·let[1] (rund′lit) *n.* A small barrel, or the wine it contains, about 18 wine gallons. Also *runlet.* [< OF *rondelet.* See ROUNDELAY.]

rund·let[2] (rund′lit) See RUNLET[1].

run-down (run′doun′) *adj.* **1** Debilitated; physically weak; tired out. **2** Dilapidated; shabby. **3** Stopped because not wound: said of a timepiece. *—n.* (run′doun′). **1** A summary; resumé. **2** In baseball, a play in which a base runner is put out when trapped between two bases.

Rund·stedt (rōōnt′shtet), **Karl Rudolf Gerd von,** 1875–1953, German field marshal in World War II.

rune (rōōn) *n.* **1** A character of the primitive runic alphabet. **2** A Finnish poem or one of its cantos. **3** *pl.* Old Norse lore expressed, or considered as if expressed, in runes; hence, early rimes or poetry in general. **4** Any obscure or mystic song, poem, verse, or saying; a mystery. [< ON *rūn* mystery, rune] **—ru′nic** *adj.*

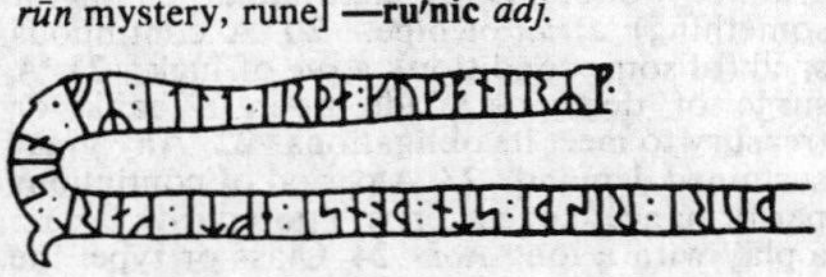

RUNES
Tomb inscription, Sweden, eleventh century.

rung[1] (rung) *n.* **1** A round crosspiece of a ladder or chair; a round; also, a spoke of a wheel. **2** *Naut.* **a** One of the handles on the rim of a ship's tiller. **b** A floor timber of a ship. **3** *Scot. & Brit. Dial.* A heavy club or staff; cudgel. [OE *hrung* crossbar]

rung[2] (rung) Past participle of RING[2].

ru·nic alphabet (rōō′nik) An old Germanic alphabet, probably originating in both the Latin and Greek, consisting originally of 24 characters, or runes, later reduced to 16 in Scandinavian writings. The earliest inscriptions in this alphabet are of the second or third century A.D. In England it was still in occasional use at the end of the Old English period, and was finally completely replaced by the Roman alphabet through the spread of Christian writings. Also called *futhark.*

runic staff A clog almanac.

run-in (run′in′) *n.* **1** A quarrel; bicker. **2** *Printing* Inserted or added matter. *—adj.* (run′in′) *Printing* That is inserted or added.

Run·jeet Singh (run′jēt siṅ′hə) See RANJIT SINGH.

run·let[1] (run′lit) *n.* A little stream; rivulet; a runnel. Also *rundlet.* See synonyms under STREAM.

run·let[2] (run′lit) See RUNDLET[1].

run·nel (run′əl) *n.* A streamlet; brooklet; rivulet. [OE *rynel* < *rinnan* run]

run·ner (run′ər) *n.* **1** One who or that which runs; especially, one who runs a race; also, a fugitive or deserter. **2** One who operates or manages anything; especially, the driver of a locomotive. **3** One who runs errands or goes about on any kind of business; a messenger, as for a bank; specifically, one who drums up or solicits patronage or business, as for a hotel. **4** That part on which an object runs or slides: the *runner* of a skate. **5** *Mech.* A device to assist sliding motion. **6** A slender fish *(Elegatis bipinnulatus)* of warm seas with single dorsal and anal pinnules; also, the jurel of the Atlantic coast of America. **7** A cursorial bird; the water rail. **8** *Bot.* **a** A slender, procumbent stem disposed to root at the end and nodes, as in strawberry; also, sometimes, the plant itself. **b** Any of various twining plants: the scarlet *runner.* **9** A smuggler. **10** A blacksnake. **11** A long, narrow rug or carpeting, used in hallways, etc. **12** A narrow strip of cloth, usually of fine quality, used on tables, dressers, etc.

run·ner-up (run′ər·up′) *n.* A contestant or team finishing in second place.

run·ning (run′ing) *adj.* **1** Such as runs: said specifically of horses inclined or trained to a running gait rather than to pacing or trotting. **2** Following one another without intermission; successive: used with words expressing periods of time: He talked for three hours *running.* **3** Continuous; repeated: said of a design: a *running* ornament, a *running* molding, etc. **4** Kept up continuously; also, passing; cursory: *running* comments, a *running* glance. **5** Characterized by easy flowing curves; cursive: a *running* hand. **6** Discharging, as pus from a sore. *—n.* **1** The act or movement of one who or that which runs: a horse trained for fast *running.* **2** That which runs or flows; the amount or quantity that runs. **3** A discharge, as from a sore. **4** Ability or power to run. **5** Competition; race; rivalry: He's out of the *running.* **6** Climbing; sending out runners, as certain plants.

running board A footboard on the side of a locomotive, street car, automobile, etc.

running expenses Daily expenses.

running fits Fright disease.

running gear 1 *Mech.* **a** The wheels and axles of any vehicle and their immediate attachments, as distinguished from the body, frame, etc., which they support. **b** Those parts of a mechanism or construction that have partially independent motion: the *running gear* of a watch. **2** *Naut.* The movable ropes and wires on a boat or ship by which sails, etc., are raised, lowered, and trimmed.

running hand Writing done with a continuous easy motion without lifting the pen from the paper and usually having the letters slanted forward.

running knot A knot made so as to slip along a noose and tighten when pulled upon.

running lights The sidelights of a vessel.

running mate 1 A horse that is teammate for another; also, a horse entered to set the pace for another entered to run in a horse race. **2** The candidate for the lesser of two offices closely linked by constitutional provisions, as the vice-presidency with the presidency.

running title *Printing* A title or headline repeated at the head of succeeding pages throughout a book or chapter. Also **running head.**

Run·ny·mede (run′i·mēd) A meadow in Surrey, England, on the Thames west of London, where King John is said to have met his barons to sign the Magna Carta in 1215.

run-off (run′ôf′, -of′) *n.* **1** That part of the rainfall in a particular area which is not absorbed directly by the soil but is drained off in rills or streams. **2** A special contest held to break a tie.

run-of-the-mill (run′əv·thə·mil′) See MILL-RUN.

run-on (run′on′, -ôn′) *n. Printing* Appended or added matter.

run-on line Enjambement.

run-out (run′out′) *n.* That portion of a motion-picture film immediately following the last frame of the picture itself.

run-round (run′round′) *n. Pathol.* A circumscribed inflammation of the skin, as on the fingers or toes; a felon: also called *run-around.*

runt (runt) *n.* **1** An unusually small, weak, or stunted animal; also, the smallest and weakest of a litter. **2** A dwarf. **3** *Scot.* An old ox or cow; a withered old man or hag. **4** *Scot. & Brit. Dial.* A stump of a tree or shrub; also, the stem or stalk of a plant. [Origin uncertain] **—runt′i·ness** *n.* **—runt′y** *adj.*

run·way (run′wā′) *n.* **1** A way or path over which something runs. **2** The channel or bed of a stream, or the path over which animals pass to and from their places of feeding or watering. **3** In lumbering, an incline down which logs are slid; a chute. **4** Any track specially laid for wheeled vehicles. Also *run.* **5** *Aeron.* An artificial landing strip for airplanes.

Run·yon (run′yən), **Damon,** 1884–1946, U.S. journalist and writer.

ru·pee (rōō·pē′) *n.* The standard monetary unit of British India: it contains 16 annas. [< Hind. *rupīya* < Skt. *rūpya* silver]

Ru·pert (rōō′pərt; *Fr.* rü·pâr′, *Ger.* rōō′pert) A masculine personal name: variant of ROBERT. Also *Ger.* **Ru·precht** (rōō′prekht). [See ROBERT] **—Rupert, Prince,** 1619–82, Royalist general in English Civil War; born in Bavaria.

ru·pi·ah (rōō·pē′ä) *n.* The principal Indonesian currency unit.

rup·ture (rup′chər) *n.* **1** The act of breaking apart or the state of being broken apart. **2** Hernia. **3** Breach of peace and concord between individuals or nations. *—v.t. & v.i.* **·tured, ·tur·ing 1** To break apart; separate into parts. **2** To affect with or suffer a rupture. See synonyms under BREAK, REND. [< F < L *ruptus,* pp. of *rumpere* break] **—rup′tur·a·ble** *adj.*

Synonyms (noun): blast, breach, break, burst, disruption, fracture. See BREACH, QUARREL[1].

ru·ral (rōōr′əl) *adj.* **1** Pertaining to the country as distinguished from the city or the town; rustic. **2** Pertaining to farming or agriculture. See synonyms under RUSTIC. [< F < L *ruralis* < *rus, ruris* country] **—ru′ral·ism** *n.* **—ru′ral·ist** *n.* **—ru′ral·ly** *adv.* **—ru′ral·ness** *n.*

rural dean Dean (def. 2).

rural free delivery A government service of house-to-house free mail delivery by carrier in rural districts, as distinguished from the general delivery service: in addresses abbreviated *R.F.D.* Often shortened to *R.D.*

ru·ral·i·ty (rōō·ral′ə·tē) *n.* **1** Ruralness. **2** A rural peculiarity. **3** A place in the country.

ru·ral·ize (rōōr′əl·īz) *v.* **·ized, ·iz·ing** *v.t.* To make rural. *—v.i.* To go into or live in the country; rusticate. **—ru′ral·i·za′tion** *n.*

Ru·rik (rōō′rik) Russian form of RODERICK. **—Rurik,** died 879, Scandinavian conqueror who founded the Russian monarchy, the **House of Rurik,** which lasted from 862 to 1598.

ruse (rōōz) *n.* An action intended to mislead or deceive; a stratagem; trick. See synonyms under ARTIFICE, PRETENSE. [< F < *ruser* dodge, detour, drive back. Related to RUSH[1].]

Ru·se (rōō′se) A city on the Danube in NE Bulgaria.

ruse de guerre (rüz də gâr′) *French* A stratagem of war.

rush[1] (rush) *v.i.* **1** To move or go swiftly or with violence. **2** To make an attack; charge: with *on* or *upon.* **3** To proceed recklessly or rashly; plunge: with *in* or *into.* *—v.t.* **4** To drive or push with haste or violence; hurry. **5** To do or perform hastily or hurriedly: to *rush* one's work. **6 a** To make a sudden assault upon. **b** To capture by such an assault. **7** *Slang* To seek the favor of with assiduous attentions. **8** In football, to move (the ball) toward the goal of the other team. See synonyms under HUSTLE. *—n.* **1** The act of rushing; a sudden turbulent movement, drive, or onset. **2** A sudden pressing demand; a run: a *rush* on foreign bonds. **3** A sudden exigency; urgent pressure: a *rush* of business. **4** A sudden flocking of people to a new region, especially to an area rumored to be rich in a precious mineral: a gold *rush.* **5** *U.S.* A

general contest or scrimmage between students from different classes, as between sophomores and freshmen. **6** In football: **a** An attempt to take the ball through the opposing linemen and toward the goal. **b** Formerly, a player in the rush line: a center *rush.* **7** In motion pictures, the first film prints of a scene or series of scenes, before editing or selection. See synonyms under CAREER. —*adj.* **1** Requiring urgency or haste: a *rush* order. **2** Characterized by much traffic, business, etc.: the *rush* hours. **3** Denoting a time or function set aside for fraternity or sorority members to meet new students to consider them for membership: *rush* week; a *rush* smoker. [<AF *russher* push, var. of *russer,* OF *ruser, reuser* push back, dodge <LL *recusare* push back. See RECUSANT.]

rush[2] (rush) *n.* **1** Any one of various grass-like, usually aquatic herbs (family *Juncaceae*). The common or **soft rush** *(Juncus effusus)* grows in marshy ground and has soft and pliant, cylindrical, leafless stems: used for mats, seats of chairs, etc. **2** A thing of little or no value. **3** A rushlight. [OE *rysc*]

Rush (rush), **Benjamin,** 1745–1813, American physician, signer for Pennsylvania of the Declaration of Independence.

rush·er (rush′ər) *n.* **1** One who rushes. **2** In football, a lineman.

rush–hold·er (rush′hōl′dər) *n.* A candlestick with a clip for supporting a rushlight.

rush hour A time when traffic or business is at its height. —**rush–hour** (rush′our′) *adj.*

rush·ing (rush′ing) *n. U.S.* The series of activities in which fraternity and sorority members meet and evaluate new college students wishing to be pledged.

rush·light (rush′līt′) *n.* A candle made by dipping a rush in tallow. Also **rush candle.**

Rush·more (rush′môr), **Mount** A mountain in the Black Hills of western South Dakota, on the side of which are carved gigantic faces of Presidents Washington, Jefferson, Lincoln, Theodore Roosevelt: in **Mount Rushmore National Memorial;** 1,220 acres; established, 1929.

rush·y (rush′ē) *adj.* **rush·i·er, rush·i·est** Abounding in or made of rushes.

ru·sine (rōō′sin, -sīn) *adj.* Of, pertaining to, or designating a genus *(Rusa)* of deer native in the East Indies. Compare SAMBUR. [<Malay *rūsa* deer]

rusine antler An antler having a simple brow tine and a simple fork at the tip of the beam.

rus in ur·be (rus′ in ûr′bē) *Latin* The country in the city.

rusk (rusk) *n.* **1** A light, sweetened bread or biscuit. **2** Bread or cake that has been crisped and browned in an oven, then often pounded fine to be eaten with milk. [<Sp. *rosca,* twisted loaf of bread]

Rus·kin (rus′kin), **John,** 1819–1900, English art critic and author.

Russ (rus) *adj.* & *n.* Russian.

Rus·sell (rus′əl), **Bertrand Arthur William,** 1872–1970, third Earl Russell, English mathematician and philosopher. —**Countess Elizabeth Mary,** 1866–1941, *née* Beauchamp, English novelist: pen name *Elizabeth.* —**George William** See Æ. —**Lord John,** 1792–1878, first Earl Russell, English statesman. —**Lillian,** 1861–1922, U. S. soprano: original name Helen Louise Leonard.

Russell diagram *Astron.* The Hertzsprung–Russell diagram.

rus·set (rus′it) *n.* **1** A color formed by combining orange and purple; popularly, any reddish– or yellowish–brown. **2** Russet cloth, clothing, etc.; hence, any coarse homespun cloth or garment; a country dress. **3** Russet leather. **4** A winter apple of greenish color, mottled with brown. —*adj.* **1** Of a reddish– or yellowish–brown color. **2** Made of russet cloth; hence, coarse; homespun; rustic. **3** Finished, but not blacked: said of leather: *russet* shoes. [<OF *rousset,* dim. of *rous* <L *russus* reddish] —**rus′set·y** *adj.*

Rus·sia The largest country in Asia; capital, Moscow; pop. 150,000,000; 6,592,800 square miles; Russia comprises the territory of Asia extending west from the Bering Sea to the Baltic sea and south from the Arctic Ocean to border of China and the Arabian Peninsula. Unified in the 9th century, Russia dissolved into independent dukedoms by 1240; its borders fluctuated through the centuries, until the formation of the U.S.S.R. in 1922. In 1991, the Soviet Union dissolved into independent nations. Russia joined with other nations to form the Commonwealth of Independent States.

Rus·sian *adj.* Pertaining to Russia, its people, or their language. —*n.* **1** An inhabitant of Russia; especially, one of any of the ethnic Slavic peoples, including the **Great Russians** of the central and northwestern region, the Ukrainians (or **Little Russians**) of the Ukraine and eastern Poland, which group includes also the Cossacks and Ruthenians, and the **White Russians** of the west, all speaking Indo-European Balto-Slavic languages, such as Russian, Polish, Lithuanian, and Lettish; also, one of any of the peoples of Russia speaking any of the Uralic languages, especially the Finno-Ugric branch; also, one of any of the native peoples of the Caucasus speaking languages unrelated to these others, as Circassian, Georgian, and the Lesghian group. **2** The language of Russia, belonging to the East Slavic branch of the Balto-Slavic languages, having a separate alphabet including several characters not found in other alphabets. Its subdivisions are **Great Russian,** the principal subdivision and standard literary language in northern and central Russia, Ukrainian or Ruthenian (or **Little Russia),** and **White Russian,** the literary language of western Russia.

Russian Church A division of the Greek Church, independent since 1589, and governed by the Holy Synod. See GREEK CHURCH.

Russian dressing Mayonnaise dressing to which chili sauce, pimientos, and chopped pickles have been added.

Russian leather A smooth, well–tanned, high–grade leather of calfskin or light cattle hide, dressed with birch oil and having a characteristic odor.

Russian Revolution See under REVOLUTION.

Russian Soviet Federated Socialist Republic The former constituent republic of the U.S.S.R., occupying 76 per cent of the U.S.S.R. and extending across northern Asia and eastern Europe; abbr. R.S.F.S.R.

Russian Turkestan See under TURKESTAN.

Russian wolfhound The borzoi.

Russo– *combining form* Russia; pertaining to the Russians: *Russophobia.* [<RUSSIA]

Rus·so·phile (rus′ə·fīl, -fil) *n.* One who favors Russia, or its principles, policy, or methods.

Rus·so·pho·bi·a (rus′ə·fō′bē·ə) *n.* Fear of the policy or influence of Russia. —**Rus′so·phobe** *n.*

rust (rust) *n.* **1** The reddish or yellow coating caused on iron and steel by oxidation, as by the action of air and moisture, consisting of ferric hydroxide, $Fe(OH)_3$, and ferric oxide, Fe_2O_3. **2** A film of oxide formed on any metal by corrosion. **3** Any of the parasitic fungi of the order *Uredinales,* living on the tissues of higher plants. **4** The diseases caused by such fungi; incorrectly, any one of several diseases not caused by these fungi. **5** Any coating or accretion formed by a corrosive or degenerative process: *rust* on salted meat. **6** A condition, affection, or tendency that destroys or weakens energy or active qualities: the *rust* of idleness. **7** Any of several shades of reddish–brown, somewhat like the color of rust, but containing more orange. —*v.t.* & *v.i.* **1** To become or cause to become rusty; undergo or cause to undergo oxidation. **2** To contract or cause to contract rust. **3** To become or cause to become weakened or impaired because of inactivity or disuse: to allow one's powers to *rust.* **4** To make or become rust–colored. [OE]

rus·tic (rus′tik) *adj.* **1** Rural; hence, plain; homely: *rustic* garments. **2** Uncultured; rude; awkward: *rustic* manners. **3** Unaffected; artless: *rustic* simplicity. **4** Pertaining to any irregular style of work or decoration appropriate to the country or to work in natural, unpolished wood. —*n.* **1** One who lives in the country; a country person of simple manners or character; also, a coarse or clownish person. **2** Rusticwork. **3** Country dialect. [<F *rustique* <L *rusticus* <*rus* country] —**rus′ti·cal·ly** *adv.*

Synonyms (adj.): agricultural, artless, awkward, boorish, bucolic, clownish, coarse, countrified, country, hoydenish, inelegant, outlandish, pastoral, plain, rude, rural, sylvan, uncouth, unpolished, unsophisticated, untaught, verdant. *Rural* refers especially to scenes or objects in the country, considered as the work of nature; *rustic* refers to their effect upon man or to their condition as affected by human agency; as, a *rural* scene; a *rustic* party; a *rustic* lass. We speak, however, of the *rural* population, *rural* simplicity, etc. *Rural* has always a favorable sense; *rustic* often an unfavorable one, as denoting lack of culture and refinement; thus, *rustic* politeness expresses that which is well–meant, but awkward. *Rustic* is, however, often used of a studied simplicity, an artistic rudeness, which is pleasing and perhaps beautiful; as, a *rustic* cottage. *Pastoral* refers to the care of flocks and to the shepherd's life with the pleasing associations suggested by the old poetic ideal of that life; as, *pastoral* poetry. *Bucolic* is kindred to *pastoral,* but is a less elevated term, and sometimes slightly contemptuous. *Antonyms:* accomplished, cultured, elegant, polished, polite, refined, urban, urbane.

rus·ti·cate (rus′tə·kāt) *v.* **·cat·ed, ·cat·ing** *v.i.* **1** To go to the country. **2** To stay or live in the country. —*v.t.* **3** To send or banish to the country. **4** *Brit.* To suspend (a student) and send away temporarily, as from a college. **5** To make rustic. **6** To construct (masonry) with rusticwork. [<L *rusticatus,* pp. of *rusticari* rusticate <*rusticus.* See RUSTIC.] —**rus′ti·ca′tion** *n.* —**rus′ti·ca′tor** *n.*

rus·tic·i·ty (rus·tis′ə·tē) *n. pl.* **·ties** **1** Rustic condition, characters, or manners; simplicity; homeliness; awkwardness. **2** A rustic trait or peculiarity. [<L *rusticitas, -tatis*]

rus·tic·work (rus′tik·wûrk′) *n.* **1** Ashlar masonry, or a method of making it, with rough surfaces, and often with deeply sunk grooves at the joints, to make them conspicuous. **2** Woodwork made of the natural limbs and roots of trees, fancifully arranged.

rus·tle[1] (rus′əl) *v.t.* & *v.i.* **·tled, ·tling** To fall, move, or cause to move with a quick succession of small, light, rubbing sounds, as dry leaves or sheets of paper. —*n.* A rustling sound. [OE *hrūxlian* make a noise. Cf. OE *gehyrstan* murmur.] —**rus′tler** *n.* —**rus′tling** *adj.* —**rus′tling·ly** *adv.*

rus·tle[2] (rus′əl) *v.t.* & *v.i.* **·tled, ·tling** **1** *Colloq.* To act with or obtain by energetic or vigorous action. **2** *U.S. Colloq.* To steal (cattle, etc.). [Blend of RUSH and HUSTLE]

rus·tler (rus′lər) *n. U.S.* **1** *Slang* Any person who is active, pushing, and bustling in any enterprise. Compare HUSTLER. **2** *Colloq.* **a** A cowboy or ranchman. **b** A cook on a ranch. **c** A cattle or horse thief.

rust·y[1] (rus′tē) *adj.* **rust·i·er, rust·i·est** **1** Covered or affected with rust. **2** Consisting of or produced by rust. **3** Having the appearance of rust; having a reddish or yellowish discoloration, as from decomposition: said especially of salted fish or meat that has become rancid. **4** Impaired by inaction or want of exercise; also, lacking nimbleness; stiff. **5 a** Weakened through neglect of use: My Latin is *rusty.* **b** Having lost skill for want of practice: *rusty* in math. **6** *Biol.* Appearing as if covered with rust; brownish–red. See synonyms under TRITE. [OE *rustig* <*rust* rust] —**rust′i·ly** *adv.* —**rust′i·ness** *n.*

rust·y[2] (rus′tē) *adj. Brit. Dial.* Restive; stubborn; obstinate.

rut[1] (rut) *n.* **1** A sunken track worn by a wheel, as in a road; hence, a groove forming a path for anything. **2** A settled habit or course of procedure; routine. —*v.t.* **rut·ted, rut·ting** To wear or make a rut or ruts in. [? Var. of ROUTE]

rut[2] (rut) *n.* **1** The sexual excitement of various animals, especially deer; estrus; also, the period during which it lasts. **2** A roaring or uproar; especially, the noise made by a rutting stag. —*v.* **rut·ted, rut·ting** *v.i.* To be in rut. —*v.t. Rare* To unite with in copulation; cover. [<F <L *rugitus* a roaring, tumult <*rugire* roar] —**rut′ting** *adj.*

ru·ta·ba·ga (rōō′tə·bā′gə) *n.* **1** A cultivated plant *(Brassica napobrassica)* allied to the common turnip. **2** Its edible, yellowish root. Also *Swedish turnip.* [<dial. Sw. *rotabagge*]

ru·ta·ceous (rōō·tā'shəs) *adj. Bot.* Of or pertaining to the rue family (*Rutaceae*) of shrubs, trees, and, rarely, herbs, including the lemon, lime, citron, etc. [< L *ruta* < Gk. *rhytē* rue]

Rut·ger (rut'gər, rōōt'gər) Dutch form of ROGER.

ruth (rōōth) *n.* Sorrow; compassion; pity; also, grief; misery; repentance; regret. [ME *reuthe, reowthe* < OE *hrēow* sad]

Ruth (rōōth, *Fr.* rüt) A feminine personal name. [< Hebrew, companion]
—**Ruth** A woman of Moab, daughter-in-law of the Israelite Naomi; she left her own people and went to Bethlehem, where she married Boaz, thus becoming an ancestress of David. Her story is told in the Old Testament book of this name.

Ru·the·ni·a (rōō·thē'nē·ə) A region of western Ukrainian S.S.R.; formerly a province of Czechoslovakia; annexed by Hungary, 1939; ceded to U.S.S.R., 1945; since 1945, the **Transcarpathian Oblast** of the Ukrainian S.S.R.; 5,000 square miles; capital, Uzhgorod: also *Carpatho-Ukraine*.

Ru·the·ni·an (rōō·thē'nē·ən) *n.* 1 One of a group of Ukrainians living in Ruthenia and eastern Czechoslovakia, formerly in Austria. 2 The East Slavic language of the Ukrainians; Ukrainian. See RUSSIAN. —*adj.* Pertaining to the Ruthenians or their language.

ru·then·ic (rōō·then'ik) *adj. Chem.* Of, pertaining to, or derived from ruthenium, especially when combined in its higher valence.

ru·the·ni·ous (rōō·thē'nē·əs) *adj. Chem.* Of, pertaining to, or derived from ruthenium, especially when combined in its lower valence.

ru·the·ni·um (rōō·thē'nē·əm) *n.* A hard, brittle, gray metallic element (symbol Ru, atomic number 44) found in platinum ores and used as a catalyst and alloying element. See PERIODIC TABLE. [< NL, after *Ruthenia*]

ruth·er·ford (ruth'ər·fərd) *n.* A unit of radioactivity larger than the curie: equal to that quantity of a radioisotope which decays at the rate of a million disintegrations per second. [after Sir Ernest *Rutherford*]

Ruth·er·ford (ruth'ər·fərd) **Sir Ernest,** 1871–1937, English physicist. —**Joseph,** 1869–1942, U.S. leader of Jehovah's Witnesses.

ruth·ful (rōōth'fəl) *adj. Archaic* 1 Full of sorrow or pity; sorrowful; merciful. 2 Causing sorrow. —**ruth'ful·ly** *adv.* —**ruth'ful·ness** *n.*

ruth·less (rōōth'lis) *adj.* Having no compassion; unrestrained by pity; merciless. —**ruth'less·ly** *adv.* —**ruth·less·ness** *n.*

ru·ti·lant (rōō'tə·lənt) *adj.* Of a shining red color; glittering. [< L *rutilans, -antis,* ppr. of *rutilare* glow red < *rutilus.* See RUTILE.]

ru·ti·lat·ed (rōō'tə·lā'tid) *adj.* Enclosing rutile needles: *rutilated* quartz.

ru·tile (rōō'til, -tēl, -tīl) *n.* An adamantine, reddish-brown, transparent to opaque titanium dioxide, TiO₂, usually containing a small quantity of iron. [< F, shining < L *rutilus* red]

Rut·land (rut'lənd) 1 A county of eastern England; 152 square miles: county town Oakham. Also **Rut'land·shire** (-shir). 2 A city in central Vermont, important as a center of the marble-cutting industry.

Rut·ledge (rut'lij), **Ann,** 1816–35, fiancée of Abraham Lincoln. —**Edward,** 1749–1800, American jurist; signer for South Carolina of Declaration of Independence. —**John,** 1739–1800, jurist; a framer of the U.S. Constitution; brother of the preceding.

rut·tish (rut'ish) *adj.* Disposed to rut; lustful; libidinous.

rut·ty (rut'ē) *adj.* Full of ruts. —**rut'ti·ness** *n.*

Ru·vu·ma (rōō·vōō'mä) A river in eastern Africa, flowing 450 miles north and east to the Indian Ocean, and forming the Tanganyika-Mozambique border: Portuguese *Rovuma.*

Ru·wen·zo·ri (rōō'wən·zôr'ē, -zō'rē) A mountain group in east central Africa between Albert and Edward lakes, on the boundary between the Belgian Congo and Uganda: identified with the *Mountains of the Moon* of ancient writers; highest peak, 16,795 feet.

Ru·y (*Sp.* rōō·ē', *Pg.* rōō'ē) Spanish and Portuguese form of RODERICK.

Ruys·dael (rois'däl, *Du.* rœis'däl), **Jacob van,** 1625?–82, Dutch painter: also spelled *Ruisdael.*

Ruy·ter (roi'tər), **Michel Adriaanszoon de,** 1607–76, Dutch admiral.

Rwan·da (rwän'də) A republic in central Africa, part of the former UN Trust Territory of Ruanda-Urundi; 10,169 square miles; pop. about 2,500,000; capital Kigali.

-ry Var. of -ERY.

Rya·zan (rē·ə·zän', *Russian* ryä·zän') A city near the Oka river in the central European Russian S.F.S.R.

Ry·binsk (ri'binsk) See SHCHERBAKOV.

Ry·binsk Reservoir (ri'binsk) The largest artificial lake of the U.S.S.R. in north central European Russian S.F.S.R. on the upper Volga; 1,800 square miles: also **Rybinsk Sea.**

Ry·der (ri'dər), **Albert Pinkham,** 1847–1917, U.S. painter.

rye¹ (ri) *n.* 1 The grain or seeds of a hardy cereal grass (*Secale cereale*) closely allied to wheat. 2 The plant. 3 Whisky distilled from rye. ♦ Homophone: *wry.* [OE *ryge* rye]

rye² (ri) *n.* In Gipsy dialect, a gentleman. ♦ Homophone: *wry.* [< Romany *rei, rae,* prob. < Skt. *rājan* a king]

Rye (ri) A municipal borough of east Sussex, England; an important Channel port before the sea receded in the early 19th century.

rye·grass (ri'gras', -gräs') *n.* Common darnel: sometimes called *raygrass.*

ryke (rik, rēk) *v.i. Scot.* To reach.

rynd (rind, rind) *n.* An iron fitting supporting an upper millstone, having a central hollow bearing which rests upon the upper pointed end of the mill spindle: also spelled *rind.* [Prob. < M Du. *rijn*]

Ryo·jun (ryō·jōōn) The Japanese name for PORT ARTHUR.

ry·ot (ri'ət) *n.* In India, a tenant; tiller of the soil; peasant. [< Hind. *raiyat* < Arabic *ra'iyah*]

Rys·wick (riz'wik) A village in southern Netherlands, near The Hague; site of the signing of a treaty by France, Germany, the Netherlands, England, and Spain, 1697: Dutch *Rijswijk.*

Ryu·kyu Islands (ryōō·kyōō) An archipelago between Kyushu and Taiwan; 1,803 square miles; chief island, Okinawa; Japanese possessions, administered by the U.S. after 1945; formally returned to Japan, May 15, 1972. Also *Nansei Islands.*

S

s,S (es) *n. pl.* **s's, S's** or **ess·es** (es'·iz) 1 The nineteenth letter of the English alphabet, from Phoenician *shin,* through Hebrew *shin,* Greek *sigma,* Roman S. 2 The sound of the letter *s,* usually a voiceless sibilant. See ALPHABET. —*symbol* 1 *Chem.* Sulfur (symbol S). 2 Anything shaped like an S.

-s¹ A variant of *-es*¹, inflectional ending of the plurals of nouns, attached to nouns not ending in a sibilant or an affricate: *books, words, cars.* It is pronounced (s) after a voiceless consonant, and (z) after a voiced consonant or a vowel.

-s² An inflectional ending used to form the third person singular present indicative of verbs not ending in a sibilant, affricate, or vowel: *reads, walks, sings.* Compare -ES².

-s³ *suffix* On; of a; at: often used in adverbs without appreciable force: *nights, Mondays, always, towards.* [OE *-es,* genitive ending]

-'s¹ An inflectional ending used to form the possessive of singular nouns and of plural nouns not ending in *-s*: a *man's* world, *women's* fashions. In plurals ending in *-s* (or *-es*) a simple apostrophe is used as a sign of the possessive: a *girls'* school, the *churches'* steeples, the *Joneses'* claim to the inheritance.

-'s² Contraction of: 1 Is: *He's* here. 2 Has: *She's* left. 3 Us: *Let's* go.

Saa·di (sä'dē), **Muslih-ud-Din,** 1184?–1291?, Persian poet. Also spelled *Sadi.*

Saa·le (zä'lə) 1 A river in central East Germany, flowing 265 miles north to the Elbe. Also **Sax·o·ni·an Saale** (sak·sō'nē·ən). 2 A river in northern Bavaria, West Germany, flowing 84 miles west, south and SW from the East Ger-

man border to the Main. Also **Fran·co·ni·an Saale** (frang·kō'nē·ən).

Saa·mi (sä'mē) *n.* Lapp.

Saar (zär) A river in NE France and western Germany, flowing 152 miles north from the Vosges Mountains to the Moselle.

Saar (zär), **The** A state and industrial region in the Saar valley, SW West Germany; 989 square miles; capital, Saarbrücken. French *Sarre,* German *Saar-land* (zär'länt). Also **Saar Basin, Saar Territory.**

Saar·brück·en (zär'brük·ən) The capital of The Saar.

Saa·re (sä're) The largest Estonian island in the Baltic, at the mouth of the Gulf of Riga; 1,046 square miles: Swedish *Ösel*: also *Sarema.* Also **Saa·re·maa** (sä're·mä). *Russian* **E·zel** (ā'zel).

Saa·ri·nen (sä'ri·nen), **Eero,** born 1910, U.S. architect. —**Eliel,** 1873–1950, U.S. architect born in Finland; father of the preceding.

Saa·ve·dra La·mas (sä·vä'thrä lä'mäs), **Carlos,** 1878–1959, Argentine lawyer and statesman.

sab (sab) *n., v.t. & v.i. Scot.* Sob.

sa·ba (sä·bä') *n.* A fine Philippine fabric made from fibers of a plant resembling the banana. [< Tagalog]

Sa·ba (sä'bä) 1 The Arab name for SHEBA. 2 An island in the eastern group of the Netherlands West Indies; 5 square miles.

sab·a·dil·la (sab'ə·dil'ə) *n.* 1 The acrid seeds of a Mexican and Central American bulbous plant (*Schoenocaulon officinale*), used as a source of veratrine, and formerly as an anthelmintic. 2 The plant. Also spelled *cebadilla, cevadilla.* [< Sp. *cebadilla,* dim. of *cebada* barley]

Sa·bah (sä'bä) A state of Malaysia in northern Borneo; 29,387 square miles; capital, Jesselton. Formerly *North Borneo.*

Sa·ba·ism (sä'bə·iz'əm) *n.* Star worship. [< Hebrew *tsābhā* (heavenly) host, army + -ISM] —**Sa'ba·ist** *n.*

Sab·a·oth (sab'ē·oth, sə·bā'ōth) *n. pl.* Armies; hosts: chiefly in the phrase *the Lord of Sabaoth. Rom.* ix 29, *James* v 4. [< LL < Gk. *Sabaōth* < Hebrew *tsebāōth,* pl. of *tsābhā* host, army]

Sa·bar·ma·ti (sä'bər·mu'tē) A river in southern Rajasthan and northern Bombay, India, flowing 250 miles south to the Gulf of Cambay.

Sa·ba·tier (sȧ·bȧ·tyā'), **Paul,** 1854–1941, French chemist.

sab·bat (sab'ət) *n.* The witches' Sabbath. Also **Sab'bat.** [< OF. See SABBATH.]

sab·ba·tar·i·an (sab'ə·târ'ē·ən) *adj.* Pertaining to the Sabbath or its strict observance. —*n.* 1 A Christian who observes Sunday with strict propriety. 2 A Christian who observes the seventh day as the Sabbath: opposed to *dominical.* [< L *sabbatarius* < *sabbatum* SABBATH] —**Sab'ba·tar'i·an·ism** *n.*

Sab·bath (sab'əth) *n.* 1 The seventh day of the week, appointed in the decalog as a day of rest to be observed by the Jews; now, Saturday. 2 The first day of the week as observed by Christians; Sunday. 3 The institution or observance of a day or time of rest. 4 The sabbatical year of the Jews. *Lev.* xxv 4. [Fusion of OE *sabat* and OF *sabbat, sabat,* both < L *sabbatum* < Gk. *sabbaton* < Hebrew *shabbāth* < *shābath* rest] —**Sab·bat'ic** or **·i·cal** *adj.* —**Sab·bat'i·cal·ly** *adv.*
— *Synonym:* Sunday. *Sabbath* carries a suggestion of rest not in *Sunday,* the first day of the week. See FIRST DAY.

Sabbath school A Sunday school.
sab·bat·i·cal (sə·bat'i·kəl) *adj.* Of the nature of the Sabbath as a day of rest; offering rest at regular intervals. Also **sab·bat'ic.** — *n.* A sabbatical year. [< *sabbatic* < F *sabbatique* < Gk. *sabbatikos* < *sabbaton* SABBATH]
sabbatical year 1 In the ancient Jewish economy, every seventh year, in which the people were required to refrain from tillage. 2 A year's vacation awarded to teachers in some American educational institutions every seven years.
sa·be (sä'bē) *SW U.S. v.i.* To understand; know. — *n.* Understanding; knowledge. [< Sp. *saber* know]
Sa·be·an (sə·bē'ən) *adj.* Of or pertaining to ancient Sheba, its people, or their language. — *n.* 1 One of an ancient people of the kingdom of Sheba in SW Arabia in the first millennium B.C.: noted for their commerce and their wealth. 2 The Southwest Semitic language of these people. Also **Sa·bae'an.** [< L *Sabaeus* < Gk. *Sabaios* < *Saba* Sheba < Arabic *Saba'* < Hebrew *Shebā*]
Sa·bel·li·an (sə·bel'ē·ən) *n.* A branch of the Italic subfamily of Indo-European languages, including the ancient Aequian, Marsian, Sabine, and Volscian. [< L *Sabellus* a Sabine]
sa·ber (sä'bər) *n.* A heavy one-edged cavalry sword, with a thick-backed blade, often curved. — *v.t.* **·bered** or **·bred, ·ber·ing** or **·bring** To strike, wound, kill, or arm with a saber. Also spelled **sabre.** [< F *sabre, sable* < MHG *sabel,* prob. < Slavic]
sa·ber-toothed (sä'bər·tōōtht') *adj.* Having very long, curved, upper canine teeth, likened to sabers.
saber-toothed tiger *Paleontol.* A large, ferocious, extinct carnivore (subfamily *Machaerodontinae*), characterized by very large, trenchant, upper canine teeth; especially, *Smilodon californicus,* common in the western hemisphere until its extinction in the Pleistocene.

SABER-TOOTHED TIGER
(About 3 feet high at the shoulders)

Sa·bi (sä'bē) A river in SE Africa, flowing 400 miles SE to the Indian Ocean: Portuguese *Save.*
Sa·bi·an (sä'bē·ən) *n.* One of an ancient religious sect dwelling in Mesopotamia and described in the Koran as monotheistic: identified by some with the Mandeans. — *adj.* Pertaining to the Sabians or to their religious worship. [< Arabic *sabi'ah* < Aramaic *tsebha'* immerse, baptize] — **Sa'bi·an·ism** *n.*
sab·i·cu (sab'ə·kōō') *n.* Horseflesh (def. 3).
sa·bin (sä'bin) *n. Physics* A unit of sound absorption, equivalent to one square foot of a completely absorbing substance. [after W. C. W. *Sabine,* 1868–1919, U. S. physicist]
sab·ine (sab'in) See SAVIN.
Sa·bine (sä'bīn) *n.* 1 One of an ancient central Italian people, conquered and absorbed by Rome in 290 B.C., whose daughters the early Romans married by force. 2 The language of these people, belonging to the Sabellian branch of the Italic languages. — *adj.* Of or pertaining to the Sabines. [< L *Sabinus*]
Sa·bine River (sə·bēn') A river in eastern Texas and western Louisiana, flowing 578 miles SE, passing through **Sabine Lake** (17 miles long) and entering the Gulf of Mexico through **Sabine Pass** (7 miles long).
Sa·bir (sa·bēr') *n.* The lingua franca of the Mediterranean ports, largely a mixture of French, Italian, and Spanish. [< *Se ti sabir,* a jargon phrase in Molière's *Bourgeois Gentilhomme* < Provençal *sabir* knowledge, science]
sa·ble (sä'bəl) *n.* 1 A carnivore (*Martes zibellina*), of northern Asia and Europe, related to the marten. ◆ Collateral adjective: *zibeline.* 2 The dressed fur of a sable, specifically, of the Asian sable. 3 *pl.* Garments made wholly or partly of this fur. 4 The color black; hence, mourning or a mourning garment. 5 *Her.* Black: represented, when uncolored, by a net-

work of lines crossing each other at right angles. — **Alaska sable** A trade name for natural or dyed skunk. — *adj.* 1 Black, especially as the color of mourning. 2 Made of or having the color of sable fur; dark-brown. See synonyms under DARK. [< OF *sable, saible* < Med. L *sabelum* < Slavic]
Sable, Cape 1 The southernmost point of the United States, at the SW tip of Florida. 2 The southernmost extremity of Nova Scotia, on an islet just south of **Cape Sable Island** (7 miles long, 3 miles wide).
sable antelope A large, black, African antelope (*Hippotragus niger*) having annular curved horns.
sa·ble-fish (sä'bəl·fish') *n. pl.* **·fish** or **·fish·es** The coalfish (def. 2).
Sable Island An island SW of Nova Scotia; 30 miles by 2 miles; opposite Cape Sable, Nova Scotia.
sa·bot (sab'ō, *Fr.* så·bō') *n.* 1 A wooden shoe, as of a French peasant. 2 A shoe having a wooden sole but flexible shank. See GETA. 3 A disk formerly attached to a projectile to cause it to maintain its position in the bore of a firearm or to take the rifling of the gun. [< F < OF *sabot,* alter. of *savate* an old shoe, ult. < Arabic *sabbāt* a sandal; infl. in form by *bot* a boot]
sab·o·tage (sab'ə·täzh, *Fr.* så·bô·tàzh') *n.* An act of malicious damage; deliberately poor workmanship intended to cause damage, obstruction of plans, aims, etc., as in secret resistance to an enemy: sometimes resorted to by workmen to secure compliance with demands. — *v.t. & v.i.* **·taged, ·tag·ing** To engage in, damage, or destroy by sabotage. [< F < *saboter* work badly, damage < *sabot* a sabot; with ref. to damage done to machinery with sabots]
sab·o·teur (sab'ə·tûr', *Fr.* så·bô·tœr') *n.* One who engages in sabotage. [< F]
sa·bra (sä'brə) *n.* Often *cap.* An Israeli born in Israel. [< Heb.]
sa·bre (sä'bər) See SABER.
sa·bre·tache (sä'bər·tash, sab'ər-) *n.* A leather pocket hung from the sword belt of a mounted man. [< F < G *säbeltasche* < *säbel* a saber + *tasche* a pocket]
sab·u·lous (sab'yə·ləs) *adj.* Gritty, like sand. Also **sab'u·lose** (-lōs). [< L *sabulosus* < *sabulum* sand] — **sab·u·los'i·ty** (-los'ə·tē) *n.*
sac (sak) *n. Biol.* A membranous pouch; a cavity or receptacle: the ink *sac* of a squid. [< F < L *saccus.* Doublet of SACK.]
Sac (sak, sôk) See SAUK.
sac·a·ton (sak'ə·tōn') *n.* A coarse perennial grass (*Sporobolus wrighti*) of the United States and Mexico, yielding hay. [< Sp. *zacatón* < *zacate, sacate* < Nahuatl *çacatl* a kind of grass]
sac·cate (sak'it, -āt) *adj.* 1 Sac-shaped. 2 Having a sac, bag, or pouch. [< Med. L *saccatus* < L *saccus* a sack]
sac·cha·rate (sak'ə·rāt) *n. Chem.* 1 A salt of saccharic acid. 2 A compound of a sugar with a metallic oxide.
sac·char·ic (sə·kar'ik) *adj. Chem.* 1 Of, pertaining to, or derived from sugar or a sweetish substance. 2 Designating a dibasic acid, $C_6H_{10}O_8$, obtained by the oxidation of glucose and other sugars.
sac·cha·ride (sak'ə·rid, -rid) *n. Chem.* Any of a class of carbohydrates containing sugar, as a *monosaccharide, polysaccharide,* etc.
sac·cha·ri·fy (sə·kar'ə·fi, sak'ər·ə·fi) *v.t.* **·fied, ·fy·ing** To convert, as starches, into sugar; impregnate with sugar. [< SACCHAR(O)- + (I)FY] — **sac·char'i·fi·ca'tion** *n.*
sac·cha·rim·e·ter (sak'ə·rim'ə·tər) *n.* A polariscope for detecting the strength or concentration of sugar in a solution. [< F *saccharimètre* < Gk. *sakchari* sugar + *metron* measure] — **sac'cha·rim'e·try** *n.*
sac·cha·rin (sak'ər·in) *n. Chem.* A white crystalline compound, $C_7H_5O_3NS$, derived from toluene. It is 300 to 500 times sweeter than cane sugar, and is used as a sweetening agent, especially by diabetics. Also spelled *saccharine.* [< Med. L *saccharum* sugar (< L *saccharon* < Gk. *sakchari, sakcharon,* ult. < Skt. *sharkarā* grit, gravel, sugar) + -IN]
sac·cha·rine (sak'ər·in, -ə·rin) *adj.* 1 Of, pertaining to, or of the nature of sugar; sweet. 2 Ingratiatingly or cloyingly sweet. — *n.* Sac-

charin. [< SACCHAR(O)- + -INE¹] — **sac'cha·rine·ly** *adv.* — **sac'cha·rin'i·ty** *n.*
sac·cha·rize (sak'ə·riz) *v.t.* **·rized, ·riz·ing** *Chem.* To convert into sugar; ferment. — **sac'cha·ri·za'tion** *n.*
saccharo- *combining form* Sugar; of or pertaining to sugar: *saccharometer.* Also, before vowels, **sacchar-.** [< Gk. *sakcharon* sugar]
sac·cha·roid (sak'ə·roid) *adj.* 1 Resembling sugar. 2 *Geol.* Having crystalline granular structure: *saccharoid* marble. Also **sac'cha·roi'dal** (-roid'l).
sac·cha·rom·e·ter (sak'ə·rom'ə·tər) *n.* A hydrometer for determining the concentration of sugar in saccharine solutions.
sac·cha·ro·my·ce·tous (sak'ə·rō·mi·sē'təs, -mi'sə-) *adj.* Of or pertaining to a genus (*Saccharomyces*) of fungi, the yeast family, commonly unicellular, but sometimes developing a septate mycelium. Several produce endogenous spores, while most of them cause alchoholic fermentation with evolution of carbon dioxide. [< NL < Gk. *sakcharon* sugar + *mykēs, -ētos* a mushroom, fungus]
sac·cha·rose (sak'ə·rōs) *adj.* Sucrose.
Sac·co (sak'ō, *Ital.* säk'kō), **Nicola,** 1891–1927, philosophical anarchist in the United States who with *Bartolomeo Vanzetti* was convicted of murder in connection with a payroll robbery, and executed. Their trial aroused international protest because it was thought to have been influenced by political considerations.
sac·cu·late (sak'yə·lāt) *adj.* Formed into a series of saclike expansions; dilated and constricted alternately. Also **sac'cu·lat'ed.**
sac·cule (sak'yōōl) *n.* 1 A little sac. 2 *Anat.* Part of the membranous labyrinth of the ear. [< L *sacculus* a sacculus]
sac·cu·lus (sak'yə·ləs) *n. pl.* **·li** (-lī) A small sac or pouch; a saccule. [< L, dim. of *saccus* a sack]
sac·er·do·tal (sas'ər·dōt'l) *adj.* 1 Pertaining to a priest or priesthood; priestly. 2 Believing in the divine authority of the priesthood. [< OF < L *sacerdotalis* < *sacerdos, -dotis* a priest < *sacer* holy + *do-,* stem of *dare* give] — **sac'er·do'tal·ly** *adv.*
sac·er·do·tal·ism (sas'ər·dōt'l·iz'əm) *n.* 1 The character and methods of the priesthood; priestcraft. 2 Zeal for priestly things.
sa·chem (sä'chəm) *n.* 1 A North American Indian hereditary chief. 2 Any chief; the head of a political party; specifically, one of the leaders of the Tammany Society in New York. See synonyms under CHIEF. [< Algonquian (Narraganset). Akin to SAGAMORE.]
sa·chet (sa·shā', *esp. Brit.* sash'ā) *n.* A small ornamental bag for perfumed powder. [< OF, dim. of *sac* < L *saccus* a sack]
Sachs (zäks), **Hans,** 1494–1576, German shoemaker, poet, and playwright; also, the hero of Wagner's *Die Meistersinger.*
Sach·sen (zäkh'sən) The German name for SAXONY.
sack¹ (sak) *n.* 1 A bag for holding bulky articles. 2 A measure or weight of varying amount. 3 A loosely hanging dress without a waistline, often worn without a belt: also spelled *sacque:* also **sack dress.** 4 *Slang* Dismissal: especially in the phrases **to get the sack, to give (someone) the sack.** 5 In baseball slang, a base. 6 *Slang* A bed; mattress. — **to be left holding the sack** *Slang* To be left to take the consequences of a bad situation. — *v.t.* 1 To put into a sack or sacks. 2 To dismiss, as a servant. [OE *sacc* < L *saccus* < Gk. *sakkos* < Hebrew *saq* sackcloth, a grain sack. Doublet of SAC.]
Sack may appear as a combining form in hyphenes or solidemes, or as the first element in two-word phrases, with the meaning of the noun (def. 1):

sack baler	sack-formed
sack baling	sackmaker
sack carrier	sackmaking
sack checker	sackman
sack cleaner	sack mender
sack cutter	sack repairer
sack emptier	sack-shaped
sack examiner	sack sorter

sack² (sak) *v.t.* To plunder or pillage (a town or city) after capturing. — *n.* 1 The pillaging of

a captured town or city. 2 Loot; booty obtained by pillage. [<MF *sac* <Ital. *sacco,* orig. plunder <Med. L *saccare* pillage <L *saccus* a sack; from the use of sacks in carrying off plunder] — **sack'er** *n.*

sack[3] (sak) *n.* Light-colored Spanish dry wine; also, any strong white wine from southern Europe. [Earlier *(wyne)seck* <F *(vin) sec* a dry (wine) <L *siccus* dry]

sack·but (sak'but) *n.* 1 A primitive instrument resembling the trombone. 2 In the Bible, a stringed instrument. [<MF *saquebute,* orig. a hooked lance for horseback fighting <OF *saquer* pull + *bouter* push]

sack·cloth (sak'klôth', -kloth') *n.* 1 A coarse cloth used for making sacks. 2 Coarse cloth or haircloth worn in penance.

sack coat A man's short, loose-fitting coat with no waist seam, for informal wear.

sack·ful (sak'fŏŏl') *n. pl.* **·fuls** Enough to fill a sack.

sack·ing (sak'ing) *n.* A coarse cloth made of hemp or flax and used for sacks; bagging.

sack posset A posset formerly brewed with sack.

sack race A race in which each contestant has a sack tied over both feet.

sack suit A man's suit having a sack coat.

Sack·ville (sak'vil), **Thomas,** 1536–1608, first Earl of Dorset and Baron Buckhurst, English poet and diplomat.

Sack·ville–West (sak'vil·west'), **V(ictoria Mary),** 1892–1962, English novelist and poet.

sacque (sak) See SACK[1] (def. 3).

sa·cral[1] (sā'krəl) *adj.* Of, pertaining to, or situated near the sacrum. —*n.* A sacral vertebra or nerve. [<NL *sacralis* <*sacrum* SACRUM]

sa·cral[2] (sā'krəl) *adj.* Pertaining to sacred rites. [<L *sacrum* a rite, orig. neut. sing. of *sacer* holy]

sac·ra·ment (sak'rə·mənt) *n.* 1 *Eccl.* A rite ordained by Christ or by the church as an outward and visible sign of an inward and spiritual grace: in the Greek Church, also called *mystery.* Traditionally they are seven in number (baptism, the Eucharist, confirmation, matrimony, orders, penance, and unction) in the Greek, Roman Catholic, and some other churches; since the Reformation only two of these (baptism and the Eucharist) are recognized by most Protestant churches. 2 *Often cap. Eccl.* **a** The Eucharist; the Lord's Supper. **b** The consecrated bread and wine of the Eucharist: often with *the.* See BLESSED SACRAMENT. 3 Any sign or token of a solemn covenant or pledge. 4 Any thing considered to have a secret or mysterious meaning. [<OF *sacrement* <LL *sacramentum* a mystery <L, an oath, pledge <*sacrare.* See SACRED.]

Synonyms: ceremony, communion, Eucharist, observance, ordinance, rite, service, solemnity. A *ceremony* is a form expressing reverence, or respect; as, religious *ceremonies,* the *ceremonies* of a coronation or of a wedding. An *observance* has more than a formal obligation, approaching a religious sacredness; a religious *observance* viewed as established by authority is called an *ordinance;* viewed as an established custom, it is a *rite.* Any religious act, especially a public act, viewed as a means of serving God is called a *service. Sacrament* and *ordinance* in the religious sense are often used interchangeably; the *ordinance* derives its sacredness from the authority that ordained it, while the *sacrament* possesses a sacredness due to something in itself, even when viewed simply as a memorial. The Lord's Supper is the Scriptural name for the *observance* commemorating the death of Christ; the word *communion* is once applied to it (1 *Cor.* x 16). *Eucharist,* called *The Sacrament,* describes the Lord's Supper as a thanksgiving *service.*

sac·ra·men·tal (sak'rə·men'təl) *n.* 1 One of certain rites, such as the use of holy water, oil, or salt, employed as adjuncts to sacraments, or regarded as analogous to a sacrament. 2 *pl.* The objects, words, or ceremonies used in administering a sacrament. —*adj.* 1 Of or pertaining to a sacrament; constituting or composing a sacrament; having the influence or efficacy of a sacrament. 2 Consecrated, as by sacred vows: the *sacramental* host of God's elect. —**sac'ra·men'tal·ism** *n.* —**sac'ra·men'tal·ist** *n.* —**sac'ra·men'tal·ly** *adv.*

sac·ra·men·tar·i·an (sak'rə·men·târ'ē·ən) *n.* One who regards the sacraments as channels of divine grace. Also **sac'ra·men'ta·rist, sac'·ra·ment·er.** —*adj.* Of or pertaining to a sacrament or sacraments, or to sacramentarians. —**sac'ra·men·tar'i·an·ism** *n.*

Sac·ra·men·tar·i·an (sak'rə·men·târ'ē·ən) *n.* One who regards the sacraments as simply symbols or signs: the name given to Calvinists and followers of Zwingli.

sac·ra·men·ta·ry (sak'rə·men'tər·ē) *n. pl.* **·ries** Any of several books containing the ritual for mass, the sacraments, and various other rites: now used only as a basis for modern rituals.

Sac·ra·men·to (sak'rə·men'tō) The capital of California, on the **Sacramento River,** the largest river in the State, flowing 382 miles south from Central Valley to Suisun Bay.

sa·crar·i·um (sə·krâr'ē·əm) *n. pl.* **·i·a** (-ē·ə) 1 Any sacred or secluded place or shrine of the ancient Romans where venerated things were deposited. 2 The sanctuary of a church. 3 In the Roman Catholic Church, a piscina. [<L <*sacer* holy, sacred]

sa·cred (sā'krid) *adj.* 1 Set apart or dedicated to religious use; hallowed: a *sacred* edifice. 2 Pertaining or related to deity, religion, or hallowed places or things. 3 Consecrated by love or reverence; dedicated to a person or purpose. 4 Entitled to reverence or respect; not to be profaned; inviolable. 5 *Rare* Set apart for evil; accursed. See synonyms under HOLY. [Orig. pp. of obs. *sacre* consecrate <OF *sacrer* <L *sacrare* <*sacer* holy] —**sa'·cred·ly** *adv.* —**sa'cred·ness** *n.*

Sacred College See COLLEGE OF CARDINALS.

sac·ri·fice (sak'rə·fīs) *n.* 1 The act of making an offering to a deity, in worship or atonement. 2 That which is sacrificed; a victim. 3 A giving up of some cherished or desired object. 4 Loss incurred or suffered without return; destruction, as of life. 5 A reduction of price that leaves little or no profit or involves loss. 6 In baseball, a sacrifice hit. —*v.* **·ficed, ·fic·ing** *v.t.* 1 To make an offering or sacrifice of, as to a god or deity in propitiation, supplication, etc. 2 To give up, yield, permit injury to, or relinquish (something valued) for the sake of something else, as a person, thing, or idea. 3 To sell at a reduced price; part with at a loss. 4 In baseball, to advance (one or more runners) by means of a sacrifice hit. —*v.i.* 5 To make a sacrifice. 6 To make a sacrifice hit. See synonyms under SURRENDER. [<OF <L *sacrificium* <*sacra* rites, orig. neut. pl. of *sacer* holy + *facere* make] —**sac'ri·fic'er** *n.* —**sac'·ri·fic'ing·ly** *adv.*

sacrifice hit In baseball, a hit by which the batter is retired but by which a base runner is advanced another base, the batter not being charged with a time at bat: when batted into the air also called **sacrifice fly.**

sac·ri·fi·cial (sak'rə·fish'əl) *adj.* Pertaining to, performing, or of the nature of a sacrifice. —**sac'ri·fi'cial·ly** *adv.*

sac·ri·lege (sak'rə·lij) *n.* The act of violating or profaning anything sacred, including sacramental vows. [<OF <L *sacrilegium* <*sacrilegus* a temple robber <*sacer* holy + *legere* gather] —**sac'ri·le'gist** (-lē'jist) *n.*

sac·ri·le·gious (sak'rə·lij'əs, -lē'jəs) *adj.* 1 Having committed, or being ready to commit, sacrilege; impious. 2 Of the nature of sacrilege. See synonyms under PROFANE. —**sac'ri·le'gious·ly** *adv.* —**sac'ri·le'gious·ness** *n.*

sa·cring bell (sā'kring) A small bell rung at the elevation during mass; the tolling of the church bell at this time; the Sanctus bell. [<*sacring,* ppr. of obs. *sacre* consecrate + BELL]

sa·crist (sā'krist) *n.* 1 A sacristan. 2 A person who takes charge of choir books and copy music; also, a sexton. [<OF *sacrist* <L *sacrista* <*sacra* holy (objects), neut. pl. of *sacer*]

sac·ris·tan (sak'ris·tən) *n.* An officer having charge of the sacristy of a church or religious house and its contents, and of the proper arrangement of all objects needed for divine service. The sacristan of a cathedral is commonly in orders. Compare SEXTON. [<Med. L *sacristanus* <L *sacrista.* Doublet of SEXTON.]

sac·ris·ty (sak'ris·tē) *n. pl.* **·ties** A room in a religious house for the sacred vessels and vestments; a vestry. [<F *sacristie* <Med. L *sacristia* <L *sacrista* a sacrist]

sacro– *combining form Med.* Near, or related to the sacrum: *sacrosciatic.* [<L *(os) sacrum* the sacral (bone)]

sac·ro·il·i·ac (sak'rō·il'ē·ak) *adj. Anat.* Pertaining to the sacrum and the ilium and to the joints or ligaments connecting them. [<SACRO- + ILIAC]

sac·ro·sanct (sak'rō·sangkt) *adj.* Peculiarly and exceedingly sacred; inviolable; preeminent for sanctity: sometimes used ironically. [<L *sacrosanctus* <*sacro,* ablative of *sacrum* a rite (<*sacer* holy) + *sanctus,* pp. of *sancire* make holy, inviolable] —**sac'ro·sanc'ti·ty** *n.*

sa·cro·sci·at·ic (sā'krō·sī·at'ik) *adj. Anat.* Of or pertaining to the sacrum and the ischium: the *sacrosciatic* ligaments, connecting the sacrum and the hip bone.

sa·crum (sā'krəm) *n. pl.* **·cra** (-krə) *Anat.* A composite bone formed by the union of the five vertebrae between the lumbar and caudal regions, constituting the dorsal part of the pelvis. [<NL <L *(os) sacrum* sacred (bone); from its being offered in sacrifices]

Sa·cy (sà·sē'), **Baron de,** 1758–1838, Antoine Isaac Silvestre, French Oriental scholar.

sad (sad) *adj.* **sad·der, sad·dest** 1 Sorrowful or depressed in spirits; expressing, or having the external appearance of grief or sorrow; unhappy; mournful; gloomy. 2 Causing sorrow or pity; distressing; unfortunate. 3 *Dial.* Heavy; soggy: said of food. 4 *Colloq.* Vexatious, mischievous, or bad: often humorously or as a mild intensive: That boy is a *sad* tease. 5 Dark-hued; somber. [OE *sæd,* orig. sated] —**sad'ly** *adv.* —**sad'ness** *n.*

Synonyms: afflicted, dejected, depressed, desolate, despondent, disconsolate, dismal, distressed, doleful, downcast, dreary, dull, gloomy, grave, heavy, lugubrious, melancholy, miserable, mournful, sober, somber, sorrowful, sorry, unhappy, woebegone, woeful. *Sad, melancholy, unhappy,* and many similar words may be used either of the personal experience of grief, sorrow, mental depression, etc., or of that which causes grief or pain; a person is *sad* on account of a *sad* event. See synonyms under BAD. *Antonyms:* see synonyms for HAPPY.

sad·den (sad'n) *v.t.* & *v.i.* To make or become sad or unhappy.

sad·dle (sad'l) *n.* 1 A seat or pad for a rider, as on the back of a horse or on a bicycle. 2 A padded cushion for a horse's back, as part of a harness or to support a pack, etc. For illustration see HARNESS. 3 The two hindquarters of a carcass, as of mutton, veal, or venison; also, the undivided loins of such a carcass. 4 Some part like or likened to a saddle, as the lower part of the back of a fowl. See illustration under FOWL. 5 *Geog.* A depression across the summit of a ridge; a pass. 6 *Meteorol.* A low-pressure area between two anticyclones; a col. 7 Something resembling a saddle in form or position, as a bearing for a car axle. —**in the saddle** In control. —*v.* **·dled, ·dling** *v.t.* 1 To put a saddle on: to *saddle* a horse. 2 To load, as with a burden. 3 To place as a burden or responsibility: with *upon.* —*v.i.* 4 To get into a saddle. [OE *sadol*]

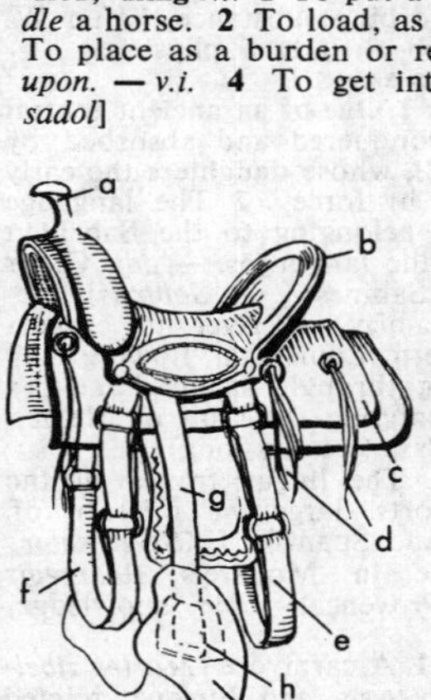

NOMENCLATURE—AMERICAN STOCK SADDLE
a. Pommel or horn.
b. Cantle.
c. Saddle.
d. Saddle strings.
e. Back cinch.
f. Front cinch.
g. Stirrup strap or leather.
h. Stirrup.
i. Tapadera or stirrup hood.

saddle bags A pair of pouches connected by a strap or band and slung over an animal's back or attached to a saddle.

saddle band A remuda.

sad·dle·bow (sad'l·bō') *n.* The arched front upper part of a saddletree.

sad·dle·cloth (sad'l·klôth', -kloth') *n.* A cloth

under and attached to a saddle, or one under the saddle of a harness.
saddle horse A horse used with or trained for the saddle.
sad·dler (sad′lər) *n.* **1** A maker of saddles, harness, etc. **2** A saddle horse.
saddle roof A roof consisting of two gables and one ridge.
sad·dler·y (sad′lər·ē) *n. pl.* **·dler·ies 1** Saddles, harness, and fittings, collectively. **2** A saddler's shop. **3** The business of a saddler.
saddle shoe A white sport shoe with a dark band of leather across the instep.
saddle soap A softening and preserving soap for leather, containing pure white soap, usually Castile, and neat's-foot oil.
sad·dle·tree (sad′l·trē′) *n.* **1** The frame of a saddle. **2** The tulip tree: so called from its saddle-shaped leaf.
Sad·du·cee (saj′ŏŏ·sē, sad′yŏŏ·sē) *n.* A member of a strict Jewish school that arose in the second century B.C., and later became skeptical and traditionalistic, adhering only to the Mosaic law. [<LL *Sadducaeus* <Gk. *Saddoukaios* <Hebrew *tsaddūqī,* appar. after *Tsaddūq* Zadok (*Ezek.* xl 46)] **—Sad′du·ce′an, Sad′du·cae′an** *adj.* **—Sad′du·cee′ism** *n.*
sa·de (sä·dā′) *n.* The eighteenth Hebrew letter: also spelled *tsade.* Also **sa·dhe′.** See ALPHABET.
Sade (säd), **Comte Donatien de,** 1740–1814, French writer and libertine: known as *Marquis de Sade.*
Sa·di (sä·dē′) See SAADI.
sad·i·ron (sad′ī′ərn) *n.* A flat iron for smoothing clothes: distinguished from a *box-iron.* [<SAD, in obs. sense "heavy" + IRON]
sad·ism (sā′diz·əm, sad′iz·əm) *n. Psychiatry* **1** Sexual gratification obtained through the infliction of pain upon others. **2** A morbid delight in being cruel. [after Comte Donatien de *Sade;* with reference to the various sexual aberrations described in his writings] **—sad·ist** (sā′dist, sad′ist) *n. & adj.* **—sa·dis·tic** (sə·dis′tik, sā-) *adj.* **—sa·dis′ti·cal·ly** *adv.*
sa·do·mas·och·ism (sā′dō·mas′ə·kiz·əm, ·maz′·) *n. Psychiatry.* A condition in which sadism and masochism are combined in one person. **—sa′do·mas′o·chist** *n.* **—sa′do·mas′o·chis′tic** *adj.*
Sa·do·va (sä′dô·vä) A town in southern Bohemia, Czechoslovakia; scene of the culminating defeat of the Austrians by Prussian forces, 1866. *German* **Sa′do·wa.**
sa·fa·ri (sə·fä′rē) *n.* **1** An expedition or journey, often on foot, as for hunting. **2** The caravan and animals employed in this; also, a day's march: also spelled *suffari.* [<Swahili <Arabic *safara* travel]
safe (sāf) *adj.* **1** Free or freed from danger or evil. **2** Having escaped injury or damage; unharmed. **3** Not hazardous; not involving risk or loss; also, conferring safety; of persons, trusty; prudent. **4** Not likely to disappoint; free from doubt or error: It is *safe* to promise. **5** Not likely to cause or do harm or injury. **6** In politics, adhering to party principles; to be depended on to support certain interests: said of a candidate; also, sure to vote for a certain candidate: said of a district. **7** In baseball, having reached base without being retired: He was ruled *safe* at second. See synonyms under SECURE. —*n.* **1** A strong iron-and-steel receptacle, usually fireproof, for protecting valuables, as money or jewels. **2** Any place of safe storage, as a room, tank, refrigerator, or box, for preserving perishable articles, as meat or fish. [<OF *sauf* <L *salvus* whole, healthy] **—safe′ly** *adv.* **—safe′ness** *n.*
safe-blow·ing (sāf′blō′ing) *n.* The act of using explosives to open a safe to be robbed. **—safe′-blow′er** *n.*
safe-break·er (sāf′brā′kər) *n.* A safe-cracker.
safe-con·duct (sāf′kon′dukt) *n. Law* **1** An official document assuring protection on a journey or voyage, as in time of war; a passport. **2** The act of conducting in safety. —*v.t.* (sāf′kən·dukt′) **1** To convoy in safety. **2** To provide with a safe-conduct.
safe-crack·er (sāf′krak′ər) *n.* One who breaks into safes to rob them.
safe-cracking (sāf′krak′ing) *n.* The breaking open of safes for robbery.
safe deposit A room, vault, or other fireproof storage place for valuables.
safe-de·pos·it box (sāf′di·poz′it) A box, safe, drawer, or other fireproof receptacle for valuable jewelry, papers, etc., generally in a bank.
safe·guard (sāf′gärd′) *n.* **1** One who or that which guards or keeps in safety, as an escort, guard, or safe-conduct. **2** A mechanical device designed to prevent accident or injury. See synonyms under DEFENSE. —*v.t.* To defend; protect; guard.
safe-hand (sāf′hand′) *n.* **1** A safe method of transmitting official secret papers. **2** A trustworthy courier.
safe hit In baseball, a fair hit by which the batter reaches first base.
safe house A house or apartment used by a spy where he or she may presume to be safe from capture or discovery.
safe·keep·ing (sāf′kē′ping) *n.* The act or state of keeping or being kept in safety; protection.
safe·light (sāf′līt′) *n.* A bulb for darkroom use providing light that will not adversely affect photosensitive film or paper.
safe·ty (sāf′tē) *n. pl.* **·ties 1** The state or condition of freedom from danger or risk. **2** Freedom from injury. **3** A device or catch designed as a safeguard, as in a firearm. **4** In football, the act or play of touching the ball to the ground behind the player's own goal line when the impetus which sent the ball over the goal line was given to it by one of his own side: also **safe′ty-touch′down′** (-tuch′doun′) **5** In baseball, a safe hit.
safety belt 1 An extensible strap encircling the user and a permanently fixed object so that the user may move freely but be safe from falling or slipping: used by linemen, window cleaners, etc. **2** *Aeron.* A strap fixed to the seat of an aircraft by which the passenger is secured against sudden shocks or turning movements. **3** A life belt.
safety bicycle A bicycle having equal or nearly equal wheels, operated by pedal cranks communicating with the driving wheel.
safety glass See under GLASS.
Safety Islands A group of three islands off the coast of French Guiana, including Devil's Island. *French* **Îles du Sa·lut** (ēl dü sȧ·lü′).
safety lamp 1 A miner's lamp having the flame surrounded by fine wire gauze, which prevents the ignition of explosive gases: called a *davy* from its inventor, Sir Humphry Davy. **2** A specially protected incandescent electric lamp.
safety lever *Mech.* **1** A device for controlling the movement of machine parts. **2** A similar contrivance for preventing the accidental discharge of a grenade, automatic pistol, etc.: also **safety catch.**
safety match A match that will ignite only when struck upon a chemically prepared surface.
safety pin 1 A pin whose point springs into place within a protecting sheath. **2** A pin which prevents the premature detonation of a hand grenade.
safety razor See under RAZOR.
safety valve 1 *Mech.* A valve in a steam boiler, etc., for automatically relieving excessive pressure. **2** Any outlet for pent-up energy or emotion.
saf·flow·er (saf′lou′ər) *n.* **1** A thistlelike herb *(Carthamus tinctorius)* about 2 feet high, with spiny heads of orange-red flowers. **2** The dried flower heads of this plant pressed into small cakes for export: also **safflower cake. 3** The reddish dyestuff obtained from the dried flowers. [<Du. *saffloer* <OF *saffleur, safour* <Ital. *saffiore;* infl. in form by SAFFRON and FLOWER]
saf·fron (saf′rən) *n.* **1** An autumn-flowering species of crocus *(Crocus sativus).* **2** The dried orange-colored stigmas of this plant used for coloring confectionery, varnishes, etc., and in parts of the Old World as a flavoring and coloring ingredient in cookery. **3** A deep yellow orange: also **saffron yellow.** —*adj.* Of the orange color of saffron. [<OF *safran* <Sp. *azafran* <Arabic *az-za′farān* the saffron]
saf·ra·nine (saf′rə·nēn, -nin) *n. Chem.* **1** Any of a class of basic compounds considered as symmetrical diamine derivatives of the azo group bases. Their salts form important dyes. **2** Any of various mixtures of safranine salts used in dyeing. See SAFFRON. Also **saf′ra·nin** (-nin). [<F *safran* SAFFRON + -INE[2]]
saf·role (saf′rōl) *n.* A colorless, poisonous, and carcinogenic oil, $C_{10}H_{10}O_2$, occurring in sassafras oil and camphor and once used in perfumes, medicines, etc. [<F *safran* SAFFRON + -OLE[1]]
saft (saft, säft) *adj. Scot.* **1** Soft. **2** Wet: said of the weather.
sag (sag) *v.* **sagged, sag·ging** *v.i.* **1** To bend or sink downward from weight or pressure, especially in the middle. **2** To hang unevenly. **3** To lose firmness or determination; weaken, as from exhaustion, age, etc. **4** To decline, as in price or value. **5** *Naut.* To drift. —*v.t.* **6** To cause to sag. —*n.* **1** A sagging, or its extent or degree; a sagging place or part, as of a roof. **2** *Naut.* A sidewise drift, as of a vessel. **3** A depressed or sunken place in flat land; a marsh. [ME *saggen,* ? <MDU. *zakken* subside, ? <dial. ON (nautical) *sakka* plummet]
sa·ga (sä′gə) *n.* **1** A medieval Scandinavian (specifically, Icelandic) prose narrative of conventionalized form dealing with legendary or historical exploits, usually of a single hero or a single family. **2** A story, sometimes poetic, having the saga form or manner, often chronicling the history of a family, as Galsworthy's *Forsyte Saga.* [<ON, history, narrative]
sa·ga·cious (sə·gā′shəs) *adj.* **1** Ready and apt to apprehend and to decide on a course. **2** Characterized by discernment, shrewdness, and wisdom. **3** Quick of scent, as a hound. [<L *sagax, sagacis* wise, foreseeing] **—sa·ga′cious·ly** *adv.* **—sa·ga′cious·ness** *n.*
Synonyms: able, acute, apt, clear-sighted, discerning, intelligent, judicious, keen, keen-sighted, keen-witted, perspicacious, quick-witted, rational, sage, sensible, sharp, sharp-witted, shrewd, wise. *Sagacious* refers to a power of tracing the hidden or recondite by slight indications, as by instinct or intuition; with reference to inferior animals it is often applied to special keenness of sense-perception as of a hound in following a trail. In human affairs *sagacious* refers to a power of ready, far-reaching, an accurate inference from observed facts, perhaps in themselves very slight, that seems like a special sense; or to a similar readiness to foresee the results of any action, a kind of prophetic common sense, especially upon human motives or conduct. *Sagacious* is a broader word than *shrewd,* and not capable of the invidious sense which the latter often bears; on the other hand, *sagacious* is less lofty than *wise* in its full sense, and more limited to practical matters. See ACUTE, ASTUTE, KNOWING, POLITIC, WISE[1]. *Antonyms*: absurd, dull, foolish, futile, ignorant, irrational, obtuse, senseless, silly, simple, sottish, stupid, unintelligent.
sa·gac·i·ty (sə·gas′ə·tē) *n.* The quality of being sagacious; discernment and judgment; shrewdness. See synonyms under ACUMEN, WISDOM. [<MF *sagacité* <L *sagax* sagacious]
sa·ga·man (sä′gə·man′, -mən) *n.* The author, singer, or narrator of a saga; a Scandinavian poet or bard. [Trans. of ON *sögumadhr* <*sögu,* genitive of *saga* a sage + *madhr* a man]
Sa·ga·mi Sea (sä·gä·mē) An inlet of the Philippine Sea in central Honshu island, Japan.
sag·a·more (sag′ə·môr, -mōr) *n.* A tribal or lesser chief among the Algonquian Indians of North America, usually inferior to *sachem.* [<Algonquian (Penobscot) *sagamo.* Akin to SACHEM.]
sage[1] (sāj) *n.* A venerable man of recognized experience, prudence, and foresight; a profoundly wise counselor or philosopher. —*adj.* **1** Characterized by or proceeding from calm, far-seeing wisdom and prudence. **2** Befitting a sage; profound; learned; also, grave; serious; shrewd. See synonyms under SAGACIOUS, WISE[1]. [<OF *saige, savie,* ult. <L *sapiens, -entis* wise, ppr. of *sapere* be wise. Doublet of SAPIENT.] **—sage′ly** *adv.* **—sage′ness** *n.*
sage[2] (sāj) *n.* **1** A plant of the mint family (genus *Salvia*), especially the common garden sage *(S. officinalis),* a stiff, shrubby perennial with gray-green leaves and purple, blue, or white flowers: used for flavoring meats, etc. **2** A light, greenish-gray color, like the color of sage leaves. **3** Any other plant of the genus *Salvia,* as the scarlet sage *(S. splendens).* **4** The Jerusalem sage (genus *Phlomis*), also of the mint family. **5** The sagebrush. [<OF

sauge < L *salvia,* ? < *salvus* safe; with ref. to its reputed healing powers]

Sage (sāj), **Russell,** 1816–1906, U.S. financier and philanthropist.

sage·brush (sāj′brush′) *n.* An aromatic, bitter, typically perennial herb or small shrub (genus *Artemisia*) of the composite family, widely distributed on the alkali plains of the western United States; especially, *A. tridentata,* the State flower of Nevada. The Old World species are called *wormwood.*

Sagebrush State Nickname of NEVADA.

sage cock See COCK OF THE PLAINS.

sage hen 1 The female of the sage cock. See GROUSE. **2** *Usually cap.* A native of Nevada: a nickname.

sage sparrow A small, pale–gray, fringilline bird of the western United States (*Amphispiza nevadensis*).

sag·gar (sag′ər) *n.* **1** A vessel of baked fireproof clay in which are fired delicate pieces of pottery that would be injured by direct exposure to the heat. **2** Clay used for making saggars. Also spelled *seggar.* Also **sag′gard** (-ərd). —*v.t.* To place or treat in a saggar, as pottery. Also **sag′ger.** [Contraction of SAFEGUARD]

Sa·ghal·ien (sə·gäl′yən) A former spelling of SAKHALIN.

Sag·i·naw (sag′ə·nô) A city in east central Michigan, a port of entry on the **Saginaw River,** which flows about 22 miles into Saginaw Bay just below Bay City.

Saginaw Bay A SW arm of Lake Huron, extending 60 miles into eastern Michigan.

Sa·git·ta (sə·jit′ə) *Astron.* A northern constellation between Aquila and Cygnus; the Arrow. See CONSTELLATION. [< L, lit., an arrow]

sag·it·tal (saj′ə·təl) *adj.* **1** Pertaining to or resembling an arrow or arrowhead. **2** *Anat.* **a** Straight: the *sagittal* suture between the two parietal bones of the skull. **b** Of or pertaining to the longitudinal plane dividing an animal into right and left halves. [< L *sagitta* an arrow] —**sag′it·tal·ly** *adv.*

Sag·it·ta·ri·us (saj′ə·târ′ē·əs) **1** A zodiacal constellation, pictured as a centaur shooting an arrow; the Archer. See CONSTELLATION. **2** The ninth sign of the zodiac, with the symbol ♐. [< L, lit., an archer < *sagitta* an arrow]

sag·it·tate (saj′ə·tāt) *adj. Bot.* Shaped like an arrowhead, as certain leaves. Also **sag′it·tat·ed, sa·git·ti·form** (sə·jit′ə·fôrm). [< L *sagitta* an arrow]

sa·go (sā′gō) *n.* **1** Any of several varieties of East Indian palm (genus *Metroxylon*). **2** The dried, powdered pith of this palm used as a thickening agent in puddings, etc. [< Malay *sāgū*]

Sa·guache (sə·wach′) See SAWATCH MOUNTAINS.

sa·gua·ro (sə·gwä′rō, -wä′-) *n. pl.* **·ros** The giant cactus of the SW United States (*Cereus giganteus*): its blossom is the State flower of Arizona. Also **sa·hua′ro** (-wä′-). [< Sp.–Piman]

Sag·ue·nay River (sag′ə·nā′) A river in southern Quebec province, Canada, flowing 110 miles east from Lake St. John to the St. Lawrence River; total length, including sections above and traversing Lake St. John, about 475 miles.

Sa·guia el Ham·ra (sä′gyä el häm′rä) A territory of Spanish West Africa; 32,047 square miles. Also **Se·kia el Hamra** (se′kyä).

sa·gum (sā′gəm) *n. pl.* **·ga** (-gə) The ancient Roman soldiers' military cloak: a symbol of war, as the toga was of peace. [< L, ? ult. < Celtic]

Sa·gun·to (sä·gōōn′tō) An ancient town in eastern Spain near the Gulf of Valencia; destroyed by Hannibal, 219 B.C.: formerly *Murviedro.* Ancient **Sa·gun·tum** (sə·gun′təm).

sag·y (sā′jē) *adj.* Flavored or seasoned with or like sage.

Sa·har·a (sə·har′ə, -hâr′ə, -hä′rə) The world's largest desert area, extending from the Atlantic to the Red Sea in northern Africa; about 3,000,000 square miles. Also **Sahara Desert.**

Sa·ha·ran·pur (sə·hä′rən·pŏŏr) A city in northern Uttar Pradesh State, India.

Sa·hib (sä′ib) *n.* Master; lord; Mr.; sir: used in India by natives in speaking of or addressing Europeans, also by Hindus and Moslems for people of rank: Raja *Sahib.* Also **Sa′heb.** [< Urdu *sāhib* < Arabic *ṣāḥib,* lit., a friend]

said[1] (sed) Past tense and past participle of

SAY[1]. —*adj. Law* Previously mentioned; aforesaid.

sa·id[2] (sä′yid, sī′id) See SAYID.

Sa·i·da (sä·ē·dä) A port in SW Lebanon: ancient *Sidon:* also *Sayida.*

Sai·du (sī′dōō) A market town in northern West Pakistan, NE of Peshawar; the capital of the former princely state of Swat.

sai·ga (sī′gə) *n.* An antelope (*Saiga tatarica*) of the Siberian steppes, resembling a sheep. [< Russian *saiga*]

Sai·gon (sī·gon′, *Fr.* sá·ē·gôṅ′) Former name of Ho Chi Minh City.

sail (sāl) *n.* **1** *Naut.* A piece of canvas, etc., attached to the mast of a vessel, to secure its propulsion by the wind: variously shaped and rigged: fore–and–aft or square *sails.* **2** Sails collectively: full *sail.* **3** A sailing vessel or craft: plural same as singular: 30 *sail* in sight. **4** A trip or passage in a sailing vessel, or in any watercraft. **5** Anything resembling a sail in form or use, as the broad part of the arm of a windmill or a bird's wing. **6** A structure rising from the deck of a submarine that houses detection gear. —**to make sail 1** To

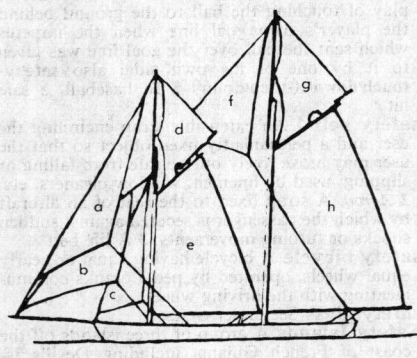

SAILS OF A
CLUB TOPSAIL SCHOONER

a. Jib topsail.   *e.* Foresail.
b. Flying jib.   *f.* Maintopmast staysail.
c. Jib.   *g.* Main club topsail.
d. Fore club topsail.   *h.* Mainsail.

unfurl a sail or sails. **2** To set out on a voyage. —**to set sail** To begin a voyage; get under way. —**under sail** Sailing; with sails spread and driven by the wind. —*v.i.* **1** To move across the surface of water by the action of wind or, by extension, steam. **2** To travel over water in a ship or boat. **3** To begin a voyage; set sail. **4** To manage a sailing craft: Can you *sail*? **5** To move, glide, or float in the air; soar. **6** To move along in a stately or dignified manner: She *sailed* by haughtily. **7** *Colloq.* To pass rapidly. **8** *Colloq.* To proceed boldly into action: with *in.* —*v.t.* **9** To move or travel across the surface of (a body of water) in a ship or boat. **10** To navigate (a ship, etc.). —**to sail into 1** To begin with energy. **2** To attack violently. —Homophone: *sale.* [OE *segl*] —**sail′a·ble** *adj.*

sail·boat (sāl′bōt′) *n.* A small boat propelled by a sail pr sails.

sail·cloth (sāl′klôth′, -kloth′) *n.* A very strong, firmly woven, cotton canvas suitable for sails: also called *duck.*

sail·fish (sāl′fish′) *n. pl.* **·fish** or **·fish·es** **1** Any of a genus (*Istiophorus*) of marine fishes allied to the swordfish, having a large and conspicuous dorsal fin likened to a sail. **2** The basking shark.

SAILFISH
(Up to 6 feet in length)

sail·ing (sā′ling) *n.* **1** The setting forth on or prosecution of a voyage: the *sailing* of a vessel. **2** The art and method of determining the direction and distance sailed by a ship at sea, the point reached, and the course to be taken; navigation; seamanship.

sailing orders Instructions given to a ship's captain, covering alldetails of a voyage.

sail·loft (sāl′lôft′, -loft′) *n.* A room where sails are cut out and sewed.

sail·or (sā′lər) *n.* **1** A seaman; mariner. **2** A sailor hat. —**sail′or·ly** *adj.*

  Synonyms: mariner, seafarer, seaman. In nautical language *sailors* and *seamen* are exclusive of officers, but in literary use all whose vocation is navigation are figuratively termed *sailors* or *seamen. Mariner* is one who navigates or assists in navigating a ship; in the United States statutes *mariner* denotes any person, from captain to cook, who serves in any capacity on a ship. *Antonym:* landsman.

sailor hat A low–crowned, flat–topped straw hat with a brim, worn by both sexes. Also *sailor.*

sail·or's–choice (sā′lərz·chois′) *n.* **1** The hogfish. **2** The pinfish. **3** A West Indian grunt (*Haemulon parra*) or related fish.

sail·plane (sāl′plān′) *n. Aeron.* A light, highly maneuverable glider requiring a relatively low speed for flight, used for soaring. —*v.i.* **·planed, ·plan·ing** To fly a sailplane.

Sai·maa (sī′mä) A lake system of SE Finland near the U.S.S.R. border; 1,699 square miles.

sain (sān) *v.t. Scot.* or *Archaic* To sign or bless with the sign of the cross to preserve against malign influence: also spelled *sane.* [OE *segnian* < L *signare* sign, make a sign of the cross < *signum* a sign]

sain·foin (sān′foin) *n.* An Old World perennial, cloverlike herb (*Onobrychis viciaefolia*) of the bean family, with variegated flowers, cultivated for forage: also called *esparcet.* Also **saint′·foin.** [< F < *sain* wholesome (< L *sanus* healthy) + *foin* hay]

saint (sānt) *n.* **1** A holy, godly, or sanctified person; in the New Testament, any Christian believer. *Eph.* i 1. **2** Such a person who has died and been canonized by certain churches, as the Roman Catholic. **3** Any one of the blessed in heaven. **4** An angel. **5** A very patient, unselfish person. —*v.t.* To canonize; venerate as a saint. —*adj.* Holy; canonized: as a title, often abbreviated to *St.* [< OF *seint, saint* < L *sanctus,* orig. holy, consecrated, pp. of *sancire* make sacred]

Saint For entries not found under *Saint,* see under ST.

Saint (sānt) *n.* A member of one of the religious bodies known as **Saints:** Latter–day *Saint.*

Saint–Bar·thé·le·my (saṅ′bár·tā·lə·mē′) An island dependency of Guadeloupe, 125 miles NW of it, in the Leeward Islands; 9 1/2 square miles.

Saint Bernard A working dog of great size and strength, originally bred in Switzerland, characterized by a massive head, and a thick, white coat combined with red or brindle: used to rescue travelers by the hospice at Great St. Bernard Pass in the Swiss Alps.

SAINT BERNARD
(About 28 inches high at the shoulder)

Saint–Cloud (saṅ·klōō′) A town in northern France, 5 miles west of Paris; former residence of French monarchs.

Saint–Cyr (saṅ·sēr′), **Marquis Laurent de Gouvion,** 1764–1830, French marshal.

Saint–Cyr–l'É·cole (saṅ·sēr·lā·kôl′) A town near Versailles in north central France; site of a national military academy.

Saint–De·nis (saṅ·də·nē′) **1** A northern suburb of Paris; burial place of many French kings. **2** The capital of Réunion island.

Sainte–Beuve (saṅt·bœv′), **Charles Augustin,** 1804–69, French poet, critic, and historian.

saint·ed (sān′tid) *adj.* **1** Canonized. **2** Of holy character; saintly.

Saintes (saṅt), **Les** See LES SAINTES.

Saint–É·tienne (saṅ·tā·tyen′) A city in SE France, SW of Lyon; a key industrial center.

Saint–Ex·u·pé·ry (saṅ·teg·zü·pā·rē′) **Antoine de,** 1900–44, French writer and aviator.

Saint–Gau·dens (sānt·gô′dənz), **Augustus,** 1848–1907, U.S. sculptor born in Ireland.

Saint–Ger·main (saṅ·zher·maṅ′) A NW suburb of Paris; scene of the signing of the peace treaty between France and Austria,

1919. Also **Saint-Germain-en-Laye** (-äṅ·lā′).

saint·hood (sānt′ho͝od) *n.* **1** The character or condition of a saint. **2** Saints collectively.

Saint-Just (saṅ·zhüst′), **Louis Antoine Léon de,** 1767–94, French revolutionist; one of the triumvirate of the Reign of Terror.

Saint-Lô (saṅ·lō′) A town of NW France; partially destroyed during the Normandy campaign of World War II.

Saint-Lou·is (saṅ·lo͞o·ē′) **1** A city at the mouth of the Senegal, capital of Senegal and of Mauritania. **2** A town on the SW coast of Réunion island.

saint·ly (sānt′lē) *adj.* Like a saint; godly; pious; holy. See synonyms under HOLY. **—saint′li·ness** *n.*

Saint-Ma·lo (saṅ·mà·lō′) A port in NW France on the **Gulf of Saint-Malo,** an inlet of the English Channel between Normandy and Brittany.

Saint-Mi·hiel (saṅ·mē·yel′) A town on the Meuse in NE France, scene of an American victory of World War I, 1918.

Saint-Na·zaire (saṅ·nà·zâr′) A port in central western France, at the mouth of the Loire.

Saint-O·mer (saṅ·tō·mâr′) A town in northern France, 22 miles SE of Calais.

Saint-Ouen (saṅ·twäṅ′) A northern suburb of Paris, on the Seine.

Saint·paul·i·a (sānt·pô′lē·ə) *n.* The African violet, much cultivated as an ornamental house plant. [<NL, after Baron Walter von *Saint Paul,* German botanist, its discoverer]

Saint-Pierre (saṅ·pyâr′), **Jacques Henri Bernardin de,** 1737–1814, French author.

Saint-Quen·tin (saṅ·kaṅ·taṅ′) A city in NE France, on the Somme.

Saint-Quentin Canal A canal in NE France, connecting the Oise with the Somme and the Scheldt; 58 miles long.

Saint-Saëns (saṅ·säṅs′), **(Charles) Camille,** 1835–1921, French composer.

Saints·bur·y (sānts′ber·ē), **George Edward Bateman,** 1845–1933, English literary critic and historian.

saint·ship (sānt′ship) *n.* Sainthood.

Saint-Si·mon (saṅ·sē·môṅ′), **Comte de,** 1760–1825, Claude Henri, founder of French socialism. **— Duc de,** 1675–1755, Louis de Rouvroy, French historian, memoirist, and diplomat.

Saint-Si·mon·ism (sānt·sī′mən·iz′əm) *n.* The socialistic principles of the Comte de Saint-Simon, advocating the state ownership of all property and the distribution of earnings based on the amount and quality of the work done by each laborer: also called *Simonianism.*

Saint-Vaast-la-Hogue (saṅ·väst′là·ôg′) A port of the NE Cotentin Peninsula, NW France; site of a French naval defeat by English and Dutch forces, 1692: also *La Hogue.*

Sai·pan (sī·pän′, -pan′, sī′pan) The largest island of the Marianas group; 47 square miles; capital, Garapan; captured from Japan by United States forces in World War II, 1944; after 1947, a district of the Trust Territory of the Pacific Islands, administered by the U.S. under the United Nations.

sair[1] (sâr) *v.t. & v.i. Scot.* To serve.

sair[2] (sâr) *adj. Scot.* Sore; sorrowful; heavy, great. **—sair′ly** *adv.*

sair·y (sâr′ē) *adj. Scot.* Sorry; sorrowful; wretched; poor. Also **sair′ie.**

Sa·ïs (sā′is) An ancient city of Lower Egypt on the Rosetta branch of the Nile. **— Sa·ite** (sā′īt) *n.* **— Sa·it·ic** (sā·it′ik) *adj.*

saith (seth) *Archaic* Present indicative third person singular of SAY[1].

sai·yid (sī′id, sä′yid) See SAYID.

sa·jou (sə·jo͞o′) *n.* Sapajou.

Sa·kai (sä·kī) A city on Osaka Bay, southern Honshu, Japan; industrial center; once a port.

Sa·kart·ve·lo (sä·kärt′ve·lô) The Georgian name for GEORGIA, U.S.S.R.

Sa·kar·ya (sä·kär′yä) A river in west central Turkey in Asia, flowing 490 miles to the Black Sea.

sake[1] (sāk) *n.* **1** Purpose of obtaining or accomplishing: preceded by *for* and followed by *of*: to open the window for the *sake* of air. **2** Interest, regard, or affectionate or reverent consideration, felt for any person or thing; account; well-being; advantage: commonly with *for* and a possessive: for your *sake,* for the *sake* of your children. [OE *saccu* a (legal) case]

sa·ke[2] (sä′kē) *n.* A fermented liquor made from rice; by extension, in Japan, any spirituous liquor. Also **sa′ki.** [<Japanese]

Sa·kel (zä′kəl), **Manfred,** 1906–57, Austrian psychiatrist; originator of insulin shock therapy.

sa·ker (sā′kər) *n.* A falcon; specifically, the Old World *Falco cherrug* or *sacer,* and the American prairie falcon (*F. mexicanus*). [< OF *sacre* <Sp. *sacro* <Arabic *ṣaqr* falcon]

Sa·kha·lin (sä′hä·lēn′, sak′ə·lēn) An island of Siberian Russian S.F.S.R. off its eastern coast; 29,700 square miles; the portion south of latitude 50° (13,930 square miles), known as **Japanese Sakhalin** or *Karafuto,* was ceded to Japan by the Treaty of Portsmouth; reoccupied by Russia after World War II. Formerly *Saghalien.*

Sa·ki (sä′kē) Pseudonym of Hector Hugh Munro, 1870–1916, English writer.

Sa·ki·shi·ma Islands (sä·kē·shē·mä) A southern group of the Ryukyu Islands; 343 square miles.

Sak·ka·ra (sə·kä′rə) A village of Upper Egypt; site of excavations of many ancient ruins: also *Saqqara.*

Sak·ti (säk′tē, sak′-; *Sanskrit* shuk′tē) See SHAKTI.

Sa·kun·ta·la (sə·ko͝on′tə·lä, shə-) The heroine of a famous Sanskrit play of this name by Kalidasa. Also *Shakuntala.*

sal (sal) *n.* Salt. [<L]

sa·laam (sə·läm′) *n.* An oriental salutation or obeisance resembling prostration, the palm of the right hand being held to the forehead; also, a respectful or ceremonious verbal greeting. — *v.t. & v.i.* To greet with or make a salaam. [<Arabic *salām,* orig. peace, in *(as)salām ('alaikum)* peace (be upon you), a salutation]

sal·a·ble (sā′lə·bəl) *adj.* Such as can be sold; marketable: also spelled *saleable.* See synonyms under VENAL[1]. **—sal′a·bil′i·ty, sal′a·ble·ness** *n.* **—sal′a·bly** *adv.*

sa·la·cious (sə·lā′shəs) *adj.* Lustful; lecherous. [<L *salax, salacis* < *salire* leap] **—sa·la′cious·ly** *adv.* **—sa·la′cious·ness, sa·lac′i·ty** (-las′ə·te) *n.*

sal·ad (sal′əd) *n.* **1** A dish of green herbs or vegetables, usually uncooked and served with a dressing, sometimes mixed with chopped cold meat, fish, etc. **2** The course consisting of such a dish. [<OF *salade* <Provençal *salada* <L *salata,* pp. of *salare* salt < *sal* salt]

sa·la·dang (sə·lä′däng) *n.* The East Indian ox (*Bos gaurus*): also called *gaur.* Also spelled *seladang.* [Var. of *seladang* <Malay *sĕladaṅ*]

salad days Days of youth, freshness, and inexperience.

salad dressing A savory sauce used on salads, as mayonnaise, or a mixture of salt, oil, and vinegar, etc.

Sal·a·din (sal′ə·din), 1137?–93, sultan of Egypt and Syria, 1174–93; defended Acre against Crusaders.

Sa·la·do (sä·lä′tħō), **Río** **1** A river of north central Argentina, flowing 1,250 miles SE from the Andes to the Paraná: also **Salado del Nor·te** (tħel nôr′tā). **2** A river of central Argentina, flowing 750 miles south from the Andes to the salt marshes near the Colorado: in its upper courses known as the **Des·a·gua·de·ro** (des′ä·gwä·tħā′rō). **3** A river in Buenos Aires province, eastern Argentina, flowing 400 miles SE from the border of Santa Fe province to the Río de la Plata.

Sa·la·jar (sä·lä′yär) An Indonesian island off SW Celebes; 259 square miles. Also **Sa·la′yar.**

Sal·a·man·ca (sal′ə·mang′kə, *Sp.* sä′lä·mäng′kä) A city in west central Spain; scene of a victory of Wellington against the French, 1812.

sal·a·man·der (sal′ə·man′dər) *n.* **1** Any of an order (*Caudata*) of tailed, lizardlike amphibians having a smooth, moist, scaleless skin and usually two pairs of limbs, as the American **tiger salamander** (*Ambystoma tigrinum*): once popularly believed able to live in fire. **2** One of the genii fabled to live in fire; an elemental fire spirit in Paracelsus' theory of elementals; hence, a creature fabled to live in fire. **3** Any person or thing that can stand great heat. **4** A large poker or other implement used around or in fire, or when red-hot. **5** A mass of hardened metal or slag remaining in the hearth of a furnace after the fires are drawn: also called *shadrach.* [<OF *salamandre* <L *salamandra* <Gk.] **—sal′a·man′drine** (-drin) *adj.*

SPOTTED SALAMANDER
(From 6 to 7 inches long over-all)

Sa·lam·bri·a (sä′läm·brē′ä, *Greek* sä′läm·brē·ä′) The former name for the PENEUS.

sa·la·mi (sə·lä′mē) *n.* A salted, spiced sausage, originally Italian. [<Ital., pl., preserved meat, salt pork, ult. <L *salare* salt < *sal* salt]

Sal·a·mis (sal′ə·mis) **1** An ancient ruined city of eastern Cyprus. **2** An island in the Saronic Gulf of the Aegean, off the coast of Attica, Greece; 39 square miles; the **Bay of Salamis,** nearly bisecting the island, was the scene of the Greek victory over the Persian fleet, 480 B.C.

sal ammoniac A white, soluble ammonium chloride. [<L *sal Ammoniacum,* lit., salt of Ammon; so called because orig. made from camel's dung near the shrine of Jupiter *Ammon* in Libya]

sal·a·ried (sal′ər·ēd) *adj.* **1** In receipt of a salary. **2** Yielding a salary.

sal·a·ry (sal′ər·ē) *n. pl.* **·ries** A periodic allowance as compensation for official or professional services. — *v.t.* **·ried, ·ry·ing** To pay or allot a salary to. [<AF *salarie* <L *salarium* money paid Roman soldiers for their salt, orig. neut. of *salarius* of salt < *sal* salt]

Synonyms (noun): allowance, compensation, earnings, fee, hire, honorarium, pay, payment, recompense, remuneration, requital, stipend, wages. An *allowance* is a stipulated amount furnished at regular intervals, as of food or of money. *Compensation* signifies a return for a service done. *Remuneration* is applied to matters of great amount or importance. *Recompense* has a still wider meaning; there are services for which affection and gratitude are the sole and sufficient *recompense*; *earnings, fees, hire, pay, salary,* and *wages* are forms of *compensation* and may be included in *compensation, remuneration,* or *recompense.* *Pay* is commercial, and signifies an exact pecuniary equivalent for a thing or service, except when the contrary is expressly stated, as when we speak of high *pay* or poor *pay.* A *wage* is what a worker receives, and is usually estimated on an hourly or daily rate. *Earnings* is often equivalent to *wages,* but may be used with reference to the real value of work done or service rendered, and even applied to inanimate things; as, the *earnings* of capital. *Hire* is distinctly mercenary or menial. *Salary* is for professional, literary, executive, or clerical work, and is usually estimated on a weekly, monthly, or annual rate. A *fee* is given for a single service or privilege, and is sometimes a gratuity. Compare REQUITE.

Sa·la·zar (sä′lə·zär′), **Antonio de Oliveira,** born 1889, Portuguese statesman; prime minister 1932–.

sale (sāl) *n.* **1** The act of selling; the exchange or transfer of property for money or its equivalent. **2** An auction or selling-off at bargain prices. **3** Opportunity of selling; demand by purchasers; market: Stocks find no *sale.* **—for sale** (or **on sale**) Offered or ready for sale. ◆ Homophone: *sail.* [OE *sala,* prob. <ON]

Synonyms: bargain, barter, change, deal, exchange, trade. A *bargain* is strictly an agreement or contract to buy and sell; (see CONTRACT) but the word is often used to denote the entire transaction and also the thing sold or purchased. *Change* and *exchange* are words of wider signification, applying only incidentally to the transfer of property or value; a *change* secures something different in any way or by any means; an *exchange* secures something as an equivalent or return, but not necessarily as payment for what is given. *Barter* is the *exchange* of one commodity, generally a portable one, for another. *Trade* in the broad sense may apply to vast businesses (as the book *trade*), but as denoting

a single transaction is used chiefly in regard to things of moderate value, when it becomes nearly synonymous with *barter. Sale* is commonly limited to the transfer of property for money, or for something estimated at a money value or considered as equivalent to so much money. A *deal* in the political sense is a *bargain,* substitution, or transfer for the benefit of certain persons or parties against all others; as, The nomination was the result of a *deal;* in business it may have a similar meaning, but it frequently signifies simply a *sale* or *exchange,* a dealing.

Sa·lé (sä·lā′) A port of NW Morocco NE of Rabat. *Arabic* **Sla** (slä).

sale·a·ble (sā′lə·bəl) See SALABLE.

Sa·lem (sā′ləm) **1** A port of entry in NE Massachusetts; the original settlement of the Massachusetts Bay Colony. **2** The capital of Oregon, on the Willamette River in the NW part of the State. **3** An Old Testament name for JERUSALEM. **4** A city in west central Madras State, India.

sal·ep (sal′ep) *n.* A farinaceous meal obtained from the dry tubers of various orchids, used as food and formerly as medicine. [<F <Turkish *sālep* <Arabic *tha'leb, sa'leb,* prob. contraction of *khasyu'th-tha'lab* orchis, lit., fox's testicles]

sal·er·a·tus (sal′ə·rā′təs) *n.* Sodium (or formerly potassium) bicarbonate, for use in cookery; baking soda. [<NL *salaëratus* aerated salt <L *sal* salt + *aër* air, gas; so called because it produces carbon dioxide]

Sa·ler·no (sä·ler′nō) A port in SW Italy on the **Gulf of Salerno,** an arm of the Tyrrhenian Sea; scene of fierce fighting in World War II between Germans and Allied landing forces, 1943. Ancient **Sa·ler·num** (sə·lûr′nəm).

sales·clerk (sālz′klûrk′) *n.* A clerk who sells goods in a store.

sales·girl (sālz′gûrl′) *n.* A woman or girl hired to sell merchandise, especially in a store.

Sa·le·sian (sə·lē′shən) *n.* A member of an order of priests and nuns founded in Italy by Don Bosco for the rescue and education of poor and neglected children and named for St. Francis de Sales, patron of the order. —*adj.* Pertaining to the spirit of St. Francis de Sales or to his works.

sales·la·dy (sālz′lā′dē) *n. pl.* **·dies** *Colloq.* A woman or girl hired to sell merchandise, especially in a store.

sales·man (sālz′mən) *n. pl.* **·men** (-mən) A man hired to sell goods, stock, etc., in a store or by canvassing.

sales·man·ship (sālz′mən·ship) *n.* **1** The work or profession of a salesman. **2** Ability or skill in selling.

sales·peo·ple (sālz′pē′pəl) *n. pl.* Salespersons.

sales·per·son (sālz′pûr′sən) *n.* A person hired to sell merchandise, especially in a store.

sales resistance An attitude or state of mind in an individual or in the buying public that resists buying certain goods because of something antipathetic in the salesman, the advertising, or in the product.

sales·room (sālz′ro͞om′, -ro͝om′) *n.* A room where merchandise is displayed for sale.

sales tax A tax on money received from sales of goods.

sales·wom·an (sālz′wo͝om′ən) *n. pl.* **·wom·en** (-wim′in) A woman or girl hired to sell merchandise, especially in a store.

Sal·ford (sôl′fərd) A county borough in SE Lancashire, England.

Sa·li·an (sā′lē·ən) *adj.* Of or pertaining to the **Sal·i·i** (sal′ ē·ī), a tribe of Franks who, in the fourth century A.D., settled on both sides of the lower Rhine, near the Zuyder Zee. —*n.* One of the Salii. Also **Salian Frank.** [<LL *Salii*]

sal·ic (sal′ik) *adj. Geol.* Belonging to a group of igneous rocks composed chiefly of silica and alumina, as the feldspars, quartz, etc. [<S(ILICA) + AL(UMINUM) + -IC]

Sal·ic (sal′ik) *adj.* **1** Characterizing a law, the **Salic Law,** derived from Germanic sources in the fifth century, and providing that males only could inherit lands: later applied to the succession to the French and Spanish thrones. **2** Pertaining to the Salian Franks. Also spelled *Salique.* [<MF *salique* <Med. L *salicus* <LL *Salii* the alii]

sal·i·ca·ceous (sal′ə·kā ′shəs) *adj. Bot.* Of or pertaining to a family *(Salicaceae)* of shrubs and trees forming the order *Salicales,* havin-galternate undivided leaves and dioecious flowers; the willow family. It includes the willows and the poplars. [<NL *salicaceus* <L *salix, -icis* a willow]

sal·i·cin (sal′ə·sin) *n.* Chem. A white, crystalline, bitter glycoside, $C_{13}H_{18}O_7$, contained in the bark of certain willows and poplars, and also made synthetically: used in medicine for rheumatism and as an antiperiodic. Also **sal′i·cine** (-sēn, -sin). [<F *salicine* <L *salix, -icis* a willow + F *-ine* - INE[2]]

sal·i·cyl·ate (sal′ə·sil′ āt, sə·lis′ə·lāt) *n. Chem.* A salt or ester of salicylic acid.

sal·i·cyl·ic (sal′ə·sil′ik) *adj.* Of, pertaining to, or derived from certain willows. [<F *salicyle* (<L *salix, -icis* a willow + F *-yle* -YL) + -IC]

salicylic acid *Chem.* A white crystalline compound, $C_7H_6O_3$, occurring naturally in many plants and also made synthetically from phenol. It is an antiseptic and is used sparingly in preserving foods, and, in the form of its salts, for treating rheumatism.

sa·li·ence (sā′lē·əns) *n.* **1** The condition of being salient or, figuratively, noteworthy. **2** A protruding feature or detail. **3** That which arrests attention because of its importance. Also **sa′li·en·cy.**

sa·li·ent (sā′lē·ənt) *adj.* **1** Standing out prominently; striking; conspicuous: a *salient* feature. **2** Extending beyond the general line; projecting. **3** Leaping; springing. —*n.* An angle pointing outwards, as of a fortification (see illustration under BASTION); projecting line or lines of trenches; a sharp curve in a military line protruding toward the enemy. [<L *saliens, -entis,* ppr. of *salire* leap] — **sa′·li·ent·ly** *adv.* —**sa′li·ent·ness** *n.*

sa·li·en·ti·an (sā′lē·en′shē·ən) *n.* Any of an order *(Salientia)* of amphibians characterized by broad, stocky bodies and the absence of tails, and having hind legs adapted for leaping, including the frogs and toads. —*adj.* Belonging or pertaining to the *Salientia.* [<NL <L *saliens.* See SALIENT.]

sa·lif·er·ous (sə·lif′ər·əs) *adj.* Containing a considerable proportion of salt in beds or as brine: *saliferous* strata. [< L *sal, salis* salt + -FEROUS]

sal·i·fy (sal′ə·fī) *v.t.* **·fied, ·fy·ing 1** To combine or impregnate with a salt. **2** To form into a salt, as with an acid. [<F *salifier* <NL *salificare* <L *sal, salis* salt + *facere* make] —**sal′i·fi′a·ble** *adj.* —**sal′i·fi·ca′tion** *n.*

sa·lim·e·ter (sə·lim′ə·tər) *n.* A salinometer. [<L *sal, salis* salt + -METER]

sa·li·na (sə·lī′nə) *n.* **1** A pool, pond, or marsh containing salt water diked in from the sea; also, a salt spring; a saltlick. **2** A saltworks or salt mine. [<Sp. <L *salinae (fodinae)* salt (pits) <*sal, salis* salt]

Sa·li·na Cruz (sä·lē′näkro͞os′) A port of Oaxaca, southern Mexico, on the Pacific coast.

sa·line (sā′līn) *adj.* Constituting, consisting of, or characteristic of salt; containing salt; salty. —*n.* **1** A metallic salt, especially a salt of one of the alkalis or of magnesium. **2** A salt solution used in the investigation of biological and physiological processes, and also in medicine, as for an injection. **3** A natural deposit of common or other soluble salt; salina. [<F *salin* <LL (assumed) *salinus* <L *sal, salis* salt]

sa·lin·i·ty (sə·lin′ə·tē) *n.* **1** The state or degree of being salt or saline. **2** The quantity of solid material dissolved in one kilogram of water: expressed in parts per thousand. Compare CHLORINITY.

sa·lin·i·za·tion (sā′lin·ə·zā′shən, -ī·zā′-) *n.* **1** The accumulation of salt. **2** The process by which a soil acquires various kinds of salts, as sodium chloride, calcium sulfate, or the ike.

sal·i·nom·e·ter (sal′ə·nom′ə·tər) *n.* A hydrometer graduated to show the percentage of salt in a solution and to measure the density of sea water. [<*salino-* (< SALINE) + -METER] —**sal′i·nom′e·try** *n.*

Sa·lique (sə·lēk′, sal′ik, sā′lik) See SALIC.

Salis·bur·y (sôlz′ber·ē, -brē) **1** A municipal borough, county town of Wiltshire, England, on the Avon River; noted for its 13th century cathedral: also *New Sarum.* **2** The capital of Zimbabwe.

Salis·bur·y (sôlz′ber·ē, -brē), **Marquis of,** 1830–1903, Robert Gascoigne Cecil, English statesman.

Salisbury Plain An undulating chalk plateauin southern Wiltshire, England; 300 square miles; site of Stonehenge.

Salisbury steak Hamburger (def. 2).

Sa·lish (sā′lish) *n.* **1** A North American Indian of Salishan stock: commonly called *Flathead.* **2** Any of the languages of the Salishan Indians.

Sa·lish·an (sā′lish·ən, sal′ish-) *adj.* Of or pertaining to a linguistic stock of North American Indians, formerly inhabiting Oregon, Washington, British Columbia, and Montana. —*n.* Any of the Salishan languages. Also **Sa′lish.**

sa·li·va (sə·lī′və) *n. Physiol.* The slightly alkaline fluid secreted by the glands of the mouth; spittle. It contains a specific amylase called ptyalin, which converts starch into maltose and is therefore considered a promoter of digestion. [<L] —**sal·i·var·y** (sal′ə·ver′ē) *adj.*

sal·i·vate (sal′ə·vāt) *v.* **·vat·ed, ·vat·ing** *v.t.* To secrete saliva. —*v.t.* To produce salivation in. [<L *salivatus,* pp. of L *salivare* <*saliva* saliva]

sal·i·va·tion (sal′ə·vā′shən) *n.* An abnormally increased flow of saliva, especially when due to the effect of drugs, as mercury.

Salk (sôk, sôlk), **Jonas Edward,** born 1914, U.S. bacteriologist; developed vaccine for poliomyelitis.

sall (sal) *v.i. Dial.* Shall. [Var. of SHALL]

salle à man·ger (sál à mäṅ·zhā′) *French* Dining-room.

sal·len·ders (sal′ən·dərz) *n. pl.* An eczematic inflammation about the hock joint of a horse. Compare MALANDERS. [<F *solandre;* ult. origin uncertain] 94,p60

sal·let (sal′it) *n.* A hemispherical helmet of the 15th century. [<OF *salade* <Ital. *celata* <L *caelata (cassis)* an engraved (helmet), orig. pp. fem. of *caelare cfl engrave]*

SALLET
Of Italian archer. 15th century.

sal·low[1] (sal′ō) *adj.* Of an unhealthy yellowish color: said chiefly of the human skin. [OE *salo*] —**sal′low·ish** *adj.* —**sal′low·ly** *adv.* —**sal′low·ness** *n.*

sal·low[2] (sal′ō) *n.* **1** A European willow with less flexible shoots than the osiers, especially the goat willow *(Salix caprea),* sometimes called the **great sallow,** and the **gray sallow** *(S. caprea cinerea).* **2** An osier; a willow shoot. [OE *sealh*]

sal·low·y (sal′ō·ē) *adj.* Fringed with or abounding in sallows.

Sal·lust (sal′əst), 86–35 B.C., Roman historian: full name *Gaius Sallustius Crispus.*

sal·ly (sal′ē) *v.i.* **·lied, ·ly·ing 1** To rush out suddenly. **2** To set out energetically. **3** To go out, as from a room or building. —*n. pl.* **·lies 1** A rushing forth, as of besieged troops against besiegers; sortie. **2** A going forth, as on a walk or excursion. **3** A sudden overflow of spirits; a witticism or bantering remark. [<OF *saillie,* orig. pp. fem. of *saillir* <L *salire* leap]

Sal·ly (sal′ē) A diminutive of SARAH; also, a feminine personal name.

sally lunn (lun) A raised and sweetened teacake resembling a muffin. [after *Sally Lunn,* pastry cook, of Bath, England, in the 18th century]

Sal·ma·cis (sal′mə·sis) In Greek mythology, a nymph of a fountain in ancient Caria, the waters of which were supposed to render effeminate all who drank of them. See HERMAPHRODITUS.

sal·ma·gun·di (sal′mə·gun′dē) *n.* **1** A dish of chopped meat, anchovies, eggs, onions, etc., mixed and seasoned. **2** Hence, any medley or miscellany; a potpourri. [<F *salmigondis,* prob. <Ital. *salami conditi* pickled meats <*salame* preserved meat, sausage + *conditi,* pp. of *condire* flavor <L, preserve, pickle]

Sal·ma·gun·di (sal′ma·gun′dē) A series of humorous and satirical papers published periodically in 1807–08 by Washington Irving and others.

sal·mi (sal′mē) *n.* A spiced dish of birds or game roasted, minced, and stewed in wine; a ragout. Also **sal·mis** (sal′mē, *Fr.* sál·mē′). [<F, prob. contraction of *salmigondis* SALMAGUNDI]

salm·on (sam′ən) *n.* **1** A clupeid fish (family *Salmonidae,* genus *Salmo),* especially *S. salar* of the North Atlantic, brownish above, silvery

on the sides, with black spots. The salmon ascends to the headwaters of rivers to spawn, and surmounts obstructions, as waterfalls of considerable height. It is a highly prized game and food fish, and has delicate reddish-orange flesh. **2** One of other salmonoid fishes, especially the quinnat, ascending rivers flowing to the North Pacific. **3** A color of a reddish- or pinkish-orange tint: also **salm′on-pink′.** *—adj.* Having the color salmon. [< AF *samoun, saumoun, salmun* < L *salmo, -onis*]

salm·on·ber·ry (sam′ən·ber′ē) *n. pl.* **·ries 1** A hardy raspberry *(Rubus spectabilis)* of the Pacific coast. **2** The cloudberry. **3** A raspberry *(R.parviflorus)* of the United States, having a white blossom.

Sal·mo·nel·la (sal′mō·nel′ə) *n.* A genus of aerobic, rodlike, preponderantly motile bacteria capable of fermenting certain carbohydrates with the formation of acid and gas; especially, *S. paratyphi,* which causes a form of paratyphoid in man. [< NL, after Daniel Elmer *Salmon,* U.S. pathologist, 1850–1914]

sal·mo·nel·lo·sis (sal′mə·ne·lō′səs) *n.* A disease caused by Salmonella bacteria, esp. paratyphoid.

Sal·mo·ne·us (sal·mō′nē·əs) In Greek mythology, a son of Aeolus and king of Elis who was destroyed by thunderbolts for claiming to be the equal of Zeus.

sal·mo·noid (sal′mə·noid) *adj.* Resembling a salmon; belonging to the salmon family. *—n.* A salmonoid.

Salmon River A river in central Idaho, flowing 425 miles NE to the Snake River.

salmon trout 1 The European sea trout *(Salmo trutta).* **2** Certain other salmonoid fish, as the namaycush or the steelhead. See TROUT.

sal·ol (sal′ōl, -ol) *n. Chem.* A colorless crystalline compound, $C_{13}H_{10}O_3$, derived from salicylic acid: used in medicine as a substitute for salicylic acid and as an antineuralgic, antirheumatic, antipyretic, and an internal antiseptic. [< SAL(ICYLIC ACID) + -OL[1]]

Sa·lo·me (sə·lō′mē) The daughter of Herodias, who asked from Herod the head of John the Baptist on a silver charger in return for her dancing. *Matt.* xiv 8.

Sal·o·mon (sal′ə·mən; *Fr.* sȧ·lô·môn′, *Hungarian* shol′o·mōn, *Polish* sä·lō′môn, *Sp.* sä′lō·mōn′) See SOLOMON. Also *Du., Ger.* **Sa·lo·mo** (sä′lō·mō), *Ital.* **Sa·lo·mo·ne** (sä′lō·mō′nā), *Pg.* **Sa·lo·mão** (sä′lō·mouṅ′).

Sal·o·mon (sal′ō·mən), **Haym,** 1740?–85, American patriot born in Poland; advanced large loans to American treasury during the Revolutionary War.

sa·lon (sə·lon′, *Fr.* sȧ·lôṅ′) *n.* **1** A room in which guests are received; a drawing-room. **2** The periodic gathering or reception of noted persons, under the auspices of some distinguished woman, especially in Paris in the 17th and 18th centuries. **3** A hall or gallery used for exhibiting works of art. **4** An exhibition of works of art. **5** An establishment devoted to some specific purpose: a beauty *salon.* [< F < Ital. *salone,* aug. of *sala* a room, hall < OHG *sal*]

Sa·lon (sə·lon′, *Fr.* sȧ·lôṅ′) *n.* An annual exhibition of works by living artists at the Grand Palais des Champs Elysées in Paris: so called because formerly held in the Salon Carré of the Louvre. Since 1891 there have been two rival Salons in Paris, the Salon of the Champs Élysées, or **Old Salon,** and the Salon of the Champ de Mars, or **New Salon,** which both exhibit in the Grand Palais.

Sa·lo·ni·ka (sä′lô·nē′kä) A port of NE Greece, in Macedonia on the **Gulf of Salonika,** an arm of the Aegean between Thessaly and Macedonia: ancient *Therma:* Greek *Thessalonike.* Also **Sa′lo·ni′ki** (-kē), **Sa′lo·ni′ca.**

sa·loon (sə·lōōn′) *n.* **1** *U.S.* A place where alcoholic drinks are sold; a bar. **2** *Brit.* In a public house, a section of the bar set aside for patrons of a higher social status than those in the public bar. **3** A large apartment or room for assemblies, public entertainment, exhibitions, etc. **4** The main cabin of a passenger ship, used by the passengers in general. **5** A salon (def. 1). **6** *Brit.* A sedan (def. 1). [< F *salon* a salon]

sa·loon-keep·er (sə·lōōn′kē′pər) *n.* One who keeps a saloon; a liquor dealer.

sa·loop (sə·lōōp′) *n. Brit.* An infusion of sassafras chips, salep, or similiar aromatic herbs, formerly used largely as a beverage, as a cure for rheumatism, etc.; sassafras tea. [Var. of SALEP]

Sal·op (sal′əp) See SHROPSHIRE. **—Sa·lo·pi·an** (sə·lō′pē·ən) *adj. & n.*

salp (salp) *n.* Any of a class (Thaliacea) of small, free-swimming, cylindrical tunicates, often having transparent bodies ringed with bands of muscle. Also **sal·pa** (sal′pə) *pl.* **·pae** or **·pas.** [< NL < L < Gk. *salpē* a kind of sea fish] **—sal′pi·form** *adj.*

Sal·pi·glos·sis (sal′pə·glos′is) *n.* A small genus of South American solanaceous, downy herbs having entire leaves and handsome variegated flowers. [< NL < Gk. *salpinx, -ingos* a trumpet + *glōssa* tongue]

sal·pin·gec·to·my (sal′pin·jek′tə·mē) *n. Surg.* The excision of a Fallopian tube; sterilization of women. [< NL *salpinx, salpingos* a Fallopian tube (< Gk., a trumpet) + -ECTOMY]

sal·pinx (sal′pingks) *n. pl.* **sal·pin·ges** (sal·pin′jēz) *Anat.* A tube in man and other mammals, especially the Eustachian or Fallopian tube. [< NL < Gk., a trumpet]

sal·si·fy (sal′sə·fē) *n.* An Old World plant *(Tragopogon porrifolius)* of the composite family, with a white, edible root: from its flavor called *oyster plant, vegetable oyster.* [< F *salsifis,* prob. < Ital. *sassefrica;* ult. origin unknown]

sal·sil·la (sal·sil′ə) *n.* Any of several tropical American plants of the amaryllis family (genus *Bomarea*), yielding edible tubers resembling those of the Jerusalem artichoke. [< Sp., dim. of *salsa* a sauce]

sal soda Sodium carbonate; washing soda. See SODA.

salt (sôlt) *n.* **1** Sodium chloride, NaCl, a widely distributed compound, used by men from time immemorial as a seasoning preservative: a necessary ingredient of food for most mammals. It is obtained by evaporation or freezing of the water of the ocean, of saline lakes and springs or wells, and by mining in beds of rock salt. ◆ Collateral adjective: *saline.* **2** *Chem.* Any compound produced when all or part of the hydrogen of an acid is replaced by an electropositive radical or a metal. Salts are usually formed by treating a metal with an acid or by the interaction of a base and an acid. Usually the salts derived from acids whose names end in *-ic* take the suffix *-ate,* and those ending in *-ous* take *-ite.* **3** *pl.* A salt used as a laxative or cathartic; also, smelling salts. **4** Piquant humor; dry wit; repartee: from the phrase *Attic salt.* **5** That which preserves, corrects, or purifies: the *salt* of criticism; seasoning. **6** A sailor: an old *salt.* **7** A saltcellar. **—below the salt** In inferior, subordinate, or servile position. **—to take with a grain of salt** To allow for exaggeration; have doubts about. *—adj.* **1** Flavored with salt; salty; briny: opposed to *sweet.* **2** Cured or preserved with salt. **3** Containing, or growing or living in or near, salt water. **4** *Obs.* Salacious; licentious; gross. *—v.t.* **1** To season with salt. **2** To preserve or cure with salt. **3** To furnish with salt: to *salt* cattle. **4** To season as if with salt; add zest or piquancy to. **5** To add something to so as fraudulently to increase the value: to *salt* a mine with gold. **—to salt away 1** To pack in salt for preserving. **2** *Colloq.* To store up; save. **—to salt out** To separate (coal-tar colors) by adding salt to solutions containing them. [OE *sealt.* Akin to SAL.] **salt′ish** *adj.* **—salt′ness** *n.*

Sal·ta (säl′tä) A province of NW Argentina; 59,743 square miles; capital, Salta.

sal·tant (sal′tənt) *adj.* Leaping; jumping; saltatory. [< L *saltans, -antis,* ppr. of *saltare* dance, freq. of *salire* leap]

sal·ta·rel·lo (sal′tə·rel′ō, *Ital.* säl′tä·rel′lō) *n. pl.* **·rel·li** (-rel′ē, *Ital.* -rel′lē) **1** A quick Italian dance, diversified by skips. **2** Music for such a dance. [< Ital., lit., a firecracker < *saltare* dance, leap < L. See SALTANT.]

sal·ta·tion (sal·tā′shən) *n.* **1** A leaping or leap, as in a dance. **2** A throbbing or palpitation, as of a blood vessel. **3 a** Mutation. **b** In evolutionary theory, the abrupt development of new species by a major mutational change. [< L *saltatio, -onis* < *saltatus,* pp. of saltare. See SALTANT.]

sal·ta·to·ri·al (sal′tə·tôr′ē·əl, -tō′rē-) *adj.* **1** Built or adapted for leaping. **2** *Zool.* Adapted for or characterized by leaping. [< SALTATORY]

sal·ta·to·ry (sal′tə·tôr′ē, -tō′rē) *adj.* **1** Of or pertaining to leaping or dancing. **2** Moving by leaps; fitted for leaping; specifically, moving the feet synchronously, as certain birds. [< L *saltatorius* < *saltator* a leaper < *saltare.* See SALTANT.]

salt cake Crude sodium sulfate, especially as obtained by the action of sulfuric acid on sodium chloride.

salt·cel·lar (sôlt′sel′ər) *n.* A small receptacle for salt; a saltshaker.

salt chuck In the Pacific Northwest, the sea.

salt·ed (sôl′tid) *adj.* **1** Treated with or as with salt for any purpose; hence, preserved. **2** Immune from infectious disease by reason of previous attack: a term used in South Africa. **3** *Colloq.* Experienced or expert.

salt·er (sôl′tər) *n.* **1** One who applies salt to cure fish, meat, etc. **2** One who manufactures or deals in salt. [OE *sealtere*]

salt·ern (sôl′tərn) *n.* A place or building where salt is manufactured. [OE *sealtærn*]

salt grass Any of certain grasses found growing on salt marshes or on alkaline western plains, as *Distichlis spicata* or some species of *Spartina.*

salt hay Hay made from salt grass.

salt-horse (sôlt′hôrs′) *n.* Salted beef; corned beef: a sailor's term. Also **salt′-junk′** (-jungk′).

sal·ti·grade (sal′tə·grād) *adj.* Adapted for leaping; said of certain insects, as grasshoppers. [< NL *Saltigradae,* group name of saltigrade spiders < L *saltus* a leap + *gradi* step]

Sal·til·lo (säl·tē′yō) The capital of Coahuila state, NE Mexico.

sal·tine (sôl·tēn′) *n.* A crisp, salty cracker.

sal·tire (sal′tir) *n. Her.* An ordinary formed by a bend and a bend sinister crossing as in St. Andrew's cross: also spelled *sautoir.* Also **sal′tier.** [< OF *sauteoir* a stirrup cord < Med. L *saltatorium* < L *saltatorius* SALTATORY]

SALTIRE
Showing cross of St. Andrew

Salt Lake See GREAT SALT LAKE.

Salt Lake City The capital and largest city of Utah, SE of Great Salt Lake; center of Mormonism.

salt·lick (sôlt′lik′) *n.* A place to which animals resort to lick salt from superficial deposits; a salt spring or dried salt pond.

salt marsh Low coastal land frequently overflowed by the tide, usually covered with coarse grass. Also **salt meadow.**

salt of the earth The fundamentally fine people of the world; those who add value to mankind. *Matt.* v 13.

Sal·ton Sink (sôl′tən) A depression in southern California; lowest part, 280 feet below sea level; in 1905 and 1906 became a shallow, saline lake, the **Salton Sea,** by an overflow of the Colorado River; originally about 450 square miles, reduced to about 300 square miles by evaporation.

salt·pan (sôlt′pan′) *n.* **1** A vessel in which salt is made by evaporating saline water. **2** A pond or basin from which salt is obtained by natural evaporation.

salt·pe·ter (sôlt′pē′tər) *n.* Niter: so called colloquially and in commerce. **—Chile saltpeter** Mineral sodium nitrate occurring in beds in a desert region near the boundary of Chile and Peru, but chiefly in Chile. Also **salt′pe′tre.** [< OF *saltpetre* < Med. L *sal petrae,* lit., salt of rock < L *sal* salt + *petra* a rock < Gk.]

salt rheum *Pathol.* One of various skin eruptions, as eczema.

salt-ris·ing (sôlt′rī′zing) *n.* Salted batter used as leaven, or bread made from it.

Salt River 1 A river in central Arizona, flowing about 200 miles west to the Gila River. **2** A river in NE Missouri, flowing 125 miles NW to the Ohio. **—to row** (or **be rowed**) **up**

Salt River *Colloq.* To suffer political defeat.
salt·shak·er (sôlt′shā′kər) *n.* A container with small apertures for sprinkling table salt.
salt spring A flow of salt water from the earth.
salt·wa·ter (sôlt′wô′tər, -wot′ər) *adj.* Of, composed of, or living in salt water.
salt well A well from which brine is obtained.
salt·works (sôlt′wûrks′) *n. pl.* **·works** An establishment where salt is made on a commercial scale: in England the form **saltwork** is preferred in describing a single factory.
salt·wort (sôlt′wûrt′) *n.* **1** Any of various maritime plants (genus *Salsola*), especially the common saltwort *(S. kali)*, used in making soda ash. **2** Any of various glassworts, as the dwarf glasswort *(Salicornia bigelovi)* of the New England coast. [Prob. trans. of Du. *zoutkruid*]
salt·y (sôl′tē) *adj.* **salt·i·er, salt·i·est** **1** Tasting somewhat like salt; of or containing salt. **2** Reminiscent of the sea; smelling of the sea. **3** Piquant; sharp; pungent, as literature, speech, etc. —**salt′i·ly** *adv.* —**salt′i·ness** *n.*
sa·lu·bri·ous (sə·lōō′brē·əs) *adj.* Conducive to health; healthful; wholesome. See synonyms under HEALTHY. [<L *salubris* <*salus* health] —**sa·lu′bri·ous·ly** *adv.* —**sa·lu′bri·ty, sa·lu′bri·ous·ness** *n.*
Sa·lu·da River (sə·lōō′də) A river in west central South Carolina, flowing 200 miles SE to the Congaree River.
sa·lu·ki (sə·lōō′kē) *n.* A very old breed of hound, having feathered ears, tail, and legs, and a greyhoundlike body; the "dog" of the Bible, known as the Royal Dog of Egypt: introduced into England in 1840. [<Arabic *salūqi* <*Salūq* an ancient Arabian city]

SALUKI
(From 23 to 28 inches high at the shoulder)

Sa·lus (sā′ləs) In Roman mythology, goddess of health and prosperity: later identified with the Greek *Hygeia.* [<L, health]
sal·u·tar·y (sal′yə·ter′ē) *adj.* **1** Calculated to bring about a sound condition by correcting evil or promoting good; corrective; beneficial. **2** Salubrious; wholesome; healthful. See synonyms under HEALTHY, USEFUL. [<F *salutaire* <L *salutaris* <*salus, salutis* health] —**sal′u·tar′i·ly** *adv.* —**sal′u·tar′i·ness** *n.*
sal·u·ta·tion (sal′yə·tā′shən) *n.* **1** The act of saluting. **2** Any form of greeting. **3** The opening words of a letter, as *Dear Sir.* [<OF *salutacion* <L *salutatio, -onis* <*salutatus,* pp. of *salutare* SALUTE]
sa·lu·ta·to·ri·an (sə·lōō′tə·tôr′ē·ən, -tō′rē-) *n.* *U.S.* In colleges and schools, the graduating student, usually the second (sometimes the first) honor man, who delivers the salutatory at commencement. [<SALUTATORY]
sa·lu·ta·to·ry (sə·lōō′tə·tôr′ē, -tō′rē) *n. pl.* **·ries** An opening oration, as at a college commencement. —*adj.* Pertaining to or consisting in greeting or welcome; specifically, relating to a salutatory address. [<L *salutatorius* pertaining to salutation <*salutare* SALUTE]
sa·lute (sə·lōōt′) *n.* **1** A greeting by display of military, naval, or other official honors, as by presenting arms, firing cannon, etc. **2** The act of or attitude assumed in giving a military salute. **3** A gesture of greeting, compliment, respect, or the like, as a bow, kiss, etc. —*v.* **·lut·ed, ·lut·ing** *v.t.* **1** To greet with an expression or sign of welcome, respect, etc.; welcome. **2** To honor in some prescribed way, as by raising the hand to the cap, presenting arms, firing cannon, etc. —*v.i.* **3** To make a salute. See synonyms under ADDRESS. [<L *salutare* <*salus, salutis* health] —**sa·lut′er** *n.*
sal·va·ble (sal′və·bəl) *adj.* Capable of being saved or salvaged. [<LL *salvare* SAVE] —**sal′va·bil′i·ty** *n.*
Sal·va·dor (sal′və·dôr′, *Sp.* säl′vä·thōr′) **1** El Salvador. **2** The capital of Bahia state, Brazil: formerly *Bahia, São Salvador.*
Sal·va·do·ri·an (sal′və·dôr′ē·ən, -dō′rē-) *adj.* Relating to El Salvador or its people. —*n.* A native or inhabitant of El Salvador. Also **Sal′va·do′ran.** [<*(El) Salvador* <Sp., the Saviour <LL *salvator* <*salvare* save]
sal·vage (sal′vij) *v.t.* **·vaged, ·vag·ing** To save, as a ship or its cargo, from wreck, capture, etc.; salve. —*n.* **1** The saving of a ship, cargo, etc., from loss; hence, any act of saving property. **2** The compensation allowed to persons by whose voluntary exertions a vessel, her cargo, or the lives of those belonging to her are saved from danger or loss: termed legally **civil salvage,** as distinguished from **military salvage,** which consists in the liberation of property from the enemy in time of war. **3** That which is saved from a wrecked or abandoned vessel or from or after a fire; hence, anything saved from destruction. [<OF *salver* SAVE] —**sal′vag·er** *n.*
sal·va·gee (sal′və·jē′) *n.* In maritime law, a person in whose favor or behalf salvage has been effected.
Sal·va·ges (səl·vä′zhēsh) See SELVAGENS.
Sal·var·san (sal′vər·san) *n.* Proprietary name for a brand of arsphenamine. [<G <LL *salvare* save + G *arsen* arsenic]
sal·va·tion (sal·vā′shən) *n.* **1** The process or state of being saved; preservation from impending evil. **2** *Theol.* Deliverance from sin and penalty, realized in a future state; redemption. **3** Any means of deliverance from danger, evil, or ruin. [<OF *sauvacion* <LL *salvatio, -onis* <*salvatus,* pp. of *salvare* SAVE]
Salvation Army A religious and charitable organization on semimilitary lines, founded by William Booth in England in 1865 as the Christian Mission, which took the title of Salvation Army in 1878.
Sal·va·tion·ist (sal·vā′shən·ist) *n.* A member of the Salvation Army.
salve[1] (sav, säv) *n.* **1** A thick, adhesive ointment for local ailments. **2** Anything that heals, soothes, or mollifies; hence, praise or flattery. —*v.t.* **salved, salv·ing** **1** To dress with salve or ointment. **2** To soothe; appease, as conscience, pride, etc. [OE *sealf*]
salve[2] (salv) *v.t.* **salved, salv·ing** To save from loss; salvage. [Back formation <SALVAGE]
sal·ve[3] (sal′vē) *interj.* Hail: literally, be well. [<L, imperative of *salvere* be well]
Sal·ve·mi·ni (säl·vä′mē·nē), **Gaetano,** 1873–1957, Italian historian active in the United States.
sal·ver (sal′vər) *n.* A tray, as of silver. [<OF *salve* <Sp. *salva,* orig. the foretasting of food, as for a king <*salvar* taste, save <LL *salvare* SAVE]
Sal·ve Re·gi·na (sal′vē ri·jī′nə) *Eccl.* **1** A hymn to the Virgin Mary, contained in the Roman Catholic breviary. **2** A translation of this. [<L, Hail, O queen; the opening words]
sal·vi·a (sal′vē·ə) *n.* Any of a genus *(Salvia)* of ornamental plants of the mint family; the sage. [<NL <L, SAGE[2]]
Sal·vi·ni (säl·vē′nē), **Tommaso,** 1829–1916, Italian actor.
sal·vo[1] (sal′vō) *n. pl.* **·vos** or **·voes** **1** A simultaneous discharge of artillery, or of two or more bombs from an aircraft. **2** A salute given by firing all the guns, as at the funeral of an officer; hence, any salute or simultaneous discharge: *salvos* of applause, a *salvo* of rockets. **3** The concentrated fire of many pieces, as in a naval engagement. **4** A successive and specified number of discharges of guns, from right to left, or left to right, at prescribed intervals. [Orig. *salva* <Ital., a salute <L *salve* SALVE[3]]
sal·vo[2] (sal′vō) *n. pl.* **·vos** **1** A saving clause; proviso. **2** An evasion, reservation, or bad excuse. **3** An expedient. [<L *salvo (jure)* (right) being reserved, ablative of *salvus* uninjured, safe]
sal vo·lat·i·le (sal vō·lat′ə·lē) Ammonium carbonate. Compare HARTSHORN. [<NL, volatile salt <L]
sal·vor (sal′vər) *n.* One who or a ship which saves or helps to save vessels or property from loss at sea; a salvager. Also **salv′er.** [<SALVE[2] + -OR]
Sal·ween (sal′wēn′) A river of eastern Tibet, SW China, and eastern Burma, flowing about 1,750 miles east, SE, and south to the Andaman Sea at Moulmein. Also **Sal′win′.**
Salz·burg (zälts′bŏŏrkh) A city in west central Austria; the birthplace of Mozart.
Sa·ma·ni (sä·mä′nē) *n. pl.* A Persian dynasty ruling from A.D. 874–1005, celebrated because of its encouragement of literature and the arts.
Sa·mar (sä′mär) One of the Visayan Islands, third largest of the Philippines; 5,050 square miles.
sam·a·ra (sam′ər·ə, sə·mâr′ə) *n. Bot.* A one-seeded indehiscent fruit, as of the elm, ash, or maple, provided with a membrane or wing; a key or key fruit. [<NL <L, elm seed]
Sa·ma·ra (sä·mä′rä) The former name for KUIBYSHEV.
Sa·ma·rang (sə·mä′räng) See SEMARANG.
Sa·mar·i·a (sə·mâr′ē·ə) **1** In the Bible, a city of Palestine, capital of the northern kingdom of Israel, or the hill on which it was built, on the site of modern Sebastye in western Jordan. **2** In the Bible, the territory occupied by the kingdom of Israel, or, later, a restricted portion of central Palestine west of the Jordan occupied by the Samaritans.
Sa·mar·i·tan (sə·mar′ə·tən) *n.* **1** One of the people of Samaria, a mixed population. II *Kings* xvii. **2** The Northwest Semitic language of this people. —**Good Samaritan** A humane, compassionate person who helps one in trouble: from the parable in *Luke* x 30–37. —*adj.* Of or pertaining to Samaria. [<LL *Samaritanus* <Gk. *Samareitēs* <*Samareia* Samaria]
sa·mar·i·um (sə·mâr′ē·əm) *n.* A hard, brittle, metallic element (symbol Sm, atomic number 62) of the lanthanide series, three of whose seven naturally occurring isotopes are weakly radioactive. See PERIODIC TABLE. [<NL <SAMAR(SKITE); so called because first found in the spectrum of samarskite]
Sam·ar·kand (sam′ər·kand′, *Russian* sä′mär·känt′) The second largest city and former capital of the Uzbek S.S.R., in the extreme eastern part; the ancient capital of Tamerlane's empire and the site of his tomb: ancient *Maracanda.* Also **Sam′ar·cand′.**
sa·mar·skite (sə·mär′skīt) *n.* An orthorhombic, vitreous, black mineral, source of several elements, as samarium, etc. [<G *samarskit,* after Col. Samarski, 19th c. Russian mine officer]
sam·ba (sam′bə, säm′bä) *n.* A dance of Brazilian origin in two-four time. —*v.i.* To dance the samba. [<Pg. <a native African name]
sam·bo (sam′bō) *n. pl.* **·bos** A half-breed of mixed Negro and Indian or Negro and mulatto blood. [<Sp. *zambo* a Negro, a mulatto, a monkey, prob. <Bantu *nzambu* a monkey]
Sam·bre (sän′br′) A river in northern France and SW Belgium, flowing 100 miles NE to the Meuse.
Sam Browne belt (sam′ broun′) A military belt, with one or two light shoulder straps running diagonally across the chest from right to left: designed by General Sir Samuel J. Browne, 1824–1901, of the British army, to carry the pistol when on horseback, and the sword when dismounted.
sam·bu·ca (sam·byōō′kə) *n.* In ancient music, a sharp-toned, triangular, stringed instrument resembling a harp: of Asian origin. Also **sam·buke** (sam′byōōk). [<L <Gk. *sambykē,* prob. <Aramaic *sabbĕkhā*]
sam·bur (sam′bər, säm′-) *n.* A rusine deer, especially *Cervus aristotelis,* of hilly districts in India, Burma, and China. Also **sam′bar.** [<Hind. *sābar* <Skt. *shambara*]
same (sām) *adj.* **1** Having individual or specific identity or quality; identical; equal: with *the.* **2** Similar in kind or quality. **3** Aforesaid; identical: said of a person or thing just mentioned or held in mind. **4** Equal in degree of preference; indifferent. **5** Unchanged; monotonous. See synonyms under IDENTICAL, SYNONYMOUS. —**all the same** **1** Nevertheless. **2** Equally significant; equally acceptable or unacceptable. —**just the same** **1** Nevertheless. **2** Exactly identical or corresponding; unchanged. —*pron.* The identical person, thing, event, etc. —*adv.* In like manner; equally: with *the.* [ME <ON *samr, sami.* Akin to OE *same* equally.]
sa·mek (sä′mek) *n.* The fifteenth Hebrew letter. Also **sa′mech, sa′mekh.** See ALPHABET.
same·ness (sām′nis) *n.* **1** Lack of change or variety; dull monotony. **2** Close similarity. **3** Identity.
Sam Hill (sam′ hil′) *U.S. Slang* Hell: a euphemism.
sam·iel (sam′yel) *n.* The simoom. [<Turkish *samyel* <*sam* poison (<Arabic *samm*) + *yel* wind]

sam·i·sen (sam'i·sen) *n.* A Japanese guitarlike instrument with three strings, played with a plectrum. [<Japanese <Chinese *san hsien* three strings]

SAMISEN

sa·mite (sā'mīt, sam'īt) *n.* A rich medieval fabric of silk, often interwoven with gold or silver. [<OF *samit* <Med. L *samitum*, var. of *examitum* <Med. Gk. *hexamiton* < *hexamitos*, woven with six threads <Gk. *hex* six + *mitos* a thread]

sam·iz·dat (säm'iz·dät') *n.* **1** In the Soviet Union, the secret publication and distribution of officially banned literature. **2** The literature that is so published and distributed. [<Russian <*sam* self + *izdat* publishing]

sam·let (sam'lit) *n.* A young salmon; a parr. [Contracted dim. of SALMON; infl. by earlier SALMONET]

Sam·nite (sam'nīt) *adj.* Of or pertaining to ancient Samnium, its people, or their language. —*n.* **1** One of the people of ancient Samnium, descended from the Sabines. **2** The Italic language of these people: also called *Oscan.* [<L *Samnis, Samnitis*]

Sam·ni·um (sam'nē·əm) An ancient country of central Italy, on the Adriatic, conquered by the Romans by 290 B.C.

Sa·mo·a (sə·mō'ə) An island group in the SW Pacific; 1,209 square miles; formerly *Navigators' Islands;* divided by the 171st meridian into: (1) **American** (or **Eastern**) **Samoa,** an unincorporated territory of the United States, comprising Tutuila, Rose, Swains, and Manua; 76 square miles; capital, Pago Pago, on Tutuila. (2) **Western Samoa,** a former trusteeship administered by New Zealand, independent 1962, and comprising Savaii, Upolu, and several smaller islands; 1,133 square miles; capital, Apia, on Upolu.

Sa·mo·an (sə·mō'ən) *adj.* Of or pertaining to Samoa, to its aboriginal Polynesian inhabitants, or to their language. —*n.* **1** A native of the Samoan islands. **2** The Polynesian language of the Samoans.

Sam·o·gi·ti·a (sam'ō·jish'ē·ə) A historical region of western Lithuania.

Sa·mos (sā'mos, *Greek* sä'môs) A Greek island in the Aegean, north of the Dodecanese; 194 square miles. —**Sa·mi·an** (sā'mē·ən) *adj. & n.*

Sam·o·thrace (sam'ə·thrās) A Greek island in the NE Aegean; 71 square miles. *Greek* **Sa·mo·thra·ki** (sä'mô·thrä'kē). —**Sam'o·thra'cian** (-thrā'shən) *adj. & n.*

sam·o·var (sam'ə·vär, sam'ə·vär') *n.* A metal urn containing a tube for charcoal for heating water, as for making tea. [<Russian, lit., self—boiler <*samo-* self + *varit* boil]

Sam·o·yed (sam'ə·yed') *n.* **1** One of a Mongoloid people inhabiting the Arctic coasts of Siberia. **2** A large dog characterized by a thick white coat of long hair, originally bred by the Samoyeds as a sled dog and for herding reindeer. —*adj.* Samoyedic. Also **Sam'o·yede** (-yed') [<Russian, lit., self-eater, i.e., a cannibal]

Sam·o·yed·ic (sam'ə·yed'ik) *adj.* Of or pertaining to the Samoyeds or their language. —*adj.* A subfamily of the Uralic languages, including the language of the Samoyeds.

samp (samp) *n.* Coarse, hulled Indian corn; also, a porridge made of it. [<Algonquian (Narraganset) *nasaump* softened with water]

sam·pan (sam'pan) *n.* A small flat-bottomed boat or skiff used along rivers and coasts of China and Japan. [<Chinese *san pan* <*san* three + *pan* board]

SAMPAN
Shown with typical lateen rig

sam·phire (sam'fir) *n.* **1** A European herb (*Crithmum maritimum*) of the parsley family, having fleshy leaves (formerly used in pickles). **2** A species (*Salicornia europaea*) of glasswort. [Earlier *sampere* <F (*l'herbe de*) *Saint Pierre* (the herb of) Saint Peter; ? infl. in form by CAMPHIRE]

sam·ple (sam'pəl) *n.* A portion, part, or piece taken or shown as a representative of the whole. —*v.t.* **·pled, ·pling** To test or examine by means of a portion or sample. [ME, aphetic var. of *asample* <OF *essample* EXAMPLE]

Synonyms (noun): case, example, exemplification, illustration, instance, specimen. A *sample* is a portion taken at random out of a quantity supposed to be homogeneous, so that the qualities found in the *sample* may reasonably be expected to be found in the whole; as, a *sample* of sugar, a *sample* of cloth. A *specimen* is one unit of a series, or a fragment of a mass, all of which is supposed to possess the same essential quality; as, a *specimen* of coinage, or of quartz. No other unit or portion may be exactly like the *specimen*, while all the rest is supposed to be exactly like the *sample*. An *instance* is a *sample* or *specimen* of action. See EXAMPLE.

sam·pler[1] (sam'plər) *n.* **1** One who tests by samples; one who exhibits samples. **2** A device for removing a portion of a substance for testing.

sam·pler[2] (sam'plər) *n.* A piece of needlework, as a sample, designed to show a beginner's skill. [Aphetic var. of OF *essamplair* <LL *examplarium* <L *exemplum* EXAMPLE]

sam·pling (sam'pling) *n.* **1** A small part of something or a number of items from a group selected for examination or analysis in order to estimate the quality or nature of the whole. **2** The act or process of making this selection.

Samp·son (samp'sən), **William Thomas,** 1840–1902, U.S. rear admiral.

sam·sa·ra (sən·sä'rə) *n.* **1** In Buddhism, the course of mundane existence; the endless cycle of birth, death and rebirth; the wheel of causation. **2** Transmigration; metempsychosis. [<Skt. *samsāra*, lit., a passage through a succession of states]

Sam·son (sam'sən, *Fr.* sän·sôn') A masculine personal name. Also **Samp'son.** Also *Pg.* **San·são** (sän·soun), *Sp.* **San·són** (sän·sōn'). [<Hebrew, the sun]

—**Samson** A Hebrew judge of great physical strength, betrayed to the Philistines by Delilah. *Judges* xiii 24.

Sam·u·el (sam'yōō·əl; *Ger.* zä'mōō·el, *Fr.* sä·mwel', *Sp.* sä'mōō·el') A masculine personal name. Also *Hungarian* **Sá·mu·el** (shä'mōō·el), *Ital.* **Sa·mue·le** (sä·mwä'lā). [<Hebrew, name of God]

—**Samuel** A Hebrew judge and prophet, I *Sam.* i 20; also, either of two historical books of the Old Testament.

Sam·u·rai (sam'ōō·rī) *n. pl.* **·rai** *Japanese* Under the Japanese feudal system, a member of the soldier class of the lower nobility, acting as a military retainer of the daimios; also, the class itself.

San (sän) A river in SE Poland, flowing 247 miles NW from the Carpathians to the Vistula.

Sa·naa (sä·nä') The capital of Yemen, Arabia. Also **Sa·na'.**

San An·to·ni·o (san an·tō'nē·ō) A city in south central Texas, the third largest in the State; a port of entry with a free port zone on the **San Antonio River,** which, rising here, flows 195 miles SE to join the Guadalupe River near its mouth on San Antonio Bay.

San Antonio Bay An inlet of the Gulf of Mexico, extending 19 miles into southern Texas.

san·a·tive (san'ə·tiv) *adj.* Healing; sanatory; health-giving. [<OF, fem. of *sanatif* <Med. L *sanativus* <L *sanatus*, pp. of *sanare* heal]

san·a·to·ri·um (san'ə·tôr'ē·əm, -tō'rē-) *n. pl.* **·to·ri·ums** or **·to·ri·a** (-tôr'ē·ə, -tō'rē·ə) **1** A health retreat, especially one in the mountains. **2** An institution for treatment of disease by curative waters or climate, or for the care of invalids. [<NL <LL *sanatorius* SANATORY]

san·a·to·ry (san'ə·tôr'ē, -tō'rē) *adj.* Promotive of health; curative [<LL *sanatorius* <L *sanatus*, pp. of *sanare* heal]

san·be·ni·to (san'bə·nē'tō) *n. pl.* **·tos** A black garment worn by a condemned heretic or a yellow cloak worn by a penitent under the Inquisition. [<Sp. *sambenito* <*San Benito* Saint Benedict; so called from its resemblance to a Benedictine's cloak.]

San Ber·nar·di·no Mountains (san bûr'nər·dē'nō) A range in SE California south of the Mojave Desert; highest peak, 11,485 feet.

San Bernardino Pass A pass in the Lepontine Alps, SE Switzerland; 6,770 feet.

San Blas (sän bläs'), **Gulf of** An inlet of the Caribbean on the north coast of Panama, east of the Panama Canal.

San·cho Pan·za (san'chō pan'zə, *Sp.* sän'chō pän'thä) In Cervantes' *Don Quixote*, a credulous peasant who acts as squire to the Don.

San Cris·to·bal (san kris·tō'bəl) One of the British Solomon Islands; 80 miles long, 25 miles wide. Also **San Cris·to'val** (-tō'vəl).

San Cris·tó·bal Island (san kris·tō'bəl) The chief island of the Galápagos group; 195 square miles; also *Chatham Island.*

sanc·ti·fied (sangk'tə·fīd) *adj.* Made holy; freed from sin; consecrated; also, sanctimonious.

sanc·ti·fy (sangk'tə·fī) *v.t.* **·fied, ·fy·ing 1** To set apart as holy or for holy purposes; consecrate. **2** To free of sin; purify or make holy. **3** To give religious sanction to; render sacred or inviolable, as a vow. **4** To render productive of or conductive to holiness or spiritual blessing. [<OF *saintifier, sanctifier* <LL *sanctificare* <L *sanctus* holy + *facere* make] —**sanc'ti·fi·ca'tion** *n.* —**sanc'ti·fi'er** *n.*

sanc·ti·mo·ni·ous (sangk'tə·mō'nē·əs) *adj.* **1** Making an ostentatious display or a hypocritical pretense of sanctity. **2** *Obs.* Saintly. —**sanc'ti·mo'ni·ous·ly** *adv.* —**sanc'ti·mo'ni·ous·ness** *n.*

sanc·ti·mo·ny (sangk'tə·mō'nē) *n.* Assumed or outward sanctity; a show of holiness or devoutness; exaggerated gravity or solemnity. See synonyms under HYPOCRISY, SANCTITY. [<OF *sanctimonie* <L *sanctimonia* holiness < *sanctus* holy]

sanc·tion (sangk'shən) *v.t.* **1** To approve authoritatively; confirm; ratify. **2** To countenance; allow. See synonyms under ABET, ALLOW, CONFIRM, RATIFY. —*n.* **1** Final and authoritative confirmation; justification or ratification. **2** A formal decree. **3** A provision for securing conformity to law, as by the enactment of rewards or penalties or both; a reward or penalty. **4** *pl.* In international law, a coercive measure adopted, usually by several nations at the same time, to force a nation which is violating international law to desist or yield to adjudication, by withholding loans, limiting trade relations, or by military force and blockade. **5** In ethics, that which makes virtue morally obligatory, or which furnishes a motive for man to seek it. [<MF <L *sanctio, -onis* ordaining something inviolable, a decree <*sanctus*, pp. of *sancire* make, sacred, decree]

sanc·ti·ty (sangk'tə·tē) *n. pl.* **·ties 1** The state of being sanctified; holiness. **2** Sacredness; solemnity. [<OF *sainteté* <L *sanctitas, -tatis* <*sanctus* holy]

Synonyms: holiness, sanctimoniousness, sanctimony. As referring to character, *sanctity* is *holiness*, while *sanctimoniousness*, or *sanctimony* is the pretense or affectation of *holiness*. Compare synonyms for HOLY.

sanc·tu·ar·y (sangk'chōō·er'ē) *n. pl.* **·ar·ies 1** A holy or sacred place; especially, a building or space, as a church, mosque, temple, or structure devoted to the worship of any deity. **2** The most sacred part of a place in a sacred structure; especially, the part of a church where the principal altar is situated; in Scripture, the holy of holies of the Jewish tabernacle and temple; also, the adytum of an ancient Greek or Roman temple. **3** A place of refuge; asylum; hence, immunity. See synonyms under REFUGE, SHELTER. [<OF *saintuarie* < LL *sanctuarium* <L *sanctus* holy]

sanc·tum (sangk'təm) *n. pl.* **·tums** or **·ta** (-tə) **1** A sacred place. **2** A private room where one is not to be disturbed. [<L, neut. of *sanctus* holy]

sanc·tum sanc·to·rum (sangk'təm sangk·tôr'əm, -tō'rəm) **1** The holy of holies. **2** A place

of great privacy: often used humorously. [<L <*sanctum*, neut. nominative sing. + *sanctorum*, neut. genitive pl. of *sanctus* holy]

Sanc·tus (sangk′təs) *n. Eccl.* **1** An ascription of praise to God, occurring at the end of the Preface in many eucharistic liturgies. **2** A musical setting for this. [<L *sanctus* holy, its thrice repeated opening word]

Sanctus bell *Eccl.* In the celebration of the Eucharist, a bell rung at the singing of the Sanctus, the elevation of the Host, etc.: also called *mass bell, sacring bell.*

San·cy (sän·sē′), **Puy de** The highest peak of the Massif Central, France; 6,817 feet.

sand (sand) *n.* **1** A hard, granular, comminuted rock material finer than gravel and coarser than dust. **2** *pl.* Sandy wastes; stretches of sandy beach. **3** *pl.* Sandy grains or particles, as those of the hourglass; hence, moments of time or life. **4** *Slang* Strength of character; endurance; grit; courage. **5** A reddish-yellow color. —*v.t.* **1** To sprinkle or cover with sand. **2** To smooth or abrade with sand or sandpaper. **3** To mix sand with: to *sand* sugar. **4** To fill with sand, as a harbor by the action of currents. [OE]

Sand (sand, *Fr.* sänd), **George** Pseudonym of Amandine Aurore Lucie Dudevant, 1803–76, *née* Dupin, French novelist.

San·da·kan (sän·dä′kän) A port of Sabah, chief town and once capital of the former North Borneo colony.

san·dal[1] (san′dəl) *n.* **1** A foot covering, consisting usually of a sole only, held to the foot by thongs. **2** A light slipper. **3** An overshoe of rubber, cut very low. **4** A strap or latchet for fastening a low shoe on the foot. **5** Sendal. [<L *sandalium* < Gk. *sandalion,* dim. of *sambalon, sandalon*] —**san′daled** *adj.*

SANDALS
a. Japanese. *c.* Greek. *b.* Roman. *d.* Egyptian.

san·dal[2] (san′dəl) *n.* Sandalwood.

sandal tree A Burmese evergreen tree (*Sandoricum koetjape*), extensively cultivated in the tropics. Its fruit is an applelike edible berry.

san·dal·wood (san′dəl·wŏŏd′) *n.* **1** The fine-grained, dense, fragrant wood of any of several East Indian trees (genus *Santalum*). **2** The similar wood of other trees, as the East Indian **red sandalwood** (*Pterocarpus santalinus*): also called *sanderswood.* [<obs. *sandal* sandalwood (<Med. L *sandalum,* ult. <Skt. *sandana*) + WOOD]

Sandalwood Island A former name for SUMBA.

san·da·rac (san′də·rak) *n.* A pale-yellow aromatic gum resin that exudes in drops from the sandarac tree: used as a lacquer and as an incense. See GUM[1]. Also **san′da·rach.** [<L *sandaraca* <Gk. *sandarakē* <an Oriental source]

sandarac tree A medium-sized North African tree (*Tetraclinis articulata*), yielding sandarac gum and a hard, dark-colored, fragrant wood susceptible of a high polish and used in ornamental work. Also **sandarach tree.**

sand·bag (sand′bag′) *n.* **1** A bag filled with or intended for holding sand: used for building fortifications, for ballast, etc. **2** A long, narrow bag filled with sand and used as a club or weapon. —*v.t.* **·bagged, ·bag·ging 1** To fill or surround with sandbags. **2** To strike or attack with or as with a sandbag. **3** To coerce in some forceful way. —**sand′bag·ger** *n.*

sand·bar (sand′bär′) *n.* A ridge of silt or sand in rivers, along beaches, etc., formed by the action of currents or tides.

sand bird Any of various birds frequenting the seashore, as a snipe or sandpiper.

sand·blast (sand′blast′, -bläst′) *n.* **1** An apparatus for propelling a jet of sand, as for engraving patterns on glass. **2** The jet of sand. **3** A sandstorm. —*v.t.* To clean or engrave by means of a sandblast.

sand·blind (sand′blīnd′) *adj.* Partially blind; having the vision affected by appearance of moving specks, etc. —**sand′blind′ness** *n.*

sand·box (sand′boks′) *n.* **1** A box with a per-

forated top, formerly used for sanding freshly written paper to avoid blotting. **2** A reservoir on a locomotive filled with sand to be poured on the rail treads in front of the forward drivers to prevent slipping. **3** A box of sand for children to play in. **4** The sandbox tree.

sandbox tree A tropical American tree (*Hura crepitans*), often cultivated for its curious woody capsules which burst with a loud report when ripe.

sand·bur (sand′bûr′) *n.* **1** A pernicious weed (*Solanum rostratum*) of the great plains of the western United States, having prickly foliage. **2** An ambrosiaceous weed (*Franseria acanthicarpa*) common in western North America. Also **sand′burr′.**

Sand·burg (sand′bûrg, san′-), **Carl,** 1878–1967, U.S. poet.

sand–cast (sand′kast′, -käst′) *v.t.* **–cast, –cast·ing** To make (a casting) by pouring metal into a mold of sand.

sand·crack (sand′krak′) *n.* A crack running down from the coronet of a horse's hoof and apt to cause lameness if neglected. See QUARTER-CRACK.

sand dab See under DAB[1].

sand dollar Any small, flat sea urchin (genus *Echinarachnius*) having a circular shell, found on sandy bottoms from New Jersey to Labrador and on the Pacific coast.

sand·ed (san′did) *adj.* **1** Filled, covered, or clogged with sand. **2** Of a sandy color; minutely speckled.

sand eel One of a family (*Ammodytidae*) of fishes with elongate bodies. Also **sand lance** or **sand launce.**

sand·er (san′dər) *n.* **1** One who or that which sands, as a locomotive sandbox. **2** A sandpapering machine.

san·der·ling (san′dər·ling) *n.* A small sandpiper (*Crocethia alba*) of arctic breeding habits, the adult gray and white in winter but having a rusty breast in summer. [<SAND + OE *yrthling* a kind of small bird, a ploughman]

san·ders·wood (san′dərz·wŏŏd′) *n.* Sandalwood (def. 2). Also **san′ders.**

sand flea 1 The chigoe. **2** A beach flea.

sand fly Any of various minute hairy flies (family *Psychodidae*) found near the seashore and in damp places: some of the genus *Phlebotomus* are carriers of the tropical disease leishmaniasis.

sand grouse An Old World bird (family *Pteroclidae*) of pigeonlike form, with long pointed wings and short feathered legs, inhabiting sandy tracts.

san·dhi (san′dē, sän′-) *n. Ling.* **1** A phonetic environment in which a word undergoes assimilative change from its absolute form under the influence of neighboring words: "Did you" becomes dij′ŏŏ) in *sandhi.* **2** The assimilative changes occurring in combined sounds in consecutive speech: "Has" becomes (s) by *sandhi* in the sentence "Jack's done that." [<Skt. *saṁdhi* a placing together]

sand–hill·er (sand′hil′ər) *n.* A poor white inhabitant of the sand-hill districts of Georgia and South Carolina; a cracker.

sand·hog (sand′hôg′, -hog′) *n.* One who works under air pressure, as in caisson-sinking, tunnel-building, etc.: also called *ground hog.*

sand hopper A flea (def. 2).

Sand·hurst (sand′hûrst) A village in Berkshire, England; seat of the Royal Military College.

San Di·e·go (san dē·ā′gō) A port and U.S. naval base in SW California, on **San Diego Bay,** a landlocked natural harbor separated from the Pacific Ocean by overlapping peninsulas.

sand lily A low-growing herb (*Leucocrinum montanum*) of the lily family, with fragrant white flowers, native in western and Pacific States: also **star lily.**

sand–lot (sand′lot′) *adj.* Of or in a vacant lot in or near an urban area: applied to games played in such lots: *sand–lot* baseball.

sand–man (sand′man′) *n.* In nursery lore, a mythical person supposed to make children sleepy by casting sand in their eyes.

sand martin The bank swallow.

sand painting An indigenous Amerindian art form practiced especially by the Navaho. Pigments of finely ground sand in five colors are trickled on a ground base of neutral-colored sand to give highly symbolic representations (usually the gods, a rainbow, lightning, etc.). Each painting, whether three or twenty feet

in diameter, has to be started at dawn and finished by sunset.

sand·pa·per (sand′pā′pər) *n.* Stout paper coated with sand for smoothing or polishing. —*v.t.* To rub or polish with sandpaper.

sand pine The smooth-barked pine (*Pinus clausa*) of sandy areas of the southern United States, especially common to the Gulf coast of Florida.

sand·pi·per (sand′pī′pər) *n.* Any of certain small wading birds (family *Scolopacidae*), mostly frequenting seashores in flocks. The two best known are the **common sandpiper** (*Actitis hypoleuca*) of Europe, and the **spotted sandpiper** (*A. macularia*) of North America. —**least sandpiper** A tiny, common, American marsh and shore bird (*Enolia minutilla*): also **sand′peep′** (-pēp′).

SANDPIPER
(From 7 to 9 inches long)

San·dring·ham (san′dring·əm) A royal estate and parish of NW Norfolk, England.

San·dro·cot·tus (san′drō·kot′əs) See CHANDRAGUPTA I.

sand·stone (sand′stōn′) *n.* A rock consisting chiefly of quartz sand cemented with silica.

sand·storm (sand′stôrm′) *n.* A high wind by which sand or dust is carried along.

San·dus·ky (san·dus′kē) A port of entry on Lake Erie in northern Ohio.

sand verbena A trailing annual or perennial plant (genus *Abronia*) with vivid red, yellow, or white flowers, native in deserts of the western United States.

sand viper 1 The hog-nosed snake. **2** The horned viper.

sand·wich (sand′wich, san′-) *n.* Two thin slices of bread, having between them meat, cheese, etc.; hence, any combination of alternating dissimilar things pressed together. —*v.t.* To place between two layers or objects; insert between dissimilar things. [after John Montagu, fourth Earl of *Sandwich,* 1718–92, who is said to have originated it in order to eat without leaving the gaming table]

Sand·wich (sand′wich) A municipal borough in Kent, England, near Dover; the most ancient of the Cinque Ports.

Sandwich Islands A former name for the HAWAIIAN ISLANDS.

sand·wich–man (sand′wich·man′, -mən, san′-) *n. pl.* **–men** (-men′, -mən) A man carrying advertising boards slung in front and behind.

sand·wort (sand′wûrt′) *n.* Any of a genus (*Arenaria*) of low, usually tufted herbs, with opposite sessile leaves and small white flowers.

sand·y (san′dē) *adj.* **sand·i·er, sand·i·est 1** Consisting of or characterized by sand; containing, covered with, or full of sand. **2** Yellowish-red: a *sandy* beard. —**sand′i·ness** *n.*

Sandy Hook A peninsula, 6 miles long, extending north from eastern New Jersey, at the entrance to New York Bay.

sane[1] (sān) *adj.* **1** Mentally sound; not deranged. **2** Proceeding from a sound mind. [<L *sanus* whole, healthy] —**sane′ly** *adv.* —**sane′ness** *n.*

    Synonyms: healthy, lucid, rational, sober, sound, underanged, unperverted. See SOBER.

sane[2] (sān) See SAIN.

San·ford (san′fərd), **Mount** The highest peak of the Wrangell Mountains in southern Alaska; 16,208 feet.

San·for·ize (san′fə·rīz) *v.t.* **·ized, ·iz·ing** To treat (cloth) by a special mechanical process so as to prevent more than slight shrinkage: a trade name. [after *Sanford* L. Cluett, inventor of the process, 1874–1968] —**San′for·ized** *adj.* —**San′for·iz′ing** *adj.* & *n.*

San Fran·cis·co (san′ frən·sis′kō) The second largest city of California, a port on **San Francisco Bay,** a landlocked inlet of the Pacific Ocean in

western California. Colloquially shortened to *Frisco.* —**San′ Fran·cis′can** *n. & adj.*

San Francisco Peaks Three peaks of an extinct eroded volcano in northern Arizona; highest peak, also highest in State, 12,655 feet.

sang[1] (sang) Past tense of SING.

sang[2] (sang) *n. Scot.* Song.

San·gal·lo (sän·gäl′lō), **Giuliano da,** 1445–1516, Italian architect and sculptor.

San·ga·mon River (sang′gə·mən) A river in central Illinois, flowing 250 miles west to the Illinois River.

san·ga·ree (sang′gə·rē′) *n.* A tropical drink of wine or brandy and water, spiced and sweetened. [<Sp. *sangria,* lit., bleeding <*sangre* blood <L *sanguis*]

San·gay (säng·gī′) An active volcano in east central Ecuador; 17,454 feet.

sang de bœuf (sän də bœf′) *French* Oxblood.

Sang·er (sang′ər), **Margaret,** 1883–1966, U.S. advocate of birth–control education.

sang–froid (sän·frwä′) *n.* Calmness amid trying circumstances; coolness; composure. [<F, lit., cold blood]

San·gha (sung′gə) *n.* **1** The assembly; one of the three jewels of the Buddhist triad; the union of the generative power of Buddha with the productive power of the female Dharma. **2** Any order or community of Buddhist monks. **3** The total body of Buddhist monks everywhere. **4** A community of Jain monks. [< Skt. *saṁgha* close contact, an assemblage < *saṁhan* strike together, unite closely]

San·gihe Islands (säng′ir) An Indonesian island group between the Celebes Sea and the Molucca Sea; total, 314 square miles. Also **San·gi Islands** (säng′ē).

San·gre·al (sang′grē·əl) *n.* The Holy Grail. Also **San·graal** (sang·gräl′). [<OF *Saint Graal* <*saint* holy (<L *sanctus*) + *graal* GRAIL]

San·gre de Cris·to Mountains (säng′grä dä krēs′tō) A mountain range in southern Colorado, the southernmost range of the Rocky Mountains; highest point, 14,363 feet.

san·gri·a (sang·grē′ə) *n.* An alcoholic drink made from red wine and fruit juice. [<Sp. *sangria* <*sangre* blood]

san·guic·o·lous (sang·gwik′ə·ləs) *adj.* Inhabiting the blood, as a parasite. [<L *sanguis* blood + *colere* inhabit]

san·guif·er·ous (sang·gwif′ər·əs) *adj.* Conducting blood, as the organs of circulation. [<L *sanguis* blood + -FEROUS]

san·gui·nar·i·a (sang·gwə·nâr′ē·ə) *n.* The bloodroot, or its medicinal preparation which is emetic. [<NL <L *(herba) sanguinaria,* fem. of *sanguinarius* SANGUINARY]

san·gui·nar·y (sang′gwə·ner′ē) *adj.* **1** Attended with bloodshed. **2** Prone to shed blood; bloodthirsty. **3** Consisting of blood. [<L *sanguinarius* <*sanguis, -inis* blood] —**san′gui·nar′i·ly** *adv.* —**san′gui·nar′i·ness** *n.*

Synonyms: blood thirsty, bloody, cruel, inhuman, murderous, sanguine, savage. *Sanguinary* applies either to the act of shedding blood or to the spirit that delights in bloodshed; *bloody* applies more directly to the actual staining with blood; we may say either a *sanguinary* or a *bloody* battle, but a *bloody* (not a *sanguinary*) field. *Sanguine* is sometimes used in poetic or elevated style in the sense of *bloody;* as, a *sanguine* stain. See BLOODY.

san·guine (sang′gwin) *adj.* **1** Of buoyant disposition; hopeful; confident; originally, having a temperament supposed to be due to active blood. **2** Having the color of blood; of, like, or full of blood. **3** *Obs.* Bloodthirsty; sanguinary. [<OF *sanguin* <L *sanguineus* < *sanguis, sanguinis* blood] —**san′guine·ly** *adv.* —**san′guine·ness n.**

Synonyms: animated, ardent, buoyant, confident, enthusiastic, hopeful. *Sanguine,* from the same root as *sanguinary,* came to denote full–blooded or plethoric, hence, *ardent, confident, hopeful,* because these qualities were supposed to be associated with fullness of blood. For the rare use of *sanguine* in direct literal sense, see synonyms under SANGUINARY.

san·guin·e·ous (sang·gwin′ē·əs) *adj.* **1** Pertaining to, consisting of, or forming blood. **2** Full–blooded; sanguine; hence, hopeful. **3** Of the color of blood. [<L *sanguineus* SANGUINE]

san·guin·o·lent (sang·gwin′ə·lənt) *adj.* Tinged or mixed with blood; bloody. [<OF <L *sanguinolentus* <*sanguis, sanguinis* blood]

San·he·drin (san′hi·drin, san′i-) *n.* **1** In ancient times, the supreme council and highest court of the Jewish nation: also **Great Sanhedrin.** **2** Figuratively, any council or assembly. Also spelled *Synedrion, Synedrium.* Also **San′·he·drim** (-drim). [<Hebrew *sanhedrin* <Gk. *synedrion,* lit., a sitting together <*syn-* together + *hedra* a seat]

san·i·cle (san′i·kəl) *n.* Any of a genus *(Sanicula)* of smooth perennial herbs of the carrot family, reputed to have medicinal roots. [<OF <Med. L *sanicula,* prob. dim. <L *sanus* healthy; with ref. to its reputed healing powers]

sa·ni·es (sā′ni·ēz) *n. Pathol.* A serous, greenish, blood–tinged fluid discharged from ulcers. [< NL <L]

San Il·de·fon·so (sän ēl′thä·fōn′sō) A town in central Spain, 38 miles NW of Madrid; site of royal palace; scene of the signing of a treaty by Spain, France, and England, 1796: also *La Granja.*

sa·ni·ous (sā′nē·əs) *adj.* **1** Of or like sanies; watery and blood–tinged. **2** Producing or discharging sanies.

san·i·tar·i·an (san′ə·târ′ē·ən) *n.* A person skilled in matters relating to sanitation and public health.

san·i·tar·i·um (san′ə·târ′ē·əm) *n. pl.* **·tar·i·ums** or **·tar·i·a** (-târ′ē·ə) A sanatorium. [<NL <L *sanitas* health]

san·i·tar·y (san′ə·ter′ē) *adj.* **1** Relating to the preservation of health. **2** Cleanly; disease-preventing. See synonyms under HEALTHY. —*n. pl.* **·tar·ies** A public watercloset or urinal. [<F *sanitaire* <L *sanitas* health <*sanus* healthy] —**san′i·tar′i·ly** *adv.*

sanitary belt A belt, usually made of elastic, that has tabs to which a sanitary napkin may be attached.

sanitary cordon See CORDON SANITAIRE.

sanitary napkin An absorbent pad used by women during menstruation.

san·i·tate (san′ə·tāt) *v.t.* **·tat·ed, ·tat·ing** To apply sanitary measures to. [Back formation <SANITATION]

san·i·ta·tion (san′ə·tā′shən) *n.* The practical application of sanitary science; the removal or neutralization of elements injurious to health. [<SANIT(ARY) + -ATION]

san·i·ta·tion·man (san′i·tā′shən·man′) *n. pl.* **·men** (-mən) A person, especially a municipal employee, whose work is the collection of refuse and trash.

san·i·tize (san′ə·tiz) *v.t.* **·tized, ·tiz·ing 1** To make sanitary, as by scrubbing, washing, or sterilizing. **2** To make acceptable or unobjectionable, as by deleting offensive parts: a *sanitized* version of the fairy tale.

san·i·ty (san′ə·tē) *n.* **1** The state of being sane or sound; soundness of mind; mental health. **2** Moderation; reasonableness. [<MF *sanité* <L *sanitas* health <*sanus* healthy]

San Ja·cin·to (san′ jə·sin′tō) A locality in eastern Texas, scene of a Texan victory against Mexico, 1836; at the mouth of the **San Jacinto River,** which flows 115 miles south to Galveston Bay.

San Joa·quin River (san′ wô·kēn′, wä·kēn′) A river of south central California, flowing 317 miles through Central Valley to the Sacramento River just above its mouth.

San Jo·sé (sän hō·zā′) **1** The capital of Costa Rica. **2** (san′hō·zā′) A city on San Francisco Bay in western California.

San José scale A scale insect *(Quadraspidiotus perniciosus)* destructive to various fruit trees: so called because it first appeared in the United States at San José, California. For illustration see INSECTS (injurious).

San Juan (san hwän′) **1** A port, capital of Puerto Rico. **2** A province of west central Argentina; 33,249 square miles; capital, San Juan.

San Juan de la Cruz (thä lä krōōth′) See JOHN OF THE CROSS, SAINT.

San Juan de los Mor·ros (thä lōs môr′rōs) The capital of Guàrico state, north central Venezuela.

San Juan Islands An American island group lying between SE Vancouver Island and the mainland of NW Washington at the northern end of Puget Sound.

San Juan Mountains A range of the Rocky Mountains in SW Colorado; highest peak, 14,306 feet.

sank (sangk) Past tense of SINK.

San·key (sang′kē), **Ira David,** 1840–1908, U.S. evangelist and hymn writer.

San·khya (säng′kyə) *n.* The oldest system of Indian philosophy, professing unqualified dualism; founded by Kapila, fabled son of Brahma. [<Skt. *Sáṁkhya* <*samkhyá* enumeration; with ref. to its enumeration of twenty–four material principles *(tattva)* and one independent immaterial principle]

Sankt Mo·ritz (zängt mō′rits) The German name for ST. MORITZ.

San Lu·is (sän lōō·ēs′) A province in west central Argentina; 29,625 square miles; capital, San Luis.

San Luis Po·to·sí (pō′tō·sē′) A state in central Mexico; 24,415 square miles; capital, San Luis Potosí.

San Ma·ri·no (mä·rē′nō) An independent republic in eastern Italy near the coast of the Adriatic Sea; 23 square miles; capital, San Marino.

San Mar·tín (mär·tēn′), **José de,** 1778–1850, South American general and statesman.

San Mi·guel Gulf (mē·gel′) The eastern part of the Gulf of Panama, adjacent to eastern Panama.

san·nup (san′up) *n.* A married male American Indian; the husband of a squaw. Also **san′·nop.** [<Algonquian (Narraganset) *sannop*]

San Pa·blo Bay (san′ pä′blō) The northern part of San Francisco Bay, California.

San Re·mo (sän rā′mō) A port and resort on the Gulf of Genoa in NW Italy.

sans (sanz, *Fr.* sän) *prep.* Without. [<OF *sens, sanz,* alter. of L *absentia* absence, infl. by *sine* without]

San Sal·va·dor (san′ sal′və·dôr, *Sp.* sän säl′vä·thôr′) The capital of El Salvador.

San Salvador Island An island in the central Bahamas, the first landing place of Columbus in the New World, 1492: also called *Watling Island.*

san·sar (sän′sər) *n.* A sarsar.

sans cé·ré·mo·nie (sän sā·rā·mô·nē′) *French* Without ceremony; informal.

sans·cu·lotte (sanz′kyōō·lot′, *Fr.* sän·kü·lôt′) *n.* **1** A revolutionary: first applied by the aristocrats as a term of contempt for those who started the revolution of 1789; later it became a popular name for one of a revolutionary mob; a Jacobin. **2** Any revolutionary republican or radical. **3** Any ragged or strangely dressed person. [<F, lit., without knee breeches] —**sans′cu·lot′tic** *adj.* —**sans′·cu·lot′·tism** *n.*

sans·cu·lot·tides (sanz′kyōō·lot′idz, *Fr.* sän′·kü·lô·tēd′) See CALENDAR (Republican).

sans doute (sän dōōt′) *French* Without doubt; unquestionably.

San Se·bas·tián (san sə·bas′chən, *Sp.* sän sā·väs·tyän′) A port on the Bay of Biscay, in northern Spain.

San·sei (sän·sā) *n. pl.* **·sei** An American citizen of Japanese descent whose grandparents settled in the United States; a third–generation Japanese American. [<Japanese, third generation]

san·se·vi·e·ri·a (san′sə·vi·ir′ē·ə) *n.* Any of a genus *(Sansevieria)* of erect perennial herbs of the lily family, native in Africa but sometimes grown as an ornamental plant. [<NL, after the Prince of *Sanseviero,* 1710–71, a Neapolitan savant]

San·skrit (san′skrit) *n.* The ancient and classical language of the Hindus of India, belonging to the Indic branch of the Indo–Iranian subfamily of Indo–European languages. It includes specifically **Vedic Sanskrit,** the language of the Vedas, and the later **classical Sanskrit** of India's great religious, philosophical, and poetic literature, still used for sacred or learned writings, and distinguished from the vernacular Prakrit. Also **San′scrit.** Abbr. *Skt.* [<Skt. *samskṛita* well–formed <*sam-* together + *kṛ* make, do] —**San′skrit·ist** *n.*

San·skrit·ic (san·skrit′ik) *adj.* **1** Of, pertaining to, or written in the ancient and sacred language of India. **2** Designating a group

of some 30 to 40 ancient and modern languages and dialects of India, embracing Sanskrit, Prakrit, Pali, Assamese, Bengali, Eastern and Western Hindi, Punjabi, Singhalese, Romany or Gipsy, etc.

San·so·vi·no (sän′sō·vē′nō), 1486?–1570, Italian sculptor and architect: original name *Jacopo Tatti.*

sans pa·reil (sän pȧ·rā′y) *French* Without equal.

sans peur et sans re·proche (sän pœr ā sän rə·prôsh′) *French* Without fear and without reproach.

sans ser·if (sanz ser′if) *Printing* A style of type without serifs.

sans-sou·ci (sän·sōō·sē′) *adj. French* Carefree; free and easy.

San Ste·fa·no (sän stā′fä·nō) A village on the Sea of Marmara west of Istanbul, in Turkey in Europe; scene of the signing of a Russo-Turkish treaty, 1878: Turkish *Yesilköy.*

San·ta An·a (sän′tä ä′nä) A city in NW El Salvador, the second largest; a coffee center and rail junction.

San·ta An·na (sän′tä ä′nä), **Antonio Lopez de**, 1795–1876, Mexican general: president and dictator of Mexico; massacred the surviving defenders of the Alamo, Mar. 6, 1836; defeated by the U.S. Army in 1847. Also **San′ta A′na.**

San·ta Bar·ba·ra Islands (sän′tə bär′bər·ə) A chain of small islands, extending 150 miles along the coast of southern California.

San·ta Cat·a·li·na (sän′tə kat′ə·lē′nə) One of the Santa Barbara Islands, 24 miles south of Los Angeles, California; 22 miles long: also *Catalina Island.*

San·ta Ca·ta·ri·na (sän′tə kä′tə·rē′nə) A maritime state in southern Brazil; 36,592 square miles; capital, Florianópolis.

San·ta Cla·ra (sän′tä klä′rä) A city in central Cuba.

San·ta Claus (sän′tə klôz′) In nursery folklore, a friend of children who brings presents at Christmas time: usually represented as a fat, jolly old man. The patron saint of children, figuring in the nursery lore of many countries and identified with *St. Nicholas.* [< dial. Du. *Sante Klaus* Saint Nicholas]

San·ta Cruz (sän′tə krōōz′, *Sp.* sän′tä krōōth′) 1 St. Croix. 2 A national territory in southern Patagonia, Argentina; 77,822 square miles; capital, Río Gallegos.

Santa Cruz de Ten·er·ife (də ten′ə·rif′, *Sp.* thä tä′nä·rē′fä) 1 One of the two provinces in the Canary Islands, comprising Tenerife, La Palma, Gomera, and Hierro; 1,238 square miles. 2 A port of NE Tenerife, capital of this province and of Tenerife island.

Santa Cruz Islands An island group north of the New Hebrides, comprising part of the British Solomon Islands protectorate; total, 370 square miles; scene of U.S. naval victory over Japanese, 1942.

San·ta Fe (sän′tə fā′) 1 The capital of New Mexico, in the northern part of the State. 2 (sän′tä fā′) A province of NE central Argentina; 51,341 square miles; capital, Santa Fe.

Santa Fe trail The trade route, important from 1821 to 1880, between Independence, Missouri, or a nearby terminus, and Santa Fe, New Mexico.

San·ta Is·a·bel (sän′tä ē′sä·bel) 1 A city on Fernando Pó island, capital of Spanish Guinea. 2 (sän′tə iz′ə·bel) One of the British Solomon Islands; 1,800 square miles: also *Ysabel.*

san·ta·la·ceous (san′tə·lā′shəs) *adj. Bot.* Of or pertaining to a family (*Santalaceae*) of apetalous shrubs, herbs, and some trees; the sandalwood family. [< NL <*Santalum*, genus name <Med. L, sandalwood]

san·tal·ic (san·tal′ik) *adj.* Of, pertaining to, or derived from sandalwood, as **santalic acid,** a red crystalline coloring matter, $C_{15}H_{14}O_5$. [< NL *santal(um)* sandalwood (<Med. L) + -IC]

San·ta Ma·ri·a (sän′tə mə·rē′ə, *Sp.* sän′tä mä·rē′ä) One of the three ships of Columbus on his maiden voyage to America.

San·ta Ma·ri·a (sän′tə mä·rē′ä) 1 An island in the SE Azores; 37 square miles. 2 An active volcano in SW Guatemala; 12,362 feet.

San·ta Mau·ra (sän′tä mou′rä) The Italian name for LEVKAS.

San·tan·der (sän′tän·der′) A port of northern Spain on the Bay of Biscay.

San·ta·rém (saṅn′tə·rāň′) The second largest city of Pará state, Brazil, on the Tapajós at its influx into the Amazon.

San·ta·ya·na (sän′tä·yä′nä), **George**, 1863–1952, U.S. philosopher and author born in Spain.

San·tee River (san·tē′) A river in east central South Carolina, flowing 143 miles SE from the junction of the Congaree and Wateree rivers, over Santee Dam (45 feet high, 7.8 miles long; completed 1941), to the Atlantic.

San·ti·a·go (sän′tē·ä′gō) 1 The capital of Chile. Also Santiago de Chi·le (thä chē′lā). 2 Santiago de Compostela. 3 Santiago de los Caballeros.

Santiago de Com·po·ste·la (thä kōm′pō·stä′lä) A city and chief pilgrimage center of NW Spain: also *Santiago.*

Santiago de Cu·ba (thä kōō′bä) 1 The second largest city of Cuba and capital of Oriente province, on the southern coast. 2 The former name for ORIENTE province, Cuba.

Santiago del Es·te·ro (thel es·tä′rō) A province of northern Argentina; 52,208 square miles; capital, Santiago del Estero.

Santiago de los Ca·bal·le·ros (thä lōs kä′vä·yä′rōs) A city in northern Dominican Republic, the second largest city of the Republic: also *Santiago.*

San·to Do·min·go (sän′tō dō·ming′gō) The capital of the Dominican Republic, a port on the south coast; the oldest continuously occupied European settlement in the Western Hemisphere: formerly *Ciudad Trujillo.*

san·ton·i·ca (san·ton′i·kə) *n.* 1 An Old World plant of the composite family, especially the European wormwood (*Artemisia maritima*). 2 The unexpanded flower heads of this plant, used as a vermifuge. [< NL <L (*herba*) *Santonica* a kind of wormwood, fem. sing. of *Santonicus* of the Santoni <*Santoni* the Santoni, a people of Aquitania]

san·to·nin (san′tə·nin) *n. Chem.* A colorless crystalline poisonous compound, $C_{15}H_{18}O_3$, contained in santonica: used in medicine as a vermifuge. Also **san′to·nine** (-nēn, -nin). [< F *santonine* <NL *santon(ica)* + -INE²]

San·to·rin (sän′tō·rēn′) A former name for THERA.

San·tos (saṅn′tōōs) A port and the second largest city in São Paulo state, SE Brazil.

San·tos–Du·mont (saṅn′tōōz·dü·môn′), **Alberto**, 1873–1932, Brazilian airship pioneer active in France.

São Fran·cis·co (souň frän·sēs′kōō) A river of eastern Brazil, flowing 1,800 miles to the Atlantic; the third largest drainage basin of Brazil; developed for hydroelectric power.

São Jor·ge (souň zhôr′zhə) An island in the central Azores; 92 square miles.

São Lu·ís (souň lōō·ēs′) A port of NE Brazil, capital of Maranhão state. Formerly São Luís do Ma·ra·nhão (thōō mä′rə·nyouň′). Also São Luiz.

São Ma·nuel (souň mə·nwel′) A river of northern Mato Grosso, Brazil, flowing 700 miles NW to the Tapajós.

São Mi·guel (souň mē·gel′) An island in the eastern Azores; 288 square miles.

Saône (sōn) A river in eastern France, flowing 268 miles SW to the Rhône at Lyon.

São Pau·lo (souňm pou′lō) A maritime state in SE Brazil; 95,428 square miles; capital, São Paulo.

São Paulo de Lo·an·da (thə lō·än′də) A former name for LUANDA.

São Pe·dro de Ri·o Gran·de do Sul (souňm pä′·thrōō thə rē′ōō graňn′də thōō sōōl′) A former name for the port of RIO GRANDE DO SUL.

Saor·stat Eir·eann (sâr′stät âr′ən, *Gaelic* ä′rôn) Gaelic name for IRISH FREE STATE.

São Sal·va·dor (souň säl′və·thôr′) The former name for Salvador, Brazil.

São Tia·go (souň tyä′gōō) Largest of the Cape Verde Islands; 383 square miles; capital, Praia. Also São Thia′go.

Saõ To·mé e Prín·ci·pe (souň tô·me′ e preň′sē·pə) A Portuguese province in the Bight of Biafra, comprising the islands of São Tomé (also São Thomé, English *St. Thomas*); 320 square miles; and Principe (English *Prince Island*); 52 square miles.

sap¹ (sap) *n.* 1 The aqueous juices of plants, which contain and transport the materials necessary to vegetable growth. 2 Any vital fluid; vitality. 3 Sapwood. 4 *Slang* A foolish, stupid, or ineffectual person. [OE *sæp*]

sap² (sap) *v.* **sapped, sap·ping** *v.t.* 1 To weaken or destroy gradually and insidiously; enervate; exhaust. 2 To approach or undermine (an enemy fortification) by digging a sap or saps. — *v.i.* 3 To dig a sap or saps; undermine an enemy fortification. See synonyms under WEAKEN. — *n.* A deep, narrow trench or tunnel dug so as to approach or undermine a fortification. [<MF *saper, sapper* <*sappe* a spade <Ital. *zappe* <*zappa* a goat; with ref. to resemblance of the handle to a goat's horns]

sap·a·jou (sap′ə·jōō, *Fr.* sȧ·pȧ·zhōō′) *n.* A South American monkey, the capuchin: often seen in captivity. Also called *sajou.* [<F <Tupian]

SAPAJOU
(Head and body about 1 1/2 feet long)

sa·pan·wood (sə·pan′wood) *n.* 1 The brownish-red dyewood obtained from a medium-sized East Indian tree (*Caesalpinia sappan*) of the bean family. 2 The tree. Also spelled *sappanwood:* also called *brazil.* [Trans. of Du. *sapanhout* < Malay *sapang* sapanwood + Du. *hout* wood]

Sa·phar (sä·fär′) See under CALENDAR (Mohammedan).

sap·head (sap′hed′) *n. Slang* A soft-headed person; simpleton. [< SAP¹ (def. 4) + HEAD] — **sap′head′ed** *adj.*

sa·phe·na (sə·fē′nə) *n. pl.* **·nae** (-nē) *Anat.* One of the two large superficial veins of the leg. [< Med. L, a vein in the leg < Arabic *ṣāfin*] — **sa·phe′nous** *adj.*

sap·id (sap′id) *adj.* Affecting the sense of taste; savory; agreeable. [< L *sapidus* < *sapere* taste] — **sa·pid′i·ty, sap′id·ness** *n.*

sa·pi·ence (sā′pē·əns) *n.* Wisdom; learning: often ironical. Also **sa′pi·en·cy.** [< OF < L *sapientia* wisdom < *sapiens, -entis* SAPIENT]

sa·pi·ent (sā′pē·ənt) *adj.* Wise; sagacious: often ironical. See synonyms under WISE¹. [< L *sapiens, -entis,* ppr. of *sapere* know, taste] — **sa′pi·ent·ly** *adv.*

sa·pi·en·tial (sā′pē·en′shəl) *adj.* Of, marked by, or expounding wisdom; especially, the *sapiential* books of the Bible, as Proverbs. — **sa′pi·en′tial·ly** *adv.*

sap·in·da·ceous (sap′in·dā′shəs) *adj. Bot.* Of or pertaining to a family (*Sapindaceae*) of mostly tropical trees, shrubs, and vines, the soapberry family, including some genera with edible fruit, as the litchi tree. [< NL <*Sapindus,* genus name <L *sapo* soap + *Indicus* Indian]

sap·less (sap′lis) *adj.* 1 Destitute of sap; withered. 2 Wanting vitality, spirit, or vivacity; insipid; dull.

sap·ling (sap′ling) *n.* 1 A young tree. 2 A youth. [Dim. of SAP¹]

sap·o·dil·la (sap′ə·dil′ə) *n.* 1 A large evergreen tree (*Achras zapota*) of the West Indies and Central America. 2 Its luscious apple-shaped fruit, the **sapodilla plum,** for which it is cultivated. Often called *mamey, marmalade tree.* Also **sa·po·ta** (sə·pō′tə), **sap′a·dil′lo, sap′o·dil′lo.** [<Sp. *zapotille,* dim of *zapota* <Nahuatl *zapotl, sapotl*]

sap·o·na·ceous (sap′ə·nā′shəs) *adj.* Of the nature of soap; soapy. [<NL *saponaceus* <L *sapo, saponis* soap]

sa·pon·i·fi·ca·tion (sə·pon′ə·fə·kā′shən) *n.* 1 The process or result of making soap. 2 *Chem.* **a** A decomposition in which an ester is changed into an acid and an alcohol. **b** The conversion of certain acid derivatives, as nitrates, acid amides, etc., into the corresponding acids.

sa·pon·i·fy (sə·pon′ə·fī) *v.t.* **·fied, ·fy·ing** To convert (a fat or oil) into soap by the action of an alkali. [<F *saponifier* <NL *saponificare* <L *sapo, saponis* soap + *facere* make] — **sa·pon′i·fi′a·ble** *adj.* — **sa·pon′i·fi′er** *n.*

sap·o·nin (sap′ə·nin) *n. Biochem.* One of several nearly white amorphous glycosides contained in various plants and characterized by their ability to form emulsions and soapy lathers. Also **sap′o·nine** (-nēn, -nin). [<F *saponine* <L *sapo, saponis* soap + F *-ine* -INE²]

sap·o·nite (sap′ə·nīt) *n.* A soft, hydrous silicate of magnesium and aluminum, found as an

amorphous soaplike mass in nodules, or filling cavities in rock. [< L *sapo, saponis* soap + -ITE[1]]

sa·por (sā′pər, -pôr) *n.* That quality of a substance affecting the sense of taste; flavor; taste. Also *Brit.* **sa′pour.** [< L, taste < *sapere* taste, know] —**sap·o·rif·ic** (sap′ə-rif′ik), **sap′o·rous** *adj.*

sap·o·ta·ceous (sap′ə-tā′shəs) *adj. Bot.* Of or pertaining to a family (*Sapotaceae*) of trees and shrubs yielding a milky juice of considerable economic importance, and also some edible fruits, as the sapodilla family. [< NL < *sapota* < Sp. *zapote* SAPODILLA]

sap·pan·wood (sə·pan′wŏŏd′) See SAPANWOOD.

sap·per (sap′ər) *n.* **1** One who or that which saps. **2** A soldier employed in making trenches, tunnels, and underground fortifications. [< SAP[2] + -ER]

Sap·phic (saf′ik) *adj.* **1** Pertaining to or in the manner of Sappho. **2** Denoting a meter or verse form used by Sappho, especially a stanza of three Sapphics followed by an Adonic. —*n.* A line of trochaic pentameter with a dactyl in the third foot: much used by Sappho, Alcaeus, Horace, and other classical poets. [< F *sapphique, saphique* < L *Sapphicus* < Gk. *Sapphikos* < *Sapphō* Sappho]

Sap·phi·ra (sa·fī′rə) Wife of Ananias. *Acts* v.

sap·phire (saf′īr) *n.* **1** Any of various gemstones consisting of corundum of a color other than red but especially blue. **2** A jewel fashioned of sapphire. **3** Deep pure blue. [< OF *sapir* < L *sapphirus, sapp(h)ir* < Gk. *sappheiros,* a gemstone < Semitic, ? ult. < Skt. *sanipriya* dear to the planet Saturn]

sap·phi·rine (saf′ər·in, -rēn) *adj.* Consisting of or like sapphire. —*n.* **1** A vitreous pale blue or green silicate of aluminum and magnesium, crystallizing in the monoclinic system. **2** Sapphire quartz. **3** A blue variety of spinel.

Sap·pho (saf′ō) Greek poetess of Lesbos; lived about 600 B.C.

Sap·po·ro (säp·pō′rō) The capital of Hokkaido island, Japan.

sap·py (sap′ē) *adj.* **·pi·er, ·pi·est 1** Full of sap; juicy. **2** *Slang* Immature; silly. **3** Vital; pithy. —**sap′pi·ly** *adv.* —**sap′pi·ness** *n.*

sa·pre·mi·a (sə·prē′mē·ə) *n. Pathol.* Blood poisoning by the products of putrefaction. Also **sa·prae′mi·a.** [< NL < Gk. *sapros* putrid + *haima* blood] —**sa·pre′mic** *adj.*

sapro- *combining form* **1** Decomposition or putrefaction: *saprogenic.* **2** Saprophytic: *saproplankton.* [< Gk. *sapros* rotten]

sap·ro·gen·ic (sap′rə·jen′ik) *adj.* **1** Productive of putrefaction. **2** Developing in or living upon putrefying matter. Also **sa·prog·e·nous** (sə·proj′ə·nəs).

sap·ro·lite (sap′rə·līt) *n. Geol.* Thoroughly decomposed, earthy rock, lying in its original place. [< SAPRO- + -LITE] —**sap′ro·lit′ic** (-lit′ik) *adj.*

sa·proph·a·gous (sə·prof′ə·gəs) *adj.* Feeding on decaying substances. [< SAPRO- + -PHAGOUS]

sap·ro·phyte (sap′rə·fīt) *n.* An organism that lives on dead or decaying organic matter, as certain fungous or other plants, various bacteria, etc. [< SAPRO- + -PHYTE] —**sap′ro·phyt′ic** (-fit′ik) *adj.*

sap·ro·plank·ton (sap′rə·plangk′tən) *n.* Plankton found on the surface of stagnant water. [< SAPRO- + PLANKTON]

sap·sa·go (sap′sə·gō) *n.* A hard green Swiss cheese flavored with melilot, used chiefly in cooking. [Alter. of G *schabzieger* < *schaben* shave, scrape + *zieger* whey]

sap·suck·er (sap′suk′ər) *n.* Any small black-and-white woodpecker (genus *Sphyrapicus*), especially the **yellow-bellied sapsucker** (*S. varius*), which damages orchard trees by exposing and devouring the sapwood.

YELLOW-BELLIED
SAPSUCKER
(About 8 1/2 inches long)

sap sugar Maple sugar.

sap·wood (sap′wŏŏd′) *n.* The layer of newly formed and functional xylem cells between the cambium and the heartwood of a woody stem. Also called *alburnum.*

Saq·qa·ra (sə·kä′rə) See SAKKARA.

sar·a·band (sar′ə·band) *n.* A stately Spanish dance in triple time, of the 17th and 18th centuries; also, the music for or in the rhythm of this dance, often used as one of the movements of the classical suite. Also **sar′a·bande.** [< F *sarabande* < Sp. *zarabanda,* ult. < Persian *sarband* a kind of dance and song]

Sa·ra·bat (sä′rä·bät′) Former name of the GEDIZ.

Sar·a·cen (sar′ə·sən) *n.* **1** Originally, a nomad Arab of the Syrian-Arabian desert, who harassed the frontiers of the Roman Empire. **2** A Moslem enemy of the Crusaders. **3** Any Arab. **4** *Obs.* A heathen; pagan. [Fusion of OE *Sarracene* and OF *Sarazin, Saracin,* both < LL *Saracenus* < LGk. *Sarakēnos,* ? < Arabic] —**Sar′a·cen′ic** (-sen′ik) or **·i·cal** *adj.*

Sar·a·gos·sa (sar′ə·gos′ə) A city of NE Spain, on the Ebro; former capital of Aragon: Spanish *Zaragoza.*

Sar·ah (sâr′ə) A feminine personal name. Also **Sar·a** (sâr′ə), *Fr.* sá·rá′, *Ital., Sp.* sä′rä, *Ger.* zä′rä). [< Hebrew *sārāh* a princess]
—Sarah The wife of Abraham. *Gen.* xvii 15.

Sa·ra·je·vo (sä′rä·yā′vō) A city in central Yugoslavia; the former capital of Bosnia where Archduke Francis Ferdinand was assassinated, June 28, 1914: also *Serajevo.*

sa·ran (sə·ran′) *n.* Any of a class of synthetic fibers and textile materials obtained by the chemical treatment of petroleum and natural brines. [Coined by Dow Chemical Co.]

Sar·a·nac Lakes (sar′ə·nak) Three lakes in NE New York, in the Adirondack Mountains, **Upper, Middle,** and **Lower Saranac,** linked by the **Saranac River,** which flows 50 miles NE to Lake Champlain at Plattsburg.

Sa·ransk (sä·ränsk′) The capital of Mordvinian Autonomous S.S.R.

Sar·a·to·ga (sar′ə·tō′gə) A former name for SCHUYLERVILLE.

Saratoga Springs A resort city in eastern New York, noted for horse-racing and mineral waters.

Saratoga trunk A very large traveling trunk used formerly by ladies. [after *Saratoga Springs*]

Sa·ra·tov (sä·rä′tôf) A port on the Volga in SE European Russian S.F.S.R.; a major industrial and natural-gas-producing center.

Sa·ra·wak (sə·rä′wäk) A State of Malaysia in NW Borneo; 47,071 square miles; capital, Kuching. —**Sa·ra·wak·ese** (sə·rä′wäk·ēz′, -ēs′) *adj.* & *n.*

sar·casm (sär′kaz·əm) *n.* **1** A keenly ironical or scornful utterance; contemptuous and taunting language. **2** The use of biting gibes or cutting rebukes. See synonyms under BANTER. [< LL *sarcasmus* < Gk. *sarkasmos* < *sarkazein* tear flesh, speak bitterly < *sarx, sarkos* flesh]

sar·cas·tic (sär·kas′tik) *adj.* **1** Characterized by or of the nature of sarcasm. **2** Taunting. Also **sar·cas′ti·cal.** —**sar·cas′ti·cal·ly** *adv.*

sarce·net (särs′nit) See SARSENET.

sarco- *combining form* Flesh; of or related to flesh: *sarcogenic.* Also, before vowels, **sarc-.** [< Gk. *sarx, sarkos* flesh]

sar·co·carp (sär′kō·kärp) *n. Bot.* The succulent part of a drupaceous fruit, as the fleshy edible part of a plum or peach. [< F *sarcocarpe* < Gk. *sarx, sarkos* flesh + *karpos* a fruit]

Sar·co·di·na (sär′kō·dī′nə) *n. pl.* A class of marine and fresh-water protozoa which move by means of pseudopodia, including both naked forms, as the *Amoebae,* and those with protective shell covering, as the *Foraminifera.* [< NL < Gk. *sarkōdēs* fleshy < *sarx, sarkos* flesh]

sar·co·gen·ic (sär′kō·jen′ik) *adj.* Flesh-producing. Also **sar·cog·e·nous** (sär·koj′ə·nəs).

sar·co·lem·ma (sär′kō·lem′ə) *n. Anat.* The elastic membrane that invests striated muscular fibers. [< NL < Gk. *sarx, sarkos* flesh + *lemma* a husk]

sar·co·ma (sär·kō′mə) *n. pl.* **·ma·ta** (-mə·tə) *Pathol.* A tumor, or group of tumors, often malig-

nant, composed of embryonal lymphoid or connective tissue in which the cell elements predominate. [< NL < Gk. *sarkōma* < *sarkaein* become fleshy < *sarx, sarkos* flesh] —**sar·co·ma·toid,** **sar·co·ma·tous** (-kō′mə·təs, -kom′ə-) *adj.*

sar·co·ma·to·sis (sär·kō′mə·tō′sis) *n. Pathol.* The formation of sarcomatous growths in the body. [< NL < Gk. *sarkōma, -ōmatos* SARCOMA + -ōsis -OSIS]

sar·coph·a·gus (sär·kof′ə·gəs) *n. pl.* **·gi** (-jī) **1** A stone coffin or tomb; hence, a large ornamental coffin of marble or stone placed in a crypt or exposed to view. **2** A kind of limestone, used by the Greeks for coffins and said to reduce flesh to dust. [< L < Gk. *sarkophagos,* orig. adj., flesh-eating < *sarx, sarkos* flesh + *phagein* eat]

sar·co·plasm (sär′kō·plaz′əm) *n. Anat.* The substance resembling hyaloplasm that lies between the columns of a striated muscle fiber.

sar·cous (sär′kəs) *adj.* Of, pertaining to, or composed of flesh or muscle. [< Gk. *sarx, sarkos* flesh]

sard (särd) *n.* The deep brownish-red variety of chalcedony, translucently blood-red: used as a gem. Also called *sardine, sardius.* [< OF *sarde* < L *sarda* < Gk. *sardios.* See SARDIUS.]

Sar·da·na·pa·lus (sär′də·nə·pā′ləs) **1** Greek form of ASHURBANIPAL. **2** A verse tragedy by Lord Byron, published in 1821 and acted (in an adaptation by Charles Kean) in 1834.

sar·dine[1] (sär·dēn′) *n.* **1** A small fish preserved in oil as a delicacy, especially the California pilchard (*Sardinia coerulea*). **2** The young of the herring or some like fish similarly prepared. [< OF < Ital. *sardina* < L < Gk. *sardēnē* < *sarda* a kind of fish, prob. < *Sardō* Sardinia]

sar·dine[2] (särd) See SARD.

Sar·din·i·a (sär·din′ē·ə) **1** An Italian island in the Mediterranean, west of Italy; 9,196 square miles; forming, with its neighboring islands, an autonomous region of Italy; 9,298 square miles; capital, Cagliari. *Italian* **Sar·de·gna** (sär·dā′nyä). **2** A former kingdom (1720–1860) of northern Italy, including the island of Sardinia with Savoy and Piedmont. —**Sar·din′i·an** *adj.* & *n.*

Sar·dis (sär′dis) An ancient city of Asia Minor, capital of Lydia; destroyed by Tamerlane. Also **Sar′des.**

sar·di·us (sär′dē·əs) *n.* **1** A sard. **2** A stone in the breastplate of the Hebrew high priest. *Ex.* xxviii 17. [< LL < Gk. *sardios, sardion* < *Sardeis* Sardis]

sar·don·ic (sär·don′ik) *adj.* Scornful or derisive; sneering; mocking; cynical. [< F *sardonique* < L *sardonius* < Gk. *sardonios* < *sardanios* bitter, scornful; infl. in form by *Sardō* Sardinia, because thought to be < *sardanē,* a bitter plant of Sardinia causing fatal, laughterlike convulsions] —**sar·don′i·cal·ly** *adv.* —**sar·don′i·cism** *n.*

sar·do·nyx (sär′də·niks) *n.* A variety of onyx, consisting of alternate layers of light-colored chalcedony and reddish carnelian. [< L < Gk., appar. < *sardios* sardius + *onyx* onyx]

Sar·dou (sär·dōō′), **Victorien,** 1831–1908, French dramatist.

Sa·re·ma (sä′re·mä) See SAARE.

Sarg (särg), **Tony,** 1882–1942, U.S. artist born in Germany; maker of marionettes: full name *Anthony Frederick Sarg.*

sar·gas·so (sär·gas′ō) *n.* Gulfweed. [< Pg. *sargaço* < *sarga,* a kind of grape]

Sargasso Sea A part of the North Atlantic, extending from the West Indies to the Azores, known for its relatively still water and its large amounts of floating seaweed.

Sar·gent (sär′jənt), **John Singer,** 1856–1925, U.S. painter.

Sar·gon II (sär′gon), died 705 B.C., king of Assyria 722–705 B.C.

sa·ri (sär′rē) *n.* A long piece of cotton or silk cloth, constituting the principal garment of Hindu women: worn round the waist, one end falling to the feet, and the other crossed over the bosom, shoulder, and sometimes over the head. Also **sa′ree.** [< Hind. *sarī, sarhī* < Skt. *sātī*]

sark (särk) *n. Scot.* A shirt or chemise; hence, a shroud. [OE *serc*]

Sark (särk) One of the Channel Islands; 2 square miles. *French Sercq* (serk).

sark·it (sär′kit) *adj. Scot.* Provided with shirts.
Sar·ma·ti·a (sär·mā′shē·ə, -shə) An ancient name for a region of NE Europe, in Poland and U.S.S.R. between the Vistula and the Volga. —Sar·ma′tian *adj. & n.* —Sar·mat′ic (-mat′ik) *adj.*
sar·men·tose (sär·men′tōs) *adj. Bot.* Having or producing sarmenta; having runners. Also sar·men·ta·ceous (sär·mən·tā′shəs), sar·men′tous. [< L *sarmentosus* full of twigs < *sarmentum.* See SARMENTUM.]
sar·men·tum (sär·men′təm) *n. pl.* ·ta(-tə) *Bot.* The slender runner of a plant, as in a vine. Also sar′ment. [< NL < L, a twig lopped off < *sarpere* prune (trees)]
Sar·mien·to (sär·myen′tō), Domingo, 1811–88, Argentine educator, journalist, and statesman.
sa·rod (sə·rōd′) *n.* A lutelike Indian stringed instrument. [< Hindi *sarod*]
sa·rong (sə·rong′) *n.* 1 A skirtlike garment of colored silk or cloth worn by both sexes in the Malay Archipelago, etc. 2 The material used for this garment. [< Malay *sārung*, prob. < Skt. *sāranga* variegated]
Sa·ron·ic Gulf (sə·ron′ik) An inlet of the Aegean in central Greece, separating Attica from Peloponnesus; 50 miles long, 30 miles wide: also *Gulf of Aegina.*
Sa·ros (sā′rôs), Gulf of An arm of the Aegean in Turkey in Europe north of Gallipoli Peninsula; 37 miles long, 22 miles wide.
Sa·roy·an (sə·roi′ən), William, born 1908, U.S. novelist and playwright.
Sar·pe·don (sär·pē′dən) In Greek mythology: 1 A son of Zeus and Europa who was allowed to live for three generations. 2 A Lycian prince and warrior killed by Patroclus in the Trojan War.
sar·ra·ce·ni·a (sar′ə·sē′nē·ə) *n.* Any of a genus of plants, having trumpetlike or pitcher-shaped leaves by which insects are entrapped and then digested by the plants; a pitcherplant. [< NL, orig. *Sarracena*, after Dr. D. *Sarrazin*, 17th–18th c. physician of Quebec who sent a specimen to the botanist Tournefort in 1700] —sar′ra·ce′ni·a′ceous (-sē′nē·ā′shəs) *adj.*
Sarre (sär) The French name for THE SAAR.
sar·rus·o·phone (sa·rus′ə·fōn) *n.* A musical instrument resembling a bassoon but with a metal tube. [after *Sarrus*, 19th c. French bandmaster, its inventor + -(O)PHONE]
sar·sa·pa·ril·la (sas′pə·ril′ə, sär′sə·pə·ril′ə) *n.* 1 The dried roots of certain tropical American climbing plants (genus *Smilax*). 2 A medicinal preparation or a beverage made from them. 3 Any one of various plants, so called from some resemblance to true sarsaparilla, as the wild sarsaparilla (*Aralia nudicaulis*). [< Sp. *zarzaparilla* < *zarza* a bramble + *parilla*, dim. of *parra* a vine]
sar·sar (sär′sər) *n.* A cold, whistling wind of Moslem lands: also spelled *sansar.* [< Arabic *ṣarṣar* a cold wind]
sarse·net (särs′nit) *n.* A fine, thin silk, used for linings: also spelled *sarcenet.* [< AF *sarzinet*, dim. of ME *sarzin* a Saracen; prob. infl. by OF *drap sarrasinois*, lit., Saracen cloth < Med. L *pannus saracenicus*]
Sar·to (sär′tō), Andrea del, 1487–1531, Florentine painter.
sar·tor (sär′tər) *n.* A tailor: a humorous or literary term. [< L, a patcher, mender < *sartus*, pp. of *sarcire* mend]
sar·to·ri·al (sär·tôr′ē·əl, -tō′rē-) *adj.* 1 Pertaining to a tailor or his work; also, pertaining to men's clothes: *sartorial* perfections. 2 *Anat.* Relating to the sartorius. —sar·to′ri·al·ly *adv.*
sar·to·ri·us (sär·tôr′ē·əs, -tō′rē-) *n. Anat.* A long, narrow muscle of the thigh that aids in flexing the knee; the longest muscle in the human body: so called from its use in crossing the legs, as in the manner in which tailors traditionally sat down to work. [< NL < L < *sartor* a or]
Sar·tre (sär′tr′), Jean Paul, born 1905, French philosopher, novelist, and dramatist.
Sar·um (sâr′əm), New See SALISBURY.
Sa·se·bo (sä·se·bō) A port on NW Kyushu island, Japan.
Sa·se·no (sä′se·nō) An Albanian island in the Strait of Otranto, at the entrance to the Bay of Valona; 2 square miles. *Albanian* Sa·zan (sä′zän).
sash[1] (sash) *n.* An ornamental band or scarf, worn as a girdle, or around the waist or over the shoulder, often as part of a uniform or as

a badge of distinction. [Orig. *shash* < Arabic *shāsh* muslin, turban]
sash[2] (sash) *n.* A frame, as of a window, in which glass is set. —*v.t.* To furnish with a sash. [Alter. of CHASSIS, taken as a pl.]
sa·shay (sa·shā′) See CHASSÉ[1].
sa·shi·mi (sä′shē·mē) *n.* In Japan, raw fish slices.
sa·sin (sā′sin) *n.* The common black buck. [< Nepalese]
Sas·katch·e·wan (sas·kach′ə·won) A province of west central Canada; 251,700 square miles; capital, Regina: abbr. *Sask.*
Saskatchewan River A river of west central Canada, flowing 340 miles east to Lake Winnipeg from the confluence of the North Saskatchewan, flowing 760 miles east, and the South Saskatchewan, flowing 550 miles NE.
sas·ka·toon (sas′kə·tōon′) *n.* A small tree (*Amelanchier alnifolia*) of the rose family, with thick leaves and a globular purple fruit; a shadbush. [< Algonquian (Cree) *misāskwatomin* < *misāskwat* the shadbush + *min* a fruit, a berry]
Sas·ka·toon (sas′kə·tōon′) A city in south central Saskatchewan province, Canada, on the South Saskatchewan River.
Sas·quatch (sas′kwach, -kwôch) *n.* A hairy, bigfooted creature supposed to live in the forests of the Pacific Northwest.
sass (sas) *Colloq. n.* Impudence; back talk. —*v.t.* To talk to impudently or disrespectfully. [Dial. alter. of SAUCE]
sas·sa·by (sas′ə·bē) *n. pl.* ·bies A large darkred South African antelope (genus *Damaliscus*), with almost black back and face. [< Bantu *tsessébe, tsessábi*]
sas·sa·fras (sas′ə·fras) *n.* 1 A tree (genus *Sassafras*) of the laurel family. 2 The bark of the roots, yielding an aromatic stimulant and an essential oil used in cosmetics. [< Sp. *sasafrás*, prob. < N. Am. Ind. name; infl. in form by Sp. *sassifragia* < L *saxifraga* saxifrage]
Sas·sa·nid (sas′ə·nid) *n. pl.* Sas·sa·nids or Sas·san·i·dae (sas·ə·nē·dē) A member of the last national dynasty of ancient Persia (226–651). —*adj.* Of or pertaining to the Sassanids. Also Sas·sa·ni·an (sə·sā′nē·ən), Sas·sa·nide. [< Med. L *Sassanidae*, pl. < *Sassan* Sasan, grandfather of Ardashir I, the first Sassanid king]
Sas·se·nach (sas′ə·nakh) *n. Scot. & Irish* A person of Saxon blood; an Englishman; a Protestant. [< Irish *sasanach*, Scottish Gaelic *Sasunnach* < Gaelic *Sasunn* a Saxon]
Sas·soon (sa·sōon′), Siegfried, 1886–1967, English poet and author.
sas·sy[1] (sas′ē) *adj.* ·si·er, ·si·est *U.S. Dial.* Saucy; impertinent.
sas·sy[2] (sas′ē) *n.* A West African tree (*Erythrophleum guineense*) with poisonous bark and juice. Also sas′sy·wood′ (-wŏŏd′). [< native W. African name, ? < E *saucy*]
sat (sat) Past tense of SIT.
Sa·tan (sā′tən) In the Bible, the great adversary of God and tempter of mankind; the Devil: identified with *Lucifer* who, in Semitic mythology, led a revolt against God, was defeated by the archangel Michael, and cast into hell as punishment for his pride. *Luke* iv 5–8; *Rev.* xii 7–9. [< Hebrew *sātān* an enemy < *sātan* oppose, plot against]
sa·tang (sä′tang′) *n. pl.* sa·tang A bronze coin and money of account in Thailand; one one-hundredth of a baht. [< Siamese *satāṅ*]
sa·tan·ic (sā·tan′ik) *adj.* Devilish; infernal; wicked. Also sa·tan′i·cal. See synonyms under INFERNAL —sa·tan′i·cal·ly *adv.*
Sa·tan·ism (sā′tən·iz′əm) *n.* Satan-worship, specifically, a cult addicted to profane mockeries of the holy rites of Christian worship. —Sa′tan·ist *n.*
sat·a·ra (sat′ər·ə, sə·tä′rə) *n.* A lustrous ribbed woolen fabric. [from *Satara*, a town about 100 miles from Bombay, India]
satch·el (sach′əl) *n.* A small handbag. [< OF *sachel* < L *saccellus*, dim. of *saccus* a sack]
sate[1] (sāt) *v.t.* sat·ed, sat·ing To satisfy the appetite of; satiate. See synonyms under SATISFY. [Appar. alter. of obs. *sade*, OE *sadian*; refashioned after L *sat, satis* enough]
sate[2] (sāt) Archaic past tense of SIT.
sa·teen (sa·tēn′) *n.* A cotton fabric woven so as to give it a satin surface: usually mercerized cotton. [Alter. of SATIN; infl. inform by VELVETEEN]

sat·el·lite (sat′ə·līt) *n.* 1 *Astron.* A smaller body attending upon and revolving round a larger one; a moon. 2 One who attends upon a person in power. 3 Any obsequious attendant. 4 A small nation politically, economically, or militarily dependent on a great power. 5 A town or community whose activities are largely determined by those of a neighboring metropolis. 6 An airfield, base, or installation dependent upon a larger one. 7 A man-made object launched from and revolving around the earth: compare SPUTNIK. [< F < L *satelles, satellitis* an attendant, a guard]

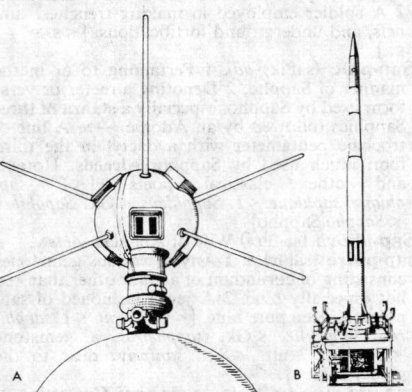

TYPE OF AMERICAN SATELLITE
A. Satellite. *B.* Rocket, which carries satellite into orbit, in position for launching.

sa·tem (sä′təm, sā′-) *n.* The eastern division of the Indo-European family of languages, including the Indo-Iranian, Armenian, Albanian, and Balto-Slavic subfamilies, in which proto-Indo-European palatal (k) is typically sibilated, as in the Avestan word *satem* "hundred." Compare CENTUM.
Sa·than (sā′tən), Sath·a·nas (sath′ə·nas) See SATAN.
sa·ti·a·ble (sā′shē·ə·bəl, -shə·bəl) *adj.* Capable of being satiated. —sa′ti·a·bil′i·ty, sa′ti·a·ble·ness *n.* —sa′ti·a·bly *adv.*
sa·ti·ate (sā′shē·āt) *v.t.* ·at·ed, ·at·ing 1 To satisfy the appetite or desire of; gratify. 2 To fill or gratify beyond natural desire; glut; surfeit. See synonyms under SATISFY. —*adj.* Filled to satiety; satiated. [< L *satiatus*, pp. of *satiare* fill < *satis* enough]
Sa·tie (sá·tē′), Erik Alfred Leslie, 1866–1925, French composer.
sa·ti·e·ty (sa·tī′ə·tē) *n. pl.* ·ties Repletion; surfeit. [< F *satiété* < L *satietas, -tatis* < *satis* enough]
sat·in (sat′ən) *n.* A silk, cotton, rayon, or acetate fabric of thick texture, with glossy face and dull back. —*adj.* Of or similar to satin; glossy; smooth. [< OF < Med. L *satinus, setinus*, ult. < L *seta* silk]
sat·i·net (sat′ə·net′) *n.* 1 A strong fabric with cotton warp and woolen filling. 2 A thin satin. Also sat′i·nette′. [< F, dim. of *satin* satin]
sat·in·flow·er (sat′ən·flou′ər) *n.* The garden flower honesty: so called from the satiny luster of its silvery silicles. Also sat′in·pod′ (-pod′).
satin spar A silky fibrous mineral, a variety either of calcite, aragonite, orgypsum.
sat·in·wood (sat′ən·wŏŏd′) *n.* 1 The satinlike wood of an East Indian tree (*Chloroxylon swietenia*) of the mahogany family. 2 The tree. 3 A West Indian tree (*Zanthoxylum flavum*) of the rue family, having a fine-textured, golden-yellow wood much used in fine cabinet work.
sat·in·y (sat′ən·ē) *adj.* Resembling or characteristic of satin; glossy.
sat·ire (sat′īr) *n.* 1 The use of sarcasm, irony, or keen wit in denouncing abuses or follies; ridicule. 2 A written composition in which vice, folly, or incapacity is held up to ridicule. See synonyms under BANTER. [< MF < L *satira, satura* a satire, earlier, a discursive verse composition on a number of subjects, orig. a medley < (*lanx*) *satura* a fruit salad, lit., a full (dish), fem. of *satur* full]

sa·tir·ic (sə·tir′ik) *adj.* Of, pertaining to, or resembling satire, especially literary satire: *satiric* verse.

sa·tir·i·cal (sə·tir′i·kəl) *adj.* **1** Given to or characterized by satire: a *satirical* writer. **2** Severely sarcastic; biting; caustic: a *satirical* laugh. **3** Satiric. —**sa·tir′i·cal·ly** *adv.* —**sa·tir′i·cal·ness** *n.*

sat·i·rist (sat′ə·rist) *n.* A writer of satire; a satirical person.

sat·i·rize (sat′ə·rīz) *v.t.* **·rized, ·riz·ing** To subject to or criticize in satire. See synonyms under RIDICULE. —**sat′i·riz′er** *n.*

sat·is·fac·tion (sat′is·fak′shən) *n.* **1** The act of satisfying, or the state of being satisfied; complete gratification. **2** The making of amends, reparation, or payment; extinguishment of a claim or obligation by payment, performance, restitution, or the rendering of an equivalent. **3** That which satisfies; atonement; compensation. [<OF *satisfactiun* <L *satisfactio, -onis* <*satisfactus*, pp. of *satisfacere* SATISFY]

Synonyms: comfort, complacence, content, contentment, enjoyment, gratification. See COMFORT, HAPPINESS, PROPITIATION, RECOMPENSE. *Antonyms*: annoyance, discontent, dislike, displeasure, dissatisfaction, disturbance, pain, sorrow, trouble, vexation.

sat·is·fac·tion–piece (sat′is·fak′shən·pēs′) *n.* A formal acknowledgment given by one who has received satisfaction of a mortgage or judgment, to authorize the entry of such satisfaction on the record.

sat·is·fac·to·ry (sat′is·fak′tər·ē) *adj.* **1** Giving satisfaction; answering fully all desires, expectations, or requirements; sufficient. **2** Making satisfaction; atoning or expiatory. See synonyms under ADEQUATE, COMFORTABLE. —**sat′is·fac′to·ri·ly** *adv.* —**sat′is·fac′to·ri·ness** *n.*

sat·is·fy (sat′is·fī) *v.* **·fied, ·fy·ing** *v.t.* **1** To supply fully with what is desired, expected, or needed; cause to have enough; gratify; content. **2** To free from doubt or anxiety; assure; convince. **3** To give what is due to. **4** To pay or discharge (a debt, obligation, etc.). **5** To answer sufficiently or convincingly, as a question or objection. **6** To fulfil the conditions or requirements of, as an equation. **7** To make reparation for; expiate. —*v.i.* **8** To give satisfaction. [<OF *satisfier* <L *satisfacere* <*satis* enough + *facere* do] —**sat′is·fi′er** *n.* —**sat′is·fy′ing** *adj.* —**sat′is·fy′ing·ly** *adv.*

Synonyms: cloy, content, fill, glut, sate, satiate, suffice, surfeit. To *satisfy* is to furnish enough to meet physical, mental, or spiritual desire. To *sate* or *satiate* is to gratify desire so fully as to extinguish it for a time. To *cloy* or *surfeit* is to gratify to the point of revulsion or disgust. *Glut* is a strong word applied to the utmost satisfaction of vehement appetites and passions; as, to *glut* a vengeful spirit with slaughter; we speak of *glutting* the market with a supply so excessive as to extinguish the demand. Much less than is needed to *satisfy* may *suffice* a frugal or abstemious person; less than a sufficiency may *content* one of a patient and submissive spirit. See INDULGE, PAY[1], REQUITE. *Antonyms*: check, deny, disappoint, refuse, restrain, restrict, starve, stint, tantalize.

sa·to·ri (sä·tō·rē) *n.* In Japanese Buddhism, enlightenment; especially, the abrupt or "sudden" enlightenment of Zen Buddhism. [<Japanese, lit., comprehension, perception]

Sat·pu·ra Range (sät·pōō′rə) A line of hills in northern India, forming the northern edge of the Deccan Plateau; highest point, 4,429 feet.

sa·trap (sā′trap, sat′rap) *n.* **1** A governor of a province in ancient Persia. **2** Any petty ruler under a despot. **3** A subordinate ruler or governor. [<L *satrapes* <Gk. *satrapēs* <O Persian *shathraparan*, lit., a protector of a province]

sa·trap·y (sā′trə·pē, sat′rə·pē) *n. pl.* **·trap·ies** The territory or the jurisdiction of a satrap. Also **sa·trap·ate** (sā′trə·pit, sat′rə-).

Sa·tsu·ma (sä·tsōō·mä) A former province of southern Kyushu island, Japan.

Satsuma ware A kind of Japanese pottery, originally made at Satsuma.

Sa·tu–Ma·re (sä′tōō·mä′rā) A city in NW Rumania near the Hungarian border.

sat·u·rant (sach′ər·ənt) *adj.* Saturating. —*n.* A substance that fully neutralizes another.

sat·u·rate (sach′ə·rāt) *v.t.* **·rat·ed, ·rat·ing 1** To soak or imbue thoroughly; fill or impregnate to the utmost capacity for absorbing or retaining. **2** *Chem.* To utilize fully the combining powers of the atoms in (a molecule). —*adj.* **1** Filled to repletion; saturated. **2** Very intense; deep: said of colors. [<L *saturatus*, pp. of *saturare* fill up <*satur* full] —**sat·u·ra·ble** (sach′ər·ə·bəl) *adj.* —**sat′u·ra′tor** or **sat′u·rat′er** *n.*

sat·u·rat·ed (sach′ə·rā′tid) *adj.* **1** Completely satisfied; replete; incapable of holding more of a substance or material: *saturated* vapor; a *saturated* solution. **2** *Chem.* Designating an organic compound having no free valences and without double or triple bonds, as paraffin, methane, and other *saturated* hydrocarbons. **3** Designating a pure color or hue, as in the spectrum; exhibiting high saturation. **4** *Geol.* Designating rocks or minerals with a maximum content of silica.

sat·u·ra·tion (sach′ə·rā′shən) *n.* **1** The act of saturating, or the state of being saturated; full impregnation. **2** The impregnation of one substance with another till no more can be received. Saturation may be by solution or by chemical combination. **3** *Meteorol.* The filling of the atmosphere with any vapor to the point of condensation. **4** The maximum magnetization of which a body is capable. **5** The degree of vividness or purity of chromatic color, as indicated by its freedom from admixture with white. **6** A massive concentration, in any given area, as of advertising, military force, etc., for a specific purpose: often used attributively: *saturation* bombing.

Sat·ur·day (sat′ər·dē, -dā) *n.* The seventh or last day of the week; the day of the Jewish Sabbath. [OE *Sæterdæg, Sæternesdæg*, trans. of L *Saturni dies* Saturn's day]

Saturday night special *U.S.* A kind of cheap, easily obtainable pistol.

Sat·urn (sat′ərn) **1** The planet next beyond Jupiter and next to Jupiter in size, remarkable for its 9 satellites and its flat, luminous, encircling rings. In astrology it was regarded as a melancholy planet. See PLANET. **2** In Roman mythology, the god of agriculture: identified with the Greek *Kronos* [OE *Sætern, Saturnus* <L *Saturnus*]

sat·ur·na·li·a (sat′ər·nā′lē·ə) *n.* Any season or period of general license or revelry: generally construed as singular: a *saturnalia* of crime. [<L. See SATURNALIA.]

Sat·ur·na·li·a (sat′ər·nā′lē·ə) *n. pl.* The feast of Saturn held at Rome in mid–December, celebrating the winter solstice, and marked by wild reveling and licentious abandon. [<L, orig. neut. pl. of *Saturnalis* of Saturn < *Saturnus* Saturn] —**Sat′ur·na′li·an** *adj.*

Sa·tur·ni·an (sə·tûr′nē·ən) *adj.* Of or pertaining to the god, or to the planet, Saturn, especially to a fabled golden age in the reign of Saturn, marked by simplicity, virtue, and happiness.

sa·tur·ni·id (sə·tûr′nē·id) *n.* Any of a family *(Saturniidae)* of large, hairy, brightly–colored moths widely distributed in most temperate regions. Many of them produce cocoons useful in the production of silk. —*adj.* Of or pertaining to the *Saturniidae*. [<NL <*Saturnia*, genus name <L *Saturnius* of Saturn < *Saturnus* Saturn]

sat·ur·nine (sat′ər·nīn) *adj.* **1** Having a grave, gloomy, or morose disposition or character; heavy; dull. **2** In old chemistry, pertaining to lead. **3** *Pathol.* Pertaining to or produced by lead. [<OF *saturnin* of Saturn, of lead, heavy <Med. L *Saturnus* lead, Saturn <L, Saturn]

Sat·ur·nine (sat′ər·nīn) *adj.* **1** Of or pertaining to the planet Saturn. **2** Born or being under the influence of the planet Saturn; hence, gloomy; heavy.

sat·urn·ism (sat′ərn·iz′əm) *n.* Lead poisoning. [<Med. L *Saturnus*. See SATURNINE.]

Sat·ya·gra·ha (sut′yə·gru′hə) *n.* **1** A movement characterized by non–violent resistance and non–cooperation, adopted in India, 1919, by the followers of M. K. Gandhi in protest against certain civil and religious abuses. **2** The non–violent force characterizing this movement, defined as an active love for one's opponents and a radical insistence on truth. [<Hind., truth–force, lit., a grasping for truth <Skt. *satya* truth + *graha* a grasping]

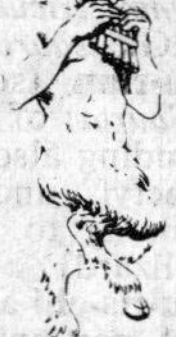
SATYR

sat·yr (sat′ər, sā′tər) *n.* **1** In Greek mythology, a woodland deity in human form, having pointed ears, pug nose, short tail and budding horns, and of wanton nature. **2** A very lascivious man. **3** Any butterfly of the family *Agapetidae*, commonly brown and gray with eyelike spots. [<L *satyrus* <Gk. *satyros*] —**sa·tyr·ic** (sə·tir′ik) or **·i·cal** *adj.*

sat·y·ri·a·sis (sat′ə·rī′ə·sis) *n. Psychiatry* A morbid lasciviousness in males. [<NL <Gk. *satyriaein* suffer from satyriasis <*satyros* a satyr]

sauce (sôs) *n.* **1** An appetizing dressing or liquid relish for food; loosely, any appetizing garnish of a meal; formerly, any condiment, as salt, pepper. **2** A dish of fruit pulp stewed and sweetened: cranberry *sauce*. **3** *Colloq.* Table vegetables, as roots or greens: also **garden sauce. 4** *Colloq.* Pert or impudent language. —*v.t.* **sauced, sauc·ing 1** To flavor with sauce; season. **2** To give zest or piquancy to. **3** *Colloq.* To be saucy to. [<OF < LL *salsa*, orig. fem. of L *salsus* salted, pp. of *salire* salt <*sal* salt]

sauce·box (sôs′boks′) *n. Colloq.* A saucy person: said generally of a child.

sauce·pan (sôs′pan′) *n.* A metal or enamel pan with projecting handle, for cooking food.

sau·cer (sô′sər) *n.* **1** A small dish for holding a cup. **2** Any small, round, shallow vessel of similar shape. [<OF *saussier* <*sauce* sauce]

sau·cy (sô′sē) *adj.* **·ci·er, ·ci·est 1** Disrespectful to superiors; impudent. **2** Piquant; sprightly; amusing. See synonyms under IMPUDENT. —**sau′ci·ly** *adv.* —**sau′ci·ness** *n.*

Sa·ud (sä·ōōd′), **King**, 1902–1969, king of Saudi Arabia 1953–1964; son of Ibn Saud: full name *Ibn Abdul Aziz al Faisal al Saud.*

Sa·u·di Arabia (sä·ōō′dē) A kingdom (1932) in the northern and central part of Arabia; 927,000 square miles; dual capitals, Mecca and Riyadh.

sauer·bra·ten (sour′brät′n, *Ger.* zou′ər·brä′tən) *n.* Beef marinated in vinegar before being braised. [<G <*sauer* sour + *braten* roast]

sauer·kraut (sour′krout′) *n.* Shredded and salted cabbage fermented in its own juice: also spelled *sourcrout*. [<G <*sauer* sour + *kraut* cabbage, vegetable, a plant]

sau·ger (sô′gər) *n.* A percoid fish, the smaller American pike perch *(Cynoperca canadensis)*, resembling the walleye. [<N. Am. Ind.]

saugh (sôkh) *n. Scot.* The sallow; the willow.

Sauk (sôk) *n.* One of a tribe of North American Indians of Algonquian stock, formerly occupying Michigan, later Wisconsin and the Mississippi valley: now on reservations in Oklahoma, Iowa, and Kansas. Also spelled *Sac*.

Saul (sôl) A masculine personal name. [<Hebrew, asked (of God)]

—**Saul** The first king of Israel. I *Sam.* ix 2.

—**Saul** The Hebrew name of the Apostle Paul. *Acts* xiii 9. Also **Saul of Tarsus.**

Sault Sainte Ma·rie (sōō′ sānt′ mə·rē′) **1** A city in northern Michigan, on St. Marys River. **2** A city opposite it in south central Ontario. Also **Sault Ste. Marie.**

Sault Sainte Marie Canals Three ship canals at the rapids in the St. Marys River, connecting Lake Superior with Lake Huron: also, *Colloq.*, *Soo Canals.*

sau·na (sou′nə, sô′-) *n.* **1** A Finnish steam bath in which the steam is produced by running water over heated stones. **2** A bath in which the bather is exposed to very hot, dry air. **3** A room or enclosure for a sauna. [< Finnish]

saun·ter (sôn′tər) *v.i.* To walk in a leisurely or lounging way; stroll. See synonyms under LINGER. —*n.* **1** A slow, aimless manner of walking. **2** An idle stroll. [ME *santren* muse, meditate; ult. origin unknown]

Sau·rash·tra (sou·räsh′trə) A former constituent State of western India, comprising most of Kathiawar peninsula and including 222

former states; merged into Bombay State, 1956; 21,062 square miles; former capital, Rajkot.

sau·rel (sôr′əl) *n.* A horse mackerel (genus *Trachurus*), especially *T. trachurus* and *T. symmetricus* of America and Europe. [<F <Gk. *sauros* a horse mackerel]

sau·rian (sôr′ē·ən) *n.* One of a suborder *(Sauria)* of reptiles, the lizards: formerly including also crocodiles, dinosaurians, pterodactyls, and other fossil forms. —*adj.* Pertaining to the *Sauria.* [<NL <Gk. *sauros* a lizard]

sau·ris·chi·an (sô·ris′kē·ən) *adj. Paleontol.* Of, pertaining to, or belonging to an order *(Saurischia)* of reptilelike dinosaurs that flourished through most of the Mesozoic era. —*n.* A member of this order. [<NL <Gk. *sauros* a lizard + *ischion* a hip]

sauro– *combining form* Lizard: *sauropod.* Also, before vowels, **saur–.** [<Gk. *sauros* a lizard]

sau·ro·pod (sôr′ə·pod) *n. Paleontol.* One of a suborder *(Sauropoda)* of amphibious four-footed dinosaurs of the Triassic, Jurassic, and Cretaceous periods. —*adj.* Of or pertaining to the *Sauropoda.* [<NL <Gk. *sauros* a lizard + *pous, podos* a foot] —**sau·rop·o·dous** (sô·rop′ə·dəs) *adj.*

–saurus *combining form Zool.* Lizard: used to form genus names: *Brontosaurus, Plesiosaurus.* Corresponding class names end in **–sauria,** family names in **–sauridae,** and individual names in **–saur** or **–saurid.** [<Gk. *sauros* a lizard]

sau·ry (sôr′ē) *n. pl.* **·ries** An edible fish *(Scomberesox saurus)* of the Atlantic, having the jaws developed into a slim beak. It travels in predatory shoals. Also **saury pike.** [<NL *saurus* <Gk. *sauros* a lizard]

sau·sage (sô′sij) *n.* **1** Finely chopped and highly seasoned meat, commonly stuffed into the cleaned and prepared entrails of some animal or artificial casings. **2** *Aeron.* A type of airship or captive observation balloon, shaped like a sausage. [<AF *saussiche* <LL *salsicia,* ult. <L *salsus.* See SAUCE.]

saus·su·rite (sô·sŏŏr′īt, sôs′yə·rīt) *n.* A tough, compact, impure form of labradorite. [after Prof. H. B. de *Saussure,* 1740–99, Swiss geologist] —**saus·su·rit·ic** (sôs′yə·rit′ik) *adj.*

saut (sät, sôt) *adj.* & *n. Scot.* Salt.

sau·té (sō·tā′, sô-) *adj.* Fried quickly with little grease. —*v.t.* **·téed, ·té·ing** To fry quickly in a little fat. [<F, pp. of *sauter* leap]

sau·terne (sō·tûrn′, sō-; *Fr.* sō·tern′) *n.* A sweet, white French wine; often, in America, any white wine, dry or sweet. Also **sau·ternes′.** [from *Sauternes,* district in SW France]

sau·toir (sō·twär′) *n. Her.* A saltire. Also **sau·toire′.** —**en sautoir** Worn saltirewise, or diagonally about the body, as a ribbon. [<F. See SALTIRE.]

sauve qui peut (sōv kē pœ′) *French* A stampede; rout; literally, save himself who can.

Sa·va (sä′vä) A river of northern Yugoslavia, flowing about 583 miles east to the Danube near Belgrade; the longest river entirely in Yugoslavia. *French* **Save** (såv), *German* **Sau** (sou).

sav·age (sav′ij) *adj.* **1** Of a wild and untamed nature; not domesticated; hence, ferocious; fierce. **2** Living in or belonging to the most primitive and rude condition of human life and society; uncivilized; uncultivated: *savage* tribes. **3** Enraged; cruel; furious: said of man or beast. **4** *Obs.* Remote from human abode; belonging to the wilderness: a *savage* trail. See synonyms under BARBAROUS, BITTER, FIERCE, GRIM, SANGUINARY. —*n.* **1** A primitive or uncivilized human being. **2** A brutal, fierce, and cruel person; a barbarian. [<OF *salvage, sauvage* <L *silvaticus, salvaticus* < *silva* a wood] —**sav′age·ly** *adv.*

Sav·age (sav′ij), **Arthur William,** 1857–1938, U. S. inventor; manufacturer of rifles, etc. —**Richard,** 1697?–1743, English poet.

Savage Island See NIUE.

sav·age·ry (sav′ij·rē) *n. pl.* **·ries** **1** The state of being savage: also **sav′age·ness.** **2** Cruelty in disposition or action; a cruel or savage act. **3** Savages collectively: also **sav′age·dom.** Also **sav′ag·ism.**

Savage's Station A battlefield near Richmond, Virginia; scene of an unsuccessful Confederate attack (1862) during the Civil War.

Sa·vai·i (sä·vī′ē) The largest island in Western Samoa; 700 square miles.

sa·van·na (sə·van′ə) *n.* **1** A tract of level land covered with low vegetation; a treeless plain. **2** Any large area of tropical or subtropical grassland, covered in part with trees and spiny shrubs. Also **sa·van′nah.** [Earlier *zavana* <Sp. <Cariban]

Sa·van·nah (sə·van′ə) A port in eastern Georgia, at the mouth of the **Savannah River,** which flows 314 miles SE to the Atlantic and forms the boundary between Georgia and South Carolina.

sa·vant (sə·vänt′, sav′ənt; *Fr.* så·väṅ′) *n.* A man of exceptional learning. See synonyms under SCHOLAR. [<F, orig. ppr. of *savoir* know <L *sapere* be wise]

Sa·vart (så·vår′), **Felix,** 1791–1841, French physician and physicist.

save[1] (sāv) *v.* **saved, sav·ing** *v.t.* **1** To preserve or rescue from danger, harm, etc. **2** To keep from being spent, expended, or lost; avoid the loss or waste of. **3** To set aside for future use; accumulate: often with *up.* **4** To treat carefully so as to avoid fatigue, harm, etc.: to *save* one's eyes. **5** To avoid the need or trouble of; prevent by timely action: A stitch in time *saves* nine. **6** *Theol.* To deliver from spiritual death or the consequences of sin; redeem. —*v.i.* **7** To avoid waste; be economical. **8** To preserve something from danger, harm, etc. **9** To admit of preservation, as food. See synonyms under DELIVER, PRESERVE, SCRIMP. [<OF *salver, sauver* <LL *salvare* save <L *salvus* safe] —**sav′a·ble** or **save′a·ble** *adj.* —**sav′a·ble·ness** *n.* —**sav′er** *n.*

save[2] (sāv) *prep.* Except; but. —*conj.* **1** Except; but. **2** *Archaic* Unless. See synonyms under BUT[1]. [<OF *sauf* being excepted, orig. safe <L *salvus*]

Sa·ve (sä′və) The Portuguese name for the SABI.

save–all (sāv′ôl′) *n.* **1** A contrivance for preventing waste; anything that saves fragments. **2** A child's savings bank. **3** An overall or pinafore.

saved (sāvd) *adj.* **1** Delivered from punishment after death. **2** Converted to religion. **3** Not spent or lost; amassed.

sav·e·loy (sav′ə·loi) *n.* A kind of highly seasoned, dried sausage made of salted pork. [Alter. of F *cervelas* <Ital. *cervellata* < *cervello* the brain <L *cerebellum.* See CEREBELLUM.]

Sav·ile (sav′il), **Sir Henry,** 1549–1622, English classical and biblical scholar.

Savile Row A street in London famous for fashionable men's tailor shops; hence, sartorially magnificent.

sav·in (sav′in) *n.* **1** A bushy shrub or small tree *(Juniperus sabina)* of the cypress family. **2** The young shoots of this plant, yielding an acrid volatile oil used in medicine. **3** The red cedar *(Juniperus virginiana).* Also called *sabine.* [OE *safine* <OF *savine* <L *(herba) Sabina* the Sabine (herb), fem. of *Sabinus*]

sav·ing (sā′ving) *adj.* **1** That saves; preserving, as from destruction. **2** Redeeming; delivering. **3** Avoiding needless waste or expense; economical; frugal. **4** Incurring no loss, if not gainful: a *saving* investment. **5** Holding in reserve; making an exception; qualifying: a *saving* clause. —*n.* **1** Preservation from loss or danger. **2** Avoidance of waste; economy. **3** The result of this; reduction in cost: a *saving* of 16 percent. **4** That which is saved; especially, in the plural, sums of money not expended. **5** *Law* Reservation; exception. See synonyms under FRUGALITY. —*prep.* **1** With the exception of; save. **2** With due respect for: *saving* your presence. —*conj.* Save. —**sav′ing·ly** *adv.* —**sav′ing·ness** *n.*

savings account An account drawing interest at a savings bank.

savings bank **1** An institution for receiving and investing savings and paying interest on deposits. **2** A container with a slot for coins.

sav·ior (sāv′yər) *n.* One who saves. Also *Brit.* **sav′iour.** [<OF *savëour* <LL *salvator, -oris* <L *salvare* SAVE]

Sav·iour (sāv′yər) *n.* He who saves men from death and sin: a title sometimes applied directly to God, but chiefly to Jesus Christ, as the Redeemer: usually with *the.* Also **Sav′ior.**

sa·voir faire (så·vwår fâr′) *French* Ability to see and to do the right thing; readiness in proper and gracious actions and speech; tact; literally, to know how to act.

sa·voir vi·vre (så·vwår vē′vr′) *French* Good breeding; good social manners; literally, to know how to live.

Sa·vo·na (sä·vō′nä) A port on the Gulf of Genoa in NW Italy.

Sav·o·na·ro·la (sav′ə·nə·rō′lə, *Ital.* sä′vō·nä·rō′lä), **Girolamo,** 1452–98, Italian monk; reformer; burned at the stake for heresy.

sa·vor (sā′vər) *n.* **1** That quality of a thing that affects the taste and smell, or both; flavor; odor. **2** Specific or characteristic quality or approach to a quality; flavor. **3** Relish; zest: The conversation had *savor.* **4** *Archaic* Character; reputation. —*v.i.* **1** To have savor; taste or smell: with *of.* **2** To have a specified savor or character: with *of.* —*v.t.* **3** To give flavor to; season. **4** To taste or enjoy with pleasure; relish. **5** To have the savor or character of. Also *Brit.* **sa′vour.** [<OF *savour* <L *sapor* taste < *sapere* taste, know] —**sa′vor·er** *n.* —**sa′vor·ous** *adj.*

Synonyms (noun): flavor, fragrance, odor, relish, scent, smell, taste. See SMELL

sa·vor·less (sā′vər·lis) *adj.* Tasteless; insipid.

sa·vor·y[1] (sā′vər·ē) *adj.* **1** Of an agreeable taste and odor; appetizing. **2** Piquant to the taste. **3** In good repute. See synonyms under DELICIOUS. —*n. Brit.* A small, hot serving of food eaten at the end or beginning of a dinner. Also *Brit.* **sa′vour·y.** [<OF *savouré,* pp. of OF *savourer* taste < *savour* SAVOR] —**sa′vor·i·ly** *adv.* —**sa′vor·i·ness** *n.*

sa·vor·y[2] (sā′vər·ē) *n.* A hardy, annual, aromatic culinary herb of the mint family *(Satureia hortensis)* used for seasoning. Also **summer savory.** [<OF *savoreie,* alter. of L *satureia*; infl. in form by OF *savour* savor]

sa·voy (sə·voi′) *n.* A variety of cabbage with wrinkled leaves and a compact head. [<F *(chou de) Savoie* (cabbage of) Savoy]

Sa·voy (sə·voi′) A region and former duchy of the kingdom of Sardinia, between Italy and France; ceded to France in 1860. *French* **Sa·voie** (så·vwå′).

Sa·voy (sə·voi′), **House of** A family of French nobles, reigning in Italy from 1861–1946. Its members were descended from Humbert I, Count of Savoy (11th century).

Sa·voy·ard (sə·voi′ərd, *Fr.* så·vwå·yår′) *n.* **1** A native or inhabitant of Savoy, France. **2** An actor or actress in the Gilbert and Sullivan operas of which most were originally produced at the Savoy Theatre in London. **3** An admirer or producer of these operas. —*adj.* **1** Of or pertaining to Savoy, France. **2** Of the Savoy Theatre, London. [<F < *Savoie* Savoy]

Sa·vu Sea (sä′vōō) That part of the Indian Ocean bounded by the islands of Flores, Sumba, and Timor.

sav·vy (sav′ē) *Slang v.i.* **·vied, ·vy·ing** To understand; comprehend. —*n.* Understanding; good sense. [Alter. of Sp. *¿Sabe (usted)?* Do (you) know? < *saber* know <L *sapere* know, taste]

saw[1] (sô) *n.* **1** A cutting instrument with pointed teeth arranged continuously along the edge of the blade: used to cut or divide wood, bone, metal, etc. See illustrations under BUCKSAW, FRET SAW, HACKSAW. **2** A machine for operating a saw or gang of saws. **3** Any tool or instrument without teeth used like a saw, as a steel disk for cutting armor plate, etc. —**circular saw** A disk having saw teeth in or on its periphery, and mounted on an arbor, with which it is rotated, usually at high speed. —*v.* **sawed, sawed** or **sawn, saw·ing** *v.t.* **1** To cut or divide with a saw. **2** To shape or fashion with a saw. **3** To cut or slice (the air, etc.) as if using a saw: The speaker *saws* the air. **4** To cause to move with a to-and-fro motion like that of a saw. —*v.i.* **5** To use a saw. **6** To cut: said of a saw. **7** To be cut with a saw: This wood *saws* easily. [OE *sagu, saga*] —**saw′er** *n.*

saw[2] (sô) *n.* A proverbial or familiar saying; old maxim. See synonyms under ADAGE. [OE *sagu.* Akin to SAGA.]

saw[3] (sô) Past tense of SEE[1].

saw[4] (sô) *v.t. Scot.* To sow.

Sa·watch Range (sə·wach′) A range of the Rocky Mountains in central Colorado; highest peak, 14,431 feet: also *Saguache.*

saw·bill (sô′bil′) *n.* A motmot.

saw·bones (sô′bōnz′) *n. Slang* A surgeon.

saw·buck (sô'buk') *n.* **1** A rack or frame consisting of two X-shaped ends joined by a connecting bar or bars, for holding sticks of wood while they are being sawed. Compare SAW-HORSE. **2** *U.S. Slang* A ten-dollar bill: so called from the resemblance of X, Roman numeral ten, to the ends of a sawbuck. [Trans. of Du. *zaagbok*]

SAWBUCK AND SAWHORSE
a. Sawbuck. *b.* Bucksaw. *c.* Sawhorse.

saw·dust (sô'dust') *n.* Small particles of wood cut or torn out by sawing.
sawed-off (sôd'ôf', -of') **1** *adj.* Having one end sawed off. **2** Short; not of average height or length: a *sawed-off* shotgun.
saw·fish (sô'fish') *n. pl.* **·fish** or **·fish·es** Any of a family (Pristidae) of large, viviparous rays found chiefly in tropical estuaries and having a long body and a snout prolonged into a flat blade with toothlike projections on each side.
saw·fly (sô'flī') *n. pl.* **·flies** A hymenopterous insect (family *Tenthredinidae*) having in the female a sawlike ovipositor for piercing plants, soft wood, etc., in which to lay eggs.
saw·grass (sô'gras', -gräs') *n.* A sedge (genus *Mariscus*) with saw-toothed leaves, growing in marshes along the Atlantic coast from North Carolina to Florida and westward.
saw·horse (sô'hôrs') *n.* A frame consisting of a long wooden bar or plank supported by four extended legs: used by carpenters. Compare SAWBUCK. **2** A packsaddle.
saw log A log of suitable size for sawing.
saw·mill (sô'mil') *n.* **1** An establishment for sawing logs with power-driven machinery. **2** A large sawing machine.
saw·munt (sô'mənt) See SAUMONT.
sawn (sôn) Alternative past participle of SAW[1].
saw palmetto Either of two palmettos (*Serenoa repens* and *Paurotis wrightii*) of the southern United States and the West Indies.
saw·pit (sô'pit') *n.* A pit over which a timber is laid to be sawed by two sawyers, one of whom stands in the pit and the other above.
saw set An instrument to give set to, or bend slightly outward, the teeth of a saw.
saw·toothed (sô'tootht') *adj.* Serrate; having teeth or toothlike processes similar to those of a saw.
saw·yer (sô'yər) *n.* **1** One who saws logs; specifically, a lumberman who fells trees by sawing, or one who works in a sawmill: also spelled *sawer*. **2** Any beetle of the genus *Monochamus* having wood-boring larvae. [Alter. of SAWER]
sax[1] (saks) *n.* **1** A chopping tool for trimming edges of roofing slates: also called *slate ax*. **2** A long knife. **3** A short, broad sword. [OE *seax* a knife]
sax[2] (saks) *n. Colloq.* A saxophone. [Short for SAXOPHONE]
sax·a·tile (sak'sə-til) *adj.* **1** Pertaining to rocks. **2** Saxicoline. [< L *saxatilis* < *saxum* a rock]
Saxe (sáks) The French name for SAXONY.
Saxe (sáks), **Comte de,** 1696–1750, Hermann Maurice, French marshal.
Saxe-Co·burg (saks'kō'bûrg) A former duchy in central Germany; united in 1826 with **Saxe-Go·tha** (-gō'thə), another duchy, to form the duchy of **Saxe-Coburg-Gotha,** which was divided between Thuringia and Bavaria in 1918.
Saxe-Mei·ning·en (saks'mī'ning-ən) A former duchy in central Germany.
Saxe-Wei·mar (saks'vī'mär) A former grand duchy in central Germany; became the duchy of **Saxe-Weimar-Ei·se·nach** (ī'zə-näkh) in 1741.
sax·horn (saks'hôrn') *n.* A brass wind instrument having a long winding tube and cup-shaped mouthpiece, used in military bands. [after Antoine Joseph *Sax*, (called *Adolphe*), 1814–94, Belgian instrument maker + HORN]

sax·ic·o·line (sak·sik'ə-lēn, -lin) *adj. Ecol.* Living or growing among rocks. Also **sax·ic'o·lous.** [< NL *saxicola* < L *saxum* rock + *colere* inhabit]
sax·i·fra·ga·ceous (sak'sə-frə-gā'shəs) *adj. Bot.* Of or pertaining to a widely distributed family (*Saxifragaceae*) of herbs, shrubs, and trees, including gooseberries and witch hazel. [< NL < L *saxifraga*. See SAXIFRAGE.]
sax·i·frage (sak'sə-frij) *n.* **1** Any plant of the genus *Saxifraga*, growing in rocky places. **2** Any of various related plants. Also called *stonebreak*. [< OF < L (*herba*) *saxifraga*, lit., stone-breaking (herb)]
Sax·o Gram·mat·i·cus (sak'sō grə·mat'i·kəs), 1150?–1220?, Danish historian.
Sax·on (sak'sən) *n.* **1** A member of a Germanic tribal group living in the southern part of what is now Schleswig-Holstein in the early centuries of the Christian era. **2** A member of any of the offshoots of this group, as those who, with the Angles and Jutes, invaded England in the fifth and sixth centuries A.D. **3** An Anglo-Saxon. **4** An inhabitant of Saxony. **5** The modern High German dialect of Saxony. **6** A Teuton. — **Old Saxon** The dialect of Low German current in the valley of the lower Elbe in the early Middle Ages. — *adj.* **1** Of or pertaining to the Saxons, or to their language. **2** Germanic; Anglo-Saxon; also, English: said of words, phrases, etc. [< F < L *Saxo, Saxonis* < WGmc.]
Sax·on·ism (sak'sən·iz'əm) *n.* A word, phrase, etc., of English, specifically Anglo-Saxon, origin.
Sax·on·ist (sak'sən·ist) *n.* An authority on pre-Norman England or the Saxon language, especially Old Saxon.
Sax·o·ny (sak'sə·nē) *n. pl.* **·nies 1** A fabric made from wool raised in Saxony, central Germany. **2** A variety of fine yarn. **3** A glossy woolen cloth.
Sax·o·ny (sak'sə·nē) **1** A former duchy, electorate, and kingdom of central Germany. **2** A former Prussian province of central Germany, constituted in 1816, largely from the territories of the kingdom of Saxony; 9,753 square miles; capital, Magdeburg. **3** A former state of east central Germany, 1918–45; 5,789 square miles; capital, Dresden. **4** A former state of SE East Germany, 1949–52; 6,561 square miles; capital, Dresden. French *Saxe*, German *Sachsen*.
Sax·o·ny-An·halt (sak'sə·nē·än'hält) A former state (1949) of east central East Germany; 9,515 square miles; capital, Halle.
sax·o·phone (sak'sə·fōn) *n.* A brass wind instrument with about 20 finger keys, tonally like, but more powerful than, a clarinet. [after Antoine Joseph *Sax* (called Adolphe), 1814–94, Belgian instrument maker, who invented it about 1840 + -PHONE] — **sax'o·phon·ist** *n.*

SAXOPHONE

sax·tu·ba (saks'too'bə, -tyoo'-) *n.* A large saxhorn. [< SAX(HORN) + TUBA]
say[1] (sā) *v.* **said, say·ing** *v.t.* **1** To pronounce or utter; speak. **2** To declare or express in words; tell; state. **3** To state positively or as an opinion: *Say* which you prefer. **4** To recite; repeat: to *say* one's prayers. **5** To report; allege. **6** To assume as possibly true or as a hypothesis: He is worth, *say*, a million. — *v.i.* **7** To make a statement; speak. — **that is to say** In other words. — *n.* **1** What one has said or has to say; testimony; word: Let him have his *say*. **2** *Colloq.* My turn to speak or choose: Now it is my *say*. **3** Authority: to have the *say*. — *interj. U.S. Colloq.* A hail or an introductory exclamation to command attention: also *Brit.* **I say!** Compare LISTEN. [OE *secgan*] — **say'er** *n.*
　Synonyms (*verb*) : allege, assert, speak.
say[2] (sa) *n.* A fine, thin serge used in the 16th century, sometimes partly of silk, later entirely of wool. [< OF *saie* < L *saga*, pl. of *sagum* a military cloak]
Say (sā), **Thomas,** 1787–1834, U.S. zoologist.
Sa·yan Mountains (sä·yän') A mountain system on the Siberia-Mongolia border.

Say·ers (sā'ərz, sârz), **Dorothy L(eigh),** 1893–1957, English author.
say·id (sī'id, sä'yid) *n.* Lord: a title applied to men who claimed to be descendants of Mohammed through his elder grandson, Husain: also spelled *said, saiyid*. Also **say'yid.** [< Arabic *sayyid*]
Sa·yi·da (sä'yə·dä) See SAIDA.
say·ing (sā'ing) *n.* An utterance; also, a maxim. See synonyms under ADAGE.
sa·yo·na·ra (sä'yō·nä'rä) *n. Japanese* goodby.
say-so (sā'sō') *n. Colloq.* **1** An unsupported assertion or decision. **2** Right or power to make decisions: He has the *say-so*.
Sb *Chem.* Antimony (symbol Sb). [< L *stibium*]
'sblood (zblud) *interj. Archaic* God's blood: an imprecation. [Short for *God's blood*]
S-brack·et (es'brak'it) *n.* In mechanical construction, a bracket or other piece in the shape of the letter S: also called *S-piece*.
Sc *Chem.* Scandium (symbol Sc).
scab (skab) *n.* **1** A crust formed on the surface of a wound or sore. **2** A contagious disease among sheep, resembling mange; scabies. **3** Any of certain plant diseases of bacterial or fungous origin, in which there is a roughened or warty exterior. **4** *Slang* A mean, paltry fellow. **5** A workman who does not belong to or will not join or act with a labor union; one who takes the place of a striker; a strikebreaker. — *v.i.* **scabbed, scab·bing 1** To form or become covered with a scab. **2** To take the place of a striker; act as a scab. [Fusion of ON *skabbr* (assumed) and OE *sceabb*; infl. in meaning by L *scabies*. See SCABIES.] — **scabbed** *adj.* — **scab'bi·ly** *adv.* — **scab'bi·ness** *n.* — **scab'by** *adj.*
scab·bard (skab'ərd) *n.* A sheath for a weapon, as for a bayonet or a sword. — *v.t.* To sheathe in or furnish with a scabbard. [< OF *escalberc*, prob. < OHG *scara* sword + *bergan* hide, protect]
scabbard fish 1 The cutlas fish (*Trichiurus lepturus*) having a long, eel-like body, found in the warm coastal waters of the United States and West Indies. **2** Any long, slender, silvery fish of the genus *Lepidopus* of European coasts.
scab·ble (skab'əl) *v.t.* **·bled, ·bling** In stoneworking, to dress or shape roughly. [Earlier *scapple* < OF *escapeler* dress timber]
scab·bling (skab'ling) *n.* A stone chip or fragment.
sca·bies (skā'bi·ēz, -bēz) *n.* The itch; especially, a contagious skin disease of sheep caused by any of certain itch mites, as *Psoroptes communis*. [< L, roughness, an itch < *scabere* scratch, scrape. Akin to SHAVE.]
sca·bi·ous[2] (skā'bē·əs) *adj.* **1** Pertaining to scabies. **2** Having scabs. [< L *scabiosus* < *scabies*. See SCABIES.]
sca·bi·ous[1] (skā'bē·əs) *n.* Any of a genus (*Scabiosa*) of herbs of the teasel family, with involucrate heads of variously colored flowers, as the sweet scabious (*S. atropurpurea*). Also **sca·bi·o'sa** (-ō'sə). [< NL < Med. L (*herba*) *scabiosa* fem. sing. of *scabiosus* SCABIOUS[1]]
sca·brous (skā'brəs) *adj.* **1** Roughened with minute points; rugged; scurfy. **2** Knotty; difficult to handle tactfully. [< LL *scabrosus* < *scabere* scratch] — **sca'brous·ly** *adv.* — **sca'brous·ness** *n.*
scac·cog·ra·phy (ska·kog'rə·fē) *n.* The literature pertaining to the science and art of chess. [< Ital. *scacchi* chess, pl. of *scacco* a square on a chessboard + -(O)GRAPHY] — **scac·chic** (skak'ik) *adj.* — **scac·cog'ra·pher** *n.*
scad (skad) *n.* A saurel. [? Var. of SHAD]
scads (skadz) *n. pl. Colloq.* A large amount or quantity. [? Var. of dial. E *scald* a large amount, great number]
Sca·fell Pike (skô·fel') A mountain in Cumberland, England, the highest peak in England; 3,210 feet.
scaff (skaf, skäf) *n. Scot. & U.S. Dial.* Food; provisions. — *v.t. & v.i.* **1** To beg for (food). **2** *U.S. Slang* To eat. Also spelled *scauff*. [Prob. < G and Du. *schaffen* provide (food)]
scaf·fold (skaf'əld, -ōld) *n.* **1** A temporary elevated structure for the support of workmen, materials, etc., as in building. **2** A raised wooden framework used for drying hay, tobacco, fish, etc. **3** A platform for the execution of criminals. **4** A stage, as for

exhibition purposes. **5** A raised wooden frame formerly used by certain North American Indians for the disposal of their dead. —*v.t.* **1** To furnish or support with a scaffold: to *scaffold* a building in order to repaint the exterior. **2** To place on a scaffold. [<OF *(e)schaffaut, escadafaut.* Related to CATAFALQUE.]

scaf·fold·ing (skaf′əl·ding) *n.* A scaffold, or system of scaffolds, or the materials for constructing them: wooden *scaffolding.* Also **scaf′fold·age.**

scaff–raff (skaf′raf′, skäf′räf′) *n. Scot.* The rabble.

scag (skag) *n. Slang* Heroin. [Origin unknown]

scagl·ia (skal′yə) *n.* An Italian calcareous rock, corresponding to the chalk of England. [<Ital., a scale, a chip of marble <Med. L *scalia* <Gmc.]

scagl·io·la (skal·yō′lə) *n.* Hard, polished plasterwork imitating marble, granite, or other stone: made of powdered gypsum and glue, colored in various ways. [<Ital. *scagliuola,* dim. of *scaglia* SCAGLIA]

scaith (skāth) *n. Scot.* Scathe; damage; mar. —**scaith′less** *adj.*

sca·lade (skə·lād′) *n.* An escalade. Also **sca·la·do** (skə·lā′dō). [<Ital. *scalada* <*scalare* scale <*scala* a ladder <L. See SCALE[2].]

scal·age (skā′lij) *n.* **1** A percentage by which something is scaled down to allow for shrinkage. **2** The amount of lumber estimated to be in a log or logs being scaled. [<SCALE[2] + -AGE]

sca·lar (skā′lər) *adj.* Completely definable by a single number or by a point on a scale: said of a quantity having magnitude but no direction, as a volume or mass: distinguished from *vector.* —*n. Math.* A pure number, especially one representing only a magnitude. [<L *scalaris* of a ladder <*scala* a ladder. See SCALE[2].]

sca·la·re (skə·lā′rē, -lä′rā) *n.* **1** A deep-bodied cichlid fish of South American rivers (genus *Pterophyllum*), noted for its striking coloration and popular as an aquarium fish: also called *angelfish.* **2** A related fish of the Amazon, the **blue scalare** *(Symphysodon discus),* with a brownish-green, disk-shaped body. [<NL <L *scalaris* of a ladder; so called because marked with dark crossbars]

sca·lar·i·form (skə·lar′ə·fôrm) *adj. Biol.* Ladderlike: said of cells or vessels. [<NL *scalariformis* <L *scalaris* of a ladder + *forma* form]

scal·a·wag (skal′ə·wag) *n.* **1** *Colloq.* A worthless fellow; scamp. **2** *U.S.* A native Southern white who became or remained a Republican during the Reconstruction period: a contemptuous term used by Southern Democrats. Compare CARPETBAGGER. Also spelled *scallawag, scallywag.* [Origin uncertain]

scald[1] (skôld) *v.t.* **1** To burn with or as with hot liquid or steam. **2** To cleanse or treat with boiling water. **3** To heat (a liquid) to a point just short of boiling. **4** To cook in a liquid which is just short of the boiling point. —*v.i.* **5** To be or become scalded. —*n.* **1** A burn or injury to the skin by a hot fluid, as steam or water. **2** An act of scalding. **3** A destructive parasitic disease of cranberries. **4** A discoloration of plant tissue due to improper conditions of growth, bad storage, etc. [<AF *escalder* <LL *excaldare* wash with hot water <*ex-* very + *calidus* hot]

scald[2] (skôld, skäld) *n.* An ancient Scandinavian bard, minstrel, or reciter of eulogies: also spelled *skald.* [<ON *skald*] —**scal·dic** (skôl′dik, skäl′-) *adj.*

scald[3] (skäld, skôld) *v.t.* & *v.i. Scot.* To scold.

scald[4] (skôld) See SCALL.

scald·head (skôld′hed′) *n. Pathol.* Favus. [<*scald,* var. of *scalled* (<SCALL) + HEAD]

scale[1] (skāl) *n.* **1** One of the thin, flat, horny, membranous or bony outgrowths of the skin of various vertebrates, as most fishes, usually overlapping and forming a nearly complete investment. **2** A scab. **3** A scale insect. **4** *Bot.* A rudimentary or metamorphosed leaf, as of a pine cone. **5** *Metall.* The coating of oxide that forms on heated iron, etc.: also, an incrustation, as on the inside of boilers. **6** Any hard, thin, scalelike formation, as a flake, husk, shell, pod, or exfoliation. —*v.* **scaled, scal·ing** *v.t.* **1** To strip or clear of scale or scales. **2** To form scales on; cover with scales. **3** To take off in layers or scales; pare off. **4** To throw (a thin, flat object) so that its edge cuts the air or so that it skips along the surface of water. —*v.i.* **5** To come off in layers or scales; peel. **6** To shed scales. **7** To become incrusted with scales. [<OF *escale* a husk <Gmc.; infl. in meaning by OF *escaille* a fish's scale, an oyster's shell <Med. L *scalia* <Gmc.] —**scal′er** *n.*

scale[2] (skāl) *n.* **1** A piece of metal, wood, or glass bearing accurately spaced lines or graduations for use in measurement, or the series of marks so used. **2** Any system of designating units of measurement or in which a fixed proportion is used in determining quantities: a *scale* of 1 inch to the mile. **3** *Math.* A system of notation in which the successive places determine the value of figures, as the decimal system. **4** Any progressive or graded series; a graduation: the social *scale.* **5** *Music* All the tones or notes of a key in regular ascending or descending order, in an octave or

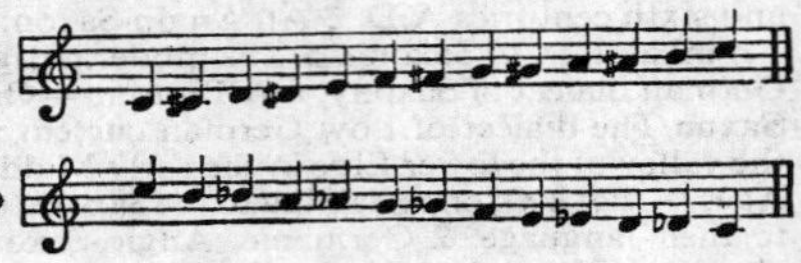

SCALE
a. Ascending. *b.* Descending.

more. **6** *Phot.* The range of light values which may be reproduced by a photographic paper. **7** An escalade. **8** A succession of steps; ladder; stairs: the original meaning. —**major scale** *Music* A scale having semitones between the 3–4 and 7–8 notes. —**minor scale** *Music* A scale having semitones between 2–3, 5–6, 7–8 notes (the harmonic form); or between 2–3, 7–8 ascending, 6–5, 3–2 descending (the melodic form). —*v.* **scaled, scal·ing** *v.t.* **1** To climb to the top of; go up by or as by means of a ladder. **2** To make according to a scale. **3** To regulate or adjust according to a scale or ratio: with *up, down,* etc. **4** To measure (logs) or estimate the amount of lumber in (standing timber). —*v.i.* **5** To climb; ascend. **6** To rise, as in steps or stages: Mountains *scaling* to the skies. [<Ital. *scala* a ladder <L <*scandere* climb] —**scal′a·ble** *adj.* —**scal′er** *n.*

scale[3] (skāl) *n.* **1** The bowl, scoop, or platform of a weighing instrument or balance. **2** The balance itself; hence, figuratively, the *scale* or *scales* of Justice. **3** *Usually pl.* Any form of weighing machine. —**to turn the scales** To determine; decide. —*v.* **scaled, scal·ing** *v.t.* **1** To weigh in scales. **2** To amount to in weight. —*v.i.* **3** To be weighed in scales. [<ON *skāl* a bowl, in pl. a weighing balance. Akin to SHALE, SHELL.]

scale board **1** A very thin, veneerlike piece of board, as for the back of a picture. **2** *Printing* A narrow strip of wood used in justifying a line of type. [<SCALE[1] + BOARD]

scale insect One of numerous small, hemipterous, plant-feeding insects (family *Coccidae*) which as adults are degenerate, sedentary, and covered with a scalelike, waxy protective shield.

scale moss Any plant belonging to the class *Hepaticae*; any of the liverworts: so called because of their scalelike leaves.

sca·lene (skā′lēn, skā·lēn′) *adj.* **1** *Geom.* **a** Having no two sides equal: said of a triangle. **b** Having the axis inclined to the base: said of a cone or cylinder. **2** *Anat.* Designating one of several deeply placed muscles attached to the cervical vertebrae and first and second ribs and acting to flex or bend the neck. Also **sca·le·nous** (skā·lē′nəs). [<LL *scalenus* <Gk. *skalēnos* uneven]

sca·le·nus (skə·lē′nəs) *n.* A scalene muscle. [<NL *(musculus) scalenus* <L, SCALENE (def. 2)]

Scales (skālz) A sign of the zodiac, called also *Libra* or *The Balance.*

scall (skôl) *n. Pathol.* **1** A cutaneous eruption of small pustular vesicles containing a purulent fluid: often epidemic among children. **2** Any scabby or scaly eruption. Also called *scald.* [<ON *skalle* a bald head]

scal·la·wag (skal′ə·wag), **scal·ly·wag** (skal′ē·wag) See SCALAWAG.

scal·lion (skal′yən) *n.* **1** A young, tender onion with a small, underdeveloped white bulb. **2** A shallot or leek. [<AF *scalun,* OF *eschalogne,* ult. <L *(caepa) Ascalonia* (onion) of Ashkelon, a Palestinian seaport]

scal·lop (skal′əp, skol′-) *n.* **1** A bivalve (genus *Pecten*) having a nearly circular shell with radiating ribs and wavy edge. **2** Its adductor muscle, which as a rule is edible and very succulent. **3** Its shell, formerly worn as a pilgrim's badge. **4** A dish or pan (originally a scallop shell) in which oysters are cooked or served. **5** One of a series of semicircular curves along an edge, as for ornament. —*v.t.* **1** To shape the edge of with scallops; ornament with scallops. **2** To bake (food) in a casserole with a liquid or sauce, often topped with bread crumbs. Also spelled *escallop, scollop.* [ME *scalop* <MF *escalope* shell <Gmc. Akin to SCALE[1].] —**scal′lop·er** *n.*

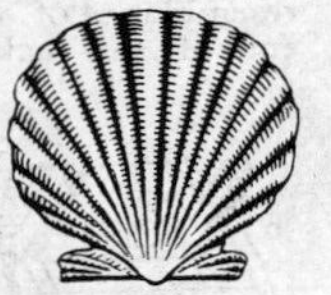

SCALLOP SHELL

scalp (skalp) *n.* **1** The skin of the top and back of the human skull, usually covered with hair; also, a portion of this, cut or torn away as a war trophy among certain North American Indians, particularly of the St. Lawrence region. **2** A similar piece taken from the head of a wild animal as an evidence that it has been killed for the collection of a bounty. **3** A political victory or defeat. **4** A denuded or bare summit, as of a hill or cliff. **5** On the stock exchange, a small profit taken by a speculator. —*v.t.* **1** To cut or tear the scalp from. **2** *Colloq.* To buy (tickets) and sell again at prices exceeding the established rate. **3** *Colloq.* To buy and sell again quickly in order to make a small profit. —*v.i.* **4** *Colloq.* To scalp bonds, tickets, etc. [ME, prob. <Scand. Cf. ON *skálpr* a sheath.] —**scalp′er** *n.*

scalp dance A ceremonial victory dance of certain North American Indians, in which the women of the tribe display the trophies and perform the dances, accompanied by the singing of the warriors.

scal·pel (skal′pəl) *n.* A small pointed knife with a very sharp, thin blade, used in dissections and in surgery. [<L *scalpellum,* dim. of *scalprum* a knife <*scalpere* cut]

scalp lock A long lock of hair left on the crown of the head by certain North American Indians, often braided and interwoven with feathers or fur: a challenge to an enemy.

scal·y (skā′lē) *adj.* **scal·i·er, scal·i·est** **1** Having a covering of scales; hence, also, exfoliated; scurfy. **2** Of the nature of a scale; squamous. **3** Incrusted, as a boiler. **4** *Slang* Mean; dishonorable. [<SCALE[1] + -Y[1]] —**scal′i·ness** *n.*

scaly ant–eater A pangolin.

scam (skam) *n. U.S. Slang* **1** A fraudulent bankruptcy planned as a swindle. **2** Any fraudulent scheme; swindle. [? Alter. of *scheme*]

Sca·man·der (skə·man′dər) Ancient name for the MENDERES (def. 2).

scam·ble (skam′bəl) *v.* **·bled, ·bling** *Brit. Dial.* *v.t.* **1** To scatter (something) to a crowd. **2** To gather confusedly. —*v.i.* **3** To scramble. **4** To stumble along. [Cf. SCRAMBLE and SHAMBLE[1]]

scam·mo·ny (skam′ə·nē) *n.* **1** A climbing plant *(Convolvulus scammonia)* of the morning-glory family, native in Asia Minor, with tuberous roots containing a milky juice. **2** The dried resin of scammony roots, used as a strong cathartic. [<L *scammonia* <Gk. *skammōnia*]

scamp[1] (skamp) *n.* A confirmed rogue; good-for-nothing fellow; rascal. [<obs. *scamp, v.,* roam, contraction of SCAMPER] —**scamp′ish, scamp′y** *adj.*

scamp[2] (skamp) *v.t.* To perform (work) carelessly or dishonestly. [Orig. dial. E, ? <ON *skemma* shorten <*skammr* short. Akin to SCANT, SKIMP.] —**scamp′er** *n.*

scam·per (skam′pər) *v.i.* To run quickly or hastily, as from danger; hurry away. —*n.* A hurried flight. [? <obs. Du. *schampen* run away <AF *escamper,* OF *eschamper* decamp, run off hurriedly, escape, ult. <L *ex* out from + *campus* a plain, battlefield] —**scam′per·er** *n.*

scam·pi (skam′pē) *n.pl.* Large shrimp, usually served in a garlic sauce. [<Ital.]

scan (skan) *v.* **scanned, scan·ning** *v.t.* **1** To examine in detail; scrutinize closely. **2** To pass

the eyes over quickly; glance at, as a page of manuscript. 3 To separate (verse) into metrical feet; ascertain the rhythm of. 4 To read (verse) aloud so as to ascertain the metrical structure. 5 In television, to pass a beam of light or electrons rapidly over every point of (a surface) so as to reproduce an image being televised. —*v.i.* 6 To scan verse. 7 To conform to metrical rules: said of verse. 8 In television, to scan a surface. See synonyms under LOOK. [<LL *scandere* scan verses <L, climb] **—scan′na·ble** *adj.* **—scan′ner** *n.*

scan·dal (skan′dəl) *n.* 1 The heedless or malicious repetition of evil reports; aspersion of character. 2 Reproach caused by outrageous or improper conduct. 3 A discreditable circumstance, event, or action; cause of reproach. 4 Injury to reputation, or general comment causing it. 5 *Law* Malicious defamation by word of mouth. 6 One whose conduct disgraces. [<AF *escandle* <L *scandalum* a cause of stumbling <Gk. *skandalon* a snare; refashioned after MF *scandale* <L *scandalum.* Doublet of SLANDER.]

Synonyms: aspersion, backbiting, calumny, defamation, detraction, obloquy, odium, reproach, slander. *Scandal* may be odious truth; *slander* is certain falsehood. *Antonyms*: applause, celebrity, credit, eulogy, fame, glory, honor, renown, repute.

scan·dal·i·za·tion (skan′dəl·ə·zā′shən, -ī·zā′-) *n.* 1 The act of offending moral feelings. 2 That which scandalizes; a scandal.

scan·dal·ize (skan′dəl·īz) *v.t.* **·ized, ·iz·ing** To shock the moral feelings of, as by improper, frivolous, or offensive conduct; outrage. **—scan′dal·iz′er** *n.*

scan·dal·ous (skan′dəl·əs) *adj.* 1 Causing, or tending to cause, scandal; being a scandal; opprobrious; disgraceful; shocking to the sense of truth, decency, or propriety. 2 Consisting of evil or malicious reports; tending to injure reputation. 3 *Law* Libelous; irrelevant. See synonyms under FLAGRANT, INFAMOUS. **—scan′dal·ous·ly** *adv.* **—scan′dal·ous·ness** *n.*

scan·dent (skan′dənt) *adj.* Climbing, or aiding to climb, as a plant. [<L *scandens, -entis,* ppr. of *scandere* climb]

Scan·der·beg (skan′dər·beg), 1403–68, Albanian chief and national hero: real name *George Castriota.*

scan·di·a (skan′dē·ə) *n. Chem.* Scandium oxide, Sc_2O_3, a colorless, amorphous powder soluble in acids. [<NL <*scandium* SCANDIUM]

Scan·di·an (skan′dē·ən) *adj.* 1 Relating to Scandia, the Scandinavian Peninsula. 2 Scandinavian. [<L *Scandia*]

scan·dic (skan′dik) *adj. Chem.* Pertaining to or derived from scandium, especially in its higher valence.

Scan·di·na·vi·a (skan′də·nā′vē·ə) The region of NW Europe occupied by Sweden, Norway, and Denmark; 315,156 square miles; Finland, Iceland, and the Faeroe Islands are often included: total area, 485,539 square miles.

Scan·di·na·vi·an (skan′də·nā′vē·ən) *adj.* Of or pertaining to Scandinavia, its people, or their languages. —*n.* 1 A native or inhabitant of Scandinavia. 2 The North Germanic group of languages. See under GERMANIC. **—Old Scandinavian** Old Norse. See under NORSE. [<L *Scandinavia,* var. of *Scadinavia* <Gmc.]

Scandinavian Peninsula The peninsula of NW Europe containing Norway and Sweden; 298,550 square miles.

scan·di·um (skan′dē·əm) *n.* A soft, silvery-white metallic element (symbol Sc, atomic number 21) widely distributed in small amounts in many minerals. See PERIODIC TABLE. [<NL <L *Scandia* Scandinavia]

scan·ning (skan′ing) *n.* 1 Scansion. 2 The process by which the electron beam of a television transmitting unit passes rapidly over every point of the image on the photosensitive screen.

scan·sion (skan′shən) *n.* The act or art of scanning verse to show its metrical parts. Compare METER[2] (def. 2). [<FF <LL *scansio, -onis* <L *scandere.* See SCAN.]

scan·so·ri·al (skan·sôr′ē·əl, -sō′rē-) *adj. Zool.* Pertaining to or adapted for climbing. Also **scan·so′ri·ous.** [<L *scansorius* <*scansus,* pp. of *scandere* climb]

scant (skant) *adj.* 1 Scarcely enough; meager in measure or quantity. 2 Being just short of the measure specified; of limited extent: often with the indefinite article even with a plural noun: a *scant* half-hour, a *scant* five yards. 3 Insufficiently supplied with something: with *of*: We were *scant* of breath. See synonyms under SCANTY. —*v.t.* 1 To restrict or limit in supply; stint. 2 To treat briefly or inadequately. See synonyms under SCRIMP. —*adv. Dial.* Scarcely; barely; not quite. [<ON *skamt,* neut. of *skammr* short] **—scant′ly** *adv.* **—scant′ness** *n.*

scant·ling (skant′ling) *n.* 1 A timber of moderate cross-section, used for studding, etc. 2 Such timbers collectively. 3 The dimensions of a timber in breadth and depth, but not in length; also, the dimensions of a stone in length, breadth, and thickness. 4 A small quantity or part; a sample. [Alter. of obs. *scantillon* <OF *eschantillon* specimen, corner-piece, chip; ? infl. in meaning by SCANT]

scant·y (skan′tē) *adj.* **scant·i·er, scant·i·est** 1 Limited in extent; small; close; cramped. 2 Restricted in quantity or number; scarcely sufficient. 3 Sparing. [<SCANT] **—scant′i·ly** *adv.* **—scant′i·ness** *n.*

Synonyms: deficient, insufficient, limited, narrow, niggardly, parsimonious, poor, scant, scarce, scrimped, scrimping, scrimpy, short, sparing, sparse. *Antonyms*: see synonyms under AMPLE.

Sca·pa Flow (skä′pə flō′, skap′ə) A sea basin and British naval base in the Orkney Islands, northern Scotland; 50 square miles: the Germans scuttled part of their own fleet here, June 21, 1919.

scape[1] (skāp) *n.* 1 *Bot.* A long, naked peduncle rising from a depressed stem, as in the dandelion. 2 *Biol.* A stemlike part, as of an insect antenna, or the shaft of a feather. 3 *Archit.* The shaft of a column, or the apophyge of a shaft. [<L *scapus* <dial. Gk. (Doric) *scapos.* Akin to SCEPTER.]

scape[2] (skāp) *n.* A scene, as of land, sea, clouds, or the like. [Back formation <LANDSCAPE]

scape[3] (skāp) *Archaic v.t. & v.i.* To escape: generally written *'scape.* —*n.* 1 An escape or means of escape. 2 A fault; an escapade. [Aphetic var. of ESCAPE]

scape·goat (skāp′gōt′) *n.* 1 The goat upon whose head Aaron symbolically laid the sins of the people on the day of atonement, after which it was led away into the wilderness. *Lev.* xvi. 2 Any animal or person on whom the bad luck or sins of an individual or group are symbolically placed, and which is then turned loose: a world-wide folk custom of great antiquity. 3 Any person bearing blame for others. [<SCAPE[3], *n.* + GOAT]

scape·grace (skāp′grās′) *n.* A mischievous or incorrigible person. [<SCAPE[3] + GRACE (def. 4)]

scape wheel An escape wheel.

scaph·oid (skaf′oid) *adj.* Boat-shaped. —*n. Anat.* A proximal bone of the wrist on the radial side; the navicular; also, a bone of the tarsus. [<NL *scaphoides* <Gk. *skaphoeidēs* <*skaphē* a boat + *eidos* form]

scapi- *combining form* A stalk or stem; a shaft: *scapiform,* resembling a scape. Also, before vowels, **scap-.** [<L *scapus* a stalk]

scap·o·lite (skap′ə·līt) *n.* Any of a definite group of tetragonal silicates, chiefly of aluminum, calcium, and sodium: also called *wernerite.* [<G *skapolith* <Gk. *skapos* a rod + *lithos* stone]

sca·pose (skā′pōs) *adj.* 1 Bearing a scape. 2 Like a scape. [<SCAPE[1] + -OSE]

scap·u·la (skap′yə·lə) *n. pl.* **·lae** (-lē) *Anat.* The shoulder blade; the superior or proximal element of the pectoral girdle in the skeleton of vertebrates. [<LL, shoulder <L *scapulae* shoulder blades]

scap·u·lar (skap′yə·lər) *n.* 1 An outer garment worn by members of certain religious orders and consisting of two strips of cloth hanging down front and back and joined across the shoulders; formerly, a monastic working dress. 2 Two small rectangular pieces of woolen cloth connected by strings: worn as a badge of membership by certain religious orders. 3 *Surg.* A bandage passing over the shoulder blade. 4 *Ornithol.* The shoulder feathers of a bird lying along the sides of the back. —*adj.* Of or pertaining to the scapula or scapulars. Also **scap′u·lar′y** (-ler′ē). [<Med. L *scapulare* <LL *scapula.* See SCAPULA.]

scar[1] (skär) *n.* 1 The mark left on the skin after the healing of a wound or sore; a cicatrix. 2 Any mark resulting from past injury: often applied figuratively to the effects on a character of crimes or sorrows. 3 The mark left on or made by an organ, as by leaves after separation from a stem or branch. 4 An indentation or mark made by use, motion, or contact. —*v.t. & v.i.* **scarred, scar·ring** To mark or become marked with a scar. [<OF *escare* <LL *eschara* a scab <Gk.] **—scar′less** *adj.*

scar[2] (skär) *n.* 1 A bare rock standing alone. 2 A cliff or rocky place on the side of a hill or mountain. Also, *Scot., scaur.* [<ON *sker*]

scar·ab (skar′əb) *n.* 1 A scarabaeid beetle, especially the large, black, dung beetle (*Scarabaeus sacer*), held sacred by the ancient Egyptians as the symbol of resurrection and fertility. 2 A gem representing this beetle and inscribed with symbols, used in ancient Egypt as an amulet. Also **scar·a·bee** (skar′ə·bē). [<MF *scarabée* <L *scarabaeus*]

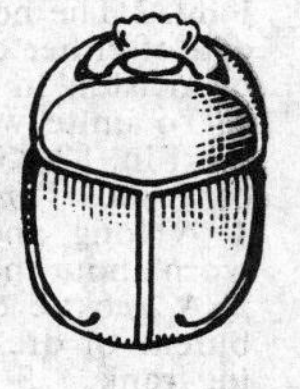

SCARAB

scar·a·bae·id (skar′ə·bē′id) *adj.* Pertaining to a large family (*Scarabaeidae*) of beetles, including cockchafers, etc. —*n.* A member of this family of beetles. Also **scar′a·bae′an, scar′a·bae′oid.** [<NL <L *scarabaeus* scarab]

scar·a·bae·us (skar′ə·bē′əs) *n. pl.* **·bae·i** (-bē′ī) 1 The scarab beetle. 2 A gem or design resembling it. Also **scar′a·be′us.** [<L]

scar·a·boid (skar′ə·boid) *adj.* Resembling or of the nature of a scarab or scarabaeid. —*n.* A scarab or scarabaeid.

scar·a·mouch (skar′ə·mouch, -mo͞osh) *n.* A boastful, cowardly character; a swaggering buffoon: so called from a character in old Italian comedy. [<F *Scaramouche* <Ital. *Scaramuccia,* lit., a skirmish <Gmc.]

Scar·bor·ough (skär′bûr·ə) A municipal borough and resort town in North Riding, eastern Yorkshire, England, on the North Sea.

scarce (skârs) *adj.* 1 Rarely met with; infrequent. 2 Not plentiful, scant; insufficient. 3 Characterized or attended by insufficiency or want. See synonyms under RARE[1], SCANTY. **—to make oneself scarce** *Colloq.* To go away, or stay away. [<AF *scars, escars,* OF *eschars* scanty, insufficient, ult. <L *excerptus.* See EXCERPT.] **—scarce′ness** *n.*

scarce·ly (skârs′lē) *adv.* 1 Only just; barely. 2 Not quite; hardly.

scarce·ment (skârs′mənt) *n.* 1 *Archit.* A plain flat ledge or set-off in a wall. 2 *Mining* A ledge or projection left in the side of a shaft, embankment, or wall, as for a ladder. [Appar. <obs. *scarce, v.,* lessen (<SCARCE) + -MENT]

scar·ci·ty (skâr′sə·tē) *n. pl.* **·ties** Scantiness; insufficiency; lack of necessities; dearth. See synonyms under WANT.

scare[1] (skâr) *v.* **scared, scar·ing** *v.t.* 1 To strike with sudden fear; frighten. 2 To drive or force by frightening: with *off* or *away*: to *scare* away an intruder. —*v.i.* 3 To take fright; become scared. See synonyms under FRIGHTEN. **—to scare up** *Colloq.* To get together hurriedly; discover; produce: *to scare up* votes, food, a group of people, etc. —*n.* 1 Sudden fright, especially from slight or imaginary cause; terror. 2 A panic (def. 2). —*adj. Colloq.* Intended or likely to scare, or to provoke alarm or concern: *scare* tactics. [<ON *skirra* frighten <*skiarr* shy] **—scar′er** *n.* **—scar′ing·ly** *adv.*

scare[2] (skâr) *n.* In golf, the smaller end of a club head at the part where, formerly, it was spliced to the handle. [<dial. E (Scottish), a joint <ON *skor*]

scare·crow (skâr′krō′) *n.* 1 Any effigy set up to scare crows and other birds from growing crops. 2 A cause of false alarm. 3 A wretched-looking person.

add,āce,câre,pälm; end,ēven; it,īce; odd,ōpen,ôrder; to͝ok,po͞ol; up,bûrn; ə = a in *above,* e in *sicken,* i in *clarity,* o in *melon,* u in *focus*; yo͞o = u in *fuse,* oi,oil; ou,pout; ch,check; g,go; ng,ring; th,thin; t͟h,this; zh,vision. Foreign sounds á,œ,ü,kh,ṅ; and ◆: see page xx. <from; + plus; ? possibly.

Synonyms: bogy, bugbear, fright, goblin, hobgoblin.
scare·head (skâr′hed′) *n.* An exceptionally large newspaper headline in very bold type for news of sensational interest.
scare·mon·ger (skâr′mung′gər, -mong′-) *n.* One who spreads an alarming rumor; an alarmist.
scarf[1] (skärf) *n. pl.* **scarfs 1** In carpentry, a lapped joint made as by notching two timbers at the ends, and bolting them together so as to form one continuous piece without increased thickness: also **scarf joint. 2** The notched end of either of the timbers so cut. **3** A cut or incision in the blubber of a whale. —*v.t.* **1** To unite with a scarf joint. **2** To cut a scarf in. [? <ON *skarfr* a notch in a timber]

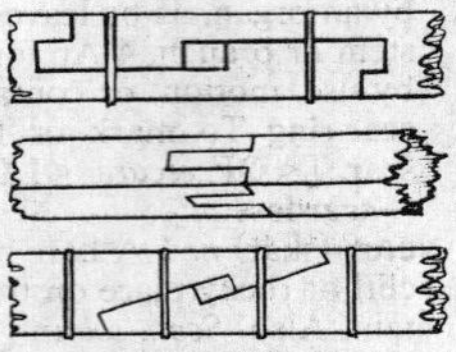

TYPES OF SCARF JOINTS

scarf[2] (skärf) *n. pl.* **scarfs** or **scarves** (skärvz) **1** A long and wide band, especially when worn about the head and neck; also, any sash. **2** A necktie or cravat. **3** A runner for a bureau or dresser. **4** An official sash, denoting rank. **5** A tippet or neckpiece. —*v.t.* **1** To cover or decorate as with a scarf. **2** To use as a scarf; wrap loosely around one. [<AF *escarpe,* OF *escharpe,* ? <*escreppe* a scrip[2]]
scarf[3] (skärf) See SCART[3].
scarf·pin (skärf′pin′) *n.* An ornamental pin worn on a tie or scarf.
scarf·skin (skärf′skin′) *n.* The epidermis; cuticle. [<SCARF[2] + SKIN]
scar·i·fi·ca·tor (skar′ə·fə·kā′tər) *n.* A surgical instrument, consisting of several lancet points, and used for making incisions in the skin to draw blood.
scar·i·fi·er (skar′ə·fī′ər) *n.* One who or that which scarifies.
scar·i·fy (skar′ə·fī) *v.t.* **·fied, ·fy·ing 1** To scratch or make slight incisions in, as the skin in surgery. **2** To criticize severely; make cutting comments on. **3** *Agric.* To stir the surface of, as soil. **4** To prune. [<MF *scarifier* <LL *scarificare* <L *scarifare* <Gk. *skariphasthai* scratch an outline, sketch <*skariphos* a stylus] —**scar′i·fi·ca′tion** *n.*
scar·i·ous (skâr′ē·əs) *adj.* **1** *Bot.* Thin, dry, membranaceous, and not green: said of plants. **2** Scaly. Also **scar′i·ose** (-ōs). [<F *scarieux* <NL *scariosus* <L *scaria* a thorny shrub]
scar·la·ti·na (skär′lə·tē′nə) *n.* Scarlet fever; popularly, a mild form of scarlet fever. [<NL <Ital. *scarlattina,* fem. dim. of *scarlatto* <Med. L *scarlatum* SCARLET]
scar·la·ti·noid (skär′lə·tē′noid, skär·lat′ə·noid) *adj.* Resembling scarlet fever. —*n. Pathol.* One of a group of erythemas closely resembling scarlet fever.
Scar·lat·ti (skär·lät′tē), **Alessandro,** 1659–1725, Italian composer. —**Domenico,** 1683–1757, Italian composer; son of preceding.
scar·let (skär′lit) *n.* **1** A brilliant red, inclining to orange. **2** A bright-red dye formerly obtained from the kermes or cochineal insect. **3** Any one of several coal-tar colors, varying from yellow to brown and used for dyeing. **4** Cloth or clothing of a scarlet color. —*adj.* **1** Brilliant-red, inclining to orange. **2** Clothed in scarlet. [<OF *escarlate* <Med. L *scarlatum,* prob. <Arabic *siqillāt* <Persian *saqalāt* a rich, scarlet cloth]
scarlet fever *Pathol.* An acute infectious fever caused by certain strains of hemolytic streptococci and characterized by a diffused scarlet rash followed by scaling off of the skin. Also *scarlatina.*
scarlet letter A scarlet "A," a badge of shame, which women convicted of adultery were once compelled to wear.
scarlet runner A tall climbing bean (*Phaseolus coccineus*) of tropical America, with vivid red flowers and long seed pods, now widely cultivated as a vegetable; a string bean.
Scarlet Woman The woman of *Rev.* xvii 4–6: an abusive epithet, first applied to pagan Rome, latterly to the Roman Catholic Church.
scarp (skärp) *n.* Any steep slope; an abrupt declivity; an escarpment. Compare illustration under BASTION. —*v.t.* To cut to a steep slope. [<AF *escarpe* <Ital. *scarpa*]
Scar·pan·to (skär·pän·tō) The Italian name for KARPATHOS.
Scarpe (skärp) A river of northern France, flowing 60 miles NE to the Scheldt.
scar·pet·ti (skär·pet′tē) *n. pl.* Rope-soled shoes used by mountain climbers. [<Ital. *scarpetto* a light shoe, dim. of *scarpa* a shoe]
Scar·ron (skȧ·rôṅ′), **Paul,** 1610–60, French poet and dramatist; first husband of Madame de Maintenon.
scart[1] (skärt) *Scot. n.* **1** A scratch; slight wound. **2** A pen or pencil mark. **3** A scrap or small irregular portion. —*v.t.* & *v.i.* To mark slightly; scratch or scrape. [ME *scratte*; of obscure origin]
scart[2] (skärt) *n. Scot.* A puny- or scrawny-looking person; also, a miserly person.
scart[3] (skärt) *n. Scot.* A cormorant. Also called *scarf.* [<ON *skarfr*]
scarves (skärvz) Alternative plural of SCARF[2].
scar·y (skâr′ē) *adj.* **scar·i·er, scar·i·est** *Colloq.* **1** Easily scared. **2** Somewhat frightened; anxious; timid. **3** Giving cause for alarm.
scat[1] (skat) *v.i.* **scat·ted, scat·ting** *Colloq.* To go away; depart: usually in the imperative. [? <*ss,* imit. of a hiss + CAT]
scat[2] (skat) *n. Slang* A type of jazz singing in which meaningless syllables are improvised on the melodic line. [Prob. <SCAT[1]]
scathe (skāth) *v.t.* **scathed, scath·ing 1** To criticize severely. **2** To injure severely; harm; blast. —*n.* Severe injury; harm; loss. Also **scath** (skath). Also, *Scot.,* *skaith.* [<ON *skatha* <*skathi* harm] —**scathe′ful** *adj.*
scathe·less (skāth′lis) *adj.* Free from harm. Also **scath′less** (skath′-).
scath·ing (skā′thing) *adj.* Damaging by scorching or blasting; withering: now usually figuratively: a *scathing* rebuke. —*n.* Harm; injury. —**scath′ing·ly** *adv.*
scato- *combining form* Dung; excrement: *scatology.* Also, before vowels, **scat-.** [<Gk. *skōr, skatos* dung]
scat·o·log·ic (skat′ə·loj′ik) *adj.* Of or pertaining to scatology; obscene. Also **scat′o·log′i·cal.**
sca·tol·o·gy (skə·tol′ə·jē) *n.* **1** The study of excrement, considered as a branch of paleontology, medicine, and psychiatry. **2** Preoccupation with filth or obscenity, as in literature. Also **scat·o·lo·gi·a** (skat′ə·lō′jē·ə). [<SCATO- + -LOGY] —**sca·tol′o·gist** *n.*
scat·o·man·cy (skat′ō·man′sē) *n.* In folklore, divination, or determination of disease, by means of feces.
scat·ter (skat′ər) *v.t.* **1** To throw about in various places; sprinkle; strew, as seed. **2** To separate and drive away in different directions; disperse; rout. **3** *Physics* To reflect (heat or light) irregularly. —*v.i.* **4** To separate and go in different directions; disperse; dissipate. See synonyms under SPREAD, SQUANDER. [ME *scateren* squander. ? Akin to SHATTER.] —**scat′ter·er** *n.*
scat·ter·brain (skat′ər·brān′) *n.* A person without concentration of mind; a heedless person. —**scat′ter-brained′** *adj.*
scat·ter·good (skat′ər·go͝od′) *n.* **1** One who wastes that which is good; a spendthrift. **2** One who or that which distributes charities.
scat·ter·ing (skat′ər·ing) *n.* **1** Dispersion. **2** *Physics* The deflection of a beam of particles or waves into a variety of directions upon collision with any obstacle preventing continuous propagation in the original direction. **3** The dispersion, over an area, of votes for candidates. —*adj.* Placed at intervals or at a distance. —**scat′ter·ing·ly** *adv.*
scat·ter·ling (skat′ər·ling) *n.* A person without a home; a vagrant. [<SCATTER + -LING[1]]
sca·tu·ri·ent (skə·cho͝or′ē·ənt) *adj. Obs.* Gushing forth, as a fountain. [<L *scaturiens, -entis,* ppr. of *scaturire* <*scatere* flow out]
scaud (skôd) *v.t. Scot.* To scald.
scauff (skôf) See SCAFF.
scaup[1] (skôp) *n.* A sea duck (genus *Aythya*) of northern regions, related to the canvasback, having the head and neck black in the male; especially, the common American bay duck (*A. marila*). Also **scaup duck.** [Short for *scaup duck* <SCAUP[2] + DUCK]
scaup[2] (skôp) *n. Obs.* & *Scot.* **1** The scalp; skull. **2** A mussel bed. [Var. of SCALP]
scaur (skär, skôr) See SCAR[2].
scav·enge (skav′inj) *v.* **·enged, ·eng·ing** *v.t.* **1** To remove filth, rubbish, and refuse from, as streets. **2** To remove exhaust gases from (the cylinder of an internal-combustion engine). **3** *Metall.* To remove impurities from (a metal or alloy). —*v.i.* **4** To act as a scavenger. **5** To search for food. [Back formation <SCAVENGER]
scav·en·ger (skav′in·jər) *n.* **1** A street-cleaner. **2** An animal that feeds on carrion, as the buzzard. [ME *scavager* <AF *scawager* <*scawage* inspection <*escauwer* inspect <Flemish *scauwen* see]
sce·nar·i·o (si·nâr′ē·ō, -när′ē·ō) *n. pl.* **·nar·i·os 1** The plot of a dramatic work, or a skeleton libretto. **2** The written plot and arrangement of incidents of a motion picture. **3** An outline or plan of a projected series of actions or events. [<Ital. <LL *scenarius* of stage scenes <L *scena.* See SCENE.]
sce·nar·ist (si·nâr′ist, -när′ist) *n.* One who writes scenarios.
scend (send) *Naut. v.i.* To heave upward, as a vessel on a wave. —*n.* The upward angular displacement of a vessel: correlative of *pitch.* Also spelled *send.* —**pitch and scend** The longitudinal rocking of a vessel. [Var. of SEND[2]; infl. in form by *ascend*]
scene (sēn) *n.* **1** A locality and all connected with it, as presented to view; a landscape. **2** The place in which the action of a drama is supposed to occur; setting or locality. **3** The place and surroundings of any event, real or imagined, as in literature or art. **4** A division of an act of a play; one comprehensive event in a play. **5** Any incident or episode that may serve as the subject of a description. **6** The painted canvas screen or screens for the background for a play. **7** Any striking exhibition or display; especially, a display of passion or excited feeling. **8** *Slang* A place or realm of a currently popular activity: the pop music *scene.* —**behind the scenes 1** Out of sight of a theater audience; backstage. **2** Privately; in secret. [<OF <L *scena, scaena* <Gk. *skēnē* tent, stage]
Synonyms: action, display, event, exhibition, incident, landscape, place, prospect, situation.
scen·er·y (sē′nər·ē) *n. pl.* **·er·ies** Natural or theatrical scenes collectively. [<Ital. *scenario.* See SCENARIO.]
sce·nic (sē′nik, sen′ik) *adj.* **1** Artistic in grouping and effect. **2** Picturesque. **3** Relating to stage scenery.
sce·nog·ra·phy (sē·nog′rə·fē) *n.* The art of making drawings in perspective. [<F *scénographie* <L *scaenographia* <Gk. *skēnographia* <*skēnē* a scene, tent + *graphein* write] —**scen·o·graph·ic** (sen′ə·graf′ik, sē′nə-) *adj.*
scent (sent) *n.* **1** An odor, pleasant or unpleasant. **2** The effluvium by which an animal can be tracked. **3** A clue aiding investigation. **4** Scraps of paper, in the game of hare and hounds, dropped by the hares in their flight to enable the hounds to follow them. **5** A fluid essence containing extracts from flowers or other fragrant bodies; perfume. **6** The sense of smell. —*v.t.* **1** To perceive by the sense of smell. **2** To form a suspicion of. **3** To cause to be fragrant; perfume. —*v.i.* **4** To hunt by the sense of smell: said of hounds. ◆ Homophone: *cent.* [<OF *sentir* discern by the senses, feel <L *sentire*] —**scent′less** *adj.*
Synonyms (noun): savor, smell.
scep·ter (sep′tər) *n.* **1** A staff or wand carried as the badge of command or sovereignty. **2** Hence, kingly office or power. —*v.t.* **1** To confer the scepter on; invest with royal power. **2** To furnish with or as with a scepter or scepters. Also **scep′tre** (-tər). [<OF *ceptre, sceptre* <L *sceptrum* <Gk. *skēptron* a staff <*skēptesthai* prop oneself, lean on]

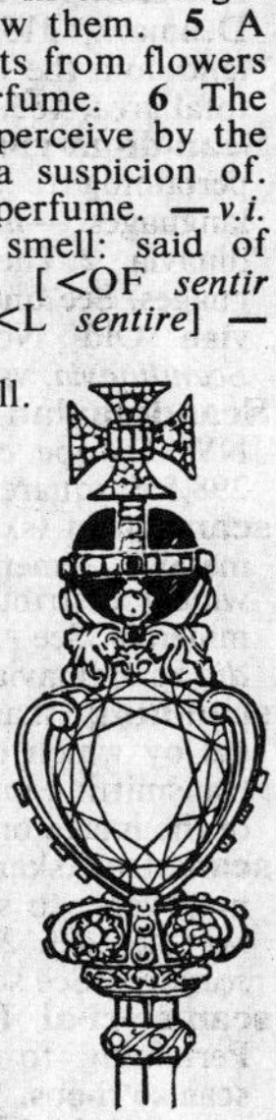

SCEPTER

scep·tic (skep′tik), **scep·ti·cal, scep·ti·cism,** etc. See SKEPTIC, etc.
Schac·a·bac (shak′ə·bak) In the *Arabian Nights,* the beggar invited to the Barmecide feast.
Schacht (shäkht), **(Horace Greeley) Hjalmar,** 1877–1970, German financier and economic expert.

Schaff·hau·sen (shäf′hou′zən) A town in northern Switzerland on the Rhine near **Schaffhausen Falls** (German *Rheinfall*), a group of several cataracts falling a total of 100 feet, now harnessed for hydroelectric power.

schanz (skhäns) *n.* A breastwork of earth and stones. —*v.t.* To protect with a schanz. [< Du. *schans*]

schap·pe (shä′pə) *n.* A fabric woven from spun silk. —*v.t.* **schapped, schap·ping** To ferment (silk) so as to remove its gum coating. [<dial. G (Swiss), a waste, impurity]

Scharn·horst (shärn′hôrst), **Gerhard von,** 1755–1813, Prussian general and military writer.

schat·chen (shät′khən) *n.* One who arranges marriages for a fee; a marriage-broker: chiefly among Russian Jews. Also **schad′chan.** [<Yiddish, a marriage broker <Hebrew *shadhkhān*]

Schaum·burg-Lip·pe (shoum′bo͝orkh·lip′ə) A former state of NW Germany, comprised in Lower Saxony, northern West Germany, 1945; 131 square miles; former capital, Bückeburg.

sched·ule (skej′o͞ol, *Brit.* shed′yo͞ol) *n.* **1** A written or printed statement, usually in tabular form, specifying the details of some matter, and often annexed to statutes, petitions, and other documents. **2** A list; catalog; an inventory. **3** A timetable; also, a detailed and timed plan for any procedure. **4** A program. —*v.t.* **·uled, ·ul·ing 1** To place in or on a schedule. **2** To make a schedule of. **3** *Colloq.* To appoint or plan for a specified time or date: He *scheduled* his appearance for five o'clock. [Alter. of ME *sedule* <OF *cedule* <LL *scedula*, dim. of L *scida, scheda* a leaf of paper <Gk. *schidē* a wood splinter <*schizein* split; infl. in form by Med. L *schedula*]

Schee·le (shā′lə), **Karl Wilhelm,** 1742–86, Swedish chemist; discovered chlorine in 1774, oxygen in 1777, and other elements.

schee·lite (shē′līt) *n.* A vitreous, variously colored, tetragonal calcium tungstate. [after K. W. *Scheele,* who discovered tungstic acid]

Schef·fel (shef′əl), **Joseph Victor von,** 1826–1886, German poet.

schef·fer·ite (shef′ə·rīt) *n.* A brown manganese pyroxene often containing iron. [after H. T. *Scheffer,* 1710–59, Swedish chemist]

Sche·her·e·za·de (shə·her′ə·zä′də, -zäd′) In the *Arabian Nights,* the bride of a sultan who had sworn to kill each of his wives after her wedding night. Scheherezade tricked the sultan into sparing her life by telling him an exciting story each night, not revealing the ending until the following day. Also **Sche·her′a·za′de.**

scheik (shēk) See SHEIK.

Scheldt (skelt) A river in northern France, Belgium, and the Netherlands, flowing 270 miles NE to North Sea: French *Escaut.* Flemish & Dutch **Schel·de** (skhel′də).

Schel·ling (shel′ing), **Friedrich Wilhelm Joseph von,** 1775–1854, German philospher. —**Schel·lin·gi·an** (she·lin′jē·ən) *adj.*

sche·ma (skē′mə) *n. pl.* **sche·ma·ta** (skē′mə·tə) **1** A scheme, synopsis, or summary. **2** A diagrammatic representation of certain relations in some system of knowledge. **3** Any figure drawn in outline; formerly, a geometric diagram. [<L. See SCHEME.]

sche·ma·tism (skē′mə·tiz′əm) *n.* **1** A particular form or disposition of anything. **2** Orderly arrangement of parts, as in a philosophic system, the classification of knowledge, etc.; design.

sche·ma·tize (skē′mə·tīz) *v.t.* **·tized, ·tiz·ing** To form into or arrange according to a scheme or schema. [<Gk. *schēmatizein* <*schēma, -atos* a form] —**sche′ma·ti·za′tion** *n.*

scheme (skēm) *n.* **1** A plan of something to be done; a plot or device for the accomplishment of an object. **2** A combination of various things according to a general plan or design; systematic arrangement. **3** A formal plan or arrangement, or a statement of such a plan; also, a table or schedule. **4** An outline drawing or sketch; diagram. **5** In astrology, a plan representing the aspects of the heavenly bodies at any given time. See synonyms under DESIGN, HYPOTHESIS, PLAN, PROJECT. —*v.* **schemed, schem·ing** *v.t.* **1** To make a scheme for; devise; plan. **2** To plan or plot in an underhand manner. —*v.i.* **3** To make schemes; plan or plot; connive. [<L *schema* a shape, figure of speech <Gk. *schēma, -atos* a form, plan] —**sche·mat·ic** (skē·mat′ik) or **·i·cal** *adj.* —**sche·mat′i·cal·ly** *adv.* —**schem′er** *n.* —**schem′ing** *adj.*

Sche·nec·ta·dy (skə·nek′tə·dē) An industrial city on the Mohawk River in eastern New York.

schenk beer (shengk) Beer fermented in 4 to 6 weeks and brewed for immediate use in the winter. [<G *schenkbier* <*schenken* pour out + *bier* beer; so called with ref. to its being put on schenk (draft) as soon as it is made, to keep it from turning sour]

scher·zan·do (sker·tsän′dō) *adv. Music* In a sportive or playful manner. [<Ital., ppr. of *scherzare* play <*scherzo.* See SCHERZO.]

scher·zo (sker′tsō) *n. pl.* **·zos** or **·zi** (-tsē) *Music* A sportive or lightsome movement, usually following a slow movement, especially in a symphony or sonata. [<Ital., a jest <G *scherz*]

Sche·ven·ing·en (skhā′vən·ing′ən) A resort town of western Netherlands just NW of The Hague on the North Sea; scene of a British naval victory over the Dutch, 1653.

Schia·pa·rel·li (skyä′pä·rel′lē), **Giovanni,** 1835–1910, Italian astronomer.

Schick (shik), **Béla,** 1877–1967, Austrian pediatrician, born in Hungary and active in the United States.

Schick test A test to determine the susceptibility of a person to diphtheria by injecting a diluted diphtheria toxin: a positive reaction gives a reddening of the skin. [after Dr. Béla *Schick,* who devised it]

Schie·dam (skhē·däm′) A town of western Netherlands, just west of Rotterdam.

schil·ler (shil′ər) *n. Mineral.* A bronzelike luster or iridescence due to the reflection of particles dispersed in certain minerals. [<G, a play of colors <*schillern* change color]

Schil·ler (shil′ər), **Johann Christoph Friedrich von,** 1759–1805, German poet and dramatist.

schil·ler·ize (shil′ə·rīz) *v.t.* **·ized, ·iz·ing** To impart schiller to. —**schil′ler·i·za′tion** *n.*

schil·ling (shil′ing) *n.* The monetary unit of Austria since 1924; a former North German silver coin. [<G]

Schip·hol (skhip′hôl) A village and international airport in western Netherlands, 6 miles SW of Amsterdam.

schip·per·ke (skip′ər·kē) *n.* A Belgian breed of dog used as a watchdog and sometimes for hunting. It is usually tailless, has a thick-set body, foxlike head, and a rather thick, short, black coat. Formerly called *Spits* or *Spitske.* [<dial. Du., a little boatman, dim. of Du. *schipper;* so called because orig. used as watchdogs on boats]

schism (siz′əm) *n.* **1** A division of a church into factions. **2** The offense of causing division in a church or a religious community. **3** An ecclesiastical body separated from a larger or older body, as from an established church. **4** The act of dividing, or the state of being divided; division. See synonyms under SECT. [<OF *cisme, scisme* <LL *schisma* <Gk., a split <*schizein* split]

schis·mat·ic (siz·mat′ik) *adj.* Relating to, having the character of, implying, or promoting schism: also **schis·mat′i·cal.** —*n.* One who makes or participates in an ecclesiastical schism: a term of opprobrium. [<OF *cismatique, scismatique* <LL *schismaticus* <L Gk. *schismatikos* <Gk. *schisma, -atos.* See SCHISM.] —**schis·mat′i·cal·ly** *adv.* —**schis·mat′i·cal·ness** *n.*

schist (shist) *n. Geol.* Any rock that readily splits or cleaves; specifically, a rock that has had a parallel or foliated structure secondarily developed in it: also spelled *shist.* [<F *schiste* <L *schistos* readily split <Gk. <*schizein* split] —**schist′ous, schist·ose** (shis′tōs) *adj.*

schis·ta·ceous (shis·tā′shəs) *adj.* Bluish-gray; of a light slaty color. [<SCHIST + -ACEOUS]

schisto- *combining form* Split: *schistosome.* Also, before vowels, **schist-.** [<Gk. *schistos* split]

schis·to·some (shis′tə·sōm) *n.* Any of a genus *(Schistosoma)* of trematode worms, including certain species parasitic in the blood of man, as the blood fluke *(S. haematobium)* common in Africa. [<NL <Gk. *schistos* split (<*schizein* split) + *sōma* a body]

schis·to·so·mi·a·sis (shis′tə·sō·mī′ə·sis) *n. Pathol.* A wasting disease caused by infestation with worms of the genus *Schistosoma,* endemic in Egypt and other parts of Africa: also called *bilharziasis.* [<NL <*Schistosoma* a schistosome]

schizo- *combining form* Split; divided: *schizophrenia.* Also, before vowels, **schiz-.** [<Gk. *schizein* split]

schiz·o·carp (skiz′ə·kärp) *n. Bot.* A split fruit; a pericarp splitting at maturity into two or more one-seeded indehiscent portions. Compare illustration under FRUIT. —**schiz′o·car′·pous, schiz′o·car′pic** *adj.*

schiz·o·gen·e·sis (skiz′ō·jen′ə·sis) *n. Biol.* Reproduction by fission.

schi·zog·o·ny (ski·zog′ə·nē) *n. Biol.* Reproduction by multiple fission, as in certain protozoa. [<NL *schizogonia* <Gk. *schizein* split + *genesthai* become]

schiz·oid (skiz′oid) *adj.* Resembling schizophrenia. —*n.* One having characteristics suggestive of schizophrenia. [<SCHIZ(OPHRENIA) + -OID]

schiz·o·my·cete (skiz′ō·mī·sēt′) *n.* One of the *Schizomycetes;* a bacterium. [<NL <Gk. *schizein* split + *mykēs, -ētos* a mushroom] —**schiz′o·my·ce′tous** *adj.*

Schiz·o·my·ce·tes (skiz′ō·mī·sē′tēz) *n. pl.* A class of widely distributed, minute, unicellular plants reproducing by fission and allied to the fungi: it comprises the bacteria and, in the Bergey classification, includes the following orders:

Eubacteriales	Simple undifferentiated forms
Actinomycetales	Moldlike bacteria
Chlamydobacteriales	Algalike iron bacteria
Caulobacteriales	Aguatic, gum-secreting bacteria
Thiobacteriales	Sulfur bacteria
Myxobacteriales	Slime-mold bacteria
Spirochaetales	Protozoanlike bacteria

schiz·o·my·co·sis (skiz′ō·mī·kō′sis) *n. Pathol.* A morbid condition or disease due to the presence of schizomycetes. [<NL]

schiz·ont (skiz′ont, skī′zont) *n.* The mature trophozoite of a sporozoan, as the malaria parasite, from which new cells, or merozoites, are liberated into the blood by schizogony. [<Gk. *schizōn, -ontos,* ppr. of *schizein* split]

schiz·o·phre·ni·a (skiz′ō·frē′nē·ə) *n.* A group of mental disorders beginning in early adulthood and characterized by disturbances of affect, behavior, and intellection and often by delusions and hallucinations. Formerly called *dementia praecox.* [<NL <Gk. *schizein* split + *phrēn* mind] —**schiz′o·phren′ic** (-fren′ik) *adj. & n.*

schiz·o·phyte (skiz′ə·fīt) *n.* One of a division or phylum *(Schizophyta)* of unicellular or simple multicellular plants which reproduce by fission or by asexual spores: it includes the bacteria and the blue-green algae. —*adj.* Of or pertaining to the *Schizophyta:* also **schiz′o·phyt′ic** (-fit′ik). [<NL <Gk. *schizein* split + *phyton* a plant]

schiz·o·pod (skiz′ə·pod) *n.* Any of a former order *(Schizopoda)* of crustaceans having a soft carapace and resembling the shrimp: now included in the subclass *Malacostraca.* [<NL <Gk. *schizopous, -podos* having parted toes <*schizein* split + *pous, podos* a foot]

schiz·o·thy·mi·a (skiz′ō·thī′mē·ə) *n. Psychiatry* A schizophrenic condition marked by introversion and a withdrawing from the world, but milder than schizophrenia. [<NL <Gk. *schizein* split + *thymos* spirit] —**schiz′o·thyme** *n.* —**schiz′o·thy′mic** *adj.*

Schle·gel (shlā′gəl), **August Wilhelm von,** 1767–1845, German philologist, poet, and literary critic. —**Friedrich von,** 1772–1829, German philosopher and critic: brother of the preceding.

Schlei·er·ma·cher (shlī′ər·mäkh′ər), **Friedrich Ernst Daniel,** 1768–1834, German theologian and philosopher.

schle·miel (shlə·mēl′) *n. Slang* An inept, easily duped person; a bungler; dolt. Also **schle·mihl′.** [<Yiddish, an unlucky person <Hebrew *Shelumiēl,* a personal name]

schlep (shlep) *Slang v.* **schlepped, schlep·ping** *v.t.* **1** To drag awkwardly; lug. — *v.i.* **2** To drag something awkwardly. **3** To proceed wearily or heavily: to *schlep* uptown. — *n.* **1** A difficult journey. **2** A stupid, awkward person. Also **schlepp.** [<Yiddish *shleppen* to drag] — **schlep′per** *n.*

Schle·si·en (shlā′zē·ən) The German name for SILESIA.

Schles·wig (shlās′vikh) **1** A city in NW Germany, former capital of Schleswig–Holstein. **2** The southern part of Jutland Peninsula, divided between Germany and Denmark: Danish *Sleswig.*

Schles·wig-Hol·stein (shlās′vikh·hōl′shtīn) A state of NW Germany (NE West Germany); 6,052 square miles; capital, Kiel.

Schley (slī), **Winfield Scott,** 1839–1911, U.S. rear admiral.

Schlie·mann (shlē′män), **Heinrich,** 1822–90, German archeologist.

schlie·re (shlē′rə) *n. pl.* **·ren** (-rən) *Geol.* In an igneous rock, an irregular, commonly not sharply bounded, portion differing in composition or texture from the general mass of the rock. [<G, lit., a streak] — **schlie′ric** *adj.*

schlie·ren (shlē′rən) *n. Physics* Any disturbance in the light path of an interferometer which alters the density of the air and thus changes the interference pattern of the light waves. [<G, pl. of *schliere,* lit., a streak]

schlock (shlok) *Slang n.* Shoddy, inferior merchandise. — *adj.* Of inferior quality; tawdry. Also spelled *shlock.* [<Yiddish] — **schlock′y** *adj.*

schmaltz (shmälts) *n. Slang* **1** Anything which is overly sentimental, as in music or literature. **2** Extreme sentimentalism. [<Yiddish <G *schmalz,* lit., melted fat] — **schmaltz′y** *adj.*

Schmidt telescope A reflecting telescope that yields undistorted images of a very wide field. [after B. *Schmidt,* died 1935, German optical designer]

Schna·bel (shna′bəl), **Artur,** 1882–1951, U.S. pianist and composer born in Austria.

schnap·per (shnap′ər, snap′-) *n.* A snapper (def. 4). [<G *schnapper* a schnapper]

schnapps (shnäps, shnaps) *n.* Holland gin; Hollands; loosely, any ardent spirits. Also **schnaps.** [<G, a dram, a nip <Du. *snaps,* lit., a gulp, mouthful]

schnau·zer (shnou′zər) *n.* A small, active terrier originally developed in Germany, having a wiry black or pepper-and-salt coat. — **miniature schnauzer** A toy terrier bred from the standard schnauzer and a pinscher. [<G *Schnauze* snout]

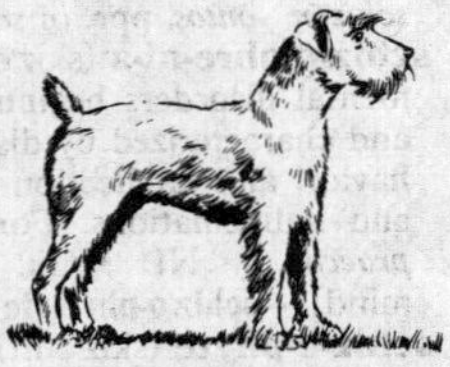

STANDARD SCHNAUZER (From 18 to 20 inches high at the shoulder)

Schnitz·ler (shnits′lər), **Arthur,** 1862–1931, Austrian playwright and novelist.

schnor·kel (shnôr′kəl) *n.* **1** An apparatus for the ventilation of a submerged submarine, consisting of retractable tubes for the intake of fresh air and the removal of the toxic gases. **2** A snorkel. [<G *schnörkel* spiral]

schnor·rer (shnôr′ər) *n.* A professional or habitual beggar. [<Yiddish <G *schnurrer* < slang *schnurren* go begging, orig. whirr, purr; with ref. to musical instruments of beggars]

schnoz·zle (shnoz′əl) *n. Slang* Nose. [<Yiddish <G *schnauze.* Akin to SNOUT.]

Scho·field (skō′fēld), **John McAllister,** 1831–1906, U.S. general.

schol·ar (skol′ər) *n.* **1** A person eminent for learning. **2** The holder of a scholarship. **3** One who learns under a teacher; a pupil. — **Rhodes scholar** A male student selected from a college or university of the United States or of any British dominion or colony, to receive one of the scholarships established by Cecil Rhodes for attendance at Oxford University, England. [Prob. fusion of OE *scolere* and OF *escoler,* both <LL *scholaris* <L *schola.* See SCHOOL[1].]

Synonyms: disciple, learner, pupil, savant, student. Historically the primary sense of a *scholar* is one who is being schooled; thence the word passes to designate one who is apt in school work, and finally one who is thoroughly schooled, master of what the schools can teach, an erudite or accomplished person: when used without qualification, the word is generally understood in this sense; as, He is manifestly a *scholar. Pupil* signifies one under the close personal supervision or instruction of a teacher or tutor.

schol·arch (skol′ärk) *n.* **1** In Greek antiquity, the head of a school of philosophy in Athens. **2** The head of any school. [<Gk. *scholarchē* < *scholē* a school + *archein* rule]

schol·ar·ly (skol′ər·lē) *adj.* Like a scholar; learned; erudite.

schol·ar·ship (skol′ər·ship) *n.* **1** Learning; erudition. **2** Maintenance or a stipend for a student awarded by an educational institution; also, the position of such a student. See synonyms under KNOWLEDGE, LEARNING.

scho·las·tic (skō·las′tik, skə-) *adj.* **1** Pertaining to or characteristic of scholars, education, or schools. **2** Pertaining to or characteristic of the medieval schoolmen. **3** Precise; pedantic. **4** Pertaining to the theological grade of students of the Jesuit order. Also **scho·las′ti·cal.** — *n.* **1** A student; pupil. **2** *Often cap.* A schoolman; an advocate of scholasticism. **3** A pedant. [<L *scholasticus* <Gk. *scholastikos* < *scholazein* be at leisure, devote leisure to study < *scholē.* See SCHOOL[1].]

scho·las·ti·cate (skō·las′tə·kāt, skə-) *n.* A general house of higher studies for Jesuit scholastics. [<NL *scholasticatus* <L *scholasticus* SCHOLASTIC]

scho·las·ti·cism (skō·las′tə·siz′əm, skə-) *n.* **1** *Often cap.* The systematized Christian logic, philosophy, and theology of medieval scholars from the 10th to the 15th centuries, based on Aristotle's *Logic* and *Metaphysics* and the writings of the early Christian fathers. See HUMANISM. **2** Any system of teaching which insists on traditional doctrines and forms. **3** A similar teaching of the present day given especially in seminaries of the Roman Catholic Church.

scho·li·ast (skō′lē·ast) *n.* A commentator; especially, an ancient grammarian or annotator of classical texts. See SCHOLIUM. [<L *scholiasta* <Gk. *scholiastēs* < *scholion* a commentary < *scholē* a school] — **scho′li·as′tic** *adj.*

scho·li·um (skō′lē·əm) *n. pl.* **·li·ums** or **·li·a** (-lē·ə) **1** An explanatory marginal note, as on a classical text by an ancient grammarian. **2** An interpolated note accompanying a mathematical proof. [<LL *scholium* <Gk. *scholion.* See SCHOLIAST.]

Schön·berg (shœn′berkh), **Arnold,** 1874–1951, Austrian composer and conductor active in the United States.

school[1] (sko͞ol) *n.* **1** An educational institution. **2** The place in which formal instruction is given; also, the instruction itself. **3** A period or session of an educational institution; a course of study at a school: *School* begins tomorrow. **4** The pupils in an educational institution. **5** A subdivision of a university devoted to a special branch of higher education: a *school* of education, medicine, etc. **6** The prescribed drill, duties, instruction, and training of any branch of the army or navy: gunnery *school,* aviation *school*; also, the manual of such instruction. **7** A body of disciples of a teacher or system; a sect, etc.; also, the system, methods, or opinions characteristic of those thus associated: the Scottish *school* of philosophy, a painting of the Flemish *school.* **8** A general style of life, manners, etc. **9** In medieval times, specifically, a seminary of logic, metaphysics, and theology; in the plural, the seats of the scholastic philosophy. **10** Any sphere or means of instruction: the *school* of example. — *v.t.* **1** To instruct in a school; train; educate. **2** To subject to rule or discipline. [OE *scōl* <L *schola* <Gk. *scholē* leisure or that which is done during leisure time, a school]

— **common school** One of the free public elementary schools in the United States.

— **consolidated school** A school, usually rural, consisting of several elementary schools and sometimes a high school, merged into one organization, for pupils from outlying districts.

— **continuation school** Comprehensively, a school for the further education of persons already employed; specifically, a school for employed boys and girls below the legal age for leaving school, attended a few hours a week on the employers' time.

— **dame school** An early form of school kept by a woman who drilled young children in their ABC's and the beginnings of reading.

— **elementary school** A school giving a course of education of from six to nine years, pupils usually entering at about six years of age.

— **finishing school** A school that prepares girls for entrance into society.

— **grammar school** **1** In graded public schools, the grades between primary and high school, grades one to eight inclusive. **2** Popularly, an elementary school. **3** *Brit.* A secondary school, often preparatory for college; originally for the teaching of Latin and Greek, but now offering broader curriculums.

— **high school** The highest division of the common schools, typically comprising grades 9, 10, 11, and 12: often preparatory for college or the vocations. — **junior high school** A school usually consisting of the 7th, 8th, and 9th grades, but sometimes of only 7th and 8th or 8th and 9th grades: also **intermediate school.** — **senior high school** A corresponding division of the public schools, consisting usually of grades 10, 11, and 12.

— **industrial school** **1** An institute for the practical development of manual and industrial skills. **2** A school for the care and training of neglected children.

— **parochial school** A school, usually elementary, supported by the parish of a church, especially by a Roman Catholic church.

— **primary school** A school for the teaching of the youngest pupils; the first grades of common schools beyond kindergarten.

— **private school** A school maintained under private or corporate management, usually for profit: in the United States, contradistinguished from *public school.*

— **public school** **1** A school maintained by public funds for the free education of the children of the community, usually covering elementary and secondary grades. **2** In England, a private or endowed school not run for profit; specifically, the exclusive endowed schools preparing students for the universities, as Eton, Harrow, etc.: so called because it serves the country at large, and not merely one community.

— **secondary school** A high school or preparatory school intermediate between the grammar school and college.

— **trade school** A vocational school designed to give a knowledge of processes and a skill of hand adequate for work in a specific trade.

— **vocational school** In general, a school training in the practical application of knowledge to business, the professions, or the technical arts and crafts.

school[2] (sko͞ol) *n.* A large number of fish, whales, etc., swimming together; shoal. — *v.i.* To swim together in a school. [<Du., a crowd, school of fishes. Akin to SHOAL[2].]

school board A legal board or committee having oversight of public schools.

school·book (sko͞ol′bo͝ok′) *n.* A book for use in school; textbook.

school·boy (sko͞ol′boi′) *n.* A boy attending school.

school bus A bus used to take children to and from school, often making numerous stops along the way and therefore distinctively marked as a warning to other motorists.

school·fel·low (sko͞ol′fel′ō) *n.* A schoolmate.

school·girl (sko͞ol′gûrl′) *n.* A girl attending school.

school·house (sko͞ol′hous′) *n.* A building in which a school is conducted.

school·ing (sko͞o′ling) *n.* **1** Instruction given at school; also, any preparatory training or discipline. **2** Price paid for instructing pupils. **3** The training of horses and riders. See synonyms under EDUCATION, NURTURE.

school·man (sko͞ol′mən) *n. pl.* **·men** (-mən) One of the theologians of the Middle Ages.

school·marm (sko͞ol′märm′) *n. Colloq.* A woman schoolteacher, especially one considered to be prudish, spinsterish, or strict. Also **school′ma′am** (-mam′).

school·mas·ter (sko͞ol′mas′tər, -mäs′-) *n.* **1** A man who teaches school. **2** One who or that which instructs or disciplines in any way:

Necessity was his *schoolmaster*. **3** A Caribbean fish *(Neomaenis apoda)* of the snapper family. See synonyms under MASTER.

school·mate (skōōl'māt') *n.* A fellow pupil; a schoolfellow.

school·mis·tress (skōōl'mis'tris) *n.* A woman who teaches school.

school·room (skōōl'rōōm', -rōōm') *n.* A room in which instruction is given.

school ship A vessel in which boys and young men are trained in seamanship.

school·teach·er (skōōl'tē'chər) *n.* One who gives instruction in a school below the college level.

school·yard (skōōl'yärd') *n.* The grounds about a school used for play.

schoon·er (skōō'nər) *n.* **1** A fore-and-aft rigged vessel having originally two masts, but now often three or more. **2** A prairie schooner. **3** A large beer glass, holding usually about a pint or more. [Appar. coined in New England < dial. *scoon* skim on water, prob. <Scand.]

SCHOONER

schoon·er–yacht (skōō'nər·yot') *n.* A yacht rigged like a schooner.

Scho·pen·hau·er (shō'pən·hou'ər), **Arthur,** 1788–1860, German philosopher. **— Scho'·pen·hau'er·i·an** *adj.*

Scho·pen·hau·er·ism (shō'pən·hou'ə·riz'əm) *n.* The philosophy (pessimistic determinism) of Arthur Schopenhauer, who taught that egoism, manifested in the "will to live," must be overcome; that the world is evil and should not be perpetuated; and that God, free will, and the immortality of the soul are illusions.

schorl (shôrl) *n.* Tourmaline, especially the black variety: also spelled *shorl.* [<G *schörl*]

schor·la·ceous (shôr·lā'shəs) *adj.* Containing black tourmaline, as granite. [<SCHORL + -ACEOUS]

schot·tische (shot'ish) *n.* A dance in 2/4 time similar to the polka, but somewhat slower; also, the music for such a dance. [<G *(der) schottische (tanz)* (the) Scottish (dance)]

Schou·ten Islands (skhou'tən, -tə) An island group off NW New Guinea, comprising part of Netherlands New Guinea; total, 1,231 square miles.

schrik (skhrik) *n. Afrikaans* Panic or sudden fright.

Schrö·ding·er (shrœ'ding·ər), **Erwin,** 1887–1961, Austrian physicist.

schtick (shtik) *n.* See SHTICK.

Schu·bert (shōō'bərt, *Ger.* shōō'bert), **Franz Peter,** 1797–1828, Austrian composer.

schuit (skoit) *n.* A Dutch vessel, sloop-rigged, used in rivers and canals. Also **schuyt.** [<Du. *schuit, schuyt* <MDu. *schute*]

schule¹ (skül, skœl) *n. Scot.* A school.

schule² (shōōl) *n. Scot.* A shovel.

Schu·man (shü·män'), **Robert,** 1886–1963, French political leader born in Luxembourg.

Schu·mann (shōō'män), **Robert,** 1810–56, German composer.

Schu·mann–Heink (shōō'män·hīngk'), **Ernestine,** 1861–1936, U.S. dramatic contralto singer born in Austria.

Schur·man (shûr'mən), **Jacob Gould,** 1854–1942, U.S. philosopher and diplomat born in Canada; president of Princeton University 1892–1920.

Schurz (shōōrts), **Carl,** 1829–1906, U.S. statesman, journalist, and general, born in Germany.

Schusch·nigg (shōōsh'nik), **Kurt von,** born 1897, Austrian statesman.

schuss (shōōs) *v.i.* To ski down a steep slope at high speed. *— n.* A straight, steep ski course, or the act of skiing this course. [<G, lit., a shot]

Schutz·staf·fel (shōōts'shtä'fəl) *n. pl.* **·feln** (-fəln) *German* Hitler's personal bodyguard, known as the Black Shirts; later, the chief section, the Elite Guard, of the Nazi militia, used to maintain order in Germany and occupied countries. Abbr. **SS.**

Schuy·ler (skī'lər), **Philip John,** 1733–1804, American statesman and soldier.

Schuy·ler·ville (skī'lər·vil) A town in eastern New York near Saratoga Springs; scene of Battle of Saratoga and General Burgoyne's surrender, October 17, 1777, in the American Revolution: formerly *Saratoga.*

Schuyl·kill River (skōōl'kil, skōō'kəl) A river in SE Pennsylvania, flowing 150 miles SE to the Delaware River.

schwa (shwä, shvä) *n.* **1** *Phonet.* A weak or obscure, central vowel sound occurring in most of the unstressed syllables in English speech. The sound, regardless of spelling, is that of the *a* in *alone,* the *o* in *lemon,* or the *u* in *circus:* written ə. **2** In Hebrew, the obscure vowel sound: written : and often transliterated by *e.* [<G <Hebrew *shewa*]

Schwab (shwäb), **Charles M.** 1862–1939, U.S. industrialist.

Schwa·ben (shvä'ben) The German name for SWABIA.

Schwann (shvän), **Theodor,** 1810–82, German physiologist.

schwan·pan (shwän'pän') See SWANPAN.

Schwarz·wald (shvärts'vält) The German name for the BLACK FOREST.

Schwein·furt (shvīn'fŏōrt) A city in NW Bavaria, West Germany.

Schwei·tzer (shvī'tsər), **Albert,** 1875–1965, Alsatian clergyman, physician, missionary, philosopher, and musicologist.

Schweitzer's reagent *Chem.* An aqueous solution of cupric hydroxide precipitated in ammonium hydroxide: used as a solvent for cellulose, especially in the cuprammonium process. Also called *cuprammonia.* [after Mathias E. *Schweitzer,* 1818–1860, German chemist]

Schweiz (shvīts) The German name for SWITZERLAND.

Schwei·zer·kä·se (shvī'tsər·kā'zə) *n. German* Swiss cheese.

Schwe·rin (shve·rēn') The capital of the former state of Mecklenburg, northern East Germany.

Schwyz (shvēts) A city of east central Switzerland near Lake Lucerne.

sci·ae·noid (sī·ē'noid) *n.* Any of a family *(Sciaenidae)* of spiny-finned, carnivorous, mostly marine fishes (order *Percomorphi*), as croakers, drums, weakfish, etc. *— adj.* Of or pertaining to the *Sciaenidae.* Also **sci·ae'nid** (-ē'nid). [<NL <L *sciaena* <Gk. *skiaina,* a kind of fish]

sci·at·ic (sī·at'ik) *adj.* Pertaining to or affecting the hip or its nerves; ischial. *— n.* A sciatic nerve or part. [<MF *sciatique* <Med. L *sciaticus,* alter. of L *ischiadicus* <Gk. *ischiadikos* < *ischion* hip, hip joint]

sci·at·i·ca (sī·at'i·kə) *n. Pathol.* **1** Neuralgia, affecting the sciatic nerve traversing the hip and thigh. **2** Any painful affection of these or adjoining parts. [<Med. L *sciatica (passio)* (the) sciatic (disease), fem. of *sciaticus* SCIATIC]

sci·ence (sī'əns) *n.* **1** Knowledge as of facts, phenomena, laws, and proximate causes, gained and verified by exact observation, organized experiment, and correct thinking; also, the sum of universal knowledge. **2** An exact and systematic statement or classification of knowledge concerning some subject or group of subjects. **3** Any department of knowledge in which the results of investigation have been systematized in the form of hypotheses and general laws subject to verification. **4** Expertness, skill, or proficiency resulting from knowledge. **5** Any one of the seven liberal arts (grammar, rhetoric, logic, arithmetic, music, geometry, astronomy): an ancient use. [<OF <L *scientia* < *sciens, -entis,* ppr. of *scire* know]

Synonyms: knowledge, art, learning, scholarship. *Knowledge* may be a medley of facts which gain real value only when coordinated and systematized by the man of *science. Art* relates to something to be done or produced by skill, *science* to something to be known. Creative *art* seeking beauty for its own sake is closely akin to fundamental *science* seeking *knowledge* for its own sake. See ART¹, KNOWLEDGE.

science fiction *n.* Fiction employing scientific ideas or devices as elements of plot or background. **— sci'ence–fic'tion** *adj.*

sci·en·tial (sī·en'shəl) *adj.* Of, characterized by,

or producing knowledge or science; also, skilful; scientific; knowing; capable.

sci·en·tif·ic (sī'ən·tif'ik) *adj.* **1** Of, pertaining to, discovered by, derived from, or used in science; of the nature of science. **2** Agreeing with the rules, principles, or methods of science; accurate; systematic; exact. **3** Versed in science or a science; eminently learned or skilful. Also **sci·en·tif'i·cal.** [<F *scientifique* <LL *scientificus* < *scientia* knowledge + *facere* make; orig. trans. of Gk. *epistēmonikos* pertaining to knowledge, science] **— sci·en·tif'i·cal·ly** *adv.*

scientific method A method of inquiry depending upon the reciprocal interplay of observable data and generalizations. It consists typically of the statement of a problem and the accumulation and analysis of relevant data that may lead to the construction of a hypothesis, in turn tested by the reliability and accuracy of deductions from it and by its consistency with other hypotheses and observed data.

sci·en·tism (sī'ən·tiz'əm) *n.* **1** Adherence to or belief in the aims and methods of scientists. **2** Uncritical or unsuitable application of scientific concepts or terms.

sci·en·tist (sī'ən·tist) *n.* One versed in science or devoted to scientific study or investigation.

Sci·en·tist (sī'ən·tist) *n.* A Christian Scientist.

sci·en·tol·o·gy (sī'ən·tol'ə·jē) *n. Often cap.* A religious and psychotherapeutic cult purporting to solve personal problems, cure mental and physical disorders, and increase intelligence. [<L *scientia* science + -LOGY] **— sci'·en·tol'o·gist** *n.*

sci–fi (sī'fī') *Colloq. n.* Science fiction. *— adj.* Science-fiction.

scil·i·cet (sil'ə·set) *adv.* Namely; to wit; that is to say: introducing a word to be supplied, or an explanation: generally abbreviated *scil., sc.,* or *ss.* [<L, contraction of *scire licet* it is permitted to know]

Scil·la (sil'ə) A town at the NE end of the Strait of Messina, southern Italy, on a small promontory supposed to be the site of the cave of the legendary Scylla.

Scil·ly Islands (sil'ē) A group of 140 islands off the SW coast of Cornwall, SW England; 6.3 square miles.

scim·i·tar (sim'ə·tər) *n.* **1** An Oriental sword or saber of extreme curve. **2** A billhook of somewhat similar form. Also **scim'e·tar, scim'i·ter:** formerly variously spelled with *si-, ci-,* etc. [<MF *cimeterre;* infl. in form by Ital. *scimitarra;* both ? <Persian *shamshīr*]

SCIMITAR

scin·coid (sing'koid) *n.* One of a family *(Scincidae)* of lizardlike viviparous reptiles (order *Squamata*) with typically smooth scales; a skink. *— adj.* Of or pertaining to the *Scincidae.* Also **scin·coi·di·an** (sing·koi'dē·ən). [< NL *scincoides* <L *scincus* skink]

scin·til·la (sin·til'ə) *n.* A spark; hence, a trace; iota: usually of something abstract: There was not a *scintilla* of truth in the remark. See synonyms under PARTICLE. [<L]

scin·til·late (sin'tə·lāt) *v.* **·lat·ed, ·lat·ing** *v.i.* **1** To give off sparks. **2** To sparkle; glitter. **3** To twinkle, as a star. *— v.t.* **4** To give off as a spark or sparks. See synonyms under SHINE. [<L *scintillatus,* pp. of *scintillare* scintillate < *scintilla* a spark] **— scin'til·lat'ing** *adj.*

scin·til·la·tion (sin'tə·lā'shən) *n.* **1** The act or state of scintillating; a sparkling, tremulous flashing or twinkling. **2** A spark or sparkle. **3** The twinkling of the stars. See synonyms under LIGHT.

sci·o·lism (sī'ə·liz'əm) *n.* Charlatanism; pretentious superficial knowledge. [<LL *sciolus* a smatterer, dim. of L *scius* knowing < *scire* know]

sci·o·list (sī'ə·list) *n.* One who has a smattering of knowledge, especially a pretender to scientific attainment. **— sci'o·lis'tic, sci'o·lous** *adj.*

sci·on (sī'ən) *n.* **1** *Bot.* A cion. **2** A child or descendant. [<OF *cion,* prob. blend of *scier* saw and L *sectio, -onis* a cutting, both <L *secare* cut]

sci·oph·i·lous (sī·of′ə·ləs) *adj. Ecol.* Shade-loving; able to live in shade; thriving in the shade. [< Gk. *skia* shade + -PHILOUS]

sci·o·phyte (sī′ə·fīt) *n.* A plant growing or adapted to live in the shade. [< Gk. *skia* shade + -PHYTE] **—sci′o·phyt′ic** (-fit′ik) *adj.*

sci·os·o·phy (sī·os′ə·fē) *n.* Any system of thought founded on beliefs which are at variance with contemporary scientific knowledge and resistant to the procedures of scientific method. [< Gk. *skia* a shadow + -SOPHY] **—sci·os′o·phist** *n.*

Sci·o·to River (sī·ō′tə, -tō) A river in central and southern Ohio, flowing 237 miles south to the Ohio River.

Scip·i·o (sip′ē·ō) Name of a great Roman family, especially including **Publius Cornelius Scipio Africanus Major,** 237–183 B.C., general; defeated Hannibal at Zama 202 B.C.: called "The Elder"; and **Publius Cornelius Scipio Aemilianus Africanus Minor,** 185–129 B.C., general; burned Carthage: called "The Younger."

sci·re fa·ci·as (sī′rē fā′shē·əs) *Law Latin* A writ (or the proceeding under it) commanding the party against whom it is issued to show cause why the plaintiff should not have advantage of or execution on a judicial record, or why a non-judicial record should not be repealed or annulled; literally, that you cause to know: abbr. *sci. fa.,* or *s. f.*

scir·rhus (skir′əs, sir′-) *n. pl.* **scir·rhi** (skir′ī) or **scir·rhus·es** *Pathol.* A hard tumor; specifically, a hard cancerous tumor. [< NL < L *scirros* < Gk. *skirrhos* a tumor < *skiros* hard] **—scir·rhos·i·ty** (ski·ros′ə·tē, si-) *n.* **—scir′rhous, scir′rhoid** *adj.*

scis·sile (sis′il) *adj.* Capable of being cut or split easily and evenly. [< L *scissilis* < *scissus,* pp. of *scindere* cut]

scis·sion (sizh′ən, sish′-) *n.* The act of cutting or splitting, or the state of being cut; hence, any division. [< OF < LL *scissio, -onis* < *scissus,* pp. of *scindere* cut]

scis·sor (siz′ər) *v.t.* & *v.i.* To cut with scissors.

scis·sor·er (siz′ər·ər) *n.* One using scissors; hence, a compiler.

scis·sors (siz′ərz) *n. pl.* & *sing.* **1** A cutting implement with handles and a pair of blades pivoted face to face: sometimes a **pair of scissors. 2** In wrestling, a hold secured by clasping the legs about the body or head of the opponent. **3** Gymnastic feats in which the movement of the legs suggests the opening and closing of scissors. [< OF *cisoires* < LL *cisoria,* pl. of *cisorium* a cutting instrument < *caedere* cut; infl. in form by L *scissor* one who cuts < *scindere* cut]

scissors kick In swimming, a kick performed usually with the side stroke, in which both legs are thrust apart, the upper leg bent at the knee while the lower is kept straight, then brought sharply together.

scis·sor·tail (siz′ər·tāl′) *n.* A flycatcher *(Muscivora forficata)* of the SW United States and Mexico having a scissorlike tail.

scis·sure (sizh′ər, sish′-) *n.* **1** A lengthwise cut; fissure. **2** Any division, rupture, or schism. [< MF < L *scissura* < *scissus.* See SCISSION.]

sci·u·rine (sī′yo͞o·rīn, -rin) *adj.* Belonging or pertaining to a family *(Sciuridae)* of rodents, including squirrels, chipmunks, woodchucks, marmots, etc. —*n.* One of the *Sciuridae.* [< L *sciurus* a squirrel < Gk. *skiouros* < *skia* a shadow + *oura* a tail + -INE[1]]

sci·u·roid (sī·yo͝or′oid) *adj.* **1** Of or pertaining to the *Sciuridae.* **2** *Bot.* Resembling a squirrel's tail, as the tufted spikes of certain cereal grasses. [< NL < L *sciurus* a squirrel + Gk. *eidos* a form]

sclaff (sklaf) *v.i.* **1** In golf, to strike the ground with the club before hitting the ball. —*v.t.* **2** In golf: **a** To strike (the ball) or make (a stroke) in this manner. **b** To drag (the club) thus. —*n.* **1** A slight slap or blow; the noise so made. **2** A light shoe; a slipper. **3** The golf stroke made by sclaffing. [< dial. E (Scottish) *sclaf* slap, shuffle; imit.]

Sclav (skläv), **Sclav·ic** (sklä′vik), etc. Obsolete forms of SLAV, etc.

scle·ra (sklir′ə) *n. Anat.* The hard, firm, fibrous outer coat of the eye, continuous with the cornea; the white of the eye. Also **scle·rot·i·ca** (sklə·rot′i·kə). See illustration under EYE. [< NL < Gk. *sklēros* hard]

scle·ren·chy·ma (sklə·reng′kə·mə) *n. Bot.* The tough, stony, thick-walled tissue composing the hard parts of plants. [< NL < Gk. *sklēros* hard + *enchyma* an infusion] **—scle·ren·chym·a·tous** (sklir′eng·kim′ə·təs) *adj.*

scle·ri·a·sis (sklə·rī′ə·sis) *n. Pathol.* Any morbid hardening or induration of parts. [< NL < Gk. *sklēriasis* < *sklēria* hardness < *sklēros* hard]

scle·rite (sklir′īt) *n.* **1** *Zool.* **a** One of the definite hard pieces of the integument of an arthropod. **b** A hard element in the integument of a polyp. **2** A spicule. [< Gk. *sklēros* hard + -ITE[1]] **—scle·rit·ic** (sklə·rit′ik) *adj.*

scle·ri·tis (sklə·rī′tis) *n. Pathol.* Rheumatic ophthalmia; inflammation of the sclera of the eye. Also **scle·ro·ti·tis** (sklir′ō·tī′tis, skler′-). [< NL < *sclera* the white of the eye] **—scle′ro·tit′ic** (-tit′ik) *adj.*

sclero- *combining form* Hardness; hard: *scleroderma.* Also, before vowels, **scler-.** [< Gk. *sklēros* hard]

scle·ro·der·ma (sklir′ō·dûr′mə, skler′-) *n. Pathol.* Hardening of the skin. [< NL < Gk. *sklēros* hard + *derma* skin]

scle·ro·der·ma·tous (sklir′ō·dûr′mə·təs, skler′-) *adj. Zool.* Provided with a horny or bony covering, as an armadillo. [< Gk. *sklēros* hard + *derma, -atos* skin]

scle·roid (sklir′oid) *adj. Biol.* Hard; sclerous; hard in texture, as the shells of nuts, etc. [< Gk. *sklēroeidēs* < *sklēros* hard + *eidos* form]

scle·ro·ma (sklə·rō′mə) *n. Pathol.* Hardening of the cellular tissue; sclerosis; scleroderma. [< NL < Gk. *sklērōma* < *sklēroein* harden < *sklēros* hard]

scle·rom·e·ter (sklə·rom′ə·tər) *n.* An instrument for determining the degree of hardness of a mineral.

scle·ro·pro·te·in (sklir′ō·prō′tē·in) *n.* Any of a class of animal proteins forming supportive tissues in the body, such as keratin, fibroin, etc. Also called albuminoid. [< SCLERO- + PROTEIN]

scle·rosed (sklə·rōst′) *adj.* Affected with sclerosis; grown abnormally hard. [< SCLEROS(IS) + -ED[2]]

scle·ro·sis (sklə·rō′sis) *n.* **1** *Pathol.* The morbid thickening and hardening of a tissue; especially, the hardening of the coats of the arteries. **2** *Bot.* The hardening of a plant cell wall by the formation of lignin in it. [< Med. L *sclirosis* < Gk. *sklērōsis* < *sklēroein* harden < *sklēros* hard] **—scle·ro′sal** *adj.*

scle·rot·ic (sklə·rot′ik) *adj.* **1** Dense; hard, as the white of the eye. **2** *Pathol.* Pertaining to or affected with sclerosis. [< NL *scleroticus* < Gk. *sklērotēs* hardness < *sklēroein.* See SCLEROMA.]

scle·ro·ti·um (sklə·rō′shē·əm) *n. pl.* **·ti·a** (-shē·ə) *Bot.* A compact horny mass of mycelium, found in certain higher fungi; especially, in the myxomycetes, a plasmodium, or part of a plasmodium, dry and hard, which for some time remains dormant. [< NL < Gk. *sklēros* hard] **—scle·ro′ti·oid** (-shē·oid), **scle·ro′tial** (-shəl) *adj.*

scle·rot·o·my (sklə·rot′ə·mē) *n. Surg.* Incision of the sclera. [< SCLER(A) + -(O)TOMY]

scle·rous (sklir′əs) *adj.* Hard or indurated; bony. [< SCLER(O)- + -OUS]

scob (skob) *n.* A defect in fabric caused by failure of the warp to interlace in the weaving. [? < Irish and Scottish Gaelic *sgolb* a splinter]

scoff (skôf, skof) *v.i.* To speak with contempt or derision; jeer: often with *at.* —*v.t.* To deride; mock. —*n.* An expression or an object of contempt or derision. See synonyms under SNEER. [ME *scof,* prob. < Scand. Cf. Dan. *skof* a jest, mockery.] **—scoff′er** *n.*

scoff·law (skôf′lô′, skof′-) *n.* One who scoffs at the law; especially, a habitual or deliberate violator of traffic, safety, or public-health regulations.

scog·ger (skog′ər) *n. Brit. Dial.* A heavy woolen garment worn for protection as a gaiter, or as a sleeve.

scold (skōld) *v.t.* To find fault with harshly. —*v.i.* To find fault harshly or continuously. —*n.* One who scolds, especially a virago: also **scold′er.** [Appar. < ON *skāld* a poet, satirist] **—scold′ing** *adj.* & *n.* **—scold′ing·ly** *adv.*

scol·e·cite (skol′ə·sīt, skō′lə-) *n.* A vitreous or silky, colorless, hydrous silicate of calcium and aluminum; a zeolite, isomorphous with natrolite. [< Gk. *skōlēx, -ēkos* a worm; so called because it sometimes curls up when heated]

sco·lex (skō′leks) *n. pl.* **sco·le·ces** (skō·lē′sēz) or **scol·i·ces** (skol′ə·sēz, skō′lə-) *Zool.* The knoblike head of a tapeworm, equipped with a circular disk of hooks and a group of two or four suckers. [< NL < Gk. *skōlēx* a worm]

sco·li·o·sis (skō′lē·ō′sis, skol′ē-) *n. Pathol.* A lateral curvature of the spine. Also **sco′li·o′ma.** [< NL < Gk. *skoliōsis* < *skolios* curved] **—sco′li·ot′ic** (-ot′ik) *adj.*

scol·lop (skol′əp), etc. See SCALLOP, etc.

scol·o·pen·drid (skol′ə·pen′drid) *n.* One of a family of chilopods *(Scolopendridae)* including the typical centipedes. [< NL < L *scolopendra* < Gk. *skolopendra* a milliped] **—scol′o·pen′drine** (-drīn, -drin) *adj.*

scom·broid (skom′broid) *adj.* Of or pertaining to a family *(Scombridae)* of acanthopterygian fishes, including mackerels, tunnies, and related genera. —*n.* One of the *Scombridae.* [< NL < L *scomber* a mackerel < Gk. *skombros*]

sconce[1] (skons) *n.* **1** A small earthwork or fort. **2** A protective shelter, covering, or screen. [< Du. *schanz* a fortress, wicker basket; infl. in form by SCONCE[2]]

sconce[2] (skons) *n.* An ornamental wall bracket for holding a candle or other light. [< OF *esconse* a dark lantern, hiding place < Med. L *sconsa,* short for L *absconsa,* pp. fem. of *abscondere* hide]

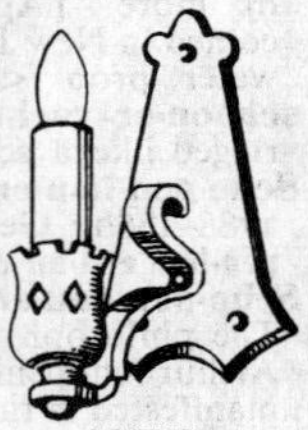
SCONCE

sconce[3] (skons) *n. Colloq.* **1** The head or skull. **2** Brains; wit. [? Special use of SCONCE[1]]

sconce[4] (skons) *Brit. n.* A light fine or penalty. —*v.t.* **sconced, sconc·ing** To fine; mulct. [? < SCONCE[3]]

scone (skōn, skon) *n. Scot.* Originally, a thin oatmeal cake, baked on a griddle; hence, a teacake or soda biscuit.

Scone (sko͞on, skōn) A village in SE Perthshire, Scotland; coronation place of Scottish kings, 1153 to 1488. **—the Stone of Scone** The stone on which early Scottish kings were crowned: brought to England by Edward I and placed under the seat of the Coronation Chair in Westminster Abbey.

scon·ner (skon′ər) *Scot. v.i.* To feel loathing or disgust. —*n.* Loathing; abhorrence. Also spelled *scunner.*

scoop (sko͞op) *n.* **1** A shovel-like instrument or large shovel with high sides for scooping. **2** A small shovel-like implement or ladle used by grocers, druggists, etc. **3** An implement for bailing, as water from a boat. **4** A spoon-shaped instrument for using in a cavity: a surgeons' *scoop.* **5** An act of scooping; a movement in a curved line convex downward. **6** The amount scooped at once: a *scoop* of water. **7** *Colloq.* A large gain, especially in speculation: He made a big *scoop* on that deal. **8** A bowl-shaped cavity; hollow excavation. **9** In newspaper slang, a news story obtained and published ahead of rival papers. —*v.t.* **1** To take or dip out with or as with a scoop. **2** To hollow out, as with a scoop; excavate. **3** To empty with a scoop. **4** *Colloq.* To heap up or gather in as if in scoopfuls; amass. **5** In newspaper slang, to obtain and publish a news story before (a rival). [Fusion of MDu. *schope* a vessel for bailing out water, and *schoppe* a shovel] **—scoop′er** *n.* **—scoop′ful′** *n.*

scoot (sko͞ot) *v.i. Colloq.* To go quickly; dart off. —*n.* The act of scooting; a darting off hurriedly. [Prob. < Scand.; cf. ON *skiōta* shoot. Akin to SHOOT.]

scoot·er (sko͞o′tər) *n.* **1** A child's vehicle consisting of a board mounted on two tandem wheels and steered by a long handle attached to the front axle: the rider stands with one foot on the board, using the other foot to push. **2** A similar vehicle powered by an internal-combustion motor and provided with a driver's seat: also *motor scooter.* **3** A sailboat so constructed that it may be sailed in water and on ice. **4** A small plow with a single shovel used for opening the soil: also *scooter plow.*

scop (skop) *n. Obs.* A bard, minstrel, or poet. [OE]

Sco·pas (skō′pəs) Greek sculptor of the fourth century B.C.

scope (skōp) *n.* **1** A range of view or action; outlook. **2** Room for the exercise of faculties or function; extent; capacity for achievement. **3** End in view; aim; purpose. **4** Length or sweep, as of a cable. **5** The range of a missile. [<Ital. *scopo* <L *scopus* <Gk. *skopos* a watcher < *skopeein* look at]

-scope *combining form* An instrument for viewing, observing, or indicating: *microscope.* [<Gk. *skopos* a watcher < *skopeein* watch]

Scopes (skōps), **John T(homas),** 1901–1970, U. S. educator; prosecuted for teaching evolution in Tennessee.

sco·po·drom·ic (skō′pə·drom′ik) *adj.* Pursuing a course in the line of sight; homing: said of guided missiles. [<Gk. *skopos* a watcher + *dromos* a running]

sco·pol·a·mine (skō·pol′ə·mēn, -min, skō′pə·lam′ēn, -in) *n. Chem.* An alkaloid, $C_{17}H_{21}O_4N$, extracted from the dried rhizomes of certain solanaceous plants, as *Scopolia carniolica*: its salts are used in medicine as a mydriatic, hypnotic, and sedative: also called *hyoscine.* [<G *scopolamin* <NL *Scopolia,* genus name of plants from which it is obtained, after G. A. *Scopoli,* 1723–88, Italian naturalist]

sco·po·line (skō′pə·lēn, -lin) *n. Chem.* A crystalline compound, $C_8H_{13}O_2N$, derived from scopolamine: also called *oscine.* [<SCOPOL(AMINE) + -INE[2]]

sco·po·phil·i·a (skō′pə·fil′ē·ə) *n. Psychiatry* Pleasure, especially of a sexual nature, derived from the act of observing, contemplating, or looking at something. Also **scop′to·phil′i·a** (skop′tə-). [<Gk. *skopos* a watcher + -PHILIA]

sco·po·pho·bi·a (skō′pə·fō′bē·ə) *n. Psychiatry* A morbid fear of being looked at. [<Gk. *skopos* a watcher + -PHOBIA]

scop·u·late (skop′yə·lit, -lāt) *adj.* Broom-shaped. [<L *scopulae* a little broom, pl. of *scopula* a broom twig, dim. of *scopa* a twig, a broom]

Sco·pus (skō′pəs), **Mount** A peak in central Palestine, NE of Jerusalem; 2,736 feet.

-scopy *combining form* Observation; viewing: *microscopy.* [<Gk. *-skopia* < *skopeein* watch]

scor·bu·tic (skôr·byōō′tik) *adj.* Relating to, like, or affected with scurvy: also **scor·bu′ti·cal.** — *n.* A person affected with scurvy. [<NL *scorbuticus* <Med. L *scorbutus* SCORBUTUS] — **scor·bu′ti·cal·ly** *adv.*

scor·bu·tus (skôr·byōō′təs) *n. Pathol.* Scurvy. [<NL <Med. L, appar. <MDu. *scheurbot, scheurbuik* < *scheuren* break, lacerate + *bot, buik* belly]

scorch (skôrch) *v.t.* **1** To change the color, taste, etc., of by slight burning; char the surface of. **2** To wither or shrivel by heat. **3** To affect painfully, as if by heat; criticize severely. — *v.i.* **4** To become scorched. **5** *Colloq.* To go at high speed. — *n.* **1** A superficial burn. **2** A mark caused by heat, as a slight burn. [Prob. related to ME *skorken* <ON *skorpna* dry up, shrivel; infl. in form by OF *escorchier* flay <L *excorticare* < *ex-* off + *cortex, -icis* bark] — **scorch′ing** *adj.* — **scorch′·ing·ly** *adv.*

scorched-earth policy (skôrcht′ûrth′) The policy of destroying all crops, industrial equipment, dwellings, etc., before an advancing enemy so as to leave nothing for his use or aid.

scorch·er (skôr′chər) *n.* **1** Something that scorches or is hot enough to scorch: Today was a *scorcher.* **2** Something severe or caustic, as criticism. **3** One who or that which moves or may move at great speed.

scor·da·to (skôr·dä′tō) *adj. Music* Out of tune; altered in tuning; made discordant. [<Ital., pp. of *scordare* be out of tune, short for *discordare* <L. See DISCORD.]

scor·da·tu·ra (skôr′dä·tōō′rä) *n. Music* An intentional changing of the normal tuning of a stringed instrument: resorted to for effect. [<Ital. *scordato* SCORDATO]

score (skôr, skōr) *n.* **1 a** A notch, cut, groove, mark, or line. **b** A notch or line used in keeping a tally or score; hence, an account or reckoning kept by notches or marks. **2** Any record, especially of indebtedness; debt; bill: to run up a *score* at a grocery. **3** Something charged or laid up against one; grudge; difference: to pay off old *scores*; an account; a credit; motive. **4** The record of the winning points, counts, or runs in competitions and games; also, the whole number of such points made by a player or side or in the game. **5** *Music* The collective notes in which a composition is written, when placed on two or more connected staffs one above another. **6** The number twenty, originally indicated by a special notch on a tally; twenty units or things: in the plural often indicating indefinitely large numbers. **7** *Psychol.* A quantitative value assigned to an individual or group response to a test or series of tests, as of intelligence or performance. — *v.* **scored, scor·ing** *v.t.* **1** To mark with notches, cuts, or lines. **2** To mark with cuts or lines for the purpose of keeping a tally or record. **3** To obliterate or cross out by means of a line drawn through: with *out.* **4** To make or gain, as points, runs, etc. **5** To count for a score of, as in games: A touchdown *scores* six points. **6** To rate or grade, as an examination paper; evaluate. **7** *Music* **a** To orchestrate. **b** To arrange or adapt for an instrument. **8** *U.S.* To criticize severely; scourge. **9** In cooking, to make superficial cuts in (meat, etc.). — *v.i.* **10** To make points, runs, etc., as in a game. **11** To keep score. **12** To make notches, cuts, etc. **13** To win an advantage; achieve a success. [OE *scoru* <ON *skor* a notch, tally] — **scor′er** *n.*

score-keep·er (skôr′kē′pər, skōr′-) *n.* One who keeps score.

Scores·by Sound (skôrz′bē, skōrz′-) An inlet and fjord system extending 200 miles into eastern Greenland from the Greenland Sea.

sco·ri·a (skôr′ē·ə, skō′rē·ə) *n. pl.* **·ri·ae** (-i·ē) Fragmentary lava; slag; refuse of ores or metals. [<L <Gk. *skōria* refuse < *skōr* dung] — **sco′ri·a′ceous** (-ā′shəs) *adj.*

sco·ri·form (skôr′ə·fôrm, skō′rə-) *adj.* Resembling scoria; in the form of dross.

sco·ri·fy (skôr′ə·fī, skō′rə-) *v.t.* **·fied, ·fy·ing** *Metall.* **1** To separate, as gold or silver, from an ore by smelting with lead, borax, etc. **2** To reduce to scoria or dross. [< SCORI(A) + -FY] — **sco′ri·fi·ca′tion** *n.*

scorn (skôrn) *n.* **1** Disdain; a feeling entertained toward someone or something as so inferior as to be unworthy of attention. **2** The expression of such a feeling; derision. **3** An object of supreme contempt. — *v.t.* **1** To hold in or treat with contempt; despise. **2** To reject with scorn; disdain; spurn. — *v.i.* **3** *Obs.* To mock; jeer. [<OF *escarn* < *escarnir* <Gmc.] — **scorn′er** *n.* — **scorn′ful** *adj.* — **scorn′ful·ly** *adv.* — **scorn′ful·ness** *n.*

Synonyms (noun): contempt, contumely, derision, despite, disdain, dishonor, mockery, scoff, scoffing, sneer, sneering, taunt. *Antonyms*: admiration, approbation, approval, attention, consideration, courtesy, deference, esteem, honor, regard, respect, reverence.

Synonyms (verb): abhor, contemn, despise, detest, disdain, spurn. *Antonyms*: see synonyms for CHERISH.

scor·pae·noid (skôr·pē′noid) *adj.* Belonging to a family *(Scorpaenidae)* of spiny-finned marine fishes. — *n.* A scorpaenoid fish: also **scor·pae′nid** (-nid). [<NL <L *scorpaena* a kind of fish + Gk. *eidos* form]

Scor·pi·o (skôr′pē·ō) **1** *Astron.* The Scorpion, a zodiacal constellation between Libra and Sagittarius, containing the brilliant red star Antares. See CONSTELLATION. **2** The eighth sign of the zodiac. Also **Scor′pi·on** (-ən), **Scor′·pi·us** (-əs). [<L, a scorpion]

scor·pi·oid (skôr′pē·oid) *adj.* **1** Scorpionlike. **2** Rolled or curled like the tail of a scorpion: specifically said of a terminal unilateral inflorescence, as in the borage family of plants. [<Gk. *skorpioeidēs* < *skorpios* a scorpion + *eidos* form]

scor·pi·on (skôr′pē·ən) *n.* **1** One of an order *(Scorpionida)* of rapacious arachnids with elongated, lobsterlike bodies and segmented tails which bear a poisonous sting: they are chiefly tropical but occur as far north as Canada. **2** The harmless pine lizard (genus *Sceloporus*) of the southern United States. **3** An instrument of chastisement; a whip or scourge. I *Kings* xii 11. **4** An ancient ballistic engine. [<OF <L *scorpio, -onis* <Gk. *skorpios*]

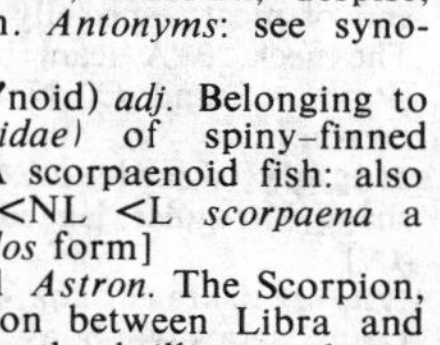

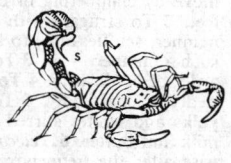

INDIAN SCORPION
s. Stinger.

scorpion fly A mecopterous insect (genus *Panorpa*) living on the banks of shaded streams and in moist woods: in the male, the end of the abdomen is upcurved like a scorpion's sting. See illustration under INSECTS (beneficial).

Scorpion's Heart *Astron.* The star Antares in the constellation Scorpio.

scot (skot) *n.* An assessment; tax; a contribution, reckoning, or fine. [Fusion of ON *skot,* OF *escot*; ? infl. by OE *sceot, scot* payment]

Scot (skot) *n.* **1** A native of Scotland; a Scotsman; formerly, a Gaelic Highlander. **2** One of a Gaelic people who migrated in the fifth century to northwestern Britain from Ireland. [OE *Scottas,* pl., the Irish <LL *Scotus, Scoti* <OIrish *Scuit*]

scot and lot An assessment in Great Britain formerly laid on all of a parish or borough, according to their ability to pay; also, figuratively, obligations of every kind.

scotch[1] (skoch) *v.t.* **1** To cut; scratch. **2** To wound so as to maim or cripple. **3** To put down; crush or suppress. **4** To dress, as stone, with a pick. — *n.* **1** A superficial cut; a scratch; a notch. **2** A line traced on the ground, as for hopscotch. [Origin uncertain]

scotch[2] (skoch) *v.t.* To block, as a wheel or log, with a chock or wedge to prevent moving or slipping. — *n.* A block put behind or under something, as a wheel, to prevent rolling or sliding. [Origin unknown]

Scotch (skoch) *n.* **1** The people of Scotland collectively: with *the.* **2** One or all of the dialects spoken by the people of Scotland. **3** Scotch whisky. — *adj.* Of or pertaining to Scotland, its inhabitants, or their language; Scottish; Scots.

◆ **Scotch, Scots, Scottish** Of these three proper adjectives, the form *Scotch* developed in the dialects of the Midland and southern England, and is accepted even in Scotland as applying to *Scotch* plaid, *Scotch* terriers, *Scotch* whisky, etc.; in Scotland and in northern England, however, the forms *Scots* and *Scottish* (earlier *Scottis*) prevailed, and are preferred as applying to the people, culture, and institutions of Scotland: *Scots* or *Scottish* English, the *Scottish* church. This distinction is now widely accepted.

Scotch broom See under BROOM.

Scotch elm The wych-elm.

Scotch grain Heavy, durable, chrome-tanned leather with pebbled grain, usually of cowhide.

Scotch·man (skoch′mən) *n. pl.* **·men** (-mən) A Scot; Scotsman.

Scotch stone See AYR STONE.

Scotch tape A rolled strip of transparent cellulose tape having an adhesive on one side: a trade name.

Scotch terrier See under TERRIER.

Scotch whisky Whisky having rather a smoky flavor and made (originally in Scotland) from malted barley.

Scotch woodcock Eggs cooked and served on toast or crackers spread with anchovy paste.

sco·ter (skō′tər) *n.* A sea duck (genera *Oidemia* and *Melanitta*) of northern regions, having the bill gibbous or swollen at the base, especially the **American scoter** *(O. americana)* also called *coot,* or **scoter duck.** [<dial. E *scote,* var. of SCOOT]

scot-free (skot′frē′) *adj.* Free from scot; untaxed; unharmed.

sco·ti·a (skō′shē·ə, -shə) *n. Archit.* A concave molding common in the bases of classical columns. [<L <Gk. *skotia* darkness < *skotos*; so called from the darkness in its concavity]

Sco·tia (skō′shə) The Medieval Latin name for SCOTLAND.

Sco·tism (skō′tiz·əm) *n.* The scholastic system and metaphysical doctrines of the Scottish philosopher John Duns Scotus (13th century): a kind of formalism. — **Sco′tist** *n.* — **Sco·tis′·tic** *adj.*

Scot·land (skot′lənd) A political division and the northern part of Great Britain; a separate

kingdom until its legislative union with England, 1707; 30,405 square miles; capital, Edinburgh.
Scotland Yard 1 The former headquarters of the London metropolitan police, situated in Great Scotland Yard, a short street in central London; removed to **New Scotland Yard,** on the Thames Embankment, 1890. 2 The police force at headquarters; specifically, the detective bureau of the London police.
scoto- *combining form* Darkness: *scotophobia.* Also, before vowels, **scot-.** [< Gk. *skotos* darkness]
sco·to·ma (skə·tō′mə) *n. pl.* **·ma·ta** (-mə·tə) *Pathol.* A defect in the field of vision; a blind or dark spot. [< LL < Gk. *skotōma* dizziness < *skotoein* darken < *skotos* darkness]
scot·o·phil·i·a (skot′ə·fil′ē·ə) *n.* A love of darkness. [< SCOTO- + -PHILIA]
scot·o·pho·bi·a (skot′ə·fō′bē·ə) *n.* A morbid fear of darkness: also called *nyctophobia.* [< SCOTO- + -PHOBIA]
sco·to·pi·a (skə·tō′pē·ə) *n. Physiol.* Adaptation of the eye for night vision. [< NL < Gk. *skotos* darkness + *ōps, ōpos* an eye] **—sco·top′ic** (-top′ik) *adj.*
Scots (skots) *adj.* Scottish. *—n.* The Scottish dialect of English. [Earlier *Scottis.* var. of SCOTTISH]
Scots·man (skots′mən) *n. pl.* **·men** (-mən) A Scot: the preferred term.
Scott (skot), **Dred,** 1795?–1858, U.S. Negro, central figure in Supreme Court decision. **—Sir George Gilbert,** 1811–78, English architect. **—Robert Falcon,** 1868–1912, English Antarctic explorer; reached South Pole, Jan. 17, 1912; perished on return journey. **—Sir Walter,** 1771–1832, Scottish novelist and poet. **—Winfield,** 1786–1866, U.S. general in the War of 1812 and Mexican and Civil Wars.
Scot·ti·cism (skot′ə·siz′əm) *n.* A form of expression or an idiom peculiar to the Scottish people.
Scot·tish (skot′ish) *adj.* Pertaining to or characteristic of Scotland, its inhabitants, or their language. *—n.* 1 The dialect of English spoken in Scotland, especially in the Lowlands; Scots. 2 The people of Scotland collectively: with *the.* [OE *Scottisc* < *Scotta* a Scot]
Scottish Gaelic The Goidelic language of the Scottish Highlands.
scoun·drel (skoun′drəl) *n.* A mean, thoroughgoing rascal; a rogue; villain. *—adj.* Scoundrelly. [Prob. dim. < AF *escoundre,* OF *escondre* abscond < L *ex-* off + *condere* hide]
scoun·drel·dom (skoun′drəl·dəm) *n.* Scoundrels collectively; scoundrelism.
scoun·drel·ism (skoun′drəl·iz′əm) *n.* The conduct or characteristics of scoundrels; rascality.
scoun·drel·ly (skoun′drəl·ē) *adj.* 1 Having the character of a scoundrel. 2 Pertaining to or characteristic of a scoundrel; rascally.
scour[1] (skour) *v.t.* 1 To clean or brighten by thorough washing and rubbing, as with sand or steel wool. 2 To remove dirt, etc., from; clean: to *scour* wool. 3 To remove by or as by rubbing away. 4 To clear by means of a strong current of water; flush. 5 To purge the bowels of. 6 To clean (wheat) before milling. *—v.i.* 7 To rub something vigorously so as to clean or brighten it. 8 To become bright or clean by rubbing. See synonyms under CLEANSE. *—n.* 1 The act of scouring. 2 A place scoured, as by running water. 3 A cleanser used in cleaning wool. 4 *Usually pl.* A watery diarrhea in cattle. [Prob. < MDu. *schuren* < OF *escurer,* ult. < L *ex-* out + *curare* take care of < *cura* care]
scour[2] (skour) *v.t.* 1 To range over or through, as in making a search. 2 To move or run swiftly over or along. *—v.i.* 3 To range about, as in making a search. 4 To move or run swiftly. [ME *scoure.* Cf. ON *skura* rush, run.]
scour·er[1] (skour′ər) *n.* 1 One who or that which cleanses, removes stains, etc. 2 A cathartic. 3 A grain scourer. [< SCOUR[1]]
scour·er[2] (skour′ər) *n.* One who prowls about the streets by night; a vagabond. [< SCOUR[2]]
scourge (skûrj) *n.* 1 A whip for inflicting suffering or punishment. 2 Any instrumentality or means for causing suffering or death; hence, severe punishment; also, a cause of suffering. *—v.t.* **scourged, scourg·ing** 1 To whip severely; lash; flog. 2 To punish severely; chastise; afflict. See synonyms under BEAT. [< AF *escorge* < LL *excoriare* flay < L *ex-* off + *corium* a hide] **—scourg′er** *n.*
Scourge of God Attila, king of the Huns.
scour·ing rush (skour′ing) Any species of horsetail, formerly much used for polishing wood and metal; scrub grass.
scour·ings (skour′ingz) *n. pl.* The residue after scouring: said especially of grain.
scouse (skous) *n.* A sailor's dish of sea biscuit and vegetables with or without meat; a hasty pudding of corn and rye meal. [Short for LOBSCOUSE]
scout[1] (skout) *n.* 1 One who or that which is engaged in scouting; specifically, a person sent out to observe and get information, as of the position or strength of an enemy in war. 2 The act of scouting. 3 At Oxford University, an undergraduate's manservant. 4 In cricket, a fielder: applied chiefly to one who fields at a distance in practice. 5 A boy scout; a girl scout. See synonyms under SPY. *—v.t.* To observe or spy upon for the purpose of gaining information; reconnoiter, as an enemy position. *—v.i.* To go or act as a scout. **—to scout around** To go in search. [< OF *escoute* a listener, listening < *escouter* listen < L *auscultare*] **—scout′er** *n.*
scout[2] (skout) *v.t.* & *v.i.* To reject with disdain; mock; jeer. See synonyms under RIDICULE. [< Scand. Cf. ON *skūta* a taunt.]
scout car A lightly armored motor car for reconnaissance work.
scout·mas·ter (skout′mas′tər, -mäs′-) *n.* The leader of a troop of Boy Scouts.
scow (skou) *n.* A large boat with a flat bottom and square ends: chiefly used as a lighter. [< Du. *schouw* a boat propelled by a pole < MDu. *schoude*]
scowl (skoul) *n.* 1 A lowering of the brows, as in anger, strong disapproval, or sullenness. 2 Gloomy aspect. *—v.i.* 1 To lower and contract the brows in anger, sullenness, or disapproval. 2 To look threatening; lower. *—v.t.* 3 To affect or express by scowling. [ME *skoul,* prob. < Scand. Cf. Dan. *skule.*] **—scowl′er** *n.* **—scowl′ing·ly** *adv.*
scrab·ble (skrab′əl) *v.* **·bled, ·bling** *v.i.* 1 To scratch, scrape, or paw, as with the hands. 2 To make irregular or meaningless marks; scribble. 3 To struggle or strive. *—v.t.* 4 To make meaningless marks on; scribble on. 5 To gather hurriedly; scrape together. *—n.* 1 The act of scrabbling; a moving on hands and feet or knees. 2 A scrambling effort. 3 A sparse growth: a *scrabble* of underbrush. [< Du. *schrabbelen* scratch]
scrag (skrag) *v.t.* **scragged, scrag·ging** *Colloq.* To use roughly; wring the neck of; specifically, to kill by hanging; garrote. [< *n.*] *—n.* 1 Something thin or lean and rough; a lean or bony piece or end of meat, especially from the neck. 2 *Slang* The neck. 3 A lean, bony person or animal. [Prob. < Scand. Cf. Norw. *skragg* a lean, feeble person.]
scrag·gly (skrag′lē) *adj.* **·gli·er, ·gli·est** Unkempt; shaggy; irregular; jagged. [Prob. < SCRAGG(Y) + -LY]
scrag·gy (skrag′ē) *adj.* **·gi·er, ·gi·est** 1 Rough. 2 Lean; scrawny; bony. [< SCRAG + -Y[1]] **—scrag′gi·ly** *adv.* **—scrag′gi·ness** *n.*
scraich (skrākh) *Scot. v.i.* To scream harshly; screech, as a fowl. *—n.* A shrill cry; scream; screech. Also **scraigh.**
scram (skram) *v.i.* **scrammed, scram·ming** *U.S. Slang* To go away; leave quickly. [Prob. short for SCRAMBLE]
scram·ble (skram′bəl) *v.* **·bled, ·bling** *v.i.* 1 To move by clambering or crawling on hands and feet. 2 To struggle with others in a disorderly manner; scuffle; also, to strive for something in such a manner. *—v.t.* 3 To mix together haphazardly or confusedly. 4 To gather or collect hurriedly or confusedly. 5 To cook (eggs) with the yolks and whites stirred together, usually with milk and butter. 6 *Telecom.* To invert or otherwise alter the frequency spectrum of (radio or wireless messages) so as to insure secrecy. *—n.* The act of scrambling; a disorderly performance or struggle. [Prob. nasalized var. of SCRABBLE]
scrambled eggs Eggs prepared by stirring together the whites and yolks while cooking, usually with milk and butter.
scram·bler (skram′blər) *n.* 1 One who or that which scrambles. 2 *Telecom.* A device for altering the frequencies of radio and wireless signals during transmission.
scran·nel (skran′əl) *Archaic adj.* Thin; lean; reedy; slight; also, harsh. *—n.* A lean person. [Prob. < Scand. Cf. Norw. *skrann* lean.]
Scran·ton (skran′tən) A city in NE Pennsylvania; an anthracite and manufacturing center.
scrap[1] (skrap) *n.* 1 A small piece cut or broken from something; fragment. 2 A brief extract. 3 *pl.* Pieces of crisp fat tissue after the oil has been expressed by cooking. 4 Old or refuse metal. See synonyms under PARTICLE. *—v.t.* **scrapped, scrap·ping** 1 To break up into scrap; make scrap of. 2 To discard; throw away. *—adj.* Having the form of scraps; discarded after use: *scrap* metal. [< ON *skrap* scrapings, scraps < *skrappa* scrape. Akin to SCRAPE.]
scrap[2] (skrap) *v.i.* **scrapped, scrap·ing** To fight; quarrel. *—n.* A scrimmage; slight disagreement; scuffle; squabble. [< SCRAPE, *n.* (def. 2)]
scrap·book (skrap′bo͝ok′) *n.* 1 A blank book in which to paste pictures, cuttings from periodicals, etc. 2 A personal notebook.
scrape (skrāp) *v.* **scraped, scrap·ing** *v.t.* 1 To rub, as with something rough or sharp, so as to abrade or to remove an outer layer or adherent matter. 2 To remove thus: with *off, away,* etc. 3 To rub (a rough or sharp object) across a surface. 4 To rub roughly across or against (a surface). 5 To dig or form by scratching or scraping. 6 To gather or accumulate with effort or difficulty; usually with *up* or *together.* *—v.i.* 7 To scrape something. 8 To rub with a grating noise. 9 To emit or produce a grating noise. 10 To draw the foot backward along the ground in bowing: to bow and *scrape.* 11 To manage or get along with difficulty. 12 To be very or overly economical. **—to scrape acquaintance** To make acquaintance without an introduction. *—n.* 1 The act or effect of scraping; also, the noise made by scraping. 2 A difficult situation; predicament. 3 A scraping or drawing back of the foot in bowing. [Prob. fusion of OE *scrapian* and ON *skrapa* scrape, erase]
scrap·er (skrā′pər) *n.* 1 Any instrument used for scraping. 2 A horse-drawn or motor-driven apparatus having a large metal scoop or scoops, for scraping up, transporting, and dumping dirt: a road *scraper,* a road leveller. 3 One who or that which scrapes. 4 A miser. 5 An unskilful player on the violin.
scrap·ie (skrā′pē) *n.* A fatal viral disease affecting the central nervous system of sheep and transmitted to other animals by feeding on affected tissue. [< SCRAPE, from the habit of affected animals of scraping against objects as if to relieve itching]
scrap·ing (skrā′ing) *n.* 1 The act of someone or something that scrapes. 2 The sound so produced. 3 Something scraped off or together.
scrap iron Old pieces of iron suitable for reworking.
scrap·ple (skrap′əl) *n.* A mixture of meal or flour boiled with scraps of pork, seasoned, and allowed to set: usually cooked by frying. [Dim. of SCRAP[1]]
scrap·py[1] (skrap′ē) *adj.* **·pi·er, ·pi·est** Composed of scraps; disconnected; fragmentary. [< SCRAP[1] + -Y[1]] **—scrap′pi·ly** *adv.* **—scrap′·pi·ness** *n.*
scrap·py[2] (skrap′ē) *adj.* **·pi·er, ·pi·est** Pugnacious; given to picking fights. [< SCRAP[2] + -Y[1]] **—scrap′pi·ly** *adv.* **—scrap′pi·ness** *n.*
scratch (skrach) *v.t.* 1 To tear or mark the surface of with something sharp or rough. 2 To scrape or dig with something sharp or rough, as the claws or nails. 3 To scrape lightly with the nails, etc., as to relieve itching. 4 To rub with a grating sound; scrape. 5 To write or draw awkwardly or hurriedly. 6 To erase or cancel by or as by scratches or marks. 7 To erase or cancel the name of (a candidate) from a political ticket, while supporting the rest of the ticket; also, to bolt (a ticket or party) in this way. 8 To withdraw (an entry) from a race, game, etc. *—v.i.* 9 To use the nails or claws, as in fighting or digging. 10 To scrape the skin, etc., lightly, as to relieve itching. 11 To make a grating noise. 12 To manage or get along with difficulty. 13 To withdraw from a game, race, etc. 14 In billiards and pool, to make

a scratch. — *n.* **1** A mark or incision made on a surface by scratching; a shallow mark, groove, furrow, or channel. **2** A slight flesh wound or cut. **3** The line from which contestants start, as in racing: to start from *scratch.* **4** The contestant who competes against an allowance: also **scratch–man.** **5** *Slang* Money. **6** A disease of horses, consisting of dry scabs or chaps on the heel: also **scratch'es. 7** In billiards, a chance shot; also, a fluke; in billiards and pool, a shot resulting in a penalty; specifically, a shot in which the cue ball goes into a pocket, leaves the table, or fails to hit an object ball. — **from scratch** From the beginning; from nothing. — **up to scratch** *Colloq.* Meeting the standard or requirement in courage, stamina, or performance; in proper or fit condition: He was never *up to scratch* in writing. — *adj.* **1** Done by chance; haphazard. **2** In sports, without handicap or allowance. **3** Made as, or used for, a first try: a *scratch* pad. **4** Chosen at random or by chance: a *scratch* team. [Prob. blend of ME *scratte* scratch (prob. <Scand.; cf. Sw. *kratta* rake) and *cracchen* scratch < MDu. *cratsen*] — **scratch'er** *n.*

scratch test *Med.* A test to determine the substances to which a person is allergic by rubbing allergens in small scratches made in his skin.

scratch·y (skrach'ē) *adj.* **scratch·i·er, scratch·i·est 1** Characterized by scratches. **2** Making a scratching noise. **3** Straggling; shaggy; rough. — **scratch'i·ly** *adv.* — **scratch'i·ness** *n.*

scrawl (skrôl) *v.t. & v.i.* To write hastily or illegibly; scribble. — *n.* Irregular or careless writing. [? < dial. E, var. of CRAWL; ? infl. in meaning by *scribble, scroll,* etc.] — **scrawl'er** *n.*

scrawl·y (skrô'lē) *adj.* **scrawl·i·er, scrawl·i·est** Consisting of or characterized by ill–formed or irregular characters.

scraw·ny (skrô'nē) *adj.* **·ni·er, ·ni·est** Lean and bony; skinny; thin. [< dial. E *scranny,* var. of SCRANNEL] — **scraw'ni·ness** *n.*

screak (skrēk) *v.i.* To creak; screech. — *n.* A screech; also, a creak. [<ON *skrǣkja;* prob. imit.]

scream (skrēm) *v.i.* **1** To utter a prolonged, piercing cry, as of pain, terror, or surprise. **2** To make a prolonged, piercing sound. **3** To laugh loudly or immoderately. **4** To use heated, hysterical language. **5** To have an effect as of screaming: This color *screams* in contrast to green. — *v.t.* **6** To utter with a scream. — *n.* A loud, shrill, prolonged cry or sound, generally denoting fear or pain. See synonyms under CALL, ROAR. [ME *scraemen,* ? <ON *skraema* scare]

scream·er (skrē'mər) *n.* **1** One who or that which screams. **2** A South American bird, related to the ducks (family *Anhimidae* or *Palamedidae*) including the **horned screamer** (*Anhima* or *Palamedea cornuta*) and the **crested screamers** (genus *Chauna*). **3** *U.S. Slang* Something calculated to call forth screams of admiration, astonishment, or the like; hence, a person of great size, strength, or skill. **4** *U.S. Slang* A sensational headline in a newspaper.

scream·ing (skrē'ming) *adj.* **1** Uttering or emitting screams. **2** Provocative of screams or of laughter: a *screaming* farce. **3** Like a scream.

scree (skrē) *n.* Debris of stones and rock fragments at the foot of a cliff or steep, rocky face: usually a sloping mass. See TALUS. [Back formation < *screes,* earlier *screethes* <ON *skridha* a landslide]

screech (skrēch) *n.* A shrill, harsh cry; shriek. — *v.t.* To utter with or as with a screech. — *v.i.* To make a prolonged, harsh, piercing sound; shriek. [Var. of obs. *scritch,* prob. < Scand. Cf. ON *skrǣkja;* prob. ult. imit.] — **screech'er** *n.* — **screech'y** *adj.*

screech owl 1 Any of various small owls (genus *Otus*) common from Canada to Brazil; especially, the small, gray *O. asio* of the eastern United States. **2** The English barn owl.

screed (skrēd) *n.* **1** A prolonged tirade; harangue. **2** A wooden strip or a strip of mortar laid on a wall at intervals, to gage the thickness of the plastering. **3** A long torn strip or shred; hence, any detached strip or fragment: the original meaning, now chiefly

Scottish. **4** *Scot.* A tearing; rent; tear; also, a drinking spree. — *v.t.* **1** To rend or tear into shreds. **2** *Scot.* To repeat glibly. [Var. of SHRED]

screen (skrēn) *n.* **1** That which separates or cuts off, shelters or protects, as a light partition. **2** A sieve or riddle, for sifting. **3** A smooth surface, as a canvas or curtain, on which motion pictures, etc., may be shown. **4** A motion picture or motion pictures collectively. **5** A plate of glass bearing very finely ruled lines, placed between the object and the camera in photographing for reproduction by the half–tone process. **6 a** *Mil.* A detachment of troops sent to deceive an enemy as to the movement of the main force. **b** *Nav.* A formation of ships arranged for the protection of heavier vessels from enemy submarines, etc. **7** *Physics* Any of various devices for confining the action of a physical agency or instrument to a definite area: a magnetic *screen.* **8** *Psychoanal.* A person who stands for someone else or others having some common characteristic, as in a dream: a form of concealment. — *v.t.* **1** To shield from observation or annoyance with or as with a screen. **2** To pass through a screen or sieve; sift. **3** To show or exhibit on a screen, as a motion picture. **4** *Psychol.* To separate from a group (those individuals showing indications of, or tendencies toward, mental or physical incapacity for specified activities): often with *out.* See synonyms under HIDE, PALLIATE, SHELTER. [Prob. <OF *escren, escrin,* prob. < OHG *skirm*] — **screen'a·ble** *adj.* — **screen'er** *n.*

screen·ing (skrēn'ing) *n.* **1** A meshlike material, as for a window screen. **2** A showing of a motion picture.

screen·ings (skrē'ningz) *n. pl.* The waste of anything passed through a sieve, as coal or defective grains; siftings.

screw (skrōō) *n.* **1** A device resembling a nail but having a slotted head and a tapering or cylindrical spiral for driving into wood with a screwdriver, or for insertion into a corresponding grooved part: called **male** or **external screw. 2** A cylindrical socket with a

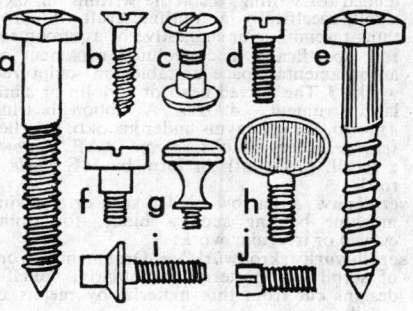

TYPES OF SCREWS
a. Lagscrew.	*f.* Shoulder screw.
b. Wood screw.	*g, h.* Thumbscrews.
c. Saw screw.	*i.* Collar screw.
d. Fillister screw.	*j.* Slotted screw.
	e. Skein screw.

spiral groove: called **female** or **internal screw. 3** Anything having the form of a screw. **4** A screw propeller. **5** A turn of or as of a screw. **6** Pressure; force. **7** *Brit. Slang* Salary; pay. **8** *Slang* A prison guard. **9** A haggler over prices; a crafty bargainer. **10** *Brit.* A worthless horse. **11** *Brit.* A small packet of tobacco. **12** *Slang* An act of sexual intercourse: a vulgar term. — **to have a screw loose** *Slang* To be mentally deranged, eccentric, etc. — **to put the screws on** (or **to**) *Slang* To exert pressure or force upon. — *v.t.* **1** To tighten, fasten, attach, etc., by or as by a screw or screws. **2** To turn or twist. **3** To force as if by the pressure of a screw; urge: to *screw* one's courage to the sticking point. **4** To twist out of shape; contort, as one's features. **5** To practice oppression or extortion on; defraud. **6** To obtain by extortion. **7** *Slang* To have sexual intercourse with: a vulgar term. **8** *Slang* To act maliciously toward; harm. — *v.i.* **9** To turn or admit of being turned as a screw. **10** To be attached or

become detached by means of a screw or screws: with *on, off,* etc. **11** To have turns like those of a screw. **12** To practice oppression or extortion. **13** *Slang* To have sexual intercourse: a vulgar term. — **to screw up** *Slang* To botch; make a mess of: He *screwed up* his career. [Appar. <OF *escroue* a nut, female screw, ? <L *scrofa* sow; infl. in OF by L *scrobis* vulva] — **screw'er** *n.*

screw·ball (skrōō'bôl') *n.* **1** In baseball, a pitch thrown with a wrist motion opposite to that used for the out–curve, and breaking sharply and often unpredictably. **2** *U.S. Slang* An unconventional or erratic person.

screw·bean (skrōō'bēn') *n.* **1** The seed of the spirally twisted pod of a species of mesquite (*Strombocarpa odorata*). **2** The tree bearing this seed.

screw·driv·er (skrōō'drī'vər) *n.* A tool for turning screws.

screwed–up (skrōōd'up') *adj. Slang* **1** Disorganized or disorderly. **2** Mentally ill or emotionally distressed.

screw jack 1 A hoisting or lifting jack operated by a screw; jackscrew. **2** A dental implement for regulating the position of the teeth.

screw log A patent log.

screw·pile (skrōō'pīl') *n.* A pile having a strong metal base with a screw thread to ensure firm penetration of hard ground or bedrock. See illustration under LIGHTHOUSE.

SCREW JACK

screw·pine (skrōō'pīn') *n.* Any of a tropical genus (*Pandanus*) of plants having a screwlike arrangement of the clustered leaves and aerial roots.

screw propeller A mechanism consisting of a revolving shaft with radiating blades set at an angle to produce a spiral action: used in propelling ships, etc.

screw thread 1 The projecting spiral ridge of uniform pitch on the outer or inner surface of a cylinder or cone, as of a screw or nut. **2** A complete revolution of any point in this ridge.

screw·worm fly (skrōō'wûrm') A shiny, blue–green blowfly (genus *Cochliomyia,* family *Calliphoridae*) about twice the size of the common housefly, whose larvae breed in living flesh; especially, *C. americana,* the destructive cattle pest of the southern and western United States.

screw·y (skrōō'ē) *adj.* **screw·i·er, screw·i·est** *Slang* Extremely irrational; crazy.

Scria·bin (skryä'bēn), **Alexander,** 1872–1915, Russian composer.

scrib·ble (skrib'əl) *v.* **·bled, ·bling** *v.t.* **1** To write hastily and carelessly. **2** To cover with careless or illegible writing or marks. — *v.i.* **3** To write in a careless or hasty manner. **4** To make illegible or meaningless marks. — *n.* **1** Hasty, careless writing. **2** Meaningless lines and marks; any scrawl. [<Med. L *scribillare,* freq. of L *scribere* write]

scrib·bler (skrib'lər) *n.* **1** One who scribbles. **2** A writer of no reputation; a petty or inferior author.

scribe (skrīb) *n.* **1** One who writes or copies manuscripts. **2** A clerk, public writer, or amanuensis. **3** An author, penman, or journalist: used humorously. **4** An ancient Jewish teacher, interpreter, or writer of the Mosaic law. **5** A pointed instrument for marking wood, bricks, etc. — *v.* **scribed, scrib·ing** *v.t.* **1** To mark or scratch with a pointed instrument. **2** To write, inscribe, or engrave. **3** In carpentry, to mark and fit closely. — *v.i.* **4** *Rare* To write; work as a scribe. [<L *scriba* < *scribere* write] — **scrib'al** *adj.*

Scribe (skrēb), **Augustin Eugène,** 1791–1861, French dramatist.

scrib·er (skrī'bər) *n.* **1** One who or that which scribes. **2** Any sharp–pointed tool used in scribing.

scrieve (skrēv) *v.i. Scot.* To glide swiftly along. [Prob. <ON *skrefa* stride]

scrim (skrim) *n.* **1** A lightweight, open–mesh, coarse cotton fabric, usually white or écru, used for draperies, etc. **2** In the theater, a

similar fabric, often painted, used as a transparency, to support artificial foliage, etc. [Origin unknown]

scrim·mage (skrim′ij) *n.* **1** A rough-and-tumble contest; fracas; formerly, a skirmish. **2** In American football, a mass play from the line of scrimmage after the ball has been placed on the ground and snapped back, the play ending when the ball is dead. **3** In Rugby football, a scrummage. **— line of scrimmage** In football, the hypothetic line, parallel to the goal lines, on which the ball rests and along which the opposing linemen take position at the start of play. *— v.t. & v.i.* **·maged, ·mag·ing** To engage in a scrimmage. Also spelled *scrummage.* [Alter. of *scrimish,* var. of SKIRMISH]

scrimp (skrimp) *v.i.* **1** To be very or overly economical; be niggardly. *— v.t.* **2** To be overly sparing toward; skimp. **3** To cut too small, narrow, etc. *— adj.* Scanty; short: also **scrimp′y.** See synonyms under SCANTY. *— n.* A miser; niggard. [?. Related to OE *scrimman* shrink, shrivel] **— scrimp′i·ness** *n.*
Synonyms (verb): contract, curtail, economize, limit, pinch, reduce, save, scant, shorten, straiten. *Antonyms:* dissipate, lavish, squander, waste.

scrim·shaw (skrim′shô) *v.t. & v.i.* To ornament (ivory, whale's teeth, etc.) by cutting or carving: a sailor's term. *— n.* A neat example of mechanical work; especially, a scrimshawed article, ornamented with fanciful carving. [?< the surname *Scrimshaw*]

scrip[1] (skrip) *n.* **1** A scrap of paper, especially one containing writing. **2** A writing; a certificate, schedule, or written list. **3** A piece of paper money less than a dollar formerly issued in the United States: also called *shinplaster.* [<SCRIPT, prob. infl. in form by SCRAP]

scrip[2] (skrip) *n.* A provisional document (or documents collectively) certifying that the holder is entitled to receive something else, as shares of stock or land. [Short for obs. *subscription receipt*]

scrip[3] (skrip) *n.* A wallet or small bag. [Prob. fusion of ON *skreppa* a bag and OF *escrepe,* in phrase *escrepe et bordon* wallet and staff]

scrip dividend A distribution of surplus to stockholders in the form of scrip or promises to pay the dividend at a certain time.

Scripps (skrips) Name of a family of U.S. newspaper publishers, including **James Edmund,** 1835–1906, born in England; his half-brother, **Edward Wyllis,** 1854–1926; and **Robert Paine,** 1895–1938, son of Edward Wyllis.

scrip·sit (skrip′sit) *Latin* He (or she) wrote (it): used after an author's name on manuscripts, etc.

script (skript) *n.* **1** Writing of the ordinary cursive form. **2** Type, or printed or engraved matter, in imitation of handwriting. **3** *Law* A writing, especially an original; in English practice, a will; codicil. **4** A piece of writing; a manuscript or typescript; especially, a prepared copy, often containing suggestions, for the use of actors in a theatrical, radio, or television performance. *— v.t. & v.i. U.S. Colloq.* To prepare a script for (a radio, television, or theatrical performance). [<OF *escript* <L *scriptum,* pp. neut. of *scribere* write]

This line is in script.

scrip·to·ri·um (skrip·tôr′ē·əm, -tō′rē-) *n. pl.* **·ri·ums** or **·ri·a** (-ē·ə) The writing-room of a monastery, where records, annals, and manuscripts were written, copied, or illuminated. [<Med. L <L *scriptus,* pp. of *scribere* write]

scrip·tur·al (skrip′chər·əl) *adj.* Relating to writing; written. **— scrip′tur·al·ly** *adv.* **— scrip′tur·al·ness** *n.*

Scrip·tur·al (skrip′chər·əl) *adj.* Pertaining to, contained in, quoted from, or warranted by the Bible; Biblical. **— Scrip′tur·al·ly** *adv.* **— Scrip′tur·al·ness** *n.*

Scrip·tur·al·ism (skrip′chər·əl·iz′əm) *n.* The quality or character of being Scriptural; also, strict or literal adherence to the Scriptures. **— Scrip′tur·al·ist** *n.*

scrip·ture (skrip′chər) *n.* **1** The sacred writings of any people. **2** Originally, anything written, as a document, book, or inscription, or its contents; a writing. [<OF *escripture* <L *scriptura* <*scriptus,* pp. of *scribere* write]

Scrip·ture (skrip′chər) *n.* **1** The books of the Old and New Testaments, including often the Apocrypha; specifically, the Bible: usually plural. **2** A text or passage from the Bible.

script·writ·er (skript′rī′tər) *n.* A writer who prepares copy for the use of a radio or television actor or announcer.

scrive (skrīv) *v.t.* **scrived, scriv·ing** **1** To engrave. **2** *Obs.* To write; scribe. [<OF *escrivre* write <L *scribere*]

scri·vel·lo (skri·vel′ō) *n. pl.* **·loes** or **·los** An elephant's tusk. [<Pg. *escrevelho,* ? var. of *escaravelho* a pin, peg]

scriv·en·er (skriv′ən·ər, skriv′nər) *n.* **1** One who prepares deeds, contracts, and other writings; a clerk or scribe. **2** Formerly, a money-lender. [<obs. *scrivein* <OF *escrivain* <Ital. *scrivano* <L *scribere* write]

scro·bic·u·late (skrō·bik′yə·lit, -lāt) *adj. Biol.* Marked with many small depressions; furrowed or pitted. Also **scro·bic′u·lat′ed** (-lā′·tid). [<L *scrobiculus,* dim. of *scrobis* a trench]

scrod (skrod) *n.* A young codfish, especially when split and prepared for broiling. [? <MDu. *schrode* a piece cut off. Akin to SHRED.]

scrof·u·la (skrof′yə·lə) *n. Pathol.* A tuberculous condition of the lymphatic glands, characterized by enlargement, suppurating abscesses, and cheeselike degeneration; the king's evil. [Orig. pl. <LL *scrofulae,* dim. pl. <*scrofa* a breeding sow; so called because sows were supposed to be subject to the disease]

scrof·u·lous (skrof′yə·ləs) *adj.* **1** Pertaining to, affected with, or of the nature of scrofula. **2** Like scrofula; hence, morally diseased. **— scrof′u·lous·ly** *adv.* **— scrof′u·lous·ness** *n.*

scrog·gy (skrog′ē) *adj. Scot. & Brit. Dial.* Stunted; dwarfed; shriveled; also, abounding with brushwood. [Prob. <Scand. Cf. Dan. *skrog* a lean carcass.]

scroll (skrōl) *n.* **1** A roll of parchment, paper, or the like, especially one containing or intended for writing; also, the writing on such a roll; specifically, an outline; draft. **2** Anything resembling or suggestive of a parchment roll; specifically, a convoluted ornament or an ornamental space or tablet on sculptured work. **3** The curved head of a violin or similar instrument. **4** *Her.* A ribbon bearing a motto. See synonyms under RECORD. [Earlier *scrowle,* alter. of obs. *scrow* <AF *escrowe* a scroll; prob. infl. in form by ME *rowle* a roll]

scroll saw A narrow-bladed saw, or a sawing machine bearing such a blade, for doing curved or irregular work.

scroll·work (skrōl′wûrk′) *n.* Ornamental work of scroll-like pattern; particularly, fanciful designs cut from thin material by means of scroll saws.

Scrooge (skrōōj), **Ebenezer** In Dickens's *Christmas Carol,* a miser whose hard nature is transformed by the revelations of human joy and sorrow given to him by three spirits that visit him on Christmas Eve.

scroop (skrōōp) *v.i.* To give forth a harsh, scraping sound or cry; creak; grate. *— n.* A harsh grating or crunching sound; harsh cry. [Imit.; infl. by SCRAPE]

scroph·u·lar·i·a·ceous (skrof′yə·lâr′ē·ā′shəs) *adj.* Of or pertaining to a family (*Scrophulariaceae*) of herbs, shrubs, and a few trees, the figwort family, including the veronica, snapdragon and digitalis. [<NL <*Scrophularia,* type genus <Med. L *scrophula* SCROFULA; so called from its supposed power to cure scrofula]

scro·tum (skrō′təm) *n. pl.* **·ta** (-tə) *Anat.* The pouch that contains the testes. [<L] **— scro′·tal** *adj.*

scrouge (skrōōj, skrouj) *v.t. Brit. Dial.* To squeeze or grind down; crowd; press. [Earlier *scruze,* blend of SCREW and SQUEEZE]

scrounge (skrounj) *v.t. & v.i.* **scrounged, scroung·ing** *Slang* **1** To hunt about and take (something); pilfer. **2** To mooch; sponge; beg. [? <dial. E *scrunge* steal, var. of SCROUGE] **— scroung′er** *n.*

scroung·y (skroun′jē) *adj.* **scroung·i·er, scroung·i·est** *Slang* **1** Given to scrounging. **2** Unkempt; unclean; grubby.

scrub[1] (skrub) *v.* **scrubbed, scrub·bing** *v.t.* **1** To rub vigorously, as with the hand or a brush, in washing. **2** To remove (dirt, etc.) by such action. **3** To cleanse (a gas). *— v.i.* **4** To rub something vigorously in washing. See synonyms under CLEANSE. *— n.* The act of scrubbing. [? <Scand. Cf. Dan. *skrubbe.*]

scrub[2] (skrub) *n.* **1** A stunted tree. **2** A thicket or tract of stunted trees or shrubs. **3** A domestic animal of inferior or impure breed. **4** A poor, insignificant person. **5** In sports, a player not on the varsity or regular team. **6** A game of baseball contrived hastily by a few players. *— adj.* **1** Undersized or stunted-looking; inferior. **2** Consisting of or participated in by untrained players or scrubs: *scrub* team; *scrub* game. [Dial. var. of SHRUB[1]]

scrub·ber (skrub′ər) *n.* **1** One who or that which scrubs. **2** Any apparatus that removes undesired material through the medium of a liquid by washing.

scrub·by (skrub′ē) *adj.* **·bi·er, ·bi·est** **1** Of stunted growth. **2** Covered with or consisting of scrub or underbrush. [<SCRUB[2]] **— scrub′·bi·ness** *n.*

scrub grass The scouring rush.

scrub·land (skrub′land′) *n.* Land covered with scrub.

scrub oak Any of various dwarf oaks of the United States, as *Quercus ilicifolia* and *Q. prinoides,* common in New England; especially, the turkey oak or *Q. laevis* of the sandy barrens of the South.

scrub pine Any of several American dwarf pines; especially, the common Jersey pine (*Pinus virginiana*) and the shore pine of California, a variety of lodgepole pine (*P. contorta*).

scrub typhus *Pathol.* Tsutsugamushi disease.

scruff (skruf) *n.* The nape or outer back part of the neck. [Earlier *scuff* (<ON *skopt* hair); infl. in form by *scruff,* var. of SCURF]

scrum (skrum) *n. Brit. Colloq.* Scrummage: an abbreviated form.

scrum·mage (skrum′ij) *v.t. & v.i.* **·maged, ·mag·ing** To scrimmage. *— n.* **1** Scrimmage. **2** In Rugby football, a formation, around the ball, of the opposing sets of forwards, each of which endeavors by superior weight or compactness to dislodge the opponent, secure and break away with the ball, or kick it out. [Var. of SCRIMMAGE] **— scrum′mag·er** *n.*

scrump·tious (skrump′shəs) *adj. Slang* **1** Elegant or stylish; fine; delightful; splendid. **2** Fastidious; overly particular; nice. [<dial. E, mean, stingy, ult. <SCRIMP; prob. infl. in meaning by SUMPTUOUS]

scrunch (skrunch) *v.t. & v.i.* To crush; squeeze; crunch. *— n.* A crunch. [Imit. alter. of CRUNCH]

scru·ple (skrōō′pəl) *n.* **1** Doubt or uncertainty regarding a question of moral right or duty; reluctance arising from conscientious disapproval. **2** An apothecaries' weight of twenty grains, or 1.295 grams (symbol: ℈). **3** A minute quantity. **4** An ancient Roman coin. *— v.t. & v.i.* **·pled, ·pling** To have scruples (about); hesitate (doing) from considerations of right or expediency. [<OF *scrupule* <L *scrupulus,* dim. of *scrupus* a sharp stone]

scru·pu·lous (skrōō′pyə·ləs) *adj.* **1** Cautious in action for fear of doing wrong; nicely conscientious. **2** Resulting from the exercise of scruples; exact; careful. See synonyms under PRECISE, SQUEAMISH. [<L *scrupulosus* <*scrupulus* a scruple] **— scru′pu·lous·ly** *adv.* **— scru′pu·lous·ness, scru′pu·los′i·ty** (-los′·ə·tē) *n.*

scru·ti·nize (skrōō′tə·nīz) *v.t.* **·nized, ·niz·ing** To observe carefully; examine in detail. See synonyms under EXAMINE. **— scru′ti·niz′er** *n.*

scru·ti·ny (skrōō′tə·nē) *n. pl.* **·nies** **1** The act of scrutinizing; close investigation. **2** A method of electing the pope by secret ballot. **3** An official examination of votes after an election. See synonyms under INQUIRY. [<LL *scrutinium* <L *scrutari* examine, appar. < *scruta* trash, rags; with ref. to a careful search, including even trash and rags]

scry·ing (skrī′ing) *n. Archaic* Crystal-gazing. [Aphetic var. of DESCRY]

scu·ba (skōō′bə, skyōō′-) *n.* A device worn by a free-swimming diver to provide a supply of air for breathing. [< *s*(*elf-*)*c*(*ontained*) *u*(*nderwater*) *b*(*reathing*) *a*(*pparatus*)]

scud (skud) *v.i.* **scud·ded, scud·ding** **1** To move, run, or fly swiftly. **2** *Naut.* To run rapidly before the wind; especially, to run before a

gale with little or no sail set. —*n.* **1** The act of scudding or moving swiftly. **2** Light clouds driven rapidly before the wind; a misty rain. **3** *Brit. Slang* A swift runner. **4** *Scot.* A slap with the open hand. **5** *pl. Scot.* Foaming beer or ale. [Prob. < Scand. (cf. Norw. *skudda* push); ? infl. in meaning by *scut,* in earlier sense of "a hare"]

Scud·der (skud′ər), **Horace,** 1838–1902, U.S. author.

Scu·dé·ry (skü·dā·rē′), **Madeleine de,** 1607–1701, French novelist.

scu·do (skōō′dō) *n. pl.* **scu·di** (skōō′dē) A former Italian and Sicilian silver or gold coin. [< Ital. < L *scutum* a shield]

scuff (skuf) *v.i.* **1** To walk with a dragging movement of the feet; shuffle. — *v.t.* **2** To scrape (the floor, ground, etc.) with the feet. **3** To make the surface of rough by rubbing or scraping. —*n.* The act of scuffing; also, the noise so made. [Prob. < ON *skūfa* shove]

scuf·fle[1] (skuf′əl) *v.i.* **·fled, ·fling 1** To struggle roughly or confusedly. **2** To drag one's feet; schuffle. — *n.* A disorderly struggle carried on by grappling, pulling, pushing, or the like; confused fracas. [Prob. freq. of SCUFF] —**scuf′fler** *n.*

scuf·fle[2] (skuf′əl) *n.* A form of hoe used by pushing in the manner of a spade. Also **scuffle hoe.** See illustration under HOE. [< Du. *schoffel* a weeding hoe]

scul·dud·der·y (skul·dud′ər·ē) *n. Scot.* Obscenity.

scull[1] (skul) *n.* **1** A long oar worked from side to side over the stern of a boat. **2** A light, short-handled spoon oar, used in pairs by one person. **3** A small boat for sculling. — *v.t.* & *v.i.* To propel (a boat) by a scull or sculls. ◆ Homophone: *skull.* [ME *sculle, skulle;* origin unknown] —**scull′er** *n.*

scull[2] (skul) *n. Scot.* A large, shallow wicker basket. ◆ Homophone: *skull.*

scul·ler·y (skul′ər·ē) *n. pl.* **·ler·ies** A room where kitchen utsensils are kept and cleaned; a back kitchen. [< OF *escuelerie* care of dishes < *escuelle* a dish < L *scutella* a tray]

scul·lion (skul′yən) *n.* **1** A servant who washes and scours dishes, pots, and kettles. **2** A low wretch. [< OF *escouillon* a mop < *escouve* a broom < L *scopae* a bundle of twigs, pl. of *scopa* a twig]

sculp (skulp) *v.t.* & *v.i. Colloq.* To sculpture. [Short for SCULPTURE]

scul·pin (skul′pin) *n.* **1** One of several broad-mouthed fishes (family *Cottidae*), of inferior food value, with large, spiny head. The **daddy sculpin** (*Acanthocothus scorpius*) is a common North Atlantic species of which the North American form is a variety. **2** A fish (*Scorpaena guttata*) having a large head and spiny fins, found in southern California. **3** *Brit.* A contemptible fellow; mischief-maker. [Prob. alter. of F *escorpene* < L *scorpaena,* a scorpionlike fish < Gk. *skorpaina* < *skorpios* a scorpion]

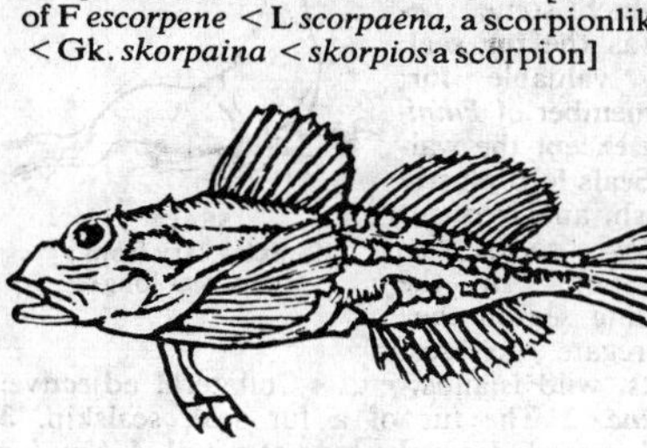

DADDY SCULPIN
(Rarely over 4 inches long)

sculp·tor (skulp′tər) *n.* One who designs sculpture by carving wood, modeling plastics, or chiseling stone. [< L < *sculpere* sculpture] —**sculp′tress** (-tris) *n. fem.*

sculp·ture (skulp′chər) *n.* **1** The art of fashioning figures of stone, wood, clay, or bronze. **2** Figures or groups carved, cut, hewn, cast, or modeled in wood, stone, clay, or metal. **3** Raised or incised lines, or markings, as upon a shell. —*v.t.* **·tured, ·tur·ing 1** To fashion, as statuary, by modeling, carving, or casting. **2** To represent or portray in sculpture. **3** To embellish with sculpture. **4** To change, as the face of a valley or canyon, by erosion and deposition. [< L *sculputra* < *sculptus,* pp. of *sculpere* carve in stone < *scalpere* cut] —**sculp′tur·al** *adj.*

sculp·tur·esque (skulp′chə·resk′) *adj.* Resembling sculpture; coldly, calmly, or grandly beautiful; statuesque; well-proportioned; majestic. —**sculp′tur·esque′ly** *adv.* —**sculp′tur·es·que′ness** *n.*

scum (skum) *n.* **1** Impure or extraneous matter that rises to the surface of boiling or fermenting liquids. **2** Minute vegetation on stagnant water. **3** Scoria or dross of molten metals; also, foam; froth. **4** Figuratively, vile element; refuse. See synonyms under WASTE. —*v.* **scummed, scum·ming** *v.t.* To take scum from; skim. —*v.i.* To become covered with or form scum. [< MDu. *schuum*] —**scum′mer** *n.* —**scum′my** *adj.*

scum·ble (skum′bəl) *v.t.* **·bled, ·bling** In drawing and painting, to soften the outlines or blend the colors of by rubbing, as with comparatively dry or opaque color. —*n.* **1** The softening or blending of colors so produced. **2** The material used in scumbling. [Freq. of SCUM]

scun·ner (skun′ər) *n.* See SCONNER.

Scun·thorpe (skun′thôrp) A municipal borough of NW Lincolnshire, England.

scup (skup) *n.* **1** A valuable sparoid food fish (*Stenotomus chrysops*) of the eastern coast of the United States; the porgy; also **scup·paug** (skup′ôg, skə·pôg′). **2** A related species (*S. aculeatus*) found southward from Cape Hatteras and on the Gulf Coast to Texas. [< Algonquian (Narraganset) *mishcup* thick-scaled < *mishe* large + *cuppi* a scale]

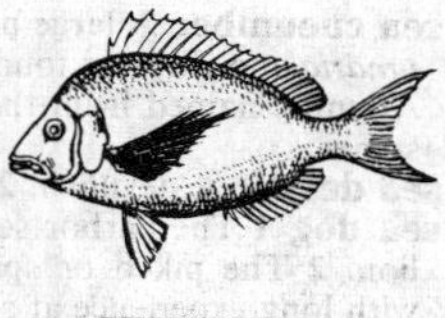

COMMON SCUP
(About 12 inches long)

scup·per[1] (skup′ər) *n. Naut.* A hole or gutter bordering a ship's deck, to let water run off. [Prob. short for *scupper hole* < OF *escope* a bailing scoop < Gmc. Akin to SCOOP.]

scup·per[2] (skup′ər) *v.t. Brit.* To put in great difficulty or danger; surprise or suprise and annihilate. [? < SCUPPER[1]]

scup·per·nong (skup′ər·nông, -nong) *n.* **1** A variety of muscadine grape cultivated in the southern United States. **2** A sweet, straw-colored wine made from this grape. [from the *Scuppernong* River in Tyrrell County, N.C.]

scurf (skûrf) *n.* **1** Loose scarfskin thrown off in minute scales, as in dandruff. **2** Any extraneous scaly matter adhering to a surface. **3** Worthless or impure coating or covering. [OE, alter. of *sceorf;* prob. infl. in form by Scand. Cf. Dan. *skurv.*] —**scurf′i·ness** *n.* —**scurf′y** *adj.*

scur·ril·i·ty (skə·ril′ə·tē) *n. pl.* **·ties 1** Coarse, vulgar abuse; a scurrilous remark. **2** The quality of being obscenely jocular. [< MF *scurrilité* < L *scurrilitas* < *scurrilis* SCURRILOUS]

scur·ri·lous (skûr′ə·ləs) *adj.* **1** Grossly offensive or vulgar; opprobrious. **2** Expressed with or given to low buffoonery. Also **scur·rile** (skûr′·il), **scur′ril.** [Earlier *scurrile* < L, neut. of *scurrilis* buffoon-like < *scurra* a buffoon] —**scur′ri·lous·ly** *adv.* —**scur′ri·lous·ness** *n.*

scur·ry (skûr′ē) *v.i.* **·ried, ·ry·ing** To move or go hurriedly; scamper. —*n. pl.* **·ries 1** The act or sound of scurrying; a precipitate movement. **2** A flurry, as of snow; whirl. **3** A short, fast run or race on horseback. [Short for HURRY-SCURRY; ? infl. by SCOUR[2]]

S-curve (es′kûrv′) *n.* A curve shaped like an *S.*

scur·vy (skûr′vē) *adj.* **·vi·er, ·vi·est 1** Meanly low or contemptible; base. **2** *Obs.* Afflicted with scurvy; also, scabby. See synonyms under BAD[1], BASE[2]. —*n. Pathol.* A disease characterized by livid spots under the skin, swollen and bleeding gums, and great prostration: caused by lack of vitamin C in the diet. [< SCURF] —**scur′vi·ly** *adv.* —**scur′vi·ness** *n.*

scurvy grass A biennial herb (*Cochlearia officinalis*) highly prized by Arctic explorers as a remedy for scurvy.

scut (skut) *n.* **1** A short or docked tail. **2** *Slang* A contemptible person. —*v.t. Obs.* To dock (an animal's tail). —*adj.* Short. [ME, a tail, a hare, prob. < Scand. Cf. Icelandic *skott* a fox's tail.]

scu·tage (skyōō′tij) *n.* A tax enacted from feudal knights instead of personal military service for their lands. [< Med. L *scutagium* < L *scutum* a shield]

Scu·ta·ri (skōō′tä·rē) **1** Üsküdar. **2** The largest city of northern Albania, at the SE end of **Lake Scutari,** a lake in SW Yugoslavia and NW Albania; 205 square miles. *Albanian* **Shko·dër** (shkô′dər), **Shko·dra** (shkô′drə). Ancient **Sco·dra** (skō′drə).

scu·tate (skyōō′tāt) *adj. Biol.* **1** Covered with horny, shieldlike plates or large scales. **2** Shaped like a shield. Also *scutellate.* See PELTATE. [< L *scutatus* provided with a shield < *scutum* a shield]

scutch (skuch) *v.t.* **1** To dress (textile fiber) by beating. **2** To separate the woody parts from the valuable fiber of (flax, etc.) by beating. —*n.* An implement for scutching hemp and flax. [Prob. < OF *escousser* shake, ? < Scand. Cf. Norw. *skoka* a scutch.] —**scutch′er** *n.*

scutch·eon (skuch′ən) *n.* **1** An escutcheon or anything shaped like it. **2** A metal plate or shield; a name plate or the like. [Aphetic var. of ESCUTCHEON]

scute (skyōōt) *n.* **1** *Zool.* A thin plate or scale, as a scale of a reptile, forming the shell on turtles, etc. **2** Scutellum. [< L *scutum* a shield]

scu·tel·late (skyōō·tel′it, skyōō′tə·lāt) *adj. Zool.* **1** Platterlike; shield-shaped. **2** Covered with transverse scales; scutate. Also **scu′tel·lat′ed** (-lā′tid). [< NL *scutellatus* < L *scutella* a platter, dim. of *scutra* a tray; infl. in meaning by L *scutum* a shield]

scu·tel·la·tion (skyōō′tə·lā′shən) *n. Ornithol.* The presence or the arrangement of the scales on a bird's tarsus and toes.

scu·tel·lum (skyōō·tel′əm) *n. pl.* **·la** (-ə) **1** *Bot.* A small shieldlike organ or part, as in the cotyledon of a plant. **2** *Ornithol.* A scale on the foot of a bird. [< NL, dim. of L *scutum* a shield] —**scu·tel′lar** *adj.*

scu·ti·form (skyōō′tə·fôrm) *adj.* Shield-shaped. [< NL *scutiformis* < L *scutum* a shield + *forma* form]

scut·ter (skut′ər) *v.i.* To scurry, scuttle. —*n.* A hasty running. [SCUTT(LE)[3] + -ER[4]]

scut·tle[1] (skut′l) *n.* **1** A small opening or hatchway with movable lid or cover, especially in the roof or wall of a house, or in the deck or side of a ship. **2** The lid closing such an opening. **3** A sea cock in the bottom of a ship. —*v.t.* **·tled, ·tling** To sink (a ship) by making holes in the bottom or by opening the sea cocks. [< MF *escoutille* a hatchway < Sp. *escotilla,* prob. < Gmc.]

scut·tle[2] (skut′l) *n.* **1** A metal vessel or hod for coal. **2** Rarely, a vessel or pail for other purposes. [OE *scutel* a disk, platter < L *scutella*]

scut·tle[3] (skut′l) *v.i.* **·tled, ·tling** To run in haste; scurry. —*n.* A hurried run or departure. [? Var. of *scuddle,* freq. of SCUD; prob. infl. in form by dial. E *scut* a hare, a short tail; with ref. to the rapid movement of the hare]

scut·tle·butt (skut′l·but) *n.* **1** A drinking fountain aboard ship; formerly, a cask containing the day's drinking water. **2** *U.S. Slang* Rumor; gossip. [Orig. *scuttled butt* a lidded cask for drinking water]

scut·tler (skut′lər) *n.* The striped lizard of the southern United States.

scu·tum (skyōō′təm) *n. pl.* **·ta** (-tə) **1** The large oval or rectangular shield of the Roman legionaries. **2** *Zool.* Some platelike piece or part in a turtle, fish, etc.; a large scale. [< L]

Scu·tum (skyōō′təm) The Shield, a zodiacal constellation. see CONSTELLATION. [< L]

scuz·zy (skuz′ē) *adj.* **·zi·er, ·zi·est** *Slang* Foul; nasty; unpleasant; filthy. —**scuz′zi·ness** *n.*

Scyl·la (sil′ə) In Greek mythology, a six-headed sea monster who dwelt in a cave on the Italian coast opposite the whirlpool Charybdis. See SCILLA. —**between Scylla and Charybdis** Between two dangers, where one cannot be avoided without incurring equally great peril from the other.

scypho- *combining form* Cup; vessel: also,

before vowels, **scyph-.** Also **scyphi-,** as in *scyphiform,* cup-shaped. [< L *scyphus* and Gk. *scyphos* a cup]

scy·pho·zo·an (sī'fə·zō'ən) *n.* Any of a class (*Scyphozoa*) of coelenterates including the sea anemones, corals, and jellyfish. —*adj.* Of or resembling the *Scyphozoa.* [< NL < Gk. *skyphos* a cup + *zōon* an animal]

Scy·ros (sī'rəs) The Latin name for SKYROS.

scythe (sīth) *n.* **1** A long curved blade for mowing, reaping, etc., fixed at an angle to a long bent handle or snath. **2** The implement so formed. **3** A curved blade attached to the axles or wheels of some ancient war chariots. —*v.t.* **scythed, scyth·ing** To cut or mow as with a scythe. [OE *sithe*]

Scyth·i·a (sith'ē·ə) An ancient region of southern Europe, generally considered as lying north of the Black Sea.

Scyth·i·an (sith'ē·ən) *n.* **1** One of an ancient nomadic and fiercely savage people dwelling along the north shore of the Black Sea and extending as far east as the Aral Sea: last known in history about 100 B.C. **2** The Iranian language of the Scythians. —*adj.* Of or pertaining to the Scythians, their land, or their language. [< L *Scythia* < Gk. *Skythia* < *Skythēs* a Scythian]

'sdeath (zdeth) *interj. Archaic* God's death: an imprecation.

Sdot Yam (sdôt yäm) A settlement in NW Israel, on the site of ancient Caesarea.

Se *Chem.* Selenium (symbol Se).

sea (sē) *n.* **1** The great body of salt water covering the larger portion of the earth's surface; the ocean. **2** A large or considerable body of oceanic water partly or almost entirely enclosed by land: the Adriatic *Sea.* **3** A large inland body of water, salt or fresh: the Dead *Sea* or the *Sea* of Galilee. **4** The swell of the ocean; the course, flow, or set of the waves. **5** Anything that resembles or suggests the sea, as something vast, boundless, or wide-spread. —**at sea 1** On the ocean. **2** At a loss what to do or think; bewildered. —**to follow the sea** To follow the occupation of a sailor. —**the high seas** The unenclosed expanse of the ocean; also, that part of the ocean beyond a country's territorial waters. —**the seven seas** All the oceans of the world: the North and the South Atlantic, the North and the South Pacific, the Indian, the Arctic, and the Antarctic oceans.◆ Homophone: *see.* [OE *sǣ*]

sea anchor A drag anchor; a heavy float or canvas bag or sail serving to hold a ship's head to the wind in order to ride out a gale or reduce drifting.

sea anemone A soft-bodied marine coelenterate (class *Anthozoa,* order *Actinaria*), that attaches itself to rocks, etc., suggesting a flower by its coloring and outspread tentacles.

sea bag A cylindrical canvas bag, fastened with a drawstring, in which sailors stow their clothes.

SEA ANEMONE
a. Tentacles contracted.
b. Tentacles extended.

sea bass 1 A dusky-brown or black serranoid food fish (*Centropristes striatus*), common from Cape Cod to Florida: also called *blackfish.* **2** A related fish of California waters (*Stereolepis gigas*). Also **black sea bass. 3** The white sea bass of California (*Cynoscion nobilis*). **4** The related shortfin sea bass (*C. parvipinnis*).

Sea·bee (sē'bē') *n.* A member of the Construction Battalions of the U.S. Navy, which build base facilities, airfields, etc. [< C(onstruction) B(attalion)]

sea bird Any web-footed bird frequenting the oceans or their coasts, as albatrosses, gulls, gannets, petrels, frigate birds, shearwaters, etc.

sea biscuit Hardtack.

sea·board (sē'bôrd', -bōrd') *adj.* Bordering on the sea. —*n.* The seashore or seacoast; also, the land or region bordering the sea. [< SEA + *board* a border, OE *bord*]

Sea·borg (sē'bôrg'), **Glenn Theodore,** born

1912, U.S. physical chemist.

sea bread An unsalted hard biscuit used at sea; hardtack.

sea bream Any of several Old World sparoid food fishes; specifically, a common migratory species (*Pagellus centrodontus*).

sea breeze A cool breeze blowing from the ocean toward the land.

sea butterfly A pteropod.

sea calf The common harbor seal (*Phoca vitulina*) of the North Atlantic.

sea captain The captain of a seagoing vessel.

sea-coast (sē'kōst') *n.* The seashore; seaboard.

sea cock A cock or valve controlling connection with the water through a vessel's hull.

sea coconut The very large and heavy bilobate fruit of a palm (*Lodoicea maldivica*) native to islands of the Indian Ocean, weighing 40 or 50 pounds and containing four nuts 18 inches long: also called *double coconut.*

sea cow 1 Any aquatic herbivorous mammal of the order *Sirenia,* sometimes attaining a length of about 25 feet; especially, the manatee or the dugong. **2** The walrus. **3** The hippopotamus.

sea craft 1 Skill in navigation. **2** Seagoing vessels.

sea cucumber A large holothurian (genera *Cucumaria* and *Thyone*) found on both coasts of the Atlantic: named from the form it commonly assumes.

sea devil 1 A devilfish. **2** An angelfish.

sea dog 1 The harbor seal or the California sea lion. **2** The piked or spiny dogfish. **3** A sailor with long experience at sea. **4** A fog dog.

sea drake 1 The male of the eider duck. **2** A cormorant.

sea drift Anything cast up by the sea; flotsam, especially vegetable or animal matter.

sea·drome (sē'drōm') *n. Aeron.* An airport established at sea for the accommodation and servicing of aircraft making overseas flights. [< SEA + -DROME]

sea duck Any duck that frequents salt water, belonging to the subfamily *Nyrocinae;* especially, the American eider duck (*Somateria mollissima dresseri*), ranging from Labrador to Maine and as far westward as the Great Lakes. See DUCK.

sea eagle 1 An eagle, related to the bald eagle, which lives principally on fish; especially, Steller's sea eagle (*Thalassoaëtus pelagicus*), found on the islands off Alaska. **2** The osprey.

sea fan A coral (*Gorgonia flabellum*) of Florida and the West Indies, with fanlike branches.

sea·far·er (sē'fâr'ər) *n.* A seaman; a mariner. See synonyms under SAILOR. [< SEA + FARER]

sea·far·ing (sē'fâr'ing) *adj.* Following the sea as a calling. —*n.* Traveling over the ocean.

sea fight A conflict between vessels on the high seas.

sea fire The phosphorescence of sea water.

sea floor The bottom of the sea.

sea flower A sea anemone or related anthozoan.

sea foam 1 Foam of the ocean. **2** Meerschaum. **3** A fluffy candy made of spun sugar.

sea food Edible fish, shellfish, etc.

sea fowl A sea bird or sea birds collectively.

sea front Land that borders on the sea; buildings, etc., that face the sea.

sea gage 1 The depth to which a vessel sinks in the water; the draft of a vessel. **2** A sounding instrument showing the depth of water by the pressure on a column of fluid. Also **sea gauge.**

sea-girt (sē'gûrt') *adj.* Surrounded by waters of the sea or ocean. [< SEA + GIRT²]

sea·go·ing (sē'gō'ing) *adj.* **1** Adapted for use on the ocean. **2** Skilful in navigation; seafaring.

sea grape A tropical American tree (*Coccolobis uvifera*) of the buckwheat family, with glossy, red-veined leaves, white flowers, and clusters of a purple fruit resembling grapes.

sea green A deep bluish green, like the color of sea water.

sea gull Any gull or large tern.

sea hog A porpoise.

sea holly A European coarse herb (*Eryngium maritimum*) of the carrot family.

sea horse 1 A teleost fish, usually 3 inches long, found in warm seas and allied to the

pipefish; especially, *Hippocampus guttatus,* having a head resembling that of a horse. **2** A hippopotamus. **3** A walrus. **4** A fabulous animal, half horse and half fish, driven by Neptune. **5** A large white-crested wave.

Sea Island cotton A valuable long-staple variety of cotton formerly grown on the Sea Islands, now also cultivated elsewhere.

Sea Islands A chain of small islands off the coasts of South Carolina, Georgia, and northern Florida.

sea kale A hardy perennial herb (*Crambe maritima*) of the mustard family, cultivated for its edible young shoots.

SEA HORSE
(From 2 to 12 inches in length)

sea king 1 A viking as a maritime leader; Norse pirate king of the Middle Ages. **2** Neptune.

seal¹ (sēl) *n.* **1** An instrument or device used for making an impression upon some tenacious substance, as wax or a wafer; also, the impression made. **2** The wax, wafer, or similar token affixed to a document as a proof of authenticity; also, an impression, scroll, ormark on the paper. **3** A substance employed to secure a letter, door, lid, wrapper, joint, etc., firmly. **4** Anything that confirms or ratifies; a pledge; authentication. **5** Any instrumentality that keeps something close, secret, or unknown. **6** The fluid filling thetrap of a drainage pipe and preventing the upward flow of gas. **7** An ornamental stamp for packages, etc. —*v.t.* **1** To affix a seal to, as to prove authenticity or prevent tampering. **2** To stamp or otherwise impress a seal upon in order to attest to weight, fineness, quality, etc. **3** To fasten or close with or as with a seal: to *seal* a letter; to *seal* a glass jar. **4** To grant or assign under seal. **5** To establish or settle finally; determine. **6** In Mormon usage, to solemnize forever, as a marriage or the adoption of a child. **7** To sign with the cross; also, to baptize or confirm. **8** To secure, set, or fill up, as with plaster. **9** To supply with a device or trap for preventing a return flow of gas or air. ◆ Homophone: *ceil.* [< OF *seel* < L *sigillum* a small picture, seal, dim. of *signum* a sign] —**seal'a·ble** *adj.*

GREAT SEAL
OF THE
UNITED STATES

seal² (sēl) *n.* **1** An aquatic carnivorous mammal (order or suborder *Pinnipedia*) mostly of high latitudes, of which some species, as the **fur seal,** yield valuable fur; any member of *Pinnipedia* except the walrus. Seals feed mostly on fish, and frequent seacoast rocks, ice floes, etc. In the breeding season they congregate on seacoasts, wild islands, etc. ◆ Collateral adjective: *phocine.* **2** The fur of a fur seal; sealskin. **3** Leather made from the hide of a seal. **4** Any fur prepared so as to look like sealskin. —*v.i.* To hunt seals. ◆ Homophone: *ceil.* [OE *seolh*]

SEAL
(Species vary from 7 to 12 feet long)

seal·ant (sē'lənt) *n.* Any substance which secures the contents of a container against contamination, evaporation, spoilage, or leakage.

sea lavender Any of a genus (*Limonium*) of mostly Old World maritime herbs bearing lavender-colored flowers.

sea lawyer A sailor given to criticizing and querying at every opportunity; a captious or argumentative person.

sea leather The skins of sharks, porpoises, and dogfishes prepared for use as leather.

sealed orders Orders given in a sealed envelope, with instructions to open at a given time or place under specified conditions; specifically, such orders given to the master of a ship before sailing.

sea legs The ability to walk aboard ship without losing one's balance.

seal·er[1] (sē′lər) *n.* 1 A person or thing that seals. 2 An officer who attests and certifies weights, materials, etc. [<SEAL[1]]
seal·er[2] (sē′lər) *n.* A person or ship employed in hunting seals. [<SEAL[2]]
seal·er·y (sē′lər·ē) *n. pl.* **·er·ies** 1 The business of hunting seals. 2 A place where seals are regularly hunted.
sea lettuce A green seaweed (genus *Ulva*) often used for food.
sea level The level continuous with that of the surface of the ocean at mean tide, between high and low water: used in reckoning altitudes.
sea lily A crinoid; a stalked marine invertebrate resembling a flower.
sealing wax A mixture of shellac and resin with turpentine and pigment that is fluid when heated but becomes solid as it cools: used for sealing papers and bottles.
sea lion One of various large, eared seals (family *Otariidae*), especially the California sea lion *(Zalophus californianus)*.
seal ring A signet ring; a finger ring containing an engraved stone.
seal·skin (sēl′skin′) *n.* 1 The under fur of the fur seal when prepared for use by removing the long hairs and dyeing dark-brown or black. 2 A coat or other article made of this fur.
sea lungwort An attractive American herb *(Mertensia maritima)* of the borage family, with white, long-stalked flowers, common to northern coasts.
Sea·ly·ham terrier (sē′lē·ham, -əm) See under TERRIER.
seam[1] (sēm) *n.* 1 A visible line of junction between parts, especially the edges of two pieces of cloth sewn together. 2 A crack; fissure; rent. 3 A ridge made in joining two pieces or left by a mold upon a casting. 4 A scar or cicatrix; also, a wrinkle. 5 A thin layer or stratum of rock. 6 A suture. — *v.t.* 1 To unite by means of a seam. 2 To mark with a cut, furrow, wrinkle, etc. 3 In knitting, to give the appearance of a seam to; purl. — *v.i.* 4 To crack open; become fissured. 5 In knitting, to form seams. ◆ Homophone: *seem.* [OE *sēam*] — **seam′er** *n.*
seam[2] (sēm) *n. Obs.* Any kind of grease; hence, fatness. ◆ Homophone: *seem.* [<OF *saim,* ult. <L *sagina* a fattening]
sea maiden *Poetic* A sea nymph or a mermaid. Also **sea maid.**
sea·man (sē′mən) *n. pl.* **·men** (-mən) 1 An enlisted man in the Navy or in the Coast Guard, graded according to his rank. 2 One skilled in the work of a ship and the ways of the sea; mariner; sailor. — **sea′man·like′** (-līk′) *adj.* — **sea′man·ly** *adj.* & *adv.*
sea·man·ship (sē′mən·ship) *n.* The skill and ability of a seaman in the operation and handling of a boat or ship.
sea·mark (sē′märk′) *n.* Any landmark that serves as a guide in navigation; a beacon; lighthouse.
Seam·as (shā′məs) Irish form of JAMES. Also **Seam′us.**
sea mew A gull, especially the European mew *(Larus canus).* [<SEA + MEW[3]]
sea mile See under MILE.
sea milkwort See under MILKWORT.
seam·less (sēm′lis) *adj.* Having no seam.
sea monster 1 Any huge, terrifying, or strange marine creature, as a devilfish or octopus. 2 A fabulous or mythical man-eating monster of the sea.
sea·mount (sē′mount′) *n.* Any of a widely distributed group of orogenic formations which rise to various heights from the ocean floor and serve as indicators of geologic processes; a submarine mountain.
sea mouse One of a family *(Aphroditidae)* of annelids with iridescent hairlike setae.
seam·ster (sēm′stər) *n.* A person employed in sewing. [OE *seamestre*]
seam·stress (sēm′stris) *n. fem.* A woman skilled in needlework, especially one whose occupation is sewing. Also spelled *sempstress.* [<OE *seamestre* a seamster + -ESS]
seam·y (sē′mē) *adj.* **seam·i·er, seam·i·est** 1 Full of seams, as the wrong side of a garment. 2 Showing the worst aspect: the *seamy* side. — **seam′i·ness** *n.*

Seán (shôn, shän) Irish form of JOHN.
Sean·ad Eir·eann (san′ad âr′ən) The Senate, or upper house, of the Irish Free State legislature. [<Irish *seanad* a senate + *Eireann* of Ireland]
sé·ance (sā′äns, *Fr.* sā·äṅs′) *n.* 1 A session or sitting. 2 A meeting of persons seeking spiritualistic manifestations. [<F <OF *seoir* sit <L *sedere*]
sean·na·chie (shan′ə·kē) *n. Scot.* A bard who preserved and repeated the traditions of the Scottish Highland tribes.
sea onion A bulbous herb *(Urginea maritima)* of the Old World, the source of squill.
sea otter A nearly extinct otter *(Enhydra lutris)* of the rocky shores of the North Pacific, about four feet long, and feeding principally on shellfish. The deep, rich fur, silvery-gray brown superficially, liver-brown beneath, is extremely valuable.
sea palm See under KELP.
sea pen A polyp (genus *Pennatula*) having a rodlike base with the polyps borne on lateral pinnae, giving the appearance of a feather.
sea·plane (sē′plān′) *n.* An airplane designed to rise from and descend upon the water.
sea·port (sē′pôrt′, -pōrt′) *n.* 1 A harbor or port on a coast accessible to seagoing ships. 2 A town located on such a harbor.
sea potato A brown alga (genus *Leathesia*) having a rounded, tuberous appearance.
sea power 1 A nation of great naval importance. 2 The naval strength of a nation.
sea purse *Zool.* The rectangular capsule enclosing the eggs or embryo of certain sharks, skates, and rays.

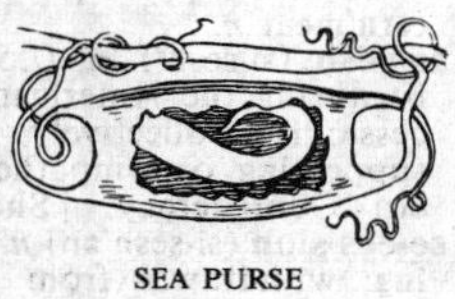
SEA PURSE

sea·quake (sē′kwāk′) *n.* An agitation of the sea from a submarine earthquake; a seismic disturbance under the sea.
sear[1] (sir) *v.t.* 1 To wither; dry up. 2 To burn the surface of; scorch. 3 To burn or cauterize, as with a hot iron; brand. 4 To make callous; harden. — *v.i.* 5 To become withered; dry up. — *adj.* Dried or blasted; withered. — *n.* A scar or brand. Also spelled *sere.* ◆ Homophones: *cere, sere.* [OE *sēarian* wither <*sear* dry]
sear[2] (sir) *n.* The pawl in a gunlock, which holds the hammer at half or full cock. ◆ Homophones: *cere, sere.* [<OF *serre* a grasp <*serrer* close, press <LL *serrare* bolt, bar <L *serare* bolt, bar <*sera* a lock; infl. in LL by L *serrare* saw]
sea raven 1 A deep-water sculpin. 2 The cormorant.
search (sûrch) *n.* 1 The act of seeking or looking diligently. 2 Investigation; inquiry. 3 A critical examination or scrutiny. 4 *Law* Right of search. — *v.t.* 1 To look through or explore thoroughly in order to find something; go over or through in making a search. 2 To subject (a person) to a search, as for concealed weapons, etc. 3 To examine with close attention; probe. 4 To penetrate or pierce: The wind *searches* my clothes. 5 To learn by examination or investigation: with *out.* — *v.i.* 6 To make a search. See synonyms under EXAMINE, HUNT. [<OF *cercher* <L *circare* go round, explore <*circus* a ring] — **search′a·ble** *adj.* — **search′er** *n.*
search·ing (sûr′ching) *adj.* 1 Investigating minutely. 2 Keenly penetrating. — **search′·ing·ly** *adv.* — **search′ing·ness** *n.*
search·light (sûrch′līt′) *n.* An apparatus containing a reflector, and so mounted that a beam of intensely brilliant light may be thrown in various directions for search or signaling; the beam of light from this apparatus.
search warrant A warrant directing an officer to search a house or other specified place for things alleged to be unlawfully concealed there.
sea risk Danger or hazard at sea; specifically, in marine insurance, a peril of the sea.
sea robin One of various gurnards, especially the American brown-finned species *(Prionotus strigatus)*.
sea room Sufficient offing or space for a vessel to be maneuvered.
sea·scape (sē′skāp′) *n.* 1 An ocean view, especially when picturesque. 2 A picture presenting a marine view. [<SEA + (LAND)SCAPE]

sea-scout·ing (sē′skou′ting) *n.* Training in seamanship and water activities given to older boy scouts, called **sea scouts.**
sea serpent A snakelike animal, of monstrous size, believed by many to inhabit the ocean in very limited numbers.
sea·shell (sē′shel′) *n.* The shell of a marine mollusk.
sea·shore (sē′shôr′, -shōr′) *n.* Land adjacent to or bordering on the ocean; the ground between high- and low-water marks.
sea·sick (sē′sik′) *adj.* Suffering from seasickness.
sea·sick·ness (sē′sik′nis) *n.* Nausea, dizziness, and prostration caused by the motion of a vessel.
sea·side (sē′sīd′) *n.* The seashore, especially as a place of resort; also, the side abutting or facing the sea.
sea snake 1 A venomous fish-eating snake (subfamily *Hydrophinae*) of tropical seas, especially of the Indian Ocean. 2 A sea serpent.
sea·son (sē′zən) *n.* 1 A division of the year as determined by the earth's position with respect to the sun, and as marked by the temperature, moisture, vegetation, etc. The ancient Greeks had three seasons, spring, summer, and winter (mentioned by Homer and Hesiod); autumn appears first in Alcman: these four seasons are still used. 2 A period of time. 3 Any of the periods into which the Christian year is divided. 4 A period of special activity: usually with the definite article: the opera or hunting *season.* 5 A fit or suitable time. 6 That which imparts relish; seasoning. See synonyms under OPPORTUNITY, TIME. — **in season** 1 In condition and obtainable for use: Clams are *in season* during the summer. 2 In good or sufficient time; opportunely. 3 To be killed or taken by permission of the law. 4 Ready to mate or breed: said of animals. — *v.t.* 1 To increase the flavor or zest of (food), as by adding spices, etc. 2 To add zest or piquancy to. 3 To render more suitable for use, especially by drying or hardening, as timber. 4 To make accustomed or inured; harden: to *season* troops by strict discipline. 5 To mitigate or soften; moderate. — *v.i.* 6 To become seasoned. [<OF *seson* <LL *satio, -onis* sowing time <L, a sowing <*satus,* pp. of *serere* sow] — **sea′son·er** *n.*
sea·son·a·ble (sē′zən·ə·bəl) *adj.* 1 Being in keeping with the season. 2 Done at the proper time. See synonyms under CONVENIENT. — **sea′son·a·ble·ness** *n.* — **sea′son·a·bly** *adv.*
sea·son·al (sē′zən·əl) *adj.* Characteristic of, or occurring at, a certain season. — **sea′son·al·ly** *adv.*
sea·son·er (sē′zən·ər) *n.* 1 One who or that which seasons or gives added relish; a seasoning. 2 *U.S.* One engaged to serve for the season on a fishing vessel.
sea·son·ing (sē′zən·ing) *n.* 1 The act or process by which something, as lumber, is rendered fit for use. 2 Something added to food to give relish; especially, a condiment; hence, figuratively, something added to increase enjoyment or to relieve monotony. 3 The gradual process of acclimation to a new country or climate.
season ticket A ticket or pass entitling the holder to daily trips on a train for a certain period or to admission to a series of entertainments.
sea squirt An ascidian.
seat (sēt) *n.* 1 That on which one sits; a chair, bench, or stool. 2 That part of a thing upon which one rests in sitting, or upon which an object or another part rests. 3 That part of the person which sustains the weight of the body in sitting, or the corresponding portion of a garment. 4 The place where anything is situated, settled, or established: the *seat* of pain, the *seat* of a government; a site. 5 A place of abode; an estate or mansion, especially a country estate. 6 The privilege or right of membership in a legislative body, stock exchange, or the like. 7 The manner of sitting, as on horseback. 8 A surface or part upon which the base of anything rests. 9 A position in a legislature or an office. — *v.t.* 1 To place on a seat or seats; cause to sit down. 2 To have seats for; furnish

with seats: The theater *seats* only 299 people. **3** To put a seat on or in; renew or repair the seat of. **4** To locate, settle, or center: usually in the passive: The French government is *seated* in Paris. **5** To fix or set firmly or in place. [<ON *sǣti.* Akin to SIT.]

sea tangle A large brown seaweed (genus *Laminaria*) of the temperate zones.

seat·ing (sē′ting) *n.* **1** The act of providing with seats. **2** Fabric for upholstering seats. **3** A fitted support or base; a seat.

SEATO (sē′tō) Southeast Asia Treaty Organization.

seat of government **1** Any city (usually the capital) of a state or nation where the administrative offices of the government are located. **2** A town where a county court sits; a county seat.

sea trout **1** A trout that descends to the sea after spawning. **2** A weakfish.

seat·stone (sēt′stōn′) *n.* Underclay.

Se·at·tle (sē·at′l) A port on Puget Sound in west central Washington.

sea urchin An echinoderm (class *Echinoidea*) having a soft rounded body covered with a variously shaped shell bearing numerous movable spines.

sea wall **1** A wall or an embankment for preventing the encroachments of the sea or for breaking the force of the waves. **2** A ridge of stones, etc., washed up by the sea. **— sea-walled** (sē′wôld′) *adj.*

sea walnut Any of various ctenophores having an ovate body somewhat resembling a walnut, especially of the genus *Pleurobrachia.*

sea·wan (sē′wən) *n.* An oblong bead made from shell; hence, wampum: used by the Algonquian Indians of North America: also spelled *sewan.* Also **sea′want** (-wənt). [<Algonquian (Narraganset) *seawohn* scattered, i.e., unstrung (shell beads)]

sea·ward (sē′wərd) *adj.* **1** Going toward the sea. **2** Blowing, as wind, from the sea. **—** *adv.* In the direction of the sea: also **sea′wards.**

sea·ware (sē′wâr′) *n.* Seaweed; especially, coarse seaweed thrown up on the beach: used for manure and other purposes. [OE *sǣwār* < *sǣ* sea + *wār* alga]

sea·way (sē′wā′) *n.* **1** A way or lane over the sea. **2** An inland waterway that receives ocean shipping. **3** The headway made by a ship. **4** A rough sea: usually in *in a seaway.*

sea·weed (sē′wēd′) *n.* Any of a widely distributed class *(Algae)* of plants growing in the sea, including the kelps, rockweeds, dulse, sea lettuce, etc.

sea·wor·thy (sē′wûr′thē) *adj.* In fit condition for a voyage: said of a vessel. See synonyms under STAUNCH. **— sea′wor′thi·ness** *n.*

sea wrack Seaweed, especially a kelp or other large species.

se·ba·ceous (si·bā′shəs) *adj. Physiol.* **1** Pertaining to, appearing like, or secreting fat. **2** Designating the compound, saclike glands in the corium of the skin. [<NL *sebaceus* <L, a tallow candle < *sebum* tallow]

se·bac·ic (si·bas′ik, -bā′sik) *adj.* **1** Of or derived from fat. **2** *Chem.* Designating a white crystalline acid, $C_{10}H_{18}O_4$, contained in various oils, from which it is obtained by distillation. [<SEBAC(EOUS) + -IC]

Se·bas·tian (si·bas′chən, *Ger.* zä·bäs′tē·än) A masculine personal name. Also *Du., Sw.* **Se·bas·ti·aan** (sä·bäs′tē·än), *Fr.* **Sé·bas·tien** (sā·bäs·tyaṅ′), *Ital.* **Se·bas·tia·no** (sä′bäs·tyä′nō), *Lat.* **Se·bas·ti·a·nus** (si·bas′tē·ā′nəs); *Pg.* **Se·bas·tião** (sā′bäs·tyouṅ′). [<Gk., venerable]

Se·bas·to·pol (si·bas′tə·pōl) A former spelling of SEVASTOPOL.

Se·bas·tye (sa·bäs′tē·yə) A town in western Jordan, on the site of ancient Samaria.

Se·bat (shi·bät′) See SHEBAT.

Seb·ha (seb′hə) The capital of Fezzan, Libya.

sebi– *combining form* Fat; fatty matter: *sebiferous:* also, before vowels, **seb–.** Also **sebo–.** [<L *sebum* tallow]

se·bif·er·ous (si·bif′ər·əs) *adj.* Secreting or producing fat or fatty matter; sebaceous: *sebiferous* glands; *sebiferous* plants. Also **se·bip·a·rous** (si·bip′ər·əs). [<SEBI- + -FEROUS]

seb·or·rhe·a (seb′ə·rē′ə) *n. Pathol.* A morbid increase of secretion from the sebaceous glands: also called *steatorrhea.* Also **seb′or·rhoe′a.** [<L *sebum* tallow + -RRHEA]

se·bum (sē′bəm) *n. Physiol.* A fatty matter secreted by the sebaceous glands. [<L, tallow]

sec (sek) *adj. French* Dry: said of wines. Also *Italian* **sec·co** (sek′kō).

se·cant (sē′kənt, -kant) *adj.* Cutting, especially into two parts; intersecting. **—** *n.* **1** *Geom.* A straight line intersecting a given curve. **2** *Trig.* **a** A line drawn from the center of a circle through one extremity of an arc to the tangent drawn from the other extremity of the same arc. **b** The ratio of this line to the radius of the circle: the reciprocal of the cosine. [<L *secans, -antis,* ppr. of *secare* cut]

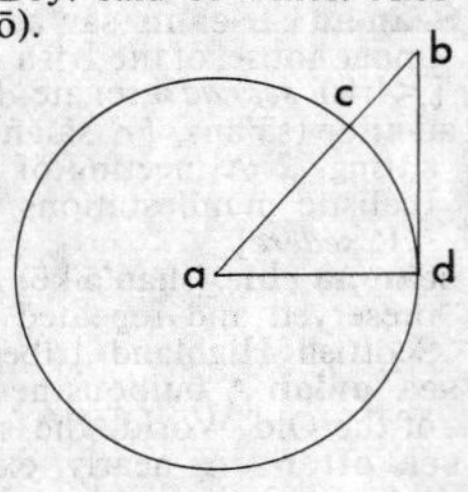

SECANT
Ratio of *ab* to *ad* is the secant of angle *a.* *ab* is the secant of arc *cd.*

sec·co painting (sek′ō) Painting done on dry plaster, as opposed to fresco painting on wet plaster. [<Ital., dry <L *siccus*]

se·cede (si·sēd′) *v.i.* **·ced·ed, ·ced·ing** To withdraw formally from a union, fellowship, or association, especially from a political or religious organization. [<L *secedere* withdraw < *se-* apart + *cedere* go] **— se·ced′er** *n.*

se·cern (si·sûrn′) *v.t.* **1** To separate; also, to distinguish. **2** *Physiol.* To secrete: said of a gland or follicle. [<L *secernere* < *se-* apart + *cernere* separate] **— se·cern′ent** *adj.* **— se·cern′ment** *n.*

se·cesh (si·sesh′) *n. U.S. Slang* A secessionist during the American Civil War; also, secessionists collectively. **—** *adj.* Belonging to, supporting, or sympathetic toward the Southern Confederacy. [Short for SECESSIONIST]

se·ces·sion (si·sesh′ən) *n.* **1** The act of seceding; withdrawal from fellowship, especially from political or religious association. **2** *Usually cap. U.S.* The withdrawal of the Southern States from the Union in 1860–61. [<L *secessio, -onis* < *secedere* SECEDE] **— se·ces′sion·al** *adj.*

se·ces·sion·ism (si·sesh′ən·iz′əm) *n. U.S.* The principles and doctrines of those who favored the withdrawal of the Southern States from the Union. **— se·ces′sion·ist** *adj.* & *n.*

seck (sek) *adj.* Barren; profitless; unenforceable by distress: said of rent. [<F *sec* <L *siccus* dry]

Seck·el (sek′əl, sik′əl) *n.* A variety of small, sweet pear. Also called *sickle pear.* [after the Pennsylvania farmer who introduced it]

se·clude (si·klōōd′) *v.t.* **·clud·ed, ·clud·ing** **1** To remove and keep apart from company or society of others; isolate. **2** To screen or shut off, as from view: usually in the past participle. [<L *secludere* < *se-* apart + *claudere* shut]

se·clud·ed (si·klōō′did) *adj.* **1** Separated; withdrawn; living apart from others. **2** Protected or screened. **— se·clud′ed·ly** *adv.* **— se·clud′ed·ness** *n.*

se·clu·sion (si·klōō′zhən) *n.* **1** The act of secluding, or the state or condition of being secluded; solitude; retirement. **2** A secluded place. [<Med. L *seclusio, -onis* <L *seclusus,* pp. of *secludere* SECLUDE]

Synonyms: privacy, retirement, retreat, secrecy, separation, solitude. See RETIREMENT, SOLITUDE. *Antonyms:* crowd, multitude, numbers, publicity, society, throng, world.

se·clu·sive (si·klōō′siv) *adj.* Having a tendency to seclusion. **— se·clu′sive·ly** *adv.* **— se·clu′sive·ness** *n.*

sec·ond[1] (sek′ənd) *n.* **1** A unit of time, 1/60 of a minute. **2** *Geom.* A unit of angular measure, 1/60 of a minute of arc. Symbol: ″ **3** In the duodecimal notation, 1/12 of an inch or prime. [<OF *seconde* <Med. L *seconda (minuta),* lit., second (minute), i.e., the result of the second operation of sexagesimal division, fem. of L *secundus* SECOND[2]]

sec·ond[2] (sek′ənd) *adj.* **1** Next in order, authority, responsibility, etc., after the first: the ordinal of *two.* **2** Ranking next to or below the first or best; of inferior quality or value; secondary; subordinate. **3** Identical in character with another or preceding one; another; other. **4** *Music* Lower in pitch, or rendering a lower part than the principal one. **—** *n.* **1** The one next after the first in position, rank, importance, or quality. **2** An attendant who supports or aids another, as in a duel. **3** *pl.* Articles of merchandise of imperfect manufacture, of second grade, or of inferior quality. **4** *Music* **a** The interval between any note and the next above or below in the diatonic scale. **b** A note separated by this interval from any other. **c** Two notes at this interval written or sounded together. **d** The resulting dissonance. **e** A second or subordinate part, instrument, or voice. **5** In parliamentary law, an utterance whereby a motion is seconded: Do I hear a *second*? **— major second** *Music* A second between whose tones is a difference of pitch of a step. **—** *v.t.* **1** To act as a supporter or assistant of; promote; stimulate; encourage. **2** In deliberative bodies, to support formally, as a motion, resolution, etc., as a prerequisite to discussion or adoption. See synonyms under AID, HELP. **—** *adv.* In the second order, place, or rank: also, in formal discourse, **sec′ond·ly.** [<OF <L *secundus* following < *sequi* follow]

Second Advent The expected second coming of Christ, to judge the world. Also **Second Coming. — Second Adventist**

sec·on·dar·y (sek′ən·der′ē) *adj.* **1** Of second rank, grade, or influence; subordinate; auxiliary; subsequent; resultant. **2** Depending on what is primary or original. **3** *Ornithol.* Of or pertaining to the secondaries of a bird's wings. **4** *Electr.* Of, pertaining to, or noting an induced current or its circuit, especially in an induction coil. **5** *Chem.* Formed by replacement of atoms or radicals in the molecules of certain organic compounds: a *secondary* alcohol. **6** *Geol.* Subsequent in origin; involving some chemical or physical change of the original mineral: contrasted with *primary.* **7** Pertaining to instruction in a secondary school. **—** *n. pl.* **·dar·ies** **1** One who acts in a secondary or subordinate capacity; an assistant; a deputy or delegate. **2** Anything of secondary size, position, or importance. **3** A secondary planet; a satellite. **4** *Ornithol.* One of the feathers that grow on the second joint or forearm of a bird's wing. See illustrations under BIRD, FOWL. **5** One of the hind wings of an insect. **— sec′on·dar′·i·ly** *adv.*

Sec·on·dar·y (sek′ən·der′ē) *n. Geol.* **1** The Mesozoic era. **2** The rocks formed in this era. **—** *adj.* Belonging to or occurring in the Mesozoic era.

secondary education High school or preparatory school education; schooling beyond the elementary or primary, and below the college, level.

secondary electron *Physics* An electron emitted from a surface by the direct impact of electrons or ions, as produced by an X-ray machine.

secondary emission *Physics* The emission of secondary electrons from a substance exposed to direct radiation, as by X-rays, etc. Also **secondary radiation.**

secondary school See under SCHOOL.

second base In baseball, the second base reached by the runner, situated between first and third base. See illustration under BASEBALL.

second childhood A time or condition of foolishness or dotage; senility.

sec·ond–class (sek′ənd·klas′, -kläs′) *adj.* **1** Ranking next below the first or best; inferior; mediocre. **2** Of, pertaining to, or belonging to a class next below the first: *second-class* mail, *second-class* standing, *second-class* ticket, etc. **—** *adv.* By second-class ticket or by using second-class conveniences: to travel *second-class.*

second class A class of mail including all periodical printed matter.

se·conde (si·kond′, *Fr.* sə·gôṅd′) *n.* The second position in fencing. [<F, fem. of *second* <OF, SECOND]

sec·ond·er (sek′ən·dər) *n.* One who seconds, supports, or approves what is attempted, moved, or proposed by another.

second fiddle **1** The part played by the second violins in an orchestral composition. **2** Any secondary status; a substitute **— to be** (or **play**) **second fiddle** To be of secondary importance in an undertaking or in the affections of another.

sec·ond–hand (sek′ənd·hand′) *adj.* **1** Having been previously owned, worn, or used by another; not new. **2** Received from another;

not direct from the original source: *second-hand* information. 3 Employed in handling or dealing in merchandise that is not new. 4 Of inferior grade; being a poor imitation: a *second-hand* statesman. — *n.* That which is second-hand or a poor imitation.

second hand The hand that marks the seconds on a clock or a watch.

sec·on·dine (sek′ən·dīn, -din) See SECUNDINE.

second mortgage A mortgage given next after and subordinate to a first mortgage.

second nature A disposition or character that is acquired and not innate; deep-seated habits that have become fixed.

se·con·do (sā·kôn′dō) *n. pl.* **·di** (-dē) *Italian* The second part in concerted music, especially in a pianoforte duet; also, the performer of this part.

sec·ond-rate (sek′ənd·rāt′) *adj.* Second in quality, size, rank, importance, etc.; second-class. — *n.* That which is mediocre or of inferior value: also **sec′ond-rat′er.**

second sight 1 The faculty or power of seeing the invisible. 2 The power of prophecy; intuition; clairvoyance. — **sec′ond-sight′ed** *adj.*

second sound *Physics* The peculiar vibratory motion, resembling that of sound waves, associated with the rapid transfer of heat by helium atoms cooled to within two degrees of absolute zero.

Second World War See WORLD WAR II in table under WAR.

sec·par (sek′pär) *n. Astron.* Parsec. [< *sec(ond of) par(allax)*]

se·cre·cy (sē′krə·sē) *n. pl.* **·cies** 1 The condition or quality of being secret or hidden; concealment. 2 The character of being secretive; secretiveness. 3 Privacy; retirement; solitude. Also **se′cret·ness.** See synonyms under SECLUSION. [Earlier *secretee* < obs. *secre* <OF *secré* secret; refashioned after *primacy, lunacy,* etc.]

se·cret (sē′krit) *adj.* 1 Kept separate or hidden from view or knowledge, or from all persons except the individuals concerned; not immediately apparent; unseen; occult. 2 Affording privacy; secluded. 3 Good at keeping secrets; close-mouthed. 4 Unrevealed or unavowed as such: a *secret* partner. 5 *U.S.* Designating defense information classified second to top-secret material with regard to required security and protection. Compare TOP-SECRET, CONFIDENTIAL (def. 4). — *n.* 1 Something not to be told. 2 A thing undiscovered or unknown. 3 An underlying reason; that which, when known, explains; key. 4 A secret contrivance. 5 Secrecy. — **in secret** In privacy; in a hidden place. [<OF *secré, secret* <L *secretus,* orig. pp. of *secernere* < *se-* apart + *cernere* separate] — **se′cret·ly** *adv.*

Synonyms (adj.): clandestine, concealed, covered, covert, furtive, hid, hidden, latent, mysterious, obscure, occult, private, recondite, retired, unknown, unrevealed, unseen, veiled. See MYSTERIOUS. *Antonyms*: aboveboard, apparent, clear, evident, manifest, obvious, plain, transparent, unconcealed, undisguised.

se·cret·age (sē′krə·tij) *n.* A process of preparing or dressing furs by means of mercury or some of its salts, in order to facilitate felting and matting; carroting. Also **se′cret·ing.** [<F *sécréter* conceal; because it was at first a secret process]

sec·re·tar·i·at (sek′rə·târ′ē·it, -at) *n.* 1 A secretary's position. 2 The place where a secretary transacts his business and preserves his official records. 3 The entire staff of secretaries in an office; especially, the department headed by a governmental secretary. Also **sec′re·tar′i·ate.** [<F *secrétariat* <Med. L *secretariatus* the office of secretary < *secretarius* SECRETARY]

Sec·re·tar·i·at (sek′rə·târ′ē·it, -at) *n.* The administrative organ of the former League of Nations and of the present United Nations, consisting of the Secretary General, his officials, and secretaries.

sec·re·tar·y (sek′rə·ter′ē) *n. pl.* **·tar·ies** 1 A person employed to deal with correspondence, keep records, and handle clerical business for a person, business, committee, or organization. 2 An executive officer presiding over and managing a department of government. 3 A writing desk with a bookcase or cabinet with pigeonholes on top. — **under-secretary** In a government department, the official who ranks next below the secretary. [<Med. L *secretarius* <L *secretum* a secret, neut. of *secretus* SECRET] — **sec′re·tar′i·al** (-târ′ē·əl) *adj.*

secretary bird A South African bird (genus *Sagittarius*), having long legs and a crested head: so named from the resemblance of its crest to quill pens stuck behind the ear. It preys on serpents.

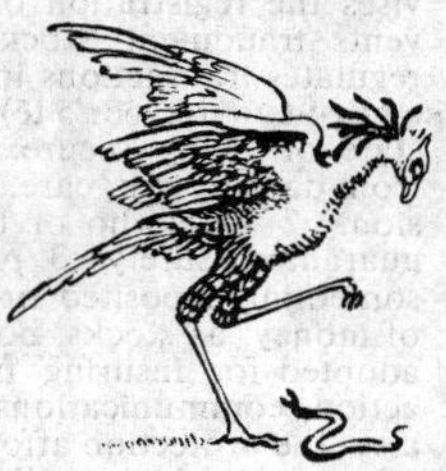

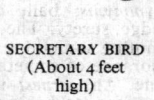

SECRETARY BIRD
(About 4 feet high)

secretary general *pl.* **secretaries general** A chief secretary; an assistant to a governor general. — **sec′re·tar′y-gen′er·al·cy** *n.*

sec·re·tar·y·ship (sek′rə·ter′ē·ship) *n.* The work or position of a secretary.

sec·re·tar·y-treas·ur·er (sek′rə·ter′ē·trezh′ər·ər) *n.* 1 A person who performs the combined duties of secretary and treasurer; especially, an official in an organization. 2 In Canada, a town or city clerk.

se·crete (si·krēt′) *v.t* **·cret·ed, ·cret·ing** 1 To remove or keep from observation; conceal; hide. 2 *Biol.* To separate or elaborate from blood or sap. [Alter. of obs. *secret, v.* conceal; refashioned after L *secretus* SECRET] — **se·cre′tor** *n.*

Synonym: conceal. *Secrete* is a stronger word than *conceal,* and is used chiefly of such material objects as may be separated from the person, or from their ordinary surroundings, and put in unlooked-for places; a man *conceals* a scar on his face, but does not *secrete* it; a thief *secretes* stolen goods; an officer may also be said to *secrete* himself to watch the thief. See HIDE.

se·cre·tin (si·krē′tin) *n. Biochem.* A hormone found in the lining of the intestinal wall and stimulating the flow of pancreatic juice. [<SECRET(ION) + -IN]

se·cre·tion (si·krē′shən) *n.* 1 *Biol.* The process by which materials are separated from blood or sap and elaborated into new substances: the *secretion* of milk, gastric juice, or urine. Secretion in animals is generally performed by glandular epithelial cells. Compare EXCRETION. 2 The substance secreted, as saliva or milk. 3 The act of concealing. 4 A deposit of mineral matter in successive coatings, filling cavities, and fissures.

se·cre·tive (si·krē′tiv) *adj.* 1 (*also* sē′krə·tiv) Inclined to secrecy; reticent. 2 Producing or causing secretion. — **se·cre′tive·ly** *adv.* — **se·cre′tive·ness** *n.*

se·cre·to·ry (si·krē′tər·ē) *adj.* Pertaining to secretion. — *n. pl.* **·ries** A secreting vessel or gland.

secret service 1 Investigation conducted secretly for a government. 2 The secret or espionage work of various government agencies in time of war.

Secret Service A section of the Department of the Treasury concerned with the suppression of counterfeiting, the protection of the president of the United States, etc.

secret society A society or association that uses secret signs, oaths, rites, or symbols.

sect (sekt) *n.* 1 A body of persons distinguished by peculiarities of faith and practice from other bodies adhering to the same general system; specifically, the adherents collectively of a particular creed or confession; a denomination, or an organized body of dissenters from an established or older form of faith. 2 Adherents of a particular philosophical system or teacher. 3 Any number of persons united in opinion or interest, as in the state or in society; a party or faction; an order. 4 A cutting in horticulture. [<OF *secte* <L *secta* a following, a faction < *sequi* follow. Doublet of SET.]

Synonyms: church, communion, denomination, heresy, heterodoxy, party, schism, school. *Heresy* or *heterodoxy* is a departure from the established doctrine; a *schism* is a division of the *church* either on matters of faith or practice; *schism* is applied also to non-religious organizations. A *sect* or *denomination* is an organized body of believers distinct in doctrine or practice, or in both, from others: *sect* is an opprobrious and *denomination* an honorable term for the same body. Within a *denomination* there may be *schools* differing on minor matters, or *parties* favoring or opposing certain persons or measures, without breach of essential and organic unity. *Church* is often used as synonymous with *denomination*; as, the Presbyterian *Church. Communion* designates those who share a common faith with reference to their spiritual unity.

-sect *combining form* Cut; divided (in a specified manner or number of parts): *vivisect.* Also **-sected,** as in *bisected.* [<L *sectus,* pp. of *secare* cut]

sec·tar·i·an (sek·târ′ē·ən) *adj.* Pertaining to a sect; bigoted. — *n.* A member of a sect, especially if bigoted.

sec·tar·i·an·ism (sek·târ′ē·ən·iz′əm) *n.* Sectarian character or tendency; excessive devotion to or zeal for a particular sect.

sec·tar·i·an·ize (sek·târ′ē·ən·īz′) *v.t.* **·ized, ·iz·ing** To make sectarian.

sec·ta·ry (sek′tər·ē) *n. pl.* **·ries** 1 A sectarian: mostly used opprobriously. 2 A dissenter from an established church; a nonconformist. 3 *Obs.* A religious sect. Also **sec′ta·rist.** [< MF *sectaire* <Med. L *sectarius* <L *secta* a sect]

sec·tile (sek′til) *adj.* Admitting of being cut or severed smoothly. [<F <L, neut. of *sectilis* < *sectus,* pp. of *secare* cut] — **sec·til·i·ty** (sek·til′ə·tē) *n.*

sec·tion (sek′shən) *n.* 1 A separate part or division; a portion of a book, treatise, or writing; a subdivision of a chapter; also, a division of law. 2 A distinct part of a country, community, etc. 3 *U.S.* An area of public land one mile square, containing 640 acres and constituting 1/36 of a township. 4 A portion of a railway company's tracks under the care of a particular set of men. 5 In a sleeping-car, a space containing two berths. 6 A tactical unit of the U.S. Army, smaller than a platoon and larger than a squad. 7 A division of an animal group, of indeterminate rank. 8 A representation, picture, or drawing of a building, machine, geological formation, etc., as if cut by an intersecting plane; also, the thing so cut or viewed. 9 A very thin slice of anything, especially for microscopic examination. 10 The character §, indicating a subdivision: used also as a reference mark. 11 The act of cutting; division by cutting, as in surgical operations. 12 The figure formed by the intersection of a plane or other surface with a solid. In mechanical drawing the following sections are distinguished: **lengthwise** or **longitudinal section,** usually representing objects as cut lengthwise through the center; **cross-section** or **transverse section,** cut crosswise; **horizontal section,** cut horizontally, and usually through the center; **oblique section,** cut at various angles. See synonyms under PART. — **frozen section** A cutting, slice, or sliced surface of a frozen part: much employed in anatomy. — *v.t.* 1 To cut or divide into sections. 2 To shade (a drawing) so as to designate a section or sections. [<MF <L *sectio, -onis* < *sectus,* pp. of *secare* cut]

-section *combining form* The act or process of cutting or dividing: *vivisection.* [<L *sectio, -onis* a cutting < *secare* cut]

sec·tion·al (sek′shən·əl) *adj.* 1 Pertaining to a section, as of a country; local; characteristic of the people of a certain section or area: a *sectional* dialect. 2 Dividing or alienating one section from another: *sectional* problems. 3 Made up of sections. — **sec′tion·al·ly** *adv.*

sectional feeling Intense consciousness of the differences between the interests of one section of a country and those of another.

sec·tion·al·ism (sek′shən·əl·iz′əm) *n.* Regard for a particular section of the country rather than the whole; sectional feeling. — **sec′tion·al·ist** *n.*

sec·tion·al·ize (sek′shən·əl·īz′) *v.t.* **·ized, ·iz·ing** 1 To make sectional. 2 To divide into sections. — **sec′tion·al·i·za′tion** *n.*

section gang A work crew assigned to a certain section of a railroad.

sec·tor (sek′tər) *n.* **1** *Geom.* A part of a circle bounded by two radii and the arc subtended by them. **2** A mathematical instrument consisting of two arms marked with various scales and hinged together at one end. **3** *Mil.* A part of a front in contact with the enemy. —*v.t.* To divide into sectors. [<LL <L, a cutter < *sectus,* pp. of *secare* cut]

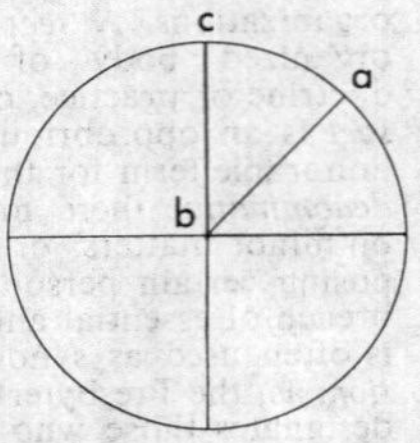

SECTOR
abc is a sector of the circle.

sec·to·ri·al (sek·tôr′ē·əl, -tō′rē-) *adj.* **1** Of or pertaining to a sector. **2** *Zool.* Adapted for cutting; carnassial.

sec·u·lar (sek′yə·lər) *adj.* **1** Of or pertaining to this world or the present life; temporal; worldly: contrasted with *religious* or *spiritual.* **2** Not under the control of the church; civil; not ecclesiastical. **3** Not concerned with religion; not sacred: *secular* art. **4** Not bound by monastic vows: opposed to *regular*: the *secular* clergy. **5** Occurring or observed but once in an age or century. **6** Lasting for ages. See synonyms under PROFANE. —*n.* **1** One in holy orders who is not bound by monastic vows. **2** A layman. [<OF *seculer* <LL *saecularis* <L, belonging to an age < *saeculum* a generation, an age]

sec·u·lar·ism (sek′yə·lə·riz′əm) *n.* Regard for worldly as opposed to spiritual matters; specifically, the belief of secularists.

sec·u·lar·ist (sek′yə·lə·rist) *n.* **1** A person who bases morality on the well–being of mankind in this world without any consideration of religious systems and forms of worship. **2** One who believes that religion should not be introduced into public education or the management of public affairs. —**sec′u·lar·is′tic** *adj.*

sec·u·lar·i·ty (sek′yə·lar′ə·tē) *n.* **1** Secularism; worldliness. **2** Any practice or interest belonging exclusively to the present life.

sec·u·lar·ize (sek′yə·lə·rīz′) *v.t.* **·ized, ·iz·ing** **1** To make secular; convert from sacred to secular uses. **2** To make worldly. **3** To change from a monastic or regular to a secular, as a monk. —**sec′u·lar·i·za′tion** *n.*

se·cund (sē′kund, sek′und) *adj. Bot.* Having the parts or organs arranged on one side only, as certain flowers; unilateral. [<L *secundus* following. See SECOND².]

Se·cun·der·a·bad (si·kun′dər·ä·bäd′) A northern suburb of Hyderabad, Andhra Pradesh, India, where conduction of malaria by mosquitoes was discovered by Sir Ronald Ross, 1898.

sec·un·dine (sek′ən·dīn, -din) *n.* **1** *Bot.* The inner, first–developed coat or integument of an ovule. **2** That which remains in the womb to be expelled after childbirth: usually in the plural. Also spelled *secondine.* [<LL *secundinae,* pl., the afterbirth <L *secundus* following. See SECOND².]

se·cun·dum na·tu·ram (si·kun′dəm nə·tyŏŏr′·əm) *Latin* According to nature.

se·cun·dum u·sum (si·kun′dəm yōō′səm) *Latin* According to usage or ritual.

se·cure (si·kyŏŏr′) *adj.* **1** Guarded against or not likely to be exposed to danger; safe. **2** Free from fear, apprehension, etc. **3** Confident; careless. **4** Assured; certain; sure: followed by *of,* sometimes by an infinitive. **5** So strong or well made as to render loss, escape, or failure impossible. —*v.* **·cured, ·cur·ing** *v.t.* **1** To make secure; protect. **2** To make firm, tight, or fast; fasten. **3** To make sure or certain; insure; guarantee. **4** To obtain possession of; get. —*v.i.* **5** To be or become secure; take precautions. See synonyms under ARREST, BIND, CATCH, GET, OBTAIN, PRESERVE, PURCHASE, RETAIN. [<L *securus* < *se-* without + *cura* care. Doublet of SURE.] —**se·cur′a·ble** *adj.* —**se·cure′ly** *adv.* —**se·cure′ment** *n.* —**se·cure′ness** *n.* —**se·cur′er** *n.*

Synonyms (adj.): assured, careless, certain, confident, defended, guarded, impregnable, insured, protected, safe, sure, unassailable, undisturbed, unmolested, unsuspecting, untroubled. See FIRM. *Antonyms*: dangerous, dubious, exposed, hazardous, imperiled, insecure, perilous, risky.

Securities and Exchange Commission An agency of the U.S. government which supervises the registration of security issues, prevents fraudulent stock manipulations, and regulates transactions in securities.

se·cur·i·ty (si·kyŏŏr′ə·tē) *n. pl.* **·ties** **1** The state of being secure; specifically, freedom from danger, risk, care, poverty, or apprehension. **2** One who or that which secures or guarantees; surety. **3** *pl.* Written promises or something deposited or pledged for payment of money, as stocks, bonds, etc. **4** Methods adopted for insuring freedom or secrecy of action, communications, etc., as in wartime; also, the protection afforded by such methods.

Synonyms: bail, collateral, earnest, gage, pledge, surety. The first four words agree in denoting something given or deposited as an assurance of something to be given, paid, or done. An *earnest* is a portion delivered in advance, as when part of the purchase money is paid, "to bind the bargain." A *pledge* or *security* may be wholly different in kind from that to be given or paid; it may greatly exceed it in value, and may be of real or personal property; a *pledge* (as here considered) is always of personal property or chattels. Every pawnshop contains unredeemed *pledges*; land, merchandise, bonds, etc., are frequently offered and accepted as *security. Collateral* is property, as stocks, bonds, etc., actually deposited as *security,* often termed *collateral security.* A person may become *security* or *surety* for another's payment of a debt, appearance in court, etc.; in the latter case, he is said to become *bail* for that person; the person accused gives *bail* for himself. *Gage* survives only as a literary word, chiefly in certain phrases; as, "the *gage* of battle."

Security Council A permanent organ of the United Nations charged with the maintenance of international peace and security and consisting of five permanent members (China, France, the U.S.S.R., the United Kingdom, and the United States) and six elected members, three of whom are replaced each year.

se·dan (si·dan′) *n.* **1** A closed automobile having one compartment for passengers and driver. **2** A closed chair, for one passenger, carried by two or more men by means of poles at the sides: also **sedan chair.** [? <Ital. *sedere* sit <L]

Se·dan (si·dan′, *Fr.* sə·dän′) A city in NE France on the Meuse; scene of the decisive French defeat in the Franco–Prussian War, 1870.

se·date (si·dāt′) *adj.* Characterized by habitual composure; staid. [<L *sedatus,* pp. of *sedare* make calm, settle < *sedere* sit] —**se·date′ly** *adv.* —**se·date′ness** *n.*

Synonyms: calm, contemplative, demure, grave, quiet, serene, serious, sober, solemn, staid, still, thoughtful, tranquil, undisturbed, unruffled. See CALM, SERIOUS, THOUGHTFUL. *Antonyms*: agitated, disturbed, excited, flighty, flurried, frolicsome, gay, lively, mad, merry.

se·da·tion (si·dā′shən) *n. Med.* The act of reducing distress, irritation, excitement, etc., particularly by administering sedatives.

sed·a·tive (sed′ə·tiv) *adj.* **1** Having a soothing tendency. **2** *Med.* Allaying irritation; assuaging pain. —*n.* Any means, as a medicine, of allaying irritation or pain.

sed·en·tar·y (sed′ən·ter′ē) *adj.* **1** Sitting much of the time; accustomed to sit much or to work in a sitting posture; hence, settled in one place, as certain tribes; sluggish; inactive. **2** Characterized by sitting. **3** Resulting from much or long sitting. **4** *Zool.* Remaining in one place; attached or fixed to an object; sessile. [<L *sedentarius* < *sedens, -entis,* ppr. of *sedere* sit] —**sed′en·tar′i·ly** *adv.* —**sed′en·tar′i·ness** *n.*

Se·der (sā′dər) *n. pl.* **Se·da·rim** (sə·där′im) or **Se·ders** In Judaism, the ceremonial dinner commemorating the Exodus, held on the eve of the first day of Passover, and traditionally on the eve of the second day by Jews outside of Israel.

sedge (sej) *n.* **1** A grasslike cyperaceous herb (genus *Carex*) with flowers densely clustered in spikes: widely distributed in marshy places. **2** Any coarse, rushlike or flaglike herb growing in a wet place. [OE *secg*] —**sedged** *adj.* —**sedg′y** *adj.*

Sedge·moor (sej′mŏŏr) A tract in Somersetshire, England; scene of the victory of James II over the Duke of Monmouth, 1685.

Sedg·wick (sej′wik), **Anne Douglas,** 1873–1935, U.S. novelist.

se·di·le (si·dī′lē) *n. pl.* **·dil·i·a** (-dil′ē·ə) A seat (usually one of three) near the altar in the chancel of a church, for officiating clergy: usually in the plural. Also **se·dil′i·um.** [<L, a seat < *sedere* sit]

sed·i·ment (sed′ə·mənt) *n.* **1** Matter that settles to the bottom of a liquid; settlings; dregs; lees. **2** *Geol.* Fragmentary material deposited by water or air. See synonyms under WASTE. [<MF *sédiment* <L *sedimentum* a settling < *sedere* sit, settle]

sed·i·men·ta·ry (sed′ə·men′tər·ē) *adj.* **1** Pertaining to or having the character of sediment. **2** *Geol.* Designating rocks, as shale and sandstone, composed of fragments of other rocks deposited after transportation from their sources, and including also rocks formed by precipitation, as gypsum, or by calcareous secretions of animals, as certain limestones. Also **sed′i·men′tal.**

sed·i·men·ta·tion (sed′ə·men·tā′shən) *n.* **1** The accumulation or deposition of sediment. **2** The depositing of an insoluble material.

se·di·tion (si·dish′ən) *n.* **1** Language or conduct directed against public order and the tranquillity of the state. **2** The incitement of such disorder, tending toward treason, but lacking an overt act. **3** Dissension; revolt. See synonyms under REVOLUTION. [<OF <L *seditio, -onis* < *sed-* aside + *itio, -onis* a going < *ire* go]

se·di·tion·ar·y (si·dish′ən·er′ē) *adj.* Seditious. —*n. pl.* **·ar·ies** One who promotes sedition: also **se·di′tion·ist.**

se·di·tious (si·dish′əs) *adj.* **1** Pertaining to, promotive of, or having the character of sedition. **2** Inclined to, taking part in, or guilty of sedition. See synonyms under REBELLIOUS, TURBULENT. [OF *seditieux* <L *seditiosus* < *seditio, -onis* SEDITION] —**se·di′tious·ly** *adv.* —**se·di′tious·ness** *n.*

Se·dl·ča·ny (sed′l·chä′nē) A village in southern Bohemia, Czechoslovakia. *German* **Sed·litz** (zed′lits). Also *Seidlitz.*

se·duce (si·dōōs′, -dyōōs′) *v.t.* **·duced, ·duc·ing** **1** To lead astray; entice into wrong, disloyalty, etc.; tempt. **2** To induce, as a woman, to surrender chastity; debauch. See synonyms under ALLURE. [<L *seducere* lead apart < *se-* apart + *ducere* lead] —**se·duc′er** *n.* —**se·duc′i·ble** or **se·duce′a·ble** *adj.*

se·duc·tion (si·duk′shən) *n.* **1** The act of seducing. **2** Something which seduces; an enticement. Also **se·duce′ment.** [<MF *séduction* <L *seductio, -onis* < *seductus,* pp. of *seducere.* See SEDUCE.]

se·duc·tive (si·duk′tiv) *adj.* Tending to seduce; enticing. —**se·duc′tive·ly** *adv.* —**se·duc′tive·ness** *n.*

se·duc·tress (si·duk′tris) *n.* A female seducer.

se·du·li·ty (si·dōō′lə·tē, -dyōō′-) *n.* The state or character of being sedulous.

sed·u·lous (sej′ōō·ləs) *adj.* Constant in application or attention; persevering in effort; assiduous. See synonyms under INDUSTRIOUS. [<L *sedulus* careful, appar. < *sedulo* sincerely < *se dolo* without guile] —**sed′u·lous·ly** *adv.* —**sed′u·lous·ness** *n.*

se·dum (sē′dəm) *n.* Any of a large genus *(Sedum)* of chiefly perennial smooth plants, the stonecrops, having very thick leaves and cymose flowers. [<L, house leek]

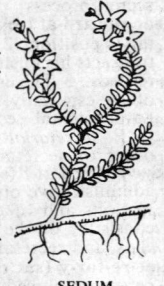

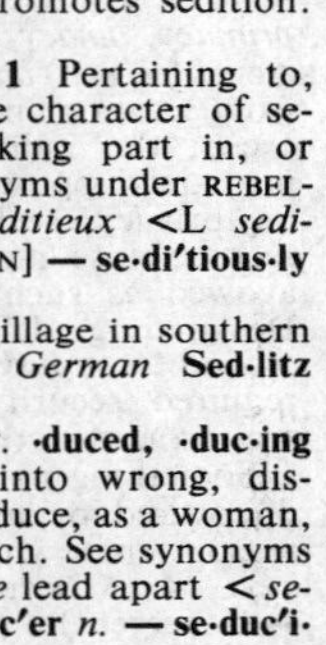
SEDUM

see[1] (sē) *v.* **saw, seen, see·ing** *v.t.* **1** To perceive with the eyes; gain knowledge or awareness of by means of one's vision. **2** To perceive with the mind; understand; comprehend. **3** To find out or ascertain; inquire about: *See* who is at the door. **4** To have experience or knowledge of; undergo: We have *seen* more peaceful times. **5** To encounter; chance to meet: I *saw* your husband today. **6** To have a meeting or interview with; visit or receive as a guest, visitor,

etc.: The doctor will *see* you now. **7** To attend as a spectator; view. **8** To accompany; escort. **9** To take care; be sure: with a clause as object: *See* that you do it! **10** In poker, to accept (a bet) or equal the bet of (a player) by betting an equal sum. — *v.i.* **11** To have or exercise the power of sight. **12** To find out; inquire: I will go and *see.* **13** To understand; comprehend. **14** To think; consider. **15** To take care; be attentive: *See* to your work. **16** To gain certain knowledge, as by awaiting an outcome: We will *see* if you are right or wrong. — **to see about 1** To inquire into the facts, causes, etc., of. **2** To take care of; attend to. — **to see through 1** To penetrate, as a disguise or deception. **2** To aid or protect, as throughout a period of difficulty or danger. See synonyms under LOOK. ◆ Homophone: *sea.* [OE *sēon*]

see[2] (sē) *n.* **1** The local seat from which a bishop, an archbishop, or the pope exercises jurisdiction; espiscopal or papal jurisdiction, authority, or rank; a bishop's or pope's office. **2** *Obs.* A seat, especially of dignity or power. — **Holy See** The pope's jurisdiction, court, or office; erected as an independent state, Feb. 11, 1929: also **See of Rome.** ◆ Homophone: *sea.* [<OF *se, sie, sed* <L *sedes* a seat]

see·catch (sē′kach′) *n. pl.* **·catch·ie** An adult male fur seal. [<Russian *sekach*]

seed (sēd) *n.* **1** The ovule from which a plant may be reproduced; the fertilized ovule containing an embryo. **2** That from which anything springs; source. **3** Offspring; children. **4** The male fertilizing element; semen; milt. **5** Any small seedlike fruit; also, any part of a plant from which it may be propagated, as bulbs, tubers, etc. **6** A young oyster fit for transplanting. **7** Race; generation; birth. **8** The seed-bearing stage; hence, overripeness. **9** *U.S. Dial.* An animal or animals used for breeding. — *v.t.* **1** To sow with seed. **2** To sow (seed). **3** To remove the seeds from: to *seed* raisins. **4** To strew (moisture-bearing clouds) with crystals, as of dry ice, silver iodide, etc., in order to initiate precipitation. **5** In sports: **a** To arrange (the drawing for positions in a tournament, etc.) so that the more skilled competitors meet only in the later events. **b** To rank (a skilled competitor) thus. — *v.i.* **6** To sow seed. **7** To grow to maturity and produce or shed seed. — **to go to seed 1** To develop and shed seed. **2** To become shabby, useless, etc. ◆ Homophone: *cede.* [OE *sǣd*] — **seed′less** *adj.*

seed·bed (sēd′bed′) *n.* **1** A bed of earth planted with seeds, especially for later transplanting. **2** A place of early growth or nurture: the *seedbed* of neurosis.

seed bud *Bot.* The germ within a seed; also, the ovule.

seed cake 1 A sweet cake containing aromatic seeds, as caraway. **2** Cottonseed-oil cake.

seed·case (sēd′kās′) *n. Bot.* A seed vessel; pericarp.

seed capsule *Bot.* A testa (def. 1).

seed coat *Bot.* The integument of a seed, usually the outer one or testa.

seed corn Corn or grain of high quality, especially maize, used or intended for seed.

seed crystal A crystallon.

seed·er (sē′dər) *n.* **1** One who or that which sows seed, as a machine. **2** A device for removing seeds from fruit.

seed leaf *Bot.* A cotyledon.

seed·ling (sēd′ling) *n.* **1** *Bot.* A plant grown from seed, as distinguished from one propagated by grafting. **2** A very small or young tree or plant.

seed money Funds used to experiment or innovate with a new venture to test its workability.

seed oyster A young oyster, especially one transplanted to another bed: also *oyster seed.*

seed pearl A small pearl, especially one used for ornamenting bags, etc., or in embroidery.

seed plant A plant which bears seeds; spermatophyte.

seeds·man (sēdz′mən) *n. pl.* **·men** (-mən) **1** A dealer in seeds. **2** A sower. Also **seed′man.**

seed·time (sēd′tīm′) *n.* The proper time for sowing seed.

seed vessel *Bot.* The part of a plant that contains the seeds; pericarp.

seed·y (sē′dē) *adj.* **seed·i·er, seed·i·est 1** Abounding with seeds; going to seed. **2** Poor and ragged; shabby. **3** Feeling or looking wretched. — **seed′i·ly** *adv.* — **seed′i·ness** *n.*

See·ger (sē′gər), **Alan,** 1888–1916, U.S. poet.

see·ing (sē′ing) *n.* The act of seeing; vision; sight. — *conj.* Taking into consideration; since; in view of the fact.

Seeing Eye A philanthropic organization located near Morristown, New Jersey, that trains and supplies dogs (**Seeing Eye dogs**) as guides and companions to the blind.

seek (sēk) *v.* **sought, seek·ing** *v.t.* **1** To go in search of; look for. **2** To strive for; try to get or obtain: to *seek* glory. **3** To endeavor or try: with an infinitive as object: He *seeks* to mislead me. **4** To ask or inquire for; request: to *seek* information. **5** To go to; betake oneself to: to *seek* a warmer climate. **6** *Obs.* or *Dial.* To search or explore. — *v.i.* **7** To make a search or inquiry. [OE *sēcan*] — **seek′er** *n.*

See·land (zā′länt) The German name for ZEALAND.

see·ly (sē′lē) *adj. Obs.* Weak; wretched; feeble. [OE *gesǣlig* punctual, happy, innocent < *sǣl* time, due time, happiness]

seem (sēm) *v.i.* **1** To give the impression of being; appear. **2** To appear to oneself: a form of reflexive use: I *seem* to hear strange voices. Compare MESEEMS. **3** To appear to exist: There *seems* no reason for hesitating. **4** To be evident or apparent: It *seems* to be raining. [<ON *sǣma* honor, conform to] — **seem′er** *n.*

seem·ing (sē′ming) *adj.* Having the appearance of reality; apparent: often implying non-reality. See synonyms under APPARENT. — *n.* Appearance; semblance; especially, false show. — **seem′ing·ly** *adv.* — **seem′ing·ness** *n.*

seem·ly (sēm′lē) *adj.* **·li·er, ·li·est** Befitting the proprieties; becoming; proper; decorous; suited to the occasion. See synonyms under BECOMING. — *adv.* Becomingly; decently; appropriately. [<ON *sǣmiligr* honorable, becoming < *sǣmr* fitting] — **seem′li·ness** *n.*

seen (sēn) Past participle of SEE.

seep (sēp) *v.i.* To soak through pores or small interstices; percolate; ooze. — *n.* A small spring; a place out of which water, oil, or other liquid oozes. [OE *sipian* soak]

seep·age (sē′pij) *n.* **1** The oozing or percolation of fluid. **2** The fluid or moisture that oozes.

seer[1] (sē′ər *for def. 1;* sir *for defs. 2 and 3*) *n.* **1** One who sees. **2** One who foretells events; a prophet. **3** One believed to have second sight. [<SEE[1] + -ER] — **seer′ess** *n. fem.*

seer[2] (sir) *n.* **1** A weight used in different parts of India, and having varying local values: also spelled *ser.* **2** A measure of capacity: used chiefly in Bombay and Ceylon. [<Hind. *ser*]

seer·suck·er (sir′suk′ər) *n.* **1** A thin linen or linen and silk fabric, usually striped in colors, with crinkled surface. **2** A similar lightweight cotton or rayon crinkled fabric made by having some of the warp threads slack and others tight. [<Hind. *shirshaker* <Persian *shīr o shakkar,* lit., milk and sugar]

see-saw (sē′sô′) *n.* **1** A sport in which persons sit or stand on opposite ends of a balanced plank and make it move up and down. **2** A plank or board balanced for this sport. **3** Any up-and-down or to-and-fro movement. **4** A crossruff. — *v.t. & v.i.* To move or cause to move on or as if on a see-saw. — *adj.* Moving to and fro; vacillating. [Reduplication of SAW[1] <*See saw sack a downe,* a sawyer's jingle]

seethe (sēth) *v.* **seethed** (*Obs.* **sod**), **seethed** (*Obs.* **sod·den, sod**), **seeth·ing** *v.i.* **1** To boil. **2** To foam or bubble as if boiling. **3** To be agitated or excited, as by rage. — *v.t.* **4** To soak in liquid; steep. **5** *Archaic* To boil. — *n.* The act of seething; turmoil. [OE *sēothan*]

Se·ges·ta (si·jes′tə) An ancient city of NW Sicily.

seg·gar (seg′ər) See SAGGAR.

seg·ment (seg′mənt) *n.* **1** A part cut off or divided from the other parts of anything; a section. **2** *Geom.* **a** A part of a figure cut off by a line or plane; especially, the part of a circle included within a chord and its arc. **b** A finite part of a divided line. **3** *Zool.* One of the serial divisions of an animal; somite; metamere; also, the portion of a limb between two joints. See synonyms under PART. — *v.t. & v.i.* To divide into segments. [<L *segmentum* <*secare* cut] — **seg·men·tal** (seg·men′təl) *adj.* — **seg·men′tal·ly** *adv.* — **seg·men·tar·y** (seg′mən·ter′ē) *adj.*

seg·men·ta·tion (seg′mən·tā′shən) *n.* **1** The act of cutting or dividing into segments. **2** The state of being so divided. **3** The cleavage of a cell into parts.

segmentation cavity *Biol.* The cavity formed by segmentation of a fertilized ovum; blastocele.

se·gno (sā′nyō) *n. pl.* **·gni** (-nyē) *Music* A sign; specifically, the musical sign *:S:* or 𝄋, indicating the beginning or end of a repeat. [< Ital. <L *signum*]

se·go (sē′gō) *n. pl.* **·gos 1** A perennial herb (*Calochortus nuttalli*) of the lily family, having white flowers lined with purple: it is the State flower of Utah. **2** Its edible bulb. Also **sego lily.** [<Shoshonean (Ute) *sigo*]

Se·go·via (sā·gō′vyä) A city of Old Castile, central Spain; remarkable for its architecture.

Se·go·via (sā·gō′vyä), **Andrés,** born 1894, Spanish classical guitarist.

seg·re·gate (seg′rə·gāt) *v.* **·gat·ed, ·gat·ing** *v.t.* **1** To place apart from others or the rest; isolate. — *v.i.* **2** To separate from a mass and gather about nuclei or along lines of fracture, as in crystallization or solidification. **3** To undergo segregation. — *adj.* **1** Separated or set apart from others; select. **2** Simple; solitary; not compound. [<L *segregatus,* pp. of *segregare* separate <*se-* apart + *grex, gregis* a flock] — **seg′re·ga′tive** *adj.* — **seg′re·ga′tor** *n.*

seg·re·ga·tion (seg′rə·gā′shən) *n.* **1** The act or process of segregating. **2** *Biol.* The separation and distribution of inherited characters in the offspring of crossbred parents. **3** The provision for separate facilities, as in housing, schools, and transportation, for whites and non-whites, especially Negroes.

se·gue (sā′gwā, seg′wā) *v.i.* **se·gued, se·gue·ing** *Music* To flow without any break into the next section or theme. [<Ital., (there) follows < *seguire* to follow]

se·gui·dil·la (sā′gē·dē′lyä) *n. Spanish* **1** A lively Spanish dance, in triple time, for two dancers. **2** The music of such a dance, or its movement, based on a stanza of four to seven lines, partly assonant. **3** *pl.* An air to which the dancers sing a group of these stanzas.

sei·cen·to (sā·chen′tō) *n.* The 17th century, in reference to Italian art and literature. [<Ital., short for *mil seicento* one thousand six hundred]

seiche (sāsh) *n.* An occasional oscillation of water above and below the mean level of lakes or landlocked seas, lasting from a few minutes to an hour or more. [< dial. F (Swiss), ? ult. <L *siccus* dry]

Seid·litz (zīd′lits) A German name for SEDLČANY: also *Sedlitz.*

Seid·litz powder (sed′lits) An aperient powder consisting of two separate parts: tartaric acid and sodium bicarbonate mixed with Rochelle salt: a mild cathartic used by dissolving separately, mixing the solutions, and drinking while effervescing: also called *Rochelle* powder. [from *Seidlitz;* so called because of its aperient property, similar to that of the water from the spring there]

seign·ior (sēn′yər) *n.* **1** A lord; in southern Europe, equivalent to English *sir.* **2** A lord or feudal lord. Also **sei·gneur** (sēn·yûr′). [< AF *segnour,* OF *seignor* <L *senior* older] — **sei·gnio·ri·al** (sēn·yôr′ē·əl, -yō′rē-) *adj.*

seign·ior·age (sēn′yər·ij) *n.* **1** Something charged or claimed as a prerogative. **2** A charge made by a government for coining bullion; also, the difference between the cost of bullion and the face value of coin made from it. **3** A royalty. Compare BRASSAGE.

seign·ior·y (sēn′yər·ē) *n.* **1** The territory or jurisdiction of a seignior; a manor. **2** Right or priority belonging to feudal superiority.

Seim (sām) A river in SW European U.S.S.R., rising in SW Russian S.F.S.R. and flowing 435 miles west to the Desna in central northern Ukrainian S.S.R., above Chernigov: also *Seym.*

seine (sān) *n.* Any long fishnet, having floats at the top edge and weights at the bottom, and

hauled by its ends to close around a body of fish. —*v.t.* & *v.i.* **seined, sein·ing** To fish or catch with a seine. [OE *segne* < L *sagena* < Gk. *sagēnē* a fishing net]

Seine (sān, *Fr.* sen) A river of NE France, flowing 482 miles NW to the English Channel between Le Havre and Honfleur.

Seine, Bay of the A bay of the Normandy coast, NW France, indented by the estuary of the Seine; 65 miles wide; 25 miles long.

seise (sēz), **sei·sin** (sē′zin) See SEIZE, SEIZIN.

seism (sī′zəm, -səm) *n.* An earthquake. [< Gk. *seismos.* See SEISMIC.]

seis·mic (sīz′mik, sīs′-) *adj.* Pertaining to, characteristic of, or produced by earthquakes. Also **seis′mal, seis′mi·cal.** [< Gk. *seismos* an earthquake < *seiein* shake]

seis·mism (sīz′miz·əm, sīs′-) *n.* The process or phenomena involved in earth movements.

seismo- *combining form* Earthquake: *seismograph.* Also, before vowels, **seism-.** [< Gk. *seismos* an earthquake]

seis·mo·gram (sīz′mə·gram, sīs′-) *n.* The record of an earthquake or earth tremor made by a seismograph.

seis·mo·graph (sīz′mə·graf, -gräf, sīs′-) *n.* An instrument for automatically recording the intensity, direction, and duration of an earthquake shock. —**seis′mo·graph′ic** *adj.* —**seis·mog·ra·pher** (sīz·mog′rə·fər, sīs-) *n.*

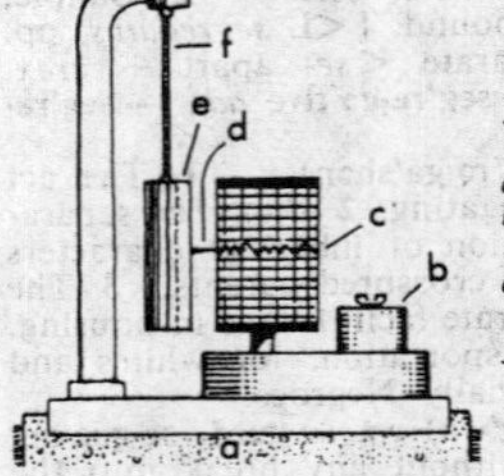

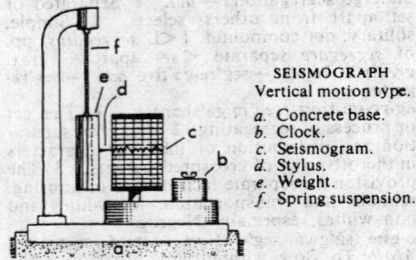

SEISMOGRAPH
Vertical motion type.
a. Concrete base.
b. Clock.
c. Seismogram.
d. Stylus.
e. Weight.
f. Spring suspension.

seis·mog·ra·phy (sīz·mog′rə·fē, sīs-) *n.* The study or description of earthquakes. [< SEISMO- + -GRAPHY]

seis·mol·o·gy (sīz·mol′ə·jē, sīs-) *n.* The science of earthquake phenomena. [< SEISMO- + -LOGY] —**seis·mo·log·ic** (sīz′mə·loj′ik, sīs′-) or **·i·cal** *adj.* —**seis′mo·log′i·cal·ly** *adv.* —**seis·mol′o·gist** *n.*

seis·mom·e·ter (sīz·mom′ə·tər, sīs-) *n.* A seismograph. —**seis·mo·met·ric** (sīz′mō·met′rik, sīs′-) or **·ri·cal** *adj.*

seis·mom·e·try (sīz·mom′ə·trē, sīs-) *n.* The scientific recording of facts regarding earthquake phenomena.

seis·mo·scope (sīz′mə·skōp, sīs′-) *n.* A simple form of seismograph; a device for indicating the time and occurrence of earthquake waves without measuring them. —**seis′mo·scop′ic** (-skop′ik) *adj.*

Seis·tan (sās·tän′) A region and inland lake depression of eastern Iran and SW Afghanistan: also *Sistan.*

seize (sēz) *v.* **seized, seiz·ing** *v.t.* **1** To take hold of suddenly and forcibly; clutch; grasp. **2** To grasp mentally; comprehend; understand. **3** To take possession of by authority or right. **4** To take possession of by or as by force: The usurper *seized* the throne. **5** To take prisoner; capture; arrest. **6** To act upon with sudden and powerful effect; attack; strike: Terror *seized* the attackers and they fled. **7** To take advantage of immediately, as an opportunity. **8** *Law* To put into legal possession: usually spelled *seise.* **9** *Naut.* To fasten or bind by turns of cord, line, or small rope; lash. —*v.i.* **10** To take a sudden or forcible hold. See synonyms under ARREST, CATCH, GRASP. [< OF *saisir, seisir* < Med. L *(ad propriam) sacire* take (into one's own possession), prob. < Gmc.] —**seiz′a·ble** *adj.*

seiz·er (sē′zər) *n.* **1** One who seizes in any sense. **2** *Law* One who takes livery of seizin: also **seiz′or, seis′or.**

sei·zin (sē′zin) *n. Law* **1** The possession of land under a claim of a freehold. **2** That which is possessed; property. **3** The act of taking possession. —**livery of seizin** The delivery of corporeal possession of lands and tenements of freehold. Also spelled *seisin.* [< OF *saisine* < *saisir.* See SEIZE.]

seiz·ing (sē′zing) *n.* **1** The act of grasping or taking forcible possession. **2** The process of fastening or binding together with turns of cord. **3** A small cord used in making such fastenings, and the fastening itself.

sei·zure (sē′zhər) *n.* **1** The act of seizing. **2** A sudden or violent attack, as of epilepsy or neuralgia; fit; spell.

se·jant (sē′jənt) *adj. Her.* Sitting with the fore limbs erect, as a lion. Also **se′jeant.** [< AF *sejant,* OF *seant,* ppr. of AF *seier,* OF *seoir* sit < L *sedere*]

Se·ja·nus (si·jā′nəs), **Lucius Aelius,** died A.D. 31, Roman favorite of Tiberius; executed.

Sejm (sām) *n. Polish* An assembly or diet having legislative power; specifically, the former Constituent Assembly of the Polish Republic.

Se·la·chi·i (si·lā′kē·ī) *n. pl.* An order or subclass of elasmobranch fishes, including the sharks, skates, dogfishes, and rays, with their immediately related fossil allies. [< NL < Gk. *selachos* a shark] —**se·la′chi·an** *adj.* & *n.* —**sel·a·choid** (sel′ə·koid) *adj.* & *n.*

sel·a·gi·nel·la (sel′ə·ji·nel′ə) *n.* One of a widely distributed genus *(Selaginella)* of flowerless branching herbs with scalelike leaves. [< NL, dim. of L *selago, -inis,* a plant like the savin]

se·lah (sē′lə) *n.* A word of unknown meaning in the Psalms and Habakkuk, usually considered as a direction to readers or musicians. [< Hebrew *selāh*]

se·lam·lik (si·läm′lik) *n.* The men's quarters in a Turkish house, where guests are received; formerly, the official visit of the Turkish sultan to a mosque on a Friday. [< Turkish *selāmliq* < Arabic *salām* health, peace]

Se·lan·gor (se·läng′gôr, -gōr) A State of Malaya, on the Strait of Malaya; 3,160 square miles; capital, Kuala Lumpur.

Sel·den (sel′dən), **John,** 1584–1654, English jurist and antiquary.

sel·dom (sel′dəm) *adv.* At widely separated intervals, as of time or space; infrequently. [OE *seldum, seldan,* dative pl. of *seld-* rare, strange]

se·lect (si·lekt′) *v.t.* To take in preference to another or others; pick out; choose. —*v.i.* To make a choice; choose. See synonyms under ALLOT, CHOOSE. —*adj.* **1** Chosen in preference to others; taken as being most fit or desirable; choice. **2** Exclusive. **3** Very particular in selecting. See synonyms under CHOICE, EXCELLENT. [< L *selectus,* pp. of *seligere* < *se-* apart + *legere* choose] —**se·lect′ness** *n.* —**se·lec′tor** *n.*

se·lec·tee (si·lek′tē′) *n.* One selected; specifically, a person called up for military service under selective service.

se·lec·tion (si·lek′shən) *n.* **1** The act of selecting; choice. **2** Anything selected; a collection made with care. **3** *Biol.* The process, natural or artificial, by which certain organisms, or any of their characteristics, are favored in the struggle for perpetuation and survival.

se·lec·tive (si·lek′tiv) *adj.* **1** Pertaining to selection; tending to select. **2** Having or characterized by good selectivity, as a radio receiver. —**se·lec·tive·ly** *adv.*

selective service Compulsory military service according to specified conditions of age, fitness, etc. —**se·lec′tive-ser′vice** *adj.*

selective transmission *Mech.* A transmission for motor vehicles effected by a single lever which directly changes the gear from one speed to another.

se·lec·tiv·i·ty (si·lek′tiv′ə·tē) *n.* **1** The state or condition of being selective. **2** *Telecom.* That characteristic of a radio receiver by which certain frequencies can be received to the exclusion of others.

se·lect·man (si·lekt′mən) *n. pl.* **·men** (-mən) One of a board of town officers, elected annually in New England, except in Rhode Island, to exercise executive authority in local affairs.

selector box A watertight metal box which contains the mechanisms controlling a set of submarine mines and operated electrically from a shore station.

sel·e·nate (sel′ə·nāt) *n. Chem.* A salt of selenic acid. [< SELEN(IC) + -ATE[3]]

Se·le·ne (si·lē′nē) In Greek mythology, goddess of the moon: identified with the Roman *Luna.* Also **Se·le′na** (-nə). [< Gk. *Selēnē,* lit., the moon]

Se·len·ga (se′leng·gä′) A river in the Mongolian People's Republic, flowing 897 miles NE to Lake Baikal.

se·len·ic (si·len′ik, -lē′nik) *adj. Chem.* Of, pertaining to, or derived from selenium, especially in its higher valence. [< SELEN(IUM) + -IC]

selenic acid *Chem.* A transparent, colorless liquid, H_2SeO_4, obtained variously, as by decomposing a selenate with hydrogen sulfide.

se·le·ni·ous (si·lē′nē·əs) *adj. Chem.* Of, pertaining to, or derived from selenium, especially in its lower valence, as the colorless, crystalline **selenious acid,** H_2SeO_3.

sel·e·nite[1] (sel′ə·nīt) *n.* A pearly, usually transparent variety of gypsum. [< L *selenites* < Gk. *selēnitēs (lithos),* lit., moonstone < *selēnē* the moon; so called because it was thought to wax and wane with the moon]

sel·e·nite[2] (sel′ə·nīt) *n.* A salt of selenious acid. [< SELEN(IUM) + -ITE[2]]

sel·e·nite[3] (sel′ə·nīt) *n. Often cap.* An imaginary inhabitant of the moon. [< Gk. *selēnitēs* < *selēnē* the moon]

se·le·ni·um (si·lē′nē·əm) *n.* A nonmetallic element (symbol Se, atomic number 34) resembling sulfur chemically and having several allotropic forms, and in the usual gray, crystalline form having the property of varying in electric resistance when exposed to light of varying intensity. See PERIODIC TABLE. [< NL < Gk. *selēnē* the moon]

selenium cell A photoelectric cell in which plates of selenium respond in accordance with the action of light upon them.

seleno- *combining form* Moon; pertaining to the moon; lunar: *selenography.* Also, before vowels, **selen-.** [< Gk. *selēnē* the moon]

sel·e·nog·ra·phy (sel′ə·nog′rə·fē) *n.* The science or study of the moon's surface. [< SELENO- + -GRAPHY] —**sel′e·nog′ra·pher** or **·phist** *n.* —**sel′e·no·graph′ic** (-nō·graf′ik) or **·i·cal** *adj.*

sel·e·nol·o·gy (sel′ə·nol′ə·jē) *n.* The science that treats of the movements and astronomical relations of the moon. [< SELENO- + -LOGY] —**se·le·no·log·i·cal** (si·lē′nō·loj′i·kəl) *adj.* —**sel′e·nol′o·gist** *n.*

Se·leu·cia (si·lo͞o′shə) **1** An ancient city on the NE Mediterranean, in extreme southern Turkey near Syria; formerly the port of Antioch. Also **Seleucia Pi·e·ri·a** (pī·ir′ē·ə) **2** An ancient city of Mesopotamia, on the Tigris, the site of which is 20 miles SE of Baghdad, Iraq. **3** An ancient city of Cilicia, SW of Tarsus, the site of modern Silifke, Turkey. Also **Seleucia Tra·che·o·tis** (trā′kē·ō′tis).

Se·leu·cid (si·lo͞o′sid) *adj.* Pertaining to the Seleucids: also **Se·leu′ci·dan, Se·leu·cid·i·an** (sē′lo͞o·sid′ē·ən). —*n.* One of the Seleucids. [< L *Seleucides* < Gk. *Seleukidēs,* a descendant of Seleucus < *Seleukos* Seleucus]

Se·leu·cids (si·lo͞o′sids) *n. pl.* The members of the dynasty that ruled Syria from 312 B.C. till the Roman conquest, 64 B.C.: named from Seleucus. Also **Se·leu′ci·dae** (-dē).

Se·leu·cus (si·lo͞o′kəs) Name of six kings of the Seleucid dynasty, especially **Seleucus Ni·ca·tor** (nī·kā′tər), 358?–280 B.C., Macedonian general under Alexander the Great, and founder of the dynasty.

self (self) *adj.* **1** Same; identical: obsolete except in the compound *selfsame.* **2** Pure; unmixed: applied especially to colors. —*n. pl.* **selves 1** An individual known or considered as the subject of his own consciousness; anything considered as having a distinct personality. **2** Personal interest or advantage. **3** Any thing, class, or attribute that, abstractly considered, maintains a distinct and characteristic individuality or identity. [OE]

Self may appear as a combining form with various meanings in solidemes and hyphemes, as shown in the list beginning at the foot of this page.

1 Of the self (the object of the root word); as in:

self-abandonment	**self-abhorrence**	**self-administer**	**self-adornment**	**self-advertise**	**self-aggrandizement**	**self-applause**
self-abasement	**self-accusation**	**self-admiration**	**self-adulation**	**self-advertisement**	**self-analysis**	**self-appreciation**
self-abasing	**self-adaptive**	**self-admission**	**self-advancement**	**self-affliction**	**self-annihilation**	**self-approbation**

self–ab·ne·ga·tion (self'ab'ni·gā'shən) *n.* The complete putting aside of self and claims of self for the sake of some person or object; self-sacrifice.

Synonyms: self-control, self-denial, self-devotion, self-renunciation, self-sacrifice. *Self-control* is holding oneself within due limits in pleasures and duties, as in all things else; *self-denial*, the giving up of pleasures for the sake of duty. *Self-renunciation* surrenders conscious rights; *self-abnegation* forgets that there is anything to surrender. A mother will care for a sick child with complete *self-abnegation*, but without a thought of *self-denial*. *Self-devotion* is whole-hearted consecration of self to a person or cause with readiness for any needed sacrifice. *Self-sacrifice* is the strongest term of all, and contemplates the gift of self as actually made. *Antonyms*: self-gratification, self-indulgence, self-will.

self–a·buse (self'ə·byoos') *n.* **1** The disparagement of one's own person or powers. **2** Masturbation.

self–ad·dressed (self'ə·drest') *adj.* Addressed to and by oneself.

self–as·sured (self'ə·shoord') *adj.* Confident in one's own abilities; self-reliant. — **self'–as·sur'ance** *n.*

self–col·ored (self'kul'ərd) *adj.* **1** Having the natural color. **2** Of but one color or tint. Also *Brit.* **self'–col'oured.**

self–com·mand (self'kə·mand', -mänd') *n.* The state of having all the faculties and powers fully and effectively at command: more positive and less repressive than *self-control.*

self–com·posed (self'kəm·pōzd') *adj.* Calm; controlling one's emotions.

self–con·ceit (self'kən·sēt') *n.* An unduly high opinion of oneself or of one's own abilities, acquirements, etc.; self-esteem; vanity; egotism. See synonyms under EGOTISM, PRIDE. — **self'–con·ceit'ed** *adj.*

self–con·fi·dence (self'kon'fə·dəns) *n.* Confidence in oneself or in one's own unaided powers, judgment, etc. See synonyms under ASSURANCE, EGOTISM. — **self'–con'fi·dent** *adj.* — **self'–con'fi·dent·ly** *adv.*

self–con·scious (self'kon'shəs) *adj.* **1** Unduly conscious that one is observed by others, or manifesting such consciousness; embarrassed by inability to forget oneself; ill at ease. **2** Conscious of one's existence. — **self'–con'scious·ly** *adv.* — **self'–con'scious·ness** *n.*

self–con·tained (self'kən·tānd') *adj.* **1** Keeping one's thoughts and feelings to oneself; uncommunicative; impassive. **2** Exercising self-control. **3** Complete and independent; bearing its own motor, as a machine; mounted on its own boiler, as a steam engine.

self–con·tra·dic·tion (self'kon'trə·dik'shon) *n.* **1** The contradicting of oneself or itself. **2** That which contradicts itself. — **self'–con'·tra·dic'to·ry** *adj.*

self–con·trol (self'kən·trōl') *n.* The act, power, or habit of having one's faculties or energies under control of the will. Compare SELF-COMMAND.

self–de·fense (self'di·fens') *n.* Defense of oneself, one's property, or one's reputation. Also **self'–de·fence'.** — **self'–de·fen'sive** *adj.*

self–de·ni·al (self'di·nī'əl) *n.* The act or power of denying oneself gratification; passive self-sacrifice. See synonyms under ABSTINENCE, SELF-ABNEGATION. — **self'–de·ny'ing** *adj.* — **self'–de·ny'ing·ly** *adv.*

self–de·ter·mi·na·tion (self'di·tûr'mə·nā'shən) *n.* **1** The principle of free will; decision by oneself without extraneous force or influence. **2** Decision by the people of a country or section as to its future political status. — **self'–de·ter'min·ing** *adj.* & *n.*

self–de·vo·tion (self'di·vō'shən) *n.* The devoting of oneself, with one's claims, wishes, or interests, to the service of a person or a cause. See synonyms under SELF-ABNEGATION. — **self'–de·vo'tion·al** *adj.*

self–driv·en (self'driv'ən) *adj.* Driven by itself; automotive.

self–ed·u·cat·ed (self'ej'oo·kā'tid) *adj.* **1** Educated through one's own efforts without the aid of instructors. **2** Educated at one's own expense. — **self'–ed'u·ca'tion** *n.*

self–es·teem (self'es·tēm') *n.* A good opinion of oneself; an overestimate of oneself. See synonyms under EGOTISM, PRIDE.

self–ev·i·dent (self'ev'ə·dənt) *adj.* Carrying its evidence or proof in itself; requiring no proof of its truth. — **self'–ev'i·dence** *n.* — **self'–ev'i·dent·ly** *adv.*

self–ex·e·cut·ing (self'ek'sə·kyoo'ting) *adj.* Containing provisions for securing its own execution independent of legislation: said of a law, etc.

self–ex·ist·ence (self'ig·zis'təns) *n.* Inherent, underived, independent existence: an attribute of God. — **self'–ex·ist'ent** *adj.*

self–ex·pres·sion (self'ik·spresh'ən) *n.* Expression of one's own temperament or emotions, as in art.

self–feed·er (self'fē'dər) *n.* A machine, boiler, or other mechanical device that feeds itself automatically. — **self'–feed'ing** *adj.*

self–fer·til·i·za·tion (self'fûr'təl·ə·zā'shən, -ī·zā'shən) *n. Biol.* Fertilization of an ovum by semen from the same animal or of a plant ovule by its own pollen.

self–gov·ern·ment (self'guv'ərn·mənt, -ər·mənt) *n.* **1** Self-control. **2** Government of a country or region by its own people; especially, government of a colony by the inhabitants rather than by the mother country. — **self'–gov'ern·ing, self'–gov'erned** *adj.*

self–hard·en·ing (self'här'də·ning) *adj. Metall.* Pertaining to or designating certain steels which will harden properly without the need for quenching.

self–heal (self'hēl') *n.* **1** A weedy, perennial herb (genus *Prunella*) with violet or purple flowers, formerly reputed to cure disease, especially the common selfheal of North America (*P. vulgaris*). **2** One of various similar plants, as the sanicle.

self–hood (self'hood) *n.* **1** The state of being an individual, or that which constitutes such a state; personality. **2** Selfishness.

self–i·den·ti·ty (self'ī·den'tə·tē) *n.* **1** The identity of a thing with itself. **2** *Psychol.* That state of consciousness by or through which the self recognizes itself as one and the same.

self–im·por·tance (self'im·pôr'təns) *n.* Pompous self-conceit. — **self'–im·por'tant** *adj.*

self–in·duced (self'in·doost', -dyoost') *adj. Electr.* Characterizing an electromotive force induced in a circuit because of variations of the current in that circuit.

self–in·duc·tion (self'in·duk'shən) *n. Electr.* The production of an induced or extra current in a circuit by the variation of the current in that circuit, especially when it is started or stopped. — **self'–in·duc'tive** *adj.*

self–in·sur·ance (self'in·shoor'əns) *n.* That proportion of the insurance risk which the insured assumes himself by the premium payments he makes.

self–in·ter·est (self'in'tər·ist, -in'trist) *n.* Personal interest or advantage, or the pursuit of it; selfishness. — **self'–in'ter·est·ed** *adj.*

self·ish (sel'fish) *adj.* **1** Caring chiefly for self or for one's own interests or comfort; influenced by personal motives to the disregard of the welfare or wishes of others. **2** Proceeding from or characterized by undue love of self. See synonyms under GREEDY. — **self'ish·ly** *adv.*

self·ish·ness (sel'fish·nis) *n.* The quality of being selfish; undue regard for one's own interest, regardless of others.

Synonym: self-love. *Self-love* is a due care for one's own happiness and well-being, which is perfectly compatible with justice, generosity, or benevolence toward others; *selfishness* is an undue or exclusive care for one's own

self–approval	self–correction	self–disposal	self–humbling	self–lashing	self–persuasion	self–scrutinizing
self–asserting	self–corruption	self–disquieting	self–humiliation	self–laudatory	self–pitiful	self–scrutiny
self–assertion	self–creation	self–dissolution	self–hypnosis	self–limitation	self–pity	self–searching
self–assertive	self–criticism	self–distrust	self–hypnotism	self–limited	self–pitying	self–serve
self–awareness	self–cure	self–doubt	self–hypnotize	self–limiting	self–pleasing	self–slaughter
self–bedizenment	self–damnation	self–easing	self–idolatry	self–loss	self–praise	self–soothing
self–betrayal	self–debasement	self–enriching	self–idolizing	self–loving	self–praising	self–study
self–blame	self–deceit	self–estimate	self–ignorance	self–maceration	self–preparation	self–subjection
self–castigation	self–deceiving	self–evacuation	self–ignorant	self–maintenance	self–presentation	self–subordination
self–chastisement	self–dedication	self–exalting	self–imitation	self–martyrdom	self–preserving	self–support
self–cognizance	self–defeating	self–examination	self–immolation	self–mastery	self–projection	self–supporting
self–commendation	self–deflation	self–exculpation	self–immurement	self–mistrust	self–protecting	self–suppression
self–committal	self–degradation	self–excuse	self–impairment	self–mortification	self–protection	self–surrender
self–comparison	self–deifying	self–expansion	self–improvement	self–murder	self–punishment	self–suspicious
self–comprehending	self–dejection	self–expatriation	self–indignation	self–murderer	self–raising	self–taxation
self–condemnation	self–delation	self–exploiting	self–indulgence	self–mutilation	self–realization	self–teacher
self–condemning	self–delusion	self–exposure	self–indulgent	self–neglect	self–recollection	self–terminating
self–conditioning	self–depreciation	self–extermination	self–indulgently	self–neglectful	self–reconstruction	self–tolerant
self–confinement	self–depreciative	self–fearing	self–indulging	self–nourishment	self–reduction	self–torment
self–confounding	self–destroying	self–flatterer	self–inspection	self–objectification	self–regulation	self–torture
self–congratulatory	self–destruction	self–flattering	self–instruction	self–observation	self–representation	self–treatment
self–conquest	self–destructive	self–flattery	self–insurer	self–offense	self–repressing	self–trust
self–conservative	self–direction	self–folding	self–integration	self–opinion	self–repression	self–trusting
self–conserving	self–disapproval	self–formation	self–intensifying	self–painter	self–reproach	self–undoing
self–consideration	self–discipline	self–glorification	self–interrogation	self–paying	self–reproachful	self–upbraiding
self–consoling	self–disclosure	self–gratification	self–introduction	self–perceiving	self–restriction	self–usurp
self–consuming	self–discovery	self–guidance	self–judgment	self–perceptive	self–revealing	self–valuing
self–contempt	self–disgrace	self–harming	self–justification	self–perfecting	self–revelation	self–vaunting
self–contradicting	self–disparagement	self–help	self–justifying	self–perfection	self–ruin	self–vindication
self–conviction	self–display	self–helpful	self–knowledge	self–perpetuation	self–satirist	self–worship

2 By oneself or itself; by one's own effort (the agent of the root word); as in:

self–abandoned	self–balanced	self–caused	self–conducted	self–corrupted	self–deprived	self–divided
self–appointed	self–beguiled	self–chosen	self–confuted	self–declared	self–destroyed	self–doomed
self–approved	self–betrayed	self–commissioned	self–constituted	self–defended	self–determined	self–elaborated
self–authorized	self–blinded	self–condemned	self–convicted	self–deluded	self–devised	self–elected

comfort or pleasure, regardless of the happiness, and often of the rights, of others. *Self-love* is necessary to high endeavor, and even to self-preservation; *selfishness* limits endeavor to a narrow circle of intensely personal aims. *Antonyms:* See synonyms under BENEVOLENCE.

self·less (self′lis) *adj.* Regardless of self; unselfish.

self·liq·ui·dat·ing (self′lik′wə·dā′ting) *adj.* Designating a business transaction in which goods in great demand are converted into cash over a short period.

self·load·ing (self′lō′ding) *adj.* Automatically reloading: said of a gun using the energy of recoil to eject and reload.

self·love (self′luv′) *n.* Love of oneself; the desire or tendency that leads one to seek to promote his own well-being. See synonym under SELFISHNESS.

self·made (self′mād′) *adj.* 1 Having attained honor, wealth, etc., by one's own efforts. 2 Made by oneself.

self·per·cep·tion (self′pər·sep′shən) *n.* Perception of one's own existence or mental states; introspection.

self·pol·li·na·tion (self′pol′ə·nā′shən) *n. Bot.* The transfer of pollen from stamens to pistils of the same flower.

self·pos·ses·sion (self′pə·zesh′ən) *n.* 1 The full possession or control of one's powers or faculties; freedom from perturbation, perplexity, or excitement. 2 Presence of mind; self-command. — **self′–pos·sessed′** *adj.*

self·pres·er·va·tion (self′prez′ər·vā′shən) *n.* 1 The protection of oneself from destruction. 2 The urge to protect oneself regarded as an instinct.

self·prof·it (self′prof′it) *n.* Self-interest.

self·pro·nounc·ing (self′prə·noun′sing) *adj.* Having marks of pronunciation and stress applied to a word without phonetic alteration of the spelling.

self·re·li·ance (self′ri·lī′əns) *n.* Reliance on one's own abilities, resources, or judgment. See synonyms under ASSURANCE. — **self′–re·li′ant** *adj.*

self·re·nun·ci·a·tion (self′ri·nun′sē·ā′shən) *n.* Renunciation of one's own rights, privileges, or claims. — **self′–re·nun′ci·a·to′ry** (-sē·ə·tôr′ē, -tō′rē) *adj.*

self·re·spect (self′ri·spekt′) *n.* Such regard for one's own character as will restrain one from unworthy action; rational self-esteem. See synonyms under PRIDE. — **self′–re·spect′ing** *adj.*

self·re·straint (self′ri·strānt′) *n.* Restraint, as of the passions, by the force of one's own will; self-control.

self·right·eous (self′rī′chəs) *adj.* Righteous in

one's own estimation; pharisaic. — **self′–right′eous·ly** *adv.* — **self′–right′eous·ness** *n.*

self·ris·ing (self′rī′zing) *adj.* 1 That rises of itself. 2 Having the leaven already added by the millers, as some flours.

self·sac·ri·fice (self′sak′rə·fīs) *n* The sacrifice or subordination of one's self or one's personal welfare or wishes, for the sake of duty or for others' good. See synonyms under SELF-ABNEGATION. — **self′–sac′ri·fic′ing** *adj.*

self·same (self′sām′) *adj.* Exactly the same; identical. See synonyms under IDENTICAL. — **self′–same′ness** *n.*

self·sat·is·fac·tion (self′sat′is·fak′shən) *n.* Satisfaction with one's own actions and characteristics; conceit; self-complacency. — **self′–sat′is·fied** *adj.* — **self′–sat′is·fy′ing** *adj.*

self·seek·ing (self′sē′king) *adj.* Given to the exclusive pursuit of one's own interests or gain. — *n.* Self-aggrandizement; selfishness. — **self′–seek′er** *n.*

self·ser·vice (self′sûr′vis) *adj.* Designating a particular type of café, restaurant, or store where patrons serve themselves.

self·start·er (self′stär′tər) *n.* 1 An internal-combustion engine, with automatic or semi-automatic starting mechanism; also, such mechanism. 2 *Slang* One who requires no outside stimulus to start or accomplish work.

self·styled (self′stīld′) *adj.* Characterized (as such) by oneself: a *self-styled* gentleman.

self·suf·fi·cient (self′sə·fish′ənt) *adj.* 1 Able to support or maintain oneself without aid or cooperation from others. 2 Having overweening confidence in oneself. Also **self′–suf·fic′ing** (-sə·fī′sing). — **self′–suf·fi′cien·cy** *n.*

self·will (self′wil′) *n.* Pertinacious adherence to one's own will or wish, especially with disregard of the wishes of others; obstinacy. — **self′–willed′** *adj.*

self·wind·ing (self′wīn′ding) *adj.* Having a magnetic, electrical, or other attachment which automatically winds a clock or other mechanism at certain times.

self·wrong (self′rông′, -rong′) *n.* Injury done to one's self.

Sel·juk (sel·jōōk′) *n.* A member of one of several Turkish dynasties which reigned over a large part of central and western Asia from the 11th to the 13th centuries. — *adj.* Pertaining to a Seljuk. Also **Sel·ju·ki·an** (sel·jōō′-kē·ən). [<Turkish *seljúq,* after *Seljúq,* a Turkish chieftain, reputed ancestor of the Seljuk dynasties]

Sel·kirk (sel′kûrk) A county of SE Scotland; 267 square miles; county burgh, Selkirk. Also **Sel′kirk·shire** (-shir).

Sel·kirk (sel′kûrk), **Alexander,** 1676–1721, Scottish sailor who was marooned on Juan Fernandez Island, Pacific Ocean, for four

years. His adventures are said to have suggested Defoe's *Robinson Crusoe.*

Selkirk Mountains A range of the Rocky Mountains in SE British Columbia.

sell¹ (sel) *v.* **sold, sell·ing** *v.t.* 1 To transfer (property) to another for a consideration; dispose of by sale. 2 To deal in; offer for sale. 3 To deliver, surrender, or betray for a price or reward: to *sell* one's honor. 4 *Colloq.* To cause to accept or approve something: They *sold* him on the scheme. 5 *Colloq.* To cause the acceptance or approval of. 6 *Slang* To deceive; cheat. — *v.i.* 7 To transfer ownership for a consideration; engage in selling. 8 To be on sale; be sold. See synonyms under CONVEY. — *n.* 1 *Slang* A trick; joke; swindle. 2 On the stock exchange, a stock that ought to be sold. ◆ Homophone: *cell.* [OE *sellan* give]

sell² (sel) *n.* 1 An elevated seat; an honorable place; also, any seat. 2 A saddle. ◆ Homophone: *cell.* [<OF *selle* <L *sella* a seat, ult. < *sedere* sit]

sell·er (sel′ər) *n.* 1 One who sells. 2 Something with a measure of salability: This book is a good *seller.*

sell·ing–plat·er (sel′ing·plā′tər) *n.* A horse that runs in a selling race.

selling race *Brit.* A horse race in which the entrants may be claimed for a set price, and the winning horse must be offered at auction. Compare CLAIMING RACE. Also **sell′er, sell′ing·er.**

sell–out (sel′out′) *n.* 1 An act of selling out. 2 *Colloq.* A performance for which all seats have been sold. 3 *Slang* A betrayal through a secret bargain or agreement.

Selt·zer (selt′sər) *n.* An effervescing mineral water. Also **Seltzer water, Sel·ters** (sel′tərz). [Alter. of G *Selterser,* from *Nieder Selters,* a village in SW Prussia, its place of origin]

sel·vage (sel′vij) *n.* 1 The edge of a woven fabric so finished that it will not ravel. 2 An edge. 3 The edge plate of a lock having an opening for a bolt. Also **sel′vedge.** [<SELF + EDGE, trans. of MDu. *selfegghe*]

Sel·va·gens (sel·vä′zhĕñsh) A group of uninhabited islets in Madeira: also *Salvages.*

selves (selvz) Plural of SELF.

se·man·tic (si·man′tik) *adj.* 1 Of or pertaining to meaning. 2 Of or relating to semantics. [<Gk. *sēmantikos* < *sēmainein* signify]

se·man·ti·cist (si·man′tə·sist) *n.* A specialist in semantics.

se·man·tics (si·man′tiks) *n. pl.* (construed as singular) 1 *Ling.* The study of the meanings of speech forms, especially of the development and changes in meaning of words and word groups. 2 *Logic* The relation between signs or symbols and what they signify or

3 To, toward, in, for, on, or with oneself; as in:

self–employed	self–honored	self–instructed	self–maimed	self–pampered	self–proclaimed	self–schooled
self–exhibited	self–idolized	self–invited	self–matured	self–performed	self–professed	self–sown
self–explained	self–illumined	self–irrecoverable	self–misused	self–perpetuated	self–punished	self–subdued
self–exposed	self–improvable	self–judged	self–mortified	self–perplexed	self–renounced	self–supported
self–extolled	self–incurred	self–justified	self–named	self–planted	self–repressed	self–sustained
self–furnished	self–inflicted	self–kindled	self–offered	self–pollinated	self–restrained	self–taught
self–hidden	self–initiated	self–limited	self–paid	self–posed	self–revealed	self–tempted

3 To, toward, in, for, on, or with oneself; as in:

self–absorbed	self–centered	self–contented	self–dissatisfied	self–injurious	self–preference	self–repellent
self–absorption	self–comment	self–delight	self–elation	self–injury	self–preoccupation	self–repose
self–aid	self–communing	self–dependence	self–enamored	self–kindness	self–prescribed	self–reproof
self–aim	self–compassion	self–dependent	self–enclosed	self–liking	self–pride	self–repulsive
self–amusement	self–compensation	self–desire	self–exultation	self–loathing	self–procured	self–resentment
self–angry	self–complacence	self–despair	self–focusing	self–oblivious	self–produced	self–resigned
self–application	self–complacency	self–directed	self–gain	self–occupied	self–profit	self–respectful
self–applied	self–complacent	self–direction	self–helpfulness	self–panegyrical	self–purifying	self–responsibility
self–assumed	self–concentration	self–disdain	self–helpless	self–penetration	self–reflection	self–rigorous
self–assuming	self–conflict	self–disgust	self–hope	self–permission	self–regard	self–sent
self–benefit	self–consistency	self–dislike	self–imposture	self–pictured	self–relation	self–tenderness
self–care	self–consistent	self–dissatisfaction	self–infliction	self–pleased	self–relying	self–vexation

4 From oneself or itself; from one's own nature or power; as in:

self–apparent	self–derived	self–explaining	self–initiative	self–moving	self–refuting	self–rewarding
self–arising	self–desirable	self–explanatory	self–intelligible	self–operative	self–renewing	self–sprung
self–born	self–developing	self–forbidden	self–interpretative	self–originating	self–resourceful	self–stability
self–coherence	self–distinguishing	self–fruition	self–issuing	self–perfect	self–resplendent	self–stimulated
self–complete	self–effort	self–healing	self–luminous	self–poise	self–restoring	self–sustaining
self–defining	self–evolving	self–inclusive	self–manifestation	self–poised	self–reward	self–warranting
		self–authority				

5 Independent; as in: **self–agency**

self–credit	self–dominance	self–entity	self–existence	self–ownership	self–rule	self–sovereignty

6 *Technol.* Automatic or automatically; as in:

self–acting	self–binder	self–cleaning	self–feed	self–lubricating	self–propelled	self–registering
self–adapting	self–burning	self–closing	self–filling	self–lubrication	self–propelling	self–regulated
self–adjustable	self–changing	self–cocking	self–inking	self–oiling	self–propulsion	self–regulating
self–adjusting	self–charging	self–cooled	self–lighting	self–primer	self–raker	self–righting
self–alining	self–checking	self–emptying	self–locking	self–priming	self–recording	self–setting

denote: also called *semasiology, semiotics.* Compare GENERAL SEMANTICS. **3** Loosely, verbal trickery, especially by adulteration or shift of meaning within a word; amphibology.

sem·a·phore (sem′ə-fôr, -fōr) *n.* An apparatus for making signals, as with movable arms, disks, flags, or lanterns. — *v.t.* To send by semaphore. [<F *sémaphore* <Gk. *sēma* a sign + *pherein* carry] — **sem′·a·phor′ic** (-fôr′ik, -for′ik) or **·i·cal** *adj.*

Se·ma·rang (sə-mä′räng) A port of northern Java: also *Samarang.*

se·ma·si·ol·o·gy (si-mä′sē·ol′ə-jē, -zē-) *n.* Semantics (def. 2). [<Gk. *sēmasia* the signification of a word < *sēma* sign + -LOGY] — **se·ma·si·o·log·i·cal** (si-mä′sē·ə·loj′i·kəl, -zē-) *adj.*

se·mat·ic (si·mat′ik) *adj.* Of the nature of a sign; warning; in animal coloration, serving to distinguish as a means of recognition or warning. [<Gk. *sēma, -atos* a sign]

sem·bla·ble (sem′blə-bəl) *adj.* **1** Resembling; similar. **2** Apparent; not real. — *n.* A thing resembling another thing. Also **sem′bla·tive.** [<OF <*sembler.* See SEMBLANCE.]

sem·blance (sem′bləns) *n.* **1** A mere show without reality; pretense. **2** Outward appearance; look; aspect. **3** A pictorial representation; likeness; resemblance. See synonyms under PRETENSE. [<OF <*sembler* seem <L *simulare, similare* simulate <*similis* like]

sem·ble (sem′bəl) *v.i.* **·bled, ·bling** It seems; it would seem: used only in law, and generally in abbreviated form, **sem.** or **semb.** [<F, it seems <*sembler.* See SEMBLANCE.]

se·mé (sə-mā′, *Fr.* se-mā′) *adj. Her.* Strewn or scattered over with small bearings, as fleurs-de-lis; powdered. [<OF, pp. of *semer* sow <L *seminare* <*semen* a seed]

se·mei·ol·o·gy (sē′mī·ol′ə-jē, sē′mē-), **se·mei·ot·ics** (sē′mī·ot′iks, sē′mē-), etc. See SEMIOLOGY, SEMIOTICS, etc.

Sem·e·le (sem′ə-lē) In Greek mythology, the mother of Dionysus by Zeus: she was destroyed by lightning when she asked to see Zeus as he appeared to the gods.

se·meme (sē′mēm) *n. Ling.* The meaning of a morpheme. [<Gk. *sēma* a sign; on analogy with *phoneme*]

se·men (sē′mən) *n.* **1** The impregnating fluid of male animals. **2** Seed. [<L <*serere* sow]

se·mes·ter (si·mes′tər) *n.* A college half-year; hence, a period of instruction, usually lasting 17 or 18 weeks. [<G <L (*cursus*) *semestris* (a period) of six months <*sex* six + *mensis* a month] — **se·mes′tral** *adj.*

sem·i (sem′ē) *n. pl.* **sem·is** *Colloq.* **1** *U.S.* A semitrailer. **2** *Brit.* A semi-detached house. — **the semis** *Colloq.* The semifinal round of competition in a sports competition.

semi– *prefix* **1** Half; partly; not fully: *semiautomatic, semicivilized.* **2** Exactly half: *semicircle.* **3** Occurring twice (in the period specified): *semiweekly.* [<L]

Semi-, meaning not fully, partially, or partial, is found in solidemes and hyphemes, as in the list beginning at the foot of this page.

sem·i·an·nu·al (sem′ē·an′yōō·əl) *adj.* Issued or occurring twice a year; half-yearly. — *n.* A publication issued twice a year. — **sem′i·an′nu·al·ly** *adv.*

sem·i·a·quat·ic (sem′ē·ə·kwat′ik, -kwot′ik) *adj. Biol.* Adapted for living or growing near water, as certain types of plants and animals.

sem·i·au·to·mat·ic (sem′ē·ô′tə·mat′ik) *adj.* Only partly automatic: said especially of guns which are self-loading but not self-firing.

sem·i·breve (sem′ē·brēv′) *n. Music* A note equal to half a breve; a whole note.

sem·i·cell (sem′ē·sel′) *n. Biol.* Half of a complete cell, usually joined to the other half by an isthmus, as in certain green algae. Compare DESMID.

sem·i·cen·ten·ni·al (sem′ē·sen·ten′ē·əl) *adj.* Occurring or celebrated at the end of fifty years from some event. — *n.* The fiftieth anniversary of an event, or its celebration.

sem·i·cir·cle (sem′ē·sûr′kəl) *n.* **1** A half-circle; an arc or a segment of 180°. **2** Anything formed or arranged in a half-circle. — **sem′i·cir′cu·lar** *adj.*

semicircular canal *Anat.* One of the three tubular structures in the inner ear of most vertebrates, which together serve as the organ of balance. See illustration under EAR.

sem·i·cir·cum·fer·ence (sem′ē·sər·kum′fər·əns, -frəns) *n.* One half of a circumference.

sem·i·civ·i·lized (sem′ē·siv′ə·līzd) *adj.* Half or partly civilized.

sem·i·co·lon (sem′ē·kō′lən) *n.* A mark (;) of punctuation, indicating a greater degree of separation than the comma.

sem·i·con·duc·tor (sem′ē·kən·duk′tər) *n. Physics* **1** One of a class of crystalline solids, as germanium, silicon, and lead sulfide, which are electronic conductors at ordinary temperatures: used in the manufacture of transistors. **2** Any substance or material having an electrical conductivity intermediate between metals and dielectrics.

sem·i·con·scious (sem′ē·kon′shəs) *adj.* Partly conscious; half-conscious.

sem·i·de·tached (sem′ē·di·tacht′) *adj.* Joined to another on one side only: said of two houses built side by side with one common wall.

sem·i·di·am·e·ter (sem′ē·dī·am′ə·tər) *n.* A radius; half of a diameter.

sem·i·di·ur·nal (sem′ē·dī·ûr′nəl) *adj.* **1** Pertaining to or continuing during a half-day; occurring or accomplished in a half-day, or once each half-day. **2** Designating either half of the arc described by a heavenly body during its rising or setting. [<SEMI- + DIURNAL]

sem·i·dome (sem′ē·dōm′) *n. Archit.* A roof structure resembling a portion, approximately half, of a dome divided vertically.

SEMIDOME

sem·i·el·lip·ti·cal (sem′ē·i·lip′ti·kəl) *adj.* Having the form of half of an ellipse that has been divided along either diameter.

sem·i·fi·nal (sem′ē·fī′nəl) *n.* **1** A competition which precedes the final in a list of sporting events. **2** One of two competitions in a tournament, the winners of each meeting in the final. — *adj.* Next before the final. — **sem′i·fi′nal·ist** *n.*

sem·i·flu·id (sem′ē·flōō′id) *adj.* Fluid, but thick and viscous. — *n.* A thick, viscous fluid. — **sem′i·flu·id′ic** (-flōō·id′ik) *adj.*

sem·i·liq·uid (sem′ē·lik′wid) *adj.* Half liquid. — *n.* A partly liquid substance.

sem·i·lu·nar (sem′ē·lōō′nər) *adj.* Resembling or shaped like a half-moon; crescentic. Also **sem′i·lu′nate** (-lōō′nāt).

semilunar bone *Anat.* The middle bone in the upper row of wrist bones.

semilunar valve *Anat.* One of the crescent-shaped pockets at the entrances to the aorta and to the pulmonary artery respectively: their function is to prevent the backward flow of blood.

sem·i·mo·bile (sem′ē·mō′bēl) *adj.* Partly mobile: said especially of military units not fully equipped with motor vehicles.

sem·i·month·ly (sem′ē·munth′lē) *adj.* Taking place twice a month. — *n. pl.* **·lies** A publication issued twice a month. — *adv.* At half-monthly intervals.

sem·i·mute (sem′ē·myōōt′) *adj.* Having imperfectly developed or partially lost speech.

sem·i·nal (sem′ə·nəl) *adj.* **1** Pertaining to or containing seeds, germs, or primal elements. **2** Having productive power; germinal; propagative. **3** Not developed; embryonic; rudimentary. [<OF <L *seminalis* <*semen, seminis* semen, a seed] — **sem′i·nal·ly** *adv.*

sem·i·nar (sem′ə·när) *n.* **1** A group of advanced students at a college or university, meeting regularly and informally with a professor for discussion of research problems. **2** The course thus conducted. [<G <L *seminarium.* See SEMINARY.]

sem·i·nar·y (sem′ə·ner′ē) *n. pl.* **·nar·ies** **1** A special school, as of theology; also, a school of higher education. **2** A seminar. **3** The place where anything is nurtured. **4** A seminary priest. — *adj.* **1** Seminal. **2** Pertaining to a seminary. [<MF *séminaire* <L *seminarium* a seed plot, orig. neut. of *seminarius* seminal <*semen, seminis* a seed, semen]

sem·i·na·tion (sem′ə·nā′shən) *n.* **1** The act of sowing or spreading; dispersion of seeds. **2** Propagation. [<L *seminatio, -onis* <*semen, seminis* a seed, semen]

sem·i·nif·er·ous (sem′ə·nif′ər·əs) *adj.* **1** Carrying or producing semen. **2** Seed-bearing. [<L *semen, seminis* a seed, semen + *ferre* bear]

sem·i·niv·o·rous (sem′ə·niv′ər·əs) *adj.* Feeding on seeds. [<L *semen, seminis* a seed, semen + -VOROUS]

Sem·i·nole (sem′ə·nōl) *n.* One of a Florida tribe of North American Indians of Muskhogean linguistic stock, an offshoot of the Creeks: now chiefly in Oklahoma, a remnant remaining in Florida. [<Muskhogean (Creek) *Simanóle,* lit., a separatist, a runaway]

sem·i·of·fi·cial (sem′ē·ə·fish′əl) *adj.* Having official authority or sanction; official to a certain extent. — **sem′i·of·fi′cial·ly** *adv.*

se·mi·ol·o·gy (sē′mē·ol′ə·jē, sem′ē-) *n.* **1** The science that relates to sign language. **2** *Med.* Symptomatology. **3** The use of signs in signaling. Also spelled *semeiology.* [<Gk. *sēmeion,* dim. of *sēma* a mark + -LOGY]

sem·i·o·paque (sem′ē·ō·pāk′) *adj.* Half-opaque; translucent but not transparent.

se·mi·ot·ic (sē′mē·ot′ik, sē′mī-) *adj.* **1** Of or pertaining to semantics (def. 2). **2** *Med.* Relating to symptomatology. Also spelled *semeiotic.* Also **se′mi·ot′i·cal.** [<Gk. *sēmeiōtikos* <*sēmeion* a sign. See SEMIOLOGY.]

se·mi·ot·ics (sē′mē·ot′iks, sē′mī-) *n. pl.* (construed as singular) **1** Semantics (def. 2). **2** *Med.* Symptomatology. Also spelled *semeiotics.* [<Gk. *sēmeiōtikos.* See SEMIOTIC.]

sem·i·o·vip·a·rous (sem′ē·ō·vip′ər·əs) *adj.* Giving birth to imperfectly developed offspring, as a marsupial.

Se·mi·pa·la·tinsk (sye·mē·pə·lä′tyinsk) A city of eastern Kazakh S.S.R., on the Irtysh.

sem·i·pal·mate (sem′ē·pal′māt, -mit) *adj. Ornithol.* Having the toes connected by webs for less than half their length, as many shore birds. Also **sem′i·pal′mat·ed.**

semipalmated plover A common plover (*Charadrius semipalmatus*) of the Atlantic coast, which breeds only in the Arctic.

sem·i·par·a·sit·ic (sem′ē·par′ə·sit′ik) *adj. Biol.*

semiaccomplishment	semiarchitectural	semibleached	semiclosure	semiconversion	semidiaphanous	semifailure
semiacquaintance	semiarid	semiblind	semicoagulated	semicooperative	semidigested	semifatalistic
semiaffectionate	semiatheist	semiblunt	semicollapsible	semicured	semidirect	semifeudalism
semiagricultural	semiattached	semiboiled	semicolonial	semicylindrical	semidomesticated	semifictional
semialcoholic	semi–autonomous	semibourgeois	semicomplete	semidangerous	semidry	semifinished
semiallegiance	semi–autonomy	semichannel	semiconceal	semidarkness	semi–Empire	semifit
semianarchist	semibald	semichaotic	semiconfident	semideaf	semienclosed	semifitting
semiangular	semibarbarian	semichivalrous	semiconfinement	semidelirious	semierect	semifixed
semianimal	semibarbarism	semi–Christian	semiconformist	semidenatured	semiemeritical	semiflexed
semianimated	semibarbarous	semiclerical	semiconnection	semidependent	semiexposed	semifluctuating
semiarborescent	semibarren	semiclosed	semiconservative	semidestructive	semiextinction	semiforeign

Partly parasitic: said especially of certain bacteria and of chlorophyll–bearing plants, as the mistletoe.

Sem·i–Pe·la·gi·an (sem′ē·pə·lā′jē·ən) *n.* One of a theological party in the fifth century which held a middle ground between the predestination doctrine of Augustine and the free–will doctrine of Pelagius. [<SEMI- + PELAGIAN]

sem·i·per·me·a·ble (sem′ē·pûr′mē·ə·bəl) *adj.* Partially permeable: said especially of osmotic membranes that separate a solvent from the dissolved substance.

sem·i·por·ce·lain (sem′ē·pôr′sə·lin, -pōr′-, -pôrs′lin, -pōrs′-) *n.* **1** A grade of porcelain having little or no translucency. **2** Earthenware resembling porcelain.

sem·i·post·al (sem′ē·pōs′təl) *adj.* Designating a postage stamp or series of stamps sold by postal authorities for more than the franking value, the additional proceeds usually going to a philanthropic purpose. — *n.* A semipostal stamp.

sem·i·pre·cious (sem′ē·presh′əs) *adj.* Designating a gem or class of gems that are not as valuable as those classified precious: *semiprecious* stones.

sem·i·qua·ver (sem′ē·kwā′vər) *n. Music* A note one sixteenth the value of a semibreve or whole note.

Se·mir·a·mis (si·mir′ə·mis) In Assyrian legend, the wife of Ninus and founder of Babylon, known for her beauty and wisdom.

sem·i·rig·id (sem′ē·rij′id) *adj. Aeron.* Partly rigid, as an airship in which an exterior stiffener supports the load. — *n.* A semirigid airship.

sem·i·round (sem′ē·round′) *adj.* Having one side round and the other flat. — *n.* A semiround object.

sem·i·skilled (sem′ē·skild′) *adj.* Partly skilled, but not enough to perform highly specialized work.

sem·i·sol·id (sem′ē·sol′id) *adj.* Partly solid; so viscous as to be nearly solid.

Sem·ite (sem′īt, sē′mīt) *n.* **1** A person believed to be or considered as a descendant of Shem. **2** One of a people of Caucasian stock, now represented by the Jews and Arabs, but originally including the ancient Babylonians, Assyrians, Arameans, Phoenicians, etc. Also *Shemite.* [<NL *Semita* <LL *Sem* Shem <Gk. *Sēm* <Hebrew *shēm*]

Se·mit·ic (sə·mit′ik) *adj.* Of or pertaining to the Semites, or to any of their languages. — *n.* A subfamily of the Hamito–Semitic family of languages, divided into three groups — **East Semitic** (Akkadian), **Northwest Semitic** (Phoenician, ancient and modern Hebrew, Aramaic, etc.), and **Southwest Semitic** (Arabic, Ethiopic, Amharic, etc.).

Se·mit·ics (sə·mit′iks) *n.* The scientific study of the history, language, and literature of the Semitic peoples.

Sem·i·tism (sem′ə·tiz′əm) *n.* **1** A Semitic word or idiom. **2** Semitic practices, opinions, or customs collectively. **3** Any political or economic policy favoring the Jews.

sem·i·tone (sem′ē·tōn′) *n. Music* An interval approximately equal to half a major tone on the scale: the smallest interval in most European music. — **sem·i·ton·ic** (sem′ē·ton′ik) *adj.*

sem·i·trail·er (sem′ē·trāl′ər) *n.* **1** A trailer having wheels only at the rear, the front end being attached to the rear of a truck tractor. **2** A tractor and its attached semitrailer considered as a unit: also called *trailer truck.*

sem·i·trans·lu·cent (sem′ē·trans·lōō′sənt, -tranz-) *adj.* Half or partly translucent. — **sem′i·trans·lu′cent·ly** *adv.*

sem·i·trans·par·ent (sem′ē·trans·pâr′ənt, -par′-) *adj.* Half or partly transparent.

sem·i·trop·i·cal (sem′ē·trop′i·kəl) *adj.* Nearly tropical.

sem·i·vit·ri·fied (sem′ē·vit′rə·fīd) *adj.* Half vitrified; partially made into glass.

sem·i·vow·el (sem′i·vou′əl) *n. Phonet.* A vowel–like sound used as a consonant, as (w), (y), and (r): also called *glide.* — **sem′i·vo′cal** (-vō′kəl) *adj.*

sem·i·week·ly (sem′ē·wēk′lē) *adj.* Issued or occurring twice a week. — *n. pl.* **·lies** A publication issued twice a week. — *adv.* At half–weekly intervals.

Sem·lin (zem·lēn′) The German name for ZEMUN.

Sem·mel·weiss (sem′əl·vīs), **Ignaz Philipp,** 1816–65, Austrian obstetrician; pioneer in prevention of puerperal fever.

Semmes (semz), **Raphael,** 1809–77, American Confederate naval officer.

sem·o·li·na (sem′ə·lē′nə) *n.* The gritty or grain–like portions of wheat retained in the bolting machine after the fine flour has been passed through. [Alter. of Ital. *semolino,* dim. of *semola* bran <L *simila* fine flour]

Sem·pach (zem′päkh) A town in central Switzerland; scene of a Swiss victory over the Austrians, 1386.

sem·per fi·de·lis (sem′pər fi·dē′lis, fi·dā′lis) *Latin* Always faithful: motto of the U.S. Marine Corps.

sem·per pa·ra·tus (sem′pər pə·rā′təs) *Latin* Always prepared: motto of the U.S. Coast Guard.

sem·per·vi·rent (sem′pər·vī′rənt) *adj.* Evergreen. [<L *semper* always + *virens, -entis,* ppr. of *virere* be green]

sem·pi·ter·nal (sem′pə·tûr′nəl) *adj.* Enduring or existing to all eternity; everlasting. See synonyms under IMMORTAL, PERPETUAL. [<OF *sempiternel* <LL *sempiternalis* <L *sempiternus* everlasting < *semper* always] — **sem′·pi·ter′ni·ty** *n.*

sem·pli·ce (sem′plē·chā) *adj. Music* Simple; unaffected: a direction to performers. [<Ital. <L *simplex, simplicis*]

sem·pre (sem′prā) *adv. Music* Always; throughout the passage or composition: *sempre* legato, piano, etc. [<Ital. <L *semper*]

semp·stress (semp′stris, sem′-) See SEAMSTRESS.

sen (sen) *n. Japanese* A Japanese copper or bronze coin, equal to 1/100 of a yen.

sen′ (sen) *v.t.* & *v.i., n. Scot.* Send[1].

sen·a·ry (sen′ər·ē) *adj.* Of or pertaining to six; containing six units. [<L *senarius* < *seni* six each < *sex* six]

sen·ate (sen′it) *n.* **1** The governing body of some universities and institutions of learning. **2** An advisory body of members of the faculty and representative students in a school or college. **3** A body of distinguished or venerable men; council; legislative body. [<OF *senat* <L *senatus,* lit., a council of old men < *senex, senis* old]

Sen·ate (sen′it) *n.* **1** The upper branch of national or state legislative bodies of the United States, and of France and other governments; especially, the **United States Senate,** composed of two Senators elected by popular vote from each State. **2** In ancient Rome, the state council, whose originally very extensive powers were curtailed under the empire: limited to 100 patricians under the kings, it consisted, under the republic, of 300 patricians, plebeians, and high officials; under Augustus, there were 600 senators.

sen·a·tor (sen′ə·tər) *n.* A member of a senate. [<OF *senateur* <L *senator* < *senex, senis* an old man, old] — **sen′a·tor·ship′** *n.*

sen·a·to·ri·al (sen′ə·tôr′ē·əl, -tō′rē-) *adj.* **1** Pertaining to or befitting a senator or senate. **2** Entitled to elect a senator, as a district. — **sen′a·to′ri·al·ly** *adv.*

se·na·tus con·sul·tum (sə·nā′təs kən·sul′təm) *Latin* A decree of the ancient Roman Senate, pronounced upon some matter of law or public policy: originally only advisory and finally authoritative as laws. Also **se·na′tus con·sult′.**

send[1] (send) *v.* **sent, send·ing** *v.t.* **1** To cause or direct to go; dispatch, as a messenger. **2** To cause to be conveyed to another place; transmit; forward: to *send* a letter. **3** To cause to issue; emit or discharge, as heat, light, smoke, etc.: with *forth, out,* etc. **4** To throw or drive by force; impel. **5** To cause to come, happen, etc.; grant: God *send* us peace. **6** To bring into a specified state or condition; drive: The decision *sent* him into bankruptcy. **7** To transmit, as a current or electromagnetic impulses. — *v.i.* **8** To dispatch an agent, messenger, or message. — **to send for** To summon by a message or messenger. — **to send in one's papers** To resign. — *n.* A messenger. [OE *sendan*] — **send′er** *n.*

Synonyms (verb): cast, delegate, depute, discharge, dispatch, dismiss, emit, fling, forward, hurl, impel, lance, launch, project, propel, sling, throw, transmit. *Send* in its most common use involves personal efficiency without personal presence; according to the adage, "If you want your business done, go; if not, *send*"; one *sends* a letter or a bullet, a messenger or a message. To *dispatch* is to *send* hastily or very promptly, ordinarily with a destination in view; to *dismiss* is to *send* away from oneself without reference to a destination; as, to *dismiss* a clerk, an application, or an annoying subject. To *discharge* is to *send* away so as to relieve a person or thing of a load; we *discharge* a gun or *discharge* the contents; as applied to persons, *discharge* is a harsher term than *dismiss.* To *emit* is to *send* forth from within, with no reference to a destination; as, The sun *emits* light and heat. *Transmit,* from the Latin, is a dignified term, often less vigorous than the Saxon *send,* but preferable at times in literary or scientific use; as, to *transmit* a charge of electricity. *Transmit* fixes the attention more on the points of departure and destination. *Antonyms*: bring, carry, convey, get, give, hand, hold, keep, receive, retain.

send[2] (send) *Naut. n.* **1** The flow or impulse of the waves. **2** Scend. — *v.i.* **1** To move by the force of waves. **2** To scend. [<SEND[1]; prob. infl. in meaning by ASCEND]

Sen·dai (sen·dī) A city on NE Honshu island, Japan.

sen·dal (sen′dəl) *n.* **1** A light, thin, silken fabric much used for dresses, etc., in the Middle Ages. **2** An article made of it. Also spelled *sandal.* [<OF *cendal, sendal,* ult. <Gk. *sidōn* fine linen]

send–off (send′ôf′, -of′) *n.* **1** The act of sending off; a start. **2** A farewell dinner or other celebration or demonstration at parting. **3** Encouragement, as in starting a career.

send–up (send′up′) *n. Brit. Slang* A parody; take–off.

Sen·e·ca (sen′ə·kə) *n.* One of a tribe of North American Indians of Iroquoian stock formerly inhabiting western New York, the largest tribe of the confederation known as the Five Nations: still numerous in New York and Ontario. [<Du. *Sennacaas* the Five Nations <Algonquian (Mohegan) *A′sinnika,* trans. of Iroquoian *Oneñiute,* short for *oneñiute′ roñnon* Oneida, lit., people of the standing rock]

Sen·e·ca (sen′ə·kə), **Lucius Annaeus,** 3? B.C.–A.D. 65, Roman Stoic philosopher, statesman, and tragic dramatist.

Sen·e·ca Lake (sen′ə·kə) One of the Finger Lakes in west central New York, extending 35 miles north and south; 67 square miles.

sen·e·ga (sen′ə·gə) *n.* **1** The dried root of an herb *(Polygala senega)* of the milkwort family, used as a stimulating expectorant, as in treating bronchitis. **2** The plant itself. Also **senega**

semifriable
semifrontier
semifunctional
semigala
semigenuflection
semi–Gnostic
semi–Gothic
semigranulate
semihard
semihigh
semihistorical
semihobo
semihostile
semihumanitarian
semihumorous
semi–idle
semi–idleness
semi–incandescent
semi–independence
semi–intoxicated
semi–intoxication
semi–invalid
semileafless
semilegendary
semiliberal
semilined
semilucent
semimilitary
semimonastic
semimonopoly
semimystical
seminationalization
seminecessary
seminervous
semioblivious
semiobscurity
semiopened
semiorganized
semiovoid
semipagan
semipanic
semiparallel
semiparalysis
semipastoral
semipeace
semiperfect
semipermanent
semiperspicuous
semipolitician
semiprivate
semiprofessional
semipublic
semiraw
semirebellion
semireligious
semiresolute
semirespectability
semirespectable
semiretirement
semiriddle
semi–Romanized
semiroyal
semirustic
semisacred
semisatiric
semiscientific
semisecrecy
semiseriousness
semisocial
semisocialism
semisoft
semispontaneity
semistagnation
semistarvation
semistarved
semisuccess
semitailored
semitrained
semitruth
semivirtue
semivital
semivoluntary
semiwarfare
semiwild

root. [<NL, alter. of SENECA; so called because thought, by the Seneca Indians, to be good for snakebites]

Sen·e·gal (sen′ə·gôl′) A river of western Africa, flowing about 1,000 miles NW from SW Guinea to the Atlantic at Saint-Louis, Senegal, forming the border between Senegal and Mauritania.

Sen·e·gal (sen′ə·gôl′), **Republic of** An independent republic of the French Community in west Africa; 76,124 square miles; capital, Dakar: formerly a French overseas territory. — **Sen′e·ga·lese′** (-gə·lēz′, -lēs′) *adj.* & *n.*

Sen·e·gam·bi·a (sen′ə·gam′bē·ə) The former name for the territory between the Senegal and Gambia rivers, in west Africa.

se·nes·cent (si·nes′ənt) *adj.* **1** Growing old. **2** Characteristic of old age. [<L *senescens, -entis,* ppr. of *senescere* grow old <*senex* old] — **se·nes′cence** *n.*

sen·e·schal (sen′ə·shəl) *n.* **1** An official in the household of a medieval prince or noble who had charge of feasts, etc.; a steward or majordomo. **2** A magistrate or governor. **3** *Brit.* A cathedral official. [<OF <Gmc. Cf. OHG *siniskalk* old servant.]

se·nile (sē′nīl, -nil) *adj.* **1** Pertaining to, proceeding from, or characteristic of old age. **2** Infirm; weak; doting. **3** *Geog.* Almost worn away to base level: a *senile* continent. [<L *senilis*< *senex* old] — **se′nile·ly** *adv.*

senile dementia *Psychiatry* The progressive deterioration of cerebral functions and mental faculties associated with old age. Also **senile psychosis.**

se·nil·i·ty (si·nil′ə·tē) *n.* Mental and physical infirmity due to old age.

sen·ior (sēn′yər) *adj.* **1** Older in years; elder; specifically, after personal names (usually in the abbreviated form *Sr.*), to denote the elder of two related persons of the same name, especially a father and his son. **2** Older in office; more advanced in service; superior in rank or dignity. **3** Pertaining to the closing year of a high school or college course. — *n.* **1** One older in years or office, or more advanced in rank or dignity than another. **2** Hence, any elderly person. **3** A member of a senior class. **4** A graduate or one of the older fellows of an English college. [<L, compar. of *senex, senis* old]

senior citizen An elderly person, especially one of or over the age of retirement.

sen·ior·i·ty (sēn·yôr′ə·tē, -yor′-) *n.* *pl.* **·ties** **1** The state of being older in years or in office; priority of age, service, or rank. **2** An assembly of seniors or, in England, senior fellows of a college.

Sen·lac (sen′lak) A hill, near Hastings, in Sussex, England; scene of the battle of Hastings, 1066.

sen·na (sen′ə) *n.* **1** The dried leaflets of any one of several leguminous plants (genus *Cassia*), used medicinally for their purgative properties; especially, the Old World species *C. acutifolia* and *C. angustifolia.* **2** Any one of the plants yielding true senna or a similar product. [<NL *senna, sena* <Arabic *sanā*]

Sen·nach·er·ib (si·nak′ər·ib), died 681 B.C.; king of Assyria 705–681 B.C.

Sen·nar (sen·när′) An ancient city in the Sudan between the White Nile and the Blue Nile, capital of a large native kingdom, 15th to 19th centuries. Also **Sen·naar′.**

sen·net (sen′it) *n.* A signal of exit or entrance sounded on a horn: chiefly as a stage direction in Elizabethan plays. [<OF *senet, sinet, signet.* Double of SIGNET.]

sen·night (sen′īt, -it) *n.* *Archaic* A week. Also **se′n′night, sev′en-night′.** [OE *seofan nihta* <*seofan* seven + *nihta,* pl. of *niht* a night]

sen·nit (sen′it) *n.* **1** Plaited cordage, of from 3 to 9 strands, used for gaskets on ships. **2** Plaited grass or straw for hatmaking. [Earlier *sinnet,* ? <SEVEN + KNIT]

se·no·pi·a (si·nō′pē·ə) *n.* An apparent restoration of normal vision in formerly myopic people who have become hypermetropic in old age. Also called *gerontopia.* [<NL <L *senex* old + Gk. *ōps, ōpos* an eye]

se·ñor (sā·nyôr′) *n.* *pl.* **·ño·res** (-nyō′rās) *Spanish* A Spanish title of courtesy; a gentleman; Mr.; sir: used before a name, like *Mr.,* or alone, like *Sir.*

se·ño·ra (sā·nyō′rä) *n.* *Spanish* A Spanish lady; Mrs.; madam.

se·ño·ri·ta (sā′nyō·rē′tä) *n.* *Spanish* A young, unmarried Spanish lady; miss.

sen·sate (sen′sāt) *adj.* Perceived or appreciated by the senses: *sensate* matters: also **sen′sat·ed.** — *v.t.* **·sat·ed, ·sat·ing** To perceive by the senses. [<LL *sensatus* gifted with sense <L *sensus* sense]

sen·sa·tion (sen·sā′shən) *n.* **1** *Physiol.* **a** That aspect of consciousness resulting from the stimulation of a nerve process beginning at any point in the body and passing through the brain, especially by those stimuli affecting any of the sense organs, as hearing, taste, touch, smell, and sight. **b** The capacity to respond to such stimulation. **2** That which produces interest or excitement; an excited condition: to cause a *sensation.* **3** A condition of mind resulting from inherent feeling; emotion. [<Med. L *sensatio, -onis* <LL *sensatus.* See SENSATE.]

Synonyms: emotion, feeling, perception, sense. *Sensation* is the mind's consciousness due to bodily response to stimuli, as heat or sound; *perception* is the cognition of some external object which causes the *sensation.* While *sensations* are connected with the body, *emotions* add the reactions of the mind. *Feeling* is a term popularly denoting what is felt, whether through the body or by the mind alone, and includes both *sensation* and *emotion.* A *sense* is an organ or faculty of *sensation* or of *perception.* See FEELING.

sen·sa·tion·al (sen·sā′shən·əl) *adj.* **1** Pertaining to emotional excitement. **2** Pertaining to physical sensation. **3** Causing excitement; startling. **4** Causing unnatural emotional excitement; melodramatic; trashy: a *sensational* story. — **sen·sa′tion·al·ly** *adv.*

sen·sa·tion·al·ism (sen·sā′shən·əl·iz′əm) *n.* **1** *Philos.* The theory that all knowledge originates in sensation, or is composed of transformed sense elements, that all consciousness is modified sensation, and all mental phenomena have a sensory basis: a branch of modern empiricism. **2** The use of melodramatic methods in writing or speaking. **3** The theory that feeling is the only criterion of good. — **sen·sa′tion·al·ist** *n.* — **sen·sa′tion·al·is′tic** *adj.*

sense (sens) *n.* **1** The faculty of sensation; sense perception. **2** Any of certain agencies by or through which an individual receives impressions of the external world; popularly, one of the five senses. **3** *Physiol.* Any receptor, or group of receptors, specialized to receive and transmit stimuli, either external, as of sight, taste, smell, etc., or internal, as of hunger, thirst, sex, equilibrium, muscular and visceral movements, etc. **4** Rational perception accompanied by feeling; realization; discriminating cognition: a *sense* of wrong. **5** Normal power of mind or understanding; sound or natural judgment: The fellow has no *sense*; often in the plural: She is coming to her *senses.* **6** Signification; import; meaning. **7** Opinion, view, or judgment of the majority: The *sense* of the meeting was manifest. **8** That which commends itself to the understanding as being in accordance with reason and good judgment: to talk *sense.* **9** Capacity to perceive or appreciate: a *sense* of color. **10** *Geom.* One of two opposite directions in which a magnitude may be described or generated. **11** Direction; trend. See synonyms under FEELING, MIND. — **the five senses** The Aristotelian division of senses into sight, hearing, smell, taste, and touch: now collectively known as the **special senses.** — **sixth sense** **1** Capacity for perception beyond the normal range of the senses; extrasensory perception. **2** Intuitive or premonitory knowledge, especially as affecting or affected by the senses. **3** Cenesthesia. — *v.t.* **sensed, sens·ing** **1** To become aware of through the senses. **2** *Colloq.* To comprehend; understand. [<MF *sens* <L *sensus* perception <*sentire* feel]

sense datum *Psychol.* That which is experienced as a result of the stimulation of a sense organ.

sense·less (sens′lis) *adj.* **1** Deprived of consciousness; unconscious. **2** Incapable of feeling or perception; insensate. **3** Devoid of sense; foolish; stupid. — **sense′less·ly** *adv.* — **sense′less·ness** *n.*

sense organ *Physiol.* A structure specialized to receive sense impressions, as the eye, nose, ear, etc.; a receptor (def. 2).

sense perception Immediate knowledge of things through the senses, as distinguished from mediate or inferred knowledge.

sense stress See SENTENCE STRESS.

sen·si·bil·i·ty (sen′sə·bil′ə·tē) *n.* *pl.* **·ties** **1** The capability of sensation; power to perceive or feel. **2** The capacity of sensation and rational emotion, as distinguished from intellect and will. **3** Susceptibility or sensitiveness to outside influences or mental impressions; sometimes, abnormal sensitiveness: often in the plural. **4** Appreciation accompanying mental apprehension; discerning judgment. **5** Delicacy or sensitiveness of an instrument. **6** Responsiveness to pathos or to artistic or esthetic values. **7** *Archaic* Sentimentality.

Synonyms: sensitiveness, sensibility, susceptibility. In popular use *sensibility* denotes sometimes capacity of feeling of any kind; as, *sensibility* to heat or cold; sometimes, a peculiar readiness to be the subject of feeling, especially of the higher feelings: as the *sensibility* of the artist or the poet. *Sensitiveness* denotes an especial delicacy of *sensibility,* ready to be excited by the slightest cause, as displayed, for instance, in the sensitive plant. *Susceptibility* is rather a capacity to receive, to contain feeling, so that a person of great *susceptibility* is capable of being readily and deeply moved; *sensitiveness* is more superficial, *susceptibility* more pervading. In physics, the *sensitiveness* of a magnetic needle is the ease with which it may be deflected, as by another magnet; its *susceptibility* is the degree to which it can be magnetized by a given magnetic force or the amount of magnetism it will hold. A person of great *sensitiveness* is quickly and keenly affected by any external influence, as by music, pathos, or ridicule, while a person of great *susceptibility* is not only touched, but moved to his utmost soul. See FEELING. *Antonyms*: coldness, deadness, hardness, insensibility, numbness, unconsciousness.

sen·si·ble (sen′sə·bəl) *adj.* **1** Possessed of good mental perception; exhibiting sound sense and judgment; discreet; judicious. **2** Capable of physical sensation; sensitive: *sensible* to pain. **3** Perceptible or appreciable through the senses: *sensible* heat. **4** Emotionally or mentally sensitive. **5** Having a perception or cognition; fully aware; persuaded. **6** Great enough to be perceived; appreciable. **7** *Obs.* Sensitive to minute changes. See synonyms under CONSCIOUS, EXPEDIENT, INTELLIGENT, PHYSICAL, SAGACIOUS. — *n.* **1** A substance capable of being felt or observed. **2** A sentient being. **3** *Music* The leading note; the seventh of a scale: also **sensible note** (or **tone**). [<OF <L *sensibilis* <*sensus,* pp. of *sentire* feel, perceive] — **sen′si·ble·ness** *n.* — **sen′si·bly** *adv.*

sen·si·tive (sen′sə·tiv) *adj.* **1** Easily affected by outside operations or influences; excitable or impressible; touchy; easily offended. **2** *Chem.* & *Phot.* Reacting readily to the proper agents or forces: paper *sensitive* to light. **3** Pertaining to or depending on the senses or sensation: *sensitive* motions. **4** Closing or moving when touched or irritated, as certain plants. **5** Liable to fluctuation. **6** *Obs.* Wise; sensible. **7** Capable of indicating minute changes or differences; delicate. See synonyms under FINE, MOBILE. [<OF *sensitif* <Med. L *sensitivus* <L *sensus.* See SENSIBLE.] — **sen′si·tive·ly** *adv.* — **sen′si·tive·ness** *n.*

sensitive plant A shrubby tropical herb (*Mimosa pudica*), whose leaves close at a touch: often cultivated in hothouses.

sen·si·tiv·i·ty (sen′sə·tiv′ə·tē) *n.* **1** The state or degree of being sensitive; sensitiveness. **2** *Physiol.* The degree of acuteness with which sensations are discriminated; irritability, as of organs: distinguished from *sensibility,* in which the mental side is more prominent. **3** The degree of responsiveness to an electric current or to radio waves. **4** *Phot.* Sensitiveness to light.

sen·si·tize (sen′sə·tīz) *v.t.* **·tized, ·tiz·ing 1** To render sensitive. **2** *Phot.* To make sensitive to light, as a plate or film. **3** *Med.* To make susceptible or hypersensitive to the action of a drug by repeated injections. [<SENSIT(IVE) + -IZE] **— sen′si·ti·za′tion** *n.* **— sen′si·tiz′er** *n.*

sen·si·tom·e·ter (sen′sə·tom′ə·tər) *n.* An apparatus by which the sensitiveness to light of a photographic film or body tissue may be tested or measured. [<SENSIT(IVE) + -(O)-METER]

sen·sor (sen′sər) *adj.* Sensory: applied to nerves and nerve organs. [Short for SENSORY]

sen·so·ri·mo·tor (sen′sə·ri·mō′tər) *adj. Physiol.* Of or pertaining to muscular and nervous responses induced by sensory stimuli. Compare IDEOMOTOR. [<SENSORY + MOTOR]

sen·so·ri·um (sen·sôr′ē·əm, -sō′rē-) *n. pl.* **·ri·a** (-ē·ə) **1** *Anat.* The nervous system, including the cerebrum, as the collective organ of sensation. **2** *Biol.* The entire sensory apparatus of an organism. [<LL <L *sensus.* See SENSIBLE.]

sen·so·ry (sen′sər·ē) *adj.* **1** Pertaining to the sensorium or to sensation. **2** Conveying or producing sense impulses. Also **sen·so·ri·al** (sen·sôr′ē·əl, -sō′rē-). [<LL *sensorium* SENSORIUM]

sen·su·al (sen′shōō·əl) *adj.* **1** Unduly indulgent to the appetites or sexual pleasure; exhibiting a predominance of the animal nature; lewd. **2** Pertaining to the body or the physical senses; also, fleshly; carnal: opposed to *spiritual.* **3** Pertaining to sensualism: usually opprobrious. See synonyms under BRUTISH. [<MF *sensuel* <LL *sensualis* <L *sensus* SENSE] **— sen′su·al·ly** *adv.*

sen·su·al·ism (sen′shōō·əl·iz′əm) *n.* **1** Sensuality. **2** *Philos.* A debased sensationalism. **3** A system of ethics predicating the pleasures of sense to be the highest good. **4** Emphasis on the sensuous elements of beauty, rather than the ideal. **— sen′su·al·ist** *n.* **— sen′su·al·is′tic** *adj.*

sen·su·al·i·ty (sen′shōō·al′ə·tē) *n.* **1** The state of being sensual, or sensual acts collectively. **2** Sensual or animal indulgence. Also **sen′su·al·ness.**

sen·su·al·ize (sen′shōō·əl·īz′) *v.t.* **·ized, ·iz·ing** To make sensual. Also *Brit.* **sen′su·al·ise′. — sen′su·al·i·za′tion** *n.*

sen·su·ous (sen′shōō·əs) *adj.* **1** Pertaining or appealing to or derived from the senses: used in a higher and purer sense than *sensual.* **2** Keenly appreciative of and aroused by beauty, refinement, or luxury. **3** Resembling imagery that appeals to the senses: a *sensuous* portrayal. [<L *sensus* SENSE + -OUS] **— sen′su·ous·ly** *adv.* **— sen′su·ous·ness** *n.*

sent (sent) Past tense and past participle of SEND.

sen·tence (sen′təns) *n.* **1** *Gram.* A word or a related group of words expressing a complete thought, whether a statement of fact (declarative), a question (interrogative), a command (imperative), or an exclamation (exclamatory). Declarative and interrogative sentences usually contain a subject (that which is spoken of) and a predicate (what is said about the subject), but either or both of these elements may be missing in an utterance that, nevertheless, conveys full meaning, as in "Where is John?" "At home." or "Look!" **— simple sentence** A sentence consisting of one independent clause, as *The dog barked.* Its subject and predicate may be simple (having one substantive or one verb) or compound (having two or more substantives or verbs), and there may be modifying words and phrases. **— compound sentence** A sentence consisting of more than one independent clause, as *The sun shone and the birds sang.* **— complex sentence** A sentence consisting of a principal clause and one or more subordinate clauses, as *After I have read it, I shall give the book to you.* **2** *Law* A final judgment; penalty pronounced upon a person convicted. **3** A determination; opinion, especially as expressed formally. **4** An instructive saying; a maxim. **5** *Music* A complete idea or period, usually consisting of several phrases, as the half of a four-line hymn tune or song. — *v.t.* **·tenced, ·tenc·ing** To pass sentence upon; condemn to punishment. See synonyms under CONDEMN. [<OF <L *sententia* an opinion < *sentire* feel, be of opinion] **— sen·ten·tial** (sen·ten′shəl) *adj.*

sen·tenc·er (sen′tən·sər) *n.* One who pronounces sentence; a judge.

sentence stress The variation in emphasis given to successive words in a sentence to stress the meaning: also called *sense stress.* Also **sentence accent.**

sen·ten·tious (sen·ten′shəs) *adj.* **1** Abounding in or giving terse expression to thought; axiomatic; sometimes, opprobriously, pompously formal, or moralizing. **2** Habitually using terse, laconic, or aphoristic language. See synonyms under TERSE. [<L *sententiosus* < *sententia* a maxim. See SENTENCE.] **— sen·ten′tious·ly** *adv.* **— sen·ten′tious·ness, sen·ten·ti·os·i·ty** (sen·ten′shē·os′ə·tē) *n.*

sen·ti·ence (sen′shē·əns, -shəns) *n.* **1** The state of being sentient. **2** Capacity for sensation or sense perception. **3** Consciousness. **4** Sensation regarded as immediate experience and so distinguished from thought or perception. Also **sen′ti·en·cy.**

sen·ti·ent (sen′shē·ənt, -shənt) *adj.* Possessing powers of sense or sense perception; having or actually experiencing sensation or feeling: opposed to *inanimate* and *vegetal.* — *n.* One capable of sensation or perception; loosely, the mind, as the seat of consciousness. [<L *sentiens, -entis,* ppr. of *sentire* feel] **— sen′ti·ent·ly** *adv.*

sen·ti·ment (sen′tə·mənt) *n.* **1** Noble, tender, or artistic feeling, or susceptibility to such feeling; sensibility; also, its verbal expression. **2** A mental attitude or response to a person, object, or idea conditioned entirely by feeling instead of reason; loosely, an exaggerated emotional reaction. **3** Idealistic, personal, or esthetic reaction as distinguished from intellectual or practical. **4** An opinion or judgment; thought as distinguished from its expression: often in the plural. **5** An expressive thought or idea dressed in appropriate language, as a toast aptly uttered. See synonyms under FEELING, IDEA. [<OF *sentement* <Med. L *sentimentum* <L *sentire* feel]

sen·ti·men·tal (sen′tə·men′təl) *adj.* **1** Characterized by sentiment or intellectual emotion; involving or exciting tender emotions or aspirations. **2** Experiencing, displaying, or given to sentiment, often in an extravagant or mawkish manner: a *sentimental* person. See synonyms under ROMANTIC. **— sen′ti·men′tal·ly** *adv.*

sen·ti·men·tal·ism (sen′tə·men′təl·iz′əm) *n.* The state of being sentimental, or its manifestation; tendency to be emotional. Also **sen′ti·men·tal′i·ty** (-men·tal′ə·tē). **— sen′ti·men′tal·ist** *n.*

sen·ti·men·tal·ize (sen′tə·men′təl·īz) *v.* **·ized, ·iz·ing** *v.t.* **1** To affect with sentiment. **2** To cherish sentimentally. — *v.i.* **3** To behave sentimentally. Also *Brit.* **sen′ti·men′tal·ise.**

sen·ti·nel (sen′tə·nəl) *n.* A sentry; hence, any watcher or guard. — *v.t.* **·neled** or **·nelled, ·nel·ing** or **·nel·ling 1** To watch over as a sentinel. **2** To protect or furnish with sentinels. **3** To station or appoint as a sentinel. [<OF *sentinelle* <Ital. *sentinella* <LL *sentinare* avoid danger < *sentire* perceive]

sen·try (sen′trē) *n. pl.* **·tries 1** A soldier placed on guard to see that only authorized persons pass his post and to give warning of approaching danger; a sentinel. **2** The watch or guard kept by a sentry. [? Short for obs. *centrenel,* var. of SENTINEL]

sentry box A small shelter or cabin to protect a sentry from the weather.

Se·nus·si (se·nōō′sē) *n. pl.* A belligerent Moslem religious sect once influential in northern Africa and Arabia, founded by Sidi Mohammed ben Ali ben Es Senussi about 1842. Also **Se·nu′si, Se·nus′sites. — Se·nus′si·an** *adj.*

Se·oul (sā·ōōl′, sōl; *Korean* syœ·ōōl) The capital of the Republic of Korea (South Korea): also *Kyongsong*: Japanese *Keijo.*

se·pal (sē′pəl) *n. Bot.* One of the individual leaves of a calyx. [<F *sépale* <NL *sepalum* <L *sep(aratus)* separate + *(pet)alum* a petal] **— sep·a·line** (sep′ə·lin, -līn), **sep′a·lous** *adj.*

sep·a·ra·ble (sep′ər·ə·bəl, sep′rə-) *adj.* Capable of being separated or divided. [<L *separabilis* < *separare* separate] **— sep′a·ra·bil′i·ty, sep′a·ra·ble·ness** *n.* **— sep′a·ra·bly** *adv.*

sep·a·rate (sep′ə·rāt) *v.* **·rat·ed, ·rat·ing** *v.t.* **1** To set asunder; disunite or disjoin; sever. **2** To occupy a position between; serve to keep apart: The Hudson River *separates* New York from New Jersey. **3** To divide into components, parts, etc. **4** To isolate or obtain from a compound, mixture, etc.: to *separate* the wheat from the chaff. **5** To consider separately; distinguish between. **6** *Law* To part by separation. — *v.i.* **7** To become divided or disconnected; draw apart. **8** To part company; withdraw from association or combination. — *adj.* (sep′ər·it, sep′rit) **1** Existing or considered apart from others; distinct; individual: *separate* rooms. **2** Disembodied; disunited from the body. **3** Separated; disjoined. — *n.* **1** An offprint. **2** *pl.* Garments to be worn in various combinations, as skirts and blouses. See synonyms under PARTICULAR. [<L *separatus,* pp. of *separare* < *se-* apart + *parare* prepare] **— sep′a·rate·ly** *adv.* **— sep′a·rate·ness** *n.*

Synonyms (verb): alienate, detach, disconnect, disengage, disjoin, dissever, disunite, divide, part, remove, sever, split, sunder, withdraw. *Antonyms*: see synonyms for MIX.

separate school *Canadian* A private school; specifically, a Roman Catholic parochial school.

sep·a·ra·tion (sep′ə·rā′shən) *n.* **1** The act or process of separating; division. **2** The state of being disconnected or apart. **3** A dividing line. **4** *Law* Relinquishment of cohabitation between husband and wife by mutual consent: distinguished from *divorce.* See synonyms under SECLUSION.

separation center A central army or navy point that handles discharges and releases of personnel except medical discharges.

sep·a·ra·tist (sep′ər·ə·tist, sep′rə-) *n.* One who advocates or upholds separation; specifically, a seceder; dissenter. Also **sep′a·ra′tion·ist. — sep′a·ra·tism** *n.*

sep·a·ra·tive (sep′ə·rā′tiv, -rə·tiv) *adj.* Tending to or inducing separation; useful in separating.

sep·a·ra·tor (sep′ə·rā′tər) *n.* **1** Any device, implement, or apparatus for dividing or separating things into their component parts. **2** A machine for separating the chaff from grain. **3** A centrifugal mechanism for separating cream from milk. **4** One who separates.

sep·a·ra·trix (sep′ə·rā′triks) *n.* A separating point or line; decimal point. [<LL *(linea) separatrix* the separating or dividing (line)]

sep·a·ra·tum (sep′ə·rā′təm) *n. pl.* **·ta** (-tə) A paper published separately from a series to which it belongs; a reprint of an article previously published as a part of a report.

Se·phar·dim (si·fär′dim) *n. pl.* The Spanish and Portuguese Jews or their descendants: distinguished from the *Ashkenazim.* Also **Se·phar′a·dim** (-ə·dim). [<Hebrew *sephārādhim* <*Sephāradh,* a country mentioned in *Ob.* iii 20, identified by the rabbis with Spain, but prob. orig. in Asia Minor] **— Se·phar′dic, Se·phar′a·dic** *adj.*

se·pi·a (sē′pē·ə) *n.* **1** A reddish-brown pigment prepared from the ink of the cuttlefish; the color of this pigment. **2** A picture done in this pigment. **3** The ink of the cuttlefish. **4** Any of a genus *(Sepia)* of decapod mollusks having an internal shell, especially the common Atlantic cuttlefish *(S. officinalis).* — *adj.* Executed in or colored like sepia; dark-brown with a tinge of red. [<L <Gk. *sēpia* a cuttlefish]

Se·pik (sā′pik) A river in NE New Guinea, in the Australian Territory of New Guinea, rising near the border of Netherlands New Guinea and flowing 700 miles NE to the Bismarck Sea.

se·pi·o·lite (sē′pē·ə·līt′) *n.* Meerschaum. [<G *sepiolith* <NL *sepium* cuttlebone (<Gk. *sēpion,* dim. of *sēpia* a cuttlefish) + Gk. *lithos* a stone]

se·poy (sē′poi) *n.* A native Indian soldier outfitted and trained in European style; especially, one employed in the former British Indian Army. [<Pg. *sipae* <Urdu *sipāhī* a soldier <Persian < *sipāh* an army]

Sepoy Mutiny The Indian Mutiny. Also **Sepoy Rebellion.**

sep·pu·ku (sep·pōō·kōō) *n. Japanese* Hara-kiri.

sep·sis (sep′sis) *n. Pathol.* **1** Poisonous putrefaction. **2** Infection of the blood by putrescent material containing pathogenic microorganisms. [<NL <Gk. *sēpsis* < *sēpein* make putrid]

sept (sept) *n.* A division of a tribe ruled by a hereditary chief, especially in ancient and

medieval Ireland; any similar social unit or group descended from a common ancestor. [Prob. <OF *septe,* var. of *secte* SECT] — **sep′tal** *adj.*

sept–[1] Var. of SEPTI–[1].

sept–[2] Var. of SEPTI–[2].

sep·ta (sep′tə) Plural of SEPTUM.

sep·tan·gle (sep′tang′gəl) *n.* A heptagon. [<LL *septangulus* <*septem* seven + *angulus* an angle] — **sep·tan·gu·lar** (sep·tang′gyə·lər) *adj.*

sep·tar·i·um (sep·târ′ē·əm) *n. pl.* **·tar·i·a** (-târ′ē·ə) *Geol.* A rock nodule or concretion, usually several feet in diameter and roughly spherical, having a compact crust and an internal mass broken up by angular radiating or intersecting cracks usually filled with a foreign mineral: also called *turtlestone.* [<NL <L *septum* an enclosure, wall] — **sep·tar′i·an** *adj.*

sep·tate (sep′tāt) *adj.* Divided by or provided with a partition or partitions; having a septum or septa. [<NL *septatus* <LL, surrounded <L *septum* an enclosure, wall]

sep·tec·to·my (sep·tek′tə·mē) *n. Surg.* Excision of a part of the nasal septum. [<SEPT–[2] + -ECTOMY]

Sep·tem·ber (sep·tem′bər) The ninth month of the year, containing 30 days; the seventh month in the old Roman calendar. — **massacre of September** The massacre in Paris in September, 1792, when 10,000 persons were put to death in prison by order of Danton: also **September massacre** or **massacres.** [<L *septem* seven]

Sep·tem·brist (sep·tem′brist) *n.* A member of the Parisian mob that massacred political prisoners in the massacre of September 2 to 6, 1792; hence, a cruel and bloodthirsty person; a butcher; murderer.

sep·te·mi·a (sep·tē′mē·ə) *n.* Septicemia. Also **sep·tae′mi·a.** [<NL <Gk. *sēptos* putrid + *haima* blood]

sep·tem·vir (sep·tem′vər) *n. pl.* **·virs** or **·vi·ri** (-vi·rī) One of seven men in Roman history associated in some office, authority, or work. [<L <*septem* seven + *vir* a man]

sep·te·nar·y (sep′tə·ner′ē) *adj.* **1** Consisting of, pertaining to, or being seven. **2** Septennial. **3** Septuple. — *n. pl.* **·nar·ies** **1** The number seven; heptad. **2** A group of seven things of any kind; anything that has some definite relation to the number seven. **3** A verse containing seven feet. Also **sep′te·nar′i·us** (sep′tə·nâr′ē·əs). [<L *septenarius* <*septeni* seven each <*septem* seven]

sep·te·nate (sep′tə·nāt) *adj.* Having seven parts, or the parts in sevens. [<L *septeni* seven each (<*septem* seven) + -ATE[1]]

sep·ten·nate (sep·ten′āt) *n.* A period of seven years; a term of office or the like lasting seven years. [<F *septennat* <L *septennis* (<*septem* seven + *annus* a year)]

sep·ten·ni·al (sep·ten′ē·əl) *adj.* **1** Recurring every seven years. **2** Continuing or capable of lasting seven years. [<L *septennium* a period of seven years <*septem* seven + *annus* a year] — **sep·ten′ni·al·ly** *adv.*

Sep·ten·tri·o (sep·ten′trē·ō) The constellation Ursa Major; the Dipper. See CONSTELLATION. Also **Sep·ten′tri·on.** [<L, sing. of *septentriones,* orig. *septem triones* the seven stars of the Big Dipper <*septem* seven + *triones,* pl. of *trio* a plow ox]

sep·ten·tri·on (sep·ten′trē·on) *adj.* Of, pertaining to, or coming from the north; boreal. — *n.* The north; northern regions. [<L *septentrionalis* <*septentrio* SEPTENTRIO] — **sep·ten′tri·o·nal** (-trē·ə·nəl) *adj.*

sep·tet (sep·tet′) *n.* **1** A group of seven singers, players, or other persons, things, or parts. **2** *Music* A composition for seven voices or instruments. Also **sep·tette′.** [<G <L *septem* seven]

septi–[1] *combining form* Seven: *septilateral.* Also, before vowels, *sept–.* [<L *septem* seven]

septi–[2] *combining form* **1** A partition; fence: *septicidal.* **2** *Med.* The nasal septum: *septectomy.* Also, before vowels, *sept–.* Also **septo–.** [<L *septum* an enclosure, wall]

sep·tic (sep′tik) *adj.* **1** Of, pertaining to, or caused by sepsis. **2** Productive of putrefaction; putrid. Also **sep′ti·cal.** — *n.* Any substance that produces or promotes putrefaction. [<LL *septicus* <Gk. *sēptikos* <*sēpein* putrefy]

sep·ti·ce·mi·a (sep′tə·sē′mē·ə) *n. Pathol.* A morbid condition of the blood due to infection by pathogenic micro-organisms; blood poisoning: also called *septemia.* Also **sep′ti·cae′mi·a.** [<NL <Gk. *sēptikos* putrefactive + *haima* blood] — **sep′ti·ce′mic** (-sē′mik) *adj.*

sep·ti·ci·dal (sep′tə·sīd′l) *adj. Bot.* Dividing at the partitions: said of the dehiscence of a plant capsule that resolves itself at maturity into its component carpels by splitting through the septa. Also **sep′ti·cide.** [<SEPTI–[2] + L *caedere* cut] — **sep′ti·ci′dal·ly** *adv.*

sep·tic·i·ty (sep·tis′ə·tē) *n.* The quality of being septic; sepsis.

septic tank A tank in which sewage is allowed to remain until purified by the action of anaerobic bacteria.

sep·tif·ra·gal (sep·tif′rə·gəl) *adj. Bot.* Breaking away from the partitions: said of a form of dehiscence in plants. [<SEPTI–[2] + L *frangere* break]

sep·ti·lat·er·al (sep′tə·lat′ər·əl) *adj.* Seven-sided. [<SETPI–[1] + LATERAL]

sep·til·lion (sep·til′yən) *n.* A cardinal number: in the French system and in the United States, 1 followed by 24 ciphers; in the English system, 1 followed by 42 ciphers. — *adj.* Numbering a septillion. [<F *septillion* <L *sept(em)* + F *(m)illion* a million] — **sep·til′lionth** *adj.* & *n.*

sep·time (sep′tēm) *n.* The seventh position of a swordsman in fencing. [<L *septimus* seventh <*septem* seven]

sep·tu·a·ge·nar·i·an (sep′cho͞o·ə·jə·nâr′ē·ən, sep′to͞o-) *n.* A person 70 years old, or between 70 and 80. [<L *septuagenarius* <*septuaginta* seventy]

sep·tu·ag·e·nar·y (sep′cho͞o·aj′ə·ner′ē, sep′to͞o-) *adj.* **1** Containing or consisting of 70. **2** Pertaining to a septuagenarian.

sep·tu·a·ges·i·ma (sep′cho͞o·ə·jes′ə·mə, sep′to͞o-) *n.* A period of 70 days. [<L *septuagesima (dies)* the seventieth (day), fem. of *septuagesimus* seventieth <*septuaginta* seventy] — **sep′tu·a·ges′i·mal** *adj.*

Sep·tu·a·ges·i·ma (sep′cho͞o·ə·jes′ə·mə, sep′to͞o-) *n.* The third Sunday before Lent. Also **Septuagesima Sunday.** [<L, seventieth, on analogy with *Quadragesima, Quinquagesima*]

Sep·tu·a·gint (sep′cho͞o·ə·jint′, sep′to͞o-) *n.* An old Greek version of the Old Testament Scriptures, made in Alexandria between 280 and 130 B.C. It is the version used by the Greek Church. [<L *septuaginta* seventy; from a tradition that it was produced for Ptolemy II in 70 days by a group of 72 scholars] — **Sep′tu·a·gin′tal** *adj.*

sep·tum (sep′təm) *n. pl.* **·ta** (-tə) *Biol.* **1** A dividing wall between two cavities: the nasal *septum.* **2** A partition, as in coral or in a spore. [<L <*sepere* enclose <*sepes* a hedge] — **sep′tal** *adj.*

sep·tu·ple (sep′to͞o·pəl, -tyo͞o-, sep·to͞o′-, -tyo͞o′-) *adj.* **1** Consisting of seven; sevenfold. **2** Multiplied by seven; seven times repeated. — *v.t.* & *v.i.* **·pled, ·pling** To multiply by seven; make or become septuple. — *n.* A number or sum seven times as great as another. [<L *septuplus* <*septem* seven]

sep·tu·pli·cate (sep·to͞o′plə·kit, -tyo͞o′-) *adj.* **1** Sevenfold. **2** Raised to the seventh power. — *v.t.* (-kāt) **·cat·ed, ·cat·ing** To multiply by seven; septuple. — *n.* (-kit) One of seven like things. [<L *septuplus,* on analogy with *duplicate, triplicate,* etc.] — **sep·tu′pli·cate·ly** *adv.* — **sep·tu′pli·ca′tion** *n.*

sep·ul·cher (sep′əl·kər) *n.* A burial place, especially one found or made in a rock or solidly built of stone; tomb; vault. **2** A receptacle for relics, especially in an altar slab; a box or urn in a chapel to receive the Holy Sacrament: also called the *repository.* — **the Holy Sepulcher** The rock-hewn tomb in which the body of Jesus was buried. — *v.t.* **·chered** or **·chred, ·cher·ing** or **·chring** To place in a grave; entomb; bury. Also **sep′ul·chre** (-kər). [<OF *sepulcre* <L *sepulcrum* a burial place, tomb <*sepultus,* pp. of *sepelire* bury]

se·pul·chral (si·pul′krəl) *adj.* **1** Pertaining to a sepulcher. **2** Suggestive of burial or the grave; dismal in color or aspect, or unnaturally low or hollow in tone; gloomy: a *sepulchral* color, a *sepulchral* voice. — **se·pul′chral·ly** *adv.*

sep·ul·ture (sep′əl·chər) *n.* **1** The act of entombing; burial. **2** A sepulcher. [<OF <L *sepultura* burial <*sepultus.* See SEPULCHER.]

se·qua·cious (si·kwā′shəs) *adj.* **1** Disposed to follow; following; attendant. **2** Logically consecutive. **3** Ductile; pliable. [<L *sequax, -acis* following, pursuing <*sequi* attend, follow] — **se·qua′cious·ly** *adv.* — **se·quac·i·ty** (si·kwas′ə·tē) *n.*

se·quel (sē′kwəl) *n.* **1** Something which follows and serves as a continuation; a development from what went before. **2** A narrative discourse which, though entire in itself, develops from a preceding one. **3** A consequence; upshot; result. [<OF *sequelle* <L *sequela* <*sequi* follow]

se·que·la (si·kwē′lə) *n. pl.* **·lae** (-lē) **1** One who or that which follows. **2** *Pathol.* A morbid condition resulting from a preceding disease. [<L, a sequel]

se·quence (sē′kwəns) *n.* **1** The process or fact of following in space, time, or thought; succession or order: also **se′quen·cy.** **2** Order of succession; arrangement. **3** A number of things following one another, considered collectively; a series. **4** An effect or consequence. **5** *Music* A regular succession of similar melodic phrases at different pitches. **6** *Eccl.* In the Eucharistic liturgy, a prose or hymn sung immediately after the gradual and before the gospel. **7** In card games, a set of three or more cards next each other in value; in poker, a straight. **8** A section of motion-picture film presenting a single episode, without time lapses or interruptions. **9** *Math.* An ordered succession of quantities, as $2x$, $4x^2$, $8x^3$, $16x^4$ . . . $2^n x^n$, a finite sequence, and $x_1, x_2, x_3, \ldots x_n, \ldots$, or x_n, an infinite sequence. See synonyms under TIME. [<MF *séquence* <L *sequentia* <*sequens, -entis,* ppr. of *sequi* follow]

sequence of tenses See under TENSE[2].

se·quent (sē′kwənt) *n.* That which follows; a consequence; result. — *adj.* **1** Following in the order of time; succeeding. **2** Consequent; resultant. [<OF <L *sequens.* See SEQUENCE.]

se·quen·tial (si·kwen′shəl) *adj.* **1** Characterized by or forming a sequence, as of parts. **2** Sequent. — **se·quen·ti·al·i·ty** (si·kwen′shē·al′ə·tē) *n.* — **se·quen′tial·ly** *adv.*

se·ques·ter (si·kwes′tər) *v.t.* **1** To place apart; separate; segregate. **2** To seclude; withdraw: often used reflexively. **3** *Law* To take (property) into custody until a controversy, claim, etc., is settled or satisfied. **4** In international law, to confiscate and control (enemy property) by preemption. [<OF *sequestrer* <LL *sequestrare* remove, lay aside <*sequester* a trustee] — **se·ques′tra·ble** *adj.*

se·ques·tered (si·kwes′tərd) *adj.* Retired; secluded.

se·ques·trant (si·kwes′trənt) *n.* **1** That which sets apart, divides, or sequesters. **2** *Chem.* A substance which forms a colorless mixture with certain metals precipitated in a solution.

se·ques·trate (si·kwes′trāt) *v.t.* **·trat·ed, ·trat·ing** **1** To seize, especially for the use of the government; confiscate. **2** To take possession of for a time, with a view to the just settlement of the claims of creditors. **3** To seclude; sequester. [<LL *sequestratus,* pp. of *sequestrare.* See SEQUESTER.] — **se·ques·tra·tion** (sē′kwes·trā′shən, sek′wəs-) *n.* — **se·ques·tra·tor** (sē′kwes·trā′tər, si·kwes′trā·tər) *n.*

se·ques·trum (si·kwes′trəm) *n. pl.* **·tra** (-trə) *Pathol.* A piece of dead bone remaining in its place, but separated from the living bone. [<NL <L, something separated, orig. neut. of *sequester* standing apart]

se·quin (sē′kwin) *n.* **1** An obsolete gold coin of the Venetian republic later introduced into Turkey: also spelled *zecchino.* **2** A spangle or coinlike ornament sewn on clothing. [◆F <Ital. *zecchino* <*zecca* the mint <Arabic *sikka* a coining-die]

se·quoi·a (si·kwoi′ə) *n.* One of a genus *(Sequoia)* of gigantic trees (family *Taxodiaceae*) of the western United States, including only two species, the redwood *(S. sempervirens)* and the mammoth or "big" tree *(S. gigantea* or *Sequoiadendron giganteum),* both natives of California. [<NL, after *Sikwayi,* 1770?–1843,

a half-breed Cherokee Indian who invented the Cherokee alphabet]

Sequoia National Park A government reservation in east central California including Mount Whitney and containing many giant sequoias and redwoods; 602 square miles; established, 1890.

ser (sir) See SEER[2].

ser– Var. of SERO–.

se·ra (sir′ə) Plural of SERUM.

sé·rac (sā·ràk′) *n. Geol.* One of the largest angular blocks or tower-shaped forms into which glacier ice breaks in passing down steep inclines. [< dial. F (Swiss), a cheese put up in cubic form; from its resemblance to the shape of this cheese]

ser·a·file (ser′ə·fīl) See SERREFILE.

se·ra·glio (si·ral′yō, -räl′-) *n.* **1** A harem. **2** Loosely, a place of debauchery. **3** The old palace of the sultans at Constantinople with its mosques, official buildings, and gardens. **4** Hence, any residence of a sultan. Also **se·rail** (se·rāl′). [<Ital. *serraglio* an enclosure, ult. <LL *serrare,* var. of L *serare* lock up <*sera* lock; used to render Turkish *serai* a palace, lodging, because of similarity of sound]

se·ra·i (se·rä′ē) *n.* **1** In the Orient, an inn or caravansary. **2** A Turkish palace. [<Turkish <Persian *sarāī*]

Se·ra·je·vo (se′rä·yā′vō) See SARAJEVO.

se·ra·pe (se·rä′pē) *n.* A shawl or blanketlike outer garment worn in Latin America, especially in Mexico: also spelled *zarape.* [<Sp.]

ser·aph (ser′əf) *n. pl.* **ser·aphs** or **ser·a·phim** (ser′ə·fim) A celestial being; an angel of the highest order. *Is.* vi 2–6. [Back formation from *Seraphim,* pl. <LL <Hebrew *sərāphīm,* ? ult. <*sāraph* burn] **— se·raph·ic** (si·raf′ik), **se·raph′i·cal** *adj.* **— se·raph′i·cal·ly** *adv.*

Seraphic Doctor Saint Bonaventura: so called because of the religious purity and fervor of his life.

ser·a·phim (ser′ə·fim) *n.* **1** Plural of SERAPH: also **ser′a·phin** (-fin). **2** *pl.* **·phims** A seraph, as in *Isaiah* vi 2, 6: an erroneous usage.

ser·a·phine (ser′ə·fēn) *n.* A coarse-toned musical instrument, a kind of harmonium, played with a keyboard. Also **ser·a·phi·na** (ser′ə·fē′·nə). [<SERAPH + -INE[1]]

Se·ra·pis (si·rā′pis) In Egyptian mythology, a god of the lower world in the form of the dead Apis. **— Se·ra′pic** *adj.*

ser·as·kier (ser′əs·kir′, si·ras′kir) *n.* A Turkish minister of war, or commander in chief. Also **se·ras·ker** (si·ras′kər), **ser·as·quier** (ser′əs·kir′). [<Turkish <Persian *ser asker* head of an army <*ser* head + Arabic *'asker* an army]

Ser·bi·a A republic founded from Yugoslavia; capital, Belgrade; formerly an independent kingdom. *Serbo-Croatian* Sr·bi·ja. — *adj. & n.* **Serb, Ser′bi·an.**

Ser·bo-Cro·a·tian *n.* **1** The South Slavic language of the former Yugoslavia, including all the old languages and dialects of Serbia, Montenegro, Bosnia, Herzegovina, Croatia, Slovonia, and Dalmatia. **2** A native of the former Yugoslavia; any person whose native tongue is Serbo-Croatian, Also spelled Servo-Croatian. Also **Ser′·bo-Cro′at** — *adj.* Of or pertaining to the people of Yugoslavia, or to their language.

Ser·bo·ni·an Bog or **Lake** (sûr·bō′nē·ən) A large marshy tract once existing near the Red Sea littoral of Lower Egypt, in which Herodotus said whole armies were engulfed; hence, a strait; difficulty; complication: also spelled *Sirbonian.*

Serbs, Croats, and Slovenes, Kingdom of the See YUGOSLAVIA.

ser·dab (sûr′dab, sûr·däb′) *n.* A secret cell within the masonry of an ancient Egyptian tomb, in which images of the deceased were deposited. [<Arabic *serdāb* a cellar <Persian, an icehouse, a grotto]

sere[1] (sir) See SEAR[1].

sere[2] (sir) *n. Ecol.* The series of changes found in a given plant formation from the initial to the ultimate stage. ◆ Homophones: *cere, sear.* [Back formation <SERIES] **— ser′al** *adj.*

se·rein (sə·raṅ′) *n. Meteorol.* A fine rain that falls sometimes from an apparently clear sky, especially in the tropics after sunset. [<F]

ser·e·nade (ser′ə·nād′) *n.* **1** An evening song, usually that of a lover beneath his lady's window; also, by extension, music performed in honor of some person in front of his residence in the open air at night. **2** The music for such a song. — *v.t. & v.i.* **·nad·ed, ·nad·ing** To entertain with a serenade. [<F *sérénade* <Ital. *serenata* <*sereno* serene, open air <L *serenus* clear, serene; infl. in meaning by L *sera (hora)* the evening (hour), fem. of *serus* late] **— ser′·e·nad′er** *n.*

ser·e·na·ta (ser′ə·nä′tə) *n. Music* **1** A dramatic cantata, often composed as a complimentary offering for a royal personage. **2** A serenade. [<Ital. See SERENADE.]

ser·en·dip·i·ty (ser′ən·dip′ə·tē) *n.* The faculty of happening upon or making fortunate discoveries when not in search of them. [Coined by Horace Walpole (1754), in *The Three Princes of Serendip* (Ceylon), the heroes of which make such discoveries]

se·rene (si·rēn′) *adj.* **1** Clear, or fair and calm; having its brightness undimmed: a *serene* sky. **2** Marked by peaceful repose; tranquil; unruffled; placid: a *serene* spirit. **3** Of exalted rank: chiefly in the titles of certain continental European princes: His *Serene* Highness. See synonyms under SEDATE. — *n. Rare* or *Poetic* **1** Clearness, or a serene or clear region. **2** Calmness; placidity. [<L *serenus*] **— se·rene′ly** *adv.* **— se·ren·i·ty** (si·ren′ə·tē), **se·rene′ness** *n.*

Se·reth (zā′ret) See SIRET.

serf (sûrf) *n.* **1** A person who is attached to the estate on which he lives; loosely, a peasant. **2** Figuratively, one in servile subjection. ◆ Homophone: *surf.* [<OF <L *servus* a slave] **— serf′dom, serf′age, serf′hood** *n.*

serge (sûrj) *n.* **1** A strong twilled fabric made of wool yarns and characterized by a diagonal rib on both sides of the cloth. **2** In the Middle Ages, a coarse woolen cloth. **3** A rayon lining fabric. ◆ Homophone: *surge.* [<OF *sarge, serge* <L *serica (lana)* (wool) of the Seres <*Seres* the Seres, an eastern Asian people]

ser·geant (sär′jənt) *n.* **1** A non-commissioned military officer ranking next above a corporal. See the table under GRADE. **2** In the United States, a police officer of rank next below a captain (sometimes lieutenant); in England, one next below an inspector. **3** *Brit.* Formerly, one who held land of the king by tenure of military service, or a squire or gentleman of less than knightly rank; one of the household officials of a sovereign. **4** A sergeant at arms. **5** A sergeant at law. **6** A constable or bailiff. **7** The sergeant fish. Also *serjeant.* **— color sergeant** A sergeant who standard. **— lance sergeant** A corporal acting carries the regimental or national colors or as sergeant. **— mess sergeant** A non-commissioned officer who plans meals, issues rations, and superintends the company mess under the mess officer. [<OF *sergent, serjant* <L *serviens,* ppr. of *servire* serve] **— ser′gean·cy, ser′geant·cy, ser′geant·ship** *n.*

sergeant at arms **1** An executive officer in a legislative body who enforces order; especially, *Brit.,* the attendant on the lord chancellor or on the speaker of the House of Commons. **2** The title of certain court or city officials who have ceremonial duties.

sergeant at law Formerly, a barrister of high order or rank taking social but not professional precedence of king's counsel.

sergeant fish **1** A large, dusky fish *(Rachycentron canadus)* of warm seas, with a broad black band suggesting a chevron on the sides. **2** The robalo.

sergeant major **1** In the U.S. Army, the principal enlisted assistant to the adjutant of a battalion or higher unit. **2** The highest non-commissioned officer in the U.S. Marine Corps.

Sergeant Major of the Army The highest enlisted rank in the U.S. Army. See the table under GRADE.

ser·geant·y (sär′jən·tē) *n. Brit.* Formerly, a tenure of lands on condition of rendering some personal or menial service directly to the king or to some nobleman; also, the service rendered.

Ser·gi·pe (sər·zhē′pə) A state in eastern Brazil on the Atlantic, 8,502 square miles; capital, Aracajú.

se·ri·al (sir′ē·əl) *adj.* **1** Of the nature of a series. **2** Published in a series at regular intervals. **3** Successive; arranged in rows or ranks: also **se·ri·ate** (sir′ē·it, -āt). — *n.* **1** A novel or other story regularly presented in successive instalments, as in a magazine, on radio or television, or in motion pictures. **2** *Brit.* A periodical. **3** A subdivision of a military unit organized for transport or for marching. ◆ Homophone: *cereal.* [<NL *serialis* <L *series* a row, order] **— se′ri·al·ly, se′ri·ate·ly** *adv.*

serial comma A comma placed before an *and* which joins the last two in a series of three or more substantives, adjectives, phrasal modifiers, or adverbs. ◆ Opinion is evenly divided as to whether the serial comma is needed. The best argument for its use, which is observed in this dictionary, is that it makes the meaning unmistakable and the relation between the various modifiers unmistakably clear: The motion was opposed by Lords Arundel, Salisbury, Somerset, and Say and Sele. If the last comma (the serial comma) were omitted here, there could be confusion as to the name of the last peer, which is *Say and Sele.*

se·ri·al·ize (sir′ē·əl·īz′) *v.t.* **·ized, ·iz·ing** To arrange or publish in serial form. **— se′ri·al·i·za′tion** *n.*

serial number A number assigned to a person, object, item of merchandise, etc., as a means of identification.

serial symmetry **1** The symmetry of serial parts. **2** Metamerism. Also **serial homology.**

se·ri·a·tim (sir′ē·ā′tim, ser′ē-) *adv.* One after another; in connected order; serially. [<Med. L <L *series,* on analogy with *gradatim*]

se·ri·a·tion (sir′ē·ā′shən) *n.* The arrangement of unorganized material or data in an orderly series.

se·ri·ceous (si·rish′əs) *adj.* **1** Lustrous like silk; silky. **2** *Bot.* Having fine, soft, appressed hairs, as the leaves of certain plants. [<L *sericeus* <*sericum* silk, orig. neut. of *sericus* silken, belonging to the Seres. See SERGE.]

ser·i·cin (ser′ə·sin) *n. Biochem.* A viscous substance formed on the surface of raw silk fiber and usually removed by boiling in soapy water. [<L *sericus* silken + -IN]

ser·i·cul·ture (ser′ə·kul′chər) *n.* The raising and care of silkworms for the production of raw silk. [Contraction of F *séricículture* <L *sericum* silk + *cultura* a raising, culture] **— ser′i·cul′tur·al** *adj.* **— ser′i·cul′tur·ist** *n.*

ser·i·e·ma (ser′i·ē′mə, -ā′mə) *n.* **1** A long-legged crested bird *(Cariama cristata)* of the plains of Brazil and Paraguay. **2** The smaller species, Burmeister's cariama *(Chunga burmeisteri)* of Argentina. [<NL *seriema, cariama* <Tupian *siriema, sariama* crested]

se·ries (sir′ēz) *n. pl.* **se·ries** **1** An arrangement of one thing after another; a connected succession of persons, books, objects, observations, etc., on the basis of like relationships. **2** *Math.* An ordered, finite or infinite arrangement of expressions, each a function of another, the sum of which is indicated, as $x_1 + x_2 + x_3 \ldots + x_n + \ldots$, or $\sum_{i=1}^{\infty} x_i$ for infinite series, and $x_1 + x_2 + x_3 \ldots + x_n$, or $\sum_{i=1}^{n} x_n$ for finite series. **3** *Chem.* A group of compounds or elements resembling one another more or less in their chemical characters and crystalline forms, or differing from each other by a constant difference of certain factors. **4** *Electr.* An arrangement of sources or utilizers of electricity, as batteries or lamps, in which the positive electrode of one is connected with the negative electrode of another. **5** *Gram.* A group of successive coordinate elements of a sentence. [<L <*serere* join, weave together]

series motor A motor whose field and armature windings are in series.

series winding *Electr.* The winding of a dynamo or an electric motor in such a way that the field-magnet coil is a part of the armature and exterior circuit. Compare SHUNT-WOUND. **— se·ries-wound** (sir′ēz·wound′) *adj.*

ser·if (ser′if) *n. Printing* A hairline; a light line or stroke crossing or projecting from the end of a main line or stroke in a letter: also spelled *ceriph.* [<Du. *schreef* a stroke, line <*schrijve* write <L *scribere*]

ser·i·graph (ser′ə·graf, -gräf) *n.* **1** An artist's color print made by serigraphy. **2** A device for testing the tensile strength and elasticity of textile fabrics, paper, leather, rubber, etc.,

under specified conditions. [<L *sericum* silk + GRAPH]

se·rig·ra·phy (si·rig′rə·fē) *n.* An adaptation of the silk-screen process in which hand-made color prints are made on any desired surface by the use of stencils painted upon or cemented to the screen, one stencil to each color, the finished print being in all details the work of an individual artist in distinction from those commercially reproduced by silk-screen printing. — **se·rig′ra·pher** *n.* — **ser·i·graph·ic** (ser′ə·graf′ik) *adj.*

ser·in (ser′in) *n.* A small greenish finch (*Serinus canarius*), related to and closely resembling the wild canary, but smaller. [<F; ult. origin unknown]

ser·ine (ser′ēn, -in) *n. Biochem.* A white crystalline amino acid, $C_3H_7NO_3$, obtained as a dissociation product of various proteins. Also **ser′in.** [<L *sericus* silken + -INE[2]; so called because originally obtained from dissociation of sericin]

se·rin·ga (si·ring′gə) *n.* Any of several Brazilian trees (genus *Hevea*) yielding rubber. [<Pg. <L *syringa* SYRINGA]

Se·rin·ga·pa·tam (sə·ring′gə·pə·tam′) A town in southern Mysore, India; former seat of the sultans of Mysore, 7 miles NE of Mysore city.

se·ri·o-com·ic (sir′ē·ō·kom′ik) *adj.* Mingling mirth and seriousness, or the comic with an appearance of gravity. Also **se′ri·o-com′i·cal.** [<*serio-* partly serious (<SERIOUS) + COMIC]

se·ri·ous (sir′ē·əs) *adj.* **1** Grave and earnest in quality, feeling, or disposition; thoughtful; sober. **2** Said, planned, or done with full practical intent; not jesting or making a false pretense; being or done in earnest. **3** Of grave importance; weighty; attended with considerable danger or loss: a *serious* matter, a *serious* accident. **4** Particularly attentive to religion. [<MF *sérieux* <LL *seriosus* <L *serius*] — **se′ri·ous·ly** *adv.* — **se′ri·ous·ness** *n.*

Synonyms: dangerous, demure, earnest, grave, great, important, momentous, sedate, sober, solemn. A *serious* person is *sedate, sober, solemn*; a *serious* purpose is *earnest*; a *serious* illness is *dangerous*; a *serious* business is *important*, and may be *momentous*. See BAD, GOOD, IMPORTANT, SEDATE. *Antonyms*: careless, gay, insignificant, jocose, jolly, light, slight, thoughtless, trifling, trivial, volatile.

ser·jeant (sär′jənt) See SERGEANT.

ser·mon (sûr′mən) *n.* **1** A discourse based on a passage or text of the Bible, delivered as part of a church service; hence, any discourse intended for the pulpit. **2** Any discourse of a serious kind; an exhortation to duty or a formal reproof. See synonyms under SPEECH. [<AF *sermun*, OF *sermon* <L *sermo, -onis* talk]

ser·mon·et (sûr′mən·et′) *n.* A brief sermon. Also **ser′mon·ette′.** [Dim. of SERMON]

ser·mon·ic (sər·mon′ik) *adj.* Pertaining to or of the nature of a sermon or sermonizing; didactic. Also **ser·mon′i·cal.**

ser·mon·ize (sûr′mən·īz) *v.t.* & *v.i.* **·ized, ·iz·ing** To compose or deliver sermons (to); address or discourse at length in a didactic manner. — **ser′mon·iz′er** *n.*

Sermon on the Mount The discourse of Jesus found recorded in *Matt.* v, vi, vii: properly distinguished from the **Sermon on the Plain,** *Luke* vi 20–49.

sero- *combining form* Connected with or related to serum: *serology.* Also, before vowels, *ser-.* [<L *serum* whey]

se·rol·o·gy (si·rol′ə·jē) *n.* The science of serums and their actions: also called *orrhology.* [SERO- + -LOGY] — **se·ro·log·i·cal** (sir′ə·loj′i·kəl) *adj.*

se·roon (si·ro͞on′) *n.* A bale of goods, as Spanish dates, figs, etc., packed in an animal's hide: also spelled *ceroon.* [<Sp. *serón* a hamper, crate <*sera* a large basket]

se·ros·i·ty (si·ros′ə·tē) *n.* **1** The condition of being serous or watery. **2** A watery or serous secretion. Also **se′rous·ness.** [<F *sérosité* <NL *serositas* <*serosus* SEROUS]

se·ro·ther·a·py (sir′ō·ther′ə·pē) *n. Med.* The treatment of disease by injecting into the veins serum from immunized animals.

se·rot·i·nous (si·rot′ə·nəs) *adj.* Produced, blossoming, or developing relatively late in the season: used also figuratively. Also **se·rot′i·nal, ser·o·tine** (ser′ə·tin, -tīn). [<L *serotinus* <*serus* late]

ser·o·to·nin (ser′ə·tō′nin) *n. Biochem.* A crystalline protein found in the serum of clotted blood and in various animals and plants: it is associated with a wide range of physiological processes, especially in the brain and blood vessels. [<SERO- + TON- + -IN]

se·rous (sir′əs) *adj.* Pertaining to, producing, or resembling serum. [<F *séreux* <L *serosus* <*serum* serum, whey]

serous fluid Any of the thin watery fluids secreted by the serous membranes.

serous membrane *Anat.* A tissue of endothelial cells lining the large cavities of the body, as the peritoneum and the pleura.

ser·ow (ser′ō) *n.* Any of a genus (*Capricornis*) of antelopes ranging from the Himalayas to Japan; especially, the large goat antelope (*C. bubalinus*). [<Tibetan]

Ser·pens (sûr′penz) *Astron.* An equatorial constellation, the Serpent, between Corona Borealis and Libra. See CONSTELLATION. [<L, a serpent]

ser·pent (sûr′pənt) *n.* **1** A scaly, limbless reptile; a snake, especially when of large size. **2** Anything of serpentine form or appearance, as a certain kind of twisting firework. **3** An obsolete musical wind instrument, bent several times in serpentine form. **4** An insinuating and treacherous person. **5** Satan. [<OF <L *serpens, -entis* a serpent, creeping thing, orig. ppr. of *serpere* creep]

serpent fence A worm fence. See under FENCE.

ser·pen·tine (sûr′pən·tēn, -tīn) *adj.* **1** Pertaining to or like a serpent; zigzag or sinuous; crawling sinuously. **2** Subtle; cunning. — *n.* A massive or fibrous, often mottled green or yellow, hydrous magnesium silicate, the fibrous varieties of which are important sources of asbestos, the massive as architecturally decorative stones. [<OF *serpentin* <L *serpentinus* <*serpens* SERPENT]

Ser·pen·to (sûr′pən·tō) *n. pl.* **·to** The Shoshone Indians: a tribe belonging to the Shoshoneans.

ser·pi·go (sər·pī′gō) *n. Pathol.* An eruption on the skin; spreading ringworm. [<Med. L <L *serpere* creep] — **ser·pig·i·nous** (sər·pij′ə·nəs) *adj.*

Ser·ra (ser′rä), **Junípero,** 1713–84, Spanish Franciscan missionary in California.

ser·ra·noid (ser′ə·noid) *adj.* Of or pertaining to the *Serranidae*, a family of fishes including the sea bass, striped bass, and their allies. — *n.* A serranoid fish. [<NL <*Serranus*, genus name (<L *serra* a saw) + Gk. *eidos* form]

ser·rate (ser′āt, -it) *adj.* Toothed or notched like a saw, as the margins of certain leaves. Also **ser′rat·ed.** [<L *serratus* <*serra* a saw]

ser·ra·tion (se·rā′shən) *n.* **1** The state of being edged as with saw teeth. **2** *Biol.* One of the projections of a serrate formation, or a series of such projections. Also **ser·ra·ture** (ser′ə·chər). [<NL *serratio, -onis* <L *serratus*, pp. of *serrare* saw <*serra* a saw]

ser·re·file (ser′ə·fīl) *n.* **1** One of the non-commisioned officers drawn up in line in the rear of a troop or squadron. **2** *pl.* The line of serrefiles. Also spelled *serafile.* [<F <*serrer* tighten (<LL *serrare* lock <L *sera* a lock) + *file* a file[1]]

ser·ried (ser′ēd) *adj.* Compacted in rows or ranks, as soldiers in company formation. [Pp. of obs. *serry* press close together in ranks <MF *serré*, pp. of *serrer.* See SERREFILE.]

ser·ri·form (ser′ə·fôrm) *adj.* Formed like a saw; saw-toothed. [<L *serra* a saw + -FORM]

ser·ru·late (ser′ə·lit, -lāt, ser′yə-) *adj.* Diminutively serrate; serrate with small, fine teeth. Also **ser′ru·lat′ed** (-lā′tid). [<L *serrula*, dim. of *serra* a saw + -ATE[1]]

ser·ru·la·tion (ser′ə·lā′shən, ser′yə-) *n.* **1** The state of being or becoming serrulate; a fine notching. **2** One of the teeth of a serrulate margin.

Ser·to·ri·us (sər·tôr′ē·əs, -tō′rē-), **Quintus,** 121?–72 B.C., Roman general; assassinated.

ser·tu·lar·i·an (sûr′cho͞o·lâr′ē·ən) *n. Zool.* One of a genus (*Sertularia*) of branching colonial hydroids common between tide lines. [<NL <L *sertula*, dim. of *serta* a garland]

se·rum (sir′əm) *n. pl.* **se·rums** or **se·ra** (sir′ə) **1** The more fluid constituent of blood, lymph, milk, and similar animal liquids. **2** The serum of the blood of an animal which has been subjected to the process of immunization; any antitoxic blood serum or lymph. **3** Whey; serum of milk. **4** Any similar secretion. [<L, whey, watery fluid]

serum sickness Illness caused by inoculation of serum.

serum therapy Serotherapy.

ser·val (sûr′vəl) *n.* An African wildcat (*Felis serval*), yellow with black spots and having a ringed tail and long legs. [<F <Pg. *lobo cerval* <*lobo* a wolf (<L *lupus*) + *cerval* a stag <L *cervus*]

ser·vant (sûr′vənt) *n.* **1** A person employed to work for another; especially, in law, one employed to render service and assistance in some trade or vocation; an employee. **2** A person hired to assist in domestic matters, sometimes living within the employer's house; hired help. **3** A slave or bondman. **4** A government official. [<OF, orig. ppr. of *servir* SERVE]

serve (sûrv) *v.* **served, serv·ing** *v.t.* **1** To work for, especially as a servant; be in the service of. **2** To be of service to; wait on. **3** To promote the interests of; aid; help: to *serve* one's country. **4** To obey and give homage to: to *serve* God. **5** To satisfy the requirements of; suffice for. **6** To perform the duties connected with, as a public office. **7** To go through (a period of enlistment, term of punishment, etc.). **8** To furnish or provide, as with a regular supply. **9** To offer or bring food or drink to (a guest, etc.); wait on at table. **10** To bring and place on the table or distribute among guests, as food or drink. **11** To operate or handle; tend: to *serve* a cannon. **12** To copulate with: said of male animals. **13** In tennis, etc., to put (the ball) in play by hitting it to one's opponent. **14** *Law* **a** To deliver (a summons or writ) to a person. **b** To deliver a summons or writ to. **15** *Naut.* To wrap (a rope, stay, etc.), as with marlin or spun yarn, so as to strengthen or protect. — *v.i.* **16** To work as or perform the functions of a servant; wait at table. **17** To perform the duties of any employment, office, etc. **18** To go through a term of service, as in the army or navy. **19** To be suitable or usable, as for a purpose; perform a function. **20** To be favorable, as weather. **21** In tennis, etc., to put the ball in play. — *n.* **1** In tennis, etc., the delivering of the ball by striking it toward an opponent. **2** The turn of the server. [<OF *servir* <L *servire* <*servus* a slave]

Synonyms: advance, aid, assist, attend, benefit, help, minister, obey, promote, subserve, succor, suffice. See ACCOMMODATE. *Antonyms*: command, control, desert, disobey, hinder, obstruct, oppose, retard, thwart, withstand.

serv·er (sûr′vər) *n.* **1** One who serves; especially, an attendant aiding a priest at low mass. **2** That which is used in serving, as a tray. **3** The male of any domestic animal used for breeding. **4** The player who serves the ball in games.

Ser·ve·tus (sər·vē′təs), **Michael,** 1511–53, Spanish physician and theologian, burned at the stake in Geneva for heresy. Also *Sp.* **Miguel Ser·ve·to** (ser·vā′tō). — **Ser·ve′tian** (-shən) *adj.* & *n.*

Ser·vi·a (sûr′vē·ə) A former name for SERBIA.

ser·vice (sûr′vis) *n.* **1** Assistance or benefit afforded another: to render a *service*; to be of *service.* **2** A useful result or product of labor which is not a tangible commodity: in the plural, often contrasted with *goods.* **3** The manner in which one is waited upon or served: The *service* in this restaurant is only fair. **4** A system of labor and material aids used to accomplish some regular work or accommodation for the public: telephone *service*, train *service*, postal *service.* **5** A division of public employment devoted to a particular function: the diplomatic *service.* **6** Employment as a public servant in government: to enter public *service.* **7** A public duty or function: jury *service.* **8** Any branch of the armed forces: to enter the *service.* **9** Military duty or assignment: to volunteer for foreign *service.*

10 Devotion to God, as demonstrated by obedience and good works. **11** A formal and public exercise of worship: to attend Sunday *services.* **12** A ritual prescribed for a particular ministration or observance: a burial *service*; a marriage *service.* **13** The music for a liturgical office or rite. **14** The state or position of a servant, especially a domestic servant. **15** A set of tableware for a specific purpose: a tea *service.* **16** Installation, maintenance, and repair of an article provided a buyer by a seller. **17** *Law* **a** The legal communication of a writ or process to a designated person. **b** Duty or work rendered by one person for another. **c** A duty rendered by a feudal tenant as recompense to his lord. **18** In tennis and similar games, the act or manner of serving a ball. **19** *Naut.* The protective cordage wrapped around a rope. **20** In animal husbandry, the copulation or covering of a female. — *adj.* **1** Pertaining to or for service. **2** Used by, or for the use of, servants or tradespeople: a *service* entrance. **3** Of, pertaining to, or belonging to a military service: a *service* flag. **4** Worn during active military service: distinguished from *dress*: a *service* cap, hat, or uniform. — *v.t.* **·viced, ·vic·ing 1** To maintain or repair: to *service* a car or radio. **2** To supply service to. [<OF *servise* <L *servitium* < *servus* a slave]

Synonyms (noun): advantage, avail, benefit, good, purpose, serviceableness, use, utility. See PROFIT, SACRAMENT, UTILITY.

Ser·vice (sûr′vis), **Robert William,** 1874–1958, Canadian writer.

ser·vice·a·ble (sûr′vis·ə·bəl) *adj.* **1** That can be made of service; beneficial; such as serves or can serve a useful purpose. **2** Capable of rendering long service; durable. **3** *Obs.* Obliging; attentive. See synonyms under GOOD, USEFUL. — **ser′vice·a·ble·ness, ser′vice·a·bil′i·ty** *n.* — **ser′vice·a·bly** *adv.*

ser·vice·ber·ry (sûr′vis·ber′ē) *n. pl.* **·ries** The Juneberry; the shadberry. [<*service,* the service tree + BERRY]

service book A book containing the offices, or forms of service, of any church that uses liturgical forms.

service cap A military uniform cap of cotton, wool, or felt, with visor.

service club An organization to promote community welfare and further the interests of its members.

service coat A single-breasted jacket worn with the U.S. Army service uniform: also called a *blouse.*

service hat A hat worn in the U.S. Army when full-dress uniform is not worn: its shape and material vary according to requirements of climate. Formerly, a khaki-colored felt hat with broad flat brim, and crown dented in four places.

ser·vice·man (sûr′vis·man′) *n. pl.* **·men** (-men′) A member of one of the armed forces. — **ser′vice·wom′an** *n. fem.*

service man A man who performs services of maintenance, supply, repair, etc.

service ribbon A distinctively colored ribbon worn on the U. S. service uniform to indicate the wearer's right to the corresponding campaign medal or decoration.

service station 1 A place for supplying automobiles with gasoline, oil, water, etc. **2** A place where adjustments and repairs can be made and parts obtained for electrical or mechanical devices.

service stripe A stripe worn on the sleeve of a uniform to denote years of service or employment, as in an army or on a police force: also *hash mark.*

service tree 1 An Old World tree *(Sorbus domestica)* with odd-pinnate leaves, panicled cream-colored flowers, and small edible fruit. **2** The American mountain ash *(S. americana).* **3** The Juneberry. [Orig. *serves,* pl. of obs. *serve,* OE *syrfe* <L *sorbus*]

service uniform The regulation uniform to be worn during routine or active service in the army or navy.

ser·vi·ette (sûr′vē·et′, -vyet′) *n.* A table napkin. [<MF, prob. < *servir* SERVE]

ser·vile (sûr′vil) *adj.* **1** Having the spirit of a slave; slavish; abject: a *servile* flatterer. **2** Pertaining to or appropriate for slaves or servants: a *servile* insurrection, *servile* employment. **3** Being of a subject class; existing in a condition of servitude. **4** Obedient; subject: with *to*: *servile* to applause. **5** *Ling.* Not belonging to the original root; serving only to modify the construction or pronunciation of a word. **6** Designating tenures of land in England subject to conditions distinguished from those of freehold, as labor instead of rent. See synonyms under BASE, OBSEQUIOUS. — *n.* **1** A slave, or one of slavish spirit; menial. **2** *Ling.* A letter, syllable, or sound used only to modify a word, and not part of its radical form. [<L *servilis* < *servus* a slave] — **ser′vile·ly** *adv.* — **ser·vil′i·ty, ser′vile·ness** *n.*

serv·ing (sûr′ving) *n.* **1** A portion of food for one person. **2** The act of one who or that which serves. — *adj.* Used for dealing out food.

ser·vi·tor (sûr′və·tər) *n.* **1** One who waits upon and serves another; an attendant; follower; servant. **2** Formerly, an undergraduate at Oxford University partly supported by a college grant and partly earning his living by service. [<OF <LL <L *servire* SERVE] — **ser′·vi·tor·ship′** *n.*

ser·vi·tude (sûr′və·to͞od, -tyo͞od) *n.* **1** The condition of a slave; slavery; bondage; now, especially, enforced service as a punishment for crime: penal *servitude.* **2** A state of subjection to any claim, demand, or control: *servitude* to vice. **3** The condition or duties of a servant; menial service. **4** The subjection of a person to a person or to a thing, or of a thing to a person or thing. **5** *Law* An easement; a right that one man may have to use the land of another for a special purpose. See synonyms under BONDAGE. [<MF <L *servitudo* < *servus* a slave]

servo– *combining form* In technical use, auxiliary: *servomechanism.* [<L *servus* a slave]

Ser·vo–Cro·a·tian (sûr′vō·krō·ā′shən) See SERBO-CROATIAN.

ser·vo·mech·a·nism (sûr′vō·mek′ə·niz′əm) *n.* Any of various relay devices which can be actuated by a comparatively weak force in the automatic control of a complex machine, instrument, operation, or process, as artillery fire, the course of an airplane or ship, etc. [<SERVO- + MECHANISM]

ser·vo·mo·tor (sûr′vō·mō′tər) *n.* An electric motor connected with and supplying power for a servomechanism.

ses·a·me (ses′ə·mē) *n.* An East Indian herb *(Sesamum indicum),* containing seeds which are used as food and as a source of the pale yellow **sesame oil,** used as an emollient. — **open sesame** A charm to secure admission, originally to the robbers' cave in the story of Ali Baba and the Forty Thieves in the *Arabian Nights.* [<F *sésame* <L *sesamum, sesama* <Gk. *sēsamon, sēsamē,* prob. < an Oriental source]

ses·a·moid (ses′ə·moid) *adj. Anat.* **1** Having the shape of a sesame seed; obovate; nodular: said specifically of certain bones, cartilages, and nodules. **2** Pertaining to a sesamoid. — *n.* A sesamoid bone or cartilage, as the kneecap. [<L *sesamoides* <Gk. *sēsamoeidēs* < *sēsamon* sesame + *eidos* form]

sesqui– *prefix* **1** One and a half; one-half more; one and a half times: *sesquicentennial.* **2** *Chem.* Indicating the presence of three atoms of one element and two of another in a compound, as chromium *sesquioxide,* Cr_2O_3. [<L *sesqui-* one-half more < *semis* half + *que* and]

ses·qui·cen·ten·ni·al (ses′kwi·sen·ten′ē·əl) *adj.* Of or pertaining to a century and a half. — *n.* A 150th anniversary, or its celebration.

ses·qui·pe·da·li·an (ses′kwi·pi·dā′lē·ən) *adj.* **1** Measuring a foot and a half. **2** Long and ponderous, as polysyllabic words. Also **ses·quip·e·dal** (ses·kwip′ə·dəl, ses′kwi·pēd′l). — *n.* A very long word. [<L *sesquipedalis* < *sesqui-* more by a half + *pes, pedis* a foot]

ses·qui·plane (ses′kwi·plān′) *n. Aeron.* A type of biplane one wing of which has half or less than half the area of the other.

ses·sile (ses′il) *adj.* **1** *Bot.* Attached by its base, without a stalk, as a leaf. **2** *Zool.* Fixed; sedentary; firmly or permanently attached. [<L *sessilis* sitting down, stunted < *sessus,* pp. of *sedere* sit] — **ses·sil′i·ty** *n.*

ses·sion (sesh′ən) *n.* **1** The sitting together of a legislative assembly, court, etc., for the transaction of business. **2** A single meeting or series of meetings of an assembly, court, or other body, for conducting business. **3** The governing body of a Presbyterian Church congregation. **4** In some educational institutions, a term. **5** *Law* The term for which a court or legislative body sits continuously for the transaction of business. **6** *pl.* The sitting of a certain court: the quarter-*sessions*; and in the United States, the Court of *Sessions,* a court of criminal jurisdiction; any one of certain courts, especially in England: general *sessions,* petty *sessions.* **7** *Obs.* The act of sitting, or the state of one who is seated. ◆ Homophone: *cession.* [<F <L *sessio, -onis* < *sessus,* pp. of *sedere* sit] — **ses′sion·al** *adj.* — **ses′sion·al·ly** *adv.*

sess·pool (ses′po͞ol′) See CESSPOOL.

ses·terce (ses′tûrs) *n. pl.* **·ter·ces** (-tûr′sēz) A coin of ancient Rome equal to 1/4 denarius: originally of silver, later of bronze. Also **ses·ter′ti·us** (-shē·əs). [<L *sestertius (nummus)* (a coin) that is two and a half < *semis* half + *tertius* third; so called because worth two and a half asses]

ses·ter·ti·um (ses·tûr′shē·əm) *n. pl.* **·ti·a** (-shē·ə) An ancient Roman money of account equivalent to 1,000 sesterces. [<L, short for *(mille) sestertium* (a thousand) sesterces, gen. pl. of *sestertius* a sesterce]

ses·tet (ses·tet′) *n.* **1** The last six lines of a sonnet; any six-line stanza. **2** *Music* A sextet. [<Ital. *sestetto* < *sesto* sixth (<L *sextus*) + *-etto,* dim. suffix]

ses·ti·na (ses·tē′nə) *n.* A verse form consisting of six stanzas of six, generally unrimed, lines each and a three-line envoy: the end words of the first stanza are progressively changed in order in the remaining five, and appear medially and terminally in the envoy. Also **ses′tine** (-tin). [<Ital. < *sesto* sixth <L *sextus*]

Ses·tos (ses′tos) A ruined town on the Dardanelles in Turkey in Europe. See ABYDOS.

set[1] (set) *v.* **set, set·ting** *v.t.* **1** To put in a certain place or position; place. **2** To put into a fixed or immovable position, condition, or state: to *set* brick; to *set* one's jaw. **3** To bring to a specified condition or state: *Set* your mind at ease; to *set* a boat adrift. **4** To restore to proper position for healing, as a broken bone. **5** To place in readiness for operation or use: to *set* a trap. **6** To adjust according to a standard: to *set* a clock. **7** To adjust (an instrument, dial, etc.) to a particular calibration or position. **8** To place knives, forks, etc., on (a table) in preparing for a meal. **9** To bend the teeth of (a saw) to either side alternately. **10** To appoint or establish; prescribe: to *set* a time or limit. **11** To fix or establish a time for: We *set* our departure for noon. **12** To assign for performance, completion, etc.; allot: to *set* a task. **13** To assign to some specific duty or function; appoint; station: to *set* a guard. **14** To cause to sit. **15** To present or perform so as to be copied or emulated: to *set* the pace; to *set* a bad example. **16** To give a specified direction to; direct: He *set* his course for the Azores. **17** To put in place so as to catch the wind: to *set* the jib. **18** To place in a mounting or frame, as a gem. **19** To stud or adorn with gems: to *set* a crown with rubies. **20** To place (a hen) on eggs to hatch them. **21** To place (eggs) under a fowl or in an incubator for hatching. **22** To place (a price or value): with *by* or *on*: to *set* a price on an outlaw's head. **23** To point (game): said of hunting dogs. **24** *Printing* **a** To arrange (type) for printing; compose. **b** To put into type, as a sentence, manuscript, etc. **25** *Music* To arrange (music) for words or write (words) to accompany music. **26** To describe (a scene) as taking place: to *set* the scene in Monaco. **27** In the theater, to arrange (a stage) so as to depict a scene. **28** In some games, as bridge, to defeat. — *v.i.* **29** To go or pass below the horizon, as the sun. **30** To wane; decline. **31** To sit on eggs, as fowl. **32** To become hard or firm; solidify; congeal. **33** To begin a journey; start: with *forth, out, off,* etc. **34** To have a specified direction; tend. **35** To hang or fit, as clothes. **36** To point game: said of hunting dogs. **37** *Bot.* To begin development or growth, as a rudimentary fruit. — **to set about** To start doing; begin. — **to set against 1** To balance; compare. **2** To make unfriendly to; prejudice against. — **to set aside 1** To place apart or to one side. **2** To reject; dismiss. **3** To declare null and void. — **to set back** To reverse; hinder. — **to set down 1** To place on a sur-

face. **2** To write or print; record. **3** To judge or consider. **4** To attribute; ascribe. **— to set forth** **1** To state or express. **2** To start, as a journey. **— to set in** **1** To begin. **2** To blow or flow toward shore, as wind or tide. **— to set off** **1** To put apart by itself. **2** To serve as a contrast or foil for; enhance. **3** To cause to explode. **— to set on** To incite or instigate; urge. **— to set out** **1** To present to view; display; exhibit. **2** To lay out or plan. **3** To begin a journey. **4** To begin any enterprise. **5** To plant. **— to set to** **1** To start; begin. **2** To start fighting. **— to set up** **1** To place in an upright position. **2** To raise. **3** To place in power, authority, etc. **4** **a** To construct or build. **b** To put together; assemble. **c** To found; establish. **5** To provide with the means to start a new business. **6** To cause to be heard: to *set up* a cry. **7** To propose or put forward (a theory, etc.). **8** To cause. **9** *Colloq.* **a** To pay for the drinks, etc., of; treat. **b** To pay for (drinks, etc.). **10** *Colloq.* To encourage; exhilarate. *— adj.* **1** Established by authority or agreement; prescribed; appointed: a *set* time; a *set* method. **2** Customary; conventional: a *set* phrase. **3** Deliberately and systematically conceived; formal: a *set* speech. **4** Fixed and motionless; rigid. **5** Fixed in opinion or disposition; obstinate. **6** Formed; built; made: with a qualifying adverb: deep-*set* eyes; a low-*set* man. **7** Ready; prepared: to get *set*. *— n.* **1** The act or condition of setting. **2** Permanent change of form, as by chemical action, cooling, pressure, strain, etc. **3** The arrangement, tilt, or hang of a garment, hat, sail, etc. **4** Carriage or bearing: the *set* of his shoulders. **5** The sinking of a heavenly body below the horizon. **6** The direction of a current or wind. **7** A young plant ready for setting out; a cutting, slip, or seedling. **8** *Mech.* The spread in opposite directions given to the alternate teeth of certain saws. **9** *Psychol.* A temporary condition assumed by an organism preparing for a particular response or activity. **10** In tennis, a group of games completed when one side wins six games, or in the event of a score tied at five games, the group of games terminated when one side wins two more games consecutively. [OE *settan* cause to sit. Akin to SIT.]

Synonyms (verb): adapt, adjust, appoint, arrange, assign, determine, dispose, establish, fix, locate, place, plant, post, prescribe, put, regulate, settle, station. See ALLOT, PLANT, PREPARE, PUT, RAISE. *Antonyms*: detach, disestablish, disturb, eradicate, loosen, overthrow, remove, transfer, unsettle, uproot.

set[2] (set) *n.* **1** A number of persons regarded as associated through status, common interests, etc.: a new *set* of customers. **2** A social group having some exclusive character; coterie; clique: the fast *set*. **3** A number of things belonging together and customarily used together: a *set* of instruments; a *set* of teeth; a *set* of dishes. **4** A number of specific things so grouped as to form a whole: a *set* of lyrics; a *set* of motives; a *set* of features. **5** A group of volumes issued together and related by common authorship or subject. **6** The number of couples needed for a square dance or country dance. **7** The group of movements that compose a square dance. **8** In motion pictures, the complete assembly of properties, structures, etc., required in a scene. **9** Radio or television receiving equipment assembled for use. See synonyms under CLASS, FLOCK. [<OF *sette* <L *secta* a sect; infl. by SET[1]. Doublet of SECT.]

Set (set) In Egyptian mythology, the animal-headed god of darkness, night, and evil; opponent and slayer of Osiris. Also *Seth*.

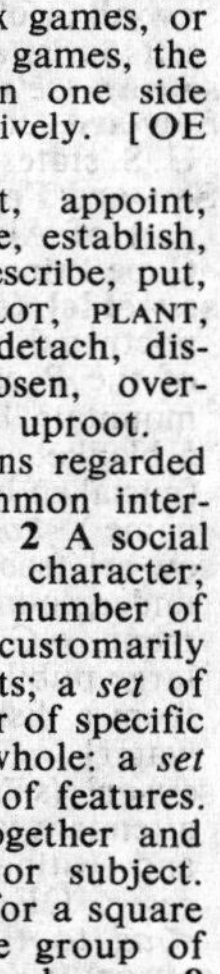

SET

se·ta (sē′tə) *n. pl.* **·tae** (-tē) *Biol.* **1** A bristle, or slender, bristlelike part or process of an organism. **2** A slender spine or prickle. **3** A coarse, rigid hair. [<L]

set–a·side (set′ə·sīd′) *n.* An amount or quantity of something put in reserve for future use.

se·ta·ceous (si·tā′shəs) *adj.* **1** Bristly; more or less covered with bristles. **2** Of the nature or form of setae. Also **se′tal** (sēt′l). [<NL *setaceus* <L *seta* a bristle]

set·back (set′bak′) *n.* **1** A check; forced return to a point already passed; a reverse in fortune or plan. **2** A countercurrent; eddy. **3** *Archit.* In mammoth buildings, the stepping of sections in such a way that, while the first section is erected on the street line, the remaining sections are erected in step formation, so as to permit of better light and ventilation in the street below.

Sète (set) A port on the Mediterranean in southern France SW of Montpellier: formerly *Cette*.

Set·e·bos (set′ə·bos) A supposed deity of the Patagonians: alluded to in Shakespeare's *The Tempest* as the power worshiped by Sycorax, the witch, mother of Caliban.

Seth (seth) A masculine personal name. [< Hebrew, appointed]

— Seth The third son of Adam. *Gen.* v 3.

— Seth The Egyptian god Set.

set–ham·mer (set′ham′ər) *n.* A hammer the head of which may be easily removed from the handle. See illustration under HAMMER.

seti– *combining form* A bristle: *setiferous*. Also, before vowels, **set–**. [<L *seta* a bristle]

se·tif·er·ous (si·tif′ər·əs) *adj.* Bearing setae; bristly. Also **se·tig·er·ous** (si·tij′ər·əs). [< SETI- + -FEROUS]

se·ti·form (sē′tə·fôrm) *adj.* Having the form of a seta; setaceous.

set–off (set′ôf′, -of′) *n.* **1** An offset or counterpoise. **2** A decorative contrast or setting. **3** A counterclaim or the discharge of a debt by a counterclaim. **4** *Archit.* A ledge; offset.

se·ton (sē′tən) *n. Surg.* A bristle, or a few threads, passed through a fold of the skin and left there to produce an issue for relief of subjacent parts. [<Med. L *seto, -onis*, appar. <*seta* silk <L, a bristle]

Se·ton (sē′tən), **Ernest Thompson**, 1860–1946, U.S. naturalist and writer born in England.

se·tose (sē′tōs) *adj.* Setaceous; bristly. Also **se′tous.** [<L *setosus* <*seta* a bristle]

set·screw (set′skrōō′) *n.* A screw used as a clamp; especially, one having a cup instead of a point: used to screw through one part and slightly into another to bind the parts tightly.

set·tee[1] (se·tē′) *n.* **1** A long wooden seat with a high back. **2** A sofa suitable for two or three people. [<SET[1] + *-ee*, dim. suffix; infl. in meaning by SEAT]

set·tee[2] (se·tē′) *n.* A Mediterranean vessel with long prow, single deck, two or three masts, and lateen sails. [<Ital. *saettia*, prob. <*saetta* an arrow]

set·ter (set′ər) *n.* **1** One who or that which sets. **2** One of a breed of medium-sized, silky-coated, lithe bird dogs of great intelligence, originally trained to indicate the presence of game birds by crouching, now by standing rigid. — **English setter** A setter, white, or white marked with black, tan, yellow, or orange, trained since the 16th century to find and point game. The most famous British strains, the Laveracks and the Llewellins, are popular in field trials and bench shows. **— Gordon setter** A setter having a black coat marked with tan, chestnut, or red, probably crossbred with black-and-tan spaniels: named for the original breeder, the Duke of Gordon, and used especially for cover shooting. — **Irish (or red) setter** A handsome, useful, and companionable golden-chestnut or red setter, probably a setter-spaniel-pointer combination: extensively bred in America and very popular.

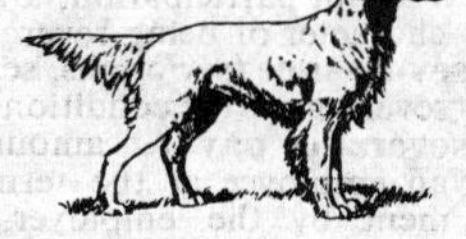

ENGLISH SETTER
(About 25 inches high at the shoulder)

set·ting (set′ing) *n.* **1** The act of anything that sets. **2** An insertion. **3** That in which something is set; a frame; environment. **4** The act of indicating game like a setter. **5** A number of eggs placed together for hatching. **6** The music adapted to a song or poem. **7** The scene or background of a play or narrative. **8** The apparent sinking of the sun, etc., below the horizon. **9** The tableware set out for one person.

set·ting–out (set′ing·out′) *n. Colloq.* The trousseau and household equipment given to a bride or newly married couple by the parents.

set·tle (set′l) *v.* **·tled, ·tling** *v.t.* **1** To put in order; set to rights; to *settle* affairs. **2** To put firmly in place; establish or fix permanently or as if permanently: He *settled* himself on the couch. **3** To free of agitation or disturbance; calm; quiet: to *settle* one's nerves. **4** To cause (sediment or dregs) to sink to the bottom. **5** To cause to subside or come to rest; make firm or compact: to *settle* dust or ashes. **6** To make clear or transparent, as by causing sediment or dregs to sink. **7** *Colloq.* To make quiet or orderly: One blow *settled* him. **8** To decide or determine finally, as an argument or difference. **9** To pay, as a debt; satisfy, as a claim. **10** To establish residents or residence in (a country, town, etc.). **11** To establish as residents. **12** To establish in a permanent occupation, home, etc. **13** To decide (a suit at law) by agreement between the litigants. **14** *Law* To make over or assign (property) by legal act: with *on* or *upon*. *— v.i.* **15** To come to rest, as after moving about or flying. **16** To sink gradually; subside. **17** To sink or come to rest, as dust or sediment. **18** To become more firm or compact. **19** To become clear or transparent, as by the sinking of sediment. **20** To take up residence; establish one's abode or home. **21** To come to a decision; determine; resolve: with *on, upon*, or *with*. **22** To pay a bill, etc. **— to settle down** **1** To start living a regular, orderly life, especially after a period of wandering or irresponsibility. **2** To apply steady effort or attention. *— n.* **1** A long seat or bench, generally of wood, with a high back, originally to direct the draft up the chimney and to provide a warm nook: often with arms and sometimes having a chest from seat to floor. **2** A wide step; platform. **3** *Obs.* A ledge. [OE *setlan* <*setl* a seat]

Synonyms (verb): adjust, allay, arrange, calm, compose, decide, determine, establish, finish, fix, pay, quiet, regulate. Compare CONFIRM, PAY[1], RATIFY, REQUITE, SET. *Antonyms*: agitate, confuse, derange, disarrange, discompose, disorder, disturb, fluster, flutter, mix, muss.

set·tle·ment (set′l·mənt) *n.* **1** The act of settling, or state of being settled; specifically, an adjustment of affairs by public authority. **2** Colonization. **3** Subsidence of a structure, or its effect. **4** An area of country newly occupied by those who intend to live and labor there; a colonized region, village, or town. **5** *Brit.* A regular or settled place of living; one's dwelling place. **6** An accounting; adjustment; liquidation in regard to amounts. **7** The conveyance of property in such form as to provide for some future object, especially the support of members of the settler's family; also, the property so settled. **8** A religious community. **9** *pl.* A collection or series of frontier dwellings and clearings: distinguished from wild, unsettled territory. **10** Formerly, Negro quarters on a southern plantation. **11** A welfare institution established in a congested part of a city, having a resident staff of workers to conduct educational and recreational activities for the community: also **settlement house.**

set·tler (set′lər) *n.* **1** One who settles; especially, one who establishes himself in a colony or new country; a colonist. **2** One who or that which settles or decides something.

set·tling (set′ling) *n.* **1** The act of settling or sinking. **2** *pl.* Dregs; sediment.

set–to (set′tōō′) *n.* A bout at fighting, fencing, arguing, or any other mode of contest. [< *set to*; see under SET]

Se·tú·bal (sə·tōō′bəl) A port of south central Portugal, on **Setúbal Bay**, an inlet of the Atlantic off the west coast of Portugal. Formerly **St. Yves** (sänt ēvz).

set·u·lose (sech′ōō·lōs) *adj.* Clothed or covered with setae or bristles. [<NL, dim. of L *seta* a bristle]

set–up (set′up′) *n.* **1** Physique; physical build; make-up. **2** Carriage of the body; bearing.

3 *U.S. Slang* A system or scheme of organization or construction; the salient elements of a situation; circumstances. 4 *U.S. Slang* A contest or match arranged to result in an easy victory; a contest in which the strength of the contestants is so unequal that the result is easily foreseen; also, the weaker of two such contestants. 5 *U.S. Colloq.* Ice, soda water, etc., provided to a customer who has brought his own liquor.

Seu·rat (sœ·rà′), **Georges,** 1859–91, French painter.

Se·van (se·vän′), **Lake** The largest lake in Transcaucasia, in central Armenian U.S.S.R.; 546 square miles. *Turkish* **Gök·cha** (gœk′chä).

Se·vas·ti·an (se·väs′tē·än′) Russian form of SEBASTIAN.

Se·vas·to·pol (si·vas′tə·pōl, sev′əs·tō′pəl, *Russian* si′väs·tô′pəl) A port and naval base in the SW Crimea, Russian S.F.S.R.: formerly *Sebastopol.*

sev·en (sev′ən) *adj.* Being one more than six. — *n.* 1 The sum of one and six. 2 The symbols (7, vii, VII) representing that number. 3 A playing card with seven spots. 4 Something composed of seven units. [OE *seofon*]

Seven against Thebes In Greek legend, the seven heroes (Adrastus, Amphiaraus, Capaneus, Hippomedon, Parthenopaeus, Polynices, and Tydeus) who unsuccessfully marched on Thebes to restore Polynices to the throne which had been usurped by his brother Eteocles: all were killed save Adrastus. See ANTIGONE, EPIGONI.

Seven Cities of Ci·bo·la (sē′bō·lä) Seven Zuñi towns sought by the early Spanish explorers as centers of hidden gold and fabulous wealth: found in what is now New Mexico by Coronado about 1540.

Seven Deadly Sins Pride, Lust, Envy, Anger, Covetousness, Gluttony, and Sloth as personified in medieval literature: also known as *cardinal sins.*

sev·en·fold (sev′ən·fōld′) *adj.* 1 Seven times as many or as great. 2 Made up of seven; septuple. 3 Folded seven times. — *adv.* In sevenfold manner or degree.

Seven Hills of Rome The group of seven hills on and around which the city of Rome was built: the Palatine, Caelian, Esquiline, Capitoline, Quirinal, Viminal, and Aventine.

seven lively arts All forms of popular entertainment; originally, motion pictures, vaudeville, popular music, popular dancing, writing in the vernacular, musical shows, comic strips. [from *The Seven Lively Arts* (1924) by Gilbert Seldes]

Seven Pines See FAIR OAKS.

Seven Seas See under SEA.

sev·en·teen (sev′ən·tēn′) *adj.* Being seven more than ten. — *n.* The sum of ten and seven, or the symbols (17, xvii, XVII) representing this number. [OE *seofontȳne*]

sev·en·teenth (sev′ən·tēnth′) *adj.* 1 Seventh in order after the tenth. 2 Being one of seventeen equal parts. — *n.* 1 One of seventeen equal parts of anything. 2 A seventeenth object or unit. [OE *seofontēotha* < *seofontȳne* seventeen]

sev·en·teen–year locust (sev′ən·tēn′yir′) A dark–bodied, wedge–shaped cicada (*Magicicada septemdecim*) native to the eastern United States: the northern variety has an underground nymphal stage of 17 years, and the southern variety of 13 years.

sev·enth (sev′ənth) *adj.* 1 Next in order after the sixth. 2 Being one of seven equal parts. — *n.* 1 One of seven equal parts; the quotient of a unit divided by seven. 2 A seventh object or unit. 3 *Music* **a** The interval between any note and the seventh note above it on the diatonic scale, counting the starting point as one. **b** A note separated by this interval from any other, considered with reference to that other; specifically, the seventh above the keynote. **c** Two notes at this interval written or sounded together. **d** The resulting dissonance. See INTERVAL (def. 5). — *adv.* In the seventh order, place, or rank: also, in formal discourse, **sev′enth·ly.** [ME *seventhe* <SEVEN + -TH, replacing OE *seofande* and *seofotha*]

sev·enth–day (sev′ənth·dā′) *adj.* 1 Pertaining to the seventh day of the week. 2 Advocating the observance of the seventh day as the Sabbath: a *Seventh–Day* Adventist.

seventh day 1 Saturday; the seventh day of the week; the Sabbath of the Jews and of some other religious groups. 2 Saturday, in the speech of the Society of Friends.

Seventh–Day Adventist See under ADVENTIST.

seventh heaven 1 The highest abode or condition of happiness. 2 The highest heaven according to various ancient systems of astronomy or in certain theologies.

sev·en·ti·eth (sev′ən·tē·ith) *adj.* 1 Tenth in order after the sixtieth. 2 Being one of seventy equal parts. — *n.* 1 One of seventy equal parts; the quotient of a unit divided by seventy. 2 A seventieth object or unit. [ME *seventithe* <SEVENTY + -TH]

sev·en·ty (sev′ən·tē) *adj.* Being ten more than sixty, or seven times ten. — *n.* *pl.* **·ties** The sum of ten and sixty, or the symbols (70, lxx, LXX) representing this number. [OE (*hund-*) *seofontig*] — **sev′en·ty·fold′** *adj.* & *adv.*

sev·en–up (sev′ən·up′) *n.* A game of cards: also called *all fours, old sledge.*

Seven Wonders of the World The seven works of man considered the most remarkable in the ancient world: generally considered to be the Egyptian pyramids, the hanging gardens of Babylon, the temple of Diana at Ephesus, the statue of Zeus by Phidias at Olympia, the Mausoleum at Halicarnassus, the Colossus of Rhodes, and the Pharos or lighthouse of Alexandria.

sev·er (sev′ər) *v.t.* 1 To put or keep apart; separate. 2 To cut or break into two or more parts. 3 To break off; dissolve, as a relationship or tie. — *v.i.* 4 To come or break apart or into pieces. 5 To go away or apart; separate. See synonyms under BREAK, CUT, REND, SEPARATE. [<AF *severer,* OF *sevrer* <L *separare* SEPARATE]

sev·er·a·ble (sev′ər·ə·bəl) *adj.* 1 Capable of being severed. 2 *Law* That can be severed from something to which it is attached or of which it forms part: said of a contract consisting of several obligations, when non–fulfilment of one obligation does not invalidate the contract.

sev·er·al (sev′ər·əl, sev′rəl) *adj.* 1 Being of an indefinite number, more than two, yet not large; divers. 2 Considered individually; pertaining to an individual; single; separate. 3 *Law* Pertaining individually and separately to each tenant or party to a bond: opposed to *joint:* a joint and *several* note. 4 Individually different; various or diverse. [<AF <Med. L *separalis* <L *separ* separate, distinct]

sev·er·al·ly (sev′ər·əl·ē, sev′rəl·ē) *adv.* 1 Individually; separately. 2 Respectively.

sev·er·al·ty (sev′ər·əl·tē, sev′rəl-) *n.* *pl.* **·ties** 1 *Law* The holding of land in one's own right without participation; a sole tenancy. 2 The character of being several or distinct.

sev·er·ance (sev′ər·əns, sev′rəns) *n.* The act of severing, or the condition of being severed.

severance pay An amount of money paid to an employee at the termination of employment by the employer, based on regular wages or salary and often related to length of service.

se·vere (si·vir′) *adj.* 1 Trying to one's powers or endurance; hard to bear. 2 Rigorous in the treatment of others; unsparing; harsh; merciless. 3 Conforming to rigid rules; marked by pure and simple excellence; accurate. 4 Serious and austere in disposition or manner; grave; sedate; austerely plain. 5 Causing sharp pain or anguish; extreme: a *severe* pain. [<MF *sévère* <L *severus*] — **se·vere′ly** *adv.*

Synonyms: austere, rigid, rigorous, stern, stiff, unrelenting. That is *severe* which is devoid of all softness, mildness, indulgence, or levity, or (in literature and art) devoid of unnecessary ornament, amplification, or embellishment of any kind; as, a *severe* style; as said of anything painful, *severe* signifies such as heavily taxes endurance or power to resist; as, a *severe* pain, fever, or winter. *Rigid* signifies primarily *stiff,* resisting any effort to change its shape, its will, or course of conduct. *Rigorous* is nearly akin to *rigid,* but is a stronger word, having reference to action or active qualities: a *rigid* rule may be *rigorously* enforced. *Strict* signifies bound or stretched tight, tense, strenuously exact. *Stern* unites harshness and authority with strictness or severity; *stern,* as said even of inanimate objects, suggests something authoritative or forbidding. *Austere* signifies severely simple or temperate, *strict* in self–restraint or discipline, and similarly *unrelenting* toward others. See ARDUOUS, AUSTERE, BAD, DIFFICULT, HARD, IMPLACABLE, MOROSE, VIOLENT.

se·ver·i·ty (si·ver′ə·tē) *n.* *pl.* **·ties** 1 The quality of being severe. 2 Harshness or cruelty of disposition or treatment; power of paining or distressing. 3 Extreme strictness in character or rigor in operation; exactness. 4 Seriousness; austerity. 5 Strict conformity to truth or law. See synonyms under ACRIMONY, VIOLENCE.

Sev·ern (sev′ərn) A river in northern Wales and western England, flowing 210 miles NE, SE, south, and SW from near Aberystwith to the Bristol Channel.

Severn River A river in NW Ontario, Canada, flowing 610 miles NE to Hudson Bay.

Se·ver·na·ya Zem·lya (sā′vir·nə·yə zim·lyä′) An archipelago in the Arctic Ocean in Krasnoyarsk territory, Russian S.F.S.R.; total, 14,300 square miles.

Se·ver·sky (si·ver′skē), **Alexander de,** 1894–1974, U.S. airplane designer and manufacturer born in Russia.

Se·ve·rus (si·vir′əs), **Lucius Septimius,** 146–211, Roman emperor; rebuilt Hadrian's Wall across northern England.

Sé·vi·gné (sā·vē·nyā′), **Madame de,** 1626–96, Marie de Rabutin–Chantal, French writer.

Se·ville (sə·vil′) A city of SW Spain; the leading city of Andalusia. *Spanish* **Se·vil·la** (sā·vēl′lyä).

Sè·vres (se′vr′) *n.* A fine porcelain originally made at Sèvres, France. Also **Sèvres ware.**

Sè·vres (se′vr′) A city of north central France on the Seine just SW of Paris.

sew (sō) *v.* **sewed, sewed** or **sewn, sew·ing** *v.t.* 1 To make, mend, or fasten with needle and thread. 2 To affect by sewing: often with *up.* — *v.i.* 3 To work with needle and thread. [OE *siwan, siowian*]

sew·age (sōō′ij) *n.* 1 The waste matter from domestic, commercial, and industrial establishments carried off in sewers. 2 Loosely, sewerage. [<SEW(ER) + -AGE]

Sew·all (sōō′əl), **Samuel,** 1652–1730, Massachusetts jurist and diarist.

se·wan (sē′wən) See SEAWAN.

Sew·ard (sōō′ərd), **William Henry,** 1801–72, U. S. statesman; secretary of state 1861–69.

Sew·ard Peninsula (sōō′ərd) The westernmost part of Alaska, extending 210 miles west to Cape Prince of Wales; 90–140 miles wide.

se·wel·lel (si·wel′el) *n.* A brown, burrowing, nocturnal, vegetarian rodent (*Aplodontia rufa*) of the Pacific coast north of California; the mountain beaver. [<Chinook *shewallal* dual, a blanket of two sewellel skins sewn together (mistaken by Lewis and Clark for the animal's name) < *ogwoolal* a sewellel]

sew·er[1] (sōō′ər) *n.* 1 A conduit, usually laid underground, to carry off drainage and excrement. ◆ Collateral adjective: *cloacal.* 2 Any large public drain. [<OF *seuwiere* a channel from a fish pond, ult. <L *ex-* off + *aqua* water]

sew·er[2] (sōō′ər) *n.* Formerly, in England, an attendant who supervised the serving of meals and seating of guests. Also **sew′ar.** [<AF *asseour,* OF *asseoir* cause to sit <L *assidere* < *ad-* to + *sedere* sit]

sew·er[3] (sō′ər) *n.* One who or that which sews.

sew·er·age (sōō′ər·ij) *n.* 1 A system of sewers. 2 Systematic draining by sewers. 3 Sewage.

sew·ing (sō′ing) *n.* 1 The act, business, or occupation of one who sews. 2 That which is sewed; material on which one is at work with needle and thread; needlework.

sewing bee A social gathering of the women and girls of a community to sew for some charitable purpose.

sewing circle 1 A group of women, usually organized within a church or other welfare organization, meeting periodically to sew for some charitable purpose. 2 A meeting of such a group. Also **sewing society.**

sewing machine A machine for stitching or sewing cloth, leather, etc.

sewing silk Finely twisted silk thread used for sewing.

sewn (sōn) Alternative past participle of SEW.

sex (seks) *n.* 1 Either of two divisions, male and female, by which organisms are distinguished with reference to the reproductive functions. 2 Males or females collectively. 3 The character of being male or female. 4 The

activity or phenomena of life concerned with sexual desire or reproduction. 5 *Colloq.* Sexual gratification. **—the fair sex** Women. [<OF *sexe* <L *sexus*, prob. orig. division]

sex- *combining form* Six: *sexpartite.* Also spelled *sexi-*. [<L *sex* six]

sex·a·ge·nar·i·an (sek′sə·jə·nâr′ē·ən) *n.* A person between sixty and seventy years of age. —*adj.* 1 Sixty years old, or between sixty and seventy. 2 Of or pertaining to a sexagenarian. [<SEXAGENARY]

sex·ag·e·nar·y (seks·aj′ə·ner′ē) *adj.* 1 Of or pertaining to the number sixty. 2 Sixty years old, or between sixty and seventy. —*n. pl.* **·nar·ies** A sexagenarian. [<L *sexagenarius* <*sexageni* sixty each <*sexaginta* sixty]

Sex·a·ges·i·ma (sek′sə·jes′ə·mə) *n.* The second Sunday before Lent. Also **Sexagesima Sunday.** [<L *sexagesima (dies)* sixtieth (day). See SEXAGESIMAL.]

sex·a·ges·i·mal (sek′sə·jes′ə·məl) *adj.* Pertaining to or founded on the number sixty. [<Med. L *sexagesimalis* <L *sexagesimus* sixtieth <*sexaginta* sixty]

sex·an·gle (seks′ang′gəl) *n.* A six-angled figure; a hexagon. [<L *sexangulus* <*sex* six + *angulus* an angle] **—sex′an′gu·lar** (-ang′gyə·lər), **sex′an′gled** *adj.* **—sex′an′gu·lar·ly** *adv.*

sex appeal 1 A physical quality or charm which attracts sexual interest. 2 *Slang* The capacity to excite interest or attention: Tax reductions have *sex appeal*.

sex cell A gamete; a sperm or ovum.

sex·cen·te·nar·y (seks·sen′tə ·ner′ē, seks′sen·ten′ər·ē) *adj.* Pertaining to or consisting of six hundred, especially six hundred years. —*n. pl.* **·nar·ies** 1 A period of six hundred years or a collection of six hundred units. 2 A six-hundredth anniversary. [<L *sexcenteni* six hundred each <*sexcenti* six hundred <*sex* six + *centum* a hundred]

sex chromosome *Biol.* A chromosome whose presence in the reproductive cells of certain plants and animals is associated with the determination of the sex of offspring. In mammals the ovum carries two X-chromosomes and sperm an X- and a Y-chromosome; females are produced by a paired XX in the fertilized ovum, males by a paired XY. Also called *allosome, heterochromosome*.

sex·en·ni·al (seks·en′ē·əl) *adj.* Happening once every six years, or lasting six years. — *n.* A sixth anniversary. [<L *sexennis, sexennium* <*sex* six + *annus* a year] **—sex·en′ni·al·ly** *adv.*

sex·fid (seks′fid) *adj. Bot.* Six-cleft, as a calyx. Also **sex′i·fid.** [< SEX- + -FID]

sex gland A gonad; either of the testes or ovaries.

sex hygiene The division of hygiene having to do with sexual conduct as related to the health of the individual and community.

sexi- Var. of SEX-.

sex·ism (seks′iz·əm) *n.* 1 Sexual prejudice or discrimination, esp. against women. 2 Behavior or beliefs that perpetuate or encourage stereotypes of social roles based on sex. [<SEX + -ISM, on analogy with *racism*] — **sex′ist** *n., adj.*

sex·less (seks′lis) *adj.* Having no sex; neuter. **—sex′less·ly** *adv.* **—sex′ less·ness** *n.*

sex linkage *Biol.* hat type of inheritance which is associated with the transmission of genes attached to the sex chromosomes. **—sex-linked** (seks′lingkt′) *adj.*

sex·ol·o·gy (seks·ol′ə·jē) *n.* The study of human sexual behavior. [<SEX + -(O)LOGY] **—sex·o·log·ic** (sek′sə·loj′ ik) or **·i·cal** *adj.* **—sex·ol′o·gist** *n.*

sex·par·tite (seks·pär′tīt) *adj.* Divided into or made up of six parts, as a groined arch or other structure. [<NL *sexpartitus* <L *sexus* six + *partitus* PARTITE]

sex·ploi·ta·tion (seks′ploi·t+210 ′shən) *n.* The commercial exploitation of interest in sex, as by means of pornography.

sex·pot (seks′pot′) *n. Slang* A very sexy woman.

sex ratio The ratio of males to females in a given population, usually expressed as the number of males per 100 females.

sext (sekst) *n.* 1 One of the canonical hours; the office for the sixth hour or noon. 2 The sixth book of the decretals. [<LL *sexta* <L *sexta (hora)* the sixth (hour), fem. of *sextus* sixth <*sex* six]

Sex·tans seks′tənz) An equatorial constellation between Leo and Hydra; the Sextant. See CONSTELLATION. [<L, a sextant]

sex·tant (seks′tənt) *n.* 1 An instrument for

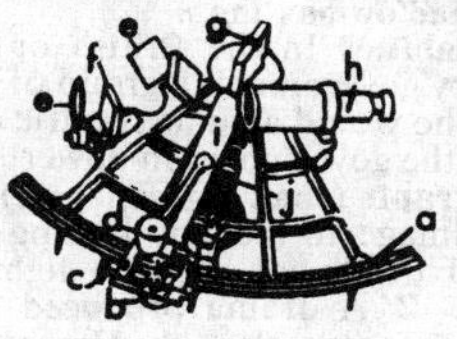

SEXTANT

a. Scale. *d.* Reading lens. *g.* Index glass.
b. Clamp screw. *e.* Glass shades. *h.* Telescope.
c. Tangent screw. *f.* Horizon glass. *i.* Movable arm.
j. Handle.

measuring angular distance between two objects, as between a heavenly body and the horizon, by a double reflection from two mirrors: used especially in determining latitude at sea. 2 The sixth part of a circle; an arc of 60 degrees. [<L *sextans, antis* the sixth part <*sextus* sixth]

sex·tar·i·us (seks·târ′ē·əs) *n. pl.* **·tar·i·i** (-târ′ē·ī) An ancient Roman measure of capacity. See CONGIUS. [<L, a sixth part <*sextus* sixth <*sex* six]

sex·tet (seks·tet′) *n.* 1 A band of six singers or players; also, a musical composition for six parts. 2 Any collection of six persons or things. Also **sex·tette′.** [Alter. of SESTET; refashioned after L *sex* six]

sex·tile (seks′til) *adj.* Indicated or measured by a distance of 60 degrees. —*n.* 1 *Astron.* The aspect of two planets at a distance of 60 degrees from each other. 2 *Stat.* One of the divisions of a frequency distribution containing exactly one sixth of the total number of cases or observations included. [<L *sextilis (mensis)* the sixth (month, i.e., August <*sextus* sixth]

sex·til·lion (seks·til′yən) *n.* A cardinal number: in the French system and in the United States, 1 followed by 21 ciphers; in the English system, 1 followed by 36 ciphers. [<F <L *sex* six + F *(m)illion* a million]

sex·to·dec·i·mo (seks′tō·des′ə·mō) *n.* Sixteenmo. [< *sextusdecimus* sixteenth <*sextus* sixth + *decimus* tenth]

sex·ton (seks′tən) *n.* 1 A janitor of a church having charge also of ringing the bell, overseeing burials, etc.; also, formerly, a gravedigger. 2 Any of certain carrion beetles (genus *Necrophorus*) that bury small dead animals by excavating the ground beneath them: also called *burying beetle*. The larvae feed on the maggots in the rotting flesh. ◆ Homophone: *sextan.* [<AF *segerstaine,* OF *secrestein* <Med. L *sacristanus.* Doublet of SACRISTAN.] **—sex′ton·ship** *n.*

sex·tu·ple (seks′too͞·pəl, -tyoo-, seks·too͞′-, -tyoo͞′-) *adj.* 1 Sixfold. 2 Multiplied by six; six times repeated. 3 *Music* Having six beats to the measure. —*v.t.* **·pled, ·pling** To make sextuple; multiply by six. —*n.* A number or sum six times as great as another. [<L *sextus* sixth < *sex* six, formed on analogy with *quadruple, quintuple*, etc.]

sex·tu·plet (seks′too͞·plit. -tyoo͞-, seks·too͞′-, -tyoo͞′-) *n.* 1 A set of six similar things. 2 One of six offspring produced at a single birth. [<SEXTUPLE on analogy with *triplet*]

sex·tu·pli·cate (seks·too͞′plə ·kit, -tyoo͞′-) *adj.* 1 Sixfold. 2 Raised to the sixth power. —*v.t.* (-kāt) **·cat·ed, ·cat·ing** To multiply by six; sextuple. —*n.* One of six like things. [<Med. L *sextuplicatus*, pp. of *sextuplicare* <*sextuplex* multiplied by six <*sex* six] **—sex·tu′pli·cate·ly** *adv.* **—sex·tu′pli·ca′tion** *n.*

sex·u·al (sek′shoo͞·əl) *adj.* 1 Of, pertaining to or peculiar to, characteristic of, or affecting sex, the sexes, or the organs or functions of sex. 2 Characterized by or having sex: opposed to *asexual.* [<LL *sexualis* <L *sexus* sex] **—sex′u·al·ly** *adv.*

sexual intercourse 1 The sexual act, especially between humans, in which the erect penis is introduced into the vagina for the ejaculation of semen and sexual gratification. 2 Any act of sexual connection, especially between humans.

sex·u·al·i·ty (sek′shoo͞·al′ə·tē) *n.* 1 The state of having, or of being distinguished by, sex. 2 Preoccupation with sex. 3 Possession of sexual power.

sexual selection In the theory of evolution, a phase of natural selection whereby characters, as bright colors, or fine song, considered especially attractive to the opposite sex, have a tendency to become perpetuated or enhanced.

sex·y (sek′sē) *adj.* **sex·i·er, sex·i·est** *Slang* 1 Provocative of sexual desire: a *sexy* dress; a *sexy* woman. 2 Concerned in large or excessive degree with sex: a *sexy* novel.

Sey·chelles (sā·shel′, -shelz′) An island group in the western Indian Ocean, comprising a British colony; 156 square miles; capital, Victoria, on Mahé.

Sey·han (sā·hän′) A river in south central Turkey in Asia, flowing 320 miles SW to the Mediterranean.

Seym (sām) See SEIM.

Sey·mour (sē′môr, -mōr), **Jane,** 1509?–37, third wife of Henry VIII of England; mother of Edward VI.

Sfax (sfäks) A port in central eastern Tunisia, on the north shore of the Gulf of Gabès; the second largest city of Tunisia.

sfer·ics (sfer′iks) *n. Meteorol.* 1 A cathode-ray tube connected with a directional antenna, used for the detection and plotting of electrical discharges in the atmosphere up to distances of several thousand miles. 2 *pl.* Atmospherics. [Short for ATMOSPHERICS]

Sfor·za (sfôr′tsä) A Milanese ducal family which flourished in the 15th century. **—Count Carlo,** 1873–1952, Italian anti-Fascist leader.

sfor·zan·do (sfôr·tsän′dō) *adj.* Music Accented more forcibly than the rhythm requires; especially, sounded, as a note or chord, with sudden explosive force: also spelled *forzando.* Also **sfor·za′to** (-tsä′tō). [<Ital., forcing <*sforzare* force]

’s Gra·ven·ha·ge (skhrä′və n·hä′khə) The Dutch name for THE HAGUE.

Shaa·ban (shä·bän′) See CALENDAR (Mohammedan).

shab·by (shab′ē) *adj.* **·bi·er, ·bi·est** 1 Threadbare; ragged; soiled or defaced, as from hard use. 2 Characterized by worn or defaced garments. 3 Mean; paltry. See synonyms under BAD[1], BASE[2]. [OE *sceabb* a scab + -Y[1]] **—shab′bi·ly** *adv.* **—shab′bi·ness** *n.*

Sha·bu·oth (shä·voo͞′ōth, shə·voo͞′əs) *n. pl.* The Jewish festival of Pentecost or Feast of Weeks. [<Hebrew *shebuōth*, lit., weeks]

shack[1] (shak) *n.* A rude cabin, as of logs. **—shack up** *Slang* 1 To live together and cohabit: said of unmarried persons. 2 To live or stay, usually briefly, at a specific place. [? <dial. Sp. (Mexican) *jacal* a wooden hut <Nahuatl *xacalli* ; prob. infl. by RAMSHACKLE]

shack[2] (shak) *n.* 1 Fallen acorns or nuts of any kind; mast. 2 Any bait picked up at sea, as dead sea birds, refuse fish, etc.: distinguished from bait regularly carried or newly caught: also **shack bait.** 3 A catch of miscellaneous, unsorted fish. [<*shack, v.,* dial. var. of SHAKE]

shack[3] (shak) *n.* A slow trot: also **shack gait.** —*v.t.* To go at a slow trot. [Short for *shack-rag*, var. of *shake-rag* a vagabond, a worthless horse <SHAKE + RAG[2]]

shack[4] (shak) *v.t.* To go after; retrieve. [Origin unknown]

shack·le (shak′əl) *n.* 1 A ring, clasp, or braceletlike fastening for encircling a limb; fetter; gyve. 2 Impediment or restraint. 3 One of various forms of fastenings, as the bow of a padlock, a clevis, or a link for coupling railway cars. See synonyms under FETTER. —*v.t.* **·led, ·ling** 1 To restrain or confine with shackles; fetter. 2 To keep or restrain from free action or speech. 3 To connect or fasten with a shackle. See synonyms under BIND. [OE *sceacul*] **—shack′ler** *n.*

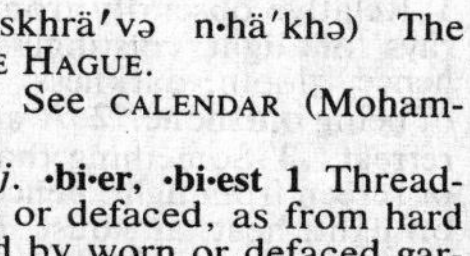

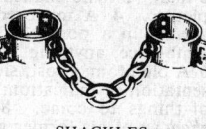

SHACKLES

shackle bolt 1 A bolt having on its end a shackle or clevis, or a bolt that is passed through the eyes of a shackle. 2 The shackle

of a padlock, chain, etc. 3 *Her.* Shackle and padlock: used as a bearing.

Shack·le·ton (shak′əl·tən), **Sir Ernest Henry,** 1874–1922, English Antarctic explorer.

shack·o (shak′ō) See SHAKO.

shad (shad) *n. pl.* **shad** A deep-bodied food fish (genus *Alosa*) related to the herring, especially the common or American shad *(Alosa sapidissima)* of the Atlantic coast, which is highly esteemed as food. [OE *sceadd*]

shad-bel·lied (shad′bel′ēd) *adj.* 1 Cutaway: said of a coat. 2 Lean and lank: said of persons.

shad·ber·ry (shad′ber′ē) *n. pl.* **·ries** The shadbush, or its fruit.

shad·bush (shad′bo͝osh′) *n.* 1 The Juneberry. 2 Other smaller and shrublike related forms of the same genus, as *Amelanchier alnifolia* of the northern and western United States. Also **shad′blow′** (-blō′). [<SHAD + BUSH[1]; so called because it flowers when the shad appear in U.S. rivers]

shad·dock (shad′ək) *n.* 1 The large, pale-yellow fruit of a tropical tree (genus *Citrus*), varying in size from the smaller grapefruit or pomelo of the United States to the pompelmous, which may be 8 inches in diameter. 2 The tree. [after Capt. *Shaddock,* commander of an East India ship, who brought the seed to the West Indies from the East Indies in 1696]

shade (shād) *v.* **shad·ed, shad·ing** *v.t.* 1 To screen from light by intercepting its rays; put in shade. 2 To make dim with or as with shade; darken; overcast. 3 To screen or protect with or as with a shade. 4 To cause to change, pass, blend, or soften, by gradations. 5 **a** To represent (degrees of shade, colors, etc.) by gradations of light or dark lines or shading. **b** To represent varying shades, colors, etc., in (a picture or painting) thus. 6 To make slightly lower, as a price. —*v.i.* 7 To change or vary by degrees. [<*n.*] —*n.* 1 Relative obscurity from interception of the rays of light: distinguished from *shadow*; hence, gloom; darkness; obscurity; the state of being outshone. 2 A shady place; secluded retreat. 3 Something that serves to intercept or screen from light; hence, a screen that shuts off light, heat, air, dust, etc. 4 A gradation of color; also, slight degree; minute difference. 5 The unilluminated part of a picture, drawing, or engraving: opposed to *light.* 6 A disembodied spirit; ghost; something unreal. 7 *pl. Slang* Sunglasses. See synonyms under SPECTER. —**the shades** The abode of departed spirits; Hades. [OE *sceadu*] —**shade′less** *adj.*

shade grass Pachysandra.

shad·fly (shad′flī′) *n. pl.* **·flies** Any of several flies that appear when the shad are running; especially, a mayfly.

shad·ing (shā′ding) *n.* 1 Protection against light or heat. 2 The lines, dots, etc., by which degrees of darkness, color, or depth are represented in a picture or painting. 3 A slight difference or variation.

sha·doof (shä·do͞of′) *n.* A water-raising device, operating on the principle of a well sweep: used in the Orient for irrigation, etc., as on the Nile. Also **sha·duf′.** [Arabic *shādūf*]

shad·ow (shad′ō) *n.* 1 A comparative darkness within an illuminated area caused by the interception of light by an opaque body. 2 The dark figure or image thus produced on a surface and representing the approximate shape of the intercepting body: the *shadow* of a man. 3 The shaded or dark portion of a picture. 4 A mirrored image: to see one's *shadow* in a pool. 5 A delusive image or semblance; anything unreal or unsubstantial. 6 A phantom; ghost; shade. 7 A faint representation or indication; a symbol: the *shadow* of things to come. 8 A remnant; vestige: *shadows* of his former glory. 9 An insignificant trace or portion: not a *shadow* of evidence. 10 *Archaic* Shelter; protection. 11 Gloom; a saddening influence. 12 An inseparable companion. 13 One who trails or follows another, as a detective or spy. See synonyms under IMAGE. —*adj.* Of or pertaining to a shadow cabinet. —*v.t.* 1 To cast a shadow upon; overspread with shadow; shade. 2 To darken or cloud; make gloomy. 3 To represent or foreshow dimly or vaguely: with *forth* or *out.* 4 To follow closely or secretly; spy on. 5 To shade in painting, drawing, etc. 6 *Archaic* To screen; shelter. [OE *sceadwe,* genitive and dative of *sceadu* a shade] —**shad′ow·er** *n.*

shad·ow·box (shad′ō·boks′) *v.i.* To spar with an imaginary opponent as a form of exercise. —**shad′ow·box′ing** *n.*

shadow cabinet In the British or other parliamentary government, a group of opposition leaders who would assume specific cabinet positions if the government in power should fall.

shad·ow·graph (shad′ō·graf, -gräf) *n.* 1 A pictorial image formed by casting a shadow, usually of the hands, upon a lighted surface or screen. 2 A drama produced by a series of these images: also **shadow play.** 3 A radiograph.

shadow test Skiascopy.

shad·ow·y (shad′ō·ē) *adj.* 1 Full of or affording shadow; dark; shady: a *shadowy* grove. 2 Like shadows in indistinctness; vague; dim. 3 Unsubstantial or illusory; unreal; ghostly. 4 Symbolic. See synonyms under DARK, IMAGINARY, VAIN. —**shad′ow·i·ness** *n.*

sha·drach (shā′drak, shad′rak) See SALAMANDER (def. 5).

Sha·drach (shā′drak, shad′rak) A Jewish captive in Babylon, who, with Meshach and Abednego, was cast into a fiery furnace by Nebuchadnezzar, but came out unscathed. *Dan.* i 7; iii 1–30.

Shad·well (shad′wel), **Thomas,** 1642?–92, English dramatist and poet.

shad·y (shā′dē) *adj.* **shad·i·er, shad·i·est** 1 Full of shade; casting a shade. 2 Shaded or sheltered. 3 Morally questionable; dubious; suspicious. 4 Quiet; hidden. See synonyms under DARK. —**to keep shady** 1 To stay in hiding; keep out of the way. 2 To hide and protect (another). —**on the shady side of** Older than; past the age of. —**shad′i·ly** *adv.* —**shad′i·ness** *n.*

shaft[1] (shaft, shäft) *n.* 1 The long narrow rod of an arrow, spear, lance, harpoon, etc. 2 An arrow. 3 Anything resembling a missile in appearance or effect: *shafts* of ridicule. 4 A beam or streak of light. 5 A long handle, as of a hammer, ax, etc. 6 *Mech.* A long and usually cylindrical bar, especially if rotating and transmitting motive power. 7 *Archit.* **a** The portion of a column between capital and base. **b** A slender column. 8 An obelisk or memorial column. 9 The vertical part of a cross. 10 The stem of a feather. 11 *Anat.* **a** A long slender portion, as the diaphysis of a bone. **b** The portion of a hair from the root to the end. 12 On a loom, one of the long laths at the ends of the heddles. 13 A thill. 14 *Slang* Malicious or abusive treatment: with *the,* especially in the phrases **to get the shaft, to give (someone) the shaft.** —*v.t. Slang* To act maliciously or abusively toward. [OE *sceaft*]

shaft[2] (shaft, shäft) *n.* 1 A narrow, vertical or inclined, excavation connected with a mine; also, a passage for light or air. 2 The tunnel of a blast furnace. 3 An opening through the floors of a building, as for an elevator. [<LG *schacht* rod, shaft; infl. by SHAFT[1]]

Shaftes·bur·y (shafts′bər·ē, shäfts′-), **Earl of,** 1621–83, Anthony Ashley Cooper, English statesman; lord chancellor 1672–73.

shaft·ing (shaf′ting, shäf′-) *n.* 1 A system of shafts or rods, as in pulleys or gearwheels, for communicating power. 2 Material from which to make shafts.

shag[1] (shag) *n.* 1 A rough coat or mass, as of hair. 2 A wild growth, as of weeds. 3 A long nap on cloth. 4 Cloth having a rough or long nap; formerly, a silk or worsted cloth having a velvet nap. 5 A cormorant. 6 A coarse, strong tobacco: also **shag tobacco.** —*v.* **shagged, shag·ging** *v.t.* 1 To make shaggy or hairy; roughen. 2 In baseball, to catch (flies) in practice. —*v.i.* 3 To become shaggy or rough. —*adj.* Shaggy: also **shag·ged** (shag′id). [OE *sceacga* rough hair, wool]

shag[2] (shag) *n.* A dance of the late 1930's, consisting of hopping quickly on alternate feet. —*v.i.* **shagged, shag·ging** To dance the shag.

shag·a·nap·pi (shag′ə·nap′ē) *Canadian* A rawhide cord or thong.

shag·bark (shag′bärk′) *n.* 1 The white hickory *(Carya ovata),* which yields high-grade nuts. 2 Its wood. Also called *shellbark.*

shag·gy (shag′ē) *adj.* **·gi·er, ·gi·est** 1 Having, consisting of, or resembling rough hair or wool; rugged; rough. 2 Covered with any rough, tangled growth; fuzzy; scrubby. 3 Unkempt; unpolished: said of manners. See synonyms under ROUGH. —**shag′gi·ly** *adv.* —**shag′gi·ness** *n.*

sha·green (shə·grēn′) *n.* 1 The rough skin of various sharks and rays: used for polishing. 2 A rough-grained Russian or Oriental leather or parchment, usually dyed green, or a pressed leather made in imitation of it. 3 Chagrin. [<F *chagrin* <Turkish *sāghrī* horse's hide]

shah (shä) *n.* An eastern king or ruler, especially of Persia. [<Persian *shāh,* short for *pādshāh.* See PADISHAH.]

Sha·hap·ti·an (shä·hap′tē·ən) *n.* A linguistic stock of North American Indians of which the Nez Percés were the chief tribe, formerly occupying the upper Columbia River valley: now on reservations in Oregon.

Shah·ja·han·pur (shä′jə·hän′po͝or) A city in Uttar Pradesh State, northern India.

Shah Je·han (shä jə·hän′), 1592–1666, Mogul emperor, 1627–58, of Delhi, celebrated for his peacock throne and as the builder of the Taj Mahal. Also **Shah Ja·han′.**

shaik (shīk) See SHEIK.

Shairp (shârp, shärp), **John Campbell,** 1819–1885, Scottish educator and critic.

shai·tan (shī·tän′) *n.* 1 In Moslem countries, the devil. 2 Any evil spirit; an evilly disposed person. 3 In India, a duststorm. Also spelled *sheitan.* [<Arabic *shaiṭān* <Hebrew *ṣāṭān.* See SATAN.]

shake (shāk) *v.* **shook, shak·en, shak·ing** *v.t.* 1 To cause to move to and fro or up and down with short, rapid movements. 2 To affect in a specified manner by or as by vigorous action: with *off, out, from,* etc.: to *shake* out a sail; to *shake* off a tackler. 3 To cause to tremble or quiver; jolt; vibrate: The blows *shook* the door. 4 To cause to stagger or totter. 5 To weaken or disturb; unsettle: I could not *shake* his determination. 6 To agitate or rouse; stir: often with *up.* 7 *Slang* To get rid of or away from. 8 *Music* To trill. 9 In dice games, to mix (the dice) before casting. —*v.i.* 10 To move to and fro or up and down in short, rapid movements. 11 To be affected in a specified way by vigorous action: with *off, out, from,* etc. 12 To tremble or quiver, as from cold or fear. 13 To become unsteady; totter. 14 *Music* To trill a note, etc. —**to shake down** 1 To cause to fall by shaking; bring down. 2 To cause to settle; make compact. 3 *Slang* To extort money from. —**to shake hands** To clasp hands as a form of greeting, agreement, etc. —*n.* 1 A shaking; concussion; agitation; vibration; shock; jolt. 2 The state of being shaken. 3 *pl. Colloq.* The chill or ague of intermittent fever. 4 A rough, unshaved shingle used to cover barns and shanties. 5 A frost or wind crack in timber; also, a tight fissure in rock. 6 An earthquake. 7 *Slang* An instant; a jiffy. 8 *Music* A trill. 9 *Colloq.* A bargain. —**to give (someone) the shake** To get rid of (someone). [OE *scacan*]

Synonyms (verb): agitate, brandish, flap, fluctuate, flutter, jar, joggle, jolt, jounce, oscillate, quake, quaver, quiver, rattle, reel, rock, shiver, shudder, sway, swing, thrill, totter, tremble, vibrate, wave, waver. A thing is *shaken* which is subjected to short and abruptly checked movements as forward and backward, up and down, from side to side, etc. A thing *rocks* that is held up from below; it *swings* if suspended from above, as a pendulum, or pivoted at the side, as a crane or a bridge draw; to *oscillate* is to *swing* with a smooth and regular returning motion; a *vibrating* motion may be tremulous or *jarring.* The pendulum of a clock may be said to *swing* or *oscillate*; a steel bridge *vibrates* under the passage of a heavy train; the term *vibrate* is also applied to molecular movements. *Jolting* is a lifting from and letting down suddenly upon an unyielding surface; a *jarring* motion is abruptly and very rapidly repeated through an exceedingly limited space; the *jolting* of the carriage *jars* the windows. *Rattling* refers directly to the sound produced by *shaking.* To *joggle* is to *shake* slightly; as, A passing touch *joggles* the desk on which one is writing. To *agitate* in its literal use is nearly the same as to *shake,* but we speak of the sea as *agitated* when we could not say it is *shaken*; in the metaphorical use *agitate* is more transitory and superficial, *shake* more fundamental and

enduring; a person's feelings are *agitated* by distressing news; his courage, his faith, his credit, or his testimony is *shaken.* Compare FLUCTUATE, QUAKE, SWAY, TREMBLE.

shake–down (shāk′doun′) *n.* **1** A bed of straw shaken down; hence, any makeshift bed. **2** *U.S. Slang* A swindle; a share of graft; extortion money. **3** A noisy, energetic dance common among Negroes of the southern United States. —*adj.* For the purpose of adjusting mechanical parts or habituating people: a *shake–down* cruise.

shak·er (shā′kər) *n.* **1** One who or that which shakes; a container for shaking something: a *saltshaker,* cocktail *shaker,* etc. **2** One who shivers or shakes; a totterer.

Shak·er (shā′kər) *n.* One of a sect practicing celibacy and communal living, introduced in America in 1774 under the leadership of Mother Ann Lee, at Lebanon, New York: so called from their characteristic bodily movements during religious meetings. Their official name is *The United Society of Believers in Christ's Second Appearing.* —**Shak′er·ism** *n.*

Shake·speare (shāk′spir), **William,** 1564–1616, English poet and dramatist. Also **Shake′spere, Shak′speare, Shak′spere.**

Shake·spear·i·an (shāk·spir′ē·ən) *adj.* Of, pertaining to, or characteristic of Shakespeare, his work, or his style. —*n.* A specialist on Shakespeare or his writings. Also **Shake·spear′e·an.**

Shake·spear·i·an·ism (shāk·spir′ē·ən·iz′əm) *n.* **1** An expression peculiar to Shakespeare. **2** Shakespearian style.

Shakespearian sonnet See under SONNET.

shake–up (shāk′up′) *n.* A change of personnel or organization, as in a government administration, a business office, etc.

Shakh·ty (shäkh′tē) A city in southern European Russian S.F.S.R.

shaking palsy *Pathol.* A chronic disorder of the central nervous system, characterized by alternations of muscular rigidity and tremor and peculiar gait: also called *paralysis agitans.*

shak·o (shak′ō) *n. pl.* **·os** A kind of high, stiff military headdress, having a peak and an upright plume: originally of fur: also spelled *shacko.* [<F *schako* <Hungarian *csákó*]

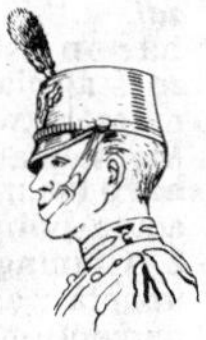

SHAKO

Shak·ti (shuk′tē) *n.* The female energy of the Hindu god, Siva: worshiped under various forms; Devi: also spelled *Sakti.* [<Skt. *śakti* power] —**Shak′tism** *n.*

Sha·kun·ta·la (shə·kōōn′tə·lə) See SAKUNTALA.

shak·y (shā′kē) *adj.* **shak·i·er, shak·i·est 1** Habitually shaking or tremulous; tottering; weak; unsound. **2** Of doubtful credit or solvency; embarrassed. —**shak′i·ly** *adv.* —**shak′i·ness** *n.*

shale[1] (shāl) *n.* A fissile argillaceous rock resembling slate, with fragile, uneven laminae. [<G *schale* shale] —**shal′y** *adj.*

shale[2] (shāl) *n.* Shell or husk. [OE *scealu*] —**shaled** *adj.*

shale oil Petroleum obtained by the distillation of bituminous shales.

shall (shal) A defective verb having a past tense **should,** an archaic present second person singular, (thou) **shalt,** past (thou) **shouldst** or **shouldest,** and no other inflected forms. It is now used only as an auxiliary followed by the infinitive without *to,* or elliptically with the infinitive unexpressed. Its function is to indicate, now chiefly in formal discourse: **1** In the first person, simple futurity, with a matter–of–fact attitude toward the action or state projected: We *shall* take only the usual precautions. (But see usage note below.) **2** In the second and third persons, futurity combined with a mood or feeling of: **a** Determination: They *shall* not pass. **b** Promise: You *shall* have whatever you need. **c** Threat: You *shall* pay for this. **d** Command: No one *shall* twice be put in jeopardy. **e** Inevitability: When earthly time *shall* end, will life survive? **3** In all persons, indefinite future time in conditional statements: If and when you or we or the divers *shall* locate the treasure, it will (or, in legal use, the mandatory *shall*) be shared out according to the agreement. **4** In all persons, futurity involving ideal certainty, in clauses following expressions of anxiety, demand, or desire: They are anxious, indeed insist, that you or I or both of us *shall* go, rather than any outsider. [OE *sceal* I am obliged, 1st person sing. of *sceolan*]

◆ **shall** vs. **will** The traditional view on the use of *shall* and *will* is that to indicate simple futurity *shall* is used in the first person, *will* in the second and third; their roles are reversed to express determination, promise, threat, command, inevitability, etc.; while in questions, the choice between them depends on which one is expected in the answer. These statements hold fairly well for legal usage, but they are too arbitrary to describe accurately the facts of current American usage in speech and writing, except at the most stilted formal level. *Shall* and *will* have had a tendency gradually to exchange roles once each century since 1500, and during the present century it has been the turn of *will* to make its way into the lead. In the important task of indicating simple future time in the first person, *will* has largely replaced *shall,* aided in doing so by the leveling effect of the contraction *'ll*: *I'll* (= *I will* or *I shall*) be free at ten. *Shall,* thus displaced, takes on one role assigned by traditional formula to *will,* and is used in the first person to express determination plus inevitability, as in General MacArthur's "I *shall* return" and Winston Churchill's ". . . and win we *shall.*" If *will* in the first person is to express determination according to the formula, it must be stressed or qualified in some way: I *will* too go out and play. In questions in the first person, *shall* is still commonly used to express the simple future, but it is also found as the hortatory *shall,* either humorously formal: *Shall* we (= *Let's*) dance? or politely threatening: *Shall* we (= *Let's*) do it my way for once. Again, *will* has won out over *shall* when it comes to giving routine or polite, as distinct from peremptory, commands: You *will* proceed to Hill 90 and occupy it. The peremptory *shall* in the second person is now usually replaced, except in legal usage, by *will* with *have to*: You *will have to* (= *shall*) go whether you want to or not. It is hazardous to try to sum up the present position of these two forms, but with the few exceptions noted, in American usage *will* now usually indicates the simple future in all persons, while *shall* expresses the future complicated by some feeling about it.

shal·loon (sha·lōōn′) *n.* A light, woven woolen fabric used for linings. [<F *chalon,* from *Châlons*–sur–Marne, France]

shal·lop (shal′əp) *n.* An open boat propelled by oars or sails. [<F *chaloupe* <Du. *sloep.* See SLOOP.]

shal·lot (shə·lot′) *n.* **1** An onionlike culinary vegetable (*Allium ascalonicum*) allied to garlic but having milder bulbs which are used in seasoning and for pickles. **2** A small onion. Also spelled *eschalot.* [<OF *eschalotte,* alter. of *eschaloigne.* See SCALLION.]

shal·low (shal′ō) *adj.* **1** Having the bottom not far below the surface or top; lacking depth; shoal. **2** Lacking intellectual depth; not wise or profound; superficial. —*n.* A shallow place in a body of water; shoal. —*v.t.* & *v.i.* To make or become shallow. [ME *schalowe.* Prob. related to SHOAL[1].] —**shal′low·ly** *adv.* —**shal′low·ness** *n.*

shalt (shalt) Archaic or poetic second person singular, present tense of SHALL: used with *thou.*

shal·war (shul′wâr) *n.* Oriental trousers or pajamas. [<Persian *shalwār*]

sham (sham) *v.* **shammed, sham·ming** *v.t.* **1** To assume or present the appearance of; counterfeit; feign. **2** To represent oneself as; pretend to be. **3** *Obs.* To delude; deceive. —*v.i.* **4** To make false pretenses; feign something. See synonyms under COUNTERFEIT, PRETEND. —*adj.* False; pretended; counterfeit; mock. See synonyms under FACTITIOUS. —*n.* **1** A pretense; imposture; deception. **2** One who affects or simulates a certain character; a pretender: also **sham′mer. 3** A deceptive imitation; simulation; counterfeit. **4** A bordered strip simulating the edge of a sheet on a made–up bed. See synonyms under HYPOCRISY. [Prob. dial. var. of SHAME]

sha·man (shä′mən, shā′-, sham′ən) *n.* **1** A priest of Shamanism; a magician. **2** Among certain northwestern North American Indians, a tribal medicine man or wizard. —*adj.* Of or pertaining to a shaman: also **sha·man·ic** (shə·man′ik). [<Russian <Tungusic *samān* <Skt. *śamaṇa* ascetic]

Sha·man·ism (shä′mən·iz′əm, shā′-, sham′ən-) *n.* A primitive religion of NE Asia and Europe holding that gods, demons, ancestral spirits, etc., work for the good or ill of mankind through the sole medium of its priests, the shamans. Certain Indians of the American Northwest have similar beliefs and practices. —**Sha′man·is′tic** *adj.* & *n.*

Sha·mash (shä′mäsh) In Assyro–Babylonian religion, the sun god, the deity controlling crops and personifying righteousness.

sham·a·teur·ism (sham′ə·tōōr′iz·əm, -ə·tər·iz′-) *n.* The practice in some sports of offering amateur athletes large fees, ostensibly for expenses, but actually as an inducement to participate. [<SHAM + AMATEURISM]

sham·ble (sham′bəl) *v.i.* **·bled, ·bling** To walk with shuffling or unsteady gait. —*n.* A shambling walk. [Origin uncertain]

sham·bles (sham′bəlz) *n. pl.* (*generally construed as singular*) **1** A place where butchers kill animals; slaughterhouse. **2** Any place of carnage or execution: The trench was a *shambles.* **3** A place marked by great destruction or disorder. **4** *Brit. Dial.* A meat market; in the singular, a table or stall in such a market. [OE *scamel* a bench, stool <L *scamellum,* dim. of *scamnum* bench, stool]

shame (shām) *n.* **1** A painful sense of guilt or degradation caused by consciousness of guilt or of anything degrading, unworthy, or immodest. **2** The restraining sense of pride, decency, or modesty. **3** That which brings reproach; a disgrace. **4** A state of ignominy; sensitiveness or susceptibility to humiliation. See synonyms under ABOMINATION, CHAGRIN. —**to put to shame 1** To disgrace; make ashamed. **2** To surpass or eclipse. —*v.t.* **shamed, sham·ing 1** To make ashamed; cause to feel shame. **2** To bring shame upon; disgrace. **3** To impel by a sense of shame: with *into* or *out of.* See synonyms under ABASH. [OE *scamu*]

shame·faced (shām′fāst′) *adj.* Easily abashed; showing shame or bashfulness in one's face; modest; bashful. [Alter. of ME *shamefast,* OE *scamfæst*abashed] —**shame·fac·ed·ly** (shām′fā′·sid·lē, shām′fāst′lē) *adv.* —**shame′fac′ed·ness** *n.*

shame·ful (shām′fəl) *adj.* **1** Deserving or bringing shame or disgrace; disgraceful; scandalous. **2** Exciting shame; indecent. See synonyms under FLAGRANT. —**shame′ful·ly** *adv.* —**shame′ful·ness** *n.*

shame·less (shām′lis) *adj.* **1** Impudent; brazen; immodest. **2** Done without shame, indicating a want of decency. See synonyms under INFAMOUS, IMMODEST, IMPUDENT. —**shame′less·ly** *adv.* —**shame′less·ness** *n.*

sham·my (sham′ē), **sham·ois** (sham′ē) See CHAMOIS (def. 2).

Sha·mo (shä′mō) A Chinese name for the GOBI DESERT.

sham·poo (sham·pōō′) *v.t.* **1** To lather, rub, and wash (the hair and scalp) thoroughly. **2** To cleanse by rubbing. —*n.* The act or process of shampooing, or a preparation used for it. [<Hind. *chāmpnā* press] —**sham·poo′er** *n.*

sham·rock (sham′rok) *n.* Any one of several trifoliate plants, accepted as the national emblem of Ireland, especially the wood sorrel (*Oxalis acetosella*), the white clover (*Trifolium repens*), and the black medic (*Medicago lupulina*). [<Irish *seamrōg,* dim. of *seamar* trefoil]

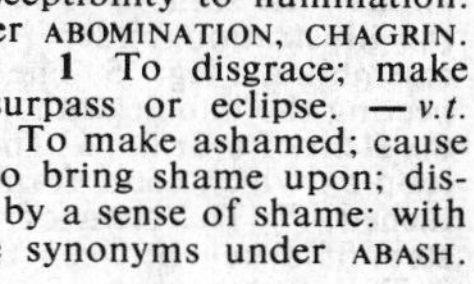

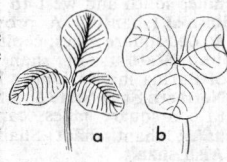

SHAMROCK
a. White clover.
b. Wood sorrel.

Shan (shan, shän) *n.* **1** One of a group of Mongoloid tribes of southern China, Assam, Burma, and Thailand. **2** The Thai language

of these tribes, closely related to Siamese. — *adj.* Of or pertaining to the Northern and Southern Shan States, their people, or their language.

shand (shand, shänd) *Scot. adj.* Worthless; mean, paltry. — *n.* Spurious coin.

shan·dry·dan (shan′drə·dan) *n. Irish* **1** A two-wheeled Irish cart, or hooded chaise: also **shan′da·ra·dan′, shan′der·y·dan′.** **2** An old-fashioned or rickety vehicle. [Origin unknown]

shan·dy·gaff (shan′dē·gaf) *n.* An alcoholic drink composed of two liquids mixed, at least one being effervescent: usually ale or beer and ginger beer. [Origin unknown]

shang·hai (shang′hī, shang·hī′) *v.t.* **·haied, ·hai·ing** **1** To drug or render unconscious and kidnap for service aboard a ship. **2** To cause to do something by force or deception. [from *Shanghai*]

Shang·hai (shang′hī′) *n.* One of a former large breed of domestic fowls, with long legs and feathered shanks, said to have originated in Shanghai, China.

Shang·hai (shang′hī′, *Chinese* shäng′hī′) A port of eastern China, the largest city on the Asian continent.

Shan·gri-la (shang′gri·lä′) *n.* **1** Any imaginary hidden utopia or paradise. **2** The reported taking-off place of the United States Army bombers that raided Tokyo April 18, 1942: a term used by Franklin Roosevelt. **3** Any secret base for air force military operations. [From the locale of James Hilton's novel *Lost Horizon*]

Shan·hai·kwan (shän′hī′gwän′) A city in NE Hopeh province, China, on the Gulf of Liaotung on the Manchurian boundary; the easternmost end of the Great Wall. Formerly called **Lin·yü** (lin′yōō′).

shank (shangk) *n.* **1** The leg proper; that part of the lower limb between the knee and the ankle. **2** A cut of meat from the leg of an animal; the shin. **3** The tarsus of a bird. See the illustration under FOWL. **4** Something resembling a leg. **5** The part of a tool connecting the handle with the working part, as the stem of a drill. **6** The projecting piece or loop by which some forms of buttons are attached. **7** The stem of an anchor. **8** The stem of a key between the bow and the bit. **9** The straight part of a hook. **10** The narrow part of a spoon handle. **11** A continuation of the tang of a tool or instrument. **12** *Printing* The body of a type. **13** The narrow part of a shoe sole in front of the heel. See illustration under SHOE. **14** *Bot.* A pedicel. **15** *Colloq.* The remainder or last part of a thing: the *shank* of the evening. — *v.i.* **1** *Bot.* To decay or fall off the stem because of disease. **2** *Scot.* To travel on foot. [OE *sceanca*]

Shan·ka·ra (shung′kə·rə), flourished about 800 A.D., Hindu religious reformer, teacher and writer; foremost exponent of Vedanta philosophy; considered an incarnation of Shiva. Also **Shan·ka·ra·char·ya** (shung′kə·rä·chär′yə).

shanks' mare One's own legs as a means of conveyance.

shan·na (shan′na, shän′nä) *Scot.* Shall not.

Shan·non (shan′ən) An international airport in southern County Clare, Ireland, on the Shannon River west of Limerick.

Shannon River (shan′ən) The chief river of Ireland, in the west central part, flowing 224 miles south and west to the Atlantic.

Shan·si (shän′sē′) A province of NE China; 50,000 square miles; capital, Taiyüan.

Shan State (shän, shan) A constituent unit of Burma in east Upper Burma, consisting of **Northern Shan State** and **Southern Shan State**; 61,090 square miles; capital, Lashio.

sha'nt (shant, shänt) Shall not: a contraction. Also **shan't.**

shan·tung (shan′tung, shan·tung′) *n.* A silk fabric similar to pongee and having the same rough, nubby surface: originally made in China of wild silk, now often made of rayon combined with cotton. [from SHANTUNG]

Shan·tung (shan′tung′, *Chinese* shän′dōōng′) A province of NE China, extending as a peninsula in the eastern part into the Yellow Sea; 55,000 square miles; capital, Tsinan.

shan·ty[1] (shan′tē) *n. pl.* **·ties** A hastily built shack or cabin; a ramshackle or rickety dwelling. See synonyms under HOUSE, HUT. [<F (Canadian) *chantier* lumberer's shack]

shan·ty[2] (shan′tē) See CHANTEY.

shan·ty·man (shan′tē·mən) *n. pl.* **·men** (-mən) One who lives in a shanty; specifically, a woodcutter or lumberman.

shan·ty·town (shan′tē·toun′) *n.* **1** That section of a city or town comprised of ramshackle or hastily constructed shacks. **2** The inhabitants collectively of such a section: All *shantytown* turned out for the parade.

Shao·hing (shou′shing′) A city in northern Chekiang province, China. Also **Shao′-hsing′.**

shape (shāp) *n.* **1** Outward form or construction; configuration; contour. **2** A developed expression or definite formulation; realization or application; embodiment; cast: to put an idea into *shape.* **3** A being, image, or appearance considered with reference to its form, generally incorporeal; ghost; phantom. **4** The character or form in which a thing appears; guise; aspect. **5** Something that gives or determines form; a pattern or mold; in millinery, a stiff frame. **6** The lines of a person's body; figure. **7** Manner of execution. **8** Condition as regarding fitness. **9** A blancmange, jelly, etc., cooled and shaped in a mold. — **to take shape** To have or assume a definite form. — *v.* **shaped, shaped** (*Rare* **shap·en), shap·ing** *v.t.* **1** To give shape to; mold; form. **2** To adjust or adapt; modify. **3** To devise; prepare. **4** To give direction or character to: to *shape* one's course of action. **5** To put into or express in words. **6** *Obs.* To appoint; ordain. — *v.i.* **7** To take shape; develop; form: often with *up* or *into.* **8** *Rare* To become adapted; conform. **9** *Rare* To happen; come about. See synonyms under MAKE. [OE *gesceap* creation] — **shap′er** *n.*

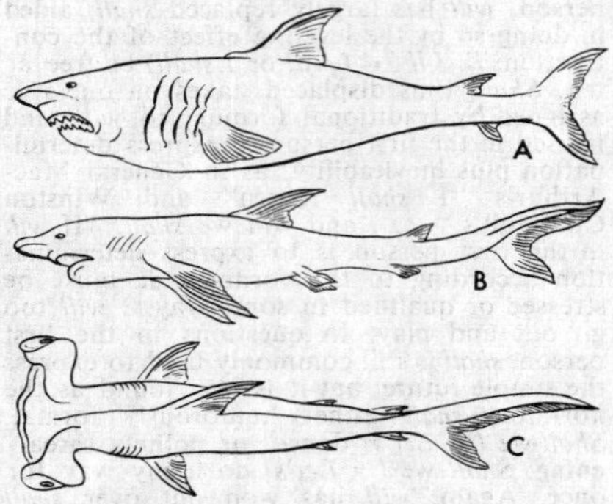

SHARKS
A. Great white shark (to 40 feet). *B.* Blue shark (to 15 feet). *C.* Hammerhead shark (to 15 feet).

shaped (shāpt) *adj.* **1** Formed. **2** Resembling in shape: used in compounds, as in leaf-*shaped,* club-*shaped,* key-*shaped.*

shaped charge An explosive charge so placed in a shell or projectile as to deliver most of its force directly through the nose of the shell instead of scattering it at random: developed especially for anti-tank guns.

shape·less (shāp′lis) *adj.* Having no definite shape; lacking symmetry; formless. — **shape′less·ly** *adv.* — **shape′less·ness** *n.*

shape·ly (shāp′lē) *adj.* **·li·er, ·li·est** Having a pleasing shape; well-formed; graceful. — **shape′li·ness** *n.*

shape-up (shāp′up′) *n.* The selection of a work crew by an employer representative, a labor union deputy, or other agent, who chooses from among a number of men assembled for a work shift: a common practice in hiring longshoremen and workers in other industries in which the relationship between an employee and a specific employer is by the day or otherwise casual.

Shap·ley (shap′lē), **Harlow,** 1885–1973, U.S. astronomer.

shard (shärd) *n.* **1** A broken piece of a brittle substance, as of an earthen vessel; a potsherd; a fragment: also spelled *sherd.* **2** *Zool.* A hard, thin shell, or a wing cover, of an insect. [OE *sceard.* Related to SHEAR.]

share (shâr) *n.* **1** A portion; allotted or equitable part. **2** Specifically, one of the equal parts into which the capital stock of a company or corporation is divided. **3** An equitable part of something enjoyed or suffered in common. **4** A plowshare: also spelled *shear.* **5** A blade of a cultivator, seeder, etc. See synonyms under PART. — *v.* **shared, shar·ing** *v.t.* **1** To divide and give out in shares or portions; apportion. **2** To enjoy or endure in common; participate in. — *v.i.* **3** To have a part; participate: with *in.* See synonyms under APPORTION. [OE *scearu* < *sceran* shear. Related to SHEAR.] — **shar′er** *n.*

share·crop·per (shâr′krop′ər) *n.* A tenant farmer who pays a share of his crop as rent for his land.

share·hold·er (shâr′hōl′dər) *n.* An owner of a share or shares of a company's stock; a stockholder.

shares·man (shârz′mən) *n. pl.* **·men** (-mən) A member of a cooperative fishing crew who shares in the risks and profits of the cruise or season. Also **share′man.**

Sha·ri (shä′rē) A river of central French Equatorial Africa, forming the principal tributary of Lake Chad and flowing 500 miles NW: French *Chari.*

shark[1] (shärk) *n.* One of a group of voracious elasmobranch fishes (order *Selachii*), mostly marine, of medium to large size, having a cartilaginous skeleton, lateral gill slits, and dun-colored bodies covered with placoid scales. Most species do not molest man; the great white shark (*Carcharodon carcharias*) is the man-eater frequenting warm seas. — *v.i.* To fish for sharks. [Origin uncertain]

shark[2] (shärk) *n.* **1** A bold and dishonest person; a rapacious swindler. **2** *Slang* A person of exceptional skill or ability in some special line. Also **shark′er.** — *v.t. Archaic* To obtain by unscrupulous or deceitful means. — *v.i.* To live by trickery or deceit. [Prob. <G *schurke* scoundrel]

shark·skin (shärk′skin′) *n.* **1** The skin of a shark. **2** A summer fabric with a smooth, almost shiny surface, made of acetate rayon and used for sports clothes; originally, a weave of woolen yarns of two colors: so called from its resemblance to sharkskin leather.

sharn (shärn) *n. Scot.* Cow dung. — **sharn′y** *adj.*

Shar·on (shar′ən), **Plain of** A part of the coastal plain of western Israel, extending 50 miles between the Hills of Ephraim and the Mediterranean.

sharp (shärp) *adj.* **1** Having a keen edge or an acute point; capable of cutting or piercing. **2** Coming to an acute angle; not obtuse; angular; abrupt: a *sharp* peak. **3** Keen of perception or discernment; also, shrewd in bargaining; artful; overreaching: *sharp* practice. **4** Ardent; quick; eager; keen, as the appetite; impetuous or fiery, as a combat or debate; vigilant or attentive. **5** Affecting the mind or senses, as if by cutting or piercing; afflictive; poignant; painful; harsh; censorious; acrimonious; rigorous; stern; sarcastic; bitter. **6** Shrill. **7** Pinching; cutting, as cold. **8** Having an acid or pungent taste. **9** Distinct, as an outline; not blurred or hazy; well-defined. **10** *Music* Being above the proper or indicated pitch; specifically, being a half-step higher than the indicated note; sharped. **11** Hard and rough; gritty, as sand. **12** *Phonet.* Surd; voiceless: opposed to *flat:* said of consonants. — *adv.* **1** In a sharp manner; sharply. **2** Promptly; exactly; on the instant: at 4 o'clock *sharp.* **3** *Music* Above the proper pitch. — *n.* **1** *Music* A character (♯) used on a natural degree of the staff to make it represent a pitch a half-step higher; the tone so indicated; on the pianoforte, the next higher key; one of the black keys: a loose use in the phrase *sharps and flats.* **2** A sewing needle of long, slender shape. **3** A cheating rogue; sharper: a *cardsharp.* **4** *Obs.* A dueling sword; rapier. — *v.t. Music* To raise in pitch, as by a half-step. — *v.i. Music* To sing, play, or sound above the right pitch. [OE *scearp*] — **sharp′ly** *adv.* — **sharp′ness** *n.*

Synonyms (*adj.*): acute, cutting, keen, penetrating, piercing, pointed. See ACID, ACUTE, ASTUTE, BITTER, CLEVER, FINE, KNOWING, SAGACIOUS, STEEP, VIOLENT. *Antonyms*: blunt, dull, dulled, edgeless, flat, obtuse, pointless, round, rounded.

Sharp (shärp), **William,** 1856?–1905, Scottish poet and novelist: pseudonym, *Fiona McLeod.*

sharp·en (shär′pən) *v.t.* & *v.i.* To make or become sharp. — **sharp′en·er** *n.*

sharp·er (shär′pər) *n.* A swindler; cheat.

sharp–eyed (shärp′īd′) *adj.* 1 Having acute eyesight. 2 Keenly observant; alert.

sharp·ie (shär′pē) *n.* A long, sharp, flat-bottomed sailboat having a center-board and one or two masts, each having a triangular sail: originally used in the oyster and scallop fisheries. [<SHARP; in allusion to its outline]

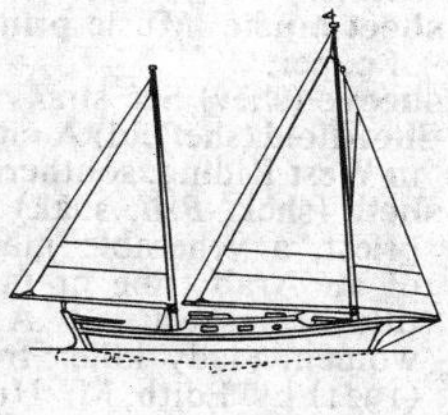
SHARPIE

Sharps·burg (shärps′bûrg) A town in NW Maryland; site of the battle of Antietam, 1862, in the Civil War.

sharp–set (shärp′set′) *adj.* 1 Set at a sharp angle; prepared like a saw for cutting. 2 Keen; eager; fierce. 3 Ravenous; hungry; thin and hungry-looking.

sharp–shinned (shärp′shind′) *adj.* Having slender shanks, somewhat angular in front: specifically said of the North American **sharp–shinned hawk** *(Accipiter velox).*

sharp·shoot·er (shärp′sho͞o′tər) *n.* 1 A skilled marksman, especially in the use of the rifle. 2 The second grade of skill in small–arms shooting, ranking next above *marksman* and below *expert*; also, a soldier having this grade. **— sharp′shoot′ing** *n.*

sharp–sight·ed (shärp′sī′tid) *adj.* Having keen vision. **— sharp′–sight′ed·ness** *n.*

sharp–tongued (shärp′tungd′) *adj.* Bitter or caustic in speech.

sharp–wit·ted (shärp′wit′id) *adj.* Acute; intelligent; discerning. See synonyms under INTELLIGENT, SAGACIOUS. **— sharp′–wit′ted·ness** *n.*

Sha·si (shä′sē′) A city on the Yangtze in south central Hupeh province, China.

Shas·ta (shas′tə), **Mount** A volcanic cone in the Cascade Range of northern California; 14,161 feet.

Shasta daisy A cultivated variety of a short-lived perennial *(Chrysanthemum maximum)* having large, white–rayed flowers.

Shas·tan (shas′tən) *adj.* & *n.* Comanchean.

Shatt–el–Ar·ab (shat′al·ar′əb) A river in SE Iraq, formed by the Tigris and Euphrates which unite 40 miles NW of Basra and flow 120 miles SE, forming the Iraq–Iran boundary from below Basra to the Persian Gulf.

shat·ter (shat′ər) *v.t.* 1 To break into pieces suddenly, as by a blow. 2 To break the health or tone of, as the body or mind; disorder; damage. 3 *Obs.* To scatter. **—** *v.i.* 4 To break into pieces; burst. See synonyms under BREAK. **—** *n. Obs.* 1 A shattered fragment; a splinter: a tree rent into *shatters.* 2 A shattered or disordered condition: His nerves are in a *shatter.* [ME *schateren.* ? Akin to SCATTER.]

shat·ter·proof glass (shat′ər·pro͞of′) See under GLASS.

shauch·le (shakh′əl, shä′khəl, shô′-) *Scot. v.t.* To put out of shape; distort, as a shoe. **—** *v.i.* To shuffle; shamble. Also **shaugh′le.**

shaul (shôl) See SHOAL[1].

shave (shāv) *v.* **shaved, shaved** or **shav·en, shav·ing** *v.i.* 1 To cut hair or beard close to the skin with a razor. **—** *v.t.* 2 To remove hair or beard from (the face, head, etc.) with a razor. 3 To cut (hair or beard) close to the skin with a razor: often with *off.* 4 To trim closely as if with a razor: to *shave* a lawn. 5 To cut thin slices from, as in preparing the surface; pare; plane. 6 To cut into thin slices: to *shave* ice. 7 To touch or scrape in passing; graze; come close to. 8 *U.S.* To buy (commercial paper) at a greater reduction than the bank discount. **—** *n.* 1 The act or operation of cutting off the beard with a razor. 2 A knife or blade, mounted between two handles, as for shaving wood: also **draw shave, spoke shave.** 3 A shaving; thin slice. 4 An extra or exorbitant discount paid for cashing a note or draft, as a premium given for an extension of time. 5 *Colloq.* The act of rushing by or barely grazing something; hence, a narrow escape: a close *shave.* 6 One who drives hard bargains. [OE *scafan* shave]

shave·ling (shāv′ling) *n.* 1 One who is shaven; opprobriously, a monk or priest. 2 A youth.

shav·en (shā′vən) Alternative past participle of SHAVE. **—** *adj.* 1 Shaved; also, tonsured. 2 Trimmed closely.

shav·er (shā′vər) *n.* 1 One who shaves; specifically, a barber. 2 A plunderer; cheat; sharper. 3 *Colloq.* A lad.

shave·tail (shāv′tāl′) *n. U.S. Slang* 1 A second lieutenant, especially one recently commissioned. 2 An untrained or intractable mule. 3 A tenderfoot. [Formerly in allusion to young, unbroken army mules with their tails bobbed]

Sha·vi·an (shā′vē·ən) *n.* An admirer of George Bernard Shaw, his books, or his theories. **—** *adj.* Of, pertaining to, or like George Bernard Shaw, or his style and methods.

shav·ie (shā′vē) *n. Scot.* A deceptive trick.

shav·ing (shā′ving) *n.* 1 The act of one who shaves; that which shaves. 2 A thin paring shaved from anything, as a board.

shaw[1] (shô) *v.t. Scot.* To show.

shaw[2] (shô) *n. Brit.* 1 A thicket; copse: also **shaugh.** 2 The leaves and tops of vegetables: usually in the plural. [OE *scaga* copse]

Shaw (shô), **George Bernard,** 1856–1950, Irish dramatist, critic, and novelist. **— Henry Wheeler,** 1818–85, U.S. humorist: pseudonym *Josh Billings.* **— Thomas Edward** See LAWRENCE, THOMAS EDWARD.

Shawan·gunk Mountains (shong′gum, -gungk) A range of the Appalachians in SE New York; about 45 miles long; highest point, 2,289 feet.

shawl (shôl) *n.* A wrap, as a square cloth, or large broad scarf, worn over the upper part of the body. [<Persian *shāl*]

shawm (shôm) *n.* An ancient, double–reed instrument; inaccurately, a cornet or horn. [<OF *chalemie* pipe <LL *calamellus,* dim. of L *calamus* reed]

Shaw·nee (shô·nē′) *n.* One of a warlike tribe of North American Indians of Algonquian stock, formerly living in Tennessee and South Carolina: now in Oklahoma. [<Algonquian (Shawnee) *Shawunogi* southerners <*shawun* south]

Shaw·wal (shô·wäl′) See under CALENDAR (Mohammedan).

shay (shā) *n.* A chaise: a back formation due to mistaking *chaise* for a plural.

Shays (shāz), **Daniel,** 1747?–1825, a captain in the American Revolution and leader of **Shays' Rebellion,** 1786–87, a popular insurrection in western Massachusetts, caused by economic distress of that time. **— Shays′ite** *n.*

Shcher·ba·kov (shchir′bə·kôf′) A city on the Volga in north central European Russian S.F.S.R.: formerly *Rybinsk.*

she (shē) *pron.* 1 The female person or being previously mentioned or understood, in the nominative case. 2 That woman or female; any woman: *She* who listens learns. **—** *n.* A female person or being: This puppy is a *she.* [OE *sēo, sīo,* fem. of *sē* the, replacing *hēo* she]

she– *combining form* Female; feminine: in hyphenated compounds: a *she*–lion.

shea (shē) *n.* A large tree *(Butyrospermum parkis)* growing only in western tropical Africa and yielding **shea butter,** used for food, illumination, and making soap. [<Mundingo *si, se*]

sheaf[1] (shēf) *n. pl.* **sheaves** (shēvz) 1 A quantity of the stalks of cut grain or the like, bound together; a bundle of straw. 2 Any collection of things, as papers, held together by a band or tie. 3 The quiverful of arrows carried by an archer, usually 24. **—** *v.t.* To bind in a sheaf; sheave. [OE *scēaf*]

sheaf[2] (shēf) See SHEAVE[2].

sheal[1] (shēl) *n. Scot. & Brit. Dial.* A shealing.

sheal[2] (shēl) *n. Brit.* A pod or shell. [Var. of SHELL]

sheal·ing (shē′ling) *n.* 1 *Brit. Dial.* A hut or cabin for the use of shepherds or sportsmen in the hills, for fishermen at the shore, etc.: also spelled *shieling.* 2 *Scot.* A shed for sheltering sheep at night in the hills. Also called *sheal.*

shealing hill *Scot.* A hill upon which grain is winnowed by the wind: also spelled *sheeling hill.*

shear (shir) *n.* 1 A two–bladed cutting instrument: obsolete except in the plural. See SHEARS. 2 *Physics* A deformation of a solid body, equivalent to a sliding over each other of adjacent laminar elements, with a progressive relative displacement: also **shearing stress.** 3 The act or result of shearing. 4 A plowshare. 5 *Naut.* Sweep; sheer. **—** *v.* **sheared** (*Archaic* **shore**), **sheared** or **shorn, shear·ing** *v.t.* 1 To cut the hair, fleece, etc., from. 2 To remove by cutting or clipping: to *shear* wool. 3 To deprive; strip, as of power or wealth. 4 To cut or clip with shears or other sharp instrument: to *shear* a cable. 5 *Dial.* To reap, as grain, with a sickle. **—** *v.i.* 6 To use shears or other sharp instrument. 7 To slide or break from a shear (def. 2). 8 To proceed by or as by cutting a way: with *through.* 9 *Dial.* To reap with a sickle. See synonyms under CUT. ◆ Homophone: *sheer.* [OE *scēara* scissors <*sceran* shear. Akin to SHARD, SHARE.] **— shear′er** *n.*

shear·ling (shir′ling) *n.* 1 The fleece from the second shearing of a sheep. 2 The sheep from which one fleece has been cut.

shears (shirz) *n. pl.* 1 Any large cutting or clipping instrument worked by the crossing of cutting edges. 2 The ways or guides, as of a lathe. 3 An apparatus for hoisting and moving heavy objects, consisting of two or more spars with lower ends spread out and upper ends jointed to receive the tackle: also **shear legs:** sometimes spelled *sheers.* 4 The side frames of a steam fire engine. [See SHEAR]

shear·wa·ter (shir′wô′tər, -wot′ər) *n.* One of several sea birds (genus *Puffinus*) related to the petrels and albatrosses, found in most seas: so called because they skim close to the water.

sheat·fish (shēt′fish′) *n. pl.* **·fish** or **·fish·es** A catfish *(Siluris glanis)* of the fresh waters of central and eastern Europe. It is the largest fresh–water fish in Europe. [OE *scēota* trout + FISH]

sheath (shēth) *n.* 1 An envelope or case, as for a sword; scabbard. 2 *Bot.* A case enclosing a part or an organ, as the lower part of the leaves in grasses. 3 *Zool.* Any covering in animals that resembles a sheath. 4 *Entomol.* An elytron of a beetle. 5 *Agric.* A bar connecting the beam and sole in a plow [OE *scǣth*] **— sheath′less** *adj.*

sheath–bill (shēth′bil′) *n.* Any of a small number of species of sea birds of the family *Chionididae,* natives of the Antarctic islands. They are pure white in plumage and have a horny sheath at the base of the bill.

sheathe (shēth) *v.t.* **sheathed, sheath·ing** 1 To put into a sheath. 2 To plunge (a sword, etc.) into flesh, as if into a sheath. 3 To incase or protect with a covering, as the hull of a ship with metal. 4 To draw in, as claws. [<SHEATH]

sheath·ing (shē′thing) *n.* 1 A casing, as of a building, or the protective covering of a ship's hull; that which sheathes; also, the material used. 2 The act of one who sheathes. 3 *Archit.* The covering or waterproof material on outside walls or roof

sheath knife A large case knife carried in a sheath attached to a belt, worn by sailors and riggers.

sheave[1] (shēv) *v.t.* **sheaved, sheav·ing** To gather into sheaves; collect. [<SHEAF]

sheave[2] (shēv) *n.* 1 A grooved pulley wheel; also, a pulley wheel and its block. 2 An eccentric, or its disk. 3 *Scot.* A slice or cut. Also spelled *sheaf, sheeve.* [Var. of SHIVE[1]]

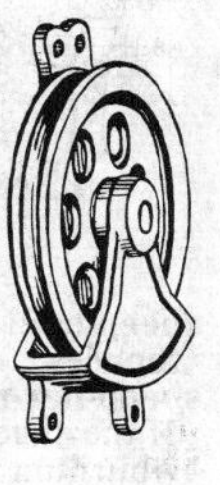
SHEAVE

sheaves (shēvz) Plural of SHEAF.

She·ba (shē′bə) The Old Testament name for a region of the SW Arabian peninsula, corresponding to modern Yemen: Arabic *Saba.*

She·ba (shē′bə), **Queen of** A queen, called Balkis in the Koran, who visited Solomon to test his wisdom. I *Kings* x 1–13.

she·bang (shi·bang′) *n. U.S. Slang* 1 A building, vehicle, saloon, theater, etc. 2 Any matter of present concern; thing; contrivance; outfit: tired of the whole *shebang.* [Var. of SHEBEEN]

She·bat (shi·bät′) See under CALENDAR (Hebrew). Also spelled *Sebat.*

she·been (shi·bēn′) *n. Irish & Scot.* A groggery; specifically, a place where liquors are sold without a license; hence, weak ale or beer. [<Irish *sibīn* little mug]

She·be·li (shi·bā′lē), **Web·be** (web′ā) See SHIBELI, WEBBE.

She·chem (shē′kem) The ancient name for NABLUS.

shed[1] (shed) *v.* **shed, shed·ding** *v.t.* **1** To pour forth in drops; emit, as tears or blood. **2** To cause to pour forth. **3** To send forth or abroad; diffuse; radiate, as light. **4** To throw off without allowing to penetrate, as rain; repel. **5** To cast off by natural process, as hair, skin, a shell, etc. — *v.i.* **6** To cast off or lose hair, skin, etc., by natural process. **7** To fall or drop, as leaves or seed. — **to shed blood** To kill. — *n.* **1** That which sheds, as a sloping surface or watershed. **2** The act of shedding: *bloodshed.* **3** A separation or division; parting: applied technically to the opening in the warp through which the shuttle is thrown in weaving, and in parts of Great Britain to the parting of the hair. See illustration under LOOM. **4** The slope of a hill. [OE *scēadan* separate, part]

shed[2] (shed) *n.* **1** A small low building, often with front or sides open; also, a lean–to: a wagon *shed.* **2** *Brit.* A storehouse; barn. **3** A temporary covering; cabin. **4** A hangar. See synonyms under HUT. [Var. of SHADE]

she'd (shēd) **1** She had. **2** She would.

shed·der (shed′ər) *n.* **1** One who sheds. **2** An animal that sheds or has lately shed its skin, as a crab.

she–dev·il (shē′dev′əl) *n.* **1** A bad–tempered and spiteful woman. **2** A female demon.

shee (shē) See SID.

sheel·ing hill (shē′ling) See SHEALING HILL.

sheen (shēn) *n.* **1** A glistening brightness, as if from reflection. **2** Bright, shining attire. See synonyms under LIGHT. — *adj.* Shining; radiant; beautiful. — *v.i.* To shine; gleam; glisten. [OE *scēne* beautiful; infl. in meaning by SHINE. Akin to G *schön* beautiful.] — **sheen′y** *adj.*

sheep (shēp) *n. pl.* **sheep 1** A medium–sized, domesticated ruminant of the genus *Ovis* (family *Bovidae*), highly prized for its flesh, wool, and skin. ◆ Collateral adjective: *ovine.* **2** Leather made from the skin of the sheep, as for bookbinding: also *sheepskin.* **3** Someone with the supposed temperament of a sheep; hence, a meek, bashful, or timid person. [OE *scēap*]

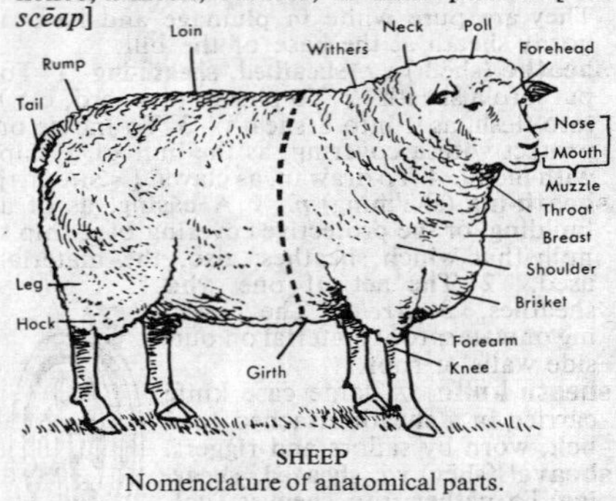

SHEEP
Nomenclature of anatomical parts.

sheep·backs (shēp′baks′) *n. pl.* Roches moutonnées.

sheep·ber·ry (shēp′ber′ē) *n. pl.* **·ries 1** One of the black, oval, edible drupes of the sweet viburnum *(Viburnum lentago).* **2** The tree itself.

sheep·cote (shēp′kōt′) *n.* A small enclosure for the protection of sheep; a sheepfold. Also **sheep′cot′** (-kot′).

sheep dip Any of several liquid disinfectants which contain creosote, nicotine, cresol, arsenic, etc., used for dipping sheep.

sheep dog 1 A dog trained to guard and control sheep; shepherd's dog: often a collie, but also a rough–coated, heavy, short–tailed dog much used by drovers in England. **2** Figuratively, a chaperon. — **old English sheep dog** A bob–tailed dog of undetermined origin, used as a sporting dog, and, in Great Britain, to herd flocks: characterized by a strong, muscular, thick–set body, covered with a very thick gray, grizzle, or blue–gray shaggy coat.

sheep·fold (shēp′fōld′) *n.* A place where sheep are enclosed at night; a pen for sheep.

sheep·herd·er (shēp′hûr′dər) *n.* A herder of sheep. — **sheep′herd′ing** *n.*

sheep·ish (shē′pish) *adj.* Foolish, as a sheep; awkwardly diffident; abashed. — **sheep′ish·ly** *adv.* — **sheep′ish·ness** *n.*

sheep laurel Lambkill.

sheep ranch A ranch and range where sheep are bred and raised. Also *Brit.* **sheep′walk′**, *Austral.* **sheep run.**

sheep's eyes Bashful, sidelong, or amorous glances.

sheeps·head (shēps′hed′) *n.* **1** A common deep–bodied sparoid food fish *(Archosargus probatocephalus)* of the Atlantic coast of the United States. **2** The Great Lakes drumfish, also found in the Mississippi region. **3** The dollar–fish. **4** A foolish or silly person.

sheep·shear·ing (shēp′shir′ing) *n.* **1** The act of shearing sheep. **2** The shearing season; an occasion at which sheep are shorn, and the feast or celebration given at the occasion. — **sheep′shear′er** *n.*

sheep·skin (shēp′skin′) *n.* **1** The skin of a sheep, tanned or untanned, or anything made from it, as parchment. **2** A document written on parchment; hence, a diploma.

sheep sorrel An herb *(Rumex acetosella)* of the buckwheat family, widely distributed in dry places, and having leaves of an acrid taste.

sheer[1] (shir) *v.i.* To swerve from a course; turn aside. — *v.t.* To cause to swerve or deviate. — *n.* **1** *Naut.* **a** The rise, or the amount of rise from a level, of the lengthwise lines of a vessel's hull. **b** A position of a vessel that enables it to swing clear of a single anchor. **2** A swerving or curving course. ◆ Homophone: *shear.* [<SHEAR]

sheer[2] (shir) *adj.* **1** Having no modifying conditions; unmitigated; absolute; downright; utter: *sheer* folly; *sheer* nonsense. **2** Exceedingly thin and fine: said of fabrics. **3** Perpendicular; steep; ascending vertically: a *sheer* precipice. **4** Pure; pellucid. **5** *Obs.* Bright; shining. See synonyms under PURE, STEEP. — *n.* Any very thin fabric used for clothes. — *adv.* Entirely; perpendicularly: also **sheer′ly.** ◆ Homophone: *shear.* [ME *schere.* Cf. ON *skærr* clear, bright and OE *scīr* bright, shining.] — **sheer′ness** *n.*

Sheer·ness (shir′nes′) An urban district and port on the Isle of Sheppey at the mouth of the Medway, in the Thames estuary, northern Kent, England.

sheers (shirz) See SHEARS (def. 3).

sheet (shēt) *n.* **1** A very thin and broad piece of any substance; that which is or can be spread, as upon a surface, or can be laid in broad folds; anything having a considerable expanse with very little thickness. **2** A large rectangular piece of linen or cotton cloth, used in making up a bed. **3** A piece of paper, especially one of a regular size; hence, a newspaper, or a leaf of a book. **4** A piece of metal or other substance hammered, rolled, fused, or cut very thin: a *sheet* of glass. **5** A broad, flat surface; superficial expanse: a *sheet* of water; a *sheet* of flame. **6** *Naut.* **a** A rope or chain from a lower corner of a sail to extend it or move it. **b** *pl.* In an open boat, the space at the bow and stern not occupied by the thwarts. The former is termed the **fore sheets** and the latter the **stern sheets. 7** A sail: a literary use. **8** *Geol.* **a** An originally horizontal or moderately inclined layer of igneous rock of small thickness as compared with its lateral extent. **b** Any superficial deposit, as of gravel left by a glacier, or of soil or ice. **9** The large, unseparated block of stamps printed by one impression of a plate. — **three sheets in the wind** *Slang* Tipsy; drunk. — *v.t.* **1** To stretch by hauling on a sheet: used only in the expression **to sheet home,** to stretch the clews of a sail to the extremities of the next lower yard. **2** To cover with or wrap in a sheet. **3** To furnish with sheets. — *v.i.* **4** To extend in a particular direction: said of the sheets of a sail. [OE *scēte* linen cloth]

sheet anchor 1 One of two anchors for use only in emergency; formerly, the main anchor. **2** A sure dependence on occasion of danger or emergency.

sheet bend *Naut.* A knot used to join two ropes' ends, made by passing one end through a loop of the other rope, carrying it around the loop, and slipping it under its own running part.

sheet·ing (shē′ting) *n.* **1** The act of sheeting, in any sense. **2** Cotton, muslin, linen, or cotton percale, for making bleached, unbleached, or colored sheets for beds.

sheet lightning Lightning appearing in sheet–like form as a momentary and broadly diffused radiance in the sky, caused by the reflection of a distant lightning flash.

sheet metal Metal rolled and pressed into sheets.

sheet music Music printed on separate sheets of paper.

sheeve (shēv) See SHEAVE[2].

Shef·field (shef′ēld) A city and county borough in West Riding, southern Yorkshire, England.

sheik (shēk, *Brit.* shāk) *n.* **1** A Moslem high priest, a venerable man; the chief or head of an Arab tribe or family: often used as a title of respect. **2** A man who fascinates women; a lady–killer: from *The Sheik,* a novel (1921) by Edith M. Hull. Also **sheikh.** Also spelled *scheik, shaik, sheyk.* [<Arabic *sheikh, shaykh,* lit., an elder, chief < *shakha* grow old]

sheik·dom (shēk′dəm) *n.* The land ruled by a sheik. Also **sheikh′dom.**

Sheik ul Is·lam (shēk′ ōōl is·läm′) Formerly, the head of the hierarchy in Turkey; the grand mufti.

shei·tan (shī·tän′) See SHAITAN.

shek·el (shek′əl) *n.* **1** An Assyrian, Babylonian, and, later, Hebrew unit of weight and money; a coin having this weight. **2** *pl. Slang* Money; riches. [<Hebrew *sheqel* < *shāqal* weigh]

She·ki·nah (shi·kī′nə) *n.* A cloud of glory which accompanied the tabernacle of the Jews, especially when over the mercy seat: a symbol and manifestation of the divine presence. [<Hebrew *shekhinah,* lit., dwelling place < *shākhan* dwell]

Shel·don (shel′dən), **Charles Monroe,** 1857–1946, U. S. clergyman and author.

shel·drake (shel′drāk′) *n.* **1** A large Old World duck of either of the genera *Tadorna* or *Casarca,* as the common sheldrake *(T. tadorna),* or the **ruddy sheldrake** *(C. rutila)* of southeastern Europe and North Africa. **2** A merganser, especially the red–breasted merganser or **salt–water sheldrake** *(Mergus serrator).* **3** The canvasback duck. [< dial. E *sheld* piebald, dappled + DRAKE]

shelf (shelf) *n. pl.* **shelves** (shelvz) **1** A board or slab set horizontally into or against a wall to support articles, as books; one of the boards in a bookcase or closet; the contents of a shelf. **2** Any flat projecting ledge, as of rock. **3** A steep–sided bank or shallow place in a body of water; a reef; shoal. **4** The stratum of bedrock met in sinking a shaft. — **on the shelf** No longer in use; discarded. [<LG *schelf* set of shelves]

Shel·i·kof Strait (shel′i·kôf) A channel between Alaska and Kodiak Island, connecting the North Pacific with the Gulf of Alaska, 130 miles long, 30 miles wide.

shell (shel) *n.* **1** A hard structure incasing an animal, as a mollusk, or an egg or fruit. **2** A mollusk; shellfish: much used in composition. **3** A hollow structure or vessel, generally thin and weak; also, a framework with its interior removed or destroyed, or one to be filled out or built upon. **4** A very light, long, and narrow racing rowboat. **5** A hollow metallic projectile filled with an explosive or chemical; especially, an artillery projectile filled with high explosive: used against materiel and fortifications and distinguished from shrapnel used against personnel. **6** The plates, etc., constituting the framework of a steam boiler or the like. **7** A metallic or paper cartridge case for breechloading small arms (see illustration under CARTRIDGE); also, any paper case used to contain the explosives of fireworks, such as torpedos. **8** *Physics* One of the orbits in which the electrons of an atom revolve. **9** A shape or outline that merely simulates a reality; hollow form; external semblance. **10** The external ear; auricle. **11** The lyre: originally a stringed tortoise shell. **12** A reserved or impersonal attitude: to come out of one's *shell.* — *v.t.* **1** To divest of or remove from a shell; strip from the husk, pod, or shell. **2** To separate from the cob, as Indian corn. **3** To bombard with shells, as a fort. **4** To cover with shells. — *v.i.* **5** To shed or become freed from the shell or pod. **6** To fall off, as a shell or scale. — **to shell out** *Colloq.* To hand over, as money. [OE *scell* shell] — **shell′er** *n.* — **shell′–less** *adj.* — **shell′y** *adj.*

she'll (shēl) She will.

shel·lac (shə·lak′) *n.* **1** A purified lac obtained as plates or cakes and extensively used in varnish, sealing wax, insulators, etc. **2** A solution, orange or white, of flake shellac

dissolved in methylated spirit: used for coating floors, woodwork, etc. —*v.t.* **·lacked,** **·lack·ing** **1** To cover or varnish with shellac. **2** *Slang* **a** To belabor; beat. **b.** To defeat utterly. Also **shel·lack'.** [<SHELL +LAC[1], trans. of F *laque en écailles* lac in fine sheets]

shel·lack·ing (shə-lak'ing) *n. Slang* **1** A beating; assault. **2** A thorough defeat.

shellac varnish Any of several varnishes containing dissolved shellac and giving a thin, hard, sometimes glossy, coat.

shell·back (shel'bak') *n.* A veteran sailor; an old salt; especially, one who has crossed the equator. [Prob. with reference to the shell of the sea turtle]

shell·bark (shel'bärk') *n.* The shagbark or one of its nuts.

shell bean Any of various beans cultivated for their edible mature seeds.

Shel·ley (shel'ē), **Mary Wollstonecraft,** 1797–1851, *née* Godwin, English novelist; wife of the following. —**Percy Bysshe,** 1792–1822, English poet.

shell·fire (shel'fīr') *n.* The firing of artillery shells.

shell·fish (shel'fish') *n. pl.* **·fish** or **·fish·es** Any aquatic animal having a shell, as a mollusk.

shell game **1** A swindling game in which the victim bets on the location of a pea covered by one of three nutshells; thimblerig. **2** Any game in which the victim cannot win.

shell·heap (shel'hēp') *n.* A kitchen midden. Also **shell'mound'** (-mound').

shell hole A hole made by an exploding shell; specifically, a craterlike depression in the ground. Also **shell crater.**

shell jacket A snugly fitted jacket, short at the back, worn in place of the tuxedo in tropical countries.

shell pink Any of several shades of light, pure pink, like the color in certain seashells.

shell·proof (shel'prōōf') *adj.* Built to resist the destructive effect of projectiles and bombs.

shell shock Combat fatigue. —**shell–shocked** (shel'shokt') *adj.*

shel·ter (shel'tər) *v.t.* To provide protection or shelter for; shield, as from danger or inclement weather. —*v.i.* To take shelter. —*n.* **1** That which covers or shields from exposure or danger; a place of safety. **2** The state of being sheltered or protected. **3** A cover from the weather, as a box for meteorological instruments, etc. **4** One who protects; a guardian. [Appar. alter. of ME *scheltrum* <OE *sceld–truma,* a body of men armed with shields, phalanx, protection] —**shel'ter·er** *n.* —**shel'ter·less** *adj.*

Synonyms (verb): cover, defend, guard, harbor, protect, screen, shield, ward. To *cover* generally means to extend completely over something; a vessel is *covered* with a lid; the head is *covered* with hair. To *shelter* is to *cover* so as to *protect* from injury or annoyance; as, The roof *shelters* from the storm. To *defend* implies the actual, *protect* implies the possible use of force or resisting power; *guard* implies sustained vigilance with readiness for conflict. *Protect* is more complete than *guard* or *defend;* an object may be faithfully *guarded* or bravely *defended* in vain, but that which is *protected* is secure. See CHERISH. Compare synonyms for DEFENSE. *Antonyms:* betray, expel, expose, refuse, reject, surrender.

Synonyms (noun): asylum, cover, covert, defense, harbor, haven, protection, refuge, retreat, sanctuary, shield. See DEFENSE. *Antonyms:* assault, attack, danger, exposure, onslaught, peril.

shelter belt Natural or artificial forest maintained as a protection from wind or snow.

shelter tent A tent large enough to accommodate two men: divided into two sections, each of which, called a **shelter half,** is carried as part of a soldier's field equipment. Also called *pup tent.*

shelt·ie (shel'tē) *n. Scot.* A Shetland pony. Also **shelt'y.**

shelve (shelv) *v.* **shelved, shelv·ing** *v.t.* **1** To place on a shelf. **2** To postpone indefinitely; put aside. **3** To retire. **4** To provide or fit with shelves. —*v.i.* **5** To incline gradually; slope. [<SHELF] —**shelv'y** *adj.*

shelves (shelvz) Plural of SHELF.

shelv·ing (shel'ving) *n.* **1** Shelves collectively. **2** Material for the construction of shelves. **3** The act of putting away on shelves; hence, putting aside; dismissing. **4** A slight inclining.

Shem (shem) The eldest son of Noah. *Gen.* v 32.

Shem·ite (shem'īt) See SEMITE.

Shen·an·do·ah (shen'ən-dō'ə) A river in Virginia and West Virginia, flowing 55 miles to the Potomac at Harper's Ferry. **The Shenandoah Valley,** part of the Great Appalachian Valley, was the scene of many battles during the Civil War.

Shenandoah National Park A region in the Blue Ridge Mountains of NW Virginia; 302 square miles; established 1935.

she·nan·i·gan (shi-nan'ə-gən) *n. Colloq.* Trickery; foolery; nonsense; also, treacherous action or a treacherous act. [Prob. <Irish *sionnach* fox]

Sheng·king (sheng'jing') A former name for LIAONING.

Shen·si (shen'sē') A province of NW central China; 75,000 square miles; capital, Sian.

Shen·stone (shen'stən, -stōn), **William,** 1714–1763, English poet.

Shen·yang (shun'yäng') A city of NE China, capital of Liaoning province; the capital city of the former Manchuria region; a major metal-fabricating center: formerly *Mukden, Fengtien.*

she·ol (shē'ōl) *n.* Hell. [<Hebrew *she'ol* cave <*shā'al* dig]

She·ol (shē'ōl) In the Old Testament, a place under the earth where the departed spirits were believed to go.

Shep·ard (shep'ərd), **Alan B., Jr.,** born 1923, U.S. naval officer; first American astronaut to make a rocket flight into space and first astronaut to control the space vehicle himself, May 5, 1961.

shep·herd (shep'ərd) *n.* **1** A keeper or herder of sheep. **2** Figuratively, a pastor, leader, or guide. —*v.t.* To watch and tend as a shepherd; guard; protect. [OE *scēaphyrde*] —**shep'herd·ess** *n. fem.*

shep·herd·clock (shep'ərd·klok') *n.* Goatbeard. Also **shep'herd's–clock'.**

shepherd dog A sheep dog, as the Scotch collie or the German shepherd dog.

shepherd kings See HYKSOS.

shep·herd's–nee·dle (shep'ərdz-nēd'l) *n.* Venus's-comb.

shep·herd's–purse (shep'ərdz-pûrs') *n.* A common herbaceous weed (*Capsella bursa-pastoris*) bearing small white flowers and notched triangular pods (whence its name).

Shep·pey (shep'ē), **Isle of** An island in the Thames estuary, northern Kent, England; 36 square miles.

sher·ard·ize (sher'ər-dīz) *v.t.* **·ized, ·iz·ing** *Metall.* To give a coating of zinc to (steel or iron) by packing in zinc dust, placing in a furnace, and subjecting to a heat sufficient to cause the zinc vapor to soak in. [after *Sherard Cowper–Coles,* died 1936, British inventor] —**sher'ard·iz·ing** *n.* & *adj.*

Sher·a·ton (sher'ə-tən) *adj.* Denoting the graceful, straight-lined style of English furniture developed by Thomas Sheraton.

Sher·a·ton (sher'ə-tən), **Thomas,** 1751–1806, English furniture maker and designer.

sher·bet (shûr'bit) *n.* **1** A flavored water ice. **2** An Oriental drink, made of fruit juice sweetened and diluted with water and sometimes cooled with snow. [<Turkish *sharbat* <Arabic *sharbah* a drink <*shariba* drink. Doublet of SIRUP.]

Sher·brooke (shûr'brŏŏk') A city in southern Quebec province, Canada.

sherd (shûrd) *n.* A fragment of pottery: often in composition: *potsherd:* also spelled *shard.* [Var. of SHARD.]

Sher·i·dan (sher'ə-dən), **Philip Henry,** 1831–1888, U.S. general in the Civil War. —**Richard Brinsley,** 1751–1816, English dramatist and politician.

she·rif (she·rēf') *n.* **1** A member of a princely Moslem family which claims descent from Mohammed through his daughter Fatima. **2** The chief magistrate of Mecca: also **grand sherif. 3** An Arab chief. Also **she·reef'.** [<Arabic *sharif* noble]

sher·iff (sher'if) *n.* The chief administrative officer of a county, who executes the mandates of courts, etc. In the United States, the sheriff is elected by the legislature or by direct vote of the citizens and must be of age, a citizen of the country, and reside in the county he represents. [OE *scir–gerēfa* shire reeve] —**sher'iff·dom** *n.*

Sher·iff·muir (sher'if-myŏŏr') A locality in southern Perthshire, Scotland; scene of a battle between the Scottish Jacobites and the English, 1715.

sher·lock (shûr'lok) *n. Slang* A detective. [after *Sherlock* Holmes]

Sher·lock Holmes (shûr'lok hōmz') A fictitious English detective, the central character of numerous stories by Arthur Conan Doyle.

Sher·man (shûr'mən), **John,** 1823–1900, U.S. statesman. —**Roger,** 1721–93, American statesman; signer of Declaration of Independence. —**William Tecumseh,** 1820–91, U.S. general in the Civil War; led march from Atlanta to the sea, 1864.

she·root (shə-rōōt') See CHEROOT.

Sher·ra·moor (sher'ə-mōōr') *n. Scot. & Brit. Dial.* The Scottish rebellion of 1715, so called because the Jacobites were stopped in their advance at Sheriffmuir; hence, any turmoil or tumult. Also **Sher'ry·moor.**

Sher·ring·ton (sher'ing-tən), **Sir Charles Scott,** 1861–1952, English physiologist.

sher·ry (sher'ē) *n. pl.* **·ries** The fortified wines of Jerez (formerly Xerez), Spain, or a wine made in imitation of these, as in California. [from *Xerez,* Spain]

sherry cobbler A mixed beverage of sherry, lemon, sugar, water, and ice.

s'Her·to·gen·bosch (ser'tō-khən-bôs') The capital of North Brabant province in south central Netherlands: French *Bois–le–Duc.*

Sher·wood (shûr'wŏŏd), **Robert Emmet,** 1896–1955, U.S. playwright.

Sherwood Forest An ancient forest, chiefly in Nottinghamshire, central England; celebrated as the home of Robin Hood and his men.

she's (shēz) **1** She is. **2** She has.

Shet·land Islands (shet'lənd) A Scottish island group NE of the Orkney Islands, comprising a county of northern Scotland (**Shetland:** also *Zetland*); 551 square miles; several hundred islands, 24 inhabited; capital, Lerwick, on Mainland, the largest island.

Shetland pony A small, hardy, shaggy breed of pony originally bred on the Shetland Islands.

Shetland sheepdog A long-haired black or brown working dog resembling a small collie, bred in the Shetland Islands.

Shetland wool Thin, very loosely twisted yarn from the wool of Shetland sheep; also, the wool.

sheuch (shükh) *n. Scot.* A ditch or open drain. Also **sheugh.**

sheuk (shœk) *Scot.* Past tense and past participle of SHAKE.

shew (shō) Older spelling of SHOW.

shew·bread (shō'bred') *n.* Unleavened bread formerly displayed in the Jewish temple: also spelled *showbread.*

she–wolf (shē'wŏŏlf') *n. pl.* **–wolves** (-wŏŏlvz') A female wolf.

Shey·enne River (shī-en') A river in North Dakota, flowing 325 miles east and south to the Red River of the North.

Shi·ah (shē'ə) *n.* **1** One of the two great sects (Sunni and Shiah) of Islam, consisting of followers of Ali, the cousin and son–in–law of Mohammed, who maintain that Ali was the first Imam and true Successor to the Prophet. **2** An adherent of Shiah: also called *Shiite:* also **Shie·ite** (shē'īt). [<Arabic *shi'i* a follower, sect]

shib·bo·leth (shib'ə-leth) *n.* A test word or pet phrase of a party; a watchword: from the Hebrew word *shibboleth,* given by Jephthah (*Judges* xii 4–6) as a test to distinguish his own men from the Ephraimites, who used the pronunciation *sibboleth.* [<Hebrew *shibbōleth* ear of corn]

Shi·be·li (shi-bā'lē), **Web·be** (web'ā) A river in Ethiopia and Somalia, flowing NE, then SE and south 1,200 miles to a swamp 25 miles inland from the Indian Ocean: also *Shebeli.* Also **Webi Shebeli, Webi Shibeli.**

Shi·de·ha·ra (shē-de-hä'rä), **Baron Kijuro,**

1872–1951, Japanese diplomat and statesman.
shied (shīd) Past tense and past participle of SHY.
shield (shēld) *n.* **1** A broad piece of defensive armor, commonly carried on the left arm; a large buckler. **2** Something that protects or defends; a defender; shelter. **3** Any device for covering or protecting something. **4** *Mil.* A screen of steel attached to a gun to protect the men who are serving it. **5** *Mining* A framework or screen of wood or iron protecting the workers: pushed forward as the work advances. **6** *Her.* The escutcheon upon which emblems of heraldry are depicted. **7** *Zool.* A platelike protective part, as the carapace of a crustacean. **8** A policeman's badge. See synonyms under DEFENSE, SHELTER. —*v.t.* **1** To protect from danger as with a shield; defend; guard. **2** *Archaic* To avert; forbid. —*v.i.* **3** To act as a shield or safeguard. See synonyms under SHELTER. [OE *sceld*] —**shield′er** *n.* —**shield′-bear′er** (-bâr′ər) *n.* —**shield′-shaped′** (-shāpt′) *adj.*

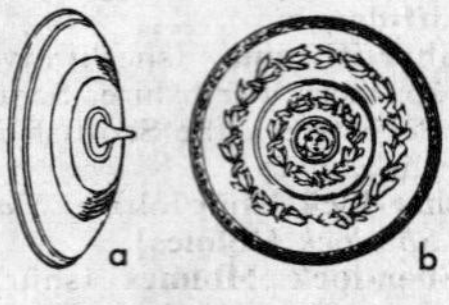

SHIELDS
a. Anglo-Saxon.
b. Greek.

shield bone *Anat.* The scapula or shoulder bone.
shield·fern (shēld′fûrn′) *n.* A fern (genus *Dryopteris*), so called from its shield-shaped sporangia.
Shield of David See MOGEN DAVID.
shiel·ing (shē′ling) *n.* A shepherd's or sportsman's hut: also spelled *shealing.* [Var. of SHEALING]
shi·er¹ (shī′ər) *n.* A horse in the habit of shying: also spelled *shyer.*
shi·er² (shī′ər), **shi·est** (shī′ist) Comparative and superlative of SHY.
shift (shift) *v.t.* **1** To change or move from one position, place, etc., to another. **2** To change for another or others of the same class. **3** To change (gears) from one arrangement to another. **4** *Ling.* To alter phonetically as part of a systematic change. —*v.i.* **5** To change position, place, etc. **6** To try varied expedients; do the best one can; manage. **7** To evade; equivocate. **8** To shift gears: The car *shifts* automatically. —*n.* **1** The act of shifting. **2** A recourse or contrivance adopted in the absence of direct means: We'll make *shift* to get along; hence, a dodge; artifice; trick; evasion. **3** *Archaic* or *Dial.* An undergarment; chemise. **4** A change of clothes. **5** A change of place, direction, or form: a *shift* in the wind; transfer, as of a burden. **6** A change of the position of the hand when playing on the fingerboard of an instrument of the viol class. **7** A relay of workers; also, the working time of each group. **8** *Physics* Any of various displacements of spectral lines caused by velocity of the light source, gravitational effect, etc. Compare EINSTEIN SHIFT, DOPPLER EFFECT. **9** *Geol.* The relative displacement of areas on opposite sides of a rock fault and outside of the zone of dislocation. **10** *Ling.* **a** A patterned phonetic or phonemic change, as the consonant *shift* described in Grimm's Law. **b** Functional shift. See synonyms under CHANGE, CONVEY. [OE *sciftan* divide] —**shift′er** *n.*
shift·less (shift′lis) *adj.* **1** Unable or unwilling to shift for oneself; inefficient or lazy. **2** Inefficiently done; showing lack of energy or resource. See synonyms under IMPROVIDENT. —**shift′less·ly** *adv.* —**shift′less·ness** *n.*
shift·y (shif′tē) *adj.* **shift·i·er, shift·i·est** **1** Full of expedients; alert; capable. **2** Artful; tricky; fickle. —**shift′i·ly** *adv.* —**shift′i·ness** *n.*
Shi·ge·mi·tsu (shē·ge·mē·tsōō), **Mamoru,** 1887–1957, Japanese diplomat.
Shi Huang Ti (shir′ hwäng′ tē′), 259–210 B.C., Chinese emperor.
Shi·ism (shē′iz·əm) *n.* The doctrine held by the Shiah or Persian branch of Moslems, showing traces of the earlier Persian faith. See SHIAH.
Shi·ite (shē′īt) *n.* A Shiah. —**Shi·it′ic** (-it′ik) *adj.*
shi·kar (shi·kär′) *Anglo-Indian v.t.* To hunt. —*n.* Hunting; sport; the chase. [<Urdu <Persian]
shi·ka·ree (shi·kä′rē) *n.* A hunter or sportsman; especially, a native attendant and guide in the chase. Also **shi·kar′ree, shi·ka′ri.** [<Urdu *shikari*]
Shi·kar·pur (shi·kär′pŏŏr) A city in NE Sind, West Pakistan.
Shi·ko·ku (shē·kō·kōō) An island of SW Japan, east of Kyushu; 7,248 square miles.
Shil·ka (shil′kə) A river in SE Siberian Russian S.F.S.R., flowing 345 miles NE to the Amur.
shill¹ (shil) *adj. Scot.* Shrill.
shill² (shil) *n. Slang* The assistant of a sidewalk peddler or gambler who makes a purchase or bet to encourage onlookers to buy or bet; a capper. [Origin unknown]
shil·le·lagh (shi·lā′lə, -lē) *n.* In Ireland, a stout cudgel made of oak or blackthorn. See synonyms under STICK. Also **shil·la′lah, shil·lea′lah, shil·le′lah.** [from *Shillelagh,* a town in Ireland famed for its oaks]
shil·ling (shil′ing) *n.* **1** A current silver coin of Great Britain, first issued in 1504; twelvepence. Compare SOLIDUS (def. 2). **2** A former denomination of money in the United States varying in value from 12 1/2 to 16 2/3 cents. —**King's shilling** An English shilling formerly handed to a recruit on his joining the British military service: considered as binding as the signing of a contract: also **Queen's shilling.** [OE *scilling*]

PINE-TREE SHILLING
Issued by Massachusetts in 1652 (actual size).

shilling side Formerly, the west side of lower Broadway, New York, where the shops carried a cheaper grade of merchandise than on the other (the dollar) side.
Shil·long (shi·lông′) The capital of Khasi and Jaintia Hills district, India.
shil·ly-shal·ly (shil′ē·shal′ē) *v.i.* **·lied, ·ly·ing** **1** To act with indecision; be irresolute; vacillate. **2** To trifle. —*adj.* Weak; hesitating. —*n.* Weak or foolish vacillation; irresolution; any trifling. —*adv.* In an irresolute manner. [Dissimilated reduplication of *shall I?*] —**shil′ly-shal′li·er** *n.*
Shi·loh (shī′lō) **1** An ancient Israelite sanctuary in central Palestine, NW of the Dead Sea. **2** A national military park in SW Tennessee; 6 square miles; scene of a Confederate defeat in the Civil War, 1862; established 1894.
shil·pit (shil′pit) *adj. Scot.* **1** Watery and insipid; weak: *shilpit* drink. **2** Sickly; puny: a *shilpit* girl.
shi·ly (shī′lē) See SHYLY.
shim (shim) *n.* In machinery, stoneworking, and railroading, a piece of metal or other material used to fill out space, as where joints are worn loose, or between something and its support. —*v.t.* **shimmed, shim·ming** To wedge up or fill out to a proper position or level by inserting a shim. [Origin uncertain]
Shi·mi·zu (shē·mē·zōō) A port on central Honshu island, Japan.
shim·mer (shim′ər) *v.i.* To shine faintly; give off or emit a tremulous light; glimmer. —*n.* A tremulous shining or gleaming; glimmer; gleam. See synonyms under LIGHT. [OE *scimerian,* prob. freq. of *scīnan* shine] —**shim′mer·y** *adj.*
shim·my (shim′ē) *n. pl.* **·mies** *U.S.* **1** *Colloq.* A chemise. **2** A jazz dance accompanied by shaking movements: also **shimmy shake.** **3** Unusual vibration, as in automobile wheels. —*v.i.* **·mied, ·my·ing** **1** To vibrate or wobble. **2** To dance the shimmy. [Alter. of CHEMISE]
Shim·o·no·se·ki (shim′ə·nō·sā′kē, *Japanese* shē·mō·nō·sä·kē) A port of SW Honshu island, Japan, on **Shimonoseki Strait,** a narrow channel between Honshu and Kyushu, connecting the Sea of Japan with the Inland Sea.
shin¹ (shin) *n.* **1** The front part of the leg below the knee; also, the shin bone. **2** The lower foreleg: a *shin* of beef. —*v.t.* & *v.i.* **shinned, shin·ning** **1** To climb (a pole) by gripping with the hands or arms and the shins or legs: usually with *up.* **2** To kick (someone) on the shins. [OE *scinu*]
shin² (shēn) *n.* The twenty-first Hebrew letter. See ALPHABET.
Shi·nar (shī′när) An ancient country along the lower Tigris and Euphrates. *Gen.* x 10.
shin bone The tibia.
shin·dig (shin′dig) *n. U.S. Slang* A dance or noisy party. [? < *a dig on the shin*]
shin·dy (shin′dē) *n. pl.* **·dies** **1** *Slang* A riotous quarrel; row; also, a dance or shindig. **2** The game of shinny. [Var. of SHINNY]
shine (shīn) *v.i.* **shone** or (*esp. for def.* **5**) **shined, shin·ing** **1** To emit light; beam; glow. **2** To gleam, as by reflected light. **3** To excel or be conspicuous in splendor, beauty, or intellectual brilliance; be preeminent. —*v.t.* **4** To cause to shine. **5** To brighten by rubbing or polishing. —**to shine up to** *Slang* To try to please. —*n.* **1** The state or quality of being bright or shining; radiance; luster; sheen. **2** Fair weather; sunshine. **3** *U.S. Colloq.* A liking or fancy. **4** *U.S. Colloq.* A smart trick or prank. **5** A gloss or polish on shoes. See synonyms under LIGHT. —**to take a shine to** *U.S. Colloq.* To become fond of. [OE *scīnan*]
Synonyms (verb): beam, coruscate, glare, gleam, glisten, glitter, glow, scintillate, sparkle.
shin·er (shī′nər) *n.* **1** One who or that which shines or causes to shine. **2** A bright or gold coin. **3** One of various silvery cyprinoid freshwater fishes (genus *Notropis*) common in North America. **4** A bristletail. **5** *Slang* A black eye from a blow.
shin·gle¹ (shing′gəl) *n.* **1** A thin, tapering piece of wood or other material, usually about 18 inches long and 4 or more inches wide, used in courses to cover roofs. **2** A small sign board, as a shingle or a brass plate, bearing the name of a doctor, lawyer, etc., and placed outside his office. **3** A short haircut. —*v.t.* **·gled, ·gling** **1** To cover (a roof, building, etc.) with or as with shingles. **2** To cut (the hair) short all over the head. [Alter. of ME *schindle* <L *scindula,* var. of *scandula* a shingle] —**shin′gler** *n.*
shin·gle² (shing′gəl) *n.* **1** Rounded, water-worn detritus, coarser than gravel, found on the seashore. **2** A place strewn with shingle, as a beach. [Cf. Norw. *singl* coarse gravel] —**shin′gly** *adj.*
shin·gle³ (shing′gəl) *v.t.* **·gled, ·gling** *Metall.* To drive out impurities from (puddled iron) by heavy blows or pressure. [Origin unknown]
shingle oak The jack oak.
shin·gles (shing′gəlz) *n. Pathol.* A skin disease, most commonly due to an infection, but also to nervous trouble, accompanied by neuralgia, with eruptions sometimes extending half round the body like a girdle: also called *herpes zoster.* [Alter. of Med. L *cingulus* <L *cingulum* girdle < *cingere* gird]
shin·ing (shī′ning) *adj.* **1** Emitting or reflecting a continuous light; gleaming; luminous. **2** Of unusual brilliance or excellence; conspicuous. —**shin′ing·ly** *adv.*
shin·leaf (shin′lēf′) *n.* A low perennial herb (*Pyrola elliptica*), with rounded evergreen root leaves, common in the woods of the northern United States. [From the use of its leaves for shinplasters]
shin·ny¹ (shin′ē) *n.* A game resembling hockey, or one of the sticks or clubs used by the players. Also **shin′ney.** [< *shin ye,* a cry used in the game]
shin·ny² (shin′ē) *v.i.* **·nied, ·ny·ing** *U.S. Colloq.* To climb using one's shins: usually with *up.*
shin·plas·ter (shin′plas′tər, -pläs′-) *n.* **1** *U.S.* **a** Fractional currency issued by other than the constituted authorities. See FRACTIONAL CURRENCY. **b** Any scrip or paper money issued by private enterprises. **2** A plaster for a sore shin.
shin·ti·yan (shin′tē·yan) *n. pl.* Wide loose trousers worn by Moslem women. [<Arabic < Turkish *chintiyan*]
Shin·to (shin′tō) *n.* The primitive religion of Japan, consisting chiefly in ancestor worship, nature worship, and the worship of many ethnic divinities, from the chief of whom the Emperor is thought to be descended, and thus himself a god: as **State Shinto,** it was the state religion of Japan, 1868–1945, and in that

period incorporated many nationalistic and militaristic elements, later minimized. Also **Shin′to·ism.** [<Japanese, way of the gods < Chinese *shin* god + *tao* way or law] —**Shin′.to·ist** *n.*

shin·y (shī′nē) *adj.* **shin·i·er, shin·i·est 1** Glistening; glossy; polished. **2** Bright; clear.

ship (ship) *n.* **1** Any vessel suitable for deep-water navigation: a *steamship*, sailing *ship*. **2** A large seagoing sailing vessel with at least three masts, carrying square-rigged sails on all three. **3** An airship or airplane. **4** Figuratively, fortune: when my *ship* comes in. —**capital ship** Any vessel of war of the first rank, as a battleship, battle cruiser, or aircraft carrier. —*v.* **shipped, ship·ping** *v.t.* **1** To transport by ship or other mode of conveyance. **2** To send by any established mode of transportation, as by rail. **3** To hire and receive for service on board a vessel, as sailors. **4** *Naut.* To receive over the side, as in rough weather: to *ship* a wave. **5** *Colloq.* To get rid of. **6** To set or fit in a prepared place on a boat or vessel, as a mast, or a rudder; also, to draw (oars) inside a boat from rowlocks. —*v.i.* **7** To go on board ship; embark. **8** To undergo shipment: Raspberries do not *ship* well. **9** To enlist as a seaman. [OE *scip*]

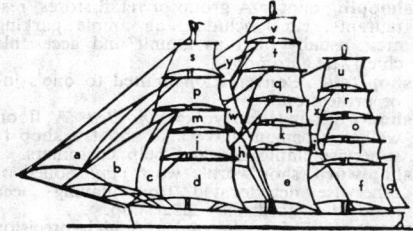

FULL-RIGGED SHIP
With double topsails and staysails.
a. Flying jib. *b.* Jib. *c.* Foretopmast staysail. *d.* Foresail. *e.* Mainsail. *f.* Crossjacksail. *g.* Spanker. *h.* Maintopmast staysail. *i.* Mizzentopmast staysail. *j.* Lower foretopsail. *k.* Lower maintopsail. *l.* Lower mizzentopsail. *m.* Upper foretopsail. *n.* Upper maintopsail. *o.* Upper mizzentopsail. *p.* Foretopgallant sail. *q.* Maintopgallant sail. *r.* Mizzentopgallant sail. *s.* Fore royal. *t.* Main royal. *u.* Mizzen royal. *v.* Main skysail. *w.* Maintopgallant staysail. *x.* Mizzentopgallant staysail. *y.* Main royal staysail.

–ship *suffix of nouns* **1** The state, condition, or quality of: *friendship*. **2** Office, rank, or dignity of: *kingship*. **3** The art or skill of: *marksmanship*. [OE *-scipe*]

ship biscuit Hardtack; sea biscuit.

ship·board (ship′bôrd′, -bōrd′) *n.* The side or deck of a ship; hence, a vessel: only in phrase **on shipboard.**

ship broker A mercantile agent who buys and sells ships, cargoes, etc. Also **ship·bro·ker** (ship′brō′kər). —**ship′bro′ker·age** *n.*

ship·build·er (ship′bil′dər) *n.* One who designs, superintends, contracts for, or works at the building of vessels. —**ship′build′ing** *n.*

ship canal A waterway or canal deep enough for seagoing vessels.

ship carpenter 1 A carpenter who builds or repairs vessels; a shipwright. **2** A carpenter attached to a vessel.

ship chandler One who deals in cordage, canvas, and other furniture of vessels.

ship fever Prison fever.

Ship·ka Pass (ship′kä) A pass in the central Balkan Mountains, central Bulgaria; elevation, 4,166 feet; scene of a defeat of the Turks by the Bulgarians, 1877.

ship·load (ship′lōd′) *n.* The quantity that a ship carries or can carry; a cargo.

ship·man (ship′mən) *n. pl.* **·men** (-mən) A sailor; mariner.

ship·mas·ter (ship′mas′tər, -mäs′-) *n.* The captain or master of a merchant ship.

ship·mate (ship′māt′) *n.* A fellow sailor.

ship·ment (ship′mənt) *n.* The act of shipping, or that which is shipped; a consignment.

ship money An impost levied by the sovereign on English maritime towns and counties, for

providing and arming a fleet for the protection of the coast: originated about 1007 and declared illegal by Parliament in 1640.

ship of the line Formerly, a man-of-war large enough to take a position in a line of battle.

ship owner A person owning a ship, ships, or shares in them. —**ship owning**

ship·pa·ble (ship′ə·bəl) *adj.* That can be shipped or transported.

ship·pen (ship′ən) *n. Scot.* A cow shed; barn. Also **ship′pon.**

ship·per (ship′ər) *n.* **1** One who or that which ships. **2** Any appliance for shifting some part of a machine, as in a loom. **3** A skipper; mariner.

ship·ping (ship′ing) *n.* **1** Ships collectively; the body of vessels belonging to a country or port; also, tonnage. **2** The act of shipping, in any sense. **3** *Obs.* A voyage.

shipping ton A freight ton. See under TON (def. 3).

ship–rigged (ship′rigd′) *adj. Naut.* Rigged as a ship; square-rigged. See illustration under SHIP.

ship·shape (ship′shāp′) *adj.* Well arranged; trim; orderly; neat. —*adv.* In a seamanlike manner; neatly.

ship's papers The documents required by international law to be carried by a ship, as bills of lading, bill of health, invoices, logbook, proofs of ownership; also, certificate of registry, crew-list, clearance, license, and shipping articles. Compare MANIFEST.

ship's time *Naut.* The time as shown by the deck clock: usually local mean time at whatever meridian a vessel happens to be.

ship·way (ship′wā′) *n.* **1** The ways on which a ship is built or examined. **2** A ship canal.

ship·worm (ship′wûrm′) *n.* One of a family (*Teredinidae*) of marine bivalves, resembling worms, especially *Teredo navalis*, which burrows into the timbers of ships, piers, wharfs, etc.: also called *borer*.

ship·wreck (ship′rek′) *n.* **1** The partial or total destruction of a ship at sea. **2** Utter or practical destruction; ruin. **3** Scattered remnants, as of a wrecked ship; wreckage. —*v.t.* **1** To wreck, as a vessel. **2** To bring to disaster; ruin; destroy.

ship·wright (ship′rīt′) *n.* A ship carpenter or builder; one who works on the wooden parts of ships.

ship·yard (ship′yärd′) *n.* An enclosure where ships are built or repaired.

shipyard eye *Pathol.* Kerato-conjunctivitis.

Shi·raz (shē·räz′) A city in SW Iran.

shire (shīr) *n.* **1** A territorial division of Great Britain; a county. **2** A county in America: used only in compounds and proper names borrowed from England. [OE *scir*]

Shi·ré (shē′rā) A river of southern Nyasaland and central Mozambique, SE Africa, flowing 250 miles south from Lake Nyasa to the Zambezi. *Portuguese* **Chi·re** (shē′rə).

shire horse One of a breed of large draft horses originating in the shires or midland counties of England. Also **Shire.**

shire town The capital of a county; county seat; county town.

shirk (shûrk) *v.t.* **1** To avoid the doing of; evade doing (something that should be done). **2** *Obs.* To obtain by trickery. —*v.i.* **3** To avoid work or evade obligation. [<*n.*] —*n.* One who shirks; also **shirk′er.** [Prob. <G *Schurke* rascal. Akin to SHARK[2].]

Shir·ley (shûr′lē), **James,** 1596–1666, English dramatist.

Shir·pu·la (shir·pōō′lə) See LAGASH.

shirr (shûr) *v.t.* **1** To gather on parallel gathering threads. **2** To bake with crumbs in a buttered dish, as eggs. —*n.* **1** A fulling or gathering by threads. **2** A rubber thread woven into a fabric to make it elastic. [Origin unknown]

shirt (shûrt) *n.* **1** A loose garment for the upper part of the body, usually having collar and cuffs and a front closing. **2** A closely fitting undergarment for the upper part of the body. **3** The inner lining of a blast furnace. —**to keep one's shirt on** *Slang* To remain calm; keep one's temper. —**to lose one's shirt** *Slang* To lose everything. [OE *scyrte* shirt, short garment. Akin to SKIRT.] —**shirt′less** *adj.*

shirt·ing (shûr′ting) *n.* Closely woven material

of cotton, linen, silk, etc., used for making shirts, blouses, dresses, etc.

shirt–waist (shûrt′wāst′) *n.* A tailored, sleeved blouse or shirt: usually worn tucked in under skirt or trousers.

Shir·wa (shir′wä) See CHILWA.

shish ke·bab (shish′ kə·bäb′) Beef or lamb, cut into cubes and cooked on skewers with onions, green peppers, and tomatoes. [<Arm. *shish kabab*]

shist (shist) See SCHIST, etc.

shit·tim·wood (shit′im·wŏŏd′) *n.* In the Bible, the wood of a species of acacia (the **shit′tah** or **shittah tree**) used in making the furniture of the Jewish tabernacle. Also **shit′tim.** [<Hebrew *shittim*, pl. of *shittāh*]

shiv (shiv) *n. Slang* In the criminal underworld, a knife or razor: often spelled *chevy*, *chiv*. Also **shive, shiv′y.** [<Romany *chiv* goad]

Shi·va (shē′və) See SIVA.

shiv·a·ree (shiv′ə·rē′) *n. U.S.* A charivari, especially in the sense of the burlesque serenade of newly-weds. [Alter. of CHARIVARI]

shive[1] (shīv) *n. Brit. Dial.* **1** A short flat cork; a thin wooden bung. **2** *Brit.* A slice cut off, as of bread. [Cf. ON *skifa* slice]

shive[2] (shīv) *n.* A thin fragment; sliver; a woody fragment separated from flax by breaking. [Back formation <SHIVER[2]]

shiv·er[1] (shiv′ər) *v.i.* To tremble, as with cold or fear; shake; vibrate; quiver. —*v.t. Naut.* To cause to flutter in the wind, as a sail. See synonyms under QUAKE. —*n.* The act of shivering; a shaking or quivering from any cause. [? Blend of SHAKE and QUIVER]

shiv·er[2] (shiv′ər) *v.t. & v.i.* To break suddenly into fragments; shatter. See synonyms under BREAK, SHAKE. —*n.* A splinter; sliver. [ME *schivere*; origin uncertain]

shiv·er·y[1] (shiv′ər·ē) *adj.* Chilly; tremulous.

shiv·er·y[2] (shiv′ər·ē) *adj.* Easily shivered; brittle.

Shi·zu·o·ka (shē·zōō·ō·kä) A city on central Honshu island, Japan.

shlock (shlok) See SCHLOCK.

shoal[1] (shōl) *n.* **1** A shallow place in any body of water. **2** A sandbank or bar, especially one seen at low water. Compare BANK and REEF. —*v.i.* **1** To become shallow. —*v.t.* **2** To make shallow. **3** To sail into a lesser depth of (water), as shown by soundings: The ship *shoaled* her water off Cape Hatteras. —*adj.* Of little depth; shallow. Also, *Scot.*, *shaul.* [OE *sceald* shallow]

shoal[2] (shōl) *n.* An assemblage or multitude; throng, as of fish. —*v.i.* **1** To throng in shoals or multitudes. **2** To school: said of fish. [OE *scolu* shoal of fish. Akin to SCHOOL[2].]

shoal duck The American eider duck: so called from Isles of Shoals, off Portsmouth, New Hampshire.

shoal·y (shō′lē) *adj.* Abounding in shoals.

shoat (shōt) *n.* **1** A young hog. **2** A worthless fellow. Also spelled *shote.* [Cf. West Flemish *schote* young pig]

shock[1] (shok) *n.* **1** A violent collision or concussion; impact; blow. **2** A sudden and violent sensation, as if causing one to shake or tremble; a stroke: a *shock* of paralysis. **3** A sudden agitation of the mind; startling emotion. **4** *Pathol.* Prostration of bodily functions, as from sudden injury. **5** The passage of a strong electric current through the body, or the phenomena it produces: characterized by involuntary muscular contractions. See synonyms under BLOW, COLLISION. —*v.t.* **1** To shake by sudden collision; jar; give a shock to. **2** To disturb the emotions or mind of; horrify; disgust. **3** To encounter with hostile intent; meet with sudden encounter. —*v.i.* **4** *Archaic* To come into violent contact; collide. [<F *choc* <*choquer* <Gmc. Cf. MDu. *schokken* collide.]

shock[2] (shok) *n.* A number of sheaves of grain, stalks of maize, or the like, stacked for drying upright in a field. —*v.t. & v.i.* To gather (grain) into a shock or shocks. [ME *schokke* <Gmc. Cf. MLG *schok.*] —**shock′er** *n.*

shock[3] (shok) *adj.* Shaggy; bushy. —*n.* **1** A coarse, tangled mass, as of hair. **2** A dog with a woolly coat. [? Var. of SHAG]

shock absorber *Mech.* **1** A device designed to absorb the energy of sudden impacts or of abrupt changes in velocity, as the springs of

an automobile, or an airplane landing gear. **2** A type of damper which absorbs motion, as of a part or mechanism, by hydraulic action, friction, etc.

shock action *Mil.* A sudden, violent attack by mobile and massed military units, as tanks, artillery, infantry with bayonets fixed, etc.

shock·er (shok′ər) *n.* **1** One who or that which shocks or startles. **2** *Brit. Colloq.* A sensational novel.

shock excitation *Electr.* The excitation of an oscillatory circuit by an impulse of different frequency, as in radio: also called *impulse excitation.*

shock·head (shok′hed′) *adj.* Having thick, bushy hair. Also **shock′-head′ed.**

shock·ing (shok′ing) *adj.* Causing a mental shock; striking as with horror or disgust; repugnant; distressing. See synonyms under AWFUL, FLAGRANT, FRIGHTFUL. **—shock′ing·ly** *adv.* **—shock′ing·ness** *n.*

shock tactics *Mil.* The use of a preponderating mass of picked troops in an attack in which hand-to-hand encounter is relied upon more than gunfire.

shock therapy *Med.* The treatment of certain nervous and mental disorders by the subcutaneous injection of drugs, as Metrazol, insulin, camphor, etc., or by electrical shocks.

shock troops *Mil.* Seasoned or picked men selected to lead an attack.

shock wave *Physics* A wave (of air, sound, etc.) having a pattern of flow which changes abruptly, with corresponding changes in temperature, pressure, and density: characteristic of bodies moving at or above the speed of sound.

shod (shod) Past tense and alternative past participle of SHOE.

shod·dy (shod′ē) *n. pl.* **·dies** **1** Reclaimed wool obtained by shredding discarded woolens or worsteds: longer fiber than mungo and better quality. **2** Fiber or cloth manufactured of inferior material or of shredded woolen rags. **3** Vulgar assumption or display; pretension; sham. **4** Refuse; waste. **—***adj.* **·di·er, ·di·est** **1** Made of or containing shoddy. **2** Sham; inferior. [Origin uncertain] **—shod′di·ly** *adv.* **—shod′di·ness** *n.*

shoe (shōō) *n. pl.* **shoes** (*Obs.* **shoon**) **1** An outer covering, usually of leather, for the human foot, usually distinguished from a *boot* by not reaching above the ankle. **2** Something resembling a shoe in position or use. **3** A rim or plate of iron to protect the hoof of an animal from wear or injury. **4** A strip of iron, steel, or other hard material fitted under a sleigh or sledge runner to receive friction. **5** A drag of iron or wood placed under the wheel of a vehicle to retard its motion in going downhill; also, the part of a brake that presses upon the wheel. **6** An iron socket or ferrule for protecting the point of a wooden pile, or the end of a handspike, pole, or staff. **7** The tread or outer covering of a pneumatic tire, as for an automobile. **8** The part of a bridge on which the superstructure rests. **9** The sliding contact plate on an electric car. **—***v.t.* **shod, shod** or **shod·den, shoe·ing** **1** To furnish with shoes or the like. **2** To furnish with a guard of metal, wood, etc., for protection, as against wear. [OE *scōh*]

PARTS OF A SHOE

a. Tongue.	*h.* Slipsole.
b. Top.	*i.* Insole.
c. Lacing.	*j.* Shank.
d. Eyelets.	*k.* Heel.
e. Vamp.	*l.* Counter.
f. Toe cap.	*m.* Backstay.
g. Outsole.	*n.* Backstrap.

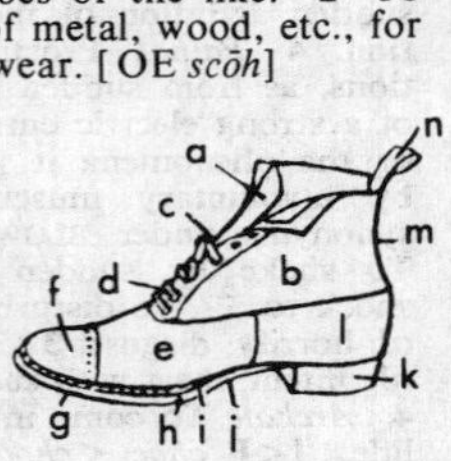

shoe·bill (shōō′bil′) *n.* A heron (*Balaeniceps rex*) of central Africa, with a huge vaulted and hooked bill.

shoe·black (shōō′blak′) *n.* A bootblack.

shoe findings Shoemakers' tools and supplies, with the exception of leather.

shoe·horn (shōō′hôrn′) *n.* A smooth curved implement of horn or other material shaped to aid in putting on a shoe.

shoe·mak·er (shōō′mā′kər) *n.* **1** One who makes shoes, boots, etc. **2** A cobbler. **—shoe′mak′ing** *n.*

sho·er (shōō′ər) *n.* One who supplies or fits on shoes; specifically, a blacksmith.

shoe·shine (shōō′shīn′) *n.* **1** The waxing and polishing of a pair of shoes. **2** The polished appearance thus given to the shoes.

shoe string A lace, cord, or ribbon for tying a shoe. Also **shoe lace.**

shoe·tree (shōō′trē′) *n.* A wooden or metal form for inserting in boots and shoes to preserve their shape or to stretch them: also called *boot-tree.*

sho·far (shō′fär) *n.* A ram's horn used in Jewish ritual, sounded on solemn occasions and in war. It is still blown on the Jewish New Year and on the Day of Atonement: also spelled *shophar.* [<Hebrew *shōphār*]

sho·gun (shō′gun, -gōōn) *n.* The hereditary commander in chief of the Japanese army until 1868: known to foreigners as the *tycoon.* [<Japanese <Chinese *chiang-chün* leader of an army] **—sho′gun·ate** (-it, -āt) *n.*

Sho·la·pur (shō′lə·pōōr) A town in central southern Bombay State, India.

shone (shōn, shon) Past tense and past participle of SHINE.

shoo (shōō) *interj.* Begone! be off! away!: used in driving away fowls. **—***v.t.* To drive away by crying "shoo." **—***v.i.* To cry "shoo." [Imit.]

shoo·fly (shōō′flī) *n. U.S.* **1** A shuffling dance; also, the music for it. **2** An enclosed child's rocker with sides representing horses, swans, etc. **3** A kind of pie with a sirupy filling made with molasses and brown sugar: also **shoofly pie.**

shoo-in (shōō′in′) *n. Colloq.* One who is virtually certain to win, as an election.

shook[1] (shŏŏk) Past tense of SHAKE.

shook[2] (shŏŏk) *n.* **1** A collection of barrel staves, shaped, chamfered, and arranged for assembling, conveniently bundled for transportation. **2** A set of boards in order for nailing together into a packing box, and conveniently bundled for transportation. **3** A shock of sheaves. [? Var. of SHOCK[2]]

shoon (shōōn) Obsolete plural of SHOE.

shoot (shōōt) *v.* **shot, shoot·ing** *v.t.* **1** To hit, wound, or kill with a missile discharged from a weapon. **2** To discharge (a missile) from a bow, rifle, etc. **3** To discharge (a weapon): often with *off*: to *shoot* a cannon. **4** To take the altitude of with a sextant, etc.: to *shoot* the sun. **5** To send forth as if from a weapon, as questions, glances, etc. **6** To pass over or through swiftly: to *shoot* rapids. **7** To go over (an area) in hunting game. **8** To emit, as rays of light. **9** To photograph; film. **10** To cause to stick out or protrude; extend. **11** To put forth in growth; send forth (buds, leaves, etc.). **12** To push into or out of the fastening, as the bolt of a door. **13** To propel, discharge, or dump, as down a chute or from a container. **14** To variegate, as with streaks of color: usually in the past participle: The morning clouds were *shot* with silver. **15** In games: **a** To score (a goal, point, etc.) by kicking or otherwise forcing the ball, etc., to the objective. **b** To play (golf, craps, pool, etc.). **c** To propel (a marble) from between the thumb and forefinger; play (marbles). **d** To cast (the dice). **16** *Slang* To inject (a drug, especially a narcotic). **—***v.i.* **17** To discharge a missile from a bow, firearm, etc.: Don't *shoot*! **18** To go off; discharge. **19** To move swiftly; dart. **20** To hunt game. **21** To jut out; extend or project. **22** To put forth buds, leaves, etc.; germinate; sprout. **23** To take a photograph. **24** To start the cameras, as in motion pictures. **25** In games, to make a play by propelling the ball, puck, etc., in a certain manner. **—to shoot at** (or **for**) *Colloq.* To strive for; attempt to attain or obtain. **—to shoot down** To bring to earth by shooting. **—to shoot off one's mouth** *Slang* To talk too freely or too much. **—to shoot up** **1** To move or grow upward quickly. **2** To strike with several or many shots. **3** *SW U.S.* To ride through (a town, etc.) shooting recklessly in all directions. **—***n.* **1** A young branch or sucker of a plant; offshoot. **2** A narrow passage in a stream; a rapid. **3** An inclined passage down which anything may be shot; a chute. **4** The act of shooting. **5** A shooting match, hunting party, etc. **6** The thrust of an arch. **7** An antler or horn just pushing up. **8** Shooting distance; range. **9** A rapid thrusting movement. [OE *scēotan*]

shoot·ing (shōō′ting) *n.* The act of one who or that which shoots.

shooting box A small house in a game district, furnishing accommodation for sportsmen. Also **shooting lodge.**

shooting gallery A place where one can go for target practice.

shooting iron *U.S. Slang* A firearm.

shooting star **1** A meteor. **2** Any of certain small perennial herbs (genus *Dodecatheon*); especially, the American cowslip (*D. meadia*) with oblong leaves and clusters of cyclamenlike flowers.

shoot-out (shōōt′out′) *n.* A battle involving an exchange of gunfire.

shop (shop) *n.* **1** A place for the sale of goods at retail: in the United States commonly called a *store.* **2** A place for making or repairing any article, or the carrying on of a craft. **3** One's own craft or business as a subject of conversation: to talk *shop.* **—***v.i.* **shopped, shop·ping** To visit shops or stores to purchase or look at goods. [OE *sceoppa* booth]

shop·boy (shop′boi′), **shop·girl** (-gûrl′) *n.* A boy or a girl who works in a shop.

sho·phar (shō′fär) See SHOFAR.

shop·keep·er (shop′kē′pər) *n.* One who keeps a shop or store; a tradesman.

shop·lift·er (shop′lif′tər) *n.* One who steals goods exposed for sale in a shop. **—shop′·lift′ing** *n.*

shop·per (shop′ər) *n.* One who purchases or inspects goods in shops. **—shop′ping** *n.*

shopping center A group of retail stores, restaurants, etc., including an ample parking area, usually built as a unit and accessible chiefly by automobile.

shop talk Conversation limited to one's job or profession.

shop·walk·er (shop′wô′kər) *n. Brit.* A floorwalker; a person who walks about a shop to supervise employees and help customers.

shop·worn (shop′wôrn′, -wōrn′) *adj.* Soiled or otherwise deteriorated from having been handled or on display in a shop.

sho·ran (shôr′an, shō′ran) *n.* A high-precision electronic navigation system which transmits pulses, usually from an aircraft or ship, to ground stations at distances determined by the elapsed time between emission and return of the pulses. [<SHO(RT) RA(NGE) N(AVIGATION)]

shore[1] (shôr, shōr) *n.* **1** The coast or land adjacent to an ocean, sea, lake, or large river. ◆ Collateral adjective: *littoral.* **2** *Law* The ground between the ordinary high-water mark and low-water mark. See synonyms under BANK[1], LAND, MARGIN. **—in shore** Near or toward the shore. **—***v.t.* **shored, shor·ing** **1** To set on shore. **2** To surround as with a shore. [ME *schore*; origin uncertain]

shore[2] (shôr, shōr) *v.t.* **shored, shor·ing** To prop, as a wall, by a vertical or sloping timber: usually with *up.* **—***n.* A beam set endwise as a prop, as against the side of a building, a ship on the stocks, etc., especially as a temporary support. See illustration under DRYDOCK. [Cf. Du. *schoor* prop, ON *skordha* stay]

shore[3] (shôr, shōr) Archaic past tense of SHEAR.

shore bird Any of various birds (suborder *Charadrii*) which frequent beaches and also the shores of inland waters.

shore·less (shôr′lis, shōr′-) *adj.* Having no shore; boundless.

shore·line (shôr′līn′, shōr′-) *n.* The line or contour of a shore.

shore patrol A detail of the U. S. Navy, Coast Guard, or Marine Corps assigned to police duties ashore.

shore·ward (shôr′wərd, shōr′-) *adj.* & *adv.* Toward the shore. Also **shore′wards.**

shor·ing (shôr′ing, shō′ring) *n.* **1** The operation of propping, as with shores. **2** Shores, collectively.

shorl (shôrl) See SCHORL.

shorn (shôrn, shōrn) Alternative past participle of SHEAR.

short (shôrt) *adj.* **1** Having little linear extension; not long; of little extent; of no great distance. **2** Being below the average stature; not tall. **3** Having little extension in time; of limited duration; brief. **4** Abrupt in manner or spirit; curt; petulant; cross. **5** Not reaching or attaining a requirement, result, or mark; deficient; inadequate; scant: often with *of.* **6** In finance or commerce, not having in possession when selling, but having to procure in time to deliver as contracted; not being in

possession of the seller, as stocks or shares; of or pertaining to short stocks or commodities: *short* sales. **7** Not comprehensive or retentive; at fault; in error; narrow: said of persons or their faculties: *short* memory. **8** Breaking easily; friable; crisp. **9** *Phonet.* **a** Relatively brief in pronunciation: said of vowels. **b** Designating a set of vowel sounds which contrast with the "long" vowels. See LONG[1] (def. 9). **10** In classical prosody, requiring a relatively short time to pronounce: said of syllables containing a short vowel (epsilon, omicron, etc.) not followed by two consonants or a double consonant. **11** In English prosody, unaccented. **12** Less than: with *of.* **13** Concise; compressed. See synonyms under LITTLE, SCANTY, TERSE, TRANSIENT. —*n.* **1** The compressed substance or pith of a matter. **2** Anything that is short; a short syllable or vowel. **3** A deficiency, as in a payment. **4** A short contract or sale; one who has sold short; a bear. **5** *pl.* Bran mixed with coarse meal or flour. **6** *pl.* Trousers with legs extending part way to the knees: worn by both men and women. **7** *pl.* A man's undergarment covering the loins and often a portion of the legs. **8** In baseball slang, a shortstop. **9** *pl.* Clippings, scraps, etc., left over in the manufacture of different products and used to make an inferior quality of the product. **10** *Electr.* A short circuit. **11** A motion picture of relatively short duration as compared with the feature attraction on a program. **—for short** For brevity: Edward was called Ed *for short.* **—in short** In a word; briefly. **—the short and the long** The whole; the entire sum and substance. —*adv.* In a short manner or method, in any sense of the adjective: to stop *short,* to turn *short,* to sell *short.* —*v.t.* & *v.i.* To short-circuit. [OE *sceort* short] **—short′ish** *adj.* **—short′ness** *n.*

Short (shôrt), **Walter Campbell,** 1880–1949, U.S. general.

short account **1** The account of a person who sells short on the stock market. **2** The open short sales as a whole.

short·age (shôr′tij) *n.* The amount by which anything is short; deficiency.

short·bread (shôrt′bred′) *n.* A rich, dry cake or cooky made with shortening.

short·cake (shôrt′kāk′) *n.* **1** A cake made short and crisp with butter or other shortening. **2** Cake or biscuit served with fruit usually between layers: strawberry *shortcake.*

short·change (shôrt′chānj′) *v.t.* **·changed, ·chang·ing** To give less change than is due to; hence, to cheat or swindle. **—short′chang′er** *n.*

short-cir·cuit (shôrt′sûr′kit) *v.t.* & *v.i.* To make a short circuit (in).

short circuit *Electr.* **1** A path of low resistance established between any two points in an electric circuit, thus shortening the distance traveled by the current. **2** Any defect in an electric circuit or apparatus which may result in a dangerous or wasteful leakage of current.

short·com·ing (shôrt′kum′ing) *n.* **1** Failure; remissness; delinquency. **2** A falling off; shortage, as of a crop.

short commons A scanty supply of food; a meager ration.

short covering The buying of stocks or securities to close out a short sale.

short-cut (shôrt′kut′) *v.t.* & *v.i.* To take a short cut (in).

short cut **1** A byway or path between two places shorter than the regular road. **2** A means or method that saves distance or time.

short-eared owl (shôrt′ird′) See under OWL.

short·en (shôr′tən) *v.t.* **1** To make short or shorter; curtail. **2** To reduce; diminish; lessen. **3** To furl or reef (a sail) so that less canvas is exposed to the wind. **4** To make brittle or crisp, as pastry, by adding shortening. —*v.i.* **5** To become short or shorter. See synonyms under ABBREVIATE, SCRIMP. **—short′en·er** *n.*

short·en·ing (shôr′tən·ing) *n.* **1** A fat, such as lard or butter, used to make pastry crisp. **2** An abbreviation. **3** The act of one who shortens.

short·fall (shôrt′fôl′) *n.* A failure to reach a certain amount, or a specific goal: an energy *shortfall.*

short·hand (shôrt′hand′) *n.* Any system of rapid writing, as stenography or phonography. —*adj.* **1** Written in shorthand. **2** Using shorthand.

short-hand·ed (shôrt′han′did) *adj.* Not having a sufficient or the usual number of assistants, workmen, or hands.

short·head (shôrt′hed′) *n.* A brachycephalic individual. **—short′-head′ed** *adj.*

short·horn (shôrt′hôrn′) *n.* One of a breed of cattle with short horns, originally from northern England.

shor·ti·a (shôr′tē·ə) *n.* Any of a genus *(Shortia)* of perennial evergreen herbs with bell-shaped, nodding, white flowers. [after C. W. *Short,* 1794–1863, U.S. botanist]

short-leaf pine (shôrt′lēf′) A pine *(Pinus echinata)* common in southeastern North America, with short needles.

short-lived (shôrt′līvd′, -livd′) *adj.* Living or lasting but a short time.

short·ly (shôrt′lē) *adv.* **1** At the expiration of a short time; quickly; soon. **2** In few words; briefly. **3** Curtly; abruptly.

short-range (shôrt′rānj′) *adj.* Limited in range, distance, or time: *short-range* opportunities.

short sale A sale for future delivery of goods or stocks not in possession at time of sale.

short shrift **1** A short time in which to confess before dying. **2** Little or no mercy or delay in dealing with a person or disposing of a matter.

short-sight·ed (shôrt′sī′tid) *adj.* **1** Unable to see clearly at a distance; myopic; near-sighted. **2** Lacking foresight. **3** Resulting from or characterized by lack of foresight. See synonyms under IMPRUDENT. **—short′-sight′ed·ly** *adv.* **—short′-sight′ed·ness** *n.*

short-spo·ken (shôrt′spō′kən) *adj.* Characterized by shortness or curtness of speech or manner; abrupt in address; gruff.

short-sta·ple (shôrt′stā′pəl) *adj.* Having a short fiber: in the United States, said of cotton fibers less than 1⅛ inches long.

short·stop (shôrt′stop′) *n.* In baseball, an infielder stationed between second and third bases.

short story A narrative prose story presenting a central theme or impression, usually subordinated to a single mood or characterization: shorter than a novel or novelette, usually under 10,000 words.

short-tem·pered (shôrt′tem′pərd) *adj.* Easily aroused to anger.

short-term (shôrt′tûrm′) *adj.* Payable a short time after issue: said of securities.

short ton See under TON.

short wave A radio wave having a length of about 100 meters or less, corresponding to a frequency ranging upwards from about 3000 kilocycles. **—short′-wave′** *adj.*

short-wind·ed (shôrt′win′did) *adj.* Affected with difficulty of breathing; becoming easily out of breath.

Sho·sho·ne (shō·shō′nē) *n.* **1** One of a large and important tribe of North American Indians of northern Shoshonean stock of the Uto-Aztecan family, formerly occupying western Wyoming, central and southern Idaho, northeastern Nevada, and western Utah. **2** The Shoshonean language of this tribe. Also **Sho·sho′ni.**

Sho·sho·ne·an (shō·shō′nē·ən, shō′shə·nē′ən) *n.* The largest branch of the Uto-Aztecan linguistic family of North American Indians, including the Comanche, Paiute, Ute, and Shoshone plateau tribes, and the Hopi Indians. —*adj.* Of or pertaining to this linguistic branch. Also **Sho·sho′ni·an.**

Shoshone Cavern A national monument on the Shoshone River SW of Cody, Wyoming; 212.4 acres; established 1909.

Shoshone Falls A cascade in the Snake River, southern Idaho; over 200 feet high.

Shoshone River A river in NW Wyoming, flowing 100 miles NE to the Bighorn River.

Shos·ta·ko·vich (shos′tə·kō′vich), **Dmitri,** 1906–75, Russian composer.

shot[1] (shot) *n.* **1** *pl.* **shot** A solid missile, as a ball of iron, or a bullet or pellet of lead, to be discharged from a firearm; also, such spherules or pellets collectively. See illustration under CARTRIDGE. **2** The act of shooting; any stroke, hit, or blow. **3** One who shoots; a marksman. **4** The distance traversed or that can be traversed by a projectile; reach; range. **5** A blast, as in mining. **6** A stroke, especially in certain games, as in billiards. **7** A conjecture; guess. **8** An attempted performance. **9** A metal sphere which a competitor puts, pushes, or slings, in a distance contest. **10** A hypodermic injection. **11** A drink of liquor. **12** An action or scene recorded on motion-picture film. **13** A picture taken with a camera. **14** *Naut.* A unit of chain length: in the United States, 15 fathoms; in Great Britain, 12½ fathoms. **15** *Obs.* Any projectile. —*v.t.* **shot·ted, shot·ting** To load or weight with shot. —*adj.* **1** Of changeable color, as when warp and weft are of different colors. **2** *Slang* More or less intoxicated. **3** *Colloq.* Completely done for; ruined. [OE *scot*]

shot[2] (shot) Past tense and past participle of SHOOT.

shot[3] (shot) *n.* A reckoning or charge, or a share of such a reckoning; scot. [Var. of SCOT]

shote (shōt) See SHOAT.

shot glass A small glass for holding or measuring out one shot of liquor.

shot·gun (shot′gun′) *n.* A light, smoothbore gun, either single-or double-barreled, adapted for the discharge of shot at short range. —*adj.* **1** Having a clear passageway straight through: a *shotgun* house. **2** Coerced with, or as with, a shotgun: a *shotgun* wedding.

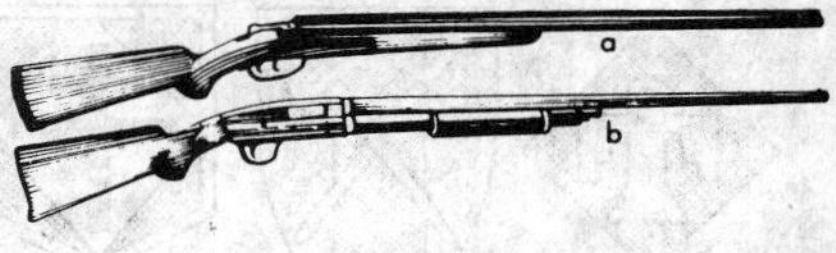

SHOTGUNS
a. Double-barrel hammerless shotgun.
b. Repeating shotgun.

shot peening A method for improving the mechanical properties of steel parts by bombarding the surfaces with metallic shot delivered under pressure or by centrifugal action.

shot-put (shot′po͝ot′) *n.* **1** An athletic contest in which a shot is thrown, or put, for distance. **2** A single put of the shot. **—shot′-put′ter** *n.*

shot·ten (shot′n) *adj.* Having spawned: said of a fish, especially a herring. [Obs. pp. of SHOOT]

should (sho͝od) Past tense of SHALL, but rarely a true past, rather chiefly used as a modal auxiliary which, while conveying varying shades of present and future time, expresses a wide range of subtly discriminated feelings and attitudes: **1** Obligation or propriety in varying degrees, but milder than *ought*: You *should* write that letter; *Should* we tell him the truth about his condition? His father thought that he *should* go; You *should* really taste that cake! **2** Condition: **a** Simple contingency, but involving less probability than *shall* or the present with future sense: If I *should* die before I wake . . . If I *should* go, he would go too. **b** Assumption: *Should* (= *Assuming that*) the space platform prove practicable, as seems almost certain, a trip to the moon will be easy. **3** Surprise at an unexpected event in the past: When I reached the station, whom *should* I run into but the detective! **4** Expectation: I *should* be at home by noon. ("I said that I *should* be home by noon" implies expectation, whereas "I said that I *would* be home by noon" implies intention.) **5** *U.S. Colloq.* Irony, in positive statement with negative force: He'll be fined heavily, but with all his money he *should* (= *need not*) worry! **6** Hesitation or deprecatory modesty, in the first person: I *should* hardly think so; We *should* like to have you come to dinner, if you are free and have nothing better to do. (Ordinarily, in American usage, but not in British, *would* is used in the first person, as well as in the second and third, before *like, prefer,* etc.: We *would,* or We'*d,* like to have you come to visit us.) See usage note under WOULD. [OE *scolde,* pt. of *sculan* owe]

shoul·der (shōl′dər) *n.* **1** The part of the trunk between the neck and the free portion of the arm or forelimb; also, the joint connecting the arm or forelimb with the body. **2** Anything which supports, bears up, or

projects like a shoulder. 3 The forequarter of various animals. 4 An enlargement, projection, or offset, as for keeping something in place, or preventing movement past the projection. 5 *Printing* The top of the shank of a type when extending above or below the face of the letter. 6 Either edge of a road or highway. 7 The angle of a bastion included between a face and the adjacent flank: also **shoulder angle.** — **shoulder to shoulder** 1 Side by side and close together. 2 With united effort; in cooperation. — **straight from the shoulder** *Colloq.* Candidly; straightforwardly. — *v.t.* 1 To assume as something to be borne; sustain; bear. 2 To push with or as with the shoulder or shoulders. 3 To fashion with a shoulder or abutment; make a shoulder on. — *v.i.* 4 To push with the shoulder or shoulders. — **to shoulder arms** To rest a rifle against the shoulder, holding the butt with the hand on the same side, the arm being held bent and close to the side. [OE *sculder* shoulder]

shoulder blade The scapula.

shoulder loop 1 A strap worn on or over the shoulder to support an article of dress. 2 A strap of cloth marked with insignia of rank, worn by army and navy officers. Also **shoulder strap.**

shoulder patch A cloth insignia worn on the upper part of the sleeve of a uniform to indicate the branch or unit to which the wearer belongs.

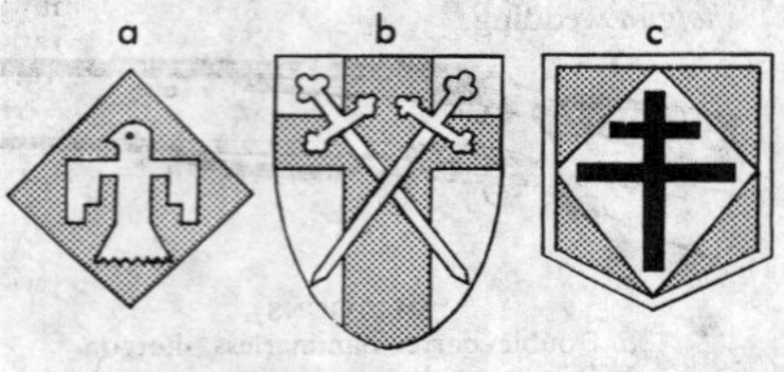

SHOULDER PATCHES
a. United States — 45th Division.
b. Great Britain — Army of Liberation.
c. France — Fighting French Commandos.

shoulder screw A screw having a shoulder, as for limiting the depth to which it may be sunk. See illustration under SCREW.

shoulder weapon Any small-arm weapon designed to be held against the shoulder in firing, as a rifle, carbine, etc.

should·na (shōōd′nə) *Scot.* Should not.

should·n't (shōōd′nt) Should not.

shout (shout) *n.* 1 A sudden and loud outcry, such as a call or command, but also expressing emotion, as of joy, exultation, courage, or derision; a loud burst of voice or voices. 2 *Austral. Slang* **a** A free drink or round of drinks. **b** One's turn to buy drinks. **c** One's turn to pay. — *v.t.* To utter with a shout; say or express loudly. — *v.i.* 1 To utter a shout; cry out loudly. 2 *Austral. Slang* To buy drinks for another or others. See synonyms under CALL, ROAR. [Origin unknown]

shout·er (shou′tər) *n.* One who shouts.

shouth·er (shōō′thər) *n. Scot.* The shoulder.

shove (shuv) *v.t. & v.i.* **shoved, shov·ing** 1 To push, as along a surface: to *shove* a boat with a pole. 2 To press forcibly (against); jostle. See synonyms under PUSH. — **to shove off** 1 To push along or away, as a boat. 2 *Colloq.* To depart. — *n.* 1 The act of pushing or shoving; strong push. 2 The woody center of flax. 3 *Can.* A forward movement of ice in a river. [OE *scūfan*] — **shov′er** *n.*

shov·el (shuv′əl) *n.* 1 A flattened scoop with a handle, as for digging, lifting earth, rock, etc. 2 *Colloq.* A shovel hat. — *v.* **·eled** or **·elled, ·el·ing** or **·el·ling** *v.t.* 1 To take up and move or gather with a shovel. 2 To toss hastily or in large quantities as if with a shovel. 3 To clear or clean with a shovel, as a path. — *v.i.* 4 To work with a shovel. [OE *scofl*]

shov·el·board (shuv′əl·bôrd′, -bōrd′) *n.* Shuffleboard.

shov·el·er (shuv′əl·ər, shuv′lər) *n.* 1 One who or that which shovels. 2 A large river duck (genus *Spatula*) with spatulate bill broadening roundly toward the end; especially, the **common shoveler** (*S. clypeata*) of the northern hemisphere: also *shovelbill.* Also **shov′el·ler.**

shovel hat A hat with broad brim turned up at the sides and projecting in front.

shov·el·head (shuv′əl·hed′) *n.* 1 A shark (*Sphyrna tiburo*) resembling the hammerhead, about 5 feet long. 2 The paddlefish. 3 The shovelnose (def. 1).

shov·el·nose (shuv′əl·nōz′) *n.* 1 A sturgeon (*Scaphirhynchus platyrhynchus*), common in the Mississippi valley, having a broad, depressed, shovel-shaped snout. 2 Any of several varieties of shark with a shovel-like nose; especially, the cow shark (*Hexanchus corinus*), found on the Pacific coast of the United States.

shov·el-nosed (shuv′əl·nōzd′) *adj.* Having a broad, flattened snout or beak.

show (shō) *v.* **showed, shown** or **showed, show·ing** *v.t.* 1 To cause or permit to be seen; present to view; exhibit; manifest; display. 2 To give in a marked or open manner; confer; bestow: to *show* favor. 3 To cause or allow (something) to be understood or known; explain; reveal; tell. 4 To cause (someone) to understand or see; explain something to; convince; teach. 5 *Law* To advance an allegation; plead: to *show* cause. 6 To make evident by logical process; prove; demonstrate. 7 To guide; lead; introduce, as into a room or building: with *in* or *up*: to *show* a caller in. 8 To indicate: The thermometer *shows* the temperature. 9 To enter in a show or exhibition. — *v.i.* 10 To become visible or known; be manifested or displayed. 11 To appear; seem. 12 To make one's or its appearance; be present. 13 *Colloq.* To give a theatrical performance; appear: to *show* in Newark. 14 *Colloq.* In racing, to be the third (horse, dog, etc.) to finish in a race. — **to show off** 1 To exhibit proudly or ostentatiously. 2 To make an ostentatious display of oneself, or of one's accomplishments. — **to show up** 1 To expose or be exposed, as faults. 2 To be evident or prominent. 3 To attend; arrive; make an appearance. 4 *Colloq.* To be better than. — *n.* 1 That which is shown; a public spectacle; a theatrical performance, circus, or motion picture; exhibition. 2 The act of showing; specifically, display; parade. 3 Pretense; semblance. 4 That which shows; an indication; promise; specifically, a sign of precious metal in a mine: a *show* of ore. 5 *Colloq.* An opportunity or chance. 6 *U.S. Colloq.* The third place in a race. — **the whole show** The center of interest or notice. [OE *scēawian*]

show·bill (shō′bil′) *n.* A poster announcing a play or show.

show biz *U.S. Slang* Show business.

show·boat (shō′bōt′) *n.* A boat, such as the old stern-wheelers on the Mississippi, on which a traveling troupe gives a theatrical performance.

show·bread (shō′bred′) See SHEWBREAD.

show business The entertainment arts, especially the theater, motion pictures, television, etc., collectively considered as an industry.

show·case (shō′kās′) *n.* A glass case for exhibiting and protecting articles for sale.

show·down (shō′doun′) *n.* 1 In poker, the play in which the hands are laid on the table face up. 2 Any action or any disclosure of facts, plans, etc., that brings an issue to a head.

show·er[1] (shou′ər) *n.* 1 A fall of rain, hail, or sleet, especially heavy rain of short duration within a local area. 2 A copious fall, as of tears, sparks, or other small objects. 3 A shower bath. 4 A variety of fireworks for simulating a shower of stars. 5 A party for the bestowal of gifts, as to a bride; also, the gifts. — *v.t.* 1 To sprinkle or wet with or as with showers. 2 To discharge in a shower; pour out. 3 To bestow with liberality. — *v.i.* 4 To fall as in a shower. 5 To take a shower bath. [OE *scūr*] — **show′er·y** *adj.*

show·er[2] (shō′ər) *n.* One who shows.

shower bath A bath in which water is sprayed on the body from an overhead, perforated nozzle.

show·folk (shō′fōk′) *n. pl.* Persons engaged in the entertainment business.

show-how (shō′hou′) *n. U.S. Colloq.* The teaching which imparts know-how: used especially in connection with the export of U.S. technological and agricultural aid and skills to backward areas of the world. [First in print in State Department publication on Point 4, Nov. 1949.]

show·ing (shō′ing) *n.* 1 Show; display, as of a quality. 2 Presentation; statement, as of a subject.

show·man (shō′mən) *n. pl.* **·men** (-mən) 1 One who exhibits or owns a show. 2 One who is skilled in presenting shows, etc. — **show′·man·ship** *n.*

Show Me State Nickname of MISSOURI.

shown (shōn) Past participle of SHOW.

show-off (shō′ôf′, -of′) *n. Colloq.* One who makes a pretentious display of himself; a swaggerer.

show·piece (shō′pēs′) *n.* 1 A prized object considered worthy of special exhibit. 2 An object on display.

show place A place exhibited for its beauty, historic interest, etc.

show ring A circular enclosure at a fair, cattle show, or other exhibition, where animals are shown to compete for prizes, or for sale.

show·y (shō′ē) *adj.* **show·i·er, show·i·est** 1 Making a great display; gaudy; gay; splendid. 2 Given to display; ostentatious. — **show′i·ly** *adv.* — **show′i·ness** *n.*

shrank (shrangk) Past tense of SHRINK.

shrap·nel (shrap′nəl) *n. pl.* **·nel** *Mil.* 1 A field artillery projectile for use against personnel, containing a quantity of metal balls and a time fuze and base charge which expel the balls in mid-air. 2 Shell fragments. [after Henry *Shrapnel*, 1761–1842, British artillery officer]

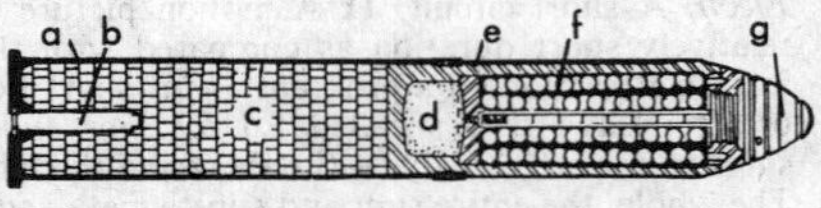

SHRAPNEL SHELL
a. Brass casing.
b. Percussion primer.
c. Smokeless powder.
d. Black powder.
e. Steel shell body.
f. Shrapnel balls.
g. Time fuze.

shred (shred) *n.* 1 A small irregular strip torn or cut off. 2 A bit; fragment; particle. See synonyms under PARTICLE. — *v.t.* **shred·ded** or **shred, shred·ding** 1 To tear or cut into shreds, as fibrous material. 2 *Brit. Dial.* To lop off; trim. [OE *scrēade* cutting]

shred·der (shred′ər) *n.* 1 One who or that which shreds. 2 A machine for cutting up corn or cane stalks, or for shredding wheat.

Shreve·port (shrēv′pôrt, -pōrt) A city on the Red River in NW Louisiana.

shrew (shrōō) *n.* 1 Any of numerous diminutive, mouse-like, insectivorous mammals (family *Soricidae*) having a long pointed snout and soft fur, as the **long-tailed shrew** (*Sorex longicauda*): also **shrew′mouse′.**

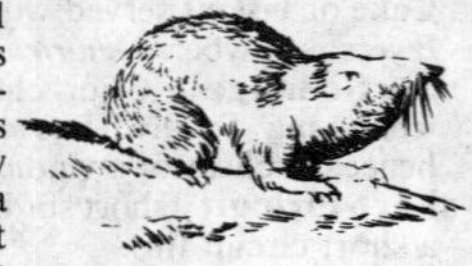

SHREW
(Species vary from 1 1/2 to 6 inches in body length)

◆ Collateral adjective: *soricine.* 2 A woman of vexatious, scolding, or nagging disposition. — *v.t. Obs.* To berate; curse. [OE *scrēawa*]

shrewd (shrōōd) *adj.* 1 Having keen insight; sharp; sagacious. 2 Artful; sly. 3 *Obs.* Keen or sharp; biting. 4 *Obs.* Shrewish; also, vexatious, vicious; dangerous. See synonyms under ACUTE, ASTUTE, INTELLIGENT, KNOWING, POLITIC, SAGACIOUS. [ME *shrewed*, pp. of *schrewen* curse < *shrew* malicious person] — **shrewd′ly** *adv.* — **shrewd′ness** *n.*

shrew·ish (shrōō′ish) *adj.* Like a shrew; ill-tempered. — **shrew′ish·ly** *adv.* — **shrew′ish·ness** *n.*

Shrews·bur·y (shrōōz′ber·ē, -bər·ē) A municipal borough and county town of Shropshire, England.

shriek (shrēk) *n.* A sharp shrill outcry or scream. — *v.i.* To utter a shriek. — *v.t.* To utter with or in a shriek. See synonyms under CALL, ROAR. [<ON *skrækja*] — **shriek′er** *n.*

shriev·al·ty (shrē′vəl·tē) *n. pl.* **·ties** The office, term, or jurisdiction of a sheriff. — **shriev′al** *adj.*

shrieve (shrēv) *n. Obs.* A sheriff. [Contraction of SHERIFF]

shrift (shrift) *n.* The act of shriving; confession; absolution. [OE *scrift*]

shrike (shrīk) *n.* Any of numerous birds (family *Laniidae*) with hooked bill, short wings, and long tail; especially, the **loggerhead shrike** (*Lanius ludovicianus*) of the southern Atlantic coast. [OE *scrīc* thrush]

shrill (shril) *adj.* **1** Having a high and piercing quality; sharp and piercing, as a sound. **2** Emitting a sharp, piercing sound. **3** *Poetic* Sharp to other senses than that of hearing; keen. —*v.t.* To cause to utter a shrill sound. —*v.i.* To make a shrill sound. —*adv.* Shrilly. [<Gmc. Cf. LG *schrell* having a sharp tone.] —**shrill'ness** *n.*

shrill·y (shril'ē) *adj. Poetic* Shrill, or somewhat shrill. —*adv.* (shril'lē) In a shrill manner.

shrimp (shrimp) *n. pl.* **shrimp** or **shrimps 1** Any of numerous diminutive, long-tailed, principally marine crustaceans (genus *Crago*), especially the edible shrimp (*C. vulgaris*) of the northern hemisphere. **2** *Slang* A small or insignificant person. [Akin to OE *scrimman* shrink]

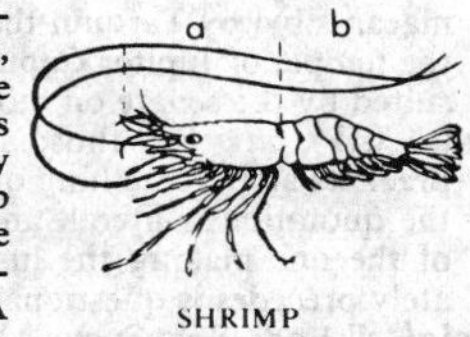

SHRIMP
a. Cephalothorax.
b. Abdomen.

shrine (shrīn) *n.* **1** A receptacle for sacred relics. **2** A place, as a tomb or a chapel, sacred to some holy personage, or considered as sanctified by the remains or presence of such. **3** A thing or spot made sacred by historic or other association. —*v.t.* **shrined, shrin·ing** To enshrine. [OE *scrīn* <L *scrinium* case, chest]

Shrine (shrīn) *n.* A secret fraternal order said to have been founded in Mecca, A.D. 646, and established in the United States in 1872: officially called *Ancient Arabic Order of Nobles of the Mystic Shrine.*

Shrin·er (shrī'nər) *n.* A member of the Shrine.

shrink (shringk) *v.* **shrank** or **shrunk, shrunk** or *less commonly* **shrunk·en, shrink·ing** *v.i.* **1** To draw together; contract, as from heat, cold, etc. **2** To diminish; become less or smaller. **3** To draw back, as from disgust, horror, or timidity; withdraw; recoil: with *from.* **4** To flinch; wince. —*v.t.* **5** To cause to shrink, contract, or draw together. See synonyms under WITHER. —*n.* **1** The act of shrinking; contraction. **2** *Slang* A psychiatrist or psychoanalyst. [OE *scrincan*] —**shrink'a·ble** *adj.* —**shrink'er** *n.*

shrink·age (shringk'ij) *n.* **1** Contraction, as of metal by cooling, or wood by drying. **2** The amount lost by contraction, depreciation, etc. **3** Decrease in value; depreciation.

shrive (shrīv) *v.* **shrove** or **shrived, shriv·en** or **shrived, shriv·ing** *v.t.* **1** To receive the confession of and give absolution to. **2** To obtain absolution for (oneself) by confessing one's sins and doing penance. —*v.i.* **3** To make confession. **4** To hear confession. [OE *scrifan,* ult. <L *scribere* write, prescribe] —**shriv'er** *n.*

shriv·el (shriv'əl) *v.t. & v.i.* **·eled** or **·elled, ·el·ing** or **·el·ling 1** To contract into wrinkles; shrink and wrinkle: often with *up.* **2** To make or become impotent; wither. [Origin uncertain. Cf. Sw. *skryvla.*]

shriv·en (shriv'ən) Alternative past participle of SHRIVE.

shroff (shrof) *n.* **1** In China and Japan, an expert detector of counterfeit money or base coin. **2** In India, a money-changer. [<Hind. *sarrāf* <Arabic]

Shrop·shire (shrop'shir, -shər) *n.* A breed of black-faced hornless sheep, noted for heavy fleece and superior mutton, originating in Shropshire.

Shrop·shire (shrop'shir, -shər) A county in western England on the border of Wales; 1,347 square miles; county town, Shrewsbury: also *Salop.*

shroud[1] (shroud) *n.* **1** A dress or garment for the dead; winding sheet. **2** Something that envelops or conceals like a garment. —*v.t.* **1** To dress for the grave; clothe in a shroud. **2** To envelop, as with a garment. **3** *Archaic* To shelter. —*v.i.* **4** *Obs.* To take shelter; go under cover; also, to gather together, as beasts, for warmth. See synonyms under MASK[1]. [OE *scrūd* a garment] —**shroud'less** *adj.*

shroud[2] (shroud) *n.* **1** *Naut.* **a** One of a set of ropes fitted in pairs and constituting part of the standing rigging of a vessel; specifically, one of the ropes, often of wire, stretched from a masthead to the sides or rims of a top, serving as means of ascent and as a lateral strengthening stays to the masts. **b** One of a pair or set of stay ropes or chains to give lateral support to a topmast, bowsprit, etc. **2** A guy, as a support for a smokestack: usually in the plural. **3** One of the supporting ropes attached to the edges of a parachute canopy. [<SHROUD[1]]

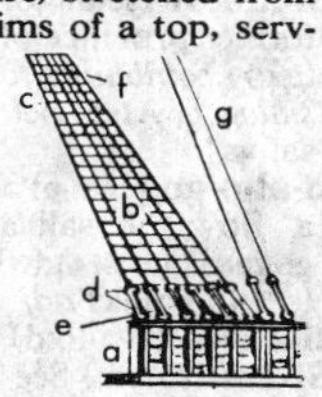

SHROUDS
a. Chain plates.
b. Shrouds.
c. Swifter.
d. Deadeyes.
e. Lanyards.
f. Ratlines.
g. Topmast backstays.

shroud-laid (shroud'lād') *adj.* Made of four strands twisted around a core: said of rope.

shrove (shrōv) Alternative past tense of SHRIVE.

Shrove·tide (shrōv'tīd') *n.* The three days immediately preceding Ash Wednesday (**Shrove Sunday, Shrove Monday, Shrove Tuesday**), on which confession is made in preparation for Lent. Compare QUINQUAGESIMA. [ME *schroftide* <stem of SHRIVE + TIDE[1], *n.* (def. 4)]

shrub[1] (shrub) *n.* A woody perennial plant of low stature, characterized by persistent stems and branches springing from the base. ◆ In popular language a shrub is a *bush.* [OE *scrybb* brushwood] —**shrub'by** *adj.*

shrub[2] (shrub) *n.* A beverage of sweetened fruit juice, sometimes with spirits. [<Arabic *sharāb.* See SHERBET.]

shrub-al·the·a (shrub'al·thē'ə) *n.* A hardy shrub (*Hibiscus syriacus*) of the mallow family: also called *rose of Sharon.*

shrub·ber·y (shrub'ər·ē) *n. pl.* **·ber·ies 1** Shrubs collectively. **2** A shrubby place; a collection of shrubs, as in a garden.

shrug (shrug) *v.t. & v.i.* **shrugged, shrug·ging** To draw up (the shoulders), as in displeasure, doubt, surprise, etc. —*n.* The act of shrugging the shoulders. [Origin uncertain]

shrunk (shrungk) Alternative past tense and past participle of SHRINK.

shrunk·en (shrungk'ən) Alternative past participle of SHRINK. —*adj.* Contracted and atrophied.

shtick (shtik) *n. U.S. Slang* An artificial or contrived device, mannerism, special area of knowledge, etc., intended to make one appear distinctive or unique; gimmick. Also spelled *schtick.* [<Yiddish <G *stück* piece, bit]

shuck (shuk) *n.* **1** A husk, shell, or pod, as of maize or peas; the outer covering of nuts. **2** A shell of an oyster or a clam. **3** *U.S. Colloq.* Something of little or no value: usually plural: not worth *shucks.* —*v.t.* **1** To remove the shucks of or from; remove the husk or shell from (corn, oysters, etc.). **2** *Colloq.* To take off or cast off, as clothes, or any outer covering. [? Metathetic alter. of HUSK] —**shuck'er** *n.*

shuck·ing (shuk'ing) *n. U.S. Colloq.* **1** A husking bee. **2** The removing of shucks, especially from corn.

shucks (shuks) *interj. U.S. Colloq.* A mild ejaculation expressing annoyance, disgust, etc.

shud·der (shud'ər) *v.i.* To tremble or shake, as from fright or cold; shiver; quake. —*n.* The act of shuddering; convulsive shiver, as from horror or fear; tremor. See synonyms under QUAKE, SHAKE. [Prob. freq. of OE *scūdan* move, shake] —**shud'der·ing** *adj.* —**shud'der·ing·ly** *adv.*

shuf·fle (shuf'əl) *n.* **1** A mixing or changing of the order of things, as of cards in a pack before each deal. **2** A hesitating, evasive, or tricky course; prevarication; artifice. **3** A scraping of the feet, as in walking; a slow, dragging gait. **4** A dance, or the step used in it, where the dancer pushes his foot along the floor at each step. —*v.* **·fled, ·fling** *v.t.* **1** To shift this way and that; mix; confuse; disorder; especially, to change the order of by mixing, as cards in a pack. **2** To move (the feet) along the ground or floor with a dragging gait. **3** To change from one place to another. **4** To make up or remove fraudulently or hastily; also, to put aside carelessly: with *up, off,* or *out.* —*v.i.* **5** To change position; shift ground. **6** To resort to indirect methods; prevaricate. **7** To dance the shuffle. **8** To scrape the feet along. **9** To scrape or struggle along awkwardly. [Prob. <LG *schuffeln* move with dragging feet, mix cards, etc.]

shuf·fle·board (shuf'əl·bôrd', -bōrd') *n.* **1** A game in which wooden or composition disks are slid by means of a pronged cue along a smooth surface toward numbered spaces. **2** The board or surface on which the game is played. Also spelled *shovelboard.*

shuf·fler (shuf'lər) *n.* **1** One who shuffles. **2** The scaup duck. **3** The coot.

shuf·fling (shuf'ling) *adj.* **1** Marked by awkward or clumsy movements. **2** Evading the truth; prevaricating.

shul (shōōl) *n.* A synagogue. [<Yiddish]

Shu·lam·ite (shōō'ləm·īt) The chief female character in the Song of Solomon, vi 13.

shun (shun) *v.t.* **shunned, shun·ning 1** To keep clear of; avoid; refrain from. **2** *Obs.* To escape; evade. **3** *Obs.* To abhor. See synonyms under ABHOR, ESCAPE. [OE *scunian*] —**shun'ner** *n.*

shun·pike (shun'pīk') *n.* A road taken by a motorist to avoid a turnpike or other express highway. —**shun'pik'ing,** *n.*

shunt (shunt) *n.* **1** A turning aside; the act of using a switch or shunt. **2** A railroad switch. **3** *Electr.* A conductor joining two points in a circuit and serving to divert part of the current. The proportion of the current diverted is regulated by the resistance of the shunt employed. —*v.t.* **1** To turn aside. **2** In railroading, to switch, as a train or car, from one track to another. **3** *Electr.* To distribute by means of shunts. **4** To evade by turning away from; put off on someone else, as a task. —*v.i.* **5** To move to one side. **6** *Electr.* To be diverted by a shunt: said of current. **7** To shift or transfer one's views or course. [Origin uncertain] —**shunt'er** *n.*

shunt-wound (shunt'wound') *adj. Electr.* Designating a type of direct-current motor in which the armature circuit and field circuit are connected in parallel: distinguished from *series-wound.*

shush (shush) *v.t.* To try to quiet; hush up, especially by making a noise like the sound (sh). [Imit.; infl. in form by HUSH]

Shu·shan (shōō'shän) Old Testament name for SUSA.

shut (shut) *v.* **shut, shut·ting** *v.t.* **1** To bring into such position as to close an opening or aperture; close, as a door, lid, or valve. **2** To close (an opening, aperture, etc.) so as to prevent ingress or egress. **3** To close and fasten securely, as with a latch or lock. **4** To forbid entrance into or exit from. **5** To keep from entering or leaving; confine or exclude; bar: with *in, out, from,* etc. **6** To close, fold, or bring together, as extended, expanded, or unfolded parts: to *shut* an umbrella. **7** To hide from view; obscure. —*v.i.* **8** To be or become closed or in a closed position. —**to shut down 1** To cease from operating, as a factory or mine; close up; stop work. **2** To lower; come down close: The fog *shut down.* **3** *Colloq.* To suppress: with *on.* —**to shut one's eyes to** To ignore. —**to shut out** In sports, to keep (an opponent) from scoring during the course of a game. —**to shut up 1** *Colloq.* To stop talking or cause to stop talking. **2** *Colloq.* To become exhausted and stop running, as a horse in a race. **3** To close all the entrances to, as a house. **4** To imprison; confine. —*adj.* **1** Made fast or closed. **2** Not sonorous; dull: said of sound. **3** *Phonet.* **a** Formed by closing the oral and nasal passages completely, preparatory to uttering certain sounds: said of certain consonants, as *t, p, k, b,* and *d.* **b** Cut off sharply by succeeding consonants: said of vowels, as *i* in *pit* and *o* in *top.* **4** *Dial.* Freed, as from something disagreeable; rid: with *of.* —*n.* **1** The act of shutting; also, the time of shutting, closing, or ending: the *shut* of day. **2** The place of shutting or closing together; specifically, the junction between welded pieces of metal. [OE *scyttan*]

Synonyms (verb): bar, beleaguer, block, blockade, close, confine, enclose, exclude, imprison, intercept, preclude, prohibit, seal, stop. *Antonyms:* expand, liberate, open, unbar, unclose, undo, unfasten.

shut·down (shut′doun′) *n.* The closing of or ceasing of work in a mine, mill, factory, or other industrial plant.

Shute (shōōt), **Nevil,** 1899–1960, English aeronautical engineer and writer: full name Nevil Shute Norway.

shut-eye (shut′ī′) *n. Slang* Sleep.

shut-in (shut′in′) *n.* An invalid who has to stay at home. —*adj.* **1** Obliged to stay at home. **2** Inclined to avoid people.

shut·off (shut′ôf′, -of′) *n. Mech.* A device for shutting something off.

shut·out (shut′out′) *n.* **1** A shutting out; especially, a lock-out. **2** In sports, a game in which one side is prevented from scoring; also, the action or the play that prevents scoring.

shut·ter (shut′ər) *n.* **1** One who or that which shuts. **2** That which shuts out or excludes; specifically, a cover, usually hinged, for closing an opening. **3** A hinged screen or cover for a window. **4** *Phot.* Any of various mechanisms for momentarily admitting light through a camera lens to the film or plate. —*v.t.* To furnish, close, or divide off with shutters.

shut·ter·bug (shut′ər·bug′) *n. Slang.* A photography enthusiast. [< SHUTTER + BUG[1]]

shut·tle (shut′l) *n.* **1** A device used in weaving to carry the weft to and fro between the warp threads. **2** A similar rotating or other device in a sewing machine or the like. **3** A transport system operating between two nearby points. —*v.t.* & *v.i.* **·tled, ·tling** To move to and fro, like a shuttle. —*adj.* Pertaining to or designating any contrivance, action, etc., intended to operate back and forth between two points: *shuttle* bombing. [OE *scytel* missile; so called because shot to and fro in weaving]

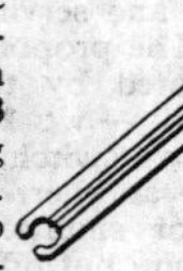

SHUTTLE (*def. 1*)

shuttle armature An H-armature.

shut·tle·cock (shut′l·kok′) *n.* A rounded piece of cork, with a crown of feathers, used in the game of badminton and of battledore and shuttlecock; the game itself. —*v.t.* To send or knock back and forth like a shuttlecock. [< SHUTTLE + COCK[1]]

shy[1] (shī) *v.i.* **shied, shy·ing 1** To start suddenly aside, as in fear: said of a horse. **2** To draw back, as from doubt or caution: with *off* or *away.* [< *adj.*] —*adj.* **shy·er, shy·est,** or **shi·er, shi·est 1** Easily frightened or startled, timorous. **2** Bashful; reserved; coy. **3** Circumspect, as from motives of caution; watchful; wary: with *of.* **4** Not easy to perceive, seize, or secure; elusive: a *shy* expression. **5** Not prolific: said of plants, trees, or, rarely, birds. **6** *Colloq.* Having a less amount of money than is called for or required. **7** Short; lacking: often with *on.* —*n.* A starting aside, as in fear. [OE *scēoh* timid. Akin to ESCHEW.] —**shy′ly** *adv.* —**shy′ness** *n.*

shy[2] (shī) *v.t.* & *v.i.* **shied, shy·ing** To throw with a swift, sidelong motion. —*n. pl.* **shies 1** A careless throw; fling, hence, a verbal fling; a sneer. **2** A trial; experiment. [Origin unknown]

shy·er (shī′ər) *n.* **1** One who shies. **2** A shying horse. Also spelled *shier.*

Shy·lock (shī′lok) In Shakespeare's *Merchant of Venice,* a revengeful usurer who endeavors to exact a pound of flesh from Antonio's body as a forfeit for non-payment of a debt; hence, any relentless creditor.

shy·ster (shīs′tər) *n.* **1** Anyone who conducts his business in an unscrupulous or tricky manner. **2** A lawyer who practices in an unprofessional manner, preys on petty criminals, etc. [? < SHY[1], in slang sense of "disreputable" + -STER]

si[1] (sē) See TI[1].

si[2] (sē) *adv.* Italian, Portuguese, and sometimes French, for "yes". [< L *sic* thus]

Si *Chem.* Silicon (symbol Si).

si·al (sī′al) *n. Geol.* A rock formation rich in silica and alumina which underlies sedimentary rock in continental land masses. —**si·al′ic** *adj.* [< SI(LICA) + AL(UMINA)]

si·a·lid (sī′ə·lid) *n.* Any member of a family of insects *(Sialidae,* order *Megaloptera),* with enlarged or elongated thorax, including the hellgrammite and related genera. —*adj.* Of or pertaining to the *Sialidae.* Also **si·al·i·dan** (sī·al′ə·dən). [< Gk. *sialis,* kind of bird]

Si·al·kot (sē·äl′kōt) A city in the NE part of the former province of Punjab, NE West Pakistan.

sialo- *combining form* Saliva; pertaining to saliva: *sialogog.* Also, before vowels, **sial-.** [< Gk. *sialon* saliva]

si·al·o·gog (sī·al′ə·gog) *n.* Any agent exciting a flow of saliva. Also **si·al′a·gogue, si·al′o·gogue.** [< SIAL(O)- + -AGOG] —**si·a·lo·gog·ic** (sī′ə·lō·goj′ik) *adj.* & *n.*

si·a·loid (sī′ə·loid) *adj.* Like or resembling saliva.

Si·am (sī·am′) See THAILAND.

Siam, Gulf of An arm of the South China Sea, separating the Malay Peninsula from Indochina; 300 to 350 miles wide, 450 miles long.

si·a·mang (sē′ə·mang) *n.* A large black gibbon (genus *Symphalangus)* found in Sumatra. [< Malay *siaman* < *iaman* black]

Si·a·mese (sī′ə·mēz′, -mēs′) *adj.* **1** Pertaining to Thailand (Siam), its people, or their language. **2** Closely connected; twin. —*n.* **1** A native or the natives of Siam, belonging to the Thai stock. **2** The Thai language of these people.

Siamese cat A breed of short-haired cat native in Siam, now extensively bred in the United States, typically fawn-colored or pale cream, with dark-tipped ears, tail, feet, and dark mask, a wedge-shaped head, and bright- or deep-blue, gently slanting eyes.

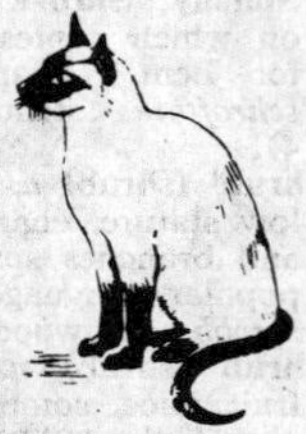

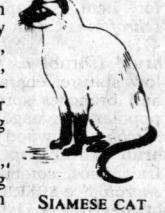

SIAMESE CAT (About 11 inches at the shoulder)

Siamese twins 1 Originally, the two Chinese males, Eng and Chang, 1811–74, born in Siam, whose bodies were joined by a fleshy band from the navel to the xiphoid cartilage. **2** Any twins joined together at birth.

Si·an (sē′än′, shē′-) **1** The capital of Shensi province, NW China: formerly *Singan.* **2** A city in northern Liaonoing province, south central Manchuria, China.

Siang (syäng, shyäng) **1** A river in Hunan province, China, flowing 715 miles NE to Tungting Lake. **2** See YÜ RIVER.

Siang·tan (syäng′tän′, shyäng′-) A city in eastern Hunan province, China.

sib (sib) *n.* **1** A blood-relation; kinsman. **2** Kinsmen collectively; relatives. —*adj.* **1** Related to blood; akin. **2** Related; similar. Also **sibb.** [OE *sibb*]

Sib·bo·leth (sib′ə·leth) See SHIBBOLETH.

Si·be·li·us (si·bā′lē·əs, -bāl′yəs; *Finnish* si·bā′lyōōs), **Jean,** 1865–1957, Finnish composer.

Si·be·ri·a A region of Russia in Asia extending from the Ural Mountains and the Caspian Sea to the Pacific Ocean in northern Asia, known for its long and difficult winters; 5,000,000 square miles. *Russian* **Si·bir** — *adj.* & *n.* Si·be′ri·an.

Siberian husky A breed of working dog of medium size with a strong, closely knit body, head resembling that of a fox, brush tail, and thick, soft outer coat.

Siberian Sea, East A section of the Arctic Ocean north of NE Siberia, east of the New Siberian Islands and west of Wrangell Island (def. 2): Russian *Vostochno-Sibirskoye More.*

sib·i·lant (sib′ə·lənt) *adj.* **1** Hissing. **2** *Phonet.* Describing those consonants which are uttered with a hissing sound, as (s), (z), (sh), and (zh). —*n. Phonet.* A sibilant consonant. [< L *sibilans, -antis,* ppr. of *sibilare* hiss] —**sib′i·lance, sib′i·lan·cy** *n.* —**sib′i·lant·ly** *adv.*

sib·i·late (sib′ə·lāt) *v.t.* **·lat·ed, ·lat·ing** To give a hissing sound to, as in pronouncing the letter *s.* [< L *sibilatus,* pp. of *sibilare* hiss] —**sib′i·la′tion** *n.*

Si·biu (si·byōō′) A city in central Rumania: German *Hermannstadt.*

sib·ling (sib′ling) *n.* A blood-relation; a relative: used in eugenics, psychology, and anthropology to denote brothers and sisters. [OE, a relative]

Si·bu·yan Sea (si·bōō′yän) A part of the Pacific in the central Philippines, bounded by Mindoro, Luzon, Masbate, and Panay.

sib·yl (sib′əl) *n.* **1** In ancient Greece and Rome, any of several women who prophesied under the supposed inspiration of some deity, chiefly of Apollo, and delivered their oracles in a frenzied state. **2** A fortune-teller; sorceress. [< L *sibylla* < Gk.]

Sib·yl (sib′əl) A feminine personal name. Also *Du.* **Si·byl·la** (sē·bil′ə), *Fr.* **Si·bylle** (sē·bē′), *Ger.* **Si·byl·le** (sē·bē′lə), *Lat.* **Si·byl·la** (si·bil′ə). [< L, soothsayer]

sib·yl·line (sib′əl·in, -ēn, -in) *adj.* **1** Pertaining to or characteristic of the sibyls; uttered or composed by sibyls; hence, prophetic; oracular; occult. **2** Exorbitant; excessive. Also **si·byl·ic** (si·bil′ik), **si·byl′lic.**

Sibylline Books A collection of nine books which were reputed to set forth the destiny of Rome. The last three were bought from the Cumaean sibyl by Tarquin the Proud and placed in the temple of Jupiter Capitolinus, and were consulted by the senate on momentous occasions.

sic[1] (sik) *adv.* So; thus: sometimes inserted in brackets after something quoted, to indicate that the quotation is literal, and that, in the opinion of the one making the insertion, what immediately precedes is questionable or incorrect. [< L]

sic[2] (sik) *adj. Scot.* Such. Also **sic′can.**

sic[3] (sik) See SICK[2].

Si·ca·ni·an (si·kā′nē·ən) *adj.* Sicilian.

sic·ca·tive (sik′ə·tiv) *adj.* Causing to dry; drying. —*n.* That which has a drying effect; a drying agent or medicine. [< LL *siccativus* < L *siccatus,* pp. of *siccare* dry < *siccus* dry]

sice (sīs) See SYCE.

Sic·el (sis′əl) *n.* **1** A member of an ancient people of Sicily. **2** The Indo-European language of the Sicels, possibly related to Ligurian or Latin. —*adj.* Of or pertaining to the Sicels or their language.

sicht (sikht) *n.* & *v. Scot.* Sight.

Si·cil·i·an Vespers (si·sil′ē·ən, -sil′yən) A general massacre of the French in Sicily (1282) by Sicilians rising against the French rule of Charles of Anjou: so called because the toll that called to Vespers on Easter Monday was the signal for attack.

Sic·i·lies (sis′ə·lēz), **The Two** See TWO SICILIES, THE.

Sic·i·ly (sis′ə·lē) The largest island in the Mediterranean, just SW of Italy (9,831 square miles); comprising with some small neighboring islands an autonomous region of Italy; 9,926 square miles; capital, Palermo: ancient *Trinacria. Italian* **Si·ci·lia** (sē·chē′lyä). —**Si·cil′i·an** *adj.* & n.

sick[1] (sik) *adj.* **1** Affected with disease; ill; ailing. **2** Of or used by ill persons: often used in combination: *sickroom.* **3** Affected by nausea; nauseated; desiring to vomit. **4** Expressive or suggestive of nausea; sickly: a *sick* laugh. **5** Impaired or unsound from any cause; weakened; out of condition. **6** Pallid; wan: said of colors. **7** Depressed and longing because of some unattained desire; languishing: *sick* for the sea. **8** Disinclined by reason of satiety or disgust; surfeited: with *of: sick* of music. **9** Exhausted, as soil; unable to produce a profitable yield; also, diseased. —*n.* Sick people collectively: with *the.* [OE *sēoc*]

sick[2] (sik) *v.t.* **1** To seek or attack: used in the imperative to order a dog to attack. **2** To urge to attack: I'll *sick* the dog on you. Also spelled *sic.* [Var. of SEEK]

sick·bay (sik′bā′) *n.* That part of a ship or of a naval base set aside for the care of the sick, including operating room, dispensary, and hospital.

sick·bed (sik′bed′) *n.* The bed upon which a sick person lies.

sick call *Mil.* **1** The daily period for reporting to the medical officer all non-hospitalized sick or injured military personnel. **2** The call or signal which announces it.

sick·en (sik′ən) *v.t.* & *v.i.* To make or become sick or disgusted. —**sick′en·er** *n.*

sick·en·ing (sik′ən·ing) *adj.* Disgusting; nauseating. —**sick′en·ing·ly** *adv.*

sick·er[1] (sik′ər) *adj.* More sick.

sick·er[2] (sik′ər) *adj. Scot.* & *Brit. Dial.* Safe; sure; also, cautious. —*adv.* Surely; securely. Also spelled *siker.* [OE *sicor* < L *securus* safe]

sick headache Headache accompanied by nausea and stomach disorders; migraine.

sick·ish (sik′ish) *adj.* **1** Somewhat sick. **2** Slightly nauseating: a sweet, *sickish* odor. See synonyms under SQUEAMISH. —**sick′ish·ly** *adv.* —**sick′ish·ness** *n.*

sick·le (sik′əl) *n.* A reaping implement with a

long, curved blade mounted on a short handle. —*v.t.* **·led, ·ling** To cut with a sickle, as grass, hay, etc. [OE *sicel* <L *secula* <*secare* cut]
Sickle A sickle-shaped group of stars in the constellation Leo.
sick·le·bill (sik′əl·bil′) *n.* Any of several birds having a strongly curved bill, as a hummingbird or the long-billed curlew *(Numenius americanus).*
sick·le-cell anemia (sik′əl·sel′) A severe, hereditary anemia occurring among the offspring of parents who both have sickle-cell trait.
sickle-cell trait A tendency in erythrocytes to become deformed into a sickle shape and to clog small blood vessels, occurring chiefly among Negroes and due to the presence of a genetic hemoglobin abnormality inherited from one parent. Also **sickl·e·mi·a** (sik′əl·ē′mē·ə).
sickle feather One of the long curved feathers in the tail of the domestic cock. See illustration under FOWL.
sickle pear A seckel.
sick·list (sik′list′) *n.* A list of those incapacitated by illness, especially in an army or navy.
sick·ly (sik′lē) *adj.* **·li·er, ·li·est 1** Habitually indisposed; ailing; unhealthy: a *sickly* child. **2** Marked by the prevalence of sickness: a *sickly* summer. **3** Nauseating; disgusting; also, mawkish; sickening. **4** Pertaining to or characteristic of the sick or sickness: a *sickly* appearance. **5** Weak- or sick-looking; faint: a *sickly* moon. —*adv.* In a sick manner; poorly. —*v.t.* **·lied, ·ly·ing** To make sickly or sickish, as in color or complexion. —**sick′li·ly** *adv.* —**sick′li·ness** *n.*
sick·ness (sik′nis) *n.* **1** Illness; the state of being sick. **2** A particular form of disease. **3** Specifically, nausea. **4** Any disordered and weakened state: the soul's *sickness.* See synonyms under DISEASE, ILLNESS.
sick-out (sik′out′) *n.* An absence from work by workers who say they are sick so they may not be penalized for an illegal strike action.
sick·room (sik′rōōm′, -rŏŏm′) *n.* A room for the sick.
sic·like (sik′līk′) *adj. Scot.* Similar; such.
sic pas·sim (sik pas′im) *Latin* Thus everywhere (as throughout a book).
sic sem·per ty·ran·nis (sik sem′pər ti·ran′is) *Latin* Thus ever to tyrants: motto of Virginia.
sic tran·sit glo·ri·a mun·di (sik tran′sit glō′·rē·ə mun′dī) *Latin* Thus passes away the glory of the world.
Sic·y·on (sish′ē·on) An ancient city NW of Corinth in Peloponnesus, southern Greece: Greek *Sikyon.*
Sid·dons (sid′nz), **Sarah,** 1755–1831, *née* Kemble, English tragic actress.
sid·dur (sid′ŏŏr) *n.* The Jewish prayer book, containing the year's prayers for weekdays, Sabbaths, fast days, and holy days. [<Hebrew *siddūr* arrangement]
side[1] (sīd) *n.* **1** Any one of the bounding lines of a surface or of the bounding surfaces of a solid object: often limited to a particular bounding line or surface, as distinguished from top, or bottom: the *side* of a box, house, or mountain. **2** A lateral part of a surface or object. **3** One of two or more contrasted surfaces, parts, or places: *inside* and *outside.* **4** Any distinct party or body of competitors or partisans; a faction. **5** An opinion, aspect, or point of view considered with respect to its opposite: my *side* of the question. **6** Family connection, especially by descent through one parent: my grandfather on my father's *side.* **7** The lateral half of a slaughtered animal or of a tanned skin or hide. **8** Either half of the human body as divided by the median plane. **9** The space beside someone. **10** A page of written or printed paper. **11** *Naut.* The part of a ship's hull from stem to stern above the waterline. **12** In billiards, a lateral spin given to the cue ball; english. **13** Abounding line of a geometrical figure. **14** *Brit. Slang* Superciliousness of manner; pretentiousness. —**off side** See OFFSIDE. —*adj.* **1** Situated at or on one side; lateral: a *side* window. **2** Being or viewed as if from one side; oblique: a *side* glance; incidental: a *side* issue. —*v.t.* **sid·ed, sid·ing 1** To provide with sides, as a building. **2** To cut into sides, as a carcass. **3** To thrust aside. —**to side with** To range oneself on the side of; take the part of. [OE]
side[2] (sīd) *adj.* **1** *Scot. & Brit. Dial.* Relatively long or wide; large: said of garments. **2** *Scot.* Far; distant.
side arms Weapons worn at the side, as swords, pistols, bayonets, etc.
side·bands (sīd′bandz′) *n. pl. Telecom.* The bands of frequencies on either side of the carrier wave within which fall the frequencies produced by modulation.
side·board (sīd′bôrd′, -bōrd′) *n.* **1** A piece of dining-room furniture for holding tableware. **2** *pl. Brit.* Sideburns.
side·burns (sīd′bûrnz′) *n. pl.* **1** Whiskers grown on the cheeks; burnsides. **2** The hair growing on the sides of a man's face below the hairline: usually worn with the rest of the beard shaved off. [Alter. of BURNSIDES]
side-by-side (sīd′bī′sīd′) *adj.* Beside or next to each other; together.
side·car (sīd′kär′) *n.* **1** A small, one-wheeled passenger car attached to the side of a motorcycle. **2** A cocktail containing equal parts of lemon juice, brandy, and curaçao or Cointreau. **3** A jaunting car.
side chain *Chem.* A group of atoms, specifically an alkyl group, attached to a carbon atom of a ring compound.
side dish A portion of food subordinate to the main dish or dishes of a course; also, the small dish in which it is served.
side-dress (sīd′dres′) *v.t. Agric.* To apply fertilizer along only one side of (a row of growing plants). —**side′-dress′ing** *n.*
side effect *Med.* A secondary, often injurious effect resulting from a drug or other form of therapy whose action is not restricted to the condition for which it was administered.
side·kick (sī′kik′) *n. U.S. Slang* A close friend; buddy.
side·light (sīd′līt′) *n.* **1** A side window. **2** A light coming from the side; hence, incidental illustration or information. **3** *Naut.* One of the colored lights (red on the port side, green on the starboard) displayed on the sides of ships at night; a running-light; also, a nightlight in the gangway of a war vessel.
side·line (sīd′līn′) *n.* **1** An auxiliary line of goods sold by a store or a commercial traveler. **2** Any additional or secondary work differing from one's main job. **3** A track or road, especially of a railroad, branching off from the main line. **4** A line used to hobble a horse by connecting the fore and hind feet of the same side: also **side′-hob′ble** (-hob′əl). **5** One of the lines bounding the two sides of a football field, tennis court, or the like; also, the area just outside these lines: often in the plural. **6** The point of view of an outsider or non-participant.
side·ling (sīd′ling) *adj.* Having a slanting or oblique position or motion; indirect. —*adv.* Sidewise; obliquely; indirectly.
side·long (sīd′lông′, -long′) *adj.* Inclining or tending to one side; lateral. —*adv.* **1** In a lateral or oblique direction. **2** Steeply inclined.
side·man (sīd′man′) *n. pl.* **·men** (-men′) One of the supporting musicians, as distinguished from the featured performers, of a band, especially a jazz band.
side meat A side of salt pork or bacon.
side·piece (sīd′pēs′) *n.* **1** A piece at or forming the side of anything. **2** The jamb or check in any finished aperture in a wall, as of a doorway.
si·de·re·al (sī·dir′ē·əl) *adj.* **1** Pertaining or relative to stars; constituted of or containing stars. **2** Measured by means of the stars: said of periods of time. [<L *sidereus* <*sidus sideris* star] —**si·de′re·al·ly** *adv.*
sidereal time See under TIME.
sid·er·ite (sid′ə·rīt) *n.* **1** A vitreous, native ferrous carbonate, $FeCO_3$; spathic iron ore: also called *chalybite.* **2** An indigo-blue variety of quartz. **3** An iron meteorite. [<L *siderites* <Gk. *sidēritēs* of iron <*sidēros* iron] —**sid′er·it′ic** (-rit′ik) *adj.*
sidero-[1] *combining form* Iron; of or pertaining to iron: *siderolite.* Also, before vowels, **sider-.** [<Gk. *sidēros* iron]
sidero-[2] *combining form* Star; stellar: *siderostat.* Also, before vowels, **sider-.** [<L *sidus, sideris* a star]
sid·er·o·lite (sid′ər·ə·līt′) *n.* **1** A spongy meteoric iron containing embedded grains of certain minerals, as chrysolite. **2** A meteorite. [<SIDERO-[1] + -LITE]
sid·er·o·scope (sid′ər·ə·skōp′) *n.* A magnetic device for detecting the presence of iron or steel particles in the eyes.
sid·er·o·sis (sid′ə·rō′sis) *n. Pathol.* **1** Abnormal deposit of iron in the tissues of the body, and especially of the lungs. **2** Any lung disease caused by the inhalation of metallic dust; pneumonoconiosis.
sid·er·o·stat (sid′ər·ə·stat′) *n. Astron.* A mirror turning by clock motion so as to reflect the light of a star in an invariable direction into a fixed telescope or other astronomical instrument. [<SIDERO-[2] + Gk. *statos* standing] —**sid′er·o·stat′ic** *adj.*
side-sad·dle (sīd′sad′l) *n.* A woman's saddle having but one stirrup and a cushioned horn on the same side, about which the right knee fits.
side show 1 A small show incidental to a larger or more important one; especially, one connected with a circus but charging an extra entrance fee; also, a minor exhibit at a fair. **2** Any subordinate issue or attraction.
side-slip (sīd′slip′) *v.i.* **-slipped, -slip·ping** To slip or skid sideways. —*n.* **1** A lateral skid, as of an automobile. **2** A downward, sidewise slipping of an airplane along the lateral axis: executed to lose altitude without a gain in forward speed.
side-split·ting (sīd′split′ing) *adj.* Having a tendency as if to split the sides with laughter; mirth-provoking.
side-step (sīd′step′) *v.* **-stepped, -step·ping** *v.i.* To step to one side; avoid responsibility. —*v.t.* To avoid, as an issue, or postpone, as a decision; evade. —*n.* **1** A step or a movement to one side, as of a pugilist. **2** A step on the side of a thing for ascending and descending. —**side′-step′per** *n.*
side stroke In swimming, a stroke made while lying on the side, the arms being thrust forward alternately, the upper arm above the water, the lower arm below the water: performed with a scissors kick.
side·swipe (sīd′swīp′) *n.* A sweeping blow along the side. —*v.t. & v.i.* **·swiped, ·swip·ing** To strike or collide with such a blow.
side·track (sīd′trak′) *v.t. & v.i.* **1** To move to a siding, as a railroad train. **2** To divert or depart from the main issue or subject; distract or be distracted. —*n.* A railroad siding; also, a branch line.
side·walk (sīd′wôk′) *n.* A path or pavement at the side of the street for the use of pedestrians.
side·wall (sīd′wôl′) *n.* The side surface of a rubber tire, between the tread and the rim.
side·ward (sīd′wərd) *adj.* Directed or moving toward or from the side; lateral. —*adv.* Toward or from the side; laterally: also **side′·wards.**
side·ways (sīd′wāz′) *adv.* **1** From one side. **2** So as to incline toward the side, or with the side forward: Hold it *sideways.* **3** Toward one side; askance; obliquely; indirectly. —*adj.* Moving to or from one side: a *sideways* glance. Also **side′way′, side′wise′.**
side wheel A wheel at the side; specifically, one of two paddle wheels on either side of a steamboat. —**side′-wheel′** *adj.* —**side′-wheel′er** *n.*

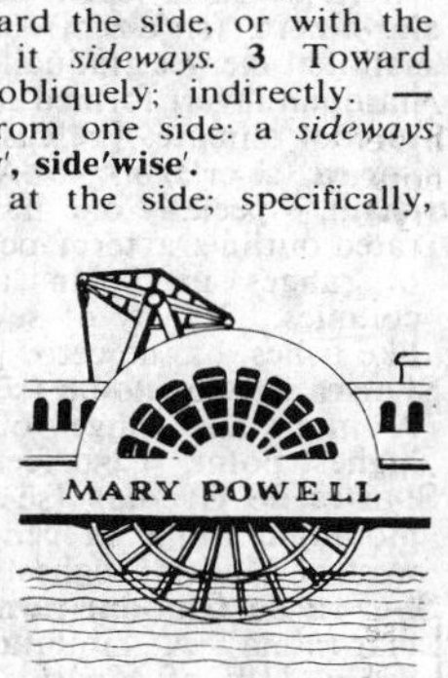

SIDE WHEEL

side-wind·er (sīd′·wīn′dər) *n.* **1** One of several small rattlesnakes found in the American Southwest, and particularly the horned rattler *(Crotalus cerastes):* so called because of its characteristic lateral motion. **2** A heavy, swinging, sideways blow with the fist.
Si·di If·ni (sē′dē ēf′nē) The capital of Ifni.
sid·ing (sī′ding) *n.* **1** A railway track by the side of the main track. **2** The boarding that covers the side of a wooden house or is prepared for that purpose: often in the plural. **3** The act of dressing timbers to correct

breadths, as in shipbuilding, or the timbers themselves. 4 The act of taking sides, as in a controversy.
si·dle (sīd'l) *v.i.* **·dled, ·dling** To move sideways, especially in a cautious or stealthy manner. —*n.* A sideways step or movement. [< obs. *sidling* sidelong] —**si'dler** *n.*
Sid·ney (sid'nē) A masculine personal name. Also *Sydney.* [<F, St. Denis]
Sid·ney (sid'nē), **Sir Philip,** 1554–86, English soldier, courtier, poet, and writer: also spelled *Sydney.*
Si·don (sīd'n) The capital of ancient Phoenicia, on the site of modern *Saida.* —**Si·do·ni·an** (sī·dō'nē·ən) *adj.* & *n.*
Sid·ra (sid'rə), **Gulf of** An inlet of the Mediterranean in the coast of Libya; 275 miles wide: ancient *Syrtis Major.*
Sie·ben·ge·bir·ge (zē'bən·gə·bir'gə) A range of hills along the Rhine south of Bonn in West Germany; highest point, 1,509 feet.
siè·cle (sye'kl') *n. French* Century; age; period.
Sie·dl·ce (she'dəl·tse) A city in eastern Poland; formerly, capital of a political subdivision of Russian Poland.
Sieg·bahn (sēg'bän), **Karl Manne Georg,** born 1886, Swedish physicist.
siege (sēj) *n.* 1 The besieging of a town or fortified place; beleaguerment. ◆ Collateral adjective: *obsidional.* 2 A steady attempt to win something; also, the protracted period spent in the effort: He laid *siege* to her heart. 3 The time during which one undergoes a protracted illness or difficulty. 4 *Obs.* A seat; chair; throne. 5 *Obs.* Rank, station. —*v.t.* **sieged, sieg·ing** To besiege. [<OF <L *sedes* seat < *sedere* sit; infl. in meaning by L *obsidium* siege]
Siege Perilous A seat at King Arthur's Round Table, fatal to all occupants save Sir Galahad, the knight destined to find the Holy Grail.
Sieg·fried (sēg'frēd, *Ger.* zēkh'frēt) The hero of the *Nibelungenlied* and several other Germanic legends. [<G, peace of victory]
Siegfried Line See LIMES.
Sieg Heil (zēkh' hīl') *German* Hail to victory: a Nazi salute.
Sie·mens (sē'mənz, *Ger.* zē'məns), **Ernst Werner von,** 1816–92, German electrical engineer, inventor, and manufacturer. —**Sir William,** 1823–83, Karl Wilhelm Siemens, German engineer who settled in England; invented the electrodynamometer; brother of the preceding.
Si·en·a (sē·en'ə, *Ital.* syä'nä) A city in Tuscany, central Italy. —**Si·en·ese** (sē'ən·ēz', -ēs') *adj.* & *n.*
si·en·ite (sī'ən·īt) See SYENITE.
Sien·kie·wicz (shen·kyā'vich), **Henryk,** 1846–1916, Polish novelist.
si·en·na (sē·en'ə) *n.* 1 A brownish orange-yellow natural clay colored with oxides of iron and manganese: used as a pigment. 2 Orange-yellow, the color of this pigment. [<Ital. *(terra di) Siena* (earth of) Siena]
sier·o·zem (sir'ə·zem) *n.* A grayish-brown soil that merges gradually into a calcareous or hardpan layer: formed usually in a temperate to cool climate. [<Russian, gray earth]
si·er·ra (sē·er'ə) *n.* 1 A mountain range or chain, especially one having a jagged or serrated outline: a term occurring in the names of ranges in Spain and former Spanish colonies. 2 Any of several large mackerel-like fishes, as the cero. [<Sp. <L *serra* saw]
Si·er·ra de Cór·do·ba (sē·er'rä thā kôr'thō·vä) A mountain range of central Argentina; highest point, 9,450 feet.
Si·er·ra de Gre·dos (sē·er'rä thā grā'thōs) A mountain range in central Spain, 25 miles west of Madrid; highest point, 8,504 feet.
Si·er·ra de Gua·dar·ra·ma (sē·er'rä thā gwä'·thär·rä'mä) A mountain range in central Spain, NW of Madrid; highest point, 7,972 feet.
Si·er·ra Le·o·ne (sē·er'rä lā·ō'nā) 1 An independent state on the west coast of Africa; 27,925 square miles, mostly on the **Sierra Leone Peninsula,** extending 25 miles into the Atlantic; capital, Freetown: formerly a British dependency. 2 An estuary in western Sierra Leone, flowing 25 miles past Freetown to the Atlantic.
Si·er·ra Ma·dre (sē·er'rä mä'thrā) A Mexican mountain chain bordering the central plateau on the east and west and divided into the **Sierra Madre del Sur** in the south, the **Sierra Madre Occidental** in the west, and the **Sierra Madre Oriental** in the east; highest point, 18,700 feet.
Si·er·ra Mo·re·na (sē·er'rä mō·rā'nä) A mountain range in southern Spain; highest point, 4,340 feet.
Si·er·ra Ne·vad·a (sē·er'ə nə·vad'ə, -vä'də; *Sp.* sē·er'rä nā·vä'thä) 1 A mountain range of eastern California, extending 400 miles north and south; highest point, 14,495 feet. 2 A mountain range in southern Spain; highest peak, 11,411 feet.
si·es·ta (sē·es'tə) *n.* A midday or afternoon nap. [<Sp. <L *sexta (hora)* sixth (hour), noon < *sex* six]
sieur (syœr) *n.* Sir; master: a former French title of respect. [<F <L *senior* older]
sieve (siv) *n.* 1 A utensil or apparatus for sifting, consisting of a frame provided with a bottom of mesh wire. 2 A garrulous person. —*v.t.* & *v.i.* **sieved, siev·ing** To sift. [OE *sife* sieve]
sieve cell *Bot.* A thin-walled, elongated cell having perforations, **sieve pores,** and sieve plates that permit communication between contiguous cells, forming sieve tubes.
sieve plate *Bot.* One of the thickened terminal sections of a sieve cell.
sieve tissue *Bot.* Phloem tissue containing or made up of vascular bundles of sieve cells.
sieve tube *Bot.* An arrangement of sieve cells in plants by means of which conduction is accomplished.
Sie·yès (syā·yes'), **Emmanuel,** 1748–1836, French revolutionist: called "Abbé Sieyès."
si·fak·a (si·fak'ə) *n.* Any of a genus *(Propithecus)* of lemuroid primates characterized by long tails, black skin, short arms, and powerful hind limbs: native in Madagascar: also called *propitheque.* [<Malagasy]
sif·fle (sif'əl) *v.t.* & *v.i.* **·fled, ·fling** To whistle; hiss. —*n.* A sibilant râle. [<F *siffler* <L *sibilare* hiss]
sift (sift) *v.t.* 1 To pass through a sieve in order to separate the fine parts from the coarse. 2 To scatter by or as by a sieve. 3 To examine carefully. 4 To separate as if with a sieve; distinguish: to *sift* fact from fiction. —*v.i.* 5 To use a sieve; sift something. 6 To fall or pass through or as through a sieve: The light *sifts* through the trees. [OE *siftan* sift] —**sift'er** *n.*
sift·ings (sif'tingz) *n. pl.* Something removed or separated by a sieve.
sigh (sī) *v.i.* 1 To draw in and exhale a deep, audible breath, as in expressing sorrow, weariness, pain, etc. 2 To make a sound suggestive of a sigh, as the wind. 3 To yearn; long. —*v.t.* 4 To express with a sigh. 5 To lament with sighs. —*n.* The act or sound of or as of sighing. [Back formation <ME *sighte,* pt. of *siken* <OE *sīcan* sigh]
sight (sīt) *n.* 1 The faculty, act, or fact of seeing; vision. 2 That which is seen; a view; spectacle; show; as used absolutely, something remarkable and strange. 3 *pl.* Things worth seeing: the *sights* of the town. 4 The range or scope of vision; limit of eyesight. 5 A point of view; estimation. 6 Insight; opportunity for investigation or study. 7 A device to assist aim, as on a gun, leveling instrument, etc. 8 An aim or observation taken with a telescope or other sighting instrument. 9 A view; glimpse. 10 The part of a drawing or painting within the marginal lines or the frame. 11 *Colloq.* A great quantity or number: a *sight* of people. —**at** (or **on**) **sight** 1 As soon as seen: to read or shoot *at sight.* 2 On presentation for payment: said of drafts, bills, and notes. —**battle sight** The position of the rear sight on a rifle in which the leaf is laid down. —**bore sight** An auxiliary sighting device with parts attached to the muzzle and breech of a gun, used to secure alinement of the axis of the bore with the axis of the gun sight. —**leaf sight** A rear sight for small arms, containing a movable peep sight and hinged to permit raising and lowering. —**peep sight** A sight attached to the breech end of a firearm, and provided with a small hole in the center for close aiming. —*v.t.* 1 To perceive with the eyes; see: to *sight* a whale. 2 To take a sight of; observe; look at through a telescope or similar instrument. 3 To furnish with sights, or adjust the sights of, as a gun. 4 To give the proper aim or elevation to, as a gun; take aim with. 5 *Colloq.* To bring to notice; present, as a bill to its drawee. —*v.i.* 6 To take aim. 7 To make an observation or sight. —*adj.* 1 Understood or performed on sight without previous familiarity or preparation. 2 Payable when presented: a *sight* draft. ◆ Homophones: *cite, site.* [OE *gesiht*]
sight-hole (sīt'hōl') *n.* A peephole.
sight·less (sīt'lis) *adj.* 1 Without the power of sight; blind. 2 Invisible. —**sight'less·ly** *adv.* —**sight'less·ness** *n.*
sight·ly (sīt'lē) *adj.* **·li·er, ·li·est** 1 Pleasant to the view; comely. 2 Affording a grand view. —**sight'li·ness** *n.*
sight-read (sīt'rēd') *v.t.* & *v.i.* **-read** (red), **-read·ing** (rē'ding) To understand or perform (something requiring interpretation or translation) on sight without previous familiarity or preparation: to *sight-read* music or a foreign language. —**sight reader** —**sight reading**
sight·see·ing (sīt'sē'ing) *n.* The visiting of objects of interest. —**sight'se'er** *n.*
sight unseen Without examing: to exchange stamps *sight unseen.*
sig·il (sij'il) *n.* A seal or signature; also, a mark or sign supposed to exercise occult power. [<L *sigillum* seal] —**sig'il·lary** (-ə·ler'ē) *adj.*
Sig·is·mund (sij'əs·mənd, sig'-; *Ger.* zē'gis·mōōnt) A masculine personal name. Also *Fr.* **Si·gis·mond** (sē·zhēs·môn'), *Ital.* **Si·gis·mon·do** (sē'jēs·mōn'dō) [<Gmc., protecting conqueror]
—**Sigismund,** 1368–1437, king of Hungary 1387–1437, Holy Roman Emperor 1411–37.
sig·ma (sig'mə) *n.* 1 The 18th letter in the Greek alphabet, written Σ (capital), σ (small initial), or ς (small final): corresponding to English *s* in *so.* As a numeral it denotes 200. 2 *Math.* The symbol signifying that the sum is to be taken of a series or sequence following. 3 Something shaped like a sigma. [<Gk. *sigma* the letter *s*]
sig·mate (sig'māt) *adj.* Having the shape or form of S or of sigma.
sig·moid (sig'moid) *adj.* 1 Shaped like the Greek capital letter sigma (Σ), or like the letter S. 2 Pertaining to the sigmoid flexure. Also **sig·moi·dal** (sig·moid'l). [<Gk. *sigmoeidēs*]
sigmoid flexure *Anat.* A fold in the colon just above the rectum.
sign (sīn) *n.* 1 A motion or action indicating thought, desire, or command; a pantomimic gesture. 2 A board, plate, or representation of any sort, generally bearing an inscription and used to indicate a place of business or resort. 3 An arbitrary mark used to express meaning, rank, condition, value, etc. 4 Any evidence of a recent presence, as tracks, droppings, etc.; a vestige; trace. 5 A mark used in place of a signature by persons unable to write. 6 *Music* Any mark used in musical notation, as a flat or sharp. 7 *Math.* A conventional mark to indicate an operation or relation, as one of the symbols +, −, ×, ÷, indicating the four fundamental operations of addition, subtraction, multiplication, and division. 8 Any indicative or significant object or event; a symbol; token. 9 In the Bible, a miraculous deed as a proof of divine commission or supernatural power; a miracle. 10 *Astron.* One of the twelve equal divisions of the zodiac, named from the constellations that formerly occupied them. See ZODIAC. 11 In hunting, a trace left by an animal; spoor. 12 *Med.* A symptom of disease that is apparent to someone other than the patient. 13 *Eccl.* The sign of the Cross: used in service books and before signatures of bishops. —*v.t.* 1 To write one's signature or initials on. 2 *Law* To acknowledge an instrument by affixing a mark or seal to. 3 To indicate or represent by a sign; stand for. 4 To mark or consecrate with a sign, especially with a cross. 5 To engage by obtaining the signature of to a contract: to *sign* a baseball player; also, to hire (oneself) out for work: often with *on.* 6 To dispose of by signature: with *off* or *away.* 7 To express or indicate with a sign. —*v.i.* 8 To make signs or signals. 9 To write one's signature or initials. —**to sign off** *Telecom.* To announce the close of a program from a broadcasting station and stop transmission. —**to sign up** To enlist, as in a branch of military service.

◆ Homophone: *sine.* [<OF *signe* <L *signum*] **— sign′er** *n.*

Synonyms (noun): emblem, indication, manifestation, mark, note, omen, pattern, presage, prognostic, signal, symbol, symptom, token, type. A *sign* is any distinctive *mark* by which a thing may be recognized or its presence known, and may be intentional or accidental, natural or artificial, suggestive, descriptive or wholly arbitrary. While a *sign* may be involuntary, and even unconscious, a *signal* is always voluntary; a ship may show *signs* of distress to the casual observer, but *signals* of distress are a distinct appeal for aid. A *symptom* is a vital phenomenon resulting from a diseased condition; in medical language a *sign* is an *indication* of any physical condition, whether morbid or healthy; thus, a hot skin and rapid pulse are *symptoms* of pneumonia; dulness of some portion of the lungs under percussion is one of the physical *signs.* See CHARACTERISTIC, EMBLEM, LETTER, MARK[1], TRACE[1].

sig·nal (sig′nəl) *n.* **1** A sign or means of communication agreed upon or understood, and used to convey information or command, as at a distance. **2** *Telecom.* A radio wave or electric current which transmits intelligence, whether direct or in code. **3** An event that incites to action or movement. **4** In some card games, a lead or play that conveys certain information to one's partner. See synonyms under SIGN. **—** *adj.* **1** Distinguished by some special sign or characteristic; notable; conspicuous. **2** Used to signal: a *signal* fire. See synonyms under EMINENT, EXTRAORDINARY. **—** *v.* **·naled** or **·nalled, ·nal·ing** or **·nal·ling** *v.t.* **1** To make signals to; inform or notify by signals. **2** To communicate by signals. **—** *v.i.* **3** To make a signal or signals. [<F <L *signalis* < *signum* sign] **— sig′nal·er** or **sig′·nal·ler** *n.*

Signal Corps A branch of the U. S. Army; a body of officers and enlisted men in charge of signaling apparatus and the transmitting of intelligence by telegraph, telephone, radio, visual signs, etc.

signal fire A fire used as a signal; a beacon fire.

signal generator An electromagnetic oscillator used to supply currents of known frequencies through a specified range in testing the performance of a radio receiver.

sig·nal·ize (sig′nəl·īz) *v.t.* **·ized, ·iz·ing** **1** To render noteworthy. **2** To point out with care.

sig·nal·ly (sig′nəl·ē) *adv.* In a signal manner; eminently.

sig·nal·man (sig′nəl·mən) *n. pl.* **·men** (-mən) **1** One who makes or interprets signals; a signaler. **2** One who operates a railroad signal.

sig·nal·ment (sig′nəl·mənt) *n.* **1** The act of signaling. **2** Description of a person for identification by peculiar or characteristic marks, as in the case of a criminal. [<F *signalement*]

signal smoke A smoke from a fire used to signal to a distance, by a system either of puffs, spirals, or clouds.

signal tower **1** Any tower from which signals are displayed. **2** A small railroad tower from which semaphore or block-system signals are controlled.

sig·na·to·ry (sig′nə·tôr′ē, -tō′rē) *adj.* Bound by the terms of a signed document; having signed: *signatory* powers. **—** *n.* One who has signed or is bound by a document; specifically, a nation so bound. [<L *signatorius* < *signatus,* pp. of *signare* sign < *signum* a sign]

sig·na·ture (sig′nə·chər) *n.* **1** The name of a person, or something representing his name, written, stamped, or inscribed by himself or by deputy, as a sign of agreement or acknowledgment. **2** *Printing* **a** A distinguishing mark, letter, or number on the first page of each form or sheet of a book, as a guide to the binder. **b** The form or sheet on which this mark is placed. **c** One of the fractional parts of a book; a folded printed sheet, usually comprising 16 pages. **3** *Music* A symbol or group of symbols at the beginning of a staff, indicating time or key. See KEY SIGNATURE, TIME SIGNATURE. **4** In radio, the musical number or sound effect that introduces or closes a given program. **5** *Zool.* A color mark resembling a letter. **6** *Med.* The part of a physician's or pharmacist's prescription that indicates how the medicine is to be taken: usually preceded by *S.* or *Sig.* [<F <Med. L *signatura* <L *signatus.* See SIGNATORY.]

sign·board (sīn′bôrd′, -bōrd′) *n.* A board on which a sign, direction, or advertisement is displayed.

sig·net (sig′nit) *n.* **1** A seal; especially, in England, one of the seals of the sovereign, used in sealing his private letters and bills of grants, etc. **2** An impression made by or as if by a seal. **—** *v.t.* To mark or make official with a signet or seal. ◆ Homophone: *cygnet.* [<F, dim. of *signe* sign <L *signum*]

sig·nif·i·cance (sig·nif′ə·kəns) *n.* **1** The character or state of being significant; expressiveness. **2** That which is signified or intended to be expressed; meaning. **3** Importance; consequence: opposed to *insignificance.* Also **sig·nif′i·can·cy.**

sig·nif·i·cant (sig·nif′ə·kənt) *adj.* **1** Having or expressing a meaning; bearing or embodying a meaning. **2** Betokening or standing as a sign for something; having some covert meaning; significative: His manner was *significant.* **3** Important, as pointing out something weighty; momentous: opposed to *insignificant.* **4** *Math.* Having value or the determining or influential value: the *significant* figures in a number. See synonyms under IMPORTANT. **—** *n.* Something bearing a meaning; specifically, a token or letter. [<L *significans, -antis,* ppr. of *significare* make a sign, mean < *signum* sign + *facere* do, make] **— sig·nif′i·cant·ly** *adv.*

sig·ni·fi·ca·tion (sig′nə·fə·kā′shən) *n.* **1** That which is signified; meaning; sense; import. **2** The act of signifying; communication. [<OF *significaciun* <L *significatio, -onis.* See SIGNIFICANT.]

sig·nif·i·ca·tive (sig·nif′ə·kā′tiv) *adj.* **1** Representing, as a sign; symbolical. **2** Conveying, or tending to convey, a meaning; significant.

sig·ni·fy (sig′nə·fī) *v.* **·fied, ·fy·ing** *v.t.* **1** To make known by signs or words; express; communicate; announce; declare. **2** Hence, to betoken in any way; mean; import. **3** To amount to; mean: What does his opinion *signify*? **4** To denote (medical use) by signature or markings. **—** *v.i.* **5** To have some meaning or importance; matter. See synonyms under ALLUDE, IMPORT. **— sig′ni·fi′er** *n.*

sign language **1** Dactylology. **2** A system of communication by means of signs, largely manual; specifically, the system used by the Plains Indians to communicate with tribes speaking other languages.

sign manual *pl.* **signs manual** **1** The personal signature of the British sovereign written at the top of state papers. **2** A sign made with the hand; also, any code consisting of manual signs.

si·gnor (sēn′yôr) *n.* **1** An Anglicized form of the Italian title **signore**, used in respectful address to a gentleman: in society equivalent to the English *sir* when no name follows, to *Mr.* with a name, and to the French *monsieur.* **2** A lord or gentleman; especially, an Italian of rank, official position, or social distinction. Also **si′gnior.** [<Ital. *signore* <L *senior* senior]

si·gno·ra (sē·nyō′rä) *n. Italian* Madam; Mrs.: a title of respectful address.

Si·gno·rel·li (sē′nyō·rel′lē), **Luca,** 1442?–1524?, Italian painter.

si·gno·ri·na (sē′nyō·rē′nä) *n. Italian* The equivalent to *miss*: diminutive of Italian *signora.*

si·gno·ri·no (sē′nyō·rē′nō) *n. Italian* A title of respectful address to a young man: diminutive of Italian *signore,* sir.

si·gno·ry (sēn′yə·rē) See SEIGNIORY.

sign·post (sīn′pōst′) *n.* A post bearing a sign; sometimes, a guideboard.

Sigs·bee (sigz′bē), **Charles Dwight,** 1845–1923, U. S. admiral.

Sig·urd (sig′ərd, *Ger.* zē′go͝ort) In the *Volsunga Saga,* the hero who slays Fafnir. He corresponds to Siegfried, the hero of the *Nibelungenlied.*

Si·kang (sē′kang′, *Chinese* shē′käng′) A former province of SW China bordering on Tibet, incorporated, 1955, in Szechwan province; 204,194 square miles; former capital, Yaan.

sike (sīk, sik) *n. Scot.* & *Brit. Dial.* **1** A gutter; rill. **2** A marshy bottom with a stream flowing through it: also spelled *syke.* [OE *sīc* streamlet]

sik·er (sik′ər) See SICKER[2].

Sikh (sēk) *n.* One of a religious and military sect founded by Guru Nanak (1469–1538) in India early in the 16th century. **—** *adj.* Of or pertaining to the Sikhs. [<Hind., lit., disciple]

Sikh·ism (sēk′iz·əm) *n.* The creed and practices of the Sikhs: it is a monotheistic system, combining the teachings of the Persian Sufis with those of Hinduism, rejecting caste, and enjoining purity of life and toleration.

Si·kho·te–A·lin Range (sē′khō·tä·ä·lēn′) A mountain range along the Sea of Japan in Russian S.F.S.R.; highest point, 5,200 feet.

Si Kiang (sē′ kyäng′, shē′ jyäng′) The Chinese name for the WEST RIVER.

Sik·kim (sik′im) A protectorate of India in the eastern Himalayas, south central Asia; 2,818 square miles; capital, Gangtok.

Si·kor·sky (si·kôr′skē), **Igor,** born 1889, U. S. aeronautical engineer born in Russia: inventor of the helicopter.

Sik·y·on (sik′ē·on) The Greek name for SICYON.

si·lage (sī′lij) *n.* Ensilage. [<ENSILAGE]

sil·ane (sil′ān) *n. Chem.* **1** A compound of silicon and hydrogen, SiH_4; silicon hydride or monosilane. **2** Any of a series of similar compounds, named according to the number of silicon atoms present in the molecule. [< SIL(ICON) + -ANE[1]]

Si·las (sī′ləs) A masculine personal name. [See SILVANUS]

sil·a·zane (sil′ə·zān) *n. Chem.* Any of a class of nitrogen-containing silicon compounds having the general formula $H_3Si(NHSiH_2)_n$-$NHSiH_3$. [<SIL(ICON) + AZ(OTE) + -ANE[1]]

sile (sīl) *Brit. Dial. v.t.* **1** To strain; skim. **2** To glide or pass through. **—** *v.i.* **3** To sink; subside. **4** To boil gently; simmer. **—** *n.* **1** A strainer. **2** Filth; sediment. [Cf. Sw. & Norw. *sila* strain]

si·le·na·ceous (sī′lə·nā′shəs) *adj.* Caryophyllaceous. [<NL *Silene,* a genus of plants <L *Silenus* Silenus + -ACEOUS]

si·lence (sī′ləns) *n.* **1** The state or quality of being silent; abstinence from speech or noise; taciturnity. **2** Absence of sound or noise; stillness. **3** Absence of note; failure to mention; oblivion; secrecy. **4** *Music* A rest. **—** *v.t.* **·lenced, ·lenc·ing** **1** To render silent; take away the authority to speak or the power of reply from. **2** To stop the motion or activity of; put to rest; quiet. **3** To force (guns, etc.) to cease firing, as by return fire, bombing, or the like. **—** *interj.* Be silent. [<F <L *silentium* < *silere* be silent]

si·lenc·er (sī′lən·sər) *n.* **1** A tubular device attached to the muzzle of a firearm rendering the discharge noiseless. **2** A muffler (def. 2). **3** A device to prevent the buzzing of telegraph or telephone wires.

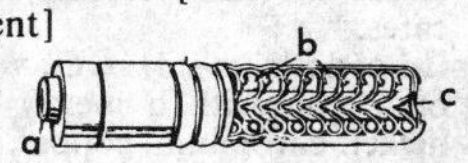

MAXIM SILENCER
a. Socket for attaching to gun.
b. Vortex chamber for gases.
c. Passage groove for bullet.

si·lent (sī′lənt) *adj.* **1** Not making any sound or noise; noiseless; still; also, unspoken; unuttered: *silent* grief. **2** Not speaking, or not given to speech; mute; taciturn. **3** Making no mention or allusion; passing by without notice or record. **4** Free from activity, motion, or disturbance; calm; quiet: a *silent* retreat. **5** Interested financially in a business, but having no authority to act: a *silent* partner. **6** Written, but not pronounced: said of a letter, as the *b* in *debt.* [<F <L *silens, -entis,* ppr. of *silere* be silent] **— si′lent·ly** *adv.* **— si′lent·ness** *n.*

silent butler A small receptacle with a handle and hinged lid, used for collecting refuse from ashtrays, etc.

si·len·ti·ar·y (sī·len′shē·er′ē) *n. pl.* **·ar·ies** **1** One appointed to keep silence and order in court. **2** A Byzantine official sworn not to divulge secrets of state; a privy councilor.

3 An observer of silence because of religious beliefs. [< LL *silentiarius*]
silent partner See under PARTNER.
silent system A system of prison discipline imposing silence on all prisoners.
si·le·nus (sī·lē′nəs) *n. pl.* **·ni** (-nī) In Greek mythology, any woodland deity resembling a satyr.
Si·le·nus (sī·lē′nəs) In Greek mythology, the foster father and teacher of Bacchus and leader of the satyrs: traditionally represented as a fat, drunken old man with pointed ears and goat's legs, riding on an ass. [< L < Gk. *Seilēnos* Silenus]
si·le·sia (si·lē′shə, sī-) *n.* **1** A glazed linen cloth first made in Prussian Silesia. **2** A thin, twilled cotton fabric for linings.
Si·le·sia (si·lē′shə, sī-) A region of east central Europe divided between north central Czechoslovakia and SW Poland; formerly a province of Prussia and a crownland of Austria; total area, about 20,000 square miles: German *Schlesien*, Polish *Śląsk*, Czech *Slezsko*. **—Si·le′sian** *adj. & n.*
si·lex (sī′leks) *n.* Silica. [< L, flint]
sil·hou·ette (sil′ōō·et′) *n.* **1** A profile drawing or portrait having its outline filled in with uniform color, commonly black: often cut out, as from cardboard. **2** The figure or likeness cast by a shadow; the outline of a solid figure. —*v.t.* **·et·ted, ·et·ting** To cause to appear in silhouette; outline; make a silhouette profile of. [after Étienne de *Silhouette*, 1709–1767, French minister of finance; in mockery of the petty economies for which he was notorious]

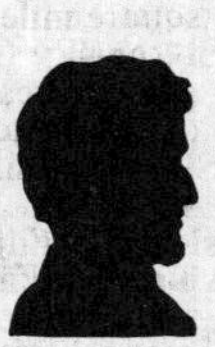
SILHOUETTE Abraham Lincoln

silic- Var. of SILICO-.
sil·i·ca (sil′i·kə) *n.* A white or colorless, extremely hard, crystalline silicon dioxide, SiO_2, the principal constituent of quartz and sand. [< NL < L *silex, silicis* flint]
silica gel A highly adsorbent colloidal silica, used for deodorizing and cleaning air, purifying blast-furnace gases, etc.
sil·i·cane (sil′i·kān) *n. Chem.* Silane.
sil·i·cate (sil′i·kit) *n. Chem.* A salt of silicic acid. The silicates are mineralogically of great importance, and make up a large part of the earth's crust.
si·li·ceous (si·lish′əs) *adj.* **1** Pertaining to, resembling, or containing silica. **2** Growing or living on siliciferous soil. Also **si·li′cious.** [< L *siliceus*]
si·lic·ic (si·lis′ik) *adj.* Pertaining to, derived from, or consisting of silica or silicon. [< SILIC- + -IC]
silicic acid *Chem.* Any of several gelatinous and easily decomposed compounds of silica and water; especially, orthosilicic acid, H_4SiO_4, associated in the formation of many metallic silicates.
sil·i·cide (sil′ə·sīd) *n. Chem.* A binary compound of silicon with a metal, such as iron, cobalt, nickel, chromium, copper, or magnesium.
sil·i·cif·er·ous sil′ə·sif′ər·əs) *adj.* Containing or producing silica; united partially with silica. [< SILIC- + -(I)FEROUS]
si·lic·i·fied wood (si·lis′ə·fīd) Wood that has been replaced by silica crystallizing out from solution so as to become a mass of quartz of the original form and structure of the wood; petrified wood. See PETRIFIED FOREST.
si·lic·i·fy (si·lis′ə·fī) *v.* **·fied, ·fy·ing** *v.t.* To convert into silica, as wood. —*v.i.* To become silica, or become impregnated with it. [< SILIC- + -(I)FY] **—si·lic′i·fi·ca′tion** *n.*
sil·i·cle (sil′i·kəl) *n.* A very short, flat silique. [< L *silicula*, dim. of *siliqua* pod]
silico- *combining form* Silicon; of, related to, or containing silicon. Also, before vowels, *silic-*, as in *silicosis*. [< L *silex, silicis* flint]
sil·i·con (sil′ə·kən) *n.* A nonmetallic element (symbol Si, atomic number 14), in nature combined chiefly with oxygen in rock and sand and forming almost 26 percent by weight of the lithosphere. See PERIODIC TABLE. [< L *silex, silicis* flint]
sil·i·cone (sil′ə·kōn) *n. Chem.* Any of various organosilicon compounds containing a silicon-carbon bond: their great physical, chemical, and electrical stability adapts them for many industrial uses as lubricants, greases, polishes, insulating resins, waterproofing materials, and for the making of a special type of synthetic rubber. [< SILICON]
sil·i·co·sis (sil′ə·kō′sis) *n. Pathol.* A pulmonary disease caused by the inhalation of finely powdered silica or quartz.
si·lic·u·lose (si·lik′yə·lōs), **si·lic·u·lous** (-ləs) *adj.* Siliquose. [< SILIQUOSE]
Si·lif·ke (si·lif·ke′) A town in central southern Turkey near the Mediterranean: ancient *Seleucia Trachea.*
si·lique (si·lēk′, sil′ik) *n. Bot.* A narrow, dry, two-valved pod or fruit characteristic of plants of the mustard family. Also **sil·i·qua** (sil′ə·kwə). [< F < L *siliqua* pod]
sil·i·quose (sil′ə·kwōs) *adj.* Silique-bearing; pertaining to or resembling a silique. Also **sil′i·quous** (-kwəs). [< NL *siliquosus* < L *siliqua* pod]
Si·lis·tri·a (si·lis′trē·ə) A city on the Danube, in NE Bulgaria. Also **Si·li·stra** (sē·lē′strä). Ancient **Du·ros·to·rum** (dōō·ros′tə·rəm, dyoo-).
silk (silk) *n.* **1** The creamy-white or yellowish, very fine natural fiber produced by various insects, especially by the larvae of silkworms, to form their cocoons. **2** A similar thread spun by other insects or arachnids. **3** Cloth, thread, or garments made of silk. **4** Anything resembling or suggestive of silk, as the fine soft styles of an ear of corn. **—to hit the silk** *Slang* To descend from an aircraft by parachute. —*adj.* Consisting of silk; silken; silky. —*v.t.* To clothe or cover with silk: grand ladies plumed and *silked.* —*v.i.* To produce the portion of the flower called silk: said of corn. [OE *seoloc*, ult. < L *sericus* silken, lit., pertaining to the Seres (Chinese), from whom silk was bought. Related to SERGE.]
silk·a·line (sil′kə·lēn′) *n.* A soft and thin mercerized cotton fabric resembling silk. Also **silk′a·lene′.**
silk cotton The silky seed covering of various species of a genus *(Bombax)* of tropical American trees, and of the West Indian god tree *(Ceiba pentandra)* or corkwood *(Ochroma pyramidale).* Its principal use is for stuffing cushions, packing, etc.
silk-cot·ton tree (silk′kot′n) Any tree producing silk cotton.
silk·en (sil′kən) *adj.* **1** Made of silk. **2** Like silk; glossy; delicate; smooth. **3** Dressed in silk; hence, luxurious.
silk hat A high cylindrical hat covered with fine silk plush: worn by men and used as a dress hat.
silk·man (silk′mən) *n. pl.* **·men** (-mən) A dealer in or a manufacturer of silk; also, an operative in a silk factory.
silk paper A granite paper made with occasional silk fibers in the pulp.
silk-screen print (silk′skrēn′) A reproduction made by the silk-screen process.
silk-screen process A printing process which forces ink through the meshes of a silk screen on which the desired pattern or design has been imposed.
silk-stock·ing (silk′stok′ing) *adj.* Wearing silk stockings; hence, wealthy; luxurious. —*n.* **1** One who wears silk stockings; a member of the wealthy class. **2** A supporter of a branch of the Whig party in the United States in the early 19th century.
silk vine A deciduous shrub of the milkweed family *(Periploca graeca)* growing in the neighborhood of the Black Sea: its bark yields periplocin. Also called *wolf's-bane.*
silk·weed (silk′wēd′) *n.* Milkweed.
silk·worm (silk′wûrm′) *n.* The larva of a moth that produces a dense silken cocoon, especially the common silkworm *(Bombyx mori),* from whose cocoon commercial silk is made.
silk·y (sil′kē) *adj.* **silk·i·er, silk·i·est** **1** Like silk in any way; soft; lustrous. **2** Made of or consisting of silk; silken. **3** Long, fine, and appressed, as hairs, or covered with such hairs, as leaves. **4** Gentle or insinuating in manner; smooth and persuasive: usually in a bad sense, implying insincerity. **—silk′i·ly** *adv.* **—silk′i·ness** *n.*
silky oak See under LACEWOOD.
sill (sil) *n.* **1** A horizontal member forming the foundation, or part of the foundation, of a structure of any kind, as at the bottom of a casing in a building; especially, a door sill or a window sill. **2** A timber in the frame of the floor of a railroad car: end *sill;* side *sill.* **3** *Geol.* A relatively thin stratum of igneous rock intruded between level or gently inclined beds of other rock. [OE *syll*]
sil·la·bub (sil′ə·bub) *n.* **1** A dish made by combining milk or cream with wine or cider, and thus forming a soft curd, which is then flavored. It may be whipped into a froth, or made solid by boiling after adding water and gelatin. **2** Figuratively, something frothy, as flowery language. Also spelled *syllabub.* [Alter. of obs. *sillibouk* < SILLY + OE *būc* belly]
Sil·lan·pää (sil′län·pa), **Frans Eemil,** 1888–1964, Finnish writer.
sil·ler (sil′ər) *adj. & n. Scot.* Silver; money.
Sil·li·man (sil′i·mən), **Benjamin,** 1779–1864, U.S. chemist and geologist.
sil·ly (sil′ē) *adj.* **·li·er, ·li·est** **1** Destitute of ordinary good sense; simple; foolish; imbecile; fatuous; sometimes, senile. **2** Characterized by or resulting from foolishness or imbecility; stupid: *silly* talk. **3** *Rare* Simple; plain; rustic. **4** *Colloq.* Stunned; dazed, as by a blow. **5** *Obs.* or *Brit. Dial.* Frail; feeble; weak; helpless. **6** *Scot.* Mentally or physically incapable; idiotic; imbecilic. **7** *Obs.* Scanty; meager. See synonyms under CHILDISH, RIDICULOUS. —*n. pl.* **·lies** *Colloq.* A silly person. [OE *gesælig* happy] **—sil′li·ly** *adv.* **—sil′li·ness** *n.*
si·lo (sī′lō) *n. pl.* **·los** **1** A structure, usually of wood or concrete, as a cylindrical pit or a tower, in which fodder, grain, or other food is stored green to be fermented and used as feed for cattle, etc. See ENSILAGE. **2** A deep cylindrical structure built underground for the housing and launching of guided missiles. —*v.t.* **·loed, ·lo·ing** To put or preserve in a silo; turn into ensilage. [< Sp. < L *sirus* < Gk. *siros* pit for corn[

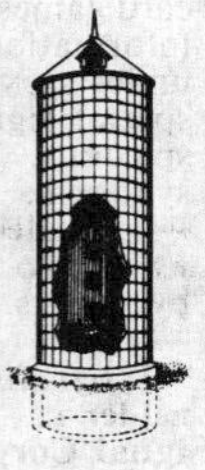
SILO Stave type, showing interior construction and pit.

Si·lo·am (si·lō′əm, sī-) A spring and pool outside Jerusalem. *John* ix 7.
sil·ox·ane (sil·ok′sān) *n. Chem.* Any of a class of oxygen-containing silicon compounds.
silt (silt) *n.* **1** An earthy sediment consisting of extremely fine particles of rock and soil suspended in and carried by water. **2** A deposit of such sediment, as at the mouth of a river. —*v.i.* **1** To become filled or choked with silt: usually with *up.* **2** To ooze; drift. —*v.t.* **3** To fill or choke with silt or mud: usually with *up.* [ME *sylte.* Cf. Dan. *sylt* salt marsh, Norw. *sylta* coast-land washed by the sea.] **—silt′y** *adj.*
sil·ta·tion (sil·tā′shən) *n.* The process of depositing silt.
sil·thi·ane (sil′thē·ān) *n. Chem.* Any of a class of sulfur-containing silicon compounds having the general formula $H_3Si(SSiH_2)_nSSiH_3$. [< SIL(ICON) + THI- + -ANE[1]]
Sil·u·res (sil′yə·rēz) *n. pl.* The pre-Celtic inhabitants of ancient Britain, occupying what is now SE Wales, described by Tacitus as of Iberian origin. [< L]
Si·lu·ri·an (si·lōōr′ē·ən, sī-) *adj.* **1** *Geol.* Of or pertaining to the period or rock system of the Paleozoic era following the Ordovician and preceding the Devonian, sometimes called the era of invertebrates: so called because first identified in southern Wales, the home of the ancient Silures. **2** Of or pertaining to the Silures. —*n.* **1** The Silurian period or system. **2** Originally, the period between the Cambrian and the Devonian.
si·lu·rid (si·lōōr′id, sī-) *n.* Any one of a large family of fishes *(Siluridae),* the catfishes, including many fresh-water food fishes of the United States. —*adj.* Of or pertaining to the *Siluridae.* Also **si·lu′roid.** [< NL *Siluridae,* name of the family < L *silurus* a river fish < Gk. *silouros*]
sil·va (sil′və), **sil·van** (sil′vən), etc. See SYLVA, etc.
Sil·va·nus (sil·vā′nəs) In Roman mythology, a god of woods and farming: also *Sylvanus.* [< L < *silva* forest]
Sil·va·nus (sil·vā′nəs, *Du., Ger.* sel·vä′nōōs), A masculine personal name. Also *Fr.* **Sil·vain** (sēl·van′) or **Sil·vie** (sēl·vē′), *Ital., Sp.* **Sil·va·no** (sēl·vä′nō) or **Sil·vio** (sēl′vyō). [< L, of the forest]
sil·ver (sil′vər) *n.* **1** A lustrous, gray, ductile, malleable metallic element (symbol Ag, atomic number 47) having great thermal and electric

conductivity, found native and in various ores, crystallizing in the isometric system, and valued as one of the precious metals. See PERIODIC TABLE. **2** The metal silver regarded as a valuable commodity or as a standard of currency. **3** Silver coin considered as money; hence, ready cash or change; money in general. **4** Articles for domestic use, as tableware, made of silver; silver plate; silverware. **5** A luster of color resembling that of silver; also, the color of silver. **6** *Phot.* Silver nitrate or one of the other salts of silver, used for sensitizing paper. —*adj.* **1** Made of or coated with silver. **2** Resembling silver; having a silvery lustre. **3** Having the soft, clear tones of a silver bell; hence, enticing; persuasive; eloquent. **4** Relating to, connected with, or producing silver. **5** Designating a 25th wedding anniversary. **6** White; hoary: said of the hair or beard. **7** Favoring the use of silver as a monetary standard. —*v.t.* **1** To coat or plate with silver. **2** To coat with some substance having a resemblance to silver; specifically, to coat with amalgam of tin and mercury, as a mirror. **3** To make silverlike; cause to glitter like silver. **4** To coat, as photographic paper, with a film of a silver salt. —*v.i.* **5** To become silver or white, as with age; to become silverlike. [OE *siolfor*] **—sil′ver·er** *n.*

silver age **1** In Latin literature, the age, following the Augustan age, of which Martial and Tacitus are representatives. **2** In classical mythology, the age of Jupiter's rule, succeeding that of Kronos or Saturn and preceding the brazen age.

sil·ver·bell (sil′vər·bel′) *n.* A small tree *(Halesia carolina)* of the southern United States, with showy white flowers: sometimes called *snowdrop tree.* Also **silverbell tree.**

sil·ver·ber·ry (sil′vər·ber′ē) *n. pl.* **·berries** A shrub *(Elaeagnus commutata)* of the northwestern United States, with silvery foliage, flowers, and edible fruit.

silver bromide *Chem.* A photosensitive compound, AgBr, of silver salts and a bromide: used in photography.

silver certificate Paper currency issued by the United States treasury and validated by silver currency or bullion.

silver chloride *Chem.* A white, curdy precipitate, AgCl, made by treating silver salts with chloride solutions: used in photography for developing and printing.

sil·ver·fish (sil′vər·fish′) *n. pl.* **·fish** or **·fish·es** **1** A silvery-white variety of the goldfish. **2** The tarpon. **3** The silversides. **4** Any of numerous primitive, flat-bodied, wingless insects (genus *Lepisma,* order *Thysanura)* having three bristlelike tails and feeding on flour, cereals, bookbindings, and other starchy matter: often called *bristletail.* **5** Any of several similar insects, as the firebrat.

silver fox **1** The red fox *(Vulpes fulva)* of the United States and Canada, in that color phase when the pelage is black with interspersed silver-tipped hairs. **2** The fur.

silver glance Silver sulfide, Ag_2S; argentite.

silver gray A slightly bluish gray, the color of silver.

sil·ver·ing (sil′vər·ing) *n.* **1** A plating or covering of silver, or an imitation of it, as applied to any surface. **2** The art or process of coating surfaces with or as with silver. **3** Sensitization of photographic paper with a silver salt.

sil·ver·ling (sil′vər·ling) *n.* **1** An old Hebrew or Persian silver coin. **2** A tarpon.

sil·ver·ly (sil′vər·lē) *adv.* In the manner of silver; brightly; with sweet tone.

silver maple White maple.

sil·vern (sil′vərn) *adj. Archaic* or *Poetic* Made of or like silver.

silver nitrate *Chem.* A white, crystalline, poisonous compound, $AgNO_3$, obtained by treating silver with nitric acid. It is widely used in industry and photography, and in medicine as an astringent, antiseptic, etc.

silver plate **1** Table utensils made of silver. **2** *U.S.* Plated silverware: a trade term.

silver point **1** A drawing implement consisting of a slender silver rod pointed at one end, or of silver wire held in an etching-needle holder. **2** The process of drawing with such an implement. **3** A drawing made with a silver point on paper coated with a white pigment, as Chinese white, characterized by delicacy of line, and often by a tarnish which is highly esteemed. **4** *Physics* The melting point of silver at normal atmospheric pressure, 960.5° C.: one of the basic points in the international temperature scale.

silver poplar The white poplar.

sil·ver·sides (sil′vər·sīdz′) *n.* **1** Any of certain small fishes (family *Atherinidae)* related to the mullets and blennies, having a silver band along each side of the body; especially, the **common silversides** *(Menidia notata)* of the coast of the eastern United States. **2** Any small cyprinoid; a fresh-water minnow. Also **sil′ver·side′.**

sil·ver·smith (sil′vər·smith′) *n.* A worker in silver; a maker of silverware.

silver standard A monetary standard or system based on silver.

Silver Star A U.S. military decoration in the form of a bronze star inset with a small raised silver star, awarded for gallantry in action: first issued in 1932, and ranking next in honor to the Distinguished Service Cross.

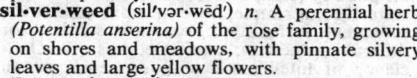

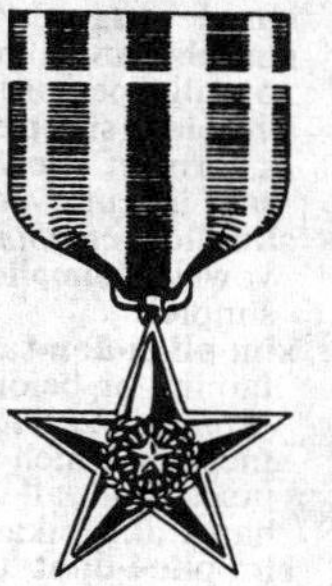
SILVER STAR

Silver State Nickname of Nevada: so called from its native silver ores.

sil·ver-tongued (sil′vər·tungd′) *adj.* Persuasive; eloquent.

sil·ver·ware (sil′vər·wâr′) *n.* Articles made of silver; silver plate; especially, tableware.

sil·ver·weed (sil′vər·wēd′) *n.* A perennial herb *(Potentilla anserina)* of the rose family, growing on shores and meadows, with pinnate silvery leaves and large yellow flowers.

sil·ver·y (sil′vər·ē) *adj.* **1** Containing or adorned with silver. **2** Resembling silver, as in luster, hue, or sound: a *silvery* laugh. **—sil′ver·i·ness** *n.*

Sil·ves·ter (sil·ves′tər) A masculine personal name. Also *Fr.* **Sil·ves·tre** (sēl·ves′tr′). *Ital.* **Sil·ves·tro** (sēl·ves′trō). [< L, forest dweller]

sil·vi·cul·ture (sil′vi·kul′chər) *n.* The art of producing and tending a forest and forest trees. See FORESTRY. [< L *silva* forest + CULTURE] **—sil′vi·cul′tur·al** *adj.* **—sil′vi·cul′tur·al·ly** *adv.* **—sil′vi·cul′tur·ist** *n.*

s'il vous plaît (sēl vōō ple′) *French* If you please; please.

si·ma (sī′mə) *n. Geol.* An igneous rock rich in silica and magnesium underlying sial formations in continental land masses. [< SI(LICA) + MA(GNESIUM)]

si·mar (si·mär′) *n.* A light, flowing robe for women. [< F *simarre* < Ital. *cimarra* < Arabic *sammūr* sable]

sim·a·ru·ba (sim′ə·rōō′bə) *n.* Any of a genus *(Simaruba)* of tropical American trees of the quassia family, having diclinous flowers and drupaceous fruits. *S. amara* yields a bark used in pharmacy. Also **sim′a·rou′ba.** [< NL < native Carib name] **—sim′a·ru·ba′ceous** or **·rou·ba′ceous** *adj.*

Sim·bor (sim·bôr′) A continental territory of Diu district, Portuguese India, on the southern coast of the Kathiawar peninsula at the mouth of the Gulf of Cambay.

Sim·chath To·rah (sim′khäs tō′rə) Literally, the rejoicing over the law; a Jewish holiday which falls on the 23rd of Tishri and closes the feast of Sukkoth. See CALENDAR (Hebrew), JEWISH HOLIDAYS. Also **Sim′hath To′rah.**

Sim·coe (sim′kō), **Lake** A lake in southern Ontario, Canada; 280 square miles.

Sim·e·on (sim′ē·ən, *Ger.* zē′mā·ōn) A masculine personal name. Also *Fr.* **Si·mé·on** (sē·mā·ôṅ′), *Pg.* **Si·ma·ão** (sē′mä·ouṅ′) or **Si·mão** (sē·mouṅ′), *Sp.* **Si·ma·on** (sē′mä·ōn′). See also SIMON. [< Hebrew, obedient]

—Simeon The second son of Jacob, or the tribe descended from him. *Gen.* xxix 33.

—Simeon A Biblical personage. See NUNC DIMITTIS.

—Simeon Sty·li·tes (stī·lī′tēz), 390?–459, Syrian ascetic and stylite.

Sim·fer·o·pol (sim′fər·ō′pəl, *Russian* sēm′fi·rô′pəl) The capital of the Crimea, SW Russian S.F.S.R., in the south central part of the peninsula.

sim·i·an (sim′ē·ən) *adj.* Like or pertaining to the apes and monkeys. —*n.* An ape or monkey. [< L *simia* ape]

sim·i·lar (sim′ə·lər) *adj.* **1** Bearing resemblance to one another or to something else; like, but not completely identical. **2** Of like characteristics, nature, or degree; of the same scope, order, or purpose. **3** *Music* Having motion in the same direction; ascending or descending together, as two parts. **4** *Geom.* Shaped alike: said of two figures, each of which may become congruous with the other by altering all its linear dimensions in one and the same ratio, its angles remaining unchanged. See synonyms under ALIKE, SYNONYMOUS. [< F *similaire* < L *similis* like]

similar fraction See under FRACTION.

sim·i·lar·i·ty (sim′ə·lar′ə·tē) *n. pl.* **·ties. 1** The quality or state of being similar. **2** The point in which the objects compared are similar. **3** *pl.* Things that coincide with or resemble each other. See synonyms under ANALOGY, APPROXIMATION.

sim·i·lar·ly (sim′ə·lər·lē) *adv.* Likewise.

sim·i·le (sim′ə·lē) *n.* A rhetorical figure expressing comparison or likeness, by the use of such terms as *like, as, so,* etc.: distinguished from *metaphor* and *comparison* proper. [< L, neut. of *similis* similar]

Synonyms: comparison, figure, illustration, image, imagery, likeness, metaphor, similitude, symbol. The *simile* carries its note of *comparison* on the surface, in the words *as, like, such as,* or similar expressions; the *metaphor* is given directly without any note of *comparison.* "God is *like* a rock" is a *simile*; "God *is* a rock" is a *metaphor.* In order that a *comparison* may become a *simile,* objects of different classes must be compared, bringing in some imaginative element. To say, "The Hudson is like the Rhine" is not *simile,* but direct and literal *comparison*; but to say, "The Hudson flows like the march of time" is to lift the river out of its class and associate it with a great elemental conception, and thus to transform the *comparison* into a *simile. Similitude* is broader in meaning than *simile* or *metaphor,* and may include direct and literal *comparison.* Compare ALLEGORY, ANALOGY, EMBLEM.

si·mil·i·a si·mil·i·bus cu·ran·tur (si·mil′ē·ə si·mil′ə·bəs kōō·ran′tər) *Latin* Like (ailments) are cured by like, i.e., by remedies that produce the effects of the disease itself: the principle of homeopathy.

si·mil·i·tude (si·mil′ə·tōōd, -tyōōd) *n.* **1** Similarity. **2** One who or that which is similar. **3** A rhetorical figure involving comparison or likeness; loosely, a metaphor or a simile. **4** *Geom.* The relation of identity between two figures irrespective of magnitude. See synonyms under ANALOGY, IMAGE, PICTURE, SIMILE. [< L *similitudo* < *similis* like]

sim·i·ous (sim′ē·əs) *adj.* Simian. Also **sim′i·oid.** [See SIMIAN]

sim·i·tar (sim′ə·tər), **sim·i·ter** See SCIMITAR.

Sim·la (sim′lə) A city of far northern central India; capital of Himachal Pradesh. Formerly the summer capital of India under British rule.

sim·lin (sim′lin) *n.* A cymlin. [Var. of SIMNEL]

sim·mer[1] (sim′ər) *v.i.* **1** To boil gently or with a singing sound; be or stay at or just below the boiling point. **2** To be on the point of breaking forth, as with rage. —*v.t.* **3** To keep at or just below the boiling point. —*n.* The state or process of simmering; figuratively, a busy pondering over something, or a state of repressed emotion. [< obs. *simper* boil; origin unknown; prob. imit.]

sim·mer[2] (sim′ər) *n. Scot.* Summer.

Simms (simz), **William Gilmore,** 1806–70, U.S. novelist and poet.

sim·nel (sim′nəl) *n. Brit.* **1** A brittle cake or bread made of fine flour. **2** A rich cake for mid-Lent Sunday, Easter, or Christmas. [< OF *simenel* < LL *siminellus* < L *simila* fine wheat flour, prob. < Gk. *semidalis,* ult. < Babylonian *samidu* fine flour]

si·mo·le·on (si·mō′lē·ən) *n. Slang* A dollar. [Origin unknown]

Si·mon (sī′mən; *Fr.* sē·môṅ′; *Ger.* zē′mōn; *Sp.*

Sw. sē·mōn′; *Hungarian* shē′mōn) A masculine personal name. Also *Ital.* **Si·mo·ne** (sē·mō′nā). See also SIMEON. [<Hebrew, obedient]
— Simon Ma·gus (mā′gəs) A Samarian magician of the first century, founder of the Simonians, a sect competing with Gentile Christianity.
— Simon Peter See PETER.
— Simon Ze·lo·tes (zē·lō′tēz) One of the twelve apostles: also called "Simon the Canaanite."

Si·mon (sī′mən) *n.* A credulous unsophisticated person: from the Mother Goose nursery rime *Simple Simon.*

Si·mon (sī′mən), **Sir John Allsebrook,** 1873–1954, first viscount Simon, English lawyer and statesman.

si·mo·ni·ac (si·mō′nē·ak) *n.* One who carries on or is guilty of simony. [<Med. L *simoniacus.* See SIMONY.] **— sim·o·ni·a·cal** (sim′ə·nī′ə·kəl) *adj.* **— sim′o·ni′a·cal·ly** *adv.*

Si·mo·ni·an (si·mō′nē·ən, sī-) *adj.* Of or pertaining to Simon Magus or his sect. **—** *n.* One of an early sect that held Simon Magus to be the Messiah.

Si·mo·ni·an·ism (si·mō′nē·ən·iz′əm, sī-) *n.* Saint-Simonism.

Si·mon·i·des of Ceos (sī·mon′ə·dēz) A Greek lyric poet of the sixth and early fifth centuries B.C.

Simon Le·gree (li·grē′) In Harriet Beecher Stowe's *Uncle Tom's Cabin,* the cruel overseer; hence, any brutal master.

si·mon–pure (sī′mən·pyŏŏr′) *adj.* Real; genuine; authentic. [after a character in a 17th c. comedy, who is impersonated by a rival; the rival is discomfited when the real Simon Pure appears]

si·mo·ny (sī′mə·nē, sim′ə-) *n.* Traffic in sacred things; the purchase or sale of ecclesiastical preferment. [<Med. L *simonia* <*Simon (Magus),* who offered Peter money for the gift of the Holy Spirit]

si·moom (si·mōōm′, sī-) *n.* A hot, dry, dust-laden, exhausting wind of the desert, as in Africa and Arabia: also spelled *samoun.* Also **si·moon′** (-mōōn′). [<Arabic *samūm* <*samma* poison]

simp (simp) *n. U.S. Slang* A simpleton.

sim·per (sim′pər) *v.i.* To smile in a silly, self-conscious manner; smirk. **—** *v.t.* To say with a simper. **—** *n.* A silly, self-conscious smile; smirk. [Prob. <Scand. Cf. Sw. and Norw. *semper* affected, coy.] **— sim′per·er** *n.* **— sim′per·ing·ly** *adv.*

sim·ple (sim′pəl) *adj.* **·pler, ·plest 1** Consisting of one thing; single; uncombined; unmingled. **2** Not complex or complicated; easy. **3** Without embellishment; plain; unadorned. **4** Free from affectation; sincere; artless; unsophisticated; also, of humble rank or condition; lowly. **5** Of weak intellect; silly; feeble-minded. **6** Not worth much consideration; insignificant; trifling; ordinary. **7** Without luxury; frugal. **8** Having nothing added; mere: the *simple* truth. **9** *Chem.* That cannot be or has not been decomposed; elementary; also, unmixed. **10** *Bot.* Not subdivided: a *simple* leaf; entire; not divided. **11** *Music* **a** Single. **b** Without overtones. **c** Not developed or elaborated: *simple* harmony. **—** *n.* **1** That which is simple; an unartificial, uncomplex, or natural thing; an element. **2** A medicinal plant, or the medicine extracted from it: from the former supposition that each single herb was or provided a specific for some disease. **3** A simpleton; a stupid or ignorant person; also, a person of humble position or birth. **4** *Eccl.* A feast of lowest rank which is merely commemorated at the canonical hours. **5** *pl. Colloq.* Foolishness; insanity: He suffers from the *simples.* [<OF <L *simplex, simplus*]
Synonyms (adj.): chaste, modest, natural, neat, plain, quiet, unadorned, unaffected, unembellished, unpretentious, unstudied, unvarnished. See CANDID, PURE. *Antonyms*: affected, artful, artificial, complex, complicated, elaborate, intricate, involved, ostentatious, pretentious, showy.

simple fraction See under FRACTION.

simple fruit *Bot.* A fruit consisting of a single enlarged and matured ovary, as the date, cherry, peach, apple, and quince.

sim·ple–heart·ed (sim′pəl·här′tid) *adj.* **1** Tender-hearted. **2** Ingenuous in disposition; open; sincere.

simple honors In bridge, three honors of the trump suit held by a player and his partner.

simple interest Interest computed on the original principal alone.

simple machine 1 Any one of certain elementary mechanical contrivances, as the lever, the wedge, the inclined plane, the screw, the wheel and axle, and the pulley. **2** A hand tool having no parts, as a hammer or chisel, or two parts working in simple combination, as shears.

sim·ple–mind·ed (sim′pəl·mīn′did) *adj.* **1** Artless or unsophisticated in character. **2** Defective in intellect; mentally imbecile. **— sim′ple–mind′ed·ly** *adv.* **— sim′ple–mind′ed·ness** *n.*

sim·pler (sim′plər) *n.* A collector or dispenser of herbs or medicinal remedies extracted from them; herbalist.

simple sentence See under SENTENCE.

Simple Simon A simpleton: from a character in an old English nursery rime of this name.

simple sugar A monosaccharide.

sim·ple·ton (sim′pəl·tən) *n.* A weak-minded or silly person.

sim·plex (sim′pleks) *adj.* **1** Simple. **2** Noting a form of telegraphy in which only one message is sent over a wire at a time. [<L, simple]

simplici– *combining form* Simple. Also, before vowels, **simplic–.** [<L *simplex, simplicis* simple]

sim·pli·ci·den·tate (sim′plə·si·den′tāt) *adj.* Pertaining or belonging to a suborder of rodents *(Simplicidentata)* with a single pair of upper incisors, which includes mice, squirrels, porcupines, and all others with the exception of hares and pikas.

sim·plic·i·dent (sim·plis′ə·dənt) *adj.* Simplicidentate. **—** *n.* A simplicidentate rodent.

sim·plic·i·ty (sim·plis′ə·tē) *n. pl.* **·ties 1** The state of being simple; freedom from admixture, ornament, formality, ostentation, subtlety, or difficulty; sincerity; unaffectedness. **2** Deficiency of intelligence or good sense, or an instance of it. See synonyms under INNOCENCE. Also **sim′ple·ness.** [<L *simplicitas, -tatis*]

sim·pli·fy (sim′plə·fī) *v.t.* **·fied, ·fy·ing** To make more simple or less complex. [<F *simplifier* <Med. L *simplificare* <L *simplex* simple + *facere* make] **— sim′pli·fi·ca′tion** *n.* **— sim′pli·fi′er** *n.*

sim·plis·tic (sim·plis′tik) *adj.* Tending to ignore or overlook underlying questions, complications, or details; overly simple: *simplistic* attitudes. **— sim·plis′ti·cal·ly** *adv.*

Sim·plon Pass (sim′plon, *Fr.* saṅ·plôṅ′) A pass over the Alps in SW Switzerland; elevation, 6,592 feet; traversed by a road built (1800–06) by Napoleon near the **Simplon Tunnel** (1906), 12 1/4 miles, the longest in the world.

sim·ply (sim′plē) *adv.* **1** In a simple manner; intelligibly; without ostentation or extravagance; without subtlety or affectation; unassumingly. **2** Merely. **3** Without sense or discretion; foolishly. **4** Really; absolutely: *simply* charming: often used ironically.

Sims (simz), **William Sowden,** 1858–1936, U. S. admiral born in Canada.

Sim·son (sim′sôn) Swedish form of SAMSON.

sim·u·la·cre (sim′yə·lā′kər) *n. Obs.* An image.

sim·u·la·crum (sim′yə·lā′krəm) *n. pl.* **·cra** (-krə) **1** That which is made in the likeness of a being or thing; an image. **2** An imaginary, visionary, or shadowy semblance. **3** A sham. [<L, image <*simulare.* See SIMULATE.]

sim·u·lant (sim′yə·lənt) *adj.* Simulating. **—** *n.* One who or that which simulates. [<L *simulans, -antis,* ppr. of *simulare.* See SIMULATE.]

sim·u·lar (sim′yə·lər) *n.* One who simulates; a pretender. **—** *adj.* **1** Given to simulation; pretending. **2** Counterfeit.

sim·u·late (sim′yə·lāt) *v.t.* **·lat·ed, ·lat·ing 1** To assume or have the appearance or form of, without the reality; counterfeit; imitate. **2** To make a pretense of. See synonyms under IMITATE, PRETEND. **—** *adj.* (-lāt, -lit) Simulated; pretended. [<L *simulatus,* pp. of *simulare* imitate <*similis* like] **— sim′u·la′tor** *n.*

sim·u·la·tion (sim′yə·lā′shən) *n.* The act of simulating; counterfeit; sham. See synonyms under PRETENSE. **— sim′u·la′tive, sim′u·la·to′ry** (-lə·tôr′ē, -tō′rē) *adj.* **— sim′u·la′tive·ly** *adv.*

si·mul·cast (sī′məl·kast′, -käst′) *v.t.* **·cast, ·cast·ing** To broadcast by radio and television simultaneously. **—** *n.* A broadcast transmitted by radio and television simultaneously. [< SIMUL(TANEOUS) + (BROAD)CAST]

si·mul·ta·ne·ous (sī′məl·tā′nē·əs, sim′əl-) *adj.* Occurring, done, or existing at the same time. [<LL *simultaneus* <L *simul* at the same time] **— si′mul·ta′ne·ous·ly** *adv.* **— si′mul·ta′ne·ous·ness, si′mul·ta·ne′i·ty** (-tə·nē′ə·tē) *n.*

simultaneous equations *Math.* A series of algebraic equations such that each will satisfy the conditions of two or more variables, as, $x + y = 7$ and $2x + 3y = 19$, where $x = 2$, $y = 5$.

si·murg (si·mŏŏrg′) *n.* In Persian mythology, an immense bird possessing great knowledge, who has witnessed the destruction of the world three times; perhaps, the roc. Also **si·murgh′.** [<Persian *simurgh*]

sin[1] (sin) *n.* **1** A lack of conformity to, or a transgression, especially when deliberate, of a law, precept, or principle regarded as having divine authority. **2** The state or condition of having thus transgressed; wickedness. **3** A particular instance of such transgression. **4** Any fault or error; an offense against a standard: a literary *sin.* **—** *v.* **sinned, sin·ning** *v.i.* **1** To commit sin, transgress, neglect, or disregard the divine law or any requirement of right, duty, or propriety; do wrong. **—** *v.t.* **2** To commit or do wrongfully: to *sin* a great sin. **3** To effect, consume, drive, etc., by sin. [OE *synn*]
Synonyms (noun): crime, criminality, delinquency, depravity, evil, guilt, ill-doing, immorality, iniquity, misdeed, offense, transgression, ungodliness, unrighteousness, vice, viciousness, wickedness, wrong, wrong-doing. *Sin,* in religious teaching, is any lack of holiness, any defect of moral purity and truth, whether in heart or life, whether of commission or of omission. *Transgression,* as its etymology indicates, is the stepping over a specific enactment, whether of God or man, ordinarily by overt act, but in the broadest sense in volition or desire. *Sin* may be either act or state; *transgression* is always an act, mental or physical. *Crime* is often used for a flagrant violation of right, but in the technical sense denotes specific violation of human law. *Depravity* denotes no act, but a perverted moral condition from which any act of *sin* may proceed. *Immorality* denotes outward violation of the moral law. Compare OFFENSE. *Antonyms*: decorum, godliness, goodness, holiness, integrity, morality, purity, right, righteousness, sinlessness, uprightness, virtue. Compare synonyms for VIRTUE.

sin[2] (sin) *adv., prep., & conj. Scot. & Brit. Dial.* Since.

Si·nai (sī′nī, -nē·ī′) A peninsula between the Mediterranean and the Red Sea, constituting the easternmost part of Egypt NW of Arabia. Also **Sinaitic Peninsula. — Si·na·ic** (sī·nā′ik), **Si·na·it·ic** (sī′nā·it′ik) *adj.*

Si·nai (sī′nī, -nē·ī′), **Mount** The mountain where Moses received the law from God: generally identified with a mountain in the southern part of Sinai. *Ex.* xix.

sin·al·bin (sin·al′bin) *n. Chem.* A white, bitter, crystalline alkaloid, $C_{30}H_{42}O_{15}N_2S_2$, found in the seeds of the white mustard. [<L *sinapi* mustard + *albus* white]

Si·na·lo·a (sē′nä·lō′ä) A state in western Mexico, on the Gulf of California; 22,580 square miles; capital, Culiacán.

Sin·an·thro·pus (sin·an′thrə·pəs, sī′nan·thrō′·pəs) *n. Paleontol.* A large-brained, well-developed hominid primate identified from extensive fossil remains discovered between 1927 and 1939 in the Pleistocene deposits of a cave near Peking, China. Also called *Peking man.* [<NL <Gk. *Sinai* Chinese + *anthropos* man]

sin·a·pine (sin′ə·pēn, -pin) *n. Chem.* A bitter, unstable alkaloid, $C_{16}H_{25}O_6N$, contained in the seed of the black mustard. Also **sin′a·pin** (-pin). [<L *sinapi* mustard + -INE[2]]

sin·a·pism (sin′ə·piz′əm) *n.* A mustard plaster. [<L *sinapismus* <Gk. *sinapismos* <*sinapi* mustard]

Sin·ar·quist (sin′är·kwist) *n.* A member of an armed fascist group *(Unión Nacional Sinarquista),* formed about 1937, pledged to destroy liberalism and democracy in Mexico and to establish an authoritarian clerical state. [< Sp. *sinarquista* <*sinarquismo* <*sin-* (<L *sine*) without + *anarquismo* anarchism] **— Sin′ar·quism** *n.* **— Sin′ar·quis′tic** *adj.*

Sin·bad (sin′bad) See SINDBAD THE SAILOR.

since (sins) *adv.* **1** From a past time, mentioned or referred to, up to the present. **2** At some time between a certain past time or

event and the present: He was willing at first, but has *since* refused. **3** In time before the present; ago; before now. — *prep.* **1** During or within the time after or later than: Things have changed *since* you left. **2** Continuously throughout the time after: He has been working *since* noon. — *conj.* **1** During or within the time after which. **2** Continuously from the time when: She has been ill *since* she arrived. **3** Because of or following upon the fact that; inasmuch as. See synonyms under BECAUSE. [ME *sithens* <OE *siththan* afterwards + *-s* (adverbial termination)]

sin·cere (sin·sir') *adj.* **1** Being in reality as it is in appearance; real; genuine: *sincere* regret. **2** Intending precisely what one says or what one appears to say; free from hypocrisy; honest in one's action or profession: a *sincere* friend. **3** *Obs.* Being without admixture; free; pure. **4** *Obs.* Blameless. **5** *Obs.* Sound; whole. See synonyms under CANDID, HONEST. [<L *sincerus* uncorrupted < *sin-* without + stem of *caries* decay] — **sin·cere'ly** *adv.*

sin·cer·i·ty (sin·ser'ə·tē) *n.* The state or quality of being sincere; honesty of purpose or character; freedom from hypocrisy, deceit, or simulation. See synonyms under INNOCENCE. Also **sin·cere'ness.**

sin·ci·put (sin'si·put) *n. Anat.* The top of the head, especially the anterior portion. Compare OCCIPUT. [<L <*semi-* half + *caput* head] — **sin·cip·i·tal** (sin·sip'ə·təl) *adj.*

Sin·clair (sin·klâr'), **Upton,** 1878–1968, U.S. author and socialist.

sind (sind) *Scot. v.t.* To rinse; wash down (food) with drink; quench. — *n.* A slight washing; a drink with or after food.

Sind (sind) A former province of West Pakistan, on the Arabian Sea; incorporated into West Pakistan province, 1955; 47,569 square miles; former capital, Hyderabad; total area of Sind and Khairpur, 56,447 square miles, divided into the Commissioners' Divisions of Hyderabad and Khairpur, 1955.

Sind·bad the Sailor (sind'bad) In the *Arabian Nights,* a traveling merchant of Baghdad, who relates the marvelous adventures that befell him on his seven voyages. Also spelled *Sinbad.*

sin·dry (sin'drē) *Scot. adj.* Sundry; several. — *adv.* Asunder.

sine[1] (sīn) *n. Trig.* **1** A function of an angle in a right triangle expressible as the ratio of the side opposite the angle to the hypotenuse. **2** A function of any acute angle expressible, when plotted in Cartesian coordinates, as the ratio of the ordinate to the distance from the point where the ordinate crosses one leg of the angle to the origin. Abbreviated *sin*, as, *sin A.*

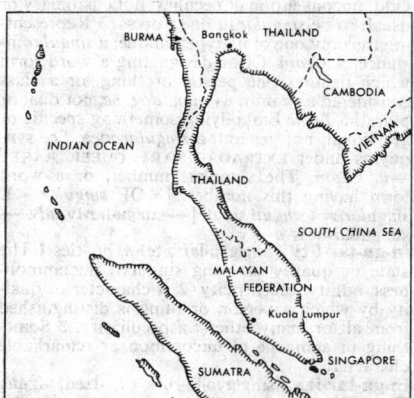

SINE
AB. Arc.
AO. Radius.
BC. Perpendicular.
$\dfrac{BC}{AO}$ is sine of the arc
AB.

See TRIGONOMETRIC FUNCTION. — **versed sine** One of the trigonometric functions, equal to one minus the cosine: also *versine.* ◆ Homophone: *sign.* [<L *sinus* bend (trans. of Arabic *jayb* bosom of a garment, sine). Doublet of SINUS.]

si·ne[2] (sī'nē) *prep. Latin* Without.

sin eater One who takes upon himself the sins of a dead person by eating food placed upon the breast of the dead: an ancient Celtic custom closely related to the scapegoat theory.

si·ne·cure (sī'nə·kyŏor, sin'ə-) *n.* **1** An office having emoluments but few or no duties. **2** A benefice without cure of souls. [<L *sine* without + *cura* care] — **si'ne·cur·ism** *n.* — **si'ne·cur·ist** *n.*

sine curve *Math.* The plane curve of the equation $y = \sin x.$ The curve has a period of $x = 2\pi$ (radians) along the abscissa and a limit along the ordinate of $y = \pm 1.$

si·ne di·e (sī'nē dī'ē) *Latin* Without a day; indefinitely: an adjournment *sine die* (that is, without setting a day for reassembling).

si·ne mo·ra (sī'nē mō'rə) *Latin* Without delay.

si·ne pro·le (sī'nē prō'lē) *Latin* Without offspring: used in genealogical tables: abbr. *s.p.*

si·ne qua non (sī'nē kwā non') *Latin* That which is indispensable; an essential: literally, without which not.

---

sin·ew (sin'yŏo) *n.* **1** A tendon or other fibrous cord. **2** Strength, or that which supplies strength. **3** *Obs.* A nerve. — *v.t.* To strengthen or knit together, as with sinews; supply with sinews. [OE *sinu, seonu*]

sin·ew·less (sin'yŏo·lis) *adj.* **1** Without sinews. **2** Without strength or vigor.

sinews of war Money as a means of carrying on war.

sin·ew·y (sin'yŏo·ē) *adj.* **1** Characteristic or consisting of a sinew or nerve. **2** Well braced with sinews; strong; brawny. See synonyms under STRONG.

sin·fo·ni·a (sin·fō'nē·ə, *Ital.* sēn'fō·nē'ä) *n. Italian* **1** A symphony. **2** The overture, in operas of early date.

sin·ful (sin'fəl) *adj.* Consisting in, suggestive of, or tainted with sin. [OE *synfull*] — **sin'·ful·ly** *adv.* — **sin'ful·ness** *n.*

Synonyms *(adj.)*: bad, criminal, depraved, evil, faulty, flagitious, immoral, iniquitous, nefarious, unholy, unrighteous, unworthy, vicious, vile, villainous, wicked, wrong. See BAD[1], CRIMINAL, IMMORAL. Compare synonyms for SIN[1]. *Antonyms:* godly, good, holy, immaculate, incorrupt, incorruptible, innocent, just, right, righteous, sinless, spotless, stainless, undefiled, unfallen, unperverted, unstained, unsullied, untainted, upright, virtuous, worthy.

sing (sing) *v.* **sang** or (*now less commonly*) **sung, sung, sing·ing** *v.i.* **1** To utter words or sounds with musical inflections of the voice. **2** To perform vocal compositions professionally or in a specified manner: She *sings* well. **3** To utter melodious sounds, as a bird. **4** To make a continuous, melodious sound suggestive of singing, as a teakettle, the wind, etc. **5** To buzz or hum; ring: My ears are *singing.* **6** To be suitable for singing. **7** To relate something in verse; hence, to compose poetry. **8** *Slang* To confess the details of a crime, and so implicate others. — *v.t.* **9** To perform (a song, etc.) vocally. **10** To chant; intone. **11** To bring to a specified condition by singing: *Sing* me to sleep. **12** To accompany or escort with songs. **13** To acclaim or relate in or as in song: Generations *sing* his deeds. — *n.* **1** The humming sound made by a bullet in flight. **2** *Colloq.* A social gathering at which songs are sung: a community *sing.* [OE *singan*] — **sing'a·ble** *adj.*

Synonyms *(verb):* carol, chant, chirp, chirrup, hum, warble. To *sing* is primarily and ordinarily to utter a succession of articulate musical sounds with the human voice. The word has come to include any succession of musical sounds; we say the bird or the rivulet *sings,* or the teakettle or the cricket *sings.* To *chant* is to *sing* in solemn and somewhat uniform cadence; *chant* is ordinarily applied to non-metrical religious compositions. To *carol* is to *sing* joyously, and to *warble* is to *sing* with trills or quavers, usually also with the idea of joy. *Carol* and *warble* are especially applied to the *singing* of birds. To *chirp* is to utter a brief musical sound, perhaps often repeated in the same way, as by certain small birds, insects, etc. To *chirrup* is to utter a somewhat similar sound; the word is often used of a brief sharp sound uttered as a signal to animate or rouse a horse or other animal. To *hum* is to utter murmuring sounds with somewhat monotonous musical cadence, usually with closed lips; we speak also of the *hum* of machinery, etc.

Si·ngan (sē'ngän') A former name for SIAN (def. 1).

Sin·ga·pore (sing'gə·pôr, -pōr, sing'ə-) **1** An island (224 square miles) off the southern end of the Malay Peninsula, comprising with adjacent islands and Christmas Island the State of Malaysia; a former part of the Straits Settlements, 1826–1946; 286 square miles. **2** Its capital, a port on **Singapore Strait,** a channel between Singapore island and the Malay Peninsula, connecting the South China Sea and the Strait of Malacca; 10 miles wide.

Sin·ga·ra·dja (sing'gə·rä'jə) The capital of Bali, and of Nusa Tenggara province, Indonesia, near the north coast of Bali; site of many Hindu temples. Also **Sin'ga·ra'ja.**

singe (sinj) *v.t.* **singed, singe·ing** **1** To burn slightly or superficially; discolor by burning;

---

scorch: to *singe* the nap of cloth. **2** To remove bristles or feathers from by passing through flame. **3** To burn the ends of (hair, etc.). See synonyms under BURN[1]. — *n.* **1** The act of singeing, especially as performed by a barber. **2** A heat that singes. **3** An injury or risk, as if from or of singeing. [OE *sengan* scorch, hiss, causative of *singan* sing; from the singing sound produced]

sing·er[1] (sing'ər) *n.* **1** One who sings, especially as a profession; also, a poet. See synonyms under POET. **2** That which produces a song-like utterance, as a songbird.

sing·er[2] (sin'jər) *n.* One who or that which singes.

Sing·er (sing'ər), **Isaac Merrit,** 1811–75, U.S. inventor; first manufacturer of the sewing machine.

Sin·gha·lese (sing'gə·lēz', -lēs') *adj.* Of or pertaining to Ceylon, to the people constituting the majority of the inhabitants of Ceylon, or to their language. — *n.* **1** One of the Singhalese people. **2** The language of the Singhalese, belonging to the Indic branch of the Indo-Iranian languages, but containing many Dravidian words: the official language of Ceylon since 1956. Also spelled *Sinhalese.* [<Skt. *Sinhala* Ceylon]

sin·gle (sing'gəl) *adj.* **1** Consisting of one only; separate; individual. **2** Having no companion or assistant; alone. **3** Unmarried; also, pertaining to the unmarried state. **4** Of or pertaining to one alone; hence, uncommon; singular; unique. **5** Consisting of only one part; simple; uncompounded. **6** In good condition; sound; also, upright; sincere. **7** Designed for use by only one person: a *single* bed. **8** Designed for use with one thing of which there might be more: a *single* harness (for one horse). **9** *Bot.* Solitary, as a flower when it is the only one on a stem: opposed to *clustered;* in popular usage, having only one row of petals: opposed to *double.* **10** *Obs.* Of medium strength; mild; not double or strong: said of malt liquors. **11** Simplex. See synonyms under PARTICULAR, SOLITARY. — *n.* **1** That which or one who is single; a unit; individual. **2** In baseball, a hit by which the batter reaches first base. **3** A hotel room for one person. **4** A golf match between two players only: opposed to *foursome.* **5** In cricket, a hit which scores one run. **6** In falconry, a talon. — *v.* **·gled, ·gling** *v.t.* **1** To choose or select (one) from others: usually with *out.* — *v.i.* **2** To go with the single-foot gait, as a horse. **3** In baseball, to make a single. [<OF <L *singulus*] — **sin'gle·ness** *n.* — **sin'gly** *adv.*

sin·gle-act·ing (sing'gəl·ak'ting) *adj.* Doing effective work in only one direction, as a motor having a reciprocating motion.

sin·gle-ac·tion (sing'gəl·ak'shən) *adj.* Designating a type of firearm of which the trigger must be cocked by one action and released by another.

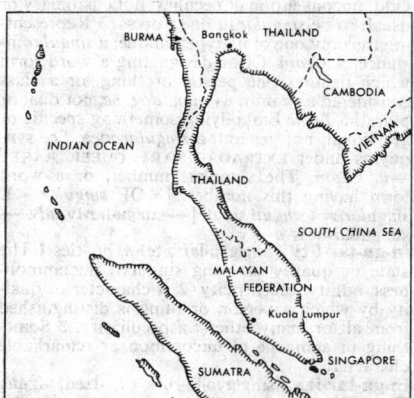

[Map showing BURMA, Bangkok, THAILAND, CAMBODIA, INDIAN OCEAN, VIETNAM, SOUTH CHINA SEA, MALAYAN FEDERATION, Kuala Lumpur, SUMATRA, SINGAPORE]

sin·gle-breast·ed (sing'gəl·bres'tid) *adj.* Having only one thickness of cloth over the breast; fastening in front with a single row of buttons, loops, or like means of engagement: said of a coat, waistcoat, etc.

sin·gle-cross (sing'gəl·krôs', -kros') *n. Genetics*

The first generation of a cross between two inbred lines.

single entry A method of bookkeeping in which the daybook and ledger are the essential books, transactions being carried to a single account only. **—sin′gle-en′try** *adj.*

single file A line of people, animals, etc., disposed one behind the other, with no two abreast.

sin·gle-foot (sing′gəl·fo͝ot′) *n.* The gait of a horse in which the footfall sequence is right hind, right fore, left hind, left fore, the support of the body being alternately upon one foot and two feet: sometimes called *amble* or *rack.* —*v.i.* To go at this gait.

sin·gle-hand·ed (sing′gəl·han′did) *adj.* **1** Without assistance; unaided. **2** Having but one hand. **3** Capable of being used with a single hand. **4** Having only one workman. Also **sin′gle-hand′.** **—sin′gle-hand′ed·ly** *adv.*

sin·gle-heart·ed (sing′gəl·här′tid) *adj.* Of sincere and frank disposition. **—sin′gle-heart′ed·ly** *adv.*

sin·gle-mind·ed (sing′gəl·mīn′did) *adj.* **1** Having but one purpose or end in view. **2** Free from duplicity; ingenuous; sincere. **—sin′gle-mind′ed·ly** *adv.* **—sin′gle-mind′ed·ness** *n.*

sin·gle-phase (sing′gəl·fāz′) *adj. Electr.* Applied to the current generated by a two-pole alternating dynamoelectric machine.

sin·gles (sing′gəlz) *n. pl.* In lawn tennis, table tennis, etc., a match with only one person on each side: opposed to *doubles.* —*adj.* Having but one player on a side: a *singles* match.

sin·gle·stick (sing′gəl·stik′) *n.* **1** A cudgel; specifically, a basket-hilted stick used in fencing. **2** The art of fencing with singlesticks; also, a bout with cudgels.

sin·gle·stick·er (sing′gəl·stik′ər) *n. Colloq.* A one-masted sailboat; a sloop.

sin·gle-sur·faced (sing′gəl·sûr′fist) *adj.* Surfaced, covered, or finished on one side only.

sin·glet (sing′glit) *n.* **1** A woolen or cotton undershirt or jersey. **2** An unlined waistcoat.

sin·gle·ton (sing′gəl·tən) *n.* **1** A single card of a suit in the hand of a player at the deal. **2** Any single thing, distinct from a pair.

sin·gle·tree (sing′gəl·trē′) *n.* A swingletree.

sin·gly (sing′glē) *adv.* **1** Without companions or associates; alone; unaided, as an individual. **2** One by one; one at a time. **3** *Obs.* Uprightly; honestly.

Sing Sing (sing′sing′) **1** A State prison near Ossining, New York. **2** The former name of OSSINING.

sing·song (sing′sông′, -song′) *n.* **1** Monotonous cadence in speaking or reading. **2** Inferior verse; doggerel. —*adj.* **1** Monotonous; droning. **2** Rising and falling in pitch.

sing·spiel (sing′spēl, *Ger.* zing′shpēl) *n.* **1** A dramatic representation in which dialog and song alternate. **2** Opera in which music is subordinated to words, especially in dramatic movement. [<G, lit., sing-play]

sin·gu·lar (sing′gyə·lər) *adj.* **1** Extraordinary; remarkable; uncommon: her *singular* beauty. **2** Odd; unconventional; peculiar; not customary or usual: to be *singular* in one's dress. **3** Representing the only one of its type; unique: a *singular* instance. **4** *Gram.* Of or designating a word form which denotes one person or thing, or a class considered as a unit, as *man, dog, he;* not dual or plural. **5** *Logic* Embodying something specific or individual; not general: a *singular* idea. See synonyms under EXTRAORDINARY, QUEER, RARE[1]. —*n. Gram.* The singular number, or a word form having this number. [<OF *singuler* <L *singularis* <*singuli* single] **—sin′gu·lar·ly** *adv.* **—sin′gu·lar·ness** *n.*

sin·gu·lar·i·ty (sing′gyə·lar′ə·tē) *n. pl.* **·ties** **1** The state or quality of being singular; uncommonness; oddity; eccentricity. **2** A character or quality by which a person or thing is distinguished from all or many others; a peculiarity. **3** Something or someone of uncommon or remarkable character.

sin·gu·lar·ize (sing′gyə·lə·rīz′) *v.t.* **·ized, ·iz·ing** To make singular; convert into the singular number.

Sin·ha·lese (sin′hə·lēz′, -lēs′) See SINGHALESE.

Sin·i·cism (sin′ə·siz′əm) *n.* Something peculiar to the Chinese, as their manners or customs. [<LL *Sinae* the Chinese]

sin·i·grin (sin′ə·grin) *n. Chem.* A white crystalline glycoside, $C_{10}H_{16}KNO_9S_2$, found principally in the seeds of the black mustard. [<NL *sinapis negra* black mustard]

sin·is·ter (sin′is·tər) *adj.* **1** Morally wrong; malevolent; evil; bad; perverse: *sinister* purposes; a *sinister* expression on the face. **2** Boding, tending toward, or attended with disaster; unlucky; inauspicious: from a superstition that omens seen on the left boded ill. **3** Situated on the left side or hand: opposed to *right* or *right-hand.* **4** *Her.* Of a shield, left as regards the wearer; hence, right as regards the observer: opposed to *dexter.* Compare illustration under ESCUTCHEON. [<F *sinistre* <L *sinister* left] **—sin′is·ter·ly** *adv.* **—sin′is·ter·ness** *n.*

sin·is·trad (sin′is·trad) *adv.* Toward the left aspect of the body: opposed to *dextrad.* [<L *sinister* left]

sin·is·tral (sin′is·trəl) *adj.* Of, pertaining to, or turned toward the left side or left hand. [<OF] **—sin·is·tral·i·ty** (sin′is·tral′ə·tē) *n.* **—sin′is·tral·ly** *adv.*

sin·is·trorse (sin′is·trôrs, sin′is·trôrs′) *adj.* **1** Sinistral. **2** Twined or twining from right to left, as the hop. Compare DEXTRORSE. [<L *sinistrorsus,* contraction of *sinistroversus* turned toward the left side <*sinister* left + *versum* turned, pp. of *vertere*] **—sin′is·tror′sal** *adj.* **—sin′is·tror′sal·ly** *adv.*

sin·is·trous (sin′is·trəs) *adj.* **1** Of, pertaining to, or directed toward the left; sinistral. **2** Sinister; unpropitious; ill-omened. [<L *sinister* left] **—sin′is·trous·ly** *adv.*

sink (singk) *v.* **sank** or **sunk, sunk** (*Obs.* **sunk·en**), **sink·ing** *v.i.* **1** To go beneath the surface or to the bottom, as of water or snow. **2** To descend to a lower level; go down, especially slowly or by degrees: The flames are *sinking.* **3** To descend toward or below the horizon, as the sun. **4** To incline downward; slope, as land. **5** To pass into a specified state: to *sink* into sleep or a coma. **6** To fail, as from ill-health or lack of strength; approach death: He's *sinking* fast. **7** To become less in force, volume, or degree: His voice *sank* to a whisper. **8** To become less in value, price, etc. **9** To decline in moral level, prestige, wealth, etc.: to *sink* into vice. **10** To penetrate a softer body: The oil *sank* into the wood. **11** To be impressed or fixed, as in the heart or mind: with *in:* I think that lesson will *sink* in. —*v.t.* **12** To cause to go beneath the surface or to the bottom. **13** To cause to fall or drop; lower: He *sank* his head upon his breast. **14** To force or drive into place: to *sink* a fence post. **15** To make (a mine shaft, well, etc.) by digging or excavating. **16** To reduce in force, volume, or degree. **17** To debase or degrade, as one's character or honor. **18** To suppress or hide; also, to omit. **19** To defeat; ruin. **20** To invest. **21** To invest and subsequently lose: I *sank* a million in that deal. —*n.* **1** A box-shaped, basinlike, porcelain or metal receptacle with a drainpipe and usually with a water supply; a cesspool or the like. **2** A place where corruption and vice gather or are rampant. **3** A natural pool, marsh, or basin in which a river terminates by evaporation or percolation. [OE *sincan*] **—sink′a·ble** *adj.*

sink boat A boat sunk to the rim in water: used in duck shooting: also called *surface boat.*

sink·er (singk′ər) *n.* **1** One who or that which sinks, or causes to sink: a die-*sinker.* **2** A weight for sinking a fishing or sounding line. **3** In baseball, a pitch that curves sharply downward as it approaches home plate.

sink·hole (singk′hōl′) *n.* A natural cavity, especially a drainage cavity, as a hole worn by water through a rock along a joint or fracture.

Sin·kiang-Ui·gur Autonomous Region (shin′jyäng′wē′go͝or′) The westernmost division of China, formerly **Sinkiang,** comprising all of northwestern China between Mongolia and Tibet; 700,000 square miles; capital, Urumchi (Tihwa): also *Chinese Turkestan.*

sinking fund The fund so instituted and invested that its gradual accumulations will wipe out a debt at maturity.

sin·less (sin′lis) *adj.* Having no sin; guiltless; innocent. See synonyms under INNOCENT, PERFECT. **—sin′less·ly** *adv.* **—sin′less·ness** *n.*

sin·ner (sin′ər) *n.* **1** One who has sinned. **2** An irreligious person.

Sinn Fein (shin fān) Literally, we ourselves; an Irish society aiming at both independence and the cultural development of the Irish people. It originated about 1905 and in 1916 became active politically, advocating republicanism and causing a revolt in the spring of that year. **—Sinn Fein′er —Sinn Fein′ism**

Sino- *combining form* Chinese; of or pertaining to the Chinese people, language, etc. See CHINO-. [<LL *Sinae* the Chinese]

si·no·a·tri·al (sī′nō·ā′trē·əl) *adj. Anat.* Of or pertaining to an area of the right auricle of the heart where the heartbeat is stimulated.

sin offering An offering made in atonement for sin.

Sin·o·log (sin′ə·lôg, -log, sī′nə-) *n.* One who studies or is versed in Sinology. Also **Sin′o·logue.** [<SINO- + Gk. *logos* discourse]

Si·nol·o·gy (sī·nol′ə·jē, si-) *n.* The systematic study or investigation of the Chinese people, language, literature, history, and characteristics. **—Sin·o·log·i·cal** (sin′ə·loj′i·kəl, sī′nə-) *adj.* **—Si·nol′o·gist** *n.*

Si·non (sī′nən) In the *Aeneid,* the Greek who induced the Trojans to drag the wooden horse into Troy.

Si·no·phile (sī′nə·fīl, sin′ə-) *n.* An admirer of the Chinese. —*adj.* Having admiration for the Chinese or things Chinese.

Si·no·phobe (sī′nə·fōb, sin′ə-) One antipathetic toward the Chinese. —*adj.* Having hostility toward the Chinese or Chinese customs.

Si·no-Ti·bet·an (sī′nō·ti·bet′n) *n.* A family of tone languages spoken over a wide area in central and SE Asia, including the languages of China, Burma, Tibet, and Indochina: characterized by monosyllabic, uninflected word-forms which indicate their syntactic roles by position only. Also called *Indochinese.*

sin·ter (sin′tər) *n.* **1** Calcareous or siliceous material deposited by springs. **2** That which is produced by sintering. —*v.t.* & *v.i. Metall.* To bring about the cohesion of (metal particles) by the combined action of heat and pressure. [<G, dross of iron]

Sint Eu·sta·ti·us (sint o͞o·stä′tē·o͞os) See under ST. EUSTATIUS.

Sint Maar·ten (sint mär′tən) See under ST. MARTIN.

Sin·tra (sēn′trə) The Portuguese spelling of CINTRA.

sin·u·ate (sin′yo͞o·it, -āt) *adj.* **1** Winding in and out, as a margin; tortuous; sinuous; wavy. **2** *Bot.* Having a sinus, or sinuses: a *sinuate* leaf. Also **sin′u·at′ed.** —*v.i.* (sin′yo͞o·āt) **·at·ed, ·at·ing** To curve in and out; turn; wind. [<L *sinuatus,* pp. of *sinuare* turn, wind <*sinus* curve] **—sin′u·ate·ly** *adv.* **—sin′u·a′tion** *n.*

Sin·ui·ju (shin·ē·jo͞o) A city of NW North Korea, on the Yalu; heavily bombed in the Korean war, 1950.

sin·u·os·i·ty (sin′yo͞o·os′ə·tē) *n.* **1** Sinuous quality. **2** A winding; deflection.

sin·u·ous (sin′yo͞o·əs) *adj.* **1** Characterized by bends or folds; winding; undulating. **2** *Bot.* Sinuate. **3** Devious; erring. [<L *sinuosus* <*sinus* bend] **—sin′u·ous·ly** *adv.* **—sin′u·ous·ness** *n.*

si·nus (sī′nəs) *n.* **1** A recess formed by a bending or folding; an opening or cavity. **2** *Anat.* **a** An air cavity in one of the cranial bones communicating with the nostrils: the frontal *sinus.* **b** A channel or receptacle for venous blood; also, a dilated part of a blood vessel. **3** *Pathol.* Any narrow opening leading to an abscess. **4** *Bot.* A recess or rounded curve between two projecting lobes or teeth of a leaf. [<L. Doublet of SINE.]

si·nu·si·tis (sī′nə·sī′tis) *n. Pathol.* Inflammation of a sinus. Also **sin·u·i·tis** (sin′yo͞o·ī′tis). [<SINUS + -ITIS]

si·nu·sot·o·my (sī′nə·sot′ə·mē) *n. Surg.* Incision of a sinus.

si·nus·oid (sī′nə·soid) *n.* **1** *Math.* sine curve. **2** *Anat.* A tiny passageway for blood in the liver.

-sion Var of -TION.

Si·on (sī′ən) See ZION.

Sion (syôn) The capital of Valais canton, SW Switzerland: German *Sitten.*

Siou·an (so͞o′ən) *n.* A large linguistic stock of North American Indians, formerly ranging from the west banks of the Mississippi to the Rocky Mountains, and comprising the languages of the Dakota or Sioux tribes proper, those of a group including the Omaha, Osage, etc., those of the Iowa, Missouri, and Oto, also Winnebago, Mandan, Crow, Catawba,

and several others now extinct. — *adj.* Of or pertaining to this linguistic stock.

Sioux (sōō) *n. pl.* **Sioux** One of a group of North American Indian tribes of Siouan linguistic stock formerly occupying the Dakotas and parts of Minnesota and Nebraska. They were Plains Indians and called themselves Dakota.

Sioux City A city on the Missouri River in western Iowa.

Sioux Falls A city in SE South Dakota.

sip (sip) *v.* **sipped, sip·ping** *v.t.* **1** To imbibe in small quantities. **2** To drink from by sips. **3** To take in; absorb. — *v.i.* **4** To drink in sips. — *n.* **1** A very small draft; a mere taste. **2** The act of sipping. [OE *sypian* drink in]

sipe (sīp) *v.i. Scot.* To seep.

si·phon (sī′fən) *n.* **1** A tube having a bend used for transferring liquids from a higher to a lower level over an intervening elevation by making use of atmospheric pressure. **2** A siphon bottle. **3** *Zool.* A tubular structure in certain aquatic animals, as the squid, for drawing in or expelling liquids. — *v.t.* To draw off by or cause to pass through or as through a siphon. — *v.i.* To pass through a siphon. Also spelled *syphon.* [<F <L *sipho, -onis* <Gk. *siphōn*] — **si′phon·al** *adj.*

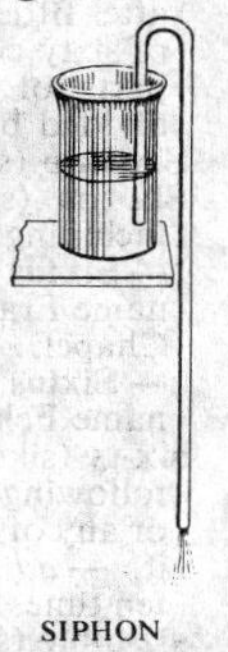

SIPHON

si·phon·age (sī′fən·ij) *n.* The use or action of a siphon.

si·pho·nap·ter·ous (sī′fə·nap′tər·əs) *adj.* Of or pertaining to the order of insects *(Siphonaptera)* including the fleas: small, flattened, wingless, bloodsucking insects with great jumping ability. [<NL *Siphonaptera,* name of the order <SIPHON + A-[4] + -PTEROUS]

siphon bottle A bottle containing aërated or carbonated water, which is expelled through a bent tube in the neck of the bottle by the pressure of the gas.

si·pho·no·phore (sī′fə·nə·fôr′, -fōr′, sī·fon′ə-) *n.* A marine organism (order *Siphonophora)* with free-swimming pelagic colonies arising by budding, as the Portuguese man-of-war. [<NL *Siphonophora,* name of the order <Gk. *siphōnophōros* tube-carrying < *siphōn* tube + *pherein* bear]

si·pho·no·stele (sī′fə·nə·stēl′, -stē′lē) *n. Bot.* The hollow tubular stem of certain plants, as ferns. [<Gk. *siphōn* tube + STELE]

sip·pet (sip′it) *n.* **1** A triangular or finger-shaped piece of toasted or fried bread used to garnish a dish of hash or minced meat; a crouton. **2** Any eatable, especially bread, cut into small pieces and soaked in some liquid: frequently used in the plural. **3** Hence, any very small quantity. [Blend of SIP and SOP in a dim. form]

Si·quei·ros (sē·kā′rōs), **David Alfaro,** born 1898, Mexican painter and muralist.

sir (sûr) *n.* **1** The conventional term of respectful address to men: used absolutely, and not followed by a proper name. **2** A title given to persons of rank or to officials: *sir* herald, *sir* clerk. **3** An influential or important person. **4** *Archaic* A title of respect for a priest. [<SIRE]

Sir (sûr) *n.* A title of baronets and knights, used before the Christian name or the full name.

Sir·bo·ni·an (sər·bō′nē·ən) See SERBONIAN.

sir·dar (sər·där′) *n.* **1** In India and Oriental countries, a chief or lord. **2** In Egypt, the commander in chief of the army. **3** In India, a head servant; a leader of palanquin-bearers; also, a body-servant or valet: also **sir·dar′-bear′er.** [<Hind. *sardār* leader < *sar* head + *dār* holding] — **sir·dar′ship** *n.*

sire (sīr) *n.* **1** A father; begetter: used also in composition: *grandsire.* The feminine correlative is *dame.* **2** The male parent of a mammal, the female parent (of lower animals) being usually termed the *dam.* **3** A form of address to a superior: now used only in addressing a king or other sovereign. **4** *Obs.* A master; lord; also, a gentleman. — *v.t.* **sired, sir·ing** To beget; procreate: now used chiefly of domestic animals. [<OF <L *senior* older. See SENIOR.]

si·ren (sī′rən) *n.* **1** One of two, or, in later Greek legend, three nymphs, living on an island, who lured sailors to destruction by their sweet singing. They are represented as birds with women's heads, later as women with birds' feet and wings. Odysseus escaped them by sealing his companions' ears with wax and having himself bound to his ship's mast. **2** Hence, a fascinating, dangerous woman; also, a sweet singer. **3** An eel-like amphibian (genus *Siren)* having well developed gills and lacking hind legs; a mud eel. **4** An apparatus having a device with a perforated rotating disk or disks through which sharp puffs of steam or compressed air are permitted to escape in such rapid succession as to produce a continued musical note or a loud whistle: used in acoustical investigations and as a warning signal. — *adj.* Of or pertaining to a siren; hence, alluring; bewitching; dangerously fascinating. Also spelled *syren.* [<L <Gk. *seirēn*]

si·re·ni·an (sī·rē′nē·ən) *n.* One of an order *(Sirenia)* of aquatic mammals, including the manatee, dugong, etc., of somewhat fishlike form with the lower jaw as in ordinary mammals, and having mostly molariform teeth for a herbivorous diet. — *adj.* Of or pertaining to the *Sirenia.* [<NL *Sirenia,* name of the order <L *siren.* See SIREN.]

Si·ret (sē·ret′) A river in eastern Rumania, flowing 270 miles SE to the Danube: also *Sereth.*

si·ri·a·sis (si·rī′ə·sis) *n. Pathol.* Sunstroke or thermic fever. [<Gk. *seiriasis* < *seirios* hot, scorching]

Sir·i·us (sir′ē·əs) The Dog Star, Alpha in the constellation of Canis Major; magnitude, −1.6. [<Gk. *seirios* hot, scorching]

sir·loin (sûr′loin) *n.* A loin of beef, especially the upper portion: also spelled *surloin.* [Alter. (after *Sir,* from a legend that the cut was knighted for its excellence) of obs. *surloyn* <OF *surlonge* < *sur-* over, above + *longe* loin <L *lumbus*]

si·roc·co (si·rok′ō) *n. pl.* **·cos** **1** A hot, dry, and dusty southerly wind blowing from the African coast to Italy, Sicily, and Spain. **2** A warm, sultry wind blowing from a warm region toward a center of low barometric pressure. **3** A southeast wind: the popular Italian name. [<Ital. *scirocco* <Arabic *sharq* the east, the rising sun < *sharaqa* rise]

Si·ros (sī′ros, *Greek* sē′rôs) See SYROS.

sir·rah (sir′ə) *n. Archaic* Fellow; sir: used in contempt or annoyance. [Var. of *sir,* after Provençal *sira*]

Sir·rah (sir′ə) See ALPHERATZ.

sir-rev·er·ence (sûr·rev′ər·əns) *interj. Obs.* Save your reverence; begging your pardon: used as an apology before any unbecoming expression. [Misspelling of *sa' reverence,* contraction of *save (your) reverence,* erroneous trans. of L *salva reverentia* with due regard for decency]

sir·up (sir′əp) *n.* A thick, sweet liquid, as the boiled juice of fruits, sugarcane, etc.: also spelled *syrup.* [<OF *sirop* <Turkish *sharbat.* Doublet of SHERBET.] — **sir′up·y** *adj.*

sir·vente (sēr·vänt′) *n.* A lyric in Provençal troubadour literature, characterized by great formal elaboration and a satirical treatment of themes of a political and courtly nature. [<F <Provençal <L *servens, -entis* ppr. of *servire* serve]

sis (sis) *n. Colloq.* Sister.

si·sal (sī′səl, sis′əl, sē′səl) *n.* **1** The strong, tough fiber obtained from the leaves of a West Indian agave *(Agave sisalina).* **2** Henequen. Also **sisal grass, sisal hemp.** [from *Sisal,* town in Yucatán, Mexico]

sis·co·wet (sis′kə·wet) *n.* **1** The namaycush. **2** The cisco. Also **sis′ka·wet, sis′ki·wit.** [<F (Canadian) *ciscoette* <Algonquian (Ojibwa) *pemitewiskawet* oily-fleshed creature]

Sis·er·a (sis′ər·ə) A Canaanite chieftain defeated by the Israelites; murdered by Jael. *Judges* iv 2; v 20, 26.

sis·er·ar·y (sis′ə·rer′ē) *n. Brit. Dial.* **1** An effective proceeding. **2** A writ of certiorari. — **with a siserary** With a vengeance; like a thunderclap. [Alter. of CERTIORARI]

sis·kin (sis′kin) *n.* A finch (genus *Spinus)* related to the goldfinch, as the **European siskin** *(S. spinus)* olive-green and yellow barred with black, or the North American **pine siskin** *(S. pinus).* [<MDu. *cijsken* <LG *zieske* <Polish *czyżik,* dim. of *czyż* finch]

Sis·ley (sēs·lē′), **Alfred,** 1839–99, French painter of English descent.

Sis·mon·di (sēs·môṅ·dē′), **Jean Charles Léonard Simonde de,** 1773–1842, Swiss historian and economist.

siss (sis) *v.i.* To hiss; sizzle. — *n.* A hissing or sizzling sound. [Imit.]

sis·si·fied (sis′i·fīd) *adj. U.S. Colloq.* Like a sissy; effeminate.

sis·sy (sis′ē) *U.S. Colloq. n. pl.* **·sies** An effeminate man or boy; a milksop; a weakling, male or female. — *adj.* Being a sissy; effeminate; sissified. [<SIS] — **sis′sy·ish** *adj.*

Si·stan (se·stän′) See SEISTAN.

sis·ter (sis′tər) *n.* **1** A female person or animal having the same parent or parents as another person or animal. Daughters of the same parents are **full** or **whole sisters,** called in law **sisters german.** Those having only one parent in common are **half-sisters.** **2** A woman or girl allied to another or others by some association: *sisters* in spirit: also used figuratively: Astronomy and astrology are *sisters.* **3** *Eccl.* A member of a sisterhood; a nun. **4** A head nurse in the ward of a hospital; also, popularly, any nurse. — **the three** (or **Fatal) Sisters** The Fates. — *adj.* Bearing the relationship of a sister or one suggestive of sisterhood. [<ON *systir*] — **sis′ter·ly** *adj.*

sis·ter·hood (sis′tər·hŏŏd) *n.* **1** A body of sisters united by some bond of fellowship or sympathy. **2** *Eccl.* **a** A community of women bound by monastic vows. **b** An association of women set apart for works of mercy and faith, sometimes bound by a revocable vow. **3** The sisterly relationship.

sis·ter-in-law (sis′tər·in·lô′) *n. pl.* **sis·ters-in-law** A sister by marriage: a sister of one's husband, a sister of one's wife, a brother's wife, or, loosely, a brother-in-law's wife.

Sis·tine (sis′tēn, -tin) *adj.* Belonging or relating to one of the five popes named Sixtus (Italian *Sisto*), particularly to Sixtus IV and Sixtus V. [<Ital. *Sistino* <*Sisto* <L *sextus* sixth]

Sistine Chapel The principal chapel in the Vatican Palace at Rome, constructed by Sixtus IV, and afterward decorated with frescos by Michelangelo and others.

Sistine choir Formerly, a select choir of thirty-two cultivated voices attached to the court of the pope.

Sistine Madonna The Madonna painted by Raphael for the Church of St. Sixtus (Italian *di San Sisto*) in 1515.

sis·troid (sis′troid) *adj. Geom.* Included by the convex sides of two intersecting curves: said of an angle and opposed to *cissoid.* [<SIS-TR(UM) + -OID]

sis·trum (sis′trəm) *n. pl.* **·tra** (-trə) or **·trums** A musical rattle used in the worship of Isis in ancient Egypt. [<L <Gk. *seistron* < *seiein* shake]

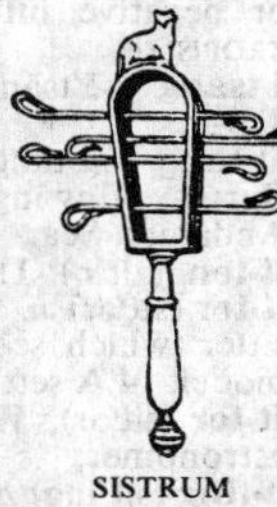

SISTRUM

Sis·y·phe·an (sis′ə·fē′ən) *adj.* **1** Of or pertaining to Sisyphus. **2** Difficult and interminable: a *Sisyphean* task.

Sis·y·phus (sis′ə·fəs) In Greek mythology, a crafty, greedy king of Corinth, condemned in Hades forever to roll uphill a huge stone that always rolled down again.

sit (sit) *v.* **sat** (*Archaic* **sate**), **sat, sit·ting** *v.i.* **1** To rest, as upon a chair, with the body bent at the hips, and the spine nearly vertical; rest upon the haunches; take or occupy a seat. **2** To perch or roost, as a bird; brood; also, to cover eggs so as to give warmth for hatching. **3** To be or remain in a seated or settled position. **4** To remain passive or inactive, or in a position of idleness or rest. **5** To assume an attitude of readiness; take a position for a special purpose; pose, as for a portrait. **6** To meet in assembly for deliberation or business; hold a session. **7** To occupy or be entitled to a seat in a deliberative body. **8** To have or exercise judicial authority. **9** To fit or be adjusted; suit: That dress *sits* well. **10** To be suffered or borne, as a burden. **11** To be situated or located; be in some position or direction: The wind *sits* in the east. — *v.t.*

12 To have or keep a seat or a good seat upon: to *sit* a horse. 13 To seat (oneself): *Sit* yourself down. **— to sit in (on)** To join: to *sit in on* a game of cards, or a business deal. **— to sit on** (or **upon**) 1 To belong to (a jury, commission, etc.) as a member. 2 To hold discussions about and look into carefully, as a case. 3 *Colloq.* To suppress or squelch. **— to sit out** 1 To sit quietly till the end of: to *sit out* an entertainment. 2 To sit aside during: They *sat out* a dance. 3 To stay longer than. **— to sit tight** *Colloq.* To wait quietly for the next move on the part of somebody else: Just *sit tight* until I get back. [OE *sittan*]

si·tar (si·tär′) *n.* A stringed instrument used in Hindu music, somewhat resembling the guitar, having a variable number of strings, some of which are plucked, others vibrating sympathetically. [<Hind. *sitār*]

sit·com (sit′kom′) *n. Slang* A situation comedy. [Blend of SIT(UATION) + COM(EDY)]

sit–down (sit′doun′) *n.* 1 A strike during which strikers refuse to leave the factory or other place of employment until agreement is reached. Also **sit–down strike.** 2 A sit–in (def. 2).

site (sīt) *n.* 1 Situation; local position. 2 A plot of ground set apart for some specific use. 3 The degree of inclination from the horizontal of a line joining the target and the muzzle of a gun: also **angle of site.** See synonyms under PLACE. ◆ Homophones: *cite, sight.* [<F <L *situs* position]

sith (sith) *adv., prep., & conj. Archaic* Since. Also **sith·ence** (sith′əns). [OE *siththan* after]

sit–in (sit′in′) *n.* 1 An organized demonstration in which a protesting group occupies an area prohibited to them, as by taking seats in a restricted restaurant, etc. 2 A form of civil disobedience in which demonstrators obstruct some activity by sitting down and refusing to move: also called *sit–down.* **— sit′–in·ner** *n.*

Sit·ka (sit′kə) A town and naval base on Baranof Island in SE Alaska.

sito– *combining form* Food; related to food: *sitotropism.* [<Gk. *sitos* food]

si·tol·o·gy (sī·tol′ə·jē) *n.* The science of foods, diet, and nutrition. **— si·to·log·ic** (sī′tə·loj′ik) or **·i·cal** *adj.*

si·tos·ter·ol (sī·tos′tə·rōl, -rol) *n. Biochem.* Any of a group of sterols found in higher plants and related to cholesterol, especially *a-sitosterol,* $C_{30}H_{50}O$, from wheat embryos. [< SITO- + STEROL]

si·to·tox·in (sī′tō·tok′sin) *n.* Any poison evolved in vegetable foods, especially in cereals, by the action of micro–organisms. [<SITO- + TOXIN]

si·to·tro·pism (sī′tō·trō′piz·əm) *n.* The automatic response of an organism to the positive or negative influence of food. [<SITO- + TROPISM]

Si·tsang (sē′tsäng′) The Chinese name for TIBET.

Sit·tang (sit′täng) A river in south central Burma, flowing 350 miles south to the Andaman Sea.

Sit·ten (zit′n) The German name for SION.

sit·ter (sit′ər) *n.* 1 One who sits. 2 A baby sitter (which see). 3 A person sitting as a model. 4 A setting hen.

Sit·ter (sit′ər), **Willem de,** 1872–1934, Dutch astronomer.

sit·ting (sit′ing) *adj.* Being in the position of a sitter; also, used for sitting: a *sitting*–room. *—n.* 1 The act or position of one who sits; hence, a seat; also, the place of or the right to a seat, as in a church. 2 A single period of uninterrupted application, as for the painting of a portrait. 3 A session or term. 4 An incubation; period of hatching; also, the number of eggs on which a bird sits at one incubation.

Sitting Bull, 1834?–90, Sioux Indian chief; defeated Custer at the battle of Little Big Horn, 1876.

sitting duck 1 A duck resting on water, and therefore an easy target for a hunter. 2 *Colloq.* Any easy target.

sit·ting–room (sit′ing·ro͝om′, -ro͞om′) *n.* A parlor; living–room.

sit·u·ate (sich′o͞o·āt) *v.t.* **·at·ed, ·at·ing** 1 To fix a site for. 2 To place in a certain position or under certain conditions or circumstances; locate. [<Med. L *situatus,* pp. of *situare* place < *situs* a place]

sit·u·at·ed (sich′o͞o·ā′tid) *adj.* 1 Having a fixed place or location; placed. 2 Placed in (usually specified) circumstances or conditions: He is *well* situated.

sit·u·a·tion (sich′o͞o·ā′shən) *n.* 1 The place in which something is situated; relative local position; locality. 2 Condition as modified or determined by surroundings; status. 3 A salaried post of employment, usually subordinate. 4 A combination of circumstances; complication; specifically, in the drama, a conjuncture, climax, or crisis. See synonyms under CIRCUMSTANCE, PLACE, SCENE. **— sit′u·a′tion·al** *adj.*

situation comedy A television or radio show typically centered about a few characters involved in comical situations and presented in separate episodes.

si·tus (sī′təs) *n.* 1 Site; situation; place. 2 A fitting or natural position, as of a part of a plant. [<L]

Sit·well (sit′wel) Name of an English literary family, including **Edith,** 1887–1964, and her brothers, **Osbert,** 1892–1969, and **Sacheverell,** born 1897, all three poets, essayists, biographers, and critics.

sitz bath (zits) 1 A small bathtub in which one bathes in a sitting posture. 2 A bath taken in such a tub. [<G *sitzbad*]

Si·va (sē′və, shē′-) The Hindu god of destruction and reproduction: forming with Brahma and Vishnu the Hindu trinity: also called *Shiva.* [<Hind. *Shiva* <Skt. *śivás* propitious]

Si·va·ism (sē′və·iz′əm, shē′-) *n.* The worship of Siva. **— Si′va·ist** *n.* **— Si′va·is′tic** *adj.*

Si·va·ji (sē·vä′jē), 1627–80, founder of the Mahratta power in India.

Si·van (sē·vän′) A Jewish month. See under CALENDAR (Hebrew). Also **Si·wan′.**

Siv·a·pi·the·cus (siv′ə·pi·thē′kəs) *n. Paleontol.* An extinct ape related to Dryopithecus. [<NL <SIVA + Gk. *pithēkos* ape]

Si·vas (sē·väs′) A city in central Turkey in Asia.

si·ver (sī′vər) *n. Scot.* An open drain; sewer.

Si·wa·lik Range (si·wä′lik) The southernmost range of the Himalayas in south central Asia; highest peak about 5,000 feet.

Si·wash (sī′wosh) *n.* 1 An Indian of the northern Pacific coast. 2 The lingua franca used between the Siwashes and white traders. [< Chinook jargon <F *sauvage* savage]

six (siks) *n.* The cardinal number following five and preceding seven, or any of the symbols (6, vi, VI) used to represent it; also, anything made up of six units or members, as a playing card with six pips. *—adj.* Being one more than five; twice three. [OE] **— six′fold′** *adj. & adv.*

six bits Seventy–five cents.

Six Nations The Iroquois confederation known as the Five Nations, plus the Tuscarora, who joined them in the 18th century. Also **Six Allied Nations.**

six·pence (siks′pəns) *n.* A British coin of the value of six English pennies.

six·pen·ny (siks′pen′ē, -pən·ē) *adj.* 1 Worth, valued at, or sold for sixpence; hence, paltry; trashy. 2 Denoting a size of nails. See -PENNY.

six·score (siks′skôr′, -skōr′) *adj.* One hundred and twenty.

six–shoot·er (siks′sho͞o′tər) *n. Colloq.* A revolver that will fire six shots without reloading. **— six′–shoot′ing** *adj.*

sixte (sikst) *n.* In fencing, a parry in which the hand is opposite the right breast and the foil is carried to the right. [<F <L *sextus* sixth]

six·teen (siks′tēn′) *n.* The cardinal number following fifteen and preceding seventeen, or any of the symbols (16, xvi, XVI) representing it. *—adj.* Being one more than fifteen; four times four. [OE *sixtēne*]

six·teen·mo (siks·tēn′mō) *n. pl.* **·mos** 1 The page size of a book or pamphlet made up of printer's sheets folded 16 leaves to the sheet, the pages being usually 4 1/2 × 6 7/8 inches. 2 A book having pages of this size. Often written *16mo.* Also called *sextodecimo.* *—adj.* Consisting of pages of this size.

six·teenth (siks′tēnth′) *adj.* 1 Sixth in order after the tenth: the ordinal of *sixteen.* 2 Being one of sixteen equal parts. *—n.* 1 One of sixteen equal parts of anything; the quotient of a unit divided by sixteen. 2 *Music* A sixteenth note.

sixteenth note *Music* A note of one sixteenth of the value of a whole note; semiquaver.

sixth (siksth) *adj.* 1 Next in order after the fifth. 2 Being one of six equal parts. *—n.* 1 One of six equal parts. 2 *Music* **a** The interval between any note and the sixth note above or below it on the diatonic scale. **b** A note separated by this interval from any other, considered with reference to that other. **c** The sixth above the keynote. **d** Two notes at this interval written or sounded together, or the resulting consonance. **— chord of the sixth** *Music* A chord consisting of a tone with its minor third and its sixth: also **sixth chord.** *—adv.* In the sixth order, place, or rank: also, in formal discourse, **sixth′ly.** [OE *sixta*; refashioned to conform to *fourth*]

sixth sense Intuitive perception supposedly not employing the five senses.

six·ti·eth (siks′tē·ith) *adj.* 1 Tenth in order after fiftieth: the ordinal of *sixty.* 2 Being one of sixty equal parts. *—n.* One of sixty equal parts of anything; the quotient of a unit divided by sixty.

Six·tine (siks′tēn, -tin) See SISTINE.

Six·tus (siks′təs) Appellation of five popes including:

— Sixtus IV, 1414–84, pope 1471–84, real name Francesco della Rovere; built the Sistine Chapel.

— Sixtus V, 1521–90, pope 1585–90, real name Felice Peretti; built the Lateran Palace.

six·ty (siks′tē) *n. pl.* **·ties** The cardinal number following fifty–nine and preceding sixty–one, or any of the symbols (60, lx, LX) representing it. *—adj.* Being one more than fifty–nine; ten times six. [OE *sixtig*]

siz·a·ble (sī′zə·bəl) *adj.* Of comparatively large or convenient size. Also **size′a·ble.** **— siz′a·ble·ness** *n.* **— siz′a·bly** *adv.*

siz·ar (sī′zər) *n.* At Cambridge University, England, and Trinity College, Dublin, a student allowed free commons, etc.: formerly required to perform menial services. [<SIZE[1] (def. 4)] **— siz′ar·ship** *n.*

size[1] (sīz) *n.* 1 Measurement or extent of a thing as compared with some standard; comparative magnitude or bulk: when unqualified, implying relative largeness. 2 One of a series of graded measures, or the magnitude between two such limits, as of hats, shoes, etc. 3 A standard of measurement; specified quantity. 4 At Cambridge University, an allotted quantity of provisions; ration. 5 Mental caliber; importance; character. 6 *Colloq.* State of affairs; true situation: That's the *size* of it. 7 Measure or amount. See synonyms under MAGNITUDE. *—v.t.* **sized, siz·ing** 1 To estimate the size of. 2 To distribute or classify according to size. 3 To cut or otherwise shape (an article) to the required size. **— to size up** *Colloq.* 1 To form an estimate, judgment, or opinion of. 2 To meet specifications. [<F *assise.* See ASSIZE.]

size[2] (sīz) *n.* 1 A solution of gelatinous material, usually glue, casein, wax, or clay, used to finish fabrics. 2 A gelatinous substance used to glaze paper, or applied to walls before papering, etc. 3 A viscous preparation used as in fixing gilding. Also *sizing.* *—v.t.* **sized, siz·ing** 1 To treat with size or any size-like substance. 2 To make plastic, as clay. [<OItal. *sisa* painter's glue, aphetic var. of *assisa,* orig., pp. of *assidere* make sit down <L *assidere.* See ASSIZE.]

sized (sīzd) *adj.* 1 Having graded dimensions or a definite size: chiefly in composition: large–*sized.* 2 Arranged according to size.

siz·ing (sī′zing) *n.* 1 Size[2], *n.* 2 The process of adding size to a fabric, yarn, etc., to give it additional strength, stiffness, smoothness, weight, etc.

siz·y (sī′zē) *adj.* Glutinous. [<SIZE[2]]

sizz (siz) *v.i.* To make a hissing sound; sizzle. [Imit.]

siz·zle (siz′əl) *v.i.* **·zled, ·zling** To burn or scorch with or as with a hissing sound; emit a hissing sound under the action of heat. *—n.* A hissing sound, as from frying or effervescence. [Freq. of SIZZ]

siz·zler (siz′lər) *n. Colloq.* Anything extremely hot, especially a summer day. [<SIZZLE]

siz·zling (siz′ling) *adj.* 1 Extremely hot. 2 That sizzles: a *sizzling* steak.

Sjael·land (shel′län) The Danish name for ZEELAND.

sjam·bok (sham′bok) *n.* A short, heavy whip of rhinoceros hide. [<Afrikaans <Du. <Malay *chamboq* <Persian *chābuq* whip]

Ska·gen (skä′gən), **Cape** The northernmost point of Jutland, Denmark, at the junction of the Skagerrak and the Kattegat: also *The Skaw.*

Skag·er·rak (skag′ə·rak, *Norw.* skäg′ûr·räk) An arm of the North Sea between Jutland and Norway; 150 miles long, 80 to 90 miles wide.

Skag·way (skag′wā) A city of SE Alaska near Chilkoot Pass: gateway to the Yukon and Klondike gold fields in the 1890's.

skail (skāl) *v.t. Brit. Dial.* **1** To scatter; spill. **2** To separate; disperse, as the members of an assembly. [Cf. ON *skilja* divide, part]

skaith (skāth) *v.t. & n. Scot.* Scathe; damage.

skald (skôld, skäld) See SCALD².

skat (skät) *n.* **1** A three-handed game played with 32 cards. Any of several varieties of the game can be chosen by the highest bidder who, alone, must oppose the other players. **2** In the game of skat, two cards dealt face down and taken into his hand by the successful bidder or otherwise treated according to rule. [<G, orig. *skart* <Ital. *scartare* discard]

skate¹ (skāt) *n.* **1** A keel-shaped metal runner attached to a plate or frame, with suitable clamps or straps for fastening it to the sole of a boot or shoe, enabling the wearer to glide rapidly over ice; also, such a runner affixed to a shoe or boot. **2** A similar contrivance with wheels instead of a runner, for use on a floor or other smooth surface; a roller skate. **3** An ice-boat runner. — *v.i.* **skat·ed, skat·ing** To glide or move over ice or some other smooth surface, on or as on skates. [<earlier *skates* <Du. *schaats* <OF *escache* stilt <Gmc.]

skate² (skāt) *n.* Any of several flat-bodied rays (genus *Raia*) with enlarged pectoral fins, ventral gill slits, and a pointed snout; especially, the **barn-door skate** *(R. laevis)* of eastern North America, or the common European **gray skate** *(R. batis).* [<ON *skata*]

skate³ (skāt) *n. Slang* **1** A miserable, contemptible person. **2** An old, worn-out horse. [Origin uncertain]

skat·er (skā′tər) *n.* **1** One who skates. **2** One of various insects with long legs that run over the surface of the water, as if skating: also called *water strider.*

skat·ole (skat′ōl) *n. Biochem.* A white crystalline compound, C_9H_9N, contained in the feces and urine, and formed in the alimentary canal by the decomposition of proteins. Also **skat′·ol.** [<Gk. *skōr, skatos* dung + -OLE]

Skaw (skô), **The** See SKAGEN, CAPE.

skean (shkēn, skēn) *n.* An early Irish double-edged dagger or short sword. Also **skeen.** [<Irish *sgian* knife]

Skeat (skēt), **Walter William,** 1835–1912, English lexicographer and philologist.

ske·dad·dle (ski·dad′l) *Colloq. v.i.* **·dled, ·dling** To flee in haste; run away; scamper. — *n.* The act of running away; hasty flight. [<dial. E, spill, scatter. Cf. Gk. *skedannynai* scatter.]

skee (skē) See SKI.

Skee·na River (skē′nə) A river in western British Columbia, Canada, flowing 360 miles south and SW to the Pacific.

skeet¹ (skēt) *n.* A variety of trapshooting in which a succession of saucer-shaped targets hurled in such a way as to resemble the flight of quail are fired at from various angles by the shooter. [Origin unknown]

skeet² (skēt) *n.* A long-handled scoop or dipper, used for wetting sails and decks. [Origin unknown]

skeet gun A short-barreled shotgun.

skeg (skeg) *n. Naut.* The after part of a vessel's keel, or a projection on or continuation of it, as for supporting the lower end of the rudder of a screw steamer. [<Du. *schegge,* prob. <Scand. Cf. ON *skegg* beard.]

skeigh (skekh, skēkh) *Scot. adj.* **1** Shy; skittish; mettlesome: said of a horse. **2** Coy; disdainful; proud: said especially of women. — *adv.* Proudly.

skein (skān) *n.* **1** A fixed quantity of yarn, thread, silk, wool, etc., wound to a certain length and then doubled and knotted. **2** A measure of length, 360 feet, or 109.73 meters. [<OF *escaigne,* prob. <Celtic. Cf. Irish *sgainne.*]

skein screw A screw with a broad shallow thread. See illustration under SCREW.

skel·dock (skel′dok) *n. Scot.* Wild mustard *(Brassica kaber).* Also **skel′lock.**

skel·e·tal (skel′ə·təl) *adj.* Of, pertaining to, forming, or like a skeleton.

skel·e·ton (skel′ə·tən) *n.* **1** The framework of an animal body, composed of bone and cartilage. The skeletal structure either surrounds and shields the vital organs, as the *exoskeleton* of a turtle, or is embedded within the body, as the *endoskeleton* of man and the vertebrates. **2** Any open framework constituting the main supporting parts of a structure: the *skeleton* of a house. **3** A mere sketch or outline of anything, especially of some literary production: the *skeleton* of an address. **4** A person or animal very thin by nature or loss of flesh; also, a band or troop whose numbers have been greatly thinned out. See synonyms under SKETCH. — **skeleton in the closet** A secret source of shame or discredit. See FAMILY SKELETON. — *adj.* Consisting merely of a framework or outline; resembling a skeleton in use or appearance; meager; emaciated. [<NL <Gk. *skeleton (sōma)* dried (body), mummy <*skeletos* dried up]

skeleton construction A construction in which the main support is an internal framework of steel, to which the outer walls are affixed, their weight being carried, story by story, by the framework.

skel·e·ton·ize (skel′ə·tən·īz′) *v.t.* **·ized, ·iz·ing** **1** To reduce to a skeleton or framework by removing soft tissues or parts; make a skeleton of. **2** To reduce greatly in size or numbers. **3** To draft in outline.

skeleton key A slender false key designed to avoid the wards of a lock, for use as a master key.

skel·lum (skel′əm) *n. Scot.* A scamp.

skelp¹ (skelp) *Brit. Dial. & Scot. v.t.* **1** To kick severely. **2** To slap with the hand; spank. **3** To cause to move rapidly. — *n.* A glancing blow with the open hand; slap.

skelp² (skelp) *n.* A strip of iron or steel; especially, one from which tubes are made. — *v.t.* To beat out into a skelp, as iron. [Origin unknown]

Skel·ton (skel′tən), **John,** 1460?–1529, English poet, scholar, and clergyman.

skep (skep) *n.* **1** A beehive, especially one made of straw. **2** A receptacle of wickerwork or wood, especially for grain; a basket. [<ON *skeppa* basket]

skep·tic (skep′tik) *n.* **1** One who questions the fundamental doctrines of religion, especially of the Christian religion. **2** One who refuses concurrence in generally accepted conclusions in science, philosophy, etc. **3** An adherent of any philosophical school of skepticism; especially, an adherent of the **Skeptic school** in ancient Greece, of which the Pyrrhonists, with their doctrine of the relativity of knowledge, were the first systematic exponents. **4** One who doubts any particular statement. — *adj.* Skeptical. Also, *Brit.,* *sceptic.* [<F *sceptique* <L *scepticus* <Gk. *skeptikos* reflective <*skeptesthai* consider]

Synonyms (noun): agnostic, atheist, deist, disbeliever, freethinker, infidel, unbeliever. The *skeptic* doubts divine revelation; the *disbeliever* and the *unbeliever* reject it, the *disbeliever* with more of intellectual dissent, the *unbeliever* (in the common acceptation) with indifference or with opposition of heart as well as of intellect. *Infidel* is an opprobrious term that is commonly applied to any decided opponent of an accepted religion. The *atheist* denies that there is a God; the *deist* admits the existence of God, but denies that the Christian Scriptures are a revelation from him; the *agnostic* denies either that we do know or that we can know whether there is a God. *Antonyms:* believer, Christian.

skep·ti·cal (skep′ti·kəl) *adj.* Doubting; questioning; of or pertaining to a skeptic or skepticism. Also, *Brit.,* *sceptical.* — **skep′ti·cal·ly** *adv.* — **skep′ti·cal·ness** *n.*

skep·ti·cism (skep′tə·siz′əm) *n.* **1** A doubting or incredulous state of mind. **2** *Philos.* The doctrine that absolute knowledge is unattainable and that judgments must be continually questioned and doubted in order to attain approximate or relative certainty: opposed to *dogmatism.* Also, *Brit.,* *scepticism.*

sker·ry (sker′ē) *n. pl.* **·ries** *Scot.* An insulated rock or reef.

sketch (skech) *n.* **1** An incomplete but suggestive delineation or presentation of anything, whether graphic or literary; an outline. **2** An artist's preliminary study, graphic or plastic, of a work of art intended for elaboration. **3** A literary or dramatic composition, short, discursive, and of slight construction. **4** A short scene, play, or musical act, especially in vaudeville. — *v.t.* To make a sketch or sketches of; outline. — *v.i.* To make a sketch or sketches. [<Du. *schets* <Ital. *schizzo* <L *schedium* improvisation <Gk. *schedios*] — **sketch′a·ble** *adj.* — **sketch′er** *n.*

Synonyms (noun): brief, delineation, draft, drawing, outline, picture, plan, skeleton. An *outline* gives only the bounding or determining lines of a figure or a scene; a *sketch* may give lines, shading and color, but is hasty and incomplete. The lines of a *sketch* are seldom so full and continuous as those of an *outline. Draft* and *plan* apply especially to mechanical drawing, of which *outline, sketch,* and *drawing* are also used; a *plan* is strictly a view from above, as of a building or machine, giving the lines of a horizontal section, originally at the level of the ground, now in a wider sense at any height; as, a *plan* of the cellar; a *plan* of the attic. A *design* is such a preliminary *sketch* as indicates the object to be accomplished or the result to be attained, and is understood to be original. One may make a *drawing* of any well-known mechanism, or a *drawing* from another man's *design;* but if he says "The *design* is mine," he claims it as his own invention or composition. In written composition an *outline* gives simply the main divisions, and is often called a *skeleton;* a somewhat fuller suggestion of illustration, treatment, and style is given in a *sketch.* A lawyer's *brief* is a succinct statement of the main facts in a case, and of the main heads of his argument on points of law, with reference to authorities. See PICTURE.

sketch·book (skech′bo͝ok′) *n.* **1** A blank book used for sketching. **2** A printed volume of literary sketches. Also **sketch book.**

sketch·y (skech′ē) *adj.* **sketch·i·er, sketch·i·est** Like or in the form of a sketch; roughly suggested without detail; hence, incomplete; superficial; slight. — **sketch′i·ly** *adv.* — **sketch′·i·ness** *n.*

skew (skyo͞o) *v.i.* **1** To take an oblique direction; move or turn aside; swerve. **2** To look obliquely or askance; squint. — *v.t.* **3** To put askew; give an oblique position or direction to. **4** To shape or form in an oblique manner; distort. — *adj.* **1** Placed or turned obliquely; twisted to one side; askew; hence, perverted in use or meaning. **2** *Stat.* Having some elements on opposite sides of a median line reversed or unbalanced; distorted: a *skew* curve. — *n.* **1** A deviation from symmetry or straightness; distortion. **2** A sidelong glance; squint. **3** A slanting coping, as at the corner of a gable. [<AF *eskiuer,* OF *eschiuver* shun <Gmc. Related to ESCHEW.] — **skew′ly** *adv.*

skew arch *Archit.* An arch whose axis is in a vertical plane making other than right angles with its abutments.

skew·back (skyo͞o′·bak′) *n. Archit.* **1** An abutment with inclined face receiving the thrust of a segmented arch. See also illustration under ARCH. **2** A cap or other casting, on the end of a truss, to receive the pull of a tie rod.

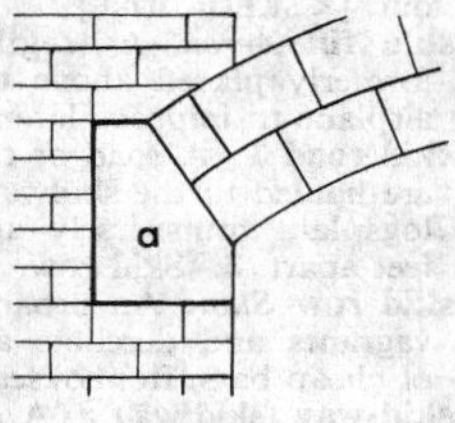

SKEWBACK
a. Skewback *(def. 1).*

skew·bald (skyo͞o′·bôld′) *adj.* Piebald, especially when the spots are white and some other color than black. [ME *skewed* piebald]

skew·er (skyo͞o′ər) *n.* **1** A long pin of wood or metal, used chiefly for fastening meat to keep it in shape while roasting. **2** Any of various articles of similar shape or use. — *v.t.* To run through or fasten with or as with a skewer. [Var. of SKIVER]

skew–gee (skyo͞o′jē) *adj. U.S. Colloq.* Crooked; off center; hence, mentally confused; uncertain.

skew·ness (skyo͞o′nis) *n.* **1** The state of being unsymmetrical or distorted. **2** *Stat.* The deviation of a frequency distribution curve from a symmetrical form.

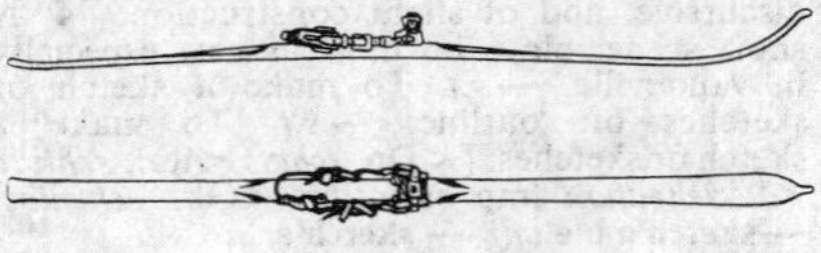

SKI
Side and top view.

ski (skē, *Norw.* shē) *n. pl.* **skis** or **ski** One of a pair of wooden runners, about 7 feet long and 3½ inches wide, attached to the feet and used in gliding over snow or ice. —*v.i.* **skied, ski·ing 1** To glide or travel on skis. **2** To engage in the sport of gliding over snow–covered inclines on skis. Also spelled *skee.* [<Norw. <ON *skidh* snowshoe] —**ski′er** *n.*

ski·a·graph (skī′ə·graf, -gräf) *n.* Roentgenogram. [<Gk. *skia* shadow + -GRAPH]

Ski·ap·o·des (skī·ap′ə·dēz) *n. pl.* In Greek mythology, an ancient people of Libya who had feet so enormous that they used them for sunshades. [<Gk. *skia* shadow + *podes,* pl. of *pous* foot]

ski·a·scope (skī′ə·skōp) *n.* An instrument for examining the refractive power of the eye by the response of the retina to lights and shadows. [<Gk. *skia* shadow + -SCOPE]

ski·as·co·py (skī·as′kə·pē) *n.* Examination of the eye by the skiascope: also called *retinoscopy, shadow test.*

skid (skid) *n.* **1** One of a pair of timbers used to support a heavy tilting or rolling object, as a cask, boat, or cannon; also, a log used as a track in sliding heavy articles about, or forming an inclined plane to ease their descent. **2** In lumbering, one of several logs used to make a track on which other logs are slid or piled; also, one of the cross–logs of a skid road. **3** A shoe or drag on a wagon wheel. **4** *Naut.* A fender hung over a vessel's side to protect it from rubbing and scraping: usually in the plural. **5** *Aeron.* A runner in an airplane's landing gear. **6** The act of skidding; a side–slip. **7** A small frame or platform upon which merchandise is stacked to be moved about or temporarily stored. —**on the skids** *Slang* Rapidly declining in prestige or power. —*v.* **skid·ded, skid·ding** *v.i.* **1** To slide instead of revolving, as a wheel which does not rotate though the vehicle is in motion. **2** To slip sideways through inability to grip the road: said of wheels, and, by extension, of vehicles. **3** *Aeron.* To slide sideways away from the center of curvature when turning, by reason of insufficient banking. —*v.t.* **4** To furnish with skids; put, drag, or haul on skids. **5** To brake or hold back with a skid. [? <ON *skidh* piece of wood]

Skid·daw (skid′ô, skid·dô′) A mountain in central Cumberland, England; 3,054 feet.

skid·doo (ski·do͞o′) *interj. Slang* Go away; get out. [<SKEDADDLE]

skid fin *Aeron.* A lengthwise vertical surface formerly placed above the upper wing of an airplane to improve lateral stability.

skid road 1 A road or track along which logs are hauled to the skidway. **2** A road made of logs laid transversely and spaced about five feet apart. **3** Skid row.

skid row *Slang* An urban section inhabited by vagrants and derelicts and consisting mainly of cheap bars, flophouses, etc.

skid·way (skid′wā′) *n.* A structure made of two logs or skids, about 10 feet apart and laid alongside a log road, on which logs are piled before loading.

skied[1] (skīd) Past tense and past participle of SKY.

skied[2] (skēd) Past tense and past participle of SKI.

skiff (skif) *n.* A light rowboat; formerly, a small sailing vessel. —**St. Lawrence skiff** A small boat, carrying centerboard and spritsail, light enough to be rowed with ease. [<F *esquif* <Ital. *schifo* <OHG *scif* ship, boat]

ski·ing (skē′ing) *n.* The act or sport of gliding on skis.

ski·jor·ing (skē·jôr′ing, -jō′ring) *n.* The sport of traveling over ice or snow on skis, towed by a horse or motor vehicle. [<Norw. *skikjöring* <*ski* ski + *kjöring* driving]

ski jump 1 A jump or leap made by a person wearing skis. **2** A course prepared for making such jumps.

skil·ful (skil′fəl) *adj.* **1** Having skill; clever; dexterous; able. **2** Showing or requiring skill. Also **skill′ful.** —**skil′ful·ly** *adv.* —**skil′ful·ness** *n.*

Synonyms: adept, adroit, apt, deft, dexterous, expert, handy, happy, proficient, skilled, trained. One is *adept* in that for which he has a natural gift, improved by practice; he is *expert* in that of which training, experience, and study have given him a thorough mastery; he is *dexterous* in that which he can do effectively with or without training, especially in work of the hand or bodily activities. A *skilled* workman is one who has thoroughly learned his trade, but he may be naturally quite dull: a *skilful* workman has some natural brightness, ability, and power of adaptation, in addition to his acquired knowledge and dexterity. See CLEVER, GOOD. *Antonyms*: awkward, bulky, clumsy, helpless, inexpert, maladroit, unskilled, untaught, untrained.

ski lift An arrangement of seats usually attached to an overhead rope or cable for carrying skiers to the top of a slope.

skill[1] (skil) *n.* **1** The familiar knowledge of any science, art, or handicraft, as shown by dexterity in execution or performance, or in its application to practical purposes; technical ability. **2** A specific art or trade; also, a gift; accomplishment. **3** *Obs.* Intellect; understanding. See synonyms under ABILITY, DEXTERITY, INGENUITY, WISDOM. [<ON *skil* knowledge] —**skill′–less** *adj.*

skill[2] (skil) *v.i. Obs.* To matter; make a difference: usually used impersonally and with a negative: It *skills* not what I do. [<ON *skilja* separate]

skilled (skild) *adj.* Possessing or requiring skill; expert; proficient. See synonyms under SKILFUL.

skil·let (skil′it) *n.* **1** A frying pan. **2** A small kettle or stew pan, often with a bail and short legs. [? <OF *escuellete,* dim. of *escuelle* porringer <L *scutella,* dim. of *scutra* dish]

skill·y (skil′ē) *adj. Scot. & Brit. Dial.* Skilful.

skim (skim) *v.* **skimmed, skim·ming** *v.t.* **1** To remove floating matter from the surface of, as with a ladle: to *skim* milk. **2** To remove thus: to *skim* cream. **3** To cover with a thin film, as of ice. **4** To move lightly and quickly across or over. **5** To cause to pass swiftly and lightly, as a coin across a pond. **6** To read or glance over hastily or superficially. —*v.i.* **7** To move quickly and lightly across or near a surface; glide. **8** To make a hasty and superficial perusal; glance: with *over* or *through.* **9** To become covered with a thin film. —*n.* **1** The act of skimming. **2** That which is skimmed off; scum. **3** Something from which floating matter has been removed, as skim milk. **4** A thin scum of ice. —*adj.* Skimmed: *skim* milk. [Var. of SCUM]

skim·ble–scam·ble (skim′bəl·skam′bəl) *adj.* Incoherent; rambling. —*n.* Meaningless talk; nonsense. Also **skim′ble–skam′ble.** [Prob. reduplication of dial. *scamble* ramble, struggle on the ground (said of horses)]

skim·mer (skim′ər) *n.* **1** A flat ladle or other utensil for skimming. **2** One who or that which skims. **3** A ternlike bird (genus *Rhynchops*) having the lower mandible compressed, that skims up the small fishes from near the surface of the water. *R. nigra* is the **black skimmer.**

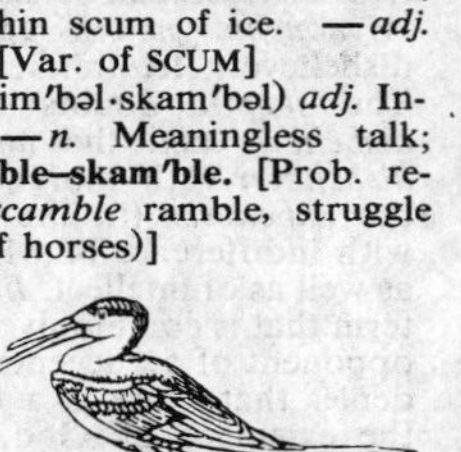

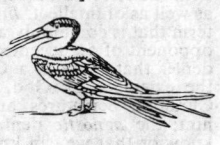

SKIMMER
(Length 16 to 20 inches; wingspread 42 to 50 inches)

skim–milk (skim′milk′) *adj.* Weak; inferior.

skim milk Milk from which the cream has been removed: often used to designate a type of inferiority.

skim·ming (skim′ing) *n.* **1** The act of one who or that which skims. **2** That which is skimmed off: usually in the plural.

skimp (skimp) *v.t. & v.i.* To scrimp or scamp. —*adj.* Scant; meager. [Prob. <ON *skemma* shorten; infl. in meaning by SCRIMP]

skimp·y (skim′pē) *adj.* **skimp·i·er, skimp·i·est 1** Carelessly done. **2** Scanty. **3** Niggardly. —**skimp′i·ly** *adv.* —**skimp′i·ness** *n.*

skin (skin) *n.* **1** The membranous external investment of an animal; the integument. ◆ Collateral adjective: *dermal.* **2** The pelt of a small animal, removed from its body, whether raw or dressed, as distinguished from the *hide* of a large animal. **3** A vessel for holding liquids, made of the skin of an animal: a wine–*skin.* **4** An outside layer, coat, or covering resembling skin, as the epidermis of a plant, fruit, etc.; rind; of pearls, the outermost layer of nacreous matter. **5** Planking or plating of a vessel. **6** A membrane resembling the integument. **7** *Slang* A mean person; skinflint; also, a sharper; blackleg. **8** One's life or physical existence: to save one's *skin.* —**by the skin of one's teeth** Very closely or narrowly; barely. —**under one's skin** Provoking; beneath the surface of control (of irritation, excitation, emotion, etc.). —*v.* **skinned, skin·ning** *v.t.* **1** To remove the skin of; flay; peel. **2** To cover with or as with skin. **3** To remove as if taking off skin: to *skin* a dollar from a roll of bills. **4** *Slang* To cheat or swindle. —*v.i.* **5** To become covered with skin; cicatrize. **6** *Slang* To make off hastily; run away: usually with *off.* [<ON *skinn*]

skin–bound (skin′bound′) *adj.* Affected with a rigid contraction of the skin and hardening of the connective tissue.

skin–deep (skin′dēp′) *adj.* Superficial. —*adv.* Superficially.

skin diving Underwater exploration in which the swimmer is equipped with a self–contained breathing apparatus, goggles, foot fins, rubber garments, etc. —**skin diver**

skin effect *Electr.* An increase of current density on the surface of an alternating–conductor, giving an increase in resistance: especially marked at high frequencies, as in radio.

skin·flint (skin′flint) *n.* A miser; one who drives a hard bargain.

skin friction 1 *Physics* The component of a fluid force tangential to a given point on a surface. **2** *Aeron.* Resistance of air particles due to friction while in contact with the moving surfaces of an airplane: also **skin drag.**

skin–game (skin′gām′) *n.* **1** A gambling game at cards in which the players have no chance of winning against the house or the bank. **2** Any swindle.

skink[1] (skingk) *n.* One of a group of lizards (family *Scincidae*) with short limbs and a conical tail; especially, the **blue–tailed skink** *(Eumeces skiltonianus)* of the United States. [<L *scincos* <Gk. *skinkos,* kind of lizard]

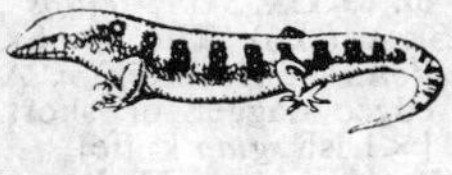

SKINK
(Up to 8 inches long)

skink[2] (skingk) *v.t. Brit. Dial.* **1** To draw or pour out. **2** To fill with liquor. [<MDu. *schenken*]

skink·er (skingk′ər) *n. Brit. Dial.* A bartender; also, an inn keeper. [<SKINK[2]]

skink·ing (skingk′ing) *adj. Scot.* Thin; sloppy.

skin·less (skin′lis) *adj.* Without skin.

skin·ner (skin′ər) *n.* **1** One who skins; a flayer of animals. **2** *U.S. Slang* A cheat; swindler. **3** A dealer in skins. **4** *U.S. Slang* A mule driver.

Skin·ner (skin′ər), **Cornelia Otis,** 1901–1979, U.S. actress and author; daughter of the following. —**Otis,** 1858–1942, U.S. actor.

skin·ny (skin′ē) *adj.* **·ni·er, ·ni·est 1** Wanting flesh; lean. **2** Consisting of or like skin. See synonyms under MEAGER. —**skin′ni·ly** *adv.* —**skin′ni·ness** *n.*

skin–tight (skin′tīt′) *adj.* Fitting closely to the skin, as a garment.

skip (skip) *v.* **skipped, skip·ping** *v.i.* **1** To move with light springing steps; caper; leap lightly. **2** To be deflected from a surface; ricochet; skim. **3** To pass from one point to another without noticing what lies between. **4** *Colloq.* To leave or depart hurriedly; flee. **5** To be advanced in school beyond the next grade in order —*v.t.* **6** To leap lightly over. **7** To cause to ricochet. **8** To pass over or by without notice. **9** *Colloq.* To leave (a place) hurriedly. —*n.* **1** A light bound or spring; especially, a hop alternating between steps in walking. **2** A passing over without notice;

omission. [Prob. <Scand. Cf. Sw. *skuppa* skip.]

skip distance That area within which signals from a radio transmitter are not received: it is between the farthest point reached by the ground wave and the nearest point at which the reflected sky wave strikes the earth.

skip·jack (skip'jak) *n.* **1** Any of various fishes that skip along the surface of the water, as the bonito. **2** Any snapping or click beetle (family *Elateridae*). **3** A Chesapeake Bay sailing vessel with a centerboard and one mast: used in dredging oysters.

skip·per[1] (skip'ər) *n.* **1** One who or that which skips. **2** The saury. **3** A butterfly of the family *Hesperiidae*: so named from its flight. **4** A cheese maggot.

skip·per[2] (skip'ər) *n.* The master or captain of a small vessel; hence, one in charge of any craft. [<Du. *schipper* < *schip* ship]

skip·pet (skip'it) *n.* A round flat box for containing and protecting the large heavy seal formerly tied to a document. [Dim. of SKEP]

skirl (skûrl, skirl) *Scot. v.i.* To shriek shrilly, as a bagpipe. — *v.t.* To play the bagpipe. — *adj.* Shrill. — *n.* A shrill cry; a squall of wind with rain or snow. [Metathetic var. of ME *scrille* <Scand. Cf. Norw. *skrylla.*]

skir·mish (skûr'mish) *v.i.* To fight in a preliminary or desultory way. — *n.* **1** A light engagement, as between small parties; desultory fighting between two armies on a skirmish line. **2** Figuratively, any light movement or operation evasive of the main contention or business. See synonyms under BATTLE. [<OF *eskermiss-*, stem of *eskermir* fence, fight <Gmc. Cf. OHG *skirman* defend < *skirm* shield. Related to SCRIMMAGE.] — **skir'mish·er** *n.*

skirmish line A line of infantry spread out in extended order for attack.

skirr (skûr) *v.t.* **1** To scour. **2** To skim over. — *v.i.* **3** To move rapidly. — *n.* A whirring sound. [Imit.]

skir·ret (skir'it) *n.* An Old World herb (*Sium sisarum*) formerly much cultivated in Europe for its white tubers, which are cooked and served like salsify. [ME *skirwhit*, prob. OF *eschervis* <Arabic *karawya.* Cf. CARAWAY.]

skirt (skûrt) *n.* **1** That part of a dress, gown, or robe that hangs from the waist downward. **2** A separate garment hanging from the waist and covering the lower portion of the body. **3** A cloth or other material that hangs or covers like a skirt: the *skirt* of a dressing table. **4** *Slang* A girl; woman. **5** The margin, border, or outer edge of anything. **6** *pl.* The border, fringe, or edge of a particular area, path, geographical feature, etc.: on the *skirts* of the town, forest, highway, etc. **7** One of the flaps or loose, hanging parts of a saddle: also **saddle skirt**. **8** *Naut.* The leech of a sail. **9** The diaphragm or midriff of a butchered animal. See synonyms under MARGIN. — *v.t.* **1** To lie along or form the edge of; to border. **2** To surround or border: with *with*. **3** To pass around or about, usually to avoid crossing: to *skirt* the town. — *v.i.* **4** To be or pass along the edge or border: to *skirt* along the coast. [ON *skyrt* shirt. Akin to SHIRT.]

ski·run·ner (skē'run'ər) *n.* One who travels on skis.

skit (skit) *n.* **1** A short literary article, theatrical sketch, etc., usually humorous or satirical. **2** A bantering jest. [<Scand.; cf. ON *skjota* shoot. Prob. akin to SHOOT.]

skite (skīt) *Scot. n.* **1** A quick, sharp slap. **2** A quick, heavy, splashing shower; dash, as of rain. **3** A trick. **4** A squire. — *v.i.* **1** To squirt. **2** To glide away quickly; scoot.

ski troops Soldiers equipped and trained for action on skis.

skit·ter (skit'ər) *v.i.* **1** To glide or skim along, touching ground or water at intervals. **2** To fish by the method known as skittering. [Freq. of SKIT]

skit·ter·ing (skit'ər·ing) *n.* A style of fishing with a hook twitched along the water.

skit·tish (skit'ish) *adj.* **1** Easily frightened, as a horse; hence, shy; timid. **2** Capricious; uncertain; unreliable. **3** Tricky; deceitful. See synonyms under RESTIVE. [<dial. E *skit* caper (said of horses)] — **skit'tish·ly** *adv.* — **skit'tish·ness** *n.*

skit·tle (skit'l) *n.* **1** *pl.* A game of ninepins, in which a flattened ball or thick rounded disk is thrown to knock down the pins. **2** One of the pins used in this game: also **skittle–pin.** — **beer and skittles** Carefree existence, consisting of drink and play; unruffled enjoyment: usually with a negative: Life is not all *beer and skittles.* [Prob. <Dan. *skyttel* a child's earthen ball]

skive[1] (skīv) *v.t.* **skived, skiv·ing** To shave or pare the surface of, as leather. [<ON *skifa* slice]

skive[2] (skīv) *n.* A gem–cutter's diamond wheel. — *v.t.* **skived, skiv·ing** To grind off, as the surface of a gem. [<Du. *schijf*]

skiv·er (skī'vər) *n.* **1** Leather split with a knife: used for bookbinding. **2** One who skives. **3** A knife or machine used in skiving.

skiv·vies (skiv'ēz) *n. pl. Slang* Men's underwear. [Origin uncertain]

sklent (sklent) *Scot. v.i.* **1** To move in a slanting manner. **2** To glance hostilely; squint. **3** To tell a lie. — *n.* **1** A slant. **2** A lie. — *adj.* Slanting.

skoal (skōl) *interj.* Hail: a toast or salutation in Scandinavian use. — *n.* The act of saluting or toasting with the word "skoal!" [<Scand. Cf. Dan. *skaal* bowl, toast, ON *skál* bowl.]

Ško·da (shkō'dä), **Emil von,** 1839–1900, Czech engineer and industrialist.

skook·um (skook'əm) *adj. U.S. Slang* Strong; powerful. [<N. Am. Ind. *skukum* powerful, evil spirit]

Skop·lje (skôp'lye) A city in SE Yugoslavia: the economic, cultural, and Islamic religious center of modern Macedonia: Turkish *Usküb.*

skreigh (skrēkh, skräkh) *v. & n. Scot.* Shriek; screech. Also **skreegh.**

Skry·mer (skrī'mər) See UTGARD–LOKI.

sku·a (skyōō'ə) *n.* A gull–like bird; a jaeger. Also **skua gull.** [<Faroese *skügver* <ON *skúfr*]

Skuld (skōōld) In Norse mythology, one of the Norns.

skul·dug·ger·y (skul·dug'ər·ē) *n. U.S.* Trickery; underhandedness. [Var. of dial. *sculduddery*; origin uncertain]

skulk (skulk) *v.i.* **1** To move about furtively or slily; lie close or keep hidden; lurk. **2** To shirk; evade work or responsibility. — *n.* **1** One who skulks. **2** A troop of foxes. [<Scand. Cf. Dan. *skulke.*] — **skulk'er** *n.*

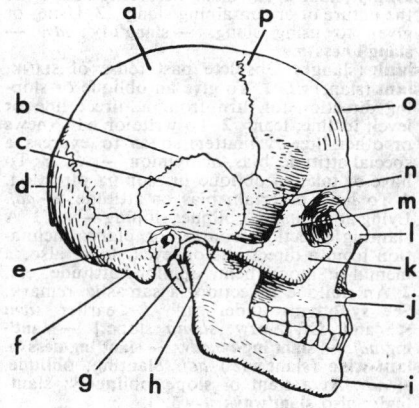

HUMAN SKULL

a.	Parietal bone.	*i.*	Inferior maxillary.
b.	Squamosal suture.	*j.*	Superior maxillary.
c.	Temporal bone.	*k.*	Malar bone.
d.	Occipital bone.	*l.*	Nasal bone.
e.	Opening of ear.	*m.*	Zygomatic bone.
f.	Mastoid process.	*n.*	Sphenoid bone.
g.	Styloid process.	*o.*	Frontal bone.
h.	Zygomatic arch.	*p.*	Coronal suture.

skull (skul) *n.* **1** The bony framework of the head of a vertebrate animal; the cranium. **2** The head considered as the seat of brain; the mind. ◆ Homophone: *scull.* [<Scand. Cf. dial. Norw. *skul* shell.]

skull and crossbones A representation of the human skull over two crossed thigh bones: used as a symbol of death, as a warning label

on poisons, etc., and as an emblem of piracy.

skull·cap (skul'kap') *n.* **1** The sinciput. **2** Any plant of the genus *Scutellaria*, especially *S. galericulata*, of wet shady places, with large blue flowers.

skull cap **1** A cap closely fitting the skull. **2** A light cap without brim or peak.

skunk (skungk) *n.* **1** A nocturnal, burrowing carnivore of North America (family *Mustelidae*), usually black with a white stripe running from the nape of the neck to a large, bushy tail: under the tail are perineal glands that secrete a liquid of very offensive odor ejected at will. The common striped skunk (*Mephitis mephitis*) of the United States is about the size of a cat, and there are spotted varieties (genus *Spilogale*). **2** *Colloq.* A low, contemptible person. — *v.t. Slang* To defeat, as in a contest, so thoroughly as to keep from scoring. [<Algonquian *seganku*]

SKUNK
(Up to 16 inches in length; tail: 7 inches)

skunk cabbage **1** A stemless perennial herb (*Symplocarpus foetidus*) of the United States, producing in the early spring a horn-shaped, brownish–purple spathe which encloses the oval spadix and emits a strong odor, especially when crushed or bruised: also called *swamp cabbage.* **2** A somewhat similar plant (*Lysichitum americanum*) of western North America. — Also **skunk'weed'** (-wēd').

sky (skī) *n. pl.* **skies** **1** The blue vault, or a part of it, that seems to bend over the earth; the firmament. **2** The upper atmosphere; especially, the region of the clouds. **3** The celestial regions or powers; heaven. **4** Climate; weather. **5** *Obs.* A cloud. — *v.t.* **skied, sky·ing** *Colloq.* In games, to bat or throw (a ball) high into the air. [<ON *sky* cloud]

sky–blue (skī'blōō') *adj.* Of the color of the sky; azure.

sky blue A blue like the color of the sky.

sky–cap (skī'kap') *n.* A porter employed at an airport.

sky·dive (skī'dīv') *v.i.* **·dived, ·div·ing** To engage in skydiving. — **sky'div'er** *n.*

sky·div·ing (skī'dī'ving) *n.* The sport of jumping from an airplane and performing various maneuvers and assuming various positions before opening the parachute.

Skye (skī), **Isle of** Largest of the Inner Hebrides Islands; 670 square miles.

Skye terrier See under TERRIER.

sky·ey (skī'ē) *adj.* Pertaining to or resembling the sky; heavenly.

sky–high (skī'hī') *adj. & adv.* Extremely high.

sky·jack (skī'jak') *v.t. Colloq.* To hijack (def. 3). [<SKY + (HI)JACK] — **sky'jack'er** *n.* — **sky'jack'ing** *n.*

sky·lark (skī'lärk') *n.* A lark (*Alauda arvensis*) that utters a sweet song as it flies. — *v.i.* To indulge in hilarious or boisterous frolic. — **sky'lark'er** *n.* — **sky'lark'ing** *n.*

sky·light (skī'līt') *n.* A window facing skyward.

sky line **1** The line where earth and sky appear to meet; horizon. **2** The outline of buildings, trees, etc., against the sky.

sky pilot *Slang* A clergyman; also, a chaplain.

sky·rock·et (skī'rok'it) *n.* A rocket that is shot high into the air, where it explodes, often with brilliant pyrotechnic effect. — *v.i.* To rise or cause to rise or ascend steeply, like a sky-rocket: used figuratively of wages, prices, etc.

Sky·ros (skē'ros) The largest island of the Northern Sporades group, in the Aegean east of Euboea; 80 square miles: Latin *Scyros.*

sky·sail (skī'səl, -sāl') *n. Naut.* A light sail above the royal in a square-rigged vessel.

sky·scrap·er (skī'skrā'pər) *n.* A very high building.

sky·ward (skī'wərd) *adv.* Toward the sky: also **sky'wards.** — *adj.* Moving or directed toward the sky.

sky wave A radio wave projected into the upper atmosphere by a transmitter and reflected back to earth from the Kennelly–Heaviside layer.

sky·writ·ing (skī'rī'ting) *n.* The forming of

words in the air by an aviator, by releasing a jet of vapor from the tail of an airplane. — **sky'writ'er** *n.*

slab[1] (slab) *n.* 1 The outside cut made from a log in sawing it into boards, planks, etc., often bearing the bark on one side. 2 A flat plate, piece, mass, or slice, as of metal, stone, chocolate, or the like. 3 *U.S. Slang* In baseball, the pitcher's plate. — *v.t.* **slabbed, slab·bing** 1 To saw slabs from, as a log; to square by removing the slabs. 2 To cover with, or form of or into slabs. [ME; origin uncertain]

slab[2] (slab) *n.* Slime; viscous mud; mire. — *adj. Archaic* Slimy; viscous. [<ON *slabb* mud]

slab·ber (slab'ər) *v.* & *n.* Slobber. [Prob. <LG. Cf. Du. *slabberen.*]

slab·by (slab'ē) *adj.* **·bi·er, ·bi·est** *Archaic* 1 Thick; viscous. 2 Sloppy; wet. [<SLAB[2]]

slab·sid·ed (slab'sī'did) *adj. U.S. Colloq.* 1 Having flat sides. 2 Lanky; gawky; ungainly.

slack[1] (slak) *adj.* 1 Hanging or extended loosely. 2 Loose or careless in performance; remiss; tardy; slovenly; slow; also, weak; loose: a *slack* mouth. 3 Lacking activity; not brisk or pressing: a *slack* season. 4 Listless; limp: a *slack* grip. 5 Flowing sluggishly, as water between the ebb and flow of the tide; also, blowing slowly, as a wind. 6 Incomplete; underdone; unfinished. See synonyms under SLOW. — *v.t.* 1 To slacken. 2 To slake, as lime. — *v.i.* 3 To be or become slack. — *n.* 1 The part of anything, as a rope, that is slack or loose; also, a slack condition; looseness. 2 A period of inactivity; a slack season. 3 An extent of water where there is no current. 4 *pl.* Loose-fitting trousers worn by both men and women as part of a casual sports costume; also, cotton or wool trousers in a military uniform. — *adv.* In a slack manner; slackly. [OE *slæc*] — **slack'ly** *adv.* — **slack'·ness** *n.*

slack[2] (slak) *n.* Small coal; screenings. [Cf. LG *slacke*]

slack[3] (slak) *n. Scot. & Brit. Dial.* 1 A dry hollow or gully. 2 A bog. 3 A common. 4 A natural slope of ground. [<ON *slakki* dip, depression]

slack-baked (slak'bākt') *adj.* Not thoroughly cooked; underdone.

slack·en (slak'ən) *v.i.* 1 To become slack, as business; diminish; retard. 2 To become less tense or tight; loosen. 3 To become slow or less intense. — *v.t.* 4 To be or become negligent of or remiss in; to avoid, as duty, especially a military duty; shirk. 5 To make slack.

slack·er (slak'ər) *n.* One who shirks his duties or avoids military service in wartime; shirker.

slae (slē) *n. Scot.* The sloe or blackthorn.

slag (slag) *n.* 1 *Metall.* **a** The fused residue separated in the reduction of ores; metallic dross. **b** A basic iron silicate that floats on the surface of molten iron. 2 Volcanic scoria. — *v.t.* & *v.i.* **slagged, slag·ging** To form into slag. [<MLG *slagge*] — **slag'gy** *adj.*

slag wool Mineral wool.

slain (slān) Past participle of SLAY.

slake (slāk) *v.* **slaked, slak·ing** *v.t.* 1 To render inoperative or harmless, especially by satisfying, as an appetite. 2 To lessen the force of in any way; quench; appease; assuage: to *slake* thirst or flames. 3 To mix with water or moist air, so that a chemical combination shall ensue. 4 To disintegrate and hydrate, as lime. 5 To make loose, slow, or less tense. — *v.i.* 6 To become disintegrated and hydrated: said of lime. 7 To slacken; become loose, slow, or less tense. 8 To ease up on one's efforts; slow down. — *n.* The act or period of slackening; an abatement. [OE *slacian* retard < *slæc* SLACK[1]]

sla·lom (slä'ləm, slā'-) *n.* In skiing, a race over a downhill, serpentine course laid out between posts and marked with flags, victory going to the skier who makes the best speed with the best grace and form. — *v.i.* To ski in or as in a slalom. [<Norw.]

slam (slam) *v.* **slammed, slam·ming** *v.t.* 1 To shut with violence and a loud noise; pull or push to loudly: to *slam* a door. 2 To put, dash, throw, or bring with violence and a loud noise; bang: to *slam* a book down. 3 *Slang* To strike with the fist. 4 *Colloq.* To take to task; criticize severely. — *v.i.* 5 To be shut, enter a place, etc., with force and noise. — *n.* 1 A closing or striking with a bang; the act or noise of slamming. 2 *Colloq.* Severe criticism. 3 A card game of the 16th century, resembling ruff. 4 In bridge, the winning of more than eleven tricks: **grand slam** is the winning of all 13 tricks; **little slam** is the winning of 12 tricks. [<Scand. Cf. dial. Norw. *slamra* slam.]

slam-bang (slam'bang') *adv.* Violently; noisily; also, recklessly. — *v.i.* To move with noise and violence.

slan·der (slan'dər) *n.* A false tale or report, or such tales or reports collectively, uttered with malice and designed or tending to injure the reputation of another; calumny; also, the utterance of such tales or reports; defamation. See synonyms under SCANDAL. — *v.t.* To injure by maliciously uttering a false report; defame; calumniate. — *v.i.* To utter slander. See synonyms under ABUSE, ASPERSE, REVILE. [<AF *esclaundre,* OF *esclandre,* ult. <L *scandalum.* Doublet of SCANDAL.] — **slan'der·er** *n.*

slan·der·ous (slan'dər·əs) *adj.* 1 Uttering slander; guilty of slander. 2 Containing slander; calumnious. — **slan'der·ous·ly** *adv.* — **slan'der·ous·ness** *n.*

slang (slang) *n.* 1 A type of popular language comprised of words and phrases of a vigorous, colorful, or facetious nature, which are invented as needed or derive from the unconventional use of the standard vocabulary. The vocabulary of slang, although usually ephemeral, may achieve wide colloquial currency, and, in the evolution of language, many words originally slang have been adopted by good writers and speakers, and ultimately taken their place as accepted English. 2 The special vocabulary of a certain class, group, or profession: college *slang.* 3 Originally, the argot or jargon of thieves and vagrants. — *v.t.* To abuse or address with slang; also, to scold. — *v.i.* To use slang. [Origin uncertain]

Synonyms: argot, cant, jargon, lingo. The language of the underworld is *argot,* stressing its secrecy; *cant* often signifies the vocabulary of a special occupational group; *jargon* emphasizes unintelligibility and cacophonous sound. *Cant,* originally the beggar's whine, then the preacher's drone, acquired, in later usage, the more common meaning of sanctimonious moralizing. *Jargon* has as its commonest sense barbarous-sounding gabble. *Lingo* commonly designates foreign-sounding speech, or a language with which we are unfamiliar.

slang·y (slang'ē) *adj.* **slang·i·er, slang·i·est** 1 Of the nature of or containing slang. 2 Using or given to using slang. — **slang'i·ly** *adv.* — **slang'i·ness** *n.*

slank (slangk) Obsolete past tense of SLINK.

slant (slant) *v.t.* 1 To give an oblique or sloping direction to; turn from a direct line or level; incline; lean. 2 To write or edit (news or other literary matter) so as to express a special attitude, bias, or opinion. — *v.i.* 3 To have or take an oblique or sloping direction. 4 To have a certain bias or attitude. — *adj.* Lying at an angle; oblique; sloping — *n.* 1 A slanting direction, course, or plane; inclination from a direct line or level; slope; also, a mental or moral bent, opinion, attitude, etc. 2 An oblique reflection; a sarcastic remark. See synonyms under TIP[1]. [<earlier *slent* <Scand. Cf. Norw. *slenta* slope.] — **slant'·ing** *adj.* — **slant'ing·ly** *adv.* — **slant'ing·ness** *n.*

slant·wise (slant'wīz') *adj.* Slanting; oblique. — *adv.* At a slant or slope; obliquely; slantingly: also **slant'ways'** (-wāz').

slap (slap) *n.* A blow delivered with the open hand or with something flat; also, an insult; slur. — *v.* **slapped, slap·ping** *v.t.* 1 To hit or strike with the open hand or with something flat; also, to rebuff; insult. 2 To put or place violently or carelessly. — *v.i.* 3 To strike or beat as if with slaps: The waves *slapped* against the dock. — *adv.* 1 Suddenly and forcibly; abruptly. 2 *Colloq.* Directly; straight: *slap* into his face. [<LG *slapp*] — **slap'per** *n.*

slap·bang (slap'bang') *adj.* & *adv. Slang* Slap-dash.

slap-dash (slap'dash') *adj.* Done or acting in a dashing or reckless way; impetuous; careless. — *n.* 1 Offhand or careless work, or thoughtless conduct. 2 Rough casting, or rough plastering. — *adv.* In a dashing or heedless manner.

slap-hap·py (slap'hap'ē) *adj. Slang* Giddy and weak-minded because of concussion of the brain; punch-drunk.

slap·jack (slap'jak) *n.* 1 A griddlecake; flapjack. 2 A children's game of cards.

slap·stick (slap'stik') *n.* 1 A flexible, double paddle formerly used in farces and pantomimes to make a loud report when an actor was struck with it. 2 The use of this apparatus, or the type of rough comedy in which it is used. — *adj.* Using or suggestive of the slapstick: *slapstick* comedy.

slash (slash) *v.t.* 1 To cut by striking violently and without attempt at accuracy; cut with long sweeping strokes; strike violently with or as with an edged instrument; slit; gash. 2 To strike with long sweeping blows of a whip; lash; scourge. 3 To make long gashes, cuts, or slits in; specifically, to slit, as a garment, so as to expose ornamental material or lining in or under the slits. 4 To criticize severely; censure harshly. 5 To cut down wastefully, as timber in a forest. 6 To reduce sharply, as salaries. — *v.i.* 7 To make a long sweeping stroke or several such strokes with or as with something sharp; cut. — *n.* 1 The act or result of slashing; a sweeping, random cut with a cutting weapon or whip; a slit or gash; specifically, an ornamental slit or cut in a garment showing some other material in or through the slit. 2 An opening or gap made in a forest. 3 The loose tops and branches of trees left in a forest after logging or a high wind. 4 A swampy thicket; low-lying boggy land: usually in the plural. 5 *Printing* A virgula. [? <OF *esclachier* break] — **slash'er** *n.*

slash·ing (slash'ing) *adj.* 1 Striking or cutting at random: a *slashing* warrior or critic. 2 *Colloq.* Of uncommonly high degree; very large; very fine, swift, etc.; exceptionally brilliant. — *n.* 1 A slash; the act of slashing; especially, the wasteful destruction of timber. 2 A region where timber trees have been cut down. 3 A mass of felled trees heaped for burning. — **slash'ing·ly** *adv.* — **slash'ing·ness** *n.*

slash pine 1 A pine *(Pinus caribae)* growing in the slashes along the southeastern coast of the United States; also, its wood. 2 The loblolly pine.

Slask (shlôṅsk) The Polish name for SILESIA.

slat[1] (slat) *n.* 1 One of a number of thin, flat, narrow strips of wood used to support the springs or mattress of a bed. 2 Any thin, narrow strip of wood or metal; a lath. 3 *Aeron.* A movable auxiliary airfoil attached to the leading edge of an airplane wing. — *v.t.* **slat·ted, slat·ting** To provide or make with slats. [<OF *esclat* splinter, chip]

slat[2] (slat) *v.* **slat·ted, slat·ting** *v.t. Dial.* 1 To throw or dash violently; fling carelessly. 2 To beat; slap. — *v.i.* 3 To flap, as sails against yards. — *n. Dial.* A sudden, sharp blow. [? <ON *sletta* slap]

slate[1] (slāt) *n.* 1 Any rock that splits readily into thin and even laminae; specifically, an argillaceous, fine-grained rock that so splits; also, an artificial material made in imitation of it. 2 A piece, slab, or plate of slate used for roofing, writing upon, etc. 3 A record of one's past performance or behavior: a clean *slate.* 4 A list of political candidates made up before their nomination or election; any prearranged list. 5 A dull bluish-gray color resembling that of slate: also **slate gray.** — *adj.* 1 Made of slate: a *slate* roof. 2 Slate-colored. — *v.t.* **slat·ed, slat·ing** 1 To roof with slate. 2 To put on a political slate or a list of any sort; hence, to register or designate as if by writing on a slate: He is *slated* for promotion. 3 To remove hair from (hides) with a slater. [<OF *esclate,* fem. of *esclat* a chip, splinter] — **slat'y** *adj.*

slate[2] (slāt) *v.t.* **slat·ed, slat·ing** 1 To censure, criticize, or review severely; berate. 2 To punish severely. [OE *slætan* bait]

slate ax See SAX[1] (def. 1).

slate pencil A pencil made of soft slate: used for writing on a slate.

slat·er[1] (slā'tər) *n.* 1 A person whose trade is to lay slates. 2 A slate-edged implement for removing hair from hides. 3 A terrestrial isopod crustacean, as the common pill bug or wood louse.

slat·er[2] (slā'tər) *n.* One who censures severely; a caustic critic.

slath·er (slath'ər) *Colloq.* or *Dial. v.t.* To daub thickly; spend or use profusely; lavish. — *n.* 1 A thick layer or spread. 2 *pl.* A lot; very

much: *slathers* of fun. [Var. of dial. E *slither* slip]

slat·ing (slā′ting) *n.* **1** The act or occupation of laying slates. **2** Slates or slate collectively. **3** A liquid for giving a slatelike surface to blackboards, etc.

slat·tern (slat′ərn) *n.* An untidy or slovenly woman. — *adj.* Untidy; slovenly. [<dial. E *slatter* slop, spill] — **slat′tern·li·ness** *n.* — **slat′tern·ly** *adj.* & *adv.*

slaugh·ter (slô′tər) *n.* **1** The act of killing; specifically, the butchering of cattle and other animals for market. **2** Wanton or savage killing, especially of human beings; massacre; carnage. **3** *Slang* A sweeping or ruinous reduction in prices. See synonyms under MASSACRE. — *v.t.* **1** To kill for the market; butcher. **2** To kill wantonly or savagely, especially in large numbers. **3** *Slang* To reduce greatly the price of; sell at a low figure. See synonyms under KILL[1]. [<ON *slātr* butcher's meat. Akin to SLAY.] — **slaugh′ter·er** *n.* — **slaugh′ter·ous** *adj.* — **slaugh′ter·ous·ly** *adv.*

slaugh·ter·house (slô′tər·hous′) *n.* A place where animals are butchered; a scene of carnage.

Slav (släv, slav) *n.* A member of any of the Slavic-speaking peoples of northern or eastern Europe, the northern group comprising the Russians, Poles, Czechs, Moravians, Sorbs or Wends, Slovaks, etc.; the southeastern group comprising the Bulgarians, Serbians, Croats, and Slovenes. Also, *Obs.*, *Sclav.* [<G *Sklave* <Med. L *Sclavus* <LGk. *Sklabos* <Slavic]

slave (slāv) *n.* **1** One whose person is held as property; a person in slavery; a bondsman; serf. **2** *Law* A person over whose life, liberty, and property someone has absolute control. **3** A person in mental or moral subjection to a habit, vice, or influence: a *slave* of tobacco. **4** One who labors like a slave; a drudge. **5** A person of slavish disposition; an abject creature. — *v.* **slaved, slav·ing** *v.i.* To work like a slave; toil; drudge. — *v.t. Rare* To enslave. [<F *esclave* <Med. L *slavus, sclavus,* orig. a Slav; because many Slavs were conquered and enslaved]

slave ant An ant enslaved by members of another species.

slave auction An auction at which slaves are sold.

Slave Coast The coastal region of western Africa extending westward from the mouths of the Niger along the Bight of Benin to Ghana: named for its former trade in slaves.

slave-driv·er (slāv′drī′vər) *n.* **1** A person hired for or charged with the overseeing of slaves at work. **2** Any severe or exacting employer.

slave·hold·er (slāv′hōl′dər) *n.* An owner of slaves. — **slave′hold′ing** *adj.* & *n.*

slav·er[1] (slav′ər) *v.t.* To dribble saliva over. — *v.i.* To dribble saliva; drool. — *n.* Saliva issuing or dribbling from the mouth. [Prob. <ON *slafra*] — **slav′er·er** *n.*

slav·er[2] (slā′vər) *n.* **1** A person or a vessel engaged in the slave trade. **2** One who procures white slaves.

Slave River A river in NE Alberta and the southern region of Mackenzie district, Northwest Territories, Canada, flowing 258 miles NW to Great Slave Lake: also *Great Slave River.*

slav·er·y (slā′vər·ē, slāv′rē) *n.* **1** Involuntary servitude; specifically, the legalized social institution in which humans are held as property or chattels; complete subjection of one person to another. **2** Mental, moral, or spiritual bondage. **3** Slavish toil; drudgery. See synonyms under BONDAGE.

Slave State Any of the United States in which slavery was not prohibited by statute before the Civil War: Alabama, Arkansas, Delaware, Florida, Georgia, Kentucky, Louisiana, Maryland, Mississippi, Missouri, North Carolina, South Carolina, Tennessee, Texas, Virginia.

slave trade The business of dealing in slaves; specifically, the bringing of Negro slaves to America for sale. — **slave′trad′er** *n.*

slav·ey (slā′vē, slav′ē) *n. Brit.* A household servant; drudge; usually, a maidservant.

Slav·ic (slä′vik, slav′ik) *adj.* Of or pertaining to the Slavs or their language. — *n.* A branch of the Balto-Slavic subfamily of the Indo-European language family, consisting of three groups — **East Slavic** (Russian or Great Russian, Ukrainian or Ruthenian or Little Russian, White Russian), **West Slavic** (Czechoslovakian, Sorbian or Wendish, Polish), **South Slavic** (Church Slavonic, Bulgarian, Serbo-Croatian, Slovenian). Also *Slavonic.*

slav·ish (slā′vish) *adj.* **1** Pertaining to or befitting a slave; servile; base. **2** Extremely hard or laborious. **3** Enslaved. See synonyms under BASE[2], OBSEQUIOUS. — **slav′ish·ly** *adv.* — **slav′ish·ness** *n.*

Slav·ism (slä′viz·əm, slav′iz·əm) *n.* The characteristics or aims of the Slavs, collectively.

Slavo- *combining form* Slavic; of or pertaining to the Slavs: *Slavophobe.* [<SLAV]

slav·oc·ra·cy (slāv·ok′rə·sē) *n. pl.* **·cies** Slaveholders or slaveholding interests as a political power, especially for the maintenance of slavery. [<SLAV(E) + -(O)CRACY] — **slav·o·crat** (slā′və·krat) *n.* — **slav′o·crat′ic** *adj.*

Sla·vo·ni·a (slə·vō′nē·ə) A region of Croatia, northern Yugoslavia, between the Sava and Drava rivers. — **Sla·vo′ni·an** *adj.* & *n.*

Sla·von·ic (slə·von′ik) *adj.* & *n.* Slavic. — **Church Slavonic** A member of the South Slavic group of the Balto-Slavic languages: now in use only as the language of the Slavic Greek Orthodox Church and certain Roman Catholic dioceses. See GLAGOL.

Slav·o·phile (släv′ə·fīl, -fil, slav′-) *n.* An admirer of the Slavs or their ideas, art, etc.

slaw[1] (slô) *n.* Cabbage sliced, shredded, or chopped, and served, usually raw, as a salad. [<Du. *sla,* short for *salade* salad]

slaw[2] (slô) *adj. Scot.* Slow.

slay (slā) *v.t.* **slew, slain, slay·ing** **1** To kill, especially by violence; put to death; destroy by, or as by, killing. **2** *Obs.* To smite; strike. See synonyms under KILL[1]. ◆ Homophones: *sleigh, sley.* [OE *slēan*] — **slay′er** *n.*

sleave (slēv) *v.t.* **sleaved, sleav·ing** To separate, as a mass of threads; disentangle. —*n.* Something tangled, matted, knotted, or unspun, as silk or thread. ◆ Homophone: *sleeve.* [OE *slǣfan* divide]

sleave silk Raw untwisted silk; floss.

slea·zy (slē′zē, slā′-) *adj.* **·zi·er, ·zi·est** **1** Lacking firmness of texture or substance. **2** Cheap; shoddy; run-down: a *sleazy* bar. [Origin uncertain] — **slea′zi·ly** *adv.* — **slea′zi·ness** *n.*

sled (sled) *n.* **1** A vehicle mounted on runners, designed for carrying people or loads over snow and ice; a sledge. **2** A small, light frame mounted on runners, used especially by children for sliding on snow and ice. — *v.* **sled·ded, sled·ding** *v.t.* To convey on a sled. — *v.i.* To ride on or use a sled. [<MLG *sledde*]

sled·der (sled′ər) *n.* **1** One who rides on or hauls with a sled. **2** An animal that draws a sled.

sled·ding (sled′ing) *n.* **1** Condition of roads admitting of the use of sleds: usually with a qualifying word: fine *sledding.* **2** The act of using a sled; use of sleds in hauling, traveling, etc. **3** State or circumstances of progress, work, etc.: We have had hard *sledding.*

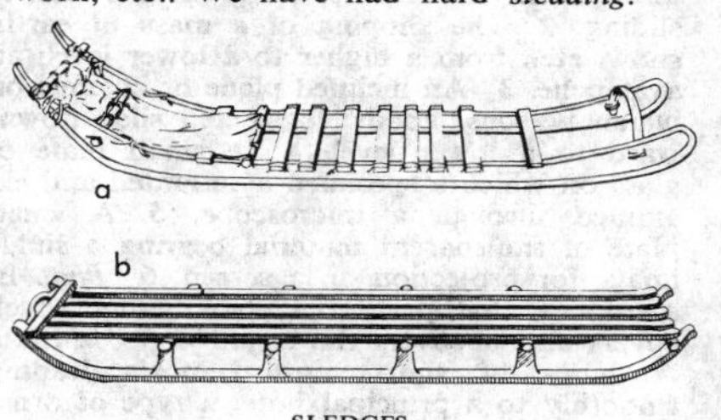

SLEDGES
a. Peary North Pole Expedition.
b. Byrd Antarctic Expedition.

sledge[1] (slej) *n.* A vehicle mounted on low runners for moving loads; especially, one designed to be drawn over snow and ice by dogs, horses, or reindeer, or one designed to be drawn on the ground by draft animals; also, a sled. — *v.t.* & *v.i.* **sledged, sledg·ing** To travel or convey on a sledge. [<MDu. *sleedse*]

sledge[2] (slej) *n.* A heavy hammer wielded with one or both hands, for blacksmiths' use, or for breaking stone, coal, etc.: also **sledge′-ham′mer** (-ham′ər). — *v.t.* **sledged, sledg·ing** To hammer, break, or strike with a sledge. [OE *slecg*]

slee (slē) *adj. Scot.* Sly; dexterous.

sleek (slēk) *adj.* **1** Smooth and glossy; polished. **2** Smooth-spoken; flattering; unctuous; insinuating. See synonyms under SMOOTH. — *v.t.* **1** To make smooth, even, or glossy; polish. **2** To soothe; mollify; also, to make less disagreeable or offensive. Also, *U.S., slick.* [Var. of SLICK] — **sleek′ly** *adv.* — **sleek′ness** *n.* — **sleek′y** *adj.*

sleek·it (slēk′it) *adj. Scot.* **1** Sleek. **2** Deceitful.

sleep (slēp) *n.* **1** A state or period of complete or partial unconsciousness, normal and periodic in man and the higher animals. In animals it is sometimes much prolonged, as in hibernation. **2** A period of slumber. **3** Any condition of inactivity, torpor, or rest; specifically, the rest of the grave; death. **4** Nyctitropism. See synonyms under REST[1]. — **to go to sleep** **1** To fall asleep. **2** To become numb, often with a tingling sensation, from retarded circulation. — *v.* **slept, sleep·ing** *v.i.* **1** To be or fall asleep; slumber. **2** To be in a state resembling sleep; to be dormant, inactive or quiet, or to rest in death. **3** To be in a benumbed state from retarded circulation of the blood: My foot *sleeps.* **4** To spin with such velocity as to be without apparent motion, as a top. **5** To undergo nyctitropism. **6** *Bot.* To assume a different position at night, as petals. — *v.t.* **7** To rest or repose in: with a cognate object: to *sleep* the sleep of the dead. **8** To provide with sleeping quarters; lodge: The hotel can *sleep* a hundred guests. See synonyms under REST[1]. — **to sleep away** (or **off** or **out**) To pass or get rid of by or as by sleep: to *sleep off* a hang-over. — **to sleep on** To postpone a decision upon. [OE *slēp*]

Sleep may appear as a combining form in hyphemes; as in:

sleep-bringing	**sleep-inducing**
sleep-compelling	**sleep-inviting**
sleep-dispelling	**sleep-loving**
sleep-disturber	**sleep-producing**
sleep-disturbing	**sleep-provoking**
sleep-filled	**sleep-resisting**

sleep·er (slē′pər) *n.* **1** One who sleeps; figuratively, a dead person. **2** A railroad sleeping-car. **3** A hibernating animal. **4** In football, a member of the backfield or an end stationed far out at either side before the ball is put in motion. **5** A heavy beam resting on or in the ground, as a support for a roadway, rails, etc.; a like support of iron or stone; also, a timber on or near the ground for the lower joists of a building. **6** A deadman. **7** *U.S. Colloq.* A play, motion picture, or book which achieves unexpected and striking success.

sleep·ing-car (slē′ping·kär′) *n.* A passenger railroad car with accommodations for sleeping.

sleeping partner See under PARTNER.

sleeping pill *Med.* A sedative; especially, one of the barbiturates taken to relieve acute or persistent insomnia.

sleeping sickness *Pathol.* **1** The terminal stage of a form of trypanosomiasis prevalent in tropical Africa: it is caused by the presence in the cerebrospinal fluid of certain trypanosomes usually transmitted by the bite of the tsetse fly, and is marked by progressive lethargy, recurrent fever and headaches, terminating in somnolence and death. **2** Epidemic encephalitis lethargica.

sleep·less (slēp′lis) *adj.* Unable to sleep; wakeful; restless; unquiet. See synonyms under VIGILANT. — **sleep′less·ly** *adv.* — **sleep′less·ness** *n.*

sleep·walk·er (slēp′wô′kər) *n.* A somnambulist. — **sleep′walk′ing** *n.*

sleep·y (slē′pē) *adj.* **sleep·i·er, sleep·i·est** **1** Inclined to sleep. **2** Drowsy; sluggish; dull; heavy. **3** Conducive to sleep. — **sleep′i·ly** *adv.* — **sleep′i·ness** *n.*

sleep·y-head (slē′pē·hed′) *n.* A sleepy person. — **sleep′y-head′ed** *adj.*

sleet (slēt) *n.* **1** A mixture of snow or hail and rain. **2** A drizzle or shower of partly frozen

rain, or rain that freezes as it falls. 3 A thin coating of ice, as on rails, wires, roads, etc. —*v.i.* To pour or shed sleet. [Akin to MLG *slote* hail] —**sleet'y** *adj.*

sleeve (slēv) *n.* 1 The part of a garment that serves especially as a covering for the arm. 2 *Mech.* **a** A tube surrounding something, as a shaft, for protection or to permit motion of itself or of the shaft. **b** A short pipe receiving the ends of two other pipes or rods; a sleeve coupling or sleeve valve. 3 *Electr.* The cylindrical contacting part of a telephone–circuit plug. —**up one's sleeve** Hidden but at hand. —*v.t.* **sleeved, sleev·ing** To furnish with a sleeve or sleeves. ◆ Homophone: *sleave.* [OE *slēfe*]

sleeve coupling *Mech.* A short tube for connecting shafts or pipes.

sleeve·less (slēv'lis) *adj.* 1 Having no sleeves. 2 *Archaic* Unprofitable; fruitless; futile: a *sleeveless* errand.

sleeve valve *Mech.* A valve consisting of a hollow slotted sleeve in the cylinder of an internal–combustion engine, operating with the piston to allow for intake or exhaust of gases.

sleigh (slā) *n.* A light vehicle with runners for use on snow and ice, adapted especially for pleasure use or travel, as distinguished from hauling. Compare SLED, SLEDGE[1]. —*v.i.* To ride or travel in a sleigh. ◆ Homophones: *slay, sley.* [<Du. *slee,* contraction of *slede* sledge] —**sleigh'er** *n.*

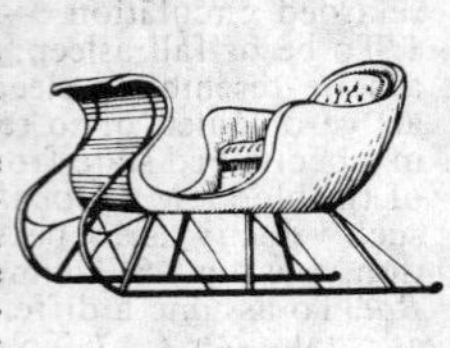

SLEIGH

sleigh·ing (slā'ing) *n.* 1 The act of riding in a sleigh. 2 The condition of the snow or ice that admits of using a sleigh.

sleight (slīt) *n.* 1 The quality of being skilful in manipulation; mechanical expertness; skill; dexterity. 2 A juggler's trick so deftly done that the manner of performance escapes observation; feat of legerdemain. 3 Craft; cunning. ◆ Homophone: *slight.* [<ON *slægdh* slyness]

sleight of hand 1 Skill in performing tricks in juggling. 2 The art or practice, or an instance, of legerdemain.

slen·dang (slen'däng) *n.* A scarf or shawl worn over the shoulders by women in the Philippines. [<Malay *sĕlendaṅ*]

slen·der (slen'dər) *adj.* 1 Having a small diameter or circumference, in proportion to the length or height; slim; thin. 2 Having little strength or vigor; feeble; frail; delicate. 3 Having slight basis or foundation; of little validity. 4 Small or inadequate; moderate; insignificant: a *slender* income or diet. 5 Meagerly or insufficiently supplied: a *slender* table. 6 Thin in sound or quality; lacking volume. 7 *Phonet.* Denoting vowels which are pronounced with a narrow opening above the tongue, as (ē); close; narrow; opposed to *broad.* See synonyms under FINE[1], LITTLE, MINUTE[2]. [ME *slendre,* prob. <OF *esclendre*] —**slen'·der·ly** *adv.* —**slen'der·ness** *n.*

slen·der·ize (slen'də·rīz) *v.t.* & *v.i.* **·ized, ·iz·ing** To make or become slender.

slept (slept) Past tense and past participle of SLEEP.

Sle·svig (sles'vikh) The Danish name for SCHLESWIG.

sleuth (sloōth) *n.* 1 *U.S. Colloq.* A detective. 2 A sleuthhound. 3 *Obs.* The track of a man or beast, as followed by the scent. —*v.t.* To follow, as a detective. —*v.i.* To play the detective. [<ON *slōdh* track, trail. Doublet of SLOT[2].]

sleuth·hound (sloōth'hound') *n.* A bloodhound.

slew[1] (sloō) Past tense of SLAY[1].

slew[2] (sloō) See SLOUGH[2].

slew[3] (sloō) *n. U.S. Colloq.* A large number, crowd, or amount; a lot: also spelled *slue.* [Cf. Irish *sluagh* a large crowd]

slew[4] (sloō) See SLUE[1].

sley (slā) *n.* 1 The reed guiding the warp threads of a loom. 2 In knitting machines, a groove, slot, or bar for directing the action of a part. —*v.t.* To separate and arrange the threads of (yarn) in a reed for weaving. ◆ Homophones: *slay, sleigh.* [OE *slege*]

Slez·sko (sles'kô) The Czech name for SILESIA.

slice (slīs) *n.* 1 A piece; especially, a thin, broad piece cut off from a larger body. 2 One of various tools or devices, used for slicing or resembling a slice in broadness and thinness; specifically, a broad knife used for serving fish, or a broad flat knife used by printers to remove ink; also, a druggist's spatula. 3 In golf, a blow delivered crosswise from right to left, causing the ball to curve to the right. —*v.* **sliced, slic·ing** *v.t.* 1 To cut or remove from a larger piece: often with *off.* 2 To cut into broad, thin pieces; divide; apportion. 3 To sunder, as with a sharp knife; split. 4 To clear out with a slice bar. 5 In golf, to hit (the ball) with a slice. —*v.i.* 6 In golf, to slice a ball. See synonyms under CUT. [<OF *esclice* < *esclicer* <OHG *slizan* slit] —**slic'er** *n.*

slice bar A thin, wide iron tool for cleaning clinkers from the grate bars of a furnace.

slick (slik) *adj.* 1 Smooth; slippery; sleek. 2 Flattering obsequious; smooth–tongued; plausible. 3 *Colloq.* Dexterously done; cleverly said; specious; tricky. 4 Smart; clever: said of people. 5 Healthy; plump: said of animals. 6 Smooth; oily, as the surface of water. 7 Glazed, as paper; also, printed on glazed paper: *slick* magazines. 8 *Slang* Agreeable; excellent: a *slick* time. —*n.* 1 A smooth place on a surface of water, as from oil or the presence of fish; also, a sleek place in the fur or hair of an animal. 2 A broad chisel for paring or slicking: also **slick chisel.** 3 *pl. U.S.* Magazines printed on glazed paper: distinguished from *pulps.* —*adv. Slang* In a slick or smooth manner; deftly; quickly. —*v.t.* 1 To make smooth, trim, glossy, or oily. 2 *Colloq.* To trim up; make presentable: often with *up.* [ME *slike* <OE *slician* make smooth]

slick·en·sides (slik'ən·sīdz) *n. pl. Geol.* Polished and scratched or striated rock surfaces, exhibited on the opposed faces of veins or faults where they have moved one upon another. [<dial. E *slicken* slick + SIDE] —**slick'en·sid'ed** *adj.* —**slick'en·sid'ing** *n.*

slick·er (slik'ər) *n.* 1 An implement for dressing leather, having a wooden handle. 2 *U.S.* A waterproof overcoat of oilskin. 3 *Colloq.* A cheat; clever person.

slid (slid) Past tense and past participle of SLIDE.

slid·den (slid'n) Alternative past participle of SLIDE.

slide (slīd) *v.* **slid, slid** or **slid·den, slid·ing** *v.i.* 1 To pass along over a surface with a smooth, slipping movement: to *slide* on ice. 2 To slip off, as scales in shedding. 3 To move or pass imperceptibly, smoothly, deftly, or easily; pass gradually or imperceptibly: The years *slide* away swiftly. 4 To move, pass, or proceed by sufferance merely; also, to take care of oneself or itself; go by default or without heed: with *let*: to let the matter *slide.* 5 *Music* To glide from tone to tone without breaking the sound. 6 To make a moral slip; err; sin. 7 To slip; lose one's equilibrium or foothold. 8 In baseball, to throw oneself along the ground toward a base, in order to avoid being tagged by the baseman. —*v.t.* 9 To cause to slide, as over a surface. 10 To move, put, enter, etc., with quietness or dexterity: with *in* or *into.* —*n.* 1 An act of sliding. 2 The slipping of a mass of earth, snow, etc., from a higher to a lower level; an avalanche. 3 An inclined plane or channel on which persons, goods, logs, etc., slide downward to a lower level. 4 A small plate of glass on which a specimen is mounted and examined through a microscope. 5 A small plate of transparent material bearing a single image for projection on a screen. 6 *Phot.* In a camera, that part of a plate holder which covers and uncovers the negative. 7 *Music* **a** A series of short musical notes leading smoothly to a principal note: a type of ornamentation. **b** A portamento. **c** In a trumpet or trombone, a U–shaped portion of the tubing which is pushed in and out to vary the pitch. 8 *Mech.* **a** A sliding part. **b** A groove, rail, etc., on which something slides. [OE *slīdan*]

slide fastener A fastening device for use on fabrics, dress goods, etc., having two rows of interlocking teeth or scoops which may be closed or separated by a sliding element: often called *zipper.*

slide·knot (slīd'not') *n.* A slipknot, particularly one made of two half–hitches on a fishing line.

Sli·dell (slī·del'), **John,** 1793–1871, American lawyer; Confederate agent to France in 1861.

Slide Mountain The highest peak of the Catskill Mountains, in SE New York, 18 miles west of Kingston; 4,204 feet.

slid·er (slī'dər) *n.* 1 One who or that which slides. 2 In baseball, a fast pitch that curves slightly at or near the strike zone.

slide rule A device consisting of a rigid ruler with a central sliding piece, both ruler and slide being graduated in a similar logarithmic scale to permit of rapid calculations.

slide valve *Mech.* 1 A sliding piece in the cylinder of a steam engine, regulated to move back and forth over the ports and connect them alternately with the boiler and the exhaust passage, thus imparting reciprocating motion to the piston. 2 A valve that slides on its seat.

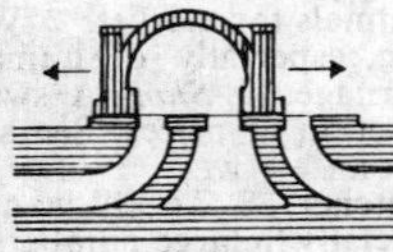

SLIDE VALVE
Arrows show reciprocal action.

sliding board A child's slide, used in play.

sliding scale 1 A schedule affecting imports, prices, or wages, varying under conditions of consumption, demand, or market price of some article. 2 Any graduated scale, as in a clinometer or slide rule, designed to move against a fixed scale in order to facilitate rapid and accurate measurements and computations.

slight (slīt) *adj.* 1 Of small importance; small in quantity, intensity, or degree; inconsiderable. 2 Slender; frail; delicate; flimsy. 3 Of weak intellect or character. 4 *Scot.* Smooth; slippery; unscrupulous. See synonyms under FINE[1], FRAGILE, INSIGNIFICANT, LITTLE, SMALL. —*v.t.* 1 To manifest intentional neglect of or disregard for; snub; omit due courtesy toward or respect for: to *slight* a friend. 2 To omit due care in the doing or performance of; do imperfectly or thoughtlessly; shirk. 3 To treat as trivial or insignificant. —*n.* An act or omission involving failure in courtesy or respect toward another; any contemptuous or neglectful action. ◆ Homophone: *sleight.* [ME. Akin to ON *slettr* smooth.] —**slight'ness** *n.*

Synonyms (noun): disregard, neglect, scorn. *Disregard* is chiefly a matter of intellectual estimate; *slight* is a matter of outward action; *neglect* may be of thought or act. *Disregard* of a thing is setting it aside as not worthy of regard. *Neglect* of a person or thing may be the result of ignorance, thoughtlessness, or preoccupation with other things; a *slight* is an intentional omission of kindness, courtesy, or attention. *Scorn* expresses mingled contempt and bitterness. See NEGLECT. *Antonyms*: esteem, honor, regard, respect, reverence.

slight·ing (slī'ting) *adj.* Conveying, containing, or characterized by a slight: a *slighting* remark. —**slight'ing·ly** *adv.*

slight·ly (slīt'lē) *adv.* In a slight manner; inconsiderably; partially; carelessly.

Sli·go (slī'gō) 1 A county of NW Ireland in Connacht province; 694 square miles. 2 Its county town, a port on **Sligo Bay,** an inlet of the Atlantic extending 7 miles into County Sligo; 10 miles wide.

sli·ly (slī'lē) *adv.* In a sly manner: also spelled *slyly.*

slim (slim) *adj.* **slim·mer, slim·mest** 1 Small in thickness in proportion to height or length, as a human figure or a tree. 2 Having little logical strength; weak. 3 Constructed unsubstantially; flimsy. 4 Lacking robustness; frail. 5 Insufficient; narrow; meager: a *slim* attendance; a *slim* chance. 6 *Brit. Dial.* Sly; crafty; worthless; bad. —*v.t.* & *v.i.* **slimmed, slim·ming** To make or become thin or thinner. [<Du. *slim* bad] —**slim'ly** *adv.* —**slim'·ness** *n.*

slime (slīm) *n.* 1 Any soft, sticky or dirty thing; hence, any offensive quality or thing. 2 Soft, moist, adhesive mud or earth; muck. 3 A mucous exudation from the bodies of certain animals, as fishes and snails, and certain plants. 4 Bitumen; asphalt. 5 *Usually pl.* A mudlike substance formed of ore in an almost impalpable powder, mixed with water. —*v.* **slimed, slim·ing** *v.t.* 1 To smear or cover with or as with slime. 2 To remove slime. 2 To remove slime from, as fishes. —*v.i.* 3 To become covered with or as with slime. [OE *slim*]

slime flux A watery or viscous flow from the injured bark of various deciduous trees, sometimes providing a medium for parasitic growths.

slime mold A fungus belonging to the class *Myxomycetes.* Also **slime fungus.**

slim·sy (slim′zē) *adj. Colloq.* **1** Utterly limp, as from fatigue or illness. **2** Lacking in stiffness or texture, as limp fabric; flimsy. Also **slimp·sy** (slimp′sē). [Blend of SLIM and FLIMSY]

slim·y (slī′mē) *adj.* **slim·i·er, slim·i·est 1** Covered or bedaubed with slime. **2** Containing slime. **3** Slimelike; foul. — **slim′i·ly** *adv.* — **slim′i·ness** *n.*

sling[1] (sling) *n.* **1** A strap or pocket with a string attached to each end, for hurling a stone or other missile by centrifugal force. **2** One of various ropes, straps, chains, or the like, for suspending or hoisting something, for holding up an injured limb, lifting and supporting an animal, in case of lameness or other need, carrying a rifle, etc. **3** *Naut.* A rope or chain by which a lower yard or a gaff is suspended; also, in the plural, the middle portion of a yard. **4** The act of slinging; a sudden throw; cast; fling. [< *v.*] — *v.* **slung, sling·ing** *v.t.* **1** To fling from or as from a sling; hurl. **2** To place or hang up in or as in a sling; move or hoist, as by a rope or tackle. — *v.i.* **3** To move at an easy gait. See synonyms under SEND[1]. [<ON *slyngva* hurl] — **sling′er** *n.*

sling[2] (sling) *n. U.S.* A drink of brandy, whisky, or gin, with sugar and nutmeg, lemon juice, and hot or cold water. — *v.i. U.S. Colloq.* To drink slings; take an alcoholic drink. [Cf. G *schlingen* swallow]

sling·shot (sling′shot′) *n.* A weapon or toy consisting of a forked stick with an elastic strap attached to the prongs for catapulting small missiles.

slink (slingk) *v.* **slunk** (*Obs.* **slank**), **slunk, slink·ing** *v.i.* To creep or steal along furtively or stealthily, as in fear. — *v.t.* To give birth to prematurely; miscarry: said of animals, especially cows. — *adj.* Produced prematurely, as a calf; too immature to be eaten. — *n.* An animal, especially a calf, prematurely born; also, its flesh, too immature for proper food. [OE *slincan* creep] — **slink′ing·ly** *adv.*

slink·y (slingk′ē) *adj.* **slink·i·er, slink·i·est 1** Sneaking; stealthy. **2** *Slang* Sinuous or feline in movement or form.

slip[1] (slip) *v.* **slipped** or **slipt, slip·ping** *v.t.* **1** To cause to move smoothly and easily; cause to glide or slide. **2** To put on or off easily, as a ring or a loose garment. **3** To convey slily or secretly. **4** To free oneself or itself from, as a fetter or bridle. **5** To let loose; unleash, as hounds. **6** To release from its fastening and let run out, as a cable. **7** To give birth to prematurely; slink; cast: said of animals. **8** To dislocate, as a bone. **9** To escape or pass unobserved: It *slipped* my mind. **10** To overlook; omit negligently: to *slip* an opportunity. — *v.i.* **11** To slide so as to cause harm or inconvenience; lose one's footing; become misplaced by failing to hold. **12** To fall into an error or fault; err. **13** To escape, as a ship. **14** To move smoothly and easily; slide; glide. **15** To get free of restraint; be unleashed. **16** To go or come stealthily or unnoticed: often with *off, away,* or *from.* — **to let slip** To say without intending to. — *n.* **1** An act of slipping; a sudden slide. **2** A lapse or error in speech, writing, or conduct; a slight mistake. **3** *U.S.* A narrow space between two wharves. **4** An artificial pier sloping down to the water, serving as a landing place. **5** An inclined plane leading down to the water, on which vessels are repaired or constructed. **6** A woman's undergarment. **7** A pillowcase. **8** A leash containing a device which permits quick release of the dog. **9** In cricket, a position on the off side a few yards behind the wicket; also, the player who stands at this position. **10** *Naut.* **a** The difference between the speed of a screw propeller and that of the ship. **b** The velocity of the back current generated by a propeller. **11** *Physics* The difference between the advance made by a propeller moving in a fluid and the advance it would make if moving in a solid substance. **12** *Mech.* **a** The relative motion of two surfaces which are meant to be immovable with respect to each other, as a belt on a pulley. **b** Allowance made for slipping or play, as between connected members of a mechanism; slippage. **13** *Geol.* A small dislocation of rock strata. — **to give (someone) the slip** To elude (someone). [<MLG *slippen*]

slip[2] (slip) *n.* **1** A cutting from a plant for planting or grafting; a cion. **2** A small, slender person, especially a youthful one. **3** A small piece of something, as of paper or cloth, rather long relative to its width; a strip. **4** A small piece of paper for jotting down memoranda, a record, etc. **5** *U.S.* A narrow pew in a church. — *v.t.* **slipped, slip·ping** To cut off for planting; make a slip or slips of. [<MDu. *slippe* < *slippen* cut]

slip[3] (slip) *n.* Liquid potter's clay, used for decorating and coating rough surfaces. [OE *slype, slypa*]

slip·cov·er (slip′kuv′ər) *n.* **1** A fitted cloth cover for a chair, couch, sofa, or other piece of furniture, that can be readily removed. **2** A paper or cloth jacket for a book.

slip·knot (slip′not′) *n.* **1** A knot so formed, by having part of the material drawn through in a bow, as to be readily untied: also called *bowknot.* **2** A running knot.

slip–on (slip′on′, -ôn′) *n.* A garment which can be easily donned or taken off. — *adj.* Denoting such a garment: a *slip–on* blouse.

slip–o·ver (slip′ō′vər) *adj.* Designating a garment easily donned by drawing over the head: a *slip–over* shirt. — *n.* A garment of this type.

slip·page (slip′ij) *n.* **1** The amount by which or distance through which anything slips, as a screw propeller. **2** The difference between actual and calculated speed, due to slipping. **3** The act of slipping; slip.

slip·per[1] (slip′ər) *n.* **1** A low, light shoe, chiefly for indoor wear, into or out of which the foot is easily slipped. **2** One who or that which slips. [<SLIP[1] + -ER[2]]

slip·per[2] (slip′ər) *adj. Archaic* Slippery; deceitful; unreliable; forgetful; voluble. [OE *slipor*]

slip·pered (slip′ərd) *adj.* Wearing slippers.

slip·per·wort (slip′ər·wûrt′) *n.* Calceolaria.

slip·per·y (slip′ər·ē) *adj.* **·per·i·er, ·per·i·est 1** Having a surface so smooth that bodies slip or slide easily on it. **2** That evades one's grasp; tricky; elusive. **3** Unreliable; undependable; tricky. **4** *Obs.* Wanton. [<SLIPPER[2] + -Y[3]] — **slip′per·i·ly** *adv.* — **slip′per·i·ness** *n.*

slippery elm 1 A tree (*Ulmus fulva*) of eastern North America. **2** Its hard wood. **3** Its mucilaginous inner bark, used in medicine as a nutritious demulcent.

slip–ring (slip′ring′) *n. Electr.* One of two or more metal rings of an electric machine serving, through contact with stationary brushes, to deliver or transmit a current.

slip–sheet (slip′shēt′) *Printing n.* A blank piece of paper interleaved between newly printed press sheets to prevent offset. — *v.t.* To insert slip–sheets in.

slip·shod (slip′shod′) *adj.* Wearing shoes or slippers down at the heels; hence, slovenly. [<SLIP[1] + SHOE]

slip·slop (slip′slop′) *n. Colloq.* **1** Sloppy victuals; any weak drink; slop. **2** A blunder, as in speaking.

slip·stream (slip′strēm′) *n. Aeron.* The stream of air driven backwards by the propeller of an aircraft: also called *race.*

slip–up (slip′up′) *n. Colloq.* A mistake; error.

slip·way (slip′wā′) *n.* A slip (def. 5).

slit (slit) *n.* A cut that is relatively straight and long; also, a long, narrow opening. [< *v.*] — *v.t.* **slit, slit·ting 1** To make a long incision in; slash. **2** To cut lengthwise into strips. See synonyms under REND. [ME *slitten* cut] — **slit′ter** *n.*

slith·er (slith′ər) *v.i.* **1** To slide; slip, as on a loose surface. **2** To glide, as a snake. — *v.t.* **3** To cause to slither. [Var. of dial. E *slidder* <OE *slidrian,* freq. of *slīdan* slide] — **slith′er·y** *adj.*

slit trench A narrow, shallow trench, similar to a foxhole.

sliv·er (sliv′ər) *n.* **1** A slender piece, as of wood, cut or torn off lengthwise; a splinter. **2** Corded textile fibers drawn into a fleecy strand. **3** A piece cut longitudinally from the side of a fish: used as bait; also, a filet. — *v.t.* & *v.i.* To cut or split into long thin pieces; splinter. [< dial. E *slive* cleave] — **sliv′er·er** *n.*

Sliv·no (slēv′nō) A city in east central Bulgaria. Also **Sliv·en** (slē′vən).

sli·vo·vitz (slē′vô·vēts) *n.* A white, dry plum brandy drunk especially in central European countries. [<Serbo–Croatian < *sliva* a plum]

Sloan (slōn), **John,** 1871–1951, U.S. painter.

slob (slob) *n.* **1** Mud; mire. **2** Slush; mushy snow. **3** *Slang* A stupid, careless, or unclean person. [<Irish *slab,* prob. <SLAB[2]]

slob·ber (slob′ər) *v.t.* **1** To wet and foul with liquids oozing from the mouth. **2** To shed or spill, as liquid food, in eating. — *v.i.* **3** To drivel; slaver. **4** To talk or act gushingly. — *n.* **1** Liquid spilled as from the mouth; slaver. **2** Gushing, sentimental talk. [Var. of SLABBER] — **slob′ber·er** *n.* — **slob′ber·y** *adj.*

slock (slok) *v.t. Brit. Dial.* To slake; drench; extinguish (a fire). Also **slock′en.**

sloe (slō) *n.* **1** A small, plumlike, astringent fruit. **2** The shrub (*Prunus spinosa*) that bears it; the blackthorn. **3** The blackhaw. **4** The wild yellow plum (*Prunus americana*); also, the Allegheny plum (*P. alleghaniensis*). ◆ Homophone: *slow.* [OE *slā*]

sloe–eyed (slō′īd′) *adj.* Having eyes dark as sloes.

sloe gin A cordial with a gin base, flavored with sloes.

slog (slog) *v.t.* & *v.i.* **slogged, slog·ging 1** To slug, as a pugilist. **2** To plod (one's way), as through deep mud. — *n.* A heavy blow. [Var. of SLUG[3]] — **slog′ger** *n.*

slo·gan (slō′gən) *n.* **1** A battle or rallying cry: originally of the Highland clans. **2** A catchword or motto adopted by a manufacturer, political party, or the like. [<Scottish Gaelic *sluagh* army + *gairm* yell]

sloid (sloid), **slojd** See SLOYD.

sloop (slōōp) *n. Naut.* A single–masted, fore–and–aft rigged sailing vessel with or without a bowsprit and carrying at least one jib: now used principally as a racing vessel. [<Du. *sloep*]

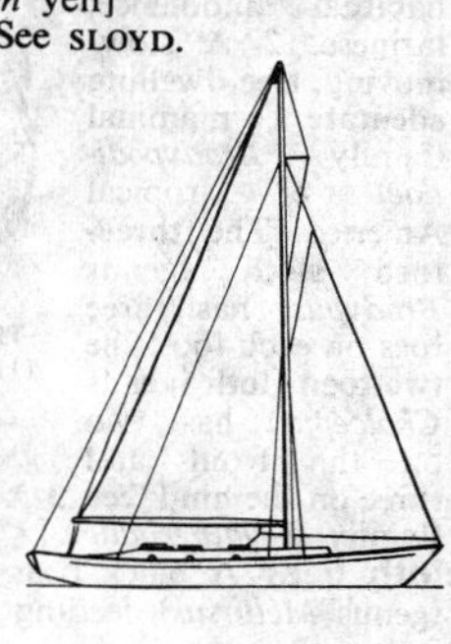

SLOOP

sloop of war In old navies, a vessel rigged either as ship, brig, or schooner, and mounting between 18 and 32 guns; later, any war vessel larger than a gunboat and carrying guns on one deck only.

slop[1] (slop) *v.* **slopped, slop·ping** *v.i.* **1** To splash or spill. **2** To walk or move through slush. — *v.t.* **3** To cause (a liquid) to spill or splash. **4** *U.S.* To feed (a domestic animal) with slops. — **to slop over 1** To overflow and splash. **2** To do or say more than is necessary, because of excess zeal, sentimentality, etc. — *n.* **1** Slush; watery mud. **2** A dash or puddle of liquid that has been slopped. **3** An unappetizing liquid or watery food. **4** Refuse liquid. **5** *pl.* Waste food or swill, as from a kitchen, used to feed cattle, pigs, etc. **6** *pl.* Distiller's mash which has been deprived of its alcohol. [ME *sloppe*]

slop[2] (slop) **1** *Obs.* A loose outer garment; a smock; in the plural, wide baggy breeches. **2** *pl.* Articles of clothing and other merchandise sold to sailors on shipboard. [ME *sloppe*]

slope (slōp) *v.* **sloped, slop·ing** *v.i.* **1** To be inclined from the level or the vertical; slant. **2** To move on an inclined path; go obliquely. **3** *Colloq.* To leave suddenly; run off. — *v.t.* **4** To cause to slope. See synonyms under TIP[1]. [< *adj.*] — *n.* **1** Any slanting surface or line; a declivity or acclivity; an inclined plane: the Atlantic *slope* of North America. **2** The degree of inclination of a line or surface from the plane of the horizon. **3** *Math.* **a** The tangent of the positive angle of less than 180° made between the *x*-axis and a tangent to a curve traced in the Cartesian coordinate system; also, the derivative of such a curve at a given point. **b** The tangent of the positive

angle of less than 180° made between the *x*-axis and a straight line traced in the Cartesian coordinate system. —*adj.* Slanting; oblique. [Aphetic var. of *aslope,* OE *aslopen,* ppr. of *a-slupan* slip away] **—slop′er** *n.* **—slop′ing** *adj.* **—slop′ing·ly** *adv.* **—slop′ing·ness** *n.*

slop·o·ver (slop′ō′vər) *n.* A breakover.

slop·py (slop′ē) *adj.* **·pi·er, ·pi·est 1** Slushy; splashy; wet. **2** Watery or pulpy; *sloppy* pudding. **3** Splashed with liquid or slops. **4** *Colloq.* Messy; slovenly; extremely untidy. **5** *Colloq.* Slipshod; careless. **6** *Colloq.* Maudlin; overly sentimental. **—slop′pi·ly** *adv.* **—slop′pi·ness** *n.*

slop·work (slop′wûrk′) *n.* **1** The manufacture of cheap ready-made clothing; also, the clothing itself. **2** Any inferior, slovenly work.

slosh (slosh) *v.t.* To throw about, as a liquid. —*v.i.* To splash; flounder: to *slosh* through a pool. —*n.* Slush. [Var. of SLUSH] **—slosh′y** *adj.*

slot[1] (slot) *n.* **1** A long narrow groove or opening; slit. **2** A comparatively long and narrow depression or cavity, particularly one that is rectangular, cut to receive some corresponding part in a mechanism. **3** The opening to receive the coin in a slot machine. **4** *Colloq.* An opening or position, as a job category or place in a sequence. **5** *Aeron.* An opening in an airplane wing to improve the conditions of airflow at high angles of flight. —*v.t.* **slot·ted, slot·ting 1** To adjust in a slot. **2** To cut a slot in; groove. [<OF *esclot* the hollow between the breasts]

slot[2] (slot) *n.* The trail of an animal, especially a deer. [<AF *esclot* <ON *slōdh.* Doublet of SLEUTH.]

sloth (slōth, slôth, sloth) *n.* **1** Disinclination to exertion; habitual indolence; laziness. **2** A slow-moving, tree-dwelling edentate mammal (family *Bradypodidae*) of tropical America. The **three-toed sloth** (genus *Bradypus*) has three toes on each foot; the **two-toed sloth** (genus *Choloepus*) has two on the front and three on the hind feet. **3** A related fossil edentate (family *Megatheriidae*). [<SLOW + -TH[1]]

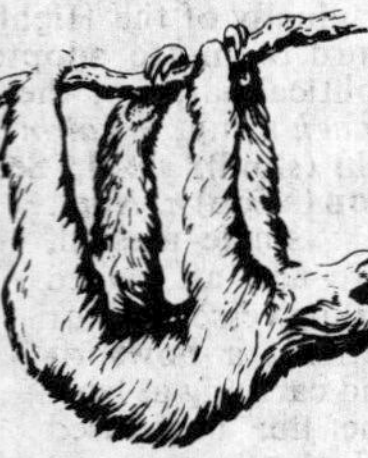

THREE-TOED SLOTH
(Head and body about 21 inches long)

sloth bear A black bear of India and Ceylon (genus *Melursus*), feeding mainly on honey and fruit.

sloth·ful (slōth′fəl, slôth′-, sloth′-) *adj.* Sluggish; lazy; indolent. See synonyms under IDLE. **—sloth′ful·ly** *adv.* **—sloth′ful·ness** *n.*

slot machine A vending machine or gambling machine having a slot in which a coin is dropped to cause operation.

slouch (slouch) *v.i.* **1** To have a downcast or drooping gait, look, or posture. **2** To hang or droop in a careless manner, as a hat. —*n.* **1** A hanging down awkwardly or carelessly; movement or appearance caused by depression or drooping. **2** An awkward or incompetent person. [Origin uncertain] **—slouch′y** *adj.* **—slouch′i·ly** *adv.* **—slouch′i·ness** *n.*

slough[1] (slou *for defs. 1 and 4;* slōō *for defs. 2 and 3*) *n.* **1** A place of deep mud or mire; bog. **2** A depression in a prairie, often dry but sometimes deeply miry, forming part of the natural drainage system. **3** A stagnant swamp, backwater, bayou, inlet, or pond in which water backs up: also spelled *slew, slue.* **4** A state of moral depravity or of despair. [OE *slōh*] **—slough′y** *adj.*

slough[2] (sluf) *n.* **1** Dead tissue separated and thrown off from the living parts, as in gangrene; also, a scab. **2** The skin of a serpent that has been or is about to be shed; cast. —*v.t.* **1** To cast off, as dead from living tissue; shed. **2** To discard; shed, as a habit or a growth; get rid of as useless or needless. —*v.i.* **3** To be cast off. **4** To cast off a slough or tissue; form a scab. [ME *slouh*] **—slough·y** *adj.*

Slough (slou) A municipal borough of SE Buckingham, England.

Slo·vak (slō′vak, slō·vak′) *n.* **1** One of a Slavic people of NW Hungary and parts of Moravia, who united with the Czechs to form the Czechoslovak republic in 1918: now in central Czechoslovakia. **2** The dialect of Czechoslovakian spoken by the Slovaks. —*adj.* Of or pertaining to the Slovaks or to their language. Also **Slo·vak·i·an** (slō·vak′ē·ən, -vä′kē·ən). [<Czech *slovák* a Slav]

Slo·vak·i·a (slō·vak′ē·ə, -vä′kē·ə) The eastern geographical region and a former province (1920–39 and 1945–49) of Czechoslovakia; an independent state, under German protection, 1939–45; divided into six administrative regions, 1949; 18,897 square miles; capital, Bratislava. *Czech* **Slo·ven·sko** (slô′ven·skô).

slov·en (sluv′ən) *n.* One who is careless of dress or of cleanliness; one habitually untidy. [Cf. Flemish *sloef* dirty] **—slov′en·li·ness** *n.* **—slov′en·ly** *adj.* & *adv.*

Slo·vene (slō′vēn, slō·vēn′) *n.* One of a group of southern Slavs now living in NW Yugoslavia. —*adj.* Of or pertaining to the Slovenes or to their language. [<G *Slowene*]

Slo·ve·ni·a (slō·vē′nē·ə) A constituent republic of NW Yugoslavia; 7,717 square miles; capital, Ljubljana: formerly part of the Austro-Hungarian Empire.

Slo·ve·ni·an (slō·vē′nē·ən) *adj.* Of or pertaining to Slovenia, its people, or their language. —*n.* The South Slavic language of the Slovenes.

slow (slō) *adj.* **1** Having relatively small velocity; not quick in motion, performance, or occurrence; not advancing or growing rapidly. **2** Behind the standard time: said of a timepiece. **3** Taking sufficient time; not precipitate or hasty: *slow* to anger. **4** Dull or tardy in comprehending; mentally sluggish: a *slow* student. **5** Lacking promptness, spirit, or liveliness; also, colloquially, dull or tedious in character. **6** Denoting a condition of a racetrack that retards the horses' speed, but in less degree than a muddy or heavy track: a *slow* track. —*v.t.* **1** To make slow or slower; cause to go at a slower pace; slacken in speed: often with *up* or *down.* **2** To retard; delay. —*v.i.* **3** To go or become slow or slower: often with *up* or *down.* —*adv.* In a slow or cautious manner or speed. ◆ Homophone: *sloe.* [OE *slāw*] **—slow′ly** *adv.* **—slow′ness** *n.*

Synonyms (adj.): deliberate, dilatory, drowsy, dull, gradual, inactive, inert, lingering, moderate, slack, sluggish, tardy. *Tardy* is applied to that which is behind the proper or desired time, especially in doing work or arriving at a place; *slow* applies to that which is a relatively long time in passing from one point to another, or in beginning or executing something. A person is *deliberate* who takes a noticeably long time to consider and decide before acting, or who acts or speaks as if he were deliberating at every point; a person is *dilatory* who lays aside, or puts off as long as possible, necessary or required action. *Gradual* signifies advancing by steps, and refers to *slow* but regular and sure progression. *Slack* refers to action that seems to indicate a lack of tension, as of muscle or of will, *sluggish* to action that seems as if reluctant to advance. See GRADUAL, HEAVY, RELUCTANT, TEDIOUS. *Antonyms*: see synonyms for IMPETUOUS, NIMBLE.

slow-down (slō′doun′) *n.* A slackening of pace.

slow match A slowly burning fuse used in firing explosives.

slow-mo·tion (slō′mō′shən) *adj.* Pertaining to or designating a motion picture filmed at greater than standard speed so that the action appears slow in normal projection.

slow·poke (slō′pōk′) *n. Slang* A person who works or moves at an exceedingly slow pace; a laggard.

slow·worm (slō′wûrm′) *n.* A blindworm.

sloyd (sloid) *n.* A system of elementary manual training originating in Sweden, having exercises graduated from the simplest use of tools to the most complete joinery: also spelled *sloid, slojd.* [<Sw. *slöjd* skill]

slub (slub) *v.t.* **slubbed, slub·bing** To twist (slivers of wool) slightly in preparation for spinning. —*n.* **1** A slightly twisted roll of cotton, wool, or silk. **2** A thick, uneven lump in yarn. [Origin unknown]

sludge (sluj) *n.* **1** Soft, water-soaked mud; mire. **2** A slush of snow or broken or half-formed ice. **3** Muddy or pasty refuse of various kinds, as that produced by the action of a rock drill and in the purification of sewage. **4** The sediment in a water tank or boiler. [<earlier *slutch.* ? Related to SLUSH.] **—sludg′y** *adj.*

slue[1] (slōō) *v.* **slued, slu·ing** *v.t.* **1** To cause to move sidewise, as if some portion were pivoted; swing, slide, or skid to the side. **2** To cause to twist or turn in its seat or fastenings: said of a boom or mast. —*v.i.* **3** To move sidewise. —*n.* The act of sluing around sidewise; a skidding or pivoting about; also, the position of a body that has slued. Also spelled *slew.* [Origin unknown]

slue[2] (slōō) See SLEW[3].

slue[3] (slōō) See SLOUGH[1] (def. 3).

slug[1] (slug) *n.* **1** A bullet or shot of irregular or oblong shape, especially as used in old muskets. **2** *Printing* **a** A strip of type metal, thicker than a lead and less than type-high, for spacing matter, etc. **b** A metal strip bearing a type-high number, abbreviated title, or the like, used as a compositor's mark. **3** A slungshot, or its metal weight. **4** Any small chunk of metal; especially, one used as a coin in automatic machines, as dial telephones. **5** *Physics* A unit of mass; the mass of a body which, when acted upon by a force of one pound, acquires an acceleration of one foot per second per second: it has the value of about 32.174 pounds or 14.59 kilograms, and is also called *geepound.* —*v.* **slugged, slug·ging** *v.i.* To take shape to fit the grooves of a rifle, as a bullet. —*v.t.* To load with slugs. [Origin uncertain. ? Akin. to SLAG.]

slug[2] (slug) *n.* **1** Any of numerous terrestrial gastropod mollusks related to snails but having only a rudimentary shell concealed in the mantle, or none at all. **2** The larva of certain insects, as the sawfly, resembling a slug. **3** A sluggard. [ME *slugge* a sluggard, ? <Scand. Cf. dial. Norw. *slugg* a large, heavy object.]

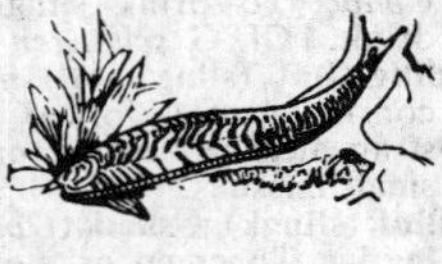

SLUG

slug[3] (slug) *Colloq. n.* **1** A heavy blow, as with the fist or a baseball bat. **2** A drink of undiluted liquor. —*v.t.* **slugged, slug·ging** To strike heavily or brutally, or without science, as with the fist or a baseball bat. [Origin uncertain] **—slug′ger** *n.*

slug·a·bed (slug′ə·bed′) *n.* One who lounges late in bed, because of laziness.

slug·gard (slug′ərd) *n.* A person habitually lazy or idle; a drone. —*adj.* Lazy; sluggish. [<SLUG[2] + -ARD]

slug·gish (slug′ish) *adj.* **1** Having little motion or power of motion; slow; inactive; torpid. **2** Habitually idle and lazy. **3** Not active; slow; stagnant: a *sluggish* season. See synonyms under HEAVY, IDLE, SLOW, TEDIOUS. **—slug′gish·ly** *adv.* **—slug′gish·ness** *n.*

sluice (slōōs) *n.* **1** Any artificial channel for conducting water, or the stream so conducted; specifically, a body of water controlled by a floodgate. **2** A floodgate. **3** A flume. **4** *Mining* A board trough having at the bottom baffles holding quicksilver to separate gold from placer dirt carried through the trough by a current of water. **5** That through which anything issues or flows. —*v.* **sluiced, sluic·ing** *v.t.* **1** To wet or drench, water or irrigate by or as by means of a sluice. **2** To wash in or by a sluice. **3** To draw out or conduct by or through a sluice. **4** To send (logs) down a sluiceway. —*v.i.* **5** To flow out or issue from a sluice. [<OF *escluse* <L *exclusa,* pp. fem. of *excludere* shut out]

sluice·gate (slōōs′gāt′) *n.* The gate of a sluice; a watergate or floodgate.

sluice·way (slōōs′wā′) *n.* An artificial channel for the passage of water; a sluice, as in mining; flume.

sluit (slōōt) *n. Afrikaans* A narrow, natural or artificial channel, through which water flows; a gully.

slum[1] (slum) *n.* A squalid, dirty, overcrowded street or section of a city, marked by the poverty and poor living conditions of its inhabitants. —*v.i.* **slummed, slum·ming** To visit slums, as for reasons of curiosity or philanthropy. [<slang E, a room; ult. origin unknown] **—slum′mer** *n.* **—slum′ming** *n.*

slum[2] (slum) *n. Slang* Slumgullion.

slum·ber (slum′bər) *v.i.* **1** To sleep, especially lightly or quietly. **2** To be inactive; stagnate. —*v.t.* **3** To spend or pass in sleeping. See synonyms under REST. —*n.* Sleep; formerly,

light sleep; more recently, complete, quiet sleep. [OE *slumerian* < *slūma*] —**slum′ber·er** *n.* —**slum′ber·ing·ly** *adv.* —**slum′ber·less** *adj.*

slum·ber·ous (slum′bər·əs) *adj.* Inviting to, being in, suggesting, or resembling slumber; soporific; drowsy; sleepy. Also **slum·brous** (slum′brəs). —**slum′ber·ous·ly** *adv.* —**slum′·ber·ous·ness** *n.*

slum·ber·y (slum′bər·ē) *adj.* Slumberous; somnolent.

slum·gul·lion (slum·gul′yən) *n.* **1** *Slang* **a** A stew made principally of meat and vegetables. **b** A weak beverage. **2** A servant, especially one who performs menial chores. **3** Refuse drainage from blubber; also, fish offal. **4** A reddish, muddy deposit in mine sluiceways. [< slang E; origin uncertain]

slum·gum (slum′gum′) *n.* The residue of propolis, cocoons, etc., after beeswax is extracted from honeycombs.

slum·lord (slum′lôrd′) *n.* A landlord of a slum dwelling. [< SLUM + (LAND)LORD]

slump (slump) *v.i.* **1** To break through a crust, as of snow or ice, and sink; sink, as a foot, into any soft material. **2** To slide with perceptible motion down a declivity: said of loose earth or rock. **3** To fall or fail suddenly, as in value or quality. **4** To stand, walk, or proceed with a stooping posture; slouch: He *slumps* badly. —*n.* **1** The act of slumping; a collapsing fall. **2** A collapse or failure; also, a sudden fall of prices: a *slump* in stocks. **3** A decline, as of interest, excitement, etc. [Prob. imit.]

slung (slung) Past tense and past participle of SLING.

slung·shot (slung′shot′) *n.* A weight attached to a thong or cord, used as a weapon.

slunk (slungk) Past tense and past participle of SLINK. —*n.* The body of a stillborn animal, especially of a calf when cut away from the mother's womb. See SLINK.

slur (slûr) *v.t.* **slurred, slur·ring 1** To slight; disparage; depreciate. **2** To pass over lightly or hurriedly; suppress; conceal: to *slur* a fact. **3** To pronounce, as a syllable, hurriedly and indistinctly. **4** *Music* **a** To sing or play as indicated by the slur. **b** To mark with a slur. **5** To smear; soil; contaminate. —*n.* **1** A disparaging remark or insinuation; also, the occasion for it, or the resulting state; a stigma. **2** *Music* **a** A curved line (⌣ or ⌢) indicating that tones so tied are to be sung to the same syllable or performed without a break between them. **b** The legato effect indicated or produced by this mark. **3** A blur. **4** A slurred pronunciation. [< dial. E, orig. fluid mud]

slurp (slûrp) *v.t.* & *v.i.* *Slang* To sip noisily. [Imit.]

slur·ry (slûr′ē) *n. pl.* **·ries 1** Any one of several watery mixtures used to make repairs in furnace linings, to neutralize poisonous chemicals, etc. **2** A mixture used in making Portland cement. [See SLUR.]

slush (slush) *n.* **1** Soft, sloppy material, as melting snow or soft mud. **2** Greasy material used for lubrication, etc. **3** The greasy refuse of cooking, especially from a ship's galley: used on shipboard for lubricating the masts. **4** A mixture of lime with white lead or tallow, for coating bright iron or steel parts of machinery to keep them from rusting. **5** Emotional talk or writing; gush; drivel. —*v.t.* **1** To cover or daub with slush, as for lubrication. **2** To fill (spaces in masonry) with mortar: usually with *up.* **3** To wash by throwing water upon, as a deck. [Origin unknown] —**slush′y** *adj.*

slush fund *U.S.* **1** Formerly, on naval vessels, money obtained from the sale of garbage and used to buy small luxuries. **2** Money collected or spent for corrupt purposes, as bribery, lobbying, propaganda, etc.

slut (slut) *n.* **1** A female dog; bitch. **2** A slatternly woman. **3** A drudge. **4** A woman of loose character; hussy. [Origin uncertain]

slut·tish (slut′ish) *adj.* Slatternly; dirty. —**slut′tish·ly** *adv.* —**slut′tish·ness** *n.*

sly (slī) *adj.* **sli·er** or **sly·er, sli·est** or **sly·est 1** Artfully dexterous in doing things secretly; cunning in evading notice or detection. **2** Playfully clever; roguish; mischievous. **3** Meanly or stealthily clever; crafty. **4** Done with or marked by artful secrecy: a *sly* trick. **5** Skilful; possessed of practical ability; wise. See synonyms under INSIDIOUS. —**on the sly** In a stealthy way; with concealment. [< ON *slægr*] —**sly′ness** *n.*

sly·boots (slī′bōōts′) *n. Colloq.* A roguish, cunning, and sly person or animal.

sly·ly (slī′lē) See SLILY.

Sm *Chem.* Samarium (symbol Sm).

smack[1] (smak) *n.* **1** A quick, sharp sound, as of the lips when separated rapidly; a noisy kiss. **2** A sounding blow or slap. **3** The sound of a snapping whip. —*v.t.* & *v.i.* To give or make a smack, as in tasting, kissing, striking, etc.; slap. [Cf. MDu. *smack* a blow]

smack[2] (smak) *v.i.* **1** To have a taste or flavor, especially as tested by smacking: usually with *of.* **2** To have, keep, or disclose a slight suggestion: with *of.* —*n.* **1** A suggestive tincture, taste, or flavor. **2** A mere taste; smattering. [OE *smæc* taste]

smack[3] (smak) *n.* A small, decked or half-decked vessel of various rig used chiefly for fishing; especially, one having a well for fish in its hold. [< Du. *smak, smacke*]

smack·ing (smak′ing) *adj.* Making a sharp sound; hence, brisk; lively: a *smacking* breeze. —*n.* A quick, sharp sound; smack.

smaik (smāk) *n. Scot.* A rascal; petty rogue.

Smal·kal·dic League (smôl·kôl′dik) See SCHMALKALDIC LEAGUE.

small (smôl) *adj.* **1** Comparatively less than another or than a standard; diminutive; little. **2** Being of slight moment, weight, or importance. **3** Lacking in moral or mental breadth; narrow; ignoble; mean; paltry. **4** Lacking in the qualities of greatness; not largely gifted. **5** Acting or transacting business in a limited way. **6** Weak in characteristic properties; mildly alcoholic: said of liquors: *small* beer. **7** Having little body or volume; slender; fine; soft, as a voice. **8** Of low degree; obscure. **9** Lacking in power or strength. —**to feel small** To feel humiliated. —*adv.* **1** In a low or faint tone: to sing *small.* **2** Into small pieces. **3** In a small way; trivially; also, timidly; to talk *small.* —*n.* **1** A small or slender part: the *small* of the back. **2** A small thing or quantity. [OE *smæl*] —**small′ness** *n.*

Synonyms (adj.): diminutive, fine, little, mean, microscopic, minute, narrow, petty, puny, tiny. See FINE[1], INSIGNIFICANT, LITTLE.

small·age (smô′lij) *n.* Celery, especially in the wild state. [< SMALL + F *ache* wild celery < L *apium* parsley]

small arms Arms that may be carried on the person, as a rifle, automatic pistol, or revolver.

small beer 1 Insipid or weak beer. **2** *Brit.* An insignificant person or thing.

small calorie See under CALORIE.

small capital A capital letter cut slightly larger than the lower-case letters of a specified type size. Abbr. *s.c., s. cap., small cap., sm. cap.*

THIS LINE IS IN CAPITAL LETTERS
THIS LINE IS IN SMALL CAPITAL LETTERS
this line is in lower-case letters

small circle The circumference formed by a plane cutting a sphere but not passing through its center.

small-clothes (smôl′klōthz′, -klōz′) *n. pl.* Close-fitting knee breeches worn by men in the 18th century. Also *smalls.*

small craft 1 Small vessels collectively. **2** Small things or persons generally.

small-fry (smôl′frī′) *n. pl.* **1** Small, young fish. **2** Young children. **3** Small or insignificant people or things.

small hours The early hours of the morning.

small·ish (smô′lish) *adj.* Somewhat small.

small-minded (smôl′mīn′did) *adj.* **1** Having a petty mind; interested in trivialities. **2** Narrow; intolerant; ungenerous.

small·mouth (smôl′mouth′) *n.* An American black bass *(Micropterus dolomieu).*

small potatoes *U.S. Colloq.* Unimportant, insignificant persons or things.

small·pox (smôl′poks′) *n. Pathol.* An acute, infectious, highly contagious disease caused by a filtrable virus and characterized by high inflammatory fever, followed by an eruption of deep-seated pustules; variola.

smalls (smôlz) *n. pl.* **1** Small-clothes. **2** *Brit. Colloq.* The first examination after matriculation; responsions: used at Oxford to denote the first university examination counting toward a degree. [< SMALL]

small stores Small, miscellaneous items, as tobacco, soap, thread, etc., stocked by a ship's store to be sold to the crew.

small sword 1 A light sword used on dress occasions. **2** The straight sword of modern fencing, introduced about 1700.

small talk Unimportant or trivial conversation.

small-time (smôl′tīm′) *adj. U.S. Slang* Petty; unimportant.

smalt (smôlt) *n.* A deep-blue glass colored with cobalt oxide: used when pulverized for painting, etc. [< F < Ital. *smalto* < Gmc.]

smalt·ite (smôl′tīt) *n.* A tin-white to steel-gray cobalt arsenide, crystallizing in the isometric system. Also **smalt·ine** (smôl′tin, -tēn). [< SMALT]

smal·to (smäl′tō) *n. pl.* **·ti** (-tē) *Italian* Colored glass, or a piece of it, employed in mosaics.

smar·agd (smar′agd) *n. Obs.* A green precious stone, as the beryl or the emerald. Also **smar′agde.** [< L *smaragdus* < Gk. *smaragdos.* Doublet of EMERALD.] —**sma·rag·dine** (smə·rag′dēn, -din) *adj.*

sma·rag·dite (smə·rag′dīt) *n.* A thin, foliated, light grass-green variety of amphibole.

smarm (smärm) *Brit. Colloq. v.t.* To smear or plaster (the hair) with oil. —*v.i.* To behave in a servilely flattering manner; toady. [Var. of dial. E *smalm* smear, plaster]

smarm·y (smär′mē) *adj. Brit. Colloq.* Unctuously flattering; oily; toadying.

smart (smärt) *v.i.* **1** To experience a stinging sensation, generally superficial, either bodily or mental. **2** To cause a stinging sensation. **3** To experience remorse. **4** To have one's feelings hurt. **5** To pay a severe penalty. —*v.t.* **6** To cause to smart. —*adj.* **1** Quick in thought or action; bright; acute; clever. **2** Impertinently witty: often used contemptuously. **3** Vigorous; emphatic; severe; brisk. **4** Causing a smarting sensation; stinging; pungent. **5** Keen or sharp, as a trade; shrewd. **6** In active health; well. **7** *Colloq.* Superior, as in speed, strength, or skill. **8** *Colloq.* Large; considerable: a *smart* crop of wheat. **9** Sprucely dressed; showy. **10** Belonging to the stylish classes; fashionable: a *smart* set. **11** Making a creditable showing: a *smart* regiment. See synonyms under CLEVER. —*n.* **1** An acute stinging sensation, as from a scratch or an irritant. **2** Any distress; poignant mental suffering. **3** *Dial.* A degree, number, or amount: with *right*: a right *smart* of people. [OE *smeortan*] —**smart′ly** *adv.* —**smart′ness** *n.*

smart al·eck (al′ik) *Colloq.* A cocky, offensively conceited person. —**smart-al·eck·y** (smärt′al′ik·ē) *adj.*

smart·en (smär′tən) *v.t.* To improve in appearance; make smart, as oneself or one's habitation: with *up.*

smart money 1 *Law* Damages awarded against a defendant because of great aggravation attending the wrong committed. **2** *Colloq.* Money paid for a release from an engagement or from a painful situation. **3** Money paid by an employer to a workman injured in his service. **4** *Brit.* Money allowed to soldiers or sailors for injuries received in the service. **5** Money bet by gamblers who supposedly know the result of a contest beforehand.

smart set Fashionable society.

smart·weed (smärt′wēd′) *n.* Any of several species of widely distributed herbs (genus *Polygonum*) having jointed stems, long, grasslike leaves, and inconspicuous, greenish flowers, especially the **common smartweed** or water pepper. Also called *knotweed.*

smart·y (smär′tē) *n. pl.* **smart·ies** *Slang.* A person affecting to be smart or witty; a smart aleck.

smash (smash) *v.t.* **1** To break in many pieces suddenly, as by a blow, pressure, or collision. **2** To flatten; crush: to *smash* a hat. **3** To dash or fling violently so as to crush or break in pieces. **4** To strike with a sudden blow. **5** To make bankrupt. **6** To destroy, as a theory. **7** In tennis, to strike (the ball) with a hard, swift, overhand stroke. —*v.i.* **8** To go bankrupt; fail, as a business, etc. **9** To

move or be moved with force; come into violent contact so as to crush or be crushed; collide; dash: The boats *smashed* together. See synonyms under BREAK. **— to go to smash** *Colloq.* To be ruined; fail. **—** *n.* **1** An act or instance of smashing, or the state of being smashed: often compounded with *up*: a *smash–up* on a railroad. **2** Any disaster or sudden break–up of any kind: a *smash* in business. **3** A beverage of spirituous liquors, usually brandy, with mint, water, sugar, and ice. **4** In tennis, a strong overhand shot. **5** *Colloq.* Something acclaimed by the public: The film is a box–office *smash.* [Prob. imit.] **— smash′er** *n.*

smash·ing (smash′ing) *adj. Colloq.* Extremely impressive; overwhelmingly good: a *smashing* success.

smash–up (smash′up′) *n.* A smash; a disastrous collision.

smat·ter (smat′ər) *v.t.* To talk of, dabble in, study, or use superficially. **—** *n.* A slight knowledge. [ME *smateren,* ? <Scand. Cf. Sw. *smattra* patter.] **— smat′ter·er** *n.*

smat·ter·ing (smat′ər·ing) *n.* **1** A superficial degree or kind of anything, especially of knowledge. **2** A little bit or a few.

smear (smir) *v.t.* **1** To spread, rub, or cover with grease, paint, dirt, etc.; bedaub. **2** To spread or apply in a thick layer or coating: to *smear* grease on an axle. **3** To sully the reputation of; defame; slander. **4** *U.S. Slang* To defeat utterly; overwhelm or stop. **5** To cover with smear (def. 3). **6** *Obs.* To anoint. **—** *v.i.* **7** To be or become smeared. **—** *n.* **1** A soiled spot; stain. **2** A small quantity of material, as blood, sputum, etc., placed on a microscope slide or bacterial culture for analysis. **3** A volatile flux for glazing ware. **4** *Obs.* Ointment; grease. **5** A slanderous attack; defamation. **6** *Slang* Anything to spread on bread, as butter, jam, etc. [OE *smerian* < *smeoru* grease]

smear·case (smir′kās′) *n. U.S.* Cottage cheese. [<G *schmierkäse*]

smear·y (smir′ē) *adj.* **smear·i·er, smear·i·est** Greasy, viscous, or staining; also, smeared. **— smear′i·ness** *n.*

smeath (smēth) *n.* A smew. Also **smee** (smē).

smed·dum (smed′əm) *n. Scot. & Brit. Dial.* **1** Fine ore particles that have passed through a wire sieve; fine coal slack. **2** Powder; especially, ground malt. **3** Vigor of mind; sense.

smeek (smēk) *v. & n. Scot.* Smoke. **— smeek′y** *adj.*

smell (smel) *v.* **smelled** or **smelt, smell·ing** *v.t.* **1** To perceive by means of the nose and its olfactory nerves. **2** To perceive the odor or perfume of; scent. **3** To test by odor or smell. **4** To discover, detect, or seek to know, as if by smelling: often with *out.* **—** *v.i.* **5** To emit an odor or perfume; give off a particular odor: frequently with *of*; also, to give indications of, as if by odor: to *smell* of treason. **6** To be malodorous. **7** To use the sense of smell. **8** To pry; investigate: with *about.* **—** *n.* **1** That special sense by means of which odors are perceived. **2** The sensation excited through the olfactory nerves. **3** That which is directly perceived by this sense; an odor; perfume. **4** A faint suggestion; hint; trace. **5** An act of smelling. [ME *smellen*]

Synonyms (noun): aroma, bouquet, fragrance, odor, perfume, savor, scent, stench, stink. *Smell* is the generic word including all the rest. *Aroma, fragrance,* and *perfume* are ordinarily pleasing; *odor, savor,* and *scent* may be so. *Odor* is nearly synonymous with *smell,* but is susceptible of more delicate use; as, the *odor* of incense. An *aroma* is a delicate and spicy *odor,* as of fine coffee; *bouquet* is said chiefly of the delicate *odor* of certain wines. We speak of the *fragrance* or *perfume* of flowers, but *fragrance* is more delicate; a *perfume* may be so strong and rich as to be repulsive by excess. There is a tendency to restrict the application of *perfume* to the artificial preparations called collectively "perfumery." *Scent* is chiefly used for the characteristic *odor* of an animal by which it is tracked or avoided by other animals; the word is also applied to any *odor,* natural or artificial, especially when faintly diffused through the air; as, the *scent* of mignonette or of new-mown hay. *Savor* is chiefly said of the appetizing *odor* evolved from articles of food by the processes of cooking. Any *smell* that is at once foul, strong, and pervasive may be called a *stench.* See SAVOR.

smell·er (smel′ər) *n.* **1** One who smells (anything). **2** *Slang* The nose. **3** A feeler, as of an animal.

smell·feast (smel′fēst′) *n. Archaic* **1** A person who frequents good tables. **2** A greedy sponger; parasite.

smelling salts Pungent or aromatic salts, or mixtures of such, often scented, used as stimulants by smelling; specifically, a preparation of ammonium carbonate.

smell·y (smel′ē) *adj.* **smell·i·er, smell·i·est** Having an unpleasant smell; malodorous.

smelt[1] (smelt) *v.t. Metall.* **1** To reduce (ores) by fusion in a furnace. **2** To obtain (a metal) from the ore by a process including fusion. **—** *v.i.* **3** To melt or fuse, as a metal. [<MDu. *smelten* melt]

smelt[2] (smelt) *n. pl.* **smelts** or **smelt** Any of certain small silvery food fishes (genus *Osmerus* or a related genus), of the northern Atlantic and Pacific. [OE]

smelt[3] (smelt) Alternative past tense and past participle of SMELL.

smelt·er (smel′tər) *n.* **1** One engaged in smelting ore. **2** An establishment for smelting: also **smelt′er·y.**

Sme·ta·na (sme′tä·nä), **Bedřich,** 1824–84, Czech composer.

Smeth·wick (smeth′wik) A county borough of southern Staffordshire, England.

smew (smyōō) *n.* A small merganser (*Mergus albellus*) of northern parts of the Old World. The male is black and white, with a white crest. Also called *smeath, smee.* [Origin unknown]

smid·die (smid′ē) *n. Scot.* A smithy. Also **smid′dy.**

smidg·en (smij′ən) *n. U.S. Colloq.* A tiny bit or part; mite; trifle.

Smig·ly–Rydz (shmēg′wē·rēts), **Edward,** 1886–1943?, Polish marshal; ruled Poland 1935–39.

smi·la·ca·ceous (smī′lə·kā′shəs) *adj. Bot.* Of or pertaining to a family (*Smilacaceae*) of herbs or woody–stemmed vines, having dioecious flowers and globular fruits. [<NL <L *smilax.* See SMILAX.]

smi·la·cin (smī′lə·sin) *n.* Parillin.

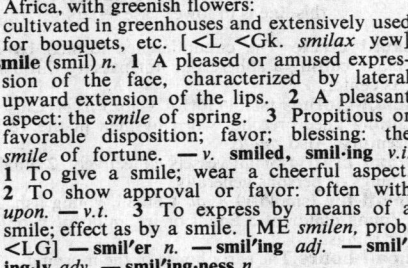

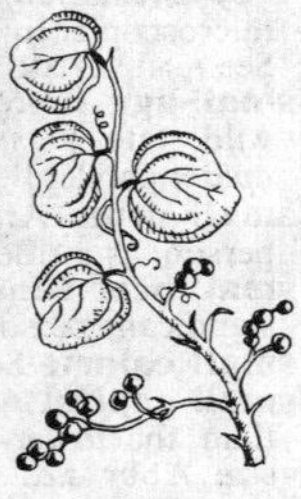
SMILAX
Greenbrier.

smi·lax (smī′laks) *n.* **1** Any of a large, widely scattered genus (*Smilax*) of shrubby or herbaceous plants having net–veined leaves, dioecious flowers in umbels, and globular fruit, especially *S. aristolochiifolia,* a source of sarsaparilla: also called *catbrier, greenbrier.* **2** A delicate twining plant (*Asparagus asparagoides*) of the lily family, from South Africa, with greenish flowers: cultivated in greenhouses and extensively used for bouquets, etc. [<L <Gk. *smilax* yew]

smile (smīl) *n.* **1** A pleased or amused expression of the face, characterized by lateral upward extension of the lips. **2** A pleasant aspect: the *smile* of spring. **3** Propitious or favorable disposition; favor; blessing: the *smile* of fortune. **—** *v.* **smiled, smil·ing** *v.i.* **1** To give a smile; wear a cheerful aspect. **2** To show approval or favor: often with *upon.* **—** *v.t.* **3** To express by means of a smile; effect as by a smile. [ME *smilen,* prob. <LG] **— smil′er** *n.* **— smil′ing** *adj.* **— smil′ing·ly** *adv.* **— smil′ing·ness** *n.*

Smiles (smīlz), **Samuel,** 1812–1904, Scottish writer and physician.

smirch (smûrch) *v.t.* **1** To soil, as by contact with grime; smear. **2** Figuratively, to defame; degrade: to *smirch* a reputation. **—** *n.* The act of smirching, or the state of being smirched; a smutch; smear; a moral stain or defect. See synonyms under BLEMISH. [ME *smorchen,* appar. <OF *esmorcher* hurt, torment]

smirk (smûrk) *v.i.* To smile in a silly, self–complacent, or affected manner. **—** *n.* An affected or artificial smile. Also *Obs.* **smerk.** [OE *smercian*] **— smirk′ing·ly** *adv.*

smit (smit) *Brit. Dial. v.t.* **1** To destroy. **2** To infect. **—** *n.* **1** A smutch; spot. **2** Infection.

smite (smīt) *v.* **smote** (*Obs.* **smit**), **smit·ten** or **smit** or **smote, smit·ing** *v.t.* **1** To strike (something). **2** To strike a blow with (something); cause to strike. **3** To cut, sever, or break by a blow: usually with *off* or *out.* **4** To strike with disaster; afflict; destroy by a catastrophe. **5** To affect powerfully with sudden feeling; in the passive, to affect with love. **6** To cause to feel regret or remorse: His conscience *smote* him. **7** To affect as if by a blow; come upon suddenly: The thought *smote* him. **8** To kill by a sudden blow. **—** *v.i.* **9** To come with sudden force; also, to knock against something: His knees *smote* together. See synonyms under BEAT. [OE *smītan*] **— smit′er** *n.*

smith (smith) *n.* **1** One who shapes metals by hammering: often used in combination: *goldsmith, tinsmith.* **2** A blacksmith. [OE]

Smith (smith), **Adam,** 1723–90, Scottish economist. **— Alfred Emanuel,** 1873–1944, U.S. politician. **— Edmund Kirby,** 1824–93, American Confederate general and educator. **— Francis Hopkinson,** 1838–1915, U.S. civil engineer, artist, and author. **— Goldwin,** 1823–1910, English historian. **— Captain John,** 1579–1631, English adventurer; president of Virginia Colony 1608. **— Joseph,** 1805–44, founder and first prophet of the Mormon Church; assassinated. **— Sydney,** 1771–1845, English clergyman and author. **— Theobald,** 1859–1934, U.S. pathologist. **— Walter Bedell,** 1895–1961, U.S. Army officer and diplomat. **— William,** 1769–1839, English geologist. **— Sir William,** 1813–93, English classical scholar. **— William Robertson,** 1846–94, Scottish theologian and author.

smith·er·eens (smith′ə·rēnz′) *n. pl. Colloq.* Fragments produced as by a blow. Also **smith′·ers.** [Cf. dial. E (Irish) *smidirin* a fragment]

smith·er·y (smith′ər·ē) *n. pl.* **·er·ies** **1** The art or trade of a smith. **2** A smith's shop; a smithy.

Smith·son (smith′sən), **James,** 1765–1829, English chemist: known in his youth as James Lewis Macie.

Smith·so·ni·an Institution (smith·sō′nē·ən) An institution founded in 1846 at Washington, D.C., from funds left by James Smithson "for the increase and diffusion of knowledge among men."

smith·son·ite (smith′sən·īt) *n.* **1** A vitreous zinc carbonate, $ZnCO_3$. **2** *Brit.* Hemimorphite. [after James *Smithson*]

Smith Sound (smith) A sea passage between Ellesmere Island and NW Greenland; 45 miles wide.

smith·y (smith′ē, smith′ē) *n. pl.* **smith·ies** A blacksmith's shop; a forge.

smit·ten (smit′n) Alternative past participle of SMITE. **—** *adj.* **1** Struck with sudden force; gravely afflicted. **2** Having the affections suddenly attracted.

smock (smok) *n.* **1** A loose outer garment of light material worn like a coat to protect one's clothes. **2** In colonial times, a woman's undergarment; chemise. **—** *v.t.* **1** To furnish with or clothe in a smock. **2** To shirr (def. 1). See SMOCKING. [OE *smoc*]

smock–frock (smok′frok′) *n.* A loose–fitting outer garment or jacket worn by laborers.

smock·ing (smok′ing) *n.* Shirred work; decorative stitching holding fullness in regular patterns.

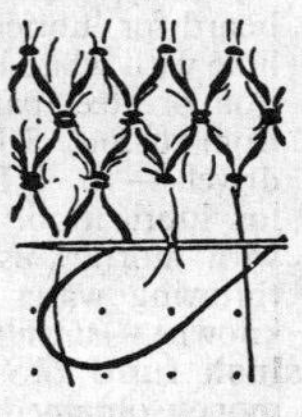
SMOCKING

smog (smog) *n. Colloq.* A combination of smoke and fog, especially as seen in and about heavy industry and manufacturing areas. [Blend of SM(OKE) + (F)OG]

smok·a·ble (smō′kə·bəl) *adj.* Capable of being smoked. **—** *n.* Something to be smoked, as a cigarette, cigar, etc.: usually in the plural.

smoke (smōk) *n.* **1** The volatilized products of the combustion of an organic compound, as coal, wood, etc., charged with fine particles of carbon or soot; less properly, fumes, steam, etc. **2** *Chem.* A colloid system of solid particles in a gas. See COLLOID SYSTEM. **3** Anything transient and unsubstantial; a useless or ephemeral result. **4** The act of smoking a pipe, cigar, etc. **5** A period of time during which one smokes tobacco. **6** *Colloq.* A cigarette, cigar, or pipeful of tobacco. **7** A chemical–warfare agent producing a smoke-like cloud; also, a smudge. **8** A column of smoke, used as a signal by the North American Indians. **9** *U.S. Slang* In baseball, speed in a pitch. **10** A cheap drink, usually of wood

alcohol. —*v.* **smoked, smok·ing** *v.i.* **1** To emit or give out smoke: The embers *smoke;* also, to emit smoke excessively or in an undesired direction, as a stove or lamp. **2** To raise dust in rapid riding or driving; hence, to travel rapidly; speed. —*v.t.* **3** To inhale and exhale the smoke of (tobacco, opium, etc.); also, to use, as a pipe, for this purpose. **4** To treat or affect with smoke; treat by the application of smoke; cure; medicate; fumigate; tinge; flavor with smoke. **5** To apply smoke to in order to drive away or expel: to *smoke* bees; hence, to force out of hiding: usually with *out:* to *smoke* out a criminal. **6** To get the scent of; hence, to suspect. **7** To change the color of (glass, etc.) by darkening with smoke. [OE *smoca*]

smoke candle A small, portable, short-burning smokepot.

smoke helmet A protective headdress, such as worn by soldiers, firemen, etc., for protection against poisonous gas fumes and smoke.

smoke·house (smōk′hous′) *n.* **1** A building or close room in which meat, fish, hides, etc., are cured by the action of smoke. **2** A building in which anything is disinfected by the use of smoke.

smoke·jack (smōk′jak′) *n.* A mechanism by which to turn a roasting spit, operated by the ascending combustion gases in a chimney.

smoke·jump·er (smōk′jum′pər) *n.* A fireman trained and equipped to fight forest fires when parachuted to the affected area by aircraft.

smoke·less (smōk′lis) *adj.* Having or emitting little or no smoke: *smokeless* powder.

smoke·pot (smōk′pot′) *n.* A small container for generating a dense cloud of smoke.

smok·er (smō′kər) *n.* **1** One who or that which smokes; one who smokes tobacco habitually. **2** A firebox for blowing smoke upon bees to quiet them. **3** A smoking car. **4** A social gathering of men. **5** A smoking jacket.

smoke screen A dense cloud of smoke emitted to screen an attack or bombardment by land or sea, or to cover a retreat. Also **smoke blanket.**

smoke·stack (smōk′stak′) *n.* **1** An upright pipe, usually of sheet or plate iron, through which combustion gases from a boiler furnace are discharged into the air. **2** The funnel of a steamboat or locomotive, or the tall chimney of a factory, etc.

smoke·tree (smōk′trē′) *n.* **1** An ornamental Old World shrub or tree *(Cotinus coggygria)* with long feathery stalks resembling smoke or mist. **2** A related American species *(C. americanus).*

smoking jacket A short coat worn instead of a regular suit coat as a lounging jacket.

smok·y (smō′kē) *adj.* **smok·i·er, smok·i·est 1** Giving forth smoke. **2** Mixed with or containing smoke: *smoky* air. **3** Liable to be filled with smoke, as a house. **4** Emitting smoke improperly and unpleasantly, as from bad draft. **5** Discolored with smoke. **6** Smoke-colored; dark-gray. **7** Covered with mist: said of certain mountains. —**smok′i·ly** *adv.* —**smok′i·ness** *n.*

Smoky Hill River A river in Colorado and Kansas, flowing 560 miles east, SE, north, and NE, joining the Republican River to form the Kansas River.

Smoky Mountains See GREAT SMOKY MOUNTAINS.

smol·der (smōl′dər) *v.i.* **1** To burn and smoke in a smothered way, showing little smoke and no flame. **2** Figuratively, to exist in a latent state; to manifest suppressed feeling: His wrath was *smoldering.* —*n.* Smother; smoke. Also spelled *smoulder.* [Dissimilated var. of ME *smorther.* See SMOTHER.]

Smo·lensk (smô·lyensk′) A city on the Dnieper in western Russian S.F.S.R.

Smol·lett (smol′it), **Tobias George,** 1721–71. English novelist and physician.

smolt (smōlt) *n.* A young salmon on its first descent from the river to the sea. [? Related to SMELT[2]]

smooch (smōōch) *n.* A smear; a smutch. —*v.t.* To smear; smudge. —*v.i. Slang* To neck. [Cf. SMUTCH]

smoor (smōōr) *Scot. v.t.* To smother. —*n.* Stifling smoke or atmosphere.

smooth (smōōth) *adj.* **1** Having a surface without irregularities; not rough; continuously even. **2** Having no impediments or obstructions; easy; free from shocks or jolts. **3** Calm and unruffled; bland; pleasant; mild. **4** Flowing melodiously: opposed to *rugged:* a *smooth* style. **5** Suave, as in speech; flattering: often implying deceit. **6** *Phonet.* Sounded without the aspirate: opposed to *rough:* a *smooth* breathing. **7** Free from hair; beardless. **8** Having no acidulous or astringent taste or quality: said of liquors. **9** Without lumps; having the elements perfectly blended: a *smooth* mayonnaise. **10** Offering no resistance to a body sliding along its surface; without friction. **11** Having the high points removed by wear, as the surface of a tire. —*adv.* Calmly; evenly. —*v.t.* **1** To make smooth or even on the surface. **2** To make easy or less difficult: to *smooth* one's path. **3** To free from obstructions. **4** To remove (an obstruction): often with *away:* to *smooth* away a mound. **5** To render less harsh or softer and more flowing: to *smooth* one's verses. **6** To soften the worst features of; palliate; extenuate: usually with *over.* **7** To make calm; mollify: to *smooth* one's feelings. —*v.i.* **8** To become smooth. Also **smooth′en.** —**to smooth (someone's) ruffled feathers** To mollify. —*n.* **1** The smooth portion or surface of anything: the *smooth* of the neck. **2** The act of smoothing. [OE *smōth*] —**smooth′er** *n.* —**smooth′ly** *adv.* —**smooth′ness** *n.*

Smooth may appear as a combining form in hyphemes; as in:

smooth-ankled	**smooth-headed**
smooth-barked	**smooth-limbed**
smooth-billed	**smooth-necked**
smooth-bodied	**smooth-paced**
smooth-browed	**smooth-polished**
smooth-cheeked	**smooth-riding**
smooth-combed	**smooth-rimed**
smooth-cut	**smooth-sculptured**
smooth-edged	**smooth-sided**
smooth-filed	**smooth-skinned**
smooth-fibered	**smooth-sliding**
smooth-flowing	**smooth-speaking**
smooth-fronted	**smooth-stalked**
smooth-gliding	**smooth-stemmed**
smooth-going	**smooth-surfaced**
smooth-grained	**smooth-tempered**
smooth-haired	**smooth-voiced**
smooth-handed	**smooth-woven**

Synonyms (adj.): even, flat, glossy, level, plain, plane, polished, sleek, undisturbed, unruffled. An *even* surface is free from any considerable irregularities, as knobs, or splinters, or abrupt changes of direction or curvature; a *smooth* surface is one that the hand may be passed over without friction or in which the eye discerns no noticeable break or flaw. That which is *polished* is brought to a very high degree of smoothness, so as to be not only frictionless to touch but lustrous to the eye. A board is sawed to an *even* surface, planed till it is *smooth,* and sandpapered till it is *polished.* A thing may be *smooth* or *polished* and yet very uneven, as a warped piece of veneering. See BLAND, BLUNT, CALM, FINE[1], LEVEL, PACIFIC. *Antonyms*: see synonyms for ROUGH.

smooth·bore (smōōth′bôr′, -bōr′) *n.* A firearm, as a shotgun, with an unrifled bore. Also **smooth bore.**

smooth breathing See under BREATHING.

smooth-faced (smōōth′fāst′) *adj.* **1** Beardless. **2** Of smooth surface, as a wall, etc. **3** Bland or mild in expression, especially with deceitful intent.

smooth-shod (smōōth′shod′) *adj.* Shod without sharp projections on the shoes, as a horse.

smör·gås·bord (smôr′gəs·bôrd, *Sw.* smœr′·gōs·bōrd) *n.* Scandinavian hors d'oeuvres. Also spelled **smor′gas·bord.** [< Sw.]

smor·zan·do (zmôr·tsän′dō) *adj. Music* Fading away; growing softer. [< Ital.]

smote (smōt) Past tense of SMITE.

smoth·er (smuth′ər) *v.t.* **1** To prevent the respiration of, as by filling or covering the mouth and nostrils; also, to kill by such means; suffocate; stifle. **2** To cover, or cause to smolder, as a fire. **3** Figuratively, to hide or suppress: to *smother* a scandal. **4** In cooking, to enclose and cook in a covered dish or under a close mass of some other substance. **5** To daub; smear. —*v.i.* **6** To be covered without vent or air, as a fire. **7** To be hidden or suppressed, as wrath. —*n.* **1** That which smothers, as stifling vapor or dust. **2** The state of being smothered; suppression; also, a smoldering fire. **3** A surging of foam or water; a welter. [Earlier *smorther.* Related to OE *smorian* suffocate] —**smoth′er·y** *adj.*

smouch (smōōch, smouch) *v.t. Dial.* To lift; pilfer.

smoul·der smōl′dər) See SMOLDER.

smout·y (smōō′tē) *adj. Scot.* Smutty; obscene. Also **smout′ie, smoot′ie.**

smudge (smuj) *v.* **smudged, smudg·ing** *v.t.* **1** To smear; soil. **2** To protect (from frost, insects, etc.) by a heavy, smoky pall. —*v.i.* **3** To cause a smudge. **4** To be smudged. —*n.* **1** A soiling, as of dry dirt or soot; smear; stain. **2** A smoky fire or its smoke for driving away insects, preventing frost, etc. **3** Paint-pot scrapings and cleanings. [Var. of SMUTCH] —**smudg′i·ly** *adv.* —**smudg′i·ness** *n.* —**smudg′y** *adj.*

smug (smug) *adj.* **smug·ger, smug·gest 1** Characterized by a smoothly self-satisfied or extremely complacent air. **2** Trim; neat; spruce, especially with suggestions of respectability or self-satisfaction. [Cf. LG *smuk* neat] —**smug′ly** *adv.* —**smug′ness** *n.*

smug-faced (smug′fāst′) *adj.* Having a prim, self-satisfied face or expression.

smug·gle (smug′əl) *v.* **·gled, ·gling** *v.t.* **1** To take (merchandise) into or out of a country without payment of lawful duties. **2** To bring in or introduce illicitly or clandestinely. —*v.i.* **3** To engage in or practice smuggling. [< LG *smuggeln*]

smug·gler (smug′lər) *n.* **1** One who smuggles. **2** A vessel used in smuggling.

smug·gling (smug′ling) *n.* The offense or practice of fraudulently and illegally importing or exporting merchandise without payment of lawful duties.

smut (smut) *n.* **1** The blackening made by soot, smoke, etc. **2** Obscenity; obscene language. **3** Any of various fungus diseases of plants, in which the affected parts change into a dusty black powder. **4** The parasitic fungus (order *Ustiliginales*) causing such a disease. —*v.* **smut·ted, smut·ting** *v.t.* **1** To blacken or stain, as with soot or smoke. **2** To affect with smut, as growing grain. **3** To remove the smut from (grain). **4** Figuratively, to pollute; defame. —*v.i.* **5** To give off smut. **6** To be or become stained. **7** To be affected with smut, as growing grain. [< LG *schmutt* dirt]

smutch (smuch) *v.* & *n.* Soil; smear; smudge. [Cf. MHG *smutzen* smear] —**smutch′y** *adj.*

Smuts (smuts), **Jan Christiaan,** 1870–1950, South African statesman and general.

smut·ty (smut′ē) *adj.* **·ti·er, ·ti·est 1** Soiled with smut; black; stained. **2** Affected by smut: *smutty* corn. **3** Obscene; coarse; indecent. —**smut′ti·ly** *adv.* —**smut′ti·ness** *n.*

Smyr·na (smûr′nə) A port of western Turkey in Asia, on the **Gulf of Smyrna,** an inlet of the Aegean 35 miles long: Turkish *Izmir.* —**Smyr′ni·ot** (-nē·ot), **Smyr′ni·ote** (-nē·ōt) *adj.* & *n.*

smyte·rie (smī′trē, smit′rē) *n. Scot.* A numerous collection of small things. Also **smy′trie.**

Smyth (smith), **Henry De Wolf,** born 1898, U.S. physicist.

Sn *Chem.* Tin (symbol Sn). [< L *stannum*]

snack (snak) *n.* **1** A sip or bite. **2** A slight, hurried meal. **3** A share of something. [Orig. a verb < MDu. *snacken* bite, snap]

snaf·fle (snaf′əl) *n.* A horse's bit without a curb, jointed in the middle. Also **snaf′fle·bit′** (-bit′). —*v.t.* **·fled, ·fling** To control with a snaffle. [< Du. *snavel* muzzle]

sna·fu (sna·fōō′) *Slang adj.* In a state of utter confusion; chaotic. —*v.t.* **·fued, ·fu·ing** To put into a confused or chaotic condition. —*n.* Anything which is confused or chaotic. [< S(ituation) n(ormal), a(ll) f(ouled) u(p)]

snag (snag) *n.* **1** A jagged or stumpy knot or protuberance, especially the stumpy base of a branch left in pruning. **2** The root or remnant of a tooth remaining in the jaw; also, a projecting tooth. **3** A branch or point of a deer's antler. **4** The trunk of a tree fixed in

add,āce,câre,pälm; end,ēven; it,īce; odd,ōpen,ôrder; tŏŏk,pōōl; up,bûrn; ə = a in *above,* e in *sicken,* i in *clarity,* o in *melon,* u in *focus;* yōō = u in *fuse,* oi,oil; ou,pout; ch,check; g,go; ng,ring; th,thin; th,this; zh,vision. Foreign sounds à,œ,ü,kh,ṅ; and ◆: see page xx. < from; + plus; ? possibly.

the bottom of a river, bayou, etc., by which boats are sometimes pierced. 5 Hence, any unsuspected or hidden obstacle or difficulty. —*v.* **snagged, snag·ging** *v.t.* 1 To injure, destroy, or impede by or as by a snag. 2 To clear of snags. 3 *Colloq.* To block; impede. —*v.i.* 4 To run upon a snag: said especially of river craft. [Prob. <Scand. Cf. dial. Norw. *snag* sharp point, projection.] **—snagged** *adj.*

snag boat A vessel equipped with machinery for removing snags from river beds.

snag chamber A watertight room or compartment in the bow of a river steamboat to keep the boat from sinking if snagged.

snag·gle-tooth (snag′əl·tōōth′) *n.* A tooth that is broken, projecting, or conspicuously out of alinement with the others. **—snag′gle-toothed′** (-tōōtht′, -tōōthd′) *adj.*

snag·gy (snag′ē) *adj.* **·gi·er, ·gi·est** 1 Full of snags, as a river. 2 Full of knots or stubs, as a tree or swamp. 3 Like a snag.

snail (snāl) *n.* 1 Any of numerous gastropod mollusks of terrestrial or aquatic habit having a spiral shell, a retractile foot, and a distinct head with eyes borne on stalks or tentacles. 2 A slow or lazy person. 3 A cinnamon roll shaped like a snail shell. [OE *snægl*]

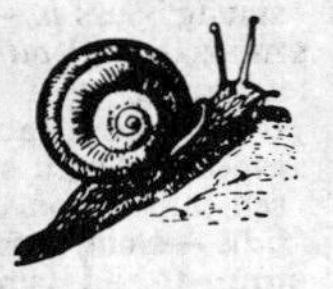

SNAIL

snail hawk The small, bluish-gray everglade kite *(Rostrhamus sociabilis plumbeus)* ranging from Florida to Mexico, that feeds on snails.

snail pace A very slow gait or advance movement. Also **snail's pace. —snail′-paced′** *adj.*

snake (snāk) *n.* 1 An ophidian reptile (suborder *Serpentes*), having a greatly elongated, scaly body, no limbs, and a specialized swallowing apparatus. The bite of most snakes is non-venomous, but some have much enlarged fangs, connected with venom glands from which a deadly poison flows into the punctures they make. ◆ Collateral adjective: *anguine.* 2 A treacherous or insinuating person. 3 A flexible, resilient wire used to clean clogged drains. etc. —*v.* **snaked, snak·ing** *v.t. Colloq.* To drag by seizing an end or limb and pulling forcibly or quickly; haul along the ground, as a log. —*v.i.* To wind or move like a snake. [OE *snaca*]

Snake (snāk) *n.* A member of any of various Shoshonean tribes of North American Indians, but especially the Walpapi and Yahuskin of eastern Oregon.

snake·bird (snāk′·bûrd′) *n.* One of several birds (genus *Anhinga*), with very long slender neck, frequenting southern swamps and feeding upon fish; the water turkey; the darter.

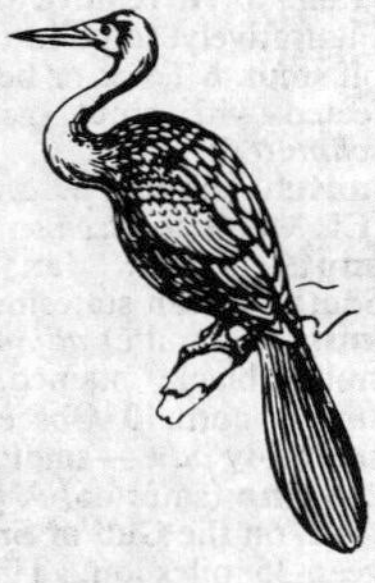

SNAKEBIRD
(Average length about 33 inches)

snake·bite (snāk′·bīt′) *n.* 1 The bite of a snake. 2 Poisoning caused by the venom of a snake.

snake charmer 1 An entertainer who charms venomous snakes by rhythmic motions of his body, and, supposedly, by music. 2 Any entertainer who handles snakes.

snake dance A ceremonial dance of the Hopi Indians of Arizona in which live rattlesnakes are carried in the mouths of the dancers. The Hopis believe the snakes to be influential with the rain gods.

snake fence A worm fence; a stake-and-rider. See under FENCE.

snake hawk The swallow-tailed kite *(Elanoides forficatus)* of North and South America.

Snake Mountains A range in eastern Nevada; highest point, 12,049 feet.

snake·mouth (snāk′mouth′) *n.* A terrestrial orchid *(Pogonia ophioglossoides)* native in eastern North America, with fragrant rose-pink flowers.

Snake River The principal tributary of the Columbia River, flowing 1,038 miles from NW Wyoming through southern Idaho, then northwards to form part of the boundary between Oregon and Idaho, to SE Washington.

snake·root (snāk′rōōt′, -rŏŏt′) *n.* 1 One of various plants having roots reputed to be effective against snakebite; especially, the bugbane; the **Seneca snakeroot** *(Polygala senega),* growing east of the Mississippi; the **Virginia snakeroot** *(Aristolochia serpentaria),* with purplish-brown flowers and fibrous roots; and the **white snakeroot** *(Eupatorium rugosum)* of Europe and the United States. 2 The root of any of these plants.

snake·skin (snāk′skin′) *n.* The skin of a snake.

snake·stone (snāk′stōn′) *n.* 1 An ammonite: so called because it resembles a fossil coiled snake. 2 Any absorbent stone-like material popularly believed to cure snakebite.

snake·weed (snāk′wēd′) *n.* The bistort.

snak·y (snā′kē) *adj.* **snak·i·er, snak·i·est** 1 Of or like a snake; serpentine; winding. 2 Insinuating; cunning; treacherous. 3 Full of snakes. **—snak′i·ly** *adv.* **—snak′i·ness** *n.*

snap (snap) *v.* **snapped, snap·ping** *v.i.* 1 To make a sharp, quick sound, as of percussion. 2 To break suddenly with a cracking noise; part with a snap. 3 To fly off or give way quickly, as when tension is suddenly relaxed. 4 To make the jaws come suddenly together in an effort to bite: often with *up* or *at.* 5 To seize or snatch suddenly: often with *up* or *at.* 6 To speak sharply, harshly, or irritably: often with *at.* 7 To emit, or seem to emit, a spark or flash of light: said of the eyes. 8 To close, fasten, etc., with a click or snapping sound, as a lock. 9 To move or act with sudden, neat gestures: He *snapped* to attention. —*v.t.* 10 To seize suddenly or eagerly, with or as with the teeth; snatch: often with *up.* 11 To sever with a snapping sound. 12 To utter, address, or interrupt harshly, abruptly, or irritably: often with *out.* 13 To cause to make a sharp, quick sound. 14 To close, fasten, etc., with a snapping sound. 15 To strike, press, etc., with a snap: to *snap* a whip. 16 To cause to move suddenly, neatly, etc. 17 To photograph instantaneously with a camera. 18 In football, to put in play: said of the ball when sent to a back by the center. **—to snap out of it** *Colloq.* 1 To recover. 2 To change one's attitude. —*n.* 1 The act of snapping, or a sharp, quick sound produced by it: the *snap* of a whip. 2 A sudden breaking of anything, or the sound so produced. 3 Any catch, fastener, or other device that closes or springs into place with a snapping sound. 4 A sudden seizing or effort to seize with or as with the teeth; a sharp shutting, as of the jaws or of a trap. 5 A quick blow of the thumb sprung from the finger or of the finger from the thumb. 6 The sudden release of the tension of a spring or elastic cord. 7 A small, thin, crisp cake, usually containing ginger; a gingersnap. 8 Brisk energy; vigor; vim; zip. 9 A brief spell; a sudden turn: said chiefly of cold weather. 10 A hasty meal; snack. 11 Any task or duty easy to perform: often in the phrase **a soft snap.** 12 A bit: It is not worth a *snap.* 13 The instantaneous taking of a photograph; also, the photograph so taken; a snapshot. 14 A stringbean. —*adj.* 1 Made or done suddenly and without consideration; offhand. 2 Contrived to take unawares and at an advantage: a *snap* policy. 3 Fastening with a snap. —*adv.* With a snap; quickly. [<MDu. *snappen* bite at]

snap·back (snap′bak′) *n.* 1 Formerly, the center in football. 2 The act of snapping back.

snap bean A wax bean.

snap·drag·on (snap′drag′ən) *n.* 1 A plant (genus *Antirrhinum)* of the figwort family, especially the **large-flowered snapdragon** *(A. majus)* having solitary axillary flowers, likened to dragons' heads. 2 Flapdragon.

snap·per (snap′ər) *n.* 1 One who or that which snaps, as a cracker. 2 A large food fish (genus *Lutianus*) of the Gulf coast, as the **red snapper** *(L. blackfordii).* 3 One of various other fishes, as the bluefish, rosefish, etc. 4 A sparoid fish *(Pagrosomus auratus),* reddish with blue bars or spots; one the most important food fishes of Australasia: also called *schnapper.* 5 A snapping turtle.

snapping beetle An elaterid beetle which by a quick, snapping movement of its body is able to right itself when on its back; especially, the eyed elater *(Alaus oculatus)* of eastern North America: also called *click beetle, skipjack.* For illustration see under INSECTS (injurious).

snapping turtle 1 A large voracious turtle of North America, especially *Chelydra serpentina,* much used as food. 2 The alligator turtle *(Macrochelys temminickii),* a related species.

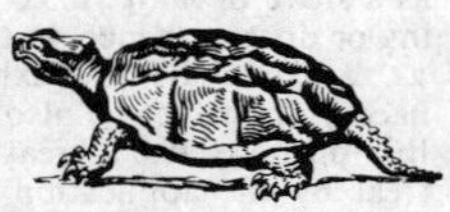

SNAPPING TURTLE
(Up to 2 feet in length; weight to 100 pounds or more)

snap·pish (snap′ish) *adj.* 1 Apt to speak crossly or tartly. 2 Disposed to snap, as a dog. See synonyms under FRETFUL. **—snap′pish·ly** *adv.* **—snap′pish·ness** *n.*

snap·py (snap′ē) *adj.* **·pi·er, ·pi·est** 1 *Colloq.* Brisk, vivid, and energetic; vivacious. 2 Smart or stylish in appearance. 3 Snappish. **—snap′pi·ly** *adv.* **—snap′pi·ness** *n.*

snap·shot (snap′shot′) *n.* A photograph taken with a small camera without timing..

snap shot A shot made without aim.

snap·weed (snap′wēd′) *n.* Any plant of the genus *Impatiens*; a touch-me-not.

snare[1] (snâr) *n.* 1 A device, as a noose, for catching birds or other animals; a gin; trap. 2 Anything by which one is brought into trouble or caused to sin; an allurement; wile. 3 *Surg.* A loop of wire used to remove tumors and other growths from the body. —*v.t.* **snared, snar·ing** 1 To catch with a snare; ensnare; entrap. 2 To capture by trickery; entice; inveigle. [<ON *snara.* Akin to SNARE[2].] **—snar′er** *n.*

snare[2] (snâr) *n.* 1 A cord to produce a rattling on a drumhead. 2 A snare drum. [<MDu., a string. Akin to SNARE[1].]

snare drum A small drum to be beaten on one head and having snares or strings of catgut stretched across the other.

snarl[1] (snärl) *n.* A sharp, harsh, angry growl; harsh or quarrelsome utterance. —*v.i.* 1 To growl harshly, as a dog. 2 To speak angrily and resentfully. —*v.t.* 3 To utter or express with a snarl. [Freq. of obs. *snar* growl] **—snarl′er** *n.* **—snarl′ing·ly** *adv.* **—snarl′y** *adj.*

snarl[2] (snärl) *n.* 1 A tangle, as of hair or yarn. 2 Any complication, perplexity, or entanglement. 3 *Colloq.* A wrangle; quarrel. 4 A knot or gnarl in wood. —*v.i.* 1 To get into a snarl or tangle; become entangled. —*v.t.* 2 To put into a snarl or tangle. 3 To confuse; entangle mentally; embarrass; make entanglements in. 4 To emboss or flute (thin metalware). [<SNARE[1]] **—snarl′er** *n.* **—snarl′y** *adj.*

snarling iron A curved tool for snarling hollow metalware, etc. Also **snarling tool.**

snash (snash, snäsh) *n. Scot.* Impertinent, abusive, or sneering language.

snatch (snach) *v.t.* 1 To seize or lay hold of suddenly, hastily, or eagerly. 2 To take or remove suddenly. 3 To take or obtain as the opportunity arises: to *snatch* a few hours of sleep. 4 *Slang* To kidnap. —*v.i.* 5 To attempt to seize swiftly and suddenly: with *at.* 6 To accept with great eagerness: with *at.* —*n.* 1 An act of snatching; a hasty grab or grasp: usually with *at.* 2 A brief period: a *snatch* of rest. 3 A small amount; fragment: *snatches* of a conversation; *snatches* of melody. 4 *Slang.* A kidnaping. [ME *snacchen.* ? Related to SNACK.] **—snatch′er** *n.*

snatch block *Naut.* A single block having an opening in one cheek to receive a rope, and usually having a swivel hook.

snatch·y (snach′ē) *adj.* Interrupted; spasmodic.

snath (snath) *n.* The long curved handle of a scythe. Also **snathe** (snāth). [Var. of dial. E *snead,* OE *snǣd*]

snaw (snô, snä) *v.* & *n. Scot.* Snow.

sneak (snēk) *v.i.* 1 To move or go in a stealthy manner. 2 To act with covert cowardice or servility. —*v.t.* 3 To put, give, transfer, move, etc., secretly or stealthily. 4 *Colloq.* To pilfer. —*n.* 1 One who sneaks; a mean, cowardly fellow. 2 *pl. Colloq.* Sneakers. 3 A stealthy movement. —*adj.* Stealthy; covert: a *sneak* attack. [Akin to OE *snīcan* creep]

sneak boat A small, shallow boat used for duck hunting. Also **sneak-box** (snēk′boks′).

sneak·er (snē′kər) *n.* 1 One who sneaks; a sneak. 2 *pl. U.S. Colloq.* Rubber-soled canvas shoes.

sneak·ing (snē′king) *adj.* 1 Cringing; meanly secret and underhand. 2 Secretly entertained

or cherished; unavowed: a *sneaking* suspicion. See synonyms under BASE[2]. — **sneak′ing·ly** *adv.*

sneak thief One who steals small miscellaneous articles, without violence, by sneaking in through unfastened doors or windows.

sneak·y (snē′kē) *adj.* **sneak·i·er, sneak·i·est** Like a sneak; sneaking. — **sneak′i·ly** *adv.* — **sneak′i·ness** *n.*

snecked (snekt) *adj.* **1** Twisted to one side of the vertical plane of the shank, as the point of a fish hook. **2** Built of rubblework. [? Related to SNATCH]

sned (sned) *v.t. Scot.* To cut; trim; lop off.

sneer (snir) *n.* **1** A grimace of contempt or derision made by slightly raising the upper lip and nostrils. **2** A mean or contemptuous insinuation; a fling. — *v.i.* **1** To make or show a sneer. **2** To express derision or contempt in speech, writing, etc. — *v.t.* **3** To utter with a sneer or in a sneering manner. See synonyms under SCOFF. [ME *sneren*; ult. origin uncertain] — **sneer′er** *n.* — **sneer′ing** *adj.* — **sneer′·ing·ly** *adv.*

Synonyms (noun): fling, gibe, jeer, scoff, taunt. A *sneer* may be simply a contemptuous facial contortion or some brief satirical utterance that throws a contemptuous sidelight on what it attacks without attempting to prove or disprove. The *jeer* and *gibe* are uttered; the *gibe* is bitter, and often sly or covert; the *jeer* is rude and open. A *scoff* may be in act or word, and is commonly directed against that which claims honor, reverence, or worship. A *fling* is careless and commonly pettish; a *taunt* is intentionally insulting and provoking; the *sneer* is supercilious; the *taunt* is defiant. See SCORN.

sneesh (snēsh) *n. Scot.* Snuff. Also **sneesh′ing.**

sneeze (snēz) *v.i.* **sneezed, sneez·ing** *v.i.* To drive air forcibly and audibly out of the mouth and nose by a spasmodic involuntary action. — *v.t.* To utter with or as with a sneeze: often with *out.* — **not to be sneezed at** *Colloq.* Of a character entitling to consideration. — *n.* An act of sneezing: also **sneez′ing.** [Misreading of ME *fnese*, OE *fnēosan* sneeze] — **sneez′er** *n.* — **sneez′y** *adj.*

sneeze gas A sternutator.

sneeze·weed (snēz′wēd′) *n.* Any plant of a genus (*Helenium*) of the composite family, especially *H. autumnale*: from the effect of the powdered leaves and flowers when snuffed up: also called *bitterweed.*

sneeze·wort (snēz′wûrt′) *n.* **1** A perennial Eurasian plant (*Achillea ptarmica*) resembling the yarrow. Its powdered dry leaves produce sneezing. **2** Sneezeweed.

snell[1] (snel) *n.* A short line of gut, horsehair, etc., bearing a fish hook, to be attached to a longer line. [Origin unknown]

snell[2] (snel) *adj.* **1** *Scot.* Sharp; keen; piercing. **2** Austere; severe. **3** Nimble; quick.

Snel·len test (snel′ən) *Med.* A test for determining visual acuity performed by reading a standard set of graded letters at a specified distance. [after Herman *Snellen*, 1834–1908, Dutch opthalmologist, who devised it]

snick (snik) *n.* **1** A small cut; nick; snip. **2** A knot in thread or the like. **3** In cricket, a glancing hit. — *v.t.* **1** To cut a nick in. **2** To hit (a ball) a glancing blow. — **to snick and snee** To thrust and cut. [Back formation < *snick or snee.* See SNICKERSNEE.]

snick·er (snik′ər) *n.* A half-suppressed or smothered laugh. — *v.i.* To utter a snicker; laugh slyly and foolishly with audible catches of the voice; giggle. — *v.t.* To utter or express with a snicker. Also *snigger.* [Imit.]

snick·er·snee (snik′ər·snē′) *n.* **1** A fight with knives. **2** A knife suitable for thrusting and cutting. Also **snick and snee, snick′-a-snee, snick or snee.** [Alter. of earlier *snick or snee* thrust or cut, ult. <Du. *steken* thrust + *snijen* cut]

snide (snīd) *adj.* Malicious or derogatory; nasty. — *n.* A snide person. [Origin unknown]

sniff (snif) *v.i.* **1** To breathe through the nose in short, quick, audible inhalations. **2** To express contempt, etc., by sniffing: often with *at.* **3** To inhale a scent in sniffs. — *v.t.* **4** To breathe in through the nose; inhale. **5** To smell or attempt to smell with sniffs: to *sniff* smoke. **6** To perceive as if by sniffs: to *sniff* peril. **7** To express (contempt) by sniffs. — *n.* **1** An act or the sound of sniffing. **2** Perception by or as by sniffing; that which is inhaled by sniffing. [Appar. back formation <SNIVEL]

snif·fle (snif′əl) *v.i.* **·fled, ·fling** **1** To snuffle. **2** To snivel or whimper; whine; sniff. — *n.* A snuffle. [Freq. of SNIFF]

snif·fy (snif′ē) *adj.* **·fi·er, ·fi·est** *Colloq.* Disposed to sniff or be disdainful or scornful.

snif·ter (snif′tər) *n.* **1** A liquor glass, pear-shaped, with a small opening to concentrate the aroma. **2** *U.S. Slang* A small drink of liquor, usually a dram. [< *snift*, var. of SNIFF]

snig·ger (snig′ər) *n.* A snicker, especially a derisive snicker. — *v.i.* To snicker, especially in derision. [Var. of SNICKER] — **snig′ger·er** *n.*

snig·gle (snig′əl) *v.t.* **·gled, ·gling** *Brit.* **1** To fish for or catch, as eels, by thrusting the bait into their hiding places. **2** To entrap, as in a net; ensnare. [< dial. E *snig* eel]

snip (snip) *v.* **snipped, snip·ping** *v.t.* To clip, remove, or cut with a short, light stroke or strokes of scissors or shears: often with *off.* — *v.i.* To cut with small, quick strokes. — *n.* **1** An act of snipping. **2** A small piece snipped off. **3** *U.S. Colloq.* A small or insignificant person or thing. **4** *pl.* Small shears for cutting metal. [<Du. *snippen*]

snipe (snīp) *n. pl.* **snipe** or **snipes** **1** A shore bird (genus *Capella*), allied to the woodcock and much esteemed as a game bird; especially, the common **European** or **whole snipe** (*C. gallinago*), and the common **American** or **Wilson's snipe** (*C. delicata*). **2** One of other snipelike birds, as the **lesser snipe** or **jack snipe** of Europe (*Limnocryptes minimus*). **3** *U.S. Slang* A cigarette or cigar butt. — *v.i.* **sniped, snip·ing** **1** To hunt or shoot snipe. **2** To shoot at or pick off individual enemies from cover or ambush. **3** *U.S. Slang* To hunt for cigarette or cigar butts. [<ON *snipa*]

snip·er (snī′pər) *n.* One who shoots an enemy from cover; a sharpshooter.

snip·er·scope (snī′pər·skōp′) *n.* An electronic optical device which may be mounted on a carbine or rifle in order to permit accurate night-firing by means of infrared rays focused on a fluorescent screen.

snip·pet (snip′it) *n.* **1** A small piece snipped off. **2** A small portion or share.

snip·pet·y (snip′it·ē) *adj.* **1** Arrogant; brusk; snippy. **2** Trivial, as if composed of little pieces snipped off; small; trifling.

snip·py (snip′ē) *adj.* **·pi·er, ·pi·est** *Colloq.* **1** Supercilious; pert; impertinent. **2** Fragmentary.

snit (snit) *n. Colloq.* An irritable or angry mood: usually preceded by *in* or *into*: The affront put him in a *snit.* [Origin unknown]

snitch (snich) *Slang v.t.* To grab quickly; steal. — *v.i.* To inform; peach: usually with *on.* [? Var. of SNATCH]

snits (snits) *n. pl.* Slices of dried fruit, especially of dried apples. [<Pennsylvania Dutch *schnitz* sections of apple]

sniv·el (sniv′əl) *v.i.* **·eled** or **·elled, ·el·ing** or **·el·ling** To cry in a snuffling manner; run at the nose; snuffle; make affectedly tearful professions. — *n.* **1** Discharge from the nose. **2** The act of sniveling. [OE (assumed) *snyflan* < *snyflung* mucus from the nose] — **sniv′el·er** *n.* — **sniv′el·ing** *adj.* & *n.*

snob (snob) *n.* **1** One who makes birth, wealth, or education the sole criterion of worth. **2** One who is cringing to superiors and overbearing with inferiors in position. **3** *Obs. Brit.* A scab; rat: said of a workingman. [Origin uncertain] — **snob′ber·y** *n.*

snob·bish (snob′ish) *adj.* Pertaining to, characteristic of, or befitting a snob or snobs. — **snob′bish·ly** *adv.* — **snob′bish·ness** *n.*

snod (snod) *Scot. v.t.* To make trim or neat; prune; tidy. — *adj.* Neat; also, sly; demure.

snood (snōōd) *n.* **1** A small meshlike cap or bag attached to the back of a hat, worn by women to keep the hair in place. **2** *Scot.* A fillet formerly worn about the hair by an unmarried woman in Scotland as an emblem of virginity. — *v.t.* To bind with a snood, as hair. [OE *snōd*]

snook (snōōk, snŏŏk) *v.i.* **1** *Scot.* To sniff. **2** To lurk. — *n.* **1** A smell; sniff; a bite. **2** *Slang* An informer.

snook·er (snŏŏk′ər) *n.* A pool game played with fifteen red object balls (one point each) and six variously colored object balls (2 to 7 points). The player pocketing a red ball may try for any varicolored ball. When all red balls have been pocketed, the varicolored balls must be played in order. Also **snooker pool.** [Origin uncertain]

snool (snōōl) *Scot. v.i.* **1** To snivel. **2** To yield submissively. — *n.* One who is meanly subservient.

snoop (snōōp) *Colloq. v.i.* To look or pry into things with which one has no business; thrust one's nose into things. — *n.* One who snoops: also **snoop′er.** [<Du. *snoepen* eat goodies on the sly] — **snoop′y** *adj.*

snoop·er·scope (snōō′pər·skōp) *n.* An optical device operating on the same principle as the sniperscope but designed for carrying in the hand or on the head.

snoot (snōōt) *n. Colloq.* A person's nose or face; also, a grimace. [Var. of SNOUT]

snoot·y (snōō′tē) *adj.* **snoot·i·er, snoot·i·est** *U.S. Colloq.* Conceited or supercilious.

snooze (snōōz) *Colloq. v.i.* **snoozed, snooz·ing** To sleep lightly; doze. — *n.* A short and light sleep. [Origin uncertain]

Sno·qual·mie Falls (snō·kwol′mē) A waterfall of 270 feet in the **Snoqualmie River,** a river flowing 45 miles west and NW in central Washington from the Cascade Range east of Seattle.

snore (snôr, snōr) *v.i.* **snored, snor·ing** To breathe in sleep through the nose and open mouth, with a hoarse rough noise and rattling vibrations of the soft palate. — *n.* An act or the noise of snoring. [Imit.] — **snor′er** *n.*

snor·kel (snôr′kəl) *n.* **1** A long ventilating tube capable of extending from a submerged submarine to the surface of the water. **2** A similar device used for underwater breathing. — *v.i.* To swim with a snorkel. [<G *Schnorkel*] — **snor′kel·er** *n.*

snort (snôrt) *v.i.* **1** To force the air violently and noisily through the nostrils, as spirited horses. **2** To express indignation, ridicule, etc., by a snort. **3** *Colloq.* To laugh with a boisterous outburst. — *v.t.* **4** To utter or express by snorting. **5** To expel by or as by a snort. — *n.* **1** The act or sound of snorting. **2** *Slang* A small drink. [ME *snorten.* ? Related to SNORE.] — **snort′er** *n.*

snot (snot) *n.* **1** Mucus from or in the nose: a vulgar usage. **2** *Slang* A low or mean fellow. [OE *gesnot*]

snot·ty (snot′ē) *adj.* **·ti·er, ·ti·est** **1** Dirtied with snot: a vulgar usage. **2** *Slang* Contemptible; mean; paltry. **3** *Slang* Impudent; proudly conceited; saucy.

snout (snout) *n.* **1** The forward projecting part of a beast's head, especially of a swine's; proboscis; muzzle. **2** Some similar anterior prolongation of the head of an animal, as the rostrum of a gastropod or that of a weevil. **3** Something resembling a hog's snout, such as the nozzle of a hose, a pipe, or the like; a blunt projection, as of rock; or, contemptuously, a person's nose. — *v.t.* To provide with a snout or nozzle. [ME *snūte.* Related to OE *snȳtan* blow the nose.]

snout beetle The curculio.

snow[1] (snō) *n.* **1** Precipitation taking the form of minute ice crystals formed from an aqueous vapor in the air when the temperature is below 32° F., and usually falling in irregular masses or flakes. ◆ Collateral adjective: *nival.* **2** A similar aggregation that resembles snow in being white or composed of flakes: a *snow* of blossoms. **3** A fall of snow; snowstorm. **4** A winter. **5** *Slang* Cocaine. **6** The pattern of snowlike drops appearing on a television screen as a result of weakened signals in a receiver. — *v.i.* **1** To fall as snow: usually used impersonally: It is *snowing.* — *v.t.* **2** To scatter or cause to fall as or like snow. **3** To cover, enclose, or

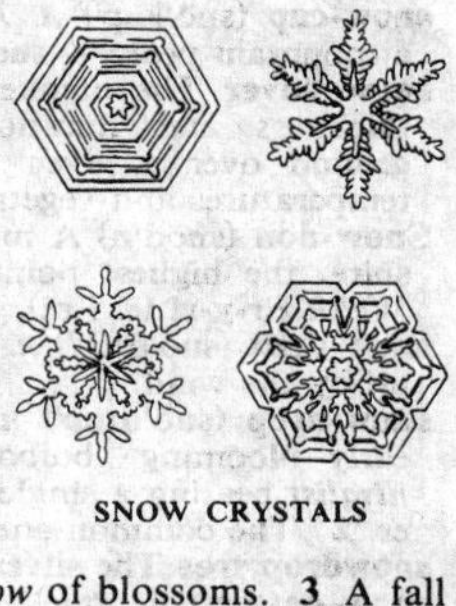

SNOW CRYSTALS

obstruct with snow: with *in, over, under,* or *up.* [OE *snāw*]

Snow may appear as a combining form in hyphemes or solidemes, or as the first element in two–word phrases; as in:

snowbank
snow–beaten
snow–blast
snow–blown
snow–bright
snow–clad
snow cloud
snow–cold
snow–colored
snow–covered
snow–crested
snow–driven
snow–field
snow–haired
snowland
snowless
snowlike
snow–lined
snow peak
snowscape
snow–tipped
snow–topped

snow[2] (snō) *n. Naut.* A two–masted square–rigged vessel characterized by having a trysail mast close behind the main mast. [<MDu. *snauw* snout]

Snow (snō), **C(harles) P(ercy),** born 1905, English physicist and novelist.

snow apple The Fameuse.

snow·ball (snō′bôl′) *n.* **1** A small round mass of snow compressed to be thrown, as in sport. **2** The guelder–rose *(Viburnum opulus)*: so called from its ball–shaped clusters of white flowers: also **snowball bush** or **tree.** —*v.i.* **1** To throw snowballs. **2** To gain in size, importance, etc., as a snowball that rolls over snow. —*v.t.* **3** To throw snowballs at.

snow·bell (snō′bel′) *n.* Any of a genus *(Styrax)* of trees and shrubs of warm regions, bearing showy white flowers in racemes; especially, *S. americana* of the SE United States.

snow·ber·ry (snō′ber′ē) *n. pl.* **·ries 1** A bushy American shrub *(Symphoricarpos albus)* having a loose, leafy cluster of snow–white berries. **2** A West Indian shrub *(Chiococca alba)* of the madder family: it produces the cainca root and is often cultivated in greenhouses for its white berries: also called *milkberry.*

snow·bird (snō′bûrd′) *n.* **1** A small finch (genus *Junco*) of northern North America, commonly seen in flocks during the winter. **2** The snow bunting. **3** *Slang* A cocaine or heroin addict.

snow blindness An impairment of vision, caused by exposure of the eye to the glare of snow. —**snow′–blind′** *adj.*

snow·blink (snō′blingk′) *n.* The dazzling scintillation of light reflected from a field of ice or snow.

snow–bound (snō′bound′) *adj.* Hemmed in or forced to remain in a place by heavy snow; snowed in.

snow bridge A natural arch formation of snow bridging a crevasse.

snow·broth (snō′brôth′, -broth′) *n.* **1** Melted snow or snow and water mixed. **2** Any very cold liquid.

snow bunting A bird (genus *Plectrophenax*), especially *P. nivalis* of northern regions, the male of which in the breeding season is snow–white with black markings. Also called *snowbird, snowflake.*

snow·bush (snō′boosh′) *n.* A California shrub ofthe genus *Ceanothus,* as *C. cordulatus,* that bears numerous small white flowers.

snow·cap (snō′kap′) *n.* A crest of snow, as on a mountain peak. —**snow′–capped′** *adj.*

snow cover The blanket of snow, variable in thickness and duration, which covers the ground over a given area, affecting ground temperatures and vegetation.

Snow·don (snōd′n) A mountain in Caernarvonshire, the highest point in Wales; 3,560 feet. *Welsh* **Er·y·ri** (er′i·rē).

snow·drift (snō′drift′) *n.* A pile of snow heaped up by the wind.

snow·drop (snō′drop′) *n.* **1** A low, European, early–blooming bulbous plant *(Galanthus nivalis)* bearing a single, white, drooping flower. **2** The common anemone.

snowdrop tree The silverbell.

snow–eat·er (snō′ē′tər) *n.* The chinook.

snow·fall (snō′fôl′) *n.* **1** A fall of snow. **2** The amount of snow that falls in a given period.

snow fence Portable fencing consisting of thin, closely placed pickets, used to prevent the drifting of snow over roads, fields, etc.

snow·flake (snō′flāk′) *n.* **1** One of the small feathery masses in which snow falls. **2** The snow bunting. **3** Any of certain plants (genus *Leucojum*) allied to and resembling the snowdrop; especially, the **spring snowflake** *(L. vernum),* the **summer snowflake** *(L. aestivum),* and the **autumn snowflake** *(L. autumnale).*

snow goose Any of certain North American geese (genus *Chen*) which breed in the Arctic, snow–white with black primary feathers.

snow leopard The ounce.

snow lily An attractive spring–blooming herb *(Erythronium grandiflorum)* of the lily family native in the Rocky Mountains.

snow line 1 The limit of perpetual snow on the sides of mountains, varying in position with the latitude, the season, and the climate. **2** The extreme distance north and south of the equator within which snow never falls. Also **snow limit.**

snow·man (snō′man′, -mən) *n. pl.* **·men** (-men′, -mən) A statue of a man, made of snow, and often having a hat, broom, scarf, etc.

snow·mo·bile (snō′mō·bēl) *n.* Any of various motor vehicles, often with caterpillar treads and steerable front runners, used for traveling over snow, ice, etc. [<SNOW + (AUTO)MOBILE]

snow pellets Snowlike particles sometimes precipitated from a cloud during showers.

snow plant A handsome, blood–red saprophytic herb *(Sarcodes sanguinea)* found in the rich humus of mountain forests in southern California, frequently covered with snow in its blooming season.

snow·plow (snō′plou′) *n.* Any large, plowlike device for turning fallen snow aside from a road or railroad, or for the removal of snow from such surfaces. Also **snow′plough′.**

snow pudding A pudding containing gelatin, sugar, and white of egg whipped into a snowlike foam.

snow·shed (snō′shed′) *n.* A timber structure, as one built over portions of a railway, as a protection from snow slides.

snow·shoe (snō′sho͞o′) *n.* A device, usually a network of sinew in a wooden frame, to be fastened on the foot by a strap across the toes, as a support in walking over snow. —*v.i.* **·shoed, ·shoe·ing** To walk on snowshoes.

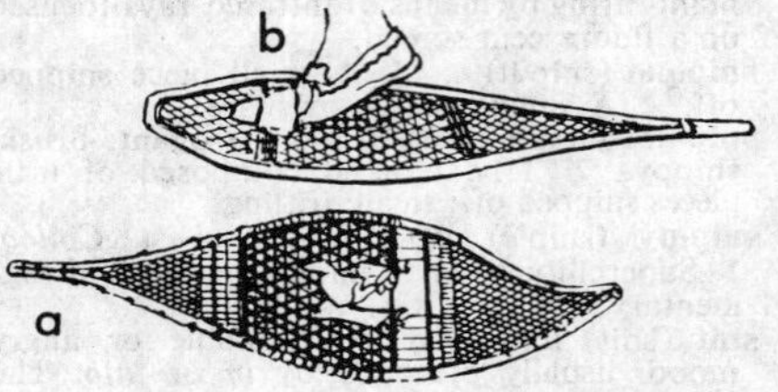

SNOWSHOES
a. Sioux Indian. *b.* Iroquois Indian.

snow·slide (snō′slīd′) *n.* An avalanche of snow.

snow·storm (snō′stôrm′) *n.* A storm with a heavy fall of snow.

snow·suit (snō′so͞ot′) *n.* A heavy outer garment worn by young children in cold weather, consisting either of one piece or of ankle–length, tight–fitting pants and a snug jacket with a hood.

snow tire An automobile tire with a heavy tread designed to provide more traction on snow or ice.

snow·y (snō′ē) *adj.* **snow·i·er, snow·i·est 1** Abounding in or full of snow. **2** Snow–white; hence, pure; unblemished; spotless: *snowy* linen. —**snow′i·ly** *adv.* —**snow′i·ness** *n.*

snowy heron The common small white egret *(Egretta thula)* of the southern United States and northern South America.

snowy owl See under OWL.

snub (snub) *v.t.* **snubbed, snub·bing 1** To treat with contempt or disdain; slight. **2** To rebuke or check with a sharp or cutting remark. **3** To stop or check, as a rope in running out, by taking a turnabout a post, etc.; also, to make fast (a boat, etc.) thus. **4** *Obs.* To clip; stunt; nip. —*adj.* Short; pug: said of the nose. —*n.* **1** An act of snubbing; a deliberate and intentional slight. **2** A sudden checking, as of a running rope or cable. **3** A snub nose. [<ON *snubba* snub] —**snub′ber** *n.*

snub–nosed (snub′nōzd′) *adj.* Having a pug or snub nose.

snuff[1] (snuf) *v.t.* **1** To draw in (air, etc.) through the nose. **2** To catch the scent of; smell; sniff; also, to examine by smelling. —*v.i.* **3** To snort; sniff. **4** To inhale air in disdain or anger. —*n.* **1** An act of snuffing; sniff; also, perception by smelling. **2** Resentment expressed by sniffing. [<MDu. *snuffen*]

snuff[2] (snuf) *n.* The charred portion of a wick. —*v.t.* **1** To crop the snuff from (a wick). **2** To put out or extinguish: with *out.* [Cf. G *schnuppe* snuff of a candle]

snuff[3] (snuf) *n.* **1** Pulverized tobacco to be inhaled into the nostrils. **2** The quantity of it taken at one time. **3** Any medicinal powder to be drawn into the nostrils. —**up to snuff** *Colloq.* **1** Meeting the usual standard, as in quality, health, etc. **2** Not easily deceived; sharp–witted. —*v.i.* To take or use snuff. [<Du. *snuf,* appar. short for *snuiftabak,* lit., tobacco to be inhaled]

snuff·box (snuf′boks′) *n.* A small box for carrying snuff about the person.

snuff color The color of snuff; yellowish brown. —**snuff′–col′ored** *adj.*

snuf·fer[1] (snuf′ər) *n.* **1** One who or that which snuffs. **2** A porpoise.

snuf·fer[2] (snuf′ər) *n.* **1** One who or that which snuffs (a candle). **2** *pl.* A scissorlike instrument for removing the snuff from a candle: also called **pair of snuffers.**

snuf·fle (snuf′əl) *v.* **·fled, ·fling** *v.i.* **1** To breathe through the nose noisily and with difficulty, as when it is obstructed by mucus. **2** To breathe noisily, as a dog following a scent. **3** To talk through the nose; snivel. —*v.t.* **4** To utter in a nasal tone. —*n.* **1** An act of snuffling, or the sound made by it. **2** *pl.* Nasal catarrh. **3** An affected nasal or emotional voice or twang; hence, cant. [Freq. of SNUFF[1]] —**snuf′fler** *n.* —**snuf′fly** *adj.*

snuff·y (snuf′ē) *adj.* **snuf·fi·er, snuf·fi·est 1** Pertaining to or like snuff. **2** Soiled with or smelling of snuff; hence, offensive; unattractive. —**snuf′fi·ly** *adv.* —**snuf′fi·ness** *adj.*

snug (snug) *adj.* **snug·ger, snug·gest 1** Closely and comfortably sheltered, covered, or situated. **2** Close or compact; having room enough, but not too much; comfortable; cozy; also, having everything closely secured; trim: said of a ship. **3** Fitting closely but comfortably, as a garment. See synonyms under COMFORTABLE. —*v.* **snugged, snug·ging** *v.t.* To make snug. —*v.i.* To snuggle; move close. —**to snug down** To make a vessel ready for a storm by reducing sail, etc. [Prob. <LG. Cf. Du. *snugger* clean, smooth.] —**snug′ly** *adv.* —**snug′ness** *n.*

snug·ger·y (snug′ər·ē) *n. pl.* **·ger·ies** A cozy and comfortable place or room.

snug·gle (snug′əl) *v.t.* & *v.i.* **·gled, ·gling** To lie or draw close; nestle; cuddle: often with *up* or *together.* [Freq. of SNUG, *v.*]

so[1] (sō) *adv.* **1** To this or that or such a degree; to this or that extent; in the same degree, quantity, or proportion: either used alone, the degree being implied or understood: Why *so* long; or followed by or preceded by a dependent expression introduced by *as, that,* or *but.* **2** In this, that, or such a manner; in the same or a like or corresponding manner; in the manner mentioned: often following a clause beginning with *as,* or preceding one beginning with *that.* **3** Just as said, directed, suggested, or implied; also, according to fact: referring to a preceding (sometimes following) statement or suggestion. **4** To an extreme degree; extremely; very. **5** The fact being thus: used as an expletive. **6** About as many or as much as stated; thereabouts: I shall stay a day or *so.* **7** At all events; in any case; at all: now only in the compounds *whosoever, whichsoever,* etc. **8** According to the truth of what is sworn to or averred: said in oaths or asseverations: *So* help me God. **9** Indeed! elliptical for *Is it so?* **10** To such an extent: used elliptically for *so much*: I love him *so*! **11** Too: used in emphatic denial: You can *so*! **12** Indicative of surprise or disapproval: *So* there you are. **13** So as to follow immediately; then; therefore. **14** Let it be that way; very well. —*conj.* **1** With the purpose that: often with *that*: They left the hotel early *so* (that) they would not encounter him. **2** In such a way that; as a consequence of which: He consented, *so* they went away. **3** *Obs.* As. —*interj.* **1** Stay still! **2** Is that so! **3** In nautical parlance, steady! [OE *swā*]

so[2] (sō) *n. Music* The fifth of the syllables used in singing the scale: also *sol.* [See GAMUT]

soak (sōk) *v.t.* **1** To place in liquid till thoroughly saturated; steep. **2** To wet thoroughly;

drench: The rain *soaks* the earth. 3 To take in through or as through pores or interstices; suck up; absorb: with *in* or *up*. 4 *Colloq.* To drink, especially to excess. 5 *U.S. Slang* **a** To charge exorbitantly. **b** To pawn. **c** To strike hard; beat. — *v.i.* 6 To remain or be placed in liquid till saturated. 7 To penetrate; pass: with *in* or *into*. 8 *U.S. Slang* To drink to excess. — *n.* 1 The process or act of soaking, or state of being soaked. 2 Liquid in which something is soaked. 3 *Slang* A hard drinker; a drinking spree. ◆ Homophone: *soke*. [OE *socian*. Akin to SUCK.]

soak·age (sō′kij) *n.* 1 The process of soaking, or the state of being soaked. 2 The quantity of liquid that soaks in or through, or seeps out.

soak·er (sō′kər) *n.* 1 One who or that which soaks. 2 *Slang* A habitual drunkard.

soak·ers (sō′kerz) *n. pl.* Short pants of absorbent material, usually wool, worn by babies over diapers.

soak·y (sō′kē) *adj.* **soak·i·er, soak·i·est** Covered or filled with moisture; steeped; soggy.

so–and–so (sō′ən·sō′) *n.* 1 An unnamed or undetermined person or thing. 2 *Colloq.* A euphemism for many offensive epithets.

soap (sōp) *n.* 1 A cleansing agent consisting of sodium or potassium salts of fatty acids, made by decomposing the glyceryl esters of fats and oils with alkalies; a detergent. *Hard* soaps are made by the use of soda, while the potash soaps are *soft*. 2 A metallic salt of one of the fatty acids. 3 *U.S. Slang* Money used for sinister purposes; hence, any means of obtaining an end. — *v.t.* To rub with soap; treat with soap. [OE *sāpe*]

soap·bark (sōp′bärk′) *n.* 1 The bark of the quillai. 2 The bark of a tropical American shrub (genus *Pithecellobium*), used as a substitute for soap. Also **soapbark tree.**

soap·ber·ry (sōp′ber′ē) *n. pl.* **·ries** 1 The fruit of any one of several trees or shrubs (genus *Sapindus*) of the family *Sapindaceae*. 2 Any one of the trees producing it, especially *S. saponaria*, of tropical America and southern Florida, the pulp of whose fruit is used in washing textile fabrics.

soap·box (sōp′boks′) *n.* 1 A box or crate for soap. 2 Any box or crate used as a platform by street orators. — **soapbox oratory** Impromptu or crude oratory, marked by vigor rather than logic. Also **soap box.**

soap·box·er (sōp′bok′sər) *n. Colloq.* A loud and ranting speaker; a street–corner orator; a tubthumper.

soap bubble 1 An inflated bubble of soapsuds, forming a hollow globule. 2 Anything attractive but unsubstantial.

soap opera A daytime television or radio drama presented serially and usually dealing with domestic themes of a highly emotional character: so called in reference to the soap commercials often presented on such programs.

soap plant Any of several plants whose bulbs are used for soap, especially a lilywort (*Chlorogalum pomeridianum*) of California.

soap·stone (sōp′stōn′) *n.* Steatite: so called from its soapy feel.

soap·suds (sōp′sudz′) *n. pl.* Soapy water, especially when worked into a foam.

soap·wort (sōp′wûrt′) *n.* A perennial herb (*Saponaria officinalis*) of the pink family having clusters of pink or whitish, often double, flowers: so called because its juice forms a lather with water. Also called *bouncing Bet.*

soap·y (sō′pē) *adj.* **soap·i·er, soap·i·est** 1 Resembling, containing, or consisting of soap. 2 Smeared with soap. 3 *Slang* Flattering.

soar (sôr, sōr) *v.i.* 1 To float aloft through the air on wings, as a bird. 2 To sail through the air without perceptibly moving the wings, as a hawk or vulture. 3 To glide without losing altitude, as an airplane. 4 To rise above any usual level: Prices will *soar* if the ceilings are removed. See synonyms under FLY[1]. — *n.* An act of soaring; a range of upward flight. [<F *essorer* <L *ex* out + *aura* breeze, air] — **soar′er** *n.*

sob (sob) *n.* A convulsive, audible inhalation of air under the impulse of painful or hysterical emotion, and usually accompanied with tears; the act or the sound of sobbing; also, any similar sound, as of the wind. Also **sob′·bing.** — *v.* **sobbed, sob·bing** *v.i.* 1 To weep with audible, convulsive catches of the breath. 2 To make a sound like a sob, as the wind. — *v.t.* 3 To utter with sobs. 4 To bring to a specified condition by sobbing: to *sob* oneself to sleep. [Imit.]

So·bat (sō′bat) A river in SE Sudan, flowing 205 miles NW from the Ethiopian border to the White Nile.

so·be·it (sō·bē′it) *n.* An amen. — *conj.* If so; if only; provided: originally **so be it.**

so·ber (sō′bər) *adj.* 1 Possessing properly controlled faculties; even–tempered; well–balanced; temperate in action or thought. 2 Grave; sedate; realizing the importance and seriousness of life. 3 Not under the influence of an intoxicant; not drunk. 4 Moderate in or abstinent from the use of intoxicating drink. 5 Of subdued or modest color. — *v.t.* & *v.i.* To make or become sober. [<OF *sobre* <L *sobrius*] — **so′ber·ly** *adv.* — **so′ber·ness** *n.*

Synonyms (adj.): abstemious, abstinent, calm, collected, cool, dispassionate, moderate, quiet, regular, sane, staid, steady, temperate, unimpassioned, unintoxicated. See SAD, SANE[1], SEDATE, SERIOUS. *Antonyms*: agitated, crazy, drunk, drunken, ecstatic, excited, extravagant, extreme, frantic, furious, immoderate, impassioned, intemperate, intoxicated, passionate, unreasonable.

So·bies·ki (sô·byes′kē), **John** See JOHN III OF POLAND.

So·bran·je (sô·brän′yə) *n.* The national assembly or legislature of Bulgaria. Also **So·bran·i·ye** (sô·brän′ē·yə), **So·bran′ye.**

so·bri·e·ty (sō·brī′ə·tē) *n. pl.* **·ties** 1 The state of being sober. 2 Moderateness in temper or conduct; sedateness; seriousness; temperance. See synonyms under ABSTINENCE. [<L *sobrietas, -tatis* <*sobrius* sober]

so·bri·quet (sō′bri·kā) *n.* A fanciful or humorous appellation; a nickname: also spelled *soubriquet*. [<F; ult. origin unknown]

sob sister *U.S. Slang* A journalist who writes mawkishly sentimental news stories.

sob story *Slang* A sad personal narrative told to elicit pity or sympathy.

soc·age (sok′ij) *n.* The feudal tenure of land by certain determinate services other than knight–service; hence, later, tenure by any fixed service other than military. [<*soc*, var. of SOKE] — **soc′ag·er** *n.*

so–called (sō′kôld′) *adj.* Called as stated; generally styled thus: usually implying a doubtful or improper form.

soc·cer (sok′ər) *n.* A form of football in which the ball is propelled toward the opponents' goal by kicking or by striking with the head or body, other than the shoulders or arms, the goalkeepers being the only players allowed to use their hands and arms in deflecting or carrying the ball: officially called *association football*. [Alter. of ASSOCIATION]

So·che (sō′che′) The Chinese name for YARKAND.

So·chi (sō′chē) A port on the Black Sea in southern Krasnodar territory, European Russian S.F.S.R.

so·cia·bil·i·ty (sō′shə·bil′ə·tē) *n.* The quality or character of being sociable. Also **so′cia·ble·ness.**

so·cia·ble (sō′shə·bəl) *adj.* 1 Inclined to seek company; social. 2 Agreeable in company; companionable; genial. 3 Characterized by or affording occasion for agreeable conversation and friendliness. See synonyms under AMICABLE, FRIENDLY. — *n.* 1 An informal social gathering: also *social*. 2 A four–wheeled open carriage with facing seats. [<F <L *sociabilis* <*socius* friend] — **so′cia·bly** *adv.*

so·cial (sō′shəl) *adj.* 1 Of or pertaining to society or its organization; relating to persons as living in society or to the public as an aggregate body: *social* life, *social* questions. 2 Disposed to hold friendly intercourse with others; sociable. 3 Constituted to live in society; having developed or fulfilled tendencies to organize in society as a race or people: *social* beings. 4 Of or pertaining to public welfare: *social* insurance. 5 Pertaining to or characteristic of persons of fashion: *social* register. 6 Living in communities: *social* ants or bees; aggregate; compound; colonial. 7 Grouping compactly, as individual plants; partly or wholly covering a large area of land: said of plant species. 8 Venereal: *social* disease: a euphemism. 9 Pertaining to or between allies or confederates, as the wars waged by Rome in 90–89 B.C., and by Athens in 357–355 B.C. against their allies. See synonyms under FRIENDLY, GOOD. — *n.* A sociable. [<L *socialis* <*socius* ally]

social climber A person who attempts to become friendly with prominent or wealthy people.

social contract *Philos.* The supposed original agreement by which individuals were united in political associations for their mutual protection, the surrender of their individual sovereignty having been made not through force but by mutual consent: a theory of Hobbes, Locke, Rousseau, etc.

Social Democrat 1 A member of the Social Democratic party of Germany, founded by Bebel and Liebknecht in 1869 and based on Marxian principles. In 1875 it was merged with Lassalle's General German Workmen's Association. Under the Republic (1918–33) it advocated the principles embedded in the Weimar Constitution. 2 A member of a similar party in other countries. — **so′cial-dem′o·crat′ic** *adj.*

social evil Prostitution.

social insurance Government insurance designed to protect wage earners against unemployment, illness, accident, or the like, and not always requiring the payment of a premium on the part of the insured.

so·cial·ism (sō′shəl·iz′əm) *n.* Public collective ownership or control of the basic means of production, distribution, and exchange, with the avowed aim of operating for use rather than for profit, and of assuring to each member of society an equitable share of goods, services, and welfare benefits: as a system of social and economic organization planned, attempted, or achieved through various methods—in **Utopian** or **Christian Socialism,** through cooperative communal groups holding all things in common (approximating the philosophic anarchism of Thoreau, Tolstoy, and Kropotkin, and the communalism and commensalism of the early and undivided church); in **Guild Socialism,** through organization of producer groups and the professions in syndicalist guilds to be represented in a federal legislative body; in **Fabian** or **British Labour Party Socialism,** through parliamentary democracy using gradualist evolutionary processes; in **Marxist–Leninist State Socialism,** through revolution, expropriation, and dictatorship of the so–called proletariat, in short, Communism. Compare MIXED ECONOMY. — **creeping socialism** Anything considered as a gradual or piecemeal encroachment upon the system of private property and free enterprise through state action: used as an epithet.

so·cial·ist (sō′shəl·ist) *n.* An advocate of socialism. — *adj.* Socialistic.

so·cial·is·tic (sō′shəl·is′tik) *adj.* Of, pertaining to, advocating, like, or practicing socialism.

Socialist Labor party A U. S. political party, originally formed in 1877 as the **Socialistic Labor party** and renamed in 1891.

Socialist party A U. S. political party formed in 1901 by the combination of a dissident group from the Socialist Labor party with the **Social Democratic party** (established in 1898 by E. V. Debs and others). After the **Social Democratic Federation,** a dissident group formed in 1936, rejoined in 1957, the name **Socialist party–Social Democratic Federation** was officially adopted.

so·cial·ite (sō′shəl·īt) *n.* A person prominent in fashionable society.

so·ci·al·i·ty (sō′shē·al′ə·tē) *n. pl.* **·ties** 1 The state or character of being social; sociability. 2 A social custom or action. 3 The instinct or tendency which is the basis of social organization.

so·cial·ize (sō′shəl·īz) *v.* **·ized, ·iz·ing** *v.t.* 1 To convert from an anti–social to a social attitude; make friendly, cooperative, or sociable. 2 To arouse to an interest in humanity. 3 To convert or adapt to social uses or needs. 4 To put under group control; especially, to

regulate according to socialistic principles. —*v.i.* 5 To take part in social activities. Also *Brit.* **so′cial·ise.** —**so′cial·i·za′tion** *n.*

socialized medicine A system proposing to supply the public with medical care at nominal cost, by regulating services and fees, by government subsidies to physicians and medical projects, or by cooperative projects.

social register A directory of persons prominent in fashionable society.

social science 1 The body of knowledge that relates to man as a member of society, or of any component part of society, as the state, family, or any systematized human institution. **2** Any field of knowledge dealing with human society, as economics, history, sociology, education, politics, ethics, etc.

social security 1 Any public system which provides welfare services for members of the community in need. **2** *U.S.* A Federal program of old-age and unemployment insurance, public assistance to the blind, disabled, and dependent, and maternal and child welfare services, administered by the **Social Security Administration.**

social service Activity intended to advance human welfare. —**so′cial-ser′vice** *adj.*

social settlement An institution or settlement, usually in the poor quarters of a large city, devoted to the aid and instruction of the poor.

social studies Social science, as a part of the curriculum in elementary and high school.

social work Any clinical, social, or recreational service for improving community welfare, as through health clinics, recreational facilities, aid to the poor and the aged, etc. —**social worker**

so·ci·e·ty (sə·sī′ə·tē) *n. pl.* **·ties 1** The system of community life, in which individuals, ordinarily in a territorial establishment, form a continuous and regulatory association for their mutual benefit and protection. **2** The body of persons composing such a community. **3** A number of persons in a community regarded as forming a class having certain common interests, status, etc.: high *society.* **4** The fashionable or cultured portion of a community, considered as constituting a class. **5** A body of persons associated for a common purpose or object; an association: a medical *society.* **6** *U.S.* In some States, an incorporated religious congregation. **7** A club or fraternity. **8** Association based on friendship or intimacy; companionship; company: to enjoy the *society* of working men. **9** *Ecol.* A group of plants or animals living together under the same physiographic conditions and influences and characterized by a principal species. See synonyms under ACQUAINTANCE, ALLIANCE, ASSOCIATION, CLASS. [<OF *societe* <L *societas, -tatis* <*socius* a friend]

Society Islands A part of French Oceania, comprising an island group south of the Tuamotu Islands; 690 square miles; capital, Papeete, on Tahiti; divided into two clusters: the *Windward Islands,* including Tahiti, Moorea, and other adjacent islands; and the *Leeward Islands,* including the major island of Raiatea.

Society of Friends A Christian religious group, founded in England by George Fox in the middle of the seventeenth century, characterized by their doctrine of "waiting upon the Spirit" for direct guidance and their repudiation of ritual, formal sacraments, oaths, and violence: commonly known as *Quakers.*

Society of Jesus See JESUIT.

So·cin·i·an (sō·sin′ē·ən) *adj.* Pertaining to either or both of the Italian theologians named Socinus or to their religious teachings, as the denial of the Trinity, of the natural depravity of man, of vicarious atonement, and of the efficacy of sacraments. —*n.* A believer in the Socinian theory. —**So·cin′i·an·ism** *n.*

socio- *combining form* **1** Society; social: *sociology.* **2** Sociology; sociological: *sociobiology.* [<F <L *socius* a companion]

so·ci·o·bi·ol·o·gy (sō′sē·ō·bī·ol′ə·jē, sō′shē-) *n.* The study of social behavior in animals and humans, as determined by the biological characteristics. —**so′ci·o·bi·ol′o·gist** *n.*

so·ci·o·cul·tur·al (sō′sē·ō·kul′chər·əl, sō′shē-) *adj.* Of or pertaining to society and culture in combination.

so·ci·o·ec·o·nom·ic (sō′sē·ō·ek′ə·nom′ik, sō′shē-, -ē′kə-) *adj.* Social and economic: considered as a unit based upon the interrelationship of social and economic factors. —**so′ci·o·ec′o·nom′i·cal·ly** *adv.*

so·ci·o·ge·net·ic (sō′sē·ō·jə·net′, -shē·ō-) *adj.* Of or pertaining to the origin, development, and preservation of human society in any of its aspects.

so·ci·o·lin·guis·tics (sō′sē·ō·ling·gwis′tiks, sō′·shē-) *n.* The study of language as a social instrument and in its social context, in which the principles and investigative techniques of both sociology and linguistics are employed. [<SOCIO- + LINGUISTICS] —**so′ci·o·lin·guis′tic** *adj.* —**so′ci·o·lin·guis′ti·cal·ly** *adv.*

so·ci·o·log·i·cal (sō′sē·ə·loj′i·kəl, -shē·ə-) *adj.* **1** Of or concerned with human social relations or conditions. **2** Of or pertaining to sociology. Also **so′ci·o·log′ic.** —**so′ci·o·log′i·cal·ly** *adv.*

so·ci·ol·o·gy (sō′sē·ol′ə·jē, sō′shē-) *n.* The science that treats of the origin and evolution of human society and social phenomena, the progress of civilization, and the laws controlling human institutions and functions. —**so′ci·ol′o·gist** *n.*

so·ci·om·e·try (sō′sē·om′ə·trē, sō′shē-) *n.* The study of the interrelationships of individuals within a community or social group, especially as expressed by attitudes of acceptance or rejection. —**so′ci·o·met′ric** (-ə·met′rik) *adj.*

so·ci·o·path (sō′sē·ə·path, sō′shē-) *n.* One who suffers from a mental disorder that causes a lack of moral restraint or responsibility toward fellow members of society.

sock[1] (sok) *n.* **1** A short stocking. **2** The light shoe worn by comic actors in the Greek and Roman drama; hence, comedy. Compare BUSKIN. [OE *socc* <L *soccus* slipper]

sock[2] (sok) *Slang v.t.* To strike or hit, especially with the fist; to punch. —*n.* A hard blow. [Origin unknown]

sock·dol·a·ger (sok·dol′ə·jər) *n. Slang* **1** That which gives the finishing stroke, or is decisive, especially in a dispute; a decisive blow, a conclusive reply or argument, or the like. **2** Something of great size; a rouser. Also **sock·dol′o·ger.** [Alter. of DOXOLOGY]

sock·et (sok′it) *n.* **1** *Mech.* A cavity or an opening specially adapted to receive and hold some corresponding piece or fixture: the *socket* for an electric-light bulb. **2** *Anat.* A cavity or hollowed depression for the reception of an organ or part. —*v.t.* To furnish with, hold by, or put into a socket. [<AF *soket,* dim. of OF *soc* a plowshare <Celtic]

sock·eye (sok′ī′) *n.* The red salmon of the Pacific coast *(Oncorhynchus nerka),* highly valued as a food fish. [Alter. of Salishan *sukkegh*]

so·cle (sō′kəl) *n. Archit.* **1** A plain, square block, higher than a plinth, supporting a statue or other work of art. **2** A base supporting a wall or a range of ornaments. [<F <Ital. *zoccolo* a pedestal, shoe <L *socculus,* dim. of *soccus* a sock]

soc·man (sok′mən) *n. pl.* **·men** (-mən) In old English law, one who holds land in socage: often spelled *sokeman.* Also **sock′man.**

Soc·ra·tes (sok′rə·tēz), 469?–399 B.C., Athenian philosopher; the chief character in the dialogs of Plato: accused of impiety and innovation, he was imprisoned, condemned to death, and forced to drink an infusion of hemlock.

So·crat·ic (sō·krat′ik) *adj.* Pertaining to or characteristic of Socrates: also **So·crat′i·cal.** —*n.* A disciple of Socrates. —**So·crat′i·cal·ly** *adv.* —**Soc·ra·tism** (sok′rə·tiz′əm) *n.* —**Soc′ra·tist** *n.*

Socratic irony A pretense of ignorance, though one may be wise, in order to expose the errors in an opponent's reasoning.

Socratic method The dialectic method of instruction by questions and answers, as adopted by Socrates in his disputations, leading either to a foreseen conclusion or to admissions damaging to an opponent.

sod[1] (sod) *n.* **1** Grassy surface soil held together by the matted roots of grass and weeds; sward; also, a piece of such soil. **2** Grassy ground; lawn; the earth or soil. —**the old Sod** Ireland. —*v.t.* **sod·ded, sod·ding** To cover with sod. [<MDu. *sode* piece of turf]

sod[2] (sod) Obsolete past tense of SEETHE.

so·da (sō′də) *n.* **1** Any of several white alkaline compounds widely used in medicine, industry, and the arts, especially sodium bicarbonate (baking soda), sodium carbonate, sodium hydroxide, and sodium oxide. **2** Soda alum. **3** Soda salts. **4** Soda water; also, a soft drink containing carbonated water, flavoring, and, sometimes, ice-cream. **5** In faro, the first card to appear face up in the dealing box before the start of play. [<Med. L <Ital. *soda (cenere)* solid (ash) <L *solidus*]

soda alum *Chem.* A double salt of sodium sulfate and aluminum.

soda ash Crude sodium carbonate.

soda biscuit 1 A biscuit leavened with sodium bicarbonate. **2** A soda cracker.

soda cracker A thin, crisp cracker made with yeast-leavened dough containing soda.

soda fountain 1 An apparatus from which soda water is drawn, usually containing receptacles for sirups, ice, and ice-cream. **2** A counter at which soft drinks and ice-cream are dispensed.

soda jerk *U.S. Slang* A clerk who serves at a soda fountain.

soda lime A mixture made from sodium hydroxide and calcium oxide.

so·da·lite (sō′də·līt) *n.* A vitreous, translucent silicate of sodium and aluminum, with some chlorine. [<SODA + -LITE]

so·dal·i·ty (sō·dal′ə·tē) *n. pl.* **·ties** A brotherhood or fraternity; especially, a brotherhood for devotional or charitable purposes. [<L *sodalitas, -tatis* <*sodalis* companion]

soda water 1 An effervescent drink consisting of water strongly charged under pressure with purified carbon dioxide gas, formerly generated from sodium bicarbonate: often flavored with a fruit sirup. **2** Alkaline water as found in natural reservoirs or springs.

sod·den (sod′n) *adj.* **1** Soaked with moisture: *sodden* ground. **2** Doughy; soggy, as bread, biscuits, etc. **3** Flabby and pale; flaccid, especially from dissipation: said of persons or their features. **4** Dull; dreary: a *sodden* life. —*v.t.* & *v.i.* To make or become sodden. [ME *sothen,* orig. pp. of SEETHE] —**sod′den·ly** *adv.* —**sod′den·ness** *n.*

Sod·dy (sod′ē), **Frederick,** 1877–1956, English chemist and physicist.

sod house A dwelling built of sod or turf walls, often having a wooden roof: used by early settlers on the prairies.

so·di·um (sō′dē·əm) *n.* A soft, light, very reactive metallic element (symbol Na, atomic number 11) constituting about 2.6% of the lithosphere, usually in the form of sodium chloride, an essential element in all living systems. See PERIODIC TABLE. [<NL <Med. L. *soda* SODA]

Sodium Am·y·tal (am′i·tôl, -tal) Proprietary name of a white, hygroscopic powder, $C_{11}H_{17}O_3N_2Na$, used in medicine as a sedative and hypnotic.

sodium benzoate *Chem.* A white, odorless, amorphous, granular or crystalline powder, $NaC_7H_5O_2$, used as an antipyretic, antirheumatic, antiseptic, as a food preservative, and to disguise taste, as of poor-quality food.

sodium bicarbonate *Chem.* A white crystalline compound, $NaHCO_3$, of alkaline taste, used in medicine and cookery; baking soda.

sodium borate *Chem.* Any sodium salt of boric acid; specifically, borax.

sodium carbonate *Chem.* A strongly alkaline compound, Na_2CO_3: in crystalline hydrated form known as washing soda, $Na_2CO_3{\cdot}10H_2O$, used in the manufacture of glass, soap, paper, etc., and in medicine and photography.

sodium chlorate *Chem.* A white crystalline compound, $NaClO_3$, used as a mordant, insecticide, weed-killer, and as an oxidizing agent.

sodium chloride Common salt, NaCl.

sodium cyanide *Chem.* A white, extremely poisonous salt of hydrocyanic acid, NaCN: used in electroplating and case hardening of metals, as a fumigant and chemical reagent.

sodium dichromate *Chem.* A red crystalline compound, $Na_2Cr_2O_7{\cdot}2H_2O$, used as a dye and in making inks.

sodium hydroxide *Chem.* A white, caustic, fusible compound, NaOH: used in various solutions in chemistry, metallurgy, as a bleaching agent, etc.; caustic soda.

sodium hypochlorite *Chem.* An oxidizing and

bleaching compound, NaOCl, used also as a decontaminating agent for war gases.

sodium hyposulfite 1 Sodium thiosulfate. 2 A colorless crystalline salt, $Na_2S_2O_4$.

sodium nitrate A white compound, $NaNO_3$, used in the manufacture of nitric acid and as a manure. It occurs abundantly in nature.

sodium oxide A gray, highly reactive compound, Na_2O; sodium monoxide.

sodium perborate *Chem.* A colorless crystalline compound, $NaBO_3 \cdot 4H_2O$, used as a bleaching agent and disinfectant.

sodium peroxide *Chem.* A yellowish solid, Na_2O_2, used in combination with other chemicals as a bleaching agent.

sodium phosphate *Chem.* A sodium salt of phosphoric acid, Na_2HPO_4, crystallizing in the presence of water: the tribasic form is used as a laxative and also as a fixing agent in textile coloring.

sodium propionate *Chem.* A colorless, crystalline, water-soluble compound, $NaC_3H_5O_2$, used in medicine as a fungicide and to retard bacterial and mold growth in foods.

sodium silicate A material used in making artificial stone and in various industrial processes: known also as *soluble glass* or *waterglass.*

sodium sulfate *Chem.* A compound, Na_2SO_4, made by the action of sulfuric acid on common salt or on Chile saltpeter. It is used in glassmaking, and in one form (Glauber's salt) is important in medicine.

sodium sulfide *Chem.* A bleaching and decontaminating agent, Na_2S, especially effective against mustard gas.

sodium sulfite *Chem.* A decontaminating agent, Na_2SO_3, effective against chlorpicrin.

sodium thiosulfate *Chem.* A crystalline salt, $Na_2S_2O_3$, used industrially and in photography as a fixing agent: also called *hypo.*

Sod·om (sod′əm) In the Bible, a city on the Dead Sea, destroyed with Gomorrah because of the wickedness of its people. *Gen.* xiii 10.

sod·om·ite (sod′əm-īt) *n.* One guilty of sodomy.

Sod·om·ite (sod′əm-īt) *n.* One of the people of Sodom.

sod·om·y (sod′əm-ē) *n.* Carnal copulation between male persons or with beasts. [<OF *sodomie* <LL *Sodoma* Sodom, to whose people this practice was imputed]

Soem·ba (sōōm′bä) The Dutch name for SUMBA.

Soem·ba·wa (sōōm-bä′wä) The Dutch name for SUMBAWA.

Soe·ra·ba·ja (sōō′rä-bä′yä) The Dutch name for SURABAYA.

so·ev·er (sō-ev′ər) *adv.* To or in some conceivable degree: used in generalizing and emphasizing what follows: a word often added to *who, which, what, where, when, how,* etc., to form the compounds *whosoever,* etc., giving them specific force. Often used separately: *how great soever* he might be.

so·fa (sō′fə) *n.* A wide seat, upholstered and having a back and raised ends. [<F <Arabic *soffah* a part of a floor raised to form a seat]

sofa bed A sofa which may be opened up to form a large bed.

so·far (sō′fär) *n.* A system for locating stranded ships or aircraft by means of underwater sound waves, set up by depth charges released by the survivors and detected by hydrophones operated from ground stations. [<SO(UND) F(IXING) A(ND) R(ANGING)]

sof·fit (sof′it) *n. Archit.* The under side of a staircase, entablature, lintel, archway, or cornice. [<F *soffite* <Ital. *soffita* <L *suffixus.* Doublet of SUFFIX.]

So·fi·a (sō-fē′ä) German, Italian, Russian, Spanish, and Swedish form of SOPHIA.

So·fi·a (sō′fē-ä, sō-fē′ə) The capital of Bulgaria, in the western part. *Bulgarian* **So·fi·ya** (sō′fē-yä).

soft (sôft, soft) *adj.* 1 Being or composed of a substance whose shape is changed easily by pressure, without fracture; impressible; pliable, ductile, or malleable; easily worked: *soft* wood: opposed to *hard.* 2 Smooth and delicate to the touch: *soft* skin. 3 Gentle in its effect upon the ear: not loud or harsh. 4 Mild in any mode of physical action; gentle; bland: a *soft* breeze; a *soft* ripple. 5 Of subdued coloring or delicate shading; not glaring

or abrupt: *soft* tints; *soft* outline. 6 Gentle; conciliatory; expressing mildness or sympathy; courteous: *soft* words. 7 Giving or enjoying rest; placid: *soft* sleep. 8 Easily or too easily touched in feeling; tender; sympathetic: a *soft* heart. 9 Incapable of bearing hardship; susceptible; tender; delicate: *soft* muscles. 10 Of yielding character; weak; effeminate. 11 *Colloq.* Of weak intellect; also, yielding to emotion; maudlin. 12 Free from mineral salts which prevent the detergent action of water and soap: said of water. 13 Bituminous, as opposed to anthracite: said of coal. 14 Describing *c* and *g* when articulated fricatively as in *cent* and *gibe*: opposed to *hard*; also, voiced and weakly articulated; also, palatalized, as certain consonants in the Slavic languages. 15 *Colloq.* Easy: a *soft* job. 16 *Scot. & Brit. Dial.* Characterized by moisture or thawing: said of the weather. See synonyms under BLAND, SUPPLE. — *n.* 1 That which is soft; softness; a soft part or material. 2 *Colloq.* One who is soft or foolish; a softy. — *adv.* 1 Softly. 2 Quietly; gently. — *interj. Archaic* Proceed softly; be quiet or slow. [OE *sôfte*] — **soft′ly** *adv. & interj.* — **soft′·ness** *n.*

sof·ta (sof′tə) *n. Turkish* A student at a Moslem mosque.

soft·back (sôft′bak′, soft′-) *adj.* Soft-cover. — *n.* A soft-cover book.

soft·ball (sôft′bôl′, soft′-) *n.* A variation of baseball, requiring a smaller diamond, a larger, softer ball, ten players on a team, and seven innings for play.

soft-boiled (sôft′boild′) *adj.* 1 Boiled, as an egg, for only a short while, so that the yolk and albumen are soft or semiliquid. 2 *Colloq.* Mild in disposition: lenient.

soft·bound (sôft′bound′, soft′-) *adj.* Soft-cover.

soft clam The common long clam (*Mya arenaria*) of the north Atlantic coast.

soft coal Bituminous coal.

soft-cov·er (sôft′kuv′ər, soft′-) *adj.* Designating a book having flexible sides, as of paper: contrasted to *hard-cover.*

soft drink A nonalcoholic beverage, as sweetened soda water, ginger ale, etc.

sof·ten (sôf′ən, sof′-) *v.t. & v.i.* To make or become soft or softer. See synonyms under ALLAY, ALLEVIATE, CHASTEN, TEMPER. — **sof′ten·er** *n.*

softening of the brain 1 *Pathol.* Degeneration of the brain tissue, especially as resulting from paresis; encephalomalacia. 2 *Colloq.* Dementia.

soft-finned (sôft′find′, soft′-) *adj. Zool.* Having fins whose membrane is supported on flexible or jointed rays: opposed to *spiny-finned.*

soft focus *Phot.* A slightly blurred effect obtained by an imperfect focusing of the lens upon a scene or object.

soft-head (sôft′hed′, soft′-) *n.* A foolish or simple person. — **soft′-head′ed** *adj.*

soft-heart·ed (sôft′här′tid, soft′-) *adj.* Tenderhearted; merciful. — **soft′heart′ed·ly** *adv.* — **soft′heart′ed·ness** *n.*

soft-ped·al (sôft′ped′l, soft′-) *v.t.* **-aled** or **-alled, -al·ing** or **-al·ling** 1 To mute the tone of by depressing the soft pedal. 2 *Colloq.* To render less emphatic; moderate; tone down.

soft pedal A pedal which mutes the tone, as in a piano.

soft sell *U.S. Colloq.* The use of subtle, noninsistent methods of salesmanship.

soft-shell (sôft′shel′, soft′-) *adj.* 1 Having a soft shell, as certain clams, or a crab or lobster after shedding its shell: also **soft′-shelled′.** 2 *U.S. Colloq.* Somewhat moderate in opinion or doctrine; somewhat liberal; not hidebound: a *soft-shell* Baptist. — *n.* A crab which has lately shed its shell: also **soft-shelled crab.**

soft-shelled turtle Any member of a family (*Trionychidae*) of turtles having a long snout and a soft, leathery shell, especially *Trionyx* (or *Amyda*) *spinifera,* common from the Gulf States to the St. Lawrence River.

soft-soap (sôft′sōp′, soft′-) *v.t.* To flatter. — **soft′-soap′er** *n.*

soft soap 1 Fluid or semifluid soap. 2 *Colloq.* Flattery; blarney.

soft·ware (sôft′wâr′, soft′-) *n.* In a digital computer, any of the programs designed to control

various aspects of the operation of the machine, such as input and output operations: distinguished from *hardware* (def. 4).

soft·wood (sôft′wood′, soft′-) *n.* 1 A coniferous tree or its wood. 2 Any soft wood, or any tree with soft wood.

soft·y (sôf′tē, sof′-) *n. pl.* **soft·ies** *Colloq.* 1 An extremely sentimental person. 2 A weak or effeminate man or boy; one not inured to hardship; a sissy.

Sog·di·an (sog′dē-ən) *n.* 1 One of an ancient Iranian people inhabiting Sogdiana. 2 Their extinct Iranian language.

Sog·di·a·na (sog′dē-ā′nə) An ancient region of central Asia comprising part of the Persian Empire; capital, Samarkand: also *Transoxiana.*

sog·gy (sog′ē) *adj.* **·gi·er, ·gi·est** 1 Saturated with water or moisture; wet and heavy; soaked. 2 Heavy: said of pastry. 3 Soft; boggy: said of land. 4 Dull; logy: said of a person or an animal. Also **sog·ged** (sog′id). [< dial. E *sog* a swamp, bog <Scand. Cf. dial. Norw. *soggjast* get wet.] — **sog′gi·ly** *adv.* — **sog′gi·ness** *n.*

Sog·ne Fjord (sông′nə) The longest and deepest fjord in Norway, in the western part; 112 miles long; an inlet of the North Sea.

So·ho (sō-hō′, sō′hō) The foreign quarter of London, noted for its restaurants.

soi-di·sant (swä-dē-zän′) *adj. French* Self-styled; pretended: usually implying false pretense.

soi·gné (swä-nyä′) *adj. French* Cared for; well-groomed.

soil[1] (soil) *n.* 1 Finely divided rock mixed with decayed vegetable or animal matter, constituting that portion of the surface of the earth in which plants grow. 2 The ground in general; native land; country. 3 A mixture of lampblack, glue, and water used in plumbing. See synonyms under LAND. [<OF *soile, sueil* <L *solium* a seat, mistaken for *solum* the ground]

soil[2] (soil) *v.t.* 1 To make dirty; smudge. 2 To disgrace; defile. 3 *Obs.* To manure. — *v.i.* 4 To become dirty. See synonyms under BLEMISH, DEFILE[1], POLLUTE, STAIN. — *n.* 1 That which soils; foul matter; a foul spot; hence, a taint. 2 Manure: confused in use with *soil*[1]. 3 A slough or marshy place in which a hunted boar takes refuge; hence, water or a wet place resorted to by other game. [<OF *soillier,* ult. <L *suculus,* dim. of *sus* a pig]

soil[3] (soil) *v.t.* 1 To feed and fatten, as stalled cattle, with freshly cut, green food. 2 To purge with green food. [? <OF *saoler, saouler* fill <L *satullare* < *satullus,* dim. of *satur* sated]

soil·age (soi′lij) *n.* Green crops for feeding animals.

soil·ure (soil′yər) *n.* Soiling, or the condition of being soiled.

soi·rée (swä-rā′, *Fr.* swà-rā′) *n.* A party or reception given in the evening. Also **soi·ree′.** [<F <*soir* evening]

Sois·sons (swä-sôn′) A city in NE France on the Aisne.

so·ja (sō′jə, sō′yə) *n.* The soybean. [<NL <Du. *soya* the soybean]

so·journ (sō′jûrn, sō-jûrn′) *v.i.* To stay or dwell temporarily; abide for a time. See synonyms under ABIDE. — *n.* (sō′jûrn) A temporary residence or stay, as of one in a foreign land. [<OF *sojorner, sojourner,* ult. <L *sub-* under + *diurnus* daily] — **so′journ·er** *n.*

soke (sōk) *n.* 1 In feudal law, a franchise, privilege, or liberty; jurisdiction; a privilege to administer justice within a certain territory, as a manor. 2 The district within which such privilege was exercised. ◆ Homophone: *soak.* [<Med. L *soca* <OE *sōcn* jurisdiction]

soke·man (sōk′mən) See SOCMAN.

Soke of Peterborough An administrative county in NE Northamptonshire, England; 83 square miles.

So·kol (sō′kôl) *n.* 1 A Czech patriotic organization of gymnasts started (1862) as a democratic fraternal body to develop strength, litheness, alertness, and fearlessness. 2 A member of this organization. [<Czechoslovakian *sokol* falcon]

So·ko·to (sō′kō-tō) A province of northern

Nigeria; 39,965 square miles; capital, Sokoto.
So·ko·tra (sō·kō′trə) See SOCOTRA.
sol[1] (sōl) *n. Music* The fifth note of the diatonic scale. [See GAMUT]
sol[2] (sol) *n.* A former French silver or copper coin, equivalent to 12 deniers. [<OF <LL *solidus,* a gold coin <L, solid]
sol[3] (sōl) *n. pl.* **so·les** (sō′lās) A Peruvian monetary unit, equivalent to 1/10 libra. [<Sp., sun]
sol[4] (sol, sōl) *n.* A colloidal suspension in a liquid. [<(HYDRO)SOL]
sol[5] (sol) *n.* In alchemy, gold. [<L, sun]
Sol (sol) **1** The sun. **2** In Roman mythology, the god of the sun. [<L]
so·la (sō′lə) See SOLUS.
sol·ace (sol′is) *v.t.* **·aced, ·ac·ing 1** To comfort or cheer in trouble, grief, or calamity; console. **2** To alleviate, as grief; soothe; assuage; mitigate. —*n.* Comfort in grief, trouble, or calamity; also, that which supplies such comfort or alleviation: also **sol′ace·ment.** [<OF *solacier, solasier* < *solas* comfort <L *solacium*] —**sol′ac·er** *n.*
so·lan (sō′lən) *n.* The gannet, a bird related to the pelicans. Also **so·land** (sō′lənd, -lən), **solan goose.** [<ON *sūla* the gannet]
sol·a·na·ceous (sol′ə·nā′shəs) *adj. Bot.* Pertaining or belonging to a widely distributed family (*Solanaceae*) of frequently narcotic poisonous plants, the nightshade family, having colorless juice and alternate simple leaves. The family includes belladonna, tobacco, eggplant, and potato. [<NL <L *solanum* nightshade]
so·lan·der (sə·lan′dər) *n.* A hinged case or box, usually in the form of a book, adapted to hold a variety of objects, as jewelry, cigarettes, writing materials, pamphlets, maps, rare books and the like. [after Daniel C. *Solander,* 1736–82, English inventor born in Sweden]
so·la·no (sō·lä′nō) *n.* A hot, violent, southeasterly wind of the Mediterranean. [<Sp. <L *sol* sun]
so·la·num (sə·lā′nəm) *n.* Any of a genus (*Solanum*) of herbs and shrubs, the nightshades, typifying the family *Solanaceae,* especially *S. tuberosum,* the common potato. [<NL <L, nightshade]
so·lar (sō′lər) *adj.* **1** Pertaining to, proceeding from, or connected with the sun. **2** Affected, determined, or measured by the sun. **3** Operated by the action of the sun's rays: a *solar* engine. [<L *solaris* < *sol* sun]
solar constant The amount of solar energy falling on one square centimeter of the earth's surface at normal incidence, having a mean value of 1.92 small calories per minute.
solar energy Energy radiated by the sun, the primary source of chemical and other forms of energy, but utilized directly in only minor applications.
so·lar·im·e·ter (sō′lə·rim′ə·tər) *n.* An instrument for measuring solar radiation.
so·lar·i·um (sō·lâr′ē·əm) *n. pl.* **·i·a** (-ē·ə) A room or enclosed porch exposed to the sun's rays, as in a sanatorium. [<L]
so·lar·i·za·tion (sō′lər·ə·zā′shən, -ī·zā′-) *n.* **1** Exposure to the sun's rays. **2** *Phot.* Injury to a sensitized film resulting from overexposure to strong light, or from overprinting.
so·lar·ize (sō′lə·rīz) *v.* **·ized, ·iz·ing** *v.t.* **1** To affect or injure by the action of the sun's rays. **2** *Phot.* To overexpose. —*v.i.* **3** *Phot.* To be overexposed.
solar month A twelfth of a solar year; the time during which the sun is passing through one of the signs of the zodiac.
solar myth A primitive etiological story explaining symbolically some natural phenomenon of the sun; also, a folk tale arising among an agricultural people explaining or symbolizing the power or influence of the sun.
solar plexus 1 *Anat.* The large network of the sympathetic nervous system, found behind the stomach, and containing important ganglia serving the abdominal viscera. **2** *Colloq.* The pit of the stomach.
solar system The sun and the heavenly bodies that revolve about it.
solar time See under TIME.
solar wind The streams of charged particles emanating outward in all directions from the surface of the sun.
solar year See under YEAR.
sol·ate (sol′āt) *v.i.* **·at·ed, ·at·ing** *Chem.* To change from a gel to a sol. [<SOL[4] + -ATE[1]] —**so·la·tion** (sə·lā′shən) *n.*
so·la·ti·um (sə·lā′shē·əm) *n. pl.* **·ti·a** (-shē·ə) **1** Compensation; solace. **2** *Law* Compensation for injury to the feelings as distinguished from pecuniary loss or physical suffering. [<L, var. of *solacium* solace]
sold (sōld) Past tense and past participle of SELL.
sol·dan (sol′dən) *n. Archaic* A ruler or sovereign of a Moslem country, especially Egypt: also spelled *suldan, soudan.* [<OF *soudan* <Arabic *sulṭān* king, sovereign]
sol·der (sod′ər) *n.* **1** A fusible metal or alloy used for joining metallic surfaces or margins: applied in a melted state, either as a **hard solder,** melting only at a red heat, or as a **soft solder,** melting below a red heat. **2** Anything that unites or cements. —*v.t.* **1** To unite or repair with solder. **2** To join together; bind. —*v.i.* **3** To work with solder. **4** To be united by or as by solder. [<OF *soldure* < *souder* make hard <L *solidare* < *solidus* firm, hard] —**sol′der·er** *n.*
sol·dier (sōl′jər) *n.* **1** A person serving in an army. **2** A private in an army, as distinguished from a commissioned officer. **3** A brave, skilful, or experienced warrior. **4** One who serves loyally in any cause. **5** *Colloq.* One who makes a show of working but does little; a shirker; malingerer. **6** *Entomol.* **a** An asexual form (neuter or worker) of a termite or white ant, in which the head and jaws are largely developed, and whose office is to defend the community. **b** A similar neuter of certain true ants. See synonyms under ARMY. —*v.i.* **1** To be a soldier; perform military service. **2** To make a show of working; shirk; malinger. [<OF < *soude* pay, wages <LL *solidus.* See SOL[2].]
sol·dier·ly (sōl′jər·lē) *adj.* Like a true soldier; brave; martial. See synonyms under WARLIKE.
soldier of fortune A military adventurer; a soldier who serves where fortune summons him.
Soldier's Medal A decoration in the form of a bronze octagon on which is displayed an eagle standing on fasces between two groups of stars: awarded to any member of the U.S. Army, or of a military organization connected with it, for heroism not involving actual conflict with the enemy.
sol·dier·y (sōl′jər·ē) *n. pl.* **·dier·ies 1** Soldiers collectively. **2** Military service.
sol·do (sol′dō, *Ital.* sôl′dō) *n. pl.* **·di** (-dē) A small Italian copper coin worth, generally, one twentieth of a lira. [<Ital. <LL *solidus,* a gold coin <L, solid]
sole[1] (sōl) *n.* **1** The bottom surface of the foot. ◆ Collateral adjectives: *plantar, volar*[2]. **2** The bottom surface of a shoe, boot, etc. **3** The lower part of a thing, or the part on which it rests when standing; especially, the bottom part of a plowshare. **4** The bottom part of the head of a golf club. —*v.t.* **soled, sol·ing 1** To furnish with a sole; resole, as a shoe. **2** In golf, to allow (the clubhead) to rest flat on the ground, just behind the ball. ◆ Homophone: *soul.* [<OF <Med. L *sola,* var. of L *solea* a sandal]
sole[2] (sōl) *n.* **1** Any of several flatfishes allied to the flounders, having a small mouth and small eyes set close together on one side of the head; especially, the common **European sole** (*Solea solea*), highly esteemed as food, and the **American sole** (genus *Achirus*), common on the Atlantic coast of the United States. **2** One of various flounders, as *Psettichthys melanostictus,* a food fish of the Pacific coast of the United States. ◆ Homophone: *soul.* [<OF <L *solea*]
sole[3] (sōl) *adj.* **1** Being alone or the only one; existing or acting without another; only; individual. **2** *Law* **a** Unmarried; single: feme *sole* (an unmarried woman). **b** Having exclusive rights; absolute: opposed to *joint*: a *sole* tenant. **3** *Archaic* Solitary. See synonyms under SOLITARY. ◆ Homophone: *soul.* [<OF *sol* <L *solus* alone]
sol·e·cism (sol′ə·siz′əm) *n.* **1** A violation of grammatical rules or of the approved idiomatic usage of language. **2** Any impropriety or incongruity. [<L *soloecismus* <Gk. *soloikismos* < *soloikos* speaking incorrectly < *Soloi,* a Cilician town whose people spoke a substandard Attic dialect] —**sol′e·cist** *n.* —**sol′e·cis′tic** or **·ti·cal** *adj.*
sol·e·cize (sol′ə·sīz) *v.i.* **·cized, ·ciz·ing** *Rare* To use solecisms. Also *Brit.* **sol′e·cise.**
sole·ly (sōl′lē) *adv.* **1** By oneself or itself alone; singly. **2** Completely; entirely. **3** Without exception; exclusively.
sol·emn (sol′əm) *adj.* **1** Characterized by majesty, mystery, or power; exciting grave or serious thought; impressive; awe-inspiring. **2** Characterized by ceremonial observances; religious; sacred. **3** Marked by gravity; serious; earnest; also, affectedly serious. **4** *Law* Done in due form of law; executed formally: a *solemn* protest. **5** *Obs.* Of great reputation, dignity, or importance. **6** *Obs.* Somber; sober: said of color. See synonyms under AWFUL, SEDATE, SERIOUS. [<OF *solemne* <L *solemnis*] —**sol′em·ness, sol′emn·ness** *n.* —**sol′emn·ly** *adv.*
so·lem·ni·ty (sə·lem′nə·tē) *n. pl.* **·ties 1** The state or quality of being solemn; solemn feeling; gravity; reverence. **2** A rite expressive of religious reverence; also, any ceremonious observance. **3** A thing of a solemn or serious nature. **4** Mock seriousness; affected gravity. **5** *Law* A formality to be seriously observed and requisite to the validity or legality of an act. See synonyms under SACRAMENT.
sol·em·nize (sol′əm·nīz) *v.t.* **·nized, ·niz·ing 1** To perform as a ceremony or solemn rite, or according to legal or ritual forms: to *solemnize* a marriage. **2** To dignify as with a ceremony; celebrate. **3** To make solemn, grave, or serious. Also *Brit.* **sol′em·nise.** See synonyms under CELEBRATE. —**sol′em·ni·za′tion** *n.* —**sol′em·niz′er** *n.*
Solemn League and Covenant See under COVENANT.
so·le·noid (sō′lə·noid) *n. Electr.* A conducting wire in the form of a cylindrical coil or helix, capable of setting up a magnetic field by the passage through it of an electric current. [<Gk. *sōlēn* a channel + -OID] —**so′le·noi′dal** *adj.* —**so′le·noi′dal·ly** *adv.*

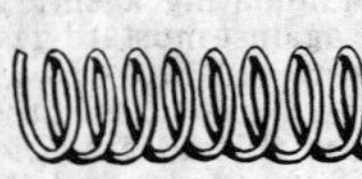

SOLENOID

So·lent (sō′lənt), **The** A strait between the Isle of Wight and Southampton, England; 3/4 to 5 miles wide, 15 miles long.
sol·er·et (sol′ə·ret′) See SOLLERET.
sole trader See FEME-SOLE TRADER.
So·leure (sô·lœr′) The French name for SOLOTHURN.
sol-fa (sōl′fä′) *Music v.t. & v.i.* **-faed, -fa·ing** To sing syllables instead of words to (notes); sing solfeggi. —*n.* **1** Syllables collectively used in solmization; the act of singing them. **2** Rarely, a scale. —**tonic sol-fa** See TONIC. [<Ital. *solfa* the gamut. See GAMUT.] —**sol′-fa′ist** *n.*
sol·fa·ta·ra (sōl′fä·tä′rä) *n. Geol.* An area or phase of volcanic action characterized by the escape of steam, various gases, and sublimates. [<Ital., a dormant crater near Naples, Italy < *solfo* sulfur] —**sol′fa·ta′ric** *adj.*
sol·feg·gio (sōl·fej′ō) *n. pl.* **·feg·gi** (-fej′ē) or **·feg·gios** *Music* **1** A singing exercise of runs, broken chords, etc., sung either to different syllables or all to the same syllable or vowel. **2** Solmization. [<Ital. < *solfa.* See SOL-FA.]
sol·fe·ri·no (sol′fe·rē′nō) *n.* **1** A bright purplish red. **2** Fuchsin. [from *Solferino*; named in honor of a battle fought there in 1859]
Sol·fe·ri·no (sōl′fā·rē′nō) A village in northern Italy; scene of a French and Sardinian victory over Austria, 1859.
so·lic·it (sə·lis′it) *v.t.* **1** To ask for earnestly; seek to obtain by persuasion or entreaty. **2** To beg or entreat (a person) persistently. **3** To influence to action; tempt; especially, to entice (one) to an unlawful or immoral act. —*v.i.* **4** To make petition or solicitation. See synonyms under ASK, PLEAD. [<OF *solliciter* <L *sollicitare* agitate]
so·lic·i·ta·tion (sə·lis′ə·tā′shən) *n.* **1** Importunity; the act of soliciting. **2** An attempt to entice.
so·lic·i·tor (sə·lis′ə·tər) *n.* **1** A person who does any kind of soliciting; especially, one who solicits gifts of money or subscriptions to magazines. **2** The legal advisor to certain branches of the public service. **3** In England, a lawyer who may advise clients or who prepares cases for presentation in court, but who may appear as an advocate in the lower courts only. See BARRISTER. Also **so·lic′i·ter.** —**so·lic′i·tor·ship′** *n.*

Solicitor General *pl.* **Solicitors General** 1 In the United States, an officer who ranks after the Attorney General, and, in the absence of the latter, acts in his place. 2 The principal law officer in some of the States, corresponding to the Attorney General in others. 3 In England, a law officer of the Crown, ranking next after the Attorney General.

so·lic·i·tous (sə·lis′ə·təs) *adj.* 1 Full of anxiety or concern, as for the attainment of something. 2 Full of eager desire; willing. See synonyms under URGENT. —**so·lic′i·tous·ly** *adv.* —**so·lic′i·tous·ness** *n.*

so·lic·i·tude (sə·lis′ə·to͞od, -tyo͞od) *n.* 1 The state of being solicitous; uneasiness of mind. 2 That which makes one solicitous. See synonyms under ANXIETY, CARE.

sol·id (sol′id) *adj.* 1 Having its constituent particles so firmly coherent as to resist stress; compact, firm, and unyielding: opposed to *fluid.* 2 Substantial; firm and stable. 3 Filling the whole of the space occupied by its apparent form; completely filled; not hollow. 4 Having no aperture or crevice; compact. 5 Manifesting strength and firmness; not weak or sickly; sound. 6 Characterized by reality; substantial or satisfactory. 7 Exhibiting united and unbroken characteristics, opinions, etc.; being or acting in unison; unanimous: the *solid* vote; This county is *solid* for the Democratic party; also, blindly or unreasonably partisan. 8 Financially sound or safe. 9 *U.S. Colloq.* Certain and safe in approval and support: They were *solid* with the boss. 10 Having or relating to the three dimensions of length, breadth, and thickness. 11 Written without a hyphen: said of a compound word. See SOLIDEME. 12 Cubic in shape: a *solid* yard. 13 Unadulterated; unalloyed: *solid* gold. 14 Carrying weight or conviction: a *solid* argument. 15 Serious; reliable; exhibiting sound judgment: a *solid* citizen. 16 Continuous; unbroken: a *solid* hour. 17 *Printing* Having no leads or slugs between the lines; not open. See synonyms under FIRM[1], HARD, IMPENETRABLE. —*n.* 1 A mass of matter of which the shape cannot be changed permanently and greatly without fracture. 2 A magnitude that has length, breadth, and thickness, as a cone, cube, pyramid, prism, or sphere. [<F *solide* <L *solidus*] —**sol′id·ly** *adv.* —**sol′id·ness** *n.*

sol·i·da·go (sol′ə·dā′gō) *n. pl.* **·gos** Any of a large North American genus (*Solidago*) of perennial plants of the composite family; a goldenrod: the State flower of Alabama, Kentucky, and Nebraska. [<NL <L *solidare* strengthen; with ref. to its alleged curative powers]

solid angle See under ANGLE.

sol·i·dar·i·ty (sol′ə·dar′ə·tē) *n. pl.* **·ties** Coherence and oneness in nature, relations, or interests, as of a race, class, etc.

sol·i·dar·y (sol′ə·der′ē) *adj.* United in nature or interests.

sol·i·deme (sol′ə·dēm) *n.* A solid compound word. Compare HYPHEME. [<SOLID + *-eme,* as in *phoneme*]

solid geometry That part of geometry which includes all three dimensions of space in its reasoning.

so·lid·i·fy (sə·lid′ə·fī) *v.t.* & *v.i.* **·fied, ·fy·ing** 1 To make or become solid, hard, firm, or compact, as water crystallizing into ice. 2 To bring or come together in unity. —**so·lid′i·fi·ca′tion** *n.*

so·lid·i·ty (sə·lid′ə·tē) *n. pl.* **·ties** 1 The quality or state of being solid; the property of occupying space; extension in the three dimensions of space; incompressibility. 2 Mental, moral, or financial soundness; substantial or reliable character or quality; firm standing; stability. 3 *Aeron.* The ratio of the total blade area of a rotor or propeller to the area of the disk swept by the blades. 4 *Geom.* Cubic contents; volume.

Solid South The Southern States of the United States, regarded as a political unit because of their support of the Democratic party.

solid state physics That branch of physics which deals with the physical properties of solids, especially as exhibited by atoms and molecules when in the solid state. It includes the study of crystal structure, elasticity, and friction, semiconductors and plastics, defects in materials, thermal properties, and a wide range of electrical and magnetic phenomena.

sol·i·dus (sol′ə·dəs) *n. pl.* **·di** (-dī) 1 A gold coin of the Byzantine Empire: first issued under Constantine, it remained the standard unit of currency during the Middle Ages, when it was called a *bezant.* 2 A medieval coin, equal to 12 denarii: often called *shilling.* 3 The sign (/) used to divide shillings from pence: 10/6 (10*s.* 6*d.*), being originally the long *ſ* written for shilling: sometimes also used instead of a horizontal line to express fractions: 3/4. See VIRGULE. [<LL]

sol·i·fid·i·an (sol′ə·fid′ē·ən) *n.* One who maintains that faith alone, without works, is the one requisite to salvation. —*adj.* Maintaining that faith alone is necessary to insure salvation; also, pertaining to such belief. [<L *solus* alone + *fides* faith]

so·lil·o·quize (sə·lil′ə·kwīz) *v.i.* **·quized, ·quiz·ing** To discourse to oneself; utter a soliloquy. Also *Brit.* **so·lil′o·quise.**

so·lil·o·quy (sə·lil′ə·kwē) *n. pl.* **·quies** A talking to oneself, regardless of the presence or absence of others; a monolog. [<LL *soliloquium* <L *solus* alone + *loqui* talk]

So·li·mões (sô′lē·moiṅzh′) The upper reaches of the Amazon river, extending from the Peruvian border to the Río Negro.

So·ling·en (zō′ling·ən) A city in North Rhine-Westphalia, West Germany.

sol·i·on (sol′ī′ən) *n. Physics* A small electrochemical cell so constructed that the movement of ions in solution serves to indicate minute changes in temperature, pressure, sound or light waves, acceleration, and other external conditions: used as an electronic control device. [< *ion(s in) sol(ution)*]

sol·ip·sism (sol′ip·siz′əm) *n.* The theory or belief that only knowledge of the self is possible, and that, for each individual, the self itself is the only thing really existent, and therefore that reality is subjective. [<L *solus* alone + *ipse* self] —**sol′ip·sist** *n.*

sol·i·taire (sol′ə·târ′) *n.* 1 A diamond or other gem set alone. 2 One of many games, especially of cards, played by one person. 3 A bird (*Pezophaps solitarius*) somewhat resembling the dodo but more slender and graceful: formerly a native of Réunion but now extinct. [<F <L *solitarius* solitary]

sol·i·tar·y (sol′ə·ter′ē) *adj.* 1 Living, being, or going alone. 2 Made, done, or passed alone: a *solitary* life. 3 Unfrequented by human beings; secluded; lonely; desolate. 4 Lonesome; lonely. 5 Single; one; sole: Not a *solitary* soul was there. —*n. pl.* **·tar·ies** A hermit; recluse; one who lives alone. [<L *solitarius* < *solus* alone] —**sol′i·tar′i·ly** *adv.* —**sol′i·tar′i·ness** *n.*

Synonyms (adj.): alone, companionless, deserted, lone, lonely, lonesome, only, single, sole, unaccompanied, unattended. *Antonyms:* manifold, many, multiplied, multitudinous, myriad, numerous.

sol·i·ter·ra·ne·ous (sol′ə·tə·rā′nē·əs) *adj.* Pertaining to the joint influence of solar and terrestrial forces, especially in relation to meteorological phenomena. [<L *sol, solis* the sun + *terra* the earth]

sol·i·tude (sol′ə·to͞od, -tyo͞od) *n.* 1 Loneliness; seclusion. 2 A deserted or lonely place; hence, a desert. [<OF <L *solitudo* < *solus* alone]

Synonyms: isolation, loneliness, privacy, retirement. See RETIREMENT, SECLUSION.

sol·ler·et (sol′ə·ret′) *n.* In medieval armor, a mounted warrior's steel shoe or one of its overlapping splints: also spelled *soleret.* [<OF, dim. of *soller, soler* a shoe <L *solea* sole of the foot]

sol·mi·zate (sol′mə·zāt) *v.i.* **·zat·ed, ·zat·ing** To sing by syllables; sol-fa.

sol·mi·za·tion (sol′mə·zā′shən) *n. Music* The use of syllables as names for the notes or tones of the scale. The syllables now commonly used are *do, re, mi, fa, sol, la, ti.* [<SOL + MI]

so·lo (sō′lō) *n. pl.* **·los** or **·li** (-lē) 1 A musical composition or passage for a single voice or instrument, with or without accompaniment. 2 Any of several card games, especially one in which the player who bids to take the highest number of tricks plays alone against the others. 3 Any performance accomplished alone or without assistance. —*adj.* 1 Composed or written for, or executed by, a single voice or instrument; performed as a solo. 2 Done by a single person alone: a *solo* flight. —*v.i.* **·loed, ·lo·ing** To fly an airplane alone, especially for the first time. [<Ital. <L *solus* alone]

So·lo (sō′lō) 1 A city in central Java: formerly *Surakarta.* 2 The longest river of Java, flowing 335 miles north, east, and NE from south central Java to the Java Sea, opposite Madura.

so·lo·ist (sō′lō·ist) *n.* One who performs a solo.

So·lo man (sō′lō) *Paleontol.* A species of early man (*Homo soloensis*) identified from a group of skulls found near the Solo river at Ngandong, Java, in 1931: it is thought to be an evolutionary advance over Pithecanthropus. Also called *Ngandong man.*

Sol·o·mon (sol′ə·mən) A masculine personal name. Also (diminutive) **Sol.** See also SALOMON. [<Hebrew, peaceful]

—**Solomon** King of Israel during the tenth century B.C.; noted for his wisdom and magnificence; a son of David.

Solomon Islands An archipelago in the SW Pacific east of New Guinea; about 16,500 square miles; the SE islands, including Guadalcanal, Santa Isabel, San Cristobal, Choiseul, New Georgia, and Malaita, comprise a British protectorate; total, 11,500 square miles; capital, Honiara, on Guadalcanal; the NW islands, including Bougainville, Buka and adjacent islands (total 4,320 square miles) are part of the Territory of Papua and New Guinea, administered by Australia.

Sol·o·mon's-seal (sol′ə·mənz·sēl′) *n.* Any one of several rather large perennial herbs of the lily family (genus *Polygonatum*), having tubular, six-toothed flowers and rootstocks marked at intervals by circular scars.

Solomon's seal A six-pointed star. See MOGEN DAVID.

So·lon (sō′lən), 638?–558? B.C., Athenian lawgiver; hence, **solon,** any wise lawmaker. —**So·lo·ni·an** (sə·lō′nē·ən) *adj.*

so long *Colloq.* Good-by.

So·lor Islands (sô·lôr′) An island group east of Flores, part of the Lesser Sunda Islands, Nusa Tenggara, Indonesia; total, 785 square miles.

So·lo·thurn (zō′lō·to͝orn) 1 A canton of NW Switzerland; 305 square miles. 2 The capital of Solothurn canton, NW Switzerland, on the Aar river: French *Soleure.*

sol·pu·gid (sol·pyo͞o′jid) *n.* A predatory, spider-like arachnid (order *Solpugida*) of warm climates that hides by day. [<L *solpuga, solipuga,* a kind of venomous ant or spider]

sol·stice (sol′stis) *n.* 1 *Astron.* The time of year when the sun is at its greatest distance from the celestial equator, either north or south, and seems to pause before returning on its course; either the **summer solstice,** about June 22 in the northern hemisphere, or the **winter solstice,** about December 22. 2 A culminating or high point; epoch; limit. [<F <L *solstitium* < *sol* sun + *sistere* cause to stand] —**sol·sti·tial** (sol·stish′əl) *adj.*

sol·u·bil·i·ty (sol′yə·bil′ə·tē) *n. pl.* **·ties** The state of being soluble, or the capability of being dissolved. Also **sol′u·ble·ness.**

sol·u·bil·ize (sol′yə·bəl·īz′) *v.t.* **·ized, ·iz·ing** *Chem.* To make soluble; specifically, to disperse (normally insoluble oils and fats) by the action of detergents and certain protein molecules. —**sol′u·bil·i·za′tion** *n.*

sol·u·ble (sol′yə·bəl) *adj.* 1 Capable of being uniformly dissolved in a liquid: Sugar is *soluble* in water. 2 Susceptible of being solved or explained. [<OF <L *solubilis* < *solvere* solve, dissolve] —**sol′u·bly** *adv.*

soluble cotton Nitrocellulose which is soluble in acetone, amyl acetate, ethanol, and certain other solvents: used in making nail polish and similar lacquers.

soluble glass Sodium silicate.

so·lum (sō′ləm) *n.* That part of a soil profile above the parent material in which the processes of soil formation take place; the soil proper. [<L *solum* ground]

so·lus (sō′ləs) *adj. Latin* Alone: used in stage directions. **—so·la** (sō′lə) *adj. fem.*
sol·ute (sol′yōōt, sō′lōōt) *n.* The substance dissolved in a solution as distinguished from the solvent.
so·lu·tion (sə·lōō′shən) *n.* **1** A homogeneous mixture formed by dissolving one or more substances, whether solid, liquid, or gaseous, in another substance, usually a liquid but sometimes a solid or a gas. **2** Any homogeneous mixture of which the solute is uniformly dispersed through the solvent, and whose composition may undergo continuous variation within certain limits. **3** The act or process by which such a mixture is made. **4** The act or process of explaining, settling, or disposing, as of a difficulty, problem, or doubt. **5** *Law* Payment or satisfaction of a claim or debt. **6** *Med.* The crisis of a disease; termination of a disease with critical signs. **7** *Math.* The answer to a problem; also, the method of finding the answer. **8** Separation; disruption: the *solution* of continuity. [< OF < L *solutio, -onis* < *solutus,* pp. of *solvere* dissolve]
solution pressure *Chem.* The pressure caused by the tendency of atoms or molecules to dissolve. In the case of metals it produces the current in a primary attery.
sol·u·tive (sol′yə·tiv) *adj.* **1** Loosening; laxative. **2** Soluble.
So·lu·tre·an (sə·lōō′trē·ən) *adj. Anthropol.* Pertaining to or characteristic of an Upper Paleolithic culture preceding the Magdalenian in western Europe: it is typified by a skilled technique in the making of bladed flint implements and by marked improvements in polychrome cave painting. Also **So·lu′tri·an.** [after *Solutré,* a village in central France, where remains were discovered]
solv·a·ble (sol′və·bəl) *adj.* **1** That may be solved. **2** That may be dissolved. **—solv′a·bil′i·ty, solv′a·ble·ness** *n.*
sol·va·tion (sol·vā′shən) *n. Chem.* A loose combination sometimes formed by the solute and solvent of a solution, as copper sulfate crystallizing from water.
Sol·vay process (sol′vā) A process of making soda by treating a concentrated solution of common salt with ammonia and carbon dioxide, yielding sodium bicarbonate, which is converted into soda by heat, carbon dioxide and water being expelled. [after Ernst *Solvay,* 1838–1922, Belgian chemist]
solve (solv) *v.t.* **solved, solv·ing** To arrive at or work out the correct explanation or solution of; find the answer to; resolve. [< L *solvere* solve, loosen] **—solv′er** *n.*
Synonyms: clear, decipher, do, elucidate, explain, guess, interpret, resolve, understand, unfold. *Antonyms*: confound, confuse, perplex.
sol·ven·cy (sol′vən·sē) *n.* The condition of being solvent.
sol·vent (sol′vənt) *adj.* **1** Having means sufficient to pay all debts; having more assets than liabilities. **2** Having the power of dissolving. —*n.* **1** That which solves. **2** A substance, generally a liquid, capable of dissolving other substances; that in which another substance is dissolved. **3** A medicine used for dissolving morbid concretions or obstructions in or upon some organ. [< L *solvens, -entis,* ppr. of *solvere* solve, loosen]
sol·vol·y·sis (sol·vol′ə·sis) *n. Chem.* Any of various double-decomposition reactions similar to hydrolysis, as the reaction of mercuric chloride with liquid ammonia to form a basic salt. [< L *solvere* loosen + Gk. *lysis* a loosening] — **sol·vo·lyt·ic** (sol′və·lit′ik) *adj.*
Sol·way Firth (sol′wā) An inlet of the Irish Sea on the boundary between England and Scotland; extends 40 miles inland; 20 miles wide at its mouth.
Sol·y·man (sol′i·mən) See SULEIMAN.
Sol·zhe·ni·tsyn (sôl′zhə·nē′tsin), **Alexander Isaevich,** born 1918, U.S.S.R. author.
so·ma (sō′mə) *n. pl.* **·ma·ta** (-mə·tə) *Biol.* The body of any organism, excluding the germ, or germ plasm. [< Gk. *sōma* body]
-soma See -SOME².
So·ma·li (sō·mä′lē) *n.* **1** A member of one of certain Hamitic tribes of Somaliland. **2** The Hamitic language of the Somalis. Also **So·mal** (sō·mäl′).
So·ma·lia (sō·mä′lyə) An independent republic in eastern Africa comprising the former United Nations Trust Territory of Somalia, administered by Italy, and British Somaliland; about 270,000 square miles; capital, Mogadishu. — **So·ma′li** *adj. & n.*
So·ma·li·land (sō·mä′lē·land), **French** A French overseas territory in eastern Africa; 8,494 square miles; capital, Djibouti.
so·ma·scope (sō′mə·skōp) *n.* A photographic device combining the principles of sonar, radar, and television to facilitate the detection of cancer and other diseases. —*v.t.* **·scope, ·scop·ing** To apply the somascope to (a patient). [< Gk. *sōma* body + -SCOPE] **—so·mas·co·py** (sō·mas′kə·pē) *n.*
so·ma·tal·gi·a (sō′mə·tal′jē·ə) *n. Pathol.* Pain due to physical causes: distinguished from *psychalgia.* [< SOMAT(O)- + Gk. *algos* a pain]
so·mat·ic (sō·mat′ik) *adj. Biol.* **1** Of or relating to the body, as opposed to the spirit; physical; corporeal. **2** Of or pertaining to the framework or walls of a body, as distinguished from the viscera; parietal. **3** Pertaining to those elements or processes of an organism which are concerned with the maintenance of the individual as distinguished from the reproduction of the species: *somatic* cells. [< Gk. *sōmatikos* < *sōma* body]
somatic cell *Biol.* A cell that assists with maintenance of the body rather than reproduction of the species: distinguished from *germ cell.*
so·mat·ics (sō·mat′iks) *n. pl. (construed as singular)* Somatology.
so·ma·tism (sō′mə·tiz′əm) *n.* Materialism. — **so′ma·tist** *n.*
somato- *combining form* Body; of, pertaining to, or denoting the body: *somatology.* Also, before vowels, **somat-.** [< Gk. *sōma, sōmatos* the body]
so·ma·to·gen·ic (sō′mə·tō·jen′ik) *adj. Biol.* Originating in the soma or body cells of an organism: said of variations due to the direct influence of environment: *somatogenic* or acquired characters. Also **so′ma·to·ge·net′ic** (-jə·net′ik). — **so′ma·to·gen′e·sis** *n.*
so·ma·tol·o·gy (sō′mə·tol′ə·jē) *n.* **1** The science of organic bodies, especially of the human body: embracing anatomy and physiology. **2** The branch of anthropology that treats of the physical nature of man. [< SOMATO- + -LOGY] — **so′ma·to·log′ic** (-tō·loj′ik), **so′ma·to·log′i·cal** *adj.* **—so′ma·to·log′i·cal·ly** *adv.* **—so′ma·tol′o·gist** *n.*
so·ma·to·plasm (sō′mə·tə·plaz′əm) *n. Biol.* The protoplasm making up the somatic cells.
so·ma·to·pleure (sō′mə·tō·plŏŏr′) *n. Biol.* In the embryonic development of vertebrates, the outer of the two layers into which the mesoblast divides, together with its investing epiblast. [< SOMATO- + Gk. *pleura* side]
so·ma·to·tro·pin (sō′mə·tō·trō′pin) *n. Biol.* The hormone that regulates bodily growth, produced in the pituitary gland.
som·ber (som′bər) *adj.* **1** Partially deprived of light or brightness; dusky; murky; gloomy. **2** Somewhat melancholy; producing or denoting gloomy feelings; depressing. Also **som′bre,** *Obs.* **som′brous.** See synonyms under DARK, SAD. [< F *sombre*; ult. origin uncertain] **—som′ber·ly** *adv.* **—som′ber·ness** *n.*
som·bre·ro (som·brâr′ō) *n. pl.* **·ros** A broad-brimmed hat, usually of felt, much worn in Spain, Latin America, and the southwestern United States: humorously called a *ten-gallon hat.* [< Sp. < *sombra* shade]
Som·bre·ro (sôm·brâr′ō) See ST. CHRISTOPHER, NEVIS, AND ANGUILLA.
some (sum) *adj.* **1** Of indeterminate quantity, number, or amount. **2** Limited in degree or amount; moderate. **3** Conceived or thought of, but not definitely known: *some* person. **4** *Logic* Part (more than one) but not all of a class. **5** *U.S. Slang* Of considerable account; worthy of notice; extraordinary: That was *some* birthday party. — *pron.* **1** A certain undetermined quantity or part; a portion. **2** Certain particular ones not definitely known or not specifically designated. — *adv.* **1** *U.S. Colloq.* In an approximate degree; as nearly as may be estimated; about: *Some* eighty people were present. **2** *Slang* Somewhat. ◆ Homophone: *sum.* [OE *sum* some]
-some¹ *suffix of adjectives* Characterized by, or tending to be (what is indicated by the main element): *blithesome, frolicsome, darksome.* [OE *-sum* like, resembling]
-some² *suffix of nouns* A body: *chromosome, merosome.* Also spelled *-soma.* [< Gk. *sōma* a body]
-some³ *suffix of nouns* A group consisting of (a specified number): *twosome, foursome.* [< SOME]
some·bod·y (sum′bod′ē, -bəd·ē) *pron.* A person unknown or unnamed: *Somebody* loves me. —*n. pl.* **·bod·ies** A person of consequence or importance: She thinks herself a *somebody.*
some·day (sum′dā′) *adv.* At some future time.
some·deal (sum′dēl′) *adv. Archaic* Somewhat.
some·how (sum′hou′) *adv.* In some way or in some manner not explained.
some·one (sum′wun′, -wən) *pron.* Some person; somebody. —*n.* A somebody.
som·er·sault (sum′ər·sôlt) *n.* A leap in which a person turns heels over head and lights on his feet. —*v.i.* To perform a somersault. Also spelled *summersault, summerset.* Also **som′er·set.** [< OF *sombresault,* alter. of *sobresault,* ult. < L *supra* above + *saltus* a leap]
Som·er·set (sum′ər·set) A maritime county in SW England; 1,613 square miles; county town, Taunton. Also **Som′er·set·shire′** (-shir′).
Som·er·vell (sum′ər·vel), **Brehon,** 1892–1955, U.S. general.
So·mes (sô·mesh′) A river in northern Rumania and NE Hungary, flowing 145 miles NW to the Tisza river; including either headstream, 250 miles.
so·mes·the·sis (sō′məs·thē′sis) *n.* A diffuse, generalized awareness of the body and of bodily sensation. Also **so′mes·the′si·a** (-thē′·zhē·ə, -zhə). [< Gk. *sōma* body + *esthesis*] **—so′mes·thet′ic** (-thet′ik) *adj.*
some·thing (sum′thing) *n.* **1** A particular thing indefinitely conceived or stated. **2** Some portion or quantity. **3** A person or thing of importance. —*adv.* Somewhat: archaic except in special phrases, as **something like.**
some·time (sum′tīm′) *adv.* **1** At some future time not precisely stated; eventually. **2** At some indeterminate time or occasion. —*adj.* Former; quondam: a *sometime* student at Oxford.
some·times (sum′tīmz′) *adv.* **1** At times; occasionally. **2** *Obs.* Formerly; once.
some·way (sum′wā′) *adv.* In some way or other; somehow. Also **some way, some′ways′.**
some·what (sum′hwot′, -hwət) *n.* **1** An uncertain quantity or degree; something. **2** An individual or thing of consequence. —*adv.* In some degree.
some·when (sum′hwen′) *adv.* At some time.
some·where (sum′hwâr′) *adv.* **1** In, at, or to some place unspecified or unknown. **2** In one place or another. **3** In or to some existent place: opposed to *nowhere.* **4** Approximately. —*n.* An unspecified or unknown place.
some·wheres (sum′hwârz′) *adv. Chiefly Dial.* Somewhere: not considered an acceptable form in standard English.
some·whith·er (sum′hwith′ər) *adv. Archaic* To some indefinite or unknown place; somewhere.
some·why (sum′hwī′) *adv.* For some reason.
some·wise (sum′wīz′) *adv.* In some way or other: obsolete except in the phrase, **in somewise.**
so·mite (sō′mīt) *n. Zool.* A serial segment of the body of an animal, especially of an annelid or arthropod. [< Gk. *sōma* body + -ITE¹] **—so·mi·tal** (sō′mə·təl), **so·mit·ic** (sō·mit′ik) *adj.*
Somme (sôm) A river in northern France, flowing 150 miles west to the English Channel; scene of battles in World War I (1916, 1918), and in World War II (1940, 1944).
som·me·lier (sô·me·lyā′) *n. French* A wine steward.
som·nam·bu·late (som·nam′byə·lāt) *v.* **·lat·ed, ·lat·ing** *v.i.* To walk or wander about while asleep. —*v.t.* To walk over or through while asleep. [< L *somnus* sleep + AMBULATE]
som·nam·bu·lism (som·nam′byə·liz′əm) *n.* The act or state of walking during sleep. Also **som·nam′bu·la′tion. —som·nam′bu·lant** (-lənt) *adj.* **—som·nam′bu·list** *n.* **—som·nam′bu·lis′tic** *adj.*
somni- *combining form* Sleep; of or pertaining to sleep: *somnifacient.* [< L *somnus* sleep]
som·ni·fa·cient (som′nə·fā′shənt) *adj.* Promoting sleep; hypnotic. —*n.* A drug which induces sleep. [< SOMNI- + -FACIENT]
som·nif·er·ous (som·nif′ər·əs) *adj.* Tending to produce sleep; soporiferous; narcotic. Also **som·nif′ic.** [< SOMNI- + -FEROUS]
som·nil·o·quy (som·nil′ə·kwē) *n.* **1** The act of talking when asleep, especially in mesmeric

sleep. 2 The words so spoken. [< SOMNI- + L *loqui* speak] —**som·nil′o·quist** *n.*

som·no·lence (som′nə·ləns) *n.* Oppressive drowsiness or inclination to sleep. Also **som′· no·len·cy.**

som·no·lent (som′nə·lənt) *adj.* 1 Inclined to sleep; drowsy. 2 Tending to induce drowsiness. [< F < L *somnolentus* < *somnus* sleep] —**som′no·lent·ly** *adv.*

Som·nus (som′nəs) In Roman mythology, the god of sleep: identified with the Greek *Hypnos.*

son (sun) *n.* 1 A male child considered with reference to either parent or to both parents. 2 Any male descendant. 3 One who occupies the place of a son, as by adoption, marriage, or regard. 4 A person regarded as a native of a particular country or place. 5 A male person who is characterized or influenced by some quality or thing or by a being representing some quality or character: a *son* of liberty; *sons* of Belial. Homophone: *sun.* [OE *sunu*]

Son (sun) Jesus Christ; the second person of the Trinity.

so·nance (sō′nəns) *n.* 1 A sound, as of music; also, a tune or air. 2 The state or quality of being sonant.

so·nant (sō′nənt) *adj.* 1 Sounding; resonant. 2 *Phonet.* Voiced: opposed to *surd, voiceless.* —*n. Phonet.* 1 A voiced speech sound. 2 A syllabic sound; in the Indo-European languages, a sonorant. [< L *sonans, -antis,* ppr. of *sonare* resound]

so·nar (sō′när) *n.* 1 A method of using underwater sound waves, at either audible or ultrasonic frequencies, for sounding, navigating, range finding, detection of submerged objects, communication, etc. 2 The equipment for accomplishing the transmission or reception of underwater sound waves. —*adj.* Of, or pertaining to, the equipment, personnel, or methods employed in underwater acoustic signaling. [< SO(UND) NA(VIGATION AND) R(ANGING)]

so·na·ta (sə·nä′tə) *n. Music* A composition for one or two instruments, written in three or four movements, each of which is distinct from the others in tempo and mood but akin to them in style and key. [< Ital. < *sonare* sound]

sonata form *Music* The outline upon which the construction of a movement, specifically the first, of a sonata, quartet, symphony, etc., is based. A movement written in sonata form falls into three sections, called *exposition,* or statement of themes, *development,* and *recapitulation.*

so·na·ti·na (son′ə·tē′nə) *n. pl.* **·ti·ne** (-tē′nä) *Music* A short or easy sonata. [< Ital., dim. of *sonata* SONATA]

son·der (zon′dər) *n. Naut.* A class of small yachts, of which the sum of the water-line length, extreme beam, and extreme draft must not be greater than thirty-two feet. Also **son′der·class′** (-klas′, -kläs′). [Short for G *sonderklasse* < *sonder* particular + *klasse* class]

sone (sōn) *n. Physics* A unit of loudness, equivalent to a simple tone having a frequency of 1,000 cycles per second at 40 decibels above the threshold of hearing. [< L *sonus* sound]

song (sông, song) *n.* 1 The rendering of vocal music; more widely, any melodious utterance, as of a bird. 2 A musical composition for the voice or for several voices. 3 A short poem whether intended to be sung or not; a lyric or ballad. 4 Poetry; verse. 5 A mere trifle: to sell something for a *song.* [OE] —**song′less** *adj.*

song and dance 1 A short theatrical act consisting of a song and dance, often having no connection with the rest of the program; especially, a vaudeville act. 2 *Colloq.* Any highly interesting or entertaining statement of no pertinence to the subject under consideration; a rigmarole.

song·bird (sông′bûrd′, song′-) *n.* A bird that utters a musical call; an oscine bird.

Song Bo (sông′ bō′) The Annamese name for the BLACK RIVER, North Vietnam.

Song Coi (sông′ koi′) The Annamese name for the RED RIVER, North Vietnam.

song·ful (sông′fəl, song′-) *adj.* Full of song or melody.

Song of Solomon A Hebrew dramatic love poem in the Old Testament, attributed to Solomon; Canticles. Also **Song of Songs.**

song sparrow A common sparrow (*Melospiza melodia*) of the eastern United States, noted for its song.

song·ster (sông′stər, song′-) *n.* 1 A person or bird given to singing; one skilled in song; a poet. 2 A book of favorite songs.

song·stress (sông′stris, song′-) *n.* A female songster.

son·ic (son′ik) *adj.* 1 Of, pertaining to, determined or affected by sound: *sonic* vibrations. 2 Having a speed approaching that of sound. [< L *sonicus* < *sonus* sound]

sonic barrier *Aeron.* The transonic barrier.

so·nif·er·ous (sō·nif′ər·əs) *adj.* Producing or conducting sound. [< L *sonus* sound + -FEROUS]

son-in-law (sun′in·lô′) *n. pl.* **sons-in-law** The husband of one's daughter.

son·net (son′it) *n.* 1 A poem of fourteen decasyllabic or (rarely) octosyllabic lines, originally composed of an octave and a sestet, properly expressing two successive phases of a single thought or sentiment. In the **Petrarchan,** or **Italian, sonnet** the rime scheme for the octave is *abbaabba,* followed by two or three other rimes in the sestet, with a slight change in thought after the octave. In the **Elizabethan,** or **Shakespearean, sonnet** the rime scheme is *ababcdcdefefgg.* 2 A short poem; an amatory lyric. See synonyms under SONG. —*v.t.* To celebrate in sonnets. —*v.i.* To compose sonnets. [< F < Ital. *sonnetto* < Provençal *sonet,* dim. of *son* a sound < L *sonus*]

son·net·eer (son′ə·tir′) *n.* A composer of sonnets. —*v.i.* To compose sonnets.

son·ny (sun′ē) *n. pl.* **·nies** *Colloq.* Youngster: a familiar form of address.

son·o·chem·is·try (son′ō·kem′is·trē) *n.* The study of the chemical changes effected by sound waves, especially ultrasound.

son of liberty Originally, one who fought against the British in the American Revolution, or a member of any of various organizations formed to oppose the Stamp Act.

son·o·gram (son′ō·gram) *n.* Echogram.

So·no·ra (sə·nôr′ä, -nō′rä) 1 A state in NW Mexico; 70,465 square miles; capital, Hermosillo. 2 A river in Sonora state, flowing 250 miles south and SW to the Gulf of California.

so·no·rant (sə·nôr′ənt, -nō′rənt) *n. Phonet.* A voiced consonant of relatively high resonance, as (l), (r), (m), and (n), capable of constituting a syllable.

so·nor·i·ty (sə·nôr′ə·tē, -nor′-) *n.* Sonorous quality or state; resonance. Also **so·no′rous·ness.**

so·no·rous (sə·nôr′əs, -nō′rəs) *adj.* 1 Productive or capable of sound vibrations; sounding. 2 Loud and full-sounding; resonant. 3 *Phonet.* Sonant. [< L *sonorus* < *sonare* resound] —**so·no′rous·ly** *adv.*

son·ship (sun′ship) *n.* The state or relation of being a son.

Sons of Liberty The various patriotic societies, or members thereof, organized to oppose British rule in the American colonies.

son·sy (son′sē) *adj. Scot. & Brit. Dial.* Having sweet, engaging looks; happy; jolly; well-conditioned. Also **son′sie.**

Soo Canals (sōō) A colloquial name for the SAULT SAINTE MARIE CANALS.

soo·chong (sōō′chong′, -jong′) See SOUCHONG.

Soo·chow (sōō′chou′, *Chinese* sōō′jō′) See SÜCHOW.

soom (sōōm) *v. & n. Scot.* Swim.

soon (sōōn) *adv.* 1 At a future or subsequent time not long distant; shortly. 2 Without delay; in a speedy manner; also, with ease; readily. 3 With willingness or readiness: usually with *would as, had as,* etc. 4 In good season; early. 5 *Obs.* At once; immediately. [OE *sōna* immediately]

soon·er (sōō′nər) *n. U.S. Slang* 1 A person who goes before the appointed time to take up free public land, and thus obtains one of the most desirable sites. 2 One who makes an unfair and premature start.

Soon·er (sōō′nər) *n. U.S.* A nickname for a native of Oklahoma.

Sooner State Nickname for OKLAHOMA.

Soong (sōōng) Name of a distinguished Chinese family influential in politics, whose members include **Tse-ven,** born 1891, banker; **Ai-ling,** born 1888, the wife of H. H. Kung; **Ching-ling,** born 1890, the widow of Sun Yat-sen, and **Mei-ling,** born 1898, the wife of Chiang Kai-shek.

soop (sōōp) *v.t. & v.i. Scot.* To sweep.

soor (sōōr) *adj. Scot.* Sour.

soot (sŏŏt, sōōt) *n.* A black substance, essentially carbon from the combustion of wood or coal, as deposited on the inside of chimneys and other surfaces in contact with smoke. —*v.t.* To soil or cover with soot. [OE *sōt*]

sooth (sōōth) *Archaic adj.* 1 True; real. 2 Soothing; smooth. —*n.* Truth. Also spelled *soth.* [OE *sōth*] —**sooth′ly** *adv.*

soothe (sōōth) *v.* **soothed, sooth·ing** *v.t.* 1 To restore to a quiet or normal state; calm. 2 To mitigate, soften, or relieve, as pain or grief. 3 *Obs.* To yield assent to; agree with. —*v.i.* 4 To afford relief; have a calming or relieving effect. See synonyms under ALLAY, TEMPER, TRANQUILIZE. [OE *sōthian* verify < *sōth* truth] —**sooth′er** *n.*

sooth·fast (sōōth′fast′, -fäst′) *adj. Archaic* 1 Truthful; also, steadfast; loyal. 2 Real; true. —**sooth′fast′ly** *adv.* —**sooth′fast′ness** *n.*

sooth·ing (sōō′thing) *adj.* Calming; quieting, as a sedative; pacifying. —**sooth′ing·ly** *adv.*

sooth·say (sōōth′sā′) *v.i.* **·said, ·say·ing** To announce the future, as a soothsayer. —**sooth′· say′ing** *n.*

sooth·say·er (sōōth′sā′ər) *n.* 1 One who claims to have supernatural insight and to be able to foretell events. 2 *Obs.* A truthful person: the original meaning.

soot·y (sŏŏt′ē, sōōt′ē) *adj.* **soot·i·er, soot·i·est** 1 Blackened or stained by soot. 2 Producing or consisting of soot. 3 Black like soot. —**soot′i·ly** *adv.* —**soot′i·ness** *n.*

sooty grouse A blue grouse (*Dendrogapus fuliginosus*).

sop (sop) *v.* **sopped, sop·ping** *v.t.* 1 To dip or soak in a liquid. 2 To drench. 3 To take up by absorption: often with *up.* —*v.i.* 4 To be absorbed; soak in. 5 To be or become saturated or drenched. —*n.* 1 Anything softened in liquid, as bread. 2 Anything given to pacify, as a bribe. 3 Any soggy mass. [OE *sopp*] —**sop′py** *adj.*

So·phi·a (sō·fī′ə, -fē′ə) A feminine personal name. Also **So·phie** (sō′fē; *Dan., Du.* sō·fē′ə, *Fr.* sō·fē′). [< Gk., wise]

soph·ism (sof′iz·əm) *n.* 1 A false argument intentionally used to deceive. 2 The doctrine or method of the sophists. See synonyms under SOPHISTRY. [< L *sophisma* < Gk., ult. < *sophos* wise]

soph·ist (sof′ist) *n.* 1 A philosopher; a learned man; a thinker. 2 One who argues cleverly but fallaciously or unnecessarily minutely. —*adj.* Pertaining to the art or method of sophists, or to sophistry. [< L *sophista* < Gk. *sophistēs,* ult. < *sophos* wise]

Soph·ist (sof′ist) *n.* 1 A member of a certain school of early Greek philosophy, preceding the Socratic school. 2 One of the later Greek teachers of philosophy and rhetoric, who acquired great skill in subtle disputation under logical forms.

soph·is·ter (sof′is·tər) *n.* 1 A student in one of the later years of a course in some English universities. At Cambridge, students of the second year are called **junior sophisters** or **junior sophs,** and the third-year men **senior sophisters.** 2 A sophist or a Sophist.

so·phis·tic (sə·fis′tik) *adj.* Pertaining to a Sophist, sophists, or sophistry. —*n.* The art or method of the Sophists. Also **so·phis′ti·cal.** —**so·phis′ti·cal·ly** *adv.* —**so·phis′ti·cal·ness** *n.*

so·phis·ti·cate (sə·fis′tə·kāt) *v.* **·cat·ed, ·cat·ing** *v.t.* 1 To make less simple or ingenuous in mind or manner; render worldly-wise or artificial. 2 To mislead or corrupt (a person). 3 To adulterate. 4 To falsify (a text, statement, etc.) by unauthorized or deceptive alterations. —*v.i.* 5 To indulge in sophistry; be sophistic. —*n.* (-kit, -kāt) A sophisticated person. [< Med. L *sophisticatus,* pp. of *sophisticare* < *sophisticus* sophistic] —**so·phis′ti·ca′tor** *n.*

so·phis·ti·cat·ed (sə·fis′tə·kā′tid) *adj.* 1 Worldly-wise; deprived of natural simplicity; disillusioned. 2 Pretentiously wise; possessing

superficial information. 3 Of a kind that appeals to the worldly-wise. 4 Very complicated in design, capabilities, etc.: said of mechanical and electronic devices.
so·phis·ti·ca·tion (sə·fis′tə·kā′shən) *n.* 1 The act of sophisticating; a quibble; a misrepresentation in reasoning or argument. 2 The state of being sophisticated. 3 Adulteration or falsification.
soph·is·try (sof′is·trē) *n. pl.* **·tries** 1 Subtly fallacious reasoning or disputation. 2 The art or methods of the Greek Sophists.
Synonyms: casuistry, chicanery, evasion, fallacy, hair-splitting, paralogism, prevarication, quibbling, sophism, subterfuge, trickery.
Soph·o·cles (sof′ə·klēz), 495?–406 B.C., Athenian tragic poet. — **Soph′o·cle′an** *adj.*
soph·o·more (sof′ə·môr, -mōr) *n.* In American high schools, colleges, and universities having a four-year course, a second-year student. [Earlier *sophomer* a dialectician < *sophom*, var. of SOPHISM (def. 1), because they studied dialectics; later infl. in meaning by Gk. *sophos* wise + *mōros* a fool]
soph·o·mor·ic (sof′ə·môr′ik, -mōr′-) *adj.* Of, pertaining to, or like a sophomore; hence, marked by a shallow assumption of learning or by empty grandiloquence; immature; callow. Also **soph′o·mor′i·cal.** — **soph′o·mor′i·cal·ly** *adv.*
So·phy (sō′fē) *n. Obs.* A title formerly given to kings of Persia: also **So′phi.** [<Persian *Safawi*, a Persian royal family]
So·phy (sō′fē) A diminutive of SOPHIA.
-sophy *combining form* Knowledge pertaining to a (specified) field: *theosophy.* [<Gk. *sophia* wisdom]
so·por (sō′pər) *n.* Deep lethargic sleep. [<L]
so·po·rif·er·ous (sō′pə·rif′ər·əs, sop′ə-) *adj.* Bringing sleep. — **so′po·rif′er·ous·ly** *adv.* — **so′·po·rif′er·ous·ness** *n.*
so·po·rif·ic (sō′pə·rif′ik, sop′ə-) *adj.* 1 Causing or tending to cause sleep. 2 Drowsy; sleepy; characterized by lethargy. — *n.* A medicine that produces sleep.
sop·ping (sop′ing) *adj.* Wet through; drenched; soaking.
sop·py (sop′ē) *adj.* **·pi·er, ·pi·est** Saturated and softened with moisture; soft and sloppy; very wet.
so·pran·o (sə·pran′ō, -prä′nō) *n. pl.* **so·pran·os** or **so·pra·ni** (sə·prä′nē) 1 A woman's or boy's voice of the highest range, usually extending from middle C upward about two octaves. 2 The music intended for such a voice; the treble. 3 A person having a treble or high-range voice, or singing such a part. — *adj.* Of or pertaining to a soprano voice or part. [<Ital. < *sopra* above <L *supra.* Related to SOVEREIGN.]
Sop·ron (shōp′rōn) A city in western Hungary near the Austrian border: German *Ödenburg.*
So·qo·tra (sō·kō′trə) See SOCOTRA.
so·ra (sôr′ə, sō′rə) *n.* A small grayish-brown North American rail *(Porzana carolina)*, esteemed as food. Also **sora rail.** [? <N. Am. Ind.]
So·ra·ta (sô·rä′tä) See ILLAMPU.
sorb (sôrb) *n.* 1 The service tree, or the rowan. 2 The fruit of either of these. [<F *sorbe* <L *sorbus* service tree]
Sorb (sôrb) *n.* A Wend.
sorb apple The fruit of the service tree.
sor·be·fa·cient (sôr′bə·fā′shənt) *adj.* Conducive to absorption; absorptive. — *n.* A medicine that promotes absorption. [<L *sorbere* absorb + -FACIENT]
Sorb·i·an (sôr′bē·ən) *adj.* Of or pertaining to the Sorbs or Wends or to their language. — *n.* 1 A Sorb or Wend. 2 The West Slavic language of the Sorbs; Wendish.
sor·bite (sôr′bīt) *n. Metall.* A mixture of ferrite and cementite forming an important constituent of tempered steels. [after H. C. *Sorby*, 1826–1908, British metallurgist]
sor·bi·tol (sôr′bə·tōl, -tol) *n. Chem.* A white, sweetish, crystalline alcohol, $C_6H_{14}O_6$, found in mountain-ash berries, cherries, apples, pears, and some other fruits: it is used as a plasticizer and moistening agent and in the manufacture of ascorbic acid. [<SORB + -IT(E)[1] + -OL[1]]
Sor·bon·ist (sôr′bən·ist) *n.* A doctor of the Sorbonne; a student at the Sorbonne.
Sor·bonne (sôr·bôn′) 1 A former theological college founded in Paris by Robert de Sorbon in 1255–59. 2 The seat of the faculties of literature and science of the University of Paris.
sor·bose (sôr′bōs) *n.* A non-fermentable monosaccharide, $C_6H_{12}O_6$, obtained from sorbitol by bacterial action and important in the synthesis of vitamin C. [<SORB + -OSE[2]]
sor·cer·er (sôr′sər·ər) *n.* A wizard; conjurer; magician. — **sor′cer·ess** *n. fem.*
sor·cer·y (sôr′sər·ē) *n. pl.* **·cer·ies** 1 Pretended employment of supernatural agencies; magic; witchcraft. 2 Any remarkable or inexplicable means of accomplishment; witchery. [<OF *sorcerie* < *sorcier* <L *sors* fate] — **sor′cer·ous** *adj.* — **sor′cer·ous·ly** *adv.*
Synonyms: divination, enchantment, incantation, magic, necromancy, spell, voodoo, witchcraft.
sor·del·li·na (sôr′del·lē′nä) *n. Italian* A kind of small bagpipe.
Sor·del·lo (sôr·del′ō, *Ital.* sôr·del′lō), 1180?–1255?, Provençal troubadour.
sor·did (sôr′did) *adj.* 1 Of, pertaining to, or actuated by a low desire for gain; mercenary. 2 Of degraded character; vile; base; squalid. 3 Of a dull, dirty, or muddy hue. 4 Foul: the old sense. See synonyms under AVARICIOUS, BASE[2]. [<L *sordidus* squalid] — **sor′did·ly** *adv.* — **sor′did·ness** *n.*
sor·di·no (sôr·dē′nō) *n. pl.* **·ni** (-nē) *Music* A mute. [<Ital.]
sore (sôr, sōr) *n.* 1 A place on an animal body where the skin or flesh is bruised, broken, or inflamed; an ulcer or diseased spot. 2 A painful memory; distressing evil; trouble; grief; controversy. — *adj.* **sor·er, sor·est** 1 Morbidly tender; having a sore or sores. 2 Pained or distressed in mind; aggrieved; touchy. 3 Arousing painful feelings; irritating; distressing. 4 Causing extreme distress; severe; also, very great; extreme: He was in *sore* need of money. 5 *Colloq.* Offended; aggrieved; angry. — *adv. Archaic* Sorely. [OE *sār*] — **sore′ness** *n.*
so·re·di·um (sə·rē′dē·əm) *n. pl.* **·di·a** (-dē·ə) *Bot.* A scalelike structure of algal cells in a lichen, enveloped in a network of hyphae and capable of independent vegetative growth. Also **so·rede** (sō′rēd). [<NL <Gk. *sōros* a heap]
sore·head (sôr′hed′, sōr′-) *U.S. Slang n.* A disgruntled or offended person. — *adj.* Dissatisfied; discontented.
sor·el (sôr′əl, sor-) See SORREL[2].
sore·ly (sôr′lē, sōr′-) *adv.* 1 Grievously; distressingly. 2 Greatly; in high degree: His aid was *sorely* needed.
sor·ghum (sôr′gəm) *n.* 1 A stout canelike tropical grass (genus *Sorghum*) cultivated for its saccharine juice and as fodder, especially any of the varieties of *Sorghum vulgare.* 2 Molasses prepared from the sweet juices of the plant. [<NL <Ital. *sorgo*, ult. <L *Syricus* of Syria, where originally grown]
sor·go (sôr′gō) *n. pl.* **·gos** *Spanish* Any variety of sorghum cultivated for its sweet juices and for forage. Also **sor′gho.**
so·ri (sôr′ī, sō′rī) Plural of SORUS.
sor·i·cine (sôr′ə·sīn, -sin, sor′-) *adj.* Pertaining or belonging to a subfamily *(Soricinae)* typical of a family *(Soricidae)* of small, mouselike mammals, the shrews, widely distributed in the northern hemisphere; shrewlike. [<NL <L *sorex, soricis* a shrew]
so·ri·tes (sō·rī′tēs, sō-) *n. Logic* A form of compound syllogism made up of successive coordinate members: Bucephalus is a horse; a horse is a quadruped; a quadruped is an animal; therefore Bucephalus is an animal. [<L <Gk. *sōreitēs* < *sōros* a heap] — **so·rit′i·cal** (-rit′i·kəl) *adj.*
sorn (sôrn) *v.i. Scot.* To force oneself on others for food and lodging. — **sorn′er** *n.*
So·ro·ca·ba (sō′rōō·kä′və) A city in SE São Paulo state, Brazil.
so·ro·che (sō·rō′chā) *n. Spanish* Mountain sickness; puna.
So·rol·la y Bas·ti·da (sō·rō′lyä ē väs·tē′thä), **Joaquín**, 1863–1923, Spanish painter.
so·ror·ate (sôr′ə·rāt, sō′rə·rāt) *n. Anthropol.* The marriage of a man with the sister or sisters of his wife, or with other close female relatives. Compare LEVIRATE. [<L *soror* a sister]
so·ror·i·cide (sə·rôr′ə·sīd) *n.* 1 The killing of a sister. 2 One who kills a sister. [<LL *sororicidium* < *soror* a sister + *caedere* kill; def. 2 <L *sororicida*]
so·ror·i·ty (sə·rôr′ə·tē, -ror′-) *n. pl.* **·ties** A sisterhood; specifically, a women's national or local association having chapters in a secondary school, college, or university. [< Med. L *sororitas, -tatis,* <L *soror* a sister]
so·ro·sis (sə·rō′sis) *n. Bot.* A type of multiple fruit consisting of a fleshy mass formed by the merging of many flowers, as in the mulberry. [<NL <Gk. *sōros* a heap]
So·ro·sis (sə·rō′sis) *n.* A women's club, the first to be organized (1868) in America; hence, **sorosis,** any women's club or society.
sorp·tion (sôrp′shən) *n.* Any process by which one substance takes up and holds the molecules of another substance, as by absorption or adsorption. [<NL *sorptio, -onis* <L *sorbere*]
sor·rel[1] (sôr′əl, sor′-) *n.* 1 Any of several low perennial herbs (genus *Rumex*) with acid leaves, especially the common sorrel *(R. acetosa).* 2 The wood sorrel (genera *Oxalis* or *Xanthoxalis*). [<F *surele* < *sur* <OHG, sour]
sor·rel[2] (sôr′əl, sor′-) *n.* 1 A reddish- or yellowish-brown color. 2 An animal of this color. 3 A buck of the third year. Also spelled *sorel.* [<OF *sorel* < *sor*, a hawk with red plumage]
sorrel tree An American tree *(Oxydendrum arboreum)* of the heath family, with drooping clusters of white flowers and sour evergreen leaves.
Sor·ren·to (sôr·ren′tō) A port on the Bay of Naples, SW Italy.
sor·row (sor′ō, sôr′ō) *n.* 1 Pain or distress of mind because of loss, injury, or misfortune, the commission of sin, or sympathy with suffering; grief. 2 An event that causes pain or distress of mind; affliction; a trial; misfortune; woe. 3 The expression of grief; lamentation; mourning. See synonyms under GRIEF, MISFORTUNE, REPENTANCE. — *v.i.* To feel sorrow; grieve; lament; be sad. See synonyms under MOURN. [OE *sorg* care] — **sor′row·er** *n.*
sor·row·ful (sor′ə·fəl, sôr′-) *adj.* Sad; unhappy; mournful. See synonyms under BAD[1], PITIFUL, SAD. — **sor′row·ful·ly** *adv.* — **sor′row·ful·ness** *n.*
sor·ry (sor′ē, sôr′ē) *adj.* **·ri·er, ·ri·est** 1 Grieved or pained; affected by sorrow from any cause. 2 Causing sorrow; melancholy; dismal. 3 Pitiable or worthless; poor; paltry. 4 Painful; grievous. See synonyms under BAD, SAD. [OE *sārig* < *sār* sore] — **sor′ri·ly** *adv.* — **sor′ri·ness** *n.*
sort (sôrt) *n.* 1 Any number or collection of persons or things characterized by the same or similar qualities; a kind; species; class; set. 2 Form of being or acting; character; nature; quality; also, manner; way; style. 3 *Printing* A character or type considered as a portion of a font: usually in the plural. 4 *Obs.* Social rank, especially high rank. 5 *Obs.* A lot; destiny. — **of sorts** Originally, of various or different kinds; now, of a poor or unsatisfactory kind: used disparagingly: an actor *of sorts.* — **sort of** Somewhat. — *v.t.* 1 To arrange or separate into grades, kinds, or sizes; classify; assort. — *v.i.* 2 To agree; be suitable; correspond. 3 To associate; consort. [<OF *sorte* <L *sors, sortis* lot, condition] — **sort′a·ble** *adj.* — **sort′a·bly** *adv.* — **sort′er** *n.*
Synonyms (noun): character, condition, degree, denomination, description, kind, nature, order, race, rank, style.
sor·tie (sôr′tē) *n. Mil.* 1 A sally of troops from a besieged place to attack the besiegers. 2 A single trip of an aircraft on an assigned military or naval mission. [<F < *sortir* go forth]
sor·ti·lege (sôr′tə·lij) *n.* The act or practice of drawing lots; divination by lot; also, sorcery. [<OF *sortilege* <LL *sortilegus* a diviner <L *sors, sortis* a lot + *legere* pick, choose]
so·rus (sôr′əs, sō′rəs) *n. pl.* **so·ri** (sôr′ī, sō′rī) *Bot.* In ferns and fernlike plants, a cluster of spore cases (sporangia); a fruit dot. [<NL <Gk. *sōros* a heap]
S O S The code signal of distress adopted by the Radiotelegraphic Convention in 1912, and used by airplanes, ships, etc.; hence, any call for assistance.
So·sno·wiec (sô·snô′vyets) A city in SW Poland, important as an industrial center.
so-so (sō′sō′) *adj.* Passable; neither very good nor very bad; mediocre. — *adv.* Indifferently; tolerably.
sos·te·nu·to (sôs′te·nōō′tō) *Music adj.* Sustained or continuous in tone; prolonged or held. — *n.* A sostenuto passage or movement.

Also **sos'ti·nen'to** (-tē·nen'tō), **sos'te·nen'do** (-te·nen'dō). [<Ital.]

sot (sot) *n.* A habitual drunkard. [OE <OF <LL *sottus* a drunkard]

so·te·ri·ol·o·gy (sə·tir'ē·ol'ə·jē) *n.* The branch of theology that treats of salvation by Jesus Christ. [<Gk. *sōtērios* <*sōtēr* savior + -LOGY] **—so·te'ri·o·log'i·cal** (-ə·loj'ə·kəl) *adj.*

soth (sōth) See SOOTH.

Soth·ern (suth'ərn), **Edward Hugh,** 1859–1933, U.S. actor.

So·thic cycle (sō'thik, soth'ik) A period of about 1,460 years, based on an ordinary year of 365 days; or 1,461 years, based on a Sothic year of the Egyptians. See under YEAR. Also **Sothic period.**

So·this (sō'this) Sirius, the Dog Star. [<Gk. <Egyptian] **—So'thic** *adj.*

So·tho (sō'thō) *n.* **1** Any of a number of Sotho languages, especially Sesotho. **2** A group of Bantu languages of Botswana, Lesotho, and the Republic of South Africa.

so·tol (sō'tōl) *n.* Any one of a genus *(Dasylirion)* of yuccalike plants found in the SW United States. [<Mexican Sp. <Nahuatl *tzotolli*]

sot·ted (sot'id) *adj.* Drunk; besotted.

sot·tish (sot'ish) *adj.* Having the manner or character of a sot; stupefied with drink; hence, stupid; doltish. **—sot'tish·ly** *adv.*

sot·to vo·ce (sot'ō vō'chē, *Ital.* sôt'tō vō'chā) Softly; in an undertone; privately; under the breath. [<Ital., under the (normal) voice]

sou (so͞o) *n.* A former French coin of varying value; now, colloquially, something trivial or negligible. [<F <LL *solidus,* a gold coin]

sou·a·ri (so͞o·ä'rē) *n.* Any of several tropical American trees (genus *Caryocar*), yielding a durable timber known as **souari wood,** and edible nuts called **souari nuts** or butternuts; especially, *C. nuciferum.* [<F *saouari* <native name]

sou·bise (so͞o·bēz') *n. French* A sauce of onions, butter, and white sauce: also **soubise sauce.**

sou·brette (so͞o·bret') *n.* **1** An actress in light comedy; originally, a pert, intriguing lady's maid. **2** A frivolous or coquettish maidservant. [<F <Provençal *soubreto* <*soubret* shy, coy] **—sou·bret'tish** *adj.*

sou·bri·quet (so͞o'bri·kā) See SOBRIQUET.

sou·car (sou·kär') *n. Anglo-Indian* A native banker: also spelled *sowcar.*

sou·chong (so͞o'chong', -shong') *n.* A variety of black tea, made from the youngest leaves of the earliest pickings, or the infusion made from it: also spelled *soochong.* [<F <Chinese *siao* small + *chung* plant]

sou·dan (sou'dən) See SOLDAN.

Sou·dan (so͞o·dän') The French name for SUDAN.

souf·fle (so͞o'fəl) *n.* A low whispering or blowing sound or murmur heard on auscultation: the respiratory *souffle.* [<F <*souffler* blow]

souf·flé (so͞o·flā') *adj.* Made light and frothy, and fixed in that condition by heat: also **souf·fléed'** (-flād'). — *n.* A light, baked dish made fluffy with beaten egg whites combined with the yolks, and often with cheese, mushrooms, or other ingredients. [<F, orig. pp. of *souffler* blow <L *sufflare* <*sub-* under + *flare* blow]

Sou·fri·ère (so͞o·frē·âr') **1** La Soufriere. **2** Either of two dormant volcanoes, one on Guadaloupe, French West Indies, the other on St. Lucia, The West Indies.

sough (suf, sou) *v.i.* To make a sighing sound, as the wind. —*n.* A deep, murmuring sound, as of wind through trees. **—to keep a calm sough** *Scot.* To be silent. [OE *swōgan* sound, roar, rustle]

sought (sôt) Past tense and past participle of SEEK.

soul (sōl) *n.* **1** The rational, emotional, and volitional faculties in man, conceived of as forming an entity distinct from, and often existing independently of, his body. **2** *Theol.* **a** The divine principle of life in man. **b** The moral or spirital part of man as related to God, considered as surviving death and liable to joy or misery in a future state. **3** The emotional faculty of man as distinguished from his intellect: He puts his *soul* into his acting. **4** Fervor; emotional force; heartiness; vitality; nobleness: His music lacks *soul.* **5** The animating principle of a thing; an essential or vital element: Justice is the *soul* of law. **6** The leading figure or inspirer of acause, movement, party, etc.: Lee was the *soul* of the Confederacy. **7** A person considered as the embodiment of a quality or attribute: He is the *soul* of generosity. **8** A living person; a human being: Every *soul* trembled at the sight. **9** The disembodied spirit of one who has died; a ghost. **10** In Christian Science, Spirit; Deity. **11** Among American blacks: **a** The awareness of a black African heritage. **b** A strongly emotional pride and solidarity based on this awareness. **c** The qualities that arouse such feelings, especially in black culture and art. **12** Soul music. **13** Soul food. —*adj.* Of or pertaining to soul (def. 11). ◆Homophone: *sole,* [OE *sawol*] **—souled** *adj.*

Synonyms: mind, spirit. The *soul* includes the intellect, sensibilities, and will; beyond what is expressed by the word *mind,* the *soul* denotes especially the moral, the immortal nature. *Spirit* is used especially in contradistinction from matter; it may in many cases be substituted for *soul,* but *soul* has commonly a fuller and more determinate meaning. In the figurative sense, *spirit* denotes animation, excitability, perhaps impatience; as, a lad of *spirit. Soul* denotes energy and depth of feeling, as when we speak of *soulful* eyes; or it may denote the very life of anything; as, the *soul* of harmony. Compare MIND.

soul brother A black male.

soul food Any of various Southern foods or dishes such as fried chicken, ham hocks, chitterlings, yams, and collard greens, traditionally eaten by Southern American blacks.

soul·ful (sōl'fəl) *adj.* Full of that which appeals to or satisfies the higher feelings; emotional; spiritual. **—soul'ful·ly** *adv.* **—soul'ful·ness** *n.*

soul·less (sōl'lis) *adj.* **1** Having no soul. **2** Heartless; unemotional. **3** Devoid of activity or expression. **— soul'less·ly** *adv.* **—soul'·less·ness** *n.*

soul music A type of popular music strongly emotional in character and influenced chiefly by the blues and gospel hymns.

soul–search·ing (sōl'sûrch'ing) *n.* A deep examination of one's motives, desires, etc.

soul sister A black female.

sou mar·qué (so͞o mär·kā') *French* **1** An 18th century copper coin of France. **2** Hence, a trifle; something of little value. Also **sou mar·kee'** (-kē'), **sou mar·quee'** (-kē').

sound[1] (sound) *n.* **1** The sensation of hearing, produced by stimulation of the auditory centers of the brain by vibratory waves propagated through the atmosphere or other elastic medium. **2** The vibrations that produce sound waves, having for the normal human ear frequencies from about 20 to 20,000 cycles per second. **3** Noise of any specified quality: the *sound* of bugles; any tone, voice, or note. **4** Significance; implication: The story has a sinister *sound.* **5** Sounding or hearing distance; earshot: We were within the *sound* of battle. **6** Mere noise without significance: full of *sound* and fury. **7** *Obs. Rumor.* —*v.i.* **1** To give forth a sound or sounds. **2** To give a specified impression; seem: The story *sounds* true. —*v.t.* **3** To cause to give forth sound. **4** To give a signal or order for or announcement of: to *sound* retreat; to *sound* the hour. **5** To utter audibly; pronounce. **6** To make known or celebrated: to *sound* a hero's fame. **7** To test or examine by sound; auscultate. **—to sound in tort** To act as or have the nature of a tort. [<OF *son* < L *sonus*]

Synonyms (noun): noise, note, tone. *Sound* is the most comprehensive word, applying to anything that is audible. *Tone* is sound considered from the point of view of quality or pitch, or as expressive of some feeling; *noise* is *sound* considered without reference to musical quality or as distinctly unmusical or discordant. In music, *tone* may denote a musical *sound* or the interval between two such *sounds,* but in the most careful usage the latter is now distinguished as the "interval." *Note* in music strictly denotes the character representing a *sound,* but in loose popular usage it denotes the *sound* also, and becomes practically equivalent to *tone.*

sound[2] (sound) *adj.* **1** Having all the organs or faculties complete and in normal action and relation; healthy. **2** Free from injury, flaw, mutilation, defect, or decay: *sound* timber. **3** Founded in truth; right; substantial; valid; legal. **4** Correct in views or processes of thought. **5** Solvent. **6** Profound, as rest; deep; unbroken; also, resting profoundly. **7** Complete and effectual; thorough. **8** Solid; stable; firm; safe; hence, trustworthy. **9** Based on good judgment. See synonyms under HEALTHY, SANE[1], STAUNCH, WISE[1]. [OE *gesund*] **—sound'ly** *adv.* **—sound' ·ness** *n.*

sound[3] (sound) *n.* **1** A long and narrow body of water, more extensive than a strait, connecting larger bodies. **2** The air bladder of a fish. [Fusion of OE *sund* sea, a swimming and ON *sund* a strait, swimming]

sound[4] (sound) *v.t.* **1** To test the depth of (water, etc.), especially by means of a lead weight at the end of a line. **2** To measure (depth) thus. **3** To explore or examine (the bottom of the sea, etc.) by means of a sounding lead adapted for bringing up adhering particles. **4** To discover or try to discover the views and attitudes of (a person) by means of conversation and round-about questions: usually with *out.* **5** To try to ascertain or determine (beliefs, attitudes, etc.) in such a manner. **6** *Surg.* To search or examine, as with a sound. —*v.i.* **7** To measure depth, as with a sounding lead. **8** To dive down suddenly and deeply, as a whale when harpooned. **9** To make investigation; inquire. — *n. Surg.* An instrument for exploring a cavity; a probe. [<OF *sonder,?* <L *sub-* under + *unda* a wave] **—sound'a·ble** *adj.*

Sound (sound), **The** See ÖRESUND.

sound barrier *Aeron.* The tansonic barrier.

sound·bite (sound'bīt'') *n.* A very brief, edited segment of a televised interview, as with an election candidate, chosen to communicate succinctly his or her position on an issue.

sound·board (sound'bôrd', -bōrd') *n.* A thin board, as in a piano or violin, forming the upper plate of a resonant box: also called *belly.*

sound·box (sound'boks') *n.* That part of a phonograph which by means of a sensitive diaphragm relays to the surrounding air the acoustic vibrations transmitted to it by the stylus in the record groove.

sound effects In motion pictures, radio, etc., the incidental and often mechanically produced sounds, as of rain, hoofbeats, fire, etc., required to heighten the illusion of reality.

sound·er (soun'dər) *n.* **1** One who or that which sounds or gives a sound. **2** An apparatus for taking soundings, as at sea. **3** A probe. **4** A telegraphic device for converting electromagnetic code impulses into sound, thus enabling messages to be interpreted.

sound·ing[1] (soun'ding) *adj.* **1** Giving forth a full sound; sonorous. **2** Having much sound with little significance; noisy and empty. **—sound'ing·ly** *adv.*

sound·ing[2] (soun'ding) *n.* **1** The act of one who or that which sounds, in any sense. **2** Measurement of the depth of water. **3** *pl.* The depth of water as sounded; also, water of such depth that the bottom may be reached by sounding.

sounding board **1** A structure or suspended dome over a pulpit or speaker's platform to amplify and clarify the speaker's voice. **2** Any device that gives force to an opinion or speech.

sounding lead The lead or other weight used on a sounding line; a plummet.

sounding line A weighted line marked at fathom intervals with pieces of leather, cloth, etc., used for determining the depth of water.

sound·less (sound'lis) *adj.* Having or making no sound; silent. **—sound'less·ly** *adv.* **—sound'·less·ness** *n.*

sound locator An apparatus for locating the position of aircraft by means of the sound waves which they emit.

sound picture A motion picture with a sound track.

sound·proof (sound'pro͞of') *adj.* Resistant to the penetration or spread of sound. — *v.t.* To make soundproof.

sound ranging A method of locating the point of origin of a sound by checking time intervals as recorded from microphones of known position.

sound spectrograph See under SPECTROGRAPH.

sound track That portion along the edge of a motion-picture film which carries the sound record.

sound truck A truck with a mounted loudspeaker.

soup (sōōp) *n.* **1** Liquid food made by boiling meat, vegetables, etc., in water: distinguished from *broth,* which is usually strained. **2** *Phot.* A developer. **3** *U.S. Slang* Nitroglycerin. —**in the soup** *U.S. Slang* In difficulties; in a quandary. —**to soup up** *U.S. Slang* To supercharge or otherwise modify (an automobile) for high speed. [<F *soupe* <Gmc.]

soup·çon (sōōp·sôAN/n′) *n. French* Literally, a suspicion; hence, a minute quantity; a taste.

soup kitchen A place where soup is served to the needy either free or at very low cost.

sou·ple (sōō′pəl) *adj. Scot.* **1** Supple. **2** Swift.

soup·spoon (sōōp′spōōn′) *n.* A spoon used in eating soup.

soup·y (sōō′pē) *adj.* **soup·i·er, soup·i·est** Like soup in appearance or consistency.

sour (sour) *adj.* **1** Sharp to the taste; acid; tart, like vinegar: designating one of the four fundamental taste sensations. **2** Having an acid or rancid taste as the result of fermentation; also, pertaining to fermentation. **3** Having a rancid, acid smell or vapor; dank. **4** Misanthropic and crabbed; cross; morose: a *sour* person, a *sour* smile. **5** Cold and wet; unpleasant: *sour* weather. **6** Acid; harsh to crops: said of land. **7** Containing sulfur compounds: said of gasoline. —*v.t & v.i.* To become or make sour. —*n.* **1** Something sour or distasteful. **2** An acid solution used in bleaching or in curing skins. **3** A treatment with such a solution. **4** A sour or acid beverage: a whisky *sour.* [OE *sūr*] —**sour′ly** *adv.* —**sour′ness** *n.*

source (sôrs, sōrs) *n.* **1** That from which any act, movement, or effect proceeds; an originator; creator; origin. **2** A place where something is found or whence it is taken or derived. **3** The spring or fountain from which a stream of water proceeds; a fountain-head; fountain. **4** A person, writing, or agency from which information is obtained. **5** The initiator of a payment, dividend, etc. [<OF, orig. pp. of *sourdre* rise <L *surgere*]
  Synonyms: beginning, fountain, fountainhead, origin, spring. See BEGINNING, CAUSE. *Antonyms:* close, completion, conclusion, end, expiration, result, termination.

sour·crout (sour′krout′) See SAUERKRAUT.

sour·dine (sōōr·dēn′) *n.* **1** A mute, especially a trumpet mute. **2** A stop on the harmonium producing a soft effect. **3** An obsolete, soft-toned musical instrument. **4** In telegraphy, a silencer. [<F <Ital. *sordino* <*sordo* <L *surdus* deaf]

sour·dough (sour′dō′) *n.* **1** *Dial.* Fermented dough for use as leaven in making bread. **2** *U.S. & Can. Slang* A pioneer or prospector; especially, an Alaskan or Canadian prospector who carries fermented dough for use in making bread.

sour gourd **1** One of a genus (*Adansonia*) of trees with huge trunk, having a woody gourdlike capsule; especially, the Australian tree (*A. gregorii*). **2** The acid fruit of this tree. **3** The Madagascar baobab.

sour grapes That which a person affects to despise, because it is beyond his attainment: in allusion to the fable of the fox and the grapes.

sour·gum (sour′gum′) *n.* Any of several species of trees of the genus *Nyssa,* especially the blackgum tree and the tupelo.

Sou·ris (sōōr′is) A river in North Dakota and Canada, flowing 435 miles SE and north from SE Saskatchewan, through northern North Dakota, to the Assiniboine river in southern Manitoba.

sour·puss (sour′poos′) *n. Slang* A person with a sullen, peevish expression or character.

sour·sop (sour′sop′) *n.* **1** A tree (*Annona muricata*) of tropical America. **2** The pulpy, somewhat acid fruit of this tree.

Sou·sa (sōō′zə), **John Philip,** 1854–1932, U.S. bandmaster and composer.

sou·sa·phone (sōō′zə·fn, -sə-) *n.* A large brass wind instrument, resembling a tuba, but circular and with flaring bell frontward: used in military bands. [after John P. *Sousa*]

souse¹ (sous) *v.t. & v.i.* **soused, sous·ing** **1** To dip or steep in a liquid. **2** To pickle. **3** *Slang* To make or get drunk. —*n.* **1** Pickled meats; especially, the ears and feet of swine, pickled

or soused in brine; formerly, any salt pickle. **2** A plunge in water. **3** Brine. **4** *Slang* A drunkard; sot. [<OF *sous* <OHG *sulza* brine]

souse² (sous) *Archaic v.* **soused, sous·ing** *v.t.* To pounce upon. —*v.i.* To swoop suddenly, as a hawk: with *on* or *upon.* [<*n.*] —*n.* A swoop, as of a hawk on its prey; a downright blow or stroke. —*adv.* Suddenly; with a plunge or swoop headlong; all over. [Var. of SOURCE, in earlier sense of 'arising']

Sousse (sōōs) A port of eastern Tunisia: ancient *Hadrumetum;* formerly *Susa.*

sou·tache (sōō·tăsh′) *n. French* **1** A very narrow, flat, decorative braid in a herringbone effect. **2** Mohair or silk rounded braid.

sou·tane (sōō·tän′) *n.* A Roman Catholic priest's cassock. [<F <Ital. *sottana* <*sotto* under <L *subtus*]

sou·ter (sōō′tər) *n. Scot.* a shoemaker; cobbler: also spelled *sowter.* Also **sou′tar.**

south (south) *n.* **1** That of the four cardinal points of the compass which is directly opposite to north, and at the right hand of an observer who faces the sunrise. **2** The direction in which the point lies. **3** A region lying in this direction. **4** A south wind. —*adj.* **1** Situated in a southern direction relatively to the observer or to any given place or point. **2** Facing toward the south. **3** Belonging to or proceeding from the south. —*v.i.* **1** To turn southward. **2** *Astron.* To cross the meridian. —*adv.* **1** Toward or at the south. **2** From the south. [OE *sūth*]

South, the **1** The portion of the United States lying south of the Mason-Dixon line, and east and south of the western and northern borders of Missouri. **2** The Confederacy.

South Africa, Republic of An independent republic at the southern end of Africa, consisting of four provinces; 472,359 square miles; seat of government, Pretoria; seat of legislature, Cape Town. Formerly *Union of South Africa.*

South African **1** Pertaining to South Africa, especially to the Republic of South Africa. **2** A native of the Republic of South Africa.

South African Dutch Afrikaans.

South African Republic Formerly, Union of South Africa.

South African War See BOER WAR in table under WAR.

South America The southern continent of the western hemisphere; about 6,900,000 square miles. —**South American.**

South·amp·ton (south·hamp′tən, sou·thamp′-) **1** An administrative county and the mainland part of Hampshire, southern England; 1,503 square miles; county town, Winchester. **2** A port and county borough of southern Hampshire, England, the major European terminal of most transatlantic shipping lines, at the head of **Southampton Water,** an inlet of **The Solent** in Southampton county, 6 miles long.

South Australia A state of southern Australia; 380,070 square miles; capital, Adelaide.

South Bass Island An island in Lake Erie, 15 miles NW of Sandusky, Ohio; site of Put-in-Bay; 3½ miles long, 1½ miles wide.

South Bend A city in northern Indiana.

south·bound (south′bound′) *adj.* Going southward. Also **south′bound′.**

south by east One point east of south on the mariner's compass. See COMPASS CARD.

south by west One point west of south on the mariner's compass. See COMPASS CARD.

South Carolina A SE State of the United States, on the Atlantic; 31,055 square miles; capital, Columbia; entered the Union May 23, 1788; one of the thirteen original States; nickname *Palmetto State:* abbr. SC —**South Carolinian**

South China Sea The arm of the Pacific between the SE Asian mainland and the Malay Archipelago.

South Dakota A State in the north central United States; 77,047 square miles; capital, Pierre; entered the Union Nov. 2, 1889; nickname *Coyote State:* abbr. SD —**South Dakotan**

South·down (south′doun′) *n.* One of a breed of hornless sheep with brown legs and faces: originally bred in the South Downs.

South Downs A range of hills in southern England, chiefly in Sussex, terminating at Beachy Head.

south·east (south′ēst′, *in nautical usage* sou′ēst′,) *n.* That point on the mariner's compass midway between south and east; any region lying toward that point on the horizon. —*adj.* Of, pertaining to, toward, or from the southeast. —*adv.* Toward or from the southeast. —**south′east′ern** *adj.* —**south′east′ern·most** *adj.* —**south′east′ward** *adj. & adv.* —**south′east′ward·ly, south′east′wards** *adv.*

southeast by east One point east of southeast on the mariner's compass. See COMPASS CARD.

southeast by south One point south of southeast on the mariner's compass. See COMPASS CARD.

south·east·er (south′ēs′tər, *in nautical usage* sou′ēs′tər) *n.* A gale from the southeast.

south·east·er·ly (south′ēs′tər·lē, *in nautical usage* sou′ēs′tər·lē) *adj. & adv.* **1** Toward the southeast. **2** From the southeast: said of wind.

South·end-on-Sea (south′end′on-sē′) A resort and county borough in SE Essex, England.

south·er¹ (sou′thər) *n.* A gale from the south.

sou·ther² (sō′thər) *n. Brit. Dial.* Solder: also spelled *sowther.*

south·er·ly (suth′ər·lē) *adj.* **1** Situated in or tending toward the south. **2** Proceeding from the south. —*adv.* Toward or from the south. —**south′er·li·ness** *n.*

southerly buster See under BUSTER.

south·ern (suth′ərn) *adj.* **1** Pertaining to the south or a place relatively in the south. **2** Proceeding from the south, as a wind. [OE *sutherne*] —**south′ern·er** *n.* —**south′ern·ly** *adv.* —**south′ern·most** *adj.*

South·ern (suth′ərn) *adj.* Of or pertaining to the South.

Southern Alps A mountain range in west central South Island, New Zealand; highest peak, 12,349 feet.

Southern Cross A southern constellation having four bright stars in the form of a cross. See CONSTELLATION.

Southern Crown A southern constellation near Sagittarius; Corona Australis.

South·ern·er (suth′ərn·ər) *n.* A native of the South.

Southern Kar·roo (ka·rōō′) A plateau region in Western Cape Province, Republic of South Africa: also *Little Karroo.*

southern lights The aurora australis.

Southern Pines A resort town in central North Carolina.

Southern Protectorate of Morocco A former Spanish protectorate on the NW coast of Africa, part of Spanish West Africa; 10,039 square miles.

Southern Rhodesia See ZIMBABWE.

Southern Territories **1** A division of southern Algeria; 769,827 square miles. **2** A former French military territory of southern Tunisia; about 17,800 square miles. *French* **Ter·ri·toires du Sud** (ter·ē·twàr′ dü süd′).

south·ern·wood (suth′ərn·wōōd′) *n.* A European plant (*Artemisia abrotanum*) allied to wormwood.

South·ey (suth′ē), **Robert,** 1774–1843, English poet; poet laureate 1813–43.

South Georgia A barren island between the Falkland Islands and Cape Horn, considered part of the Falkland Island Dependencies in the South Atlantic; 1,600 square miles. See FALKLAND ISLAND DEPENDENCIES.

South Holland A province of western Netherlands; 1,085 square miles; capital. The Hague. *Dutch* **Zuid·hol·land** (zoit′hô′länt).

south·ing (sou′thing) *n.* **1** The difference of latitude measured toward the south between any position and the last one determined. **2** *Astron.* **a** The passage across the meridian, in its diurnal motion, of a celestial object that culminates south of the zenith. **b** The attainment of this position, or the time at which it is reached. **3** Deviation or progression toward the south.

South Island The largest island of the New Zealand group; 58,093 square miles.

South Jutland The southern part of the Jutland peninsula, northern Germany and southern Denmark, coextensive with the former duchy of Schleswig.

South Korea See under KOREA.

south·land (south′land′) *n.* A land or region situated to the south. —**south′land′er** *n.*

South Mountain The northernmost part of the Blue Ridge, in western Pennsylvania, Maryland, and northern Virginia; highest peak, 2,145 feet; scene of a Union victory in the Civil War, Sept. 14, 1862.

South Orkney Islands An island group in the South Atlantic NE of the Palmer Peninsula; 240 square miles; claimed by Great Britain and by Argentina; administered by Great Britain as a dependency of the Falkland Islands.

South Os·se·tia (o·sē′shən) An autonomous region of northern Russian Georgia; 1,428 square miles.

south·paw (south′pô′) *Slang n.* **1** In baseball, a left-handed pitcher. **2** Any left-handed person or player. —*adj.* Left-handed.

South Platte River A river in Colorado and Nebraska, flowing 450 miles east and NE to join the North Platte, forming the Platte River.

South Pole The southern extremity of the earth's axis; the 90th degree of south latitude, from which all terrestrial directions are north.

South·port (south′pôrt, -pōrt) A county borough on the Irish Sea in SW Lancashire, England, north of Liverpool.

south·ron (suth′rən, south′-) *adj.* Southern. —*n.* A person who lives in the south. [Alter. of dial. E *southern*, var. of SOUTHERN; infl. in form by *Saxon, Briton,* etc.]

South·ron (suth′rən, south′-) *n. Scot.* An Englishman or native of southern Britain: formerly used by the Scots as a term of derision: also *Suthron*.

South Sandwich Islands An island group in the South Atlantic, included in the Falkland Island Dependencies; 130 square miles.

South Sea Islands The islands of the South Pacific Ocean.

South Seas 1 The South Pacific Ocean. **2** The seas of the world south of the Equator.

South Shetland Islands An archipelago in the South Atlantic, between South America and Antarctica; claimed by Great Britain, Argentina, and Chile; administered by Great Britain as a dependency of the Falkland Islands; 1,800 square miles.

South Shields A port and county borough of NE Durham, England, at the mouth of the Tyne on the North Sea.

south-south·east (south′south′ēst′, *in nautical usage* sou′sou′ēst′) *n.* That point on the mariner's compass midway between south and southeast. —*adj. & adv.* Midway between south and southeast. See COMPASS CARD.

south-south·west (south′south′west′, *in nautical usage* sou′sou′ēst′) *n.* That point on the mariner's compass midway between south and southwest. —*adj. & adv.* Midway between south and southwest. See COMPASS CARD.

South Vietnam A region comprising the former French colony of Cochin China and the southern part of the former Empire of Annam, now part of the Socialist Republic of Vietnam. See VIETNAM.

south·ward (south′wərd, *In nautical usage* suth′ərd) *adj.* Situated in or toward the south. —*adv.* In a southerly direction: also **south′ward·ly, south′wards.** —*n.* The direction of south; also, a region south to the south.

South·wark suth′ərk A borough of London, England, on the south bank of the Thames.

South·well (south′wel, suth′əl) A town in central Nottinghamshire, England; known for its Norman cathedral.

south·west (south′west′, *in nautical usage* sou′west′) *n.* That point on the mariner's compass midway between south and west; any region lying toward that point on the horizon. —*adj.* Of, pertaining to, facing, or toward the southwest; blowing from the southwest. —*adv.* Toward or from the southwest. —**south′west′ern, south′west′ern·most** *adj.* —**south′west′ward** *adj. & adv.* —**south′-west′ward·ly, south′west′wards** *adv.*

Southwest, the The SW part of the United States: generally including Oklahoma, Texas, New Mexico, Arizona, and southern California.

South-West Africa A self-governing territory on the Atlantic, now NAMIBIA; 317,887 square miles; capital, Windhoek: formerly *German Southwest Africa.*

southwest by south One point south of southwest on the mariner's compass. See COMPASS CARD.

southwest by west One point west of southwest on the mariner's compass. See COMPASS CARD.

south·west·er (south′wes′tər, *in nautical usage* sou′wes′tər) *n.* **1** A wind, gale, or storm from the southwest. **2** A waterproof hat of oilskin, canvas, etc., with a broad brim behind to protect the neck: worn in stormy weather. Also **sou′west′er.**

south·west·er·ly (south′wes′tər·lē, *in nautical usage* sou′west′tər·lē) *adj. & adv.* **1** Toward the southwest. **2** From the southwest: said of wind.

Southwest Semitic See under SEMITIC.

South Yemen, People's Republic of A republic on the southern coast of the Arabian peninsula, containing most of the territory of the former Aden and Aden Protectorate; about 110,000 square miles; capital Medina al-Eshaab.

sou·ve·nir (soo′və·nir′, soo′və·nir) *n.* A token of remembrance; memento. [<F, remember <L *subvenire* come to mind]

sov·er·eign (sov′rin, suv′-) *n.* **1** One who possesses supreme authority, especially a person or a determine body of persons in whom the supreme power of the state is vested; a monarch. **2** An English gold coin equivalent to one pound sterling or twenty shillings, first issued by Henry VII. **3** A former gold coin of Austria. See synonyms under MASTER. —*adj.* **1** Exercising or possessing supreme jurisdiction or power; royal. **2** Free, independent, and in no way limited by external authority or influence: a *sovereign* state. **3** Possessing supreme excellence of greatness; preeminent; paramount. **4** Superior in efficacy; potent: a *sovereign* remedy. See synonyms under IMPERIAL, PREDOMINANT. Also, *Poetic, sovran.* [<OF *soverain,* ult. <L *super* above. Related to SOPRANO.] —**sov′er·eign·ly** *adv.*

sov·er·eign·ty (sov′rin·tē, suv′-) *n. pl.* ·**ties 1** The state of being sovereign; supreme authority. **2** The ultimate, supreme power in a state. **3** A sovereign state. **4** The status or dominion of a sovereign. Also, *Poetic, sovranty.* —**popular sovereignty** The theory that the right to legislate and choose a government belongs to the body of the people.

So·vetsk (so·vyetsk′) A city on the Neman River in western European Russia: formerly *Tilsit.*

So·vet·ska·ya Ga·van (so-vyet′ska·yə gä′və n·y′) A port and naval base on the Sea of Japan, in southeast Asiatic Russia.

so·vi·et (sō′vē·et, sō′vē·et) *n.* **1** In the Soviet Union, any of the legislative bodies existing at various governmental levels. See SUPREME SOVIET. **2** Any of various similar legislative bodies. [<Russian *sovyet* a council]

So·vi·et (sō′vē·et, sō′vē·et) *adj.* Of or pertaining to the Soviet Union.

Soviet Central Asia The areas of Central Asia formerly belonging to the Soviet Union (U.S.S.R.), now comprising the independent cuntries of: Kazakstan, Kyrgyzstan, Tajikistan, Turkmenistan, and Uzbekistan; 1,541,530 square miles: also *Central Asia.*

soviet congress The administrative body of each constituent republic of the Union of Soviet Socialist Republics, empowered to adopt its own constitution based on the Union constitution: autonomous republics are governed by executive committees elected by the local Congress of Soviets.

so·vi·et·ism (sō′vē·ə·tiz′əm) *n.* The policies and principles of, or government by peoples' councils or congress, especially as practiced in Soviet Russia. —**so′vi·et·ist** *n.*

so·vi·et·ize (sō′vē·ə·tīz′) *v.t.* ·**ized,** ·**iz·ing** To bring under a soviet form of government. —**so′vi·et·i·za′tion** *n.*

so·vi·et·ol·o·gist (sō′vē·ə·tol′ə·jist) *n.* A student of the policies and history of the Soviet Union. —**so′vi·et·ol′o·gy** *n.*

Soviet Russia See RUSSIAN SOVIET FEDERATED SOCIALIST REPUBLIC.

sov·ran (sov′rən, suv′-), **so·ran·ty** (sov′rən·tē, suv′-), etc. See SOVEREIGN, etc.

sow¹ (sō) *v.* **sowed, sown** or **sowed, sow·ing** *v.t.* **1** To scatter (seed) over land for growth. **2** To scatter seed over (land). **3** To spread abroad; disseminate; implant; to *sow* the seeds of distrust. **4** To cover or sprinkle. —*v.i* **5** To scatter seed. See synonyms under PLANT. [OE *sāwan*] —**sow′er** *n.* —**sow′ing** *n.*

sow² (sou) *n.* **1** A female hog. **2** *Metall* **a** The connection between pieces of pig iron before breaking up. **b** The conduit to the pig bed for molten metal. [OE *sū, sugu*]

so·war (sō·wär′, -wôr′) *n. Anglo-Indian* Formerly, in the British-Indian army, an Indian trooper of the calvary; a mounted orderly.

sow-bel·ly (souo′bel′ē) *n. U.S. Colloq.* Salt pork.

sow·bread (sou′bred) *n.* The cyclamen.

sow bug A small crustacean (family *Oniscidae*) found under logs and stones; a wood louse.

sow·car (sou·kär′) See SOUCAR.

sow·ens (sō′ənz) *n. Scot.* **1** Sour porridge made from the husks of oatmeal.

sowth (sooth) *v.t. & v.i Scot.* To hum or whistle (an air) softly.

sow·ther (sou′thər) See SOUTHER².

sow thistle Any of a genus (*Sonchus*) of spiny plants, especially the common sow thistle.

soy (soi) *n.* **1** A small, erect herb (*Glycine soja*) of the bean family, growing in India and China and cultivated for forage. **2** Its edible bean, a source of oil, flour, and other products: also **soy·a** (soi′ə), **soy′bean′.** **3** A sauce prepared in China and Japan from soybeans that have been fermented and steeped in brine: also **soy sauce.** [<Japanese *soy, shoy,* short for *shōyu* soy]

so·zin (sō′zin) *n. Biochem.* Any protein normally contained in the body of an animal and forming a natural protection against germs. Also **so′zine.** [<Gk. *sōzein* save + -IN]

spa (spä) *n.* Any locality frequented for its mineral springs; a mineral spring. [from SPA]

Spa (spä) A resort town in eastern Belgium.

Spaak (späk), **Paul Henri,** 1899–1972, Belgian and international statesman.

Spaatz·(späts), **Carl,** 1891–1974, U.S. general.

space (spās) *n.* **1** An interval between points or objects; a limited portion of extension; distance; area. **2** The abstract possibility of extension; that which is characterized by illimitable dimension; continuous boundless extension in all directions. **3** An interval of time; period; hence, a little while. **4** An occasion or opportunity. **5** *Printing* A piece of type metal, less than type-high, used for spacing between lines; specifically, one less than one en in width. **6** One of the degrees of a musical staff. **7** One of the intervals during the transmission of a telegraph message when the key is open or not in contact. **8** Reserved accommodations, as on a train or airplane. **9** *Math.* A system of continuous, unlimited, corresponding points in a series; an ordered set of infinite numbers. **10** Outer space. See synonyms under PLACE. —*v.t.*

spaced, spac·ing 1 To separate by spaces. **2** To divide into spaces. [<OF *espace* <L *spatium*] —**space′less** *adj.* —**spac′er** *n.*

Space, meaning for, pertaining to, or concerned with travel in outer space, may appear as a combining form in solidemes or as the first element in two–word phrases; as in:

space age	**spaceman**	**space sociology**
space crew	**space patrol**	**space suit**
spaceflight	**space rocket**	**space vehicle**

space band *Printing* In Linotype operation, an adjustable wedge–shaped metal strip used for spacing.

space–cab·in simulator (spās′kab′in) A chamber built to resemble the cabin of a spaceship, for testing human or animal reactions under physiological conditions simulating those in actual space travel.

space charge *Physics* **1** An electric charge uniformly distributed through a given space. **2** A grouping of electrons around the filament of a vacuum tube, imparting a negative charge which inhibits the free emission of other electrons.

space·craft (spās′kraft′, -kräft′) *n.* **1** Any vehicle, manned or unmanned, designed for flight in outer space. **2** Spacemanship.

spaced–out (spāst′out′) *adj. U.S. Slang* Dazed or drugged, as by the use of narcotics.

space·flight (spās′flīt′) *n.* Flight in outer space by a man–made object or vehicle.

space lattice *Physics* The characteristic arrangement of the atoms or structural units in a crystal, such that corresponding units are separated by constant intervals along any straight line drawn through their centers.

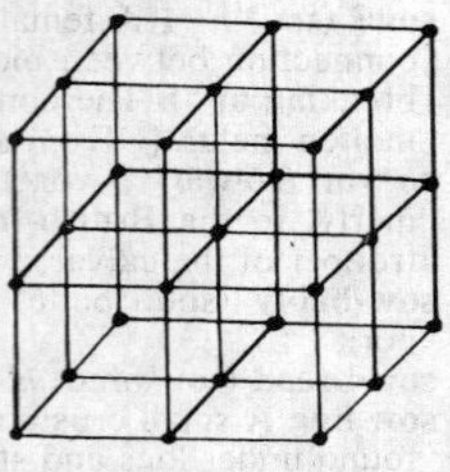

SPACE LATTICE

space·man·ship (spās′mən·ship) *n.* The science and art of space travel, especially as regards the design, construction, fueling, launching, and operation of vehicles and missiles equipped for flight beyond the earth's atmosphere.

space medicine The branch of aviation medicine which deals with the biological, physiological, and psychological aspects of travel in outer space.

space·port (spās′pôrt′, -pōrt′) *n.* A base for rockets and other spacecraft, including the equipment necessary for their testing, storage, maintenance, launching, etc.

space probe A spacecraft designed and equipped to obtain information of phenomena and conditions in outer space.

space·ship (spās′ship′) *n.* Any of various vehicles designed for the transport of men and materials through outer space, especially between and among the planets.

space shuttle A vehicle used for transferring passengers and freight from earth to an orbiting space station.

space station A large, usually manned satellite orbiting the earth, used for observation, experiments, as a relay station, etc.

space time A four–dimensional continuum within which may be precisely located any magnitude having both extension and duration: it consists of three spatial coordinates and one coordinate of time. Also **space–time continuum.**

space travel Travel in regions above the earth's atmosphere or beyond its gravitational field, whether within or outside of the solar system.

spa·cial (spā′shəl) See SPATIAL.

spac·ing (spā′sing) *n.* **1** The arrangement of spaces. **2** A space or spaces, as in a line of print.

spa·cious (spā′shəs) *adj.* **1** Of indefinite or vast extent. **2** Affording ample room; capacious. See synonyms under LARGE. —**spa′·cious·ly** *adv.* —**spa′cious·ness** *n.*

Spack·le (spak′əl) *n.* A dry powder which, in the form of a paste, is used for filling cracks, holes, and other surface defects before painting and decorating: a trade name. —*v.t.* **·led, ·ling** To apply Spackle to (a crack, etc.).

spade[1] (spād) *n.* **1** An implement used for digging in the ground, ditching, cutting turf, etc., heavier than a shovel and having a flatter blade. **2** A tool or implement resembling a spade; specifically, a large chisel–like implement for flensing whales. **3** A heavy piece of metal at the end of a gun–carriage trail which helps to keep the carriage in position when the gun recoils. —**to call a spade a spade** To call a thing by its right name; speak the plain, uncompromising truth. —*v.t.* **spad·ed, spad·ing** To dig or cut with a spade. [OE *spadu*] —**spade′ful** *n.* —**spad′er** *n.*

spade[2] (spād) *n.* **1** A figure, resembling a heart with a triangular handle, on a playing card. **2** A card so marked. **3** The suit of cards so marked: usually in the plural. [<Sp. *espada* a sword <L *spatha* <Gk. *spathē*]

spade·fish (spād′fish′) *n. pl.* **·fish** or **·fish·es 1** A spiny–finned food fish *(Chaetodipterus faber)* of the Atlantic coast from Massachusetts to the West Indies. **2** The paddlefish.

spade·work (spād′wûrk′) *n.* **1** Work done with a spade. **2** Any preliminary work necessary to get a project under way.

spa·di·ceous (spā·dish′əs) *adj.* **1** Of or like a spadix. **2** Of a clear brown or bay color.

spa·dix (spā′diks) *n. pl.* **spa·di·ces** (spā·dī′sēz) *Bot.* A spike or head of flowers with a fleshy axis, usually enclosed within a spathe. [<Gk. *spadix* <*spaein* break]

spae (spā) *v.t. Scot.* To foretell; divine. —**spae′·man** (-mən), **spae′wife′** (-wīf′) *n.*

spa·ghet·ti (spə·get′ē) *n.* **1** A cordlike food paste, in size between macaroni and vermicelli. **2** Insulated cloth tubing through which wire is passed, as in a radio circuit. [<Ital., pl. dim. of *spago* a small cord]

spa·gyr·ic (spə·jir′ik) *adj.* Alchemical. Also **spa·gir′ic, spa·gyr′i·cal.** [<NL *spagyricus;* prob. coined by Paracelsus]

spa·hi (spä′hē) *n.* **1** Formerly, a Turkish corps of irregular cavalry; a member of such a corps. **2** One of a native Algerian cavalry corps in the French service. Also **spa′hee.** [<Turkish *sipāhi* <Persian *sipāh* an army. Cf. SEPOY.]

Spain (spān) A nominal monarchy in SW Europe; continental Spain alone, 189,626 square miles; including the Balearic and Canary Islands, 194,368 square miles; capital, Madrid: Spanish *España.*

spake (spāk) Archaic past tense of SPEAK.

Spa·la·to (spä′lä·tō) The Italian name for SPLIT.

spall (spôl) *v.t.* To break up; chip; prepare for sorting, as ore. —*v.i.* To chip at the edges, as a stone under pressure. —*n.* A chip, splinter, or flake, as from a stone. [ME *spalle.* ? Related to MLG *spalden* split.]

Spal·lan·za·ni (späl′län·dzä′nē), **Lazzaro,** 1729–99, Italian naturalist; disproved theory of spontaneous generation.

spal·la·tion (spa·lā′shən) *n.* **1** The act or process of reducing to fragments. **2** *Physics* The splitting of an atomic nucleus into numerous parts instead of the two or three characteristic of ordinary fission. [<SPALL + -ATION]

spal·peen (spal·pēn′, spal′pēn) *n.* A wandering harvester; hence, a good–for–nothing. [<Irish *spailpín* laborer]

span[1] (span) *v.t.* **spanned, span·ning 1** To measure, especially with the hand with the thumb and little finger extended. **2** To encircle or grasp with the hand, as in measuring. **3** To stretch across; extend over or from side to side of: This road *spans* the continent. **4** To provide with something that stretches across or extends over. [<*n.*] —*n.* **1** The extreme space over which the hand can be expanded: 9 inches, or 22.86 centimeters. **2** Any small interval or distance, in space or in time. **3** *Archit.* The space or distance between the supports of an arch, abutments of a bridge, etc. **4** That which spans. **5** *Aeron.* The maximum lateral distance from tip to tip of airplane wings. [OE *spann*]

span[2] (span) *v.* **spanned, span·ning** *v.t.* To bind; make fast; fetter. —*v.i.* To match in color and size: said of horses. —*n.* **1** A rope or chain used as a fastening on a ship. **2** A pair of matched horses or oxen. **3** In South Africa, a team of oxen or bullocks, of two or more yokes. [<MDu. *spannen* fasten, join, draw together]

span[3] (span) Archaic past tense of SPIN.

Span·dau (shpän′dou) A district of western Berlin, Germany: formerly an independent city.

span·drel (span′drəl) *n. Archit.* **1** The triangular space between the outer curve of an arch and the rectangular figure formed by the moldings or framework surrounding it. **2** The space between the shoulders of two adjoining arches. See illustration under ARCH. Also **span′dril.** [Dim. of AF *spaundre,* prob. <OF *espandre* expand]

spa·ne·mi·a (spə·nē′mē·ə) *n. Pathol.* Poverty of blood; anemia. Also **spa·nae′mi·a.** [<NL <Gk. *spanos* lacking + *haima* blood] —**spa·ne′mic** (-nē′mik, -nem′ik) *adj.*

spang (spang) *v.t. Brit. Dial.* To throw or bang down. —*v.i. Brit. Dial.* To spring. —*adv. U.S. Colloq.* Abruptly; straight: He ran *spang* into the wall.

span·gle (spang′gəl) *n.* **1** A small bit of brilliant tin or other metal foil, or other substances, used for decoration in dress, as in theatrical costume. **2** Any small sparkling object. —*v.* **·gled, ·gling** *v.t.* To adorn with or as with spangles; cause to glitter. —*v.i.* To sparkle as spangles; glitter. [Dim. of MDu. *spang* a clasp, brooch] —**span′gly** *adj.*

Span·iard (span′yərd) *n.* **1** A native or citizen of Spain. **2** A prickly bush of New Zealand *(Aciphylla colensoi).*

span·iel (span′yəl) *n.* **1** A small or medium–sized dog having large pendulous ears and long silky hair: used especially for hunting small game in the fields, retrieving water birds, etc. **2** One who follows like a dog; an obsequious follower. [<OF *espaignol* Spanish (dog)]

—**Blenheim spaniel** A variety of English toy spaniel having a white coat with rich chestnut or ruby–red markings: originally bred at Blenheim, England, from cocker spaniels sent to the Duke of Marlborough from China: formerly used for woodcock shooting, now usually a pet.

—**Clumber spaniel** A small, stout–bodied, short–legged spaniel having a straight silky coat usually white with lemon markings: named from Clumber, the estate of the second Duke of Newcastle, where they were bred.

—**cocker spaniel** The smallest of the sporting spaniels, of solid or various coloring, characterized by sturdy body and rather short legs: an excellent retriever, especially in thick covers and swamps, and named for its special skill in woodcock hunting.

—**English springer spaniel** A spaniel of moderate size, strongly built, with a long and broad skull, deep chest, and wavy or flat coat; usually liver and white or tan, black and white or tan, etc.: named for its characteristic method of flushing game.

—**field spaniel** A black or varicolored spaniel used for hunting small game, having a long, low body, short legs, and a larger, stronger appearance than the cocker.

—**Irish water spaniel** A sporting dog of a breed developed in Ireland, having a curly, waterproof, liver–colored coat: used especially as a duck retriever.

—**Japanese spaniel** A breed of toy dog, thought to have originated in China, squarely built with small–boned feathered legs, a proportionately large head, and a long, straight coat which may be black and white or red and white.

—**King Charles spaniel** An English toy spaniel, originating in the Far East at an unknown date, having a long, silky, black–and–tan coat, feathery ears and feet, rounded head, and a short, turned–up nose.

—**Sussex spaniel** A field spaniel bred in Sussex county, England, somewhat slow in speed, having a very keen nose, massive muscular body, heavy head, rather large ears, long back, short large–boned legs, and a thick coat of a rich, golden–liver color.

—**Welsh springer spaniel** A dark, rich red–and–white sporting spaniel of uncertain origin, found chiefly in Wales and the west of England: larger than the cocker, and an excellent watchdog.

Span·ish (span′ish) *adj.* Pertaining to Spain, the Spaniards, or their language. —*n.* **1** The Romance language of Spain, Spanish America, and the Philippine Islands. **2** The inhabitants of Spain collectively: with *the.*

Spanish America The parts of the western hemisphere in which Spanish is the common language: Mexico, the countries of Central America, except British Honduras, the countries of South America except Brazil and

the Guianas, and most of the Caribbean islands: also *Hispanic America.*

Span·ish–A·mer·i·can (span′ish-ə-mer′ə-kən) *adj.* **1** Pertaining to the parts of America where Spanish is the vernacular tongue or is in common use. **2** Designating or pertaining to the war between the United States and Spain, 1898. — *n.* One of Spanish blood living in America, especially Central or South America; a citizen of a Spanish–American country.

Spanish–American War See table under WAR.

Spanish Armada See under ARMADA.

Spanish cedar Cedar (def. 4).

Spanish dagger Any of various species of yucca, with sword–shaped leaves. Also **Spanish bayonet.**

Spanishfly A bright-green blister beetle (*Lytta vesicatoria*) of the Mediterranean region, used in the preparation of the drug canthari-din. See illustration under INSECTS (beneficial).

SPANISH DAGGER

Spanish Guinea A Spanish colony in western Africa, divided into the two districts of Fernando Pó and Río Muni (continental Guinea, together with Annobon, Corisco, Great Elobey, and Little Elobey); total area, 10,853 square miles; capital, Santa Isabel, on Fernando Pó.

Spanish mackerel 1 The chub. **2** The cero.

Spanish Main 1 The mainland of Spanish America, especially the coastal region of northern South America between Panama and the mouth of the Orinoco. **2** That part of the Caribbean comprising the course of Spanish merchantmen formerly sailing between the eastern and western hemispheres.

Spanish Morocco Formerly, a Spanish protectorate on the coastal strip of Morocco north of French Morocco; incorporated in Morocco, 1956; 10,808 square miles; former capital, Tetuán.

Spanish moss A long, pendent, epiphytic plant (*Tillandsia* or *Dendropogon usneoides*) that grows upon trees of the southern United States near the seacoast: not a true parasite: sometimes called *long moss, Florida moss.* Also **Spanish beard.**

Spanish needles 1 A smooth annual plant (*Bidens bipinnata*) of the composite family, with bipinnate leaves and spiny achenia. **2** The barbed, prickly fruit of this plant.

Spanish onion A large, fleshy variety of onion, usually mild flavored.

Spanish paprika A cultivated variety of paprika, widely used as a condiment.

Spanish Peaks Two peaks in the Sangre de Cristo Mountains of southern Colorado; 13,623 feet and 12,683 feet.

Spanish Sahara A subdivision of Spanish West Africa, comprising Río de Oro and Saguia el Hamra; 105,409 square miles.

Spanish West Africa The Spanish possessions in NW Africa: Spanish Sahara (Río de Oro and Saguia el Hamra), Ifni, and the Southern Protectorate of Morocco; 116,189 square miles.

spank (spangk) *v.t.* To slap or strike, especially on the buttocks with the open hand as a punishment. — *v.i.* To move briskly. — *n.* A smack on the buttocks; a spanking. [Imit.]

spank·er (spangk′ər) *n.* **1** One who or that which spanks. **2** *Naut.* A fore–and–aft sail extended by a boom and a gaff from the mizzenmast of a ship or bark. **3** Any person or thing uncommonly large or fine. **4** One who or that which proceeds rapidly.

spank·ing (spangk′ing) *adj.* **1** Moving or blowing rapidly; swift; dashing; lively; strong. **2** *Brit. Colloq.* Uncommonly large or fine. — *n.* A series of slaps on the buttocks; the act of administering such punishment.

span·less (span′lis) *adj.* That cannot be spanned.

span·ner (span′ər) *n.* **1** One who or that

which spans. **2** *Brit.* A hand–tool used to turn nuts, bolts, etc.: a form of wrench. **3** A measuring worm. [def. 2 <G]

span–new (span′nōō′, -nyōō′) *adj. Dial.* Really or freshly new. [<ON *spān-nyr* < *spānn* chip + *nyr* new]

span worm A measuring worm.

spar[1] (spär) *n.* **1** *Naut.* A round timber for extending a sail, as a mast, yard, or boom. **2** A similar heavy, round timber forming part of a derrick, crane, etc., or used for various other purposes. **3** *Aeron.* That part of an airplane wing which carries the ribs. **4** *Naut.* A spar buoy: see under BUOY. — *v.t.* **sparred, spar·ring 1** To furnish with spars. **2** *Archaic* To fasten, as with a bolt. [<ON *sparri* a beam]

spar[2] (spär) *v.i.* **sparred, spar·ring 1** To box, especially with care and adroitness. **2** To bandy words; wrangle. **3** To fight, as cocks, by striking with spurs. — *n.* The act or practice of boxing, as by pugilists; a boxing match: also **spar′ring.** [<OF *esparer* <Ital. *sparare* kick <L *parare* prepare]

spar[3] (spär) *n.* A vitreous, crystalline, easily cleavable, lustrous mineral. [<MDu. Akin to OE *spær* gypsum.]

Spar (spär) *n.* A member of the women's reserve of the United States Coast Guard. Also **SPAR.** [<L *s(emper) par(atus)* always ready, the motto of the U.S. Coast Guard]

spar·a·ble (spar′ə-bəl) *n.* A species of small headless nail used by shoemakers in soling boots. [Alter. of *sparrow bill;* so called from resemblance in shape]

spar buoy *Naut.* See under BUOY.

spar deck *Naut.* The light upper deck of a vessel extending from bow to stern: including the quarter–deck and the forecastle; the deck on which extra spars are stowed.

spare (spâr) *v.* **spared, spar·ing** *v.t.* **1** To refrain from injuring, molesting, or killing; treat with mercy or lenience. **2** To free or relieve (someone) from (pain, expense, etc.): *Spare* us the sight. **3** To use frugally; refrain from using or exercising: *Spare* the rod and spoil the child. **4** To dispense or dispense with; do without: Can you *spare* a dime? — *v.i.* **5** To be frugal; live or act economically. **6** To be lenient or forgiving; show mercy. — *adj.* **spar·er, spar·est 1** That can be spared or used at will; disposable; available. **2** Held in reserve; additional; extra; surplus. **3** Having little flesh; thin; lean. **4** Not lavish or abundant; scanty. **5** Economical; chary; stingy; parsimonious. See synonyms under MEAGER. — *n.* **1** That which has been saved or stored away; something unused. **2** A .duplicate; an item kept as a substitute in case the original breaks down, as an automobile tire or a mechanical part. **3** In bowling, the act of overturning all the pins with the first two balls; also, the score thus made. [OE *sparian*] — **spare′ly** *adv.* — **spare′ness** *n.* — **spar′er** *n.*

spare·rib (spâr′rib′) *n.* A piece of meat, especially pork, consisting of ribs somewhat closely trimmed.

sparge (spärj) *v.t. & v.i.* **sparged, sparg·ing** To scatter; sprinkle; shower. — *n.* A sprinkling. [<OF *espargier* <L *spargere* sprinkle]

sparg·er (spär′jər) *n.* **1** A sprinkler or sprinkling apparatus. **2** In brewing, a hot–water sprinkler for use in a mashing tub.

spar·ing (spâr′ing) *adj.* **1** Scanty; slight. **2** Frugal; stingy. **3** Merciful; forbearing. See synonyms under SCANTY. — *n.* The act of one who spares; frugality; parsimony. See synonyms under FRUGALITY. — **spar′ing·ly** *adv.* — **spar′ing·ness** *n.*

spark[1] (spärk) *n.* **1** An incandescent particle thrown off from a red–hot or burning body or struck from a flint. **2** Any glistening or brilliant point or transient luminous particle. **3** Anything that kindles or animates. **4** *Electr.* **a** The luminous effect of a disruptive electric discharge, or the discharge itself. **b** A small transient arc or an incandescent particle thrown off from such an arc. **5** A small diamond, or bit of diamond used as in cutting glass. **6** A small trace or indication. — *v.i.* **1** To give off sparks; sparkle; scintillate. **2** In an internal–combustion engine, to have the electric ignition operating. — *v.t.* **3** To bring

into action or being; activate or cause: The shooting *sparked* a revolution. [OE *spearca*]

spark[2] (spärk) *n.* **1** A man fond of gallantry. **2** A lover; suitor; gallant. — *v.t. & v.i.* To play the spark (to); woo; court. [Special use of SPARK[1]]

spark arrester 1 A sievelike device for catching sparks, as on a locomotive. **2** *Electr.* An apparatus to prevent injurious sparking at the opening of a circuit made and broken frequently.

spark coil *Electr.* An induction coil used with an internal–combustion engine, wireless telegraph equipment, etc., to secure sparking.

spark·er (spärk′ər) *n.* **1** One who or that which sparks. **2** An electrical spark arrester.

spark gap *Electr.* **1** An arrangement of two electrodes between which a disruptive electric charge may pass. **2** The space so covered.

spark generator *Electr.* Any device capable of generating a sufficiently high voltage to discharge a spark across a spark gap.

spark·ish (spärk′ish) *adj.* **1** Jaunty; sprightly; airy; gay. **2** Showy; fine; well–dressed.

spark killer *Electr.* A device, usually a condenser, or condenser and resistance in series, for reducing harmful sparking at frequently interrupted points in a circuit. Also **spark suppressor.**

spar·kle (spär′kəl) *v.i.* **-kled, -kling 1** To give off flashes of light; scintillate; glitter. **2** To emit sparks. **3** To effervesce. **4** To be brilliant or vivacious: His words *sparkle* with wit. See synonyms under SHINE. — *n.* A spark; gleam. See synonyms under LIGHT[1]. [Freq. of SPARK[1]]

spar·kler (spär′klər) *n.* **1** Something that sparkles. **2** A sparkling gem. **3** A thin, rod-like firework that emits sparks. **4** A person who shines with spirit or vivacity.

spar·kling (spär′kling) *adj.* Giving out sparks or flashes; glittering; figuratively, brilliant; vivacious. — **spar′kling·ly** *adv.* — **spar′kling·ness** *n.*

spark plug A device for igniting the charge in an internal–combustion engine by means of an electric current.

Sparks (spärks), **Jared,** 1789–1866, U.S. editor and historian.

spark transmitter *Telecom.* A radio transmitter which obtains its alternating current from the discharge of a condenser across a spark gap.

spar·ling (spär′ling) *n.* **1** A smelt, parr, or other young fish. **2** A young herring. [<OF *esperlinge* <Gmc.]

spar·oid (spär′oid, spar′-) *adj.* Of or pertaining to a family (*Sparidae*) of spiny–finned marine fishes allied to the grunts and including the porgy, sheepshead, etc. — *n.* A sparoid fish; the sea bream. [<L *sparus* <Gk. *sparos* gilthead + -OID]

spar·row (spar′ō) *n.* **1** Any of various small, plainly colored, passerine birds (family *Fringillidae*) related to the finches, grosbeaks, and buntings; especially, the European house sparrow (*Passer domesticus*), known in the United States as the **English sparrow. 2** Some other singing bird like or likened to the house sparrow, as the song sparrow. [OE *spearwa*]

sparrow bill A sparable.

spar·row·grass (spar′ō·gras′, -gräs′) *n. Dial.* Asparagus: a corruption. Also **spar′ry·grass′** (spar′ē-).

sparrow hawk 1 A small falconine bird that preys on sparrows, as the kestrel, or the **eastern sparrow hawk** (*Falco sparverius*). **2** A small European hawk (*Accipiter nisus*) that preys on other birds.

spar·ry (spär′ē) *adj.* **·ri·er, ·ri·est** Of, abounding in, or like spar.

sparse (spärs) *adj.* Scattered at considerable distances apart; thinly diffused; not dense. [<L *sparsus,* pp. of *spargere* sprinkle, scatter] — **sparse′ly** *adv.* — **sparse′ness, spar·si·ty** (spär′sə·tē) *n.*

Spar·ta (spär′tə) An ancient city in the Peloponnesus, southern Greece; capital of ancient Laconia: also *Lacedaemon.*

Spar·ta·cist (spär′tə·sist) *n.* A member of a party of extreme socialists in Germany (1918–19): name derived from the pseudonym *Spartacus* used by their leader, Karl Liebknecht. Also **Spar′ta·cide** (-sīd).

Spar·ta·cus (spär′tə·kəs) Thracian leader of slaves in the gladiatorial war against Rome 73–71 B.C.

Spar·tan (spär′tən) *adj.* Pertaining to Sparta or the Spartans; heroically brave and enduring. — *n.* A native or citizen of Sparta; hence, one of exceptional valor and fortitude. — **Spar′tan·ism** *n.*

spar·te·ine (spär′ti·ēn, -tē·in) *n. Chem.* A colorless, oily, poisonous alkaloid, $C_{15}H_{26}N_2$, contained in the common broom: it resembles digitalis in action. [<Gk. *spartos* broom + -INE[2]]

spasm (spaz′əm) *n.* **1** Any sudden or convulsive action or effort, as of the body, mind, or nature, especially such a one as is abnormal or temporary. **2** *Pathol.* Any involuntary convulsive contraction of muscles: when manifested by alternate contractions and relaxations it is a **clonic spasm;** when persistent and steady, it is a **tonic spasm.** [<L *spasma, spasmus* <Gk. *spasmos* < *spaein* draw, pull]

spas·mod·ic (spaz·mod′ik) *adj.* **1** Of the nature of a spasm; convulsive. **2** Violent, or impulsive and transitory. Also **spas·mod′i·cal.** — **spas·mod′i·cal·ly** *adv.*

spas·mol·y·sis (spaz·mol′ə·sis) *n. Med.* The checking or relief of spasms. — **spas·mo·lyt·ic** (spaz′mə·lit′ik) *adj.*

spas·mo·phil·i·a (spaz′mə·fil′ē·ə) *n. Pathol.* A constitutional tendency to spasms and convulsions. — **spas′mo·phil′ic** *adj.*

spas·tic (spas′tik) *adj.* Of, pertaining to, or characterized by spasms; spasmodic; tetanic: *spastic* hemiplegia. — *n.* A person afflicted with spastic seizures. [<L *spasticus* <Gk. *spastikos* < *spaein* draw, pull] — **spas′ti·cal·ly** *adv.*

spat[1] (spat) Past tense and past participle of SPIT[1].

spat[2] (spat) *n.* **1** Spawn of shellfish; specifically, spawn of the oyster. **2** A young oyster, or young oysters collectively. — *v.i.* **spat·ted, spat·ting** To spawn, as oysters. [? Related to SPIT[1]]

spat[3] (spat) *n.* **1** A slight blow; slap. **2** A splash, as of rain; spatter. **3** A petty dispute. — *v.* **spat·ted, spat·ting** *v.i.* **1** To strike with a slight sound; slap. **2** To engage in a petty quarrel. — *v.t.* **3** To slap. [Prob. imit.]

spat[4] (spat) *n.* A short gaiter worn over a shoe and fastened underneath with a strap: usually in the plural. [Short for SPATTERDASH]

spate (spāt) *n.* **1** A freshet; overflow. **2** A sudden, violent rainstorm; also, a waterspout. **3** A sudden or vigorous outpouring, as of words, feeling, etc. Also **spait.** [Origin uncertain]

spa·tha·ceous (spə·thā′shəs) *adj. Bot.* Bearing or of the nature of a spathe. Also **spa·thal** (spā′thəl).

spathe (spāth) *n. Bot.* A large bract or pair of bracts sheathing a flower cluster, as a spadix. [<L *spatha* <Gk. *spathē* broadsword] — **spa·those** (spā′thōs, spath′ōs) *adj.*

spath·ic (spath′ik) *adj. Mineral.* Of, pertaining to, or resembling spar. Also **spath·ose** (spath′ōs). [<G *spath* spar]

spa·tial (spā′shəl) *adj.* Pertaining to space; involving or having the nature of space. Also *spacial.* [<L *spatium* space] — **spa·ti·al·i·ty** (spā′shē·al′ə·tē) *n.* — **spa′tial·ly** *adv.*

spa·ti·o-tem·po·ral (spā′shē·ō·tem′pər·əl) *adj.* Of or pertaining to both space and time.

spat·ter (spat′ər) *v.t.* **1** To scatter in drops or splashes, as mud or paint. **2** To splash with such drops; bespatter. **3** To defame. — *v.i.* **4** To throw off drops or splashes; sputter. **5** To fall in a shower, as raindrops. — *n.* **1** The act of spattering, or the matter spattered; a splash. **2** A pattering noise, as of falling rain. [OE *spat-*, stem of *spatlian* spit out + -ER[4]]

spat·ter·dash (spat′ər·dash′) *n.* A legging reaching to the knee, worn as a protection from mud, especially when riding: used chiefly in the plural. — **spat′ter·dashed′** *adj.*

spat·ter·dock (spat′ər·dok′) *n.* The yellow pondlily (*Nuphar advena*).

spat·u·la (spach′ŏŏ·lə) *n.* **1** A knifelike instrument with a flat, flexible blade, used to spread plaster, cake icing, etc. **2** *Med.* An instrument used to press the tongue down or aside, as in examinations. [<L, dim. of *spatha.* See SPATHE.] — **spat′u·lar** *adj.*

spat·u·late (spach′ŏŏ·lit, -lāt) *adj.* **1** Shaped like a spatula. **2** *Bot.* Oblong, with an attenuated base, as many leaves.

spav·in (spav′in) *n.* A disease of the hock joint of horses, occurring either as an infusion of lymph within the joint (**blood spavin** or **bog spavin**) or as a bony deposit stiffening the joint (**bone spavin**). Also *Scot.* **spa·vie** (spā′vē, spav′ē). [<OF *espavain, esparvain*; ult. origin uncertain] — **spav′ined** *adj.*

spawn (spôn) *n.* **1** *Zool.* The eggs of fishes, amphibians, mollusks, etc., especially in masses. **2** Derisively, the offspring of any animal; also, outcome or results; product; yield. **3** The spat of the oyster. **4** Very small fish; fry. **5** *Bot.* The mycelium of mushrooms or other fungi. [< *v.*] — *v.i.* **1** To produce spawn; deposit eggs or roe. **2** To come forth as or like spawn. — *v.t.* **3** To produce (spawn). **4** To give rise to; originate. **5** To bring forth abundantly or in great quantity. **6** To plant with spawn or mycelium. [<AF *espaundre*, OF *espendre* <L *expandere.* Doublet of EXPAND.]

spay (spā) *v.t.* To remove the ovaries from (a female animal). [<AF *espeier,* OF *espeer* cut with a sword < *espee* a sword <L *spatha*]

speak (spēk) *v.* **spoke** (*Archaic* **spake**), **spo·ken** (*Archaic* **spoke**), **speak·ing** *v.i.* **1** To employ the vocal organs in ordinary speech; utter words. **2** To express or convey ideas, opinions, etc., in or as in speech: to *speak* about a matter; Actions *speak* louder than words. **3** To make a speech; deliver an address. **4** To converse. **5** To make a sound; also, to bark, as a dog. — *v.t.* **6** To express or make known in or as in speech. **7** To utter in speech: to *speak* words of love. **8** To use or be capable of using (a language) in conversation. **9** To speak to. **10** *Naut.* To hail and exchange communications with (a vessel) at sea. — **to speak daggers** To express hatred. — **to speak for 1** To speak in behalf of; represent officially. **2** To lay claim to; bespeak; engage. [OE *specan, spreccan*]

Synonyms: announce, articulate, converse, declaim, declare, deliver, dictate, enunciate, express, pronounce, say, talk, tell, utter. See TALK.

speak–eas·y (spēk′ē′zē) *n. pl.* **–eas·ies** A saloon where liquor is sold contrary to law.

speak·er (spē′kər) *n.* **1** One who speaks; an orator. **2** The presiding officer in any one of various legislative bodies. **3** A volume of oratorical selections, for declamation. **4** A loudspeaker. — **speak′er·ship** *n.*

speak·ing (spē′king) *adj.* **1** Having the power of effective speech; uttering speech. **2** Expressive; vivid; telling; lifelike. — *n.* **1** The act of utterance; vocal expression. **2** Oratory; public declamation. — **speak′ing·ly** *adv.*

spean (spēn) *v.t. Brit. Dial.* To wean. [<MDu. *spene* a teat]

spear (spir) *n.* **1** A weapon consisting of a pointed head on a long shaft. **2** A similar instrument, barbed and usually forked, as for spearing fish. **3** A spearman. **4** A leaf or slender stalk, as of grass: sometimes called a *spire.* — *v.t.* **1** To pierce or capture with a spear. — *v.i.* **2** To pierce as a spear does. **3** To send forth spears or spires, as a plant. [OE *spere* spear] — **spear′er** *n.*

spear·fish (spir′fish′) *n. pl.* **·fish** or **·fish·es** A powerful marine fish (genus *Tetrapturus*) with a long snout, related to the swordfish.

spear·head (spir′hed′) *n.* **1** The point of a spear or lance. **2** The military units which lead in a massed attack on enemy positions. — *v.t.* To be in the lead of (an attack, etc.).

spear·man (spir′mən) *n. pl.* **·men** (-mən) A man armed with a spear. Also **spears′man.**

spear·mint (spir′mint′) *n.* An aromatic herb (*Mentha spicata*) similar to peppermint.

spear side *Archaic* The male branch of a family: opposed to the female or *distaff* or *spindle side.* Also **spear half.**

spear·wort (spir′wûrt′) *n.* Any of several species of crowfoot having lance–shaped or linear leaves, especially, the **lesser spearwort** (*Ranunculus flammula*).

spe·cial (spesh′əl) *adj.* **1** Having some peculiar or distinguishing characteristic or characteristics; out of the ordinary; uncommon; particular. **2** Designed for or assigned to a specific purpose; limited or specific in range, aim, or purpose. **3** Of or pertaining to, constituting, or designating a species; specific; distinguishing; differential. **4** Unique; singular; exceptional. **5** Extra or additional, as a dividend. **6** Intimate; esteemed; beloved: a *special* favorite. See synonyms under PARTICULAR. — *n.* **1** A person or thing made, detailed for, or appropriated to a specific service or occasion, as a train, a newspaper edition, etc. **2** A featured dish or course in a restaurant or cafeteria. **3** A temporary sale. **4** A television show that is not regularly scheduled but is produced for a single presentation. [<OF *especial* <L *specialis* < *species* kind, species] — **spe′cial·ly** *adv.*

special delivery *U.S.* Mail delivery by special courier in advance of regular delivery: a postal service obtained for an additional fee.

Special Drawing Rights International monetary credit that can be drawn by member nations from the International Monetary Fund to be used in lieu of gold: also called *paper gold.* Abbr. *SDR, S.D.R., SDRs, S.D.R.s.*

spe·cial·ism (spesh′əl·iz′əm) *n.* The confining of oneself to a particular line of work.

spe·cial·ist (spesh′əl·ist) *n.* A person devoted to some one line of study, occupation, or professional work. — **spe′cial·is′tic** *adj.*

spe·ci·al·i·ty (spesh′ē·al′ə·tē) *n. pl.* **·ties 1** A specific or individual characteristic; peculiarity. **2** Specialty (defs. 3, 4, 5). ◆ In British usage, this form is preferred instead of *specialty.*

spe·cial·i·za·tion (spesh′əl·ə·zā′shən, -ī·zā′-) *n.* **1** The act or process of specializing; also, the state of being or becoming specialized. **2** *Biol.* The development of an organ or part for a special function; differentiation.

spe·cial·ize (spesh′əl·īz) *v.* **·ized, ·iz·ing** *v.i.* **1** To concentrate on one particular activity or subject; engage in a specialty. **2** *Biol.* To take on a special form or forms by specialization or adaptation. — *v.t.* **3** To adapt for some special use or purpose; endow with a particular character. **4** *Biol.* To develop by specialization or adaptation, as an organ or part. **5** To endorse, as a check, to a payee. **6** To mention specifically. Also *Brit.* **spe′cial·ise.**

special pleading 1 *Law* **a** A pleading made with reference to some new or particular matter instead of the general issue. **b** The allegation of new or special matter in reply to the opposing party's averments, rather than an offer of a direct denial. **2** A presentation of the favorable aspects of an argument while avoiding or suppressing the unfavorable.

spe·cial·ty (spesh′əl·tē) *n. pl.* **·ties 1** The state of being special or of having peculiar characteristics. **2** An individual characteristic; peculiarity; distinguishing mark. **3** An occupation or study limited to one particular line. **4** An article dealt in exclusively or chiefly, or a manufactured product of peculiar character. **5** *Law* A sealed contract; deed. — **specialty of the house** A featured dish or course in a restaurant.

spe·ci·a·tion (spē′shē·ā′shən) *n. Biol.* The formation of a species by the action of evolutionary processes upon plant and animal organisms.

spe·cie (spē′shē) *n.* Coined money; coin. See synonyms under MONEY. — **in specie 1** In coin. **2** *Law* In kind; in the shape mentioned; in sort. [<L (*in*) *specie* (in) kind]

spe·cies (spē′shēz, -shiz; *Lat.* spē′shi·ēz) *n. pl.* **·cies 1** *Biol.* A category of animals or plants subordinate to a genus but above a breed, race, strain, or variety. The species name follows immediately after the name of the genus to which it belongs, and with it forms the scientific name of the individual plant or animal, as *Oreamnos americanus,* the Rocky Mountain goat. **2** A group of individuals or objects agreeing in some common attribute or attributes and designated by a common name. **3** A mental image considered as having the likeness of some object in nature. **4** A kind; sort; variety; form. **5** *Eccl.* **a** The visible form of bread or of wine retained by the eucharistic elements after consecration. **b** The consecrated elements of the Eucharist. **6** *Obs.* Specie; coin. [<L, form, kind. Doublet of SPICE.]

spec·i·fi·a·ble (spes′ə·fī′ə·bəl) *adj.* Such as can be specified.

spe·cif·ic (spi·sif′ik) *adj.* **1** Distinctly and plainly set forth; definite or determinate; particular; explicit. **2** Of, pertaining to, or distinguishing a species: a *specific* name of an animal. **3** Peculiar; special. **4** Having some distinct medicinal or pathological property;

distinguishable or determinate: a *specific medicine*, a *specific germ*. **5** Having or designating a particular property, composition, ratio, or quantity serving to identify a given substance or phenomenon in relation to some arbitrary but constant standard of comparison: *specific heat*, *specific volume*, etc. **6** Denoting a customs duty chargeable upon imported merchandise by quantity, weight, or number, without regard to value: contrasted with *ad valorem duty*. Also *Rare* **spe·cif´i·cal.** — *n.* Anything specific or adapted to effect a specific result, as a medicine specially indicated to cure or prevent some particular disease. [<L *specificus* < *species* kind, class + *facere* make] — **spec·i·fic·i·ty** (spes´ə-fis´ə-tē) *n.*

spe·cif·i·cal·ly (spi-sif´ik-lē) *adv.* **1** In a specific manner; explicitly; particularly; definitely. **2** As to or in respect to species: *specifically* distinct. **3** In a particular sense or case.

spec·i·fi·ca·tion (spes´ə-fə-kā´shən) *n.* **1** The act of specifying. **2** A definite and complete statement, as in a contract; also, one detail in such a statement. **3** In patent law, the detailed statement of an inventor's scheme, setting forth the nature of the invention and the precise method of constructing and applying it. **4** A specific description of certain dimensions, types of material, etc., to be used in a construction or engineering project; also, any item in this description.

specific gravity *Physics* The ratio of the mass of a body to that of an equal volume of some standard substance, water in the case of solids and liquids, and air or hydrogen in the case of gases.

specific heat *Physics* The amount of heat required to raise the temperature of a given quantity of a substance one degree.

specific impulse The thrust in pounds produced in one second by the burning with its oxidizer of one pound of a specified fuel, as in a rocket motor or jet engine.

spec·i·fy (spes´ə-fī) *v.t.* **·fied, ·fy·ing 1** To mention specifically; state in full and explicit terms. **2** To embody in a specification. [<OF *specifier* <L *species* kind, species + *facere* make]

spec·i·men (spes´ə-mən) *n.* **1** One of a class of persons or things regarded as representative of the class; an example; sample. **2** *Biol.* A plant or an animal, entire or in part, prepared and kept as an example to illustrate a species or variety. **3** A sample for urinalysis. **4** *Colloq.* A person of pronounced or curious type; a character; a case: *What a* specimen! See synonyms under EXAMPLE, SAMPLE. [<L <*specere* look at]

spe·ci·os·i·ty (spē´shē-os´ə-tē) *n.* *pl.* **·ties 1** One who or that which is specious; a thing that appears just and plausible at first view but actually is not. **2** *Obs.* The state of being beautiful.

spe·cious (spē´shəs) *adj.* **1** Apparently good or right, but without merit; plausible: *specious reasoning*. **2** Pleasing or attractive in appearance, but deceptive; fair–seeming: a *specious promise*. **3** Beguiling, but lacking in sincerity: a *specious hypocrite*. **4** *Archaic* Showy; pleasing to the view. See synonyms under OSTENSIBLE. [<L *speciosus* fair] — **spe´cious·ly** *adv.* — **spe´cious·ness** *n.*

speck (spek) *n.* **1** A small spot; a little stain or discoloration. **2** Any very small thing; a particle. See synonyms under BLEMISH. — *v.t.* To mark with spots or specks; speckle. [OE *specca*]

speck·le (spek´əl) *v.t.* **·led, ·ling** To mark with specks or speckles. — *n.* A diminutive spot; speck.

speck·led (spek´əld) *adj.* **1** Dotted with specks or spots. **2** Of motley appearance or mixed character.

specs (speks) *n. pl. Colloq.* Spectacles. Also **specks.**

spec·ta·cle (spek´tə-kəl) *n.* **1** That which is exhibited to public view; a grand display; pageant; parade; show. **2** An unwelcome or deplorable exhibition; a painful sight. **3** *pl.* A pair of eyeglasses, with hinged bows to secure them before the eyes: used to correct defects in vision, or to protect the eyes, as from glare. **4** *pl.* A marking on animals resembling

a pair of spectacles. — **compound spectacles** *Optics* **1** Spectacles having supplementary colored glasses hinged to them for use when desired. **2** Supplementary lenses of greater power, similarly hinged. **3** Bifocals; trifocals. [<F <L *spectaculum* <*spectare*, freq. of *specere* see]
Synonyms: display, exhibition, pageant, parade, scene, show, sight. See SIGHT.

spec·ta·cled (spek´tə-kəld) *adj.* **1** Wearing spectacles. **2** Having markings resembling a pair of spectacles: the *spectacled* cobra.

spec·tac·u·lar (spek-tak´yə-lər) *adj.* Characterized by grand scenic display; exciting wonder by dramatic or unusual display. — *n.* **1** An imposing exhibition. **2** In television, a lavish dramatic or musical production of 90 minutes duration, especially designed for reproduction in color. **3** An elaborate, illuminated sign. — **spec·tac´u·lar·ly** *adv.* — **spec·tac·u·lar·i·ty** (-lar´ə-tē) *n.*

spec·ta·tor (spek´tā-tər, spek-tā´-) *n.* **1** One who beholds; an eyewitness; an onlooker. **2** One who is present at and views a show, game, spectacle, etc. [<L <*spectare* look at]
Synonyms: beholder, bystander, onlooker, observer, witness.

Spec·ta·tor (spek´tā-tər, spek-tā´-), **The** An English periodical, conducted by Joseph Addison and Richard Steele from March, 1711, to Dec., 1712; revived by Addison, June–Dec., 1714.

spec·ter (spek´tər) *n.* A phantom of the dead or of a disembodied spirit; especially, one of a grisly or horrible nature; ghost; apparition. Also **spec´tre.** [<F *spectre* <L *spectrum* vision]
Synonyms: apparition, phantom, ghost, shade, spirit.

specter of the Brocken See BROCKEN.

spec·tra (spek´trə) Plural of SPECTRUM.

spec·tral (spek´trəl) *adj.* **1** Pertaining to a specter; ghostly. **2** Pertaining to the spectrum or to spectra. See synonyms under GHASTLY. — **spec´tral·ly** *adv.* — **spec·tral·i·ty** (spek-tral´ə-tē) *n.*

spectro– *combining form* **1** Radiant energy, as exhibited in the spectrum: *spectroscope*. **2** Spectroscope; spectroscopic: *spectrobolometer*. [<SPECTRUM]

spec·tro·bo·lom·e·ter (spek´trō-bō-lom´ə-tər) *n.* A bolometer combined with a spectroscope for measuring the heat of different parts of the spectrum.

spec·tro·chem·is·try (spek´trō-kem´is-trē) *n.* The study of chemical phenomena and properties by means of spectrum analysis. — **spec´tro·chem´i·cal** *adj.*

spec·tro·gram (spek´trə-gram) *n.* The record of a spectrograph.

spec·tro·graph (spek´trə-graf, -gräf) *n. Physics* **1** An apparatus for photographing a spectrum or for forming a representation of the spectrum in any way. **2** A photograph of a spectrum. — **sound spectrograph** An electronic instrument designed to record the frequencies of speech sounds as measured in cycles per second, and the amplitude at any given frequency: used in acoustic phonetics.

spec·tro·he·li·o·gram (spek´trō-hē´lē-ə-gram´) *n.* A photograph made by the spectroheliograph.

spec·tro·he·li·o·graph (spek´trō-hē´lē-ə-graf´, -gräf´) *n.* An instrument for photographing the sun with its prominences by means of monochromatic light.

spec·trom·e·ter (spek-trom´ə-tər) *n.* **1** An instrument by means of which the angular deviation of a ray of light produced by a prism or by a refraction grating can be determined, or a wavelength of a ray of light can be accurately measured. **2** A spectroscope provided with such an instrument. — **spec·tro·met·ric** (spek´trō-met´rik) *adj.*

spec·tro·pho·tom·e·ter (spek´trō-fō-tom´ə-tər) *n.* An instrument for determining the relative intensity of two spectra or of the corresponding bands of color in two spectra.

spec·tro·ra·di·om·e·ter (spek´trō-rā´dē-om´ə-tər) *n.* A form of spectrometer for determining the distribution of the intensity of any type of radiation, especially in the infrared region of the spectrum. — **spec´tro·ra´di·om´e·try** *n.*

spec·tro·scope (spek´trə-skōp) *n.* An optical instrument for forming and analyzing spectra emitted by bodies or substances. — **spec´tro·scop´ic** (-skop´ik) or **·i·cal** *adj.* — **spec´tro·scop´i·cal·ly** *adv.*

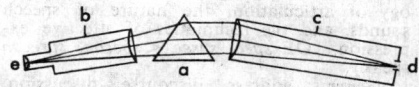

PRINCIPLE OF SIMPLE SPECTROSCOPE
a. Prism. *b.* Telescope for viewing prism through eyepiece *(e).* *c.* Collimator with slit *(d).*

spec·tros·co·py (spek·tros´kə-pē) *n.* **1** The branch of physical science treating of the phenomena observed with the spectroscope. **2** The art of using the spectroscope. — **spec·tros´co·pist** *n.*

spec·trum (spek´trəm) *n.* *pl.* **·tra** (-trə) **1** The continuously varying band of color observed when a beam of white light is passed through a prism which separates each component of the light according to frequencies ranging from low for red to high for violet: also **visible spectrum, chromatic spectrum.** **2** An image formed by radiant energy directed through a spectroscope and brought to a focus in which each wavelength corresponds to a specific band or line in a progressive series characteristic of the emitting source. **3** An after–image. [<L, a vision]

spectrum analysis The investigation or qualitative analysis of bodies or substances by means of their spectra; spectroscopy.

spec·u·la (spek´yə-lə) Plural of SPECULUM.

spec·u·lar (spek´yə-lər) *adj.* **1** Pertaining to or assisted by a speculum or a mirror; reflecting. **2** *Obs.* Affording a view; aiding vision. [<L *specularis* < *speculum* mirror]

specular iron A lustrous, crystalline variety of hematite.

specular pig iron Spiegeleisen.

spec·u·late (spek´yə-lāt) *v.i.* **·lat·ed, ·lat·ing 1** To form conjectures regarding anything without experiment; theorize; conjecture. **2** To make an investment involving a risk, but with hope of gain. [<L *speculatus*, pp. of *speculari* look at, examine < *specere* see]

spec·u·la·tion (spek´yə-lā´shən) *n.* **1** The act of theorizing or conjecturing; speculating. **2** A theory or conjecture. **3** A conclusion reached by or based upon conjecture. **4** An investment involving risk with hope of large profit. **5** The act of engaging in risky business transactions that offer a possibility of large profit. **6** *Archaic* Vision; observation; intuition. See synonyms under HYPOTHESIS, THOUGHT[1].

spec·u·la·tive (spek´yə-lā´tiv, -lə-tiv) *adj.* **1** Of, pertaining to, engaged in, or given to speculation: opposed to *experimental*. **2** Strictly theoretical or purely scientific: opposed to *practical*. **3** Engaging in or involving financial speculation. **4** *Archaic* Pertaining to vision or observation; affording a good view. **5** *Archaic* Prying; observing. — **spec´u·la´tive·ly** *adv.* — **spec´u·la´tive·ness** *n.*

spec·u·la·tor (spek´yə-lā´tər) *n.* One who speculates, in any sense. — **spec´u·la·to´ry** (-lə-tôr´ē, -tō´rē) *adj.*

spec·u·lum (spek´yə-ləm) *n.* *pl.* **·la** (-lə) or **·lums 1** A mirror of polished metal or of glass coated with a metal film used for telescope reflectors and other optical instruments. **2** *Med.* An instrument that dilates a passage of the body for examination. **3** *Ornithol.* A specially colored, typically iridescent area on the wings of certain birds, as ducks. [<L, a mirror < *specere* see]

sped (sped) Alternative past tense and past participle of SPEED.

Spee (shpā), **Count Maximilian von,** 1861–1914, German rear admiral in World War I.

speech (spēch) *n.* **1** The faculty of expressing thought and emotion by spoken words; the power of speaking. **2** The act of speaking, involving the production of meaningful combinations of distinctive speech sounds. **3** That which is spoken; conversation; talk; a saying or remark. **4** A public address; a discourse. **5** A characteristic manner of

speaking: His *speech* is loud and unpleasant. **6** A particular language, idiom, or dialect: American *speech.* **7** Any audible or visible method of communication, including cries, gestures, and sign language. **8** The study of oral communication, including the physiology of articulation, the nature of speech sounds, and the techniques of effective expression. [OE *spec, sprec* < *specan, sprecan* speak]

Synonyms: address, discourse, discussion, disquisition, dissertation, eloquence, harangue, oration, oratory, sermon. *Speech* is the general word for utterance of thought in language. A *speech* is the simplest mode of delivering one's sentiments; an *oration* is an elaborate and prepared *speech*; a *harangue* is a vehement appeal to passion, or a *speech* that has something disputatious and combative in it. A *discourse* is a set *speech* on a definite subject intended to convey instruction. See LANGUAGE. *Antonyms*: hush, silence, stillness.

speech clinic A place where speech disorders are corrected by training and re-education.

speech community All the speakers of a given language or dialect in both contiguous and geographically distributed areas.

speech defect The manifestation or end product of a speech disorder.

speech disorder Disorganization or impairment of speech caused either by physical defect or by mental disorder, such as aphasia, stuttering, etc.

speech·i·fy (spē'chə·fī) *v.i.* **·fied, ·fy·ing** To make speeches: often used derisively. — **speech'i·fi'er** *n.*

speech·less (spēch'lis) *adj.* **1** Unable to speak or temporarily deprived of speech because of physical weakness or strong emotion, etc.: *speechless* with rage. **2** Mute; dumb. **3** Silent; reticent. **4** *Archaic* Unspoken in words: the *speechless* message in her eyes. **5** Unaccompanied by speech: *speechless* joy. **6** *Archaic* Inexpressible. — **speech'less·ly** *adv.* — **speech'less·ness** *n.*

speech·mak·er (spēch'mā'kər) *n.* One who delivers a speech or speeches. — **speech'mak'·ing** *n.*

speech sound An articulation which functions in oral communication.

speed (spēd) *n.* **1** The act or state of moving or progressing swiftly; rapidity of motion; celerity; swiftness. **2** *Physics* **a** Rate of motion, especially as considered without reference to direction: a scalar quantity distinguished from *velocity.* **b** Rate of performance, as shown by the ratio of work done to time spent. **3** *Mech.* A transmission gear in a motor vehicle. **4** *Phot.* In a camera lens, the minimum time required for an effective exposure under given conditions, expressed as the ratio of focal length to effective aperture. **5** *Slang* One of the amphetamines taken illicitly, especially by injection. **6** *Archaic* Good luck; success; prosperity. — *v.* **sped** or **speed·ed, speed·ing** *v.i.* **1** To move or go with speed. **2** *Obs.* To prosper. **3** *Obs.* To fare in a specified manner. — *v.t.* **4** To promote the forward progress of; cause to move or go with speed. **5** To promote the success of. **6** To wish Godspeed to: *Speed* the parting guest. — **to speed up** To accelerate in speed or action. See synonyms under FLY[1]. — *adj.* Having, pertaining to, characterized by, regulating, or indicating speed: used chiefly in compounds:

speed-cone	**speed-lathe**	**speed-test**
speed-gage	**speed-pulley**	**speed-trap**
speed-gear	**speed-recorder**	

[OE *spēd* power]

speed·boat (spēd'bōt') *n.* A motorboat capable of high speed.

speed·er (spē'dər) *n.* Someone or something that speeds; specifically, a motorist who drives at a speed exceeding a safe or legal limit.

speed indicator **1** An instrument showing the rotation speed of a machine or part of a machine. **2** A speedometer.

speed·ing (spē'ding) *adj.* Moving with speed. — *n.* Travel at high speed; especially, by motor vehicles, travel at an unsafe or reckless speed or above a specified speed limit.

speed limit A legally set maximum speed at which vehicles may travel on certain stretches of roads or through specified districts.

speed·om·e·ter (spi·dom'ə·tər) *n.* A device for indicating the speed of a vehicle or the distance traveled.

speed·ster (spēd'stər) *n.* **1** A speeder. **2** An automobile, usually having two seats, designed for speed.

speed-up (spēd'up') *n.* An acceleration in work, output, movement, etc.

speed·way (spēd'wā') *n.* A specially reserved or prepared road for vehicles traveling at high speed.

speed·well (spēd'wel) *n.* One of various low herbs (genus *Veronica*) of the figwort family, bearing blue or white flowers, especially the common speedwell (*V. arvensis*) and the **germander speedwell** (*V. chamaedrys*), with bright-blue flowers: also called *birdseye.*

speed·y (spē'dē) *adj.* **speed·i·er, speed·i·est** **1** Characterized by speed. **2** Without delay. See synonyms under NIMBLE, SWIFT[1]. — **speed'·i·ly** *adv.* — **speed'i·ness** *n.*

speed·y-cut (spē'dē·kut') *n.* An injury on the side of the knee or carpus of a horse caused by a blow from the shoe of the foot of the opposite leg when trotting or moving at any other rapid gait.

speel (spēl) *v.t.* & *v.i.* *Scot.* To climb.

speer (spir) *v.t.* & *v.i.* *Scot.* To inquire; ask: also spelled *spier.* — **to speer at** To question.

speer·ing (spir'ing) *n.* *Scot.* Inquiry; news; information.

speiss (spīs) *n.* An impure mixture consisting of the arsenides of certain metals, as copper, iron, and nickel, that concentrate in smelting certain ores. Also *Ger.* **spei·se** (shpī'zə). [<G *speise* amalgam]

spe·le·an (spi·lē'ən) *adj.* **1** Dwelling in a cave or caves. **2** Of or pertaining to a cave or caverns. Also **spe·lae'an.** [<L *spelaeum* <Gk. *spēlaion* a cave]

spe·le·ol·o·gy (spē'lē·ol'ə·jē) *n.* **1** The scientific study of caves in their physical, geological, and biological aspects. **2** The exploration of caves as a sport or profession. [<L *spelaeum* a cave + -LOGY] — **spe'le·o·log'i·cal** (-ə·loj'i·kəl) *adj.* — **spe'le·ol'o·gist** *n.*

spell[1] (spel) *v.* **spelled** or **spelt, spell·ing** *v.t.* **1** To pronounce or write the letters of (a word); especially, to do so correctly. **2** To form or be the letters of: C-a-t *spells* cat; hence, to compose; make up. **3** To read with difficulty; hence, to puzzle out and learn: sometimes with *over* or *out.* **4** To signify; mean: Extravagance *spells* disaster. — *v.i.* **5** To form words out of letters, especially correctly. [<OF *espeler* <Gmc. Akin to SPELL[2].]

spell[2] (spel) *n.* A formula used as a charm; incantation; charm; hence, fascination. — *v.t.* **spelled, spell·ing** To cast a spell upon; fascinate; bewitch. [OE, story, statement. Akin to SPELL[1].]

spell[3] (spel) *n.* **1** A period of time, usually of short length. **2** *Colloq.* A continuous period characterized by a certain type of weather. **3** *Colloq.* A short distance. **4** *Colloq.* A fit of illness, debility, etc. **5** A turn of duty in relief of another. **6** A period of work or employment. **7** *Austral.* A period of relaxation; rest. — *v.t.* **1** To relieve temporarily from some work or duty. **2** *Austral.* To give a rest to, as a horse. — *v.i.* **3** To take a rest. [OE *gespelia* a substitute, one who spells another]

spell·bind (spel'bīnd') *v.t.* **·bound, ·bind·ing** To bind or enthral, as if by a spell.

spell·bind·er (spel'bīn'dər) *n.* One who casts a spell over others; specifically, a political orator.

spell·bound (spel'bound') *adj.* Bound as by a spell; fascinated.

spell·er (spel'ər) *n.* **1** One who spells. **2** A spelling book.

spell·ing (spel'ing) *n.* **1** The act of one who spells. **2** The art of correct spelling; orthography. **3** The way in which a word is spelled.

spelling bee A gathering at which contestants engage in spelling words, those who spell wrongly usually being retired until only one remains.

spelling book A book of exercises for training students to spell.

Spell·man (spel'mən), **Francis Joseph,** 1889–1967, U. S. cardinal; archbishop of New York.

spelt[1] (spelt) Alternative past tense and past participle of SPELL[1].

spelt[2] (spelt) *n.* A species of wheat (*Triticum spelta*) or any of its winter or spring varieties. [OE]

spel·ter (spel'tər) *n.* Zinc: a commercial term. — **brazing spelter** See BRAZING SOLDER. [Var. of PEWTER]

spe·lun·ker (spē·lung'kər) *n.* An enthusiast in the exploration and study of caves; a speleologist. [<L *spelunca* a cave]

Spe·mann (shpā'män), **Hans,** 1869–1941, German zoologist.

spence (spens) *n.* *Brit. Dial.* **1** A pantry or larder. **2** The parlor of a cottage. [<OF *despense* <L *dispendere* DISPENSE]

spen·cer[1] (spen'sər) *n.* A trysail.

spen·cer[2] (spen'sər) *n.* **1** A man's short jacket of the early 19th century. **2** A similar outer garment for women, usually tight-fitting and often knitted or fur-trimmed. [after 2nd Earl *Spencer,* 1758–1834, English nobleman]

Spen·cer (spen'sər), **Herbert,** 1820–1903, English philosopher.

Spen·cer Gulf (spen'sər) An inlet of the Indian Ocean in South Australia; 200 miles long; 80 miles wide.

Spen·ce·ri·an (spen·sir'ē·ən) *adj.* **1** Pertaining to Herbert Spencer, or to his doctrine. **2** Pertaining to a system of freehand penmanship devised by P. R. Spencer about 1855. — *n.* A follower of Herbert Spencer and his system.

Spen·cer·ism (spen'sə·riz'əm) *n.* The doctrine of Herbert Spencer that the universe has evolved through mechanical forces from relative simplicity to relative complexity; synthetic philosophy. Also **Spen·ce·ri·an·ism** (spen·sir'ē·ən·iz'əm).

spend (spend) *v.* **spent, spend·ing** *v.t.* **1** To pay out or disburse (money). **2** To expend by degrees; use up. **3** To apply or devote, as thought or effort, to some activity, purpose, etc. **4** To pass: to *spend* one's life in jail. **5** To lose: now chiefly in the nautical phrase **to spend a mast.** **6** To emit, as a milt or spawn. — *v.i.* **7** To pay out or disburse money, etc. **8** *Obs.* To be wasted or exhausted. See synonyms under SQUANDER. [OE *aspendan* <L *expendere* EXPEND] — **spend'er** *n.*

Spen·der (spen'dər), **Stephen,** born 1909, English poet and critic.

spend·thrift (spend'thrift') *n.* One who is wastefully lavish of money: also **spend'er.** — *adj.* Excessively lavish; wasteful; prodigal.

Speng·ler (speng'glər, *Ger.* shpeng'lər), **Oswald,** 1880–1936, German philosopher of history.

Spen·ser (spen'sər), **Edmund,** 1552–99, English poet.

Spen·se·ri·an (spen·sir'ē·ən) *adj.* Of or pertaining to Edmund Spenser or to his style.

Spenserian sonnet See under SONNET.

Spenserian stanza A nine-line stanza consisting of eight lines of ten syllables and one of twelve syllables and riming *ababbcbcc*: used by Edmund Spenser in *The Faerie Queene.*

spent (spent) Past tense and past participle of SPEND. — *adj.* **1** Worn out or exhausted. **2** Deprived of force: a *spent* bullet or cannon ball.

Sper·lon·ga (sper·lông'gä) A village and port of south central Italy; site of a cave containing numerous ancient statues.

sperm[1] (spûrm) *n.* **1** The male fertilizing fluid; semen. **2** A male reproductive cell; spermatozoon. [<Gk. *sperma* a seed < *speirein* sow]

sperm[2] (spûrm) *n.* **1** A sperm whale. **2** Spermaceti. **3** Sperm oil. [Short for SPERMACETI]

-sperm *combining form Bot.* A seed (of a specified kind): *gymnosperm.* [<Gk. *sperma, spermatos* a seed]

sper·ma·ce·ti (spûr'mə·sē'tē, -set'ē) *n.* A white, waxy substance separated from the oil contained in the head of the sperm whale: used for making candles, ointments, etc. [<F <L *sperma ceti* seed of a whale]

sper·ma·ry (spûr'mər·ē) *n.* *pl* **·ries** The sperm-generating gland of the male; testis.

sper·ma·the·ca (spûr'mə·thē'kə) *n.* *pl.* **·cae** (-sē) *Zool.* A receptacle for receiving and retaining spermatozoa in the females of many invertebrates, as insects, worms, and mollusks. [<L *sperma* a seed + THECA] — **sper'·ma·the'cal** (-thē'kəl) *adj.*

sper·mat·ic (spûr·mat'ik) *adj.* Of or pertaining to sperm or a spermary.

spermatic cord *Anat.* The cord, made up of the spermatic duct and its accompanying vessels and nerves, that passes from the testis through the inguinal canal into the abdominal cavity.

spermatic fluid *Physiol.* Semen.

spermatic sac *Anat.* The scrotum.

sper·ma·tid (spûr'mə·tid) *n. Biol.* A cell resulting from the division of the secondary spermatocytes, and developing into a spermatozoon.

sper·ma·ti·um (spûr·mā'shē·əm) *n.* *pl.* **·ti·a** (-shē·ə) *Bot.* **1** A minute spore in certain lichens and fungi: formerly regarded as a non-motile male gamete. **2** A non-motile gamete which, in the red algae, unites with the carpogonium. [<NL <Gk. *spermation,* dim. of *sperma* a seed]

spermato- *combining form* **1** Seed; pertaining to seeds: *spermatophyte.* **2** Spermatozoa; of or related to spermatozoa: *spermatophore.* Also spelled *spermo-.* Also, before vowels, **spermat-.** [<Gk. *sperma, spermatos* a seed]

sper·ma·to·cyte (spûr'mə·tə·sīt') *n. Biol.* A primary cell from which spermatozoa are developed through primary and secondary divisions, resulting in the spermatids.

sper·ma·to·gen·e·sis (spûr'mə·tə·jen'ə·sis) *n. Biol.* The development of spermatozoa. — **sper·ma·to·ge·net·ic** (spûr'mə·tō·jə·net'ik) *adj.*

sper·ma·to·go·ni·um (spûr'mə·tə·gō'nē·əm) *n.* *pl.* **·ni·a** (-nē·ə) *Biol.* One of the cells of the seminal tubules that produce the spermatozoa. — **sper·ma·to·go'ni·al** *adj.*

sper·ma·toid (spûr'mə·toid) *adj.* Resembling sperm.

sper·ma·to·phore (spûr'mə·tə·fôr', -fōr') *n. Zool.* A capsule or case containing spermatozoa, as in many mollusks, worms, and other invertebrates. — **sper'ma·toph'o·ral** (-tof'ər·əl) *adj.*

sper·ma·to·phyte (spûr'mə·tə·fīt') *n.* Any plant of a phylum or division (*Spermatophyta*) of the most highly developed plants; a flowering and seed–bearing plant. — **sper'ma·to·phyt'ic** (-fit'ik) *adj.*

sper·ma·tor·rhe·a (spûr'mə·tə·rē'ə) *n. Pathol.* Excessive or frequent seminal discharge without sexual excitement. Also **sper'ma·tor·rhoe'a.**

sper·ma·to·zo·id (spûr'mə·tə·zō'id) *adj.* Resembling a spermatozoon. — *n.* **1** A spermatozoon. **2** *Bot.* A motile male germ cell in plants. Also **sper'ma·to·zo'oid** (-zō'oid).

sper·ma·to·zo·on (spûr'mə·tə·zō'on) *n.* *pl.* **·zo·a** (-zō'ə) *Biol.* The male fertilizing element of an animal, usually in the form of a nucleated cell with a long flagellate process or tail by which it swims actively about. [< SPERMATO- + Gk. *zōion* an animal] — **sper'ma·to·zo'al, sper'ma·to·zo'ic** *adj.*

sper·mic (spûr'mik) *adj.* Of or pertaining to sperm or semen; spermatic.

sper·mine (spûr'mēn, -min) *n. Biochem.* A colorless, crystalline, strongly basic compound, $C_{10}H_{26}N_4$, salts of which are contained in semen and other animal tissues. [<SPERM + -INE²]

sperm·ism (spûr'miz·əm) *n.* The old theory that the spermatozoon alone is responsible for the development of the future animal. **sperm·ist** (spûr'mist) *n.* A believer in spermism.

spermo- See SPERMATO-.

sper·mo·go·ni·um (spûr'mə·gō'nē·əm) *n.* *pl.* **·ni·a** (-nē·ə) *Bot.* In fungi, a cup– or flask–shaped receptacle bearing a great number of spermatia.

sperm oil Oil obtained from the head and blubber cavities of the sperm whale.

sperm·o·phile (spûr'mə·fīl, -fil) *n.* A squirrel-like burrowing rodent (*Citellus* and related genera), as the striped gopher or the suslik.

-spermous *combining form* Having (a specified number or kind of) seeds; –seeded: *polyspermous.* Also **–spermal, –spermic.** [<SPERM + -OUS]

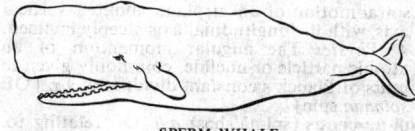

SPERM WHALE
(Up to 80 feet in length)

sperm whale A large, toothed whale (*Physeter catodon*) of warm seas, having a huge truncate head containing a reservoir of sperm oil; the cachalot.

Sper·ry (sper'ē), **Elmer Ambrose,** 1860–1930. U. S. engineer and inventor.

sper·ry·lite (sper'i·līt) *n.* A metallic tin–white platinum arsenide, PtAs₂, crystallizing in the isometric system. [after F. L. *Sperry,* Canadian mineralogist + -LITE]

spet (spet) *Obs. v.t. & v.i.* To spit. — *n.* Spittle. [OE *spætan*]

spetch·es (spech'iz) *n. pl.* The offal of skins, hides, etc., used for making glue. [Origin uncertain]

spew (spyōō) *v.t. & v.i.* To vomit; throw up. — *n.* That which is spewed; vomit. [OE *spīwan*]

Spey·er (shpī'ər) A city in SE Rhineland–Palatinate, West Germany; former capital of Rhine Palatinate; English *Spires.*

Spe·zia (spe'tsyä) La Spezia, a port on the Gulf of Spezia, an inlet of the Gulf of Genoa in NW Italy.

sphac·e·late (sfas'ə·lāt) *v.i.* **·lat·ed,** **·lat·ing** *Pathol.* To become gangrenous; decay; die. [<Gk. *sphakelos* gangrene] — **sphac'e·la'tion** *n.*

sphag·num (sfag'nəm) *n.* Any of a genus (*Sphagnum*) of whitish–gray mosses constituting the family *Sphagnaceae,* the bog or peat mosses: used as packing and in surgical dressings. [<Gk. *sphagnos,* kind of moss] — **sphag'nous** *adj.*

sphal·er·ite (sfal'ə·rīt) *n.* A resinous to adamantine native zinc sulfide, ZnS, crystallizing in the isometric system; zinc blende. [<Gk. *sphaleros* deceptive + -ITE¹]

sphene (sfēn) *n.* An adamantine, variously colored silicate of calcium and titanium, crystallizing in the monoclinic system: also called *titanite.* [<F *sphène* <Gk. *sphēn* wedge]

sphe·nic (sfē'nik) *adj.* Wedge–shaped.

sphenic number See under NUMBER.

spheno- *combining form* **1** Wedge–shaped: *sphenogram.* **2** *Med.* Pertaining to the sphenoid bone. Also, before vowels, **sphen-.** [<Gk. *sphēn, sphēnos* a wedge]

sphe·no·don (sfē'nə·don) *n.* A lizardlike reptile (*Sphenodon punctatum*), the sole surviving representative of the order *Rhynchocephalia;* the hatteria or tuatara of New Zealand. [<NL <Gk. *sphēn, sphēnos* a wedge + *odous, odontos* a tooth]

sphe·no·gram (sfē'nə·gram) *n.* A cuneiform character or symbol.

sphe·noid (sfē'noid) *n.* **1** *Mineral.* In the tetragonal and orthorhombic crystal systems, a hemihedral form enclosed by four faces, each of which cuts all three axes. **2** The sphenoid bone. — *adj.* Wedge–shaped: the *sphenoid* bone. [<SPHEN(O)- + -OID] — **sphe·noi·dal** (sfi·noid'l) *adj.*

sphenoid bone *Anat.* An irregular, compound bone situated at the base of the skull.

sphe·ra·di·an (sfi·rā'dē·ən) *n.* A steradian.

spher·al (sfir'əl) *adj.* **1** Shaped like a sphere; spherical; rounded; symmetrical. **2** Of or pertaining to a sphere. **3** Belonging to or relating to the celestial sphere; harmonious.

sphere (sfir) *n.* **1** The surface described by a semicircle making one complete rotation on its diameter as a fixed axis; a globular figure enclosed by a surface, every point of which is equidistant from a point within called the center. **2** An approximately globular body; a globe; ball; orb. **3** One of the heavenly bodies; a planet, sun, or star. **4** The apparent outer dome of the heavens on which the heavenly bodies appear to lie. **5** In old astronomy, one of the concentric and transparent globes believed to revolve about the earth and carry the various heavenly bodies, their movement supposedly producing mysteriously beautiful music. **6** Compass or field of activity, endeavor, influence, etc.; range; scope; province. **7** Social rank or position. — *v.t.* **sphered, spher·ing** **1** To place in or as in a sphere; encircle; encompass. **2** To set among the celestial spheres. **3** To make spherical. [<OF *espere* <L *sphaera* < Gk. *sphaira* a ball]

-sphere *combining form* **1** Denoting an enveloping spherical mass: *hydrosphere, atmosphere.* **2** A sphere–shaped body: *oosphere.* **3** Denoting a spherical form: *planisphere.* [<Gk. *sphaira* a ball, sphere]

sphere of influence A country or region, usually backward politically or economically undeveloped, in which a state or states claim and are allowed exclusive rights to colonize, exploit natural and economic resources, or eventually annex.

spher·ic (sfer'ik) *adj.* Pertaining to a sphere or spheres; spherical.

spher·i·cal (sfer'i·kəl) *adj.* **1** Shaped like a sphere; globular. **2** Pertaining to a sphere or spheres. **3** Pertaining to the heavenly bodies; celestial. See synonyms under ORBICULATE, ROUND¹ — **spher'i·cal·ly** *adv.* — **spher'i·cal·ness** *n.*

spherical aberration See under ABERRATION.

spherical angle See under ANGLE.

spherical coordinate system *Math.* A three-dimensional system for indicating the shape of a solid by means of a sphere with the pole at the center. A point is located in terms of its distance along its radius vector from the pole, and in terms of two angles—the colatitude, or angle the radius vector forms with the vertical or polar axis of the sphere; and the longitude, or angle the radius vector makes with a fixed, vertical plane or initial meridian axis.

spherical sailing Navigation in which calculations are based upon a consideration of the spherical or spheroidal shape of the earth: distinguished from *plane sailing.*

spherical triangle *Math.* A spherical polygon the three sides of which are arcs of great circles of a sphere.

spherical trigonometry *Math.* The study of spherical triangles.

sphe·ric·i·ty (sfi·ris'ə·tē) *n.* *pl.* **·ties** The state of being a sphere; spherical form; roundness.

spher·ics (sfer'iks) *n.* **1** The geometry and trigonometry of figures on the surface of a sphere. **2** Atmospherics.

sphe·roid (sfir'oid) *n. Geom.* A body having nearly the form of a sphere; an ellipsoid. — **sphe·roi·dal** (sfi·roid'l), **sphe·roi·dic** or **·di·cal** *adj.* — **sphe·roi'dal·ly** *adv.*

sphe·roi·dic·i·ty (sfir'oi·dis'ə·tē) *n.* The state or character of being a spheroid. Also **sphe·roi·di·ty** (sfi·roi'də·tē).

sphe·rom·e·ter (sfi·rom'ə·tər) *n.* An instrument for measuring curvature or radii of spherical and other curved surfaces. [<SPHERE + -(O)METER]

spher·ule (sfer'ōōl) *n.* A small or minute sphere; globule. — **spher·u·lar** (sfer'ōō·lər) *adj.*

spher·u·lite (sfer'ōō·līt) *n.* A radiating spherical group of minute acicular crystals common in acidic glassy rocks. [<SPHERULE + -ITE¹] — **spher·u·lit'ic** (-lit'ik) *adj.*

spher·y (sfir'ē) *adj. Poetic* **1** Like a sphere or star. **2** Of or relating to the celestial spheres.

sphinc·ter (sfingk'tər) *n. Anat.* A muscle that surrounds an opening or tube and serves to close it. [<LL <Gk. *sphinktēr* <*sphingein* close] — **sphinc'ter·al** *adj.*

sphinx (sfingks) *n.* *pl.* **sphinx·es** or **sphin·ges** (sfin'jēz) **1** In Egyptian mythology, a wingless monster with a lion's body and the head of a man (*androsphinx,* or simply *sphinx*), or of a ram (*criosphinx*), or of a hawk (*hieracosphinx*); also, any monumental representation of such a creature. **2** In Greek mythology, a winged monster with a woman's head

SPHINX (def. 2)

and breasts and a lion's body, that destroyed those unable to guess her riddle. See OEDIPUS. **3** A mysterious or enigmatical person. **4** A large, stout-bodied, swift-flying moth. — **the Sphinx** The colossal androsphinx at Gizeh, having the body of a couchant lion, representing Harmachis, the Egyptian god of the morning, and dating to the IV dynasty. [<L <Gk. *Sphinx* <*sphingein* close, strangle]

sphinx moth A hawk moth.

sphra·gis·tics (sfrə·jis'tiks) *n.* The study of signet rings or engraved seals, including their

authenticity, age, history, etc. [<Gk. *sphragistikos* of sealing <*sphragis* seal] **—sphra·gis'tic** *adj.*

sphyg·mic (sfig'mik) *adj. Physiol.* Pertaining to the pulse; pulsatory. [<Gk. *sphygmikos* < *sphygmos* pulse]

sphygmo– *combining form* Pulse; of or related to the pulse: *sphygmogram.* Also, before vowels, **sphygm–.** [<Gk. *sphygmos* pulse]

sphyg·mo·gram (sfig'mə·gram) *n.* A series of connected curves traced by a sphygmograph.

sphyg·mo·graph (sfig'mə·graf, -gräf) *n.* An instrument that, when applied over the heart or an artery, notes and records the character of the pulse and its rate, force, and variations: also called *pulsimeter.* **—sphyg'mo·graph'ic** *adj.* **—sphyg·mog·ra·phy** (sfig·mog'rə·fē) *n.*

sphyg·moid (sfig'moid) *adj. Physiol.* Pulselike.

sphyg·mo·ma·nom·e·ter (sfig'mō·mə·nom'ə·tər) *n.* An instrument for measuring the pressure of the blood in the arteries. Also **sphyg·mom'e·ter** (-mom'ə·tər).

sphyg·mo·scope (sfig'mə·skōp) *n.* An apparatus designed to make the pulse beat visible and to exhibit the varying pressures of the blood in the arteries during circulation.

sphyg·mus (sfig'məs) *n.* The pulse. [<NL <L <Gk. *sphygmos* pulse]

spi·ca (spī'kə) *n. pl.* **·cae** (-sē) **1** An ear of grain; a spike. **2** *Surg.* A bandage having a reversed spiral form, somewhat resembling an ear of wheat. [<L, spike, ear of grain]

Spi·ca (spī'kə) *Astron.* A spectroscopic binary star, Alpha in the constellation Virgo; magnitude, 1.21.

spi·cate (spī'kāt) *adj.* **1** *Bot.* Arranged in spikes: said of flowers. **2** *Ornithol.* Having a spur, as the legs of some birds. Also **spi'cat·ed.** [<L *spicatus* <*spica* spike]

spic·ca·to (spēk·kä'tō) *adj. & adv. Music* Detached; not legato. [<Ital., pp. of *spiccare* detach]

spice (spīs) *n.* **1** An aromatic, pungent vegetable substance, as cinnamon, cloves, etc., used to flavor food and beverages. **2** Such substances collectively. **3** That which gives zest or adds interest. **4** An aromatic odor; an agreeable perfume. **5** *Obs.* Sort; kind; species: the original meaning; also, a specimen. —*v.t.* **spiced, spic·ing** To season with spice; hence, to add zest or piquancy to. [< OF *espice* <L *species.* Doublet of SPECIES.] **—spic'er** *n.*

spice·ber·ry (spīs'ber'ē) *n. pl.* **·ries** **1** A small tree *(Eugenia rhombea)* found in the West Indies and Florida. **2** The black or orange fruit of this tree. **3** The wintergreen or checkerberry.

spice·bush (spīs'bo͝osh') *n.* An aromatic American shrub *(Lindera benzoin)* of the laurel family, the leaves of which have been used for tea, and the drupes, when powdered, for allspice. Also **spice'wood'** (-wo͝od').

Spice Islands A former name for the MOLUCCA ISLANDS.

spic·er·y (spī'sər·ē) *n. pl.* **·er·ies** **1** Spices collectively. **2** *Obs.* A place where spices are kept. **3** Spicy property or character; also, that which has spiciness.

spick (spik) *n. U.S. Slang* A Spanish-speaking person: an offensive term. Also **spic, spig** (spig).

spick–and–span (spik'ən·span') *adj.* **1** Neat and clean. **2** Perfectly new, or looking as if new. [Prob. <*spick,* var. of SPIKE[1] + SPAN-NEW]

spic·ule (spik'yo͞ol) *n.* **1** A small, slender, sharp-pointed body; a spikelet. **2** *Zool.* One of the small, needlelike, calcareous growths supporting the soft tissues of certain invertebrates, as sponges, radiolarians, etc. Also **spic·u·la** (spik'yə·lə). [<L *spiculum,* dim. of *spicum* point, spike] **—spic'u·lar, spic'u·late** (-lāt, -lit) *adj.*

spic·u·lum (spik'yə·ləm) *n. pl.* **·la** (-lə) **1** A spicule. **2** *Zool.* Any small, dartlike organ, as the spines of a sea urchin. [<L]

spic·y (spī'sē) *adj.* **spic·i·er, spic·i·est** **1** Containing, flavored, or fragrant with spices. **2** Producing spices. **3** Highly flavored; pungent; having zest; hence, somewhat improper; risqué. See synonyms under RACY. **—spic'i·ly** *adv.* **—spic'i·ness** *n.*

spi·der (spī'dər) *n.* **1** Any one of a large number of wingless arachnids (order *Araneae*) having an unsegmented abdomen and capable of spinning silk in the construction of webs for the capture of prey such as flies or other insects. **2** A long-handled iron frying pan, often having legs. **3** A portable electric switching apparatus for use in motion-picture studios. **4** A three-legged iron stool for the support of pots and pans over a fire; a trivet. **5** An apparatus for pulverizing the ground during cultivation. **6** *Electr.* The central part of an armature core. **7** *Naut.* **a** An iron hoop around the mast of a ship for the attachment of shrouds. **b** A magnifying glass for a ship's compass. **8** Any of several vehicles of different types having unusually light frames. [OE *spithra* <*spinnan* spin]

spider crab Any of a genus *(Libinia)* of decapod crustaceans with long legs, retractable eyes, and spiny growths on the carapace, especially *L. emarginata,* common on the Atlantic coast of North America.

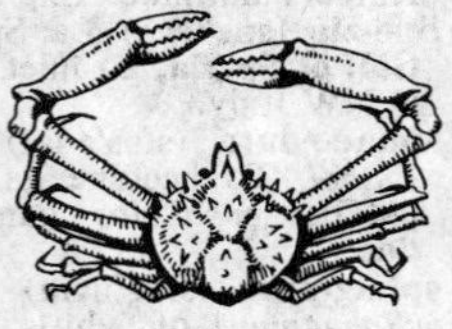

SPIDER CRAB
(Up to 10 inches in breadth)

spi·der·flow·er (spī'dər·flou'ər) *n.* A cleome.

spider monkey An arboreal American monkey (genus *Ateles*) of slender form, with very long limbs, thumbs absent or vestigial, and a long prehensile tail: range from Mexico to Paraguay.

spider phaeton A type of carriage of light construction, having a covered seat in front, and a rear seat for a footman or attendant.

spi·der·wort (spī'dər·wûrt') *n.* **1** Any species of a genus *(Tradescantia)* of plants, especially *T. virginiana,* an American perennial with deep-blue, three-petaled flowers in umbels. **2** Any plant of the same family *(Commelinaceae).*

spi·der·y (spī'dər·ē) *adj.* Spiderlike.

S–piece (es'pēs') *n.* An S-bracket.

spied (spīd) Past tense and past participle of SPY.

spie·gel·ei·sen (spē'gəl·ī'zən) *n.* A white, very hard and brittle cast iron containing manganese, largely used in the manufacture of steel: when more than about 20 percent of manganese is in the alloy it is called *ferromanganese.* Also **spie'gel, spiegel iron.** [<G <*spiegel* a mirror + *eisen* iron]

spiel (spēl) *U.S. Slang v.i.* To talk; orate. —*n.* A speech, especially a long speech. [<G, a game, play <*spielen* play]

spi·er[1] (spī'ər) *n. Brit. Dial.* A spy; scout.

spier[2] (spir) See SPEER.

spif·fy (spif'ē) *adj. Slang* Smartly dressed; spruce. [<dial. E *spiff* a dandy]

spi·ge·li·a (spī·jē'lē·ə) *n.* Pinkroot: used as a vermifuge. [<NL, after Adrian van den *Spiegel,* 1578–1625, Flemish anatomist]

spig·ot (spig'ət) *n.* **1** A plug or faucet for the bunghole of a cask. **2** A turning plug fitting into a faucet, or the faucet itself. [ME *spigote.* Prob. akin to SPIKE[1].]

spike[1] (spīk) *n.* **1** A stout piece of metal, like a large nail, but thicker in proportion. **2** A projecting, pointed piece of metal, or any similar object, as in the soles of shoes to keep the wearer from slipping. **3** A very high heel on a woman's shoe, narrow at the bottom. **4** A steel pin for plugging cannon vents. **5** A straight, unbranched antler, as of a young deer. **6** A young mackerel. —*v.t.* **spiked, spik·ing** **1** To fasten with spikes. **2** To set or provide with spikes. **3** To block the vent of (a cannon) with a spike, rendering it useless. **4** To block; put a stop to. **5** To pierce with or impale on a spike. **6** In baseball, to injure (another player) with the spikes on one's shoes. **7** *Colloq.* To add spirituous liquor to. [ME <Scand. Cf. ON *spikr* a nail.]

spike[2] (spīk) *n.* **1** An ear of corn, barley, wheat, or other grain. **2** *Bot.* A flower cluster in which there are numerous flowers arranged closely on an elongated common axis. [<L *spica* ear of grain]

spike lavender See under LAVENDER.

spike·let (spīk'lit) *n. Bot.* A small spike bearing few flowers and forming the compound inflorescence of cereal grasses and sedges.

spike·nard (spīk'nərd, -närd) *n.* **1** An ancient fragrant and costly ointment prepared mainly from a plant of the same name. **2** A perennial East Indian herb *(Nardostachys jatamansi)* of the valerian family. **3** An American herb *(Aralia racemosa)* of the ginseng family. [<L *spica* spike + *nardus* nard]

spik·er (spī'kər) *n.* One who or that which spikes; specifically, a workman who drives spikes in railroad ties.

spik·y (spī'kē) *adj.* **spik·i·er, spik·i·est** **1** Resembling a spike; pointed. **2** Having spikes.

spile[1] (spīl) *n.* **1** A large timber driven into the ground to serve as a foundation; a pile. **2** A wooden pin or plug used as a vent in a cask; a spigot. **3** A spout driven into a sugar-maple tree to lead the sap to a bucket. —*v.t.* **spiled, spil·ing** **1** To pierce for and provide with a spigot. **2** To drive spiles into. [<MDu., skewer, splinter]

spile[2] (spīl) *v.t. & v.i. Dial.* To spoil.

spil·i·kin (spil'i·kin) *n.* **1** A jackstraw; one of the thin straws used in playing jackstraws. **2** *pl.* The game of jackstraws. Also **spil'li·kin.** [Dim. of SPILL[2]]

spil·ing (spī'ling) *n.* Spiles collectively; piling.

spill[1] (spil) *v.* **spilled** or **spilt, spill·ing** *v.t.* **1** To allow or cause to fall or run out or over, as a liquid or a powder. **2** To shed, as blood. **3** *Naut.* To empty (a sail) of wind. **4** *Colloq.* To cause to fall, as from a horse. **5** *Colloq.* To divulge; make known, as a secret. —*v.i.* **6** To fall or run out or over: said of liquids, etc. **—to spill the beans** *Colloq.* To divulge, especially a secret. —*n.* **1** *Colloq.* A fall to the ground, as from a horse or vehicle; tumble. **2** *Colloq.* A downpour, as of rain. **3** A crack, seam, or other defect in iron or steel castings, forgings, etc. [OE *spillan* destroy] **—spill'·age** *n.* **—spill'er** *n.*

spill[2] (spil) *n.* **1** A slip of wood, or rolled strip of paper, used for lighting lamps, etc.; a lamplighter. **2** A slender peg, pin, or bar of wood or metal; especially, a slender plug for stopping a hole in a cask; a spile. [Var. of SPILE[1]]

spill·way (spil'wā') *n.* **1** A passageway in or about a dam to release the water in a reservoir. **2** The paved upper surface of a dam over which surplus water escapes.

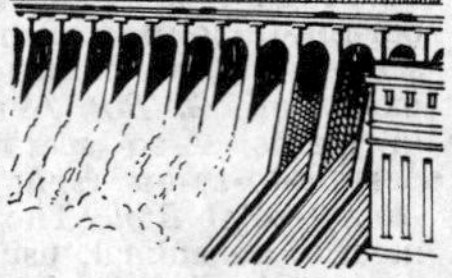

SPILLWAY

spil·o·site (spil'ə·sīt) *n.* A greenish schistous rock spotted with chlorite, produced by the shearing of a basic amygdaloid. [<Gk. *spilos* spot + -ITE[1]]

spilt (spilt) Alternative past tense and past participle of SPILL[1].

spilth (spilth) *n.* That which is spilled or poured out profusely; effusion; excess of supply.

spin (spin) *v.* **spun** (*Archaic* **span**), **spun, spin·ning** *v.t.* **1** To draw out and twist into threads; also, to draw out and twist fiber into (threads, yarn, etc.). **2** To make or produce as if by spinning. **3** To form (a net, etc.) from filaments of a viscous substance extruded from the body: said of spiders, silkworms, etc. **4** To tell, as a story or yarn. **5** To protract; prolong, as a period of time by delays or a story by additional details: with *out.* **6** To cause to whirl rapidly: to *spin* a top. —*v.i.* **7** To make thread or yarn. **8** To extrude filaments of a viscous substance from the body: said of spiders, etc. **9** To whirl rapidly; rotate. **10** To seem to be whirling, as from dizziness: My head is *spinning.* **11** To move rapidly. **12** To fish with a spoon bait or swivel. —*n.* **1** An act or instance of spinning; a rapid whirling. **2** Any rapid movement or action. **3** *Aeron.* The downward spiral motion of an airplane about a vertical axis, with its longitudinal axis steeply inclined. **4** *Physics* The angular momentum of an atomic particle or nuclide, commonly given in units of Planck's constant divided by 2π. [OE *spinnan* spin]

spi·na·ceous (spi·nā'shəs) *adj.* Of, relating to, or resembling spinach or plants allied to it.

spin·ach (spin'ich, -ij) *n.* **1** An edible garden pot herb *(Spinacia oleracea)* of the goosefoot family. **2** Its fleshy, edible leaves. Also **spin'·age.** [<OF *espinage* <LL *spinacia* <Arabic *isbānah*; infl. in form by L *spina* a thorn]

spi·nal (spī'nəl) *adj.* **1** Pertaining to the backbone; vertebral. **2** Pertaining to a spine, spines, or spinous processes. **3** Dependent upon or functioning with a spinal cord, as the vertebrates.

spinal canal *Anat.* The tubular cavity on the dorsal side of the spinal column, in which the spinal cord and its membranes are lodged.
spinal column *Anat.* The series of articulated vertebrae which, with their associated structures, enclose the spinal cord and provide dorsal support for the ribs; the backbone or spine.
spinal cord *Anat.* That portion of the central nervous system enclosed by the spinal column. It is composed of an inner region of gray matter and an outer, larger region of white matter, the whole divided into the cervical, thoracic, lumbar, sacral, and coccygeal areas.
spi·nate (spī′nāt) *adj.* Spinelike, or bearing spines or thorns. Also **spi′nat·ed.**
spin·dle (spin′dəl) *n.* **1** A rod having a slit or catch in the top and a whorl of wood or metal at its lower end, formerly used in hand spinning, and on which was wound the thread from the distaff. **2** The slender rod in a spinning wheel by the rotation of which the thread is twisted and wound on a spool or bobbin on the same rod; also, a small rod or pin bearing the bobbin of a spinning machine or a shuttle. **3** *Mech.* A rotating rod, pin, axis, arbor, or shaft, especially when small and bearing something that rotates: the *spindle* of a lathe. **4** The pin on which rotates a fusee in a watch, or the fusee itself. **5** The tapering end of a vehicle axle that enters the hub. **6** A small shaft passing through the lock of a door and bearing the knobs or handles. **7** *Biol.* A spindle-shaped structure of elongated achromatic fibers formed during the mitosis of a cell. **8** A measure of length for cotton or linen yarn, varying according to the number of hanks or cuts: generally 18 hanks, or 15,120 yards. **9** *Naut.* An iron pile or pipe, surmounted by a lantern or other conspicuous object, placed on a rock or shoal for the guidance of seamen. **10** A hydrometer. **11** A needlelike rod mounted on a weighted base, for impaling bills, checks, etc. —*v.* **·dled, ·dling** *v.i.* **1** To grow into a long, slender stalk or body; become extremely long and slender. —*v.t.* **2** To form into or as into a spindle. **3** To provide with a spindle. **4** To puncture with or impale on a spindle (def. 11), as a bill, memorandum, etc. [OE *spinel* <*spinnan* spin]
spin·dle-leg·ged (spin′dəl·leg′id, -legd′) *adj.* Having long, slender legs. Also **spin′dle-shanked′** (-shangkt′).
spin·dle-legs (spin′dəl·legz′) *n.* **1** Long, slender legs. **2** *Colloq.* A person having long, slender legs. Also **spin′ dle-shanks′** (-shangks′).
spindle side The female or distaff side of a family.
spindle tree A European shrub or low-spreading tree *(Euonymus europaeus),* so called from the use of its compact wood in making spindles, slender pins, skewers, etc.
spin·dling (spind′ling) *adj.* Long and thin; disproportionately slender. —*n.* A spindling person or plant shoot.
spin·dly (spind′lē) *adj.* Of a slender, lanky growth or form, suggesting weakness.
spin·drift (spin′drift) *n.* Blown spray or scud: also called *spoondrift.* [Alter. of *spoondrift* <*spoon,* var. of SPUME + DRIFT]
spine (spīn) *n.* **1** The spinal column of a vertebrate; backbone. **2** *Zool.* Any of various hard, pointed outgrowths on the bodies of certain animals, as the porcupine and starfish; a spicule; the fin ray of a fish. **3** *Bot.* A stiff, short-pointed woody process on the stems of certain plants, as the honey locust; thorn. **4** The back of a bound book. **5** A projecting eminence or ridge. **6** Any slender, thornlike process, as of a vertebra or nerve. **7** The central ridge on the underside of a horse's hoof. [<OF *espine* <L *spina* spine, thorn]
spi·nel (spi·nel′, spin′əl) *n.* A hard isometric mineral of various colors and composition, some of mwhich are used as gemstones. [<F *spinelle* <Ital. *spinella,* dim. of L *spina* spine]
spine·less (spīn′lis) *adj.* **1** Having no spine or backbone; invertebrate. **2** Lacking spines. **3** Having a very flexible backbone; limp. **4** Figuratively, lacking decision of character or steadfastness. —**spine′less·ness** *n.*
spi·nes·cent (spi·nes′ənt) *adj.* **1** *Bot.* Bearing spines; spinous; terminating in a spine. **2** *Zool.* Tending to become spinous, as certain animals during the period of racial decline. —**spi·nes′cence** *n.*
spin·et (spin′it) *n.* **1** A small keyboard musical instrument of the harpsichord class. **2** A small upright piano. [Perhaps after G. *Spinetti,* 16th-century Venetian inventor]
Spin·garn (spin′gärn), **Joel Elias,** 1875–1939, U.S. poet and critic.
spini- *combining form* A spine; thorn: *spiniferous.* [<L *spina* a thorn]
spi·nif·er·ous (spī·nif′ər·əs) *adj.* Bearing or producing spines. Also **spi·nig′er·ous** (-nij′ər·əs).
spin·i·fex (spin′i·feks, spī′ni-) *n.* An Australian grass (genus *Spinifex*) with pointed leaves.
spin·na·ker (spin′ə·kər) *n.* *Naut.* A large jib-shaped sail sometimes carried on the mainmast of a racing vessel, opposite the mainsail, and used when sailing before the wind. The foot slides on a spar called the **spinnaker boom** [? <*spinx,* a mispronunciation of *Sphinx,* the name of the first vessel to carry this kind of sail]
spin·ner (spin′ər) *n.* **1** One who or that which spins, as a spider or a machine. **2** In angling, a whirling spoon bait. **3** *Aeron.* A streamlined fairing fitted over the boss of an airplane propeller and revolving with it. See illustration under AIRPLANE. **4** A play in football wherein the ball carrier spins around to conceal the direction of the play from his opponents.
spin·ner·et (spin′ə·ret) *n.* **1** An organ, as of spiders and silkworms, for spinning silk. **2** A metal plate pierced with holes through which filaments of plastic material are forced, as in the making of rayon fibers.
spin·ner·y (spin′ər·ē) *n.* pl. **·ner·ies** A spinning mill.
spin·ney (spin′ē) *n.* A small wood or thicket. Also **spin′ny.** [<OF *espinei* <LL *spinetum* <L *spina* a thorn]
spin·ning (spin′ing) *n.* **1** The action of, or activities involved in, converting fibers into thread or yarn. **2** The product of spinning. —*adj.* **1** That spins, in any sense. **2** Of or used in the processs of spinning.
spinning gland A gland that secretes silk or a silky substance, as in silkworms.
spinning house A house of correction for prostitutes: so called because the inmates were formerly forced to spin yarn, etc.
spinning jenny A framed mechanism for spinning more than one strand of yarn at a time: also called *jenny.*
spinning mill A mill or factory devoted to spinning.
spinning mule A kind of spinning jenny.
spinning wheel A household implement formerly used for spinning yarn or thread, consisting of a rotating spindle operated by a treadle and flywheel.

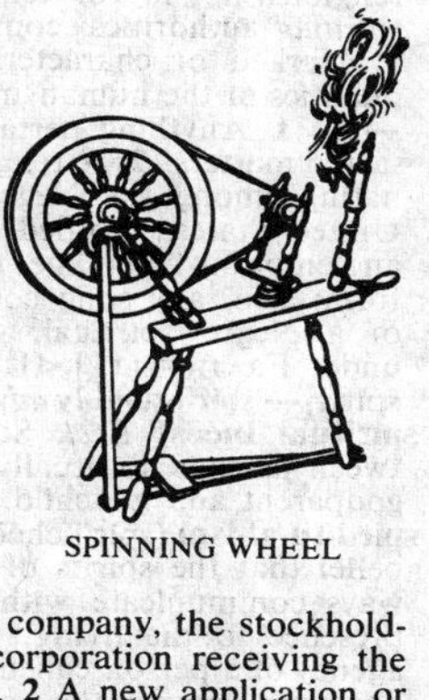

SPINNING WHEEL

spin-off (spin′ôf′,-of′) *n.* **1** Action of a corporation in divesting itself, tax free, of a segment or division of its operations by transfer to a new, independently owned and managed company, the stockholders of the original corporation receiving the new shares pro rata. **2** A new application or incidental result, especially if beneficial; offshoot or by-product; also, such applications or results considered collectively: commercial *spin-off* from the government's aerospace program: also **spin′off′.**
spi·nose (spī′nōs) *adj.* Bearing, armed with, or having many spines. [<L *spinosus* <*spina* a thorn] —**spi′nose·ly** *adv.*
spi·nos·i·ty (spī·nos′ə·tē) *n. pl.* **·ties 1** The state of being spinous or spinose. **2** A spinous part or thing.
spi·nous (spī′nəs) *adj.* **1** Spinelike; prickly. **2** Spinose.
Spi·no·za (spi·nō′zə), **Baruch,** 1632–77, Dutch philosopher and pantheist: also known as *Benedict Spinoza.*
Spi·no·zism (spi·nō′ziz·əm) *n.* Philos. A system of absolute monism developed from Cartesianism by Spinoza. This system regards the entire universe as one infinite and universal substance, namely, God. —**Spi·no′zist** *n.* —**Spin·o·zis·tic** (spin′ō·zis′tik) *adj.*
spin·ster (spin′stər) *n.* **1** An unmarried woman, especially when no longer young; an old maid. **2** *Law* In England, a woman who has never married: a legal title. **3** A woman who spins; a spinner. [ME <SPIN + -STER] —**spin′ster·hood** *n.* — **spin′ster·ish** *adj.*
spin·thar·i·scope (spin·thar′ə·skōp) *n.* A device for showing the radioactivity of a substance by the scintillations of the alpha rays emitted from a minute particle of the substance and thrown against a fluorescent screen. [<Gk. *spintharis* spark + SCOPE] —**spin·thar′i·scop′ic** (-skop′ik) *adj.*
spi·nule (spī′nyo͞ol, spin′yo͞ol) *n.* A small spine; spicule. Also **spin·u·la** (spin′yə·lə). [<L *spinula,* dim. of *spina* spine]
spin·u·les·cent (spin′yə·les′ənt, spī′nyə-) *adj.* Furnished with or producing spinules; spiny.
spin·u·lose (spin′yə·lōs, spī′nyə·lōs) *adj.* Having spinules. Also **spin′u·lous** (-ləs).
spin·y (spī′nē) *adj.* **spin·i·er, spin·i·est 1** Having spines; thorny. **2** Difficult; perplexing. —**spin′i·ness** *n.*
spiny ant-eater The echidna.
spin·y-finned (spī′nē·find′) *adj.* Characterized by fins bearing one or more sharp, unsegmented rays, as the perch, mackerel, and bass. Also **spine′-finned′.**
spiny lobster One of various large-bodied marine crustaceans (genus *Palinurus*) with spiny shells but lacking claws; especially, the California spiny lobster *(P. interruptus),* valued as a sea food. Also called *crayfish.*
Spi·on Kop (spē′ən kop) A hill in Kwa Zulu/Natal Province, Union of South Africa; scene of a battle in the Boer War, 1900.
spir- *Var. of* SPIRO-.
spir·a·cle (spir′ə·kəl, spī′rə-) *n.* **1** *Zool.* **a** An aperture or orifice for the passage of air or water in the respiration of terrestrial arthropods, as the grasshopper and locust. **b** A breathing hole, as the blowhole or nostril of a cetacean. **2** A minute cone formed on a stream of lava by escaping gases. **3** Any opening to admit or expel air; an airhole. [<OF <L *spiraculum* airhole <*spirare* breathe]
spi·rae·a (spī·rē′ə) *n.* Any of a genus *(Spiraea)* of ornamental shrubs of the rose family, having alternate simple or pinnate leaves and small, white or pink flowers; especially, an American variety, the meadowsweet. Also **spi·re′a.** [<L, meadowsweet <Gk. *speiraia* < *speira* coil]
spi·ral (spī′rəl) *adj.* **1** Winding about and constantly receding from a center. **2** Winding and advancing; helical. **3** Winding and rising in a spire, as some springs. —*n.* **1** *Geom.* Any plane curve formed by a point that moves around a fixed center and continually increases its distance from it. **2** A curve winding like a screw thread. **3** Something wound as a spiral or having a spiral shape, as a spring or a whorled shell. **4** A sharp or disproportionate rise, as in prices. **5** *Aeron.* A flight of an airplane in a spiral path. **6** In football, the motion of a ball rotating on its long axis. —*v.* **·raled** or **·ralled, ·ral·ing** or **·ral·ling** *v.t.* **1** To cause to take a spiral form or course. —*v.i.* **2** To take a spiral form or course. **3** To rise sharply or disproportionately, as prices, costs, etc. [<Med. L *spiralis* <L *spira* SPIRE[2]] —**spi′ral·ly** *adv.*
spiral binding A binding consisting of a wire in spiral form looped through holes in the covers on either side.
spiral nebula *Astron.* An extragalactic system of celestial bodies exhibiting a spiral configuration, known to be composed of aggregates of stars resembling the Milky Way, as the *spiral nebula* in Andromeda.
spiral of Archimedes *Math.* The polar curve traced by a point starting at the pole and moving along its radius vector at a constant velocity while the radius vector moves at a constant angular velocity.

add,āce,câre,pälm; end,ēven; it,īce; odd,ōpen,ôrder; to͝ok,po͞ol; up,bûrn; ə = a in *above,* e in *sicken,* i in *clarity,* o in *melon,* u in *focus;* yo͞o = u in *fuse;* oi,oil; ou,pout; ch,check; g,go; ng,ring; th,thin; th,this; zh,vision. Foreign sounds á,œ,ü,kh,ń; and ◆: see page xx. < from; + plus; ? possibly.

spi·rant (spī′rənt) *n.* & *adj. Phonet.* Fricative.

spire[1] (spīr) *n.* **1** The tapering or pyramidal roof of a tower; a pinnacle; also, loosely, a steeple. **2** A slender stalk or blade. **3** The summit or tapering end of anything; a sharp point. — *v.* **spired, spir·ing** *v.t.* **1** To furnish with a spire or spires. — *v.i.* **2** To shoot or point up in or as in a spire. **3** To put forth a spire or spires; sprout. [OE *spīr* a stalk, stem] — **spired** *adj.*

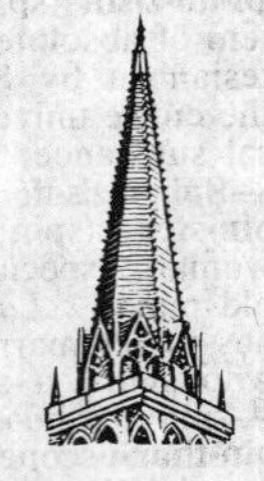

SPIRE

spire[2] (spīr) *n.* **1** A spiral or a single turn of one; whorl; twist. **2** The portion of a spiral formed by a single revolution about the central point. **3** *Zool.* The convoluted portion of a spiral shell. [<F <L *spira* <Gk. *speira* coil] — **spired** *adj.*

spi·reme (spī′rēm) *n. Biol.* **1** The stage in the division of a cell during which the chromatin appears like a skein of filaments. **2** One of these filaments. Also **spi′rem** (-rem). [<Gk. *speirēma* a coil]

Spires (spīrz) The English name for SPEYER.

spi·rif·er·ous (spī·rif′ər·əs) *adj.* **1** Bearing spiral appendages. **2** Having a spire, as a univalve. Also **spi·rig′er·ous** (-rij′ər·əs). [<L *spira* coil + -(I)FEROUS]

spir·il·lo·sis (spir′ə·lō′sis) *n.* **1** *Pathol.* Any disease caused by the presence of spirilla in the body. **2** A disease of domestic fowls caused by a spirochete transmitted by a tick. [<SPIRILLUM + -OSIS]

spi·ril·lum (spī·ril′əm) *n. pl.* **·ril·la** (-ril′ə) Any of a genus *(Spirillum)* of flagellate bacteria with cells in spirally twisted and rigid filaments. See illustration under BACTERIUM. [<NL, dim. of L *spira* a coil]

spir·it (spir′it) *n.* **1** The principle of life and energy in man and animals, at one time regarded as being composed of an especially refined substance, such as breath or warm air, separable from the body, mysterious in nature, and ascribable to a divine origin. **2** An entity conceived of as that part of a human being that is incorporeal and invisible and is characterized by intelligence, personality, self-consciousness, and will; the mind: opposed to *body.* **3** The substance or universal aspect of reality, regarded as independent of and opposed to matter. **4** In the Bible, the creative, animating power or divine influence of God. *Joel* ii 28. **5** A rational, supernatural being without a material body, as an angel, demon, elf, fairy, etc.; specifically, such a being with a certain character or a particular abode or area of activity: an evil *spirit.* **6** A disembodied soul regarded as manifested to the senses, often as visible or having some kind of immaterial body: a ghost; specter: Hamlet saw his father's *spirit.* **7** A person regarded with reference to any peculiar activity, characteristic, or temper: a leading *spirit* in the community. **8** *Usually pl.* A state of mind; mood; temper: Success raised his *spirits.* **9** Vivacity or energy; ardor; dash; fire: an attack made with *spirit.* **10** Ardent loyalty or devotion: school *spirit.* **11** True intent or meaning as opposed to outward, formal signification: to keep the *spirit* of the law. Compare LETTER (def. 5). **12** The emotional or affective faculty of man; the heart: Great poetry stirs the *spirit.* **13** The characteristic temper or disposition of a period or of a movement: the *spirit* of the Reformation. **14** *pl.* A strong alcoholic liquor or liquid obtained by distillation. **15** *Usually pl. Chem.* **a** The essence or distilled extract of a substance: *spirits* of turpentine. **b** Ethanol. **16** *Often pl.* In pharmacy, a solution of a volatile principle in alcohol; a tincture; essence: *spirits* of ammonia. **17** In dyeing, a solution of a tin salt in acid. **18** In alchemy, one of four substances, mercury, sal ammoniac, sulfur, and arsenic (or orpiment). **19** In medieval physiology, one of the three degrees of spirit inherent in the human body: **natural spirit,** located in the liver and underlying the processes of nutrition, growth, and reproduction; **vital spirit,** located in the heart, which circulated heat and life through the body; **animal spirit,** located in the brain, which guided reason and conveyed the powers of motion and sensation to and through the nerves. **20** *Obs.* Breathed air; breeze; wind. **21** *Obs.* The breath; life. See synonyms under CHARACTER, COURAGE, MIND, SPECTER. — *v.t.* **1** To carry off secretly or mysteriously, as if by the agency of a spirit: with *away, off,* etc. **2** To infuse with spirit or animation; inspirit; encourage: often with *up.* — *adj.* **1** Of or pertaining to ghosts or the belief in the existence of departed souls; spiritualistic. **2** Operated by the burning of alcohol: a *spirit* lamp. [<OF *espirit* <L *spiritus* breathing < *spirare* breathe. Doublet of SPRITE.]

Spir·it (spir′it) *n.* In Christian theology, the Holy Spirit.

spir·it·ed (spir′it·id) *adj.* Full of spirit; animated: used in various compound adjectives: high-*spirited,* mean-*spirited.* See synonyms under RACY. — **spir′it·ed·ly** *adv.* — **spir′it·ed·ness** *n.*

spir·it·ing (spir′it·ing) *n.* Movement as of a spirit; hence, something dexterously done; the work or ministering of a spirit; inspiration; encouragement.

spir·it·ism (spir′i·tiz′əm) *n.* **1** Loosely, spiritualism. **2** *Rare* Animism; the theory that inanimate objects possess spirits. — **spir′it·ist** *n.* — **spir′it·is′tic** *adj.*

spirit lamp A lamp that burns alcohol: used in laboratory work, etc.

spir·it·less (spir′it·lis) *adj.* Lacking in enthusiasm, energy, or courage; lacking in the sense of well-being. — **spir′it·less·ly** *adv.* — **spir′it·less·ness** *n.*

spirit level An instrument for adjusting any deviation from the horizontal or perpendicular by reference to the position of a bubble of air in a tube of alcohol or other liquid.

spi·ri·to·so (spir′i·tō′sō, *Ital.* spē′rē·tō′sō) *Music adj.* Spirited; animated. — *adv.* With spirit. [<Ital. < *spirito* spirit]

spir·it·ous (spir′i·təs) *adj.* **1** Like spirits; refined. **2** Spirituous. **3** Spirited; ardent.

spirit rapping The professed communication with the spirits of departed persons by raps, as on a table; also, the rapping believed to be made by spirits.

spirits of hartshorn See under AMMONIA.

spirits of turpentine Oil of turpentine.

spirits of wine Rectified alcohol.

spir·i·tu·al (spir′i·chōō·əl) *adj.* **1** Of or pertaining to spirit, as distinguished from matter; having the nature of spirit; consisting of spirit; incorporeal. **2** Pertaining to or affecting the immaterial nature or soul of man. **3** Of or pertaining to God, his Spirit, or his law, or to the soul as acted upon by the Holy Spirit; holy; pure; not carnal. **4** Sacred or religious; not lay or temporal; ecclesiastical: *spiritual* authorities: contrasted with *secular.* **5** Marked or characterized by the highest qualities of the human mind; intellectualized. — *n.* **1** Anything pertaining to spirit or to sacred matters. **2** A religious folk song originating among the Negroes of the southern United States, typified by colorful rhythm and emotion: sometimes in narrative or ballad form; also, any song composed in imitation of a Negro spiritual. — **the Spirituals** See under FRATICELLI. [<L *spiritualis* < *spiritus* spirit] — **spir′i·tu·al·ly** *adv.* — **spir′i·tu·al·ness** *n.*

spiritual incest *Eccl.* Sexual intercourse between persons spiritually related, as between godparent and godchild.

spir·i·tu·al·ism (spir′i·chōō·əl·iz′əm) *n.* **1** The belief that the spirits of the dead in various ways communicate with and manifest their presence to the living, usually through the agency of a person called a medium; also, the doctrines and practices of those so believing. **2** The doctrine that there are beings not cognizable by the senses or characterized by the properties of matter, and that are therefore spiritual, as distinguished from material: opposed to *materialism.* **3** The doctrine that man is an immortal spirit and as such may know, love, or worship God. **4** A non-materialistic philosophy, a form of idealism which identifies ultimate reality as one universal conscious mind. **5** The state or character of being spiritual. — **spir′i·tu·al·ist** *n.* — **spir′i·tu·al·is′tic** *adj.*

spir·i·tu·al·i·ty (spir′i·chōō·al′ə·tē) *n. pl.* **·ties** **1** The state of being spiritual. **2** That which belongs to the church or to an ecclesiastic: opposed to *temporality.*

spir·i·tu·al·ize (spir′i·chōō·əl·īz′) *v.t.* **·ized, ·iz·ing** **1** To make spiritual; free of grossness or materialism: to *spiritualize* the thoughts. **2** To imbue with spirit; animate. **3** To treat as having a spiritual meaning or sense. Also *Brit.* **spir′i·tu·al·ise′.** — **spir′i·tu·al·i·za′tion** *n.* — **spir′i·tu·al·iz′er** *n.*

spir·i·tu·al·ty (spir′i·chōō·əl·te) *n. pl.* **·ties** Ecclesiastical bodies collectively; the clergy.

spiritual wife Among the Mormons, a woman who has been married for eternity in accordance with the doctrine of the Mormon gospel; hence, **spiritual wifeism, spiritual wifehood.**

spir·i·tu·el (spir′i·chōō·el′, *Fr.* spē·rē·tü·el′) *adj.* Characterized by esprit, or wit, and by the higher and finer qualities of the mind generally. [<F] — **spir′i·tu·elle′** *adj. fem.*

spir·i·tu·ous (spir′i·chōō·əs) *adj.* **1** Containing alcohol. **2** Intoxicating; distilled. **3** *Obs.* Spiritlike; ethereal. **4** *Rare* Lively. — **spir′i·tu·ous·ness** *n.*

spir·i·tus (spir′i·təs) *n. pl.* **·tus** **1** A breathing or an aspirate. In Greek grammar the rough breathing is called **spiritus asper,** the smooth **spiritus lenis.** See BREATHING. **2** Any liquid product of distillation; especially, alcoholic liquor. See SPIRIT. [<L, a breathing]

spirit writing Visible but automatic writing done without the conscious will of the writer, and believed to be a manifestation of spirit guidance; pneumatography.

spiro-[1] *combining form* Breath; respiration: *spirograph.* Also, before vowels, *spir-.* [<L *spirare* breathe]

spiro-[2] *combining form* Spiral; coiled: *spirochete.* Also, before vowels, *spir-.* [<Gk. *speira* a coil]

spi·ro·chete (spī′rə·kēt) *n.* **1** Any of a genus *(Spirochaeta)* of typically saprophytic bacteria commonly found in water and sewage, and characterized by spiral flexible filaments with apparently rotary movements. See illustration under BACTERIUM. **2** Any of various other similar micro-organisms of the order *Spirochaetales,* including those which cause syphilis and relapsing fever. Also **spi′ro·chaete.** [<Gk. *speira* coil + *chaitē* bristle] — **spi′ro·che′tal** *adj.*

spi·ro·che·to·sis (spī′rə·kē·tō′sis) *n.* **1** *Pathol.* Infection by spirochetes. **2** An infectious septicemia in chickens caused by a spirochete *(Borrelia anserina).*

spi·ro·graph (spī′rə·graf, -gräf) *n.* An instrument for recording the breathing movement. [<SPIRO-[1] + -GRAPH] — **spi′ro·graph′ic** *adj.* — **spi·rog·raph·y** (spī·rog′rə·fē) *n.*

spi·ro·gy·ra (spī′rə·jī′rə) *n.* Any of a genus *(Spirogyra)* of bright-green, fresh-water algae forming dense masses or beds of growth in slow-running or stagnant water, and characterized by having the chlorophyll bands winding spirally to the right. [<SPIRO-[2] + Gk. *gyros* ring, coil]

spi·roid (spī′roid) *adj.* Resembling a spiral.

spi·rom·e·ter (spī·rom′ə·tər) *n.* An instrument for measuring the capacity of the lungs. [<SPIRO-[1] + -METER] — **spi·ro·met·ric** (spī′rə·met′rik) *adj.* — **spi·rom′e·try** *n.*

spirt (spûrt) See SPURT.

spir·u·la (spir′yə·lə, spir′ōō-) *n. pl.* **·lae** (-lē) Any of a genus *(Spirula)* of cephalopods with an internal spiral chambered shell having whorls detached and in the same plane. [<NL <Gk. *speira* coil]

spir·y[1] (spīr′ē) *adj.* **1** Pertaining to or having the form of a spire. **2** Abounding in spires, as a city.

spir·y[2] (spīr′ē) *adj.* Having the form of a spiral; coiled; whorled.

spis·sat·ed (spis′ā·tid) *adj.* Thickened. [<L *spissatus,* pp. of *spissare* thicken]

spit[1] (spit) *v.* **spat** or **spit, spit·ting** *v.t.* **1** To eject (saliva, blood, etc.) from the mouth. **2** To throw off, eject, or utter with violence. **3** To light, as a fuse. — *v.i.* **4** To eject saliva from the mouth. **5** To make a noise like that made in ejecting saliva. **6** To fall in scattered drops or flakes, as rain or snow. — *n.* **1** Spittle; saliva. **2** An act of spitting or expectorating. **3** A frothy, spitlike secretion of the spittle insect; also, a spittle insect. **4** A light, scattered fall or short, driving flurry of snow or rain. **5** *Colloq.* Exact image; likeness; counterpart: He's the *spit* of John. [OE *spittan*] — **spit′ter** *n.*

spit[2] (spit) *n.* **1** A pointed rod on which meat is turned and roasted before a fire. **2** A

point of low land, or a long, narrow shoal, extending from a shore into the water. — *v.t.* **spit-ted, spit-ting** To transfix or impale with or as with a spit. [OE *spitu* spit]

spit-al (spit′l) *n. Obs.* A hospital. Also **spital house, spit′tle, spittle house.**

spit-ball (spit′bôl′) *n.* **1** Paper chewed in the mouth and shaped into a ball for use as a missile. **2** In baseball, a pitched ball wet with saliva, and rotating deceptively in its course: no longer permitted by the rules. — **spit′ball′er** *n.*

spitch-cock (spich′kok) *v.t.* To split and broil, as a bird or fish. — *n.* An eel split and broiled. [Origin unknown]

spite (spīt) *n.* **1** Malicious bitterness prompting to vexatious acts; mean hatred; grudge. **2** That which is done in spite. **3** *Archaic* Trouble; bad luck: a Shakespearean usage. See synonyms under ENMITY, HATRED. — **in spite of** (or **spite of**) Formerly, in contempt of; now, notwithstanding. — *v.t.* **spit-ed, spit-ing** **1** To show one's spite toward; vex maliciously; thwart. **2** *Obs.* To fill with spite; offend; vex. [Short for DESPITE]

spite fence *U.S.* A fence or wall put up to spite a neighbor, usually of such a nature as to detract from the desirability or value of the adjoining property: now illegal.

spite-ful (spīt′fəl) *adj.* **1** Filled with spite. **2** Prompted by spite. See synonyms under MALICIOUS. — **spite′ful-ly** *adv.* — **spite′ful-ness** *n.*

spit-fire (spit′fīr′) *n.* A quick-tempered person who is given to saying spiteful things.

Spit-head (spit′hed′) *n.* A roadstead between the Isle of Wight and southern England, at Portsmouth.

Spits-ber-gen (spits′bûr′gən) A group of Norwegian islands in the Arctic Ocean, east of Greenland and north of Norway, and comprising most of Svalbard; 23,658 square miles. Also **Spitz′ber-gen.**

Spits (spits), **Spits-ke** (spits′kē) See SCHIPPERKE.

Spit-te-ler (shpit′ə·lər), **Carl,** 1845-1924, Swiss writer; pseudonym *Felix Tandem.*

spit-ter (spit′ər) *n.* **1** A young deer whose antlers have emerged, but have not branched. **2** One who cooks meat on a spit.

spit-ting image (spit′ing) *Colloq.* An exact likeness or counterpart. Also **spit and image.**

spitting snake A venomous snake of South Africa (*Sepedon haemachates*) related to the cobras, that is able to eject its poison for some distance; the ringhals.

spit-tle (spit′l) *n.* **1** The fluid secreted by the mouth; saliva; spit. **2** The salivalike matter in which the larvae of spittle insects live. [OE *spātl*; infl. in form by *spit*[1]]

spittle insect A froghopper.

spit-toon (spi·tōōn′) *n.* A receptacle for spit; a cuspidor.

spitz (spits) *n.* One of a breed of small dogs with a tapering muzzle; a Pomeranian. Also **spitz dog.** [<G, short for *spitzhund*]

Spitz-en-burg (spit′sən·bûrg) *n.* A variety of apple, yellow and red in color, prized for its delicate flavor. [Prob. <Du. *spits* a point + *berg* a hill; so called because it is pointed and was found on an upstate New York hillside]

spiv (spiv) *n.* **1** *Brit. Colloq.* A flashy chiseler, sharper, or one who lives by his wits. **2** A low and common thief.

spiv-er-y (spiv′ər·ē) *n. Brit. Colloq.* The obtaining of a livelihood by the least possible personal effort, relying on government subsidy, sinecures, or private income.

splake (splāk) *n. Canadian* A hybrid fish, a cross between the speckled trout and the lake trout: also called *mendigo.*

splanch-nic (splangk′nik) *adj. Anat.* Pertaining to or supplying the viscera: a *splanchnic nerve.* [<Gk. *splanchnikos* <*splanchnon* entrail]

splanchno- *combining form Anat. & Med.* The viscera; of or related to the viscera. Also, before vowels, **splanchn-.** [<Gk. *splanchnon* entrail]

splanch-nol-o-gy (splangk·nol′ə·jē) *n.* The anatomy and physiology of the viscera. [<SPLANCHNO- + -LOGY]

splash (splash) *v.t.* **1** To dash or spatter (a liquid, etc.) about. **2** To spatter, wet, or soil with a liquid dashed about. **3** To make with

splashes: to *splash* one's way. **4** To decorate with splashed ornament. — *v.i.* **5** To make a splash or splashes. **6** To move, fall, or strike with a splash or splashes. — *n.* **1** The act or noise of splashing. **2** The result of splashing; a spot made by a liquid or color splashed on. **3** In logging, a head of water released suddenly from a splash dam to drive a body of logs. [Var. of PLASH[1]]

splash-board (splash′bôrd′, -bôrd′) *n.* **1** Any of various devices to protect against splashes, especially a dashboard for a vehicle. **2** A board for closing the spillway or sluice of a dam. Also **splash′wing** (-wing′).

splash-down (splash′doun′) *n.* The setting down of a spacecraft or a part of it in the seas following its flight.

splash-er (splash′ər) *n.* **1** One who or that which splashes. **2** A piece of oilcloth, toweling, rug, or other device to protect a surface against splashing, as at the back of a washstand or over a wheel.

splash-y (splash′ē) *adj.* **1** Slushy; wet. **2** Marked by or as by splashes; blotchy. **3** *Colloq.* Sensational; showy: They made a *splashy* appearance.

splat (splat) *n.* A thin, broad piece of wood, as that forming the middle of a chair back. [Origin uncertain]

splat-ter (splat′ər) *v.t. & v.i.* To spatter or splash. — *n.* A spatter; splash. [Blend of SPLASH and SPATTER]

splay (splā) *adj.* Spread out; displayed; broad; clumsy; clumsily formed: a *splay* mouth. — *n. Archit.* A slanted surface or beveled edge, as of the sides of a doorway or window, or of a joist. — *v.t.* **1** To make with a splay; bevel or chamfer away a corner or angle of, as a window opening. **2** To open to sight; spread; cut open; display. **3** In farriery, to dislocate. — *v.i.* **4** To spread out; open. **5** To slant; slope. [Aphetic var. of DISPLAY]

splay-foot (splā′fōōt′) *n.* **1** Abnormal flatness and turning outward of the feet. **2** A foot so deformed. — **splay′-foot′ed** *adj.*

spleen (splēn) *n. Anat.* **1** A highly vascular, flattened, ductless organ found near the stomach of most vertebrates, which effects certain modifications in the blood. ◆ Collateral adjective: *lienal.* **2** This organ regarded as the seat of various emotions. **3** Ill temper; spitefulness: to vent one's *spleen.* **4** *Archaic* Lowness of spirits; melancholy; hypochondria. **5** *Obs.* Mode or state of mind; also, caprice; a fit of pique. **6** *Obs.* Violent mirth. [<L *splen* <Gk. *splēn*] — **spleen′ish** *adj.* — **spleen′y** *adj.*

spleen-ful (splēn′fəl) *adj.* Affected with spleen; peevish; ill-tempered. — **spleen′ful-ly** *adv.*

spleen-wort (splēn′wûrt′) *n.* Any of a genus (*Asplenium*) of hardy and cultivated ferns with simple or compound fronds: so called from the use formerly made of some species in disorders of the spleen.

splen-dent (splen′dənt) *adj.* **1** Shining; lustrous. **2** Illustrious. [<L *splendens, -entis,* ppr. of *splendere* shine]

splen-did (splen′did) *adj.* **1** Magnificent; imposing. **2** Inspiring to the imagination; glorious; illustrious. **3** Giving out or reflecting brilliant light; shining. **4** *Colloq.* Very good; excellent: a *splendid* offer. See synonyms under FINE[1], BRIGHT. [<L *splendidus* <*splendere* shine] — **splen′did-ly** *adv.* — **splen′did-ness** *n.*

splen-di-de men-dax (splen′di-dē men′daks) *Latin* Splendidly false; nobly untruthful.

splen-dif-er-ous (splen-dif′ər·əs) *adj. Colloq.* Exhibiting great splendor; very magnificent: a facetious usage. [<SPLEND(OR) + -(I)FEROUS]

splen-dor (splen′dər) *n.* **1** Exceeding brilliance from emitted or reflected light. **2** Magnificence. **3** Conspicuous greatness of achievement; preeminence. Also *Brit.* **splen′dour.** [<L, brightness <*splendere* shine] — **splen′dor-ous, splen′drous** *adj.*

sple-net-ic (spli-net′ik) *adj.* **1** Pertaining to the spleen. **2** Fretfully spiteful; peevish. See synonyms under MOROSE. Also **sple-net′i-cal, splen-i-tive** (splen′ə·tiv). — *n.* **1** One suffering from disease of the spleen. **2** A peevish person. — **sple-net′i-cal-ly** *adv.*

splen-ic (splen′ik, splē′nik) *adj.* Of, in, or pertaining to the spleen.

sple-ni-tis (spli-nī′tis) *n. Pathol.* Inflammation of the spleen.

sple-ni-um (splē′nē·əm) *n. pl.* **·ni-a** (-nē·ə) **1** *Surg.* A compress or bandage. **2** *Anat.* The rounded posterior end of the corpus callosum. [<NL <Gk. *splēnion* a bandage] — **sple′ni-al** *adj.*

sple-ni-us (splē′nē·əs) *n. pl.* **·ni-i** (-nē·ī) *Anat.* A large, thick muscle of the back of the neck, extending in two parts from the skull to the vertebral spines in the cervical and upper thoracic region. [<NL <Gk. *splēnion* a bandage] — **sple′ni-al** *adj.*

spleno- *combining form Anat. & Med.* The spleen; of or related to the spleen. Also, before vowels, **splen-,** as in *splenitis.* [<Gk. *splēn, splēnos* the spleen]

spleu-chan (splōō′khan) *n. Scot. & Irish* A small bag or wallet to hold tobacco, etc.: sometimes used as a purse. [<Irish *spliúcán* a leather pouch]

splice (splīs) *v.t.* **spliced, splic-ing** **1** To unite, as two ropes or parts of a rope, so as to form one continuous piece, by intertwining the strands. **2** To connect, as timbers, by beveling, scarfing, or overlapping at the ends. **3** *Slang* To join in marriage: usually in the passive. — **to splice the main brace** To serve or take a glass of grog: chiefly jocular. — *n.* **1** A union at the ends of joined parts, especially of ropes, made by intertwining the strands. **2** The place at which two parts are spliced. [<MDu. *splissen*]

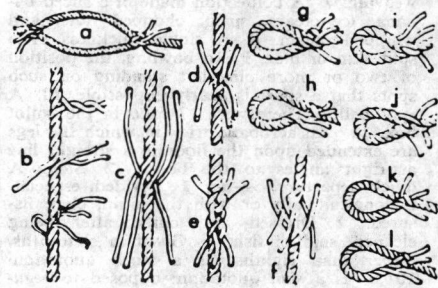

SPLICES
a. Cut splice.   *d-f.* Short splices.
b-c. Long splices.   *g-l.* Eye splices.

splic-er (splī′sər) *n.* **1** One who makes splices. **2** An implement by which a splice is made in a rope; a fid for splicing.

spline (splīn) *n.* **1** *Mech.* A metal key permanently set into a slot in one of two connected rotating mechanical parts, as a shaft and a pulley, and engaging with a similar slot cut in the other, thus permitting both parts to have relative lengthwise motion, but not to rotate upon each other: also called *feather, feather key.* **2** A long, flexible strip of wood or hard rubber, used by mechanical draftsmen to lay down ship lines, railway curves, or similar work. **3** A thin strip or tongue of wood or metal used in matching grooved planks, making partitions, filling air spaces, etc. — *v.t.* **splined, splin-ing** **1** To make a slot or groove in for a spline. **2** To fit with a spline. [? Related to SPLINT] — **splined** *adj.*

splint (splint) *n.* **1** A thin, flat piece split off; a splinter. **2** A thin, flexible strip of split wood used for basket-making, chair bottoms, etc. **3** In plate armor, one of the flexibly adjusted overlapping laminae. **4** *Surg.* An appliance, as of wood or metal, used for keeping a fractured limb or other injured part in a fixed position. **5** A splint bone. **6** An osseous tumor on the splint bone of a horse, due to inflammation of the periosteum; also, a bony callosity resulting from disease of the splint bones. — *v.t.* To confine, support, or brace, as a fractured limb, with or as with splints. [<MDu. *splinte*]

splint armor Armor made of overlapping metal plates.

splint bone 1 One of the small rudimentary bones of the metacarpus or metatarsus of the horse and related animals. Compare illustration under HORSE. **2** The fibula.

splin-ter (splin′tər) *n.* A thin, sharp piece of wood, glass, metal, etc., split or torn off.

lengthwise; a sliver. —*v.t. & v.i.* To split into thin sharp pieces or fragments; shatter; shiver. [<MDu.] —**splin'ter·y** *adj.*

splin·ter·proof (splin'tər·prōōf') *adj.* Resistant to the penetration of splinters: said especially of shelters affording protection from machine-gun fire and shell fragments.

split (split) *v.* **split, split·ting** *v.t.* **1** To separate into parts by force, especially into two approximately equal parts. **2** To break or divide lengthwise or along the grain; rive; separate into layers. **3** To divide into groups or factions; disrupt, as a political party. **4** To divide and distribute by portions or shares. —*v.i.* **5** To break apart; divide lengthwise or along the grain. **6** To become divided or disunited through disagreement, etc. **7** To share something with others. **8** *Slang* To leave quickly or abruptly. —**to split hairs** To make fine distinctions; be unnecessarily precise or subtle. —**to split off 1** To break off by splitting. **2** To separate by or as by splitting. —**to split the difference** To divide equally a sum in dispute. —**to split up 1** To separate into parts and distribute. **2** To cease association; separate. —*n.* **1** The act or result of splitting; a longitudinal fissure; cleft; rent. **2** Separation of an aggregate body into factions; rupture; schism: a *split* in the church. **3** A sliver; splinter. **4** A share or portion, as of loot or booty. **5** A six-ounce bottle of an alcoholic beverage or of mineral water. **6** A split osier, used in certain phases of basket weaving. **7** A confection made of a sliced banana, ice-cream, sirup, chopped nuts, and whipped cream. **8** A single thickness of a split skin or hide. **9** In bowling, the position of two or more pins left standing on such spots that a spare is nearly impossible. **10** A split ballot: There were 47 *splits* in the ballot box. **11** An acrobatic trick in which the legs are extended upon the floor in a straight line at right angles to the body. **12** *Slang* A quick departure. —*adj.* **1** Divided, especially longitudinally or with the grain; cleft; fissured. **2** Dressed and cured after being cleaned: said of fish. **3** Given in sixteenths, rather than eighths, as a stock quotation: 10 1/16 is a *split* quotation: opposed to *regular.* **4** Divided: a *split* ballot. [<MDu. *splitten*] —**split'ter** *n.*

Split (splēt) The chief Dalmatian city of southern Croatia, Yugoslavia; a major port on the Adriatic: Italian *Spalato.*

split decision In boxing, a decision in which only two of three officials agree on the winner.

split infinitive See under INFINITIVE.

split-lev·el (split'lev'əl) *adj.* Designating a type of dwelling in which the floors of adjoining parts are at different levels, connected by short flights of stairs, permitting a compact arrangement of living and service rooms.

split product *Chem.* Any product of a decomposition, as of a protein into amino acids.

split saw A ripsaw.

split ticket 1 A ballot on which the voter has distributed his vote among candidates of different parties. **2** A ballot containing names of candidates of more than one party or party faction. Compare STRAIGHT TICKET.

split·ting (split'ing) *adj.* Acute or extreme in kind or degree: a *splitting* pain.

splotch (sploch) *n.* A discolored spot, as of ink, etc.; a daub; splash; spot. —*v.t.* To soil or mark with a splotch or splotches. [Cf. OE *splot* spot] —**splotch'y** *adj.*

splurge (splûrj) *Colloq. n.* **1** An ostentatious display. **2** An extravagant expenditure. —*v.i.* **splurged, splurg·ing 1** To show off; be ostentatious. **2** To spend money lavishly or wastefully. [Imit.] —**splurg'y** *adj.*

splut·ter (splut'ər) *v.i.* **1** To make a series of slight, explosive sounds, or throw off small particles, as meat frying in fat. **2** To speak hastily, confusedly, or incoherently, as from surprise or indignation. —*v.t.* **3** To utter excitedly or confusedly; sputter. **4** To spatter or bespatter. —*n.* A noise as of spluttering; bustle; confused stir. [Blend of SPLASH and SPUTTER] —**splut'ter·er** *n.*

spode or **Spode** (spōd) *n.* Fine porcelain or china made at the works founded by Josiah Spode (1754–1827) in Staffordshire, England.

spod·u·mene (spoj'oo·mēn) *n.* A vitreous, transparent to translucent lithium-aluminum silicate, belonging to the pyroxene group and crystallizing in the monoclinic system. [<Gk. *spodoumenos,* ppr. of *spodoesthai* be burned to ashes <*spodos* ashes]

spoil (spoil) *v.* **spoiled** or **spoilt, spoil·ing** *v.t.* **1** To impair or destroy the value, usefulness, or beauty of; injure: to *spoil* a book. **2** To weaken or impair the character or personality of, especially by overindulgence: Spare the rod and *spoil* the child. **3** *Obs.* To take property from by force; despoil. **4** *Obs.* To seize by force. —*v.i.* **5** To lose normal or useful qualities; specifically, to become tainted or decayed, as food. **6** *Obs.* To plunder; rob. See synonyms under CORRUPT, DECAY, DEFILE[1], INDULGE, PAMPER. —**to be spoiling for** To long for; crave: He is *spoiling for* a fight. —*n.* **1** Plunder seized by violence; booty; loot. **2** *pl.* The emoluments of public office as the objects of political contests and rewards of political service. **3** The act of pillaging; spoliation. **4** An object to be forcibly seized and taken away. **5** *Obs.* Ruin; destruction. **6** Material removed in digging trenches or excavations. **7** *Obs.* Damage; waste. See synonyms under PLUNDER. [<OF *espoillier* <L *spoliare* <*spolium* booty]

spoil·age (spoi'lij) *n.* **1** Spoiled material collectively. **2** Something that is or has been spoiled. **3** The process of spoiling. **4** The state of being spoiled.

spoil·er (spoi'lər) *n.* **1** One who takes spoil; a robber; despoiler. **2** One who or that which causes to spoil; a corrupter.

spoil-five (spoil'fīv') *n.* A card game played by 2 to 10 persons, in which each player tries to take the pool or to spoil it, taking being accomplished by winning, spoiling by preventing the other players from winning, three out of five possible tricks in a deal.

spoils·man (spoilz'mən) *n. pl.* **·men** (-mən) One who advocates the spoils system or works for a political party for spoils.

spoil-sport (spoil'spôrt', -spōrt') *n.* A person whose actions or attitudes spoil the pleasures of others.

spoils system The theory, or the practice of a political party after a victorious campaign, of making public offices the rewards of partisan services.

Spo·kane (spō·kan') The second largest city in Washington, located on a falls in the **Spokane River,** a river which flows 100 miles west from western Idaho to the Columbia River in eastern Washington.

spoke[1] (spōk) *n.* **1** One of the members of a wheel which serve to support the rim (or felly) by connecting it to the hub. **2** One of the radial handles of a ship's steering wheel. **3** A stick or bar for insertion in a wheel to prevent it from turning, as in descending a hill. **4** A rung of a ladder. —**to put a spoke in (someone's) wheel** To hinder or prevent (someone's) action. —*v.t.* **spoked, spok·ing 1** To provide with spokes. **2** To fasten (a wheel) with a stick or spoke to prevent its turning. [OE *spāca*]

spoke[2] (spōk) Past tense and archaic past participle of SPEAK.

spo·ken (spō'kən) Past participle of SPEAK. —*adj.* **1** Uttered orally, as opposed to written. **2** Speaking or having a specified kind of speech: smooth-*spoken.*

spoke·shave (spōk'shāv') *n.* A wheelwright's tool having a blade set between two handles, used with a drawing motion in rounding and smoothing wooden surfaces.

spokes·man (spōks'mən) *n. pl.* **·men** (-mən) One who speaks in the name and behalf of another or others. —**spokes'wom'an** (-wŏŏm'-ən) *n. fem.*

Spo·le·to (spō·lā'tō) A town of central Italy, site of extensive Roman ruins and several medieval churches, including an 11th century cathedral. Ancient **Spo·le·ti·um** (spō·lē'shē·əm).

spo·li·a·tion (spō'lē·ā'shən) *n.* **1** The act of despoiling; specifically, the plundering of neutral commerce by a belligerent. **2** *Law* Destruction; mutilation; alteration; specifically, the erasure, alteration, mutilation, or destruction of a paper to prevent its being used as evidence. **3** In English canon law, the taking of the fruits of a benefice under a pretended but illegal title, or a writ or suit brought on such grounds. **4** *Law* The destruction of a ship's papers so as to conceal its nationality, the character of its trade, cargo, etc. [<L *spoliatio,* -*onis* <*spoliare* despoil] —**spo'li·a'tor** *n.*

spo·li·a·tive (spō'lē·ā'tiv) *adj.* Tending to abstract from or lessen; in medicine, resulting in a considerable loss of blood.

spon·da·ic (spon·dā'ik) *adj.* **1** Pertaining to or of the nature of a spondee; composed of spondees. **2** Having a spondee in a position where another kind of metrical foot is usual. Also **spon·da'i·cal.** [<L *spondaicus* <Gk. *spondeiakos* <*spondē.* See SPONDEE.]

spon·dee (spon'dē) *n.* A metrical foot consisting of two long syllables or, in English verse, of two accented syllables. [<F *spondée* <Gk. *spondeios (pous)* libation (meter) <*spondē* a libation; because used in the solemn chants accompanying a libation]

spon·du·lics (spon·dōō'liks) *n. U.S. Slang* Cash money. Also **spon·du'licks, spon·du'lix.**

spon·dy·li·tis (spon'də·lī'tis) *n. Pathol.* Pott's disease.

spondylo- *combining form Anat. & Med.* A vertebra; of or pertaining to vertebrae. Also, before vowels, **spondyl-.** [<Gk. *spondylos* a vertebra]

sponge (spunj) *n.* **1** Any of a phylum *(Porifera)* of fixed, usually marine organisms characterized by a highly porous body without specialized internal organs. **2** The skeleton or network of elastic fibers that remains after the removal of the living matter from certain sponges and that readily absorbs liquids: used as an absorbent, for bathing, etc. **3** Some spongelike implement or substance that serves as an absorbent, as a swabbing implement for cleaning a cannon bore after discharge. **4** Leavened dough, or dough in the process of leavening and before kneading. **5** A porous, spongelike form assumed by finely divided metals, as iron and platinum. **6** *Surg.* An absorbent pad, as of sterilized gauze, used in operations, etc., to absorb blood or other fluid matter. **7** One who consumes or absorbs a great deal, as of food or drink. **8** *Colloq.* A person who lives at the expense of another or others; a parasite. —**to throw** (or **toss) up** (or **in) the sponge** *Colloq.* To yield; give up; abandon the struggle. —*v.* **sponged, spong·ing** *v.t.* **1** To wipe, wet, or clean with a sponge. **2** To wipe out; expunge; erase. **3** To absorb; suck in, as a sponge does. **4** *Colloq.* To get by mean device or at another's expense. —*v.i.* **5** To be absorbent. **6** To gather or fish for sponges. **7** *Colloq.* To live at the expense of others. See synonyms under CLEANSE. [OE <L *spongia,* ult. <Gk. *spongos.* Akin to FUNGUS.]

sponge cake A cake of sugar, eggs, and flour, containing no shortening and beaten very light.

spong·er (spun'jər) *n.* **1** One who or that which sponges in any sense. **2** A person or vessel that gathers sponges. **3** A human parasite.

spon·gi·form (spun'jə·fôrm, spon'-) *adj.* Resembling a sponge in form or structure.

spon·gin (spun'jin) *n. Biochem.* A protein from the skeletal tissue of sponges and corals.

spon·gi·o·blast (spon'jē·ə·blast') *n. Biol.* **1** An epithelial cell of the embryonic neural tube which becomes transformed into a cell of the tissue lining the central cavities of the brain and spinal cord. **2** A spongoblast. [<Gk. *spongia,* var. of *spongos* a sponge + -BLAST]

spon·go·blast (spon'gō·blast) *n. Biol.* An ameboid cell in the mesenchyme of sponges by which spongin is secreted. Also **spon·gin·blast** (spun'jin·blast, spon'-). [<Gk. *spongos* a sponge + -BLAST]

spong·y (spun'jē) *adj.* **1** Having the nature or character of a sponge; elastic, compressible, and porous. **2** Having the quality of imbibing fluids; absorptive. **3** Existing in a condition of fine division and loose coherence. **4** *Obs.* Wet; soaked. Also **spon·gi·ose** (spun'jē·ōs). —**spong'i·ness** *n.*

spon·sal (spon'səl) *adj.* Relating to marriage or to a spouse. [<L *sponsus,* pp. of *spondere* promise]

spon·sion (spon'shən) *n.* **1** The act of becoming surety or sponsor for another. **2** In international law, an undertaking on behalf of his state by a public officer not specifically empowered to enter into it.

spon·son (spon'sən) *n.* **1** A curved projection from the hull of a vessel or seaplane, to give greater stability or increase the surface area. **2** A similar protuberance on a ship or

tank, for storage purposes or for the training of a gun. **3** An air tank built into the side of a canoe, to improve stability and prevent sinking. [Appar. alter. of EXPANSION]

spon·sor (spon′sər) n. **1** One who makes himself responsible for a statement by, or the debt or duty of, another; a surety. **2** One who makes the required professions and promises for an infant at baptism and becomes responsible for its religious training; a godfather or godmother. **3** A business firm or enterprise that assumes all the costs of a radio or television program which advertises its product or service. —v.t. To act as sponsor for; answer or vouch for. —**spon·so·ri·al** (spon·sôr′ē·əl, -sō′rē-) adj. —**spon′sor·ship** n.

spon·ta·ne·i·ty (spon′tə·nē′ə·tē) n. pl. ·ties **1** Spontaneous quality. **2** The tendency to action or behavior independent of external forces, conditions, or influences.

spon·ta·ne·ous (spon·tā′nē·əs) adj. **1** Arising from inherent qualities or tendencies without external efficient cause; done or acting from one's own impulse, prompting, or desire. **2** Not having material causation outside itself. **3** Generated or produced without human labor; wild or sporadic; indigenous. **4** Biol. Apparently arising independently of external stimulus, influence, or conditions. [<LL spontaneus <L sponte of free will] —**spon·ta′ne·ous·ly** adv. —**spon·ta′ne·ous·ness** n.

Synonyms: automatic, instinctive, involuntary, unbidden, voluntary, willing. That is spontaneous which is freely done, with no external compulsion and, in human actions, without special premeditation or distinct determination of the will; that is voluntary which is freely done with distinct act of will; that is involuntary which is independent of the will, and perhaps in opposition to it; a willing act is not only in accordance with will, but with desire. Thus voluntary and involuntary, which are antonyms of each other, are both partial synonyms of spontaneous. An infant's smile in answer to that of its mother is spontaneous; the smile of a pouting child wheedled into good humor is involuntary. In physiology the action of the heart and lungs is involuntary action; the growth of the hair and nails is spontaneous; the action of swallowing is voluntary up to a certain point, beyond which it becomes involuntary or automatic.

spontaneous combustion The oxidation of a substance with such rapidity as to engender heat sufficient to ignite it, as masses of oiled rags, finely powdered ores, coal, and certain metals.

spontaneous generation Biol. Abiogenesis.

spon·toon (spon·tōōn′) n. A half-pike usually armed with a hook, carried by infantry officers in the 18th century: also spelled espontoon. [<F sponton <Ital. spontone pike <puntone a point]

spoof (spōōf) Colloq. v.t. & v.i. To deceive or hoax; joke. —n. Deception; humbug; hoax. [after a nonsensical game invented by Arthur Roberts, 1852–1933, English comedian]

spook (spōōk) Colloq. n. A ghost; an apparition; specter. —v.t. **1** To haunt (a person or place). **2** To frighten, disturb, or annoy. **3** To startle or frighten (an animal) into flight, stampeding, etc. [<Du.] —**spook′ish** adj.

spook·y (spōō′kē) adj. **spook·i·er, spook·i·est** Colloq. **1** Of or like a spook; ghostly; eerie. **2** Frightened; nervous; skittish. —**spook′i·ly** adv. —**spook′i·ness** n.

spool (spōōl) n. **1** A small cylinder, commonly of wood and with a flange at each end and an axial bore, upon which thread or yarn is or may be wound. **2** The quantity of thread held by a spool; also, the spool and the thread upon it. **3** Anything resembling a spool in shape or purpose. —v.t. To wind on a spool. [<MLG spole]

spoon (spōōn) n. **1** A utensil having a shallow, generally ovoid bowl and a handle, used in preparing, serving, or eating food. **2** Something resembling a spoon or its bowl. **3** A metallic lure attached to a fishing line: also **spoon bait, trolling spoon. 4** A concave overhanging extension on a torpedo tube to keep the launched torpedo in a straight course.

5 A wooden golf club with lofted face and comparatively short, stiff shaft, used by some players for approaching. —v.t. **1** To lift up or out with a spoon. **2** To hollow out like the bowl of a spoon. **3** In certain games, to play or hit (the ball) with little force up into the air; in croquet, to shove or scoop (the ball) with the mallet. —v.i. **4** To fish with a spoon. **5** In certain games, to spoon the ball. **6** Colloq. To make love, especially openly and demonstratively. [OE spōn sliver, chip]

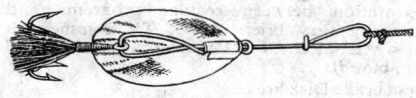
SPOON BAIT

spoon·bill (spōōn′bil′) n. **1** A wading bird (genera Platalea or Ajaia) related to the ibises, having the bill broad and flattened. **2** The shoveler (def. 2). **3** The paddlefish. —**spoon′-billed′** adj.

spoon·bread (spōōn′bred′) n. A quick bread made of cornmeal, eggs, milk, and shortening, baked soft enough to be served with a spoon: also called batter bread.

spoon·drift (spōōn′drift) n. Spindrift.

spoon·er·ism (spōō′nə·riz′əm) n. The unintentional transposition of sounds or of parts of words in speaking, as in "half-warmed fish" for "half-formed wish". [after William A. Spooner, 1844–1930, of New College, Oxford, who was renowned for such slips of the tongue]

spoon·feed (spōōn′fēd′) v.t. -fed (fed), -feed·ing (fē′ding) **1** To feed with a spoon. **2** To pamper; spoil. **3** To present (information) in such a manner that little or no thought, initiative, etc., is required of the recipient. **4** To instruct or inform (a person) in this manner.

spoon·ful (spōōn′fōōl′) n. pl. ·fuls As much as a spoon will hold; especially, a teaspoonful.

spoon hook A fish hook with a bright, revolving, spoon-shaped piece of metal attached.

spoon·y (spōō′nē) Colloq. adj. **spoon·i·er, spoon·i·est** Sentimental or silly, as in lovemaking; soft. —n. pl. **spoon·ies** A foolish, demonstrative lover; sentimental simpleton. Also **spoon′ey.**

spoor (spōōr) n. **1** A track; trail. **2** Footprint or other trace of a wild animal. —v.t. & v.i. To track by or follow a spoor. [<Du.]

Spor·a·des (spôr′ə·dēz, Greek spô·rä′thes) **1** Loosely, all the Greek islands in the Aegean, exclusive of the Cyclades. **2** Anciently, the islands of the SE Aegean, off western Asia Minor, including the Dodecanese, Icaria, Samos, and, in some usages, Chios and Lesbos. **3** Strictly, the **Northern Sporades,** a group of Greek islands in the western Aegean, off the coasts of Euboea and Thessaly, the chief of which is Skyros: Greek Voriai Sporades.

spo·rad·ic (spô·rad′ik, spō-) adj. **1** Occurring here and there; occasional. **2** Separate; isolated. **3** Not widely diffused; neither epidemic nor endemic: said of disease. Also **spo·rad′i·cal.** [<Med. L sporadicus <Gk. sporadikos < sporas scattered] —**spo·rad′i·cal·ly** adv. —**spo·rad′i·cal·ness** n.

spor·a·do·sid·er·ite (spôr′ə·dō·sid′ər·īt, spō′rə-) n. A meteorite consisting of a typically crystalline mass with disseminated particles of nickel-iron alloy. [<SPORADIC + SIDERITE]

spo·ran·gi·o·spore (spô·ran′jē·ə·spôr′, spō·ran′jē·ə·spôr′) n. Bot. A spore produced within a sporangium.

spo·ran·gi·um (spô·ran′jē·əm, spō-) n. pl. ·gi·a (-jē·ə) Bot. A sac in which asexual spores are produced endogenously, as in certain algae and fungi. Also called spore case. [<SPOR(O)- + Gk. angeion a vessel] —**spo·ran′gi·al** adj.

spore (spôr, spōr) n. **1** Bot. The reproductive body in flowerless plants, but containing no embryo. They are free, usually single-celled and highly resistant bodies, produced externally or in some closed sac or cavity, and are capable of developing at once or after a time into an independent organism or individual. **2** A minute body that develops into a new

individual; any minute organism; a germ. —v.i. **spored, spor·ing** To develop spores: said of plants. [<Gk. spora seed, sowing] —**spo·ra·ceous** (spô·rā′shəs, spō-) adj.

spore case A sporangium.

spore fruit Bot. An ascocarp; any plant structure producing spores.

spo·rif·er·ous (spô·rif′ər·əs, spō-) adj. Bearing spores.

sporo– combining form Seed; spore: sporophyte. Also, before vowels, **spor–.** [<Gk. spora a seed]

spo·ro·carp (spôr′ə·kärp, spō′rə-) n. Bot. **1** A many-celled form of fruit produced from a fertilized archicarp in certain of the lower cryptogams, especially red algae and ascomycetous fungi: also called cystocarp. **2** The sporogonium in mosses.

spo·ro·cyst (spôr′ə·sist, spō′rə-) n. Zool. **1** An asexual form of a trematode worm that develops directly from the embryo and in which mouth and intestinal tract are wanting. **2** An encysted organism, especially a protozoan, that gives rise to spores.

spo·ro·cyte (spôr′ə·sīt, spō′rə-) n. Biol. The mother cell from which spores are produced.

spo·ro·gen·e·sis (spôr′ə·jen′ə·sis, spō′rə-) n. Biol. **1** Reproduction by spores. **2** Sporogony. —**spo·rog·e·nous** (spô·roj′ə·nəs, spō-) adj.

spo·ro·go·ni·um (spôr′ə·gō′nē·əm, spō′rə-) n. pl. ·ni·a (-nē·ə) Bot. An elongated stalk having upon its summit a capsule in which the asexual spores of liverworts and mosses are produced.

spo·rog·o·ny (spô·rog′ə·nē, spō-) n. Biol. Spore formation; specifically, in sporozoans, the development of spores from a mature zygote. [<SPORO- + -GONY]

spo·ro·phore (spôr′ə·fôr, spō′rə·fōr) n. **1** A spore-bearer or seed-bearer. **2** Bot. In fungi, a branch from the thallus which bears the spores.

spo·ro·phyll (spôr′ə·fil, spō′rə-) n. Bot. The leaf, or modified leaf, which bears the sporangia. Also **spo′ro·phyl.**

spo·ro·phyte (spôr′ə·fīt, spō′rə-) n. Bot. The spore-bearing individual or generation in certain plants which reproduce by alternation of generations.

spo·ro·tri·cho·sis (spôr′ə·tri·kō′sis, spō′rə-) n. Pathol. A chronic disease caused by a fungus (genus Sporotrichum) and marked by the formation of ulcerated lesions in the lymph nodes or subcutaneous tissue. [<NL Sporotrichum, genus of fungi + -OSIS]

–sporous combining form Having (a specified number or kind of) spores: homosporous. [<SPOR(O)- + -OUS]

spo·ro·zo·an (spôr′ə·zō′ən, spō′rə-) adj. Designating or belonging to a class (Sporozoa) of parasitic protozoans developing by asexual and sexual stages and reproducing by sporulation, as the malaria parasite. —n. One of the class Sporozoa. [<SPORO- + Gk. zōion animal]

spo·ro·zo·ite (spôr′ə·zō′īt, spō′rə-) n. Zool. An aggregation of protoplasm of a sporozoan zygote, segmented off as a minute sickle-shaped germ: the initial phase of the malaria parasite in its host.

spor·ran (spor′ən) n. A skin pouch, generally with the fur on, worn in front of the kilt by Highlanders. [<Scottish Gaelic sporan <LL bursa purse]

sport (spôrt, spōrt) n. **1** That which amuses in general; diversion; pastime. **2** A particular game or play pursued for diversion, especially an outdoor or athletic game, as baseball, football, track, tennis, swimming, etc. **3** A spirit of jesting or raillery. **4** That with which one sports; a toy; plaything. **5** Mockery; an object of derision: to make sport of someone; also, a laughingstock; butt. **6** Biol. An animal or plant, or one of its parts, that exhibits sudden and spontaneous variation from the normal type; a mutation. **7** Bot. A bud variation. **8** Colloq. One whose interest in sport lies chiefly in gambling; a gamester or gambler. **9** Colloq. One who lives a fast, gay, or flashy life. **10** A person characterized by his observance of the rules of fair play, or by his ability to get along with others: a good sport. **11** Archaic Amorous fondling; wanton dalliance. —v.i. **1** To amuse oneself; play; frolic.

2 To participate in games. 3 To make sport or jest; trifle. 4 *Bot.* **a** To vary suddenly or spontaneously from the normal type; mutate. **b** To display bud variation. 5 *Archaic Dial.* To make love in a sportive or trifling manner. —*v.t.* 6 *Colloq.* To display or wear ostentatiously; show off. 7 *Obs.* To amuse; divert. See synonyms under FRISK. —*adj.* Of, pertaining to, or fitted for sports; also, appropriate for informal outdoor wear: a *sport* coat: also **sports.** [Aphetic var. of DISPORT] —**sport'er** *n.* —**sport'ful** *adj.* —**sport'ful·ly** *adv.* —**sport'ful·ness** *n.*

Synonyms (noun): amusement, diversion, entertainment, frolic, fun, gaiety, gambol, game, jollity, joviality, merriment, merrymaking, mirth, pastime, play, pleasure, prank, recreation. See ENTERTAINMENT, FROLIC.

sport·ing (spôr'ting, spōr'-) *adj.* 1 Pertaining to, engaged in, or used in connection with athletic games or field sports. 2 Characterized by the spirit of sportsmanship; conforming to the codes or standards of sportsmanship. 3 Interested in or associated with sports for gambling or betting: a *sporting* man. —**sport'ing·ly** *adv.*

sporting chance *Colloq.* A chance involving the risk of loss.

spor·tive (spôr'tiv, spōr'-) *adj.* 1 Relating to or fond of sport or play; frolicsome. 2 Interested in, active in, or related to sports. 3 *Obs.* Wanton or amorous. —**spor'tive·ly** *adv.* —**spor'tive·ness** *n.*

sports car A low, rakish automobile, usually seating two persons, and built for high speed and maneuverability.

sports·cast·er (spôrts'kas'tər, -käs'-, spōrts'-) *n. U.S.* One who broadcasts sports events, news, and comment.

sport shirt A shirt for informal wear, often cut square at the bottom so as to be worn inside or outside slacks. Also **sports shirt.**

sports·man (spôrts'mən, spōrts'-) *n. pl.* **·men** (-mən) 1 One who pursues field sports, especially hunting and fishing. 2 A professional gambler; also, one who bets on horse races. 3 One who abides by a code of fair play in games or in daily practice.

sports·man·like (spôrts'mən·līk', spōrts'-) *adj.* Pertaining to sportsmen; honorable; generous; conforming to the rules of sportsmanship. Also **sports'man·ly.**

sports·man·ship (spôrts'mən·ship, spōrts'-) *n.* 1 The art or practice of field sports. 2 Honorable or sportsmanlike conduct.

sports·wear (spôrts'wâr', spōrts'-) *n.* Clothes made for informal or outdoor activities.

sports·wom·an (spôrts'wŏŏm'ən, spōrts'-) *n. pl.* **·wom·en** (-wim'in) A woman who participates in sports.

sport·y (spôr'tē, spōr'-) *adj.* **sport·i·er, sport·i·est** *Colloq.* Relating to or characteristic of a sport; hence, gay, loud, or dissipated. —**sport'i·ly** *adv.* —**sport'i·ness** *n.*

spor·u·late (spôr'yə·lāt, spor'-) *v.i.* **·lat·ed, ·lat·ing** To form spores.

spor·u·la·tion (spôr'yə·lā'shən, spor'-) *n. Biol.* The act or condition of spore formation, especially by multiple cell division after encystment.

spor·ule (spôr'yōōl, spor'-) *n.* A spore; sometimes, a little spore. [Dim. of SPORE]

spot (spot) *n.* 1 A particular place of small extent; a definite locality. 2 Any small portion of a surface differing as in color from the rest; blot. 3 A stain or blemish on character; a fault; a reproach. 4 A congenital birthmark. 5 A food fish *(Leiostomus xanthurus)* of the Atlantic coast of the United States, marked with a spot above each pectoral fin; the oldwife. 6 One of the figures or pips with which a playing card is marked; also, a card having (a certain number of) such marks: the five *spot* of clubs. 7 *Slang* A currency note having a specified value: a ten *spot.* 8 *Chiefly Brit.* A portion or bit: a *spot* of tea. 9 *Slang* Position or situation: He was in a good *spot.* 10 *U.S. Slang* A spotlight. See synonyms under BLEMISH, PLACE. —**in a spot** *Slang* In a difficult or embarrassing situation; in trouble. —**in spots** Now and then, in some respects: He is bright *in spots.* —**to go to the spot** To satisfy a definite need or craving. —**to hit the spot** *Slang* To gratify an appetite or need. —**on the spot** 1 At once; immediately. 2 At the very place. 3 *Slang* **a** In danger of death. **b** Accountable or in danger of being held accountable for some action. —*v.* **spot·ted, spot·ting** *v.t.* 1 To mark or soil with spots. 2 To decorate with spots; dot. 3 To place on a designated spot; locate; station. 4 *Colloq.* To recognize or detect; see. 5 *Colloq.* To yield (an advantage or handicap) to someone: We *spotted* them five points. —*v.i.* 6 To become marked or soiled with spots. 7 To make a stain or discoloration. 8 *Mil.* To observe the effect of gunfire to obtain data for improving its accuracy. See synonyms under STAIN. —*adj.* 1 Being on the place or spot. 2 Paid or prepared for payment on delivery; also, ready for instant delivery following sale. 3 *Telecom.* Designed for presentation between regular programs and usually very brief: a *spot* TV commercial. [< ME < LG. Cf. MDu. *spotte* a spot.] —**spot'ta·ble** *adj.*

spot brake Disk brake.

spot cash Immediate payment on actual delivery.

spot·less (spot'lis) *adj.* Free from spot, stain, or impurity. See synonyms under INNOCENT, PERFECT, PURE. —**spot'less·ly** *adv.* —**spot'less·ness** *n.*

spot·light (spot'līt') *n.* 1 A circle of powerful light thrown on the stage to bring an actor or actors into clearer view. 2 The apparatus that produces such a light. 3 A pivoted automobile lamp. 4 Notoriety; publicity.

Spot·syl·va·ni·a (spot'sil·vā'nē·ə) A village in NE Virginia; scene of a 13-day battle in the Civil War, May, 1864. Formerly called **Spotsylvania Courthouse.**

spot·ted (spot'id) *adj.* 1 Discolored in spots; stained; soiled. 2 Characterized or marked by spots. 3 Blazed: said of trees, trails, etc.

spotted adder The house snake.

spotted crake A small European rail *(Porzana porzana)*, allied to the American sora.

spotted cranesbill A North American woodland herb *(Geranium maculatum)* covered more or less densely with long white hairs and having lavender, rose, or sometimes white flowers. Also called *alumroot, wild geranium.*

spotted fever *Pathol.* 1 Meningitis. 2 Typhus. 3 Rocky Mountain spotted fever.

spotted sandpiper See under SANDPIPER.

spot·ter (spot'ər) *n.* 1 One who or that which spots. 2 *Colloq.* A private detective. 3 An observation balloon. 4 A device on a railroad car that marks irregularities along the track. 5 In drycleaning, one who removes spots.

spot·ty (spot'ē) *adj.* **·ti·er, ·ti·est** 1 Having many spots. 2 Occurring in spots; unevenly distributed. —**spot'ti·ly** *adv.* —**spot'ti·ness** *n.*

spous·al (spou'zəl) *adj.* Pertaining to marriage. See synonyms under MATRIMONIAL. *n.* Marriage; espousal.

spouse (spouz, spous) *n.* A partner in marriage; one's husband or wife. —*v.t.* **spoused, spous·ing** *Obs.* To wed; marry; espouse. [< OF *espous, espouse* < L *sponsus,* pp. of *spondere* promise, betroth]

spout (spout) *v.i.* 1 To pour out copiously and forcibly, as a liquid under pressure. 2 To discharge a fluid either continuously or in jets. 3 *Colloq.* To speak or orate pompously; declaim. —*v.t.* 4 To cause to pour or shoot forth. 5 To utter grandiloquently or pompously. 6 *Brit. Slang* To pawn or pledge. —*n.* 1 A tube, trough, etc., for the discharge of a liquid. 2 A continuous stream of fluid. 3 Formerly, the shoot or lift in a pawnbroker's shop. 4 *Brit. Slang* A pawnbroker's shop. [ME *spoute*; origin uncertain] —**spout'er** *n.*

sprag (sprag) *n.* A billet of wood used to prevent a vehicle from slipping backward, or in mining as a prop to support coal when undermined. [Origin uncertain]

Sprague's pipit (sprāgz) The Missouri skylark.

sprain (sprān) *n.* 1 A violent straining or twisting of the ligaments surrounding a joint. 2 The condition due to such strain. [< *v.*] —*v.t.* To cause a sprain in; wrench the muscles of (a joint). [< OF *espreindre* squeeze < L *exprimere.* See EXPRESS]

sprang (sprang) Alternative past tense of SPRING.

sprat (sprat) *n.* 1 A herringlike fish *(Clupea sprattus)* found in shoals on the Atlantic coast of Europe. 2 The young of the herring. [OE *sprott*]

sprawl (sprôl) *v.i.* 1 To sit or lie with the limbs stretched out ungracefully. 2 To be stretched out ungracefully, as the limbs. 3 To move with awkward motions of the limbs. 4 To spread out in a straggling manner, as handwriting, vines, etc. —*v.t.* 5 To cause to spread or extend awkwardly or irregularly. —*n.* 1 The act or position of sprawling; an awkward recumbent posture or movement. 2 An unplanned or disorderly group, as of houses, spread out over a broad area: urban *sprawl;* a vast *sprawl* of lights. [OE *spreawlian* move convulsively] —**sprawl'er** *n.*

spray[1] (sprā) *n.* 1 Water or other liquid dispersed in fine particles. 2 An instrument for discharging small particles of liquid; an atomizer. [< *v.*] —*v.t.* 1 To disperse (a liquid) in fine particles. 2 To apply spray to, as with an atomizer. —*v.i.* 3 To send forth or scatter spray. 4 To go forth as spray. [Akin to MDu. *sprayen* sprinkle] —**spray'er** *n.*

spray[2] (sprā) *n.* 1 A small branch bearing dependent branchlets or flowers. 2 Any ornament, pattern, etc., resembling a collection of twigs or flowers. [ME; origin uncertain]

spread (spred) *v.* **spread, spread·ing** *v.t.* 1 To open or unfold to full width, extent, etc., as wings, sail, a map, etc. 2 To distribute over a surface, especially in a thin layer; scatter or smear. 3 To cover with a layer of something: to *spread* toast with marmalade. 4 To force apart or farther apart: The heavy train has *spread* the rails. 5 To extend over a period of time; prolong: He *spread* the payments over a six-month period. 6 To make more widely known, active, etc.; promulgate or diffuse: to *spread* a rumor; to *spread* contagion. 7 To set (a table, etc.), as for a meal. 8 To arrange or place on a table, etc., as a meal or feast. 9 To set forth or record in full. —*v.i.* 10 To be extended or expanded; increase in size, width, etc. 11 To be distributed or dispersed, as over a surface or area; scatter. 12 To become more widely known, active, etc. 13 To be forced farther apart; separate. —*n.* 1 The act of spreading: the *spread* of the gospel. 2 An open extent or expanse. 3 The limit or extent of expansion of some designated object, as of sail or a bird's wings. 4 *Aeron,.* The maximum distance from tip to tip of an airplane wing. 5 A cloth or covering for a bed, table, or the like. 6 *Colloq.* An informal feast or banquet; also, a table with a meal set out on it. 7 Anything used to spread on bread: a cheese *spread.* 8 Two pages of a magazine or newspaper facing each other and covered by related material; also, print spread across two or more columns or on facing pages for advertising or display. 9 In finance and commerce, a straddle. 10 Diffusion; dispersion. —*adj.* Having a broad surface; expanded; outstretched. [OE *sprǣdan*]

Synonyms (verb): circulate, diffuse, disperse, disseminate, distribute, divulge, expand, extend, promulgate, propagate, scatter. See PUBLISH, STRETCH. *Antonyms*: check, confine, condense, contract, restrain.

spread-ea·gle (spred'ē'gəl) *adj.* 1 Having the arms and legs spread wide apart. 2 Extravagant; bombastic: applied especially to patriotic American oratory. —*v.* **-ea·gled, -ea·gling** *v.t.* To lash to the mast or shrouds in spread-eagle position as a punishment: a former practice. —*v.i.* To deliver an oration in bombastic, patriotic style. —**spread'-ea'gle·ism** *n.*

spread eagle 1 The figure of an eagle with extended wings: used as an emblem of the United States. 2 Any position or movement resembling this, as a figure in skating. 3 Extravagant speech; especially, American bombastic, patriotic oratory.

spread·er (spred'ər) *n.* 1 One who or that which spreads, as a small knife for spreading butter. 2 A bar of wood, metal, etc., to keep stays or wires apart, etc. 3 *Agric.* An implement for spreading hay, manure, etc.

spread·sheet (spred'shēt') *n.* A kind of computer program that processes numerical data for financial calculations of various kinds.

spreck·le (sprek'əl) *n.* & *v. Scot. & Brit. Dial.* Speckle.

spree (sprē) *n.* 1 A drinking spell; drunken carousal. 2 A gay frolic. See synonyms under FROLIC. Compare SPORT. [Origin uncertain]

Spree (sprā, shprā) A river of eastern Germany, flowing 250 miles north to the Havel River.

sprig (sprig) *n.* 1 A shoot or sprout of a tree or plant; an ornament in this form. 2 An offshoot from an ancestral stock; a young man. 3 One of various small, pointed implements.

4 A brad without a head. 5 A small, wedge-shaped piece of metal used to hold glass in a window sash. — *v.t.* **sprigged, sprig·ging** 1 To ornament with a design of sprigs. 2 To form (twigs or plants) into sprays. 3 To fasten with sprigs or brads. 4 To pluck sprigs from. [ME *sprigge*; origin uncertain] — **sprig′ger** *n.*

sprig·gy (sprig′ē) *adj.* **·gi·er, ·gi·est** Abounding in sprigs or small branches.

spright (sprīt) See SPRITE.

spright·ly (sprīt′lē) *adj.* **·li·er, ·li·est** Full of animation and spirits; vivacious; lively. — *adv.* Spiritedly; briskly; gaily. — **spright′li·ness** *n.*
Synonyms: airy, animated, brisk, bustling, cheerful, lively, nimble, spry, vivacious. The *sprightly* display a cheerful, pleasing lightness and quickness, spiritlike; *lively* has a similar meaning, as abounding in cheerful life. The *brisk* and *bustling* are full of stir, the former generally to some purpose. See ACTIVE, AIRY, CHEERFUL, HAPPY, NIMBLE, VIVACIOUS, VIVID.

spring (spring) *v.* **sprang** or **sprung, sprung, spring·ing** *v.i.* 1 To move or rise suddenly and rapidly; leap; dart: He *sprang* across the creek; The cat *sprang* into the air. 2 To move suddenly as by elastic reaction; snap: The jaws of the heavy trap *sprang* shut. 3 To move as if with a leap: An angry retort *sprang* to his lips. 4 To rise up suddenly, as birds from cover. 5 To work or snap out of place, as a mechanical part. 6 To become warped or bent, as boards. 7 To explode: said of a mine. 8 To rise above surrounding objects. 9 To come into being: New towns have *sprung* up. 10 To originate; proceed, as from a source. 11 To develop; grow, as a plant. 12 To be descended: He *springs* from good stock. 13 *Poetic* To begin to appear, as light or dawn. — *v.t.* 14 To cause to spring or leap. 15 To cause to act, close, open, etc., unexpectedly or suddenly, as by elastic reaction: to *spring* a trap. 16 To cause to happen, become known, or appear suddenly: to *spring* a surprise. 17 To leap over; vault. 18 To start (game) from cover; flush. 19 To explode (a mine). 20 To warp or bend; split. 21 To cause to snap or work out of place. 22 To force into place, as a beam or bar. 23 To suffer (a leak). 24 *Slang* To obtain the release of (a person) from prison or custody. See synonyms under LEAP, RISE. — *n.* 1 *Mech.* An elastic body or contrivance that yields under stress, and returns to its normal form when the stress is removed. 2 Elastic quality or energy. 3 The act of flying back from a position of tension; recoil. 4 An energy or power; a cause of action; impelling motive. 5 The act of leaping up or forward suddenly; a jump; bound. 6 The season in which vegetation starts anew; in the north temperate zone, the three months of March, April, and May; in the astronomical year, the period from the vernal equinox to the summer solstice. 7 A flow or fountain, as of water; hence, any source or origin of continued supply; a flow of curative water. 8 A crack or break, as of a plank, beam, or spar, or a thing sprung or warped. 9 *Archit.* The commencement of curvature in an arch. 10 A hinge. See illustration under HINGE. 11 *Scot.* A quick, lively tune. See synonyms under BEGINNING, CAUSE, SOURCE. — *adj.* 1 Pertaining to the season of spring. 2 Resilient; acting like or having a spring. 3 Hung on springs. [OE *springan*]

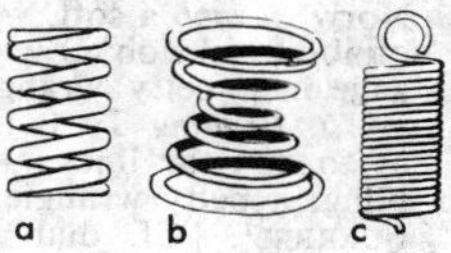

SPRING
a. Compression coil.
b. Double spiral.
c. Extension coil.

spring·al[1] (spring′əl) *n.* An engine like the ballista, used in medieval warfare: also *espringal.* Also **spring′ald** (-əld). [<AF *springalde,* OF *espringale* < *espringuer* spring < Gmc.]

spring·al[2] (spring′əl) *n. Scot.* A youth.

spring balance A weighing device, often used in classroom experiments, consisting essentially of a spring with a hook at one end to which objects to be weighed may be hung.

spring·beau·ty (spring′byōō′tē) *n. pl.* **·ties** One of a genus *(Claytonia)* of perennial wild flowers of the purslane family; especially, *C. virginica* of the eastern United States, with pink-tinged white flowers. See CLAYTONIA.

spring·board (spring′bôrd′, -bōrd′) *n.* 1 An elastic board used to aid in leaping; a springy board secured at one end, used to give impetus to a dive into the water below. Also *diving board.* 2 A short board inserted by one end in a notch in a tree, on which a workman stands when felling large trees.

spring·bok (spring′bok) *n.* A small South African gazelle *(Antidorcas marsupialis)* noted for its ability to leap high in the air. Also **spring′·buck′** (-buk′). [< Afrikaans]

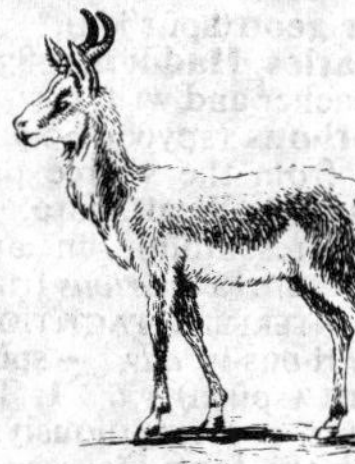

SPRINGBOK
(About 2 feet high at the shoulder)

spring chicken 1 A young chicken, 10 weeks to 10 months old, especially tender for cooking: so called because usually hatched in the spring. 2 *Colloq.* A young, immature, or unsophisticated person.

springe (sprinj) *n.* A snare or noose, arranged with a spring to catch small game. [ME *sprenge.* Related to SPRING.]

spring·er (spring′ər) *n.* 1 One who or that which springs. 2 *Archit.* The bottom stone of an arch, lying upon the impost (see illustration under ARCH); the lowest stone in the coping of a gable; a rib in a groined roof or vault. 3 A spaniel valuable for flushing birds. See under SPANIEL. 4 The springbok. 5 The grampus. 6 A spring chicken.

spring fever The listlessness and restlessness that overtakes a person with the first warm days of spring.

Spring·field (spring′fēld) 1 The capital of Illinois. 2 A city in southern Massachusetts; site of a U. S. arsenal. 3 A city in SW Missouri. 4 A city in SW Ohio.

Springfield rifle A magazine-fed, bolt-action, .30-caliber U. S. Army rifle. Also **Springfield.** [from the U. S. arsenal at *Springfield,* Mass.]

spring·halt (spring′hôlt′) *n.* A stringhalt.

spring·head (spring′hed′) *n.* A fountainhead; source.

spring hinge A hinge the leaves of which are connected with a spring to insure automatic closing.

spring·house (spring′hous′) *n.* A small building constructed over a spring, and used for keeping milk, meats, etc., cool.

spring·ing (spring′ing) *n.* 1 The act of one who or that which springs. 2 *Archit.* A springer: also **springing line.**

spring·let (spring′lit) *n.* A small spring; streamlet or rill.

Springs (springz) A city of southern Transvaal province, Republic of South Africa.

spring·tail (spring′tāl′) *n.* Any of certain very small wingless insects (order *Collembola*) having a tail comprised of two united parts, which bends beneath it and enables it to jump.

spring tide 1 A high tide occurring under the combined attraction of sun and new or full moon. 2 Any great wave of feeling, etc.

spring·time (spring′tīm′) *n.* The season of spring. Also **spring′tide′** (-tīd′).

spring water Water found in or obtained from a spring.

spring·y (spring′ē) *adj.* **spring·i·er, spring·i·est** 1 Elastic. 2 Spongy; wet. — **spring′i·ly** *adv.* — **spring′i·ness** *n.*

sprin·kle (spring′kəl) *v.* **·kled, ·kling** *v.t.* 1 To scatter in drops or small particles. 2 To besprinkle; specifically, to apply drops of water to, as a form of baptism: opposed to *immerse.* — *v.i.* 3 To fall or rain in scattered drops. — *n.* A falling in drops or particles, or that which so falls; a sprinkling; hence, a small quantity. [ME *sprenkelen.* Akin to LG *sprinkeln* scatter.]

sprin·kler (spring′klər) *n.* 1 A nozzle or other device for spraying water on lawns, built either as a portable apparatus or as a unit in a stationary network fed by underground pipes. 2 An outlet in a sprinkler system.

sprinkler system An arrangement of pipes distributed through a building, with outlets suitably placed for sprinkling water or other extinguishing fluid to put out fire: often with automatic temperature control.

sprin·kling (spring′kling) *n.* 1 That which is sprinkled. 2 A small number or quantity. 3 A mottling. 4 The act of scattering drops of liquid.

sprint (sprint) *n.* A short race run at top speed. [< *v.*] — *v.i.* To run fast, as in a sprint. [ME *sprenten* <Scand. Cf. ON *spretta* run.] — **sprint′er** *n.*

sprit[1] (sprit) *n. Naut.* 1 A small spar reaching diagonally from a mast to the peak of a fore-and-aft sail. 2 *Brit.* A pole used for propelling a boat. 3 A bowsprit. [OE *sprēot* pole]

sprit[2] (sprit) *n. Scot.* A rush or rushlike plant. — **sprit′tie** *adj.*

sprite (sprīt) *n.* 1 A fairy, elf, or goblin. 2 A disembodied spirit; a ghost. Also spelled *spright.* [<OF *esprit* <L *spiritus.* Doublet of SPIRIT.]

sprit·sail (sprit′səl, sprit′sāl′) *n. Naut.* A sail extended by a sprit.

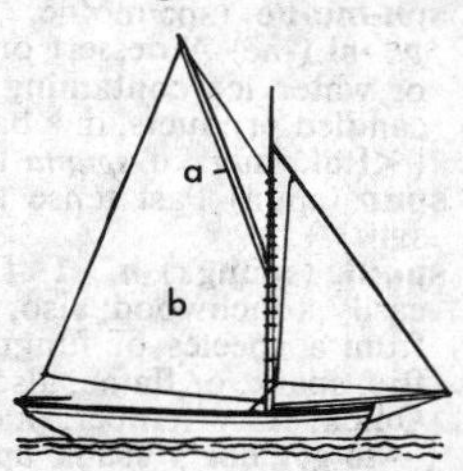

SPRITSAIL
a. Sprit. *b.* Spritsail.

sprock·et (sprok′it) *n. Mech.* 1 A projection, as on the periphery of a wheel, for engaging with the links of a chain. 2 A wheel bearing such projections: also **sprocket wheel.** [Origin uncertain]

sprout (sprout) *v.i.* 1 To put forth shoots; begin to grow; germinate. 2 To develop or grow rapidly. — *v.t.* 3 To cause to sprout. 4 To remove shoots from. — *n.* 1 A new shoot or bud on a plant; hence, something like or suggestive of a sprout; a scion. 2 *pl.* Brussels sprouts. — **a course of sprouts** A period of training. [OE *sprūtan*]

sprout·ling (sprout′ling) *n.* A little sprout.

spruce[1] (sprōōs) *n.* 1 Any of a genus *(Picea)* of evergreen trees of the pine family, having a sharp-pointed pyramidal crown, needle-shaped leaves, and pendulous cones; especially, the ornamental **Norway spruce** *(P. abies),* and the **Engelmann spruce** *(P. engelmanni)* of the Pacific coast. 2 The wood of any of these trees. 3 Any of certain other coniferous trees, as the Douglas fir. [Earlier *pruce* Prussian <*Pruce* Prussia <Med. L *Prussia*; so called because first known as a product of Prussia]

spruce[2] (sprōōs) *adj.* 1 Having a smart, trim appearance. 2 Fastidious. See synonyms under NEAT[1]. — *v.* **spruced, spruc·ing** *v.t.* To make spruce; dress or arrange neatly: often with *up.* — *v.i.* To make oneself spruce: usually with *up.* [Special use of SPRUCE[3]] — **spruce′ly** *adv.* — **spruce′ness** *n.*

spruce[3] (sprōōs) *n.* A kind of superior Prussian leather. Also **spruce leather.** [See SPRUCE[1]]

spruce beer A slightly fermented beverage made by boiling leaves and twigs of spruce with sugar or molasses.

sprue[1] (sprōō) *n.* 1 In founding, a channel connecting with the gate through which the melted metal is poured into the mold; also, dross. 2 A pouring hole in a mold; gate. [Origin uncertain]

sprue[2] (sprōō) *n. Pathol.* 1 A disease of tropical regions marked by anemia, emaciation, and gastrointestinal disturbances; psilosis. 2 Thrush. [<Du *spruw*]

sprug (sprug) *n. Scot. & Brit. Dial.* The common sparrow.

sprung (sprung) Past participle and alternative past tense of SPRING.

sprung rhythm In prosody, a rhythm involving feet of varying number of syllables but of equal time length, the stress usually falling on the first syllable: a term coined by Gerard Manley Hopkins.

sprung weight In automobiles, the weight supported by the suspension system: opposed to *unsprung weight.*

spry (sprī) *adj.* **spri·er** or **spry·er, spri·est** or **spry·est** Quick and active; agile. See synonyms under ACTIVE, SPRIGHTLY. [<dial. E *sprey* <Scand. Cf. Sw. *sprygg* active.] —**spry′ly** *adv.* —**spry′ness** *n.*

spud (spud) *n.* **1** A spadelike tool with narrow blade or prongs for removing the roots of weeds by digging or cutting. **2** *Colloq.* A potato. —*v.t.* **spud·ded, spud·ding** To remove, as weeds, with a spud. [ME *spudde* <Scand. Cf. Dan. *spyd* a spear.]

spud·der (spud′ər) *n.* A tool for removing bark from trees; also, one who uses such an implement.

spul·yie (spül′yē) *Scot. n.* The act of despoiling; spoil; booty. Also **spul′yie·ment.** —*v.t.* & *v.i.* To plunder. Also **spuil′zie, spul′zie** (-yē).

spume (spyo͞om) *n.* Froth, as on an agitated or effervescing liquid; foam; scum. —*v.i.* **spumed, spum·ing** To foam; froth. [<F <L *spuma* foam] —**spu′mous** *adj.* —**spum′y** *adj.*

spu·mes·cent (spyo͞o·mes′ənt) *adj.* Resembling or producing froth or foam; spumy. —**spu·mes′cence** *n.*

spu·mo·ne (spə·mō′nē, *Ital.* spo͞o·mō′nā) *n. pl.* **·ni** (-nē) A dessert or mousse of ice-cream or water ice containing fruit, nuts, or other candied products, in a base of whipped cream. [<Ital., aug. of *spuma* froth <L *spuma*]

spun (spun) Past tense and past participle of SPIN.

spunk (spungk) *n.* **1** Dry wood that burns easily; touchwood; also, a kind of tinder made from a species of fungus; punk. **2** A small fire, spark, or flame; also, a match. **3** *Colloq.* Quick, fiery temper; mettle; pluck; courage. —**to get one's spunk up** To become defiant or angry; also, to take heart; show courage. —*v.i.* To take fire; flare up; kindle. [<Irish *sponnc* tinder <L *spongia* sponge]

spunk·ie (spungk′ē) *Scot. n.* **1** The ignis fatuus. **2** A small flame. **3** Liquor; whisky. —*adj.* Spunky.

spunk·y (spungk′ē) *adj.* **spunk·i·er, spunk·i·est** *Colloq.* Spirited; courageous; also, touchy. —**spunk′i·ly** *adv.* —**spunk′i·ness** *n.*

spun rayon Yarns or fabrics made from short rayon fibers instead of from one long filament.

spun silk **1** Short fibers of silk from cocoons which the worms have pierced, and which cannot be reeled. **2** Yarn or cloth made from these fibers.

spun yarn *Naut.* A two- to four-stranded, left-handed line made from loosely twisted rope yarn: used for seizings, etc.

spur (spûr) *n.* **1** A pricking or goading instrument worn on a horseman's heel, and bearing a sharp point or a series of points on a rotating wheel. **2** Anything that incites or urges; instigation; incentive. **3** A part or attachment projecting like or suggestive of a spur, as a crag or mountain peak, a steel gaff fastened to a gamecock's leg, the ergot of rye, etc. **4** A stiff, sharp spine, as on the legs of some insects and the wings of some birds; especially, the spine on the tarsus of the domestic cock. See illustration under FOWL. **5** *Archit.* A buttress or other offset from a wall; also, a claw or the like projecting upon the plinth at the four angles of the base of a column. **6** In carpentry, a brace reinforcing a rafter or post; a strut. **7** *Bot.* A tubular expansion of a foliaceous part, usually some part of the flower, as in the columbine and larkspur. **8** A branch of a lode, railroad, etc. —**on the spur of the moment** Hastily; prompted by an impulse. —*v.* **spurred, spur·ring** *v.t.* **1** To prick or urge with or as with spurs. **2** To furnish with spurs. **3** To injure or gash with the spur, as a gamecock. —*v.i.* **4** To spur one's horse. **5** To hasten; hurry. [OE *spura*] —**spur′rer** *n.*

Synonyms (verb): goad, impel, incite, instigate, provoke, rouse, stimulate, sting, stir, urge. *Antonyms*: check, deter, discourage, dissuade, hold, moderate, rein, restrain.

spur·gall (spûr′gôl′) *n.* A galled place on a horse's side, caused by the spur. —*v.t.* To injure or gall with a spur.

spurge (spûrj) *n.* **1** Any of several shrubs (genus *Euphorbia*) having fertile flowers with 3-lobed ovaries on long pedicels and yielding a milky juice of bitter taste. **2** One of various related plants of the spurge family (*Euphorbiaceae*). [<OF *espurge* < *espurgier* purge <L *expurgare* < *ex-* out + *purgare* cleanse]

spur gear *Mech.* **1** A spur wheel. **2** Spur gearing.

spur gearing *Mech.* Gearing composed of spur wheels.

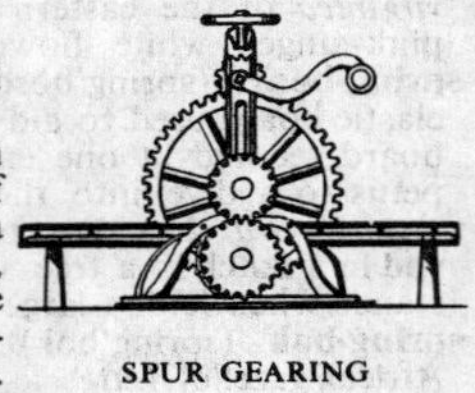

SPUR GEARING

spurge laurel An evergreen shrub of Europe and Asia (*Daphne laureola*), with oblanceolate leaves and yellowish-green flowers.

Spur·geon (spûr′jən), **Charles Haddon,** 1834–92, English Baptist preacher and writer.

spu·ri·ous (spyo͝or′ē·əs) *adj.* **1** Not proceeding from the source pretended; not genuine; false. **2** Illegitimate. **3** Apparent, but not real; resembling in appearance but not in structure: a *spurious* fruit. See synonyms under COUNTERFEIT, FACTITIOUS. [<L *spurius*] —**spu′ri·ous·ly** *adv.* —**spu′ri·ous·ness** *n.*

spurn (spûrn) *v.t.* **1** To reject with disdain; refuse contemptuously; scorn. **2** To strike with the foot; kick. —*v.i.* **3** To reject something with disdain. See synonyms under SCORN. —*n.* The act of spurning; also, a kick. [OE *spurnan* kick, reject] —**spurn′er** *n.*

spurred (spûrd) *adj.* Wearing or having spurs; having sharp spikes, claws, or shoots.

spur·ri·er (spûr′ē·ər) *n.* A maker of spurs.

spur·ry (spûr′ē) *n. pl.* **·ries** Any of several low annual herbs (genus *Spergula*); especially, the **corn spurry** (*S. arvensis*), which is a common weed. Also **spur′rey.** [<Du. *spurrie*]

spurt (spûrt) *n.* **1** A sudden gush of liquid. **2** Any sudden outbreak, as of anger. **3** An extraordinary effort of brief duration; a sudden rise in activity or price. **4** A brief period. —*v.i.* **1** To come out in a jet; gush forth. **2** To make a sudden and extreme effort. —*v.t.* **3** To force out in a jet; squirt. Also spelled *spirt.* [Var. of earlier *spirt*, metathetic var. of *sprit* <OE *spryttan* come forth]

spur·tle (spûr′təl) *n. Scot.* A stirring stick for porridge.

spur track A short side track connecting with the main track of a railroad. Also **spur.**

spur wheel A toothed wheel having external radial teeth on the periphery; a spur gear.

sput·nik (spo͝ot′nik, sput′-) *n.* A Russian artificial earth satellite: the first to be recorded in world history, called Sputnik I, containing various scientific instruments, was launched October 4, 1957, to an initial height of 560 miles, orbiting at a mean velocity of 18,000 miles per hour. [<Russian, a satellite; lit., that which travels with something else]

sput·ter (sput′ər) *v.i.* **1** To throw off solid or fluid particles in a series of slight explosions. **2** To emit particles of saliva from the mouth, as when speaking excitedly. **3** To speak rapidly or confusedly. —*v.t.* **4** To throw off or emit in small particles. **5** To utter in a confused or excited manner. —*n.* **1** The act or sound of sputtering; especially, excited talk; jabbering. **2** That which is thrown out in sputtering. **3** Trouble; fuss. [Freq. of SPOUT, *v.*] —**sput′ter·er** *n.*

spu·tum (spyo͞o′təm) *n. pl.* **·ta** (-tə) Saliva; spittle; expectorated matter. [<L < *spuere* spit]

Spuy·ten Duy·vil Creek (spīt′n dī′vəl) A narrow stream in New York City, connecting the Hudson and Harlem rivers and separating Manhattan Island from the mainland on the north; used as a ship canal.

spy (spī) *n. pl.* **spies** **1** One who enters an enemy's military lines covertly to get information; a secret agent. **2** One who watches others secretly: often used contemptuously. **3** A peep; glance; hence, an eye. **4** The act of watching secretly. —*v.* **spied, spy·ing** *v.i.* **1** To keep watch closely or secretly; act as a spy. **2** To make careful examination; pry: with *into.* —*v.t.* **3** To observe stealthily and with hostile intent: usually with *out.* **4** To catch sight of; see; espy. **5** To discover by careful or secret investigation: with *out.* **6** To examine or scrutinize carefully. [<OF *espie* < *espier* espy <Gmc.]

Synonyms (noun): emissary, scout. The *scout* and the *spy* are both employed to obtain information of the numbers, movements, etc., of an enemy. The *scout* lurks on the outskirts of the hostile army with such concealment as the case admits of, but without disguise; a *spy* enters in disguise within the enemy's lines. A *scout*, if captured, has the rights of a prisoner of war; a *spy* is held to have forfeited all rights, and is liable, in case of capture, to capital punishment. Soldiers not in disguise or military aviators are not considered *spies,* even while passing through or over hostile territory. An *emissary* is rather political than military, sent to influence opponents secretly rather than to bring information concerning them.

spy·glass (spī′glas′, -gläs′) *n.* A small field glass or telescope.

Spy·ri (shpē′rē), **Johanna,** 1827–1901, *née* Heusser, Swiss author of *Heidi.*

squab (skwob) *n.* **1** A young pigeon, especially when an unfledged nestling. **2** A fat, short person. **3** A soft, stuffed cushion; sofa; ottoman. —*adj.* **1** Fat and short; low and bulky; squat. **2** Unfledged or but half-fledged; half-grown, as a pigeon, or figuratively, any fowl. [<dial. E <Scand. Cf. dial. Norw. *skvabb* a soft, wet mass.]

squab·ble (skwob′əl) *v.* **·bled, ·bling** *v.i.* To engage in a petty wrangle or scuffle; quarrel. —*v.t. Printing* To twist (composed type) so as to mix the lines. —*n.* The act of squabbling; a petty wrangle. See synonyms under QUARREL[1]. [Cf. dial. Sw. *skvabbel* dispute, argue] —**squab′bler** *n.*

squab·by (skwob′ē) *adj.* **·bi·er, ·bi·est** Short and fat. Also **squab′bish.**

squad (skwod) *n.* **1** A small group of persons organized for the performance of a specific function; a small detachment of troops or police; specifically, the smallest tactical unit in the infantry of the U. S. Army. **2** Hence, a team: a football *squad.* —*v.t.* **squad·ded, squad·ding** **1** To form into a squad or squads. **2** To assign to a squad. [<F *escouade* <OF *esquadre* a square <Ital. *squadra* <L *quattuor* four]

squad car An automobile used by police for patrolling, and equipped with radiotelephone for communicating with headquarters.

squad·ron (skwod′rən) *n.* **1** An assemblage of war vessels smaller than a fleet; one of the divisions of a fleet. **2** A division of a cavalry regiment. **3** The basic unit of the United States Air Force, usually consisting of two or more flights operating as a unit. **4** Any regularly arranged or organized body, as of men. —*v.t.* To arrange in a squadron or squadrons. [<Ital. *squadrone,* aug. of *squadra* SQUAD]

squail (skwāl) *n.* A disk used in the game of squails.

squails (skwālz) *n. pl.* A game played with small wooden disks on a table, the object being to approach as nearly as possible to a mark at the center of the board, by snapping the disks from the edge. [Origin uncertain]

squal·id (skwol′id) *adj.* Having a foul, mean, or poverty-stricken appearance; dirty, neglected, and wretched. See synonyms under BASE[2]. [<L *squalidus* < *squalere* be foul] —**squal′id·ly** *adv.* —**squal′id·ness, squa·lid·i·ty** (skwo·lid′ə·tē) *n.*

squall[1] (skwôl) *n.* A loud, screaming outcry. —*v.i.* To cry loudly; scream; bawl. [Cf. ON *skvala* shout, bawl] —**squall′er** *n.*

squall[2] (skwôl) *n.* A sudden, violent burst of wind, often accompanied by rain or snow. —*v.i.* To blow a squall; be squally. [Cf. Sw. *skval-regn* a sudden rainstorm]

squall cloud A grayish cloud rolling beneath an approaching thunderstorm.

squall line *Meteorol.* A cold front characterized along its edge by a sharp change of wind and the occasional formation of line squalls.

squall·y (skwô′lē) *adj.* **squall·i·er, squall·i·est** **1** Stormy; blustering. **2** *Colloq.* Threatening a squall or trouble of any kind.

squal·or (skwol′ər) *n.* The state of being squalid, or the filth of thriftless poverty. [<L < *squalere* be foul]

squa·lus (skwā′ləs) *n.* Any of a genus (*Squalus*) of cartilaginous fishes (class *Chondrichthyes*), including the spiny dogfish or shark (*S. acanthias*) common in shore waters of the Atlantic. [<L, large marine fish]

squa·ma (skwā′mə) *n. pl.* **·mae** (-mē) A thin, scalelike structure; a scale. [<L] —**squa′·mate** (-māt) *adj.*

Squa·ma·ta (skwə·mā′tə) *n. pl.* An order of reptiles, including lizards, chameleons, and serpents. [<NL <L *squama* a scale]

squa·ma·tion (skwə·mā′shən) n. 1 The state of being scaly. 2 The arrangement of epidermal scales.

squa·mo·sal (skwə·mō′səl) adj. 1 Like a scale; squamous. 2 Anat. Relating to the squamous portion of the temporal bone or the analogous bone in lower animals. — n. The squamosal bone.

squa·mous (skwā′məs) adj. 1 Covered with scales; scaly; scalelike. 2 Anat. Designating the vertical plate of the temporal bone. Also **squa′mose** (-mōs). [< L squamosus < squama a scale] — **squa′mous·ly** adv. — **squa′mous·ness** n.

squam·u·lose (skwam′yə·lōs, skwā′myə-) adj. Bot. Provided with small bracts or scales, as a plant; minutely squamate.

squan·der (skwon′dər) v.t. 1 To spend (money, time, etc.) wastefully; lavish profusely; dissipate. 2 Obs. To scatter. — n. Prodigality; the act of squandering. [Cf. dial. E squander scatter] — **squan′der·er** n. — **squan′der·ing·ly** adv.

Synonyms (verb): dissipate, expend, lavish, scatter, spend, waste. Antonyms: economize, hoard, hold, husband, preserve, reserve, save.

squan·tum¹ (skwon′təm) n. Among North American Indians, especially the Narragansets, a spirit or god; an evil spirit.

squan·tum² (skwon′təm) n. In New England, a picnic or shore dinner; a chowder party; hence, any merrymaking or frolic. [from Squantum, Mass., after Tisquantum, a Massachuset chief]

square (skwâr) n. 1 A parallelogram having four equal sides and four right angles. 2 Any object, part, or surface that is square or nearly so, as a pane of glass, or one of the spots on a checkerboard. 3 An instrument by which to measure or lay out right angles, consisting usually of two legs or branches at right angles to each other, in L-shape or T-shape (in the latter case called a T-square). 4 An open area in a city or village, left between streets at their intersection or formed by their expansion. 5 A town or city block; also, the distance between one street and the next. 6 Math. The product of a number or quantity multiplied by itself. 7 Formerly, a body of troops formed in a four-sided array. 8 Obs. A standard or pattern; rule. 9 Slang A person not conversant with developments in the popular arts, especially the latest fashions in jazz, slang, etc. — **on the square** 1 At right angles. 2 On equal terms. 3 Colloq. In a fair and honest manner. 4 In Freemasonry, in good standing: said of members. — **out of square** 1 Not at right angles; obliquely. 2 Incorrectly; askew; out of order. — adj. 1 Having four equal sides and four right angles; loosely, approaching a square in form. 2 Formed with or characterized by a right angle; rectangular. 3 Adapted to forming squares or computing in squares: a square measure. 4 Direct; fair; just; equitable; honest. 5 Having debit and credit balanced; even; settled. 6 Absolute; complete; unequivocal. 7 Having a broad, stocky frame; hence, strong, sturdy. 8 Colloq. Solid; full; satisfying: a square meal. 9 Naut. At right angles to the mast and keel: said of the yards of a square-rigged ship. 10 Math. Raised to the second power; squared: 10 square equals 100. 11 Steady: said of a horse's gait. 12 Mech. Having the cylinder bore equal, or nearly equal, to the piston stroke: said of engines. See synonyms under JUST¹. — v. **squared**, **squar·ing** v.t. 1 To make square; form with four equal sides and four right angles. 2 To shape or adjust so as to form a right angle, or a right angle with something else. 3 To mark with or divide into squares. 4 To test for the purpose of adjusting to a straight line, right angle, or plane surface. 5 To bring to a position suggestive of a right angle: Square your shoulders. 6 To make satisfactory settlement or adjustment of: to square accounts. 7 To make (the score of a game or contest) equal.

8 To cause to conform; adapt; reconcile: to square one's opinions to the times. 9 Math. a To multiply (a number or quantity) by itself. b To determine the contents of in square measure. c To find the square equivalent of: to square a circle. 10 Slang To bribe: to square a jockey. — v.i. 11 To be at right angles. 12 To conform; agree; harmonize. 13 In golf, to make the ·scores equal. 14 Obs. To squabble; quarrel. — **to square away** 1 Naut. To set (the yards) at right angles to the keel. 2 To square up. — **to square off** To assume a position for attack or defense; prepare to fight. — **to square up** To adjust satisfactorily. — adv. 1 So as to be square, or at right angles. 2 Honestly; fairly. 3 Directly; firmly. [< OF esquire, esquarre, ult. < L quattuor four] — **square·ness** n.

square bracket Bracket (def. 4).

square dance Any dance, as a quadrille, in which the couples form sets in squares.

squared circle Colloq. A boxing ring; the prize ring. Also **squared ring**.

square deal Colloq. 1 In card games, an honest deal. 2 Hence, fair or just treatment.

square·head (skwâr′hed′) n. U.S. Slang 1 A Scandinavian. 2 A German.

square knot A common knot, formed of two overhand knots: also called reef knot. See illustration under KNOT.

square league An old Spanish land measure equal to 4,438 acres.

square·ly (skwâr′lē) adv. 1 In a direct or straight manner: He looked her squarely in the eyes. 2 Honestly; fairly. 3 U.S. Plainly; unequivocally. 4 In a square form: squarely built. 5 At right angles (to a line or plane).

square meal Colloq. A full and substantial meal.

square measure A unit or system of units for measuring areas, as in the following table of principal customary standards. See also METRIC SYSTEM.

144 square inches (sq. in.; in²)	= 1 square foot (sq. ft.; ft²)
9 square feet	= 1 square yard (sq. yd.; yd²)
30.25 square yards	= 1 square rod (sq. rd.; rd²)
160 square rods	= 1 acre (A.)
640 acres	= 1 square mile (sq. mi.)

square number See under NUMBER.

square piano See under PIANO¹.

squar·er (skwâr′ər) n. 1 One who squares. 2 Archaic A brawler.

square-rigged (skwâr′rigd′) adj. Naut. Having the principal sails extended by horizontal yards; ship-rigged: distinguished from fore-and-aft-rigged. Compare illustrations under BARK, BRIG, SHIP.

square-rig·ger (skwâr′rig′ər) n. A square-rigged ship.

square root Math. A number or quantity that, multiplied by itself, produces the given number or quantity: 4 is the square root of 16; a second root. See under CUBE¹, ROOT¹.

square sail Naut. A quadrilateral sail usually rigged on a yard set at right angles to the mast.

square shooter Colloq. An upright person; one who acts honestly and justly.

square-toed (skwâr′tōd′) adj. Having the toes square, as the shoes worn by the Puritans; hence, exact; punctilious.

square-toes (skwâr′tōz′) n. An old-fashioned, exact person.

squaring a log Sawing a log so as to give it four equal sides.

squaring the circle Quadrature of the circle.

squar·rose (skwar′-ōs, skwo·rōs′) adj. 1 Biol. Rough with projecting scalelike processes. 2 Bot. Crowded and rigid: squarrose leaves. Also **squar·rous** (skwar′əs). [< L squarrosus scurfy]

SQUARES
a. T-square.
b. Steel square.
c. Try square.

SQUARING A LOG

squash¹ (skwosh) v.t. 1 To beat or press into a pulp or soft mass; crush. 2 To quell or suppress. — v.i. 3 To be smashed or squashed. 4 To make a splashing or sucking sound. — n. 1 A soft or overripe object; also, a crushed mass. 2 The sudden fall of a heavy, soft, or bursting body; also, the sound made by such a fall. 3 The sucking, squelching sound made by walking through ooze or mud. 4 Either of two games played on an indoor court with rackets and a ball. In one (**squash rackets**) a slow rubber ball is used; in the other (**squash tennis**), a livelier, smaller ball. 5 A beverage of which one ingredient is a fruit juice: lemon squash. — adv. With a squelching, oozy sound. [< OF esquasser, ult. < L ex- thoroughly + quassare crush] — **squash′er** n.

squash² (skwosh) n. 1 The edible fruit of various trailing annuals (genus Cucurbita) of the gourd family. 2 The plant that bears it. [< Algonquian. Cf. Massachuset askootasquash, lit., eaten raw.]

squash bug A large, brownish-black, evil-smelling North American hemipterous insect (Anasa tristis) which is destructive to squash vines.

squash·y (skwosh′ē) adj. **squash·i·er**, **squash·i·est** Soft and moist; easily squashed. — **squash′i·ly** adv. — **squash′i·ness** n.

squat (skwot) v. **squat·ted** or **squat**, **squat·ting** v.i. 1 To sit on the heels or hams, or with the legs near the body. 2 To crouch or cower down, as to avoid being seen. 3 To settle on a piece of land without title or payment. 4 To settle on government land in accordance with certain government regulations that will eventually give title. — v.t. 5 To cause (oneself) to squat. — adj. 1 Short and thick; squatty. 2 Being in a squatting position. — n. A squatting attitude or position. [< OF esquatir < es- thoroughly (< L ex-) + quatir press down < L coactus, pp. of cogere force < co- together + agere drive]

squat tag A game of tag in which the players cannot be tagged while squatting.

squat·ter (skwot′ər) n. 1 One who or that which squats; specifically, one who settles on land without permission or right, as on public or unimproved land. 2 In the United States and Australia, one who settles on government land subject to regulations with a view to obtaining title.

squatter sovereignty 1 The political theory that the people or settlers of a Territory had the right to make their own laws, specifically whether or not slavery should be permitted; popular sovereignty. 2 The right of settlers to the lands they have settled.

squat·ty (skwot′ē) adj. Disproportionately short and thick.

squaw (skwô) n. 1 An American Indian woman or wife. 2 Colloq. Any woman or girl. [< Algonquian, woman]

squaw·bush (skwô′bŏŏsh′) n. 1 Any shrub of the genus Cornus; especially, the red-osier dogwood. 2 The cranberry tree.

squaw·fish (skwô′fish′) n. pl. ·fish or ·fish·es 1 A cyprinoid fish (genus Ptychocheilus) found in the rivers of the northern Pacific coast. 2 A surf fish.

squawk (skwôk) v.i. 1 To utter a shrill, harsh cry, as a parrot. 2 Slang To utter loud complaints or protests. — n. 1 The harsh cry of certain birds; also, the act of squawking. 2 Slang A loud protest or complaint. 3 The black-crowned night heron (Nycticorax nycticorax). [Prob. imit.] — **squawk′er** n.

squaw man 1 Among the American Indians, a man who lives and works among the women. 2 A white man married to an Indian woman and in possession of tribal rights on that account.

squaw·root (skwô′rōōt′, -rŏŏt′) n. 1 A yellowish-brown leafless North American herb (Conopholis americana) parasitic on roots. 2 One of certain other plants, as the blue cohosh.

squaw vine The partridgeberry.

squeak (skwēk) n. 1 A thin, sharp, penetrating sound. 2 Colloq. A narrow margin; the least amount; a hairbreadth: in the phrase **a narrow** (or **close**) **squeak**. — v.i. 1 To make a squeak. 2 Colloq. To let out information; squeal. 3 To succeed or otherwise progress

after narrowly averting failure or reversal: He just managed to *squeak* through. —*v.t.* **4** To utter or effect with a squeak. **5** To cause to squeak. [ME *squeke,* prob. <Scand. Cf. Sw. *sqväka* croak.] **—squeak′er** *n.*

squeak·y (skwē′kē) *adj.* **squeak·i·er, squeak·i·est** Making a squeaking noise. **—squeak′i·ly** *adv.* **—squeak′i·ness** *n.*

squeal (skwēl) *v.i.* **1** To utter a sharp, shrill, somewhat prolonged cry. **2** *Slang* To turn informer; betray an accomplice or a plot. —*v.t.* **3** To utter with a squeal. —*n.* A shrill, prolonged cry, as of a pig. [Imit.] **—squeal′er** *n.*

squeam·ish (skwē′mish) *adj.* **1** Easily disgusted or shocked; unduly scrupulous. **2** Easily nauseated. [<earlier *squeamous* <AF *escoymous;* ult. origin unknown] **—squeam′ish·ly** *adv.* **—squeam′ish·ness** *n.*

Synonyms: affected, dainty, difficult, fastidious, finical, foolish, hypercritical, overnice, oversensitive, particular, prudish, qualmish, scrupulous, sickish.

squee·gee (skwē′jē) *n.* **1** A wooden implement having a stout straight-edged strip of rubber or leather inserted in its blade, used for removing water from wet decks or floors, window panes, etc. **2** *Phot.* A smaller similar implement, made in the same way or in the form of a roller, used for pressing a film closer to its mount, or for squeezing the moisture from a print. —*v.t.* **1** To smooth down, as a photographic film, with a squeegee. **2** To cleanse with a squeegee. Also spelled *squilgee, squillagee.* [<*squeege,* var. of SQUEEZE]

squeeze (skwēz) *v.* **squeezed, squeez·ing** *v.t.* **1** To press hard upon; compress. **2** To extract something from by pressure: to *squeeze* oranges. **3** To draw forth by pressure; express: to *squeeze* juice from apples. **4** To force or push; cram. **5** To oppress, as with burdensome taxes. **6** To exert pressure upon (someone) to act as one desires, as by blackmailing. **7** To take a squeeze (def. 4) of. —*v.i.* **8** To apply pressure. **9** To force one's way; push: with *in, through,* etc. **10** To be pressed; yield to pressure: These lemons *squeeze* well. See synonyms under JAM[1]. **—to squeeze out** To force out of business, or ruin financially, by unscrupulous methods. —*n.* **1** The act or process of squeezing; pressure. **2** A firm grasp of someone's hand; a hearty handclasp; also, an embrace; hug. **3** Something, as juice, extracted or expressed. **4** A facsimile, as of a coin or inscription, produced by pressing some soft substance upon it. **5** *Colloq.* A crowded social gathering. **6** *Colloq.* Pressure exerted for the extortion of money or favors; also, financial pressure. [? <OF *es-* thoroughly (<L *ex-*) + ME *queisen,* OE *cwēsan* crush]**—squeez′a·ble** *adj.*

squeeze play In baseball, a play in which the batter bunts the ball so that a man on third base may score by starting while the pitcher is about to deliver the ball.

squeez·er (skwē′zər) *n.* One who or that which squeezes; especially, a mechanical device for applying pressure on fruit.

squeez·ing (skwē′zing) *n.* **1** The act or process of squeezing. **2** *Often pl.* That which is squeezed out. **3** A crowding together.

squelch (skwelch) *v.t.* **1** To crush; squash. **2** *Colloq.* To subdue utterly; silence, as with a crushing reply. —*v.i.* **3** To make a splashing or sucking noise, as when walking in deep mud. **4** To walk with such a sound. —*n.* **1** A noise made when walking in wet boots. **2** A heavy fall or blow. **3** *Colloq.* A squelcher. [Prob. imit.]

squelch·er (skwel′chər) *n.* **1** One who or that which squelches. **2** *Colloq.* A silencing retort; crushing reply.

sque·teague (skwi·tēg′) *n.* A weakfish. [<Algonquian (Narraganset) *pesukwiteaug* they make glue]

squib (skwib) *n.* **1** A roll or case filled with gunpowder, to be thrown or rolled swiftly, finally exploding like a rocket. **2** A tubular case filled with gunpowder and connected with an electric circuit, used for firing a charge in a blasthole, igniting a smokepot, or the like. **3** A broken firecracker that burns with a spitting sound. **4** A short speech or writing in a witty or satirical vein; a mild lampoon. **5** An undistinguished or petty person. —*v.* **squibbed, squib·bing** *v.i.* **1** To write or use squibs. **2** To fire a squib. **3** To explode or sound like a squib. **4** To move quickly or restlessly. —*v.t* **5** To attack with squibs; lampoon. **6** To fire or use as a squib. [Origin unknown]

squid (skwid) *n. pl.* **squid** or **squids** Any of various predaceous marine cephalopod mollusks having a long, slender body, ten tentacles, a vestigial internal shell, and an ink sac. Some species are esteemed as food. —*v.i.* **squid·ded, squid·ding** *Aeron.* to assume a narrow, squidlike shape, as a parachute under excess wind or air pressure. [Origin uncertain]

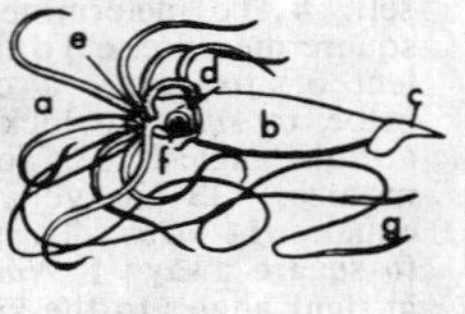

SQUID
a. Arm. *b.* Body. *c.* Fluke. *d.* Eye. *e.* Mouth. *f.* Siphon. *g.* Tentacles.

squig·gle (skwig′əl) *Colloq. n.* A meaningless scrawl. —*v.i.* To wriggle. [Blend of SQUIRM and WRIGGLE]

squil·gee (skwil′jē, skwil·jē′) See SQUEEGEE.

squill[1] (skwil) *n.* **1** A bulbous plant *(Urginea maritima)* of the lily family, growing in the Mediterranean region; the sea onion. **2** Its bulb, dried and sliced, the white variety having diuretic and expectorant properties, and the red variety yielding a rat poison. **3** Any plant of the genus *Scilla,* the more common ones usually called by some other name, as the common English bluebell or wild hyacinth. [<L *squilla* <Gk. *skilla* sea onion]

squill[2] (skwil) *n.* Any of a genus *(Squilla)* of burrowing crustaceans having the form and appearance of a mantis: sometimes called *mantis shrimp.* Also **squil·la** (skwil′ə). [<L *squilla* shrimp]

squil·la·gee (skwil′ə·jē) See SQUEEGEE.

squinch (skwinch) *n.* *Archit.* A small stone arch or series of arches, or of projecting courses, across an interior angle of a square tower, to support an oblique side of an octagonal spire or lantern. [Alter. of obs. *scunch,* abbreviation of *scuncheon* <OF *escoinson*]

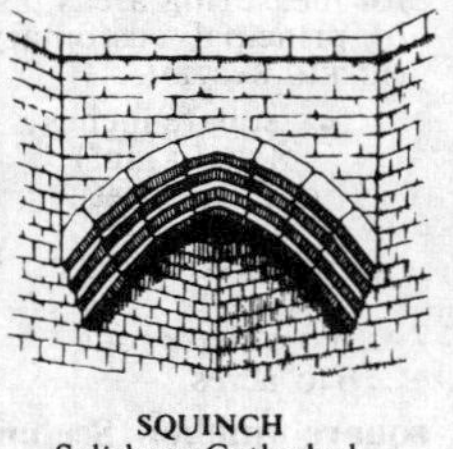

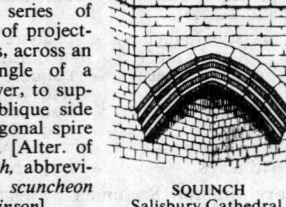

SQUINCH
Salisbury Cathedral, England.

squin·ny (skwin′ē) *v.i.* & *n. Obs.* Squint. Also **squin′y.** [Var. of SQUINT]

squint (skwint) *v.i.* **1** To look with half-closed eyes, as into bright light. **2** To look with a side glance; look askance. **3** To be cross-eyed. **4** To incline or tend: with *toward,* etc. —*v.t.* **5** To hold (the eyes) half shut, as in glaring light. **6** To cause to squint. —*adj.* **1** Having the optic axes not coincident; affected with strabismus: said of the eyes. **2** Looking obliquely or askance; indirect. —*n.* **1** *Pathol.* An affection of the eyes in which their axes are differently directed; strabismus. **2** The act or habit of squinting. **3** Hence, an indirect leaning, tendency, or drift. **4** A hagioscope. [Origin uncertain] **—squint′er** *n.*

squint-eye (skwint′ī′) *n.* Strabismus, or one afflicted with it.

squint-eyed (skwint′īd′) *adj.* **1** Affected with strabismus; cross-eyed. **2** Looking sidewise; aiming in two directions. **3** Apt to see awry; malignant; evil.

squire (skwīr) *n.* **1** A knight's attendant; an armorbearer. **2** A title of dignity, office, or courtesy ranking in England below that of *knight,* and applied in the United States especially to rural or village lawyers and justices of the peace; also, in England, a landed proprietor. **3** A gentleman who acts as the escort of a lady in public; a gallant. —*v.t.* & *v.i.* **squired, squir·ing** To attend or serve (someone) as a squire or escort. [Aphetic var. of ESQUIRE]

squire·ar·chy (skwīr′är·kē) *n. pl.* **·chies** **1** English country gentleman collectively; also, any body of squires. **2** Government by squires. Also **squir′ar·chy.**

squire·ling (skwīr′ling) *n.* A petty squire. Also **squire′let** (-lit).

squirm (skwûrm) *v.i.* **1** To bend and twist the body; wriggle; writhe. **2** To show signs of pain or distress. —*n.* A squirming motion; a wriggle. [Origin uncertain] **—squirm′er** *n.* **—squirm′y** *adj.*

squir·rel (skwûr′əl, *Brit.* skwir′əl) *n.* **1** Any of various slender rodents (family *Sciuridae*) with a very long bushy tail, living mainly in trees and feeding chiefly on nuts, but occasionally on eggs and small birds. The **red squirrel** *(Sciurus hudsonicus),* the **gray squirrel** *(S. carolinensis),* and the **fox squirrel** *(S. niger)* are North American types. ◆ Collateral adjective: *sciurine.* **2** One of various sciuroid rodents, as the **rock squirrel** *(Otospermophilus grammurus)* of the western United States. **3** The fur of a squirrel. [<Of *esquireul* <LL *scurellus,* dim. of L *sciurus* <Gk. *skiouros* <*skia* shadow + *oura* tail]

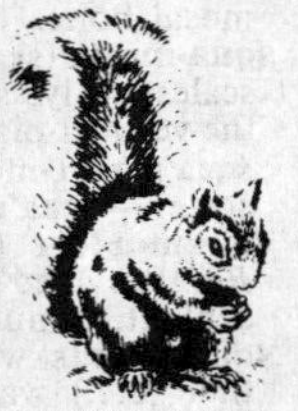

GRAY SQUIRREL
(Body to 10 inches; tail to 8 inches)

squirrel corn A smooth and delicate plant *(Dicentra canadensis)* of the northern United States, having white or cream-colored flowers with the spurs rounded and yellow tubers resembling grains of corn.

squirrel glider A flying phalanger *(Petaurus norfolcensis)* of Australia.

squirrel monkey A marmoset.

squirt (skwûrt) *v.i.* **1** To come forth in a thin stream or jet; spurt out. **2** To eject water, etc., thus. —*v.t.* **3** To eject (water or other liquid) forcibly and in a jet. **4** To wet or bespatter with a squirt or squirts. —*n.* **1** The act of squirting or spurting; also, a jet of liquid squirted forth. **2** A syringe or squirt gun. **3** *Colloq.* A conceited, brainless fellow. [Cf. LG *swirtjen*] **—squirt′er** *n.*

squirt gun An instrument or toy shaped like a gun and used for squirting.

squirting cucumber The fruit of a procumbent branching herb *(Ecballium elaterium)* of the gourd family, which, when ripe, ejects its seeds and juice.

squish (skwish) *v.t.* & *v.i. Colloq.* To squash. **—***n.* A squashing sound. [Var. of SQUASH[1]] **—squish′y** *adj.*

Sr *Chem.* Strontium (symbol Sr).

Sri·nag·ar (srē·nug′ər) The capital of Jammu and Kashmir State, NW India; site of extensive eighth century Buddhist ruins.

St. For entries not found under *St.,* see under SAINT.

-st See -EST[2].

stab (stab) *v.* **stabbed, stab·bing** *v.t.* **1** To pierce with a pointed weapon; wound, as with a dagger. **2** To thrust (a dagger, etc.), as into a body. **3** To penetrate; pierce. —*v.i.* **4** To thrust or lunge with a knife, sword, etc. **5** To inflict a wound thus. See synonyms under PIERCE. —*n.* A thrust made with any pointed weapon. [? <Irish *stob* push, thrust, fix a stake <*stob* a stake] **—stab′ber** *n.*

Sta·bat Ma·ter (stä′bät mä′tər, stā′bat mā′tər) *Latin* A 13th century hymn commemorating the agony of Mary at the crucifixion of Christ and so called from its opening words: literally, the mother was standing.

sta·bile (stā′bil, stab′il) *adj.* **1** Not kept in motion. **2** *Med.* **a** Not affected by moderate heat. **b** Denoting a form of electrotherapy in which one of the electrodes is kept stationary on a part. Compare LABILE. —*n.* An amorphous piece of stationary sculpture. Compare MOBILE. [<L *stabilis.* See STABLE[1].]

sta·bil·i·ty (stə·bil′ə·tē) *n. pl.* **·ties** **1** The condition of being stable; steadiness. **2** The quality or character of being steady or constant; steadfastness of purpose or resolution. **3** *Physics* The state of being in stable equilibrium, or the degree of such equilibrium as measured by the force with which a body tends to maintain its condition of rest or steady motion. **4** *Aeron.* The ability of an aircraft to resume equilibrium when disturbed. **5** A vow to continue in the same profession and order, taken by some Benedictine monks. **6** *Obs.* Rigidity: opposed to *fluidity.* [<L *stabilitas, -tatis* <*stabilis.* <*stare* stand. See STABLE[1].]

sta·bi·lize (stā′bə·līz) *v.t.* **·lized, ·liz·ing** **1** To make firm or stable. **2** To keep steady; keep from fluctuating, as money or currency: to *stabilize* prices. **3** *Aeron.* To secure or maintain the equilibrium of (an aircraft) by means of fixed surfaces, gyroscopes, etc. [<L

stabilis steady + -IZE] **— sta′bi·li·za′tion** *n.*
sta·bi·liz·er (stā′bə·lī′zər) *n.* **1** *Aeron.* An automatic balancing device; especially, one which steadies the flight of an airplane. See illustration under AIRPLANE. **2** *Chem.* A substance which increases the stability of another substance or compound, especially one which reduces the spontaneous combustion of an explosive.
sta·ble[1] (stā′bəl) *adj.* **1** Standing firmly in place; not easily moved, shaken, or overthrown; fixed. **2** Marked by fixity of purpose; steadfast; inflexible. **3** Having durability or permanence; abiding. **4** *Chem.* Not easily decomposed: said of compounds. **5** *Physics* Resisting forces which tend to cause or distort motion. See synonyms under FIRM, PERMANENT. [<F <L *stabilis* < *stare* stand] **— sta′bly** *adv.* **— sta′ble·ness** *n.*
sta·ble[2] (stā′bəl) *n.* **1** A building set apart for lodging and feeding horses or cattle. **2** Specifically, race horses belonging to a particular stable; also, the owner and personnel of a particular stable collectively. **—** *v.t.* & *v.i.* **·bled, ·bling** To put or lodge in a stable. [<OF *estable* <L *stabulum* < *stare* stand]
sta·ble·boy (stā′bəl·boi′) *n.* A boy employed in a stable.
sta·ble·man (stā′bəl·man′, -mən) *n. pl.* **·men** (-men′, -mən) One who works in a stable; a hostler; groom.
sta·bling (stā′bling) *n.* **1** The act of one who stables. **2** Room or accommodation in a stable.
stab·lish (stab′lish) *v.t. Archaic* To establish. [Aphetic var. of ESTABLISH]
stac·ca·to (stə·kä′tō) *adj.* **1** *Music* Played, or to be played, in an abrupt, disconnected manner: opposed to *legato.* **2** Marked by abrupt, sharp emphasis: a *staccato* style of speaking. [<Ital., pp. of *staccare* detach]
stack (stak) *n.* **1** A large, orderly pile of unthreshed grain, hay, or straw, usually conical. **2** Any systematic pile or heap, as a pile of poker chips purchased or won by a player. **3** A group of rifles (usually three) set upright and supporting one another. **4** A case composed of several rows of bookshelves one above the other. **5** *pl.* That part of a library where most of the books are shelved. **6** A vertical main smoke flue, especially of a furnace or boiler; a chimney; smokestack; also, a collection of such chimneys or flues. **7** *Brit.* A measure of fuel (coal or wood), equal to 108 cubic feet or 4 cubic yards. **8** *Colloq.* A great amount; plenty. **—** *v.t.* To gather or place in a pile; pile up in a stack: to *stack* arms; to *stack* firewood. **— to stack the cards** **1** To arrange cards in the pack in a manner favorable to the dealer. **2** To have an unfair advantage secured beforehand. [<ON *stakkr*]
stack·er[1] (stak′ər) *n. Agric.* An attachment or apparatus for depositing straw from a threshing machine on a wagon or on a stack.
stack·er[2] (stak′ər) *v.* & *n. Scot.* Stagger.
stac·te (stak′tē) *n.* One of the spices, of uncertain composition, anciently used by the Jews in preparing incense. *Ex.* xxx 34. [<L, oil of myrrh <Gk. *staktē* < *stazein* drip]
stac·tom·e·ter (stak·tom′ə·tər) *n.* A tube having a minute orifice in one end, for measuring a liquid in drops: also called *stalagmometer.* [<Gk. *staktos* trickling + -METER]
stad·dle (stad′l) *n. Brit. Dial.* **1** Anything that serves as a foundation or support; a prop; staff; crutch. **2** *Agric.* A raised platform or frame, or an arrangement of short posts, for a stack of hay or straw, to keep it dry and free from vermin. [OE *stathol* base]
stad·hold·er (stad′hōl·dər) *n.* Formerly, a viceroy or governor of a province or town of the Netherlands as the representative of the sovereign; specifically, the chief magistrate of the Netherlands, a hereditary office in the family of the princes of Orange. Also **stadt′·hold·er** (stat′-). [<Du. *stadhouder* lieutenant < *stad* place + *houder* holder]
sta·di·a (stā′dē·ə) *n.* **1** A temporary surveying station. **2** A form of sighting instrument for measuring distances used in connection with a vertical graduated rod (**stadia rod**). **3** The rod alone or the method of using it. [Prob. <F *stade* a stage, a measure of length <L *stadium.* See STADIUM.]
sta·di·um (stā′dē·əm) *n. pl.* **·di·a** (-dē·ə), *for def.* **2 ·di·ums** **1** In ancient Greece, a course for footraces, with banked seats for spectators, as at Olympia and Athens, where games were held. **2** A similar modern structure in which athletic games are played: the *stadium* at Harvard. **3** An ancient Greek measure of length, equaling 606.75 feet. **4** A degree of progress or development. **5** *Med.* A given stage or period in the course of a disease. [<L <Gk. *stadion,* a measure of length]
Staël (stäl), **Madame de,** 1766–1817, Baronne de Staël-Holstein, *née* Anne Louise Germaine Necker, French writer; famous for her salon.
staff[1] (staf, stäf) *n. pl.* **staves** (stāvz) or **staffs** *for defs. 1–3,* **staffs** *for defs. 4–6.* **1** A stick or piece of wood carried for some special purpose, as an aid in walking or climbing, or as a cudgel or weapon, or as an emblem of authority. **2** A shaft or pole that forms a support or handle: the *staff* of a spear; a *flagstaff.* **3** A stick used in measuring or testing, as a surveyors' leveling rod. **4** *Mil.* **a** A body of officers not having command but attached in an executive or advisory capacity to an army or navy unit as assistants to the officer in command. The central body is known as the **general staff.** **b** The personnel of a military establishment, as the officers in charge of construction, ordnance, repairs, equipment, provisions, medicine and surgery, the paymasters, and engineers. **5** A body of persons associated in carrying out some special enterprise under the supervision of a manager or chief: the editorial *staff* of a newspaper. **6** *Music* The combined lines and spaces used to represent the pitches of tones. The staff has always five long horizontal lines and the accompanying long spaces, but is enlarged as the occasion may require, by short lines above or below and the short spaces they bring. See synonyms under STICK. **—** *v.t.* To provide (an office, etc.) with a staff: to *staff* a management group. [OE *stæf* stick]
staff[2] (staf, stäf) *n.* A composition of plaster, fiber, etc., for temporary buildings, statues, etc. [Prob. <G *staffieren* fill, decorate]
Staf·fa (staf′ə) An islet of the Inner Hebrides group, NW Argyll, Scotland, on which is Fingal's Cave.
staff officer An officer serving on a staff.
Staf·ford (staf′ərd) A county in west central England; 1,153 square miles; county town, Stafford. Also **Staf′ford·shire** (-shir). Shortened form **Staffs.**
stag (stag) *n.* **1** The male of the red deer *(Cervus elaphus),* especially the matured male. **2** The male of other large deer, as the caribou, and of certain other animals. **3** A castrated bull or boar. **4** *Scot.* A colt: also spelled *staig.* **5** *U.S. Slang* A man, especially when not in the company of women. **6** *U.S. Slang* A social gathering for men only. **—** *adj. U.S. Slang* Of or for men only: a *stag* party. **—** *v.i.* **stagged, stag·ging** *Slang* **1** *Brit.* To turn informer; squeal. **2** *U.S.* To attend a social affair unaccompanied by a woman. [OE *stagga*]

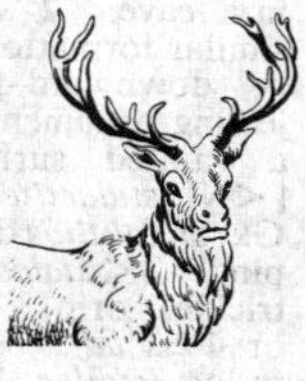

STAG HEAD
Showing antlers.

stag beetle A large, lamellicorn beetle (family *Lucanidae*), the male of which has the jaws enormously developed and branched like the antlers of a stag; specifically, the European *Lucanus cervus* and the American *L. dama:* also called *pinchbug.* They are injurious to trees.
stage (stāj) *n.* **1** The raised platform, with its scenery and mechanical appliances, on which the performance in a theater or hall takes place. **2** The theater. **3** The drama. **4** The dramatic profession. **5** The field or plan of action of some notable event: to set the *stage* for a counter-offensive. **6** A definite portion of a journey. **7** The distance traveled between two stopping points. **8** One of the regular stopping places on the route of a stagecoach or postrider. **9** A stagecoach. **10** A step in some development, progress, or process. **11** *Med.* A definite period in the course of a disease, characterized by a certain group of symptoms. **12** *Biol.* Any of the periods of growth in animals or plants: the larval *stage* of insects. **13** *Electronics* One of the radio elements in cascade amplification. **14** A water level: The river rose to flood *stage.* **15** A horizontal section or story of a building. **16** An elevated platform or scaffold for the use of workmen. **17** The horizontal shelf on a microscope which supports the slide or object to be examined. **18** Any raised platform or floor. **19** *Geol.* The stratigraphic subdivision next below a series, corresponding to an *age* in the time scale. **20** *Aerospace* One of the separate propulsion units of a rocket vehicle. Each becomes operational after the preceding one reaches burnout and is jettisoned. **—** *v.t.* **staged, stag·ing** **1** To put or exhibit on the stage. **2** To plan, conduct, or carry out: to *stage* a rally. **3** To organize, perform, or carry out so as to appear authentic, legitimate, or spontaneous when actually not so: The entire incident was *staged* for the benefit of press photographers. [<OF *estage,* ult. <L *status,* pp. of *stare* stand]
stage·coach (stāj′kōch′) *n.* A large four-wheeled vehicle having a regular route from town to town.
stage·craft (stāj′kraft′, -kräft′) *n.* Skill in writing or staging plays.
stage door A door to a theater used by actors and stagehands which leads to the stage or behind the scenes.
stage-door Johnny (stāj′dôr′) *U.S. Slang* A man who frequents stage doors seeking the companionship of actresses.
stage·hand (stāj′hand′) *n.* A worker in a theater who handles scenery and props, etc.
stage-man·age (stāj′man′ij) *v.t.* **·aged, ·ag·ing** **1** To be a stage manager for. **2** To plan, organize, or direct, especially so as to create a desired impression.
stage manager One who superintends the stage during the production of a play.
stag·er (stā′jər) *n.* **1** One who has had long experience at anything; an old hand: often **old stager.** **2** *Archaic* An actor.
stage-set·ting (stāj′set′ing) *n.* **1** The scene or background of a stage presentation. **2** The act of arranging scenery.
stage-struck (stāj′struk′) *adj.* Possessed of the idea of becoming an actor or an actress; enamored of theatrical life.
stage whisper A loud whisper, as one uttered on the stage for the audience to hear.
stag·fla·tion (stag′flā′shən) *n. Econ.* Inflation combined with abnormally slow economic growth, resulting in high unemployment. [<STAG(NATION) + (IN)FLATION)]
stage·y (stā′jē) See STAGY.
stag·gard (stag′ərd) *n.* The male of the red deer in its fourth year. Also **stag′gart** (-ərt). [<STAG + -ARD]
stag·ger (stag′ər) *v.i.* **1** To move unsteadily; totter; reel. **2** To begin to give way; become less confident or resolute; waver; hesitate. **—** *v.t.* **3** To cause to stagger. **4** To affect strongly; overwhelm, as with surprise or grief. **5** To place in alternating rows or groups. **6** To arrange so as to prevent congestion or confusion, as by distributing: to *stagger* lunch hours. **7** *Aeron.* To adjust (two surfaces, as the wings of a biplane) so that the edge of one extends beyond the other. **—** *n.* **1** The act of staggering; a reeling motion. See STAGGERS. **2** *Aeron.* The amount of advance of the leading edge of one wing of a biplane over that of the other. [< obs. *stacker* <ON *stakra*] **— stag′ger·er** *n.* **— stag′ger·ing·ly** *adv.*
stag·ger·bush (stag′ər·bo͝osh′) *n.* A shrub *(Lyonia mariana),* 2 to 4 feet high, with white or pale-red flowers, common to Tennessee and the North Atlantic seaboard: poisonous to stock.
stag·gers (stag′ərz) *n. pl. (construed as singular)* **1** Any of various diseases of domestic animals, as horses, characterized by vertigo, staggering, and sudden falling, due to disorder of the brain and spinal cord: also called *blind staggers.* **2** A giddy sensation.

stag·hound (stag′hound′) *n.* One of a breed of nearly extinct, large hounds, somewhat resembling the foxhound, formerly used for hunting deer, wolves, etc.: also called *buckhound, deerhound.*

stag·ing (stā′jing) *n.* **1** A scaffolding or temporary platform. **2** The act of putting a play upon the stage. **3** The business of driving or running stagecoaches; also, traveling by stagecoach.

Sta·gi·ra (stə·jī′rə) A city of ancient Macedonia, on the Chalcidice peninsula, NE Greece, near the Strymonic Gulf; birthplace of Aristotle. Also **Sta·gi·rus** (stə·jī′rəs).

Stag·i·rite (staj′ə·rīt) *n.* A native of Stagira; specifically, Aristotle. —*adj.* Of or pertaining to Stagira; also, Aristotelian.

stag·nant (stag′nənt) *adj.* **1** Standing still; not flowing: said of water, as in a pool; hence, foul from long standing. **2** Lacking briskness or activity, as life or business; dull; inert; sluggish. [<F <L *stagnans, -antis,* pp. of *stagnare* stagnate <*stagnum* a pool] —**stag′nan·cy** *n.* —**stag′nant·ly** *adv.*

stag·nate (stag′nāt) *v.i.* **·nat·ed, ·nat·ing** **1** To be or become stagnant. **2** To become dull or inert. [<L *stagnatus,* pp. of *stagnare.* See STAGNANT.]

stag·na·tion (stag·nā′shən) *n.* **1** The condition of being stagnant: the *stagnation* of water; *stagnation* in trade. **2** *Physiol.* Accumulation and retardation of a circulating fluid in the body.

St. Agnes' Eve The evening of January 20th, when, by old superstition, a girl might have prevision of her future husband. Also **St. Agnes's Eve.**

stag·y (stā′jē) *adj.* **stag·i·er, stag·i·est** Having a theatrical manner; of or suited to the stage. Also spelled *stagey.* —**stag′i·ly** *adv.* —**stag′i·ness** *n.*

staid (stād) *adj.* Fixed; steady and sober; sedate. See synonyms under SOBER, SEDATE. [Orig. pt. and pp. of STAY[1]] —**staid′ly** *adv.* —**staid′ness** *n.*

staig (stag) See STAG (def. 4).

stain (stān) *n.* **1** A discoloration from foreign matter; a spot; smirch; blot. **2** The act of discoloring, or the state of being discolored. **3** A dye or thin pigment used in staining. **4** A chemical reagent for coloring microscopic specimens. **5** A moral taint; tarnish. [<*v.*] —*v.t.* **1** To make a stain upon; discolor; soil. **2** To color by the use of a dye or stain. **3** To bring a moral stain upon; blemish. **4** To impregnate, as a microscopic specimen, with a substance whose reaction colors some part without affecting others, thus rendering form or structure visible. —*v.i.* **5** To take or impart a stain. [Aphetic var. of DISTAIN] —**stain′a·ble** *adj.* —**stain′er** *n.* —**stain′less** *adj.* —**stain′less·ly** *adv.*

Synonyms (verb): blot, color, discolor, disgrace, dishonor, dye, soil, spot, sully, tarnish, tinge, tint. To *color* is to impart a color desired or undesired, temporary or permanent, or, in the intransitive use, to assume a color in any way. To *dye* is to impart a color intentionally and with a view to permanence, and especially so as to pervade the substance or fiber of that to which it is applied. To *stain* is primarily to *discolor,* to impart a color undesired and perhaps unintended, and which may or may not be permanent. *Stain* is, however, used of giving an intended and perhaps pleasing color to wood, glass, etc., by an application of coloring matter which enters the substance a little below the surface, in distinction from painting, in which coloring matter is spread upon the surface; *dyeing* is generally said of wool, yarn, cloth, or similar materials which are dipped into the *coloring* liquid. To *tinge* is to *color* slightly. It may be used of giving a slight flavor, or a slight admixture of one ingredient or quality with another that is more pronounced. See BLEMISH, DEFILE[1], POLLUTE. Compare FOUL.

stained glass See under GLASS.

stainless steel A steel alloy made resistant to corrosion and atmospheric influences by the addition of from 10 to 30 percent chromium, and other ingredients.

stair (stâr) *n.* **1** A step, or one of a series of steps, for mounting or descending from one level to another. **2** A series of steps: usually in the plural. ◆ Homophone: *stare.* [OE *stǣger*]

stair·case (stâr′kās′) *n.* A flight or set of stairs, usually from one floor to another, complete with the supports, balusters, etc.

stair·head (stâr′hed′) *n.* The top of a staircase.

stair·way (stâr′wā′) *n.* A flight of stairs.

stair·well (stâr′wel′) *n.* A vertical shaft enclosing a staircase.

stake (stāk) *n.* **1** A stick or post, as of wood sharpened for driving into the ground: used as a boundary mark, sign of ownership, to support the rails of a fence, etc. **2** A post to which a person is bound to be burned alive; hence, death by burning at the stake. **3** An upright, set in a socket at the edge of the floor of a car or wagon, to confine loose material. **4** Something wagered or risked, as the money bet on a race. **5** A prize in a contest: sometimes in the plural. **6** An interest in an enterprise; contingent gain or loss. **7** An organizational unit of the Mormon Church, consisting of several wards. **8** A grubstake. —**at stake** In hazard or jeopardy; in question: My whole future was *at stake.* —**to pull up stakes** To wind up one's business in a place and move on; move out. —*v.t.* **staked, stak·ing** **1** To fasten or support by means of a stake; tether to a stake. **2** To mark the boundaries of with stakes: often with *off* or *out.* **3** *Colloq.* To put at hazard; wager; risk. **4** *Colloq.* To grubstake; also, to supply with working capital; finance. ◆ Homophone: *steak.* [OE *staca*]

stake-and-rid·er (stāk′ən·rī′dər) *n.* A split rail fence having the ends of the rails or riders laid at an angle across each other and supported by pairs of stakes: also called *snake fence.* —**staked′-and-rid′ered** *adj.*

Staked Plain See LLANO ESTACADO.

Sta·kha·no·vism (stä·khä′no·viz′əm) *n.* The efficiency system of Stakhanovite competition and awards. [after Aleksei G. *Stakhanov,* a Russian miner who originated it in 1935]

Sta·kha·no·vite (stä·khä′no·vīt) *n.* In the U.S.S.R., a worker awarded special privileges and bonuses for having displayed marked efficiency and initiative.

sta·lac·ti·form (stə·lak′tə·fôrm) *adj.* Resembling or having the form of a stalactite.

sta·lac·tite (stə·lak′tīt) *n.* **1** An elongated, downward-hanging form in which certain minerals, especially calcium carbonate, are sometimes deposited by slow dripping, as in a cave. **2** Any similar formation. **3** A downward-projecting ornament of a vaulted surface. [<NL *stalactites* <Gk. *stalaktitos* dripping <*stalassein* trickle, drip] —**stal·ac·tit·ic** (stal′ək·tit′ik) or **·i·cal** *adj.*

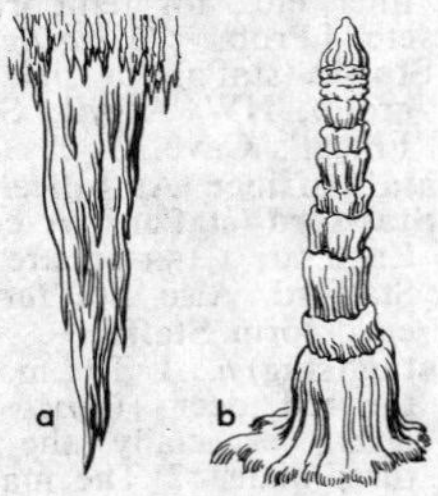

STALACTITE (*a*)
STALAGMITE (*b*)

sta·lag (stal′ag, *Ger.* shtä′läkh) *n.* A German prison camp for captured enlisted men. [<G, contraction of *stammlager* <*stamm* base + *lager* camp]

sta·lag·mite (stə·lag′mīt) *n.* **1** An incrustation, usually cylindrical, or conical, on the floor of a cavern: the counterpart of a stalactite, often fusing with it into the stalactite column. **2** Any similar formation. [<NL *stalagmites* <Gk. *stalagmos* a dripping <*stalassein* drip] —**stal·ag·mit·ic** (stal′əg·mit′ik) or **·i·cal** *adj.*

stal·ag·mom·e·ter (stal′əg·mom′ə·tər) *n.* A stactometer.

St. Al·bans (sānt′ ôl′bənz) A city in southern Hertfordshire, England: scene of a Yorkist victory in the Wars of the Roses, 1455; site of one of the oldest inhabited houses in England: Roman *Verulamium.*

stale[1] (stāl) *adj.* **1** Having lost freshness; slightly changed or deteriorated by standing, as air, vapid wine or beer, old bread, etc. **2** Lacking in interest from age or familiarity; worn out; trite: a *stale* joke. **3** In poor condition from prolonged activity, as from overstudy or, in athletics, from overtraining: especially in the phrase **gone stale.** **4** Inactive; dull: said of a stock market after a period of overactivity. **5** *Law* In courts of equity, impaired in legal force, due to long neglect in pressing or asserting a claim or to a change in the condition or situation of the parties. See synonyms under TRITE. —*v.i.* **staled, stal·ing** To become stale or trite. [Origin uncertain] —**stale′ly** *adv.* —**stale′ness** *n.*

stale[2] (stāl) *n.* The urine of cattle or horses. —*v.i.* **staled, stal·ing** To urinate: said of horses and cattle. [Prob. <MLG *stal* horse urine]

stale[3] (stāl) *n. Obs.* **1** A prostitute; drab. **2** A snare; trap. **3** Concealment; stealth; also, theft. [? <AF *estale, estal* a decoy]

stale·mate (stāl′māt′) *n.* **1** In chess, a position in which a player, not in check, can make no move without putting his king in check. The result is a drawn game. **2** Hence, any tie or deadlock. —*v.t.* **·mat·ed, ·mat·ing** **1** To put into a condition of stalemate. **2** To bring to a standstill. [<AF *estale* a fixed position + MATE[2]]

Sta·lin (stä′lin, -lēn) **1** See VARNA. **2** A city in Transylvania, central Rumania: Rumanian *Brașov,* German *Kronstadt.* **3** See STALINO.

Sta·lin (stä′lin, -lēn), **Joseph,** 1879–1953, U.S.S.R. statesman: real name *Iosif Dzhugashvili.*

Sta·li·na·bad (stä′lyi·nä·bät′) The capital of Tadzhik S.S.R., in the eastern part: formerly *Dyushambe.*

Sta·lin·grad (stä′lin·grad, *Russian* stä′lyin·grät′) A city on the lower Volga in SE European Russian S.F.S.R.; scene of a battle and ultimate Russian victory over German forces in World War II, Sept., 1942, to Jan., 1943: formerly *Tsaritsyn.*

Sta·li·ni·ri (stä′lyi·nyē′rē) The capital of the South Ossetian Autonomous Region, north central Georgian S.S.R. Formerly **Tskhin·va·li** (tskhin′vä·lē).

Sta·lin·ism (stä′lin·iz′əm) *n.* The doctrines or practices of Stalin; especially, communism involving a rigid implementation of government policy, through coercion, intimidation, and ruthless suppression of opposition, and characterized by ardent patriotism focused upon the Soviet Union and its leader. —**Sta′lin·ist** *n.*

Sta·li·no (stä′lyi·no) A city in the Donbas in SE Ukrainian S.S.R.: formerly *Yuzovka*: also *Stalin.*

Stalin Peak **1** The highest peak of the Carpathians and of Czechoslovakia; 8,737 feet: formerly *Gerlachovka.* **2** The highest point in the U.S.S.R., in SE Tadzhik S.S.R.; 24,590 feet: formerly *Garmo Peak.* **3** The highest peak of the Rhodope Mountains and of Bulgaria, in SW Bulgaria: formerly *Mus Allah.*

Sta·linsk (stä′lyinsk) A city on the Tom river in SW Asiatic Russian S.F.S.R.: formerly *Novo Kuznetsk.*

stalk[1] (stôk) *n.* The stem or axis of a plant, especially when herbaceous. **2** Any support on which an organ is borne, as a pedicel. **3** A supporting part or stem: the jointed *stalk* of a sea lily, the *stalk* of a quill. **4** Any stem or main axis, as of a goblet. [ME *stalke,* dim. of OE *stæla* stem of a plant] —**stalked** *adj.* —**stalk′less** *adj.*

stalk[2] (stôk) *v.i.* **1** To approach game, etc., stealthily. **2** To walk in a stiff, dignified manner: also used figuratively: Murder *stalked* through the streets. **3** *Obs.* To go stealthily; creep. —*v.t.* **4** To approach (game, etc.) stealthily. **5** To pace through: Famine *stalked* the countryside. —*n.* **1** The act of stalking game. **2** A stately step or walk. [OE *bestealcian* move stealthily] —**stalk′er** *n.*

stalk·ing-horse (stô′king·hôrs′) *n.* **1** A horse behind which a hunter conceals himself in stalking game. **2** Anything serving to conceal one's intention.

stalk·y (stô′kē) *adj.* **stalk·i·er, stalk·i·est** **1** Long and slender, like a stalk. **2** Consisting of stalks.

stall (stôl) *n.* **1** A compartment in which a horse or bovine animal is confined and fed. **2** A small booth or compartment in a street, market, etc., for the sale or display of small articles. **3** A partially enclosed seat, as in the orchestra of a theater or the choir of a cathedral. **4** A working compartment in a coal mine. **5** A space set aside for the parking of an automobile. **6** A sheath or covering for a finger or thumb; a cot. **7** *Aeron.* The condition of an airplane which has lost the relative speed necessary for control; the act of stalling. **8** *Colloq.* An evasion or argument made to postpone action or decision. —*v.t.* **1** To place or keep in a stall. **2** To keep in a stall for fattening,

as cattle. 3 To bring to a standstill; stop the progress or motion of, especially unintentionally. 4 To cause to stick fast in mud, snow, etc. — *v.i.* 5 To come to a standstill; stop, especially unintentionally. 6 To stick fast in mud, snow, etc. 7 *Colloq.* To make delays; be evasive: to *stall* for time. 8 To live or be kept in a stall. 9 *Aeron.* To go into a stall. [OE *steall*]

stall-feed (stôl′fēd′) *v.t.* **-fed, -feed·ing** To feed (cattle) in a stall or stable; fatten. — **stall′-fed′** *adj.*

stal·lion (stal′yən) *n.* An uncastrated male horse. [<OF *estalon* <OHG *stal* stable]

stal·wart (stôl′wərt) *adj.* 1 Strong and brawny; robust. 2 Resolute: determined; unwavering. 3 Brave; courageous. — *n.* 1 An uncompromising partisan, as in politics. 2 *U.S.* A member of a conservative faction of the Republican party (1874–85) which opposed civil service reform and liberal policies toward the South. [Var. of STALWORTH] — **stal′wart·ly** *adv.* — **stal′wart·ness** *n.*

stal·worth (stôl′wərth) *adj. Obs.* Stalwart. [OE *stǣlwierthe* serviceable < *stǣl* place + *wierthe* worth]

stam·bou·line (stam′bə·lēn′) *n.* A coat for formal occasions, worn by officials in Turkey. [from *Stamboul*, var. of *Stambul*]

Stam·bul (stäm·bo͞ol′) 1 Istanbul. 2 The old part of the city of Istanbul. Also **Stam·boul′.**

sta·men (stā′mən) *n. pl.* **sta·mens,** *Rare* **stam·i·na** (stam′ə·nə) *Bot.* The pollen-bearing floral organ of a flower, standing inside the floral envelopes and consisting of two parts: the *filament*, or support, and the *anther*, or pollen sac. [<L, warp, thread < *stare* stand]

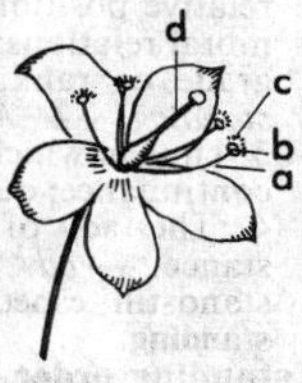

STAMEN (*a*, *b*, *c*)
a. Filament.
b. Anther.
c. Pollen.
d. Pistil.

Stam·ford (stam′fərd) 1 A municipal borough in SW Lincolnshire, England; a 14th century center of learning, at that time comparable to Oxford. 2 A city on Long Island Sound in SW Connecticut.

stam·i·na (stam′ə·nə) *n.* 1 Supporting vitality; strength; vigor; physical or moral capacity to endure or withstand hardship or difficulty. 2 The supporting part of a body. [<L, pl. of *stamen* warp, thread. See STAMEN.]

stam·i·nal (stam′ə·nəl) *adj.* 1 Of or pertaining to a stamen. 2 Relating to or furnishing stamina or lasting strength and vigor; essential.

stam·i·nate (stam′ə·nit, -nāt) *adj. Bot.* 1 Having stamens but no pistils, as certain flowers. 2 Having stamens.

stamini- *combining form Bot.* Stamen; of or pertaining to stamens: *staminiferous*, bearing stamens. Also, before vowels, **stamin-.** [<L *stamen, -inis* a fiber, thread]

stam·i·no·di·um (stam′ə·nō′dē·əm) *n. pl.* **·di·a** (-dē·ə) *Bot.* An abortive or sterile stamen, or an organ resembling one. Also **stam′i·node** (-nōd). [<NL <L *stamen, -inis* a stamen + Gk. *eidos* form]

stam·i·no·dy (stam′ə·nō′dē) *n. Bot.* The conversion of other parts of a flower, such as bracts, sepals, petals, or pistils, into stamens.

stam·mel (stam′əl) *n.* A linsey-woolsey of a dull-scarlet color; also, a dull scarlet. — *adj.* Of or pertaining to stammel or its color; dull-red. [<OF *estamel* < *estamine* <L *stamen* thread]

stam·mer (stam′ər) *v.t.* & *v.i.* To speak or utter with a halting articulation, commonly with nervous repetitions or prolongations of a sound or syllable, and involuntary pauses: to *stammer* an apology. — *n.* A halting, defective utterance. [OE *stamerian*] — **stam′·mer·er** *n.*

Synonym: stutter. *Stammer* and *stutter* are virtually interchangeable in general use. Frequently, however, *stammer* is associated with nervousness. excitement, or embarrassment, while *stutter* is reserved by the speech therapists for a particular speech disorder of obscure origin.

stamp (stamp) *v.t.* 1 To strike heavily with the sole of the foot. 2 To bring down (the foot) heavily and noisily. 3 To affect in a specified manner by or as by stamping with the foot: to *stamp* a fire out; to *stamp* out opposition. 4 To make marks or figures upon by means of a die, stamp, etc. 5 To imprint or impress with a die, stamp, etc. 6 To fix or imprint permanently: The deed was *stamped* on his memory. 7 To assign a specified quality to; characterize; brand: to *stamp* a story false. 8 To affix an official seal, stamp, etc., to. 9 To crush, break, or pulverize, as ore. — *v.i.* 10 To strike the foot heavily on the ground. 11 To walk with heavy, resounding steps. See synonyms under IMPRESS[1], INSCRIBE. — *n.* 1 A characteristic mark made by stamping; a device or design impressed upon any object, as by a die. 2 An implement or machine for stamping; specifically, a die having a pattern as for coinworking; any instrument for impressing a mark, design, or copy upon any object or surface: a hand *stamp.* 3 The weight or block as in an ore mill, which by its impact crushes the ore; by extension, the stamping mill itself. 4 A cutting tool for making articles of outline corresponding to the cutting edges: operated by pressure or by blows. 5 Any characteristic mark, as a label or imprint; a brand. 6 Hence, figuratively, characteristic quality or form; kind; sort: I dislike men of his *stamp.* 7 The act of stamping. 8 A printed device prepared and sold by a government, for attachment, as to a letter **(postage stamp)**, commodity **(revenue stamp)**, etc., as proof that the tax or fee has been paid; also, a trading stamp. See synonyms under MARK[1]. — **trading stamp** A stamp of fixed value given by a tradesman to a purchaser and exchangeable, in quantities, for goods selected from a premium list. [ME *stampen.* Akin to OE *stempan* pound.]

Stamp Act An act of the British Parliament, passed in March, 1765, and repealed in March, 1766, which required the American colonists to affix to various legal and commercial papers, as well as to pamphlets, newspapers, vellum, parchment, or paper, a government stamp varying in price from a halfpenny up to £10.

stam·pede (stam·pēd′) *n.* 1 A sudden starting and rushing off through panic: said primarily of a herd of cattle, horses, etc. 2 Any sudden, impulsive, tumultuous running movement of a crowd, as of a mob. 3 A movement or rush of people toward a certain region or object, as a gold rush or for homestead sites. 4 The sudden unplanned movement to support a certain candidate at a political convention, as from common impulse. — *v.* **·ped·ed, ·ped·ing** *v.t.* To cause a stampede or panic in. — *v.i.* To rush or flee in a stampede. [<Am. Sp. *estampida* crash < *estampar* stamp] — **stam·ped′er** *n.*

stamp·er (stam′pər) *n.* 1 One who stamps, in any sense. 2 One who cancels stamps, as in a post office. 3 Any tool or machine for stamping.

stamping ground 1 A place where horses or other animals gather in numbers. 2 A favorite resort; a habitual gathering place.

stamp mill A machine for pulverizing rock for the purpose of extracting the ore it contains.

stance (stans) *n.* 1 Mode of standing; posture. 2 In golf, the position of a player's feet, with reference to the ball and to each other, when making a stroke. 3 *Scot.* A position; a station; hence, a site; foundation. [<OF *estance* <L *stans, stantis,* ppr. of *stare* stand]

stanch (stanch, stänch) *v.t.* 1 To stop or check the flow of (blood, etc.). 2 To stop the flow of blood from (a wound). 3 *Obs.* To quench; quell; put an end to. Also spelled *staunch.* — *adj.* & *n.* Staunch. [<OF *estanchier* halt, bring to a stop, make stand, ult. <L *stare* stand] — **stanch′er** *n.*

◆ The spelling *stanch* is preferred for the verb in both England and the United States, and *staunch* for the adjective. Many writers use one or the other spelling for both.

stan·chion (stan′shən) *n.* 1 An upright bar forming a principal support. 2 A vertical bar or pair of bars used to confine cattle in a stall. — *v.t.* 1 To provide with stanchions. 2 To support or confine with stanchions. [<OF *estanchon* < *estance* situation, position. See STANCE.]

stand (stand) *v.* **stood, stand·ing** *v.i.* 1 To assume or maintain an erect position on the feet: distinguished from *sit, lie, kneel,* etc. 2 To be in a vertical position; be erect. 3 To measure a specified height when standing: He *stands* six feet. 4 To assume a specified position: to *stand* aside. 5 To be situated; have position or location; lie. 6 To have or be in a specified state, condition, or relation: We *stand* ready to fight; He *stood* in fear of his life. 7 To assume an attitude for defense or offense: *Stand* and fight! 8 To be or remain firm or resolute, as in determination. 9 To be consistent; accord; agree. 10 To remain unimpaired, unchanged, or valid: My decision still *stands.* 11 To collect and remain; also, to be stagnant, as water. 12 To be of a specified rank or class: He *stands* third. 13 To stop or pause; halt. 14 To scruple; hesitate. 15 *Naut.* To take a direction; steer: The brig *stood* into the wind. 16 To point, as a hunting dog. 17 *Brit.* To be a candidate, as for election. — *v.t.* 18 To place upright; set in an erect position. 19 To put up with; endure; tolerate. 20 To be subjected to; undergo: He must *stand* trial. 21 To withstand; resist. 22 *Colloq.* To pay for; bear the expense of: to *stand* a treat. — **to stand a chance** (or **show**) To have a chance or likelihood, as of success. — **to stand by** 1 To stay near and be ready to help or operate. 2 To help; support. 3 To abide by; make good; adhere to. 4 To remain passive and watch, as when help is needed. 5 *Telecom.* To wait, as for the continuance of an interrupted transmission. — **to stand clear** To remain at a safe distance. — **to stand down** *Law* To leave the witness stand. — **to stand for** 1 To represent; symbolize. 2 To put up with; tolerate. — **to stand from under** To move from beneath, as something about to fall. — **to stand in** *Colloq.* To cost. — **to stand in for** To act as a substitute for. — **to stand off** *Colloq.* 1 To keep at a distance. 2 To fail to agree or comply. — **to stand on** 1 To be based on or grounded in; rest. 2 To insist on or demand observance of: to *stand on* ceremony. 3 *Naut.* To keep on the same tack or course. — **to stand on one's own (two) feet** (or **legs**) To be independent; manage one's own affairs. — **to stand out** 1 To stick out; project or protrude. 2 To be prominent; appear in relief or contrast. 3 To refuse to consent or agree; remain in opposition. — **to stand over** 1 To remain near and watch, as a subordinate. 2 To be postponed. — **to stand pat** 1 In poker, to play one's hand as dealt, without drawing new cards. 2 To resist change. See STAND-PATTER. — **to stand to reason** To conform to reason. — **to stand up** 1 To stand erect. 2 To withstand wear, criticism, analysis, etc. 3 *Slang* To fail, usually intentionally, to keep an appointment with. — **to stand up for** To side with; take the part of. — **to stand up to** To confront courageously; face. — **to stand up with** To be best man or bridesmaid for. — *n.* 1 A structure upon which persons or things may stand, or on which articles may be kept or displayed. 2 A small table on which things may be placed conveniently. 3 A rack or other piece of furniture on which hats may be hung, or canes, umbrellas, etc., supported: a hall *stand.* 4 A stall, counter, or the like, where merchandise is displayed: a *bookstand.* 5 A structure upon which persons may sit or stand, as a platform, or a series of raised seats: a *bandstand*, a judges' *stand*; also, a small platform in court from which a witness testifies. 6 Any place where or in which something stands; position; place; specifically, the place of one's customary occupation; an assigned or chosen location. 7 The act of standing, especially of standing firmly: to make a *stand* against the enemy. 8 Cessation from motion or progress; a standstill. 9 A complete set; outfit: chiefly in the phrase **stand of arms.** 10 A growth on the field, as of corn or grass. 11 A tree grown from seed; also, a young tree left when others are cut down.

12 The growing trees in a forest or in part of a forest. **13** In the theater, a stop made while on tour to give a performance; also, the place: a one-night *stand.* **14** *Obs.* A troop; force. **15** A curved metal bar attached to the base of a force pump and serving as a fulcrum for the brake which moves the piston up and down. **16** In prosody, an epode: so called because it was originally sung while the chorus stood still. [OE *standan*] **— stand′er** *n.*
Synonyms (verb): abide, continue, endure, halt, pause, remain, stay, stop. See REST[1]. *Antonyms*: decline, droop, drop, fail, faint, falter, flee, fly, sink, succumb, yield.

stan·dard (stan′dərd) *n.* **1** A flag, ensign, or banner, used as a distinctive emblem of a government, body of men, or special cause: the *standard* of freedom or revolt. **2** A figure or an image adopted as the emblem of a nation. **3** A long, narrow flag carried by mounted and motorized units of the U. S. Army. **4** Any established measure of extent, quantity, quality, or value. **5** Any type, model, or example for comparison; a criterion of excellence; test: a *standard* of conduct or taste. **6** In coinage, the established proportion by weight of fine metal and alloy. **7** An upright timber, post, pole, or beam, especially as a support. **8** *Bot.* **a** Any tree, shrub, bush, or herb not dwarfed by grafting, and growing on a vigorous upright stem without support of a wall or trellis. **b** The vexillum (def. 2). **9** A heavy or stationary article of furniture. See synonyms under EXAMPLE, IDEAL, RULE. **— National Bureau of Standards** A branch of the U. S. Department of Commerce that maintains scientific, technical, and industrial standards, and acts as a research and testing agency for the government. **—** *adj.* **1** Having the accuracy or authority of a standard; serving as a gage, test, or model; hence, of recognized excellence or authority: a *standard* book or author. **2** Designating or belonging to the form of a language which, through its use in a region of economic and cultural importance, has gained acceptance and social prestige among all the speakers of the language. ◆ In this dictionary, words and meanings not considered to be at the level of the standard language are appropriately labeled colloquial, slang, dialectal, or illiterate. [<OF *estandard* banner <Gmc.]

stan·dard-bear·er (stan′dərd·bâr′ər) *n.* **1** An officer or soldier of a regiment or other military body who carries the flag or ensign. **2** Hence, one who leads, as a candidate; specifically, a presidential nominee.

stan·dard·bred (stan′dərd·bred′) *n.* A breed of horse notable for its trotters and pacers: descendent from the thoroughbred stallion *Messenger,* imported from England in 1788.

stan·dard-bred (stan′dərd·bred′) *adj.* Bred so as to be of a required strain, quality, or pedigree, as poultry, horses, etc.

standard candle *Physics* A candela.

standard cell *Electr.* A voltaic cell which serves as a standard of electromotive force.

standard deviation *Stat.* The square root of the arithmetic average of the squares of all the deviations from the mean value of a series of observations.

standard dollar See under DOLLAR.

standard gage **1** A gage for determining whether tools, etc., are of a recognized standard size. **2** A railroad track width of 56 1/2 inches, considered as standard. **3** A railroad having such a gage, or a locomotive or car made to run on this gage. **— stan′dard-gage′** (-gāj′) *adj.*

stan·dard·ize (stan′dər·dīz) *v.t.* **·ized, ·iz·ing** To make to or regulate by a standard: to *standardize* equipment. **— stan′dard·i·za′tion** *n.* **— stan′dard·iz′er** *n.*

standard lamp **1** Any of several standard lighting units used in photometric determinations. **2** In the United States, the pentane-burning lamp, equal to 10 international candles, or the Hefner lamp, burning amyl acetate, equal to 0.9 international candle.

standard time Civil time as reckoned from a certain meridian officially established as standard over a large area. Reckoning from the meridian of Greenwich, each time zone, comprising a sector of 15 degrees of longitude, is considered to represent a time interval of one hour, although in practice these zones are adjusted to meet various geographic and other regional conditions, as along the International

STANDARD TIME IN PRINCIPAL CITIES

Referred to noon in Washington, D.C. *(Time Zone +5)* and in Greenwich, England *(Time Zone 0).* Times have been calculated to the even hour, disregarding a few deviations (up to 30 minutes) resulting from local time-zone adjustments. All hours are for the same day except as indicated by (*) when the time is for the *following* day. Compare the table under TIME ZONE for explanation of the plus and minus factor in column 4.

(1) *City*	(2) *When* NOON *Washington Time*	(3) *When* NOON *Greenwich Time*	(4) *Time Zone Number*
Alexandria	7 P.M.	2 P.M.	−2
Amsterdam	5 P.M.	NOON	0
Athens	7 P.M.	2 P.M.	−2
Auckland	*4 A.M.	11 P.M.	−11
Baghdad	8 P.M.	3 P.M.	−3
Bangkok	MIDNIGHT	7 P.M.	−7
Belfast	5 P.M.	NOON	0
Berlin	6 P.M.	1 P.M.	−1
Bogotá	NOON	7 A.M.	+5
Bombay	10 P.M.	5 P.M.	−5
Boston	NOON	7 A.M.	+5
Brussels	5 P.M.	NOON	0
Bucharest	7 P.M.	2 P.M.	−2
Budapest	6 P.M.	1 P.M.	−1
Buenos Aires	1 P.M.	8 A.M.	+4
Cairo	7 P.M.	2 P.M.	−2
Calcutta	11 P.M.	6 P.M.	−6
Cape Town	6 P.M.	1 P.M.	−1
Caracas	1 P.M.	8 A.M.	+4
Chicago	11 A.M.	6 A.M.	+6
Copenhagen	6 P.M.	1 P.M.	−1
Delhi	10 P.M.	5 P.M.	−5
Denver	10 A.M.	5 A.M.	+7
Detroit	11 A.M.	6 A.M.	+6
Dublin	5 P.M.	NOON	0
Geneva	6 P.M.	1 P.M.	−1
Greenwich	5 P.M.	NOON	0
Halifax	1 P.M.	8 A.M.	+4
Havana	1 P.M.	8 A.M.	+4
Hong Kong	*1 A.M.	8 P.M.	−8
Istanbul	7 P.M.	2 P.M.	−2
Jakarta	MIDNIGHT	7 P.M.	−7
Johannesburg	7 P.M.	2 P.M.	−2
LeHavre	5 P.M.	NOON	0
Leningrad	7 P.M.	2 P.M.	−2
Lima	NOON	7 A.M.	+5
Lisbon	5 P.M.	NOON	0
Liverpool	5 P.M.	NOON	0
London	5 P.M.	NOON	0
Madrid	6 P.M.	1 P.M.	−1
Manila	*1 A.M.	8 P.M.	−8
Melbourne	*3 A.M.	10 P.M.	−10
Mexico City	11 A.M.	6 A.M.	+6
Montreal	NOON	7 A.M.	+5
Moscow	7 P.M.	2 P.M.	−2
New York	NOON	7 A.M.	+5
Oslo	6 P.M.	1 P.M.	−1
Ottawa	NOON	7 A.M.	+5
Paris	5 P.M.	NOON	0
Peking	*1 A.M.	8 P.M.	−8
Philadelphia	NOON	7 A.M.	+5
Quebec	NOON	7 A.M.	+5
Río de Janeiro	2 P.M.	9 A.M.	+3
Rome	6 P.M.	1 P.M.	−1
St. Louis	11 A.M.	6 A.M.	+6
San Francisco	9 A.M.	4 A.M.	+8
Shanghai	*1 A.M.	8 P.M.	−8
Singapore	MIDNIGHT	7 P.M.	−7
Stockholm	6 P.M.	1 P.M.	−1
Sydney	*3 A.M.	10 P.M.	−10
Teheran	8 P.M.	3 P.M.	−3
Tokyo	*2 A.M.	9 P.M.	−9
Toronto	NOON	7 A.M.	+5
Vancouver	9 A.M.	4 A.M.	+8
Vienna	6 P.M.	1 P.M.	−1
Vladivostok	*2 A.M.	9 P.M.	−9
Warsaw	6 P.M.	1 P.M.	−1
Washington	NOON	7 A.M.	+5
Winnipeg	11 A.M.	6 A.M.	+6
Yokohama	*2 A.M.	9 P.M.	−9
Zurich	6 P.M.	1 P.M.	−1

Date Line. See table above. In the conterminous United States the four standard time zones are the Eastern, Central, Mountain, and Pacific, using respectively the mean local time of the 75th, 90th, 105th, and 120th meridians west of Greenwich, and being 5, 6, 7, and 8 hours slower or earlier than Greenwich time. Canada has in addition a fifth zone, the Atlantic (or Provincial), based on the local time of the 60th meridian, which is 4 hours earlier than Greenwich time. See also TIME ZONE.

standard wavelength *Physics* The wavelength of the red cadmium line observed in dry air at 15 degrees Celsius and 760 millimeters of mercury: equal to 6438.4696 angstrom units.

stand-by (stand′bī′) *n. pl.* **-bys** Any person or thing that can be relied on in time of stress or emergency.

stand·ee (stan·dē′) *n. Colloq.* A person who must stand for lack of chairs or seats, as at a theater or on a train.

stand-fast (stand′fast′, -fäst′) *n.* That which stands firm and strong; a solid or settled position. **—** *adj.* Firm; settled.

stand-in (stand′in′) *n.* **1** A position of influence or favor; a pull. **2** A person who relieves a motion-picture player from tedious waiting intervals and substitutes for him in hazardous actions.

stand·ing (stan′ding) *adj.* **1** Remaining erect; not prostrated or cut down, as grain. **2** Continuing for regular or permanent use; remaining the same indefinitely; not special or temporary: a *standing* rule, a *standing* army. **3** Stagnant; not flowing: *standing* water. **4** Begun while standing: distinguished from *running*: a *standing* high jump. **5** Established; permanent: the *standing* church. **—** *n.* **1** Place; relative position, as in social, commercial, or moral relations; repute; grade; especially, high grade or rank; good reputation: a man of *standing.* **2** A place to stand in; station. **3** Time in which something stands or goes on; continuance; duration: a feud of long *standing.* **4** The act of one who stands; erectness; stance. **—** *adv.* At or to a sudden stop or standstill, especially in the phrase **to bring up standing.**

standing order **1** A military order always in force and not subject to change or modification. **2** In parliamentary procedure, a general regulation governing the manner in which the business of a body shall be conducted: in force from session to session until rescinded or voided.

standing rigging *Naut.* The heavy ropes or cables which support the masts and fixed spars of a ship.

standing room Place in which to stand, as in a building, theater, etc., where the seats are all occupied.

stand·ish (stan′dish) *n.* A receptacle for pens and ink. [<STAND + DISH]

Stan·dish (stan′dish), **Miles,** 1584?–1656, English soldier and emigrant in the "Mayflower"; military leader of the Pilgrims; subject of Longfellow's *The Courtship of Miles Standish.*

stand-off (stand′ôf′, -of′) *n.* **1** A draw or tie, as in a game. **2** A counterbalancing or neutralization. **3** A feeling or state of indifference or coldness; aloofness. **4** A postponement. **— stand′-off′ish** *adj.*

stand oil Linseed or other oil heated for several hours at a temperature of about 300° C. to thicken it and remove coagulated impurities: used in varnishes and paints.

stand-out (stand′out′) *n.* **1** Someone or something that is outstanding, excellent, etc. **2** *Colloq.* One who stubbornly refuses to agree, consent, or cooperate.

stand-pat (stand′pat′) *adj.* Characterized by or pertaining to the policy of opposition to change; conservative.

stand-pat·ter (stand′pat′ər) *n.* In U. S. politics, one who adheres obstinately to a policy or party; specifically, a politician who advocates maintaining the existing tariff schedules; a conservative. **— stand′-pat′tism** *n.*

stand·pipe (stand′pīp′) *n.* A vertical pipe, as at a reservoir, into which the water is pumped to give it a head; a water tower.

stand·point (stand′point′) *n.* A position from which things are viewed or judged; point of view; basal principle.

St. An·drews (sānt an′drōōz) A port and burgh in eastern Fifeshire, Scotland; the rules of golf are established at a famous course nearby, founded 1754.

St. Andrew's cross The oblique cross; also, a saltire. See under CROSS.

stand·still (stand′stil′) *n.* A pause; cessation of motion or action; halt; rest. **—** *adj.* In a state of rest or inactivity; standing still.

stand-up (stand′up′) *adj.* **1** Having an erect

position: a *stand-up* collar. **2** Done, consumed, etc., while standing.

Stan·ford revision (stan′fərd) *Psychol.* A modification of the Binet–Simon scale designed to cover a wider range of mental age and to provide a constant number of tests, usually six, for each year group. [from *Stanford* University, Calif., where it was originated]

stang[1] (stang) *Scot. & Brit. Dial. v.t.* To sting. — *v.i.* To throb with pain. — *n.* A sting; throbbing pain.

stang[2] (stang) Obsolete past tense of STING.

stan·hope (stan′hōp) *n.* A light, open, one-seated carriage. [after Fitzroy *Stanhope*, 1787–1864, English clergyman, for whom it was first made]

stan·iel (stan′yəl) *n.* The kestrel. Also **stan·nel** (stan′əl). [OE *stāngella* < *stān* stone + *gellan* scream]

sta·nine (stā′nīn) *n. Psychol.* A composite weighted score of aptitudes and performance based on a scale of nine: it is a form of frequency distribution about a median of 5, 1 being lowest and 9 highest: originally developed to test air crews in the U.S. Army Air Forces. [STA(NDARD SCALE OF) NINE]

Sta·ni·slav (stä′ni·släf) A city in western Ukrainian S.S.R., formerly, 1919–45, in Poland. *German* **Stan·is·lau** (stän′is·lou), *Polish* **Sta·ni·sła·wow** (stä′nē·swä′vŏŏf).

Stan·is·lav·sky (stä′ni·släf′skē), **Constantin**, 1863–1938, Russian actor, director, and producer: real name *Konstantin Sergeyevich Alekseyev*.

stank[1] (stangk) Past tense of STINK.

stank[2] (stangk) *n. Brit. Dial.* A pool; reservoir; pond; ditch; dam. [OF *estanc* < L *stagnum* < *stagnare* stagnate. See STAGNANT.]

Stan·ley (stan′lē) A masculine personal name. [OE, stone lea]

Stan·ley (stan′lē), **Arthur Penrhyn**, 1815–81, English author and divine. — **Sir Henry Morton**, 1841–1904, British journalist and explorer active in the United States; sent out to find David Livingstone in Africa; original name *John Rowlands*. — **Wendell Meredith**, born 1904, U.S. biochemist.

Stanley, Mount See RUWENZORI.

Stanley Falls The seven cataracts of the upper Congo river, near the equator; total fall, 200 feet.

Stanley Pool A lakelike expansion of the Congo river on the border between SW Belgian Congo and SE French Equatorial Africa; 320 square miles.

stan·na·ry (stan′ər·ē) *n. pl.* **·ries** A tin mine or region of tin mines. [Med. L *stannaria* < L *stannum* tin]

stan·nic (stan′ik) *adj. Chem.* Of, pertaining to, or containing tin, especially in its higher valence. [L *stannum* tin]

stannic acid *Chem.* Any of three compounds derived from stannic chloride by the action of alkalis.

stannic chloride *Chem.* A thin, colorless liquid, SnCl₄, made by exposing metallic tin to the action of chlorine: used as a mordant in dyeing.

stannic oxide *Chem.* A white, amorphous, pulverulent compound, SnO_2, found native or formed by heating the lower (stannous) oxide in air: extensively used as a polishing agent called *putty powder.*

stannic sulfide *Chem.* A yellow compound, SnS_2, precipitated from a solution of a stannic salt by hydrogen sulfide: used in bronzing.

stan·nif·er·ous (stə·nif′ər·əs) *adj.* Yielding or containing tin. [L *stannum* tin + -FEROUS]

stan·nite (stan′īt) *n.* A granular, metallic, steel-gray to iron-black mineral containing tin, copper, iron, sulfur, and sometimes zinc; tin pyrites. [L *stannum* tin + -ITE[1]]

stan·nous (stan′əs) *adj. Chem.* Of, pertaining to, or containing tin, especially in its lower valence. [L *stannum* tin + -OUS]

stan·num (stan′əm) *n.* Tin. [L]

Sta·no·voi Range (stä′nô·voi′) A mountain chain in SE Siberian Russian S.F.S.R.; highest point, 8,143 feet; forms the watershed between the Lena and Amur river basins. Also **Sta·no·vy Range** (stä·nô′vē).

St. Anthony's fire *Pathol.* Erysipelas.

St. Anthony's nut An earthnut (*Conopodium denudatum*), fed to pigs: so called because St.

Anthony was once a swineherd: also called *pignut, groundnut.*

Stan·ton (stan′tən), **Edwin McMasters**, 1814–1869, U.S. statesman; secretary of war 1862–1868. — **Elizabeth Cady**, 1815–1902, U.S. woman-suffrage leader.

stan·za (stan′zə) *n.* A certain number of lines of verse grouped in a definite scheme of meter and sequence; a metrical division of a poem: often incorrectly called a *verse.* [Ital., room, stanza < L *stans, stantis* standing. See STANCE.] — **stan·za·ic** (stan·zā′ik) *adj.*

sta·pe·li·a (stə·pē′lē·ə) *n.* Any of a genus (*Stapelia*) of fleshy African plants of the milkweed family, having leafless toothed stems and showy, starlike, ill-smelling, purple or yellowish flowers sometimes a foot in diameter; a carrion flower. [NL, after J. B. van *Stapel*, died 1636, Dutch botanist]

sta·pes (stā′pēz) *n. Anat.* The innermost ossicle of the middle ear of mammals. See illustration under EAR. [LL *stapes* a stirrup] — **sta·pe·di·al** (stə·pē′dē·əl) *adj.*

staphylo– *combining form* **1** *Anat.* The uvula: *staphyloplasty.* **2** *Med.* Staphylococcic. Also, before vowels, **staphyl–**. [Gk. *staphylē* bunch of grapes]

staph·y·lo·coc·cus (staf′ə·lō·kok′əs) *n. pl.* **·coc·ci** (-kok′sī) Any of a genus (*Staphylococcus*) of typically parasitic bacteria occurring singly, in pairs, or in irregular clusters; especially, *S. aureus*, an infective agent in boils, furuncles, and suppurating wounds. See illustration under BACTERIUM. [NL < Gk. *staphylos* bunch of grapes + *kokkos* a berry] — **staph′y·lo·coc′cic** (-kok′sik) *adj.*

staph·y·lo·plas·ty (staf′ə·lō·plas′tē) *n.* Reparative surgery of the soft palate and uvula. — **staph′y·lo·plas′tic** *adj.*

staph·y·lor·rha·phy (staf′ə·lôr′ə·fē, -lor′-) *n. Surg.* The operation of uniting a cleft palate. Also **staph′y·lor′a·phy.** [STAPHYLO- + -RHAPHY]

sta·ple[1] (stā′pəl) *n.* **1** A principal commodity or production of a country or region; a well-established article of commerce. **2** A chief element or main constituent of something. **3** The carded or combed fiber of cotton, wool, or flax. **4** Raw material. **5** A commercial emporium; mart. **6** Hence, a source of supply; storehouse. — *adj.* **1** Regularly and constantly produced or sold; hence, main; chief. **2** Commercially established; having regular commercial channels. **3** Marketable. — *v.t.* **·pled, ·pling** To sort or classify according to length, as wool fiber. [OF *estaple* market, support < Gmc.]

sta·ple[2] (stā′pəl) *n.* A U-shaped piece of metal with pointed ends, or a loop of thin wire, driven into wood, fabrics, paper, etc., to serve as a fastening. — *v.t.* **·pled, ·pling** To fix or fasten by a staple or staples. [OE *stapol* post, prop]

sta·pler[1] (stā′plər) *n.* **1** A sorter of wool according to its staple. **2** A merchant who participated in one of the monopolies formerly granted by royal authority.

sta·pler[2] (stā′plər) *n.* A wire-stitching machine that binds pamphlets, books, etc.

star (stär) *n.* **1** *Astron.* One of a class of self-luminous celestial bodies, exclusive of comets, meteors, and nebulae, but including the sun. The stars are classified according to their relative brightness in what are known as magnitudes, the first being the brightest and the sixth the faintest visible to the naked eye. The table below gives the names of the principal navigational stars and their apparent magnitudes, with the constellation in which each may be found. ◆ Collateral adjectives: *astral, sidereal, stellar.* **2** Loosely, any heavenly body; a planet. **3** A conventional figure having five or more radiating points: used as an emblem or device, as on the shoulder strap of a general. **4** An asterisk (*). **5** A white spot on the forehead of a horse or bovine animal. **6** An actor or actress who plays the leading part; hence, anyone who shines prominently in a calling or profession: a literary *star.* **7** A heavenly body considered as influencing one's fate; hence, fortune; destiny. — **binary star** A pair of stars revolving about a common center. Three types have been noted: *eclipsing,* in which the mem-

bers successively eclipse each other; *spectroscopic,* in which the members are distinguishable only by shifts in their spectral lines; and *visual,* in which the members may be distinguished through the telescope. — **dark star** An invisible star, non-shining or dimly shining: known only through relation to visible stars, as during eclipsing action. — **double star** Two stars so near to each other as to be almost indistinguishable except through a telescope. — **dwarf star** Any of a class of stars which have reached their greatest temperature and are in the phase of contraction, with luminosity passing from bluish to orange. — **giant star** Any of a class of stars of great mass and high luminosity which are passing through the early stages of their evolution. — **variable star** Any of several groups of stars whose apparent magnitude varies at different times. The cause may be external, as with binary stars, one of which regularly eclipses the other; or internal, as with true variable stars whose periodic fluctuations in light are caused by internal changes. See CEPHEID VARIABLE, NOVA. — *v.* **starred, star·ring** *v.t.* **1** To set or adorn with spangles or stars. **2** To mark with an asterisk. **3** To transform into a star. **4** To present as a star in a play or motion picture. — *v.i.* **5** To shine brightly as a star; be prominent or brilliant. **6** To play the leading part; be the star. — *adj.* **1** Of or pertaining to a star or stars. **2** Prominent; brilliant: a *star* football player. [OE *steorra*]

TABLE OF PRINCIPAL STARS

Star	*Constellation*	*Magnitude*
Achernar	Eridanus	0.60
Acrux	Crucis	1.05
Aldebaran	Taurus	1.06
Alpheratz	Andromeda	2.15
Altair	Aquila	0.89
Antares	Scorpio	1.22
Arcturus	Boötes	0.24
Betelgeuse	Orion	1.20
Canopus	Argo	−0.86
Capella	Auriga	0.21
Deneb	Cygnus	1.33
Fomalhaut	Piscis Austrinus	1.29
Peacock	Pavo	2.12
Polaris	Ursa Minor	2.12
Pollux	Gemini	1.21
Procyon	Canis Minor	0.48
Regulus	Leo	1.34
Rigel	Orion	0.34
Rigil Kentaurus	Centaurus	0.06
Sirius	Canis Major	−1.58
Spica	Virgo	1.21
Vega	Lyra	0.14

star apple 1 The edible fruit of a West Indian tree (*Chrysophyllum cainito*), resembling an apple in size and appearance, and having ten cells and as many seeds disposed stellately around its center. **2** The tree itself.

star·board (stär′bərd) *Naut. n.* The right-hand side of a vessel as one looks from stern to bow: opposed to *larboard, port.* — *adj.* Of or pertaining to the right of the observer on a vessel when facing the bow. — *adv.* Toward the starboard side. — *v.t.* To put, move, or turn (the helm) to the starboard side. [OE *steorbord* steering side]

star boarder The senior boarder in a boarding house, or one who pays more than the others, considered as entitled to special privileges.

starch (stärch) *n.* **1** *Biochem.* A white, odorless, tasteless, amorphous, powdery carbohydrate (C₆H₁₀O₅)ₙ, insoluble in cold water, alcohol, and other liquids, found in the seeds, pith, or tubers of most plants. Starch is an exceedingly important component of vegetable foods, reacting with certain digestive enzymes to produce maltose and dextrin; it is also used in the commercial production of glucose, for stiffening linen, and for many industrial purposes. **2** Stiffness or formality; a stiff or formal manner. **3** *U.S. Slang* Energy; vigor. — *v.t.* To apply starch to; stiffen with or as with starch. [ME *sterche* < OE *stercan* stiffen < *stearc* stiff. Related to STARK.]

Star Chamber A former English court which met in secret and dispensed justice without jury, and which was noted for its arbitrary

and inquisitorial proceedings: abolished by Parliament in 1641; hence, any arbitrary or secret tribunal. [Prob. because it met in Westminster Palace in a chamber whose ceiling was decorated with stars]

starch gum Dextrin.

starch sugar Dextrose.

starch·y (stär′chē) *adj.* **starch·i·er, starch·i·est 1** Stiffened with starch; stiff; figuratively, prim; formal; precise: also **starched. 2** Formed of or combined with starch; farinaceous. **—starch′i·ly** *adv.* **—starch′i·ness** *n.*

star cluster *Astron.* Any of numerous groupings of stars associated in the same region of space, as the Pleiades and Coma Berenices: they are classified as open or galactic, and globular.

star-crossed (stär′krôst′, -krost′) *adj.* Astrologically ill-fated; unfortunate; ill-starred: a *star-crossed* love affair.

star·dom (stär′dəm) *n.* The status of a movie or theatrical star.

star drift *Astron.* A common proper motion of stars in the same region of the heavens: noticed in close groups of stars and in pairs of widely separated stars.

stare (stâr) *v.* **stared, star·ing** *v.i.* **1** To gaze fixedly, usually with the eyes open wide, as from admiration, fear, or insolence. **2** To be conspicuously or unduly apparent; glare. **3** To stand on end, as hair. —*v.t.* **4** To stare at. **5** To affect in a specified manner by a stare: to *stare* a person into silence. See synonyms under LOOK. —*n.* A steady, fixed gaze with wide-open eyes. ◆ Homophone: *stair.* [OE *starian*] **—star′er** *n.*

sta·re de·ci·sis (stā′rē di·sī′sis) *Law Latin* The doctrine that precedents are law and should be followed; literally, to stand by decisions.

star facet One of eight triangular facets adjoining the table in the crown of a brilliant-cut gem. For illustration see DIAMOND.

star·fish (stär′fish′) *n.* *pl.* **·fish** or **·fish·es** Any of various radially symmetrical echinoderms (class *Asteroidea*), commonly with a star-shaped body having five or more arms. Starfish feed mainly on mollusks, including oysters.

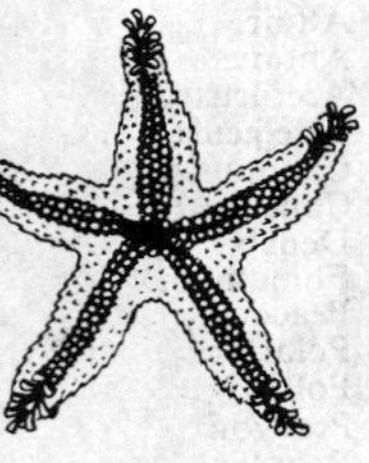

STARFISH
Ventral side showing tube feet.

star·flow·er (stär′flou′ər) *n.* **1** Any of various plants with conventionally star-shaped flowers; especially, a low perennial *(Trientalis borealis)* with one or more white star-shaped flowers. **2** A starwort. **3** A star of Bethlehem.

star-gaze (stär′gāz′) *v.i.* **-gazed, -gaz·ing 1** To gaze at or study the stars. **2** To daydream.

star-gaz·er (stär′gā′zər) *n.* **1** One who gazes at or studies the stars; especially, an astrologer or astronomer. **2** A marine carnivorous fish with eyes small and near the front of the top of the head, as *Uranoscopus scaber* of the Mediterranean, and *Astroscopus anoplus* of the Atlantic coast of the United States.

star-gaz·ing (stär′gā′zing) *adj.* Given to watching the stars. —*n.* **1** The act or practice of watching or studying the stars. **2** An absent-minded state; abstraction.

star·grass (stär′gras′, -gräs′) *n.* Any of various grasslike plants (genus *Hypoxis*) of the amaryllis family, with starlike flowers.

stark (stärk) *adj.* **1** Stiff or rigid, as in death. **2** *Obs.* Stubborn; inflexible. **3** Severe; tempestuous, as weather; strict or grim, as a person; also, deserted or barren, as a landscape. **4** *Obs.* Strong and powerful. **5** Without ornamentation; blunt; complete; utter; downright: *stark* misery. **6** Naked: short for *stark naked.* —*adv.* **1** In a stark manner. **2** Completely; utterly: *stark* mad. [OE *stearc* stiff. Related to STARCH.] **—stark′ly** *adv.*

Stark (shtärk), **Johannes,** 1874–1957, German physicist.

Stark (stärk), **John,** 1728–1822, American Revolutionary general.

stark naked Entirely without clothing. [Alter. of ME *stert-naked* <OE *steort* tail + *nacod* naked; infl. in form by STARK]

star·less (stär′lis) *adj.* Being without stars or starlight.

star·let (stär′lit) *n.* **1** A small star. **2** *Colloq.* A young movie actress aspiring to stardom.

star·light (stär′līt) *n.* The light given by a star or stars. —*adj.* Lighted by or only by the stars: also **star′lit′** (-lit′).

star·like (stär′līk′) *adj.* Like a star; bright; luminous; shining.

star lily The sand lily.

star·ling[1] (stär′ling) *n.* Any of several Old World passerine birds (genus *Sturnus*). The common starling *(S. vulgaris)* is brown glossed with black, with metallic purple and green reflections and a buff tip to each feather. It is often caged. [OE *stærling* < *stær* starling]

star·ling[2] (stär′ling) *n.* **1** An enclosure of close piling, as around a pier of a bridge for protection. **2** One of the piles of such an enclosure. [OE *statholung* foundation]

Starn·ber·ger·see (shtärn′ber′gər·zā′) A lake SW of Munich, in southern Bavaria, West Germany; 22 square miles: also *Würmsee.*

star·nose (stär′nōz′) *n.* A North American mole *(Condylura cristata)* having a radiate arrangement of fleshy processes around the end of the nose. Also **star-nosed mole.**

star of Bethlehem 1 The large star by which the three Magi were guided to the manger in Bethlehem where the child Jesus lay. **2** An Old World plant *(Ornithogalum umbellatum)* of the lily family, having white stellate flowers striped with green on the outside: naturalized in the eastern United States.

star of David The six-pointed star used as a symbol by the Hebrews; the mogen David.

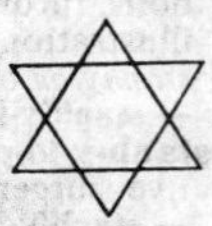

STAR OF DAVID

star of Jerusalem Goatbeard.

starred (stärd) *adj.* **1** Spangled with stars; marked with stars or a star; specifically, marked with an asterisk. **2** Affected by astral influence: chiefly in composition: ill-*starred.* **3** Presented or advertised as the star of a play or motion picture; featured.

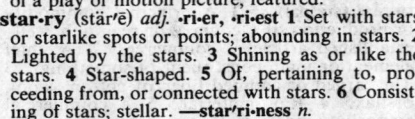

star·ry (stär′ē) *adj.* **·ri·er, ·ri·est 1** Set with stars or starlike spots or points; abounding in stars. **2** Lighted by the stars. **3** Shining as or like the stars. **4** Star-shaped. **5** Of, pertaining to, proceeding from, or connected with stars. **6** Consisting of stars; stellar. **—star′ri·ness** *n.*

star·ry-eyed (stär′ē·īd′) *adj.* Given to fanciful wishes or yearnings.

Stars and Bars The first flag authorized by the Congress of the Southern Confederacy, consisting of a field of three bars, red, white, and red, and a blue canton with a circle of white stars, one for each State of the Confederacy.

Stars and Stripes The flag of the United States of America, a field of thirteen horizontal stripes, alternate red and white, and blue union with as many white stars as States: with the definite article.

star sapphire A sapphire that reveals a six-pointed star of light reflected from interior crystal faces when specially cut to present a convex surface without facets.

star·shell (stär′shel′) *n.* An artillery shell that explodes in mid-air with a shower of bright light: used for illuminating objectives, signaling, etc.

star shower A meteoric shower.

star-span·gled (stär′spang′gəld) *adj.* Spangled with stars or starlike spots or points: said especially of the United States flag.

Star-Spangled Banner, The 1 The flag of the United States. **2** A poem written by Francis Scott Key in 1814 during the bombardment by the British of Fort McHenry, Md., and adopted by Congress in 1931 as the national anthem of the United States. The music to which it is sung is that of an old English drinking song. *To Anacreon in Heaven.*

start[1] (stärt) *v.i.* **1** To make an involuntary, startled movement, as from fear or surprise. **2** To move suddenly, as with a spring, leap, or bound; jump. **3** To make a beginning or start; set out. **4** To begin; commence: The play *starts* at eight o'clock. **5** To protrude; seem to bulge: His eyes *started* from his head. **6** To be displaced or dislocated; become loose, warped, etc.: The rivets have *started.* —*v.t.* **7** To set in motion: to *start* an engine; to *start* a rumor. **8** To begin; commence: to *start* a lecture. **9** To set up; establish. **10** To introduce (a subject) or propound (a question). **11** To displace or dislocate; loosen, warp, etc.: The collision *started* the ship's seams. **12** To rouse from cover; cause to take flight; flush, as game. **13** To draw the contents from; tap, as a cask. **14** *Archaic* To startle. See synonyms under INSTITUTE. **—to start in** To begin. **—to start off** To begin a journey; set out. **—to start out 1** To start off. **2** To make a beginning or start. **—to start up 1** To rise or appear suddenly. **2** To begin or cause to begin operation, as an engine. **—to start with** In the first place; to begin with. —*n.* **1** A quick, startled movement or feeling; a sudden quickening of sense, pulse, or nerve at something unexpected. **2** A setting out or going forth; beginning. **3** A temporary or spasmodic action or attempt; a brief, intermittent effort: by fits and *starts.* **4** *Archaic* A sudden impulse or effusion; burst; sally: *starts* of wit. **5** Advantage or distance in advance at the outset; lead: I had a *start* of five miles in the race. **6** Impetus at the beginning of motion or, figuratively, of a course of action: to get a *start* in business. **7** A loosened place or condition; crack: a *start* in a ship's planking. See synonyms under BEGINNING. [ME *sterten* start, leap, fusion of ON *sterta* overturn and OE *styrtan* start, jump]

start[2] (stärt) *n.* **1** The sharp point of an antler. **2** A tail-like piece. **3** The tail of a bird or animal: the original sense, now obsolete except in compounds: a *redstart.* [OE *steort* tail]

start·er (stär′tər) *n.* **1** One who or that which starts; specifically, one who sees to it that buses, trolleys, etc., leave on schedule. **2** A self-starter. **3** A competitor at the start of a race. **4** A person who gives the signal for the start of a race.

star thistle An Old World weed *(Centaurea calcitrapa)* with spiny heads of tubular flowers, naturalized in the United States; also, another species *(C. solstitialis)* with yellow flowers.

star·tle (stär′təl) *v.* **·tled, ·tling** *v.t.* To arouse or excite suddenly; cause to start involuntarily; alarm. —*v.i.* To be aroused or excited suddenly; take alarm. —*n.* A sudden fright or shock; a scare. [OE *steartlian* kick, struggle] **—star′tler** *n.*

star·tling (stärl′ling) *adj.* Rousing sudden surprise, alarm, or the like. **—star′tling·ly** *adv.*

star·va·tion (stär·vā′shən) *n.* **1** The act of starving. **2** The state of being starved.

starve (stärv) *v.* **starved, starv·ing** *v.i.* **1** To die or perish from lack of food. **2** To suffer from extreme hunger. **3** To suffer from lack or need: to *starve* friendship. **4** *Dial.* To die of cold. **5** *Obs.* To die. —*v.t.* **6** To cause to die of hunger; deprive of food. **7** To bring to a specified condition by starving: to *starve* an enemy into surrender. [OE *steorfan* die] **—starv′er** *n.*

starve·ling (stärv′ling) *n.* A person or animal that is starving, starved, or emaciated. —*adj.* **1** Starving; emaciated; hungry. **2** Failing to meet needs; inadequate: a *starveling* religion. See synonyms under MEAGER.

star·wort (stär′wûrt′) *n.* A stitchwort.

stase (stās) *n.* *Ecol.* A deposit of fossil plants which has not moved from its original position, often occurring as a series of layers of related species. [<Gk. *stasis.* See STASIS.]

stash (stash) *v.t.* *Slang* To hide or conceal (money or valuables), for storage and safekeeping: often with *away.* [? Blend of STORE + CACHE]

sta·sis (stā′sis, stas′is) *n.* *Pathol.* **1** Stoppage of the blood in its circulation, especially in the small vessels and capillaries: caused by abnormal resistance of the capillary walls, rather than by any lessening of the heart's action. **2** Retarded movement of the intestinal contents due to obstruction or muscular malfunction. [<NL <Gk., a standing < *histanai* stand]

stat- Var. of STATO-.

-stat *combining form* A device which stops or makes constant: *thermostat, rheostat.* [<Gk. *-statēs* causing to stand < *histanai* stand]

state (stāt) *n.* **1** Mode of existence as determined by circumstances, external or internal; nature; condition; situation. **2** Frame of mind; mood: a *state* of anxiety. **3** Mode or style of living; station; especially, grand and ceremonious style; pomp; formality. **4** A sovereign political community organized under a distinct government recognized and

conformed to by the people as supreme, and having jurisdiction over a given territory; a nation. **5** One of a number of political communities or bodies politic united to form one sovereign state; specifically, one of the United States: in this sense usually written **State.** **6** *pl.* The legislative bodies of a nation; estates. **7** Authority of government; the territorial, political, and governmental entity comprising a state or nation. **8** *Obs.* A person of rank; a noble. **9** *Obs.* An estate; order; class of persons. See synonyms under PEOPLE. — **Department of State** An executive department of the U.S. government (established in 1789), headed by the Secretary of State, which supervises the conduct of foreign affairs, directs the activities of all diplomatic and consular representatives, protects national interests abroad, and assists in the formulation of policies in relation to international problems. Also **State Department.** — **to lie in state** To be placed on public view, with ceremony and honors, before burial. — *adj.* **1** Of or pertaining to the state, nation, or government: *state* papers. **2** Intended for use on occasions of ceremony. — *v.t.* **stat·ed, stat·ing 1** To set forth explicitly in speech or writing; assert; declare. **2** To fix; determine; settle. **3** *Law* To make known specifically; declare as a matter of fact. See synonyms under AFFIRM, ALLEGE, ASSERT, RELATE. [Aphetic var. of OF *estat* <L *status* condition, state < *stare* stand; defs. 4, 5, and 7 directly <L, as in *status rei publicae* the state of the republic. Doublet of STATUS.] — **sta·tal** (stā′tal) *adj.*

state·craft (stāt′kraft′, -kräft′) *n.* The art of conducting affairs of state.

stat·ed (stā′tid) *adj.* Established; regular; fixed. See synonyms under HABITUAL. — **stat′ed·ly** *adv.*

State flower A flower or plant adopted by popular consent or official designation as the floral emblem of one of the United States.

State·hood (stāt′ho͝od) *n.* The condition or status of one of the United States as opposed to that of a Territory.

State House A building used for sessions of a State legislature and for other public purposes; a State capitol.

state·less (stāt′lis) *adj.* **1** Without nationality: a *stateless* person. **2** Without a state or community of states: a *stateless* society.

state·ly (stāt′lē) *adj.* **·li·er, ·li·est** Dignified; lofty. See synonyms under AWFUL, GRAND, HAUGHTY, SUBLIME. — *adv.* Loftily: also **state′·li·ly.** — **state′li·ness** *n.*

state·ment (stāt′mənt) *n.* **1** A summary of facts; narration; the act of stating. **2** That which is stated. **3** *Law* A formal narration of facts filed as the foundation for judicial proceeding; a pleading. **4** A summary of the assets and liabilities of a bank or firm, showing the balance due. **5** A report sent, usually at monthly intervals, to a debtor of a business firm or to a depositor in a bank. See synonyms under REPORT.

Stat·en Island (stat′n) An island SW of the mouth of the Hudson River, at the entrance to New York Harbor, coextensive with the borough of Richmond, New York City; 57 square miles.

State prison A prison built and controlled by a State, usually for felons.

stat·er[1] (stā′tər) *n.* One who makes a statement.

sta·ter[2] (stā′tər) *n.* Any of several standard coins of the ancient Greek city-states, made variously of gold, silver, and electrum, and differing widely in value. [<Gk. *statēr*]

State rights 1 The rights and powers not delegated to the United States by the Constitution, nor prohibited by it to the States: reserved by the Constitution to the respective States, or to the people of the States, under the Tenth Amendment. **2** That construction of the Constitution which makes these rights and powers as large as possible. **3** The doctrine that the States, being sovereign, have the right to judge and nullify an act of the Federal government. See NULLIFICATION. Also **States' rights.**

state·room (stāt′ro͞om′, -ro͝om′) *n.* **1** A small private room having sleeping accommodations on a passenger boat. **2** A private sleeping compartment on a railroad car.

State's attorney *U.S.* A lawyer appointed by a State to represent it in court.

state's evidence 1 One who confesses himself guilty of a crime and testifies as a witness against his accomplices. **2** Evidence produced by the State in criminal prosecutions. Also, in Great Britain, Canada, Australia, etc., *king's* or *queen's evidence.*

States General A general as opposed to a provincial legislature: the name of the legislative body of the Netherlands and that of France before the Revolution.

state·side (stāt′sīd′) *adj.* Of or in the continental United States. — *adv.* In or to the continental United States.

states·man (stāts′mən) *n. pl.* **·men** (-mən) One skilled in the science of government; a political leader of distinguished ability; also, one engaged in government matters, or influential in state affairs or policy. — **states′man·like′, states′man·ly** *adj.* — **states′man·ship** *n.*

state socialism A political theory advocating government ownership of utilities and industries for the purpose of equalizing income.

States of the Church A part of central Italy which, before the unification of Italy in 1870, was under the sovereignty of the pope: also *Papal States.*

States' Rights party A political party founded during May, 1948, in Jackson, Miss., by southern Democrats who were opposed to the civil rights program of the regular Democratic party. It nominated Gov. James Strom Thurmond of South Carolina as its candidate for president. Popularly called *Dixiecrats.*

states·wom·an (stāts′wo͝om′ən) *n. pl.* **·wom·en** (-wim′in) A woman engaged or skilled in the conduct of government affairs.

state-wide (stāt′wīd′) *adj.* Throughout a state.

stat·ic (stat′ik) *adj.* **1** Pertaining to bodies at rest or forces in equilibrium: opposed to *dynamic.* **2** *Physics* Acting as weight, but not moving: *static* pressure. **3** *Electr.* Pertaining to electricity at rest, or to stationary electric charges. **4** At rest; quiescent; dormant; not active. **5** Of or pertaining to non-active elements. **6** In art, simply posed; monumental. **7** Treating of fixed or stable conditions rather than of fluctuations of sales: said of capital or goods. Also **stat′i·cal.** — *n. Electr.* A condition in which electromagnetic waves produced by atmospheric disturbances affect a radio receiving set, interfering with normal reception. [<Gk. *statikos* causing to stand < *histanai* stand] — **stat′i·cal·ly** *adv.*

stat·ics (stat′iks) *n. pl.* (*construed as singular*) The science of bodies at rest and of the relations required to produce equilibrium. Compare DYNAMICS.

static tube *Aeron.* A small closed tube with openings around the side, facing into the wind on an airplane and designed to measure the static pressure of the air.

sta·tion (stā′shən) *n.* **1** A place where a person or thing usually stands or is; an assigned location. **2** The headquarters of some official person or body of men: a police *station.* **3** An established building or place serving as a starting point, stage, stopping place, or post; specifically, a building for the accommodation of passengers or freight, as on a railroad or bus line; terminal; depot. **4** Social condition; rank; standing. **5** *Mil.* A military post; the place to which an individual, unit, or ship is assigned for duty. **6** The administrative offices, studios, and technical installations of a radio broadcasting unit operating on its assigned frequency. **7** *Mining* A recess in a shaft or passage of a mine. **8** *Austral.* A cattle or sheep run with its appertaining buildings and grounds. **9** In surveying, a point around or from which measurements of angles or distances are made; also, the distance adopted for the standard length. **10** *Eccl.* **a** A stopping place, as a church, shrine, etc., for a solemn religious procession, at which certain prayers are said. **b** A Station of the Cross. — *v.t.* To assign to a station; set in position. [<F <L *statio, -onis* < *status,* pp. of *stare* stand]

Synonym (noun): depot. Properly, a train stops at a *station* to take on and discharge passengers or freight. Freight is kept in a *depot,* which is a storage room or a storehouse. However, the *station* and the *depot* were so often located in one building in the early days of railroads that the word *depot,* which formerly was thought to be more elegant but now has less dignity than *station,* came to be used for both. See PLACE.

sta·tion·ar·y (stā′shən·er′ē) *adj.* **1** Remaining in one place. **2** Fixed: opposed to *portable.* **3** Exhibiting no change of character or condition. — *n. pl.* **·ar·ies** One who or that which is stationary; especially, a member of a stationary military force. ◆ Homophone: *stationery.*

sta·tion·er (stā′shən·ər) *n.* **1** A dealer in stationery and kindred wares. **2** *Obs.* A bookseller; publisher. [<Med. L *stationarius* stationary, having a fixed location (for business)]

Stationers' Company A guild incorporated in London in 1577 comprising printers, bookbinders, booksellers, etc., which until 1911 in England exercised a copyright monopoly requiring all publications to be registered at its office, **Stationers' Hall.**

sta·tion·er·y (stā′shən·er′ē) *n.* Writing materials in general; paper, pens, pencils, ink, notebooks, etc. — *adj.* Dealing in or pertaining to stationery. ◆ Homophone: *stationary.*

station house A police station.

sta·tion·mas·ter (stā′shən·mas′tər, -mäs′-) *n.* The person having charge of a bus or railroad station.

Stations of the Cross The fourteen images or pictures ranged in a church or on church property, which form in series the representation of the successive scenes of the Passion of Christ, and before which devotions are performed.

station wagon An automotive vehicle with one or more rows of removable or folding seats located behind the front seat and with a hinged tailgate for admitting luggage, or the like.

stat·ism (stā′tiz·əm) *n.* **1** A theory of government which holds that the returns from group or individual enterprise are vested in the state, as in communism. **2** Loosely, adherence to state sovereignty, as in a republic. **3** *Obs.* Statecraft.

stat·ist (stā′tist) *n.* **1** An adherent of statism. **2** A statistician. **3** *Obs.* A statesman; politician.

sta·tis·tic (stə·tis′tik) *adj.* Statistical. — *n.* **1** Any element entering into a statistical statement or array, as the mean, the standard deviation, number of cases, etc. **2** Statistics. [<G *statistik* <Med. L *statisticus* statesmanlike, ult. <L *status.* See STATE.]

stat·is·ti·cian (stat′is·tish′ən) *n.* One skilled in collecting and tabulating statistical data.

sta·tis·tics (stə·tis′tiks) *n.* **1** Quantitative data, collectively, pertaining to any subject or group, especially when systematically gathered and collated; specifically, such data relating to a large body of people: *statistics* of population: construed as plural. **2** The science that deals with the collection, tabulation, and systematic classification of quantitative data, especially with reference to frequency distribution and as a basis for inference and induction respecting probable future trends: construed as singular. — **sta·tis′ti·cal** *adj.* — **sta·tis′ti·cal·ly** *adv.*

Sta·tius (stā′shəs), **Publius Papinius,** A.D. 45?–96?, Roman poet.

stato- *combining form* Position: *statoscope.* Also, before vowels, *stat-.* [<Gk. *statos* standing, fixed < *histanai* stand]

stat·o·blast (stat′ə·blast) *n. Zool.* One of the chitinous internal buds developed in freshwater sponges and on the funiculus of freshwater polyzoans.

stat·o·cyst (stat′ə·sist) *n. Anat.* One of the sacs in the labyrinth of the internal ear, provided with sensitive hairs and otoliths which are believed to aid in maintaining body equilibrium.

stat·o·lith (stat′ə·lith) *n.* **1** *Bot.* A starch grain or other minute particle in a plant cell, believed to influence the response of a plant organ to the action of gravity. **2** *Anat.* An otolith.

sta·tor (stā′tər) *n.* The stationary portion of a dynamo, turbine, or other power generator.

Compare ROTOR. [<NL <L, a supporter < *status.* See STATE.]

stat·o·scope (stat′ə·skōp) *n.* **1** *Meteorol.* A very sensitive form of aneroid barometer having a large reservoir of air, for indicating minute fluctuations in pressure. **2** *Aeron.* A device which indicates small variations in air pressure: used to show changes in altitude of an aircraft.

stat·u·ar·y (stach′o͞o·er′ē) *n. pl.* **·ar·ies** **1** Statues collectively. **2** One who makes statues; a sculptor. **3** The art of making statues. —*adj.* Of or suitable for statues. [<L *statuaria* < *statua* statue. See STATUE.]

stat·ue (stach′o͞o) *n.* A representation of a human or animal figure in marble, bronze, etc., especially when nearly life-size or larger, and preserving the proportions in all directions: distinguished from *painting* or *relief.* See synonyms under IMAGE. —*v.t.* **·ued, ·u·ing** To make a statue of. [<F <L *statua* < *status,* pp. of *stare* stand]

Statue of Liberty National Monument The site of Bartholdi's giant bronze statue *Liberty Enlightening the World* (presented to the U.S. by France, unveiled 1886) on Liberty Island in Upper New York Bay; 10 acres; established 1924. The statue is over 150 feet high and depicts a crowned woman holding aloft a burning torch.

stat·u·esque (stach′o͞o·esk′) *adj.* Resembling a statue, as in grace, pose, or dignity. [<STATUE + -ESQUE] —**stat′u·esque′ly** *adv.* —**stat′u·esque′ness** *n.*

stat·u·ette (stach′o͞o·et′) *n.* A statue not more than half life-size. [<F, dim. of *statue*]

stat·ure (stach′ər) *n.* **1** The natural height of an animal body, especially of a human body. **2** The height of anything, especially of a tree. **3** Development; growth: used figuratively: moral *stature.* [<OF <L *statura* < *status.* See STATE.]

sta·tus (stā′təs, stat′əs) *n.* **1** State, condition, or relation. **2** Relative position or rank. [<L. Doublet of STATE.]

sta·tus quo (stā′təs kwō, stat′əs) The condition or state in which (a person or thing is or has been): often used with the definite article: to maintain the *status quo.* Also **status in quo.** [<L]

sta·tus quo an·te bel·lum (stā′təs kwō an′tē bel′əm) *Latin* The state of affairs existing before the war.

stat·u·ta·ble (stach′o͞o·tə·bəl) *adj.* Statutory; agreeing or conforming with statute. —**stat′u·ta·bly** *adv.*

stat·ute (stach′o͞ot) *n.* **1** *Law* A legislative enactment duly sanctioned and authenticated by constitutional rule; act of Parliament, Congress, etc.; also, any authoritatively declared rule, ordinance, decree, or law. **2** The act of a corporation or its founder, intended as a permanent rule or law: the *statutes* of a university. See synonyms under LAW[1]. —*adj.* Consisting of or regulated by statute. [<F *statut* <LL *statutum,* neut. of L *statutus,* pp. of *statuere* set, found, constitute]

statute law The law as set forth in statutes.

statute mile See under MILE.

statute of limitations A statute which imposes time limits upon the right of action in certain cases, as by obliging a creditor to demand payment of a debt within a specified time.

stat·u·to·ry (stach′ə·tôr′ē, -tō′rē) *adj.* Pertaining to a statute; created by or dependent upon legislative enactment.

St. Augustine (sānt ô′gəs·tēn) A city on the Atlantic in NE Florida; oldest permanent town in the United States; founded by Spain in 1565.

staum·rel (stôm′rəl) *Scot. adj.* Half-witted. —*n.* A half-wit.

staunch (stônch, stänch) *adj.* **1** Firm in principle; constant; faithful; loyal; trustworthy: a *staunch* friend. **2** Stout; sound; tight; seaworthy: a *staunch* ship; having firm constitution or construction; strong and vigorous; hearty. —*v.t.* To stanch. —*n. Brit. Dial.* A floodgate; weir; dam. Also spelled *stanch.* [<OF *estanche* watertight, reliable < *estanchier* make stand. See STANCH.] —**staunch′ly** *adv.* —**staunch′ness** *n.*

Synonyms (adj.): firm, seaworthy, sound, stout, strong, taut, tight, trim, trustworthy, trusty. See FAITHFUL. *Antonyms*: crazy, leaky, rotten, unseaworthy, untrustworthy.

stau·ro·lite (stôr′ə·līt) *n.* A brown to brownish-black native silicate of iron and aluminum, found in prismatic crystals and sometimes used as a gem. [<Gk. *stauros* cross + -LITE; from the crosslike twin crystals] —**stau′ro·lit′ic** (-lit′ik) *adj.*

stau·ro·scope (stôr′ə·skōp) *n. Optics* An instrument used to determine the directions of the planes of vibration of polarized light in crystals. [<Gk. *stauros* cross + -SCOPE] —**stau′ro·scop′ic** (-skop′ik) *adj.*

Sta·vang·er (stä·väng′ər) A port in SW Norway; a fishing and industrial center; site of an 11th century cathedral.

stave (stāv) *n.* **1** A curved strip of wood, forming a part of the sides of a barrel, tub, or the like; hence, any narrow strip of material used for a like purpose: iron *staves.* **2** A straight board forming part of a curb, as about a well. **3** *Music* A staff. **4** A stanza; verse. **5** A rod, cudgel, or staff. **6** A rung of a rack or ladder. —*v.* **staved** or **stove, stav·ing** *v.t.* **1** To break in the staves or strakes of (a cask or a boat); crush the shell or surface of; smash. **2** To make (a hole) by crushing or collision. **3** To furnish with staves. **4** To ward off, as with a staff; keep at a distance: usually with *off*: to *stave* off hunger. —*v.i.* **5** To be broken in, as a vessel's hull. [Back formation < *staves,* pl. of STAFF]

staves (stāvz) **1** Alternative plural of STAFF. **2** Plural of STAVE.

staves·a·cre (stāvz′ā′kər) *n.* **1** A tall larkspur *(Delphinium staphisagria)* of southern Europe. **2** Its seeds, yielding a poisonous alkaloid formerly used as a purgative and antispasmodic. [<OF *stafisagre* <Med. L *staphis agria* <Gk. *staphis* raisin + *agrios* wild]

Stav·ro·pol (stav·rô′pəl) A city on the Volga in southern European Russian S.F.S.R.: formerly (1935–43) *Voroshilovsk.*

staw (stô) *Scot.* Past tense of STEAL.

stay[1] (stā) *v.i.* **1** To cease motion; stop; halt. **2** To continue in a specified place, condition, or state: to *stay* indoors; to *stay* healthy. **3** To remain temporarily as a guest, resident, etc.: Where are you *staying*? **4** To pause; wait; tarry. **5** *Colloq.* To have endurance; stand up; last. **6** *Colloq.* To keep pace with a competitor, as in a race. **7** In poker, to remain in a hand by meeting an ante, bet, or raise. **8** *Archaic* To cease. **9** *Archaic* To stand firm. —*v.t.* **10** To bring to a stop; halt; check. **11** To hinder; delay. **12** To put off; postpone. **13** To satisfy the demands of temporarily; quiet; appease: to *stay* the pangs of hunger. **14** To remain for the duration of: I will *stay* the night. **15** To remain till or beyond the end of: with *out*: to *stay* out one's welcome. **16** *Archaic* To quell, as strife. **17** *Obs.* To wait for. See synonyms under ABIDE, HINDER[1], OBSTRUCT, PERSIST, REPRESS, REST[1], STAND. —*n.* **1** The act or time of staying; continuance in a place; sojourn; visit. **2** That which checks or stops; specifically, a suspension of judicial proceedings. **3** Staying power; endurance; persistence. **4** A state of rest; standstill. See synonyms under RESPITE, REST. [<AF *estaier,* OF *ester* <L *stare* stand] —**stay′er** *n.*

stay[2] (stā) *v.t.* **1** To be a support to; prop or hold up. **2** To support mentally; comfort; sustain. **3** To cause to depend or rely, as for support: with *on* or *upon.* —*n.* **1** Anything which props or supports; a prop, buttress, or the like. **2** *pl.* A corset. [<OF *estayer*]

stay[3] (stā) *Naut. n.* **1** A large, strong rope, often of wire, used to support, steady, or fasten a mast or spar. **2** Any rope supporting a mast or funnel; a guy rope. —**in stays** In the act of turning about on another tack. —*v.t.* **1** To support with a stay or stays, as a mast. **2** To put (a vessel) on the opposite tack. —*v.i.* **3** To tack: said of vessels. [OE *stæg*]

stay-at-home (stā′at·hōm′) *adj.* Given to remaining at home; not in the habit of traveling. —*n.* A person accustomed to staying home.

staying power The ability to endure.

stay·sail (stā′səl, -sāl′) *n. Naut.* A sail, usually triangular, extended on a stay.

St. Ber·nard (sānt bər·närd′, *Fr.* saṅ ber·nȧr′) Either of two passes in the Alps: (1) **Great St. Bernard,** between Switzerland and Italy, east of Mont Blanc; elevation 8,120 feet; **St. Bernard hospice,** founded in the 11th century for the rescue of snowbound travelers, is at its summit. (2) **Little St. Bernard,** between France and Italy, south of Mont Blanc; elevation, 7,180 feet; site of a 10th century hospice for travelers.

St. Chris·to·pher (kris′tə·fər), **Ne·vis** (nē′vis, nev′is) **and An·guil·la** (ang·gwil′ə) A British colony, and a federating unit of The West Indies (federation), formerly a presidency of the British Leeward Islands, comprising the islands of **St. Christopher** (commonly *St. Kitts*); 68 square miles; *Nevis*; 50 square miles; and *Anguilla*; 34 square miles; capital, Basseterre, on St. Kitts.

St. Clair (klâr), **Lake** A lake between southern Ontario, Canada, and SE Michigan; 460 square miles; connected with Lake Huron by the **St. Clair River,** a river which flows 40 miles south, forming part of the boundary between Ontario, Canada, and Michigan.

St. Croix (sānt kroi′) The largest of the Virgin Islands of the United States; 82 square miles; capital, Christiansted: also *Santa Cruz.*

St. Croix River **1** A river forming the boundary between NW Wisconsin and eastern Minnesota and flowing 164 miles SW and south, through **Lake St. Croix** (a natural widening of the river extending 24 miles south) to the Mississippi River. **2** A river forming the boundary between Maine and New Brunswick and flowing 75 miles south and east to Passamaquoddy Bay.

stead (sted) *n.* **1** Place of another person or thing: preceded by *in*: Serfdom came *in* the *stead* of slavery. Compare INSTEAD. **2** Place or attitude of support; use; avail; service: in the phrase **to stand one in stead** or **in good stead.** **3** A steading or farm: used chiefly in compounds: *homestead, Hempstead.* **4** *Archaic* Position; condition; place, in general. —*v.t. Archaic* To be of advantage to; help; benefit; support. [OE *stede* place]

stead·fast (sted′fast′, -fäst′, -fəst) *adj.* **1** Firmly fixed in faith or devotion to duty; constant; unchanging. **2** Directed fixedly at one point or to one end, as the gaze or purpose; steady. Also spelled *stedfast.* See synonyms under FIRM, INFLEXIBLE, PERMANENT. [OE *stedefæst*] —**stead′fast′ly** *adv.* —**stead′fast′ness** *n.*

stead·ing (sted′ing) *n. Brit. Dial.* A farmhouse, sheds, and offices; a farmstead.

stead·y (sted′ē) *adj.* **stead·i·er, stead·i·est** **1** Stable in position; firmly supported; fixed. **2** Moving or acting with uniform regularity; constant; unfaltering: a *steady* light; hence, not readily disturbed or upset: *steady* nerves. **3** Free from intemperance and dissipation; industrious, sober, and reliable: *steady* habits. **4** Constant in mind or conduct; not wavering; steadfast; also, regular: a *steady* customer. **5** Uninterrupted; continuous: a *steady* flow of conversation. **6** *Naut.* Having the direction of the ship's head unchanged. See synonyms under FIRM, SOBER. —*v.t.* & *v.i.* **stead·ied, stead·y·ing** To make or become steady. —*interj.* **1** *Naut.* Keep her steady: an order to a helmsman to keep the ship's head pointed in the same direction. **2** Not so fast; keep calm: an order enjoining self-control or composure. —*n. Slang* A sweetheart or steady companion. [<STEAD + -Y[3]] —**stead′i·er** *n.* —**stead′i·ly** *adv.* —**stead′i·ness** *n.*

steak (stāk) *n.* **1** A slice of meat, as of beef, usually broiled or fried; specifically, beefsteak. **2** Meat, chopped for cooking like a steak: hamburger *steak.* ◆ Homophone: *stake.* [<ON *steik*]

steal (stēl) *v.* **stole, sto·len, steal·ing** *v.t.* **1** To take from another without right, authority, or permission, and usually in a secret manner. **2** To take or obtain in a surreptitious, artful, or subtle manner: He has *stolen* the hearts of the people. **3** To move, place, or convey stealthily: with *away, from, in, into,* etc. **4** In baseball, to reach (a base) without the aid of a hit or error. —*v.i.* **5** To commit theft; be a thief. **6** To move secretly or furtively. —*n.* **1** The act of stealing or that which is stolen; a theft. **2** In baseball, the act of stealing a base. **3** Any financial transaction or other deal that benefits no one but the originators. ◆ Homophones: *steel, stele.* [OE *stelan*] —**steal′er** *n.* —**steal′ing** *n.*

Synonyms (verb): abstract, embezzle, extort, filch, pilfer, pillage, plunder, purloin, rob, swindle. To *steal* is, in law, to commit simple *larceny*; but the word may be applied to any

furtive, covert, or surreptitious taking of anything, whether material or immaterial. To *pilfer* is to *steal* petty articles. *Filch* especially emphasizes the secrecy and slyness of the act, and is ordinarily applied to things of little value, but may apply to the most precious, as in Shakespeare, "he that *filches* from me my good name." To *purloin* is etymologically to carry far away, and is commonly applied to the dishonest removal of articles of value or importance. To *rob* is, in law, to take feloniously from the person by force or fear, as in highway robbery; it is also applied to the felonious taking of articles of value from places as well as persons generally with suggestion of force and violence. To *abstract* is to take secretly and feloniously from among other things belonging to another. To *embezzle* is to appropriate fraudulently to oneself funds received and held in trust. To *swindle* is to cheat grossly, commonly by false pretenses, but is not a recognized legal offense under that name; one form of *swindling*, "obtaining money by false pretenses," is an indictable offense, but much *swindling* may be carried on under the forms of law. To *plunder* is to take property from an enemy in time of war, and is not a crime at law. See ABSTRACT. *Antonyms*: refund, repay, restore, return, surrender.

steal·age (stē′lij) *n.* Losses suffered from stealing.

stealth (stelth) *n.* **1** The quality or habit of acting secretly; a concealed manner of acting; a secret or clandestine act, movement, or proceeding. **2** *Obs.* Theft or the thing stolen. [ME *stelthe, stalthe* <OE *stelan* steal]

stealth·y (stel′thē) *adj.* **stealth·i·er, stealth·i·est** Moving or acting secretly or slily; done or characterized by stealth; furtive. — **stealth′i·ly** *adv.* — **stealth′i·ness** *n.*

steam (stēm) *n.* **1** Water in the form of vapor. **2** The gas or vapor into which water is changed by boiling. **3** The visible mist into which aqueous vapor is condensed by cooling. **4** Any kind of vaporous exhalation. **5** Energy, force, or power derived from water vapor under pressure, as in cooking, heating, etc. **6** *Colloq.* Vigor; force; speed. — **to let off steam** *Colloq.* To give expression to pent-up emotions or opinions. — *v.i.* **1** To give off or emit steam or vapor. **2** To rise or pass off as steam. **3** To become covered with condensed water vapor: often with *up*. **4** To generate steam. **5** To move or travel by the agency of steam. — *v.t.* **6** To treat with steam, as in softening, cooking, cleaning, etc. — *adj.* **1** Of, driven, or operated by steam: a *steam* gage, *steam* shovel. **2** Containing or conveying steam: a *steam* boiler. **3** Treated by steam. [OE *stēam*]

steam·boat (stēm′bōt′) *n.* A boat or vessel propelled by steam.

steam boiler A closed vessel used in generating steam.

steam chest The box or chest through which steam is delivered from a boiler to an engine cylinder. Also **steam box.**

steam engine An engine that derives its motive force from the action of steam, usually by pressure against a piston sliding within a closed cylinder.

steam·er (stē′mər) *n.* **1** Something propelled or worked by steam, as a steamship. **2** A vessel in which something is steamed, as for cooking, washing, etc.

steamer trunk A trunk small enough to fit under a berth in a ship's cabin.

steam·fit·ter (stēm′fit′ər) *n.* A man who sets up or repairs steampipes and their fittings. — **steam′fit′ting** *n.*

steam point *Physics* The boiling point of water at standard atmospheric pressure; 100° C.: one of the fixed points of the international temperature scale.

steam roller 1 A road-rolling machine driven by steam. **2** Any force that ruthlessly overcomes opposition. — **steam′roll′er** *adj.*

steam·ship (stēm′ship′) *n.* A large vessel used for ocean traffic and propelled, usually, by one or more screws operated by steam; a steamer.

steam shovel A steam-operated shovel for digging and excavation.

steam table A long table with openings in which containers of food are placed to be kept warm by hot water or steam circulating beneath them.

steam·tight (stēm′tīt′) *adj.* Preventing the escape of steam.

steam turbine A turbine operated by steam power.

steam·y (stē′mē) *adj.* **steam·i·er, steam·i·est** Consisting of, like, or full of steam; misty. — **steam′i·ly** *adv.* — **steam′i·ness** *n.*

Ste. Anne de Beau·pré (sänt an′ də bō-prā′) A village and shrine on the north bank of the St. Lawrence River, 21 miles NE of Quebec, Canada.

ste·ap·sin (stē-ap′sin) *n. Biochem.* A lipase contained in pancreatic juice. [<STEA(RIN) + (pe)PSIN]

ste·a·rate (stē′ə-rāt) *n. Chem.* A salt or ester of stearic acid.

ste·ar·ic (stē-ar′ik, stir′ik) *adj. Chem.* **1** Of, pertaining to, or derived from stearin. **2** Designating a white fatty acid, $C_{17}H_{35}COOH$, contained in the more solid animal fats and in many vegetable oils. [<F *stéarique* <Gk. *stear* suet]

ste·a·rin (stē′ə-rin, stir′in) *n. Chem.* A white, crystalline ester of glycerol and stearic acid, $C_3H_5(C_{18}H_{35}O_2)_3$, obtained from various animal and vegetable fats: more correctly called *glyceryl stearate* or *tristearin*. **2** Stearic acid, especially as combined with palmitic acid for making candles, etc. **3** Fat in solid form. Also **ste′a·rine** (-rin, -rēn). [<Gk. *stear* suet]

ste·a·rop·tene (stē′ə-rop′tēn) *n. Chem.* A solid crystalline compound that separates from a volatile oil on standing or exposure to cold. Compare ELAEOPTENE. [<STEAR(IC) + (ELAE)OPTENE]

ste·ar·rhe·a (stē′ə-rē′ə) *n. Pathol.* Steatorrhea. [<Gk. *stear* suet + -RRHEA]

ste·a·tite (stē′ə-tīt) *n. Massive* talc; soapstone: found in extensive beds and quarried for hearths, sink linings, coarse utensils, etc. See TALC. [<L *steatitis* <Gk. *stear, steatos* suet, tallow] — **ste′a·tit′ic** (-tit′ik) *adj.*

ste·a·to·py·gi·a (stē′ə-tō-pī′jē-ə, -pij′ē-ə) *n.* Abnormal growth of fat on the buttocks: noted especially in women among the Bushmen and Hottentots of Africa. Also **ste′a·to·py′ga** (-pī′gə). [<NL <Gk. *stear, steatos* suet, fat + *pygē* buttock] — **ste′a·to·py′gous** (-pī′gəs) *adj.*

ste·a·tor·rhe·a (stē′ə-tə-rē′ə) *n. Pathol.* **1** Seborrhea. **2** Excess fat in the stools. Also **ste′a·tor·rhoe′a.** [<Gk. *stear, steatos* suet + -RRHEA]

stech (stekh) *v.t. & v.i. Scot.* To cram; stuff.

sted·fast (sted′fast′, -fäst′, -fəst) See STEADFAST.

steed (stēd) *n.* A horse; especially, a spirited war horse: now chiefly a literary use. [OE *stēda* studhorse]

Steed (stēd), **Henry Wickham,** 1871–1956, English journalist.

steek (stēk) *Scot. v.t. & v.i.* To shut; close. — *n.* A stitch.

steel (stēl) *n.* **1** A tough alloy of iron containing carbon in variable amounts up to about 2.0 percent, malleable under proper conditions, and greatly hardened by sudden cooling. Commercial grades are classified, on the basis of carbon content, as: **mild** or **soft steel,** with up to about 0.30 percent of carbon; **medium steel,** 0.30 to 0.60 percent of carbon, and **high** or **hard steel,** containing more than 0.60 percent of carbon. The addition of other components gives a large range of alloys having special properties, as **chrome steel, nickel steel,** etc. **2** Something made of steel, as an implement or weapon; a sword; a knife sharpener. **3** Hardness of character; steel-like nature or quality. **4** A strip or band of steel, as for stiffening a corset. **5** The quotation for shares in a steel company. — *adj.* Made or composed of steel; also, resembling steel; hence, hard; obdurate; adamant; unyielding. — *v.t.* **1** To cover with steel; plate, edge, point, or face with steel. **2** To make hard or strong like steel; make unfeeling or unyielding; harden: to *steel* one's heart against misery. ◆ Homophones: *steal, stele.* [OE *stēl*]

steel-blue (stēl′blōō′) *adj.* Having a color similar to the bluish tinge of certain steels.

steel blue A steel-blue color.

steel-die printing (stēl′dī′) Intaglio printing.

Steele (stēl), **Sir Richard,** 1672–1729, English dramatist and essayist.

steel engraving 1 The art and process of engraving on a steel plate. **2** The impression made from such a plate.

steel gray Any of several shades of dark, dull gray, like the color of finished steel.

steel-head (stēl′hed′) *n.* **1** A species of migratory trout *(Salmo gairdneri),* found from California to Alaska. **2** The black spotted trout *(S. purpuratus)* of the western United States, especially in its adult marine stage.

steel·ing (stē′ling) *n.* **1** The coating of an engraved copper plate with a protective film of iron by electrolysis to increase its durability. **2** Casehardening.

steel·mak·er (stēl′mā′kər) *n.* A maker of steel; especially, the operator or owner of a steel mill.

steel wool Steel fibers matted together for use as an abrasive or in cleaning, polishing, and finishing utensils and the like.

steel·work (stēl′wûrk′) *n.* **1** Any article or construction of steel. **2** *pl.* A shop or factory where steel is made or fabricated. — **steel′work′ing** *n.*

steel·work·er (stēl′wûr′kər) *n.* One who works in a steel mill.

steel·y (stē′lē) *adj.* **steel·i·er, steel·i·est** Made of, resembling, or containing steel; suggesting steel; figuratively, having a steel-like hardness: a *steely* obduracy; a *steely* gaze. — **steel′i·ness** *n.*

steel·yard (stēl′yärd′, -yərd) *n.* A simple device for weighing, consisting of a scaled beam, counterpoise, and hooks, the article to be weighed being hung at the short end, and the counterpoise weight on the long arm. Also **steel′yards.** [from *Steelyard,* formerly, the London headquarters for Hanseatic traders; a mistranslation of MLG *stalhof* a court where samples of goods are displayed]

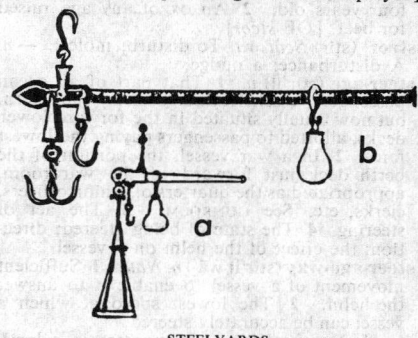

STEELYARDS
a. Pompeian. *b.* Modern.

Steen (stān), **Jan,** 1626–79, Dutch painter.

steen·bok (stān′bok, stēn′-) See STEINBOK.

steep[1] (stēp) *adj.* **1** Making a large angle with the plane of the horizon; precipitous. **2** *Colloq.* Exorbitant; excessive; high, as a price. — *n.* A cliff; hill; precipice; a precipitous place. [OE *stēap*] — **steep′ly** *adv.* — **steep′ness** *n.*

Synonyms (adj.): abrupt, high, precipitous, sharp, sheer. *High* is used of simple elevation; *steep* is said only of an incline where the vertical measurement is sufficiently great in proportion to the horizontal to make it difficult of ascent. *Steep* is relative; an ascent of 100 feet to the mile on a railway is a *steep* grade; a rise of 500 feet to the mile makes a *steep* wagon road; a roof is *steep* when it makes with the horizontal line an angle of more than 45°. A *sharp* ascent or descent is one that makes a sudden, decided angle with the plane from which it starts; a *sheer* ascent or descent is perpendicular, or nearly so; *precipitous* applies to that which is of the nature of a precipice, and is used especially of a descent; *abrupt* is as if broken sharply off, and applies to either acclivity or declivity. See HIGH. *Antonyms*: easy, gentle, gradual, level, low, slight.

steep[2] (stēp) *v.t.* **1** To soak in a liquid, as for

softening, cleansing, etc. **2** To saturate; imbue thoroughly: *steeped* in crime. — *v.i.* **3** To undergo soaking in a liquid. — *n.* **1** The process of steeping, or the state of being steeped. **2** A liquid or bath in which anything is or is to be steeped; especially, a fertilizing liquid for seeds. [ME *stepen,* ? <Scand. Cf. ON *steypa* pour.] — **steep′er** *n.*

steep·en (stē′pən) *v.t.* & *v.i.* To make or become steep or steeper.

stee·ple (stē′pəl) *n.* A lofty structure rising above the tower of a church; a spire. [OE *stēpel, stȳpel*]

stee·ple·bush (stē′pəl·bo͝osh′) *n.* An erect shrub *(Spirae tomentosa)* of the rose family, with dense terminal clusters of rose-colored flowers; the hardhack.

stee·ple·chase (stē′pəl·chās′) *n.* **1** A race on horseback across country, in which obstacles are to be leaped: originating from a race to see which of several riders could first reach a distant church steeple. **2** A race over a course artificially prepared, as with hedges, rails, and water jumps. **3** Any cross-country run. — **stee′ple·chas′ing** *n.*

stee·ple·chas·er (stē′pəl·chā′sər) *n.* A person who takes part in a steeplechase; also, a horse used in or trained for steeplechasing.

stee·ple·jack (stē′pəl·jak′) *n.* A man whose occupation is to climb steeples and other tall structures to inspect or make repairs. [<STEEPLE + obs. *jack* workman]

steer[1] (stir) *v.t.* **1** To direct the course of (a vessel or vehicle) by means of a rudder, steering wheel, or other device. **2** To follow (a course). **3** To direct; guide; control. — *v.i.* **4** To direct the course of a vessel, vehicle, etc. **5** To undergo guiding or steering: The car *steers* easily. **6** To follow a course: to *steer* for land. — **to steer clear of** To avoid; keep away from. — *n. U.S. Slang* A tip; piece of advice. [OE *stēoran*] — **steer′a·ble** *adj.* — **steer′er** *n.*

steer[2] (stir) *n.* **1** A young male of the ox kind, especially when castrated and from two to four years old. **2** An ox of any age raised for beef. [OE *stēor*]

steer[3] (stir) *Scot. v.t.* To disturb; molest. — *n.* A disturbance; a nudge.

steer·age (stir′ij) *n.* **1** That part of an ocean passenger vessel, formerly near the stern, but now usually situated in the forward lower decks, allotted to passengers paying the lowest fares. **2** In a war vessel, the portion of the berth deck just forward of the wardroom, appropriated as the quarters of junior officers, clerks, etc. See GUNROOM. **3** The act of steering. **4** The state of being steered; direction; the effect of the helm on a vessel.

steer·age·way (stir′ij·wā′) *n. Naut.* **1** Sufficient movement of a vessel to enable it to answer the helm. **2** The lowest speed at which a vessel can be accurately steered.

steering committee A committee in a legislature or other assemblage that arranges or directs the course of the business that is to be considered.

steering gear *Mech.* Any arrangement of parts for converting action on the steering wheel into corresponding motion of the rudder of a ship, or, on an automotive vehicle, of the steering axle and its connected members.

steering wheel *Mech.* **1** A vertical wheel with handles along the rim, by which motion is communicated to the rudder of a ship by the wheel ropes or other connections. **2** A hand wheel for guiding an automobile or other heavy vehicle.

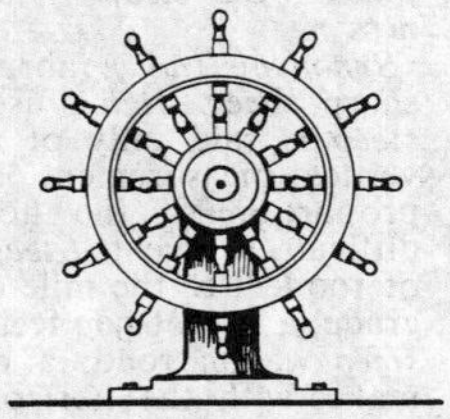

SHIP'S STEERING WHEEL

steers·man (stirz′mən) *n. pl.* **·men** (-mən) One who steers a boat; a helmsman.

steer·y (stir′ē) *Scot. n.* A stir; bustle. — *adj.* Busy; bustling.

steeve[1] (stēv) *n.* A derrick or a spar with a block at one end used in stowing cargo. [<*v.*] — *v.t.* **steeved, steev·ing** **1** To stow, as cargo in the hold of a vessel, by using a steeve or a jackscrew. **2** *Scot.* To pack; cram. [<F *estiver* <L *stipare* compress]

steeve[2] (stēv) *Naut. n.* The angular elevation of a bowsprit from the horizontal: also **steev′ing.** — *v.t.* & *v.i.* **steeved, steev·ing** To set or be set upward at an angle with the horizon. [? <OF *estive* tail of a plough <L *stiva*]

Stef·ans·son (stef′ən·sən), **Vilhjalmur,** 1879–1962, U.S. Arctic explorer, born in Canada of Icelandic parentage.

Stef·fens (stef′ənz), **(Joseph) Lincoln,** 1866–1936, U.S. journalist.

steg·o·my·ia (steg′ə·mī′ə) *n.* Any of a former genus *(Stegomyia)* of mosquitos; especially, the yellow-fever mosquito *(S. fasciata* or *S. calopus),* which is now called *Aëdes aegypti.* [<NL <Gk. *stegos* a roof + *myia* fly]

steg·o·sau·rus (steg′ə·sôr′əs) *n. pl.* **·sau·ri** (-sôr′ī) *Paleontol.* Any of a genus *(Stegosaurus)* of herbivorous armored dinosaurs of great size which flourished in the western United States during the Upper Jurassic and Lower Cretaceous periods. [<NL <Gk. *stegos* roof + -SAURUS]

Stei·er·mark (shtī′ər·märk) The German name for STYRIA.

stein (stīn) *n.* A beer mug, holding usually a pint; also, the quantity of beer it contains. [<G]

Stein (shtīn), **Baron vom und zum,** 1757–1831, Heinrich Friedrich Karl, Prussian statesman.

Stein (stīn), **Gertrude,** 1874–1946, U.S. writer, resident in France.

Stein·am·ang·er (shtīn′äm·äng′ər) See SZOMBATHELY.

Stein·beck (stīn′bek), **John Ernst,** 1902–1968, U.S. novelist.

stein·bok (stīn′bok) *n.* A small fawn-colored African antelope *(Raphicerus campestris)*: also spelled *steenbok.* Also **stein′buck′** (-buk′). [<Du. *steenbok* <*steen* stone + *bok* buck]

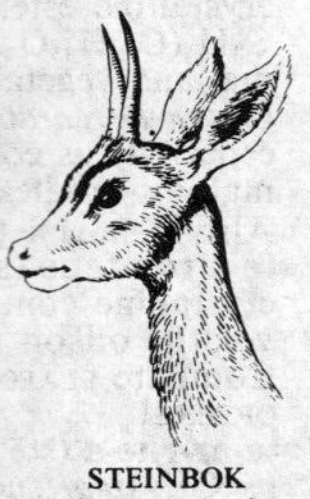

STEINBOK
(About 20 inches shoulder height)

Stein·metz (stīn′mets), **Charles Proteus,** 1865–1923, U.S. electrical engineer born in Germany.

St. E·li·as (sānt i·lī′əs), **Mount** A peak (18,008 feet) in the **St. Elias Mountains** in SW Yukon and SE Alaska; filled by the world's most extensive glacier system apart from the polar ice caps; highest point, 19,850 feet.

ste·le[1] (stē′lē) *n. pl.* **·lae** (-lē) or **·les** (-lēz) An upright sculptured slab or tablet of stone, either sepulchral or intended for public use, as for laws, decrees, treaties, milestones, etc. Also **ste·la** (stē′lə). [<L *stela* <Gk. *stēlē*] — **ste′lar, ste′lene** (-lēn) *adj.*

stele[2] (stēl) *n. Bot.* An axial cylinder of vascular tissue in plants, sometimes more than one. ◆ Homophones: *steal, steel.* [<STELE[1]] — **ste′lic** *adj.*

Stel·la (stel′ə) A feminine personal name. [<L, star]

stel·lar (stel′ər) *adj.* **1** Of or pertaining to the stars; astral. **2** Of or pertaining to an actor or actress who plays a principal role, or to other persons prominent in the arts. [<LL *stellaris* <L *stella* star]

stel·lar·a·tor (stel′ə·rā′tər) *n. Physics* A device for the study of controlled thermonuclear reactions, consisting essentially of a series of magnetizing coils surrounding a hollow glass tube in which ionized gases may be briefly heated to temperatures of several million degrees. [<STELLAR + -ATOR; from the great temperatures developed]

stel·late (stel′it, -āt) *adj.* Star-shaped or starlike; radiating. See illustration under FROST. Also **stel·lat·ed** (stel′ā·tid). [<L *stellatus,* pp. of *stellare* cover with stars <*stella* star] — **stel′late·ly** *adv.*

stel·lif·er·ous (ste·lif′ər·əs) *adj.* Abounding with stars. [<L *stella* star + -(I)FEROUS]

stel·li·form (stel′ə·fôrm) *adj.* Star-shaped. [<NL *stelliformis* <L *stella* star + *forma* form]

Stell·ite (stel′īt) *n.* A class of hard cobalt alloys containing varying amounts of tungsten and chromium: used chiefly in the manufacture of cutting tools: a trade name.

stel·lu·lar (stel′yə·lər) *adj.* Bespangled with fine stars; shaped like or resembling little stars. [<LL *stellula* little star]

St. El·mo's fire or **light** (sānt el′mōz) A luminous charge of atmospheric electricity sometimes appearing on the masts and yardarms of ships, on church steeples, etc.: also called *corposant.*

stem[1] (stem) *n.* **1** The ascending axis or stalk of a plant, as distinguished from the descending axis or *root*; the main body or stalk of a tree, shrub, or other plant, rising above the ground or other rooting place. **2** The relatively slender growth supporting the fruit, flower, or leaf of a plant; a stalk, peduncle, pedicel, or petiole. ◆ Collateral adjective: *cauline.* **3** A bunch of bananas. **4** The main line of descendants from a particular ancestor. **5** An ethnic line; race. **6** The long, slender, usually cylindrical portion of an instrument: a pipe *stem.* **7** The slender upright support of a goblet, wineglass, vase, etc. **8** A shaft, as of a hair or feather. **9** In a watch, the small projecting rod used for winding the mainspring. **10** In some locks, the central circular part about which the key turns. **11** *Printing* The upright stroke of a type face or letter. **12** *Music* The line attached to the head of a written musical note. **13** *Ling.* The element common to all the members of a given inflection or related groups of words. A stem often consists of more than one morpheme, as the Latin stem *luci-* "light" in *lucifer* "lightbearer" is composed of the root *luc-* plus the thematic vowel *-i-*. **14** *Electr.* The air-sealed, tubular glass section at the base of an incandescent lamp, serving to lead the filaments into the evacuated bulb. See illustration under INCANDESCENT. — *v.* **stemmed, stem·ming** *v.t.* **1** To remove the stems of or from. **2** To supply with stems. — *v.i.* **3** To be descended or derived: to *stem* from John Alden. [OE *stemm, stemn, stæfn* stem of a tree, prow of a ship] — **stem′less** *adj.*

stem[2] (stem) *n. Naut.* **1** A nearly upright timber or metal piece uniting the two sides of a vessel at the fore-end. **2** The bow or prow of a vessel. — **from stem to stern** From end to end; hence, thoroughly. — *v.* **stemmed, stem·ming** *v.t.* **1** To resist or make progress against, as a current: said of a vessel. **2** To stand firm or make progress against (any opposing force): to *stem* the tide of public opinion. **3** To strike with the stem (of a vessel). [<STEM[1], in obs. sense "a tree trunk"]

stem[3] (stem) *v.t.* **stemmed, stem·ming** **1** To stop, hold back, or dam up, as a current; stanch. **2** To make tight, as a joint; to plug. [<ON *stemma* stop]

stem·mer (stem′ər) *n.* **1** One who stems. **2** In tobacco manufacture, one who takes out the main stem from the tobacco plant in making strips. **3** A device for stemming fruits, as grapes.

stem·son (stem′sən) *n. Naut.* A curved supporting timber bolted to the stem and keelson of a vessel near the bow. [<STEM[2] + (KEEL)SON]

stem turn In skiing, a turn made by placing the points of the skis nearly together and the ends wide apart, then placing the weight on the outside ski.

stem·ware (stem′wâr′) *n.* Drinking vessels with stems, as goblets, taken collectively.

stem-wind·er (stem′wīn′dər) *n.* **1** A watch wound by turning the crown of the stem. **2** *U.S. Slang* A very superior person or thing.

stem-wind·ing (stem′wīn′ding) *adj.* Wound by turning a knob on an outside stem connected with inside mechanism.

stench (stench) *n.* A foul or offensive odor; stink. See synonyms under SMELL. [OE *stenc*]

sten·cil (sten′səl) *n.* **1** A thin sheet or plate in which a pattern is cut by means of spaces or dots, through which applied paint or ink penetrates to a surface beneath. **2** A decoration or the like produced by stenciling. — *v.t.* **·ciled** or **·cilled, ·cil·ing** or **·cil·ling** To mark with a stencil. [Prob. ME *stansel* decorate with many colors <OF *estenceler,* ult. <L *scintilla* a spark] — **sten′cil·er** or **sten′cil·ler** *n.*

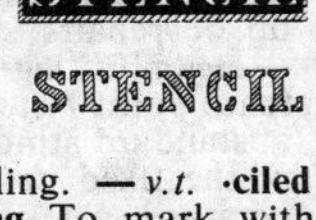

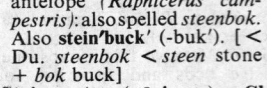

Sten·dhal (stän·däl′) Pen name of *Marie Henri Beyle,* 1783–1842, French novelist.

steno- *combining form* Tight; narrow; contracted: *stenography.* Also, before vowels, **sten-**. [<Gk. *stenos* narrow]

sten·o·graph (sten′ə·graf, -gräf) *n.* **1** A character or writing in shorthand. **2** A keyboard machine for printing in shorthand.

ste·nog·ra·pher (stə·nog′rə·fər) *n.* One who writes stenography or is skilled in shorthand; especially, a writer of phonography. Also **ste·nog′ra·phist.**

ste·nog·ra·phy (stə·nog′rə·fē) *n.* **1** The art of writing by the use of contractions or arbitrary symbols; shorthand. **2** Loosely, phonography. **—sten·o·graph·ic** (sten′ə·graf′·ik) or **·i·cal** *adj.* **—sten′o·graph′i·cal·ly** *adv.*

sten·o·morph (sten′ə·môrf) *n. Ecol.* A plant form that is abnormally undersized because of a cramped habitat. **—sten′o·mor′phic** *adj.*

sten·o·phyl·lous (sten′ō·fil′əs) *adj. Bot.* Characterized by narrow leaves, as certain plants.

ste·no·sis (sti·nō′sis) *n. Pathol.* Narrowing of a duct or canal in the body. [<NL <Gk. *stenōsis* < *stenos* narrow]

sten·o·ther·mal (sten′ō·thûr′məl) *adj. Ecol.* Adapted to a limited range of temperature variations: said especially of certain plants. **—sten′o·ther′my** *n.*

sten·o·trop·ic (sten′ə·trop′ik) *adj. Ecol.* Having a narrow range of adaptability to environmental changes: said of plant and animal species.

sten·o·type (sten′ə·tīp) *n.* A letter or combination of letters representing a word or phrase, especially in shorthand.

Sten·o·type (sten′ə·tīp) *n.* A keyboard-operated machine used in stenotypy: a trade name.

sten·o·typ·y (sten′ə·tī′pē) *n.* A system of shorthand representing, by ordinary letters or type, shortened forms of words or phrases.

stent[1] (stent) *Scot. v.t.* To assess for taxation; rate; tax. **—***n.* A tax, levy, or due.

stent[2] (stent) *n., v.t. & v.i. Brit. Dial.* Stint.

stent[3] (stent) *adj. Scot.* Drawn tight; taut.

sten·tor (sten′tôr) *n.* **1** One who possesses an uncommonly strong, loud voice. **2** Any of a genus *(Stentor)* of fresh-water protozoans (class *Ciliata*) having contractile trumpet-shaped bodies capable of attachment by their lower ends. [after *Stentor*]

Sten·tor (sten′tôr) In the *Iliad,* a herald famous for his loud voice.

sten·to·ri·an (sten·tôr′ē·ən, -tō′rē-) *adj.* Extremely loud.

step (step) *n.* **1** An act of progressive motion that requires one of the supporting limbs of the body to be thrust in the direction of the movement, and to reassume its function of support; a pace. **2** The distance passed over in making such a motion; in military quick-time marching, 30 inches. **3** Any short distance; a space easily traversed. **4** That upon which the foot rests in ascending or descending, as a stair or ladder rung. **5** A single action or proceeding regarded as leading to something: a *step* toward emancipation. **6** An advance or promotion that forms one of a series, especially in military usage; grade; degree. **7** The manner of stepping; walk; gait; also, the sound of a footfall. **8** A footprint; track. **9** *pl.* Progression by walking; walk. **10** A combination of foot movements in dancing, forming a pattern that may be repeated, varied, or elaborated: the tango *step.* **11** An interval measuring a difference of musical pitch, corresponding to a degree of the scale or staff. **12** A socket, supporting framework, pocket, or the like: the *step* of a mast. **13** A steplike projection or part, as of the bit of a key. **14** *Mech.* The radial distance between the face of one pulley and that of another stepped on the same shaft. **15** A break in the contour of a float or hull, as of a seaplane, designed to lessen resistance and improve control. **16** A stage in cascade amplification. **—in step** In agreement or synchronism when marching, dancing, etc.; walking evenly with another by taking corresponding steps. **—out of step** Not in step. **—to take steps** To adopt measures, as to attain an end. **—***v.* **stepped, step·ping** *v.i.* **1** To move forward or backward by taking a step or steps. **2** To go by foot; walk a short distance: to *step* across the street. **3** To move with measured, dignified, or graceful steps. **4** To move or act quickly or briskly: The old man was *stepping* down the road. **5** To pass into a situation, circumstance, etc., as if in a single step: He *stepped* into a fortune. **—***v.t.* **6** To take (a pace, stride, etc.). **7** To perform the steps of: to *step* a quadrille. **8** To place or move (the foot) in taking a step. **9** To measure by taking steps: often with *off:* to *step* off five yards. **10** To cut or arrange in steps. **11** *Naut.* To place the lower end of (a mast) in its step. **—to step down 1** To decrease gradually, or by steps or degrees. **2** To resign from an office or position; abdicate. **—to step in** To begin to take part; intervene. **—to step on** (or **upon**) **1** To put the foot down on; tread upon. **2** To put the foot on so as to activate, as a brake or treadle. **3** *Colloq.* To reprove or subdue. **—to step on it** To hurry; hasten. **—to step out 1** To go outside, especially for a short while. **2** *Colloq.* To go out for fun or entertainment. **3** To step down (def. 2). **4** To walk vigorously and with long strides. **—to step up** To increase; raise. ◆ Homophone: *steppe.* [OE *stæpe*]

step- *combining form* Related through the previous marriage of a parent or spouse, but not by blood: *stepchild.* [OE *steop-* < stem of *astypan, astepan* bereave, orphan]

step·broth·er (step′bruth′ər) *n.* The son of one's step-parent by a former marriage.

step·child (step′chīld′) *n.* The child of one's husband or wife by a former marriage.

step·dame (step′dām′) *n. Archaic* A stepmother.

step·daugh·ter (step′dô′tər) *n.* A female stepchild.

step-down (step′doun′) *adj.* **1** That decreases gradually. **2** *Electr.* Converting a small current of high voltage into a large one of low voltage: said of the usual form of transformer: opposed to *step-up.* **3** Designating a ratio-reducing gear.

step·fa·ther (step′fä′thər) *n.* The husband of one's mother other than one's own father.

Steph·a·nie (stef′ə·nē) A feminine personal name: feminine of STEPHEN. Also **Steph′a·na,** *Fr.* **Sté·pha·nie** (stā·fà·nē′).

Ste·phen (stē′vən) A masculine personal name: often spelled *Steven.* Also *Sw.* **Ste·fan** (stā′·fän), *Ital.* **Ste·fa·no** (stā·fä′nō), *Russian* **Ste·pan** (stā·pän′), *Dan., Ger.* **Ste·phan** (shtā′·fän). [<Gk., crown]

—Stephen The first Christian martyr. *Acts* vii 60.

—Stephen I, 975?–1038, first king of Hungary: known as *St. Stephen.*

—Stephen of Blois, 1097?–1154, king of England 1135–54.

Ste·phen (stē′vən), **Sir Leslie,** 1832–1904, English biographer and critic.

Ste·phens (stē′vənz), **Alexander Hamilton,** 1812–83, U. S. statesman; vice president of the Confederate States. **—James,** 1882–1950, Irish poet and novelist.

Ste·phen·son (stē′vən·sən), **George,** 1781–1848, English engineer; invented the locomotive. **—Robert,** 1803–59, English engineer; son of the preceding.

step-in (step′in′) *n.* **1** An undergarment like short drawers, without actual legs: also **step′-ins′.** **2** A pumplike shoe. **—***adj.* Put on, as undergarments or shoes, by being stepped into.

step·lad·der (step′lad′ər) *n.* A set of portable steps with, usually, a hinged frame at the back, which may be extended to support the steps in an upright position.

step·moth·er (step′muth′ər) *n.* The wife of one's father, other than one's own mother.

Step·ney (step′nē) A metropolitan borough of eastern London, including the districts of Whitechapel and Limehouse.

step-par·ent (step′pâr′ənt) *n.* A stepfather or stepmother.

steppe (step) *n.* A vast plain devoid of forest; specifically, one of the extensive plains in Russia and Siberia. ◆ Homophone: *step.* [<Russian *step′*]

step·per (step′ər) *n.* **1** One who or that which steps: The horse is a high *stepper.* **2** *Slang* A dancer.

Steppes (steps), **The** See KIRGHIZ STEPPE.

step·ping·stone (step′ing·stōn′) *n.* **1** A stone affording a footrest, as for crossing a stream, etc. **2** That by which one advances or rises: *steppingstones* to fortune.

step·re·la·tion (step′ri·lā′shən) *n.* A person related through the remarriage of a parent or spouse and not by blood. **—step′re·la′tion·ship** *n.*

step·sis·ter (step′sis′tər) *n.* The daughter of one's step-parent by a former marriage.

step·son (step′sun′) *n.* A male stepchild.

step-up (step′up′) *adj.* **1** Increasing by stages: a *step-up* transformer: opposed to *step-down.* **2** Designating a ratio-increasing gear.

step·wise (step′wīz′) *adv.* In the manner of steps; step by step.

-ster *suffix of nouns* **1** One who makes or is occupied with: often with pejorative force: *songster, prankster.* **2** One who belongs or is related to: *gangster.* **3** One who is: *youngster.* [OE *-estre,* feminine suffix]

ste·ra·di·an (sti·rā′dē·ən) *n.* The unit of measurement for solid angles; that solid angle which, on a sphere, encloses a surface equivalent to the square of the radius: also called *spheradian.* [<Gk. *stereos* solid + RADIAN]

ster·co·ra·ceous (stûr′kə·rā′shəs) *adj.* Consisting of or pertaining to excrement or dung: *stercoraceous* vomiting.

stercori- *combining form* Dung; excrement: *stercoricolous*: also, before vowels, **stercor-.** Also **sterco-.** [<L *stercus, stercoris* dung]

ster·co·ric·o·lous (stûr′kə·rik′ə·ləs) *n.* Living in manure, as some insects.

ster·cu·li·a·ceous (stûr·kyōō′lē·ā′shəs) *adj. Bot.* Designating or belonging to a family *(Sterculiaceae)* of chiefly tropical herbs, shrubs, and trees, including the cacao and the colanut tree. [<NL <L *Sterculius,* the deity of manuring < *stercus* dung]

stere (stir) *n.* A measure of capacity in the metric system, equal to one cubic meter. See METRIC SYSTEM. [<F *stère* <Gk. *stereos* solid]

ster·e·o (ster′ē·ō, stir′-) *n. pl.* **·e·os 1** A stereophonic record player, record, tape, etc. **2** Stereophonic sound. **3** A stereotype (defs. 1 & 3). **4** A stereoscopic method; also, a stereoscopic photograph. **—***adj.* **1** Stereophonic. **2** Stereotyped. **3** Of or pertaining to the stereoscope.

stereo- *combining form* Solid; firm; hard: *stereoscope.* Also, before vowels, **stere-.** [<Gk. *stereos* hard]

ster·e·o·bate (ster′ē·ə·bāt′, stir′-) *n. Archit.* A substructure, continuous base, or solid platform without columns, as distinguished from a *stylobate,* which has them. [<STEREO- + Gk. *batēs* that which steps] **—ster′e·o·bat′ic** (-bat′ik) *adj.*

ster·e·o·chem·is·try (ster′ē·ō·kem′is·trē, stir′-) *n.* The branch of chemistry that treats of the spatial arrangement of atoms and molecules.

ster·e·o·chro·my (ster′ē·ō·krō′mē, stir′-) *n.* The art or process of painting with pigments mixed with waterglass. [<STEREO- + Gk. *chrōma* color] **—ster′e·o·chro′mic** *adj.*

ster·e·o·com·pa·ra·graph (ster′ē·ō·kom′pər·ə·graf′, -gräf′, stir′-) *n.* A mapmaking device utilizing data provided by stereoscopic photographs. [<STEREO- + COMPARE + -GRAPH]

ster·e·og·no·sis (ster′ē·og·nō′sis, stir′-) *n.* Perception of shape, solidity, and weight, especially by the sense of touch. [<STEREO- + Gk. *gnōsis* knowing] **—ster′e·og·nos′tic** (-nos′tik) *adj.*

ster·e·o·gram (ster′ē·ə·gram′, stir′-) *n.* **1** A picture or diagram giving the impression of a solid in relief, or two pictures of an object combined so as to produce the effect of a solid, as in a stereoscopic picture. **2** A stereograph.

ster·e·o·graph (ster′ē·ə·graf′, -gräf′, stir′-) *n.* **1** A photograph or pair of photographs representing objects so that they appear solid; a stereoscopic photograph. **2** An instrument for making projections of solid objects.

ster·e·og·ra·phy (ster′ē·og′rə·fē, stir′-) *n.* **1** The art of representing solids on a plane by means of lines; perspective. **2** The branch of geometry that treats of solids and of the construction of regularly bounded solids. **—ster′·e·o·graph′ic** (-ə·graf′ik) or **·i·cal** *adj.* **—ster′e·o·graph′i·cal·ly** *adv.*

ster·e·o·i·som·er·ism (ster′ē·ō·ī·som′ə·riz′əm, stir′-) *n. Chem.* An isomerism which depends on the spatial arrangement of the atoms or groups in an organic compound. **—ster′e·o·i′so·mer′ic** (-ī′sō·mer′ik), **ster′e·o·mer′ic** *adj.*

ster·e·ome (ster′ē·ōm, stir′-) *n. Bot.* The solid supporting elements of the fibrovascular tissues of plants. [<Gk. *stereōma* solid body < *stereos* solid]

ster·e·om·e·try (ster′ē·om′ə·trē, stir′-) *n.* The art of measuring the volume and other spatial elements of solids. [<STEREO- + -METRY] **— ster′e·o·met′ric** (-ō·met′rik) or **·ri·cal** *adj.* **— ster′e·o·met′ri·cal·ly** *adv.*

ster·e·o·phone (ster′ē·ə·fōn′, stir′-) *n.* Any sound-transmitting system equipped with stereophonic devices.

ster·e·o·phon·ic (ster′ē·ə·fon′ik, stir′-) *adj.* **1** Pertaining to, designed for, or characterized by the perception of sound by both ears; binaural. **2** Denoting a system of sound transmission in which two or more microphones or loudspeakers are so placed as to give the effect of hearing with both ears simultaneously, as in wide-screen motion pictures and certain types of radio receivers. **— ster′e·o·phon′i·cal·ly** *adv.*

ster·e·o·phon·ics (ster′ē·ə·fon′iks, stir′-) *n. pl.* *(construed as singular)* The branch of acoustics which investigates the stereophonic reproduction of sound and develops its practical applications.

ster·e·o·phon·ism (ster′ē·ə·fō′niz·əm, stir′-) *n.* The condition of being stereophonic; binaural hearing.

ster·e·oph·o·ny (ster′ē·of′ə·nē, stir′-) *n.* The art and techniques of designing, producing, and applying stereophonic devices for the recording and transmission of sound.

ster·e·op·sis (ster′ē·op′sis, stir′-) *n.* Vision characterized by stereoscopy; stereoscopic vision. [<STERE(O)- + -OPSIS]

ster·e·op·ti·con (ster′ē·op′ti·kon, stir′-) *n.* A double magic lantern arranged to combine two images of the same object or scene, or used to bring one image after another on the screen by the alternate use of the lanterns; a projection lantern. [<STEREO- + Gk. *optikos* of sight]

ster·e·o·scope (ster′ē·ə·skōp, stir′-) *n.* An instrument for blending into one image two pictures of an object from slightly different points of view, so as to produce upon the eye the impression of relief and solidity. [<STEREO- + -SCOPE] **— ster′e·o·scop′ic** (-skop′ik) or **·i·cal** *adj.* **— ster′·e·o·scop′i·cal·ly** *adv.*

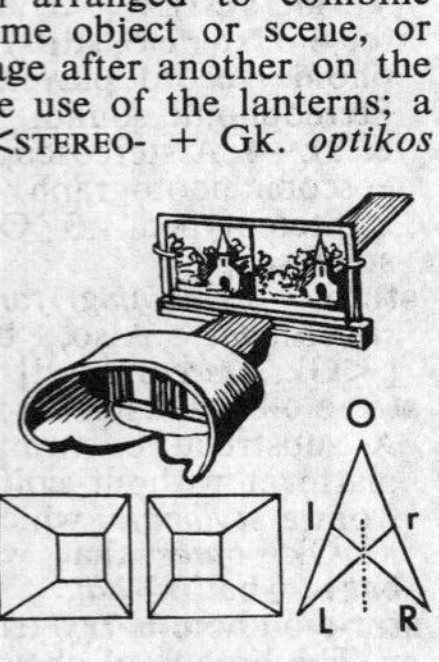

STEREOSCOPE

Line of sight, *Ll* and *Rr*, of the eyes, combines the images of points *l* and *r* at *O*. A card (at dotted line) shuts off two side images otherwise seen along *Rl* at *l* and *Lr* at *r*.

ster·e·os·co·py (ster′ē·os′kə·pē, stir′-) *n.* **1** The art of making or using stereoscopes and stereoscopic slides. **2** The viewing of objects as in three dimensions. **— ster′e·os′co·pism** *n.* **— ster′e·os′co·pist** *n.*

ster·e·o·ski·ag·ra·phy (ster′ē·ō·skī·ag′rə·fē, stir′-) *n.* Stereoscopic photography by means of X-rays. [<STEREO- + SKIAGRAPHY]

ster·e·o·tro·pism (ster′ē·ot′rə·piz′əm, stir′-) *n.* Involuntary response of an organism to contact with a foreign body. Also **ster′e·o·tax′is** (-ō·tak′sis) **— ster′e·o·trop′ic** (-trop′ik) *adj.*

ster·e·o·type (ster′ē·ə·tīp′, stir′-) *n.* **1** A plate taken in type metal from a matrix, as of paper, reproducing the surface from which the matrix was made. **2** Stereotypy. **3** Anything made or processed in this way. **4** A conventional or hackneyed expression, custom, or mode of thought. **—** *v.t.* **·typed, ·typ·ing 1** To make a stereotype of. **2** To fix firmly or unalterably.

ster·e·o·typed (ster′ē·ə·tīpt′, stir′-) *adj.* Formalized as if produced from a stereotype; hackneyed; without originality.

ster·e·o·typ·er (ster′ē·ə·tī′pər, stir′-) *n.* **1** One who makes stereotype plates. **2** A stereotype-making machine for making embossed plates from which printing for the blind is done. Also **ster′e·o·typ′ist. — ster′e·o·typ′ic** (-tip′ik), **ster′e·o·typ′i·cal** *adj.*

ster·e·o·typ·y (ster′ē·ə·tī′pē, stir′-) *n.* The art or act of making stereotypes. Also **ster′e·o·typ′er·y** (-tī′pər·ē).

ster·e·o·vi·sion (ster′ē·ō·vizh′ən, stir′-) *n.* Three-dimensional vision.

ster·ic (ster′ik, stir′-) *adj. Chem.* Denoting relative position in space: said of the component atoms in a molecule. Also **ster′i·cal.** [<Gk. *stereos* solid]

ster·il·ant (ster′əl·ənt) *n.* **1** That which makes sterile or induces sterility. **2** *Agric.* Any of various chemical compounds whose use as weed-killers renders the soil infertile for one or more growing seasons.

ster·ile (ster′əl) *adj.* **1** Having no reproductive power; barren. **2** *Bot.* Producing no pistil or no spores; incapable of germinating, as certain plants. **3** Lacking productiveness or fertility; hence, useless; being without result: *sterile* soil. **4** Containing no pathogenic bacteria or other micro-organisms; aseptic: a *sterile* fluid. **5** Destitute of attractiveness or suggestiveness: said especially of literary work: *sterile* verse. [<L *sterilis* barren] **— ster′ile·ly** *adv.* **— ste·ril·i·ty** (stə·ril′ə·tē), **ster′ile·ness** *n.*

ster·il·i·za·tion (ster′əl·ə·zā′shən, -ī·zā′-) *n.* **1** The act or process of making sterile. **2** The condition of being sterile. **3** The deliberate procedure of destroying reproductive power by surgical means.

ster·il·ize (ster′əl·īz) *v.t.* **·ized, ·iz·ing 1** To deprive of productive or reproductive power, especially by surgical operation on the Fallopian tubes or on the vas deferens. **2** To destroy bacteria in; free from germs. **3** To make barren; exhaust the productiveness of. **4** To make powerless. **— ster′il·iz′er** *n.*

ster·let (stûr′lit) *n.* A small sturgeon *(Acipenser ruthenus)* found in the Black, Caspian, and Azov seas, and in rivers of Russia, yielding superior caviar and isinglass. [<Russian *sterlyad′*]

ster·ling (stûr′ling) *n.* **1** The official standard of fineness for British coins: for silver (**sterling silver**), 0.925 until 1920, 0.500 since then; for gold, 0.91666 or 11/12. **2** Sterling silver, 0.925 fine, as used in manufacturing articles, as tableware, etc.; also, an article or articles made of it. **3** A former silver penny of England and Scotland, in circulation as early as the 12th century. **—** *adj.* **1** Made of or payable in sterling: pounds *sterling.* **2** Made of sterling silver. **3** Having accepted worth; genuine; hence, valuable; esteemed: *sterling* qualities. See synonyms under GOOD. [Prob. OE *steorra* star + -LING; because a star was stamped on some of the coins]

stern[1] (stûrn) *adj.* **1** Proceeding from or marked by severity or harshness; unyielding: a *stern* command. **2** Having an austere disposition; strict; severe: a *stern* judge. **3** Inspiring fear; repelling. **4** Resolute; stout: a *stern* resolve. See synonyms under AUSTERE, GRIM, HARD, SEVERE. [OE *styrne*] **— stern′ly** *adv.* **— stern′ness** *n.*

stern[2] (stûrn) *n.* **1** *Naut.* The aft part of a ship, boat, etc. **2** The buttocks or tail part of an animal: now chiefly humorous. **3** The hindmost part of any object. **—** *adj.* Situated at or belonging to the stern. [<ON *stjoren* steering, rudder < *styra* steer]

Stern (stûrn), **Otto,** born 1888, U. S. physicist born in Germany.

ster·nal (stûr′nəl) *adj.* Pertaining to the breastbone or sternum.

stern chase *Naut.* A chase in which the pursuing vessel follows in the other's course.

stern chaser A cannon mounted in the stern to fire at a pursuing ship.

Sterne (stûrn), **Laurence,** 1713–68, English clergyman and novelist.

stern·fore·most (stûrn′fôr′mōst′, -məst, -fōr′-) *adv.* Hind side foremost; moving with the stern in advance; backward; hence, awkwardly.

stern·most (stûrn′mōst′, -məst) *adj.* Farthest to the rear or stern.

sterno- *combining form Anat.* & *Med.* The sternum: *sternotomy,* cutting through the sternum. Also, before vowels, **stern-.** [<L *sternum* breast]

stern·post (stûrn′pōst′) *n. Naut.* The main vertical post of the stern frame of a vessel, to which the rudder is attached.

stern·sheets (stûrn′shēts′) *n. Naut.* The inside stern portion of a boat; the space in a boat abaft the thwarts.

stern·son (stûrn′sən) *n. Naut.* An inner sternpost attached to the center keelson, to strengthen the stern frame. Also **stern′knee′** (-nē′), **stern′son-knee′.** [<STERN + (KEEL)-SON]

ster·num (stûr′nəm) *n. pl.* **·na** (-nə) or **·nums 1** *Anat.* The breastbone which forms the ventral support of the ribs in most vertebrates. **2** *Zool.* The ventral portion of a somite in an arthropod, as an insect or crustacean. [<L <Gk. *sternon* breast]

ster·nu·ta·tion (stûr′nyə·tā′shən) *n.* **1** The act of sneezing. **2** A sneeze or the noise produced by it. [<L *sternutatio, -onis* < *sternutare,* freq. of *sternuere* sneeze]

ster·nu·ta·tor (stûr′nyə·tā′tər) *n.* One of a class of chemical-warfare agents having a strongly irritant effect upon the nasal and respiratory passages, with resulting physical exhaustion; a sneeze gas.

ster·nu·ta·to·ry (stər·nyōō′tə·tôr′ē, -tō′rē, -nōō′-) *adj.* Causing or tending to cause sneezing: also **ster·nu′ta·tive** (-tə·tiv). **—** *n. pl.* **·ries** Any substance tending to cause sneezing, as snuff.

stern·ward (stûrn′wərd) *adj.* & *adv.* Toward the stern; astern. Also **stern′wards.**

stern·way (stûrn′wā′) *n. Naut.* Backward or sternforemost movement of a vessel: opposed to *headway.*

stern-wheel·er (stûrn′hwē′lər) *n.* A steamboat of small draft propelled by one large paddle wheel at the stern.

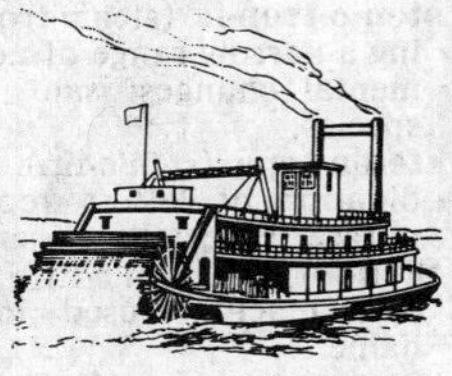

STERN-WHEELER

ster·oid (ster′oid) *n. Biochem.* Any of a sizable group of organic compounds widely distributed in nature, including the sterols, the bile acids, and the sex hormones. [<STER(OL) + -OID]

ster·ol (ster′ōl, -ol) *n. Biochem.* Any of a class of complex, chiefly unsaturated, solid alcohols widely distributed in plant and animal tissue, as cholesterol. [Contraction of CHOLESTEROL]

Ster·o·pe (ster′ə·pē) One of the Pleiades: also called *Asterope.*

ster·tor (stûr′tər) *n.* A deep snore or snoring. [<NL <L *stertere* snore]

ster·tor·ous (stûr′tər·əs) *adj.* Characterized by snoring; accompanied by a snoring sound: *stertorous* breathing. **— ster′tor·ous·ly** *adv.* **— ster′tor·ous·ness** *n.*

ster·ule (ster′ōōl, -yōōl) *n.* A small glass container holding a sterile solution. Compare AMPOULE. [<STER(ILE) + -ULE]

stet (stet) Let it stand: a direction used in proofreading to indicate that a word, letter, etc., marked for omission or correction is to remain. **—** *v.t.* **stet·ted, stet·ting** To cancel a former correction or omission of by marking with the word *stet.* Compare DELE. [<L, 3rd person sing. subjunctive of *stare* stand, stay]

stetho- *combining form* The breast or chest; pectoral: *stethoscope.* Also, before vowels, **steth-.** [<Gk. *stēthos* breast]

ste·thom·e·ter (ste·thom′ə·tər) *n.* An instrument to measure the expansion of the chest in breathing. [<STETHO- + -METER]

steth·o·scope (steth′ə·skōp) *n. Med.* An apparatus for auscultation, of various forms, sizes, and materials, adapted for conveying the sounds of the body to the examiner's ear or ears. **— steth′o·scop′ic** (-skop′ik), **steth′·o·scop′i·cal** *adj.* **— steth′o·scop′i·cal·ly** *adv.* **— ste·thos·co·py** (ste·thos′kə·pē) *n.*

Stet·son (stet′sən) *n.* A hat; especially, one of felt with high crown and wide brim: a trade name. [after John Batterson *Stetson,* 1830–1906, U. S. hatmaker]

Stet·tin (stet′in, *Ger.* shte·tēn′) A port on the Oder in NW Poland, formerly the capital of Pomerania. *Polish* **Szcze·cin** (shche·tsēn′).

Stet·tin·i·us (stə·tin′ē·əs, -tin′yəs), **Edward Riley,** 1900–49, U. S. industrialist and statesman; secretary of state December 1944–June 1945.

Steu·ben (stōō′bən, *Ger.* shtoi′bən), **Baron Friedrich Wilhelm von,** 1730–94, Prussian general; served in American Revolutionary War.

St. Eu·sta·tius (sānt yōō·stā′shəs, -shē·əs) An island in the eastern group of the Netherlands West Indies; 8 square miles. *Dutch* **Sint Eu·sta·ti·us** (sint ōō·stä′tē·ōōs).

Steve (stēv) Familiar shortening of STEPHEN. Also **Ste′vie.**

ste·ve·dore (stē′və·dôr, -dōr) *n.* One whose business is stowing or unloading the holds of vessels. **—** *v.t.* & *v.i.* **·dored, ·dor·ing** To load

or unload (a vessel or vessels). [<Sp. *estivador* <*estivar* stow <L *stipare* compress, stuff]

stevedore knot A knot used by stevedores to prevent unreeving.

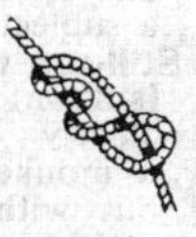

STEVEDORE KNOT

Ste·ven (stē′vən) See STEPHEN.

Ste·vens (stē′vənz), **Thaddeus,** 1792–1868, U.S. statesman; abolitionist. —**Wallace,** 1879–1955, U.S. poet and businessman.

Ste·ven·son (stē′vən·sən), **Adlai Ewing,** 1900–1965, U.S. lawyer and political leader. —**Robert Louis,** 1850–94, Scottish novelist and essayist.

ste·vi·o·side (stē′vē·ə·sīd) *n. Chem.* A glycoside extracted from the dried leaves of a small South American shrub *(Stevia rebaudiana)* and having a sweetness 300 times that of cane sugar. [<STEVI(A) the genus of the shrub + (GLYC)OSIDE]

stew (stōō, styōō) *v.t. & v.i.* **1** To boil slowly and gently; seethe; keep or be at the simmering point. **2** *Colloq.* To worry. —*n.* **1** Stewed food, especially a preparation of meat or fish cooked by stewing. **2** *Colloq.* Mental agitation; worry. **3** *pl. Archaic* A brothel. **4** *Obs.* A room heated for bathing or drying purposes. [<OF *estuver,* prob. ult. <L *ex-* out + Gk. *typhos* steam, vapor]

stew·ard (stōō′ərd, styōō′-) *n.* **1** A person entrusted with the management of estates or affairs not his own; an administrator. **2** A person put in charge of the domestic affairs of an establishment. **3** On shipboard, a petty officer in charge of the service of provisions, or a man who waits on table and takes care of passengers' rooms. **4** *Brit.* A fiscal officer in certain ancient guilds. [OE *stīweard* <*stī* hall, sty + *weard* ward, keeper] —**stew′ard·ess** *n. fem.* —**stew′ard·ship** *n.*

Stew·art (stōō′ərt, styōō′-), **Dugald,** 1753–1828, Scottish philosopher.

Stewart Island An island of New Zealand south of South Island; 670 square miles.

stewed (stōōd, styōōd) *adj.* **1** Cooked by stewing. **2** *Slang* Drunk.

stew pan A cooking vessel used for stewing.

stey (stā) *adj. Scot.* **1** Steep. **2** Haughty; lofty.

St. Fran·cis River (sānt fran′sis) **1** A river in southern Quebec, Canada, flowing 150 miles SW to the St. Lawrence. **2** A river in SW Missouri and NE Arkansas, flowing 470 miles south to the Mississippi.

St. Gall (sānt gôl′) **1** A canton in NE Switzerland; 778 square miles. **2** Its capital, site of a seventh century Benedictine abbey. *German* **Sankt Gal·len** (zängt gäl′ən). Also **Saint Gal·len** (sānt gal′in).

St. George's (sānt jôr′jiz) The capital of Grenada, The West Indies (federation); former administrative capital of the Windward Islands. Also **St. George.**

St. George's Channel A strait between SE Ireland and Wales, connecting the Irish Sea with the Atlantic Ocean; 100 miles long, 50 to 95 miles wide.

St. George's cross The Greek cross, used on the British flag. See under CROSS.

St. Gott·hard (sānt got′ərd, *Fr.* saṅ gô·tȧr′) A mountain group in the Lepontine Alps, south central Switzerland; highest peak 10,483 feet; site of the **St. Gotthard Pass,** at 6,929 feet, and of the **St. Gotthard tunnel,** extending 9 1/4 miles at an elevation of 3,786 feet.

St. He·le·na (sānt hə·lē′nə) An island in the South Atlantic, 1,200 miles west of Africa, to which Napoleon was exiled from 1815–21; 47 square miles; comprising a British crown colony with the dependencies of Ascension Island and the Tristan da Cunha group; 133 square miles; capital, Jamestown, on St. Helena.

St. Hel·ens (sānt hel′ənz) A county borough in SW Lancashire, England.

St. Hel·ier (sānt hel′yər) Capital of Jersey, Channel Islands.

sthe·ni·a (sthē′nē·ə, sthi·nī′ə) *n.* Unusual energy or vigor; excited force: opposed to *asthenia.* [<NL <Gk. *sthenos* strength]

sthen·ic (sthen′ik) *adj.* **1** Exhibiting activity or energy, especially in morbid states. **2** Having power to inspire or animate; indicating vigor. [<Gk. *sthenos* strength]

Sthe·no (sthē′nō, sthen′ō) One of the Gorgons.

stiac·cia·to (styät·chä′tō) *n.* Sculpture or a piece of sculpture in lower relief than bas-relief, as the very low relief used on coins. —*adj.* Of or pertaining to this kind of sculpture; in very low relief. [<Ital., crushed, flattened, pp. of *stiacciare*]

stib·ble (stib′əl) *n. Scot.* Stubble. Also **stib′bul.**

stib·bler (stib′lər) *n. Scot.* **1** A gleaner. **2** A minister without a ministerial charge.

stib·ine (stib′ēn, -in) *n. Chem.* A colorless poisonous gas, SbH_3, resembling arsine, formed by decomposing antimony or any of its compounds in the presence of hydrogen. [<STIB(IUM) + -INE[2]]

stib·i·um (stib′ē·əm) *n.* Antimony. [<L <Gk. *stibi*] —**stib′i·al** *adj.*

stib·nite (stib′nīt) *n.* A metallic steel–gray antimony sulfide, Sb_2S_3, crystallizing in the orthorhombic system: the most important ore of antimony. [<STIB(I)N(E)+ -ITE[2]]

stich (stik) *n.* **1** A line of the Bible. **2** A line of poetry; a verse: used often in composition: *hemistich.* [<Gk. *stichos* row]

stich·ic (stik′ik) *adj.* **1** Relating to or consisting of stichs. **2** Metrically the same throughout: said of verses.

sti·chom·e·try (sti·kom′ə·trē) *n.* **1** The measurement of the text of a manuscript by lines of measured length into which it is divided; also, the appendix stating the number of lines. **2** The practice of writing prose in line lengths corresponding to the sense of the phrasal cadence. [<Gk. *stichos* line + -METRY] —**stich·o·met·ric** (stik′ə·met′rik) or **·ri·cal** *adj.*

sti·chom·y·thy (sti·kom′ə·thē) *n.* The arrangement of a dialog in alternate lines of verse: characteristic of ancient Greek drama, poetry, and disputation: also spelled *stychomythia.* [<Gk. *stichos* line + *mythos* speech] —**stich·o·myth·ic** (stik′ə·mith′ik) *adj.*

-stichous *combining form* Having (a specified number of) rows: *tristichous.* [<Gk. *stichos* a row, line]

stich·wort (stich′wûrt′) See STITCHWORT.

stick (stik) *n.* **1** A piece of wood that is long, compared with its cross–section; a stiff shoot or branch cut from a tree or bush and used as a rod, wand, staff, club, etc.; also, sometimes one much bigger: a *stick* of timber. **2** *Brit.* A cane. **3** Anything resembling a stick in form: a *stick* of candy or dynamite. **4** *Printing* **a** A composing stick. **b** As much type as a composing stick will hold: about two inches in depth. **c** Copy which will fill this space in a newspaper column: also **stick′ful′.** **5** A piece of wood of any size, cut for fuel, lumber, or timber. **6** *Aeron.* The control lever of an airplane which operates the elevators and ailerons. **7** A poke, stab, or thrust with a stick or pointed instrument. **8** *Archaic* A difficulty or obstacle; hesitation; stop. **9** The state of being stuck together; adhesion. **10** In sports, a baseball bat, hockey stick, racing hurdle, etc. **11** A timber tree. **12** *Colloq.* A stiff, inert, or dull person. **13** *Slang* Any alcoholic ingredient in an otherwise non–alcoholic drink. **14** A revolver or rifle. **15** *Colloq.* The mast of a ship. **16** *Mil.* A group of bombs released consecutively in a straight line crossing the target area. **17** A stalk, as of asparagus. **18** *Colloq.* A conductor's baton. —**the sticks 1** A timber forest. **2** *Colloq.* The backwoods; an obscure rural district. —*v.* **stuck** or (*for defs.* **15, 16**) **sticked, stick·ing** *v.t.* **1** To pierce, stab, or penetrate with a pin, knife, or other pointed object. **2** To kill or wound by piercing; stab. **3** To thrust or force, as a sword or pin, into or through something else. **4** To force the end of (a nail, etc.) into something so as to be fixed in place: to *stick* a nail in a wall. **5** To fasten in place with or as with pins, nails, etc.: to *stick* a ribbon on a dress. **6** To cover with objects piercing the surface: a paper *stuck* with pins. **7** To fix on a pointed object; impale; transfix. **8** To put or thrust: He *stuck* his hand into his pocket. **9** To fasten to a surface by or as by an adhesive substance. **10** To bring to a standstill; obstruct; halt: usually in the passive: We were *stuck* in Rome. **11** *Colloq.* To smear with something sticky. **12** *Colloq.* To baffle; puzzle. **13** *Slang* To impose upon; cheat. **14** *Slang* To force great expense, an unpleasant task, responsibility, etc., upon. **15** To provide with sticks or brush on which to grow, as a vine. **16** *Printing* To set or compose (type). —*v.i.* **17** To be or become fixed in place by being thrust in: The pins are *sticking* in the cushion. **18** To become or remain attached by or as by adhesion; adhere; cling. **19** To come to a standstill; become blocked or obstructed; stop; halt. **20** To be baffled or disconcerted. **21** To hesitate; scruple: with *at* or *to.* **22** To persist; persevere, as in a task or undertaking: with *at* or *to.* **23** To remain firm or resolute; be faithful, as to an ideal or bargain. **24** To be extended; protrude: with *from, out, through, up,* etc. —**to be stuck on** *Colloq.* To be enamored of. —**to stick around** *Slang* To remain near or near at hand. —**to stick by** To remain faithful to; be loyal to. —**to stick it out** To persevere to the end. —**to stick up** *Slang* To stop and rob. —**to stick up for** *Colloq.* To take the part of; support; defend. [OE *sticca*]

stick·ball (stik′bôl′) *n.* A kind of baseball played on streets or in vacant lots, with a rubber ball and a narrow stick or a broom handle for a bat.

stick·er (stik′ər) *n.* **1** One who holds tenaciously to anything. **2** One who or that which fastens with or as with paste. **3** A paster. **4** *Colloq.* Anything that confuses or silences a person; a puzzle. **5** A prickly stem, thorn, or bur.

sticking plaster An adhesive material for covering slight cuts, etc.; a court plaster.

stick insect An orthopterous insect (family *Phasmidae*), typically wingless and characterized by a long, sticklike body, as the green or pinkish *Timema* of the Pacific coast.

stick–in–the–mud (stik′in·thə·mud′) *n. Colloq.* A person too sluggish or lacking in initiative to take any progressive action.

stick·it (stik′it) *adj. Scot.* Stuck; unsuccessful; having failed in or given up something.

stickit minister *Scot.* A probationer who fails to qualify for a license, or a licentiate without pastoral charge.

stick·le[1] (stik′əl) *v.i.* **·led, ·ling 1** To contend about trifling matters. **2** To insist or hesitate for petty reasons. [ME *stightlen* set in order, freq. of OE *stihtan* arrange, dispose]

stick·le[2] (stik′əl) *n.* A prickle; spine: obsolete except in compounds. [OE *sticel* sting]

stick·le·back (stik′əl·bak′) *n.* A small fresh- or salt–water fish (genera *Gasterosteus* and *Eucalia*) of northern regions, having sharp dorsal spines. The male builds nests for the reception of the eggs laid by the female.

stick·ler (stik′lər) *n.* **1** One who contends over trifles. **2** *Obs.* A referee.

stick·pin (stik′pin′) *n.* An ornamental pin for a necktie.

stick·seed (stik′sēd′) *n.* Any of a genus *(Lappula)* of coarse weeds, whose prickly seeds stick in clothing, the wool of sheep, etc.

stick shift A gearshift operated by hand rather than automatically, located either on the floor or on the steering column.

stick·tight (stik′tīt′) *n.* A coarse herb (genus *Bidens*) of the composite family with prickly achenes; a bur marigold.

stick–to–it·ive (stik·tōō′it·iv) *adj. Colloq.* Persevering; dogged; pertinacious. —**stick–to′–it·ive·ly** *adv.* —**stick–to′–it·ive·ness** *n.*

stick–up (stik′up′) *n. Slang* **1** A robbery or hold–up. **2** A robber who intimidates his victims with a weapon, compelling them to hold their hands in the air.

stick·weed (stik′wēd′) *n.* Ragweed.

stick·y (stik′ē) *adj.* **stick·i·er, stick·i·est 1** Adhering to a surface; adhesive. **2** Warm and humid. See synonyms under ADHESIVE. —**stick′i·ly** *adv.* —**stick′i·ness** *n.*

Stieg·litz (stēg′lits), **Alfred,** 1864–1946, U.S. photographer and art patron.

stiff (stif) *adj.* **1** Resisting the action of a bending force; not flaccid, limp, pliant, or flexible; rigid. **2** Not easily moved; acting with difficulty or friction. **3** Not natural, graceful, or easy; constrained and awkward; formal. **4** Not liquid or fluid; thick; viscous. **5** Taut; tightly drawn. **6** Having a strong, steady movement: a *stiff* breeze. **7** Firm in resistance; obstinate; stubborn. **8** Difficult to achieve, understand, or accept; harsh; severe: a *stiff* penalty. **9** High; dear: a *stiff*

price. 10 Firm in prices; strong and steady: a *stiff* market. 11 *Naut.* Heeling over but little, while carrying much sail; not crank: a *stiff* ship. 12 *Scot.* & *Brit. Dial.* Lusty; strong; sturdy. 13 Dense; not porous, as soil. 14 Strong; potent: a *stiff* drink. 15 Difficult; arduous: a *stiff* climb. 16 *Obs.* Formidable; serious: said of news. See synonyms under INFLEXIBLE, SEVERE. — *n. Slang* 1 A corpse. 2 An awkward or unresponsive person; especially, a bore. 3 A man; fellow: *working* stiff; also, a roughneck. 4 A hobo. 5 An accomplice in dishonest dealings; also, a prospective victim. [OE *stīf*] — **stiff′ly** *adv.* — **stiff′ness** *n.*

stiff·en (stif′ən) *v.t.* & *v.i.* To make or become stiff or stiffer.

stiff·en·er (stif′ən·ər) *n.* One who or that which stiffens. — **bow stiffener** *Aeron.* A rigid structural member to reinforce the bow of a dirigible or other airship: also **nose stiffener.**

stiff–necked (stif′nekt′) *adj.* Not yielding; stubborn; incorrigible; obstinate.

sti·fle[1] (stī′fəl) *v.* **·fled, ·fling** *v.t.* 1 To kill by stopping respiration; suffocate; choke. 2 To keep back; suppress or repress, as sobs. — *v.i.* 3 To die of suffocation. 4 To experience difficulty in breathing, as in a stuffy room. [<ON *stīfla* stop up, choke] — **sti′·fler** *n.* — **sti′fling** *adj.* — **sti′fling·ly** *adv.*

sti·fle[2] (stī′fəl) *n.* 1 The stifle joint. 2 Any abnormal condition of the stifle joint or stifle bone. [Origin unknown]

stifle bone The patella or kneepan of a horse, situated at the stifle joint, formerly thought of as stopping or damming up the joint.

sti·fled (stī′fəld) *adj.* Having some disease of the stifle joint; affected with stifle.

stifle joint The joint in the upper leg of a horse or a dog. See illustration under DOG, HORSE.

stig·ma (stig′mə) *n. pl.* **stig·ma·ta** (stig′mə·tə, stig·mä′tə) or (*for defs.* **1–3,** *usually*) **stig·mas** 1 A mark of infamy, or token of disgrace; blemish; a blot on one's good name. 2 Formerly, a brand made with a branding iron on slaves and criminals. 3 *Bot.* That part of a pistil which receives the pollen. 4 *Biol.* **a** A mark or spot, as on the wings of certain insects. **b** An aperture, as the gill slit of a tunicate. 5 A small mark or scar; a birthmark. 6 *Pathol.* A small red or bleeding spot on the skin caused by nervous tension or by capillary congestion. 7 *pl.* The wounds that Christ received during the Passion and Crucifixion; also, marks on the body corresponding to these wounds: said to be miraculously impressed on certain persons as a token of divine favor. 8 One of the characteristic signs or marks of a disease. See synonyms under BLEMISH. [<L, mark, brand <Gk., pointed end, mark < *stizein* prick, brand]

stig·mas·ter·ol (stig·mas′tər·ōl, -ol) *n. Biochem.* A sterol, $C_{29}H_{47}OH$, obtained chiefly from the calabar bean, and in lesser amounts from soybean oil. [<STIGMA + STEROL]

stig·mat·ic (stig·mat′ik) *adj.* 1 Of, pertaining to, or marked with a stigma or stigmata. 2 Infamous; ignominious or vicious; hence, deformed. 3 Anastigmatic. Also **stig·mat′i·cal** — *n.* One marked with or bearing a stigma or stigmata.

stig·ma·tism (stig′mə·tiz′əm) *n.* 1 The state of being affected with stigmas. 2 *Optics* The quality or condition of a lens or of the cornea of the eye through which rays of light are accurately focused.

stig·ma·tist (stig′mə·tist) *n.* One bearing miraculous stigmata.

stig·ma·tize (stig′mə·tīz) *v.t.* **·tized, ·tiz·ing** 1 To characterize or brand as ignominious. 2 To mark with a stigma. 3 To cause stigmata to appear on. Also *Brit.* **stig′ma·tise.** [<Med. L *stigmatizare* <Gk. *stigmatizein* mark < *stigma* pointed end, mark] — **stig′ma·ti·za′·tion** *n.* — **stig′ma·tiz′er** *n.*

Sti·kine River (sti·kēn′) A river in NW British Columbia and SE Alaska flowing 335 miles SW to the Pacific from the **Stikine Mountains,** a range in northern British Columbia; highest point 8,200 feet.

stilb (stilb) *n.* A unit of illumination, equal to one candle per square centimeter. [<Gk. *stilbein* glitter]

stil·bene (stil′bēn) *n. Chem.* A crystalline unsaturated hydrocarbon, $C_{14}H_{12}$, used in making dyestuffs. [<Gk. *stilbein* glitter + -ENE]

stil·bes·trol (stil′bəs·trōl, -trol) *n. Chem.* A synthetic sex hormone, $C_{18}H_{20}O_2$, similar in action to but more potent than the naturally occurring estrogens. [<STILB(ENE) + ESTR(ONE) + -OL[1]]

stil·bite (stil′bīt) *n.* A vitreous native hydrous silicate of aluminum, calcium, and sodium crystallizing in the monoclinic system. [<Gk. *stilbein* glitter + -ITE[1]]

stile[1] (stīl) *n.* A step, or series of steps, on each side of a fence or wall to aid in surmounting it; loosely, a turnstile. ◆ Homophone: *style.* [OE *stigel* < *stīgan* climb]

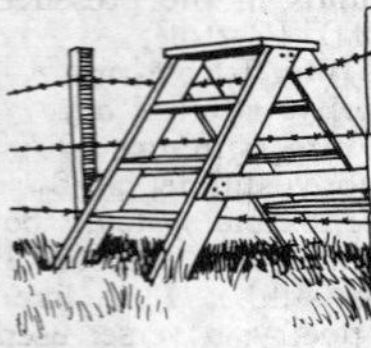

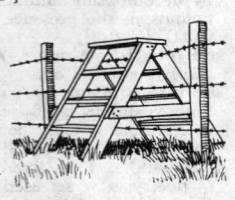

STILE
Over wire fence.

stile[2] (stīl) *n.* One of the vertical sidepieces in a door or a window sash. ◆ Homophone: *style.* [< Du. *stijl* doorpost]

sti·let·to (sti·let′ō) *n. pl.* **·tos** or **·toes** 1 A small dagger with a slender blade. 2 A small, sharp–pointed instrument, as of bone, for puncturing eyelets. — *v.t.* To pierce with a stiletto; stab. Also **sti·let′, sti·lette′.** [<Ital., dim. of *stilo* dagger <L *stilus.* See STYLE[1].]

Stil·i·cho (stil′ə·kō), **Flavius,** 359?–408, Roman general and statesman.

still[1] (stil) *adj.* 1 Being without movement; motionless. 2 Free from disturbance or agitation; peaceful; tranquil. 3 Making no sound; silent. 4 Low in sound; hushed. 5 Subdued; soft. 6 Dead; inanimate. 7 Having no effervescence: opposed to *sparkling*: said of wines. 8 *Phot.* Showing no movement. See synonyms under CALM, PACIFIC, SEDATE. — *n.* 1 Absence of sound or noise; stillness; calm. 2 A still-life picture. 3 *Phot.* A still photograph; especially, one taken with a still camera on a motion–picture set, for advertising, promotion, etc. 4 A still alarm. — *adv.* 1 Now as previously; up to this or that time; yet: He is *still* here. 2 After or in spite of something; all the same; nevertheless. 3 In increasing degree; even more; even yet: *still* more. 4 *Poetic* & *Dial.* Always; constantly. See synonyms under BUT[1], NOTWITHSTANDING, YET. — *conj.* Nevertheless. — *v.t.* 1 To cause to be still or calm. 2 To silence or hush. 3 To quiet or allay, as fears. — *v.i.* 4 To become still. See synonyms under ALLAY, REPRESS, TRANQUILIZE. [OE *stille*] — **still′ness** *n.*

still[2] (stil) *n.* 1 An apparatus in which a substance is vaporized by heat, and the vapor then liquefied in a condenser and collected: used especially for distilling liquors. 2 A distillery: also **still house.** — *v.t.* & *v.i.* To distil. [<L *stillare* drip < *stilla* a drop]

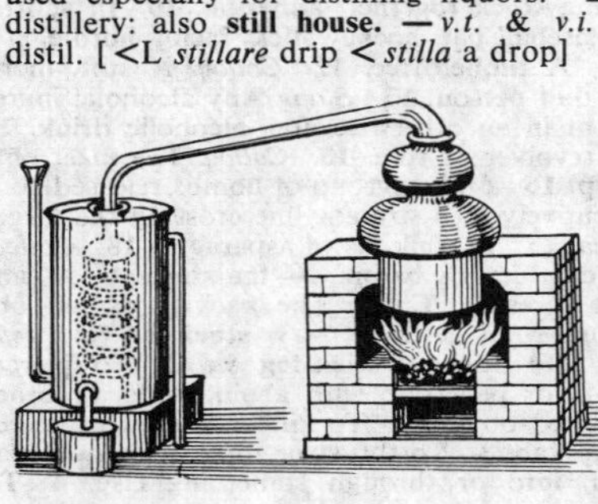

STILL

Still (stil), **Andrew Taylor,** 1828–1917, U.S. physician; founder of osteopathy.

still alarm A fire alarm given by telephone or other call without sounding the regular signal apparatus.

still·birth (stil′bûrth′) *n.* The bringing forth or birth of a dead child.

still·born (stil′bôrn′) *adj.* Dead at birth.

still–hunt (stil′hunt′) *v.t.* & *v.i.* To hunt (game) stealthily; stalk. — *n.* 1 The hunting of game by stealth. 2 The cautious, guarded pursuit of anything; specifically, secret or underhand methods in politics.

stil·li·form (stil′ə·fôrm) *adj.* Drop–shaped. [<NL *stilliformis* <L *stilla* drop + *forma* shape]

still–life (stil′līf′) *n.* 1 In painting, the representation of fruit, flowers, lifeless animals, and inanimate objects. 2 A picture of such a subject.

Still·son wrench (stil′sən) A wrench closely resembling a monkey wrench, but with one serrated jaw capable of slight angular movement about the other, so that the grip is increased by pressure on the handle: a trade name.

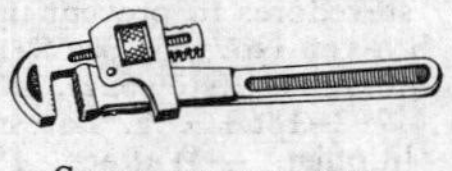

STILLSON WRENCH

Still·wa·ter (stil′wô′tər, -wot′ər) A village near Saratoga Springs, eastern New York; scene of several battles of the Revolutionary War, 1777.

still·y (stil′ē) *adj.* Still; silent, calm. — *adv.* (stil′lē) Calmly; quietly; without noise.

stilt (stilt) *n.* 1 One of a pair of slender poles made with a projection to support the foot above the ground in walking. 2 A tall post or pillar used as a support for a dock or building. 3 Any of several long–legged, three–toed birds (genera *Himantopus* and *Cladorhynchus*) related to the avocet, inhabiting ponds and fresh– and salt–water marshes. The American stilt (*H. mexicanus*) is mostly white with back, wings, crown, and nape a greenish black. The Old World stilt (*H. candidus*) is white except for wings and back. 4 *Scot.* A crutch. — *v.t.* To raise on stilts. — *v.i. Scot.* To hobble on crutches. [ME *stilte,* ? <LG. Cf. MLG *stelte.*]

stilt·ed (stil′tid) *adj.* Artificially elevated in manner; bombastic; inflated. — **stilt′ed·ly** *adv.* — **stilt′ed·ness** *n.*

stilted arch *Archit.* An arch whose curve springs from a level some distance above that of the impost.

Stil·ton cheese (stil′tən) A rich cheese permeated when ripe with a blue–green mold: originally made at Stilton, England. Also **Stil′ton.**

stilt–walk·er (stilt′wô′kər) *n.* One who walks or runs on stilts.

Stil·well (stil′wel), **Joseph Warren,** 1883–1946, U. S. general.

stime (stīm) *n. Scot.* A particle of light; a glimpse.

stim·part (stim′pərt) *n. Scot.* The fourth of a peck.

Stim·son (stim′sən), **Henry Lewis,** 1867–1950, U. S. statesman; secretary of war 1911–13, 1940–45; secretary of state 1929–33.

stim·u·lant (stim′yə·lənt) *n.* 1 Anything that quickens or promotes the activity of some physiological process, as a drug. 2 Popularly, an alcoholic beverage. — *adj.* Acting as a stimulant; serving to stimulate. [<L *stimulans, -antis,* ppr. of *stimulare.* See STIMULATE.]

stim·u·late (stim′yə·lāt) *v.* **·lat·ed, ·lat·ing** *v.t.* 1 To rouse to activity or to quickened action by some agency or motive; spur. 2 To arouse, or to increase action in, by applying some form of stimulus: to *stimulate* the skin. 3 To affect by intoxicants. — *v.i.* 4 To act as a stimulant. See synonyms under ENCOURAGE, PIQUE[1], SPUR, STIR[1]. [<L *stimulatus,* pp. of *stimulare* prick, goad < *stimulus* a goad] — **stim′u·lat′er, stim′u·la′tor** *n.* — **stim′u·la′·tion** *n.*

stim·u·la·tive (stim′yə·lā′tiv) *adj.* Having the power or tendency to stimulate. — *n.* A stimulus.

stim·u·lus (stim′yə·ləs) *n. pl.* **·li** (-lī) 1 Anything that rouses the mind or spirits; an incentive; a stimulant; a sting; a spur, or goad. 2 *Physiol.* **a** Any agent or form of excitation which influences the activity of an organism as a whole or in any of its parts. **b** That which initiates an impulse, as in a nerve or muscle, or produces an altered state of consciousness, as by arousing new or stronger sensations. [<L]

sti·my (stī′mē) See STYMIE.

sting (sting) *v.* **stung** (*Obs.* **stang**), **stung, sting·ing** *v.t.* 1 To pierce or prick painfully, as with a sharp, poisonous organ: The bee *stung* me. 2 To cause to suffer sharp, smarting pain from or as from a sting: The blow *stung* his cheek. 3 To cause to suffer mentally; pain: His heart was *stung* with remorse. 4 To stimulate or rouse as if with a sting; goad; spur. 5 *Slang* To impose upon; get the better of; also, to overcharge. — *v.i.* 6 To have or use a sting, as a bee. 7 To suffer or cause a sharp, smarting pain. 8 To suffer or cause

mental distress; pain. See synonyms under INCENSE[1], PIQUE[1], SPUR. —*n.* **1** *Zool.* A sharp offensive or defensive organ, as of a bee or wasp, capable of inflicting a painful and especially a poisonous wound. **2** The act of stinging; the wound made by a sting, or the pain caused by it. **3** Any sharp, smarting sensation; stinging quality: the *sting* of remorse. **4** A keen stimulus; spur; goad. **5** *Bot.* One of the sharp-pointed hairs of a nettle; a stinging hair. **6** The point of an epigram. **7** *Colloq.* A confidence game; swindle. [OE *stingan*] **—sting′ing·ly** *adv.*

sting-and-ling (sting′ən·ling′) *adv. Scot.* As a whole: forcibly.

sting·a·ree (sting′ə·rē, sting′ə·rē′) *n.* A sting-ray. [Alter. of STINGRAY]

stinge (stinj) *v.i.* **stinged, stinge·ing** To act in a miserly, stingy way. [Back formation <STINGY]

sting·er (sting′ər) *n.* **1** One who or that which stings. **2** A plant or animal that stings. **3** An insect's sting. **4** A cocktail made of brandy and white crème de menthe.

stinging hair *Bot.* One of the hairs of a nettle, charged at the base with an irritating fluid which is injected beneath the skin when touched.

stin·go (sting′gō) *n. Brit. Slang* **1** A strong ale or beer. **2** Zest; vim. [<STING; from the sharpness of the taste]

sting·ray (sting′rā) *n.* Any of a family *(Dasyatidae)* of bottom-dwelling rays having a long, whiplike tail bearing one or more serrated venomous spines. Also called *stingaree.* [<STING + RAY[2]]

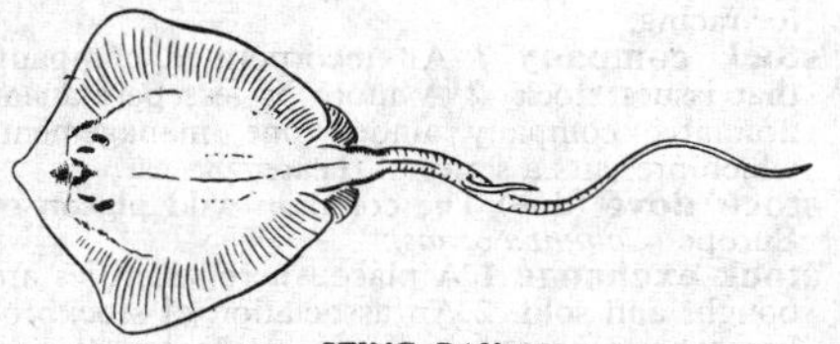

STING RAY
(Body about 20 inches in length; the stinger, 8 to 15 inches)

stin·gy[1] (stin′jē) *adj.* **·gi·er, ·gi·est 1** Extremely penurious or selfish; miserly. **2** Scanty, as from penurious giving. See synonyms under AVARICIOUS. [<dial. E *stinge* a sting] **—stin′gi·ly** *adv.* **—stin′gi·ness** *n.*

sting·y[2] (sting′ē) *adj. Colloq.* Stinging; piercing. **—sting′i·ly** *adv.*

stink (stingk) *n.* A strong, foul odor; stench. See synonyms under SMELL. —*v.* **stank** or **stunk, stunk, stink·ing** *v.i.* **1** To give forth a foul odor. **2** To be extremely offensive or hateful. —*v.t.* **3** To cause to stink. **—to stink out** To drive from a den, hideaway, etc., by a foul or suffocating odor. [OE *stincan* smell] **—stink′ing** *adj.* **—stink′ing·ly** *adv.*

stink·ard (stingk′ərd) *n.* **1** A mean, detestable fellow. **2** The dogfish.

stink·ball (stingk′bôl′) *n.* A jar containing a mixture of various compounds, as gunpowder, asafetida, etc., formerly used for throwing from one warship to another when at close quarters: also called *stinkpot.* Also **stink′bomb′** (-bom′).

stink·bug (stingk′bug′) *n.* Any of a family *(Pentatomidae)* of hemipterous insects, including mostly rather large, broad, flattened bugs which emit a sickening, sweetish odor when disturbed.

stink·er (stingk′ər) *n.* **1** One who or that which stinks, as a stinkball. **2** The fulmar or other petrel that feeds on carrion. **3** *Slang* An unpleasant, disgusting, or irritating person.

stink·horn (stingk′hôrn′) *n.* Any of an order *(Phallales)* of basidiomycetous, ill-smelling fungi, especially the carrion fungus *(Ithyphallus impudicus).*

stinking hellebore Helleboraster.

stinking smut The bunt disease of wheat.

stink·pot (stingk′pot′) *n.* **1** A stinkball. **2** The musk turtle.

stink·stone (stingk′stōn′) *n.* Any kind of rock that gives off a fetid odor under percussion, as certain limestones.

stink·weed (stingk′wēd′) *n.* The jimsonweed or stramonium.

stink·wood (stingk′wŏŏd′) *n.* **1** Any of various trees having wood of a disagreeable odor. **2** The wood.

Stin·nes (shtin′əs), **Hugo,** 1870–1924, German industrialist.

stint (stint) *v.t.* **1** To limit, as in amount or share; be stingy with: Don't *stint* yourself. **2** *Archaic* To stop. —*v.i.* **3** To be frugal or sparing. **4** *Archaic* To stop. —*n.* **1** A fixed amount, as of work; a task to be performed within a specified time; allowance. **2** A bound; restriction. **3** A small sandpiper. **4** *Obs.* A cessation. See synonyms under TASK, TOIL[1]. [ME *stynten* cause to stop <OE *styntan* stupefy <*stunt* stupid] **—stint′er** *n.* **—stint′ing** *adj.* **—stint′ing·ly** *adv.*

stipe (stīp) *n.* **1** *Zool.* A stalk or support. **2** *Bot.* **a** A stalklike support of a gynoecium or carpel. **b** The petiole or support of a fern's frond. **c** The stem supporting the cap of a mushroom or similar fungus. See illustration under MUSHROOM. [<F <L *stipes* branch]

sti·pel (stī′pəl) *n. Bot.* A secondary or small stipule standing at the base of a leaflet. [<NL *stipella,* dim. of *stipes* a branch] **—sti·pel·late** (stī·pel′it, stī′pəl·it, -āt) *adj.*

sti·pend (stī′pend) *n.* **1** An allowance or salary; a fixed payment for services, especially a salary that affords a bare livelihood. **2** *Scot.* A clergyman's salary. **3** *Eccl.* In the Roman Catholic Church, an offering given to a priest for saying a mass with a special intention. See synonyms under SALARY. [<L *stipendium* tax, tribute <*stips* coin, payment in coin + *pendere* weigh, pay ut]

sti·pen·di·ar·y (stī·pen′dē·er′ē) *adj.* **1** Receiving a stipend. **2** Paying tribute; owing feudal service; performing services for a fixed payment. —*n. pl.* **·ar·ies 1** One who receives a stipend, as a clergyman. **2** A person owing feudal service. **3** A province paying a special tribute to a Roman emperor, instead of a tax. [<L *stipendiarius* <*stipendium* STIPEND]

sti·pes (stī′pēz) *n.* **1** A stipe. **2** *Entomol.* The subbasal, central, and usually the largest part of an insect's maxilla. [<L] **—sti′pi·form** (-pə·fôrm), **stip·i·ti·form** (stip′ə·tə·fôrm′) *adj.*

stip·i·tate (stip′ə·tāt) *adj.* Having or borne on a stipe; stalked. [<NL *stipitatus* <L *stipes* stock]

stip·ple (stip′əl) *v.t.* **·pled, ·pling** To draw, paint, or engrave with dots or short touches instead of lines, so as to produce a shaded effect. —*n.* In painting, etching, etc., a method of representing light and shade by employing dots instead of lines, or the effect thus produced: also **stip′pling.** [<Du. *stippelen* <*stippen* speckle <*stip* dot] **—stip′pler** *n.*

stip·u·lar (stip′yə·lər) *adj. Bot.* **1** Growing on stipules. **2** Of, resembling, or pertaining to stalks or stems.

stip·u·late[1] (stip′yə·lāt) *v.* **·lat·ed, ·lat·ing** *v.t.* **1** To specify as the terms of an agreement, contract, etc. **2** To specify as a requirement or condition for agreement. **3** To promise; guarantee. —*v.i.* **4** To demand something as a requirement or condition: with *for.* **5** To make an agreement. [<L *stipulatus,* pp. of *stipulari* bargain] **—stip′u·la′tor** *n.*

stip·u·late[2] (stip′yə·lit, -lāt) *adj.* Furnished with stipules. Also **stip′u·lat′ed** (-lā′tid).

stip·u·la·tion (stip′yə·lā′shən) *n.* **1** The act of stipulating, or the condition of being stipulated. **2** An agreement or contract. See synonyms under CONTRACT. **—stip′u·la·to′ry** (-lə·tôr′ē, -tō′rē) *adj.*

stip·ule (stip′yŏŏl) *n. Bot.* One of a pair of leaflike appendages at the base of the petiole of certain leaves. [<L *stipula* stalk]

stir[1] (stûr) *v.* **stirred, stir·ring** *v.t.* **1** To agitate so as to alter the relative position of the particles or components of, as soup with a spoon. **2** To cause to move, especially slightly or irregularly; disturb: The tide *stirred* the boat. **3** To move vigorously; bestir: *Stir* yourself! **4** To rouse, as from sleep, indifference, or inactivity; stimulate. **5** To incite; provoke; often with *up.* **6** To affect strongly; move with emotion. —*v.i.* **7** To move, especially slightly: The log wouldn't *stir.* **8** To be active; move about: They heard him *stirring* in his room. **9** To take place; happen. **10** To undergo stirring: This molasses *stirs* easily. —*n.* **1** The act of stirring, or state of being stirred; activity. **2** Public interest; excitement; to-do; commotion. **3** A poke; nudge. [OE *styrian*] **—stir′rer** *n.*

Synonyms (verb): agitate, animate, arouse, awake, awaken, excite, incite, instigate, move, prompt, provoke, rouse, stimulate, wake. See ACTUATE, INFLUENCE, SPUR. *Antonyms*: see synonyms for ALLAY, ALLEVIATE.

stir[2] (stûr) *n. Slang* A jail; prison. [Origin uncertain]

stir·a·bout (stûr′ə·bout′) *n. Brit.* A porridge made of oatmeal or cornmeal stirred in boiling milk or water; a hasty pudding.

stirk (stûrk) *n.* **1** A yearling ox or cow. **2** *Scot.* A stupid fellow. [OE *stirc* calf <*stēor* steer]

Stir·ling (stûr′ling) A county in central Scotland; 451 square miles; county town, Stirling. Also **Stir′ling·shire** (-shir).

stir·pi·cul·ture (stûr′pə·kul′chər) *n.* The breeding of special races or strains of animals and plants. [<L *stirps, stirpis* stem, stock + CULTURE] **—stir′pi·cul′tur·al** *adj.* **—stir′pi·cul′tur·ist** *n.*

stirps (stûrps) *n. pl.* **stir·pes** (stûr′pēz) **1** Race; family. **2** A stock as regards lineage: a source of property-descent: Descent per *stirpes* (as a family) is distinguished from descent per capita (as an individual). **3** *Biol.* The number of organic units existing in and determining the development of a fertilized ovum. [<L]

stir·ring (stûr′ing) *adj.* **1** Stimulating; inspiring. **2** Full of activity or stir; lively. See synonyms under VIVID. **—stir′ring·ly** *adv.*

stir·rup (stûr′əp, stir′-) *n.* **1** A loop, as an inverted U-shaped piece of metal or wood with flat footpiece, suspended from a saddle to support the rider's foot in and after mounting. **2** A loop or metal strap, as for supporting a beam. **3** *Naut.* A rope on a ship depending from a yard and having at its end an eye or thimble to carry a footrope. [OE *stigrāp* mounting rope]

stirrup bone *Anat.* The stapes.

stir·rup-cup (stûr′əp·kup′, stir′-) *n.* A cup of liquor, as that taken by a mounted horseman on departing; hence, a farewell drink.

stirrup leather The strap by which the stirrup iron is hung from the saddle. Also **stirrup strap.**

stitch[1] (stich) *n.* **1** A single passage of a threaded needle or other implement through fabric and back again, as in sewing or embroidery, or, in surgery, through skin or flesh. **2** A single turn of thread or yarn around a needle or other implement, as in knitting or crocheting; also, the link or loop resulting from such a turn. **3** Any peculiar or individual arrangement of a thread or threads used in sewing, embroidery, or crocheting: a chain *stitch.* **4** A sharp sudden pain, especially in the back or side. **5** A ridge between two furrows. **6** *Colloq.* A garment: I haven't a *stitch* to wear. **—to be in stitches** *Colloq.* To laugh uproariously; be overcome with laughter. —*v.t.* **1** To join together with stitches. **2** To ornament with stitches. —*v.i.* **3** To make stitches; sew. [OE *stice* prick, stab]

stitch[2] (stich) *n. Brit. Dial.* **1** A space passed over; a span of time; distance. **2** A fragment. [OE *stycce* piece]

stitch·er (stich′ər) *n.* One who or that which stitches; especially, a machine for that purpose, as in bookbinding.

stitch·wort (stich′wûrt′) *n.* Any of various plants (genus *Stellaria*), especially the common chickweed: also called *starwort, stichwort.* [OE *sticwyrt* <*stice* prick + *wyrt* plant]

stith·y (stith′ē, stith′ē) *n. pl.* **stith·ies 1** A smithy or forge. **2** An anvil. —*v.t.* **stith·ied, stith·y·ing** *Archaic* To forge on an anvil. [<ON *stedhi*]

stive (stīv) *v.t. Obs.* To stow closely; cram; stifle. [<OF *estiver* <L *stipare* crowd]

sti·ver (stī′vər) *n.* **1** A small Dutch coin, 1/20 of a guilder. **2** Anything of little value. [<Du. *stuiver*]

St. James's Palace (sānt jām′ziz) The Tudor palace in Pall Mall, London, residence of the British sovereigns from Henry VIII to the accession of Victoria: the British royal court is still called the **Court of Saint James's.**

St. John (sānt jon′) **1** One of the Virgin Islands of the United States; 19 square miles. **2** A port on the Bay of Fundy, in southern New Brunswick, Canada. **3** St. John's, Leeward Islands.

St. John (sānt jon′, sin′jən), **Henry** See BOLINGBROKE.

St. John, Lake A lake in south central Quebec, Canada; 375 square miles.

St. John River A river flowing 400 miles NE and east through northern Maine and western New Brunswick to the Bay of Fundy, forming part of the boundary between Maine and New Brunswick.

St. John's (jonz) **1** The capital and largest city of Newfoundland, a port on the SE coast. **2** The capital of Antigua, The West Indies (federation), and former administrative capital of the Leeward Islands.

St. John's bread See CAROB.

St. Johns River A river in NE Florida, flowing 285 miles north and east to the Atlantic.

St. Johns-wort (sānt jonz′wûrt′) Any of a genus *(Hypericum)* of herbs and shrubs, mostly of the northern hemisphere, usually having large yellow or purplish flowers, considered to be typical of the family Guttiferae. Also **St.-John's-wort, Saint Johnswort.**

St. Jo·seph (sānt jō′zif) A city in NW Missouri on the Missouri River.

St. Kitts (sānt kits′) See ST. CHRISTOPHER, NEVIS, AND ANGUILLA.

St. Lau·rent (saṅ lô·räṅ′), **Louis,** 1882–1973, Canadian prime minister 1948–57.

St. Law·rence Island (sānt lôr′əns, lor′-) An island of western Alaska in the Bering Sea; 90 miles long, 8 to 22 miles wide.

St. Lawrence River A river of SE Canada, the outlet of the Great Lakes system, flowing 744 miles NE from the NE end of Lake Ontario to the **Gulf of St. Lawrence,** an inlet of the North Atlantic between Newfoundland and eastern Canada; together with the Great Lakes and the St. Marys River it forms a waterway about 2,350 miles long, from the western end of Lake Superior to the Atlantic.

St. Lou·is (sānt lōō′is, lōō′ē) A city in eastern Missouri, on the Mississippi River below the influx of the Missouri; a major center of transportation, industry, and commerce.

St. Lu·ci·a (sānt lōō′shē·ə, lōō·sē′ə, lōō′shə) A British colony in the Windward Islands, a federating unit of The West Indies (federation); 233 square miles; capital, Castries.

St. Mar·tin (sānt mär′tin) An island in the NW Leeward Islands; the southern part, *Dutch* **Sint Maar·ten** (sint mär′tən), 13 square miles, in the Netherlands Antilles; the northern part, *French* **Saint-Mar·tin** (saṅ·mär·taṅ′), 20 square miles, a dependency of Guadeloupe; total 33 square miles.

St. Mar·y·le·bone (sānt mâr′ē·lə·bōn′) See MARYLEBONE.

St. Mar·ys River (sānt mâr′ēz) **1** A river flowing 63 miles SE from Lake Superior to Lake Huron and forming the boundary between northern Michigan and Ontario. **2** A river in SE Georgia and NE Florida, flowing 175 miles south, east, and north from the Okefinokee Swamp to the Atlantic, and forming part of the Georgia-Florida border.

St. Mau·rice River (sānt môr′is, mor′is; *Fr.* saṅ mô·rēs′) A river in Quebec province, Canada, flowing 325 miles SE and south to the St. Lawrence.

St. Mo·ritz (sānt môr′its, mō′rits) A resort town in SE Switzerland; elevation, 6,080 feet: German *Sankt Moritz. French* **Saint-Mo·ritz** (saṅ·mô·rēts′).

sto·a (stō′ə) *n. pl.* **sto·ae** (stō′ē) or **sto·as** In Greek architecture, a covered colonnade, portico, cloister, or promenade. [< Gk., porch]

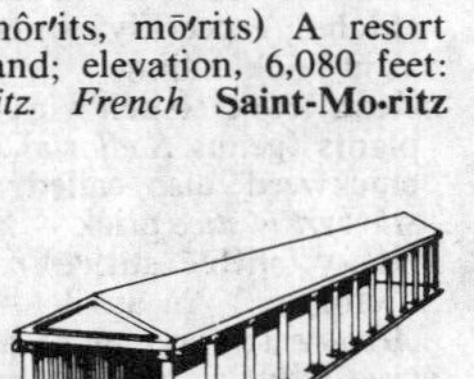

STOA

stoat[1] (stōt) *n.* The ermine, especially in its summer coat, red-brown above, yellow below. [ME *stote;* origin uncertain]

stoat[2] (stōt) *v.t.* To sew with an invisible stitch that passes only half-way through the cloth. [Origin unknown] **—stoat′ing** *n.*

stob (stob) *Dial. n.* A stake or post, usually short; also, the stump of a tree. —*v.t.* To stab. [Var. of STUB]

stoc·ca·do (stə·kā′dō, -kä′-) *n. Archaic* A stabbing or thrusting movement with a rapier. Also **stoc·ca′ta** (-tə). [< Ital. *stoccata* < *stocco* rapier]

sto·chas·tic (stō·kas′tik) *adj.* **1** Of, pertaining to, characterized by, or skilled in conjecture; conjectural. **2** *Physics* Subject to the laws of probability; not predictable within a given time limit or spatial framework, as the disintegration of a single radioactive element: the *stochastic* phenomena of microphysics. **3** Denoting the process of selecting, from among a group of theoretically possible alternatives, those elements or factors whose combination will most closely approximate a desired result: a *stochastic* model. [< Gk. *stochastikos* < *stochazesthai* guess at < *stochos* mark, aim]

stock (stok) *n.* **1** The trunk or main stem of a tree or other plant, as distinguished from a branch or root. **2** A line of familial descent. **3** The original progenitor of a family line. **4** An ethnic group; race. **5** *Ling.* A family of languages. **6** A related group or family of plants or animals. **7** *Bot.* **a** A rhizome. **b** A stem upon which a graft is made. **8** *Zool.* A zooid which reproduces by generation. **9** Livestock: in Australia, cattle, not livestock in general. **10** A quantity of something acquired or kept for future use: to lay in a *stock* of provisions. **11** The merchandise or goods which a trader or merchant has on hand. **12** In card games and dominoes, the part of the pack or group of dominoes that is left on the table and drawn from. **13** The broth from boiled meat or fish used in preparing soups, etc. **14** Raw material: paper *stock.* **15** *pl.* A timber frame with holes for confining the ankles and often the wrists, formerly used in punishing petty offenders. **16** *pl.* The timber frame on which a vessel rests during construction. **17** *pl.* A frame for confining an animal for shoeing or veterinary treatment. **18** *Naut.* An anchor crossbar. **19** The wooden block suspending a bell. **20** In firearms: **a** The rear wooden portion of a rifle, musket, or shotgun, to which the barrel and mechanisms are secured. **b** The arm on rapid-fire guns connecting the shoulder piece to the slide. **c** The handle of a pistol or similar firearm. **d** That member of a gun carriage which usually bears the prolonge and trails along the ground. **21** The handle of certain instruments, as of a whip or fishing rod. **22** A theatrical stock company. **23** The collection of dramas produced by a theatrical stock company. **24** A broad stiffened band, formerly worn as a cravat. **25** *Geol.* The rounded mass of plutonic rock rising above ground level: also called *boss.* **26** *Mech.* An adjustable wrench used for grasping and turning thread-cutting dies. **27** An ornamental garden plant, as the gilliflower, or common stock *(Mathiola incana).* **28** In finance: **a** The capital or fund raised by a corporation through the sale of shares, which entitle the holder to interest or dividends and to part ownership of the corporation. The stockholder may not claim repayment of the principal, though he may sell his shares to other investors at the current market value. **b** The proportional part of this capital credited to an individual stockholder and represented by the number of shares he owns. **c** A certificate showing ownership of a specific number of shares. **—common stock** The stock of a corporation which entitles the holder to dividends, or a share in the profits, only after all other obligations have been met and dividends have been rendered to the owners of preferred stock. Direction of a corporation is usually vested in the owners of common stock. **—debenture stock** *Brit.* A debenture of a corporation or public body issued in the form of stock, the certificates of which are usually transferable but not redeemable and entitle the holder to a perpetual annuity. **—no-par stock** Stock issued without a face value on the certificate and sold at whatever price it will command on the market. **—preferred stock** The stock of a corporation which gives the holder prior claim to dividends up to a certain amount. **—to take stock 1** To take an inventory. **2** To make a careful estimate or appraisal. **—to take stock in** To have trust or belief in; give credence to. —*v.t.* **1** To furnish with stock; supply with cattle, as a farm, or with merchandise, as a store. **2** To keep for sale: to *stock* black ink. **3** To put aside for future use. **4** To provide with a handle or stock. **5** *Obs.* To put (a person) in the stocks for punishment. —*v.i.* **6** To lay in supplies or stock: often with *up.* **7** To send out new shoots; sprout. —*adj.* **1** Kept continually ready or constantly brought forth, like old goods: a *stock* joke. **2** Kept on hand: a *stock* size. **3** Banal; commonplace: a *stock* phrase. **4** Used for breeding purposes: a *stock* mare. **5** Employed in handling or caring for the stock: a *stock* clerk. —*adv.* Motionlessly; like a stump or block of wood: used in combination: *stockstill.* [OE *stocc*]

Synonyms (noun): accumulation, capital, fund, hoard, material, provision, store, supply. See STICK.

stock·ade (sto·kād′) *n.* **1** A line of stout posts, stakes, etc., set upright in the earth to form a fence or barrier; also, the area thus enclosed. **2** Specifically, a strong, high barrier of upright posts, stakes, etc., formerly used by American settlers as a defense against Indians. **3** A breakwater of piling, as for protecting a pier. —*v.t.* **·ad·ed, ·ad·ing** To surround or fortify with a stockade. [< OF *estocade, estacade* < *estaque* a stake < Gmc.]

stock·breed·er (stok′brē′dər) *n.* One who breeds and raises livestock.

stock·breed·ing (stok′brē′ding) *n.* The breeding and raising of livestock.

stock·bro·ker (stok′brō′kər) *n.* One who buys and sells stocks or securities for others. **—stock′bro′ker·age, stock′bro′king** *n.*

stock car 1 An automobile, as one selected at random, typifying the regular factory stock. **2** Such an automobile, usually a sedan, modified for racing.

stock company 1 An incorporated company that issues stock. **2** A more or less permanent dramatic company under one management, which presents a series of theater pieces.

stock dove (duv) The common wild pigeon of Europe *(Columba oenas).*

stock exchange 1 A place where securities are bought and sold. **2** An association of stockbrokers who transact business in stocks, bonds, and other shares.

stock farm A farm which specializes in the breeding of livestock.

stock fish Cod, haddock, or the like, cured by splitting and drying in the air, unsalted.

stock·hold·er (stok′hōl′dər) *n.* One who holds certificates of ownership in a company or corporation.

Stock·holm (stok′hōm, *Sw.* stôk′hôlm) The capital of Sweden, a port on the east coast, on the Baltic Sea; called "the Venice of the North" because of its waterways.

stock·i·net (stok′i·net′) *n.* **1** An elastic knitted fabric used chiefly for undergarments. **2** A style of knitting in which the rows are alternately knitted and purled: also **stockinet stitch.** Also **stock′i·nette′.** [Alter. of *stockinget* < STOCKING + -ET]

stock·ing (stok′ing) *n.* **1** A close-fitting woven or knitted covering for the foot and lower leg. **2** Something resembling such a covering. [< STOCK, in obs. sense of "a stocking" + -ING[3]] **—stock′ing·less** *adj.*

stock in trade 1 The goods which a storekeeper has for sale. **2** Resources, either material or spiritual.

stock·ish (stok′ish) *adj.* Like a stock or block of wood; stupid.

stock·job·ber (stok′job′ər) *n.* A dealer or speculator in stocks in his own interest; also, a stockbroker. **—stock′job′ber·y, stock′job′bing** *n.*

stock·man (stok′mən) *n. pl.* **·men** (-mən) **1** A man having charge of stock. **2** One who raises or owns livestock; a cattleman.

stock market 1 A stock exchange. **2** The business transacted in such a place: The *stock market* was active. **3** The rise and fall of prices of securities.

stock·pile (stok′pīl′) *n.* A storage pile of materials or supplies. Also **stock pile.** —*v.t.* & *v.i.* **·piled, ·pil·ing** To accumulate a supply or stockpile (of).

Stock·port (stok′pôrt, -pōrt) A county borough of NE Cheshire, England.

stock·pot (stok′pot′) *n.* A pot for preparing and keeping soup stock.

stock·rais·ing (stok′rā′zing) *n.* Breeding and raising of livestock. **—stock′-rais′er** *n.*

stock·room (stok′rōōm′, -rōōm′) *n.* A room where reserve stocks of goods are stored.

stock·still (stok′stil′) *adj.* Still as a stock or post; motionless.
Stock·ton (stok′tən), **Frank,** 1834–1902, U.S. author; full name Francis Richard Stockton. —**Richard,** 1730–81, American statesman; signer of the Declaration of Independence.
Stock·ton–on–Tees (stok′tən·on·tēz′) A port and borough in SE Durham, England.
stock·whip (stock′wip′) *Austral.* A whip used by stockmen, usually of kangaroo hide with a seven– to eight–foot lash and a cord or horsehair cracker.
stock·work (stok′wûrk′) *n. Geol.* An irregular mass of rock interlaced by a network of small ore–bearing veins.
stock·y (stok′ē) *adj.* **stock·i·er, stock·i·est** Short and stout; thick–set. —**stock′i·ly** *adv.* —**stock′·i·ness** *n.*
stock·yard (stok′yärd′) *n.* A large yard with pens, stables, etc., where cattle are kept ready for shipping, slaughter, etc.
stodge (stoj) *v.* **stodged, stodg·ing** *v.t.* To render dull and heavy by stuffing with food. —*v.i.* To become muddy or marshy. [<dial. E *stodge* fill to distention]
stodg·y (stoj′ē) *adj.* **stodg·i·er, stodg·i·est** **1** Distended; crammed full; bulky; lumpy. **2** Stupid; dull; heavy. **3** Indigestible; satiating. **4** Sticky; muddy. **5** Thick–set; clumsy and stiff. —**stodg′i·ly** *adv.* —**stodg′i·ness** *n.*
sto·gy (stō′gē) *n. pl.* **·gies** **1** A stout, coarse boot or shoe. **2** A long, slender, inexpensive cigar: also **sto′gie.** [Earlier *stoga* <(CONE)-STOGA (WAGON), because their drivers wore heavy boots and smoked coarse cigars]
sto·ic (stō′ik) *n.* A person apparently unaffected by pleasure or pain. —*adj.* Indifferent to pleasure or pain; impassive; uncomplaining. Also **sto′i·cal.** —**sto′i·cal·ly** *adv.* —**sto′i·cal·ness** *n.*
Sto·ic (stō′ik) *n.* A member of a school of Greek philosophy founded by Zeno about 308 B.C., holding the pantheistic beliefs that the world is a manifestation of a divine mind, that there is no reality but matter, even the human soul being doomed to dissolution, that wisdom lies in being superior to passion, joy, grief, etc., and in submission to the divine will. —*adj.* Of or pertaining to the Stoics or Stoicism. [<L *Stoicus* <Gk. *Stoikos* <*Stoa (Poikilē)* (Painted) Porch, the colonnade at Athens where Zeno taught]
stoi·chi·ol·o·gy (stoi′kē·ol′ə·jē) *n.* T Also **stoe′·chi·ol′o·gy, stoi′·chei·ol′o·gy.** [<Gk. *stoicheion* element + -LOGY] —**stoi′chi·o·log′·i·cal** (-ə·loj′i·kəl) *adj.*
stoi·chi·om·e·try (stoi′kē·om′ə·trē) *n.* The branch of chemistry that treats of the proportions of elements or compounds involved in reactions, and the methods of calculating them. Also **stoe′chi·om′e·try, stoi′chei·om′e·try.** [<Gk. *stoicheion* element + -METRY] —**stoi′chi·o·met′ric** (-ə·met′rik) or **·ri·cal** *adj.*
sto·i·cism (stō′ə·siz′əm) *n.* Indifference to pleasure or pain; stoicalness. See synonyms under APATHY.
Sto·i·cism (stō′ə·siz′əm) *n.* The doctrines of the Stoics.
stoit (stōt, stoit) *v.i. Scot. & Irish* **1** To walk in a reeling, stumbling manner: also **stoit′er, stoit′ur.** **2** To rebound; bounce. **3** To leap from the water: said of certain fish.
stoke[1] (stōk) *v.t. & v.i.* **stoked, stok·ing** To supply (a furnace) with fuel; stir up or tend (a fire or furnace). [Back formation <STOKER]
stoke[2] (stōk) *n. Physics* A unit of kinematic viscosity, equivalent to 1 poise in a fluid having a density of 1 gram per cubic centimeter referred to a specified temperature. [after Sir George G. *Stokes,* 1819–1903, English mathematician and physicist]
stoke·hold (stōk′hōld′) *n. Naut.* **1** The furnace room of a steamer. **2** The space in front of the furnaces from which they are stoked.
stoke·hole (stōk′hōl′) *n.* **1** The space about the mouth of a furnace; the fireroom. **2** The mouth of a furnace. **3** A stokehold.
Stoke–on–Trent (stōk′on·trent′) A county borough in NW Stafford, England. Also **Stoke′–up·on′–Trent′.**
Stoke Po·ges (pō′jis) A village in SE Buckinghamshire, England; generally regarded as the scene of Gray's *Elegy.*
stok·er (stō′kər) *n.* **1** One who or that which supplies fuel to a furnace, especially of a steam boiler, as in a ship or locomotive; a fireman on a locomotive, ship, etc. **2** A device for feeding coal to a furnace. [<Du. <*stoken* stir a fire <*stok* stick]
Stokes mortar A light, muzzleloading mortar for high–angle, short–range fire. [after Sir Frederick W. S. *Stokes,* 1860–1927, English inventor]
Sto·kow·ski (stə·kôf′skē, -kou′skē), **Leopold,** 1882–1977, U.S. orchestra conductor born in England.
stole[1] (stōl) *n.* **1** *Eccl.* A long, narrow band, usually of decorated silk or linen, worn about the shoulders by priests and bishops, and over the left shoulder only by deacons, when officiating; loosely, any ecclesiastical vestment. **2** A fur, scarf, or garment resembling a stole, worn by women. **3** In ancient Rome, a long outer garment worn by matrons. [OE <L *stola* a robe <Gk. *stolē* a garment] —**stoled** *adj.*
stole[2] (stōl) Past tense of STEAL.
sto·len (stō′lən) Past participle of STEAL.
stol·id (stol′id) *adj.* Having or expressing no power of feeling or perceiving; impassible; dull. See synonyms under BRUTISH, HEAVY. [<L *stolidus* dull]—**sto·lid·i·ty** (stə·lid′ə·tē), **stol′id·ness** *n.* —**stol′id·ly** *adv.*
sto·lon (stō′lon) *n.* **1** *Bot.* **a** A trailing branch that is capable of taking root. **b** A runner or rootstock by which grasses may propagate. **2** *Zool.* A prolongation of the body of various animals, as corals. [<NL <L *stolo, stolonis*]
sto·ma (stō′mə) *n. pl.* **sto·ma·ta** (stō′mə·tə, stom′ə·tə) **1** A minute orifice; pore. **2** *Biol.* An aperture in the walls of blood vessels or in serous membranes, or in the epidermis of leaves, young stems, etc. [<Gk. *stoma* mouth]
–stoma See -STOME.
stom·ach (stum′ək) *n.* **1** The pouchlike, highly vascular dilation of the alimentary canal, situated in most vertebrates between the esophagus and the small intestine, and serving as one of the principal organs of digestion. ◆ Collateral adjective: *gastric.* **2** Any digestive cavity, as of an invertebrate. **3** The abdomen; belly: an anatomically incorrect use. **4** Desire for food; appetite; hence, any desire or inclination. **5** Temper; spirit. **6** *Obs.* Pride; haughtiness. —*v.t.* **1** To accept without apparent opposition; to put up with; endure. **2** To take into and retain in the stomach; digest. **3** *Obs.* To resent. [<OF *estomac* <L *stomachus* <Gk. *stomachos* gullet, stomach <*stoma* a mouth]
stomach ache Pain in the stomach, as from indigestion or inflammation.
stom·ach·er (stum′ək·ər) *n.* A former ornamental article of dress for the breast and stomach.
sto·mach·ic (stō·mak′ik) *adj.* **1** Pertaining to the stomach. **2** Strengthening the activity of the stomach. Also **stom·ach·al** (stum′ək·əl), **sto·mach′i·cal.** —*n.* Any medicine strengthening or stimulating the stomach.
stomach tooth *Dent.* A lower canine tooth of the first dentition: so called because its emergence is frequently accompanied by digestive disturbances.
stomach worm Any of various nematode worms which are parasitic in the stomachs of man and animals, especially the sheep stomach worm *(Haemonchus contortus).*
stom·ach·y (stum′ək·ē) *adj.* **1** Having a paunch. **2** *Brit. Dial.* Spirited; haughty; proud; also, choleric; resentful.
sto·ma·ta (stō′mə·tə, stom′ə·tə) Plural of STOMA.
sto·ma·tal (stō′mə·təl, stom′ə-) *adj.* Of or pertaining to stomata.
sto·mat·ic (stō·mat′ik) *adj.* **1** Of or pertaining to the mouth. **2** Of, pertaining to, or like a stoma.
sto·ma·tif·er·ous (stō′mə·tif′ər·əs, stom′ə-) *adj.* Bearing stomata. [<STOMAT(O)- + -(I)FEROUS]
sto·ma·ti·tis (stō′mə·tī′tis, stom′ə-) *n. Pathol.* Inflammation of the mouth.
stomato– *combining form* The mouth; of or pertaining to the mouth: *stomatoplasty.* Also, before vowels, **stomat–.** [<Gk. *stoma, stomatos* the mouth]
sto·ma·tol·o·gy (stō′mə·tol′ə·jē, stom′ə-) *n.* The science treating of the mouth and of its diseases.
sto·ma·to·plas·ty (stō′mə·tə·plas′tē, stom′ə-) *n.* Plastic surgery of the mouth.
sto·ma·to·pod (stō′mə·tə·pod′, stom′ə-) *n.* Any of an order *(Stomatopoda)* of crustaceans having abdominal gills and legs near the mouth, including the squills. —**sto′ma·top′o·dous** (-top′ə·dəs) *adj.*
sto·ma·tous (stō′mə·təs, stom′ə-) *adj.* Having a stoma or stomata.
–stome *combining form* Mouth; mouthlike opening: *peristome.* Also spelled *-stoma.* [<Gk. *stoma* the mouth]
sto·mo·de·um (stō′mə·dē′əm, stom′ə-) *n. pl.* **·de·a** (-dē′ə) *Biol.* The invagination of the ectoderm, or outer layer of the embryo, that forms the mouth. Also **sto′mo·dae′um.** [<NL <Gk. *stoma* mouth + *hodaios* on the way <*hodos* way] —**sto′mo·de′al** or **·dae′al** *adj.*
–stomous *combining form* Having a (specified kind of) mouth: *microstomous.* Also **–stomatous.** [<Gk. *stoma, stomatos* the mouth]
stomp (stomp) *Dial. v.t. & v.i.* To stamp; tread heavily (upon). —*n.* A dance involving a heavy and lively step. [Var. of STAMP]
–stomy *combining form Surg.* An operation to form an artificial opening for or into (a specified organ or part): *colostomy, ileostomy.* [<Gk. *stoma* the mouth]
stone (stōn) *n.* **1** A small piece of rock, as a cobble or pebble. **2** Rock, or a piece of rock hewn or shaped; a milestone; a gravestone; hard, concreted mineral or earthy matter. **3** A precious stone; gem. **4** Anything resembling a stone in shape or hardness: a *hailstone.* **5** *Pathol.* A stony concretion in the bladder, or a disease characterized by such concretions. **6** *Bot.* The hard covering of the kernel in a fruit. **7** *(pl.* **stone)** *Brit.* A measure of weight, avoirdupois, usually 14 pounds. **8** A testicle: usually in the plural. **9** *Printing* An imposing table for type, whether made of stone or metal. —*adj.* **1** Made of stone: a *stone* ax. **2** Made of coarse hard earthenware: a *stone* bottle. **3** Characterized by the use of stone implements: the *Stone* Age. —*v.t.* **stoned, ston·ing** **1** To hurl stones at; pelt or kill with stones. **2** To remove the stones or pits from. **3** To furnish or line, as a well, with stone. **4** To castrate; geld, as a hog. **5** *Obs.* To make hard or unyielding, as the heart. [OE *stān*] —**ston′er** *n.*
Stone (stōn), **Harlan Fiske,** 1872–1946, U.S. educator; Supreme Court justice 1941–46. —**Lucy,** 1818–93, U.S. suffragist: wife of *Henry Broun Blackwell.*
Stone Age The earliest known period of the cultural evolution of mankind, marked by the creation and use of stone implements and weapons, preceding the Bronze Age, and subdivided into the Eolithic, Paleolithic, and Neolithic periods.
stone–blind (stōn′blīnd′) *adj.* Blind as a stone; totally blind.
stone·boat (stōn′bōt′) *n. U.S.* A runnerless plank sled used for transporting rocks or similar heavy objects or, when weighted, dragged across a field to break clods of earth, etc.; also, a platform swung under the axles of a wagon.
stone·break (stōn′brāk′) *n.* Saxifrage.
stone–broke (stōn′brōk′) *adj. Colloq.* Without any money; having no funds. Also **ston′y–broke′.**
stone·chat (stōn′chat′) *n.* A small thrushlike European bird (genus *Saxicola*) with upper parts black and breast dark–reddish. [<STONE + CHAT[1] (def. 2); from its cry suggesting the knocking together of pebbles]
stone coal Hard or anthracite coal.
stone color Bluish gray. —**stone′–col′ored** *adj.*
stone·crop (stōn′krop′) *n.* A low spreading mosslike herb *(Sedum acre)* with small fleshy leaves and yellow flowers.
stone·cut·ter (stōn′kut′ər) *n.* One who or that which cuts stone; specifically, a machine for facing stone. —**stone′cut′ting** *n.*
stoned (stōnd) *adj.* **1** Having the stones removed: *stoned* peaches. **2** *U.S. Slang* Intoxicated, as by liquor, marihuana, or a narcotic.
stone–deaf (stōn′def′) *adj.* Completely deaf.
stone fly A plecopteran.
stone fruit A fruit having a stone; a drupe.

Stone·henge (stōn'henj) A prehistoric megalithic structure on Salisbury Plain, SE Wiltshire, England. It consists primarily of circles of dressed stones, some with lintels, the main structure dating probably from 1500 B.C.

STONEHENGE

stone lily A fossil sea lily or other crinoid.

stone·ma·son (stōn'mā'sən) n. One whose occupation or trade is to prepare and lay stones in building. —**stone'ma'son·ry** n.

stone·mint (stōn'mint') n. Dittany (def. 1).

Stone Mountain A granite dome (1,686 feet) of NW central Georgia; a Confederate monument is carved on one side.

stone parsley An Old World herb of the parsley family, especially a British perennial (*Sison amomum*) with cream-colored flowers and aromatic seeds.

stone roller 1 A cyprinoid fish (*Campostoma anomalum*) of North America. **2** A North American sucker (*Catastomus nigricans*).

Stones River A river of central Tennessee, flowing 39 miles NW to the Cumberland River; scene of a Union victory in the Civil War, 1862–63.

stone's throw (stōnz) **1** The distance a stone may be cast by hand. **2** A short distance.

stone·still (stōn'stil') adj. Perfectly motionless.

stone·wall (stōn'wôl') v.i. **1** In cricket, to play on the defensive so as to secure a draw. **2** *Austral.* To oppose by a policy of obstruction; filibuster: a political term. **3** *U.S. Slang* To act in a calculatedly obstructive way, as by lying or failing to respond to inquiry. —v.t. **4** *U.S. Slang* To respond to by stonewalling.

stone wall A wall built of stone; especially, a fence built of stones.

Stone·wall Jack·son (stōn'wôl' jak'sən) See JACKSON, THOMAS JONATHAN.

stone·ware (stōn'wâr') n. A variety of very hard, glazed pottery, made from siliceous clay or clay mixed with flint or sand.

stone·work (stōn'wûrk') n. **1** Work concerned with cutting or setting stone; work made of stone. **2** pl. A place where stone is shaped or stoneware is made. —**stone'work'er** n.

stone·wort (stōn'wûrt') n. Any of a genus (*Chara*) of green algae growing submerged in fresh or brackish waters and often incrusted with deposits of calcium carbonate.

ston·ish (stŏn'ish) v.t. *Obs.* To astonish. [Aphetic var. of ASTONISH] —**ston'ish·ment** n.

ston·y (stō'nē) adj. **ston·i·er, ston·i·est 1** Abounding in stone. **2** Made or consisting of stone. **3** Hard as stone; hence, unfeeling or inflexible. **4** Converting into stone; petrifying; cold and stiff. **5** *Slang* Stone-broke; having no money. —**ston'i·ly** adv. —**ston'i·ness** n.

stony coral A coral having a calcareous skeleton.

ston·y-heart·ed (stō'nē-här'tid) adj. Hard-hearted; unfeeling; pitiless.

Stony Point A village in SE New York; scene of an American victory in the Revolutionary War, July, 1779.

stood[1] (stŏŏd) Past tense and past participle of STAND.

stood[2] (stŏŏd) *Illit. & Dial.* Stayed: He should have *stood* in bed.

stooge (stŏŏj) *Colloq.* n. **1** An actor placed in the audience to heckle a comedian on the stage. **2** An actor who feeds lines to the principal comedian, acts as a foil for his jokes, etc. **3** Anyone who acts as or is the tool or dupe of another. —v.i. **stooged, stooging** To act as a stooge: usually with *for*. [Origin unknown]

stook (stŏŏk, stŏŏk) n. A collection of sheaves set together in the field; a shock of corn. —v.t. To set up in stooks.[Cf. MLG *stuke* a bundle] —**stook'er** n.

stool (stŏŏl) n. **1** A backless and armless seat intended for one person. **2** A low bench or portable support for the feet or for the knees in kneeling. **3** A seat used in defecating; a privy. **4** The matter evacuated from the bowels. **5** *Bot.* **a** A plant from which young plants are produced, as from runners. **b** A stump or root of any kind from which suckers or sprouts shoot up. **c** The shoots from such a root or stump. **6** A decoy, as a bird or likeness of one. —v.i. **1** To send up shoots or suckers. **2** To decoy wild fowl with a stool or stools. **3** To void feces. **4** *U.S. Slang* To be a stool pigeon; inform. [OE *stōl*]

stool pigeon 1 A living or artificial pigeon attached to a stool or perch to decoy others. **2** Any decoy, as a person employed to decoy others into a gambling house, etc. **3** *U.S. Slang* An informer or spy, especially for the police.

stoop[1] (stŏŏp) v.i. **1** To bend or lean the body forward and down; bow; crouch. **2** To stand or walk with the upper part of the body habitually bent forward; slouch. **3** To bend; lean; sink: said of trees, cliffs, etc. **4** To lower or degrade oneself; condescend; deign. **5** To pounce or swoop, as a hawk on prey. **6** *Obs.* To submit: yield. —v.t. **7** To bend (one's head, shoulders, etc.) forward. **8** *Obs.* To humble or subdue. See synonyms under BEND[1]. —n. **1** An act of stooping; a downward and forward bending of the body; also, a habitual forward inclination of the head and shoulders. **2** A decline from dignity or superiority. **3** A swoop, as of a bird of prey. [OE *stūpian*]

stoop[2] (stŏŏp) n. *U.S.* **1** Originally, a platform at the door of a house approached by steps and having seats. **2** A small porch or platform at the entrance to a house. [< Du. *stoep*]

stoop[3] (stŏŏp) n. *Brit. Dial.* A post set in the ground; a pillar. [< ON *stolpi*]

stoop[4] (stŏŏp) See STOUP.

stop (stop) v. **stopped** or (*chiefly Poetic*) **stopt,** **stop·ping** v.t. **1** To bring (something in motion) to a halt; arrest the progress of: to *stop* an automobile. **2** To prevent the doing or completion of: to *stop* a revolution. **3** To prevent (a person) from doing something; restrain. **4** To keep back, withhold, or cut off, as wages or supplies. **5** To cease doing; desist from; discontinue: *Stop* that! **6** To intercept in transit, as a letter. **7** To block up, obstruct, or clog (a passage, road, etc.): often with *up*. **8** To fill in, cover over, or otherwise close, as a hole, cavity, etc. **9** To close (a bottle, barrel, etc.) with a cork, plug, or other stopper. **10** To stanch (a wound, etc.). **11** To order a bank not to pay or honor: to *stop* a check. **12** To defeat; also, to kill. **13** *Music* To press down (a string) on the fingerboard, or to close (a finger hole) in order to vary pitch. **14** To punctuate. **15** In boxing, etc., to parry. —v.i. **16** To come to a halt; cease progress or motion. **17** To cease doing something; pause or desist. **18** To come to an end. See synonyms under ABIDE, ARREST, CEASE, END, HINDER[1], OBSTRUCT, REST[1], SHUT, STAND, SUSPEND. —**to stop off** To stop for a brief stay before continuing on a trip or journey. —**to stop over** *Colloq.* **1** To stay at a place temporarily. **2** To interrupt a journey; make a stopover. —n. **1** The act of stopping, or the state of being stopped; a halt; pause; cessation; end. **2** That which stops or limits the range or time of a movement: a camera *stop*; an obstruction or obstacle; a hindrance. **3** *Music* The pressing down of a string or the closing of an aperture on a musical instrument, to change the pitch of the tone emitted; a key, lever, or handle for stopping a string or an aperture; a fret for a guitar. **4** *Music* In an organ, a set of pipes or reeds producing tones of the same quality, and arranged in regular musical progression. **5 a** *Brit.* A punctuation mark; a period. **b** In cables, etc., a period. **6** In joinery, a block, pin, or the like to check sliding motion, as of a drawer. **7** *Naut.* A small line for lashing or fastening anything temporarily on a ship. **8** *Phonet.* **a** Complete blockage of the breath stream (implosion), as with the lips or tongue, followed by a sudden release (explosion). **b** A consonant so produced; a plosive: opposed to *continuant.* The stops in English are the bilabials (p) and (b), the alveolars (t) and (d), and the velars (k) and (g); the nasals (m) and (n) may also be included in this category. **9** In dogs, the short incline between the forepart of the skull and the face. See illustration under DOG. **10** pl. A card game in which certain cards, called **stop cards,** terminate play when they appear: a variety of *newmarket.* [OE -*stoppian,* as in *forstoppian* stop up]

stop·cock (stop'kok) n. A faucet or short pipe having a valve for stopping or regulating the passage of liquid, gas, etc.

stope (stōp) *Mining* n. An excavation from which the ore is removed, either above or below a level, in a series of steps. —v.t. & v.i. **stoped, stop·ing** To excavate in stopes. [Appar. related to STEP]

stop·gap (stop'gap') n. That which stops a gap; also, an expedient.

stop key A key so made that when inserted in one side of a lock no key may be used on the other.

stop knob The knob by which a set of organ pipes is opened.

stop light 1 A red light on a traffic sign, directing a motorist or pedestrian to stop. **2** A red light on the rear of a motor vehicle which shines upon application of the brakes.

stop-loss (stop'lôs', -los') adj. Intended to prevent further loss, in a brokerage account, from falling prices on financial markets.

stop net A small net joined to a seine, to increase its length or prevent the escape of fish.

stop order An order to an agent or stockbroker to buy or sell a stock at the market only when it reaches a specified price.

stop-out (stop'out') n. *U.S.* A student who interrupts his college education for a year in order to pursue some other activity.

stop·o·ver (stop'ō'vər) adj. Giving permission to stop over, as a railway ticket. —n. A stopover check, the act of stopping over, or permission to stop over, as from one train to a later train. Also **stop'—off.**

stop·page (stop'ij) n. **1** The act of stopping or the state of being stopped. **2** A deduction from pay to repay something.

stop payment An order to a bank to refuse payment on a certain check.

stop·per (stop'ər) n. **1** One who or that which stops up or closes. **2** A plug or cork, as in a bottle. **3** In card games, as bridge, a card that can be used to stop an opponent's successful play of cards of one suit. —v.t. To secure or close with a stopper.

stop·ple (stop'əl) n. A stopper, plug, cork, or bung. —v.t. **·pled, ·pling** To close with or as with a stopple. [ME *stoppel,* prob. < *stoppen* stop]

stop sign A sign in a traffic system, instructing a pedestrian or vehicle to stop.

stop thrust In fencing, a slight thrust designed to frustrate the attack of an opponent.

stop·watch (stop'woch') n. A watch which has a hand indicating fractions of a second and which may be stopped or started by the pressure of a spring: used for timing races, etc.

stop·way (stop'wā') n. *Aeron.* An extension of an airfield runway to permit safe landing in the event of engine failure during take-off.

stor·age (stôr'ij, stō'rij) n. **1** The depositing of articles in a warehouse for safekeeping. **2** Space for storing goods. **3** A charge for storing. **4** A section of a computer in which data is held for later use; memory.

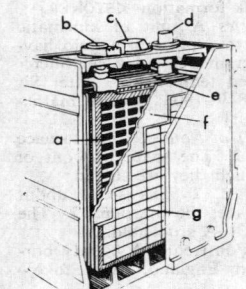

STORAGE BATTERY
a. Positive plate.
b. Positive terminal.
c. Vent cap or plug.
d. Negative terminal.
e. Electrolyte space.
f. Separator.
g. Negative plate.

storage battery A connected group of two or more electrolytic cells for the generation of electric energy by the passage of a current which, on being reversed in direction, serves to recharge the cells for another period of use.

sto·rax (stôr'aks, stō'raks) n. **1** A fragrant

balsam obtained from the wood and inner bark of either of two trees (*Liquidambar orientalis*, or *L. styraciflua*) of Asia Minor: used in medicine and as a perfume. **2** A gum resin obtained from certain trees of a family (*Styracaceae*), especially *Styrax officinalis*. [<L <Gk. *styrax*]

store (stôr, stōr) *v.t.* **stored**, **stor·ing 1** To put away for future use; to accumulate. **2** To furnish or supply; provide. **3** To place in a warehouse or other place of deposit for safekeeping. — *n.* **1** That which is stored or laid up against future need; hence, a large amount at hand. **2** *pl.* Supplies, as of ammunition, arms, or clothing; necessary articles, especially of food. **3** A place where commodities are stored; warehouse. **4** *U.S.* A place where merchandise of any kind is kept for sale; a shop. See synonyms under HEAP, STOCK. — **department store** A large retail establishment selling various types of merchandise and service, and organized by departments. — **in store** Set apart for the future; forthcoming; impending. — **to set store by** To value or esteem; regard. [Aphetic var. of earlier *astore* <OF *estorer* erect, equip, store <L *instaurare* restore, erect]

store·house (stôr′hous′, stōr′-) *n.* A building in which goods are stored; a warehouse; depository.

store·keep·er (stôr′kē′pər, stōr′-) *n.* **1** A person who keeps a retail store or shop; a shopkeeper. **2** One who has charge of receiving and distributing stores; especially, one in charge of naval or military stores.

store·room (stôr′rōōm′, -rōōm′, stōr′-) *n.* A room in which things are stored, as supplies.

sto·rey (stôr′ē, stō′rē) See STORY[2].

sto·ried[1] (stôr′ēd, stō′rēd) *adj.* Having or consisting of stories, as a building: usually in compounds: a six-*storied* house. Also **sto′·reyed.**

sto·ried[2] (stôr′ēd, stō′rēd) *adj.* **1** Having a notable history. **2** Related in a story. **3** Ornamented with designs representing scenes from history or story.

sto·ri·ette (stôr′ē·et′, stō′rē-) *n.* A short story or tale.

stork (stôrk) *n.* A wading bird with a long neck and long legs (family *Ciconiidae*), related to the herons and ibises, especially the Old World **migratory** or **white stork** (*Ciconia ciconia*), which often nests on buildings. [OE *storc*]

WHITE STORK
(About 20 inches tall)

stork's·bill (stôrks′bil′) *n.* **1** Heronbill. **2** Any species of pelargonium.

storm (stôrm) *n.* **1** A disturbance of the atmosphere, generally a great whirling motion of the air, accompanied by rain, snow, etc. **2** In the Beaufort scale, a wind force of the 11th degree. **3** Figuratively, a furious flight or shower of objects, especially of missiles. **4** A violent outburst, as of passion or excitement: a *storm* of applause or rage. **5** *Mil.* A violent and rapid assault on a fortified place. **6** A violent commotion, as in politics, society, or domestic life. — *v.i.* **1** To blow with violence; rain, snow, hail, etc., heavily: used impersonally: It *stormed* all day. **2** To be very angry; rage. **3** To move or rush with violence or rage: He *stormed* about the room. — *v.t.* **4** *Mil.* To take or try to take by storm. [OE] *Synonyms* (noun): agitation, disturbance, tempest. A *storm* is properly a *disturbance* of the atmosphere, with or without rain, snow, hail, or thunder and lightning. Thus we have *rainstorm*, *snowstorm*, etc., and by extension, *magnetic storm*, etc. A *tempest* is a *storm* of extreme violence, always attended with some precipitation, as of rain, from the atmosphere. In the moral and figurative use *tempest* commonly implies greater intensity. We speak of *agitation* of feeling, *disturbance* of mind, a *storm* of passion, a *tempest* of rage. See WIND. *Antonyms*: calm, hush, peace, serenity, stillness, tranquility.

Storm may appear as a combining form in hyphemes or solidemes, or as the first element in two-word phrases:

storm area	storm god	storm-rocked
storm-beaten	storm goddess	storm shutter
storm blast	storm gust	storm-swept
storm-boding	storm jacket	stormtight
stormbound	storm lane	storm-tossed
storm-bringer	stormlike	storm-washed
storm cloud	storm path	stormwind
storm coat	storm-rent	storm-worn

Storm (shtôrm), **Theodor Woldsen**, 1817–88, German poet and novelist.

storm·belt (stôrm′belt′) *n.* A strip of territory along which storms most frequently move.

storm cellar A cyclone cellar.

storm center 1 *Meteorol.* The center or place of lowest pressure and comparative calm in a cyclonic storm. **2** The central point of a heated argument; the focus of any trouble or turmoil.

storm door A strong outer door for added protection during storms and inclement weather.

Stor·month (stôr′mənth), **James**, 1825–82, Scottish lexicographer.

storm petrel Any of certain petrels of the North Atlantic; especially, *Hydrobates pelagicus*, thought to portend storm. Also **stormy petrel.**

storm·proof (stôrm′prōōf′) *adj.* Capable of keeping out storms.

storm trooper A member of the Nazi party militia unit, the *Sturmabteilung.*

storm warning A signal, as a flag or light, used to warn mariners of coming storm. Also **storm signal.**

storm window An extra window outside the ordinary one as a protection against storms or for greater insulation against cold.

storm·y (stôr′mē) *adj.* **storm·i·er**, **storm·i·est 1** Characterized by storms; boisterous; also, turbulent; violent: a *stormy* life. **2** Accompanying storms; also, passionate. See synonyms under BLEAK[1]. [OE *stormig*] — **storm′·i·ly** *adv.* — **storm′i·ness** *n.*

Stor·thing (stôr′ting′, stōr′-) *n.* The Norwegian parliament. Also **Stor′ting′.** [<Norw. < *stor* great + *thing* meeting]

sto·ry[1] (stôr′ē, stō′rē) *n. pl.* **·ries 1** A narrative or recital of an event, or a series of events, whether real or fictitious. **2** A narrative, usually of fictitious events, intended to entertain a reader or hearer; a short tale. **3** An account or allegation of the facts relating to a particular person, thing, or incident: He tells a more plausible *story* of the conflict. **4** A news article in a newspaper or magazine. **5** The material for a news article. **6** An anecdote. **7** *Colloq.* A lie; falsehood. **8** The series of events in a novel, play, etc. **9** Celebrated or romantic legend or history: to live on in *story.* — *v.t.* **·ried**, **·ry·ing 1** To relate as a story. **2** To adorn with designs representing scenes from history, legend, etc. [<OF *estoire* <L *historia.* Doublet of HISTORY.]

Synonyms (noun): allegory, anecdote, incident, narrative, recital, record, relation, tale. *Tale* is nearly synonymous with *story*, but is somewhat archaic; it is used for an imaginative, legendary, or fictitious *recital*, especially if of ancient date: as, a fairy *tale*; also, for an idle or malicious report; as, Do not tell *tales.* See FICTION, HISTORY, REPORT.

sto·ry[2] (stôr′ē, stō′rē) *n. pl.* **·ries** A division in a building comprising the space between two successive floors; a floor; habitable rooms on the same level; also, a horizontal architectural division of a building: also spelled *storey.* [Special use of STORY[1]; ? from earlier sense of "a tier of painted windows or sculptures that narrated an event"]

Sto·ry (stôr′ē, stō′rē), **Joseph**, 1779–1845, U.S. jurist. — **William Wetmore**, 1819–95, U.S. sculptor; son of preceding.

story board 1 A bulletin board in a newspaper office on which are posted reportorial assignments to specific stories. **2** The set of original drawings illustrating each stage in the sequence of a motion picture, television program, animated cartoon, etc.

sto·ry·tell·er (stôr′ē·tel′ər, stō′rē-) *n.* **1** One who relates stories or anecdotes. **2** *Colloq.*

A prevaricator; liar; fibber. — **sto′ry·tell′ing** *n. & adj.*

stoss (stos, *Ger.* shtōs) *adj. Geol.* Facing the direction whence a glacier moves. [<G *stoss* a thrust, push]

sto·tin·ka (stô·ting′kä) *n. pl.* **·ki** (-kē) A small copper coin of Bulgaria; one one-hundredth of a lev. [<Bulgarian]

stound (stound) *n. Obs.* **1** A short time. **2** A sharp pain; pang; heavy blow. — *v.i. Scot.* To ache; hurt. [OE *stund*]

stoup (stōōp) *n.* **1** *Eccl.* A basin for holy water at the entrance of a church. **2** *Scot.* A pail; bucket; flagon; cup; also, its contents. **3** A measure for liquids: a pint *stoup.* Also spelled *stoop*, *stowp.* [<ON *staup* bucket]

stour[1] (stour) *n. Obs.* **1** A battle; conflict. **2** Dust in motion; chaff. Also **stoure.** [<OF *estour* tumult] — **stour′ie**, **stour′y** *adj.*

stour[2] (stour) *Scot. adj.* **1** Sturdy; also, harsh; rough; surly. **2** Grievous; painful. — *n.* Pressure of circumstances.

stout (stout) *adj.* **1** Strong or firm of structure or material; sound; tough. **2** Determined; resolute. **3** Fat; bulky; thick-set. **4** Strong in effects or active qualities; substantial; solid. **5** Having muscular strength; robust. **6** Proud; stubborn. See synonyms under CORPULENT, STAUNCH, STRONG. — *n.* **1** A stout person. **2** A dress or suit made for a stout person.

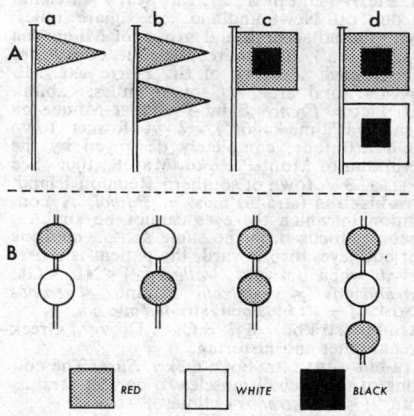

STORM WARNINGS
A. Daylight signals.　　B. Night signals.
a. Small-craft warning.　b. Gale.　c. Whole gale.
d. Hurricane.

3 A strong, very dark porter or ale: also **brown stout.** [<OF *estout* bold, strong <Gmc. Cf. MDu. *stolt* bold.] — **stout′ly** *adv.* — **stout′·ness** *n.*

stout·heart·ed (stout′här′tid) *adj.* Brave; courageous. — **stout′heart′ed·ly** *adv.* — **stout′·heart′ed·ness** *n.*

Sto·va·ine (stō′və·ēn, stō·vā′in) *n.* Proprietary name for a local anesthetic, $C_{14}H_{21}NO_2 \cdot HCl$, used especially intraspinally: invented by E. F. A. Fourneau, born 1872, French chemist.

stove[1] (stōv) *n.* **1** An apparatus, usually of metal, in which fuel is consumed for heating or cooking. **2** A drying room or box used in some factories. **3** An artificially heated greenhouse. **4** A pottery kiln. [OE *stofa* a heated room]

stove[2] (stōv) Alternative past tense and past participle of STAVE.

stove·pipe (stōv′pīp′) *n.* **1** A pipe, usually of thin sheet iron, for conducting the smoke and gases of combustion from a stove to a chimney flue. **2** *U.S. Colloq.* A tall silk hat: also **stovepipe hat.**

sto·ver (stō′vər) *n.* Fodder or feed for cattle; cornstalks. [<OF *estover.* See ESTOVERS.]

stow[1] (stō) *v.t.* **1** To place or arrange compactly; pack. **2** To fill by packing. **3** To have room for; hold: said of a room, receptacle, etc. **4** *Slang* To stop; cease. **5** *Obs.* To furnish lodging for. — **to stow away 1** To put in a place of safekeeping, hiding, etc. **2** To be a stowaway. [OE *stōwian* < *stōw* a place]

stow[2] (stō) *v.t. Scot. & Brit. Dial.* To lop or cut off; crop.

stow³ (stō) *n. Scot. & Brit. Dial.* A stump or shoot of a tree; also, a slice; cut.

Stow (stō), **John,** 1525?–1605, English historian and antiquary.

stow·age (stō′ij) *n.* 1 The act or manner of stowing, or the state of being packed away. 2 Space for stowing goods. 3 Charge for stowing goods. 4 The goods stowed.

stow·a·way (stō′ə·wā′) *n.* One who conceals himself, as on a vessel, to obtain free passage.

Stowe (stō), **Harriet Beecher,** 1811–96, U.S. author; wrote *Uncle Tom's Cabin.*

stowp (stōōp) See STOUP.

STP (es′tē′pē′) *n.* A hallucinogenic drug chemically related to mescaline and amphetamine. [<*STP,* a trade name for a gasoline additive supposed to increase engine power]

St. Pat·rick's Day (sānt pat′riks) March 17. See under PATRICK.

St. Paul (sānt pôl′) The capital of Minnesota, in the SE part of the State, on the Mississippi River: one of the Twin Cities.

St. Pe·ter (sānt pē′tər), **Lake** An expansion of the St. Lawrence River in southern Quebec, Canada; 130 square miles.

St. Pe·ters·burg (sānt pē′tərz·bûrg) 1 The capital of the former Russian Empire; renamed *Petrograd* in 1914 and *Leningrad* in 1924. 2 A city on Tampa Bay, western Florida.

St. Pierre (sānt pyâr′, *Fr.* saṅ pyâr′) An island group off Newfoundland; 10 square miles; with the adjacent island group of **Mi·que·lon** (mē·kə·lôṅ′), 83 square miles, it constitutes the French territory of **St. Pierre and Miquelon;** total area, 93 square miles; capital, St. Pierre. *French* **Saint-Pierre-et-Mi·que·lon** (saṅ·pyâr′ā·mē·kə·lôṅ′). 2 A former town in Martinique, completely destroyed by the eruption of Mont Pelée on May 8, 1902. See PELÉE. 3 A town of southern Réunion Island.

stra·bis·mus (strə·biz′məs) *n. Pathol.* A condition in which the eyes cannot be simultaneously focused on the same spot: when one or both eyes turn inward, the patient is *cross-eyed:* when outward, *walleyed.* [<NL <Gk. *strabismos* <*strabizein* squint <*strabos* twisted] —**stra·bis′mal, stra·bis′mic** *adj.*

Stra·bo (strā′bō), 63? B.C.–A.D. 24?, Greek geographer and historian.

stra·bot·o·my (strə·bot′ə·mē) *n. Surg.* The cutting of the eyeball muscles to correct strabismus. [<Gk. *strabos* oblique + -TOMY]

Stra·chey (strā′chē), **(Evelyn) John,** 1901–1963, English politician and writer. —**(Giles) Lytton,** 1880–1932, English author.

strad·dle (strad′l) *v.* **·dled, ·dling** *v.i.* 1 To stand, walk, or sit with the legs spread apart. 2 To stand wide apart: said of the legs. 3 *Colloq.* To appear to favor both sides of an issue; refuse to commit oneself. —*v.t.* 4 To stand, walk, or sit with the legs on either side of. 5 To spread (the legs) wide apart. 6 *Colloq.* To appear to favor both sides of (an issue). 7 *Mil.* To fire shots both beyond and in front of (a target) so as to determine the range. —*n.* 1 A going, standing, or sitting with legs wide apart; the space between the feet or legs of one who straddles. 2 A noncommittal or vacillating position in any issue. 3 A stock transaction in which the holder obtains the privilege of either delivering or calling for a stock at a fixed price. 4 A long position in some stocks while being short in others. 5 *Mil.* Successive range settings that have bracketed the target. [Freq. of STRIDE] —**strad′dler** *n.* —**strad′dling·ly** *adv.*

Stra·di·va·ri (strä′dē·vä′rē), **Antonio,** 1644–1737, violin-maker of Cremona, Italy. Also **Strad·i·var·i·us** (strad′i·vâr′ē·əs).

Strad·i·var·i·us (strad′i·vâr′ē·əs) *n.* One of the famous violins produced by the fine workmanship of Antonio Stradivari.

strafe (strāf, sträf) *v.t.* **strafed, straf·ing** 1 To attack (troops, emplacements, etc.) with machine-gun fire from low-flying airplanes. 2 To bombard or shell heavily. 3 *Slang* To punish. —*n.* A heavy bombardment. [<G *strafen* punish] —**straf′er** *n.*

Straf·ford (straf′ərd), **Earl of,** 1593–1641, Thomas Wentworth, English statesman; beheaded.

strag·gle (strag′əl) *v.i.* **·gled, ·gling** 1 To wander from the road, main body, etc.; stray. 2 To wander aimlessly about; ramble. 3 To occur at irregular intervals. [? Freq. of obs. *strake* move, go about] —**strag′gler** *n.*

strag·gly (strag′lē) *adj.* **·li·er, ·li·est** Scattered or spread out irregularly.

straight (strāt) *adj.* 1 Extending uniformly in the same direction without curve or bend. 2 Free from kinks; not curly, as hair. 3 Not stooped or inclined; erect, as in posture. 4 Not deviating from truth, fairness, or honesty; accurate; honest; upright; reliable; also, candid. 5 Free from obstruction; uninterrupted; unbroken. 6 Correctly kept, ordered, or arranged. 7 Sold without discount for number or quantity taken. 8 *Colloq.* Adhering without reservation or exception to a particular party or policy; representing the regular or older organization; accepting the whole, as of a plan, party, or policy: a *straight* ticket. 9 In poker, consisting of five cards forming a sequence: a *straight* flush. 10 Having nothing added; unmixed; undiluted: *straight* whisky. 11 *Slang* Conforming to what is accepted as usual, normal, or conventional, especially according to middle-class standards. 12 *Slang* Heterosexual. —*n.* 1 A straight part or piece. 2 The part of a racecourse between the winning post and the last turn. 3 In poker, a numerical sequence of five cards not of the same suit, or a hand containing this. 4 A straight line. 5 *Slang* A conventional person. 6 *Slang* A heterosexual. —*adv.* 1 In a straight line or a direct course. 2 Closely in line; correspondingly. 3 At once; straightway. ◆ Homophone: *strait.* [ME *stregt* <OE *streht,* pp. of *streccan* stretch] —**straight′ly** *adv.* —**straight′ness** *n.*

straight angle See under ANGLE.

straight-arm (strāt′ärm′) *v.t.* In football, to ward off (an opposing tackler) with the outstretched arm.

straight·a·way (strāt′ə·wā′) *adj.* Having no curve or turn; straightforward. —*n.* A straight course or track. —*adv.* At once; straightway.

straight·edge (strāt′ej′) *n.* A bar of wood or metal having one edge true to a straight line: used for ruling, etc. —**straight′-edged′** *adj.*

straight·en (strāt′n) *v.t.* 1 To make straight. 2 To lay out (a corpse). —*v.i.* 3 To become straight. —**to straighten out** To restore order to; set right; rectify. —**to straighten up** 1 To free from disorder; make neat; tidy. 2 To stand in erect posture. 3 To reform; become honorable or honest. —**straight′ener** *n.*

straight face A sober, expressionless, or unsmiling face. —**straight-faced** (strāt′fāst′) *adj.*

straight flush See under FLUSH.

straight·for·ward (strāt′fôr′wərd) *adj.* Proceeding in a straight course or direct manner; frank. See synonyms under CANDID, CLEAR, HONEST, JUST¹, PLAIN¹. —**straight′for′ward·ly** *adv.* —**straight′for′ward·ness** *n.*

straight·for·wards (strāt′fôr′wərdz) *adv.* In a straight course or direct manner.

straight-line (strāt′līn′) *adj. Mech.* Designating a linkage or similar apparatus intended to copy or generate motion in a straight or nearly straight line.

straight man *U.S. Colloq.* An entertainer who acts as a foil for a comedian.

straight-out (strāt′out′) *adj.* 1 Showing the true sentiments or feelings; unreserved; also, shown without reserve. 2 Real; genuine.

straight ticket 1 A political party ballot or ticket that presents the regular party candidates without addition or change. 2 A ballot cast for all the candidates of one party. Compare SPLIT TICKET.

straight·way (strāt′wā′) *adv.* Immediately; straightaway.

straik¹ (strāk) *v.t. Scot.* To stroke.

straik² (strāk) *Scot.* Past participle of STRIKE.

strain¹ (strān) *v.t.* 1 To pull or draw tight; stretch. 2 To exert to the utmost. 3 To injure by overexertion; sprain; also, to wrench or twist. 4 To deform in structure or shape as a result of pressure or stress. 5 To stretch beyond the true intent, proper limit, etc.: to *strain* a point. 6 To embrace tightly; hug. 7 To pass through a strainer (def. 2). 8 To remove by filtration. 9 *Mech.* To alter in size or shape by applying external force. 10 *Obs.* To force; constrain. —*v.i.* 11 To make violent efforts; strive. 12 To be or become wrenched or twisted. 13 To filter, trickle, or percolate. See synonyms under STRETCH. —**to strain at** 1 To push or pull with violent efforts. 2 To strive for. 3 To scruple or balk at accepting. —*n.* 1 An act of straining or the state of being strained; a violent effort or exertion. 2 The injury due to excessive tension or effort. 3 *Physics* Change of shape or size of a body, especially of a solid, produced by the action of a stress; deformation, temporary or permanent; thrust; force. [<OF *estrein-,* stem of *estreindre* <L *stringere* bind tight]

strain² (strān) *n.* 1 Line of descent, or the individuals, collectively, in that line; race; stock. 2 Inborn or hereditary disposition; natural tendency; trace; an element or admixture: to have a heroic *strain* in one's character. 3 *Biol.* A special line of individuals belonging to a certain race or species and maintained at a high standard of perfection by selection: said of animals or plants. 4 *Rare* Distinguishing nature or quality; kind; sort. 5 A section, in hymn tunes, divided off by a double bar; a melody; tune; air. 6 A distinctive portion of a poem; also, a composition in verse. 7 Prevailing tone, style, or manner; mood. [? Var. of ME *strene,* OE *strēon* offspring]

strain·er (strā′nər) *n.* 1 One who or that which strains. 2 A utensil or device, containing meshes or porous parts, through which liquids are passed to separate them from coarse particles. 3 A device used for tightening, strengthening, or stretching.

straining arch Any arch erected to exert a corrective strain or to resist a destructive strain in a building.

straining beam A tie beam receiving a lengthwise pulling stress, and connecting the rafters of a roof with the tops of the queenposts. Also **straining piece.**

strait (strāt) *adj.* 1 Of small transverse dimensions; narrow. 2 *Archaic* Restricted as to space or room; close; tight. 3 Destitute, as of money; needy. 4 *Archaic* Strict; rigorous. 5 *Obs.* Difficult; hard-pressed. —*n.* 1 A narrow passage of water connecting two larger bodies of water. 2 Any narrow pass or passage. 3 A position of perplexity or distress; necessity: frequently plural. 4 *Obs.* An isthmus. ◆ Homophone: *straight.* [<OF *estreit* <L *strictus,* pp. of *stringere* bind tight. Doublet of STRICT.] —**strait′ly** *adv.* —**strait′ness** *n.*

strait·en (strāt′n) *v.t.* 1 To make strait or narrow; contract; restrict. 2 To embarrass, as in finances; also, to distress; hamper. Also **strait.** See synonyms under SCRIMP.

strait·ened (strāt′nd) *adj.* 1 Contracted; narrowed. 2 Suffering privation or hardship, especially from pecuniary difficulties.

strait·jack·et (strāt′jak′it) *n.* 1 A tight jacket of strong canvas, for confining the arms of violent mental patients or prisoners. 2 Anything that unduly confines or restricts. —*v.t.* To confine in or as if in a straightjacket.

strait-laced (strāt′lāst′) *adj.* 1 Tightly laced, as stays; encased in tight corsets. 2 Strict, especially in morals or manners.

Straits (strāts), **The** The Bosporus and the Dardanelles considered as a single passage from the Mediterranean to the Black Sea.

Straits Settlements A former British crown colony comprising Singapore, Penang, Malacca, and Labuan: dissolved, 1946.

strake (strāk) *n. Naut.* A breadth of planking or a line of plating on a vessel's hull from stem to stern: also spelled *streak.* [Appar. akin to STRETCH; infl. in meaning by STREAK]

Stral·sund (shträl′zŏŏnt) A port on the Baltic Sea in northern East Germany, in the former state of Mecklenburg.

stra·min·e·ous (strə·min′ē·əs) *adj.* 1 Straw-colored. 2 Strawlike; chaffy. [<L *stramineus* <*stramen* straw]

stra·mo·ni·um (strə·mō′nē·əm) *n.* 1 The jimsonweed. 2 A drug prepared from the dried leaves and flowering tops of this plant, used as a sedative, especially in asthma. Also **stram·o·ny** (stram′ə·nē). [<NL <Med. L *stramonia,* ? ult. <Tatar *turman,* a medicine for horses]

strand¹ (strand) *n.* A shore or beach; especially, that portion of an ocean shore between high and low tides. See synonyms under BANK¹. —*v.t. & v.i.* 1 To drive or run aground. 2 To leave or be left in straits or difficulties: usually in the passive. [OE *strand*]

strand² (strand) *n.* 1 One of the principal twists or members of a rope. 2 A fiber, hair, or the like. 3 Wires twisted into a cable.

4 Anything plaited or twisted. — *v.t.* 1 To break a strand of (a rope). 2 To make by twisting strands. [? <OF *estran* <Gmc.]

strand line A line marking the boundary between the shore and the ocean, especially a line higher than the present one.

strang (strang) *adj. Scot.* Strong.

strange (strānj) *adj.* 1 Previously unknown, unseen, or unheard of; unfamiliar. 2 Not according to the ordinary way; unaccountable; remarkable. 3 Pertaining to another or others; of a different class, character, or kind. 4 Foreign; alien. 5 Distant in manner; reserved; shy. 6 Inexperienced; unskilled; unaccustomed. See synonyms under ALIEN, EXTRAORDINARY, ODD, QUEER, RARE[1]. — *adv.* Strangely. [<OF *estrange* <L *extraneus* foreign < *extra* on the outside. Doublet of EXTRANEOUS.] — **strange′ly** *adv.* — **strange′·ness** *n.*

stran·ger (strān′jər) *n.* 1 One who is not an acquaintance. 2 An unfamiliar visitor; guest. 3 A foreigner. 4 One unversed in or unacquainted or unfamiliar with something specified: with *to.* 5 *Law* Any person who is neither a party to a transaction nor privy to it. See synonyms under ALIEN. [<OF *estrangier* < *estrange.* See STRANGE.]

stran·gle (strang′gəl) *v.* **·gled, ·gling** *v.t.* 1 To choke to death; throttle; suffocate; stifle. 2 To repress; suppress. — *v.i.* 3 To suffer or die from strangulation. [<F *estrangler* <L *strangulare* <Gk. *strangalaein* < *strangalē* a halter < *strangos* twisted] — **stran′gler** *n.*

strangle hold 1 In wrestling, a hold which chokes one's opponent: usually forbidden. 2 Any influence or power that chokes freedom or progress.

stran·gles (strang′gəlz) *n. pl.* An infectious bacterial disease of the horse characterized by fever and inflammation of the respiratory mucous membrane.

stran·gu·late (strang′gyə·lāt) *v.t.* **·lat·ed, ·lat·ing** 1 To strangle. 2 *Pathol.* To compress, contract, or obstruct, especially so as to cut off circulation of the blood or flow of fluid. — *adj.* Strangulated. [<L *strangulatus,* pp. of *strangulare.* See STRANGLE.]

stran·gu·lat·ed (strang′gyə·lā′tid) *adj. Pathol.* Characterized by strangulation.

strangulated hernia *Pathol.* A form of hernia in which the protruded organ or part is so tightly constricted as to cut off normal circulation of the blood, with possible necrosis and mortification.

stran·gu·la·tion (strang′gyə·lā′shən) *n.* 1 The act of strangling or the state of being strangled. 2 *Pathol.* The state of being strangulated; constriction of a part, as of the intestine in strangulated hernia, to cut off circulation.

stran·gu·ry (strang′gyə·rē) *n. Pathol.* Difficult and painful urination. [<L *stranguria* <Gk. *strangouria* < *stranx, strangos* a drop + *ouron* urine]

strap (strap) *n.* 1 A long, narrow, and flexible strip of leather or the like, usually having a buckle or other fastener, for binding about objects. 2 A razor strop. 3 A shoulder strap. 4 Something made of, resembling, or used as a strap. 5 A thin metal band or plate. — *v.t.* **strapped, strap·ping** 1 To fasten or bind with a strap. 2 To beat with a strap. 3 To sharpen or strop. 4 *Scot.* To hang. 5 To embarrass financially. [Var. of STROP] — **strap′less** *adj.*

strap hinge A hinge having long leaves, designed for attaching to the flat surfaces of a door and jamb. See illustration under HINGE.

strap·pa·do (strə·pā′dō, -pä′dō) *n. pl.* **·does** 1 A former punishment in which one was drawn up by a rope attached usually to the wrists, and let fall to the length of the rope; also, the machine used. 2 Erroneously, a beating with a strap. [<Ital. *strappata* a pulling, orig. fem. pp. of *strappare* pull]

strap·pan (strap′ən) *adj. Scot.* Tall and handsome; strapping.

strap·per (strap′ər) *n.* 1 One who uses a strap or straps. 2 One who bolts the straps to rails. 3 *Colloq.* A strong, tall person. 4 One who grooms horses.

strap·ping (strap′ing) *adj. Colloq.* Large and muscular; robust.

Stras·bourg (stras′bûrg, sträz′-; *Fr.* stràz·bōōr′) A city in NE France, the chief city of Alsace. *German* **Strass·burg** (shträs′bŏŏrkh).

strass (stras) *n.* A lead glass of great brilliance used in the manufacture of gems; paste. [after Josef *Strasser,* 18th century German jeweler]

strasse (stras) *n.* Refuse of silk left in making skeins. [<F *strasse* <Ital. *straccio* rag, something torn < *stracciare* tear, lacerate]

stra·ta (strā′tə, strat′ə) Plural of STRATUM.

strat·a·gem (strat′ə·jəm) *n.* 1 A maneuver designed to deceive or outwit an enemy in war. 2 A deception; any device for obtaining advantage. See synonyms under ARTIFICE. [<F *stratagème* <L *strategema* <Gk. *stratēgēma* piece of generalship < *stratēgos* a general < *stratos* army + *agein* lead]

stra·tal (strāt′l) *adj.* Pertaining to, derived from, characteristic of, or caused by a stratum or strata.

stra·te·gic (strə·tē′jik) *adj.* Of or pertaining to strategy; characterized by, used in, or having relation to strategy. Also **stra·te′gi·cal, strat·e·get·ic** (strat′ə·jet′ik) or **·i·cal.** — **stra·te′gi·cal·ly, strat′e·get′i·cal·ly** *adv.*

strategic material Any of several, chiefly raw, materials essential to national defense and industry, especially those that are wholly lacking or in insufficient supply within a nation's boundaries and have to be obtained from sources outside the country: the stockpiling of *strategic materials.*

stra·te·gics (strə·tē′jiks) *n. pl. (construed as singular)* The art or science of strategy; generalship.

strat·e·gist (strat′ə·jist) *n.* One versed in strategy, or skilled in managing affairs.

strat·e·gy (strat′ə·jē) *n. pl.* **·gies** 1 The science and art of conducting a military campaign by the combination and employment of means on a broad scale for gaining advantage in war; generalship: distinguished from *tactics.* 2 The use of stratagem or artifice, as in business, politics, etc. 3 Skill in management. [<F *stratégie* <Gk. *stratēgia* < *stratēgos* general. See STRATAGEM.]

Strat·ford-on-A·von (strat′fərd·on·ā′von) A town on the Avon river in SW Warwickshire, England; birthplace and place of burial of Shakespeare.

strath (strath) *n. Scot.* A wide, open valley; a river course.

Strath·clyde and Cum·bri·a (strath′klīd; kum′·brē·ə) An early medieval British kingdom comprising territory now in southern Scotland and northern England.

Strath·co·na and Mount Royal (strath·kō′·nə), **Lord,** 1820–1914, Donald Alexander Smith, Canadian railroad builder and administrator born in Scotland.

Strath·more (strath′môr) A plain extending 100 miles across Scotland, south of the Grampians, between Dumbarton and the North Sea coast of Kincardine.

strati– *combining form* A stratum; of or pertaining to a stratum or to strata: *stratiform.* Also, before vowels, **strat–.** [<L *stratum* a covering]

stra·tic·u·late (strə·tik′yə·lit, -lāt) *adj. Geol.* Arranged in thin layers or strata: said of sedimentary rocks and certain minerals, as the agate. [<NL *straticulum,* dim. of L *stratum* a layer + -ATE[1]] — **stra·tic′u·la′tion** *n.*

strat·i·form (strat′ə·fôrm) *adj.* 1 *Geol.* Having the form of or constituting a stratum. 2 *Anat.* Denoting a fibrous cartilage enclosed in a channel in a bone as a support for tendons. 3 *Meteorol.* Resembling a stratus. [<STRATI- + -FORM]

strat·i·fy (strat′ə·fī) *v.* **·fied, ·fy·ing** *v.t.* 1 To form or arrange in strata. 2 To preserve (seeds) by spreading in alternating layers of earth and sand. — *v.i.* 3 To form in strata. 4 To be formed in strata. [<F *stratifier* <Med. L *stratificare* <L *stratum* layer + *facere* make] — **strat′i·fi·ca′tion** *n.*

stra·tig·ra·phy (strə·tig′rə·fē) *n.* 1 The order and relative position of the strata of the earth's crust. 2 The study or description of such strata; stratigraphic geology. [< STRATI- + -GRAPHY] — **strat·i·graph·ic** (strat′·ə·graf′ik) or **·i·cal** *adj.* — **strat′i·graph′i·cal·ly** *adv.*

stra·toc·ra·cy (strə·tok′rə·sē) *n. pl.* **·cies** Government by the military. [<Gk. *stratos* army + -CRACY] — **strat·o·crat·ic** (strat′ə·krat′ik) *adj.*

stra·to·cu·mu·lus (strā′tō·kyōō′myə·ləs) *n. pl.* **·li** (-lī) *Meteorol.* Large rolls or globular masses of cloud, gray to dark in color, disposed in waves, groups, or bands, and often covering the whole sky: also called *cumulo-stratus.* See table under CLOUD. [< *strato-* (<STRATUS) + CUMULUS]

strat·o·pause (strat′ə·pôz) *n. Meteorol.* The zone of transition between the stratosphere and the mesosphere.

strat·o·sphere (strat′ə·sfir, strā′tə-) *n. Meteorol.* The portion of the atmosphere lying above the troposphere and beginning at a height of about six miles. In it the systematic fall of temperature with increasing altitude, characteristic of the region below it, ceases, often giving place to a more or less uniform temperature. — **strat′o·spher′ic** (-sfer′ik) *adj.*

stra·tum (strā′təm, strat′əm) *n. pl.* **·ta** (-tə) or **·tums** 1 A natural or artificial layer, bed, or thickness. 2 *Geol.* A more or less homogeneous layer of rock, often in two or more beds, and serving to identify a geological group, system, or series. 3 *Biol.* A sheet or layer of tissue. 4 Something corresponding to a stratum of the earth: a low *stratum* of society. [<L, orig. neut. of *stratus,* pp. of *sternere* spread]

stra·tus (strā′təs, strat′əs) *n. pl.* **·ti** (-tī) *Meteorol.* A cloud of foglike appearance, low-lying and arranged in a uniform layer. See table under CLOUD. [<L, orig. pp. of *sternere* spread]

Straus (strous, *Ger.* shtrous), **Oscar,** 1870–1954, Austrian composer.

Strauss (strous, *Ger.* shtrous), **David Friedrich,** 1808–74, German rationalistic theologian. — **Johann,** 1804–49, Austrian composer of dance music. — **Johann,** 1825–99, Austrian composer; son of the preceding. — **Richard,** 1864–1949, German composer.

Stra·vin·sky (strə·vin′skē, *Russian* strä·vēn′·skē), **Igor Fëdorovich,** 1882–1971, U. S. composer born in Russia.

straw (strô) *n.* 1 A dry or ripened stalk. 2 Stems or stalks of grain, collectively, after the grain has been thrashed out. 3 A mere trifle or slight indication. 4 A slender tube, originally a wheat straw, now made of paper, glass, etc., used to suck up a beverage. — **the last straw** The final test of patience or endurance; the culminating element in any state of circumstances. — **straw in the wind** A sign or indication of the course of future events. — *adj.* 1 Like or of straw; of straw color. 2 Of no value; worthless; sham. 3 Made of straw. [OE *strēaw* straw] — **straw′y** *adj.*

straw·ber·ry (strô′ber′ē, -bər·ē) *n. pl.* **·ries** 1 The edible fruit of any plant of the genus *Fragaria,* technically neither a fruit nor a berry, but an enlarged fleshy achene receptacle. 2 The plant that bears this fruit, a stemless perennial of the rose family, with radical trifoliolate leaves, usually white flowers on scapes, and slender runners by which it propagates: also **strawberry vine.** [OE *strēaw* straw + BERRY]

strawberry bass The calico bass.

strawberry blond A person having reddish-blond hair; a red-headed person.

strawberry bush 1 An upright or straggling shrub *(Euonymus americanus)* of the United States and Canada, with rough, warty, depressed crimson pods and scarlet aril. 2 The wahoo or burningbush.

strawberry festival A sociable gathering, church bazaar, etc., at which strawberries are served.

strawberry shrub A shrub (genus *Calycanthus),* named for the strawberrylike fragrance of its purple or dark-red flowers.

strawberry tomato The ground cherry.

strawberry tree A small evergreen tree *(Arbutus unedo)* of southern Europe, having racemose white flowers and edible fruit resembling strawberries.

straw·board (strô′bôrd′, -bōrd′) *n.* Coarse board, made of straw, used for paper boxes and book covers.

straw boss *U.S. Colloq.* In construction work, logging, etc., an under-foreman.

straw color A pale-yellow color, as of clean ripe straw. — **straw′-col′ored** (-kul′ərd) *adj.*
straw man 1 A figure of a man made of straw. 2 A position, as in debate, set forth as one's opponent's view but typically misrepresenting it so that it may be convincingly refuted. 3 A person used to misrepresent or otherwise conceal the real nature of an activity or undertaking.
straw vote A vote taken at a chance gathering to test the strength of opposing candidates; an unofficial test vote.
straw wine A sweet wine made from grapes dried or partly dried in the sun on straw.
straw worm The larva of a caddis fly.
stray (strā) *v.i.* 1 To wander from the proper course, an area, group, etc.; straggle; roam. 2 To wander about; rove. 3 To deviate from right or goodness; go astray. See synonyms under RAMBLE, WANDER. — *adj.* 1 Having strayed; straying. 2 Irregular; occasional; casual; unrelated. — *n.* 1 A domestic animal that has strayed; an estray. 2 A person who is lost or wanders aimlessly. 3 The act of straying or wandering. 4 *pl. Electronics* Electromagnetic waves, affecting a radio receiver, produced by atmospheric electric discharges and electrical storms. [<OF *estraier* wander about, ult. <L *extra vagare* wander outside] — **stray′er** *n.*
streak (strēk) *n.* 1 A long, narrow, somewhat irregularly shaped mark, line, or stripe: a *streak* of lightning. 2 A not very marked characteristic; a vein; trace; dash: a *streak* of meanness; also, a transient mood; whim. 3 *Mineral.* The color of the line of powder left when a mineral is rubbed on an unglazed porcelain plate known as a **streak plate.** 4 A strake. 5 A layer or strip: meat with a *streak* of fat and a *streak* of lean. 6 *Bacteriol.* The application of an inoculum in a thin stripe, as across the surface of a culture. 7 *Slang* The act or an instance of streaking (*v.* def. 3). — *v.i.* 1 To form a streak or streaks. 2 To move, run, or travel at great speed. 3 *Slang* To appear naked in a public place, usually briefly and especially while running, as for a thrill. — *v.t.* 4 To mark with a streak; form streaks in or on. 5 *Slang* To appear naked in (a public place), usually briefly and especially while running, as for a thrill. [OE *strica.* Akin to STRIKE.] — **streaked** *adj.* — **streak′er** *n.*
streak·y (strē′kē) *adj.* **streak·i·er, streak·i·est** 1 Marked with or occurring in streaks; streaked. 2 Variable in character; not uniform. — **streak′i·ly** *adv.* — **streak′i·ness** *n.*
stream (strēm) *n.* 1 A current or flow of water or other fluid. 2 Anything continuously flowing, moving, or passing, as people. 3 A continuous course or advance; drift; current. 4 Anything issuing out or flowing from a source; a ray. — **on stream** In full commercial production, as an oil refinery, chemical plant, etc. — *v.i.* 1 To pour forth or issue in a stream. 2 To pour forth a stream: eyes *streaming* with tears. 3 To move in continuous succession; proceed uninterruptedly, as a crowd. 4 To float with a waving movement, as a flag. 5 To move with a trail of light, as a meteor. 6 In mining or dyeing, to wash in running water. [OE *strēam*] — **stream′y** *adj.*
Synonyms (noun): brook, channel, course, creek, current, drift, eddy, flow, flume, flux, race, rill, river, rivulet, run, runlet, runnel, streamlet, tide, watercourse.
stream·er (strē′mər) *n.* 1 An object that streams forth, or hangs extended. 2 A flag, pennant, or ensign; a long, narrow flag or standard. 3 A stream or shaft of light, such as shoots up from the horizon into or across the sky in the aurora borealis. 4 A newspaper headline that runs across the whole page.
stream·let (strēm′lit) *n.* A rivulet.
stream·line (strēm′līn′) *n.* 1 The course of a fluid relative to a solid body past which it is moving, especially a course free of turbulence or eddies. 2 Any shape or contour designed to lessen air resistance. — *adj.* 1 Designating an uninterrupted flow or drift. 2 Denoting a form, body, or the like so constructed as to permit an uninterrupted flow of fluid around it: a *streamline* flow, a *streamline* shape, a *streamline* body for a motor car. — *v.t.* **·lined, ·lin·ing** 1 To design with a streamline shape. 2 To make more simple, efficient, or up to date, especially by reorganization.
stream·lin·er (strēm′lī′nər) *n.* A fast, streamlined train.
stream of consciousness *Psychol.* The uninterrupted series of individual conscious states moving continuously as though in a stream. Also **stream of thought.**
stream-of-con·scious·ness technique (strēm′·əv·kon′shəs·nis) A method of writing fiction in which an author objectifies the inward thoughts, feelings, and sometimes sensations of the characters to supplement or replace dialog and narrated action.
streek (strēk) *Scot. v.t.* 1 To stretch or extend; hence, to lay out, as a corpse. 2 To stretch forth; stretch. — *n.* Extent; progress.
street (strēt) *n.* 1 A public way, with buildings on one or both sides, in a city, town, or village. 2 The highway on which buildings front; also, the roadway for vehicles, between sidewalks. 3 *Colloq.* The people living, habitually gathering, or doing business in a street. — *adj.* 1 Working in the streets: a *street* musician; a *street* beggar. 2 Opening onto the street: a *street* door. 3 Performed or taking place on the street: *street* crime; *street* fair. 4 Habituated to the ways of life in the streets, especially in cities: *street* people. See synonyms under ROAD, WAY. [OE *strǣt* <LL *strata (via)* paved (road)]
Street may appear as a combining form in hyphemes or as the first element in two-word phrases, with the following meanings:
1 Of or pertaining to a street or streets:

street-cleaner	**street-sprinkler**
street-cleaning	**street-sprinkling**
street directory	**street-sweeper**
street layer	**street-sweeping**
street name	**street-widening**

2 In the streets:

street beggar	**street music**	**street-pacing**
street-bred	**street musician**	**street peddler**
street fight	**street noise**	**street singer**

3 On or abutting a street:

street corner	**street entrance**	**street gate**
street door	**street floor**	**street lamp**

street Arab A homeless or outcast child who lives in the streets; a gamin.
street car A passenger car that runs on rails laid on the surface of the streets.
street people People, especially young people of the early 1970s, typically without a permanent home and having a life style like that of hippies, marked by the rejection of family life and other middle-class values and by the use of drugs for pleasure.
street-walk·er (strēt′wô′kər) *n.* A prostitute who solicits in the streets. — **street′-walk′ing** *n. & adj.*
strength (strength) *n.* 1 The quality or property of being strong; power; muscular force; physical vitality. 2 The capacity of material bodies to sustain the application of force without yielding or breaking; solidity; tenacity; toughness. 3 Power in general; operative energy; ability to do or bear. 4 Binding force or validity, as of a law. 5 Vigor or force of style. 6 Available numerical force in a military unit or other organization. 7 Degree of intensity; vehemence: *strength* of passion. 8 The degree in which a thing possesses its distinctive properties or essential elements; concentration. 9 Potency, as of a drug, chemical, or liquor. 10 Rising prices; firmness of prices. 11 One regarded as an embodiment of sustaining or protecting power; in archaic or poetic use, a fortress. See synonyms under POWER, PROWESS. [OE *strengthu* < *strang* strong]
strength·en (streng′thən) *v.t.* 1 To make strong. 2 To encourage; hearten. — *v.i.* 3 To become or grow strong or stronger. See synonyms under CONFIRM. — **strength′en·er** *n.*
stren·u·ous (stren′yōō·əs) *adj.* 1 Eagerly pressing or urgent; earnest. 2 Necessitating or marked by strong effort or exertion. [<L *strenuus.* Akin to Gk. *strēnēs* strong.] — **stren′u·ous·ly** *adv.* — **stren′u·os′i·ty** (-os′ə·tē), **stren′u·ous·ness** *n.*
streph·o·sym·bo·li·a (stref′ō·sim·bō′lē·ə) *n.* 1 *Pathol.* A defect of vision in which objects are seen in reverse, as in a mirror. 2 *Psychol.* A condition marked by an inability to differentiate between certain oppositely oriented letters, as *b, d; p, q,* resulting in difficulty in learning to read. [<NL <Gk. *strephein* twist + *symbolon* sign, symbol]
strep·to·coc·cus (strep′tə·kok′əs) *n. pl.* **·coc·ci** (-kok′sī) Any of a genus *(Streptococcus)* of Gram-positive, typically non-motile ovoid or spherical bacteria, grouped in long chains, and dividing in one plane, including highly pathogenic species causing many diseases, as pneumonia, erysipelas, etc. See illustration under BACTERIUM. [<NL <Gk. *streptos* twisted + COCCUS] — **strep′to·coc′cal** (-kok′əl), **strep′to·coc′cic** (-kok′sik) *adj.*
strep·to·my·cin (strep′tō·mī′sin) *n.* A potent antibiotic isolated from a moldlike organism *(Streptomyces griseus)*, effective against certain pathogenic bacteria. [<Gk. *streptos* twisted + *mykēs* fungus]
strep·to·thri·cin (strep′tō·thrī′sin, -thris′in) *n.* A bactericidal substance isolated from a soil fungus *(Actinomyces lavendulae)*: used therapeutically in certain intestinal infections. [<NL *Streptothrix,* former genus name <Gk. *streptos* twisted + *thrix* hair + -IN]
Stre·se·mann (shtrā′zə·män), **Gustav,** 1878–1929, German statesman.
stress (stres) *n.* 1 Special weight, importance, or significance. 2 *Physics* Force exerted between contiguous portions of a body or bodies and generally expressed in pounds per square inch; strain; tension. 3 *Mech.* A force or system of forces which tends to produce deformation in a body on which it acts. 4 Influence exerted forcibly; pressure; compulsion. 5 In pronunciation and oral reading, the relative force with which a sound, syllable, or word is uttered. See also METRICAL STRESS, RHETORICAL STRESS. — *v.t.* 1 To subject to mechanical stress, as a timber. 2 To put stress or emphasis on; accent, as a syllable. 3 To put into straits or difficulties; distress. [<OF *estrece* < *estrecier* constrain <L *strictus,* pp. of *stringere* draw tight] — **stress′ful** *adj.* — **stress′less** *adj.*
-stress *suffix of nouns* Feminine form of -STER: *songstress.* [<-STER + -ESS]
stretch (strech) *v.t.* 1 To extend or draw out, as to full length or width. 2 To extend or draw out forcibly, especially beyond normal or proper limits: The weight has *stretched* the cable; to *stretch* the truth. 3 To cause to reach, as from one place to another or over an area; extend: They *stretched* telegraph wires across the continent. 4 To put forth, hold out, or extend (the hand, an object, etc.): often with *out:* to *stretch* out the hands in appeal. 5 To draw tight; tighten. 6 To strain or exert to the utmost: to *stretch* every nerve. 7 *Slang* To fell with a blow. — *v.i.* 8 To reach or extend over an area or from one place to another: The road *stretches* on and on. 9 To become extended, especially beyond normal or proper limits. 10 To extend one's body or limbs, as in relaxing or reaching for something. 11 To lie down and extend one's limbs to full length: usually with *out.* — *n.* 1 An act of stretching, or the state of being stretched; tension. 2 Extent or reach of that which stretches; scope; especially, an overstrain. 3 A continuous extent of space or time. 4 In racing, the straight part of the track; the straight-away. 5 Direction. 6 *Slang* A term of imprisonment. — *adj.* Capable of being stretched; elastic: said especially of clothing and fabrics: *stretch* socks. [OE *streccan* stretch] — **stretch′a·ble** *adj.* — **stretch′i·ness** *n.* — **stretch′y** *adj.*
Synonyms (verb): elongate, exaggerate, expand, extend, lengthen, reach, spread, strain, tighten.
stretch·er (strech′ər) *n.* 1 One who or that which stretches; any device for stretching, as a device for loosening the fit of gloves, shoes, etc., a frame for drying curtains, sweaters, etc., in shape. 2 A frame, as of stretched canvas, for carrying the wounded or dead; a litter. 3 In masonry, a brick or stone lying lengthwise of a course. 4 A tie beam in the frame of a building.
stretch·er-bear·er (strech′ər·bâr′ər) *n.* One who carries one end of a stretcher or litter. Also **stretch′er·man′** (-man′).
stretch-out (strech′out′) *n.* 1 A system of industrial operation in which employees are required to perform more work per unit of time worked, as by tending additional machines, usually without proportionate increase in pay. 2 A slow-down practiced by employees so as to make the work last longer: see CA′ CANNY.
stret·to (stret′tō) *n. pl.* **·ti** (-tē) or **·tos** *Music*

1 A portion of a fugue, near the close, in which the answer crowds closely on the subject. 2 In an oratorio or operatic piece, the portion at the close accelerated in time to produce a climax: also **stret′ta** (-tä). [<Ital., lit., drawn tight <L *strictus*. See STRESS.]

strew (stro͞o) *v.t.* **strewed, strewed** or **strewn, strew·ing** 1 To spread about loosely or at random; scatter; sprinkle. 2 To cover with something scattered or sprinkled. 3 To be scattered over (a surface). [OE *strēawian*]

stri·a (strī′ə) *n. pl.* **stri·ae** (strī′ē) 1 A narrow streak, stripe, or band of distinctive color, structure, or texture, often parallel with others. 2 *Geol.* A small groove, channel, or ridge on a rock surface, due to the action of glacier ice. [<L, a groove]

stri·ate (strī′āt) *adj.* 1 Having fine linear markings; grooved. 2 Constituting a stria or striae. Also **stri′at·ed.** —*v.t.* **·at·ed, ·at·ing** To mark with striae. [<L *striatus*, pp. of *striare* groove <*stria* a groove]

stri·a·tion (strī·ā′shən) *n.* 1 The act of striating, or the state of being striated. 2 A striate form or appearance. 3 One of a series of parallel striae, as in a muscle or mineral.

stri·a·ture (strī′ə·chər) *n.* 1 The manner in which striae are disposed or arranged; striation. 2 A stria.

strick (strik) *n. Brit. Dial.* 1 A bunch of fibers, as flax, hackled or ready for hackling. 2 A bundle of silk fibers prepared for the second combing. [Prob. <STRICKEN (def. 4)]

strick·en (strik′ən) *adj.* 1 Wounded, especially by a missile: a *stricken* hare. 2 Struck down; afflicted, as by calamity or disease: *stricken* with polio. Compare STRIKE *v.* 3 Advanced or far gone, as in age: *stricken* in years. 4 Having the contents leveled off even with the top of a container. [OE *stricen*, pp. of *strican* strike]

strick·le (strik′əl) *n.* 1 A straightedge used for striking off an even measure of grain. 2 A template or curved piece of wood used in smoothing a sand or loam mold to form a core. 3 A straightedge, to which emery is applied, for sharpening rotary knives. —*v.t.* **·led, ·ling** To shape or smooth with a strickle. [OE *stricel*]

strict (strikt) *adj.* 1 Observing or enforcing rules exactly; also, containing exact or severe rules or provisions; exacting. 2 Strenuously enjoined and maintained; rigidly observed. 3 Exactly defined, distinguished, or applied; not indefinite or loose. 4 Stretched tight; not lax; tense. 5 Close, narrow, and upright; straight: said of the panicles of certain plants. See synonyms under AUSTERE, PRECISE. [<L *strictus*, pp. of *stringere* draw tight. Doublet of STRAIT.] —**strict′ly** *adv.* —**strict′ness** *n.*

stric·tion (strik′shən) *n.* Constriction. [<L *strictio, -onis* <*strictus*. See STRICT.]

stric·ture (strik′chər) *n.* 1 Severe criticism. 2 *Pathol.* A morbid contraction of some duct or channel of the body. 3 *Obs.* Strictness. [<L *strictura* <*strictus* strict]

strid·den (strid′n) Past participle of STRIDE.

strid·dle (strid′l) *v.t.* & *v.i. Brit. Dial.* To straddle. Also **strid′dul.** [Freq. of STRIDE; infl. in meaning by STRADDLE]

stride (strīd) *n.* 1 A long and sweeping or measured step; also, the space passed over by such a step. 2 In animal locomotion, an act of progressive motion, completed when all the feet are returned to the same relative positions they occupied at the beginning of the movement. 3 A stage of progress. —**to hit one's stride** To attain one's normal speed. —**to make rapid strides** To make quick progress. —**to take (something) in one's stride** To do (something) without undue effort as part of one's normal activity. —*v.* **strode, strid·den, strid·ing** *v.i.* 1 To walk with long steps, as from haste or pride. 2 *Archaic* To straddle. —*v.t.* 3 To walk through, along, etc., with long steps. 4 To pass over with a single stride. 5 To straddle; bestride. [OE *strīdan* stride] —**strid′er** *n.*

stri·dent (strīd′nt) *adj.* Giving a loud and harsh sound; shrill; grating. [<L *stridens, -entis*, ppr. of *stridere* creak] —**stri′dence, stri′den·cy** *n.* —**stri′dent·ly** *adv.*

stri·dor (strī′dər) *n.* 1 A harsh, shrill, creaking, screechy, or grating noise. 2 *Pathol.* A harsh grating noise, particularly one heard in laryngeal obstruction. [<L]

strid·u·late (strij′o͞o·lāt) *v.i.* **·lat·ed, ·lat·ing** To make a shrill, creaking noise, as a locust, cicada, or the like. [<NL *stridulatus*, pp. of *stridulare* <*stridulus* rattling <*stridere* rattle, rasp] —**strid′u·la′tion** *n.* —**strid′u·la·to′ry** (-lə·tôr′ē, -tō′rē), **strid′u·lous** *adj.* —**strid′u·lous·ly** *adv.* —**strid′u·lous·ness** *n.*

strife (strīf) *n.* 1 Angry contention; fighting. 2 Any contest for advantage or superiority; rivalry. 3 The act of striving; strenuous endeavor. See synonyms under BATTLE, FEUD[1], QUARREL[1]. [<OF *estrif* <*estriver*. See STRIVE.]

strig·il (strij′əl) *n.* 1 In ancient Greece and Rome, a scraper, as of metal, bone, or ivory, used for scraping the skin, as at the bath. 2 *Archit.* One of a group of wavy flutings carved on flat or curved surfaces, as in Roman architecture. [<L *strigilis* scraper]

strig·i·la·tion (strij′ə·lā′shən) *n.* 1 The application of a strigil to the skin. 2 The friction thus caused.

strig·il·lose (strij′ə·lōs) *adj.* Diminutively or minutely strigose. [<NL *strigilla*, dim. of *striga* a furrow]

stri·gose (strī′gōs, stri·gōs′) *adj.* 1 *Bot.* Rough with short, sharp, appressed stiff hairs or bristles, as a leaf; hispid. 2 *Zool.* Marked with stripes or striae. [<NL *strigosus* <L *striga* a furrow]

strike (strīk) *v.* **struck, struck** (*chiefly Archaic* **strick·en**), **strik·ing** *v.t.* 1 To come into violent contact with; hit; crash into: The car *struck* the wall. 2 To hit with a blow; deal a blow to; smite: It *struck* him in the face. 3 To deal (a blow, etc.). 4 To cause to hit forcibly: He *struck* his hand on the table. 5 To attack; assault: We *struck* the enemy on his left flank. 6 To remove, separate, or take off by or as by a blow: with *off, from*, etc.: *Strike* it from the record. 7 **a** To ignite (a match, etc.). **b** To produce (a light, etc.) thus. 8 To form by stamping, printing, etc.; impress; coin. 9 To announce; sound: The clock *struck* two. 10 To fall upon; reach; catch: A sound of crying *struck* his ear. 11 To arrive at; come upon: to *strike* a trail. 12 To discover; find: to *strike* oil. 13 To affect suddenly or in a specified manner: He was *struck* speechless. 14 To come to the mind of; occur to: An idea *strikes* me. 15 To impress in a specified manner; seem to: He *strikes* me as an honest man. 16 To attract the attention of; impress: The dress *struck* her fancy. 17 To assume; take up: to *strike* an attitude. 18 To cause to enter or penetrate deeply or suddenly: to *strike* dismay into one's heart. 19 To lower or haul down; take or let down, as a sail, or a flag in token of surrender. 20 To cease working at in order to compel compliance to a demand, etc. 21 In the theater, to dismantle (a set or scene). 22 To make level (a measure of grain, etc.); strickle. 23 To make and confirm, as a bargain. 24 To harpoon (a whale). 25 To hook (a fish that has taken the lure) by a sharp pull on the line. 26 To arrive at by reckoning: to *strike* a balance. —*v.i.* 27 To come into violent contact; crash; hit. 28 To deal or aim a blow or blows. 29 To make an assault or attack. 30 To sound from a blow or blows. 31 To be indicated by the sound of blows or strokes: Noon has just *struck*. 32 To ignite. 33 To run aground, as on a reef or shoal: The ship *struck* and heeled over. 34 To lower a flag in token of surrender or in salute. 35 To come suddenly or unexpectedly; chance: with *on* or *upon*: to *strike* upon an unknown path. 36 To take a course; start and proceed: to *strike* for home. 37 To move quickly; dart. 38 To cease work in order to enforce demands, etc. 39 To snatch at or swallow the lure: said of fish. —**to strike camp** To take down the tents of a camp. —**to strike down** 1 To fell with a blow. 2 To affect disastrously; incapacitate completely. —**to strike dumb** To astonish; amaze. —**to strike hands** To clasp hands, especially in confirming a bargain. —**to strike home** 1 To deal an effective blow. 2 To have telling effect. —**to strike it rich** 1 To find a valuable vein or pocket of ore. 2 To come into wealth or good fortune. —**to strike off** 1 To remove or take off by or as by a blow or stroke. 2 To cross out or erase by or as by a stroke of the pen. 3 To deduct. —**to strike out** 1 To strike off (def. 2). 2 To aim a blow or blows. 3 To originate; devise; contrive. 4 To begin; start. 5 In baseball: **a** To put out (the batter) by pitching three strikes. **b** To be put out because of taking three strikes. —**to strike up** 1 To begin to play, sing, or sound, as a band or musical instrument. 2 To start up; begin, as a friendship. —*n.* 1 An act of striking or hitting; a blow. 2 In baseball, an unsuccessful attempt by the batter to hit the ball; a pitched ball that passes over home plate above the level of the batter's knees and below that of his shoulders; a foul bunt; any foul tip held by the catcher; any ball hit foul except when there have been two strikes. 3 In bowling, the knocking down by a player of all the pins with the first bowl in any frame. 4 The quitting of work by a body of workers to enforce some demand. 5 A new or unexpected discovery, as of oil or ore. 6 Any unexpected or complete success. 7 A straight-edged implement for leveling something, as grain in a measure; strickle. 8 *Geol.* The direction, referred to the meridian, of a horizontal line in a given structural plane, or of the intersection of the structural plane with a horizontal surface. 9 In coining, the quantity of coin or the number of medals made or struck at one time. 10 Full measure; hence, excellence. 11 The act of attempting to obtain money or some valuable thing, as by simple request, or by the introduction of a bill in a legislative body for the purpose of being bought off. 12 The sudden rise and taking of the bait by a fish; a bite. —**general strike** Concerted cessation of work on the part of the employees of all or nearly all industries, including public utilities, in a certain town, region, or nation. —**sit-down strike** See SIT-DOWN. [OE *strīcan* stroke, move. Akin to STREAK.]

strike·break·er (strīk′brā′kər) *n.* 1 One who takes the place of a workman on strike. 2 A person who supplies workmen to take the place of strikers. —**strike′break′ing** *n.*

strike fault *Geol.* A fault lying parallel with the strike of the rocks through which it cuts.

strike figure A percussion figure.

strike-out (strīk′out′) *n.* An instance of striking out, especially in baseball.

strik·er (strī′kər) *n.* 1 One who or that which strikes. 2 In certain torpedoes, a plunger which strikes the priming cap and ignites the charge. 3 An employee who is on strike. 4 One whose business is to strike something in a mechanical occupation, as in forging. 5 *U.S. Colloq.* One who makes a blackmailing strike in politics. 6 In the U. S. Navy, an apprentice in training for a specific technical rating: a radioman *striker*. 7 Formerly, the engineer's apprentice on a river steamboat. 8 In the U. S. Army, a soldier assigned to run errands and do odd jobs for an officer.

strik·ing (strī′king) *adj.* Notable; impressive. See synonyms under EXTRAORDINARY. —**strik′·ing·ly** *adv.* —**strik′ing·ness** *n.*

Strind·berg (strind′bûrg, *Sw.* strēn′ber·y′), **John August,** 1849–1912, Swedish dramatist and novelist.

string (string) *n.* 1 A slender line, thinner than a cord and thicker than a thread, used for tying or lacing; twine; also, a slender strip, as of cloth or leather; the cord of a bow; prepared wire or catgut for musical instruments. 2 A stringlike organ or formation; a fibrous vegetable formation; an animal nerve or tendon. 3 A thin cord upon which anything is strung; a row or series of things connected by a small cord: a *string* of pearls. 4 A connected series or succession as of things, acts, or events: sometimes implying unusual length: a *string* of carriages; a *string* of lies. 5 *U.S. Colloq.* A drove or small collection of stock, especially of saddle horses. 6 *pl.* Stringed instruments, especially those of an orchestra; those who play on these. 7 In billiards, the score; the buttons, strung on a wire, by which the score is kept; the string line; the act of stringing. 8 *Archit.* **a** A string-course, as of bricks. **b** A stout inclined plank, notched and set edgewise as a support for the steps of a wooden stairway; a ramp or sidepiece of

solid–built stairs. **9** In sports, a group of contestants ranked as to skill. **10** The conditions, limitations, or restrictions attached to any proposition, gift, or donation, whereby the terms may not be binding, or whereby the donor retains some control. **— to pull strings** To manipulate or influence others, secretly or underhandedly, to gain some advantage. **—** *v.* **strung, string·ing** *v.t.* **1** To thread, as beads, on or as on a string. **2** To fit with a string or strings, as a guitar. **3** To bind, fasten, or adorn with a string or strings. **4** To tighten the strings of (a musical instrument). **5** To brace; strengthen. **6** To make tense or nervous. **7** To arrange or extend like a string. **8** To remove the strings from (vegetables). **9** *Colloq.* To hang: usually with *up.* **—** *v.i.* **10** To extend, stretch, or proceed in a line or series. **11** To form into strings. **12** In billiards, to drive the cue ball from within the string against the farther cushion and back. **— to string along** *Slang* **1** To follow with trust or confidence. **2** To fool; deceive; cheat. **3** To keep (someone) waiting or on tenterhooks. [OE *streng* string]

string bass The double bass.

string bean **1** Any of several varieties of beans (genus *Phaseolus*) cultivated for their edible pods, especially *P. vulgaris.* **2** The pod itself. **3** *Colloq.* A tall, skinny person.

string·board (string′bôrd′, -bōrd′) *n. Archit.* A board serving as a stringpiece in which the ends of steps of a staircase are set.

string–course (string′kôrs′, -kōrs′) *n. Archit.* A horizontal molding or ornamental course, often projecting along the face of a building.

stringed (stringd) *adj.* **1** Furnished with strings. **2** Produced from stringed instruments. **3** Tied with string.

strin·gen·do (strin·jen′dō) *adj. Music* Hastening the tempo as toward a climax; accelerando. [<Ital., ppr. of *stringere* draw tight <L]

strin·gent (strin′jənt) *adj.* **1** Keeping one closely to strict requirements; rigid; severe, as regulations. **2** Hampered by obstructing conditions or scarcity of money; close or tight: The money market is very *stringent.* **3** Convincing; forcible. [<L *stringens, -entis,* ppr. of *stringere* draw tight] **— strin′gen·cy, strin′gent·ness** *n.* **— strin′gent·ly** *adv.*

string·er (string′ər) *n.* **1** A heavy timber, generally horizontal, supporting other members of a structure, and usually running in the direction of the greatest length of the collection of supported members. **2** Any horizontal framing timber, as a tie beam; a stringpiece. **3** A lengthwise timber on which rails are laid, as distinguished from a *cross–tie* or *sleeper.* **4** A news reporter employed on a free–lance basis, often in out–of–town or foreign locations. **5** A person having a specific rating as to excellence, skill, etc.: used in combination: a *second–stringer.*

string·halt (string′hôlt′) *n.* A convulsive movement of the hind legs of a horse: also called *springhalt.* **— string′halt′ed, string′halt′y** *adj.*

string line In billiards, a line passing across the table through the cue spot.

string·piece (string′pēs′) *n.* A heavy supporting timber, horizontal or inclined, forming the margin or edge of a framework, as of a floor or staircase; a stringer, or stringboard.

string·y (string′ē) *adj.* **string·i·er, string·i·est** **1** Containing fibrous strings. **2** Forming in strings, as thick glue; ropy. **3** Having tough sinews. **4** Tall and wiry in build. **— string′·i·ly** *adv.* **— string′i·ness** *n.*

strip[1] (strip) *n.* **1** A narrow piece, comparatively long, as of cloth, wood, etc. **2** A number of stamps attached in a row. **3** A narrow piece of land; a minor civil division in Maine. **4** An act of destruction or spoliation. **5** A comic strip. **— Cherokee strip** A strip of land formerly leased to the Cherokee Indians but now part of Oklahoma. **—** *v.t.* **stripped, strip·ping** To cut or tear into strips. [? <MLG *strippe* a strap]

strip[2] (strip) *v.* **stripped** (*Rare* **stript**), **strip·ping** *v.t.* **1** To pull the covering, clothing, etc., from; denude; lay bare. **2** To pull off (the covering or clothing). **3** To rob or plunder; spoil. **4** To make bare or empty. **5** To remove; take away. **6** To deprive of something; divest: He was *stripped* of his rank. **7** To separate the leaves of (tobacco) from the stalks. **8** To milk (a cow) dry by a downward stroke and compression of the thumb and forefinger. **9** *Mech.* To damage or break the teeth, thread, etc., of (a gear, bolt, or the like). **—** *v.i.* **10** To remove one's clothing; undress. **11** *Mech.* To suffer breaking or jamming of the teeth or thread. [ME <OE *-strȳpan,* as in *bestrȳpan* despoil, plunder]

stripe[1] (strīp) *n.* **1** A line, band, or long strip of material of different color or finish from the adjacent surface. **2** Distinctive quality or character; kind; sort; also, a certain kind of religious or political belief or opinion: a man of Democratic *stripe.* **3** Striped cloth. **4** *pl.* Prison uniform. **5** A piece of material or braid on the sleeve of a uniform to indicate rank, etc.; a chevron; a service or wound stripe. **—** *v.t.* **striped, strip·ing** To mark with a stripe or stripes. [<MDu.]

stripe[2] (strīp) *n.* **1** A blow struck with a whip or rod, as in flogging. **2** A weal or welt on the skin caused by such a blow. See synonyms under BLOW[2]. [Prob. <LG. Cf. Du. *strippen* whip.]

striped (strīpt, strī′pid) *adj.* Having stripes; marked with stripes.

striped bass See under BASS[1] (def. 1).

striped snake A garter snake.

striped squirrel A chipmunk.

strip·er (strī′pər) *n. U.S. Colloq.* A person who wears stripes on his or her sleeves: a one–*striper* or ensign in the Navy.

strip·ling (strip′ling) *n.* A mere youth; a lad. [<STRIP[1] + -LING]

strip–mine (strip′mīn′) *v.t.* **–mined, –min·ing** **1** To extract (material, as coal) from a strip mine. **—** *v.i.* **2** To work a strip mine. **— strip miner — strip mining**

strip mine A mine, especially a coal mine, the seams of which are close to the surface of the earth, and which is worked by stripping away the topsoil and the material beneath it.

strip·per (strip′ər) *n.* **1** One who or that which strips. **2** *Slang* A female performer of a strip–tease. **3** A partially depleted oil well producing few barrels a day: also **stripper well.** **4** An owner or operator of a strip mine; also, a worker on a strip mine.

strip·ping (strip′ing) *n.* **1** The act or process of one who or that which strips. **2** *pl.* The milk drawn from a cow by stripping. **3** The operation of strip mines; strip mining.

strip–tease (strip′tēz′) *n.* In burlesque, a gradual disrobing by a female performer. **— strip′–teas′er** *n.*

strip·y (strī′pē) *adj.* **strip·i·er, strip·i·est** Being in or suggesting stripes or streaks; having or marked with stripes.

strive (strīv) *v.i.* **strove, striv·en** (striv′ən) or **strived, striv·ing** **1** To make earnest effort. **2** To engage in strife; contend; fight. **3** To vie; emulate. See synonyms under CONTEND, ENDEAVOR, STRUGGLE. [<OF *estriver,* prob. <Gmc.] **— striv′er** *n.*

strobe (strōb) *n.* **1** A stroboscope. **2** An electronically controlled device that emits light in very brief, brilliant flashes, used in photography, in the theater, etc.: also **strobe light.**

strob·ic (strō′bik) *adj.* **1** Resembling a top. **2** Seeming to spin: said of concentric circles that appear to spin when moved. [<Gk. *strobos* whirling]

stro·bi·la (strō·bī′lə) *n. pl.* **·lae** (-lē) *Zool.* **1** A stage in the life cycle of a jellyfish characterized by a series of annular plates each of which separates as a new organism. **2** The segmented body of a tapeworm. [<NL <Gk. *strobilē* plug of lint shaped like a fir cone <*strobilos* fir cone, anything twisted <*strobos* twisted, ult. <*strephein* twist]

strob·i·la·ceous (strob′ə·lā′shəs) *adj.* **1** Resembling or relating to a strobile or cone. **2** Producing strobiles.

strob·i·late (strob′ə·lāt) *v.i.* **·lat·ed, ·lat·ing** To divide metamerically; undergo strobilation.

strob·i·la·tion (strob′ə·lā′shən) *n. Zool.* Asexual reproduction by division, as in jellyfish and tapeworms; metameric division.

strob·ile (strob′il) *n. Bot.* **1** A multiple fruit consisting of an oblong, oval, or conical mass of dry imbricated scales, as in the pines, spruces, firs, etc.; a cone. **2** A cone–shaped mass of sporophylls producing spore cases, as in the horsetails, clubmosses, etc. Also **strob′il.** [See STROBILA]

strob·o·scope (strob′ə·skōp) *n.* An instrument for observing or studying periodic motion by rendering the moving body visible only at certain points of its path. [<Gk. *strobos* twisting + -SCOPE] **— strob′o·scop′ic** (-skop′·ik) or **·i·cal** *adj.* **— strob·os·co·py** (strob·os′·kə·pē) *n.*

strob·o·tron (strob′ə·tron) *n.* A low–pressure electron tube filled with a rare gas or a mixture of rare gases and used in stroboscopic photography, or to transmit supersonic impulses by means of its periodic discharges.

strode (strōd) Past tense of STRIDE.

stroke (strōk) *n.* **1** The act or movement of striking; a knock; an impact. **2** One of a series of recurring movements, as of oars, a piston, etc.; also, the rate, extent, or manner of such movement. **3** Stroke oar. **4** A single movement, as of the hand, arm, or some instrument, by which something is made or done. **5** A single movement of some instrument, as of a pen or pencil. **6** A blow or any ill effect caused as if by a blow: a *stroke* of misfortune, a *sunstroke.* **7** *Pathol.* An attack of paralysis or apoplexy. **8** A blow or the sound of a blow of a striking mechanism, as of a clock. **9** A sudden or brilliant mental act; feat; coup: a great *stroke* of diplomacy, a *stroke* of wit. **10** A pulsation, as of the heart. **11** A mark or dash of a pen or tool. **12** A light caressing movement; a stroking. See synonyms under BLOW[2], MISFORTUNE. **—** *v.t.* **stroked, strok·ing** **1** To pass the hand over gently or caressingly, or with light pressure. **2** To set the pace for (a rowboat or its crew); act as stroke for. **3** To sound (time), as a gong or clock. [ME *strok, strak* <OE *strācian* strike]

stroke oar **1** The aftmost oar of a boat, whose movement sets the rate of rowing. **2** The person who rows with this oar: also **stroke–oars·man** (strōk′ôrz′mən, -ōrz′-), **strokes·man** (strōks′mən). **3** The position occupied by such an oarsman.

stroll (strōl) *v.i.* **1** To walk in a leisurely or idle manner; saunter. **2** To go from place to place. **—** *n.* An idle or leisurely walk; a wandering. See synonyms under RAMBLE. [Origin uncertain]

stroll·er (strō′lər) *n.* **1** One who strolls; especially, a strolling showman or player. **2** A tramp. **3** A small, light baby carriage, often collapsible.

stro·ma (strō′mə) *n. pl.* **·ma·ta** (-mə·tə) **1** *Physiol.* The ground substance or connective tissue that forms the framework of an organ or cell. **2** *Bot.* In fungi, the union of mycelial threads into a dense crust on or in which the sporophores are borne. [<Gk. *strōma* bed] **— stro·mat·ic** (strō·mat′ik) *adj.*

Strom·bo·li (strôm′bō·lē) The northernmost of the Lipari Islands in the Tyrrhenian Sea; 5 square miles; site of an active volcano, 3,040 feet.

stro·mey·er·ite (strō′mī·ər·īt) *n.* A metallic, lustrous, steel–gray native sulfide of copper and silver, crystallizing in the orthorhombic system. [after F. *Stromeyer,* 1786–1835, German chemist]

strong (strông, strong) *adj.* **1** Physically or bodily powerful; muscular; vigorous. **2** Healthy; robust: a *strong* constitution. **3** Morally powerful; firm; resolute; courageous. **4** Mentally powerful or vigorous. **5** Especially competent or able (in a certain subject or field): *strong* in mathematics. **6** Abundantly or richly supplied (with something): *strong* in trumps; *strong* in literary interest. **7** Solidly made or constituted; not easily destroyed, injured, or strained: *strong* walls, paper, etc. **8** Powerful as a rival or combatant: a *strong* team, army, etc. **9** Easy to defend; difficult to capture: a *strong* hill position. **10** In numerical force: an army 20,000 *strong.* **11** Well able to exert influence, authority, etc.: a *strong* government. **12** Financially sound: a *strong* bank. **13** Powerful in effect: *strong* poison, medicine, etc. **14** Concentrated; not diluted or weak: *strong* coffee. **15** Containing much alcohol: a *strong* drink. **16** Powerful in flavor or odor; also, rank; unpleasant: a *strong* breath. **17** Intense in degree or quality; not mild: a *strong* pulse; *strong* light, heat, etc. **18** Loud and firm: a *strong* voice. **19** Firm; tenacious: a *strong* grip; a *strong* opinion. **20** Deeply earnest; fervid: a *strong* desire. **21** Cogent; convincing: *strong* evidence. **22** Distinct; marked; definite: a *strong* resemblance. **23** Extreme; high–handed: *strong* measures. **24** Emphatic; not moderate: *strong* language. **25** Moving

with great force: said of a wind, stream, or tide; specifically, *Meteorol.*, designating a breeze (No. 6) or a gale (No. 9) on the Beaufort scale. **26** Characterized by steady or rising prices: a *strong* market. **27** *Phonet.* Stressed; accented, as a syllable. **28** *Gram.* In Germanic languages: **a** Of verbs, indicating changes in tense by means of ablaut vowel alteration in the stem, rather than by the addition of inflectional endings; as, English *drink, drank, drunk; write, wrote, written*; German *singen, sang, gesungen*: also called *irregular.* **b** Of nouns and adjectives (in German and Old English), showing distinctive declensional endings for case, number, and gender. For example, in German, a descriptive adjective is used in the strong form when not preceded by a limiting word *(guter Mann)* or when preceded by one having no distinctive case and gender inflection *(mein guter Mann).* Compare WEAK (def. 12). —*adv.* Strongly: usually employed in combination: *strong*-talking. Many self-explaining compound adjectives have *strong* as the first element: *strong*-armed, *strong*-smelling, etc. [OE] —**strong'ly** *adv.*

Synonyms (adj.): cohesive, compact, hardy, robust, sinewy, stalwart, stout, stubborn, sturdy, tenacious, vigorous. See FIRM, HEALTHY.

strong-arm (strông'ärm', strong'-) *Colloq. adj.* Using physical or coercive power: *strong-arm* tactics. —*v.t.* **1** To use physical force upon; assault. **2** To coerce; compel.

strong·bark (strông'bärk', strong'-) *n.* A small tree *(Bourreria ovata),* native to the West Indies and Florida. The wood is brown, hard, and strong; the berries are edible.

strong·box (strông'boks', strong'-) *n.* A strongly built chest or safe for keeping valuables.

strong drink Alcoholic liquors.

strong·hold (strông'hōld', strong'-) *n.* A place that nature or man has made strongly defensible; hence, a refuge.

strong·man (strông'man', strong'-) *n.* A political leader having considerable or preeminent power, as from a military coup or other extra-legal means.

strong-mind·ed (strông'mīn'did, strong'-) *adj.* Having a determined, vigorous mind. —**strong'-mind'ed·ly** *adv.* —**strong'-mind'ed·ness** *n.*

strong·room (strông'rōōm', -rŏŏm', strong'-) *n.* A room especially equipped for the safekeeping of valuables.

strong-willed (strông'wild', strong'-) *adj.* Having a strong will; decided; often, obstinate.

stron·gyle (stron'jil) *n.* Any of an order *(Strongyloidea)* of parasitic nematode worms, many of them very injurious to man and certain animals; especially, the hookworm and the gapeworm. [<Gk. *strongylos* round]

stron·ti·a (stron'shē·ə) *n. Chem.* **1** A grayish-white, infusible strontium monoxide, SrO. **2** Strontium hydroxide, $Sr(OH)_2$. [<NL <STRONTIUM]

stron·ti·an·ite (stron'shē·ən·īt') *n.* A vitreous, native strontium carbonate, $SrCO_3$, occurring in various forms and colors.

stron·ti·um (stron'shē·əm, -shəm, -tē·əm) *n.* A hard yellowish metallic element (symbol Sr, atomic number 38) of the alkaline earth group, usually occurring with barium and never in the free state. See PERIODIC TABLE. [<NL, from *Strontian,* Argyll, Scotland, where first discovered] —**stron'tic** (-tik) *adj.*

strontium 90 A radioactive isotope of strontium of mass number 90, having a half-life of 28 years, present in used reactor fuel and in the fallout from nuclear explosions, where it constitutes a special hazard because its chemical similarity to calcium results in its being metabolized and accumulated in bone and other living tissues and secretions such as milk.

strop (strop) *n.* **1** A strip of leather or canvas on which to sharpen a razor; also, a rectangular implement with strops on it. **2** A strap. —*v.t.* **stropped, strop·ping** To sharpen on a strop. [OE *stropp* <L *struppus* <Gk. *strophos* a band, cord]

stro·phan·thin (strō·fan'thin) *n.* A bitter, poisonous, crystalline glycoside contained in certain varieties of a tropical plant (genus *Strophanthus*) and resembling digitalis in its action on the heart. [<NL *Strophanthus,* a genus name (<Gk. *strophos* cord + *anthos* flower) + -IN]

stro·phe (strō'fē) *n.* **1** In ancient Greek poetry, the verses sung by the chorus in a play while moving from right to left. **2** In classical prosody, the lines of an ode comprising a stanza and alternating with the antistrophe. **3** The first of two alternating metrical systems in a poem. [<Gk. *strophē* a turning, twist <*strephein* turn] —**stroph·ic** (strof'ik, strō'fik) or **·i·cal** *adj.*

stroph·i·ole (strof'ē·ōl, strō'fē-) *n. Bot.* An aril-like appendage attached to the base of certain seeds. [<L *strophiolum,* dim. of *strophium* a band <Gk. *strophos* cord <*strephein* twist] —**stroph'i·o·late'** (-lāt'), **stroph'i·o·lat'ed** *adj.*

stroph·u·lus (strof'yə·ləs) *n. Pathol.* Any of various types of miliaria common in children: also called *tooth rash, red gum.* [<NL, dim. of Gk. *strophos* a cord. See STROPHE.]

stross·ers (stros'ərz) *n. pl. Obs.* Trousers.

stroud (stroud) *n.* A coarse, heavy, woolen material used for blankets; also, a blanket made of this material, formerly used for trading with North American Indians. [from *Stroud,* England]

strove (strōv) Past tense of STRIVE.

strow (strō) *v.t. Obs.* To strew.

struck (struk) Past tense and past participle of STRIKE.

struck jury A jury specially selected by a process in which each party strikes twelve names from a list of forty-eight eligible persons, and the remaining twenty-four are summoned as the panel from which the jury of twelve men is drawn.

struck measure A measure, as of meal, smoothed down: opposed to *heaped measure.*

struck mine, plant, etc. A mine, manufacturing plant, etc., in which work has been stopped by a strike.

struc·tur·al (struk'chər·əl) *adj.* **1** Of, pertaining to, possessing, characterized, or caused by structure. **2** *Geol.* Having a form, position, or character determined by the preexistent structure of the earth's crust; tectonic. **3** *Biol.* Morphological. **4** *Chem.* Pertaining to or denoting the spatial arrangements of atoms in a molecule: a *structural* formula. **5** Used in or essential to construction. —**struc'tur·al·ly** *adv.*

structural iron **1** Shapes of iron used in constructing buildings, bridges, etc. **2** Iron cast in shapes for this purpose.

structural steel **1** Steel prepared after the manner of structural iron for use in building. **2** Rolled steel adapted for use in construction: of considerable toughness and strength.

struc·ture (struk'chər) *n.* **1** That which is constructed; a combination of related parts, as a building or machine. **2** *Biol.* The arrangement and functional union of parts, tissues, and organs of a plant or animal. **3** *Geol.* **a** The spatial arrangement of rock strata in a larger formation. **b** The gross physical characteristics of a rock. **4** *Chem.* The disposition of atoms within a molecule or of molecules in a compound. **5** The manner of construction or organization: the social *structure* of a primitive society. **6** *Archaic* The act of constructing. —*v.t.* **·tured, ·tur·ing** **1** To form into an organized structure; build. **2** To conceive as a structural whole; ideate: He *structured* the plan before proposing it. See synonyms under FRAME. [<F <L *structura* <*structus,* pp. of *struere* build]

stru·del (strōōd'l, *Ger.* shtrōō'dəl) *n.* A kind of pastry made of a thin sheet of dough, spread with fruit or cheese, nuts, etc., rolled, and baked. [<G, lit., eddy]

strug·gle (strug'əl) *n.* A violent effort or series of efforts; a labored contest; sometimes, a war; battle. See synonyms under ENDEAVOR. [<*v.*] —*v.* **·gled, ·gling** *v.i.* **1** To contend with an adversary in physical combat; fight. **2** To put forth violent efforts; strive: to *struggle* against odds. **3** To make one's way by violent efforts: to *struggle* through mud. —*v.t.* **4** To accomplish with a struggle. [ME *strogelen;* origin unknown] —**strug'gler** *n.* —**strug'gling·ly** *adv.*

Synonyms (verb): battle, contend, contest, endeavor, fight, labor, strain, strive, toil, try, vie, wrestle, writhe.

Struld·brug (struld'brug) *n.* One of a class of immortal human beings, described in Swift's *Gulliver's Travels* (Voyage to Laputa), who became senile after the age of eighty, gradually losing all power of communication and becoming wards of the state.

strum (strum) *v.t.* & *v.i.* **strummed, strum·ming** To play (on a stringed instrument) without expression; thrum. —*n.* The act of strumming. [Prob. imit.] —**strum'mer** *n.*

stru·ma (strōō'mə) *n. pl.* **·mae** (-mē) **1** *Pathol.* **a** Scrofula. **b** Goiter. **2** *Bot.* A wenlike cushion or swelling of or on an organ, as at the base of the capsule in certain mosses. [<L <*struere* build] —**stru·mat·ic** (strōō·mat'ik), **stru'mose** (-mōs), **stru'mous** (-məs) *adj.*

Stru·ma (strōō'mä) A river in SW Bulgaria and NE Greece, flowing 215 miles SE to the Aegean: Greek *Strymon.*

strum·pet (strum'pit) *n.* A whore; harlot. [? Ult. <OF *strupe* concubinage <L *stuprum* dishonor]

strung (strung) Past tense and past participle of STRING.

strunt (strunt, strōōnt) *Scot. v.i.* **1** To strut. **2** To be sullen. —*n.* **1** A sullen mood; umbrage. **2** Spirituous liquor; whisky and water; toddy. —**to take the strunt** To be or become sulky.

strut (strut) *n.* **1** A proud or pompous step or walk. **2** A compression member in a framework, keeping two others from approaching nearer together, as the vertical members of the wing truss of a biplane. **3** An instrument used in adjusting the plaits of a ruff. —*v.* **strut·ted, strut·ting** *v.i.* To walk pompously, conceitedly, and affectedly. —*v.t.* To brace or support, as a framing or structure, by compression pieces, as struts or posts. [OE *strūtian* be rigid, stand stiffly] —**strut'ter** *n.* —**strut'ting** *adj.* —**strut'ting·ly** *adv.*

Stru·thi·on·i·dae (strōō'thē·on'i·dē) *n. pl.* A family of large, terrestrial, swift-running ratite birds; the ostriches, especially *Struthio camelus* of Africa and Arabia. [<NL <L *struthio* <Gk. *strouthiōn* ostrich]

stru·thi·ous (strōō'thē·əs) *adj.* **1** Like an ostrich. **2** Pertaining to the *Struthionidae.* [<L *struthio* an ostrich]

strych·nine (strik'nin, -nēn, -nīn) *n.* A white, crystalline, bitter, extremely poisonous alkaloid, $C_{21}H_{22}N_2O_2$, contained in various plants (genus *Strychnos*) of the logania family, especially *S. nuxvomica.* Its salts are used in medicine, chiefly as a neural stimulant; a large dose produces tetanic spasms. Also **strych'ni·a** (-nē·ə), **strych'nin** (-nin). [<F <L *strychnos* <Gk., nightshade]

strych·nin·ism (strik'nin·iz'əm) *n. Pathol.* The morbid condition resulting from the excessive or improper use of strychnine.

Stry·mon (strī'mən) The Greek name for the STRUMA.

Stry·mon·ic Gulf (strī·mon'ik) **1** An inlet of the northern Aegean in Greek Macedonia; 14 miles wide, 17 miles long. **2** The entire section of the Aegean between Thasos and Akti: also *Gulf of Orfani.*

St. Si·mons Island (sānt sī'mənz) One of the Sea Islands off the coast of SE Georgia; about 13 miles long, 3 to 7 miles wide; site of a national monument and of a decisive battle between England and Spain, 1742.

St. Swith·in's Day (sānt swith'ənz) July 15th, the day that commemorates St. Swithin, a former patron saint of Winchester Cathedral, England: rain occurring on this day is said to foretell wet weather for the following 40 days. Also **St. Swith'un's Day.**

St. Thom·as (sānt tom'əs) **1** An island of the Virgin Islands of the United States; 28 square miles; capital, Charlotte Amalie. **2** The English name for SÃO TOMÉ.

Stu·art (stōō'ərt, styōō'-) Name of the royal family of Scotland, 1371–1603, and of Great Britain, 1603–1714: also spelled *Stewart.* —**Charles Edward,** 1720–88, English prince, grandson of James II: called "Bonnie Prince Charlie" and the "Young Pretender." —**James Edward,** 1688–1766, English prince, son of James II: called the "Old Pretender."

Stuart (sto͞o′ərt, styo͞o′-), **Gilbert Charles,** 1755–1828, U. S. portrait painter. — **James Ewell Brown,** 1833–64, American Confederate cavalry general: nickname *Jeb.*

stub (stub) *n.* **1** The part of a tree trunk, bush, etc., that remains when the main part is cut down. **2** Any short projecting part or piece; a remnant, as of a pencil, candle, cigarette, cigar, or broken tooth. **3** In a checkbook or the like, one of the inner ends upon which a memorandum is entered, and which remains when the check is detached; also, the detachable coupon of a theater or other ticket. **4** Anything blunt, short, or stumpy, as a worn horseshoe nail or a stub pen. **5** *Obs.* A log; block; blockhead. **6** The title of a row in a statistical table; also, the first or reading column in such a table. — *v.t.* **stubbed, stub·bing 1** To strike, as the toe, against a low obstruction or projection. **2** To grub up, as roots; root out. **3** To clear or remove the stubs or roots from. — *adj.* Thick-set; stocky. [OE *stubb*]

stub·bed (stub′id, stubd) *adj.* **1** Made into or resembling a stub. **2** Full of stubs. **3** Sturdy; blunt in manner; stout and rough; rugged. — **stub′bed·ness** *n.*

stub·ble (stub′əl) *n.* **1** The stubs of grain stalks, sugarcane, etc., covering a field after the crop has been cut. **2** The field itself. **3** Any surface or growth resembling stubble, as short bristly hair or beard. [<OF *stuble,* ult. <L *stipula* stalk] — **stub′bled** *adj.* — **stub′·bly** *adj.*

stub·born (stub′ərn) *adj.* **1** Inflexible in opinion or intention; unreasonably obstinate. **2** Not easily handled, bent, or overcome; intractable: *stubborn* facts. **3** Characterized by perseverance or persistence: *stubborn* fighting. See synonyms under HARD, INFLEXIBLE, OBSTINATE, PERVERSE, STRONG. [Prob. OE *stubb* a stump] — **stub′born·ly** *adv.* — **stub′·born·ness** *n.*

Stubbs (stubz), **William,** 1825–1901, English bishop and historian.

stub·by (stub′ē) *adj.* **·bi·er, ·bi·est 1** Short, stiff, and bristling: a *stubby* beard. **2** Short and thick; like a stub: a *stubby* pencil. **3** Having many stubs. — **stub′bi·ly** *adv.* — **stub′bi·ness** *n.*

stub nail 1 A short thick nail. **2** An old horseshoe nail.

stub pen A very blunt-pointed pen for writing.

stuc·co (stuk′ō) *n. pl.* **·coes** or **·cos 1** A fine plaster for walls or their relief ornaments, usually of Portland cement, sand, and a small amount of lime. **2** Any plaster or cement used for the external coating of buildings. — *adj.* Stucco-coated. — *v.t.* **·coed, ·co·ing** To apply stucco to; decorate with stucco. [<Ital. <Gmc. Akin to OHG *stucchi* crust.] — **stuc′·co·er** *n.*

stuck (stuk) Past tense and past participle of STICK.

stuck-up (stuk′up′) *adj. Colloq.* Conceited; very vain; supercilious and arrogant; snobbish. — **stuck′-up′ness** *n.*

stud[1] (stud) *n.* **1** A short intermediate post, as in a building frame; a post to which laths are nailed; a scantling. **2** A knob, round-headed nail, or small protuberant ornament, as an ornamental button in a shirt front. **3** A crosspiece in a link, as in a chain cable. **4** A small pin such as is used in a watch. **5** Stud poker. — *v.t.* **stud·ded, stud·ding 1** To set thickly with small points, projections, or knobs. **2** To be scattered or strewn over: Daisies *stud* the meadows. **3** To support or stiffen by means of studs or upright props. [OE *studu* post]

stud[2] (stud) *n.* **1** A collection of horses and mares for breeding. **2** The place where they are kept. **3** A collection of horses for riding, hunting, or racing. **4** A stallion: also *studhorse.* — *adj.* **1** Of or pertaining to a stud. **2** Kept for breeding: a *stud* mare. [OE *stōd*]

stud book A record of the pedigree of a stud, or of thoroughbred racing stock collectively.

stud·die (stud′ē) *n. Brit. Dial.* An anvil; a stithy. [Prob. var. of STITHY]

stud·ding (stud′ing) *n.* **1** Studs or joists collectively, or material from which to make them. **2** The height of a room from floor to ceiling.

stud·ding·sail (stun′səl, stud′ing·sāl′) *n. Naut.* A light auxiliary sail set out beyond one of the principal sails by extensible booms during a following wind.

student (sto͞od′nt, styo͞od′nt) *n.* **1** A person engaged in a course of study; especially, one in a secondary school, college or university. **2** One who closely examines or investigates; one devoted to study. See synonyms under SCHOLAR. [<OF *estudiant* <L *studens, -entis,* ppr. of *studere* be eager, apply oneself, study]

student lamp A reading lamp easily adjustable for direction or distance of light rays.

student nurse One who is in training in a hospital school of nursing.

stu·dent·ship (sto͞od′nt·ship, styo͞od′nt-) *n.* **1** A scholarship. **2** The condition of being a student.

stud·fish (stud′fish′) *n. pl.* **·fish** or **·fish·es** Any of several minnows (genus *Fundulus*) having the sides studded with orange or brown spots, as *Fundulus stellifer* of the Alabama River.

stud·horse (stud′hôrs′) *n.* A stallion kept for breeding. Also **stud horse.**

stud·ied (stud′ēd) *adj.* **1** Deliberately and intentionally designed or undertaken; planned; premeditated: a *studied* insult. **2** Acquired or prepared by study. **3** *Rare* Learned; versed. — **stud′ied·ly** *adv.* — **stud′ied·ness** *n.*

stu·di·o (sto͞o′dē·ō, styo͞o′-) *n. pl.* **·di·os 1** The workroom of an artist, photographer, etc. **2** A place where motion pictures are filmed. **3** A room or rooms where radio or television programs are broadcast or recorded. [<Ital. <L *studium* zeal <*studere* apply oneself, be diligent]

studio couch A backless couch with a bed frame underneath which may be drawn out and made level with the couch to form a double bed or twin beds.

stu·di·ous (sto͞o′dē·əs, styo͞o′-) *adj.* **1** Given to study; devoting oneself to the acquisition of knowledge. **2** Earnest in the use of means; assiduous: *studious* to please. **3** Done with deliberation; studied: *studious* politeness. **4** Favorable to study; for study: *studious* halls. [<L *studiosus* <*studium* zeal. See STUDIO.] — **stu′di·ous·ly** *adv.* — **stu′di·ous·ness** *n.*

stud poker A game of poker in which the cards of the first round are dealt face down and the rest face up, betting opening on the second round.

stud·work (stud′wûrk′) *n.* **1** Walls of brickwork between studs. **2** Studded leather armor. **3** Anything set or supported with studs.

stud·y (stud′ē) *v.* **stud·ied, stud·y·ing** *v.t.* **1** To apply the mind in acquiring a knowledge of: to *study* physics. **2** To examine; search into: to *study* a problem. **3** To look at attentively; scrutinize: to *study* one's reflection in a mirror. **4** To endeavor to memorize, as a part in a play. **5** To give thought and attention to, as something to be done or devised: often with *out.* — *v.i.* **6** To apply the mind in acquiring knowledge. **7** To follow a regular course of instruction; be a student. **8** To muse; meditate. See synonyms under CONSIDER, EXAMINE, MUSE. — **to study up on** To acquire more complete information concerning, as by investigation. — *n. pl.* **stud·ies 1** The act of studying; the process of acquiring information; application of the mind to books, to art or science, etc. **2** A particular instance or form of mental work. **3** Something to be studied; a branch or department of knowledge. **4** A specific product of studious application. **5** In art, a first sketch; a student's art exercise. **6** A carefully elaborated literary treatment of a subject. **7** A room devoted to study, reading, etc. **8** A studious state of mind; profound thought; absent-mindedness: in a brown *study.* See BROWN STUDY. **9** Earnest endeavor; thoughtful care or its object: Our *study* is to please you. **10** *Music* A composition designed to aid development in technical facility; an étude. See synonyms under EDUCATION, INQUIRY, LEARNING, REFLECTION, TASK, THOUGHT[1]. [<OF *estudier* <*estudie* a study <L *studium* zeal. See STUDIO.] — **stud′·i·a·ble** *adj.*

study hall In a school, a large room equipped and reserved for study.

stuff (stuf) *v.t.* **1** To fill completely; pack; cram full. **2** To fill (an opening, etc.) with something forced in; plug. **3** To obstruct or stop up; choke. **4** To fill or expand with padding, as a cushion. **5** To fill (a fowl, roast, etc.) with stuffing. **6** In taxidermy, to fill the skin of (a bird, animal, etc.) with a material preparatory to mounting. **7** To fill too full; overload; distend. **8** To fill or cram with food: He *stuffed* himself with oysters. **9** To fill with knowledge, ideas, or attitudes, especially unsystematically: His head is *stuffed* with prejudices. **10** To force or cram, as into a small space. **11** To fill the pores of (a skin or pelt) with a preservative of oil and tallow. — *v.i.* **12** To eat to excess; gluttonize. — **to stuff a ballot box** To put fraudulent votes into a ballot box. [<*n.*] — *n.* **1** The material out of which something may be shaped or made; hence, raw or unwrought material. **2** Figuratively, the fundamental element of anything, material or spiritual. **3** Possessions generally, especially household goods. **4** A worthless collection of things; rubbish; hence, worthless ideas: often used as an interjection: *Stuff* and nonsense! **5** Woven material, especially of wool. **6** Any textile fabric. **7** Any one of various substances, mixtures, or compounds prepared for use, as paper pulp; in leathermaking, dubbing or stuffing. **8** A medicinal mixture or potion. **9** *Scot.* Luggage; belongings; corn; grain. **10** *Slang* Money; means. **11** In journalism, copy ready for the printer or engraver. [<OF *estoffe,* prob. <L *stuppa* tow] — **stuff′er** *n.*

stuffed shirt *Colloq.* A pretentious person; especially, a pompous boob.

stuff·ing (stuf′ing) *n.* **1** The material with which anything is stuffed. **2** A mixture, as of bread or cracker crumbs with meat and seasoning, used in stuffing fowls, etc., for cooking. **3** The process of stuffing anything.

stuff·ing box *Mech.* A device consisting of a chamber affording passage and lengthwise or rotary motion of a piece, as of a piston rod or shaft, while preventing leakage about the moving part by using packing material to fill the free space.

stuffing nut The nut which encloses a stuffing box.

stuff·y (stuf′ē) *adj.* **stuff·i·er, stuff·i·est 1** Badly ventilated. **2** Impeding respiration. **3** *U.S. Colloq.* Angry; sulky. **4** Old-fashioned; stodgy; stiffly precise; strait-laced. — **stuff′·i·ly** *adv.* — **stuff′i·ness** *n.*

Stu·ka (sto͞o′kə, *Ger.* shto͞o′kä) *n.* A German dive bomber: contraction of *Sturzkampfflugzeug.*

stull (stul) *n. Mining* A cross-timbering or platform in an excavation, especially in a stope to support workmen or to protect workers from falling stones. [Prob. <G *stollen* post, prop]

Stülp·na·gel (shtülp′nä·gəl), **Otto von,** 1880–1948, German general.

stul·ti·fy (stul′tə·fī) *v.t.* **·fied, ·fy·ing 1** To cause to appear absurd; give an appearance of foolishness to. **2** To bring to naught; nullify. **3** *Law* To allege to be of unsound mind. [<LL *stultificare* make foolish <L *stultus* foolish + *facere* make] — **stul′ti·fi·ca′tion** *n.* — **stul′ti·fi′er** *n.*

stum (stum) *n.* **1** Unfermented or partly fermented grape juice. **2** Wine revived, as by adding must, to produce increased fermentation; must. — *v.t.* **stummed, stum·ming 1** To stop fermentation in by some admixture. **2** To revive (wine), as by adding must, so as to increase fermentation. [<Du. *stom* must, lit., silent]

stum·ble (stum′bəl) *v.* **·bled, ·bling** *v.i.* **1** To miss one's step in walking or running; trip. **2** To walk or proceed unsteadily or in a blundering manner. **3** To happen upon something by chance: with *across, on, upon,* etc. **4** To fall into sin or error. — *v.t.* **5** To cause to stumble. — *n.* The act of stumbling; hence, a blunder; false step. [Cf. Norw. *stumla* stumble in the dark] — **stum′bler** *n.* — **stum′bling** *adj.* — **stum′bling·ly** *adv.*

stum·bling·block (stum′bling·blok′) *n.* Any obstacle or hindrance; something that may cause one to err: now only figurative.

stump (stump) *n.* **1** That portion of the trunk of a tree left standing when the tree is felled. **2** The part of anything, as of a limb, that remains when the main part has been removed; a stumplike part; a stub. **3** *pl. Colloq.* The legs: chiefly in the phrase **to stir one's stumps. 4** A place or platform where a stump speech is made; hence, any place or platform from which speeches are made; also,

political haranguing. 5 *Colloq.* A challenge; a dare. 6 In cricket, any one of the three posts (the **off stump,** the **middle stump,** and the **leg stump**) forming the wicket. 7 A pencil-like soft leather or rubber bar, with conical ends, used to soften drawings of crayon or charcoal or to apply powdered pigments. 8 A short, thick–set person or animal. 9 A heavy step; a clump. **— to be up a stump** To be in trouble or in a dilemma. **— to take the stump** To electioneer in a political campaign. — *adj.* 1 Being or resembling a stump; stumpy. 2 Of or pertaining to political oratory or campaigning: a *stump* speaker, *stump* speech. — *v.t.* 1 To reduce to a stump; truncate; lop. 2 To remove stumps from (land). 3 To canvass (a district) by making political speeches: The candidate *stumped* the State. 4 *Colloq.* To challenge, as to a contest; dare; defy. 5 *Colloq.* To bring to a halt by real or fancied obstacles; nonplus; baffle. 6 To strike against an obstacle; stub, as one's toe. 7 To shade (a drawing) by rubbing with a stump (def. 7). — *v.i.* 8 To go about on or as on stumps; hence, to walk heavily, noisily, and stiffly; hobble. [<MLG]

stump·age (stum′pij) *n.* 1 Standing timber considered with reference to its value for cutting; also, its price. 2 A tax on lumber cut, rated by the amount cut and the price.

stump·er (stum′pər) *n.* 1 One who or that which stumps. 2 A political speaker. 3 Any problem, situation, etc., beyond one's powers of decision.

stump·y (stum′pē) *adj.* **stump·i·er, stump·i·est** 1 Full of stumps. 2 Like a stump; short and thick. **— stump′i·ness** *n.*

stun (stun) *v.t.* **stunned, stun·ning** 1 To render unconscious or incapable of action by a blow, fall, etc. 2 To astonish; astound. 3 To daze or overwhelm by loud or explosive noise. — *n.* A stupefying blow, shock, or concussion; also, the condition of being stunned. [<OF *estoner* resound, stun <L *ex-* thoroughly + *tonare* thunder, crash]

Stun·dist (shtōōn′dist) *n.* A member of a Russian body of Christians originating among peasants about 1860. As fundamentalists, the Stundists rejected forms and ceremonies, took only the Bible as their guide, and emphasized brotherly love and the need to labor: they were subjected to persecution. [<Russian *shtundist′* <G *stunde* hour, lesson] **— Stun′dism** *n.*

stung (stung) Past tense and past participle of STING.

stunk (stungk) Past participle and alternative past tense of STINK.

stun·ner (stun′ər) *n.* 1 One who or that which stuns. 2 *Slang* A person or thing of extraordinary or surprising qualities, such as beauty.

stun·ning (stun′ing) *adj.* 1 Rendering unconscious. 2 *Colloq.* Surprising; impressive; wonderful; beautiful. **— stun′ning·ly** *adv.*

stun·sail (stun′səl) *n.* *Naut.* A studdingsail. Also **stun's'le.** [Contraction of STUDDINGSAIL]

stunt[1] (stunt) *v.t.* To check the natural development of; dwarf; cramp. — *n.* 1 A check in growth, progress, or development. 2 A stunted animal or thing. [OE *stunt* dull, foolish; prob. infl. in meaning by ON *stuttr* short] **— stunt′ed** *adj.* **— stunt′ed·ness** *n.*

stunt[2] (stunt) *U.S. Colloq.* *n.* 1 A sensational feat, as of bodily skill. 2 Any remarkable feat, enterprise, or undertaking. — *v.i.* To perform a stunt or stunts. — *v.t.* To perform stunts with (an airplane, etc.). [Prob. <G *stunde* lesson; orig. college slang]

stunt man In motion pictures, a man employed to perform dangerous actions, such as falling, jumping, etc., often as a temporary substitute for an actor.

stu·pa (stōō′pə) *n.* Tope[4]. [<Skt., heap]

stupe (stōōp, styōōp) *n.* *Med.* A compress or medicated cloth to be applied to a wound. [<L *stupa, stuppa* tow]

stu·pe·fa·cient (stōō′pə·fā′shənt, styōō′-) *adj.* Having power to stupefy; stupefying: also **stu′pe·fac′tive.** (-fak′tiv). — *n.* Anything that stupefies, as a narcotic. [<L *stupefaciens, -entis,* ppr. of *stupefacere* stun. See STUPEFY.]

stu·pe·fac·tion (stōō′pə·fak′shən, styōō′-) *n.* The act of stupefying or state of being stupefied; stupor. See synonyms under STUPIDITY.

stu·pe·fy (stōō′pə·fī, styōō′-) *v.t.* **·fied, ·fy·ing** 1 To dull the senses or faculties of; stun. 2 To amaze; astound. [<F *stupéfier* <L *stupefacere* stun <*stupere* be stunned + *facere* make] **— stu′pe·fied** *adj.* **— stu′pe·fi′er** *n.*

stu·pen·dous (stōō·pen′dəs, styōō-) *adj.* Of prodigious size, bulk, or degree; characterized by any highly impressive feature: a *stupendous* structure, a *stupendous* error. See synonyms under IMMENSE. [<L *stupendus* amazed, orig. gerundive of *stupere* be benumbed, stunned] **— stu·pen′dous·ly** *adv.* **— stu·pen′dous·ness** *n.*

stu·pid (stōō′pid, styōō′-) *adj.* 1 Very slow of apprehension or understanding; dull–witted; sluggish. 2 Affected with stupor; stupefied: *stupid* from drink. 3 Marked by, or resulting from, lack of understanding, reason, or wit; senseless; doltish: *stupid* acts. See synonyms under ABSURD, BRUTISH, FLAT[1], HEAVY. [<L *stupidus* struck dumb <*stupere* be stunned] **— stu′pid·ly** *adv.* **— stu′pid·ness** *n.*

stu·pid·i·ty (stōō·pid′ə·tē, styōō-) *n.* The state, quality, or character of being stupid; great mental dulness. [<L *stupiditas, -tatis* <*stupidus.* See STUPID.]

Synonyms: apathy, dulness, insensibility, obtuseness, slowness, sluggishness, stupefaction, stupor. *Stupidity* is sometimes loosely used for temporary *dulness* or partial *stupor,* but chiefly for innate and chronic *dulness* and *sluggishness* of mental action, *obtuseness* of apprehension, etc. *Apathy* may be temporary, and be dispelled by appeal to the feelings or by the presentation of an adequate motive, but *stupidity* is inveterate and often incurable. Compare APATHY, IDIOCY, STUPOR. *Antonyms*: acuteness, alertness, animation, brilliancy, cleverness, intelligence, keenness, quickness, readiness, sagacity, sense, sensibility.

stu·por (stōō′pər, styōō′-) *n.* 1 A condition of the body in which the senses and faculties are suspended or greatly dulled, as by drugs or intoxicants. 2 Extreme intellectual or moral dulness; gross stupidity. [<L <*stupere* be stunned] **— stu′por·ous** *adj.*

Synonyms: apathy, asphyxia, coma, fainting, insensibility, lethargy, swoon, swooning, syncope, unconsciousness. The *apathy* of disease is a mental state of morbid indifference; *lethargy* is a morbid tendency to heavy and continued sleep, from which the patient may perhaps be momentarily aroused. *Coma* is a deep, abnormal sleep, from which the patient cannot be aroused, or is aroused only with difficulty, a state of profound *insensibility* perhaps with full pulse and deep, stertorous breathing, and is due to brain–oppression. *Syncope* or *swooning* is a sudden loss of sensation and of power of motion, with suspension of pulse and of respiration, and is due to failure of heart action, as from sudden nervous shock or intense mental emotion. *Insensibility* is a general term denoting loss of feeling from any cause, as from cold, intoxication, or injury. *Stupor* is especially profound and confirmed *insensibility,* properly comatose. *Asphyxia* is a special form of *syncope* resulting from partial or total suspension of respiration, as in strangulation or drowning. See STUPIDITY.

stupp (stup, *Ger.* shtōōp) *n.* A deposit of finely divided metallic mercury, as in the condensers of mercury smelters. Also **stup.** [<G]

stur·dy[1] (stûr′dē) *adj.* **·di·er, ·di·est** 1 Possessing rugged health and strength; hardy; enduring; vigorous; lusty: *sturdy* health, *sturdy* blows. 2 Firm and unyielding; resolute: a *sturdy* defense. See synonyms under POWERFUL, STRONG. [<OF *estourdi* dazed, reckless <*estourdir* stun, amaze <LL *exturdire* deafen; ult. origin uncertain] **— stur′di·ly** *adv.* **— stur′di·ness** *n.*

stur·dy[2] (stûr′dē) *n.* A disease of sheep; gid. [Special use of STURDY[1]] **— stur′died** *adj.*

stur·geon (stûr′jən) *n.* A large ganoid fish of northern regions (family *Acipenseridae*), with coarse, edible flesh, especially *Acipenser sturio,* the common sturgeon of both coasts of the Atlantic, which ascends rivers. Sturgeons are the principal source of isinglass and caviar. [<AF *sturgeon,* OF *sturgiun* <Med. L *sturio, -onis* <OHG *sturjo*]

Stur·gis (stûr′jis), **Russell,** 1836–1909, U.S. architect and writer.

stur·ine (stûr′ēn, -in) *n.* A bactericidal protamine from the sperm of sturgeons. [<STUR(GEON) + (PROTAM)INE]

Stur·lu·son (stûr′lə·sən, stōōr′-), **Snorri** See SNORRI STURLUSON.

Sturm·ab·teil·ung (shtōōrm′äp·tī′lōōng) *n.* *pl.* **·teil·ung·en** *German* Literally, storm detachment; a political militia of the Nazi party, organized to keep order at Nazi mass meetings. After 1934, as *Brown Shirts,* the organization became a national army of political soldiers in charge of pre– and post–military indoctrination.

Sturm und Drang (shtōōrm′ ōōnt dräng′) *German* Storm and stress: used to designate the late 18th century period of German literary romanticism.

sturt (stûrt) *Brit. Dial.* *v.t.* 1 To annoy; vex; trouble. 2 To startle. — *v.i.* 3 To start with fear; be frightened. — *n.* 1 Vexation. 2 Strife; wrath. 3 Unrest. [Prob. var. of START[1]]

sturt·in (stûr′tin) *adj.* *Scot.* Frightened; overwhelmed.

stut·ter (stut′ər) *v.t.* & *v.i.* To utter or speak with spasmodic repetition, blocking, and prolongation of sounds and syllables, especially those in initial position in a word. — *n.* The act or habit of stuttering. See synonyms under STAMMER. [Freq. of ME *stutten* stutter] **— stut′ter·er** *n.* **— stut′ter·ing** *adj.* & *n.* **— stut′ter·ing·ly** *adv.*

Stutt·gart (stut′gärt, *Ger.* shtōōt′gärt) A city in SW West Germany, capital of Baden-Württemberg.

Stuy·ve·sant (stī′və·sənt), **Peter,** 1592–1672, last Dutch governor of New Amsterdam 1647–64.

St. Val·en·tine's Day (sānt val′in·tīnz) See under VALENTINE.

St. Vin·cent (sānt vin′sənt) A British colony of the Windward Islands; 150 square miles including dependencies in the Grenadines; capital, Kingstown; a component unit of The West Indies (federation).

St. Vincent, Cape The SW extremity of Portugal and of continental Europe. *Portuguese* **Ca·bo de São Vi·cen·te** (kä′bōō thə souṅ vē·sāṅn′tə).

St. Vi·tus's dance (sānt vī′təs·iz) *Pathol.* Chorea. Also **St. Vitus dance.**

sty[1] (stī) *n.* *pl.* **sties** 1 A pen for swine. 2 Any filthy habitation or place of bestiality or debauchery. — *v.t.* & *v.i.* **stied, sty·ing** To keep or live in a sty or hovel. [OE *stī, stig*]

sty[2] (stī) *n.* *pl.* **sties** *Pathol.* A small, inflamed swelling of a sebaceous gland on the edge of the eyelid. Also **stye.** [<obs. *styanye* <OE *stīgend,* ppr. of *stīgan* rise + *ye* eye]

stych·o·myth·i·a (stik′ə·mith′ē·ə) See STICHOMYTHY.

Styg·i·an (stij′ē·ən) *adj.* 1 Pertaining to the river Styx; hence, infernal; dark and gloomy. 2 Inviolable, like the oath, "By the Styx." [<L *Stygius* <Gk. *Stygios* <*Styx* the Styx, prob. <*stygein* hate]

style (stīl) *n.* 1 Manner of expressing thought, in writing or speaking; distinctive or characteristic form of expression: a florid *style*; the *style* of Mark Twain. 2 A good or suitable mode of expression: His writing lacks *style.* 3 A particular form of composition, construction, or appearance, as in art, music, etc.: the Gothic *style*; the American *style* of automobile. 4 The manner in which some action or work is performed: The horse ran in fine *style.* 5 A good or exemplary manner of performing: a team with *style.* 6 A mode of conduct or behavior; a way of living: to live in makeshift *style.* 7 A fashionable manner or appearance: to live in *style.* 8 A particular fashion in clothing. 9 A particular type or fashion suitable for or agreeable to a person: That coat is not my *style.* 10 *Printing* The

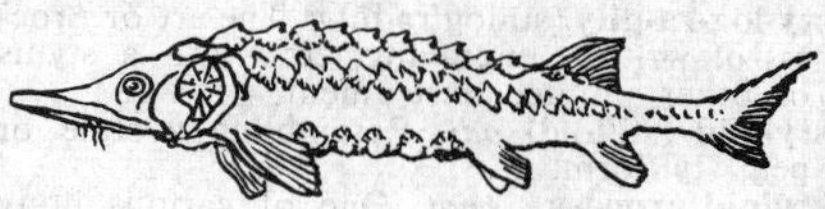

STURGEON
(Length up to 10 feet)

conventions of typography, design, etc., observed in a given printing office. **11** The legal or official title or appellation of a person, organization, etc. **12** A stylus (in any sense). **13** The gnomon of a sundial. **14** *Surg.* A slender probe with a blunt point: also called *stylet.* **15** *Bot.* The prolongation of a carpel or ovary, bearing the stigma. **16** *Zool.* A stylet. **17** A system of arranging the length of the calendar years so as to average that of the true solar year: called **New Style,** when following the arrangement made by Pope Gregory XIII (Gregorian calendar) and used in nearly all Christian countries; and **Old Style** when following the Julian calendar. England adopted the New Style by act of Parliament in 1752. Since 1900 New Style has been 13 days later than Old Style. See synonyms under AIR[1], CUSTOM, DICTION, MANNER, NAME. — *v.* **styled, styl·ing** *v.t.* **1** To name; give a title to. **2** To make consistent in typography, spelling, punctuation, etc., as copy to be printed; stylize. — *v.i.* **3** In ornamentation, to use a style or stylus. ◆ Homophone: *stile.* [<OF <L *stilus, stylus* writing instrument] — **sty′lar, sty′li·form** *adj.* — **styl′er** *n.*

sty·let (stī′lit) *n.* **1** Any slender pointed instrument, as a poniard or stiletto. **2** *Surg.* A style. **3** *Zool.* Any pointed, bristlelike process or appendage. [<F <Ital. *stiletto.* See STILETTO.]

sty·li·form (stī′lə·fôrm) *adj.* Resembling or shaped like a stylus. [<L *styliformis* <L *stylus* a stylus + *forma* a form]

styl·ish (stī′lish) *adj.* Having style; especially, very fashionable. — **styl′ish·ly** *adv.* — **styl′ish·ness** *n.*

styl·ist (stī′list) *n.* **1** One who is a master of literary or rhetorical style. **2** An adviser concerning style in clothes, interior decoration, etc.

sty·lis·tic (stī·lis′tik) *adj.* Pertaining to style, especially literary style. — *n.* Stylistics. — **sty·lis′ti·cal·ly** *adv.*

sty·lis·tics (stī·lis′tiks) *n. pl.* (*construed as singular*) The art or study of literary expression.

sty·lite (stī′līt) *n.* One of a class of early religious ascetics who lived most of the time on the tops of pillars, without shelter. The practice was originated by Simeon Stylites in A.D. 420. [<Gk. *stylitēs* <*stylos* column]

styl·ize (stī′līz) *v.t.* **·ized, ·iz·ing** To conform to a distinctive mode or style; conventionalize. Also *Brit.* **styl′ise.** — **styl′i·za′tion** *n.* — **styl′iz·er** *n.*

stylo- *combining form* **1** A pillar: *stylobate.* **2** *Bot. & Zool.* A style; of or related to a style: *stylopodium.* **3** *Anat.* Denoting relationship to a styloid process. Also, before vowels, **styl-.** [<Gk. *stylos* a column, pillar]

sty·lo·bate (stī′lə·bāt) *n. Archit.* A continuous base for two or more columns, in contradistinction to a pedestal, which is a base for only one column or object. Compare STEREOBATE. [<L *stylobates* <Gk. *stylobatēs* <*stylos* pillar + *-batēs* a treader <*bainein* walk, step]

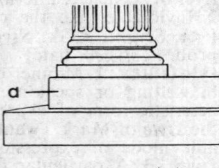

STYLOBATE (*a*)

sty·lo·graph (stī′lə·graf, -gräf) *n.* A fountain pen from which ink is fed to a conical writing point. Also **stylographic pen.** — **sty′lo·graph′ic** or **·i·cal** *adj.*

sty·log·ra·phy (stī·log′rə·fē) *n.* The art or process of writing, engraving, etc., with a stylus or other pointed instrument.

sty·loid (stī′loid) *adj.* Resembling a style or peg; styliform.

styloid process *Anat.* One of various bony processes, as the spine that projects from the base of the temporal bone; a projection on the head of the fibula; the pointed lower extremity of either the radius or the ulna; the proximal end of the third metacarpal bone.

sty·lo·lite (stī′lə·līt) *n. Geol.* A small columnar body of the same composition as the surrounding rock. — **sty′lo·lit′ic** (-lit′ik) *adj.*

sty·lo·po·di·um (stī′lə·pō′dē·əm) *n.* *pl.* **·di·a** (-dē·ə) *Bot.* The fleshy disk that bears the style in umbelliferous flowers. [<NL]

sty·lus (stī′ləs) *n.* **1** An ancient writing instrument, having one end pointed for writing on wax tablets and the other end blunt for erasure. **2** A pointed instrument for marking or engraving, as on carbons, stencils, etc. **3** The needle of a phonograph or of a sound-recording instrument. [<L]

sty·mie (stī′mē) *n.* A condition obtaining in golf when an opponent's ball lies in the line of the player's putt on the green, the balls being more than six inches apart. — *v.t.* **·mied, ·my·ing** **1** To block (an opponent) by or as by a stymie. **2** To baffle or perplex. Also spelled *stimy.* [Origin uncertain]

Stym·pha·lus (stim·fā′ləs) A district of NE Arcadia, central Peloponnesus, Greece.

styp·sis (stip′sis) *n.* The application or the action of a styptic. [<LL <Gk., a contraction <*styphein* contract]

styp·tic (stip′tik) *adj.* **1** Causing contraction of living tissues, as blood vessels. **2** Preventing hemorrhage; astringent: a *styptic* pencil. Also **styp′ti·cal.** — *n.* A substance or agent that arrests bleeding. [<L *stypticus* <Gk. *styptikos* <*stypsis* a contraction. See STYPSIS.]

Styr (stir) A river in western Ukrainian S.S.R., flowing 280 miles north to the Pripet River.

Sty·ra·ca·ce·ae (stī′rə·kā′si·ē) *n. pl.* An order of gamopetalous trees or shrubs yielding resins and gums, the storax family, having alternate simple leaves and usually white racemed flowers with a corolla of 4 to 8 united petals. They are found in all parts of the world. [<NL <L *styrax* storax] — **sty′ra·ca′ceous** (-shəs) *adj.*

sty·rene (stī′rēn, stir′ēn) *n. Chem.* A colorless aromatic hydrocarbon, C_8H_8, contained in liquid storax, from which it may be derived by distillation. [<L *styrax* storax + -ENE]

Styr·i·a (stir′ē·ə) A province and former duchy in central and SE Austria; 6,324 square miles; capital, Graz: German *Steiermark.*

Sty·ro·foam (stī′rə·fōm) *n.* A lightweight, rigid, cellular material formed from a synthetic hydrocarbon polymer: a trade name.

stythe (stīth) *n.* Chokedamp. [OE *stith* harsh]

Styx (stiks) In Greek mythology, the river of hate, one of the five rivers surrounding Hades.

su·a·ble (sōō′ə·bəl) *adj.* Legally subject to civil process; able to be sued. — **su′a·bil′i·ty** *n.*

Sua·kin (swä′kēn) A port on the Red Sea in NE Sudan.

sua·sion (swā′zhən) *n.* The act of persuading; persuasion: archaic except in the phrase **moral suasion.** [<OF <L *suasio, -onis* <*suadere* persuade] — **sua·sive** (swā′siv), **sua·so·ry** (swā′sər·ē) *adj.*

suave (swäv, swāv) *adj.* Smooth and pleasant in manner; bland; gracious. [<F <L *suavis* sweet] — **suave′ly** *adv.* — **suave′ness** *n.*

suav·i·ty (swä′və·tē, swav′ə-) *n. pl.* **·ties** **1** The state of being suave; urbanity. **2** Something that is suave, bland, or agreeable. [<F *suavité* <L *suavitas, -tatis* <*suavis* sweet]

sub (sub) *n. Colloq.* Short for: **1** A substitute. **2** A subordinate or subaltern. **3** A subway. **4** A submarine.

sub- *prefix* **1** Under; beneath; below; as in:

subaquatic	subfloor
subastral	subfluvial
subcoastal	subsurface
subcurrent	subtext

2 *Anat.* Situated under or beneath, or on the ventral side of; as in:

subabdominal	submuscular
subalar	subnasal
subapical	subneural
subauricular	subnodal
subaxial	subocular
subcerebellar	suboptic
subclavicular	suboral
subcortical	suborbital
subcostal	subpelvic
subcranial	subphrenic
subcuticular	subpleural
subdental	subpubic
subdermal	subpulmonary
subdiaphragmatic	subrectal
subdorsal	subretinal
subepiglottic	subspinal
subgenital	subspinous
subgingival	substernal
subglottic	subungual
subintegumental	suburethral
subintestinal	subvaginal
submammary	subvertebral

3 Almost; nearly; slightly; imperfectly: chiefly in scientific terms; as in:

subacid	subfluid
subacidity	subhorizontal
subacidulous	subinflammation
subacrid	sublateral
subacuminate	sublinear
subalkaline	subluminous
subangular	submedial
subastringent	submetallic
subaudible	subnarcotic
subcalcareous	suboval
subcarbureted	subparallel
subcentral	subparalytic
subconcave	subpolar
subconchoidal	subsaline
subconical	subserrate
subcolumnar	subsibilant
subconvex	subtetanic
subcubical	subtypical
subdelirium	subvertical
subfebrile	subvirile

4 Lower in rank or grade; secondary; subordinate; as in:

subadministration	subholding
subadministrator	sub–idea
subagency	sublessee
subagent	sublessor
subassociation	sublieutenancy
subcantor	sublieutenant
subcause	submeaning
subchanter	submediator
subclerk	submortgage
subcommission	subofficer
subconstellation	subpart
sub–echo	subrector
sub–editor	subrent
sub–element	subsecretary
subflavor	subtone
subforeman	subvicar
subfunction	subworker

5 Forming a subdivision; as in:

sub–branch	submember
sub–bureau	suboffice
subcavity	subprovince
subclass	subscience
subclassification	subsegment
subcorporation	subseries
subcouncil	subshaft
subdepartment	subtype
subdialect	subunit
subdistrict	subzone

6 *Math.* Denoting a ratio, the inverse of a given ratio: The *subtriplicate* ratio is the inverse of the ratio of the cube. **7** *Chem.* **a** Present (in a compound) in less than normal amount: *subchloride, suboxide.* **b** Designating a basic salt compound: *subacetate, subcarbonate.*

Also: *suc-* before *c,* as in *succumb; suf-* before *f,* as in *suffer; sug-* before *g,* as in *suggest; sum-* before *m,* as in *summon; sup-* before *p,* as in *support; sur-* before *r,* as in *surrogate; sus-* before *c, p, t,* as in *susceptible, suspect, sustain.* [<L *sub-* <*sub* under]

sub·a·cute (sub′ə·kyōot′) *adj.* **1** Somewhat acute. **2** Intermediate between acute and chronic: said of a disease. — **sub′a·cute′ly** *adv.*

sub·aer·i·al (sub′âr′ē·əl, -ā·ir′-) *adj.* Of, pertaining to, or formed at the earth's surface, in open air: contrasted with *aerial, submarine,* and *subterranean.*

su·bah (sōō′bä) *n.* **1** A province or governmental district of India. **2** A subahdar. Also **su′ba.**

su·bah·dar (sōō′bä·där′) *n.* The chief native officer of a company of sepoys in the former British East–Indian Army: also spelled *subah.* Also **su′ba·dar′.** [<Urdu *sūbahdār* <Persian <Arabic *sūbah* a province + Persian *dār* a possessor, master]

sub·al·pine (sub·al′pīn, -pin) *adj.* **1** Lower than alpine. **2** Of or pertaining to mountainous regions near but below the timber line.

sub·al·tern (sub·ôl′tərn) *adj.* **1** *Brit. Mil.* Ranking below a captain. **2** Of inferior rank or position; subordinate, as a species to a genus, or as a particular proposition under a universal. — *n.* **1** A person of subordinate rank or position. **2** *Brit. Mil.* An officer ranking below a captain. **3** (sub′əl·tûrn) *Logic* A specific class as included under a general one, or a particular statement as deducible from a

universal one. [< MF *subalterne* < LL *subalternus* < L *sub-* under + *alternus* alternate]

sub·al·ter·nant (sub'ôl·tûr'nənt) *adj.* Universal, as opposed to *particular.* —*n.* A universal proposition in its relation to the particular proposition containing the same terms. [< NL *subalternans, -antis,* ppr. of Med. L *subalternare* subordinate < LL *subalternus.* See SUBALTERN.]

sub·al·ter·nate (sub·ôl'tər·nit, -al'-) *adj.* 1 Subordinate; subaltern. 2 Successive, or succeeding by turns. 3 *Bot.* Alternate, with a tendency to become opposite. —*n.* A particular as opposed to a universal proposition. [< Med. L *subalternatus,* pp. of *subalternare.* See SUBALTERNANT.]

sub·al·ter·na·tion (sub·ôl'tər·nā'shən, -al'-) *n.* A succession; a subordination.

sub·ant·arc·tic (sub'ant·ärk'tik, -är'tik) *adj.* Denoting or pertaining to a region contiguous to that within the Antarctic Circle.

sub·a·que·ous (sub·ā'kwē·əs) *adj.* 1 Being, formed, or operating under water; submarine. 2 Occurring under or in water; adapted for use under water. 3 Having an appearance like that produced under water.

sub·ar·id (sub·ar'id) *adj.* Partly arid; moderately dry.

sub·a·tom·ic (sub'ə·tom'ik) *adj.* Within the atom.

sub·au·di·tion (sub'ô·dish'ən) *n.* 1 The understanding or supplying of something not expressed. 2 A thought thus understood or supplied.

sub·ax·il·lar·y (sub·ak'sə·ler'ē) *adj.* 1 *Bot.* Lying under or beneath the axil. 2 *Anat.* Beneath the armpit.

sub·base (sub'bās) *n.* 1 *Archit.* The lowest member of a base or pedestal. 2 A subdivision of a main base, as in a field of military operations. 3 The section of a base line between two fixed points, as the line connecting two microphones in a sound-ranging system.

sub·base·ment (sub'bās'mənt) *n.* An underground story, or any one of several below the first or true basement.

sub·bass (sub'bās') *n.* In an organ, a 16-foot or 32-foot pedal stop. Also **sub'-base'.**

sub·cal·i·ber (sub·kal'ə·bər) *adj. Mil.* Of smaller caliber than the firearm from which it is to be fired: said of a projectile. A tube or disk is used to make up the deficit. Also **sub·cal'i·bre.**

sub·car·ti·lag·i·nous (sub·kär'tə·laj'ə·nəs) *adj. Anat.* 1 Beneath cartilage or under tissue. 2 Partly cartilaginous.

sub·ce·les·tial (sub'si·les'chəl) *adj.* 1 Lower than celestial; beneath the heavens; mundane. 2 Directly beneath the zenith. —*n.* A subcelestial being.

sub·cel·lar (sub'sel'ər) *n.* A cellar under another cellar.

sub·chlo·ride (sub·klôr'īd, -klō'rīd, -rid) *n.* A basic chloride: copper *subchloride,* Cu₂Cl₂.

sub·class (sub'klas') *n. Biol.* A plant or animal division intermediate between a class and an order; superorder.

sub·cla·vi·an (sub·klā'vē·ən) *Anat. adj.* 1 Situated beneath the clavicle. 2 Of or pertaining to the subclavian vessels. —*n.* A subclavian nerve, muscle, vein, etc. [< NL *subclavius* < L *sub-* under + *clavis* a key]

subclavian artery *Anat.* The large main artery that passes under the clavicle to convey blood to the arm.

subclavian groove *Anat.* A groove made by the subclavian artery or vein on the first rib.

subclavian vein *Anat.* That portion of the main venous trunk of the arm that lies under the clavicle.

sub·cli·max (sub·klī'maks) *n.* 1 A stage prior to or below the climax. 2 *Ecol.* a Any stage in the development of a plant or animal community determined by agencies other than climate which prevent attainment of the normal climax. b Any community so acted upon. —**sub·cli·mac·tic** (sub'klī·mak'tik) *adj.*

sub·clin·i·cal (sub·klin'ə·kəl) *adj.* Not able to be diagnosed by ordinary clinical tests: a *subclinical* infection.

sub·com·mit·tee (sub'kə·mit'ē) *n.* An undercommittee; part of a committee appointed for special work.

sub·con·scious (sub·kon'shəs) *adj.* 1 Only dimly conscious; not clearly discerned by the conscious subject; lacking intellectual clearness. 2 *Psychol.* Denoting such phenomena of mental life as are not attended by full consciousness, as the many automatic processes involved in the performance of familiar actions. —*n.* 1 That portion of mental activity not directly in the focus of consciousness but sometimes susceptible to recall by the proper stimulus. 2 *Psychoanal.* The preconscious. —**sub·con'scious·ly** *adv.* —**sub·con'scious·ness** *n.*

sub·con·ti·nent (sub·kon'tə·nənt) *n.* A great land mass forming part of a continent but having considerable geographical independence, as India.

sub·con·tract (sub·kon'trakt) *n.* A contract subordinate to another contract and assigning part of the work to a third party. —*v.t. & v.i.* (sub'kən·trakt') To make a subcontract (for); arrange for part or all of (work) to be performed by a third party.

sub·con·trac·tor (sub'kən·trak'tər, -kon'trak-) *n.* One who enters into a contract with a contractor to do work embraced in the latter's contract.

sub·cor·tex (sub·kôr'teks) *n. pl.* **·ti·ces** (-tə·sēz) *Anat.* That part of the brain which underlies the cortex. [< NL < L *sub-* under + *cortex* bark]

sub·cul·ture (sub·kul'chər) *n.* 1 *Bacteriol.* A culture of bacteria or other material derived from a preexisting culture. 2 *Sociol.* A group having specific patterns of behavior that set it off from other groups within a culture or society.

sub·cu·ta·ne·ous (sub'kyoo·tā'nē·əs) *adj.* 1 Situated, found, or applied beneath the skin. 2 Hypodermic. [< LL *subcutaneus* < L *sub-* under + *cutis* skin] —**sub'cu·ta'ne·ous·ly** *adv.*

sub·dea·con (sub·dē'kən) *n.* A member of the order of the ministry next below that of deacon, who assists at the Eucharist. [< AF *soudiakene, subdiacne* < Med. L *subdiaconus* (< *sub-* under + *diaconus* deacon), trans. of LGk. *hypodiakonos*] —**sub·dea'con·ate** (-it) *n.*

sub·dean (sub'dēn') *n.* An assistant or substitute dean. [< OF *soudeien* < *sou-* SUB- + *deien* a dean]

sub·dean·er·y (sub·dē'nər·ē) *n. pl.* **·er·ies** The office of a subdean.

sub·deb·u·tante (sub'deb·yoo·tänt', -deb'yoo-tant) *n.* A young girl the year before she becomes a debutante.

sub·del·e·gate (sub·del'ə·gāt, -git) *n.* One who represents a delegate. —*v.t.* (-gāt) **·gat·ed, ·gat·ing** 1 To appoint as a subdelegate. 2 To delegate (authority, etc.) to another.

sub·de·pot (sub·dē'pō, -dep'ō) *n.* An auxiliary depot located near a base of operations.

sub·di·ac·o·nate (sub'dī·ak'ə·nit, -nāt) *adj.* Of or pertaining to the office, rank, or order of subdeacon: also **sub'di·ac'o·nal.** —*n.* The office, rank, or order of subdeacon. [< Med. L *subdiaconatus* < *subdiaconus.* See SUBDEACON.]

sub·dis·ci·pline (sub·dis'ə·plin) *n.* A subdivision of a course of learning.

sub·di·vide (sub'di·vīd') *v.t. & v.i.* **·vid·ed, ·vid·ing** 1 To divide (a part) resulting from a previous division; divide again. 2 To divide (land) into lots for sale or improvement. [< LL *subdividere* < L *sub-* under + *dividere* DIVIDE]

sub·di·vi·sion (sub'di·vizh'ən) *n.* 1 Division following upon division. 2 A part, as of land, resulting from subdividing. See synonyms under PART.

sub·dom·i·nant (sub·dom'ə·nənt) *n. Music* The tone next below the dominant; fourth tone or degree of a major or minor scale. —*adj.* Less important than the dominant.

sub·duce (sub·doos', -dyoos') *v.t.* **·duced, ·duc·ing** *Obs.* 1 To withdraw; take away. 2 To take as a part from a whole; subtract. Also **sub·duct'** (-dukt'). [< L *subducere* < *sub-* from + *ducere* lead] —**sub·duc'tion** (-duk'shən) *n.*

sub·duc·tion (sub·duk'shən) *n. Geol.* The sinking of one tectonic plate beneath the edge of another.

sub·due (sub·doo', -dyoo') *v.t.* **·dued, ·du·ing** 1 To gain dominion over, as by war or force; subjugate; vanquish. 2 To overcome by training, influence, or persuasion; tame. 3 To repress (emotions, impulses, etc.). 4 To reduce the intensity of; soften, as a color or sound. 5 To bring (land) under cultivation. [< OF *soduire* seduce < L *subducere* SUBDUCE: infl. in meaning by L *subdere* overcome] —**sub·du'a·ble** *adj.* —**sub·du'al** *n.* —**sub·du'er** *n.*

Synonyms: beat, break, bridle, conquer, control, crush, master, overbear, overcome, overpower, overwhelm, reduce, repress, subject, suppress, train, vanquish. See CHASTEN, CONQUER, REPRESS.

sub·el·a·phine (sub·el'ə·fīn, -fin) *adj. Zool.* Designating a modified form of elaphine antlers. For illustration see ANTLER.

sub·en·try (sub'en'trē) *n.* An entry made on a list beneath a major entry.

sub·e·qua·to·ri·al (sub·ē'kwə·tôr'ē·əl, -tō'rē-) *adj.* 1 Nearly equatorial. 2 Denoting or belonging to a region adjoining the equatorial region.

su·ber (soo'bər) *n.* Cork. [< L] —**su·be·re·ous** (soo·bir'ē·əs) *adj.*

su·ber·ic (soo·ber'ik) *adj.* Of, pertaining to, or derived from cork.

suberic acid *Chem.* A white crystalline diacid, C₈H₁₄O₄, obtained by the action of nitric acid on cork and on various fatty oils.

su·ber·in (soo'bər·in) *n.* A waxlike, fatty substance formed in cork cells.

su·ber·i·za·tion (soo'bər·ə·zā'shən, -ī·zā'-) *n. Bot.* The transformation of plant cell walls into suberin or cork tissue.

su·ber·ize (soo'bə·rīz) *v.t.* **·ized, ·iz·ing** To make corky, as cell walls.

su·ber·ose (soo'bər·ōs) *adj.* 1 Corky. 2 Of or pertaining to suberin. Also **su'ber·ous** (-əs).

sub·fam·i·ly (sub·fam'ə·lē, -fam'lē) *n. pl.* **·lies** 1 A division of plants or animals next below a family but above the genus. 2 *Ling.* A division of languages below a family and above a branch.

sub·ge·nus (sub·jē'nəs) *n. pl.* **·gen·e·ra** (-jen'ər·ə) A primary subdivision of a genus including one or more species with common characters. —**sub'ge·ner'ic** (-ji·ner'ik) *adj.*

sub·gla·cial (sub·glā'shəl) *adj.* Deposited or formed at the bottom of or beneath a glacier.

sub·group (sub'group') *n.* 1 An inferior order, or one of the biological divisions of an order. 2 *Chem.* A group that is included within a superior group, as in the periodic table of the elements.

sub·head (sub'hed') *n.* 1 A heading or title of a subdivision: also **sub·head'ing.** 2 An official next below the head in a college or school.

sub·hu·man (sub·hyoo'mən) *adj.* 1 Less than or imperfectly human. 2 *Anthropol.* Below the level of the primate type represented by *Homo sapiens.*

sub·hu·mid (sub·hyoo'mid) *adj.* Intermediate between semiarid and humid: said especially of a climate with sufficient precipitation to support a moderate to dense growth of tall and short grasses.

Su·bic (soo'bik) A municipality of central Luzon, Philippines, at the head of **Subic Bay,** an inlet of the South China Sea near Bataan Peninsula; site of U.S. landing in World War II, January, 1945.

sub·in·ci·sion (sub'in·sizh'ən) *n.* 1 A cutting beneath or under. 2 Among certain primitive peoples, a slitting open of the urethra of the penis.

sub·in·dex (sub·in'deks) *n. pl.* **·in·dices** (-in'də·sēz) An indicative figure, letter, or sign following and usually underneath a figure, letter, or sign: in Mₙ, X₂, Y₄, the subindices are n, 2, and 4.

sub·in·feu·date (sub'in·fyoo'dāt) *v.t. & v.i.* **·dat·ed, ·dat·ing** To sublet by subinfeudation. Also **sub'in·feud'.**

sub·in·feu·da·tion (sub'in·fyoo·dā'shən) *n.* 1 The granting of lands by a feudal vassal to a tenant who thus becomes his vassal. 2 The feud or fief resulting from subinfeudation. —**sub·in·feu·da·to·ry** (sub'in·fyoo'də·tôr'ē, -tō'rē) *adj.*

sub·in·trant (sub·in'trənt) *adj.* 1 Occurring

or entering secretly. 2 *Pathol.* Anticipating a recurrence of, as a paroxysm, a malarial fever, etc. [<L *subintrans, -antis,* ppr. of *subintrare* <*sub-* secretly + *intrare* enter] —**sub·in′·trance** (-trəns) *n.*

sub·ir·ri·gate (sub·ir′ə·gāt) *v.t.* **·gat·ed, ·gat·ing** To irrigate through underground pipes, etc. —**sub′ir·ri·ga′tion** *n.*

su·bi·to (sōō′bē·tō) *adv. Music* Quickly; suddenly. [<Ital. <L *subitus,* pp. of *subire* come or go stealthily <*sub-* secretly + *ire* go]

sub·ja·cent (sub·jā′sənt) *adj.* 1 Situated underneath. 2 Being at a lower elevation. [<L *subjacens, -entis,* ppr. of *subjacere* < *sub-* under + *jacere* lie] —**sub·ja′cen·cy** *n.*

sub·ject (sub′jikt) *adj.* 1 Being under the power of another; owing or yielding obedience to sovereign authority. 2 Exposed to some agency or tendency: *subject* to headache; a climate *subject* to storms. 3 Being under discretionary authority: a treaty *subject* to ratification. —*n.* 1 One who is under the governing power of another, as of a ruler or government, especially of a monarch. 2 One who or that which is employed or treated in a specified way, as a body for dissection, a person used in hypnotic experiments, one attacked by or liable to any disease. 3 Something upon which thought or the artistic constructive faculty is employed, as a theme of consideration or the general idea or plan of an artistic work. 4 *Gram.* The word, phrase, or clause of a sentence about which something is stated or asked in the predicate. 5 *Music* The melodic phrase on which a composition or a part of it is based. 6 A branch of learning. 7 The originating clause or motive. 8 The ego or self; that of which qualities or attributes are affirmed; substance; essential being; the thinking, feeling agent. 9 *Logic* In a proposition, that term about which something is affirmed or denied. See PROPOSITION. See synonyms under TOPIC. —*v.t.* (səb·jekt′) 1 To bring under dominion or control; subjugate. 2 To cause to undergo some experience or action. 3 To offer for consideration or approval; submit. 4 To make liable; expose: His inheritance was *subjected* to heavy taxation. 5 *Obs.* To place beneath. See synonyms under CONQUER, SUBDUE. [<OF *suget, sujet* <L *subjectus,* pp. of *subjicere* <*sub-* under + *jacere* throw; refashioned after L]

Synonyms (adj.): dependent, disposed, exposed, inferior, liable, obnoxious, prone, subordinate. *Antonyms*: clear, exempt, free, supreme, uncontrolled, unrestrained.

sub·jec·tion (səb·jek′shən) *n.* The act of making subject or bringing into a state of subjection.

sub·jec·tive (səb·jek′tiv) *adj.* 1 Relating to, or conditioned by, mental states or the ego; proceeding from or taking place within the thinking subject: opposed to *objective.* 2 Pertaining to the real nature or essence or substance of a person or thing; inherent; essential. 3 Peculiar to an individual; fanciful; illusory. 4 Inclined to be submissive; obedient. 5 *Gram.* Designating that case of the substantive used to denote its function as subject of a finite verb. 6 In literature and art, giving prominence to the subject or author as treating of his inner experience and emotion. 7 Introspective. —**sub·jec′tive·ly** *adv.* —**sub·jec′·tive·ness, sub·jec·tiv·i·ty** (sub′jek·tiv′ə·tē) *n.*

◆ *Subjective* and *objective,* paired words, are strictly speaking neither synonyms nor antonyms. In scholasticism and philosophies of idealism they are both concerned with the object perceived, but represent different approaches to it. *Objective* signifies the relating of mental states to an object, that is, to something outside the perceiving mind which is recognized as having an existence outside that mind. *Subjective* relates to a feeling, attitude, or cognition that is recognized as being a construct within the mind of the perceiver, even though it takes the external object as its point of departure. Different individuals may receive different *subjective* impressions from the same *objective* fact. See INHERENT, OBJECTIVE.

sub·jec·tiv·ism (səb·jek′tiv·iz′əm) *n.* 1 The doctrine that knowledge is merely subjective and relative and is derived from one's own consciousness. 2 The doctrine that we know directly no external object. 3 The doctrine that there is no objective standard, test, or measure of truth; relativism. 4 The doctrine that individual feeling is the standard by which to judge right and wrong. —**sub·jec′tiv·ist** *n.* —**sub·jec′tiv·is′tic** *adj.*

subject matter The object of consideration or study; the subject of thought.

sub·join (sub·join′) *v.t.* To add at the end; attach; affix. See synonyms under ADD. [<MF *subjoindre* <L *subjungere* <*sub-* in addition + *jungere* join]

sub·join·der (sub·join′dər) *n.* Something subjoined. [<SUBJOIN, on analogy with *rejoinder*]

sub ju·di·ce (sub jōō′di·sē) *Latin* Under judicial consideration.

sub·ju·gate (sub′jōō·gāt) *v.t.* **·gat·ed, ·gat·ing** 1 To bring under dominion; conquer; subdue. 2 To make subservient in any way; enslave. See synonyms under CONQUER. [<L *subjugatus,* pp. of *subjugare* <*sub-* under + *jugum* a yoke] —**sub′ju·ga′tion** *n.* —**sub′ju·ga′·tor** *n.*

sub·junc·tion (səb·jungk′shən) *n.* 1 The act of subjoining, or the state of being subjoined. 2 That which is subjoined. [<LL *subjunctio, -onis* <L *subjungere* SUBJOIN]

sub·junc·tive (səb·jungk′tiv) *Gram. adj.* Of or pertaining to that mood of the finite verb that is used to express a future contingency, a supposition implying the contrary, a mere supposition with indefinite time, or a wish or desire. In English the forms of the subjunctive mood are introduced by conjunctions of condition, doubt, contingency, possibility, etc., as *if, though, lest, unless, that, till,* or *whether,* but verbs in conditional clauses are not always in the subjunctive mood, for the use of these conjunctions with the indicative is very common. —*n.* 1 The subjunctive mood. 2 A verb form or construction in this mood. [<L *subjunctivus* <*subjunctus,* pp. of *subjungere* SUBJOIN]

sub·king·dom (sub·king′dəm) *n.* A phylum.

sub·lap·sar·i·an (sub′lap·sâr′ē·ən) *n.* A believer in the predestinarian view held by moderate Calvinists that God foresaw the fall of man and decreed to save some by election. —*adj.* Relating to the sublapsarians or to their tenets. [<NL *sublapsarius* <L *sub-* consequent upon, under + *lapsus* a fall] —**sub′·lap·sar′i·an·ism** *n.*

sub·la·tion (sub·lā′shən) *n. Med.* The detachment, displacement, or removal of a part. [<L *sublatio, -onis* <*sublatus,* pp. to *tollere* lift up, take away]

sub·lease (sub·lēs′) *v.t.* **·leased, ·leas·ing** To obtain or let (property) on a sublease. —*n.* (sub′lēs′) A lease of property from a tenant or lessee.

sub·let (sub·let′, sub′let′) *v.t.* **·let, ·let·ting** 1 To let to another (property held on a lease); underlet. 2 To let (work that one has contracted to do) to a subordinate contractor.

sub·le·thal (sub·lē′thəl) *adj.* Having an effect short of death: a *sublethal* dose of poison.

sub·li·mate (sub′lə·māt) *v.* **·mat·ed, ·mat·ing** *v.t.* 1 *Chem.* To convert from a solid to a vapor by heat, and then solidify again by cooling, with no apparent intermediate liquefaction. 2 To refine; purify. 3 *Psychol.* To convert the energy of (primitive impulses) into acceptable social and cultural manifestations. —*v.i.* 4 To undergo or engage in sublimation. —*adj.* Sublimated; refined. —*n. Chem.* The product of sublimation, especially when regarded as purified by the process. [<L *sublimatus,* pp. of *sublimare* <*sublimis* SUBLIME]

sub·li·ma·tion (sub′lə·mā′shən) *n.* 1 The act or process of sublimating. 2 That which has been sublimated; the pure essence of a thing. 3 *Psychol.* The transfer of psychic energy into socially acceptable channels of endeavor.

sub·lime (sə·blīm′) *adj.* 1 Characterized by elevation, nobility, or awe; grand; solemn. 2 Preeminent for nobility of character or attainment; majestic; noble: said of persons. 3 Being of the highest degree; supreme; utmost. 4 *Poetic* Of lofty bearing; haughty; proud; elated. —*n.* That which is sublime, in any sense: usually with the definite article. —*v.* **·limed, ·lim·ing** *v.t.* 1 To make sublime; ennoble. 2 To purify by sublimating. —*v.i.* To become sublimated. [<L *sublimis* lofty, prob. <*sub-* up to, under + *limen* a lintel] —**sub·lime′ly** *adv.* —**sub·lim′er** *n.* —**sub·lim·i·ty** (sə·blim′ə·tē), **sub·lime′ness** *n.*

Synonyms (adj.): beautiful, exalted, grand, lofty, magnificent, majestic, stately. *Sublime* represents the ultimate, the quintessence, and is seldom applied to persons. What is *beautiful* attracts, but what is *sublime* transcends the beautiful and inspires awe rather than simple delight. *Majestic* refers exclusively to superficial effect which makes an impression but has no connection with moral greatness. *Magnificent* denotes the possession at once of greatness, splendor, and richness; as, *magnificent* array. See GRAND. *Antonyms*: base, contemptible, insignificant, little, mean, petty, ridiculous.

Sublime Porte See PORTE.

sub·lim·i·nal (sub·lim′ə·nəl) *adj. Psychol.* 1 Below the threshold of consciousness: opposed to *supraliminal*: said of psychophysical changes of too small intensity to produce definite sensations or a clear awareness: a *subliminal* stimulus. 2 Belonging to the subconscious. [<SUB- + L *limen, liminis* a threshold, trans. of G *unter der Schwelle (des Bewusstseins)* under the threshold (of consciousness)]

sub·lin·gual (sub·ling′gwəl) *adj.* 1 Situated beneath the tongue. 2 Of or pertaining to the salivary gland situated beneath the tongue.

sub·lit·to·ral (sub·lit′ər·əl) *adj.* 1 Close to the seashore. 2 Pertaining to or designating the area between low–tide mark and a depth of 20 fathoms or of 40 meters.

sub·lu·nar·y (sub′lōō·ner′ē, sub·lōō′nər·ē) *adj.* 1 Situated beneath the moon: also **sub·lu·nar** (sub·lōō′nər). 2 Terrestrial; earthly. [<NL *sublunaris* <L *sub-* under + *luna* the moon]

sub·ma·chine gun (sub′mə·shēn′) A lightweight, gas–operated gun, automatic or semi–automatic in action, designed for firing from the shoulder or hip. —**Thompson submachine gun** An air–cooled, .45–caliber submachine gun with automatic firing action: also called *Tommy gun*: named for its inventor, John T. *Thompson,* 1860–1940, U.S. Army officer.

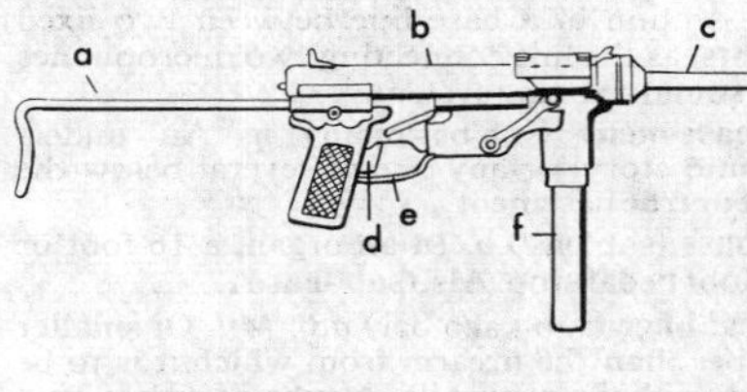

SUBMACHINE GUN
a. Stock. *b.* Housing. *c.* Barrel. *d.* Trigger. *e.* Trigger guard. *f.* Clip.

sub·mar·gin·al (sub·mär′jən·əl) *adj.* 1 Below the margin. 2 Below economic sufficiency: *submarginal* land. 3 *Biol.* Situated close to the margin of an organ or structure.

submarginal land *Agric.* Land of such low degree of fertility or productivity as to be incapable of furnishing an economic return.

sub·ma·rine (sub′mə·rēn′) *adj.* Existing, done, or operating beneath the surface of the sea: a *submarine* mine: contrasted with *subaerial.* —*n.* (sub′mə·rēn) A boat designed to operate both on, and at various depths below, the surface of the sea, and now often powered by a reactor using nuclear fuel.

submarine chaser A small patrol vessel designed for action against submarines.

sub·mar·i·ner (sub·mar′ə·nər) *n.* A trained and qualified member of a submarine crew.

sub·max·il·lar·y (sub·mak′sə·ler′ē) *Anat. adj.* 1 Of, pertaining to, or situated beneath the lower jaw. 2 Of or pertaining to one of the salivary glands situated near the angle of the lower jaw. —*n. pl.* **·lar·ies** The lower jaw bone: also **sub·max·il·la** (sub′mak·sil′ə).

sub·me·di·ant (sub·mē′dē·ənt) *n. Music* The sixth tone of a major or minor scale.

sub·men·tal (sub·men′təl) *adj.* 1 *Anat.* Situated beneath the chin: the *submental* artery. 2 Of or pertaining to the submentum.

sub·men·tum (sub·men′təm) *n. Entomol.* The basal sclerite of the labium of an insect, between the gula and the mentum. [<NL <L *sub-* under + *mentum* the chin]

sub·merge (səb·mûrj′) *v.* **·merged, ·merg·ing** *v.t.* 1 To place under or plunge into water. 2 To cover; hide. —*v.i.* 3 To sink or dive beneath the surface of water. Also **sub·merse′**

(-mûrs′). See synonyms under IMMERSE. [<L *submergere,* var. of *summergere* <*sub-* under + *mergere* plunge] — **sub·mer′gence, sub·mer′·sion** (-mûr′shən, -zhən) *n.*
sub·mer·gi·ble (səb·mûr′jə·bəl) *adj.* Capable of being submerged. — **sub·mer′gi·bil′i·ty** *n.*
sub·mersed (səb·mûrst′) *adj.* **1** *Bot.* Growing under water. **2** Submerged. [<L *submersus,* pp. of *submergere* SUBMERGE]
sub·mers·i·ble (səb·mûr′sə·bəl) *adj.* That may be submerged. — *n.* A submarine.
sub·mi·cron (sub·mī′kron) *n.* A particle of from 50 to 1,000 angstroms in diameter.
sub·mi·cro·scop·ic (sub·mī′krə·skop′ik) *adj.* Below the limit of vision in a microscope.
sub·mine (sub′mīn′) *n.* A small, electrically actuated mine located near a submarine mine and used in the training of navy personnel.
sub·min·i·a·ture camera (sub′min′ē·ə·chŏŏr) A miniature camera using 16-mm. film for taking still photographs.
sub·min·i·a·tur·ize (sub·min′ē·ə·chə·rīz′) *v.t.* **·ized, ·iz·ing** To reduce, as certain delicate instruments, to the smallest size compatible with efficient use and service, as in the design and production of hearing aids. — **sub·min′i·a·tur·i·za′tion** *n.*
sub·miss (səb·mis′) *adj. Archaic* Submissive; soft; subdued. [<L *submissus,* pp. of *submittere* SUBMIT]
sub·mis·sion (səb·mish′ən) *n.* **1** The act of submitting; a yielding to the power or authority of another; obedience. **2** The state or quality of being submissive; the spirit of subjection or obedience; an acquiescent temper; humility; resignation; meekness. **3** The act of referring, or the agreement to refer, a matter of controversy to arbitration. **4** *Archaic* Acknowledgment of error.
Synonyms: obedience, patience, resignation, subjection, submissiveness. See PATIENCE.
sub·mis·sive (səb·mis′iv) *adj.* Willing or inclined to submit; yielding; obedient; docile. See synonyms under DOCILE, HUMBLE, OBSEQUIOUS, PASSIVE, SUPPLE. — **sub·mis′sive·ly** *adv.* — **sub·mis′sive·ness** *n.*
sub·mit (səb·mit′) *v.* **·mit·ted, ·mit·ting** *v.t.* **1** To place under or yield to the authority, will, or power of another; surrender. **2** To present for the consideration, decision, or approval of others; refer. **3** To present as one's opinion; suggest. — *v.i.* **4** To give up; surrender. **5** To be obedient or submissive; be acquiescent. See synonyms under BEND¹, DEFER, OBEY. [<L *submittere,* var. of *summittere* <*sub-* underneath + *mittere* send] — **sub·mit′tal** *n.* — **sub·mit′ter** *n.*
sub·mon·tane (sub·mon′tān) *adj.* **1** Situated at the foot of a mountain or mountain range. **2** Beneath a mountain. — **sub·mon′tane·ly** *adv.*
sub·mul·ti·ple (sub·mul′tə·pəl) *n. Math.* A number or quantity that is contained in another without remainder; an aliquot part. — *adj.* Contained in something an exact number of times. [<LL *submultiplus* <*sub-* opposite of, lesser + *multiplus* MULTIPLE]
sub·nor·mal (sub·nôr′məl) *adj.* **1** Below the normal. **2** *Psychol.* Of less than normal intelligence. — *n.* **1** *Math.* That portion of the axis of a curve included between the ordinate of one of its points and the normal to that point. **2** A subnormal individual. — **sub·nor·mal·i·ty** (sub′nôr·mal′ə·tē) *n.*
sub·o·ce·an·ic (sub′ō·shē·an′ik) *adj.* Occurring, formed, or happening beneath the ocean floor.
sub·or·der (sub′ôr′dər) *n.* **1** *Biol.* A category of animals or plants next below an order. **2** A subordinate architectural order modifying the principal order, generally for decoration. — **sub·or·di·nal** (sub·ôr′də·nəl) *adj.*
sub·or·di·nar·y (sub·ôr′də·ner′ē) *n. pl.* **·nar·ies** *Her.* One of a class of armorial charges usually considered less honorable than the ordinaries. Among them are the *bordure, flanch, orle, tressure,* etc.
sub·or·di·nate (sə·bôr′də·nit) *adj.* **1** Belonging to an inferior order in a classification; secondary; minor. **2** Subject or subservient to another; inferior in any way. **3** Dependent; joining dependent words to others. See synonyms under AUXILIARY, SUBJECT. — *n.* One who is subordinate; an inferior in rank or official position. — *v.t.* (-nāt) **·nat·ed, ·nat·ing** **1** To make subordinate; assign to a lower order or rank; hence, to hold as of less importance. **2** To make subject or subservient. [<L *subordinatus,* pp. of *subordinare* <*sub-* under + *ordinare* order] — **sub·or′di·nate·ly** *adv.* — **sub·or′di·nate·ness** *n.* — **sub·or′di·na′tion** *n.*
subordinate conjunction See under CONJUNCTION.
sub·or·di·na·tion·ism (sə·bôr′də·nā′shən·iz′əm) *n. Theol.* The doctrine that the second and third persons of the Trinity are inferior to the first person. — **sub·or′di·na′tion·ist** *n.*
sub·or·di·na·tive (sə·bôr′də·nā′tiv) *adj.* Having a tendency to or expressive of subordination.
sub·orn (sə·bôrn′) *v.t.* **1** To bribe or procure (someone) to commit perjury. **2** To incite or instigate to an evil act, especially a criminal act. **3** *Obs.* To decorate or adorn. [<L *subornare* <*sub-* secretly + *ornare* equip] — **sub·orn′er** *n.* — **sub·or·na·tion** (sub′ôr·nā′shən) *n.*
Su·bo·ti·ca (sōō′bô·ti·tsä) A city in northern Serbia, Yugoslavia: German *Maria Theresiopel,* Hungarian *Szabadka.* Also **Su′bo′ti·tsa.**
sub·ox·ide (sub·ok′sīd) *n. Chem.* An oxide having the minimum amount of oxygen.
sub·phy·lum (sub·fī′ləm) *n. Biol.* A primary division of a phylum, superior to the class.
sub·plinth (sub′plinth′) *n. Archit.* A block or base supporting a plinth; a second or lower plinth.
sub–plot (sub′plot′) *n.* A plot subordinate to the principal one in a novel, play, etc.
sub·poe·na (sə·pē′nə, səb-) *n.* A judicial writ requiring a person to appear at a specified time and place under penalty for default. — *v.t.* To notify or summon by writ or subpoena. Also **sub·pe′na.** [<Med. L <L *sub poena* <*sub* under + *poena* penalty]
sub–port (sub′pôrt′, -pōrt′) *n.* An auxiliary port, equipped to handle traffic diverted from the main port.
sub–post (sub′pōst′) *n.* An administrative subdivision of a military post.
sub·pre·fect (sub·prē′fekt) *n.* A subordinate prefect; in France, the administrative officer of an arrondissement. — **sub·pre′fec·ture** (-fek·chər) *n.*
sub·prin·ci·pal (sub·prin′sə·pəl) *n.* **1** A vice principal. **2** A rafter or brace next to or auxiliary to one of the main timbers of the frame. **3** *Music* An open diapason sub–bass in an organ.
sub·ra·mose (sub·rā′mōs) *adj. Bot.* **1** Branching moderately, as a plant. **2** Having few branches. [<NL *subramosus* <L *sub-* somewhat, under + *ramosus* RAMOSE]
sub·re·gion (sub′rē′jən) *n.* A subdivision of a region, especially with reference to the distribution of animals. — **sub·re′gion·al** *adj.*
sub·rep·tion (səb·rep′shən) *n.* **1** A procuring of some favor or reward by means of a fraudulent concealment or suppression of the truth. **2** Inference resulting from concealment, or misrepresentation of essential elements or facts. [<L *subreptio, -onis* <*subreptus,* pp. of *subripere* <*sub-* secretly + *rapere* snatch, seize]
sub·ro·gate (sub′rō·gāt) *v.t.* **·gat·ed, ·gat·ing** **1** To substitute (one thing) for another. **2** To substitute (one person) for another when attributing or assigning rights or appointing to an office. [<L *subrogatus,* pp. of *subrogare* substitute <*sub-* in place of + *rogare* ask]
sub·ro·ga·tion (sub′rō·gā′shən) *n.* **1** The succession or substitution of one person or thing by or for another. **2** *Law* The putting of a person who (as a surety) has paid the debt of another in the place of the creditor to whom he has paid it.
sub ro·sa (sub rō′zə) *Latin* Confidentially; in secret: literally, under the rose: because, in Egypt, the rose was the emblem of Horus, (Roman Harpocrates), mistakenly regarded by the Greeks and Romans as the god of silence, for he was often depicted as a child with finger on mouth.
sub·scap·u·lar (sub·skap′yə·lər) *adj. Anat.* Situated underneath the scapula. Also **sub·scap′u·lar′y** (-ler′ē). [<NL *subscapularis* <L *sub-* under + *scapula* a shoulder blade]
sub·scribe (səb·skrīb′) *v.* **·scribed, ·scrib·ing** *v.t.* **1** To write, as one's name, at the end of a document; sign. **2** To sign one's name to as an expression of assent, acceptance, etc.; attest to by signing. **3** To promise, especially in writing, to pay or contribute (a sum of money). — *v.i.* **4** To write one's name at the end of a document. **5** To give sanction, support, or approval; agree. **6** To promise to pay or contribute money. **7** To agree to receive and pay for an article, as a periodical, usually by written agreement: with *to.* [<L *subscribere* <*sub-* underneath + *scribere* write] — **sub·scrib′er** *n.*
sub·script (sub′skript) *adj.* **1** Written following and slightly beneath, as a small letter: iota *subscript.* **2** *Math.* Of a subindex. — *n.* A subscript sign, symbol, or letter. Compare SUPERSCRIPT. [<L *subscriptus,* pp. of *subscribere.* See SUBSCRIBE.]
sub·scrip·tion (səb·skrip′shən) *n.* **1** The act of subscribing; signature; hence, consent, confirmation, or agreement. **2** That which is subscribed; a signed paper or statement. **3** A signature written at the end of a document. **4** A signed acceptance of religious articles. **5** The individual or total sum or number subscribed for any purpose. **6** A formal agreement or undertaking evinced by signature, as payment of a certain price for the receipt of a magazine, book, ticket, etc. **7** *Archaic* Submission; obedience. **8** The part of a doctor's prescription which gives directions for compounding the ingredients. **9** The sale of books, magazines, tickets, etc., by mail or by personal canvass. — **to take up a subscription** To collect money (for some special purpose or cause) from a large number of people. — **sub·scrip′tive** *adj.* — **sub·scrip′tive·ly** *adv.*
subscription list A list of the names of people and the amounts they have subscribed, as for a periodical, a charity, or other cause.
sub·sec·tion (sub·sek′shən, sub′sek′shən) *n.* A subdivision of a section.
sub·sec·tor (sub·sek′tər, sub′sek′tər) *n.* A portion of a military sector or coastal frontier marked out for convenience in operations.
sub·se·quence (sub′sə·kwəns) *n.* **1** The condition of being subsequent. **2** The act of following. Also **sub′se·quen·cy.**
sub·se·quent (sub′sə·kwənt) *adj.* **1** Following in time, place, or order, or as a result. **2** Succeeding; consequent. [<L *subsequens, -entis,* ppr. of *subsequi* <*sub-* next below + *sequi* follow] — **sub′se·quent·ly** *adv.* — **sub′se·quent·ness** *n.*
sub·serve (səb·sûrv′) *v.t.* **·served, ·serv·ing** **1** To be of use or help in furthering (a process, cause, etc.); serve; promote. **2** To serve as a subordinate to (a person). See synonyms under SERVE. [<L *subservire* <*sub-* under + *servire* SERVE]
sub·ser·vi·ent (səb·sûr′vē·ənt) *adj.* **1** Adapted to promote some end or purpose; being of service; useful as a subordinate. **2** Hence, acting in the interests of another; servile; obsequious; truckling. — *n.* One who or that which subserves. See synonyms under BASE². [<L *subserviens, -entis,* ppr. of *subservire* SUBSERVE] — **sub·ser′vi·ent·ly** *adv.* — **sub·ser′vi·ent·ness, sub·ser′vi·ence, sub·ser′vi·en·cy** *n.*
sub–shrub (sub′shrub′) *n.* An undershrub or very small shrub. — **sub′–shrub′by** *adj.*
sub·side (səb·sīd′) *v.i.* **·sid·ed, ·sid·ing** **1** To sink to a lower level. **2** To become less violent or agitated; become calm or quiet; abate. **3** To sink to the bottom, as sediment; settle. See synonyms under ABATE, FALL. [<L *subsidere* <*sub-* under + *sidere* settle <*sedere* sit]
sub·sid·ence (səb·sīd′ns, sub′sə·dəns) *n.* **1** The settling of heavy parts to the bottom; precipitation. **2** The sinking of water or other liquids to a lower or usual level: *subsidence* of a flood. **3** A gradual settling into a quiet or inactive state. **4** A gradual settling of the earth to a lower level, because of ground movements or underground workings. [<L *subsidentia* sediment <*subsidere* SUBSIDE]
sub·sid·i·ar·y (səb·sid′ē·er′ē) *adj.* **1** Assisting in an inferior capacity; supplementary; auxiliary; secondary. **2** Of, pertaining to, or in the nature of a subsidy; helping by a subsidy. — *n. pl.* **·ar·ies** **1** One who or that which furnishes supplemental aid or supplies; an auxiliary; assistant. **2** *Music* A theme subordinate to or dependent on the main theme

or subject. [<L *subsidiarius* <*subsidium* <*subsidere* SUBSIDE] **— sub·sid′i·ar′i·ly** *adv.*

subsidiary coin Coin of small denomination, legal tender only to a limited amount; in the United States, any coin worth less than a dollar.

subsidiary company A company controlled by another company which owns the greater part of its shares.

sub·si·dize (sub′sə·dīz) *v.t.* **·dized, ·diz·ing 1** To furnish with a subsidy; grant a regular allowance or pecuniary aid to. **2** To obtain the assistance of by a subsidy: now often implying bribery. Also *Brit.* **sub′si·dise. — sub′si·di·za′tion** *n.* **— sub′si·diz′er** *n.*

sub·si·dy (sub′sə·dē) *n. pl.* **·dies 1** Pecuniary aid directly granted by government to an individual or private commercial enterprise deemed beneficial to the public. **2** Formerly, an aid or tax granted by the House of Commons to the king for urgent needs of the kingdom. **3** Any financial assistance afforded by one individual or government to another. [<AF *subsidie,* OF *subside* <L *subsidium* auxiliary forces, aid <*subsidere* SUBSIDE]

Synonyms: aid, allowance, bonus, bounty, gift, grant, indemnity, pension, premium, reward, support, subvention, tribute. A nation grants a *subsidy* to an ally, pays a *tribute* to a conqueror. An *indemnity* is a single reparation demanded for a specific injury, while a *tribute* may be exacted indefinitely. A nation may also grant a *subsidy* to its own citizens as a means of promoting the public welfare; as, a *subsidy* to a steamship company. The somewhat rare term *subvention* is especially applied to a *grant* of governmental aid to a literary or artistic enterprise. The word *bounty* may be applied to almost any regular or stipulated *allowance* by a government to a citizen or citizens; as, a *bounty* for enlisting in the army, a *bounty* for killing wolves, a land *bounty* to encourage settlement of sparsely populated areas. A *bounty* is reward for a single act; a *pension* is earned by long service.

sub·sist (səb·sist′) *v.i.* **1** To have existence or reality; continue to exist. **2** To remain alive; manage to live. **3** To continue unchanged; abide. **4** To have existence in or by something; inhere. **—** *v.t. Obs.* **5** To provide with food and clothing; support. See synonyms under LIVE. [<MF *subsister* <L *subsistere* <*sub-* under + *sistere* cause to stand <*stare* stand] **— sub·sist′er** *n.*

sub·sis·tence (səb·sis′təns) *n.* **1** The act of subsisting. **2** That on which one subsists; sustenance; means of support; livelihood. **3** The state of being subsistent; inherent quality. **4** That which subsists; real being. **5** A basis; a logical substance; hypostasis. Also **sub·sis′ten·cy.** [<LL *subsistentia* <*subsistere* SUBSIST]

subsistence department A former department of the army that provided and had charge of subsistence stores: these are now purchased and issued by the Quartermaster Corps: also called *commissary department.*

sub·sis·tent (səb·sis′tənt) *adj.* **1** That subsists or is inherent. **2** Existing; having real being or action. **3** Having subsistence.

sub·soil (sub′soil′) *n.* The stratum of earth next beneath the surface soil. **—** *v.t.* To turn up the subsoil of; plow with a subsoil plow. **— sub′soil′er** *n.*

subsoil plow *Agric.* A plow specially designed for loosening or turning up the subsoil.

sub·so·lar (sub·sō′lər) *adj.* **1** Situated directly beneath the sun, as at high noon at the equinoxes; also, between the tropics. **2** Mundane; earthly.

sub·son·ic (sub·son′ik) *adj.* **1** Designating those sound waves beyond the lower limits of human audibility, or with frequencies of less than about 25 cycles per second; infrasonic. **2** Of, pertaining to, characterized, or operated by such waves. Compare SUPERSONIC.

sub·spe·cies (sub·spē′shēz, -shiz) *n. Biol.* A subdivision of a species, variously ranked but usually distinguished by minor differences in characteristics and by having a particular geographic range within a larger area. [<NL <L *sub-* under + *species* an appearance, sort]

sub·stance (sub′stəns) *n.* **1** The material of which anything is made or constituted. **2** The essential part of anything said or written, put into a brief, condensed statement; the gist or purport. **3** The vital part of that which is spiritual or emotional. **4** Material possessions; wealth; property. **5** That which gives stability or solidity; confidence; ground. **6** *Philos.* The essential nature that underlies phenomena; the permanent cause underlying outward manifestations; that in which qualities or attributes inhere. **7** In Christian Science, Spirit. **8** Any particular kind of material. **9** Essential components or characteristic elements of ideas: The tenets are the same in *substance.* See synonyms under MASS[1]. [<OF <L *substantia* <*substare* be present <*sub-* under + *stare* stand]

sub·stan·dard (sub·stan′dərd) *adj.* **1** Below the standard. **2** Lower than the established rate or authorized requirements.

sub·stan·tial (səb·stan′shəl) *adj.* **1** Solid; strong; firm. **2** Of real worth and importance; of considerable value; valuable. **3** Considerable and sure. **4** Possessed of wealth or sufficient means; responsible. **5** Of or pertaining to substance; having real existence; not illusory; actual; permanent; lasting. **6** Containing or conforming to the essence of a thing; giving the correct idea; essential; material; fundamental. **7** Ample and nourishing. **—** *n.* **1** That which has substance; a reality. **2** The more important part. **— sub·stan′ti·al′i·ty** · (-shē·al′ə·tē), **sub·stan′tial·ness** *n.* **— sub·stan′tial·ly** *adv.*

sub·stan·tial·ism (səb·stan′shəl·iz′əm) *n. Philos.* The doctrine that substantial realities are the sources or underlying ground of all phenomena, material and mental; the doctrine that matter is a real substance. **— sub·stan′tial·ist** *n.*

sub·stan·ti·ate (səb·stan′shē·āt) *v.t.* **·at·ed, ·at·ing 1** To establish, as a position or a truth, by substantial evidence; verify. **2** To give form to; embody. **3** To make substantial, existent, or real; give substance to. See synonyms under CONFIRM, RATIFY. [<NL *substantiatus,* pp. of *substantiare* establish <L *substantia* SUBSTANCE] **— sub·stan′ti·a′tion** *n.* **— sub·stan′ti·a′tive** *adj.*

sub·stan·ti·val (sub′stən·tī′vəl) *adj.* **1** Of or pertaining to a substantive. **2** Self-existent. **— sub′stan·ti′val·ly** *adv.*

sub·stan·tive (sub′stən·tiv) *n.* **1** A noun. **2** Anything used in place of a noun, as a verbal form, phrase, or clause. **3** One who or that which is independent; a self-subsisting person or thing. **—** *adj.* **1** Capable of being used as a noun. **2** Expressive of or denoting existence: The verb "to be" is called the *substantive* verb. **3** Having substance or reality; hence, lasting. **4** Being an essential part or constituent. **5** Relating to what is essential. **6** Having distinct individuality. **7** Independent in resources; self-supporting, as a country. **8** Of considerable amount; substantial. **9** In dyeing, not needing a mordant. [<OF *substantif* <LL *substantivus* <L *substantia* SUBSTANCE] **— sub′stan·tive·ness** *n.*

substantive dye See under DYE.

sub·stan·tiv·ize (sub′stən·tiv·īz′) *v.t.* **·ized, ·iz·ing** To treat or use as a substantive: The adjective "meek" is *substantivized* in "Blessed are the meek."

sub·sta·tion (sub′stā′shən) *n.* A subsidiary station, as an electric power station for switching, transforming, or converting purposes, a branch post office, etc.

sub·stit·u·ent (səb·stich′ōō·ənt) *n. Chem.* A radical, atom, or group, substituting or replacing another in a chemical reaction. **—** *adj.* Of a substituting atom or molecule. [<L *substituens, -entis,* ppr. of *substituere* SUBSTITUTE]

sub·sti·tute (sub′stə·tōōt, -tyōōt) *v.* **·tut·ed, ·tut·ing** *v.t.* **1** To put in the place of another person or thing. **2** To take the place of. **—** *v.i.* **3** To act as a substitute. **4** *Chem.* To exchange one constituent of a compound for, or replace it with, another. See synonyms under CHANGE. **—** *n.* **1** One who or that which takes the place or serves in lieu of another. **2** In the American Civil War, one hired to serve in the place of a man drafted into military service. **3** Any substance or material adapted to replace another in a given product or process, or for a specified purpose: Gelatin is a *substitute* for agar, synthetic rubber for cork, etc.: also called *alternative, replacement.* See synonyms under DELEGATE. [<L *substitutus,* pp. of *substituere* <*sub-* in place of + *statuere* set up]

sub·sti·tu·tion (sub′stə·tōō′shən, -tyōō′-) *n.* **1** The act of substituting, or the state of being substituted. **2** *Chem.* Any reaction which involves the replacement of certain elements or radicals by others: said especially of organic compounds. **— sub′sti·tu′tion·al** *adj.* **— sub′sti·tu′tion·al·ly** *adv.*

sub·sti·tu·tive (sub′stə·tōō′tiv, -tyōō′-) *adj.* Acting or tending to act as a substitute; admitting of substitution.

sub·strate (sub′strāt) *n.* **1** *Biochem.* The material or substance acted upon by an enzyme or ferment. **2** A substratum. [<SUBSTRATUM]

sub·stra·tum (sub·strā′təm, -strat′əm) *n. pl.* **·stra·ta** (-strā′tə, -strat′ə) **1** An underlying stratum or layer, as of earth or rock; subsoil. **2** That which forms the foundation or groundwork. **3** Matter or mind considered as the ground of qualities and phenomena; the substance possessing attributes. **4** The substance in which something takes root, as vegetable or animal tissue. [<NL <L, pp. neut. of *substernere* spread underneath <*sub-* underneath + *sternere* strew] **— sub·stra′tive** *adj.*

sub·struc·tion (sub·struk′shən) *n.* A foundation. [<F <L *substructio, -onis* <*substruere* <*sub-* underneath + *struere* build] **— sub·struc′tion·al** *adj.*

sub·struc·ture (sub·struk′chər, sub′struk′-) *n.* **1** A structure serving as a foundation of a building, etc. **2** Groundwork. **3** The earthen roadway supporting railroad tracks. **— sub·struc′tur·al** *adj.*

sub·sume (səb·sōōm′) *v.t.* **·sumed, ·sum·ing 1** To place in some particular class; classify. **2** To include, as the specific or individual in the general. [<NL *subsumere* <L *sub-* underneath + *sumere* take] **— sub·sum′a·ble** *adj.*

sub·sump·tion (səb·sump′shən) *n.* **1** The act of subsuming. **2** That which is subsumed; an assumption; especially, the minor premise of a syllogism as stated after the major premise. **3** Formerly, a narrative of an alleged crime giving minute particulars. [<NL *subsumptio, -onis* <*subsumere* SUBSUME] **— sub·sump′tive** *adj.*

sub·tan·gent (sub·tan′jənt) *n. Geom.* The portion of the axis of a curve cut off between the tangent to a given point and the ordinate of that point. [<NL *subtangens, -entis* <L *sub-* under + *tangens,* ppr. of *tangere* touch]

sub·tem·per·ate (sub·tem′pər·it) *adj.* **1** Pertaining to the colder parts of the temperate zone. **2** Slightly temperate.

sub·ten·ant (sub·ten′ənt) *n.* A person who rents or leases from a tenant; a sublessee. **— sub·ten′an·cy** *n.*

sub·tend (sub·tend′) *v.t.* **1** *Geom.* To extend under or opposite to, as the chord of an arc or the side of a triangle opposite to an angle. **2** *Bot.* To enclose in its axil: A leaf *subtends* a bud. [<L *subtendere* <*sub-* underneath + *tendere* stretch]

sub·tense (sub·tens′) *Geom. n.* **1** A line that subtends an arc or angle. **2** The chord of an arc. **—** *adj.* Pertaining to or used in estimating distance by measuring the subtended angle. [<NL *subtensa (linea)* (a) subtended (line), pp. fem. of L *subtendere* SUBTEND]

subter- *prefix* Under; less than: opposed to *super-*: *subteraqueous.* [<L *subter* below, beneath]

sub·ter·a·que·ous (sub′tə·rā′kwē·əs, -rak′wē-) *adj.* Situated beneath the surface of the water. Also **sub′ter·ra′que·ous.** [<L (assumed) *subteraqueus* <*subter-* beneath + *aqua* water]

sub·ter·fuge (sub′tər·fyōōj) *n.* That to which one resorts for escape or concealment; an evasion of an issue; a plan to avoid censure; a false excuse. See synonyms under ARTIFICE, SOPHISTRY. [<L *subterfugium* <*subterfugere* <*subter-* below, in secret + *fugere* flee, take flight]

sub·ter·nat·u·ral (sub′tər·nach′ər·əl) *adj.* Below the norms of nature.

sub·ter·rane (sub′tə·rān) *n.* **1** A basal or underlying terrane. **2** An underground room; a cave. [<L *subterraneus* <*sub-* under + *terra* the earth]

sub·ter·ra·ne·an (sub′tə·rā′nē·ən) *adj.* **1** Situated or occurring below the surface of the earth: contrasted with *subaerial* and *surficial*; underground. **2** Hidden. Also **sub′ter·ra′ne·al, sub′ter·ra′ne·ous, sub′ter·rene′** (-tə·rēn′).

sub·ter·res·tri·al (sub′tə·res′trē·əl) *adj.* Subterranean; lower than the terrestrial. —*n.* A creature that lives underground.

sub·tile (sut′l, sub′til) *adj.* **1** Having fine structure; delicately formed; ethereal. **2** Characterized by material rarity; rarefied; refined; hence, penetrating; pervasive. **3** Subtle. [< OF *subtil,* alter of *soutil* SUBTLE; refashioned after L] —**sub′tile·ly** *adv.* —**sub′tile·ness** *n.*

Synonym: subtle. *Subtile* and *subtle* have been constantly used as interchangeable by good writers; but there is a present tendency to distinguish them by making *subtile* an attribute of things and *subtle* a characteristic of mind. *Subtle,* the later form of the word, is used preferably when the derogatory sense of crafty is to be expressed. See ACUTE, ASTUTE, FINE[1].

sub·til·i·ty (sub·til′ə·tē) *n.* The quality or state of being subtile; thinness; fineness.

sub·til·ize (sut′l·īz, sub′tə·līz) *v.* **·ized, ·iz·ing** *v.t.* **1** To make subtle or subtile; refine. **2** To make acute; sharpen, as the senses. **3** To discuss or argue subtly. —*v.i.* **4** To make subtle distinctions; use subtlety. [<Med. L *subtilizare* <L *subtilis* SUBTLE] —**sub′til·i·za′tion** *n.*

sub·til·ty (sut′l·tē, sub′təl·tē) *n. pl.* **·ties 1** Refinement or niceness, or an instance of it; a nicety. **2** Subtlety.

sub·ti·tle (sub′tīt′l) *n.* A subordinate or explanatory title, as in a book, play, or document; a book title repeated, as on top of the first page of the text.

sub·tle (sut′l) *adj.* **1** Characterized by cunning, craft, or artifice; wily; crafty. **2** Keen; penetrative; discriminating: *subtle* humor; overrefined. **3** Apt; skilful. **4** Executed with nice art; ingenious; clever. **5** Insidious; secretly active. **6** Hard to understand; abstruse. **7** Of delicate texture. **8** Subtile. See synonyms under ACUTE, ASTUTE, FINE[1], INSIDIOUS, SUBTILE. [<OF *soutil* <L *subtilis* fine, orig. closely woven < *sub-* under + *tela* a web] —**sub′tle·ness** *n.* —**sub′tly** *adv.*

sub·tle·ty (sut′l·tē) *n. pl.* **·ties 1** The state or quality of being subtle. **2** The ability to make fine distinctions; keenness of perception. **3** Something subtle, as a nice distinction.

sub·ton·ic (sub·ton′ik) *adj. Phonet.* Sonant or voiced, as certain consonants. —*n.* **1** *Phonet.* A subtonic sound. **2** *Music* The seventh of the scale; a semitone below the tonic.

sub·tor·rid (sub·tôr′id, -tor′-) *adj.* Subtropical.

sub·tract (səb·trakt′) *v.t.* & *v.i.* To take away or deduct, as a portion from the whole, or one quantity from another. [<L *subtractus,* pp. of *subtrahere* < *sub-* away + *trahere* draw] —**sub·tract′er** *n.*

sub·trac·tion (səb·trak′shən) *n.* **1** The act or process of subtracting; a deducting; something deducted. **2** *Math.* The operation of finding the difference between two quantities (symbol −).

sub·trac·tive (səb·trak′tiv) *adj.* **1** Serving or tending to diminish. **2** *Math.* Having the minus sign; to be subtracted.

subtractive process *Phot.* A method of making two or more negatives through filters which exclude all but a desired color: used in color printing and engraving.

sub·tra·hend (sub′trə·hend) *n. Math.* That which is to be subtracted from a number or quantity (the minuend) to give the difference. [<L *subtrahendus (numerus)* (the number) to be subtracted, gerundive of *subtrahere* SUBTRACT]

sub·trans·lu·cent (sub′trans·lo͞o′sənt, -tranz-) *adj.* Not fully translucent, as certain gemstones and other minerals.

sub·treas·ur·y (sub·trezh′ər·ē) *n. pl.* **·ur·ies 1** A branch of the U. S. Treasury Department maintained for receipt and safekeeping of government revenues: established in 1840 and abolished in 1920. **2** The building that housed such a branch. —**sub·treas′ur·er** *n.*

sub·trop·i·cal (sub·trop′i·kəl) *adj.* **1** Of, pertaining to, or designating regions adjacent to the tropical zone. **2** Designating either of two irregular belts of high atmospheric pressure roughly between 30° and 40° latitude, north and south. Also **sub·trop′ic.**

sub·trop·ics (sub·trop′iks) *n. pl.* Subtropical regions.

su·bu·late (so͞o′byə·lāt, -lit) *adj. Biol.* Shaped like an awl; slender and tapering to a point. [<NL *subulatus* <L *subula* an awl]

sub·um·brel·la (sub′um·brel′ə) *n. Zool.* The under surface of the swimming bell of a jellyfish, or that surface situated in the region of the mouth. —**sub·um·bral** (sub·um′brəl), **sub′·um·brel′lar** *adj.*

sub·urb (sub′ûrb) *n.* A place adjacent to a city; in the plural, collectively, environs; outskirts; outlying residential districts; purlieus. [<OF *suburbe* <L *surburbium* < *sub-* near to + *urbs, urbis* a city]

sub·ur·ban (sə·bûr′bən) *adj.* Of or pertaining to a suburb; dwelling or located in a place which is a combination of the rural and urban. —*n.* A suburbanite.

sub·ur·ban·ite (sə·bûr′bən·īt) *n.* A resident of a suburb.

sub·ur·bi·a (sə·bûr′bē·ə) *n.* **1** The social and cultural world of suburbanites. **2** Suburbs or suburbanites collectively.

sub·ur·bi·car·i·an (sə·bûr′bə·kâr′ē·ən) *adj.* Being in the suburbs (of Rome): applied to the six sees that compose the province of the pope as metropolitan. [<LL *suburbicarius* <L *suburbium* SUBURB]

sub·vene (səb·vēn′) *v.i.* **·vened, ·ven·ing** To come or happen so as to be of aid or support, especially by preventing something; intervene. [<L *subvenire* come to one's assistance < *sub-* up from under + *venire* come]

sub·ven·tion (səb·ven′shən) *n.* **1** The act of subvening; giving of succor; aid. **2** That which aids, especially a grant, as of money; subsidy. See synonyms under SUBSIDY. [<OF *subvencion* <LL *subventio, -onis* <L *subvenire.* See SUBVENE.] —**sub·ven′tion·ar′y** (-er′ē) *adj.*

sub·ver·sion (səb·vûr′shən, -zhən) *n.* **1** The act of subverting, or the state of being subverted; a demolition; overthrow. **2** A cause of ruin. Also **sub·ver′sal** (-səl). See synonyms under RUIN. [<OF <LL *subversio, -onis* <L *subvertere* SUBVERT]

sub·ver·sive (səb·vûr′siv) *adj.* Tending to subvert or overthrow. —*n.* A person who engages in subversion.

sub·vert (səb·vûrt′) *v.t.* **1** To overthrow from the very foundation; destroy utterly. **2** To corrupt; undermine the morals or character of. [<OF *subvertir* <L *subvertere* overturn < *sub-* up from under + *vertere* turn] —**sub·vert′er** *n.* —**sub·vert′i·ble** *adj.*

Synonyms: destroy, extinguish, overthrow, overturn, supersede, supplant. To *supersede* implies the putting of something that is preferred in the place of that which is removed; to *subvert* does not imply substitution. To *supplant* is more often personal, signifying to take the place of another, usually by underhand means; one is *superseded* by authority, *supplanted* by a rival. See ABOLISH. *Antonyms*: conserve, perpetuate, preserve, sustain, uphold.

sub·vit·re·ous (sub·vit′rē·əs) *adj.* Having a luster resembling that of glass, but less brilliant.

sub·way (sub′wā) *n.* **1** An artificial passage below the surface of the ground; specifically, one for traffic, water and gas mains, electric cables, etc. **2** An underground railroad, usually electrically operated; also, a tunnel for such a railroad.

suc– Assimilated var. of SUB–.

suc·ce·da·ne·um (suk′si·dā′nē·əm) *n. pl.* **·ne·ums** or **·ne·a** (-nē·ə) One who or that which is a substitute. [<NL, neut. sing. of L *succedaneus* < *succedere* succeed, replace] —**suc′ce·da′ne·ous** *adj.*

suc·ceed (sək·sēd′) *v.i.* **1** To come next in order or sequence; follow; ensue. **2** To come after another into office, ownership, etc.; be the successor: often with *to.* **3** To be successful; accomplish what is attempted or intended; also, formerly, to achieve an end in a specified manner: They *succeeded* badly. **4** *Law* To devolve: said of an estate. —*v.t.* **5** To be the successor or heir of. **6** To come after in time or sequence; follow. [<OF *succeder* <L *succedere* go under, follow after < *sub-* under + *cedere* go] —**suc·ceed′er** *n.*

Synonyms: achieve, attain, flourish, prevail, prosper, thrive, win. To *win* implies that someone loses, but one may *succeed* where no one fails. A solitary swimmer *succeeds* in reaching the shore; if we say he *wins* the shore we place him in competition with the water. Many students may *succeed* in study; a few *win* the special prizes for which all compete. See FOLLOW.

suc·cen·tor (sək·sen′tər) *n.* **1** A deputy precentor; subcantor; subchanter. **2** The leading bass or bass soloist in a church or cathedral choir. [<LL <L *succinere* sing to < *sub-* subordinately + *canere* sing]

suc·cès d'es·time (sük·se′ des·tēm′) *French* Success marked by the praise of critics but not by widespread popular approval: said of a play, book, etc.

suc·cess (sək·ses′) *n.* **1** A favorable or prosperous course or termination of anything attempted; prosperous or advantageous issue. **2** A successful person or affair. **3** *Obs.* The outcome or result, favorable or unfavorable. **4** *Obs.* Succession. See synonyms under VICTORY. [<L *successus* < *succedere* SUCCEED]

suc·cess·ful (sək·ses′fəl) *adj.* **1** Of persons, obtaining what one desires or intends; especially, having reached a high degree of worldly prosperity. **2** Of things, terminating in or meeting with success; resulting favorably: said of a course of action, etc. See synonyms under AUSPICIOUS, FORTUNATE, HAPPY. —**suc·cess′ful·ly** *adv.* —**suc·cess′ful·ness** *n.*

suc·ces·sion (sək·sesh′ən) *n.* **1** The act of following in order, or the state of being successive; a following consecutively. **2** A group of things that succeed in order; a series, either in time or in place; sequence. **3** The act or right of legally or officially coming into a predecessor's office, possessions, etc.; also, the order of so succeeding, or that which is or is to be so taken. **4** The right or act of succeeding to a throne. **5** Descendants collectively; issue. See synonyms under TIME. —**suc·ces′sion·al** *adj.* —**suc·ces′sion·al·ly** *adv.*

suc·ces·sive (sək·ses′iv) *adj.* Following in succession; consecutive. —**suc·ces′sive·ly** *adv.* —**suc·ces′sive·ness** *n.*

suc·ces·sor (sək·ses′ər) *n.* One who or that which follows in succession; especially, a person who succeeds to a throne, property, or office.

suc·ci·nate (suk′si·nāt) *n. Chem.* A salt of succinic acid. [<SUCCIN(IC) + -ATE[3]]

suc·cinct (sək·singkt′) *adj.* **1** Reduced or comprised within a narrow compass; terse; concise. **2** Supported by an encircling silken thread, as a butterfly chrysalis. **3** *Archaic* Encircled or held in position by or as by a girdle. See synonyms under TERSE. [<L *succinctus,* pp. of *succingere* < *sub-* underneath + *cingere* gird] —**suc·cinct′ly** *adv.* —**suc·cinct′ness** *n.*

suc·cinc·to·ri·um (suk′singk·tôr′ē·əm, -tō′rē-) *n. pl.* **·to·ri·a** (-tôr′ē·ə, -tō′rē·ə) A band or scarf embroidered with an Agnus Dei, worn pendent from the girdle: used by the pope on solemn occasions. [<LL <L *sub-* under + *cinctorium* a girdle < *cinctus,* pp. of *cingere* gird]

suc·cin·ic (sək·sin′ik) *adj.* Derived from or found in amber. [<F *succinique* <L *succinum* amber]

succinic acid *Chem.* Either of two white crystalline isomeric compounds, $C_4H_6O_2$, contained in amber and in certain plants, and also made synthetically.

suc·cor (suk′ər) *n.* **1** Help or relief rendered in danger, difficulty, or distress. **2** One who or that which affords relief. —*v.t.* To go to the aid of; help; rescue. See synonyms under AID, HELP, SERVE. Also *Brit.* **suc′cour.** [<OF *sucurs* <Med. L *succursus* <L *succurrere* < *sub-* up from under + *currere* run] —**suc′·cor·a·ble** *adj.* —**suc′cor·er** *n.*

suc·co·ry (suk′ər·ē) *n.* Chicory. [Alter. of *cicoree, sichorie,* earlier vars. of CHICORY; infl. in form by MDu. *sukerie* chicory]

suc·co·tash (suk′ə·tash) *n.* A dish of Indian corn kernels and beans boiled together. [<Algonquian (Narraganset) *misickquatash* an ear of corn]

Suc·coth (so͝ok′ōth, so͝ok′ōs) See SUKKOTH.

suc·cu·bus (suk′yə·bəs) *n. pl.* **·bi** (-bī) One of a class of demons in female form fabled to have intercourse with men in their sleep. [<Med. L <LL *succuba* a strumpet <L *succubare* < *sub-* underneath + *cubare* lie]

suc·cu·lent (suk′yə·lənt) *adj.* **1** *Bot.* Juicy;

fleshy, as the tissues of certain plants. 2 Rich or vigorous: a *succulent* theme. [<L *succulentus* <*succus* juice] —**suc′cu·lence, suc′cu·len·cy** *n.* —**suc′cu·lent·ly** *adv.*

suc·cumb (sə·kum′) *v.i.* **1** To give way; yield, as to force or persuasion. **2** To die. [<OF *succomber* <L *succumbere* <*sub-* underneath + *cumbere* lie] —**suc·cum′bent** (-bənt) *adj.*

suc·cuss (sə·kus′) *v.t.* To shake suddenly or forcibly. [<L *succussus,* pp. of *succutere* < *sub-* up from under + *quatere* shake] —**suc·cus′sive** *adj.*

suc·cus·sion (sə·kush′ən) *n.* **1** The act of shaking. **2** *Med.* A vigorous shaking of the patient to detect liquids in the thorax or other cavities of the body. Also **suc·cus·sa·tion** (suk′ə·sā′shən). —**suc·cus·sa·to·ry** (sə·kus′ə·tôr′ē, -tō′rē) *adj.*

such (such) *adj.* **1** Of that kind; of the same or like kind: often with *as* or *that* completing the comparison: *Such* wit *as* this is rare. **2** Specifically, being the same as what has been mentioned or indicated: *Such* was the king's command. **3** Being the same in quality: Let the truthful continue *such.* **4** Being the same as something understood by the speaker or the hearer, or purposely left indefinite: a concise and elliptical use by which specification is avoided: the chief of *such* a clan. **5** So extreme, unpleasant, or the like: an emphatic or expletive use: We have come to *such* a pass. —*pron.* **1** Such a person or thing, or (more commonly) such persons or things: by ellipsis of the noun: The friend of *such* as are in trouble. **2** The same; the aforesaid: I bring good tidings, for *such* the general sent. —*adv.* So: *such* destructive criticism. [OE *swelc, swilc, swylc*]

such-and-such (such′ən·such′) *adj.* Being a particular person, thing, or time, not specifically named: He visited *such-and-such* a place. Also **such and such.**

such·like (such′līk′) *adj.* Of a like or similar kind. —*pron.* Persons or things of that kind: mosses, ferns, and *suchlike.*

Sü·chow (shü′jō′) **1** A city in SW Shantung province, China: formerly (1912–45) *Tungshan.* **2** A former name for IPIN.

suck (suk) *v.t.* **1** To draw into the mouth by means of a partial vacuum created by action of the lips and tongue. **2** To draw in or take up in a manner resembling this; inhale; absorb: The sponge *sucked* the water up. **3** To draw liquid or nourishment from with the mouth: to *suck* a lemon; also, to take into and hold in the mouth as if to do this: to *suck* one's thumb. **4** To consume by licking, or by holding in the mouth: to *suck* candy. **5** To bring to a specified state or condition by sucking: He *sucked* the lemon dry. —*v.i.* **6** To draw in liquid, air, etc., by suction. **7** To suckle. **8** To draw in air instead of water, as a defective pump does. **9** To make a sucking sound. —*n.* **1** The act of sucking; suction. **2** That which is sucked or comes by sucking. **3** A slight draft or drink. **4** A mother's milk. **5** A whirlpool or powerful eddy. [OE *sūcan*] —**suck′ing** *adj.* —**suck′ing·ly** *adv.*

suck·er (suk′ər) *n.* **1** One who or that which sucks; a suckler, as a suckling pig or a newly born whale. **2** A North American fresh-water fish (family *Catostomidae*), related to the cyprinoids, having the mouth usually protractile with thick and fleshy lips adapted for sucking in food. **3** *Zool.* An organ by which an animal adheres to other bodies; a suctorial organ. **4** *Slang* A toady; sponger; parasite; hanger-on. **5** *U.S. Slang* A foolish fellow; dolt; one easily deceived; a gull. **6** A piston, as of a syringe or a suction pump; a tube or pipe used for suction. **7** *Bot.* **a** A shoot or branch originating on a subterranean portion of a stem. **b** A shoot or sprout arising from the root near or remote from the trunk of certain trees. **8** A haustorium. **9** A sweetmeat; also, sugar. —*v.t.* To strip of suckers or shoots. —*v.i.* To form or send out suckers or shoots. [<SUCK]

Sucker State Nickname for ILLINOIS.

suck·fish (suk′fish′) *n. pl.* **·fish** or **·fish·es 1** A remora. **2** A fish *(Caularchus maeandricus)* of the Pacific coast, with a ventrally placed sucker by which it attaches itself to stones, shells, etc.

suck·le (suk′əl) *v.* **·led, ·ling** *v.t.* **1** To give suck to, as at the breast. **2** To bring up; nourish. —*v.i.* **3** To take nourishment at the breast; suck. [ME *sucklen,* freq. of *suken* SUCK] —**suck′ler** *n.*

suck·ling (suk′ling) *n.* **1** An unweaned mammal. **2** A young, inexperienced person.

Suck·ling (suk′ling), **Sir John,** 1609–42, English poet and dramatist.

su·crate (so͞o′krāt) *n. Chem.* A compound in which sucrose or some analogous carbohydrate combines with a base to form a salt: calcium *sucrate.* [<F <*sucre* sugar + *-ate* -ATE[3]]

su·cre (so͞o′krā) *n.* The monetary unit of Ecuador. [<Sp., after Antonio José de *Sucre*]

Su·cre (so͞o′krā) The nominal capital of Bolivia. La Paz is the seat of government.

Su·cre (so͞o′krā), **Antonio José de,** 1795?–1830, South American soldier; first president of Bolivia.

su·crose (so͞o′krōs) *n. Chem.* **1** Any one of the group of carbohydrates, including cane sugar, milk sugar, maltose, etc., having the common composition $C_{12}H_{22}O_{11}$, and deviating the plane of polarized light to the right. **2** Cane sugar as obtained from the sugarcane, maple, beet, etc. Also called *saccharose.* [<F *sucre* sugar + *-ose* -OSE[2]]

suc·tion (suk′shən) *n.* **1** The act or process of sucking. **2** The production of a partial vacuum in a space connected with a fluid or gas under pressure. **3** The tendency of a fluid to fill a vacuum contiguous with it. [<OF <L *suctio, -onis*<*sugere* suck]

suction pump A pump operating by suction, consisting of a piston working up and down in a cylinder, both equipped with valves: the most common form of house pump. Compare illustration under FORCE PUMP.

suction stop *Phonet.* A click, as in the Bushman and Hottentot languages. See CLICK (def. 3).

Suc·to·ri·a (suk·tôr′ē·ə, -tō′rē·ə) *n. pl.* A class or subclass of aquatic protozoans having in the adult stage long hollow tentacles for piercing and sucking. [<NL <L *suctus,* pp. of *sugere* suck]

suc·to·ri·al (suk·tôr′ē·əl, -tō′rē·əl) *adj.* **1** Adapted for sucking or for adhesion. **2** *Zool.* Living by sucking; having organs for sucking.

sud (so͝od) *v. Scot.* Should.

su·dan (so͞o·dan′) *adj. Chem.* Designating any of a class of diazo compounds widely used as red and yellow dyes. [from *Sudan*]

Su·dan (so͞o·dan′) A region extending across Africa from the Atlantic Ocean to the Red Sea, south of the Sahara: formerly *Nigritia.*

Sudan, Republic of the An independent country in NE Africa; 967,500 square miles; capital, Khartoum.

Su·da·nese (so͞o′də·nēz′, -nēs′) *adj.* Of or pertaining to the Sudan or its people. —*n. pl.* **·nese** One living in the Sudan; the people of the Sudan collectively, including Negro and Negroid peoples, Hamites and certain Arab tribes.

Su·dan·ic (so͞o·dan′ik) *n.* A family of languages spoken in central Africa from the Atlantic to the Indian oceans, including Dinka, Ewe, Nubian, and Yoruba. —*adj.* Of or pertaining to this family.

su·dar·i·um (so͞o·dâr′ē·əm) *n. pl.* **·dar·i·a** (-dâr′ē·ə) **1** A handkerchief or cloth for drying or removing perspiration; specifically, the sweat cloth or handkerchief of St. Veronica, said to have been miraculously impressed with the features of Jesus when she wiped his face on his way to crucifixion. **2** The napkin about the head of Christ in the tomb. *John* xx 7. **3** Any miraculous picture of Christ; a veronica. **4** A sudatory (def. 2). Also **su·da·ry** (so͞o′·dər·ē). [<L <*sudor, -oris* sweat]

su·da·tion (so͞o·dā′shən) *n.* Morbid or excessive sweating. [<L *sudatio, -onis* <*sudatus,* pp. of *sudare* sweat]

su·da·to·ry (so͞o′də·tôr′ē, -tō′rē) *adj.* **1** Producing perspiration; sudorific. **2** Perspiring. —*n. pl.* **·ries 1** An agent that causes sweating; a sudorific. **2** A sweating bath; specifically, a hot-air room in a Roman bath: also **su′da·to′ri·um.** [<L *sudatorius*]

sudd (sud) *n.* A floating mass of vegetation that frequently obstructs navigation on the White Nile. [<Arabic <*sudd* obstruct]

sud·den (sud′n) *adj.* **1** Happening quickly and without warning: *sudden* death. **2** Hurriedly or quickly contrived, used, or done; hasty. **3** Come upon unexpectedly; causing surprise. **4** Quick-tempered; precipitate; rash. See synonyms under IMPETUOUS, SWIFT[1]. —*n.* The state of being sudden, or that which is sudden: obsolete except in a few phrases. —**all of a sudden, all on a sudden, on a sudden** Without warning; on the spur of the moment. [< AF *sodein,* OF *soudain* <L *subitaneus* < *subitus,* pp. of *subire* come or go stealthily < *sub-* secretly + *ire* go] —**sud′den·ly** *adv.* —**sud′den·ness** *n.*

sudden death 1 Death that occurs suddenly or instantaneously, esp. violently. **2** *Sports* An extra period played in order to break a tie score, in which the first score ends the game.

Su·der·mann (zo͞o′dər·män), **Hermann,** 1857–1928, German dramatist and novelist.

Su·de·ten·land (so͞o·dāt′n·land, *Ger.* zo͞o·dā′·tən·länt) The border district of Bohemia and Moravia, Czechoslovakia; 8,976 square miles.

Su·de·tes (so͞o·dē′tēz) A mountainous system along the German-Czechoslovak and Polish-Czechoslovak border; highest point, 5,259 feet. Also **Su·det·ic Mountains** (so͞o·det′ik).

su·dor (so͞o′dôr) *n.* Visible perspiration; sweat. [<L] —**su·dor·al** (so͞o′dər·əl) *adj.*

su·dor·if·er·ous (so͞o′də·rif′ər·əs) *adj.* Secreting or producing sweat. [<NL *sudoriferus* <L *sudor, -oris* sweat + *ferre* carry] —**su′dor·if′·er·ous·ness** *n.*

su·dor·if·ic (so͞o′də·rif′ik) *adj.* Causing perspiration. —*n.* A medicine that produces or promotes sweating. [<NL *sudorificus* <L *sudor, -oris* sweat + *facere* make]

suds (sudz) *n. pl.* **1** Soapy water worked up into bubbles and froth; foam; lather. **2** *Slang* Beer: so called from its foamy properties. [Prob. <MDu. *sudde, sudse* a marsh, marsh water] —**suds′y** *adj.*

sue (so͞o) *v.* **sued, su·ing** *v.t.* **1** *Law* **a** To institute proceedings against for the recovery of some right or the redress of some wrong. **b** To prosecute (an action). **c** To seek a grant from (a court). **2** To endeavor to persuade by entreaty; beg; urge; petition. **3** To seek to win in marriage; woo. —*v.i.* **4** To institute legal proceedings. **5** To make entreaty. **6** *Archaic* To pay court; woo. [<AF *suer,* OF *suivre,* ult. <L *sequi* follow] —**su′er** *n.*

Sue (so͞o) Diminutive of SUSANNA.

Sue (so͞o, *Fr.* sü), **(Marie Joseph) Eugène,** 1804–57, French novelist.

suède (swād) *n.* Undressed kid: often attributively: *suède* gloves. [<F *Suède* Sweden, in phrase *gants de Suède* Swedish gloves]

suède fabric A woven or knitted fabric of cotton, rayon, or wool, finished to resemble suède leather: used for sports coats and jackets, linings, gloves, etc.

su·et (so͞o′it) *n.* The fatty tissues about the loins and kidneys of sheep, oxen, etc.: used in cookery and for making tallow. [Dim. of AF *sue,* OF *seu* <L *sebum* tallow, fat] —**su′et·y** *adj.*

Sue·to·ni·us (swi·tō′nē·əs), **Gaius Tranquillus,** A.D. 70?–140?, Roman historian.

Su·ez (so͞o·ez′, so͞o′ez) A port in NE Egypt at the northern end of the **Gulf of Suez,** the NW arm of the Red Sea (about 180 miles long, 20 miles wide).

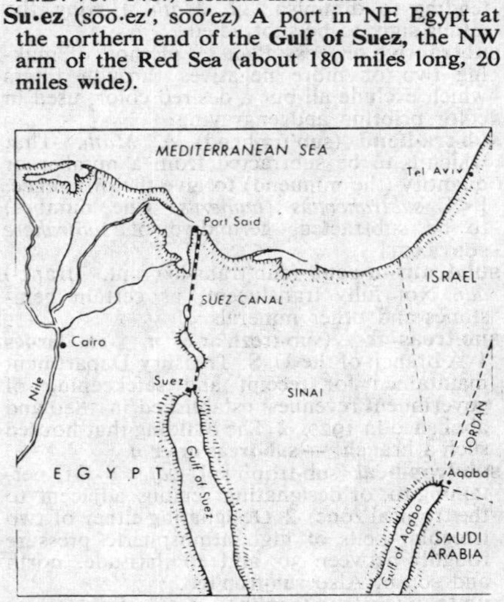

Suez, Isthmus of The neck of land joining Asia and Africa; between the Gulf of Suez and the Mediterranean; 72 miles wide at its narrowest point; traversed by the **Suez Canal,** a ship canal 107 miles long, 197 feet wide,

constructed (1859–69) by Ferdinand de Lesseps.

suf– Assimilated var. of SUB–.

suf·fa·ri (sə·fä′rē) See SAFARI.

suf·fer (suf′ər) v.i. **1** To feel pain or distress. **2** To be affected injuriously; suffer loss or injury. **3** To undergo punishment; especially, to be put to death. **4** Archaic To tolerate or endure pain, injury, etc. — v.t. **5** To have inflicted on one; sustain, as an injury or loss. **6** To undergo; pass through, as change. **7** To bear; endure: He cannot suffer more pain. **8** To allow; permit: Will he suffer us to leave? See synonyms under ALLOW, ENDURE, PERMIT. [< AF suffrir, OF sofrir, ult. < L sufferre < sub– up from under + ferre bear] — suf′fer·er n.

suf·fer·a·ble (suf′ər·ə·bəl, suf′rə·) adj. Such as can be suffered or endured; endurable. — suf′fer·a·ble·ness n. — suf′fer·a·bly adv.

suf·fer·ance (suf′ər·əns, suf′rəns) n. **1** Permission given or implied by failure to prohibit; negative consent. **2** In customs, a permit for the shipment of certain kinds of goods to specified ports. **3** The act or state of suffering; wretchedness; experience of pain or evil; power to endure. **4** Patience or endurance under suffering; submission; submissiveness. **5** Rare Loss; injury; damage. See synonyms under PATIENCE. [< AF, OF surrance < LL sufferentia < sufferre SUFFER]

suf·fer·ing (suf′ər·ing, suf′ring) n. **1** The state of anguish or pain of one who suffers; the bearing of pain, injury, or loss. **2** The pain so borne; distress; loss; injury. See synonyms under AGONY, PAIN. — suf′fer·ing·ly adv.

suf·fice (sə·fīs′) v. ·ficed, ·fic·ing v.i. To be sufficient or adequate; meet the requirements or answer the purpose. — v.t. To satisfactory or adequate for; satisfy. See synonyms under SATISFY, SERVE. [< OF suffis-, stem of suffire < L sufficere < sub– under + facere make] — suf·fic′er n.

suf·fi·cien·cy (sə·fish′ən·sē) n. pl. ·cies **1** The state of being sufficient. **2** That which is sufficient; especially, adequate pecuniary means or income; a competency. **3** Full capability or qualification; efficiency. **4** Conceit; self-sufficiency. See synonyms under COMFORT.

suf·fi·cient (sə·fish′ənt) adj. **1** Being all that is needful; adequate; enough. **2** Archaic Capable; competent. **3** Obs. Financially competent; responsible. See synonyms under ADEQUATE, AMPLE, ENOUGH. [< OF < L sufficiens, -entis, ppr. of sufficere SUFFICE] — suf·fi′cient·ly adv.

suf·fix (suf′iks) n. **1** Ling. A letter or letters added to the end of a word or root, and functioning as a formative, derivative, or inflectional element, as -er in shorter, -ful in faithful, -s and -es in dogs, boxes, -ed in loved, -ness in kindness, etc. Compare COMBINING FORM, PREFIX. **2** Any added title or the like. **3** Math. A subindex. — v.t. To add as a suffix; append. [< NL suffixum < L suffixus, pp. of suffigere < sub– underneath + figere fix. Doublet of SOFFIT.] — suf′fix·al adj. — suf·fix·ion (sə·fik′shən) n.

suf·flate (sə·flāt′) v.t. ·flat·ed, ·flat·ing Obs. To blow up or inflate. [< L sufflatus, pp. of sufflare < sub– up from under + flare blow] — suf·fla′tion n.

suf·fo·cant (suf′ə·kənt) n. Any substance or agent that produces suffocation.

suf·fo·cate (suf′ə·kāt) v. ·cat·ed, ·cat·ing v.t. **1** To kill by obstructing respiration in any manner. **2** To obstruct or oppress, as by an inadequate supply of air. **3** To stifle; extinguish; smother, as a fire. — v.i. **4** To become choked or stifled; die from suffocation. [< L suffocatus, pp. of suffocare < sub– under + fauces throat] — suf′fo·cat′ing·ly adv. — suf·fo·ca′tion n. — suf′fo·ca′tive adj.

Suf·folk (suf′ək) n. **1** A breed of hardy, chestnut-colored English working horse, smaller and freer from feather than the Shire and Clydesdale breeds. It is heavy in body and has rather short legs. Also **Suffolk punch**. **2** A breed of hornless, short-wool Southdown sheep, with black face and legs: preeminent for the quality of its mutton. [from Suffolk, England]

Suf·folk (suf′ək) A county in eastern England; 1,507 square miles; administratively divided into **East Suffolk** (879 square miles; county town, Ipswich) and **West Suffolk** (628 square miles; county town, Bury St. Edmunds).

suf·fra·gan (suf′rə·gən) Eccl. n. An auxiliary or assistant bishop, who assists a bishop in the administration of the diocese, or is consecrated for service in a limited portion of the diocese: also **suffragan bishop**. — adj. Of or pertaining to a suffragan; assisting; auxiliary; subordinate to an archiepiscopal see. [< AF, OF < Med. L suffraganeus < L suffragari vote for, support] — suf′fra·gan·ship′ n.

suf·frage (suf′rij) n. **1** A vote in support of some measure or candidate; hence, approbation; assent. **2** Voting; also, the right or privilege of voting; franchise: also **political suffrage**. **3** Eccl. Any short intercessory prayer or petition. — **woman suffrage** Political suffrage as belonging to or exercised by women. In the United States suffrage was granted to women in 1920 by the 19th amendment to the Constitution: also **female suffrage**. [< OF < L suffragium a voting tablet, vote]

suf·fra·gette (suf′rə·jet′) n. Colloq. A woman who advocated female suffrage; specifically, a member of a militant organization demanding it. [< SUFFRAGE + -ETTE] — suf′fra·get′tism n.

suf·fra·gist (suf′rə·jist) n. **1** A voter. **2** An advocate of some particular form of suffrage, especially of woman suffrage.

suf·fru·tex (suf′rə·teks) n. Bot. **1** An undershrub; a small plant having a decidedly woody stem. **2** An herb with a permanent woody base. [< NL < L sub– under, less than + frutex, -icis a shrub] — suf′fru·tes′cent (-tes′ənt) adj.

suf·fru·ti·cose (sə·frōō′tə·kōs) adj. Bot. Somewhat shrubby; woody; shrubby or woody at base and herbaceous above. [< NL suffruticosus < suffrutex, -icis. See SUFFRUTEX.]

suf·fu·mi·gate (sə·fyōō′mə·gāt) v.t. ·gat·ed, ·gat·ing To fumigate from or as from underneath. [< L suffumigatus, pp. of suffumigare < sub– up from under + fumigare FUMIGATE]

suf·fu·mi·ga·tion (sə·fyōō′mə·gā′shən) n. **1** The act of suffumigating. **2** The act of burning perfumes. **3** A fume or vapor.

suf·fuse (sə·fyōōz′) v.t. ·fused, ·fus·ing To overspread, as with a vapor, fluid, or color. [< L suffusus, pp. of suffundere < sub– underneath, up from under + fundere pour] — suf·fu·sive (sə·fyōō′siv) adj.

suf·fu·sion (sə·fyōō′zhən) n. **1** The act of welling up or spreading over. **2** The state of being suffused; a blush. **3** That which suffuses: a suffusion of blood.

Su·fi (sōō′fē) n. A follower of a system of Moslem philosophical and devotional mysticism, especially in Persia. [< Arabic sufī. lit., a man of wool < sūf wool] — Su′fic, Su·fis·tic (sōō·fis′tik) adj.

Su·fism (sōō′fiz·əm) n. The doctrine of the Sufis, which has inspired a mass of symbolical religious poetry.

sug– Assimilated var. of SUB–.

sug·ar (shōōg′ər) n. **1** A sweet crystalline disaccharide having the formula $C_{12}H_{22}O_{11}$, obtained chiefly from the juice of the sugarcane or sugar beet; called, according to its source, **beet sugar, cane sugar, date sugar, grape sugar, maple sugar**, etc. ◆ Collateral adjective: saccharine. **2** Any of a large class of sweet, soluble, optically active carbohydrates which are ketone or aldehyde derivatives of the higher alcohols. They are widely distributed in plants and animals, play an important role in nutrition, and are generally classified on the basis of chemical structure as monosaccharides, disaccharides, trisaccharides. **3** Flattering or honeyed words, especially if used to disguise or soften an unpleasant or severe reality. **4** Slang Sweet one: a pet name. — v.t. **1** To sweeten, cover, or coat with sugar. **2** To make agreeable or less distasteful, as by flattery. — v.i. **3** U.S. & Can. To make maple sugar. **4** To form or produce sugar; granulate. [< OF sucre < Med. L succarum, ult. < Arabic sukkar. Prob. related to SACCHARIN.]

sugar apple The sweetsop.

sugar beet Any sugar-producing variety of the common garden beet.

sug·ar·ber·ry (shōōg′ər·ber′ē) n. pl. ·ries The hackberry.

sug·ar·bird (shōōg′ər·bûrd′) n. **1** Any bird that sucks the nectar of flowers, as the honey creepers, honey-eaters, sunbirds, etc. **2** The evening grosbeak (Hesperiphona vespertina): so named by North American Indians from its fondness for maple sugar.

sugar bush A grove of sugar-maple trees: sometimes designating a grove of 200 or more trees.

sugar camp The collection of cabins and other buildings in a sugar bush where the maple sap is boiled.

sug·ar·cane (shōōg′ər·kān′) n. A tall, stout, perennial grass (Saccharum officinarum) of tropical regions with a solid jointed stalk rich in sugar.

sug·ar·coat (shōōg′ər·kōt′) v.t. **1** To cover with sugar. **2** To cause to appear attractive or less distasteful. — sug′ar·coat′ed adj. — sug′ar·coat′ing n.

sugar corn Sweet corn (def. 1).

sug·ar·cured (shōōg′ər·kyōord′) adj. Cured by using sugar in the curing process: said of ham and pork.

sugar daddy U.S. Slang A wealthy old man who gives a young woman presents in return for her favors.

sug·ared (shōōg′ərd) adj. Sugar-coated; honeyed; pleasant; sweetened.

sug·ar·house (shōōg′ər·hous′) n. **1** A building in which the juices are extracted from sugarcane, sugar beets, etc., and made into raw sugar; a sugar refinery. **2** A building in which sugar is stored. **3** A building in a sugar camp in which maple sap is boiled.

sugaring off 1 The boiling of maple sap until it crystallizes into sugar. **2** The time of year at which this is done. **3** A community social gathering to take part in making maple sugar.

sugaring over Making palatable the unpalatable, especially facts.

sugar loaf 1 A conical mass of hard refined sugar. **2** A conical hat or hill. — sug′ar·loaf′ adj.

Sugar Loaf Mountain A peak in Río de Janeiro, Brazil, at the entrance to Guanabara Bay; 1,296 feet: Portuguese Pão de Açúcar.

sugar maple The maple (Acer saccharum) of eastern North America from the sap of which maple sugar is made: also called hard maple, rock maple.

sugar of lead Lead acetate.

sugar of milk Lactose.

sugar orchard An orchard of sugar maples.

sugar pine A tall pine (Pinus lambertiana) of the Pacific coast, bearing very large cones and having wood much used in construction work.

sug·ar·plum (shōōg′ər·plum′) n. **1** A small sweetmeat; a small ball or disk of candy; a bon-bon. **2** The shadbush.

sugar tree The sugar maple.

sug·ar·y (shōōg′ər·ē) adj. **1** Composed of or as of sugar; sweet. **2** Fond of sugar. **3** Figuratively, honeyed; alluring. **4** Granular. — sug′ar·i·ness n.

sug·gan (sug′ən) n. **1** A type of rope made of twisted straw. **2** A saddle, collar, or bolster so made. **3** A heavy bed coverlet. [< Irish sūgān]

sug·gest (səg·jest′, sə·jest′) v.t. **1** To bring or put forward for consideration, action, or approval; propose. **2** To arouse in the mind by association or connection; connote: Hallowe'en suggests witches and black cats. **3** To give a hint or indirect suggestion of; intimate: This poem suggests a great deal of care and thought. **4** To act as or provide a motive for; prompt: The success of his novel suggested a sequel. See synonyms under ALLUDE, IMPORT. [< L suggestus, pp. of suggerere < sub– underneath + gerere carry] — sug·gest′er n.

sug·gest·i·bil·i·ty (səg·jes′tə·bil′ə·tē, sə–) n. **1** Psychol. Responsiveness to suggestion, normal in children and diminishing in adults, but heightened or abnormal in hypnosis, light sleep, and certain nervous conditions. **2** Readiness to believe and agree without reflection; compliancy of mind and will.

sug·gest·i·ble (səg·jes′tə·bəl, sə–) adj. **1** That can be suggested. **2** Easily led; yielding, especially to hypnosis: a suggestible patient.

sug·ges·tion (səg·jes′chən, sə·jes′-) *n.* **1** The act of suggesting. **2** A hint; insinuation. **3** The spontaneous calling up of an idea in the mind by a connected idea. **4** *Psychol.* **a** The inducing in a person of some idea, impulse, action, or mode of behavior through a stimulus, verbal or other, coming from another person but independent of critical argument or rational persuasion, as in hypnosis. **b** The idea, impulse, etc., so induced.

Synonyms: hint, innuendo, insinuation, intimation. A *suggestion* brings something before the mind less directly than by formal or explicit statement, as by a partial statement, an incidental allusion, an illustration, a question, or the like. *Suggestion* is often used of an unobtrusive statement of one's views or wishes to another, leaving consideration and any consequent action entirely to that person's judgment, and is hence, in many cases, the most respectful way in which to convey one's views to a superior or a stranger. An *intimation* is a *suggestion* in brief utterance, or sometimes by significant act, gesture, or token, of one's meaning or wishes; in the latter case it is often the act of a superior. A *hint* is still more limited in expression and more remote, and is always covert, but frequently with good intent; as, to give one a *hint* of danger or of opportunity. *Insinuation* and *innuendo* usually imply discredit; an *insinuation* is a covert or partly veiled injurious utterance; an *innuendo* is commonly secret as well as sly, as if pointing to something derogatory. See COUNSEL.

sug·ges·tive (səg·jes′tiv, sə-) *adj.* **1** Fitted or tending to suggest; stimulating to thought or reflection. **2** Hinting at indecent thoughts; suggesting the improper. **—sug·ges′tive·ly** *adv.* **—sug·ges′tive·ness** *n.*

sugh (so͝okh) *n. Scot.* A rushing sound; sough.

Su·grue (sə·gro͞o), **Thomas,** 1907–53, U.S. newspaperman, critic, and writer.

su·i·ci·dal (so͞o′ə·sīd′l) *adj.* Self-destructive; ruinous; pertaining to, or leading to, suicide; fatal to one's prospects or interests. **—su′i·ci′dal·ly** *adv.*

su·i·cide (so͞o′ə·sīd) *n.* **1** The intentional taking of one's own life. **2** Self-inflicted political, social, or commercial ruin. **3** One who commits self-murder. *—v.i.* **·cid·ed, ·cid·ing** *Colloq.* To commit suicide. [< NL *suicidium* < L *sui* of oneself + *caedere* kill]

su·i gen·e·ris (so͞o′ī jen′ər·is) *Latin* Literally, of his (her, its) particular kind; forming a kind by itself; unique.

su·i ju·ris (so͞o′ī jo͝or′is) *Latin* In one's own right; having legal capacity to act for oneself.

su·int (so͞o′int, swint) *n.* Natural wool grease from wool-washings: it consists of fatty substances combined with potash salts. [< F < *suer* sweat < L *sudare*]

Suisse (swēs) The French name for SWITZERLAND.

Sui·sun Bay (sə·so͞on′) The easternmost arm of San Francisco Bay.

suit (so͞ot) *n.* **1** A set of outer garments or armor to be worn together. **2** A set of garments consisting of a coat and trousers or skirt, made of the same fabric. **3** An outfit or garment for a particular purpose: a bathing *suit*; a space *suit.* **4** A group of things of like kind or pattern composing a series or set: now usually *suite.* **5** In card-playing, any one of the four sets of thirteen cards each that make up a pack, as spades, hearts, diamonds, or clubs. **6** *Law* A proceeding in a court of law or chancery in which a plaintiff demands the recovery of a right or the redress of a wrong: a term rarely applied to criminal prosecution. **7** *Archaic* Entreaty; petition; supplication. **8** The courting or courtship of a woman. See synonyms under PRAYER. **—to follow suit. 1** To play a card identical in suit to the card led. **2** To do as somebody or something else has done; follow an example. *—v.t.* **1** To meet the requirements of, or be appropriate to; be in accord with; befit. **2** To please; satisfy. **3** To render appropriate or accordant; accommodate; adapt. **4** *Archaic* To furnish with clothes. *—v.i.* **5** To be befitting; agree; correspond. **6** To be or prove satisfactory. **7** *Obs.* To clothe oneself. See synonyms under ACCOMMODATE, ADAPT. [< AF *siwte,* OF *sieute,* ult. < L *sequi* follow. Doublet of SUITE.]

suit·a·ble (so͞o′tə·bəl) *adj.* Capable of suiting; appropriate; applicable; proper. See synonyms under APPROPRIATE, BECOMING, CONVENIENT, EXPEDIENT, GOOD. **—suit′a·bil′i·ty, suit′a·ble·ness** *n.* **—suit′a·bly** *adv.*

suit·case (so͞ot′kās′) *n.* A flat, rectangular valise used for carrying clothing, etc.

suite (swēt; *for def.* 3, *also* so͞ot) *n.* **1** A succession of things forming a series; a set of things having a certain dependence upon each other and intended to go or be used together. **2** A number of connected apartments. **3** A set of furniture. **4** A collection of pictures illustrating consecutive events. **5** *Music* A form of instrumental composition formerly consisting of a series of dances, but now often written for an orchestra and varying freely in its construction and movements. **6** A retinue; a company of attendants or followers. ◆ Homophone: *sweet.* [< F < OF *sieute.* Doublet of SUIT.]

suit·ing (so͞o′ting) *n.* Cloth from which to make entire suits of clothes.

suit·or (so͞o′tər) *n.* **1** One who institutes a suit in court. **2** A wooer. **3** A petitioner. [< AF *seutor* < LL *secutor, -oris* < L *secutus,* pp. of *sequi* follow]

Sui·yü·an (swā′yü′än′) A former province of northern China, incorporated in the Inner Mongolian Autonomous Region, June, 1954; 135,000 square miles; capital, Kweisui.

Su·khu·mi (so͞o′kho͞o·mē) A port on the Black Sea, capital of Abkhaz Autonomous S.S.R.

su·ki·ya·ki (so͞o′kē·yä′kē, -yak′ē) *n.* A Japanese dish, usually cooked rapidly at the table, made of meat in thin slices, vegetables, and condiments. [< Japanese]

Suk·koth (so͝ok′ōth, so͝ok′ōs) *n. pl.* The feast of Tabernacles, a Jewish holiday beginning on the 15th of Tishri (late September-October): originally a harvest festival: also spelled *Succoth.* Also **Suk′kos, Suk′kot.** [< Hebrew *sūkōth* tabernacles, booths]

Suk·kur (so͝ok′ko͝or) A city in SE central West Pakistan, on the Indus.

Su·ky (so͞o′kē) Diminutive of SUSANNA.

Su·la Islands (so͞o′lə) An Indonesian island group between the Banggai and the Obi island groups; total, 1,873 square miles. *Dutch* **Soe·la** (so͞o′lä).

sul·cate (sul′kāt, -kit) *adj. Biol.* Having long narrow furrows or channels; grooved; fluted. Also **sul′cat·ed.** [< L *sulcatus,* pp. of *sulcare* plow < *sulcus* a furrow] **—sul·ca′tion** *n.*

sul·cus (sul′kəs) *n. pl.* **·ci** (-sī) **1** A narrow channel or furrow. **2** *Anat.* One of a large number of shallow grooves on the surface of the mammalian brain. [< L]

sul·dan (sul′dən) See SOLDAN.

Su·lei·man (sü′lā·män′) Name of three Turkish rulers: also spelled *Solyman.*

—Suleiman the Magnificent, 1496?–1566, Ottoman sultan 1520–66; added extensive territories to the Turkish Empire in Europe and encouraged arts and science.

sul·fa (sul′fə) See SULFA DRUG.

sulfa- *combining form Chem.* Sulfur; related to or containing sulfur: also spelled *sulpha-.* Also, before vowels, **sulf-,** as in *sulfarsenide.* See also SULFO-. [< SULFUR]

sul·fa·di·a·zine (sul′fə·dī′ə·zēn) *n. Chem.* A white, crystalline, relatively non-toxic derivative of sulfanilamide, $C_{10}H_{10}N_4SO_2$, used in the treatment of infections due to streptococci, pneumococci, and staphylococci.

sul·fa drug (sul′fə) *Chem.* Any of a group of organic compounds consisting mainly of substituted sulfanilamide derivatives and having a wide range of therapeutic effects in the treatment of bacterial infections.

sul·fa·gua·ni·dine (sul′fə·gwä′nə·din, -dēn, -gwan′ə-) *n. Chem.* A white, crystalline, relatively non-toxic sulfonamide, $C_7H_{10}N_4O_2S$, used in the treatment of certain infections.

sul·fal·de·hyde (sul·fal′də·hīd) *n. Chem.* An oily, liquid compound, C_3H_6S, sometimes used as a hypnotic.

sul·fa·nil·a·mide (sul′fə·nil′ə·mīd, -mid) *n. Chem.* A colorless, crystalline sulfonamide, $C_6H_8N_2O_2S$, originally widely developed and used as a chemotherapeutic agent in the treatment of various bacterial infections. [< SULF(A)- + ANIL(INE) + AMIDE]

sul·fa·pyr·i·dine (sul′fə·pir′ə·dēn, -din) *n. Chem.* A white, crystalline derivative of sulfanilamide, $C_{11}H_{11}N_3O_2S$, once widely used in the treatment of various infections.

sulf·ar·se·nide (sulf·är′sə·nīd, -nid) *n. Chem.* A compound of the arsenide and sulfide of a metal or metals.

sulf·ars·phen·a·mine (sulf′ärs·fen′ə·mēn, -fen·am′in) *n. Chem.* A yellow, almost odorless, water-soluble powder containing from 18 to 20 percent arsenic: used in the treatment of syphilis.

sul·fate (sul′fāt) *n. Chem.* A salt of sulfuric acid. Sulfates are widely distributed in nature and are important in the arts and in medicine. *—v.* **·fat·ed, ·fat·ing** *v.t.* **1** To form a sulfate of; treat with a sulfate or sulfuric acid. **2** *Electr.* To form a coating of lead sulfate on (the plate of a secondary battery). **3** To make (red lead) into lead sulfate by the action of sulfuric acid. *—v.i.* **4** To become sulfated. Also **sul′phate.** [< F < NL *sulfas, -atis* a sulfate < L *sulfur* sulfur]

sulfate process A method for manufacturing tough kraft paper by introducing sulfate of soda in the digesters containing the wood pulp.

sul·fa·thi·a·zole (sul′fə·thī′ə·zōl) *n. Chem.* A sulfanilamide derivative, $C_9H_9N_3O_2S_2$, considered particularly effective in treating certain pneumococcal and staphylococcal infections.

sul·fa·tize (sul′fə·tīz) *v.t.* **·tized, ·tiz·ing** To turn (ores, etc.) into sulfate, by roasting. Also **sul′pha·tize.**

sulf·hy·dryl (sulf·hī′dril) *n. Chem.* The univalent thiol radical SH: also called *mercapto.* [< SULF(A)- + HYDR- + -YL]

sul·fide (sul′fīd) *n. Chem.* A compound of sulfur with an element or radical. Also **sul′fid** (-fid), **sul′phide, sul′phid.** [< SULF(A)- + -IDE]

sul·fi·nyl (sul′fə·nil) *n. Chem.* Thionyl. [< *sulfine,* var. of SULFONIUM + -YL]

sul·fite (sul′fīt) *n. Chem.* A salt or ester of sulfurous acid. Also **sul′phite.** [< SULF(A)- + -ITE[2]] **—sul·fit′ic** (-fit′ik) *adj.*

sulfite process The production of chemical wood pulp by the use of calcium sulfite.

sulfo- *combining form Chem.* **1** Sulfur; containing sulfur. **2** Denoting the replacement of oxygen by sulfur in a compound. **3** Indicating the presence of the sulfonic or sulfonyl group. Also spelled *sulpho-.* Compare THIO-. [< SULFUR]

Sul·fo·nal (sul′fə·nal, sul′fə·nal′) *n.* Proprietary name for a brand of sulfonmethane used in medicine as a sedative and hypnotic.

sul·fon·a·mide (sul·fon′ə·mīd, sul′fən·am′īd, -id) *n. Chem.* Any group of organic compounds containing the univalent radical SO_2NH_2, especially those derived from para-aminobenzene-sulfonamide, p-$H_2N{\cdot}C_6H_4{\cdot}SO_2NH_2$, used in the treatment of certain bacterial infections. [< SULFON(E) + AMIDE]

sul·fo·nate (sul′fə·nāt) *v.t.* **·nat·ed, ·nat·ing** *Chem.* **1** To form into a sulfonic acid. **2** To subject to the treatment of sulfonic acid. *—n.* A salt or ester of sulfonic acid. [< SULFON(E) + -ATE[3]] **—sul′fo·na′tion** *n.*

sul·fone (sul′fōn) *n. Chem.* Any of several compounds consisting of two organic radicals in combination with the sulfonyl group and corresponding to the formula R_2SO_2. [< G *sulfon*] **—sul·fon·ic** (sul·fon′ik) *adj.*

sul·fon·eth·yl·meth·ane (sul′fōn·eth′il·meth′ān) *n. Chem.* A colorless crystalline compound, $C_8H_{18}O_4S_2$, used as a hypnotic and sedative: a form of sulfonmethane. [< SULFON(E) + ETHYL + METHANE]

sulfonic acid *Chem.* Any of several compounds consisting of an organic radical in combination with the sulfonic radical and corresponding to the formula $R{\cdot}SO_2OH$: used in organic synthesis.

sul·fo·ni·um (sul·fō′nē·əm) *n. Chem.* The ion, H_3S, resulting from the addition of a proton to hydrogen sulfide. [< SULF(A) + (AMM)ONIUM]

sul·fon·meth·ane (sul·fōn·meth′ān) *n. Chem.* A white, crystalline, organic compound, $C_7H_{16}O_4S_2$, used in medicine as a sedative and hypnotic. [< SULFON(E) + METHANE]

sul·fo·nyl (sul′fə·nil) *n. Chem.* The bivalent radical SO_2; also called *sulfuryl.* [< SULFON(E) + -YL]

sul·fur (sul′fər) *n.* **1** A chemically active, nonmetallic element (symbol S, atomic number 16), under usual conditions consisting of pale yellow crystals but known in many other allotropic forms, and representing an essential constituent of living organisms. See lisiting under PERIODIC TABLE. **2** Any of various yellowish pieridine butterflies, as the

common North American **clouded sulfur** (*Colias philodice*) or the **cloudless sulfur** (*Callidryas eubule*). — **flowers of sulfur** A fine yellow powder obtained by the distillation of sulfur. — *v.t.* To treat or fume, as a wine cask or a hive, with sulfur or with sulfurous acid. Also **sul'phur.** [<AF *sulfre*, OF *soufre* <L *sulfur, -uris*]

sul·fu·rate (sul'fyə-rāt, -fə-) *v.t.* **·rat·ed, ·rat·ing** To sulfurize. [<SULFUR + -ATE[1]]

sul·fur-bot·tom (sul'fər-bot'əm) *n.* A very large baleen whale (*Sibbaldius musculus*) found in Atlantic and Pacific waters, having a yellowish belly and attaining an average length of 60-80 feet, with a maximum of about 100 feet.

SULFUR-BOTTOM

sulfur dioxide *Chem.* A colorless, gaseous compound, SO_2, with a sharp odor and readily soluble in water: used in the manufacture of sulfuric acid, in bleaching, as a preservative, etc.

sul·fu·re·ous (sul-fyoor'ē-əs) *adj.* Of or like sulfur. [<L *sulfureus* < *sulfur* sulfur]

sul·fu·ret (sul'fyə-ret) *v.t.* **·ret·ed** or **·ret·ted, ·ret·ing** or **·ret·ting** To sulfurize. — *n.* (-rit) A sulfide. [<F *sulfuret* a sulfide <NL *sulfuretum* <L *sulfur*] — **sul'fu·ret'ed** or **sul'fu·ret'ted** *adj.*

sul·fu·ric (sul-fyoor'ik) *adj. Chem.* Pertaining to or derived from sulfur, especially in its higher valence.

sulfuric acid *Chem.* A colorless, exceedingly corrosive, oily liquid, H_2SO_4, essentially a combination of sulfur trioxide and water, extensively employed in the manufacture of soda, batteries, guncotton, and in almost all chemical operations. Formerly called *vitriol.*

sul·fur·ize (sul'fyə-rīz, -fə-) *v.t.* **·ized, ·iz·ing** 1 To impregnate, treat with, or subject to the action of sulfur. 2 To bleach or fumigate with sulfur. — **sul'fur·i·za'tion** *n.*

sul·fur·ous (sul'fər-əs, sul·fyoor'əs) *adj.* 1 *Chem.* Of, pertaining to, or derived from sulfur: specifically applied to compounds that contain sulfur in its lower valence. 2 Fiery; hellish; blasphemous, as language.

sulfurous acid *Chem.* A compound corresponding to the formula H_2SO_3, and known only in solution and by its salts.

sulfur point *Physics* The boiling point of pure liquid sulfur at standard atmospheric pressure, 444.60° C.: one of the fixed points of the international temperature scale.

sulfur trioxide *Chem.* A compound, SO_3, formed by the union of sulfur dioxide and oxygen in the presence of a catalytic agent. With water, sulfur trioxide forms sulfuric acid; hence, it is often called **sulfuric anhydride.**

sul·fur·y (sul'fər-ē) *adj.* Resembling or suggesting sulfur; sulfureous.

sulfur yellow A light greenish-yellow color of very high brilliance, like the color of refined sulfur.

sul·fur·yl (sul'fər·il, -fyə·ril) *n.* Sulfonyl. [< SULFUR + -YL]

sulfuryl chloride *Chem.* A colorless, very pungent liquid compound, SO_2Cl_2, used in the manufacture of dyes, drugs, and poison gas.

sulk (sulk) *v.i.* To be sulky or morose. — *n.* A sulky mood or humor: often plural. [Back formation <SULKY]

sulk·y[1] (sul'kē) *adj.* **sulk·i·er, sulk·i·est** 1 Sullenly cross; doggedly or resentfully ill-humored. 2 Stunted; sluggish; dismal. See synonyms under MOROSE. [? OE (*ā*)*solcen* slothful, orig. pp. of (*ā*)*seolcan* be weak, slothful] — **sulk'i·ly** *adv.* — **sulk'i·ness** *n.*

sulk·y[2] (sul'kē) *n. pl.* **sulk·ies** A light, two-wheeled, one-horse vehicle for one person. — *adj.* Resembling this vehicle: a *sulky* plow. [<SULKY[1]; so called because one rides alone] — **sull** (sul) *v.i. Dial.* To sulk. [<SULLEN]

Sul·la (sul'ə), **Lucius Cornelius,** 138–78 B.C., Roman general and dictator.

sul·lage (sul'ij) *n.* 1 Mud or silt deposited by flowing water. 2 Refuse; sewage. [<AF *souiller, soillier* SOIL²; infl. in form by *sully*]

sul·len (sul'ən) *adj.* 1 Obstinately and gloomily ill-humored; morose; glum. 2 Depressing; somber: *sullen* clouds. 3 Slow; sluggish: a *sullen* tread. 4 Melancholy. 5 Ill-omened; threatening. See synonyms under GRIM. [Earlier *solein,* appar. <AF < *sol* SOLE³] — **sul'len·ly** *adv.* — **sul'len·ness** *n.*

Sul·li·van (sul'ə·vən), **Sir Arthur Seymour,** 1842–1900, English composer (often in collaboration with W. S. Gilbert). — **Harry Stack,** 1892–1949, U.S. psychiatrist, editor, and writer. — **John L(awrence),** 1858–1918, U.S. pugilist. — **Louis Henri,** 1856–1924, U.S. architect.

Sul·li·vant (sul'ə·vənt), **William Starling,** 1803–73, U.S. botanist.

sul·ly (sul'ē) *v.* **·lied, ·ly·ing** *v.t.* To mar the brightness or purity of; soil; defile; tarnish. — *v.i.* To become soiled or tarnished: also figuratively. See synonyms under DEFILE, STAIN. — *n. pl.* **·lies** Anything that tarnishes; a stain; spot; blemish. [<MF *souiller* SOIL²]

Sul·ly (sul'ē, *Fr.* sü·lē'), **Duc de,** 1560–1641, Maximilien de Béthune, French statesman. — **Thomas,** 1783–1872, U.S. portrait painter born in England.

Sul·ly-Prud·homme (sü·lē'·prü·dôm'), **René François Armand,** 1839–1907, French poet and critic.

sulph– For all words so spelled, see the forms beginning SULF–.

sulpha– Var. of SULFA–.

sulpho– Var. of SULFO–.

sul·tan (sul'tən) *n.* 1 The ruler of a Moslem country. 2 A gallinule with deep-blue or purple plumage and white lower tail coverts. *Ionornis martinica* is the purple gallinule or sultan of the warmer parts of America. 3 A small white-crested variety of the domestic fowl, originating in Turkey, having heavily feathered legs and feet. 4 Formerly, any ruler. — **the Sultan** The title of the sovereign of Turkey: office abolished, 1922. [<F <Med. L *sultanus* <Arabic *sultān* a sovereign, dominion]

sul·tan·a (sul·tan'ə, -tä'nə) *n.* 1 A sultan's wife, daughter, sister, or mother: also **sul·tan·ess** (sul'tən·is). 2 The mistress of a king or prince. 3 A variety of raisin from the district of Smyrna, Asia Minor. 4 Sultan (def. 3): also **sul·tan'a-bird'.** [<Ital., fem. of *sultano* a sultan <Arabic *sultān*]

sul·tan·ate (sul'tən·āt, -it) *n.* The authority or territorial jurisdiction of a sultan. Also **sul'tan·ship.**

sul·try (sul'trē) *adj.* **·tri·er, ·tri·est** 1 Hot, moist, and still; close: said of weather. 2 Emitting an oppressive heat; burning; hot with anger. 3 Showing or suggesting passion; sensual. [<obs. *sulter,* var. of SWELTER] — **sul'tri·ly** *adv.* — **sul'tri·ness** *n.*

Su·lu (soo'loo) *n.* 1 A member of the chief Moro tribe occupying the Sulu Archipelago. 2 The Indonesian language of this tribe, closely related to Tagalog. — **Su·lu'an** *adj. & n.*

Sulu Archipelago An island group between Basilan and the NE coast of Borneo, comprising a province of the Philippines; 1,086 square miles; capital, Jolo.

Sulu Sea An arm of the Pacific Ocean between the SW Philippines and Borneo; over 400 miles long, east to west.

sum (sum) *n.* 1 The result obtained by addition. 2 The entire quantity, number, or substance; the whole; all: the *sum* total of my means; the *sum* and substance of the case. 3 Any indefinite amount: said chiefly of money. 4 A problem in arithmetic propounded for solution. 5 The summit; topmost or highest point; also, the maximum; the complement. 6 A summary; the pith or essence. See synonyms under AGGREGATE. — *v.* **summed, sum·ming** *v.t.* 1 To present in brief; recapitulate succinctly: usually with *up:* to *sum up* evidence. 2 To add into one total; ascertain the sum of: often with *up.* 3 To ascertain the sum of (the terms of a series). — *v.i.* 4 To make a summation or recapitula-

tion: generally with *up.* ◆ Homophone: *some.* [<AF, OF *summe, somme* <L *summa* (*res*) highest (thing), fem. of *summus* highest]

sum– Assimilated var. of SUB–.

su·mac (soo'mak, shoo'-) *n.* 1 Any of a genus (*Rhus*) of woody, erect, or root-climbing plants (family *Anacardiaceae*), with panicles of small flowers, small drupaceous fruits, and yielding a resinous or milky juice; especially, the **smooth sumac** (*R. glabra*) used in medicine. 2 The poison sumac. 3 The dried and powdered leaves of certain species of sumac, used for tanning and dyeing, especially of **tanner's sumac** (*Rhus coriaria*). Also **su'mach.** [<OF <Med. L *sumach* <Arabic *summāq*]

Su·ma·tra (soo·mä'trə) An Indonesian island south of the Malay Peninsula, comprising, with adjacent islands, six provinces of Indonesia; 163,557 square miles; chief city, Palembang. — **Su·ma'tran** *adj. & n.*

Sum·ba (soom'bä) One of the Lesser Sunda Islands, SE of Sumbawa, in south central Nusa Tenggara province, Indonesia; 4,300 square miles: formerly *Sandalwood Island:* Dutch *Soemba.*

Sum·bar (soom'bär) A river in SW Turkmen S.S.R. and Iran, flowing 150 miles west to its confluence with the Atrek river, on the U.S.S.R.–Iran border.

Sum·ba·wa (soom·bä'wä) One of the Lesser Sunda Islands, east of Lombok, in NW central Nusa Tenggara province, Indonesia; 5,965 square miles: Dutch *Soembawa.*

sum·bul (sum'bəl) *n.* Muskroot. Also **sum'bal, sum'bul-root'** (-root', -root'). [<F <Arabic *sunbul*] — **sum·bu·lic** (sum-boo'lik) *adj.*

sumbul tree See under AMMONIAC².

Su·mer (soo'mər) A region and ancient country of Mesopotamia, later the southern division of Babylonia; the sites of its once great cities are in south central Iraq.

Su·me·ri·an (soo·mir'ē·ən) *adj.* Of or pertaining to ancient Sumer, its people, or their language. — *n.* 1 One of an ancient non-Semitic people formerly occupying a part of lower Babylonia: culturally important in the Near East from about 3300–1800 B.C. 2 The agglutinative, unclassified language of these people, written in cuneiform characters and preserved on rocks and clay tablets the earliest of which date from about 4000 B.C. Also **Su·mir'i·an.**

sum·less (sum'lis) *adj.* Too great for computation; incalculable; without number.

sum·ma cum lau·de (sum'ə kum lô'dē, soom'ə koom lou'de) See under CUM LAUDE.

sum·mand (sum'and) *n.* That which is added; any of the numbers forming part of a sum. [<Med. L *summandus* (*numerus*) (the number) to be added < *summare* add <L *summa.* See SUM.]

sum·ma·rize (sum'ə·rīz) *v.t.* **·rized, ·riz·ing** To make a summary of; sum up; epitomize. Also *Brit.* **sum'ma·rise. — sum'ma·ri·za'tion** *n.* **sum'ma·riz'er** *n.*

sum·ma·ry (sum'ər·ē) *adj.* 1 Giving the substance or sum; greatly condensed; concise. 2 Performed without ceremony or delay; instant; offhand: used specifically in law. — *n. pl.* **·ries** An abridgment or epitome; abstract; compendium. See synonyms under ABRIDGMENT. [<Med. L *summarius* <L *summarium* a summary < *summa.* See SUM.] — **sum·ma·ri·ly** (sum'ər·ə·lē, *emphatic* sə·mer'ə·lē) *adv.* — **sum'ma·ri·ness** *n.* — **sum'ma·rist** *n.*

sum·mate (sum·āt') *v.t. & v.i.* **·mat·ed, ·mat·ing** 1 To arrive at the sum of (a series). 2 To sum up. [Back formation <SUMMATION]

sum·ma·tion (sum·ā'shən) *n.* 1 The act or operation of obtaining a sum; the computation or statement of an aggregate sum or result; addition. 2 A speech or a portion of a speech summing up the principal points. [<NL *summatio, -onis* <Med. L *summare* add < *summa.* See SUM.]

sum·mer[1] (sum'ər) *n.* 1 The hottest or warmest season of the year: including June, July, and August, in the northern hemisphere. In the southern hemisphere the summer occurs during the months of the northern winter. ◆ Collateral adjective: *estival.* 2 Figuratively, a year of life, especially of early or happy life; a bright and prosperous period. — **Indian summer** A period of mild weather occurring in

the autumn, with hazy atmosphere usually along the horizon, and a clear sky. It corresponds to the English St. Luke's or St. Martin's summer. —**St. Luke's summer** or **little summer of St. Luke** A short period of warm weather in England expected for a few days beginning with St. Luke's day, the 18th of October. —**St. Martin's summer** A season of mild weather about St. Martin's day, the 11th of November, corresponding to the American Indian summer. —*v.t.* To keep or care for through the summer. —*v.i.* To pass the summer. —*adj.* Of, pertaining to, or occurring in summer. [OE *sumor, sumer*] — **sum′mer·ly** *adj. & adv.*

sum·mer² (sum′ər) *n.*

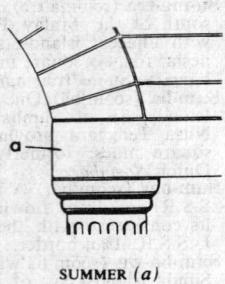

SUMMER (*a*)

Archit. **1** A heavy horizontal timber or girder serving as a support for some superstructure in a building, etc.; a lintel. **2** A large stone, as on a column or pilaster, for supporting one or more arches, or any similar structure. **3** A horizontal beam resting upon the walls or external frame of a building, and supporting the ends of joists. [< OF *somier* a pack horse, beam < LL *saumarius* < L *sagmarius* < *sagma* a pack saddle < Gk.]

summer flounder A flounder (*Paralichthys dentatus*) of the Atlantic coast of North America.

sum·mer·house (sum′ər·hous′) *n.* A rustic structure, as in a garden, for rest or shade.

summer house A house or cottage in the country or at the seashore, used during the summer.

sum·mer·sault (sum′ər·sôlt), **sum·mer·set** (sum′ər·set) See SOMERSAULT.

summer squash Any of various squashes derived from the variety *Cucurbita pepo melopepo* and picked as vegetables before mature, while their rinds and seeds are tender.

sum·mer·time (sum′ər·tīm′) *n.* Summer; the summer season. Also **sum′mer·tide′.**

sum·mer·y (sum′ər·ē) *adj.* Pertaining to or resembling summer.

sum·mit (sum′it) *n.* **1** The highest part; the top; vertex. **2** The highest degree; maximum. **3** The highest level or office, as of a government or business organization. **4** A meeting of executives of the highest level, as heads of government. — *adj.* Of or involving those at the highest level: a *summit* conference. [< OF *sommette*, dim. of *som* a summit, top < L *summum*, neut. of *summus* highest]

Synonyms: acme, apex, cap, climax, crown, height, peak, pinnacle, top, vertex. *Antonyms*: abyss, base, bottom, chasm, deep, depth, gorge, gulf, pit, vale, valley.

sum·mit·ry (sum′it·rē) *n.* **1** Meetings of officials of the highest rank, as heads of government. **2** The use or dependency upon such meetings to solve international problems.

sum·mon (sum′ən) *v.t.* **1** To order to come; send for. **2** To call together; cause to convene, as a legislative assembly. **3** To order (a person) to appear in court by a summons. **4** To call forth or into action; arouse: usually with *up*: to *summon* up courage. **5** To bid or call on for a specific act: The garrison was *summoned* to surrender. See synonyms under ARRAIGN, CONVOKE. [< AF, OF *somondre* < L *summonere* suggest, hint < *sub-* secretly + *monere* warn] —**sum′mon·er** *n.*

sum·mons (sum′ənz) *n.* **1** A call to attend or act at a particular place or time. **2** *Law* A notice to a defendant summoning him to appear in court: either a judicial writ or process, or a notice signed by the plaintiff or his attorney; any citation issued to a party to an action to appear before a court or judge at chambers. See WRIT OF SUMMONS. **3** A notice to a person requiring him to appear in court as a witness or as a juror. **4** A military demand to surrender. **5** Any signal or sound that is a peremptory call. [< AF *somonse*, OF *sumunse* < *somondre* SUMMON]

sum·mum bo·num (sum′əm bō′nəm) *Latin* The chief, supreme, or highest good.

Sum·ner (sum′nər), **Charles,** 1811–74, U.S.

statesman and abolitionist. —**James Batcheller,** 1887–1955, U.S. biochemist. —**William Graham,** 1840–1910, U.S. sociologist.

su·mo (sōō′mō) *n.* A highly stylized form of wrestling popular in Japan. [< Japanese *sumō*]

sump (sump) *n.* **1** *Mining* **a** A depression sunk below the lowest level in a mine shaft, to receive water and form a pool from which it may be pumped. **b** A sump winze. **2** *Mech.* The lowest part of the crankcase of an internal-combustion engine, acting as a reservoir for lubricating oil. **3** A cesspool or other reservoir for drainage. [< MDu. *somp, sump* a marsh. Akin to SWAMP.]

sump·ter (sump′tər) *n.* A pack animal; beast of burden. [< OF *sometier* a driver of a pack horse, ult. < L *sagma*. See SUMMER².]

sump·tu·ar·y (sump′chōō·er′ē) *adj.* Pertaining to expense; limiting or regulating expenditure, as some laws. [< L *sumptuarius* < *sumptus* expenditure < *sumere* take]

sumptuary law 1 A law limiting or regulating expenditure in order to prevent extravagance and inflation. **2** A law regulating private life on moral or religious grounds.

sump·tu·ous (sump′chōō·əs) *adj.* Involving or showing lavish expenditure; hence, luxurious; magnificent. [< OF *sumptueux, somptueux* < L *sumptuosus* < *sumptus*. See SUMPTUARY.] — **sump′tu·ous·ly** *adv.* —**sump′tu·ous·ness** *n.*

sump·weed (sump′wēd′) *n.* Marsh elder.

sun (sun) *n.* **1** The heavenly body that is the center of attraction and the main source of light and heat in the solar system, with a mean distance from the earth of about 93,000,000 miles and a diameter of 864,000 miles. Its mass is 332,000 times that of the earth, but its density only about one-fourth. **2** Any star, especially one that is the center of a system revolving around it. **3** The light and heat radiated from the sun; sunshine. **4** Anything brilliant and magnificent, or that is a source of splendor. **5** The time of the earth's revolution round the sun; a year. **6** The daily appearance of the sun; a day; also, the time of its appearance or shining; sunrise. —**a place in the sun** A dominant position in international affairs; hence, a position in the spotlight; publicity. —*v.* **sunned, sun·ning** *v.t.* **1** To expose to the light or heat of the sun. **2** To warm or dry (something) in the sun. —*v.i.* **3** To bask in the sun; expose oneself to the light or heat of the sun. ◆ Homophone: *son.* [OE *sunne*]

Sun may appear as a combining form in hyphemes or solidemes, or as the first element in two-word phrases, with the following meanings:

1 Of the sun; of sunshine:

sun blaze	sun-loving
sun-eclipsing	sun-worship
sun glare	sun-worshipper
sunland	sun-worshiping

2 By or with the sun:

sun-bake	sun-filled
sun-baked	sun-flooded
sun-blind	sun-gilt
sun-blinded	sun-heated
sun-blistered	sun-kissed
sun-brown	sunlit
sun-browned	sun-scorched
sun-cracked	sun-scorching
sun-dappled	sun-streaked
sun-dried	sun-warmed
sun-dry	sun-withered

sun bath Exposure to direct sunlight.

sun-bathe (sun′bāth′) *v.i.* **-bathed, -bath·ing** To bask in the sun, especially as a method of tanning the skin. —**sun′-bath′er** *n.* —**sun′-bath′ing** *n.*

sun·beam (sun′bēm′) *n.* **1** A ray or beam of the sun; light from the sun in a visible path. **2** *pl.* Sunlight.

sun bear A small arboreal bear (*Helarctos malayanus*), inhabiting forests of southeastern Asia. Also called *honey bear.*

Sun-belt (sun′belt′) *n. U.S.* The southeastern and southwestern states of the United States, ranging from Virginia south to Florida and west to California.

sun·bird (sun′bûrd′) *n.* **1** A brilliantly colored oriental singing bird (family *Nectariniidae*) resembling the hummingbird. **2** A sun bittern.

sun bittern Either of two birds of Central and

South America (genus *Eurypyga*) related to the rails and herons, having a slender neck and bill, long wings and tail, and moderately long legs.

sun-bon·net (sun′bon′it) *n.* A bonnet of light material with projecting brim and sometimes a cape covering the neck.

sun-burn (sun′bûrn′) *n.* Discoloration or inflammation of the skin, produced by exposure to the sun. —*v.t. & v.i.* To affect or be affected with sunburn. —**sun′burnt′, sun′burned′** *adj.*

sun-burst (sun′bûrst′) *n.* **1** A strong burst of sunlight, as through rifted clouds. **2** A brooch or pin with jewels so set around a larger central gem as to suggest sun rays.

sun compass A compass serving to establish Greenwich time in relation to the position of the sun: used chiefly in polar regions, where the magnetic compass is unreliable.

sun-dae (sun′dē) *n.* A refreshment consisting of ice-cream and crushed fruit, flavoring, sirup, nuts, etc. [Prob. < *Sunday*, prob. so called because orig. sold only on that day]

Sun-da Islands (sun′də, *Du.* sōōn′dä) An Indonesian island group of the Malay Archipelago, between the Indian Ocean and the Java Sea; divided into *Greater Sunda Islands*, including Sumatra, Java, Borneo, and Celebes, and *Lesser Sunda Islands*, the smaller islands east of Java. Dutch **Soen′da.**

sun dance The greatest ceremonial dance of the Plains Indians, usually a summer solstice ceremony, comprising fast days, dance days, secret rites, and a public performance.

Sun-da Strait (sun′də, *Du.* sōōn′dä) The channel between Java and Sumatra, connecting the Java Sea with the Indian Ocean, 16 to 70 miles wide.

Sun-day (sun′dē, -dā) *n.* The first day of the week; the Lord's day; the Christian Sabbath: sometimes used attributively. See synonyms under SABBATH. [OE *sunnan dæg* < *sunnan* of the sun + *dæg* a day; trans. of LL *dies solis* day of the sun]

Sun-day (sun′dē, -dā), **Billy,** 1862–1935, U.S. preacher and evangelist; full name *William Ashley Sunday.*

Sun-day-go-to-meet-ing (sun′dē-gō′tə-mē′ting) *adj. Colloq.* Best: *Sunday-go-to-meeting* clothes or manners.

Sunday school A school, generally attached to some church, in which religious instruction is given on Sunday, especially to the young; also, the pupils, or teachers and pupils, collectively: also called *Sabbath school.*

sun-der (sun′dər) *v.t.* To break apart; disunite; sever. —*v.i.* To be parted or severed. See synonyms under BREAK, CUT, REND, SEPARATE. —*n.* Division into parts; separation. —**in sunder** Apart; separate from other parts. Compare ASUNDER. [OE *syndrian, sundrian*] —**sun′der·ance** *n.*

Sun-der-land (sun′dər-lənd) A port and county borough in NE Durham, England.

sun-dew (sun′dōō′, -dyōō′) *n.* Any of a genus (*Drosera*) of marsh plants that exude a viscid liquid from the tips of the hairs on the leaves. Insects are caught by the secretions and are utilized by the plant for its own nutrition.

sun-di·al (sun′dī′əl) *n.* A device that measures time and shows the time of day by means of the shadow of a style or gnomon thrown on a dial.

sun disk The winged disk. See under DISK.

sun-dog (sun′dôg′, -dog′) *n.* **1** A parhelion, appearing near the sun, sometimes with a luminous train, due to the presence of ice crystals in the air; a mock sun. **2** A small rainbow lying near the horizon.

SUNDIAL

sun-down (sun′doun′) *n.* **1** Sunset: originally colloquial, like *sunup*, but now in good literary usage. **2** A broad-brimmed hat worn by women. [? Contraction of *sun-go-down*]

sun-down-er (sun′dou′nər) *n.* **1** *Colloq.* A tramp. **2** *Austral.* A vagrant who seeks food and lodging at back-country ranches, often about the time of sundown. **3** *Slang* A strict,

rigidly uncompromising ship's officer; originally, a ship's captain who granted liberty only until sundown.

sun·dries (sun'drēz) *n. pl.* Items or things too small or too numerous to be separately specified. [<SUNDRY]

sun·drops (sun'drops') *n.* Any of several American species of evening primrose (genus *Oenothera*), having large yellow flowers, and blooming in the daytime.

sun·dry (sun'drē) *adj.* Of an indefinite small number; various; several; miscellaneous. See synonyms under MANY. [OE *syndrig* separate, private]

sune (sōōn) *adv. Scot.* Soon.

sun·fish (sun'fish') *n. pl.* **·fish** or **·fish·es** 1 A large pelagic plectognath fish (genus *Mola*), having a deep compressed body truncate behind, as *Mola mola* of warm and tropical seas. It has tough and leathery flesh. 2 Any of several North American freshwater perchlike fishes (family *Centrarchidae*) of the genus *Lepomis,* as the pumpkinseed.

SUNFISH (*def. 1*)
(Up to 8 feet in length)

sun·flow·er (sun'flou'ər) *n.* Any of a genus (*Helianthus*) of tall, stout, rough herbs of the composite family, with large leaves and circular heads of flowers, those in the center tubular and usually purple, and those on the margin strap–shaped and bright–yellow; especially, the common sunflower (*H. annuus*), the source of an edible oil, and the State flower of Kansas.

Sunflower State Nickname of KANSAS.

sung (sung) Past participle and occasional past tense of SING.

Sung (sōōng) *n.* A dynasty in Chinese history, 960 to 1280, noted for its achievements in art and philosophy.

Sun·ga·ri (sōōng'gä·rē') The largest river of Manchuria, flowing 1,150 miles NW to the Amur river. *Chinese* **Sung·hwa** (sōōng'hwä').

Sung·kiang (sōōng'jyäng') A former province of NE Manchuria region, NE China, incorporated in Heilungkiang province; 75,000 square miles; capital, Harbin.

sun·glass (sun'glas', -gläs') *n.* 1 A burning glass; a glass used for concentrating the rays of the sun. 2 *pl.* Spectacles that protect the eyes from the glare of the sun by their colored lenses.

sun·glow (sun'glō') *n.* 1 The rose tint or faint yellow of the sky that precedes sunrise or follows sunset. 2 The warm glow of the sun.

sun·god (sun'god') *n.* In the religions of some primitive agricultural peoples, a deity conceived of as life–giving and beneficent, and symbolized by the sun, as the ancient Egyptian Ra, ancient Irish Lug, Inti of the Incas, etc.: not to be confused with personifications of the sun in many cosmogonic myths (Greek Helios, for instance) which are mere explanatory etiological tales and do not posit a sun cult.

sunk (sungk) Past participle and alternative past tense of SINK.

sunk·en (sung'kən) Obsolete past participle of SINK. — *adj.* 1 Lying at the bottom of a body of water: a *sunken* ship. 2 Located beneath a surface. 3 Lower than the surrounding or usual level: *sunken* gardens. 4 Deeply depressed or fallen in: *sunken* cheeks.

sun·ket (sung'kit, sōōng'-) *n. Scot.* A dainty; tidbit.

sunk fence A ditch having a retaining wall on one side to divide lands; a ha–ha.

sunk·ie (sungk'ē) *n. Scot.* A low stool or small seat.

sunk panel A panel so depressed as to form a recess below the surface of its frame.

sun lamp 1 A lamp giving illumination of high intensity, usually reflected by parabolic mirrors: used in motion–picture studios. 2 A lamp radiating ultraviolet rays: used for therapeutic treatments and as a protec-

tion against airborne bacteria in operating rooms, etc.

sun·less (sun'lis) *adj.* Dark; cheerless. — **sun'less·ness** *n.*

sun·light (sun'līt') *n.* The light of the sun.

sun·lit (sun'lit') *adj.* Lighted by the sun.

sunn (sun) *n.* An East Indian shrub (*Crotalaria juncea*) of the bean family, with bright–yellow flowers and tough, durable fiber: used for making cordage, bagging, and other coarse textiles: also called *Bombay* or *Madras hemp.* Also **sunn hemp.** [<Hind. *san*]

Sun·na (sōōn'ə) *n.* A path or manner of life; that part of the orthodox Moslem creed or law based on traditions of the Prophet's words and deeds: regarded by a numerous sect as of equal importance with the Koran, which it supplements; hence, the theory and practice of orthodox Islam. Also **Sun'nah.** [<Arabic *sunnah,* lit., a form, way]

Sun·nite (sōōn'īt) *n.* An orthodox Moslem of the sect accepting Sunna (tradition) and the Koran as of equal authority, and acknowledging the first four caliphs as rightful successors of the Prophet: opposed to *Shiah.* Also **Sun·ni** (sōōn'ē).

sun·ny (sun'ē) *adj.* **·ni·er, ·ni·est** 1 Filled with the light and warmth of the sun; exposed to the sun. 2 Bright like the sun; of the sun or sunshine; hence, genial; cheery: a *sunny* smile. See synonyms under BRIGHT, CHEERFUL, HAPPY. — **sun'ni·ly** *adv.* — **sun'ni·ness** *n.*

sunny side 1 The side, as of a hill, facing the sun. 2 The cheerful view of any situation, question, etc.

sun parlor A room enclosed in glass and having a sunny exposure.

sun pillar A column of variously tinted light sometimes seen projecting vertically above or below the sun at sunrise or sunset. It is caused by the reflection of sunlight from small snow crystals.

sun·rise (sun'rīz') *n.* 1 The daily first appearance of the sun above the horizon, with the atmospheric phenomena just preceding and following. 2 The time at which the sun rises. 3 The east; Orient.

sun·room (sun'rōōm', -rōōm') *n.* A room built to admit a profusion of sunlight.

sun·scald (sun'skôld') *n.* A diseased condition of plants induced by exposure to intense sunlight.

sun·scorch (sun'skôrch') *n.* A scorched or burnt condition of plants.

sun·set (sun'set') *n.* 1 The apparent daily descent of the sun below the horizon. 2 The time when the sun sets; the early evening. 3 The colors in the sky when the sun sets. 4 The west; Occident. 5 Figuratively, the ending or decline, as of life.

sun·shade (sun'shād') *n.* Something used as a shade or protection from the rays of the sun, as a parasol, an awning, etc.

sun·shine (sun'shīn') *n.* 1 The shining light of the sun; the direct rays of the sun. 2 The warmth of the sun's rays. 3 The place where the rays fall. 4 Figuratively, brightness; any cheering influence. — **sun'shin'y** *adj.*

Sunshine State Nickname of NEW MEXICO.

sun·spot (sun'spot') *n.* 1 *Astron.* One of many dark irregular spots appearing periodically on the surface of the sun: believed to have connection with terrestrial magnetic storms. 2 An incandescent sun lamp used in color photography.

sun·stone (sun'stōn') *n.* A variety of feldspar; aventurine.

sun·stroke (sun'strōk') *n. Pathol.* A sudden onset of high fever induced by exposure to the sun and often marked by convulsions and coma; insolation. — **sun'struck'** (-struk') *adj.*

sun tan A bronze–colored condition of the skin, produced by exposure to the sun. — **sun'–tanned'** (-tand') *adj.*

sun·tans (sun'tanz') *n. pl.* The lightweight summer uniform made of khaki worn by U. S. Army personnel: officially known as *cotton khakis,* and often called *khakis.* They are worn in the Navy by officers.

sun·up (sun'up') *n.* Sunrise. [<SUN + UP: on analogy with *sundown*]

Sun Valley A resort village in south central Idaho; altitude, 6,000 feet.

sun·ward (sun'wərd) *adj.* Facing toward the

sun. — *adv.* Toward the sun: also **sun'wards.**

sun·wise (sun'wīz') *adv.* With the sun; in the direction of the sun; clockwise.

Sun Yat–sen (sōōn' yät'sen'), 1865?–1925, Chinese statesman; president of China 1911–1912.

su·o ju·re (sōō'ō jōōr'ē) *Latin* In one's own right.

su·o lo·co (sōō'ō lō'kō) *Latin* In its own or proper place.

Su·o·mi (sōō·ō'mē) *n. pl.* 1 The people of Finland; the Finns. 2 The language of the Finns; Finnish. — **Su·o'mic** *adj.* & *n.*

Su·o·mi (sōō·ō'mē) The Finnish name for FINLAND.

sup¹ (sup) *v.t. & v.i.* **supped, sup·ping** To take (fluid food) in successive mouthfuls, a little at a time; sip. — *n.* A mouthful or taste of liquid or semiliquid food. [OE *sūpan* drink]

sup² (sup) *v.* **supped, sup·ping** *v.i.* To eat supper. — *v.t. Obs.* To furnish with or invite to supper. [<OF *soper, super*; ult. origin unknown]

sup- Assimilated var. of SUB-.

supe (sōōp) *n. Slang* A supernumerary actor. [Short for SUPERNUMERARY]

su·per¹ (sōō'pər) *n. Colloq.* Shortened form of SUPERINTENDENT.

su·per² (sōō'pər) *n. Slang* Shortened form of SUPERNUMERARY (def. 2).

su·per³ (sōō'pər) *n.* 1 An article of superior size or quality; also, such size or quality. 2 In bookbinding, a thin, starched cotton fabric used in reinforcement. — *adj.* 1 *Slang* First-rate; superfine. 2 Showing excessive loyalty: a *super* American. — *v.t.* To reinforce (a book) with super. [Short for SUPERIOR, SUPERFINE, etc.]

super– *prefix* 1 Above in position: over: *superstructure, superimpose.* 2 *Anat. & Zool.* Situated above, or on the dorsal side of: *superorbital.* 3 Above or beyond; more than: *supersonic, supersensible.* 4 Excessively: *supersaturate.* 5 *Med.* Exceeding the normal: *superacidity.* 6 *Chem.* Denoting a high proportion of the ingredient indicated (now superseded by PER-, BI-): *superphosphate.* 7 Surpassing in power or size all others of its class: *superhighway, supermarket.* In this sense the prefix is sometimes doubled to intensify the degree of superiority: a *super–supernavy* a navy far superior to any other. 8 Extra; additional: *supertax.* [<L *super–* < *super* above, beyond]

In the following list of words *super–* denotes excess or superiority, as *supercritical* excessively critical, *superexcellence* superior excellence.

superabhor	superbold
superabominable	superbrave
superabsurd	superbusy
superaccession	supercandid
superaccommodating	supercapable
superaccomplished	supercatastrophe
superaccumulate	supercatholic
superachievement	supercaution
superacquisition	superceremonious
superacute	superchivalrous
superadaptable	supercivil
superadequate	supercivilized
superadmiration	superclassified
superadorn	supercolossal
superaffluence	supercombination
superagency	supercommendation
superaggravation	supercommercial
superagitation	supercompetition
superambitious	supercomplex
superangelic	supercomprehension
superappreciation	supercompression
superarbitrary	superconfident
superarduous	superconformist
superarrogant	superconformity
superaspiration	superconfusion
superastonish	supercongestion
superattachment	superconservative
superattraction	supercontrol
superattractive	supercordial
superbelief	supercritic
superbeloved	supercritical
superbenefit	supercultivated
superbenevolent	supercurious
superbenign	supercynical
superbias	superdainty
superblessed	superdanger
superblunder	superdeclamatory

superdeficit
superdejection
superdelicate
superdemand
superdemonic
superdesirous
superdevelopment
superdevilish
superdevotion
superdiabolical
superdifficult
superdiplomacy
superdistribution
superdividend
superdonation
supereconomy
supereffective
supereffluence
superelastic
superelated
superelegance
supereligible
supereloquent
superemphasis
superendorsement
superendow
superenforcement
superenrolment
superestablishment
superesthetic
superethical
superevident
superexacting
superexalt
superexaltation
superexcellence
superexcellent
superexcitation
superexcited
superexcitement
superexiguity
superexpansion
superexpectation
superexpenditure
superexpressive
superexquisiteness
superextension
superfecundity
superfeminine
superfervent
superfoliation
superfolly
superformal
superformation
superformidable
superfriendly
superfructified
superfulfilment
supergaiety
supergallant
supergenerosity
superglorious
supergoodness
supergovernment
supergratification
supergravitation
superhandsome
superhearty
superhero
superheroic
superhistorical
superhypocrite
superideal
superignorant
superillustrate
superimpending
superimpersonal
superimportant
superimprobable
superimproved
superincentive
superinclination
superinclusive
superincomprehensible
superindependent
superindifference
superindignant
superindividualism
superindividualist
superindulgence
superindustrious
superinference
superinfinite
superinfirmity
superinfluence
superingenious
superinitiative

superinjustice
superinquisitive
superinsistent
superintellectual
superintolerable
superjurisdiction
superjustification
superknowledge
superlaborious
superlenient
superlie
superlogical
superloyal
superlucky
superluxurious
supermagnificently
supermanhood
supermarvelous
supermasculine
supermechanical
supermediocre
supermental
supermentality
supermetropolitan
supermishap
supermodest
supermoisten
supermorose
supermundane
supermystery
supernecessity
supernegligent
supernotable
supernumerous
superobedience
superobese
superobjectionable
superobligation
superobstinate
superoffensive
superofficious
superofficiousness
superopposition
superoratorical
superordinary
superorganize
superornamental
superoutput
superpatient
superpatriotic
superpatriotism
superperfection
superpious
superplease
superpolite
superpositive
superpraise
superprecise
superpreparation
superproduce
superprosperous
superpublicity
superpure
superpurgation
superradical
superrational
superrefined
superreform
superreliance
superremuneration
superrespectable
superresponsible
superrestriction
superreward
superrighteous
superromantic
supersacrifice
supersafe
supersagacious
supersanguine
supersarcastic
supersatisfaction
superscholarly
superscientific
supersensitive
supersensitiveness
supersensuousness
supersentimental
superserious
supersevere
supersignificant
supersimplify
supersmart
supersolemn
supersolemnly
supersolicitation
superspecialize

superspiritual
superspirituality
superstimulation
superstoical
superstrain
superstrenuous
superstrict
superstrong
superstylish
supersufficient
supersurprise
supersweet
supertension
superthankful
superthorough

supertoleration
supertragic
supertrivial
superugly
superunity
superurgent
supervexation
supervigilant
supervigorous
supervirulent
supervital
superwise
superworldly
superwrought
superzealous

su·per·a·ble (soo′pər·ə·bəl) *adj.* That can be surmounted, overcome, or conquered. [<L *superabilis* < *superare* overcome < *super* over]

su·per·a·bound (soo′pər·ə·bound′) *v.i.* To abound to excess or to an unusual extent. [<LL *superabundare* <L *super-* exceedingly + *abundare* overflow]

su·per·a·bun·dant (soo′pər·ə·bun′dənt) *adj.* Excessive; more than sufficient. See synonyms under REDUNDANT. [<LL *superabundans, -antis,* ppr. of *superabundare.* See SUPERABOUND.] — **su′per·a·bun′dance** *n.* — **su′per·a·bun′dant·ly** *adv.*

su·per·a·cid·i·ty (soo′pər·ə·sid′ə·tē) *n. Med.* An excess of acid, especially in the gastric juices; hyperacidity.

su·per·add (soo′pər·ad′) *v.t.* To add in addition to something already added. [<LL *superaddere* < *super-* over and above + *addere* ADD] — **su′per·ad·di′tion** (-ə·dish′ən) *n.*

su·per·al·tar (soo′pər·ôl′tər) *n. Eccl.* **1** A consecrated slab laid on an unconsecrated altar when mass is said in oratories or temporary chapels. **2** Sometimes, incorrectly, a retable. [<Med. L *superaltare* <L *super-* over + *altare* an altar]

su·per·an·nu·ate (soo′pər·an′yoo·āt) *v.t.* ·**at·ed,** ·**at·ing** **1** To retire or retire and pension on account of age: chiefly in past participle. **2** To set aside or discard as obsolete or too old. [<Med. L *superannuatus* more than a year old (said of cattle) <L *super annum* < *super* beyond + *annus* a year] — **su′per·an′nu·at′ed** *adj.* — **su′per·an′nu·a′tion** *n.*

su·per·aq·ual (soo′pər·ak′wəl, -ā′kwəl) *adj.* Of, pertaining to, or denoting those soils lying just above the water table, from which they derive the greater part of their moisture. [<L *super* above + *aqua* water]

su·perb (soo·pûrb′, sə-) *adj.* **1** Having grand, impressive beauty; majestic; imposing: a *superb* edifice. **2** Luxurious; rich and costly; elegant. **3** Very good; supremely fine. [<L *superbus* proud < *super-* over] — **su·perb′ly** *adv.* — **su·perb′ness** *n.*

su·per·bomb (soo′pər·bom′) *n.* A hydrogen bomb.

su·per·cal·en·der (soo′pər·kal′ən·dər) *n.* A calender having a number of polished rollers for giving a high finish to paper. See CALENDER[1]. — *v.t.* To give a high finish to (paper). — **su′·per·cal′en·dered** *adj.*

su·per·car·go (soo′pər·kär′gō) *n. pl.* ·**goes** or ·**gos** An agent on board ship in charge of the cargo and its sale and purchase. [Alter. of obs. *supracargo* <Sp. *sobrecargo* < *sobre-* over (<L *super-*) + *cargo* CARGO]

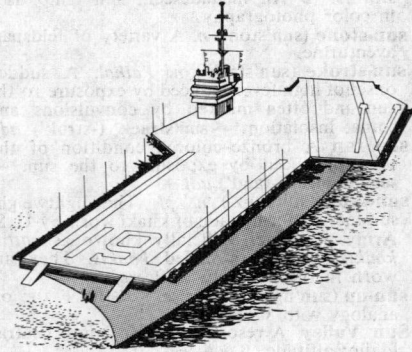

SUPERCARRIER OF THE FORRESTAL CLASS

su·per·car·ri·er (soo′pər·kar′ē·ər) *n.* An aircraft-carrier of exceptional size.

su·per·charge (soo′pər·chärj′) *v.t.* ·**charged,** ·**charg·ing** **1** To adapt (an engine) to develop more power, as by fitting with a supercharger. **2** To charge to excess; overload. — *n.* (soo′pər·chärj′) **1** An excess charge, in any sense. **2** *Her.* One charge or device borne on another.

su·per·charg·er (soo′pər·chär′jər) *n.* A compressor for supplying air or combustible mixture to an internal-combustion engine at a pressure greater than that developed by the suction of the pistons alone.

su·per·cil·i·ar·y (soo′pər·sil′ē·er′ē) *adj.* **1** Of or pertaining to the eyebrow. **2** Situated over the eyebrow; supraorbital: the *superciliary* arches. [<NL *superciliaris* <L *supercilium* an eyebrow < *super-* above + *cilium* an eyelid]

su·per·cil·i·ous (soo′pər·sil′ē·əs) *adj.* Exhibiting haughty contempt or indifference; arrogant. See synonyms under HAUGHTY. [<L *superciliosus* < *supercilium.* See SUPERCILIARY.] — **su′per·cil′i·ous·ly** *adv.* — **su′per·cil′i·ous·ness** *n.*

su·per·class (soo′pər·klas′, -kläs′) *n. Biol.* A division of plants or animals below a phylum but above a class.

su·per·co·lum·nar (soo′pər·kə·lum′nər) *adj. Archit.* **1** Erected above a colonnade or another column. **2** Having one order placed above another.

su·per·con·duc·tiv·i·ty (soo′pər·kon·duk·tiv′ə·tē) *n. Electr.* The property, exhibited by certain metals and alloys, of becoming almost perfect conductors of electricity when their temperatures fall below transition points in the neighborhood of absolute zero. — **su′per·con·duc′tive** (-kən·duk′tiv) *adj.* — **su′per·con·duc′tor** *n.*

su·per·cool (soo′pər·kool′) *v.t.* To cool, as a liquid, below the freezing point without solidification.

su·per·dom·i·nant (soo′pər·dom′ə·nənt) *n. Music* The tone just above the dominant; the sixth or submediant.

su·per–du·per (soo′pər·doo′pər) *Slang adj.* Superlative: an intensive formation. — *n.* Anything especially fine. [Reduplication of SUPER[3]]

su·per·e·go (soo′pər·ē′gō, -eg′ō) *n. Psychoanal.* A largely unconscious element of the personality, regarded as dominating the conscious ego, for which it acts principally in the role of conscience and critic.

su·per·em·i·nent (soo′pər·em′ə·nənt) *adj.* Excelling or surpassing others; of a superior or remarkable quality; supremely exalted. [<L *supereminens, -entis,* ppr. of *supereminere* rise above < *super-* above + *eminere* rise. See EMINENT.] — **su′per·em′i·nence** *n.* — **su′per·em′i·nent·ly** *adv.*

su·per·er·o·gate (soo′pər·er′ə·gāt) *v.i.* ·**gat·ed,** ·**gat·ing** To do more than is required or ordered. [<L *supererogatus,* pp. of *supererogare* < *super-* over and above + *erogare* pay out < *ex-* out + *rogare* ask]

su·per·er·o·ga·tion (soo′pər·er′ə·gā′shən) *n.* The performance of an act in excess of the demands or requirements of duty. — **works of supererogation** Good deeds done by saints of the Roman Catholic Church in excess of the requirements of divine law; also, voluntary good deeds performed by men over and above God's commandments.

su·per·e·rog·a·to·ry (soo′pər·ə·rog′ə·tôr′ē, -tō′rē) *adj.* Of, pertaining to, or of the nature of supererogation; superfluous. Also **su′per·e·rog′a·tive.**

su·per·fam·i·ly (soo′pər·fam′ə·lē, -fam′lē) *n. pl.* ·**lies** *Biol.* A division of plants or animals ranking next above the family but below an order or suborder.

su·per·fe·cun·da·tion (soo′pər·fē′kən·dā′shən, -fek′ən-) *n. Physiol.* The successive impregnation of two or more ova.

su·per·fe·male (soo′pər·fē′māl) *n. Biol.* A supersexual organism, characterized in the fruit fly by a ratio of 3 X-chromosomes to 2 sets of autosomes.

su·per·fe·tate (soo′pər·fē′tāt) *v.i.* ·**tat·ed,** ·**tat·ing** *Physiol.* To conceive again prior to the birth of an embryo or fetus already conceived. [<L *superfetatus,* pp. of *superfetare* < *super-* over and above + *fetus* a foetus]

su·per·fe·ta·tion (soo′pər·fi·tā′shən) *n.* **1** *Physiol.* **a** The second impregnation of a female already pregnant. **b** The progeny resulting from such second impregnation; hence,

any unusual additional growth. 2 *Bot.* Fertilization of the same ovule by two or more kinds of pollen. Also **su′per·foe·ta′tion.**

su·per·fi·cial (so͞o′pər·fish′əl) *adj.* 1 Of, pertaining to, lying near, or forming the surface; affecting only the surface. 2 Of or pertaining to only the ordinary and the obvious; not profound; shallow: a *superficial* writer. 3 Marked by partial knowledge; cursory; hasty; slight: *superficial* treatment of a subject. 4 Not real or genuine. 5 Square: said of measure. [<LL *superficialis* <L *superficies* SUPERFICIES] — **su′per·fi′ci·al′i·ty** (-fish′ē·al′ə·tē), **su′per·fi′cial·ness** *n.* — **su′per·fi′cial·ly** *adv.*

su·per·fi·ci·ar·y (so͞o′pər·fish′ē·er′ē) *adj.* 1 Belonging or pertaining to the superficies; superficial. 2 *Law* Situated on another's land, or resulting from such situation.

su·per·fi·ci·es (so͞o′pər·fish′i·ēz, -fish′ēz) *n. pl.* **·ci·es** 1 A surface or its area; superficial area. 2 External appearance; exterior part. [<L *super-* over + *facies* a face]

su·per·fine (so͞o′pər·fīn′) *adj.* 1 Of surpassing fineness and delicacy; of the best quality. 2 Overrefined; unduly elaborate; overnice. [<MF *superfin* <*super-* over (<L) + *fin* FINE[1]] — **su′per·fine′ness** *n.*

su·per·flu·id (so͞o′pər·flo͞o′id) *n. Physics* A peculiar state of matter noted in helium cooled to within a degree of absolute zero: it is characterized by an exceptional heat conductivity, a ready permeation of very dense substances, and the ability to flow upward against gravity: also called *quantum liquid.* — *adj.* (so͞o′pər·flo͞o′id) Of or pertaining to such a state.

su·per·flu·i·ty (so͞o′pər·flo͞o′ə·tē) *n. pl.* **·ties** 1 The state of being superfluous; superabundance. 2 That, or that part, which is superfluous. See synonyms under EXCESS. [<OF *superfluité* <Med. L *superfluitas, -tatis* <L *superfluus* excessive <*super-* over + *fluere* flow]

su·per·flu·ous (so͞o·pûr′flo͞o·əs) *adj.* 1 Exceeding what is needed; excessively abundant; surplus. 2 *Music* Augmented: sometimes said of an interval. 3 *Archaic* Supererogatory; officious. 4 *Obs.* Overfed, overequipped, or oversupplied. See synonyms under REDUNDANT, WASTE. [<L *superfluus.* See SUPERFLUITY.] — **su·per′flu·ous·ly** *adv.* — **su·per′flu·ous·ness** *n.*

Su·per·for·tress (so͞o′pər·fôr′tris) *n.* A heavy, four-engine bombing plane; the B-29: a trade name. Also **Su′per·fort′.**

su·per·fuse (so͞o′pər·fyo͞oz′) *v.* **·fused, ·fus·ing** *v.t.* To pour so as to cover something else, as cod-liver oil on wine. — *v.i.* To be poured over or on something. [<L *superfusus,* pp. of *superfundere* <*super-* over + *fundere* pour] — **su′per·fu′sion** (-fyo͞o′zhən) *n.*

su·per·gla·cial (so͞o′pər·glā′shəl) *adj. Geol.* Resting upon or deposited from the surface of a glacier.

su·per·heat (so͞o′pər·hēt′) *v.t.* 1 To heat to excess; overheat. 2 To raise the temperature of (a vapor not in contact with its liquid) above the saturation point for a given pressure. 3 To heat (a liquid) above the boiling point for a given pressure, but without conversion into vapor. — *n.* (so͞o′pər·hēt′) The degree to which steam has been superheated, or the heat so imparted.

su·per·heat·er (so͞o′pər·hē′tər) *n.* A mechanical contrivance for superheating steam, as by causing it to traverse small tubes in the lower part of a chimney.

su·per·het·er·o·dyne (so͞o′pər·het′ər·ə·dīn′) *adj. Electronics* Pertaining to or designating a type of radio reception in which the modulated incoming signals have the frequency of their carrier waves changed to an intermediate (inaudible) frequency, and are then rectified to reproduce the original sounds. — *n.* A radio receiving set for this method of reception. [<SUPER(SONIC) + HETERODYNE]

su·per·high·way (so͞o′pər·hī′wā′) *n.* A highway for high-speed traffic, generally with four or more traffic lanes divided by a safety strip.

su·per·hu·man (so͞o′pər·hyo͞o′mən) *adj.* 1 Above the range of human power or skill; above and beyond what is human; miraculous; divine. 2 Beyond normal human ability or power. See synonyms under SUPERNATURAL. — **su′per·hu·man′i·ty** (-hyo͞o·man′ə·tē) *n.* — **su′per·hu′man·ly** *adv.*

su·per·im·pose (so͞o′pər·im·pōz′) *v.t.* **·posed, ·pos·ing** 1 To lay or impose upon something else. 2 To add to something else. — **su′per·im′po·si′tion** (-im′pə·zish′ən) *n.*

su·per·in·cum·bent (so͞o′pər·in·kum′bənt) *adj.* Resting or lying upon something else. [<L *superincumbens, -entis,* ppr. of *superincumbere* <*super-* over + *incumbere* rest on. See INCUMBENT.] — **su′per·in·cum′bence** or **·ben·cy** *n.*

su·per·in·duce (so͞o′pər·in·do͞os′, -dyo͞os′) *v.t.* **·duced, ·duc·ing** To introduce additionally; bring in or cause as an addition. [<LL *superinducere* cover over, add <L *super-* over + *inducere* INDUCE] — **su′per·in·duc′tion** (-duk′·shən) *n.*

su·per·in·tend (so͞o′pər·in·tend′) *v.t.* To have the charge and direction of; manage; supervise. [<LL *superintendere* <*super-* over + *intendere* aim at. See INTEND.]

su·per·in·ten·dence (so͞o′pər·in·ten′dəns) *n.* Direction and management; guiding and controlling supervision. See synonyms under OVERSIGHT.

su·per·in·ten·den·cy (so͞o′pər·in·ten′dən·sē) *n. pl.* **·cies** 1 The office or rank of a superintendent. 2 Superintendence.

su·per·in·ten·dent (so͞o′pər·in·ten′dənt) *n.* 1 One whose function is to superintend some particular work, office, or undertaking: a school *superintendent,* road *superintendent.* 2 The person charged with supervising maintenance and repair in an office or apartment building. — *adj.* Of or pertaining to superintendence or a superintendent; superintending. [<LL *superintendens, -entis,* ppr. of *superintendere* superintend]

Synonyms (noun): conductor, curator, custodian, director, guardian, inspector, intendant, manager, master, overseer, superior, supervisor, warden.

su·pe·ri·or (sə·pir′ē·ər, so͞o-) *adj.* 1 Surpassing in quantity, quality, or degree; more excellent; preferable; in an absolute sense, of great excellence: a *superior* man. 2 Of higher grade, rank, or dignity. 3 Too great or dignified to be under the influence of something specified; serenely unaffected or indifferent: with *to*: *superior* to envy. 4 Locally higher; more elevated; upper. 5 Situated relatively nearer the top of the head when the body is standing erect: opposed to *inferior.* 6 *Bot.* Situated above or over another organ or part, as an ovary when free from the calyx, or, in an axillary flower, a petal or lip which is the one next to the main axis of the plant. 7 *Printing* Set above the level of the line: said of type; thus, in C^4D^n, 4 and n are *superior.* 8 *Logic* Of wider application; generic: said of terms, conceptions, and propositions. 9 Supercilious; affecting superiority: a *superior* smile. See synonyms under EXCELLENT, PARAMOUNT, PREDOMINANT. — *n.* 1 One who surpasses another in rank or excellence. 2 The ruler of an ecclesiastical order or house, as an abbey, convent, or monastery. 3 *Printing* A superior letter or character. See synonyms under SUPERINTENDENT. [<OF <L, compar. of *superus* on high, above <*super* above] — **su·pe·ri·or·i·ty** (sə·pir′ē·ôr′ə·tē, -or′-, so͞o-) *n.* — **su·pe′ri·or·ly** *adv.*

Su·pe·ri·or (sə·pir′ē·ər, so͞o-) A port and industrial city in Wisconsin at the western end of Lake Superior.

Superior, Lake The northernmost, westernmost, and largest of the Great Lakes, in the United States and Canada; 31,820 square miles; length, 350 miles; width, 160 miles.

superior court See under COURT.

su·per·ja·cent (so͞o′pər·jā′sənt) *adj.* Lying or resting immediately upon or above something else; overlying. [<LL *superjacens, -entis,* ppr. of *superjacere* <*super-* above + *jacere* lie]

su·per·la·tive (sə·pûr′lə·tiv, so͞o-) *adj.* 1 Elevated to the highest degree; consummate; of supreme excellence or eminence. 2 *Gram.* Expressing or involving the extreme degree: said of a form of comparison of adjectives or adverbs: The *superlative* degree of "wise" is "wisest." See COMPARISON (def. 2). 3 Excessive. — *n.* 1 That which is of the highest possible excellence or superior to all others. 2 *Gram.* The highest degree of comparison of the adjective or adverb; any word or phrase in the superlative degree. [<OF *superlatif* <LL *superlativus* <L *superlatus* excessive < *super-* above + *latus,* pp. to *ferre* carry] — **su·per′la·tive·ly** *adv.* — **su·per′la·tive·ness** *n.*

su·per·lu·nar (so͞o′pər·lo͞o′nər) *adj.* Being above or beyond the moon; celestial. Also **su′per·lu′na·ry.**

su·per·male (so͞o′pər·māl′) *n. Biol.* A supersexual individual having, in the fruit fly, a ratio of 1 X-chromosome to 3 sets of autosomes.

su·per·man (so͞o′pər·man′) *n. pl.* **·men** (-men′) 1 A hypothetical superior being, characterized by perfection of physique, capacity for power, and a moral nature beyond good and evil, regarded as the product of evolutionary survival of the fittest; the *Ubermensch* of Nietzsche. 2 An intellectually and morally improved man; a superior man; one possessing superhuman powers. [Trans. of G *übermensch*]

su·per·mar·ket (so͞o′pər·mär′kit) *n.* A large store or market selling food and household supplies and operating generally on a self-service, cash-and-carry basis. Also **super market.**

su·per·mo·ron (so͞o′pər·môr′on, -mō′ron) *n. Psychiatry* A mentally deficient person ranking above the moron; one only slightly deficient mentally.

su·per·nal (so͞o·pûr′nəl) *adj.* 1 Heavenly; celestial. 2 Placed or located above; lofty; overhead; towering. 3 Coming from above or from the sky. [<OF <L *supernus* <*super* over] — **su·per′nal·ly** *adv.*

su·per·na·tant (so͞o′pər·nā′tənt) *adj.* 1 Floating uppermost, above something, or on the surface. 2 *Chem.* Denoting a liquid from which a precipitate has been thrown down. [<L *supernatans, -antis* <*super-* above + *natare* swim] — **su′per·na·ta′tion** (-nā·tā′·shən) *n.*

su·per·na·tion·al (so͞o′pər·nash′ən·əl) *adj.* Pertaining to all mankind, rather than to one nation only. — **su′per·na′tion·al·ism** *n.* — **su′·per·na′tion·al·ist** *n.*

su·per·nat·u·ral (so͞o′pər·nach′ər·əl) *adj.* 1 Existing or occurring through some agency beyond the known forces of nature. 2 Lying outside the sphere of natural law, whether psychic or physical. 3 Believed to be miraculous or caused by the immediate exercise of divine power. 4 Pertaining to the miraculous. — *n.* That which is outside the accepted and known order of nature; that which transcends nature. [<Med. L *supernaturalis* <L *super-* above + *natura* NATURE] — **su′per·nat′u·ral·ly** *adv.* — **su′per·nat′u·ral·ness** *n.*

Synonyms (adj.): miraculous, preternatural, superhuman. The *supernatural* is above or superior to the known powers of nature; the *preternatural* is aside from or beyond what we have been accustomed to regard as the result of natural law, often in the sense of inauspicious; as, a *preternatural* gloom. *Miraculous* is more emphatic and specific than *supernatural,* as referring to the direct personal intervention of divine power. *Miraculous* might be termed "extranatural," rather than *supernatural.* All that is beyond human power is *superhuman*; as, Prophecy gives evidence of *superhuman* knowledge; the word is sometimes applied to remarkable manifestations of human power, surpassing all that is ordinary. *Antonyms*: common, natural, ordinary, usual.

su·per·nat·u·ral·ism (so͞o′pər·nach′ər·əl·iz′əm) *n.* 1 The quality of being supernatural. 2 Belief in the supernatural; especially, the doctrine that there is a power not to be identified with nature, but which is the ground of its existences and is manifested in its forces, laws, and events: opposed to *naturalism.* 3 The doctrine of spiritual revelation together with the belief in Providence, the efficacy of prayer, and related doctrines: opposed to *rationalism.* Also spelled *supranaturalism.* — **su′per·nat′u·ral·ist** *adj.* & *n.* — **su′per·nat′u·ral·is′tic** *adj.*

su·per·nor·mal (so͞o′pər·nôr′məl) *adj.* 1 *Psychol.* Above the normal in characteristics, properties, or intelligence: a *supernormal*

child. 2 Pertaining to or designating phenomena incapable of rigorous scientific explanation but conceivably in accord with still undiscovered natural laws.

su·per·nu·mer·ar·y (sōō′pər·nōō′mə·rer′ē, -nyōō′-) *adj.* 1 Being beyond a fixed or standard number. 2 Beyond a customary or necessary number; superfluous. —*n. pl.* **·ar·ies** 1 A person or thing in excess of the regular, necessary, or customary number. 2 A stage performer, as in mob scenes or processions, without any speaking part: often contracted to *supe* or *super.* [<LL *supernumerarius* a soldier added to a legion after it is complete <L *super numerum* < *super* over + *numerus* a number]

su·per·or·der (sōō′pər·ôr′dər) *n. Biol.* A plant or animal division intermediate between a class and an order.

su·per·pa·tri·ot (sōō′pər·pā′trē·ət, -ot) *n.* A person who is or claims to be a great patriot, often one whose patriotic fervor is marked by a readiness to regard dissent as unpatriotic or subversive. —**su′per·pa′tri·ot′ic** *adj.* —**su′per·pa′tri·ot·ism** *n.*

su·per·phos·phate (sōō′pər·fos′fāt) *n. Chem.* 1 An acid phosphate. 2 Any fertilizing material mostly consisting of soluble phosphates: *superphosphate* of lime.

su·per·phys·i·cal (sōō′pər·fiz′i·kəl) *adj.* Beyond or above the physical.

su·per·pose (sōō′pər·pōz′) *v.t.* **·posed, ·pos·ing** 1 To lay over or upon something else, as one layer upon another. 2 *Geom.* To suppose (one figure) to be placed upon another so that all like parts coincide. Compare SUPERIMPOSE. 3 *Physics* To combine additively, as forces or wave amplitudes. [<F *superposer* < *super-* over + *poser* POSE[1]] —**su′per·pos′a·ble** *adj.* —**su′per·po·si′tion** (-pə·zish′ən) *n.*

su·per·pow·er (sōō′pər·pou′ər) *n.* One of a few great, dominant nations characterized by superior economic or military strength and by large population.

su·per·pres·sure (sōō′pər·presh′ər) *n.* 1 Excessive pressure under given conditions. 2 *Aeron.* The amount by which the pressure within the gas cell of a dirigible exceeds atmospheric pressure.

su·per-roy·al (sōō′pər·roi′əl) *n.* A size of ledger paper, 20 by 28 inches.

su·per·sat·u·rate (sōō′pər·sach′ōō·rāt) *v.t.* **·rat·ed, ·rat·ing** 1 To saturate to excess or beyond the normal point. 2 To cause (a solution) to contain more of a dissolved substance than can be held under normal conditions of temperature. —**su′per·sat′u·ra′tion** *n.*

su·per·scribe (sōō′pər·skrīb′) *v.t.* **·scribed, ·scrib·ing** To write or engrave on the outside or on the upper part of; inscribe with a name or address; specifically, to address, as a letter. [<LL *superscribere* <L *super-* over + *scribere* write]

su·per·script (sōō′pər·skript′) *adj.* Written above or overhead: opposed to *subscript.* —*n.* 1 Superscription. 2 *Math.* An index or other mark following and above a letter or figure, as a^3, c'. [<LL *superscriptus,* pp. of *superscribere* SUPERSCRIBE]

su·per·scrip·tion (sōō′pər·skrip′shən) *n.* 1 The act of superscribing an address on a letter. 2 An upper or outer inscription, as a title or a direction; especially, an address on a letter. 3 That portion of a medical prescription that begins with the word *recipe* (generally abbreviated ℞, and meaning "take"). [<OF <LL *superscriptio, -onis* < *superscribere.* See SUPERSCRIBE.]

su·per·sede (sōō′pər·sēd′) *v.t.* **·sed·ed, ·sed·ing** 1 To take the place of, as by reason of superior worth, right, or appropriateness; replace; supplant. 2 To put something in the place of; set aside; suspend; annul. See synonyms under SUBVERT. [<OF *superceder* <L *supersedere* sit over, forbear < *super-* above + *sedere* sit] —**su′per·sed′er** *n.* —**su′per·se′dure** (-sē′jər), **su′per·ses′sion** (-sesh′ən) *n.*

su·per·se·de·as (sōō′pər·sē′dē·əs) *n. Law* A proceeding, as a writ, that operates to supersede or check proceedings. [<L, you shall desist]

su·per·sen·si·ble (sōō′pər·sen′sə·bəl) *adj.* Being above or beyond the range of the senses; supersensual; psychical. —**su′per·sen′si·bly** *adv.*

su·per·sen·su·al (sōō′pər·sen′shōō·əl) *adj.* 1 Being above the senses; supersensible. 2 Spiritual; ideal. Also **su′per·sen′so·ry** (-sen′sər·ē).

su·per·ser·vice·a·ble (sōō′pər·sûr′vis·ə·bəl) *adj.* Trying needlessly or disagreeably to be of service; officious. —**su′per·ser′vice·a·bly** *adv.*

su·per·sex (sōō′pər·seks′) *n. Biol.* A sterile organism having a mixture of male and female characteristics due to a disturbed ratio of autosomes to X-chromosomes, as in the fruit fly. —**su′per·sex′u·al** (-sek′shōō·əl) *adj.*

su·per·son·ic (sōō′pər·son′ik) *adj. Aeron.* Of, pertaining to, or characterized by a speed greater than that of sound: distinguished from *ultrasonic.*

su·per·son·ics (sōō′pər·son′iks) *n. pl. (construed as singular)* The science which treats of the phenomena of supersonic speed, with especial reference to their practical applications to aircraft, guided missiles, rockets, etc.: distinguished from *ultrasonics.*

su·per·star (sōō′pər·stär′) *n.* A public performer, as an actor, singer, or professional athlete, regarded as one of the best or most popular. —**su′per·star′dom** *n.*

su·per·state (sōō′pər·stāt′) *n.* A state established as the governing power of a union or federation of subordinate states.

su·per·sti·tion (sōō′pər·stish′ən) *n.* 1 A belief founded on irrational feelings, especially of fear, and marked by credulity; also, any rite or practice inspired by such belief. 2 Specifically, a belief in a religious system regarded (by others than the believer) as without reasonable support; also, any of its rites. 3 Credulity regarding or reverence for the occult or supernatural, as belief in omens, charms, and signs; loosely, any unreasoning or unreasonable belief or impression. 4 *Obs.* Undue scrupulousness. See synonyms under FANATICISM. [<OF <L *superstitio, -onis* excessive fear of the gods, amazement, dread < *superstare* < *super-* over + *stare* stand still]

su·per·sti·tious (sōō′pər·stish′əs) *adj.* 1 Disposed to believe in or be influenced by superstitions. 2 Of, pertaining to, or manifesting superstition. —**su′per·sti′tious·ly** *adv.* —**su′per·sti′tious·ness** *n.*

su·per·stra·tum (sōō′pər·strā′təm, -strat′əm) *n. pl.* **·stra·ta** (-strā′tə, -strat′ə) A layer superimposed upon another; a superficial stratum.

su·per·struct (sōō′pər·strukt′) *v.t.* To build or erect upon a foundation.

su·per·struc·ture (sōō′pər·struk′chər) *n.* 1 Any structure or any part of a structure above the basement or considered in relation to its foundation. 2 The sleepers, rails, etc., of a railway, as distinguished from the roadbed. 3 *Naut.* The parts of a ship's structure, especially of a warship, above the main deck. Compare SUBSTRUCTURE.

su·per·sub·tle (sōō′pər·sut′l) *adj.* Extremely subtle; oversubtle.

su·per·tank·er (sōō′pər·tangk′ər) *n.* A very large tanker capable of carrying a vast cargo, as of oil.

su·per·tax (sōō′pər·taks′) *n.* An extra tax in addition to the normal tax; especially, a graded additional tax on incomes above certain amounts; a surtax.

su·per·ton·ic (sōō′pər·ton′ik) *n. Music* The tone above the tonic or keynote; the second.

su·per·vene (sōō′pər·vēn′) *v.i.* **·vened, ·ven·ing** 1 To follow closely upon something; come as something extraneous or additional. 2 To take place; happen. See synonyms under HAPPEN. [<L *supervenire* < *super-* over and above + *venire* come] —**su′per·ven′ient** (-vēn′yənt) *adj.* —**su′per·ven′tion** (-ven′shən) *n.*

su·per·vise (sōō′pər·vīz) *v.t.* **·vised, ·vis·ing** To have a general oversight of; superintend; oversee. [<Med. L *supervisus,* pp. of *supervidere* <L *super-* over + *videre* see]

su·per·vi·sion (sōō′pər·vizh′ən) *n.* 1 The act of supervising; superintendence. 2 The authority to direct or supervise.

su·per·vi·sor (sōō′pər·vī′zər) *n.* 1 One who supervises or oversees; a superintendent; an inspector. 2 *U.S.* A township officer in administrative charge of its business; one of a board of such officers constituting a body having charge of the business of a county; a borough officer who has charge of road repairs, etc. 3 A person supervising teachers of special subjects in a school. 4 *Obs.* A beholder. —**su′per·vi′sor·ship** *n.* —**su′per·vi′so·ry** (-zər·ē) *adj.*

su·pi·nate (sōō′pə·nāt) *v.t. & v.i.* **·nat·ed, ·nat·ing** 1 To make or become supine. 2 To turn, as the hand or forelimb, so that the palm is upward or forward. [<L *supinatus,* pp. of *supinare* throw (someone) on the back < *supinus* SUPINE]

su·pi·na·tion (sōō′pə·nā′shən) *n. Physiol.* 1 The act of turning the palm of the hand, or the corresponding surface of the forelimb, upward. 2 The position of a limb so turned: opposed to *pronation.* 3 The act or state of lying supine.

su·pi·na·tor (sōō′pə·nā′tər) *n. Anat.* A muscle of the forearm by which supination is effected.

su·pine[1] (sōō·pīn′) *adj.* 1 Lying on the back, or with the face turned upward. 2 Having no interest or care; inactive; indolent; negligent; indifferent; listless. 3 Having an inclined position; sloping, as a hill. [<L *supinus* < *sup-*, root of *super* above] —**su·pine′ly** *adv.* —**su·pine′ness** *n.*

su·pine[2] (sōō′pīn) *n.* In Latin grammar, one of two parts of the verb, generally regarded as verbal nouns. The **first** or **former supine,** an accusative form in *-um,* is used after verbs of motion to express purpose, as in *Processit libatum* He went forth to sacrifice; the **second** or **latter supine,** an ablative form in *-u,* is used for specification, as in *Mirabile dictu*! Wonderful to relate! [<L *supinum (verbum)* (a) supine (word), neut. of *supinus* SUPINE[1]]

sup·per (sup′ər) *n.* The last meal of the day: frequently used of an evening banquet. [<OF *soper, super* sup, dine] —**sup′per·less** *adj.*

sup·plant (sə·plant′, -plänt′) *v.t.* 1 To take the place of; displace. 2 To take the place of (someone) by scheming, treachery, etc. 3 To replace (one thing) with another; remove; uproot. See synonyms under ABOLISH, SUBVERT. [<OF *supplanter* <L *supplantare* trip up < *sub-* up from below + *planta* the sole of the foot] —**sup·plan·ta·tion** (sup′lan·tā′shən) *n.* —**sup·plant′er** *n.*

sup·ple (sup′əl) *adj.* 1 Easily bent; flexible; pliant: a *supple* bow. 2 Yielding to the humor or wishes of others; especially, servilely compliant; obsequious. 3 Of the mind, showing adaptability; elastic; easily changing. —*v.t. & v.i.* **·pled, ·pling** To make or become supple. [<OF *supple, sople* <L *supplex, -icis* submissive, lit., bending under < *sub-* under + stem of *plicare* fold] —**sup′ple·ly** *adv.* —**sup′ple·ness** *n.*

Synonyms (adj.): compliant, elastic, fawning, flexible, limber, lissom, lithe, lithesome, obsequious, pliable, pliant, soft, submissive, willowy, yielding. See ACTIVE, OBSEQUIOUS. *Antonyms*: firm, fixed, inflexible, obstinate, pertinacious, rigid, stiff, stubborn, unbending, unyielding.

sup·ple·jack (sup′əl·jak) *n.* 1 Any of various woody climbers with tough and lithe stems; specifically, a high-climbing vine (genus *Berchemia*) of the southern United States. 2 A walking stick made from the wood of such a plant.

sup·ple·ment (sup′lə·ment) *v.t.* To make additions to; provide for what is lacking in. —*n.* (-mənt) 1 Something added that supplies a deficiency; especially, an addition to a publication. 2 A supplementary angle. See synonyms under APPENDAGE. [<L *supplementum* < *supplere* SUPPLY[1]]

sup·ple·men·tal (sup′lə·men′təl) *adj.* Like a supplement; supplementing; additional. Also **sup·ple·to·ry** (sup′lə·tôr′ē, -tō′rē).

sup·ple·men·ta·ry (sup′lə·men′tər·ē) *adj.* Supplemental.

supplementary angle See under ANGLE.

sup·pli·ance (sup′lē·əns) *n.* The act of supplicating; an urgent petition or prayer.

sup·pli·ant (sup′lē·ənt) *adj.* 1 Entreating earnestly and humbly; beseeching. 2 Manifesting entreaty or submissive supplication. —*n.* One who supplicates. [<MF, ppr. of *supplier* <L *supplicare* SUPPLICATE] —**sup′pli·ant·ly** *adv.* —**sup′pli·ant·ness** *n.*

sup·pli·cant (sup′lə·kənt) *n.* One who supplicates; a suppliant. —*adj.* Asking or entreating humbly; beseeching. [<L *supplicans, -antis,* ppr. of *supplicare* SUPPLICATE]

sup·pli·cate (sup′lə·kāt) *v.* **·cat·ed, ·cat·ing** *v.t.* 1 To ask for humbly or by earnest prayer. 2 To beg something of; entreat. —*v.i.* 3 To beg or pray humbly; make an earnest request. See synonyms under ASK, PRAY. [<L *supplicatus,* pp. of *supplicare* supplicate < *sub-* under + *plicare* bend, fold] —**sup′pli·ca′tion** *n.* —**sup′pli·ca·to′ry** (-kə·tôr′ē, -tō′rē) *adj.*

sup·ply[1] (sə·plī′) *v.* **·plied, ·ply·ing** *v.t.* 1 To give or furnish (something needful or desirable):

to *supply* milk for a city. **2** To furnish with what is needed: to *supply* an army with ammunition. **3** To provide for adequately; satisfy: to *supply* a demand. **4** To make up for; make good or compensate for, as a loss or deficiency. **5** To fill (the place of another); also, to fill (an office, etc.) or occupy (a pulpit) as a substitute. — *v.i.* **6** To take the place of another temporarily. See synonyms under ACCOMMODATE, GIVE, PROVIDE. — *n. pl.* **·plies** **1** That which is or can be supplied; the available aggregate of things needed or demanded. **2** The amount of a commodity offered at a given price or available for meeting a demand. **3** Accumulated stores reserved for distribution, as for an army or a fleet: usually in the plural: He was cut off from his base of *supplies.* **4** A grant of money to the crown or for the public service; appropriation: usually in the plural. **5** An amount sufficient for a given use; store or quantity on hand. **6** A substitute or temporary incumbent. **7** *Obs.* Reinforcements. **8** The act of supplying. See synonyms under STOCK. [<OF *sopleer, soupleier* <L *supplere* < *sub-* up from under + *ple-*, root of *plenus* full] — **sup·pli′er** *n.*

sup·ply[2] (sup′lē) *adv.* In a supple manner; supplely. [<SUPPLE]

sup·port (sə·pôrt′, -pōrt′) *v.t.* **1** To bear the weight of, especially from underneath; hold in position; keep from falling, sinking, etc. **2** To bear or sustain (weight, etc.). **3** To keep (a person, the mind, etc.) from failing or declining; strengthen. **4** To serve to uphold or corroborate (a statement, theory, etc.); substantiate; verify. **5** To provide (a person, institution, etc.) with maintenance; provide for. **6** To give approval or assistance to; uphold; advocate; aid. **7** To endure or tolerate: I cannot *support* his insolence. **8** To carry on; keep up; maintain: to *support* a war. **9** In the theater: **a** To act (a role or part). **b** To act in a subordinate role to. — *n.* **1** The act of supporting. **2** One who or that which supports. **3** Subsistence. See synonyms under SUBSIDY. [<OF *supporter* <L *supportare* convey <*sub-* up from under + *portare* carry] — **sup·por′tive** *adj.*

Synonyms (verb): bear, carry, maintain, prop, sustain, uphold. *Support* and *sustain* alike signify to hold up or keep up, to prevent from falling or sinking; but *sustain* has a special sense of continuous exertion or strength, as when we speak of *sustained* endeavor or a *sustained* note; a flower is *supported* by the stem or a temple roof by arches; the foundations of a great building *sustain* an enormous pressure; to *sustain* life implies a greater exigency and need than to *support* life; to say one is *sustained* under affliction emphasizes the severity of the trial and the completeness of the *upholding* more than if we say he is *supported.* To *bear* is the most general word, denoting all holding up or keeping up of any object, whether in rest or motion; it refers to something that is a tax upon strength or endurance; as, to *bear* a strain; to *bear* pain or grief. To *maintain* is to keep in a state or condition, especially in an excellent and desirable condition; as, to *maintain* health, reputation, position, etc. *Maintain* is a word of more dignity than *support*; a man *supports* his family; a state *maintains* an army or navy. To *prop* is always partial, signifying to add support to something that is insecure. See ABET, AID, ENDURE, KEEP, LEAN, PROP. *Antonyms*: abandon, betray, demolish, desert, destroy, drop, overthrow, wreck.

sup·port·a·ble (sə·pôr′tə·bəl, -pōr′-) *adj.* That may be supported or borne; bearable; endurable. — **sup·port′a·ble·ness, sup·port′a·bil′i·ty** *n.* — **sup·port′a·bly** *adv.*

sup·port·er (sə·pôr′tər, -pōr′-) *n.* **1** One who or that which supports, in any sense. **2** One who countenances or supports; an adherent. **3** *Her.* One of a pair representing living objects, standing on the dexter and sinister sides of a shield, as if supporting it. **4** An elastic or other support for some part of the body.

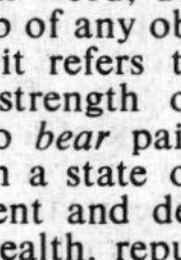

SUPPORTER (*def. 3*)

sup·pos·a·ble (sə·pō′zə·bəl) *adj.* That may be supposed. — **sup·pos′a·ble·ness** *n.* — **sup·pos′a·bly** *adv.*

sup·pos·al (sə·pō′zəl) *n.* The act or an instance of supposing; supposition.

sup·pose (sə·pōz′) *v.* **·posed, ·pos·ing** *v.t.* **1** To think or imagine to oneself as true; believe or believe probable; think; presume. **2** To assume as true for the sake of argument or illustration. **3** To require to exist as true; imply as cause or consequence; involve as an inference: Design in creation *supposes* the existence of a God. **4** To expect: I am *supposed* to follow. **5** To presuppose; assume. — *v.i.* **6** To make a supposition. [<OF *suposer* < *sup-* under (<L *sub-*) + *poser* POSE[1]] — **sup·pos′er** *n.*

Synonyms: conjecture, deem, guess, imagine, surmise, think. To *suppose* is temporarily to assume a thing as true, either with the expectation of finding it so or for the purpose of ascertaining what would follow if it were so. To *conjecture* is to put together the nearest available materials for a provisional opinion, always with some expectation of finding the facts to be as *conjectured.* To *imagine* is to form a mental image of something as existing, while its actual existence may be unknown, or even impossible. To *think,* in this application, is to hold as the result of thought what is admitted not to be matter of exact or certain knowledge; as, I do not know, but I *think* this to be the fact: a more conclusive statement than would be made by the use of *conjecture* or *suppose.* See GUESS. *Antonyms*: ascertain, conclude, discover, know, prove.

sup·posed (sə·pōzd′) *adj.* Accepted as genuine; believed; often, falsely imagined. — **sup·pos·ed·ly** (sə·pō′zid·lē) *adv.*

sup·po·si·tion (sup′ə·zish′ən) *n.* **1** The act of supposing, or that which is supposed; conjecture. **2** A hypothetical proposition made for the purpose of explaining certain facts, relating them, or of deducing consequences from them; hypothesis. See synonyms under FANCY, GUESS, HYPOTHESIS, IDEA, THOUGHT. [<Med. L *suppositio, -onis* <L, a substitute < *suppositus,* pp. of *supponere* suppose, substitute < *sub-* under + *ponere* place] — **sup′po·si′tion·al** *adj.* — **sup′po·si′tion·al·ly** *adv.*

sup·po·si·tious (sup′ə·zish′əs) *adj.* Supposed or assumed; hypothetical; also, imaginary.

sup·pos·i·ti·tious (sə·poz′ə·tish′əs) *adj.* Put in the place of or made to represent, in order to deceive or defraud; spurious. See synonyms under COUNTERFEIT. [<L *suppositus.* See SUPPOSITION.] — **sup·pos′i·ti′tious·ly** *adv.* — **sup·pos′i·ti′tious·ness** *n.*

sup·pos·i·tive (sə·poz′ə·tiv) *adj.* Including or implying supposition; supposed. — *n.* A conjunction introducing a supposition, as *if,* or *provided.* — **sup·pos′i·tive·ly** *adv.*

sup·pos·i·to·ry (sə·poz′ə·tôr′ē, -tō′rē) *n. pl.* **·ries** *Med.* A solid, readily fusible, medicated preparation for introduction into some canal, cavity, or internal organ. [<LL *suppositorium,* orig. neut. sing. of *suppositorius* placed underneath or up <L *suppositus.* See SUPPOSITION.]

sup·press (sə·pres′) *v.t.* **1** To put an end or stop to; quell; crush, as a rebellion. **2** To stop or prohibit the activities of, as a rival political group; abolish. **3** To withhold from knowledge or publication, as a book, news, etc. **4** To repress, as a groan or sigh. **5** To stop (a hemorrhage, etc.). See synonyms under ABOLISH, HIDE, REPRESS, RESTRAIN, SUBDUE. [<L *suppressus,* pp. of *supprimere* < *sub-* under + *premere* press] — **sup·press′er, sup·pres′sor** *n.* — **sup·press′i·ble** *adj.*

sup·pres·sion (sə·presh′ən) *n.* **1** The act of suppressing, or the state of being suppressed. **2** *Psychoanal.* The deliberate exclusion from consciousness and action of ideas, memories, or emotions, especially those regarded as unpleasant or as socially unacceptable.

sup·pres·sive (sə·pres′iv) *adj.* Tending to suppress.

sup·pu·rate (sup′yə·rāt) *v.i.* **·rat·ed, ·rat·ing** To form or generate pus; maturate. [<L *suppuratus,* pp. of *suppurare* < *sub-* under + *pus, puris* pus]

sup·pu·ra·tion (sup′yə·rā′shən) *n.* **1** The act or process of suppurating. **2** Pus.

sup·pu·ra·tive (sup′yə·rā′tiv) *adj.* Tending to or producing suppuration. — *n.* A remedy promoting suppuration.

supra– *prefix* Above; beyond: *supraliminal.* Used to form adjectives and often the equivalent of *super–* which is preferred in general words. [<L *supra-* < *supra* above, beyond]

In anatomical and zoological terms *supra–* means above in position, on the dorsal side of; as in:

supra–abdominal	**suprahepatic**	**supranasal**
supra–auditory	**supralabial**	**supra–ocular**
supracaudal	**supramaxillary**	**supraspinal**

su·pra·lap·sar·i·an (sōō′prə·lap·sâr′ē·ən) *n.* A high Calvinist or holder of the doctrine that predestination preceded creation and the fall of man in the divine order of decrees. See INFRALAPSARIAN. [<NL *supralapsarius* <L *supra-* before + *lapsus* a fall] — **su′pra·lap·sar′i·an·ism** *n.*

su·pra·lim·i·nal (sōō′prə·lim′ə·nəl) *adj. Psychol.* Above the threshold of normal consciousness or sensation: opposed to *subliminal.*

su·pra·mo·lec·u·lar (sōō′prə·mə·lek′yə·lər) *adj.* **1** Containing more than one molecule. **2** Of greater complexity than a molecule.

su·pra·mun·dane (sōō′prə·mun′dān, -mun·dān′) *adj.* Being or placed beyond, or superior to, the world; supernatural; celestial.

su·pra·na·tion·al (sōō′prə·nash′ə·nəl) *adj.* Of or concerning several or a number of nations; involving more than one nation. — **su′pra·na′tion·al·ism** *n.*

su·pra·nat·u·ral·ism (sōō′prə·nach′ər·əl·iz′əm) See SUPERNATURALISM.

su·pra·or·bi·tal (sōō′prə·ôr′bi·təl) *adj. Anat.* Situated above the orbit of the eye. [<NL *supraorbitalis* <L *supra-* above + *orbita* ORBIT]

su·pra·pro·test (sōō′prə·prō′test) *n. Law* Acceptance or payment of a bill of exchange by one not a party to it after protest for non-acceptance or non-payment. [<Ital. *sopra protesta* upon protest < *sopra* (<L *supra* above) + *protesta* <L *protestari* PROTEST]

su·pra·re·nal (sōō′prə·rē′nəl) *Anat. adj.* Situated above the kidneys, or pertaining to the ductless glands above the kidneys. — *n.* A suprarenal gland.

suprarenal gland *Anat.* A ductless gland lying outside the upper or anterior part of either kidney in most vertebrates: also called *adrenal gland.*

su·pra·ren·a·lin (sōō′prə·ren′ə·lin) *n.* Epinephrine. [<SUPRARENAL + -IN]

su·pra·ster·ol (sōō′prə·ster′ōl, -ol) *n. Biochem.* One of two inactive sterols produced as end products by the ultraviolet irradiation of ergosterol. [<SUPRA- + STEROL]

su·pra·tem·po·ral (sōō′prə·tem′pər·əl) *Anat. adj.* Situated in the upper part of the temporal bone or region. — *n.* A supratemporal bone.

su·prem·a·cy (sə·prem′ə·sē, sōō-) *n. pl.* **·cies** The state of being supreme; supreme power or authority. See synonyms under PRECEDENCE, VICTORY. — **royal supremacy** The judicial and executive supremacy of a sovereign as the head of the Christian church within his realm: used especially of English sovereigns.

su·preme (sə·prēm′, sōō-) *adj.* **1** Highest in power or authority; dominant. **2** Highest in degree, importance, or estimation; most extreme or momentous; utmost: *supreme* devotion. **3** Ultimate; last and greatest. See synonyms under ABSOLUTE, FIRST, IMPERIAL, PARAMOUNT, PREDOMINANT. — **the Supreme Being** God; the Deity. — *n.* **1** The supreme or highest point; acme. **2** One who is above the rest; a superior; chief. [<L *supremus* highest, superl. of *superus* that is above < *super* above] — **su·preme′ly** *adv.* — **su·preme′ness** *n.*

su·prême (sü·prem′) *n. French* **1** An especially choice portion of breast of fowl, fish, etc.: a culinary term. **2** A rich cream sauce.

Supreme Bench The United States Supreme Court.

Supreme Court See under COURT.

supreme sacrifice The sacrifice of one's life.

Supreme Soviet The Russian Congress consisting of two legislative chambers, the Soviet (Council) of the Union and the Soviet (Council) of Nationalities, which have equal rights and whose members are elected for a period of four years.

Supreme War Council An international body with headquarters at Versailles, composed of representatives of the Entente nations, of their

allies, and of the United States, established at the end of World War I, to determine the terms of peace. This was accomplished by the signing of the Treaty of Versailles, June 28, 1919.
Sur (sŏŏr, sür) A port of SW Lebanon, on the Mediterranean; site of ancient Tyre: also *Tyre. Arabic* **El Sur.**
sur-[1] *prefix* A form of the Latin *super-* found in words which came into English through Old French. [<OF *sur-* <L *super-* SUPER-]
sur-[2] Assimilated var. of SUB-.
su·ra (sŏŏr′ə) *n.* A chapter or section of the Koran. [<Arabic *sūrah,* lit., a step, degree]
Su·ra·ba·ya (sōō′rä·bä′yä) A port and industrial city of NE Java: Dutch *Soerabaja.* Also **Su′ra·ba′ja.**
su·rah (sŏŏr′ə) *n.* A soft, usually twilled, silk fabric, used for women's wear, ties, etc.: now sometimes mixed with rayon. Also **surah silk.** [from *Surat,* India]
Su·ra·jah Dow·lah (sə·rä′jə dou′lə), 1728?–1757, nawab of Bengal; executed by the British. Also *Siraj-ud-daula.*
Su·ra·kar·ta (sŏŏr′ə·kär′tə) Former name for SOLO.
su·ral (sŏŏr′əl) *adj. Anat.* Of or pertaining to the calf of the leg. [<NL *suralis* <L *sura* the calf of the leg]
sur·ance (sŏŏr′əns, shŏŏr′-) *n. Obs.* Assurance. [<OF < *sur* SURE; infl. in meaning by ASSURANCE]
Su·rat (sōō·rat′, sŏŏ′rət) A port on the Gulf of Cambay, northern Bombay State, India; the first British settlement in India, 1612.
sur·base (sûr′bās′) *n. Archit.* A molding or border above the dado and base of a pedestal or above the baseboard of a room. [<SUR-[1] + BASE[1]]
sur·based (sûr′bāst′) *adj. Archit.* **1** Having a surbase, as a pedestal. **2** Flattened; depressed. **3** Having the rise of the curve less than half the span: a *surbased* arch.
sur·cease (sûr·sēs′, sûr′sēs) *n.* Absolute cessation; end. — *v.t.* & *v.i.* **·ceased, ·ceas·ing** To cease entirely or finally; end. [<AF *sursise* omission, orig. pp. of *surseoir* refrain <L *supersedere* SUPERSEDE]
sur·charge (sûr′chärj′) *n.* **1** An excessive burden, load, or charge. **2** In chancery law, the showing of an omission of items in an account for which credit ought to be allowed: opposed to *falsification.* **3** An additional or excessive amount charged, especially an unlawful charge; an overcharge. **4** A new valuation or something additional printed on a postage or revenue stamp; also, a stamp so imprinted. — *v.t.* (sûr·chärj′) **·charged, ·charg·ing 1** To charge (a person) too much; overcharge. **2** To show an omission of credits in (an account), or of something for which credit should have been allowed. **3** To overload. **4** To fill to excess. **5** To imprint a surcharge on (postage stamps). [<F < *surcharger* < *sur-* over + *charger* <OF *chargier* CHARGE] — **sur·charg′er** *n.*
sur·cin·gle (sûr′sing·gəl) *n.* **1** A girth or strap encircling the body of a beast of burden, for holding a saddle, etc. **2** A girdle, as of a cassock. — *v.t.* **·gled, ·gling** To gird or fasten with a surcingle. [<OF *surcengle* < *sur-* over + L *cingulum* a belt]
sur·coat (sûr′kōt′) *n.* An outer coat or garment; in the Middle Ages, a loose robe or cloaklike garment worn over armor. [<OF *surcot* < *sur-* over + *cot, cote* a coat]
sur·cu·lose (sûr′kyə·lōs) *adj. Bot.* Producing or having suckers: said of plants. [<L *surculosus* < *surculus* a twig, sucker, dim. of *surus* a twig]
surd (sûrd) *n.* **1** *Math.* An irrational number or quantity, especially an indicated root that can only be approximated, as $\sqrt{2}$. **2** *Phonet.* A speech sound made without vibration of the vocal cords. — *adj.* **1** *Math.* Incapable of being expressed in rational numbers; irrational. **2** *Phonet.* Voiceless: opposed to *sonant, voiced.* [<L *surdus* deaf, silent]
sure (shŏŏr) *adj.* **1** Not liable to change or failure; firm; unyielding; stable; infallible. **2** Fit, proper, or deserving to be depended on; reliable; trustworthy. **3** Free from doubt; certain; positive. **4** Certain of obtaining, attaining, or retaining something: with *of.* **5** Safe; secure from danger or harm. **6** Bound to happen. — *adv. Colloq.* Surely; certainly. — **to be sure** Indeed; certainly. — **to make sure** To make certain; secure. [<OF *sur* <L *securus.* Doublet of SECURE.] — **sure′ness** *n.*
Synonyms (adj.): actual, assured, aware, certain, clear, confident, indisputable, positive, real. See AUTHENTIC, FAITHFUL, SECURE.
sure-e·nough (shŏŏr′i·nuf′) *U.S. Colloq. adj.* Real; genuine. — *adv.* Really; surely.
sure-fire (shŏŏr′fīr′) *adj. Colloq.* Reliable; sure or certain to succeed, win, or come out as expected.
sure-foot·ed (shŏŏr′fŏŏt′id) *adj.* Not liable to fall or stumble; figuratively, not liable to err.
sure·ly (shŏŏr′lē) *adv.* **1** Without doubt; certainly. **2** Securely; safely.
sure thing A certainty; any project or undertaking bound to succeed.
sure·ty (shŏŏr′tē, shŏŏr′ə·tē) *n. pl.* **·ties 1** A person who engages to be responsible for the debt, default, or miscarriage of another; bail. **2** An individual or corporation that, in consideration of the payment of a premium, acts as security for a principal (as a State, city, bank, etc.), against possible loss through the act of an associate or employee who is required to furnish such security. **3** A pledge of money deposited, or of credit given, to secure against loss or damage; security for payment or performance. **4** That which gives security or confidence; ground or basis of certainty or security. **5** The state of being sure; sureness; security; safety; certainty. **6** A sponsor. See synonyms under CERTAINTY, SECURITY. [<OF *surte* <L *securitas, -atis* < *securus* SECURE] — **sure′ty·ship** *n.*
surf (sûrf) *n.* **1** The swell of the sea that breaks upon a shore. **2** The foam caused by the billows. — *v.i.* To ride the surf on a surfboard; engage in surfing. ◆ Homophone: *serf.* [Earlier *suff,* ? var. of SOUGH] — **surf′y** *adj.*
sur·face (sûr′fis) *n.* **1** The exterior part or face of anything that has length, breadth, and thickness. **2** That which has length and breadth, but not thickness; a superficies. **3** A superficial aspect; external view or appearance. **4** That portion of the side of a fortification which is bounded by the angle of the nearest bastion and the prolongation of the flank. — *v.* **·faced, ·fac·ing** *v.t.* **1** To put a surface on; especially, to make smooth, even, or plain. — *v.i.* **2** To mine at or near the surface. **3** To rise to the surface, as a submarine. [<F < *sur-* above + *face* FACE] — **sur′fac·er** *n.*
sur·face-ac·tive (sûr′fis·ak′tiv) *adj. Chem.* Pertaining to or denoting any of a class of substances which have the property of reducing the surface tension of a liquid in which they are dissolved: said especially of detergents.
surface boat A sink boat.
surface mail Mail sent by land or sea rather than by air.
surface noise The mechanical noise produced by friction of the needle against the granular surface of a phonograph record.
surface plate *Mech.* A plate having a very accurate surface: used for testing other surfaces.
surface tension *Physics* That property of a liquid by virtue of which the surface molecules exhibit a strong inward attraction, thus forming an elastic skin which tends to contract to the minimum area.
sur·fac·tant (sûr·fak′tənt) *n. Chem.* A surface-active agent or a solute which tends to reduce the surface tension of the solvent, as a soap or detergent. [<SURF(ACE)-ACT(IVE) + -ANT]
surf·bird (sûrf′bûrd′) *n.* A ploverlike bird *(Aphriza virgata)* of the Pacific coast of America from Alaska to Chile.
surf·board (sûrf′bôrd′, -bōrd′) *n.* A long, narrow board used in surfing. Compare AQUAPLANE.
surf·boat (sûrf′bōt′) *n.* A boat of extra strength and buoyancy, for launching and landing through surf. — **surf′boat′man** (-mən) *n.*
surf duck One of various scoters or sea ducks, especially the surf scoter. Also **surf coot.**
sur·feit (sûr′fit) *v.t.* **1** To feed to fullness or satiety; overfeed. **2** To supply to satiety. — *v.i.* **3** To partake of food or drink to excess; overeat. **4** To overindulge. See synonyms under SATISFY. — *n.* **1** The act of surfeiting oneself; excess in eating or drinking; also, the excessive quantity partaken of. **2** The result of such excess; satiety; superfluity. **3** The state of being surfeited; oppressive fullness of the system caused by excess in eating or drinking. [<OF *sorfait* < *surfaire* overdo < *sur-* above + *faire* make <L *facere*]
surf·er (sûrf′ər) *n.* One who engages or is adept in the sport of surfing. Also **surf·rid·er** (sûrf′rī′dər).
surf fish Any of a family *(Embiotocidae)* of viviparous sea fishes, perchlike in form, numerous near shore all along the northern Pacific coast of North America.
sur·fi·cial (sûr·fish′əl) *adj. Geol.* Originally belonging to or being on the surface, as of the earth: contrasted with *subterranean.* [< SURFACE]
surf·ing (sûrf′ing) *n.* A water sport in which a person standing on a surfboard is borne by the surf toward the shore. Also **surf·rid·ing** (sûrf′rī′ding).
surf scoter A North American scoter *(Melanitta perspicillata).* The adult male is black with a white spot on the forehead and the nape. Also **surf′er.**
surge (sûrj) *v.* **surged, surg·ing** *v.i.* **1** To rise high and roll onward, as waves; swell or heave. **2** To move or go in a manner suggestive of this: The mob *surged* through the square. **3** To increase or vary suddenly, as an electric current. **4** To slip, as a rope on a windlass. — *v.t.* **5** To cause to move in surges. **6** To let go suddenly, as a rope or cable. — *n.* **1** A large swelling wave; billow; also, such billows collectively. **2** The act of surging; a heaving and rolling motion, as of great waves. **3** *Naut.* The tapered drum of a capstan or windlass around which the rope surges. **4** *Electr.* A sudden fluctuation of voltage due to lightning, switching, etc. See synonyms under WAVE. ◆ Homophone: *serge.* [<OF *sourge-,* stem of *sourdre* rise <L *surgere*] — **surg′er** *n.* — **surg′y** *adj.*
sur·geon (sûr′jən) *n.* **1** One who practices surgery. **2** A medical officer in the military or naval service; a ship's doctor. **3** A surgeon fish. [<AF *surgien,* var. of OF *cirugien.* See CHIRURGEON.]
sur·geon·cy (sûr′jən·sē) *n. pl.* **·cies** The office, duties, or rank of a surgeon.
surgeon fish A West Indian fish *(Teuthis hepatus)* having erectile lancetlike spines at the sides of the tail.
Surgeon General 1 Chief officer of the Medical Department in the United States Army or Navy. **2** Chief medical officer of the United States Public Health Service.
surgeon's knot A knot used in tying ligatures, stitching up wounds, etc. See illustration under KNOT.
sur·ger·y (sûr′jər·ē) *n. pl.* **·ger·ies 1** The branch of medical science that relates to body injuries, deformities, and morbid conditions that require being remedied by operations or instruments. **2** A place where surgical treatment or advice is regularly given; a surgeon's office; an operating room. **3** The work of a surgeon. **4** The treatment of diseases or injuries to nonhuman organisms by like methods: tree *surgery.* [<OF *surgerie,* contraction of *serurgerie,* ult. <LL *chirurgia* <Gk. *cheirourgia* a handicraft < *cheir, cheiros* the hand + *ergein* work]
sur·gi·cal (sûr′ji·kəl) *adj.* **1** Of or pertaining to surgery. **2** Designating a degree of anesthesia deep enough to permit major surgical operations. — **sur′gi·cal·ly** *adv.*
Su·ri·ba·chi (sŏŏr′ə·bä′chē), **Mount** An extinct volcano (546 feet) in southern Iwo Jima; scene of an American victory over the Japanese in World War II, February, 1945.
su·ri·cate (sŏŏr′ə·kāt) *n.* A small burrowing viverrine carnivore *(Suricata tetradactyla)* of South Africa, having only four toes: often domesticated. [<F *surikate* <Afrikaans, ? < a native South African name]
Su·ri·nam (sŏŏr′ə·näm′) Part of the Kingdom of the Netherlands, on the NE coast of South America; 55,129 square miles; capital, Paramaribo: also called *Dutch Guiana, Netherlands Guiana. Dutch* **Su·ri·na·me** (sü′rē·nä′mə).
Surinam River A river in central Surinam, flowing 300 miles north to the Atlantic near Paramaribo.
sur·loin (sûr′loin) *n.* Sirloin: the older spelling.
sur·ly (sûr′lē) *adj.* **·li·er, ·li·est 1** Persistently rude and ill-humored; crabbed; cross; gruff. **2** Characterized by rudeness or gruffness, as a reply. **3** *Obs.* Haughty. See synonyms under HAUGHTY, MOROSE. [Earlier *sirly* like a lord

< *sir* a lord + *-ly* like] — **sur′li·ly** *adv.* — **sur′li·ness** *n.*

Sur·ma (so͝or′mä) A river in Manipur and SE Assam, NE India, and East Pakistan, flowing 320 miles north and west to the Meghna River, and forming numerous arms, especially in Assam.

sur·mise (sər·mīz′) *v.* **·mised, ·mis·ing** *v.t.* To infer on slight evidence; guess. — *v.i.* To make a conjecture thus. See synonyms under GUESS, SUPPOSE, SUSPECT. — *n.* (sər·mīz′, sûr′mīz) A conjecture made on slight evidence; supposition. See synonyms under GUESS, HYPOTHESIS. [<OF, an accusation, pp. fem. of *surmettre* accuse < *sur-* upon + *mettre* put <L *mittere* send]

sur·mount (sər·mount′) *v.t.* **1** To overcome; prevail over (a difficulty, etc.). **2** To mount to the top or cross to the other side of; get over, as an obstacle or mountain. **3** To be or lie over or above. **4** To place something above or on top of; cap. **5** *Obs.* To surpass; exceed. See synonyms under CONQUER. [<OF *surmunter* <Med. L *supermontare* <L *super-* over + *mons, montis* a hill, mountain] — **sur·mount′a·ble** *adj.* — **sur·mount′a·ble·ness** *n.* — **sur·mount′er** *n.*

sur·mul·let (sər·mul′it) See MULLET[1] (def. 2).

sur·name (sûr′nām′) *n.* A name subjoined to a given or Christian name; hence, a family name. — *v.t.* (sûr′nām′, sûr·nām′) **·named, ·nam·ing** To give a surname to; call by a surname. [Alter. of obs. *surnoun* <OF *surnom* < *sur-* above, beyond + *nom* a name <L *nomen, -inis;* infl. in form by NAME] — **sur′·nam′er** *n.*

sur·pass (sər·pas′, -päs′) *v.t.* **1** To go beyond or past in degree or amount; exceed; excel. **2** To transcend; be beyond the reach or powers of. [<MF *surpasser* < *sur-* above + *passer* PASS] — **sur·pass′a·ble** *adj.*

Synonyms: eclipse, outdo, outstrip, transcend. See BEAT, LEAD. *Antonyms*: fail, yield.

sur·pass·ing (sər·pas′ing, -päs′-) *adj.* Preeminently excellent. — *adv. Poetic* Surpassingly. — **sur·pass′ing·ly** *adv.* — **sur·pass′ing·ness** *n.*

sur·plice (sûr′plis) *n. Eccl.* A loose white vestment with full sleeves, worn over the cassock by the clergy of the Anglican, Moravian, and Roman Catholic churches, and also by choristers in a vested choir. [<AF *surpliz,* OF *sourpeliz* < Med. L *superpellicium (vestimentum)* an overgarment < *super-* over + *pellicia* a fur garment < *pellis* skin]

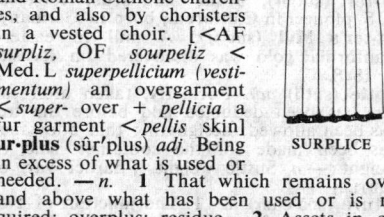

SURPLICE

sur·plus (sûr′plus) *adj.* Being in excess of what is used or needed. — *n.* **1** That which remains over and above what has been used or is required; overplus; residue. **2** Assets in excess of liabilities. **3** Excess of net assets above the face value of shares of a corporation. **4** A small unorganized tract of land in Maine set apart by State authority. See synonyms under EXCESS. [<OF <Med. L *superplus* < *super-* over and above + *plus* more]

sur·plus·age (sûr′plus·ij) *n.* **1** That which is over and above; surplus; overplus. **2** *Law* Matter in an instrument not necessary to the meaning; irrelevant matter.

sur·print (sûr′print′) *v.t.* To print again on or over (matter once printed). — *n.* That which is surprinted.

sur·pris·al (sər·prī′zəl) *n.* The act of surprising; surprise. Also *Rare* **sur·priz′al.**

sur·prise (sər·prīz′) *v.t.* **·prised, ·pris·ing** **1** To cause to feel wonder or astonishment because unusual or unexpected. **2** To come upon suddenly or unexpectedly; take unawares. **3** To attack suddenly and without warning; capture by surprise. **4** To lead unawares, as into doing something not intended: with *into.* **5** To elicit in this manner: They *surprised* the truth from him. — *n.* **1** The act of surprising; a coming upon unawares. **2** A surprised state; astonishment. **3** Something that causes surprise, as a sudden and unexpected event, fact, or gift. Also *Rare* **sur·prize′.** [<OF *surpris,* pp. of *surprendre* < Med. L *superprendere* <L *super-* over + *prehendere* take] — **sur·pris′er** *n.*

surprise party A prearranged social gathering of persons, usually at a friend's home, but without previous notice to him.

sur·pris·ing (sər·prī′zing) *adj.* Causing wonder or astonishment; amazing. — **sur·pris′ing·ly** *adv.* — **sur·pris′ing·ness** *n.*

sur·re·al·ism (sə·rē′əl·iz′əm) *n.* A movement in 20th century literature and art which attempts to express and exhibit the workings of the subconscious mind, especially as manifested in dreams and uncontrolled by the reason or any conscious process: characterized by the incongruous and startling arrangement and presentation of subject matter. [<F *surréalisme* < *sur-* beyond, above + *réalisme* realism < *réal* REAL] — **sur·re′al·ist** *adj.* & *n.* — **sur·re′al·is′tic** *adj.* — **sur·re′al·is′ti·cal·ly** *adv.*

sur·re·but·tal (sûr′ri·but′l) *n. Law* A plaintiff's evidence or presentation of evidence, to support or maintain a surrebutter.

sur·re·but·ter (sûr′ri·but′ər) *n.* In common-law pleading, the plaintiff's reply to a defendant's rebutter. [<SUR-[1] + REBUTTER; on analogy with *surrejoinder*]

sur·reined (sə·rānd′) *adj. Obs.* Overridden; worn out. [? <SUR-[1] + *reined,* pp. of REIN]

sur·re·join·der (sûr′ri·join′dər) *n. Law* The plaintiff's answer to the defendant's rejoinder. [<SUR-[1] + REJOINDER]

sur·ren·der (sə·ren′dər) *v.t.* **1** To yield possession of or power over to another; give up because of demand or compulsion. **2** To give up; abandon, as hope. **3** To give up or relinquish, especially in favor of another; resign. **4** To give (oneself) over to a passion, influence, etc. — *v.i.* **5** To give oneself up, as to an enemy in warfare; yield. — *n.* The act of surrendering one's person to another, or the possession of something to another. [< AF *surrender,* OF *surrendre* < *sur-* over + *rendre* RENDER] — **sur·ren′der·er,** *Law* **sur·ren′der·or** *n.*

Synonyms (verb): abandon, alienate, capitulate, cede, give, relinquish, sacrifice, yield. A state *cedes* territory for a consideration, *surrenders* it to a conqueror; a military commander *abandons* an untenable position or unavailable stores. We *relinquish* a claim, *sacrifice* something precious through error, friendship, or duty, *yield* to convincing reasons, a stronger will, winsome persuasion, or superior force. To *yield* is to give place or give way under pressure, and hence under compulsion; it implies more softness or concession than *surrender.* See ABANDON.

surrender value The reserve value of an insurance policy payable to the insured or to the beneficiary when the policy is discontinued.

sur·rep·ti·tious (sûr′əp·tish′əs) *adj.* **1** Accomplished by secret or improper means; clandestine. **2** Acting secretly or by stealth. [<L *surreptitius, subrepticius* < *subreptus,* pp. of *subripere* steal < *sub-* secretly + *rapere* snatch] — **sur′rep·ti′tious·ly** *adv.* — **sur′rep·ti′tious·ness** *n.*

sur·rey (sûr′ē) *n.* A light pleasure vehicle, having two seats, both facing forward, four wheels, and sometimes a top. [Prob. from *Surrey,* England]

Sur·rey (sûr′ē) A county in SE England; 722 square miles; county town, Guildford.

Sur·rey (sûr′ē), **Earl of,** 1516?–47, Henry Howard, English courtier, soldier, and poet: executed for treason.

sur·ro·gate (sûr′ə·gāt) *n.* **1** One who or that which is substituted for another; a substitute. **2** *Brit.* A deputy appointed by an ecclesiastical judge to act in his place. **3** A probate judge. — *v.t.* **·gat·ed, ·gat·ing** **1** To put in the place of another; substitute; subrogate. **2** To appoint (another) to succeed oneself. [<L *surrogatus* < *subrogatus,* pp. of *subrogare* < *sub-* in place of another + *rogare* ask]

sur·round (sə·round′) *v.t.* **1** To extend completely around; be on all sides of; encircle: Chairs *surrounded* the table. **2** To place something completely around; enclose. **3** To shut in or enclose, as enemy troops, on all sides so as to cut off communication or retreat; beset; invest. — *n.* That which surrounds; the surrounding area. [<AF *surunder,* OF *soronder* overflow <LL *superundare* < *super-* over + *undare* rise in waves < *unda* a wave]

Synonyms: compass, encompass, environ, invest. See EMBRACE.

sur·round·ing (sə·roun′ding) *n.* **1** That which surrounds, or any part of it; environment; conditions of life: usually in the plural. **2** The act of one who surrounds. — *adj.* Encompassing; enveloping.

sur·sum cor·da (sûr′səm kôr′də) *Latin* **1** *Eccl.* **a** Lift up your hearts: the opening words of the Preface in the mass. **b** A translation of this, used in other eucharistic liturgies. **2** A cry of encouragement, exhortation, etc.

sur·tax (sûr′taks′) *n.* An extra or additional tax; specifically, a graduated income tax over and above the usual or fixed income tax, levied on the amount by which net income exceeds a certain sum. — *v.t.* To assess with an extra or additional tax. [<F *surtaxe* < *sur-* above + *taxe* < *taxer* TAX]

Sur·tees (sûr′tēz), **Robert Smith,** 1803–1864, English novelist and editor.

sur·tout[1] (sər·to͞ot′, -to͞o′; *Fr.* sür·to͞o′) *n.* A long, close-fitting overcoat. [<F < *sur-* above + *tout* all <L *totus*]

sur·tout[2] (sür·to͞o′) *adv. French* Above all; chiefly; especially.

Su·ru·ga Bay (so͞o·ro͞o·gä) An inlet of the Philippine Sea in central Honshu, Japan; 35 miles long, 15 to 35 miles wide.

sur·veil·lance (sər·vā′ləns, -vāl′yəns) *n.* The act of watching, or the state of being watched; a very close watch; a spying supervision. See synonyms under OVERSIGHT. [<F < *surveiller* superintend < *sur-* over + *veiller* watch <L *vigilare*]

sur·veil·lant (sər·vā′lənt, -vāl′yənt) *adj.* Exercising surveillance; watching; watchful. — *n.* One who keeps watch so as to control; an overseer or a spy.

sur·vey (sər·vā′) *v.t.* **1** To look at in its entirety; view as from a height. **2** To look at carefully and minutely; scrutinize; inspect. **3** To determine accurately the area, contour, or boundaries of by measuring lines and angles according to the principles of geometry and trigonometry. — *v.i.* **4** To survey land. See synonyms under LOOK. — *n.* (sûr′vā, sər·vā′) **1** The operation, act, process, or results of finding the contour, area, boundaries, etc., of a surface. **2** A department or corps for carrying on such operations; also, an area that has been surveyed. **3** A general or comprehensive view; an overlooking. **4** A scrutinizing view; inspection. [<AF *survey-,* stem of *surveier,* OF *sorveir* <Med. L *supervidere* < *super-* over + *videre* look]

sur·vey·ing (sər·vā′ing) *n.* **1** The science and art of determining the area and configuration of portions of the surface of the earth and representing them on maps. **2** The work of one who makes surveys.

sur·vey·or (sər·vā′ər) *n.* **1** One who surveys lands, roads, mines, oil fields, etc.; especially, one engaged in the business of land surveying. **2** One who examines a thing for the purpose of ascertaining its condition, quality, or character; an inspector, as of customs. **3** A customs officer who examines merchandise brought into a port.

sur·vey·or·ship (sər·vā′ər·ship) *n.* The office of a surveyor.

surveyor's level A form of spirit level with telescope and tripod attachment, for use in surveying.

surveyor's measure A system of measurement used in surveying and based on the chain as a unit.

sur·viv·al (sər·vī′vəl) *n.* **1** The act of surviving; an outliving. **2** Something surviving. **3** *Sociol.* The persistence in a society of customs and beliefs originating under circumstances not fully understood or no longer valid. **4** One who or that which lives longer than others. Also *Archaic* **sur·viv′ance.**

survival of the fittest Natural selection.

sur·vive (sər·vīv′) *v.* **·vived, ·viv·ing** *v.i.* To live or continue beyond the death of another, the occurrence of an event, etc.; remain alive or in existence. — *v.t.* To live or exist beyond the death, occurrence, or end of; outlive; outlast. See synonyms under LIVE.

[<AF *survivre,* OF *sorvivre* <LL *supervivere* < *super-* above, beyond + *vivere* live] **— sur·viv′ing** *adj.* **— sur·vi′vor, sur·viv′er** *n.*

sur·vi·vor·ship (sər·vī′vər·ship) *n.* **1** The state of surviving. **2** *Law* The right of a surviving party, having a joint interest with others in property, to take the whole estate.

sus– Assimilated var. of SUB–.

Su·sa (sōō′sə) **1** An ancient city of Persia, capital of Elam, the site of which is in SW Iran: Old Testament *Shushan. Persian* **Shush** (shōōsh). **2** A former name for SOUSSE, Tunisia.

Su·san·na (sōō·zan′ə; *Dan., Du., Sw.* sōō·zä′nä, *Ital.* sōō·zän′nä, *Sp.* sōō·sä′nä) A feminine personal name. Also **Su·san** (sōō′zən), **Su·san·nah** (-zä′nə). [Hebrew, a lily]
— Susanna A Jewish captive in Babylon, falsely accused of adultery, whose life Daniel saved; also, the book of the Old Testament Apocrypha containing the story of Susanna.

sus·cep·ti·bil·i·ty (sə·sep′tə·bil′ə·tē) *n. pl.* **·ties** **1** The state or quality of being susceptible to influences or of easily receiving impressions. **2** The ability to receive or be impressed by deep emotions or strong feelings; sensibility. **3** *Physics* The ratio of the magnetization of a material to the magnetic force producing it.

sus·cep·ti·ble (sə·sep′tə·bəl) *adj.* **1** Yielding readily; capable of being influenced, acted on, or determined; unresistant; open; liable: usually with *of* or *to.* **2** Having delicate sensibility; sensitive; impressionable; easily affected. [<Med. L *susceptibilis* <L *suscipere* receive, undertake < *sub-* under + *capere* take] **— sus·cep′ti·ble·ness** *n.* **— sus·cep′ti·bly** *adv.*

sus·cep·tive (sə·sep′tiv) *adj.* Receptive; sensitive to; susceptible. **— sus·cep′tive·ness, sus·cep·tiv·i·ty** (sus′ep·tiv′ə·tē) *n.*

Su·si·an (sōō′zē·ən) *n.* The Elamite language.

Su·si·a·na (sōō′zē·ā′nə, -an′ə) See ELAM.

Su·sie, Su·sy (sōō′zē) Diminutives of SUSANNA.

sus·lik (sōōs′lik) *n.* A sciuroid rodent (*Citellus citellus*) of NE Europe and NW Asia, with a very short tail; a pouched marmot; spermophile. [<Russian]

sus·pect (sə·spekt′) *v.t.* **1** To think (a person) guilty as specified on little or no evidence. **2** To have distrust of; doubt: They *suspected* my motives. **3** To have an inkling or suspicion of; think possible: The police *suspect* arson. **—** *v.i.* **4** To have suspicions. **—** *adj.* (sus′pekt) Suspected; exciting suspicion. **—** *n.* (sus′pekt) A person suspected of a crime or other action. [<F *suspecter* <L *suspectus,* pp. of *suspicere* look under, mistrust < *sub-* from under + *specere* look] **— sus·pect′er** *n.*
Synonyms (verb): conjecture, distrust, doubt, mistrust, surmise. See DOUBT, GUESS.

sus·pend (sə·spend′) *v.t.* **1** To bar for a time from a privilege, office, or function as a punishment; debar. **2** To cause to cease for a time; interrupt; withhold temporarily: to *suspend* payments on a debt. **3** To hold in a state of indecision or abeyance; withhold or defer action on: to *suspend* a sentence. **4** To hang from a support so as to allow free movement. **5** To sustain in a body of nearly the same specific gravity; keep in suspension, as dust motes in the air. **—** *v.i.* **6** To stop for a time. **7** To fail to meet obligations; stop payment. [<OF *suspendre* <L *sub-* under + *pendere* hang]
Synonyms: debar, defer, delay, discontinue, fail, hang, hinder, intermit, interrupt, stay, stop, withhold. See ADJOURN. *Antonyms*: begin, continue, expedite, prolong, protract.

suspended animation Temporary loss of a vital force, simulating death.

sus·pend·er (sə·spen′dər) *n.* **1** One who or that which suspends. **2** One of a pair of straps for supporting the trousers: usually in the plural, **pair of suspenders.** **3** *Brit.* A garter.

sus·pense (sə·spens′) *n.* **1** The state of being uncertain, undecided, or insecure; anxiety. **2** The state of being suspended or stopped temporarily. **3** *Obs.* Cessation. See synonyms under DOUBT. [<OF *suspens, suspense* delay, abeyance <Med. L *suspensum,* orig. pp. neut. of L *suspendere* SUSPEND]

suspense account An account in which charges or credits are entered temporarily pending determination of their proper place.

sus·pen·sion (sə·spen′shən) *n.* **1** The act of suspending or hanging. **2** The state of deferment. **3** *Physics* A uniform dispersion of the fine particles of a solid in a liquid which does not dissolve them. Compare BROWNIAN MOVEMENT, COLLOID. **4** Cessation of payments in business; a going into liquidation: the *suspension* of a bank. **5** Any device used for the purpose of suspension, as in a compass. **6** *Mech.* A system of flexible or absorbent members, as springs in a vehicle, intended to insulate the chassis and body against road shocks transmitted by the wheels. **7** *Music* The prolongation of any note of a chord into the succeeding chord, causing at first dissonance which disappears by resolution; the note so prolonged. **8** The act of debarring from an office or its privileges.

suspension bridge See under BRIDGE.

suspension point One of a series of dots used to indicate the omission of words or sentences.

sus·pen·sive (sə·spen′siv) *adj.* **1** Tending to suspend or to keep in suspense. **2** Having the power of suspending operation: a *suspensive* veto. **— sus·pen′sive·ly** *adv.*

sus·pen·sor (sə·spen′sər) *n.* **1** A suspensory bandage. **2** *Bot.* The thread or chain of cells, in flowering plants and certain cryptogams, which produces at its extremity the developing embryo.

sus·pen·so·ry (sə·spen′sər·ē) *adj.* Suspending; sustaining; delaying. **—** *n. pl.* **·ries** A truss, bandage, or supporter.

suspensory ligament *Anat.* A fibrous membrane sustaining the lens of the eye.

sus·pi·cion (sə·spish′ən) *n.* **1** Conjecture; doubt; mistrust; imagining something wrong without proof or clear evidence. **2** *Colloq.* The least particle, as of a flavor. See synonyms under DOUBT. **—** *v.t. Dial.* To suspect. [<AF *suspecioun,* OF *sospeçon* <Med. L *suspectio, -onis* <L *suspicere.* See SUSPECT.] **— sus·pi′cion·al** *adj.*

sus·pi·cious (sə·spish′əs) *adj.* **1** Inclined to suspect. **2** Questionable. **3** Indicating suspicion. See synonyms under ENVIOUS, EQUIVOCAL. **— sus·pi′cious·ly** *adv.* **— sus·pi′cious·ness** *n.*

sus·pire (sə·spīr′) *v.i.* **·pired, ·pir·ing** **1** To sigh. **2** To breathe. [<L *suspirare* < *sub-* up from below + *spirare* breathe] **— sus·pi·ra·tion** (sus′pə·rā′shən) *n.*

Sus·que·han·na (sus′kwə·han′ə) A river in New York, Pennsylvania, and Maryland, flowing 444 miles south to Chesapeake Bay.

Sus·sex (sus′iks) **1** A county in SE England; administratively divided into **East Sussex** (829 square miles; county town, Lewes) and **West Sussex** (628 square miles; county town, Chichester). **2** A former Anglo-Saxon kingdom in southern England.

Sussex spaniel See under SPANIEL.

sus·tain (sə·stān′) *v.t.* **1** To keep from sinking or falling, especially by bearing up from below; uphold; support. **2** To endure without yielding; withstand. **3** To have inflicted on one; undergo; suffer, as loss or injury. **4** To keep up the courage, resolution, or spirits of; comfort. **5** To keep up or maintain; keep in effect or being: to *sustain* friendly relations. **6** To maintain by providing with food, drink, or other necessities; support. **7** To uphold or support as being true or just. **8** To prove the truth or correctness of; corroborate; confirm. See synonyms under AID, ASSENT, CARRY, CONFIRM, ENDURE, HELP, KEEP, PRESERVE, PROP, SUPPORT. [<OF *sustein-,* stem of *sustenir, sostenir* <L *sustinere* < *sub-* up from under + *tenere* hold] **— sus·tain′a·ble** *adj.* **— sus·tain′·er** *n.* **— sus·tain′ment** *n.*

sustaining program A radio or television program that has no commercial sponsor but is paid for by the network or station.

sus·te·nance (sus′tə·nəns) *n.* **1** The act or process of sustaining; especially, maintenance of life or health; subsistence. **2** That which sustains; especially, that which supports life; food. **3** Livelihood; means of support. See synonyms under FOOD, NUTRIMENT. [<AF *sustenaunce,* OF *sostenance* < *sostenir* SUSTAIN]

sus·ten·tac·u·lar (sus′ten·tak′yə·lər) *adj. Anat.* Supporting; sustaining. [<L *sustentaculum* a support < *sustentare* hold up, intens. of *sustinere* SUSTAIN]

sus·ten·ta·tion (sus′ten·tā′shən) *n.* **1** The act or process of sustaining; specifically, support of life; maintenance. **2** That which provides the means of support. **3** Upkeep or maintenance of an estate, building, etc. **4** Physical support. **5** Preservation on a certain level. [<OF *sustentacion* <L *sustentatio, -onis* < *sustentatus,* pp. of *sustentare* hold up < *sustinere* SUSTAIN] **— sus′ten·ta′tive** *adj.*

sus·ten·tion (sə·sten′shən) *n.* **1** Support. **2** The act of being sustained. [<SUSTAIN; on analogy with *retention, detention,* etc.]

su·sur·rant (sōō·sûr′ənt) *adj.* Softly murmuring; rustling; whispering. [<L *susurrans, -antis,* ppr. of *susurrare* whisper < *susurrus* a humming, whispering]

su·sur·rate (sōō·sûr′āt) *v.i.* **·rat·ed, ·rat·ing** To speak softly; whisper. [<L *susurratus,* pp. of *susurrare.* See SUSURRANT.] **— su·sur·ra·tion** (sōō′sə·rā′shən) *n.*

su·sur·rus (sōō·sûr′əs) *n.* A gentle sibilant murmur; whisper; rustling. [<L, a humming, whispering]

Suth·er·land (suth′ər·lənd) A county in northern Scotland; 2,028 square miles; county seat, Dornoch. Also **Suth′er·land·shire** (-shir).

Sutherland Falls Falls in SW South Island, New Zealand; 1,904 feet.

Suth·ron (suth′rən) See SOUTHRON.

Sut·lej (sut′lej) A river in SW Tibet, central Himachal Pradesh, and northern Punjab State, northern India and West Pakistan, flowing 850 miles SW to the Indus river on the former SW border of Bahawalpur.

sut·ler (sut′lər) *n.* A peddler who follows an army to sell goods and food to the soldiers. [<Du. *soeteler* a petty tradesman < *soetelen* perform mean duties] **— sut′ler·ship** *n.*

su·tra (sōō′trə) *n.* **1** A formulated doctrine, often so short as to be unintelligible without a key; literally, a rule or precept. **2** In Sanskrit literature, a short grammatical rule. **3** *pl.* A collection of writings or aphorisms, as the dialogs of the Buddha, the Laws of Manu. **4** In Buddhism, an extended writing, usually in verse, and often in dialog form, embodying important religious and philosophical propositions, sometimes directly, sometimes in highly allegorical or metaphorical language. Also **sut·ta** (sōōt′ə). [<Skt. *sūtra* a thread, rule < *siv* sew]

sut·tee (su·tē′, sut′ē) *n.* Formerly, the sacrifice of a Hindu widow on the funeral pyre of her husband: now forbidden; also, the widow so immolated. [<Hind. *satī* <Skt., a faithful wife, fem. of *sat* good, wise, orig. ppr. of *as* be] **— sut·tee′ism** *n.*

Sut·ter (sut′ər), **John Augustus,** 1803–80, U. S. pioneer in California, born in Germany.

Sut·ter's Mill (sut′ərz) A mill in eastern California: gold was discovered on its site in 1848.

sut·tle (sut′l) *adj.* Formerly, taken after the tare has been deducted and before the tret has been allowed; designating that allowance has been made for the container: said of weight. **—** *n.* Suttle weight. [Earlier var. of SUBTLE]

su·ture (sōō′chər) *n.* **1** The junction of two contiguous surfaces or edges along a line by or as by sewing. **2** *Anat.* The interlocking of two bones at their edges, as in the skull. **3** *Zool.* The line of junction between contiguous parts. **4** *Bot.* The line of dehiscence in plants. **5** *Surg.* **a** The act or operation of uniting parts by or as by stitching. **b** The sewing together of the cut or cleft edges of divided parts. **c** The thread, silver wire, or other material used in this operation. **—** *v.t.* **·tured, ·tur·ing** To unite by means of sutures; sew together. [MF <L *sutura* < *sutus,* pp. of *suere* sew] **— su′tur·al** *adj.* **— su′tur·al·ly** *adv.*

su·um cui·que (sōō′əm kī′kwē, kwī′-) *Latin* To each his own.

Su·va (sōō′vä) A port on the south coast of Viti Levu, capital of the Fiji Islands.

Su·vo·rov (sōō·vô′rôf), **Count Alexander Vasilievich,** 1729–1800, Russian field marshal.

Su·wal·ki (sōō·vä′ōō·kē) A town of NE Poland; formerly in Russia.

Su·wan·nee River (sōō·wô′nē, -won′ē) A river in Georgia and Florida, flowing 250 miles south, west, and SW to the Gulf of Mexico: also *Swanee.*

su·ze·rain (sōō′zə·rān, -rin) *n.* **1** One invested with superior or paramount authority; formerly, a feudal lord. **2** A nation having paramount control over a locally autonomous region. **—** *adj.* Sovereign; supreme. [<F *sus* above <L *susum, sursum* upwards; on analogy with *souverain* a sovereign] **— su′ze·rain·ty** *n.*

Su·zu·ki (sōō·zōō·kē), **Daisetz Teitaro,** 1870–1966, Japanese scholar, author, and teacher, active in the U. S.; leading authority on Zen Buddhism, especially as its expositor to the West.
Su·zy (sōō′zē) Diminutive of SUSANNA.
Sval·bard (väl′bär) An archipelago in the Arctic Ocean, including Spitsbergen and other smaller islands and comprising a possession of Norway; 23,951 square miles; administrative capital, Longyear City on West Spitsbergen.
sva·raj (svä·räj′) See SWARAJ.
Sved·berg (svā′berkh), **The (Theodor),** born 1884, Swedish chemist.
svelte (svelt) *adj.* Slender; slim; willowy. [<F *svelte* <Ital. *svelto* <L *ex-* out + *vellere* pluck]
Sverd·lovsk (sverd·lôfsk′) A city in the central Ural Mountains in western Asiatic Russian S.F.S.R.: formerly *Ekaterinburg.*
Sver·drup (svar′drōōp), **Otto,** 1855–1930, Norwegian Arctic explorer.
Sver·drup Islands (svar′drōōp) An archipelago of northern Franklin District, Northwest Territories, in the Arctic Ocean.
Sve·rige (svā′ryə) The Swedish name for SWEDEN.
Sviz·ze·ra (svēt·tsä′rä) The Italian name for SWITZERLAND.
swab (swob) *n.* **1** One of various utensils consisting essentially of a soft absorbent substance on the end of a handle: used for cleaning, etc. **2** A mop for cleaning decks, floors, etc. **3** A sailor who uses such a mop; a menial; a worthless person. **4** A cylindrical brush for cleaning firearms. **5** *Med.* **a** A bit of sponge or cloth for cleansing the mouth of, or used as a means of applying nourishment or medicine to, a sick person. **b** A specimen of mucus, etc., taken for examination; also, the cotton–wound wire used in obtaining it. — *v.t.* **swabbed, swab·bing** To clean or apply with a swab. Also spelled *swob.* [Back formation <SWABBER]
swab·ber (swob′ər) *n.* **1** One who uses a swab. **2** One fit only for swabbing. **3** A swab. [<MDu. *zwabber* < *zwabben* do dirty work, swab]
Swa·bi·a (swā′bē·ə) A region and former duchy of SW West Germany, which contains the Black Forest; the eastern section comprises an administrative province of SW Bavaria; 3,818 square miles; capital, Augsburg: German *Schwaben.* — **Swa′bi·an** *adj.* & *n.*
swad·dle (swod′l) *v.t.* **·dled, ·dling** To wrap with a bandage; especially, to wrap (an infant) with a long strip of linen or flannel; swathe. — *n.* A swaddling band. [OE *swæthel* swaddling clothes, a bandage < *swathian* swathe]
swaddling clothes **1** Bands or strips of linen or cloth wound around a newborn infant. **2** A time of immaturity, or the limitations that restrict the immature. Also **swaddling bands, swaddling clouts.**
Swa·de·shi (swə·dā′shē) *n.* A former political movement originating in Bengal, India, advocating the boycott of British goods as one means of obtaining swaraj or home rule. [<Skt. *svadeśin* native, national < *svadeśa* native country]
swag (swag) *n.* **1** *Slang* Property obtained by robbery or theft; plunder; booty. **2** *Austral.* A swagman's bundle or pack. **3** Baggage; luggage. **4** A swaying; a lurch. — *v.i.* **swagged, swag·ging** **1** *Brit. Dial.* To swing heavily. **2** *Austral.* To tramp, bearing a swag. **3** To sag; sway; lurch. [Prob. <Scand. Cf. dial. Norw. *svagga* sway.]
swag·bel·ly (swag′bel′ē) *n.* A person having a protuberant abdomen. [<SWAG, *v.* (def. 3) + BELLY] — **swag′bel′lied** *adj.*
swage (swāj) *n.* **1** A tool or form, often one of a pair, for shaping metal by hammering or pressure. **2** An ornamental border or molding. **3** A groove on an anvil for use in shaping metal. **4** A swage block. — *v.t.* **swaged, swag·ing** To shape (metal) with or as with a swage or swage block. [<OF *souage*; ult. origin uncertain]
swage block A heavy iron block or anvil having grooves or holes for shaping metal, heading bolts, etc.: also called *swage.*
swag·ger (swag′ər) *v.i.* **1** To walk with a proud or insolent air; strut. **2** To boast; bluster. — *n.* Braggadocio; expression of superiority in words or deeds. — *adj.* Showy or ostentatious in style, manner, or appearance. [Appar. freq. of SWAG] — **swag′ger·er** *n.* — **swag′ger·ing·ly** *adv.*
swagger coat A sports coat without a belt.
swagger stick A short canelike stick; specifically, one carried by a British soldier when off duty: also called *swanking stick.*
swagger suit A short flared coat and a skirt that matches.
swag·man (swag′man′) *n. pl.* **·men** (-men′) *Austral.* One who seeks work, carrying his bundle or swag.
Swa·hi·li (swä·hē′lē) *n. pl.* **·hi·li** **1** One of a Bantu people of Zanzibar and the adjacent coast, having an admixture of Arab blood. **2** These people collectively: with *the.* **3** The agglutinative language of the Swahili, belonging to the Bantu family of languages. [<Arabic, coastal < *sawāḥil,* pl. of *sāḥil* a coast] — **Swa·hi′li·an** *adj.*
swain (swān) *n.* **1** A youthful rustic; a lover. **2** *Obs.* A squire; a male servant. [<ON *sveinn* a boy, servant] — **swain′ish** *adj.* — **swain′ish·ness** *n.*
swaird (swârd) *n. Scot.* Sward.
swale[1] (swāl) *n.* **1** Low, marshy ground. **2** *Dial.* Shade; a shady place. Also **swail.** [Prob. <Scand. Cf. ON *svalr* cool.]
swale[2] (swāl) See SWEAL.
swall (swäl) *v.* & *n. Scot.* Swell.
swal·low[1] (swol′ō) *v.t.* **1** To cause (food, etc.) to pass from the mouth into the stomach by means of muscular action of the gullet or esophagus. **2** To take in or engulf in a manner suggestive of this; absorb; envelop: often with *up.* **3** To put up with or endure; submit to, as insults. **4** *Colloq.* To believe credulously. **5** To refrain from expressing or giving vent to; suppress. **6** To take back; recant: to *swallow* one's words. — *v.i.* **7** To perform the act or the motions of swallowing. See synonyms under ABSORB. — *n.* **1** That which is swallowed at once; a small amount; a mouthful. **2** The gullet; throat; gorge. **3** The act of swallowing; appetite; inclination. **4** The channel in a hoisting block for the passage of the rope. **5** An abyss; whirlpool; also, a pit. [OE *swelgan* swallow] — **swal′low·er** *n.*
swal·low[2] (swol′ō) *n.* **1** Any of various small, widely distributed passerine birds (family *Hirundinidae*) with short, broad, depressed bill, long, pointed wings, and forked tail: noted for swiftness of flight and migratory habits, as the common **bank swallow** *(Riparia riparia),* the American **tree swallow** *(Iridoprocne bicolor),* and the **barn swallow** *(Hirundo erythrogaster).* ◆ Collateral adjective: *hirundine.* **2** A similar bird, as the swift. [OE *swealwe*]
swallow dive A swan dive.
swal·low·tail (swol′ō·tāl′) *n.* **1** *Colloq.* A man's dress coat with two long, tapering skirts or tails. **2** A butterfly (family *Papilionidae*) having a posterior, tail–like prolongation on each hind wing. —**swal′low–tailed′** *adj.*
swal·low·wort (swol′ō·wûrt′) *n.* **1** A twining perennial herb *(Cynanchum vincetoxicum)* with greenish–white flowers and roots, the latter formerly used in medicine. **2** The common celandine: said to blossom with the arrival of the swallows and to wither when they depart. **3** One of several plants of the milkweed family.
swam (swam) Past tense of SWIM.
swa·mi (swä′mē) *n.* **1** Master; lord: used by Hindus as a title of respect. **2** A Hindu teacher, especially a religious teacher; a pundit. **3** Loosely, a yogi or fakir. Also **swa′my.** [<Hind. *svāmi* lord, master <Skt. *swāmin*]
swamp (swomp, swômp) *n.* A tract or region of low land saturated with water; a wet bog. Also **swamp′land′** (-land′). ◆ Collateral adjective: *paludal.* — *v.t.* **1** To drench or submerge with water or other liquid. **2** To overwhelm with difficulties; crush; ruin. **3** *Naut.* To sink or fill (a vessel) with water. — *v.i.* **4** To sink in water, a swamp, etc. [Cf. LG *swampen* quake (said of a bog). Akin to SUMP.] — **swamp′y, swamp′ish** *adj.*
swamp angel **1** A person who lives in a swamp; a swamper. **2** The hermit thrush.
Swamp Angel A 200–pound Parrott gun used in the siege of Charleston, S.C., in 1863: so called because it was mounted in a swamp.
swamp blackbird The redwing (def. 1).
swamp boat A small, flat–bottomed, blunt–prowed boat powered by an engine with an airplane propeller mounted high in the stern: used in swampy or boggy areas.
swamp cabbage Skunk cabbage.
swamp·er (swom′pər, swôm′-) *n.* **1** One who lives in a swamp or in a swampy district. **2** One who clears a way in a swamp or forest for skidding logs; also, one who clears away underbrush, fallen trees, and other debris for logging operations.
swamp fever **1** Malaria. **2** An infectious anemia of equine animals, caused by a filtrable virus.
Swamp Fox Sobriquet of FRANCIS MARION.
swamp hare A rabbit *(Sylvilagus aquaticus)* frequenting the swamps of the southern United States.
swamp honeysuckle The swamp azalea *(Azalea viscosa)* of the SE United States.
swamp land **1** Land covered with swamps. **2** Fertile, arable land in a swamp.
swamp law Lynch law.
swamp locust The water locust.
swamp maple The red maple of North America *(Acer rubrum).*
swamp oak **1** An oak *(Quercus bicolor)* common in swamps of the eastern United States: also **swamp white oak.** **2** The pin oak.
swamp owl **1** The short–eared owl. **2** The barred owl. See under OWL.
swamp pine Any of certain pines common in swamps or swampy regions; especially, the loblolly pine and the slash pine.
swamp privet See under PRIVET.
swamp sparrow An American sparrow *(Melospiza georgiana)* resembling the song sparrow, inhabiting the swamps of the southern and eastern United States.
swamp willow The pussy willow.
swan[1] (swon, swôn) *n.* **1** A large, web-footed, long–necked bird (subfamily *Cygninae*), allied to but heavier than the goose, and noted for its grace on the water, as the whooper, the trumpeter swan, and the common North American whistling swan *(Cygnus columbiana).* The male is a *cob,* and the female is a *pen.* **2** Figuratively, a poet or singer. [OE]

TRUMPETER SWAN (Body length from 4 to 4 1/2 feet)

swan[2] (swon, swôn) *v.i. U.S. Dial.* Swear: chiefly in the phrase *I swan,* an exclamation of amazement. [Prob. < dial. E (Northern) *Is' wan,* lit., I shall warrant, used as euphemism for *swear*]
Swan (swon, swôn) The constellation Cygnus. See under CONSTELLATION.
swan dive A fancy dive performed with head tilted back and arms held like the wings of a swallow until near the water: also called *swallow dive.*
Swa·nee River (swô′nē, swon′ē) See SUWANNEE RIVER.
swang (swang) Dialectal past tense of SWING.
swan·herd (swon′hûrd′, swôn′-) *n.* One who tends swans; especially, a royal officer of England having charge of marking the swans on the Thames which belong to the crown. Also **swan′mas′ter.** Compare SWAN–UPPING.
swank (swangk) *v.* & *n. Slang* Swagger; bluster. — *adj. Slang* **1** Ostentatiously fashionable; pretentious. **2** *Scot.* Slim; pliant; agile; jolly; lively. Also **swank′y.** [< dial. E. Appar. akin to MLG *swank* flexible, MHG *swanken* sway.] — **swank′i·ly** *adv.* — **swank′i·ness** *n.*
swank·ie (swangk′ē) *n. Scot.* An active, clever lad: sometimes said of a lass. Also **swank′y.**
swanking stick A swagger stick.
swan maiden In many ancient folk myths, a beautiful fairy maiden able to transform herself into a swan by means of a magic robe,

add,āce,câre,pälm; end,ēven; it,īce; odd,ōpen,ôrder; tŏŏk,pōōl; up,bûrn; ə = a in *above,* e in *sicken,* i in *clarity,* o in *melon,* u in *focus;* yōō = u in *fuse;* oi,oil; ou,pout; ch,check; g,go; ng,ring; th,thin; th,this; zh,vision. Foreign sounds à,œ,ü,kh,ṅ; and ◆: see page xx. < from; + plus; ? possibly.

ring, or chain, and living under an enchantment or tabu affecting her life with a human lover.

swan-neck (swon'nek', swôn'-) *n.* Any of several mechanical contrivances resembling in outline the neck of a swan.

swan·ner·y (swon'ər-ē, swôn'-) *n. pl.* **·ner·ies** A place where swans are bred or kept.

swan·pan (swän'pän') *n.* A Chinese abacus or frame of beads to aid reckoning: also spelled *schwanpan, shwanpan.* [<Chinese *suan p'an* a reckoning board]

Swan River (swon, swôn) A river in SW Western Australia, flowing 240 miles NW and SW to the Indian Ocean at Fremantle.

swan's-down (swonz'doun', swônz'-) *n.* 1 The down of a swan: used for trimming, powder puffs, etc. 2 Canton or cotton flannel. 3 A soft, thick, fine woolen cloth resembling down. Also **swans'down'.**

Swan·sea (swon'sē) A port and industrial county borough in SW Glamorganshire, southern Wales.

swan·skin (swon'skin', swôn'-) *n.* 1 The unplucked skin of a swan. 2 A soft, fine-twilled flannel or cotton fabric having a soft nap. — *adj.* Made of swanskin.

swan-song (swon'sông', -song', swôn'-) *n.* A last or dying work, as of a poet or composer: in allusion to the ancient fable that the swan sings a last song before dying.

swan-up·ping (swon'up'ing, swôn'-) *n. Brit.* The annual inspection and marking on the beak of the royal and other privileged young swans or cygnets on the Thames; also, the annual expedition for this purpose.

swap (swop) *v.t. & v.i.* **swapped, swap·ping** *Colloq.* To exchange (one thing for another); trade. — **to swap lies** To exchange tales; tell stories. — *n.* The act of swapping. Also spelled *swop.* [ME *swappen* strike (a bargain), slap; prob. ult. imit. of the sound of clapping the hands, as in bargaining]

swa·raj (swə-räj') *n.* 1 Formerly in British India, self-government; by extension, cultural and political development under native influence as distinguished from such development under British influence. 2 Home rule: the watchword of the Indian Nationalists; the party itself. Also spelled *svaraj.* [Skt. *svarāj* self-ruling <*sva-* own + *rāj* rule] — **swa·raj'ist** *n.* — **swa·raj'ism** *n.*

sward (swôrd) *n.* 1 Land thickly covered with grass; turf. 2 *Obs.* A skin; rind. Also **swarth** (swôrth). — *v.t. & v.i.* To cover or become covered with sward. [OE *sweard* a skin]

sware (swâr) Obsolete past tense of SWEAR.

swarm[1] (swôrm) *n.* 1 A large number or body of insects or small living things of any kind. 2 A hive of bees; also, a large number of bees leaving the parent stock at one time, to take up new lodgings, accompanied by a queen. 3 A crowd or throng of persons, animals, or things, especially when in motion or advancing under pressure. 4 *Biol.* A collection of free-swimming unicellular organisms, especially zoospores. See synonyms under FLOCK. — *v.i.* 1 To leave the hive in a swarm: said of bees. 2 To come together, move, or occur in great numbers. 3 To be crowded or overrun; teem: with *with.* 4 *Biol.* To come forth in a swarm. — *v.t.* 5 To fill with a swarm or crowd; throng. [OE *swearm*]

swarm[2] (swôrm) *v.t. & v.i.* To climb (a tree, etc.) by clasping it with the hands and limbs. [Orig. nautical cant. Prob. akin to SWARM[1].]

swarm·er (swôr'mər) *n.* 1 A swarm spore. 2 An insect that swarms, as a bee or gnat; one who or that which swarms.

swarm spore *Biol.* 1 A zoospore. 2 A flagellate spore. 3 A ciliated sponge embryo.

swart (swôrt) *adj.* 1 Swarthy; also, poetically, absolutely black. 2 Malignant; gloomy. Also **swarth** (swôrth). [OE *sweart*] — **swart'ness** *n.*

swart·back (swôrt'bak') *n. Scot.* The great black-backed gull (*Larus marinus*).

swarth[1] (swôrth) *n.* 1 *Obs.* Sward (*n.* def. 1). 2 *Dial.* An unripe crop of hay. [OE *swearth*]

swarth[2] (swôrth) *n. Dial.* The apparition of a person about to die; a wraith. [? Var. of SWART]

swarth·y (swôr'thē) *adj.* **swarth·i·er, swarth·i·est** Having a dark hue; of dark or sunburned complexion; tawny; swart. Also **swart'y.** See synonyms under DARK. [Var. of obs. *swarty* <SWART] — **swarth'i·ly** *adv.* — **swarth'i·ness, swarth'ness** *n.*

swarve[1] (swôrv) *v.t. & v.i. Obs.* To swerve. [<dial. var. of SWERVE]

swarve[2] (swôrv) *v.t. & v.i.* To climb. [Origin uncertain. Prob. akin to SWARM[2].]

swarve[3] (swôrv) *v.i.* To swoon. [?<ON *svarfa* upset]

swash (swosh, swôsh) *v.i.* 1 To move or wash noisily, as waves. 2 To swagger. — *v.t.* 3 To splash (water, etc.). 4 To splash or dash water, etc., upon or against. — *n.* 1 The splash of a liquid. 2 A narrow channel through which tides flow. 3 A bar over which the waves pass freely. 4 Swill or wet refuse for pigs. 5 A swaggerer or his behavior. 6 *Slang* Worthless sentimental literature; trash. [Imit.]

swash·buck·ler (swosh'buk'lər, swôsh'-) *n.* A swaggering soldier; a bravo[2]. [<SWASH + BUCKLER; with ref. to striking one's own or one's opponent's shield with a sword] — **swash'buck'ler·ing** *n.* — **swash'buck'ling** *adj. & n.*

swash·er (swosh'ər, swôsh'-) *n.* A blusterer; braggart; bully.

swash·ing (swosh'ing, swôsh'-) *adj.* 1 Splashing. 2 Swaggering; blustering. 3 Crushing; violent.

swash letters Italic special letters having a top or bottom flourish on the side where there is most blank space.

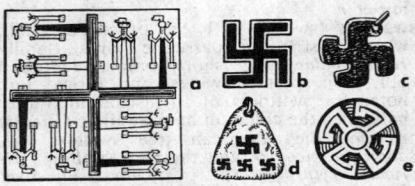

SWASH LETTERS

swas·ti·ka (swos'ti-kə) *n.* 1 A primitive religious ornament or symbol, originally in the form of a gammadion, but variously modified, the most typical being a Greek cross with the ends of the arms bent at right angles, and prolonged to the length of the upright arms, clockwise, or counterclockwise. See *b* in illustration. It dates back to the Bronze Age in Europe, and still exists as a religious symbol in India, Persia, China, Japan, and among North, Central, and South American Indians: believed to be a token of good luck or blessing. 2 The emblem of the Nazis: as *b* in illustration. See HAKENKREUZ. Compare FYLFOT. Also **swas'ti·ca.** [<Skt. *svastika* <*svastí* well-being, fortune <*sú* good + *astí* being <*as* be]

SWASTIKA
a. Navaho Indian.   c. Caucasian.
b. Indian.   d. Siberian.
e. Pima Indian.

swat (swot) *v.t.* **swat·ted, swat·ting** To hit with a sharp blow. — *n.* A smart blow. Also spelled *swot.* [Var. of SQUAT, in dial. sense of "squash"]

Swat (swot) *n. pl.* **Swa·ti** (swä'tē) One of an East Indian Moslem people of Indo-European linguistic stock, dwelling in northern West Pakistan. Also **Swa'ti.**

Swat (swot) 1 A former princely state, in the former North-West Frontier Province, northern West Pakistan; 4,000 square miles; capital, Saidu. 2 A river in northern West Pakistan, flowing about 200 miles south, SW, and SE to the Kabul.

swatch (swoch) *n.* A strip, as of cloth, especially one cut off for a sample. [<dial. E (Northern), a cloth tally]

swath (swoth, swôth) *n.* 1 A row or line of cut grass. 2 The space cut by a machine or implement in a single course. 3 The width of grass cut by the sweep of a scythe. Also spelled *swathe.* — **to cut a wide swath** To accomplish much; hence, to make a fine impression. [OE *swæth* a track]

swathe[1] (swäth, swāth) *v.t.* **swathed, swath·ing** 1 To bind or wrap, as in bandages; swaddle. 2 To envelop; enwrap; surround. — *n.* A bandage for swathing. [OE *swathian*] — **swath'er** *n.*

swathe[2] (swäth) See SWATH.

Swa·tow (swä'tou') An industrial city and former treaty port on the South China Sea in eastern Kwangtung province, China.

swat·ter[1] (swot'ər) *n.* 1 One who or that which crushes with a blow. 2 A perforated rubber or meshed wire device for killing flies. 3 A hard-hitting baseball player.

swat·ter[2] (swot'ər) *v.i. Dial.* To splash water about, as geese and ducks in drinking. [Imit.]

sway (swā) *v.i.* 1 To swing from side to side or to and fro; oscillate. 2 To bend or incline to one side; lean; veer. 3 To tend in opinion, sympathy, etc. 4 To have influence or control; rule. — *v.t.* 5 To cause to swing from side to side. 6 To cause to bend or incline to one side. 7 *Naut.* To swing into place; hoist, as a yard or mast. 8 To cause (a person, opinion, etc.) to tend in a given way; influence. 9 To cause to swerve; deflect or divert, as from a course of action. 10 *Archaic* a To wield, as a weapon or, especially, a scepter. b To rule over; govern. See synonyms under GOVERN, INFLUENCE, SHAKE. — *n.* 1 Power exercised in governing; dominion; control. 2 The act of swaying, literal or figurative; a sweeping, swinging, or turning from side to side. 3 Momentum; inclination; bias. 4 Overpowering force or influence. [Prob. fusion of ON *sveigja* bend and LG *swajen* be moved to and fro by the wind]

sway·back (swā'bak') *n.* 1 A hollow or unnaturally sagging condition of the back, as in a horse. 2 An animal with a swayback.

sway·backed (swā'bakt') *adj.* 1 Having a sagged or hollow back. 2 Hence, strained or weakened, as by overwork.

Swa·zi (swä'zē) *n.* One of a tribe belonging to the Bantu peoples, and dwelling in Swaziland, Africa.

Swa·zi·land (swä'zē-land) An independent member of the Commonwealth of Nations, between Mozambique and South Africa; 6,704 sq. mi.; capital, Mbabane. See map of SOUTH AFRICA.

sweal (swēl) *v.i. Brit. Dial.* 1 To melt and run down, as the tallow of a candle. 2 To burn away slowly; waste away. Also spelled *swale.* [OE *swelan, swēlan* burn]

swear (swâr) *v.* **swore** (*Obs.* **sware**), **sworn, swear·ing** *v.i.* 1 To make a solemn affirmation with an appeal to God or to some deity, or with invocation of something held sacred, as in attestation of truth or proof of good intentions: He *swore* by all the gods. 2 To make a vow; utter a solemn promise. 3 To use profanity; invoke or mention sacred beings or things irreverently or blasphemously; curse. 4 *Law* To give testimony under oath. — *v.t.* 5 To affirm or assert solemnly by invoking sacred beings or things. 6 To promise with an oath or solemn affirmation; vow. 7 To declare or affirm upon oath: to *swear* treason against a man. 8 To take or utter (an oath). 9 To administer a legal oath to. — **to swear by** 1 To appeal to by oath. 2 To have complete confidence in. — **to swear in** To administer a legal oath to. — **to swear off** *Colloq.* To promise to renounce or give up: to *swear off* drink. — **to swear out** To obtain (a warrant for arrest) by making a statement or charge under oath. [OE *swerian*] — **swear'er** *n.*

swear·word (swâr'wûrd') *n.* A word used in profanity or cursing.

sweat (swet) *v.* **sweat** or **sweat·ed, sweat·ing** *v.i.* 1 To exude or excrete sensible moisture from the pores of the skin; perspire. 2 To exude moisture in drops; ooze. 3 To gather and condense moisture in drops on its surface. 4 To pass through pores or interstices in drops. 5 To ferment, as tobacco leaves. 6 *Colloq.* To work hard; toil; drudge. 7 *Colloq.* To suffer: You will *sweat* for that! — *v.t.* 8 To exude (moisture) from the pores. 9 To gather or condense drops of (moisture). 10 To soak or stain with sweat. 11 To cause to sweat. 12 To cause to work hard. 13 *Colloq.* To force (employees) to work for low wages and under unfavorable conditions. 14 *Slang* To extort money from. 15 To heat (solder, etc.) until it melts. 16 To join, as metal objects, by applying heat after binding together with solder. 17 *Metall.* To heat so as to extract an element that is easily fusible; also, to extract thus. 18 To force moisture from, as wood in a charcoal kiln. 19 To subject to fermentation, as hides or tobacco. 20 To remove particles of (coins) illegally, as

by shaking them in a bag. **21** *Slang* To subject to torture or rigorous interrogation for the purpose of extracting information; put through the third degree. **—to sweat (something) out** *Slang* To wait through anxiously and helplessly: to *sweat out* a long delay. **—n. 1** Sensible perspiration of animals, or any gathering of moisture in minute drops like those of perspiration on the skin. **2** The act or state of sweating; specifically, sweating induced by drugs or artificial means. **3** Figuratively, hard labor; drudgery. **4** *Colloq.* Fuming impatience; worry; hurry. **5** The act or process of causing to sweat, as a short rapid exercise given to a horse or the process of sweating hides or bricks. **6** *Obs.* The sweating sickness. [< OE *swǣtan* < *swāt* sweat] **—sweat'i·ly** *adv.* **—sweat'i·ness** *n.* **—sweat'y** *adj.*

sweat·band (swet'band') *n.* A band, usually of leather, inside the crown of a hat to protect it from sweat.

sweat·box (swet'boks') *n.* **1** A device for sweating such products as hides and dried fruits. **2** Any very hot, close room. **3** *Colloq.* Formerly, a narrow cell where an unruly prisoner was confined; now, any place of confinement; specifically, a place where a prisoner is questioned or put through the third degree.

sweat·ed (swet'id) *adj.* **1** Saturated or covered with sweat; that has been made to perspire. **2** Employed in hard work for low pay; overworked and underpaid: *sweated* labor.

sweat·er (swet'ər) *n.* **1** One who or that which sweats; specifically, an employer who underpays and overworks his employees. **2** A jerseylike knitted garment with or without sleeves. **3** A medicine that induces sweating; a sudorific.

sweat gland *Anat.* One of the convoluted tubules that secrete sweat, found in subcutaneous tissue and terminating externally in a small orifice or pore.

sweating sickness *Pathol.* A febrile infective disease epidemic in England in the 15th and 16th centuries, characterized by profuse sweating; miliaria. Also **sweating fever.**

sweat shirt A collarless pull-over sweater, sometimes lined with fleece: used by athletes.

sweat·shop (swet'shop') *n.* A place where work is done under poor conditions, for insufficient wages, and for long hours.

Swede (swēd) *n.* **1** A native or naturalized inhabitant of Sweden. **2** A Swedish turnip; the rutabaga.

Swe·den (swē'd'n) A kingdom in NE Europe, in the eastern part of the Scandinavian peninsula; 173,577 square miles; capital, Stockholm: Swedish *Sverige*.

Swe·den·borg (swē'd'n-bôrg, *Sw.* svā'dən·bôr'y'), **Emanuel**, 1688–1772, Swedish mystic, philosopher, and scientist. **—Swe'den·bor'gi·an** (-bôr'jē·ən) *adj. & n.*

Swe·den·bor·gi·an·ism (swē'dən·bôr'jē·ən·iz'·əm) *n.* The system of philosophy or the theology developed by Emanuel Swedenborg, or from his writings, which teaches that Jesus Christ is the only God, and emphasizes a symbolic interpretation of the Bible. The Swedenborgian church, first organized in London in 1783, is called the *New Church,* or the *New Jerusalem Church.* Also **Swe'den·borg'ism** (-bôrg'iz·əm).

Swed·ish (swē'dish) *adj.* Pertaining to Sweden, the Swedes, or their language. **—n. 1** The North Germanic language of Sweden, including Old Swedish (the pre-Reformation language), Modern Swedish, and several dialects. **2** The inhabitants of Sweden collectively: with *the.*

Swedish clover Alsike.

Swedish massage Massage given in combination with Swedish movements.

Swedish movements A system of muscular movements employed in treating certain diseases or developing the body.

Swedish turnip The rutabaga.

swee·ny (swē'nē) *n.* Atrophy of the shoulder muscles of a horse. [Perhaps < dial. G *schweine* atrophy]

sweep (swēp) *v.* **swept, sweep·ing** *v.t.* **1** To collect, remove, or clear away with a broom, brush, etc. **2** To clear or clean with or as with a broom

or brush: to *sweep* a floor; to *sweep* the plains of buffalo. **3** To touch or brush with a motion as of sweeping: Her dress *swept* the ground; to *sweep* the strings of a harp. **4** To pass over or through swiftly, as in searching: His eyes *swept* the sky. **5** To cause to move with an even, continuous action: He *swept* the cape over her shoulders. **6** To move, carry, bring, etc., with strong or continuous force: The flood *swept* the bridge away. **7** To move over or through with strong or steady force: The gale *swept* the bay. **8** To drag the bottom of (a body of water, etc.). **—v.i. 9** To clean or brush a floor or other surface with a broom, etc. **10** To move or go strongly and evenly, especially with speed: The train *swept* by. **11** To walk with or as with trailing garments: She *swept* into the room. **12** To trail, as a skirt. **13** To extend with a long reach or curve: The road *sweeps* along the lake shore on the north. See synonyms under CLEANSE. **—n. 1** The act or result of sweeping. **2** The motion of a long stroke or movement: a *sweep* of the hand. **3** The act of clearing out or getting rid of; hence, removal from office or place: a clean *sweep* of the officeholders; also, a clearance. **4** A turning of the eye or of optical instruments over the field of vision. **5** The winning of a great success, as in an election. **6** The range, area, or compass reached by sweeping, as extent of stroke, range of vision, etc.; direction or extent of motion; hence, a curve or bend, as of a scythe blade, etc. **7** One who or that which sweeps. **8** A piece, as of a machine, along which something sweeps. **9** *Brit.* A chimneysweeper. **10** A long, heavy oar. **11** A well sweep. **12** A curved roadway or approach before a building. **13** *pl.* Sweepings, as of a place where precious metals are worked. **14** *Physics* An irreversible process in which a substance settles to thermal equilibrium or tends to do so. **15** In card games, a winning of all the points in a hand, as by taking of all the tricks in whist; in casino, the taking or capture of all the cards on the table. **16** *Colloq.* Sweepstakes. [ME *swepen,* alter. of *swopen* brush away < OE *swāpen*] **—sweep'er** *n.*

sweep·back (swēp'bak') *n. Aeron.* **1** The backward inclination of the leading edge of an airplane wing. **2** The acute angle between the line of this inclination and the lateral axis of the airplane.

sweep·ing (swē'ping) *adj.* **1** Carrying off or clearing away with a driving movement. **2** Carrying all before it; covering a wide area; comprehensive. **3** General and thoroughgoing. **—n. 1** The action of one who or that which sweeps. **2** *pl.* Things swept up; refuse. **—sweep'ing·ly** *adv.* **—sweep'ing·ness** *n.*

sweep·stakes (swēp'stāks') *n. pl.* **·stakes 1** A gambling arrangement by which all the sums staked may be won by one or by a few of the betters, as in a horse race. **2** A race for all the stakes. **3** A prize in a sporting contest comprising several stakes. **4** A lottery which offers sweepstakes as prizes. Also **sweep'stake'.**

sweep ticket A ticket which gives the holder a chance to win in a sweepstakes.

sweep·y (swē'pē) *adj.* **sweep·i·er, sweep·i·est 1** Having a sweeping, swaying, or trailing motion. **2** Sweeping in curves, as a river.

sweer (swir) *adj. Dial.* **1** Heavy; lazy; indolent. **2** Reluctant; unwilling. [OE *swǣr*]

sweet (swēt) *adj.* **1** Agreeable to the sense of taste; having a flavor like that of sugar; especially, containing or due to sugar in some form. **2** Fresh, as opposed to *salt, sour,* or *rancid;* not fermented or decaying. **3** Gently pleasing to the senses; agreeable to the smell; pleasing in sound; melodious; fair; restful. **4** Agreeable or delightful to the mind; arousing gentle, pleasant emotions. **5** Having gentle, pleasing, and winning qualities; marked by kindness and amiability; dear; beloved. **6** Easy; smooth; noiseless: said of machines or contrivances. **7** Sound; rich; productive: said of soil. **8** Not dry: said of wines. **9** *Chem.* Free from acid, etc. **—n. 1** The quality of being sweet; sweetness. **2** Something sweet: chiefly in the plural, as confections, preserves, candy. **3** A beloved person; darling. **4** Something agreeable or pleasing; pleasure. **5** A sweet smell; perfume. **6** *Brit.* A dessert. ◆ Homophone: *suite.* [OE *swēte*] **—sweet'ly** *adv.* **—sweet'ness** *n.*

Synonyms (adj.): honeyed, luscious, nectared, saccharine, sugared, sugary.

Sweet (swēt), **Henry,** 1845–1912, English philologist.

sweet alyssum A widely cultivated perennial crucifer (*Lobularia maritima*) native to the Mediterranean region, having small, very fragrant white or purple flowers. Also called *alyssum.*

sweet basil Basil (def. 1).

sweet bay 1 Laurel (def. 1). **2** A highly ornamental tree or shrub (*Magnolia virginiana*), with evergreen or deciduous leaves and large handsome flowers.

sweet birch Black birch.

sweet·bread (swēt'bred') *n.* The pancreas (**stomach sweetbread**) or the thymus gland (**neck sweetbread** or **throat sweetbread**) of a calf or other animal, when used as food. [< SWEET + BREAD, in obs. sense of "a morsel"]

sweet·bri·er (swēt'brī'ər) *n.* A stout prickly rose (*Rosa eglanteria*) with aromatic leaves. Also **sweet'bri'ar.**

sweet cicely 1 A small European perennial (*Myrrhis odorata*) having white fragrant flowers. **2** A related American herb (genus *Osmorhiza*) with white or purplish flowers and fleshy aromatic root.

sweet clover Melilot.

sweet corn 1 Any of several varieties of Indian corn rich in sugar, and shriveling when ripe. **2** Indian corn in the milky stage.

sweet·en (swēt'n) *v.t.* **1** To make sweet or sweeter. **2** To make more endurable; lighten. **3** To make pleasant or gratifying. **4** In poker, to increase the chips in (the pot). **5** To add gilt-edge securities to others so as to increase the value of (collateral for a loan). **—v.i. 6** To become sweet or sweeter. **—sweet'en·er** *n.*

sweet·en·ing (swēt'n·ing) *n.* **1** The act of making sweet. **2** That which sweetens. **—long sweetening** Molasses; treacle. **—short sweetening** Sugar.

sweet fennel Finochio.

sweet fern 1 A shrub of the northern United States and Canada (genus *Comptonia*) with long, fernlike, fragrant leaves. **2** Any of several ferns (genus *Dryopteris*).

sweet·flag (swēt'flag') *n.* A marsh-dwelling plant (*Acorus calamus*), with sword-shaped leaves and a thick creeping rootstock with an aromatic flavor; the calamus.

sweet·gale (swēt'gāl') *n.* A branching shrub (*Myrica gale*), with both fertile and sterile flowers in short scaly catkins, and resinous, dotted, fragrant leaves. [< SWEET + GALE²]

sweet·gum (swēt'gum') *n.* **1** A balsamiferous tree (*Liquidambar styraciflua*) of Atlantic North America, the wood of which is sometimes used to imitate mahogany. **2** The balsam or gum yielded by it.

sweet·heart (swēt'härt') *n.* One who is particularly loved by or as a lover; a lover.

sweet·ing (swē'ting) *n.* **1** A sweet apple. **2** A sweetheart; dear one; darling.

sweet·ish (swē'tish) *adj.* Somewhat sweet; slightly sweet; also, nauseatingly sweet. **—sweet'ish·ly** *adv.* **—sweet'ish·ness** *n.*

sweet·leaf (swēt'lēf') *n.* The horse sugar.

sweet marjoram Marjoram.

sweet·meat (swēt'mēt') *n.* **1** A confection, preserve, or the like. **2** A candy or crystallized fruit. **3** *pl.* Very sweet candy, cakes, etc.

sweetness and light The essence of esthetic and moral culture, consisting of sympathy, appreciation, open-mindedness, and capacity to enlighten or be enlightened: phrase taken from Swift and popularized by Matthew Arnold.

sweet pea An ornamental annual climber (*Lathyrus odoratus*) of the bean family cultivated for its fragrant, varicolored flowers.

sweet pepper A mild variety of capsicum used for pickling and as a vegetable.

sweet potato 1 A perennial tropical vine (*Ipomoea batatas*) of the morning-glory family, with rose-violet or pink flowers and a fleshy tuberous root. **2** The root itself,

eaten as a vegetable. 3 *Colloq.* An ocarina.

sweets (swēts) *n. pl.* **1** Sweet things to eat, as puddings, cakes, tarts, jellies, etc. **2** The pleasures and gratifying things in life: the *sweets* of success.

sweet·sop (swēt′sop′) *n.* **1** A tropical American tree *(Annona squamosa)* allied to the custard apple. **2** Its egg-shaped, scaly fruit; the sugar apple.

sweet–talk (swēt′tôk′) *Colloq. v.t.* **1** To persuade by coaxing or flattering. —*v.i.* **2** To flatter or coax someone. —**sweet talk**

sweet tooth *Colloq.* A fondness or appetite for candy or sweets.

sweet william A perennial species of pink *(Dianthus barbatus)* with large lanceolate leaves and closely clustered, showy flowers.

swell (swel) *v.* **swelled, swelled** or **swol·len, swell·ing** *v.i.* **1** To increase in bulk or dimension, as by inflation with air or by absorption of moisture; dilate; expand. **2** To increase in size, amount, degree, etc. **3** To grow in volume or intensity, as a sound. **4** To rise in waves or swells, as the sea. **5** To bulge; protrude or belly, as a sail. **6** To become puffed up with pride. **7** To grow within one: My anger *swells* at the sight. —*v.t.* **8** To cause to increase in size or bulk. **9** To cause to increase in amount, extent, or degree. **10** To cause to bulge; belly. **11** To puff with pride. **12** *Music* To sing or play with combined crescendo and diminuendo. —*n.* **1** The act, process, or effect of swelling; expansion. **2** The long continuous body of a wave; a billow; hence, a rise of, or undulation in, the land. **3** A bulge or protuberance. **4** *Music* The union of crescendo and diminuendo; also, the signs (< >) indicating it. **5** A device by which the loudness of a musical instrument, as an organ, may be increased or diminished. **6** *Slang* A person of the ultrafashionable set. See synonyms under WAVE. —*adj. Slang* **1** Of or pertaining to swells or ultrafashionable people; hence, in the height of fashion; smart. **2** First-rate; distinctive. [OE *swellan*]

Synonyms (verb): bulge, dilate, distend, enlarge, expand, increase, inflate. See PUFF. *Antonyms*: contract, decrease, dwindle, shrink.

swell·box (swel′boks′) *n.* A chamber containing the pipes of the organ and having a front of movable slats which muffle the sound or allow it to be heard clearly.

swell·fish (swel′fish′) *n. pl.* **·fish** or **·fish·es** A puffer or globefish.

swell·head (swel′hed′) *n. Slang* A conceited person.

swell·ing (swel′ing) *n.* **1** The act of expanding, inflating, or augmenting. **2** *Pathol.* Morbid enlargement of a part of the body. **3** A protuberance. —*adj.* Increasing; bulging.

swell mob *Brit. Slang* Well-dressed pickpockets collectively.

swel·ter (swel′tər) *v.i.* **1** To suffer from oppressive heat; perspire from heat. —*v.t.* **2** To cause to swelter. **3** *Obs.* To exude. —*n. Rare* A hot, sweltering condition; oppressive humid heat. [Freq. of obs. and dial. *swelt* be faint, die <OE *sweltan* die]

swel·ter·ing (swel′tər·ing) *adj.* **1** Oppressive; overpoweringly hot. **2** Overcome by heat. Also **swel′try** (-trē). —**swel′ter·ing·ly adv.**

swept (swept) Past tense and past participle of SWEEP.

swept·back (swept′bak′) *adj. Aeron.* Having the front edge (of a wing) tilted backward at an angle with the lateral axis of an airplane. Also called *backswept.*

swept·wing (swept′wing′) *n.* A sweptback wing. —*adj.* Having a sweptback wing.

swerve (swûrv) *v.t. & v.i.* **swerved, swerv·ing** To turn or cause to turn aside from a course or purpose; deflect. See synonyms under FLUCTUATE, WANDER. —*n.* The act of swerving; a sudden turning aside. [OE *sweorfan* file or grind away]

swev·en (swev′ən) *n. Obs.* A dream. [OE *swefn* sleep, a dream]

swift[1] (swift) *adj.* **1** Traversing space or performing movements in a brief time; rapid; quick. **2** Capable of quick motion; fleet; speedy. **3** Passing rapidly, as time or events; also, coming without warning; unexpected. **4** Acting with readiness; prompt. —*adv.* Quickly: a poetic use. [OE] —**swift′ly** *adv.* —**swift′ness** *n.*

Synonyms (adj.): expeditious, fast, fleet, flying, hasty, quick, rapid, speedy, sudden. See IMPETUOUS, NIMBLE. *Antonyms*: deliberate, dilatory, dull, lingering, slow, sluggish, tardy.

swift[2] (swift) *n.* **1** A bird of swallowlike form (family *Micropodidae*), possessing extraordinary powers of flight, including the builders of edible birds' nests (genus *Collocalia*) and the common American swift *(Chaetura pelagica).* **2** One of various small lizards (genera *Sceloporus* and *Uta*) common in the western United States. **3** A reel having an adjustable diameter for winding yarn, etc. **4** The main cylinder of a carding machine; also, a similar part in other machines. [< SWIFT[1]]

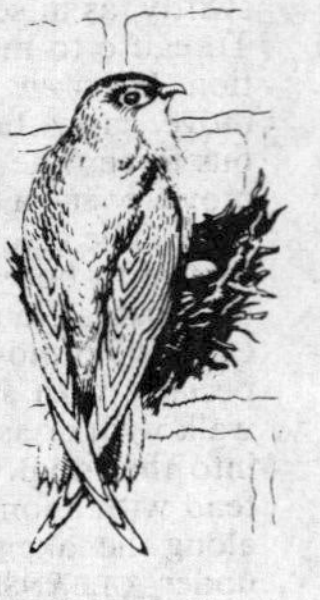

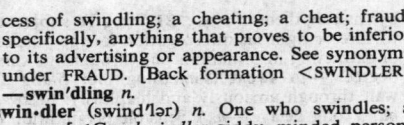

CHIMNEY SWIFT
(About 9 1/2 inches long)

Swift (swift), **Jonathan,** 1667–1745, English satirist born in Dublin: called "Dean Swift."

swift·er (swif′tər) *v.t.* To make taut, as shrouds of a ship, by means of a block and tackle. —*n. Naut.* **1** A rope around the extremities of the capstan bars to connect and steady them, and to give a hold for extra men. **2** One of the forward lower shrouds. **3** A rope for encircling a boat, to strengthen her or prevent chafing of her sides. [<obs. *swift* tie with ropes drawn taut, prob. <Scand. Cf. ON *svifta* reef (a sail).]

swift lizard The fence lizard.

swig[1] (swig) *n. Colloq.* A deep draft. —*v.t. & v.i.* **swigged, swig·ging** *Colloq.* To drink swigs (of). [Origin unknown]

swig[2] (swig) *Naut. v.t.* **swigged, swig·ging** To tighten (a rope that is fast at both ends) by hauling at right angles to its lead. —*n.* **1** A hauling on the bight of a rope fast at both ends. **2** A tackle having diverging ropes. [Akin to SWAG]

swill (swil) *v.t.* **1** To drink greedily and to excess. **2** *Brit.* To drench, as with water; rinse; wash. —*v.i.* **3** To drink to excess; tope. —*n.* **1** Liquid food for domestic animals; especially, the mixture of liquid and solid food given to swine; garbage. **2** Liquor drunk greedily or grossly; loosely, liquor in general. [OE *swillan, swillian* wash]

swim[1] (swim) *v.* **swam** (*Dial.* **swum**), **swum, swim·ming** *v.i.* **1** To move through water by working the legs, arms, fins, etc. **2** To be supported on water or other liquid; float. **3** To move with a smooth or flowing motion, as if swimming in water. **4** To be immersed in or covered with liquid; be flooded; overflow. —*v.t.* **5** To cross or traverse by swimming. **6** To cause to swim. See synonyms under FLOAT. —*n.* **1** The action or pastime of swimming. **2** A gliding, swaying motion or movement. **3** The air bladder of a fish; the sound: also **swim bladder, swimming bladder.** **4** *Colloq.* The current of affairs, especially of fashionable life: in the *swim.* [OE *swimman*] —**swim′mer** *n.*

swim[2] (swim) *v.i.* To be dizzy; reel; have a giddy sensation; seem to go round. —*n.* A sudden dizziness; temporary unconsciousness; swoon. [OE *swima* dizziness]

swim·mer·et (swim′ə·ret) *n. Zool.* One of a series of fringed, typically biramous abdominal appendages of a crustacean, adapted for swimming, for aid in respiration, and for carrying the eggs on females. [Dim. of *swimmer*]

swim·ming[1] (swim′ing) *n.* The act of one who swims. —*adj.* **1** Used for swimming; having the capacity of swimming. **2** Watery; flooded with tears, as the eyes. [<SWIM[1]]

swim·ming[2] (swim′ing) *adj.* Affected by dizziness. [<SWIM[2]]

swimming hole A deep hole in a shallow running stream, used for swimming.

swim·ming·ly (swim′ing·lē) *adv.* In a swimming manner; easily, rapidly, and successfully.

swim·suit (swim′so͞ot′) *n.* A garment designed to be worn while swimming.

Swin·burne (swin′bûrn), **Algernon Charles,** 1837–1909, English poet and critic.

swin·dle (swin′dəl) *v.* **·dled, ·dling** *v.t.* **1** To cheat of money or property by deliberate fraud; defraud. **2** To obtain by such means. —*v.i.* **3** To practice fraud; be a swindler. See synonyms under STEAL. —*n.* The act or process of swindling; a cheating; a cheat; fraud; specifically, anything that proves to be inferior to its advertising or appearance. See synonyms under FRAUD. [Back formation <SWINDLER] —**swin′dling** *n.*

swin·dler (swind′lər) *n.* One who swindles; a rogue. [<G *schwindler* giddy-minded person, cheat <*schwindeln* act thoughtlessly]

swindle sheet *U.S. Slang* An expense account.

swine (swīn) *n. pl.* **swine 1** An omnivorous mammal (family *Suidae*) having a long mobile snout and cloven hoofs. **2** A domesticated hog. **3** A low, greedy, stupid, or vicious person. [OE *swin*]

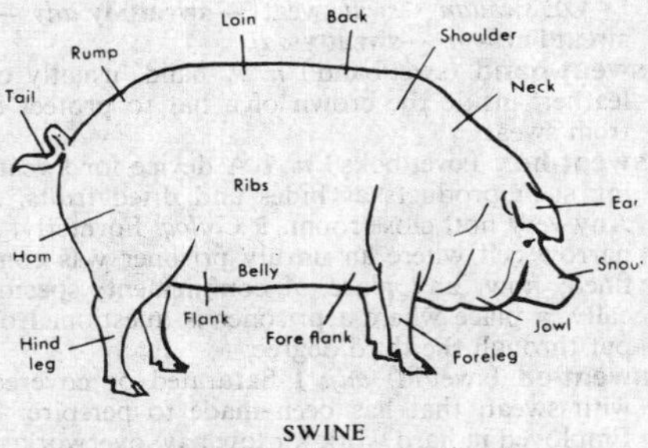

SWINE
Nomenclature of anatomical parts.

swine fever Hog cholera.

swine·herd (swīn′hûrd′) *n.* A tender of swine.

Swi·ne·mün·de (svē′nə·mün′də) The German name for ŚWINOUJŚCIE.

swine·pox (swīn′poks′) *n.* A form of chicken pox affecting swine.

swing (swing) *v.* **swung** (*Dial.* **swang**), **swung, swing·ing** *v.i.* **1** To move to and fro or backward and forward rhythmically, as something suspended; oscillate. **2** To move in a swing (def. 3). **3** To move with an even, swaying motion; walk with vigorous strides. **4** To turn; pivot: We *swung* around and went home. **5** To be suspended; hang. **6** *Colloq.* To be executed by hanging. **7** *Slang* To be very up-to-date and sophisticated, especially in one's amusements and pleasures. **8** *Colloq.* To sing or play with or to have a compelling, usually jazzlike rhythm. **9** *Slang* To be sexually promiscuous. —*v.t.* **10** To cause to move to and fro or backward and forward. **11** To cause to move with a sweeping or circular motion, as a sword, ax, etc.; brandish; flourish. **12** To cause to turn on or as on a pivot or central point. **13** To lift or hoist: They *swung* the mast into place. **14** *Colloq.* To bring to a successful conclusion; manage successfully. **15** *Colloq.* To arrange, sing, or play in the style of swing music. —*n.* **1** The action of swinging. **2** A free swaying motion. **3** A contrivance of hanging ropes with a seat on which a person may move to and fro through the air as a pastime. **4** Free course or scope; full liberty or license. **5** Compass; sweep. **6** The movement or rhythm characterizing certain styles of prose and poetry. **7** That which swings or is swung; a swinging blow or stroke. **8** The course of a career or period of activity. **9** Swing music. **10** *Colloq.* A trip or tour. [OE *swingan* scourge, beat up]

swing back *Phot.* **1** A camera back provided with a hinge to allow free movement in any direction so as to minimize distortion of perspective or focus. **2** A camera so equipped.

swing bridge A bridge constructed to rotate in a horizontal plane to permit the passage of large vessels, etc.

swinge[1] (swinj) *v.t.* **swinged, swinge·ing** *Archaic* To flog; chastise. [OE *swengan* shake, beat]

swinge[2] (swinj) *v.t.* **swinged, swinge·ing** *Dial.* To singe. [? Alter. of SINGE]

swinge·ing (swin′jing) *adj. Colloq.* Very large; heavy; extravagant. [<SWINGE[1]]

swing·er (swing′ər) *n.* **1** *Slang* A lively and up-to-date person. **2** *Slang* A person who indulges freely in sex.

swing·ing (swing′ing) *adj. Slang* **1** Lively and compelling in effect: a *swinging* jazz quartet. **2** Lively and modern.

swinging door A door that will open in either direction and swing shut when not held.

swin·gle (swing′gəl) *n.* **1** A large, knifelike

wooden implement for beating flax: also **swing′-knife. 2** The short wooden bar of a flail; a swiple. —*v.t.* **·gled, ·gling** To cleanse, as flax, by beating with a swingle; scutch. [< MDu. *swinghel.* Akin to SWING.]

swin·gle·tree (swing′gəl·trē′) *n.* A horizontal crossbar, to the ends of which the traces of a harness are attached; a whiffletree or singletree. See illustration under HARNESS. Also **swing·tree** (swing′trē′), **swin′gle·bar′** (-bär′).

SWINGLETREE
a. a. Swingletrees.
b. Traces.
c. Double-tree.
d. Plow beam.

swing music 1 A development of jazz after about 1935 which achieved its effects by large bands of musicians, contrapuntal styles, and arranged ensemble playing rather than improvised solo performances. **2** The particular rhythmic quality in such music. Also called *swing.*

swing shift An evening work shift, usually lasting from about 4 p.m. to midnight.

swin·ish (swī′nish) *adj.* Of or like swine; degraded; sensual; beastly. See synonyms under BRUTISH. —**swin′ish·ly** *adv.* —**swin′ish·ness** *n.*

swink (swingk) *v.i. Archaic & Brit. Dial.* To toil hard; drudge. [OE *swincan*]

Swin·ner·ton (swin′ər·tən), **Frank (Arthur)**, born 1884, English novelist and critic.

Swi·no·ujś·cie (shve′nô·ōō′əsh·che) A port of NW Poland: German *Swinemünde.*

swipe (swīp) *v.t.* **swiped, swip·ing 1** *Colloq.* To give a strong blow; strike with a full swing of the arm. **2** *Slang* To steal; snatch. —*n. Colloq.* **1** A hard blow, especially in field games. **2** A well sweep, lever, pump handle, or the like. [Var. of SWEEP]

swipes (swīps) *n. pl. Brit. Slang* Poor, spoiled, or weak beer; small beer; beer in general. [< SWIPE, in obs. sense of "drink hastily"]

swip·le (swip′əl) *n.* That part of a threshing flail that strikes the grain; a swingle. Also **swip′ple.** [ME *swepelles* a broom. Akin to SWEEP.]

swirl (swûrl) *v.t. & v.i.* To move or cause to move along in irregular eddies; whirl. —*n.* **1** A whirling along, as in an eddy; whirl. **2** A curl or twist; spiral. [<dial. E (Scottish) *swyrle.* Prob. akin to Dan. Norw. *svirla* whirl.]

swirl·y (swûr′lē) *adj.* **1** Full of swirls. **2** *Scot.* Tangled; knotty; gnarled: also **swirl′ie.**

swish (swish) *v.i.* **1** To move with a sweeping motion and whistling sound, as a whip. —*v.t.* **2** To cause to swish. **3** To thrash; flog. —*n.* **1** A hissing, swishing sound, as of a lash through the air, or the swing of a silk skirt. **2** A movement producing such a sound. **3** An implement, as a broom, used with such a movement. [Imit.]

swiss (swis) *n. Often cap.* A sheer, crisp cotton fabric, similar to muslin, and often dotted or figured, when it is called *dotted swiss.*

Swiss (swis) *adj.* Pertaining to Switzerland; characteristic of Switzerland. —*n. pl.* **Swiss** A native or naturalized inhabitant of Switzerland.

Swiss chard Chard (def. 2).

Swiss cheese A pale-yellow cheese with many large holes, made in, or similar to that made in, Switzerland.

Swiss guards Mercenary soldiers from Switzerland formerly used as bodyguards by European monarchs, now as guards at the Vatican.

Swiss steak A thick cut of steak floured and cooked, often with a sauce of tomatoes and onions.

switch (swich) *n.* **1** A small flexible rod; light whip. **2** A tress of human or false hair, fastened together at one end and used by women in building a coiffure. **3** A mechanism for shifting a railway train or other rail vehicles from one track to another. **4** The act or operation of switching, shifting, or changing. **5** The end of the tail in certain animals, as a cow. **6** *Electr.* A device to make or break a circuit, or transfer a current from one conductor to another. **7** A connecting trench between two lines of defensive trenches. **8** A blow with a switch. See synonyms under STICK. —*v.t.* **1** To whip or lash with or as with a switch. **2** To move, jerk, or whisk suddenly or sharply: The woman *switched* her skirts aside. **3** To turn aside or divert; shift. **4** To exchange: They *switched* plates. **5** To shift, as a railroad car, to another track. **6** *Electr.* To connect or disconnect with a switch. —*v.i.* **7** To turn aside; change; shift. **8** To be shifted or turned. **9** *Dial.* To walk with a jerky or uneven gait. [Earlier *swits.* Akin to LG *zwuske* a thin rod.]

switch·back (swich′bak′) *n.* **1** A railway ascending or descending a steep incline in a series of zigzag tracks. **2** A zigzag mountain road. **3** A railroad at amusement resorts in which the cars are hoisted to a starting point and descend along a circuitous route by gravity.

switch·board (swich′bôrd′, -bōrd′) *n.* A panel or arrangement of panels bearing switches for connecting and disconnecting electric circuits, as a telephone exchange.

switch·er (swich′ər) *n.* **1** A switch-tender. **2** One who or that which switches.

switch hitter In baseball, a batter who bats either right- or left-handed.

switch·man (swich′mən) *n. pl.* **·men** (-mən) One who handles railway switches.

switch plant A plant in which green shoots take the place of absent or reduced leaves.

switch·yard (swich′yärd′) *n.* A railroad yard for the assembling and breaking up of trains.

swith (swith) *adv. Scot.* or *Obs.* Strongly; very much; quickly. —*interj.* Begone! quick! Also **swithe** (swith).

swith·er (swith′ər) *Dial. & Scot. v.i.* To doubt; hesitate; fear. —*n.* **1** A state of doubt or hesitation. **2** A fright; perspiration; faint.

Swith·in (swith′in), **Saint,** died A.D. 862, bishop of Winchester. See under ST. SWITHIN'S DAY.

Swit·zer (swit′sər) *n.* **1** A Swiss. **2** Specifically, Swiss mercenary soldier. Also **Swiss·er** (swis′ər).

Swit·zer·land (swit′sər·lənd) A republic in central Europe; 15,940 square miles; capital, Bern: French *Suisse,* German *Schweiz,* Italian *Svizzera,* Latin *Helvetia.* Also **Swiss Confederation.**

swiv·el (swiv′əl) *n.* **1** A coupling device, link, ring, or pivot that permits either half of a mechanism, as a chain, to rotate independently. **2** A rest on a boat's gunwale, on which a gun may be swept or swung in a horizontal plane. **3** Anything that turns on a pin or headed bolt. **4** A cannon that swings on a pivot: also **swivel gun. 5** The shuttle of a ribbon loom. —*v.* **·eled** or **·elled, ·el·ing** or **·el·ling** *v.t.* **1** To turn on or as on a swivel. **2** To provide with or secure by a swivel. —*v.i.* **3** To turn or swing on or as on a swivel. [ME *swyuel* <OE *swif-,* stem of *swīfan* move]

swiv·et (swiv′it) *n. Colloq.* Hurry; anxiety; eager, nervous haste or excitement: Don't be in such a *swivet.* Also **swiv′vet.** [Cf. obs. *swive* copulation <OE *swīfan* move] —**swiv′et·ty** *adj.*

swiz·zle (swiz′əl) *n.* One of various compounded intoxicating drinks; specifically, a drink made with rum or other spirit, sugar, bitters, and ice. —*v.t. & v.i.* **·zled, ·zling** *Slang* To guzzle. [Origin unknown] —**swiz′zler** *n.*

swizzle stick 1 A stick, usually with prongs set at right angles to one end, used to mix swizzle by whirling between the palms of the hands. **2** A slender rod of glass, plastic, etc., used to mix drinks.

swob (swob), **swob·ber** (swob′ər) See SWAB, etc.

swol·len (swō′lən) Alternative past participle of SWELL.

swoon (swoon) *v.i.* To fall in a faint; faint. —*n.* The act of swooning; a fainting fit. See synonyms under STUPOR. Also, *Obs., swoun, swound.* [ME *swounen,* back formation < *swoweninge* SWOONING]

swoon·ing (swoon′ning) *n.* A fainting fit; swoon. —*adj.* Fainting. [ME *swoweninge* <OE *geswōgen* unconscious]

swoop (swoop) *v.i.* To drop or descend suddenly, as a bird pouncing on its prey. —*v.t.* To take or seize suddenly, as with a swoop. —*n.* A sweeping down or pouncing down, as by a bird of prey: often figuratively. [Var. of obs. *swope* <OE *swāpan* sweep; prob. infl. in form by dial. E *soop* sweep <ON *sōpa*]

swop (swop) See SWAP.

sword (sôrd, sōrd) *n.* **1** A weapon consisting of a long blade fixed in a hilt: used for cutting or thrusting, as a rapier, scimitar, or claymore. **2** The power of the sword; sovereignty; the power of life and death; especially, military as opposed to civil power. **3** War; also, the cause of death or ruin. **4** An end bar from which the lay of a hand loom hangs; also, the upright support of the lay of a power loom. —**at swords' points** Very unfriendly; hostile; ready for a fight. —**to put to the sword** To kill with a sword; slaughter in battle. [OE *sweord*]

sword bayonet A bayonet having the shape of a sword and used like one. See illustration under BAYONET.

sword·bill (sôrd′bil′, sōrd′-) *n.* A tropical American hummingbird (genus *Ensifera*) with a very long, slender bill.

sword cane A cane made to carry a sword or dagger.

sword·craft (sôrd′kraft′, -kräft′, sōrd′-) *n.* **1** Dexterity or skill in the use of the sword. **2** Exercise of authority by the sword, or by military power.

sword dance 1 A dance among or over naked swords laid on the ground. **2** A dance in which the female dancers pass under a double line of swords crossed over their heads by the men.

sword·er (sôr′dər, sōr′-) *n. Obs.* One skilled in the use of, or who fights with, a sword; hence, a cut-throat.

sword·fish (sôrd′fish′, sōrd′-) *n. pl.* **·fish** or **·fish·es** A large fish of the open sea (genus *Xiphias*) having the bones of the upper jaw consolidated to form an elongated swordlike process.

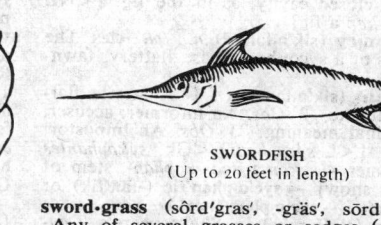

SWORDFISH
(Up to 20 feet in length)

sword·grass (sôrd′gras′, -gräs′, sōrd′-) *n.* **1** Any of several grasses or sedges (especially genus *Mariscus,* formerly *Cladium*) with sharp or serrated edges. **2** The sword lily.

sword·knot (sôrd′not′, sōrd′-) *n.* Formerly, a loop of leather used to fasten the hilt of a sword to the wrist; now, a tassel of cord or ribbon tied to a sword hilt.

sword lily A gladiolus.

sword play 1 Attack and defense with the sword. **2** Skill in fighting with the sword or in fencing; fencing. —**sword′-play′er** *n.*

swords·man (sôrdz′mən, sōrdz′-) *n. pl.* **·men** (-mən) **1** One skilled in the use of or armed with a sword. **2** A soldier. Also **sword′-man.** —**swords′man·ship, sword′man·ship** *n.*

swore (swôr, swōr) Past tense of SWEAR.

sworn (swôrn, swōrn) Past participle of SWEAR.

swot[1] (swot) *Brit. Slang v.i.* **swot·ted, swot·ting** To sweat or work hard over a task; grind. —*n.* Hard work; also, one who works hard, especially in studying. [Dial. var. of SWEAT]

swot[2] (swot) See SWAT[1].

swoun (swoun), **swound** (swound) See SWOON.

swounds (zwoundz, zoundz), **swouns** (zwounz, zounz) See ZOUNDS.

swum (swum) Past participle and dialectal past tense of SWIM.

swung (swung) Past tense and past participle of SWING.

swy (swī) *n. Austral. Slang* The game of two-up. Also **swy′-up** (swī′up). [G *zwei* two]

sy- Var. of SYN-.

Syb·a·ris (sib′ə·ris) An ancient Greek city on the Gulf of Tarentum in southern Italy, famous

as a center of luxurious living; founded in 720 B.C.; destroyed, 510 B.C.

syb·a·rite (sib′ə·rīt) *n.* A luxurious person; epicure; voluptuary. [<L *Sybarita* <Gk. *Sybaritēs* <*Sybaris* Sybaris]

Syb·a·rite (sib′ə·rīt) *n.* A native or citizen of Sybaris.

Syb·a·rit·ic (sib′ə·rit′ik) *adj.* **1** Of or pertaining to Sybaris or the Sybarites. **2** Hence, given to luxury; voluptuous. Also **Syb′a·rit′i·cal.** — **Syb′a·rit′i·cal·ly** *adv.* — **Syb·a·rit·ism** (sib′ə·rīt·iz′əm) *n.*

sy·bo (sī′bō) *n. pl.* **·boes** The cibol or Welsh onion. [< dial. E (Scottish), var. of CIBOL]

syc·a·mine (sik′ə·min) *n.* The mulberry tree *(Morus nigra)* of the New Testament. [<LL *sycaminus* <Gk. *sykaminos* a mulberry tree <Aramaic *shiqmīn*, pl. <Hebrew *shiqmah*]

syc·a·more (sik′ə·môr, -mōr) *n.* **1** A medium-sized bushy tree of Syria and Egypt *(Ficus sycomorus)* allied to the common fig. **2** Any of various plane trees widely distributed in the United States, especially the American sycamore *(Platanus occidentalis)* and the buttonwood of California. **3** An ornamental shade tree of Europe and Asia *(Acer pseudo-platanus)*; the sycamore maple. Also *Obs.* **syc′o·more.** [<OF *sicamor* <LL *sycomorus* <Gk. *sykomoros* < *sykon* a fig + *moron* a mulberry]

syce (sīs) *n.* A groom; a man servant: also spelled *sice, saice.* [<Hind. *sā'is* <Arabic < *sūs* tend a horse]

sy·cee (sī·sē′) *n.* Pure uncoined silver ingots of various weight and size: used by the Chinese as a medium of exchange. Also **sycee silver.** — *adj.* Pure; unalloyed. [< dial. Chinese (Cantonese) *sai sze*, var. of Chinese *si szĕ* fine silk; so called because if pure it may be drawn out into fine threads]

sy·con (sī′kon) *adj. Zool.* Designating a type of sponge having an infolded body wall provided with radial canals for the reception of water, as in the typical genus *Sycon.* [<NL <Gk. *sykon* a fig]

sy·co·ni·um (sī·kō′nē·əm) *n. pl.* **·ni·a** (-nē·ə) *Bot.* An aggregate or multiple fruit in which many flowers have been developed on a fleshy receptacle, which is a flattened disk or forms a nearly closed cavity, as in the fig. [<NL <Gk. *sykon* a fig]

syc·o·phan·cy (sik′ə·fən·sē) *n. pl.* **·cies** The practices of a sycophant; base flattery; fawning.

syc·o·phant (sik′ə·fənt) *n.* **1** A servile flatterer; parasite. **2** *Obs.* An informer; accuser: the original meaning. **3** *Obs.* An impostor; deceiver. [<L *sycophanta* <Gk. *sykophantēs* an informer < *sykon* a fico + *phan-*, stem of *phainein* show] — **syc′o·phan′tic** (-fan′tik) or **·ti·cal** *adj.* — **syc′o·phan′ti·cal·ly** *adv.*

Syc·o·rax (sik′ō·raks) In Shakespeare's *Tempest*, Caliban's mother, a witch.

sy·co·sis (sī·kō′sis) *n. Pathol.* An inflamed staphylococcic infection of the skin involving the hair follicles, generally of the face and scalp. ◆ Homophone: *psychosis.* [<NL <Gk. *sykōsis* a fig-shaped ulcer < *sykon* a fig]

Syd·ney (sid′nē) A masculine personal name. Also *Sidney.* [from a surname, orig. <AF *St. Denis.* See DENIS]

Syd·ney (sid′nē) **1** The chief port and capital of New South Wales, Australia. **2** A port on Cape Breton Island, NE Nova Scotia, Canada.

Syd·ney (sid′nē), **Sir Philip** See SIDNEY.

Sy·e·ne (sī·ē′nē) The ancient name for ASWAN. — **Sy·e·nit·ic** (sī′ə·nit′ik) *adj.*

sy·e·nite (sī′ə·nīt) *n.* An igneous granular rock composed principally of feldspar and containing little or no quartz: also spelled *sienite.* [<F *syénite* <L *syenites (lapis)* (stone) of Syene <*Syene* Syene <Gk. *Syēnē*] — **sy′e·nit′ic** (-nit′ik) *adj.*

syke (sīk) *n. Scot.* A small stream from a bog: also spelled *sike.*

Syk·tyv·kar (sik′tif·kär′) The capital of Komi Autonomous S.S.R., in NE central European Russian S.F.S.R.

syl- Assimilated var. of SYN-.

syl·la·bar·y (sil′ə·ber′ē) *n. pl.* **·bar·ies** A list of characters representing syllables; the syllabic characters, collectively, of a language, as Chinese or Japanese, answering the function of an alphabet in writing. [<NL *syllabarium*, neut. of Med. L *syllabarius* < *syllaba* SYLLABLE]

syl·lab·ic (si·lab′ik) *adj.* **1** Of, pertaining to, or consisting of a syllable or syllables. **2** *Phonet.* Designating a consonant capable of forming a complete syllable without a vowel, as *l* in *middle* (mid′l) and *n* in *sudden* (sud′n). See SONORANT. **3** Having every syllable distinctly pronounced. **4** Designating a type of poetry based on a definite number of syllables per line rather than on stress or rhythm. Also **syl·lab′i·cal.** — *n. Phonet.* A syllabic consonant; a sonorant. — **syl·lab′i·cal·ly** *adv.*

syl·lab·i·cate (si·lab′ə·kāt) *v.t.* **·cat·ed, ·cat·ing** To form or divide into syllables. Also **syl·lab′i·fy.** — **syl·lab′i·ca′tion, syl·lab′i·fi·ca′tion** *n.*

syl·la·bism (sil′ə·biz′əm) *n.* **1** The use of characters representing syllables instead of letters in a written language. **2** The theory of syllables; division into syllables.

syl·la·bist (sil′ə·bist) *n.* One skilled in syllabicating.

syl·la·bize (sil′ə·bīz) *v.t.* **·bized, ·biz·ing** To divide (words) or form (letters) into syllables.

syl·la·ble (sil′ə·bəl) *n.* **1** *Phonet.* A word or part of a word uttered in a single vocal impulse, and consisting of a vowel (or diphthong) alone or with one or more consonants, or of a syllabic consonant. An **open syllable** is one ending in a vowel, as the first syllable of *si·lent* (sī′lənt); a **closed syllable** is one ending in a consonant, as the first and third syllables of *cat·a·pult* (kat′ə·pult). **2** A part of a written or printed word corresponding, more or less, to the spoken division. In this dictionary, syllable breaks are indicated by centered dots. **3** The smallest particle of expression; the least detail, mention, or trace: Please don't repeat a *syllable* of what you've heard here. — *v.* **·bled, ·bling** *v.t.* **1** To pronounce the syllables of; utter; speak. **2** *Obs.* To syllabicate. — *v.i.* **3** To pronounce syllables. [<AF *sillable*, OF *sillabe* <L *syllaba* <Gk. *syllabē* < *syllambanein* < *syn-* together + *lambanein* take]

syl·la·bub (sil′ə·bub) See SILLABUB.

syl·la·bus (sil′ə·bəs) *n. pl.* **·bus·es** or **·bi** (-bī) A concise statement of the main points of a subject; outline, as of a course of study; schedule; epitome; abstract; specifically, a short statement at the beginning of a brief of the legal points involved. [<NL <Med. L *syllabos*, a misprint for L *sittybas*, accusative pl. of *sittyba* label on a book <Gk.]

syl·lep·sis (si·lep′sis) *n. pl.* **·ses** (-sēz) A figure of speech, common in classical Greek and Roman literature, by which an adjective or a verb is made to modify or govern two nouns, but must be understood in a different sense for each noun. This figure conveys a double meaning, often with humorous effect, as in Pope's comment on Queen Anne: Dost sometimes *counsel take* —and sometimes *tea.* Compare ZEUGMA. [<LL *syllepsis* <Gk. *syllēpsis* < *syn-* together + *lēpsis* a taking < *lēb-, lab-*, stem of *lambanein* take] — **syl·lep′tic** *adj.*

syl·lo·gism (sil′ə·jiz′əm) *n.* **1** *Logic* **a** A formula of argument consisting of three propositions. The first two propositions, called *premises*, have one term in common furnishing a logical connection between the two other terms, which are then linked in the third proposition, called the *conclusion.* Example: All men are mortal *(major premise)*; kings are men *(minor premise)*; therefore, kings are mortal *(conclusion).* In this example, the *major term* is "mortal," the *minor term* is "kings," and the *middle term* is "men." **b** Deductive reasoning. **2** A subtle or crafty argument. [<OF *silogime* <L *syllogismus* <Gk. *syllogismos* < *syllogizesthai* SYLLOGIZE]

syl·lo·gis·tic (sil′ə·jis′tik) *adj.* Pertaining to, or having the nature or form of, a syllogism: also **syl′lo·gis′ti·cal.** — *n.* The art of reasoning by syllogism; the department of logic dealing with syllogisms: also **syl′lo·gis′tics.** — **syl′lo·gis′ti·cal·ly** *adv.*

syl·lo·gize (sil′ə·jīz) *v.t.* & *v.i.* **·gized, ·giz·ing** To reason or argue by syllogisms. [<OF *silogiser* <Med. L *syllogizare* <Gk. *syllogizesthai* < *syn-* together + *logizesthai* calculate, infer < *logos* discourse] — **syl′lo·gi·za′tion** (-jə·zā′shən) *n.*

sylph (silf) *n.* **1** Originally, in the system of Paracelsus, a being, male or female, mortal but without a soul, living in and on the air, and intermediate between material and immaterial beings. **2** A slender, graceful young woman or girl. **3** A South American hummingbird *(Cyanolesbia gorgo)*, with a long, forked, brilliantly colored tail. [<NL *sylphes*, pl., ? coined by Paracelsus]

sylph·id (sil′fid) *n.* A young or diminutive sylph. — *adj.* Having qualities suggesting a sylph: also **sylph·i·dine** (sil′fə·din, -dīn). [<F *sylphide*, dim. of *sylphe* <NL *sylphes* SYLPH]

sylph·like (silf′līk′) *adj.* Like a sylph; slender; graceful. Also **sylph′ish, sylph′y.**

syl·va (sil′və) *n. pl.* **·vas** or **·vae** (-vē) **1** The forest trees, collectively, of a territory or region. **2** A treatise on forest trees, or a description or list of the forest trees of a certain region. Also spelled *silva.* [<L *silva* a forest]

syl·van (sil′vən) *adj.* **1** Of, pertaining to, or located in a forest or woods. **2** Composed of or abounding in trees or woods. **3** Characteristic of a forest or wood; rustic. — *n.* **1** In mythology, a spirit or deity of the forest. **2** *Archaic* or *Poetic* A person or animal dwelling in the woods. [<MF *sylvain* a sylvan <L *sylvanus, silvanus* < *silva* a wood]

syl·van·ite (sil′vən·īt) *n.* A metallic, steel-gray to silver-white telluride of gold or silver, crystallizing in the monoclinic system: when the crystals are arranged in patterns suggesting runic symbols, it is called *graphic gold, graphic tellurium.* [from (TRAN)SYLVAN(IA) + -ITE[1]]

Syl·va·nus (sil·vā′nəs) See SILVANUS.

Syl·ves·ter (sil·ves′tər) Silvester; a masculine personal name. Also *Sp.* **Syl·ves·tre** (sēl·ves′·trā). [<L, living in the wood]

syl·ves·tral (sil·ves′trəl) *adj.* Adapted to growing in woody and shady places, as certain plants; also, relating to the woods; wild. [<L *silvester, silvestris* < *silva* a forest]

Syl·vi·a (sil′vē·ə) A feminine personal name. [<L, of the forest]

Syl·vi·an fissure (sil′vē·ən) *Anat.* A deep fissure that separates the temporal lobe of the cerebrum from the parietal and frontal lobes. [<F *sylvien*, after François de la Boë *Sylvius*, 1614–72, Flemish anatomist]

syl·vite (sil′vīt) *n.* A vitreous, native potassium chloride, crystallizing in the isometric system. Also **syl′vin** (-vin), **syl′vine** (-vin, -vīn), **syl′·vin·ite.** [<NL *(sal digestivus) sylvii* (digestive salt) of Sylvius + -ITE[1]]

sym- Assimilated var. of SYN-.

sym·bi·ont (sim′bī·ont, -bē-) *n. Biol.* An organism living in a state of symbiosis. Also **sym′·bi·on.** [<Gk. *symbioōn, -ontos*, ppr. of *bioein.* See SYMBIOSIS.] — **sym′bi·on′tic** *adj.*

sym·bi·o·sis (sim′bī·ō′sis, -bē-) *n. Biol.* The consorting together or partnership of dissimilar organisms, as of the algae and fungi in lichens. The term ordinarily connotes an association which is mutually advantageous. Compare CONSORTISM. [<NL <Gk. *symbiōsis* a living together, companionship < *symbioein* live together < *symbios* a companion, living together < *syn-* together + *bios* life] — **sym′bi·ot′ic** (-ot′ik) or **·i·cal** *adj.* — **sym′bi·ot′i·cal·ly** *adv.*

sym·bol (sim′bəl) *n.* **1** Something chosen to stand for or represent something else, usually because of a resemblance in qualities or characteristics; an object used to typify a quality, abstract idea, etc.: The oak is a *symbol* of strength. **2** A character, mark, abbreviation, conventional sign, or letter indicating something, as a quantity in mathematics, a substance in chemistry, a planet or celestial body, a quality, operation, relationship, etc. **3** A confession of faith; creed. **4** The disguised representation of an unconscious trend involving a person, object, act, etc. See synonyms under EMBLEM, LETTER, MARK, SIGN, SIMILE. ◆ Homophone: *cymbal.* [<LL *symbolum* <Gk. *symbolon* a mark, token < *symballein* put together < *syn-* together + *ballein* throw]

sym·bol·ae·og·ra·phy (sim′bəl·ē·og′rə·fē) *n.* The drawing up or framing of legal instruments. Also **sym′bol·e·og′ra·phy.** [<Gk. *symbolaiographia* < *symbolaiographos* a notary < *symbolaion* a mark, contract + *graphein* write]

sym·bol·ic (sim·bol′ik) *adj.* **1** Of or pertaining to a symbol or symbols; expressed by a symbol. **2** Serving as signs of relation or connection; relational; connective: distinguished from *presentive*: said of certain classes of words, as prepositions and conjunctions. **3** Characterized by or involving the use of symbols: *symbolic* poetry. Also **sym·bol′i·cal.** — **sym·bol′i·cal·ly** *adv.* — **sym·bol′i·cal·ness** *n.*

symbolical books Books containing the symbols or confessions of faith of a church, religious body, or inspired writer.

symbolic logic A development of formal logic in which the ambiguity of verbal propositions and of operations upon them is reduced to a minimum by the rigorous use of symbols each of which has only one referent within the given context. Also called *mathematical logic.*

sym·bol·ics (sim·bol′iks) *n. pl. (construed as singular)* The science or study of symbols or of ancient symbolic rites or creeds.

sym·bol·ism (sim′bəl·iz′əm) *n.* **1** Representation by symbols; treatment or interpretation of things as symbolic; also, the quality of being symbolic. **2** A system of symbols or symbolical representation. **3** The theories and practice of a group of symbolists. **4** Artistic imitation as a means of suggesting or expressing ideal or intangible states or ideas; also, the expression or representation of the invisible by conventional signs or figures.

sym·bol·ist (sim′bəl·ist) *n.* **1** One who uses symbols; one versed or ardent in the interpretation or use of symbols; especially, one who regards the elements in the Eucharist as mere symbols. **2** One of a class of French and Belgian writers and artists of the late 19th century, including Verlaine, Mallarmé and Maeterlinck, who sought to exalt the metaphysical by suggesting ideas and emotions by patterns of color and form and by symbolic meanings of objects, words, and sound.

sym·bol·is·tic (sim′bəl·is′tik) *adj.* **1** Expressed by symbols; characterized by the use of symbols. **2** Of or pertaining to symbolism; symbolic. Also **sym′bol·is′ti·cal.**

sym·bol·ize (sim′bəl·īz) *v.* **·ized, ·iz·ing** *v.t.* **1** To be typical of; represent symbolically; typify. **2** To represent by a symbol or symbols. **3** To treat as symbolic or figurative. — *v.i.* **4** To use symbols. **5** *Psychol.* To transfer emotional values from one person, object, or act to another. Also *Brit.* **sym′bol·ise.** — **sym′bol·i·za′tion** *n.*

sym·bol·o·gy (sim·bol′ə·jē) *n.* The art of representing by, or of interpreting, symbols. [< SYMBO(L) + -LOGY]

sym·met·al·ism (sim·met′l·iz′əm) *n.* A money system in which the unit of coinage is composed of two or more metals combined. [< SYM- + METAL + -ISM]

sym·met·ri·cal (si·met′ri·kəl) *adj.* **1** Exhibiting symmetry; having harmonious proportions or a correspondence in shape and size of parts; well-balanced; regular: a *symmetrical* structure. **2** *Biol.* Having parts or organs on one side corresponding to those on the other. **3** *Bot.* Regular as to number or shape of parts: said especially of a flower when the parts or divisions in each cycle (that is, the sepals, petals, stamens, and pistils) are of the same number or multiples of the same. **4** *Chem.* Denoting an arrangement of atoms of a molecule at equal relative intervals when graphically represented. **5** *Med.* Affecting corresponding organs or parts similarly. Also **sym·met′ric.** [< SYMMETRY] — **sym·met′ri·cal·ly** *adv.* — **sym·met′ri·cal·ness** *n.*

sym·me·trist (sim′ə·trist) *n.* A student or advocate of symmetry.

sym·me·trize (sim′ə·trīz) *v.t.* **·trized, ·triz·ing** To make symmetrical or proportional. — **sym′me·tri·za′tion** *n.*

sym·me·try (sim′ə·trē) *n. pl.* **·tries** **1** Corresponding arrangement or balancing of the parts or elements of a whole in respect to size, shape, and position on opposite sides of an axis or center; hence, loosely, congruity; harmony; also, an instance of such arrangement. **2** The element of beauty in nature or art that results from such arrangement and balancing. **3** *Biol.* Regular arrangement of parts or organs in an animal body so that a division will give halves corresponding in shape, size, function, relative position, etc.; similarity of structure. **4** *Bot.* Equality of number in the whorls of a flower, as of sepals, petals, etc. **5** *Math.* An arrangement of pairs of points in a general system such that the set of lines joining them together is divided into equal parts by a line, a plane, or a point. **6** *Mineral.* The symmetrical distribution of non-parallel but equivalent direc-

tions (faces, edges, etc.) in a crystal with reference to certain planes or lines called **planes** or **axes of symmetry.** [< MF *symmetrie* < LL *symmetria* < Gk. < *symmetros* measured together < *syn-* together + *metron* a measure]

Synonyms: agreement, conformity, harmony, order, parity, proportion, regularity, shapeliness. See HARMONY. *Antonyms:* deformity, discordance, disproportion, shapelessness.

Sym·onds (sim′əndz), **John Addington,** 1840–1893, English author.

Sy·mons (sī′mənz), **Arthur,** 1865–1945, English poet and critic born in Wales.

sym·pa·thec·to·my (sim′pə·thek′tə·mē) *n. Surg.* The operation of interrupting some portion of the sympathetic nervous system, as by transection or resection of a nerve pathway. [< SYMPATH(ETIC) + -ECTOMY]

sym·pa·thet·ic (sim′pə·thet′ik) *adj.* **1** Pertaining to, expressing, or proceeding from sympathy. **2** Having a fellow feeling for others; sympathizing; compassionate. **3** Being in accord or harmony; congenial. **4** Referring to sounds produced by responsive vibrations. **5** *Anat.* Designating the entire autonomic nervous system. Also **sym′pa·thet′i·cal.** See synonyms under HUMANE. [< NL *sympatheticus* < Gk. *sympathētikos* < *sympatheia.* See SYMPATHY.] — **sym′pa·thet′i·cal·ly** *adv.*

sympathetic ink An ink that is colorless and invisible until brought out by heat, light, or chemical action: also called *invisible ink.*

sympathetic nervous system *Anat.* That part of the autonomic nervous system which serves the viscera, glands, heart, blood vessels, and smooth muscles. It consists of a chain of ganglia on each side of the spinal column between the cervical and the sacral regions, connected with nerve plexuses, and in general produces effects opposite to those coming from the parasympathetic system.

sym·path·i·co·to·ni·a (sim·path′i·kō·tō′nē·ə) *n. Physiol.* Increased dominance of the sympathetic nervous system over other body functions, marked by vascular spasm and high blood pressure. [< NL < E *sympathic,* var. of SYMPATHETIC + Gk. *tonos* tension] — **sym·path′i·co·ton′ic** (-ton′ik) *adj.*

sym·pa·thin (sim′pə·thin) *n. Biochem.* A substance liberated by the stimulation of certain fibers of the sympathetic nervous system and acting as a chemical mediator in associated nerve impulses. [< SYMPATH(ETIC) + -IN]

sym·pa·thism (sim′pə·thiz′əm) *n.* Suggestibility; the state of being susceptible to hypnotic or other influences.

sym·pa·thize (sim′pə·thīz) *v.i.* **·thized, ·thiz·ing** **1** To share the sentiments or ideas of another; have the same feelings as another: with *with.* **2** To feel or express compassion, as for another's sorrow or affliction: with *with.* **3** To be in harmony or agreement. Also *Brit.* **sym′pa·thise.** See synonyms under CONSOLE. — **sym′pa·thiz′er** *n.* — **sym′pa·thiz′ing·ly** *adv.*

sym·pa·thy (sim′pə·thē) *n. pl.* **·thies** **1** The quality of being affected by the state of another with feelings correspondent in kind; a fellow feeling; a mutual affinity or susceptibility; reaction to such relationship. **2** A feeling of compassion for another's sufferings; pity; commiseration. **3** An agreement of affections or inclinations, or a conformity of natural temperaments, which makes persons agreeable to one another; congeniality; accord. **4** That quality of inanimate things by virtue of which they attract or influence one another, or are supposed to do so; affinity: a sense once much used in alchemy and astrology: the *sympathy* of the lodestone for iron. See synonyms under BENEVOLENCE, PITY. [< L *sympathia* < Gk. *sympatheia* < *sympathēs* feeling compassion with another < *syn-* together + *pathos* a feeling, passion]

sympathy strike A strike in which the strikers support the demands of another group of workers but demand nothing for themselves.

sym·pa·try (sim′pə·trē) *n. Ecol.* The distribution of plant and animal species in coextensive areas. [< SYM- + L *patria* fatherland]

sym·pet·al·ous (sim·pet′l·əs) *adj. Bot.* Gamopetalous. [< NL *Sympetalae,* a division of dicotyledons < Gk. *syn-* together + *petalon* a leaf, petal]

sym·phon·ic (sim·fon′ik) *adj.* **1** Relating to or having the form of a symphony: also **sym·pho·net·ic** (sim′fə·net′ik). **2** Agreeing in sound; harmonious.

symphonic poem *Music* A composition in free form for symphony orchestra, composed either as a unit (as Liszt's *Les Préludes* or Strauss's *Death and Transfiguration*) or as a short series of pieces (as Debussy's *La Mer*), and following a descriptive, literary, or "program" outline; a tone poem: a form developed by Liszt in the 19th century.

sym·pho·ni·ous (sim·fō′nē·əs) *adj.* According in sound; harmonious; concordant; agreeing; sounding together or in harmony. — **sym·pho′ni·ous·ly** *adv.*

sym·pho·nize (sim′fə·nīz) *v.t. & v.i.* **·nized, ·niz·ing** To harmonize.

sym·pho·ny (sim′fə·nē) *n. pl.* **·nies** **1** A harmonious or agreeable mingling of sounds, whether vocal, instrumental, or both; figuratively, any concord or agreeable blending: *symphonies* in gray. **2** *Music* A composition for orchestra, consisting usually of four movements, of which one or more generally follow sonata form, and which are of diverse individuality united by homogeneous elements. **3** A symphony orchestra. [< OF *simphonie* < L *symphonia* < Gk. *symphōnia* < *syn-* together + *phōnē* a sound]

symphony orchestra A large orchestra composed usually of the string, brass, woodwind, and percussion sections needed to present symphonic works.

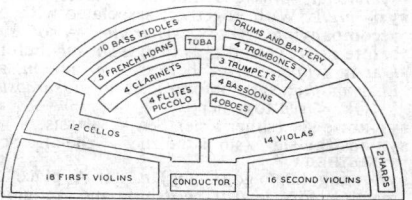

TRADITIONAL SEATING PLAN OF
MODERN SYMPHONY ORCHESTRA

sym·phy·sis (sim′fə·sis) *n. pl.* **·ses** (-sēz) **1** *Anat.* A junction of two parts of the skeleton, formed either by a growing together (*synostosis*) or by the intervention of cartilage (*synchondrosis*). **2** *Bot.* The union of similar parts, or of parts normally separate. [< NL < Gk., a growing together, esp. of the bones < *syn-* together + *phyein* grow]

sym·plec·tic (sim·plek′tik) *adj. Geol.* Denoting a rock texture formed by the intermingling of two different minerals. [< Gk. *symplektikos* plaiting together < *symplekein* < *syn-* together + *plekein* plait]

Sym·pleg·a·des (sim·pleg′ə·dēz) In Greek mythology, twin rocks forming a gateway to the Black Sea and supposed to swing together and crush whatever tried to pass between them. [< L < Gk. *(petrai) Symplēgades* the clashing (rocks) < *symplēgas, -ados* striking together < *syn-* together + *plēssein* strike]

sym·po·di·um (sim·pō′dē·əm) *n. pl.* **·di·a** (-dē·ə) *Bot.* A false axis or stem of a plant, morphologically made up of a series of superposed branches imitating a simple stem; a pseudaxis. [< NL < Gk. *syn-* together + *podion,* dim. of *pous, podos* a foot] — **sym·po′di·al** *adj.* — **sym·po′di·al·ly** *adv.*

sym·po·si·ac (sim·pō′zē·ak) *adj.* Pertaining to, of the nature of, or occurring at a symposium; specifically, denoting convivial songs, glees, etc.: also **sym·po′si·al.** — *n.* A symposium. [< LL *symposiacus* < Gk. *symposiakos* < *symposion.* See SYMPOSIUM.]

sym·po·si·arch (sim·pō′zē·ärk) *n.* **1** The master or director of an ancient Greek symposium; hence, the master of a feast; a toastmaster. **2** Familiarly, a ruling spirit of a social or convivial company. [< Gk. *symposiarchos* < *symposion* a symposium (def. 3) + *archos* a ruler]

sym·po·si·um (sim·pō′zē·əm) *n.* **1** A meeting for discussion of a particular subject. **2** A

collection of comments or opinions brought together; especially, a series of several brief essays or articles on the same subject by different writers, as in a magazine. **3** In ancient Greece, an after-dinner drinking party, characterized by conversation, music, dancing, and other amusements. **4** Any similar social gathering. Also called *symposiac.* Also **sym·po′si·on** (-zē·on). [<L <Gk. *symposion* < *syn-* together + *posis* a drinking < *po-*, stem of *pinein* drink]

symp·tom (simp′təm) *n.* **1** *Pathol.* An organic or functional condition indicating the presence of disease, especially when regarded as an aid in diagnosis. **2** That which serves to point out the existence of something else; any sign, token, or indication. See synonyms under SIGN. [<L *symptoma* <Gk. *symptōma* a chance, a disease < *sympiptein* happen to < *syn-* together + *piptein* fall]

symp·to·mat·ic (simp′tə·mat′ik) *adj.* **1** Pertaining to, of the nature of, or constituting a symptom or symptoms; indicative: Fever is *symptomatic* of inflammation. **2** According to symptoms: a *symptomatic* classification of diseases. Also **symp′to·mat′i·cal.** [<F *symptomatique* <LL *symptomaticus* <Gk. *symptōmatikos* < *symptōma, -atos* a symptom] — **symp′to·mat′i·cal·ly** *adv.*

symp·tom·a·tol·o·gy (simp′təm·ə·tol′ə·jē) *n.* **1** The branch of medicine that has for its object the observation and classification of symptoms. **2** The combined symptoms of a disease: also *semeiology, semeiotics.* Compare DIAGNOSIS. [<NL *symptomatologia* <Gk. *symptōma, -atos* a symptom + *logos* study]

syn– *prefix* With; together; associated with or accompanying: *syntax, syndrome.* Also: *sy–* before *sc, sp, st,* and *z,* as in *system; syl–* before *l,* as in *syllable; sym–* before *b, p,* and *m,* as in *sympathy; sys–* before *s,* as in *syssarcosis.* [<Gk. < *syn* together]

syn·aer·e·sis (si·ner′ə·sis) See SYNERESIS.

syn·aes·the·sia (sin′is·thē′zhə, -zhē·ə) See SYNESTHESIA.

syn·a·gog (sin′ə·gôg, -gog) *n.* **1** A place of meeting for Jewish worship and religious instruction. **2** A Jewish congregation or assemblage for religious instruction and observances. **3** The Jewish religion or communion. Also **syn′a·gogue.** [<OF *sinagoge* <LL *synagoga* <Gk. *synagōgē* an assembly, synagog < *synagein* bring together < *syn-* together + *agein* lead, bring] — **syn′a·gog′i·cal** (-goj′i·kəl), **syn′a·gog′al** (-gôg′əl, -gog′əl) *adj.*

syn·a·le·pha (sin′ə·lē′fə) *n.* The blending into a single syllable of two successive vowels of different syllables; especially, the suppression of a final vowel or diphthong before one that begins the next word: *th′ Omnipotent* for *the Omnipotent.* Compare APOCOPE. Also **syn′a·le′·phe** (-lē′fē), **syn′a·loe′pha, syn′a·loe′phe.** [<LL <Gk. *synaloiphē* < *synaleiphein* smear together < *syn-* together + *aleiphein* anoint]

syn·al·gi·a (si·nal′jē·ə) *n. Pathol.* Sympathetic pain transmitted to a remote organ through associated nerves. [<NL <Gk. *synalgeein* share in suffering < *syn-* together + *algeein* feel bodily pain < *algos, -eos* bodily pain] — **syn·al′gic** *adj.*

syn·an·ther·ous (si·nan′thər·əs) *adj. Bot.* Having the stamens cohering by their anthers, as in composite flowers. [<NL *Synanthereae,* former family name <Gk. *syn-* together + NL *anthera* an anther]

syn·apse (si·naps′) *n. Physiol.* The junction point of two neurons, across which a nerve impulse passes. [<NL *synapsis* <Gk., a junction < *syn-* together + *hapsis* a joining < *haptein* join]

syn·ap·sis (si·nap′sis) *n.* **1** *Biol.* The conjugation of maternal and paternal chromosomes preceding maturation, or the reduction division in the nucleus; syndesis. **2** A synapse. [<NL. See SYNAPSE.] — **syn·ap′tic** *adj.* — **syn·ap′ti·cal·ly** *adv.*

syn·ar·thro·sis (sin′är·thrō′sis) *n. pl.* **·ses** (-sēz) *Anat.* A joint that permits no motion between the parts articulated. Also **syn′ar·thro′di·a** (-dē·ə). [<NL <Gk. *synarthrōsis* < *syn-* together + *arthrōsis* a jointing < *arthron* a joint] — **syn′ar·thro′di·al** *adj.* — **syn′ar·thro′·di·al·ly** *adv.*

syn·ax·is (si·nak′sis) *n.* A congregation assembled for public worship, especially for celebrating the Lord's Supper. [<LL <Gk. < *synagein.* See SYNAGOG.]

sync (singk) See SYNCH.

syn·carp (sin′kärp) *n. Bot.* An aggregate fruit composed of several more or less coherent carpels, as in the blackberry, or a multiple fruit, as in the fig. Also **syn·car·pi·um** (sin·kär′pē·əm). [<NL *syncarpium* <Gk. *syn-* together + *karpos* a fruit]

syn·car·pous (sin·kär′pəs) *adj. Bot.* Characterized by or characteristic of a syncarp; consisting of united carpels: contrasted with *apocarpous.*

syn·cat·e·gor·e·mat·ic (sin·kat′ə·gôr′ə·mat′ik, -gor′-) *adj.* Pertaining to words that can only form parts of terms, as adverbs, prepositions, and conjunctions: opposed to *categorematic.* Also **syn·cat′e·gor′e·mat′i·cal.** [<Gk. *synkatēgorēmatikos* < *synkatēgorēma* < *synkatēgorein* predicate jointly < *syn-* together + *katēgoreein.* See CATEGORY.]

synch (singk) *Slang v.i.* & *v.t.* To synchronize or cause to be synchronized. — *n.* The state of being synchronous; synchronization: usually in the phrases **in synch** and **out of synch.** [<SYNCHRONIZATION]

syn·chon·dro·sis (sing′kən·drō′sis) See under SYMPHYSIS. [<NL <Gk. *synchondrōsis* < *syn-* together + *chondros* cartilage]

syn·chro·mesh (sing′kro·mesh′) *n. Mech.* **1** A gear system by which driving and driven members are brought to the same speed before engaging. **2** The mechanism by which this uniform speed of gears is obtained. [<SYNCHRO(NIZED) + MESH]

syn·chron·ic (sin·kron′ik) *adj.* **1** Synchronous. **2** *Ling.* Pertaining to the study of some aspect of a language at a given stage in its development: *synchronic* grammar. Also **syn·chron′i·cal.** See DIACHRONIC. [<LL *synchronus* SYNCHRONOUS] — **syn·chron′i·cal·ly** *adv.*

syn·chro·nic·i·ty (sing′krə·nis′ə·tē) *n.* The temporal coincidence of two or more events linked together by meaning, but without any causal connection; meaningful cross-connection between separate causal chains. [Trans. of G *synchronizität;* used by C. G. Jung]

syn·chro·nism (sing′krə·niz′əm) *n.* **1** The state of being synchronous. **2** Coincidence in time of different events or phenomena; simultaneousness. **3** A tabular grouping of historic personages or events according to their dates. **4** In art, representation in the same picture of events having differing dates. [<LL *synchronismus* <Gk. *synchronismos* < *synchronos* SYNCHRONOUS] — **syn′chro·nis′·tic** or **·ti·cal** *adj.* — **syn′chro·nis′ti·cal·ly** *adv.*

syn·chro·nize (sing′krə·nīz) *v.* **·nized, ·niz·ing** *v.i.* **1** To occur at the same time; coincide. **2** To move or operate in unison. — *v.t.* **3** To cause (timepieces) to agree in keeping or indicating time. **4** To cause to operate in unison: to *synchronize* video and audio portions. **5** To assign the same date or period to; make contemporaneous. [<SYNCHRONISM] — **syn′·chro·ni·za′tion** *n.* — **syn′chro·niz′er** *n.*

synchronized shifting A change in the speed of an automotive vehicle by means of synchromesh gearing.

syn·chron·o·scope (sin·kron′ə·skōp) *n.* A synchroscope. [<SYNCHRON(ISM) + -(O)SCOPE]

syn·chro·nous (sing′krə·nəs) *adj.* **1** Occurring at the same time; coincident. **2** Happening at the same rate. **3** *Physics* Having the same period or rate of vibration: *synchronous* currents. Also **syn′chro·nal.** [<LL *synchronus* <Gk. *synchronos* < *syn-* together + *chronos* time] — **syn′chro·nous·ly** *adv.* — **syn′chro·nous·ness** *n.*

synchronous converter *Electr.* A machine adapted for the conversion of direct into alternating current or vice versa.

synchronous machine *Electr.* A machine whose normal speed of operation is exactly proportional to the frequency of the current to which it is connected, as a motor or generator.

synchronous speed *Electr.* The speed of an alternating-current machine as determined by the frequency of the circuit.

syn·chro·scope (sing′krə·skōp) *n. Electr.* An apparatus for visually indicating the degree of synchronization in the working, speed, etc., of two or more engines, as in an airplane. Also *synchronoscope.* [<SYNCHRO(NISM) + -SCOPE]

syn·chro·tron (sing′krə·tron) *n. Physics* An accelerator in which the particles being accelerated travel in nearly constant orbits, the change in orbital period being compensated by a synchronous change in the frequency of the alternating voltage providing the acceleration. [<SYNCHRO(NIZE) + (ELEC)TRON]

syn·clas·tic (sin·klas′tik) *adj.* Having the same kind of curvature in all directions; concave or convex in every direction: said of a surface: opposed to *anticlastic.* [<SYN- + Gk. *klastos* broken < *klaein* break]

syn·cli·nal (sin·klī′nəl) *adj.* **1** Sloping downward on each side toward a common line or point. **2** *Geol.* Dipping downward on each side toward the axis of the fold, as rock strata: opposed to *anticlinal.* Also **syn·clin·i·cal** (sin·klin′i·kəl). — *n.* A syncline. [<Gk. *synklinein* < *syn-* together + *klinein* incline]

syn·cline (sing′klīn) *n. Geol.* **1** A trough or structural basin toward which rocks dip. **2** A synclinal fold. [<Gk. *synklinein.* See SYNCLINAL.]

syn·clit·ism (sing′klə·tiz′əm) *n. Med.* The lateral turning of the fetal head in a natural presentation at childbirth, thus bringing the cranial planes into parallelism with the planes of the maternal pelvis. [<Gk. *syn-* together + *klitikos* < *klinein* incline, turn aside] — **syn·clit′ic** *adj.*

syn·co·pate (sing′kə·pāt) *v.t.* **·pat·ed, ·pat·ing** **1** To contract, as a word, by syncope. **2** *Music* To treat or modify, as a tone, by syncopation. [<LL *syncopatus,* pp. of *syncopare* affect with syncope < *syncope* SYNCOPE]

syn·co·pa·tion (sing′kə·pā′shən) *n.* **1** The act of syncopating or state of being syncopated; also, that which is syncopated; a dance or rhythm in syncopated time. **2** *Music* The beginning of a tone on an unaccented beat and its continuation through the following accented beat, or the beginning of a tone on the last half of a beat and continuing it through the first half of the next beat; also, the tone so treated, generally receiving an accent. **3** Any music featuring syncopation, as ragtime, jazz, etc. **4** Syncope of a word, or an example of it.

syn·co·pe (sing′kə·pē) *n.* **1** The elision of a sound or syllable in the middle part of a word, as *e′er* for *ever.* **2** *Music* Syncopation. **3** *Pathol.* Sudden faintness; swooning, with loss of sensation, motion, and consciousness. See synonyms under STUPOR. [Earlier *sincopis* <OF *sincopin,* ult. <LL *syncope* <Gk. *synkopē* < *syn-* together + *kop-,* stem of *koptein* strike, cut; refashioned after LL] — **syn′co·pal, syn·cop·ic** (sin·kop′ik) *adj.*

syn·cra·sy (sing′krə·sē) *n.* The blending, harmonizing, or massing of different or antagonistic elements. [<Gk. *synkrasis* a commixture < *syn-* together + *krasis* a mixing < *kerannynai* mix]

syn·cre·tism (sing′krə·tiz′əm) *n.* **1** A tendency or effort to reconcile and unite various systems of philosophy or religious opinion on the basis of tenets common to all and against a common opponent. **2** *Ling.* The fusion of two or more inflectional forms which were originally different, as of two cases. [<F *syncrétisme* <NL *syncretismus* <Gk. *synkrētismos* a union of two parties against a third < *synkrētizein* combine] — **syn′cre·tist** *n.* — **syn′cre·tis′tic** or **·ti·cal, syn·cret·ic** (sin·kret′ik) *adj.*

syn·cre·tize (sing′krə·tīz) *v.t.* **·tized, ·tiz·ing** To attempt to blend and reconcile, as various religions or philosophies. [<NL *syncretizare* <Gk. *synkrētizein* combine]

syn·cri·sis (sing′krə·sis) *n.* A figure of speech formed by comparison of opposite persons or things. [<LL <Gk. *synkrisis* < *synkrinein* compare < *syn-* together + *krinein* separate]

sync signal (singk) *Telecom.* The electromagnetic signal pulses by which the scanning process in television is synchronized for proper transmission and reception.

syn·cyt·i·um (sin·sit′ē·əm, -sish′əm) *n. pl.* **·cyt·i·a** (-sit′ē·ə, -sish′ə) *Biol.* **1** A multinucleate cell, or a mass of non-cellular, undifferentiated protoplasm. **2** Plasmodium. [<NL <Gk. *syn-* together + *kytos* a hollow] — **syn·cyt′i·al** *adj.*

syn·dac·tyl (sin·dak′til) *adj. Anat.* Having two or more digits either of the hand or of the foot wholly or partly united; web-footed: also **syn·dac′tyle, syn·dac′ty·lous.** — *n.* A mammal or bird which is syndactyl. [<F *syndactyle* <Gk. *syn-* together + *daktylos* a finger]

syn·dac·tyl·ism (sin·dak′til·iz′əm) *n.* **1** The condition of being syndactyl. **2** The union of two or more digits or toes.

syn·de·sis (sin′də·sis) *n. pl.* **·ses** (-sēz) Synapsis.

syndesmo- *combining form Anat.* A ligament; of or pertaining to a ligament or ligaments: *syndesmology.* Also, before vowels, **syndesm-.** [<Gk. *syndesmos* a ligament]

syn·des·mol·o·gy (sin′des·mol′ə·jē) *n.* The study of the anatomy and physiology of the ligaments.

syn·des·mo·sis (sin′des·mō′sis) *n. Anat.* The joining of two portions of the skeleton by means of ligamentous tissue. [<NL <Gk. *syndesmos* a ligament] **—syn′des·mot′ic** (-mot′ik) *adj.*

syn·det·ic (sin·det′ik) *adj.* Serving to unite or connect; connective, as a word. Also **syn·det′i·cal.** [<Gk. *syndetikos* <*syndeein* bind together <*syn-* together + *deein* bind] **—syn·det′i·cal·ly** *adv.*

syn·dic (sin′dik) *n.* A civil magistrate or officer representing a government or a community; also, one chosen to transact business for others: used also collectively for a body of officers or a council. [<F *syndic, syndique* a delegated representative <LL *syndicus* an advocate, delegate <Gk. *syndikos* a defendant's advocate <*syn-* together + *dikē* judgment] **—syn′di·cal** *adj.*

syn·di·cal·ism (sin′di·kəl·iz′əm) *n.* A social and political theory proposing the taking over of the means of production by syndicates of workers, preferably by means of the general strike, with consequent political control and the disappearance of the bourgeois state. [<F *syndicalisme* <*syndical* of a labor union <*(chambre) syndicale* a labor union <*syndic* a syndic] **—syn′di·cal·ist** *n.* **—syn′di·cal·is′tic** *adj.*

syn·di·cate (sin′də·kit) *n.* **1** An association of individuals united to negotiate some business or to prosecute some enterprise requiring large capital. **2** A combination of persons associated for purchasing manuscripts and selling them again to a number of periodicals, as newspapers, for simultaneous publication. **3** The office or jurisdiction of a syndic; syndics collectively: the original meaning. *—v.t.* (-kāt) **·cat·ed, ·cat·ing 1** To combine into or manage by a syndicate. **2** To sell for publication in many newspapers or magazines. [<F *syndicat* office of a syndic <*syndic.* See SYNDIC.]

syn·drome (sin′drōm) *n.* **1** *Med.* An aggregate or set of concurrent symptoms together indicating the presence and nature of a disease. **2** A group of traits regarded as being characteristic of a certain type, condition, etc. [<NL <Gk. *syndromē* <*syn-* together + *dramein* run] **—syn·drom·ic** (sin·drom′ik) *adj.*

syne (sīn) *adv. Scot.* **1** Since; ago: auld lang *syne.* **2** Afterward. **3** Then; moreover.

sy·nec·do·che (si·nek′də·kē) *n.* A figure of speech in which a part is put for a whole or a whole for a part, an individual for a class, or a material for the thing, as a *roof* for a *house, marble* for a *statue.* [<LL <Gk. *synekdochē* <*synekdechesthai* take something with something else <*syn-* together + *ekdechesthai* take from <*ek-* from + *dechesthai* take] **—syn·ec·doch·ic** (sin′ek·dok′ik), **syn′ec·doch′i·cal** *adj.*

sy·ne·cious (si·nē′shəs) See SYNOECIOUS.

syn·e·col·o·gy (sin′ə·kol′ə·jē) *n.* The study of plant and animal communities in relation to their environment; the ecology of organisms taken collectively. [<SYN- + ECOLOGY]

Syn·e·dri·on (sin·ē′drē·ən), **Syn·e·dri·um** (-drē·əm) See SANHEDRIN.

syn·er·e·sis (si·ner′ə·sis) *n.* **1** The coalescence of two vowels or syllables generally pronounced separately, as *seest* for *see-est*: opposed to *dieresis*; crasis. Compare SYNIZESIS. **2** *Chem.* The contraction of a gel, with the expulsion of water or other liquids, as in the clotting of blood. Also spelled *synaeresis.* [<LL *synaeresis* <Gk. *synairesis* a drawing together <*syn-* together + *haireein* take]

syn·er·get·ic (sin′ər·jet′ik) *adj.* Working together; cooperative, as the flexor muscles of the leg. [<Gk. *synergētikos* <*synergeein* cooperate <*syn-* together + *ergeein* work]

syn·er·gism (sin′ər·jiz′əm) *n.* **1** The doctrine that human effort cooperates with divine grace in the salvation of the soul. **2** *Med.* The mutually cooperating action of separate substances which together produce an effect greater than that of any component taken alone, as certain drug mixtures. [<NL *synergismus* <Gk. *synergos* working together <*synergeein.* See SYNERGETIC.]

syn·er·gist (sin′ər·jist) *n.* **1** One holding to synergism. **2** A cooperating organ, part, or medicine. **—syn′er·gis′tic** or **·ti·cal** *adj.*

syn·er·gy (sin′ər·jē) *n.* **1** Combined and correlated force; united action. **2** *Med.* Correlation or concurrence of action between different organs in health or disease, or between different drugs. Also **syn·er·gi·a** (si·nûr′jē·ə). [<NL *synergia* <Gk. *synergos.* See SYNERGISM.] **—syn·er′gic** *adj.*

syn·e·sis (sin′ə·sis) *n. Gram.* Construction in accordance with the sense rather than the syntax, as the use of a plural form of a verb with a collective noun to emphasize the individuals in the group. [<Gk., a joining together, understanding <*synienai* perceive <*syn-* together + *hienai* send]

syn·es·the·sia (sin′is·thē′zhə, -zhē·ə) *n. Physiol.* **1** Transferred sensation; sensation produced at a point different from the point of stimulation. **2** The producing of a subjective response normally associated with one sense by stimulation of another sense, as of a color from hearing a certain sound. Also spelled *synaesthesia.* [<NL *synaesthesia* <Gk. *synaisthēsis* joint perception <*synaisthanesthai* perceive simultaneously <*syn-* together + *aisthanesthai* perceive, feel] **—syn′es·thet′ic** (-thet′ik) *adj.*

syn·fu·el (sin′fyōō′əl) *n.* Synthetic fuel.

syn·ga·my (sing′gə·mē) *n. Biol.* The union of male and female gametes in fertilization. [<SYN- + -GAMY] **—syn·gam·ic** (sin·gam′ik), **syn′ga·mous** *adj.*

Synge (sing), **John Millington,** 1871–1909, Irish dramatist and poet.

syn·gen·e·sis (sin·jen′ə·sis) *n. Biol.* **1** Sexual reproduction. **2** The theory that the sexually fertilized germ contains within itself the germs of all future generations: opposed to *epigenesis.* [<NL <Gk. *syn-* together + *genesis* GENESIS] **—syn·ge·net·ic** (sin′jə·net′ik) *adj.*

syn·i·ze·sis (sin′ə·zē′sis) *n.* **1** In Greek prosody, the union in pronunciation of two vowels that cannot form a diphthong, so as to pass for one syllable: differing from *contraction* in not being made in the written word, but only in pronunciation. Compare SYNERESIS. **2** *Biol.* The contractile massing of the chromatin during meiotic cell division: associated with *synapsis.* **3** *Med.* Contraction of the pupil of the eye. Also **syn′e·zi′sis** (-zī′sis). [<LL <Gk. *synizēsis* <*synizanein* sink down <*syn-* together + *izanein* settle down, sit <*izein* seat, sit]

syn·od (sin′əd) *n.* **1** An ecclesiastical council, stated or special, local or general; hence, any deliberative assembly. **2** *Astron.* A conjunction (def. 2). [OE *synoth* <LL *synodus* <Gk. *synodos,* lit., a coming together <*syn-* together + *hodos* a way; refashioned after MF *synode* <LL]

Syn·od (sin′əd) *n.* **1** One of certain ecclesiastical councils distinguished by their extent or locality. **2** In the Presbyterian churches, a council intermediate between presbyteries and General Assembly. **3** In the Dutch Reformed, German Reformed, and Lutheran churches in the United States, a supreme council, known as **General Synod,** and also a more limited one, known as **Particular** or **District Synod.**

syn·od·i·cal (si·nod′i·kəl) *adj.* **1** Of, pertaining to, or of the nature of a synod; transacted in a synod. **2** *Astron.* Pertaining to the conjunction of two heavenly bodies one of which revolves round the other, or to the interval between two successive conjunctions: a *synodical* month. Also **syn·od·al** (sin′ə·dəl), **sy·nod′ic.** **—sy·nod′i·cal·ly** *adv.*

sy·noe·cious (si·nē′shəs) *adj. Bot.* Having male and female organs, either stamens and pistils or antheridia and archegonia, in the same inflorescence or receptacle, as in most composite plants and many mosses: also spelled *synecious.* [<Gk. *synoikia* living together <*syn-* together + *oikos* a house; formed on analogy with *dioecious, monoecious,* etc.]

syn·o·nym (sin′ə·nim) *n.* **1** A word having the same or almost the same meaning as some other; hence, one of a number of words that have one or more meanings in common: opposite of *antonym.* **2** The equivalent of a word in another language. **3** *Biol.* A scientific name, as of a genus or species, superseded or discarded, as by the law of priority or because of incorrect application. Also **syn′o·nyme.** [<LL *synonymum* <Gk. *synōnymon,* neut. of *synōnymos* having like meaning or name <*syn-* together + *onyma, onoma* a name] **—syn′o·nym′ic** or **·i·cal** *adj.* **—syn′o·nym′i·ty** *n.*

sy·non·y·mize (si·non′ə·mīz) *v.t.* **·mized, ·miz·ing** To give the synonyms of; express by words of similar or equivalent meaning.

sy·non·y·mous (si·non′ə·məs) *adj.* Being a synonym or synonyms; equivalent or similar in meaning; closely related or nearly alike in significance. Also **syn·o·ny·mat·ic** (sin′ə·ni·mat′ik), **syn′o·nym′ic** (-nim′ik) or **·i·cal.** **—sy·non′y·mous·ly** *adv.*

Synonyms: alike, correspondent, corresponding, equivalent, identical, interchangeable, like, same, similar, synonymic. In the strictest sense, *synonymous* words scarcely exist; rarely, if ever, are any two words in any language *equivalent* or *identical* in meaning; where a difference in meaning cannot be easily shown, a difference in usage, often involving connotation, usually exists, so that the words are not *interchangeable.* By *synonymous* words we usually understand words that coincide or nearly coincide in some part of their meaning, and may hence within certain limits be used interchangeably, while outside of these limits they may differ very greatly in meaning and use. To consider *synonymous* words *identical* is fatal to accuracy; to forget that they are *similar,* to some extent *equivalent,* and sometimes *interchangeable,* is destructive of freedom and variety.

sy·non·y·my (si·non′ə·mē) *n. pl.* **·mies 1** The quality of being synonymous; the expressing or extending of an idea by the use of synonyms. **2** The science or systematic collection and study of synonyms; the use and nice discrimination of synonyms: also **syn·o·nym·ics** (sin′ə·nim′iks). **3** A book treating of or discriminating the meaning of synonyms or of allied terms. **4** An index, list, or collection of synonyms, as in scientific nomenclature. [<LL *synonymia* <Gk. *synōnymia* <*synōnymos.* See SYNONYM.]

sy·nop·sis (si·nop′sis) *n. pl.* **·ses** (-sēz) A general view, as of a subject or its treatment; an abstract; syllabus; a summary. See synonyms under ABRIDGMENT. [<LL <Gk., a general view <*syn-* together + *opsis* a view]

sy·nop·tic (si·nop′tik) *adj.* **1** Giving a general view. **2** Presenting the same or a similar point of view; containing parts that, when compared, are virtually identical: said of the first three Gospels **(Synoptic Gospels)** as distinguished from the fourth. Also **sy·nop′ti·cal.** [<NL *synopticus* <Gk. *synoptikos* <*synopsis* a synopsis] **—sy·nop′ti·cal·ly** *adv.*

syn·os·to·sis (sin′os·tō′sis) See under SYMPHYSIS. Also **syn·os·te·o·sis** (si·nos′tē·ō′sis). [Contraction of *synosteosis* <NL <Gk. *syn-* together + *osteon* a bone]

sy·nou·si·acs (si·nōō′shē·aks, -nou′-) *n.* That branch of knowledge pertaining to societies: a term used in cataloging, as in libraries. [<Gk. *synousia* society <*synousa,* ppr. fem. of *syneinai* be with <*syn-* together + *einai* be]

sy·no·vi·a (si·nō′vē·ə) *n. Physiol.* The viscid, transparent, albuminous fluid secreted in the interior of joints and at other points where lubrication is necessary. [<NL *sinovia, synovia, synophia;* coined by Paracelsus, appar. <Gk. *syn-* together + L *ovum* an egg <Gk. *ōon*] **—sy·no′vi·al** *adj.*

syn·o·vi·tis (sin′ō·vī′tis) *n. Pathol.* Inflammation of a synovial membrane.

syn·sep·a·lous (sin·sep′ə·ləs) *adj. Bot.* Gamosepalous. [<SYN- + SEPAL + -OUS]

syn·tax (sin′taks) *n.* **1** The arrangement and interrelationship of words in grammatical

constructions. 2 The branch of linguistics dealing with this. [<F *syntaxe* <LL *syntaxis* <Gk. <*syntassein* join together <*syn-* together + *tassein* arrange] — **syn·tac·tic** (sin·tak′tik) or **·ti·cal** *adj.* — **syn·tac′ti·cal·ly** *adv.*

syn·tech·nic (sin·tek′nik) *adj. Ecol.* Denoting resemblance among dissimilar animal forms due to influences of common environment. See CONVERGENCE (def. 7). [<Gk. *syntechnos* practicing the same art <*syn-* together + *technē* an art]

syn·the·sis (sin′thə·sis) *n. pl.* **·ses** (-sēz) **1** The assembling of separate or subordinate parts into a new form; also, the complex whole resulting from this. **2** *Ling.* The combination of radical and formative or inflectional elements in one word, as in *un-think-ing, home-wards.* **3** *Logic* **a** Combination of separate elements into a whole, as of species into genera: contrasted with *analysis.* **b** A process of reasoning from the whole to a part, from the general to the particular; deductive reasoning. **4** *Surg.* The operation of reuniting broken or divided parts, as of bones. **5** *Chem.* **a** The building up of compounds from a series of reactions involving elements, radicals, or simpler compounds. **b** The preparation by such means of organic compounds which have specific properties or are identical in certain respects with naturally occurring substances. Compare ANALYSIS. [<L <Gk. <*syntithenai* <*syn-* together + *tithenai* place] — **syn′the·sist** *n.*

syn·the·size (sin′thə·sīz) *v.t.* **·sized, ·siz·ing** **1** To unite or produce by synthesis. **2** To apply synthesis to. Also *Brit.* **syn′the·sise.**

syn·thet·ic (sin·thet′ik) *adj.* **1** Pertaining to or of the nature of synthesis; characterized by or consisting in synthesis; specifically, tending to reduce particulars to inclusive wholes: a *synthetic* mind. **2** *Chem.* Produced by the synthesis of simpler materials or substances: *synthetic* rubber. **3** Artificial; spurious. **4** *Ling.* Describing a language that utilizes inflectional affixes for the expression of relationships between words, as in Latin; inflectional: opposed to *analytic.* Also **syn·thet′i·cal.** —*n.* **1** Anything produced by synthesis. **2** *Chem.* A synthesized compound adapted for use as a substitute for some other material or substance. [<F *synthétique* <NL *syntheticus* <Gk. *synthetikos* <*synthetos* compounded <*syntithenai* <*syn-* together + *tithenai* place] — **syn·thet′i·cal·ly** *adv.*

synthetic philosophy Spencerism: so called by Spencer as being an attempt to combine all the sciences into a connected whole.

syn·to·nize (sin′tə·nīz) *v.t.* **·nized, ·niz·ing** *Electr.* **1** To place in resonance with each other, as radio frequencies. **2** To tune or tone together, as electrical instruments. [<SYNTON(Y) + -IZE] — **syn·ton·ic** (sin·ton′ik) or **·i·cal** *adj.* — **syn·ton′i·cal·ly** *adv.* — **syn′·to·ni·za′tion** *n.*

syn·to·ny (sin′tə·nē) *n. Electr.* **1** The harmonizing or tuning of particular transmitters and receivers each to the other. **2** Resonance. [<Gk. *syntonia* agreement <*syn-* together + *tonos* a tone]

syn·u·ra (sin·yŏŏr′ə) *n. pl.* **·u·rae** (-yŏŏr′ē) Any of a genus (*Synura*) of flagellate protozoans, uniting in subspherical clusters and discharging oil globules. They are common in swamp waters and render drinking water unpalatable by giving it a cucumberlike flavor. [<NL <Gk. *synouros, synoros* bordering on <*syn-* together + *oros* a boundary]

sy·pher (sī′fər) *v.t.* To make a lap joint with (two chamfered or beveled plank edges) so as to leave a flush surface. [Var. of CIPHER] — **sy′pher·ing** *n.*

syph·i·lis (sif′ə·lis) *n. Pathol.* An infectious, chronic, venereal disease caused by a spirochete (*Treponema pallidum*) transmissible by direct contact or congenitally. It usually progresses by three stages of increasing severity: primary, secondary, and tertiary. [after *Syphilis, sive Morbus Gallicus,* a Latin poem by Fracastoro, published in 1530, the hero of which, *Syphilus,* a shepherd, was the first sufferer from the disease] — **syph′i·loid, syph′·i·lous** *adj.*

syph·i·lit·ic (sif′ə·lit′ik) *adj.* Relating to or affected with syphilis. —*n.* A person suffering from syphilis. [<NL *syphiliticus* <*syphilis* SYPHILIS]

syph·i·lol·o·gy (sif′ə·lol′ə·jē) *n.* The science of syphilis, its cognate diseases, and their treatment. [<SYPHIL(IS) + -(O)LOGY] — **syph′i·lol′o·gist** *n.*

syph·i·lo·pho·bi·a (sif′ə·lə·fō′bē·ə) *n. Psychiatry* A morbid fear of syphilis. [<SYPHIL(IS) + -(O)PHOBIA] — **syph′i·lo·pho′bic** *adj.*

syphon (sī′fən) See SIPHON.

Syr·a·cuse (sir′ə·kyŏŏs) **1** A port of SE Sicily: Italian *Siracusa.* Ancient **Syr·a·cu·sae** (sir′ə·kyŏŏ′sē, -zē). **2** A city in central New York. — **Syr′a·cu′san** *adj. & n.*

Syr Dar·ya (sir där′yä) A river in SW Asiatic U.S.S.R. flowing about 1,327 miles NW to the Aral Sea: ancient *Jaxartes.*

sy·ren (sī′rən) See SIREN.

Syr·ette (si·ret′) *n.* A miniature syringe; especially, a small disposable tube for the emergency administration of morphine, for use on the battlefield, by paratroopers, etc.: a trade name.

Syr·i·a (sir′ē·ə) *n.* **1** A former republic, 1941–1958, south of Asia Minor on the NE coast of the Mediterranean, a part of the United Arab Republic from 1958–61; 72,234 square miles; capital, Damascus. *Arabic* **Esh Shan.** **2** A former French mandated territory, 1920–1941, roughly comprising Syria (def. 1) and Lebanon. **3** An ancient country including Syria (def. 1), Lebanon, Palestine (def. 2), and adjacent districts of western Asia.

Syr·i·ac (sir′ē·ak) *n.* The language of the Syrians, belonging to the eastern Aramaic subgroup of the Northwest Semitic languages. [<L *Syriacus* <Gk. *Syriakos* <*Syria* Syria]

Syr·i·an (sir′ē·ən) *adj.* Of or pertaining to Syria, ancient or modern. —*n.* **1** A native of Syria, especially one of the native Semitic people of Arabic, Phoenician, and Aramean descent. **2** One who is a member of the Christian church in Syria. [<OF *sirien* <L *Syrius* a Syrian <Gk. *Syrios* <*Syria* Syria]

Syrian Desert An arid wasteland of SW Asia between the lands along the eastern Mediterranean and the Euphrates valley.

sy·rin·ga (si·ring′gə) *n.* **1** Any of a genus (*Philadelphus*) of ornamental shrubs of the saxifrage family having cream-colored flowers resembling those of the orange in form and fragrance, especially the Lewis mock orange (*P. lewisii*), the State flower of Idaho. **2** Any of a genus (*Syringa*) of ornamental shrubs of the olive family having panicles of showy white or purple flowers; the lilacs. [<NL <Gk. *syrinx, -ingos* a pipe]

SYRINGA
(Plant to 10 feet)

syr·inge (sir′inj, si·rinj′) *n. Med.* An instrument used to withdraw a fluid from a reservoir and eject it in one or more jets or streams. The simplest forms are valveless single-acting devices; other forms consist of an elastic bag supplied with flexible inlet and outlet pipes each having a suitable check valve. —*v.t.* **·inged, ·ing·ing** To spray or inject by a syringe; cleanse or treat with injected fluid. [<Med. L *siringa* <Gk. *syrinx, -ingos* a tube, a pipe]

sy·rin·go·my·e·li·a (si·ring′gō·mī·ē′lē·ə) *n. Pathol.* A morbid condition of the spinal cord, due to the presence of liquid in abnormally formed cavities. [<NL <Gk. *syrinx, -ingos* a tube + *myelos* marrow]

syr·inx (sir′ingks) *n.* **1** *Ornithol.* A special modification of the windpipe serving as the song organ in birds. **2** A tube, pipe, or fistula. **3** Panpipes. [<Gk., a pipe] — **sy·rin·ge·al** (si·rin′jē·əl) *adj.*

Syr·inx (sir′ingks) In Greek mythology, a nymph pursued by Pan and changed into a reed, from which Pan made his pipes.

Sy·ros (sī′rəs) One of the Cyclades group, SW of Tenos; 33 square miles. Also *Siros.* Latin **Sy′rus.**

syr·phus fly (sûr′fəs) A fly of *Syrphus* or a related genus (family *Syrphidae*). The group is large and widely distributed, and contains many species which deceptively resemble bees and wasps. The larvae of many feed upon harmful plant lice. For illustration see INSECTS (beneficial). Also **syr·phid** (sûr′fid), **syr′phi·an.** [<NL <Gk. *syrphos* a gnat]

Syr·tis Ma·jor (sir′tis mā′jər) The ancient name for the GULF OF SIDRA.

Syrtis Minor An ancient name for the GULF OF GABÈS.

syr·up (sir′əp), **syr·up·y** See SIRUP, etc.

sys- Assimilated var. of SYN-.

sys·sar·co·sis (sis′är·kō′sis) *n. Anat.* The union of bones by means of muscles. [<NL <Gk. *syssarkōsis* <*syssarkoein* unite by or cover over with flesh] — **sys′sar·co′sic, sys′sar·cot·ic** (-kot′ik) *adj.*

sys·tal·tic (sis·tal′tik) *adj. Physiol.* Alternately contracting and dilating: the *systaltic* motion of the heart; pulsatory. Compare PERISTALSIS. [<LL *systalticus* <Gk. *systaltikos* depressing <*systellein* draw together <*syn-* together + *stellein* send]

sys·tem (sis′təm) *n.* **1** Orderly combination or arrangement, as of parts or elements, into a whole; specifically, such combination according to some rational principle; any methodical arrangement of parts. **2** In science and philosophy, an orderly collection of logically related principles, facts, or objects. **3** Any group of facts and phenomena regarded as constituting a natural whole and furnishing the basis and material of scientific investigation and construction: the solar *system.* **4** The connection or manner of connection of parts as related to a whole, or the parts collectively so related; a whole as made up of constitutive parts: a railroad *system.* **5** The state or quality of being in order or orderly; orderliness; method: He works with *system.* **6** *Physiol.* An assemblage of organic structures composed of similar elements and combined for the same general functions: the nervous *system;* also, the entire body, taken as a functional whole. **7** *Physics* An aggregation of matter in, or tending to approach, equilibrium. **8** *Mineral.* One of the six divisions into which all crystal forms may be grouped, depending upon the relative lengths and mutual inclinations of the assumed crystal axes. **9** *Geol.* A category of rock strata next below a group and above a series and corresponding with a period in the time scale. [<LL *systema* a musical interval <Gk. *systēma, -atos* an organized whole <*syn-* together + *histanai* stand, set up]

Synonyms: manner, method, mode, order, regularity, rule. *Order* in this connection denotes a fact or a result; as, These papers are in *order. Method* denotes a process; *rule* an authoritative requirement or an established course of things; *system,* not merely a law of action or procedure, but a comprehensive plan; *manner* refers to the external qualities of actions, and to those often as settled and characteristic; we speak of a *system* of taxation, a *method* of collecting taxes, the *rules* by which assessments are made; or we say, As a *rule* the payments are heaviest at a certain time of year; a just tax may be made odious by the *manner* of its collection. *Regularity* applies to even disposition of objects or uniform recurrence of acts in a series. There may be *regularity* without *order,* as in the recurrence of paroxysms of disease or insanity; there may be *order* without *regularity,* as in the arrangement of furniture in a room, where the objects are placed at varying distances. *Order* commonly implies the design of an intelligent agent or the appearance or suggestion of such design; *regularity* applies to an actual uniform disposition or recurrence with no suggestion of purpose, and as applied to human affairs is less intelligent and more mechanical than *order.* See BODY, FRAME, HABIT, HYPOTHESIS. *Antonyms*: chaos, confusion, derangement, disarrangement, disorder, irregularity.

sys·tem·at·ic (sis′tə·mat′ik) *adj.* **1** Of, pertaining to, of the nature of, or characterized by system. **2** Acting by system or method; methodical: *systematic* thieving. **3** Forming a system; systematized. **4** Carried out with organized regularity. **5** Taxonomic: *systematic* botany. Also **sys′tem·at′i·cal.** [<LL *systematicus* <LGk. *systēmatikos* <*systēma, -atos* a system] — **sys′tem·at′i·cal·ly** *adv.*

sys·tem·at·ics (sis′tə·mat′iks) *n. pl.* (*construed as singular*) **1** The art or principles of classification and nomenclature. **2** *Biol.* The science of the classification of organisms; taxonomy.

sys·tem·a·tism (sis′tə·mə·tiz′əm) *n.* **1** Systematic arrangement or classification. **2** Adherence to or reduction of principles, etc., to a system.

sys·tem·a·tist (sis'tə·mə·tist) *n.* **1** One who reduces things to systems, as a taxonomist. **2** One who forms or adheres to a system or to a systematic view of things.

sys·tem·a·tize (sis'tə·mə·tīz') *v.t.* **·tized, ·tiz·ing** To reduce to a system; dispose methodically. See synonyms under REGULATE. Also **sys'tem·ize**, *Brit.* **sys'tem·a·tise'**. —**sys'tem·a·ti·za'tion, sys'tem·i·za'tion** *n.* —**sys'tem·a·tiz'er, sys'tem·iz'er** *n.*

sys·tem·ic (sis·tem'ik) *adj.* **1** Of or pertaining to system or a system; systematic. **2** *Physiol.* Pertaining to or affecting the body as a whole: a *systemic* poison. —**sys·tem'i·cal·ly** *adv.*

systems analysis The technique of reducing complex processes, as of industry, government, research, etc., to basic operations that can be treated quantitatively and reordered into sequences amenable to control. —**systems analyst**

sys·to·le (sis'tə·lē) *n.* **1** *Physiol.* The regular contraction of the heart, especially of the ventricles, that impels the blood outward. Compare DIASTOLE. **2** The shortening of a syllable that is naturally or by position long. [<NL <Gk *systolē* a contraction <*systellein*. See SYSTALTIC.] —**sys·tol·ic** (sis·tol'ik) *adj.*

syz·y·gy (siz'ə·jē) *n.* pl. **·gies** **1** *Astron.* One of two opposite points in the orbit of a celestial body when it is in conjunction with or opposition to the sun; especially, the points on the moon's orbit when the moon is most nearly in line with

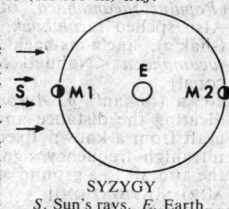

SYZYGY
S. Sun's rays. *E.* Earth. *M1, M2.* Syzygy of the moon.

the earth and the sun. **2** The union of parts or organisms. **3** A dipody or group of two feet in one verse. [<LL *syzygia* <Gk., a yoke, conjunction <*syzygos* yoked, paired <*syn-* together + *zeugnynai* yoke <*zygon* a yoke] —**syz·zyg·i·al** (si·zij'ē·əl) *adj.*

Sza·bad·ka (sô'bôd·kô) The Hungarian name for SUBOTICA.

Sze·chwan (se'chwän', su'-) A province of SW and central western China; 338,136 square miles; capital, Chengtu.

Sze·ged (se'ged) A city of southern Hungary. Formerly **Sze·ge·din** (se'ge·din).

Sze·ming (su'ming') A former name for AMOY.

Szent-Gyor·gyi von Nagy·ra·polt (sent'·dyûr'dyē fonnod'y'ro'pōlt), Albert, born 1893, Hungarian biochemist.

Szi·lard (si·lärd') Leo, 1898–1964, U.S. physicist born in Hungary.

Szom·bat·hely (som'bôt·hāy') A city of western Hungary: German *Steinamanger*.

T

t, T (tē) *n.* pl. **t's, T's** or **ts, Ts, tees** (tēz) **1** The twentieth letter of the English alphabet, from Greek *tau* (a modification of Phoenician *tau*) and Latin *T.* **2** The sound of the letter *t*, the voiceless alveolar stop. See ALPHABET. —*symbol* Anything shaped like a T. —**to a T** Precisely; with exactness: probably in allusion to a T-square.

T (tē) *adj.* Shaped or having a cross-section like a **T**, as *T-* beam, *T-* pipe, etc. —*n.* Anything having the shape of a T.

't Contraction for IT: used initially, as in *'tis*, and finally, as in *on't*.

-t Inflectional ending used to indicate past participles and past tenses, as in *bereft, lost, spent*: equivalent to *-ed*.

Ta *Chem.* Tantalum (symbol Ta).

Taal (täl) *n.* A form of Dutch spoken in South Africa; Afrikaans. [<Du., speech, language]

Ta·al (tä·äl'), Mount An active volcano (984 feet) on an island in **Lake Taal** (94 square miles) in southern Luzon, Philippines.

tab (tab) *n.* **1** A flap, strip, tongue, or appendage of something, as a garment. **2** *Colloq.* Tally: to keep *tab*. **3** *Aeron.* An auxiliary airfoil attached to the control surface of an airplane. [Origin uncertain]

tab·a·cin (tab'ə·sin) *n.* *Chem.* A waxy, lemon-yellow, poisonous glycoside extracted from the leaves of Kentucky tobacco. [<F *tabac* tobacco + -IN]

tab·a·nid (tab'ə·nid) *n.* Any of a family (*Tabanidae*) of large, bloodsucking insects; a horsefly or deerfly. —*adj.* Of the *Tabanidae*. [<NL, family name <L *tabanus* a horsefly]

tab·ard (tab'ərd) *n.* **1** Formerly, a short, sleeveless or short-sleeved, outer garment. **2** A knight's cape or cloak, worn over his armor and emblazoned with his own arms; also, a similar garment worn by a herald and embroidered with his lord's arms. **3** A banner attached to a trumpet or bugle. [<OF *tabard*, ult. <L *tapete* tapestry]

tab·a·ret (tab'ə·rit) *n.* A strong, silk upholstery fabric with varicolored stripes of satin or moiré. [Prob. <TABBY]

Ta·bas·co (tə·bas'kō) *n.* A pungent sauce made from the red-pepper plant (genus *Capsicum*): a trade name.

Ta·bas·co (tə·bas'kō, *Sp.* tä·väs'kō) A state in SE Mexico; 9,782 square miles; capital, Villahermosa.

tab·by (tab'ē) *n.* pl. **·bies** **1** Any of several plain-woven fabrics, as a striped or watered taffeta, or a moreen. **2** A garment made of a watered fabric. **3** A brindled or striped cat; popularly, any domestic cat, especially a female. **4** A gossiping old maid. **5** A building material of equal parts of lime and shells, and gravel, mixed with water. —*adj.* **1** Watered; mottled, as a fabric; also, brindled, as a cat. **2** Made of tabby. **3** Woven in the same way as fabric that is to be watered. —*v.t.* **·bied, ·by·ing** To give a wavy or watered appearance to (silk, etc.) by pressure between hot rollers; water; calender. [<F *tabis, atabis* <Arabic *'attābi* <*'Attabi*, name of a quarter of Baghdad where it was manufactured]

tab·er·nac·le (tab'ər·nak'əl) *n.* **1** A tent or similar structure; slight shelter, fixed or portable. **2** Specifically, the portable sanctuary used by the Jews in the wilderness; later, the Jewish temple; hence, any house of worship, especially one of large size and not of specially ecclesiastical architecture: in England, the place of worship of some nonconformists. **3** The human body as the dwelling place of the soul. **4** The ornamental receptacle for the consecrated eucharistic elements, or for the pyx. **5** An ornamental recess or a structure sheltering something. **6** A socket or hinged post to unstep or lower a mast. —*v.i.* **·led, ·ling** To dwell in a tent; hence, to dwell transiently: The soul *tabernacles* in the body. [<OF <L *tabernaculum*, dim. of *taberna* shed] —**tab·er·nac·u·lar** (tab'ər·nak'yə·lər) *adj.*

ta·bes (tā'bēz) *n.* *Pathol.* **1** Emaciation with general languor, progressive atrophy, and hectic fever; a decline. **2** Locomotor ataxia: also **tabes dor·sa·lis** (dôr·sā'lis). [<L, a wasting away <*tabere* waste away] —**ta·bes·cence** (tə·bes'əns) *n.* —**ta·bes'cent, ta·bet'ic** (-bet'ik) *n. & adj.* —**tab·id** (tab'id) *adj.*

Tab·i·tha (tab'i·thə) A feminine personal name. [<Aramaic, gazelle] —**Tabitha** A woman of Joppa noted for her good works. *Acts* ix 36.

Tab·las (tab'läs) The largest island in the Romblon group, central Philippines; 265 square miles.

tab·la·ture (tab'lə·chər) *n.* **1** *Anat.* One of the plates of bony tissue that form the walls of the cranium. **2** A tablelike painting or design. [<F <L *tabula* board]

ta·ble (tā'bəl) *n.* **1** An article of furniture with a flat horizontal top upheld by one or more supports. **2** Such a table around which persons sit for a meal: to set the *table*. **3** The food served or entertainment provided at a meal or dinner. **4** The company of persons at a table. **5** A gaming table, as for roulette, dice, etc. **6** A collection of related numbers, values, signs, or items of any kind, arranged for ease of reference or comparison, often in parallel columns: a *table* of logarithms; a *table* of statistics. **7** A synoptical statement; list: *table* of contents. **8** A tableland; plateau. **9** *Geol.* A horizontal stratum of rock. **10** The flat facet cut across the top of a precious stone. **11** *Archit.* **a** A raised horizontal surface or band of molding on a wall; a string-course.

b A raised or sunken panel on a wall. **12** In palmistry, the quadrangle formed by four lines of the hand. **13** In backgammon: **a** Either of the two leaves of a backgammon board. **b** *pl. Obs.* Backgammon. **14** *Anat.* One of the flat bony plates forming the inner or outer part of the cranium. **15** A tablet or slab bearing an inscription; especially, one of those which bore the Ten Commandments or certain Roman laws. —**to turn the tables** To thwart an opponent's action and turn the situation to his disadvantage. —*v.t.* **·bled, ·bling** **1** To place on a table, as a playing card. **2** To postpone discussion of (a resolution, bill, etc.) until a future time, or for an indefinite period. **3** *Rare* To make into or enter in a list or table; tabulate. [Fusion of OF *table* and OE *tabule*, both <L *tabula* board]

tab·leau (tab'lō, ta·blō') *n.* pl. **·leaux** (-lōz) or **·leaus** (-lōz) **1** Any picture or picturesque representation; especially, an unexpected situation produced suddenly and dramatically. **2** A tableau vivant. [<F, dim. of *table*. See TABLE.]

ta·bleau vi·vant (tá·blō'vē·vän') pl. **ta·bleaux vi·vants** (tá·blō' vē·vän') *French* A picturelike scene represented by silent and motionless persons standing in appropriate attitudes: also called *living picture*.

Table Bay An inlet of the Atlantic in Western Cape Province, Republic of South Africa: the harbor of Cape Town.

table book An ornamental book to be kept on a table.

ta·ble-chair (tā'bəl·châr') *n.* An armchair or small bench having a hinged back which when tilted up forms a table-top: also called *chair-table*.

ta·ble·cloth (tā'bəl·klôth', -kloth') *n.* A cloth, often white, covering a table at meals.

tab·le d'hôte (tab'əl dōt', tä'bəl) pl. **tab·les d'hôte** (tab'əlz dōt, tä'bəlz) **1** A common table for guests, as at a hotel. **2** A complete meal of several specified courses, served in a restaurant at a fixed price. [<F, lit., table of the host]

ta·ble·land (tā'bəl·land') *n.* A broad, level, elevated region, usually treeless; a plateau; specifically, a precipitous mesa.

table linen Tablecloths, napkins, doilies, etc., made of linen, cotton, etc.

ta·ble·mount (tā'bəl·mount') *n.* A guyot.

Table Mountain A flat-topped mountain in Western Cape Province, near Cape Town, Republic of South Africa; 3,550 feet.

ta·ble·spoon (tā'bəl·spoon', -spoon') *n.* A large spoon, larger than a dessertspoon, with a capacity of 15 cc. or three times the capacity of a teaspoon: used for serving food.

ta·ble·spoon·ful (tā'bəl·spoon·fool', -spoon-) **·fuls** As much as a tablespoon will hold:

usually reckoned as equivalent to half a fluid ounce, 15 cc., or three teaspoonfuls.

tab·let (tab′lit) *n.* **1** A thin leaf or sheet of solid material, as ivory or wood, for writing, painting, or drawing. **2** One of a set of leaves pivoted or joined together at one end and used for writing; also, a set of such leaves; hence, a pad, as of writing paper or note paper. **3** A small table or flat surface, especially one designed for or containing an inscription or design. **4** A small, flat or nearly flat piece of some prepared substance, as chocolate or soap. **5** A definite portion or weight of drug brought by pressure and the addition of a gum into a solid form; a troche or lozenge; also, an electuary. **6** A flat or tablelike surface. [<OF *tablete*, dim. of *table*. See TABLE.]

table tennis A game resembling tennis in miniature, played indoors with a small celluloid ball and wooden paddles on a large table; Ping-pong.

ta·ble·ware (tā′bəl·wâr′) *n.* Ware for table use; dishes, knives, forks, spoons, etc., collectively: called **table furniture** when napery is included.

tab·loid (tab′loid) *n.* A newspaper, one half the size of an ordinary newspaper, in which the news is presented by means of pictures and concise reporting. —*adj.* **1** Compact; concise; condensed. **2** Sensational: *tabloid* journalism. [<TABL(ET) + -OID]

Tab·loid (tab′loid) *n.* Proprietary name for any of various medical preparations and drugs in concentrated or condensed tablet form.

ta·boo (tə·bōō′, ta-) See TABU.

ta·bor (tā′bər) *n.* A small drum or tambourine on which a fife-player beats his own accompaniment; a timbrel. —*v.i.* To beat or play on a timbrel or small drum; beat lightly and repeatedly. Also spelled *taber*. Also **ta′bour.** [<OF *tabour*, prob. <Persian *tabīrah* drum] —**ta′bor·er** *n.*

Ta·bor (tā′bər), **Mount** A mountain near Nazareth in Galilee, northern Israel; 1,929 feet.

tab·o·ret (tab′ər·it, tab′ə·ret′) *n.* **1** A small tabor. **2** A stool or small seat, usually without arms or back. **3** An embroidery frame. **4** A needle case. Also **tab′ou·ret.** [<F *tabouret*, dim. of *tabour* TABOR]

tab·o·rine (tab′ə·rēn, tab·ə·rēn′) *n.* A small tabor, tambourine, or side drum. Also **tab′o·rin, tab′ou·rine.** [<OF *tabourin*, dim. of *tabour* TABOR]

Ta·briz (tä·brēz′) A city in NW Iran: ancient *Tauris*: also *Tebriz*.

ta·bu (tə·bōō′, ta-) *n.* **1** Among primitive peoples, especially the Polynesians, a religious and social interdict against the touching or mentioning of a certain person, thing, or place, the uttering of a certain name, or the performing of a certain action, because it is considered sacred, protective, dangerous, unclean, or possessed of mysterious powers. **2** The system or practice of such interdicts or prohibitions. **3** Any restriction or ban founded on custom or social convention. —*adj.* **1** Consecrated or prohibited by tabu. **2** Banned or forbidden by social authority or convention. —*v.t.* **1** To place under tabu. **2** To exclude; ostracize. Also spelled *taboo*. [<Tonga]

tab·u·lar (tab′yə·lər) *adj.* **1** Pertaining to or consisting of a table or list. **2** Computed from or with a mathematical table. **3** Having a flat surface; tablelike. [<L *tabularis* < *tabula* table] —**tab′u·lar·ly** *adv.*

tab·u·la ra·sa (tab′yōō·lə rä′sə) *Latin* **1** An empty or clean tablet; a clean slate. **2** The concept of the mind of a newborn child as a blank, to be written on by experience.

tab·u·lar·ize (tab′yə·lə·rīz′) *v.t.* **·ized, ·iz·ing** To arrange in tabular form, or in a table or tables; tabulate. —**tab′u·lar·i·za′tion** *n.*

tab·u·late (tab′yə·lāt) *v.t.* **·lat·ed, ·lat·ing** **1** To arrange in a table or list: to *tabulate* results. **2** To form with a tabular surface. —*adj.* **1** Having a flat surface or surfaces; broad and flat. **2** *Zool.* Having tabulated horizontal plates extending across the visceral cavity: said of certain corals. [<L *tabula* table + -ATE[1]] —**tab′u·la′tion** *n.*

tab·u·la·tor (tab′yə·lā′tər) *n.* **1** One who or that which tabulates. **2** A device built into a typewriter with which statistical matter may be speedily written in tabulated form. **3** An automatic high-speed accounting machine for tabulating reports.

tac·a·ma·hac (tak′ə·mə·hak′) *n.* **1** A yellowish resinous substance with a strong odor, derived from various trees and used as incense. **2** Any of the trees producing this substance, especially the balsam poplar (*Populus tacamahaca*) of the United States. Also spelled *tacmahack*. Also **tac′a·ma·hac′a** (-hak′ə), **tac′a·ma·hack′.** [<Sp. *tacamaca, tacamahaca* <Nahuatl *tecomahca*, lit., fetid copal]

ta·can (ta·kan′) *n. Aeron.* A system for indicating the distance and bearing of an aircraft from a known fixed point by means of ultrahigh-frequency signals transmitted from the aircraft to a ground station. [<TAC(TICAL) A(IR) N(AVIGATION)]

tace (tās) *n.* Tasset.

ta·cet (tā′set) *Latin* Literally, it is silent: a musical direction for silence.

tache (tach) *n. Archaic* A hook or fastening; a clasp; buckle. Also **tach.** [<OF *tache* nail, fastening. Doublet of TACK.]

tach·e·om·e·ter (tak′ē·om′ə·tər) *n.* **1** A tachymeter. **2** A tachometer. [<Gk. *tachos, tacheos* speed + -METER] —**tach′e·om′e·try** *n.*

tach·i·na fly (tak′ə·nə) A fly (family *Tachinidae*) often resembling the house fly, whose larvae develop as parasites in the caterpillar or other insect. For illustration see under INSECTS (beneficial). [<NL *tachina* <Gk. *tachinos* swift]

Ta Ch'ing (dä′ jing′) The Manchu dynasty of China. See MANCHU.

tach·i·nid (tak′ə·nid) *n.* A tachina fly. —*adj.* Of or pertaining to the *Tachinidae*.

ta·chis·to·scope (tə·kis′tə·skōp) *n.* An apparatus for giving a brief but accurately measurable exposure to visual objects, for the purpose of determining the speed and conditions of their apperception. [<Gk. *tachistos* swiftest + -SCOPE]

tach·o·graph (tak′ə·graf, -gräf) *n.* **1** A registering tachometer. **2** The record it makes. [<Gk. *tachos* swiftness + -GRAPH]

ta·chom·e·ter (tə·kom′ə·tər) *n.* **1** An instrument for measuring linear and angular velocity, as of a machine, the flow of a current, blood, etc. **2** A device for indicating the speed of rotation of an engine, etc. [See TACHEOMETER]

ta·chom·e·try (tə·kom′ə·trē) *n.* The art or science of using a tachometer. —**tach·o·met·ric** (tak′ə·met′rik) *adj.*

tachy- *combining form* Speed; swiftness: *tachycardia*. [<Gk. *tachys* swift]

tach·y·car·di·a (tak′i·kär′dē·ə) *n. Pathol.* Abnormal rapidity of the heartbeat, usually indicating a pulse rate above 100 per minute. —**tach′y·car′di·ac** *adj.* & *n.*

tach·y·graph (tak′ə·graf, -gräf) *n.* **1** A tachygraphic manuscript or symbol. **2** A tachygrapher.

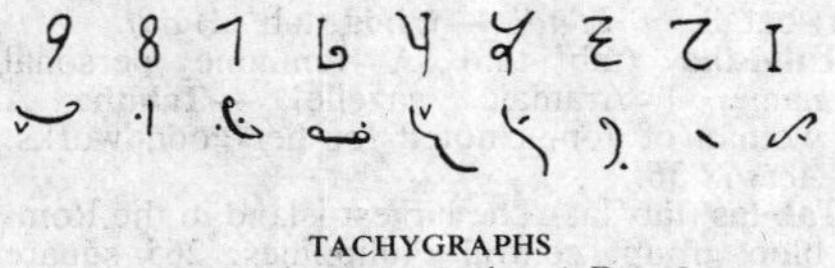

TACHYGRAPHS
Numerals: *Upper* Arabic, A.D. 976; *Lower* Modern Shorthand.

ta·chyg·ra·pher (tə·kig′rə·fər) *n.* **1** One who writes in shorthand; a stenographer. **2** One of the shorthand writers of the ancient Greeks and Romans. Also **ta·chyg′ra·phist.**

ta·chyg·ra·phy (tə·kig′rə·fē) *n. Archaic* Stenography; shorthand. —**tach·y·graph·ic** (tak′ə·graf′ik) or **·i·cal** *adj.* —**tach′y·graph′i·cal·ly** *adv.*

tach·y·lyte (tak′ə·līt) *n.* A pitch-black basaltic glass which is rapidly decomposed by acids. [<TACHY- + -LYTE[1]; so called because easily decomposed] —**tach′y·lyt′ic** (-lit′ik) *adj.*

ta·chym·e·ter (tə·kim′ə·tər) *n.* **1** A surveying instrument for stadia surveying, having a level, telescope, vertical arc or circle, horizontal compass, and stadia wires. **2** A tachometer.

ta·chym·e·try (tə·kim′ə·trē) *n.* The art or science of using, or measuring with, the tachymeter. —**tach·y·met·ric** (tak′ə·met′rik) *adj.*

ta·chys·ter·ol (tə·kis′tə·rōl, -rol) *n. Biochem.* One of the substances formed by the ultraviolet irradiation of ergosterol, and the immediate predecessor of calciferol. [<TACHY- + STEROL]

tac·it (tas′it) *adj.* **1** Existing, inferred, or implied without being directly stated; implied by silence or silent acquiescence. **2** *Law* Not expressed but understood by provision or operation of the law. **3** Silent; emitting no sound; noiseless. ◆ Homophone: *tasset*. [<F *tacite* <L *tacitus*, pp. of *tacere* be silent] —**tac′it·ly** *adv.* —**tac′it·ness** *n.*

Synonyms: implicit, implied, understood, unexpressed, unspoken.

tacit mortgage A lien in the nature of a mortgage created by operation of law.

tac·i·turn (tas′ə·tûrn) *adj.* Habitually silent or reserved; disinclined to conversation. [<L *taciturnus* <L *tacere* be silent] —**tac′i·tur′·ni·ty** *n.* —**tac′i·turn·ly** *adv.*

Synonyms: close, dumb, mute, reserved, reticent, silent, uncommunicative. *Dumb, mute*, and *silent* refer to fact or state; *taciturn* refers to habit and disposition. The talkative person may be stricken *dumb* with terror; the obstinate may remain *mute*; one may be *silent* through preoccupation or set purpose; but the *taciturn* person is averse to the utterance of thought or feeling and to communication with others. One who is *silent* does not speak at all; one who is *taciturn* speaks when compelled, but in a grudging way. *Reserved* suggests more of method and intention than *taciturn*, applying often to some special time or topic. *Reserved* is thus closely equivalent to *uncommunicative*, but is a somewhat stronger word, often suggesting pride or haughtiness, as when we say one is *reserved* toward strangers. *Antonyms*: communicative, free, garrulous, loquacious, talkative, unreserved.

Tac·i·tus (tas′ə·təs), **Gaius Cornelius**, A.D. 55?– after 117, Roman historian.

tack[1] (tak) *n.* **1** A small sharp-pointed nail, commonly with tapering sides and a flat head. **2** *Naut.* **a** A rope which holds down the weather clew of a course. **b** The weather clew of a square sail. **c** The lower forward corner of a fore-and-aft sail. **d** A rope by which the lower outer corner of a studdingsail is pulled to the end of the boom. **e** The direction in which a vessel sails when sailing close-hauled, considered in relation to the position of her sails: the starboard *tack* when the wind is coming from the right-hand side. **f** The distance or the course run at one time in such direction. **g** The act of tacking. **h** Any veering of a vessel to one side, as to take advantage of a side wind. **3** A change of policy; a new course of action. **4** A fastening; in needlework, a temporary stitch. **5** In Scots law, a contract; a lease; also, leased land. **6** The saddle, bridle, martingale, etc., used in riding horseback. —*v.t.* **1** To fasten or attach with tacks. **2** To secure temporarily, as with tacks or long stitches. **3** To attach as supplementary; append. **4** *Naut.* **a** To bring (a vessel) momentarily into the wind so as to go on the opposite tack. **b** To navigate (a vessel) to windward by making a series of tacks. —*v.i.* **5** *Naut.* **a** To tack a vessel. **b** To go on the opposite tack, or sail to windward by a series of tacks: said of vessels. **6** To change one's course of action; veer. [<AF *taque*, OF *tache* a nail <Gmc. Doublet of TACHE.] —**tack′er** *n.*

tack[2] (tak) *n.* Food in general: usually used contemptuously, and often in compounds: *hardtack*. [Origin uncertain]

tack·et (tak′it) *n. Scot.* A hobnail or clout.

tack hammer A small hammer for driving tacks.

tack·le (tak′əl, *in nautical usage* tā′kəl) *n.* **1** A rope, pulley, or combination of ropes and pulleys, used for hoisting or moving objects. **2** *Naut.* A mechanism for raising and lowering heavy weights, or managing sails and spars, as on shipboard. **3** A windlass or winch, together with ropes and hooks. **4** The instruments collectively used in any work or sport; gear; equipment: fishing *tackle*. **5** Formerly, the implements of war; weapons. **6** The act of tackling, or seizing and stopping, especially in

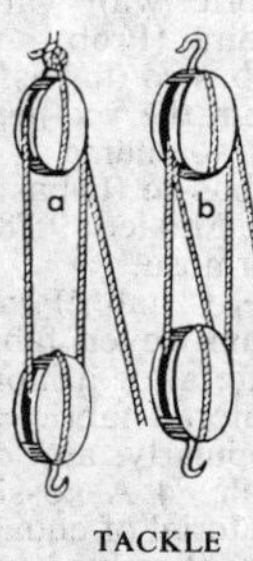

TACKLE
a. Gun.
b. Luff.

football. **7** In football, either of two linemen stationed between the guard and end: called **right** and **left tackle.** **8** A ship's rigging collectively. — *v.t.* **·led, ·ling** **1** To harness (a horse). **2** To deal with; undertake to master, accomplish, or solve: to *tackle* a task or a problem. **3** To seize suddenly and forcefully, usually in order to stop or throw to the ground: to *tackle* a fleeing burglar. **4** In football, to seize and stop (an opponent carrying the ball). [<MLG *takel* < *taken* seize] — **tack′ler** *n.*

tack·ling (tak′ling) *n. Naut.* Tackle, collectively.

tack·y[1] (tak′ē) *adj.* **tack·i·er, tack·i·est** Having adhesive properties; sticky: said especially of surfaces covered with partly dried varnish. Also **tack′ey.** [Prob. <TACK[1], *v.* (def. 2)]

tack·y[2] (tak′ē) *adj. U.S. Colloq.* Unfashionable; plain; in bad taste; common. [Cf. dial. G *taklig* untidy]

tac·ma·hack (tak′mə·hak) See TACAMAHAC.

Tac·na (täk′nä) A department of southern Peru on the Pacific; 4,920 square miles.

tac·node (tak′nōd) *n. Math.* A point of osculation. [<L *tactus,* pp. of *tangere* touch + NODE]

ta·co (tä′kō) *n. pl.* **·cos** A fried tortilla folded around any of several fillings, as chopped meat or cheese. [<Sp., wad]

Ta·co·ma (tə·kō′mə) A port on Puget Sound in western Washington.

Ta·con·ic Mountains (tə·kon′ik) A range of the Appalachian system in New England and New York; highest point, 3,816 feet.

tac·o·nite (tak′ə·nīt) *n. Geol.* A variously tinted ferruginous chert enclosing the iron ores of the Mesabi district in Minnesota. [from *Tacon(ic Mountains)* + -ITE[1]]

tact (takt) *n.* **1** A quick or intuitive appreciation of what is fit, proper, or right; fine or ready mental discernment shown in saying or doing the proper thing, or especially in avoiding what would offend or disturb; skill or facility in dealing with men or emergencies; adroitness; cleverness; address. **2** The sense of touch; feeling; also, a touch or touching. **3** A perception or feeling, other than tactile, of the qualities of things. See synonyms under ADDRESS. [<L *tactus* a touching < *tangere* touch]

tact·ful (takt′fəl) *adj.* Possessing or manifesting tact; considerate. — **tact′ful·ly** *adv.* — **tact′ful·ness** *n.*

tac·tic (tak′tik) *n.* **1** A detail of tactics. **2** *Colloq.* A device or strategem: a clever *tactic.*

tac·ti·cal (tak′ti·kəl) *adj.* **1** Pertaining to or of the nature of tactics. **2** Exhibiting adroit maneuvering. — **tac′ti·cal·ly** *adv.*

tactical unit A military combat unit, running in size from the squad through the army group.

tac·ti·cian (tak·tish′ən) *n.* An expert in tactics; an adroit maneuverer.

tac·tics (tak′tiks) *n. pl.* **1** The science and art of military and naval evolutions; specifically, the art of handling troops in the presence of the enemy or for immediate objectives, as distinguished from *strategy*: construed as singular. **2** Any maneuvering or adroit management to effect an object. [<Gk. *taktika,* pl. of *taktikos* suitable for arranging or organizing < *tassein, tattein* arrange, order]

tac·tile (tak′til, -təl) *adj.* **1** Pertaining to the organs or sense of touch; caused by or consisting of contact; tactual. **2** That may be touched; tangible. [<F <L *tactilis* < *tactus* touch. See TACT.]

tac·til·i·ty (tak·til′ə·tē) *n.* Tangibility.

tac·tion (tak′shən) *n.* **1** The act of touching. **2** The state of being in contact. [<L *tactio, -onis* < *tactus,* pp. of *tangere* touch]

tact·less (takt′lis) *adj.* Without tact. — **tact′less·ly** *adv.* — **tact′less·ness** *n.*

tac·tom·e·ter (tak·tom′ə·tər) *n.* An esthesiometer. [<L *tactus* touch + -METER]

tac·tu·al (tak′cho͞o·əl) *adj.* **1** Pertaining to the sense or the organs of touch. **2** Derived from or caused by touch. [<L *tactus* touch. See TACT.] — **tac′tu·al·ly** *adv.*

Ta·cu·ba·ya (tä′ko͞o·bä′yä) A western section of Mexico City; site of the national astronomical observatory.

tad (tad) *n.* A little boy or girl; young child. [Prob. short for TADPOLE]

Tad·de·o (täd·dā′ō) Italian form of THADDEUS.

Ta·de·o (tä·thā′ō) Spanish form of THADDEUS.

tad·pole (tad′pōl) *n.* The aquatic larva of an amphibian, as a frog or toad, breathing by external gills and having a tail with extended membrane giving it a fishlike form. See FROG. [ME *taddepol* < *tadde* toad + *poll* head]

Ta·dzhik *n. pl.* **-dzhik** One of a people of Iranian descent inhabiting Tadzhikistan and other republics.

Tadzhikistan (also **Tajikistan**) A republic formed after the dissolution of the U.S.S.R., with five regions and provinces; capital, Dushanbe: 55,300 square miles.

tae (tā) *n. Scot.* **1** A toe. **2** The prong of a fork.

tae·di·um vi·tae (tē′dē·əm vī′tē) *Latin* Weariness of life.

Tae·dong (tī·do͝ong) A river of central and SW North Korea, flowing 245 miles SW to the Yellow Sea at Korea Bay near Chinnampo.

Tae·gu (tī·go͞o) A city in SE South Korea. *Japanese* **Tai·kyu** (tī·kyo͞o).

Tae·jon (tī·jôn) A city of SW central South Korea. *Japanese* **Tai·den** (tī·den).

tael (tāl) *n.* **1** An Oriental weight varying from 1 to 2 1/2 ounces, commonly about 1 1/3 ounces. **2** A Chinese monetary unit of varying value. [<Pg. <Malay *tahil*]

ta'en (tān) *Scot.* Taken: a contraction.

tae·ni·a (tē′nē·ə) *n.* **1** In classical antiquity, a band, ribbon, or fillet for containing the hair. **2** *Archit.* A band or fillet between the Doric frieze and the architrave. **3** *Anat.* A band or strip of tissue, especially one of several ribbonlike arrangements of white substance in the brain, or one of the three longitudinal muscular bands of the colon. **4** *Zool.* A tapeworm (genus *Taenia*). Also spelled *tenia.* [<L <Gk. *tainia* fillet, tape]

tae·ni·a·cide (tē′nē·ə·sīd′), **tae·ni·a·fuge** (tē′nē·ə·fyo͞oj′), etc. See TENIACIDE, etc.

taf·fer·el (taf′ər·əl, -ə·rel) *n. Naut.* **1** A taffrail. **2** Originally, the upper part of a vessel's stern. [<MDu. *tafereel* panel, picture, dim. of *tafel* table, panel <L *tabula* board]

taf·fe·ta (taf′ə·tə) *n.* A fine, glossy, uncorded, somewhat stiff silk fabric: a term variously applied at different times, as to certain silk-and-linen or silk-and-wool mixtures, now also to rayon. — *adj.* Made of or resembling taffeta; also, lacy; filmy; delicate. [<OF *taffetas* <Med. L *taffeta* <Persian *tāftah* < *tāftan* twist]

taff·rail (taf′rāl′) *n. Naut.* **1** The rail around a vessel's stern. **2** The upper part of a vessel's stern. [Alter. of TAFFEREL, after RAIL[1]]

taffrail log A screw log.

taf·fy (taf′ē) *n.* **1** A confection made of brown sugar or molasses, mixed with butter, boiled down, and pulled into long ropes until it cools sufficiently to hold its shape: also spelled *toffee, toffy.* **2** *Colloq.* Flattery; blarney. [Origin unknown]

taf·i·a (taf′ē·ə) *n.* A spirituous liquor resembling rum, distilled in the West Indies from impure molasses or from refuse sugar. Also **taf′fi·a.** [< native name, prob. ult. <Malay *tāfia* spirit distilled from molasses]

Ta·fi·lelt (tä·fē′lelt) The largest Saharan oasis in SE Morocco; 200 square miles. Also **Ta·fi′lalt, Ta·fi′let** (-let).

Taft (taft), **Lorado,** 1860–1936, U. S. sculptor. — **Robert A.,** 1899–1953, U. S. lawyer and politician; son of W. H. Taft. — **William Howard,** 1857–1930, U. S. statesman; president of the United States 1909–13.

tag[1] (tag) *n.* **1** Something tacked on or attached to something else; appendage. **2** A label tied or tacked on, as to a trunk; loosely, any label. **3** A loose, ragged edge of anything; tatter. **4** The tail or tip of the tail of any animal. **5** A matted and ragged lock of wool on a sheep; a loose lock of hair. **6** A worthless leaving; remnant; ort. **7** A flap or loop, as for drawing on a boot. **8** An aglet. **9** A decorative flourish, as on a signature. **10** In angling, a piece of bright material surrounding the shank of the hook in an artificial fly. **11** A lamb or yearling sheep. **12** A well-known quotation or saying, as in a song, poem, or book. **13** The refrain of a song or poem; also, the final lines of a speech in a play; catchword; cue. **14** The crowd; rabble: often in the phrases **rag and tag** and **rag, tag, and bobtail.** — *v.* **tagged, tag·ging** *v.t.* **1** To supply, adorn, fit, mark, or label with a tag. **2** To shear away tags from (sheep). **3** To follow closely or persistently. — *v.i.* **4** To follow closely at one's heels: The little boy *tagged* along. [Prob. <Scand. Cf. Sw. *tagg* spike, tooth, Norw. *tagge* tooth.]

tag[2] (tag) *n.* A juvenile game in which the object of the players is to keep from being caught or touched by one, the tagger (usually called "it"), who chases them for that purpose. — *v.t.* **tagged, tag·ging** To overtake and touch, as in the game of tag. [<TAG[1]]

Ta·ga·log *n.* **1** A member of a Malay people native to the Philippines, especially Luzon. **2** The principal native language of the Philippines, belonging to the Indonesian subfamily of the Austronesian family of languages.

Ta·gan·rog A port of SW Russia, on the **Gulf of Taganrog,** a NE arm of the Sea of Azov.

tag day A day on which contributions are solicited for eleemosynary and other institutions: so called from the custom of giving a tag to each donor.

tagged atom *Physics* A radioisotope which betrays its presence in any part of a system into which it has been introduced.

tag·ger (tag′ər) *n.* **1** One who or that which tags or is tagged. **2** *pl.* Very thin tin plate.

tag·lock (tag′lok′) *n.* Daglock. [Var. of DAGLOCK]

tag·meme (tag′mēm) *n. Ling.* The smallest unit of grammatical form having meaning. [<Gk. *tagma* arrangement + *-eme,* on analogy with *phoneme* and *morpheme*] — **tag·me′mics** *n.*

Ta·gore (tə·gôr′, -gōr′, tä′gôr), **Sir Rabindranath,** 1861–1941, Hindu philosopher and poet.

ta·gua nut (tä′gwä) The ivory nut. [< native Colombian name]

Ta·gus (tā′gəs) A river in west central Spain and central Portugal, flowing 566 miles SW to the Atlantic at Lisbon: Spanish *Tajo,* Portuguese *Tejo.*

Ta·hi·ti (tä·hē′tē, tī′tē) The largest island of the Society group; 600 square miles; capital, Papeete; formerly *Otaheite.*

Ta·hi·ti·an (tä·hē′tē·ən, -shən) *adj.* Of or relating to Tahiti, its people, or their language. — *n.* **1** One of the native Polynesian people of Tahiti. **2** The Polynesian language of the Tahitians.

Ta·hoe (tä′hō, tā′-), **Lake** A lake on the boundary between California and Nevada; 195 square miles; elevation, 6,225 feet.

tah·sil·dar (tä′sēl·där′) *n.* An Indian officer of customs; a tax-collector. Also **tah′seel·dar′.** [<Hind. *tahsīldār* <Arabic *tahsīl* a collection + Persian *dār* holder]

Tai (tī) See THAI.

Tai·an (tī′än′) A city of western Shantung province, China.

Tai·chung (tī′cho͝ong′) A city in west central Taiwan; an agricultural and industrial center.

tai·ga (tī′gə) *n.* The far northern coniferous forest of Siberia and by extension of Eurasia and America, extending to the northern limit of trees. [<Russian]

Tai·ho·ku (tī·hō·ko͞o) The Japanese name for TAIPEH.

tail[1] (tāl) *n.* **1** The hindmost part or rear end of an animal's body, especially when prolonged beyond the rest of the body. ◆ Collateral adjective: *caudal.* **2** Any slender, flexible, terminal prolongation of the body of a structure: the *tail* of a shirt or kite. **3** *Astron.* The luminous sheaf extending from the nucleus of a comet. **4** The hind, back, or inferior portion of anything. **5** *pl. Colloq.* The reverse side of a coin. **6** The lower end of a stream or pool. **7** Anything of tail-like appearance; a body of persons in single file; a queue; also, a retinue or suite. **8** A pigtail. **9** *Aeron.* One of several fixed horizontal or vertical surfaces of an airplane structure placed at some distance to the rear of the main bearing surfaces. **10** The rear portion of a bomb, projectile, rocket, or guided missile, usually equipped with vanes. **11**

The bottom of a printed page. 12 *pl. Colloq.* A man's full-dress suit; also, a swallow-tailed coat. 13 The back end of a wagon. 14 *Colloq.* The trail or course taken by a fugitive: The police were on his *tail.* — *v.t.* 1 To furnish with a tail. 2 To cut off the tail of. 3 To be the tail or end of: to *tail* a procession. 4 To join (one thing) to the end of another. 5 To insert and fasten by one end, as a beam into a wall: with *in* or *on.* 6 *Colloq.* To follow secretly and stealthily; shadow. — *v.i.* 7 To extend or proceed in a line. 8 *Colloq.* To follow close behind. 9 To diminish gradually: His voice *tailed* off. 10 To be inserted and fastened at one end, as a beam. 11 *Naut.* To swing or go aground stern foremost: The ship *tailed* into the wind. — *adj.* 1 Rearmost; hindmost: the *tail* end. 2 Following; coming from behind: a *tail* wind. ◆ Homophone: *tale.* [OE *tægl*] — **tail′less** *adj.*

tail² (tāl) *Law adj.* Restricted; limited; abridged; restricted in succession to particular heirs: an estate *tail.* — *n.* A cutting off, abridgment, or limitation of ownership; an entail: an estate in *tail.* ◆ Homophone: *tale.* [<OF *taillié,* pp. of *taillier* cut]

Tai Lake (tī) One of China's largest lakes, on the Kiangsu–Chekiang border, between Shanghai and Nanking; 40 miles long, 30 miles wide. *Chinese* **T'ai Hu** (tī′hōō′).

tail beam Tailpiece (def. 4).

tail coverts *Ornithol.* The feathers that lie at the base of the tail feathers above and below.

tail·first (tāl′fûrst′) *adv.* Backward; with the hind side foremost. Also **tail′fore′most** (-fôr′·mōst, -fōr′-).

tail·gate (tāl′gāt′) *n.* 1 A hinged or vertically sliding board or gate closing the back end of a truck, wagon, etc. Also **tail·board** (tāl′bôrd′, -bōrd′). 2 One of the gates at the lower level of a canal lock. — *v.t.* & *v.i.* **·gat·ed, ·gat·ing** *U.S. Slang* To drive too close behind for safety: impatient drivers *tailgating* in a no-passing zone.

tail gun A gun mounted in the tail section of an airplane.

tail–heav·y (tāl′hev′ē) *adj.* Having too much weight at the rear: a *tail–heavy* airplane: opposed to *nose–heavy.*

tail·ing (tā′ling) *n.* 1 Refuse or residue from grain after milling, or from ground ore after washing: usually plural. 2 The inner, covered portion of a projecting brick or stone.

taille (tāl, *Fr.* tä′y′) *n.* In feudal France, a tax levied by a king or lord from which nobles and clergy were exempt. [<OF < *taillier* cut]

tail light A light attached to the rear of a vehicle. Also **tail lamp.**

tai·lor (tā′lər) *n.* One who makes to order or repairs men's or women's outer garments. — *v.i.* 1 To do a tailor's work. — *v.t.* 2 To fit with garments: He is well *tailored.* 3 To work at or make by tailoring: to *tailor* a coat. ◆ Collateral adjective: *sartorial.* [<OF *tailleor* < *taillier* cut <LL *taliare* split, cut, prob. <L *talea* rod]

tailor bee Any of certain leaf-cutting bees (family *Megachilidae*) that line their nests with pieces of leaves.

tai·lor·bird (tā′lər·bûrd′) *n.* A bird (genus *Sutoria*) of Asia and Africa, related to the warblers, that stitches leaves together to form a receptacle for its nest. See illustration under NEST.

tai·lor·ing (tā′lər·ing) *n.* 1 A tailor's trade or occupation. 2 The making or altering of a garment by a tailor. 3 The style and fit resulting from the work of a tailor.

tai·lor–made (tā′lər·mād′) *adj.* Made by a tailor: said especially of women's clothes of a plain, close-fitting, usually heavier type, as for walking, etc.: opposed to *ready–made.* — *n. Colloq.* A commercially prepared cigarette, as opposed to one which is rolled by hand.

tail·piece (tāl′pēs′) *n.* 1 Any endpiece or appendage. 2 In a violin or similar instrument, a piece of wood, as ebony, at the sounding-board end, having the strings fastened to it. 3 *Printing* An ornamental design on the lower blank portion of a short page. 4 A piece inserted by tailing, as a floor timber.

tail·race (tāl′rās′) *n.* 1 That part of a millrace below the water wheel, bearing away the spent water. 2 *Mining* The channel for water to remove tailings.

tail·skid (tāl′skid′) *n. Aeron.* A runner fixed beneath the tail of an airplane.

tail·spin (tāl′spin′) *n.* 1 *Aeron.* The descent of an airplane along a helical path at a steep angle, either by accident or with power of recovery by manipulation of the controls. 2 *Colloq.* A sudden, sharp, emotional upheaval, often resulting in loss of control: He went into a *tailspin* over her.

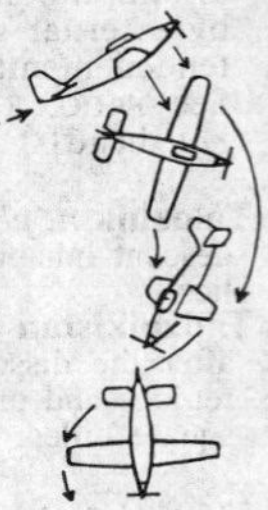
TAILSPIN

tail·stock (tāl′stok′) *n.* That standard or stock of a lathe through which passes the non-rotating spindle or dead center.

tail wind A wind blowing in the same general direction as the flight of an aircraft or course of a ship.

Tai·mir Peninsula (tī·mir′, tī′mir) A large peninsula of northern Asiatic Russian S.F.S.R., extending 700 miles NE to SW, between the Kara and Laptev seas. Also **Tai·myr′.**

tain¹ (tān) *n.* 1 Very thin plate. 2 Tinfoil suitable for backing mirrors. [Prob. aphetic var. of F *étain* tin]

tain² (tôn) *n.* Literally, a cattle raid; by extension, any of numerous Old Irish epics about a cattle raid. [<Irish *táin*]

Tai·nan (tī′nän′) A city of west central Taiwan.

Tai·na·ron (te′nä·rôn), **Cape** See MATAPAN, CAPE.

Tain Bo Cuail·gne (tôn bō kōōl′nyē) The Cattle Raid of Cooley: title of the most famous epic in the Ulster cycle of Old Irish literature, and the oldest epic of all western Europe, embodying the life and exploits of Cuchulain and his single-handed defense of Ulster against the hosts of Connacht. [<Irish *táin* cattle raid + *bo* cow (<L *bos* ox) + *Cuailgne* Cooley, a hill district in County Louth]

Taine (tān, *Fr.* ten), **Hippolyte Adolphe,** 1828–93, French literary critic and historian.

Tai·no (tī′nō) *n. pl.* **·nos** 1 A member of an extinct tribe of Indian aborigines of the West Indies, especially Haiti, probably the first encountered by Columbus. 2 The Arawakan language of this tribe.

taint (tānt) *v.t.* 1 To imbue with an offensive, noxious, or deteriorating quality or principle; infect with decay; render corrupt or poisonous. 2 To render morally corrupt or vitiated; contaminate; pollute. 3 *Obs.* To tincture; tinge. — *v.i.* 4 To be or become tainted. See synonyms under POLLUTE. — *n.* 1 A trace or germ of decay; a cause or result of corruption. 2 A moral stain or blemish; spot. [Fusion of aphetic form of ATTAINT and F *teint,* pp. of *teindre* tinge, color <L *tingere*]

Tai·pei (tī′pā′) The capital of Taiwan, in the northern part: Japanese *Taihoku.* Also **Tai′·peh′, T'ai′–pei′.**

Tai·ping (tī′ping′) *n.* An insurgent in the **Taiping Rebellion** in China (1850–64) led by one Hung-siu-tsuen, who sought to replace the Manchu dynasty with a native dynasty called the T'ai-p'ing Chao (Great Peace Dynasty): suppressed with the aid of a corps of Chinese led by Charles George Gordon. [<Chinese, great peace]

Tai·ping (tī′ping′) A tin-mining center and city in Perak state, NW Malaya.

Tai·sho (tī·shō) The title of the reign (1912–26) of Yoshihito, emperor of Japan. [<Japanese, great righteousness]

Tai·wan (tī′wän′) An island off the coast of SE China, comprising a province, and, together with the Pescadores, the National Republic of China; 13,890 square miles; capital, Taipei; ceded to Japan, 1895–1945; formerly *Formosa.* — **Tai′wan′ese′** (-ēz, -ēs) *n.* & *adj.*

Tai·yü·an (tī′yü·än′) The capital of Shansi province, China.

Ta'iz (ta·iz′) 1 A province of SW Yemen. 2 The capital of Ta'iz province, residence of the Imam of Yemen and the second capital of the country.

taj (täj) *n. Persian* A diadem or crown; a headdress of distinction; specifically, a tall cap worn by Moslem dervishes.

Ta·jik (tä·jēk′, -jik′) See TADZHIK.

Ta·jik S.S.R. (tä·jēk′, -jik′) See TADZHIK S.S.R.

Taj Ma·hal (täj′ mə·häl′, täzh′) A mausoleum of white marble built (1631–45) by the emperor Shah Jehan at Agra, India, containing the tombs of his favorite wife and of himself.

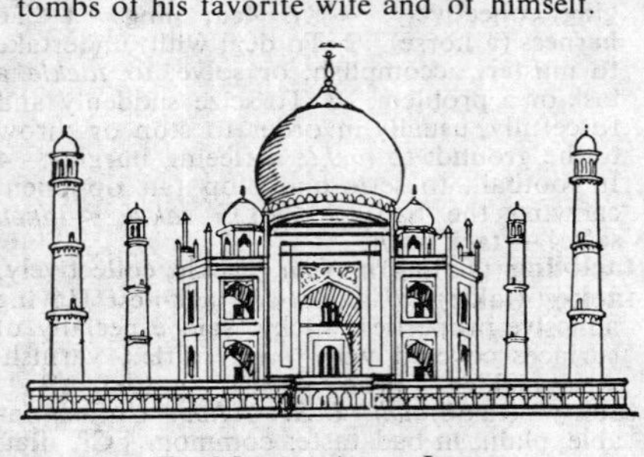
TAJ MAHAL, AGRA, INDIA.

Ta·jo (tä′hō) The Spanish name for the TAGUS.

Ta·ju·mul·co (tä′hōō·mōōl′kō) An extinct volcano in SW Guatemala; highest point in central America; 13,816 feet.

Ta·ka·mat·su (tä·kä·mät·sōō) A port in northern Shikoku, Japan.

Ta·ka·o·ka (tä·kä·ō·kä) A port of north central Honshu, Japan, a rice-trading and manufacturing center.

take (tāk) *v.* **took, tak·en, tak·ing** *v.t.* 1 To lay hold of; grasp. 2 To get possession of; seize. 3 To seize forcibly; capture; catch. 4 To catch in a trap or snare. 5 To gain in competition; win. 6 To choose; select. 7 To obtain by purchase; buy. 8 To rent or hire; lease: to *take* lodgings. 9 To receive regularly by payment; subscribe to, as a periodical. 10 To assume occupancy of: to *take* a chair. 11 To assume the responsibilities or duties of: to *take* office. 12 To bring or accept into some relation to oneself: He *took* a wife. 13 To assume as a symbol or badge: to *take* the veil. 14 To impose upon oneself; subject oneself to: to *take* a vow. 15 To remove or carry off: with *away.* 16 To remove from the proper place; misappropriate; steal. 17 To remove by death. 18 To subtract or deduct. 19 To be subjected to; undergo: to *take* a beating. 20 To submit to; accept passively: to *take* an insult. 21 To become affected with; contract: He *took* cold. 22 To affect: The fever *took* him at dawn. 23 To captivate; charm or delight: The dress *took* her fancy. 24 To conduct oneself in response to; react to: How did she *take* the news? 25 To undertake to deal with; contend with; handle: to *take* an examination. 26 To consider; deem: I *take* him for an honest man. 27 To understand; comprehend. 28 To strike in a specified place; hit: The blow *took* him on the forehead. 29 *Colloq.* To aim or direct: He *took* a shot at the target. 30 To carry with one; transport; convey: *Take* your umbrella! 31 To lead: This road *takes* you to town. 32 To escort; conduct: Who *took* her to the dance? 33 To receive into the body, as by eating, inhaling, etc.: *Take* a deep breath. 34 To accept, as something offered, due, or given; have conferred on one: to *take* a bribe; to *take* a degree. 35 To let in; admit: The ship is *taking* water; The car will *take* only six people. 36 To indulge oneself in; enjoy: to *take* a nap. 37 To perform, as an action: to *take* a stride. 38 To avail oneself of (an opportunity, etc.). 39 To put into effect; adopt: to *take* measures; to *take* advice. 40 To use up or consume; require as necessary; demand: The piano *takes* too much space; That *takes* a lot of nerve. 41 To make use of; apply: They *took* clubs to him; to *take* pains. 42 To travel by means of: to *take* a train to Boston. 43 To go to; seek: to *take* cover. 44 To ascertain or obtain by measuring, computing, etc.: to *take* a census. 45 To obtain or derive from some source; adopt or copy. 46 To obtain by writing; write down or copy: to *take* notes. 47 To obtain a likeness or representation of, as by drawing or photographing; also, to obtain (a likeness, picture, etc.) in such a manner. 48 To experience; feel: to *take* pride in an achievement. 49 To conceive or feel: She *took* a dislike to him. 50 To become impregnated with; absorb: The cloth will not *take* the pattern. 51 *Slang* To cheat; deceive. 52 *Gram.* To require by construction or usage: The verb

takes a direct object. —*v.i.* **53** To get possession. **54** To engage; catch, as mechanical parts. **55** To begin to grow; germinate. **56** To have the intended effect: The vaccination *took*. **57** To become popular; gain favor or currency, as a play. **58** To admit of being photographed: His face *takes* well. **59** To detract: with *from*. **60** To become (ill or sick). **61** To make one's way; go. See synonyms under ABSTRACT, ASSUME, CARRY, CATCH. —**to take after** **1** To resemble. **2** To follow as an example. —**to take amiss** To be offended by. —**to take at one's word** To believe. —**to take back** **1** To regain. **2** To retract. —**to take breath** To pause, as from working. —**to take down** **1** To pull down, as a building. **2** To dismantle; disassemble. **3** To humble. **4** To write down; make a record of. —**to take heart** To gain courage or confidence. —**to take in** **1** To admit; receive. **2** To lessen in size or scope. **3** To furl or brail (sail). **4** To include; embrace. **5** To understand. **6** To cheat or deceive. **7** To visit as part of a tour: Did you *take in* the Louvre? **8** To receive into one's home for pay, as lodgers or work. —**to take in vain** To use profanely or blasphemously, as the name of a deity. —**to take it** **1** To assume; understand. **2** To endure hardship, abuse, etc. —**to take off** **1** To remove, as a coat. **2** To carry away. **3** To kill. **4** To deduct. **5** To mimic; burlesque. **6** To rise from the ground or water in starting a flight, as an airplane. **7** To leave; depart. —**to take on** **1** To hire; employ. **2** To undertake to deal with; handle. **3** *Colloq.* To exhibit violent emotion. —**to take out** **1** To extract; remove. **2** To obtain from the proper authority, as a license or patent. **3** To lead or escort. —**to take over** **1** To assume control of. **2** To convey. —**to take place** To happen. —**to take stock** **1** To make an inventory. **2** To estimate probability, position, etc.; consider. —**to take the field** To begin a campaign or game. —**to take to** **1** To betake oneself to: to *take to* one's bed. **2** To develop the practice of, or an addiction to: He *took to* drink. **3** To become fond of; be attracted by. —**to take to heart** To be deeply affected by. —**to take up** **1** To raise or lift. **2** To make smaller or less; shorten or tighten. **3** To pay, as a note or mortgage. **4** To accept as stipulated: to *take up* an option. **5** To begin or begin again; resume. **6** To reprove or criticize. **7** To occupy, engage, or consume, as space or time. **8** To acquire an interest in or devotion to: to *take up* a cause. —**to take up with** *Colloq.* To become friendly with; associate with. —*n.* **1** The act of taking, or that which is taken. **2** An uninterrupted run of the camera and sound apparatus in recording any portion of a motion picture. **3** *Slang* The money collected; receipts. **4** The quantity collected at one time: the *take* of fish. [OE *tacan* <ON *taka*]

take-down (tāk′doun′) *adj.* Fitted for being taken apart or down easily: a *take-down* shack; a *take-down* rifle. —*n.* **1** Any article so constructed as to be taken apart easily. **2** The part of a take-down mechanism by means of which it is taken apart or down. **3** *Colloq.* The act of humiliating any one; humiliation.

take-home pay (tāk′hōm′) The remainder of one's wages or salary after tax and other payroll deductions.

take-in (tāk′in′) *n. Colloq.* An act of cheating or hoaxing.

take-off (tāk′ôf′, -of′) *n.* **1** *Colloq.* A satirical representation; caricature. **2** In horsemanship and athletics, the spot at which the feet leave the ground in leaping. **3** *Aeron.* The act of rising from and leaving the ground or water in an aircraft flight.

tak·er (tā′kər) *n.* One who takes; specifically, one who accepts a wager; also, a collector: a ticket *taker*.

take-up (tāk′up′) *n.* **1** *Mech.* A device for taking up lost motion or drawing in the slack of a thing, as in a loom. **2** The act of tightening or taking up.

tak·ing (tā′king) *adj.* **1** Fascinating; captivating. **2** *Colloq.* Contagious; infectious. —*n.* **1** The act of one who takes. **2** The thing or things taken; in fishing, a catch; haul; in the plural, receipts, as of money. **3** *Obs.* Agitation; perplexity; distress. —**tak′ing·ly** *adv.* —**tak′ing·ness** *n.*

Ta·kla·ma·kan (tä′klä′mä′kän′) A desert in the SW third of the Sinkiang-Uigur Autonomous Region, NW China. Also **Ta′kla′ Ma′kan′**.

Ta·ku (tä′kōō′) A port on the Gulf of Chihli, eastern Hopeh province, NE China.

tal·a·poin (tal′ə·poin) *n.* **1** A Buddhist priest or monk. **2** A West African monkey (*Cercopithecus talapoin*) of the guenon group, smallest of the Old World monkeys. [<Pg. *talapões*, pl. of *talapão* <Burmese *tala poi* our master]

ta·lar (tā′lər) *n. Archaic* A cloak or robe reaching to the ankles. [<L *talaris* of the ankles < *talus* ankle]

ta·lar·i·a (tə·lâr′ē·ə) *n. pl. Latin* Winged boots or sandals, or wings springing directly from the ankles: used in antique art as attributes of Mercury, Perseus, etc.

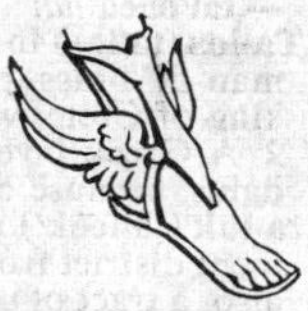

TALARIA

Ta·laud Islands (tä′lout) An Indonesian island group NE of Celebes; 495 square miles. Also **Ta·laur Islands** (tä′·lour).

Ta·la·ve·ra de la Rei·na (tä′lä·vā′rä thā lä rā′nä) A city of central Spain on the Tagus river; scene of a battle between Wellington and Joseph Bonaparte, 1809.

tal·bot (tôl′bət, tal′-) *n.* A sleuthhound, supposed to be related to the bloodhound. [after *Talbot*, English family name]

talc (talk) *n.* A soft, hydrous magnesium silicate, $H_2Mg_3(SiO_3)_4$, used in making paper, soap, toilet powder, lubricants, etc. Soapstone and French chalk are varieties of talc. —*v.t.* **talcked** or **talced, talck·ing** or **talc·ing** To treat with talc: to *talc* a photographic plate. [<F <Med. L *talcum* <Arabian *talq* <Persian *talk*]

Tal·ca (täl′kä) A city of central Chile; birthplace of Chile's independence, 1818; destroyed by earthquake, 1928.

talc·ose (tal′kōs) *adj.* Composed of or containing talc. Also **talc′ous** (tal′kəs).

tal·cum (tal′kəm) *n.* Talc. [<Med. L. See TALC.]

talcum powder Finely powdered and purified talc, used as a dusting agent, filter, and for the relief of chafed skin and prickly heat.

tale (tāl) *n.* **1** That which is told or related; a story; recital. **2** Hence, a connected narrative or account, whether oral or written, of an actual, legendary, or fictitious event or series of events. **3** An idle or malicious report; a piece of gossip. **4** A deliberately untrue story; a lie; falsehood. **5** *Archaic* A counting or enumeration; reckoning; numbering. **6** *Archaic* That which is counted; an amount; total; sum. **7** *Obs.* Speech; talk; also, the language of a country. ◆ Homophone: *tail*. [OE *talu* speech, narrative. Akin to TELL, TALK.]

tale·bear·er (tāl′bâr′ər) *n.* One who tells mischievous tales about other persons. —**tale′·bear′ing** *adj.* & *n.*

tal·ent (tal′ənt) *n.* **1** Mental endowments or capacities of a superior character; marked mental ability; also, mental ability in general. **2** A particular and uncommon aptitude for some special work or activity; a faculty or gift: a usage founded on a Scriptural parable (*Matt.* xxv 14–30), mental power being considered as a divine trust. **3** People of skill or ability, collectively: the *talent* of stage, screen, and radio. **4** *U.S. Slang* In horse-racing circles, those who make bets or take odds on their individual judgment and responsibility: distinguished from the bookmakers. **5** An ancient weight and denomination of money, varying in weight and value among different nations and in different periods. **6** *Obs.* Inclination; disposition. See synonyms under ABILITY, GENIUS. [OE *talente* appetite, will, inclination <L *talentum*, a sum of money <Gk. *talanton* weight, thing weighed]

tal·ent·ed (tal′ən·tid) *adj.* Having mental ability; gifted. See synonyms under CLEVER.

talent scout One whose business it is to discover talented or exceptionally gifted people, especially those suitable for dramatic or motion-picture careers.

ta·ler (tä′lər) *n.* A former German silver coin, the prototype of all dollars, issued in Bohemia and first dated 1518; a dollar: also spelled *thaler*. [<G. See DOLLAR.]

ta·les (tā′lēz) *n. pl.* **·les** (-lēz) *Law* **1** Persons to be summoned for jury duty to make up a deficiency when the regular panel is exhausted by challenges. **2** The writ for summoning such persons. [<L *tales (de circumstantibus)* such (of the bystanders), pl. of *talis* such a one; the phrase is from the writ summoning them]

tales·man (tālz′mən) *n. pl.* **·men** (-mən) One summoned to make up a jury when the regular panel is exhausted. [<TALES + MAN]

tale·tel·ler (tāl′tel′ər) *n.* **1** One who tells stories, etc.; a raconteur. **2** A talebearer. —**tale′tell′ing** *adj.* & *n.*

Ta·lien (dä′lyen′) The Chinese name for DAIREN.

tal·i·grade (tal′ə·grād) *adj. Zool.* Walking on the outer surface of the foot. [<L *talus* ankle + -GRADE]

tal·i·on (tal′ē·ən) *n.* Retaliation, as a form of justice. [<F <L *talio, -onis* < *talis* such]

tal·i·ped (tal′ə·ped) *adj.* Suffering from or afflicted with talipes; clubfooted. —*n.* A clubfooted person. [See TALIPES]

tal·i·pes (tal′ə·pēz) *n. Pathol.* **1** Malformation of the foot. **2** A clubfoot. [<NL <L *talus* ankle + *pes, pedis* foot]

tal·i·pom·a·nus (tal′ə·pom′ə·nəs) *n. Pathol.* Clubhand. [< *talipo-* (<TALIPES) + L *manus* a hand]

tal·i·pot (tal′ə·pot) *n.* A stately and valuable East Indian palm (*Corypha umbraculifera*) crowned by large leaves often used as fans, umbrellas, and as a house covering. Also **talipot palm.** [<Bengali *tālipāt* palm leaf <Skt. *tālī* fan palm + *pattra* leaf]

tal·is·man (tal′is·mən, -iz-) *n. pl.* **·mans** **1** Something supposed to produce or capable of producing extraordinary effects; a charm. **2** An astrological charm or symbol supposed to benefit or protect the possessor, especially by exerting magical or occult influence; in a wider sense, any amulet. [<F <Sp. <Arabic *ṭilsam, ṭilasm* magic figure <LGk. *telesma* a sacred rite <Gk. *teleein* initiate < *telos* end, completion]

Synonyms: amulet, charm. An *amulet* or *talisman* is strictly a material object; a *charm* may be a movement or a form of words. An *amulet* is ordinarily worn upon the person as a protection against disease, injury, or death. A *talisman* is any object supposed to work wonders, like Aladdin's lamp, whether kept in one's possession or not.

tal·is·man·ic (tal′is·man′ik) *adj.* Exerting magical or occult power. Also **tal′is·man′i·cal.**

talk (tôk) *v.i.* **1** To express or exchange thoughts in audible words; communicate by speech; speak or converse. **2** To communicate by means other than speech: to *talk* with one's fingers. **3** To speak irrelevantly; prate; chatter. **4** To confer; consult. **5** To gossip. **6** To make sounds suggestive of speech. **7** *Colloq.* To give information; inform. —*v.t.* **8** To express in words; utter. **9** To use in speaking; converse in: to *talk* Spanish. **10** To converse about; discuss: to *talk* business. **11** To bring to a specified condition or state by talking: to *talk* one into doing something. **12** To pass or spend, as time, in talking. —**to talk back** To answer impudently. —**to talk big** *Slang* To brag; boast. —**to talk down** To silence by talking; outtalk. —**to talk down to** To speak to (an audience of lower or supposedly lower intelligence than one's own) in simple, obvious words; speak to patronizingly. —**to talk shop** To talk about one's work. —**to talk up** **1** To discuss, especially so as to promote; praise; extol. **2** *Colloq.* To speak loudly or boldly. —*n.* **1** The act of talking; conversation; speech, especially when informal. **2** Report, rumor: We heard *talk* of war. **3** That which is talked about; a topic; theme; subject of conversation. **4** A conference for discussion or deliberation; a council. **5** Mere words; verbiage. **6** A language, dialect, or lingo; an argot:

baseball *talk.* See synonyms under CONVERSATION. [ME *talken,* prob. freq. of *talen,* OE *talian* reckon, speak. Related to TELL, TALE.]

Synonyms (verb): chat, chatter, converse, discourse, speak. To *talk* is to utter a succession of connected words, ordinarily with the expectation of being listened to. To *speak* is to give articulate utterance even to a single word; the officer *speaks* the word of command, but does not *talk* it. To *chat* is ordinarily to utter in a familiar, conversational way; to *chatter* is to *talk* in an empty, ceaseless way like a magpie. See SPEAK.

talk·a·thon (tô′kə·thon′) *n. Colloq.* A prolonged session of talking, debating, etc. [< TALK + (MAR)ATHON]

talk·a·tive (tô′kə·tiv) *adj.* Given to much talking. See synonyms under GARRULOUS. — **talk′a·tive·ly** *adv.* — **talk′a·tive·ness** *n.*

talk·er (tô′kər) *n.* One who talks; also, a loquacious person.

talk·ie (tô′kē) *n. Colloq.* A motion picture with spoken words and sound effects. Also **talking picture.**

talking machine A phonograph.

talk·ing-to (tô′king·tōō′) *n. pl.* **·tos** *Colloq.* A scolding; berating.

talk show A television or radio show in which a well-known personality interviews invited guests, often celebrities, in TV usually before a live audience.

talk·y (tô′kē) *adj.* **talk·i·er, talk·i·est** Talkative.

tall (tôl) *adj.* **1** Having more than average height; high or lofty: a *tall* building. **2** Having specified height: He is five feet *tall.* **3** *Colloq.* Inordinate; extravagant; boastful: *tall* talk; also, unbelievable; remarkable: a *tall* story. **4** *Colloq.* Large; excellent; grand: a *tall* dinner. **5** *Obs.* Handsome; fine; proud. **6** *Obs.* Brave; sturdy; spirited. — *adv. Colloq.* Proudly; handsomely: He walks *tall.* [OE *getæl* swift, prompt] — **tall′ness** *n.*

tal·lage (tal′ij) *n.* In old English law, any form of assessment or taxation for raising revenue, including subsidies and customs. — *v.t.* **·laged, ·lag·ing** To tax. [<OF *taillage* < *taille* a tax, a cutting < *taillier* cut. See TAILOR.]

Tal·la·has·see (tal′ə·has′ē) The capital of Florida, in the northern part.

tall·boy (tôl′boi′) *n.* **1** *Brit.* A highboy. **2** A variety of chimney pot.

Tal·ley·rand-Pé·ri·gord (tal′ē·rand·pā′ri·gôr, *Fr.* tà·le·räṅ′pā·rē·gôr′), **Charles Maurice de,** 1754–1838, French statesman.

Tal·linn (täl′lin) The capital of Estonia, a port in the NW part, on the Gulf of Finland: German *Reval,* Russian *Revel.* Also **Tal′lin.**

tall·ish (tô′lish) *adj.* Rather tall.

tal·lith (tal′ith, tä′lis) *n.* A fringed mantle of fine linen, originally covering the head and falling over the shoulders, now worn around the shoulders by Jews engaged in prayer. [< Hebrew *tallīth* cover, sheet, robe]

tall oil A fatty resinous liquid obtained as a by-product from wood pulp: it is used as an emulsifying agent in various manufacturing processes. [<Sw. *tallöl* pine oil]

tal·low (tal′ō) *n.* **1** A mixture of the harder animal fats, as of beef or mutton, refined for use in candles, soaps, oleomargarine, etc. **2** A vegetable fat obtained from the bayberry. — *v.t.* **1** To smear with tallow. **2** To fatten. [ME *talgh,* prob. <MLG *talg, talch*] — **tal′low·y** *adj.*

tal·ly (tal′ē) *n. pl.* **·lies** **1** A piece of wood on which notches or scores are cut as marks of number. **2** A score or mark; hence, a reckoning; account. **3** A counterpart; duplicate. **4** A mark indicative of tale or number: used to denote one in a series. **5** A label; tag. — *v.* **·lied, ·ly·ing** *v.t.* **1** To score on a tally; mark; record. **2** To reckon; count; estimate: often with *up.* **3** To mark or cut corresponding notches in; cause to correspond. — *v.i.* **4** To correspond; agree precisely; fit: His story *tallies* with yours. **5** To keep score. [<AF *tallie* <L *talea* rod, cutting] — **tal′li·er** *n.*

tal·ly·ho (tal′ē·hō′) *interj.* A huntsman's cry to hounds when the quarry is sighted. — *n.* **1** The cry of "tallyho." **2** A four-in-hand coach. — *v.t.* To urge on, as hounds, with the cry of "tallyho." — *v.i.* To cry "tallyho." [Alter. of F *taïaut,* a hunting cry]

tal·ly·man (tal′ē·mən) *n. pl.* **·men** (-mən) **1** One who keeps a count or a tally, especially of votes. **2** One who keeps a record of number, volume, and measurement, as of timber.

Tal·mi gold (tal′mē) Gold shell. [<G, orig. a trade name]

Tal·mud (tal′mud, täl′mōōd) *n.* The body of Jewish civil and religious law (and related commentaries and discussion) not comprised in the Pentateuch, commonly including the Mishna and the Gemara, but sometimes limited to the latter. [<Hebrew *talmūdh* instruction < *lāmadh* learn] — **Tal·mud′ic** or **·i·cal** *adj.* — **Tal′mud·ist** *n.*

tal·on (tal′ən) *n.* **1** The claw of a bird or other animal, especially of a bird of prey: often applied figuratively, as to a grasping human hand. **2** A projection on the bolt of a lock on which the key presses in shooting the bolt. **3** In card games, the part of a pack left on the table after the deal; the stock. **4** The heel of a sword blade. [<OF, spur <L *talus* heel] — **tal′oned** *adj.*

Ta·los (tā′los) In Greek mythology: **1** A giant man of brass presented by Zeus to Minos, king of Crete, who used him as a watchman. **2** A Greek inventor killed by his uncle, Daedalus, because of jealousy. Also **Ta′lus** (-ləs).

ta·luk (tä·lōōk′) *n.* In parts of India, a government district from which a revenue is derived; also, a tract of proprietary land; an estate. [< Arabic *ta'alluq* estate]

ta·lus (tā′ləs) *n. pl.* **·li** (-lī) **1** *Anat.* The astragalus. **2** A slope, as of a tapering wall. **3** *Geol.* The sloping mass of rock fragments below a cliff. Compare SCREE. **4** The slope given to the face of an earthwork or other fortification. [<L, ankle, heel]

tam (tam) *n.* A tam-o'-shanter.

tam·a·ble (tā′mə·bəl) *adj.* Capable of being tamed. Also **tame′a·ble.**

ta·ma·le (tə·mä′lē) *n.* A Mexican dish made of crushed Indian corn and meat, seasoned with red pepper, wrapped in corn husks, dipped in oil, and cooked by steam. Also **ta·mal** (tə·mäl′). [<Am. Sp. *tamales,* pl. of *tamal* < Nahuatl *tamalli*]

Tam·al·pais (tam′əl·pī′əs), **Mount** A peak in western California, across the Golden Gate from San Francisco; 2,604 feet.

ta·man·dua (tə·man′dwə, tä′män·dwä′) *n.* A small arboreal ant-eater *(Tamandua tetradactyla)* of Central and South America. Also **tam·an·du** (tam′ən·dōō). [<Pg. <Tupian < *taixi* ant + *mondê* catch]

tam·a·rack (tam′ə·rak) *n.* **1** The American larch *(Larix laricina)* common all over northern North America. **2** Its wood: also called *hackmatack.* **3** The lodgepole pine of the Pacific coast. [<Algonquian]

ta·ma·rau (tä′mə·rou′) *n.* A small, dark-brown, short-horned buffalo (genus *Anoa*) of the island of Mindoro, standing about 40 inches high. Also spelled *timarau.* [< native name]

tam·a·rin (tam′ə·rin) *n.* One of various squirrel-like marmosets of Guiana and the Amazon valley; especially, the **silky tamarin** *(Leontocebus rosalia).* [<F < native Cariban name]

tam·a·rind (tam′ə·rind) *n.* **1** A tropical tree *(Tamarindus indica)* of the bean family, with hard yellow wood, pinnate leaves, and showy yellow flowers striped with red. **2** The fruit of this tree, a flat pod with soft acid pulp used in preserves and as a laxative drink. [<Sp. *tamarindo* <Arabic *tamr hindi* Indian date]

tam·a·risk (tam′ə·risk) *n.* An evergreen shrub (genus *Tamarix*) of the Mediterranean region, western Asia, and India, with slender branches bearing small, pinkish-white flowers in racemes. [<LL *tamariscus,* var. of L *tamarix* a tamarisk]

ta·ma·sha (tə·mä′shə) *n.* In India, any form of public procession, display, or entertainment; a show. [<Arabic *tamāsha* sightseeing, walking around]

Ta·ma·tave (tä′mä·täv′) A port of Madagascar, on the Indian Ocean, chief port of Malagasy Republic.

Ta·ma·u·li·pas (tä′mä·ōō·lē′päs) A state of NE Mexico, bordering on the United States and the Gulf of Mexico; 30,731 square miles; capital, Ciudad Victoria.

Ta·ma·yo (tä·mä′yō), **Rufino,** born 1899, Mexican painter.

tam·bac (tam′bak) See TOMBAC.

Tam·bo·ra (täm′bō·rä) A volcano on northern Sumbawa; 9,255 feet.

tam·bour (tam′bōōr) *n.* **1** A drum. **2** A light wooden frame, usually circular, on which material for embroidering may be stretched; also, a fabric embroidered on such a frame. **3** A palisade for defending an entrance to a fortified work. — *v.t.* & *v.i.* To embroider on a tambour. [<F <Arabic *ṭambūr* a stringed instrument; prob. infl. in meaning by OF *tabour* a tabor]

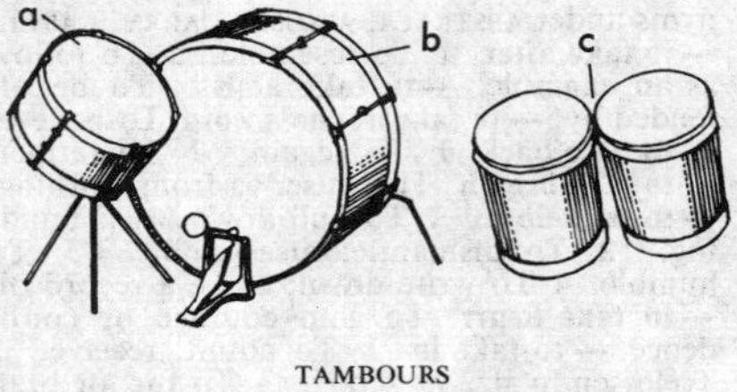

TAMBOURS
a. Snare drum. *b.* Bass drum. *c.* Bongo drums.

tam·bou·rin (tam′bə·rin) *n.* **1** A long, narrow, oblong drum, originating in Provence. **2** A gay, 18th century Provençal dance, or the music accompanying it. [<F, dim. of *tambour*]

tam·bou·rine (tam′bə·rēn′) *n.* A musical instrument like the head of a drum, with jingles in the rim, played by striking it with the hand; a timbrel. [<F]

Tam·bov (täm·bôf′) A city in south central European Russian S.F.S.R.

tame (tām) *adj.* **tam·er, tam·est** **1** Having lost its native wildness or shyness; domesticated. **2** In agriculture, brought under or produced by cultivation: *tame* hay or land. **3** Docile; tractable; hence, subdued or subjugated; spiritless; also, gentle; harmless. **4** Lacking in effectiveness; uninteresting; dull; flat; insipid. See synonyms under DOCILE, FLAT, MEAGER. — *v.t.* **tamed, tam·ing** **1** To make tame; domesticate. **2** To bring into subjection or obedience; conquer or take the spirit or heart from; render spiritless. **3** To tone down; soften, as glaring colors. See synonyms under RECLAIM. [OE *tam*] — **tame′ly** *adv.* — **tame′·ness** *n.* — **tam′er** *n.*

ta·mein (tä·mīn′) *n.* A draped garment, similar to an Indian sari, worn by Burmese women. [<Burmese *thamein*]

tame·less (tām′lis) *adj.* Untamable. — **tame′·less·ness** *n.*

Tam·er·lane (tam′ər·lān), 1336?–1405, Tatar conqueror of Asia: also called *Timour, Timur.* Also **Tam·bur·laine** (tam′bər·lān).

Tam·il (tam′əl, tum′əl) *n.* **1** One of an ancient Dravidian people, and still the most numerous of the inhabitants of southern India and northern Ceylon. **2** Their language, the oldest and most widely used of the Dravidian languages.

tam·is (tam′is) *n.* **1** A strainer of cloth or gauze. **2** A fabric used for straining. Also **tam′my.** [<F, sieve]

Tam·ma·ny (tam′ə·nē) *n.* A fraternal society in New York City (founded 1789) serving as the central organization of the city's Democratic party: more commonly **Tammany Hall,** from its meeting place. The name has often been associated with political bossism. Also called **Tammany Society.** [Alter. of *Tamanend,* lit., the affable, name of a 17th c. Delaware Indian chief noted for his friendliness toward white men]

Tam·mer·fors (täm′mər·fôrs′) The Swedish name for TAMPERE.

Tam·mer·kos·ki (täm′mer·kos′kē) The Finnish name for TAMPERE.

Tam·muz (täm′mōōz, *in Biblical usage* tam′uz) **1** In Babylonian mythology, the husband of Ishtar and god of agriculture, whose annual death and resurrection symbolize the cycle of months. **2** A Hebrew month. See CALENDAR (Hebrew). Also spelled *Thammuz.* Also **Tam·uz** (tam′uz). [<Hebrew]

tam-o'-shan·ter (tam′ə·shan′tər) *n.* A Scottish cap with a tight headband and a full, flat top, sometimes with a pompon or tassel. [after TAM O' SHANTER]

Tam o' Shan·ter (tam′ ə shan′tər) In Robert Burns's poem *Tam o' Shanter,* the hero, a drunken farmer, who fancies himself pursued by witches.

tamp (tamp) *v.t.* **1** To force down or pack closer by firm, repeated blows. **2** To ram

down, as a packing on a charge in a blasthole, in order to increase the explosive effect. — *n.* A tamper. [Back formation <TAMPION]

Tam·pa (tam′pə) A port of entry on **Tampa Bay,** an arm of the Gulf of Mexico in central western Florida.

tam·pa·la (tam′pə·lə) *n.* A horticultural variety of an Asian plant (*Amaranthus tricolor*), cultivated in the United States and esteemed for its edible, spinachlike leaves. [<Hind.]

tam·pan (tam′pan) *n.* A soft-bodied tick (genus *Argas*) of cosmopolitan distribution, a dangerous bloodsucking parasite of poultry whose bite is often injurious to men. Also called *miana bug.* [< native S. African name]

tam·per[1] (tam′pər) *v.i.* **1** To meddle; interfere: usually with *with.* **2** To make changes, especially so as to damage, corrupt, etc.: with *with*: to *tamper* with a manuscript. **3** To use corrupt measures, as bribery; scheme or plot. [Var. of TEMPER] — **tam′per·er** *n.*

tamp·er[2] (tam′pər) *n.* **1** One who tamps. **2** An instrument for tamping. **3** *Physics* A reflector (def. 4).

Tam·pe·re (täm′pe·re) A city in SW Finland: Swedish *Tammerfors*, Finnish *Tammerkoski.*

Tam·pi·co (tam·pē′kō, *Sp.* täm·pē′kō) A port on the Gulf of Mexico in SE Tamaulipas state, NE Mexico.

Tampico fiber Istle.

tam·pi·on (tam′pē·ən) *n.* A tompion. [<F *tampon*, nasal var. of *tapon, tape* a bung < Gmc.]

tam·pon (tam′pon) *n. Med.* A plug of cotton or lint for insertion in a wound or body cavity. — *v.t.* To plug up, as a wound, with a tampon. [See TAMPION]

tam-tam (tum′tum′) *n.* **1** A type of drum, used in the East Indies and western Africa. See TOM-TOM. **2** A Chinese gong. — *v.i.* To play on a tam-tam. [<Hind.; imit. in origin]

tan (tan) *v.* **tanned, tan·ning** *v.t.* **1** To convert into leather, as hides or skins, by treatment with an infusion of tannin obtained from the bark of the oak, hemlock, etc. **2** To make durable or hard, as fishnets or sails. **3** To bronze, as the skin, by exposure to sunlight. **4** *Colloq.* To thrash; flog. — *v.i.* **5** To become tanned, as hides or the skin. — *n.* **1** *Chem.* **a** Tanbark. **b** Tannin. **2** A yellowish-brown color tinged with red. **3** A dark or brown coloring of the skin, resulting from exposure to the sun: a coat of *tan.* — *adj.* **1** Of a yellowish- or reddish-brown; tan-colored. **2** Used in or pertaining to tanning. [OE *tannian* <Med. L *tannare* < *tanum* tanbark, prob. <Celtic. Cf. Breton *tann* oak.]

Ta·na (tä′nä) A river in SE Kenya, Africa, flowing about 500 miles east and south to the Indian Ocean.

Ta·na (tä′nä), **Lake** A lake in northern Ethiopia, source of the Blue Nile; the largest lake in Ethiopia; about 1,400 square miles: also *Tsana.*

tan·a·ger (tan′ə·jər) *n.* Any of a family (*Thraupidae*) of arboreal oscine American birds related to the finches and noted for the brilliant plumage of the male. Most of the species are tropical, but a few migrate to the United States, especially the **scarlet tanager** (*Piranga erythromelas*) and the **western tanager** (*P. ludoviciana*). [<NL *tanagra* <Pg. *tangara* <Tupian] — **tan′a·grine** (-grēn) *adj.*

Tan·a·gra (tan′ə·grə, tə·nag′rə) A village in eastern Boeotia, east central Greece; known for the terra-cotta figurines excavated there.

Tan·a·is (tan′ə·is) An ancient name for the DON (def. 1).

Ta·na·na·rive (tä·nä·nä·rēv′) The capital of Malagasy Republic, in the central part: English *Antananarivo.* Also **Ta·na′na·ri′vo** (-rē′vō).

Ta·na·na River (tä′nä·nä′) A river of western Yukon and central and eastern Alaska, flowing 600 miles from near the Alaskan border to the Yukon River in central Alaska.

tan·bark (tan′bärk′) *n.* **1** The bark of certain trees, especially oak or hemlock, containing tannin in quantity, and used in tanning leather. **2** Spent bark from the tan vats, used on circus arenas, racetracks, etc.

Tan·cred (tang′krid), 1078?-1112, Norman hero of the first crusade.

tan·dem (tan′dəm) *adv.* One in front of or before another: said of two or more persons or things so arranged, and of horses harnessed in single file instead of abreast. — *n.* **1** Two or more horses harnessed and driven in single file; also, such a turnout, including both horses and vehicle. **2** A bicycle with seats for two persons, one behind the other: also **tandem bicycle. 3** Any arrangement of two or more persons or things placed one before another. — *adj.* Consisting of or being two arranged one before another. [<L, at length (of time); used in puns in sense of "lengthwise"]

Tan·djung·pi·nang (tän·jōong′pē·näng′) A seaport SE of Singapore, capital of the Riouw Archipelago province of Indonesia.

Tan·djung·pri·ok (tän′jōong·prē′ôk) See TANJUNGPRIOK.

Ta·ney (tä′nē), **Roger Brooke,** 1777-1864, U. S. jurist; chief justice of Supreme Court 1836-64.

tang[1] (tang) *n.* **1** A slender shank or tongue projecting from some metal part, as the end of a sword blade or of a chisel, for inserting into or fixing upon a handle, hilt, etc.; also, a tonguelike part, as of a belt buckle. **2** A penetrating taste, flavor, or odor, sometimes a disagreeable one; also, a trace; hint: a *tang* of pepper. **3** Any distinct quality, other than one that is sweet. — *v.t.* To provide with a tang. [<ON *tongi* a point, dagger]

tang[2] (tang) See TWANG.

Tang (täng) A Chinese dynasty, 618-907, under which China enjoyed its greatest period of literature and art.

Tan·gan·yi·ka (tan′gən·yē′kə, tang′-) A region of Tanzania in eastern Africa; 361,800 square miles; capital, Dar es Salaam.

Tan·gan·yi·ka (tan′gən·yē′kə, tang′-), **Lake** A lake in the Great Rift Valley of east central Africa, SW of Victoria Nyanza; 12,700 square miles; 400 miles long; the longest and deepest (4,700 feet) lake in Africa, second deepest fresh-water body in the world.

tan·ge·lo (tan′jə·lō) *n. pl.* **·los 1** A loose-skinned orangelike fruit, a hybrid of the tangerine and the pomelo. **2** The tree (genus *Citrus*) on which it grows. [<TANG(ERINE) + (POM)ELO]

tan·gen·cy (tan′jən·sē) *n. pl.* **·cies** The state of being tangent. Also **tan′gence.**

tan·gent (tan′jənt) *adj.* **1** *Geom.* Meeting at a point or along a line without further coincidence or intersection: said of either or both of two lines or surfaces so touching. **2** Touching; in contact. — *n.* **1** *Geom.* **a** A line tangent to a curve at any point. **b** The straight line through two coincident points of a curve. **c** The length of a tangent line from the point of contact to the axis of abscissas. **2** *Trig.* One of the functions of an angle; the quotient of the ordinate divided by the abscissa. **3** A sharp change in course or direction. — **to fly (or go) off on a tangent** *Colloq.* To make a sharp or sudden change in direction or course of action. [<L *tangens, -entis,* ppr. of *tangere* touch]

tan·gen·tial (tan·jen′shəl) *adj.* **1** Of, pertaining to, or moving in the direction of a tangent. **2** Touching slightly. **3** Divergent. Also **tan·gen′tal** (-jen′təl). — **tan·gen′ti·al′i·ty** (-shē·al′ə·tē) *n.* — **tan·gen′tial·ly** *adv.*

tan·ger·ine (tan′jə·rēn′) *n.* **1** A small, juicy orange with a loose, easily removed skin; a variety of mandarin (def. 2). **2** A slightly burnt-orange color, like the color of the tangerine. [from *Tangier*]

Tan·ger·ine (tan′jə·rēn′) *adj.* Of or pertaining to Tangier, Morocco. — *n.* A native or inhabitant of Tangier.

tan·gi·ble (tan′jə·bəl) *adj.* **1** Perceptible by touch; also, within reach by touch. **2** Figuratively, capable of being apprehended by the mind; of definite shape; not elusive or unreal: *tangible* evidence. **3** *Law* Perceptible to the senses; corporeal; material: *tangible* property. See synonyms under EVIDENT, PHYSICAL. — *n.* **1** That which is tangible. **2** *pl.* Material assets. [<F <L *tangibilis* < *tangere* touch] — **tan′gi·bil′i·ty, tan′gi·ble·ness** *n.* — **tan′gi·bly** *adv.*

Tan·gier (tan·jir′) A port on the northernmost coast of Morocco; formerly an international zone (**Tangier International Zone;** 225 square miles). French **Tan·ger** (tän·zhä′).

tan·gle[1] (tang′gəl) *v.* **·gled, ·gling** *v.t.* **1** To twist or involve in a confused and not readily separable mass. **2** To complicate; ensnare as in a tangle; trap; enmesh. — *v.i.* **3** To be or become entangled. — **to tangle with** *Colloq.* To embroil oneself with. — *n.* **1** A confused intertwining, as of threads or hairs; a snarl. **2** Hence, a state of confusion or complication; a jumbled mess. **3** A state of perplexity or bewilderment. [Nasalized var. of obs. *tagle* <Scand. Cf. dial. Sw. *taggla* disorder.] — **tan′gler** *n.*

tan·gle[2] (tang′gəl) *n.* **1** An edible seaweed (genus *Laminaria*). **2** *Scot.* A tall, lean person. [<ON *thöngull*]

tan·gle·ber·ry (tang′gəl·ber′ē) *n. pl.* **·ries** The blue huckleberry (*Gaylussacia frondosa*) of the eastern United States: also called *dangle-berry.*

tan·gly (tang′glē) *adj.* Consisting of or being in a tangle.

tan·go (tang′gō) *n. pl.* **·gos 1** Any of several Latin-American dances, originally from Argentina, in 2/4 time and characterized by deliberate gliding steps and low dips. **2** Any syncopated tune or melody to which the tango may be danced. — *v.i.* To dance the tango. [<Am. Sp., fiesta <Sp., gipsy dance]

tan·gram (tang′grəm) *n.* A Chinese puzzle consisting of a square card or board cut by straight incisions into different-sized pieces (5 triangles, a square, and a rhomboid) to be combined into a variety of figures. [Arbitrary coinage, after ANAGRAM]

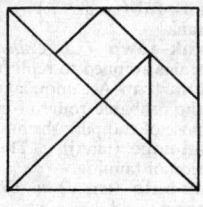

tang·y (tang′ē) *adj.* **tang·i·er, tang·i·est** Having a tang in taste or odor; pungent.

TANGRAM

Ta·nim·bar Islands (tə·nim′bär, tan′im·bär) An Indonesian island group in the Banda Sea; total, 2,172 square miles: also *Timorlaut.*

Ta·nis (tä′nis) An ancient city of Lower Egypt in the Nile delta: Old Testament *Zoan.*

tan·ist (tan′ist, thôn′-) *n.* Among the ancient Celts, the heir apparent to a chieftainship, elected in the lifetime of a chief from among the chief's kinsmen. [<Irish *tánaiste* second, heir presumptive]

tan·ist·ry (tan′ist·rē, thôn′-) *n.* The succession and life tenure relating to a tanist.

tan·jib (tun·jéb′) *n.* A kind of fine muslin fabric made in India. [<Bengali <Persian *tan-zib,* lit., ornament of the body]

Tan·jore (tan·jōr′, -jôr′) A city in SE Madras State, India.

Tan·jung·pri·ok (tän′jōong·prē′ôk) A port of NW Java, the principal port of Indonesia and port for Jakarta: also *Tandjungpriok.*

U. S. ARMY TANK M 48 A 2

tank (tangk) *n.* **1** A large vessel, basin, or receptacle for holding a fluid. **2** Any natural pool or pond. **3** *Mil.* A heavily armored combat vehicle of the Caterpillar tractor type, propelled by internal-combustion engines and mounting guns of various calibers.

—*v.t.* To place or store in a tank. [<Pg. *tanque,* aphetic var. of *estanque* <L *stagnum* pool] — **tank′less** *adj.* —**tank′like′** *adj.*

tan·ka[1] (tang′kə) *n.* **1** A Japanese verse form consisting of five lines, of which the first and third have five syllables, and the rest seven. **2** A poem imitating the Japanese tanka in verse form. [<Japanese]

tan·ka[2] (tang′kə) *n. pl.* **·ka** A descendant of an aboriginal race living on watercraft at Canton, China. [<Chinese *tankia* <*tan* egg + *chia* family, people]

tank·age (tangk′ij) *n.* **1** The act, process, or operation of putting in tanks. **2** The price for storage in tanks. **3** The capacity or contents of a tank. **4** Slaughterhouse waste, as bones and entrails, from which the fat has been rendered: used, when dried, as a fertilizer or coarse feed.

tank·ard (tangk′ərd) *n.* A large, one-handled drinking cup, usually made of pewter or silver, often with a cover. [<MDu. *tanckaert* <Med. L *tancardus,* prob. metathetic var. of L *cantharus* tankard, large goblet]

tank destroyer A motor vehicle equipped with an anti-tank gun.

tank·er (tangk′ər) *n.* A cargo vessel especially constructed for the transport of oil and gasoline.

tank farming Hydroponics. —**tank farmer**

tank·ful (tangk′fo͞ol′) *n.* The quantity that fills a tank.

tank town *U.S. Colloq.* A small town where trains stopped to refill from a water tank.

tank trap A camouflaged ditch excavated along the probable route of enemy tanks for the purpose of trapping them.

tan·nage (tan′ij) *n.* The act, process, or operation of tanning.

tan·nate (tan′āt) *n. Chem.* A salt or ester of tannic acid.

tanned (tand) Past tense and past participle of TAN.

Tan·nen·berg (tän′ən·berkh) A village in NE Poland; scene of major Russian defeat by German forces, 1914.

tan·ner[1] (tan′ər) *n.* One who tans hides.

tan·ner[2] (tan′ər) *n. Brit. Colloq.* A sixpence. [Origin unknown]

tan·ner·y (tan′ər·ē) *n. pl.* **·ner·ies** A place where leather is tanned.

Tann·häu·ser (tän′hoi·zər) A German minnesinger and crusader of the 13th century, identified with a legendary knight who gives himself up to revelry with Venus and her court, then makes a trip to Rome to seek absolution; hero of an opera by Wagner.

tan·nic (tan′ik) *adj.* Pertaining to or derived from tannin or tanbark.

tan·nif·er·ous (ta·nif′ər·əs) *adj.* Having or yielding tannin. [<TANNI(N) + -FEROUS]

tan·nin (tan′in) *n. Chem.* Any of a group of amorphous, brownish-white, astringent compounds that form shiny scales when extracted, as with water, from gallnuts, sumac, etc. Their principal applications in the arts are in the preparation of ink and the manufacture of leather. Also **tannic acid.** [<F *tanin* <*tan* tan]

tan·ning (tan′ing) *n.* **1** The art or process of converting hides into leather. **2** A bronzing, as of the skin, by exposure to the sun, etc.

tan·rec (tan′rek) See TENREC.

tan·sy (tan′zē) *n. pl.* **·sies** Any of a genus *(Tanacetum)* of coarse perennial herbs; especially, a species *(T. vulgare)* with yellow flowers and a strongly aromatic and bitter taste, used in medicine for its tonic properties. [<OF *tanesie,* aphetic var. of *athanasie* <LL *athanasia* <Gk., immortality]

tan·ta·late (tan′tə·lāt) *n. Chem.* A salt of tantalic acid.

tan·tal·ic (tan·tal′ik) *adj.* **1** Pertaining to tantalum; containing tantalum in its higher valence. **2** Designating a colorless crystalline acid, $HTaO_3$, derived from tantalum oxide, Ta_2O_5.

tan·ta·lite (tan′tə·līt) *n.* An iron-black ferrous tantalate, $FeTa_2O_6$, having a submetallic luster.

tan·ta·lize (tan′tə·līz) *v.t.* **·lized, ·liz·ing** To tease or torment by repeated frustration of hopes or desires. Also *Brit.* **tan′ta·lise.** [from *Tantalus*] — **tan′ta·li·za′tion** *n.* —**tan′ta·liz′er** *n.* —**tan′·ta·liz′ing·ly** *adv.*

tan·ta·lum (tan′tə·ləm) *n.* A very hard, heavy, gray, faintly radioactive metallic element (symbol Ta, atomic number 73), nonirritating and unaffected by body liquids, used in alloys and surgical appliances. See PERIODIC TABLE. [<TANTALUS; from its inability to absorb water]

Tan·ta·lus (tan′tə·ləs) In Greek mythology, a rich king, son of Zeus and father of Pelops and Niobe, who was punished in Hades for revealing the secrets of Zeus by being made to stand in water that receded when he tried to drink, and under fruit-laden branches he could not reach.

tan·ta·mount (tan′tə·mount) *adj.* Having equivalent value, effect, or import; equivalent: with *to.* [<AF *tant amunter* amount to as much <L *tantus* as much + OF *amonter* amount. See AMOUNT.]

tan·ta·ra (tan′tə·rä′, tan·tar′ə, -tä′rə) *n.* A quick succession of notes from a horn; also, a hunting cry. [Imit.]

tan·tiv·y (tan·tiv′ē) *adj.* Swift; rapid. —*n. pl.* **·tiv·ies 1** A hunting cry indicating that the chase is at full speed. **2** *Obs.* A rapid, rushing movement. —*adv.* Swiftly; with all speed. [Prob. imit. of the horse's gallop]

tant mieux (täṅ myœ′) *French* So much the better.

tan·to (tän′tō) *adv. Italian* So much; too much: especially in the musical direction **non tanto,** not too much.

tant pis (täṅ pē′) *French* So much the worse.

tan·trum (tan′trəm) *n.* A petulant fit of passion. [Origin unknown]

Tan·zan·i·a (tan′zə·nē′ə) An independent member of the Commonwealth of Nations consisting of a federation of Tanganyika and Zanzibar in eastern Africa; 362,800 square miles; capital, Dar es Salaam.

Tao·ism (dou′iz·əm, tou′-) *n.* One of the principal religions or philosophies of China, founded about 500 B.C. by Lâo-tse, who taught that happiness could be acquired through obedience to the requirements of man's nature and the simplification of social and political relations, in accordance with the Tao, or Way, the basic principle of the cosmos from which all of nature proceeds. [<Chinese *tao* way, road] —**Tao′ist** *adj.* & *n.* —**Tao·is′tic** *adj.*

Ta·os (tä′ōs) A resort town in northern New Mexico.

tap[1] (tap) *n.* **1** An arrangement for drawing out liquid, as beer from a cask. **2** A faucet or cock; spigot; also, a plug or stopper to close an opening in a cask or other vessel. **3** Liquor drawn from a tap; also, a particular liquor or quality of liquor contained in casks. **4** *Brit.* A place where liquor is served; a bar; taproom. **5** A tool for cutting internal screw threads. **6** A point of connection for an electrical circuit. **7** The act or an instance of wiretapping. —**on tap 1** Contained in a cask; ready for tapping: beer *on tap.* **2** Provided with a tap. **3** Available; ready. —*v.t.* **tapped, tap·ping 1** To provide with a tap or spigot. **2** To pierce or open so as to draw liquid from: to *tap* a sugar-maple tree. **3** To draw (liquid) from a container. **4** To make connection with: to *tap* a gas main. **5** To make connection with secretly: to *tap* a telephone wire. **6** To make an internal screw thread in with a tap: to *tap* a nut. [OE *tæppa*]

tap[2] (tap) *v.* **tapped, tap·ping** *v.t.* **1** To touch or strike gently. **2** To make or produce by tapping. **3** To apply leather to (the sole or heel of a shoe) in repair. —*v.i.* **4** To strike a light blow or blows, as with the finger tip. —*n.* **1** A gentle or playful blow. **2** Leather, etc., affixed to a shoe sole or heel; also, a metal plate on the toe or heel of a tap-dancer's shoe. **3** *pl.* A military signal by trumpet or beat of drum, sounded after tattoo, for the extinguishing of all lights in soldiers' quarters: often played after a military burial. [<OF *taper*]

ta·pa (tä′pä) *n.* The bark of the Asian paper-mulberry tree *(Broussonetia papyrifera),* used in making a kind of cloth, **tapa cloth.** [<native Polynesian name]

tap·a·der·a (tap′ə·dâr′ə) *n.* The leather hood of the stirrup of a Mexican saddle. Also **tap′a·der′o.** [<Sp., cover <*tapar* stop up]

Ta·pa·jós (tä′pə·zhôs′) A river of central and NE Brazil, flowing 500 miles NE from SW Pará state to the Amazon at Santerém.

tap·a·lo (tap′ə·lō) *n. pl.* **·los** A scarf or shawl of coarse cloth worn in Latin-American countries. [<Am. Sp., lit., cover it, imperative of *tapar* cover + *lo* it]

tap-dance (tap′dans′, -däns′) *v.i.* To dance or perform a tap dance. —**tap′-danc′er** *n.*

tap dance A dance, usually solo, in which the dancer emphasizes his steps by tapping the floor with the heels or toes of shoes or clogs designed to make audible the rhythm.

tape (tāp) *n.* **1** A narrow, stout strip of woven fabric. **2** Any long, narrow, flat strip of paper, metal, or the like, as the magnetic strip used in a tape recorder. **3** A tapeline. **4** Red tape. **5** A string or thread stretched breast-high across the finishing point of a racetrack and broken by the winner of the race. —*v.t.* **taped, tap·ing 1** To wrap or secure with tape; also, to bandage: to *tape* a boxer's hands. **2** To measure with or as with a tapeline. **3** To record on magnetic tape. [OE *tæppe* strip of cloth] —**tap′er** *n.*

tape deck An assembly of magnetic head, tape reels, and drive for tape recording and playback.

tape·line (tāp′līn′) *n.* A tape for measuring distances. Also **tape measure.**

ta·per (tā′pər) *n.* **1** A small candle; a burning wick or other light substance giving but feeble illumination. **2** A gradual diminution of size in an elongated object: the *taper* of a mast; also, any tapering object, as a cone. —*v.t.* & *v.i.* **1** To make or become smaller or thinner toward one end. **2** To lessen gradually; diminish: with *off.* —*adj.* Growing small by degrees in one direction. ◆ Homophone: *tapir.* [OE, dissimilated var. of Med. L *papyrus* taper, wick <L, papyrus; from the use of the pith of the papyrus as a wick]

tape-re·cord (tāp′ri·kôrd′) *v.t.* To tape (*v.* def. 3).

tape recorder An electromagnetic apparatus which records by the effect of sound waves upon the particles adhering to a magnetic tape: in the playback the magnetic patterns are reconverted into the original electrical impulses and sound waves.

tap·es·try (tap′is·trē) *n. pl.* **·tries 1** A loosely woven, ornamental fabric used for hangings, in which the woof is supplied by a spindle, the design being formed by stitches across the warp. **2** Loosely, a fabric imitating this process. —*v.t.* **·tried, ·try·ing** To adorn with tapestry. [<OF *tapisserie* <*tapis* carpet <L *tapete* <Gk. *tapētion,* dim. of *tapēs* rug]

tapestry carpet A carpet in which the fabric is woven after the designs are first printed.

ta·pe·tum (tə·pē′təm) *n. pl.* **·ta** (-tə) **1** *Bot.* A nutrient layer of cells lining the sporangium or the anther of certain plants. **2** *Zool.* A membranous layer, especially the iridescent portion of the choroid coat in certain animals whose eyes shine in the dark. **3** *Anat.* A layer of fibers of the corpus callosum. [<LL <L *tapete* carpet]

tape·worm (tāp′wûrm′) *n.* Any of various cestode worms (class *Cestoda*) with segmented, ribbonlike bodies, parasitic on the intestines of vertebrates; especially, the common pork tapeworm *(Taenia solium)* of man.

taph·e·pho·bi·a (taf′ə·fō′bē·ə) *n. Psychiatry* A morbid fear of being buried alive. [<Gk. *taphē* a grave + -PHOBIA] —**taph′e·pho′bic** *adj.*

taph·on·o·my (taf·on′ə·mē) *n.* The scientific study of the natural processes affecting the formation and modification of fossils. [<Gk. *taphē* grave + -NOMY] —**taph′o·nom′ik** (taf′ə·nom′ik) *adj.*

tap house An inn; tavern; also, a barroom.

tap·i·o·ca (tap′ē·ō′kə) *n.* A nutritious starchy substance having irregular grains, obtained from cassava. [<Sp. <Tupi *tipioca* juice of the cassava <*ty* juice + *pŷa* heart + *ocô* be removed]

ta·pir (tā′pər) *n.* A large, ungulate, herbivorous, typically nocturnal mammal (family *Tapiridae*), having short stout limbs and flexible proboscis, with the nostrils near the end. The tapir of South and Central America is brownish-black, that of the Malay Peninsula black and white. ◆ Homophone: *taper.* [<Sp. <Tupi *tapy′ra* tapir]

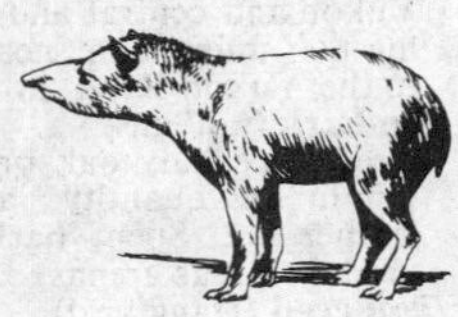

BRAZILIAN TAPIR
(From 3 to 3 1/2 feet high)

tap·is (tap′ē, tap′is; *Fr.* tá·pē′) *n.* Tapestry, formerly used as a cover of a council table: now only in the phrase **on the tapis** (up for consideration). [<F. See TAPESTRY.]

ta·pis·sier (tá·pē·syā′) *n. French* 1 A tapestry-maker. 2 An upholsterer. — **ta·pis·sière** (tá·pē·syâr′) *n. fem.*

Tap·pan Zee (tap′ən zā′) An expansion of the Hudson River in SE New York above New York City; 10 miles long and 3 miles wide.

tap·per (tap′ər) *n.* One who or that which taps, in any sense.

tap·pet (tap′it) *n. Mech.* A projecting arm of a mechanism, to operate an unattached part automatically, as to impart the motion of a cam to a valve. [<TAP²]

tappet rod *Mech.* A reciprocating rod bearing one or more tappets.

tap·ping (tap′ing) *n.* 1 The act of one who or that which taps in any sense. 2 Something taken by tapping, or running from a tap.

tap·pit (tap′it) *adj. Scot.* Having a tuft; crested.

tap·pit-hen (tap′it·hen′) *n.* 1 A hen having a topknot. 2 An Engish pewter measure for liquors, holding three quarts: named for the knob on the lid resembling a hen's topknot. [<dial. E (Scottish) *tappit* topped + HEN]

tap·poon (tə·pōōn′) *n.* A semicircular gate of heavy sheet iron, serving as a temporary dam for a small irrigating ditch. [<Sp. *tapón* plug < *tapar* stop up]

tap·room (tap′rōōm′, -rōōm′) *n.* A bar; bar-room.

tap·root (tap′rōōt′, -rōōt′) *n. Bot.* The principal descending root of a plant. — **tap′root′ed** *adj.*

taps (taps) See TAP² (*n.* def. 3).

tap·sal·tee·rie (tap′səl·tir′ē) *adv. Scot.* Upside down and in confusion; topsy-turvy.

tap·ster (tap′stər) *n.* One who draws and serves liquor; a bartender. [OE *tæppestre* barmaid]

Tap·ti (täp′tē) A river of west central India, flowing 450 miles west from west central Madhya Pradesh to the Gulf of Cambay just below Surat.

Ta·pu·ya (tä·pōō′yä) *n.* A Tapuyan Indian.

Ta·pu·yan (tä·pōō′yən) *n.* A large linguistic stock of South American Indians; Ge. — *adj.* Of or pertaining to this stock.

Ta·qua·rí (tä·kwə·rē′) 1 A river in south central Mato Grosso, Brazil, flowing 350 miles SW from the Goiás border to the Paraguay river near the Bolivian border. 2 A river in NE Río Grande do Sul, Brazil, flowing 200 miles west and south to the Jacuí river.

tar¹ (tär) *n.* 1 A dark, oily, viscid mixture of hydrocarbons, especially phenols, obtained by the dry distillation of resinous woods, coal, etc. 2 Coal tar. Compare ASPHALT, PITCH¹. — *v.t.* **tarred, tar·ring** To cover with or as with tar. — **to tar and feather** To smear with tar and then cover with feathers: an old form of punishment. — *adj.* Made of, derived from, or resembling tar. [OE *teru*]

tar² (tär) *n. Colloq.* A sailor. [Short for TARPAULIN]

Tar·a (tar′ə) A village of central County Meath, Ireland; seat of the ancient Irish kings until the sixth century.

tar·a·did·dle (tar′ə-did′l) See TARRADIDDLE.

Ta·ra·na·ki (tä′rä·nä′kē) The Maori name for EGMONT.

tar·an·tass (tar′ən·tas′) *n.* A large four-wheeled vehicle on longitudinal bars in place of springs and mounted on a sledge in winter. Also **tar′an·tas′**. [<Russian *tarantas*]

tar·an·tel·la (tar′ən·tel′ə) *n.* A lively Neapolitan dance in 6/8 time: once thought to be a remedy for tarantism; also, the music written for it. [<Ital., dim. of *Taranto* Taranto; infl. by *tarantola* a tarantula]

tar·ant·ism (tar′ən·tiz′əm) *n.* A nervous and hysterical disorder characterized by stupor and hypochondria which, it was supposed, could be cured only by inordinate dancing and music; dancing disease. Formerly prevalent in southern Italy, it was believed to follow the bite of a tarantula. [<Ital. *tarantismo* <*Taranto* Taranto]

Ta·ran·to (tä′rän·tō) A port in SE Italy on the Gulf of Taranto, an arm of the Ionian Sea forming the instep of the Italian boot: ancient *Tarentum*.

TARANTULA
(Body from 2 to 3 1/2 inches)

ta·ran·tu·la (tə·ran′-chōō·lə) *n. pl.* **·las** or **·lae** (-lē) 1 A large, hairy, venomous spider (*Lycosa tarentula*) of southern Europe, still popularly but erroneously supposed to cause tarantism by its bite. 2 Any of various large, hairy American spiders (family *Theraphosidae*), especially of the genus *Eurypelma* of the SW United States, dreaded for their painful but not dangerous bite. [<Med. L <Ital. *tarantola* <*Taranto* Taranto]

tarantula hawk A large wasp (genus *Pepsis*) which paralyzes tarantulas with its sting and places them in its nest as food for its young. Also **tarantula killer.**

Ta·ra·pon (tä′rä·pōn) *n.* Micronesian.

Ta·ra·wa (tä·rä′wä, tä′rä·wä) The island head-quarters of the Gilbert Islands and capital of the Gilbert and Ellice Islands colony; 8 square miles; scene of a United States victory over Japanese forces in World War II, November, 1943.

ta·rax·a·cum (tə·rak′sə·kəm) *n.* 1 Any of a genus (*Taraxacum*) of composite plants that includes the dandelion. 2 A medicinal preparation from the dried root of the common dandelion, used as a diuretic and laxative. [<NL <Arabic *tarakhshaqūq* bitter herb]

Tar·bell (tär′bel), **Ida Minerva,** 1857–1944, U. S. author.

tar·boosh (tär·bōōsh′) *n.* A brimless, usually red, felt cap with colored silk tassel, worn by Moslems. Also **tar·bush′.** [<Arabic *ṭarbūsh*]

tar camphor Naphthalene.

Tar·de·noi·si·an (tär′də·noi′zē·ən) *adj.* Of, pertaining to, or designating a subdivision of the Mesolithic culture epoch of the late Paleolithic period, related to the Azilian and characterized by small flint implements. [from *Fère-en-Tardenois*, town in NE France where remains were discovered]

TARBOOSH

Tar·dieu (tár·dyœ′), **André Pierre Gabriel Amédée,** 1876–1945, French statesman: pseudonym *George Villiers.*

tar·di·grade (tär′də·grād) *adj.* 1 Slow in motion or action; stepping or walking slowly. 2 Of or pertaining to a group (*Tardigrada*) of slow-moving microscopical arthropods, the water bears, found especially in water and damp moss. — *n.* One of the *Tardigrada.* [<F <L *tardigradus* < *tardus* slow + *gradi* walk]

tar·do (tär′dō) *adj. Music* Slow: a direction to performers. [<Ital.]

tar·dy (tär′dē) *adj.* **·di·er, ·di·est** 1 Not coming at the appointed time; dilatory; late. 2 Slow; reluctant. See synonyms under SLOW, TEDIOUS. [<F *tardif* <L *tardus* slow] — **tar′di·ly** *adv.* — **tar′di·ness** *n.*

tare¹ (târ) *n.* 1 An unidentified weed that grows among wheat, supposed to be the darnel; hence, a seed of wickedness. *Matt.* xiii 25. 2 Any one of various species of vetch; especially, the common vetch (*Vicia sativa*). ◆ Homophone: *tear¹.* [? <F *tare* defect, rejectable thing. See TARE².]

tare² (târ) *n.* 1 An allowance made to a buyer of goods by deducting from the gross weight of his purchase the weight of the container. 2 *Chem.* An empty flask or vessel used as a counterweight. — *v.t.* **tared, tar·ing** To weigh, as a vessel or package, in order to determine the amount of tare. ◆ Homophone: *tear¹.* [<F <Arabic *ṭarḥah* < *ṭaraḥa* reject, throw away]

Ta·ren·tum (tə·ren′təm) Ancient name for TARANTO.

targ (tärg) *n.* A device for indicating on a plotting board the changing positions of a target. [Back formation <TARGET]

targe¹ (tärj) *n.* A shield; rarely, a target. [<OF <OE *targa* <ON]

targe² (tärj) *v.t. Scot.* 1 To censure severely; thrash. 2 To cross-question rigidly. 3 To subject to strict discipline.

tar·get (tär′git) *n.* 1 An object presenting a surface that may be used as a mark or butt, as in rifle or archery practice; anything that is shot at. 2 One who or that which is made an object of attack or a center of attention or observation; a butt: He was the *target* of the crowd's sneers. 3 A small, variously shaped and colored signal, usually placed near a railroad track, to indicate the position of the switches. 4 The vane or sliding sight on a surveyor's rod. 5 *Electronics* That electrode of a vacuum tube on which cathode rays are focused and from which X-rays are emitted. 6 A small round shield or buckler; a targe. [OE *targette, targuete,* dim. of *targe* shield. See TARGE¹.]

tar·get·eer (tär′gə·tir′) *n.* A soldier armed with a shield.

Tar·gum (tär′gum, *Hebrew* tär·gōōm′) *n. pl.* **Tar·gums** or *Hebrew* **Tar·gu·mim** (tär′gōō·mēm′) One of various ancient paraphrases of portions of the Hebrew scriptures in Aramaic or Chaldee. [<Aramaic *targūm* interpretation] — **Tar′gum·ic** or **·i·cal** *adj.* — **Tar′gum·ist** *n.*

Tar·heel (tär′hēl′) *n. Colloq.* A native of the pine barrens of North Carolina; hence, any North Carolinian. Also **Tar Heel.**

Tarheel State Nickname of NORTH CAROLINA.

Ta·ri·fa (tä·rē′fä) A port on the Strait of Gibraltar in southern Spain.

tar·iff (tar′if) *n.* 1 A schedule of articles of merchandise with the rates of duty to be paid for their importation or exportation. 2 A duty, or duties collectively. 3 The law by which duties are imposed; also, the principles governing their imposition. 4 Any schedule of charges. — *v.t.* 1 To make a list or table of duties or customs on. 2 To fix a price or tariff on. [<Ital. *tariffa* <Arabic *ta'rif* information <*'arafa* know, inform]

Ta·rim (tä′rēm′) The principal river of the Sinkiang-Uigur Autonomous Region, NW China, flowing 1,300 miles east from the west central part, forming the northern boundary of the Taklamakan desert.

Tark·ing·ton (tär′king·tən), **Booth,** 1869–1946, U. S. novelist.

tar·la·tan (tär′lə·tən) *n.* A thin, open-mesh transparent muslin, slightly stiffened and often rather coarse. [<F *tarlatane*; ult. origin unknown]

Tar·mac (tär′mak) *n.* A paving material made from coal tar: a trade name.

tarn (tärn) *n.* A small mountain lake. [ME *terne* <ON *tjörn*]

Tarn (tärn) A river in south central France, flowing 235 miles west from the Cévennes to the Garonne below Montauban.

tar·nal (tär′nəl) *U.S. Slang adj.* Eternal; infernal; hence, damned. — *adv.* Very; damn. [Alter. of ETERNAL] — **tar′nal·ly** *adv.*

tar·na·tion (tär·nā′shən) *interj.* & *n. Dial.* Damnation: a euphemism. [Blend of TAR(NAL) + (DAM)NATION]

tar·nish (tär′nish) *v.t.* 1 To dim the luster of. 2 To dim the purity of; stain; disgrace. — *v.i.* 3 To lose luster, as by oxidation; become blemished. See synonyms under DEFILE¹, STAIN. — *n.* 1 Loss of luster; hence, a blemish. 2 The thin film of color on the exposed surface of a metal or mineral. [<OF *terniss-*, stem of *ternir* < *terne* dull, wan] — **tar′nish·a·ble** *adj.*

tarnished plant bug A common, brown-marked hemipterous insect (*Lygus pratensis*) of North America, which attacks many fruits and vegetables. For illustration see INSECTS (injurious).

Tar·no·pol (tär·nô′pôl) The Polish name for TERNOPOL.

Tar·nów (tär′nōōf) A city in southern Poland, 45 miles east of Cracow.

ta·ro (tä′rō) *n. pl.* **·ros** 1 Any one of several tropical plants (genus *Colocasia*) of the arum family, grown for their edible, cormlike rootstocks. 2 The rootstock of this plant. [<native Polynesian name]

tar·ot (tar′ō, -ət) *n.* One of a set of playing

cards with grilled or checkered backs used in Italy as early as the 14th century; also, a game played with such cards in which 22 are trumps and the other 56 are the usual Italian playing cards: used by fortune-tellers and gipsies in foretelling future events. [<F <Ital. *tarocco* < *taroccare* wrangle, play at cards; ult. origin obscure]

tar·pau·lin (tär-pô′lin, tär′pə-) *n.* 1 A waterproof canvas, impregnated with tar, for covering merchandise. 2 A sailor's wide-brimmed storm hat. 3 *Rare* A sailor. [<TAR[1] + PALL[1] + -ING[1]]

Tar·pe·ia (tär-pē′ə) The daughter of the governor of the citadel of Rome, who treacherously opened its gates to the Sabines on condition of receiving what they wore on their arms, meaning their golden bracelets. As they entered they crushed her with their shields instead. — **Tar·pe′ian** *adj.*

Tarpeian Rock A cliff upon the Capitoline Hill at Rome, from which state criminals were hurled to their death.

tar·pon (tär′pon, -pən) *n. pl.* **·pon** or **·pons** A large marine game fish with conspicuous silvery scales (*Tarpon atlanticus*) of the West Indies and the coast of Florida. [Origin unknown]

Tar·quin (tär′kwin) Anglicized name of two legendary kings of Rome, **Lucius Tarquinius Priscus** and **Lucius Tarquinius Superbus,** respectively fifth and seventh kings, of the sixth century B.C.

tar·ra·did·dle (tar′ə-did′l) *n. Colloq.* A prevarication; lie: also spelled *taradiddle.* [Origin uncertain]

tar·ra·gon (tar′ə-gon) *n.* 1 A European perennial plant (*Artemisia dracunculus*) allied to wormwood, and cultivated for its aromatic leaves which are used as seasoning. 2 The leaves of this plant. [<Sp. *taragona* <Arabic *ṭarkhun* <Gk. *drakōn* dragon]

Tar·ra·go·na (tar′ə-gō′nə) 1 A province in Catalonia, NE Spain; 2,425 square miles. 2 A manufacturing city, capital of Tarragona province, and formerly of a Roman province.

tar·ri·ance (tar′ē-əns) *n. Archaic* A tarrying; delay. [<TARRY + -ANCE]

tar·ri·er (tar′ē-ər) *n.* One who or that which tarries.

tar·row (tar′ō) *v.i. Scot.* 1 To show reluctance or hesitation; delay; tarry. 2 To feel loathing.

tar·ry[1] (tar′ē) *v.* **·ried, ·ry·ing** *v.i.* 1 To put off going or coming; linger. 2 To remain in the same place; abide; stay. 3 To wait. — *v.t.* 4 *Archaic* To wait for; await: to *tarry* his coming. See synonyms under ABIDE. — *n.* Sojourn; stay. [ME *tarien* vex, hinder, delay; fusion of OE *tergan* vex + OF *targer* delay <LL *tardicare* <L *tardare* delay <*tardus* slow]

tar·ry[2] (tär′ē) *adj.* Covered with tar; like tar.

tar·sal (tär′səl) *adj.* 1 Of, pertaining to, or situated near the tarsus or ankle. 2 Of or pertaining to the tarsi of the eye. See TARSUS.

Tar·shish (tär′shish) In the Bible, an ancient maritime country, often identified with Tartessus, in southern Spain. I *Kings* x 22.

tar·si·er (tär′sē-ər) *n.* A small, arboreal, insectivorous East Indian primate (*Tarsius spectrum*) of nocturnal habits, with large eyes and ears, long tail, and adhesive pads on elongated digits: it is the sole member of the suborder *Tarsioidea.* [<F < *tarse* tarsus; so called from its unusually long tarsal bones]

TARSIER
(Size of a small rat)

tarso– *combining form* 1 The tarsus; pertaining to the tarsus. 2 The tarsus of the eye; pertaining to the tarsal plate: *tarsoplasty,* plastic surgery of the eyelid. Also, before vowels, **tars–.** [<Gk. *tarsos* flat of the foot, edge of the eyelid]

tar·so·met·a·tar·sus (tär′sō-met′ə-tär′səs) *n. pl.* **·si** (-sī) *Ornithol.* The so-called tarsus of birds; the bone reaching from the tibia to the toes, consisting of the confluent proximal tarsal and metatarsal bones. [<NL]

tar·sus (tär′səs) *n. pl.* **·si** (-sī) 1 *Anat.* **a** The

ankle, or, in man, the group of seven bones of which it is composed. **b** A plate of connective tissue in the eyelid. 2 *Zool.* **a** The shank of a bird's leg. **b** The distal part of the leg of certain arthropods. [<NL <Gk. *tarsos* flat of the foot, any flat surface]

Tar·sus (tär′səs) 1 A port near the NE Mediterranean in southern Turkey in Asia; anciently, the capital of Cilicia, and the birthplace of St. Paul. 2 A river in southern Turkey, flowing 95 miles south from the Taurus mountains to the Mediterranean below Tarsus: ancient *Cydnus.*

tart[1] (tärt) *adj.* 1 Having a sharp, sour taste. 2 Figuratively, severe; cutting; caustic: a *tart* remark. See synonyms under BITTER. [OE *teart*] — **tart′ly** *adv.* — **tart′ness** *n.*

tart[2] (tärt) *n.* 1 A small pastry shell with fruit or custard filling, and without a top crust, as distinguished from a pie. 2 In England, an uncovered fruit pie. 3 *Slang* A girl or woman of loose morality. [<OF *tarte*]

tar·tan[1] (tär′tən) *n.* 1 A woolen fabric having varicolored lines or stripes at right angles, forming a distinctive pattern; a woolen plaid; the characteristic dress of the Scottish Highlanders, each clan having its particular pattern or patterns; hence, any similar pattern; a plaid. 2 A garment made of tartan. — *adj.* Made of tartan; also, striped or checkered in a manner similar to the Scottish tartans. [? <OF *tiretaine* linsey-woolsey]

tar·tan[2] (tär′tən) *n.* 1 A Mediterranean vessel having one mast with a large lateen sail. 2 A variety of long, covered carriage. [<F *tartane* <Arabic *ṭarīdah,* kind of ship]

tar·tar (tär′tər) *n.* 1 An acid substance deposited from grape juice during fermentation as a pinkish sediment; crude potassium bitartrate. See ARGOL, CREAM OF TARTAR. 2 *Dent.* A yellowish incrustation on the teeth, chiefly calcium phosphate. [<F *tartre* <LL *tartarum* <Med. Gk. *tartaron,* ? <Arabic]

Tar·tar (tär′tər) *n.* 1 Tatar. 2 A person of intractable or savage temper; also, especially in the phrase **to catch a Tartar,** an opponent who turns out to be unexpectedly formidable: also **tar′tar.** — *adj.* Of or pertaining to the Tatars of Tartary. [<F *Tartare* <LL *Tartarus* <Persian *Tātar* Tatar; prob. infl. by L *Tartarus* Hell]

Tar·tar (tär′tər) *Obs.* Tartarus.

Tar·tar·e·an (tär-târ′ē-ən) *adj.* Of or pertaining to Tartarus.

tartar emetic *Chem.* A white, crystalline, poisonous tartrate of antimony and potassium, $K(SbO)C_4H_4O_6\cdot 1/2H_2O$, with a sweet, afterward disagreeable, metallic taste: used in medicine, chiefly as an emetic, and in dyeing as a mordant.

tar·tar·e·ous (tär-târ′ē-əs) *adj.* Resembling tartar.

tar·tare sauce (tär′tər) A fish sauce consisting of mayonnaise, capers, chopped olives, and pickles. Also **tar′tar sauce.**

Tar·tar·i·an (tär-târ′ē-ən) *adj.* Of or pertaining to the Tatars or Tartary.

tar·tar·ic (tär-tar′ik, -tär′ik) *adj.* Pertaining to or derived from tartar or tartaric acid.

tartaric acid *Chem.* Any one of four isomeric organic compounds, $HOOC(CHOH)_2COOH$, differing from each other in their optical properties, especially the dextrorotatory form, occurring in the free state or as a potassium or calcium salt, as in grape juice, various unripe fruits, etc.

tar·tar·ize (tär′tə-rīz) *v.t.* **·ized, ·iz·ing** To impregnate or treat with tartar, cream of tartar, or tartar emetic. — **tar′tar·i·za′tion** *n.*

tar·tar·ous (tär′tər-əs) *adj.* Pertaining to or derived from tartar.

Tartar sable The kolinsky.

Tar·ta·rus (tär′tər-əs) 1 In Greek mythology, the abyss below Hades where Zeus confined the Titans. 2 Hades.

Tar·ta·ry (tär′tər-ē) A region of Asia and eastern Europe, mostly in central and western Asiatic Russian S.F.S.R., Soviet Central Asia, southern European Russian S.F.S.R., and Ukrainian S.S.R., ruled by the Tatars, under Mongol leadership, in the 13th and 14th centuries A.D. At its greatest extent, under Genghis Khan, it reached the Pacific; after his death, the Asian portion became known as **Great Tartary,** or **Asiatic Tartary,** while the European portion, ruled by the Golden

Horde, became **Little Tartary,** or **European Tartary:** also *Tatary.*

Tar·tes·sus (tär-tes′əs) An ancient city and region in the SW part of the Iberian Peninsula near the Pillars of Hercules, often identified with Biblical Tarshish.

tart·let (tärt′lit) *n.* A small tart.

tar·trate (tär′trāt) *n. Chem.* A salt or ester of tartaric acid.

tar·trat·ed (tär′trā-tid) *adj. Chem.* Containing or combined with tartaric acid.

Tar·tu (tär′tōō) A city in SE central Estonia: German *Dorpat,* Russian *Yurev.*

tar·tufe (tär-tōōf′, *Fr.* tår-tüf′) *n.* Any hypocrite or toady. Also **tar·tuffe′.** [after TARTUFE]

Tar·tufe (tär-tōōf′, *Fr.* tår-tüf′) In Molière's comedy of the same name, the chief character, a person of pretended devoutness. Also **Tar·tuffe′.**

Tar·ve·si·um (tär-vē′sē-əm) The ancient name for TREVISO.

Tar·zan (tär′zan, tär-zan′) The hero of a series of novels by Edgar Rice Burroughs (1875–1950): an English child of noble birth abandoned in the African jungle, raised by apes, and possessing incredible strength, agility, and a knowledge of the speech of animals. Also **Tarzan of the Apes.**

Tash·kent (täsh-kent′) The largest city of Soviet Central Asia, capital of Uzbek S.S.R. Also **Tash·kend′** (-kend′).

ta·sim·e·ter (tə-sim′ə-tər) *n.* An electrical apparatus for detecting changes in pressure by the resulting variations in the conductivity of a solid, and so measuring changes, as in length, temperature, or moisture, that produce alteration of pressure. [<Gk. *tasis* extension (<*teinein* stretch) + -METER] — **tas·i·met·ric** (tas′ə-met′rik) *adj.* — **ta·sim′e·try** *n.*

task (task, täsk) *n.* 1 A specific amount of labor or study imposed by authority or required by duty or necessity. 2 Any work voluntarily undertaken and imposed on oneself. 3 An exhausting or vexatious employment; burden. 4 A specific military mission. 5 *Obs.* A tax; duty. — **to take to task** To reprove; lecture. — *v.t.* 1 To assign a task to. 2 To overtax with labor; burden. 3 To censure; reprimand. 4 *Obs.* To tax. [<AF *tasque* <LL *tasca, taxa* <L *taxare* appraise. Related to TAX.]

Synonyms (noun): business, drudgery, job, labor, lesson, stint, toil, work. See TOIL[1].

task·er (tas′kər, täs′-) *n.* 1 A reaper. 2 A thresher of grain. 3 A laborer who performs allotted work.

task force 1 *Mil.* A tactical unit drawn from different branches of the armed services assigned to execute a specific mission. 2 Any group assigned to handle a specific task.

task·mas·ter (task′mas′tər, täsk′mäs′tər) *n.* One who assigns tasks; figuratively, one who or that which loads with heavy burdens.

Tas·lan (taz′lan) *n.* A mechanical process for imparting bulk and texture to any standard textile yarn without altering basic chemical properties: a trade name.

Tas·man (täs′mən), **Abel Janszoon,** 1603?–1659?, Dutch navigator who discovered Tasmania and New Zealand.

Tas·ma·nia (taz-mā′nē-ə) An island state in the Commonwealth of Australia, south of Victoria; 26,215 square miles; capital, Hobart; formerly *Van Diemen's Land.* — **Tas·ma′ni·an** *adj.* & *n.*

Tasmanian devil A ferocious burrowing carnivorous marsupial (*Sarcophilus harrisii*) of the dasyure family, with white markings on the black fur.

Tasmanian wolf The thylacine. Also **Tasmanian tiger.**

Tas·man Sea (taz′mən) The arm of the South Pacific Ocean between SE Australia and Tasmania on the west and New Zealand on the east.

tass (tas) *n. Scot.* A drinking cup, or its contents.

Tass (täs, tas) *n.* Russian news agency: from the initials of *Telegrafnoe Agentstvo Sovetskovo Soyuza* (Telegraph Agency Soviet Union).

tas·sel[1] (tas′əl) *n.* 1 A pendent ornament, for curtains, cushions, and the like, consisting of a tuft of loosely hanging threads or cords; formerly, a clasp for holding a cloak. 2 Something resembling a tassel, as the pendent head of some plants or flowers, or the

pyramidal inflorescence on a stalk of Indian corn. —*v.* **·seled** or **·selled, ·sel·ing** or **·sel·ling** *v.t.* **1** To provide or adorn with tassels. **2** To form in a tassel or tassels. **3** To remove the tassels from (Indian corn). —*v.i.* **4** To put forth tassels, as Indian corn. [< OF, clasp]

tas·sel[2] (tas′əl) *n.* The tercel.

tas·set (tas′it) *n.* One of a series of overlapping metal plates pendent from the cuirass to protect the waist and thighs: often called *tace.* Also **tasse.** ◆ Homophone: *tacit.* [< F *tassette,* dim. of OF *tasse* a pouch]

tas·sie (tas′ē) *n. Scot.* A drinking cup.

Tas·so (täs′sō), **Torquato,** 1544–95, Italian epic poet.

taste (tāst) *v.* **tast·ed, tast·ing** *v.t.* **1** To perceive the flavor of (something) by taking into the mouth or touching with the tongue. **2** To take a little of (food or drink); eat or drink a little of. **3** To test the quality of (a product) thus: His business is *tasting* tea. **4** *Archaic* To have a relish for; like. **5** *Obs.* To prove or try by or as by touch. —*v.i.* **6** To take a small quantity into the mouth; take a taste: usually with *of.* **7** To have experience or enjoyment; be or become acquainted through experience: with *of:* to *taste* of great sorrow. **8** To have specified flavor when in the mouth: Sugar *tastes* sweet. —*n.* **1** The sensation excited when a soluble substance comes into contact with any of the taste buds; also, the quality thus perceived; flavor. **2** *Physiol.* Any of the four fundamental sensations, salt, sweet, bitter, or sour, excited alone or in any combination by the sole action of the gustatory nerves. **3** A small quantity tasted, eaten or sipped; a sample: often used figuratively. **4** Special fondness and aptitude for a pursuit; bent; inclination: a *taste* for music. **5** The power or faculty of apprehending and appreciating the beautiful in nature, art, and literature; critical perception or discernment. **6** Style or form with respect to the rules of propriety or etiquette: She behaves in very poor *taste.* **7** Individual preference or liking: That tie suits my *taste.* **8** The act of tasting. **9** *Obs.* The act of examining or testing. See synonyms under RELISH, SAVOR. [< OF *taster* taste, try, feel, prob. ult. < L *taxare* touch, handle, appraise] —**tast′a·ble** *adj.*

taste bud *Physiol.* One of the clusters of cells situated in the mucous membrane chiefly of the tongue and containing sensitive receptors for the discriminatory perception of taste.

taste·ful (tāst′fəl) *adj.* **1** Conforming to taste. **2** Possessing good taste. **3** Savory: a rare use. —**taste′ful·ly** *adv.* —**taste′ful·ness** *n.*

Synonyms: artistic, dainty, delicate, delicious, elegant, esthetic, esthetical, exquisite, fastidious, fine, nice. That which is *elegant* is made so not merely by nature, but by art and culture. *Nice* and *delicate* both refer to exact adaptation to some standard; as regards matters of taste, *delicate* is a higher and more discriminating word than *nice,* and is always used in a favorable sense; a *delicate* distinction is one worth observing; a *nice* distinction may be so, or may be overstrained and unduly subtle. *Esthetic* or *esthetical* refers to beauty or the appreciation of the beautiful, especially from the philosophic point of view. *Exquisite* denotes the utmost perfection of the *elegant* in minute details; we speak of an *elegant* garment, an *exquisite* lace. *Exquisite* is also applied to intense keenness of any feeling; as, *exquisite* pain. *Antonyms:* clumsy, coarse, deformed, disgusting, displeasing, distasteful, fulsome, gaudy, grotesque, harsh, hideous, horrid, inartistic, inharmonious, meretricious, offensive, rude, tawdry.

taste·less (tāst′lis) *adj.* **1** Having no flavor; insipid; dull. **2** Having lost the sense of taste. **3** Devoid of esthetic taste. **4** Lacking, or showing a lack of, good taste. —**taste′less·ly** *adv.* —**taste′less·ness** *n.*

taste·mak·er (tāst′mā′kər) *n.* A person who establishes standards of style or who shapes public opinion.

tast·er (tās′tər) *n.* **1** One who tastes; specifically, one who tests the quality of for trade: a tea-*taster.* **2** A device to assist in testing or sampling. **3** A pipette, or a small, flat, circular metal vessel used in testing wines.

tast·y (tās′tē) *adj.* **tast·i·er, tast·i·est** *Colloq.* **1** Having a fine flavor; savory. **2** Tasteful. —**tast′i·ly** *adv.* —**tast′i·ness** *n.*

tat[1] (tat) *v.* **tat·ted, tat·ting** *v.t.* To make, as an edging, by tatting. —*v.i.* To make tatting. [Back formation < TATTING] —**tat′ter** *n.*

tat[2] (tat) *n.* A tap or blow: in the phrase **tit for tat.** [? Var. of TAP[2], *n.*]

ta·ta·mi (tä·tä′mē) *n. pl.* **-mi, -mis** A floor covering in a Japanese dwelling, made of rice straw matting.

Ta·tar (tä′tər) *n.* **1** One belonging to any of the Turkic peoples of eastern, western, and Ural Asiatic Russian S.F.S.R. and Soviet Central Asia; also, one of the Turkic Tatars of the Tatar Republic, the Crimea, the Kalmuck area, and the northern Caucasus. **2** Any of the Turkic languages of the Tatars, as Uzbek. **3** Originally, any of the Tungus of Manchuria and Mongolia. —*adj.* Of or pertaining to the Tatars. Also *Tartar.* [< Persian]

Ta·tar Autonomous Soviet Socialist Republic (tä′tər) An administrative division of east central European Russian S.F.S.R.; 26,100 square miles; capital, Kazan.

Ta·tar·i·an (tä·târ′ē·ən) *adj.* Of or pertaining to the Tatars: also **Ta·tar·ic** (tä·tar′ik). —*n.* A Tatar.

Ta·ta·ry (tä′tər·ē) See TARTARY.

Tate (tāt), **Nahum,** 1652–1715, English dramatist; poet laureate 1692–1715.

ta·tie (tā′tē) *n. Brit. Dial.* A potato. Also **ta′ter, ta′ty.**

Tat·ler (tat′lər), **The** An English periodical, published thrice weekly by Sir Richard Steele from 1709 to 1711, chiefly written by Steele, occasionally by Addison: predecessor of *The Spectator.*

tat·ou·ay (tat′o͞o·ā, tä·to͞o′ī) *n.* A large South American armadillo (genus *Cabassous*). [< Sp. *tatuay* < Guarani *tatu-aí* < *tatu* armadillo + *aí* worthless; so called because it is inedible]

Ta·tra (tä′trä), **High** The highest group of the central Carpathian Mountains, in northern Czechoslovakia; highest peak, 8,737 ft.

tat·ter (tat′ər) *n.* **1** A torn and hanging shred; rag. **2** *pl.* Ragged clothing. —*v.t.* To make ragged; tear into tatters. —*v.i.* To become ragged. [< Scand. Cf. ON *tötturr* rags.]

tat·ter·de·mal·ion (tat′ər·di·māl′yən, -mal′-) *n.* A person wearing ragged clothes; a ragamuffin. —*adj.* Ragged. [Origin unknown]

tat·tered (tat′ərd) *adj.* **1** Torn into tatters. **2** Clothed in rags; ragged.

Tat·ter·sall check (tat′ər·sôl) A check or plaid design of dark lines on a light ground: used especially in men's vests. Also **Tattersall plaid.** [From a pattern on blankets used in the London market of Richard *Tattersall,* 18th century horse merchant]

tat·ting (tat′ing) *n.* A lacelike threadwork, made by hand; also, the act or process of making it. [Origin unknown]

tat·tle (tat′l) *v.* **·tled, ·tling** *v.i.* **1** To talk idly; prate; chatter. **2** To tell tales about others; gossip. —*v.t.* **3** To reveal by gossiping. See synonyms under BABBLE. —*n.* **1** Idle talk or gossip. **2** Prattling speech, as of children. [Prob. < MDu. *tatelen*] —**tat′tling·ly** *adv.*

tat·tler (tat′lər) *n.* **1** One who tattles; a talebearer; tattletale. **2** Any long-billed bird of the genus *Totanus,* as the redshank and the yellowlegs. **3** The willet. **4** The wandering tattler *(Heteroscelus incanus),* a shore bird of the Pacific coast of the United States.

tat·tle·tale (tat′l·tāl′) *n.* A talebearer; tattler. —*adj.* Revealing; betraying.

tat·too[1] (ta·to͞o′) *v.t.* **1** To prick and mark (the skin) in patterns with indelible pigments. **2** To mark the skin with (designs, etc.) in this way. —*n. pl.* **·toos** A pattern or picture so made. [< Polynesian. Cf. Tahitian, Tongan *tatau,* Marquesan *tatu* < *ta* mark.] —**tat·too′er** *n.* —**tat·too′ing** *n.*

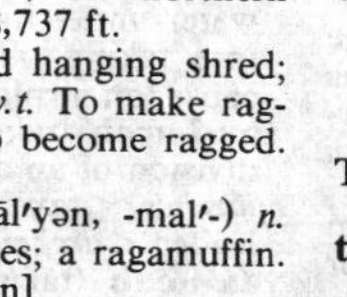

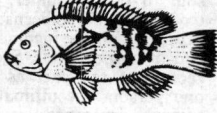

TATTOOING ON MAORI CHIEFTAIN

tat·too[2] (ta·to͞o′) *n.* **1** A continuous beating or drumming. **2** In military or naval usage, a signal by drum or bugle to repair to quarters, usually occurring about 9 p.m. [Var. of earlier *taptoo* < Du. *taptoe* < *tap* tap, faucet + *toe* shut]

tat·ty (tat′ē) *n. pl.* **·ties** *Anglo-Indian* An East Indian matting usually hung in doorways and window openings, and kept wet to cool the air. Also **tat′tie.** [< Hind. *taṭṭī*] —**tat′tied** *adj.*

tau (tou) *n.* **1** The nineteenth letter in the Greek alphabet: (Τ,τ) equivalent to the English *t.* As a numeral it denotes 300. **2** A lepton having a mass approximately 20 times that of a muon. [< Gk.]

tau cross See under CROSS.

taught (tôt) Past tense and past participle of TEACH.

taunt[1] (tônt) *n.* **1** A sarcastic, biting speech or remark; insulting reproach. **2** *Obs.* A butt of contemptuous reproach. See synonyms under SCORN, SNEER. —*v.t.* **1** To reproach with sarcastic or contemptuous words; mock; upbraid. **2** To tease in any way; provoke with taunts. See synonyms under MOCK, RIDICULE, SCOFF. [? < OF *tanter,* var. of *tenter* provoke, tempt. See TEMPT.] —**taunt′er** *n.* —**taunt′ing·ly** *adv.*

taunt[2] (tônt) *adj. Naut.* Unusually tall: said of masts. [Aphetic var. of ATAUNT]

Taun·ton (tän′tən, tôn′-) The county town of Somerset, England; in the west central part.

tau particle *Physics* A rare, unstable atomic particle of the meson group, positively charged and with a mass about 1,000 times that of the electron.

taupe (tōp) *n.* **1** A mole. **2** The color of moleskin; dark gray, often tinged with brown, purple, or yellow. ◆ Homophone: *tope.* [< F < L *talpa* mole]

Tau·ric Cher·so·nese (tô′rik kûr′sō·nēz, -nēs) An ancient name for the CRIMEA.

tau·ri·form (tôr′ə·fôrm) *adj.* Shaped like a bull. [< L *tauriformis* < *taurus* bull + *forma* shape]

tau·rine[1] (tôr′ēn) *adj.* **1** Of or like a bull. **2** Related to or connected with the constellation or sign Taurus. [< L *taurinus* < *taurus* a bull]

tau·rine[2] (tôr′ēn, -in) *n. Chem.* A colorless crystalline compound, $C_2H_7NSO_3$, contained in the bile and muscles of oxen and other animals: also derived synthetically. [< L *taurus* bull + -INE[2]]

Tau·ris (tôr′is) **1** The Tauric Chersonese. **2** The ancient name for TABRIZ.

tauro- *combining form* Bull; ox; bovine. Also, before vowels, **taur-.** [< Gk. *tauros* a bull]

tau·ro·cho·lic acid (tôr′ə·kō′lik, -kol′ik) *Chem.* A bitter crystalline compound, $C_{26}H_{45}NSO_7$, contained in the bile of man and some animals, as the ox. [< TAURO- + Gk. *cholē* bile]

tau·rom·a·chy (tô·rom′ə·kē) *n.* The art of bullfighting. Also **tau·ro·ma·chi·a** (tôr′ə·mā′kē·ə). [< Gk. *tauromachia* < *tauros* a bull + *machesthai* fight]

Tau·rus (tôr′əs) **1** A zodiacal constellation, the Bull, containing the Hyades, the Pleiades, and Aldebaran. **2** The second sign of the zodiac, which the sun enters April 20. See CONSTELLATION, ZODIAC. [< L, bull]

Tau·rus (tôr′əs) A mountain range in southern Turkey; highest point, 12,251 feet: Turkish *Toros Dağlari.*

Taus·sig (tou′sig), **Frank William,** 1859–1940, U.S. political economist.

taut (tôt) *adj.* **1** Hard-drawn; stretched tight. **2** In proper shape; ready; tidy. **3** Tense; tight: *taut* muscles. **4** *Obs.* Filled to distention; firm. [ME *toyt, toht;* origin uncertain] —**taut′ly** *adv.* —**taut′ness** *n.*

taut·ed (tô′tid) *adj. Scot.* Tangled; tousled; matted: said of wool or hair.

taut·en (tôt′n) *v.t.* & *v.i.* To make or become taut; tighten.

tauto- *combining form* Same; identical: *tautomerism.* Also, before vowels, **taut-.** [< Gk. *tauto* the same]

tau·tog (tô·tôg′, -tog′) *n.* A blackish, edible, labroid fish *(Tautoga onitis)* of the North American Atlantic coast. Also **tau·taug′.** [< Algonquian *tautauog,* pl. of *tautau,* a kind of blackfish]

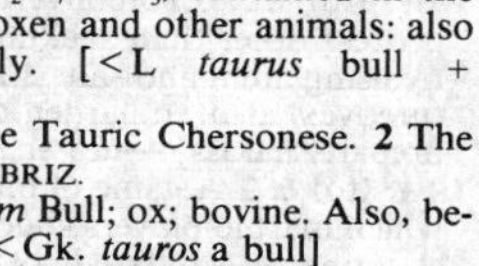

TAUTOG
(About 16 inches long)

tau·tol·o·gism (tô·tol′ə·jiz′əm) *n.* Use of needlessly repetitious

speech, or an instance of it; pleonasm. —**tau·tol′o·gist** *n.*

tau·tol·o·gize (tô·tol′ə·jīz) *v.i.* **·gized, ·giz·ing** To repeat needlessly the same idea in different words.

tau·tol·o·gy (tô·tol′ə·jē) *n. pl.* **·gies** Unnecessary repetition of the same idea in different words; pleonasm; also, an instance of such repetition; as, He is writing his own autobiography. See REDUNDANCE. [<LL *tautologia* <Gk. <*tauto* the same + *logos* discourse] —**tau·to·log·ic** (tô′tə·loj′ik) or **·i·cal** *adj.* —**tau′to·log′i·cal·ly** *adv.*

tau·to·mer·ic (tô′tə·mer′ik) *adj.* Having the property of tautomerism.

tau·tom·er·ism (tô·tom′ə·riz′əm) *n. Chem.* The property, exhibited by certain substances and compounds when subjected to appropriate chemical reaction, of assuming either of two interconvertible atomic structures, **tau·to·mers** (tô′tə·mərz), which are in equilibrium with each other. [<TAUTO- + Gk. *meros* part]

tau·tom·er·i·za·tion (tô·tom′ər·ə·zā′shən, -ī·zā′-) *n. Chem.* Conversion into a tautomeric structure.

tau·to·nym (tô′tə·nim) *n.* An instance of tautonymy.

tau·ton·y·my (tô·ton′ə·mē) *n. pl.* **·mies** *Biol.* **1** The possession by two or more distinct plants or animals of the same generic and specific names: prohibited by the rules of scientific nomenclature. **2** Identity of the generic, specific, and subspecific names of a given plant or animal, as *Bison bison bison*: a permitted practice. [<TAUTO- + Gk. *onyma* name] —**tau·to·nym·ic** (tô′tə·nim′ik) *adj.*

tav (täv) *n.* The twenty-second Hebrew letter. Also **taw.** See ALPHABET.

tav·ern (tav′ərn) *n.* **1** A public house where travelers and other guests are accommodated with lodging, food, and drink. **2** A house licensed to retail liquors to be drunk on the premises. [<OF *taverne* <L *taberna* hut, booth]

tav·ern·er (tav′ər·nər) *n. Archaic* A tavernkeeper; also, one who frequents taverns.

taw[1] (tô) *v.t.* **1** To convert into leather by some process other than soaking in tanning liquor, as by using alum and salt. **2** *Brit. Dial.* To beat; torture; vex; also, to harden or prepare. [OE *tawian* prepare, harass] —**taw′er** *n.*

taw[2] (tô) *n.* **1** A game of marbles. **2** The line from which marble-players shoot. **3** A marble used for shooting. —*v.i.* To shoot a marble or come to the mark before shooting. [<Scand. Cf. ON *taug* string.]

taw·dry (tô′drē) *adj.* **·dri·er, ·dri·est** Showy without elegance; excessively ornamental; gaudy. —*n.* Cheap, pretentious finery. [Short for *tawdry lace,* alter. of *St. Audrey's lace,* a type of silk neckpiece sold at St. Audrey's Fair at Ely, England] —**taw′dri·ly** *adv.* —**taw′dri·ness** *n.*

taw·ie (tô′ē) *adj. Scot.* Docile; tame: said of a horse, etc.

Taw·ney (tô′nē), **R(ichard) H(enry),** 1880–1962. English economist and historian.

taw·ny (tô′nē) *adj.* **·ni·er, ·ni·est** Tan-colored; brownish-yellow. Also **taw′ney.** [<AF *taune* <OF *tanné,* pp. of *tanner* tan] —**taw′ni·ness** *n.*

taw·pie (tô′pē) *n. Scot.* A foolish young woman.

taws (tôz) *Scot. n.* A whip made of a leather strap cut into thongs or of several thongs on a handle. —*v.t.* To flog; scourge. Also **tawse.**

tax (taks) *n.* **1** A compulsory contribution levied upon persons, property, or business for the support of government; by extension, any proportionate assessment, as on the members of a society. **2** A heavy demand on one's powers or resources; an onerous duty or requirement; a burden. —**direct tax** A tax, as on property or income, which the taxpayer cannot shift to another person. —**excise tax** An internal-revenue tax on domestic manufactures, levied before they are sold to the consumer. The term has been extended to include license duties. —**income tax** A tax levied on the income or profits of individuals and of corporations. See CAPITAL LEVY. —**indirect tax** A tax, such as a customs duty, paid by one person but ultimately shifted to the consumer. —**nuisance tax** A tax which yields little benefit in proportion to the amount of discontent it causes. —**single tax** A tax to be obtained from a single source, especially from a levy on land and natural resources, as a substitute for all other forms of taxation. The theory was first proposed by John Locke, and was elaborated and popularized in the 19th century by Henry George. [<*v.*] —*v.t.* **1** To impose a tax on; subject to taxation. **2** *Law* To settle or fix (amounts) as duly chargeable in any judicial matter: to *tax* costs. **3** To subject to a severe demand; impose a burden or load upon; task: He *taxes* my patience. **4** To make an accusation against; charge; also, to blame; censure: usually with *with.* [<OF *taxer* <L *taxare* estimate, appraise. Related to TASK.] —**tax′a·bil′i·ty, tax′a·ble·ness** *n.* —**tax′a·ble** *adj.* —**tax′a·bly** *adv.* —**tax′er** *n.*

Synonyms (noun): assessment, custom, demand, duty, exaction, excise, impost, rate, rating, toll, tribute.

Tax may appear as a combining form in hyphemes or solidemes, or as the first element in two-word phrases, with the meaning of definition 1:

tax-assessor	**tax-evader**	**tax payment**
tax burden	**tax-evading**	**tax proposal**
tax-burdened	**tax-exempt**	**tax receipt**
tax claim	**tax-free**	**tax-repeal**
tax-collecting	**tax-laden**	**tax revenue**
tax-collector	**tax law**	**tax-ridden**
tax-cut	**tax levy**	**tax-supported**
tax-dodger	**taxman**	**tax system**
tax-dodging	**tax-paid**	**taxwise**

tax·a·ceous (tak·sā′shəs) *adj. Bot.* Designating or belonging to a widely distributed family *(Taxaceae)* of typically evergreen shrubs and trees, the yew family, having one or two integuments and drupelike or, rarely, cone fruits. [<NL <L *taxus* yew]

tax·a·tion (tak·sā′shən) *n.* The act of taxing; the amount assessed as a tax.

Tax·co (tas′kō, *Sp.* täs′kō) A resort city in Guerrero, SW Mexico. Officially **Tax·co de Al·ar·cón** (täs′kō thā äl′är·kōn′).

tax·gath·er·er (taks′gath′ər·ər) *n.* A collector of taxes. —**tax′gath′er·ing** *n.* & *adj.*

tax·i (tak′sē) *n.* A taxicab. —*v.* **tax·ied, tax·i·ing** or **tax·y·ing** *v.i.* **1** To ride in a taxicab. **2** To move along the ground or on the surface of the water under its own power, as an airplane before taking off or after landing. —*v.t.* **3** To cause (an airplane) to taxi. [<TAXI(CAB)]

tax·i·arch (tak′sē·ärk) *n.* The commander of a division of an ancient Greek army. [<Gk. *taxiarchēs* <*taxis* division of an army + *archos* leader <*archein* rule]

tax·i·cab (tak′sē·kab′) *n.* A passenger vehicle, usually an automobile fitted with a taximeter, available for hire. [Short for *taximeter cab*]

taxi dancer *U.S.* A girl employed by a dance hall or cabaret to dance with patrons for a certain fee. [<*taxi-* hired, as in *taxicab* + DANCER]

tax·i·der·mist (tak′sə·dûr′mist) *n.* One who practices taxidermy.

tax·i·der·my (tak′sə·dûr′mē) *n.* The art or process of stuffing and mounting the skins of dead animals for preservation or exhibition. [<Gk. *taxis* arrangement + *derma* skin] —**tax′i·der′mal, tax′i·der′mic** *adj.*

tax·i·me·ter (tak′si·mē′tər) *n.* **1** An instrument for measuring distances and recording fares. **2** A taxicab equipped with a taximeter. [<F *taximètre* <*taxe* tariff + *mètre* a meter]

tax·ine (tak′sēn, -sin) *n. Chem.* A yellow-white, poisonous alkaloid, $C_{37}H_{51}O_{10}N$, from the needles and seed of the English yew *(Taxus baccata).* It produces convulsion and paralyzes the heart. Also **tax·in** (tak′sin). [<L *taxus* yew + -INE[2]]

tax·i·plane (tak′sē·plān′) *n.* An airplane available for hire as a public vehicle.

tax·is (tak′sis) *n.* **1** *Surg.* A methodical application of manual pressure, as on a hernial tumor, for restoring the parts to their normal place. **2** *Zool.* The involuntary movement of an organism or cell, as a zoospore, in response to an external stimulus; specifically, a movement involving locomotion or change of place. Compare TROPISM. **3** In ancient Greece, a body of troops of varying size. **4** *Obs.* Order; arrangement, as of words in a sentence. [<Gk., arrangement <*tassein* arrange]

-taxis *combining form* Order; disposition; arrangement: *thermotaxis.* Also spelled **-taxy.** [<Gk. *taxis* arrangement]

tax·ite (tak′sīt) *n.* A volcanic rock which has crystallized in such manner as to have a clastic appearance. [<Gk. *taxis* arrangement + -ITE[1]] —**tax·it·ic** (tak·sit′ik) *adj.*

tax·on·o·mist (tak·son′ə·mist) *n.* One versed in taxonomy. Also **tax·on′o·mer.**

tax·on·o·my (tak·son′ə·mē) *n.* **1** The department of knowledge that embodies the laws and principles of classification. **2** *Biol.* The systematic arrangement of plant and animal organisms according to accepted diagnostic criteria which determine their assignment to each of the following major groups, beginning with the most inclusive: kingdom, phylum or division, class, order, family, genus, and species. [<F *taxonomie* <Gk. *taxis* arrangement + *nomos* law] —**tax·o·nom·ic** (tak′sə·nom′ik) or **·i·cal** *adj.* —**tax′o·nom′i·cal·ly** *adv.*

tax·pay·er (taks′pā′ər) *n.* **1** One who pays any tax. **2** A building, the rental from which is intended to cover merely the taxes on the land.

tax title The title conveyed to a purchaser of property sold for non-payment of taxes.

Ta·yg·e·ta (tā·ij′ə·tə) One of the Pleiades.

Tay·lor (tā′lər), **Bayard,** 1825–78, U.S. writer. —**Frederick Winslow,** 1856–1915, U.S. engineer; developed scientific shop management. —**Jeremy,** 1613–67, English bishop and author. —**(Joseph) Deems,** 1885–1966, U.S. composer. —**Laurette,** 1887–1946, *née* Cooney, U.S. actress. —**Myron,** 1874–1959, U.S. lawyer and diplomat. —**Tom,** 1817–80, English dramatist. —**Zachary,** 1784–1850, U.S. general; 12th president of the United States 1849–50.

Tay River (tā) The largest river in Scotland, flowing 118 miles SW and SE from eastern Perthshire, near the Argyll border, to the **Firth of Tay,** an estuary of the North Sea extending 25 miles into central Scotland.

taz·za (tät′tsä) *n. Italian* A flat ornamental cup, especially one supported on a high foot.

Tb *Chem.* Terbium (symbol Tb).

T-base (tē′bās′) *n.* Two strips of wood nailed together in the form of a T and serving as a base for the tripod of a machine-gun.

Tbi·li·si (tpi′li·sē) The Georgian name for TIFLIS.

Tc *Chem.* Technetium (symbol Tc).

Tchad (chäd) The French name for CHAD.

Tchai·kov·sky (chī·kôf′skē), **Peter (Pëtr) Il·ich,** 1840–93, Russian composer.

tchick (chik) *n.* A sound made by pressing the tongue against the roof of the mouth and sucking it back, as in urging a horse. —*v.i.* To make a *tchick.* [Imit.]

Te *Chem.* Tellurium (symbol Te).

tea (tē) *n.* **1** An evergreen Asian shrub or small tree *(Thea sinensis),* having a compact head of leathery, toothed leaves and white or pink flowers. **2** The prepared leaves of this plant, or an infusion of them used as a beverage. The difference between **black tea** and **green tea** is the result of manipulation, the latter being withered by steaming, thus retaining the green color, while leaves simply dried turn black. **3** Any infusion, decoction, solution, or extract to be used as a beverage or medicinally: beef *tea.* **4** The leaves of a particular variety of plant, prepared for making a beverage, or for medicinal purposes: senna *tea.* **5** A light evening or afternoon meal; also, a social gathering at which tea is served. [<Chinese *ch'a,* dial. Chinese *t'e*]

Tea may appear as a combining form in hyphemes or solidemes, or as the first element in two-word phrases; as in:

tea-blending	**tea-making**
teabox	**tea merchant**
teacart	**tea-packer**
tea china	**tea-packing**
tea crop	**tea plant**
tea dealer	**tea-planter**
tea-drinker	**tea-planting**
tea-drinking	**tea-producer**
tea-farming	**tea-producing**
tea-grower	**tea table**
tea-growing	**tea-taster**
tea leaf	**teatime**
tea-loving	**tea tray**
tea-maker	**teaware**

tea bag A small porous sack of cloth or paper

containing tea leaves, which is immersed in water to make tea.

tea ball **1** A perforated metal ball, filled with tea leaves, to be dropped or suspended in boiling water to make tea. **2** A tea bag.

tea·ber·ry (tē′ber′ē) *n. pl.* **·ries** **1** The wintergreen, whose leaves are sometimes mixed with or used as tea. **2** The berry of this plant.

tea biscuit A biscuit or cracker, usually short and sweetened, served with tea.

tea caddy See CADDY[1] (def. 1).

teach (tēch) *v.* **taught, teach·ing** *v.t.* **1** To impart knowledge to by lessons; give instruction to; guide by precept or example; instruct: to *teach* a class. **2** To give instruction in; make known; communicate the knowledge of: to *teach* French. **3** To train by practice or exercise. —*v.i.* **4** To follow the profession of teaching. **5** To impart knowledge or skill. [OE *tǣcan, tǣcean*]

Synonyms: discipline, drill, educate, enlighten, indoctrinate, inform, initiate, instruct, nurture, school, train, tutor. To *teach* is to communicate knowledge; to *instruct* is to impart knowledge with special method and completeness; *instruct* has also an authoritative sense nearly equivalent to command. To *educate* is to draw out or develop the mental powers. To *train* is to direct to a certain result powers already existing. *Train* is used in preference to *educate* when the reference is to the inferior animals or to the physical powers of man; as, to *train* a horse; to *train* the hand or eye. To *discipline* is to bring into habitual and complete subjection to authority. To *nurture* is to furnish the care and sustenance necessary for physical, mental, and moral growth; *nurture* is a more tender word than *educate.* See INFORM[1], LEARN.

teach·a·ble (tē′chə·bəl) *adj.* **1** Capable of being taught; willing to learn; docile. **2** Capable of being imparted by teaching. See synonyms under DOCILE. **—teach′a·bil′i·ty, teach′a·ble·ness** *n.* **—teach′a·bly** *adv.*

teach·er (tē′chər) *n.* One who teaches; specifically, one whose occupation is to teach others. See synonyms under MASTER.

teacher bird **1** The ovenbird. **2** The North American red-eyed vireo. [Imit. of its cry]

teachers' institute See under INSTITUTE.

teach-in (tēch′in′) *n.* An extended meeting, as at a college or university, during which faculty and students participate in lectures, discussions, etc., on a controversial issue, often as a form of social protest.

teaching (tē′ching) *n.* **1** The profession of a teacher. **2** That which is taught. See synonyms under DOCTRINE, EDUCATION, NURTURE.

teach·ing machine Any of various manually-operated devices that present educational material in a series of steps designed to enable each student to learn at a rate commensurate with his ability.

tea cozy See COZY. *n.*

tea·cup (tē′kup′) *n.* **1** A small cup suitable for serving tea. **2** As much as a teacup will hold: also **tea′cup·ful′** (-fo͝ol′).

tea·house (tē′hous′) *n.* In the Orient, a public place serving tea and other light refreshments.

teak (tēk) *n.* **1** A large East Indian tree *(Tectona grandis)* of the vervain family, yielding a very hard, durable timber highly prized for shipbuilding. **2** The wood of this tree. [<Malayalam *tēkka*]

tea·ket·tle (tē′ket′l) *n.* A kettle with a spout, used for boiling water for culinary purposes.

teal (tēl) *n.* **1** Any of several small, short-necked river ducks (genera *Nettion* and *Querquedula*); especially, the common teal *(N. crecca)* of the Old World and the similar North American **green-winged teal** *(N. carolinense)* having grayish wing coverts and the head slightly crested. **2** A darkish, dull-blue color with a greenish cast. [ME *tele*]

team (tēm) *n.* **1** Two or more beasts of burden harnessed together: often including harness and vehicle; also, a single horse and vehicle. **2** A set of workers, or players competing in a game: a baseball *team.* **3** *Dial.* A flock; brood. **4** *Obs.* Race; lineage. —*v.t.* **1** To convey with a team. **2** To harness together in a team. —*v.i.* **3** To drive a team as a business. **4** To form a team: work as a team: to *team* up. —*adj.* Of or pertaining to a team. ◆Homophone: *teem.* [OE *tēam* offspring, succession, row. Related to TEEM[1].] **—team′ing** *n.*

team boat A paddle-wheel ferryboat propelled by horse power.

team·mate (tēm′māt′) *n.* A fellow player on a team.

team play Cooperation.

team·ster (tēm′stər) *n.* **1** One who drives or owns a team. **2** One who drives a truck or other commercial vehicle.

team teaching *U.S.* A method of organizing instruction in schools so that students in a given course are taught by several teachers, each of whom sometimes teaches the whole group and sometimes a part of it.

team·work (tēm′wûrk′) *n.* **1** Work done by or requiring to be done by or with a team of horses: distinguished from manual labor. **2** Unity of action by the players on an athletic team to further the success of the team. **3** Cooperation.

tea party A social gathering at which tea and light sandwiches or cakes are the principal refreshments.

tea·pot (tē′pot′) *n.* A vessel with a spout and handle in which tea is made and from which it is served.

tea·poy (tē′poi) *n.* A small three- or four-legged table for holding a tea service. [<Hind. *tipāī* <*tīm* three + Persian *pāē* foot]

tear[1] (târ) *v.* **tore, torn, tear·ing** *v.t.* **1** To pull apart, as cloth; part or separate by pulling; rip; rend. **2** To make by rending or tearing: to *tear* a hole in a dress. **3** To injure or lacerate, as skin. **4** To divide; disrupt: a party *torn* by dissension. **5** To distress or torment; anguish: The sight *tore* his heart. —*v.i.* **6** To become torn or rent. **7** To move with haste and energy. See synonyms under REND. —*n.* **1** A fissure made by tearing; a rent; an act of tearing. **2** *Slang* A carouse; a spree; frolic. **3** A rushing motion: to start off with a *tear,* also, any violent outburst, as of anger, enthusiasm, etc. ◆Homophone: *tare.* [OE *teran*]

tear[2] (tir) *n.* **1** A drop of the saline liquid secreted by the lacrimal gland, for moistening the eye. **2** Something resembling or suggesting a drop of the lacrimal fluid. **3** A drop of any liquid. **4** A droplike portion, as of glass, amber, etc. **5** *pl.* Sorrow; lamentation. ◆Homophone: *tier.* [OE *tēar*] **—tear′less** *adj.* **—tear′y** *adj.*

Tear may appear as a combining form in hyphemes or solidemes, with the meaning of definition 1:

tear-blinded	**tear-marked**
tear-dimmed	**tear-moistened**
tear-filled	**tear-provoking**
tear-freshened	**tear-shedding**
tear-glistening	**tear-stained**
tear-kissed	**tear-swollen**

tear·drop (tir′drop′) *n.* A tear.

tear·ful (tir′fəl) *adj.* **1** Weeping abundantly. **2** Causing tears. **—tear′ful·ly** *adv.* **—tear′ful·ness** *n.*

tear gas (tir) A lacrimator.

tear·ing (târ′ing) *adj. Colloq.* **1** Rushing along as in a hurry or rage. **2** Tremendous; mighty.

tear-jerk·er (tir′jûr′kər) *n. U.S. Slang* A story, play, or motion picture charged with sentimental sadness.

tea·room (tē′ro͞om′, -ro͝om′) n. A restaurant serving tea and other refreshments.

tea rose **1** Any of numerous garden roses thought to be tea-scented, primarily hybrids bred from the Chinese *Rosa odorata.* **2** A yellowish-pink color of many hues.

tear-sheet (târ′shēt′) *n.* A page torn or cut from a magazine, book, or newspaper, containing matter of particular interest.

Teas·dale (tēz′dāl), **Sara,** 1884–1933, U.S. poet.

tease (tēz) *v.* **teased, teas·ing** *v.t.* **1** To annoy or harass with continual importunities, raillery, etc.; pester. **2** To scratch or dress in order to raise the nap, as cloth with teasels. **3** To tear or pull apart with instruments, as tissues in examination. **4** To comb or card, as wool or flax; also, to pick or shred, as hard-packed tobacco. **5** To comb (hair) in such a way as to form fluffy layers and give an effect of fullness. —*v.i.* **6** To annoy a person in a facetious or petty way. See synonyms under AFFRONT. —*n.* **1** One who or that which teases. **2** The act of teasing or the state of being teased. [OE *tǣsan* tease, pluck, pull about] **—teas′ing** *n.* & *adj.* **—teas′ing·ly** *adv.*

tea·sel (tē′zəl) *n.* **1** A coarse, prickly Old World herb (genus *Dipsacus*) of which the flower head is covered with hooked bracts, especially the **fuller's teasel** *(D. fullonum).* **2** The rough bur of this plant, or a mechanical substitute: used in dressing cloth. —*v.t.* **·seled** or **·selled, ·sel·ing** or **·sel·ling** To use a teasel on; raise the nap of with a teasel. Also **tea′zel, tea′zle.** [OE *tǣsel*] **—tea′sel·er** or **tea′sel·ler** *n.*

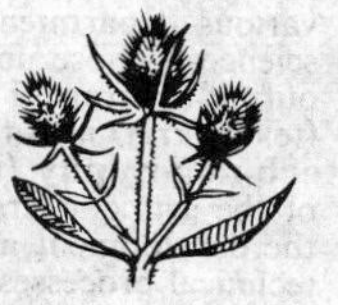

TEASEL (Plant to 5 feet or more)

teas·er (tē′zər) *n.* **1** One who or that which teases, as a machine used for teasing wool. **2** Anything tempting or whetting the appetites. **3** The border at the front of the stage. Compare BORDER.

tea service The articles used in serving tea: a silver *tea service.* Also **tea set.**

tea·shop (tē′shop′) *n.* **1** A tearoom. **2** *Brit.* A lunchroom.

tea·spoon (tē′spo͞on′, -spo͞on′) *n.* **1** A small spoon used for stirring tea, etc. **2** As much as a teaspoon will hold, 1/3 of a tablespoon, usually 1 1/3 fluid drams: also **tea′spoon·ful′** (-fo͝ol′).

teat (tēt) *n.* The protuberance on the breast or udder of most female mammals, through which the milk is drawn; a nipple; pap; dug. [<OF *tete* <Gmc.]

tea wagon A table on wheels for use in serving tea or refreshments.

Te·bet (tā·vāth′, tā′ves) A Hebrew month. Also **Te·beth′.** See CALENDAR (Hebrew).

Te·briz (tə·brēz′) See TABRIZ.

tech·ne·ti·um (tek·nē′shē·əm) *n.* An intensely radioactive metallic element (symbol Tc, atomic number 43) produced synthetically on earth but found in the spectra of certain stars, the most stable of its isotopes having a half-life of 2.6 million years. See PERIODIC TABLE. [<NL <Gk. *technētos* artificial]

tech·nic (tek′nik) *n.* **1** Technique. **2** *pl.* The theory of an art or of the arts; specifically, the study of the techniques of an art. **3** *pl.* Technical rules, methods, etc. **4** *pl.* Technology. —*adj.* Technical.

tech·ni·cal (tek′ni·kəl) *adj.* **1** Pertaining to some particular art, science, or trade. **2** Peculiar to a specialized field of knowledge. **3** Of or pertaining to the mechanical arts. **4** Employing a specialized vocabulary, as in a treatise or textbook. **5** Considered in terms of an accepted body of rules and regulations: a *technical* defeat. **6** Designating a money market in which prices are for the most part determined by speculation or manipulation. [<Gk. *technikos* <*technē* art] **—tech′ni·cal·ly** *adv.* **—tech′ni·cal·ness** *n.*

tech·ni·cal·i·ty (tek′ni·kal′ə·tē) *n. pl.* **·ties** **1** The state of being technical. **2** The use of technical terms. **3** A technical point peculiar to some profession, art, trade, etc. **4** A petty distinction; quibble. Also **tech′nism.**

technical knockout In boxing, a victory awarded when one fighter has been beaten so severely that the referee discontinues the fight. Abbr. *t.k.o., T.K.O.,* or *TKO*

tech·ni·cian (tek·nish′ən) *n.* **1** One skilled in the handling of instruments or in the performance of tasks requiring specialized training. **2** A rating in the armed services including those qualified for technical work; also, one having such a rating.

Tech·ni·col·or (tek′ni·kul′ər) *n.* A process used in making color motion pictures: a trade name. Also **tech′ni·col·or.**

tech·nique (tek·nēk′) *n.* Working methods or manner of performance, as in art, science, etc. [<F <Gk. *technikos.* See TECHNICAL.]

techno- *combining form* **1** Art; skill; craft: *technology.* **2** Technical; technological. Also, before vowels, **techn-.** [<Gk. *technē* an art, skill]

tech·noc·ra·cy (tek·nok′rə·sē) *n. pl.* **·cies** **1** A

community governed by experts in applied and theoretical science; national government by organized technologists and engineers. 2 A non-political fact-finding body of experts in the various departments of applied and theoretical sciences, whose aim is to re-evaluate industrial output in terms of energy factors. **—tech′no·crat** (tek′nə·krat) *n.* **—tech′no·crat′ic** *adj.*

tech·nog·ra·phy (tek·nog′rə·fē) *n.* 1 Description of the arts and crafts. 2 The scientific study of the development and geographic distribution of technical processes.

tech·nol·a·tor (tek·nol′ə·tər) *n.* One who has an excessive admiration for or belief in technology, especially in relation to social problems; immoderate worship of techniques, gadgets, machinery, and the like. [<TECHNO- + Gk. *latris* servant <*latron* pay, hire] **—tech·nol′a·try** *n.*

tech·no·lith·ic (tek′nə·lith′ik) *adj. Anthropol.* Pertaining to or designating those stone implements which were deliberately fashioned for some intended purpose.

tech·no·log·i·cal (tek′nə·loj′i·kəl) *adj.* Of, pertaining to, associated with, produced or affected by technology, especially in relation to improvements resulting from the application of technical advances in industry, manufacturing, commerce, and the arts. Also **tech′no·log′ic.** **—tech′no·log′i·cal·ly** *adv.*

tech·nol·o·gy (tek·nol′ə·jē) *n.* 1 Theoretical knowledge of industry and the industrial arts. 2 The application of science to the arts. 3 That branch of ethnology which treats of the development of the arts. **—tech·nol′o·gist** *n.*

tech·y (tech′ē) *adj.* **tech·i·er, tech·i·est** Peevishly sensitive; irritable; touchy. Also spelled *tetchy.* [<OF *teche* mark, quality] **—tech′i·ly** *adv.* **—tech′i·ness** *n.*

tec·tol·o·gy (tek·tol′ə·jē) *n.* The branch of morphology that treats of the manner in which organic forms are built up. [<Gk. *tektōn* carpenter, builder + -LOGY] **—tec·to·log·i·cal** (tek′tə·loj′i·kəl) *adj.*

tec·ton·ic (tek·ton′ik) *adj.* 1 Of or pertaining to building or construction. 2 *Geol.* **a** Characteristic of or relating to the structure of the earth's crust, especially as due to deformation. **b** Denoting the forces producing such structures. [<L *tectonicus* <Gk. *tektonikos* <*tektōn* carpenter]

tec·ton·ics (tek·ton′iks) *n. pl. (construed as singular)* 1 The science or art of constructing functionally beautiful buildings or things. 2 The geology of earth structure.

tec·tri·ces (tek·trī′sēz, tek′tri-) *n. pl. of* **tec·trix** (tek′triks) *Ornithol.* The wing coverts of a bird. [<NL <L *tectus,* pp. of *tegere* cover] **—tec·tri′cial** (-trish′əl) *adj.*

Te·cum·seh (ti·kum′sə), 1768?–1813, Shawnee chief, an ally of Britain in the War of 1812, during which he was killed.

ted (ted) *v.t.* **ted·ded, ted·ding** To turn over and strew about, or spread loosely for drying, as newly mown grass. [Prob. <Scand. Cf. ON *tethja* spread manure.]

Ted (ted), **Ted·dy** (ted′ē) Diminutives of EDWARD, THEODORE.

ted·der (ted′ər) *n.* 1 One who or that which teds. 2 *Agric.* A machine for spreading hay to dry.

ted·dy (ted′ē) *n. pl.* **·dies** A short undergarment combining chemise and drawers in one. [Origin unknown]

ted·dy bear (ted′ē) A toy bear, usually covered with plush. Also **Teddy bear.** [after *Teddy,* a nickname of Theodore Roosevelt]

Te De·um (tē dē′əm) 1 An ancient Christian hymn beginning with these words. 2 The music to which this hymn is set. 3 Any thanksgiving service in which it is sung. [<L *Te Deum (laudamus)* (we praise) Thee, O God]

te·di·ous (tē′dē·əs) *adj.* 1 Causing weariness; wearisome; boring. 2 *Obs.* Moving slowly. [<LL *taediosus* <L *taedium* tedium, weariness] **—te′di·ous·ly** *adv.* **—te′di·ous·ness** *n.*

Synonyms: dilatory, dreary, dull, fatiguing, irksome, monotonous, slow, sluggish, tardy, tiresome, wearisome. See WEARISOME. *Antonyms*: active, alert, animated, brilliant, energetic, exciting, lively, prompt, quick, stirring, vigorous, vivid.

te·di·um (tē′dē·əm) *n.* Tediousness; wearisomeness. [<L *taedium* <*taedere* vex, weary]

tee[1] (tē) *n.* 1 The letter T. 2 Something resembling the form of the letter T. 3 *Mining* The point of the meeting of two veins lying nearly at right angles to each other without intersecting. —*adj.* T-shaped. [OE *te* <L *te,* name of the letter T]

tee[2] (tē) *n.* 1 A little cone, as of damp sand or of wood, on which a golf ball is placed in making the first play to a hole. 2 The teeing ground in golf. —*v.t. & v.i.* **teed, tee·ing** To place (the ball) on a tee before striking it. **—to tee off** To strike (the ball) in starting play. [Prob. <TEE[3]]

tee[3] (tē) *n.* In certain games, a mark toward which the balls, quoits, etc., are directed, as in curling. **—to a tee** Exactly; as precisely as possible. [? <TEE[1]]

tee[4] (tē) *n.* A finial in the form of a conventionalized umbrella, used on pagodas, etc. [<Burmese *h′ti* umbrella]

teem[1] (tēm) *v.i.* 1 To be full, as if at the point of producing; be full to overflowing; abound. 2 *Obs.* To bear young. —*v.t.* 3 To produce or bring forth, as offspring: often figuratively. ◆ Homophone: *team.* [OE *tieman,* prob. <*tēam* progeny. Related to TEAM.] **—teem′er** *n.*

teem[2] (tēm) *v.i.* To pour; come down heavily: said of rain. —*v.t. Obs.* To pour out; empty. ◆ Homophone: *team.* [<ON *tœma* empty]

teem·ing[1] (tē′ming) *adj.* 1 Prolific; fecund; fruitful; productive. 2 Full; overflowing. 3 Produced in great quantity. See synonyms under FERTILE.

teem·ing[2] (tē′ming) *adj.* Raining heavily.

teen[1] (tēn) *n. Scot. & Brit. Dial.* Grief; trouble; also, provocation; vexation; anger. [OE *tēona* injury, vexation] **—teen′ful** *adj.*

teen[2] (tēn) *adj.* Teen-age.

-teen *suffix* Plus ten: used in cardinal numbers from 13 to 19 inclusive: *fifteen.* [OE *-tēne* <*tēn* ten]

teen age The age from 13 to 19 inclusive; hence, adolescence. **—teen′-age** *adj.*

teen-ag·er (tēn′ā′jər) *n.* A person of teen age.

teens (tēnz) *n. pl.* The numbers that end in *-teen*; the years of one's age from 13 to 19 inclusive.

tee·ny (tē′nē) *adj.* **·ni·er, ·ni·est** *Colloq.* Tiny. [Var. of TINY]

teen·y·bop·per (tē′nē·bop′ər) *n. Slang* A modern, hip teen-ager, especially a girl. [<Negro slang *teenybop, teenybopper* a teenage or tough teen-ager <TEEN(-AGE) + -Y[3] + *bop* fight (Cf. BOP[1]) + -ER[1]]

tee·pee (tē′pē) See TEPEE.

tee shirt (tē) See T-SHIRT.

Tees River (tēz) A river in northern England, flowing 70 miles east from eastern Cumberland, between Durham and York, to the North Sea.

tee·ter (tē′tər) *v.i.* 1 To see-saw. 2 To walk or move with a swaying or tottering motion. 3 To vacillate; waver. —*v.t.* 4 To cause to teeter. —*n.* 1 An oscillating motion. 2 A see-saw. 3 The spotted sandpiper: so called from its jerky motions. [<dial. E *titter,* prob. <ON *titra* tremble, shiver]

teeter board A see-saw.

tee·ter-tot·ter (tē′tər·tot′ər) *n.* A see-saw. [<TEETER + TOTTER]

teeth (tēth) Plural of TOOTH.

teethe (tēth) *v.i.* **teethed, teeth·ing** To cut or develop teeth.

teeth·ing (tē′thing) *n.* The process of developing and cutting teeth; dentition.

teething ring A ring of hard rubber, bone, or ivory for a teething baby to bite on.

tee·to·tal (tē·tōt′l) *adj.* 1 Pertaining to total abstinence from intoxicants. 2 Total; entire. [<TOTAL, with emphatic repetition of initial letter] **—tee·to′tal·ism** *n.* **—tee·to′tal·ly** *adv.*

tee·to·tal·er (tē·tōt′l·ər) *n.* One who abstains totally from intoxicants as beverages. Also **tee·to′tal·ist, tee·to′tal·ler.**

tee·to·tum (tē·tō′təm) *n.* 1 A kind of top having lettered and numbered sides: used in the game of put and take. 2 A child's toy, often four-sided, pierced by a peg and spun by the fingers. Also spelled *tetotum*: sometimes called *toddle-top.* [<*T-totum* <*T* + L *totus* all; from the fact that the side marked with a T wins the entire stake]

Tef·lon (tef′lon) *n.* A chemically resistant, heat-stable plastic polymer of fluorine and ethylene having wide application in industry and electronics: a trade name.

teg·men (teg′mən) *n. pl.* **·mi·na** (-mə·nə) 1 A covering or coat. 2 *Bot.* The soft inner covering of a seed. Also **teg′u·men** (-yə·min). [<L <*tegere* cover] **—teg′mi·nal** *adj.*

Teg·nér (teng·nâr′) **Esaisas,** 1782–1846, Swedish poet: also **Teng′ner.**

Te·gu·ci·gal·pa (tä·gōō′sē·gäl′pä) The capital of Honduras, in the SW part of the country.

teg·u·la (teg′yə·lə) *n. pl.* **·lae** (-lē) A tile. [<L *tegula* roof tile <*tegere* cover]

teg·u·lar (teg′yə·lər) *adj.* 1 Pertaining to or resembling tiles. 2 Arranged like tiles. 3 Formed of overlapping plates or scales. Also **teg′u·lat′ed.** **—teg′u·lar·ly** *adv.*

teg·u·ment (teg′yə·mənt) *n.* A covering or envelope; an integument. [<L *tegumentum* <*tegere* cover] **—teg·u·men·ta·ry** (teg′yə·men′tər·ē), **teg′u·men′tal** *adj.*

te-hee (tē·hē′) *v.i.* **-heed, -hee·ing** To laugh frivolously or with derision; titter; giggle. —*interj.* An imitative exclamation. —*n.* A restrained laugh; titter. [Imit.]

Te·he·ran (te′ə·rän′, -ran′; *Persian* te·hrän′) The capital of Iran, in the north central part; Roosevelt, Churchill, and Stalin conferred here in November, 1943. Also **Te·hran′.**

Teh·ri (tā′rē) A district of northern Uttar Pradesh State, India; 4,516 square miles; before 1949 a princely state; capital, Tehri. Also **Teh′ri-Garh·wal′** (-gûr·wäl′).

Te·huan·te·pec (te·wän′te·pek′), **Isthmus of** The narrowest part of southern Mexico (125 miles wide) between the **Gulf of Tehuantepec,** an arm of the Pacific Ocean, about 300 miles long, NW to SE, on the coast of southern Mexico, and the Gulf of Campeche.

Te·huan·te·pec Winds (te·wän′te·pek′) *n. pl.* Violent NE winds striking the Gulf of Tehuantepec in winter and early spring.

Te·huel·che (te·wel′che) *n.* One of a group of tribes of South American Indians inhabiting Patagonia, noted for their great height. **—Te·huel′che·an** (-chē·ən) *adj.*

te ig·i·tur (tē ij′ə·tər) The prayer or paragraph beginning the canon of the mass in Latin liturgies. [<L, thee therefore]

teil (tēl) *n.* 1 The linden. 2 The terebinth pistache *(Pistacia terebinthus)* of the Bible. Also called *teyl tree.* [<OF <L *tilia* lime tree]

teind (tēnd) *n. Scot.* A tithe or tithes.

Te·jo (tā′zhōō) The Portuguese name for the TAGUS.

Te·ju·co (tə·zhōō′kōō) A former name for Diamantina, Brazil.

tek·non·y·my (tek·non′ə·mē) *n. Anthropol.* The custom of renaming a parent after his or her child. [<Gk. *teknon* child + *onyma, onoma* name]

tek·tite (tek′tīt) *n. Geol.* Any of numerous small, rounded, glassy objects found in scattered geographical areas and thought to originate in collisions with cosmic bodies. [<Gk. *tēktos* molten + -ITE[1]]

tel- Var. of TELO-[1].

te·la (tē′lə) *n. pl.* **·lae** (-lē) 1 A tissue or weblike membrane. 2 *Anat.* One of the thin membranes **(tela choroidea),** prolongations of the pia mater, that cover the third and fourth ventricles of the brain. [<L, web]

tel·aes·the·sia (tel′əs·thē′zhə, -zhē·ə) See TELESTHESIA.

tel·a·mon (tel′ə·mon) *n. pl.* **tel·a·mo·nes** (tel′ə·mō′nēz) *Archit.* A male figure used as a pillar to support an entablature, etc. Compare ATLANTES, CARYATID. [<L <Gk. *telamōn* <*tlēnai* bear]

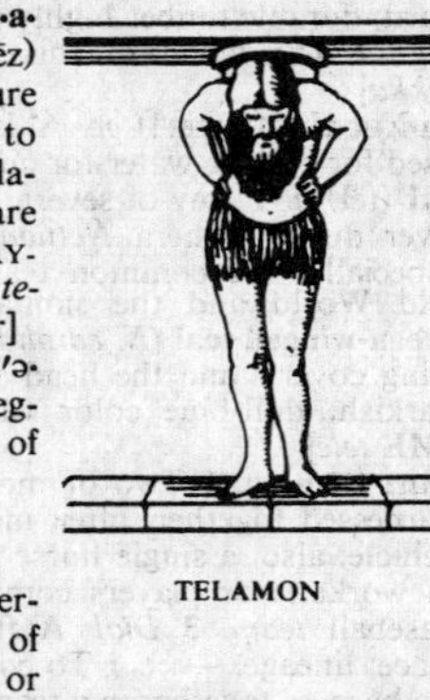

TELAMON

Tel·a·mon (tel′ə·mon) In Greek legend, the father of Ajax.

tel·an·gi·ec·ta·sia (tel·an′jē·ek·tā′zhə, -zhē·ə) *n. Pathol.* Permanent dilatation of the small arteries or capillaries, producing a vascular tumor: often seen in the form of maternal birthmarks; wine spots. Also **tel·an·gi·ec·ta·sis** (tel′ən·jē·ek′tə·sis). [<NL <Gk. *telos* end + *angeion* vessel + *ekstasis* dilatation] **—tel·an′gi·ec·tat′ic** (-tat′ik) *adj.*

tel·au·to·gram (tel·ô′tə·gram) *n.* A record made by a telautograph.

tel·au·to·graph (tel·ô′tə·graf, -gräf) *n.* An electromagnetically operated device for reproducing writing or drawings at a distance.

Tel A·viv (tel′ə·vēv′) The largest city of Israel, on the Mediterranean: since 1950 includes Jaffa.

tel·e (tel′ē) *n. Psychoanal.* The development between two or more persons of a relationship based on the gradual recognition of mutual attractions or repulsions either within or between social groups. [<Gk. *tēle* far off]

tele- *combining form* 1 Far off; operating at a distance: *telegraph.* 2 Television; related to or transmitted by television: *telecast.* Also spelled *telo-.* Also, before vowels, **tel-**. [<Gk. *tēle* far]

tel·e·car·di·o·gram (tel′ə·kär′dē·ə·gram′) *n.* A cardiogram electrically produced at a distance from the subject.

tel·e·cast (tel′ə·kast, -käst) *v.t. & v.i.* **·cast** or **·cast·ed**, **·cast·ing** To broadcast by television. — *n.* A program broadcast by television.

tel·e·com·mu·ni·ca·tion (tel′ə·kə·myōō′nə·kā′shən) *n.* 1 The art and science of communicating at a distance, especially by means of electromagnetic impulses, with or without wires, as in radio, radar, television, telegraphy, telephony, etc. Also **tel′e·com·mu′ni·ca′tions.** 2 Any message so transmitted.

tel·e·du (tel′ə·dōō) *n.* A small, short-tailed East Indian mammal (genus *Mydaus*) which resembles the skunk in color and in its ability to emit a fetid odor when disturbed. [<Malay]

tel·e·fi·nal·ist (tel′ə·fī′nəl·ist) *n.* One who believes in final causes or the working out of a final purpose in life or the universe; a teleologist, especially one who seeks scientific proof of the existence of God.

tel·e·ga (te·le′gä) *n. Russian* A rude four-wheeled wagon without springs, used in Russia.

tel·e·gen·ic (tel′ə·jen′ik) *adj.* Videogenic.

tel·eg·no·sis (tel′əg·nō′sis) *n.* Knowledge of remote happenings by other than normal sensory means, as by clairvoyance. [<TELE- + Gk. *gnōsis* knowing]

Te·leg·o·nus (tə·leg′ə·nəs) In Greek legend, the son of Odysseus and Circe, who unknowingly killed his father in Ithaca and married Penelope, his father's wife.

te·leg·o·ny (tə·leg′ə·nē) *n. Biol.* The alleged influence of a previous sire on the progeny of the same mother from subsequent matings with other males. [<TELE- + -GONY] — **tel·e·gon·ic** (tel′ə·gon′ik), **te·leg′o·nous** *adj.*

tel·e·gram (tel′ə·gram) *n.* A message sent by telegraph. [<TELE- + -GRAM]

tel·e·graph (tel′ə·graf, -gräf) *n.* Any of various devices, systems, or processes for transmitting messages or signals to a distance, especially any form of such apparatus utilizing electromagnetic impulses transmitted by conducting wires between sending and receiving points. — *v.t.* 1 To send (a message) by telegraph. 2 To communicate with by telegraph. — *v.i.* 3 To transmit a message by telegraph. [<TELE- + -GRAPH]

te·leg·ra·pher (tə·leg′rə·fər) *n.* One who is employed in sending telegrams or is skilled in telegraphy. Also **te·leg′ra·phist.**

tel·e·graph·ic (tel′ə·graf′ik) *adj.* Of or pertaining to the telegraph; transmitted by means of telegraphy. Also **tel′e·graph′i·cal.** — **tel′e·graph′i·cal·ly** *adv.*

te·leg·ra·phone (tə·leg′rə·fōn) *n.* An instrument for recording and reproducing sound, similar in principle to the tape recorder but adapted for connection with a transmitter or microphone. [<TELE- + -GRA(PH) + -PHONE]

tel·e·graph·o·scope (tel′ə·graf′ə·skōp) *n.* An instrument for transmitting and reproducing a picture telegraphically. [<TELE- + GRAPHO- + -SCOPE]

te·leg·ra·phy (tə·leg′rə·fē) *n.* 1 The process of conveying messages by telegraph. 2 The art or science of the construction and operation of telegraphs.

Tel·e·gu (tel′ə·gōō) See TELUGU.

tel·e·ki·ne·sis (tel′ə·ki·nē′sis) *n.* 1 Movement of an object or inanimate body without apparent external cause. 2 The alleged power of a spiritualist medium to bring about such movements without direct or observable contact. — **tel′e·ki·net′ic** (-net′ik) *adj.*

tel·e·lec·tric (tel′i·lek′trik) *adj.* Denoting the transmission, as of music, to a distance by electricity. [<TEL(E)- + ELECTRIC]

Te·lem·a·chus (tə·lem′ə·kəs) In Greek legend, son of Odysseus and Penelope, who helped his father kill his mother's suitors.

tel·e·mark (tel′ə·märk) *n.* In skiing, a turn effected by shifting the weight to one advanced ski and turning its tip inward: used to change direction or stop quickly. [from *Telemark*, Norway]

tel·e·me·chan·ics (tel′ə·mə·kan′iks) *n.* 1 The theory and practice of operating mechanisms from a distance. 2 Remote control operation, as by electromagnetic and radio impulses.

te·lem·e·ter (tə·lem′ə·tər, tel′ə·mē′tər) *n.* 1 An apparatus for determining distances by the measurement of angles. 2 An electrical apparatus for indicating or measuring various quantities and for transmitting the data to a distant point. — **te·lem′e·try** *n.* — **tel·e·met·ric** (tel′ə·met′rik) *adj.*

tel·e·mo·tor (tel′ə·mō′tər) *n.* A hydraulic or electrical device by which power is applied at a distance, especially in operating the steering gear of a vessel by turning the wheel on the bridge.

tel·en·ceph·a·lon (tel′en·sef′ə·lon) *n. Anat.* The terminal division of the neural tube of the embryo from which are developed the cerebral hemispheres and olfactory lobes; the endbrain. [<TEL(E)- + ENCEPHALON] — **tel·en·ce·phal·ic** (tel′en·si·fal′ik) *adj.*

teleo- Var. of TELO-[1].

tel·e·ol·o·gy (tel′ē·ol′ə·jē, tē′lē-) *n.* 1 The branch of cosmology that treats of final causes. See FINAL CAUSE. 2 The philosophical and biological doctrine of design which holds that the phenomena of organic life and development can be explained by conscious or purposive causes directed to definite ends and not by mechanical causes; vitalism as opposed to *mechanism.* 3 The explanation of nature in terms of utility or purpose, especially divine purpose; the study of a creative design in the processes of nature. [<NL *teleologia* <Gk. *telos, teleos* end + *logos* discourse] — **tel·e·o·log·i·cal** (-ə·loj′i·kəl) or **tel·e·o·log′ic** *adj.* — **tel′e·o·log′i·cal·ly** *adv.* — **tel′e·ol′o·gist** *n.*

tel·e·ost (tel′ē·ost, tē′lē-) *n.* Any of a large and widely distributed group or order (*Teleostei*) of fishes having true bones: distinguished from cyclostomes and elasmobranchs. — *adj.* Of, pertaining to, or having the characteristics of the teleosts. Also **tel·e·os′te·an.** [<Gk. *telos* end + *osteon* bone]

te·lep·a·thy (tə·lep′ə·thē) *n.* The supposed communication of one mind with another at a distance by other than normal sensory means; thought-transference. [<TELE- + -PATHY] — **tel·e·path·ic** (tel′ə·path′ik) *adj.* — **tel′e·path′i·cal·ly** *adv.* — **te·lep′a·thist** *n.*

tel·e·phone (tel′ə·fōn) *n.* An instrument for reproducing sound or speech at a distant point, by the electromagnetic transmission of variable audio frequencies over a conducting wire or other communication channel. — **wireless telephone** A radiotelephone. — *v.* **·phoned**, **·phon·ing** — *v.t.* 1 To send by telephone, as a message. 2 To communicate with by telephone. — *v.i.* 3 To communicate by telephone. [<TELE- + -PHONE] — **tel′e·phon′er** *n.*

telephone receiver That part of a telephone in which a diaphragm is caused to vibrate by electric impulses, converting the varying current into sound.

tel·e·phon·ic (tel′ə·fon′ik) *adj.* 1 Of or pertaining to the telephone. 2 Conveying sound to a great distance. Also **tel′e·phon′i·cal.** — **tel′e·phon′i·cal·ly** *adv.*

tel·e·pho·no·graph (tel′ə·fō′nə·graf, -gräf) *n.* A combination of a phonograph and a telephone receiver by which telephone messages can be recorded and then reproduced. — **tel′e·pho′no·graph′ic** *adj.*

te·leph·o·ny (tə·lef′ə·nē) *n.* The art or process of communicating by telephone, with or without wires directly connecting the terminal points.

tel·e·pho·to (tel′ə·fō′tō) *adj.* 1 Denoting a combination of lenses which produces a large image of a distant object in a camera; tele-photographic. 2 Pertaining to telephotography.

tel·e·pho·to·graph (tel′ə·fō′tə·graf, -gräf) *n.* 1 A picture transmitted by wire or radio. 2 A picture made with a telephoto lens. — **tel′e·pho′to·graph′ic** *adj.*

tel·e·pho·tog·ra·phy (tel′ə·fə·tog′rə·fē) *n.* 1 The art of producing photographic images of distant objects on a larger scale than is possible with an ordinary camera. 2 The reproduction of photographs or other picture material by radio or wire communication.

tel·e·plasm (tel′ə·plaz′əm) *n.* Ectoplasm (def. 2). [<TELE- + -PLASM]

tel·e·print·er (tel′ə·prin′tər) *n.* A teletypewriter.

Tel·e·prompt·er (tel′ə·promp′tər) *n.* A prompting device for television whereby a prepared script, unseen by the audience, is shown to a speaker or performer, enlarged line by line: a trade name.

tel·e·ra·di·o (tel′ə·rā′dē·ō) *n. pl.* **·di·os** Television and radio taken collectively, especially with reference to their use as advertising media. — *adj.* Pertaining to or by means of teleradio. [<TELE- (def. 2) + RADIO]

tel·e·ran (tel′ə·ran) *n. Telecom.* A system of air navigation which combines the principles of television and radar, the information being gathered by ground stations and transmitted to all aircraft within range. [<TELE- (def. 2) + R(ADAR) A(IR) N(AVIGATION)]

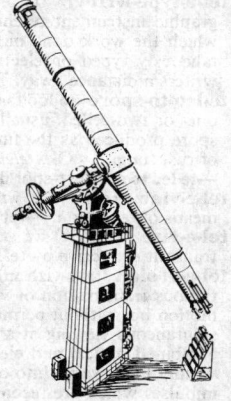

REFRACTING TELESCOPE Yerkes Observatory 40 inch.

tel·e·scope (tel′ə·skōp) *n.* 1 An optical instrument for enlarging the image of a distant object, consisting of an object glass for collecting light beams from the object and an eyepiece for viewing the image. The **refracting telescope** transmits the rays to a focus through a combination of lenses called the object glass; the **reflecting telescope** brings them to a focus by reflection from a concave mirror. 2 A valise or traveling bag that shuts with one section inside the other, and thus can be extended, like a telescope. — *v.* **·scoped**, **·scop·ing** *v.t.* 1 To drive or slide together so that one part fits into another in the manner of the sections of a small telescope. 2 To crush by driving something into or upon. 3 To represent in a compressed or shortened form, as a period of time. — *v.i.* 4 To crash or be forced into one another, as railroad cars in a collision. [<TELE- + -SCOPE]

telescope word A blend (def. 2).

tel·e·scop·ic (tel′ə·skop′ik) *adj.* 1 Pertaining to the telescope. 2 Visible only through a telescope. 3 Far-seeing. 4 Having sections that slide within or over one another. Also **tel′e·scop′i·cal.** — **tel′e·scop′i·cal·ly** *adv.*

tel·e·scop·tics (tel′ə·skop′tiks) *n. pl.* (construed as singular) The art of designing, constructing, and using telescopes.

te·les·co·py (tə·les′kə·pē) *n.* The art of using or making telescopes. — **te·les′co·pist** *n.*

tel·e·script (tel′ə·skript) *n.* A script written or adapted for a television program. [<TELE- (def. 2) + SCRIPT]

tel·e·set (tel′ə·set) *n.* A television receiving set.

tel·e·sis (tel′ə·sis) *n. Sociol.* Satisfactory progress toward an intended purpose, especially as the result of skilled direction of forces and intelligent planning. [<NL <Gk. *telein* fulfil < *telos, teleos* end]

tel·e·spec·tro·scope (tel′ə·spek′trə·skōp) *n.* 1 A combined telescope and spectroscope. 2 A spectroscope for attachment to a telescope.

tel·e·ster·e·o·scope (tel′ə·ster′ē·ə·skōp′, -stir′-) *n.* An optical instrument that presents images of objects at a distance from the observer in enhanced relief.

tel·es·the·sia (tel′is·thē′zhə, -zhē·ə) *n.* Susceptibility to stimuli coming from a distance and beyond the normal range of the senses: also spelled *telaesthesia.* [< NL < Gk. *tēle* far + *aisthēsis* feeling] **—tel′es·thet′ic** (-thet′ik) *adj.*

tel·e·stich (tel′ə·stik, tə·les′tik) *n.* An acrostic in which the significant letters are at the ends of the lines. [< Gk. *telos* end + *stichos* line]

tel·e·ther·a·py (tel′ə·ther′ə·pē) *n. Med.* 1 Treatment by radiation administered in massive doses at a distance from the body. 2 The prescribing of medical treatment by telephone, letter, etc.: also called **absent treatment.**

tel·e·ther·mom·e·ter (tel′ə·thûr·mom′ə·tər) *n.* Any apparatus used to indicate the temperature of a distant point, as a thermocouple. **—tel′e·ther·mom′e·try** *n.*

tel·e·thon (tel′ə·thon) *n.* A long telecast, usually to raise funds for a charity. [< TELE- + (MARA)THON]

tel·e·tran·scrip·tion (tel·ə·tran·skrip′shən) *n.* A method for transcribing television programs on films for subsequent presentation; also, the transcription itself.

tel·e·type (tel′ə·tīp) *v.t.* & *v.i.* **·typed, ·typ·ing** To communicate (with) by teletypewriter or Teletype. *—n.* A teletypewriter. **—tel′e·typ′er** *n.*

Tel·e·type (tel′ə·tīp) *n.* A teletypewriter: a trade name.

tel·e·type·writ·er (tel′ə·tīp′rī′tər) *n.* A telegraphic instrument resembling a typewriter, by which the work done on one machine is simultaneously typed on electrically connected typewriters a distance away.

te·leu·to·spore (tə·lo͞o′tə·spôr, -spōr) *n. Bot.* The one- or two-celled, usually stalked, thick-walled spore produced as the final stage in the growth of rust fungi. [< Gk. *teleutē* fulfilment + SPORE] **—te·leu′to·spor′ic** (-spôr′ik, -spor′ik) *adj.*

tel·e·view (tel′ə·vyo͞o) *v.t.* & *v.i.* To observe by means of television. **—tel′e·view′er** *n.*

tel·e·vise (tel′ə·vīz) *v.t.* & *v.i.* **·vised, ·vis·ing** To transmit or receive by television.

tel·e·vi·sion (tel′ə·vizh′ən) *n.* The exact and continuous transmission of visual images, still or in motion but without permanent recording, for instantaneous viewing at a distance: effected by a combined optical and electrical system for converting light waves into corresponding electrical impulses which are reconverted into their visual form in a receiving set. **—tel′e·vi′sion·al, tel′e·vi′sion·ar′y** (-vizh′ən·er′ē) *adj.*

tel·ex (tel′iks) *n.* 1 A communication system using teletypewriters connected by wire through exchanges which operate automatically. 2 A message sent by such a system. *—v.t.* To send by telex. [< TEL(ETYPEWRITER) + EX(CHANGE)]

tel·fer (tel′fər) See TELPHER.

tel·ford (tel′fərd) *adj.* Designating a road made of large broken stone packed with smaller pieces, covered with a layer of finely broken stone or gravel, and rolled hard and smooth. *—n.* A road having such a surface. [after Thomas *Telford,* 1757–1834, Scottish engineer]

tel·ford·ize (tel′fər·dīz) *v.t.* **·ized, ·iz·ing** To make or cover (a road) with a telford surface.

tel·har·mo·ni·um (tel′här·mō′nē·əm) *n.* An instrument by which an operator at a central station playing on a keyboard controlling alternating electric currents is able to produce music at a distance. [< TEL(E)- + HARMONIUM] **—tel′har·mon′ic** (-mon′ik) *adj.* **—tel·har′mo·ny** (-här′mə·nē) *n.*

tel·ic (tel′ik, tē′lik) *adj.* Connected with, tending toward, or denoting a purpose; teleological. [< Gk. *telikos* < *telos* end] **—tel′i·cal·ly** *adv.*

te·li·o·stage (tē′lē·ə·stāj′, tel′ē-) *n. Bot.* The last stage in the life cycle of rust fungi. [< TELIUM + STAGE]

te·li·um (tē′lē·əm, tel′ē-) *n. Bot.* The sorus of the teliostage of the rust fungi. [< NL < Gk. *telos, teleos* end] **—te′li·al** *adj.*

tell (tel) *v.* **told, tell·ing** *v.t.* 1 To relate in detail; narrate, as a story. 2 To make known by speech or writing; communicate. 3 To make known; reveal; disclose: to *tell* secrets. 4 To decide; ascertain: I cannot *tell* who is to blame. 5 To utter; express in words: to *tell* a lie. 6 To give a command to; bid; order: I *told* him to go home. 7 To let know; inform. 8 *Colloq.* To inform or assure emphatically: It's cold out, I *tell* you! 9 To count; enumerate: to *tell* one's beads. *—v.i.* 10 To give an account or description: usually with *of.* 11 To disclose something; inform: with *on.* 12 To serve as indication or evidence: with *of*: Their rags *told* of their poverty. 13 To produce a marked effect: Every blow *told.* See synonyms under AFFIRM, ASSERT, INFORM[1], PUBLISH, RELATE, SPEAK. **—all told** Everyone or everything being counted; in all. **—to tell off** 1 To count and set apart. 2 *Colloq.* To reprimand severely. *—n. Dial.* 1 Something told; story; say. 2 Account; story; explanation: according to his *tell.* **—to hear tell** *Colloq.* To hear (something) spoken of: I've *heard tell* of his accomplishments. [OE *tellan.* Akin to TALE, TALK.] **—tell′a·ble** *adj.*

Tell (tel), **William** A legendary Swiss hero in the struggle for independence from Austria. He refused to salute the governor's cap, which had been set up as a symbol of Austrian authority, and was forced to shoot an apple off his son's head with bow and arrow.

Tell el A·mar·na (tel el ə·mär′nə) Site of the ruins of an ancient city on the east bank of the Nile, Upper Egypt; Ikhnaton's capital, built about 1360 B.C.

tell·er (tel′ər) *n.* 1 One who relates or informs. 2 A person who receives or pays out money, as in a bank. 3 A person appointed to collect and count ballots in a legislative body or other assembly.

Tel·ler (tel′ər), **Edward,** born 1908, U.S. atomic physicist born in Hungary.

tell·ing (tel′ing) *adj.* Producing a great effect; impressive; effective; striking. See synonyms under VIVID. **—tell′ing·ly** *adv.*

tell·tale (tel′tāl′) *adj.* 1 Tattling; talebearing. 2 Betraying. *—n.* 1 One who improperly gives information concerning the private affairs of others; a tattler. 2 That which conveys information, especially in an involuntary way; a token. 3 An instrument or device, usually automatic, for giving information as to number, position, condition, etc. 4 A row of dangling straps or ropes suspended above a railway track to warn anyone standing on a car roof of the approach of a low overhead structure. 5 A clock to record the times of coming and going, as of workmen, or as a watchman's clock. 6 An index showing the position of a vessel's helm. 7 A yellowlegs or tattler.

telltale sandpiper The yellowlegs.

tel·lu·rate (tel′yə·rāt) *n. Chem.* A salt of telluric acid.

tel·lu·ri·an (te·lo͝or′ē·ən, tel·yo͝or′-) *adj.* Of or pertaining to the earth or its inhabitants. *—n.* An inhabitant of the earth. [< L *tellus, -uris* the earth]

tel·lu·ric (te·lo͝or′ik, tel·yo͝or′-) *adj.* 1 Of or pertaining to the earth; terrestrial; earthly. 2 *Chem.* Derived from or containing tellurium, especially in its higher valence.

telluric acid *Chem.* A weak acid, H_6TeO_4, obtained by oxidizing tellurium. It is analogous to sulfuric acid.

tel·lu·ride (tel′yə·rīd, -rid) *n. Chem.* A compound of tellurium with an element or an organic radical: *telluride* of lead.

tel·lu·rite (tel′yə·rīt) *n.* 1 A white or yellow native tellurium dioxide, TeO_2. 2 *Chem.* A salt of tellurous acid.

tel·lu·ri·um (te·lo͝or′ē·əm, tel·yo͝or′-) *n.* A brittle element (symbol Te, atomic number 52) having some metallic properties, rarely found native. See PERIODIC TABLE. [< NL < L *tellus, -uris* the earth]

tel·lu·rize (tel′yə·rīz) *v.t.* **·rized, ·riz·ing** To cause to combine with tellurium.

tel·lur·nick·el (tel·ər·nik′əl) *n.* Melonite. [< TELLUR(IUM) + NICKEL]

tel·lu·rous (tel′yər·əs, te·lo͝or′əs, tel·yo͝or′-) *adj. Chem.* Of, pertaining to, or derived from tellurium, especially in its lower valence: *tellurous* acid, H_2TeO_3.

Tel·lus (tel′əs) In Roman mythology, the goddess of the earth: identified with the Greek *Gaea.* Also **Tellus Mater.**

tel·ly (tel′ē) *n. pl.* **tel·lies** *Chiefly Brit. Colloq.* Television.

telo-[1] *combining form* Final; complete; perfect: *telophase*: also, before vowels, *tel-.* Also *teleo-.* [< Gk. *telos* end]

telo-[2] Var. of TELE-.

tel·o·blast (tel′ə·blast) *n. Zool.* A large cell at the growing end of the embryo, in annelids, etc., which produces rows of smaller cells. [< TELO-[1] + -BLAST]

tel·o·dy·nam·ic (tel′ə·dī·nam′ik, -di-) *adj.* Of, related to, or employed in the transmission of power to a distance, specifically by cables and pulleys. [< TELO-[2] + DYNAMIC]

tel·o·lec·i·thal (tel′ə·les′ə·thəl) *adj. Biol.* Having the nutritive part of the yolk at one pole: said of ova, as of birds, with unequal or partial segmentation. [< TELO-[1] + LECITHAL]

tel·o·phase (tel′ə·fāz) *n. Biol.* The closing phase of mitosis, when the cell divides and the daughter nuclei are formed. [< TELO-[1] + PHASE]

tel·pher (tel′fər) *n.* A light car suspended from cables and usually propelled by electricity: used for aerial transportation. *—v.t.* To transport by telpher. Also spelled *telfer.* [< TEL(E)- + Gk. *pherein* bear] **—tel′pher·ic** *adj.* **—tel′pher·age** (-ij) *n.*

tel·son (tel′sən) *n. Zool.* The last abdominal segment of the body of an arthropod, as of a lobster, shrimp, or scorpion. [< Gk. *telson* boundary]

Tel·star (tel′stär′) One of several U.S. communication satellites, the first of which was launched July 10, 1962.

Tel·u·gu (tel′o͞o·go͞o) *n. pl.* **·gu** 1 A Dravidian language, spoken by more than 30 million people, most important in literary culture. 2 One of a Dravidian people of Telugu speech, inhabiting NW Andhra Pradesh, India. *—adj.* Of or pertaining to the Telugu or to Telugu. Also spelled *Telegu.*

tem·blor (tem·blôr′) *n. pl.* **·blors** or **·blo·res** (-blô′rās) An earthquake. [< Sp.]

Tem·bu·land (tem′bo͞o·land) A district of eastern Cape of Good Hope Province, Republic of South Africa; 3,448 square miles; capital, Umtata.

tem·e·rar·i·ous (tem′ə·râr′ē·əs) *adj.* Unreasonably adventurous; rash; reckless. [< L *temerarius* < *temere* rashly] **—tem′e·rar′i·ous·ly** *adv.* **—tem′e·rar′i·ous·ness** *n.*

te·mer·i·ty (tə·mer′ə·tē) *n.* Venturesome or foolish boldness; rashness; disregard of personal danger or consequences. [< L *temeritas, -tatis* < *temere* rashly]

Synonyms: audacity, foolhardiness, hardihood, hastiness, heedlessness, precipitancy, precipitation, presumption, rashness, recklessness, venturesomeness. *Rashness* applies to the actual impulsive rushing into danger without counting the cost; *temerity* denotes the needless exposure of oneself to peril because of lack of foresight. *Rashness* is used chiefly of bodily acts, *temerity* often of mental or social matters. We say it is amazing that one should have had the *temerity* to make a statement which could be readily proved a falsehood; in such use *temerity* is often closely allied to *hardihood, audacity,* or *presumption. Venturesomeness* dallies on the edge of danger and experiments with it; *foolhardiness* rushes in for want of sense, *heedlessness* for want of attention, *rashness* for want of reflection, *recklessness* from disregard of consequences. *Antonyms*: care, caution, circumspection, cowardice, hesitation, timidity, wariness.

Tem·es·vár (te′mesh·vär) The Hungarian name for TIMISOARA.

Tem·pe (tem′pē), **Vale of** A valley, about 5 miles long, between Mount Olympus and Mount Ossa in Thessaly, Greece: famous for its beauty and in ancient times regarded as sacred to Apollo. *Greek* **Tem·be** (tem′bē).

Tem·pel·hof (tem′pəl·hof, *Ger.* tem′pəl·hōf) A southern district of West Berlin, Germany; site of the city's chief airport.

tem·per (tem′pər) *n.* 1 Heat of mind or passion; disposition to become angry; also, a fit of anger. 2 Quality of mind with reference to the passions, emotions, or affections; disposition. 3 Composure of mind; equanimity; self-command; calmness: used only in the phrases **to keep,** or **to lose, one's temper.** 4 *Metall.* The condition of a metal as regards hardness and brittleness, especially when due to heating and sudden cooling. 5 Consistency due to mixture, as of mortar, etc. 6 Lime or an equivalent used in clarifying sugar. 7 An alloy, as that added to tin to make pewter. 8 *Obs.* Constitutional condition, resulting, according to the

ancients, from the proportion in which the four humors were mixed. **9** *Archaic* A mean; medium. [<*v.*] — *v.t.* **1** To bring to a state of moderation or suitability, as by addition of another quality; free from excess; moderate; mitigate: to *temper* justice with mercy. **2** To bring to the proper consistency, texture, etc., by moistening and working: to *temper* clay. **3** To bring (metal) to a required hardness and elasticity by heating and suddenly cooling. **4** *Music* To adjust the tones of (an instrument) by temperament; tune. **5** *Obs.* To adjust. — *v.i.* **6** To be or become tempered. [Fusion of OE *temprian* mingle, regulate and OF *temprer*, *tremper* soak, temper (steel), both <L *temperare* combine in due proportion. For sense development of noun defs. 1, 2, and 3, see def. 8.] — **tem′per·a·bil′i·ty** *n.* — **tem′per·a·ble** *adj.* — **tem′per·er** *n.*
Synonyms (noun): constitution, disposition, frame, grain, humor, mood, nature, organization, temperament. See ANGER, CHARACTER.
Synonyms (verb): accommodate, adapt, adjust, appease, assuage, attemper, calm, fit, moderate, modify, mollify, pacify, qualify, restrain, soften, soothe.

tem·per·a (tem′pər·ə, *Ital.* tem′pä·rä) *n.* **1** A painting medium which is essentially an emulsion prepared by any of numerous recipes, and composed characteristically of oil usually thickened, with or without a resin such as dammar varnish, and egg and water. **2** The method of painting by this medium, which falls into three principal divisions: *unvarnished tempera*, *varnished tempera*, and *tempera*, as underpainting for oil glazes: widely used in the Renaissance and revived in modern times, sometimes in combination with oil techniques. [<Ital. <*temperare* temper <L]

tem·per·a·ment (tem′pər·ə·mənt, -prə-) *n.* **1** The characteristic physical and mental peculiarities of an individual as manifested in his reactions. **2** *Music* The tuning of an instrument so that the intervals of the scale shall follow a suitable law of succession. **3** Mental constitution; make-up; disposition. **4** Adjustment or compromise. **5** *Obs.* Temperature. See synonyms under CHARACTER, TEMPER. [<L *temperamentum* proper mixture <*temperare* mix in due proportions]

tem·per·a·men·tal (tem′pər·ə·men′təl, -prə-) *adj.* **1** Of or pertaining to temperament. **2** Having a strongly marked temperament. **3** Sensitive; easily excited; changeable. — **tem′per·a·men′tal·ly** *adv.*

tem·per·ance (tem′pər·əns) *n.* **1** The state or quality of being temperate; habitual moderation, especially in the indulgence of any appetite. **2** Specifically, the principle and practice of total abstinence from intoxicants. **3** *Obs.* Calmness; self-control. See synonyms under ABSTINENCE. — *adj.* **1** Of or pertaining to public places where alcoholic beverages are not sold. **2** Of, relating to, practicing, or promoting total abstinence from intoxicants. [<OF <L *temperantia*, orig. neut. pl. of *temperans*, -*antis*, ppr. of *temperare* mix in due proportions]

temperance pledge A pledge not to indulge in alcoholic drinks.

tem·per·ate (tem′pər·it) *adj.* **1** Observing moderation or self-control; specifically, by extension, not indulging in intoxicating liquors. **2** Moderate as regards temperature; free from extremes of heat or cold; mild. **3** Characterized by moderation or the absence of extremes; not excessive. **4** Calm; restrained; self-controlled. **5** *Music* Tempered: said of an interval or scale. See synonyms under SOBER. [<L *temperatus*, pp. of *temperare* mix in due proportions] — **tem′per·ate·ly** *adv.* — **tem′per·ate·ness** *n.*

temperate zone See ZONE (def. 1).

tem·per·a·ture (tem′pər·ə·chər, -prə-) *n.* **1** Condition as regards heat or cold. **2** The degree of heat in a body or substance, as measured on the graduated scale of a thermometer. See table below. **3** Sensible heat of the human body; also, excess of this above the normal. **4** *Obs.* Constitution; temperament; mixture; temperateness; temperance. [<L *temperatura* due measure <*temperatus*. See TEMPERATE.]

To convert from Fahrenheit to Celsius (Centigrade): Subtract 32 from the Fahrenheit reading, multiply by 5, and divide the product by 9. *Example:* 65° F. −32 = 33; 33 × 5 = 165; 165 ÷ 9 = 18.3° C. To convert from Celsius to Fahrenheit: Multiply the Celsius reading by 9, divide the product by 5, add 32. *Example:* 30° C. × 9 = 270; 270 ÷ 5 = 54; 54 + 32 = 86° F.

CONVERSION TABLE

Fahrenheit	Celsius	Fahrenheit	Celsius
500	260.0	−10	−23.3
400	204.4	−20	−28.9
300	149.0	−30	−34.4
212	100.0	−40	−40.0
200	93.3	−50	−45.6
100	37.8	−60	−51.1
90	32.2	−70	−56.7
80	26.7	−80	−62.2
70	21.1	−90	−67.8
60	15.6	−100	−73.3
50	10.0	−200	−129.0
40	4.4	−300	−184.0
32	0.0	−400	−240.0
30	−1.1	*−459.4	−273.0
20	−6.6		
10	−12.2		
0	−17.8	*Absolute zero	

temperature coefficient *Physics* The amount of change in some specified physical quantity per unit change in temperature: it may be positive or negative and is usually expressed as the quotient of the change observed after a rise of 1° C. divided by the constant value of the quantity at 0° C.

temperature gradient The rate of change in temperature with change in altitude or other variable factors.

tem·pered (tem′pərd) *adj.* **1** Having temper or a temper, in any sense; mostly in compounds: quick-*tempered*, ill-*tempered*. **2** *Music* Adjusted in pitch to some mean temperament. **3** Moderated by admixture. **4** Having the right degree of hardness and elasticity: well-*tempered* steel.

tem·per·pin (tem′pər·pin′) *n.* **1** A wooden screw used to regulate the motion of a spinning wheel. **2** A tuning peg of a violin.

tem·pest (tem′pist) *n.* **1** An extensive and violent wind, usually attended with rain, snow, or hail. **2** A violent commotion or agitation; a fierce tumult. See synonyms under STORM. — *v.t.* To agitate violently; affect as a tempest does. [<OF *tempeste* <L *tempestas* space of time, weather <*tempus* time]

tem·pes·tu·ous (tem·pes′chŏŏ·əs) *adj.* Stormy; turbulent; violent. [<OF *tempestueux* <LL *tempestuosus* <L *tempestas* weather. See TEMPEST.] — **tem·pes′tu·ous·ly** *adv.* — **tem·pes′tu·ous·ness** *n.*

tem·plar (tem′plər) *n.* A law student or a barrister who has apartments in the buildings known as the Inner and the Middle Temple in London. [<OF *templier* <Med. L *templarius* <L *templum.* See TEMPLE.]

Tem·plar (tem′plər) *n.* A Knight Templar.

tem·plate (tem′plit) *n.* **1** A pattern or gage, as of wood or metal, used as a guide in shaping something or in checking the accuracy of work. **2** In building, a stout stone or timber for distributing weight or thrust. **3** A wedge for a building block under a ship's keel. Also spelled *templet.* [<F *templette* stretcher, dim. of *temple* small timber <L *templum*]

tem·ple [1] (tem′pəl) *n.* **1** A stately edifice consecrated to one or more deities and forming a seat of their worship. **2** An edifice dedicated to public worship; especially, in the United States, a Reform synagog. **3** In France, a Protestant church. **4** Figuratively, any place considered as occupied by God; specifically, a sanctified human body. **5** A building erected and dedicated for the administration of Mormon ordinances; a Mormon church. — **the Temple 1** Either of two medieval establishments in London and Paris, once occupied by the Knights Templar. In London, since 1185, the district lying between Fleet Street and the Thames river, the site of the **Inner** and **Middle Temple.** See INNS OF COURT. **2** Any of three successive sacred

edifices built in Jerusalem for the worship of Jehovah. [OE *tempel* <L *templum* temple]

tem·ple [2] (tem′pəl) *n.* The region on each side of the head above the cheek bone. [<OF <L *tempora*, pl. of *tempus* temple]

tem·ple [3] (tem′pəl) *n.* An attachment to a loom that serves to keep the last woven part of the fabric stretched and to prevent chafing of the warp. [<F <L *templum* a small timber]

Tem·ple (tem′pəl), **Sir William,** 1628–99, English statesman, diplomat, and writer. — **William,** 1881–1944, English prelate; archbishop of Canterbury 1942–44.

Temple Bar A historic three-arched gateway in London marking the western boundary of the city proper and on which the heads of traitors and other malefactors were exposed. It was dismantled in 1878 but re-erected at Waltham Cross, in Essex, in 1888.

tem·pled (tem′pəld) *adj.* Honored with or enshrined in a temple: a *templed* god.

tem·plet (tem′plit) See TEMPLATE.

tem·po (tem′pō) *n.* pl. **·pos** or **·pi** (-pē) **1** *Music* Relative speed at which a composition is rendered; time; rhythm of a tune. **2** Characteristic manner or style; rate of speed or activity in general. [<Ital. <L *tempus* time]

tem·po·la·bile (tem′pō·lā′bil) *adj. Biol.* Subject to decay or destruction within a certain period of time, as a serum. [<L *tempus* time + *labilis* perishable]

tem·po·ral [1] (tem′pər·əl) *adj.* **1** Pertaining to affairs of the present life, as contrasted with those of a future life; earthly, as opposed to heavenly. **2** Pertaining to or limited by time; transitory, as opposed to eternal. **3** Related to or concerned with worldly affairs; worldly; material, as opposed to spiritual. **4** Pertaining to civil law or authority; lay; secular: contrasted with *clerical.* **5** *Gram.* Of, pertaining to, or denoting time: *temporal* conjunctions. See synonyms under PROFANE. — **lords temporal** English, Scottish, and Irish lay peers with seats in the House of Lords. [<OF *temporel* <L *temporalis* <*tempus*, *temporis* time] — **tem′po·ral·ly** *adv.* — **tem′po·ral·ness** *n.*

tem·po·ral [2] (tem′pər·əl) *adj. Anat.* Of, pertaining to, or situated at the temple or temples: the *temporal* bone. [<L *temporalis* <*tempora*. See TEMPLE[2].]

tem·po·ral [3] (tem′pər·äl′) *n. SW U.S.* A field or portion of land; a farm, especially one not requiring irrigation. [<Sp. *temporal* storm, tempest; ? < *terreno de temporal* land where heavy rains fall]

temporal bone *Anat.* A compound bone situated at the side of the head in man and other mammals, and containing the organ of hearing.

tem·po·ral·i·ty (tem′pə·ral′ə·tē) *n.* pl. **·ties 1** *Usually pl.* A temporal or material matter, interest, revenue, etc.; specifically, an ecclesiastical possession or revenue. **2** The state of being temporal or temporary: opposed to *perpetuity.*

tem·po·ra mu·tan·tur (tem′pər·ə myōō·tan′tər) *Latin* The times are changed.

tem·po·rar·y (tem′pə·rer′ē) *adj.* **1** Lasting or intended to be used for a short time only; transitory; of passing interest: opposed to *permanent.* **2** *Obs.* Contemporary. See synonyms under TRANSIENT. [<L *temporarius* <*tempus, temporis* time] — **tem′po·rar′i·ly** *adv.* — **tem′po·rar′i·ness** *n.*

TEMPLE OF HORUS, EDFU, BEGUN 237 B.C.
Greco-Egyptian style.

tem·po·rize (tem′pə·rīz) *v.i.* **·rized, ·riz·ing 1** To act evasively so as to gain time or put off decision or commitment. **2** To give real or apparent compliance to the circumstances;

comply. **3** To parley so as to gain time: with *with.* **4** To effect a compromise; negotiate: with *with* or *between.* Also *Brit.* **tem′po·rise.** [<F *temporiser* <L *temporis* time] —**tem′po·ri·za′tion** *n.* —**tem′po·riz′er** *n.* —**tem′po·riz′·ing·ly** *adv.*

tempt (tempt) *v.t.* **1** To attempt to persuade (a person) to do wrong, as by promising pleasure or gain. **2** To be attractive to; invite: Your offers do not *tempt* me. **3** To provoke or risk provoking: to *tempt* fate. **4** *Obs.* To test; prove. See synonyms under ALLURE. [<OF *tempter, tenter* <L *temptare, tentare* test, try, prob. intens. of *tendere* stretch] —**tempt′·a·ble** *adj.* —**tempt′er** *n.* —**tempt′ress** *n. fem.*

temp·ta·tion (temp·tā′shən) *n.* **1** That which tempts, especially to evil. **2** The state of being tempted, or enticed to evil; the act of tempting or testing. **3** A state of mental conflict between heavenly and infernal influences.

tempt·ing (temp′ting) *adj.* Alluring; attractive; seductive. —**tempt′ing·ly** *adv.* —**tempt′·ing·ness** *n.*

tem·pu·ra (tem·po͝or′ə, tem′po͝or′ə, -po͞o·ra′) *n.* A Japanese dish of seafood or vegetables, dipped in batter and deep-fried. [<Jap., fried food]

tem·pus fu·git (tem′pəs fyo͞o′jit) *Latin* Time flies.

ten (ten) *n.* **1** The cardinal number following nine and preceding eleven, or any of the symbols or combinations of symbols (10, x, X) used to represent it. **2** Anything containing or representing ten units or members; a playing card marked with ten pips; also, a ten-dollar bill. —*adj.* Being or consisting of one more than nine; decennary. [OE]

ten– Var. of TENO–.

ten·a·ble (ten′ə·bəl) *adj.* Capable of being held, maintained, or defended. [<F <*tenir* hold <L *tenere*] —**ten′a·bil′i·ty, ten′a·ble·ness** *n.* —**ten′a·bly** *adv.*

ten·ace (ten′ās) *n.* The combination in the same hand of the best and third best cards **(major tenace)** or of the second and fourth best cards **(minor tenace)** of any suit. [<Sp. *tenaza* pincers, tongs <*tenaz* tenacious <L *tenax, tenacis.* See TENACIOUS.]

te·na·cious (ti·nā′shəs) *adj.* **1** Having great cohesiveness of parts; tough. **2** Adhesive; sticky. **3** Holding or tending to hold strongly, as opinions, rights, etc.: followed by *of;* hence, stubborn; obstinate; unyielding; persistent. **4** Apt to retain; strongly retentive, as memory. See synonyms under STRONG. [<L *tenax, tenacis* holding fast <*tenere* hold, grasp, embrace] —**te·na′cious·ly** *adv.* —**te·na′·cious·ness** *n.*

te·nac·i·ty (ti·nas′ə·tē) *n.* **1** The state or quality of being tenacious. **2** That quality of a body in consequence of which it resists being pulled or forced apart.

te·nac·u·lum (ti·nak′yə·ləm) *n. pl.* **·la** (-lə) *Surg.* A hooked instrument for seizing and holding parts of the body, as arteries, during surgical operations. [<LL, holder <L *tenax, tenacis.* See TENACIOUS.]

te·naille (te·nāl′) *n.* A low outwork, usually with one or two reentering angles, in the main ditch between two bastions. —*v.t.* To equip with tenailles. Also **te·nail′.** [<F <LL *tenacula,* pl. of *tenaculum.* See TENACULUM.]

ten·an·cy (ten′ən·sē) *n. pl.* **·cies** **1** The holding of lands or tenements by any form of title; occupancy. **2** The period of holding or occupying lands, tenements, or office; temporary possession. **3** A habitation or dwelling place held of another.

ten·ant (ten′ənt) *n.* **1** One who holds or possesses lands or property by any kind of title; especially, one who holds under another; a lessee. **2** A defendant in an action concerning real property. **3** A dweller in any place; an occupant. —*v.t.* To hold as tenant; occupy. —*v.i.* To be a tenant. [<F, orig. ppr. of *tenir* hold <L *tenere*] —**ten′ant·a·ble** *adj.* —**ten′ant·less** *adj.*

tenant farmer One who farms land owned by another and pays rent usually in a share of the crops.

ten·ant–right (ten′ənt·rīt′) *n.* A customary right belonging to a tenant, even if not specifically stipulated, as a right to continuous occupancy without increase of rent, or a right to compensation for improvements.

ten·ant·ry (ten′ən·trē) *n. pl.* **·ries** **1** Tenants collectively. **2** Tenantship; tenancy.

Te·nas·se·rim (tə·nas′ər·im) A former administrative division of SE Burma extending in a narrow strip of coast 400 miles down the Malay Peninsula to the Isthmus of Kra; 31,588 square miles; capital, Moulmein.

ten–cent store (ten′sent′) See FIVE– AND TEN–CENT STORE.

tench (tench) *n.* A European fresh-water cyprinoid fish *(Tinca tinca),* very tenacious of life, and having small, deeply embedded scales. [<F *tenche* <LL *tinca* tench]

Ten Commandments See under COMMANDMENT.

tend[1] (tend) *v.i.* **1** To have an aptitude, tendency, or disposition; incline: He *tends* to talk too much. **2** To have influence toward a specified result; lead or conduce: Education *tends* to refinement. **3** To go in a certain direction. [<OF *tendre* <L *tendere* extend, tend]

tend[2] (tend) *v.t.* **1** To attend to the needs or requirements of; take care of; minister to: to *tend* a fire. **2** To watch over; look after: to *tend* children. **3** To watch (a vessel at anchor) with the intention of so managing her when the tide changes as to prevent fouling the anchor and chain. —*v.i.* **4** To be in attendance; serve or wait: with *on* or *upon.* **5** *Colloq.* To give attention or care: with *to.* [Aphetic var. of ATTEND]

ten·dance (ten′dəns) *n.* **1** The act of tending; attendance; service. **2** *Archaic* Attendants collectively. Also **ten′dence.**

Ten Degree Channel A passage from the Bay of Bengal to the Andaman Sea between the Andaman and Nicobar Islands, along 10° N; about 90 miles wide.

ten·den·cy (ten′dən·sē) *n. pl.* **·cies** **1** The state of being directed toward some purpose, end, or result; inclination; bent; aptitude. **2** That which tends to produce some specified effect. **3** Bias; propensity. **4** Trend of a speech; purpose of a story. See synonyms under AIM, DIRECTION, INCLINATION. [<Med. L *tendentia,* orig. neut. pl. of *tendens, -entis,* ppr. of *tendere* extend, tend]

ten·den·tious (ten·den′shəs) *adj.* Having a purposed aim or intentional tendency. [<G *tendenziös* <*tendenz* tendency <Med. L *tendentia.* See TENDENCY.] —**ten·den′tious·ly** *adv.* —**ten·den′tious·ness** *n.*

Ten·denz (ten·dens′) *n. German* Tendency or drift; partisan or biased attitude, as in a work of literature or art; angle; slant.

ten·der[1] (ten′dər) *adj.* **1** Yielding easily to force that tends to crush, bruise, break, or injure; soft or delicate. **2** Easily chewed or cut: said of food, especially meat. **3** Delicate or weak; not strong or hardy. **4** Youthful and delicate; not strengthened by maturity: a *tender* age. **5** Characterized by or expressive of a delicate sensibility; kind; affectionate; gentle: *tender* mercy; a *tender* father. **6** Capable of arousing sensitive feelings; touching: *tender* memories; a *tender* sight. **7** Susceptible to spiritual or moral feelings: a *tender* conscience. **8** Painful if touched; easily pained: a *tender* sore. **9** Of delicate effect or quality; soft: a *tender* light. **10** Requiring deft or delicate treatment; ticklish; touchy: a *tender* subject. **11** *Naut.* Careening too easily under sail: said of a ship. See synonyms under BLAND, FRAGILE, FRIENDLY, HUMANE, MERCIFUL. —*v.t.* To make tender; soften. [<OF *tendre* <L *tener, teneris*] —**ten′der·ly** *adv.* —**ten′·der·ness** *n.*

ten·der[2] (ten′dər) *v.t.* **1** To present for acceptance, as a resignation; offer. **2** *Law* To proffer, as money, in payment, in discharge of a debt, or to fulfil a contract. —*n.* **1** The act of tendering; an offer; specifically, in law, a formal offer of satisfaction. **2** That which is offered as payment, especially money: legal *tender.* [<F *tendre* <L *tendere* extend, tend] —**ten′der·er** *n.*

tend·er[3] (ten′dər) *n.* **1** A vessel used to bring supplies, passengers, and crew back and forth between a larger vessel and a nearby shore; also, a vessel which services another at sea. **2** A boat used to carry provisions, etc., to whalers and lighthouses. **3** A vehicle attached to the rear of a steam locomotive to carry fuel and water for it. **4** One who tends or ministers to. [<TEND[2]]

ten·der·foot (ten′dər·fo͝ot′) *n. pl.* **·foots** or **·feet** (-fēt′) *U.S.* **1** A newcomer in the West; one not yet inured to the hardships of or not yet experienced in the life of the plains, the mining camp, etc.; a greenhorn: opposed to *longhorn.* **2** Any inexperienced person. **3** A boy scout in the beginning class or group. —*adj.* Inexperienced; also, made up of inexperienced people: a *tenderfoot* gang.

ten·der–heart·ed (ten′dər·här′tid) *adj.* Having deep or quick sensibility, as to love, pity, etc.; compassionate; sympathetic; easily impressed by sorrow or pain. —**ten′der–heart′·ed·ly** *adv.* —**ten′der–heart′ed·ness** *n.*

ten·der·ize (ten′də·rīz) *v.t.* **·ized, ·iz·ing** To make tender, as meat.

ten·der·iz·er (ten′də·rī′zər) A substance, as papain, for softening the tough fibers and connective tissues of meat in order to make it more palatable.

ten·der·loin (ten′dər·loin′) *n.* The tender part of the loin of beef, pork, etc., lying close to the ventral side of the lumbar vertebrae. —**the tenderloin district** **1** A former district of New York City, coinciding with a certain police precinct from 23rd to 42nd streets, west of Broadway, where vice flourished and police corruption was common. **2** Hence, any district in any city which is noted for its night life, a high incidence of crime, and police leniency.

ten·di·nous (ten′də·nəs) *adj.* **1** Of, pertaining to, resembling, or formed by a tendon. **2** Having or full of tendons; sinewy. [<F *tendineux* <Med. L *tendo, -inis.* See TENDON.]

ten·don (ten′dən) *n. Anat.* One of the bands of tough, fibrous connective tissue forming the termination of a muscle and serving to transmit its force to some other part; a sinew. [<F <Med. L *tendo, -inis* <Gk. *tenōn* a sinew <*tenein* stretch]

tendon of Achilles *Anat.* Achilles' tendon.

ten·dril (ten′dril) *n. Bot.* One of the slender, leafless, coiling organs which serve a climbing plant as a means of attachment to a wall, tree trunk, or other supporting surface. [<F *tendrillon,* dim. of *tendron* sprout <*tendre* tender; infl. in meaning by F *tendre* stretch] —**ten′dril·lar, ten′dril·ous** *adj.*

ten·e·brae (ten′ə·brē) *n. pl.* The matins and lauds of Thursday, Friday, and Saturday of Holy Week, sung on the afternoon or evening of the preceding days. [<L, shadows]

ten·e·brif·ic (ten′ə·brif′ik) *adj.* Making dark or gloomy. [<L *tenebrae* darkness + -FIC]

ten·e·brous (ten′ə·brəs) *adj.* Gloomy; dark; obscure. [<L *tenebrosus* <*tenebrae* darkness] —**ten′e·bros′i·ty** (-bros′ə·tē) *n.*

Ten·e·dos (ten′ə·dos, *Gk.* ten′ə·dôs) A Turkish island in the Aegean near the western entrance to the Dardanelles; 15 square miles: Turkish *Bozcaada.*

ten·e·ment (ten′ə·mənt) *n.* **1** A room, or set of rooms, designed for one family. See TENEMENT HOUSE. **2** *Law* Anything of a permanent nature that may be held by one person of another as property, as land, houses, offices, rents, franchises, etc. **3** A house or building; especially, a dwelling house rented or intended for rent; a tenement house. **4** Figuratively, an abode. [<OF <LL *tenementum* tenure <L *tenere* hold] —**ten′e·men′ta·ry** (-men′tər·ē), **ten′e·men′tal** (-men′təl) *adj.*

tenement house A building or house, usually of inferior type and situated in the poorer sections of a city, rented, leased, or let, to be occupied as the home of three or more families living independently of one another, or by more than two families on a floor, all having a common right in stairways, yards, etc.

te·nen·dum (ti·nen′dəm) *n. Law* The clause in a deed in which, before the abolition of feudal tenures, the tenure was defined: now part of the habendum clause. See HABENDUM. [<L, that which must be held, gerundive of *tenere* hold]

Ten·er·ife (ten′ə·rif′, -rēf′; *Sp.* tā′nā·rē′fā) The largest of the Canary Islands; 794 1/2 square miles; capital, Santa Cruz de Tenerife; contains the **Peak of Tenerife** (also *Teyde*), a dormant volcano and the highest peak on Spanish soil; 12,200 feet. Also **Ten′er·iffe′.**

te·nes·mus (ti·nes′məs, -nez′-) *n. Pathol.* A painful straining and ineffectual effort to evacuate the bladder or the bowels. [<NL <L *tenesmos* a straining <Gk. *teneismos* <*teinein* stretch] —**te·nes′mic** *adj.*

ten·et (ten′it, tē′nit) *n.* An opinion, principle,

dogma, or doctrine that a person or organization believes or maintains as true. See synonyms under DOCTRINE. [<L, he holds < *tenere* hold]

ten·fold (ten′fōld′) *adj.* Made up of ten; ten times as many or as much; ten times repeated; decuplicate. —*adv.* In a tenfold manner or degree.

Ten·gri Khan (teng′grē khän′) The second highest peak of the Tien Shan, in NE Kirghiz S.S.R.; 22,949 feet. Also **Khan Tengri.**

Ten·gri Nor (teng′grē nôr′, nōr′) The Mongolian name for NAM TSO.

te·ni·a (tē′nē·ə) See TAENIA.

te·ni·a·cide (tē′nē·ə·sīd′) *n.* A substance which destroys tapeworms, as the oleoresin of certain ferns, carbon tetrachloride, etc.: also spelled **taeniacide.** Also **te′ni·a·fuge′** (-fyŏŏj′) [<L *taenia* <Gk. *tainia* tapeworm + -CIDE] —**te′ni·a·ci′dal** *adj.*

te·ni·a·sis (ti·nī′ə·sis) *n. Pathol.* Any morbid or toxemic condition due to the presence of tapeworms in the body: also spelled *taeniasis.* [<Gk. *tainia* tapeworm + -IASIS]

Ten·iers (ten′yərz, *Flemish* te·nirs′), **David,** 1582–1649, Flemish painter: called "the Elder." —**David,** 1610–90, Flemish painter: called "the Younger"; son of preceding.

Ten·nes·se·an (ten′ə·sē′ən) *n.* A native or inhabitant of Tennessee. —*adj.* Of or pertaining to Tennessee.

Ten·nes·see (ten′ə·sē′) A State in the SE United States; 42,246 square miles; capital, Nashville; entered the Union June 1, 1796; nicknamed *Volunteer State:* abbr. TN

Tennessee River A river of the east central United States, rising in eastern Tennessee and flowing 652 miles SW, NW, and north through Alabama, Tennessee, and Kentucky to the Ohio River at Paducah, Kentucky.

Tennessee Valley Authority A Federal corporation established in 1933 by the U.S. government to take custody of the Wilson Dam and associated plants at Muscle Shoals in Tennessee, developing and operating them in the national interest, with special reference to electric power, irrigation, fertilizers, and flood control. Abbr. *TVA, T.V.A.*

Ten·niel (ten′yəl), **Sir John,** 1820–1914, English illustrator and cartoonist.

ten·nis (ten′is) *n.* A game played by striking a ball to and fro with rackets over a net stretched perpendicularly across a space called a court. It has two forms, **court tennis,** played indoors in a specially prepared building, and **lawn tennis,** played out–of–doors on a court of grass, clay, concrete, etc. [<AF *tenetz* take, receive, imperative of *tenir* hold; from the call of the server]

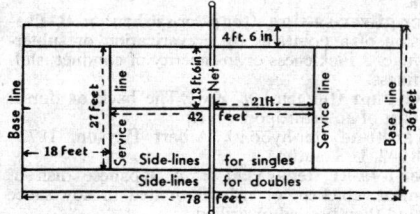

TENNIS COURT — PLAN AND DIMENSIONS

Ten·ny·son (ten′ə·sən), **Alfred,** 1809–92, Lord Tennyson, English poet laureate 1850–92.

Ten·ny·so·ni·an (ten′ə·sō′nē·ən) *adj.* Relating to or characteristic of Alfred Tennyson, or his verse or style.

teno— *combining form Med.* Tendon; related to a tendon, or to tendons: *tenotomy:* also, before vowels, **ten—.** Also **tenonto—.** [<Gk. *tenōn* a tendon]

Te·noch·ti·tlán (tā·nōkh′tē·tlän′) The capital of the ancient Aztec Empire, on the site of Mexico City.

ten·on (ten′ən) *n.* A projection on the end of a timber, etc., for inserting in a socket to form a joint. —*v.t.* **1** To form a tenon on. **2** To join by a mortise and tenon. [<F <*tenir* hold]

ten·o·ni·tis (ten′ə·nī′tis) *n. Pathol.* Inflammation of a tendon. [<NL <Gk. *tenōn* a tendon]

ten·or (ten′ər) *n.* **1** A settled course or manner of progress. **2** Course of thought; general purport. **3** *Law* The purport or substance and effect of a document; an exact transcript, as of a record. **4** General character and tendency; nature. **5** The highest adult male voice (except the falsetto); a singer having such a voice, or a part to be sung by it. **6** An instrument playing the part intermediate between the bass and the alto; especially, the viola. **7** In bell ringing, the lowest bell, irrespective of peal. —*adj.* **1** Of or pertaining to a tenor. **2** Having a relation to other instruments that the tenor bears to other musical parts: a *tenor* violin. [<OF *tenour* <L *tenor* a course <*tenere* hold; in def. 5, so called because this voice originally sang or "held" the melody]

ten·or·ite (ten′ə·rīt) *n.* Native oxide of copper, occurring in minute black scales; black copper. [after Prof. G. *Tenore,* president (1841) of Naples Academy]

te·nor·rha·phy (ti·nôr′ə·fē, -nor′-) *n. Surg.* Suture of the ends of a divided tendon. [<TENO- + -RRHAPHY]

te·not·o·my (ti·not′ə·mē) *n. Surg.* The operation of cutting a tendon. [<TENO- + -TOMY]

ten·pen·ny (ten′pen′ē, -pə·nē) *adj.* **1** Valued at tenpence. **2** Designating the size of nails three inches long. See —PENNY.

ten·pin (ten′pin′) *n.* One of the pins used in the game of tenpins.

ten·pins (ten′pinz′) *n.* A game, played in a bowling alley, in which the players attempt to bowl down ten pins set up at the far end of the alley.

ten·rec (ten′rek) *n.* One of several insectivorous mammals of Madagascar; especially, the spiny-coated, tailless *Tenrec ecaudatus,* from 12 to 16 inches long: also spelled *tanrec.* [<F <Malagasy *trāndraka*]

Ten·sas River (ten′sô) A river in eastern Louisiana, flowing 175 miles south and SW to the Ouachita River in east central Louisiana.

tense[1] (tens) *adj.* **1** Stretched tight; taut. **2** Under mental or nervous strain; strained. **3** *Phonet.* Pronounced with the tongue and its muscles taut, as (ē) and (ōō); narrow: opposed to *lax.* —*v.t. & v.i.* **tensed, tens·ing** To make or become strained or drawn tight. [<L *tensus,* pp. of *tendere* stretch] —**tense′ly** *adv.* —**tense′ness** *n.*

tense[2] (tens) *n.* A form of a verb that relates it to time viewed either as finite past, present, or future, or as non–finite. —**sequence of tenses** In inflected languages, the customary choice of tense for a verb that follows another in a sentence, particularly in reported or indirect discourse. ◆ The general principle of sequence of tenses in English is that present follows present and past follows past. Thus, the tense of the subordinate clause tends to shift back to agree with the tense of the main verb. "He *wants* to go," becomes, in indirect discourse, "They said that he *wanted* to go." However, if continued, habitual, future, or universal action is expressed, the present tense may be retained in the subordinate clause: They told me that he *is* still in town; Columbus proved that the world *is* round. The present tense is also retained in the subordinate clause for emphasis: They just learned he *is* going after all. In subordinate clauses of purpose the general rule of tense sequence holds true: We *are working* so that we *can* go to Europe; We *worked* so that we *could* go to Europe. In conditional sentences expressing a simple fact or open question, the main and subordinate verbs remain independent: If he *said* that, I *can't* prove it. However, sequence of tenses is strictly observed in a highly improbable or contrary–to–fact statement. Time present is then expressed by the use of the past tense: If he *had* any sense, he *wouldn't drive* that car. Time past is expressed by the past perfect tense: If I *had had* my wits about me, I *would have* telephoned immediately. [<OF *tens* <L *tempus* time, tense]

ten·si·ble (ten′sə·bəl) *adj.* **1** Extensible. **2** Capable of being made tense; tensile.

ten·sile (ten′sil, *Brit.* ten′sīl) *adj.* **1** Of or pertaining to tension. **2** Capable of extension. **3** Producing tones from stretched strings: said of instruments. [<NL *tensilis* <L *tensus.* See

TENSE[1].] —**ten·sil·i·ty** (ten·sil′ə·tē) *n.*

tensile strength *Physics* The resistance of a material to forces of rupture and longitudinal stress: usually expressed in pounds or tons per square inch.

ten·sim·e·ter (ten·sim′ə·tər) *n.* An instrument for measuring the tension of gases; a manometer. [<*tensi-* (<TENSION) + -METER]

ten·si·om·e·ter (ten′sē·om′ə·tər) *n.* A device for determining tensile strength. [See TENSIMETER]

ten·sion (ten′shən) *n.* **1** The act of stretching; the condition of being stretched tight. **2** Mental strain; intense nervous anxiety. **3** Any strained relation, as between governments. **4** *Physics* **a** Stress on a material caused by pulling: opposed to *compression,* and distinguished from *torsion.* **b** The condition of a body when acted on by such stress. **5** The expansive force of a gas. **6** A regulating device, as that on a sewing machine to regulate the tightness of the thread. **7** *Electr.* Electromotive force; also, electric potential. [<L *tensio, -onis* <*tensus.* See TENSE[1].] —**ten′sion·al** *adj.*

ten·si·ty (ten′sə·tē) *n.* The state of being tense; tension.

ten·sive (ten′siv) *adj.* **1** Caused by or causing tension. **2** Causing a sensation of stiffness or contraction.

ten·sor (ten′sər, -sôr) *n.* **1** *Anat.* A muscle that stretches a part. **2** *Math.* A vector quantity which may be fully described only with reference to more than three components. [<NL <L *tensus.* See TENSE[1].]

ten–strike (ten′strīk′) *n.* **1** In bowling, the knocking down by a player of all the pins at one bowl: also called *strike.* **2** *U.S. Colloq.* Hence, a stroke of unexampled success; a very profitable bargain.

tent[1] (tent) *n.* A shelter of canvas or the like, supported by poles and fastened by cords to pegs (called **tent pegs**) driven into the ground. —*v.t.* To cover with or as with a tent. —*v.i.* To pitch a tent; camp out. [<F *tente* <LL *tenta,* orig. neut. pl. of *tentus,* pp. of *tendere* stretch. Cf. L *tentorium* awning.]

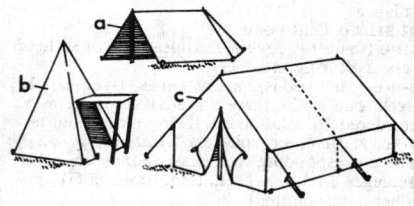

TENTS
a. Pup tent. *b.* Pyramid tent. *c.* Wall tent.

tent[2] (tent) *Surg. n.* A small roll, as of lint, placed in a wound or orifice to prevent its closing. —*v.t.* To keep open with a tent; also, to probe. [<F *tente* <*tenter* test, probe <L *tentare*]

tent[3] (tent) *Scot. v.t.* **1** To pay attention to; observe. **2** To hinder; prevent. **3** To attend upon; look after. —*n.* **1** Attention; note; heed. **2** An open–air wooden pulpit. —**tent′·less** *adj.*

tent[4] (tent) *n.* A deep–red wine obtained chiefly from Spain. [<Sp. *tinto* deep–colored <L *tinctus* dyed. See TINT.]

ten·ta·cle (ten′tə·kəl) *n.* **1** *Zool.* A protruding flexible process or appendage (usually of the head) of invertebrate animals, functioning as an organ of touch, prehension, or motion. Some examples are the hollow fleshy processes about the mouth of a polyp communicating with the body cavity, the eyestalks of a gastropod, and the arms of a cuttlefish, especially one of the two longer arms of a decapod. **2** *Bot.* A sensitive glandular hair, as on the leaves of the sundew. **3** Something resembling a tentacle; a tendril. Also **ten·tac·u·lum** (ten·tak′yə·ləm). [<L *tentaculum* <*tentare* touch, try] —**ten·tac′u·lar** *adj.*

tent·age (ten′tij) *n.* **1** The supply of tents available for any purpose. **2** Tents collectively.

ten·ta·tion (ten·tā′shən) *n.* The act or process of adjusting by experimentation until a desired

effect is secured. [<F <L *tentatio, -onis* <*tentare* try. See TEMPT.]

ten·ta·tive (ten′tə·tiv) *adj.* **1** Used in making a trial; provisional or conjectural; experimental and subject to change. **2** *Med.* Based on subjective and objective symptoms: said of a diagnosis subject to change. —*n.* An experiment; conjecture. [<Med. L *tentativus* <L *tentatus,* pp. of *tentare* try, probe] **—ten′ta·tive·ly** *adv.* **—ten′ta·tive·ness** *n.*

tent caterpillar The gregarious larva of several North American moths (family *Lasiocampidae*) that spins a large silken web which shelters the colony, especially the **orchard caterpillar** (genus *Malacosoma*).

tent·ed (ten′tid) *adj.* **1** Overspread or covered with or sheltered by tents: the *tented* field. **2** Resembling a tent.

tented arch A fingerprint pattern in which the skin ridges have an upward thrust in the shape of a tent, arranging themselves on both sides of a spine or axis.

ten·ter[1] (ten′tər) *n.* **1** A frame or machine for stretching cloth to prevent shrinkage while drying. **2** *Obs.* A tenterhook. —*v.t.* To stretch on or as on a tenter. —*v.i.* To be or admit of being stretched thus. [<L *tentus* extended. See TENT[1].]

tent·er[2] (ten′tər) *n. Brit.* One who especially attends to anything; particularly, one who attends to machinery in a factory. [<TENT[3]]

ten·ter·hook (ten′tər·ho͝ok′) *n.* A sharp hook for holding cloth while being stretched on a tenter. **—to be on tenterhooks** To be in a state of anxiety or suspense.

tenth (tenth) *adj.* **1** Next in order after the ninth. **2** Designating one of ten equal parts. —*n.* **1** One of ten equal parts. **2** *Music* An interval compounded of an octave and a third; a note separated from another by this interval. **3** An organ stop tuned a tenth above the diapasons. **4** A tax of one tenth of one's income; a tithe. [ME *tenthe*] **—tenth′ly** *adv.*

ten·tie (ten′tē) adj. Scot. Attentive; cautious. Also **ten′ty.**

tent pegging A cavalry exercise in British military tournaments in which the horseman, riding at full speed, endeavors to uproot a tent peg with his lance.

tent stitch Petit point.

te·nue (tə·nü′) *n. French* **1** Appearance or style of dress. **2** Bearing; manner.

ten·u·is (ten′yo͞o·is) *n. pl.* **·u·es** (-yo͞o·ēz) In Greek, one of the three voiceless stops, κ, π, τ, considered in relation to their voiced counterparts, γ, β, δ, or voiceless fricatives, χ, φ, θ; also, corresponding voiceless sounds in other languages, as *k, t, p.* [<L, thin, trans. of Gk. *psilos* bare, unaspirated]

ten·u·ous (ten′yo͞o·əs) *adj.* **1** Thin; slim; delicate; also, weak; flimsy. **2** Having slight density; rare: opposed to *dense.* See synonyms under FINE. [<L *tenuis* thin] **—ten′u·ous·ly** *adv.* **—ten′u·ous·ness, ten·u·i·ty** (ten·yo͞o′ə·tē, ti·no͞o′-) *n.*

ten·ure (ten′yər) *n.* **1** A holding, as of land. **2** The act of holding in general, or the state of being held. **3** The term during which a thing is held, as an office. **4** The conditions or manner of holding. See synonyms under OCCUPATION. [<F <*tenir* hold <L *tenere*] **—ten·u·ri·al** (ten·yo͝or′ē·əl) *adj.* **—ten·u′ri·al·ly** *adv.*

te·nu·to (te·no͞o′tō) *adj. Music* Sustained; held for the full time. [<Ital.]

te·nu·to-mark (te·no͞o′tō·märk′) *n. Music* A horizontal stroke over a note or chord that is to be held for its full value.

Te·o·bal·do (tā′ō·bäl′dō) Italian form of THEOBALD.

te·o·cal·li (tē′ə·kal′ē, *Sp.* tā′ō·kä′yē) *n.* **1** A temple peculiar to the ancient Mexicans and Central Americans, usually erected on a truncated pyramid. **2** A mound of similar form. Also **te·o·pan** (tā′ō·pän′). [<Sp. <Nahuatl, house of the god <*teotl* a god + *calli* house]

Te·o·do·ri·co (*Ital.* tā′ō·dō·rē′kō, *Sp.* -thō-) Italian and Spanish form of THEODORIC.

Te·o·do·ro (*Ital.* tā′ō·dō′rō, *Sp.* -thō′rō) Italian and Spanish form of THEODORE. **—Te′o·do′ra** (-rä) *fem.*

Te·o·fi·lo (tā·ō′fē·lō) Italian and Spanish form of THEOPHILUS.

te·o·sin·te (tē′ə·sin′tē) *n.* A stout, hardy perennial grass *(Euchlaena mexicana),* closely allied to Indian corn, and used for fodder. [<Sp. <Nahuatl *teocentli,* lit., divine maize <*teotl* a god + *centli* corn]

te·pee (tē′pē) *n.* A conical tent of the North American Plains Indians, usually covered with skins or other material: also spelled *teepee, tipi.* [<Dakota *tipi* <*ti* dwell + *pi* used for]

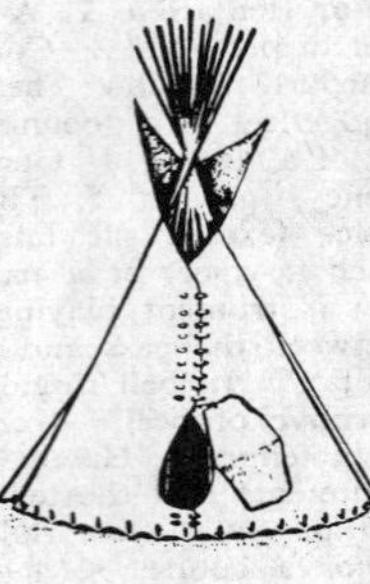

TEPEE
Western Plains Indian.

tep·e·fy (tep′ə·fī) *v.t.* & *v.i.* **·fied, ·fy·ing** To make or become tepid. [<L *tepefacere* make tepid <*tepere* be lukewarm + *facere* make] **—tep′e·fac′tion** (-fak′·shən) *n.*

teph·rite (tef′rīt) *n.* An ash-gray to black volcanic rock, essentially an alkaline andesite, with either nepheline or leucite. [<L *tephritis* <Gk. *tephra* ashes]

te·phro·sin (tə·frō′sin) *n. Chem.* A white crystalline compound, $C_{23}H_{22}O_7$, extracted from the leaves of a leguminous plant *(Tephrosia vogeli),* from derris, and cube: used as a fish poison. [<NL <Gk. *tephros* ash-colored <*tephra* ashes]

te·phro·sis (tə·frō′sis) *n.* Cremation; incineration. [<NL <Gk. *tephrōsis* <*tephra* ashes]

tep·id (tep′id) *adj.* Moderately warm; lukewarm, as a liquid. [<L *tepidus* <*tepere* be lukewarm] **—te·pid·i·ty** (tə·pid′ə·tē), **tep′id·ness** *n.* **—tep′id·ly** *adv.*

tep·i·dar·i·um (tep′ə·dâr′ē·əm) *n. pl.* **·dar·i·a** (-dâr′ē·ə) In the Roman baths, the intermediate apartment between the cold- and the hot-bath rooms. [<L <*tepidus.* See TEPID.]

te·qui·la (tə·kē′lə) *n.* A Mexican alcoholic liquor made from the maguey. [from *Tequila,* Jalisco, Mexico]

ter- *combining form* Three; third; threefold; three times: *tercentenary.* [<L *ter* thrice]

tera- *combining form* One trillion: *teravolt.*

ter·a·phim (ter′ə·fim) *n. pl. sing.* **ter·aph** (ter′əf) or **ter·a·phim** Images, small idols, or household gods consulted as oracles by some of the ancient Hebrews: used as a plural or collective singular in the Bible. [<Hebrew *terāphīm*]

ter·a·tism (ter′ə·tiz′əm) *n. Biol.* A monstrosity; especially, a malformed human or animal fetus. [<Gk. *teras* monster]

terato- *combining form* A wonder; monster: *teratogeny.* Also, before vowels, **terat-.** [<Gk. *teras, teratos* a wonder]

ter·a·to·gen (ter′ə·tə·jən, tə·rat′ə·jən) *n. Biol.* An agent, esp. a drug, that produces monsters or abnormal organisms.

ter·a·tog·e·ny (ter′ə·toj′ə·nē) *n. Biol.* The production of monsters or abnormal organisms. Also **ter′a·to·gen′e·sis** (-tō·jen′ə·sis). [<TERATO- + -GENY] **—ter′a·to·gen′ic** (-tō·jen′ik) *adj.*

ter·a·toid (ter′ə·toid) *adj.* Like a monstrosity; abnormal. [<TERAT(O)- + -OID]

ter·a·tol·o·gy (ter′ə·tol′ə·jē) *n.* The branch of biology and medicine treating of abnormal growths or monstrosities. [<TERATO- + -LOGY] **—ter′a·to·log′ic** (-tō·loj′ik) or **·i·cal** *adj.* **—ter′a·tol′o·gist** *n.*

Te·rau·chi (te·rä·o͞o·chē), **Count Juichi,** 1879–1946, Japanese general.

ter·bi·a (tûr′bē·ə) *n. Chem.* Oxide of terbium, Tb_2O_3.

ter·bi·um (tûr′bē·əm) *n.* A silvery gray metallic element (symbol Tb, atomic number 65) belonging to the lanthanide series, occurring in gadolinite and other rare earths. See PERIODIC TABLE. [<NL <*Ytterby,* a town in Sweden] **—ter′bic** *adj.*

terbium metal One of a group in the lanthanide series of elements, including gadolinium, europium, and terbium.

Ter Borch (tûr bôrkh), **Gerard,** 1617?–81, Dutch painter.

Ter·cei·ra (tûr·sâr′ə) The easternmost island of the central Azores; 153 square miles.

ter·cel (tûr′səl) *n.* A male falcon, especially the peregrine falcon: also spelled *tassel.* Also **terce·let** (tûrs′lit). [<OF <L *tertius* third; said to be so called because every third egg in a falcon's nest was thought to produce a male]

ter·cen·te·nar·y (tûr·sen′tə·ner′ē, tûr′sen·ten′·ər·ē) *adj.* Of or pertaining to a period of 300 years or to a 300th anniversary. —*n. pl.* **·nar·ies** The 300th anniversary. Also *tricentennial.* Also **ter·cen·ten·ni·al** (tûr′sen·ten′ē·əl).

ter·cet (tûr′sit, tûr·set′) *n.* **1** *Music* A triplet. **2** A group of three lines riming together or connected with adjacent triplets by double or triple rime. [<F <Ital. *terzetto,* dim. of *terzo* <L *tertius* a third]

ter·e·bene (ter′ə·bēn) *n. Chem.* A colorless, aromatic liquid hydrocarbon mixture of terpenes from oil of turpentine: used as an antiseptic and expectorant. [<TEREB(INTH) + (TERP)ENE]

te·reb·ic (te·reb′ik, -rē′bik) *adj. Chem.* Of, pertaining to, or derived from a white crystalline acid, $C_7H_{10}O_4$, derived from oil of turpentine. [<TEREBINTH]

ter·e·binth (ter′ə·binth) *n.* A small tree *(Pistacia terebinthus)* with winged pinnate leaves resembling those of the common ash but smaller: the original source of turpentine. [<L *terebinthus* <Gk. *terebinthos*]

ter·e·bin·thine (ter′ə·bin′thin) *adj.* Of or pertaining to the terebinth or turpentine. Also **ter′e·bin′thic.**

te·re·do (tə·rē′dō) *n.* One of a genus *(Teredo)* of marine mollusks (family *Teredinidae*); a shipworm. [<L, borer <Gk. *terēdōn* <*terein* rub hard, bore]

Ter·ence (ter′əns), 190?–159 B.C., Roman playwright: full name *Publius Terentius Afer.*

Te·re·sa (tə·rē′sə; *Ital., Sp.* tā·rā′sä) Italian and Spanish form of THERESA.

Te·re·sian (ti·rē′shən) *n.* A Carmelite friar or nun of the order founded by St. Teresa of Ávila in 1562.

Te·re·si·na (tā′rə·zē′nə) The capital of Piauí state, Brazil.

te·rete (tə·rēt′, ter′ēt) *adj.* Cylindrical and slightly tapering; round in cross-section. [<L *teres, teretis* round, rounded off <*terere* rub]

Te·reus (tir′yo͞os, tir′ē·əs) In Greek mythology, a Thracian king who was transformed into a hoopoe by the gods after he had raped his sister-in-law. See PHILOMELA.

ter·fa (tûr′fə) *n.* An edible fungus (genera *Terfezia* and *Tirmania*) of the deserts of North Africa, having a subterranean fruit body resembling truffles and eaten by the Arabs. [<Arabic *tirfāsh* truffle]

ter·gal (tûr′gəl) *adj.* Of or pertaining to the tergum; dorsal.

ter·gem·i·nate (tər·jem′ə·nit) *adj. Bot.* Having three pairs of forked leaflets. [<TER- + GEMINATE]

ter·gi·ver·sate (tûr′ji·vər·sāt′) *v.i.* **·sat·ed, ·sat·ing** **1** To be evasive; equivocate or prevaricate. **2** To change sides, attitudes, etc.; become a renegade; apostatize. [<L *tergiversatus,* pp. of *tergiversari* <*tergum* back + *versare* turn] **—ter′gi·ver·sa′tor** *n.*

ter·gi·ver·sa·tion (tûr′ji·vər·sā′shən) *n.* **1** Evasion of a point, as by prevarication or subterfuge. **2** Fickleness or insincerity of conduct; shiftiness.

ter·gum (tûr′gəm) *n. Zool.* The back or dorsal part of an arthropod. [<L]

Ter·hune (tər·hyo͞on′), **Albert Payson,** 1872–1942, U.S. author.

ter·i·ya·ki (ter′i·yä′kē) *n.* A Japanese dish of meat, chicken, or fish marinated in soy sauce and then broiled or grilled.

term (tûrm) *n.* **1** A word or expression used to designate some definite thing; a technical expression: a scientific *term.* **2** Any word or expression conveying some conception or thought: a *term* of reproach; to speak in general *terms.* **3** *pl.* The conditions or stipulations according to which something is to be done or acceded to: the *terms* of sale; peace *terms.* **4** *pl.* Mutual relations; footing: usually preceded by *on* or *upon*: England was on friendly *terms* with France. **5** *Math.* **a** The antecedent or consequent of a ratio. **b** The numerator or denominator of a fraction. **c** One of the quantities of an algebraic expression that are connected by the plus and minus signs. **d** One of the quantities which compose a series or progression. **6** *Logic* **a** In a proposition, either of the two parts, the subject and predicate, which are joined by a copula. **b** Any of the three elements of a syllogism, each of which appears twice. In a syllogism, the **major term** is the predicate of both the major premise and the conclusion. The **minor term** is the subject of both

the minor premise and the conclusion. See SYLLOGISM. **7** A fixed period or definite length of time: a *term* of office. **8** One of the periods of the year appointed for holding instruction in colleges and schools. **9** *Law* **a** One of the prescribed periods of the year during which a court may hold a session. **b** A specific extent of time during which a termor may hold an estate. **c** A space of time allowed a debtor to meet his obligation. **10** *Med.* The time for childbirth. **11** *Archaic* An utmost limit; boundary. **12** *Archit.* A pillar of tapering form, ending in a sculptured head or bust. —*v.t.* To designate by means of a term; name or call. [<OF *terme* <L *terminus* a limit]

Synonyms (noun): article, condition, expression, member, name, phrase, word. *Term* in its figurative use always retains something of its literal sense of a boundary or limit. The *articles* of a contract or other instrument are simply the portions into which it is divided for convenience; the *terms* are the essential statements on which its validity depends—as it were, the landmarks of its meaning or power; a *condition* is a contingent *term*, which may become fixed upon the happening of some contemplated event. In logic a *term* is one of the essential members of a proposition, the boundary of statement in some one direction. Thus in general use *term* is more restricted than *word*, *expression*, or *phrase*; a *term* is a *word* that limits meaning to a fixed point of statement or to a special class of subjects; as, when we speak of the definition of *terms*, that is of the key *words* in any discussion; or we say "that is a legal or scientific *term*." See BOUNDARY, DICTION.

ter·ma·gant (tûr′mə·gənt) *n.* A scolding or abusive woman; shrew. —*adj.* Violently abusive and quarrelsome; vixenish. [<TERMAGANT] —**ter′ma·gan′cy** *n.*

Ter·ma·gant (tûr′mə·gənt) An idol or imaginary deity of very turbulent, overbearing character that the medieval romances represented Moslems as worshiping. Also **Ter′·ma·gaunt, Ter′ma·gund** (-gənd).

Ter·man–Mer·rill test (tûr′mən·mer′il) *Psychol.* An extension of the Stanford revision intelligence test which includes ages down to two years and adds many more items at upper levels, with a choice of two alternative scales.

term day **1** A designated day; specifically, quarter-day. **2** At hiring fairs, the day from which the contract of service dates.

term·er (tûr′mər) *n.* **1** *Law* A termor. **2** *Colloq.* A prisoner serving a certain term: usually with an ordinal: a first-*termer.*

ter·mes (tûr′mēz) *n.* A termite.

ter·mi·na·ble (tûr′mə·nə·bəl) *adj.* That may be terminated; limitable; not perpetual. —**ter′·mi·na·bil′i·ty, ter′mi·na·ble·ness** *n.* —**ter′mi·na·bly** *adv.*

ter·mi·nal (tûr′mə·nəl) *adj.* **1** Pertaining to or creative of a boundary, limit, or terminus: a *terminal* railroad station. **2** Pertaining to the delivery or storage of freight or baggage: *terminal* charges. **3** Pertaining to a term or name. **4** Situated at or forming the end of a series or part. **5** *Bot.* Borne at the end of a stem or branch. **6** Of, pertaining to, or occurring in or at the end of a period of time; of a fixed period. —*n.* **1** That which terminates; a terminating point or part; termination; end. **2** *Electr.* One of the two free ends of a conductor, particularly if proceeding from an electric source, as a battery or dynamo. **3** *Archit.* A terminal figure or pedestal; terminus. **4** The edges or planes that form the end of a crystal. **5** A railroad terminus. **6** *pl.* Charges for the use of terminal facilities, or for the handling of freight at railroad terminuses. **7** *Physiol.* The end structure or end of a neuron or nerve fiber. [<F <LL *terminalis* <L *terminus* boundary] —**ter′mi·nal·ly** *adv.*

Ter·mi·na·li·a (tûr′mə·nā′lē·ə) *n. pl. Latin* The ancient Roman festival of Terminus, celebrated on Feb. 23 by the decoration of the boundary markers between private properties, and the offering of sacrifices.

terminal rime The riming of a word or group of syllables at the end of a verse with that at the end of another verse in the same stanza or poem.

terminal velocity *Physics* The velocity acquired by a freely falling body when the resistance of the medium equals the weight of the body.

ter·mi·nate (tûr′mə·nāt) *v.* **·nat·ed, ·nat·ing** *v.t.* **1** To put an end or stop to. **2** To form the conclusion of; finish. **3** To bound or limit. —*v.i.* **4** To have an end; come to an end. See synonyms under ABOLISH, CEASE, END. [<L *terminatus*, pp. of *terminare* end, limit < *terminus* a limit]

ter·mi·na·tion (tûr′mə·nā′shən) *n.* **1** The act of setting bounds or limits. **2** The act of ending or concluding. **3** That which bounds or limits; close; end; limit in time or space. **4** Outcome; result; conclusion. **5** The final letters or syllable of a word; a suffix. See synonyms under BOUNDARY, END.

ter·mi·na·tion·al (tûr′mə·nā′shən·əl) *adj.* Of, pertaining to, or formative of a syllable or other termination; formed by suffixes.

ter·mi·na·tive (tûr′mə·nā′tiv) *adj.* Designed or tending to terminate; determining; definitive; bounding; conclusive. —**ter′mi·na′tive·ly** *adv.*

ter·mi·na·tor (tûr′mə·nā′tər) *n.* **1** One who or that which terminates. **2** *Astron.* The boundary between the illuminated and dark portions of the moon or of a planet.

ter·mi·ner (tûr′mə·nər) *n. Law* The act or function of determining. See OYER AND TERMINER. [<AF *terminour* <F *terminer* end <L *terminare. See* TERM.]

ter·mi·nism (tûr′mə·niz′əm) *n.* **1** *Theol.* The doctrine that God has ordained a limit in the life of each man and of mankind beyond which the opportunity for salvation is lost. **2** A form of nominalism; specifically, the doctrine of William of Ockham, who stated that universals are abstract terms or predicables, rather than either real existents or mere vocal sounds. [<L *terminus* term]

ter·mi·nol·o·gy (tûr′mə·nol′ə·jē) *n.* **1** The study or the use of terms. **2** The technical terms used in a science, art, trade, etc. **3** Nomenclature. [<L *terminus* + -LOGY] —**ter′mi·no·log′i·cal** (-nə·loj′i·kəl) *adj.* —**ter′·mi·no·log′i·cal·ly** *adv.* —**ter′mi·nol′o·gist** *n.*

ter·mi·nus (tûr′mə·nəs) *n. pl.* **·nus·es** or **·ni** (-nī) **1** The final point or goal; end; terminal. **2** The farthermost station on a railway; also, the town in which such station is situated. **3** A boundary or border; also, a boundary mark. See synonyms under END. [<L]

Ter·mi·nus (tûr′mə·nəs) In Roman mythology, the god of boundaries and landmarks.

ter·min·us ad quem (tûr′mə·nəs ad kwem) *Latin* The end or limit to which; the goal; the terminating point of an argument, period, etc.

ter·mi·nus a quo (tûr′mə·nəs ā kwō) *Latin* The starting point.

ter·mite (tûr′mīt) *n.* A white ant. Also *termes.* For illustration see INSECTS (injurious). [<L *termes, termitis*]

term·less (tûrm′lis) *adj.* **1** Of boundless extent or duration. **2** Independent of conditions; unconditional. **3** *Archaic* Incapable of being expressed by terms; indescribable.

term·ly (tûrm′lē) *adj.* Happening or done every term. —*adv.* Periodically.

term·or (tûr′mər) *n. Law* A person who holds lands or tenements for a definite number of years or for life.

tern[1] (tûrn) *n.* Any of several gull-like birds (subfamily *Sterninae*), having the bill pointed and the mandibles co-terminal, smaller than most gulls, with wings more pointed, and the tail usually deeply forked; especially, the common tern *(Sterna hirundo)* of the Atlantic coasts, white with a black cap, and the **least** or **minute tern** *(S. antillarum).* ◆ Homophones: *terne, turn.* [< Scand. Cf. Dan. *terne* tern.]

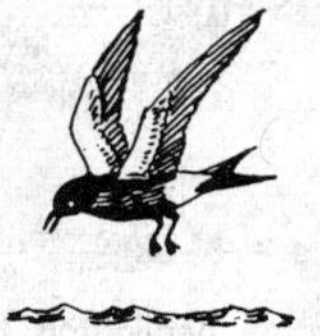

BLACK TERN (Body length about 10 inches; wingspread, 25 inches)

tern[2] (tûrn) *n.* **1** That which is composed of three; specifically, three numbers in a lottery that, when drawn together, secure a large prize. **2** In New England, a three-masted schooner. ◆ Homophones: *terne, turn.* [<L *terni* by threes < *ter* thrice]

ter·na·ry (tûr′nər·ē) *adj.* **1** Formed or consisting of three; grouped in threes. **2** *Math.* Containing three variables; also, pertaining to systems of notation, having three as a base, or radix. **3** *Chem.* Having three separate parts, as atoms, elements, etc. **4** *Metall.* Made of an alloy which contains three metals. —*n. pl.* **·ries** A group of three; a triad. [<L *ternarius* < *terni* by threes]

ter·nate (tûr′nāt) *adj.* **1** Classified or arranged in threes. **2** *Bot.* Trifoliolate; consisting of threes. [<NL *ternatus* <L *terni* by threes] —**ter′nate·ly** *adv.*

Ter·na·te (ter·nä′tā) An Indonesian island of the northern Moluccas; 41 square miles.

terne (tûrn) *v.t.* **terned, tern·ing** To cover with a thin layer of lead and tin. —*n.* Terne plate. ◆ Homophones: *tern, turn.* [<F *terne* dull; from the resulting finish]

terne plate Steel plate with a coating of lead and tin, having a dull finish and inferior in quality to standard tin plate.

Ter·ni (ter′nē) A city in Umbria, central Italy.

ter·ni·on (tûr′nē·ən) *n.* **1** A set of three. **2** A section of a book composed of three sheets in double folds, or 12 pages. [<L *terni* by threes]

Ter·no·pol (tûr·nō′pəl, *Russian* tyir·nô′pəl) A city in western Ukrainian S.S.R.: *Polish* **Tar·no·pol** (tär·nô′pəl).

Ter·pan·der (tər·pan′dər) Greek poet and musician of the seventh century B.C.

ter·pene (tûr′pēn) *n. Chem.* Any of a class of isomeric hydrocarbons, $C_{10}H_{16}$, contained chiefly in the essential oils of coniferous plants. [<*terp(entin)*, earlier form of TURPENTINE + -ENE]

ter·pin·e·ol (tər·pin′ē·ōl, -ol) *n. Chem.* A colorless, unsaturated, tertiary alcohol, $C_{10}H_{17}OH$, derived from the essential oils of various plants and also made synthetically: it has an odor of lilacs and is used in perfumery. [< *terpin*, earlier form of TERPENE + -OL[1]]

ter·pi·nol (tûr′pə·nōl, -nol) *n.* An oily, colorless, liquid mixture of various terpenes, having an odor of hyacinth. [See TERPINEOL]

Terp·sich·o·re (tûrp·sik′ə·rē) The Muse of dancing. [<Gk. *Terpsichorē* < *terpsichoros* delighting in the dance < *terpsis* enjoyment + *choros* dance] —**Terp·si·cho·re·an** (tûrp′·si·kə·rē′ən) *adj.*

terp·si·cho·re·an (tûrp′si·kə·rē′ən) *adj.* Of or relating to dancing: also **terp′si·cho·re′al.** —*n. Colloq.* A dancer.

ter·ra (ter′ə) *n. Latin* The earth; earth.

ter·ra al·ba (ter′ə al′bə) **1** Pipe clay. **2** The pigment made from ground gypsum. **3** Magnesia. **4** A grade of kaolin used as an adulterant of paints. [<L, white earth]

ter·race (ter′is) *n.* **1** An artificial raised level space, as of lawn, having one or more vertical or sloping sides; also, such levels collectively. **2** A raised level supporting a row of houses, or the houses occupying such a position. **3** The flat roof of an Oriental or Spanish house. **4** A relatively narrow step in the face of a steep natural slope. **5** An open gallery; balcony. —*v.t.* **·raced, ·rac·ing** To form into or provide with a terrace or terraces. [<OF <Ital. *terraccia* <L *terra* earth]

ter·ra cot·ta (ter′ə kot′ə) **1** A hard, durable, kiln-burnt clay, reddish-brown in color and usually unglazed: widely used as a structural material and also, in glazed and colored forms, for tiles, building façades, etc. **2** A statue or figure made of this clay. **3** A brownish-orange color resembling that of terra cotta. [<Ital., cooked earth]

ter·ra fir·ma (ter′ə fûr′mə) Solid ground, as distinguished from the sea or the air. [<L]

ter·rain (te·rān′, ter′ān) *n.* **1** Battleground, or a region suited for defense, fortifications, etc. **2** A piece or plot of ground; a region or territory viewed with regard to its suitability for some particular purpose. **3** A terrane. [<F <L *terrenum* < *terrenus* earthen < *terra* earth]

ter·ra in·cog·ni·ta (ter′ə in·kog′nə·tə) **1** An unknown land or region. **2** An unexplored field of study or knowledge. [<L]

Ter·ra·my·cin (ter′ə·mī′sin) *n.* Proprietary name for an antibiotic isolated from a soil mold *(Streptomyces rimosus)*, of value in the

treatment of a wide variety of pathogenic infections.

ter·rane (te·rān′, ter′ān) *n.* **1** *Geol.* A continuous formation or continuous series of related formations; an area of particular rocks. **2** A tract or region considered with reference to some special purpose. [<F *terrain.* See TERRAIN.]

ter·ra·pin (ter′ə·pin) *n.* One of the several North American edible tortoises (family *Testudinidae*); especially, the diamond-back terrapin. [<Algonquian]

DIAMOND–BACK
TERRAPIN
(Shell from 4 to 7 inches)

ter·ra·que·ous (te·rā′kwē·əs) *adj.* Composed of, living in, or consisting of, both land and water. [<L *terra* earth, land + AQUEOUS]

ter·rar·i·um (te·râr′ē·əm) *n. pl.* **·rar·i·ums** or **·rar·i·a** (-râr′ē·ə) **1** A small enclosure or box with glass sides for live lizards, growing plants, etc. **2** A vivarium for land animals. [<L *terra* earth + -ARIUM, on analogy with *aquarium*]

ter·raz·zo (ter·rät′sō) *n.* Flooring made of small pieces of marble or colored stone set in concrete. Also **ter·raz′zo Ve·ne·zia·no** (vā′nā·tsyä′nō). [<Ital. <L *terra* earth]

terre (târ) *n. French* Earth. See TERRA.

Terre·bonne (ter′bon′, -bôn′), **Bayou** A lagoon in SE Louisiana, flowing 55 miles south to **Terrebonne Bay**, a shallow inlet of the Gulf of Mexico SW of New Orleans.

ter·reen (te·rēn′) See TERRINE.

Ter·re Haute (ter′ə hōt′) A city in western Indiana, on the Wabash River.

ter·rene[1] (te·rēn′) *adj.* **1** Pertaining to earth; earthy. **2** Earthly; worldly; mundane. — *n.* **1** The surface of the earth. **2** The earth; a land or terrain. [<L *terrenus* < *terra* earth]

ter·rene[2] (te·rēn′) See TERRINE.

terre·plein (ter′plān) *n.* **1** The upper surface of a rampart behind the parapet, on which the guns are mounted. **2** An embankment with a level top. [<F *terre* earth + *plein* level]

ter·res·tri·al (tə·res′trē·əl) *adj.* **1** Belonging to the earth: opposed to *celestial* or *cosmic.* **2** Pertaining to land or earth: *terrestrial* magnetism. **3** *Biol.* Living on or growing in the earth or land: opposed to *aquatic, aerial,* etc. **4** Belonging to or consisting of land, as distinct from water, trees, etc. **5** Worldly; mundane. — *n.* An inhabitant of the earth. [<L *terrestris* <L *terra* land] — **ter·res′tri·al·ly** *adv.* — **ter·res′tri·al·ness** *n.*

ter·ret (ter′it) *n.* **1** One of two metal rings projecting from the saddle of a harness, through which the reins are passed. **2** A ring for attaching a leash to a dog's collar, etc. Also **ter′rit.** [ME *toret* <F *touret* small wheel, dim. of *tour* a turn]

terre–ten·ant (ter′ten′ənt) *n. Law* **1** The person who is in actual possession of lands. **2** The owner or holder of the legal estate in lands. Also spelled **ter–tenant.** [<AF *terre tenaunt* holding land <F *terre* (<L *terra* land) + *tenaunt* holding, ppr. of *tenir* hold <L *tenere*]

terre–verte (ter′vert′) *n.* **1** An earthy silicate resembling glauconite and used as a green pigment by artists. **2** Glauconite. [<F *terre verte* green earth]

ter·ri·ble (ter′ə·bəl) *adj.* **1** Of a nature to excite terror; appalling. **2** *Colloq.* Characterized by excess; severe; extreme. **3** Inspiring awe. See synonyms under AWFUL, FORMIDABLE, FRIGHTFUL, GRIM. [<F <L *terribilis* < *terrere* terrify] — **ter′ri·ble·ness** *n.* — **ter′ri·bly** *adv.*

ter·ric·o·lous (te·rik′ə·ləs) *adj. Biol.* Living on or in the ground. Also **ter·ric′o·line** (-lēn, -lin). [<L *terricola* earth dweller < *terra* earth + *colere* dwell]

ter·ri·er[1] (ter′ē·ər) *n.* A small, active, wiry dog of several breeds, formerly used to hunt burrowing animals and noted for the courage and eagerness with which it "goes to earth" in pursuit of its quarry. See AIREDALE, DANDIE DINMONT, SCHNAUZER. [<OF <L *terrarius* pertaining to earth. See TERRIER[2].]

— **Bedlington terrier** A liver-colored or blue terrier with muscular body, long neck, narrow skull, and thick coat. It is very game in attacking badgers, foxes, or vermin. [<*Bedlington,*

---

shire in Northumberland County, England]

— **Boston terrier** A small, non-sporting terrier of dark brindle color marked with white, crossbred from the English bulldog and the white English terrier, and having a square skull, short tail, and short, smooth coat.

— **bull terrier** A white terrier first crossbred from the bulldog and the white English terrier, then crossed with the Spanish pointer. It has a muscular, well-balanced body, long head, flat skull, and short, stiff coat.

— **Cairn terrier** A small, stocky, alert terrier of Scotland, having a broad head, a rough outer coat of any color except white, pointed

Welsh Terrier   Airedale   Lakeland Terrier   Irish Terrier

West Highland White Terrier   Cairn Terrier   Yorkshire Terrier   Skye Terrier

Norwich Terrier   Dandie Dinmont   Boston Terrier   Bull Terrier

Scottish Terrier   Schnauzer   Wire-haired Fox Terrier   Smooth-haired Fox Terrier

Bedlington Terrier   Manchester Terrier   Sealyham Terrier   Kerry Blue Terrier

ears, and a black nose: used as a retriever and to exterminate vermin.

— **Clydesdale terrier** A straight-eared, silky-haired dog, with tiny, erect ears and short legs, bred from but smaller than the Skye terrier.

— **fox terrier** A small white terrier, either smooth or wire-haired: formerly bred for bringing the fox out of his burrow, now usually a pet.

— **Irish terrier** A small, red or golden-red, rough-haired terrier having a rather long

---

body built on racing lines: used for hunting small or big game and vermin and also for retrieving in water.

— **Kerry blue terrier** A breed of terrier originating in County Kerry, Ireland, having a long straight back, straight legs, long head, and soft, wavy, bluish-black coat: used to hunt and retrieve small game and as a herd dog, watchdog, and companion.

— **Lakeland terrier** A courageous breed of terrier having a dense, harsh coat of black, blue, or grizzle and tan: originally from Cumberland County, England, and used in hunting the otter or the fox.

— **Lhasa terrier** A breed of terrier native to Tibet, with a heavy yellow, black, white, or brown coat, straight forelegs, and tail curled over its back.

— **Manchester terrier** A small, speedy, short-haired, black-and-tan terrier, originally bred in Manchester, England, and known at one time as **Black-and-Tan terrier.**

— **Norwich terrier** A breed of small, wire-haired terrier, native in England, and usually red, black-and-tan, or grizzled: used in hunting.

—**Scottish terrier** A Scotch breed of small, wire-haired, alert, and intelligent terrier, having a compact body, short legs, small eyes and skull, and gray, brindled, grizzled, black, sandy, or wheaten coat. Also **Scotch terrier, Scottie.**

—**Sealyham terrier** A terrier of mixed ancestry, native of Sealyham, Wales, with short legs, a wide skull, square jaws, and wiry coat, usually solid white, but sometimes marked with lemon or brown on ears and head: used in hunting badger, fox, and otter.

—**Skye terrier** The smallest, lowest-set, and longest-bodied of all useful terriers, unrivaled for acute scent, hearing, sight, and alacrity. Its coat is long and straight, usually blue, gray, or fawn with black points.

—**Welsh terrier** An old breed of rough-haired, black-and-tan terrier, a native of Wales, having a broader head than a fox terrier and a flat skull: used for hunting otter, fox, and badger.

—**West Highland white terrier** A breed of small terrier, with long, low, compact body, short legs, and a pure white, coarse, wiry outer coat: said to have existed in Scotland prior to 1600 A.D.

—**Yorkshire terrier** A toy breed, among the smallest of all varieties of terriers. It has semi-erect ears and a coat of long, silky, dark steel-blue hair, with golden tan on chest and head. At first a pet of the working classes, especially of weavers, it later became a fashionable pet.

ter·ri·er[2] (ter′ē·ər) *n. Law* **1** A land survey setting forth in detail the number of acres, names of tenants, etc., in a given district: the *terrier* of glebe lands. **2** A book containing the lists of the lands either of a private person or a corporation; a rent roll. [<OF, list of tenants <LL *terrarius* a roll describing landed property <L, pertaining to land < *terra* land]

ter·rif·ic (tə·rif′ik) *adj.* **1** Arousing or calculated to arouse great terror or fear. **2** *Colloq.* Excessive; extreme; tremendous. See synonyms under AWFUL, FRIGHTFUL. —**ter·rif′i·cal·ly** *adv.*

ter·ri·fy (ter′ə·fī) *v.t.* **·fied, ·fy·ing** To fill with extreme terror. See synonyms under FRIGHTEN. [<L *terrificare* < *terrificus* causing fear < *terrere* frighten + *facere* make]

ter·rig·e·nous (te·rij′ə·nəs) *adj.* **1** Produced from or of the earth. **2** *Geol.* Derived from the land: said of marine deposits formed of material washed from the land, as contrasted with those of organic, chemical, or other origin, formed in the sea. **3** Earthborn. Also **ter·ri·gene** (ter′ə·jēn). [<L *terrigenus* < *terra* earth + *gignere* be born]

ter·rine (te·rēn′) *n.* **1** An earthenware jar containing some delicacy for the table and sold with its contents: a *terrine* of preserved ginger. **2** A kind of ragout or stew. Also spelled *terreen, terrene.* [<F <LL *terrineus* made of earth <L *terra* earth. Doublet of TUREEN.]

ter·ri·to·ri·al (ter′ə·tôr′ē·əl, -tō′rē-) *adj.* **1** Pertaining to a territory or territories; limited to a particular territory. **2** Designating military forces intended for territorial defense. **3** Belonging to a particular locality. **4** Organized or intended primarily for national defense: a *territorial* reserve. —**ter′ri·to′ri·al·ly** *adv.*

Ter·ri·to·ri·al (ter′ə·tôr′ē·əl, -tō′rē-) *adj.* Of or pertaining to any or all of the Territories of the United States: the *Territorial* system. —*n.* A member of the Territorial Army in Great Britain who enlisted for home defense but volunteered for overseas service in World War I.

ter·ri·to·ri·al·ism (ter′ə·tôr′ē·əl·iz′əm, -tō′rē-) *n.* The organizations, theories, or doctrines of the territorial systems. —**ter′ri·to′ri·al·ist** *n.*

ter·ri·to·ri·al·i·ty (ter′ə·tôr′ē·al′ə·tē, -tō′rē-) *n.* Territorial condition, status, or position.

ter·ri·to·ri·al·ize (ter′ə·tôr′ē·əl·īz′, -tō′rē-) *v.t.* **·ized, ·iz·ing** **1** To enlarge by annexation of territory. **2** To reduce to the political status of a territory. **3** To distribute among certain territories. —**ter′ri·to′ri·al·i·za′tion** *n.*

territorial jurisdiction *Law* The sovereign jurisdiction exercised by a state over all lands, waters, persons, and properties within its boundaries.

territorial system **1** A system of church government in which all inhabitants of a territory are required to belong to the same religion as the civil ruler. **2** Local organization for militia service. **3** Landlordism; a system giving predominance to landowners.

territorial waters The belt of sea under a state's territorial jurisdiction: formerly, the range of a cannon shot, or three miles: now often controversial. Also **territorial sea.**

ter·ri·to·ry (ter′ə·tôr′ē, -tō′rē) *n. pl.* **·ries** **1** The domain over which a sovereign state exercises jurisdiction. **2** Any considerable tract of land; a region; district; figuratively, sphere; province. **3** An area assigned for a special purpose: the *territory* of a commercial traveler. [<L *territorium* < *terra* earth]

Ter·ri·to·ry (ter′ə·tôr′ē, -tō′rē) *n. U.S.* A region having a certain degree of self-government, but not having the status of a State. Alaska and Hawaii were formerly Territories.

ter·ror (ter′ər) *n.* **1** An overwhelming impulse of fear; extreme fright or dread. **2** That which or one who causes extreme fear. **3** *Colloq.* An intolerable nuisance: That child is a holy *terror.* See synonyms under ALARM, FEAR, FRIGHT. [<F *terreur* <L *terror* fright < *terrere* frighten]

ter·ror·ism (ter′ə·riz′əm) *n.* **1** The act of terrorizing. **2** A system of government that seeks to rule by intimidation. **3** Unlawful acts of violence committed in an organized attempt to overthrow a government.

ter·ror·ist (ter′ər·ist) *n.* **1** One who adopts or supports a policy of terrorism. **2** A Jacobin or Republican of the French Revolution of 1789, especially during the Reign of Terror. **3** A member of political extremist groups in czarist Russia. **4** An alarmist; a scaremonger. —**ter′ror·is′tic** *adj.*

ter·ror·ize (ter′ə·rīz) *v.t.* **·ized, ·iz·ing** **1** To reduce to a state of terror; terrify. **2** To coerce through intimidation. Also *Brit.* **ter′ror·ise.** —**ter′ror·i·za′tion** *n.* —**ter′ror·iz′er** *n.*

ter·ry (ter′ē) *n. pl.* **·ries** **1** The loop raised for the nap in weaving pile fabrics. **2** A pile dressmaking fabric in which the loops are uncut: also **terry cloth.** **3** A looped cotton fabric, very water-absorbent, used chiefly for towels and beach robes. [Prob. <F *tiré,* pp. of *tirer* draw <L *trahere*]

Ter·ry (ter′ē), **Dame Ellen,** 1848–1928, English actress.

terse (tûrs) *adj.* **1** Elegantly concise; short and to the point. **2** Rubbed to a polish; clean; polished; refined. [<L *tersus,* pp. of *tergere* rub off, rub down] —**terse′ly** *adv.* —**terse′ness** *n.*

Synonyms: brief, compact, compendious, concise, condensed, laconic, pithy, sententious, short, succinct. Anything *short* or *brief* is of relatively small extent. That which is *concise* is trimmed down, and that which is *condensed* is, as it were, pressed together, so as to include as much as possible within a small space. That which is *compendious* gathers the substance of a matter into a few weighty and effective words. *Succinct* writing is taut and lean without extraneous detail. *Summary* implies compression to the utmost, often to the point of abruptness; as, a *summary* statement or a *summary* dismissal. That which is *terse* has an elegant and finished completeness within the smallest possible compass. A *sententious* style is one abounding in maxims or short, pithy phrases. A *pithy* utterance gives the gist of a matter effectively, whether in rude or elegant style. *Antonyms*: diffuse, lengthy, long, prolix, tedious, verbose, wordy.

ter-ten·ant (ter′ten′ənt) See TERRE-TENANT.

ter·tial (tûr′shəl) *Ornithol. adj.* Of or pertaining to the third row of flight feathers in a bird's wing. —*n.* A tertiary feather. [<L *tertius* third < *ter* thrice]

ter·tian (tûr′shən) *adj.* Recurring every third day, reckoned inclusively, hence every alternate day. —*n. Pathol.* A disease, the paroxysms of which return every other day; a tertian fever. [<L *(febris) tertiana* tertian (fever) < *tertius* third]

ter·ti·ar·y (tûr′shē·er′ē, -shə·rē) *adj.* **1** Third in point of time, number, degree, or standing. **2** Tertial. **3** *Eccl.* Pertaining to the third order of a religious body. **4** *Chem.* **a** Having three substituted atoms or radicals: a *tertiary* amine. **b** Denoting a radical in which three bonds of the combining carbon atoms are directly connected with three other carbon atoms: *tertiary* butyl. —*n. pl.* **·ar·ies** **1** *Ornithol.* One of the feathers attached to the humerus joint of the wing of a bird. **2** Any member of the third order of a monastic body. [<L *tertiarius* < *tertius* third]

Ter·ti·ar·y (tûr′shē·er′ē, -shə·rē) *Geol. adj.* Of or pertaining to the earlier of the two geological periods or systems comprising the Cenozoic era, following the Cretaceous and succeeded by the Quaternary. —*n.* The Tertiary period or system, characterized by the rise of mammals.

ter·ti·um quid (tûr′shē·əm kwid) *Latin* **1** A third something; an indefinite or undefined thing related in some way to two definite or known things. **2** A mediating factor between essentially opposite things.

Ter·tul·li·an (tər·tul′ē·ən) Anglicized name of Quintus Septimius Florens Tertullianus, A.D. 160?–230?, Latin church father.

Te·ru·el (tā′rōō·el′) **1** A province in NE Spain; 6,710 square miles. **2** The capital city of Teruel province; scene of fierce fighting in the Spanish Civil War, 1937.

ter·va·lent (tûr′və·lənt, tər·vā′lənt) *adj. Chem.* Trivalent.

ter·za-ri·ma (ter′tsä·rē′mä) *n. pl.* **ter·ze-ri·me** (ter′tsā·rē′mā) A form of Italian triplet, in iambic decasyllables or hendecasyllables, in which the middle line of the first triplet rimes with the first and third lines of the following triplet: used by Dante in the *Divine Comedy.* [<Ital., third or triple line]

ter·zet·to (ter·tset′tō) *n. pl.* **·ti** (-tē) *Music* A short composition for three performers or singers; a trio. [See TERCET]

Tesch·en (tesh′ən) A territory and former principality in southern Poland and eastern Silesia, Czechoslovakia; 850 square miles; incorporated in Germany, 1939–45. *Czech* **Tě·šín** (tye′shēn), *Polish* **Cie·szyn** (che′shin).

Te·sho La·ma (te′shō lä′mə) See under DALAI LAMA.

Tes·la (tes′lə), **Nikola,** 1857–1943, U. S. electrical inventor born in Yugoslavia.

Tes·lin Lake (tez′lin, tes′-) A lake between NW British Columbia and southern Yukon, Canada; about 200 square miles; 80 miles long, 1 to 3 miles wide.

tes·sel·late (tes′ə·lāt) *v.t.* **·lat·ed, ·lat·ing** To construct in the style of checkered mosaic; lay or adorn with squares or tiles, as pavement. [<L *tessellatus* checkered < *tessella,* dim. of *tessera* cube. See TESSERA.] —**tes′sel·lat′ed** *adj.*

tes·sel·la·tion (tes′ə·lā′shən) *n.* **1** Tessellated work. **2** The art or act of doing such work.

tes·ser·a (tes′ər·ə) *n. pl.* **·ser·ae** (-ər·ē) **1** A small square, as of stone, glass, etc., used in mosaic work. **2** A small object, often a square or cube, as of bone or wood, used as a die in gambling or as a token, voucher, or the like. [<L <dial. Gk. (Ionic) *tesseres* four]

tes·ser·act (tes′ər·akt) *n. Math.* **1** A construct intended to illustrate graphically or in the form of a model the general appearance of a four-dimensional figure. **2** A hypercube bounded by 8 cubes or cells, with 16 vertices, 24 faces, and 32 edges. [<dial. Gk. (Ionic) *tesseres* four + *aktis* ray]

Tes·sin (te·sēn′) See TICINO.

test[1] (test) *v.t.* **1** To subject to a test or trial; try. **2** *Chem.* **a** To refine, as gold or silver, by means of lead, as in the process of cupellation. **b** To examine by means of some reagent, as in testing for sulfuric acid. —*v.i.* **3** *Chem.* To undergo testing; also, to show specified qualities or properties under testing: The alcohol *tested* 75 percent. See synonyms under EXAMINE. [<*n.*] —*n.* **1** Subjection to conditions that disclose the true character of a person or thing in relation to some particular quality. **2** An examination made for the purpose of proving or disproving some matter in doubt, as mental

condition. 3 A criterion or standard of judgment. 4 An oath or other confirmatory evidence of principles or belief. 5 *Chem.* **a** A reaction by means of which the identity of a compound or one of its constituents may be determined. **b** Its agent or the result. 6 An earthen vessel similar to a cupel, formerly used in testing metals. 7 A series of questions, problems, etc., intended to measure the extent of knowledge, aptitudes, intelligence, and other mental traits: an intelligence *test.* See synonyms under PROOF. [<OF, a cupel, pot <L *testum* an earthen vessel < *testa* potsherd, shell] — **test′a·ble** *adj.*

test[2] (test) *n.* 1 *Zool.* A rigid external case or covering of many invertebrates, as a sea urchin or mollusk; a shell. 2 *Bot.* A testa. [<L *testa* shell]

test[3] (test) *v.t.* To attest. [<OF *tester* bequeath <L *testari* be a witness. See TESTAMENT.]

tes·ta (tes′tə) *n. pl.* **·tae** (-tē) 1 *Bot.* The outer, usually hard and brittle coat or integument of a seed. 2 *Zool.* A test. [See TEST[2]]

tes·ta·ce·an (tes·tā′shē·ən, -shən) *adj.* Pertaining or belonging to an order *(Testacea)* of rhizopods enclosed in a single-chambered cell. [<NL <L *testaceum* shellfish < *testaceus.* See TESTACEOUS.]

tes·ta·ceous (tes·tā′shəs) *adj.* 1 Of or derived from shells or shellfish. 2 Having a hard shell. 3 Dull brick-red or brownish-yellow. [<L *testaceus* of shell, brick < *testa* a shell]

tes·ta·cy (tes′tə·sē) *n. Law* The state of being testate or of having left a will at death: opposed to *intestacy.*

tes·ta·ment (tes′tə·mənt) *n.* 1 The written declaration of one's last will: usually **last will and testament.** In strictness, a testament differs from a will in that it bequeaths personal property only, but the words are commonly used interchangeably. 2 In Biblical use, a covenant; dispensation. [<F <L *testamentum* < *testari* testify < *testis* a witness] — **tes′ta·men′tal** *adj.*

Tes·ta·ment (tes′tə·mənt) *n.* 1 One of the two volumes of the Bible, distinguished as the **Old** and the **New Testament.** 2 Specifically, a volume containing the New Testament.

tes·ta·men·ta·ry (tes′tə·men′tər·ē) *adj.* 1 Derived from, bequeathed by, or set forth in a will. 2 Appointed or provided by, or done in accordance with, a will. 3 Pertaining to a will, or to the administration or settlement of a will; testamental. 4 *Often cap.* Pertaining to a Testament.

tes·tate (tes′tāt) *adj.* Having made a will before decease. [<L *testatus,* pp. of *testari* be a witness. See TESTAMENT.]

tes·ta·tor (tes·tā′tər, tes′tā·tər) *n.* 1 The maker of a will. 2 One who has died leaving a will. [<L] — **tes·ta′trix** (-triks) *n. fem.*

test·er[1] (tes′tər) *n.* One who tests; a device for testing.

tes·ter[2] (tes′tər) *n.* A flat canopy over a tomb, pulpit, or bed. [<OF *testiere* < *teste* head <L *testa* shell, skull]

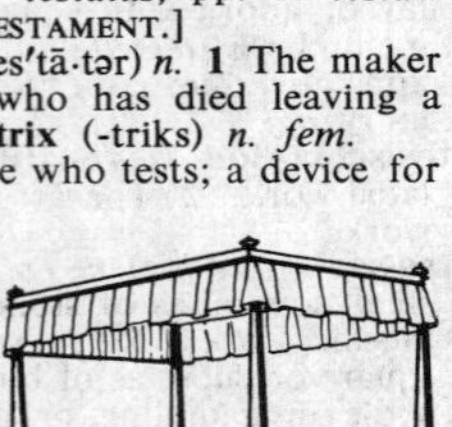

TESTER

tes·ter[3] (tes′tər) *n. Obs.* A silver coin of the Tudor period, originally equal to twelve pence, later worth sixpence. [<OF *teston* coin < *teste* head. See TESTER[2].]

tes·ti·cle (tes′ti·kəl) *n. Biol.* One of the two genital glands of the male in which the spermatozoa and certain internal secretions are formed; a testis. [<L *testiculus,* dim. of *testis* testicle]

tes·tic·u·late (tes·tik′yə·lit, -lāt) *adj.* 1 Shaped or formed like a testicle. 2 Solid and ovate, like the roots of certain orchids. 3 Having organs like testicles. [<L *testiculus* + -ATE[1]]

tes·tif·i·cate (tes·tif′ə·kāt) *n.* In Scots law, a solemn written assertion. [<L *testificatus,* pp. of *testificari* bear witness. See TESTIFY.]

tes·ti·fi·ca·tion (tes′tə·fə·kā′shən) *n.* 1 The act of testifying or the giving of testimony. 2 The testimony given. — **tes′ti·fi·ca′tor** *n.*

tes·ti·fy (tes′tə·fī) *v.* **·fied, ·fy·ing** *v.i.* 1 To make solemn declaration of truth or fact. 2 *Law* To give testimony; bear witness. 3 To serve as evidence or indication: Her rags *testified* to her poverty. — *v.t.* 4 To bear witness to; affirm positively. 5 *Law* To state or declare on oath or affirmation. 6 To be evidence or indication of. 7 To make known publicly; declare. See synonyms under AFFIRM, AVOW. [<L *testificari* < *testis* witness + *facere* make] — **tes′ti·fi′er** *n.*

tes·ti·mo·ni·al (tes′tə·mō′nē·əl) *n.* 1 A formal token of regard. 2 A written certificate; an acknowledgment of services or worth; a letter of recommendation. — *adj.* Pertaining to or constituting testimony or a testimonial. [<L *testimonialis* < *testimonium.* See TESTIMONY.]

tes·ti·mo·ny (tes′tə·mō′nē) *n. pl.* **·nies** 1 A statement or affirmation of a fact, as before a court; evidence; proof. 2 The aggregate of proof offered in a case. 3 The act of testifying; attestation. 4 Public declaration regarding some experience. 5 The Decalog; the Old Testament Scriptures. [<L *testimonium* < *testis* a witness] — **tes′ti·mo′nied** *Obs. adj.*

Synonyms: affidavit, affirmation, attestation, deposition, proof, witness. *Testimony,* in legal as well as in common use, denotes the statements of witnesses. *Deposition* and *affidavit* denote *testimony* reduced to writing. The *deposition* differs from the *affidavit* in that the latter is voluntary and without cross-examination, while the former is made under interrogatories and subject to cross-examination. *Evidence* is a broader term, including the *testimony* of witnesses and all facts of every kind that tend to prove a thing true; we have the *testimony* of a traveler that a fugitive passed this way; his footprints in the sand are additional *evidence* of the fact. Compare PROOF.

tes·tis (tes′tis) *n. pl.* **·tes** (-tēz) A testicle. [<L]

test meal A meal of prescribed materials and quantity taken as a preliminary to a subsequent examination of the contents of the stomach.

tes·ton (tes′tən, tes·tōōn′) *n. Obs.* 1 A European silver coin: so called from the head on the obverse side. 2 A French coin of the 16th century. 3 An English silver coin; a tester. Also **tes·toon** (tes·tōōn′). [<F <Ital. *testone,* aug. of *testa* head <L, skull]

tes·tos·ter·one (tes·tos′tə·rōn) *n. Biochem.* A male sex hormone, $C_{19}H_{28}O_2$, isolated as a white crystalline substance from the testes, and also made synthetically. [<TESTIS + STER(OL) + -ONE]

test paper 1 *Chem.* A paper saturated with some reagent that readily changes color when exposed to certain others, as litmus paper. 2 A list of questions, problems, etc., for the testing of students.

test pilot An aviator who flies airplanes of new design to test their performance under various conditions.

test tube A glass tube, open at one end, and usually with a rounded bottom, used in making chemical or biological tests.

tes·tu·di·nal (tes·tōō′də·nəl, -tyōō′-) *adj.* Pertaining to or like a turtle or tortoise shell: also **tes·tu′di·nate.** [<L *testudo, -inis* tortoise]

Tes·tu·din·i·dae (tes′tōō·din′i·dē, -tyōō-) *n. pl.* A family of reptiles having a dorsal shell or carapace constituted chiefly by the vertebrae and ribs and a ventral shell or plastron; tortoises and turtles. [<NL <L *testudo, -inis* tortoise]

tes·tu·do (tes·tōō′dō, -tyōō′-) *n. pl.* **·di·nes** (-də·nēz) 1 A shed or screen used by the Romans for the protection of soldiers in siege operations. 2 A protecting cover formed by soldiers in ranks by overlapping their shields above their heads. [<L < *testa* shell]

Tes·tu·do (tes·tōō′dō, -tyōō′-) *n.* A genus typical of land tortoises. [<L]

tes·ty (tes′tē) *adj.* **·ti·er, ·ti·est** Having an irritable disposition; touchy. See synonyms under FRETFUL. [<AF *testif* heady <OF *teste* head <L *testa* skull] — **tes′ti·ly** *adv.* — **tes′ti·ness** *n.*

te·tan·ic (ti·tan′ik) *adj.* Relating to or productive of tetanus: also **te·tan′i·cal.** — *n.* A drug capable of causing convulsions, as strychnine or nux vomica.

tet·a·nize (tet′ə·nīz) *v.t.* **·nized, ·niz·ing** To affect with tetanic spasms. — **tet′a·ni·za′tion** *n.*

tet·a·nus (tet′ə·nəs) *n.* 1 *Pathol.* An acute infectious disease caused by a bacillus *(Clostridium tetani)* and characterized by rigid spasmodic contraction of various voluntary muscles, especially that form affecting the muscles of the jaw, called *lockjaw.* 2 *Physiol.* A state of contraction in a muscle excited by a rapid series of shocks. [<L <Gk. *tetanos* spasm < *teinein* stretch]

tet·a·ny (tet′ə·nē) *n. Pathol.* 1 Intermittent tetanic spasms, usually due to defective metabolism. 2 Tetanus.

tetarto- *combining form* Four; fourth. Also, before vowels, **tetart-.** [<Gk. *tetartos* fourth < *tettares* four]

te·tar·to·he·dral (ti·tär′tō·hē′drəl) *adj.* Possessing one fourth of the planes necessary for true symmetry: said of crystals.

tetch·y (tech′ē) See TECHY.

tête-à-tête (tāt′ə·tāt′, *Fr.* tet·à·tet′) *adj.* Being face to face; literally, head to head; hence, confidential, as between two persons. — *n.* 1 A private interview; a confidential chat between two persons. 2 An S-shaped sofa on which two persons may face each other. — *adv.* In private or personal talk. [<F]

tête-bêche (tet·besh′) *adj. French* Literally, head to foot: said of a pair of stamps so printed that one is reversed in relation to the other.

tête-de-pont (tet·də·pôṅ′) *n. pl.* **têtes-de-pont** (tet·də·pôṅ′) *French* A bridgehead.

teth (teth) *n.* The ninth Hebrew letter. See ALPHABET.

teth·er (teth′ər) *n.* 1 Something used to check or confine, as a rope for fastening an animal. 2 The range, scope, or limit of one's powers or field of action. — **at the end of one's tether** At the extreme end or limit of one's resources. — *v.t.* To fasten or confine by a tether. [ME *tethir* <Scand. Cf. ON *tiodhr* a tether.]

Te·thys (tē′this) In Greek mythology, a Titaness, sister and wife of Oceanus and mother of the Oceanids.

Te·ton Range (tē′ton, tēt′n) A range of the Rocky Mountains, chiefly in NW Wyoming; highest peak, 13,776 feet.

te·to·tum (tē·tō′təm) See TEETOTUM.

tetra- *combining form* Four; fourfold: *tetrachord.* Also, before vowels, **tetr-.**

tet·ra·ba·sic (tet′rə·bā′sik) *adj. Chem.* 1 Containing four atoms of hydrogen replaceable by a base or basic radicals: said of certain acids. 2 Denoting a compound with four atoms of a univalent metal or the equivalent.

tet·ra·brach (tet′rə·brak) *n.* A Greek or Latin word or foot made up of four short syllables. [<Gk. *tetrabrachys* < *tessares, tettares* four + *brachys* short]

tet·ra·cene (tet′rə·sēn) *n. Chem.* A yellow, solid, nitrogen compound, $C_2H_8N_{10}$, used as a sensitizer or combustion initiator in priming compositions. Also *tetrazine.*

tet·ra·chlo·ride (tet′rə·klôr′īd, -id, -klō′rīd, -rid) *n. Chem.* A compound containing four atoms of chlorine. Also **tet′ra·chlo′rid** (-klôr′id, -klō′rid).

tet·ra·chord (tet′rə·kôrd) *n. Music* 1 A scale series of half an octave. 2 The interval of a perfect fourth. [<Gk. *tetrachordon* a musical instrument < *tetras* group of four + *chordē* string] — **tet′ra·chor′dal** *adj.*

te·trac·id (te·tras′id) *Chem. adj.* Denoting a base which is capable of combination with four molecules of a monobasic acid to form a salt or ester. — *n.* A base having four replaceable hydroxyl radicals. [<TETR(A)- + ACID]

tet·ra·cy·cline (tet′rə·sī′klin) *n. Chem.* A nitrogenous compound, $C_{22}H_{24}N_2O_8$, isolated as a yellow, odorless, crystalline powder from certain species of a soil bacillus (genus *Streptomyces*). It forms the base of several antibiotics, as Aureomycin and Terramycin. [< *tetracyclic,* containing four atomic rings + -INE[2]]

tet·rad (tet′rad) *n.* 1 A collection of four, or the number four. 2 An atom, radical, or element that is quadrivalent. 3 *Biol.* The group of four chromatids into which two bivalent chromosomes divide in the last stages of meiosis. 4 A crystal having an axis showing fourfold symmetry. [<Gk. *tetras, -ados* group of four]

te·trad·y·mite (te·trad′ə·mīt) *n.* A soft, metallic, pale steel-gray, bismuth telluride, Bi_2Te_3, crystallizing in the rhombohedral system. [<G *tetradymit* <Gk. *tetradymos* fourfold; from its occurring in compound twin crystals]

tet·ra·dyn·a·mous (tet′rə·din′ə·məs, -dī′nə-) *adj. Bot.* Having six stamens, of which four,

arranged in opposite pairs, are longer than the other two and inserted above them, as in flowers of the mustard family. [< TETRA- + Gk. *dynamis* power]

tet·ra·eth·yl·lead (tet′rə·eth′il·led′) *n.* An extremely toxic liquid compound, $Pb(C_2H_5)_4$, having an antiknock effect when added in small amounts to motor fuels. Also **tetraethyl lead.** Also called *lead tetraethyl.*

tet·ra·gon (tet′rə·gon) *n. Geom.* A plane figure having four angles; a quadrangle. [< Gk. *tetragōnon* a quadrangle < *tetra-* four + *gōnia* angle]

tet·rag·o·nal (tet·rag′ə·nəl) *adj.* **1** Being or pertaining to a tetragon; having four angles; quadrangular. **2** Belonging to or designating a crystal system characterized by four alternately dissimilar planes of symmetry intersecting at angles of 45 degrees and a fifth symmetrical plane at right angles to the others.

tet·ra·gram (tet′rə·gram) *n.* A word of four letters.

Tet·ra·gram·ma·ton (tet′rə·gram′ə·ton) *n.* In Hebrew texts, the group of four letters (JHVH, JHWH, YHVH, or YHWH) representing the holy and ineffable name of God. The common transliteration Jehovah is the result of a combination of the Tetragrammaton with the vowel points of *Adonai* "my Lord," which is substituted in reading the name. [< Gk. *tetragrammaton* < *tetra-* four + *gramma* a letter < *graphein* write]

tet·ra·he·dral (tet′rə·hē′drəl) *adj.* **1** Of or pertaining to a tetrahedron. **2** Made up of or having four sides. [< Gk. *tetraedros.* See TETRAHEDRON.]

tet·ra·he·drite (tet′rə·hē′drīt) *n.* A steel-gray, fine-grained mineral, usually a sulfide of copper and antimony but having other elements, found in tetrahedral crystals. [< TETRAHEDRON]

tet·ra·he·dron (tet′rə·hē′drən) *n. pl.* **·dra** (-drə) **1** *Geom.* A solid bounded by four plane triangular faces. **2** An anti-tank obstacle shaped like a pyramid. [< Gk. *tetraedron,* neut. of *tetraedros* < *tetra-* four + *hedra* base]

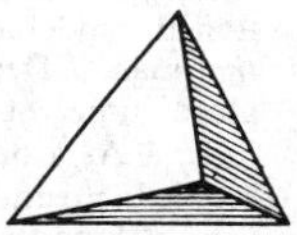

TETRAHEDRON

te·tral·o·gy (te·tral′ə·jē) *n. pl.* **·gies 1** A group of four dramas, three tragic and one satyric, presented together at the festivals of Dionysus at Athens. **2** Hence, any series of four related dramatic, fictional, or operatic works. [< Gk. *tetralogia* < *tetra-* four + *logos* word, speech]

te·tram·er·ous (te·tram′ər·əs) *adj.* **1** Having four parts. **2** *Bot.* Having the parts or organs in four; arranged in fours or multiples of four: often written *4-merous.* **3** *Zool.* Having four joints; having four-jointed tarsi. Also **te·tram′·er·al.** [< Gk. *tetramerēs* four-parted < *tetra-* four + *meros* part]

te·tram·e·ter (te·tram′ə·tər) *adj.* Having four measures. In classical trochaic, iambic, and anapestic verse a measure consists of two feet (a dipody); hence, a trochaic tetrameter contains eight feet to the line. In English, a tetrameter has four feet or measures. —*n.* A verse (line) thus composed. [< LL *tetrametrus* < Gk. *tetrametros* < *tetra-* four + *metron* measure]

tet·ra·morph (tet′rə·môrf) *n.* The union of the four attributes of the four Evangelists in one composite figure, winged, and standing on winged wheels of fire, the wings being full of eyes. [< Gk. *tetramorphon* four-shaped < *tetra-* four + *morphē* form]

tet·ra·pet·al·ous (tet′rə·pet′l·əs) *adj. Bot.* Having four petals.

tet·ra·pod (tet′rə·pod) *adj.* Four-footed. [< NL *tetrapodus* < Gk. *tetrapous, tetrapodos* four-footed < *tetra-* four + *pous* foot]

te·trap·o·dy (te·trap′ə·dē) *n. pl.* **·dies** A group of four feet, as a colon, meter, or verse containing that number. [< Gk. *tetrapodia* < *tetrapous.* See TETRAPOD.] **—tet·ra·pod·ic** (tet′rə·pod′ik) *adj.*

te·trap·ter·ous (te·trap′tər·əs) *adj. Biol.* Having four wings, as certain fruits and insects. [< NL *tetrapterus* < Gk. *tetrapteros* four-winged < *tetra-* four + *pteron* wing]

tet·ra·py·lon (tet′rə·pī′lon). *n. Archit.* A structure having four gateways or penetrated by two intersecting passages, as some arches. [< Gk. *tetrapylos* with four gates < *tetra-* four + *pylē* a gate]

tet·rarch (tet′rärk, tē′trärk) *n.* **1** The governor of one of four divisions of a country or province. **2** A tributary prince under the Romans; a subordinate ruler. **3** Anciently, in the Greek army, the commander of a subdivision of a phalanx. [< LL *tetrarcha* < L *tetrarches* < Gk. *tetrarchēs* < *tetra-* four + *archos* ruler] **—tet·rar·chy** (tet′rär·kē, tē′trär-), **tet·rarch·ate** (tet′rär·kāt, -kit, tē′trär-) *n.*

tet·ra·seme (tet′rə·sēm) *n.* A long syllable or a foot equal to four short syllables. [< TETRA- + Gk. *sēma* sign] **—tet′ra·se′mic** *adj.*

tet·ra·spore (tet′rə·spôr, -spōr) *n. Bot.* An asexual spore produced by certain algae: named from the fact that often four are produced together from a mother cell.

tet·ra·stich (tet′rə·stik) *n.* A poem or stanza of four lines; a quatrain. [< TETRA- + Gk. *stichos* row, line] **—tet′ra·stich′ic** *adj.*

te·tras·ti·chous (te·tras′tə·kəs) *adj. Bot.* Four-ranked; having organs, as leaves on a stem, arranged in four vertical rows or ranks.

tet·ra·style (tet′rə·stīl) *adj.* Having four pillars. —*n. Archit.* **1** A temple having four columns in the front or end row. **2** Any building or structure having four pillars in a row or rows. [< L *tetrastylos* < Gk. < *tetra-* four + *stylos* column]

tet·ra·syl·la·ble (tet′rə·sil′ə·bəl) *n.* A word of four syllables. **—tet′ra·syl·lab′ic** or **·i·cal** *adj.*

tet·ra·tom·ic (tet′rə·tom′ik) *adj. Chem.* **1** Containing four atoms. **2** Containing four replaceable univalent atoms or molecules. **3** Quadrivalent.

tet·ra·va·lent (tet′rə·vā′lənt) *adj. Chem.* Quadrivalent.

tet·ra·zine (tet′rə·zēn, -zin) *n. Chem.* Tetracene.

Te·traz·zi·ni (tā′trät·tsē′nē), **Luisa,** 1874?–1940, Italian coloratura soprano active in the United States.

tet·rode (tet′rōd) *n. Electronics* A vacuum tube containing four elements, the fourth usually being an additional grid interposed between the first grid and the plate. [< TETR(A)- + -ODE[1]]

te·trox·ide (te·trok′sīd, -sid) *n. Chem.* An oxide containing four atoms of oxygen to the molecule. Also **te·trox′id** (-sid). [< TETR(A)- + OXIDE]

tet·ryl (tet′ril) *n. Chem.* A yellowish, crystalline nitrogen compound, $C_7H_5N_5O_8$, used as an explosive in boosters and detonators. [< TETR(A)- + -YL]

tet·ter (tet′ər) *n. Pathol.* A vesicular skin disease, as eczema. [OE *teter*]

Te·tuán (tā·twän′) A port on the Mediterranean Sea in NE Morocco; former capital of Spanish Morocco.

Tet·zel (tet′səl), **Johann,** 1465–1519, German Dominican monk, opponent of Luther. Also spelled *Tezel.*

Teu·cer (to͞o′sər, tyo͞o′-) In Greek legend: **1** The half-brother of Ajax, who founded Salamis in Cyprus: noted as an archer. **2** The first king of Troy.

Teu·cri·a (to͞o′krē·ə, tyo͞o′-) See TROAS.

Teu·cri·an (to͞o′krē·ən, tyo͞o′-) *adj.* **1** Trojan. **2** Of or pertaining to Teucer.

teugh (to͝okh, tyo͝okh) *adj. Scot.* Tough. Also **teuch. —teugh′ly** *adv.* **—teugh′ness** *n.*

Teu·to·bur·ger Wald (toi′tō·bo͝or′gər vält) A range of hills in western Germany; highest point, 1,465 feet; scene of a German victory by Arminius over the Roman army commanded by Varus, 9 A.D.

Teu·ton (to͞ot′n, tyo͞ot′n) *n.* **1** One of an ancient German tribe that dwelt in Jutland north of the Elbe, appearing in history as **Teu·to·nes** (to͞o′tə·nēz, tyo͞o′-), together with the **Cim·bri** (sim′brī), a possibly related tribe, in 113 B.C. **2** One belonging to any of the Teutonic peoples; especially, a German.

Teu·ton·ic (to͞o·ton′ik, tyo͞o-) *adj.* **1** Of or pertaining to the Teutons; especially, designating the blond peoples of northern Europe, formerly including the Angles, Saxons, Danes, Normans, Norwegians, the Goths, Franks, Lombards, Vandals, etc.; now embracing also the English, Germans, Dutch, etc. **2** Of or pertaining to that subfamily of Indo-European languages now called *Germanic,* including Gothic, the Scandinavian languages, and all the High and Low German languages and dialects, among which are German, Dutch, Flemish, and English. —*n.* The Germanic subfamily of languages.

Teutonic Knights The Knights of St. Mary's Hospital at Jerusalem, an order of military monks deriving their name and office from a German hospital founded at Jerusalem in 1128. One of the three great military orders founded during the Crusades to convert the heathen, help pilgrims, and nurse the sick, the knights later moved to eastern Europe and during the Middle Ages became the spearhead of German expansion toward Slavic and Baltic territories. Their costume was a white mantle with a black cross. See HOSPITALER, KNIGHT TEMPLAR.

Teu·ton·ism (to͞ot′n·iz′əm, tyo͞ot′n-) *n.* **1** A custom or mode of expression peculiar to Germans or Teutons; Germanism: also **Teu·ton·i·cism** (to͞o·ton′ə·siz′əm, tyo͞o-). **2** A belief in the superiority of the Teutonic race. **3** Teutonic character and civilization. **—Teu′ton·ist** *n.*

Teu·ton·ize (to͞ot′n·īz, tyo͞ot′n-) *v.t.* & *v.i.* **·ized, ·iz·ing** To make or become Teutonic or German. **—Teu′ton·i·za′tion** *n.*

Te·ve·re (tā′vā·rā) The Italian name for the river TIBER.

Tewkes·bur·y (to͞oks′ber·ē, -bər·ē, tyo͞oks′-) A municipal borough in NW Gloucestershire, England; scene of the final defeat of the Lancastrian forces in the Wars of the Roses, 1471.

Tex·ar·kan·a (teks′är·kan′ə) A dual city in NE Texas and SW Arkansas, with two municipal governments.

tex·as (tek′səs) *n. U.S.* The uppermost structure on a river steamboat, containing the pilot house, officers' cabins, etc.; often, a row of staterooms behind the pilot house, or having the pilot house set on top of it. [from *Texas;* so called from the former custom of naming staterooms after the States, those of the officers being the largest]

Tex·as (tek′səs) *n.* A Caddo Indian.

Tex·as (tek′səs) A State in the SW United States, bordering on Mexico and the Gulf of Mexico; 267,339 square miles; capital, Austin; entered the Union Dec. 29, 1845; nicknamed *Lone Star State*: abbr. TX **—Tex′an** *n.* & *adj.*

Texas cattle Cattle bred from the old longhorn stock of early Texas.

Texas fever A destructive cattle disease caused by a blood parasite transmitted by the cattle tick, *Margaropus annulatus.* Also **Texan fever.**

Texas leaguer *U.S. Colloq.* In baseball, a looping fly ball that falls safe between an infielder and an outfielder.

Texas Ranger 1 A member of the mounted State police force of Texas. **2** Originally, one of a band of armed and mounted men organized in Texas to fight Indians and keep order on the frontiers.

Texas sparrow A plain, olive-backed fringilline bird *(Arremonops rufivirgatus)* found in Mexico and southern Texas.

Texas tower A radar station having several tall towers erected on a platform which may be moored permanently in the sea as part of a radar-warning network.

Texas trail The old Chisholm cattle trail from Red River, Texas, to Abilene, Kansas.

Tex·o·ma (tek·sō′mə), **Lake** A reservoir in northern Texas and southern Oklahoma created by damming the Red River; one of the largest in the U.S.; 227 square miles.

text (tekst) *n.* **1** The actual or original words of an author; the body of matter on a written or printed page, as distinguished from notes, commentary, illustrations, etc. **2** A written or printed version of the matter of an author's works: the folio *text* of Shakespeare. **3** Any one of various recensions that are taken to represent the authentic words, or portion of the words, of the original Scriptures. **4** A verse of Scripture, particularly when cited as the basis of a discourse or sermon. **5** Any subject of discourse; a topic; theme. **6** One of several styles of letters or types. **7** A textbook. [< OF *texte* < L *textus* fabric, structure < *texere* weave]

text·book (tekst′bŏŏk′) *n.* A book used as a standard work or basis of instruction in any branch of knowledge; schoolbook; manual.

tex·tile (teks′til, -tīl) *adj.* **1** Pertaining to weaving or woven fabrics. **2** Such as may be woven; manufactured by weaving. —*n.* **1** A woven fabric; textile material. **2** Material capable of being woven. [< L *textilis* < *textus* fabric. See TEXT.]

tex·tu·al (teks′chōō·əl) *adj.* **1** Pertaining to, contained in, or based on the text of a book, especially of the Scriptures; literal; word for word. **2** Versed in texts. [< OF *textuel* < *texte.* See TEXT.] —**tex′tu·al·ly** *adv.*

tex·tu·al·ism (teks′chōō·əl·iz′əm) *n.* **1** Rigid adherence to the letter of a text. **2** The method or principles of textual criticism.

tex·tu·al·ist (teks′chōō·əl·ist′) *n.* **1** A close adherent to the letter of a text. **2** One who is versed in or cites texts readily.

tex·tu·ar·y (teks′chōō·er′ē) *adj.* **1** Contained in a text. **2** Of, belonging to, or adhering to a text. —*n. pl.* **·ar·ies** A textualist.

tex·ture (teks′chər) *n.* **1** The arrangement or character of the threads, etc., of a woven fabric. **2** The mode of union or disposition of elementary constituent parts, as in a photograph, or surface of paper, etc.; minute structure or make; structural order. **3** The structure, especially as regards detail, of a work of art. **4** Any woven fabric; a web. [< L *textura* < *textus* fabric. See TEXT.] —**tex′tur·al** *adj.* —**tex′tur·al·ly** *adv.*

Tey·de (tā′thā) See PEAK OF TENERIFE under TENERIFE.

teyl tree (tēl) See TEIL.

Tez·el (tet′səl) See TETZEL.

T-group (tē′grōōp) *n.* A group of people, often business or industrial personnel, who meet with a trained leader whose function is to guide them to a more insightful awareness of themselves and others through the free and uninhibited expression of their thoughts, feelings, etc. [< *t(raining) group*]

Th *Chem.* Thorium (symbol Th).

-th[1] *suffix of nouns* **1** The act or result of the action expressed in the root word: *growth.* **2** The state or quality of being what is indicated in the root word: *health.*

-th[2] *suffix* Used in ordinal numbers: *tenth.* Also, after vowels, *-eth,* as in *fortieth.* [OE *-tha, -the*]

-th[3] See -ETH[1].

Thack·er·ay (thak′ər·ē), **William Makepeace,** 1811–63, English novelist.

Thad·de·us (thad′ē·əs) A masculine personal name. Also **Thad′dae·us,** *Ger.* **Thad·dä·us** (tä·dā′ōōs), *Polish* **Ta·de·usz** (tä·dā′ōōsh), *Pg.* **Thad·de·o** (täd·dā′ōō). [< Aramaic, praise]

Thai (tī) *n.* **1** The people collectively of Thailand, Laos, and parts of Burma, including the Laos, Shan, and Siamese. **2** A family of languages spoken by these people: considered by some a branch of the Sino-Tibetan family. —*adj.* Of or pertaining to the Thai, their culture, or their languages. Also spelled *Tai.*

Thai·land (tī′land) A constitutional monarchy in SE Asia; 198,404 square miles; capital, Bangkok: formerly *Siam.* *Thai* **Mu·ang Thai** (mōō′äng tī′).

thal·a·men·ceph·a·lon (thal′ə·men·sef′ə·lon) *n. Anat.* Diencephalon. [< THALAM(US) + ENCEPHALON]

tha·lam·ic (thə·lam′ik) *adj.* Of or pertaining to a thalamus, especially to the optic thalamus.

thal·a·mus (thal′ə·məs) *n. pl.* **·mi** (-mī) **1** *Anat.* The optic thalamus. **2** *Bot.* The receptacle of a flower. [< L < Gk. *thalamos* chamber]

thal·as·se·mi·a (thal′ə·sē′mē·ə) *n.* Any of a group of mild-to-fatal anemias accompanied by varying bone deformities, enlargement of the spleen and other signs, resulting from an inborn error in the synthesis of globin; limited largely to persons of Mediterranean origin. [< Gk. *thalassa* sea + -EMIA **thal′as·se′mic** *adj.*

tha·las·sic (thə·las′ik) *adj.* **1** Of or pertaining to the seas. **2** Pelagic; oceanic. [< Gk. *thalassa* sea]

thalasso- *combining form* The sea; of or pertaining to the sea: *thalassophobia.* Also, before vowels, **thalass-.** Also **thalassi-.** [< Gk. *thalassa* the sea]

thal·as·sog·ra·phy (thal′ə·sog′rə·fē) *n.* Oceanography. [< THALASSO- + -GRAPHY]

tha·las·so·pho·bi·a (thə·las′ə·fō′bē·ə) *n.* Morbid fear of the sea. [< THALASSO- + -PHOBIA]

tha·ler (tä′lər) See TALER.

Tha·les of Miletus (thā′lēz), 640?–546? B.C., Greek philosopher and scientist.

Tha·li·a (thə·lī′ə) **1** The Muse of comedy and pastoral poetry. **2** One of the three Graces. [< L < Gk. *Thaleia* < *thallein* bloom]

Tha·lic·trum (thə·lik′trəm) *n.* A genus of perennial herbs of the crowfoot family, the meadow rues. [< L < Gk. *thaliktron* < *thallein* bloom]

thal·i·do·mide (thə·lid′ə·mīd) *n. Med.* A mild sedative, illegalized when its use by pregnant women resulted in birth anomalies.

thal·lic (thal′ik) *adj. Chem.* Of, pertaining to, or derived from thallium, especially in its higher valence.

thal·line (thal′ēn, -in) *n. Chem.* A white, crystalline, synthetic alkaloid, $C_{10}H_{13}NO$: its salts are used as antipyretics and antiseptics.

thal·li·um (thal′ē·əm) *n.* A soft, heavy, toxic metallic element (symbol Tl, atomic number 81) resembling lead. See PERIODIC TABLE. [< NL < Gk. *thallos* a green shoot; from the bright green line in its spectrum, which led to its discovery]

thal·loid (thal′oid) *adj.* Resembling a thallus. Also **thal·loi·dal** (thə·loid′l).

thal·lo·phyte (thal′ə·fit) *n.* Any plant belonging to a major division or phylum of plants *(Thallophyta),* comprising the bacteria, fungi, algae, and lichens. Many of the forms are unicellular and those more highly developed are without true roots, stems, or leaves. [< *thallo-* (< THALLUS) + -PHYTE] —**thal′lo·phyt′ic** (-fit′ik) *adj.*

thal·lous (thal′əs) *adj. Chem.* Derived from thallium, especially in its lower valence. Also **thal·li·ous** (thal′ē·əs).

thal·lus (thal′əs) *n. pl.* **·lus·es** or **·li** (-ī) *Bot.* A plant body without true root, stem, or leaf, as in thallophytes. [< L, a shoot < Gk. *thallos* < *thallein* bloom]

Thames (temz) A river of southern England, rising in the Cotswold Hills, south central Gloucestershire, and flowing 209 miles east through London to the North Sea between northern Kent and southern Essex; the principal river of England.

Thames River 1 (temz) A river in SE Ontario, Canada, flowing SW 160 miles to Lake St. Clair. **2** (thāmz, tāmz) A river and estuary in SE Connecticut, flowing about 15 miles south to Long Island Sound.

Tham·muz (täm′mōōz, tam′uz) See TAMMUZ.

than (t͟han, *unstressed* t͟hən) *conj.* **1** When, as, or if compared with: after an adjective or adverb to express comparison between what precedes and what follows: I am stronger *than* he (is); I know her better *than* (I know) him. **2** Except; but: used after *other, else,* etc: no other *than* you. *Than* is sometimes considered a preposition in the one phrase, *than whom*: an eminent judge *than whom* no other is more just. [OE *thanne* then]

than·age (thā′nij) *n.* **1** In early English law, the state, jurisdiction, or office of a thane. **2** The land held by a thane or the tenure by which he held it. Also spelled *thenage.* [< AF *thaynage* < OE *thegn* a thane]

thanato- *combining form* Death; of or pertaining to death: *thanatophobia.* Also, before vowels, **thanat-.** [< Gk. *thanatos* death]

than·a·toid (than′ə·toid) *adj.* Resembling death; deadly.

than·a·to·pho·bi·a (than′ə·tə·fō′bē·ə) *n.* Morbid fear of death. [< THANATO- + PHOBIA] — **than′a·to·pho′bic** *adj.*

than·a·top·sis (than′ə·top′sis) *n.* A musing or meditation upon death; a view of death. [< THANAT(O)- + -OPSIS]

Than·a·tos (than′ə·tos) **1** In Greek mythology, the god of death: identified with the Roman *Mors.* **2** *Psychoanal.* The death instinct: opposed to *Eros,* the life instinct.

thane (thān) *n.* **1** Originally, a warrior companion of an English king before the Conquest. **2** Later, a man who ranked above an ordinary freeman or ceorl (churl) but below an earl or nobleman. **3** *Scot.* The chief of a clan; a baron; one of the old nobility in the service of the king. Also spelled *thegn.* [OE *thegn*]

Than·et (than′it), **Isle of** An island comprising the NE corner of Kent county, England; 10 miles long, 5 miles wide.

thank (thangk) *v.t.* **1** To express gratitude to; give thanks to. **2** To hold responsible; blame: often used ironically. [OE *thancian* < *thanc* thanks, thought]

thank·ful (thangk′fəl) *adj.* **1** Deeply sensible of favors received; grateful. **2** Done or made to express thanks; manifesting thanks. —**thank′ful·ly** *adv.* —**thank′ful·ness** *n.*

thank·it (thangk′it) *Scot.* Past participle of THANK.

thank·less (thangk′lis) *adj.* **1** Not feeling or expressing gratitude; ungrateful; unresponsive. **2** Not gaining or likely to gain thanks; unthanked; unappreciated. —**thank′less·ly** *adv.* — **thank′less·ness** *n.*

thanks (thangks) *n. pl.* Expressions of gratitude; grateful acknowledgement. —*interj.* My thanks to you; I thank you. —**thanks to 1** Thanks be given to. **2** Because of.

thanks·giv·ing (thangks′giv′ing) *n.* **1** The act of giving thanks, as to God; the expression of gratitude. **2** A form of words or worship in recognition of divine mercies. **3** A public celebration in recognition of divine favor. **4** A day set apart for such celebration.

Thanksgiving Day *U.S.* The fourth Thursday in November, set apart as an annual festival of thanksgiving to God for the year's blessings. Also **Thanksgiving.**

Thant (thänt, tänt), **U,** 1909–, Burmese statesman; secretary general of the United Nations 1961–71.

Thap·sus (thap′səs) An ancient ruined town on the coast of eastern Tunisia; scene of Julius Caesar's defeat of Cato the Younger, 46 B.C.

Thar Desert (tär) A sandy waste in NW India (much of western Rajasthan and southern Punjab) and West Pakistan; over 15,000 square miles: also *Indian Desert.*

Tha·sos (thā′sos) A Greek island in the north Aegean Sea; 170 square miles.

that (t͟hat, *unstressed* t͟hət) *adj. pl.* **those 1** Pertaining to some person or thing previously mentioned, understood, or specifically designated: *that* man. **2** Denoting something more remote in place, time, or thought: correlative to *this.* —*pron.* **1** As a demonstrative, the person or thing implied, mentioned, or understood; or the person or thing there or in the second place: *That* is the dress I like. **2** As a relative, who or which: used as a correlative to *such* or *so.* ◆ In earlier English, *that* was the relative pronoun, *who, what,* and *which* being only interrogatives until they gradually assumed the force of relatives, and in some uses superseded *that.* When the relative clause qualifies or makes an addition to the main clause, *who* or *which* is generally preferred, whereas *that* usually introduces a restrictive clause. Thus we say: Washington, *who* was the first president, is often called Father of his Country. But: *The* Washington *that* emigrated to this country was his ancestor. —*adv.* **1** *Colloq.* In such a manner or degree; so. **2** To that extent: I can't see *that* far. —*conj.* *That* is used primarily to connect a subordinate clause with its principal clause, with the following meanings: **1** As a fact that: introducing a fact: I tell you *that* it is so. **2** So that; in order that: I tell you *that* you may know. **3** For the reason that; seeing that; because: She wept *that* she was growing old. **4** As a result: introducing a result, consequence, or effect: He bled so profusely *that* he died. **5** At which time; when: It was only yesterday *that* I saw him. **6** Introducing an exclamation: O *that* he would come! See synonyms under BUT. —**so that 1** To the end that. **2** With the result that. **3** Provided. See THOSE. [OE *thæt,* neut. of *se* the]

thatch (thach) *n.* **1** A covering of reeds, straw, etc., arranged on a roof so as to shed water. **2** Any of various palms whose leaves are used for thatching, especially those of the genera *Thrinax* and *Sabal.* **3** Any of certain tall, coarse American grasses (genus *Spartina*) of the northern Atlantic coasts. —*v.t.* To cover with a thatch. [OE *thæc* cover] —**thatch′er** *n.* —**thatch′y** *adj.*

thatch·ing (thach′ing) *n.* **1** The act or process of covering a roof with a thatch. **2** Material used for a thatch.

thaumato- *combining form* A wonder; a miracle: *thaumatology.* Also, before vowels, **thaumat-.** [< Gk. *thauma, -atos* a wonder]

thau·ma·tol·o·gy (thô′mə·tol′ə·jē) n. The scientific study of miracles. [<THAUMATO- + -LOGY]

thau·ma·trope (thô′mə·trōp) n. An optical toy or instrument in which pictures on opposite sides of a card appear to blend together when the card is rapidly twirled. [<Gk. *thauma* wonder + -TROPE]

thau·ma·turge (thô′mə·tûrj) n. One who performs wonders or miracles; a wonder-worker; magician. Also **thau′ma·tur′gist.** [<Gk. *thaumatourgos* < *thauma* wonder + *ergon* work]

thau·ma·tur·gy (thô′mə·tûr′jē) n. Magic; the performance or working of wonders or miracles. — **thau′ma·tur′gic** or **-gi·cal** adj.

thaw (thô) v.i. **1** To melt or dissolve; become liquid or semi-liquid, as snow or ice. **2** To rise in temperature so as to melt ice and snow: said of weather and used impersonally. **3** To become less cold and unsociable. — v.t. **4** To cause to thaw. See synonyms under MELT. — n. **1** The act of thawing, or the state of being thawed. **2** Warmth of weather such as melts things frozen; also, figuratively, state of warmer feeling or expression. [OE *thawian*] — **thaw′er** n.

Thax·ter (thaks′tər), **Celia,** 1835-94, *née* Laighton, U. S. poet.

Thay·er (thā′ər), **Sylvanus,** 1785-1872, U.S. Army officer: called "Father of West Point." — **William Roscoe,** 1859-1923, U.S. historian and biographer.

the[1] (stressed *thē;* unstressed *before a consonant* *thə;* unstressed *before a vowel* *thi*) *definite article* or *adj.* *The* is opposed to the indefinite article *a* or *an,* and is used, especially before nouns, to render the modified word more particular or individual. It is used specifically: **1** When reference is made to a particular person, thing, or group: *The* natives are getting restless; He left *the* room. **2** To give an adjective substantive force, or render a notion abstract: *the* quick and *the* dead; *the* doing of the deed. **3** Before a noun to make it generic: *The* dog is a friend of man. **4** With the force of a possessive pronoun: He kicked me in *the* (my) leg. **5** To give distributive force: equivalent to *a, per, each,* etc.: a dollar *the* volume. **6** *Scot. & Irish* To designate the head of a clan or group: *the* MacIntosh. **7** To designate a particular one as emphatically outstanding: usually stressed in speech and italicized in writing: He is *the* officer for the command. **8** As part of a title: *The* Duke of York. [OE *the,* later form of *sē*]

the[2] (thə) *adv.* By that much; by so much; to this extent: *the* more, *the* merrier: used to modify words in the comparative degree. [OE *thȳ,* oblique case of *sē* the]

the- Var. of THEO-.

the·a·ceous (thē·ā′shəs) adj. Bot. Designating a family (*Theaceae*) of shrubs and trees having alternate, simple leaves, large flowers, and a typically capsular fruit; the tea family. [<NL < *Thea,* genus name < dial. Chinese *t′e* tea; incorrectly taken by Linnaeus as "divine herb" <Gk. *thea* a goddess]

the·an·throp·ic (thē′ən·throp′ik) adj. **1** Being both divine and human. **2** Having or pertaining to a nature both divine and human. Also **the′an·throp′i·cal.** [<Gk. *theanthrōpos* < *theos* god + *anthrōpos,* -ōpou man]

the·an·thro·pism (thē·an′thrə·piz′əm) n. **1** The doctrine of the manifestation of God in man, or of the union of the divine and human in Christ. **2** The ascription of human characteristics to a deity; anthropomorphism. **3** Belief in the possibility of the combination in one being of a nature both human and divine. — **the·an′thro·pist** n.

the·ar·chy (thē′är·kē) n. pl. **·chies** **1** Government by God or by a god. **2** A theocracy. **3** A body or class of deities. [<Gk. *thearchia* < *theos* god + *archein* rule]

the·a·ter (thē′ə·tər) n. **1** A building especially adapted to dramatic, operatic, or spectacular representations; playhouse. **2** The theatrical world and everything relating to it. **3** A room or hall arranged with seats that rise as they recede from a platform, especially adapted to lectures, surgical demonstrations, etc. **4** Any place of semicircular form with seats rising by easy gradations. **5** Any place or region that is the scene of events: a *theater* of opera-

tions in war. Also **the′a·tre.** [<OF *theatre* <Gk. *theatron* < *theasthai* behold]

the·a·ter-go·er (thē′ə·tər·gō′ər) n. One who frequents theaters. Also **the′a·tre-go′er.** — **the′a·ter-go′ing, the′a·tre-go′ing** n.

the·a·ter-in-the-round (thē′ə·tər·in·thə·round′) n. An arena theater.

The·a·tin (thē′ə·tin) n. **1** A member of a congregation founded in 1524 by Bishop Carafa and St. Cajetan. **2** A member of an order of nuns founded by Ursula-Benincasa, who died in 1618. Also **The′a·tine** (-tēn, -tin). [<NL *theatinus,* from *Teate,* ancient name of Chieti, Italy]

the·at·ri·cal (thē·at′ri·kəl) adj. **1** Pertaining to the theater or to dramatic performances. **2** Designed for show, display, or effect; showy; artificial. **3** Suited to dramatic presentation. **4** Like the manner of actors; histrionic. Also **the·at′ric.** — n. pl. Dramatic performances: especially when given by amateur performers. [<LL *theatricus* <Gk. *theatrikos* < *theatron.* See THEATER.] — **the·at′ri·cal·ly** adv. — **the·at′ri·cal·ness** n.

the·at·ri·cal·ism (thē·at′ri·kəl·iz′əm) n. Theatrical or melodramatic manner or style.

the·at·rics (thē·at′riks) n. pl. (construed as singular) The art of bringing about effects appropriate for dramatic performances.

The·ba·id (thē′bā·id, thi·bā′-) n. A Latin epic by Statius, narrating the story of the siege of Boeotian Thebes.

The·ba·id (thē′bā·id, thi·bā′-) The territory about Thebes in either Egypt or Greece.

the·ba·ine (thē′bə·ēn, thi·bā′ēn, -in) n. Chem. A silvery-white, poisonous, crystalline alkaloid, $C_{19}H_{21}O_3N$, found in opium and resembling strychnine in action: also called *paramorphine.* Also **the′ba·in** (-in). [from Egyptian *Thebes,* where a kind of opium was produced + -INE[2]]

Thebes (thēbz) **1** The ancient capital of Upper Egypt; Luxor and Karnak occupy part of its site on the Nile: Greek *Diospolis.* **2** The chief city of ancient Boeotia, Greece; destroyed in 336 B.C. by Alexander the Great: also **The·bae** (thē′bē). **3** A commercial city in east central Greece on the site of ancient Thebes; important in the Middle Ages: Greek **The·vai** or **Thi·vai** (thē′vā). — **The·ban** (thē′bən) adj. & n.

the·ca (thē′kə) n. pl. **·cae** (-sē) **1** A sheath or case. **2** Anat. The investment of the spinal cord formed by the dura mater, sometimes called **theca vertebralis.** **3** Bot. A spore case, sac, or capsule. [<L <Gk. *thēkē* case] — **the′cal** adj.

the·cate (thē′kit, -kāt) adj. Having a sheath; sheathed.

thé dan·sant (tā′ dän·sän′) pl. **thés dan·sants** (tā′ dän·sän′) *French* Literally, a dancing tea; an afternoon tea at which there is dancing.

thee (thē) pron. **1** The objective case of *thou.* **2** Thou: used generally by Quakers with a verb in the third person singular: *Thee* knows my mind. [OE *thē,* accusative case of *thū* thou]

theek (thēk) v.t. Brit. Dial. To thatch. [Scottish var. of THATCH] — **theek′ing** n.

Thee·lin (thē′lin) n. Proprietary name for a brand of estrone.

Thee·lol (thē′lōl, -lol) n. Proprietary name for a brand of estriol.

theft (theft) n. **1** The act of thieving; larceny. **2** Rare That which is stolen. [OE *thēoft, thīefth*]

the·gith·er (thi·gith′ər) adv. Scot. Together.

thegn (thān) See THANE.

the·ine (thē′ēn, -in) n. Chem. The alkaloid found in the tea plant: chemically identical with caffeine. Also **the′in** (-in). [<F *théine* <NL *thea* tea < dial. Chinese *t′e*]

their (thâr) pronominal adj. The possessive case of the pronoun *they* employed attributively; belonging or pertaining to them: *their* homes. [ME <ON *theirra* of them]

theirs (thârz) pron. **1** The possessive case of *they,* used predicatively; belonging or pertaining to them: That house is *theirs.* **2** The things or persons belonging or relating to them: our country and *theirs.* — **of theirs** Belonging or pertaining to them; their: the double possessive. [<THEIR + -s, on analogy with *his*]

the·ism[1] (thē′iz·əm) n. **1** Belief in, or in the existence of, God, a god, or gods: opposed to *atheism.* **2** Belief in a personal God as creator and supreme ruler of the universe, who transcends his creation but works in and through it in revealing himself to men. Compare DEISM, PANTHEISM. **3** Belief in one god; monotheism: opposed to *polytheism.* **4** Formerly, deism. **5** *Philos.* The doctrine that one supreme reality, intrinsically complete and perfect, is the final ground and source of everything other than itself: a doctrine resembling monotheism and some types of monism, but opposed to atheism, agnosticism, deism, materialism, pantheism, and polytheism. [<Gk. *theos* god] — **the′ist** n. — **the·is′tic** or **·ti·cal** adj. — **the·is′ti·cal·ly** adv.

the·ism[2] (thē′iz·əm) n. Pathol. The toxic effects of excessive tea-drinking. [<NL *thea* tea. See THEINE.]

Theiss (tīs) The German name for TISZA.

Thé·lème (tā·lem′), **Abbey of** An abbey described by Rabelais in *Gargantua,* and having only one rule, "Do what you like."

the·li·tis (thi·lī′tis) n. Pathol. Inflammation of the nipple. [<NL <Gk. *thēlē* teat + -ITIS]

Thel·ma (thel′mə) A feminine personal name. [<Gk., nursling]

The·lon River (thi·lon′) A river in Northwest Territories, Canada, rising in eastern Mackenzie district and flowing about 550 miles north, NE, and east to NW Hudson Bay on the central eastern coast of Keewatin district.

them (them, *unstressed* thəm) pron. The objective case of *they.* [ME *theim* <ON, to them]

the·mat·ic (thē·mat′ik) adj. **1** Of, constituting, or pertaining to a theme or themes. **2** *Ling.* Constituting a stem. Also **the·mat′i·cal.** — **the·mat′i·cal·ly** adv.

theme (thēm) n. **1** A subject of discourse; a topic to be discussed or developed in speech or writing; hence, any topic. **2** An essay or dissertation; loosely, a brief composition in any form, written as an exercise. **3** *Ling.* The stem of a word, to which are attached the inflectional endings, consisting of the root unmodified or with some internal change and, often, a thematic vowel common to the particular stem class. **4** A melodic subject usually developed with variations in a musical composition. **5** One of the administrative divisions of the Byzantine Empire. See synonyms under TOPIC. [<OF *teme* <L *thema* <Gk. *the-,* stem of *tithenai* place]

theme song 1 A melody used throughout a dramatic presentation to furnish the key to the mood. **2** A strain of music which, from repetition, identifies a daily or periodical radio or television presentation, a dance band, etc.

The·mis (thē′mis) In Greek mythology, a goddess of law and justice, daughter of Uranus and Gaea. [<Gk., law]

The·mis·to·cles (thi·mis′tə·klēz), 527?-460? B.C., Athenian statesman and soldier.

them·selves (them′selvz′, *unstressed* thəm-) pron. Emphatic or reflexive form of THEY, THEM: the plural of HIMSELF, HERSELF, ITSELF.

then (then) adv. **1** At that time. **2** Soon or immediately afterward; next in space or time. **3** At another time: often introducing a sequential statement following *now,* at *first,* etc. — conj. **1** For that reason; as a consequence; accordingly. **2** In that case: I will *then,* since you won't. — adj. Being or acting in, or belonging to, that time: the *then* secretary of state. — n. A specific time already mentioned or understood; that time. [OE *thanne*]

then·age (then′ij) See THANAGE

the·nar (thē′när) n. Anat. **1** The palm of the hand. **2** The prominence on the palm at the base of the thumb. — adj. Of or pertaining to the palm of a hand or the sole of a foot: also **the′nal.** [<Gk. *thenar* palm of the hand]

thence (thens) adv. **1** From that place. **2** From the circumstance, fact, or cause; therefore. **3** From that time; after that time. **4** *Archaic* Away from there; elsewhere; absent. [ME *thannes* <OE *thanon* from there + -s[3]]

thence·forth (thens′fôrth′, -fōrth′, thens′fôrth′, -fōrth′) adv. From that time on; thereafter.

thence·for·ward (thens′fôr′wərd) *adv.* 1 Thenceforth. 2 From that place or time forward. Also **thence′for′wards.**

theo– *combining form* God; of or pertaining to God, a god, or gods: *theophany, theodicy.* Also, before vowels, *the–.* [<Gk. *theos* a god]

The·o·bald (thē′ə·bôld, tib′əld; *Dan.* tā′ō·bäl, *Ger.* tā′ō·bält, *Sw.* tā′ō·bäld) A masculine personal name. Also *Lat.* **The·o·bal·dus** (tā′ō·bôl′dəs), *Pg.* **The·o·bal·do** (tā′ōō·bäl′thōō), *Sp.* **The·u·de·bal·do** (tā′ōō·thä·väl′thō). [<Gmc., bold patriot]

The·o·bro·ma (thē′ə·brō′mə) *n.* A genus of small trees indigenous in tropical America, especially *Theobroma cacao,* source of the cocoa and chocolate of commerce, now cultivated also in the Old World tropics. [<NL <Gk. *theos* god + *brōma* food]

the·o·bro·mine (thē′ə·brō′mēn, -min) *n. Chem.* A bitter, colorless, crystalline alkaloid, $C_7H_8N_4O_2$, resembling caffeine, contained in cacao beans: used in medicine as a diuretic and myocardial stimulant. [<THEOBROM(A) + -INE[2]]

the·o·cen·tric (thē′ə·sen′trik) *adj.* Having God for its center; proceeding from and returning to God.

the·oc·ra·cy (thē·ok′rə·sē) *n. pl.* **·cies** 1 A state, polity, or group of people that claims a deity as its ruler, as ancient Israel after the Exodus. 2 Government of a state by a god, or by a priestly class claiming to have divine authority, as in the Papacy. [<Gk. *theokratia* < *theos* god + *krateein* rule] — **the·o·crat·ic** (thē′ə·krat′ik) *or* **·i·cal** *adj.*

the·oc·ra·sy (thē·ok′rə·sē) *n.* 1 The mingling of several deities or divine attributes in one personality. 2 The mystical intimacy or union of the soul with God. [<LGk. *theokrasia* <Gk. *theos* god + *krasis* mingling]

the·o·crat (thē′ə·krat) *n.* 1 A theocratic or divine ruler. 2 An advocate of theocracy.

The·oc·ri·tus (thē·ok′rə·təs) Greek pastoral poet of the third century B.C.

the·od·i·cy (thē·od′ə·sē) *n. pl.* **·cies** 1 Justification of the divine providence by the attempt to reconcile the existence of evil with the goodness and sovereignty of God: a term established by Leibnitz in 1710. 2 The branch of philosophy that treats of the being, perfections, and government of God and the immortality of the soul. [<F *théodicée* <Gk. *theos* god + *dikē* justice]

the·od·o·lite (thē·od′ə·līt) *n.* One of several surveying and astronomical instruments for measuring horizontal and vertical angles by means of a small telescope turning on both a horizontal and a vertical axis. [An arbitrary formation] — **the·od·o·lit·ic** (-lit′ik) *adj.*

The·o·dore (thē′ə·dôr, -dōr) A masculine personal name. Also *Dan., Ger., Sw.* **The·o·dor** (tā′ō·dôr), *Fr.* **Thé·o·dore** (tā·ō·dôr′), *Gk.* **The·o·do·ros** (thē·o′dō·ros), *Du.* **The·o·do·rus** (tā′ō·dōr′əs). [<Gk., gift of God] — **The·o·do·ra** (thē′ə·dôr′ə) *fem.*

The·od·o·ric (thē·od′ər·ik) A masculine personal name. Also **The·od′e·rick, The·od′o·rick,** *Fr.* **Thé·o·do·ric** (tā·ō·dō·rēk′), *Ger.* **The·o·do·rich** (tā·ō′dō·rikh), *Lat.* **The·o·do·ri·cus** (tā′ō·də·ri′kəs). [<Gmc., ruler of the people] — **Theodoric,** 454?–526, king of the Ostrogoths; invaded and conquered Italy.

The·o·do·si·us (thē′ə·dō′shē·əs), 346?–395, Roman emperor 379–395.

the·og·o·ny (thē·og′ə·nē) *n.* The generation or genealogy of the gods, especially as recited in ancient poetry. [<Gk. *theogonia* < *theos* god + *gonos* generation < *gignesthai* be born] — **the·o·gon·ic** (thē′ə·gon′ik) *adj.* — **the·og′o·nist** *n.*

the·o·log (thē′ə·lôg, -log) *n.* A theological student. Also **the′o·logue.** [<L *theologus* one who treats of the gods < *theos* god + *logos* discourse < *legein* speak]

the·o·lo·gi·an (thē′ə·lō′jē·ən, -jən) *n.* One versed in theology, especially that of the Christian church; a professor of divinity; a divine.

the·o·log·i·cal (thē′ə·loj′i·kəl) *adj.* 1 Pertaining or relating to theology. 2 Linked to, based on, or referring to divine revelation. 3 Pertaining to the exposition or expounders of theology. Also **the′o·log′ic.** — **the·o·log′i·cal·ly** *adv.*

theological virtues See under VIRTUE.

the·ol·o·gize (thē·ol′ə·jīz) *v.* **·gized, ·giz·ing** *v.t.* To devise or fit (something) into a system of

theology. — *v.i.* To reason theologically. Also *Brit.* **the·ol′o·gise.**

the·ol·o·gy (thē·ol′ə·jē) *n. pl.* **·gies** 1 The study of religion, culminating in a synthesis or philosophy of religion; also, a critical survey of religion, especially of the Christian religion. 2 A body of doctrines concerning God, including his attributes and relations with man; especially, such a body of doctrines as set forth by a particular church or religious group: Catholic *theology.* [<OF *theologie* <LL *theologia* <Gk. < *theos* god + *logos* discourse]

the·om·a·chy (thē·om′ə·kē) *n.* 1 A combat with the gods, as that waged by the Titans. 2 A battle among the gods. [<Gk. *theomachia* < *theos* god + *machē* combat]

the·o·mor·phic (thē′ə·môr′fik) *adj.* Having the form or likeness of God. [<Gk. *theomorphos* < *theos* god + *morphē* form]

the·o·mor·phism (thē′ə·môr′fiz·əm) *n.* The doctrine that man has the likeness or form of God.

the·o·pa·thet·ic (thē′ō·pə·thet′ik) *adj.* Pertaining to or of the nature of theopathy: *theopathetic* mysticism. Also **the·o·path·ic** (thē′ə·path′ik).

the·op·a·thy (thē·op′ə·thē) *n.* Religious emotion aroused by meditation on God; mystical ecstasy. [<Gk. *theopathia* the suffering of God < *theos* a god + *path-,* stem of *paschein* suffer]

the·oph·a·ny (thē·of′ə·nē) *n. pl.* **·nies** A manifestation or appearance of a deity or of the gods to man. [<L *theophania* <Gk. < *theos* god + *phainein* show]

The·oph·i·lus (thē·of′ə·ləs, *Du., Ger.* tā·ō′fē·lōōs) A masculine personal name. Also *Fr.* **Thé·o·phile** (tā·ō·fēl′), *Pg.* **The·o·phi·lo** (tā·ō′fē·lōō). [<Gk., lover of God]

The·o·phras·tus (thē′ə·fras′təs), 372?–287? B.C., Greek philosopher.

the·o·phyl·line (thē′ə·fil′ēn, -in) *n. Chem.* A white, bitter, crystalline alkaloid, $C_7H_8O_2N_4$, obtained from tea leaves and also made synthetically: it is an isomer of theobromine. [<NL *thea* tea + Gk. *phyllon* leaf + -INE[2]]

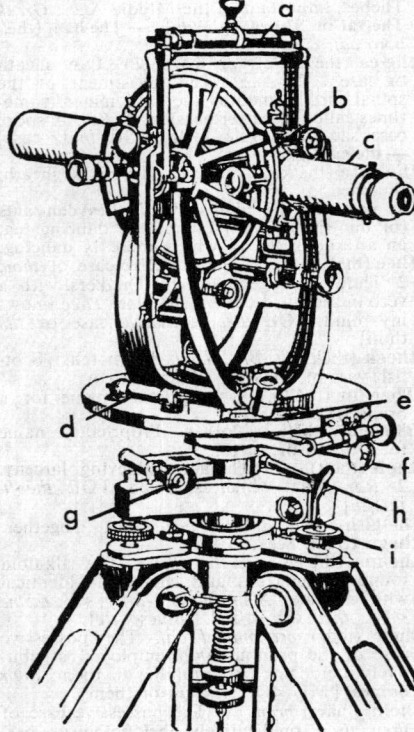

THEODOLITE
a. Striding level. *b.* Vertical limb and vernier. *c.* Telescope. *d.* Plate bubble. *e.* Horizontal limb and vernier. *f.* Clamp and tangent screw. *g.* Lower clamp screw. *h.* Tangent screw. *i.* Leveling screw.

the·or·bo (thē·ôr′bō) *n.* A 17th century lute

having two necks. [<F *théorbe* <Ital. *tiorba,* prob. after the name of the inventor]

the·o·rem (thē′ər·əm, thir′əm) *n.* 1 A proposition demonstrably true or acknowledged as such. 2 *Math.* **a** A proposition setting forth something to be proved. **b** A proposition that has been proved or assumed to be true. **c** A rule or statement of relations formulated in symbols. [<F *théorème* <Gk. *theōrēma* sight, theory < *theōreein* look at] — **the·o·re·mat·ic** (thē′ər·ə·mat′ik), **the′o·rem′ic** (-ə·rem′ik) *adj.*

the·o·ret·ic (thē′ə·ret′ik) *n.* 1 Theory, as distinct from practice. 2 *pl.* Theoretical matters; specifically, the theoretical aspect of a science. — *adj.* Theoretical.

the·o·ret·i·cal (thē′ə·ret′i·kəl) *adj.* 1 Of, relating to, or consisting of theory. 2 Relating to knowledge or pure science without reference to its application: compare EXPERIMENT (def. 3). 3 Existing only in theory; hypothetical. 4 Addicted to theorizing; unaffected by practical considerations; hence, impractical; visionary. Also *theoretic.* — **the′o·ret′i·cal·ly** *adv.*

the·o·re·ti·cian (thē′ər·ə·tish′ən) *n.* One who deals with the speculative, hypothetical, or ideal rather than with the practical and executive aspects of a subject.

the·o·rist (thē′ər·ist) *n.* One who theorizes.

the·o·rize (thē′ə·rīz) *v.i.* **·rized, ·riz·ing** To form or express theories; speculate. Also *Brit.* **the′o·rise.** — **the·o·ri·za′tion** *n.* — **the′o·riz′er** *n.*

the·o·ry (thē′ər·ē, thir′ē) *n. pl.* **·ries** 1 A plan or scheme existing in the mind only, but based on principles verifiable by experiment or observation. 2 A body of the fundamental principles underlying a science or the application of a science: the *theory* of relativity. 3 Abstract knowledge of any art, as opposed to the practice of it. 4 A proposed explanation or hypothesis designed to account for any phenomenon. 5 Loosely, mere speculation or hypothesis; an individual idea or guess. 6 *Math.* An arrangement of results, or a body of theorems, presenting a systematic view of some subject: the *theory* of functions. 7 The science of musical composition, as distinguished from the art of execution. See synonyms under HYPOTHESIS, IDEA. [<F *théorie* <Gk. *theōria* view, speculation < *theōreein* look at]

the·os·o·phy (thē·os′ə·fē) *n.* Mystical speculation applied to deduce a philosophy of the universe. In its modern phase, a system that claims to embrace the essential truth underlying all systems of religion, science, and philosophy. Its doctrines resemble closely those of Buddhism and Brahmanism, teaching the existence of an omnipotent, infinite, eternal, and immutable principle transcending the power of human conception, and the identity of all souls, through the cycle of incarnation with a universal spirit. [<Med. L *theosophia* <Gk. < *theosophos* wise in divine matters < *theos* god + *sophos* wise] — **the·o·soph·ic** (thē′ə·sof′ik) *or* **·i·cal** *adj.* — **the′o·soph′i·cal·ly** *adv.* — **the·os′o·phist** *n.*

The·o·to·co·pu·li (tā′ō·tō·kō′pōō·lē), **Domenico** See GRECO, EL.

The·ra (thir′ə, thē′rə) The southernmost island of the Cyclades in the Aegean; 31 square miles: formerly *Santorin.*

ther·a·peu·tic (ther′ə·pyōō′tik) *adj.* 1 Having healing qualities; curative. 2 Pertaining to therapeutics. Also **ther′a·peu′ti·cal.** [<NL *therapeuticus* <Gk. *therapeutikos* < *therapeutēs* an attendant < *therapeuein* serve, take care of < *therapōn* an attendant] — **ther′a·peu′ti·cal·ly** *adv.*

therapeutic dose That quantity of a drug which will produce the greatest beneficial effect in the given instance; the optimal dose.

ther·a·peu·tics (ther′ə·pyōō′tiks) *n. pl.* (construed as singular) 1 The department of medical science that treats of remedies for disease and their application. 2 The art and science of healing. — **ther′a·peu′tist** *n.*

ther·a·py (ther′ə·pē) *n. pl.* **·pies** 1 The treatment of disease by drugs or other curative processes: chiefly used in compounds: *hydrotherapy.* 2 Healing or curative quality. [<NL *therapia* <Gk. *therapeia* < *therapeuein* take care of. See THERAPEUTIC.] — **ther′a·pist** *n.*

there (thâr) *adv.* 1 In or at that place; in a place other than that of the speaker: opposed to *here.* 2 To, toward, or into that place; thither. 3 At that stage or point of action

or proceeding. 4 In that respect, relation, or connection. [OE *thǣr*]

◆ *There* is also used: as a pronominal expletive introducing a clause or sentence, the subject usually following the verb: *There* once lived three bears; with independent phrases or clauses, as an equivalent of *that*, expressing encouragement, approval, etc.: *There's* a little dear; as an exclamation expressing triumph, etc.: *There*! I told you so.

there·a·bout (thâr′ə·bout′) *adv.* Near that number, quantity, degree, place, or time; approximately. Also **there′a·bouts′**.

there·af·ter (thâr′af′tər, -äf′-) *adv.* 1 Afterward; from that time on. 2 Accordingly.

there·a·gainst (thâr′ə·genst′) *adv.* Against or in opposition to that thing; on the other hand.

there·at (thâr′at′) *adv.* At that event, place, or time; at that incentive; upon that.

there·by (thâr′bī′) *adv.* 1 Through the agency of that. 2 Connected with that. 3 Conformably to that. 4 Nearby; thereabout. 5 By it or that; into possession of it or that: How did you come *thereby*?

there·for (thâr′fôr′) *adv.* For this, that, or it; in return or requital for this or that: We return thanks *therefor*.

there·fore (thâr′fôr′, -fōr′) *adv.* & *conj.* For that or this reason; on that ground or account; hence; consequently: He did not run fast enough; *therefore* he lost the race.

Synonyms (conj.): accordingly, because, consequently, hence, since, then, thence, whence, wherefore. *Therefore* is the most precise and formal word for expressing the direct conclusion of a chain of reasoning; *then* carries a similar but slighter sense of inference, which it gives incidentally rather than formally; as, If this is true, *then* we can go. *Consequently* denotes a direct result, but more frequently of a practical than a theoretical kind; as, Important matters demand my attention; *consequently* I shall not sail today. *Accordingly* denotes correspondence, which may or may not be consequence; it is often used in narration; as, The soldiers were eager and confident; *accordingly* they sprang forward at the word of command. *Thence* is a word of more sweeping inference than *therefore*, applying not merely to a single set of premises but often to all that has gone before, including the reasonable inferences that have not been formally stated. *Wherefore* is the correlative of *therefore*, and *whence* of *hence* or *thence*, appending the inference or conclusion to the previous statement without a break. Compare synonyms for BECAUSE.

there·from (thâr′frum′, -from′) *adv.* From this, that, or it; from this or that time, place, state, event, or thing.

there·in (thâr′in′) *adv.* 1 In that place. 2 In that time, matter, or respect.

there·in·af·ter (thâr′in·af′tər, -äf′-) *adv.* In a subsequent part of that (book, document, speech, etc.).

there·in·to (thâr′in·too͞′) *adv.* Into this, that, or it.

Ther·e·min (ther′ə·min) *n.* A musical instrument played by manual interference with two sets of radio-frequency waves issuing from a pair of oscillators adapted for tone variation and volume control: a trade name. [after Léon *Thérémin*, born 1896, Russian-French inventor]

there·of (thâr′uv′, -ov′) *adv.* 1 Of or relating to this, that, or it. 2 From or because of this or that cause or particular; therefrom.

there·on (thâr′on′, -ôn′) *adv.* 1 On this, that, or it. 2 Thereupon; thereat.

there's (thârz) There is: a contraction.

The·re·sa (tə·rē′sə, -res′ə) A feminine personal name. Also *Fr.* **Thé·rèse** (tā·rez′). [<Gk., harvester]

— Saint Theresa of Ávila, 1515–82, Spanish Carmelite nun and mystic: also *Teresa.*

there·to (thâr′too͞′) *adv.* 1 To this, that, or it. 2 In addition; furthermore. Also **there′·un·to′** (-un·too͞′).

there·to·fore (thâr′tə·fôr′, -fōr′) *adv.* Before this or that; previously to that.

there·un·der (thâr′un′dər) *adv.* 1 Under this or that. 2 Less, as in number. 3 In a lower or lesser status or rank.

there·up·on (thâr′ə·pon′, -ə·pôn′) *adv.* 1 Upon that; upon it. 2 Following upon or in consequence of that. 3 Immediately following; at once.

there·with (thâr′with′, -with′) *adv.* 1 With this, that, or it. 2 Thereupon; thereafter; immediately afterward.

there·with·al (thâr′with·ôl′) *adv.* 1 With all this or that; besides. 2 *Obs.* Therewith; with this, that, or it.

the·ri·a·ca (thi·rī′ə·kə) *n.* 1 An ancient antidote for the bite of venomous creatures, containing numerous drugs mixed with honey. 2 Molasses; treacle. Also **the·ri·ac** (thir′ē·ak). [<LL *theriaca*, an antidote for poison <Gk. *thēriakos* pertaining to wild beasts < *thērion*, dim. of *thēr* wild beast] — **the·ri′a·cal** *adj.*

the·ri·an·thro·pism (thir′ē·an′thrə·piz′əm) *n.* Representation of preternatural beings in combined forms of man and beast, especially in primitive polytheistic worship: the religions of *therianthropism*. [<Gk. *thērion* wild beast + *anthrōpos*, *-ōpou* man] — **the′ri·an·throp′ic** (-an·throp′ik) *adj.*

the·ri·o·mor·phic (thir′ē·ə·môr′fik) *adj.* Beastlike in form: *theriomorphic* gods. Also **the′ri·o·mor′phous.** [<Gk. *thērion* wild beast + *morphē* form]

therm (thûrm) *n.* 1 A unit of heat used as a basis for the sale of illuminating gas in England, equal to 100,000 British thermal units. 2 One thousand great calories. 3 The great calorie. 4 The lesser calorie. Also **therme.** [<Gk. *thermē* heat]

therm– Var. of THERMO–.

Ther·ma (thûr′mə) Ancient name for THESSALONIKE.

ther·mae (thûr′mē) *n. pl.* 1 Hot springs or baths. 2 Specifically, the public baths of the ancient Romans; also, the bathhouses. [<L <Gk. *thermai*, pl. of *thermē* heat]

ther·mal (thûr′məl) *adj.* 1 Pertaining to, determined by, or measured by heat. 2 Hot or warm. Also **ther′mic.** — **ther′mal·ly** *adv.*

thermal barrier *Aeron.* The limit imposed upon the operating speed of jet engines, rockets, motors, and the like by temperatures above the melting point of their materials.

thermal death Heat death.

thermal diffusion 1 The diffusion of heat. 2 *Physics* A method for the separation of isotopes by passing a gas through a vertical tube containing an electrically heated wire which produces a concentration of the heavier components at the bottom and of the lighter components at the top.

therm·an·es·the·sia (thûr′mən·is·thē′zhə, -zhē·ə) *n. Pathol.* Loss of ability to recognize sensations of heat or cold; absence of temperature sense. Also **therm′an·aes·the′sia.** [< THERM(O)- + ANESTHESIA]

therm·el (thûr′mel) *n.* A thermocouple or group of thermocouples when used to determine temperatures. [<Gk. *thermē* heat]

therm·es·the·sia (thûr′mis·thē′zhə, -zhē·ə) *n. Physiol.* The ability to recognize changes of temperature; temperature sensitivity. Also **therm′aes·the′sia.** [<THERM(O)- + ESTHESIA]

Ther·mi·dor (thûr′mə·dôr′, *Fr.* ter·mē·dôr′) See under CALENDAR (Republican). [<F <Gk. *thermē* heat + *dōron* gift]

therm·i·on (thûrm′ī′ən, thûr′mē·ən) *n. Physics* An electrically charged particle emitted by a heated body: it may be either positive or negative. [<THERM(O)- + ION] — **therm·i·on·ic** (thûr′mē·on′ik) *adj.*

therm·i·on·ics (thûr′mē·on′iks) *n. pl. (construed as singular)* The science and practical application of thermionic phenomena.

thermionic tube A vacuum tube emitting thermions from a heated electrode. Also *Brit.* **thermionic valve.**

therm·is·tor (thər·mis′tər) *n. Electr.* A small, compact thermometric device consisting of a semiconducting material having a large temperature coefficient of resistance: widely used in the measurement of microwave power, of temperatures, and as a protective device in circuits. [<THERM(O)- + (RES)ISTOR]

ther·mit (thûr′mit) *n.* A mixture composed of finely divided aluminum and oxide of iron, chromium, or manganese. When such a mixture is brought to a sufficient temperature, the oxygen of the oxide unites with the aluminum, producing an intense heat. Also **ther′mite** (-mīt). [<Gk. *thermē* heat]

thermo– *combining form* Heat; of, related to, or caused by heat: *thermolysis, thermostat.* Also, before vowels, *therm–*. [<Gk. *thermos* heat, warmth]

ther·mo·bar·o·graph (thûr′mō·bar′ə·graf, -gräf) *n.* An apparatus for measuring the pressure and temperature of a gas simultaneously.

ther·mo·ba·rom·e·ter (thûr′mō·bə·rom′ə·tər) *n.* 1 An apparatus for measuring atmospheric pressure by the boiling point of water: used in determining altitudes. 2 A form of barometer that can be inverted and made to serve as a thermometer.

ther·mo·cau·ter·y (thûr′mō·kô′tər·ē) *n.* Cautery by means of heated wires or points.

ther·mo·chem·is·try (thûr′mō·kem′is·trē) *n.* The branch of chemistry that treats of the relations between chemical reactions and the evolution and absorption of heat observed to accompany them. — **ther′mo·chem′i·cal** (-kem′·i·kəl) *adj.* — **ther′mo·chem′ist** *n.*

ther·mo·cline (thûr′mō·klīn) *n.* A gradient indicating marked changes in temperature with depth, especially between discontinuous layers of ocean waters.

ther·mo·coup·le (thûr′mō·kup′əl) *n.* A pair of dissimilar metals so joined as to produce a thermoelectric effect when the contact surfaces are at different temperatures. Also **ther′mo·e·lec′tric couple.**

ther·mo·dy·nam·ics (thûr′mō·dī·nam′iks, -di-) *n. pl. (construed as singular)* That branch of physical science which treats of the relations between heat and energy, especially the convertibility of one into the other and the mechanical work involved. — **ther′mo·dy·nam′ic** or **·i·cal** *adj.* — **ther′mo·dy·nam′i·cist** (-nam′ə·sist) *n.*

ther·mo·e·lec·tric (thûr′mō·i·lek′trik) *adj.* Of or pertaining to thermoelectricity. Also **ther′mo·e·lec′tri·cal.** — **ther′mo·e·lec′tri·cal·ly** *adv.*

ther·mo·e·lec·tric·i·ty (thûr′mō·i·lek′tris′ə·tē) *n.* Electricity generated by differences of temperature, especially between two different metals in contact when one of the junctions is heated.

ther·mo·e·lec·tro·mo·tive (thûr′mō·i·lek′trə·mō′tiv) *adj.* Of, pertaining to, or designating electromotive force caused by difference of temperature.

ther·mo·gal·va·nom·e·ter (thûr′mō·gal′və·nom′·ə·tər) *n.* A combination of a galvanometer and a thermocouple used to measure minute variations of temperature.

ther·mo·gen·e·sis (thûr′mō·jen′ə·sis) *n.* The production of heat, especially of animal heat by organic action. — **ther′mo·gen′ic, ther·mog·e·nous** (thər·moj′ə·nəs), **ther′mo·ge·net′ic** (-jə·net′ik) *adj.*

ther·mo·gram (thûr′mə·gram) *n.* The record made by a thermograph.

ther·mo·graph (thûr′mə·graf, -gräf) *n.* An instrument for recording temperature variations; a self-registering thermometer.

ther·mog·ra·phy (thər·mog′rə·fē) *n.* 1 Photography by means of heat waves emitted by an object which has been coated with luminescent paint and exposed to ultraviolet light. 2 *Printing* Any process of reproducing written or printed characters that employs heat. — **ther·mo·graph·ic** (thûr′mə·graf′ik) *adj.*

ther·mo·hal·ine (thûr′mō·hal′ēn, -īn, -in) *adj.* Pertaining to or characterized by variations in the temperature and salinity of sea water. [<THERMO- + Gk. *hals* salt + -INE[1]]

ther·mo·junc·tion (thûr′mō·jungk′shən) *n.* The point of contact between the pair of conductors forming a thermocouple.

ther·mo·kin·e·mat·ics (thûr′mō·kin′ə·mat′iks) *n. pl. (construed as singular)* The study of heat in motion or of the motive power of heat.

ther·mo·la·bile (thûr′mō·lā′bil) *adj. Biochem.* Decomposed, destroyed, affected, or liable to be adversely affected by heat, as some enzymes and toxins: opposed to *thermostable.* [<THERMO- + LABILE]

ther·mo·lu·mi·nes·cence (thûr′mō·loo͞′mə·nes′·əns) *n.* 1 The emission of light from a substance or material under the action of

add, āce, câre, pälm; end, ēven; it, īce; odd, ōpen, ôrder; to͝ok, po͞ol; up, bûrn; ə = a in *above*, e in *sicken*, i in *clarity*, o in *melon*, u in *focus*; yo͞o = u in *fuse*; oi, oil; ou, pout; ch, check; g, go; ng, ring; th, thin; th, this; zh, vision. Foreign sounds à, œ, ü, kh, ṅ; and ◆: see page xx. < from; + plus; ? possibly.

heat. 2 A luminous effect in rock crystals from which electrons displaced by radioactivity have been released at definite temperatures, with or without pressure: sometimes indicative of the age of sedimentary rocks. — **ther′mo·lu′mi·nes′cent** *adj.*

ther·mol·y·sis (thər·mol′ə·sis) *n.* 1 *Chem.* The resolution of a compound substance into its component elements by the application of heat. 2 *Physiol.* The dissipation of heat from the animal body by physical processes. [< THERMO- + -LYSIS] — **ther·mo·lyt·ic** (thûr′mə·lit′ik) *adj.*

ther·mo·mag·net·ic (thûr′mō·mag·net′ik) *adj.* Of or pertaining to the relations between heat and magnetism.

ther·mom·e·ter (thər·mom′ə·tər) *n.* An instrument for measuring the temperature of a substance, body, or space. The ordinary thermometer consists of a graduated glass capillary tube or stem with a bulb containing mercury which expands or contracts as the temperature rises or falls. The **differential thermometer** has two air bulbs connected by a U–tube, containing colored liquid, so that when the bulbs are exposed to different temperatures a shifting of the liquid in the tube will be caused by the difference of expansion of air in the bulbs. A **resistance thermometer** indicates, by means of the change in electrical conductivity of wires with temperature, the temperature of any given wire or its environment. — **clinical thermometer** A thermometer accurately calibrated for determining body temperature, especially of a person. [<THERMO- + METER]

ther·mom·e·try (thər·mom′ə·trē) *n.* The measurement of temperature, or the art thereof, by means of the thermometer; specifically, the use of the thermometer in medical diagnosis. — **ther·mo·met·ric** (thûr′mō·met′rik) or **·ri·cal** *adj.* — **ther′mo·met′ri·cal·ly** *adv.*

ther·mo·mo·tor (thûr′mō·mō′tər) *n.* A heat engine; especially, a hot–air engine. Compare MOTOR.

ther·mo·nu·cle·ar (thûr′mō·nōō′klē·ər, -nyōō′-) *adj. Physics* Pertaining to or characterized by the mass–energy reactions involving the fusion of light atomic nuclei subjected to very high temperatures, especially with reference to stellar energy and the hydrogen bomb.

ther·mo·pen·e·tra·tion (thûr′mō·pen′ə·trā′shən) *n.* Diathermy.

ther·mo·phil·ic (thûr′mō·fil′ik) *adj.* Fond of heat: used mainly of certain bacteria. Also **ther′mo·phile** (-fil, -fīl). [<THERMO- + Gk. *philos* loving]

ther·mo·pile (thûr′mō·pīl) *n.* A group of thermocouples acting jointly to produce electric energy, especially when used with a galvanometer to measure heat.

ther·mo·plas·tic (thûr′mō·plas′tik) *adj.* Plastic in the presence of or under the application of heat: said especially of certain synthetic molding materials. — *n.* A thermoplastic substance or material.

Ther·mop·y·lae (thər·mop′ə·lē) A narrow mountain pass in Greece; scene of a battle, 480 B.C., in which the Spartans under the command of Leonidas held off the Persians under Xerxes and finally died to the last man rather than yield.

ther·mos bottle (thûr′məs) A container shaped like a bottle or flask, having two walls separated by a vacuum which serves to insulate the contents so that they retain their temperature.

ther·mo·scope (thûr′mə·skōp) *n.* An instrument for detecting changes or differences of temperature without accurately measuring them. [<THERMO- + -SCOPE] — **ther′mo·scop′ic** (-skop′ik) or **·i·cal** *adj.*

ther·mo·set·ting (thûr′mō·set′ing) *adj.* Having the property of assuming a fixed shape after being molded under heat, as certain phenol and other synthetic resins.

ther·mo·si·phon (thûr′mō·sī′fən) *n.* A device consisting of siphon tubes to increase or induce circulation by making use of temperature differential in a water–cooling system, as in that of an internal–combustion engine.

ther·mo·sta·ble (thûr′mō·stā′bəl) *adj.* 1 Resistant to heat, as certain plastics and chemicals. 2 *Biochem.* Unaffected by moderate heats; denoting immune substances, as certain toxins or ferments, which may be heated to 55° C. without loss of special properties: opposed to *thermolabile.* Also **ther′mo·sta′bile.** — **ther′·mo·sta·bil′i·ty** (-stə·bil′ə·tē) *n.*

ther·mo·stat (thûr′mə·stat) *n.* A device for the automatic regulation of temperature by means of a relay utilizing the expansion and contraction caused by temperature changes in certain metals: used for actuating fire alarms, opening or closing dampers, regulating steam pressures, etc. [<THERMO- + Gk. *statos* standing] — **ther′mo·stat′ic** *adj.* — **ther′mo·stat′i·cal·ly** *adv.*

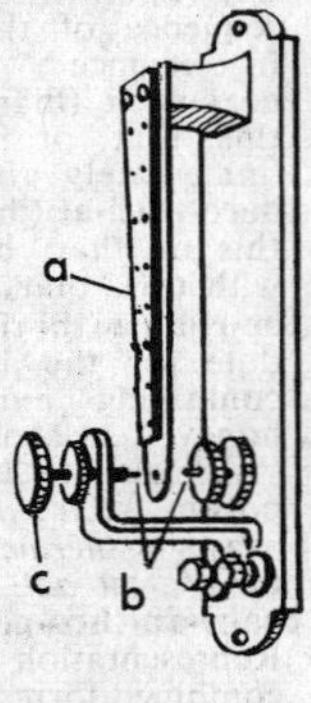

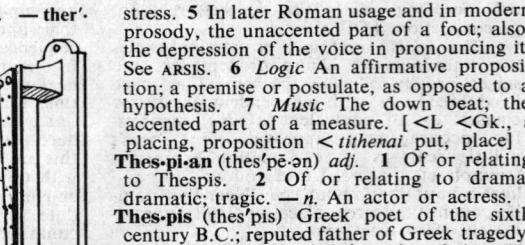

THERMOSTAT
a. Bimetal bar.
b. Contact points.
c. Control knob.

ther·mo·stat·ics (thûr′mō·stat′iks) *n. pl. (construed as singular)* The science that deals with the equilibrium of heat.

ther·mo·tank (thûr′mō·tangk′) *n.* A tank or box in which steam, water, air, or the like circulates through pipes and thus heats or cools the air passing through the tank.

ther·mo·tax·is (thûr′mō·tak′sis) *n. Biol.* 1 The regulation or normal adjustment of the animal heat in an organism. 2 The determination of movement by heat. — **ther′mo·tax′ic, ther′mo·tac′tic** (-tak′tik) *adj.*

ther·mo·ten·sile (thûr′mō·ten′sil) *adj.* Relating to variation of tensile strength caused by temperature.

therm·o·ther·a·py (thûr′mō·ther′ə·pē) *n. Med.* The treatment of disease by the application of heat.

ther·mot·ics (thər·mot′iks) *n. pl. (construed as singular)* The science of heat. [<Gk. *thermotēs* heat]

ther·mot·ro·pism (thər·mot′rə·piz′əm) *n. Biol.* 1 The property or phenomenon of movement in growing plants or other organisms brought about by the influence of heat or cold. 2 The attraction or repulsion from a source of heat evinced by some bacteria. — **ther·mo·trop·ic** (thûr′mō·trop′ik) *adj.*

the·roid (thir′oid) *adj.* Resembling or like a beast. [<Gk. *thēroeidēs* < *thēr, thēros* a wild beast + *eidos* form]

the·ro·phyte (thir′ə·fīt) *n. Bot.* An annual plant which completes its life cycle in one vegetative season. [<Gk. *theros* summer + -PHYTE]

the·ro·pod (thir′ə·pod) *n.* Any of a suborder *(Theropoda)* of saurischian dinosaurs of the Triassic and Cretaceous periods, including the true carnivorous types, as *Allosaurus* and *Tyrannosaurus.* — *adj.* Of or pertaining to the *Theropoda.* [<NL *Theropoda* <Gk. *thēr, thēros* a wild beast + *pous, podos* foot] — **the·rop·o·dan** (thi·rop′ə·dən) *adj.* & *n.*

Ther·si·tes (thər·sī′tēz) In the *Iliad,* an ugly and scurrilous Greek soldier in the Trojan War, killed by Achilles for troublemaking.

ther·sit·i·cal (thər·sit′i·kəl) *adj.* Characteristic of Thersites; hence, loud and scurrilous; abusive.

the·sau·ric (thi·sôr′ik) *adj.* Encyclopedic; having or containing large stores of miscellaneous information.

the·sau·ro·sis (thē′sô·rō′sis) *n. Pathol.* A condition marked by the storage in the body of excessive amounts of normal or foreign substances. [<Gk. *thēsauros* treasure + -OSIS]

the·sau·rus (thi·sôr′əs) *n. pl.* **·sau·ri** (-sôr′ī) 1 A place where treasure is laid up; a storehouse. 2 A repository of words or knowledge; hence, a lexicon or cyclopedia. [<L <Gk. *thēsauros* treasure house. Doublet of TREASURE.]

these (thēz) Plural of THIS.

The·seus (thē′sōōs, -sē·əs) In Greek mythology, the chief hero of Attica, son of Aegeus and king of Athens, celebrated for many adventures, chiefly the killing of the Minotaur, and for unifying Attica with Athens as its capital. See ARIADNE, HIPPOLYTUS, PHAEDRA, PIRITHOUS. — **The′se·an** (-sē·ən) *adj.*

the·sis (thē′sis) *n. pl.* **·ses** (-sēz) 1 A proposition. 2 Specifically, a formal proposition, advanced and defended by argumentation. 3 A formal treatise on a particular subject, especially, a dissertation presented by a candidate for an academic degree. 4 In early prosody, that part of a foot which had the ictus or stress. 5 In later Roman usage and in modern prosody, the unaccented part of a foot; also, the depression of the voice in pronouncing it. See ARSIS. 6 *Logic* An affirmative proposition; a premise or postulate, as opposed to a hypothesis. 7 *Music* The down beat; the accented part of a measure. [<L <Gk., a placing, proposition < *tithenai* put, place]

Thes·pi·an (thes′pē·ən) *adj.* 1 Of or relating to Thespis. 2 Of or relating to drama; dramatic; tragic. — *n.* An actor or actress.

Thes·pis (thes′pis) Greek poet of the sixth century B.C.; reputed father of Greek tragedy.

Thes·sa·lo·ni·an (thes′ə·lō′nē·ən) *n.* 1 A native or inhabitant of modern Thessalonike or of ancient Thessalonica. 2 *pl.* Either of two epistles in the New Testament (**First** and **Second Thessalonians**) written by St. Paul to the Christians of Thessalonica. — *adj.* Of or pertaining to Thessalonike.

Thes·sa·lo·ni·ke (thes′ä·lô·nē′kē) The Greek name for SALONIKA. Ancient **Thes·sa·lo·ni·ca** (thes′ə·lō·nī′kə, -lon′i·kə).

Thes·sa·ly (thes′ə·lē) A division of north central Greece; 5,399 square miles; chief town, Larissa. — **Thes·sa·li·an** (the·sā′lē·ən) *adj.* & *n.*

the·ta (thā′tə, thē′tə) *n.* The eighth letter in the Greek alphabet (Θ, ϑ, θ): equivalent in classical Greek to *t* + *h,* as in *right–hand,* but in modern Greek to spirant *th,* as in *thin.* [<Gk. *thēta*]

thet·ic (thet′ik) *adj.* 1 In ancient prosody, beginning with, bearing, relating to, or of the nature of a thesis. 2 Characterized by positive statement; arbitrary; dogmatic. Also **thet′i·cal.** [<Gk. *thetikos* fit for placing < *thetos* placed < *the-,* stem of *tithenai* place] — **thet′i·cal·ly** *adv.*

The·tis (thē′tis) In Greek mythology, a Nereid, wife of Peleus and mother of Achilles: by dipping Achilles into the Styx, she made him invulnerable, except in the right heel, by which she had held him.

the·ur·gy (thē′ûr·jē) *n. pl.* **·gies** 1 Divine or supernatural intervention in human affairs. 2 The working of miracles through divine or supernatural aid. 3 Magic, as practiced by the Neo–Platonists, by means of which miraculous effects were supposedly produced through the intervention of beneficent spirits; white magic. [<Gk. *theourgia* < *theourgos* divine worker < *theos* god + *ergon* work] — **the·ur·gic** (thē·ûr′jik), **the·ur′gi·cal** *adj.* — **the·ur′gi·cal·ly** *adv.* — **the′ur·gist** *n.*

thew (thyōō) *n.* 1 A sinew or muscle, especially when strong or well–developed. 2 *pl.* Bodily strength or vigor. [ME *theawes* good qualities, strength <OE *thēau* habit, characteristic quality] — **thew′y** *adj.*

thew·less (thyōō′lis) *adj. Scot.* 1 Having no thews; inactive; weak. 2 Spiritless; inert.

they (thā) *pron.* 1 The persons, beings, or things previously mentioned or understood: the nominative plural of *he, she, it.* 2 People in general; men: *They* say rain is expected. [<ON *their,* pl. of *sā* this, that]

they'd (thād) Contraction of: 1 They had. 2 They would.

they'll (thāl) They will: a contraction.

they're (thâr) They are: a contraction.

they've (thāv) They have: a contraction.

thi– Var. of THIO–.

thi·a·mine (thī′ə·mēn, -min) *n. Biochem.* A white crystalline compound, $C_{12}H_{18}ON_4SCl_4$; vitamin B_1, found in various natural sources, as cereal grains, green peas, liver, egg yolk, etc., and also made synthetically. Thiamine is the anti–beriberi vitamin. Also **thi′a·min** (-min). [<THI- + -AMINE]

thi·a·zine (thī′ə·zēn, -zin) *n. Chem.* One of a class of organic ring compounds of one atom of nitrogen, one of sulfur, and four of carbon. Also **thi′a·zin** (-zin). [<THI- + -AZINE]

thi·a·zole (thī′ə·zōl) *n. Chem.* A colorless, stable, liquid compound, C_3H_3NS, whose derivatives yield dyestuffs and certain sulfa drugs. Also **thi′a·zol** (-zōl, -zol). [<THI- + AZOLE]

Thi·bault (tē·bō′), **Jacques Anatole** See FRANCE, ANATOLE.

Thi·baut (tē·bō′) French form of THEOBALD.

Thi·bet (ti·bet′) See TIBET.

thick (thik) *adj.* 1 Having relatively large depth or extent from one surface to its opposite; having the dimension that is commonly least, comparatively great; not thin: distinguished from *long* and *broad.* 2 Having a

specified dimension of this kind, whether great or small: an inch *thick.* **3** Arranged compactly; close: a *thick* forest; also, following at brief intervals; frequent, as blows, raindrops, etc. **4** Set or furnished closely or abundantly with objects; abounding. **5** Having considerable density or consistency; dense; hence, turbid; impure; heavy. **6** Overcharged with vapor; foggy; misty. **7** Lacking quickness of apprehension; dull; stupid. **8** Indistinct; muffled: a *thick* sound; also, guttural; husky; throaty. **9** *Colloq.* Very friendly; intimate. **10** *Colloq.* Excessive; going too far; being beyond the bounds of what is tolerable. — *adv.* In a thick manner; placed or following closely. — **to lay it on thick** *Colloq.* **1** To overstate; exaggerate. **2** To praise fulsomely. — *n.* **1** The dimension of thickness; the thickest part. **2** The thickest or most intense time or place of anything: the *thick* of the fight. — **through thick and thin** Through good times and bad; loyally; through good fortune and adversity. [OE *thicce*] — **thick′ly** *adv.*

Synonyms (adj.): close, cloudy, compact, condensed, dense, dull, foggy, gross, hazy, inspissate, misty, muddy, turbid. See BLUNT.

thick·en (thik′ən) *v.t.* & *v.i.* **1** To make or become thick or thicker. **2** To make or become more intricate or intense: The plot *thickens.* — **thick′en·er** *n.*

thick·en·ing (thik′ən·ing) *n.* **1** The act of making or becoming thick. **2** Something added to a liquid to increase its consistency. **3** That or that part which is or has been thickened.

thick·et (thik′it) *n.* A thick growth, as of underbrush, through which a passage is not easily effected; a coppice; jungle. [OE *thiccet* < *thicce* thick]

thick·head (thik′hed′) *n.* A stupid person; numskull. Also **thick′skull′** (-skul′).

thick·ish (thik′ish) *adj.* Somewhat thick.

thick·ness (thik′nis) *n.* **1** The state or quality of being thick. **2** The dimension or measure of a solid other than its length or width. **3** A sheet, layer, etc., as of paper.

thick-set (thik′set′) *adj.* **1** Having a short, thick body; stout. **2** Set like a thicket; closely planted. — *n.* **1** A thicket; also, a thick hedge. **2** A fustianlike fabric with a velveteen nap.

thick-skinned (thik′skind′) *adj.* **1** Having a thick skin; pachydermatous. **2** Insensitive; callous to hints or insults.

thick-wit·ted (thik′wit′id) *adj.* Stupid; obtuse; dense.

thief (thēf) *n. pl.* **thieves** (thēvz) **1** One who takes something belonging to another; one who steals. **2** *Law* One guilty of simple or compound larceny, embezzlement, or swindling. **3** That which causes loss: Procrastination is the *thief* of time. See synonyms under ROBBER. [OE *thēof*]

Thiers (tyâr), **Louis Adolphe,** 1797–1877, French statesman and historian.

thieve (thēv) *v.* **thieved, thiev·ing** *v.t.* To take by theft; purloin; steal. — *v.i.* To be a thief; commit theft. [OE *thēofian*]

thieve·less (thēv′lis) *adj. Scot.* **1** Ungracious; hard. **2** Listless.

thiev·er·y (thē′vər·ē) *n. pl.* **·er·ies** The practice or act of thieving; theft; also, an instance of thieving.

thiev·ish (thē′vish) *adj.* **1** Addicted to thieving. **2** Acting by stealth; furtive. **3** Relating to or like a thief. **4** Partaking of the nature of theft. — **thiev′ish·ly** *adv.* — **thiev′ish·ness** *n.*

thigh (thī) *n.* **1** The leg between the hip and the knee of man or the corresponding portion in other animals. ◆ Collateral adjective: *femoral.* **2** The femur of an insect. [OE *thēoh*]

thigh bone The femur.

thig·mo·tax·is (thig′mə·tak′sis) *n. Biol.* Stereotropism. [<Gk. *thigma* touch + -TAXIS] — **thig′mo·tac′tic** (-tak′tik) *adj.* — **thig′mo·tac′·ti·cal·ly** *adv.*

thig·mot·ro·pism (thig·mot′rə·piz′əm) *n. Biol.* Involuntary response to mechanical stimulation of any kind, as displayed by many insects and by the tendrils, leaves, etc., of certain plants. [<Gk. *thigma* touch + TROPISM] — **thig·mo·trop·ic** (thig′mə·trop′ik) *adj.*

thill (thil) *n.* One of the shafts of a vehicle, between which a horse is harnessed. [OE *thille* board]

thim·ble (thim′bəl) *n.* **1** A caplike cover with a pitted surface, worn in sewing to protect the end of the finger that pushes the needle. **2** *Mech.* A sleeve through which a bolt passes, or which unites two rods, tubes, or the like. **3** *Naut.* **a** A metal anti-chafing ring forming a guard over a loop or eye in a sail. **b** The metal piece about which a rope is bent and spliced to the main body of the rope to form an eye. [OE *thȳmel* < *thūma* thumb]

thim·ble·ber·ry (thim′bəl·ber′ē) *n. pl.* **·ries** Any of certain American raspberries or blackberries having a thimble-shaped fruit; especially, the blackcap raspberry, the **fragrant thimbleberry** *(Rubus odoratus),* and the **western thimbleberry** *(R. parviflorus).*

thim·ble·rig (thim′bəl·rig′) *n.* **1** A swindling trick in which a pea or ball is shifted by sleight of hand from one to another of three inverted thimble-shaped cups. **2** A gambler who operates a thimblerig. — *v.t.* **·rigged, ·rig·ging** To cheat by or as by thimblerig. — **thim′ble·rig′ger** *n.*

thim·ble·weed (thim′bəl·wēd′) *n.* Any of various plants (genus *Rudbeckia*) with thimble-shaped receptacles, as the rudbeckia and the American wood anemone.

thin (thin) *adj.* **thin·ner, thin·nest** **1** Having opposite surfaces relatively close to each other; being of little depth or width; not thick. **2** Lacking roundness or plumpness of figure; lean; slender. **3** Having the component parts or particles scattered or diffused; not dense or abundant; sparse; rare: *thin* ranks, *thin* gas. **4** Having little body or substance; of a loose texture; hence, insufficient to conceal or cover: *thin* clothing; flimsy: a *thin* excuse. **5** Having little or no consistency, as a liquid: *thin* molasses. **6** Lacking in essential ingredients or qualities: *thin* blood. **7** Having little volume or richness; shrill or metallic, as a voice. **8** Not abundantly supplied or furnished; bare; scant: a *thin* table. **9** Not having sufficient contrasts of shade to print well: said of a photographic negative. **10** Lacking vigor or force; feeble; superficial: *thin* wit. See synonyms under FINE[1], GAUNT, MEAGER. — *v.t.* & *v.i.* **thinned, thin·ning** To make or become thin or thinner. [OE *thynne*] — **thin′ly** *adv.* — **thin′ness** *n.*

thine (thīn) *pron.* **1** The possessive case of thou, used predicatively; belonging or pertaining to thee: *Thine* is the kingdom. **2** The things or persons belonging or pertaining to thee. — **of thine** Belonging or relating to thee; thy: the double possessive. — *pronominal adj. Archaic* Thy: *thine* eyes. [OE *thīn,* genitive of *thū* thou]

thing[1] (thing) *n.* **1** That which exists or is conceived to exist as a separate entity; an entity; being. **2** That which is designated, as contrasted with the word or symbol used to denote it. **3** A matter or circumstance; an affair; concern: *Things* have changed. **4** An act or deed; transaction: That was a shameless *thing* to do. **5** A statement or expression; utterance: to say the right *thing.* **6** An idea; opinion; notion: Stop putting *things* in her head. **7** A quality; attribute; characteristic: Kindness is a precious *thing.* **8** An inanimate object, as distinguished from a living organism. **9** An organic being: usually with a qualifying word: Every living *thing* dies. **10** An object that is not or cannot be described or particularized: The *thing* disappeared in the shadows. **11** A person, regarded in terms of pity, affection, or contempt: that poor *thing;* You stupid *thing*! **12** *pl.* Possessions; belongings: to pack one's *things.* **13** *pl.* Clothes; especially, outer garments: Take off your *things* and stay awhile. **14** A piece of literature, art, music, etc.: He read a few *things* by Byron. **15** The proper or befitting act or result: with *the:* That was not the *thing* to do. **16** The important or remarkable point: with *the:* The *thing* we learned from the war was this. **17** *Law* A subject or property or dominion, as distinguished from a person. — **to do one's (own) thing** *Slang* To express oneself by doing what one wants to do or can do well or is in the habit of doing. — **to see things** To have hallucinations. [OE, thing, cause, assembly. Akin to THING[2].]

thing[2] (ting) *n.* A Scandinavian legislative or judicial body: the *Storthing,* the Norwegian parliament: also spelled *ting.* [<ON, assembly. Akin to THING[1].]

thing·a·ma·bob (thing′ə·mə·bob′) *n. Colloq.* A thing the specific name of which is unknown or forgotten; a dingus. Also **thing′um·a·bob′, thing′um·bob.**

thing·a·ma·jig (thing′ə·mə·jig′) *n. Colloq.* A thingamabob. Also **thing′um·a·jig′.**

T-hinge (tē′hinj′) *n.* A hinge the two sections of which have the form of the letter T. See illustration under HINGE.

thing in itself *Philos.* A noumenon; the ultimate, metaphysical reality behind the physical phenomena perceived by the senses, which, according to Kant, can never be known: the English rendering of the German *Ding an sich.*

think[1] (thingk) *v.* **thought** (thôt), **think·ing** *v.t.* **1** To produce or form in the mind; conceive mentally: to *think* evil thoughts. **2** To examine in the mind; meditate upon, or determine by reasoning: He was *thinking* what to do next; to *think* a plan through. **3** To believe; consider: I *think* him guilty. **4** To expect; anticipate: They did not *think* to meet us. **5** To bring to mind; remember; recollect: I cannot *think* what he said. **6** To have the mind preoccupied by: to *think* business morning, noon, and night. **7** To intend; purpose: Do they *think* to rob me? — *v.i.* **8** To use the mind or intellect in exercising judgment, forming ideas, etc.; engage in rational thought; reason. **9** To have a particular opinion, sentiment, or feeling: I don't *think* so. — **to think better of** **1** To abandon a course of action; alter one's intentions: I was going to call but I *thought better of* it. **2** To form a better opinion of. — **to think fit, proper, right,** etc. To regard as worth doing. — **to think nothing of** **1** To have a low opinion of; ignore. **2** To consider easy to do. — **to think of** **1** To bring to mind; remember; recollect. **2** To conceive in the mind; invent; imagine. **3** To have a specified opinion or attitude toward; regard. **4** To be considerate of; have regard for. — **to think over** To reflect upon; ponder. — **to think up** To devise, arrive at, or invent by thinking. — *n.* An act of thinking; a thought. [OE *thencean;* influenced in form by THINK[2]]

think[2] (thingk) *v.i.* To seem; appear: now obsolete except with the pronoun as indirect object in the combinations *methinks, methought.* [OE *thyncan* seem]

think·a·ble (thingk′ə·bəl) *adj.* Susceptible of being thought; conceivable; hence, possible to be believed.

think·er (thingk′ər) *n.* **1** One who thinks. **2** A person of powerful mind who devotes himself to abstract thought.

think·ing (thingk′ing) *adj.* **1** Exercising the mental capacities. **2** Capable of such exercise; rational. — *n.* **1** Mental action; thought. **2** The product of such action, as an idea. See synonyms under REFLECTION, THOUGHT. — **think′ing·ly** *adv.*

think tank *Colloq.* **1** A group of people **(think tankers),** usually academics, business executives, or government employees, organized for the investigation and study of social, scientific, and technological problems. **2** The place in which such a group works.

thin·ner (thin′ər) *n.* **1** One who or that which thins. **2** A liquid, as turpentine or petroleum spirits, mixed with paint in order to give it a proper consistency for working.

thin·nish (thin′ish) *adj.* Somewhat thin.

thin-skinned (thin′skind′) *adj.* **1** Having a thin skin. **2** Hence, easily hurt or offended; sensitive.

thio- *combining form Chem.* Containing sulfur; denoting a compound of sulfur, especially one in which sulfur has displaced oxygen: *thiocyanic.* Also, before vowels, sometimes *thi-.* Compare SULFURO-. [<Gk. *theion* sulfur]

thi·o·a·ce·tic (thī′ō·ə·sē′tik, -ə·set′ik) *adj. Chem.* Designating a yellow, fuming, pungent acid, C_2H_4OS, used in ammonia solutions as a precipitant of metals. [<THIO- + ACETIC]

thi·o·al·co·hol (thī′ō·al′kə·hôl) *n. Chem.* Thiol.

thi·o·al·de·hyde (thī′ō·al′də·hīd) *n. Chem.* An aldehyde containing sulfur as a substitute for oxygen.

thi·o·bac·te·ri·um (thī′ō·bak·tir′ē·əm) *n.* Any

of an order *(Thiobacteriales)* of bacteria which utilize the sulfur of decaying organic matter.

thi·o·car·bam·ide (thī′ō·kär·bam′īd, -id, -kär′·bə·mīd) *n.* Thiourea. [<THIO- + CARBAMIDE]

thi·o·cy·a·nate (thī′ō·sī′ə·nāt) *n. Chem.* A salt or ester of thiocyanic acid.

thi·o·cy·an·ic (thī′ō·sī·an′ik) *adj. Chem.* Designating or pertaining to a colorless liquid acid, HSCN, soluble in water and having a pungent odor. [<THIO- + CYANIC]

thi·o·gen (thī′ə·jen) *n.* A bacterial organism producing sulfur. [<THIO- + -GEN]

Thi·o·kol (thī′ə·kōl, -kol) *n.* A synthetic material consisting of organic polysulfides and resembling natural rubber in its physical properties: a trade name.

thi·ol (thī′ōl, -ol) *n. Chem.* Any of a class of sulfur compounds which are analogs of the alcohols and have the general formula RSH, in which R is a hydrocarbon radical: used largely in compounding, as *ethanethiol,* C_2H_5SH. Formerly called *mercaptan.* [<THI- + -OL[1]]

thi·on·ic (thī·on′ik) *adj. Chem.* **1** Of, pertaining to, containing, or derived from sulfur. **2** Denoting any of a group of unstable acids having the general formula $H_2S_nO_6$. [<Gk. *theion* sulfur]

thi·o·nine (thī′ə·nēn, -nin) *n. Chem.* A dark-green thiazine derivative, $C_{12}H_9N_3S$, made by synthesis, with a glistening metallic luster that yields purplish colors to silk and wool. Also **thi′o·nin** (-nin). [<Gk. *theion* sulfur + -INE[2]]

thi·o·nyl (thī′ə·nil) *n. Chem.* The bivalent sulfur radical SO: also called *sulfinyl.* [<Gk. *theion* sulfur + -YL]

thi·o·phene (thī′ə·fēn) *n. Chem.* A colorless liquid hydrocarbon, C_4H_4S, with an odor resembling that of benzene, found in coal tar and also made by synthesis. Also **thi′o·phen** (-fen). [<THIO- + PH(ENYL) + -ENE]

thi·o·sin·am·ine (thī′ō·sin·am′in, -sin′ə·mēn) *n. Chem.* A crystalline compound, $C_4H_8N_2S$, formed by the union of allyl mustard oil and alcohol with ammonia: used in photography. Also **thi′o·sin·am′in** (-am′in). [<THIO- + Gk. *sin(api)* mustard + AMINE]

Thi·o·spi·ril·lum (thī′ō·spī·ril′əm) *n.* A genus of motile, sulfur-containing bacteria found in fresh or salt water. [<THIO- + SPIRILLUM]

thi·o·sul·fate (thī′ō·sul′fāt) *n. Chem.* A salt of thiosulfuric acid.

thi·o·sul·fu·ric (thī′ō·sul·fyŏŏr′ik) *adj. Chem.* Designating or pertaining to an unstable acid, $H_2S_2O_3$, known chiefly by its salts, which have extensive applications in bleaching and photography.

thi·o·u·re·a (thī′ō·yŏŏ·rē′ə) *n. Chem.* A white, solid compound, NH_2CSNH_2, prepared from urea by replacement of oxygen by sulfur: used in organic synthesis, in photography, and as an insecticide: also called *thiocarbamide.* [<THIO- + UREA]

thir (thir, thir) *pron. Scot.* These.

third (thûrd) *adj.* **1** Next in order after second: the ordinal of *three.* **2** Being one of three equal parts. —*n.* **1** One of three equal parts of anything. **2** The person or thing coming after the second, as in a series. **3** *pl. Law* The third part of a husband's personal estate, allotted to the widow in case of his dying intestate and leaving an heir; also, loosely, a dower. **4** A unit of time or of an arc, equal to one sixtieth of a second. **5** *Music* **a** The interval between any note and the next note but one above it on a diatonic scale, known as a **major third** when such interval is two whole steps or degrees of the staff, and as a **minor third** when it is a step and a half. **b** A note separated by this interval from any other, considered in relation to that other; specifically, the third above the keynote. **c** Two notes at this interval written or sounded together, or the consonance so produced. **6** In baseball, the third base. —*adv.* In the third order, rank, or place: also, in formal discourse, **third′ly.** [OE *thridda* < *thrī* three]

third base In baseball, the third base reached by the runner, at the left-hand angle of the infield. Compare illustration under BASEBALL.

third class **1** In the U.S. postal system, a classification of mail that includes all miscellaneous printed matter but not newspapers and periodicals legally entered as second class. **2** A classification of accommodations on some ships and trains, usually the cheapest and least luxurious available; formerly, on a ship, steerage; also, the passengers traveling in this classification.

third degree **1** *Colloq.* Severe or brutal examination of a prisoner by the police for the purpose of securing information or a confession; hence, any brutal treatment. **2** In Freemasonry, the degree of Master Mason.

third estate The commons or common people; the third political class of a kingdom, following the nobility and the clergy. See under ESTATE.

third eyelid The nictitating membrane.

Third Order *Eccl.* A confraternity, generally for laymen, associated with a religious order and following a modified rule. [after the *Third Order* of St. Francis, founded 1221]

third person The person or thing spoken of, or the grammatical form indicating such person or thing.

third rail An insulated rail placed as a conductor on the track of an electric railway, from which the current is taken by means of a contact device, the running rails acting as return conductors. —**third′-rail′** *adj.*

Third Reich See under REICH.

third world **1** Any or all of the underdeveloped countries in the world, especially such countries in Asia or Africa that are not aligned with either the Communist or non-Communist nations. **2** Those not resident in the countries of the third world but collectively identified with their peoples, as because of ideology, ethnic background, or disadvantaged status. Also **Third World.**

thirl (thûrl) *v.t. Scot. & Brit. Dial.* **1** To thrill. **2** To drill or bore. [OE *thyrlian* < *thȳrel* hole < *thurh* through]

thirl·age (thûr′lij) *n.* A feudal obligation upon certain tenants or the inhabitants of certain districts to bring their grain to a certain mill for grinding; also, the fee for such grinding. Also **thirl.** [Metathetic var. of obs. *thrillage* < obs. *thrill* enthrall <OE *thræl* thrall]

thirst (thûrst) *n.* **1** A distressful feeling of dryness in the throat and mouth, accompanied by an increasingly urgent desire for liquids. **2** The physiological condition which produces this feeling. **3** Any eager desire; a longing or craving: a *thirst* for glory. See synonyms under APPETITE. —*v.i.* **1** To feel thirst; be thirsty. **2** To have an eager desire or craving; long; yearn. [OE *thurst*] —**thirst′er** *n.*

thirst·y (thûrs′tē) *adj.* **thirst·i·er, thirst·i·est** **1** Affected with thirst. **2** Lacking moisture; arid; parched. **3** Eagerly desirous. **4** *Colloq.* Causing thirst. [OE *thurstig*] —**thirst′i·ly** *adv.* —**thirst′i·ness** *n.*

thir·teen (thûr′tēn′) *n.* The cardinal number preceding fourteen and following twelve, or any of the symbols (13, xiii, XIII) which represent it. —*adj.* Consisting of or being one more than twelve. [OE *thrēotēne*]

thir·teenth (thûr′tēnth′) *adj.* **1** Third in order after the tenth: the ordinal of *thirteen.* **2** Being one of thirteen equal parts. —*n.* **1** One of thirteen equal parts. **2** The next one after the twelfth.

thir·ti·eth (thûr′tē·ith) *adj.* **1** Tenth in order after the twentieth: the ordinal of *thirty.* **2** Being one of thirty equal parts. —*n.* **1** One of thirty equal parts of anything. **2** The tenth in order after the twentieth.

thir·ty (thûr′tē) *n.* The cardinal number preceding thirty-one and following twenty-nine; thrice ten; also, any of the symbols (30, xxx, XXX) used to represent it. —*adj.* Consisting of or being ten more than twenty, or thrice ten; tricennial. [OE *thrītig*]

thir·ty-sec·ond note (thûr′tē·sek′ənd) *Music* A note having one thirty-second of the time of a whole note; a demisemiquaver.

thir·ty-two·mo (thûr′tē·tōō′mō) *n. pl.* **·mos** A sheet of paper folded so as to make 32 leaves about 3 1/8 by 4 3/4 inches; hence a book or pamphlet having 32 leaves to the sheet. —*adj.* Having 32 leaves to a sheet. Commonly written *32mo.*

Thirty Years' War See table under WAR.

this (t͟his) *adj. pl.* **these** **1** That is near or present, either actually or in thought: *This* house is for sale; I shall be there *this* evening. **2** That is understood or has just been mentioned: *This* offense justified my revenge. **3** That is nearer than or contrasted with something else: opposed to *that*: *This* tree is still alive, but that one is dead; He ran *this* way and that. **4** These: used of a number or collection considered as a whole: He has been dead *this* fourteen nights. —*pron.* **1** The person or thing near or present, being understood or just mentioned: *This* is where I live; *This* is the guilty man. **2** The person or thing nearer than or contrasted with something else: opposed to *that*: *This* is a better painting than that. **3** The idea, statement, etc., about to be made clear: I will say *this*: he is a hard worker. —*adv.* To this degree; thus or so: I was not expecting you *this* soon. [OE]

This·be (thiz′bē) See PYRAMUS AND THISBE.

this·tle (this′əl) *n.* **1** One of various vigorous prickly plants (genera *Carduus, Cirsium, Cnicus,* and *Onopordum*) with cylindrical or globular heads of tubular purple flowers; especially, the **bull thistle** *(Cirsium lanceolatum)* of Scotland, and the **Canada thistle** *(Cirsium canadense).* **2** Any of several prickly plants of other genera. [OE *thistel*] —**this′·tly** *adj.*

thistle butterfly A butterfly *(Vanessa cardui)* resembling the painted beauty but having usually four eyespots on the under side of each wing: also called *painted lady.*

this·tle·down (this′əl·doun′) *n.* The pappus of a thistle; the ripe silky fibers from the dry flower of a thistle.

thith·er (thith′ər, t͟hith′-) *adv.* **1** To that place; in that direction: opposed to *hither.* **2** *Archaic* To that end, point, or result. —*adj.* Situated or being on the other side; farther; more distant: the *thither* bank of the river. [OE *thider*]

thith·er·to (thith′ər·tōō′, t͟hith′-) *adv.* Up to that time.

thith·er·ward (thith′ər·wərd, t͟hith′-) *adv.* In that direction; toward that place. Also **thith′·er·wards.**

thix·ot·ro·py (thik·sot′rə·pē) *n. Chem.* The property possessed by certain gels of liquefying under the action of vibrating forces. [<Gk. *thixis* touch + *tropē* turning] —**thix·o·trop·ic** (thik′sə·trop′ik) *adj.*

tho (t͟hō) See THOUGH.

thole[1] (thōl) *n.* A pin or pair of pins serving as a fulcrum for an oar in rowing. Also **thole pin.** [OE *thol* pin]

thole[2] (thōl) *v.t. & v.i. Archaic* To endure; suffer; tolerate. [OE *tholian* suffer]

Thom·as (tom′əs; *Dan., Du., Ger., Sw.* tō′mäs; *Fr.* tō·mä′) A masculine personal name. [< Hebrew, twin]

—**Thomas** One of the Twelve Apostles, known for his doubting disposition. *John* xx 25.

—**Thomas à Becket** See BECKET.

—**Thomas à Kempis** See KEMPIS.

—**Thomas of Er·cel·doune** (ûr′səl·dōōn), 1220?–97, Scottish seer and poet: best known as *Thomas the Rhymer.*

Tho·mas (tō·mä′), **Ambroise,** 1811–96, French composer.

Tho·mas (tom′əs), **Dylan,** 1914–53, Welsh poet and author. —**George Henry,** 1816–70, U.S. general. —**Norman,** 1884–1968, U.S. socialist leader and writer. —**Seth,** 1785–1859, U.S. clock manufacturer. —**Theodore,** 1831?–1905, U.S. orchestra conductor born in Germany.

Tho·mism (tō′miz·əm, thō′-) *n.* The doctrine of St. Thomas Aquinas, who attempted to combine Aristotelian metaphysics, ontology, logic, and method with Christian theology into one comprehensive system, including theology, natural philosophy, esthetics, ethics, psychology, and politics. He held that human reason was the faculty by which men apprehended many truths, but that the divinely revealed truths necessary for salvation could be known only through faith; that reason was distinct from faith, though not opposed to it when rightly used; and that reason served faith by preparing men's minds to receive revealed truth, by expounding and systematizing that truth, and by defending it against attack. The system of dogmatic theology constructed by St. Thomas remains the standard within the Roman Catholic Church, and has had a wide influence in many other communions. —**Tho′·mist** *adj. & n.* —**Tho·mis′·tic** or **·ti·cal** *adj.*

Thomp·son (tomp′sən), **Benjamin** See RUMFORD, COUNT. —**Francis,** 1859–1907, English poet.

Thomp·son River (tomp′sən) A river in southern British Columbia, Canada, flowing 304

miles west and south to the Fraser River.

Thompson submachine gun See under SUB-MACHINE GUN.

Thom·son (tom′sən), **Sir George Paget**, 1892–1975, English physicist; son of Sir Joseph John. —**James**, 1700–48, Scottish poet. —**James**, 1834–82, Scottish poet: pseudonym B.V. —**Sir John Arthur**, 1861–1933, Scottish biologist. — **Sir Joseph John**, 1856–1940, English physicist. —**William**, 1824–1907, English mathematical physicist and inventor.

thong (thông, thong) n. **1** A narrow strip, properly of leather, as for tying or fastening. **2** A whiplash. [OE thwang thong]

Thor (thôr, tôr) In Norse mythology, the god of war, thunder, and strength, and son of Odin: he destroyed the enemies of the gods with his magic hammer Mjollnir. A variant of the name Thor is preserved in the first element of *Thur*sday.

tho·rac·ic (thô·ras′ik, thō-) adj. Of, relating to, or situated in or near the thorax. [< NL thoracicus < Gk. thōrax the chest]

thoracic duct Anat. The canal emptying into the left subclavian vein which collects the lymph from parts of the body below the diaphragm.

thoraco- combining form Med. & Surg. The thorax or the chest; of or related to the thorax: thoracotomy. Also, before vowels, **thorac-**. [< Gk. thōrax the chest]

tho·ra·co·plas·ty (thôr′ə·kō·plas′tē, thō′rə-) n. Surg. An operation for the removal and replacement of several ribs in order to provide a thoracic cavity within which the underlying lung is kept permanently collapsed: used in the treatment of tuberculosis. [< THORACO- + -PLASTY]

tho·ra·cot·o·my (thôr′ə·kot′ə·mē, thō′rə-) n. Surg. Incision of the wall of the chest. [< THORACO- + -TOMY]

tho·rax (thôr′aks, thō′raks) n. pl. **tho·rax·es** or **tho·ra·ces** (thôr′ə·sēz, thō′rə-) **1** Anat. The part of the body between the neck and the abdomen, enclosed by the ribs. **2** Entomol. The middle region of the body of an insect, between the head and the abdomen. **3** Zool. The corresponding region of the body in other arthropods. [< L < Gk. thōrax]

THORAX
a Manubrium.
b Gladiolus.
c Ensiform cartilage.
d Clavicle.
e Scapula.
f Sternal ribs.
g False ribs.
h Floating ribs.
i Costal arch.
j Costal cartilage.

Tho·reau (thôr′ō, thō′rō, thə·rō′), **Henry David**, 1817–1862, U.S. author.

Tho·rez (tô·rez′), **Maurice**, 1900–1964, French Communist.

tho·ri·a (thôr′ē·ə, thō′rē·ə) n. A white, very heavy oxide of thorium, ThO₂, used with zirconia and other earths in the mantle of Welsbach's incandescent lamp. [< NL < thorium THORIUM]

tho·ri·a·nite (thôr′ē·ə·nīt, thō′rē-) n. A black radioactive mineral composed chiefly of thorium, cerium, and uranium oxides.

tho·rite (thôr′īt, thō′rīt) n. A vitreous, yellow to black, thorium silicate, ThSiO₄. [< THOR(IUM) + -ITE¹]

tho·ri·um (thôr′ē·əm, thō′rē-) n. A gray, radioactive metallic element (symbol Th, atomic number 90) of the actinide series, about as abundant as lead in the lithosphere. See PERIODIC TABLE. [after Thor] —**tho·ric** adj.

thorium series The succession of radioactive nuclides stemming from the decay of thorium of mass number 232 and terminating in the stable lead isotope of mass number 208.

thorn (thôrn) n. **1** An indurated, leafless spine or sharp-pointed process from a branch. **2** One of various other sharp processes, as the spine of a porcupine. **3** Any of various thorn-bearing shrubs or trees; especially, any of a genus (Crataegus) of rosaceous plants, as the hawthorn. **4** Anything or anyone that occasions discomfort,

pain, or annoyance; a vexation. **5** The name of the Old English rune ρ ; also, the corresponding Icelandic character: equivalent originally to th, both voiced and unvoiced, but finally only to the unvoiced sound, as in thorn, from which it derives its name. Y or y is sometimes used as a makeshift for it in early English, as in the contraction yᵉ. Compare EDH. —v.t. To pierce or prick with a thorn. [OE] —**thorn′less** adj.

Thorn (thôrn) The German name for TORUN.

thorn apple 1 Jimsonweed: so called from its spiny capsule. **2** Any plant of the same genus. **3** The fruit of the hawthorn; a haw.

thorn·back (thôrn′bak′) n. **1** A European ray (Raia clavata) whose back is studded with short stout spines. **2** The common European spider crab (Maia squinado). **3** Any of certain American skates or sticklebacks. **4** Brit. Slang. An old maid.

thorn·bill (thôrn′bil′) n. Any of certain brightcolored hummingbirds of South America (genera Rhamphomicron and Chalcostigma) characterized by a long, sharp bill.

thorn broom The furze.

Thorn·dike (thôrn′dīk), **Ashley**, 1871–1933, U.S. educator. —**Edward Lee**, 1874–1949, U.S. psychologist; brother of the preceding. —**Lynn**, 1882–1965, U.S. historian; brother of the preceding. —**Dame Sybil**, 1882–1976, English actress.

thorn tree 1 The hawthorn. **2** The honey locust.

thorn·y (thôr′nē) adj. **thorn·i·er**, **thorn·i·est 1** Full of thorns; spiny. **2** Sharp like a thorn, literally or figuratively; painful; vexatious; presenting difficulties or trials. —**thorn′i·ness** n.

tho·ron (thôr′on, thō′ron) n. An isotope of radon emanating from thorium, having mass number 220 and a half-life of 54.5 seconds. [< NL THOR(IUM) + -on, as in neon]

thor·ough (thûr′ō, thûr′ə) adj. **1** Carried to completion; thoroughgoing: a thorough search; also, carrying (a task) to completion; persevering: a very thorough worker. **2** Marked by careful attention throughout; not superficial; hence, complete; perfect. **3** Completely (such and such); through and through: a thorough nincompoop. **4** Painstakingly conforming to a standard. **5** Obs. Going or passing through. See synonyms under RADICAL. —adv. & prep. Obs. Through. Also Obs. **thor′o**. [Emphatic var. of THROUGH] — **thor′ough·ly** adv. —**thor′ough·ness** n.

Thor·ough (thûr′ō) n. The administrative policy of Charles I's minister, the Earl of Strafford: so called by himself as being a method of carrying through his ideas in spite of all opposition.

THOROUGH-BASS
The numbers under the bass indicate the notes of the chords in the treble.

thor·ough·bass (thûr′ō·bās′) n. Music **1** A bass part accompanied by shorthand marks, as numerals, below the staff, to indicate the general harmony: now disused. **2** Loosely, the science of harmony or the art of harmonic composition.

thorough brace A strong leather strap extending under each side of the body of a carriage and serving as a support and a spring. —**thor′ough·braced** adj.

thor·ough·bred (thûr′ō·bred′, thûr′ə-) n. **1** Pure stock. **2** Colloq. A person of culture and good breeding. —adj. **1** Belonging to the strain of horses known as Thoroughbred. **2** Bred from pure stock. **3** Possessing the traits of a thoroughbred.

Thor·ough·bred (thûr′ō·bred′, thûr′ə-) n. A horse whose ancestry is recorded in the English Stud Book, and which is therefore descended from one of three Eastern sires: the Byerly Turk, the Darley Arabian, or the Godolphin.

thor·ough·fare (thûr′ō·fâr′, thûr′ə-) n. **1** A frequented way or course; especially, a road or street through which the public have unob-

structed passage; highway. **2** A traveling or passing through, or the right or possibility of doing so; a passage: now chiefly in the phrase no thoroughfare. **3** An outlet to an enclosed place, as to a court. **4** Any place through which much traffic passes, as a strait, river, or other waterway. See synonyms under ROAD, WAY. [ME thurghfare < OE thurh through + faru going]

thor·ough·go·ing (thûr′ō·gō′ing, thûr′ə-) adj. **1** Characterized by extreme thoroughness or efficiency. **2** Unmitigated: a thoroughgoing scoundrel.

thor·ough·paced (thûr′ō·pāst′, thûr′ə-) adj. **1** Perfectly trained, as a horse. **2** Hence, thoroughgoing; accomplished: a thorough-paced villain.

thor·ough·pin (thûr′ə·pin′) n. Dropsical swelling of the sheath of the tendon of a flexor muscle connected with the hock of a horse: it appears on both sides of the leg, as if the latter had been pierced by a pin. Also **thor′ough·shot** (-shot′).

thor·ough·wort (thûr′ō·wûrt′, thûr′ə-) n. **1** A stout, hairy herb, the boneset, 2 to 5 feet high, with white flowers, common in the United States and Canada. **2** Any other eupatorium.

thorp (thôrp) n. A hamlet; small cluster of houses in the country: now chiefly in names of places. Also **thorpe**. [OE. Akin to DORP.]

THOROUGHWORT
(Plant to 5 feet high)

Thors·havn (tôrs′houn′) Capital of the Faeroe Islands, in the central part of the group.

Thor·vald·sen (tôr′väl·sən), **Albert Bertel**, 1770–1844, Danish sculptor. Also **Thor′·wald·sen**.

those (thōz) adj. & pron. Plural of THAT. [OE thās]

Thoth (thōth, tōt) In Egyptian mythology, the god of wisdom, inventor of art, science, and letters: identified with the Greek Hermes Trismegistus: represented with the head of an ibis or a dog.

Thoth·mes (thōth′mēz, tōt′mes) Any of several Egyptian kings, between 1587–1328 B.C.: also Thuthmose.

thou (thou) pron. The person spoken to, as denoted in the nominative case: archaic except in Biblical, homiletic, elevated, or poetic language, in prayers to a deity, or in certain dialects. [OE thū]

THOTH

though (thō) conj. **1** Notwithstanding the fact that: introducing a clause expressing an actual fact. **2** Conceding or granting that; even if: introducing a clause assumed or admitted as supposedly true. **3** And yet; still; however: introducing a modifying clause or statement added as an afterthought: I am well, though I do not feel very strong. **4** Notwithstanding what has been done or said; nevertheless: But they have, though. As used in this sense, though is sometimes regarded as a conjunctive adverb. Also spelled tho. Compare HOWEVER. See synonyms under BUT¹. [Prob. fusion of OE thēah and ON thō]

thought¹ (thôt) n. **1** The act or process of using the mind actively and deliberately; meditation; cogitation. **2** The product of thinking; an idea, concept, judgment, opinion, or the like. **3** Intellectual activity of a specific kind: Greek thought. **4** Consideration; attention; heed: to take thought on how to do something. **5** Intention or idea of doing something; plan; design: All thought of returning was abandoned. **6** Expectation; an-

add, āce, câre, pälm; end, ēven; it, īce; odd, ōpen, ôrder; tŏŏk, pōōl; up, bûrn; ə = a in above, e in sicken, i in clarity, o in melon, u in focus ; yōō = u in fuse, oi, oil; ou, pout; ch, check; g, go; ng, ring; th, thin; th, this; zh, vision. Foreign sounds á, œ, ü, kh, ṅ; and ◆: see page xx. < from; + plus; ? possibly.

ticipation: He had no *thought* of finding her there. 7 A trifle; a small amount: Be a *thought* more cautious. [<THOUGHT[2]]

Synonyms: cogitation, conception, conclusion, consideration, contemplation, deliberation, fancy, idea, imagination, judgment, meditation, musing, notion, opinion, reflection, reverie, speculation, study, supposition, thinking, view. See IDEA, MIND, REFLECTION.

thought[2] (thôt) Past tense and past participle of THINK. [OE *thōht*]

thought·ful (thôt′fəl) *adj.* 1 Full of thought; meditative: a *thoughtful* face. 2 Showing, characterized by, or employed in thought; promotive of thought. 3 Attentive; careful; especially, manifesting regard for others; considerate: often with *of* or an infinitive: *thoughtful* of one's reputation; *thoughtful* to lay up a store for winter. **— thought′ful·ly** *adv.* **— thought′ful·ness** *n.*

Synonyms: attentive, careful, circumspect, considerate, heedful, mindful, provident. An *attentive* person waits upon another to supply what is needed or desired. A *thoughtful* person provides in advance for needs and wishes not yet manifested. A *considerate* person carefully spares another all that would harm, grieve, or annoy; one who is *circumspect* carefully avoids all that might compromise himself. See SEDATE. *Antonyms*: careless, gay, giddy, heedless, inadvertent, inattentive, inconsiderate, neglectful, negligent, reckless, remiss.

thought·less (thôt′lis) *adj.* 1 Manifesting lack of thought or care; heedless; also, giddy. 2 Stupid. See synonyms under IMPROVIDENT, IMPRUDENT. **— thought′less·ly** *adv.* **— thought′·less·ness** *n.*

thought–trans·fer·ence (thôt′trans·fûr′əns) *n.* Telepathy.

thou·sand (thou′zənd) *n.* The cardinal number following 999; one hundred times ten, or any of the symbols (1,000, m, M) used to represent it; also, loosely, an indefinitely large number. — *adj.* Consisting of a hundred times ten; millenary. [OE *thusend*] **— thou′sand·fold′** (-fōld′) *adj.* & *adv.*

Thousand Islands A group of 1,500 islets in an expansion of the upper St. Lawrence River, near Lake Ontario.

thou·sandth (thou′zəndth) *adj.* 1 Last in a series of a thousand: an ordinal numeral. 2 Being one of a thousand equal parts. — *n.* 1 One of a thousand equal parts. 2 The next in order after the 999th.

thowe (thō) *n. Scot.* Thaw. Also **thow.**

thow·less (thou′lis) *adj. Scot.* Inactive; lazy; without ambition or energy. See THEWLESS.

Thrace (thrās) An ancient region, later a Roman province, NE of Macedonia in the eastern part of the Balkan Peninsula: modern Thrace is divided into a Greek division (3,315 square miles); and a Turkish division corresponding to Turkey in Europe. Ancient **Thra·cia** (thrā′shə).

Thra·cian (thrā′shən) *adj.* Pertaining to Thrace or its people. — *n.* 1 One of the people of Thrace. 2 The Indo-European language of the ancient Thracians, related to Phrygian. 3 A gladiator who fought in the native dress of the Thracians. See illustration under GLADIATOR.

Thracian Chersonese An ancient name for GALLIPOLI PENINSULA.

thral·dom (thrôl′dəm) *n.* 1 The state of being a thrall. 2 Figuratively, any sort of bondage or servitude. See synonyms under BONDAGE. Also **thrall′dom.**

Thrale (thrāl), **Mrs.** See PIOZZI, HESTER LYNCH.

thrall (thrôl) *n.* 1 A person in bondage; a slave; serf; hence, figuratively, one controlled by a passion or vice. 2 The condition of bondage; thraldom. — *v.t. Archaic* To reduce to thraldom; enslave. — *adj.* Held in subjection; enslaved. [OE *thræl* <ON]

thrang (thräng) *Scot. adj.* Occupied fully; busy. — *n.* A throng; crowd.

thrash (thrash) *v.t.* 1 To thresh, as grain. 2 To beat as if with a flail; flog; whip. 3 To defeat utterly. — *v.i.* 4 To move or swing about with flailing, violent motions. 5 *Naut.* To work to windward, against the tide, etc. See synonyms under BEAT. **— to thrash out** To discuss fully and to a conclusion. — *n.* 1 The act of thrashing. 2 In swimming, a kick used with the crawl and back strokes. [Dial. var. of THRESH]

thrash·er[1] (thrash′ər) *n.* 1 One who or that which thrashes. 2 *Agric.* A threshing machine. 3 The thresher shark.

thrash·er[2] (thrash′ər) *n.* Any of several long-tailed American songbirds (genus *Toxostoma*) resembling the thrushes and related to the mockingbirds, especially the common eastern **brown thrasher** (*T. rufum*), colored foxy-red with black spots. [<dial. E *thresher* <THRUSH[1]]

thrash·ing (thrash′ing) *n.* A sound beating or whipping.

thra·son·i·cal (thrā·son′i·kəl) *adj.* Characterized by boasting or ostentation; bragging; boastful. [<L *Thraso*, a braggart soldier in Terence's *Eunuch* <Gk. *Thrason* < *thrasus* rash] **— thra·son′i·cal·ly** *adv.*

Thras·y·bu·lus (thras′ə·byōō′ləs) Greek patriot and naval commander, died 389 B.C.

thrave (thrāv) *n. Scot. & Brit. Dial.* 1 Twenty-four sheaves of grain. 2 An indefinite number; a company; throng; also, a bundle.

thraw[1] (thrô) *Scot. n.* 1 A wrench or twist. 2 A throe. — *v.t.* 1 To twist or wrench. 2 To thwart; frustrate. — *adj.* Awry.

thraw[2] (thrô) *v. & n. Scot. & Brit. Dial.* Throw.

thrawn (thrôn) *adj. Scot.* 1 Wrenched; awry; twisted; crooked. 2 Obstinate; contrary.

thread (thred) *n.* 1 A very slender cord or line composed of two or more yarns or filaments, as of flax, cotton, silk, or other fibrous substance, twisted together. 2 A filament of any substance, as of metal, glass, or tissue; a hair. 3 A fine stream or beam: a *thread* of light. 4 A fine line of color. 5 Anything suggestive of a thread; something that runs a continuous course through a series, serving to give sequence to the whole: the *thread* of his discourse. 6 *Mining* A very thin seam or vein of ore. 7 *Mech.* The spiral ridge of a screw. 8 Thread of life. — *v.t.* 1 To pass a thread through the eye of: to *thread* a needle. 2 To arrange or string on a thread, as beads. 3 To cut a thread on or in, as a screw. 4 To make one's way through or over: to *thread* a maze. 5 To make (one's way) carefully. 6 To be present throughout; pervade. — *v.i.* 7 To make one's way carefully; step. 8 To drop from a fork or spoon in a fine thread: said of boiling sirup when it has reached a certain consistency. — *adj.* Pertaining to, resembling, or made of thread; filar. [OE *thrǣd*] **— thread′er** *n.* **— thread′like′** *adj.*

thread·bare (thred′bâr′) *adj.* 1 Worn so that the threads show, as a rug or garment. 2 Clad in worn garments. 3 Commonplace; hackneyed. See synonyms under COMMON, TRITE. **— thread′bare′ness** *n.*

thread feather *Ornithol.* An extremely slender feather, having the vane rudimentary or absent; filoplume.

thread·fin (thred′fin′) *n.* A fish of tropical seas (family *Polynemidae*), having three or more threadlike rays below the pectoral fins. Also **thread′fish′.**

thread mark A marking made in paper currency by running colored silk fibers in with the pulp, as a safeguard against counterfeiting. Compare GRANITE PAPER, SILK PAPER.

Thread·nee·dle Street (thred′nēd′l) A short street in London faced by the Bank of England. **— The Old Lady of Threadneedle Street** The Bank of England.

thread of life The course of existence, represented by the ancient Greeks and Romans as a thread being spun and cut off by the three Fates, Atropos being the one who cut it.

thread·worm (thred′wûrm′) *n.* A threadlike nematode worm; a pinworm or filaria.

thread·y (thred′ē) *adj.* 1 Resembling a thread; filamentous; tenuous. 2 Consisting of, containing, or covered with thread.

threap (thrēp) *v.t. & v.i. Scot. & Brit. Dial.* To contradict; dispute; also, to rebuke; insist. Also **threep.**

threat (thret) *n.* 1 A declaration of an intention to inflict injury or pain; a menace. 2 An announcement or omen of impending danger or evil. 3 A menace or danger of any sort. — *v.t. Archaic* To threaten. [OE *thrēat* crowd, oppression]

threat·en (thret′n) *v.t.* 1 To utter menaces or threats against. 2 To be menacing or dangerous to. 3 To be ominous or portentous of. 4 To utter threats of (injury, vengeance, etc.). — *v.i.* 5 To utter threats. 6 To have a menacing aspect; lower: The rising waters seemed to *threaten.* [OE *thrēatnian* urge, compel] **— threat′en·er** *n.* **— threat′en·ing·ly** *adv.*

Synonym: menace. *Threaten* is applied alike to vast and trivial matters; *menace* only to those of moment. Either persons or things may *threaten*; *menace* is chiefly used of persons or of things personified. One may *threaten* by word or act; *menace* is for the most part limited to actions or concrete things; one *threatens* another with death; he *menaces* him with a revolver.

three (thrē) *n.* 1 The cardinal number following two and preceding four, or any of the symbols (3, iii, III) used to represent it. 2 Any group of three persons or things; a playing card with three pips. — *adj.* Being one more than two; ternary. [OE *thrī*]

three–base hit (thrē′bās′) A fair hit in baseball that enables the batter to reach third base without the help of an error. Also **three′–bag′ger** (-bag′ər).

three–cent piece (thrē′sent′) A copper and nickel coin of the United States from 1865–1890.

three–col·or (thrē′kul′ər) *adj.* Pertaining to or denoting a process of color printing based on three primary colors, each of which is transferred to the printing surface from a separate, accurately registered plate.

three–deck·er (thrē′dek′ər) *n.* 1 A vessel having three decks or gun decks. 2 Any structure having three levels. 3 A sandwich made with three slices of bread.

three·fold (thrē′fōld′) *adj.* Made up of three; three times as many or as great; triplicate. — *adv.* Triply; in a threefold manner or degree.

three–mile limit (thrē′mīl′) See under LIMIT.

three·pence (thrip′əns, threp′-, thrup′-) *n. Brit.* 1 The sum of three pennies. 2 A small coin of Great Britain, made of alloy, formerly of silver, worth three pennies: also **threepenny bit.**

three·pen·ny (thrip′ə·ni, threp′-, thrup′-, thrē′pen′ē) *adj. Brit.* 1 Worth or costing threepence. 2 Hence, of little value.

three–phase (thrē′fāz′) *adj. Electr.* Designating a combination of alternating currents or circuits each of which differs in phase by one third of a cycle or 120 degrees.

three–piled (thrē′pīld′) *adj.* 1 Having a triple pile or nap: said of velvet; also, figuratively, costly or extravagant. 2 Clad in or wearing such velvet; hence, wealthy. 3 Piled in a set or sets of three.

three–ply (thrē′plī′) *adj.* Consisting of three thicknesses, strands, layers, etc.

three–point landing (thrē′point′) 1 *Aeron.* A perfect airplane landing, with the front wheels and tail skid or wheel touching the ground simultaneously. 2 Any successful outcome.

three–quar·ter binding (thrē′kwôr′tər) A style of bookbinding having the strip of leather over the back and corners projecting to a greater width than in half-binding.

Three Rivers The English name for TROIS RIVIÈRES, Canada.

three R's See under R.

three·score (thrē′skôr′, -skōr′) *adj.* & *n.* Sixty.

three·some (thrē′səm) *adj.* Performed by three; triple: a *threesome* reel. — *n.* A golf match in which one ball plays against two, the latter playing one ball between them alternately.

three–square (thrē′skwâr′) *adj.* Having three plane faces of equal width: said especially of certain files of triangular cross-section.

threm·ma·tol·o·gy (threm′ə·tol′ə·jē) *n.* The science of breeding animals and plants. [< Gk. *thremma, -atos* a nursling + -LOGY]

thren·o·dy (thren′ə·dē) *n. pl.* **·dies** An ode or song of lamentation; a dirge. Also **thren′ode** (-ōd). [<Gk. *thrēnōidia* < *thrēnos* lament + *ōidē* song] **— thre·no·di·al** (thri·nō′dē·əl), **thre·nod·ic** (thri·nod′ik) *adj.* **— thren′o·dist** *n.*

thre·o·nine (thrē′ə·nēn, -nin) *n. Biochem.* A crystalline amino acid, $C_4H_9NO_3$, isolated as a product of the hydrolysis of certain proteins and regarded as an essential to proper nutrition.

thresh (thresh) *v.t.* 1 To beat stalks of (ripened grain) with a flail or machine so as to separate the grain from the straw or husks. 2 To beat; flog. — *v.i.* 3 To thresh grain. 4 To move or thrash about. **— to thresh out** (**or over**) To discuss fully and to a conclusion. — *n.* The act of threshing; a threshing. [OE *therscan*] **— thresh′ing** *n.*

thresh·er (thresh′ər) *n.* **1** One who or that which threshes; specifically, a machine for threshing. **2** A large shark *(Alopias vulpes)* of warm seas, having the dorsal lobe of the tail extremely long, supposedly for splashing the water to round up its prey: also **thresher shark.**

thresh·old (thresh′ōld, -hōld) *n.* **1** The plank, timber, or stone lying under the door of a building; doorsill. **2** The entrance, entering point, or beginning of anything: the *threshold* of the 20th century. **3** *Physiol.* The point at which a stimulus, as of a nerve or muscle, just produces a response; especially, the minimum degree of stimulation necessary for conscious perception: the *threshold* of consciousness: also called *limen.* ◆ Collateral adjective: *liminal.* [OE *therscold*]

threw (thro͞o) Past tense of THROW.

thrice (thrīs) *adv.* **1** Three times. **2** In a threefold manner; hence, fully; repeatedly. [ME *thries* <OE *thriwa* thrice + -s[3]]

thrift (thrift) *n.* **1** Care and wisdom in the management of one's resources; frugality. **2** A flourishing condition; vigorous growth, as of a plant. **3** Any of a genus *(Armeria,* formerly *Statice)* of tufted herbs of the north temperate zone growing on mountains and the seashore; especially, the common thrift *(A. maritima),* having white or pink flower heads. **4** *Obs.* The state of one who thrives; prosperity. **5** *Scot.* & *Brit. Dial.* Effort; occupation; work. [<ON. Akin to THRIVE.] — **thrift′less** *adj.* — **thrift′less·ly** *adv.* — **thrift′less·ness** *n.*

Synonyms: gain, profit, prosperity. See FRUGALITY.

thrift·y (thrif′tē) *adj.* **thrift·i·er, thrift·i·est** **1** Displaying thrift or good management; economical; frugal. **2** Prosperous; thriving. **3** Growing vigorously. See synonyms under PRUDENT. — **thrift′i·ly** *adv.* — **thrift′i·ness** *n.*

thrill[1] (thril) *v.t.* **1** To cause to feel a sudden wave of emotion; move to great or tingling excitement. **2** To cause to vibrate or tremble. — *v.i.* **3** To feel a sudden wave of emotion or excitement. **4** To vibrate or tremble; quiver. See synonyms under SHAKE. — *n.* **1** A tremor of feeling or excitement. **2** A pulsation. **3** *Med.* An abnormal vibratory or tremulous resonance perceived in auscultation; fremitus. [Metathetic var. of THIRL[1]] — **thrill′ing** *adj.* — **thrill′ing·ly** *adv.*

thrill[2] (thril) See TRILL[1].

thrill·er (thril′ər) *n.* **1** One who or that which thrills. **2** *Colloq.* An exciting book, play, or motion picture.

thrip (thrip) *n. Brit. Slang* A threepenny piece.

thrips (thrips) *n.* A small insect (order *Thysanoptera*), many species of which are injurious to grain and plants. [<L <Gk., woodworm]

thrive (thrīv) *v.i.* **throve** (thrōv) or **thrived, thrived** or **thriv·en** (thriv′ən), **thriv·ing** **1** To prosper; be successful, especially by being thrifty. **2** To grow with vigor; flourish. See synonyms under FLOURISH, SUCCEED. [<ON *thrīfast,* orig. reflexive of *thrīfa* grasp. Akin to THRIFT.] — **thriv′er** *n.* — **thriv′ing·ly** *adv.*

throat (thrōt) *n.* **1** The anterior part of the neck, extending from the back of the mouth and containing the epiglottis, larynx, trachea, and pharynx. **2** Anything resembling a throat; an entrance, inlet, or orifice: the *throat* of a bottle. **3** *Naut.* The end of a gaff nearest the mast. — *v.t.* **1** *Rare* To utter in a guttural tone. **2** To provide with a throat; channel; groove. [OE *throte*]

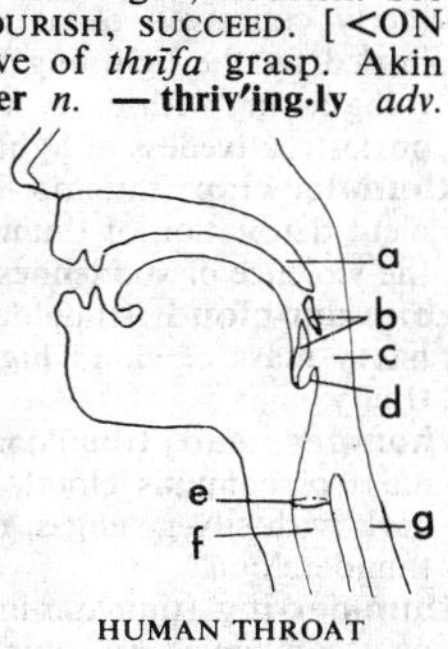

HUMAN THROAT
a. Soft palate.
b. Tonsils.
c. Pharynx.
d. Epiglottis.
e. Vocal cords.
f. Larynx.
g. Esophagus.

throat·latch (thrōt′lach′) *n.* A strap passing under the neck of a draft animal and aiding in holding a bridle or halter in place.

throat·y (thrō′tē) *adj.* **throat·i·er, throat·i·est** Uttered in the throat; guttural. — **throat′i·ly** *adv.* — **throat′i·ness** *n.*

throb (throb) *v.i.* **throbbed, throb·bing** **1** To beat or pulsate rhythmically, as the heart; especially, to beat rapidly or violently; palpitate. **2** To feel or show emotion. — *n.* **1** The act or state of throbbing. **2** A pulsation or beat, especially one caused by excitement or emotion. [? Imit.] — **throb′ber** *n.*

throe (thrō) *n.* **1** A violent pang or pain; agony: said especially of the pains of death and childbirth. **2** Any agonized or agonizing activity. See synonyms under AGONY, PAIN. — *v.t.* & *v.i.* **throed, throe·ing** *Rare* To put in, suffer, or undergo agony. ◆ Homophone: *throw.* [ME *throwe,* prob. fusion of OE *thrōwian* suffer and *thrāwan* twist, throw]

throm·bin (throm′bin) *n. Biochem.* The enzyme present in blood serum that reacts with fibrinogen to form fibrin in the process of clotting. [<THROMBUS]

throm·bo·cyte (throm′bə·sīt) *n.* A blood platelet. [<Gk. *thrombos* clot + -CYTE]

throm·bo·gen (throm′bə·jen) *n. Biochem.* Prothrombin. [<Gk. *thrombos* clot + -GEN]

throm·bo·plas·tin (throm′bō·plas′tin) *n. Biochem.* A complex substance present in the blood and other animal tissues, which reacts with calcium ions to give prothrombin. Also **throm′bo·kin′ase** (-kin′ās, -kī′nās). [<Gk. *thrombos* clot + -PLAST + -IN] — **throm′bo·plas′tic** *adj.*

throm·bo·sis (throm·bō′sis) *n. Pathol.* Local coagulation of blood in the heart, arteries, veins, or capillaries, forming by its clot an obstruction to circulation. [<NL <Gk. *thrombōsis* < *thrombos* clot] — **throm·bot′ic** (-bot′ik) *adj.*

throm·bus (throm′bəs) *n. pl.* **·bi** (-bī) *Pathol.* The blood clot formed in thrombosis. [<Gk. *thrombos* clot, lump]

throne (thrōn) *n.* **1** The royal chair occupied by a sovereign on state occasions. **2** The chair of state of a pope or of some other dignitary, as a cardinal, archbishop, or bishop. **3** Royal estate or dignity; sovereign power. **4** One invested with sovereign power; sometimes, the rank or authority of any high dignitary. **5** *pl.* The third of the nine orders of angels in the celestial hierarchy. — *v.t.* & *v.i.* **throned, thron·ing** To place or sit on a throne; enthrone; exalt. [<OF *trone* <L *thronus* <Gk. *thronos* seat]

throng (thrông, throng) *n.* **1** A multitude of people crowded closely together. **2** Any numerous collection. — *v.t.* **1** To crowd into and occupy fully; jam. **2** To press or crowd upon. — *v.i.* **3** To collect or move in a throng. See synonyms under JAM[1]. [OE *gethrang*]

Synonyms (noun): concourse, crowd, host, jam, mass, multitude, press. A *crowd* is a company of persons filling to excess the space they occupy and pressing inconveniently upon one another; the total number in a *crowd* may be great or small. *Throng* implies that the persons are numerous as well as pressed or pressing closely together; there may be a dense *crowd* in a small room, but there cannot be a *throng. Host* and *multitude* both imply vast numbers, but a *multitude* may be diffused over a great space so as to be nowhere a *crowd; host* is a military term, and properly denotes an assembly too orderly for crowding. *Concourse* signifies a spontaneous gathering of many persons moved by a common impulse, and suggests less massing and pressure than is indicated by the word *throng.* Compare ASSEMBLY, COMPANY.

throp·ple (throp′əl) *n. Scot.* & *Brit. Dial.* The windpipe or throttle.

thros·tle (thros′əl) *n.* **1** *Scot.* A thrush, as the song thrush. **2** A machine for twisting and winding fibers from roves. [OE. Related to THRUSH[1].]

throt·tle (throt′l) *n.* **1** The throat or windpipe. **2** *Mech.* A valve controlling the supply of steam to a steam engine, or of vaporized fuel to the cylinders of an internal-combustion engine: also **throttle valve. 3** The lever which operates the throttle valve: also **throttle lever.** — *v.t.* **·tled, ·tling** **1** To press or constrict the windpipe or throat of; strangle; choke or suffocate. **2** To silence, stop, or suppress by or as by choking. **3** To reduce or shut off the flow of (steam, or fuel in an internal-combustion engine). **4** To reduce the speed of by means of a throttle; slow down. — *v.i.* **5** To suffocate; choke. [Dim. of ME *throte* throat] — **throt′tler** *n.*

through (thro͞o) *prep.* **1** From end to end, side to side, or limit to limit of; into at one side, end, or point, and out of at another. **2** Covering, entering, or penetrating all parts of; throughout; also, over the surface of. **3** From the first to the last of; during the time or period of. **4** In the midst of; here and there upon or in. **5** By way of: He departed *through* the door. **6** By means of; by the instrumentality or aid of. **7** Having reached the end of, especially with success: He got *through* his examinations easily. **8** On account of; because or as a result of. See synonyms under BY. — *adv.* **1** From one end, side, surface, etc., to or beyond another. **2** From beginning to end. **3** To a termination or conclusion, especially a successful one: to pull *through.* **4** Completely; entirely: He is wet *through.* — **through and through** Thoroughly; completely. — *adj.* **1** Going from beginning to end without stops or with very few stops, and without reshipment or change: a *through* train; also, pertaining to or serving an entire distance or route: a *through* ticket. **2** Extending from one side or surface to another. **3** Unobstructed; open; clear: a *through* road. **4** Arrived at an end; finished: Are you *through* with my pen? **5** At the end of all relations or dealings: He is *through* with his old friends. Also spelled *thru.* [OE *thurh*]

through·ith·er (thro͞o′ith′ər) *Scot. adj.* Disorderly; harum-scarum. — *adv.* Pell-mell. Also **through′-oth′er** (-uth′ər), **throu·ther** (thro͞o′thər).

through·ly (thro͞o′lē) *adv. Archaic* Thoroughly.

through·out (thro͞o·out′) *adv.* Through or in every part: The house was searched *throughout.* — *prep.* All through; everywhere in: *throughout* the nation.

through·put (thro͞o′po͝ot′) *n.* The quantity of raw materials which may be processed for intended final use in a given time, as in an oil refinery or a chemical plant.

throve (thrōv) Past tense of THRIVE.

throw (thrō) *v.* **threw** (thro͞o), **thrown, throw·ing** *v.t.* **1** To propel through the air by means of a sudden straightening or whirling of the arm. **2** To propel or hurl: The mortar *threw* shells into the town. **3** To put hastily or carelessly: He *threw* a coat over his shoulders. **4** To direct or project (light, shadow, a glance, etc.). **5** To bring to a specified condition or state by or as by throwing: to *throw* the enemy into a panic. **6** To cause to fall; overthrow: The horse *threw* its rider. **7** In wrestling, to force the shoulders of (an opponent) to the ground. **8** To cast (dice). **9** To make (a specified cast) with dice. **10** To cast off or shed; lose: The horse *threw* a shoe. **11** *Colloq.* To lose purposely, as a race. **12** To give birth to (young): said of domestic animals. **13** To move, as a lever or switch, in connecting or disconnecting a circuit, mechanism, etc.; also, to connect or disconnect in this manner. **14** *Slang* To give (a party, etc.). **15** In card games, to play or discard. **16** In ceramics, to shape on a potter's wheel. **17** To spin (filaments, as of silk) into thread. — *v.i.* **18** To cast or fling something. — **to throw away** **1** To cast off; discard. **2** To waste; squander. — **to throw back** To revert to ancestral characteristics. — **to throw cold water on** To discourage. — **to throw in** **1** To cause (gears or a clutch) to mesh or engage. **2** To contribute; add. **3** To join with others. — **to throw off** **1** To cast aside; reject; spurn. **2** To rid oneself of. **3** To do or utter in an offhand manner. **4** To disconnect, as a machine; release. — **to throw oneself at** To strive to gain the affections or love of. — **to throw oneself into** To engage or take part in vigorously. — **to throw oneself on** (or **upon**) To entrust oneself to; rely on. — **to throw open** **1** To open suddenly or completely, as a door. **2** To free from restrictions or

obstacles. **—to throw out 1** To put forth; emit. **2** To cast out or aside; discard; reject. **3** To utter as if accidentally: to *throw out* hints. **4** In baseball, to retire (a runner) by throwing the ball to the base toward which he is advancing. **—to throw over 1** To overturn. **2** To discard. **—to throw together** To put together hastily or roughly. **—to throw up 1** To erect hastily. **2** To give up; relinquish. **3** To vomit. **4** *Colloq.* To mention or repeat, as a fault or taunt. *—n.* **1** An act of throwing or hurling; a cast; fling. **2** The distance over which a missile may be thrown: a stone's *throw.* **3** A cast of dice, or the resulting number; hence, a hazard; venture. **4** *Mech.* **a** The radius of the circle described by a crank, cam, or the like. **b** The travel or extent of reciprocating motion obtainable, as from a crank, piston, slide valve, etc. **5** A scarf used for draping an easel or picture frame; also, a woman's scarf or boa. **6** *Geol.* **a** A faulting, or dislocation of rock strata. **b** The amount of vertical displacement produced by dislocation of strata. **7** The sudden fluctuation of a magnetic needle when the force is suddenly changed. **8** The distance from a motion-picture projector to the screen. **9** In wrestling, a flooring of one's opponent so that both his shoulders touch the mat simultaneously for ten seconds. ◆ Homophone: *throe.* [OE *thrāwan* turn, twist, curl] **—throw′er** *n.*

throw·back (thrō′bak′) *n.* **1** *Biol.* **a** Reversion to an earlier ancestral or primitive type, phase, or condition of physical being or development. **b** An example of such reversion. **2** Anything returned for revision, correction, redirection, etc.

throw·ster (thrō′stər) *n.* **1** A thrower of dice; gamester. **2** One who throws silk.

thru (thrōō) See THROUGH.

thrum[1] (thrum) *v.* **thrummed, thrum·ming** *v.t.* **1** To play on or finger (a stringed instrument) idly and without expression. **2** To drum or tap monotonously or listlessly. **3** To recite or repeat in a droning, monotonous way. *—v.i.* **4** To thrum a stringed instrument. **5** To sound when played thus, as a guitar. **6** *Scot.* To purr. *—n.* Any monotonous drumming. [Prob. imit.]

thrum[2] (thrum) *n.* **1** The fringe of warp threads remaining on a loom beam after the web has been cut off; also, one of such threads. **2** Any loose thread or fringe, or a tuft of filaments or fibers; a tassel. **3** *pl.* Coarse or waste yarn. **4** *pl. Naut.* Bits of rope yarn for sewing on canvas to make chafing gear or collision mats. **5** *Bot.* A threadlike organ or part of a flower; stamen. **6** *Scot.* A bit; particle: I don't care a *thrum.* **7** *Scot.* A tangle. *—v.t.* **thrummed, thrum·ming. 1** To cover or trim with thrums or similar appendages. **2** *Naut.* To insert bits of rope yarn in (canvas) to produce a rough surface or mat to be used to prevent chafing. [OE *-thrum* ligament, as in *tungethrum* the ligament of the tongue]

thrum·my (thrum′ē) *adj.* **·mi·er, ·mi·est** Made of or with thrums or resembling a thrum; shaggy; rough.

thrush[1] (thrush) *n.* Any one of many migratory, passerine birds of the family *Turdidae,* having typically a long and slightly graduated tail, long wings, and spotted under parts. The robin, **hermit thrush** *(Hylocichla guttata),* **wood thrush** *(H. mustelina),* and the European **song thrush** *(Turdus philomelus)* are examples. ◆ Collateral adjective: *turdine.* [OE *thrysce*]

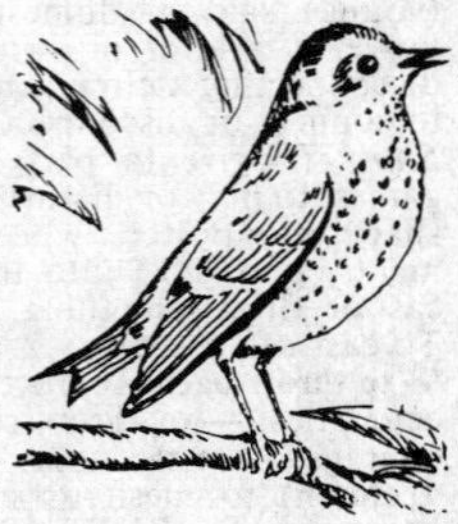

WOOD THRUSH
(To 8 1/2 inches in length)

thrush[2] (thrush) *n.* **1** *Pathol.* A vesicular disease of the mouth, lips, and throat caused by a fungus *(Monilia albicans)*: generally confined to infants. **2** A disease of a horse's foot characterized by suppuration. Also called *sprue.* [Cf. Dan. *tröske,* Sw. *trosk* a mouth disease]

thrust (thrust) *v.* **thrust, thrust·ing** *v.t.* **1** To push or shove with force or sudden impulse. **2** To pierce with a sudden forward motion; stab, as with a sword or dagger. **3** To interpose; put in. *—v.i.* **4** To make a sudden push or thrust. **5** To force oneself on or ahead; push one's way; crowd: with *through, into, on,* etc. See synonyms under DRIVE, PUSH. *—n.* **1** A sudden and forcible push, especially with a long, pointed weapon: distinguished from *cut.* **2** A vigorous attack; sharp onset. **3** *Engin.* A stress or strain tending to push a member of a structure outward or sidewise: the *thrust* of an arch. **4** The driving force exerted by certain propulsive devices, as a jet or rocket engine, an airplane's or ship's propeller, etc. **5** Salient force or meaning: the *thrust* of his remarks. **6** *Geol.* A rock fault due to horizontal compression; also, the plane of such a fault. [<ON *thrȳsta*] **—thrust′er** *n.*

thrust fault *Geol.* A fault resulting from horizontal compression in which the hanging wall appears to have moved upward, with a corresponding shortening of the entire rock mass: opposed to *gravity fault.* Also called *reverse fault.*

thru·way (thrōō′wā′) *n.* A long-distance express highway.

Thu·cyd·i·des (thōō·sid′ə·dēz, thyōō-), 471?–399? B.C., Athenian statesman and historian. **—Thu·cyd′i·de′an** (-dē′ən) *adj.*

thud (thud) *n.* A dull, heavy sound, as of a hard body striking upon a comparatively soft one; also, the blow causing such a sound; a thump. *—v.i.* **thud·ded, thud·ding** To make a thud. [OE *thyddan* strike, thrust, press]

thug (thug) *n.* **1** Formerly, one of an organization of religious, professional assassins in northern India. **2** Any cutthroat or ruffian. [<Hind. *thag* <Skt. *sthaga* swindler] **—thug′ger·y** *n.* **—thug′gish** *adj.*

thug·gee (thug′ē) *n.* The system of secret assassination formerly practiced by thugs in India.[<Hind. *thagī*]

thu·ja (thōō′jə) *n.* Any of a genus *(Thuja)* of evergreen trees and shrubs of the pine family, including the arborvitae, source of the medicinal **oil of thuja.** Also spelled *thuya.* [<NL <Gk. *thyia,* an African tree]

Thu·le (thōō′lē, tōō′-) **1** In ancient geography, the northernmost limit of the habitable world: identified with Iceland or Mainland in the Shetland Islands. See ULTIMA THULE. **2** A settlement in NW Greenland; site of a major United States military installation.

thu·li·a (thōō′lē·ə) *n. Chem.* Oxide of thulium, Tm_2O_3, found in samarskite. [<THULIUM]

thu·li·um (thōō lē·əm) *n.* A soft, silvery-gray metallic element (symbol Tm, atomic number 69), the least abundant of the lanthanide series. See PERIODIC TABLE. [from THULE]

thumb (thum) *n.* **1** The inner digit of a limb when set apart from and apposable to the other fingers; especially, the short, thick digit on the radial side of the human hand; the pollex. **2** *Ornithol.* The first radial digit of the wing of certain birds. **3** The division in a glove or mitten that covers the thumb. **4** *Archit.* An ovolo. **—all thumbs** *Colloq.* Clumsy with the hands; not deft. **—thumbs down** A sign of negation or disapproval. **—under one's thumb** Under one's influence or power. *—v.t.* **1** To press, rub, soil, or wear with the thumb in handling, as the pages of a book. **2** To perform with or as with the thumbs; hence, to do or handle clumsily. **3** To run through the pages of (a book, manuscript, etc.,) rapidly and perfunctorily. **4** To solicit or obtain (a ride) in an automobile by standing by the road and indicating with the thumb the direction one wishes to go; also, to make (one's way) thus: He *thumbed* his way to New York. [OE *thūma*]

thumb-in·dex (thum′in′deks) *v.t.* To provide with a thumb index.

thumb index A series of scalloped indentations cut along the right-hand edge of a book and labeled to indicate its various sections.

thumb·kin (thum′kin) *n.* A thumbscrew or pair of thumbscrews.

thumb·ling (thum′ling) *n.* A diminutive being; dwarf. Compare FINGERLING.

thumb·nail (thum′nāl′) *n.* **1** The nail of the thumb. **2** Anything as small and essentially complete as a thumbnail. *—adj.* Small and essentially complete: a *thumbnail* sketch.

thumb·nut (thum′nut′) *n.* A threaded nut having one or more wings or projections for screwing by the thumb and fingers; wing-nut. See illustration under NUT.

thumb·print (thum′print′) *n.* An impression or print made by the thumb.

thumb·screw (thum′skrōō′) *n.* **1** A screw to be turned by thumb and fingers. See illustration under SCREW. **2** An instrument of torture for compressing the thumb or thumbs.

thumb·stall (thum′stôl) *n.* A covering or sheath, as of leather, for the thumb.

thumb·tack (thum′tak′) *n.* A broad-headed tack that may be pushed in with the thumb.

Thum·mim (thum′im) See under URIM.

thump (thump) *n.* A blow with a blunt or heavy object; also, the sound made by such a blow; a dull thud. See synonyms under BLOW. *—v.t.* **1** To beat or strike so as to make a heavy thud or thuds. **2** *Colloq.* To beat or defeat severely. *—v.i.* **3** To strike with a thump. **4** To make a thump or thumps; pound or throb. [Imit.] **—thump′er** *n.*

thump·ing (thum′ping) *adj.* **1** That thumps. **2** *Colloq.* Huge; whopping.

thumps (thumps) *n. pl.* **1** Hiccups in a horse. **2** A lung disease in swine, caused by infestation with the larvae of a roundworm (genus *Ascaris*). [<THUMP; from the sound of the contractions of the diaphragm]

Thun (tōōn) A town on the Aar river in central Switzerland. *French* **Thoune** (tōōn).

Thun (tōōn), **Lake of** An expansion of the Aar river in central Switzerland; 10 miles long; 18 square miles. *German* **Thu·ner·see** (tōō′nər·zā).

thun·der (thun′dər) *n.* **1** The sound that accompanies lightning, caused by the sudden heating and expansion of the air along the path of the lightning flash. **2** Any loud, rumbling or booming noise, suggestive of thunder. **3** An awful denunciation or threat; a vehement or powerful utterance, oratorical or other. **4** *Rare* A lightning stroke; thunderbolt. **—to steal one's thunder** To take for one's own use anything especially popular or effective originated by another: said especially of an argument. *—v.i.* **1** To give forth a peal or peals of thunder: used impersonally: It *thunders.* **2** To make a noise like thunder. **3** To utter vehement denunciations or threats. *—v.t.* **4** To utter or express with a noise like or suggestive of thunder: The cannon *thundered* defiance. [OE *thunor*] **—thun′der·er** *n.*

thun·der·a·tion (thun′də·rā′shən) *interj.* & *n. Slang* Damnation: a euphemism. [<THUNDER + (DAMN)ATION]

thun·der·bird (thun′dər·bûrd′) *n.* An enormous bird believed to produce thunder by flapping its wings, lightning by opening and closing its eyes, and rain by allowing a huge lake to run off its back: common to the folklore of the North American Indians of the Plains and the Canadian forests.

thun·der·bolt (thun′dər·bōlt′) *n.* **1** One electric discharge accompanied by a clap of thunder: formerly conceived of as a molten ball or bolt hurled by the lightning flash. **2** Any person or thing acting with or as with the force and speed or destructiveness of lightning.

thun·der·clap (thun′dər·klap′) *n.* **1** A sharp, violent detonation of thunder. **2** Anything having the violence or suddenness of a clap of thunder.

thun·der·cloud (thun′dər·kloud′) *n.* A dark, heavy mass of cloud highly charged with electricity.

thun·der·head (thun′dər·hed′) *n.* A rounded mass of cumulus cloud, either silvery-white or dark with silvery edges, often developing into a thundercloud.

thun·der·ing (thun′dər·ing) *adj.* **1** Giving forth, or accompanied by, thunder. **2** Unusually great or extreme; superlative.

thun·der·ous (thun′dər·əs) *adj.* Producing or emitting thunder or a sound like thunder. Also **thun′drous** (-drəs). **—thun′der·ous·ly** *adv.*

thun·der·peal (thun′dər·pēl′) *n.* A clap of thunder.

thun·der·show·er (thun′dər·shou′ər) *n.* A shower of rain with thunder and ightning.

thunder snake The house snake: so called because forced out of its hole by heavy rain.

thun·der·squall (thun′dər·skwôl′) *n.* A squall accompanied by thunder.

thun·der·stone (thun′dər·stōn′) *n.* **1** *Archaic* A thunderbolt. **2** A stone or rock supposed to have accompanied a thunderbolt. **3** A belemnite.

thun·der·storm (thun′dər·stôrm′) *n.* A local storm accompanied by lightning and thunder.

thun·der·stroke (thun′dər·strōk′) *n.* A stroke of lightning.

thun·der·struck (thun′dər·struk′) *adj.* **1** Struck by lightning. **2** Amazed, astonished, or confounded, as with fear, surprise, or the like. Also **thun′der·strick′en** (-strik′ən).

thun·der·y (thun′dər·ē) *adj. Colloq.* Thunderous; indicative of, or accompanied by thunder.

Thur·ber (thûr′bər), **James Grover,** 1894–1961, U.S. humorous artist and writer.

thu·ri·ble (thoor′ə·bəl) *n.* A censer. [< L *thuribulum* < *thus, thuris* frankincense]

thu·ri·fer (thoor′ə·fər) *n.* A censer-bearer; an acolyte or altar boy who carries a thurible. [< L < *thus, thuris* frankincense + *ferre* bear, carry]

thu·rif·er·ous (thoo·rif′ər·əs) *adj.* Yielding or bearing incense.

Thu·rin·gi·a (thoo·rin′jē·ə, -jə) A former state of central Germany in southwestern East Germany; 6,022 square miles; capital, Weimar; formerly a region of central Germany including several duchies and principalities. *German* **Thü·rin·gen** (tü′ring·ən).

Thu·rin·gi·an (thoo·rin′jē·ən) *adj.* **1** Of or relating to Thuringia or its inhabitants. **2** *Geol.* Denoting the upper division of the Permian in Europe. —*n.* **1** One of an ancient Teutonic tribe which occupied a kingdom in central Germany until the sixth century, when they were conquered by the Franks. **2** A citizen or inhabitant of modern Thuringia.

Thuringian Forest A wooded mountain range of central Germany; highest point, 3,222 feet. *German* **Thü·ring·er Wald** (tü′ring·ər vält).

Thurs·day (thûrz′dē, -dā) *n.* The fifth day of the week. [Fusion of OE *Thunres dæg* day of Thunor and ON *Thōrsdagr* day of Thor; trans. of LL *dies Jovis* day of Jove]

Thursday Island An island of NE Australia in Torres Strait, comprising a municipality of Queensland; 1½ miles long, 1 mile wide.

thus (thus) *adv.* **1** In this or that or the following way or manner. **2** To such degree or extent; so: *thus far.* **3** In these circumstances or conditions; in this case; therefore. [OE]

thu·ya (thoo′yə) See THUJA.

thwack (thwak) *v.t.* To strike with something flat; whack. —*n.* A blow with some flat or blunt instrument. [Prob. *thwack* smack; infl. in form by *whack*] —**thwack′er** *n.*

thwart (thwôrt) *v.t.* **1** To prevent the accomplishment of, as by interposing an obstacle; also, to prevent (one) from accomplishing something; foil; frustrate; balk. **2** *Obs.* To move or place over or across. See synonyms under BAFFLE, HINDER¹. —*n.* An oarsman's seat extending athwart a boat. —*adj.* **1** Lying, moving, or extending across something; transverse. **2** *Obs.* Perverse or cross-grained; ill-natured. —*adv. & prep.* Athwart. [< ON *thvert,* neut. of *thverr* transverse] —**thwart′er** *n.*

Thwing (twing), **Charles Franklin,** 1853–1937, U.S. educator.

thy (thī) *pronominal adj.* The possessive case of the pronoun *thou* used attributively; belonging or pertaining to thee: *Thy* kingdom come. [Apocopated var. of THINE]

Thy·es·te·an banquet (thī·es′tē·ən) A cannibal feast: so called from the feast at which Thyestes was served his own sons. See ATREUS.

Thy·es·tes (thī·es′tēz) In Greek legend, son of Pelops and brother of Atreus. —**Thy·es′te·an, Thy·es′ti·an** *adj.*

thy·la·cine (thī′lə·sīn, -sin) *n.* A nearly extinct, carnivorous, doglike marsupial (*Thylacinus cynocephalus*) of Tasmania, grayish-brown with dark transverse bands on the hinder part of the back: also called Tasmanian wolf, zebra wolf. [< NL < Gk. *thylax, thylakos* pouch]

THYLACINE
(About 18 inches high at
the shoulder)

thyme (tīm) *n.* Any of a genus (*Thymus*) of small shrubby plants of the mint family, having aromatic leaves and cultivated for seasoning in cookery; especially, the **wild thyme** (*T. serpyllum*). [< F *thym* < L *thymum* < Gk. *thymon*] —**thym′y** *adj.*

thym·e·la·e·a·ceous (thim′ə·lē·ā′shəs) *adj. Bot.* Designating a family (*Thymelaeaceae*) of apetalous trees or shrubs having very tough bark; the mezereon family. [< NL, family name < L *thymelaea* < Gk. *thymelaia* < *thymon* thyme + *elaia* olive tree]

thym·ic¹ (tī′mik) *adj.* Pertaining to or derived from thyme.

thy·mic² (thī′mik) *adj.* Of, pertaining to, or derived from the thymus.

thy·mol (tī′mōl, -mol, thī′-) *n. Chem.* A crystalline compound, $C_{10}H_{13}OH$, contained in certain volatile oils, as those of thyme and horsemint, and also made synthetically: used as an antiseptic. [< THYME + -OL²]

thymol iodide *Chem.* A reddish-brown mixture of iodine derivatives and thymol, used as a deodorant and antiseptic.

thy·mus (thī′məs) *n. Anat.* A lymphoid organ of glandular character and unknown function, developed in the region of the neck in many vertebrates. In man and other mammals it lies at the root of the neck, just above the heart, and is most prominent in the young. It is the neck sweetbread of calves and lambs. [< NL < Gk. *thymos*]

thy·re·oid (thī′rē·oid) *adj.* Thyroid.

thyro- *combining form Med & Surg.* The thyroid; of or related to the thyroid: *thyrotropin.* Also, before vowels, **thyr-.** Also **thyreo-.** [< Gk. *thyreoeidēs* thyroid]

thy·ro·hy·oid (thī′rō·hī′oid) *adj. Anat.* Having a relationship to the thyroid gland and the hyoid bone: the *thyrohyoid* ligament. See illustration under LARYNX. [< THYRO- + HYOID]

thy·roid (thī′roid) *adj.* **1** Relating or pertaining to the thyroid cartilage or the thyroid gland. **2** Shaped like a shield; also, having a shield-shaped marking. —*n.* **1** The thyroid cartilage or gland. **2** The dried and powdered thyroid gland of certain domesticated food animals, used in the treatment of myxedema, goiter, obesity, and other disorders. [< Gk. *thyreoeidēs* shield-shaped < *thyreos* large shield + *eidos* form]

thyroid cartilage *Anat.* The largest cartilage of the larynx, composed of two blades whose juncture in front forms the Adam's apple.

thy·roid·ec·to·my (thī′roid·ek′tə·mē) *n. Surg.* Excision of the thyroid gland. [< THYROID + -ECTOMY]

thyroid gland *Anat.* A bilobate endocrine gland situated in front of and on each side of the trachea, close to the larynx. It secretes thyroxin, vitally important in growth and in the prevention of such disorders as goiter, cretinism, etc.

thy·roid·i·tis (thī′roid·ī′tis) *n. Pathol.* Inflammation of the thyroid gland.

thy·ro·tox·i·co·sis (thī′rō·tok′sə·kō′sis) *n. Pathol.* A morbid or diseased condition resulting from excessive activity of the thyroid gland, as in exophthalmic goiter. [< THYRO- + TOXICOSIS] —**thy′ro·tox′ic** (-tok′sik) *adj.*

thy·rot·ro·pin (thī·rot′rə·pin) *n. Biochem.* A hormone from the anterior lobe of the pituitary gland, regarded as having an affinity for the thyroid gland. [< THYRO- + -TROP(E) + -IN]

thy·rox·in (thī·rok′sin) *n. Biochem.* A white, odorless, crystalline compound, $C_{15}H_{11}O_4NI_4$, obtained as the hormone of the thyroid gland and also made synthetically: used in the treatment of thyroid disorders. Also **thy·rox′ine** (-sēn, -sin). [< THYR(O)- + OXY- + -IN] —**thy·rox·in·ic** (thī′rok·sin′ik) *adj.*

thyr·soid (thûr′soid) *adj. Bot.* Resembling or shaped like a thyrsus. Also **thyr·soi·dal** (thûr·soid′l).

thyr·sus (thûr′səs) *n. pl.* **·si** (-sī) **1** A staff wreathed in ivy and crowned with a pine cone or a bunch of ivy leaves with grapes or berries: an attribute of Dionysus and the satyrs. **2** *Bot.* A branched panicle in which the middle branches are longer than those above or below them, as in the lilac and grape. [< L *thyrsos*]

thy·sa·nu·ran (thī′sə·noor′ən, -nyoor′-, this′ə-) *adj.* Designating or belonging to an order (*Thysanura*) of primitive wingless insects, including

the silverfish and the firebrat. —*n.* One of the *Thysanura.* [< NL, name of the order < Gk. *thysanos* fringe + *oura* tail] —**thy′sa·nu′rous** *adj.*

thy·self (thī·self′) *pron.* Emphatic or reflexive form of the second person singular pronouns *thee* and *thou:* I love thee for *thyself.*

Thys·sen (tis′ən), **Fritz,** 1873–1951, German industrialist.

ti¹ (tē) *n. Music* In solmization, a syllable representing the seventh note of the diatonic scale: formerly called *si.* [See GAMUT.]

ti² (tē) *n.* One of several Asian trees (genus *Cordyline*) of the lily family, especially the **ti palm** (*C. terminalis*) of eastern Asia, having many foliage forms. [< Polynesian]

Ti *Chem.* Titanium (symbol Ti).

Ti·a Jua·na (tē′ə wä′nə) See TIJUANA.

ti·ar·a (tī·âr′ə, tē·är′ə, -ar′ə) *n.* **1** The pope's triple crown, emblematic of his claim to spiritual and temporal authority; hence, the papal dignity. Compare MITER. **2** The upright headdress worn by the ancient Persian kings. **3** A coronet or form of headdress denoting princely rank; also, anything in imitation of it worn for personal adornment. **4** A Phrygian cap for men and women, long, conical, and falling over the brow: found in Greco-Roman art as the attribute of Paris, Mithras, and others. [< L < Gk. *tiara* Persian headdress]

**PAPAL
TIARA**

Tib·bett (tib′it), **Lawrence,** 1896–1960, U.S. baritone.

Ti·ber (tī′bər) A river of central Italy, flowing 251 miles south from the Apennines through Rome to the Tyrrhenian Sea, SE of Rome: Italian *Tevere.*

Ti·be·ri·as (tī·bir′ē·əs), **Lake** See GALILEE, SEA OF.

Ti·be·ri·us (tī·bir′ē·əs), 42 B.C.–A.D. 37, second emperor of Rome, A.D. 14–37: full name Tiberius Claudius Nero Caesar.

Ti·bes·ti Massif (ti·bes′tē) The highest mountain group of the Sahara and of western equatorial Africa, lying mostly in NW Chad, partly in Libya and in Niger; highest point, 11,204 feet.

Ti·bet (ti·bet′) A former independent theocracy of central Asia, south of the Sinkiang-Uigur Autonomous Region, China, and north of India, Nepal, Sikkim, and Bhutan; incorporated, 1950–1957, in China, as the **Tibetan Autonomous Region**; about 470,000 square miles; capital, Lhasa: Chinese *Sitsang:* also *Thibet.* Tibetan **Pö** (pœ).

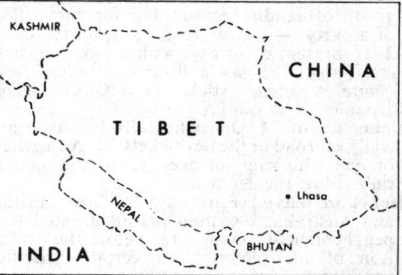

Ti·bet·an (ti·bet′n) *adj.* Of or pertaining to Tibet, the Tibetans, or to their language, religion, or customs. —*n.* **1** One of the native Mongoloid people of Tibet, now intermixed with Chinese and various peoples of India. **2** The Sino-Tibetan language of Tibet. Also spelled *Thibetan.*

Tibetan lion dog The Lhasa apso.

tib·i·a (tib′ē·ə) *n. pl.* **tib·i·ae** (tib′i·ē) or **tib·i·as** **1** *Anat.* The inner and larger of the two bones of the leg below the knee; the shin bone. See illustration under FOOT. **2** *Entomol.* The fourth or penultimate joint of the leg of an insect, between the femur and the tarsus. **3** An ancient flute or pipe provided with holes

for the fingers, originally made of an animal's leg bone. [<L] — **tib′i·al** *adj.*

Ti·bul·lus (ti-bul′əs), **Albius**, 54?–18 B.C., Roman elegiac poet.

Ti·bur (tī′bər) Ancient name of TIVOLI.

tic (tik) *n.* **1** An involuntary spasm or twitching of muscles, usually of the face and sometimes of neurotic origin. **2** Tic douloureux. [<F]

ti·cal (ti-käl′, -kôl′, tē′kəl) *n.* **1** The former name for the baht, a Thai unit of currency. **2** A Thai unit of weight, equivalent to about half an ounce: also called *baht.* [<Malay *tikal*]

tic dou·lou·reux (tik dōō′lōō-rōō′, *Fr.* tēk′ dōō·lōō·rœ′) *Pathol.* An acutely painful neuralgia of the face with paroxysmal muscular twitchings. [<F, painful tic]

Ti·ci·no (tē-chē′nō) A river of Switzerland and Italy, flowing 150 miles south through Lake Maggiore to the Po below Pavia. Ancient **Ti·ci·nus** (ti-sī′nəs).

tick¹ (tik) *n.* **1** A light recurring sound made by a watch, clock, or similar mechanism. **2** *Brit. Colloq.* The length of time occupied by one tick of a watch or clock: I'll be through in five *ticks.* **3** A mark, as a dot or dash, used in checking off something. — *v.i.* To make or sound a tick or ticks; make a recurrent clicking sound, as a running watch or clock. — *v.t. Brit.* To mark or check with ticks. — **to tick off** *Brit. Colloq.* To tell off. [Prob. imit.]

tick² (tik) *n.* **1** One of numerous flat, leathery, bloodsucking arachnids (order *Acarida*) that attack the skin of man and other animals; especially, the **cattle tick** (*Margaropus annulatus*), causative agent of Texas fever. **2** Any of certain two-winged or wingless parasitic insects (family *Hippoboscidae*), as the **sheep ticks** and **bat ticks.** [Cf. LG *tieke*, G *zecke* a tick]

tick³ (tik) *n.* **1** The stout outer covering of a mattress; also, the material for such covering. **2** *Colloq.* Ticking. [Earlier *teke, tyke*, ult. <L *teca, theca* <Gk. *thēke* a case]

tick⁴ (tik) *n. Brit. Colloq.* Credit; trust: to buy something on *tick.* [Short for TICKET]

tick·er (tik′ər) *n.* **1** One who or that which ticks. **2** A telegraphic receiving instrument which records stock quotations on a paper ribbon (**ticker tape**). **3** *Slang* A watch. **4** *Slang* The heart.

tick·et (tik′it) *n.* **1** A note or notice; a memorandum; also, a slip of paper containing a notice or memorandum. **2** A card with words or characters on it showing that the holder is entitled to something, as transportation in a public vehicle, admission to a theater, or the like. **3** A certificate or license, as of an airplane pilot or the captain of a ship. **4** A label or tag for attachment or identification. **5 a** A list of candidates of a single party on a ballot: the Democratic *ticket.* **b** The group of candidates running for the offices of a party. — *v.t.* **1** To fix a ticket to; label. **2** To present or furnish with a ticket or tickets. [<MF *etiquet* a little note <OF *estiquette* < *estiquer* stick, fix <OLG *stekan.* Doublet of ETIQUETTE.]

ticket agent 1 One who sells tickets, especially railroad or theater tickets. **2** An agency, or one who runs an agency, for the sale of railroad or theater tickets.

ticket of leave Formerly, in Great Britain and Australia, a written permit granted to a penal convict to be at large before the expiration of his sentence on certain specified conditions.

tick fever Any of several fevers caused by ticks, especially the Texas fever of cattle, and Rocky Mountain spotted fever, transmitted to man by the bite of a wood tick.

tick·ing (tik′ing) *n.* A strong, closely woven cotton or linen fabric: used for mattress covering, awnings, etc. [<TICK³ + -ING¹]

tick·le (tik′əl) *v.* **·led, ·ling** *v.t.* **1** To excite the nerves of by touching or scratching on some sensitive spot, producing a thrilling sensation resulting in spasmodic laughter or twitching; titillate. **2** To arouse or excite agreeably; please: Compliments *tickle* our vanity. **3** To amuse or entertain; delight. **4** To move, stir, or get by or as by tickling. — *v.i.* **5** To have or experience a thrilling or tingling sensation: My foot *tickles.* — *n.* The sensation produced by tickling; titillation; also, the

touch or action producing such sensation. [ME *tikelen,* ? metathetic var. of ON *kitla* tickle]

tick·le-grass (tik′əl·gras′, -gräs′) *n.* Rough bent grass (*Agrostis hiemalis*).

tick·ler (tik′lər) *n.* **1** One who or that which tickles. **2** A memorandum book or file, as of bills receivable, notes due, etc.

tickler coil In radio, a coil of the regenerative type coupled in series with the plate circuit and employed to intensify sound on a receiving circuit by means of a feedback action.

tick·lish (tik′lish) *adj.* **1** Sensitive to tickling. **2** Liable to be upset; unstable; also, easily offended; sensitive. **3** Attended with risk; difficult; delicate. — **tick′lish·ly** *adv.* — **tick′lish·ness** *n.*

Tick·nor (tik′nər), **George**, 1791–1871, U.S. historian and educator.

tick·seed (tik′sēd′) *n.* **1** The coreopsis. **2** The tick trefoil. [<TICK² + SEED]

tickseed sunflower A square-stemmed species of bur marigold (genus *Bidens*), with a panicle of large-rayed yellow flowers.

tick-tack (tik′tak′) *n.* **1** A recurrent sound like that of the ticking of a clock. **2** Anything that makes a tapping or rattling noise; specifically, a device for making a rattling noise against a window or door, worked from a distance: used in playing pranks. [Imit. reduplication of TICK¹]

tick-tack-toe (tik′tak·tō′) *n.* A game for two players, who alternately put circles or crosses in the spaces of a figure formed by two sets of parallel lines crossing at right angles. Each player tries to get a row of three circles or crosses before his opponent does.

tick-tock (tik′tok′) *n.* The oscillating sound of a clock. — *v.i.* To make this sound. [Imit.]

tick trefoil Any of several leguminous plants (genus *Desmodium*) whose leaves and pods cling to the coats of animals and to clothing. [<TICK² + TREFOIL]

tick·y tack·y (tik′ē tak′ē) *Slang* **1** Shoddy, inferior materials: rows of little houses built of *ticky tacky.* **2** Dull, tedious uniformity. — **tick′y-tack′y** *adj.*

Ti·con·der·o·ga (tī′kon·də·rō′gə) A town on Lake George in New York; site of **Fort Ticonderoga**, captured from the French in 1759 and from the British by the American revolutionists in 1775.

tid·al (tīd′l) *adj.* **1** Of, pertaining to, or influenced by the tides; periodically flowing and ebbing: a *tidal* river. **2** Dependent on the rise of the tide as to time of starting or leaving: a *tidal* steamship.

tidal wave 1 Any great incoming rise of waters along a shore, caused by windstorms at sea or by excessively high tides. **2** A tsunami. **3** A great movement in popular feeling or in the affairs of men.

tid·bit (tid′bit′) *n.* A choice bit, as of food. Also, *Brit., titbit.* [< dial. E *tid* a small object + BIT¹]

tid·dle·dy-winks (tid′l-dē-wingks′) *n.* A game in which the players attempt to snap little disks of bone, ivory, or the like, from a plane surface into a cup. Also **tid′dly-winks′** (tid′lē-). [Prob. < *tiddly,* a child's word for *little*]

tide¹ (tīd) *n.* **1** The periodic rise and fall of the surface of the ocean, and of the waters connected with the ocean, caused by the attraction of moon and sun. In each lunar day of 24 hours and 51 minutes there are two high tides and two low tides, alternating at equal intervals of flood and ebb. **Spring tides** are high tides above the average, occurring when the moon is new or full; **neap tides** are high tides below the average, occurring when the moon is in the first or third quarter. See FLOOD, EBB. **2** Anything that comes like the tide at flood; the time at which something is most flourishing. **3** The natural drift or tendency of events; also, a current; stream. **4** Season; time; especially, a season of the ecclesiastical year: used chiefly in composition and in the phrase *time and tide*: Christmastide. **5** *Archaic* A suitable or favorable occasion; opportunity. See synonyms under STREAM. — *v.* **tid·ed,** **tid·ing** *v.i.* **1** To ebb and flow like the tide. **2** To float with the tide. — *v.t.* **3** To carry or help like a boat buoyed up by the tide: Charity *tided* us over the depression. **4** To surmount; survive; endure, as a difficulty: with *over*: to *tide* over hard times. [OE *tīd* a period, season] — **tide′less** *adj.*

tide² (tīd) *v.i. Archaic* To betide; happen. [OE *tīdan*]

tide-land (tīd′land′) *n.* Land alternately covered and uncovered by the tide.

tide-rip (tīd′rip′) *n.* Riptide. [<TIDE¹ + RIP²]

tide-waiter (tīd′wā′tər) *n.* A customs officer who boards vessels entering port, to enforce customs regulations.

tide-wa·ter (tīd′wô′tər, -wot′ər) *n.* Water which inundates land at high tide; also, water affected by the tide on the seacoast or in a river; hence, loosely, the seacoast. — *adj.* Pertaining to the tidewater; also, situated on the seacoast: the *tidewater* country.

tide-way (tīd′wā′) *n.* A channel where the tide runs.

ti·dings (tī′dingz) *n. pl.* (sometimes construed as singular) A report or information; news. [OE *tīdung,* infl. in meaning by ON *tithindi* news, a message]

Synonyms: advice, information, intelligence, news. *News* is the most general of these words, signifying something that has either just happened or just become known. *Advices* are communications of fact by a trusted informant with the design of guiding or influencing the action of the recipient; the word signifies *news* with a practical purpose and value. *Intelligence* is *news* or *information,* often secret *information,* specifically communicated, usually in certain form. See NEWS.

ti·dy (tī′dē) *adj.* **·di·er, ·di·est 1** Marked by neatness and order; trim. **2** Of an orderly disposition. **3** *Colloq.* Moderately large; considerable: a *tidy* sum. **4** *Colloq.* Tolerable; fairly good. See synonyms under NEAT¹. — *v.t.* & *v.i.* **ti·died, ti·dy·ing** To make (things) tidy; put (things) in order. — *n. pl.* **·dies** A light, detachable covering, to protect the back or arms of a chair or sofa. [ME *tidi* <OE *tīd* time] — **ti′di·ly** *adv.* — **ti′di·ness** *n.*

ti·dy-tips (tī′dē-tips′) *n. pl.* **·tips** Any of a genus (*Layia*) of ornamental annual plants of California, having yellow flower heads tipped with white; especially, *L. elegans.*

tie (tī) *v.* **tied, ty·ing** *v.t.* **1** To fasten with cord, rope, etc., the ends of which are then drawn into a knot. **2** To draw the parts of together or into place by a cord or band fastened with a knot: to *tie* one's shoes. **3** To form (a knot). **4** To form a knot in, as string. **5** To fasten, attach, or join in any way. **6** To restrain or confine; restrict; bind. **7 a** To equal (a competitor) in score or achievement. **b** To equal (a competitor's score). **8** *Colloq.* To unite in marriage. **9** *Music* To unite by a tie. — *v.i.* **10** To make a tie or connection. **11** To make the same score; be equal. See synonyms under BIND. — **to tie down** To hinder; restrict. — **to tie up 1** To fasten with rope, string, etc. **2** To wrap, as with paper, and then fasten with string, cord, etc. **3** To moor (a vessel). **4** To block; hinder. **5** To have or be already committed, in use, etc., so as to be unavailable. — *n.* **1** A flexible bond or fastening secured by drawing the ends into a knot or loop. **2** Any bond or obligation, mental, moral, or legal: *ties* of affection. **3** An exact equality in number, as of a score, votes, etc.; hence, a contest which neither side wins; a draw. **4** Something that is tied or intended for tying, as a shoelace, necktie, or the like. **5** *Engin.* A structural member fastening parts together and receiving tensile stress: distinguished from a *strut.* **6** *Music* A curved line placed over or under two musical notes of the same pitch on the staff to make them represent one tone length. **7** *pl.* Low shoes fastened with lacings: Oxford *ties.* **8** One of a set of timbers laid crosswise on the ground as supports for railroad tracks. [OE *tīgan* bind < *tēah,* *tēag* a rope]

tie beam A timber that serves as a tie in a roof, etc.

Tie·bout (tē′bout) Dutch form of THEOBALD.

tie-dye (tī′dī′) *v.t.* **-dyed, -dye·ing** To create designs on fabric by tying parts of it in clumps that will not absorb the dye. — *n.* **1** The process of decorating fabrics by tie-dying. **2** Fabric so decorated; also, a design so made.

tie-in (tī′in′) *n.* Connection; association.

tie-in sale A sale in which the buyer, in order to get the article he wants, is required to buy a second article.

tie-man·nite (tē′mə-nīt) *n.* A metallic, steel-to lead-gray, opaque mercuric selenide, HgSe.

[<G *tiemannit,* after W. *Tiemann,* 19th c. German mineralogist, its discoverer]

Tien Shan (tyen′ shän′) A mountain chain of central Asia, chiefly in the Tadzhik S.S.R., Kirghiz S.S.R., and Sinkiang-Uigur Autonomous Region, China; highest point, 24,406 feet.

Tien·tsin (tin′tsin′, *Chinese* tyen′jin′) A port near the Gulf of Chihli, NE China; formerly included in Hopeh Province; since 1935, an independent municipality under direct control of the central government; the leading transportation and industrial center of northern China.

Tie·po·lo (tye′pō·lō), **Giovanni Battista,** 1696?–1770?, Venetian painter.

tier[1] (tir) *n.* A rank or row in a series of things placed one above another. —*v.t.* & *v.i.* To place or rise in tiers. ◆ Homophone: *tear.* [Earlier *tire* <OF, a sequence < *tirer* draw, elongate]

ti·er[2] (tī′ər) *n.* **1** One who or that which ties; also, that used for or in tying. **2** A child's apron.

tierce (tirs) *n.* **1** A former liquid measure equivalent in the United States to 42 wine gallons; a third of a pipe or butt. **2** A cask holding this amount, intermediate between a hogshead and a barrel. **3** In card games, a sequence of three cards of the same suit. **4** In fencing, the third standard position from which a guard, parry, or thrust can be made. **5** *Eccl.* The third canonical hour, nine a.m., or the office or service of that hour: often called *undernsong.* **6** *Music* An interval of a third. **7** A set of three. [<OF *tierce, terce* a third <L *tertia,* fem. of *tertius*]

Tier·ra del Fue·go (tyer′ä del fwā′gō) **1** An archipelago at the southern tip of South America, belonging to Chile and to Argentina; separated from the mainland by the Strait of Magellan; total, 27,476 square miles: 7,996 square miles in Argentina, the rest in Chile. **2** The largest island of the group; 18,000 square miles: 7,750 square miles in Argentina, the rest in Chile.

tiers é·tat (tyâr zā·tà′) *French* The third estate, especially in prerevolutionary France.

tie-up (tī′up′) *n.* **1** A situation, resulting from a strike, the breakdown of machinery, etc., in which further progress or operation is impossible: a *tie-up* in traffic. **2** *Dial.* The part of a barn where cows and oxen are kept.

tiff[1] (tif) *n.* **1** A peevish display of irritation; a pet; huff. **2** A light quarrel; a spat. —*v.i.* To be in or have a tiff. [Prob. imit.]

tiff[2] (tif) *Obs. n.* A small draft of liquor; a sip; drink. —*v.t.* To sip; taste. [Cf. ON *thefr* a smell, taste]

tiff[3] (tif) *v.i. Anglo-Indian* To take tiffin or lunch. [Back formation < *tiffing* TIFFIN]

tif·fa·ny (tif′ə·nē) *n. pl.* **·nies** **1** A very thin transparent cotton gauze. **2** Formerly, a very thin silk. [<OF *tifinie, tiphanie* Epiphany <LL *theophania* THEOPHANY; ? so called because its transparency manifests the wearer]

Tif·fa·ny (tif′ə·nē), **Charles Lewis,** 1812–1902, U. S. jeweler.

tif·fin (tif′ən) *Anglo-Indian n.* Midday luncheon. —*v.i.* To lunch; tiff. [Appar. < *tiffing,* ppr. of TIFF[2]]

Tif·lis (tif′lis, *Russian* tif·lēs′) The capital of Georgian S.S.R., on the Kura River: Georgian *Tbilisi.*

ti·ger (tī′gər) *n.* **1** A large carnivorous feline mammal (*Felis tigris*) of Asia, with vertical black wavy stripes on a tawny body and black bars or rings on the limbs and tail. **2** One of several other large ferocious animals, as the South American jaguar or the African leopard; also, the thylacine of Tasmania. **3** A fierce, cruel person. **4** *U.S.* An additional cheer or yell (often the word "tiger") given at the conclusion of a round of cheering. [<OF *tigre* <L *tigris* <Gk., ?< Avestan *tīghri* an arrow, a dart]

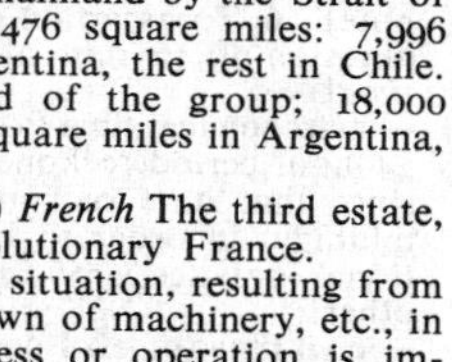

BENGAL TIGER
(About 6 1/2 feet long; tail, 3 feet)

tiger beetle Any of certain very active, predacious beetles (genus *Cicindela*) having spotted or striped wings, which dart upon their prey from a concealment. For illustration see INSECTS (beneficial).

tiger cat **1** A wildcat, resembling, but smaller than, the tiger, as the Asian **marbled tiger cat** (*Felis marmorata*), the African serval, the American ocelot, and the margay. **2** A domestic cat having striped markings.

ti·ger-eye (tī′gər·ī′) *n.* **1** A gemstone, usually the mineral crocidolite altered by oxidation, showing a beautiful chatoyant luster. One variety is called *hawk's-eye.* Also **ti′ger's-eye′.** **2** A tiger cat.

ti·ger·ish (tī′gər·ish) *adj.* Of, pertaining to, or resembling the tiger or its habits; predacious; bloodthirsty: also spelled *tigrish.*

tiger lily **1** A tall cultivated lily (*Lilium tigrinum*) from China, with nodding orange flowers spotted with black. **2** Any of various lilies with similar flowers, especially the leopard lily (*L. pardalinum*).

tiger moth A stout-bodied moth (family *Arctiidae*) with striped or spotted wings.

tight (tīt) *adj.* **1** So closely held together or constructed as to be impervious to fluids; not leaky: a *tight* roof; a *tight* vessel. **2** Firmly fixed or fastened in place; secure. **3** Fully stretched, so as not be slack; taut; tense: *tight* as a drum. **4** Strict; stringent: a *tight* schedule. **5** Fitting closely; especially, fitting too closely: said of a garment, shoe, cork, etc. **6** *Colloq.* Difficult to cope with; troublesome: a *tight* spot; a *tight* squeeze. **7** *Colloq.* Parsimonious; tight-fisted; close. **8** Characterized by a feeling of constriction: a *tight* cough. **9** *Slang* Drunk; intoxicated. **10** Evenly matched: said of a race or contest. **11** Difficult to obtain because of scarcity or financial restrictions: said of money or of commodities. **12** Straitened from lack of money or commodities: a *tight* market. **13** Yielding very little or no profit: said of a bargain. —*adv.* **1** Firmly; securely: Hold me *tight.* **2** Closely; with much constriction: The dress fits too *tight.* —**to sit tight** To remain firm in one's position; refrain from budging. [ME *thight,* appar. <Scand. Cf. ON *thēttr* dense.] —**tight′ly** *adv.* —**tight′ness** *n.*

-tight *combining form* Impervious to: *water-tight.*

tight·en (tīt′n) *v.t.* & *v.i.* To make or become tight or tighter. —**tight′en·er** *n.*

tight-fist·ed (tīt′fis′tid) *adj.* Stingy; parsimonious.

tight-lipped (tīt′lipt′) *adj.* Having the lips held tightly together; hence, unwilling to talk; reticent or secretive.

tight·rope (tīt′rōp′) *n.* A tightly stretched rope on which acrobats perform. —*adj.* Pertaining to or performing on a tightrope: a *tightrope* walker.

tights (tīts) *n. pl.* Skin-fitting garments, commonly for the legs and lower torso.

tight·wad (tīt′wod′) *n. U. S. Slang* A skinflint; miser. [<TIGHT + WAD[1]]

Tig·lath-pi·le·ser (tig′lath·pi·lē′zər, -pī-) Any of several Assyrian kings and conquerors; especially, Tiglath-pileser III, reigned 745–727 B.C.

tig·lic (tig′lik) *adj. Chem.* **1** Derived from croton oil. **2** Designating a white, crystalline, poisonous acid, $C_5H_8O_2$, contained as an ester in croton oil. Also **tig·lin·ic** (tig·lin′ik). [<NL (*Croton*) *tiglium* the croton oil plant, prob. ult. <Gk. *tilos* thin feces; so called because of its purgative properties]

Ti·gré (tē·grā′) *n.* A modern Semitic language of Ethiopia, descended from the ancient Ethiopian.

Ti·gré (tē·grā′) A province of northern Ethiopia, bordering on Eritrea; formerly an independent kingdom; about 26,000 square miles; capital, Makale. Also **Ti·gre** (tēg′r′).

ti·gress (tī′gris) *n.* A female tiger.

Ti·gri·ña (tē·grē′nyä) *n.* A Southwest Semitic language spoken in Ethiopia.

Ti·gris (tī′gris) A river of SW Asia, flowing about 1,150 miles SE from east central Turkey in Asia through Iraq to the Euphrates NW of Basra.

ti·grish (tī′grish) See TIGERISH.

Ti·hwa (dē′hwä′) See URUMCHI.

Ti·jua·na (tē·hwä′nä) A border town in NW Lower California, Mexico: also *Tia Juana.*

tike (tīk) *n.* **1** A low-bred dog; a cur. **2** *Scot.* An uncouth fellow; a boor. **3** *Colloq.* A small child. Also spelled *tyke.* [<ON *tīk* a bitch]

Ti·ki (tē′kē) In Maori mythology, the creator of the first man.

til (til, tēl) *n.* Sesame. [<Hind. <Skt. *tilá*]

Til·burg (til′bûrg, *Du.* til′bûrkh) A city in North Brabant province, south Netherlands.

til·bur·y (til′ber·ē) *n. pl.* **·bur·ies** A form of gig seating two persons. [after *Tilbury,* an early 19th c. London coachmaker who invented it]

Til·da (til′də) Diminutive of MATILDA.

til·de (til′də, -dē) *n.* **1** A sign (~) used in Spanish over *n* to indicate nasal palatalization or the sound of *ny,* as in *cañon,* canyon. **2** The same sign (usually called **til**) used in Portuguese over a vowel or the first vowel of a dipthong to indicate nasalization, as in *lã, Camões.* [<Sp. <L *titulus* superscription, title]

Til·den (til′dən), **Samuel Jones,** 1814–86, U. S. statesman.

Til·dy (til′dē), **Zoltán,** 1889–1961, Hungarian politician; president of Hungary 1946–48.

tile (tīl) *n.* **1** A thin piece or plate of baked clay, sometimes decorated, used for covering roofs, floors, etc., and as an ornament. **2** A short earthenware pipe, used in forming sewers. **3** Tiles collectively; tiling. **4** *Colloq.* A high silk hat. —*v.t.* **tiled, til·ing** **1** To cover with tiles. **2** To secure against intrusion; specifically, in Freemasonry, to place the doorkeeper or tiler at the door of (a lodge) to keep out unauthorized persons. [OE *tigule, tigele,* ult. <L *tegula* < *tegere* cover]

tile·fish (tīl′fish′) *n. pl.* **·fish** or **·fishes** A large marine fish (*Lopholatilus chamaeleonticeps*) of the western Atlantic, marked with large yellow spots, and esteemed as food. [<NL (*Lophola*)*til*(*us*), genus name; infl. by *tile,* because its markings resemble ornamental tiles]

til·er (tī′lər) *n.* **1** A maker or layer of tiles. **2** The doorkeeper of a Masonic lodge.

til·i·a·ceous (til′ē·ā′shəs) *adj. Bot.* Designating or belonging to a widely distributed family (*Tiliaceae*) of trees, shrubs, and herbs, the linden family, having clusters of often fragrant flowers. [<NL <L *tiliaceus* <*tilia* the linden tree]

til·ing (tī′ling) *n.* **1** The act, operation, or system of using tiles for roofing or drainage. **2** Tiles collectively. **3** Something made of or faced with tiles.

till[1] (til) *v.t.* & *v.i.* To put and keep (soil) in order for the production of crops, as by plowing, harrowing, hoeing, sowing, etc.; cultivate. [OE *tilian* strive, acquire] —**till′a·ble** *adj.*

till[2] (til) *prep.* **1** To the time of; up to; until: He slept *till* noon. **2** Before: with the negative: He couldn't leave *till* today. **3** *Scot.* & *Brit. Dial.* To; unto; as far as. —*conj.* **1** Up to such time as; until: *till* death do us part. **2** Before: with the negative: They couldn't go *till* the carriage came for them. [OE *til* <ON, to]

till[3] (til) *n.* A drawer, compartment, or tray; a money drawer. [Earlier *tille,* prob. <ME *tillen, tyllen* draw]

till[4] (til) *n. Geol.* An unassorted, commingled, and chiefly unstratified mass of clay, sand, pebbles, and boulders, deposited by masses of ice. [Var. of ME *thill,* ? <OE *thille* a board, flooring]

till·age (til′ij) *n.* The cultivation of land. See synonyms under AGRICULTURE. [<TILL[1] + -AGE]

til·land·si·a (ti·land′zē·ə) *n.* Any of a genus (*Tillandsia*) of mainly epiphytic bromeliaceous plants of tropical America and the southern United States, having narrow, entire, often scurfy leaves, and flowers in a terminal spike. [<NL, after Elias *Tillands,* 18th c. Swedish botanist]

till·er[1] (til′ər) *n.* One who or that which tills; a plowman; a farmer. [<TILL[1]]

till·er[2] (til′ər) *n.* **1** A lever to turn a rudder. **2** A means of guidance. [<OF *telier* stock

of a crossbow <Med. L *telarium* a weaver's beam <L *tela* a web; prob infl. in meaning by ME *tillen* draw]

till·er[3] (til'ər) *n.* **1** A shoot from the base of a stem; sucker. **2** A sapling. — *v.i.* To put forth stems from the root; send forth new shoots. [Prob. OE *telgor* a twig <*telga* a branch]

til·lot (til'ət) *n. Brit.* A type of cloth used for wrapping fabric. Also **til'let.** [Earlier *tillet,* appar. <OF *tellette,* var. of *teilete, toilete* a wrapper of cloth. See TOILET.]

Til·lot·son (til'ət·sən), **John,** 1630–94, English theologian.

Til·ly (til'ē), **Count von,** 1559–1632, Johann Tserklaes, Flemish general of the imperial league in the Thirty Years' War.

til·ly–val·ly (til'ē·val'ē) *interj. Brit.* Nonsense; bosh. Also **til'ly–fal'ly** (-fal'ē). [Origin unknown]

Til·sit (til'zit) A former name for SOVETSK.

tilt[1] (tilt) *v.t.* **1** To cause to rise at one end or side; incline at an angle; slant; lean; tip. **2** To aim or thrust, as a lance. **3** To charge or overthrow in a tilt or joust. **4** To hammer or forge with a tilt hammer. — *v.i.* **5** To incline at an angle; lean. **6** To contend with the lance; engage in a joust. See synonyms under TIP[1]. — *n.* **1** An inclination from the vertical or horizontal position; slant; slope; also, the act of inclining, or the state of being inclined. **2** A medieval sport in which mounted knights, charging with lances, endeavored to unseat each other. **3** Any encounter resembling or suggestive of that between two tilting knights; hence, a quarrel; dispute; altercation; also, a thrust or blow, as with a lance. **4** A tilt hammer. **5** A seesaw. **6** The American black–necked stilt. — **at full tilt** At full speed; at full charge. [ME *tylten* be overthrown, totter <OE *tealt* unsteady] — **tilt'er** *n.*

tilt[2] (tilt) *n.* A canvas canopy or awning on a boat, wagon, booth, or the like. — *v.t.* To furnish or cover with an awning or tilt. [Var. of ME *tild, teld,* OE *teld* a tent]

tilth (tilth) *n.* **1** The act of tilling; cultivation of soil; tillage. **2** That part of the surface soil affected by tillage; cultivated land. [OE < *tilian* till]

tilt hammer A trip hammer.

tilt roof A round–topped roof: so called from its resemblance to the canopy or tilt of a covered wagon.

tilt–up (tilt'up') *n.* The spotted sandpiper: so called from its teetering habits.

tilt·yard (tilt'yärd') *n.* A courtyard or other place for tilting.

Tim (tim) Diminutive of TIMOTHY.

Ti·ma·ga·mi (ti·mä'gə·mē), **Lake** A lake in east central Ontario, Canada; 90 square miles.

ti·ma·rau (tē'mə·rou') See TAMARAU.

Tim·a·ru (tim'ə·rōō) A port on eastern South Island, New Zealand.

tim·bal (tim'bəl) *n.* **1** A kettledrum. **2** *Entomol.* The drumlike, sound–producing, folding membrane of the shrilling organ of a male cicada or harvest fly. Also spelled *tymbal.* [<F. *timbale,* appar. alter. of *attabale* <Sp. *atabal* ATABAL]

tim·bale (tim'bəl, *Fr.* tan̓·bàl') *n.* **1** A dish made of chicken, fish, cheese, or vegetables, pounded fine and mixed with the white of eggs, sweet cream, etc., cooked in a drum–shaped mold, then turned out and served with sauce. **2** A small cup made of fried pastry, in which food may be served. [<F. See TIMBAL.]

tim·ber (tim'bər) *n.* **1** Wood suitable for building purposes, prepared for use. **2** Growing or standing trees; also, woodland. **3** A single piece of squared wood prepared for use or already in use. **4** Any principal beam in a vessel's framing. **5** The wooden part or handle of any implement. **6** Loosely, the materials for any structure; hence, also, human material: That boy has good *timber* in him. See synonyms under STICK. — *v.t.* To provide or shore with timber. [OE] — **tim'ber·er** *n.*

tim·bered (tim'bərd) *adj.* **1** Covered with growing trees; wooded. **2** Constructed of timber.

tim·ber·head (tim'bər·hed') *n. Naut.* **1** An end of a timber projecting above the deck, and used for attaching lines, etc. **2** An upright post fastened to the deck at the point where a timber's end would come.

timber hitch *Naut.* A knot by which a rope is fastened around a spar.

tim·ber·ing (tim'bər·ing) *n.* **1** Timberwork; timbers collectively. **2** The act or process of furnishing with timber.

tim·ber·land (tim'bər·land') *n.* Land covered with forests.

timber line **1** The upper limit of tree growth on mountains and in arctic regions; the line above which no trees grow. **2** The boundary line of a tract of timber. — **tim'ber–line'** (-līn') *adj.*

timber wolf The large gray or brindled wolf (*Canis occidentalis*) of the forests of the northern United States and Canada: distinguished from the *coyote* or *prairie wolf.*

TIMBER WOLF
(About 4 feet long; 26 inches high)

tim·ber·work (tim'bər·wûrk') *n.* Work constructed of wood, especially the framing of a structure.

tim·bre (tim'bər, tam'-; *Fr.* tan̓'br') *n.* **1** The inherent quality of tone which serves to distinguish one musical instrument or voice from another and renders it unique: sometimes called *tone color.* **2** In acoustics, the character or quality of a sound that is produced by the relative number and strength of its harmonics: distinguished from *intensity* (amplitude of vibrations) and *pitch* (frequency of vibrations). **3** *Phonet.* The degree of resonance of a voiced sound, especially a vowel. [<F <OF, a small bell, sound of a bell, orig. a timbrel <L *tympanum* a kettledrum <Gk. *tympanon*]

tim·brel (tim'brəl) *n.* An ancient Hebrew instrument resembling a tambourine. [Dim. of earlier *timbre* a timbrel <OF. See TIMBRE.]

tim·breled (tim'brəld) *adj.* Chanted to the accompaniment of a timbrel. Also **tim'brelled.**

Tim·buk·tu (tim·buk'tōō, tim'buk·tōō') A town of central French Sudan, French West Africa, near the Niger; formerly a major center of the slave trade: French *Tombouctou.*

time (tīm) *n.* **1** The general idea, relation, or fact of continuous or successive existence; infinite duration or its measure. **2** A definite portion of duration; a moment; period; season. **3** A considerable period marked off by some special characteristics; era. **4** The portion of duration allotted to some specific purpose, as that allotted to human life or to any particular life, military service, a prison sentence, etc. **5** The length of an apprenticeship. **6** Period of gestation. **7** A portion of duration available or sufficient for, or allotted to, some special purpose or event; also, leisure: I have no *time* to read. **8** Indefinite duration viewed in the concrete as measurable and terminable, but not precisely limited: You build for *time,* we for eternity. **9** A general term indicating a subdivision of one of the grander divisions of geological history. **10** A point in duration; date; occasion; especially, the hour of death or of travail: Your *time* has come! **11** A portion of duration considered as having some quality or experience of its own, personal or general: in the latter sense usually in the plural: *Times* are hard. **12** A system of reckoning or measuring duration, especially with reference to the rotation and revolution of the earth, or to the movements of the celestial bodies. See also DAYLIGHT–SAVING TIME, STANDARD TIME, and lists given below. **13** A case of recurrence or repetition: many a *time,* three *times* a day. **14** The temporal relation of a verb. **15** *Music* **a** The characteristic tempo suited to a particular style of composition. **b** The division of musical composition into measures of equal length; rhythm: common *time,* triple *time.* Rhythms which are divisible by two are called **duple** or **common time,** as 2/2, 2/4, 2/8, 4/2, 4/4, 4/8, etc. Rhythms which are divisible by three are called **triple time,** as 3/2, 3/4, 3/8. **Compound triple times** are 9/4, 9/8, 9/16, 5/4, and 5/8. **16** A measured interval in verse; a unit of duration in rhythmical utterance; a mora. **17** One of the Aristotelian unities of the drama. See under UNITY. **18** Period during which work has been, or remains to be done; also, the amount of pay due one, especially on an hourly rate: *time* and a half for overtime. **19** Rate of movement, as in dancing, marching, etc.; tempo. **20** *pl.* In arithmetic, the fact or process of being multiplied or added to or by: Five *times* four is twenty; also, the multiplication sign ×. **21** Fit or proper occasion: This is no *time* to quibble. — **at the same time** **1** At the same moment. **2** Despite that; however; nevertheless. — **at times** Now and then. — **to bring to time** To call to account; discipline; force to conform. — **to have a time** To experience unusual pleasure, difficulty, etc. — **high time** The expiration of, or a time past the expiration of, a period of which something should have been accomplished. — **in time** **1** While time permits or lasts; before it is too late. **2** In the progress of time; ultimately. — **to keep time** **1** To indicate time correctly, as a clock; run in time, as a train. **2** To make regular or rhythmic movements in unison with another or others. **3** To render a musical composition in proper time or rhythm. **4** To make a record of the number of hours worked by an employee or employees. — **to make a time** To make a fuss or to–do. — **to make time** **1** To gain time; especially, to make up for lost time by extra speed, as a train. **2** To perform, achieve, or arrive in a certain time: to *make* good *time.* **3** *Slang* To impress or influence favorably: with *with.* — **on time** **1** Promptly; according to schedule: The train left *on time.* **2** Paid for, or to be paid for, later or in instalments. — *adj.* **1** Of or pertaining to time. **2** Devised so as to operate, explode, etc., at a specified time: a *time* bomb, *time* lock. **3** Payable at, or to be paid for at, a future date. — *v.t.* **timed, tim·ing** **1** To regulate as to time. **2** To cause to correspond in time: They *timed* their steps to the music. **3** To choose or arrange the time or occasion for: He *timed* his arrival for five o'clock. **4** To mark the rhythm or measure of. **5** To assign metrical or rhythmic qualities to (a syllable or note). **6** To ascertain or record the speed or duration of: to *time* a horse or a race. [OE *tīma*]

— **astronomical time** Prior to Jan. 1, 1925, the 24–hour period reckoned from noon to noon: since that date reckoned from midnight to midnight in order to bring civil and navigational practice into conformity with each other.

— **civil time** (or **civil day**) The 24–hour period extending from midnight to midnight: generally divided into two sections of 12 hours each, but in navigation, aeronautics, and other technical uses reckoned from 0 (midnight) to 24 hours. The same reckoning now applies to *astronomical time.*

— **Greenwich mean time** See CIVIL TIME.

— **Greenwich time** Time as reckoned from the zero meridian of Greenwich, England. To each hour in advance of, or behind, Greenwich time there corresponds a difference of 15 degrees longitude east or west of the Greenwich meridian.

— **local time** Time, whether sidereal or solar, as reckoned from a local meridian other than the standard meridian.

— **mean time** Time reckoned from the hour angle of the mean sun; the *mean solar day* is the 24–hour interval between two successive lower transits of the mean sun across the meridian of a place and corresponds exactly with civil time.

— **sidereal time** Time computed from the hour angle of a fixed point on the celestial sphere known as the first point in Aries, coincident with the vernal equinox; the *sidereal day* is the interval between two successive upper transits of the vernal equinox across the meridian.

— **solar time** Time reckoned from the hour angle of the central point of the sun's disk; the *apparent solar day* is the slightly variable interval between two successive lower transits of the sun across the meridian of a place, noon being the moment of upper transit or the hour angle plus 12 hours.

— **zone time** Time corresponding to that within a zone of 7 1/2 degrees on either side of a meridian; used in the determination of a ship's longitude.

Synonyms (noun): age, date, duration, epoch, era, period, season, sequence, succession. *Sequence* and *succession* apply to events viewed as following one another; *time* and *duration* denote something conceived of as enduring while events take place and acts are

done. According to the necessary conditions of human thought, events are contained in *time* as objects are in space, *time* existing before the event, measuring it as it passes, and still existing when the event is past. *Duration* and *succession* are more general words than *time* ; we can speak of infinite or eternal *duration* or *succession*, but *time* is commonly contrasted with eternity. *Time* is measured or measurable *duration*.

time and again Frequently. Also **time after time**.

time belt A time zone.

time-card (tīm′kärd′) *n.* A card for recording the time of arrival and departure of an employee.

time clock A clock equipped for automatically recording times of arrival and departure, or for actuating release mechanisms, as on vault doors, etc.

time exposure *Phot.* A film exposure made at spaced intervals by two separate manual operations of the shutter instead of automatically.

time-hon·ored (tīm′on′ərd) *adj.* Observed or honored from former times; claiming veneration as of long existence. See synonyms under AN-CIENT[1]. Also *Brit.* **time′-hon′oured.**

time immemorial A considerable and indefinite length of time; specifically, in law, time beyond legal memory, now reckoned at twenty years: the period of the statute of limitations relating to reality.

time-keep·er (tīm′kē′pər) *n.* **1** One who or that which keeps time. **2** One who declares the time in a race, game, athletic match, etc., or records the hours worked by employees. **3** A railroad train starter. **4** A timepiece.

time-less (tīm′lis) *adj.* **1** Independent of, or unaffected by, time; unending. **2** *Archaic* Untimely. **3** Not assigned or limited to any special time, era, or epoch; without a date. See synonyms under ETERNAL. —**time′less·ly** *adv.* —**time′less·ness** *n.*

time lock A lock, having a clock mechanism attached, so devised as to prevent its being unlocked before a specified time.

time·ly (tīm′lē) *adj.* **·li·er, ·li·est 1** Being or occurring in good or proper time; opportune; seasonable; also, well-timed. **2** *Archaic* Early. —*adv.* Opportunely; seasonably; early. —**time′li·ness** *n.*

time·e·o Dan·a·os et do·na fe·ren·tes (tim′ē·ō dan′ā·ōs et dō′nə fə·ren′tēz) *Latin* I fear the Greeks, even when they bring gifts; hence, the motives of a foe offering a gift are suspect.

time·ous (tī′məs) *adj. Scot.* Seasonable; timely.

time-out (tīm′out′) *n.* **1** A short recess requested by a team during play. **2** Any interval of rest taken during the course of a regular period of work. Also **time out.**

time out of mind Longer than is known or can be remembered; time immemorial.

time-piece (tīm′pēs′) *n.* A chronometer; a clock, or watch.

tim·er (tī′mər) *n.* **1** A timekeeper, or one who gives or officially records time. **2** A stopwatch, as for timing a race. **3** A device attached in an adjustable form to an internal-combustion engine so as to time the spark automatically.

time-sav·ing (tīm′sā′ving) *adj.* Calculated or devised to save time by facilitating work: Vacuum cleaners are *time-saving* devices.

time-serv·er (tīm′sûr′vər) *n.* One who yields to the apparent demands of the time, without reference to principle; a temporizer. Also **time′pleas′er** (-plē′zər). —**time′-serv′ing** *adj. & n.*

time-shar·ing (tīm′shâr′ing) *n.* **1** simultaneous use of a single large computer by many people at one time through individual terminals. **2** Joint use of a condominium or other vacation property, whereby each user occupies the property for a specified portion of the year.

time signature *Music* A sign placed at the beginning of a composition, immediately after the key signature, to indicate the rhythm or time.

Times Square A square in New York City formed by the intersection of Broadway and Seventh Avenue, extending from 42nd to 45th street; by extension, the area around it, the city's entertainment district.

time-ta·ble (tīm′tā′bəl) *n.* A tabular statement of the times at which certain things, as arrivals and departures of trains, boats, and high and low tides, etc., are to take place.

time-work (tīm′wûrk′) *n.* Work paid for on the basis of a set wage per hour, day, week, etc. —**time′work′er** *n.*

time-worn (tīm′wôrn′, -wōrn′) *adj.* Showing the ravages of time; affected by time.

time zone One of the 24 established divisions or sectors into which the globe is divided for convenience in reckoning standard time from the meridian of Greenwich: each sector represents 15 degrees of longitude, or a time interval of 1 hour. See table below. See also STANDARD TIME.

WORLD TIME ZONES

Each zone comprises (with certain geographic adjustments) an area 7½ degrees on each side of the reference longitude from Greenwich, and the zone number is equivalent to the number of hours later (−) or earlier (+) than Greenwich time. The places given in parentheses are for convenience of reference.

	Zone No. East of Greenwich	Longitude from Greenwich	Zone No. West of Greenwich
	0 (Greenwich)	0°	0 (Greenwich)
−	1 (Berlin)	15°	+ 1 (Iceland)
−	2 (Leningrad)	30°	+ 2 (Azores)
−	3 (Baghdad)	45°	+ 3 (Rio de Janeiro)
−	4 (Bokhara)	60°	+ 4 (Halifax)
−	5 (Bombay)	75°	+ 5 (Washington)
−	6 (Lhasa)	90°	+ 6 (Chicago)
−	7 (Singapore)	105°	+ 7 (Denver)
−	8 (Manila)	120°	+ 8 (Vancouver)
−	9 (Kyoto)	135°	+ 9 (Dawson)
−	10 (Melbourne)	150°	+10 (Tahiti)
−	11 (Kamchatka)	165°	+11 (Nome)
−	12 (Fiji Is.)	180°	+12 (Samoa)

(International Date Line)

tim·id (tim′id) *adj.* Shrinking from danger or publicity; easily frightened; shy; lacking self-confidence. See synonyms under FAINT, PUSILLANIMOUS. [< L *timidus* < *timere* fear] —**ti·mid·i·ty** (ti·mid′ə·tē), **tim′id·ness** *n.* —**tim′id·ly** *adv.*

tim·ing (tī′ming) *n.* **1** In music, oratory, acting, etc., the act or art of regulating the speed of performance, utterance, etc., so as to accentuate the impressiveness of certain parts; also, the effect produced by such regulation. **2** In certain sports, as swimming, boxing, etc., the regulation of the speed of a blow or stroke so that it reaches its highest effectiveness at just the right moment.

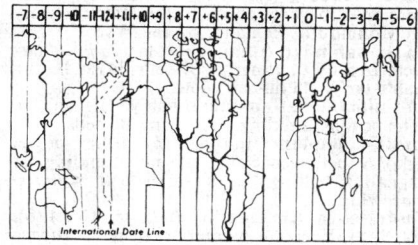

WORLD TIME ZONES
The system of keeping standard time at sea has been adopted by most of the world's navies.

Ti·mi·soa·ra (tē′mē·shwä′rä) A city in western Rumania: Hungarian *Temesvár.*

ti·moc·ra·cy (ti·mok′rə·sē) *n. pl.* **·cies 1** A state in which the honor attaching to the position of ruler becomes an object of contention, and is sought by the ambitious with intrigue, rather than accepted as a trust. **2** A state in which honors are bestowed according to property owned. [< OF *tymocracie* < Med. L *timocratia* < Gk. *timokratia* < *timē* honor + *kratein* rule] —**ti·mo·crat·ic** (tī′mə·krat′ik) or **·i·cal** *adj.*

ti·mol·o·gy (tī·mol′ə·jē) *n. Philos.* A study or theory of value or excellence, especially of inherent rather than relative value. [< Gk. *timē* honor, valuation + -LOGY] —**ti·mo·log·ic** (tī′mə·loj′ik) or **·i·cal** *adj.* —**ti·mol′o·gist** *n.*

Ti·mon (tī′mən) An Athenian of the fifth century B.C.; called "the Misanthrope"; hero of Shakespeare's *Timon of Athens.*

Ti·mor (tē′môr, ti·môr′) The largest and easternmost of the Lesser Sunda Islands; divided into *Indonesian Timor,* included in Nusa Tenggara province, in the western portion; 5,765 square miles; capital, Kupang: formerly *Netherlands Timor,* and into *Portuguese Timor,* a Portuguese province, in the eastern portion; 5,761 square miles, including the exclave of Ambeno and the islands of Atauro and Jaco; capital, Dili.

Timor Archipelago See LESSER SUNDA ISLANDS.

Ti·mor-laut (tē′môr-lout) See TANIMBAR ISLANDS. Also **Ti·mor-laoet** (tē′môr-lout′).

tim·or·ous (tim′ər·əs) *adj.* **1** Fearful of danger; timid. **2** Indicating or produced by fear. See synonyms under PUSILLANIMOUS. [< OF *timoureus, temeros* < Med. L *timorosus,* ult. < L *timor, -oris* fear] —**tim′or·ous·ly** *adv.* —**tim′or·ous·ness** *n.*

Timor Sea An arm of the Indian Ocean between northern Australia and Timor.

Ti·mo·shen·ko (tē′mō·sheng′kō), **Semion Konstantinovich,** 1895–1970, Russian marshal in World War II.

tim·o·thy (tim′ə·thē) *n.* A perennial fodder grass (*Phleum pratense*) having its flowers in a long, dense, cylindrical, spikelike panicle. Also **timothy grass.** [after *Timothy* Hanson, who took the seed from New York to the Carolinas about 1720]

Tim·o·thy (tim′ə·thē) A masculine personal name. Also *Dan., Du., Ger., Sw.* **Ti·mo·the·us** (tē·mō′tē·ōōs), *Fr.* **Ti·mo·thée** (tē·mō·tā′), *Ital., Sp.* **Ti·mo·te·o** (tē′mō·tā′ō), *Pg.* **Ti·mo·the·o** (tē′mō·tā·ōō). [< Gk., honoring a god] —**Timothy** A convert and companion of the apostle Paul; also, either of two pastoral epistles in the New Testament, addressed to Timothy and attributed to Paul.

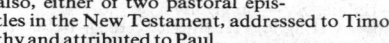

TIMOTHY
(Plant to 6 feet high)

Ti·mour, Ti·mur (ti·mōōr′, tē-) See TAMERLANE.

tim·pa·ni (tim′pə·nē) *n. pl. sing.* **·pa·no** (-pə·nō) Kettledrums; a set of kettledrums in an orchestra: also spelled *tympani.* [< Ital., pl. of *timpano* < L *tympanum* a drum < Gk. *tympanon*] —**tim′pa·nist** *n.*

tim·pa·num (tim′pə·nəm) See TYMPANUM.

tin (tin) *n.* **1** A metallic element (symbol Sn, atomic number 50) having at least two allotropic forms, the more common being a soft, lustrous, white metal used in making alloys and protective coatings. See PERIODIC TABLE. **2** Tin plate. **3** An article of tinware; a box or container made of tin. **4** *Brit.* A tin container for preserved foods; a can. **5** *Slang* Money. —*v.t.* **tinned, tin·ning 1** To coat or cover with tin or tin plate. **2** To pack or put up in tins. —*adj.* Made of tin [OE]

Ti·na (tē′nə) Diminutive of CHRISTINA.

tin·a·mou (tin′ə·mōō) *n.* Any of certain South American birds (family *Tinamidae*), resembling quails, and hunted as game birds. [< F < Cariban *tinamu*]

tin·cal (ting′kəl, -käl, -kôl) *n.* Native borax. [< Malay *tinkal* < Persian *tinkāl, tinkar* < Skt. *tankana* borax]

tinct (tingkt) *v.t.* To tinge; tint. —*adj. Poetic* Slightly tinged. —*n.* **1** *Poetic* A tint. **2** *Obs.* A tincture; specifically, the elixir vitae. [< L *tinctus,* pp. of *tingere* dye, color]

tinc·to·ri·al (tingk·tôr′ē·əl, -tōr′ē-) *adj.* **1** Of or pertaining to color or hue. **2** Affording or imbuing with tint or color. [< L *tinctorius* < *tinctus.* See TINCT.]

tinc·ture (tingk′chər) *n.* **1** A solution, usually in alcohol, of some principle used in medicine. **2** A tinge of color; tint. **3** A slight flavor superadded; modicum; spice. **4** That part of a substance which is extracted by a solvent. **5** One of the metals, colors, or furs used in heraldic description. —*v.t.* **·tured, ·tur·ing 1** To impart a slight hue or tinge to. **2** To imbue with flavor, odor, etc. **3** To imbue with a specified moral or mental quality. [< L *tinctura* a dyeing < *tinctus.* See TINCT.]

tin·der (tin′dər) *n.* Any readily combustible substance, as charred linen or touchwood,

that will ignite (without explosion) on contact with a spark. [OE *tynder*] —**tin′der·y** *adj.*

tin·der·box (tin′dər·boks′) *n.* **1** A portable metallic box containing tinder, and usually flint and steel to ignite it. **2** A highly inflammable mass of material. **3** A person with an easily excitable temper.

tine (tīn) *n.* A spike or prong, as of a fork or of an antler. [OE *tind*] —**tined** *adj.*

tin·e·a (tin′ē·ə) *n.* **1** Any of a genus (*Tinea*) of small, narrow-winged moths, including the case-making clothes moth (*T. pellionella*). **2** *Pathol.* Ringworm; any fungous skin disease. [<NL <L, a moth, gnawing worm]

tin·e·id (tin′ē·id) *adj.* Of or pertaining to a family (*Tineidae*) of moths. —*n.* One of the *Tineidae.* [<NL <*Tinea* TINEA]

tin·foil (tin′foil′) *n.* Tin or an alloy of tin made into thin sheets for use as wrapping material and in decoration.

ting[1] (ting) *n.* A single high metallic sound, as of a small bell. —*v.t.* & *v.i.* To give forth or cause to give forth a ting. [Imit.]

ting[2] (ting) See THING[2].

ting-a-ling (ting′ə·ling′) *n.* The sound of a little bell.

tinge (tinj) *v.t.* **tinged, tinge·ing** or **ting·ing** **1** To imbue with a faint trace of color; impart a tint to. **2** To impart a slight characteristic quality of some other element to. See synonyms under STAIN. —*n.* **1** A faint trace of added color. **2** A quality or peculiar characteristic imparted to something by the slight admixture of some foreign element. [<L *tingere* dye]

tin·gle (ting′gəl) *v.* **·gled, ·gling** *v.i.* **1** To experience a prickly, stinging sensation, as the skin from exposure to cold, or the ears from a sharp blow. **2** To cause such a sensation. —*v.t.* **3** To cause to tingle. —*n.* **1** A prickly, stinging sensation; a tingling. **2** A jingle or tinkling. [Appar. var. of TINKLE] —**tin′gler** *n.* —**tin′gly** *adj.*

Ting·ley (ting′lē), **Katherine,** 1847–1929, *née* Wescott, U. S. theosophist.

tin·horn (tin′hôrn′) *Slang* *n.* **1** A pretentious person without any real ability, power, influence, etc. **2** A gambler who bets with low stakes. —*adj.* **1** Resembling or characteristic of a cheap gambler. **2** Pretentious. [With ref. to the fine appearance, but poor quality, of a tin horn]

Tin·i·an (tin′ē·ən, tē′nē·än′) One of the southern Marianas Islands; 39 square miles.

tink (tingk) *v.i.* To make a single or separate tinkling sound; chink. —*n.* A tinkle or tinkling. [Imit.]

tink·er (tingk′ər) *n.* **1** An itinerant mender of domestic tin utensils, as pots and pans. **2** Loosely, one who does repairing work of any kind; a jack-of-all-trades. **3** A clumsy workman; a botcher. **4** The act of roughly repairing; hasty workmanship. **5** A young mackerel about two years old. **6** The chub mackerel. **7** The razor-billed auk. —*v.i.* **1** To work as a tinker. **2** To work in a clumsy, makeshift fashion on anything. **3** To potter; fuss. —*v.t.* **4** To mend as a tinker. **5** To repair clumsily or inexpertly. [Var. of earlier *tinekere* a worker in tin]

tinker's damn *Slang* Any useless or worthless article: commonly in the phrase *not worth a tinker's damn.* Also **tinker's dam.** [<TINKER + DAMN; with ref. to the reputed profanity of tinkers]

tin·kle (ting′kəl) *v.* **·kled, ·kling** *v.i.* **1** To produce slight, sharp, metallic sounds, as a small bell. —*v.t.* **2** To cause to tinkle. **3** To summon or signal by a tinkling. —*n.* A sharp, clear, tinkling sound. [Freq. of TINK] —**tin′kling** *adj.* & *n.* —**tin′kly** *adj.*

tin lizzie *U.S. Slang* The Model T automobile.

tin·ner (tin′ər) *n.* **1** A miner employed in tin mines. **2** A maker of or dealer in tinware; a tinsmith.

tin·ni·tus (ti·nī′təs) *n. Pathol.* A subjective ringing, rushing, or buzzing sound in the ears, not caused by any external stimulus. [<NL <L *tinnire* ring]

tin·ny (tin′ē) *adj.* **·ni·er, ·ni·est** **1** Pertaining to, composed of, or abounding in tin. **2** Sounding as if a tin pan were being struck: a *tinny* sound. **3** Tasting of tin, as food from a can. —**tin′ni·ly** *adv.* —**tin′ni·ness** *n.*

tin-pan (tin′pan′) *adj.* Noisy; clanging; inharmonious; tinny. Also **tin′-pan′ny.**

tin-pan alley (tin′pan′) **1** A street or section of a city frequented by musicians and song writers and occupied by publishers of popular music: originally used to designate a section of New York where cheap, tinny-sounding pianos were supposedly heard in publishers' offices. **2** The composers and publishers of popular music, collectively.

tin-plate (tin′plāt′) *v.t.* **-plat·ed, -plat·ing** To plate with tin. —**tin′-plat′er** *n.*

tin plate Sheet iron or steel plated with tin.

tin·sel (tin′səl) *n.* **1** Very thin glittering bits of brass, copper, and other cheap metals, used for display and to ornament articles of dress; also, the thin metal from which they are cut. **2** A fabric in which such spangles or bits of metal are woven, or to which they are attached; also, a fabric or yarn containing gold or silver thread. **3** Anything sparkling and showy, with little real worth; superficial adornment and brilliancy. —*adj.* **1** Made or covered with tinsel. **2** Of tinsel-like qualities; superficially brilliant; tawdry. —*v.t.* **·seled** or **·selled, ·sel·ing** or **·sel·ling** **1** To adorn or decorate with or as with tinsel. **2** To give a metallic appearance to (ceramic ware) by washing with a metallic substance. [<MF *étincelle* <OF *estincelle* <L *scintilla* a spark]

tin·smith (tin′smith′) *n.* One who works with tin or tin plate.

tin spirits *Chem.* A solution of a tin salt in acid, used in dyeing.

tin·stone (tin′stōn′) *n.* Cassiterite.

tint[1] (tint) *n.* **1** A variety of color; tincture; specifically, a tendency toward or slight admixture of a different color; tinge: red with a blue *tint.* **2** A gradation or shading of a color made by dilution with white to lessen its chroma and saturation. **3** Any color having a brilliance higher than that of median gray. **4** In engraving, an effect of light, shade, texture, etc., produced by the spacing of lines or by hatching. **5** An impression from a block bearing a design to be printed in a faint color as a background: used on checks as a safeguard against erasure. —*v.t.* **1** To give a tint to; tinge. **2** In engraving, to form a tint upon. See synonyms under STAIN. [Alter. of TINCT; ? infl. in form by Ital. *tinta* color] —**tint′er** *n.*

tint[2] (tint) *Scot.* Past tense and past participle of TINE[2].

Tin·tag·el Head (tin·taj′əl) A promontory with castle ruins in western Cornwall, England; traditionally, the birthplace of King Arthur.

Tin·tern Abbey (tin′tərn) The ruins of a Cistercian abbey founded in the 12th century in Monmouth, England, on the Wye.

tin·tin·nab·u·lar (tin′ti·nab′yə·lər) *adj.* Characterized by tinkling, as of bells. Also **tin′tin·nab′u·lar′y, tin′tin·nab′u·lous.**

tin·tin·nab·u·la·tion (tin′ti·nab′yə·lā′shən) *n.* The pealing, tinkling, or ringing of bells.

tin·tin·nab·u·lum (tin′ti·nab′yə·ləm) *n. pl.* **·la** (-lə) A bell; especially, a small tinkling or signaling bell. [<L, a small bell < *tintinnare* ring]

Tin·to·ret·to (tin′tə·ret′ō, *Ital.* tēn′tō·ret′tō), 1518–94, Venetian painter: real name *Jacopo Robusti.*

tin·type (tin′tīp′) *n.* A photograph taken on a sensitized film supported on a thin sheet of enameled tin or iron; a ferrotype.

tin·ware (tin′wâr′) *n.* Household articles, collectively, made of tin plate.

tin·work (tin′wûrk′) *n.* **1** Articles made of tin; work with tin. **2** *pl.* A place or establishment where tin is manufactured or mined.

ti·ny (tī′nē) *adj.* **·ni·er, ·ni·est** Very small; minute; wee. See synonyms under LITTLE, MINUTE[2], SMALL. [<obs. *tine* a small amount, bit + -Y[3]; ult. origin unknown]

-tion *suffix of nouns* **1** Action or process of: *rejection.* **2** Condition or state of being: *completion.* **3** Result of: *connection.* Also *-ation, -cion, -ion, -sion, -xion.* [<F *-tion* <OF *-cion* <L *-tio, -tionis*]

tip[1] (tip) *n.* A slanting or inclined position; a tilt. —*v.* **tipped, tip·ping** *v.t.* **1** To cause to lean by lowering or raising one end or side; cant; tilt. **2** To overturn or upset: often with *over.* —*v.i.* **3** To become tilted; slant. **4** To overturn; topple: with *over.* [ME *tipen* overturn; origin uncertain] —**tip′per** *n.*

Synonyms (verb): cant, careen, heel, incline, lean, list, slant, slope, tilt. To *tilt* or *tip* is to throw out of a horizontal position by raising one side or end or lowering the other. *Slant* and *slope* are said of things somewhat fixed or permanent in a position out of the horizontal or perpendicular: the roof *slants,* the hill *slopes. Incline* is a more formal word for *tip,* and also for *slant* or *slope.* To *cant* is to set slantingly; in many cases *tip* and *cant* might be interchanged, but *tip* is more temporary, often momentary; one *tips* a pail so that the water flows over the edge; a mechanic *cants* a table by making or setting one side higher than the other. *Careen, heel,* and *list* are used of vessels which from any cause, as leakage, shifting of cargo, etc., are off an even keel.

tip[2] (tip) *v.t.* **tipped, tip·ping** **1** To strike lightly, or with something light; tap. **2** In baseball, to strike (the ball) a light, glancing blow. —*n.* A tap; light blow. [Earlier *tippe,* prob. <LG. Cf. Du. *tippen* tap.]

tip[3] (tip) *n.* **1** A small gift of money for services rendered, given to a servant, waiter, porter, or the like. **2** A friendly, helpful hint; specifically, secret information presumed to increase a better's or speculator's chance of winning. [< *v.*] —*v.* **tipped, tip·ping** *v.t.* **1** To give a small gratuity to. **2** *Colloq.* To give secret information to, as in betting and speculation: often with *off.* —*v.i.* **3** To give tips. [Orig. < thieves' cant, ? <TIP[2]] —**tip′·per** *n.*

tip[4] (tip) *n.* **1** The point or extremity of anything tapering; end: the *tip* of the tongue. **2** A piece or part made to form the end of anything, as a nozzle, ferrule, etc. **3** The upper part of a hat crown; also, the lining in the upper part of the crown. —*v.t.* **tipped, tip·ping** **1** To furnish with a tip. **2** To form the tip of. **3** To cover or adorn the tip of. [Prob. <MDu., a point]

ti palm See TI[2].

tip·cart (tip′kärt′) *n.* A cart having a body that can be tipped for unloading.

tip·cat (tip′kat′) *n.* A game played with a stick or bat and a small piece of wood pointed at the ends and called a *cat,* which the batter hits lightly into the air and then hits again, trying to drive it as far as possible; also, the cat. [<TIP[1] + CAT]

ti·pi (tē′pē) See TEPEE.

tip-off (tip′ôf′, -of′) *n. Colloq.* A hint or warning.

Tip·pe·ca·noe (tip′ē·kə·nōō′) The nickname of William Henry Harrison: from his victory over Tecumseh's Indians at Tippecanoe River in 1811. The name provided the presidential campaign slogan, **Tippecanoe and Tyler too,** for Harrison and his vice-presidential running mate, John Tyler, in 1840.

Tip·pe·ca·noe River (tip′ē·kə·nōō′) A river in north central Indiana, flowing 166 miles NW, west, and SW to the Wabash River near Lafayette; scene of General W. H. Harrison's victory over Indians, 1811.

Tip·per·ar·y (tip′ə·râr′ē) A county of NE Munster province, Ireland; 1,643 square miles; county town, Clonmel.

tip·pet (tip′it) *n.* **1** An outdoor covering for the neck, or neck and shoulders, hanging well down in front. **2** *Eccl.* A long scarf worn by clergymen in the Anglican Church. **3** A ruff of feathers on birds, etc. [Prob. dim. of TIP[4]]

tip·ple[1] (tip′əl) *v.t.* & *v.i.* **·pled, ·pling** To drink (alcoholic beverages) frequently and habitually. —*n.* Liquor consumed in tippling. [Cf. Norw. *tipla* drip, tipple] —**tip′pler** *n.*

tip·ple[2] (tip′əl) *n.* **1** An apparatus for tipping loaded cars. **2** The place where such tipping is done. [< dial. E *tipple* topple, freq. of TIP[1]]

tip·py (tip′ē) *adj.* **·pi·er, ·pi·est** *Colloq.* Shaky; unsteady; apt to tip over. [<TIP[1] + -Y[3]]

tip·staff (tip′staf′, -stäf′) *n.* **1** *pl.* **·staffs** In England, a sheriff's subordinate; bailiff; constable; also, a court crier. **2** *pl.* **·staves** (-stāvz′) A staff having a metal tip: a badge of office. [<TIP(PED) STAFF]

tip·ster (tip′stər) *n. Colloq.* One who sells tips for betting, as on a race. [<TIP[3]]

tip·sy (tip′sē) *adj.* **·si·er, ·si·est** **1** Befuddled with drink, but not really drunk; partially intoxicated; high. **2** Tippy; shaky; also, crooked; askew. [<TIP[1]] —**tip′si·ly** *adv.* —**tip′si·ness** *n.*

tip·toe (tip′tō′) *n.* **1** The tip of a toe, or the tips of all the toes collectively. **2** Topmost height; also, alertness of expectation: usually in the phrase **to be on tiptoe** or **a-tiptoe,** to be

eagerly expectant. —*v.i.* **·toed, ·toe·ing** To walk on tiptoe; go stealthily. —*adj.* **1** Standing on tiptoe. **2** Quiet; gentle; stealthy. —*adv.* On tiptoe, in any sense.

tip-top (tip′top′) *Colloq. adj.* Best of its kind; first-rate. —*n.* The highest point, quality, or degree; the very top; the best. —*adv.* In a tip-top manner. [< TIP[4] + TOP[1]] **—tip′-top′per** *n.*

Ti·pu Sa·hib (ti′po͞o sä′hib), 1753?–99, sultan of Mysore; fought against the British 1775–79. Also **Tip′poo Sa′hib.**

Ti·rach Mir (tē′rəch mēr′) See TIRICH MIR.

ti·rade (tī′rād, tə·rād′) *n.* **1** A prolonged declamatory outpouring, as of censure. **2** *Music* A diatonic run, filling the interval between two musical notes. [< F < Ital. *tirata* a volley, pp. of *tirare* fire, pull]

ti·rail·leur (tir′ə·lûr′, *Fr.* tē·rá·yœr′) *n.* A sharpshooter; skirmisher. [< F]

Ti·ra·na (tē·rä′nə) The capital of Albania, in the central part. Also **Ti·ra′në.**

tire[1] (tīr) *v.* **tired, tir·ing** *v.t.* **1** To reduce the strength of, as by toil; weary; fatigue. **2** To reduce the interest or patience of, as with tediousness. —*v.i.* **3** To become weary or exhausted. **4** To lose patience, interest, etc. **—to tire of** To become weary of or impatient with. **—to tire out** To weary completely. —*n. Dial.* The sensation of fatigue; weariness. [OE *tiorian, tēorian*]

Synonyms (verb): exhaust, fag, fatigue, harass, jade, weary. To *tire* is to reduce one's strength in any degree by exertion; one may be *tired* just enough to make rest pleasant, or even unconsciously *tired,* becoming aware of the fact only when he ceases the exertion. One who is *fatigued* suffers from painful lack of strength as the result of overtaxing; an invalid may be *fatigued* with very slight exertion; when one is *wearied,* the painful lack of strength is the result of long-continued demand or strain; one is *exhausted* when the strain has been so severe and continuous as utterly to consume the strength, so that further exertion is for the time impossible. One is *fagged* by drudgery; he is *jaded* by incessant repetition of the same act until it becomes increasingly difficult or well-nigh impossible; as, a horse is *jaded* by a long and unbroken journey. See WEAR[1].

tire[2] (tīr) *n.* **1** A band or hoop surrounding the rim of a wheel. **2** A flexible tube, usually of inflated rubber, set in a rim and protected by an outer covering: used on automobiles, bicycles, etc., to reduce vibration. —*v.t.* **tired, tir·ing** To furnish with a tire; put a tire on. Also, *Brit.,* *tyre.* [Special use of TIRE[4]]

tire[3] (tīr) *Archaic v.t.* **1** In falconry, to rend and devour; draw; pull. —*v.i.* **2** To prey. **3** To be preoccupied; dote; gloat. [< OF *tirer*; ult. origin uncertain]

tire[4] (tīr) *Obs. v.t.* To attire; dress; adorn. —*n.* **1** A tiara; headdress. **2** Attire. [Aphetic var. of ATTIRE]

tire[5] (tīr) *n.* A volley of cannon; a broadside. [< OF *tir* < *tirer* draw, shoot; ult. origin uncertain]

tired (tīrd) *adj.* Weary; exhausted; jaded; fatigued. [Orig. pp. of TIRE[1]] **—tired′ly** *adv.* **—tired′ness** *n.*

tire·less (tīr′lis) *adj.* Proof against fatigue; untiring. See synonyms under INDEFATIGABLE. [< TIRE[1] + -LESS] **—tire′less·ly** *adv.* **—tire′·less·ness** *n.*

Ti·re·si·as (tī·rē′sē·əs) In Greek mythology, a Theban soothsayer, blinded by Athena whom he saw bathing: in recompense she gave him power to foretell the future. **—Ti·re′si·an** *adj.*

tire·some (tīr′səm) *adj.* Tending to tire, or causing one to tire; tedious. See synonyms under TEDIOUS, TROUBLESOME, WEARISOME. **—tire′some·ly** *adv.* **—tire′some·ness** *n.*

tire·wom·an (tīr′wo͝om′ən) *n. pl.* **·wom·en** (-wim′in) *Obs.* A lady's maid; an abigail. Also **tir′ing-wom′an.** [< TIRE[4] + WOMAN]

Ti·rich Mir (tē′rich mēr′) The highest mountain in the Hindu Kush, in extreme NW West Pakistan near the border of Afghanistan; 25,263 feet: also *Tirach Mir.*

tiring room *Archaic* A dressing-room, especially in a theater. [< *tiring,* ppr. of TIRE[4] + ROOM]

tirl (tûrl) *Scot. v.t.* To cause to produce a vibrating or thrilling noise, as by plucking a string. —*n.* A vibrating or thrilling noise.

tirl·ing pin (tûr′ling) *Scot.* A vertical twisted iron bar passed through a loose ring and fastened to a door: formerly used as a knocker.

Tir·no·vo (tir′nô·vô) A city in northern Bulgaria; scene of the declaration of the country's independence, 1908: also *Trnovo.*

ti·ro (tī′rō) See TYRO.

Ti·rol (ti·rōl′, tir′ōl, tī′rōl) An autonomous province of western Austria in the eastern Alps north of Italy; 4,883 square miles; capital, Innsbruck: also *Tyrol.* **—Ti·ro′le·an** *adj.* & *n.*

Tir·o·lese (tir′ō·lēz′, -lēs′) *adj.* Of or pertaining to Tirol or its inhabitants. —*n. pl.* **·lese** A native of Tirol. Also *Tyrolese.*

Tir·pitz (tir′pits), **Alfred von,** 1849–1930, German admiral.

tir·ri·vee (tir′ə·vē) *n. Scot.* A burst of ill-humor; fit of passion; tantrum.

Tir·so de Mo·li·na (tir′sō thā mō·lē′nä), 1571?–1648, Spanish dramatist: real name Gabriel Téllez.

Ti·ruch·i·rap·pal·li (ti·ro͞och′ē·räp′ə·lē) A city in east central Madras State, India: also *Trichinopoly.*

'tis (tiz) It is: a contraction.

Ti·sa (tē′sä) The Czech and Rumanian name for the Tisza.

ti·sane (ti·zan′, *Fr.* tē·zàn′) *n.* a slightly medicated decoction, usually of herbs, prepared for the sick; a ptisan. [< F < L *ptisana* a ptisan]

Tish·ri (tish′rē) The first month of the Hebrew calendar. See CALENDAR (Hebrew). Also **Tis·ri** (tiz′rē). [< Hebrew < Aramic *tishrī* < *sherā* begin; infl. by Babylonian *tashritu* the seventh month, first month of the second half of the year]

Ti·siph·o·ne (ti·sif′ə·nē) In Greek mythology, one of the three Furies. [< L < Gk. *Tisiphonē* vengeful destruction]

tis·sue (tish′o͞o) *n.* **1** Any light or gauzy textile fabric, usually of silk; originally, cloth interwoven with gold or silver thread. **2** *Biol.* One of the elementary aggregates of cells and their products, developed by plants and animals for the performance of a particular function: connective *tissue.* **3** A connected or interwoven series; chain; fabrication: a *tissue* of lies. **4** Tissue paper. —*v.t.* **·sued, ·su·ing** *Rare* **1** To make into tissue. **2** To adorn with tissue; weave. [< OF *tissu* a rich stuff, orig. pp. of *tistre* weave < L *texere*]

tissue culture The science and art of growing body tissues in a culture medium.

tis·sued (tish′o͞od) *adj.* **1** Clad in tissue. **2** Variegated.

tissue paper Very thin, unsized, almost transparent paper for wrapping delicate articles, protecting engravings, etc.

Ti·sza (ti′so) A river flowing 800 miles from the Carpathian Mountains, in SW Ukrainian S.S.R., south through Hungary and Yugoslavia to the Danube north of Belgrade: German *Theiss,* Czech and Rumanian *Tisa.*

tit[1] (tit) *n.* **1** A titmouse. **2** One of various other small birds, as a titlark, etc. [Short for TITMOUSE, TITLARK, etc.]

tit[2] (tit) *n.* A light blow; tap: chiefly in the phrase *tit for tat.* [Var. of TIP[2]]

tit[3] (tit) *n.* Teat; breast; nipple. [OE *titt*]

tit[4] (tit) *n.* **1** A small or worn-out horse; a nag. **2** *Slang* A young woman or girl: a disrespectful term. [ME, a little thing, ? < Scand. Cf. dial. Norw. *titta* little girl.]

ti·tan (tīt′n) *n.* Any person having gigantic strength or size; a giant. —*adj.* Titanic. [after *Titan*] **—ti′tan·ess** *n. fem.*

Ti·tan (tīt′n) **1** In Greek mythology, one of a race of giant gods, children of Uranus and Gaea, who were vanquished and succeeded by the Olympian gods, who imprisoned them in Tartarus. **2** Helios: so called by some Latin poets.

ti·tan·ate (tī′tə·nāt) *n. Chem.* A salt or ester of titanic acid. [< TITAN(IC)[2] + -ATE[3]]

Ti·tan·esque (tīt′n·esk′) *adj.* Of or befitting the Titans; gigantic.

Ti·tan·ess (tīt′n·is) A female Titan.

Ti·ta·ni·a (ti·tā′nē·ə, tī-) Queen of fairyland and wife of Oberon in Shakespeare's *A Midsummer Night's Dream.*

ti·tan·ic[1] (tī·tan′ik) *adj.* Gigantic; huge; tremendous. [< Gk. *titanikos* < *Titanes* the Titans]

ti·tan·ic[2] (tī·tan′ik, ti-) *adj. Chem.* Of or pertaining to titanium, especially in its higher valence. [< TITAN(IUM) + -IC]

Ti·tan·ic (tī·tan′ik) *adj.* Pertaining to, characteristic of, or resembling the Titans.

titanic acid *Chem.* **1** A white pulverulent titanium dioxide, TiO_2, found native as rutile, etc.: a common constituent of iron ores: also **titanic oxide.** **2** One of various weak acids derived from titanium ioxide.

ti·tan·if·er·ous (tī′tən·if′ər·əs) *adj.* Containing or yielding titanium. [< TITAN(IUM) + -(I)FEROUS]

Ti·tan·ism (tīt′n·iz′əm) *n.* Defiance of, or rebellion against, constituted authority or social conventions: a characteristic attributed to the Titans in Greek mythology.

ti·tan·ite (tī′tən·īt) *n.* Sphene. [< G *titanit* < *titanium* titanium]

ti·ta·ni·um (tī·tā′nē·əm) *n.* An abundant, light, strong, lustrous metallic element (symbol Ti, atomic number 22), never found uncombined, used in certain alloys. See PERIODIC TABLE. [< NL < L *Titani* the Titans < Gk. *Titanes*; named on analogy with *uranium*]

titanium tetrachloride *Chem.* A colorless liquid compound, $TiCl_4$, used as a smoke-producing agent in warfare.

Ti·tan·om·a·chy (tī′tən·om′ə·kē) *n.* In Greek mythology, the war of the Titans against the Olympian gods. [< Gk. *Titanomachia* < *Titan* a Titan + *machē* a battle]

ti·tan·o·there (tī′tən·ə·thir′, tī·tā′nə-, ti-) *n. Paleontol.* Any of an extinct family *(Titanotheridae)* of large, odd-toed ungulates resembling the rhinoceros and common in the Lower Eocene of the Tertiary period. [< NL < Gk. *Titan* a Titan + *thērion,* dim. of *thēr* a wild beast]

ti·tan·ous (tī′tən·əs, tī·tan′əs, ti-) *adj. Chem.* Of or pertaining to titanium, especially in its lower valence. [< TITAN(IUM) + -OUS[2]]

tit·bit (tit′bit′) See TIDBIT.

Tite (tēt) French form of TITUS.

ti·ter (tī′tər, tē′-) *n. Chem.* **1** The strength or concentration of a solution as determined by titration. **2** The temperature at which a molten fatty acid or wax solidifies. Also spelled *titre.* [< F *titre* the fineness of gold or silver alloy]

tit for tat Retaliation in kind; blow for blow. [? Alter. of *tip for tap*; ? infl. in form by MF *tant pour tant* tit for tat]

tith·a·ble (tī′thə·bəl) *adj.* Liable to be tithed, as property.

tithe (tīth) *n.* **1** A tax or assessment of one tenth, especially when payable in kind; loosely, any ratable tax. **2** Specifically, in England, a tenth part of the yearly proceeds arising from lands and from the personal industry of the inhabitants, for the support of the clergy and the church. **3** The tenth part of anything; hence, a small part. —*v.t.* **tithed, tith·ing 1** To give or pay a tithe, or tenth part of. **2** To tax with tithes. [ME *tithe, tethe,* OE *tēotha, tēogotha* a tenth] **—tith′er** *n.*

tith·ing (tī′thing) *n.* **1** The act of levying tithes. **2** A tenth part. **3** In old English law, a civil division composed of ten freeholders and their families.

tith·ing·man (tī′thing·mən) *n. pl.* **·men** (-mən) **1** Anciently, in England, the chief of a tithing; more recently, a constable. **2** In the New England colonies, an officer for enforcing Sunday observance and order.

Ti·tho·nus (ti·thō′nəs) In Greek mythology, a son of Laomedon who was loved by Eos. She persuaded Zeus to grant him immortality but neglected to request for him eternal youth, so that Tithonus shriveled as he grew older and older, and was finally changed into a grasshopper. [< L < Gk. *Tithōnos*]

ti·ti[1] (tē′tē) *n.* **1** An evergreen or small tree *(Cliftonia monophylla)* with fragrant white flowers, native in swamps of the southern United States. **2** Any of a genus *(Cyrilla)* of related trees of tropical America; especially, the **white titi** *(C. racemiflora).* [< Sp. < Aymaran]

ti·ti[2] (tē·tē′) *n.* One of several small South American monkeys (genus *Callicebus*). [< Sp. *tití* < Guarani *titi*]

ti·tian (tish′ən) *n.* A reddish-yellow color

much used by Titian, especially in painting women's hair. —*adj.* Having or pertaining to the color of titian. [after *Titian*]

Ti·tian (tish'ən), 1477–1576, Venetian painter: real name *Tiziano Vecellio.*

Ti·ti·ca·ca (tē'tē·kä'kä), **Lake** The largest lake in South America, in the Andes between SE Peru and west central Bolivia; 3,200 square miles; elevation, 12,500 feet; the highest large lake in the world.

tit·il·lant (tit'ə·lənt) *n.* An excitant. [< L *titillans, -antis,* ppr. of *titillare* tickle]

tit·il·late (tit'ə·lāt) *v.t.* **·lat·ed, ·lat·ing 1** To cause a tickling sensation in. **2** To excite pleasurably in any way. [< L *titillatus,* pp. of *titillare* tickle]

tit·il·la·tion (tit'ə·lā'shən) *n.* **1** The act of titillating, or the state of being titillated. **2** Any momentary exciting or gratifying sensation. —**tit'il·la'tive** *adj.*

tit·i·vate (tit'ə·vāt) *v.t.* & *v.i.* **·vat·ed, ·vat·ing** *Colloq.* To put on decorative touches; smarten; dress up: also spelled *tittivate.* [Earlier *tidivate, tiddivate.* ? < TIDY, on analogy with *cultivate*] —**tit'i·va'tion** *n.*

tit·lark (tit'lärk') *n.* A pipit. [ME *tit* a little thing + LARK]

ti·tle (tīt'l) *n.* **1** *Law* **a** The means whereby the owner of lands has the just possession of his property; the union of possession, the right of possession, and the right of property in lands and tenements; also, the legal evidence of one's right of property, or the means by or source from which one's right to property has accrued: *title* by purchase. **b** The distinguishing form of words that heads or opens a legal document or statute; also, the opening clause containing the name of the court in which any action is pending, together with the names of the parties, etc. **2** A claim based on an acknowledged or alleged right: What is his *title* to credence? **3** A section or division of a statute, legal document, treatise, or the like. **4** An inscription that serves as a name for designating something, as a book or legal document. **5** A name; descriptive designation. **6** An appellation significant of office, rank, etc.; especially, a designation of nobility. **7** In or near Rome, a church or parish headed by a cardinal: so called because dedicated to or named after the title of some martyr or saint. **8** A source of maintenance, as a patrimony, or a place of duty, especially with income attached, a right or nomination to which is a canonical prerequisite to ordination. **9** In some sports, supremacy; championship: to play for the *title.* See synonyms under NAME. —*v.t.* **·tled, ·tling 1** To give a name to; entitle; call. **2** To confer an honorary title upon; ennoble. [< OF < L *titulus* a label, an inscription. Doublet of TITTLE.] —**ti'tle·less** *adj.*

ti·tled (tīt'ld) *adj.* Having a title, especially of nobility.

ti·tle·hold·er (tīt'l·hōl'dər) *n.* One who possesses a title, especially a championship title. Also **ti'tlist.** —**ti'tle·hold'ing** *adj.*

title page A page containing the title of a work and the names of its author and its publisher.

title role The character in a play, opera, or motion picture for whom it is named.

tit·man (tit'mən) *n. pl.* **·men** (-mən) *U.S. Colloq.* **1** The smallest pig in a litter; the runt of a litter of pigs. **2** A man small or stunted either physically or mentally. [ME *tit* a little thing + MAN]

tit·mouse (tit'mous') *n. pl.* **·mice** (-mīs') Any of several small oscine birds (family *Paridae*) related to the nuthatches; especially, the **tufted titmouse** *(Baeolophus bicolor)* of the United States, having a conspicuous crest. [Alter. of ME *titmose* < *tit-* little + *mose,* alter. of OE *mase* a titmouse; infl. in form by MOUSE]

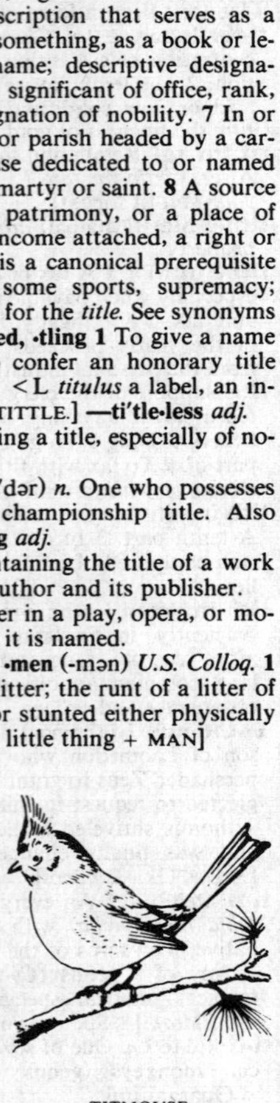

TITMOUSE
(About 5 1/2 inches long)

Ti·to (tē'tō) Italian, Spanish, and Portuguese form of TITUS.

Ti·to (tē'tō), **Marshal,** 1891?–1980, Yugoslav guerrilla leader in World War II; premier 1945–53; president 1953–80; real name *Josip Broz.*

Ti·to·grad (tē'tô·gräd) The capital of Montenegro in southern Yugoslavia: formerly **Pod·go·ri·ca** (pod'gô·rē'tsä).

Ti·to·ism (tē'tō·iz'əm) *n.* The assertion by a Communist state of its national interests in opposition to Soviet domination, such as occurred under Marshal Tito in Yugoslavia.

ti·trate (tī'trāt, tit'rāt) *v.t.* & *v.i.* **·trat·ed, ·trat·ing** *Chem.* To determine the strength of (a solution) by means of standard solutions or by titration. [< F *titrer* < *titre.* See TITER.]

ti·tra·tion (tī·trā'shən, ti-) *n. Chem.* The process of determining the strength or concentration of a given solution by adding to it measured amounts of a standard solution until the desired chemical reaction has been effected.

ti·tre (tī'tər, tē'-) See TITER.

tit·ter (tit'ər) *v.i.* To laugh in a suppressed way, as from nervousness or in ridicule; snicker; giggle. —*n.* The act of tittering; a giggling. [Imit.] —**tit'ter·er** *n.* —**tit'ter·ing·ly** *adv.*

tit·tie (tit'ē) *n. Scot.* A sister. Also **tit'ty.**

tit·tle (tit'l) *n.* **1** The minutest quantity; iota. **2** Originally, a very small mark in writing, as the dot over an *i,* etc.; any diacritical mark. [< L *titulus.* Doublet of TITLE.]

tit·tle-tat·tle (tit'l·tat'l) *n.* **1** Foolish or trivial talk; gossip. **2** An idle, trifling or tattling talker. —*v.i.* **·tled, ·tling** To talk foolishly or idly; gossip; chatter. [Reduplication of TATTLE]

tit·tup (tit'əp) *v.i.* **·tuped** or **·tupped, ·tup·ing** or **·tup·ping** To act in a restless or lively manner; dance along; prance. —*n.* A prancing or curveting action, indicating gaiety or frolicsomeness; a caper. [Appar. imit. of hoof beats]

tit·u·ba·tion (tich'ōō·bā'shən, tit'yə-) *n. Pathol.* A stumbling; tottering; a disturbance of equilibrium resulting in the stumbling gait characteristic of spinal disease. [< L *titubatio, -onis* < *titubatus,* pp. of *titubare* stagger]

tit·u·lar (tich'ōō·lər, tit'yə-) *adj.* **1** Existing in name or title only; nominal. **2** Pertaining to a title. **3** Bestowing or taking title. See TITLE (def. 8). —*n.* One having a title in virtue of which he holds an office or benefice, whether he performs its duties or not; in ecclesiastical law, one holding a sinecure title. Also **tit'u·lar'y** (-ler'ē). [< L *titulus* a title] —**tit'u·lar·ly** *adv.*

Ti·tus (tī'təs) A masculine personal name. [< L, safe]

—**Titus** A disciple of the apostle Paul; also, the epistle in the New Testament addressed to Titus and attributed to Paul.

—**Titus,** A.D. 40?–81, emperor of Rome A.D. 79–81: full name *Titus Flavius Sabinus Vespasianus.*

Ti·u (tē'ōō) In Teutonic mythology, god of war and sky: identified with the Norse *Tyr.*

Tiv·o·li (tiv'ə·lē, *Ital.* tē'vō·lē) A town in central Italy NE of Rome: ancient *Tibur.*

tiz·zy[1] (tiz'ē) *n. pl.* **·zies** *Slang* A bewildered or excited state of mind; a dither. [Origin unknown]

tiz·zy[2] (tiz'ē) *n. pl.* **·zies** *Brit. Slang* A sixpence. [Prob. alter. of TESTER[3]; infl. in form by slang *tilbury* a sixpence]

Tji·la·tjap (chē·lä'chäp) A port of southern Java, Indonesia. Also **Chi·la'chap.**

Tji·re·bon (chē're·bôn') A port of NW central Java, Indonesia, SE of Jakarta: also *Cheribon.*

Tl *Chem.* Thallium (symbol Tl).

Tlax·ca·la (tläs·kä'lä) A state of central Mexico; 1,555 square miles; capital, Tlaxcala.

Tlem·cen (tlem·sen') A city of NW Algeria. Also **Tlem·sen'.**

Tlin·git (tling'git) *n. pl.* North American Indians belonging to any of eighteen tribes comprising the Koluschan linguistic stock, and inhabiting the Alexander Archipelago of SE Alaska. They are seafaring people of fairly advanced culture. Also **Tlin·kit** (tling'kit).

Tm *Chem.* Thulium (symbol Tm).

tme·sis (tmē'sis, mē'sis) *n.* The separation of the elements of a compound word by an intervening word, as in the phrase *to us ward,* meaning "toward us." [< L < Gk. *tmēsis* a cutting < *temnein* cut]

TNT (tē'en'tē') *n.* **1** Trinitrotoluene. **2** *Colloq.* Any explosive and dangerous circumstance, force, or person. Also **T.N.T.** [< T(RI)N(ITRO)-T(OLUENE)]

to (tōō, *unstressed* tə) *prep.* **1** In a direction toward or terminating in: going *to* town. **2** Opposite, in contact with, or near: face *to* face; Hold me *to* your breast. **3** Intending or aiming at; having as an object or purpose: Come *to* my rescue. **4** Resulting in; having as a condition or effect: frozen *to* death; flattered *to* his ruin. **5** Belonging in connection or accompaniment with; denoting the relation of things made to go together or between which there is correspondence: the key *to* the barn; March *to* the music. **6** In honor of: Drink *to* me only with thine eyes. **7** In comparison, correspondence, or agreement with: often denoting ratio: 9 is *to* 3 as 21 *to* 7; four quarts *to* the gallon. **8** Until; approaching as a limit; denoting the end of a period of time, or a time not reached: *to* my dying day; five minutes *to* one. **9** For the utmost duration of; as far as: a miser *to* the end of his days. **10** In respect of; concerning: blind *to* her charms; a speech *to* the point. **11** In close application toward: Buckle down *to* work; Fall *to* dinner. **12** For; with regard for: The contest is open *to* everyone. **13** Noting an indirect or limiting object after verbs, adjectives, or nouns, and designating the recipient of the action: taking the place of the dative case in other languages: Give the ring *to* me; That fact is not apparent *to* me. **14** By: known *to* the world. **15** From the point of view of: It seems *to* me. **16** *Dial.* At or in (a place): He is not *to* home now. **17** *Colloq.* With: The land was planted *to* potatoes. **18** About; involved in: That's all there is *to* it. ◆ *To* also serves to indicate the infinitive, and is often used elliptically for it: You may come if you care *to.* See synonyms under AT, INTO. —*adv.* **1** To or toward something. **2** In a direction, position, or state understood or implied; especially, shut or closed: Pull the door *to.* **3** Into a normal condition; into consciousness: She soon came *to.* **4** *Naut.* With head to the wind: said of a sailing vessel: to lie *to.* **5** Upon the matter at hand; into action or operation: They fell *to* with good will. **6** Nearby; at hand. —**to and fro** In opposite or different directions; back and forth. [OE *tō*]

toad (tōd) *n.* **1** A tailless, jumping, insectivorous amphibian (family *Bufonidae*), resembling the frog but without teeth in the upper jaw, and resorting to water only to breed. **2** Some similar amphibian; especially, the **Surinam toad** *(Pipa pipa)* or the European **midwife toad** *(Alytes obstetricans).* **3** Any person regarded scornfully or contemptuously. [OE *tādige*]

TOAD
(Species vary from 2 to 6 inches)

toad-eat·er (tōd'ē'tər) *n.* A fawning parasite; a sycophant. [Orig. an assistant to a charlatan, who ate, or pretended to eat, toads (held to be poisonous) to show the efficacy of a patent medicine]

toad·fish (tōd'fish') *n. pl.* **·fish** or **·fish·es** Any of a family *(Batrachoididae)* of fishes with scaleless skin and mouth and head resembling those of a toad.

toad·flax (tōd'flaks') *n.* **1** A common, showy perennial weed *(Linaria vulgaris)* of the figwort family, having terminal spikes of spurred yellow flowers marked with an orange spot: also called *butter-and-eggs.* **2** Any other plant of the genus *Linaria.* [So called because spotted like toads and having a flaxlike foliage]

toad spit Cuckoo spit. Also **toad spittle.**

toad·stone[1] (tōd'stōn') *n. Dial.* A volcanic rock, generally decomposed, occurring in limestone in Derbyshire, England. [? So called from a resemblance of its markings to those of a toad]

toad·stone[2] (tōd'stōn') *n.* A natural or artificial stone resembling a toad in color and form, and long believed to be formed in a toad: worn as a talisman. [< TOAD + STONE; trans. of L *batrachites* < Gk.]

toad·stool (tōd'stōōl') *n.* **1** Any one of many umbrella-shaped fungi, growing on decaying vegetable matter, common in woods and damp places; a mushroom. **2** *Colloq.* A poisonous mushroom.

toad·y (tō′dē) *n. pl.* **toad·ies** An obsequious flatterer; a fawning, servile person; a toadeater. — *v.t.* & *v.i.* **toad·ied, toad·y·ing** To act the toady (to). ◆Homophone: *tody*. [Short for TOAD EATER] — **toad′y·ish** *adj.* — **toad′y·ism** *n.*

to-and-fro (tōō′ən·frō′) *adj.* Moving back and forth; undulating; alternating. — *n.* Motion back and forth.

toast[1] (tōst) *v.t.* 1 To brown before or over a fire; especially, to brown (bread or cheese) before a fire or in a toaster. 2 To warm thoroughly before a fire. — *v.i.* 3 To become warm or toasted. — *n.* Sliced bread browned in a toaster or at a fire; toasted bread. [< OF *toster* roast, grill < L *tostus* < *torrere* parch, roast]

toast[2] (tōst) *n.* 1 The act of drinking to someone's health or to some sentiment. 2 The person or sentiment named in thus drinking: She was the *toast* of the town. — *v.t.* To drink to the health of or in honor of. — *v.i.* To drink a toast or toasts. [< TOAST[1] in obs. sense of "a spiced piece of toast put in a drink to flavor it"]

toast·er[1] (tōs′tər) *n.* A device for making toast.

toast·er[2] (tōs′tər) *n.* One who proposes a toast.

toast·mas·ter (tōst′mas′tər, -mäs′tər) *n.* A person who, at public dinners, announces the toasts, calls upon the various speakers, etc. — **toast′ mis′tress** (-mis′tris) *n. fem.*

to·bac·co (tə·bak′ō) *n. pl.* **·cos** or **·coes** 1 An annual plant of the nightshade family (genus *Nicotiana*), especially *N. tabacum*, the chief source of the tobacco of commerce, originally of tropical America, but now cultivated in various parts of the world. 2 Its leaves prepared in various ways, as for smoking, chewing, snuffing, etc. 3 The use of tobacco for smoking. 4 The various products prepared from tobacco leaves, as cigarettes, cigars, etc. [< Sp. *tabaco* < Cariban, a tube or pipe in which the natives smoked tobacco]

TOBACCO
(Plant to 8 feet or more)

tobacco heart *Pathol.* A cardiac disorder brought about by excessive smoking and characterized by a rapid or uneven pulse; nicotinism.

to·bac·co·nist (tə·bak′ə·nist) *n. Brit.* One who deals in tobacco.

tobacco worm Either of two large green worms (*Protoparce sexta* and *P. quinquemaculata*) with white stripes and a slender horn at the rear end of the body, destructive to tobacco plants.

To·ba·go (tō·bā′gō) See TRINIDAD AND TOBAGO.

To·bi·as (tō·bī′əs, tō-; *Dan., Du., Ger., Sp.* tō·bē′äs) A masculine personal name. Also **To·bi′ah** (-bī′ə), *Fr.* **To·bie** (tō·bē′), *Ital.* **To·bi·a** (tō·bē′ä). [< Hebrew, the Lord is (my) good]

To·bit (tō′bit) A pious Hebrew captive in Nineveh, hero of the Apocryphal book of the Old Testament bearing his name.

to·bog·gan (tə·bog′ən) *n.* 1 A light sledlike vehicle, consisting of a long thin board or boards curved upward at the forward end: used for transporting goods or coasting, especially on prepared slides. 2 A luge. — *v.i.* 1 To coast on a toboggan. 2 To move downward swiftly: Wheat prices *tobogganed*. [< dial. F (Canadian) *tabagan* a sled < Algonquian. Cf. Micmac *tobākun*.] — **to·bog′gan·er, to·bog′gan·ist** *n.*

toboggan slide A slope prepared for coasting with toboggans: often a winding track with banked curves.

To·bol (tò·bôl′y′) A river in northern Kazakh S.S.R. and SW Asiatic Russian S.F.S.R., flowing 1,042 miles NE from the Ural Mountains of NW central Kazakh S.S.R., near the Russian border, to the Irtish River at Tobolsk.

To·bolsk (tô·bôlsk′) A city in SW Asiatic Russian S.F.S.R., at the junction of the Tobol and Irtish rivers.

To·bruk (tō·brōōk′, tō′brōōk) A port of eastern Cyrenaica, Libya; scene of several battles of

World War II, 1941–42. *Italian* **To·bruch** (tō′·brook).

to·by (tō′bē) *n. pl.* **·bies** 1 A mug or jug for ale or beer, often made in the form of an old man wearing a three-cornered hat. 2 *Colloq.* A form of stogie cigar. [< TOBY]

TOBY JUG

To·by (tō′bē) Diminutive of TOBIAS.

To·can·tins (tō′kän·tēns′) A river in north central and north Brazil, flowing 1,640 miles north to the Pará River.

toc·ca·ta (tə·kä′tə, *Ital.* tôk·kä′tä) *n. Music* A rapid free composition for piano, organ, or other keyboard instrument, often preceding a fugue. [< Ital., lit., a touching, orig. pp. fem. of *toccare* touch]

To·char·i·an (tō·kâr′ē·ən, -kär′-) *n.* 1 One of an ancient cultured people known to the Greeks and Chinese as having inhabited central Asia in the first Christian millennium: conquered by the Uigurs. 2 The language of the Tocharians, belonging to the centum division of the Indo-European language family: unknown before 1904, when it was brought to light through manuscripts of the seventh century found in ruined temples in Chinese Turkestan. Two dialects have been distinguished, usually referred to as *Tocharian A* and *Tocharian B*. Also spelled *Tokharian*.

toch·er (tokh′ər) *Scot.* & *Brit. Dial. n.* The dowry of a bride. — *v.t.* To give a dowry to; dower. [< Irish *tochar* an assigned portion < *tochuirim* I put to, assign < *chuirim* I put]

toco- *combining form* Child; pertaining to children or to childbirth: *tocology*. Also, before vowels, **toc-.** [< Gk. *tokos* child, childbirth]

to·col·o·gy (tō·kol′ə·jē) *n.* The science and art of midwifery; obstetrics: also spelled *tokology*. [< TOCO- + -LOGY]

to·coph·er·ol (tō·kof′ə·rōl, -rol) *n.* Any of a group of chemically related compounds occurring naturally in many vegetable oils and including some that exhibit the biological activity of vitamin E. [< TOCO- + Gk. *pherein* bear + -OL[1]; so called because thought to be effective against sterility]

Tocque·ville (tōk·vēl′), **Alexis Charles Henri Maurice Clérel de,** 1805–59, French statesman and political writer.

toc·sin (tok′sin) *n.* 1 A signal sounded on a bell; alarm. 2 An alarm bell. [< MF < OF *toquassen* < Provençal *tocasenh* < *tocar* strike, touch + *senh* a bell < LL *signum* a signal bell < L, a sign]

tod[1] (tod) *n.* 1 A bushy clump. 2 A former weight for wool, about 28 pounds. [ME *todde*, prob. < LG. Cf. East Frisian *todde* small load]

tod[2] (tod) *n. Scot.* & *Brit. Dial.* A fox.

to·day (tə·dā′) *adv.* 1 On or during this present day. 2 At the present time; nowadays. — *n.* The present day, time, or age. Also **to-day′.** ◆ Collateral adjective: *hodiernal.* [OE *tō dæg* < *tō* to + *dæg* a day]

Todd (tod), **Sir Alexander R.,** born 1907, English chemist.

tod·dle (tod′l) *v.i.* **·dled, ·dling** To walk unsteadily and with short steps, as a little child. — *n.* The act of toddling; a child's walk; also, a stroll. [? Freq. of TOTTER] — **tod′dler** *n.*

tod·dy (tod′ē) *n. pl.* **·dies** 1 A drink made with spirits, hot water, sugar, and a slice of lemon. 2 The sap or juice that flows from the incised spathes of certain East Indian palms; also, a spirituous liquor distilled from it. The principal palms yielding toddy are called **toddy palms,** as the wild date of India (*Phoenix sylvestris*). [< Hind. *tārī* toddy (def. 2) < *tār* palm tree < Skt. *tāla* a palmyra]

Tod·le·ben (tōt′lā·bən) See TOTLEBEN.

to-do (tə·dōō′) *n. Colloq.* Confusion or bustle, as on account of something disturbing; a demonstration; a fuss. [OE *to-dōn* < *to-* asunder + *dōn* do, put]

Todt (tōt), **Fritz,** 1891–1942, German military engineer.

to·dy (tō′dē) *n. pl.* **·dies** Any of numerous very small insectivorous West Indian birds (genus *Todus*) related to the kingfishers; especially, the **green tody** (*Todus godus*) of Jamaica, bright green with a scarlet throat. ◆Homophone: *toady.* [< F *todier* < L *todus*, a kind of small bird]

toe (tō) *n.* 1 One of the digits of the foot; also, the forward part of the foot, as distinguished from the *heel*. 2 That portion of a shoe, boot, sock, stocking, skate, or the like that covers, or corresponds in position with, the toes. 3 The lower end or projection of something, resembling or suggestive of a toe. 4 *Mech.* **a** A pivot or journal in a bearing. **b** A horizontally projecting arm on a stem, as for operating a valve, raised by a cam or lifted. 5 The end of the head of a golf club. 6 In a railroad switch, the space between the rails at the unchanneled end of a frog. — **on one's toes** Alert; wide-awake. — **to tread on (someone's) toes** To offend (a person); trespass on (someone's) feelings, opinions, prejudices, etc. — *v.* **toed, toe·ing** *v.t.* 1 To touch with the toes: to *toe* the line. 2 To kick with the toe. 3 To furnish with a toe. 4 To drive (a nail or spike) obliquely; also, to attach (beams, etc.) end to end, by nails driven thus. 5 To strike (a golf ball) with the toe of the club. — *v.i.* 6 To stand or walk with the toes pointing in a specified direction: to *toe* out. — **to toe the mark** To touch a certain line or mark with the toes preparatory to starting a race; hence, to abide by the rules; conform to discipline or a standard. [OE *tā*] — **toe′less** *adj.*

toe cap A cap covering for the tip or toe of a boot or shoe. See illustration under SHOE.

toe crack A sandcrack.

toed (tōd) *adj.* 1 Having toes: chiefly in composition: pigeon-*toed.* 2 Fastened or fastening by obliquely driven nails; also, driven obliquely, as a nail.

toe-dance (tō′dans′, -däns′) *v.i.* **-danced, -danc·ing** To dance on tiptoe; perform a toe dance. — **toe′-danc′er** *n.*

toe dance A dance performed on tiptoe.

toe·hold (tō′hōld′) *n.* 1 In climbing, a small space which supports the toes. 2 Any means of entrance, support, or the like; a footing: The Marines gained a *toehold* on the island. 3 A hold in which a wrestler bends back the foot of his opponent.

toe·nail (tō′nāl′) *n.* 1 A nail growing on the toe. 2 A nail driven obliquely to hold the foot of a stud or brace. — *v.t.* To fasten with obliquely driven nails.

toff (tof, tôf) *n. Brit. Slang* A dandy; also, a gentleman. [Earlier *tuft* < TUFT (def. 3)]

tof·fee, tof·fy (tôf′ē, tof′ē) See TAFFY.

toft (tôft, toft) *n. Brit.* 1 Land once occupied as a messuage, on which the buildings have decayed or been burned; a homestead. 2 A hillock or knoll. [OE, a homestead < ON *topt, tupt*]

to·fu (tō′fōō) *n.* A soft, cheeselike, protein-rich food made from soybean milk curds. [< Jap.]

tog (tog) *Colloq. n.* 1 A coat. 2 *pl.* Clothes; outfit: football *togs.* — *v.t.* **togged, tog·ging** To dress; clothe: often with *up* or *out.* [Short for vagabond's cant *togemans, togman* coat, cloak < F *toge* a toga < L *toga*]

to·ga (tō′gə) *n. pl.* **·gas** or **·gae** (-jē) 1 The distinctive outer garment worn in public by a citizen of ancient Rome. 2 Any gown or cloak characteristic of a calling or profession: the lawyer's *toga.* [< L *tegere* cover]

to·gaed (tō′gəd) *adj.* Robed in the toga; hence, classical and stately. Also **to·gat·ed** (tō′gā·tid).

to·ga vi·ri·lis (tō′gə vi·rī′lis) *Latin* The toga assumed by a male citizen of ancient Rome at the age of 14 as a token of manhood.

ROMAN TOGA

to·geth·er (tōō·geth′ər, tə-) *adv.* 1 Into union or contact with each other; conjointly. 2 In the same place or at the same spot; with each other; in company. 3 At the same moment of time; simultaneously. 4 Without cessation or intermission. 5 With one another; mutually. [OE *tōgædere, tōgadore < tō* to + *gædre* together. Akin to GATHER.]

to·geth·er·ness (tōō·geth′ər·nis, tə-) *n.* The state of being associated or united.

tog·ger·y (tog′ər·ē) *n. pl.* **·ger·ies** *Colloq.* Togs collectively; clothes.

tog·gle (tog′əl) *n.* **1** A pin, or short rod, properly attached in the middle, as to a rope, and designed to be passed through a hole or eye and turned. **2** A toggle iron. **3** A toggle joint. —*v.t.* **·gled, ·gling** To fix, fasten, or furnish with a toggle or toggles. [Prob. nautical var. of dial. *tuggle,* appar. freq. of TUG]

toggle iron A harpoon, as for killing whales, so arranged as to turn crosswise when it enters the animal's body. Also **toggle harpoon.**

toggle joint *Mech.* A joint having a central hinge like an elbow, and operable by applying the power at the junction, thus changing the direction of motion and giving indefinite mechanical pressure.

TOGGLE JOINT Level Type

toggle switch *Electr.* A switch in the form of a projecting lever whose movement through a small arc opens or closes an electric circuit.

To·gliat·ti (tō·lyät′tē), **Palmiro,** 1893–1964, leader of the Italian Communist party.

To·go (tō′gō) An independent republic in western Africa; 22,008 square miles; capital, Lomé: formerly French Togoland, a United Nations Trust Territory. —**To′go·lese′** (-lēs, -lēz) *adj.* & *n.*

To·go (tō·gō), **Count Heihachiro,** 1847–1934, Japanese admiral; defeated the Russian fleet at the battle of Tsushima, 1905.

To·go·land (tō′gō·land), **British** See GHANA.

Togoland, French See TOGO.

toil[1] (toil) *n.* **1** Fatiguing work; labor; hence, any oppressive task. **2** Any notable work accomplished by labor. **3** *Obs.* Strife; struggle. —*v.i.* **1** To work arduously; labor painfully and tiringly. **2** To progress or make one's way with slow and labored steps. —*v.t.* **3** To accomplish or obtain by toil. See synonyms under STRUGGLE. [<AF *toil* a dispute, OF *tooil* trouble <AF *toiler* strive, OF *tooillier* soil, agitate <L *tudiculare* stir about < *tudicula* a machine for bruising olives, dim. of *tudes* a mallet] —**toil′er** *n.*

Synonyms (noun): drudgery, labor, stent, stint, task, travail, work. *Work* is exertion of body or mind that taxes the powers for the accomplishment of some end. The term is a broad one; *work* may be light and pleasant, or severe and exhausting. *Labor* is always strenuous; it is hard *work. Toil* is still more severe. One may enjoy *work* and be cheerful in *labor,* but *toil* oppresses. *Drudgery* is often applied to menial service, but also to any *work* that is not only hard, but dull and mechanical. A *task* is a definite amount of *work* appointed and required by another; yet we sometimes speak of a *task* which one imposes upon himself; this in popular language is called a *stint* or *stent.* See TASK, WORK. *Antonyms*: amusement, ease, idleness, leisure, play, recreation, relaxation, repose, rest.

toil[2] (toil) *n.* A net, snare, or other trap: now generally used figuratively and commonly in the plural. [<MF *toiles* nets < *toile* cloth <OF *teile* <L *tela* a web]

toile (twäl) *n.* A sheer linen fabric; also, a fine cretonne with scenic designs printed in one color. [<F. See TOIL[2].]

toi·let (toi′lit) *n.* **1** A fixture in the shape of a bowl, used for urination and defecation. **2** A lavatory or watercloset; also, a bathroom. **3** The act or process of dressing oneself; formerly, especially of dressing the hair. **4** Attire; toilette; also, a toilette or costume. —*adj.* Used in dressing or grooming: *toilet* articles. [<F *toilette* orig. a cloth dressing gown, dim. of *toile* cloth. See TOIL[2].]

toi·let·ry (toi′lit·rē) *n. pl.* **·ries** Any of the several articles used in making one's toilet, as soap, comb, brush, etc.

toi·lette (toi·let′, *Fr.* twà·let′) *n.* **1** The act or process of grooming oneself, usually including bathing, hair-dressing, application of cosmetics and perfume, and costuming. **2** A person's actual dress or style of dress; also, any specific costume or gown: an elaborate *toilette.* [<F. See TOILET.]

toilet water A scented liquid containing a small amount of alcohol, used in or after the bath, after shaving, etc.

toil·ful (toil′fəl) *adj.* Replete with toil; laborious. —**toil′ful·ly** *adv.*

toil·some (toil′səm) *adj.* Accomplished with fatigue; involving toil. See synonyms under ARDUOUS, DIFFICULT. —**toil′some·ly** *adv.*

toil·worn (toil′wôrn′, -wōrn′) *adj.* Exhausted by toil; showing the effects of toil.

toit (toit) *v.i. Brit. Dial.* **1** To dawdle; saunter. **2** To totter. Also spelled *toyte.* [Origin uncertain]

To·jo (tō·jō), **Hideki,** 1885–1948, Japanese general and statesman in World War II.

To·kay (tō·kā′) *n.* **1** A white or reddish-blue grape from Tokay, Hungary. **2** A wine made from it. [from *Tokay,* a town in northern Hungary]

To·ke·lau (tō′kə·lou′) A New Zealand island group north of Samoa; 4 square miles: also *Union Islands.*

to·ken (tō′kən) *n.* **1** Anything indicative of some other thing; a visible sign; indication; evidence: in *token* of respect. **2** A symbol: This gift is a *token* of my affection. **3** *Obs.* A signal. **4** Some tangible proof or evidence of a statement or of one's identity, authority, etc. **5** A memento; keepsake; souvenir. **6** A characteristic mark or feature. **7** A piece of metal issued as currency and having a face value greater than its actual value. **8** A piece of metal issued by a transportation company and good for one fare. See synonyms under EMBLEM, MARK[1], SIGN, TRACE[1]. —*v.t.* To evidence by a token; betoken. —*adj.* Done or given as a token, especially in partial fulfillment of an obligation or engagement: a *token* payment. [OE *tācen, tācn*]

to·kened (tō′kənd) *adj. Obs.* Marked by spots: the *tokened* pestilence. [<TOKEN, in obs. sense "a spot on the body indicating disease"]

to·ken·ism (tō′kən·iz·əm) *n.* The policy of attempting to meet certain obligations or conditions by symbolic or token efforts.

To·khar·i·an (tō·kâr′ē·ən, -kär′-) See TOCHARIAN.

to·kol·o·gy (tō·kol′ə·jē) See TOCOLOGY.

To·ku·shi·ma (tō·kōō·shē·mä) A port of eastern Shikoku, Japan.

To·ky·o (tō′kē·ō, *Japanese* tō·kyō) The capital of Japan, a port on **Tokyo Bay,** an inlet of the Philippine Sea in central Honshu, Japan: formerly *Edo* or *Yedo.* Also **To′ki·o.**

to·la (tō′lä) *n. Anglo-Indian* A weight, about 180 grains, for gold and silver; the weight of one rupee. [<Hind. <Skt. *tulā* a balance, weight < *tul-* weigh]

to·lan (tō′lan) *n.* A white crystalline unsaturated hydrocarbon, $C_{14}H_{10}$, prepared by synthesis. Also **to·lane** (tō′lān). [<TOL(UENE) + -ANE[2]]

tol·booth (tōl′bōōth′, -bōōth′) See TOLLBOOTH.

told (tōld) Past tense and past participle of TELL.

tole[1] (tōl) *v.t.* **toled, tol·ing 1** *Dial.* To draw as with a lure; entice; decoy. **2** *Obs.* To pull; drag; draw. Also spelled *toll.* [Var. of TOLL[2]]

tole[2] (tōl) *n.* A metalware, enameled or lacquered in various colors and frequently gilded: esteemed as an ornamental material. Also **tôle.** ◆ Homophone: *toll.* [<F *tôle* sheet iron, dial. var. of *table* a table]

To·le·do (tə·lē′dō) *n. pl.* **·dos** A sword or sword blade from Toledo, Spain. Also **to·le′do.**

To·le·do (tə·lē′dō) **1** A city in NW Ohio near Lake Erie. **2** (*Sp.* tō·lā′thō) An ancient city of central Spain on the Tagus.

tol·er·a·ble (tol′ər·ə·bəl) *adj.* **1** Passably good; commonplace. **2** Endurable; capable of being borne. **3** Allowable. **4** *Colloq.* In passably good health. [<OF <L *tolerabilis* able to endure < *tolerare* endure] —**tol′er·a·ble·ness** *n.* —**tol′er·a·bly** *adv.*

tol·er·ance (tol′ər·əns) *n.* **1** The character, state, or quality of being tolerant. **2** Indulgence or forbearance in judging the opinions, customs, or acts of others; freedom from bigotry or from racial or religious prejudice. **3** The act of enduring, or the capacity for endurance. **4** *Mech.* A fractional allowance for variations from the specified standard weight, dimensions, etc., of mechanical constructions. **5** A legally permissible variation from the standard of weight, fineness, etc., of coins: also called *remedy.* **6** *Med.* Natural or acquired ability to endure without ill effects large or increasing amounts of specified substances, particularly drugs.

tol·er·ant (tol′ər·ənt) *adj.* **1** Of a long-suffering disposition. **2** Indulgent; liberal. **3** *Med.* Capable of taking with impunity unusual or excessive doses of dangerous drugs. [<F <L *tolerans, -antis,* ppr. of *tolerare* endure] —**tol′er·ant·ly** *adv.*

tol·er·ate (tol′ə·rāt) *v.t.* **·at·ed, ·at·ing 1** To allow to be or be done without active opposition. **2** To concede, as the right to opinions or participation. **3** To bear, sustain, or be capable of enduring or sustaining. **4** *Med.* To endure, as a poisonous amount of dose, with impunity. See synonyms under ABIDE, ALLOW, ENDURE, PERMIT. [<L *toleratus,* pp. of *tolerare* endure] —**tol′er·a′tive** *adj.* —**tol′er·a′tor** *n.*

tol·er·a·tion (tol′ə·rā′shən) *n.* **1** The act or practice of tolerance. **2** The recognition of the rights of the individual to his own opinions and customs, as in matters pertaining to religious worship, when they do not interfere with the rights of others or with decency and order. **3** The spirit and desire to be tolerant in matters of opinion; forbearance; freedom from bigotry or race prejudice.

tol·i·dine (tol′ə·dēn, -din) *n. Chem.* One of several isomeric bases, $(CH_3 \cdot C_6H_3 \cdot NH_2)_2$, derived from dimethyl benzidine: one form is used in making dyes. Also **tol′i·din** (-din). [<TOL(UOL) + (BENZ)IDINE]

To·li·ma (tō·lē′mä), **Ne·va·da del** (nā·vä′thä thel) A volcano in the Andes Mountains of west central Colombia; 18,438 feet; last eruption, 1829.

toll[1] (tōl) *n.* **1** A fixed compensation for some privilege granted or service rendered, especially for one granted in a general or public way, as passage on a bridge or turnpike, or that taken by a miller for grinding grain (commonly a portion of the grain). **2** The right to levy such charge. **3** Something taken or elicited like a toll; price: The train wreck took a heavy *toll* of lives. **4** A due charged for the privilege of shipping or landing goods. **5** A charge for transportation of goods, especially by rail or canal. **6** A charge for a long-distance telephone call. See synonyms under TAX. —*v.t.* To take as a toll. —*v.i.* To take or exact a toll. ◆ Homophone: *tole.* [OE, ? <LL *toloneum* <L *telonium* <Gk. *telōnion* a customhouse < *telōnes* a tax collector < *telos* a tax]

toll[2] (tōl) *v.t.* **1** To cause (a bell) to sound slowly and at regular intervals. **2** To announce thus; especially, to announce (a death, funeral, etc.) by tolling. **3** To call or summon by tolling. **4** To decoy (game, especially ducks). **5** *Rare* To entice. —*v.i.* **6** To sound slowly and at regular intervals. —*n.* The sound of a bell rung slowly and with single, regularly repeated strokes. ◆ Homophone: *tole.* [Prob. <TOLL[1], in obs. sense of "pull, draw"]

toll·age (tō′lij) *n.* **1** A charge in the nature of a toll. **2** The toll itself.

toll·bar (tōl′bär′) *n.* A tollgate, properly one with a single bar.

toll·booth (tōl′bōōth′, -bōōth′) *n.* **1** *Scot.* A jail; prison: also spelled *tolbooth.* **2** A toll-house.

toll bridge A bridge at which toll for passage is paid.

toll call A long-distance telephone call, charged for at more than local rates.

toll collector A collector of tolls.

toll·er (tō′lər) *n.* **1** One who tolls a bell. **2** A bell used for tolling. **3** A small dog trained to toll or decoy ducks.

Tol·ler (tôl′ər), **Ernst,** 1893–1939, German dramatist and politician.

toll·gate (tōl′gāt′) *n.* A gate at the entrance to a bridge, or on a road, at which toll is paid.

toll·house (tōl′hous′) *n.* A toll collector's lodge adjoining a tollgate.

toll·keep·er (tōl′kē′pər) *n.* One who keeps a tollgate.

toll line A telephone line or channel, as between two central offices in different exchanges, for the use of which a toll is charged; a long-distance circuit.

Tol·stoy (tol′stoi, tōl′-; *Russian* tol·stoi′), **Count Leo Nikolaevich,** 1828–1910, Russian novelist and social reformer. Also **Tol′stoi.**

Tol·tec (tol′tek, tōl′-) *n.* One of certain ancient Nahuatlan tribes that dominated central and southern Mexico about A.D. 900–1100 and through contact with Mayan culture founded the highly civilized Nahua culture of the Aztecs: referred to in Aztec and Mayan legend. See NAHUA. —*adj.* Of or pertaining to the Toltecs. [<Nahuatl *Tolteca*] —**Tol′tec·an** *adj.*

to·lu (tə·lōō′) *n.* Balsam of Tolu. [<Sp. *tolú,*

from Santiago de *Tolu*, a seaport in Colombia]

tol·u·ate (tol′yŏŏ-āt) *n. Chem.* A salt or ester of a toluic acid. [<TOLU(IC) + -ATE³]

To·lu·ca (tō-lŏŏ′kä) The capital of Mexico state, central Mexico. Also **Toluca de Ler·do** (thä ler′thō)

tol·u·ene (tol′yŏŏ-ēn) *n. Chem.* A limpid hydrocarbon, $C_6H_5CH_3$, of the aromatic series, homologous with benzene, and obtained from coal tar by distillation: it is used in making dyestuffs and explosives. [<TOLU + -ENE; so called because orig. obtained from toluene]

to·lu·ic (tə-lŏŏ′ik, tol′yŏŏ-ik) *adj. Chem.* Designating or pertaining to any one of four isomeric acid derivatives of toluene, $C_8H_8O_2$, occurring as white crystalline compounds. [< TOLU(ENE) + -IC]

tol·u·ide (tol′yŏŏ-id, -id) *n. Chem.* One of a series of compounds obtained from toluene by substituting a tolyl radical for hydrogen in the amino group. Also **tol′u·id** (-id). [< TOLU(ENE) + -IDE]

to·lu·i·dine (tə-lŏŏ′ə-dēn, -din) *n. Chem.* One of three isomeric compounds, C_7H_9N, homologous with aniline and derived from the nitro–compounds of toluene. Also **to·lu′i·din** (-din). [<TOLUID(E) + -INE²]

tol·u·ol (tol′yŏŏ-ōl, -ol) *n. Chem.* Crude commercial toluene. Also **tol′u·ole** (-ōl). [<TOLU + (BENZ)OL]

tol·u·yl (tol′yŏŏ-il) *n. Chem.* The univalent acid radical C_8H_7O. [<TOLU(IC) + -YL]

tol·yl (tol′il) *n. Chem.* The univalent radical $C_6H_4CH_3$, derived from toluene; cresyl. [< TOL(UIC) + -YL]

tom (tom) *n.* **1** The male of various animals, especially the cat. **2** *U. S. Slang* An Uncle Tom; a servile Negro. —*adj.* Male: a *tom* pheasant. [from the personal name *Tom*]

Tom (tom) Diminutive of THOMAS.

Tom (tom) A river in SW central Asiatic Russian S.F.S.R., flowing 440 miles west and NW, from east Stalinsk to the Ob river NW of Tomsk.

tom·a·hawk (tom′ə-hôk) *n.* A war weapon used by the Algonquian Indians of North America, originally a carved club about three feet long, having a knob of solid wood on the end in which a piece of bone or metal was inserted; later, the light ax or hatchet–shaped weapon with an iron blade obtained in trade with Europeans. Tomahawks were either thrown or wielded in the hand. —*v.t.* To strike or kill with a tomahawk. [Algonquian *tamahak*, short for *tamahaken* a cutting utensil < *tamahaken* he uses for cutting < *tamaham* he cuts]

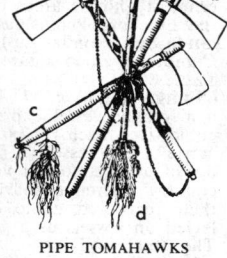

PIPE TOMAHAWKS
a. Cree. *b.* Iroquois.
c. Omaha. *d.* Osage.

tom·al·ley (tom′al-ē) *n.* The liver of the lobster, turning green when cooked: considered a great delicacy. Also **to·mal·ly** (tə-mal′ē). [Prob. <Cariban]

to·man (tō-män′) *n.* A Persian gold coin of varying value: formerly a money of account. [<Persian *tūmān, tumān, tuman* <Turki, lit., ten thousand]

Tom–and–Jer·ry (tom′ən-jer′ē) *n.* A drink made with brandy, rum, beaten egg, hot milk or water, sugar, and nutmeg. [after Corinthian *Tom* and *Jerry* Hawthorn, two main characters in *Life in London*, 1821, by Pierce Egan, 1772–1849, English writer on sports and sports jargon]

To·más (tō-mäs′) Spanish form of THOMAS.

to·ma·tin (tə-mä′tin, -mä′-) *n.* An antibiotic extracted from the leaves and plants of the tomato plant and also from the leaf juices of potatoes and green peppers. [<TOMAT(O) + -IN]

to·ma·to (tə-mä′tō, -mä′-) *n. pl.* **·toes** **1** The pulpy edible berry, yellow or red when ripe, of a tropical American perennial plant (*Lycopersicon esculentum*) of the nightshade family, highly esteemed as a vegetable. **2** The plant

itself. **3** *U.S. Slang* A girl or woman. [<Sp. *tomate* <Nahuatl *tomatl*]

tomato fruitworm The bollworm.

tomb (tŏŏm) *n.* **1** A place for the burial of the dead; a vault; grave. **2** A place where the dead lie. **3** Death itself. **4** A tombstone. —*v.t.* To entomb; bury; inter. [<AF *tumbe*, OF *tombe* <LL *tumba* <Gk. *tymbos* a mound]

tom·bac (tom′bak) *n.* Any of several copper-and–zinc alloys used to make gongs and bells in the East, and cheap jewelry in Europe: often spelled *tambac*. Also **tom′back, tom′-bak**. [<F <Pg. <Malayan *tambāga* copper <Skt. *tāmraka*]

Tom·big·bee River (tom-big′bē) A river in NE Mississippi and SW Alabama, flowing 384 miles SE and south to a junction with the Alabama River, forming the Mobile River, 30 miles north of Mobile Bay.

Tom·bouc·tou (tôn-bŏŏk-tŏŏ′) The French name for TIMBUKTU.

tom·boy (tom′boi′) *n.* A girl of romping and boisterous conduct; hoyden. [<TOM + BOY] — **tom′boy′ish** *adj.* — **tom′boy′ish·ness** *n.*

Tombs (tŏŏmz), **the** Formerly, the New York City police prison: so called from the funereal appearance of the building in which it was housed until 1948; also, loosely, the prison which replaced the original Tombs.

tomb·stone (tŏŏm′stōn′) *n.* A stone, usually inscribed, marking a place of burial.

Tomb·stone (tŏŏm′stōn′) A city in SE Arizona; formerly the site of the richest gold mines in Arizona.

tom·cat (tom′kat′) *n.* A male cat. [after *Tom*, a male cat, hero of *The Life and Adventures of a Cat*, 1760, a very popular anonymous work]

tom·cod (tom′kod′) *n.* Any of several small edible fishes (genus *Microgadus*) common on the Atlantic coast of North America. [<TOM + COD]

Tom Collins A drink consisting of gin, lemon or lime juice, sugar, and carbonated water.

Tom, Dick, and Harry Any persons taken at random from the crowd: used disparagingly, and often preceded by *every*.

tome (tōm) *n.* A volume, particularly if large; originally, one of a series of volumes. [<MF <L *tomus* <Gk. *tomos* a fragment, volume < *temnein* cut]

–tome *combining form* A cutting instrument (of a specified kind): *microtome*. [<Gk. *tomos* a cutting < *temnein* cut]

to·men·tose (tə-men′tōs, tō′men-tōs) *adj. Biol.* Covered with matted woolly hairs; flocculent. Also **to·men′tous** (-təs). [<L *tomentosus* < *tomentum* a stuffing for cushions]

to·men·tum (tə-men′təm) *n. pl.* **·ta** (-tə) **1** *Anat.* A network of small blood vessels of the pia mater where applied to the brain or spinal cord. **2** *Bot.* A form of pubescence composed of matted woolly hairs. [<L. See TOMENTOSE.]

tom·fool (tom′fŏŏl′) *n.* **1** An idiotic or silly person. **2** An amusing trifler. —*adj.* Ridiculous; very stupid. [after *Tom Fool*, a name formerly applied to mental defectives]

tom·fool·er·y (tom′fŏŏ′lər-ē) *n. pl.* **·er·ies** **1** Nonsensical behavior. **2** Kickshaws. Also **tom′fool′ish·ness**.

tom·ful·ler (tom′fŏŏl′ər) *n.* Sour or fermented hominy prepared as food: originally a Choctaw Indian dish. Also **tom′ful′la** (-fŏŏl′ə), **tom fuller.** [<Choctaw *tahfula* hominy]

Tom·ma·si·ni (tôm′mä-zē′nē), **Vicenzo**, 1880–1950, Italian composer.

tom·my¹ (tom′ē) *n. pl.* **·mies** *Slang* A roll; a loaf or piece of bread. [< *brown Tommy* < *Tommy Brown*, appar. a personification of brown bread]

tom·my² (tom′ē) *n. pl.* **·mies** Provisions or goods given instead of money in payment of wages; also, the system of paying workmen partly or entirely in kind. [Short for *tommyshop*, a store run on the truck system]

tom·my³ (tom′ē) *n. pl.* **·mies** A Tommy Atkins; a British soldier: also **Tom′my.** [Short for TOMMY ATKINS]

Tom·my (tom′ē) Diminutive of THOMAS.

Tommy At·kins (at′kinz) A British private of the regular army. [after *Thomas Atkins*, a name used on specimen forms in the official

regulations of the British Army after 1815]

Tommy gun A Thompson submachine gun. [<*Tommy*, dim. of *Thompson* + GUN]

to·mo·dro·mic (tō′mə-drō′mik, -drom′ik) *adj.* Having a flight path which cuts athwart a moving target; heading to cut or intercept: said of guided missiles. [<Gk. *tomos* cutting (< *temnein* cut) + *dromos* a running < *dramein* run]

to·mog·ra·phy (tō-mog′rə-fē) *n. Med.* X-ray photography of a predetermined plane of the body, with a blurring or elimination of details in other planes. [<Gk. *tomos* a slice (< *temnein* cut) + (PHOTO)GRAPHY]

to·mor·row (tə-môr′ō, -mor′ō) *adv.* On or for the next day after today. — *n.* The next day after today; the morrow. Also **to–mor′row.** [OE *tō morgen* < *tō* to + *morgen* morning, morrow]

tom·pi·on (tom′pē-ən) *n. Mil.* A stopper, as the plug put into the mouth of a cannon, to exclude moisture, etc.: also called *tampion*. [Var. of TAMPION]

Tomsk (tomsk, *Russian* tômsk) A city in west central Siberia, Russian S.F.S.R.

Tom Thumb In English folklore, the son of a plowman, as big as his father's thumb, who undergoes many adventures, including being swallowed by a cow and a giant.

— **General Tom Thumb** The stage name of Charles Sherwood Stratton, 1838–83, a dwarf exhibited by P. T. Barnum.

tom·tit (tom′tit′) *n.* **1** A tit; titmouse. **2** Any of various small birds, as a chickadee or a wren. [<TOM + TIT¹]

tom–tom (tom′tom′) *n.* **1** The native drum of India, Africa, etc., variously shaped, and usually beaten with the hands. **2** A percussion instrument of monotonous tone, used in some modern orchestras for special effects. **3** A copper or copper–alloy disk–shaped instrument sounded with a felt–covered hammer or stick; a Chinese gong. Also spelled *tam–tam.* [<Hind. *tamtam*, imit. of the instrument's sound]

–tomy *combining form* **1** *Surg.* A cutting of a (specified) part or tissue: *osteotomy*. **2** A (specified) kind of cutting or division: *dichotomy*. [<Gk. *tomē* a cutting < *temnein* cut]

ton¹ (tun) *n.* **1** Any of several large measures of weight; particularly, the **short ton** of 2000 pounds avoirdupois, commonly used in the United States and Canada; the **long ton** of 2240 pounds of Great Britain; or the **metric ton** of 1000 kilograms. **2** A unit for reckoning the displacement or weight of vessels, 35 cubic feet of sea water weighing about one long ton: called **displacement ton. 3** A unit for reckoning the freight–carrying capacity of a ship, usually equivalent to 40 cubic feet of space but varying with the cargo: called **freight ton, measurement ton. 4** A unit for reckoning the internal capacity of merchant vessels for purposes of registration, equivalent to 100 cubic feet or 2.832 cubic meters: called **register ton.** [Var. of TUN; infl. in form by OF *tonne* a cask]

ton² (tôn) *n. French* Tone; style; the prevailing fashion; vogue.

ton– Var. of TONO–.

–ton *suffix* Town: used in place names: *Charleston, Brockton.* [OE *-tun* < *tun* a town]

to·nal (tō′nəl) *adj.* Of or pertaining to tone or tonality. — **to′nal·ly** *adv.*

to·nal·ite (tō′nəl·it) *n.* A quartz–mica diorite. Also **to′nal·yte.** [from *Tonale*, in the Tirol, where it was first described]

to·nal·i·ty (tō-nal′ə-tē) *n. pl.* **·ties** **1** *Music* The quality and peculiarity of a tonal system; the melodic and harmonic relations between the tones of a scale or system of tones; a key or mode. **2** The general color scheme or collective tones of a painting. **3** Tonicity.

to–name (tŏŏ′nām′) *n. Scot.* **1** Some special distinguishing name; nickname. **2** A surname. [OE *tō-nama*]

to·na·pha·si·a (tō′nə-fā′zhē-ə, -zhə) *n. Psychiatry* Inability to recall a familiar tune; musical aphasia. [<NL <L *tonus* TONE + Gk. *aphasia* inability to speak]

tone (tōn) *n.* **1** Sound in relation to quality, volume, duration, and pitch. **2** *Physics* A sound having a definite pitch, and due to vibration of a sounding body. The pitch of a

tone depends on rate of vibration and its force on amplitude of vibration; its timbre is a complex resultant of concomitant vibration. If the vibration is simple harmonic motion the tone is pure; if there are complex components, the one of lowest pitch is the **fundamental tone** and the other components, in a simple ratio to the lowest, are **partial tones** or *overtones.* The combined result of all the partial tones gives the quality or *timbre* of the tone. **3** *Music* **a** The timbre, or peculiar characteristic sound, as of a voice or instrument. **b** The interval corresponding to one degree of the scale or staff; two semitones: sometimes called a **major tone** or **whole tone,** in distinction from a *semitone.* **4** A predominating disposition; especially, a frame or condition of mind; mood. **5 a** Characteristic style or tendency; tenor; quality: a want of moral *tone.* **b** Style or distinction; elegance: The party had *tone.* **6** Vocal inflection as expressive of feeling: a *tone* of pity. **7** *Ling.* A musical intonation or modulation of the voice by which a word or phrase may be changed in meaning or function: Peking Chinese distinguishes four *tones.* **8** *Phonet.* **a** The acoustical pitch, or change in pitch, of a phrase or sentence: In English, a questioning is indicated by a rising *tone.* **b** Special stress or accent given to one syllable of a word, or to one of the words in a sentence or phrase. **9** The prevailing effect of a picture, due to the management of chiaroscuro and to the effect of light upon the quality of color. **10** A shade, hue, tint, or degree of a particular color, or some slight modification of it: a deep *tone* of yellow; red with a purplish *tone.* **11** *Phot.* The shade or color of a photographic positive picture; also, the color of a negative film. **12** *Physiol.* The general condition of the body with reference to the vigorous and healthy discharge of its functions. See synonyms under SOUND[1]. —*v.* **toned, ton·ing** *v.t.* **1** To give tone to; modify in tone. **2** To tune or modify with reference to musical quality, as an instrument. **3** To intone in monotonous recitative; intone. **4** To alter the color or increase the brilliancy of (a photographic print) by a chemical bath. —*v.i.* **5** To assume a certain tone or hue. **6** To blend or harmonize, as in tone or shade. —**to tone down 1** To subdue the tone of (a painting). **2** To moderate in quality or tone. —**to tone up 1** To raise in quality or strength. **2** To elevate in pitch. **3** To gain in vitality. [<OF *ton* <L *tonus* <Gk. *tonos* a pitch of voice, a stretching < *teinein* stretch] —**ton'er** *n.*

Tone (tōn), **Wolfe,** 1763–98, Irish revolutionist and author.

tone color Timbre.

tone·less (tōn'lis) *adj.* Having no tone; without tone. —**tone'less·ly** *adv.* —**tone'less·ness** *n.*

tone poem A symphonic poem.

to·net·ic (tō·net'ik) *adj. Ling.* Tonic. [<TONE + (PHON)ETIC]

tong[1] (tông, tong) *v.t.* To gather, collect, or seize with tongs. —*v.i.* To use or fish with tongs. [<TONGS]

tong[2] (tông, tong) *n.* A Chinese closed society; in the United States, a secret society composed of Chinese. [<Chinese *t'ang* a hall, meeting place]

ton·ga (tong'gə) *n. Anglo-Indian* A light two-wheeled cart for four persons, in use in the country districts of India. [<Hind. *tāngā*]

Ton·ga (tong'gə) *n.* A Polynesian language spoken in the Tonga Islands.

Ton·ga Islands (tong'gə) An island group SE of the Fiji Islands in the South Pacific, comprising an independent Polynesian kingdom under British protection; total, 270 square miles; capital, Nukualofa: also *Friendly Islands.*

Ton·ga·land (tong'gə·land) A region of Zululand on the Mozambique border.

Ton·ga·re·va (tông'ä·rā'vä) See PENRHYN.

tongs (tôngz, tongz) *n. pl. (sometimes construed as singular)* **1** An implement for grasping, holding, or lifting objects, consisting usually of a pair of pivoted levers: also called **pair of tongs. 2** One of various grasping mechanisms. [OE *tang, tange*]

tongue (tung) *n.* **1** A protrusile, freely moving organ situated in the mouth of most vertebrates and supported by the hyoid bone: most completely developed in mammals, where it is important in taking in and masticating food, as one of the organs of taste, and in man as an organ of speech. ◆ Collateral adjective: *lingual.* **2** An organ or part of the mouth of various insects and fishes, having a similar shape or function. **3** An animal's tongue, as of beef, prepared as food. **4** The power of speech or articulation: to lose one's *tongue.* **5** Manner or style of speaking: a smooth *tongue.* **6** Mere speech, as contrasted with fact or deed. **7** Utterance; talk; discourse. **8** A language, vernacular, or dialect. **9** *Archaic* A people or race, regarded as having its own language: a Biblical use. **10** Anything resembling an animal tongue in appearance, shape, or function. **11** A slender projection of land, as a cape or small promontory. **12** A long narrow bay or inlet of water. **13** A jet of flame. **14** A strip of leather for closing the gap in the front of a laced shoe. **15** The fastening pin of a brooch or buckle. **16** *Music* The free or vibrating end of a reed in a wind instrument. **17** The clapper of a bell. **18** The harnessing pole of a horse-drawn vehicle. **19** The pointed, movable rail in a street railway switch. **20** *Mech.* Any flange or projecting part of a machine or mechanical device. **21** A projecting edge or tenon of a board for insertion into a corresponding groove of another board, thus forming a **tongue-and-groove joint. 22** A spike on a sword blade on which the hilt is secured. **23** The movable arm of a bevel. **24** A small, young sole. See synonyms under LANGUAGE. —**gift of tongues** See under GIFT. —**to hold one's tongue** To keep silent. —**with tongue in cheek** With mental reservations; facetiously; insincerely. —*v.* **tongued, tongu·ing** *v.t.* **1** To use the tongue in playing (a wind instrument) so as to produce marcato or staccato effects; also, to modify the sound of (a flute, cornet, etc.) by the use of the tongue. **2** To touch or lap with the tongue. **3 a** To cut a tongue on (a board). **b** To join or fit by a tongue-and-groove joint. **4** *Poetic* To utter; articulate. **5** *Archaic* To reproach; chide. —*v.i.* **6** To use the tongue in playing a wind instrument. **7** To talk or prattle. **8** To extend as a tongue. [OE *tunge.* Akin to LANGUAGE.]

TONGUE AND GROOVE

tongued (tungd) *adj.* Having a tongue: chiefly in compounds: four-*tongued.*

tongue·grass (tung'gras', -gräs') *n.* Peppergrass.

tongue·less (tung'lis) *adj.* Having no tongue; hence, speechless.

tongue-tie (tung'tī') *n.* Abnormal shortness of the frenum of the tongue, whereby its motion is impeded or confined. —*v.t.* **1** To deprive of speech or the power of speech, or of distinct articulation. **2** To bewilder or amaze so as to render speechless. —**tongue'-tied'** *adj.*

tongue-twist·er (tung'twis'tər) *n.* A word or phrase difficult to articulate quickly: "Miss Smith's fish-sauce shop" is a *tongue-twister.*

tongue worm A hemichordate animal.

ton·ic (ton'ik) *adj.* **1** Having power to invigorate or build up; bracing. **2** Pertaining to tone or tones; specifically, in music, pertaining to the keynote. **3** In art, denoting the general color effect and the light and shade in a picture or scene. **4** *Physiol.* **a** Of or pertaining to tension, especially muscular tension. **b** Rigid; unrelaxing: *tonic* spasm. **5** *Ling.* **a** Of or pertaining to musical intonations or modulations of words, sentences, etc. **b** Designating languages which distinguish words of identical or very similar form by variations in tone or pitch, as Chinese. **6** *Phonet.* **a** Stressed, as a syllable. **b** *Obs.* Voiced. —*n.* **1** *Med.* A drug that gradually restores the normal tone of organs from a condition of debility. **2** Whatever imparts vigor or tone. **3** The basic note of a key; keynote. [<Gk. *tonikos* < *tonos* sound, tone]

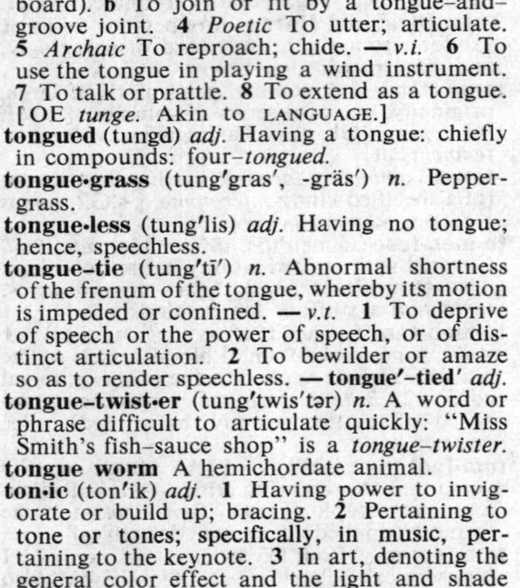

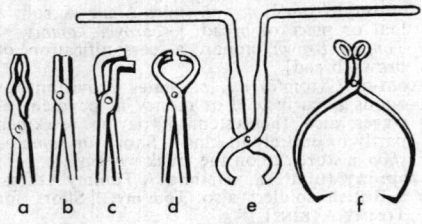

TONGS
a, b, c, d. Blacksmith's tongs.
e. Rail tongs. *f.* Ice tongs.

tonic accent 1 An accent that is spoken or pronounced rather than written. **2** *Phonet.* Emphasis placed on a syllable or sound by raising or changing the pitch of the voice.

to·nic·i·ty (tō·nis'ə·tē) *n.* **1** The state of being tonic; tone. **2** *Physiol.* The peculiar elastic condition of healthy tissue; tonus. **3** Health and vigor generally.

tonic sol-fa A system of teaching, writing, and reading music, especially vocal music, that lays particular stress on the tonal relations of the various elements of the key. The initials of the syllables used in solmization are employed to write its scale. [<TONIC + SOL[1] + FA]

to·night (tə·nīt') *adv.* **1** In or during the present or coming night. **2** *Obs.* Last night. —*n.* The night that follows this day; also, the present night. Also **to-night'.** [OE *tō niht* < *tō* to + *niht* night]

Ton·ite (tōn'īt) *n.* A blasting explosive of the guncotton class, with addition of barium nitrate and dinitrobenzene: a trade name.

Tonk (tongk) **1** A former princely state of the Rajputana States, India; merged with Rajasthan, 1948; 2,543 square miles. **2** A city of SE Rajasthan, India, formerly the capital of Tonk state.

Ton·ka bean (tong'kə) **1** An odoriferous seed obtained from a tropical American tree *(Dipteryx odorata),* and used for the adulteration of vanilla, flavoring of tobacco, snuff, etc. **2** The tree from which it is obtained. [Prob. <Negro name for the bean in Guiana]

Ton·kin (ton'kin, tong'-) A former name for northern North Vietnam, once a powerful independent kingdom, later a French protectorate; 44,670 square miles; capital, Hanoi. Also **Tong'king, Ton'king.** —**Ton'kin·ese'** *adj.* & *n.*

Tonkin, Gulf of An arm of the South China Sea between North Vietnam and the southernmost Chinese areas of Hainan island and the Luichow Peninsula.

Ton·le Sap (ton'lā sap) A lake in central Cambodia; 1,000 square miles: French *Grand Lac.*

ton·nage (tun'ij) *n.* **1** The cubic capacity of a merchant vessel expressed in tons of 100 cubic feet each. **2** The freight-carrying capacity of a vessel. **3** The aggregate freightage of a collection of vessels, especially of a country's merchant marine, as represented by their registered cubic capacity. **4** A tax levied on vessels at a given rate per ton. **5** The total weight of materials produced, mined, or transported. [<OF < *tonne* a ton, tun]

ton·neau (tu·nō') *n. pl.* **·neaus** (-nōz') or **·neaux** (-nōz') The rear part of an early type of automobile or vehicle, with low sides enclosing the seats, and a door at the rear or the side; also, the whole body of an automobile having such a rear part. [<F, lit., a barrel]

tono- *combining form* **1** Tension; pressure: *tonoplast.* **2** *Music* Tone; pitch: *tonometer* (def. 2). Also, before vowels, *ton-.* [<Gk. *tonos* tension < *teinein* stretch]

ton·o·graph (ton'ə·graf, -gräf, tō'nə-) *n.* A recording tonometer. [<TONO- + GRAPH]

to·nom·e·ter (tō·nom'ə·tər) *n.* **1** An instrument to measure strains within a liquid that tend to pull the particles asunder. **2** An accurately pitched tuning fork or set of forks; any instrument for determining the pitch of a tone. **3** An instrument for measuring tension in the eyeball or varying pressure of the blood.

to·nom·e·try (tō·nom'ə·trē) *n.* The art of using a tonometer. —**ton·o·met·ric** (ton'ə·met'rik, tō'nə-) *adj.*

ton·o·plast (ton'ə·plast) *n. Biol.* An inner plasmic membrane lining the vacuole of a cell and controlling the osmotic pressure. [<TONO- + -PLAST]

ton·o·scope (ton'ə·skōp, tō'nə-) *n.* An instrument by which a player or singer can observe departures from pitch or tone.

ton·sil (ton'səl) *n. Anat.* One of two oval lymphoid organs situated on either side of the passage from the mouth to the pharynx. [<L *tonsillae* the tonsils] —**ton'sil·lar, ton'sil·ar** *adj.*

ton·sil·lec·to·my (ton'sə·lek'tə·mē) n. Surg. Removal of a tonsil. [<TONSIL + -ECTOMY]

ton·sil·li·tis (ton'sə·lī'tis) n. Pathol. Inflammation of the tonsils. —**ton'sil·lit'ic** (-lit'ik) adj.

ton·sil·lo·tome (ton·sil'ə·tōm) n. An instrument used for cutting away a portion of the tonsils. [<TONSILLO- (<TONSIL) + -TOME]

ton·sil·lot·o·my (ton'sə·lot'ə·mē) n. Surg. The operation of cutting away the tonsils or a part of them. [<tonsillo- (<TONSIL) + -TOMY]

ton·so·ri·al (ton·sôr'ē·əl, -sō'rē-) adj. Pertaining to a barber or to barbering: chiefly used in the humorous phrase, tonsorial artist. [<L tonsorius <tonsor, -oris a barber < tonsus, pp. of tondere shear, clip]

ton·sure (ton'shər) n. 1 The shaving of the head, or of the crown of the head, as of a priest or monk, or the state of being thus shaven; hence, the priestly office. 2 That part of a priest's or monk's head left bare by shaving. —v.t. **·sured**, **·sur·ing** To shave the head of. [<OF <L tonsura a shearing <tonsus. See TONSORIAL.] —**ton'sured** adj.

ton·tine (ton'tēn, ton·tēn') n. 1 A form of collective life annuity, the individual profits of which increase as the number of survivors diminishes, the final survivor taking the whole. 2 The subscribers to such an annuity, collectively. 3 The share of a single subscriber. [<F, after Lorenzo Tonti, a Neapolitan banker who introduced it into France in about 1653]

to·nus (tō'nəs) n. 1 Tonicity. 2 Physiol. **a** The ability of a muscle to contract in response to a stimulus. **b** A condition of prolonged muscular spasm. [<L, TONE]

ton·y (tō'nē) adj. **ton·i·er**, **ton·i·est** Colloq. Aristocratic; high-toned; fashionable; stylish; swell. [<TONE (def. 5b)]

too (tōō) adv. 1 In addition; likewise; also: beautiful and good too. 2 In excessive quantity or degree; more than sufficiently: too long and too technical. 3 In a degree beyond expression or endurance; extremely: I am too happy for you. 4 Colloq. Indeed: an intensive, often used to reiterate a contradicted statement: You are too going! [Stressed var. of OE tō tō]

took (tōōk) Past tense of TAKE.

Tooke (tōōk), (**John**) **Horne**, 1736–1812, English politician and philologist.

tool (tōōl) n. 1 A simple mechanism or implement, as a hammer, saw, spade, or chisel, used chiefly in the direct manual working, moving, shaping, or transforming of material. 2 A power-driven apparatus, as a lathe, used for cutting and shaping the parts of a machine. 3 The cutting or shaping part of such an apparatus. 4 A bookbinder's hand stamp used in lettering or ornamenting book covers. 5 A person used to carry out the designs of others or another; a dupe. 6 Law Any instrument or apparatus necessary to the efficient prosecution of one's profession or trade. —v.t. 1 To shape, mark, or ornament with a tool. 2 To provide with tools. 3 Colloq. To drive, as an automobile, or convey (a person) by driving. 4 In bookbinding, to ornament or impress designs upon with a roller bearing a pattern. —v.i. 5 To work with a tool or tools. 6 Colloq. To drive or travel in a vehicle. [OE tōl]

Synonyms (noun): apparatus, appliance, implement, instrument, machine, mechanism, utensil. A tool is both contrived and used for extending the force of an intelligent agent to something that is to be operated upon. An instrument is anything through which power is applied and a result produced; in general usage, the word is of considerably wider meaning than tool; as, a piano is a musical instrument. Instruments is the word usually applied to tools used in scientific pursuits; as, we speak of a surgeon's or an optician's instruments. An implement is a mechanical agency considered with reference to some specific purpose to which it is adapted; as, an agricultural implement, implements of war. Implement is a less technical term than tool. A utensil is that which may be used for some special purpose; the word is especially applied to articles used for domestic or agricultural purposes; as, kitchen utensils, farming utensils.

Mechanism is a word of wide meaning, denoting any combination of mechanical devices for united action. A machine in the most general sense is any mechanical instrument for the conversion of motion; in this sense a lever is a machine; but in more commonly accepted usage a machine is distinguished from a tool by its complexity, and by the combination and coordination of powers and movements to produce results.

tool·ing (tōōl'ing) n. 1 The ornamentation or work done with tools. 2 The application of a tool or tools to any work.

tool·mak·er (tōōl'mā'kər) n. A maker of tools.

toom (tōōm) adj. Scot. & Brit. Dial. Empty; void; futile. [OE tōm]

Toombs (tōōmz), **Robert Augustus**, 1810–85, American Confederate general.

toon[1] (tōōn) n. 1 The fine, close-grained red wood of an East Indian tree (Toona ciliata) of the mahogany family, used for furniture, boxes, and construction. 2 The tree itself. [<Hind. tun, tūn <Skt. tunna]

toon[2] (tōōn) n. Scot. Hamlet; town.

toot (tōōt) v.i. 1 To blow a horn, whistle, etc., especially with short blasts. 2 To give forth a blast or toot, as a horn. 3 To make a similar sound. —v.t. 4 To sound (a horn, etc.) with short blasts. 5 To sound (a blast, etc.). —n. 1 A short note or blast on a horn. 2 Slang A spree; especially, a drinking spree. [? <MLG tuten; prob. orig. imit.] —**toot'er** n.

tooth (tōōth) n. pl. **teeth** (tēth) 1 One of the hard, dense structures in the mouth of a vertebrate, used for seizing and chewing food, as offensive and defensive weapons, etc. It consists chiefly of dentine or ivory, invested on the outer surface and crown with enamel, and a root embedded in the gum, with a small opening leading into a pulp cavity richly supplied with blood vessels and nerves. ◆ Collateral adjective: dental. 2 One of various hard calcareous or chitinous bodies of the oral or gastric regions of invertebrates. 3 Any one of various small toothlike projections.

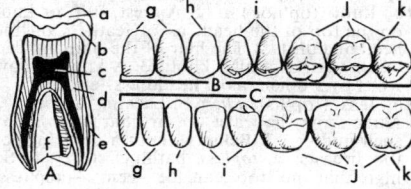

TEETH OF HUMAN ADULT
A. Cross-section of a molar.
B. Left upper jaw. C. Left lower jaw.
A. a. Crown. b. Enamel. c. Pulp cavity. d. Dentine.
e. Cement. f. Roots.
B. & C. g. Incisors. h. Canines. i. Bicuspids.
j. Molars. k. Wisdom teeth.

4 Zool. A process near the hinge of a bivalve shell. 5 Bot. One of the processes in the peristome of a moss. 6 Something resembling a tooth in form or use; specifically, a projecting point, pin, tine, or cog, as on a saw, comb, fork, rake, or gearwheel. 7 Appetite, liking, or taste (for something): She has a sweet tooth. 8 pl. That part which opposes, as in the gnawing, biting, or piercing manner of a tooth; the face of opposition, especially when involving resistance or risk: the teeth of the wind; He disobeyed them in their teeth. 9 pl. Means of enforcement: to put teeth into a law. 10 In paper or painting grounds, coarseness; irregularity of surface. —**armed to the teeth** Completely or heavily armed. —**by the skin of one's teeth** Barely; by the narrowest possible margin. —**in the teeth of** Directly against, counter to, or in defiance of. —**to put teeth into** To provide (something) with strength or power. —**to show one's teeth** To display a disposition to fight; threaten. —**to throw** (or **cast**) **in one's teeth** To fling at one, as a challenge or taunt. —v.t. 1 To supply with teeth, as a rake or saw. 2 To give a serrated edge to; indent. —v.i. 3 To become interlocked, as gearwheels; to gear. [<ON tōth, tōdh]

tooth·ache (tōōth'āk') n. 1 Pain in a tooth

or the teeth, generally due to caries exposing the nerve. 2 Neuralgia of the teeth or of the jaw bone.

tooth and nail By biting and scratching; hence, fiercely; with all possible strength and effort: to fight tooth and nail.

tooth·brush (tōōth'brush') n. A small brush used for cleaning the teeth.

toothed (tōōtht, tōōthd) adj. 1 Having teeth, notches, cogs, or jags. 2 Bot. Dentate. 3 Coarse; irregular of surface: said of paper or painting grounds.

tooth·less (tōōth'lis) adj. 1 Being without teeth. 2 Incapable of biting; harmless.

tooth·paste (tōōth'pāst') n. A paste used in cleaning the teeth.

tooth·pick (tōōth'pik') n. A small sliver of wood or metal, used for removing particles of food from between the teeth. 2 U.S. Slang A bowie knife: sometimes **Arkansas toothpick**.

tooth·pow·der (tōōth'pou'dər) n. A powder used in cleaning the teeth.

tooth rash Strophulus.

tooth·shell (tōōth'shel') n. A burrowing mollusk (genus Dentalium), having a long, very slender tubular shell.

tooth·some (tōōth'səm) adj. Having a pleasant taste. —**tooth'some·ly** adv. —**tooth'some·ness** n.

tooth·wort (tōōth'wûrt') n. 1 Any of a genus (Dentaria) of spring-blooming herbs of the mustard family, with compound toothed leaves and terminal clusters of white or purplish flowers. 2 Any of a genus (Lathraea) of small, parasitic plants having rootstocks covered with white scales instead of leaves.

tooth·y (tōō'thē) adj. **tooth·i·er**, **tooth·i·est** Having large or prominent teeth.

too·tle (tōōt'l) v.i. **·tled**, **·tling** To toot lightly or continuously, especially on the flute, as in double-tonguing. —n. The act of, or sound produced by, tootling. [Freq. of TOOT]

toot·sy (tōōt'sē) n. pl. **·sies** Slang The foot of a child or woman: an endearing or humorous term. Also **toot'sy-woot'sy** (-wōōt'sē). [Child's term for a foot]

too·zie (tōō'zē) See TOWZIE.

top[1] (top) n. 1 The uppermost or highest part, end, side, or surface of anything. 2 That end or part of anything, regarded as the higher or upper extremity: the top of the street. 3 A lid or cover: a bottle top. 4 The roof of a vehicle, as an automobile. 5 The crown of the head: from top to toe. 6 pl. The aboveground part of a plant producing root vegetables. 7 The highest degree or reach: at the top of one's voice; the top of one's ambition. 8 The highest or most prominent place or rank: at the top of one's profession. 9 One who is highest in rank or position: the top of one's class. 10 The choicest or best part: the top of the crop. 11 In bridge, the highest card in a suit. 12 In billiards, tennis, golf, etc.: **a** A stroke in which the player hits the ball above the center or on the upper half. **b** The forward spinning motion imparted to the ball by such a stroke. 13 Naut. A platform at the head of the lower section of a ship's mast, used as a place to stand and for extending the topmast rigging. 14 Chem. The most volatile part of a substance in distillation. 15 Scot. **a** The hair on one's head. **b** A bird's crest. **c** A horse's forelock. **d** A bunch of hair, wool, flax, etc. See synonyms under SUMMIT. —**to blow one's top** Slang 1 To break out in a rage; flare up. 2 To go insane. —adj. 1 Of or pertaining to the top. 2 Forming or comprising the top or upper part. 3 Highest in rank or quality; chief: top authors. 4 Greatest in amount or degree: top prices. —v. **topped**, **top·ping** v.t. 1 To remove the top or upper end of; prune. 2 To provide with a top, cap, etc. 3 To form the top of. 4 To reach or pass over the top of; surmount. 5 To surpass or exceed. 6 Chem. To take away the most volatile part of by distillation. 7 In golf, tennis, etc.: **a** To hit the upper part of (the ball) in making a stroke. **b** To make (a stroke) thus. —v.i. 8 To top someone or something. —**to top off** 1 To put something on the top of. 2 To complete; finish. [OE]

top[2] (top) n. A toy of wood or metal, with a point on which it is made to spin, as by the

unwinding of a string, a spring, etc. [OE]

top– Var. of TOPO–.

to·paz (tō′paz) *n.* **1** A native fluosilicate of aluminum, often found in yellow prismatic crystals valued as gemstones. **2** The yellow sapphire, a highly prized corundum of Ceylon: also called **Oriental topaz.** **3** Citrine (def. 2). **4** Either of two large tropical American hummingbirds *(Topaza pyra* and *T. pella)* with brilliant green–and–gold plumage. **5** A brownish–gold color, the color of the mineral. [<OF *topaze, topace* <L *topazus* <Gk. *topazos*]

to·paz·o·lite (tō·paz′ə·līt) *n.* A variety of andradite, yellow or sometimes green. [<Gk. *topazos* topaz + -LITE]

top·boot (top′bo͞ot′) *n.* A boot with a high top, sometimes ornamented with materials different from the rest of the boot. **— top′–boot′ed** *adj.*

top buggy A buggy with a top that may be raised or folded back.

top·coat (top′kōt′) *n.* A lightweight overcoat.

top–drawer (top′drôr′) *adj. Colloq.* Of the highest standard or merit.

top–dress (top′dres′) *v.t. Agric.* To apply manure on the top of, instead of plowing it into, a field.

top dressing *Agric.* A dressing of manure not to be plowed under the surface of a field.

tope[1] (tōp) *v.t.* **toped, top·ing** To drink (alcoholic beverages) excessively and frequently. ◆ Homophone: *taupe.* [? Related to earlier *top* tilt, turn over]

tope[2] (tōp) *n. Dial.* A small European shark or dogfish (genus *Galeorhinus*). ◆ Homophone: *taupe.* [? <dial. E (Cornish); ult. origin unknown]

tope[3] (tōp) *n. Anglo–Indian* A grove, especially a mango grove. ◆ Homophone: *taupe.* [< Tamil *tōppu*]

tope[4] (tōp) *n. Anglo–Indian* A round Buddhist shrine, dome, or tower, constructed to contain relics of the Buddhas, to indicate some sacred site, or for the burial of priests: also called *stupa.* ◆ Homophone: *taupe.* [<Hind. *top,* prob. <Pali *thūpo* <Skt. *stūpa*]

to·pec·to·my (tō·pek′tə·mē, tə-) *n. Surg.* An operation in which certain prefrontal cortical areas of the brain are removed. [<TOP(O)- + -ECTOMY]

to·pee (tō·pē′, tō′pē) See TOPI.

to·pek (tō′pek) *n.* A North American Indian or Eskimo hut of weeds, twigs, and animal skins. [<Eskimo *toopik, tupek* a tent]

To·pe·ka (tə·pē′kə) The capital of Kansas, on the Kansas River in the NE part.

to·pep·o (tə·pep′ō) *n. pl.* **·pep·oes** **1** A hybrid plant obtained by crossing the Chinese pepper with a variety of tomato, cultivated for its edible fruit. **2** The fruit itself. [<TO(MAT)O + PEP(PER)]

top·er (tō′pər) *n.* A habitual drunkard; sot. [<TOPE[1]]

top·flight (top′flīt′) *adj.* Of the highest quality; outstanding; superior.

top·full (top′fo͝ol′) *adj. Rare* Brimful.

top·gal·lant (tə·gal′ənt, top′gal′ənt) *n. Naut.* **1** The mast, sail, yard, or rigging immediately above the topmast and topsail. **2** The parts of a deck that are higher than the rest. *— adj.* Pertaining to the topgallants. [<TOP[1] + GALLANT; with ref. to "making a gallant show" compared with the lower tops]

toph (tōf) *n.* Tufa. Also **tophe.** [<L *tophus, tofus*]

top·ham·per (top′ham′pər) *n. Naut.* **1** Spars and rigging usually kept aloft. **2** The light upper sails and rigging. **3** Casks, cables, rigging, etc., encumbering the deck. [<TOP[1] + HAMPER[1], *n.*] **— top′–ham′pered** *adj.*

top hat A high silk hat for men.

top·heav·y (top′hev′ē) *adj.* Having the top or upper part too heavy for the lower part; ill–proportioned; impracticable. **— top′heav′i·ness** *n.*

To·phet (tō′fet) **1** In the Old Testament, a place in the valley of Hinnom, near Jerusalem, where the Jews were said to sacrifice their children to Moloch: later used as a place for burning the city's refuse. **2** A place of endless perdition; hell. Also **To′pheth** (-fet). [<Hebrew *tōpheth,* ? an altar]

top–hole (top′hōl′) *adj. Brit. Slang* First–rate; excellent.

to·phus (tō′fəs) *n. pl.* **·phi** (-fī) **1** *Dent.* Tartar of the teeth. **2** *Pathol.* A deposit of urates around and at the surface of joints in persons affected with gout. **3** *Mineral.* Any natural calcareous tufa. [<L, tufa]

to·pi (tō·pē′, tō′pē) *n.* A hat or helmet, especially a light helmet made of pith: also spelled *topee.* [<Hind. *topī*]

to·pi·ar·y (tō′pē·er′ē) *adj.* Arranged or trimmed in, or making use of, fantastic shapes of shrubs and evergreen trees, as in gardening, etc. *— n. pl.* **·ar·ies** A topiary garden. [<L *topiarius* concerning ornamental gardening < *topia opera* ornamental gardening <Gk. *topion,* dim. of *topos* a place]

top·ic (top′ik) *n.* **1** A subject of discourse or of a treatise; any matter treated of in speech or writing; a theme for discussion. **2** *pl.* In rhetorical invention, the part that treats of the selection and arrangement of the proofs; also, the places or classes in which the various kinds of proofs are to be found. **3** A subdivision of an outline or a treatise. *— adj. Obs.* Topical. [<L *topica* <Gk. *(ta) topica,* lit., (matters) concerning commonplaces, title of a work by Aristotle, neut. pl. of *topikos* of a place < *topos* a place, commonplace]

Synonyms (noun): division, head, issue, matter, motion, point, proposition, question, subject, theme. Since a *topic* for discussion is often stated in the form of a *question, question* has come to be extensively used to denote a debatable *topic,* especially of a practical nature; as, the labor *question.* In deliberative assemblies the *motion* or other matter for consideration is known as the *question*; a member is required to speak to the *question.* In speaking or writing the general *subject* or *theme* may be termed the *topic,* but it is more usual to apply the latter term to the subordinate *divisions, points,* or *heads* of discourse; as, To enlarge on this *topic* would carry me far from my *subject.*

top·i·cal (top′i·kəl) *adj.* **1** Pertaining to a topic. **2** Of the nature of merely probable argument. **3** Belonging to a place or spot; local. **4** Pertaining to matters of present interest: a *topical* song. **5** *Med.* Local. **— top′i·cal·ly** *adv.*

top kick *Slang* A top sergeant.

top·knot (top′not′) *n.* **1** A crest, tuft, or knot on the top of the head, as of feathers on the head of a bird. **2** The hair of the human head when worn as a high knot. **3** A knot or bow worn by women, as a headdress, etc.

top·less (top′lis) *adj.* **1** Lacking a top. **2** Nude from the waist up, or characterized by such nudity. **3** Being without a covering for the breasts: a *topless* bathing suit. **4** So high that no top can be seen. **— top′less·ness** *n.*

top–loft·y (top′lôf′tē, -lof′tē) *adj.* **1** Towering very high. **2** Very proud or haughty; inflated; pompous. **— top′–loft′i·ness** *n.*

top·mast (top′məst, top′mast′, -mäst′) *n. Naut.* The mast next above the lower mast.

top minnow Any of a family *(Poeciliidae)* of small, typically viviparous fishes which feed near the surface of the water, especially *Gambusia affinis,* widely used to combat mosquitoes.

top·most (top′mōst′) *adj.* Being at the very top.

top–notch (top′noch′) *adj. Colloq.* Excellent; best. **— top′–notch′er** *n.*

topo– *combining form* A place or region; regional: *topography.* Also, before vowels, *top–.* [<Gk. *topos* a place]

to·pog·ra·pher (tə·pog′rə·fər) *n.* An expert in topography.

to·pog·ra·phy (tə·pog′rə·fē) *n.* **1** The detailed description of particular places. **2** The art of representing on a map the physical features of a place. **3** The physical features, collectively, of a region. **4** Topographic surveying. [<TOPO- + -GRAPHY] **— top·o·graph·ic** (top′ə·graf′ik) or **·i·cal** *adj.* **— top′o·graph′i·cal·ly** *adv.*

to·pol·o·gy (tə·pol′ə·jē) *n.* **1** The branch of geometry which studies those properties of figures or solid bodies which remain invariant under all continuous deformation: also called *analysis situs.* **2** *Med.* The relation between the forward part of the fetus and the birth canal. [<TOPO- + -LOGY] **— top·o·log·ic** (top′ə·loj′ik) or **·i·cal** *adj.*

top·o·nym (top′ə·nim) *n.* **1** *Anat.* The name of a region of the body, as distinguished from an organ. **2** Any name derived from the name of a place. [<TOPO- + Gk. *onoma, onyma* a name] **— top′o·nym′ic** or **·i·cal** *adj.*

to·pon·y·my (tə·pon′ə·mē) *n. pl.* **·mies** **1** The nomenclature of anatomical regions. **2** The science or study of place names, or a register of place names.

top·o·type (top′ə·tīp) *n. Biol.* A plant or animal specimen selected from the locality typical of the species. [<TOPO- + TYPE]

top·per (top′ər) *n.* **1** One who or that which cuts off the top of something. **2** *Slang* One who or that which is of supreme quality. **3** *Slang* A high silk hat.

top·ping (top′ing) *adj.* **1** Towering high above; eminent; distinguished. **2** Making great pretensions; arrogant; domineering. **3** *Brit. Colloq.* Excellent; first–rate. *— n.* **1** The act of one who tops, in any sense. **2** That which forms the top of anything.

topping lift *Naut.* A rope extending from the lower masthead to the outer end of a boom, for hoisting or supporting the boom.

top·ple (top′əl) *v.* **·pled, ·pling** *v.t.* **1** To push over and cause to totter or fall by its own weight; overturn. *— v.i.* **2** To totter and fall, as by its own weight. **3** To lean or jut out, as if about to fall. [Freq. of TOP[1], *v.*]

tops (tops) *adj. Slang* Excellent; first–rate.

top·sail (top′səl, top′sāl′) *n. Naut.* **1** In a square–rigged vessel, a square sail set next above the lowest sail of a mast. **2** In a fore–and–aft–rigged vessel, a square or triangular sail carried above the gaff of a lower sail.

top–se·cret (top′sē′krit) *adj. U.S.* Designating defense information requiring the strictest measures of secrecy and safeguard. Compare SECRET (*adj.* def. 5), CONFIDENTIAL (def. 4).

top sergeant *Colloq.* The first sergeant of a company, battery, or troop.

top·side (top′sīd′) *n. Naut.* The portion of a ship above the main deck. *— adv.* To or on the upper parts of a ship: He is going *topside.*

top·soil (top′soil′) *n.* The surface soil of land: distinguished from *subsoil.* *— v.t.* To remove the surface soil of (an area or region).

top·stone (top′stōn′) *n.* A capstone.

Top·sy (top′sē) In *Uncle Tom's Cabin,* a young Negro slave girl who, when questioned about her origins, replied that she had "just growed."

top·sy–tur·vy (top′sē·tûr′vē) *adv.* Upside–down; hind side before; in utter confusion. *— adj.* Being in an upset or disordered condition; upside–down. *— n.* A state of confusion; disorder; chaos. [Earlier *topsy–tervy, topsy–tirvy,* prob. <TOP[1] + obs. *terve, tirve* turn, overturn] **— top′sy–tur′vi·ly** *adv.* **— top′·sy–tur′vi·ness** *n.* **— top′sy–tur′vy·dom** *n.*

toque (tōk) *n.* **1** A small, close–fitting, brimless hat worn by women. **2** The tall conical headdress formerly worn by the doges of Venice. **3** A black velvet cap, ornamented with eagle's plumes and furnished with a band and brim: worn by both sexes in France before the Restoration. Also **to·quet** (tō·kā′). [<F, a cap <Sp. *toca* <Basque *tauka,* a kind of cap]

tor (tôr) *n.* A high, rocky hill; a jutting rock. [OE *torr* <Celtic]

to·rah (tôr′ə, tō′rə) *n.* In Hebrew literature, a law; also, counsel or instruction proceeding from a specially sacred source. Also **to′ra.** [<Hebrew *tōrāh* an instruction, law < *yārāh* throw, show, instruct]

To·rah (tôr′ə, tō′rə) *n.* The Mosaic law; the Pentateuch.

tor·bern·ite (tôr′bərn·īt) See under URANITE. [<G *torbernit, torberit* <NL *torbernus,* after *Torber* Bergmann, 18th c. Swedish chemist]

torc (tôrk) See TORQUE[2].

torch (tôrch) *n.* **1** A source of light, as from flaming pine knots, or from some material dipped in tallow or oil, and fixed at the end of a handle or pole. **2** Anything that illuminates or brightens: the *torch* of science. **3** A portable device giving off an intensely hot flame and used for burning off paint, melting solder, etc. **4** *Brit.* A flashlight. **— to carry a** (or **the**) **torch for** *Slang* To continue to love (someone), though the love is unrequited. [<OF *torche,* ult. <L *torquere* twist; so called because early torches were made of twisted tow dipped in pitch]

torch·bear·er (tôrch′bâr′ər) *n.* **1** One who carries a torch. **2** One who imparts knowledge, truth, etc. **3** *Colloq.* One loud in his praise of a friend.

torch·light (tôrch′līt′) *n.* The light of a torch or torches. *— adj.* Lighted by torches: a *torchlight* rally.

torchlight procession A parade of persons

carrying torches, usually a political demonstration.
tor·chon lace (tôr′shon, *Fr.* tôr·shôn′) **1** A coarse, durable bobbin lace in simple geometrical designs made of linen thread. **2** An imitation of this made by machine. [<F *torchon* a dishcloth < *torcher* wipe]
torch singer One who sings torch songs.
torch song A popular love song, slow and melancholy, expressing sadness and hopeless yearning. [< phrase "carry a torch for." See under TORCH.]
torch·wood (tôrch′wo͝od′) *n.* **1** Any of a genus *(Amyris)* of tropical American shrubs and small trees, especially *A. balsamifera.* **2** Its bright-burning, fragrant wood.
Tor·de·sil·las (tôr′thā·sē′lyäs) A village in NW Spain; scene of the signing of a treaty between Spain and Portugal setting the line of demarcation for colonial expansion, 1494.
tore[1] (tôr, tōr) Past tense of TEAR[1].
tore[2] (tôr, tōr) *n.* Torus (defs. 1 and 4). [<F *tore* <L *torus* a torus]
tor·e·a·dor (tôr′ē·ə·dôr′, *Sp.* tō′rā·ä·thôr′) *n.* One who engages in a bullfight, especially on horseback; a bullfighter: also spelled *toreador.* [<Sp. < *torear* fights bulls < *toro* a bull <L *taurus*]
to·re·ro (tō·rā′rō) *n. pl.* **·ros** (-rōs) *Spanish* A bullfighter, usually on foot.
to·reu·tics (tə·ro͞o′tiks) *n. pl. (construed as singular)* The art of working in ornamental relief or intaglio, especially in metal. [<Gk. *toreutikos* < *toreuein* work in relief, bore] **— to·reu′tic** *adj.*
tor·ic (tôr′ik, tor′-) *adj.* Of, pertaining to, or resembling a torus; segmental.
toric lens *Optics* A lens in which one of the surfaces is a segment of a torus: used for eyeglasses because of its special refracting powers.
to·ri·i (tôr′i·ē, tō′ri·ē) *n.* The gateway of a Shinto temple or of a shrine: properly comprising two uprights with one straight crosspiece, and another above with a concave lintel. [<Japanese]

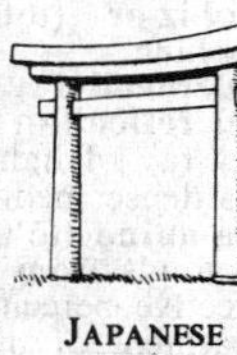
JAPANESE TORII

To·ri·no (tō·rē′nō) The Italian name for TURIN.
tor·ment (tôr′ment) *n.* **1** Intense bodily pain or mental anguish; agony; torture. **2** One who or that which torments. **3** The inflicting of torture. **4** *Archaic* Any device for inflicting torture, as the rack; also, the torture inflicted. **5** Hell. See synonyms under AGONY, PAIN. **—** *v.t.* (tôr·ment′) **1** To subject to excruciating physical or mental suffering; torture. **2** To make miserable; afflict or vex grievously. **3** To harass or tease. **4** To distort; also, to throw into violent agitation. See synonyms under PERSECUTE. [<AF *turment,* OF *torment, tourment* <L *tormentum* a rack, orig. a machine for hurling missiles by means of torsion < *torquere* twist] **— tor·ment′ing·ly** *adv.* **— tor·ment′ing·ness** *n.*
tor·men·til (tôr′men·til) *n.* A slender, trailing, Old World herb *(Potentilla erecta),* with yellow flowers. Its root, a powerful astringent, has been used in treating diarrhea and dysentery, and also in tanning. [<OF *tormentille* < Med. L *tormentilla,* dim. of L *tormenium* TORMENT; so called because used as a pain killer]
tor·men·tor (tôr·men′tər) *n.* **1** One who or that which torments. **2** A movable panel of sound-insulating material for controlling the acoustics on a sound stage outside of the field of the camera. **3** A movable piece of theater scenery at either side and back of the proscenium arch to mask sidelights and downstage entrances and exits. Also **tor·ment′er.**
torn (tôrn, tōrn) Past participle of TEAR[1].
tor·na·do (tôr·nā′dō) *n. pl.* **·does** or **·dos** **1** A whirling wind of exceptional violence, usually associated with thunderstorms and accompanied by a pendulous, funnel-shaped cloud marking the narrow path of greatest destruction. **2** A violent thunderstorm or squall of the west coast of Africa. **3** A hurricane or violent windstorm of the tropical Atlantic. See synonyms under CYCLONE. [Alter. of *ternado,* prob. alter. of Sp. *tronada* a thunderstorm < *tronar* thunder <L *tonare;* infl. in form by Sp. *tornar* turn, because characterized by shifting or whirling winds] **— tor·nad′ic** (-nad′ik) *adj.*
Tor·ne (tôr′nə, tōr′-) A river in northern Sweden and northern Finland, flowing 250 miles SE and south from Lake Torne to its confluence with the Muonio, and thence along the Swedish-Finnish border to the Gulf of Bothnia.
Torne, Lake A lake near the Norwegian border in extreme NW Sweden; 124 square miles; 40 miles long, 1 to 6 miles wide.
to·roid (tôr′oid, tō′roid) *n.* **1** *Geom.* **a** A surface generated by the rotation of any closed plane curve, as a circle or ellipse, about an axis lying in its plane. **b** The solid produced by such a surface. **2** *Electr.* An electromagnetic coil wound upon a ring of circular cross-section. [<TOR(US) + -OID] **— to·roi′dal** *adj.*
To·ron·to (tə·ron′tō) The capital of Ontario province, Canada, on Lake Ontario; a leading industrial center.
To·ros Dağ·la·ri (tô·rôs′ dä′lä·rē′) The Turkish name for the Taurus range.
to·rose (tôr′ōs, tō′rōs, tō·rōs′, tō-) *adj.* **1** Having protuberances; bulging. **2** *Bot.* Knobby; cylindrical and swollen at intervals. Also **to·rous** (tôr′əs, tō′rəs). [<L *torosus* < *torus* a swelling] **— to·ros·i·ty** (tō·ros′ə·tē) *n.*
tor·pe·do (tôr·pē′dō) *n. pl.* **·dos** or **·does** **1** A device or apparatus containing an explosive to be fired by concussion or otherwise. **2** A self-propelling, cigar-shaped projectile for carrying a powerful detonating charge under water to a hostile vessel. **3** A submarine mine. **4** A cartridge placed on a railway track and exploded by the weight of a train passing over it, the report serving as a warning signal to the train crew. **5** A cartridge exploded in an oil or gas well to start or increase the flow. **6** A toy of gravel and a fulminating powder wrapped in paper, and exploded by being dashed against some hard surface. **7** A ray fish *(Torpedo ocellata)* having an electric apparatus with which it stuns or kills its prey; a crampfish; numbfish. **8** *Colloq.* A gangster, especially an armed bodyguard prepared to attack or kill without warning. **— aerial torpedo** A torpedo projectile, moving under its own power and usually released from low-flying aircraft at fixed or floating targets. **—** *v.t.* **·doed, ·do·ing** To damage or sink (a vessel) with a torpedo or torpedos. [<L, stiffness, numbness < *torpere* be numb]
torpedo boat A small, swift, lightly armed and armored surface vessel equipped with one or more tubes for the discharge of torpedos.
tor·pe·do-boat destroyer (tôr·pē′dō·bōt′) A small, swift, lightly armed war vessel; a destroyer.
torpedo tube A tube in a torpedo boat or other war vessel, through which torpedos are launched.
tor·pid[1] (tôr′pid) *adj.* **1** Having lost sensibility or power of motion, partially or wholly, as a hibernating animal. **2** Dormant; numb. **3** Sluggish; apathetic; dull. See synonyms under LIFELESS, NUMB. [<L *torpidus* < *torpere* be numb] **— tor·pid·i·ty** (tôr·pid′ə·tē), **tor′pid·ness** *n.* **— tor′pid·ly** *adv.*
tor·pid[2] (tôr′pid) *n.* **1** An eight-oared, clinker-built racing boat for the second crew at Oxford University; also, one of its crew. **2** *pl.* The Lenten races in which such boats take part. [<TORPID[1]; so called because the second crew consisted of awkward or very young oarsmen]
tor·por (tôr′pər) *n.* **1** Complete or partial insensibility; stupor. **2** Apathy; torpidity. [<L < *torpere* be numb] **— tor·po·rif·ic** (tôr′·pə·rif′ik) *adj.*
tor·quate (tôr′kwit, -kwāt) *adj. Zool.* Having a torque or ring, as of color, about the neck; collared. [<L *torquatus* having a collar < *torques.* See TORQUES.]
Tor·quay (tôr·kē′) A port and municipal borough in southern Devon, England.
torque[1] (tôrk) *n.* **1** *Mech.* **a** Anything that causes or tends to cause torsion in a body; the moment of forces that causes rotation or twisting. **b** The rotary force in a mechanism. **c** The degree of smoothness in the conversion of reciprocating into rotary motion. **2** *Optics* The rotatory effect upon the plane of polarization produced by the passage of light through certain liquids and crystals. [<L *torquere* twist]
torque[2] (tôrk) *n.* A necklace, armlet, or collar of wire, usually twisted: worn especially by ancient Gauls and Britons: also spelled *torc.* [<L *torques.* See TORQUES.]
Tor·que·ma·da (tôr′kwə·mä′də, *Sp.* tôr′kā·mä′thä), **Tomás de,** 1420–98, Dominican monk; first inquisitor general of Spain.
tor·ques (tôr′kwēz) *n. Zool.* A natural ring or collar, of feathers or hair, on the neck of a bird or other animal. [<NL <L, a twisted collar < *torquere* twist]
tor·re·a·dor (tôr′ē·ə·dôr′) See TOREADOR.
Tor·re An·nun·zia·ta (tôr′rā än′no͞on·tsyä′tä) A port on the Bay of Naples, southern Italy; destroyed by an eruption of Vesuvius, 1631, and rebuilt.
tor·re·fy (tôr′ə·fī, tor′-) *v.t.* **·fied, ·fy·ing** To dry or roast by exposure to heat, as ores or drugs. Also **tor′ri·fy.** [<MF *torréfier* <L *torrefacere* < *torrere* dry, parch + *facere* make] **— tor′re·fac′tion** (-fak′shən) *n.*
Tor·rens (tôr′ənz, tor′-), **Lake** A salt lake in SE central South Australia, often dry; 120 miles long; 2,230 square miles.
tor·rent (tôr′ənt, tor′-) *n.* **1** A stream of water flowing with great velocity or turbulence. **2** Any similar stream, as of lava. **3** Any abundant or tumultuous flow: a *torrent* of rain; a *torrent* of abuse. **—** *adj.* Like a torrent; pouring forth with violence. [<OF <L *torrens, -entis,* lit., boiling, burning, ppr. of *torrere* parch]
tor·ren·tial (tô·ren′shəl, to-) *adj.* **1** Of, pertaining to, or resulting from the action of a torrent or torrents. **2** Figuratively, suggestive of a torrent in rapidity and volume; outpouring; overpowering: *torrential* passion. **— tor·ren′tial·ly** *adv.*
Tor·re·ón (tôr′rā·ôn′) A city in Coahuila, northern Mexico; an industrial center.
Tor·res Strait (tôr′əs, -iz, tor′-) A strait between Australia and New Guinea; 95 miles wide; connects the Arafura and Coral seas.
Tor·res Ve·dras (tôr′rizh vā′thrəsh) A town north of Lisbon in western Portugal; Wellington's headquarters in the Peninsula campaign, 1810.
Tor·rey (tôr′ē, tor′ē), **John,** 1796–1873, U.S. botanist.
Tor·ri·cel·li (tôr′rē·chel′lē), **Evangelista,** 1608–1647, Italian physicist; discovered the principle of the barometer. **— Tor·ri·cel·li·an** (tôr′·i·sel′ē·ən, -chel′ē·ən) *adj.*
Torricellian tube A vertical glass tube containing mercury or other fluid, sealed at the top and having the lower end in a container of the same fluid. [after E. TORRICELLI]
Torricellian vacuum The vacuum above the fluid in a Torricellian tube or in the top of a barometer tube.
tor·rid (tôr′id, tor′-) *adj.* **1** Exposed to the full force of the sun's heat; sultry. **2** Having power to parch or burn; scorching; burning; hot and dry. [<L *torridus* < *torrere* parch] **— tor·rid·i·ty** (tô·rid′ə·tē, to-), **tor′rid·ness** *n.* **— tor′rid·ly** *adv.*
torrid zone See under ZONE.
tor·sade (tôr·säd′) *n.* **1** A molded ornament resembling a twisted cable. **2** A twisted cord for draperies. [<F <Med. L *torsus,* var. of L *tortus,* pp. of *torquere* twist]
tor·si·bil·i·ty (tôr′sə·bil′ə·tē) *n.* Capacity for undergoing torsion, measured by the amount of torsion produced.
tor·sion (tôr′shən) *n.* **1** The act of twisting, or the state of being twisted. **2** *Mech.* Deformation of a body, as a thread or rod, by twisting, one end being held fast while the other is subjected to a torque around its length as an axis. **3** The force with which a twisted cord or cable tends to return to its former position: distinguished from *tension.* [<OF <LL *torsio, -onis,* var. of L *tortio, -onis* < *tortus,* pp. of *torquere* twist] **— tor′sion·al** *adj.* **— tor′sion·al·ly** *adv.*
torsion balance An instrument for determining very minute forces by measuring the angle through which an arm turns before the resisting force of torsion acts upon the supporting wire or filament.

torsion bar A solid or laminated bar or rod, anchored on one end, which acts as a spring when subjected to torsion (def. 2). — **tor′sion–bar′** *adj.*

torsk (tôrsk) *n.* **1** A gadoid fish; the cusk. **2** The codfish. [<Norw. <ON *thorskr,* prob. < base of *thurr* dry. Akin to THIRST.]

tor·so (tôr′sō) *n. pl.* **·sos** or **·si** (-sē) **1** The trunk of a human body. **2** In sculpture, a statue deprived of head and limbs. **3** Any fragmentary or defective thing. [<Ital., a stalk, core, trunk of a body <L *thyrsus* a stalk <Gk. *thyrsos* a thyrsus]

tort (tôrt) *n. Law* Any private or civil wrong by act or omission for which a civil suit can be brought, but not including breach of contract. [<OF <L *tortus.* See TORSION.]

torte (tôrt, *Ger.* tôr′tə) *n.* A rich cake variously made of butter, eggs, fruits, and nuts. [<G]

tort–fea·sor (tôrt′fē′zər) *n. Law* One who has committed a tort; a wrongdoer. [<OF *tortfesor, tortfaiseur* < *tort* a wrong, tort + *fesor, faiseur* a doer < *faire* do <L *facere*]

tor·ti·col·lis (tôr′tə·kol′is) *n. Pathol.* A spasmodic affection of the muscles of the neck which draws the head to one side; wryneck. [<NL <L *tortus* twisted + *collum* neck] — **tor′ti·col′lar** *adj.*

tor·tile (tôr′til) *adj.* Twisted up into a coil. [<L *tortilis* < *tortus* twisted. See TORSION.] — **tor·til·i·ty** (tôr·til′ə·tē) *n.*

tor·til·la (tôr·tē′yä) *n.* A flat cake made of coarse cornmeal and baked on a hot sheet of iron or a slab of stone: the customary substitute for bread in Mexico. [<Sp., dim. of *torta* a cake <LL, a twisted loaf <L, pp. fem. of *torquere* twist]

tor·tious (tôr′shəs) *adj. Law* Of the nature of or implying a tort; wrongful. [<AF *torcious* < *torcion, tortion,* var. of OF *torsion* torsion; infl. in meaning by TORT] — **tor′tious·ly** *adv.*

tor·tive (tôr′tiv) *adj. Obs.* Twisted. [<L *tortivus* < *tortus.* See TORSION.]

tor·toise (tôr′təs) *n.* **1** A turtle; chelonian; specifically, one of a terrestrial or fresh–water species, or a terrestrial as distinguished from an aquatic species. **2** A testudo. — **giant tortoise** Any of several species of very large herbivorous land tortoises (family *Testudinidae*), especially those found on the Galápagos Islands, which may reach a length of four feet and weigh 600 pounds. [Earlier *tortuce* < Med. L *tortuca,* ult. <L *tortus* twisted; so called from its crooked feet]

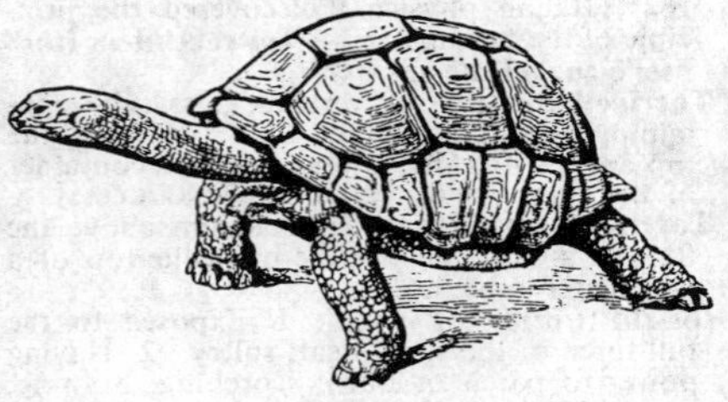

GIANT TORTOISE
(Largest specimens: up to 5 1/2 feet long by 4 1/2 feet wide)

tortoise beetle A small, iridescent beetle (family *Chrysomelidae*) having a tortoiselike form.

tortoise plant Elephant foot.

tortoise shell **1** The shell of a marine turtle, especially of the hawkbill, valuable in the arts. **2** A cat having fur mottled with black and yellow like the shell of a tortoise. — **tor′toise–shell′** *adj.*

Tor·to·la (tôr·tō′lə) The chief island of the British Virgin Islands; 21 square miles; capital, Road Town.

tor·tri·cid (tôr′trə·sid) *n.* Any of a large family (*Tortricidae*) of small, usually bright–colored moths with rectangular fore wings, including many important pests of fruit and forest trees. — *adj.* Of or pertaining to the *Tortricidae.* [<NL <*Tortrix,* type genus <L *tortus.* See TORSION.]

Tor·tu·ga (tôr·tōō′gə) An island off the northern coast of Haiti, to which it belongs; 70 square miles; a 17th century pirate stronghold. *French* **Île de la Tor·tue** (ēl′ də lä tôr·tü′).

tor·tu·os·i·ty (tôr′chōō·os′ə·tē) *n.* **1** The quality or state of being tortuous, or an instance of it. **2** A bend or twist; winding.

tor·tu·ous (tôr′chōō·əs) *adj.* **1** Consisting of or abounding in irregular bends or turns; twisting. **2** Figuratively, morally irregular or crooked; not straightforward; devious. [<AF <L *tortuosus* < *tortus.* See TORSION.] — **tor′tu·ous·ly** *adv.* — **tor′tu·ous·ness** *n.*

tor·ture (tôr′chər) *n.* **1** Infliction of or subjection to extreme physical pain. **2** A former judicial mode of getting evidence by inflicting pain. **3** Great mental suffering; agony. **4** Something that causes severe pain. **5** A violent perversion or straining. See synonyms under AGONY, PAIN. — *v.t.* **·tured, ·tur·ing** **1** To inflict extreme pain upon; cause to suffer keenly in body or mind; specifically, to put to judicial torture. **2** To twist or turn into an abnormal form; distort; wrench. [<OF <L *tortura,* lit., a twisting < *tortus.* See TORSION.] — **tor′tur·er** *n.*

tor·u·lose (tôr′ə·lōs) *adj. Bot.* Having alternate swellings and constrictions like the vegetative growth of *Torula,* a genus of fungus. Also **tor′u·lous** (-ləs). [<NL *Torula,* dim. of *torus* a torus]

To·ruń (tô′rōōn·y′) A port on the Vistula in north central Poland: German *Thorn.*

to·rus (tôr′əs, tō′rəs) *n. pl.* **to·ri** (tôr′ī, tō′rī) **1** *Archit.* A large convex molding, nearly semicircular in cross–section: used in bases as the lowest molding, or in columns above the plinth. **2** *Anat.* A rounded ridge, as on the occipital bone of the skull. **3** *Bot.* The swollen end of a flowerstalk which bears the floral leaves; the receptacle. **4** *Geom.* The surface or solid generated by the rotation of a conic section about an axis in its own plane. [<L, lit., a swelling]

to·ry (tôr′ē, tō′rē) *n. pl.* **·ries** *Obs.* **1** A freebooter among the outlawed Irish in the 17th century. **2** Any outlaw or bandit. [<Irish *tōruidhe* a robber, a pursuer < *tōir* pursue]

To·ry (tôr′ē, tō′rē) *n. pl.* **To·ries** **1** A historical English political party, successor to the Cavaliers and opponent of the Whigs; since about 1832 called the Conservative party. **2** One who at the period of the American Revolution adhered to the cause of British sovereignty over the colonies. **3** A very conservative person: also **tory.** — **To′ry·ism** *n.*

Tos·ca·na (tôs·kä′nä) The Italian name for TUSCANY.

Tos·ca·ni·ni (tos′kə·nē′nē, tôs′-; *Ital* tôs′kä·nē′nē), **Arturo,** 1867–1957, Italian orchestra conductor active in the United States.

tosh (tosh) *n. Brit. Colloq.* Nonsense; rubbish; bosh. [? Alter of BOSH]

toss (tôs, tos) *v.t.* **1** To throw, pitch, or fling about. **2** To make restless; agitate; disturb. **3** To throw with the hand, especially with the palm of the hand upward; pitch. **4** To lift with a quick motion, as the head. **5** To bandy about, as something discussed. **6** To toss up with. See TO TOSS UP, below. — *v.i.* **7** To be moved or thrown about; be flung to and fro, as a ship in a storm. **8** To throw oneself from side to side; roll about restlessly, as in sleep. **9** To go quickly or angrily, as with a toss of the head. **10** To toss up a coin. — **to toss** (or **peak**) **oars** To raise the oars out of the rowlocks to a vertical position. — **to toss off** **1** To drink at one draft. **2** To utter, write, or do in an offhand manner. — **to toss up** To throw a coin into the air to decide a wager or choice by the way in which it falls. — *n.* **1** The act of tossing; specifically, a gentle throwing from the hand; a pitch; also, the distance over which a thing is tossed. **2** A quick upward or backward movement of the head; any quick jerk. **3** The state of being tossed about; excitement; agitation. **4** A toss–up or wager. **5** *Scot.* A belle; a toast. [Prob. <Scand. Cf. dial. Norw. *tossa* spread, strew.] — **toss′er** *n.*

toss·pot (tôs′pot′, tos′-) *n.* A toper; drunkard.

toss–up (tôs′up′, tos′-) *n. Colloq.* **1** The throwing up, as of a coin, to decide a bet, etc. **2** An even or fair chance.

tot[1] (tot) *n.* A little child; toddler; also, anything small or trifling. [Prob. <Scand. Cf. ON *tuttr* a dwarf.]

tot[2] (tot) *v.t. Colloq.* To add; total: with *up* or *together.* [Short for TOTAL]

to·tal (tōt′l) *n.* The whole sum or amount; the whole, especially when considered as an aggregate of parts or elements. See synonyms under AGGREGATE, MASS[1]. — *adj.* **1** Constituting or comprising a whole, without diminution or division; being a total: the sum *total.* **2** Extending throughout the whole; comprising everything; complete; perfect: a *total* loss. — *v.* **·taled** or **·talled, ·tal·ing** or **·tal·ling** *v.t.* **1** To ascertain the total of. **2** To come to or reach as a total; amount to. — *v.i.* **3** To amount: often with *to.* [<OF <Med. L *totalis* <L *totus* all] — **to′tal·ly** *adv.*

total abstinence See under ABSTINENCE.

total depravity The condition defined by the doctrine that human nature has no tendency to piety or spirituality, but has the opposite tendency, every faculty having an innate taint: one of the five points of Calvinism. Compare ORIGINAL SIN.

total emission *Physics* The maximum emission of electrons from the cathode of a thermionic or vacuum tube.

to·tal·i·sa·tor (tōt′l·ə·zā′tər, -ī·zā′-) *n. Brit.* A machine used at racetracks for totaling the bets, reckoning the resulting pay–off odds, and recording these on a large scoreboard visible to the grandstand; a pari–mutuel. Also **to′tal·i·za′tor.**

to·tal·i·tar·i·an (tō·tal′ə·târ′ē·ən) *adj.* Designating or characteristic of a government controlled exclusively by one party or faction, which suppresses all opposition and criticism and controls and regiments all social, cultural, and economic activity in the country to advance its political aims. — *n.* An adherent of totalitarian government. [<TOTALIT(Y) + -ARIAN] — **to·tal′i·tar′i·an·ism** *n.*

to·tal·i·ty (tō·tal′ə·tē) *n.* **1** An aggregate of parts or individuals. **2** The state of being whole or entire. **3** *Astron.* The state or period of an eclipse while it is total. Also **to′tal·ness.** See synonyms under AGGREGATE, MASS[1].

to·tal·ize (tōt′l·īz) *v.t.* **·ized, ·iz·ing** To collect into or ascertain as an aggregate; make total. — **to′tal·i·za′tion** *n.*

to·tal·iz·er (tōt′l·ī′zər) *n.* A pari–mutuel machine.

total recall *Psychol.* Hypermnesia.

total reflection *Optics* The complete reflection of a ray of light passing from a denser to a less dense medium.

to·ta·quine (tō′tə·kwin) *n.* A mixture of the alkaloids from cinchona bark, including an effective percentage of quinine: used in the treatment of malaria. [<NL *totaquina* <L *tota,* fem. of *totus* all + Quechua *(quin)quina* cinchona bark]

tote (tōt) *Colloq. v.t.* **tot·ed, tot·ing** **1** To carry or bear on the person, as a burden. **2** To carry, transport, or haul, as supplies. **3** In arithmetic, to carry. **4** To wear habitually: He *totes* a gun. — *n.* **1** The act of toting. **2** A load or haul. [Prob. <West African] — **tot′er** *n.*

to·tem (tō′təm) *n.* **1** Among many primitive peoples, especially the North American Indians, an animal, plant, or other natural object believed to be ancestrally related to a tribe, clan, or family group or to be its tutelar spirit. **2** The representation of such an animal, plant, or object taken as an emblem or symbol. **3** The name or symbol of a person, clan, or tribe. [<Algonquian. Cf. Ojibwa *ototeman* his relations.] — **to·tem·ic** (tō·tem′ik) *adj.*

to·tem·ism (tō′təm·iz′əm) *n.* **1** Belief in totems and the practices associated therewith. **2** The system of dividing a tribe into sibs or clans according to their totems. — **to′tem·ist** *n.* — **to′tem·is′tic** *adj.*

totem pole A post or pole, usually of cedar and sometimes as much as 50 feet high, carved or painted with totemic symbols, erected outside an Indian house or as a memorial to a deceased, especially among the Indians of the NW American coast. Also **totem post.**

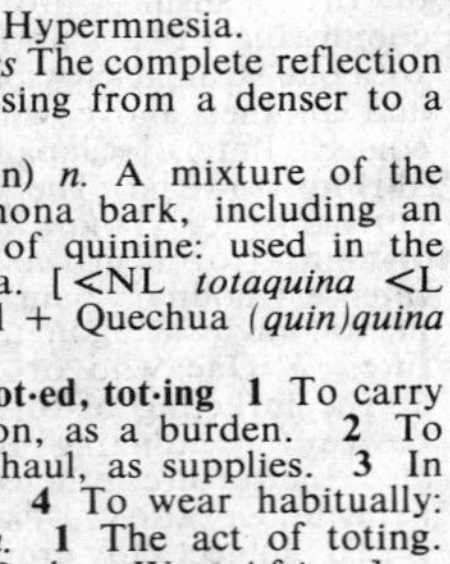

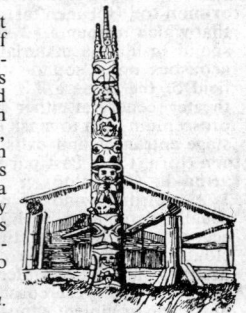

TOTEM POLE
Haida Indians, Queen Charlotte Islands, B.C.

toth·er (tuth′ər) *pron. Colloq.* The other; other. Also **t′oth′er.** [ME *the tother* < *thet other* the other]

toti– *combining form* Whole; wholly: *totipalmate.* [<L *totus* whole]

to·ti·pal·mate (tō′ti·pal′māt) *adj. Ornithol.* Wholly webbed; having all four toes joined by a web, as pelicans. [<TOTI- + PALMATE] —**to′ti·pal·ma′tion** (-pal·mā′shən) *n.*

to·tip·o·tence (tō·tip′ə·təns) *n. Biol.* Power to regenerate the whole of an organism, or some one part, from a fragment. [<TOTI- + *potence,* var. of POTENCY] —**to·tip′o·tent** *adj.*

Tot·le·ben (tôt′lā·bən, tot·lā′-), **Count Franz Eduard Ivanovich,** 1818–84, Russian general and engineer. Also *Todleben.*

Tot·ten·ham (tot′n·əm) A municipal borough of SE Middlesex, and northern suburb of London, England.

tot·ter (tot′ər) *v.i.* **1** To walk feebly and unsteadily. **2** To shake or waver, as if about to fall; be unsteady. —*n.* The act of tottering. See synonyms under SHAKE. [Prob. <Scand. Cf. Norw. *totra, tutra* quiver.] —**tot′ter·er** *n.* —**tot′ter·y** *adj.*

tot·ter·ing (tot′ər·ing) *adj.* Unsteady; that totters; variable. —**tot′ter·ing·ly** *adv.*

to·tum (tō′təm) *Latin* The whole; all.

tou·can (tōō′kan, tōō·kän′) *n.* A large, fruit-eating bird of tropical America (family *Rhamphastidae*) with brilliant plumage and an immense thin-walled beak. [<F <Pg. *tucano* <Tupian *tucana*]

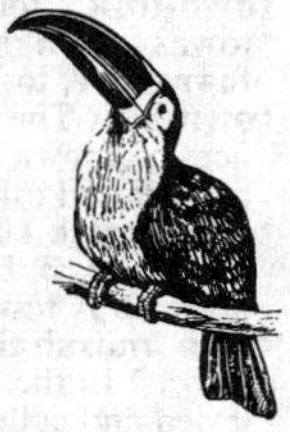

TOUCAN (About 12 inches over-all)

touch (tuch) *v.t.* **1** To place the hand, finger, etc., in contact with. **2** To be in or come into contact with. **3** To bring into contact with something else. **4** To hit or strike lightly; tap. **5** To lay the hand or hands on. **6** To border on; adjoin. **7** To come to; reach. **8** To attain to; equal. **9** To mark or delineate lightly, as with a brush or pen. **10** To modify by adding fine strokes or lines; retouch. **11** To color slightly: The sun *touched* the clouds with gold. **12** To affect injuriously; taint: Vegetables *touched* by frost. **13** To affect by contact; act upon: The drill could not *touch* the steel. **14** To affect the emotions of; soften; move. **15** To move to anger; irritate. **16** To strike the strings or keys of (a musical instrument); play on. **17** To play (a tune). **18** To relate to; concern: This quarrel *touches* you. **19** To treat or discuss in passing; deal with. **20** To have to do with, use, or partake of: I will not *touch* this food. **21** *Slang* To borrow money from. **22** *Slang* To steal. **23** *Geom.* To be tangent to. **24** *Obs.* To test, as gold with a touchstone. —*v.i.* **25** To touch someone or something. **26** To come into or be in contact. See synonyms under REACH. —**to touch at** To stop briefly at (a port or place) in the course of a journey or voyage. —**to touch off** **1** To cause to explode; detonate; fire. **2** To cause to happen or occur. —**to touch on** (or **upon**) **1** To relate to; concern. **2** To treat briefly or in passing. —**to touch up** **1** To strike or prod gently; rouse. **2** To add finishing touches or corrections to. —*n.* **1** The act or process of touching or coming in contact with (something). **2** The act or state of being touched. **3** That one of the special senses that gives the impression of contact with external material objects or their impact upon the body. ◆ Collateral adjective: *tactile.* **4** The sensation conveyed by touching something: a smooth *touch.* **5** *Med.* **a** Examination by feeling; palpation. **b** Digital examination of the vagina in obstetrics. **6** A stroke; hit; blow: to give a ball a slight *touch.* **7** A stroke of wit, ridicule, etc.: He felt the *touch* of her wit. **8** In art, any slight or delicate effort or effect, as of a brush, pen, or chisel; a light stroke or mark: to apply the finishing *touches* to a painting. **9** Any slight detail or effort given to anything, as to a literary work. **10** The manner or style in which an artist, workman, or author executes his work: a master's *touch*; a freedom of *touch.* **11** A trace; tinge; hint; infusion: a *touch* of irony; a *touch* of autumn. **12** A slight attack or twinge: a *touch* of rheumatism; a *touch* of remorse. **13** A small quantity or dash: to apply a *touch* of perfume. **14** Close communication, contact, or sympathy: to keep in *touch* with; to lose *touch* with. **15** A test; trial: to put something to the *touch* of proof. **16** *Music* **a** In the pianoforte, the resistance made to the fingers by the keys. **b** The manner in which a player presses the keyboard. **17** In Rugby football and soccer, the ground just outside the touch lines. **18** An official stamp impressed upon ware made of gold, silver, or pewter, to testify to its fineness. **19** *Obs.* A touchstone, or the method of assaying by the use of a touchstone. **20** *Slang* A sum of money obtained, usually from a friend or acquaintance, by borrowing or mooching. **21** *Slang* A request for such a sum of money: to make a *touch.* **22** *Slang* A person who is an easy mark for a loan or gift of money: usually with an attributive word: a soft *touch*; an easy *touch.* [<OF *tochier, tuchier*; prob. ult. imit.] —**touch′a·ble** *adj.* —**touch′a·ble·ness** *n.* —**touch′er** *n.*

touch-and-go (tuch′ən·gō′) *adj.* **1** Risky; precarious. **2** Hasty and casual; perfunctory.

touch and go **1** An uncertain, risky, or precarious state of things; a narrow escape. **2** An instantaneous or rapid action.

touch·back (tuch′bak′) *n.* In football, the act of touching the ball to the ground behind the player's own goal line when the impetus that sent the ball over the goal line was given to it by an opponent.

touch·down (tuch′doun′) *n.* A scoring play in football in which the ball is held on or over the opponent's goal line and is there declared dead.

tou·ché (tōō·shā′) *French adj.* In fencing, touched by the point of an opponent's foil. —*interj.* You've scored a point! That argument struck home!: an exclamation used to indicate an opponent's success.

touched (tucht) *adj.* **1** That has been subjected to contact. **2** Slightly unbalanced in mind; crack-brained.

touch·hole (tuch′hōl′) *n.* The orifice in old-fashioned cannon or firearms through which the powder was ignited.

touch·ing (tuch′ing) *adj.* Appealing to the susceptibilities; affecting; pathetic. See synonyms under PITIFUL. —*n.* **1** The act of one who touches. **2** The sense of touch. —*prep.* With regard to; concerning; with respect to. —**touch′ing·ly** *adv.* —**touch′ing·ness** *n.*

touch lines The side boundary lines of a Rugby football or soccer field.

touch-me-not (tuch′mē·not′) *n.* **1** Any plant of the genus *Impatiens,* as the garden balsam (*I. balsamina*): so called from the explosive discharge of the seeds by the ripe capsules when touched. **2** The squirting cucumber **3** *Pathol.* Lupus.

touch paper Paper made slow-burning by saturation with saltpeter: used for firing explosives, as in pyrotechny.

touch·stone (tuch′stōn′) *n.* **1** A fine-grained dark stone, as jasper, formerly used to test the fineness of gold by the color of the streak made on the stone. **2** A criterion or standard by which the qualities of something are tested.

Touch·stone (tuch′stōn) A witty clown in Shakespeare's *As You Like It.*

touch-up (tuch′up′) *n.* A finishing touch or retouch.

touch·wood (tuch′wŏŏd′) *n.* **1** Wood, decayed or thoroughly dried, for use as tinder; punk. **2** Dried fungi or fungous growth; amadou.

touch·y (tuch′ē) *adj.* **touch·i·er, touch·i·est** **1** Apt to take offense on very little provocation; irascible; also, apt or liable to take fire, as tinder. **2** In art, done with short, light touches of the brush or pencil instead of with firm, unbroken lines. See synonyms under FRETFUL. —**touch′i·ly** *adv.* —**touch′i·ness** *n.*

tough (tuf) *adj.* **1** Susceptible of great tension or strain without breaking; also, of a close texture. **2** Not easily separated; tenacious; viscid; ropy. **3** Possessing great physical endurance: a *tough* constitution. **4** Possessing moral or intellectual endurance; steadfast; persistent; also, stubborn. **5** Irreclaimably vicious; disreputable; vulgar. **6** Difficult to accomplish; laborious; also, severe. **7** Hard to believe; incredible. —*n.* A lawless person; a rowdy; ruffian. [OE *tōh*] —**tough′ly** *adv.* —**tough′ness** *n.*

tough·en (tuf′ən) *v.t.* & *v.i.* To make or become tough or tougher. —**tough′en·er** *n.*

Toul (tōōl) A town in NE France; besieged and captured by the Germans in the Franco-Prussian War, 1870.

Tou·lon (tōō·lôn′) A French port and naval base on the Mediterranean 29 miles SE of Marseille.

Tou·louse (tōō·lōōz′) A city of southern France, on the Garonne, capital of the Haute-Garonne department.

Tou·louse-Lau·trec (tōō·lōōz′lō·trek′), **Henri Marie Raymond de,** 1864–1901, French painter and lithographer.

toun (tōōn) *n. Scot.* A town; also, a farmhouse.

tou·pee (tōō·pā′, -pē′) *n.* **1** A little tuft or lock of hair. **2** A curl or lock of hair worn as a false front or at the top of a wig. **3** A wig worn to cover baldness or a bald spot. [<F *toupet* <OF *toup, top* a tuft of hair, prob. <Gmc.]

tour (tŏŏr) *n.* **1** A round trip or journey or a rambling excursion. **2** A passing around; circuit for inspection or sightseeing. **3** A turn or shift, as of service. See synonyms under JOURNEY. —**grand tour** A tour of the principal cities of Europe, customary in the 17th and 18th centuries for young English gentlemen as a supplement to their education· chiefly used in the expression *to make the grand tour.* —*v.t.* **1** To make a tour of; travel. **2** To present on a tour: to *tour* a play. —*v.i.* **3** To go on a tour. [<MF <OF *tor, tors* <L *tornus* a lathe <Gk. *tornos*; infl. in meaning by OF *tourner* TURN]

tou·ra·co (tŏŏr′ə·kō) See TURACOU.

Tou·raine (tōō·ren′) A region and former province of west central France; capital, Tours.

tour·bil·lion (tŏŏr·bil′yən) *n.* **1** A whirling wind or a vortex, or something resembling them. **2** A kind of rocket with a spiral flight. [<MF *tourbillon* a whirlwind <OF *torbeillon* <L *turbo, -inis*]

Tour·coing (tŏŏr·kwan′) A city in northern France near the Belgian border in the Nord department.

tour de force (tŏŏr də fôrs′) *French* A feat of remarkable strength or skill.

tour·ing (tŏŏr′ing) *adj.* Used for touring; that tours.

touring car A large, open automobile with a capacity for five or more passengers and baggage, built especially for touring. Also *Brit.* **tour′er.** —**convertible touring car** A touring car with folding top and disappearing or removable windows.

tour·ism (tŏŏr′iz·əm) *n.* **1** Traveling as a recreation. **2** Touring groups; tourists. **3** The organization and guidance of tourists. —**tour·is′tic** *adj.*

tour·ist (tŏŏr′ist) *n.* One who makes a tour or a pleasure trip. —*adj.* Of or suitable for tourists.

tourist camp A roadside group of cabins for the accommodation of transients, usually automobilists.

tourist class A class of accommodations for steamship passengers, lower than cabin class.

tour·ma·line (tŏŏr′mə·lēn, -lin) *n.* A complex borosilicate of aluminum, with a vitreous to resinous luster and found commonly black or brownish or bluish-black, but sometimes blue, green, red, or colorless. The transparent variety, when cut, is esteemed as a gemstone. Also spelled *turmaline.* Also **tour′ma·lin** (-lin). [<F, ult. <Singhalese *tōramalli* carnelian]

Tour·nai (tŏŏr·nā′) A town in SW Belgium on the Sabeldt; a manufacturing and quarrying center. Also **Tour·nay′.**

tour·na·ment (tûr′nə·mənt, tŏŏr′-) *n.* **1** In medieval times, a pageant in which two opposing parties of men in armor contended on horseback, with blunted weapons, in mock combat. **2** The jousts, sports, or contests in which such combatants engaged. **3** A comparatively recent sport of skilled horsemen, who tilt at rings suspended in the air, seeking to bear them off on their lances. **4** Any contest of skill involving a number of competitors and a series of games: a chess *tournament.* **5** An encounter, as of arms: Don Quixote's

tournament with the barber. Also *tourney.* [< OF *torneiement, tornoiement* < *torneier, tornoier* tourney, ult. < L *tornare.* See TURN.]

Tour·neur (tûr′nər), **Cyril,** 1575?–1626, English dramatist.

tour·ney (tûr′nē, to͝or′-) *v.i.* To take part in a tournament; tilt. —*n.* A tournament. [< OF *torneier.* See TOURNAMENT.]

tour·ni·quet (to͝or′nə·ket, -kā, tûr′-) *n. Surg.* A bandage, etc., for stopping the flow of blood through an artery by compression. [< F < *tourner* TURN]

tour·nure (to͞or·nür′) *n. French* **1** The curving shape of a figure; outline; contour. **2** A light pad or cushion formerly worn by women to give the effect of well-rounded hips; a bustle; also, the drapery at the back of a gown.

tour of duty *Mil.* The hours or period of time during which a member of the armed services is on official duty, or assigned to a particular duty: the 24-hour *tour of duty* as officer of the day.

Tours (to͝or) A city in west central France between the Loire and the Cher above their confluence; scene of Charles Martel's defeat of the Saracens, 732.

touse (touz) *Dial. & Scot. v.t.* **1** To stir up, as a row. **2** To tousle; dishevel; rumple. —*n.* Disturbance. [ME *tusen, tousen,* prob. < Gmc.] —**tous′er** *n.*

tou·sle (tou′zəl) *v.t.* **·sled, ·sling** To disarrange or disorder, as the hair or dress. —*n.* **1** *Scot.* A tussle; also, a rude dalliance. **2** A tousled mass or mop of hair. Also **tou′zle.** [Freq. of TOUSE]

tous-les-mois (to͞o·lā·mwä′) *n.* The edible, starchlike tubers of a perennial herb of the West Indies and South America *(Canna edulis),* used in making baby food and as a substitute for arrowroot. [< F, all the months, every month; so called because edible the year round]

Tous·saint l'Ou·ver·ture (to͞o·saN′ lo͞o·ver·tür′), **Dominique François,** 1743–1803, Negro general; liberator of Haiti.

tou·sy (tou′zē) See TOWSY.

tout (tout) *Colloq. v.i.* **1** To solicit patronage, customers, votes, etc. **2** To spy on a race horse so as to gain information for betting; act as a tout. —*v.t.* **3** To solicit; importune. **4 a** To spy on (a race horse) to gain information for betting. **b** To sell information concerning (a race horse). —*n.* **1** One who touts. **2** In horse-racing, a spy who sells information regarding horses entered for a race. **3** One who solicits business. **4** A spy for a robber. [OE *tōtian, tȳtan* peep, look out]

tout à fait (to͞o tȧ fe′) *French* Entirely; quite.

tout à l'heure (to͞o tȧ lœr′) *French* Instantly; just now; presently.

tout au con·traire (to͞o tō kôN·trâr′) *French* Quite to the contrary; quite the reverse.

tout à vous (to͞o tȧ vo͞o′) *French* Wholly yours; sincerely yours; at your service.

tout de suite (to͞ot swēt′) *French* Immediately; at once.

tout en·sem·ble (to͞o täN säN′bl′) *French* **1** All in all; everything considered. **2** The general effect.

tout·er (tou′tər) *n.* **1** One who plies or solicits customers or supporters obtrusively: a *touter* for a candidate for election. **2** *Colloq.* A runner.

tout le monde (to͞o lə môNd′) *French* All the world; everybody.

to·va·risch (to·vä′rish) *n. Russian* Comrade.

tow[1] (tō) *n.* A short, coarse hemp or flax fiber prepared for spinning. [Prob. OE *tōw-* for spinning, as in tōwlic pertaining to spinning]

tow[2] (tō) *v.t.* To pull or drag by a rope or chain; drag or pull along. See synonyms under DRAW. —*n.* **1** The act of towing, or the state of being towed. **2** That which is towed, as barges by a tugboat. **3** That which tows. **4** A rope or cable used in towing; towline. **—to take in tow** To take in charge for or as for towing; take under protection; take charge of. [OE *togian*]

tow·age (tō′ij) *n.* **1** The service of, or charge for, towing. **2** The act of towing. [< TOW[1]]

to·ward (tôrd, tōrd, tə·wôrd′) *prep.* **1** In the direction of; facing. **2** With respect to; regarding: his attitude *toward* women. **3** In anticipation of or as a contribution to; for: He is saving *toward* his education. **4** Near in point of time; approaching; about: arriving *toward* evening. **5** Tending to result in; designed or likely to achieve: a struggle *toward* mutual understanding. Also **to·wards′.** See synonyms under AT. —*adj.* (tôrd, tōrd) *Archaic* or *Rare* **1** Ready to do or learn; apt. **2** Docile. **3** In progress: used predicatively. **4** Impending or imminent. [OE *tōweard* < *tō* to + *-weard* -ward] **—to·ward′ness** *n.*

to·ward·ly (tôrd′lē, tōrd′-) *Archaic adj.* **1** Ready to do or learn; compliant; docile. **2** Favorable; promising; propitious.

tow·a·way (tō′ə·wā) *n.* The act of towing away a vehicle, especially one illegally parked. —*adj.* Of or pertaining to the towing away of such vehicles: the city *towaway* policy.

tow·boat (tō′bōt′) *n.* A tugboat.

tow·el (toul, tou′əl) *n.* **1** A cloth or paper for drying anything by wiping. **2** An altar cloth. —*v.t.* **·eled** or **·elled, ·el·ing** or **·el·ling** To wipe or dry with a towel. [< OF *toaille,* prob. < OHG *dwahila* a washcloth < *dwahan* wash]

tow·el·ing (tou′ling, tou′əl·ing) *n.* Material, as crash, for towels. Also *Brit.* **tow′el·ling.**

tow·er (tou′ər) *n.* **1** A structure very tall in proportion to its other dimensions, and frequently forming part of a large building; properly, a structure larger than a pinnacle, and less tapering than a steeple. **2** A tall, wooden, movable structure from which besiegers formerly stormed a fortress. **3** A place of security or defense; fortified place; citadel. —*v.i.* **1** To rise or stand like a tower; extend to a great height. **2** To fly directly upward, as some birds. [Fusion of OE *torr* (< L *turris*) and OE *tūr* < OF *tor, tur* < L *turris*]

tow·ered (tou′ərd) *adj.* **1** Furnished with towers for ornament or defense. **2** Rising like a tower.

tow·er·ing (tou′ər·ing) *adj.* **1** Like a tower; lofty; hence, very high or great: also **tow′er·y.** **2** Rising or increasing to a high pitch of violence or intensity; furious. See synonyms under HIGH.

Tower of London A group of buildings comprising a fortress and palace on the north bank of the Thames, built in 1078 around the original tower (the White Tower) and used as a royal residence, a political prison, and a museum.

tower of silence A circular tower with central well, having a high outer wall, and inner platform on which the Parsees expose the bodies of their dead to be eaten by vultures, so that the bodies may be dissipated without polluting the earth: also called *dakhma, dokhma.*

tow·head (tō′hed′) *n.* **1** A head of very light-colored or flaxen hair, or a person having such hair. **2** *U.S.* A wooded sandbar or newly formed island in a river. [< TOW[1] + HEAD] **—tow′-head′ed** *adj.*

tow·hee (tou′hē, tō′-) *n.* An American bird related to the buntings and the sparrows, especially the **Alabama towhee** *(Pipilo erythrophthalmus)* and the **green-tailed towhee** *(Oberholseria chlorura)* of the western United States. Also **towhee bunting.** [Imit. of one of its notes]

tow·line (tō′līn′) *n.* A line, rope, or chain used in towing.

tow·mont (tō′mənt) *n. Scot.* A twelvemonth. Also **tow′mond** (-mənd).

town (toun) *n.* **1** Any considerable collection of dwellings and other buildings larger than a village and comprising a geographical and political community unit, but not incorporated as a city. **2** The local government of such a community; also, the voters, the representatives, or the inhabitants collectively. **3** A subdivision of a county, usually rural, that may include a number of villages and towns; a township. **4** In New England, a local unit governing itself through a town meeting. **5** *Brit.* Originally, a collection of dwellings enclosed for security within some form of fortification; subsequently, any collection of dwelling houses larger than a village. ◆ Collateral adjective: *oppidan.* **6** A closely settled urban district as contrasted with the open country: *town* and country. **7** The city or town nearest to where one lives: a trip to *town;* also, the downtown or business section of a city or town. **8** A group of prairie-dog burrows. **—on the town 1** Dependent on municipal charity. **2** *Slang* On a round of pleasure in the city. **—to go to town** *Slang* To succeed in the highest degree. **—to paint the town red** *Slang* To carouse. —*adj.* **1** Of or pertaining to, like, situated in, or for use in town: *town* clothes. **2** Supported by town funds: a *town* library. [OE *tūn, tuun* an enclosure, group of houses]

Town may appear as a combining form in hyphemes or solidemes, or as the first element in two-word phrases:

town-absorbing	**town-hating**
town-born	**town jail**
town-bound	**town-keeping**
town-bred	**town life**
town car	**town lot**
town church	**town-loving**
town dweller	**town-made**
town-dwelling	**town park**
town-flanked	**town-tied**
town-goer	**town-trained**
town-going	**town-weary**

town clerk An official who keeps the records of a town.

town crier A person appointed to make proclamations through the streets of a town.

town farm A farm maintained by town or township funds for the poor or indigent.

town·folk (toun′fōk′) *n.* People who live in towns or in a particular town or city. Also **towns′folk′, towns′peo′ple** (-pē′pəl).

town hall The building containing the public offices of a town and used for meetings of the town council and other official business.

town house 1 A residence in a town or city. **2** A town hall. **3** *U.S. Obs.* **a** An almshouse; workhouse. **b** A town prison.

town marshal 1 An officer of a town police force. **2** In the American colonies, an officer who levied and collected taxes, fines, etc.

town meeting 1 A general assemblage of the people of a town. **2** An assembly of qualified voters for the purpose of transacting town business; also, the voters assembled.

town·ship (toun′ship) *n.* **1** *U.S.* **a** A territorial subdivision of a county with certain corporate powers of municipal government for local purposes; also, the corporation or government thereof. **b** In New England, a local political unit governed by a town meeting. **2** A unit of area in surveys of U.S. public lands, normally six miles square, subdivided into 36 sections of one square mile each. **3** *Brit.* Anciently, an organized group of families forming the political unit of early society which existed prior to the parish. [OE *tūnscipe* < *tūn* a village, group of houses]

towns·man (tounz′mən) *n. pl.* **·men** (-mən) **1** A resident of a town; also, a fellow citizen. **2** In New England, a town officer; a selectman. **3** In a school or college town, one who lives in the town as contrasted with a student or teacher in the school or college.

towns·wom·an (tounz′wo͝om′ən) *n. pl.* **·wom·en** (-wim′in) A woman living in a town.

tow·path (tō′path′, -päth′) *n.* A path along a river or canal used by men, horses, or mules towing boats; a towing path.

tow·rope (tō′rōp′) *n.* A heavy rope or cable used in towing. Also called *towline.*

tow truck (tō) A truck equipped to tow other vehicles.

tow·y (tō′ē) *adj.* Composed of, like, or containing tow. [< TOW[1]]

tow·zie (tou′zē) *adj. Scot.* Disheveled; rumpled; shaggy: also spelled *toozie, tousy.* Also **tow′sie.**

tox·al·bu·min (tok′sal·byo͞o′min) *n. Biochem.* Any protein substance having toxic properties, as snake venom, ricin, certain bacterial cultures, etc. [< TOX(IC) + ALBUMIN]

tox·a·phene (tok′sə·fēn) *n.* A waxy chlorinated hydrocarbon, $C_{10}H_{10}Cl$, used as a pesticide. [< TOX(IC) + PHEN(YL)]

tox·e·mi·a (tok·sē′mē·ə) *n. Pathol.* A poisoned condition of the body caused by the absorption of bacterial toxins from a local source of infection and their distribution by the blood. Also **tox·ae′mi·a.** [< NL < Gk. *toxicon* a poison + *haima* blood] **—tox·e′mic, tox·ae′mic** *adj.*

tox·ic (tok′sik) *adj.* **1** Pertaining to poison; poisonous. **2** Due to or caused by poison or a toxin. Also **tox′i·cal.** [< Med. L *toxicus* poisoned, poisonous < L *toxicum* a poison, orig. a poison for arrows < Gk. *toxicon (pharmakon)* (a poison) for arrows < *toxa* arrows < *toxon* a bow] —**tox′i·cal·ly** *adv.*

tox·i·cant (tok′sə·kənt) *adj.* **1** Possessing poisonous qualities. **2** Producing a poisonous effect. —*n.* A toxic substance; poison; also, an intoxicant. [< LL *toxicans, -antis,* ppr. of

toxicare smear with poison <L *toxicum.* See TOXIC.]

tox·i·ca·tion (tok'sə·kā'shən) *n.* **1** The act of poisoning. **2** The state of being poisoned. **3** Poisoning.

tox·ic·i·ty (tok·sis'ə·tē) *n.* **1** The quality of being toxic. **2** The degree or intensity of virulence of a poison.

toxico– *combining form* Poison; of or pertaining to poison, or to poisons: *toxicology.* Also, before vowels, **toxic–.** [<Gk. *toxicon* poison]

tox·i·co·gen·ic (tok'sə·kō·jen'ik) *adj.* **1** Producing poisons or toxins. **2** Generated or formed by toxic matter.

tox·i·col·o·gy (tok'sə·kol'ə·jē) *n.* The science that treats of the origin, nature, properties, and effects of poisons, of their detection in the organs or tissues, of their antidotes, and of the treatment of diseases due to poisoning. [<F *toxicologie*] — **tox'i·co·log'i·cal** (-kō·loj'i·kəl) *adj.* — **tox'i·co·log'i·cal·ly** *adv.* — **tox'i·col'o·gist** *n.*

tox·i·co·ma·ni·a (tok'sə·kō·mā'nē·ə, -mān'yə) *n.* A morbid desire to take poison. [<TOXICO- + -MANIA]

tox·i·co·pho·bi·a (tok'sə·kō·fō'bē·ə) *n.* A morbid fear of poison or of being poisoned: also called *iophobia, toxiphobia.* [<TOXICO- + -PHOBIA] — **tox'i·pho'bic** *adj.*

tox·i·co·sis (tok'sə·kō'sis) *n. pl.* **·ses** (-sēz) *Pathol.* A morbid condition due to the effect of toxins generated within the system or administered from without. [<NL <L *toxicum* poison]

tox·in (tok'sin) *n.* **1** Any of a class of more or less unstable poisonous compounds elaborated by animal, vegetable, or bacterial organisms and acting as causative agents in many diseases, usually after an incubation period. **2** Any toxic matter generated in living or dead organisms. Also **tox·ine** (tok'sēn). [<TOX(IC) + -IN]

tox·is·ter·ol (tok·sis'tər·ōl, -ol) *n. Biochem.* A toxic compound produced by the excessive irradiation of ergosterol and intermediate between calciferol and suprasterol. [<TOXI(C) + STEROL]

tox·o·phil (tok'sə·fil) *adj. Biol.* Having an affinity for or being in harmony with a toxin. Also **tox'o·phile** (-fīl, -fil). [< *toxo-* (<TOXIN) + -PHIL]

tox·o·plas·mo·sis (tok'sō·plaz·mō'sis) *n.* A diseased condition resulting from the presence of or infection by sporozoan parasites (genus *Toxoplasma*) which act principally upon the nervous system of certain animals and sometimes of man. [<NL <*Toxoplasma,* genus name]

toy (toi) *n.* **1** An article constructed for the amusement of children; a plaything; hence, any trifling or diverting object; an ornament; trinket. **2** Any diminutive object imitating a larger one and fitted for entertainment and instruction. **3** *Obs.* Wanton play; dalliance. **4** A small dog bred to extreme smallness and kept as a pet: also **toy dog. 5** *Scot.* A head covering for women that hangs loosely over the shoulders; a toy-mutch. **6** *Obs.* A dance tune. **7** *Archaic* A quaint utterance, idle tale, or anecdote; fancy; jest. See synonyms under GAUD. — *v.i.* To trifle; play. — *adj.* Resembling a toy; of miniature size. [Prob. fusion of ME *toye* flirtation, sport + Du. *tuig* tools, stuff] — **toy'er** *n.* — **toy'ish** *adj.*

To·ya·ma (tō·yä·mä) A port of north central Honshu, Japan.

toy-mutch (toi'much) *n. Scot.* Toy (def. 5).

Toyn·bee (toin'bē), **Arnold Joseph,** born 1889, English historian.

to·yo (tō'yō) *n.* A shiny, rice-paper straw. [<Japanese]

To·yo·ha·shi (tō·yō·hä·shē) A city of southern Honshu, Japan; a manufacturing center.

to·yon (tō'yən) *n.* An evergreen shrub (*Photinia arbutifolia*) indigenous to the Pacific coast of North America, having white flowers, followed by persistent berries of a bright red color; California holly. [<Sp. *tollón* < N. Am. Ind. (Mexican)]

toy shop A shop where toys are displayed for sale.

tra·be·at·ed (trā'bē·ā'tid) *adj. Archit.* **1** Having an entablature. **2** Having beams or long stones as lintels instead of an arch. Also **tra'·**

be·ate (-it, -āt). [Irregularly formed <L *trabs, trabis* a beam]

tra·be·a·tion (trā'bē·ā'shən) *n. Archit.* **1** The state of being trabeated. **2** An entablature.

tra·bec·u·la (trə·bek'yə·lə) *n. pl.* **·lae** (-lē) **1** A small supporting band or bar. **2** *Anat.* The interwoven bands of connective tissue that form the supporting framework of an organ, as the spleen. **3** *Bot.* A row or plate of sterile cells extending across the cavity in the sporangium of a moss. [<L, dim. of *trabs, trabis* a beam] — **tra·bec'u·lar** *adj.*

Tra·ben–Trar·bach (trä'bən–trär'bäkh) A town in Rhineland–Palatinate, West Germany, on the Mosel; a wine center.

Trab·zon (träb·zôn') The Turkish name for TREBIZOND.

trace¹ (trās) *n.* **1** A vestige or mark left by some past event or agent, especially when regarded as a sign or clue. **2** A barely detectable quantity, quality, token, or characteristic; touch. **3** *Chem.* A proportion or ingredient too small to be weighed (often abbreviated *tr.*): *a trace of soda.* **3** An imprint or mark indicating the passage of a person or thing, as a footprint, etc. **4** A path or trail through woods or forest beaten down by men or animals. **5** A lightly drawn line; something traced. **6** The point or line on a map or on the ground indicating the position of a trench, an aircraft flight path, etc. **7** The path of a tracer bullet. **8** *Psychol.* An engram. — *v.* **traced, trac·ing** *v.t.* **1** To follow the tracks, course, or development of. **2** To follow (tracks, a course of development, etc.). **3** To discover or ascertain by examination or investigation; find out or determine. **4** To draw; sketch. **5** To copy (a drawing, etc.) on a superimposed transparent sheet. **6** To form (letters, etc.) with careful strokes. **7** To mark with an impressed design; chase. **8** To imprint (a pattern or design). **9** To mark or record by a curved or broken line. **10** To go or move over, along, or through. — *v.i.* **11** To make one's way; proceed. **12** To have its origin; go back in time. [<OF *tracier,* ult. <L *tractus* a dragging, a track <*trahere* draw] — **trace'a·ble** *adj.* — **trace'a·bil'i·ty, trace'a·ble·ness** *n.* — **trace'a·bly** *adv.* — **trace'·less** *adj.*

Synonyms (noun): footmark, footprint, footstep, mark, memorial, remains, remnant, sign, token, track, vestige. A *vestige* is always slight compared with that whose existence it recalls; as, Scattered mounds containing human implements are *vestiges* of a former civilization. A *vestige* is always a part of that which has passed away; a *trace* may be merely the *mark* it has made, or some slight evidence of its presence or of the effect it has produced; as, *Traces* of game were observed by the hunter. See CHARACTERISTIC, MARK¹.

trace² (trās) *n.* **1** One of two side straps or chains for connecting the collar of a harness with the swingletree. **2** *Mech.* A link or connecting bar hinged at each end to other pieces of a mechanism, to transmit motion from one part to another. — **to kick over the traces** To throw off control; become unmanageable. — *v.t.* **traced, trac·ing** To fasten, as with traces. [<OF *traiz, trais,* pl. of *trait* a dragging, a leather harness <L *tractus.* See TRACE¹.]

trac·er (trā'sər) *n.* **1** One who or that which traces. **2** One of various instruments used in tracing drawings, etc. **3** An inquiry forwarded from one point to another, to trace missing mail matter, etc. **4** *Surg.* An instrument for laying bare and tracing the course of nerves, muscles, etc. **5** One who searches for lost property, as on railroads. **6** *Mil.* **a** A chemical incorporated in certain types of ammunition used for ranging, signaling, or incendiary purposes. **b** A tracer bullet. **7** *Med.* A radioisotope introduced into the body for the purpose of following the processes of metabolism, the course or location of a disease, etc. **8** A message that describes a person or thing wanted, as by the police. [<TRACE¹]

tracer bullet A bullet which leaves a line of smoke or fire in its wake, thus indicating its course for correction of aim.

trac·er·y (trā'sər·ē) *n. pl.* **·er·ies 1** Ornamental

stonework formed of ramifying lines. **2** Any work resembling this.

tra·che·a (trā'kē·ə) *n. pl.* **·che·ae** (-ki·ē) **1** *Anat.* The duct, composed of membrane and incomplete cartilaginous rings, by which air passes from the larynx to the bronchi and the lungs; the windpipe. **2** *Zool.* One of the passages by which air is conveyed from the exterior in air–breathing arthropods, as insects and arachnids. **3** *Bot.* A duct or vessel in plants, particularly one having spiral markings. [<Med. L <LL *trachia* <Gk. (*artēria*) *tracheia* a rough (artery), fem. of *trachys* rough] — **tra'che·al** *adj.*

tracheal tissue *Bot.* Plant tissue consisting of tracheae or tracheids: one of the chief constituents of xylem.

tra·che·id (trā'kē·id) *n. Bot.* An elongated, taper–pointed, woody plant cell, especially when marked with bordered pits and serving for support, as in the pine family. [<G *tracheïde* <Med. L *trachea* the trachea] — **tra·che·i·dal** (trə·kē'ə·dəl) *adj.*

tra·che·i·tis (trā'kē·ī'tis) *n. Pathol.* Inflammation of the trachea or windpipe. [<NL <Med. L *trachea* the trachea]

tracheo– *combining form* The trachea; of or pertaining to the trachea: *tracheotomy.* Also, before vowels, **trache–.** [<TRACHEA]

tra·che·os·co·py (trā'kē·os'kə·pē) *n. Med.* Instrumental inspection of the windpipe. — **tra'che·o·scop'ic** (-ō·skop'ik) *adj.* — **tra'che·os'co·pist** *n.*

tra·che·ot·o·my (trā'kē·ot'ə·mē) *n. Surg.* The operation of making an incision into the windpipe. — **tra'che·ot'o·mist** *n.*

trach·le (träkh'əl) *Scot. v.t.* To trail or draggle; fatigue; exhaust. — *n.* Any exercise involving or resulting in unusual fatigue; a burdensome work. Also spelled *trauchle.* [Corruption of DRAGGLE]

tra·cho·ma (trə·kō'mə) *n. Pathol.* A contagious virus disease of the eye characterized by hard papillary elevations or granular excrescences on the inner surface of the eyelids, with inflammation of the lining; granular conjunctivitis. [<NL <Gk. *trachōma, -atos* roughness < *trachys* rough] — **tra·chom·a·tous** (trə·kom'-ə·təs) *adj.*

trachy– *combining form* Rough; uneven: *trachycarpous,* bearing rough fruit. Also, before vowels, **trach–.** [<Gk. *trachys* rough]

tra·chyte (trā'kīt, trak'īt) *n.* A light–colored, rough volcanic rock having a porphyritic texture, composed essentially of alkaline feldspar and one or more secondary minerals. [<F <Gk. *trachytēs* ruggedness < *trachys* rough]

trac·ing (trā'sing) *n.* **1** The act of one who traces. **2** An ornamentation produced by etching, drawing, or tracing. **3** A copy made by tracing on transparent paper. **4** A record made by a self–registering instrument.

track (trak) *n.* **1** A mark or trail left by the passage of anything; the *track* of a storm. **2** A footprint or series of footprints. **3** Any regular path; course: the *track* of a comet round the sun. **4** Any kind of race-course; also, sports performed on such a course; track athletics. **5** A set of rails or a rail on which something may travel; specifically, the pair of metal rails on which a railway train or tramway runs; also, the rail or pair of rails with its ties, bolts, etc.; by extension, the whole trackway. **6** A trace or vestige. **7** A sequence of events; a succession of ideas. **8** Awareness of the progress or sequence; count; record: to keep *track* of. **9** Tread (def. 2). See synonyms under MARK¹, ROAD, TRACE¹, WAY. **10** A course or trail leading to a desired goal: to be on the right *track.* **11** One of a pair of endless metal belts by means of which certain vehicles, as tanks, are capable of moving over a variety of surfaces. **12** In education, any of two or more classes covering the same course of study, segregated according to the students' preparation or ability and taught at correspondingly different levels. — **to make tracks** To hurry; run away in haste. — **in one's tracks** Right where one is; on the spot. — **to jump the track 1** To leave the rails, as a railroad engine or car. **2** To depart from any usual course or procedure. — *v.t.* **1** To

follow the tracks of; trail. **2** To discover and follow up or out, by means of marks or indications. **3** To make tracks upon or with: to *track* snow through a house. **4** To traverse, as on foot: to *track* the wild forests. **5** To furnish with rails or tracks. —*v.i.* **6** To measure a certain distance between wheels. **7** To have the wheels equal in span or gage to the wheels of another vehicle. **8** To run in the same track; be in alinement. —*adj.* Pertaining to or performed on a track. [<OF *trac,* prob. <Gmc. Cf. Du. *trek* pull.] —**track′er** *n.* —**track′·a·ble** *adj.*

track·age (trak′ij) *n.* **1** Railroad tracks collectively. **2** The right of one company to use the track system of another company. **3** The charge for this right. **4** A towing, especially of a vessel in a canal, with a rope from the towpath.

track boat A boat towed from a path along the shore.

track detector *Physics* A device for showing the ionization paths of subatomic particles, as the cloud chamber.

track events The races at an athletic meet: distinguished from *field events.* Also **track athletics.**

track·less (trak′lis) *adj.* **1** Unmarked by footsteps; pathless: the *trackless* desert. **2** Leaving no traces: a *trackless* fugitive. **3** Not running on tracks or rails.

trackless trolley A trolley bus.

track·man (trak′mən) *n. pl.* **·men** (-mən) *U. S.* A person employed to inspect regularly the condition of a section of railroad track. Also **track·walk·er** (trak′wôk′ər).

track meet An athletic contest made up of track events.

track record *Colloq.* A record of achievements.

track·way (trak′wā′) *n.* The permanent way of a railroad.

tract[1] (trakt) *n.* **1** An extended area, as of land or water. **2** Continued duration, as of time. **3** *Anat.* An extensive region of the body, especially one comprising a system of parts or organs: the alimentary *tract.* [<L *tractus* a drawing out, duration < *trahere* draw. Doublet of TRAIT.]

tract[2] (trakt) *n.* **1** A short treatise, as on some question of religion or morals; a propaganda leaflet. **2** An anthem sometimes substituted for the Alleluia: so styled because, instead of being treated antiphonally, it is sung *tractim* (continuously) and as a solo: also **trac′tus.** [Short for TRACTATE]

tract·a·ble (trak′tə·bəl) *adj.* **1** Easily led or controlled; manageable; docile. **2** Readily worked or handled; malleable. See synonyms under DOCILE. [<L *tractabilis* < *tractare* handle, freq. of *trahere* draw] —**tract′a·bly** *adv.* —**tract′a·ble·ness, tract′a·bil′i·ty** *n.*

Trac·tar·i·an (trak·târ′ē·ən) *n.* One of the authors of the series of 90 pamphlets called *Tracts for the Times.* —*adj.* Pertaining to the Tractarians or to their teachings.

Trac·tar·i·an·ism (trak·târ′ē·ən·iz′əm) *n.* The tenets or principles expressed in *Tracts for the Times* (1833–41) by the leaders of the religious movement known as the Oxford Movement which sought to link the Anglican Church more closely to the Roman Catholic Church and opposed liberalism in theology.

trac·tate (trak′tāt) *n.* A short treatise; a tract. [<L *tractatus* a handling, treatise, pp. of *tractare.* See TRACTABLE.]

trac·tile (trak′til) *adj.* That can be drawn out; ductile. [<L *tractilis* < *tractus.* See TRACE[1].] —**trac·til′i·ty** *n.*

trac·tion (trak′shən) *n.* **1** The act of drawing, as by motive power over a surface. **2** The state of being drawn, or the power employed. **3** *Physiol.* Contraction, as of a muscle. **4** Adhesive or rolling friction, as of wheels on a track. [<Med. L *tractio, -onis* <L *tractus.* See TRACE[1].] —**trac′tion·al** *adj.*

trac·tive (trak′tiv) *adj.* Having or exerting traction.

trac·tor (trak′tər) *n.* **1** A machine or instrument for pulling or drawing. **2** A powerful, motor-driven vehicle, usually having heavy treads, used, as on farms, to draw a plow, reaper, etc. **3** An automotive vehicle with a driver's cab, used to haul trailers, etc. **4** A traction engine. **5** *Aeron.* **a** An airplane with the propeller or propellers situated in front of the supporting surface to pull it through the air: also **tractor airplane. b** The propeller of a tractor airplane. [<NL <L *tractus.* See TRACE[1].]

trad (trad) *adj. Slang* Traditional: *trad* jazz.

trade (trād) *n.* **1** A business, particularly a skilled or specialized handicraft; a craft. **2** Mercantile traffic; commerce. **3** A bargain; deal; also, an exchange; specifically, a corrupt bargain in patronage between political–party leaders. **4** The people following a particular calling. **5** The amount of business or exchange done in a particular place; a firm's customers. **6** Customary pursuit; occupation. **7** *Brit.* **a** The submarine service of the Royal Navy. **b** The liquor traffic. **8** *Obs.* A trail or track. **9** *Obs.* A course, path, passage, or way. **10** *Obs.* Custom, habit, or practice. **11** A trade wind: usually in the plural. See synonyms under BUSINESS, SALE, TRAFFIC. —*v.* **trad·ed, trad·ing** *v.t.* To dispose of by bargain and sale; now, especially, to barter; exchange. —*v.i.* To engage in commerce or in business transactions of bargain and sale. —**to trade in** To give in exchange as payment or part payment. —**to trade off** To get rid of by exchange or trading. —**to trade on** To take advantage of. [<MLG, a track. Akin to TREAD.]

trade acceptance A bill of exchange drawn by the seller of goods on the purchaser who accepts the draft by writing across the face of it when and where it is payable.

trade book An edition of a book designed for ordinary sale to the general public, as distinguished from a textbook, limited or de luxe edition, etc.

trade dollar See under DOLLAR.

trade–in (trād′in′) *n.* Something given or accepted in payment or part payment for something else; an exchange.

trade journal A periodical publishing news and discussions of a particular trade or business.

trade–last (trād′last′, -läst′) *n. Colloq.* A favorable remark that one has heard and offers to repeat to the person complimented in return for a similar remark.

trade·mark (trād′märk′) *n.* A name, symbol, design, device, or word, or any combination thereof, used by a merchant or manufacturer to identify his goods and distinguish them from those made or sold by others. A trademark may or may not be legally registered as such —*v.t.* **1** To label with a trademark. **2** To register as a trademark. —**trade′marked′** *adj.*

trade name **1** The name by which an article, process, service, or the like is designated in trade. **2** A name given by a manufacturer to designate a proprietary article, sometimes having the status of a trademark or of a copyrighted and patented proprietary name. **3** A style or a name of a business house acquired by purchase from a retiring firm or trader.

trade–off (trād′ôf′, -of′) *n.* **1** A giving up of something, as an objective or advantage, in exchange for something else: a *trade–off* of higher pay for longer vacations. **2** The relationship that characterizes such an exchange; a compromise or adjustment between opposing elements or positions: the *trade–off* between taxation and improved public services.

trad·er (trā′dər) *n.* **1** One who trades. **2** Any vessel employed in a particular trade. **3** A member of a stock exchange who trades for himself, and not for customers.

trade rat A pack rat.

trad·es·can·ti·a (trad′əs·kan′shē·ə, -shə) *n.* Any of a genus (*Tradescantia*) of perennial American herbs, often having grasslike leaves and showy flowers with ephemeral petals. [<NL, after John *Tradescant,* died in 1638, English traveler and naturalist]

trade school See under SCHOOL.

trades·folk (trādz′fōk′) *n. pl.* People engaged in retail trade; shopkeepers or salespeople. Also **trades′peo′ple**

trades·man (trādz′mən) *n. pl.* **·men** (-mən) **1** A retail dealer; shopkeeper. **2** *Brit.* A mechanic.

trades·wom·an (trādz′wo͝om′ən) *n. pl.* **·wom·en** (-wim′in) A woman engaged in trade or the sale of goods.

trade union An organized association of workmen formed for the protection and promotion of their common interests, especially with regard to wages, hours, and working conditions. Also **trades union.** —**trade′–un′ion·ism** *n.* —**trade′–un′ion·ist** *n.*

trade wind Either of two steady winds blowing in the same course toward the equator from about 30° N and S latitude, one from the northeast on the north, the other from the southeast on the south side of the equatorial line.

trad·ing (trā′ding) *adj.* **1** Carrying on trade. **2** Corrupt; venal: said of officials. **3** *Obs.* Pursuing a steady course.

trading post A building or small settlement in unsettled territory where a trader or trading company has set up a station for barter (usually in furs) with North American Indians or other natives.

trading stamp See under STAMP.

tra·di·tion (trə·dish′ən) *n.* **1** The transmission of knowledge, opinions, doctrines, customs, practices, etc., from generation to generation, originally by word of mouth and by example. **2** That which is so transmitted; a body of beliefs and usages handed down from generation to generation; also, any particular story, belief, or usage so handed down; hence, remembrance, or recollection existing as by transmission. **3** That body of Christian doctrine, handed down through successive generations and held by some churches to belong to the deposit of faith, even if it may not be found in the Holy Scripture. **4** Among the Jews, an unwritten code said to have been revealed to Moses on Mount Sinai at the time of the delivery of the Decalog and handed down through the oral teaching of prophets and doctors of the law. **5** The record of the acts and utterances of Mohammed, known as the *Sunna.* **6** A custom so long continued that it has almost the force of a law. **7** *Law* Delivery of possession. [<OF *tradicion* <L *traditio, -onis* a delivery, surrender < *traditus,* pp. of *tradere* deliver < *trans-* across + *dare* give. Doublet of TREASON.] —**tra·di′tion·er, tra·di′tion·ist** *n.*

tra·di·tion·al (trə·dish′ən·əl) *adj.* **1** Relating to or depending on tradition. **2** Characterizing a school of English Biblical critics who hold the Greek texts of the New Testament to be the foundation of the true text. Also **tra·di′tion·ar′y** (-er′ē). —**tra·di′tion·al·ist** *adj.* & *n.* —**tra·di′tion·al·is′tic** *adj.* —**tra·di′tion·al·ly** *adv.*

tra·di·tion·al·ism (trə·dish′ən·əl·iz′əm) *n.* **1** A system of faith founded on tradition. **2** Adherence to tradition; especially, undue reverence for tradition in religious matters.

trad·i·tive (trad′ə·tiv) *adj. Obs.* Traditional. [Appar. <MF *traditif* <L *traditus.* See TRADITION.]

trad·i·tor (trad′ə·tər) *n. pl.* **trad·i·to·res** (trad′ə·tôr′ēz, -tō′rēz) A traitor among the early Christians at the time of the Roman persecutions. [<L, a deliverer, betrayer < *tradere.* See TRADITION.]

tra·duce (trə·do͞os′, -dyo͞os′) *v.t.* **·duced, ·duc·ing** To misrepresent wilfully the conduct or character of; defame; slander. See synonyms under ASPERSE, REVILE. [<L *traducere* transport, bring into disgrace < *trans-* across + *ducere* lead] —**tra·duc′er** *n.* —**tra·duc′i·ble** *adj.* —**tra·duc′ing·ly** *adv.* —**tra·duc·tion** (trə·duk′shən) *n.*

tra·du·cian·ism (trə·do͞o′shən·iz′əm, -dyo͞o′-) *n.* The doctrine that the soul, equally with the body, is produced and begotten by the parent or parents: distinguished from *creationism* and *preexistence.* [<LL *traducianus* <L *tradux, -icis* a shoot for propagation < *traducere.* See TRADUCE.] —**tra·du′cian·ist** *n.* —**tra·du′cian·is′tic** *adj.*

Tra·fal·gar (trə·fal′gər, *Sp.* trä′fäl·gär′), **Cape** A headland on the Atlantic coast of SW Spain; scene of a naval battle in which Nelson, though fatally wounded, defeated the French and Spanish fleets, 1805.

traf·fic (traf′ik) *n.* **1** The exchange of goods, wares, etc.; the business of buying and selling, between individuals or communities; trade. **2** The business of transportation, as by railroad. **3** The subjects of transportation collectively; the things carried. **4** A business procedure; transaction; hence, intercourse. **5** The passing of pedestrians and vehicles along a road; the flow of telephone messages, etc. **6** Unlawful or improper trade: *traffic* in stolen goods. —*v.i.* **·ficked, ·fick·ing** **1** To engage in buying and selling; do business, especially

illegally: with *in.* 2 To have dealings: with *with.* [<MF *trafic, trafique* <Ital. *traffico* < *trafficare* <L *trans-* across + Ital. *ficcare* thrust in <L *figere* fasten] —**traf′fick·er** *n.*

Synonyms (noun): business, commerce, trade. *Commerce* is the broadest and noblest term of this group. *Trade* may be local; *commerce* is always extended and is between members of distinct communities, states, or nations; as, foreign, interstate, or intrastate *commerce*; foreign, domestic, or free–port *trade. Traffic* is local, as between different parts of one city or between two or more cities. *Trade* may be largely by letter or telegram, etc.; *traffic* involves the actual passing to and fro of persons or commodities and may be applied directly to persons when considered as in some way a source of gain: the passenger *traffic* of a railroad. *Traffic* always suggests stir and bustle: the din of *traffic*; one may say dull *trade,* but scarcely dull *traffic.* Compare synonyms for BUSINESS.

Traffic may appear as a combining form in hyphemes or as the first element in two–word phrases, with the following meanings:

1 Of or pertaining to the flow of roadway traffic:

traffic accident **traffic congestion**
traffic artery **traffic–laden**
traffic–congested **traffic lane**

2 Of or pertaining to the laws or regulation of roadway traffic:

traffic cop **traffic signal**
traffic court **traffic violation**
traffic policeman **traffic violator**

traf·fic·a·tor (traf′ə·kā′tər) *n.* A traffic signal. [<TRAFFIC + -ATOR]

traffic circle A circular intersection, where traffic is maintained in one direction, so constructed as to allow vehicles to enter or leave it at any of the converging roads, or to change course, without interruption of the flow of traffic.

traffic light A signal light which, by changing color, directs the flow of traffic along a road or highway.

trag·a·canth (trag′ə·kanth) *n.* 1 A white or reddish gum obtained from various species of Old World leguminous herbs (genus *Astragalus*), especially *A. gummifer* of SW Asia: used in pharmacy and the arts. 2 Any of the shrubs yielding this gum. [<MF *tragacante* <L *tragacantha* <Gk. *tragakantha* a tragacanth shrub < *tragos* a male goat + *akantha* a thorn]

tra·ge·di·an (trə·jē′dē·ən) *n.* 1 An actor in tragedy. 2 A writer of tragedies.

tra·ge·di·enne (trə·jē′dē·en′) *n.* An actress of tragedy. [<F]

trag·e·dy (traj′ə·dē) *n. pl.* **·dies** 1 A form of drama in which the protagonist, having some quality of greatness (and, in Greek, Roman, and Renaissance tragedy, in high place) comes to disaster through some flaw (which may be a noble fault) in his nature that interacts with the fabric of events (the plot) to bring about his inevitable downfall or death, the action being managed in a way to produce pity and fear in the spectator and to effect a catharsis of these feelings. The failure to achieve this leads to **tragedy manquée,** which falls short of true tragedy. To the outcome of death or madness usual in ancient and Renaissance tragedy, modern tragedy adds the possibility of frustration and unfulfilment from which there seems no escape. Opposed to *comedy.* 2 A fatal event or course of events; murder, especially one involving dramatic incidents. 3 A very terrible or sorrowful fate or end. 4 The art or theory of acting or composing tragedy. [<OF *tregedie, tragedie* <L *tragoedia* <Gk. *tragōidia* appar. < *tragos* a goat + *ōidē* a song; semantic development uncertain]

Trag·e·dy (traj′ə·dē) Tragedy personified, especially as Melpomene.

trag·ic (traj′ik) *adj.* 1 Involving death or calamity; causing suffering; fatal; terrible. 2 Pertaining to or having the nature of tragedy. 3 Appropriate to or like tragedy, especially in drama. Also **trag′i·cal.** [<L *tragicus* <Gk. *tragikos* pertaining to tragedy < *tragos* a goat] —**trag′i·cal·ly, trag′ic·ly** *adv.* —**trag′·i·cal·ness** *n.*

trag·i·com·e·dy (traj′i·kom′ə·dē) *n. pl.* **·dies** A drama in which tragic and comic scenes are intermingled. [<MF *tragi–comédie* <LL *tragicomoedia* <L *tragico–comoedia* < *tragicus* TRAGIC + *comoedia* COMEDY] —**trag′i·com′ic** or **·i·cal** *adj.* —**trag′i·com′i·cal·ly** *adv.*

trag·o·pan (trag′ə·pan) *n.* An Asian pheasant (genus *Tragopan*) of which the horned pheasant, having gorgeous ocellated plumage, is a variety. [<NL <L, a fabulous bird <Gk. < *tragos* a goat + *Pan* Pan]

tra·gus (trā′gəs) *n. pl.* **·gi** (-jī) *Anat.* A flattened, somewhat conical eminence of the auricle in front of the opening of the external ear. [<LL <Gk. *tragos* the hairy part of the ear, a he–goat; so called because of the hairs on it]

traik (trāk) *Scot. v.i.* 1 To wander idly or with fatigue; tramp; trudge. 2 To go astray. —*n.* 1 The flesh of sheep that have died from disease or accident. 2 A stroll or saunter; also, a wearisome tramp or journey: also spelled *trake.*

traik·et (trā′kit) *adj. Scot.* Overfatigued; tired out. Also **traik′it.**

trail (trāl) *v.t.* 1 To draw along lightly over a surface; also, to drag or draw after: to *trail* a robe. 2 To follow the trail of; trace; track. 3 *Mil.* To carry, as a rifle, by grasping it in the right hand just above the balance, with the muzzle to the front and the butt nearly touching the ground. 4 To tread or force down, as grass into a pathway. 5 *Naut.* To allow (the oars) to drift alongside the boat. —*v.i.* 6 To hang or float loosely. 7 To grow along the ground or over rocks, bushes, etc., in a loose, creeping way. 8 To follow behind loosely; stream. 9 To saunter leisurely along; move heavily. 10 To lag behind; straggle; remain in the rear. —*n.* 1 The track left by anything that has moved or been drawn or dragged over any surface. 2 The track or indications followed by a huntsman or by a dog in hunting; the scent. 3 The path worn by persons or by animals; particularly, a route made by repeated passage through a wilderness. 4 Anything drawn behind or in the wake of something; a train; specifically, the train of a dress or gown. 5 *Mil.* The inclined stock of a gun carriage, or extension of the stock that rests on the ground when the piece is not limbered up: when divided longitudinally into two parts, it is called a **split trail.** —**to hit** (or **take**) **the trail** To set out on a journey. [<AF *trailler* haul, tow a boat <L *tragula* a dragnet < *trahere* draw]

trail·er (trā′lər) *n.* 1 One who or that which trails. 2 A vehicle without automotive power designed to be coupled with a cab or tractor and used to haul freight, household goods, etc. 3 A vehicle usually drawn by an automobile or truck and equipped to serve as living quarters. 4 A preview (def. 2).

trailer truck A semitrailer (def. 2).

trailing arbutus An evergreen perennial (*Epigaea repens*) of the heath family, bearing clusters of fragrant pink flowers; the mayflower: the State flower of Massachusetts.

trailing edge *Aeron.* The rear edge of an airfoil or propeller blade.

trail rope 1 A guiderope. 2 A rope used for dragging or towing. 3 A rope attached to a horse's halter or tied around its neck, but allowed to drag while the horse grazes. 4 *Mil.* A prolonge.

train (trān) *n.* 1 Anything drawn out to a length, or any series of things drawn along. 2 A continuous line of coupled railway cars. 3 A series, succession, or set of connected things; a sequence; especially, an assemblage of people or objects drawn up processionally or in orderly disposition. 4 A retinue or body of retainers; suite. 5 Something pulled along with and in the track of another. 6 An extension of a dress skirt, trailing behind the wearer. 7 Proper order; due course. 8 *Mech.* A series of parts acting upon each other, as for transmitting motion: also called *drive train, power train.* 9 *Mil.* **a** The variation of the axis of a gun in a horizontal plane. **b** Collectively, the men, animals, and vehicles attached to a military body for the transportation of its ammunition, supplies, etc. 10 A succession or line of wagons and pack animals en route. 11 A line of gunpowder or other combustible laid to conduct fire to a charge, mine, or the like. See synonyms under PROCESSION. —*v.t.* 1 To bring to a requisite standard, as of conduct or skill, by protracted and careful instruction; specifically, to mold the character of; educate; instruct: sometimes with *up.* 2 To render skilful or proficient, as a mechanic or soldier. 3 To make obedient to orders or capable of performing tricks, as an animal. 4 To bring into a required physical condition by means of a course of diet and exercise: to *train* a man for a boat race. 5 To lead into taking a particular course; develop into a fixed shape: to *train* a plant on a trellis. 6 To put or point in an exact direction; bring to bear; aim, as a cannon. 7 *Obs.* To mislead; entice. 8 *Obs.* To draw along; trail. —*v.i.* 9 To undergo a course of training. 10 To give a course of training; drill. See synonyms under LEARN, SUBDUE, TEACH. [Fusion of OF *traïne* a dragging and *traïn* a series, procession, both < *traïner, trahiner* draw <L *trahere*] —**train′·a·ble** *adj.* —**train′less** *adj.*

Train may appear as a combining form in hyphemes or solidemes, or as the first element in two–word phrases, with the meaning of definition 2:

train caller **train schedule**
train conductor **train service**
train crew **train signal**
train flagman **train staff**
train foreman **train stop**
train inspector **train ticket**
train–lighting **traintime**
train line **train trip**
train recorder **trainway**
train reporter **train whistle**
train robber **train wreck**

train·a·si·um (trā·nā′zē·əm) *n.* A structure of bars crossing and intersecting one another to form ladders, tunnels, etc.: used in developing the muscles, as in military training. [<TRAIN + (GYMN)ASIUM]

train·band (trān′band′) *n.* A militia organization, especially one in London, England, during the Stuart period (17th century). [Short for *trained band*]

train·bear·er (trān′bâr′ər) *n.* An attendant who holds the long train of a dress or robe.

trained nurse One who has been trained in and graduated from a nurses' training school.

train·ee (trā·nē′) *n.* One who undergoes training.

train·er (trā′nər) *n.* 1 One who trains. 2 One who directs and superintends a course of physical training, or who supervises the physical condition of members of an athletic team. 3 An apparatus or device used in training: a Link *trainer.* 4 One who trains a cannon; specifically, in the U. S. Navy, the member of the gun's crew who gives direction to the gun. 5 One who trains animals for shows, contests, animal acts, etc.

train·ing (trā′ning) *n.* 1 Systematic instruction and drill. 2 The condition of being physically fit for the performance of an athletic exercise or contest; also, the act or science of bringing one to such a condition. See synonyms under EDUCATION, LEARNING, NURTURE.

training school A school for practical instruction and drill; specifically, a school in which students receive special vocational or technical instruction and practice.

training ship A vessel on which apprentice seamen and cadets are educated in seamanship, navigation, etc.

train·man (trān′mən) *n. pl.* **·men** (-mən) A railway employee serving on a train; especially, a brakeman.

train·mas·ter (trān′mas′tər, -mäs′-) *n.* A railroad official supervising some division or subdivision of a rail line.

train oil Oil obtained from the fat of whales, especially from the right whale, and from cod livers, etc. [Earlier *trane* <MDu. *traen* extracted oil]

traipse (trāps) *v.i.* **traipsed, traips·ing** *Colloq.* To walk about in an idle or aimless manner; go on foot: also spelled *trapes.* [Earlier *trapass.*

prob. <OF *trapasser*, var. of *trespasser* TRESPASS]

trait (trāt) *n.* **1** A distinguishing feature or quality of mind or character. **2** A line, stroke, or touch. See synonyms under CHARACTERISTIC. [<F <MF *traict* <L *tractus*. Doublet of TRACT[1].]

trai·tor (trā′tər) *n.* **1** One who betrays a trust; especially, one who commits treason. **2** Hence, one who acts deceitfully and falsely. [<OF *traitre, traitor* <L *traditor*. See TRADITOR.] —**trai′tor·ism** *n. Obs.* —**trai′tress** (-tris) *n. fem.*

trai·tor·ous (trā′tər·əs) *adj.* **1** Inclined to treason. **2** Involving treason. See synonyms under PERFIDIOUS. —**trai′tor·ous·ly** *adv.* —**trai′tor·ous·ness** *n.*

Tra·jan (trā′jən), A.D. 56–117, Roman emperor 98–117: full name *Marcus Ulpius Trajanus.* —**Tra·jan·ic** (trā·jan′ik) *adj.*

tra·ject (trə·jekt′) *v.t.* To throw or cast over, through, or across, as a beam of light; transmit. [<L *trajectus*, pp. of *trajicere* < *trans-* over + *jacere* throw] —**tra·jec′tion** *n.*

tra·jec·to·ry (trə·jek′tər·ē) *n. pl.* **·ries** **1** The path described by an object or body moving in space. **2** The path of a projectile after leaving the muzzle of a gun. **3** *Geom.* **a** A curve which cuts a set of curves at the same angle. **b** A surface which passes through a given set of points. [<Med. L *trajectorius* <L *trajectus*. See TRAJECT.]

trake (trāk) See TRAIK (*n.* def. 2).

tral·a·ti·tion (tral′ə·tish′ən) *n. Obs.* The use of a word or expression in a figurative sense; metaphor. [<L *tralatio, -onis* < *tralatus, translatus*, pp. to *transferre* TRANSFER]

tral·a·ti·tious (tral′ə·tish′əs) *adj.* **1** Traditional; legendary. **2** Not literal; figurative; metaphorical.

Tra·lee (trə·lē′) The county town of County Kerry, Ireland, in the western part.

tram[1] (tram) *n.* **1** *Brit.* A tramway. **2** A street railway car for passengers; a tramcar. **3** A four-wheeled vehicle for conveying coals to or from a pit's mouth. —*v.t.* **trammed, tram·ming** To convey in a tramcar. [Short for TRAMROAD]

tram[2] (tram) *n.* **1** A trammel. **2** *Mech.* Accuracy or trueness of adjustment. Compare TRAMMEL. —*v.t.* **trammed, tram·ming** To use a trammel in adjusting (any part). [Short for TRAMMEL]

tram[3] (tram) *n.* A thick silk thread used for the cross threads of the best silks and velvets. Also **trame.** [<F *trame* <OF *traime* a woof, machination <L *trama* a woof]

tram·car (tram′kär′) *n. Brit.* A car or carriage that runs on a tramway; particularly, a street car; a tram. [<TRAM[1] + CAR]

tram·line (tram′līn′) *n. Brit.* A street-car line.

tram·mel (tram′əl) *n.* **1** That which limits freedom or activity; an impediment; hindrance. **2** A fetter, shackle, or bond, particularly one of such kind as is used in teaching a horse to amble. **3** An instrument whose parts slide on a rod, especially one bearing pointers, for use as a compass, or for describing ellipses. **4** A gage for adjusting machine parts. **5** A two-piece hook, adjustable for length, used to suspend cooking pots from a fireplace crane. **6** A net formed of three layers, the central one being of finer mesh in order to catch the fish which pass through either of the others: also **trammel net.** —*v.t.* **·meled** or **·melled, ·mel·ing** or **·mel·ling** **1** To hinder or obstruct; restrict. **2** To entangle in or as in a snare; imprison. Also **tram′el** or **tram′ell.** [<OF *tramail* a net <LL *tramaculum, tremaculum* <L *tri-* three + *macula* a mesh] —**tram′mel·er** or **tram′mel·ler** *n.*

tra·mon·tane (trə·mon′tān, tram′ən·tān) *adj.* **1** Situated beyond the mountains; ultramontane; hence, barbarous; foreign. **2** Coming from the other side of the mountains. —*n.* A foreigner or barbarian; originally, a resident beyond the mountains. [<Ital. *tramontana* north wind, polestar <L *transmontanus* beyond the mountains < *trans-* over + *mons, montis* a mountain]

tramp (tramp) *v.i.* **1** To walk or wander, especially as a tramp or vagabond. **2** To walk heavily or firmly. —*v.t.* **3** To walk or wander through. **4** To walk on heavily; trample. —*n.* **1** A heavy continued tread. **2** The sound produced by continuous and heavy marching or walking. **3** A long stroll on foot. **4** One who walks from place to place; a vagrant; vagabond. **5** A steam vessel that goes from port to port picking up freight wherever it can be obtained: also **tramp steamer.** **6** A metal plate on a shoe to protect it from wear or from a spade in digging. [ME *trampen* <Gmc. Cf. LG *trampen.*]

tramp·er (tram′pər) *n.* One who or that which tramps; specifically, a vagabond.

tram·ple (tram′pəl) *v.* **·pled, ·pling** *v.t.* To tread on heavily; injure, violate, or encroach upon by or as by tramping. —*v.i.* To tread heavily or ruthlessly; tramp. —*n.* The act or sound of treading under foot. [ME *trampelen*, freq. of *trampen* TRAMP] —**tram′pler** *n.*

tram·po·line (tram′pə·lin) *n.* **1** An acrobatic performance on stilts. **2** A heavy mat or net used in acrobatic exhibitions. Also **tram′po·lin.** [<Ital. *trampoli* stilts]

trampoline trainer A section of strong canvas stretched on a frame, on which a person may bound or spring: used in training for body control and acrobatics.

tram·road (tram′rōd′) *n.* A road with wheel tracks of stone, wood, or metal; especially, a railroad in a mine. [< dial. E *tram* a rail, wagon shaft (prob. <LG *traam* a beam, shaft) + ROAD]

tram·way (tram′wā′) *n. Brit.* **1** A street railroad. **2** A roadway having plates or rails on one part of it on which wheeled vehicles may run. **3** A system of cars suspended from cables, often operating in counterbalancing pairs: also called **aerial tramway.**

trance[1] (trans, träns) *n.* **1** A state in which the soul seems to have passed out of the body; an ecstasy; rapture. **2** *Psychol.* A condition between sleep and waking characterized by dissociation, involuntary movements, and automatisms of behavior, as in hypnosis and mediumistic seances. **3** A dreamlike state marked by bewilderment and an insensibility to ordinary surroundings. **4** A state of deep abstraction. See synonyms under DREAM. —*v.t.* **tranced, tranc·ing** To entrance, usually in a figurative sense; enchant. [<OF *transe* passage, dread of coming evil < *transir* pass, die, benumb <L *transire*. See TRANSIENT.]

trance[2] (trans, träns) *n. Scot.* A passage or hallway; an alley, courtyard, or close.

tran·gam (trang′gəm) *n. Obs.* A worthless person or thing; a knick-knack or trinket. Also **tran·kum** (trang′kəm). [Origin uncertain]

tran·quil (trang′kwil) *adj.* **·quil·er** or **·quil·ler, ·quil·est** or **·quil·lest** **1** Free from agitation or disturbance; calm: said of persons. **2** Quiet and motionless: said of things. See synonyms under CALM, PACIFIC, SEDATE. [<L *tranquillus* quiet] —**tran′quil·ly** *adv.* —**tran′quil·ness** *n.*

tran·quil·ize (trang′kwəl·īz) *v.t.* & *v.i.* **·ized, ·iz·ing** To make or become tranquil. Also **tran′quil·lize,** *Brit.* **tran′quil·lise.** —**tran′quil·i·za′tion** *n.*

Synonyms: allay, appease, assuage, calm, compose, hush, lull, moderate, pacify, quell, quiet, soothe, still. See ALLAY. *Antonyms*: agitate, alarm, arouse, disturb, excite, inflame, rouse, stimulate, stir.

tran·quil·iz·er (trang′kwəl·ī′zər) *n.* **1** One who or that which tranquilizes. **2** *Med.* An ataractic drug. Also **tran′quil·liz′er.**

tran·quil·li·ty (trang·kwil′ə·tē) *n.* The state of being tranquil; rest; quiet. Also **tran·quil′i·ty.** See synonyms under APATHY, REST.

trans- *prefix* **1** Across; beyond; through; on the other side of; as in:

transarctic	**transequatorial**
transborder	**transfrontier**
transchannel	**transisthmian**
transdesert	**transpolar**

In adjectives and nouns of place, the prefix may signify "on the other side of" (opposed to *cis-*) or "across; crossing." Through long usage, certain of these are written as solid words, as *transalpine, transatlantic*; otherwise, words in this class, unless by contrary official usage, are properly written with a hyphen, as in:

trans-American	**trans-Germanic**
trans-Andean	**trans-Himalayan**
trans-Arabian	**trans-Iberian**
trans-Baltic	**trans-Mediterranean**
trans-Canadian	**trans-Siberian**

2 Through and through; changing completely; as in:

transcolor	**transfashion**

3 Surpassing; transcending; beyond; as in:

transconscious	**transmundane**
transempirical	**transnational**
transhuman	**transphysical**
transmaterial	**transrational**
transmental	

4 *Anat.* Across; transversely; as in:

transcortical	**transocular**
transduodenal	**transthoracic**
transfrontal	**transuterine**

[<L <*trans* across, beyond, over]

trans·act (trans·akt′, tranz-) *v.t.* To carry through; accomplish; do. —*v.i. Rare* To do business. [<L *transactus*, pp. of *transigere* drive through, accomplish < *trans-* through + *agere* drive, do] —**trans·ac′tor** *n.*

Synonyms: accomplish, act, conduct, do, negotiate, perform, treat. There are many acts that one may *do, accomplish*, or *perform* unaided; what he *transacts* is by means of or in association with others; one may *do* a duty, *perform* a vow, *accomplish* a task, but he *transacts* business, since that always involves the agency of others. To *negotiate* and to *treat* are likewise collective acts, but *negotiate* implies deliberation with adjustment of mutual claims and interests, while *transact* implies execution. Nations may *treat* of peace without result, but when a treaty is *negotiated* peace is secured; the citizens of the two nations are then free to *transact* business with one another.

trans·ac·tion (trans·ak′shən, tranz-) *n.* **1** The management of any affair. **2** Something transacted; an affair; a business deal. **3** *pl.* Published reports, as of a society. —**trans·ac′tion·al** *adj.*

Synonyms: act, action, affair, business, deed, doing, proceeding. A man's *acts* or *deeds* may be exclusively his own; his *transactions* involve the agency or participation of others. A *transaction* is something completed; a *proceeding* is or is viewed as something in progress; but since *transaction* is often used to include the steps leading to the conclusion, while *proceedings* may result in *action*, the dividing line between the two words becomes sometimes quite faint. Both *transactions* and *proceedings* are used of the records of a deliberative body, especially when published. See ACT.

Trans-A·lai Range (trans′ä·lī′) A branch of the Pamir-Alai mountain system on the Kirgiz-Tadzhik S.S.R. border; highest point, 23,382 feet.

trans·al·pine (trans·al′pin, -pīn, tranz-) *adj.* **1** On the other side of the Alps, especially from Rome. **2** Crossing or extending across the Alps. **3** Of or pertaining to the country or the people beyond the Alps. —*n.* A native of or a resident beyond the Alps. [<L *transalpinus* < *trans-* across + *alpinus* alpine < *Alpes* the Alps]

Transalpine Gaul The section of Gaul on the northern side of the Alps.

trans·at·lan·tic (trans′ət·lan′tik, tranz′-) *adj* **1** On the other side of the Atlantic. **2** Across or crossing the Atlantic.

trans·berke·li·an (trans·bûrk′lē·ən) *adj. Physics* Of or pertaining to unstable radioactive elements beyond berkelium, atomic No. 97, as californium, einsteinium, fermium, mendelevium, and nobelium. [<TRANS- + BERKEL(IUM) + -IAN]

trans·ca·lent (trans·kā′lənt) *adj.* Permitting or facilitating the passage of heat. [<TRANS- + L *calens, -entis*, ppr. of *calere* be hot] —**trans·ca′len·cy** *n.*

Trans·cas·pi·a (trans·kas′pē·ə) A former administrative division of Russian Turkestan, roughly coextensive with the Turkmen S.S.R., in which it was incorporated in 1924; capital, Ashkhabad. Also **Trans·cas′pi·an Region.**

Trans·cau·ca·sia (trans′kô·kā′zhə, -shə) A region of southeastern U.S.S.R., between the Caucasus mountains on the north and Iran and Turkey in Asia on the south, comprising the republics of Armenia, Azerbaijan, and Georgia, and from 1922 to 1936 constituting the **Transcaucasian Socialist Federated Soviet Republic.** —**Trans′cau·ca′sian** *adj.* & *n.*

trans·cei·ver (tran·sē′vər) *n. Electronics* A radio unit, usually for portable or mobile service, containing equipment for both transmission and reception. [<TRANS(MITTER) + (RE)CEIVER]

tran·scend (tran·send′) *v.t.* **1** To rise above in excellence or degree. **2** To overstep or exceed, as a limit. — *v.i.* **3** To be surpassing; excel. See synonyms under SURPASS. [<L *transcendere* surmount < *trans-* beyond, over + *scandere* climb] — **tran·scend′i·ble** *adj.*

tran·scen·dent (tran·sen′dənt) *adj.* **1** Of very high and remarkable degree; surpassing; superexcellent. **2** *Philos.* In Kantianism, lying beyond the bounds of all possible human experience; hence, beyond knowledge. **3** *Theol.* Pertaining to God as exalted above the universe; beyond limitation; hence, perfect. See synonyms under EXCELLENT, TRANSCENDENTAL. — *n.* That which is transcendent or surpassingly great or remarkable. [<L *transcendens, -entis,* ppr. of *transcendere* TRANSCEND] — **tran·scen′dence** *n.* — **tran·scen′dent·ly** *adv.* — **tran·scen′dent·ness** *n.*

tran·scen·den·tal (tran′sen·den′təl) *adj.* **1** Of very high degree; transcendent. **2** Pertaining to or being a transcendent; not included in any of the categories. See CATEGORY. **3** *Philos.* **a** In Kant's system, of an a priori character; transcending experience but not knowledge. **b** Rising above the common notions of men; with the Cartesians, pertaining to body and spirit alike. **4** Wildly speculative; above, beyond, or contrary to common sense. **5** *Math.* That cannot be formed by the five fundamental operations of algebra, each performed a finite number of times. — **tran′scen·den′tal·ly** *adv.*

Synonyms: instinctive, intuitive, original, primordial, transcendent. *Intuitive* truths are those which are in the mind independently of all experience, not being derived from experience nor limited by it. All *intuitive* truths or beliefs are *transcendental.* But *transcendental* is a wider term than *intuitive,* including all within the limits of thought that is not derived from experience, as the ideas of space and time. *Transcendent, transcendental,* and *intuitive* are opposed to *empirical*; or, according to the philosophy of Kant, *transcendent* is opposed to *immanent,* and *transcendental* to *empirical.* See MYSTERIOUS.

tran·scen·den·tal·ism (tran′sen·den′təl·iz′əm) *n.* **1** The state or quality of being transcendental. **2** In common usage, that which, in philosophy or religion, is vague, visionary, or sublimated. **3** *Philos.* The doctrine that man can attain knowledge which goes beyond or transcends appearances or phenomena. In the Kantian sense, transcendentalism affirmed the existence of a priori principles of cognition. The New England movement, as represented by Emerson and others, has been characterized by the exaltation of the spiritual in a general sense over the material, and the immanence of the divine in all creation. — **tran′scen·den′tal·ist** *n.* & *adj.*

transcendental number See under NUMBER.

trans·con·ti·nen·tal (trans′kon·tə·nen′təl) *adj.* Extending or passing across a continent.

tran·scribe (tran·skrīb′) *v.t.* **·scribed, ·scrib·ing** **1** To write over again; copy or recopy in handwriting or typewriting from an original or from shorthand notes. **2** *Telecom.* To make an electrical recording of for use on a later radio program. **3** To adapt (a musical composition) for a change of instrument or voice. [<L *transcribere* < *trans-* over + *scribere* write] — **tran·scrib′a·ble** *adj.* — **tran·scrib′er** *n.*

tran·script (tran′skript) *n.* **1** A copy made directly from an original. **2** Any copy. **3** A copy of a student's academic record, listing courses taken and grades received. See synonyms under DUPLICATE. [Fusion of OF *transcrit* (pp. of *transcrire* transcribe <L *transcribere*) and L *transcriptus,* pp. of *transcribere* TRANSCRIBE]

tran·scrip·tion (tran·skrip′shən) *n.* **1** The act of transcribing; a copying. **2** A copy; transcript. **3** *Telecom.* An electrical recording made for the purpose of a later radio broadcast. **4** *Music* The adaptation of a composition for some instrument or voice other than that for which it was written. — **tran·scrip′tion·al, tran·scrip′tive** *adj.*

trans·cul·tu·ra·tion (trans·kul′chə·rā′shən) *n.* *Anthropol.* **1** The processes, resulting in the development of new cultural phenomena and the disappearance of old, involved in the transition of a group or a people from one culture context to another. **2** The transition itself. [<TRANS- + *culturation* development of a culture <CULTUR(E) + -ATION] — **trans·cul′tu·ra′tive** *adj.*

trans·cur·rent (trans·kûr′ənt) *adj.* Passing or extending transversely.

trans·duc·er (trans·doo͞′sər, -dyoo͞′-, tranz-) *n.* *Physics* Any device whereby the energy of one power system may be transmitted to another system, whether of the same or a different type. [<L *transducere,* var. of *traducere.* See TRADUCE.]

tran·sect (tran·sekt′) *v.t.* To dissect transversely. [<TRANS- + L *sectus,* pp. of *secare* cut] — **tran·sec′tion** (-sek′shən) *n.*

tran·sept (tran′sept) *n.* *Archit.* One of the lateral members or projections between the nave and choir of a cruciform church: commonly distinguished as the *north* and *south transepts.* [<Med. L *transeptum,* short for L *transversum septum* < *transversus* TRANSVERSE + *septum* an enclosure] — **tran·sep′tal** *adj.*

trans·e·unt (tran′sē·ənt) *adj.* Proceeding from and operating beyond itself on another, as a physical cause: opposed to *immanent.* [<L *transiens, transeuntis.* See TRANSIENT.]

trans·fer (trans·fûr′, trans′fər) *v.* **·ferred, ·fer·ring** *v.t.* **1** To carry, or cause to pass, from one person, place, etc., to another. **2** To make over possession of to another. **3** To convey (a drawing) from one surface to another, as by specially prepared paper. — *v.i.* **4** To transfer oneself. **5** To be transferred. **6** To change from one car or line to another on a transfer. **7** To shift one's enrollment as a student from one educational institution to another. See synonyms under CONVEY. — *n.* (trans′fər) **1** The act of transferring, or the state of being transferred. **2** That which is transferred; specifically, in art, lithography, etc., a design conveyed or to be conveyed, as by copying ink or pressure, in reverse, from one surface to another. **3** A place, method, or means of transfer. **4** A ticket, entitling a passenger on one car or boat to ride on another, as on a connected line, with or without paying an additional fare; also, the place where such transfer is made. **5** A delivery of title or property from one person to another. **6** The exchange of a person from one organization to another, from one military division to another, from one school to another, etc. **7** An order transferring money or securities. [<OF *transferer* <L *transferre* < *trans-* across + *ferre* carry] — **trans·fer′a·bil′i·ty** *n.* — **trans·fer′a·ble** *adj.*

trans·fer·al (trans·fûr′əl) *n.* The act or an instance of transferring. Also **trans·fer′ral.**

trans·fer·ee (trans′fə·rē′) *n.* **1** *Law* The person to whom a transfer is made. **2** One who is transferred.

trans·fer·ence (trans·fûr′əns) *n.* **1** Transfer. **2** *Psychoandl.* **a** The reproduction of the repressed or forgotten experiences of early childhood, accompanied by a transfer of emotions from the original object or person to another. **b** Displacement (def. 7). [<NL *transferentia* <L *transferens, -entis,* ppr. of *transferre* TRANSFER] — **trans·fer·en·tial** (trans′fə·ren′shəl) *adj.*

trans·fer·or (trans·fûr′ər) *n.* The vender or conveying party in a transfer.

Trans·fig·ur·a·tion (trans′fig·yə·rā′shən) *n.* **1** The supernatural transformation of Christ on the mount as recorded in the Gospels. *Matt.* xvii 1–9. **2** A festival commemorating this: August 6.

trans·fig·ure (trans·fig′yər) *v.t.* **·ured, ·ur·ing** **1** To change the outward form or appearance of. **2** To make glorious. See synonyms under CHANGE. [<L *transfigurare* change the shape of < *trans-* across + *figura* shape] — **trans′fig·ur·a′tion, trans·fig′ure·ment** *n.*

trans·fi·nite (trans·fī′nīt) *adj.* **1** Beyond the finite. **2** *Math.* Of, pertaining to, or characterizing the properties of a set of numbers whose cardinality is not expressible by any finite number.

trans·fix (trans·fiks′) *v.t.* **1** To pierce through; impale. **2** To fix in place by impaling. **3** To make motionless, as with horror, amazement, etc. See synonyms under PIERCE. [<L *transfixus,* pp. of *transfigere* < *trans-* through, across + *figere* fasten] — **trans·fix′ion** (-fik′shən) *n.*

trans·flu·ent (trans′floo͞·ənt) *adj.* **1** Flowing across or through. **2** *Her.* Flowing through the arches of a bridge. [<L *transfluens, -entis,* ppr. of *transfluere* < *trans-* across + *fluere* flow]

trans·flux (trans′fluks) *n.* A flowing or running through, across, or beyond.

trans·form (trans·fôrm′) *v.t.* **1** To give a different form to; change the character of. **2** To alter the nature of; convert. **3** *Math.* To change (one expression or operation) into another equivalent to it or having similar properties. **4** *Electr.* **a** To change the potential or the type of, as a current from higher to lower voltage, or from alternating to direct. **b** To alter the energy form of, as electrical into mechanical. **5** In alchemy, to transmute. — *v.i.* **6** To be or become changed in form or character. See synonyms under CHANGE. [<L *transformare* < *trans-* over + *formare* form < *forma* a form] — **trans·form′a·ble** *adj.*

trans·for·ma·tion (trans′fər·mā′shən) *n.* **1** A change. **2** The act of transforming or the state of being transformed. **3** A wig or partial wig worn by a woman.

trans·form·a·tive (trans·fôr′mə·tiv) *adj.* Having power or a tendency to transform.

trans·form·er (trans·fôr′mər) *n.* **1** One who or that which transforms. **2** *Electr.* A device for altering the strength and potential of a current; especially, a form of induction coil used in alternating–current systems of electrical distribution, by which a current of high voltage is transformed to one of lower voltage, or vice versa: classed accordingly either as **step–down** or **step–up transformers.**

trans·form·ism (trans·fôr′miz·əm) *n.* *Biol.* **1** The theory of the development of one species from another through gradual modifications and without the intervention of special acts of creation. **2** Any doctrine or example of evolution.

trans·fuse (trans·fyoo͞z′) *v.t.* **·fused, ·fus·ing** **1** To pour, as a fluid, from one vessel to another. **2** To cause to be imparted or instilled. **3** *Med.* To transfer (blood) from one person or animal to another. [<L *transfusus,* pp. of *transfundere* < *trans-* across + *fundere* pour] — **trans·fus′er** *n.* — **trans·fus′i·ble, trans·fu·sive** (trans·fyoo͞′siv) *adj.*

trans·fu·sion (trans·fyoo͞′zhən) *n.* **1** The act of pouring from one vessel into another; hence, transference; transmission. **2** *Med.* **a** The transfer of blood from one person or animal to the veins or arteries of another. **b** A similar transfer of any other fluid, as a saline solution.

trans·gress (trans·gres′, tranz-) *v.t.* **1** To break over the bounds of, as a law; violate. **2** To pass beyond or over (limits); exceed; trespass. — *v.i.* **3** To break a law; sin. See synonyms under BREAK. [Appar. <OF *transgresser* <L *transgressus,* pp. of *transgredi* < *trans-* across + *gradi* step] — **trans·gress′i·ble** *adj.* — **trans·gress′ing·ly** *adv.* — **trans·gres′sor** *n.*

trans·gres·sion (trans·gresh′ən, tranz-) *n.* **1** The act of transgressing; sin. **2** An overpassing. **3** *Geol.* An overlap. See synonyms under OFFENSE, SIN[1].

trans·gres·sive (trans·gres′iv, tranz-) *adj.* Apt to transgress; faulty; culpable. — **trans·gres′sive·ly** *adv.*

tran·shape (tran·shāp′) See TRANSSHAPE.

tran·ship (tran·ship′), **tran·ship·ment** (tran·ship′mənt) See TRANSSHIP, etc.

trans·hu·mance (trans·hyoo͞′məns) *n.* The moving of cattle or other animals to more suitable places as the seasons change, especially of herds to and from mountain pastures. [<F < *transhumer* <Sp. *trashumar* <L *trans-* across + *humare* cover with earth < *humus* earth] — **trans·hu′mant** *adj.*

tran·sience (tran′shəns) *n.* The quality of existing for a short time only; also, something that is transient: the *transience* of life. Also **tran′sien·cy.**

tran·sient (tran′shənt) *adj.* **1** Passing before the vision in a brief time; of short duration; brief; hasty. **2** Not permanent; temporary; casual. **3** *Obs.* Proceeding from one place or object to another; imparted. — *n.* One who

or that which is transient; specifically, a lodger or boarder who remains for a short time. [<L *transiens, -euntis,* ppr. of *transire* <*trans-* across + *ire* go] — **tran′sient·ly** *adv.* — **tran′sient·ness** *n.*

Synonyms (*adj.*): brief, ephemeral, evanescent, fleeting, flitting, flying, fugitive, momentary, passing, short, temporary, transitory. A thing is *transient* which in fact is not lasting; a thing is *transitory* which by its very nature must soon pass away; a thing is *temporary* which is intended to last or be made use of but a little while; as, a *transient* joy; this *transitory* life; a *temporary* chairman. That which is *ephemeral,* literally lasting but for a day, is looked upon as at once slight and perishable, and the word carries often a suggestion of contempt; with no solid qualities or worthy achievement a pretender may sometimes gain an *ephemeral* popularity. That which is *fleeting* is viewed as in the act of passing swiftly by, and that which is *fugitive* as eluding attempts to detain it; that which is *evanescent* is in the act of vanishing even while we gaze, as the hues of the sunset. *Antonyms:* abiding, enduring, eternal, everlasting, immortal, imperishable, lasting, permanent, perpetual, persistent, undying, unfading.

tran·si·gent (tran′sə·jənt) *n.* A person who is willing to compromise or to be brought to terms. [<L *transigens, -entis,* ppr. of *transigere* settle. See TRANSACT.]

tran·sil·i·ent (tran·sil′ē·ənt) *adj.* Leaping or passing abruptly from one thing or condition to another; saltatory; spanning; extending over. [<L *transiliens, -entis,* ppr. of *transilire* <*trans-* across + *salire* leap] — **tran·sil′i·ence** *n.*

trans·il·lu·mi·nate (trans′i·lo͞o′mə·nāt, tranz′-) *v.t.* **·nat·ed, ·nat·ing** *Med.* To cause light to pass through (an organ or part of the body) to reveal its condition.

tran·sis·tor (tran·zis′tər, -sis′-) *n. Electronics* **1** A semiconductor device having three terminals and the property that the current between one pair of them is a function of the current between another pair. **2** A transistorized radio. [<TRANS(FER) (RES)ISTOR]

tran·sis·tor·ize (tran·zis′tər·īz, -sis′-) *v.t.* **·ized, ·iz·ing** To equip with transistors instead of vacuum tubes, as a radio, hearing aid, etc.

tran·sit (tran′sit, -zit) *n.* **1** The act of passing over or through; passage. **2** The act of carrying across or through; conveyance. **3** A specific passage or route; also, a traveler through a country. **4** *Astron.* **a** The passage of one heavenly body over the disk of another. **b** The moment of passage of a celestial body across the meridian: when in that half of the meridian containing the zenith it is *superior* or *upper* transit; when in that half containing the nadir it is *inferior* or *lower* transit. **5** A transit compass. See synonyms under JOURNEY, MOTION. [<L *transitus* <*transire* cross. See TRANSIENT.]

transit compass A surveying instrument resembling a theodolite, for measuring horizontal angles. Also **transit theodolite.**

transit instrument **1** An astronomical telescope mounted in the plane of the meridian and turning on a fixed east-and-west axis: used to determine the time of passage of an object over the meridian. **2** A transit compass.

tran·si·tion (tran·zish′ən) *n.* **1** Passage from one place, condition, or action to another; change. **2** *Music* A passing modulation, an abrupt change of key, or a passage leading from one theme to another. **3** The time, period, or place of such passage; also, its product or result . See synonyms under CHANGE, MOTION. — **tran·si′tion·al, tran·si′tion·ar′y** (-er′ē) *adj.* — **tran·si′tion·al·ly** *adv.*

transition point *Physics* A single point or temperature at which different phases of a substance can exist together.

tran·si·tive (tran′sə·tiv) *adj.* **1** *Gram.* Having, requiring, or terminating upon a direct object; also, expressing an action performed by a subject or agent, that passes over to or takes effect on some person or thing as its object. **2** Having the power of passing; effecting transition. —*n. Gram.* A transitive verb. [<LL *transitivus* <L *transitus* transit. See TRANSIT.] —**tran′si·tive·ly** *adv.* —**tran′si·tive·ness, tran′si·tiv′i·ty** *n.*

transitive verb A verb whose action, performed by a subject or agent, requires or terminates upon a direct object. The verbs in the following are transitive: *catch* the ball; he *shot* the gun; they *shot* the traitor; cats *climb* trees; we *speak* French.

tran·si·to·ry (tran′sə·tôr′ē, -tō′rē) *adj.* Existing for a short time only; transient. See synonyms under TRANSIENT. [<OF *transitoire* <L *transitorius* having, allowing passage through <*transitus.* See TRANSIT.] — **tran′si·to′ri·ly** *adv.* — **tran′si·to′ri·ness** *n.*

Trans-Jor·dan (trans·jôr′dən, tranz-) An Arab territory included in the Hashemite Kingdom of the Jordan; 34,758 square miles; capital, Amman; a former British mandate. Formerly called **Trans·jor·da·ni·a** (trans′jôr·dā′·nē·ə, tranz′-).

Transkei (trans·kā′) District in Eastern Cape Province, Republic of South Africa; 16,554 square miles; capital Umtata.

trans·late (trans·lāt′, tranz-, trans′lāt, tranz′-) *v.* **·lat·ed, ·lat·ing** *v.t.* **1** To give the sense or equivalent of, as a word or an entire work, in another language; change into another language. **2** To interpret; explain in other words. **3** To remove, as an ecclesiastic, from one office to another. **4** To change into another form; transform. **5** To convey or remove from one place to another, as a human being from earth to heaven without natural death. **6** *Archaic* To transport; enrapture. **7** *Mech.* To impart to (any body) motion in which all the parts follow the same direction. **8** To retransmit, as a message, by means of a telegraphic relay. —*v.i.* **9** To act as a translator; also, to admit of translation: This book *translates* easily. **10** To give form to ideas. See synonyms under INTERPRET. [? <OF *translater* <L *translatus,* pp. to *transferre* TRANSFER] —**trans·lat′a·ble** *adj.* —**trans·lat′a·ble·ness** *n.*

trans·la·tion (trans·lā′shən, tranz-) *n.* **1** The act of translating, or the state of being translated. **2** A transfer from one language to another; a turning of a foreign literary composition into the vernacular; a reproduction of a work in a language different from the original. **3** *Mech.* Motion in which all the parts of a body follow the same direction: distinguished from *rotation.* **4** Automatic resending of a telegraphic message to a more distant point. See synonyms under DEFINITION. —**trans·la′tion·al** *adj.*

trans·la·tor (trans·lā′tər, tranz-, trans′lā·tər, tranz′-) *n.* **1** One who translates; also, an interpreter. **2** A telegraph repeater. —**trans·la·to·ri·al** (trans′lə·tôr′ē·əl, -tō′rē-, tranz′-) *adj.*

Trans·lei·tha·ni·a (trans′li·thā′nē·ə, -li·tä′-) A region in Hungary east of the Leitha river.

trans·lit·er·ate (trans·lit′ə·rāt, tranz-) *v.t.* **·at·ed, ·at·ing** To represent, as a word, by the alphabetic characters of another language having the same sound: distinguished from *translate.* [<TRANS- + L *litera* a letter] —**trans·lit′er·a′tion** *n.*

trans·lo·cate (trans·lō′kāt, tranz-) *v.t.* **·cat·ed, ·cat·ing** To cause to shift from one place or position to another.

trans·lo·ca·tion (trans′lō·kā′shən, tranz′-) *n.* **1** A shift in position. **2** *Genetics* The attachment of a part of a chromosome to another chromosome, with resulting changes in the arrangement of the genes.

trans·lu·cent (trans·lo͞o′sənt, tranz-) *adj.* Allowing the passage of light, but not permitting a clear view of any object; semitransparent. See synomyms under CLEAR, TRANSPARENT. [<L *translucens, -entis,* ppr. of *translucere* <*trans-* through, across + *lucere* shine] —**trans·lu′cence, trans·lu′cen·cy** *n.* —**trans·lu′·cent·ly** *adv.*

trans·lu·nar (trans-lo͞o′nər, tranz-) *adj.* **1** Situated beyond the moon. **2** Ethereal; visionary. Also **trans·lu′na·ry** (-nər·ē). [<TRANS- + L *luna* the moon]

trans·lu·vi·al (trans·Lo͞o′vē·əl, tranz-) *adj.* Pertaining to or characterized by progressive leaching, with some erosion: said of soils. [<TRANS- + (AL)LUV(IUM) + -IAL]

trans·ma·rine (trans′mə·rēn′, tranz′-) *adj.* **1** Beyond the sea. **2** Born or found overseas. **3** Crossing the sea. [<L *transmarinus* <*trans-* across + *mare* the sea]

trans·mi·grant (trans·mī′grənt, trans-, trans′·mə-, tranz′-) *adj.* Passing from one place or condition to another. —*n.* An emigrant or an immigrant. [<L *transmigrans, -antis,* ppr. of *transmigrare* TRANSMIGRATE]

trans·mi·grate (trans·mī′grāt, tranz-, trans′·mə-, tranz′-) *v.i.* **·grat·ed, ·grat·ing** **1** To migrate, as from one place or condition to another; pass from one country or jurisdiction to another. **2** To pass into another body, as the soul at death. [<L *transmigratus,* pp. of *transmigrare* <*trans-* across + *migrare* migrate] —**trans·mi′gra·tor** *n.* —**trans·mi·gra·to·ry** (trans·mī′grə·tôr′ē, -tō′rē, tranz-) *adj.*

trans·mi·gra·tion (trans′mī·grā′shən, -mə-, tranz′-) *n.* The act of transmigrating; especially, the assumed passing of the soul from one body, after death, to another; metempsychosis. —**trans′mi·gra′tion·ism** *n.*

transmigration of souls The doctrine that souls pass into other bodies after death.

trans·mis·si·ble (trans·mis′ə·bəl, tranz-) *adj.* That may be transmitted. Also **trans·mit′ti·ble** (-mit′ə·bəl). —**trans·mis′si·bil′i·ty** *n.*

trans·mis·sion trans·mish′ən, tranz-) *n.* **1** The act of transmitting. **2** The state of being transmitted. **3** That which is transmitted. **4** *Mech.* **a** A device that transmits power from the engine of an automobile to the driving wheels and varies the speed ratios between them. The principal types are **automatic transmission,** in which the speed ratios are automatically selected and engaged (see also FLUID DRIVE), and **manual transmission,** in which the speed ratios are selected and engaged by hand. **b** The gears for changing speed. [<L *transmissio, -onis* <*transmissus,* pp. of *transmittere* TRANSMIT]

Trans-Mis·sis·sip·pi (trans′mis′ə·sip′ē, tranz′-) *adj.* Of or pertaining to the region west of the Mississippi River.

trans·mis·sive (trans·mis′iv, tranz-) *adj.* **1** Derivable. **2** Tending to transmit; capable of sending or being sent through. **3** Derived; transmitted.

trans·mit (trans·mit′, tranz-) *v.t.* **·mit·ted, ·mit·ting** **1** To send from one place or person to another; forward or convey; dispatch. **2** To pass on by heredity; transfer. **3** To serve as a medium of passage for; conduct. **4** To send out by means of radio waves. **5** To cause (light, sound, etc.) to pass through a medium. **6** *Mech.* To convey (force, motion, etc.) from one part or mechanism to another. See synonyms undre CARRY, CONVEY, SEND[1]. [<L *transmittere* <*trans-* across + *mittere* send] —**trans·mit′tal** *n.*

trans·mit·tance (trans·mit′ns, tranz-) *n.* **1** The act or process of transmitting. **2** *Physics* That proportion of radiant energy transmitted by a body upon which it is impinging. Compare OPACITY.

trans·mit·ter (trans·mit′ər, tranz-) *n.* **1** One who or that which transmits. **2** A telegraphic sending instrument. **3** That part of a telephone into which a person talks. **4** That part of a radio or television system which produces, modulates, and transmits radiofrequency waves.

trans·mog·ri·fy (trans·mog′rə·fī, tranz-) *v.t.* **·fied, ·fy·ing** To convert into a different shape; transform. [A humorous coinage; ? alter. of TRANSMIGRATE] —**trans·mog′ri·fi·ca′tion** *n.*

trans·mon·tane (trans·mon′tān, tranz-, trans′·mon·tān′, tranz′-) *adj.* Situated beyond a mountain. [Fusion of OF *transmontane,* alter. of *tramontane* polestar, north pole and L *transmontanus* TRAMONTANE]

trans·mu·ta·tion (trans′myo͞o·tā′shən, tranz′-) *n.* **1** The act of transmuting. **2** In alchemy, the supposed change of a baser metal into one of greater value, as of lead into gold. **3** *Physics* The change of one element into another through alteration of its nuclear structure, as in radioactivity or by bombardment with high-energy particles, etc. **4** *Biol.* Successive change of form; transformism. See synomyms under CHANGE. —**trans′mu·ta′tion·al, trans·mut·a·tive** (trans·myo͞o′tə·tiv, tranz-) *adj.*

trans·mute (trans·myo͞ot′, tranz-) *v.t.* **·mut·ed, ·mut·ing** To change in nature or form; alter in essence. Also **trans·mu′tate.** See synonyms under CHANGE. [<L *transmutare* <*trans-* across + *mutare* change] —**trans·mut′a·ble** *adj.* —**trans·mut′a·bil′i·ty, trans·mut′a·ble·ness** *n.* —**trans·mut′a·bly** *adv.* —**trans·mut′er** *n.*

trans·nep·tu·ni·an (trans′nep·to͞o′nē·ən, -tyo͞o′-, tranz′-) *adj. Astron.* Beyond the planet Neptune. [<TRANS- + NEPTUN(E) + -IAN]

trans·nor·mal (trans·nôr′məl, tranz-) *adj.* Supernormal.

trans·o·ce·an·ic (trans′ō·shē·an′ik, tranz′-) *adj.* **1** Lying beyond or over the ocean. **2** Crossing the ocean.

tran·som (tran′səm) *n.* **1** A horizontal piece framed across an opening; a lintel. **2** A window above such a bar, especially a small window above a door. **3** A horizontal construction dividing a window into stages. **4** A tie beam. **5** *Naut.* A beam running across and forming part of the stern frame of a ship. **6** The horizontal crossbar of a gallows or cross. [<L *transtrum* a crossbeam <*trans* across] **—tran′somed** *adj.*

transom window 1 A window divided into stages by transoms. **2** A window over a door transom and often hinged to it.

tran·son·ic (tran·son′ik) *adj. Aeron.* Of, pertaining to, or characterized by speeds between the subsonic and supersonic.

transonic barrier *Aeron.* A barrier to flight encountered by aircraft not designed to exceed subsonic speed: caused by turbulence of the airflow around different parts of the plane. Also called *sonic barrier, sound barrier.*

Trans·ox·i·an·a (trans·ok′sə·an′ə) See SOGDIANA.

trans·pa·cif·ic (trans′pə·sif′ik) *adj.* **1** Crossing the Pacific Ocean. **2** Situated across or beyond the Pacific.

trans·pa·dane (trans′pə·dān) *adj.* Being beyond the river Po, from Rome as a standpoint. [<L *transpadanus trans-* across + *padamus* of the Po <*Padus* the river Po]

Transpadane Gaul The section of Gaul in Italy north of the river Po.

trans·par·en·cy (trans·pâr′ən·sē, -par′-) *n. pl.* **·cies 1** The quality of being transparent. **2** Something, as a picture on glass, intended to be viewed by shining a light through it. **3** *Phot.* The light-transmitting power of a sensitized negative. **4** Simplicity. Also **trans·par′ence.**

trans·par·ent (trans·pâr′ənt, -par′-) *adj.* **1** Admitting the passage of light, and of clear views of objects beyond; pervious to light: *transparent* glass: distinguished from *translucent.* **2** Figuratively, easy to see through or understand; hence without guile; frank. **3** Diaphanous. **4** Luminous; bright. [<Med. L *transparens, -entis* <L *trans-* across + *parere* appear, be visible] **—trans·par′ent·ly** *adv.* **—trans·par′ent·ness** *n.*

Synonyms: clear, diaphanous, limpid, lucid, pellucid, translucent. Whatever offers no obstruction to the vision is *clear; limpid, lucid,* and *pellucid* refer to a shining, sparkling clearness. A *transparent* body allows the forms and colors of objects beyond to be seen through it; a *translucent* body allows light to pass through, but may not permit forms and colors to be distinguished; plate glass is *transparent,* ground glass is *translucent. Limpid* refers to a liquid clearness, or that which suggests it; as, *limpid* streams. see CANDID, CLEAR, EVIDENT, MANIFEST, PLAIN.[1] *Antonyms:* cloudy, dark, dim, obscure, opaque, turbid.

transparent velvet A soft, lightweight velvet suitable for draping, having a silk or rayon back and a rayon pile.

tran·spic·u·ous (tran·spik′yo͞o·əs) *adj.* Transparent. [<Med. L *transpicuus*<L *transpicere* look, see through <*trans-* through + *specere* look]

trans·pierce (trans·pirs′) *v.t.* **·pierced, ·piercing** To pierce through; penetrate completely. [<MF *transpercer* <*trans-* (<L, across, through) + *percer* pierce]

tran·spi·ra·tion (tran′spə·rā′shən) *n.* A transpiring or exhalation, as through a porous substance or through the tissues of a plant.

tran·spire (tran·spīr′) *v.* **·spired, ·spiring** *v.t.* **1** *Physiol.* To send off through the excretory organs, as of the skin and lungs; exhale. *—v.i.* **2** *Physiol.* To be emitted, as through the skin; be exhaled, as moisture or odors. **3** To become known. **4** *Colloq.* To happen; occur. [<F *transpirer* <L *trans-* across, through + *spirare* breathe]

trans·plant (trans·plant′, -plänt′) *v.t.* **1** To remove and plant in another place. **2** To remove and settle or establish for residence in another place. **3** *Surg.* To transfer (an organ or tissue) from its original site to another part of the body or to another individual. *—n.* (trans′plant′, -plänt′) **1** That which is transplanted, as a seedling or an organ of the body. **2** A transplanting. [<LL *transplantare* <L *trans-* across + *plantare* plant] **—trans′plan·ta′tion** *n.* **—trans·plant′er** *n.*

trans·pond·er (trans·pon′dər) *n. Electronics* A device that receives a signal from one telecommunication circuit and transmits the corresponding signal to another circuit: used in conjunction with an interrogator. Also called *pulse repeater.* [<TRANS(MITTER) + (RES)PONDER]

trans·po·ni·ble (trans·pō′nə·bəl) *adj.* Transposable. [<L *transponere* transpose (<*trans-* across + *ponere* put) + -IBLE] **—trans·po′ni·bil′i·ty** *n.*

trans·pon·tine (trans·pon′tin, -tīn) *adj.* Situated on the other side of a bridge: said of London south of the Thames. [<TRANS- + L *pons, pontis* a bridge]

trans·port (trans·pôrt′; -pōrt′) *v.t.* **1** To carry or convey from one place to another. **2** To carry into banishment, especially beyond the sea. **3** To carry away with emotion. **4** *Obs.* To take out of the world; kill. See synonyms under CARRY, CONVEY, RAVISH. *—n.* (trans′·pôrt, -pōrt) **1** The state of being transported, as with rapture. **2** *pl.* The varied and recurrent emotions that charaterize such a state. **3** Transportation. **4** A vessel, rolling stock, or other means of conveyance used by a government to transport troops, military supplies, etc. **5** The act of transporting convicts. **6** A deported convict. **7** *Aeron.* An airplane used to transport passengers, mail, etc. See synonyms under ENTHUSIASM, RAPTURE. [<MF *transporter* <L *transportare* <*trans-* across + *portare* carry] **—trans·port′er** *n.*

trans·port·a·ble (trans·pôr′tə·bəl, -pōr′-) *adj.* **1** That may be transported. **2** Rendering liable to transportation (def. 2). **—trans·port′a·bil′i·ty** *n.*

trans·por·ta·tion (trans′pər·tā′shən) *n.* **1** The act of transporting; conveyance. **2** The sending away of a convict to a remote place. **3** Vehicles used in transporting; also, charge for conveyance. **4** A ticket, pass, or other printed matter entitling a passenger to travel on a railroad train, street car, etc.

trans·port·ing (trans·pôr′ting, -pōr′-) *adj.* Enrapturing; ravishing; ecstatic. **—trans·port′·ing·ly** *adv.*

trans·pose (trans·pōz′) *v.t.* **·posed, ·pos·ing 1** To reverse the order or change the place of; interchange. **2** *Math.* To transfer (a term) with a changed sign from one side of an algebraic equation to the other, so as not to destroy the equality of the members. **3** To change in place or order, as a word in a sentence. **4** *Music* To write or play in a different key. **5** To transport. **6** *Obs.* To transform. [<OF *transposer* <L *trans-* over + OF *poser.* See POSE[1].] **—trans·pos′a·ble** *adj.* **—trans·pos′er** *n.*

trans·po·si·tion (trans′pə·zish′ən) *n.* **1** The act of transposing, or the state of being transposed. **2** That which has been transposed. Also **trans·po·sal** (trans·pō′zəl). **—trans′po·si′tion·al** *adj.*

trans·sex·u·al (trans·sek′sho͞o·əl, -sek′shəl) *n.* A person who is genetically and physically of one sex but who identifies psychologically with the other and may seek treatment by surgery or with hormones to bring the physical sexual cahracteristics into conformity with the psychological preference. *—adj.* Of, for, or characteristic of transsexuals. **—trans·sex′u·al·ism** *n.*

trans·shape (trans·shāp′) *v.t.* **·shaped, ·shap·ing** To change the shape of: also spelled *transhape.*

trans·ship (trans·ship′) *v.t. & v.i.* **·shapped, ·ship·ping** To transfer from one conveyance or line to another: also spelled *tranship.* **—trans·ship′ment** *n.*

tran·sub·stan·ti·ate (tran′səb·stan′shē·āt) *v.t.* **·at·ed, ·at·ing 1** To change from one substance into another; transmute; transform. **2** *Theol.* To change the substance of (the bread and wine of the Eucharist) into the body and blood of Christ. [<Med. L *transubstantiatus,* pp. of *transubstantiare* <L *trans-* over + *substantia* substance]

tran·sub·stan·ti·a·tion (tran′səb·stan′shē·ā′·shən) *n.* **1** *Theol.* The conversion of the substance of the eucharistic elements into that of Christ's body and blood: a doctrine of the Greek and Roman Catholic churches. Compare CONSUBSTANTIATION, IMPANATION. **2** A change of anything into something essentially different. **—tran′sub·stan′ti·a′tion·al·ist** *n.*

tran·su·date (tran′so͞o·dāt) *n.* **1** The fluid that transudes. **2** The act or process of transuding. Also **tran′su·da′tion** (-dā′shən). [<NL *transudatus,* pp. of *transudare* TRANSUDE]

tran·sude (tran·so͞od′) *v.i.* **·sud·ed, ·sud·ing** To pass through the pores or tissues, as of a membrane. [<NL *transudare* <L *trans-* across, through + *sudare* sweat] **—tran·su′·da·to′ry** (-de·tôr′ē, -tō′rē) *adj.*

trans·u·ra·ni·an (trans′yo͞o·rā′nē·ən, tranz′-) *adj. Physics* Of or pertaining to those radioactive elements having an atomic number greater than that of uranium. Also **trans′u·ran′ic** (-ran′ik), **trans′u·ra′ni·um.** [<TRANS- + URAN(IUM) + -IAN]

Trans·vaal (trans·väl′, tranz-) Previous province of Republic of South Africa; now divided into Eastern and Northern Transvaal and Gauteng Provinces; 110,450 square miles; seat of government, Pretoria.

trans·val·ue (trans·val′yo͞o, tranz-) *v.t.* **·ued, ·u·ing 1** To appraise the value of, as conduct, morals, beliefs, and the like, in accordance with principle at variance with accepted or conventional standards. **2** *Psychoanal.* To attach to an idea or complex of ideas a disproportionate emotional value, as in dreams, schizophrenia, etc. **—trans′val·u·a′tion** *n.*

trans·ver·sal (trans·vûr′səl, tranz-) *adj.* Transverse. *—n. Geom.* A straight line intersecting a system of lines.

trans·verse (trans·vûrs′, tranz-) *adj.* **1** Lying or being across; athwart. **2** *Anat.* Placed across the long axis of a part: a *transverse* muscle. *—n.* (*also* trans′vûrs, tranz′-) **1** That which is transverse **2** *Geom.* That axis of a conic section which passes through its foci. [<L *transversus* lying across, pp. of *transvertere* <*trans-* across + *vertere* turn] **—trans·verse′ly** *adv.*

transverse process *Anat.* A long process extending laterally from a vertebra.

transverse wave *Physics* A wave whose component particles oscillate in a direction perpendicular to the line of propagation.

trans·ves·tite (trans·ves′tit, tranz-) *n.* One who wears the clothes of the opposite sex. [<L *trans-* over + *vestire* to clothe + -ITE] **—trans·ves′tism, trans·ves′ti·tism** (-ves′tə·tiz′·əm) *n.*

Tran·syl·va·ni·a (tran′sil·vā′nē·ə) A region and former province in central Rumania; 24,000 square miles; formerly the eastern part of Hungary. **—Trans′syl·va′ni·an** *adj. & n.*

trap¹ (trap) *n.* **1** A device for catching game or other animals, as a pitfall or a baited device so arranged that a slight disturbance causes it to close or fall and thus kill or capture the victim. **2** A contrivance for hurling clay pigeons or glass balls into the air for sportsmen to shoot at. **3** Any artifice by which a person may be betrayed or taken unawares. **4** *Mech.* A U- or S-bend in a pipe, etc., for stopping return flow, as of noxious gas, **5** A trap door. **6** *Colloq.* A light, two-wheeled carriage suspended by springs. **7** A rattltrap. **8** *pl.* Traps. **9 a** The game of trap ball. **b** A pivoted piece of wood, resembling a low shoe, used in the game of trap ball to throw a ball into the air. **10** In some games, especially golf, an obstacle or hazard: a water *trap,* sand *trap.* **11** *U.S. Slang* The mouth: Shut your *trap.* *—v.* **trapped, trap·ping** *v.t.* **1** To catch in a trap; ensnare. **2** To provide with a trap. **3** To stop or hold by some obstruction: said of a liquid. *—v.i.* **4** To set traps for game; be a trapper. [OE *treppe, træppe*]

trap² (trap) *n.* **1** *pl. Colloq.* Personal effects, as luggage; also, household goods. **2** A trapping. *—v.t.* **trapped, trap·ping** To adorn with trappings; bedeck. [Orig. a cloth covering

for a horse, alter. of OF *drap* a cloth, covering <Med. L *drappus*; ult. origin uncertain]

trap[3] (trap) *n. Geol.* A dark, fine-grained igneous rock, often of columnar structure, as basalt, dolerite, etc.: also called *traprock.* [<Sw. *trapp* <*trappa* a stair; so called from the steplike arrangement of this rock in other rock]

tra·pan (trə·pan′) See TREPAN[2].

Tra·pa·ni (trä′pä·nē) An Italian port on the NW tip of Sicily: ancient *Drepanum.*

trap ball 1 A game in which a player strikes one end of a trap with a bat and thus flips a ball into the air for other players to try to catch. **2** The ball used in this game. See TRAP[1] (*n.* def. 9).

trap door A door, hinged or sliding, to cover an opening, as in a floor or roof.

trap-door spider (trap′dôr′, -dōr′) A large spider (family *Ctenizidae*) that inhabits a vertical, tubular pit in the ground, covered by a circular trap door hinged at one side to the silken lining of the tube, especially *Bothriocyrtum californica* of the SW United States.

trapes (trāps) See TRAIPSE.

tra·peze (trə·pēz′, tra-) *n.* **1** A short swinging bar, suspended by two ropes, for various gymnastic exercises. **2** *Geom.* A trapezium. [<F *trapèze* <NL *trapezium* a trapezium]

tra·pe·zi·form (trə·pē′zə·fôrm) *adj.* Having the form of a trapezium. [<TRAPEZI(UM) + -FORM]

tra·pe·zi·um (trə·pē′zē·əm) *n. pl.* **·zi·a** (-zē·ə) **1** *Geom.* **a** A four-sided plane figure of which no two sides are parallel. **b** In England, a quadrilateral of which two sides are parallel; a trapezoid. **2** *Anat.* **a** The bone of the distal row of the carpus situated on the radial side at the base of the thumb. **b** A band of transverse fibers found in the pons Varolii of the brain. **3** *Astron.* The four brightest stars in the nebula of Orion, at the angles of a trapezium. [<NL <Gk. *trapezion,* dim. of *trapeza* a table, lit., a four-footed (bench) <*tetra-* four + *peza* foot]

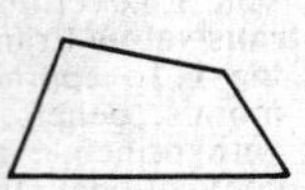
TRAPEZIUM

tra·pe·zi·us (trə·pē′zē·əs) *n. Anat.* Either of a pair of large, flat, triangle-shaped muscles on the upper back and neck.

trap·e·zo·he·dron (trap′ə·zō·hē′drən, trə·pē′-) *n. pl.* **·dra** (-drə) A crystal figure bounded by six, eight, or twelve faces, each having unequal intercepts on all axes. [<NL <*trapezium* a trapezium + Gk. *hedra* a base]

trap·e·zoid (trap′ə·zoid) *n.* **1** *Geom.* **a** A quadrilateral of which two sides are parallel. **b** In England, a plane quadrilateral of which no two sides are parallel; a trapezium. **2** *Anat.* An irregular bone in the second row of the carpus, at the end of the forefinger. [<NL *trapezoïdes* <Gk. *trapezoeidēs* tablelike <*trapeza* a table + *eidos* a form] **—trap′e·zoi′dal** *adj.*

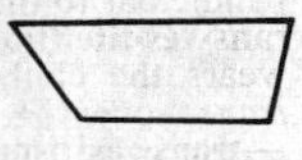
TRAPEZOID

trap·fall (trap′fôl′) *n.* A trap door yielding under pressure of feet.

trap line 1 The ensnaring filament in a spider's web. **2** A series of traps set out at approximately equal distances.

trap net A fishing net having a funnel-shaped entrance into an oblong net pen from which egress is almost impossible.

trap·pe·an (trap′ē·ən, trə·pē′ən) *adj.* Of or pertaining to traprock. Also **trap′pous, trap·pose** (trap′ōs). [<TRAP[3]]

trap·per (trap′ər) *n.* One whose occupation is the trapping of fur-bearing animals.

trap·ping (trap′ing) *n.* **1** An ornamental housing or harness for a horse. **2** *pl.* Adornments of any kind; embellishments; superficial dress. See synonyms under CAPARISON. [<TRAP[2]]

trap·pist (trap′ist) *n.* A nunbird. [<TRAPPIST]

Trap·pist (trap′ist) *n.* A member of an ascetic order of monks, a branch of the Cistercians, founded at Soligny-la-Trappe, France, and noted for silence and abstinence. [<F *Trappiste,* from *La Trappe,* name of their first abbey, established 1664]

trap·rock (trap′rok′) *n.* Trap[3].

traps (traps) *n. pl.* Percussion instruments, such as drums, cymbals, etc. [<TRAP[1] (def. 8)]

trap·shoot·ing (trap′shōō′ting) *n.* The sport of shooting pigeons, or artificial substitutes sent up from spring traps. See TRAP[1] (*n.* def. 2). **—trap′shoot′er** *n.*

trash[1] (trash) *n.* **1** Worthless or waste matter of any kind; rubbish. **2** That which is broken or lopped off, as loppings of trees. **3** The lowest grade of tobacco. **4** The dry refuse of sugarcane after the juice has been expressed. **5** A worthless person, or one of ill repute. *—v.t.* **1** To free from trash. **2** To strip of leaves; prune; lop. **3** To regard as trash; discard. [Cf. dial. Norw. *trask* lumber, trash, baggage]

trash[2] (trash) *n.* **1** Something fastened to an animal's neck to serve as a check. **2** A clog; collar; leash; any hindrance. *—v.t.* To keep in check with a leash, trash, or halter. [<OF *trachier,* var. of *tracier.* See TRACE[1].]

trash·trie (trash′trē) *n. Scot.* Trash.

trash·y (trash′ē) *adj.* **trash·i·er, trash·i·est 1** Consisting of or like trash; worthless. **2** Cheap; inferior: said of literature. **3** Covered with underbrush or waste: said of land. **—trash′i·ly** *adv.* **—trash′i·ness** *n.*

Tra·si·me·no (trä′sē·mē′nō), **Lake** A lake in central Italy, 10 miles in diameter; 50 square miles; here Hannibal defeated the Romans, 217 B.C.: also *Lake of Perugia.* Ancient **Tras·i·me·nus** (tras′i·mē′nəs).

trass (tras) *n.* A gray, yellow, or whitish earth, related to pozzuolana, common in volcanic districts: used in preparation of a hydraulic cement. [<G <Du. *tras* <earlier *taras.* Akin to TERRACE.]

trat·to·ri·a (trä′tə·rē′ə) *n. pl.* **·ri·as, ·ri·e** (-rē′ā) A restaurant, esp. one with reasonable prices. [<Ital.]

trauch·le (troukh′əl) See TRACHLE.

trau·ma (trô′mə, trou′-) *n. pl.* **·mas** or **·ma·ta** (-mə·tə) **1** *Pathol.* Any injury to the body caused by shock, violence, etc.; a wound. **2** *Psychiatry* A severe emotional shock having a deep, often lasting effect upon the personality. **3** A traumatism. [<NL <Gk. *trauma, -atos* a wound]

trau·mat·ic (trô·mat′ik) *adj.* **1** Of or pertaining to trauma. **2** Connected with or resulting from shock, a wound, or wounds. [<LL *traumaticus* <Gk. *traumatikos* <*trauma, -atos* a wound] **—trau·mat′i·cal·ly** *adv.*

trau·ma·tism (trô′mə·tiz′əm) *n. Pathol.* **1** The general condition of the system resulting from a severe wound or external injury. **2** The injury or wound itself; a trauma. Also **trau′ma·to′sis** (-tō′sis).

trau·ma·tize (trô′mə·tīz) *v.t.* **-tized, -tiz·ing** To cause trauma to the body or the mind.

trau·ma·to·pho·bi·a (trô′mə·tə·fō′bē·ə) *n.* A morbid fear of injury. [<*traumato-* (<Gk. *trauma* a wound) + -PHOBIA]

trau·mat·ro·pism (trô·mat′rə·piz′əm) *n. Biol.* The growth or involuntary movement of an organism as determined by an injury. [<TRAUMA + TROPISM]

trav·ail[1] (trav′āl, trə·vāl′) *v.t.* **1** To weary. *—v.i.* **2** To suffer the pangs of childbirth. **3** To toil; labor. *—n.* **1** Labor in childbirth. **2** Anguish or distress encountered in achievement. **3** Hard or agonizing labor. **4** Physical agony. See synonyms under TOIL[1]. [<OF <*travaillier* labor, toil, ult. <LL *trepalium* a three-pronged instrument of torture <*tres, tria* three + *palus* a stake]

tra·vail[2] (trá·vá′y′) *n. pl.* **·vails** (-vá′y′) *French* A travois.

Trav·an·core-Co·chin (trav′ən·kôr′kō′chin, koch′in) A former constituent state of SW India; mostly incorporated in Kerala State, 1956; 9,144 square miles; capital, Trivandrum.

trave (trāv) *n. Obs.* **1** A frame to confine a beast of burden while being shod. **2** A crossbeam; transom. [<OF <L *trabs, trabis* a beam]

trav·el (trav′əl) *v.* **trav·eled** or **·elled, trav·el·ing** or **·el·ling** *v.i.* **1** To go from one place to another or from place to place; make a journey or tour. **2** To proceed; advance. **3** To go about from place to place as a traveling salesman. **4** *U.S. Colloq.* To move with speed. **5** To pass or be transmitted, as light, sound, etc. **6** *Mech.* To move in a fixed path, as part of a mechanism. *—v.t.* **7** To move or journey across or through; traverse. *—n.* **1** The act of traveling; a journeying: chiefly in the plural. **2** *pl.* A narration of things experienced or observed in traveling. **3** A moving or progress of any kind. **4** *Mech.* Movement or length of stroke. **5** The passage of people and vehicles to, over, or past a certain place. **6** Tourists, collectively. **7** Distance traveled; mileage. See synonyms under JOURNEY. [Var. of TRAVAIL[1]] **—trav′el·ing** or **·el·ling** *adj.* & *n.*

trav·eled (trav′əld) *adj.* **1** Having made many journeys, especially to distant lands. **2** Experienced as the result of travel. **3** Frequented or used by travelers: a *traveled* district. Also **trav′elled.**

trav·el·er (trav′əl·ər, trav′lər) *n.* **1** One who travels or journeys from place to place. **2** An animal or thing considered with reference to its mode or speed of movement. **3** A traveling salesman; specifically, a drummer: also **commercial traveler. 4** *Naut.* **a** A metal ring or thimble running freely on a rope, rod, or spar. **b** A bar affixed to the deck, along which a ring or thimble slides. **5** A traveling crane or other moving device for transporting heavy objects. **6** In the theater, an overhead rod or pipe in the flys of the stage from which small spotlights are suspended and made available for unusual lighting effects. **7** The rings and track for drawn curtains. Also **trav′el·ler.**

traveler's tree Ravenala.

trav·el·ing (trav′əl·ing, trav′ling) *adj.* **1** Designed or used for travel: a *traveling* bag. **2** Itinerant: a *traveling* tinker. **3** Portable; movable. **4** *Mech.* **a** Running or sliding along a fixed course, as a ring or thimble. **b** Constructed with a part that travels.

traveling crane A hoisting and transporting apparatus which moves along a supporting frame or bridge, the frame itself moving on tracks. Compare illustration under GANTRY.

traveling man A commercial traveler; a traveling salesman.

trav·e·log (trav′ə·lôg, -log) *n.* A lecture or discourse on or an account of travel, usually illustrated pictorially. Also **trav′e·logue.** [<TRAVEL, on analogy with *monolog, dialog,* etc.]

trav·erse (trav′ərs, trə·vûrs′) *v.* **·ersed, ·ers·ing** *v.t.* **1** To pass over, across, or through. **2** To move back and forth over or along. **3** To examine carefully; survey or scrutinize. **4** To oppose; thwart. **5** To turn (a gun, lathe, etc.) to right or left; swivel. **6** *Law* To make denial of; in legal pleading, to deny and tender issue upon, as a matter of fact alleged by the opposite party; impeach the validity of an inquest of office. **7** *Naut.* To brace (a yard) fore and aft. *—v.i.* **8** To move back and forth. **9** To move across; cross. **10** To turn; swivel. **11** In fencing, to slide one's blade toward the hilt of an opponent's sword while maintaining pressure on it. *—n.* (trav′ərs) **1** A part, as of a machine or structure, that traverses, as a crosspiece, crossbeam, transom, or the like. **2** *Archit.* A gallery or loft communicating with opposite sides of a building. **3** Something serving as a screen or barrier. **4** *Geom.* A transversal. **5** The act of traversing or traveling; a journey; passage. **6** *Mech.* Sidewise travel, as of the tool in a slide rest. **7** The act of traversing or denying; a denial; in legal pleading, a formal denial. **8** *Naut.* A zigzag track of a vessel while beating to windward. **9** A short line surveyed from a main line, to establish the position of a side point. **10** *Mil.* A bank of earth thrown up, as from a trench, to afford protection from gunfire. **11** Something that obstructs, vexes, or thwarts. **12** A path cut transversely in the side of a cliff or mountain; also, the cliff across which a path is cut. **13** A sled having a long board connecting two or more sleds or two or more sets of runners. *—adj.* (trav′ərs) Transverse; lying or being across. *—adv.* (trav′ərs, trə·vûrs′) Transversely; crosswise. [<OF *traverser* <LL *traversare, transversare* <L *transversus* TRANSVERSE] **—trav′ers·a·ble** *adj.* **—trav·er·sal** (trav′ər·səl, trə·vûr′səl) *n.* **—trav′ers·er** *n.*

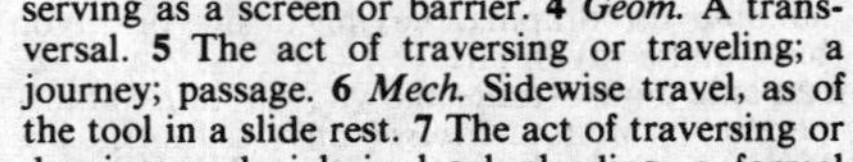
TRAVERSE *(def. 13)*

Trav·erse (trav′ərs), **Lake** A lake on the

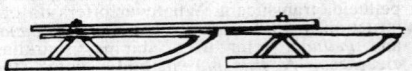

**boundary of South Dakota and Minnesota; 26 miles long, 3 miles wide.

traverse jury A trial jury. [<TRAVERSE (v. def. 3) + JURY]

trav·er·tine (trav′ər·tin, -tēn, -tīn) n. A porous, light–yellow, crystalline calcium carbonate deposited in solution from ground or surface waters: a form of limestone used for building purposes. Also **trav′er·tin** (-tin). [<Ital. travertino, tivertino <L Tiburtinus Tiburtine <Tibur, -urtis of Tibur <Tibur Tibur]

trav·es·ty (trav′is·tē) n. pl. ·ties 1 A grotesque imitation; burlesque. 2 In literature, a burlesque treatment of a lofty subject. See synonyms under CARICATURE. — v.t. ·tied, ·ty·ing To make a travesty on; burlesque; parody. [<MF travesti, pp. of (se) travestir disguise (oneself) <Ital. travestire disguise]

tra·vois (tra·voi′) n. pl. ·vois (-voiz′) or ·vois·es (-voi′ziz) A primitive sled constructed of two poles which serve as shafts for a dog or other draft animal and which drag on the ground, bearing a frame for the load: used by North

TRAVOIS

American Indians and lumbermen in logging: also spelled travail. Also **tra·voise** (-voiz′). [< dial. F (Canadian), alter. of F travail, a frame in which horses are held while being shod <OF]

trawl (trôl) n. 1 A stout line, sometimes over a mile long, anchored and buoyed, and having hanging from it many lines frequently spaced and bearing baited hooks: also called trotline. 2 A great net shaped like a flattened bag, for towing on the bottom of the ocean by a boat. — v.t. To drag, as a net to catch fish. — v.i. To fish with a trawl line, trawl net, or the like. [Cf. MDu. traghel a dragnet; prob. infl. by trail] — **trawl′ing** n.

trawl·er (trô′lər) n. 1 A person engaged in trawling. 2 A vessel used for trawling.

trawl·ey (trô′lē) See TROLLEY (def. 4).

tray (trā) n. 1 A flat shallow utensil or bowl with raised edges, for various uses. 2 A shallow box without a cover, used in trunks and otherwise. 3 A kind of flat board with a low rim, made of wood, metal, or other material, and used for carrying or holding articles; also, its contents. ◆ Homophone: trey. [OE treg, trig a wooden board]

treach·er·ous (trech′ər·əs) adj. 1 Traitorous; perfidious. 2 Having a good appearance, but bad in character or nature; untrustworthy; affording unsafe footing: a treacherous path. See synonyms under INSIDIOUS, PERFIDIOUS, ROTTEN. — **treach′er·ous·ly** adv. — **treach′er·ous·ness** n.

treach·er·y (trech′ər·ē) n. pl. ·er·ies Violation of allegiance, confidence, or plighted faith; perfidy; treason. See synonyms under FRAUD. [<OF trecherie, tricherie <tricher, trechier cheat]

trea·cle (trē′kəl) n. 1 The sirup obtained in refining sugar. 2 Molasses. 3 A saccharine fluid of certain plants. 4 Originally, a compound used as an antidote. 5 Obs. A panacea. [<OF triacle <L theriaca <Gk. thēriakē a remedy for poisonous bites <thērion, dim. of thēr a wild beast] — **trea′cly** adj.

tread (tred) v. trod (Archaic trode), trod·den or trod, tread·ing v.t. 1 To step or walk on, over, along, etc.: to tread the floor. 2 To press with the feet; trample: to tread grass. 3 To accomplish in walking or in dancing: to tread a measure. 4 To copulate with: said of male birds. — v.i. 5 To place the foot down; walk. 6 To press the ground or anything beneath the feet: usually with on. — **to tread water** In swimming, to keep the body erect and the head above water by moving the feet up and down as if walking. — n. 1 The act or manner of treading; a walking or stepping. 2 That on which something treads or rests in moving, or which affords space for or as for treading. 3 The part of a wheel that bears upon the ground or rails. 4 The outer surface of an automobile tire, or the distance between opposite wheels. 5 The part of a

rail on which the wheels bear. 6 The cicatricle or chalaza of an egg. 7 The impression made by a foot, a tire, etc. 8 The flat part of a step in stairs. [OE tredan] — **tread′er** n. — **tread′ing** n.

tread·le (tred′l) n. A lever operated by the foot, usually to cause rotary motion. — v.i. ·led, ·ling To work a treadle. Also spelled treddle. [OE tredel <tredan tread] — **tread′ler** n.

tread·mill (tred′mil′) n. 1 A mechanism rotated by the walking motion of one or more persons: formerly used as a prison punishment. 2 A somewhat similar mechanism operated by a quadruped. 3 Toilsome effort; monotonous routine.

tread·way (tred′wā′) n. The roadway in certain types of bridges.

trea·son (trē′zən) n. 1 Betrayal, treachery, or breach of allegiance or of obedience toward the sovereign or government. Treason against the United States is declared by the Constitution (Article 3, section 3) to "consist only in levying war against them, or in adhering to their enemies, giving them aid and comfort." 2 A breach of faith; treachery. See synonyms under FRAUD. [<AF treyson, OF traïson <L traditio, -onis a betrayal, delivery. Doublet of TRADITION.]

trea·son·a·ble (trē′zən·ə·bəl) adj. Of, involving, or characteristic of treason. — **trea′son·a·ble·ness** n. — **trea′son·a·bly** adv.

trea·son·ous (trē′zən·əs) adj. Full of treason; treasonable. — **trea′son·ous·ly** adv.

treas·ure (trezh′ər) n. 1 The precious metals; money; jewels. 2 Riches accumulated or possessed; a stock or store of anything; wealth. 3 Something very precious. See synonyms under WEALTH. — v.t. ·ured, ·ur·ing 1 To lay up in store; accumulate. 2 To retain carefully, as in the mind: generally with up. 3 To set a high value upon; prize. See synonyms under CHERISH. [<OF tresor <L thesaurus. Doublet of THESAURUS.]

Treasure Island An artificial island in San Francisco Bay, used as a naval base; 400 acres.

treas·ur·er (trezh′ər·ər) n. 1 One who has the care of treasure or of a treasury. 2 An officer legally authorized to receive, care for, and disburse public revenues upon lawful orders. 3 A similar custodian of the funds of a society or a corporation.

Treasure State Nickname of MONTANA.

treas·ure-trove (trezh′ər·trōv′) n. 1 Law Money, plate, or the like, found hidden in the earth, etc., the owner being unknown. 2 Any wealth–yielding discovery; loosely, treasure; riches. [<AF tresor trové <tresor TREASURE + trové, pp. of trover find]

treas·ur·y (trezh′ər·ē) n. pl. ·ur·ies 1 The place of receipt and disbursement of public revenue, or of funds belonging to a corporation. 2 A repository, especially of words, as a dictionary or thesaurus. — **Department of the Treasury** An executive department of the U. S. government (established in 1789), headed by the Secretary of the Treasury, which superintends and manages the national finances, controls the coinage and printing of money, and supervises the Coast Guard (except when it is a part of the Navy, in wartime or when the president directs), the Bureau of Narcotics, and the Secret Service. Also **Treasury Department.** [<OF tresorie <tresor TREASURE]

Treasury note A demand note on which the face value is printed, issued by the Treasury: a legal tender for all debts, public and private, unless otherwise expressly stipulated.

treat (trēt) v.t. 1 To conduct oneself toward in a specified manner: He treated her shamefully. 2 To look upon or regard in a specified manner: They treat the matter as a joke. 3 To subject to chemical or physical action, as for altering or improving. 4 To give medical or surgical attention to. 5 To deal with in writing or speaking; handle. 6 To deal with or develop (a subject in art) in a specified manner or style. 7 To pay for the entertainment, food, or drink of. — v.i. 8 To handle a subject in writing or speaking: usually with of. 9 To carry on negotiations; negotiate. 10 To pay for another's enter-

tainment. See synonyms under TRANSACT. — n. 1 Something that gives unusual pleasure. 2 Entertainment of any kind furnished gratuitously to another. 3 Colloq. One's turn to pay for refreshment or entertainment, especially for drinks. [<OF tretier, traitier <L tractare. See TRACTABLE.] — **treat′a·ble** adj. — **treat′er** n. — **treat′ing** n.

trea·tise (trē′tis) n. 1 An elaborate, formal, and systematic literary composition presenting a serious subject in all its parts: distinguished from an essay in being longer, more exhaustive, and less popular, and from a monograph in being more full and complete. 2 Obs. A story; tale. [<AF tretiz, OF traitier TREAT]

treat·ment (trēt′mənt) n. 1 The act, mode, or process of treating anything, as a raw material, substance, or product. 2 Med. The management of illness, by the use of drugs, dieting, or other means designed to bring relief or effect a cure. 3 In motion pictures and television, an expanded synopsis of a story, used in planning, writing, or marketing a play or scenario.

trea·ty (trē′tē) n. pl. ·ties 1 A formal agreement or compact, duly concluded and ratified, between two or more states. 2 Obs. The act of negotiating for an agreement; also, the agreement so made. 3 Obs. An entreaty. [<AF treté, OF traitié, pp. of traitier TREAT]

treaty port Any of several sea and river ports, especially in China, in which foreigners were permitted to reside, purchase property, and erect business establishments: abolished by various treaties.

Treb·bia (treb′byä) A river in NW Italy, flowing 70 miles NE from the Apennines NE of Genoa to the Po river near Piacenza; on its banks Hannibal defeated the Romans, 218 B.C.

Treb·i·zond (treb′i·zond) 1 A province of NW Turkey; 1,753 square miles; an empire of Asia Minor from 1204 to 1461. 2 Its capital, a port on the Black Sea. Turkish Trabzon.

treb·le (treb′əl) v.t. & v.i. ·led, ·ling To multiply by three; triple. — adj. 1 Threefold; triple. 2 Soprano. — n. 1 Music The soprano; the highest register of the compass of an instrument; a soprano singer. 2 High, piping sound; a musical instrument of treble pitch; a violin. [<OF <L triplus. Doublet of TRIPLE.] — **treb′le·ness** n. — **treb′ling** n. — **treb′ly** adv.

treb·u·chet (treb′yoo·shet) n. A medieval catapultlike device for throwing heavy missiles. The missile, on the long arm of a lever, was hurled with great force by the sudden descent of a heavy weight on the short arm. Also **treb′uck·et** (-uk·it). [<OF <trebucher trip, fall]

tre·cen·to (trā·chen′tō) n. Italian The 14th century, as producing a particular style of Italian literature and art (in literature, Petrarchism); the early Italian style.

tred·dle (tred′l) See TREADLE.

tree (trē) n. 1 A perennial woody plant having usually a single self–supporting trunk, with branches and foliage growing at some distance above the ground, the whole ranging from about ten feet to as high as 300 feet. ◆ Collateral adjective: arboreal. 2 Any shrub or plant that assumes treelike shape or dimensions. 3 Something whose outline resembles that of a tree: a genealogical tree; a branching diagram; a treelike group of crystals. 4 A timber or heavy piece of wood, as in a framing: usually in composition: axletree, boot–tree, etc. 5 A gibbet; also, a cross. — **up a tree** Colloq. In a position from which there is no retreat; cornered; caught; also, in an embarrassing position. — v.t. **treed, tree·ing** 1 To force to climb or take refuge in a tree: to tree an opossum. 2 Colloq. To get the advantage of; corner. 3 To stretch, as a boot, on a boot–tree. [OE trēow, trīow, trēo]

Tree may appear as a combining form in hyphemes or solidemes, or as the first element in two–word phrases; as in:

tree–bordered   tree–clad   tree–covered
tree–boring   tree–climbing   tree–crowned

tree-dotted	tree-hopping	tree protector
tree-dwelling	tree-inhabiting	tree-pruning
tree-feeding	tree insulator	tree-ripened
tree-fringed	tree-lined	tree-sawing
tree-garnished	tree-locked	tree-shaded
tree-girt	tree-loving	tree-skirted
tree guard	tree-marked	tree-spraying
tree-haunting	tree-planted	tree tag
tree-hewing	tree planter	treetop
tree holder	tree-planting	tree-trimmer

Tree (trē), **Sir Herbert Beerbohm**, 1853–1917, English actor and impresario.

tree fern Any of various ferns (families *Cyatheaceae* and *Dicksoniaceae*) with large fronds and woody trunks that often attain a treelike size.

tree frog An arboreal amphibian (family *Hylidae*), having the toes dilated with viscous, adhesive disks. Also **tree toad**.

TREE FROG
(Species vary from 1 to 5 inches)

tree heath An evergreen shrub of southern Europe (*Erica arborea*) about 4 feet high, with white flowers: also called *brier*.

tree kangaroo Any of various kangaroos (genus *Dendrolagus*) of Australia and New Guinea adapted for tree-dwelling.

tree·nail (trē'nāl', tren'əl, trun'əl) n. A wooden peg or nail of dry, hard wood which swells when wet, used for fastening timbers, especially in shipbuilding: also *trenail, trunnel*.

tree of heaven A large ornamental tree (*Ailanthus altissima*) of eastern Asia. It has large green flowers, those on the male trees being very ill-scented; ailanthus.

tree of knowledge of good and evil In the Bible, a tree in Eden whose fruit Adam and Eve were forbidden to eat. *Gen.* iii 3, 6. Also **tree of knowledge**.

tree of life 1 Arborvitae. 2 In the Bible: **a** A tree in the garden of Eden whose fruit conferred immortality. *Gen.* iii 22. **b** A similar tree in heaven. *Rev.* xxii 2.

Tree–Plant·er State (trē'plan'tər, -plän'-) Nickname of NEBRASKA.

tree ring A growth ring.

tree sparrow A North American sparrow (*Spizella arborea*) which nests in Canada and migrates southward in winter: also called *Canada sparrow*.

tree surgeon One skilled in tree surgery.

tree surgery The treatment of disease conditions and decay in trees by operative methods.

tref (trāf) adj. Unclean. See KOSHER. Also **tre·fa** (trā'fə). [<Yiddish *tréf* impure, forbidden <Hebrew *teréphāh* an animal torn by wild beasts, lit., that which is torn < *ṭāraf* tear]

tre·foil (trē'foil) n. 1 Any one of the clovers (genus *Trifolium*), so called from the trifoliolate leaves. 2 Certain other plants with trifoliolate leaves, as the black medic. 3 A three-lobed architectural ornamentation. [< AF *trifoil* < *trefeuil* < L *trifolium*]

tre·ha·la (tri-hä'lə) n. Biochem. A carbohydrate substance forming the pupal case of certain weevils (genus *Larixus*) and deposited upon Asian plants of the genus *Echinops*. [<NL <Turkish *tiġálah*]

tre·ha·lose (trē'hə-lōs) n. Biochem. A crystalline disaccharide, $C_{12}H_{22}O_{11}$, elaborated by many fungi and stored as a food reserve instead of starch. [TREHAL(A) + -OSE²]

treil·lage (trā'lij) n. A trellis. [< MF *treille* a bower, trellis, arbor <L *trichila, tricla*]

Treitsch·ke (trīch'kə), **Heinrich von**, 1834–96, German historian and political writer.

trek (trek) v. **trekked, trek·king** v.i. 1 In South Africa, to travel by ox wagon. 2 To travel; migrate. — v.t. 3 In South Africa, to draw (a vehicle or load): said of an ox. — n. 1 An organized migration, as for the founding of a colony. 2 A journey; also, a stage in a journey. 3 The act of pulling. — **Great Trek** The migration of the Boers of Cape Colony across the Vaal, Orange, and Drakenburg rivers (1835–38) which led to the formation of the Orange Free State and the South African Republic. Also spelled *treck*. [<Du. *trekken* draw, travel <MDu. *trecken*,

intensive of *tréken* <OHG *trechan* draw] — **trek'ker** n.

trel·lis (trel'is) n. 1 A crossbarred grating or lattice, used as a screen or a support for vines, etc. 2 A summerhouse or other structure of trelliswork. — v.t. 1 To interlace so as to form a trellis. 2 To furnish with or fasten on a trellis. [<OF *treliz, trelis* <L *trilix, trilicis* of three threads < *tri-* three + *licium* a thread]

trel·lis·work (trel'is-wûrk') n. Latticework.

trem·a·tode (trem'ə-tōd) n. One of a class (*Trematoda*) of typically parasitic flatworms, including the liver flukes. [<NL <Gk. *trematōdēs* perforated < *trēma, -atos* a hole + *eidos* form] — **trem'a·toid** (-toid) adj.

trem·ble (trem'bəl) v.i. **·bled, ·bling** 1 To shake involuntarily, as with fear or weakness; be agitated. 2 To have slight, irregular vibratory motion, as from some jarring force; quiver; shake. 3 To feel anxiety or fear. 4 To quaver, as the voice. See synonyms under QUAKE, SHAKE. — n. 1 The act or state of trembling. 2 *pl.* A debilitating disease of cattle and sheep, possibly caused by eating certain plants, and communicated to man as the milk sickness. [<OF *trembler* <LL *tremulare* < *tremulus* tremulous < *tremere* tremble, shake] — **trem'bler** n. — **trem'bling** adj. & n. — **trem'bling·ly** adv. — **trem'bly** adj.

tre·men·dous (tri-men'dəs) adj. 1 Causing or fitted to cause astonishment by its magnitude, force, etc.: a *tremendous* blow; awe-inspiring; terrible. 2 Colloq. Extraordinarily big; remarkable. See synonyms under FORMIDABLE. [<L *tremendus* to be trembled at < *tremere* tremble] — **tre·men'dous·ly** adv. — **tre·men'dous·ness** n.

trem·e·tol (trem'ə-tōl, -tol) n. An oily, poisonous alcohol isolated from certain plants, as the white snakeroot, and believed to be the cause of trembles in sheep. [<L *tremere* tremble + -OL¹]

trem·o·lite (trem'ə-līt) n. A light-colored calcium-magnesium amphibole, $CaMg_3Si_4O_{12}$. [from *Tremola*, Switzerland, where it was first found + -ITE¹]

trem·o·lo (trem'ə-lō) n. pl. **·los** *Music* 1 A vibrating, beating, or throbbing sound produced vocally or instrumentally. 2 The mechanism for causing this effect in organ tones. [<Ital., trembling <L *tremulus*. See TREMBLE.]

trem·or (trem'ər, trē'mər) n. 1 A quick, vibratory movement caused by an external impulse; a shaking; also, a succession of such movements. 2 Any involuntary quivering or trembling of the body or limbs; a shiver. 3 *Pathol.* An involuntary and continued quivering or shaking of the whole or some part of the body: a form of paralysis. 4 Any trembling, quivering effect. See synonyms under FEAR. [<OF, fear, a trembling <L *tremere* tremble]

trem·u·lant (trem'yə-lənt) adj. Trembling; tremulous: also **trem'u·lent**. — n. A tremolo. [<LL *tremulans, -antis*, ppr. of *tremulare* TREMBLE]

trem·u·lous (trem'yə-ləs) adj. 1 Characterized or affected by trembling: *tremulous* speech. 2 Showing timidity and irresolution. 3 Characterized by mental excitement. [<L *tremulus*. See TREMBLE.] — **trem'u·lous·ly** adv. — **trem'u·lous·ness** n.

tre·nail (trē'nāl, tren'əl, trun'əl) See TREENAIL.

trench (trench) n. 1 A long narrow excavation in the ground; ditch. 2 A long irregular ditch, lined with a parapet of the excavated earth, to protect troops: often with a descriptive word: *communication, reserve, shelter*, or *supply trench*. — v.t. 1 To dig a trench or trenches in. 2 *Mil.* To fortify with trenches; construct trenches against. 3 To cut deep furrows in; ditch. 4 To confine in a trench, as water; entrench. — v.i. 5 To cut or dig trenches. 6 To cut; carve. 7 To encroach. [<OF *trenche* a cutting, gash <*trenchier* cut, ult. <L *truncare* lop off <*truncus* a tree trunk]

Trench (trench), **Richard Chenevix**, 1807–86, English prelate, poet, and philologist.

trench·ant (tren'chənt) adj. 1 Cutting deeply and quickly; sharp: a *trenchant* sword. 2 Figuratively, clear, vigorous, and effective; cutting, as sarcasm. [<OF, ppr. of *trenchier*. See TRENCH.] — **trench'an·cy** n. — **trench'ant·ly** adv.

trench coat A loose-fitting overcoat of rain-

proof fabric with removable lining, several pockets, and a belt.

trench·er¹ (tren'chər) n. 1 A wooden plate formerly used at table; originally, a square piece of board used to cut food on. 2 *Archaic* The food served on trenchers; hence, the table or its pleasures. 3 *Obs.* A thick slice of bread used as a platter. [<AF *trenchour*, OF *tranchouoir* < *trancher*. See TRENCH.]

trench·er² (tren'chər) n. 1 One who digs trenches. 2 One who carves. [<TRENCH, v. + -ER¹]

trench·er·man (tren'chər-mən) n. pl. **·men** (-mən) 1 A feeder; eater; especially, one who enjoys food. 2 A table companion: also **trench'er·mate** (-māt'). 3 A hanger-on; parasite.

trench fever *Pathol.* A remittent rickettsial fever transmitted by body lice and characterized by headache, nausea, high temperature, profuse sweating, muscular pains, and neuralgic pains in the legs. It attacked soldiers assigned to prolonged service in trenches during World War I.

trench foot *Pathol.* A disease of the feet caused by continued dampness and cold, and characterized by discoloration, weakness, and sometimes gangrene.

trench knife A double-edged steel knife with a long blade, used in hand-to-hand combat.

trench mortar Any of various portable, muzzleloading mortars designed for firing a projectile at a high trajectory. Also **trench gun**.

trench mouth *Pathol.* A mildly contagious disease of the mouth, gums, and sometimes the larynx and tonsils, caused by a soil bacillus: Vincent's angina.

TRENCH MORTAR
A. Shell. B. 8 mm. mortar.
a. Base plate. b. Tube. c. Sight. d. Bipod.

trend (trend) v.i. To have or take a general course or direction; incline. — n. General course or direction; bent. [OE *trendan* roll]

trend·y (tren'dē) adj. *Slang* **trend·i·er, trend·i·est** In step with current fashion; voguish. — n. pl. **trend·ies** *Chiefly Brit.* A trendy person or thing. — **trend'i·ness** n.

Treng·ga·nu (treng-gä'noō) A State of Malaya in the southern part on the South China Sea; 5,050 square miles; capital, Kuala Trengganu.

Trent (trent) A city in northern Italy on the Adige: ancient *Tridentum*. Italian **Tren·to** (tren'tō).

Trent (trent) The third longest river of England, flowing 170 miles SE and NE from NW Staffordshire, to a confluence with the Ouse, forming the Humber.

Trent, Council of A council of the Roman Catholic Church, held at intervals in Trent, Italy, from 1545 to 1563: it condemned the leading doctrines of the Reformation.

trente-et-qua·rante (tränt-tā-kȧ-ränt') n. A gambling game played with cards laid out in two rows on a table, the top row representing "black" and the lower, "red." The players, who play against the bank, win if the row of cards they have chosen totals, in pips, nearer 31 than the other. Compare ROUGE ET NOIR. [<F, thirty and forty]

Tren·ti·no (tren-tē'nō) A district around Trent, Italy: that part of the southern Tirol under Italian control.

Tren·ton (tren'tən) The capital of New Jersey, on the Delaware River at the west central border of the State.

Trent River (trent) A river in SE Ontario, Canada, flowing 150 miles south and east to Lake Ontario.

tre·pan¹ (tri-pan') n. 1 An early form of the trephine. 2 A large rock-boring tool. — v.t. **·panned, ·pan·ning** 1 *Mech.* To use a trepan upon. 2 *Surg.* To subject to the operation of trephining. 3 To cut a hole partly through, as the back of a brush, for the insertion of bristles. Also **trep·a·nize** (trep'ə·nīz). [<OF, a borer <Med. L *trepanum* a crown saw <Gk. *trypanon* a borer < *trypaein*

bore] **— trep·a·na·tion** (trep′ə·nā′shən) *n.* **— tre·pan′ner** *n.*

tre·pan[2] (tri·pan′) *Obs.* & *Archaic v.t.* To ensnare. — *n.* A snare; trick; also, a trickster. Also spelled *trapan.* [< thieves' cant *trapan* <TRAP; prob. infl. in form by *trepan*[1]]

tre·pang (tri·pang′) *n.* An East Indian holothurian or sea cucumber, especially *Holothuria marmorata* or a related species: a Chinese delicacy esteemed for soups: also called *bêche-de-mer.* [<Malay *trīpang*]

tre·phine (tri·fīn′, -fēn′) *n. Surg.* A cylindrical saw for removing a piece of bone from the skull, to relieve pressure, etc. — *v.t.* **·phined, ·phin·ing** To operate on with a trephine. [Earlier *trafine* <L *tres fines* three ends; infl. in form by *trepan*[1]]

trep·i·da·tion (trep′ə·dā′shən) *n.* **1** A state of agitation from fear. **2** An involuntary trembling. **3** *Obs.* Confused haste. **4** *Obs.* A vibrating or vibration, as of leaves. Also **tre·pid·i·ty** (tri·pid′ə·tē). See synonyms under FEAR. [<L *trepidatio, -onis* < *trepidatus,* pp. of *trepidare* hurry, be alarmed < *trepidus* alarmed]

trep·o·neme (trep′ə·nēm) *n.* Any of a genus (*Treponema*) of corkscrew-shaped bacteria parasitic in the blood and tissues of animals. *T. pallidum* is the morbific agent of syphilis. [<NL <Gk. *trepein* turn + *nēma* thread] **— trep′o·nem′a·tous** (-nem′ə·təs) *adj.*

tres·pass (tres′pəs, -pas′) *v.i.* **1** *Law* To violate wilfully and forcibly the personal or property rights of another; commit a trespass: with *on* or *upon.* **2** To pass the bounds of propriety or rectitude, to the injury of another; intrude offensively; encroach: with *on* or *upon.* **3** To violate a positive law, rule, or custom: with *against.* — *n.* **1** Any voluntary transgression of law or rule of duty; any offense done to another. **2** *Law* Any wrongful act accompanied with force, either actual or implied, as wrongful entry on another's land, whereby another is injuriously treated; also, an action for trespass. See synonyms under AGGRESSION, ATTACK, OFFENSE. [<OF *trespasser* pass beyond, across <Med. L *transpassare* <L *trans-* across, beyond + *passare* PASS] **— tres′pass·er** *n.*

tress (tres) *n.* **1** A lock, curl, or ringlet of human hair, especially when abundant: applied also, figuratively, to adornment suggesting tresses. **2** *pl.* The hair of a woman or girl, especially when worn loose. [<OF *tresce* <LL *tricia;* ult. origin uncertain] **— tress′y** *adj.*

-tress *suffix* Used in feminine nouns corresponding to masculine nouns in *-ter, -tor:* a contracted form of *-teress, -toress.* Compare -ER[1], -ESS.

tressed (trest) *adj.* Wearing or arranged in tresses; braided; also, curled.

tres·sure (tresh′ər) *n. Her.* A bearing around the edge of a shield; modified or double orle, generally ornamented with fleurs-de-lis. Also **tres′sour.** [<OF *tresseor, tressure* < *tresce* a tress] **— tres′sured** *adj.*

tres·tle (tres′əl) *n.* **1** A beam or bar supported by four divergent legs, for bearing platforms, etc. **2** An open braced framework for supporting the horizontal stringers of a railway bridge, etc. **3** In carpentry, an intervening stud. **4** A trestletree. **5** *pl.* The props of a vessel on the ways. [<OF *trestel* <L *transtrum.* See TRANSOM.]

tres·tle·tree (tres′əl·trē′) *n. Naut.* One of a pair of pieces at right angles to a lower mast, to support the crosstrees, etc.

tres·tle·work (tres′əl·wûrk′) *n.* **1** Trestles collectively. **2** A bridge made of trestles or braced framework, especially of wood. Also **tres′tling.**

tret (tret) *n.* A former allowance to purchasers for waste due to transportation. [<AF, OF *tret,* var. of *traict.* See TRAIT.]

Tre·vel·yan (tri·vel′yən), **George Macaulay,** 1876–1962, English historian; son of the following. **— Sir George Otto,** 1838–1928, English historian and statesman.

Treves (trēvz) The English name for TRIER. *French* **Trèves** (trev).

trev·et (trev′it) See TRIVET.

trev·is (trev′is) *n.* **1** A bar or beam. **2** A crosspiece; partition. [Var. of TRAVERSE]

Tre·vi·so (trā·vē′zō) A city 16 miles NW of Venice in NE Italy: ancient *Tarvisium.*

trews (trōōz) *n. Scot.* Close-fitting tartan trousers. Also spelled *trooz.*

trey (trā) *n.* A card, domino, or die having three spots or pips. ◆ Homophone: *tray.* [<OF *trei, treis* <L *tres* three]

trez tine (trez) The royal tine. Also **tres tine, trey tine.** [Prob. <L *tres* three + TINE[1]]

tri- *prefix* **1** Three; threefold; thrice: *tricycle, trisect.* **2** *Chem.* Containing three (specified) atoms, radicals, groups, etc.: *trioxide, trisulfide.* **3** Occurring every three (specified) intervals, or three times within a (specified) interval: *triweekly.* [<L *tri-* threefold < *tres* three]

tri·a·ble (trī′ə·bəl) *adj.* **1** That may be tried or tested. **2** *Law* That may undergo a judicial examination or determination. **— tri′a·ble·ness** *n.*

tri·ac·id (trī·as′id) *n. Chem.* An acid containing three hydroxyl radicals which are replaceable by acid radicals.

tri·ad (trī′ad) *n.* **1** A group of three persons or things. **2** *Music* A chord of three tones or notes; often the common chord, consisting of a fundamental tone with its third and fifth higher. A **major triad** has a major third and a perfect fifth; a **minor triad** has a minor third and a perfect fifth. **3** *Chem.* **a** A trivalent atom or radical. **b** One of a group of three elements having similar chemical properties, as chlorine, bromine, and iodine. [<L *trias, -adis* <Gk. *trias, -ados* < *treis* three] **— tri·ad′ic** *adj.* & *n.*

tri·age (trī′ij, trē·äzh′) *n. Med.* The sorting out of a group of sick and wounded persons and classifying them according to a system of priorities for the treatment of mass casualties under conditions of limited medical resources and personnel. [<OF < *trier* pick out, sort]

tri·ag·o·nal (trī·ag′ə·nəl) *adj.* Having three angles; triangular. [Var. of TRIGONAL, on analogy with *tetragonal, pentagonal,* etc.]

tri·al (trī′əl, trīl) *n.* **1** The act of testing or proving by experience or use. **2** The state of being tried or tested by suffering: the hour of *trial.* **3** Experimental treatment or action performed to determine a result: to learn by *trial* and error. **4** An experience, person, or thing that puts strength, patience, or faith to the test. **5** An attempt or effort to do something; a try: to make a *trial.* **6** The examination, before a tribunal having assigned jurisdiction, of the facts or law involved in an issue in order to determine that issue. **7** A former method of determining guilt or innocence by subjecting the accused to physical tests of endurance, as by ordeal or by combat with his accuser. **8** *Brit.* An academic or licensing examination. See synonyms under ENDEAVOR, MISFORTUNE, PROOF. **— on trial** In the process of being tried or tested. — *adj.* **1** Of or pertaining to a trial or trials. **2** Made or performed in the course of trying or testing: a *trial* trip. **3** Used in testing: a *trial* specimen. [<AF < *trier* TRY]

trial balance In double-entry bookkeeping, a draft or statement of the debit and credit footings or balances of each account in the ledger.

trial balloon **1** A balloon released in order to test atmospheric and meteorological conditions, as wind velocities, air currents, etc. **2** Any tentative plan or scheme advanced to test public reaction.

trial jury A jury impaneled to try a civil or criminal case: also called *petit* or *petty jury.*

tri·a·morph (trī′ə·môrf) *n.* Any mineral or other substance that crystallizes in three different forms. [<L *tres, tria* three + Gk. *morphē* form] **— tri′a·mor′phous** *adj.*

tri·an·gle (trī′ang′gəl) *n.* **1** *Geom.* A figure, especially a plane figure, bounded by three sides, and having three angles. **2** Something resembling such a figure in shape or arrangement. **3** A flat drawing implement for making parallel or diagonal lines, etc. **4** A group or set of three; a triad. **5** A situation involving three persons: the eternal *triangle.* **6** *Music* A musical instrument of percussion, consisting of a resonant bar bent into a triangle and open at one corner, sounded by being struck with a small metal rod. [<OF <L *triangulum* < *triangulus* three-cornered < *tri-* three + *angulus* an angle]

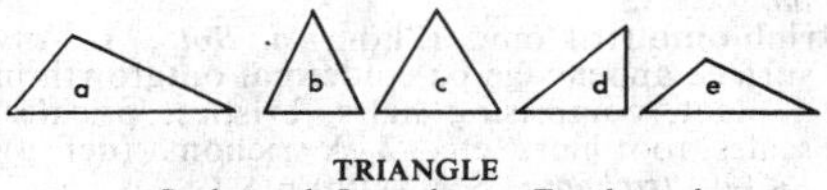

TRIANGLE
a. Scalene. *b.* Isosceles. *c.* Equilateral.
d. Right-angled. *e.* Obtuse.

tri·an·gu·lar (trī·ang′gyə·lər) *adj.* **1** Pertaining to, like, or bounded by a triangle: also **tri′an·gled.** **2** Concerned with or pertaining to three things, parties, or persons. [<LL *triangularis* <L *triangulum* a triangle] **— tri·an′gu·lar′i·ty** (-lar′ə·tē) *n.* **— tri·an′gu·lar·ly** *adv.*

triangular number See under NUMBER.

tri·an·gu·late (trī·ang′gyə·lāt) *v.t.* **·lat·ed, ·lat·ing** **1** To divide into triangles. **2** To survey by triangulation. **3** To give triangular shape to. — *adj.* Marked with triangles. [<L *triangulum* a triangle + -ATE[1]]

tri·an·gu·la·tion (trī·ang′gyə·lā′shən) *n.* The laying out and accurate measurement of a network of triangles, especially on the surface of the earth, as in surveying.

Tri·an·gu·lum (trī·ang′gyə·ləm) *Astron.* A zodiacal constellation. See CONSTELLATION. [<L, a triangle]

tri·ap·si·dal (trī·ap′sə·dəl) *adj. Archit.* Distinguished by or constructed with three apses. [<TRI- + L *apsis, -idis* an apse + -AL]

tri·ar·chy (trī′är·kē) *n. pl.* **·chies** Government by three persons, or a country so governed; a triumvirate. [<Gk. *triarchia* < *tri-* three + *archein* rule]

Tri·as·sic (trī·as′ik) *adj. Geol.* Of or pertaining to the lowest of the three geological periods comprised in the Mesozoic era. — *n.* The Triassic period or rock system, following the Permian and succeeded by the Jurassic. Also **Tri·as** (trī′əs). [<LL *trias.* See TRIAD.]

tri·at·ic stay (trī·at′ik) *Naut.* A device consisting of two pendants connected by a span, and attached respectively to the foremast head and mainmast head of a ship: used principally for hoisting boats in and out of a vessel.

tri·a·tom·ic (trī′ə·tom′ik) *adj. Chem.* **1** Containing only three atoms in the molecule. **2** Containing three replaceable univalent atoms. **3** Trivalent.

tri·ax·i·al (trī·ak′sē·əl) *adj.* Having three axes.

tri·a·zine (trī′ə·zēn, -zin, trī·az′ēn, -in) *n. Chem.* **1** One of three heterocyclic compounds, $C_3H_3N_3$, each having three carbon and three nitrogen atoms in the ring. **2** Any of their derived compounds. Also **tri·a·zin** (trī′ə·zin, trī·az′in). [<TRI- + AZ(O)- + -INE[2]]

tri·a·zo·ic (trī′ə·zō′ik) *adj. Chem.* Hydrazoic. [<TRI- + -AZ(O)- + -IC]

tri·a·zole (trī′ə·zōl, trī·az′ōl) *n.* One of four five-membered ring compounds, $C_2H_3N_3$, in which nitrogen atoms have replaced two CH groups. [<TRI- + AZ(O)- + OLE[1]]

trib·ade (trib′əd) *n.* A female homosexual, especially one who assumes the role of the male; a Lesbian. [<MF <L *tribas, -adis* <Gk. *tribas, -ados* < *tribein* rub]

trib·a·dism (trib′ə·diz′əm) *n.* Homosexual practices between females; Lesbianism.

tri·bal·ism (trī′bəl·iz′əm) *n.* Tribal organization, culture, or relations.

tri·ba·sic (trī·bā′sik) *adj. Chem.* **1** Containing three atoms of hydrogen replaceable by a base or basic radical: said of certain acids. **2** Having three hydroxyl groups in the molecule.

tribe (trīb) *n.* **1** A division, class, or group of people, varying ethnologically according to the circumstances from which their separation or distinction is supposed to originate. **2** Among primitive peoples, a group or aggregation of persons, usually consanguineous and endogamous, under one chief, characterized by its own culture, and having a name, a dialect, a government, and usually a territory of its own: Kaffir *tribes.* **3** In ancient states, an ethnic, hereditary, or political division of a united people: the *tribes* of Athens or of Israel. **4** A division of freeholders with a right to vote in certain of the ancient Roman councils. The Latins, Sabines, and Etruscans

probably represented primitive clan divisions, to which Servius Tullius added a fourth when making his territorial division of Rome. Outside the city the spread of tribal organizations was coincident with the founding of new colonies. 5 A number of persons of any class or profession taken together: often derogatory or contemptuous: the theatrical *tribe.* 6 *Biol.* A group of plants or animals of indefinite rank. 7 Among stockbreeders, the descendants of a particular female bearer through females. See synonyms under PEOPLE. [Fusion of OF *tribu* (<L *tribus* a tribe) and L *tribus*] — **tri′bal** *adj.* — **tri′bal·ly** *adv.*

tribes·man (trībz′mən) *n. pl.* **·men** (-mən) A member of a tribe.

trib·o·e·lec·tric (trib′ō·i·lek′trik) *adj.* Of, pertaining to, or characterized by frictional electricity, as when a glass rod is rubbed with flannel. [< *tribo-* (<Gk. *tribein* rub) + ELECTRIC] — **trib′o·e·lec·tric′i·ty** (-i·lek′tris′ə·tē) *n.*

triboelectric series A grouping of substances in such order that each one may be positively electrified by rubbing with those below it in the series.

trib·o·lu·mi·nes·cence (trib′ō·lo͞o′mə·nes′əns) *n.* Luminescence produced by crushing or grinding certain substances, as glass. [< *tribo-* (<Gk. *tribein* rub) + LUMINESCENCE] — **trib′·o·lu′mi·nes′cent** *adj.*

tri·brach (trī′brak, trib′rak) *n.* In ancient prosody, a foot composed of three short syllables, two of which belong to the thesis and one to the arsis. [<L *tribrachys* <Gk. < *tri-* three + *brachys* short]

tri·brom·eth·a·nol (trī′brom·eth′ə·nōl, -nol) *n. Chem.* A white crystalline compound, $C_2H_3Br_3O$, with an ethereal odor, used as a general anesthetic. Also **tri·bro′mo·eth′a·nol** (trī·brō′mō-).

tri·brom·phe·nol (trī′brom·fē′nōl, -nol) *n. Chem.* A colorless crystalline compound, $C_6H_3Br_3O$: used in medicine as an antiseptic.

trib·u·la·tion (trib′yə·lā′shən) *n.* A condition of affliction and distress; suffering; also, that which causes it. See synonyms under GRIEF, MISFORTUNE. [<OF *tribulacion* <LL *tribulatio, -onis* <L *tribulatus,* pp. of *tribulare* thrash < *tribulum* a threshing floor < *tri-*, root of *terere* rub, grind]

tri·bu·nal (tri·byo͞o′nəl, trī-) *n.* 1 A court of justice; any judicial body, as a board of arbitrators. 2 The seat set apart for judges, magistrates, etc. [<L < *tribunus* TRIBUNE]

trib·u·nate (trib′yə·nit, -nāt) *n.* The office or dignity of a tribune. Also **trib·une·ship** (trib′·yo͞on·ship).

trib·une[1] (trib′yo͞on, *Brit.* trī′byo͞on) *n.* 1 In Roman history, a magistrate chosen by the plebeians to protect them against patrician oppression. 2 One of various civil or military officers of later times; any champion of the people: as the title of a newspaper, often pronounced tri·byo͞on′. [<L *tribunus,* lit., head of a tribe < *tribus* a tribe] — **trib′u·nar′y** (-yə·ner′ē), **trib′u·ni′cial** (-yə·nish′əl), **trib′u·ni′cian** *adj.*

trib·une[2] (trib′yo͞on) *n.* 1 A raised floor for a Roman magistrate's chair. 2 A bishop's throne. 3 A rostrum or platform. [<MF <Ital. *tribuna* <L *tribunal* a tribunal]

trib·u·tar·y (trib′yə·ter′ē) *adj.* 1 Bringing supply; contributory; subsidiary: a *tributary* stream. 2 Offered or due as tribute; having the character of tribute: a *tributary* payment. 3 Paying tribute; hence, subordinate, as a state. —*n. pl.* **·tar·ies** 1 A person or state paying tribute; a dependent. 2 A stream flowing into another; an affluent. [<L *tributarius* < *tributum.* See TRIBUTE.] — **trib′u·tar′i·ly** *adv.* — **trib′u·tar′i·ness** *n.*

trib·ute (trib′yo͞ot) *n.* 1 Money or other valuables paid by one state or ruler to another as an acknowledgment of submission or as the price of peace and protection, or by virtue of some treaty; also, the taxes imposed to raise money to make such payment. 2 The obligation or necessity of making such gift or payment; the state of being tributary. 3 Anything given, paid, or rendered as by a subordinate to a superior; figuratively, that which is due to worth, affection, or duty; contribution; tax; gift; offering; meed: I must render my *tribute* of praise. See synonyms under SUBSIDY, TAX. [<L *tributum,* neut. of *tributus,* pp. of *tribuere* pay, allot]

trice (trīs) *v.t.* **triced, tric·ing** To raise with a rope; also, to tie or lash: usually with *up.* —*n.* An instant: only in the phrase *in a trice.* [< MDu. *trisen* hoist]

tri·cen·ni·al (trī·sen′ē·əl) *adj.* Of or pertaining to the number thirty; taking place every thirtieth year. [<L *tricennium* a period of thirty years < *tricies* thirty times + *annus* a year]

tri·cen·ten·ni·al (trī′sen·ten′ē·əl) *adj.* & *n.* Tercentenary.

tri·ceps (trī′seps) *n. Anat.* A muscle having three heads; specifically, the large muscle at the back of the upper arm, of which the function is to extend the forearm. [<L *triceps, -cipitis* three-headed < *tri-* three + *caput, capitis* a head]

trich- Var. of TRICHO-.

tri·chi·a·sis (tri·kī′ə·sis) *n. Pathol.* 1 A condition of ingrowing hairs about an orifice, especially ingrowing eyelashes. 2 The presence of hairlike filaments in the urine. [<LL *trichiasis* <Gk. < *trichiaein* be hairy < *thrix, trichos* hair]

tri·chi·na (tri·kī′nə) *n. pl.* **·nae** (-nē) A small nematode parasitic worm *(Trichinella spiralis)* that in its larval stage sometimes infests the muscles of man, swine, and other mammals. [<NL <Gk. *trichinos* of hair < *thrix, trichos* hair]

trich·i·nize (trik′ə·nīz) *v.t.* **·nized, ·niz·ing** To infect with trichinae. — **trich′i·ni·za′tion** *n.*

Trich·i·nop·o·ly (trich′ə·nop′ə·lē) See TIRUCHIRAPPALI.

trich·i·no·sis (trik′ə·nō′sis) *n. Pathol.* The disease produced by trichinae in the intestines and muscles of the body. Also **trich′i·ni′a·sis** (-nī′ə·sis). [<TRICHINA + -OSIS] — **trich′i·nosed, trich′i·not′ic** (-not′ik), **trich′i·nous** *adj.*

trich·ite (trik′īt) *n.* 1 *Mineral.* A microscopic crystallite, curved, bent, or zigzag in form, found in volcanic rocks. 2 *Bot.* One of the needle-shaped, radial crystals occurring in starch grains. 3 *Zool.* A rodlike organ surrounding the mouth and gullet of certain ciliate protozoa. [<G *trichit* <Gk. *thrix, trichos* hair] — **tri·chit·ic** (tri·kit′ik) *adj.*

tri·chlo·ride (trī·klôr′īd, -id, -klō′rīd, -rid) *n. Chem.* Any compound having three chlorine atoms in its molecule. Also **tri·chlo·rid** (trī·klôr′id, -klō′rid).

tri·chlo·ro·eth·yl·ene (trī·klôr′ō·eth′əl·ēn, -klō·rō-) *n. Chem.* A colorless, odorless, volatile liquid, C_2HCl_3, used in organic synthesis, in chemical manufactures, and as a general anesthetic. Also **tri′chlor·eth′yl·ene** (trī′klôr-).

tricho- *combining form* Hair; of or resembling a hair or hairs: *trichocyst*: also, before vowels, *trich-* Also **trichi-**. [<Gk. *thrix, trichos* a hair]

trich·o·bac·te·ri·a (trik′ō·bak·tir′ē·ə) *n.* A group of bacteria which includes forms possessing flagella.

trich·o·cyst (trik′ə·sist) *n. Biol.* 1 A stinging capsule containing a protrusible hairlike body: found in various protozoans. 2 A thread cell. — **trich′o·cys′tic** *adj.*

trich·o·gyne (trik′ə·jīn, -jin) *n. Bot.* The slender threadlike portion of the procarp in red algae which receives the male fertilizing bodies. [<TRICHO- + Gk. *gynē* a woman, female]

trich·oid (trik′oid) *adj.* Having the form or appearance of hair. [<Gk. *trichoeidēs* < *thrix, trichos* a hair + *eidos* form]

tri·chol·o·gy (tri·kol′ə·jē) *n.* The sum of knowledge concerning the hair.

tri·cho·ma (tri·kō′mə) *n. pl.* **·ma·ta** (-mə·tə) 1 *Pathol.* a Entropion. b Matted and crusted hair; plica polonica. 2 *Bot.* One of the threads or filaments of filamentous algae: also spelled *trichome.* [<NL <Gk. *trichōma* growth of hair < *trichoein* cover with hair < *thrix, trichos* hair] — **tri·chom′ic** (-kom′ik) *adj.*

trich·ome (trik′ōm, trī′kōm) *n. Bot.* 1 Any surface appendage or epidermal outgrowth in a plant, comprising hairs, bristles, prickles, scales, root hairs, etc. 2 A trichoma (def. 2). [<Gk. *trichōma.* See TRICHOMA.]

Tri·chop·ter·a (tri·kop′tər·ə) *n. pl.* An order of insects including the caddis flies. The aquatic larvae of most species construct cases of sand or other material; the adults are mothlike, with two pairs of hairy wings and well-developed compound eyes. [<NL <Gk. *thrix, trichos* hair + *pteron* a wing]

tri·cho·sis (tri·kō′sis) *n. Pathol.* Any morbid condition of the hair. [<NL <Gk. *trichōsis* growth of hair < *trichoein.* See TRICHOMA.]

tri·chot·o·my (trī·kot′ə·mē) *n.* 1 Division into three parts. 2 *Logic* The threefold division of a genus or class. 3 *Theol.* The division of human nature into body, soul, and spirit. [<Gk. *tricha* threefold + -TOMY] — **trich·o·tom·ic** (trik′ə·tom′ik), **tri·chot′o·mous** *adj.* — **tri·chot′o·mous·ly** *adv.*

tri·chro·ism (trī′krō·iz′əm) *n.* The property of a crystal of transmitting light of different colors in three different directions. [<Gk. *trichroos* of three colors < *tri-* three + *chroia* color, skin] — **tri·chro·ic** (trī·krō′ik) *adj.*

tri·chro·mat·ic (trī′krō·mat′ik) *adj.* Of, pertaining to, having, or using three colors, as the normal eye, the three-color process in photography and printing, etc. Also **tri′chrome, tri·chro·mic** (trī·krō′mik). [<TRI- + CHROMATIC] — **tri·chro′ma·tism** (-mə·tiz′əm) *n.*

trick (trik) *n.* 1 A device for getting an advantage by deception; a petty artifice. 2 A malicious, injurious, or annoying act: a dirty *trick.* 3 A practical joke; prank: the *tricks* of schoolboys. 4 A particular habit or manner; characteristic; trait; also, a vicious habit. 5 A peculiar skill or knack. 6 An act of legerdemain; a feat of jugglery: conjurer's *tricks.* 7 In card games, the whole number of cards played in one round. 8 The turn of one sailor at the helm; a turn or spell of duty; a railroad or factory shift. 9 *Colloq.* A toy; trifle; plaything; a child. See synonyms under ARTIFICE, FRAUD. — **to do** (or **turn**) **the trick** *Slang* To produce the desired result. —*v.t.* 1 To deceive or cheat; delude. 2 To dress or array; adorn: with *up* or *out.* —*v.i.* 3 To practice trickery or deception. See synonyms under DECEIVE. [<AF *trique,* OF *triche* deceit < *trichier* cheat, prob. ult. <L *tricare, tricari* trifle, play tricks < *tricae* trifles, tricks] — **trick′er** *n.* — **trick′less** *adj.*

trick·er·y (trik′ər·ē) *n. pl.* **·er·ies** 1 The practice of tricks; artifice; stratagem; wiles. 2 Dressing up; decorations. See synonyms under DECEPTION.

trick·ing (trik′ing) *n.* The act of dressing up; also, ornaments. —*adj. Obs.* Given to tricks; tricky.

trick·ish (trik′ish) *adj.* Apt to be tricky; partaking of trickery. — **trick′ish·ly** *adv.* — **trick′·ish·ness** *n.*

trick·le (trik′əl) *v.* **·led, ·ling** *v.i.* 1 To flow or run drop by drop or in a very thin stream. 2 To move, come, go, etc., slowly or bit by bit. —*v.t.* 3 To cause to trickle. —*n.* The act or state of trickling, or that which trickles. [ME *triklen,* prob. alter. of *striklen,* freq. of *striken* strike] — **trick′ly** *adj.*

trick·let (trik′lit) *n.* A tiny rill. [Dim. of TRICKLE]

trick·ster (trik′stər) *n.* One who plays tricks; a cheat.

trick·sy (trik′sē) *adj.* 1 Fond of tricks or pranks; mischievous; playful. 2 Given to artifice or stratagem; cunning; crafty. 3 Tending to elude or deceive; illusory. 4 Neat; trim; spruce; smartly attired. — **trick′si·ness** *n.*

trick-track (trik′trak′) *n.* A form of backgammon; specifically, an old form in which pegs as well as pieces were used. Also **tric′-trac′.** [<F *trictrac* <MF, a clicking noise; imit. of the sound of the pieces during a game]

trick·y (trik′ē) *adj.* **trick·i·er, trick·i·est** 1 Disposed to or characterized by trickery; deceitful. 2 Vicious, as an animal. 3 Intricate; requiring or showing adroitness or skill in making: *tricky* clothes. See synonyms under INSIDIOUS. Also *Scot.* **trick′ie.** — **trick′i·ly** *adv.* — **trick′i·ness** *n.*

tri·clin·ic (trī·klin′ik) *adj.* Describing a crystal form having three unequal and dissimilar axes with oblique intersections. [<TRI- + Gk. *klinein* incline + -IC]

tri·clin·i·um (trī·klin′ē·əm) *n. pl.* **·i·a** (-ē·ə) 1 In Roman antiquity, a dining table of four sides, three sides of which were provided with low couches upon which guests could recline. 2 The Roman dining-room. [<L <Gk. *triklinion,* dim. of *triklinos* a dining-room with three couches < *tri-* three + *klinē* a couch]

tri·col·or (trī′kul′ər) *adj.* Having or characterized by three colors: also **tri′col′ored.** —*n.* 1 A flag of three colors; the French national flag of blue, white, and red vertical bands.

2 The tricolor cockade of the French Revolutionists. Also *Brit.* **tri'col'our.** [<F *tricolore* <LL *tricolor* <L *tri-* three + *color* color]
tri·corn (trī'kôrn) *n.* A hat with the brim turned up on three sides, worn during the 17th and 18th centuries by both men and women: used improperly in the form *tricorne* for the two-cornered hat of the French gendarmes. See BICORN. — *adj.* Three-horned; three-pronged; having three hornlike processes. [<F *tricorne* <L *tricornis* three-horned < *tri-* three + *cornu* a horn]
tri·cor·nered (trī'kôr'nərd) *adj.* Three-cornered.
tri·cos·tate (trī·kos'tāt) *adj. Biol.* Having three ribs or costae. [<TRI- + L *costa* a rib + -ATE[1]]
tri·cot (trē'kō, *Fr.* trē·kō') *n.* 1 A hand-knitted or woven fabric, or a machine-made imitation thereof. 2 A soft ribbed cloth. 3 A tight-fitting garment worn by ballet dancers. [<F, knitting < *tricoter* knit, ? ult. <LG *striken* make movements]
tri·crot·ic (trī·krot'ik) *adj. Med.* Having three distinct rhythmic waves in succession, as the pulse: also **tri·cro·tous** (trī'krə·təs). [<TRI- + Gk. *kroteein* knock, beat] — **tri·crot·ism** (trī'krə·tiz'əm) *n.*
tri·cus·pid (trī·kus'pid) *adj.* 1 Having three cusps or points, as a molar tooth or a valve of the heart. 2 Of or pertaining to the tricuspid valve. Also **tri·cus'pi·dal.** [<L *tricuspis, -idis* three-pointed < *tri-* three + *cuspis, -idis* a point]
tri·cus·pi·date (trī·kus'pə·dāt) *adj.* Three-pointed: a *tricuspidate* leaf.
tricuspid valve *Anat.* A three-segmented valve which controls the flow of blood from the right atrium to the right ventricle of the heart.
tri·cy·cle (trī'sik·əl) *n.* 1 A three-wheeled vehicle of the velocipede class. 2 A motorcycle with three wheels. [<F <*tri-* three + Gk. *kyklos* a circle]
tri·cy·clic (trī·sī'klik, -sik'lik) *adj.* Having or characterized by three cycles or identical units of structure: a *tricyclic* chemical compound.
tri·dac·tyl (trī·dak'til) *adj. Anat.* Possessing three fingers or toes. [<Gk. *tridaktylos* < *tri-* three + *daktylos* a digit]
tri·dec·ane (trī·dek'ān) *n. Chem.* A light, colorless, liquid hydrocarbon, $C_{13}H_{28}$, of the methane series, having an odor like turpentine. [<TRI- + DECANE]
tri·dent (trīd'nt) *n.* 1 A three-pronged implement or weapon, the emblem of Neptune (Poseidon); hence, dominion over the sea. 2 The three-pronged spear with which the Roman retiarius was armed. 3 A fishspear with three prongs. 4 *Geom.* A plane cubic curve somewhat resembling a three-pronged spear. — *adj.* Having three teeth or prongs: also **tri·den·tate** (trī·den'tāt), **tri·den'tat·ed.** [<L *tridens, -dentis* < *tri-* three + *dens, dentis* a tooth]
Tri·den·tine (trī·den'tin, -tīn, tri-) *adj.* 1 Pertaining to Trent or to the Council of Trent. 2 Adhering to the decrees of the Council of Trent. — *n.* A Roman Catholic: from the fact that the creed (**Tridentine Creed**) of the Roman Catholic Church as now held was formulated by the Council of Trent. [<Med. L *Tridentinus* <*Tridentum* Trent]
Tri·den·tum (trī·den'təm) The ancient name for TRENT, Italy.
tri·di·men·sion·al (trī'di·men'shən·əl) *adj.* Of three dimensions; having length, breadth, and thickness. — **tri'di·men'sion·al'i·ty** *n.*
tri·di·ur·nal (trī'dī·ûr'nəl) *adj.* Occurring every three days or lasting three days.
tri·e·cious (trī·ē'shəs) See TRIOECIOUS.
tried (trīd) *adj.* 1 Tested; trustworthy, as a friend or a formula. 2 Freed of impurities, as metal or oil. 3 Rendered, as fat.
tri·en·ni·al (trī·en'ē·əl) *adj.* 1 Taking place every third year. 2 Lasting three years. — *n.* 1 A ceremony or event observed or celebrated every three years; a third anniversary. 2 A plant lasting three years. — **tri·en'ni·al·ly** *adv.*
tri·en·ni·um (trī·en'ē·əm) *n. pl.* **·en·ni·ums** or **·en·ni·a** (-en'ē·ə) A period of three years. [<L < *tri-* three + *annus* a year]
Trier (trir) A city of Rhineland-Palatinate, West Germany, on the Moselle river in the central western part near Luxembourg: English *Treves,* French *Trèves.*
tri·er·arch (trī'ər·ärk) *n.* In Greek antiquity, the captain of a trireme; also, at Athens, one who alone or with others fitted out and maintained a trireme. [<L *trierarchus* <Gk. *triērarchos* < *triērēs* a trireme + *archein* rule]
tri·er·ar·chy (trī'ər·är'kē) *n. pl.* **·chies** 1 The command of a trireme. 2 The fitting out and maintaining of a trireme. 3 The body of trierarchs collectively. [<Gk. *triērarchia* < *triērarchos* TRIERARCH]
Tri·este (trē·est', *Ital.* trē·es'tā) An Italian port on the **Gulf of Trieste,** a NE inlet of the Gulf of Venice; formerly an Austrian port and later part of the Free Territory of Trieste.
Trieste, Free Territory of A former free territory, including the city of Trieste and adjoining portions of Istria, constituted by the Italian-Allied peace treaty of 1947; 298 square miles; in 1954 the smaller part (81 square miles, including the city of Trieste) reverted to Italy, and the larger (217 square miles) passed to Yugoslavia.
tri·e·ter·ic (trī'ə·ter'ik) *adj.* Happening every other year. [<L *trietericus* <Gk. *trietērikos* < *trietēris* a festival celebrated every other year < *tri-* three + *etos* a year]
tri·fa·cial (trī·fā'shəl) *adj.* Trigeminal (def. 2).
tri·fid (trī'fid) *adj.* Divided into three parts or sections; three-cleft. [<L *trifidus* < *tri-* three + *fid-*, stem of *findere* split]
tri·fle (trī'fəl) *v.* **·fled, ·fling** *v.i.* 1 To treat something as of no value or importance; dally: with *with.* 2 To act or speak frivolously or idly; jest. 3 To play; toy. 4 To pass time idly; idle. — *v.t.* 5 To pass (time) in an idle and purposeless way. — *n.* 1 Anything of very little value or importance. 2 A light confection, usually made of alternate layers of macaroons or ladyfingers with sugared fruit, covered with a custard and topped with meringue or whipped cream. 3 A variety of pewter. — **a trifle** Slightly; to a small extent: a *trifle* short. [<OF *truffler,* var. of *truffer* deceive, jeer at < *trufle,* dim. of *trufe* a cheating, mockery; ult. origin unknown] — **tri'fler** *n.*
tri·fling (trī'fling) *adj.* 1 Frivolous. 2 Insignificant. See synonyms under CHILDISH, IDLE, INSIGNIFICANT, LITTLE, RIDICULOUS, VAIN. — **tri'fling·ly** *adv.*
tri·fo·cal (trī·fō'kəl) *adj.* 1 Having three foci. 2 *Optics* Pertaining to or describing a lens ground in three segments, for near, intermediate, and far vision respectively.
tri·fold (trī'fōld) *adj.* Triple.
tri·fo·li·ate (trī·fō'lē·it, -āt) *adj. Bot.* Having three leaves or leaflike processes. Also **tri·fo'li·at'ed.** [<TRI- + FOLIATE]
tri·fo·li·o·late (trī·fō'lē·ə·lāt') *adj. Bot.* Having three leaflets.
tri·fo·li·um (trī·fō'lē·əm) *n.* Any of a genus (*Trifolium*) of small plants of the bean family, the clovers, with trifoliolate leaves, and purple, red, white, or yellow flowers. [<NL <L < *tri-* three + *folium* a leaf]
tri·fo·ri·um (trī·fôr'ē·əm, -fō'rē-) *n. pl.* **·fo·ri·a** (-fôr'ē·ə, -fō'rē·ə) *Archit.* A gallery above the arches of the nave in a church. [<Med. L <L *tri-* three + *foris* a door] — **tri·fo'ri·al** *adj.*

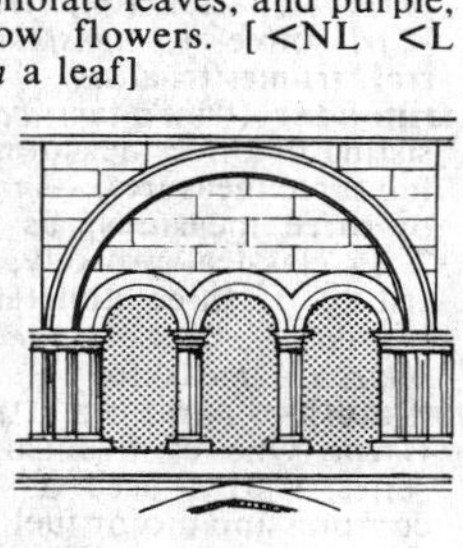
TRIFORIUM

tri·formed (trī'fôrmd') *adj.* 1 Having three forms or shapes. 2 Consisting of three parts or divisions. Also **tri'·form.** — **tri·form'i·ty** *n.*
tri·fur·cate (trī·fûr'kāt) *adj.* Three-forked; trichotomous. Also **tri·fur'cat·ed.** — **tri·fur·ca·tion** (trī'fər·kā'shən) *n.*
trig[1] (trig) *adj.* 1 Characterized by tidiness; trim; neat. 2 Strong; sound; firm. 3 In a depreciative sense, correct; precise; prim. 4 Faithful; trustworthy; dependable. 5 Active; alert. 6 Full; inflated. — *v.t.* **trigged, trig·ging** To make trig or neat; dress finely or smartly: often with *out* or *up.* [<ON *tryggr* true, trusty] — **trig'ly** *adv.* — **trig'ness** *n.*
trig[2] (trig) *v.t.* **trigged, trig·ging** 1 To check, as with a skid; obstruct; stop. 2 To shore; prop. — *n.* A check or brake, as a skid or drag for a wheel. [? <ON *tryggja* make firm]
tri·gem·i·nal (trī·jem'ə·nəl) *adj.* 1 Being in three parts; threefold; triple. 2 Of or pertaining to the trigeminus: *trigeminal* neuralgia. — *n.* The trigeminus. [<L *trigeminus* born three at a time < *tri-* three + *geminus* a twin]
tri·gem·i·nus (trī·jem'ə·nəs) *n. pl.* **·ni** (-nī) *Anat.* The fifth cranial or trifacial nerve, the great nerve of sensation for the face and head. [<NL <L. See TRIGEMINAL.]
trig·ger[1] (trig'ər) *n.* 1 The fingerpiece of a gunlock or pistol-lock, for releasing the hammer. 2 A catch or other small lever doing similar service in a trap or other mechanism. — **quick on the trigger** 1 Quick to shoot. 2 Quick to act in response to a suggestion; quick-witted; alert. — *v.t.* To cause or precipitate. [Earlier *tricker* <Du. *trekker* < *trekken* pull, tug at]
trig·ger[2] (trig'ər) *n. Dial.* A skid or trig. [< TRIG[2] + -ER]
trig·ger·fish (trig'ər·fish') *n. pl.* **·fish** or **·fish·es** A plectognath fish (genus *Balistes*) found mainly in the tropical Pacific region, with an ovate body covered with large, rough scales: named from the triggerlike second spine of the dorsal fin.

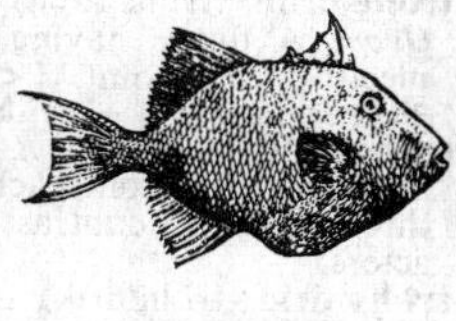
TRIGGERFISH
(About 12 inches long)

tri·glyph (trī'glif) *n. Archit.* An ornament in a Doric frieze consisting of a tablet with three parallel vertical channels or glyphs, and standing on each side of the metopes. [<L *triglyphus* <Gk. *triglyphos* thrice grooved < *tri-* three + *glyphē* a carving < *glyphein* carve, engrave]
tri·glyph·ic (trī·glif'ik) *adj.* 1 Pertaining to or consisting of triglyphs. 2 Having three groups of characters or carvings. Also **tri'·glyph·al, tri·glyph'i·cal.**
tri·go (trē'gō) *n. Spanish* Wheat.
tri·gon (trī'gon) *n.* 1 A triangle; especially, the triangle of reference used in trilinear coordinates. 2 One of four parts of the zodiac, each consisting of three signs. 3 In Greek and Roman antiquity, a lyre or harp of triangular form. [<L *trigonum* <Gk. *trigōnon,* orig. neut. of *trigōnos* three-angled < *tri-* three + *gōnia* an angle]
trig·o·nal (trig'ə·nəl) *adj.* 1 Pertaining to or in the form of a trigon; triangular; three-cornered. 2 Characterized, in the hexagonal crystal system, by having a principal (vertical) axis of threefold symmetry. Also **trig'o·nous.** — **trig'o·nal·ly** *adv.*
trig·o·nom·e·ter (trig'ə·nom'ə·tər) *n.* 1 An instrument for solving triangles mechanically. 2 *Obs.* An expert in trigonometry.
trigonometric functions Certain functions of an angle or arc used in trigonometry. The most commonly used are: sine, cosine, tangent, cotangent, secant, cosecant. In illustration *A* the functions of the angle θ are defined as ratios or fractions. They are:

$$\text{sine } \theta = \frac{AB}{AC} \qquad \text{cosecant } \theta = \frac{AC}{AB}$$
$$\text{cosine } \theta = \frac{CB}{AC} \qquad \text{secant } \theta = \frac{AC}{CB}$$
$$\text{tangent } \theta = \frac{AB}{CB} \qquad \text{cotangent } \theta = \frac{CB}{AB}$$

The functions may be represented also as lines by constructing the reference triangle in a circle whose radius is taken as unity, and drawing additional lines as in *B.* The *sine* is then AB, the *cosine* CB, the *tangent* ED, the *cotangent* GF, the *secant* CE, and the *cosecant* CF.

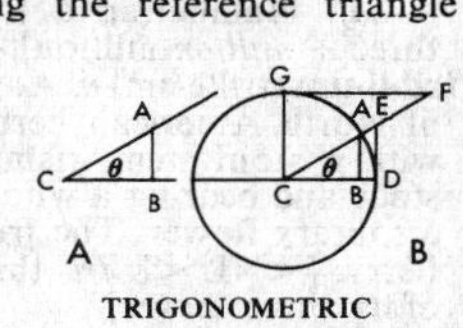

TRIGONOMETRIC FUNCTIONS

These are all spoken of as the sine, cosine, etc., of the arc AD as well as of the angle θ. Other, less common, trigonometric functions are: versed sine, coversed sine, exsecant, and

haversine. These functions are expressed as follows:

versed sine θ (or versine θ) = 1 – cosine θ
coversed sine θ (or versed cosine θ) = 1 – sine θ
exsecant θ = secant θ – 1
haversine θ = 1/2 versine θ

trig·o·nom·e·try (trig′ə·nom′ə·trē) *n.* The branch of mathematics that treats of the relations of the sides and angles of triangles and of the methods of applying these relations in the solution of problems involving triangles: widely used in navigation, surveying, etc. [<NL *trigonometria* <Gk. *trigōnon* a triangle + *metron* measure] —**trig·o·no·met·ric** (trig′ə·nō·met′rik) or **·ri·cal** *adj.* —**trig′o·no·met′ri·cal·ly** *adv.*

tri·graph (trī′graf, -gräf) *n.* A group of three letters representing one articulate sound: *eau* in *beau*; also, the sound thus represented. [<TRI- + -GRAPH] —**tri·graph′ic** *adj.*

tri·he·dron (trī·hē′drən) *n.* *pl.* **·dra** (-drə) *Geom.* A figure having three plane surfaces meeting at a point. [<NL <Gk. *tri-* three + *hedra* a base] —**tri·he′dral** *adj.*

tri·hy·brid (trī·hī′brid) *n. Biol.* A hybrid whose parents differ from each other in respect to three pairs of contrasting Mendelian characters.

tri·hy·dric (trī·hī′drik) *adj. Chem.* Pertaining to or designating a compound containing three hydroxyl groups. Also **tri·hy·drox·y** (trī′hī·drok′sē). [<TRI- + HYDR(OXYL) + -IC]

tri·ju·gate (trī′jo͞o·gāt, trī·jo͞o′gāt, -git) *adj. Bot.* Having three pairs of leaflets. Also **tri·ju·gous** (trī′jo͞o·gəs, trī·jo͞o′gəs). [<L *trijugus* threefold <*tri-* three + *jugum* a yoke]

tri·lat·er·al (trī·lat′ər·əl) *adj.* Having three sides. [<L *trilaterus* <*tri-* three + *latus, lateris* a side] —**tri·lat′er·al·ly** *adv.*

tril·by (tril′bē) *n.* A soft felt hat with indented crown: informal wear for men in Great Britain. [after *Trilby*, a novel (1894) by George Du Maurier, in which such hats are described]

tri·lin·e·ar (trī·lin′ē·ər) *adj.* Pertaining to, referring to, or bounded by three lines.

tri·lin·gual (trī·ling′gwəl) *adj.* Derived from, composed of, or using three languages: a *trilingual* discourse. Also **tri·lin′guar.** [<L *trilinguis* <*tri-* three + *lingua* a tongue]

tri·lit·er·al (trī·lit′ər·əl) *adj.* Consisting of three letters. —**tri·lit′er·al·ism** *n.*

trill[1] (tril) *v.t.* **1** To sing or play in a quavering or tremulous tone. **2** *Phonet.* To articulate with a trill. —*v.i.* **3** To utter, make, or give forth a quavering or tremulous sound. **4** *Music* To execute a trill or shake. —*n.* **1** A tremulous utterance of successive tones, as of certain insects or birds; a warble. **2** *Music* A quick alternation of two notes either a tone or a semitone apart; shake. **3** *Phonet.* A rapid vibration of a speech organ, as of the tip of the tongue against the alveolar ridge or the uvula against the back of the tongue, as in the articulation of *rr* in Spanish. **4** A consonant or word so uttered. Also spelled *thrill.* [<Ital. *trillare*, prob. <Gmc.]

trill[2] (tril) *v.t.* & *v.i. Archaic* **1** To flow or cause to flow in a trickle, as tears. **2** To turn or roll; also, to quiver. [ME *trillen* <Scand. Cf. Sw. & Norw. *trilla* roll.]

tril·ling (tril′ing) *n.* A compound crystal made up of three individuals. [Cf. Dan. *trilling* a triplet]

tril·lion (tril′yən) *n.* A cardinal number; in the French and United States system of numeration, 1 followed by 12 zeros; in the English and German system, 1 followed by 18 zeros. —*adj.* Numbering a trillion. [<MF <*tri-* three + *million* million] —**tril′lionth** *adj.* & *n.*

tril·li·um (tril′ē·əm) *n.* Any of a genus *(Trillium)* of North American herbs of the lily family, with a stout stem, rising from a short rootstock and bearing a whorl of three leaves and a solitary flower. The fruit is a red or purple berry. [<NL <L *tri-* three; so called because of its three leaves]

tri·lo·bate (trī·lō′bāt, trī′lə·bāt) *adj.* **1** Three-lobed. **2** *Bot.* Having three lobes, as some leaves. Also **tri·lo′bal, tri·lo′bat·ed, tri′lobed.**

tri·lo·bite (trī′lə·bīt) *n. Paleontol.* Any of a subclass or group *(Trilobita)* of early Paleozoic marine arthropods related to the crustaceans, having a flattened body divided into a variable number of segments covered by a hard dorsal shield marked in three lobes. [<NL *Trilobites* <Gk. *tri-* three + *lobos* a lobe] —**tri′lo·bit′ic** (-bit′ik) *adj.*

tri·loc·u·lar (trī·lok′yə·lər) *adj.* Having three cells or chambers. [<TRI- + L *loculus* a small receptacle, dim. of *locus* a place]

tril·o·gy (tril′ə·jē) *n.* *pl.* **·gies** A group of three literary or dramatic compositions, each complete in itself, but continuing the same general subject. [<Gk. *trilogia* <*tri-* three + *logos* a discourse]

trim (trim) *v.* **trimmed, trim·ming** *v.t.* **1** To put in or restore to order; make neat by clipping, pruning, etc. **2** To remove by cutting: usually with *off* or *away.* **3** To put ornaments on; decorate. **4** In carpentry, to smooth; dress. **5** *Colloq.* **a** To chide; rebuke. **b** To punish or thrash; beat. **c** To defeat. **d** To cheat; victimize. **6** *Naut.* **a** To adjust (sails or yards) for sailing. **b** To cause (a ship) to sit well in the water by adjusting cargo, ballast, etc. **7** *Aeron.* To bring (an airplane) to level or balanced flight by adjusting control surfaces. **8** *Obs.* To furnish; equip. —*v.i.* **9** *Naut.* **a** To be or remain in equilibrium: said of a ship. **b** To adjust sails or yards for sailing. **10** To act so as to appear to favor opposing sides in a controversy. —*n.* **1** State of adjustment or preparation; fitting condition; orderly disposition: All was in good *trim.* **2** Condition as to general appearance; dress; style. **3** *Naut.* Fitness for sailing: said of a vessel in reference to disposition of ballast, masts, cargo, etc. **4** *Naut.* Actual or comparative degree of immersion: said of a vessel. **5** Particular character or nature; kind; stripe. **6** The moldings, etc., as about the doors of a building; also, the hardware trimmings of a house, such as hinges, window fastenings, etc. **7** Ornament; trapping; dress. **8** Material rejected or cut out, as sections from a motion-picture film. **9** In advertising, window dressing or display. **10** The interior furnishings of an automobile body. **11** *Aeron.* The position of an aircraft relative to balanced flight. —*adj.* **trim·mer, trim·mest** **1** Adjusted to a nicety; being in perfect order; handsomely equipped or of stylish and smart appearance; spruce; precise; jaunty. **2** Excellently fit; nice; pretty; fine. See synonyms under NEAT[1], STAUNCH. —*adv.* In a trim manner: also **trim′ly.** [OE *trymman* arrange, strengthen <*trum* steadfast, strong] —**trim′ness** *n.*

tri·mer (trī′mər) *n. Chem.* A compound formed by the union of three molecules of another compound or substance, as benzene from acetylene. [<TRI- + Gk. *meros* a part]

trim·er·ous (trim′ər·əs) *adj.* **1** Composed of three similar parts. **2** *Bot.* Three-parted. **3** *Entomol.* Having three joints, as the tarsus of an insect: often written 3-*merous.* [<TRI- + Gk. *meros* a part]

tri·mes·ter (trī·mes′tər) *n.* A three-month period; quarter. [<F *trimestre* <L *trimestris* <*tri-* three + *mensis* a month] —**tri·mes′·tral, tri·mes′tri·al** *adj.*

trim·e·ter (trim′ə·tər) *adj.* In prosody, consisting of three measures or of lines containing three measures. —*n.* **1** A verse consisting of three measures, as the iambic trimeter. **2** In classical prosody, a line or verse consisting of three dimeters, or six feet. [<L *trimetrus* <Gk. *trimetros* <*tri-* three + *metron* a measure]

tri·meth·yl·pen·tane (trī′meth·il·pen′tān) *n. Chem.* One of five isomers of the pentane series, C_8H_{18}, used as a solvent and high-compression motor fuel. Also called *isooctane.* Compare OCTANE NUMBER. [<TRI- + METHYL + PENTANE]

tri·met·ric (trī·met′rik) *adj.* **1** Trimeter. **2** Orthorhombic. Also **tri·met′ri·cal.**

trimetric projection *Geom.* A three-dimensional geometric projection in which each dimension is measured on a separate scale and according to arbitrarily assigned angles.

tri·met·ro·gon (trī·met′rə·gon) *n.* A high-speed system of aerial topographic photography, in which a unit of three cameras takes simultaneous pictures of one area, from three positions, one vertical and two at matching oblique angles. —*adj.* Of or pertaining to this system or camera unit. [<TRI- + METRO- + -GON]

trim·mer (trim′ər) *n.* **1** One who or that which trims. **2** A time-server. **3** *Brit.* One who keeps the balance between opposing political parties by throwing his support from one to the other. **4** A small horizontal beam, as in a floor, into which the ends of one or more joists are framed. **5** A tool or machine with which to trim; specifically, a large table with power saw used to trim lumber for buildings.

trim·ming (trim′ing) *n.* **1** Something added for ornament or to give a finished appearance or effect. **2** Material attached to a garment, etc., for ornamentation or effect. **3** *pl.* Articles or equipment; fittings, as the hardware of a house. **4** *pl.* The usual or proper accompaniments or condiments of an article or food. **5** *pl.* That which is removed by trimming, cutting, or clipping; in shearing, wool from the shanks. **6** A severe reproof or a chastisement; flogging; beating. **7** *Colloq.* A defeat. **8** The act of one who trims.

tri·mo·lec·u·lar (trī′mə·lek′yə·lər) *adj. Chem.* Having, consisting of, or pertaining to three molecules.

tri·month·ly (trī·munth′lē) *adj.* & *adv.* Done or occurring every third month.

tri·morph (trī′môrf) *n.* **1** A substance existing or occurring in three forms. **2** One of the forms in which such a substance exists. [<Gk. *trimorphos* having three forms <*tri-* three + *morphē* a form]

tri·mor·phism (trī·môr′fiz·əm) *n.* **1** *Bot.* The existence on the same plant of three distinct forms of flowers as regards the relative lengths of stamens and pistils. **2** *Mineral.* The property of crystallizing in three series of fundamentally different forms with the same ultimate chemical composition. **3** *Zool.* Difference of species in form, color, etc., characterizing three distinct types. —**tri·mor′phic, tri·mor′phous** *adj.*

Tri·mur·ti (tri·mo͝or′tē) *n.* In Hindu mythology, the triad of the Vedas, consisting of Brahma (the Creator), Vishnu (the Preserver), and Siva (the Destroyer). [<Skt. *trimūrti* <*tri-* three + *mūrti* shape]

Tri·na·cri·a (tri·nā′krē·ə, trī-) Ancient name for SICILY. —**Tri·na′cri·an** *adj.*

tri·nal (trī′nəl) *adj.* **1** Of or pertaining to three. **2** Having three parts; threefold. [<LL *trinalis* <L *trinus* three each <*tres, tria* three]

tri·na·ry (trī′nər·ē) *adj.* Made up of three parts or proceeding by threes; ternary. [<LL *trinarius* of three kinds <L *trinus.* See TRINAL.]

Trin·co·ma·lee (tring′kō·mə·lē′) **1** A port of NE Ceylon, capital of its eastern province and of Trincomalee district. **2** A district of NE Ceylon; 1,165 square miles.

trin·dle (trin′dəl) *n.* **1** One of several forked pieces of wood or metal between the cords and boards of a book to flatten its front and back edges before cutting. **2** *Brit. Dial.* A wheel, especially of a barrow. **3** A large wooden tub. —*v.t.* **1** *Brit. Dial.* To trundle; roll. —*v.i. Brit. Dial.* **2** To travel easily and rapidly. **3** To roll; advance by rolling. Also **trin′tle** (-təl). [ME *trindel*, var. of OE *trendel* a circle]

trine[1] (trīn) *adj.* **1** Threefold; triple: also *trinal.* **2** In astrology, relating to or situated in trine; auspicious. —*n.* **1** A compound in three parts or elements; a trio; triad. **2** *Her.* A charge composed of three objects. **3** In astrology, the aspect of two planets when 120° apart. —*v.t. Obs.* In astrology, to place or join in trine. [<OF *trin, trine* <L *trinus.* See TRINAL.]

trine[2] (trīn) *v.i. Obs.* To proceed; go. [<Scand. Cf. OSw. *trina* tramp.]

Trine (trīn) *n.* The Trinity.

Trin·i·dad and To·ba·go (trin′ə·dad, tō·bā′gō, *Span.* trē′nē·thäth′) An independent member of the Commonwealth of Nations, in the West Indies NE of Venezuela, comprising the islands of **Trinidad;** 1,864 square miles; and **Tobago;** 116 square miles; capital, Port-of-Spain, on Trinidad.

Tri·nil man (trē′nil) *Paleontol.* Pithecanthropus. [from *Trinil*, Java, where remains were found]

Trin·i·tar·i·an (trin′ə·târ′ē·ən) *adj.* **1** Of or pertaining to the Trinity. **2** Holding or professing belief in the Trinity: distinguished from *Unitarian.* —*n.* A believer in the doctrine of the Trinity. [<NL *trinitarius* <LL *trinitas* TRINITY] —**Trin′i·tar′i·an·ism** *n.*

tri·ni·trate (trī·nī′trāt) *n. Chem.* A nitrate containing three nitric-acid radicals in combination: bismuth *trinitrate.*

tri·ni·tro·ben·zene (trī·nī′trō·ben′zēn) *n. Chem.* A yellow crystalline compound, $C_6H_3(NO_2)_3$,

occurring in three forms, one of which is highly explosive.

tri·ni·tro·cre·sol (trī·nī′trō·krē′sōl, -sol) *n. Chem.* A yellow crystalline organic compound, $C_8H_8N_3O_7$, used as an explosive. [<TRI- + NITRO- + CRESOL]

tri·ni·tro·phe·nol (trī·nī′trō·fē′nōl, -nol) *n.* Picric acid. [<TRI- + NITROPHENOL]

tri·ni·tro·tol·u·ene (trī·nī′trō·tol′yo͞o·ēn) *n. Chem.* A high explosive, $C_7H_5N_3O_6$, made by treating toluene with nitric acid: used for filling high explosive shells, for it melts readily and can be poured safely and rapidly: also called *TNT, trotyl.* Also **tri·ni′tro·tol′u·ol** (-yo͞o·ōl, -ol). [<TRI- + NITRO- + TOLUENE]

trin·i·ty (trin′ə·tē) *n. pl.* **·ties 1** In art, a symbolic representation of the Trinity. **2** The state or character of being three; also, any union of three parts or elements in one; a trio; triad. [<OF *trinite* <LL *trinitas* <L, a triad < *trinus.* See TRINAL.]

Trin·i·ty (trin′ə·tē) *n.* **1** *Theol.* A threefold personality existing in the one divine being or substance; the union in one God of Father, Son, and Holy Spirit as three infinite persons. **2** Trinity Sunday.

Trinity, Cape A cliff on the lower Saguenay River, SE central Quebec, Canada; 1,500 feet high.

Trinity River A river in Texas, flowing 510 miles SE to **Trinity Bay,** the NE arm of Galveston Bay.

Trinity Sunday *Eccl.* The eighth Sunday after Easter, observed as a festival in honor of the Trinity. Also *Trinity.*

trin·ket (tring′kit) *n.* **1** Any small ornament, as of jewelry. **2** Any small article forming part of an outfit. **3** A trifle; a trivial object; a toy. **4** *Obs.* A knife. See synonyms under GAUD. [<AF *trenquet,* OF *trenchet* a toy knife, ornament, < *trenchier.* See TRENCH.]

trin·kums (tring′kəmz) *n. pl. Scot. & Brit. Dial.* Small ornaments; trinkets. Also **trin′·kum-tran′kums** (-trang′kəmz). [Appar. alter. of TRINKET]

tri·no·dal (trī·nōd′l) *adj. Bot.* Having three nodes or nodal points.

tri·no·mi·al (trī·nō′mē·əl) *adj.* **1** *Biol.* Of, having, or employing three terms or names—the generic, the specific, and the subspecific or varietal, as *Lynx rufus texensis,* the Texas bobcat. **2** *Math.* Consisting of three terms connected by plus or minus signs or both. —*n.* **1** An algebraic expression consisting of three terms connected by plus or minus signs or both, as $3x + y - 27z$. **2** A trinomial name. Also **tri·nom′i·nal** (-nom′ə·nəl), **tri·on′·y·mal** (-on′ə·məl). [<TRI- + (BI)NOMIAL]

tri·o (trē′ō, *for def. 1 also* trī′ō) *n. pl.* **tri·os 1** Any three things grouped or associated together. **2** *Music* **a** A composition for three performers. **b** The second part of a minuet or scherzo, of a march, and of dance forms generally. **c** A group of three musicians who render trios. [<F <Ital. < *tre* three <L *tres, tria*]

tri·ode (trī′ōd) *n. Electronics* A three-element vacuum tube, containing an anode, cathode, and a control grid or electrode. [<TRI- + (ELECTR)ODE]

tri·oe·cious (trī·ē′shəs) *adj. Bot.* Having in different plants of the same species male, female, and hermaphrodite flowers: also spelled *triecious.* Also **tri·oi′cous** (-oi′kəs). [<NL *Trioecia,* order name <Gk. *tri-* three + *oikos* a house] —**tri·oe′cious·ly** *adv.*

tri·o·let (trī′ə·lit) *n.* A stanza of eight lines on two rimes, the first line repeated as the fourth and seventh and the second as the eighth. Its rime scheme is *abaaabab.* [<F, dim. of *trio* TRIO]

Tri·o·nal (trī′ə·nal) *n.* Proprietary name for a brand of sulfonethylmethane.

tri·ose (trī′ōs) *n. Biochem.* A monosaccharide whose molecule contains three atoms of carbon and three of oxygen. [<TRI- + -OSE[2]]

tri·ox·ide (trī·ok′sīd, -sid) *n. Chem.* An oxide containing three atoms of oxygen in combination: iron *trioxide,* Fe_2O_3. Also **tri·ox′·id** (-sid).

trip (trip) *n.* **1** A short journey; excursion; jaunt. **2** A misstep or stumble occasioned by losing the balance or striking the foot against an object. **3** An active, nimble step or movement. **4** The number of fish caught in an excursion. **5** A single tack to windward. **6** *Mech.* A pawl or similar device that trips, or the action of such a device. **7** A sudden catch, especially of the legs and feet, as of a wrestler. **8** A blunder; mistake. **9** *Slang* **a** The hallucinations and other sensations experienced by a person taking a psychedelic drug. **b** Any intense, usually personal experience. See synonyms under JOURNEY. —*v.* **tripped, trip·ping** *v.i.* **1** To stumble. **2** To move quickly with light or small steps; saunter. **3** To commit an error; make a false step; go astray. **4** *Mech.* To run past the nicks or dents in the ratchet escape wheel of a timepiece. **5** *Slang* To experience the effects of a psychedelic drug: often with *out.* —*v.t.* **6** To cause to stumble: often with *up.* **7** To detect and expose in an error; defeat the purpose of. **8** To perform (a dance) lightly. **9** *Mech.* To set free or in operation by releasing a stay, catch, trigger, etc. **10** *Naut.* **a** To loosen, as an anchor, from the bottom by a long rope or cable. **b** To hoist (the topmast) so as to prepare it for being lowered. **c** To tilt (a yard) similarly. [OF *treper, triper* leap, trample, ? <MDu. *trippen* trip, hop]

tri·pal·mi·tin (trī·pal′mə·tin) *n.* Palmitin.

tri·par·tite (trī·pär′tīt) *adj.* **1** Divided into three parts or divisions; threefold: a *tripartite* leaf: also **tri·part·ed** (trī′pär·tid). **2** *Law* Pertaining to or executed between three parties. **3** *Math.* Homogeneous in three sets of variables. [<L *tripartitus* < *tri-* three + *partitus,* pp. of *partiri* divide] —**tri·par′tite·ly** *adv.*

tri·par·ti·tion (trī′pär·tish′ən) *n.* Division into three parts, into thirds, or among three.

tripe (trīp) *n.* **1** A part of the stomach of a ruminant, as the ox, used for food. **2** *Colloq.* Contemptible or worthless stuff; an inferior, mean, or offensive thing. [<OF *tripe, trippe* <Arabic *tharb* entrails, a net]

tri·pe·dal (trī′pə·dəl, trī·pēd′l, trip′ə·dəl) *adj.* Having three feet; three-footed. [<L *tripedalis* < *tri-* three + *pes, pedis* foot]

tri·per·son·al (trī·pûr′sən·əl) *adj.* Consisting of or relating to three persons.

tri·per·son·al·i·ty (trī·pûr′sən·al′ə·tē) *n. Theol.* The state or quality of existing in three persons in one Godhead; trinity.

tri·pet·al·ous (trī·pet′l·əs) *adj. Bot.* Having three petals.

trip hammer A heavy power hammer that is raised or tilted by a cam and then allowed to drop: also called *tilt hammer.*

tri·phase (trī′fāz) *adj. Electr.* Having or employing three phases, as in an alternating current.

tri·phen·yl·meth·ane (trī·fen′əl·meth′ān) *n. Chem.* A hydrocarbon, $(C_6H_5)_3CH$, occurring in colorless leaflets: used in organic synthesis and in the manufacture of dyes. [<TRI- + PHENYL + METHANE]

tri·phib·i·an (trī·fib′ē·ən) *adj.* Describing a joint military and naval operation which utilizes terrestrial, marine, and aerial weapons.

triph·thong (trif′thông, -thong, trip′-) *n.* **1** A combination of three vowel sounds in one syllable, as in one pronunciation of *fire.* **2** A trigraph composed of vowels, as in *beau.* [<TRI- + (DI)PHTHONG] —**triph·thon′gal** *adj.*

triph·y·lite (trif′ə·līt) *n.* A greenish-gray, bluish, transparent to translucent phosphate of iron and lithium, crystallizing in the orthorhombic system. Also **triph′y·line** (-lin, -lēn). [<TRI- + Gk. *phylē* a tribe + -ITE[1]; so called because it contains three bases]

tri·pin·nate (trī·pin′āt) *adj. Bot.* Thrice pinnate, as when the pinnae of a bipinnate leaf become again pinnate in certain ferns. Also **tri·pin′nat·ed.** —**tri·pin′nate·ly** *adv.*

tri·pin·nat·i·fid (trī′pə·nat′ə·fid) *adj. Bot.* Tripinnately cleft. [<TRIPINNATE + -FID]

tri·plane (trī′plān′) *n.* An airplane having three supporting surfaces arranged one above the other.

trip·le (trip′əl) *v.* **·led, ·ling** *v.t.* **1** To make threefold in number or quantity. —*v.i.* **2** To be or become three times as many or as large. **3** In baseball, to make a triple. —*adj.* **1** Consisting of three things united or of three parts; threefold. **2** Multiplied by three; thrice said or done. **3** *Archaic* Third. —*n.* **1** A set or group of three. **2** In baseball, a three-base hit. [<MF <L *triplus* <Gk. *triploos* threefold. Doublet of TREBLE.] —**trip′ly** *adv.*

Triple Alliance 1 An alliance between England, Holland, and Sweden against Louis XIV of France, formed in 1668. **2** A league between England, France, and Holland, formed in 1717, but called **Quadruple** when joined by Austria in 1718, designed to secure the succession to the crown of England for the house of Hanover, that of France for the house of Bourbon, and to prevent the union of France and Spain under one crown. **3** An alliance formed in 1795 between Austria, Great Britain, and Russia against France. **4** A Dreibund.

Triple Entente A friendly understanding formed between Great Britain, France, and Russia prior to World War I to counteract the Dreibund.

trip·le-ex·pan·sion (trip′əl·ik·span′shən) *adj.* Designating a compound steam engine constructed with three cylinders of graduated sizes in which the steam is successively expanded.

triple measure *Music* A measure of three beats, the first accented, the second and third unaccented.

trip·le-nerved (trip′əl·nûrvd′) *adj. Bot.* Three-nerved; having three principal nerves arising from or near the base, as certain leaves.

triple play In baseball, a play during which three men are put out.

trip·let (trip′lit) *n.* **1** A group of three of a kind. **2** One of three children born at one birth. **3** A group of three rimed lines. **4** *Music* A group of three notes performed in the time of two. **5** A bicycle for three. [<TRIPLE, on analogy with *doublet*]

trip·le·tail (trip′əl·tāl′) *n.* A large edible marine fish (*Lobotes surinamensis*) of warm seas, with soft dorsal and anal fins extended backward, suggesting additional tails.

triple time See under TIME.

triple voile Ninon.

tri·plex (trī′pleks, trip′leks) *adj.* Having three parts; threefold. —*n. Music* Triple measure. [<L < *tri-* three + *plicare* fold]

trip·li·cate (trip′lə·kit) *adj.* Threefold; made in three copies. —*n.* A third thing corresponding to two others of the same kind or three similar things collectively: a document signed in *triplicate.* —*v.t.* (-kāt) **·cat·ed, ·cat·ing** To make three times as much or as many; treble. [<L *triplicatus,* pp. of *triplicare* triple < *triplex* TRIPLEX] —**trip′li·cate·ly** *adv.*

trip·li·ca·tion (trip′lə·kā′shən) *n.* **1** The act of triplicating. **2** That which is triplicated or made threefold, or is in three layers.

tri·plic·i·ty (tri·plis′ə·tē) *n. pl.* **·ties 1** Threefold character. **2** A group or combination of three; a triad; a triplet. **3** In astrology, a combination of three of the twelve signs of the zodiac. [<LL *triplicitas, -tatis* <L *triplex, -icis* TRIPLEX]

trip·lite (trip′līt) *n.* A brown or black, translucent to opaque, fluophosphate of iron and manganese. [<G *triplit* <Gk. *triploos* triple; with ref. to its three cleavages]

trip·lo·blas·tic (trip′lə·blas′tik) *adj. Biol.* Having or characterized by three germ layers, as the embryos of the higher animals. [<Gk. *triploos* triple + BLASTIC]

trip·loid (trip′loid) *adj.* **1** Trebled. **2** *Genetics* Noting the occurrence in certain cells of three times the basic number of chromosomes. —*n.* A triploid cell or organism. [<NL *triploides* <Gk. *triploos* threefold + *eidos* form]

trip·loi·dy (trip·loi′dē) *n.* The condition of being triploid.

trip·lo·pi·a (trip·lō′pē·ə) *n. Pathol.* A defect of vision in which objects are seen tripled. [<NL <Gk. *triploos* threefold + *ōps, ōpos* eye]

tri·pod (trī′pod) *n.* **1** A utensil or article having three feet or legs. **2** A three-legged stand, as for supporting a camera, compass, or other instrument. [<L *tripus, -podis* <Gk. *tripous* < *tri-* three + *pous* foot]

trip·o·dal (trip′ə·dəl) *adj.* **1** Of the nature or form of a tripod. **2** Having three feet or legs. Also **tri·po·di·al** (tri·pō′dē·əl, trī-), **tri·pod′ic** (-pod′ik).

trip·o·dy (trip′ə·dē) *n. pl.* **·dies** A verse or meter having three feet. [< TRI- + (DI)PODY]

trip·o·li (trip′ə·lē) *n.* Rottenstone. [from *Tripoli,* Libya, where it is found]

Trip·o·li (trip′ə·lē) **1** One of the two capitals (with Bengasi) and the largest city of Libya, a port on the central Mediterranean and the capital of Tripolitania province: Phoenician *Oea.* **2** A port of NW Lebanon on the Mediterranean: ancient **Trip·o·lis** (trip′ə·lis). —**Tri·pol·i·tan** (tri·pol′ə·tən) *adj. & n.* —**Trip′o·line** (-lin) *adj.*

Trip·o·li·ta·ni·a (trip′ə·li·tā′nē·ə) The western province of Libya, on the Mediterranean; 82,990 square miles; capital, Tripoli; a former Barbary State. Ancient **Trip′o·lis.** —**Trip′o·li·ta′ni·an** *adj. & n.*

tri·pos (trī′pos) *n.* **1** An honors examination held at Cambridge University, England, especially in mathematics. **2** *Obs.* A tripod. [Appar. alter. of L *tripus* TRIPOD]

trip·per (trip′ər) *n.* **1** One who trips in any sense. **2** *Brit. Colloq.* One who makes trips; a tourist or traveler. **3** *Mech.* A trip or tripping mechanism, as a device on a railroad track which operates a catch on a passing train to give a signal or alarm.

trip·pet (trip′it) *n. Mech.* A cam, toe, or projecting piece, designed to strike some other piece at fixed intervals. [< TRIP, *v.*]

trip·ping (trip′ing) *n.* **1** The act of one who or that which trips. **2** A light dance. —*adj.* Light; nimble; easy; stepping. —**trip′ping·ly** *adv.*

trip·tane (trip′tān) *n. Chem.* A hydrocarbon compound, C_7H_{16}, derived from butane and having a very high octane number. [Contraction of *tripentane* < TRI- + PENTANE]

triptane number An improved measure of the efficiency of a motor fuel, expressed in terms of a blend of normal heptane and triptane, each containing a specified amount of tetraethyl lead.

trip·ter·ous (trip′tər·əs) *adj. Bot.* Having three wings or winglike processes, as certain seeds. [< TRI- + Gk. *pteron* a wing, on analogy with *dipterous*]

Trip·tol·e·mus (trip·tol′ə·məs) In Greek mythology, a hero said to have given mankind the secret of the cultivation of grain. Also **Trip·tol′e·mos** (-mos).

trip·tych (trip′tik) *n.* **1** A picture, carving, or work of art on three panels side by side. **2** Three pictures associated in their subjects and placed side by side in compartments. **3** A writing tablet in three sections, made of various laminate materials. Also **trip′ty·ca** (-ti·kə), **trip′ty·chon** (-ti·kon). [< Gk. *triptychos* threefold < *tri-* three + *ptyx, ptychos* a fold < *ptyssein* fold]

tri·pu·di·ate (trī·pyōō′dē·āt) *v.i.* **·at·ed, ·at·ing** To dance, especially in a measured way. [< L *tripudiatus,* pp. of *tripudiare* < *tripudium* a religious dance, prob. < *tri-* three + *pes, pedis* foot] —**tri·pu′di·a′tion** *n.*

Tri·pu·ra (tri′pōō·rä) A union territory of NE India; 4,032 square miles; capital, Agartala.

tri·quet·rous (trī·kwet′rəs, -kwē′trəs) *adj.* **1** Three-sided. **2** Having three acute or salient angles. **3** Three-cornered, as certain stems and bones. [< L *triquetrus*]

tri·ra·di·ate (trī·rā′dē·āt) *adj.* Having three rays or radiate branches: the *triradiate* sulcus of the brain. Also **tri·ra′di·al, tri·ra′di·at′ed.** —**tri·ra′di·al·ly, tri·ra′di·ate′ly** *adv.*

tri·reme (trī′rēm) *n.* An ancient Greek or Roman warship with three banks of oars. [< L *triremis* < *tri-* three + *remus* an oar]

tri·sac·cha·ride (trī·sak′ə·rīd, -rid) *n. Biochem.* Any of a class of saccharides which yield three monosaccharide molecules when subjected to hydrolysis, as raffinose. Also **tri·sac′cha·rid** (-rid).

Tris·ag·i·on (tris·ag′ē·on, -ā′gē-) *n.* A hymn, probably of Hebrew origin, in the liturgy of the Greek and Oriental churches, beginning with a threefold invocation of the Deity as Holy. Also **Tris·ag′i·um, Tris·hag′i·on.** [< Gk. *trisagion,* orig. neut. of *trisagios* thrice holy < *tris* thrice (< *treis* three) + *hagios* holy]

tri·sect (trī·sekt′) *v.t.* To divide into three parts, especially, as in geometry, into three equal parts. [< TRI- + L *sectus,* pp. of *secare* cut] —**tri·sect′ed** *adj.* —**tri·sec′tion** (-sek′shən) *n.* —**tri·sec′tor** *n.*

tri·sec·trix of MacLaurin (trī·sek′triks) *Math.* The plane curve of the equation $x^3 + xy^2 + ay^2 - 3ax^2 = 0$. Symmetric about the *x*-axis, passing through the origin and asymptotic to the line $x = -a$, the trisectrix is so named because it can be employed to trisect an angle. [after Colin *MacLaurin,* 1698–1746, Scottish mathematician]

tri·seme (trī′sēm) *n.* A syllable or foot consisting of or equivalent to three morae or short syllables, as the tribrach, iambus, and trochee. —*adj.* Consisting of or equal to three morae or short syllables: also **tri·se·mic** (trī·sē′mik). [< Gk. *trisēmos* < *tri-* three + *sēma* a sign]

tri·sep·al·ous (trī·sep′əl·əs) *adj. Bot.* Having three sepals.

tri·sep·tate (trī·sep′tāt) *adj. Biol.* Having three septa.

tri·se·ri·al (trī·sir′ē·əl) *adj.* **1** Arranged in three series or rows. **2** *Bot.* Tristichous. Also **tri·se′ri·ate** (-it, -āt). —**tri·se′ri·al·ly, tri·se·ri·a·tim** (trī·sir′ē·ā′tim) *adv.*

tris·kel·i·on (tris·kel′ē·ən) *n. pl.* **·kel·i·a** (-kel′ē·ə) A symbolic figure charaterized by three lines or three human legs radiating from a common center. It is used as the arms of the Isle of Man. Also **tris·cele** (tris′sēl), **tris·kele** (tris′kēl). [< Gk. *triskelēs* of three legs < *tri-* three + *skelos* a leg]

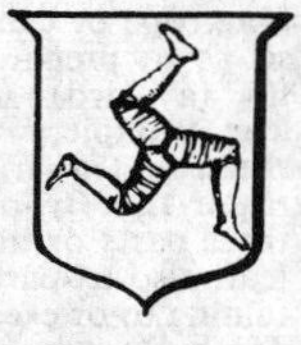

TRISKELION

Tris·me·gis·tus (tris′mə·jis′·təs, triz′-) See HERMES TRISMEGISTUS.

tris·mus (triz′məs, tris′-) *n. Pathol.* Tetanic spasm causing rigid closure of the jaws; lockjaw. [< NL < Gk. *trismos* a gnashing of teeth, a grinding] —**tris′mic** *adj.*

tris·oc·ta·he·dron (tris·ok′tə·hē′drən) *n. pl.* **·dra** (-drə) **1** A solid having 24 equal faces corresponding by threes to the faces of an octahedron. **2** A holohedral isometric crystal included under 24 equal isosceles triangular faces with eight planes meeting at the extremities of the rectangular axes: also **trigonal trisoctahedron. 3** An isometric holohedron included under 24 similar and equal trapeziform faces; a trapezohedron: also **tetragonal trisoctahedron.** [< Gk. *tris* thrice (< *treis* three) + OCTAHEDRON.] —**tris·oc′ta·he′dral** *adj.*

tri·sper·mous (trī·spûr′məs) *adj. Bot.* Having three seeds.

tri·spo·rous (trī·spôr′əs, -spō′rəs) *adj. Bot.* Having three spores. Also **tri·spor′ic** (-spôr′ik, -spor′ik). [< TRI- + -SPOROUS]

Tris·tan (tris′tän, -tən) In medieval legend, a knight sent to Ireland to bring back the princess Iseult the Beautiful as a bride for his uncle, King Mark of Cornwall. Iseult and Tristan mistakenly drink a magic love potion, and ultimately die together. In some versions, Tristan is later married to Iseult of the White Hand, daughter of the Duke of Brittany. Also **Tris·tram** (tris′trəm).

Tris·tan da Cun·ha (tris·tän′ dä kōōn′yä) A British island group in the South Atlantic, midway between South America and the Cape of Good Hope; administered with St. Helena; 40 square miles.

triste (trēst) *adj. French* Sorrowful; sad.

tris·tesse (trēs·tes′) *n. French* Sadness; melancholy.

trist·ful (trist′fəl) *adj. Archaic* Sad; gloomy; sorrowful. [< obs. *trist* sad < OF *triste* < L *tristis*] —**trist′ful·ly** *adv.*

tris·tich (tris′tik) *n.* A strophe or system of three lines; triplet. Compare COUPLET, DISTICH. [< TRI- + (DI)STICH]

tris·ti·chous (tris′tə·kəs) *adj.* **1** Three-ranked. **2** *Bot.* Having parts, as leaves, arranged in three vertical rows. [< Gk. *tristichos* three-rowed < *tri-* three + *stichos* a row]

tri·stim·u·lus (trī·stim′yə·ləs) *adj.* **1** Having, pertaining to, or caused or characterized by three distinct stimuli. **2** In color analysis, designating an instrument or method for measuring a color stimulus in terms of three selected primary stimuli.

tri·sty·lous (trī·stī′ləs) *adj. Bot.* Having three styles.

tri·sul·fide (trī·sul′fīd, -fid) *n. Chem.* A sulfide containing three atoms of sulfur in combination. Also **tri·sul′fid** (-fid), **tri·sul′phide, tri·sul′phid.**

tri·syl·la·ble (trī·sil′ə·bəl) *n.* A word of three syllables. —**tri·syl·lab·ic** (trī′si·lab′ik) or **·i·cal** *adj.* —**tri′syl·lab′i·cal·ly** *adv.*

tri·tag·o·nist (trī·tag′ə·nist) *n.* In Greek drama, the actor who played the third part; hence, also, a third-rate actor. [< Gk. *tritagōnistēs* < *tritos* third + *agōnistēs* a contender, actor < *agōnizesthai* contend < *agōn* a contest]

trit·an·o·pi·a (trit′ən·ō′pē·ə) *n. Pathol.* Impairment of vision for blue and yellow; blue blindness. Also **trit′an·op′si·a** (-op′sē·ə). [< NL < Gk. *tritos* third + ANOPIA] —**trit′an·op′tic** (-op′tik) *adj.*

trite (trīt) *adj.* **1** Used so often as to be hackneyed; made commonplace by repetition. **2** *Archaic* Worn-out; frayed. [< L *tritus,* pp. of *terere* rub] —**trite′ly** *adv.* —**trite′ness** *n.*

Synonyms: common, commonplace, hackneyed, musty, rusty, stale, stereotyped, threadbare, worn. See COMMON. *Antonyms:* bright, brilliant, fresh, new, original, racy, striking, telling, vivid.

tri·the·ism (trī′thē·iz′əm) *n. Theol.* The doctrine of the separate existence of three Gods: sometimes opprobriously applied to belief in the distinct personality of the Father, the Son, and the Holy Spirit. [< TRI- + Gk. *theos* a god] —**tri′the·ist** *n.* —**tri′the·is′tic** or **·ti·cal** *adj.*

tri·thing (trī′thing) *n.* In English law, a riding. See RIDING[2]. [OE *thrithing* < ON *thridhungr* a third part]

trit·i·ca·le (trit′ə·kā′lē) *n.* A hybrid grain produced for its high protein content by crossing wheat and rye. [< L *triticum* wheat + *secale* rye]

Trit·i·cum (trit′ə·kəm) *n.* A widely distributed and important genus of cereal grasses, the wheats, especially *T. aestivum* and its numerous cultivated varieties. [< NL < L, wheat]

trit·i·um (trit′ē·əm, trish′ē·əm) *n.* An unstable isotope of hydrogen having atomic mass 3 and a half-life of about 12.5 years. [< NL < Gk. *tritos* third]

tri·ton[1] (trīt′n) *n.* Any of a genus *(Triton)* of marine gastropods with many gills and a trumpet-shaped shell. [< NL < L, Triton]

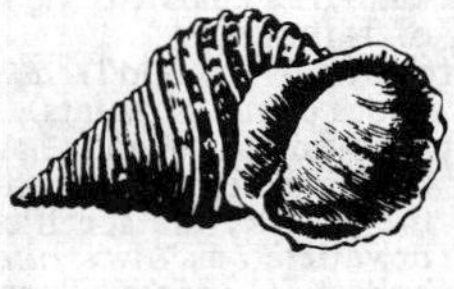

TRITON

tri·ton[2] (trī′ton) *n.* The nucleus of an atom of tritium. [< TRIT(IUM) + (ELECTR)ON]

Tri·ton (trīt′n) **1** In Greek mythology: **a** A son of Poseidon (Neptune) and Amphitrite, represented with a man's head and upper body and a dolphin's tail. **b** One of a race of attendants of the sea gods. **2** *Her.* A merman; also, a Neptune holding a trident. —**Tri′ton·ess** *n. fem.*

tri·tone (trī′tōn) *n. Music* An augmented fourth, as containing three whole tones. [< Med. L *tritonus* < Gk. *tritonos* < *tri-* three + *tonos.* See TONE.]

trit·u·rate (trich′ə·rāt) *v.t.* **·rat·ed, ·rat·ing** To reduce to a fine powder or pulp by grinding or rubbing; pulverize. —*n.* **1** That which has been triturated. **2** A trituration (def. 3). [< LL *trituratus,* pp. of *triturare* thresh < L *tritura* a rubbing, threshing < *tritus.* See TRITE.] —**trit·u·ra·ble** (trich′ər·ə·bəl) *adj.* —**trit′u·ra′tor** *n.*

trit·u·ra·tion (trich′ə·rā′shən) *n.* **1** The act of triturating; reduction to a very fine powder by grinding or rubbing, as in a mortar. **2** The process of reducing to a pulp. **3** A triturated preparation, especially one in which 10 parts of a medicinal substance are triturated with 90 parts of milk sugar: also *triturate.*

tri·umph (trī′əmf) *v.i.* **1** To win a victory; be victorious. **2** To be successful. **3** To rejoice over a victory; exult. **4** To celebrate a triumph, as a victorious Roman general. —*v.t.* **5** *Obs.* To conquer. See synonyms under REJOICE. —*n.* **1** In Roman antiquity, the religious pageant of the entry of a victorious consul, dictator, or pretor into Rome: given only for a decisive victory over a foreign enemy. **2** Exultation over victory. **3** The condition of being victorious; victory. **4** *Obs.* A trump card. **5** *Obs.* Any public spectacular display, procession, or pageant. See synonyms under HAPPINESS, VICTORY. [< OF *triumpher* < L *triumphare* < *triumphus* a triumph < Gk. *thriambos* a processional hymn to Dionysus] —**tri′umph·er** *n.*

tri·um·phal (trī·um′fəl) *adj.* 1 Of, pertaining to, or of the nature of a triumph. 2 Celebrating a victory.
triumphal arch A large monumental arch erected in ancient or modern times to commemorate any great victory or achievement.
tri·um·phant (trī·um′fənt) *adj.* 1 Exultant for or as for victory. 2 Crowned with victory; victorious. 3 *Obs.* Of supreme magnificence or beauty; glorious. 4 *Obs.* Triumphal. [<L *triumphans, -antis,* ppr. of *triumphare* TRIUMPH] — **tri·um′phant·ly** *adv.*
tri·um·vir (trī·um′vər) *n. pl.* **·virs** or **·vi·ri** (-və·rī) One of three men united in public office or authority, as in ancient Rome. [<L < *trium virorum* of three men < *tres, trium* three + *vir* a man] — **tri·um′vi·ral** *adj.*
tri·um·vi·rate (trī·um′vər·it, -və·rāt) *n.* 1 A group or coalition of three men who unitedly exercise authority or control; government by triumvirs. 2 The office of a triumvir; also, the triumvirs collectively. 3 A group of three men; a trio. [<L *triumviratus* < *triumvir* TRIUMVIR]
tri·une (trī′yōōn) *adj.* Three in one: said of the Godhead. — *n.* A group of three things united; a triad; a trinity in unity. [<TRI- + L *unus* one]
Tri·u·ni·tar·i·an (trī·yōō′nə·târ′ē·ən) *n.* A Trinitarian. [<TRIUNIT(Y) + -ARIAN]
tri·u·ni·ty (trī·yōō′nə·tē) *n.* Trinity.
tri·va·lent (trī·vā′lənt, triv′ə·lənt) *adj. Chem.* Having a valence or combining value of three. [<TRI- + L *valens, -entis,* ppr. of *valere* be strong] — **tri·va′lence, tri·va′len·cy** *n.*
tri·valve (trī′valv′) *adj.* Having three valves, as a shell. — *n.* A trivalve shell.
Tri·van·drum (tri·van′drəm) A port on the Malabar Coast, capital of Kerala State, SW India, in the SW part of the State.
triv·et (triv′it) *n.* A short, usually three-legged stand for holding cooking vessels in a fireplace, a heated iron, or a hot dish on a table: also *trevet.* [OE *trefet* <L *tripes, -pedis* three-footed < *tri-* three + *pes, pedis* a foot]
triv·i·a (triv′ē·ə) *n. pl.* Insignificant or unimportant matters; trifles. [<NL <L *trivialis* TRIVIAL]
triv·i·al (triv′ē·əl) *adj.* 1 Of little value or importance; trifling; insignificant. 2 Such as is found everywhere or every day; ordinary; commonplace. 3 Occupied with trifles; of low ability or wit; unscholarly. See synonyms under CHILDISH, INSIGNIFICANT, LITTLE, RIDICULOUS, VAIN, VENIAL. [<L *trivialis* of the crossroads, commonplace < *trivium* a crossing of three roads < *tri-* three + *via* a road] — **triv′i·al·ism** *n.* — **triv′i·al·ly** *adv.*
triv·i·al·i·ty (triv′ē·al′ə·tē) *n. pl.* **·ties** 1 The state or quality of being trivial: an age of *triviality*: also **triv′i·al·ness.** 2 A trivial matter; a trivialism.
triv·i·um (triv′ē·əm) *n.* In medieval schools, the course in the liberal arts embracing grammar, logic, and rhetoric. Compare QUADRIVIUM. [<Med. L <L. See TRIVIAL.]
tri·week·ly (trī·wēk′lē) *adj.* & *adv.* 1 Occurring three times a week. 2 Sometimes, done or occurring every third week.
-trix *suffix* A feminine termination of agent nouns the masculine form of which is *-tor*: *testatrix.* See -OR[1]. [<L *-trix*]
Tr·no·vo (tûr′nô·vô) See TIRNOVO.
troak (trōk) See TROKE.
Tro·as (trō′as) The region of western Asia Minor on the Aegean surrounding the ancient city of Troy: also *Teucria.* Also **the Tro′ad** (-ad).
Tro·bri·and Islands (trō′brē·änd) A volcanic island group off the eastern tip of New Guinea; a dependency of the Australian Trust Territory of Papua and New Guinea; total, 175 square miles.
tro·car (trō′kär) *n. Surg.* A sharp-pointed instrument used with a cannula to drain off internal fluids. Also **tro′char.** [<F *troquart, trois-quarts* < *trois* three + *carre* face; so called because of its triangular shape]
tro·cha (trō′chä) *n.* 1 A path; road. 2 An obstruction on a road, to hinder an enemy; a military cordon. [<Sp.]
tro·cha·ic (trō·kā′ik) *adj.* Pertaining to, containing, or composed of trochees: a *trochaic* foot or verse. — *n.* A trochaic verse or line. [<MF *trochaïque* <L *trochaicus* <Gk. *trochaikos* < *trochaios* TROCHEE]
tro·chal (trō′kəl) *adj.* 1 Shaped like a wheel; rotiform. 2 Trochilic. [<Gk. *trochos* a wheel]
tro·chan·ter (trō·kan′tər) *n.* 1 *Anat.* One of several bony processes on the upper thigh bone. 2 *Entomol.* The small second segment of an insect's leg. [<MF <Gk. *trochantēr* < *trechein* run]
tro·che (trō′kē) *n.* A medicated lozenge, usually circular. [Alter. of obs. *trochisk* <MF *trochisque* a lozenge <L *trochiscus* <Gk. *trochiskos* a small wheel, a lozenge < *trochos* a wheel < *trechein* run]
tro·chee (trō′kē) *n.* In prosody, a foot comprising a long and short syllable (—⌣), or, in modern verse, an accented syllable followed by an unaccented one. [<L *trochaeus* <Gk. *trochaios (pous)* a running (foot) < *trechein* run]
Troch·el·min·thes (trok′əl·min′thēz) *n. pl.* A phylum of minute, transparent, aquatic protozoans which move by means of cilia, including the wheel animalcules. [<NL <Gk. *trochos* a wheel + *helmins, helminthos* a worm]
tro·chil·ic (trō·kil′ik) *adj.* 1 Of the nature of or pertaining to rotary motion. 2 Capable of such motion. [<Gk. *trochilos* a pulley, taken as var. of *trochos* a wheel < *trechein* run]
troch·i·lus (trok′ə·ləs) *n. pl.* **·li** (-lī) 1 The crocodile bird: also **tro·chil** (trō′kil, trok′il), **troch′i·los** (-los). 2 A hummingbird (family *Trochilidae*). 3 One of various small warblers or warblerlike birds. [<L *trochilus* a crocodile bird <Gk. *trochilos* < *trechein* run]
troch·le·a (trok′lē·ə) *n. pl.* **·le·ae** (-li·ē) *Anat.* A grooved pulleylike surface, permitting smooth motion, as between the humerus and ulna. [<L, a pulley <Gk. *trochilia, trochileia* < *trechein* run]
troch·le·ar (trok′lē·ər) *adj.* 1 *Anat.* Of, pertaining to, or situated near a trochlea. 2 Of the nature of a pulley. 3 Short, cylindrical, compressed, and contracted in the middle of its circumference like a pulley block. [<NL *trochlearis* <L *trochlea* TROCHLEA]
troch·le·ar·i·form (trok′lē·ar′ə·fôrm) *adj.* Having the form of a pulley; trochlear.
tro·choid (trō′koid) *adj.* Rotating upon its own axis; pivotal: also **tro·choi′dal.** — *n. Math.* A plane curve traced by a point on a circle or on its extended radius as the circle rolls, without slipping, on a straight line: when the point is on the circumference of the circle, the curve traced is a cycloid. [<Gk. *trochoeidēs* round, wheel-like < *trochos* a wheel + *eidos* form, shape] — **tro·choi′dal·ly** *adv.*
troch·o·phore (trok′ə·fôr, -fōr) *n. Zool.* A pear-shaped larval form of certain aquatic invertebrates, as annelids, brachiopods, and mollusks. Also **troch′o·sphere** (-sfir). [<Gk. *trochos* a wheel + -PHORE]
trock (trok) See TROKE.
trod (trod) Past tense and alternative past participle of TREAD.
trod·den (trod′n) Past participle of TREAD.
trode (trōd) Archaic past tense of TREAD.
trog·lo·dyte (trog′lə·dīt) *n.* 1 A prehistoric cave man. 2 Figuratively, a hermit; anyone of primitive or degenerate habits. 3 An anthropoid ape, as the gorilla. 4 The wren. [<L *troglodyta* <Gk. *trōglodytēs* < *trōglē* a hole + *dyein* go into] — **trog′lo·dyt′ic** (-dit′ik), **trog′lo·dyt′i·cal** *adj.*
tro·gon (trō′gon) *n.* A tropical American bird (family *Trogonidae*) noted for its resplendent plumage. [<NL <Gk. *trōgōn,* ppr. of *trōgein* gnaw]
troi·ka (troi′kə) *n.* A Russian vehicle drawn by a team of three horses driven abreast; also, the team, or both team and vehicle together. [<Russian]
Troi·lus (troi′ləs, trō′i·ləs) In Greek legend, a son of Priam killed by Achilles; in medieval legend, Chaucer's *Troilus and Criseyde,* and Shakespeare's *Troilus and Cressida,* Cressida's lover.
troilus butterfly The green-clouded or spicebush swallowtail butterfly (*Papilio troilus*) of eastern North America. [after *Troilus*]
Trois Ri·vières (trwȧ rē·vyâr′) A city on the St. Lawrence River at the mouth of the St. Maurice River in southern Quebec, Canada: English *Three Rivers.*
Tro·jan (trō′jən) *n.* 1 A native of Troy. 2 A brave, persevering person; one who works earnestly or suffers courageously. 3 *Colloq.* A jolly fellow; boon companion. — *adj.* Of or pertaining to ancient Troy. Also called *Dardan, Dardanian.* [Earlier *Troyan, Troian* <L *Troianus* < *Troja* Troy]
Trojan horse 1 In classical legend, a large, hollow wooden horse, described in Vergil's *Aeneid,* filled with Greek soldiers and left at the Trojan gates: when it was brought within the walls the soldiers emerged at night and admitted the Greek army, who burned the city: also called *wooden horse.* 2 *Mil.* The infiltration of military men into a potentially hostile region for the purpose of nullifying resistance against attack: compare FIFTH COLUMN.
Trojan War In Greek legend, the ten years' war waged by the confederated Greeks under their king, Agamemnon, against the Trojans to recover Helen, the wife of Menelaus, who had been abducted by Paris: celebrated especially in the *Iliad* and the *Odyssey.* See APPLE OF DISCORD.
troke (trōk) *Scot. n.* 1 Exchange; also, articles of trade; small wares; truck. 2 Familiar intercourse or acquaintance. — *v.t.* & *v.i.* To exchange; barter. Also spelled *troak, trock.*
troll[1] (trōl) *v.t.* 1 To cause to roll; revolve. 2 To sing in succession, as in a round or catch. 3 To sing in a full, hearty manner. 4 To fish for with a moving lure, as from a moving boat. 5 To move (the line or lure) in fishing. 6 *Obs.* To pass around, as a bottle or decanter. — *v.i.* 7 To roll; turn. 8 To sing a tune, etc., in a full, hearty manner. 9 To be uttered in such a way. 10 To fish with a moving lure. 11 *Obs.* To move about; ramble. — *n.* 1 A catch or round. 2 A rolling movement or motion; hence, repetition or routine. 3 In fishing, a spoon or other lure. [? <OF *troller* quest, wander <Gmc. Cf. MHG *trollen* walk with short steps.] — **troll′er** *n.*
troll[2] (trōl) *n.* In Scandinavian folklore, a giant; later, a friendly but often mischievous dwarf. Also **trold** (trōld). [<ON]
trol·ley (trol′ē) *n. pl.* **·leys** 1 A grooved metal wheel for rolling in contact with an electric conductor (the **trolley wire**), to convey the current to an electric vehicle. 2 In a subway system, a bow or shoe adapted to the same purpose attached to a current-taker operating through a slot in the track: also **trolley wheel.** 3 A car or system so operated. 4 A small truck or car for conveying material, as in a factory, mine, etc.: also spelled *trawley.* 5 A small cart for serving food and drink: tea *trolley.* 6 *Brit. Dial.* A small hand or donkey cart. 7 A parcels carrier. 8 The mechanism of a traveling crane. 9 A small car running on tracks and worked by a lever operated by hand: used by workmen on a railway. — *v.t.* & *v.i.* To convey or travel by trolley. Also spelled *trolly.* [<TROLL[1]]
trolley bus A passenger conveyance operating without rails, propelled electrically by current taken from an overhead wire by means of a trolley: also called *trackless trolley.* Also **trolley coach.**
trolley car A car arranged with a trolley and motor for use on an electric railway operated by the trolley system.
trolley line A system of street cars propelled on the trolley system; also, the road itself.
trol·ley·man (trol′ē·man′) *n. pl.* **·men** (-men′) A man who operates a trolley; especially, a conductor or motorman.
trolley pole A pole on a trolley car carrying the trolley wheel.
troll·ing (trō′ling) *n.* The method or act of fishing by dragging a hook and line, as behind a boat and near the surface: usually with a spoon bait or the like. [<TROLL[1]]
trolling bait Spoon bait. Also **trolling hook, trolling spoon.**
trolling rod A strong fishing rod for trolling.
trol·lop (trol′əp) *n.* 1 A slatternly woman. 2 A prostitute. [<dial. E (Scottish) <ME

trollen roll about; prob. infl. in meaning by *trull*] **—trol′lop·ish, trol′lop·y, trol′lop·ing** *adj.*

Trol·lope (trol′əp), **Anthony,** 1815–82, English novelist.

trol·ly (trol′ē) *n.* *pl.* **·lies** *n.* & *v.* Trolley.

Trom·be·tas (trōn̄m·bā′təs) A river of NW Pará state, Brazil, flowing 470 miles south and east to the Amazon.

trom·bic·u·li·a·sis (trom·bik′yə·lī′ə·sis) *n.* *Pathol.* Infestation with mites of the genus *Trombicula,* the chiggers. Also **trom·bic′u·lo′·sis** (-lō′sis). [<NL *Trombicula* + -IASIS]

trom·bone (trom′bōn, trom·bōn′) *n.* A powerful brass wind instrument of the trumpet family possessing a complete chromatic scale. It consists of a cupped mouthpiece and a long tube bent twice upon itself, the outer bend being a U-shaped slide, by the motion of which the length of the vibrating air column may be so adjusted as to produce any note within its compass. [<Ital., aug. of *tromba* a trumpet] **— trom′bon·ist** *n.*

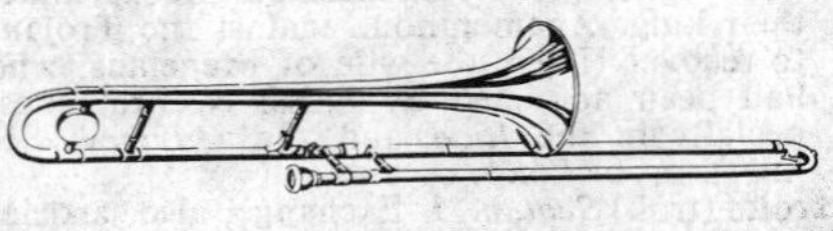

TROMBONE

trom·mel (trom′əl) *n.* *Metall.* A perforated steel plate, usually cylindrical in form, used for sifting or screening rock, ore, etc. [<G, a drum]

trom·o·ma·ni·a (trom′ə·mā′nē·ə, -mān′yə) *n.* Delirium tremens. [<NL <Gk. *tromos* a trembling + *mania* madness]

Tromp (trômp), **Cornelius van,** 1629–91, Dutch admiral; son of the following. **— Marten Harpertzoon,** 1597–1653, Dutch admiral.

trompe (tromp) *n.* **1** *Metall.* An apparatus that supplies a blast of air, as to a forge, by the action of a thin column of water falling through a large, long tube and thus carrying air by entanglement. **2** An arched and vaulted structure that supports a portion of a building. Also **tromp.** [<F, lit., a trumpet]

Trom·sö (trom′zō, *Norw.* trōms′œ, tro͝oms′œ) A port on eastern **Tromsö Island,** an islet of NW Norway (8 square miles).

tro·na (trō′nə) *n.* A vitreous, gray or white, monoclinic hydrous sodium carbonate, $Na_2CO_3HNaCO_3 \cdot 2H_2O$. [<Sw., appar. <Arabic *trōn,* short for *natrūn* NATRON]

Trond·heim (trôn′hām) A port on **Trondheim Fiord,** in Norway: formerly *Nidaros.* Formerly spelled **Trond·hjem** (trôn′yem).

troop (tro͞op) *n.* **1** An assembled company; gathering; a herd or flock. **2** *Usually pl.* A body of soldiers; soldiers collectively. **3** The cavalry unit of formation, corresponding to a company of infantry. **4** A body of Boy Scouts consisting of four patrols of eight scouts each. **5** Formerly, a troupe; a company of actors. See synonyms under ARMY. **—** *v.i.* **1** To move along or gather as a troop or as a crowd. **2** *Archaic* To associate; consort. **—** *v.t.* **3** To form into troops. **4** *Brit. Mil.* To carry ceremoniously before troops: to *troop* the colors. ◆ Homophone: *troupe.* [<OF *trope* <LL *troppus* a flock <Gmc.]

troop·er (tro͞o′pər) *n.* **1** A cavalryman. **2** A mounted policeman. **3** A troop horse; charger. **4** A troopship.

troop·i·al (tro͞o′pē·əl) *n.* Any American bird of the family *Icteridae,* including the blackbirds, orioles, bobolinks, and meadowlarks, especially *Icterus icterus* of South America and the West Indies, mostly black varied with yellow and white. Also spelled *troupial.* [<F *troupiale* < *troupe* <OF *trope* TROOP; so called because it goes in flocks]

troop·lift (tro͞op′lift′) *n.* **1** The troop-carrying capacity of a nation's passenger ships, merchant marine, or aviation. **2** The actual transport of troops.

troop·ship (tro͞op′ship′) *n.* A ship for carrying troops; a transport.

troost·ite (tro͞os′tīt) *n.* A variety of willemite in large reddish crystals. [after Gerhard *Troost,* 1776–1850, U.S. mineralogist]

trooz (tro͞oz) See TREWS.

trop (trō) *adv.* *French* Too much; too many; too.

tro·pa·co·caine (trō′pə·kō·kān′, -kō′kān, -kō′·kə·ēn) *n.* *Chem.* A white crystalline compound, $C_{15}H_{19}O_2N$, obtained from Java coca leaves and also made synthetically from atropine and hyoscine: used as an anesthetic. [<*(benzoyl-pseudo)trop(eine),* its chemical name + COCAINE]

Tro·pae·o·lum (trō·pē′ə·ləm) *n.* A genus of tropical American plants with alternate leaves and bright-colored flowers supposed to resemble ancient trophies. Many species, known as *nasturtiums,* are cultivated. [<NL <Gk. *tropaion* a trophy; so called from the resemblance of the leaf and flower to a shield and helmet]

tro·pae·um (trō·pē′əm) *n.* In Greek antiquity, a monument of victory, composed of captured arms, set up by the Greeks at a place where they had defeated an enemy. Also **tro·pai·on** (trō·pā′on). [<L, TROPHY]

-tropal *combining form* -tropic.

tro·par·i·on (trō·pâr′ē·on) *n.* *pl.* **·par·i·a** (-pâr′·ē·ə) In the Greek Church, a stanza of, or the several stanzas constituting, a hymn. [<Gk., dim. of *tropos.* See TROPE.]

trope (trōp) *n.* **1** The figurative use of a word. **2** Loosely and less properly, a figure of speech; figurative language in general. **3** A short distinguishing cadence interpolated in Gregorian melodies. **4** An interpolated phrase that was occasionally inserted in various parts of the mass prior to the 16th century. [<F <L *tropus* a figure of speech <Gk. *tropos* a turn < *trepein* turn]

-trope *combining form* **1** One who or that which turns or changes: *allotrope.* **2** Turning; turned in a (specified) way: *hemitrope.* [<Gk. *tropos* a turning < *trepein* turn]

tro·pe·ine (trō′pē·in, -ēn) *n.* *Chem.* An ester of tropine, from which it is formed by the action of certain organic acids. Also **tro′pe·in** (-in). [Alter. of TROPINE]

tro·pe·o·lin (trō·pē′ə·lin) *n.* *Chem.* Any of several orange azo dyes formed by the action of diazosulfuric acids on phenols. Also **tro·pae′·o·lin.** [<TROPAEOL(UM) + -IN; so called because their hues resemble those of the flower]

troph·al·lax·is (trof′ə·lak′sis) *n.* *Biol.* The free exchange of food substances among individuals, considered as an essential factor in the life cycle of certain insects, especially army ants. [<NL <Gk. *trophē* food + *allaxis* an exchange] **— troph′al·lac′tic** (-lak′tik) *adj.*

troph·ic (trof′ik) *adj.* Pertaining to nutrition and its processes. Also **troph′i·cal.** [<Gk. *trophikos* < *trophē* nourishment < *trephein* nourish] **— troph′i·cal·ly** *adv.*

tro·phied (trō′fēd) *adj.* Adorned with trophies.

tropho- *combining form* Nutrition; nourishment; of or pertaining to food or nutrition: *trophoplasm.* Also, before vowels, **troph-.** [<Gk. *trophē* food, nourishment < *trephein* feed, nourish]

troph·o·blast (trof′ə·blast) *n.* *Biol.* The ectodermal layer of cells in the embryo that establishes relation with the uterus and is concerned in the nutrition of the embryo and fetus. Also **troph′o·derm** (-dûrm). [<TROPHO- + -BLAST] **— troph′o·blas′tic** *adj.*

troph·o·gen·e·sis (trof′ə·jen′ə·sis) *n.* *Biol.* The production of variations among plants and animals by differences in food and nutrition, as distinguished from genetic factors. Also **tro·phog·e·ny** (trō·foj′ə·nē). **— troph′o·gen′ic** *adj.*

troph·o·plasm (trof′ə·plaz′əm) *n.* *Biol.* **1** The nutritive or vegetative substance of the cell, as distinguished from the idioplasm. **2** Formerly, a cytoplasmic substance distinguished from the archiplasm. **— troph′o·plas′mic** *adj.*

troph·o·ther·a·py (trof′ə·ther′ə·pē) *n.* *Med.* The treatment of disease by diet therapy.

tro·phot·ro·pism (trō·fot′rə·piz′əm) *n.* *Bot.* The movement or curvature, as toward or away from nutrient substances, induced in a growing plant by the influence of the chemical nature of its surroundings. **— troph·o·trop·ic** (trof′ə·trop′ik) *adj.*

troph·o·zo·ite (trof′ə·zō′īt) *n.* *Zool.* A parasitic sporozoan at the stage of entering the blood cell of its host, feeding on the nutritive material in the blood. [<TROPHO- + Gk. *zōion* an animal + -ITE[1]]

tro·phy (trō′fē) *n.* *pl.* **·phies** **1** Anything taken from an enemy and displayed or treasured in proof of victory; hence, a memento of victory or success: *trophies* of the chase. **2** An ancient Roman memorial of victory in imitation of the Greek tropaeum, but a permanent structure, decorated with arms or beaks of ships suspended over the undecorated parts. **3** An ornamental group of objects hung together on a wall, or any collection of objects typical of some event, art, industry, or branch of knowledge. **4** A memento or memorial. **5** *Archit.* A group of arms and armor carved in marble or cast in bronze rising from a circular or quadrangular stepped base. [<MF *trophée* <L *trophaeum, tropaeum* <Gk. *tropaion* < *tropē* a defeat, turning < *trepein* turn, rout]

-trophy *combining form* A (specified) kind of nutrition or nurture: *hypertrophy.* Corresponding adjectives end in *-trophic.* [<Gk. *trophē.* See TROPHO-.]

trop·ic (trop′ik) *n.* **1** *Geog.* Either of two parallels of latitude at a distance from the equator, north and south, equal to the obliquity of the ecliptic, or 23° 27′, on which the sun is seen in the zenith on the days of its greatest declination: called respectively **tropic of Cancer** and **tropic of Capricorn.** **2** *Astron.* **a** Either of two corresponding parallels of declination in the celestial sphere similarly named, and respectively 23° 27′ north or south from the celestial equator. **b** Either of the two points in the celestial sphere where the sun reaches its maximum distance north or south of the celestial equator; a solstice. **3** *pl.* The regions of the earth's surface between the tropics of Cancer and Capricorn, where the sun crosses the zenith twice in the course of the year: with the definite article; the torrid zone. **—** *adj.* Of or pertaining to the tropics; tropical. [<L *tropicus* <Gk. *tropikos (kyklos)* the tropical (circle), pertaining to the turning of the sun at the solstice < *tropē.* See TROPHY.]

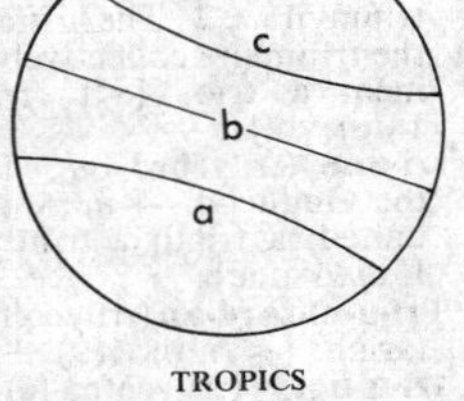

TROPICS
a. Tropic of Capricorn.
b. Equator.
c. Tropic of Cancer.

-tropic *combining form* Having a (specified) tropism; turning or changing in a (particular) way, or in response to a (given) stimulus: *chemotropic, phototropic.*

trop·i·cal (trop′i·kəl) *adj.* **1** Of, pertaining to, or characteristic of the tropics. **2** Of the nature of a trope or metaphor; changed from the original to a figurative meaning. **— trop′i·cal·ly** *adv.*

trop·i·cal·ize (trop′i·kəl·īz′) *v.t.* **·ized, ·iz·ing** To adapt, as clothing, war equipment, ships, etc., for service in tropical areas. **— trop′i·cal·i·za′tion** *n.*

tropic bird A long-winged, oceanic, tern-like bird (genus *Phaëthon*), found mostly in the tropics, having the two middle tail feathers elongated.

tro·pine (trō′pēn, -pin) *n.* *Chem.* A colorless crystalline alkaloid, $C_8H_{15}NO$, with a tobacco odor, formed when atropine is hydrolyzed. Also **tro′pin** (-pin). [<ATROPINE]

tro·pism (trō′piz·əm) *n.* *Biol.* **1** The involuntary response of an organism, or of any of its parts, to an external stimulus. **2** Any automatic reaction to a stimulus. [<Gk. *tropē* a turning] **— tro·pis·tic** (trō·pis′tik) *adj.*

-tropism *combining form* A (specified) tropism; a tendency to turn or change in response to a (given) stimulus: *chemotropism, phototropism.* Corresponding adjectives end in *-tropic.* [<TROPISM]

tro·pist (trō′pist) *n.* **1** One given to the use of tropes. **2** One who interprets and explains a text, especially Scripture, tropically or figuratively.

tro·pol·o·gy (trō·pol′ə·jē) *n.* **1** The use of tropical or figurative language. **2** Consideration or treatment of the Scriptures both literally and figuratively, or as having a double sense. **3** A treatise on figures of speech. [<LL *tropologia* <Gk. < *tropos* TROPE + *logos* discourse] **— trop·o·log·ic** (trop′ə·loj′ik) or **·i·cal** *adj.* **— trop′o·log′i·cal·ly** *adv.*

trop·o·pause (trop′ə·pôz) *n.* *Meteorol.* A transition zone in the atmosphere between the troposphere and the stratosphere at which the fall of temperature with increasing height

abruptly ceases. [<TROPO(SPHERE) + Gk. *pausis* a ceasing]

tro·poph·i·lous (trō·pof′ə·ləs) *adj. Ecol.* Adapted to extreme conditions of moisture or of heat: said of plants. [<Gk. *tropos* a turning, change + *philos* loving; with ref. to adaptation to seasonal changes]

trop·o·phyte (trop′ə·fīt) *n. Ecol.* Any of the plants that adapt themselves to seasonal changes of dryness or cold and also of moisture: they form the highest type of temperate-zone plants, as the deciduous trees. [<Gk. *tropos* a turning, change + -PHYTE] — **trop′o·phyt′ic** (-fit′ik) *adj.*

trop·o·sphere (trop′ə·sfir) *n. Meteorol.* The region of the atmosphere from the earth's surface to the tropopause, having a height of from six to twelve miles and characterized by decreasing temperature with increasing altitude. [<F *troposphère* <Gk. *tropos* a turning + F *sphère* <L *sphaera* SPHERE]

trop·po (trop′ō, *Ital.* trôp′pō) *adv. Music* Too much: andante ma non *troppo* (andante but not too much). [<Ital.]

-tropous *combining form* Turned in a specified way: *anatropous*. Corresponding nouns end in *-tropy.*

-tropy *combining form* **1** -tropism. **2** A state of being turned. See -TROPOUS. [<Gk. *tropē* a turning <*trepein* turn]

Tros·sachs (tros′aks, -əks) A valley in Perthshire, central Scotland: scene of Scott's *The Lady of the Lake.*

trot[1] (trot) *n.* **1** A progressive motion of a quadruped, in which each diagonal pair of legs is alternately lifted, thrust forward, and placed upon the ground almost simultaneously, the body of the animal being entirely unsupported twice during each stride; the sound of this gait. **2** A race for trotters. **3** A little child; toddler: a term of endearment. **4** Steady going or movement, implying persistence and diligence: I have been on the *trot* all day. **5** *Colloq.* A literal translation of a foreign-language text, used as an aid in study or in examination; a crib; pony. — *v.* **trot·ted, trot·ting** *v.i.* **1** To go at a trot. **2** To go quickly; hurry. — *v.t.* **3** To cause to trot. **4** To ride at a trotting gait. — **to trot out** To bring forth for inspection, approval, etc. [<OF < *troter* <OHG *trottôn* tread]

trot[2] (trot) *n. Archaic* An old woman: a derogatory term. [<AF *trote*; ult. origin uncertain]

troth (trôth, trōth) *n.* **1** Good faith; fidelity; also, the act of pledging fidelity; especially, betrothal. **2** Truth; verity. — *v.t. Archaic* To betroth; pledge. [ME *trowthe, trouthe,* var. of OE *trēowth* truth]

troth·plight (trôth′plīt′, trōth′-) *Archaic v.t.* To betroth; affiance. — *n.* Betrothal. — *adj.* Betrothed: also **troth′-plight′ed.** [<TROTH + PLIGHT[2]]

trot·line (trot′līn′) *n.* A trawl line.

Trot·sky (trot′skē), **Leon,** 1879–1940, Russian Bolshevist leader; exiled 1929; murdered: real name *Lev Davidovitch Bronstein.*

Trot·sky·ism (trot′skē·iz′əm) *n.* The doctrines of Trotsky and his followers; especially, his belief in "permanent revolution" or the theory that Communism to succeed must be international. — **Trot′sky·ist** *n.*

Trot·sky·ite (trot′skē·īt) *n.* An adherent of any of the various factions of the Communist party originally led by Leon Trotsky, who opposed Stalinism and supported international Communism.

trot·ter (trot′ər) *n.* **1** One who or that which trots; a trotting horse; specifically, a horse trained to trot for speed. **2** *Colloq.* An animal's foot: a pig's *trotters.*

tro·tyl (trō′til) *n.* Trinitrotoluene. [<(TRINI)TROT(OLUENE) + -YL]

trou·ba·dour (trōō′bə·dôr, -dōr, -dŏŏr) *n.* One of a class of lyric poets, sometimes including wandering minstrels and jongleurs, originating in Provence in the 11th century and flourishing in southern France, northern Italy, and eastern Spain during the 12th and 13th centuries. Compare TROUVÈRE. See synonyms under POET. [<MF <Provençal *trobador* <*trobar* compose, invent, find; ult. origin uncertain]

Trou·betz·koy (trōō·bets′koi), **Princess** See RIVES, AMÉLIE.

trou·ble (trub′əl) *n.* **1** The state of being distressed, annoyed, or confused; also, grief; affliction; disturbance. **2** A person, circumstance, or event that occasions difficulty or perplexity; the vexation thus occasioned; annoyance; worry; civil unrest or agitation. **3** Toilsome exertion; pains. **4** Any serious or permanent diseased condition: lung *trouble.* See synonyms under ANXIETY, CARE, GRIEF, MISFORTUNE, PAIN. — *v.* **·led, ·ling** *v.t.* **1** To cause mental agitation to; distress; worry. **2** To agitate or disturb; stir up or roil, as water. **3** To inconvenience or incommode. **4** To annoy or pester; bother. **5** To cause physical pain or discomfort to; afflict. — *v.i.* **6** To take pains; bother. **7** To worry. See synonyms under PERPLEX. [<OF *truble, turble* <*turbler* <L *turbula,* dim. of *turba* a crowd] — **troub′ler** *n.* — **troub′ling·ly** *adv.*

troub·le·mak·er (trub′əl·mā′kər) *n.* One who habitually stirs up trouble.

troub·le·shoot·er (trub′əl·shōō′tər) *n.* **1** A mechanic; a repairman. **2** One who locates difficulties and seeks to remove them. **3** A person trained to find and eliminate trouble in the operation of a machine, process, or the like; a maintenance man. — **troub′le·shoot′· ing** *n.*

troub·le·some (trub′əl·səm) *adj.* **1** Causing trouble; vexatious; burdensome; trying; afflictive: a *troublesome* business. **2** Marked by violence; tumultuous. **3** Greatly agitated or disturbed; troublous. — **troub′le·some·ly** *adv.* — **troub′le·some·ness** *n.*

Synonyms: afflictive, annoying, arduous, burdensome, difficult, galling, harassing, hard, importunate, intrusive, irksome, laborious, painful, perplexing, teasing, tiresome, trying, vexatious, wearisome. *Antonyms:* amusing, cheering, easy, entertaining, grateful, gratifying, helpful, light, pleasant.

troub·lous (trub′ləs) *adj.* **1** Marked by commotion or tumult; full of trouble: *troublous* times. **2** Uneasy; restless. **3** *Obs.* Troublesome.

trou-de-loup (trōō′də·lōō′) *n. pl.* **trous-de-loup** (trōō′də·lōō′) *Usually pl.* A conical pit having a vertical central stake with a pointed top, used as a defense against cavalry. [<F *trou* a hole + *de* of + *loup* a wolf]

trough (trôf, trof; *Dial.* trôth, troth) *n.* **1** A long, narrow, open receptacle for conveying a fluid or for holding food or water for animals. **2** A long, narrow channel or depression, as between ridges on land or waves at sea. **3** A gutter for rain water fixed under the eaves of a building. [OE *trog*]

trounce (trouns) *v.t.* **trounced, trounc·ing** **1** To beat or thrash severely; punish. **2** *Colloq.* To defeat. [<OF *tronce* a thick piece of wood <L *truncus* stem, trunk] — **trounc′ing** *n.*

troupe (trōōp) *n.* A company of actors or other performers. — *v.i.* **trouped, troup·ing** To travel as one of a company of actors or entertainers. ♦ **Homophone:** *troop.* [<MF <OF *trope* TROOP] — **troup′er** *n.*

troup·i·al (trōō′pē·əl) See TROOPIAL.

trou·sers (trou′zərz) *n. pl.* A man's garment, covering the body from the waist to the ankles or knees and divided so as to make a separate covering for each leg. Also **trow′sers.** [Blend of obs. *trouse* breeches (<Irish *triubhas*) and DRAWERS]

trousse (trōōs) *n.* **1** A collection of small implements in a sheath or case. **2** A case containing knives, tweezers, etc., fastened to the belt: a surgeon's *trousse.* [<F. See TRUSS.]

trous·seau (trōō·sō′, trōō′sō) *n. pl.* **·seaux** (-sōz′, -sōz) **1** A bride's outfit, especially of clothing. **2** *Obs.* A bundle; truss. [<F < *trousse* a packed collection of things. See TRUSS.]

trout (trout) *n.* **1** A salmonoid fish mostly found in fresh waters and highly esteemed as a game and food fish. The **brown trout** or **river trout** (*Salmo trutta*), attaining a length of 30 inches, is common in Europe; the **cutthroat trout** (*S. clarkii*), and the **rainbow trout** or steelhead (*S. gairdnerii*) are species of western North America. The **speckled trout** or **brook trout** (*Salvelinus fontinalis*) is common in eastern North America. **2** A fish resembling, or supposed to resemble, the

above, as the greenling. [OE *truht* <LL *tructus, tructa* <Gk. *trôktēs* a nibbler < *trôgein* gnaw]

trou·vère (trōō·vâr′) *n.* One of a class of poets flourishing in northern France from the 11th to the 14th centuries, distinguished from the troubadours of southern France by the prevailingly narrative and epic character of their works, which include chansons de geste, fabliaux, romances, and chronicles. Also **trou·veur** (trōō·vûr′). [<F <OF *trovere* < *trover* find, compose; ult. origin uncertain]

Trou·ville (trōō·vēl′) A port and resort in northern France, 9 miles south of Le Havre.

tro·ver (trō′vər) *n. Law* An action to recover the value of personal property of the plaintiff wrongfully withheld or converted by another to his own use: originally an action of trespass against one who found the goods of another, and refused to give them up; the finding, however, became a fiction. [<OF, find; ult. origin uncertain]

trow (trō) *v.t. & v.i.* **1** *Archaic* To suppose; think; believe. **2** *Obs.* To wonder. [Fusion of OE *truwian* < *truwa* faith and *trēowan* believe < *trēowe* true]

trow·el (trou′əl, troul) *n.* **1** A flat-bladed, sometimes pointed implement having an offset handle: used by masons, plasterers, and molders. **2** A small concave scoop with a handle: used in digging about small plants, potting them, etc. **3** A molder's smoothing tool. — *v.t.* **·eled** or **·elled, ·el·ing** or **·el·ling** To apply, dress, or form with a trowel. [<OF *truele* <LL *truella* <L *trulla,* dim. of *trua* a stirring spoon, ladle] — **trow′el·er** or **trow′el·ler** *n.*

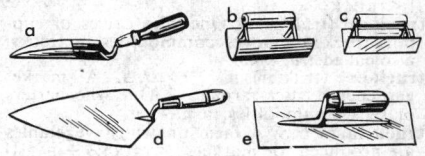

TYPES OF TROWELS
a. Garden. *b.* Circle. *c.* Corner.
d. Brick. *e.* Plastering.

trowel bayonet A spade-shaped bayonet.

trowth (trōth) *n. Scot.* **1** Truth. **2** Troth.

troy (troi) *n.* A system of weights in which 12 troy ounces make a pound, used by jewelers in England and the United States. See under WEIGHT. Also **troy weight.** [from *Troyes;* with ref. to a weight used at a fair held there]

Troy (troi) **1** The site of nine superimposed ruined cities in NW Asia Minor: the seventh stratum, a Phrygian city of perhaps about 1200 B.C., the scene of the *Iliad,* was also called *Ilium, Ilion.* **2** A city on the Hudson River in eastern New York.

Troy coach A type of passenger coach commonly used in travel in the United States before the building of railroads, seating nine inside, having room for driver, six passengers, and baggage outside, and drawn by four to six horses. [from *Troy,* N. Y.]

Troyes (trwä) A city in NE central France, on the Seine river; a major textile center.

tru·an·cy (trōō′ən·sē) *n. pl.* **·cies** The state or habit of being truant; an act of playing truant. Also **tru′ant·ry.**

tru·ant (trōō′ənt) *n.* One who absents himself, especially from school, without leave. — *v.i.* To play the truant. — *adj.* **1** Playing truant; idle. **2** Relating to or characterizing a truant. [<OF, a vagabond, prob. <Celtic]

truant officer *U. S.* An official who investigates truancy from school.

truce (trōōs) *n.* **1** An agreement between belligerents for a temporary suspension of hostilities; an armistice. **2** Temporary cessation or intermission. [Plural of ME *trew,* OE *truwa* faith, a promise. Akin to TRUE, TRUST.]

Tru·cial O·man (trōō′shəl ō·män′) A region on the eastern coast of the Arabian peninsula extending along the **Trucial Coast,** a nearly 400-mile section between Oman and Qatar,

and consisting largely of seven **Trucial Sheikdoms** bound by treaties with Great Britain; about 32,300 square miles.

truck[1] (truk) *n.* **1** One of several forms of strong vehicles, variously constructed, for moving bulky articles, freight, etc.; a dray; a stout automotive vehicle on rubber tires able to carry heavy loads. **2** A two-wheeled barrowlike vehicle with a forward lip and no sides, for use in moving barrels, boxes, etc., by hand. **3** A two-, three-, four-, or sometimes six-wheeled vehicle used about railway stations, for moving trunks, etc.: distinguished as **baggage truck, freight truck,** or **wagon truck. 4** Any of numerous small, flat-topped cars moved by pushing or pulling and used in stores. **5** *Brit.* An open or platform freight car. **6** *Naut.* A disk at the upper extremity of a mast or flagpole through which the halyards of signals are run. **7** A wheel: the original sense, now rare, and usually implying a small tireless wheel. — *v.t.* **1** To carry on a truck. — *v.i.* **2** To carry goods on a truck. **3** To drive a truck. [Appar. <L *trochus* a hoop <Gk. *trochos* a wheel < *trechein* run]

truck[2] (truk) *v.t.* & *v.i.* To exchange or barter; also, to peddle. — *n.* **1** Commodities for sale. **2** *U.S.* Garden produce for market: often in compounds: *truck* farming, etc. **3** *Colloq.* Rubbish; worthless articles collectively. **4** Barter. **5** *Colloq.* Intercourse; dealings: I will have no *truck* with him. [<OF *troquer* barter; origin unknown]

truck·age[1] (truk′ij) *n.* **1** Money paid for conveyance of goods on trucks. **2** Such conveyance. [<TRUCK[1] + -AGE]

truck·age[2] (truk′ij) *n.* Exchange; barter. [<TRUCK[2] + -AGE]

truck·er[1] (truk′ər) *n.* One who drives or supplies trucks or moves commodities in trucks: also called *truckman.*

truck·er[2] (truk′ər) *n.* **1** *U.S.* A market gardener; a truck farmer. **2** One who barters or sells commodities; a hawker.

truck farm *U.S.* A farm on which vegetables are produced for market. [<TRUCK[2] + FARM] — **truck farming**

truck·head (truk′hed′) *n.* The terminal to which supplies are brought by truck and from which they are distributed to the required points. [< TRUCK[1] + HEAD; on analogy with *railhead*]

truck house Formerly, a building used to store articles used in trading with the Indians. Also **trucking house.**

truck·ing[1] (truk′ing) *n.* The act or business of transportation by trucks.

truck·ing[2] (truk′ing) *n.* **1** Exchanging or bartering; dealings; intercourse. **2** *U.S.* Cultivation of vegetables for market; truck farming.

truck·le (truk′əl) *v.* **·led, ·ling** *v.i.* **1** To yield meanly or weakly: with *to.* **2** To roll on truckles or casters. — *v.t.* **3** To cause to roll on truckles or casters. [< *n.*] — *n.* **1** A small wheel. **2** *Dial.* A trundle bed. [<AF *trocle, trokle* <L *trochlea.* See TROCHLEA.] — **truck′ler** *n.* — **truck′ling·ly** *adv.*

truckle bed A trundle bed.

truck·man[1] (truk′mən) *n.* **1** A truck driver. **2** One engaged in the business of trucking.

truck·man[2] (truk′mən) *n. pl.* **·men** (-mən) A dealer in truck; one who trucks or trades.

truck system The practice of paying wages to workmen in goods instead of money.

truc·u·lence (truk′yə·ləns) *n.* Savageness of character, behavior, or aspect. Also **truc′u·len·cy.**

truc·u·lent (truk′yə·lənt) *adj.* **1** Of savage character; awakening terror; cruel; ferocious. **2** Scathing; harsh; violent: said of writing or speech. [<L *truculentus* < *trux, trucis* fierce] — **truc′u·lent·ly** *adv.*

Tru·deau (trōō′dō), **Edward Livingston,** 1848–1915, U.S. physician, pioneer in tuberculosis treatment. — (trōō·dō′), **Pierre Elliott,** born 1919, Canadian statesman; prime minister 1968–: full name *Joseph Phillippe Pierre Ives Elliotte Trudeau.*

trudge (truj) *v.i.* **trudged, trudg·ing** To walk wearily or laboriously; plod. — *n.* A tiresome walk or tramp. [Earlier *tredge, tridge*; origin uncertain] — **trudg′er** *n.*

trudg·en stroke (truj′ən) In swimming, a former racing stroke similar to the crawl stroke but performed with a frog kick or a scissors kick. Also **trudgen, trudgeon stroke.** [after John *Trudgen,* 19th c. British swimmer, who introduced the stroke into England, 1873]

Tru·dy (trōō′dē) Diminutive of GERTRUDE.

true (trōō) *adj.* **tru·er, tru·est 1** Faithful to fact or reality; not false or erroneous: a *true* judgment or proposition. **2** Being real or natural; genuine, not counterfeit: a *true* specimen, *true* gold. **3** Faithful to friends, promises, or principles; loyal; steadfast: *true* love, a *true* friend. **4** Conformable to an existing standard type or pattern; exact: a *true* copy. **5** Accurate, as in shape, dimensions, or position: a *true* fit, a *true* circle. **6** Faithful to the requirements of law or justice; legitimate: the *true* king. **7** Faithful to truth; trustful; honest: a *true* man. **8** Faithful to the promise or predicted event; correctly indicative: a *true* sign. **9** *Biol.* **a** Possessing all the attributes of a developed organ or structure of its class; complete. **b** Of pure strain or pedigree: a *true* collie dog. **c** Conformed to the structure of the type; properly so called: said of a plant or animal, as distinguished from others improperly so called: a *true* locust. **10** Exactly correspondent in pitch or key; in perfect tune: His voice is *true.* See synonyms under AUTHENTIC, CORRECT, FAITHFUL, GOOD, HONEST, JUST[1], MORAL, RIGHT, PURE. — *n.* **1** Truth; covenant; pledge. **2** *pl.* **trues** or **truce** *Obs.* An armistice or truce. — **in** (or **out of**) **true** In (or not in) line of adjustment: said of a mark or part, as in a drawing or a machine. — *adv.* **1** In truth; truly. **2** In a true and accurate manner: The wheel runs *true.* **3** Conformably to the ancestral type: in the phrase *to breed true.* — *v.t.* **trued, tru·ing** To bring to conformity with a standard or requirement; form or adjust, as with geometrical precision: to *true* a frame or a tool. [OE *trēowe.* Akin to TRUCE, TRUST.] — **true′ness** *n.*

true bill *Law* **1** The endorsement by a grand jury on a bill of indictment which they find to be sustained by the evidence. **2** A bill so endorsed.

true·blue (trōō′blōō′) *n.* **1** Originally, a fast blue color or dye; hence, constancy or unchangingness. **2** In the 17th century, a Scotch Presbyterian or Covenanter, so called from the blue adopted as the distinctive color of his political party. **3** A person of uncompromising faithfulness or loyalty as to party, sect, friendship, or principle. — *adj.* Staunch; faithful; dependable; genuine.

true copy An exact, verbatim transcript of any document, report, etc.; especially, one certified as correct by a qualified authority.

true level A surface that is everywhere perpendicular to a plumb line, as that of a liquid at rest.

true·love (trōō′luv′) *n.* **1** One truly beloved; a sweetheart: used also adjectively. **2** *Obs.* Truelovers' knot. **3** The herb-Paris, so called because its four leaves are set together in the form of a truelovers' knot.

true·lov·ers' knot (trōō′luv′·ərz) A complicated double knot, a symbol of fidelity in love.

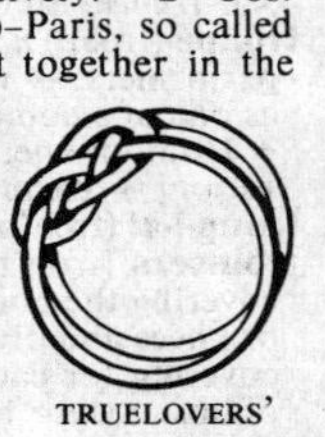

TRUELOVERS' KNOT

true·pen·ny (trōō′pen′ē) *n. Archaic* **1** Originally, a coin of genuine metal. **2** A trusty or genuine person; an honest fellow.

true rib See under RIB.

true time Mean time, or mean solar time.

true toxin An endotoxin.

truf·fle (truf′əl, trōō′fəl) *n.* Any of various fleshy underground fungi (genus *Tuber*), regarded as a choice table delicacy. [<OF *trufe, truffe,* prob. <Ital. *truffa,* ult. <L *tuber* a tuber]

tru·ism (trōō′iz·əm) *n.* An obvious or self-evident truth; a platitude. See synonyms under AXIOM.

Tru·jil·lo (trōō·hē′yō), **Ciudad** See CIUDAD TRUJILLO.

Tru·jil·lo Mo·li·na (trōō·hē′yō mō·lē′nä), **Rafael,** 1891–1961, Dominican general; president of the Dominican Republic 1930–38, 1942–57; assassinated.

Truk (truk, trŏŏk) An island group in the eastern Caroline Islands; total, 40 square miles.

trull (trul) *n.* A prostitute; drab. [<G *trulle, trolle.* ? Akin to TROLL[1].]

tru·ly (trōō′lē) *adv.* **1** In conformity with fact. **2** With accuracy. **3** With loyalty or fidelity. **4** *Archaic* Surely; verily. **5** Lawfully; legally.

Tru·man (trōō′mən), **Harry S,** 1884–1972, president of the United States 1945–1953.

Trumbull (trum′bəl), **John,** 1750–1831, American poet and satirist. — **John,** 1756–1843, American painter. — **Jonathan,** 1710–85, American statesman.

trump[1] (trump) *n.* **1** In various card games, a card of the suit selected to rank above all others temporarily. **2** The suit thus determined: usually in the plural. **3** *Colloq.* A very acceptable and agreeable person; good fellow. — *v.t.* **1** To take (another card) with a trump. **2** To surpass; excel; beat. — *v.i.* **3** To play a trump. — **to trump up** To make up or invent for a fraudulent purpose. [Alter. of TRIUMPH]

trump[2] (trump) *n.* **1** *Poetic* A trumpet. **2** *Scot.* A jew's-harp. [<OF *trompe* <Gmc.]

trump·er·y (trum′pər·ē) *n. pl.* **·er·ies 1** Worthless finery. **2** Rubbish; nonsense. **3** Deceit; trickery. See synonyms under GAUD. — *adj.* Having a showy appearance, but valueless. [<OF *tromperie* < *tromper* TRUMP[1], *v.*]

trum·pet (trum′pit) *n.* **1** A soprano wind instrument with a flaring bell and a long metal tube. The tube was formerly always straight, but now may recurve singly or doubly. **2** A powerful reed stop in an organ. **3** Something resembling a trumpet in form. **4** A tube for collecting and conducting sounds to the ear; an ear trumpet. **5** A loud penetrating sound like that of a trumpet; trumpeting. **6** *pl.* A pitcherplant *(Sarracenia flava)* of the southern United States having trumpet-shaped leaves. **7** *Obs.* A trumpeter. — *v.t.* **1** To sound or proclaim by or as by trumpet; publish abroad. — *v.i.* **2** To blow a trumpet. **3** To give forth a sound as if from a trumpet. [<OF *trompette,* dim. of *trompe* TRUMP[2]]

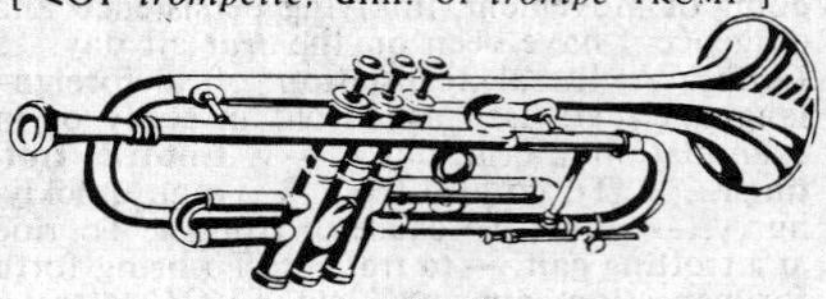

TRUMPET

trumpet creeper A woody vine *(Campsis radicans)* of the southern United States, with scarlet trumpet-shaped flowers. Also **trumpet vine.**

trum·pet·er (trum′pit·ər) *n.* **1** One who sounds a trumpet. **2** One who publishes something loudly abroad. **3** A large South American bird, related to the cranes; especially, the golden-breasted trumpeter *(Psophia crepitans),* often domesticated. **4** A large North American wild swan *(Cygnus buccinator),* having a clarionlike cry: now very scarce: also **trumpeter swan. 5** One of a breed of domestic pigeons.

trumpet flower Any of various plants having trumpet-shaped flowers, as the trumpet creeper, the trumpet honeysuckle.

trumpet honeysuckle A twining honeysuckle *(Lonicera sempervirens)* with oblong leaves and trumpet-shaped flowers, scarlet without and yellow within.

trumpet tree A West Indian and South American tree *(Cecropia peltata)* whose hollow branches are used for musical instruments. Also **trum′pet·wood′** (-wŏŏd′).

trum·pet·weed (trum′pit·wēd′) *n.* **1** The joe-pye weed. **2** The boneset.

trun·cate (trung′kāt) *v.t.* **·cat·ed, ·cat·ing** To cut the top or end from. — *adj.* **1** Truncated. **2** *Biol.* Appearing as though cut or broken squarely off, as the end of certain leaves and shells, the tail of certain birds, the caudal fin of some fishes, etc. [<L *truncatus,* pp. of *truncare* < *truncus* TRUNK] — **trun·ca·tion** (trung·kā′shən) *n.*

trun·ca·ted (trung′kā·tid) *adj.* **1** Cut off; shortened. **2** Describing a cone or pyramid whose vertex is cut off by a plane usually parallel to the base. **3** *Mineral.* Having the edges or angles cut off, as certain crystals. **4** *Biol.* Truncate.

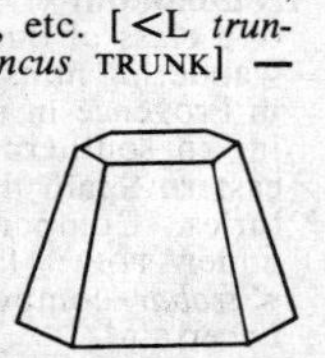

TRUNCATED PYRAMID

trun·cheon (trun′chən) *n.* **1** A short, heavy stick; a club; staff. **2** The baton of a military officer or marshal. **3** A tree

whose branches have been lopped off to hasten growth; tree trunk: the original meaning. **4** *Obs.* A short club or cudgel; a spear shaft. **5** *Brit.* A policeman's club. — *v.t.* To beat as with a truncheon; cudgel. [<OF *truncun, tronchon* a stump, ult. <L *truncus* TRUNK]

trun·dle (trun'dəl) *n.* **1** A small broad wheel, as of a caster. **2** The act, motion, or sound of trundling. **3** A trundle bed. **4** A lantern wheel. **5** *Obs.* A small low-wheeled vehicle; truck. — *v.t.* & *v.i.* **·dled, ·dling** **1** To roll along, as a hoop. **2** To rotate. [Var. of TRINDLE] — **trun'dler** *n.*

trundle bed A bed with very low frame resting upon casters, so that it may be rolled under another bed: also called *truckle bed.*

trun·dle·tail (trun'dəl·tāl') *n. Obs.* A curly-tailed dog; also, a curly tail.

trunk (trungk) *n.* **1** The main stem or stock of a tree, as distinguished from its branches or roots. **2** The human body, apart from the head, neck, and limbs; the torso. **3** *Entomol.* The thorax. **4** *Anat.* The main stem of a nerve, blood vessel, or lymphatic. **5** The main line of a communication or transportation system. **6** The circuit connecting two telephone exchanges. **7** The main body, line, or stem of anything, as distinct from its appendages. **8** A proboscis, as of an elephant. **9** A large box or case used for packing and carrying clothes or other articles, as for a journey. **10** A large compartment at the rear of an automobile, used for storage. **11** *pl.* A close-fitting garment covering the loins and often part of the thighs, worn by male swimmers, athletes, etc. **12** *pl. Obs.* Trunk hose. **13** *Mech.* **a** A trough, chute, or conduit. **b** A large hollow piston in which a connecting rod moves. **14** *Naut.* **a** The well for the centerboard of a vessel. **b** A casing connecting the hatchways of two or more decks and forming a shaft. **c** Any structure placed on the upper deck of a ship, as for shelter. **15** *Archit.* The shaft of a column. See synonyms under BODY. — *adj.* Being or belonging to a trunk or main body: a *trunk* railroad. [<OF *tronc* <L *truncus* stem, trunk, orig. adj., mutilated; def. 8 infl. in meaning by F *trompe* a trumpet]

trunk engine A steam engine having a trunk or open cylinder attached to the piston in place of the usual piston rod, permitting direct attachment of the connecting rod to the piston head.

trunk·fish (trungk'fish') *n. pl.* **·fish** or **·fish·es** A plectognath fish (family *Ostraciidae*) of warm seas, characterized by a body covering of hard, bony plates.

TRUNKFISH
(Rarely to 10 inches)

trunk hose Full breeches worn by gentlemen in the 16th and early 17th centuries, extending from the waist to the middle of the thigh: originally one piece with the hose. Also **trunk breeches.**

trunk line The main line of a transportation or communication system, as distinguished from a branch line.

trunk sleeve A sleeve made very full at the top after the manner of trunk hose.

trun·nel (trun'əl) *n.* A treenail. [Var. of TREENAIL]

trun·nion (trun'yən) *n.* **1** One of two opposite cylindrical projections from the sides of a cannon, forming an axis on which it is elevated or depressed. **2** A similar support on which the cylinders of some engines oscillate. [<F *trognon* the core of a fruit, a stump, trunk; ult. origin unknown]

Tru·ro (troor'ō) **1** A municipal borough in SW Cornwall, England. **2** A port of central Nova Scotia, Canada.

truss (trus) *n.* **1** *Med.* A bandage or support for a rupture. **2** A braced framework of ties, beams, or bars, usually arranged in a series of triangles, as for the support of a roof, airplane, or bridge. **3** A bundle, especially of hay or straw. In England, 56 pounds of old or 60 pounds of new hay make a *truss*; 36 pounds make a *truss* of straw. **4** *Naut.* A heavy iron piece by which a lower yard is attached to a

mast. **5** *Bot.* A compact terminal cluster of flowers. **6** *Archit.* A projection from the face of a wall, used to support a cornice; a large corbel; a bracket or modillion. **7** A pack; package. — *v.t.* **1** To tie or bind; fasten: often with *up.* **2** To support by a truss; brace, as a roof. **3** To fasten the wings of (a fowl) with skewers or twine before cooking. **4** To fasten, tighten, or tie around one, as a garment or laces. **5** To hang, as a criminal: with *up.* [<OF *trusse, trousse* <*trousser, trusser* pack up, bundle, prob. <L *torca* a bundle <*torques.* See TORQUES.] — **truss'er** *n.*

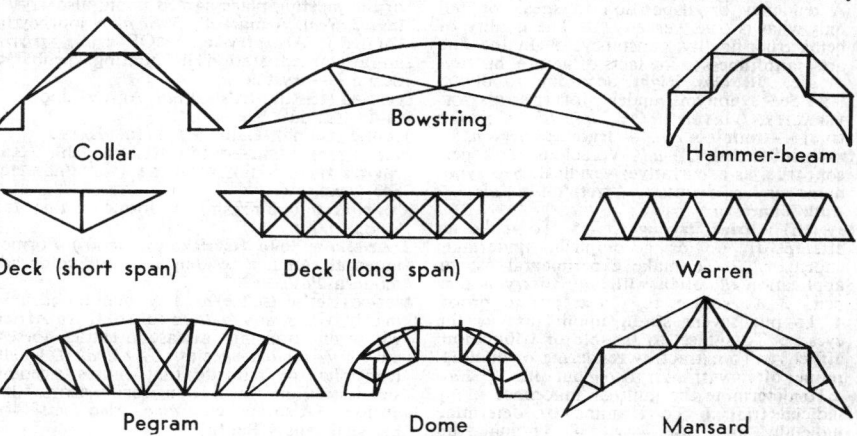

Collar

Bowstring

Hammer-beam

Deck (short span)

Deck (long span)

Warren

Pegram

Dome

Mansard

TYPES OF TRUSSES

truss bridge A bridge stiffened, supported, or formed by a truss or construction of trusses.

truss·ing (trus'ing) *n.* **1** A system of diagonal tension rods and struts for strengthening or stiffening a structure, as a railway car or a vessel's hull. **2** Trusses collectively. **3** The act of one who trusses. **4** A bracing with ties, struts, or the like.

trust (trust) *n.* **1** A confident reliance on the integrity, veracity, or justice of another; confidence; faith; also, the person or thing so trusted. **2** Something committed to one's care for use or safekeeping; a charge; responsibility. **3** The state or position of one who has received an important charge. **4** A confidence in the reliability of persons or things without careful investigation. **5** Credit, in the commercial sense. **6** *Law* The confidence, or the obligation arising from the confidence, reposed in a person (called the *trustee*) to whom the legal title to property is conveyed for the benefit of another (the *cestui que trust*), that he will faithfully apply the property according to such confidence; also, the beneficial title or ownership of property of which the legal title is in another. ◆ Collateral adjective: *fiducial.* **7** The property or thing held in trust; also, the relation subsisting between the holder and the property so held. **8** A permanent combination, now illegal, for the purpose of controlling the production, price, etc., of some commodity or the management, profits, etc., of some business; also, a trust company. Compare CARTEL, CORNER, MONOPOLY, POOL[2], SYNDICATE. **9** Confident expectation; belief; hope. **10** Custody; care; keeping. **11** *Obs.* Trustworthiness. — *v.t.* **1** To have trust in; rely upon. **2** To commit to the care of another; entrust. **3** To commit something to the care of: with *with.* **4** To allow to do something without fear of the consequences. **5** To expect with confidence or with hope. **6** To believe. **7** To allow business credit to. — *v.i.* **8** To place trust or confidence; rely: with *in.* **9** To hope: with *for.* **10** To allow business credit. — **to trust to** To depend upon; confide in. — *adj.* Held in trust: *trust* property, *trust* money. [<ON *traust*, lit., firmness. Akin to TRUCE, TRUE.] — **trust'er** *n.* — **trust'less** *adj.*

Synonyms (noun): assurance, belief, confidence, credence, expectation, faith, hope. See ASSURANCE, BELIEF, FAITH.

Synonyms (verb): believe, commit, confide, hope. See COMMIT, LEAN[1]. *Antonyms:* despair, disbelieve, discredit, distrust, doubt, mistrust, suspect.

trust company An incorporated institution empowered by its charter to accept and execute trusts, as provided by law, to receive deposits of money and other personal property and issue obligations therefor, and to lend money on real and personal securities.

trus·tee (trus·tē') *n.* **1** One who holds property in trust; especially, in popular usage, one of a body of men, often elective, who hold the property and manage the affairs of a church or public institution. **2** One in whose hands property is attached by a trustee process. — *v.t.* **·teed, ·tee·ing** **1** *Law* To attach by trustee process (the property of a debtor in the hands of a third person). **2** To place (property) in the care of a trustee.

trustee process A statutory remedy whereby a creditor may reach property or assets of his debtor in the hands of a third person.

trus·tee·ship (trus·tē'ship) *n.* **1** The post or function of a trustee. **2** Supervision and control of a trust territory by a country or countries commissioned by the United Nations; also, the territory so controlled.

trust·ful (trust'fəl) *adj.* Disposed to trust. — **trust'ful·ly** *adv.* — **trust'ful·ness** *n.*

trust fund Money, securities, or similar property held in trust.

trust·ing (trus'ting) *adj.* Having trust; trustful. — **trust'ing·ly** *adv.* — **trust'ing·ness** *n.*

trust officer An administrator of a trust company or the trust department of a bank.

Trust Territory An area, usually a former colonial possession, governed by a member state of the United Nations as an Administering Authority reporting to the United Nations Trusteeship Council functioning under the authority of the General Assembly with the exception that the trusteeships of the areas designated as strategic are supervised by the Security Council after first being approved the trust agreements. Trust Territories include former League of Nations mandates. Also **trust territory, UN Trust Territory.** The independence of the Cameroons, Somaliland, Tanganyika, and Togoland in 1960–61 and of Western Samoa in 1962 reduced the Trust Territories to:

Trust Territory	*Administered by*
Nauru	Australia on behalf of Australia, New Zealand, and the United Kingdom
(Papua and) New Guinea	Australia
Ruanda–Urundi	Belgium
Trust Territory of the Pacific Islands (a strategic territory)	United States

trust·wor·thy (trust'wûr'thē) *adj.* Worthy of confidence; reliable. See synonyms under AUTHENTIC, FAITHFUL, HONEST, RELIABLE, STAUNCH. — **trust'wor'thi·ly** (-wûr'thə·lē) *adv.* — **trust'wor'thi·ness** *n.*

trust·y (trus'tē) *adj.* **trust·i·er, trust·i·est** **1** Faithful to duty or trust. **2** Staunch; firm. **3** *Obs.* Trustful. See synonyms under FAITHFUL, HONEST, JUST[1], RELIABLE, STAUNCH. — *n. pl.* **trust·ies** A trustworthy person; especially,

a convict who has been found serviceable and reliable and to whom special liberties are granted. — **trust′i·ly** adv. — **trust′i·ness** n.

truth (trooth) n. pl. **truths** (troothz, trooths) 1 The state or character of being true in relation to being, knowledge, or speech. 2 Conformity to fact or reality. 3 Conformity to rule, standard, model, pattern, or ideal. 4 Conformity to the requirements of one's being or nature; steadfastness; sincerity. 5 That which is true; a statement or belief which corresponds to the reality. 6 A fact as the object of correct belief; reality. 7 A tendency or disposition to speak or tell only what is true; veracity. 8 The quality of being true; fidelity; constancy. 9 In the fine arts, faithfulness to the facts of nature, history, or life. 10 Obs. Right, according to divine law. See synonyms under FIDELITY, JUSTICE, VERACITY, VIRTUE. [OE tréowth < treowe true] — **truth′less** adj. — **truth′less·ness** n.

truth·ful (trooth′fəl) adj. Veracious, as a person; true, as a narrative; veridical. See synonyms under CANDID. — **truth′ful·ly** adv. — **truth′ful·ness** n.

try (trī) v. **tried**, **try·ing** v.t. 1 To make an attempt to do or accomplish; undertake; endeavor. 2 To make experimental use or application of: often with out: to try a new pen. 3 To subject to a test; put to proof. 4 To put severe strain upon; tax, as the eyes. 5 To subject to trouble or tribulation; afflict. 6 To extract by rendering or melting; refine: often with out: to try out oil. 7 Law a To determine the guilt or innocence of by judicial trial. b To examine or determine judicially, as a case. — v.i. 8 To make an attempt; put forth effort. 9 To make an examination or test. See synonyms under CHASTEN, ENDEAVOR, EXAMINE, STRUGGLE. — **to try on** To put on (a garment) to test it for fit or appearance. — **to try out** To attempt to qualify: He tried out for the football team. — n. pl. **tries** 1 The act of trying; trial; experiment. 2 In Rugby football, the act of touching the ball down behind an opponent's goal, which scores three points. [< OF trier sift, pick out, prob. < LL tritare thresh < L tritus. See TRITE.] — **tri′er** n.

try·ing (trī′ing) adj. Testing severely; hard to endure. See synonyms under ARDUOUS, DIFFICULT, TROUBLESOME.

trying plane A long plane used to true up the edges of boards to be joined; a jointer. Also **try plane.**

try·lon (trī′lon) n. A three-sided pylon: used as part of the main gateway to the New York World's Fair, 1939. [< TR(I)- + (P)YLON]

try·ma (trī′mə) n. pl. **-ma·ta** (-mə·tə) Bot. A drupelike, commonly two-celled fruit with a bony nucleus and a fleshy, leathery, or fibrous dehiscent or separating exocarp, as the hickory nut and walnut. [< NL < Gk. tryma, trymē a hole < tryein wear away]

try·out (trī′out′) n. U.S. Colloq. A test of ability, as of an actor or athlete, often in competition with others.

tryp·a·no·some (trip′ə·nə·sōm′) n. Any of a genus (Trypanosoma) of flagellate infusorians infesting the blood of man and some lower animals. They destroy the red corpuscles, and cause serious and even fatal diseases, as the sleeping sickness. Also **tryp′a·no·so′ma** (-sō′mə). [< Gk. trypanon a borer + -SOME²]

tryp·a·no·so·mi·a·sis (trip′ə·nō·sō·mī′ə·sis) n. Pathol. Any disease caused by the presence in the body of trypanosomes. Also **tryp′a·no·so′ma·to′sis** (-sō′mə·tō′sis). [< TRYPANOSOME + -IASIS]

tryp·ars·am·ide (trip′är·sam′id, -īd, trip·är′sə·mid, -mīd) n. Chem. A colorless crystalline compound, $C_8H_{10}O_4N_2AsNa$, used in the treatment of trypanosomiasis and certain forms of syphilis. [< TRYP(ANOSOME) + ARS(ENIC) + AMIDE]

tryp·sin (trip′sin) n. Biochem. A proteolytic enzyme contained in the pancreatic juice. [< G < Gk. tripsis a rubbing (< tribein rub) + (PEP)SIN] — **tryp′tic** (-tik) adj.

tryp·sin·o·gen (trip·sin′ə·jen) n. Biochem. The substance secreted by the pancreas and converted into trypsin by the action of intestinal enzymes. [< trypsino- < TRYPSIN + -GEN]

tryp·to·phan (trip′tə·fan) n. Biochem. A crystalline amino acid, $C_{11}H_{12}O_2N_2$, contained in variable amounts in most proteins and associated with the digestive functions. Also **tryp′-**

to·phane (-fān). [< tryptic (< TRYPSIN) + -phan, var. of -PHANE]

try·sail (trī′səl, -sāl′) n. Naut. A small sail bent to a gaff abaft the foremast and mainmast of a ship: also called spencer. [< nautical phrase (at) try lying to in a storm + SAIL]

try square A carpenter's square having usually a wooden stock and a steel blade.

tryst (trist, trīst) v.t. 1 To agree to meet. 2 To appoint (a time), as for meeting. 3 To arrange for in advance; engage. 4 Obs. To trust. — v.i. 5 To agree upon some place or time of meeting. — n. 1 An appointment to meet, or the meeting place agreed upon: also **tryst′ing.** 2 Scot. A market. 3 Scot. A journey in company. Also **tryste.** [< OF triste, tristre an appointed station in hunting, prob. < Scand.] — **tryst′er** n.

tryst·ed (tris′tid, trī′stid) adj. Agreed upon.

tsa·de (tsä·dä′) See SADE.

Tsa·na (tsä′nä), **Lake** See TANA, LAKE.

tsar (tsär), **tsar·e·vitch** (tsär′ə·vich), **tsa·rev·na** (tsä·rev′nä), **tsa·ri·na** (tsä·rē′nä) etc. See CZAR, etc.

Tsa·ri·tsyn (tsä·rē′tsin) A former name for STALINGRAD.

Tsar·sko·e Se·lo (tsär′skə·yə sye·lô′) Former imperial summer residence near Leningrad: modern Pushkin.

tset·se (tset′sē, tsē′tsē) n. 1 A small bloodsucking fly (Glossina morsitans) of southern Africa whose bite transmits disease in cattle, horses, etc. 2 A related species (G. palpalis), which transmits the parasite that causes sleeping sickness. For illustration see INSECTS (injurious). Also spelled tzetze. Also **tsetse fly.** [< Afrikaans < Bantu]

Tshi (chwē, chē) See TWI.

T–shirt (tē′shûrt′) n. 1 A cotton undershirt with short sleeves: so called because T-shaped. 2 A sleeveless jersey or sweater of similar cut for outer wear. Also spelled tee shirt. Also **T shirt.**

Tsi·nan (jē′nän′) A port in NE China, capital of Shantung province; a former treaty port: also Chinan.

Tsing·hai (ching′hī′) A province of NW China; 318,450 square miles; capital, Sining: also Chinghai.

Tsing·tao (ching′dou′) A port in eastern Shantung province, China.

Tsi·tsi·har (tsē′tsē′här′) A city in former north central Manchuria, NE China, former capital of Heilungkiang province.

Tso·ne·can (tsō·nā′kən) n. A linguistic stock of South American Indians, including all the Tehuelchan tribes, and, possibly, the Onas of Tierra del Fuego. By some linguists called **Cho·ne·an** (chō′nē·ən).

T–square (tē′skwâr′) n. An instrument by which to measure or lay out right angles or parallel lines, consisting usually of a flat strip with a shorter head at right angles to it and slightly offset so that it may be slid along the edge of a drawing board.

Tsu·ga·ru Strait (tsoo·gä·roo′) The passage from the Sea of Japan to the Pacific between Honshu and southern Hokkaido, Japan; 15 to 25 miles wide.

tsu·na·mi (tsoo·nä′mē) n. An extensive and often very destructive ocean wave caused by a violent submarine earthquake: erroneously called a tidal wave. [< Japanese, a storm wave < tsu port, harbor + nami wave]

Tsu·shi·ma (tsoo·shē·mä) A Japanese island in Korea Strait; 271 square miles, including 42 offshore islets; scene of a naval battle in the Russo–Japanese War in which the Russian fleet was destroyed, 1905.

tsu·tsu·ga·mu·shi disease (tsoo·tsoo′gä·moo′shē) Pathol. A rickettsial fever endemic in Japan and the Orient, caused by a microorganism (Rickettsia orientalis) transmitted to man by the infected larvae of a mite (genus Trombicula): also called Japanese river fever, river fever, scrub typhus. [< Japanese tsutsugamush, a small Japanese mite < mushi a bug]

Tu·a·mo·tu Archipelago (too′ä·mō′too) An island chain extending 1,300 miles south of the Marquesas Islands in eastern French Oceania; 330 square miles: also Low Archipelago: formerly Paumotu Archipelago.

Tuan (twän) n. Sir; mister: courteous Malayan form of address for a European. [< Malay]

Tua·reg (twä′reg) n. 1 A member of the nomadic Berber tribes of the central and

western Sahara. 2 The Berber dialect spoken by these people.

tu·a·ta·ra (too′ä·tä′rä) n. A sphenodon. Also **tu′a·te′ra** (-tä′rä). [< Maori < tua on the farther side, the back + tara the spine]

Tu·a·tha De Da·naan (thoo′ə·hə dä dä′nôn) In ancient Irish mythology, a race of gods who ruled in Ireland until their defeat by the Milesians: now conceived of as fairies. See DANU. [< OIrish, people of Danu]

tub (tub) n. 1 A broad, open–topped vessel, usually of wood, and formed with staves, bottom, hoops, and handles on the side. 2 A bathtub. 3 Brit. Colloq. A bath taken in a tub. 4 The amount that a tub contains. 5 Anything resembling a tub, as a broad, clumsy boat: contemptuous or humorous. 6 A small cask. 7 A bucket for bringing ore or coal up a shaft; also, an underground tram. 8 A keeve. 9 A sweating in a tub. — v.t. & v.i. **tubbed, tub·bing** To wash, bathe, or place in a tub. [< MDu. tubbe] — **tub′ba·ble** adj. — **tub′ber** n.

tu·ba (too′bə, tyoo′-) n. pl. **·bas** or **·bae** (-bē) 1 A large bass instrument of the saxhorn family. 2 An ancient Roman war trumpet. 3 A powerful reed stop in an organ. [< L, a war trumpet]

tu·bal (too′bəl, tyoo′-) adj. 1 Relating to a tube. 2 Anat. Pertaining to the Fallopian tube.

Tu·bal–cain (too′bəl·kān, tyoo′-) The first artificer in brass and iron. Gen. iv 22.

tu·bate (too′bāt, tyoo′-) adj. Of the form of or provided with a tube; tubular. [< NL tubatus < L tubus a pipe]

TUBA

tub·by (tub′ē) adj. **·bi·er**, **·bi·est** 1 Resembling a tub in form; round and fat; corpulent. 2 Lacking resonance when struck; sounding dull or wooden, as a musical instrument.

tube (toob, tyoob) n. 1 A long hollow cylindrical body of metal, glass, rubber, etc., generally used for the conveyance of something through it; a pipe. 2 The principal part of a gun. 3 Any similar device having a tube or tubelike part, as a telescope. 4 Biol. Any elongated hollow part or organ, as the united part of a gamopetalous corolla or a gamosepalous calyx. 5 A subway or a tunnel. 6 An electron, thermionic, or vacuum tube. 7 The tubular space enclosing lines of magnetic force or induction. 8 A collapsible metal cylinder for containing paints, toothpaste, glue, and the like. — v.t. **tubed, tub·ing** 1 To fit or furnish with a tube. 2 To enclose in a tube or tubes. 3 To make tubular. [< F < L tubus a tube] — **tube′less** adj. — **tub′er** n.

Tube may appear as a combining form in hyphemes or solidemes, with the meaning of noun definition 1:

tube–drawing	tube–rolling
tube–drilling	tube–scraping
tube–fed	tube–shaped
tube–filling	tubesmith
tubemaker	tube–straightening
tubemaking	tubework

tube foot Zool. An ambulacral sucker; one of the small vascular locomotor processes exserted through the ambulacral pores of echinoderms.

tu·ber (too′bər, tyoo′-) n. 1 Bot. A short, thickened portion of an underground stem, as in the potato or artichoke. 2 Anat. A swelling or prominence; tubercle. [< L, a swelling]

tu·ber·cle (too′bər·kəl, tyoo′-) n. 1 A small rounded eminence or nodule. 2 Bot. A minute swelling on the roots of leguminous plants, which contains a micro–organism believed to absorb nitrogen from the air for the use of the plant. 3 Pathol. A small granular tumor formed within an organ from morbid or infected matter: in the lungs, the seat of pulmonary consumption. 4 Anat. A small knoblike excrescence, especially on the skin or on a bone. [< L tuberculum, dim. of tuber a swelling] — **tu·ber·cu·loid** (too·bûr′kyə·loid, tyoo′-) adj.

tubercle bacillus The rod-shaped, Gram-positive bacterium (Mycobacterium tuberculosis) which is the cause of tuberculosis in man.

tu·ber·cu·lar (tŏŏ·bûr′kyə·lər, tyŏŏ-) *adj.* 1 Affected with tubercles; nodular. 2 Tuberculous. —*n.* One affected with tuberculosis.

tu·ber·cu·late (tŏŏ·bûr′kyə·lit, -lāt) *adj.* 1 Nodular. 2 Affected with tubercles; tuberculous. Also **tu·ber′cu·lat′ed.** [<NL *tuberculatus* <L *tuberculum* TUBERCLE] —**tu·ber′cu·la′tion** *n.*

tu·ber·cu·lin (tŏŏ·bûr′kyə·lin, tyŏŏ-) *n.* Bacteriol. A sterile liquid prepared from attenuated cultures of the tubercle bacillus, used especially as a test for tuberculosis in children and animals. Also **tu·ber′cu·line** (-lin, -lēn). [<L *tuberculum* TUBERCLE + -IN]

tuberculo- *combining form* 1 Tuberculosis; of or pertaining to tuberculosis; tuberculous. 2 The tubercle bacillus. Also, before vowels, **tubercul-.** [<L *tuberculum*, dim. of *tuber* a swelling]

tu·ber·cu·lo·sis (tŏŏ·bûr·kyə·lō′sis, tyŏŏ-) *n.* Pathol. A communicable disease caused by infection with the tubercle bacillus, characterized by the formation of tubercles within some organ or tissue: when affecting the lungs, known as **pulmonary tuberculosis.** [<NL <L *tuberculum* TUBERCLE + -OSIS]

tu·ber·cu·lous (tŏŏ·bûr′kyə·ləs, tyŏŏ-) *adj.* Of, pertaining to, or affected with tuberculosis.

tu·ber·if·er·ous (tŏŏ′bə·rif′ər·əs, tyŏŏ′-) *adj.* Bearing or producing tubers. [<TUBER + -(I)FEROUS]

tu·ber·oid (tŏŏ′bər·oid, tyŏŏ′-) *adj.* Resembling a tuber.

tube·rose¹ (tŏŏb′rōz′, tyŏŏb′-, tŏŏ·bə·rōs′, tyŏŏ-) *n.* A bulbous plant (*Polianthes tuberosa*) of the amaryllis family, bearing a long raceme of fragrant white flowers. [<NL *Tuberosa*, species name <L *tuberosus* knobby <*tuber* a swelling]

tube·rose² (tŏŏ′bər·ōs, tyŏŏ′-) *adj.* Tuberous. [<TUBER + -OSE]

tu·ber·os·i·ty (tŏŏ′bə·rôs′ə·tē, tyŏŏ′-) *n. pl.* **ties** 1 The state of being tuberous. 2 A swelling or protuberance. 3 Anat. A large, rough eminence on a bone, as for the attachment of a muscle.

tu·ber·ous (tŏŏ′bər·əs, tyŏŏ′-) *adj.* 1 Bearing projections or prominences. 2 Resembling tubers. 3 Bot. Bearing tubers.

tuberous root Bot. One of the tuberlike parts of a multiple or fascicled fleshy root, as in the dahlia.

tu·bi·form (tŏŏ′bə·fôrm, tyŏŏ′-) *adj.* Having the form of a tube; tubular. [<*tubi-* (<TUBE) + -FORM]

tub·ing (tŏŏ′bing, tyŏŏ′-) *n.* 1 Tubes collectively. 2 A piece of tube or material for tubes. 3 Material for pillowcases. 4 The act of making tubes.

Tü·bing·en (tü′bing·ən) A university town in the state of Baden-Württemberg, SW Germany, on the Neckar.

Tub·man (tub′mən), **William Vacanarat**, 1895–1971, Liberian statesman: president of Liberia 1944–1971.

tub·thump·er (tub′thum′pər) *n.* U.S. Colloq. A noisy speaker; a soapbox orator.

Tu·bu·ai Islands) (tŏŏ′bŏŏ·ī′) An island group south of the Society Islands, comprising a part of Rench Oceania; 115 square miles: also *Austral Islands.*

tu·bu·lar (tŏŏ′byə·lər, tyŏŏ′-) *adj.* 1 Having the form of a tube; tube-shaped. 2 Made up of or provided with tubes. 3 Pertaining to or sounding as if produced in a tube. [<L *tubulus* TUBULE]

tu·bu·late (tŏŏ′byə·lāt) *v.t.* **·lat·ed, ·lat·ing** 1 To shape or fashion into a tube. 2 To furnish with a tube. —*adj.* Shaped like or into a tube; also, provided with a tube: also **tu′bu·lat′ed.** [<L *tubulatus* tubular <*tubulus* TUBULE] —**tu′bu·la·tor** *n.*

tu·bu·la·tion (tŏŏ′byə·lā′shən, tyŏŏ′-) *n.* 1 The formation of a tube. 2 The arrangement of a set of tubes.

tu·bule (tŏŏ′byŏŏl, tyŏŏ′-) *n.* A minute tube. [<L *tubulus*, dim. of *tubus* a tube] —**tu′bu·li·form′** *adj.*

tu·bu·li·flo·rous (tŏŏ′byə·lə·flôr′əs, -flō′rəs, tyŏŏ′-) *adj.* Bot. Having tubular florets: said of composite plants with all the florets tubular. [<*tubuli-* (TUBULE) + -FLOROUS]

tu·bu·lous (tŏŏ′byə·ləs, tyŏŏ′-) *adj.* 1 Tube-shaped; tubular. 2 Bot. Having tubular florets.

3 Consisting of or containing small tubes. Also **tu′bu·lose** (-lōs).

tu·bu·lure (tŏŏ′byə·lŏŏr, tyŏŏ′-) *n.* The short open tube of a retort, receiver, or bell jar. [<F <L *tubulus* TUBULE]

Tu·ca·na (tŏŏ·kā′nə, tyŏŏ-) Astron. A southern constellation. See CONSTELLATION.

tu·chun (dŏŏ′jŭn′) *n.* Chinese Formerly, the military governor of a Chinese province. —**tu′chun·ate** *n.* —**tu′chun·ism** *n.*

tuck¹ (tuk) *n.* 1 A fold made in a garment usually horizontal. 2 A flap forming a continuation of one side of a book cover, and inserted in a loop or pocket in the other side. 3 Naut. That part of a vessel's hull where the after planks meet. 4 Brit. Slang Food. 5 U.S. Slang Stamina; determination. [<v.] —*v.t.* 1 To fold under; thrust or press in the ends or edges of. 2 To wrap or cover snugly. 3 To thrust or press into a close place; cram; hide. 4 To make tucks in, by folding and stitching. —*v.i.* 5 To contract; draw together. 6 To make tucks, [Fusion of OE *tūcian* ill-treat, lit., tug and MDu, *tucken* pluck]

tuck² (tuk) Scot. & Obs. *n.* 1 A stroke; tap; beat, as of a drum. 2 A flourish, as of a trumpet. —*v.t. & v.i.* To beat; tap, as a drum. [<AF *toker*, OF *toucher* touch]

tuck³ (tuk) *n.* Archaic A long narrow sword; rapier. [<AF *etoc*, OF *estoc* <*estoquier* <Du. *stocken* pierce]

Tuck (tuk), Friar A jovial priest, associate and confessor of Robin Hood.

tuck·a·hoe (tuk′ə·hō) *n.* An underground fungus (*Poria cocos*) with a brown edible sclerotium: found in the southern United States: also *Indian bread* or *Virginia truffle.* [<Algonquian (Virginian) *tockawhoughe*]

tuck·er¹ (tuk′ər) *n.* 1 One who or that which tucks. 2 A covering, formerly worn over the neck and shoulders by women. 3 Austral. Food. [<TUCK¹]

tuck·er² (tuk′ər) *v.t.* Colloq. To weary completely; exhaust: usually with *out.* [Freq. of TUCK¹, *v.*]

tuck·er·bag (tuk′ər·bag) *n.* Austral. A cloth bag in which food is carried by tramps, travelers, etc.

tuck·et (tuk′it) *n.* Archaic A flourish on a trumpet. [Dim. of TUCK²]

Tuc·son (tŏŏ·son′, tŏŏ′son) A city in SE Arizona; a factory, rail, and mining center.

Tu·cu·mán (tŏŏ′kŏŏ·män′) A city in NW Argentina; an agricultural and industrial center.

-tude *suffix of nouns* Condition or state of being: gratitude. [<F *-tude* <L *-tudo*]

Tu·dor (tŏŏ′dər, tyŏŏ′-) *adj.* 1 Of or pertaining to the **Tudors,** an English royal family descended from Sir Owen Tudor, a Welshman who married Catherine of Valois, widow of Henry V. See the table of sovereigns under ENGLAND. 2 Designating or pertaining to the architecture, poetry, etc., developed during the reigns of the Tudors.

Tudor architecture The latest phase of the Perpendicular style, developed under the Tudors to make houses more livable. it employed large windows, many fireplaces, large bays, steep roofs, flattened arches, much carving, and paneling. The house plan was generally a quadrangle, an H or an E.

Tues·day (tŏŏz′dē, -dā, tyŏŏz′-) *n.* The third day of the week; the day after Monday. [OE *tīwesdæg* day of Tiw <*Tiw,* an ancient Teutonic deity + *dæg* a day; trans. of LL *dies Martis* Mars's day]

tu·fa (tŏŏ′fə, tyŏŏ′-) *n.* 1 A variety of calcium carbonate with cellular structure, as deposited from springs and streams. 2 Tuff. [<Ital. *tufa, tufo* <L *tofus, tophus*] —**tu·ffa·ceous** (tŏŏ·fā′shəs, tyŏŏ′-) *adj.*

tuff (tuf) *n.* A volcanic rock composed of material varying in size from fine sand to coarse gravel; used for building. [<MF *tufe, tuffe* <Ital. *tufo* TUFA] —**tuff·a′ceous** *adj.*

tuft (tuft) *n.* 1 A collection or bunch of small, flexible parts, as hair, grass, or feathers, held together at the base. 2 A clump or knot; frequently, a cluster of threads drawn tightly through a quilt, mattress, or upholstery to secure the stuffing. 3 A gold tassel formerly worn by titled undergraduates at Oxford and

Cambridge universities; also, a student who wears such a tuft. —*v.t.* 1 To separate or form into tufts. 2 To cover or adorn with tufts. —*v.i.* 3 To form tufts. [<OF *tuffe,* prob. <Gmc.] —**tuft′er** *n.* —**tuft′y** *adj.*

tuft·ed (tuf′tid) *adj.* 1 Having, or adorned with, a tuft; crested: the *tufted* duck. 2 Forming a tuft or dense cluster; cespitose.

tuft·hunt·er (tuft′hun′tər) *n.* Archaic 1 Originally, a student at Oxford or Cambridge who sought association with titled students distinguished by gold tufts on their hats. 2 One who seeks the acquaintance of persons of rank; a snob; sycophant; parasite. —**tuft′·hunt′ing** *n. & adj.*

tug (tug) *v.* **tugged, tug·ging** *v.t.* 1 To pull at with effort; strain at. 2 To pull, draw, or drag with effort. 3 To tow with a tugboat. —*v.i.* 4 To pull strenuously: to *tug* at an oar. 5 To strive; toil; struggle. See synonyms under DRAW. —*n.* 1 An act of tugging; a violent pull. 2 A strenuous contest; a struggle; wrestle. 3 A tugboat. 4 A trace of a harness; also, Scot., rawhide: formerly used in making traces. 5 Brit. A colleger or member of the king's foundation at Eton College. 6 Brit. Dial. A high-wheeled cart for carrying logs, etc., slung beneath its axles. [ME *toggen,* intens. of OE *tēon* tow; infl. by ON *toga* draw] —**tug′ger** *n.*

tug·boat (tug′bōt′) *n.* A small, compact, ruggedly built vessel operated by steam or other power and designed for towing: also called *towboat.*

Tu·ge·la (tŏŏ·gā′lə) A river in Kwa Zulu/Natal, Republic of South Africa, flowing 300 miles east from near the Basutoland and Orange Free State borders, through the **Tugela Falls** (2,810 feet) to the Indian Ocean.

Tug·gurt (tŏŏ·gŏŏrt′) A territory of NE Southern Territories, Algeria; 52,094 square miles; capital, Tuggurt: French *Touggourt.*

tug of war 1 A contest in which a number of persons at one end of a rope pull against a like number at the other end, each side endeavoring to drag the other across a line marked between. 2 A laborious effort; supreme contest.

Tui·le·ries (twē′lər·ēz, Fr. twēl·rē′) A palace of the French kings in Paris: begun in 1564 and burned in 1871; site occupied by the **Tuileries Gardens,** a public park near the Louvre.

tuille (twēl) *n.* In armor, a steel protection for the thighs, attached by straps to the tassets. [<MF <OF *tieule* <L *tegula* a tile]

tu·i·tion (tŏŏ·ish′ən, tyŏŏ-) *n.* 1 The act or business of teaching or any branch of learning; instruction. 2 The charge or payment for instruction. 3 Archaic Guardianship; care. See synonyms under EDUCATION, learning, nurture. [<AF *tuycioun,* OF *tuicion* <L *tuitio, -onis* a guard, guardianship <*tuitus,* pp. of *tueri* look at, watch] —**tu·i′tion·al, tu·i′tion·ar′y** (-er′ē) *adj.*

Tu·la (tŏŏ′lä) 1 A city of west central European Russian S.F.S.R. 2 A city in Hidalgo state, central Mexico; site of the ancient capital of the Toltecs: officially **Tula de Al·len·de** (thä ä·yen′dä).

tu·la·re·mi·a (tŏŏ′lə·rē′mē·ə) *n.* A disease of rodents, especially rabbits, caused by a micro-organism (*Pasteurella tularensis*) which may be transmitted to man by flies and certain insects, producing an undulant fever; rabbit fever. Also **tu′la·rae′mi·a.** [<NL, from *Tulare* County, California + Gk. *haima* blood]

tu·le (tŏŏ′lē) *n.* A large bulrush (*Scirpus acutus*) of the sedge family growing on damp or flooded land in the southwestern United States. [<Sp. <Nahuatl *tullin*]

tu·lip (tŏŏ′lip, tyŏŏ′-) *n.* 1 Any of numerous hardy bulbous herbs (genus *Tulipa*) of the lily family, bearing variously colored bell-shaped flowers. 2 A bulb or flower of this plant. [<F *tulipe* <OF *tulipan* <Turkish *tuliband* <Persian *dulband* a turban]

tu·lip·o·ma·ni·a (tŏŏ′lip·ə·mā′nē·ə, -mān′yə, tyŏŏ′-) *n.* A craze for the acquisition of cultivation of tulips; specifically, that which arose in Holland early in the 17th century and which spread into wild speculation like

an epidemic. [< *tulipo-* (< TULIP) + -MANIA] — **tu′lip·o·ma′ni·ac** *n.*

tu·lip·tree (to͞o′lip·trē′, tyo͞o′-) *n.* **1** A large magnoliaceous tree *(Liriodendron tulipifera)* of the eastern United States, with greenish cup-shaped flowers. **2** Any of various other trees having tuliplike flowers.

tu·lip·wood (to͞o′lip·wo͝od′, tyo͞o′-) *n.* **1** The wood of the tuliptree. **2** Any of several ornamental cabinet woods yielded by various trees: so called from their color or markings. **3** Any of the trees themselves.

Tul·la·more (tul′ə·môr′, -mōr′) The county town of County Offaly, Ireland.

tulle (to͞ol, *Fr.* tül) *n.* A fine, silk, open-meshed material, used for veils, etc. [< F, from *Tulle,* a city in SW France, where first made]

Tul·ly (tul′ē) See CICERO, MARCUS TULLIUS.

Tul·sa (tul′sə) A city in NE Oklahoma, on the Arkansas River.

tum·ble (tum′bəl) *v.* **·bled, ·bling** *v.i.* **1** To roll or toss about. **2** To perform acrobatic feats, as somersaults, etc. **3** To fall violently or awkwardly. **4** To move in a careless or headlong manner; stumble. **5** *Colloq.* To understand; comprehend: with *to.* **6** *Metall.* To smooth, clean, or polish, as castings, by friction with each other or with a polishing material, in a rotating box or barrel. — *v.t.* **7** To toss carelessly; cause to fall. **8** To throw into disorder or confusion; disturb; rumple. —*n.* **1** The act of tumbling; a fall. **2** A state of disorder or confusion. [ME *tumbel,* freq. of *tumben,* OE *tumbian* fall, leap] —**tum′bling** *n.*

tum·ble·bug (tum′bəl·bug′) *n.* A scarabaeid beetle that rolls up a ball of dung to enclose its eggs.

tum·ble-down (tum′bəl·doun′) *adj.* Rickety, as if about to fall in pieces; dilapidated.

tumble gear *Mech.* A type of reversing gear comprising a rocking frame adapted to bring either of two idlers into mesh with the driving gear.

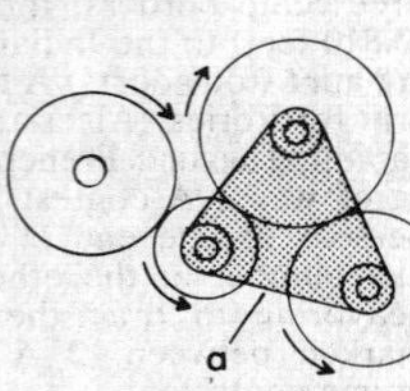

TUMBLE GEAR
a. Rocking frame.

tum·ble-home (tum′bəl·hōm′) *n. Naut.* The inward inclination of a vessel's hull above the line of extreme breadth.

tum·bler (tum′blər) *n.* **1** A drinking glass without a foot; also, its contents. The base was formerly rounded, so that the glass would not stand upright. **2** One who or that which tumbles; especially, an acrobat or contortionist. **3** One of a breed of domestic pigeons noted for the habit of turning forward somersaults during flight. **4** A greyhound used formerly in coursing. **5** In a lock, a latch that engages a bolt and prevents its being shot in either direction unless the tumbler is raised by the key bit. **6** In a firearm lock, a piece attached to the hammer and receiving the thrust of the mainspring. **7** A tumbling box. **8** *Mech.* **a** A piece of metal that projects from a revolving or rocking shaft and communicates motion to another piece. **b** The rocking frame in a tumble gear. **9** *Scot.* A light cart. **10** A child's toy, so formed and weighted as to rock at the slightest touch.

tum·ble·weed (tum′bəl·wēd′) *n.* Any of various plants which, when withered, break from the root and are driven about by the wind, widely scattering their seed.

tumbling box *Metall.* A box, usually cylindrical and mounted on a horizontal shaft, in which articles, as castings, are cleaned by friction against each other and the walls of the box. Also **tumbling barrel.**

tum·brel (tum′bril) *n.* **1** *Obs.* A two-wheeled military covered cart for carrying tools, ammunition, etc. **2** A farmer's cart; especially, a boxlike cart for carrying and dumping dung. **3** A rude cart in which prisoners were taken to the guillotine during the French Revolution. **4** Formerly, a ducking stool set on wheels. Also **tum′bril.** [< OF *tomberel* < *tomber* fall, ult. < Gmc.]

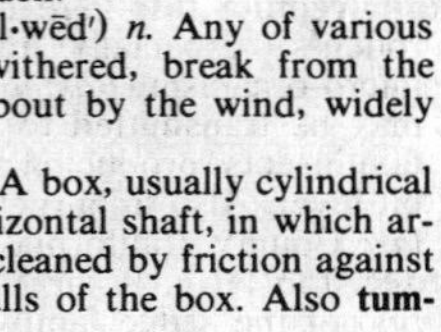
TUMBREL

tu·me·fa·cient (to͞o′mə·fā′shənt, tyo͞o′-) *adj.* Producing or tending to produce tumefaction; causing a swelling.

tu·me·fac·tion (to͞o′mə·fak′shən, tyo͞o′-) *n.* **1** Any puffing up of a part, especially as in a tumor. **2** A swelling; puffiness. **3** The act of tumefying; state of being tumefied.

tu·me·fy (to͞o′mə·fī, tyo͞o′-) *v.t.* & *v.i.* **·fied, ·fy·ing** To swell or puff up. [< MF *tuméfier* < L *tumefacere* < *tumere* swell + *facere* make]

Tu·men (to͞o′mun′) A river on the Korea-Manchuria border, flowing 324 miles east to the Sea of Japan.

tu·mer·os·i·ty (to͞o′mə·ros′ə·tē) *n.* The state or quality of being swollen.

tu·mes·cence (to͞o·mes′əns, tyo͞o-) *n.* **1** The state or quality of being swollen. **2** The act or process of becoming tumid, as an organ or part of the body. **3** That which is swollen.

tu·mes·cent (to͞o·mes′ənt, tyo͞o-) *adj.* **1** Swelling; somewhat tumid. **2** Beginning to swell. [< L *tumescens, -entis,* ppr. of *tumescere,* inceptive of *tumere* swell]

tu·mid (to͞o′mid, tyo͞o′-) *adj.* **1** Swollen; enlarged; protuberant. **2** Inflated or pompous in style; bombastic. **3** Bursting; teeming. [< L *tumidus* < *tumere* swell] —**tu′mid·ly** *adv.*

tu·mid·i·ty (to͞o·mid′ə·tē, tyo͞o-) *n.* The state or character of being tumid. Also **tu·mid·ness** (to͞o′mid·nis, tyo͞o′-).

tu·mor (to͞o′mər, tyo͞o′-) *n.* **1** *Pathol.* A local swelling on or in any part of the body, especially from some autonomous morbid growth of tissue which may or may not become malignant; a neoplasm. **2** *Obs.* High-sounding words or style; bombast. **3** *Obs.* A swelling of any kind, as of water. Also *Brit.* **tu′mour.** —**fatty tumor** Lipoma. [< OF *tumour* < L *tumor* a swelling < *tumere* swell] —**tu′mor·ous** *adj.*

tump (tump) *n. Dial.* A little mound or hill, as about a plant; a barrow. [Cf. Welsh *twmp*] — **tump′y** *adj.*

tump·line (tump′līn′) *n. Canadian* A strap passing across the forehead and helping support a load on the back: also called *metump.* Also **tump.** [Prob. < Am. Ind.]

Tu·muc-Hu·mac Mountains (to͞o·mo͞ok′o͞o·mäk′) A range on the border between Brazil and French Guiana and Surinam; highest point, 2,800 feet.

tu·mu·lar (to͞o′myə·lər, tyo͞o′-) *adj.* Having the form of a mound.

tu·mu·lose (to͞o′myə·lōs, tyo͞o′-) *adj.* Full of mounds or hills. Also **tu′mu·lous.** [< L *tumulosus* < *tumulus* a mound] —**tu′mu·los′i·ty** (-los′ə·tē) *n.*

tu·mult (to͞o′mult, tyo͞o′-) *n.* **1** The commotion, disturbance, or agitation of a multitude; an uproar; turbulence; hubbub. **2** Any violent commotion or agitation, as of the mind. [< OF *tumulte* < L *tumultus* < *tumere* swell]

Synonyms: agitation, bluster, bustle, commotion, confusion, disorder, disturbance, ferment, flurry, hubbub, hurly-burly, noise, outbreak, racket, riot, turbulence, turmoil, uproar. See NOISE, QUARREL[1], REVOLUTION. *Antonyms:* calmness, peace, quiet, repose, tranquillity.

tu·mul·tu·ous (to͞o·mul′cho͞o·əs, tyo͞o-) *adj.* **1** Characterized by tumult; disorderly. **2** Causing or affected by tumult or agitation; agitated or disturbed. Also **tu·mul′tu·ar′y** (-er′ē). See synonyms under NOISY, TURBULENT, VIOLENT. — **tu·mul′tu·ous·ly, tu·mul′tu·ar′i·ly** *adv.* — **tu·mul′tu·ous·ness, tu·mul′tu·ar′i·ness** *n.*

tu·mu·lus (to͞o′myə·ləs, tyo͞o′-) *n. pl.* **·li** (-lī) A sepulchral mound, often of great size. Compare BARROW[2], CAIRN. [< L, a mound < *tumere* swell]

tun (tun) *n.* **1** A large cask. **2** A brewers' fermenting vat. **3** The amount of malt liquor fermented at one operation; a brew. **4** A varying measure of capacity, usually equal to 252 gallons. —*v.t.* **tunned, tun·ning 1** To put into a cask or tun. **2** To add to a liquor, as for flavoring. [OE *tunne*]

tu·na[1] (to͞o′nə) *n.* A tunny. Also **tuna fish.** [< Am. Sp., ult. < L *thunnus* TUNNY]

tu·na[2] (to͞o′nə) *n.* **1** A tropical American prickly pear *(Opuntia tuna),* or its edible fruit. **2** One of a number of other prickly pears. [< Am. Sp., prob. < Taino]

tun·a·ble (to͞o′nə·bəl, tyo͞o′-) *adj.* **1** That may be put in tune. **2** Being in tune. **3** *Obs.* Tuneful; musical. Also **tune′a·ble.** —**tun′a·ble·ness** *n.* — **tun′a·bly** *adv.*

Tun·bridge Wells (tun′brij) A municipal borough in SW Kent, England.

tun·dra (tun′drə, to͝on′-) *n.* A rolling, treeless, often marshy plain of Siberia, arctic North America, etc. [< Russian < Lapp]

tune (to͞on, tyo͞on) *n.* **1** A melodious succession of musical tones adjusted to some measure and constituting one whole; a melody or air. **2** A setting for a hymn or psalm used in worship. **3** The state or quality of being in the proper pitch or key. **4** Concord or unison. **5** Suitable temper or humor; state of mind. **6** *Obs.* A musical tone or sound. —**to change one's tune** To assume a different manner or style. —**to the tune of** To the serious or exorbitant amount of: *to the tune of* a thousand dollars. —*v.* **tuned, tun·ing** *v.t.* **1** To adjust to a musical standard; put in tune; attune. **2** To adapt to a particular tone, expression, or mood. **3** To bring into harmony or accord. **4** To utter or express musically; sing. —*v.i.* **5** To be in harmony. —**to tune in** To adjust a radio receiver to the frequency of (a station, broadcast, etc.). —**to tune out** To adjust a radio receiver to exclude (interference, a station, etc.). —**to tune up 1** To bring (musical instruments) to a common pitch. **2** To adjust (a machine, engine, etc.) to proper working order. [Var. of TONE] —**tun′ing** *adj.* & *n.*

tune·ful (to͞on′fəl, tyo͞on′-) *adj.* Musically disposed; melodious; musical —**tune′ful·ly** *adv.* — **tune′ful·ness** *n.*

tune·less (to͞on′lis, tyo͞on′-) *adj.* **1** Not being in tune. **2** Not employed in making music; silent. **3** Lacking in rhythm, melody, etc. —**tune′less·ly** *adv.* —**tune′less·ness** *n.*

tun·er (to͞o′nər, tyo͞o′-) *n.* **1** One who or that which tunes. **2** One who puts musical instruments, as pianos, in tune. **3** *Telecom.* A radio receiver without audio-frequency amplifiers, speaker, etc.

tune-up (to͞on′up′, tyo͞on′-) *n. Colloq.* An adjustment to bring a motor or other device into proper operating condition.

Tung (do͝ong) A river of SE China, flowing 250 miles SW and west from southern Kiangsi province to a delta in east central Kwangtung province, emptying into the Canton River.

Tung·chow (to͞ong′jō′) A former name for NANTUNG.

tung oil (tung) A yellow, ill-smelling oil extracted from the seeds of the Chinese **tung tree** *(Aleurites fordi),* now cultivated in the U.S.: used in paints, varnishes, etc., as a highly effective drying agent, and also as a waterproofing agent. [< Chinese *t'ung* the tung tree]

tung·state (tung′stāt) *n. Chem.* A salt of tungstic acid: sodium *tungstate.*

tung·sten (tung′stən) *n.* A gray, brittle, metallic element (symbol W, atomic number 74) having about the same density as gold and the highest melting point of any metal, much used in the manufacture of filaments for electric lamps and tools. See PERIODIC TABLE. [< Sw. < *tung* weighty + *sten* stone] —**tung·sten·ic** (tung·sten′ik) *adj.*

tungsten lamp An incandescent electric lamp having a filament of metallic tungsten.

tungsten steel A hard, tenacious steel that contains tungsten.

tung·stic (tung′stik) *adj. Chem.* Of, pertaining to, derived from, or containing tungsten, especially in its highest valence. [< TUNGST(EN) + -IC]

tungstic acid *Chem.* Either of two acids consisting of tungsten oxide combined with water, and uniting with bases to form salts; especially, the yellow crystalline monohydrate, H_2WO_4.

tung·stite (tung′stīt) *n.* A yellow or yellowish-green native tungsten trioxide, WO_3. Also **tungstic ocher.**

Tung·ting (do͝ong′ting′), **Lake** A lake in NE Hunan province, SE central China; one of the largest lakes in China; 1,450 square miles.

Tun·gus (to͝on·go͞oz′) *n.* **1** One of a Mongoloid people of the Tungusic group inhabiting eastern Siberia. **2** The language of the Tungus, belonging to the Manchu-Tungusic subfamily of Altaic languages: also *Tungusic.* Also **Tun·guz′.**

Tun·gus·i·an (to͝on·go͞oz′ē·ən) *adj.* Of or per-

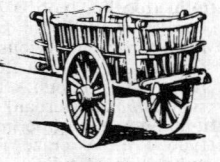

taining to the Tungus or their language. —*n.* One of the Tungus.

Tun·gus·ic (tŏŏn·gōōz′ik) *adj.* **1** Of, pertaining to, or denoting a group of tribes including the Tungus and Manchus. **2** Tungusian. —*n.* The Tungus language.

Tun·gus·ka (tŏŏn·gōōs′kä) Any of three rivers in north central Asiatic Russian S.F.S.R., known as the **Upper Tunguska** (see ANGARA), the **Stony** (or **Middle**) **Tunguska**, flowing 975 miles NW and west to the Yenisei, and the **Lower Tunguska**, flowing 1,587 miles north and NW to the Yenisei.

tu·nic (tōō′nik, tyōō′-) *n.* **1** Among the ancient Greeks and Romans, a body garment, with or without sleeves, reaching to the knees: worn usually without a girdle. **2** A modern outer garment gathered at the waist, as a short overskirt or a blouse. **3** A surcoat worn over armor. **4** A tunica. **5** *Bot.* Any loose membranous skin enveloping an organ, as a seed coat. **6** *Brit.* The undercoat worn by soldiers, policemen, etc. **7** A bishop's tunicle; a dalmatic. [< F *tunique* < L *tunica* < Semitic]

tu·ni·ca (tōō′nə·kə, tyōō′-) *n. pl.* **·cae** (-sē) *Biol.* A covering or investing part; a mantle of tissue, as of the kidney, ovaries, etc.; tunic. [< NL < L, a tunic]

tu·ni·cate (tōō′nə·kit, -kāt, tyōō′-) *n.* Any of a subphylum (Tunicata or Urochordata) of small marine chordates characterized by the presence of a notochord and tail in the larval stage only and by the secretion of a tough envelope, or tunic, enclosing the body of the adult, as ascidians and salps. —*adj.* **1** Pertaining to or resembling a tunicate. **2** Covered with a tunic or tunica. **3** *Bot.* Having concentric coats, as an onion. [< NL *tunicata* < L *tunicata* (*animalia*) coated (animals), neut. pl. of *tunicatus*, pp. of *tunicare* clothe with a tunic < *tunica* a tunic]

tu·ni·cle (tōō′ni·kəl, tyōō′-) *n.* **1** A light or fine tunic. **2** A slight natural covering. **3** A short ecclesiastical vestment. [< L *tunicula*, dim. of *tunica* a tunic]

tuning fork A fork-shaped piece of steel which vibrates with a definite frequency when struck: used to measure the pitch of musical tones.

Tu·nis (tōō′nis, tyōō′-) **1** A former Barbary state of northern Africa. **2** The capital and chief port of Tunisia, on the Mediterranean.

Tu·ni·sia (tōō·nish′ə, -nish′ē·ə, -nē′zhə, tyōō-) A republic in northern Africa, proclaimed July, 1957; 48,195 square miles; capital, Tunis; formerly, *Tunis.*

Tu·ni·sian (tōō·nish′ən, -nē′zhən, tyōō-) *adj.* Of or relating to Tunisia, or Tunis, or their inhabitants. —*n.* **1** An inhabitant or native of Tunisia or Tunis. **2** The speech of Tunisia, a North Arabic dialect.

tunk·et (tung′kit) *n. U.S. Dial.* Hell: a euphemistic expletive. [Origin unknown]

tun·nage (tun′ij) *n. Brit.* Tonnage.

tun·nel (tun′əl) *n.* **1** An artificial subterranean passageway or gallery, especially one under a hill, etc., as for a railway. **2** Any similar passageway under or through something. **3** A funnel. **4** The main flue or shaft of a chimney or the like. **5** An adit or level in a mine. —*v.* **·neled** or **·nelled**, **·nel·ing** or **·nel·ling** *v.t.* **1** To make a tunnel through. **2** To shape or make in the form of a tunnel: to *tunnel* a passage. —*v.i.* **3** To make a tunnel. [Fusion of OF *tonnelle* a partridge net and *tonel*, dim. of *tonne* a cask] —**tun′nel·er** or **tun′nel·ler** *n.*

tunnel disease Decompression sickness.

tun·ny (tun′ē) *n. pl.* **·nies 1** A large, oily, marine fish (family *Thunnidae*) related to

GREAT TUNNY

the mackerel, especially the **great tunny** (*Thunnus thynnus*) of warm seas, sometimes weighing 1,500 pounds. **2** One of various related fishes, as

the albacore and the California horse mackerel (*Trachurus symmetricus*). [< OF *thon* < L *thunnus* < Gk. *thynnos*]

Tu·ol·um·ne River (tōō·ol′ə·mē) A river in central California, flowing 110 miles west to the San Joaquin River.

tup (tup) *n.* **1** A ram, or male sheep. **2** The striking part of a power hammer. —*v.t. & v.i.* **tupped**, **tup·ping** To copulate with (a female): said of the ram. [ME *tupe, tope*, prob. < Scand. Cf. Norw. & Sw. *tupp* a cock.]

tu·pe·lo (tōō′pə·lō) *n. pl.* **·los 1** One of several trees of Asia and the southeastern United States (genus *Nyssa*), especially the sourgum or blackgum. **2** The wood of any of these trees. [< Muskhogean]

Tu·pi (tōō·pē′) *n. pl.* **Tu·pis** or **Tu·pi 1** A member of any of a group of South American Indian tribes, comprising the northern branch of the Tupian stock, and occupying the Amazon, Tapajós, and Xingú valleys. **2** The language spoken by the Tupis, used as a lingua franca along the Amazon: also called *Neengatu*. [< Tupian, a comrade]

Tu·pi·an (tōō·pē′ən) *adj.* Of or pertaining to the Tupis or their language. —*n.* A large linguistic stock of South American Indians of some one hundred tribes of the Tupis and Guaranis, scattered throughout the continent (except in Venezuela): also **Tu·pi′-Gua·ra·ni′** (-gwä′rä·nē′).

tuque (tōōk, tyōōk) *n.* A Canadian cap consisting of a knitted cylindrical bag with tapered ends, worn by thrusting one end inside the other, for tobogganing, etc. [< dial. F (Canadian) < F *toque* TOQUE]

tu quo·que (tōō kwō′kwē, tyōō) *Latin* A retort in kind from a person assailed: also used attributively; literally, thou also.

tu·ra·cou (tōō′rä·kōō′) *n.* An African bird (*Turacus fischeri*) related to the cuckoo, remarkable for its red-and-green plumage: also called *touraco*. [< F *touraco* < native West African name]

Tu·ra·ni·an (tōō·rā′nē·ən, tyōō-) *adj.* Of or pertaining to a large family of agglutinative languages of Europe and northern Asia, neither Indo-European nor Semitic, specifically known as the Ural-Altaic languages, or any of the people who speak them. —*n.* **1** One whose mother tongue is a Ural-Altaic language; a person of Ural-Altaic stock. **2** The Ural-Altaic languages collectively. **3** Theoretically, one of an unknown nomadic people who antedated the Aryans in Europe and Asia. [< Persian *Tūrān*, a country north of the Oxus River]

tur·ban (tûr′bən) *n.* **1** An Oriental head covering consisting of a sash or shawl, twisted about the head or about a cap. **2** Any similar headdress. **3** A round-crowned brimless hat for women or children. [< F *turban, turbant* < Pg. *turbante* < Turkish *tülbend*, dial. alter. of *dülbend* < Persian *dulband* < *dul* a turn + *band* a band] —**tur′baned** (-bənd) *adj.*

tur·ba·ry (tûr′bər·ē) *n. pl.* **·ries 1** In English law, the liberty of digging turf or peat upon another's ground. **2** A place where turf or peat is dug. [< AF *turberie*, OF *tourberie* < *tourbe* peat < LG *turf, turv* turf]

tur·bel·lar·i·an (tûr′bə·lâr′ē·ən) *n.* Any of a class (Turbellaria) of motile aquatic flatworms having a ciliated epidermis and sometimes brilliantly colored: includes the planarians. [< NL < L *turbellae* a tumult, pl. dim. of *turba* a crowd]

tur·beth (tûr′bəth), **tur·bith** See TURPETH.

tur·bid (tûr′bid) *adj.* **1** Having the sediment or lees stirred up; cloudy; muddy. **2** Being in a state of confusion; disturbed. See synonyms under THICK. [< L *turbidus* < *turbare* trouble < *turba* crowd] —**tur′bid·ly** *adv.* —**tur′bid·ness, tur·bid·i·ty** (tûr·bid′ə·tē) *n.*

tur·bi·dim·e·ter (tûr′bə·dim′ə·tər) *n.* An instrument for measuring the turbidity of a liquid. [< TURBIDI(TY) + -METER]

tur·bi·nal (tûr′bə·nəl) *adj.* Spirally coiled; turbinate; top-shaped. —*n.* A turbinate bone or cartilage. [< L *turbo, -inis* a whirlwind, top]

tur·bi·nate (tûr′bə·nit, -nāt) *adj.* **1** Top-shaped; also, spinning like a top. **2** *Zool.* Tapering from a broad base to the apex, as certain spiral shells. **3** *Anat.* Pertaining to one of the thin, curved bones on the walls of the nasal passages. Also **tur′bi·nat·ed**. [< L *turbinatus* < *turbo, -inis* a whirlwind]

tur·bi·na·tion (tûr′bə·nā′shən) *n.* **1** A conelike formation. **2** The act, state, or condition of spinning like a top.

tur·bine (tûr′bin, -bīn) *n.* An engine consisting of one or more rotary units, mounted on a shaft and usually provided with a series of curved vanes, actuated by the reaction, impulse, or suction of steam, water, gas, or other fluid under pressure. [< F < L *turbo, -inis* a whirlwind, top]

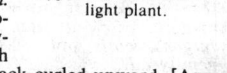

TURBINE
Type used in an electric-light plant.

tur·bit (tûr′bit) *n.* One of a breed of domestic pigeons having a small head with the feathers at the back curled upward. [Appar. < L *turbo, -inis* a top; so called with ref. to its shape]

turbo- *combining form* A turbine; related to or operated by a turbine or turbines: *turbojet.* [< L *turbo* a top]

tur·bo·fan (tûr′bō·fan′) *n. Aeron.* **1** A compressor having ducted fans which supply air to a jet engine. **2** The engine using such a fan.

tur·bo·gen·er·a·tor (tûr′bō·jen′ə·rā′tər) *n.* An electric power-generating machine adapted for direct coupling to a steam turbine.

tur·bo·jet (tûr′bō·jet′) *n. Aeron.* **1** A gas turbine which drives the air compressor and auxiliaries of certain types of jet engines. **2** The engine itself.

tur·bo·prop (tûr′bō·prop′) *n. Aeron.* **1** A gas turbine connecting directly with the propeller. **2** An engine having such a turbine. [< TURBO- + PROP(ELLER)]

tur·bo·su·per·charg·er (tûr′bō·sōō′pər·chär′jər) *n. Aeron.* A compact, highly efficient supercharging device utilizing exhaust gases, for use on aircraft engines operating at very high altitudes.

tur·bot (tûr′bət) *n. pl.* **·bot** or **·bots 1** A large European flatfish (*Psetta maxima*) esteemed as food. **2** One of various related flatfishes. [< AF *turbut*, OF *tourbout*, ? < OSw. *törnbut* < *törn* a thorn + *but* the butt]

tur·bu·lence (tûr′byə·ləns) *n.* **1** The state or condition of being violently disturbed, restless, or confused. **2** *Physics* The irregular flow of a gas or fluid caused by an obstacle or by friction, as of a ship or airplane in rapid motion. **3** *Meteorol.* A disturbed condition of the atmosphere due to irregular wind currents. Also **tur′bu·len·cy**.

tur·bu·lent (tûr′byə·lənt) *adj.* **1** Being in violent agitation or commotion. **2** Inclined to rebel; insubordinate. **3** Having a tendency to disturb or throw into confusion. [< MF < L *turbulentus* full of disturbance < *turbare*. See TURBID.] —**tur′bu·lent·ly** *adv.*

Synonyms: agitated, blustering, boisterous, disorderly, disturbed, insurgent, mutinous, obstreperous, rebellious, refractory, riotous, seditious, tumultuous, wild. See NOISY, VIOLENT.

Tur·co (tûr′kō) *n. pl.* **·cos** An Algerian light-infantryman serving in the French army; an Algerian tirailleur. [< F < Sp., a Turk]

Tur·co·man (tûr′kə·mən) See TURKOMAN.

tur·di·form (tûr′də·fôrm) *adj.* Thrushlike in form or structure. [< L *turdus* a thrush + -FORM]

tur·dine (tûr′din, -dīn) *adj.* **1** Belonging or pertaining to a large and widely distributed family (Turdidae) of singing birds, including thrushes and bluebirds. **2** Pertaining to the subfamily (Turdinae) which includes the true thrushes. [< NL, subfamily name < L *turdus* a thrush]

tu·reen (tŏŏ·rēn′, tyŏŏ-) *n.* A deep, covered dish, as for soup. [Earlier *terrene* < F *terrine*. Doublet of TERRINE.]

---

add, āce, câre, pälm; end, ēven; it, īce; odd, ōpen, ôrder; tŏŏk, pōōl; up, bûrn; ə = a in *above*, e in *sicken*, i in *clarity*, o in *melon*, u in *focus*; yōō = u in *fuse*, oi, oil; ou, pout; ch, check; g, go; ng, ring; th, thin; th, this; zh, vision. Foreign sounds á, œ, ü, kh, ṅ; and ◆: see page xx. < from; + plus; ? possibly.

Tu·renne (tü·ren'), **Viscount de**, 1611–75. Henri de la Tour d'Auvergne, French general and marshal.

turf (tûrf) n. pl. **turfs** (Archaic **turves**) 1 A mass of matted roots of grass and other fine plants filling the upper stratum of certain soils; a sod. 2 Peat. 3 Loosely, a grass plot. 4 A racecourse; horse-racing: in the phrase **the turf.** 5 Slang a A home territory, especially that of a youthful street gang, defended against invasion by rival gangs. b Any place regarded possessively as the center of one's activity or interest: Philadelphia is his turf. — v.t. To cover with turf; sod. [OE] — **turf'y** adj.

Tur·fan (tōōr'fän') A depression in eastern Sinkiang-Uigur Autonomous Region, NW China, lowest point of the Chinese mainland (940 feet below sea level); center of an ancient Indo-Iranian civilization (A.D. 200–400) and site of the capital of a Uigur empire (about 800–1200).

turf·man (tûrf'mən) n. pl. **·men** (-mən) A man who is devoted to or connected with horse-racing.

Tur·ge·nev (tōōr·gä'nyef), **Ivan Sergeyevich**, 1818–83, Russian novelist. Also **Tur·ge'niev.**

tur·gent (tûr'jənt) adj. Obs. Turgid. [<L turgens, -entis, ppr. of turgere swell] — **tur'gent·ly** adv.

tur·ges·cence (tûr·jes'əns) n. 1 The process of swelling up; the state of being swollen. 2 Hence, empty pompousness; inflation. Also **tur·ges'cen·cy.** [<Med.L turgescentia <L turgescens, -entis, ppr. of turgescere, inceptive of turgere swell] — **tur·ges'cent** adj. — **tur·ges'cent·ly** adv.

tur·gid (tûr'jid) adj. 1 Unnaturally distended, as by contained air or liquid; swollen. 2 Figuratively, inflated; bombastic; tumid: a turgid tale of woman wronged. [<L turgidus < turgere swell] — **tur'gid·ly** adv.

tur·gid·i·ty (tûr·jid'ə·tē) n. 1 The state or quality of being turgid. 2 Biol. The internal pressure of a cell against its enclosing membrane. Also **tur·gid·ness** (tûr'jid·nis).

tur·gite (tûr'jīt) n. A fibrous, earthy iron ore, found as a reddish-black or dark-red ferric hydroxide. [from Turginsk, a copper mine in the Ural Mountains]

tur·gor (tûr'gər) n. 1 The state of being turgid; turgidity. 2 Physiol. The normal condition of the blood vessels and of cells distended by their protoplasmic contents: also **vital turgor.** [<LL <L turgere swell]

Tur·got (tür·gō'), **Anne Robert Jacques**, 1727–81, French statesman, financier, and economist.

Tu·rin (tōōr'in, tyōōr'-, tōō·rin', tyōō-) A city on the Po river in NW Italy; capital of the kingdom of Sardinia until 1860 and of Italy until 1864; a major industrial and transportation center: Italian **Torino.**

Turk (tûrk) n. 1 A native or inhabitant of Turkey; an Ottoman. 2 One of any of the peoples speaking any of the Turkic languages, and ranging from the Adriatic to the Sea of Okhotsk: believed to be of the same ultimate extraction as the Mongols. 3 Loosely, a Moslem. 4 A Turkish horse.

Turk·cap lily (tûrk'kap') See under LILY.

Tur·ke·stan A region of central Asia that extended from the Caspian Sea to the Gobi Desert and was divided by the Pamir and Tien Shan mountain systems, incorporating the Kazakh, Kirghiz, Tadzhik, Turkmen, and Uzbek S.S.R. (called Soviet Central Asia) during the era of the Soviet Union; and Chinese Turkestan, comprising the Sinkiang-Uigur Autonomous Region.

tur·key (tûr'kē) n. pl. **·keys** 1 A large American bird (family Meleagridae) related to the pheasant, having the head naked and the tail extensible upward and sideward; especially, the American domesticated turkey (Meleagris gallopavo): much esteemed as food. 2 A guinea fowl. 3 U.S. Slang A play (occasionally, a motion picture) that is a failure. [Short for turkey cock the guinea fowl, from Turkey; later applied erroneously to the American bird]

Tur·key (tûr'kē) A republic of Asia Minor and SE Europe; 296,108 square miles (Turkey in Asia, known as Anatolia, 287,043 square miles, Turkey in Europe, 9,065 square miles); capital, Ankara.

turkey buzzard A sooty-black vulture of tropical America (Cathartes aura), with a naked red head and neck.

Turkey carpet A hand-made Turkish carpet or one having a Turkish design and texture. Also **Turkish carpet.**

turkey cock 1 A male turkey. 2 One who struts and behaves in a pompous, conceited manner.

turkey gobbler A turkey cock.

TURKEY BUZZARD
(Length, 30 inches; wingspread, 6 feet)

turkey red 1 A brilliant red pigment, or its color. 2 Cotton cloth dyed with this permanent bright red.

tur·key-trot (tûr'kē-trot') n. A dance consisting of a stop-step, glide, and turn to syncopated music, the feet being kept well apart and a swinging motion being given to the shoulders: popular in the early 20th century.

turkey vulture The turkey buzzard.

Tur·ki (tōōr'kē) adj. 1 Of or pertaining to any of the languages included in the Turkic subfamily of Altaic languages. 2 Of or pertaining to any of the peoples speaking any of these languages, as the Osmanlis and Chuvashes of Turkey, NW Persia, Transcaucasia, etc., and the Asian Tatar tribes, as the Uigurs, Uzbeks, Kipchaks, Turkomans, etc., of Mongolia and Turkestan. — n. 1 The Turkic languages. 2 A member of any of the Turki peoples.

Turk·ic (tûr'kik) n. A subfamily of the Altaic family of languages, including Osmanli or Turkish, Azerbaijani, Uzbek, Chuvash, Yakut, etc. — adj. Pertaining to this linguistic subfamily, or to any of the peoples speaking these languages.

Turk·ish (tûr'kish) adj. 1 Of or pertaining to Turkey or the Turks. 2 Of or relating to the Turkic subfamily of Altaic languages, especially to Osmanli. — n. The Altaic language of Turkey; Osmanli.

Turkish bath A bath originating in the East in which sweating is induced by exposure to high temperature, usually in a room heated by steam, followed by washing, rubbing, kneading, or the like.

Turkish delight A sweetmeat of Turkish origin, usually consisting of cubes having a gelatinous consistency coated with powdered sugar and having any of various fruit flavors. Also **Turkish paste.**

Turkish Empire The Ottoman Empire.

Turkish pound A Turkish lira. Symbol £T.

Turkish towel A heavy, rough towel with loose, uncut pile. Also **turkish towel.**

Turk·ism (tûr'kiz·əm) n. 1 The religion, or the social or political system, characteristic of the Turks. 2 Any distinctive peculiarity of Turkish speech or custom.

Tur·k·man n. pl. **·mans** 1 A member of the ethnic group in Turkmenistan, descended from the nomadic tribes that inhabited the land during the Persian Empire. Also spelled **Turcoman, Turk'·man.** [Persian Turkuman one like a Turk]

— **Turk·me·ni·an** (tûrk·mē'nē·ən) adj. & n. — **Turk·o·man·ic** (tûr'kə·man'ik) adj.

Turk·men (tûrk'men) n. The Turkic language of the Turkomans.

Turk·me·ni·stan A country of Central Asia bordering Iran and Afghanistan to the south and Kazakhstan and Uzbekistan to the north; capital, Ashkhabad; pop. 3,714,000.

Turkmen Soviet Socialist Republic A former republic of the U.S.S.R. in Central Asia; 189,370 square miles; capital, Ashkhabad.

Turks and Cai·cos Islands (tûrks, kā'kos) An archipelago SE of the Bahamas, comprising a dependency of Jamaica in The West Indies; 202 square miles.

Turk's-cap lily (tûrks'kap') See under LILY.

Turk's-head (tûrks'hed') n. An ornamented knot of turbanlike form.

Tur·ku (tōōr'kōō) A city of SW Finland, on the Gulf of Bothnia: Swedish Åbo.

tur·ma·line (tûr'mə·lēn) See TOURMALINE.

tur·mer·ic (tûr'mər·ik) n. 1 The root of an East Indian plant (Curcuma longa) of the ginger family, used as a condiment, aromatic stimulant, dyestuff, etc. 2 The plant. 3 Any of several plants resembling turmeric.

— adj. Of, pertaining to, or saturated with turmeric. [Earlier tarmaret, ? <F terre mérite deserving earth <Med.L terra merita; ult. origin uncertain]

turmeric paper A paper, yellow from saturation with the extract of turmeric, used as a test for alkalis, turning it brown, and for boric acid, turning it red-brown: also called curcuma paper.

tur·moil (tûr'moil) n. Confused motion; disturbance; tumult. See synonyms under TUMULT. — v.t. & v.i. Archaic To be or cause to be in a state of turmoil. [? <OF tremouille hopper of a mill <L tremere tremble; prob. infl. in form by turn and moil]

turn (tûrn) v.t. 1 To give a rotary motion to; cause to rotate, as about an axis. 2 To change the position of, as by rotating: to turn a trunk on its side. 3 To move so that the upper side becomes the under: to turn a page. 4 To bring the subsoil of to the surface, as by plowing or spading. 5 To alter (a garment) by reversing the material: to turn a cuff. 6 To reverse the arrangement or order of; cause to be upside down. 7 To upset mentally; dement or distract; infatuate. 8 To revolve mentally; ponder: often with over. 9 To sprain or strain: to turn one's ankle in running. 10 To nauseate (the stomach). 11 To shape (an object revolving in a lathe, etc.) in rounded form by application of a cutting tool. 12 To give rounded or curved form to. 13 To give graceful or finished form to: to turn a phrase. 14 To perform by revolving: to turn cartwheels. 15 To bend, curve, fold, or twist. 16 To bend or blunt (the edge of a knife, etc.). 17 To change or transform; convert: to turn water into wine. 18 To translate: to turn French into English. 19 To exchange for an equivalent: to turn stocks into cash. 20 To adapt to some use or purpose; apply: to turn information to good account. 21 To cause to become as specified: The sight turned him sick. 22 To change the color of. 23 To make sour or rancid; ferment or curdle. 24 To change the direction of. 25 To direct or aim; point. 26 To change the direction or focus of (thought, attention, etc.). 27 To deflect or divert: to turn a blow. 28 To repel: to turn a charge. 29 To go around or to the other side of: to turn a corner. 30 To pass or go beyond: to turn twenty-one. 31 To cause or compel to go; send; drive: to turn a beggar from one's door. 32 To keep circulating in trade: to turn goods or money. 33 Obs. To pervert. — v.i. 34 To move around an axis or center; rotate; revolve. 35 To move completely or partially on or as if on an axis: He turned and ran. 36 To change position; also, to roll from side to side, as in bed. 37 To take a new direction: We turned north. 38 To reverse position; become inverted. 39 To reverse direction or flow: The tide has turned. 40 To change the direction or focus of one's thought, attention, etc.: Let us turn to the next problem. 41 To depend; hinge: with on or upon. 42 To be affected with giddiness; whirl, as the head. 43 To become upset or nauseated, as the stomach. 44 To change attitude, sympathy, or allegiance: to turn on one's neighbors. 45 To rebel; act in retaliation: The worm turns; to turn on one's persecutors. 46 To become transformed; change: The water turned into ice. 47 To become as specified: His hair turned gray. 48 To change color: said especially of leaves. 49 To become sour, rancid, or fermented, as milk or wine. 50 Naut. To tack or put about. 51 Obs. To vacillate. See synonyms under BEND, CHANGE, REVOLVE. — **to turn against** To become or cause to become opposed or hostile to. — **to turn an honest dollar** (or **penny**) To earn money honestly. — **to turn down** 1 To diminish the flow, volume, etc., of: Turn down the gas. 2 Colloq. a To reject or refuse, as a proposal, or request. b To refuse the request, proposal, etc., of. — **to turn in** 1 To fold or double. 2 To bend or incline inward. 3 To deliver; hand over. 4 Colloq. To go to bed. — **to turn off** 1 To stop the operation, flow, use, etc. 2 To leave the direct road; make a turn. 3 To deflect or divert. 4 Brit. To dismiss; discharge. — **to turn on** 1 To set in operation, flow, etc.: to turn on an engine. 2 Slang

To take or experience the mental and perceptual effects of taking a psychedelic drug, as marijuana, LSD, etc. 3 *Slang* To arrange for (someone) to take or be affected by such a drug. 4 *Slang* To evoke in (someone) a profound or rapt response, as though under the influence of a psychedelic drug: Baroque music really *turned* him *on.* — **to turn out** 1 To turn inside out. 2 To eject or expel; put out. 3 To dismiss or discharge. 4 To turn off (def. 1). 5 To bend or incline outward. 6 To produce by work or toil; make. 7 To come or go out, as for duty or service. 8 To prove (to be); be found. 9 To become or result. 10 To equip or fit; dress. 11 *Colloq.* To get out of bed. — **to turn over** 1 To change the position of; invert. 2 To upset; overturn. 3 To hand over; transfer or relinquish. 4 To do business to the amount of. 5 To invest and get back (capital). 6 To use in trade or exchange; buy and then sell: to *turn over* merchandise. — **to turn tail** To run away; flee. — **to turn to** 1 To set to work. 2 To seek aid from. 3 To refer or apply to. — **to turn up** 1 To bring or fold the under side upward. 2 To bend or incline upward. 3 To bring or be brought to view by plowing, digging, etc.; find or be found. 4 To increase the flow, volume, etc., of. 5 To put in an appearance; arrive. — *n.* 1 The act of turning, or the state of being turned. 2 A change to another direction, motion, or position: a *turn* of the tide. 3 A deflection or deviation from a course; a bend; a change in policy or trend: a *turn* of fortune. 4 The point at which a change takes place: a *turn* for the better in a crisis or an illness. 5 Motion about or as about a center; a rotation or revolution: the *turn* of a crank. 6 Favorable, fitting, or regular time or chance in some succession or rotation, or the work it offers; a job; also, a round; spell: one's *turn* to read, a *turn* of work. 7 Characteristic form or style; distinguishing shape; mold; cast: the *turn* of an ankle or sentence. 8 Disposition; tendency; manner: a humorous *turn*; a knack or special ability: a *turn* for study. 9 A deed performed, regarded as aiding or injuring another: an ill *turn*; also, an advantage proposed or gained: It served his *turn.* 10 A walk, drive, or trip to and fro; promenade: a *turn* in the park. 11 A trip back and forth in taking a load of anything: *turns* made to a mill; also, the load so taken. 12 A round in a skein or coil. 13 *Music* An instrumental or vocal embellishment formed by a group of four notes rapidly performed, the first a tone above and the third a tone below the principal tone, which occupies the second and fourth positions. In an **inverted turn** the tones are reversed in order. 14 *Colloq.* A spell of dizziness or faintness; a shock to the nerves, as from alarm: It gave her quite a *turn.* 15 A variation or difference in type or kind. 16 A short theatrical act of any description; also, in sport, a contest; a bout. 17 A twist, as of a rope, around a tree or post. 18 A transaction on the stock exchange, involving purchase and sale, or the reverse; also, any business transaction. 19 In infantry drill, a maneuver in which a line of troops changes the direction of its front, usually in preparation for marching. — **at every turn** On every occasion; constantly. — **by turns** 1 In alternation or sequence. 2 At intervals. — **in turn** One after another; in proper order or sequence. — **out of turn** Not in proper order or prescribed order or sequence. — **to a turn** Just right; perfectly or exactly: said especially of cooked food, in allusion to the turning of the spit in roasting. — **to take turns** To act, play, etc. in proper order. ◆ Homophones: *tern, terne.* [Fusion of OE *tyrnan* and *turnian* and OF *turner,* all <L *tornare* turn in a lathe <*turnus* a lathe <Gk. *tornos*]

turn·a·bout (tûrn′ə·bout′) *n.* 1 One who overturns things; a radical. 2 A merry-go-round. 3 A turn-about-face.

turn-a·bout-face (tûrn′ə·bout′fās′) *n.* A change from one loyalty or viewpoint to another; adoption of new opinions or policy: also *turnabout.*

turn·a·round (tûrn′ə·round′) *n.* 1 The time required for maintenance, refueling, discharging or loading cargo, etc., during a round trip of a truck, ship, aircraft, etc. 2 A space, as in a driveway, large enough for the turning around of a vehicle. 3 A shift or reversal of a trend, procedure, development, etc.

turn·buck·le (tûrn′buk′əl) *n. Mech.* A form of coupling so threaded that when connected lengthwise between two metal rods it may be turned so as to regulate the distance between them.

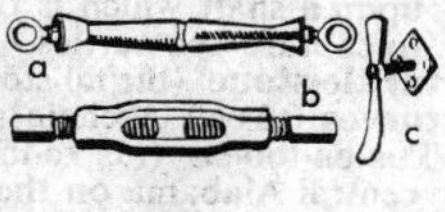

TURNBUCKLES
a. Insulated for electric wires.
b. Type for metal tie rods.
c. For window shutters.

turn·coat (tûrn′kōt′) *n.* One who goes over to the opposite side or party; a renegade.

turn-down (tûrn′doun′) *adj.* Folded down, as a collar; also, capable of being turned down.

turned comma *Printing* An inverted comma, as a single initial quotation mark.

turn·er¹ (tûr′nər) *n.* One who turns; specifically, one who fashions objects with a lathe.

turn·er² (tûr′nər) *n.* A gymnast; a member of a turnverein. [<G <*turnen* engage in gymnastics <F *turner* turn]

Tur·ner (tûr′nər), **Frederick Jackson,** 1861–1932, U.S. historian. — **Joseph Mallord William,** 1775–1851, English painter.

turn·er·y (tûr′nər·ē) *n. pl.* **·er·ies** 1 A place where lathework is carried on. 2 The act or process of turning, or articles and ornamentation made with a lathe.

turn·hall (tûrn′hôl′) *n.* A building in which gymnasts, especially members of a turnverein, practice; a gymnasium. Also *German* **Turn·hal·le** (to͝orn′häl′ə). [<G *turnhalle* <*turnen* exercise + *halle* a hall]

turn indicator In motor vehicles, any device, as a flashing light, which enables the driver to signal his intention to turn.

turn·ing (tûr′ning) *n.* 1 The act of one who turns. 2 The art of shaping wood, metal, etc., in a lathe. 3 Any deviation from a straight or customary course; a winding; bend.

turning point 1 The point of a decisive change in direction of action; a crisis. 2 The point at which the direction of a motion is reversed. 3 A marked object toward which a surveying instrument is sighted from each of two positions in the process of leveling.

tur·nip (tûr′nip) *n.* 1 The fleshy globular edible root of either of two brassicaceous biennial herbs, *Brassica rapa* and the rutabaga. 2 Either of the plants. [Earlier *turnepe,* ? <F *tour* a turn, rotation (<L *tornus* a lathe) + ME *nepe* <L *napus* a turnip; with ref. to its round shape]

tur·nix (tûr′niks) *n.* One of a genus *(Turnix)* of small three-toed birds with short tails found in warm regions of the Old World. [<NL, short for L *coturnix* a quail]

turn·key (tûrn′kē′) *n.* One who has charge of the keys of a prison; a jailer. — *adj.* Of, pertaining to, or being, by prearrangement with a buyer, a product or service in complete readiness for use when purchased: a *turnkey* housing project.

turn-off (tûrn′ôf′, -of′) *n. Colloq.* A road, path, or way branching off from a main thoroughfare.

turn·out (tûrn′out′) *n.* 1 An act of turning out or coming forth. 2 An assemblage of persons; attendance. 3 A quantity produced; output. 4 Array; equipment; outfit. 5 A railroad siding. 6 The movement of a vehicle from a line of traffic to pass other vehicles. 7 A section of narrow road widened to permit vehicles to pass one another. 8 A carriage or wagon with its horses and equipage. 9 *Brit.* A labor strike; also, a striker.

turn·o·ver (tûrn′ō′vər) *n.* 1 The act or process of turning over; an upset or overthrow, as of a vehicle. 2 A change or revolution: a *turnover* in affairs. 3 A small pie or tart made by covering half of a circular crust with fruit, jelly, or the like, and turning the other half over on top. 4 The amount of business accomplished, or of work achieved; turnout. 5 A completed commercial transaction or course of business; also, the money receipts of a business for a given period. 6 The rate at which persons hired by a given establishment within a given period are replaced by others; also, the number of persons hired. — *adj.* 1 Designed for turning over or reversing. 2 Capable of being turned over or folded down. 3 Made with a part folded down: a *turnover* collar.

turn·pike (tûrn′pīk′) *n.* 1 A road on which there are tollgates. 2 Loosely, any highway: also **turnpike road.** 3 A tollbar or tollgate. 4 *Obs.* A turnstile. See synonyms under ROAD. [ME *turnpyke* a spiked road barrier <TURN, *v.* + *pyke* PIKE¹]

turn·sole (tûrn′sōl′) *n.* 1 Any of several plants supposed to turn their flowers toward the sun; especially, the heliotrope and the sunflower. 2 Litmus. 3 One of various other blue coloring matters obtained from certain lichens and herbs. [<OF *tournesole* <Ital. *tornasole* <*tornare* turn (<L) + *sole* the sun <L *sol*]

turn·spit (tûrn′spit′) *n.* 1 One who turns a spit; a menial. 2 A dog formerly used in a treadmill to turn a roasting spit.

turn·stile (tûrn′stīl′) *n.* 1 A kind of gate or closure consisting of a vertical post and horizontal arms which by revolving permit persons, but not cattle, to pass; also, one that permits persons to pass in one direction only. 2 A similar device for registering the number of persons entering a building or for automatically admitting passengers to subways, buses, etc., on the deposit of fares.

turn·stone (tûrn′stōn′) *n.* A ploverlike migratory bird (genus *Arenaria*) of northern regions: so called from its habit of turning over stones to obtain its food; especially, the **ruddy turnstone** *(A. interpres)* and the **black turnstone** *(A. melanocephala)* of North America.

turn·ta·ble (tûrn′tā′bəl) *n.* 1 A rotating platform arranged to turn a section of a bridge in order to open a passage for ships. 2 Such a platform to turn a locomotive, car, etc.: also *Brit.* **turn′plate′** (-plāt′). 3 A small rotating disk in a microscope. 4 A rotating table in a show window. 5 The disk which carries a phonograph record.

turn·up (tûrn′up′) *n.* 1 That which is turned up, as part of a garment. 2 A particular card or die turned up in games of chance. 3 Pure chance; a toss-up; an unexpected phenomenon. 4 *Colloq.* A boxing contest; hence, a fight or row; commotion. — *adj.* Turned up.

turn·ver·ein (to͝orn′fe·rīn) *n.* An association of turners or gymnasts; an athletic club. [<G <*turnen* exercise + *verein* a club]

tur·pen·tine (tûr′pən·tīn) *n.* 1 A resinous, oily mixture of various pinenes exuding from any one of several coniferous trees, especially the longleaf pine *(Pinus palustris).* 2 The semifluid resin of the terebinth: also **Chian turpentine.** — **oil of turpentine** The colorless essential oil formed when turpentine is distilled with steam and consisting of a mixture of terpenes: widely used in industry, medicine and the arts. — *v.t.* **·tined, ·tin·ing** 1 To put turpentine with or upon; saturate with turpentine. 2 To obtain crude turpentine from (a tree). [<OF *turbentine* <L *terebinthinus* of the terebinth tree <*terebinthus* the terebinth <Gk. *terebinthos*]

turpentine tree The peebeen.

tur·peth (tûr′pith) *n.* 1 The root of an East Indian plant (genus *Ipomoea*) allied to the one yielding the common jalap, similar to it in properties: also **vegetable turpeth.** 2 A lemon-yellow basic mercuric sulfate, $HgSO_4 \cdot 2HgO$, used in medicine as an emetic: also **turpeth mineral.** Also called *turbeth, turbith.* [<OF *turbit* <Med. L *turbithum* <Arabic *turbid* <Persian]

Tur·pin (tûr′pin), **Richard,** 1706–39, English highwayman: known as *Dick Turpin.*

tur·pi·tude (tûr′pə·to͞od, -tyo͞od) *n.* Inherent baseness; vileness; depravity, or any action showing depravity. [<MF <L *turpitudo, -inis* <*turpis* vile]

tur·quoise (tûr′koiz, -kwoiz) *n.* 1 A blue or green hydrous aluminum phosphate, $H_5Al_2PO_8$, colored by copper: found massive, and in its highly polished blue varieties esteemed

as a gemstone. **2** A light, greenish blue, the color of the turquoise: also **turquoise blue**. Also spelled *turkois*. Also *Obs.* **tur·quois** (tûr·koiz′). [<MF *(pierre) turquoise* Turkish (stone) <OF *turqueise*, fem. of *turqueis* Turkish; so called because first imported through Turkey]

tur·rel (tûr′əl) *n. Obs.* An auger used by coopers. [? Dim. of OF *tour* a turn <L *tornus* a lathe]

tur·ret (tûr′it) *n.* **1** A small tower, often merely ornamental, rising above a larger structure, as on a castle. **2** *Mil.* A rotating armed tower, large enough to contain a powerful gun or guns and gunners, forming part of a man-of-war or a fort; a similar enclosed structure in a tank or a bombing or combat airplane. **3** The clerestory of a railway car. **4** In ancient warfare, a high wooden structure, supported on slides or wheels, intended to enable besiegers to surmount the walls against which it was pushed. **5** *Mech.* In a lathe, a cylinder fitted with sockets or chucks for the reception of various tools, any one of which may be presented in succession in the axial line of the work: also **turret head.** [<OF *torete*, dim. of *tor* TOWER]
tur·ret·ed (tûr′it·id) *adj.* **1** Provided with turrets. **2** Having the form of a turret. **3** *Zool.* Having a long spire, as certain shells.
turret lathe A power-driven metalworking machine having a rotating turret head holding various tools, each of which in turn processes the material.
tur·ri·cal (tûr′i·kəl) *adj.* Of, pertaining to, or like a turret. [<L *turris* a tower]
tur·ric·u·late (tə·rik′yə·lit, -lāt) *adj.* **1** Having or resembling a turret or turrets. **2** Turreted or having a spire: said of shells. [<L *turricula*, dim. of *turris* a tower + -ATE¹] •

tur·tle¹ (tûr′təl) *n.* **1** Any of numerous reptiles (order *Chelonia*) having a horny, toothless beak, and characterized by a short, stout body covered above and below with a bony carapace and plastron respectively, into which all the members may be drawn for protection; a tortoise; specifically, a marine species as distinguished from a terrestrial or fresh-water species. **2** The flesh of certain varieties of turtle, served as food. **3** A stout frame in the form of a segment of a cylinder, used to hold the type in a type-revolving web press. —**green turtle** An important food turtle (*Chelonia*

TURTLES
a. Wood turtle. *b.* Emyd. *c.* Trionychid.

mydas) of wide distribution in tropical and semitropical seas: so called from the greenish color of its flesh. — **to turn turtle** To overturn; capsize. —*v.i.* **·tled, ·tling** To hunt for or catch turtles. [Appar. alter. of Sp. *tortuga* <Med. L *tortuca* TORTOISE; infl. in form by TURTLE²]
tur·tle² (tûr′təl) *n. Archaic* A turtle dove. [OE <L *turtur*]
tur·tle·back (tûr′təl·bak′) *n.* **1** *Naut.* An arched covering, resembling the shell of a turtle, built over the main deck of a ship as protection against heavy seas: usually at the bow or stern. Also **turtle deck. 2** *Archeol.* A rude, chipped stone implement whose facets resemble the sculptured carapace of a turtle. [<TURTLE¹ + BACK]
turtle dove 1 An Old World dove (genus *Streptopelia*), noted for its affection for its mate and young. **2** One of other pigeons, as the mourning dove. [<TURTLE² + DOVE]
tur·tle·head (tûr′təl·hed′) *n.* Any species of a genus (*Chelone*) of hardy American herbs of

the figwort family, with large white or purple flowers.
turtle neck A high collar that fits snugly about the neck, usually rolled or turned over double: used especially on athletic sweaters. —**tur′tle-neck′** *adj.*
tur·tle·peg (tûr′təl·peg′) *n.* A small, sharp, steel spike attached to a line and loosely mounted upon a shaft which is thrown like a harpoon to capture sea turtles.
tur·tle·stone (tûr′təl·stōn′) *n.* Septarium.
turves (tûrvz) Archaic plural of TURF.
Tus·ca·loo·sa (tus′kə·lōō′sə) A city of west central Alabama on the Black Warrior River.
Tus·can (tus′kən) *adj.* **1** Pertaining to Tuscany. **2** Designating the Tuscan order of architecture. —*n.* **1** A native or naturalized inhabitant of Tuscany. **2** Any Italian dialect used in Tuscany; especially, the one spoken in Florence, used by Dante, who thus set the pattern for what has become the standard literary Italian language.
Tuscan Archipelago An Italian island group in the Tyrrhenian Sea between the coast of Tuscany and Corsica; total, 115 square miles.
Tuscan order A Roman order of architecture resembling Roman Doric but having bolder moldings, no decorated details, and no triglyphs.
Tus·ca·ny (tus′kə·nē) A region and former duchy of west central Italy; 8,876 square miles; chief city, Florence: Italian *Toscana.*
Tus·ca·ro·ra (tus′kə·rôr′ə, -rō′rə) *n. pl.* **·ra** or **·ras** One of a tribe of North American Indians of Iroquoian stock formerly living in North Carolina, now surviving in New York and Ontario. They joined the Five Nations in 1722.
Tus·cu·lum (tus′kyə·ləm) An ancient ruined city of Latium, SE of Rome. — **Tus′cu·lan** *adj.*
tush¹ (tush) *interj.* An exclamation expressing disapproval, impatience, etc.
tush² (tush) See TUSK.
tushed (tusht) *adj.* Having tushes or tusks.
tusk (tusk) *n.* **1** A long, pointed tooth, as in the boar, walrus, or elephant. **2** A sharp, projecting, toothlike point. **3** A shoulder on a tenon, to strengthen it at its base; also, a tenon having such a shoulder. —*v.t.* **1** To gore with the tusks. **2** To root up with the tusks. Also **tush.** [Metathetic var. of OE *tux*] —**tusked** (tuskt) *adj.* —**tusk′less** *adj.* —**tusk′like′** *adj.*
tusk·er (tus′kər) *n.* An elephant or wild boar with developed tusks.
tusk tenon A tenon strengthened by a step or steps, or by a shoulder. [<TUSK (def. 3) + TENON]
tus·sah (tus′ə) *n.* **1** A wild and semi-domesticated Asian silkworm (*Antheraea paphia*) which spins large cocoons of brownish or yellowish silk. **2** The silk, or the tough, durable fabric woven from it. Also **tus′sa, tus·sar** (tus′ər), **tus′seh, tus′ser, tus·sore** (tus′ôr, -ōr), **tus′sur.** [<Hind. *tasar* <Skt. *tasara, trasara,* lit., a shuttle]
tus·sis (tus′is) *n. Pathol.* A cough: bronchial *tussis.* [<NL <L] —**tus′sal, tus′sive** *adj.*
tus·sle (tus′əl) *v.t. & v.i.* **·sled, ·sling** To fight or struggle in a vigorous, determined way; engage in a tussle. —*n.* A disorderly struggle, as in sport; scuffle. [Var. of TOUSLE]
tus·sock (tus′ək) *n.* **1** A tuft or clump of grass or sedge. **2** A tuft of hair or feathers. Also **tus′suck.** [Prob. dim. of obs. *tusk* a tuft of hair, ? <TUSK] —**tus′sock·y** *adj.*
tussock moth Any of various robust, medium-sized moths (family *Lymantriidae*) whose larvae bear tufts of hairs and are very destructive of broad-leaved deciduous trees, as the gipsy moth.
tut (tut) *interj.* An exclamation to check rashness or express impatience: often repeated.
Tut-ankh-a-men (tōōt′ängk·ä′mın) Egyptian pharaoh who reigned 1358–1350 B.C.
tu·te·lage (tōō′tə·lij, tyōō′-) *n.* **1** The state of

being under a tutor or guardian. **2** The act or office of a guardian; guardianship. **3** The act of tutoring; instruction. [<L *tutela* a watching, guardianship <*tutus* safe <*tueri* watch, guard]
tu·te·lar (tōō′tə·lər, tyōō′-) *adj.* **1** Invested with guardianship. **2** Pertaining to a guardian. Also **tu′te·lar·y** (-ler′ē).
tu·te·nag (tōō′tə·nag, tyōō′-) *n.* **1** A white alloy, with varying proportions of copper, zinc, and nickel. **2** Zinc or spelter. Also **tu′te·nague:** sometimes spelled *teutenag.* [<Pg. *tutanaga, tutenaga* <Marathi *tuttināg* <Skt. *tuttha* copper sulphate + *nāga* tin, lead]
Tu·to·caine (tōō′tə·kān) *n.* Proprietary name for an ivory-colored, odorless, crystalline compound, $C_{14}H_{22}O_2N_2$, used as a local anesthetic.
tu·tor (tōō′tər, tyōō′-) *n.* **1** One who instructs another in one or more branches of knowledge; a private teacher. **2** A college teacher who gives individual instruction. **3** *Brit.* A college official entrusted with the tutelage and care of undergraduates assigned to him. **4** *Law* A guardian of a minor or of a woman. —*v.t.* **1** To act as tutor to; instruct; teach; train. **2** To have the guardianship of. **3** To treat severely or sternly, as a tutor might; discipline. —*v.i.* **4** To do the work of a tutor. **5** To be tutored or instructed. See synonyms under TEACH. [<AF, OF *tutour* <L *tutor* a watcher, guardian <*tutus.* See TUTELAGE.] —**tu·to·ri·al** (tōō·tôr′ē·əl, -tō′rē-, tyōō′-) *adj.*
tu·tor·age (tōō′tər·ij, tyōō′-) *n.* The office of a tutor; tutorship.
tutorial system A system of education, generally collegiate, in which each student is assigned to a tutor, who directs his studies and has general supervision over his instruction.
tu·tor·ship (tōō′tər·ship, tyōō′-) *n.* **1** The office of a tutor or of a guardian. **2** Tutelage.
tu·toy·er (tü·twà·yā′) *v.t. French* To speak to with the French singular pronoun *tu, te, toi* instead of the more formal plural pronoun *vous;* address intimately.
tut·ti (tōō′tē) *Music adj.* All: a term used to indicate that all performers are to take part: contrasted with *solo.* —*n.* A composition, piece, movement, or passage to be performed by all the voices and instruments together: contrasted with *solo.* [<Ital., pl. of *tutto* all]
tut·ti-frut·ti (tōō′tē·frōō′tē) *n.* A confection, chewing gum, ice-cream, etc., made with different fruits. —*adj.* Having fruit flavors. [<Ital., all fruits]
tut·ty (tut′ē) *n.* An impure zinc oxide obtained as a sublimate in the flues of zinc-smelting furnaces: used as a polishing powder. [<OF *tutie* <Arabic *tūtiya* oxide of zinc, ? <Persian]
tu·tu (tü·tü′) *n. French* A short, full, projecting skirt consisting of many layers of sheer fabric, worn by ballet dancers.
Tu·tu·i·la (tōō′tōō·ē′lä) The chief island of the American Samoan group; 40 square miles; capital, Pago Pago.
tu·um (tōō′əm) *pron. Latin* Yours; thine: used in the phrase *meum and tuum,* mine and thine.
Tu·va Autonomous Region (tōō′və) An administrative division of southern Asiatic Russian S.F.S.R.; 66,100 square miles; formerly *Tannu-Tuva People's Republic.* Also **Tu·vin·i·an Autonomous Region** (tōō·vin′ē·ən).
tu·whit tu·whoo (tōō·hwit′ tōō·hwōō′) The cry of an owl. [Imit.]
tux·e·do (tuk·sē′dō) *n. pl.* **·dos 1** A man's semi-formal dinner coat without tails. **2** The suit of which the coat is a part. Also **Tux·e′do.** [from *Tuxedo* Park, N.Y.; so called because first worn at the country club there]
Tuxt·la (tōōst′lä) The capital of Chiapas state, southern Mexico, in the west central part of the state. Also **Tuxtla Gu·tiér·rez** (gōō·tyär′räs).
tu·yère (twē·yâr′, twir′; *Fr.* tü·yâr′) *n. Metall.* The pipe through which air is forced into a furnace or forge: also spelled *twyere.* [<F, a nozzle <*tuyau* a pipe]
Tver (tver) A former name for KALININ.
twa (twä, twô) *adj. Scot.* Two.
twad·dle (twod′l) *v.t. & v.i.* **·dled, ·dling** To talk foolishly and pretentiously. See synonyms under BABBLE. —*n.* Pretentious, silly talk; also, a twaddler. [Prob. alter. of TWATTLE] —**twad′dler** *n.*
twain (twān) *adj. Archaic* Two: rare except in poetic usage. See synonyms under BOTH. —*n.* **1** A couple; two. **2** In river navigation, two

fathoms or twelve feet. [OE *twēgen,* masculine of *twa* two]

Twain (twān), **Mark** See MARK TWAIN.

twal (twäl, twôl) *adj. Scot.* Twelve. Also **twall.**

twal·pen·nies (twäl′pen′ēz, twôl′-) *n. pl. Scot.* Twelvepence: in old Scots currency, equal to one penny sterling. **— twal′pen′nie, twal′·pen′ny** *adj.*

twang (twang) *v.t.* & *v.i.* **twanged, twang·ing** **1** To make or cause to make a sharp, vibrant sound, as a bowstring. **2** To utter or speak with a harsh, nasal sound. **—** *n.* **1** A sharp, vibrating sound, as of a tense string plucked. **2** A sharp, nasal sound of the voice. **3** A sound resembling either of the foregoing. Also *tang.* [Imit.] **— twang′y** *adj.*

twan·gle (twang′gəl) *v.t.* & *v.i.* **·gled, ·gling** To twang. **—** *n.* A twang. [Freq. of TWANG] **— twan′gler** *n.*

Twan·kay (twang′kā) *n.* A variety of green tea. Also **twan·ky** (twang′kē). [from Chinese *T'un ch'i,* a town in Anwhei province, where originally grown]

twa·some (twä′səm, twô′-) *Scot. adj.* Twosome. **—** *n.* Two persons in company; a pair.

twat·tle (twot′l) *v.t.* & *v.i.* **·tled, ·tling,** *n.* Twaddle. [Short for *twittle–twattle,* var. of TITTLE–TATTLE]

tway·blade (twā′blād) *n.* Any one of various hardy terrestrial orchids (genera *Listera* or *Liparis*) with two radical leaves: also spelled *twyblade.* [< archaic *tway* two, var. of TWAIN + BLADE]

tweak (twēk) *v.t.* To pinch and twist sharply; twitch. **—** *n.* A twisting pinch; twitch. [Var. of dial. *twick,* OE *twiccan* twitch] **— tweak′y** *adj.*

tweed (twēd) *n.* **1** A soft woolen fabric with a homespun surface: often woven in two or more colors to effect a check or plaid pattern. **2** A tweed suit or coat. **— Harris tweed** A homespun woolen cloth, usually of mixed colors, made at Harris in the Hebrides. [Alter. of dial. E (Scottish) *tweel,* var. of TWILL; prob. infl. in form by *Tweed* river, which flows through the district where it is woven]

Tweed (twēd) A river in Peeblesshire, Scotland, forming part of the boundary of England and Scotland and flowing 97 miles NE to the North Sea.

Tweed (twēd), **William Marcy,** 1823–78, U.S. politician: called "Boss Tweed."

Tweed·dale (twēd′dāl) See PEEBLES.

twee·dle[1] (twēd′l) *v.* **·dled, ·dling** *v.t.* **1** To play (a musical instrument) casually or carelessly. **2** To wheedle; cajole. **—** *v.i.* **3** To produce a series of shrill tones. **4** To play a musical instrument casually or carelessly. **—** *n.* A sound resembling the tones of a violin. [Imit. of the sound of a reed pipe]

twee·dle[2] (twēd′l) *v.* **·dled, ·dling** *v.t.* To handle carelessly. **—** *v.i.* To wriggle. [Var. of TWIDDLE]

twee·dle·dum and twee·dle·dee (twēd′l·dum′, twēd′l·dē′) Two things between which there is the slightest possible distinction: from John Byrom, *On the Feuds between Handel and Bononcini* (1723). [Orig. imit. of low– and high–pitched musical instruments, respectively]

Tweedledum and Tweedledee Twin brothers of almost identical appearance in Lewis Carroll's *Through the Looking–Glass.*

Tweed Ring The political group, headed by William M. ("Boss") Tweed and other Tammany Hall politicians, which controlled New York city government (1865–71) and plundered millions of dollars. **— Tweed′ism** *n.*

Tweeds·muir (twēdz′myŏŏr), **Baron** See BUCHAN, JOHN.

'tween (twēn) Contraction of BETWEEN.

tweet (twēt) *v.i.* To utter a thin, chirping note. **—** *n.* A twittering or chirping. Also **tweet′–tweet′.** [Imit.]

tweet·er (twē′tər) *n. Electronics* A loudspeaker used to reproduce the treble register in high–fidelity sound equipment: distinguished from *woofer.* [<TWEET]

tweeze (twēz) *v.t.* **tweezed, tweez·ing** *Colloq.* To handle, pinch, pluck, etc., with tweezers. [Back formation <TWEEZERS]

tweez·ers (twē′zərz) *n. pl.* **1** Small pincers for tiny objects: often called **a pair of tweezers.** **2** *Obs.* A set of surgeon's instruments; also, a surgeon's instrument case. [Alter. of *tweezes,* pl. of *tweeze,* earlier *etweese* a case of small instruments <F *étuis,* pl. of *étui* ÉTUI]

twelfth (twelfth) *adj.* **1** Second in order after the tenth: the ordinal of *twelve.* **2** Being one of twelve equal parts. **—** *n.* **1** One of twelve equal parts; the quotient obtained by dividing by twelve. **2** *Music* An interval compounded of an octave and a fifth. [OE *twelfta*]

Twelfth–cake (twelfth′kāk′) *n.* A cake prepared for a Twelfth–night festival. [Short for *Twelfth–night cake*]

Twelfth–day (twelfth′dā′) *n.* The festival of the Epiphany, the twelfth day after Christmas.

Twelfth–night (twelfth′nīt′) *n.* The eve (Jan. 5th) of Twelfth–day, or the evening before Epiphany; sometimes, the evening (Jan. 6th) of Epiphany. **—** *adj.* Of or pertaining to Twelfth–night.

Twelfth·tide (twelfth′tīd′) *n.* Twelfth–day; the twelfth day after Christmas; Epiphany.

twelve (twelv) *adj.* Consisting of twice six: a cardinal numeral. **—** *n.* The sum of ten and two, or the symbols (12, xii, XII) representing it. **— the Twelve** The twelve apostles. See APOSTLE (def. 1). [OE *twelf*]

Twelve Apostles **1** A governing body of the Mormon Church, composed of twelve high officials. **2** The twelve disciples of Jesus: more commonly *the Twelve.*

twelve·mo (twelv′mō) *adj.* & *n.* Duodecimo.

twelve·month (twelv′munth′) *n.* A year.

twelve–tone (twelv′tōn′) *adj. Music* Of, pertaining to, or composed in a system or technique developed by Arnold Schönberg, in which any particular series of twelve tones containing all twelve of the tones of the chromatic scale is used in various permutations as the basis of composition, usually without reference to a fixed tonal center; dodecaphonic.

twen·ti·eth (twen′tē·ith) *adj.* **1** Tenth in order after the tenth: the ordinal of *twenty.* **2** Being one of twenty equal parts. **—** *n.* One of twenty equal parts; the quotient of a unit divided by twenty. [OE *twentigotha* < *twentig* twenty]

twen·ty (twen′tē) *adj.* **1** Consisting of twice ten; vicenary. **2** *Archaic* A considerable but indefinite number. **—** *n. pl.* **·ties** The sum of ten and ten, or the symbols (20, xx, XX) representing it. [OE *twentig*] **— twen′ty·fold′** *adj.*

Twenty–fourth Amendment An amendment to the Constitution of the United States prohibiting the denial or abridgment of the right to vote in elections for Federal office by reason of failure to pay any poll tax or other tax: ratified in 1964.

twen·ty–one (twen′tē·wun′) *n.* Vingt–et–un: a card game.

twerp (twûrp) *n. Slang* A small, contemptible person. [Cf. obs. *twirk* twitch, var. of TWIRL]

Twi (twē) *n.* A Sudanic language spoken by African Negroes in Ghana: also called *Ashanti:* also spelled *Tshi.*

twi– *prefix* Two; double; twice: *twibil.* Also spelled *twy–.* [OE, double < *twa* two]

twi·bil (twī′bil) *n.* **1** An ax with two cutting edges. **2** A double–bladed battle–ax. **3** A garden tool like an ax; a mattock. Also **twi′·bill.** [OE < *twi–* two + *bill* an ax]

twice (twīs) *adv.* **1** Two times. **2** In double measure; doubly. [OE *twiges,* gen. of *twiga* twice]

twice–laid (twīs′lād′) *adj.* **1** Made from the yarns of old or used rope. **2** Made from remnants or refuse.

twic·er (twī′sər) *n. Brit.* A printer who is both compositor and pressman.

Twick·en·ham (twik′ən·əm) A municipal borough on the Thames, 11 miles SW of London, England; home of Alexander Pope.

twid·dle (twid′l) *v.* **·dled, ·dling** *v.t.* **1** To twirl idly; toy or play with. **—** *v.i.* **2** To revolve or twirl. **3** To toy with something idly. **4** To be busy about trifles. **—** *n.* A gentle twirling, as of the fingers. [Prob. <ON *tridla* stir; ? infl. in meaning by TWIRL and FIDDLE] **— twid′·dler** *n.*

twi·er (twī′ər) Altered form of TUYÈRE.

twig[1] (twig) *n.* A small shoot or branchlet of a tree. ◆ Collateral adjective: *viminal.* [OE *twigge*] **— twig′less** *adj.*

twig[2] (twig) *v.* **twigged, twig·ging** *Slang v.t.* **1** To observe closely; notice or watch. **2** To comprehend; understand. **—** *v.i.* **3** To understand. [Cf. Irish *tuigim* I understand]

twig[3] (twig) *n. Archaic* The fashion: an old fop in good *twig.* [? <obs. *twig* act vigorously; ult. origin uncertain]

twig blight **1** Any of various bacterial or fungous infections of plants which attack the twigs, resulting in extreme decay. **2** Dieback.

twig borer The larva of a lepidopterous insect *(Anarsia lineatella)* which bores into the twigs of certain fruit trees, as the peach, plum, and apricot, with destructive effect.

twigged (twigd) *adj.* Having shoots or twigs.

twig·gen (twig′ən) *adj.* Made of twigs; wicker.

twig girdler See GIRDLER (def. 3).

twig·gy (twig′ē) *adj.* Like, or abounding in, twigs.

twi·light (twī′līt′) *n.* **1** The light diffused over the sky after sunset and before sunrise (especially, in popular use, the former) which is caused by the reflection of sunlight from the higher portions of the atmosphere. **2** Any faint light; shade; obscurity: the *twilight* of the groves. **3** Indistinct apprehension or perception: the *twilight* of doubt or barbarism. **4** A hazy or obscure condition following the waning of past glory, achievements, etc.: the *twilight* of the gods. **—** *adj.* **1** Pertaining or peculiar to twilight; crepuscular. **2** Imperfectly or faintly lighted; shaded; dim. [ME *twyligt* <OE *twi–* (< *twa* two) + LIGHT; used in sense of "the light between the two," i.e., between day and night]

twilight arch The arch that bounds the brightest region of twilight.

twilight of the gods See RAGNARÖK.

twilight sleep *Med.* A light or partial anesthesia, induced artificially, as by injection of morphine and scopolamine, in which the patient loses the power to remember present events and sensations: sometimes used to relieve childbirth pains. [Trans. of G *dämmerschlaf*]

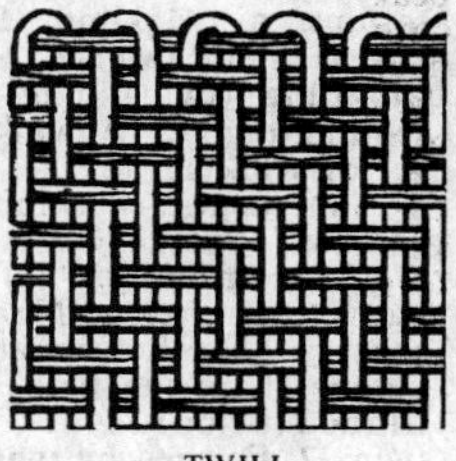

TWILL
Enlarged to show weave.

twill (twil) *n.* **1** One of the three foundation systems of weaves, in which the shuttle carries the woof thread over one and under two or more warp threads, producing the characteristic diagonal ribs or lines in fabrics. **2** A fabric woven with a twill; twilled cloth. **—** *v.t.* To weave (cloth) so as to produce diagonal lines or ribs on the surface. [Var. of ME *twile,* OE *twili* a twilled fabric < *twi–* < *twa* two, partial trans. of L *bilix* having a double thread]

twilled (twild) *adj.* Woven so as to produce a diagonal rib or line; ribbed or ridged.

twin (twin) *n.* **1** One of two young produced at the same birth. **2** The counterpart or exact mate of another. **3** An intergrowth of two or more crystals of the same substance according to some definite law, a single plane or axis usually being common to the different individuals. **— the Twins** Castor and Pollux, the two brightest stars in the constellation Gemini; also, the constellation. **—** *adj.* **1** Being, or standing in the relation of, a twin or twins. **2** Consisting of, forming, or being one of a pair of similar and closely related objects; double; twofold. **— the Twin Cities** St. Paul and Minneapolis. **—** *v.* **twinned, twin·ning** *v.i.* **1** To bring forth twins. **2** To be matched or equal; agree. **3** *Archaic* To be born as a twin. **—** *v.t.* **4** To bring forth as twins. **5** To couple; match. **6** *Scot.* To separate: also **twine** (twīn). [Fusion of OE *twinn, getwinn* (< *twi–* < *twa* two) and ON *tvinnr, tvennr* double]

twin bed One of a pair of single beds.

twin·ber·ry (twin′ber′ē, -bər·ē) *n. pl.* **·ries** **1** The partridgeberry. **2** A North American shrub *(Lonicera involucrata)* with elliptic leaves, yellowish–red flowers, and shining black berries.

twin–born (twin′bôrn′) *adj.* Brought forth at the same birth; born as a twin or twins.

twine[1] (twīn) *v.* **twined, twin·ing** *v.t.* **1** To twist together, as threads. **2** To form by such twisting. **3** To coil or wrap about something. **4** To encircle by winding or wreathing. **5** To enfold; embrace. — *v.i.* **6** To interlace; become twined. **7** To proceed in a winding course; meander. See synonyms under BEND, TWIST. — *adj.* Of or like twine. — *n.* **1** A string composed of two or more strands twisted together; loosely, any small cord. **2** The act of twining or entwining. **3** A form or conformation produced by twining. **4** An interweaving or interlacing. **5** *Obs.* A twisting about rapidly; spin. [OE *twīn* a twisted double thread < *twi-* double < *twa* two] — **twin'er** *n.*

twin·flow·er (twin'flou'ər) *n.* A trailing evergreen plant (genus *Linnaea*) of the honeysuckle family, as the Old World *L. borealis,* with fragrant rose or white bell-shaped flowers growing in pairs, and its American variety, *L. borealis americana.*

twinge (twinj) *v.t.* & *v.i.* **twinged, twing·ing** To affect with or suffer a sudden pain or twinge. — *n.* A sharp, darting, local pain; twitch; also, a mental pang. See synonyms under PAIN. [OE *twengan* pinch]

twi-night (twī'nīt') *adj.* Beginning in the late afternoon and continuing, under artificial light, into the night, as baseball games or other outdoor contests. [Blend of TWILIGHT and NIGHT]

twin·kle (twing'kəl) *v.* **·kled, ·kling** *v.i.* **1** To shine with fitful, intermittent gleams, as a star. **2** To be bright, as with amusement: Her eyes *twinkled.* **3** To wink or blink; open and shut with a quick, involuntary motion. **4** To move rapidly to and fro; flicker: *twinkling* feet. — *v.t.* **5** To emit or cause to flash out, as gleams of light. **6** To move (the eyelids) quickly and repeatedly. — *n.* **1** A tremulous gleam of light; sparkle; glimmer. **2** A quick or repeated movement of the eyelids; also, a wink or sparkle of the eye. **3** An instant; a twinkling. See synonyms under LIGHT[1]. [OE *twinclian*] — **twin'kler** *n.*

twin·kling (twing'kling) *n.* **1** The act of scintillating. **2** A wink or twinkle. **3** The act of winking, or the time required for it. **4** A moment. See synonyms under LIGHT.

twin-leaf (twin'lēf') *n.* A small perennial herb (*Jeffersonia diphylla*) of the barberry family native in eastern North America, having solitary white flowers and leaves divided into kidney-shaped leaflets.

twinned (twind) *adj.* **1** Produced at one birth; twin. **2** Formed by twinning, as a crystal.

twin·ning (twin'ing) *n.* **1** The production of two young at one birth; the bearing of twins. **2** Close union or combination; coupling of two related objects. **3** The formation of twin crystals, each the counterpart of the other.

twin-screw (twin'skro͞o') *adj.* Of a vessel, having two propeller shafts, one on each side of the keel, and two propellers, normally turning in opposite directions. — *n.* (twin'skro͞o') Such a vessel.

twirl (twûrl) *v.t.* & *v.i.* **1** To whirl or rotate. **2** In baseball, to pitch. — *n.* **1** A whirling motion, or a quick twisting action, as of the fingers. **2** A curl; twist; coil. [Alter. of ME *tirlen,* var. of *trillen* TRILL[2]; appar. infl. by *whirl*] — **twirl'er** *n.*

twist (twist) *v.t.* **1** To wind (strands, etc.) around each other. **2** To form by such winding: to *twist* thread. **3** To give spiral, circular, or semicircular form to, as by turning at either end. **4** To force out of natural shape; distort or contort. **5** To distort the meaning of. **6** To confuse; perplex. **7** To wreathe, twine, or wrap. **8** To cause to revolve or rotate. **9** To impart spin to (a ball) so that it moves in a curve. — *v.i.* **10** To become twisted. **11** To move in a winding course; meander or bend. **12** To squirm; writhe. — *n.* **1** The act, manner, or result of twisting or turning on an axis. **2** The state of being twisted. **3** *Physics* **a** A torsional strain. **b** The angle of torsion, as of a rod or bar. **4** A curve; turn; bend; winding: This path is full of *twists* and turns. **5** A contortion or twisting of a facial or bodily feature: a smile with a certain *twist.* **6** A wrench; strain, as of a joint or limb: He fell and gave his ankle a *twist.* **7** A peculiar or perverted inclination, bent, or attitude: the *twist* of a criminal's mind. **8** A distortion; deviation; wresting: a *twist* of meaning. **9** Thread or cord made of tightly twisted or braided strands. **10** *Naut.* One of the strands of a rope. **11** A twisted roll of bread. **12** Tobacco twisted in the form of a large cord. **13** In baseball, billiards, tennis, etc.: **a** A spin or whirling motion given to a ball by a certain stroke or throw. **b** The stroke or throw producing such a spin. **c** The act or knack of imparting such a spin. [ME *twisten* divide in two, combine two, prob. <OE *-twist* a rope, as in *mæst-twist* a rope to stay a mast < *twi-* double < *twa* two]

Synonyms (verb): bend, contort, crook, encircle, entwine, twine, wreathe. To *twist* is to bend a thing somewhat spirally upon itself. To *twine* is to *bend* it around some other object. Wrestlers *twine* their arms about each other, but if a combatant's arm is *twisted* it is likely to disable him. An iron shaft may be *twisted* out of shape, but not *twined*; the groove of a rifle barrel is *twisted,* not *twined*; a wreath is *twined* around one's temples, but not *twisted.* Compare BEND, PERVERT.

twist drill *Mech.* A drill or bit whose body is cut with deep spiral grooves to carry out the chips.

twisted pine The lodge-pole pine.

twist·er (twis'tər) *n.* **1** One who or that which twists. **2** A ball, as in cricket, bowled with a twist. **3** In baseball, a curve; also, one who pitches a curve. **4** *U. S.* A tornado.

Twist·or (twis'tər) *n. Electronics* A device for increasing the storage capacity of digital computers, consisting of a grid of copper wires and segments of magnetic wire twisted to change the magnetization from longitudinal to helical: a trade name.

twit (twit) *v.t.* **twit·ted, twit·ting** To taunt, reproach, or annoy by reminding of a mistake, fault, etc. — *n.* A taunting allusion; reproach. [Aphetic var. of ME *atwite,* OE *ætwitan* taunt < *æt-* at + *witan* accuse] — **twit'ter** *n.*

twitch (twich) *v.t.* **1** To pull sharply; pluck with a jerky movement. **2** In lumbering, to drag or skid (logs) along the ground with a chain. — *v.i.* **3** To tug or move with a quick, spasmodic jerk, as a muscle. — *n.* **1** A sudden involuntary contraction of a muscle. **2** A sudden jerk or pull. [ME *twicchen.* Akin to OE *twiccian* pluck.] — **twitch'ing·ly** *adv.*

twitch·grass (twich'gras', -gräs') *n.* Couch-grass.

twit·ter[1] (twit'ər) *v.i.* **1** To utter a series of light chirping or tremulous notes, as a bird. **2** To titter. **3** *Brit. Dial.* To be excited; tremble. — *v.t.* **4** To utter or express with a twitter. — *n.* **1** A succession of light, tremulous sounds. **2** *Bot.* A disease of plants caused by insects. [Imit.]

twit·ter[2] (twit'ər) *v.t.* To taunt; upbraid. [Freq. of TWIT]

twit·ter[3] (twit'ər) *v.t.* Spin or twist unevenly. [<earlier *twit,* a fault or entanglement in thread; ult. origin uncertain]

'twixt (twikst) *prep. Poetic* Betwixt: an abbreviated form.

two (to͞o) *adj.* Being one more than one, or a unit taken once again; binary: a cardinal numeral. See synonyms under BOTH. — *n.* **1** The sum of one and one: a cardinal number. **2** Any symbol or set of symbols (2, ii, II) for this number. — **in two** Bisected; bipartite; asunder; apart. [OE *twā, tū*]

two-base hit (to͞o'bās') In baseball, a hit in which the batter reaches second base without benefit of an error. Also **two'-bag'ger.**

two-bit (to͞o'bit') *adj. U.S. Slang* Cheap; small-time: a *two-bit* gambler.

two bits *U.S. Colloq.* Twenty-five cents.

two-by-four (to͞o'bī·fôr', -fōr') *adj.* **1** Measuring two inches by four inches. **2** *U.S. Slang* Of trifling size or significance; narrow or limited. — *n.* (to͞o'bī·fôr', -fōr') A piece of lumber measuring two inches by four inches before finishing: much used in building.

two-cy·cle (to͞o'sī'kəl) *adj.* Designating a type of internal-combustion engine in which the piston completes its work in two strokes.

two-edged (to͞o'ejd') *adj.* Having an edge on each side; cutting both ways.

two-faced (to͞o'fāst') *adj.* **1** Having two faces. **2** Double-dealing; insincere; of dissimulating tendency. — **two'-fac'ed·ly** (-fā'sid·lē, -fāst'lē) *adv.*

two·fer (to͞o'fər) *U.S. Slang n.* **1** An article advertised or sold at two for the price of one. **2** A free coupon which entitles the holder to two theater tickets for the price of one if presented at the box office of the designated attraction. — *adj.* Offering two of anything for the price of one: a *twofer* sale. [Alter. of *two for (one)*]

two·fold (to͞o'fōld') *adj.* Double. — *adv.* In a twofold manner or degree; doubly.

two-hand·ed (to͞o'han'did) *adj.* **1** Requiring both hands at once. **2** Constructed for use by two persons. **3** Ambidextrous. **4** Having two hands.

two-mast·er (to͞o'mas'tər, -mäs'-) *n.* A ship with two masts.

two-name (to͞o'nām') *adj.* Bearing two names or signatures.

two-name paper A negotiable paper, bearing either two signatures or one signature and one endorsement.

two·pence (tup'əns) *n. Brit.* **1** Money of account of the value of two pennies. **2** A silver coin of the same value, now issued only for alms money, distributed by order of the British sovereign on Maundy Thursday. **3** A trifle; small amount.

two·pen·ny (tup'ən·ē) *adj. Brit.* **1** Of the price or value of twopence. **2** Cheap; worthless.

two-phase (to͞o'fāz') *adj. Electr.* Diphase.

two-ply (to͞o'plī') *adj.* **1** Made of two united webs; woven double: a *two-ply* carpet. **2** Made of two strands or two thicknesses of material.

Two Sic·i·lies (sis'ə·lēz), **The** A kingdom formed by the union of Sicily with Naples in 1130; incorporated with Italy in 1861.

two·some (to͞o'səm) *n.* **1** Two persons together. **2** A match with one player on each side. — *adj.* **1** Performed or participated in by two, as a dance. **2** Comprising two or a pair.

two-spot (to͞o'spot') *n.* **1** A playing card having two pips; a deuce. **2** *U.S. Slang* An unimportant person. **3** *U.S. Slang* A two-dollar bill. **4** *U.S. Slang* A two-year prison sentence.

two-step (to͞o'step') *n.* A round dance consisting of a sliding step in 2/4 time; also, the music for it.

two-time (to͞o'tīm') *v.t.* **-timed, -tim·ing** *Slang* To be unfaithful to (someone), especially in love; delude; deceive. — **two'-tim'er** *n.*

two-up (to͞o'up') *n. Austral.* A gambling game in which two, or sometimes three, pennies are tossed: also called *swy.*

two-way (to͞o'wā') *adj.* **1** Having an arrangement that will permit a fluid to be directed in either of two channels: specifically said of cocks and valves. **2** *Math.* Having a double mode of variation. **3** Permitting traffic in either direction: a *two-way* street.

twy- See TWI-.

twy·blade (twī'blād) See TWAYBLADE.

twy·ere (twī·ir') See TUYÈRE.

-ty[1] *suffix of nouns* The state or condition of being: *sanity.* [<F *-té* <L *-tas*]

-ty[2] *suffix* Ten; ten times: used in numerals, as *thirty, forty,* etc. [OE *-tig* ten]

Tyb·alt (tib'əlt) A masculine personal name. See THEOBALD.
— **Tybalt** In Shakespeare's *Romeo and Juliet,* nephew to Lady Capulet; kills Mercutio and is killed by Romeo.

Ty·burn (tī'bərn) A former place of execution in London, England.

Ty·che (tī'kē) In Greek mythology, the goddess of chance: identified with the Roman *Fortuna.*

ty·coon (tī·ko͞on') *n.* **1** *U. S. Colloq.* A wealthy and powerful industrial or business leader. **2** A shogun. [<Japanese *taikun* a mighty lord <Chinese *ta* great + *kiun* a prince]

Ty·deus (tī'dyo͞os, -dē·əs) The father of Diomedes and one of the Seven against Thebes.

Ty·di·des (ti·dī'dēz) In Greek mythology, Diomedes, son of Tydeus.

ty·ing (tī'ing) *n.* The act of fastening, or a fastening, as a ribbon or cord.

tyke (tīk) *n.* **1** A tike. **2** *Brit. Dial.* A man from the county of Yorkshire. [Var. of TIKE]

Ty·ler (tī'lər), **John,** 1790–1862, president of the United States 1841–45. — **Wat,** died 1381, English rebel; opposed taxation.

ty·lo·sis (tī·lō'sis) *n. pl.* **·ses** (-sēz) **1** *Bot.* A bladderlike enlargement of a plant cell, intruding within the cavity of a vessel from the wall of a contiguous growing cell. **2** The formation of calluses, especially on the skin. **3** The callus so formed. [<Gk. *tylōsis* < *tylos* a lump, callus]

tym·bal (tim'bəl) See TIMBAL.

tymp (timp) *n. Metall.* A water-cooled block

of refractory material or of cast iron, as the top of the opening between the crucible and the forehearth of a blast furnace. [Short for TYMPAN]

tym·pan (tim′pən) n. 1 Printing A thickness (or, more usually, several thicknesses), as of paper, on the impression surface of a printing press: used to improve the quality of the presswork. 2 Archit. A tympanum. 3 A membrane or other thin sheet tightly stretched. 4 A drum. [<OF <L tympanum. See TYMPANUM.]

tym·pa·ni (tim′pə·nē) See TIMPANI.

tym·pan·ic (tim·pan′ik) adj. 1 Like or of the nature of a drum. 2 Of or pertaining to the middle ear.

tympanic bone Anat. An incomplete bony ring that surrounds the external auditory canal.

tympanic membrane Anat. The drumhead membrane separating the middle ear from the external ear; the eardrum. See illustration under EAR.

tym·pa·nist (tim′pə·nist) n. One who beats or plays upon a tympan; a drummer.

tym·pa·ni·tes (tim′pə·nī′tēz) n. Pathol. Swelling of the abdomen due to accumulation of gas. [<LL <Gk. tympanitēs <tympanon. See TYMPANUM.] — **tym′pa·nit′ic** (-nit′ik) adj.

tym·pa·ni·tis (tim′pə·nī′tis) n. Pathol. Inflammation of the mucous membrane lining the tympanum. [<NL <L tympanum a drum]

tym·pa·num (tim′pə·nəm) n. pl. ·na (-nə) 1 Anat. The middle ear; also, the tympanic membrane. 2 Archit. An ornamental space, as over a doorway, bounded by an arch or within the coping of a pediment. 3 A large drum wheel fitted with buckets for raising water from a flowing stream. 4 An ancient form of drum. 5 Electr. The diaphragm in a telephone. Also spelled timpanum. [<NL <L, a drum <Gk. tympanon <typtein beat]

tym·pa·ny (tim′pə·nē) n. pl. ·nies Tympanites. [<Med. L tympanias <Gk. <tympanon a drum]

Tyn·dale (tin′dəl), **William**, 1484–1536, English priest and religious reformer; translated New Testament; executed for heresy.

Tyn·dall (tin′dəl), **John**, 1820–93, English physicist born in Ireland.

Tyndall effect Physics The scattering of light due to its passage through a medium containing minute suspended particles in continuous rapid motion. Also **Tyndall cone**. [after John Tyndall]

Tyn·dal·li·za·tion (tin′dəl·ə·zā′shən, -ī·zā′-) n. Med. A form of sterilization in which heat is applied intermittently in order to destroy spores in their less resistant adult form. [after John Tyndall]

Tyn·dar·e·us (tin·dâr′ē·əs) In Greek mythology, a king of Sparta and husband of Leda.

Tyne (tīn) A river in Northumberland and Durham, England, flowing 30 miles south to the North Sea at **Tyne·mouth** (tīn′məth, tin′-), a port with a 7th century priory.

typ- Var. of TYPO-.

ty·pal (tī′pəl) adj. Typical.

type (tīp) n. 1 Something that represents or symbolizes something else; an image; emblem; symbol. 2 Theol. That by which something is prefigured. 3 An object representative of, or embodying the characteristics of, a class or group. 4 Biol. **a** The general plan of an organism, with special reference to those structural and physiological characteristics which make it representative of a group, species, class, etc. **b** An individual considered as representative of members of the next higher category in a biological system of classification: the type of a genus, family, order, etc. 5 A variety of some physiological substance as determined by specific differences in properties and in mode of action when compared with another variety of the same substance: a blood type. 6 Printing A piece or block of metal or of wood, bearing on its upper surface, usually in relief, a letter or character for use in printing; also, such pieces collectively. See AGATE, PICA, POINT SYSTEM. 7 A distinctive sign; stamp; mark. 8 A plan to which proposed work or action should conform, as in fine arts; a standard or model. 9 In coinage, the characteristic device on

either side of a medal or coin. See synonyms under EMBLEM, EXAMPLE, LETTER, MODEL, SIGN. — v. **typed**, **typ·ing** v.t. 1 To assign to a particular type or role, as an actor. 2 To determine the type of; identify: to type a blood sample. 3 To typewrite. 4 To represent; typify. 5 To prefigure. — v.i. 6 To typewrite. [<MF <L typus <Gk. typos an impression, figure, type <typtein strike]

-type combining form 1 Representative form; stamp; type: prototype. 2 Used in or produced by printing, photography, or other duplicating processes, or by type: Linotype, collotype. [<Gk. typos stamp]

type·face (tīp′fās′) n. Printing 1 Face (def. 8). 2 A set of type of a particular design.

type foundry An establishment in which metal type is made. — **type founder** — **type founding**

type genus Biol. A genus that combines the essential characteristics of the higher group (as a family) to which it belongs; the representative genus after which a family is named.

type-high (tīp′hī′) adj. Printing Designating the standard height of type (height-to-paper) from base to the level of the printing surface; in the United States, 0.918 of an inch: also **letter-high**.

type line One of the innermost ridges that circumscribe the pattern area of a fingerprint and assist in its identification.

type metal The alloy of which type is made, usually of lead, tin, and antimony.

type·script (tīp′skript′) n. Matter which has been typewritten: also called typoscript. [<TYPE(WRITTEN) + SCRIPT]

type·set·ter (tīp′set′ər) n. 1 A compositor. 2 A machine for composing type. — **type′set′ting** n. & adj.

type species Biol. The plant or animal species regarded as most typical of the genus to which its name is given; a genotype.

type specimen Biol. The individual plant or animal on whose description the distinguishing characters of a species are based.

type·write (tīp′rīt′) v.t. & v.i. ·wrote, ·writ·ten, ·writ·ing To write with a typewriter. Also type.

type·writ·er (tīp′rī′tər) n. 1 A machine for producing printed characters as a substitute for writing: it usually has a keyboard, a depression of the keys serving to impress a type upon the paper through the medium of an inked ribbon. 2 A typist.

type·writ·ing (tīp′rī′ting) n. 1 The act or operation of using a typewriter. 2 Work done by such process.

ty·pha (tī′fə) n. 1 The cat-tail. 2 A fiber resembling kapok prepared from the spikes of the cat-tail, used in life preservers, pillows, etc. [<NL <typhē a cat-tail]

typh·li·tis (tif·lī′tis) n. Pathol. Inflammation of the cecum. [<NL <Gk. typhlos blind] — **typh·lit′ic** (-lit′ik) adj.

typhlo- combining form 1 Blindness; of or pertaining to blindness, or to the blind: typhlology. 2 Anat. & Med. The cecum; related to the cecum: typhlotomy, a cutting into the cecum. Also, before vowels, **typhl-**. [<Gk. typhlos blind]

typh·lol·o·gy (tif·lol′ə·jē) n. The branch of medicine and pathology that deals with blindness. [<TYPHLO- + -LOGY]

typh·lo·sis (tif·lō′sis) n. Blindness. [<NL <Gk. typhlōsis <typhlos blind]

typho- combining form Typhus; typhoid: typhogenic. Also, before vowels, **typh-**. [<Gk. typhos smoke, stupor]

Ty·pho·eus (tī·fō′yoos) In Greek mythology, a giant with a hundred snake heads, killed by Zeus's thunderbolt. — **Ty·pho·e·an** (tī·fō′ē·ən) adj.

ty·pho·gen·ic (tī′fə·jen′ik) adj. Producing typhus.

ty·phoid (tī′foid) adj. 1 Pertaining to or resembling typhoid fever: also **ty·phoi′dal**, **ty′·phose** (-fōs). 2 Resembling typhus. — n. Typhoid fever. [<TYPH(US) + -OID]

typhoid bacillus A motile, flagellated, Gram-negative bacterium (Eberthella or Salmonella typhosa), usually introduced into the body by food or drink: the bacillus that causes typhoid fever.

typhoid carrier A person who, with few or

none of the clinical symptoms of infection, carries the typhoid bacillus and can communicate it to others in its active form. Also **ty·pho·phore** (tī′fə·fôr, -fōr).

typhoid fever Pathol. An acute, infectious fever caused by the typhoid bacillus and characterized by severe intestinal disturbances, a typical eruption of bright rose-red spots on the chest and abdomen, and great physical prostration.

ty·phoi·din (tī-foi′din) n. Bacteriol. A culture of the typhoid bacillus, used as a test for passive or active infection. [<TYPHOID + -IN]

ty·pho·ma·lar·i·al (tī′fō·mə·lâr′ē·əl) adj. Pathol. Describing a fever resembling that of typhoid but believed to be malarial in origin. [<TYPHO- + MALARIAL]

ty·pho·ma·ni·a (tī′fə·mā′nē·ə, -mān′yə) n. Pathol. The delirious state associated with typhoid fever or typhus. Also **ty·pho·ni·a** (tī-fō′nē·ə).

Ty·phon (tī′fon) In Greek mythology, a monster overcome and buried by Zeus under Mount Etna.

ty·phoon (tī·foon′) n. A tropical storm of cyclonic force and peculiar violence, occurring in the western Pacific and the China Sea. See synonyms under CYCLONE. [<dial. Chinese tai feng, lit., big wind; infl. by obs. typhon a whirlwind (<Gk. typhōn a hurricane) and by obs. tuphan, tufan a typhoon <Arabic tūfān, ? ult. from the same Gk. source]

ty·phus (tī′fəs) n. Pathol. An acute, contagious, rickettsial disease caused by a micro-organism (Rickettsia prowazeki) and marked by high fever with eruption of red spots, cerebral disorders, and extreme prostration; typhus fever: also called Brill's disease. **Epidemic typhus** is transmitted by the bite of the body louse, and **endemic** or **murine typhus** by the bite of the rat flea. [<NL <Gk. typhos smoke, a stupor <typhein smoke] — **ty′phous** adj.

typ·i·cal (tip′i·kəl) adj. 1 Having the nature or character of a type; constituting a type or pattern; symbolic. 2 Conforming to the essential features of a species, group, class, etc.; characteristic. Also **typ′ic**: also typal. See synonyms under NORMAL. [<Med. L typicalis <L typicus <Gk. typikos <typos TYPE] — **typ′i·cal·ly** adv. — **typ′i·cal·ness** n.

typ·i·fy (tip′ə·fī) v.t. ·fied, ·fy·ing 1 To represent by a type; signify, as by an image or token. 2 To constitute a type or serve as a characteristic example of. — **typ′i·fi·ca′tion** (-fə·kā′shən) n. — **typ′i·fi′er** n.

typ·ist (tī′pist) n. One who uses a typewriting machine.

typo- combining form Type; of or related to type: typography. Also, before vowels, **typ-**. [<Gk. typos stamp, type]

ty·po·graphed (tī′pə·graft, -gräft) adj. Printed from type, or from plates in which the design is raised above the level of the body of the plate.

ty·pog·ra·pher (tī·pog′rə·fər) n. A printer.

ty·po·graph·i·cal (tī′pə·graf′i·kəl) adj. Pertaining to, concerned with, or effected by typography or printing. Also **ty′po·graph′ic**. — **ty′·po·graph′i·cal·ly** adv.

ty·pog·ra·phy (tī·pog′rə·fē) n. 1 The arrangement of composed type. 2 The style and appearance of printed matter. 3 The act or art of composing and printing from types. [<TYPO- + -GRAPHY]

ty·pol·o·gy (tī·pol′ə·jē) n. The study of types, as in systems of classification. [<TYPO- + -LOGY]

ty·po·script (tī′pō·skript) See TYPESCRIPT.

Ty·poth·e·tae (tī·poth′ə·tē, tī′pə·thē′tē) n. pl. An association of master printers; hence, by extension, **ty·poth′e·tae**, printers collectively: used in the names of organized groups of printers. [<NL <Gk. typos TYPE + tithenai set, put]

Tyr (tür, tir) In Norse mythology, the god of war and son of Odin: identified with the Teutonic Tiu: also spelled Tyrr.

ty·ra·mine (tī′rə·mēn′, tir′ə-) n. Chem. A white, crystalline, nitrogenous compound, $C_8H_{11}ON$, found in ergot, ripe cheese, and putrefying animal tissue: the hydrochloride is used in medicine. [<TYR(OSINE) + AMINE]

ty·ran·ni·cal (ti·ran′i·kəl, tī-) adj. Of or like a

tyrant; harsh; despotic; arbitrary. Also **ty·ran′ ·nic**. See synonyms under ABSOLUTE, ARBITRARY. —**ty·ran′ni·cal·ly** adv. —**ty·ran′ni·cal·ness** n.

ty·ran·ni·cide (tir·ran′ə·sīd, tī-) n. 1 The slayer of tyrant. 2 The slaying of a tyrant. [<F <L tyrannicida <tyrannus a tyrant + caedere kill; def. 2 <L tyrannicidium]

tyr·an·nize (tir′ə·nīz) v. **·nized, ·niz·ing** v.i. 1 To exercise power cruelly or unjustly. 2 To rule as a tyrant; have absolute power. —v.t. 3 To treat tyrannically; domineer. Also Brit. **tyr′ an·nise**. [<MF tyranniser <LL tyrannizare <Gk. tyrannizein <tyrannos a tyrant] —**tyr′ an·niz′er** n.

tyr·an·no·saur·us (tir·ran′ə·sôr′əs, tī-) n. Paleontol. A carnivorous dinosaur (Tyrannosaurus rex) inhabiting North America in the Cretaceous period: it was characterized by its huge bulk, massive jaws, and ability to walk erect on its hind legs. [<NL <Gk. tyrannos a tyrant + sauros a lizard]

tyr·an·nous (tir′ə·nəs) adj. Despotic, tyrannical. See synonyms under ARBITRARY. —**tyr′ an·nous·ly** adv. —**tyr′an·nous·ness** n.

tyr·an·ny (tir′ə·nē) n. pl. **·nies** 1 Absolute power arbitrarily or unjustly administered; despotism. 2 An arbitrarily cruel exercise of power; a tyrannical act. 3 In Greek history, the office or the administration of a tyrant. 4 Severity; roughness. [<OF tirannie <L tyrannia <tyrannus a tyrant]

ty·rant (tī′rənt) n. 1 One who rules oppressively or cruelly; a despot. 2 One who exercises absolute power without legal warrant, whether ruling well or ill: the original meaning in ancient Greece. [<OF tiran, tyran <L tyrannus <Gk. tyrannos a master, a usurper]

tyrant flycatcher Any American flycatcher (family Tyrannidae), as the kingdom, pewee, etc.

Ty·ras (tī′rəs) The ancient name for BELGOROD-DNESTROVSKI.

tyre (tīr) See TIRE[2].

Tyre (tīr) A port and capital of ancient Pheonicia, on the site of modern Sur in SW Lebanon.

Tyr·i·an (tir′ē·ən) adj. 1 Of or pertaining to Tyre. 2 Having the color of Tyrian dye: purple. —n. A native of Tyre.

Tyrian dye 1 A purple or crimson dyestuff obtained by the ancient Greeks and Romans from certain mollusks of the genus Murex. 2 A violet-purple color of high saturation and low brilliance. Also **Tyrian purple**.

ty·ro (tī′rō) n. pl. **·ros** One who is in the rudiments of any study or the preliminary stage of any occupation; a beginner; novice; also spelled tiro. [<Med. L <L tiro a recruit]

Ty·rol (ti·rōl′, tir′ōl, tī′rōl) See TIROL.

Ty·ro·lese (tir′ə·lēz′, -lēs′) See TIROLESE.

Ty·ro·lienne (tē·rō·lyen′) n. A ländler. [<F, fem. of tyrolien Tyrolean]

Ty·rone (ti·rōn′) A county of Ulster, western Northern Ireland; 1,218 miles; county town, Omagh.

ty·ro·sin·ase (tī′rō·si·nās′, tir′ō-) n. Biochem. A plant and animal enzyme which converts tyrosine into dark pigments, as melanin. [<TYROSIN(E) + -ASE]

ty·ro·sine (tī′rə·sēn, -sin, tir′ə-) n. Biochem. A white crystalline amino acid, $C_9H_{11}O_3N$, formed by the hydrolysis of many plant and animal proteins [<Gk. tyros cheese + -INE[2]]

ty·ro·sin·o·sis (tī′rō·sin·ō′sis, tir′ō-) n. Pathol. A disorder caused by defective metabolism of tyrosine in the body. [<TYROSINE(E) + -OSIS]

ty·ro·thri·cin (tī′rō·thrī′sin, -thris′in) n. An antibiotic isolated from a soil bacterium (Bacillus brevis): similar to gramicidin and used therapeutically in localized infections. [<TYRO-(SINE) + Gk. thrix, trichos a hair + -IN]

Tyrr (tür, tir) See TYR.

Tyr·rhe·ni·an Sea (ti·rē′nē·ən) The part of the Mediterranean between Italy, Sardinia, Corsica, and Sicily. [Gk. Tyrrhēnia Tuscany]

Tyr·tae·us (tûr·tē′əs) Greek poet of the seventh century B.C.

Tyu·men (tyo͞o·men′, Russian tyo͞o·myän′y′) A city in western Asiatic Russia, on the Tura.

Tyu·zen·zi (cho͞o·zen·jē) See CHUZENJI.

tzar (tsär), **Tza·ri·na** (tsä·rē′nä), etc. See CZAR, etc.

tzet·ze (tset′zē) See TSETSE.

U

u, U (yo͞o) n. pl. **u's, U's** or **Us** (yo͞oz) 1 The twenty-first letter of the English alphabet: from Greek upsilon. In Roman it was written V and had both consonant and vowel value. In English U was formerly the uncial or cursive form of V; gradually V came to be preferred in initial position in writing, and, as the sound at the beginning of a word is ordinarily consonantal, U was finally restricted to vowel use. 2 Any sound of the letter u. See ALPHABET. —symbol 1 Chem. Uranium (symbol U). 2 Anything shaped like a U.

Uau·pés (wou·pás′) A river in SE Colombia and NW Brazil, flowing 500 miles SE to the Río Negro: also Vaupés.

U·ban·gi (o͞o·bäng′gē) A river of central Africa, flowing 1,400 miles from Zaire to the Congo river.

U·ban·gi-Sha·ri (o͞o·bäng′gē·shä′rē) See CENTRAL AFRICAN REPUBLIC.

U·be (o͞o′bē, Japanese o͞o-be) A city of SW Honshu island, Japan.

Ü·ber·mensch (ü′bər·mensh) n. German The superman, in Nietzsche's terminology.

u·bi·e·ty (yo͞o·bī′ə·tē) n. The state of being in a place; local relation. [<NL ubietas, -tatis <L ubi where]

u·biq·ui·tar·i·an (yo͞o·bik′wə·târ′ē·ən) n. One who has ubiquitous existence.

U·biq·ui·tar·i·an (yo͞o·bik′wə·târ′ē·ən) n. A believer in the omnipresence of the human nature of Christ and, as a consequence, in his necessary actual bodily presence in the Eucharist. Also **U·bi·quar·i·an** (yo͞o′bə·kwâr′ ē·ən), **U′bi·quist, U′biq′ui·tist.**

U·biq·ui·tar·i·an·ism (yo͞o·bik′wə·târ′ē·ən·iz′əm) n. The tenets of the Ubiquitarians. Also **U·biq·ui·tism** (yo͞o·bik′wə·tiz′əm).

u·biq·ui·tous (yo͞o·bik′wə·təs) adj. Existing, or seeming to exist, everywhere at once; omnipresent. Also. **u·biq′ui·tar′y** (-ter′ē). —**u·biq′ ui·tous·ly** adv. —**u·biq′ui·tous·ness** n.

u·biq·ui·ty (yo͞o·bik′qə·tē) n. 1 The state of being in an indefinite number of places at once; omnipresence real or seeming. 2 The state of existing always without beginning or end. [<F ubiquité <L ubique everywhere]

u·bi su·pra (yo͞o′bī so͞o′prə) Latin Where (mentioned) above.

U-boat (yo͞o′bōt′) n. A German submarine. [<G U-boot, contraction of Unterseeboot, lit., undersea boat]

U-bolt (yo͞o′bōlt′) n. A bolt bent like the letter U, and fitted with a screw and nut at each end.

U·che·an (yo͞o·chē′ən) n. A North American Indian linguistic stock, consisting only of the Yuchi tribe.

U·dai·pur (o͞o·dī′po͞or, o͞o′dī-) 1 A former princely state of the Rajputana States, India; since 1948 merged with the State of Rajasthan: 13,170 square miles: also Mewar. 2 A city of southern Rajasthan, India; formerly capital of Udaipur state.

U·dall (yo͞o′d'l), Nicholas, 1506?–56, English scholar and dramatist; also Uvedale.

U·day Shan·kar (o͞o′dī shän·kär′), born 1900, Indian dancer.

ud·der (ud′ər) n. A large, pendulous, milk-secreting gland having nipples or teasts for the suckling of offspring, as in cows. [OE ūder]

U·di·ne (o͞o′dē·nä) A city in NE Italy.

Ud·murt Republic (o͞od′mo͞ort, o͞od·mo͞ort′) An autonomous republic in east central European Russia; 16,300 square miles; capital, Izhevsk.

u·do (o͞o′dō) n. A bushy plant (Aralia cordata) of Japan and China which, when young, yields edible shoots. [<Japanese]

u·dom·e·ter (yo͞o·dom′ə·tər) n. A pluviometer. [<L udus moist + -METER] —**u·do·met·ric** (yo͞o′də·met′rik) adj. —**u·dom′e·try** n.

Ue·le (we′lā) A river of NE Belgian Congo, flowing 700 miles north, NW, and west to a confluence with the Bomu at the border of French Equatorial Africa, forming the Ubangi: also Welle.

U·fa (o͞o·fä′) 1 A city on the Byelaya river in eastern European Russia; capital of Bashkir Republic. 2 A river in eastern European Russia, flowing 599 miles NW and SW from the southern Urals to the Byelaya river at Ufa.

UFO Unidentified flying object: an official U.S. Air Force designation. Compare FLYING SAUCER.

U·gan·da (yo͞o·gan′də, o͞o·gän′dä) An independent member of the Commonwealth of Nations in east central Africa; 93,981 square miles; capital, Kampala.

ugh (ukh, u, o͞okh, o͞o) interj. An exclamation of repugnance or disgust. [Imit.]

ug·li·fy (ug′lə·fī) v.t. **·fied, ·fy·ing** To make ugly. —**ug′li·fi·ca′tion** (-fə·kā′shən) n.

ug·ly (ug′lē) adj. **·li·er, ·li·est** 1 Displeasing to the esthetic feelings, as from lack of grace or proportion; distasteful in appearance: ill-looking; unsightly. 2 Repulsive to the moral sentiments: revolting. 3 Bad in character or consequences, as a rumor or a wound. 4 Colloq. Ill-tempered: quarrelsome. 5 Portending storms; threatening: said of the weather. [<ON uggligr dreadful <uggr fear] —**ug′li·ly** adv. —**ug′li·ness** n.

ugly duckling 1 In Hans Christian Andersen's story. The Ugly Duckling, a young swan hatched by a duck, belittled and persecuted by all the ducks for his strange appearance, until he grew into the most beautiful bird on the pond. 2 Any ill-favored or unpromising child who unexpectedly grows into a beauty or a wonder.

U·go (o͞o′gō) Italian form of HUGH. Also **U′go· li′no** (-lē′nō).

U·gri·an (o͞o′grē·ən, yo͞o′-) n. 1 A member of any of the Finno-Ugric peoples of Hungary and western Siberia, including the Ostyaks, Voguls, and Magyars. 2 Ugric. —adj. Of or pertaining to the Ugrians, their culture, or their languages.

U·gric (o͞o′grik, yo͞o′-) n. A branch of the Finno-Ugric subfamily of Uralic languages, comprising Magyar (Hungarian), Ostyak, and Vogul. —adj. Of or pertaining to any of these languages.)

U·gro-Al·ta·ic (o͞o′grō·al·tā′ik, yo͞o′grō-) n. & adj. Ural-Altaic.

ug·some (ug′səm) adj. Scot. Disgusting.

uh·lan (o͞o′län, o͞o·län′, yo͞o′län) n. 1 A cavalryman and lancer of a type originating in eastern Europe, formerly prominent in European armies, notably the German. 2 One of a body of Tatar militia. Also spelled ulan. [<G <Polish <Turkish ōghlān lad, servant]

Uh·land (o͞o′länt), Johann Ludwig, 1787–1862, German poet.

Ui·gur (wē′go͞or) n. 1 One of a Turkic people who ruled in Mongolia and East Turkestan from the eight to the twelfth century, now the majority of the population of Chinese Turkestan. 2 The Turkic language of the Uigurs.

2 The Turkic language of these people. — **Ui·gu·ri·an** (wē·gŏŏr′ē·ən), **Ui·gu·ric** (wē·gŏŏr′ik) adj.

u·in·tah·ite (yŏŏ·in′tə·īt) n. A variety of asphalt common in Utah: often called gilsonite. Also **u·in′ta·ite.** [from Uinta Mountains]

U·in·ta Mountains (yŏŏ·in′tə) A range in NE Utah and SW Wyoming; highest point, 13,498 feet (the highest point in Utah).

uit (oit, œit) prep. Afrikaans Out; out of.

uit·land·er (īt′län·dər, oit′-; Afrikaans œit′·län·dər) n. Afrikaans A foreigner; formerly, in the South African Republic, a foreign white resident.

uit·span (œit′spän) v. & n. Afrikaans Outspan.

U·ji·ji (ŏŏ·jē′jē) A port on Lake Tanganyika in western Tanganyika, Africa.

U·j·pest (ŏŏ′ē·pesht) A city on the Danube in central Hungary: German Neupest.

u·kase (yŏŏ′kās, yŏŏ·kāz′) n. **1** Formerly, an edict or decree of the imperial Russian government. **2** Any official decree. [< Russian ukaz]

U·kraine A country in eastern Europe, off the Black Sea; capital, Kiev; pop. 52,000,000; 233,100 sq. miles; originally known as **Rus,** the Ukraine was controlled by the Mongols in the 13th century, Lithuania in the 14th and 15th centuries, and Poland in the 16th century; it had a short period of independence before being absorbed by Russia, then the U.S.S.R.; Ukraine declared its independence from the U.S.S.R. in 1991. [Ukrainian Ukrayina].

U·krain·i·an adj. Of or pertaining to the Ukraine, its people, or their language. — n. **1** A native or inhabitant of the Ukraine. **2** An East Slavic language spoken in the Ukraine.

u·ku·le·le (yŏŏ′kə·lā′lē, Hawaiian ŏŏ′kŏŏ·lā′lā) n. A guitarlike musical instrument having four strings. [< Hawaiian, flea < uku insect + lele jump; from the movements of the fingers in playing]

UKULELE

U·lan (ŏŏ′län, ŏŏ·län′, yŏŏ′lən) See UHLAN.

U·lan Ba·tor (ŏŏ′län bä′tôr) The capital of the Mongolian People's Republic: formerly Urga: Chinese Kulun.

U·lan Ho·to (ŏŏ′län khŏ′tō) The capital of Inner Mongolian Autonomous Region, northern China, in the NE part of the Region: Chinese Wulanhaote: formerly Wangyehmiao. Also Khoto.

ul·cer (ul′sər) n. **1** Pathol. An open sore on an external or internal surface of the body, usually accompanied by disintegration of tissue with the formation of pus. **2** Figuratively, a corroding fault or vice; corruption; evil. [< L ulcus, ulceris]

ul·cer·ate (ul′sə·rāt) v.t. & v.i. ·at·ed, ·at·ing To make or become ulcerous. [< L ulceratus, pp. of ulcerare < ulcus, ulceris ulcer] — **ul′cer·a′tive** adj.

ul·cer·a·tion (ul′sə·rā′shən) n. **1** The forming of an ulcer, or the condition of being affected with ulcers. **2** An ulcer, or ulcers collectively.

ul·cer·ous (ul′sər·əs) adj. **1** Resembling an ulcer. **2** Affected with ulcers. — **ul′cer·ous·ly** adv. — **ul′cer·ous·ness** n.

–ule suffix of nouns Small; little: used to form diminutives: granule. [< F -ule < L -ulus, -ula, -ulum, diminutive suffix]

u·le·ma (ŏŏ′lə·mä′) n. **1** In Moslem countries, a council or college of learned officials (priests, judges, or scholars) who are trained in Moslem religion and law, and interpret the Koran. **2** Hence, any Moslem scholar. [< Turkish 'ulema < Arabic 'ulamā, pl. of 'alim wise < 'alama know]

–ulent suffix of adjectives Abounding in; full of (what is indicated in the main element): opulent, truculent. Corresponding nouns are formed in **–ulence,** as in opulence, truculence. [< L -ulentus]

Ul·fi·las (ul′fi·ləs), A.D. 311?–383, bishop of the Goths; translated the Bible into Gothic: also spelled Wulfila. Also **Ul′fi·la** (-lə).

U·li·thi (ŏŏ·lē′thē) An atoll of the western Caroline Islands; 19 miles long, 10 miles wide.

ul·lage (ul′ij) n. The quantity that a vessel, as a wine cask, lacks of being full; wantage. [< AF ulliage, OF ouillage < ouiller fill up (to the bunghole) < ueil eye, bunghole < L oculus eye]

Ulls·wa·ter (ulz′wô′tər, -wot·ər) The second largest English lake, in Cumberland and Westmoreland; 3 square miles.

Ulm (ŏŏlm) A city on the Danube River in central eastern Baden-Württemberg, SW West Germany.

ul·ma·ceous (ul·mā′shəs) adj. Bot. Designating or belonging to a family (Ulmaceae) of shrubs and trees of the order Urticales, the elm family, widely distributed in temperate and tropical regions, and characterized by alternate simple leaves, apetalous bisexual or unisexual flowers, and a compressed fruit. [< NL, family name < L ulmus elm]

ul·na (ul′nə) n. pl. ·nae (-nē) or ·nas Anat. In vertebrates above dishes fishes, that one of the two long bones of the forearm or foreleg which forms a joint with the radius and is on the same side as the little finger or fifth digit. [< L, elbow] — **ul′nar** adj.

–ulose suffix of adjectives Marked by or abounding in: widely used in scientific and technical terms: ramulose. Compare –ULOUS (def. 2). [< L -ulosus, adjective suffix]

U·lot·ri·chi (yŏŏ·lot′rə·kī) n. pl. In the classification of Huxley, a subdivision of the human species, characterized by woolly or crispy hair. Also **U·lot′ri·ches** (-kēz). [< NL Ulotriches < Gk. oulothrix, oulotrichos woolly-haired < oulos woolly + thrix hair] — **u·lot′ri·chous** (-kəs) adj.

–ulous suffix of adjectives **1** Tending to do or characterized by (what is indicated by the main element): tremulous, ridiculous. **2** Full of: meticulous, populous. Compare –ULOSE. [< L -ulus and -ulosus, adjective suffixes]

Ul·pi·an (ul′pē·ən), A.D. 170?–228, Roman jurist; full name Domitius Ulpianus.

ul·ster (ul′stər) n. A very long, loose overcoat, sometimes belted at the waist: made originally of frieze from Ulster, Ireland.

Ul·ster (ul′stər) A former province of northern Ireland comprising the nine counties listed below; 8,331 square miles. In 1925 six of the counties (Antrim, Armagh, Downe, Fermanagh, Londonderry, Tyrone: 5,238 square miles) became Northern Ireland and three (Cavan, Donegal, Monaghan: 3,093 square miles) the Province of Ulster of the Republic of Ireland. — **Ul′ster·man** (-mən) n.

Ulster cycle The older and more famous of the two cycles of Old Irish epic and romance. The manuscripts date from the seventh and eighth centuries, but celebrate the Ireland and Irish heroes of the first century, and depict a civilization of barbaric splendor that dates back centuries earlier. See FENIAN CYCLE, TAIN BO CUAILGNE.

ul·te·ri·or (ul·tir′ē·ər) adj. **1** More remote; not so pertinent as something else to the matter spoken of: applied to immaterial things: ulterior considerations; also, intentionally unrevealed; hidden: ulterior motives. **2** Following; succeeding; later in time, or secondary in importance. **3** Lying beyond or on the farther side of a certain bounding line. [< L, compar. of ulter beyond] — **ul·te′ri·or·ly** adv.

ul·ti·ma (ul′tə·mə) n. The last syllable of a word. [< L, fem. of ultimus last]

ul·ti·mate (ul′tə·mit) adj. **1** Beyond which there is no other; last of a series; final. **2** Fundamental or essential; hence, not susceptible of further analysis; elementary; primary. **3** Most distant; farthest; extreme. **4** Mech. Designating the maximum strength of a body, or a strain of the least intensity sufficient to cause rupture. — n. **1** The final result; last step; conclusion. **2** A fundamental or final fact. [< LL ultimatus, orig. pp. of ultimare come to an end < ultimus farthest, last, superl. of ulter beyond] — **ul′ti·mate·ness** n.

ul·ti·mate·ly (ul′tə·mit·lē) adv. In the end; at last; finally.

ul·ti·ma Thu·le (ul′tə·mə thŏŏ′lē, tŏŏ′lē) **1** Farthest Thule: in ancient geography, the northernmost habitable regions of the earth. **2** Any distant, unknown region. **3** The farthest possible point, degree, or limit.

ul·ti·ma·tum (ul′tə·mā′təm, -mä′-) n. pl. ·tums or ·ta (-tə) **1** A final statement, as concerning terms or conditions; in diplomacy, the final terms offered by one party, as during negotiations concerning a treaty, the rejection of which by the other party will result in breaking off all negotiation; loosely, a last proposal, offer, concession, or demand. **2** Anything ultimate. [< NL < LL, neut. of ultimatus. See ULTIMATE.]

ul·ti·mo (ul′tə·mō) adv. Latin In the last month; shortened to ult., following a date: the 15th ult.: distinguished from proximo (prox.) or instant (inst.).

ul·ti·mo·gen·i·ture (ul′tə·mō·jen′ə·chər) n. The rule whereby the youngest son takes the inheritance: the opposite of primogeniture. [< L ultimus last + GENITURE]

ul·tra (ul′trə) adj. Going beyond the bounds of moderation; extreme; extravagant. — n. One who holds extreme opinions; a radical. [< L, beyond, on the other side]

ultra– prefix **1** On the other side of; beyond in space (compare TRANS–); as in:

ultra–Arctic	ultra–Neptunian
ultra–equinoctial	ultra–stellar
ultra–galactic	ultra–terrene
ultra–lunar	ultra–terrestrial
ultra–Martian	ultra–zodiacal

2 Going beyond the limits of; surpassing; as in:

ultra–atomic	ultra–molecular
ultra–centenarian	ultra–natural
ultra–human	ultra–total

3 Beyond what is usual or natural; excessively; as in:

ultra–affected	ultra–moderate
ultra–agnostic	ultra–modest
ultra–ambitious	ultra–mulish
ultra–Anglican	ultra–nominalistic
ultra–believing	ultra–ornate
ultra–benevolent	ultra–orthodox
ultra–Christian	ultra–orthodoxy
ultra–classical	ultra–partisan
ultra–confident	ultra–physical
ultra–conservatism	ultra–positivistic
ultra–conservative	ultra–precision
ultra–cooperative	ultra–Protestant
ultra–cosmopolitan	ultra–Protestantism
ultra–credulous	ultra–prudent
ultra–democratic	ultra–purist
ultra–despotic	ultra–Puritan
ultra–discipline	ultra–radical
ultra–educationist	ultra–refined
ultra–episcopal	ultra–refinement
ultra–evangelical	ultrareligious
ultra–exclusive	ultra–revolutionary
ultrafashionable	ultra–revolutionist
ultra–fastidious	ultra–ritualism
ultra–federalist	ultra–romanticist
ultra–feudal	ultra–royalism
ultra–filtration	ultra–royalist
ultra–Gallican	ultra–scientific
ultra–German	ultra–sensual
ultra–honorable	ultra–sentimental
ultra–intellectual	ultra–servile
ultra–legality	ultra–Spartan
ultra–liberal	ultra–spiritual
ultra–liberalism	ultra–splendid
ultra–logical	ultra–sterile
ultra–loyal	ultra–strict
ultra–manners	ultra–theological
ultra–maternal	ultra–virtuous

ul·tra·cen·tri·fuge (ul′trə·sen′trə·fyo͞oj) *n.* A centrifuge whose rotor, sometimes driven by blasts of hydrogen, will exert a force of about one million times gravity: used for high precision scientific and laboratory work. —**ul′tra·cen′tri·fu·ga′tion** (-fyo͞o·gā′shən) *n.*

ul·tra·crit·i·cal (ul′trə·krit′i·kəl) *adj.* Unduly critical.

ul·tra·fil·ter (ul′trə·fil′tər) *n. Chem.* A filter having extremely minute pores, as a living membrane or a film of gelatin on filter paper: used to sift out colloidal particles which pass through ordinary filters. —**ul′tra·fil·tra′tion** (-fil·trā′shən) *n.*

ul·tra-high frequency (ul′trə·hī′) Any wave frequency between 300 and 3,000 megahertz. Abbr. *uhf, UHF.*

ul·tra·ist (ul′trə·ist) *n.* One who in opinions or conduct goes beyond moderation; a radical; an extremist. —*adj.* Radical; extreme: also **ul′tra·is′tic.** —**ul′tra·ism** *n.*

ul·tra·ma·rine (ul′trə·mə·rēn′) *n.* **1** A deep, usually purplish-blue, permanent pigment made by treating the powdered mineral lapis lazuli. **2** A similar pigment made largely by synthesis from kaolin, silica, soda, sulfur, and charcoal: also called *new blue, French blue.* **3** The color of ultramarine. —*adj.* Being beyond or across the sea. [<Med. L *ultramarinus* <L *ultra* beyond + *marinus* marine]

ul·tra·mi·crom·e·ter (ul′trə·mī·krom′ə·tər) *n.* A micrometer designed for measurements requiring a high order of precision and accuracy.

ul·tra·mi·cro·scope (ul′trə·mī′krə·skōp) *n.* An optical instrument for detecting objects too small to be seen with an ordinary microscope, by means of an intense beam of light thrown from the side upon the spot to be examined.

ul·tra·mi·cro·scop·ic (ul′trə·mī′krə·skop′ik) *adj.* **1** Too minute to be seen by an ordinary microscope. **2** Relating to the ultramicroscope. Also **ul′tra·mi′cro·scop′i·cal.** —**ul′tra·mi·cros′co·py** (-mī·kros′kə·pē) *n.*

ul·tra·mod·ern (ul′trə·mod′ərn) *adj.* Excessively or inordinately new or modern; extreme in modern tendencies or ideas. —**ul′tra·mod′ern·ism** *n.* —**ul′tra·mod′ern·ist** *n.* —**ul′tra·mod′ern·is′tic** *adj.*

ul·tra·mon·tane (ul′trə·mon′tān) *adj.* **1** Situated beyond the mountains: opposed to *cismontane;* beyond or south of the Alps, i.e., Italian or papal. **2** In politics or ecclesiastical matters, supporting the policy of the papal court. —*n.* **1** One who resides beyond the Alps. **2** One who supports the papal policy in political or ecclesiastical matters. [<Med. L *ultramontanus* <L *ultra* beyond + *montanus* pertaining to a mountain <*mons, montis* mountain]

Ul·tra·mon·ta·nism (ul′trə·mon′tə·niz′əm) *n.* The policy of Roman Catholics who wish to see all power in the church in the hands of the pope, in opposition to those desiring a more independent development of the national churches; curialism: opposed to *Gallicanism.*

ul·tra·mun·dane (ul′trə·mun′dān) *adj.* Extending beyond the world, the solar system, or the present life. [<L *ultramundanus*]

ul·tra·na·tion·al·ism (ul′trə·nash′ən·əl·iz′əm) *n.* Extreme devotion to or support of national, as opposed to international, interests or considerations. —**ul′tra·na′tion·al** *adj.* —**ul′tra·na′tion·al·ist** *n.* & *adj.* —**ul′tra·na′tion·al·is′tic** *adj.*

ul·tra·pho·tic (ul′trə·fō′tik) *adj. Physics* Denoting wavelengths of radiant energy beyond the visible region of the spectrum, as ultraviolet and infrared.

ul·tra·son·ic (ul′trə·son′ik) *adj. Physics* Pertaining to or designating sound waves having a frequency above the limits of audibility, or in excess of about 20 kilocycles per second: distinguished from *supersonic.*

ul·tra·son·ics (ul′trə·son′iks) *n. pl. (construed as singular)* The study of acoustic phenomena in the frequency range above that of audibility.

ul·tra·sound (ul′trə·sound′) *n. Physics.* Sound having a frequency above the limits of audibility, or in excess of 20 kilocycles per second.

ul·tra·trop·i·cal (ul′trə·trop′i·kəl) *adj.* **1** Situated beyond the tropics. **2** Hotter than the tropics.

ul·tra·vi·o·let (ul′trə·vī′ə·lit) *adj. Physics* Lying beyond the violet end of the visible spectrum: said of high-frequency light waves more refrangible than the violet and having wavelengths ranging from about 3,900 angstroms to the upper limits of X-rays. Compare INFRARED.

ul·tra vi·res (ul′trə vī′rēz) *Latin* **1** *Law* Beyond the lawful capacity or powers: said especially of corporations as to acts or contracts not within the scope of the powers conferred upon them and which are *ipso facto* void: applied also to the acts which although within their powers have been done without their required consent, as in the case of powers delegated to directors. **2** Figuratively, not permissible; forbidden: a colloquial use.

ul·tra·vi·rus (ul′trə·vī′rəs) *n.* A filtrable virus. [<NL]

U·lugh Muz·tagh (o͞o′lo͞o mo͞oz·tä′) A peak on the east central border of the Sinkiang-Uigur and the Tibetan autonomous regions, western China; 25,340 feet.

ul·u·lant (yo͞ol′yə·lənt, ul′-) *adj.* Howling; hooting. [<L *ululans, -antis,* ppr. of *ululare* howl]

ul·u·late (yo͞ol′yə·lāt, ul′-) *v.i.* **·lat·ed, ·lat·ing** To howl, hoot, or wail. [<L *ululatus,* pp. of *ululare* howl] —**ul′u·la′tion** *n.*

Ul·ya·novsk (o͞ol·yä′nôfsk) A port on the Volga in east central European Russian S.F.S.R.

U·lys·ses (yo͞o·lis′ēz, *Ger.* o͞o·lü′ses) A masculine personal name. Also *Fr.* **U·lysse** (ü·lēs′), *Ital.* **U·lis·se** (o͞o·lēs′sā). [<Gk., the hater] —**Ulysses** Odysseus.

um·bel (um′bəl) *n. Bot.* An indeterminate inflorescence in which a number of nearly equal pedicels radiate from a small area at the top of a very short axis, giving an umbrellalike appearance. [<L *umbella* a parasol, dim. of *umbra* shadow. Related to UMBRELLA.]

um·bel·late (um′bə·lit, -lāt) *adj.* Disposed in or resembling umbels. Also **um′bel·lar, um′bel·lat′ed.** [<NL *umbellatus*]

um·bel·let (um′bə·lit) *n.* An umbellule.

um·bel·lif·er·ous (um′bə·lif′ər·əs) *adj.* **1** Bearing umbels. **2** Designating or pertaining to an important and widely distributed family *(Umbelliferae)* of herbs and some shrubs, the parsley or carrot family, comprising many plants used as food, for flavoring, and in medicine. [<NL, family name <L *umbella* parasol + *ferre* bear]

um·bel·lu·late (um·bel′yə·lit, -lāt) *adj.* Having or disposed in umbellules.

um·bel·lule (um′bəl·yo͞ol, um·bel′-) *n. Bot.* A small or secondary umbel. [<NL *umbellula,* dim. of L *umbella* parasol]

um·ber[1] (um′bər) *n.* A chestnut- to liver-brown hydrated ferric oxide, containing some manganese oxide and clay: used as a pigment; also, the color. When in its natural state it is known as **raw umber,** and when heated, so as to produce a reddish-brown, as **burnt umber.** —*adj.* Of or pertaining to umber; of a dusky hue; brownish. —*v.t.* To color with umber; darken, as by staining. [<F *(terre d')ombre* <Ital. *ombra,* prob. <L *Umbra,* fem. of *Umber* of Umbria, where originally found; ? infl. in Ital. by *ombra* shadow, shade <L *umbra*]

um·ber[2] (um′bər) *n.* **1** Shade; hence, some indefinite dark color. **2** The grayling. [<F *ombre* <L *umbra* shade]

Um·ber·to (o͞om·ber′tō) Italian form of HUMBERT.

um·bil·i·cal (um·bil′i·kəl) *adj.* **1** Pertaining to or situated near the umbilicus. **2** Placed near the navel; central. —*n.* **1** A long, flexible tube that serves as a connecting device, conduit for air, power, communication, etc., for an astronaut or aquanaut when outside the craft. **2** A similar device used as a source of fuel, etc., for a spacecraft before launching. [<LL *umbilicalis* <L *umbilicus* navel]

umbilical cord *Anat.* The ropelike tissue connecting the navel of the fetus with the placenta.

um·bil·i·cate (um·bil′ə·kit, -kāt) *adj.* **1** Resembling a navel, as by having a central depression or mark. **2** Having an umbilicus or navel-shaped depression, as a shell. Also **um·bil′i·cat′ed.** —**um·bil′i·ca′tion** *n.*

um·bil·i·cus (um·bil′ə·kəs, um′bə·lī′kəs) *n. pl.* **·ci** (-sī) **1** *Anat.* The depression at the middle of the abdomen where the umbilical cord of the fetus was attached; the navel. **2** *Zool.* An indention or depression at the axial base of a spiral shell, as in many gastropods. **3** *Ornithol.* Either of the apertures (inferior and superior) of the calamus of a feather. **4** *Bot.* A navel-shaped depression; a hilum. [<L]

um·bil·i·form (um·bil′ə·fôrm) *adj.* Navel-shaped. [<*umbili-* (<UMBILICUS) + -FORM]

um·ble pie (um′bəl) See HUMBLE PIE.

um·bles (um′bəlz) *n. pl.* The entrails of a deer; humbles. [Var. of NUMBLES]

um·bo (um′bō) *n. pl.* **um·bo·nes** (um·bō′nēz) or **·bos** **1** The boss or projecting spike in the center of a shield. **2** *Zool.* An elevation, boss, or knob, as the prominence of a bivalve shell near the hinge, or the plate of an echinoderm. **3** *Bot.* The top of the cap of certain fungi. **4** *Anat.* The surface of the tympanic membrane at the point of attachment to the malleus. [<L] —**um′bo·nal, um·bon·ic** (um·bon′ik) *adj.*

um·bo·nate (um′bə·nit, -nāt) *adj.* Having an umbo or bosslike protuberance. Also **um′bo·nat′ed.**

um·bra (um′brə) *n. pl.* **·brae** (-brē) **1** That region of a shadow from which the direct light is entirely cut off. **2** *Astron.* **a** In an eclipse, that part of the shadow of the earth or moon within which the moon or the sun is entirely hidden. See PENUMBRA. **b** The inner dark portion of a sunspot. [<L, shadow]

um·brage (um′brij) *n.* **1** Resentment, as at being obscured by another. **2** A sense of injury; offense: now usually in **to give** (or **take**) **umbrage.** **3** That which gives shade, as a leafy tree. **4** *Poetic* Shade or shadow cast. See synonyms under PIQUE. [<F *ombrage* <L *umbraticus* shady <*umbra* shade]

um·bra·geous (um·brā′jəs) *adj.* **1** Shady or shaded; forming or providing shade. **2** Quick to take offense; peevish; suspicious. [<F *ombrageux* <*ombrage.* See UMBRAGE.] —**um·bra′geous·ly** *adv.* —**um·bra′geous·ness** *n.*

um·brel·la (um·brel′ə) *n.* **1** A light portable canopy on a folding frame, carried as a protection against sun or rain. **2** *Zool.* The contractile, jellylike portion of the body of a medusa expanded like a bell or umbrella. **3** Something serving as a cover or shield, or as a means of linking together various things under a common designation or sponsoring agency: the expanding *umbrella* of nuclear power; various theater groups appearing under the *umbrella* of UNESCO. —*adj.* Being or serving as an umbrella (def. 3): an *umbrella* organization; an *umbrella* statement. [<Ital. *ombrella,* alter. (after *ombra* shade) of L *umbella* parasol. Related to UMBEL.]

umbrella bird Any of several South American birds (genus *Cephalopterus*), the male of which has a broad crest likened to an umbrella. *C. ornatus* has lustrous black plumage with an umbrellalike crest of blue, hairlike feathers.

umbrella leaf A smooth perennial herb *(Diphylleia cymosa)* of the barberry family, with a single large peltate leaf, one to two feet across, and a terminal cyme of white flowers. It is found in the southern United States.

umbrella palm A palm *(Hedyscepe canterburyana)* having pinnate leaves, native to Lord Howe Island in the British Solomons.

umbrella tree **1** A small magnolia *(Magnolia tripetala)* of the southern United States, with fragrant white flowers and oval leaves 16 to 30 inches long, crowded in an umbrellalike whorl at the ends of the branches. **2** Any one of several other trees with large, round cordate leaves.

um·brel·la·wort (um·brel′ə·wûrt′) *n.* A typically North American herb (genus *Allionia*) with the flowers enclosed in a three- or four-parted involucre.

Um·bri·a (um′brē·ə) An ancient and modern region of central Italy between the Tiber and the Adriatic; 3,270 square miles; capital, Perugia.

Um·bri·an (um′brē·ən) *adj.* Of Umbria, or its people. —*n.* **1** A native or inhabitant of Umbria. **2** The extinct language of ancient Umbria, belonging to the Osco-Umbrian branch of the Italic languages.

um·brif·er·ous (um·brif′ər·əs) *adj.* Affording or making a shade; umbrageous. [<L *umbrifer* <*umbra* shade + *ferre* bear] —**um·brif′er·ous·ly** *adv.*

u·mi·ak (ōō′mē·ak) *n. Eskimo* A large, open boat, about 30 feet long and 8 feet wide, made by drawing skins over a wooden frame: also spelled *oomiak*. Also **u′mi·ack.**

um·laut (ōōm′lout) *n.* **1** *Ling.* **a** The change in quality of a vowel sound caused by its partial assimilation to a vowel or semi-vowel (often later lost) in the following syllable; vowel mutation: primarily a phenomenon of the Germanic languages. English plurals showing internal vowel modification, such as *feet* and *geese*, are a result of this process. **b** A vowel which has been so altered, as *ä, ö,* and *ü* in German. **2** In German, the two dots (¨) put over a vowel modified by umlaut: short for **umlaut-mark.** —*v.t.* To modify by umlaut or mutation. [<G, change of sound <*um* about + *laut* sound]

Um·nak Island (ōōm′nak) One of the Fox Islands in the Aleutian Islands; 83 miles long, 2 to 18 miles wide.

um·pir·age (um′pīr·ij, -pə·rij) *n.* The office or function of an umpire. Also **um′pire·ship.**

um·pire (um′pīr) *n.* **1** *Law* A person called upon to settle a disagreement in opinion between arbitrators. **2** In general, anything by which a question in controversy is settled. **3** In various games, as baseball, a person chosen to enforce the rules of the game, and in case of controversy to settle disputed points. See synonyms under JUDGE. —*v.t. & v.i.* **·pired, ·pir·ing** To decide as umpire; act as umpire (of or in). [Aphetic alter. of ME *noumpere* <OF *nonper* odd, uneven (i.e., third) <*non* not + *per* even, equal]

ump·teen (ump′tēn′) *adj. Slang* Indeterminately large in number; very many. —**ump′-teenth′** *adj.*

Um·ta·ta (ōōm·tä′tə) A city in NE Cape of Good Hope Province, Republic of South Africa.

UN See UNITED NATIONS.

un-[1] *prefix* Not; opposed to. [OE] ◆ Un-[1] is used to express negation, lack, incompleteness or opposition. It is freely attached to adjectives and adverbs, less often to nouns. See UN-[2].

un-[2] *prefix* Back. [OE *un-, on-,* and-] ◆ Un-[2] is used to express reversal of the action of verbs, or to form verbs from nouns indicating removal from the state or quality expressed by the noun, or sometimes to intensify the force of negative verbs. Beginning at the foot of this page will be found a partial list of words which are formed with un-[1] and un-[2]. Other compounds of these prefixes, with strongly positive, specific, or special meanings, will be found in vocabulary place. In the verbs in the list *un-* gives the sense of reversal: *unchain* "to loose the chains of." In the nouns and the adjectives usually it has negative or privative force. Thus, *unburdened* may be regarded as an adjective meaning "not burdened," or as a participle of the verb *unburden,* meaning "relieved of a burden." *In-* as a prefix of adjectives expresses in usage more of negation, *un-* more of mere lack or privation: a child's *unartistic* speech, a writer's *inartistic* diction. In general, *in-* is more confined to words of Latin origin.

Pronunciations may be ascertained by consulting the second element in its vocabulary place.

un·a·ble (un·ā′bəl) *adj.* **1** Lacking the necessary power or resources; not able: usually used with an infinitive: *unable* to walk. **2** Lacking mental capacity; incompetent.

3 *Obs.* Feeble; helpless. —**un·a·bil·i·ty** (un′ə·bil′ə·tē) *Obs. n.* —**un·a′bly** *Obs. adv.*

un·a·bridged (un′ə·brijd′) *adj.* Not abridged; not being a shorter or condensed version of another work; original and complete in itself: an *unabridged* dictionary.

un·ac·com·mo·dat·ed (un′ə·kom′ə·dā′tid) *adj.* **1** Not made suitable; ill-adapted or -adjusted. **2** Being without accommodations or conveniences.

un·ac·com·mo·dat·ing (un′ə·kom′ə·dā′ting) *adj.* Not disposed to accommodate; unobliging.

un·ac·com·plished (un′ə·kom′plisht) *adj.* **1** Having fallen short of accomplishment; not done or finished. **2** Lacking accomplishments.

un·ac·count·a·ble (un′ə·koun′tə·bəl) *adj.* **1** Impossible to be accounted for; inexplicable; hence, remarkable; extraordinary. **2** Exempt from supervision or control; irresponsible. —**un′ac·count′a·ble·ness** *n.* —**un′ac·count′a·bly** *adv.*

un·ac·count·ed-for (un′ə·koun′tid·fôr′) *adj.* Unexplained; not accounted for.

un·ac·cus·tomed (un′ə·kus′təmd) *adj.* **1** Not made familiar by use or by practice: *unaccustomed* to hardship. **2** Not familiar or well known; strange: an *unaccustomed* sight. —**un′ac·cus′tomed·ness** *n.*

un·ad·vised (un′əd·vīzd′) *adj.* **1** Not advised; not having received advice. **2** Rash or imprudent; lacking consideration. —**un′ad·vis′ed·ly** (-vī′zid·lē) *adv.* —**un′ad·vis′ed·ness** *n.*

un·af·fect·ed (un′ə·fek′tid) *adj.* **1** Not showing affectation; natural; sincere; real. **2** Not influenced or changed. See synonyms under SIMPLE. —**un′af·fect′ed·ly** *adv.* —**un′af·fect′ed·ness** *n.*

Un·a·las·ka Island (un′ə·las′kə, ōō′nə-) One of the SW Fox Islands of the Aleutian Islands; 30 miles long, 6 to 30 miles wide.

un·al·ien·a·ble (un-āl′yən·ə·bəl) *adj. Obs.* Inalienable.

un·al·loyed (un′ə·loid′) *adj.* Free from alloy or admixture; pure; also, figuratively, perfectly complete; absolute: *unalloyed* content.

un-A·mer·i·can (un′ə·mer′ə·kən) *adj.* Not having characteristics of persons or things native to the United States; lacking in patriotism and national feeling toward the United States; not consistent with American ideals, objectives, spirit, etc.

U·na·mu·no y Ju·go (ōō′nä·mōō′nō ē hōō′gō), **Miguel de,** 1864–1936, Spanish philosopher and novelist.

un·a·neled (un′ə·nēld′) *adj. Obs.* Not having received extreme unction. [<UN-[1] + ANELE]

u·na·nim·i·ty (yōō′nə·nim′ə·tē) *n.* The state of being unanimous; complete agreement in opinion or purpose. See synonyms under HARMONY. [<OF *unanimité* <L *unanimitas, -tatis* <*unanimus.* See UNANIMOUS.]

u·nan·i·mous (yōō·nan′ə·məs) *adj.* **1** Sharing the same views or sentiments; consentient; harmonious. **2** Establishing or expressive of unanimity; showing or resulting from the assent of all concerned: the *unanimous* voice of the jury. [<L *unanimus, unanimis* <*unus* one + *animus* mind] —**u·nan′i·mous·ly** *adv.* —**u·nan′i·mous·ness** *n.*

un·ap·peal·a·ble (un′ə·pē′lə·bəl) *adj.* **1** Admitting no appeal to a higher court: an *unappealable* case. **2** That cannot be appealed from; conclusive; final.

un·ap·pro·pri·at·ed (un′ə·prō′prē·ā′tid) *adj.* Not set apart for special use; not taken possession of by or formally granted to a particular person or company.

un·ap·proved (un′ə·prōōvd′) *adj.* **1** Not re-

garded with approval; not approved. **2** *Obs.* Not verified by proof; not proved.

un·apt (un·apt′) *adj.* **1** Not likely or inclined. **2** Not suitable or qualified. **3** Not ready-witted. —**un·apt′ly** *adv.* —**un·apt′ness** *n.*

un·ar·gued (un·är′gyōōd) *adj.* **1** Not argued; undebated. **2** Undisputed. **3** *Obs.* Not censured: a Latinism.

un·arm (un·ärm′) *v.t.* To disarm; deprive of weapons.

un·armed (un·ärmd′) *adj.* **1** Not armed; without weapons. **2** Having no sharp, hard projections, as spines, prickles, plates, etc.: said of plants and animals.

un·as·sum·ing (un′ə·sōō′ming) *adj.* Unpretentious; modest. —**un′as·sum′ing·ly** *adv.*

un·at·tached (un′ə·tacht′) *adj.* **1** Not attached. **2** *Law* Not held or seized, as in satisfaction of a judgment. **3** In the armed forces, not assigned to a regiment or company.

u·nau (yōō·nô′, -nô′, ōō·nou′) *n.* The common two-toed sloth of Brazil (genus *Choloepus*). [<F <Tupian]

u·na vo·ce (yōō′nə vō′sē) *Latin* Unanimously; with one voice.

un·a·void·a·ble (un′ə·voi′də·bəl) *adj.* **1** That cannot be avoided; inevitable. **2** That cannot be made null and void; not voidable. See synonyms under NECESSARY.

un·a·ware (un′ə·wâr′) *adj.* **1** Giving no heed; not cognizant, as of something specified. **2** *Poetic* Carelessly unmindful; inattentive; heedless. —*adv. Obs.* Unawares.

un·a·wares (un′ə·wârz′) *adv.* **1** Unexpectedly. **2** Without premeditation; unwittingly.

un·backed (un·bakt′) *adj.* **1** Never having borne a rider, as a horse; unbroken. **2** Left without backers or support; not supported financially; also, in sports, not wagered on. **3** Without a back, as a stool.

un·baked (un·bākt′) *adj.* **1** Not baked; insufficiently baked. **2** Immature; crude.

un·bal·ance (un·bal′əns) *v.t.* **·anced, ·anc·ing** **1** To deprive of balance. **2** To disturb or derange.

un·bal·anced (un·bal′ənst) *adj.* **1** Not in a state of equilibrium. **2** In bookkeeping, not adjusted so as to balance. **3** Lacking mental balance; unsound; erratic.

un·bal·last·ed (un·bal′əs·tid) *adj.* **1** Not steadied by ballast. **2** Not firm; wavering.

un·bar (un·bär′) *v.* **·barred, ·bar·ring** *v.t.* To remove the bar from. —*v.i.* To become unlocked or unbarred; open.

un·barbed (un·bärbd′) *adj.* **1** Not fitted or made with barbs. **2** *Obs.* Untrimmed; unbarbered.

un·bat·ed (un·bā′tid) *adj. Archaic* **1** Not bated or blunted by having a button on the point, as a lance or other thrusting weapon. **2** Unabated; undiminished.

un·bear (un·bâr′) *v.t.* **·beared, ·bear·ing** To free from the pressure of the checkrein, as a horse.

un·be·com·ing (un′bi·kum′ing) *adj.* **1** Not becoming; unsuited to the wearer, place, or surroundings: an *unbecoming* robe. **2** Not befitting; not worthy of. **3** Not decorous; improper. —**un′be·com′ing·ly** *adv.* —**un′be·com′ing·ness** *n.*

un·be·known (un′bi·nōn′) *adj.* Unknown: used with *to.* Also **un′be·knownst′** (-nōnst′).

un·be·lief (un′bi·lēf′) *n.* **1** Absence of positive belief; incredulity. **2** A refusal to believe; belief in a contrary proposition; disbelief, as in religion. **3** In Scriptural use, lack of faith in God's promises. See synonyms under DOUBT.

unabashed	unacquitted	unallowable	unanswered	unasked	unattested	unawaked
unabated	unadaptable	unalterable	unappalled	unaspirated	unattracted	unawakened
unabetted	unadjustable	unaltered	unapparent	unaspiring	unattractive	unawed
unabolished	unadjusted	unaltering	unappeasable	unassailable	unauspicious	unbaptized
unabsolved	unadorned	unambiguous	unappeased	unassailably	unauthentic	unbearable
unacademic	unadulterated	unambitious	unappetizing	unassailed	unauthentical	unbeaten
unaccented	unadvisable	unamiable	unappreciative	unassignable	unauthenticated	unbefitting
unacceptable	unadvisably	unamusing	unapproachable	unassigned	unauthorized	unbelievable
unaccepted	unaesthetic	unanalytic	unapproachably	unassisted	unavailable	unbeloved
unacclimated	unafraid	unanalyzable	unapproached	unassoiled	unavailably	unbeneficed
unacclimatized	unaggressive	unanimated	unarmored	unassumed	unavailing	unbenighted
unaccompanied	unagitated	unannealed	unarrested	unattainable	unavenged	unbenign
unaccredited	unaided	unannounced	unartful	unattained	unavouched	unbeseeming
unacknowledged	unalleviated	unanswerable	unartistic	unattempted	unavowed	unbesought
unacquainted	unallied	unanswerably	unashamed	unattended	unavowedly	unbespoken

un·be·liev·er (un′bi-lē′vər) *n.* **1** One who withholds belief. **2** One who has no religious faith. **3** One having a religion different from that of the speaker or writer; specifically, a non-Christian. See synonyms under SKEPTIC.

un·be·liev·ing (un′bi-lē′ving) *adj.* **1** Doubting; skeptical; incredulous. **2** Disbelieving, particularly in regard to religious matters. — **un′·be·liev′ing·ly** *adv.* — **un′be·liev′ing·ness** *n.*

un·belt (un-belt′) *v.t.* **1** To remove the belt of. **2** To remove from the belt; ungird.

un·bend (un-bend′) *v.* **·bent**, **·bend·ing** *v.t.* **1** To relax, as from exertion or formality: to *unbend* the mind. **2** To straighten (something bent or curved). **3** To relax, as a bow, from tension. **4** *Naut.* **a** To loose; untie, as a rope. **b** To detach or remove (a sail) from a spar or stay. — *v.i.* **5** To become free of restraint or formality; relax. **6** To become straight or nearly straight again.

un·bend·ing (un-ben′ding) *adj.* Not bending easily; stiff; hence, unyielding; resolute; firm, as character. — *n.* Relaxation. — **un·bend′ing·ly** *adv.* — **un·bend′ing·ness** *n.*

un·bi·ased (un-bī′əst) *adj.* Having no bias; especially, having no mental bias; not prejudiced or warped; impartial. Also **un·bi′assed.** — **un·bi′ased·ly** *adv.* — **un·bi′ased·ness** *n.*

un·bid·den (un-bid′n) *adj.* **1** Not commanded; not invited: an *unbidden* guest. **2** Not called forth; spontaneous: *unbidden* thoughts. Also **un·bid′.**

un·bind (un-bīnd′) *v.t.* **·bound**, **·bind·ing 1** To free from bindings; undo; hence, to release. **2** To remove, as something that binds; unfasten. See synonyms under RELEASE. [OE *unbindan*]

un·bit·ted (un-bit′id) *adj.* Not furnished with or restrained by a bit or bridle; uncontrolled.

un·blenched (un-blencht′) *adj. Obs.* Not dismayed or confounded.

un·blessed (un-blest′) *adj.* **1** Not having been blessed or admitted to blessedness or divine favor. **2** Unhappy. **3** Unhallowed or unholy; evil.

un·blood·y (un-blud′ē) *adj.* **1** Not stained by blood; hence, not attended with slaughter, as a conflict. **2** Not of a bloodthirsty disposition.

un·blush·ing (un-blush′ing) *adj.* Not blushing; immodest; shameless. — **un·blush′ing·ly** *adv.*

un·bod·ied (un-bod′ēd) *adj.* **1** Having no body; immaterial. **2** Disembodied.

un·bolt (un-bōlt′) *v.t.* To release, as a door, by withdrawing a bolt; unlock; open. — *v.i. Obs.* To remove a bolt or bar; hence, to expose something to view; make explanation.

un·bolt·ed[1] (un-bōl′tid) *adj.* Not fastened by bolts; not bolted.

un·bolt·ed[2] (un-bōl′tid) *adj.* **1** Not separated by bolting; not sifted: *unbolted* flour. **2** *Obs.* Gross; coarse.

un·boned (un-bōnd′) *adj.* **1** Without bones. **2** Not having had the bones removed.

un·bon·net (un-bon′it) *v.t. & v.i.* To remove the bonnet or other covering from (the head); uncover. — **un·bon′net·ed** *adj.*

un·born (un-bôrn′) *adj.* **1** Not yet born; of a future time or generation; future. **2** Not in existence.

un·bos·om (un-bōoz′əm, -bōō′zəm) *v.t.* To reveal, as one's thoughts or secrets; disclose or give vent to: often used reflexively. — *v.i.* To say what is troubling one; tell one's thoughts, feelings, etc. — **un·bos′om·er** *n.*

un·bound·ed (un-boun′did) *adj.* **1** Having no bounds; of unlimited extent; very great; boundless. **2** Having no boundary, as a line that returns into itself or a closed surface. **3** Going beyond bounds; unrestrained. — **un·bound′ed·ly** *adv.* — **un·bound′ed·ness** *n.*

un·bowed (un-boud′) *adj.* Not bent; not bowed or subdued; proud in defeat or adversity.

un·brace (un-brās′) *v.t.* **·braced**, **·brac·ing 1** To free from bands or braces. **2** To free from tension; loosen. **3** To weaken; make feeble.

un·breathed (un-brĕthd′) *adj.* **1** Not breathed; hence, not whispered, or spoken; not communicated to another. **2** *Obs.* Unexercised; not practiced.

un·bred (un-bred′) *adj.* **1** Devoid of good breeding; ill-bred. **2** Not taught; untrained: sometimes followed by *to*: *unbred* to spinning. **3** *Obs.* Unbegotten; not born.

un·bri·dled (un-brīd′ld) *adj.* **1** Having no bridle on: an *unbridled* horse. **2** Without restraint; unrestrained; unruly: an *unbridled* tongue; *unbridled* license. — **un·bri′dled·ly** *adv.* — **un·bri′dled·ness** *n.*

un·bro·ken (un-brō′kən) *adj.* **1** Not broken; whole; entire: an *unbroken* seal. **2** Unviolated: *unbroken* faith; an *unbroken* promise. **3** Uninterrupted; regular; smooth: *unbroken* sleep; an *unbroken* prairie. **4** Not weakened; strong; firm. **5** Not broken to harness or service, as a draft animal. **6** Not disarranged or thrown out of order. Also *Obs.* **un·broke**′. — **un·bro′ken·ly** *adv.* — **un·bro′ken·ness** *n.*

un·buck·le (un-buk′əl) *v.t. & v.i.* **·led**, **·ling** To unfasten the buckle or buckles (of).

un·build (un-bild′) *v.t.* **·built**, **·build·ing** To demolish; destroy.

un·bur·den (un-bûr′dən) *v.t.* To free from a burden; relieve. Also *Archaic* **un·bur′then** (-thən).

un·but·ton (un-but′n) *v.t.* To unfasten the button or buttons of.

un·caged (un-kājd′) *adj.* **1** Not locked up in a cage; free. **2** Released from a cage; freed.

un·called (un-kôld′) *adj.* Not in response to a summons; without being asked or demanded.

un·called-for (un-kôld′fôr′) *adj.* Unnecessary; gratuitous; not justified by circumstances; discourteous.

un·can·ny (un-kan′ē) *adj.* **1** Exciting superstitious fear; weird; unnatural; eerie. **2** So good as to seem almost supernatural in origin: *uncanny* accuracy. **3** *Scot.* Dangerous; severe, as a wound. — **un·can′ni·ly** *adv.* — **un·can′ni·ness** *n.*

un·cap (un-kap′) *v.* **·capped**, **·cap·ping** *v.t.* To take off the cap or covering of. — *v.i.* To remove the hat or cap, as in respect.

un·ca·pa·ble (un-kā′pə·bəl) *adj. Obs.* Incapable.

un·caused (un-kôzd′) *adj.* Existing without a cause; not caused; not created: an *uncaused* deity.

un·cer·e·mo·ni·ous (un′ser·ə·mō′nē·əs) *adj.* Informal; abrupt; discourteous. — **un′cer·e·mo′ni·ous·ly** *adv.*

un·cer·tain (un-sûr′tən) *adj.* **1** Not certain; that cannot be relied upon; variable; changeful; fitful; erring: an *uncertain* friend; *uncertain* weather; an *uncertain* shot. **2** That cannot be certainly predicted; being of doubtful issue. **3** Not having certain knowledge or assured conviction. **4** Not surely or exactly known: a lady of *uncertain* age. **5** Having no exact or precise significance: *uncertain* phraseology. See synonyms under EQUIVOCAL, PRECARIOUS, VAGUE. — **un·cer′tain·ly** *adv.*

un·cer·tain·ty (un-sûr′tən·tē) *n. pl.* **·ties 1** The state of being uncertain; doubt: also **un·cer′tain·ness. 2** A doubtful matter; a contingency. See synonyms under DOUBT.

uncertainty principle *Physics* A statement of the impossibility of exactly determining at any given instant or by a single operation more than one magnitude or quantity, as the velocity, position, etc., of an electron: also called *indeterminacy principle.*

un·chain (un-chān′) *v.t.* To release from a chain; set free.

un·chanc·y (un-chan′sē) *adj. Scot.* **1** Unpropitious; unlucky. **2** Ill-timed; inopportune. **3** Unsafe; dangerous.

un·charged (un-chärjd′) *adj.* **1** Not loaded. **2** Not attacked or accused. **3** Not required or asked to pay a price or meet an expense. **4** Having no electrical charge.

un·char·i·ta·ble (un-char′ə·tə·bəl) *adj.* Not charitable; harsh in judgment; censorious. — **un·char′i·ta·ble·ness** *n.* — **un·char′i·ta·bly** *adv.*

un·chris·tian (un-kris′chən) *adj.* **1** Unbecoming to a Christian. **2** Foreign to Christianity; hence, uncharitable, ungracious, rude, etc. **3** Non-Christian; pagan.

un·church (un-chûrch′) *v.t.* **1** To deprive of membership in a church; expel from a church. **2** To excommunicate. **3** To deny the validity of the sacraments and order of, as a sect.

un·cial (un′shəl, -shē·əl) *adj.* Pertaining to or consisting of a form of letters found in manuscripts from the fourth to the eighth century, and resembling modern capitals but more rounded. — *n.* **1** An uncial letter. **2** An uncial manuscript. [<L *uncialis* inch-high < *uncia* inch, ounce]

a ᴇ᾽ɴϲoʏκᴀιᴀʏᴛѡϻoɴѡᴀᴋι
b ᴇᴛϲoɴʟoǫᴜᴇʙᴀɴᴛᴜιϩ

UNCIALS

a. Greek uncials — fifth century.
b. Latin uncials — circa A.D. 700.

un·ci·form (un′sə·fôrm) *adj.* Shaped like a hook; hooklike. — *n.* The unciform bone. [<L *uncus* hook + -FORM]

unciform bone *Anat.* A bone of the distal row of the wrist on the ulnar side, articulating with the fourth and fifth metacarpals.

unciform process *Anat.* **1** A projection upon the anterior surface of the unciform bone. **2** The uncinate process.

un·ci·na·ri·a·sis (un′si·nə·rī′ə·sis) *n. Pathol.* Ancylostomiasis. [<NL <*Uncinaria,* genus name <L *uncinus* a hook, barb, dim. of *uncus* hook]

un·ci·nate (un′sə·nit, -nāt) *adj. Biol.* Hooked or bent at the end; having a hooked appendage. Also **un′ci·nal, un′ci·nat·ed.** [<L *uncinatus* <*uncinus,* dim. of *uncus* hook]

uncinate process *Anat.* A hooklike process on the ethmoid bone.

UNCINATE APPENDAGES

un·cir·cum·cised (un-sûr′kəm·sīzd) *adj.* Not circumcised; Gentile; heathen.

un·cir·cum·ci·sion (un′sûr·kəm·sizh′ən) *n.* **1** The state of being uncircumcised. **2** Those not circumcised; in Scripture, the Gentiles.

un·civ·il (un-siv′əl) *adj.* **1** Wanting in civility; discourteous; ill-bred. **2** *Obs.* Uncivilized. See synonyms under BLUFF, HAUGHTY. — **un·civ′il·ly** *adv.*

un·civ·i·lized (un-siv′ə·līzd) *adj.* Destitute of civilization; barbarous. See synonyms under BARBAROUS.

un·clad (un-klad′) *adj.* Without clothes; naked.

un·clasp (un-klasp′, -kläsp′) *v.t.* **1** To release

unbetrayed	unbought	unbrotherly	uncanonical	unchanged	uncholeric	unclothe
unbetrothed	unbound	unbruised	uncarbureted	unchanging	unchosen	unclothed
unbewailed	unboundable	unbrushed	uncared-for	unchangingly	unchristened	uncloud
unbias	unbraid	unburied	uncarpeted	unchaperoned	unclaimed	unclouded
unblamable	unbranched	unburnt	uncastrated	uncharted	unclass	uncloyed
unblamably	unbranching	unbusinesslike	uncaught	unchartered	unclassic	uncoated
unblamed	unbranded	unbuttoned	uncensored	unchary	unclassifiable	uncocked
unbleached	unbreakable	uncage	uncensured	unchaste	unclassified	uncoerced
unblemished	unbreathable	uncalculate	uncertified	unchastened	uncleaned	uncoffined
unblest	unbreech	uncalculating	unchainable	unchastised	uncleansed	uncollectable,
unblissful	unbreeched	uncalendered	unchained	unchastity	uncleared	uncollectible
unboastful	unbribable	uncanceled	unchallenged	unchecked	uncleavable	uncollected
unbookish	unbridgeable	uncandid	unchambered	unchewed	unclipped	uncolonized
unborrowed	unbridged	uncandidly	unchangeable	unchilled	unclog	uncolored
unbottomed	unbridle	uncanonic		unchivalrous	unclogged	uncombed

from a clasp. **2** To release the clasp of. — *v.i.* **3** To become released from a clasp.

un·cle (ung'kəl) *n.* **1** The brother of one's father or mother; also, the husband of one's aunt. ◆ Collateral adjective: *avuncular.* **2** An elderly man: used in direct address. **3** *Colloq.* A pawnbroker. [<F *oncle* <L *avunculus* a mother's brother, orig. dim. of *avus* grandfather]

un·clean (un·klēn') *adj.* **1** Not clean; foul. **2** Characterized by impure thoughts; unchaste; depraved. **3** Ceremonially impure. See synonyms under FOUL. — **un·clean'ness** *n.*

un·clean·ly¹ (un·klen'lē) *adj.* **1** Lacking cleanliness. **2** Impure; indecent; not chaste. [< UN-¹ + CLEANLY, *adj.*] — **un·clean'li·ness** *n.*

un·clean·ly² (un·klēn'lē) *adv.* In an unclean manner. [<UNCLEAN + -LY²]

un·clear (un·klir') *adj.* **1** Not clear. **2** Not easily understandable; confused or muddled: His point was *unclear* to me.

un·clench (un·klench') *v.t.* & *v.i.* To relax or open from a clenched condition. Also **un·clinch'** (-klinch').

Uncle Re·mus (rē'məs) In Joel Chandler Harris's folk tales, an old southern Negro who tells the stories of Br'er Rabbit, Br'er Fox, and others to a small white boy.

Uncle Sam The personification of the government of the United States or of the people of the United States: represented as a tall, lean man with chin whiskers, wearing a plug hat, blue swallow–tailed coat, and red–and–white striped pants. See BROTHER JONATHAN.

Uncle Tom 1 The chief character in Harriet Beecher Stowe's *Uncle Tom's Cabin*, a faithful, elderly Negro slave. **2** *U.S. Slang* A Negro who toadies or truckles to white men: a contemptuous term.

un·clew (un·klōō') *v.t.* **1** *Naut.* To unfurl. **2** *Archaic* To unroll; undo; also, to ruin.

un·cloak (un·klōk') *v.t.* **1** To remove the cloak or covering from. **2** To unmask; expose. — *v.i.* **3** To remove one's cloak or outer garments.

un·close (un·klōz') *v.t.* & *v.i.* **·closed, ·clos·ing** **1** To open or set open. **2** To reveal; disclose. — **un·closed'** *adj.*

un·co (ung'kō) *Scot.* & *Brit. Dial. adj.* Being out of the ordinary; strange; weird; reserved. — *n.* **1** Anything out of the common or surprising; hence, a strange person or thing. **2** *pl.* News. — *adv.* Remarkably or excessively.

un·cock (un·kok') *v.t.* **1** To release and let down the hammer of (a firearm) without exploding the charge. **2** To restore to usual position, as a hat.

un·coft (un·koft') *adj. Scot.* Unbought.

un·coil (un·koil') *v.t.* & *v.i.* To unwind or become unwound.

un·coined (un·koind') *adj.* **1** Not fabricated; natural. **2** Not minted.

un·com·fort·a·ble (un·kum'fər·tə·bəl, -kumpf'·tə·bəl) *adj.* **1** Not at ease; feeling discomfort. **2** Causing uneasiness or disquietude, physical or mental; disquieting. — **un·com'·fort·a·bly** *adv.*

un·com·mer·cial (un'kə·mûr'shəl) *adj.* **1** Not engaged or versed in commerce. **2** Conflicting with the spirit of commerce.

un·com·mit·ted (un'kə·mit'id) *adj.* **1** Not committed; specifically, not performed or done. **2** Not entrusted. **3** Not bound by a pledge.

un·com·mon (un·kom'ən) *adj.* Unusual; remarkable. See synonyms under EXTRAORDINARY, ODD, RARE. — **un·com'mon·ly** *adv.*

un·com·mu·ni·ca·tive (un'kə·myōō'nə·kə·tiv,

-nə·kā'tiv) *adj.* Not communicative; not disposed to talk, either to express oneself or to give information; reserved; taciturn.

Un·com·pah·gre Peak (un'kəm·pä'grē) A mountain in SW central Colorado, the highest of the San Juan Mountains; 14,306 feet.

un·com·pro·mis·ing (un·kom'prə·mī'zing) *adj.* Making or admitting of no compromise; inflexible; strict. — **un·com'pro·mis'ing·ly** *adv.* — **un·com'pro·mis'ing·ness** *n.*

un·con·cern (un'kən·sûrn') *n.* Absence of or freedom from concern or anxiety; indifference. See synonyms under APATHY.

un·con·cerned (un'kən·sûrnd') *adj.* Undisturbed; not anxious; indifferent. — **un'con·cern'ed·ly** (-sûr'nid·lē) *adv.* — **un'con·cern'ed·ness** *n.*

un·con·di·tion·al (un'kən·dish'ən·əl) *adj.* Limited by no conditions; absolute. See synonyms under ABSOLUTE. — **un'con·di'tion·al·ly** *adv.*

unconditional surrender The unconditional acceptance of military defeat by a warring enemy power, subject only to terms to be subsequently imposed by the victors.

un·con·di·tioned (un'kən·dish'ənd) *adj.* **1** Not restricted; unconditional. **2** In metaphysics, not limited by conditions of space or time; free from relation; unrelated; absolute. **3** *Psychol.* Not having a reaction or reflex developed by a specified condition or conditions; not acquired; natural. **4** Admitted to a school, college, or higher class without condition.

un·con·form·a·ble (un'kən·fôr'mə·bəl) *adj.* **1** Not conforming or conformable; inconsistent. **2** *Geol.* Showing unconformity. — **un'con·form'a·bil'i·ty, un'con·form'a·ble·ness** *n.* — **un'con·form'a·bly** *adv.*

un·con·form·i·ty (un'kən·fôr'mə·tē) *n. pl.* **·ties 1** Want of conformity; nonconformity. **2** *Geol.* **a** A lack of continuity between groups of stratified rocks in contact, indicative of a gap in the stratigraphic record. **b** The contact layer between such groups.

un·con·scion·a·ble (un'kon'shən·ə·bəl) *adj.* **1** Going beyond customary or reasonable bounds. **2** Not governed by sense or prudence; unconscientious; devoid of conscience. **3** *Law* Inequitable. — **un·con'scion·a·ble·ness** *n.* — **un·con'scion·a·bly** *adv.*

un·con·scious (un·kon'shəs) *adj.* **1** Temporarily deprived of consciousness. **2** Not cognizant; unaware: with *of: unconscious* of his charm. **3** Not known or felt to exist; not produced or accompanied by conscious effort: *unconscious* thought. **4** Not endowed with consciousness or a mind. — *n. Psychoanal.* That extensive area of the psyche which is not in the immediate field of awareness and whose content, when consisting of repressed material, may affect the personality through dreams, morbid fears and compulsions, forms of behavior, etc.: with *the.* — **un·con'scious·ly** *adv.* — **un·con'scious·ness** *n.*

un·con·sol·i·dat·ed (un'kən·sol'ə·dā'tid) *adj. Geol.* Not compact or solid, as rock or soil material in a form of loose aggregation.

un·con·sti·tu·tion·al (un'kon·sti·tōō'shən·əl, -tyōō'-) *adj.* Contrary to or violative of the constitution or fundamental law of a state. — **un'con·sti·tu'tion·al'i·ty** *n.* — **un'con·sti·tu'tion·al·ly** *adv.*

un·con·trol·la·ble (un'kən·trō'lə·bəl) *adj.* Beyond control; ungovernable. See synonyms under REBELLIOUS, VIOLENT. — **un'con·trol'la·ble·ness, un'con·trol'la·bil'i·ty** *n.* — **un'con·trol'la·bly** *adv.*

un·con·ven·tion·al (un'kən·ven'shən·əl) *adj.* Not adhering to conventional rules; informal; free. — **un'con·ven'tion·al'i·ty** *n.* — **un'con·ven'tion·al·ly** *adv.*

un·con·vert·ed (un'kən·vûr'tid) *adj.* **1** Not converted. **2** *Theol.* Impenitent; without saving faith.

un·cork (un·kôrk') *v.t.* To draw the cork from.

un·count·ed (un·koun'tid) *adj.* **1** Not counted. **2** Beyond counting; innumerable.

un·cou·ple (un·kup'əl) *v.* **·led, ·ling** *v.t.* **1** To disconnect or unfasten. **2** To set loose; unleash (dogs). — *v.i.* **3** To break loose. — **un·coup'led** *adj.*

un·couth (un·kōōth') *adj.* **1** Marked by awkwardness or oddity; outlandish; ungainly; unrefined; rough. **2** Not common; not well-known. **3** Mysterious; alarming. See synonyms under AWKWARD, BARBAROUS, RUSTIC. [OE *uncūth* unknown < *un-* not + *cūth,* pp. of *cunnan* know] — **un·couth'ly** *adv.* — **un·couth'ness** *n.*

un·cov·e·nant·ed (un·kuv'ə·nən·tid) *adj.* **1** Not bound by a covenant or promise; not having entered into a covenant or league. **2** Not guaranteed by a covenant: used specifically to describe divine grace or mercy not promised by a covenant.

un·cov·er (un·kuv'ər) *v.t.* **1** To remove the covering from. **2** To make known; reveal; disclose. **3** In military tactics, to expose successively, as lines of formation. — *v.i.* **4** To remove a covering; raise or remove the hat, as in token of respect.

un·cov·ered (un·kuv'ərd) *adj.* **1** Not covered; devoid of covering. **2** Not covered by collateral security.

un·cre·ate (un'krē·āt') *v.t.* **·at·ed, ·at·ing** To deprive of existence.

un·cre·at·ed (un'krē·ā'tid) *adj.* **1** Not yet created or brought into being. **2** *Philos.* Not created; self-existent.

unc·tion (ungk'shən) *n.* **1** The act of anointing, as with oil. **2** *Eccl.* **a** A ceremonial anointing with oil, as in consecration or dedication. **b** The sacramental rite of anointing the sick, reserved in the Roman Catholic Church for those in danger of death: also called **extreme unction. 3** The act of treating medicinally by anointing. **4** A substance used in anointing, as an unguent or a salve; something that soothes or palliates. **5** The quality or characteristic of speech, especially in religious discourse, that awakens or is intended to awaken deep sympathetic feeling; sometimes, effusive or affected emotion. [<F *onction* <L *unctio, -onis* <*ungere* anoint] — **unc'tion·less** *adj.*

unc·tu·ous (ungk'chōō·əs) *adj.* **1** Having the characteristics of an unguent; greasy. **2** Characterized by deep sympathetic feeling. **3** Characterized by affected emotion; hence, oily–tongued; unduly suave. **4** Being greasy or soapy to the touch, as certain minerals. **5** Soft; rich in organic matter, as certain soils. **6** Having plasticity, as clay. [<Med. L *unctuosus* <L *unctum* ointment, orig. neut. pp. of *ungere* anoint] — **unc'tu·ous·ly** *adv.* — **unc'·tu·ous·ness** *n.* — **unc'tu·os'i·ty** (-chōō·os'ə·tē) *n.*

un·cut (un·kut') *adj.* **1** Not cut. **2** In bookbinding, having untrimmed margins. **3** Unground, as a gem.

un·damped (un·dampt') *adj. Physics* Pertaining to or designating those electromagnetic oscillations which continue without change in amplitude: *undamped* radio waves.

un·daunt·ed (un·dôn'tid, -dän'-) *adj.* Not daunted; fearless; intrepid. See synonyms

uncombinable	uncomplimentary	unconfinedly	unconquered	uncontradictable	uncorrected	uncrossed
uncombinably	uncompounded	unconfirmed	unconscientious	uncontradicted	uncorroborated	uncrowded
uncombined	uncomprehended	unconfused	unconsecrated	uncontrite	uncorrupt	uncrown
uncomely	uncomprehending	unconfusedly	unconsenting	uncontrolled	uncorrupted	uncrowned
uncomforted	uncomprehensible	unconfuted	unconsidered	uncontrolledly	uncorruptly	uncrystalline
uncomforting	uncompressed	uncongeal	unconsoled	uncontroverted	uncorruptness	uncrystallizable
uncommanded	uncompromised	uncongealable	unconsonant	uncontrovertible	uncountable	uncrystallized
uncommissioned	uncomputed	uncongealed	unconstant	uncontrovertibly	uncourteous	uncultivable
uncompanionable	unconcealable	uncongenial	unconstituted	unconversant	uncourtliness	uncultivated
uncomplaining	unconcealed	uncongeniality	unconstrained	unconvinced	uncourtly	uncultured
uncomplaisant	unconceded	uncongenially	unconstricted	unconvincing	uncredited	uncumbered
uncomplaisantly	unconcerted	unconnected	unconsumed	uncooked	uncrippled	uncurb
uncompleted	unconciliated	unconnectedly	uncontaminated	uncooperative	uncritical	uncurbable
uncompliable	uncondemned	unconquerable	uncontending	uncoordinated	uncriticizable	uncurbed
uncomplicated	unconfined	unconquerably	uncontested	uncorked	uncross	uncurdled

under BRAVE. **—un·daunt'ed·ly** *adv.* **—un·daunt'ed·ness** *n.*

un·dé (un'dā) *adj. Her.* Wavy; undulating: said of an ordinary or of the lines dividing the shield. Also **un'dée, un'dy** (-dē). [<OF <L *unda* wave]

un·dec·a·gon (un-dek'ə-gon) *n.* A figure that has eleven angles and eleven sides. [<L *undecim* eleven + -GON]

un·de·ceiv·a·ble (un'di-sē'və-bəl) *adj.* **1** That cannot be deceived. **2** *Obs.* Not deceitful.

un·de·ceive (un'di-sēv') *v.t.* **·ceived, ·ceiv·ing** To free from deception, error, or illusion.

un·de·ceived (un'di-sēvd') *adj.* **1** Not deceived. **2** Freed from error or deception.

un·de·cen·ni·al (un'di-sen'ē-əl) *adj.* **1** Pertaining to a period of eleven years or to the eleventh year. **2** Lasting eleven years, or occurring or celebrated on the eleventh year or every eleven years. Also **un'de·cen'na·ry** (-sen'ər-ē). [<L *undecim* eleven + *annus* year]

un·de·cid·ed (un'di-sī'did) *adj.* **1** Not having the mind made up. **2** Not decided upon; not determined. See synonyms under IRRESOLUTE. **—un'de·cid'ed·ly** *adv.*

un·decked (un-dekt') *adj.* **1** Having no ornaments; not decked out. **2** Having no deck, as a vessel.

un·dec·u·ple (un-dek'yə-pəl) *adj.* **1** Consisting of eleven. **2** Having eleven parts or members; elevenfold. **3** Taken by elevens. **—** *n.* A number or sum eleven times as great as another. **—** *v.t.* & *v.i.* **·pled, ·pling** To multiply by eleven; make or become eleven times as large. [<L *undecim* eleven, on analogy with *decuple*]

un·de·cu·pli·cate (un'də-kyōō'plə-kit, -kāt) *adj.* **1** Elevenfold. **2** Raised to the eleventh power. **—** *v.t.* & *v.i.* **·cat·ed, ·cat·ing** To multiply by eleven; undecuple. **—** *n.* One of eleven like things. **—un'de·cu'pli·cate·ly** *adv.* **—un'de·cu'pli·ca'tion** *n.*

un·de·mon·stra·tive (un'di-mon'strə-tiv) *adj.* Not demonstrative; not characterized by show of feeling.

un·de·ni·a·ble (un'di-nī'ə-bəl) *adj.* **1** That cannot be denied; indisputably true; obviously correct: an *undeniable* fact. **2** Unquestionably good; excellent: His reputation was *undeniable.* **—un'de·ni'a·bly** *adv.*

un·der (un'dər) *prep.* **1** Beneath, so as to have something directly above; covered by: layer *under* layer. **2** In a place lower than; at the foot or bottom of: *under* the hill. **3** Beneath the shelter of: *under* the paternal roof. **4** Beneath the concealment, guise, or assumption of: *under* a false name. **5** Less than in number, degree, age, value, or amount: *under* 10 tons. **6** Inferior to in quality, character, or rank. **7** Beneath the domination of; owing allegiance to; subordinate or subservient to: *under* the Nazi flag. **8** Subject to the guidance, tutorship, or direction of: He studied *under* Mendelssohn. **9** Subject to the moral obligation of: a statement *under* oath; subject to the sanction of; with the liability or certainty of incurring: *under* penalty of the law. **10** Subject to the influence or pressure of: *under* the circumstances; swayed or impelled by: *under* fear of death. **11** Driven or propelled by: *under* sail, *under* steam. **12** Included in the group or class of; found in the matter titled or headed: See *under* History. **13** Being the subject of: *under* medical treatment. **14** During the period of; in the reign of; pending the administration of. **15** By virtue of; authorized, substantiated, attested, or warranted by: *under* his own signature. **16** In conformity to or in accordance with; having regard to. **17** Planted or sowed with: an acre *under* wheat. See synonyms under BENEATH. **—** *adv.* **1** In or into a position below

something; underneath. **2** In or into an inferior or subordinate degree or rank. **3** So as to be covered or hidden; in or into concealment. **4** Less than the required or appointed amount. **— to go under** To fail or collapse, as a business venture. **—** *adj.* **1** Situated or moving under something else; lower or lowermost: an *under* layer. **2** *Zool.* Ventral: the *under* side of a rattlesnake. **3** Subordinate; lower in rank or authority. **4** Insufficient; less than usual, standard, or prescribed. **5** Held in subjection or restraint: used predicatively: Hold your emotions *under*. [OE]

under- *combining form* **1** Below in position; situated or directed beneath; on the underside; as in:

underarch	underjaw
underbody	underlip
underbridge	undermark
underbud	undernamed
undercasing	underpart
undercellar	underpier
undercurved	underprop
underdraw	undershore
undereaten	undersole
underfeathering	underspread
underfill	understroke
underfire	undersurface
undergnaw	undersweep
undergore	underthrust

2 Below a surface or covering; lower; as in:

underbodice	undergarb
undercloth	underglow
undercrust	undergown
underdish	undergrove
underdrawers	underjacket
underdress	underlife
underearth	underpetticoat
underflooring	underregion

3 Inferior in rank or importance; subordinate; subsidiary; as in:

under-agent	under-officer
under-captain	under-secretary
under-chief	under-secretaryship
under-clerk	under-servant
under-god	under-treasurer

4 Insufficient; less than is usual or proper; as in:

underact	underpowered
underbill	underpraise
undercapitalize	underprize
underclothed	underproportioned
underconsumption	underripe
underdeveloped	undersailed
underexercise	undersaturated
undergrow	underspecified
underload	understaffed
undermanned	understimulus
underniceness	understocked
underofficered	undertaxed
underpeopled	undertrained
underpopulated	

5 At a lower rate; less in degree or amount; as in:

underprice	underspend

6 Subdued; hidden; as in:

underbreath	undernote
underfeeling	underthought
undermelody	undervoice

un·der·a·chieve (un'dər·ə·chēv') *v.i.* **·chieved, ·chiev·ing** To fail to achieve the approximate level of performance, especially in school studies, commensurate with one's abilities as indicated by testing. **—un'der·a·chieve'ment, un'der·a·chiev'er** *n.*

under a cloud Overshadowed by reproach or distrust.

un·der·age (un'dər·āj') *adj.* Not of a requisite age; immature.

un·der·arm (un'dər·ärm') *adj.* Situated or placed under the arm: the *underarm* section of a blouse. **—** *n.* The armpit.

un·der·arm (un'dər·ärm') *adj.* In various sports, as tennis, baseball, etc., delivered with the hand lower than the elbow.

un·der·bel·ly (un'dər·bel'ē) *n. pl.* **·lies 1** The lower region of the belly. **2** Any similar unprotected part: the soft *underbelly* of Europe.

un·der·bid (un'dər·bid') *v.t.* **·bid, ·bid·ding 1** To bid lower than, as in a competition. **2** In auction bridge, to fail to bid the full value of (a hand). **—un'der·bid'der** *n.*

un·der·bred (un'dər·bred') *adj.* **1** Of impure breed; not thoroughbred. **2** Lacking in good breeding. See synonyms under VULGAR.

un·der·brush (un'dər·brush') *n.* Small trees and shrubs growing beneath forest trees; undergrowth. Also **un'der·bush'** (-bŏŏsh').

un·der·buy (un'dər·bī') *v.t.* **·bought, ·buy·ing 1** To buy at a price lower than that paid by (another). **2** To pay less than the value for.

un·der·car·riage (un'dər·kar'ij) *n.* **1** The framework supporting the body of a structure, as an automobile. **2** The principal landing gear of an aircraft.

un·der·charge (un'dər·chärj') *v.t.* **·charged, ·charg·ing 1** To make an inadequate charge for. **2** To load with an insufficient charge, as a gun. **—** *n.* (un'dər·chärj') An inadequate or insufficient charge.

un·der·class (un'dər·klas, -kläs) *n. Sociol.* The group in a society so hopelessly poverty-stricken and so unorganized as to be beneath any apparent social class structure.

un·der·class·man (un'dər·klas'mən, -kläs'-) *n. pl.* **·men** (-mən) A freshman or sophomore in a school or college.

un·der·clay (un'dər·klā') *n.* A layer of clay underlying a coal seam, often containing the roots of ancient coal-forming plants: also called *seatstone.*

un·der·clothes (un'dər·klōz', -klōŧHz') *n. pl.* Clothes designed for underwear, or to be worn next the skin. Also **un'der·cloth'ing.**

un·der·coat (un'dər·kōt') *n.* **1** A coat worn under another. **2** Underfur. **3** A layer of paint, varnish, etc., beneath another layer: also **un'der·coat'ing.** **—** *v.t.* To provide with an undercoat (def. 3).

un·der·cool (un'dər·kōōl') *v.t.* To supercool.

un·der·cov·er (un'dər·kuv'ər) *adj.* Secret; surreptitious; specifically, engaged in spying or secret investigation: an *undercover* man.

under cover Secretively; surreptitiously.

un·der·cov·ert (un'dər·kuv'ərt) *n. Ornithol.* A wing covert.

un·der·croft (un'dər·krôft', -kroft') *n.* A subterranean chamber, vault, or passage. [<UNDER + obs. *croft* vault, ult. <L *crypta* crypt]

un·der·cur·rent (un'dər·kûr'ənt) *n.* **1** A current, as of water or air, below another or below the surface. **2** A hidden drift or tendency, as of popular sentiments.

un·der·cut (un'dər·kut') *n.* **1** The act or result of cutting under. **2** The tenderloin. **3** A slanting cut in a sawed log. **4** A notch cut in the side of a tree so that it will fall toward that side when sawn through. **5** Any part that is cut away below: the *undercut* of a carriage. **6** In sports, a cut or backspin imparted to the ball by an underhand or downward stroke. **—** *v.t.* (un'dər·kut') **·cut, ·cut·ting 1** To cut under. **2** To cut away a lower portion of so as to leave a part overhanging: The river *undercut* its banks. **3** To work or sell for lower

uncured	undecaying	undefended	undenominational	undeserved	undestroyed	undiminishable
uncurious	undecipherable	undefensible	undenounced	undeservedly	undetachable	undiminished
uncurl	undecipherably	undefiled	undependable	undeservedness	undetached	undimmed
uncurled	undeciphered	undefinable	undeplored	undeserving	undetected	undiplomatic
uncurrent	undeclared	undefined	undeposed	undesignated	undeterminable	undisbanded
uncursed	undeclinable	undeformed	undepraved	undesigned	undeterred	undiscerned
uncurtained	undeclined	undelayable	undepreciated	undesignedly	undeveloped	undiscernedly
uncushioned	undecomposable	undelayed	undepressed	undesignedness	undeviating	undiscernible
undamaged	undecomposed	undelineated	undeputed	undesirability	undevoured	undiscernibly
undangered	undecorated	undeliverable	underived	undesirable	undifferentiated	undiscerning
undated	undefaceable	undelivered	underivedness	undesirably	undiffused	undischarged
undaughterly	undefaced	undemocratic	underogating	undesired	undigested	undisciplined
undazzled	undefacedness	undemonstrable	underogatory	undesirous	undignified	undisclosed
undebatable	undefeatable	undemonstrably	undescribed	undesisting	undilated	undisconcerted
undecayed	undefeated	undenied	undescried	undespairing	undiluted	undiscordant

payment than (a rival). **4** In golf, to impart backspin to (the ball) by striking it obliquely downward. **5** In tennis, to use an underhand stroke in cutting (the ball). **6** To lessen or destroy the effectiveness or impact of; undermine. — *adj.* **1** Having the parts in relief cut under. **2** Done by undercutting.

un·der·de·vel·oped (un′dər·di·vel′əpt) *adj.* **1** Not sufficiently developed. **2** Below a normal or adequate standard in the development of industry, resources, agriculture, etc.: an *underdeveloped* country.

un·der·do (un′dər·dōō′) *v.t.* & *v.i.* **·did, ·done, ·do·ing** To do less than is expected or needed.

un·der·dog (un′dər·dôg′, -dog′) *n.* **1** The dog that is losing, has lost, or is at a disadvantage in a dogfight. **2** The weaker or worsted person. **3** Anyone in a position of inferiority.

un·der·done (un′dər·dun′) *adj.* **1** Insufficiently done. **2** Not cooked to the full.

un·der·drive (un′dər·drīv′) *n. Mech.* A gearing device which turns a drive shaft at a speed less than that of the engine: opposed to *overdrive.*

un·der·em·ployed (un′dər·əm·ploid′) *adj.* Unable to get a full–time or regular job; employed part of the time or working too few hours. — **un′der·em·ploy′ment** *n.*

un·der·es·ti·mate (un′dər·es′tə·māt) *v.t.* **·mat·ed, ·mat·ing** To put too low an estimate or valuation upon (things or people). See synonyms under DISPARAGE. — *n.* (-mit) **1** An insufficiently high opinion. **2** An estimate below the just value or expense. — **un′der·es′ti·ma′tion** *n.*

un·der·ex·pose (un′dər·ik·spōz′) *v.t.* **·posed, ·pos·ing** *Phot.* To expose (a film) less than is required for proper development. — **un′der·ex·posed′** *adj.* — **un′der·ex·po′sure** (-spō′zhər) *n.*

un·der·feed (un′dər·fēd′) *v.t.* **·fed, ·feed·ing** **1** To feed insufficiently. **2** To supply fuel for (an engine) from beneath.

under fire Engaged in a battle; exposed to fire; being attacked: said of troops.

un·der·foot (un′dər·fo͝ot′) *adv.* **1** Beneath the feet; down on the ground; immediately below. **2** In the way.

un·der·fur (un′dər·fûr′) *n.* The coat of dense, fine hair forming the main part of a pelt.

un·der·gar·ment (un′dər·gär′mənt) *n.* A garment to be worn under the ordinary outer garments.

un·der·gird (un′dər·gûrd′) *v.t.* **·girt** or **·gird·ed, ·gird·ing** To fasten or gird, as by something that passes underneath.

un·der·glaze (un′dər·glāz′) *adj.* Used in or suitable for porcelain decoration: said of painting in vitrifiable pigment before the glaze is applied.

un·der·go (un′dər·gō′) *v.t.* **·went, ·gone, ·go·ing** **1** To be subjected to; have experience of; suffer. **2** To bear up under; endure. **3** *Obs.* To exist under. See synonyms under ENDURE.

un·der·grad·u·ate (un′dər·graj′ōō·it) *n.* A student of a university or college who has not taken the bachelor's degree.

un·der·ground (un′dər·ground′) *adj.* **1** Situated, done, or operating beneath the surface of the ground. **2** Hence, done in secret; clandestine. — *n.* **1** That which is beneath the surface of the ground, as a passage or space. **2** A railway operated in a system of tunnels beneath the ground. **3** A group secretly organized to resist or oppose those in control of a government or country. **4** An avant-garde movement in art, cinema, journalism, etc., generally considered to be in opposition to conventional culture or society and whose works are usually experimental, erotic, or radical in style, content, or purpose: used with *the.* — *adv.* (un′dər·ground′) **1** Beneath the surface of the ground: to work *underground.* **2** Secretly.

Underground Railroad A system of cooperation among anti–slavery people, before 1861, for assisting fugitive slaves to escape to Canada and the free States.

un·der·grown (un′dər·grōn′) *adj.* Not fully grown; undersized.

un·der·growth (un′dər·grōth′) *n.* **1** A growth of smaller plants among larger ones; specifically, a thicket or coppice in or as in a forest. **2** Condition of being undergrown. **3** A close growth of hair beneath and finer than the outer growth of a pelt.

un·der·hand (un′dər·hand′) *adj.* **1** Done or acting in a treacherously secret manner; unfair; sly. **2** In baseball, cricket, etc., underarm. — *adv.* Underhandedly; slily.

un·der·hand·ed (un′dər·han′did) *adj.* Clandestinely carried on; underhand. — **un′der·hand′ed·ly** *adv.* — **un′der·hand′ed·ness** *n.*

un·der·hung (un′dər·hung′) *adj.* **1** *Anat.* Protruding from beneath, as a lower jaw: said of persons, dogs, etc., with a jaw protruding beyond the upper jaw. **2** Underslung.

un·der·laid (un′dər·lād′) *adj.* **1** Laid underneath; supporting. **2** Supported by or having something lying or placed underneath.

un·der·lay (un′dər·lā′) *v.t.* **·laid, ·lay·ing** **1** To place (one thing) under another. **2** To furnish with a base or lining. **3** *Printing* To support or raise by underlays. — *n.* (un′dər·lā′) **1** *Printing* A piece of paper, etc., placed under certain parts of a printing form, to bring them to the proper level. **2** *Mining* An inclination, as of a lode. **3** A wager made at odds unfavorable to the better: opposed to *overlay.*

un·der·lease (un′dər·lēs′) *n.* A lease of premises by a lessee; sublease.

un·der·let (un′dər·let′) *v.t.* **·let, ·let·ting** **1** To lease (premises already held on lease); sublet. **2** To lease at less than the usual rate.

un·der·lie (un′dər·lī′) *v.t.* **·lay, ·lain, ·ly·ing** **1** To lie below or under. **2** To be the ground or support of: the principle that *underlies* a scheme. **3** To constitute a first or prior claim or lien over: A first mortgage *underlies* a second. **4** To be subject, answerable, or liable to. [OE *underlicgan*]

un·der·line (un′dər·līn′) *v.t.* **·lined, ·lin·ing** **1** To mark with a line underneath; underscore. **2** To emphasize. — *n.* A line underneath, as beneath a printed or written word or syllable to indicate emphasis or stress.

un·der·lin·en (un′dər·lin′ən) *n.* Linen underwear; any underwear.

un·der·ling (un′dər·ling) *n.* A subordinate; an inferior; a servile person.

un·der·ly·ing (un′dər·lī′ing) *adj.* **1** Lying under: *underlying* strata. **2** Hence, figuratively, fundamental: *underlying* principles. **3** Prior in claim or lien. See UNDERLIE (def. 3).

un·der·men·tioned (un′dər·men′shənd) *adj.* Mentioned below in a writing.

un·der·mine (un′dər·mīn′, un′dər·mīn) *v.t.* **·mined, ·min·ing** **1** To excavate beneath; dig a mine or passage under: to *undermine* a fortress. **2** To weaken by wearing away at the base. **3** To weaken or impair secretly or by degrees: to *undermine* the influence or the health of someone. See synonyms under WEAKEN. — **un′der·min′er** *n.*

un·der·most (un′dər·mōst′) *adj.* Having the lowest place or position.

un·der·neath (un′dər·nēth′, -nēth′) *adv.* **1** In a place below. **2** On the under or lower side. See synonyms under BENEATH. — *prep.* **1** Beneath; under; below. **2** Under the form or appearance of. **3** Under the authority of; in the control of. — *adj.* Lower. — *n.* The lower or under part or side. [OE *underneothan*]

un·der·nour·ish (un′dər·nûr′ish) *v.t.* To provide with nourishment insufficient in amount or quality for proper health and growth. — **un′·der·nour′ish·ment** *n.*

un·dern·song (un′dərn·sông′, -song′) *n.* Tierce (def. 5). [OE *undern* midday, midday meal + SONG]

un·der·pants (un′dər·pants′) *n. pl.* An undergarment worn over the loins and sometimes extending over the thighs or lower legs.

un·der·pass (un′dər·pas′, -päs′) *n.* A passage beneath; the section of a way or road that passes under railway tracks or under another road.

un·der·pay (un′dər·pā′) *v.t.* **·paid, ·pay·ing** To pay insufficiently.

un·der·pin (un′dər·pin′) *v.t.* **·pinned, ·pin·ning** **1** To support, as a wall or structure, from below, especially when a previous support is removed, by inserting a prop or pier. **2** To corroborate; support.

un·der·pin·ning (un′dər·pin′ing) *n.* **1** Material or framework used to support a wall or building from below. **2** *Often pl.* Something used or functioning as a basis or foundation.

un·der·pitch (un′dər·pich′) *adj. Archit.* Designating a main vault intersected by another at a lower level. [<UNDER- + PITCH², *n.* (def. 3)]

un·der·plant (un′dər·plant′, -plänt′) *v.t. Rare* To plant young trees under (existing trees).

un·der·plot (un′dər·plot′) *n.* **1** A subsidiary literary or dramatic plot; an episode. **2** A piece of roguery or trickery; an underhand action. — **un′der·plot′ter** *n.*

un·der·priv·i·leged (un′dər·priv′ə·lijd) *adj.* At a social or economic disadvantage; specifically, through economic cause, not privileged to enjoy certain rights theoretically possessed by all members of a community or state.

un·der·pro·duc·tion (un′dər·prə·duk′shən) *n.* Production below capacity or below requirements; abnormally low production. Compare OVERPRODUCTION.

un·der·proof (un′dər·pro͞of′) *adj.* Having less strength than proof spirit.

un·der·prop (un′dər·prop′) *v.t.* **·propped, ·prop·ping** To prop from below; support.

un·der·quote (un′dər·kwōt′) *v.t.* **·quot·ed, ·quot·ing** **1** To undersell or offer to undersell, as goods or stocks. **2** To underbid.

un·der·rate (un′dər·rāt′) *v.t.* **·rat·ed, ·rat·ing** To rate too low; underestimate. See synonyms under DISPARAGE.

un·der·run (un′dər·run′) *v.t.* **·ran, ·run, ·run·ning** **1** To run or pass beneath. **2** *Naut.* To examine (a line, hawser, etc.) from below by drawing a boat along beneath it.

un·der·score (un′dər·skôr′, -skōr′) *v.t.* **·scored, ·scor·ing** To draw a line below, as for indicating emphasis; underline. — *n.* (un′dər·skôr′, -skōr′) A line drawn beneath a word, etc., as for emphasis.

un·der·sea (un′dər·sē′) *adj.* Existing, carried on, or adapted for use beneath the surface of the sea: *undersea* exploration; an *undersea* oil well. — *adv.* Beneath the surface of the sea: also **un′der·seas′.**

un·der·sell (un′dər·sel′) *v.t.* **·sold, ·sell·ing** **1** To sell at a lower price than. **2** To sell for less than the real value. — **un′der·sell′er** *n.*

un·der·set[1] (un′dər·set′) *v.t.* **·set, ·set·ting** **1** To prop up; support. **2** *Brit.* To underlet; sublet.

undiscouraged	**undismissed**	**undistracted**	**undouble**	**undutiful**	**uneliminated**	**unendorsed**
undiscoverable	**undispatched**	**undistraught**	**undoubting**	**undutifully**	**unelucidated**	**unendowed**
undiscoverably	**undispelled**	**undistressed**	**undrained**	**undutifulness**	**unemancipated**	**unendurable**
undiscovered	**undispensed**	**undistributed**	**undramatic**	**undyed**	**unembarrassed**	**unenduring**
undiscredited	**undisputable**	**undisturbed**	**undramatical**	**uneatable**	**unembellished**	**unenforceable**
undiscriminating	**undisputed**	**undisturbedly**	**undramatized**	**uneaten**	**unemotional**	**unenforced**
undiscussed	**undissected**	**undisturbedness**	**undrape**	**unecclesiastic**	**unemphatic**	**unenfranchised**
undisguised	**undissembling**	**undiversified**	**undraped**	**uneclipsed**	**unemphatical**	**unengaged**
undisguisedly	**undisseminated**	**undiverted**	**undreaded**	**uneconomic**	**unemptied**	**unengaging**
undisheartened	**undissolved**	**undivested**	**undreamed,**	**uneconomical**	**unenclosed**	**un–English**
undishonored	**undissolving**	**undivided**	**undreamt**	**unedible**	**unencumbered**	**unenjoyable**
undisillusioned	**undistilled**	**undivorced**	**undreamed–of**	**unedifying**	**unendangered**	**unenjoyed**
undismantled	**undistinguishable**	**undivulged**	**undried**	**uneducable**	**unendeared**	**unenlightened**
undismayed	**undistinguished**	**undomestic**	**undrilled**	**uneducated**	**unended**	**unenlivened**
undismembered	**undistinguishing**	**undomesticated**	**undrinkable**	**uneffaced**	**unending**	**unenriched**

add, āce, câre, pälm; end, ēven; it, īce; odd, ōpen, ôrder; to͝ok, po͞ol; up, bûrn; ə = a in *above,* e in *sicken,* i in *clarity,* o in *melon,* u in *focus*; yo͞o = u in *fuse*; oi, oil; ou, pout; ch, check; g, go; ng, ring; th, thin; th, this; zh, vision. Foreign sounds à, œ, ü, kh, ṅ; and ◆: see page xx. < from; + plus; ? possibly.

un·der·set² (un'dər·set') *n.* An undercurrent.

un·der·set·ter (un'dər·set'ər) *n.* **1** An underpinning prop or support. **2** *Brit.* One who sublets.

un·der·set·ting (un'dər·set'ing) *n.* Any underpinning; also, a base or pedestal.

un·der·shap·en (un'dər·shā'pən) *adj.* Below normal size; imperfectly formed.

un·der–sher·iff (un'dər·sher'if) *n.* A deputy sheriff, especially one upon whom the sheriff's duties devolve in his absence.

un·der·shirt (un'dər·shûrt') *n.* A garment worn beneath the shirt, generally of cotton, wool and cotton, or silk.

un·der·shot (un'dər·shot') *adj.* **1** Propelled by water that flows underneath: said of a water wheel. **2** Projecting; having a projecting lower jaw or teeth: said especially of a bulldog.

un·der·shrub (un'dər·shrub') *n.* A small shrub or plant, with shrubby base.

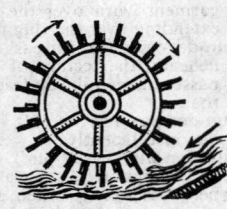

UNDERSHOT WATER WHEEL

un·der·side (un'dər·sīd') *n.* The lower or under side or surface.

un·der·sign (un'dər·sīn') *v.t.* To sign at the foot of; subscribe: used chiefly in the past participle. **— the undersigned** The subscriber or subscribers to a document.

un·der·sized¹ (un'dər·sīzd') *adj.* Of less than the normal or average size.

un·der·sized² (un'dər·sīzd') *adj.* Insufficiently sized, as paper.

un·der·skirt (un'dər·skûrt') *n.* **1** A skirt worn beneath another; a petticoat. **2** The foundation skirt of a draped gown.

un·der·sleeve (un'dər·slēv') *n.* A sleeve worn beneath another, especially when of contrasting color and showing through slashes or openings.

un·der·slung (un'dər·slung') *adj.* Having the springs fixed to the axles from below, instead of resting upon them: said of certain automobiles.

un·der·soil (un'dər·soil') *n.* Subsoil.

un·der·song (un'dər·sông', -song) *n.* **1** A subordinate strain or subdued melody. **2** An underlying meaning.

un·der·sparred (un'dər·spärd') *adj. Naut.* Having too few, too short, or too slight spars or masts.

un·der·spin (un'dər·spin') *n.* In golf, a backward spin imparted to the ball.

un·der·stand (un'dər·stand') *v.* **·stood, ·stand·ing** *v.t.* **1** To come to know the meaning or import of; apprehend. **2** To perceive the nature or character of: I do not *understand* her. **3** To have comprehension or mastery of: Do you *understand* German? **4** To be aware of; realize: She *understands* her position. **5** To have been told; believe: I *understand* that she went home. **6** To take or suppose to mean; infer: How am I to *understand* that remark? **7** To accept as a condition or stipulation: It is *understood* that the tenant will provide his own heat. **8** To supply in thought when unexpressed, as the subject of a sentence. **— v.i. 9** To have understanding; comprehend. **10** To be informed; believe. See synonyms under APPREHEND, KNOW, PERCEIVE, SOLVE. **— to understand each other** To be in agreement; be privately in sympathy with each other. [OE *understandan* < *under-* under + *standan* stand] **— un'der·stand'a·ble** *adj.* **— un'der·stand'a·bly** *adv.*

un·der·stand·ing (un'dər·stan'ding) *n.* **1** The act of one who understands, or the resulting state; intellectual apprehension; mental discernment; comprehension. **2** The power by which one understands. **3** The sum of the mental powers by which knowledge is acquired, retained, and extended; the power of apprehending relations and making inferences from them. **4** The facts or elements of a case as apprehended by any one intelligence; an individual view of a case; opinion. **5** An agreement between two or more persons; an informal or confidential compact; also, the subject of such compact; the thing agreed on; sometimes, an arrangement or settlement of differences, or of disputed points: That was not our *understanding*; They have come to an *understanding*. **— adj.** Possessing comprehension and good sense. **— un'der·stand'ing·ly** *adv.* **— un'der·stand'ing·ness** *n.*

Synonyms (noun): apprehension, comprehension, discernment, intellect, intelligence, judgment, mind, perception, reason. See INTELLECT, MIND, WISDOM.

un·der·state (un'dər·stāt') *v.* **·stat·ed, ·stat·ing** *v.t.* **1** To state with less force than the truth warrants or allows. **2** To state, as a number or dimension, as less than the true one. **— v.i. 3** To make an understatement.

un·der·state·ment (un'dər·stāt'mənt) *n.* A statement covering less than the truth or fact.

un·der·stood (un'dər·stood') Past tense and past participle of UNDERSTAND. **— adj.** Taken for granted; agreed upon by all.

un·der·strap·per (un'dər·strap'ər) *n.* An underling; a subordinate agent.

un·der·strap·ping (un'dər·strap'ing) *adj.* Subordinate; inferior.

un·der·stra·tum (un'dər·strā'təm, -strat'əm) *n. pl.* **·stra·ta** (-strā'tə, -strat'ə) An underlying stratum; substratum, literal or figurative.

un·der·stud·y (un'dər·stud'ē) *v.t. & v.i.* **·stud·ied, ·stud·y·ing** **1** To study (a part) in order to be able, if necessary, to take the place of the actor playing it. **2** To act as an understudy to (another actor). **— n. pl.** **·stud·ies** **1** An actor or actress who can take the place of another actor in a given role when necessary. **2** A person prepared to perform the work or fill the position of another.

un·der·take (un'dər·tāk') *v.* **·took, ·tak·en, ·tak·ing** *v.t.* **1** To take upon oneself; agree or attempt to do; begin. **2** To contract to do; pledge oneself to. **3** To guarantee or promise. **4** To take under charge or guidance. **5** *Obs.* To enter into combat with. **— v.i. 6** To make oneself responsible or liable; be surety with *for.* See synonyms under ENDEAVOR.

un·der·tak·er (un'dər·tā'kər *for def. 1;* un'dər·tā'kər *for def. 2*) *n.* **1** One who undertakes any work or enterprise; especially, a contractor. **2** One whose business it is to arrange for burying the dead and to conduct funerals.

un·der·tak·ing (un'dər·tā'king; *for def. 3* un'·dər·tā'king) *n.* **1** The act of one who undertakes any task or enterprise. **2** The thing undertaken; an enterprise; task. **3** The management of funerals; the business of an undertaker. **4** An engagement, promise, or guaranty.

under tenant A tenant of a tenant; one who holds premises by a lease from one who is himself a lessee.

under the rose Sub rosa.

under the weather *Colloq.* **1** Depressed by unpleasant weather; hence, somewhat ill; indisposed. **2** Inebriated; drunk. **3** In financial straits.

under the yoke In subjection.

un·der·thrust (un'dər·thrust') *n. Geol.* **1** A deformation of the earth's crust in which a mass of rock is pushed beneath an overlying mass. **2** The intruded rock mass itself.

un·der·tint (un'dər·tint') *n.* A subdued tint.

un·der·tone (un'dər·tōn') *n.* **1** A tone of lower pitch or loudness than is usual; the tone of a subdued voice; sometimes, a whisper. **2** A subdued shade of a color, as when spread thinly on a white surface; also, a color upon which other colors have been imposed and which is seen through them, modifying their effect. **3** A meaning or suggestion implied but not expressed. **4** An underlying stability in the price level of some stocks.

un·der·took (un'dər·took') Past tense of UNDERTAKE.

un·der·tow (un'dər·tō') *n.* **1** The flow of water beneath and in a direction opposite to the surface current. **2** The backward undercurrent below the surf.

un·der·trick (un'dər·trik') *n.* In certain card games, a trick required to make the number declared, but not taken.

un·der·trump (un'dər·trump') *v.t.* To play to (a previous card in the same trick) a trump lower than one already played by another player; also, to trump with too low a trump, and so be overtrumped.

un·der·val·ue (un'dər·val'yoo) *v.t.* **·ued, ·u·ing** **1** To value too lightly; underrate; underestimate. **2** *Obs.* To hold inferior: with *to* before the object compared. See synonyms under DISPARAGE. **— un'der·val'u·a'tion** *n.*

un·der·vest (un'dər·vest') *n. Brit.* An undershirt.

un·der·waist (un'dər·wāst') *n.* A waist to be worn under another waist.

un·der·wa·ter (un'dər·wô'tər, -wot'ər) *adj.* **1** Being, occurring, or used below the surface of a body of water: *underwater* research. **2** Below the water line of a ship. **— n.** The region or environment below the surface of water. **— adv.** Below the surface of water.

un·der·way (un·dər·wā') *adv.* **1** In progress: The meeting was already *underway.* **2** Into operation or motion: to get the fund drive *underway.* Also **under way.**

un·der·wear (un'dər·wâr') *n.* Garments worn underneath the ordinary outer garments.

un·der·weight (un'dər·wāt') *adj.* Having less than the normal weight. **— n.** Insufficiency of weight; also, weight below normal.

un·der·went (un'dər·went') Past tense of UNDERGO.

un·der·wing (un'dər·wing') *n. Entomol.* One of the posterior pair of wings in an insect.

underwing moth A large noctuid moth (genus *Catocala*), whose front wings are an inconspicuous brown or gray.

un·der·wood (un'dər·wood') *n.* Low trees and brush growing among large forest trees.

un·der·work (un'dər·wûrk') *v.t.* **1** To work for lower wages than. **2** To exact too little work from. **3** *Obs.* To weaken or injure by underhand contrivances; undermine. **— v.i. 4** To do too little work. **— n.** (un'dər·wûrk') Subordinate, unimportant, or routine work.

un·der·world (un'dər·wûrld') *n.* **1** In Greek and Roman mythology, the abode of the dead; Hades; Orcus. **2** In later folklore, sometimes a beautiful country under the earth or sea; also, fairyland, sometimes entered through a well. **3** The antipodes; also, all beneath the horizon. **4** The sublunary world; the earth. **5** The debased, criminal, or degenerate components of the social order; the world of crime and vice; gangsterdom.

un·der·write (un'dər·rīt') *v.* **·wrote, ·writ·ten, ·writ·ing** *v.t.* **1** To write beneath; subscribe. **2** In finance, to execute and deliver (a policy of insurance on specified property, especially

unenrolled	unescapable	unexcused	unexplored	unfashionable	unfeigningly	unfittingly
unenslaved	unessayed	unexecuted	unexported	unfashioned	unfelt	unfixed
unentangled	unestablished	unexercised	unexposed	unfastened	unfeminine	unfixedness
unentered	unesthetic	unexhausted	unexpressed	unfatherly	unfenced	unflagging
unenterprising	unestimated	unexpanded	unexpunged	unfathomable	unfermented	unflattered
unentertaining	unethical	unexpectant	unexpurgated	unfathomed	unfertile	unflattering
unenthralled	unexaggerated	unexpended	unextended	unfatigued	unfertilized	unflavored
unenthusiastic	unexalted	unexpert	unexterminated	unfavored	unfetter	unflickering
unentitled	unexamined	unexpiated	unextinguishable	unfeared	unfettered	unfoiled
unenviable	unexcavated	unexpired	unextinguished	unfearing	unfilial	unforbearing
unenvied	unexcelled	unexplainable	unfadable	unfeasible	unfilled	unforbid
unenvious	unexchangeable	unexplained	unfaded	unfed	unfilmed	unforbidden
unenvying	unexcited	unexplicit	unfading	unfederated	unfiltered	unforced
unequipped	unexciting	unexploded	unfallen	unfeignedly	unfinished	unforcedly
unerased	unexcluded	unexploited	unfaltering	unfeignedness	unfired	unfordable

marine property); insure; assume (a risk) by way of insurance. **3** To engage to buy, at a determined price and time, all or part of the stock in (a new enterprise or company) that is not subscribed for by the public; loosely, to guarantee or assume responsibility for, as an enterprise. **4** To undertake to pay, as a subscription or written pledge of money. — *v.i.* **5** To act as an underwriter; especially, to issue a policy of insurance. [OE *under-writan*, trans. of L *subscribere*]

un·der·writ·er (un'dər·rī'tər) *n.* **1** A body corporate or a person in the insurance business; one who sets up the premium for a risk. **2** One who underwrites (def. 3) an issue of stocks, bonds, or the like.

un·de·sign·ing (un'di·zī'ning) *adj.* Without ulterior purpose or selfish plan; artless; sincere.

un·de·ter·mined (un'di·tûr'mind) *adj.* **1** Not decided or fixed. **2** Not determined.

un·did (un·did') Past tense of UNDO.

un·dine (un·dēn', un'dēn, -dīn) *n. Med.* A small glass cup or flask for irrigating the eye. [<L *unda* wave + -INE¹; from its wavy profile]

Un·dine (un·dēn', un'dēn, -dīn) A water nymph without a soul, which she later received by marrying a mortal and bearing a child: heroine of a book (1811) by Baron de la Motte Fouqué, German author. [<G <NL *Undina* <L *unda* wave]

un·di·rect·ed (un'di·rek'tid, -dī-) *adj.* **1** Unguided, or uninformed as to direction. **2** Not addressed: said of a letter.

un·dis·posed (un'dis·pōzd') *adj.* **1** Not sold, settled, placed, or otherwise decided: frequently with *of*. **2** *Obs.* Disinclined. — **un'·dis·pos'ed·ness** (-pō'zid·nis) *n.*

un·do (un·dōō') *v.t.* **·did, ·done, ·do·ing** **1** To cause to be as if never done; reverse, annul, or cancel. **2** To loosen or untie. **3** To unfasten and open. **4** To bring to ruin; destroy. **5** *Obs.* To solve, as a riddle. [OE *undōn*] — **un·do'er** *n.*

un·do·ing (un·dōō'ing) *n.* **1** Reversal of what has been done. **2** Destruction; ruin; cause of ruin. **3** The action of unfastening, loosening, opening, etc. **4** *Psychoanal.* The abolition of painful experiences by the unconscious, resulting in obliviousness to the unacceptable fact.

un·done¹ (un·dun') *adj.* **1** Untied; unfastened. **2** Ruined. [Orig. pp. of UNDO]

un·done² (un·dun') *adj.* Not done. [<UN-¹ + DONE]

un·doubt·ed (un·dou'tid) *adj.* **1** Assured beyond question; being beyond a doubt. **2** Not viewed with distrust; unsuspected. See synonyms under INCONTESTABLE. — **un·doubt'ed·ly** *adv.*

un·draw (un·drô') *v.t. & v.i.* **·drew, ·drawn, ·draw·ing** To draw open, away, or aside.

un·dress (un·dres') *v.t.* **1** To divest of clothes; strip. **2** To remove the dressing or bandages from, as a wound. **3** To divest of special attire; disrobe. — *v.i.* **4** To remove one's clothing. — *n.* **1** Ordinary attire; negligée, as opposed to full or evening dress; specifically, the military or naval uniform worn by officers when not on parade or at functions necessitating full dress. **2** Comfortable, informal clothing. **3** Nudity: in a state of *undress*. — *adj.* (un'dres') Pertaining to everyday attire; hence, informal.

un·dressed (un·drest') *adj.* **1** Not dressed. **2** Not treated or dressed: said of kid leather.

Und·set (ŏon'set), **Sigrid**, 1882–1949, Norwegian novelist.

und so wei·ter (ŏont zō vī'tər) *German* And so forth; et cetera; abbreviated *u.s.w.*

un·due (un·dōō', -dyōō') *adj.* **1** Excessive; disproportionate. **2** Not justified by law; illegal. **3** Not due; in process of becoming due, but not yet demandable. **4** Not appropriate; improper.

un·du·lant (un'dyə·lənt, -də-) *adj.* Undulating; fluctuating. [<L *undul(atus)* + -ANT]

undulant fever *Pathol.* A persistent and wasting infectious disease of wide distribution, caused by a bacterium (genus *Brucella*) which is usually transmitted to man in the milk of cows and goats. The disease is marked by fluctuating or recurrent fever, with swelling of the joints, neuralgic pains, profuse perspiration, and enlargement of the spleen: also called *brucellosis, Malta fever, Mediterranean fever*.

un·du·late (un'dyə·lāt, -də-) *v.* **·lat·ed, ·lat·ing** *v.t.* **1** To cause to move like a wave or in waves. **2** To give a wavy appearance to. — *v.i.* **3** To move like a wave or waves. **4** To have a wavy form or appearance. — *adj.* (-lit, -lāt) **1** Wavy. **2** Having wavelike markings, as of color. See synonyms under FLUCTUATE. [<L *undulatus* undulated, ult. < *unda* wave]

un·du·lat·ing (un'dyə·lā'ting, -də-) *adj.* Having the appearance of waves; vibrating; wavy.

un·du·la·tion (un'dyə·lā'shən, -də-) *n.* **1** The act of undulating; a waving or sinuous motion; a wave. **2** An appearance as of waves; a gentle rise and fall. **3** *Physics* The continuous propagation of waves through a medium. — **un'du·la·to'ry** (-lə·tôr'ē, -tō'rē) *adj.*

un·du·la·tus (un'dyə·lā'təs, -də-) *n. Meteorol.* A variety of stratocumulus cloud characterized by elongated wavelike undulations, sometimes in different directions. [<NL <L. See UNDULATE.]

un·du·lous (un'dyə·ləs, -də-) *adj.* Undulatory; undulating.

un·du·ly (un·dōō'lē, -dyōō'-) *adv.* **1** Excessively. **2** In violation of a moral or of a legal standard; unjustly.

un·dy·ing (un·dī'ing) *adj.* Immortal.

un·earned (un·ûrnd') *adj.* Not earned by labor; also, undeserved.

unearned increment See under INCREMENT.

un·earth (un·ûrth') *v.t.* **1** To dig or root up from the earth. **2** To reveal; discover.

un·earth·ly (un·ûrth'lē) *adj.* **1** Not earthly; sublime. **2** Supernatural; terrifying; weird; terrible. **3** Ridiculously unconventional; inconvenient, or unpleasant; preposterous: at this *unearthly* hour. — **un·earth'li·ness** *n.*

un·ease (un·ēz') *n.* Mental or emotional discomfort, dissatisfaction, anxiety, etc.

un·eas·y (un·ē'zē) *adj.* **·eas·i·er, ·eas·i·est** **1** Deprived of ease; disturbed; unquiet. **2** Not affording ease or rest; uncomfortable; causing discomfort. **3** Showing embarrassment or constraint; strained. **4** *Obs.* Difficult. — **un·eas'i·ly** *adv.* — **un·eas'i·ness** *n.*

un·em·ploy·a·ble (un'əm·ploi'ə·bəl) *adj.* Not employable. — *n.* A person who, because of illness, age, mental or physical incapacity, or other reason, cannot be employed.

un·em·ployed (un'əm·ploid') *adj.* **1** Having no occupation; out of work. **2** Not put to use or turned to account; uninvested: *unemployed* resources. See synonyms under IDLE, VACANT. — *n.* A jobless person: with *the, unemployed* persons collectively. — **un·em·ploy'ment** *n.*

un·en·cum·bered funds (un'en·kum'bərd) **1** Funds not designated for any specific use: general funds. **2** Funds not pledged in connection with present or future obligations.

un·e·qual (un·ē'kwəl) *adj.* **1** Not having equivalent or equal extension, duration, or properties; not equal in strength, ability, wealth, status, or other respects. **2** Inadequate for the purpose; insufficient: with *to*. **3** Not balanced; disproportional; inequitable; unfair. **4** Wanting in uniformity; varying; irregular. **5** *Bot.* Unsymmetrical; *unequal* distribution. **6** Involving poorly matched competitors or contestants: an *unequal* contest. — **un·e'qual·ly** *adv.*

un·e·qualed (un·ē'kwəld) *adj.* Not equaled or matched; unrivaled; supreme. Also **un·e'qualled.**

un·e·quiv·o·cal (un'i·kwiv'ə·kəl) *adj.* Understandable in only one way; distinct; plain. See synonyms under ABSOLUTE, CLEAR, PLAIN. — **un'e·quiv'o·cal·ly** *adv.*

un·err·ing (un·ûr'ing, -er'-) *adj.* Making no mistakes; not erring: also, sure; accurate; infallible. — **un·err'ing·ly** *adv.*

UNESCO (yōō·nes'kō) The United Nations Educational, Scientific and Cultural Organization, established November, 1946, to "advance mutual knowledge and understanding of peoples," promote popular education, and assist in the diffusion of knowledge. Also **Unesco.**

un·es·sen·tial (un'ə·sen'shəl) *adj.* **1** Not absolutely required; not of prime importance. **2** Unimportant. **3** Void of essence, real or apparent. — **un'es·sen'tial·ly** *adv.*

un·e·vac·u·a·ble (un'i·vak'yōō·ə·bəl) *adj.* Not capable of being removed or evacuated, as in a military action or air raid.

un·e·ven (un·ē'vən) *adj.* **1** Not even, smooth, or level; rough. **2** Not level, parallel, or perfectly horizontal. **3** Not divisible by two without remainder; odd: said of numbers. **4** Not uniform; variable; spasmodic. **5** *Obs.* Not having correspondence; not balanced; not fair or just; also, ill-suited; not matched. See synonyms under IRREGULAR, ROUGH. — **un·e'ven·ly** *adv.* — **un·e'ven·ness** *n.*

un·e·vent·ful (un'i·vent'fəl) *adj.* Devoid of noteworthy events; quiet.

un·ex·am·pled (un'ig·zam'pəld) *adj.* So great, remarkable, or striking as to have no precedent or analogy; without a parallel example.

un·ex·cep·tion·a·ble (un'ik·sep'shən·ə·bəl) *adj.* That cannot be objected to; irreproachable. — **un'ex·cep'tion·a·ble·ness** *n.* — **un'ex·cep'tion·a·bly** *adv.*

un·ex·cep·tion·al (un'ik·sep'shən·əl) *adj.* **1** Being no exception; ordinary. **2** Subject to no exception: *unexceptional* orders.

un·ex·pect·ed (un'ik·spek'tid) *adj.* Coming without warning; not expected: said especially of things of such a kind that one would not naturally expect them; sudden; strange and unforeseen. — **the unexpected** Unexpected things or events collectively; that which is unforeseen. — **un'ex·pect'ed·ly** *adv.* — **un'ex·pect'ed·ness** *n.*

un·ex·pe·ri·enced (un'ik·spir'ē·ənst) *adj.* **1** Not experienced; not had, undergone, possessed, or known: *unexperienced* pain. **2** Lacking experience; inexperienced.

un·ex·pres·sive (un'ik·spres'iv) *adj.* **1** Not having expression; inexpressive. **2** *Obs.* Inexpressible. — **un'ex·pres'sive·ly** *adv.*

un·fail·ing (un·fā'ling) *adj.* **1** Giving or constituting a supply that never fails; inexhaustible: an *unfailing* spring. **2** Always fulfilling

unforeboding	unformulated	unfrozen	ungird	ungraded	unhandled	unhealthful
unforeknown	unforsaken	unfulfilled	ungirded	ungrafted	unhandsome	unheated
unforeseeable	unfortified	unfurnished	ungirt	ungrained	unhang	unheeded
unforeseeing	unfought	unfurrowed	ungladdened	ungrammatical	unhanged	unheedful
unforeseen	unfound	ungallant	unglazed	ungrammatically	unharassed	unheeding
unforetold	unframed	ungalled	unglossed	ungratified	unhardened	unheedingly
unforfeited	unfranchised	ungarnished	unglove	ungrounded	unharmed	unhelped
unforged	unfraternal	ungartered	ungloved	ungrudging	unharming	unhelpful
unforgetful	unfraught	ungathered	unglue	unguided	unharmonious	unheralded
unforgetting	unfree	ungenial	ungot	unhackneyed	unharnessed	unheroic
unforgivable	unfreedom	ungenteel	ungovern	unhailed	unharrowed	unhesitating
unforgiven	unfreezable	ungentle	ungowned	unhalved	unharvested	unhewn
unforgiving	un–French	ungentlemanly	ungowned	unhammered	unhasty	unhindered
unforgot	unfrequent	ungently	ungraced	unhampered	unhatched	unhired
unforgotten	unfrequently	un–get-at-able	ungraceful	unhandicapped	unhealed	unhistoric

requirements; not falling short of need, hope, or expectation. **3** Sure; infallible. —**un·fail'·ing·ly** *adv.* —**un·fail'ing·ness** *n.*

un·fair (un·fâr') *adj.* **1** Marked by dishonesty or fraud; showing partiality or prejudice; not fair: *unfair* dealing. **2** Not compatible with law and justice; illegal: *unfair* competition. **3** *Obs.* Not pleasing or comely. See synonyms under BAD. [OE *unfæger* ugly] —**un·fair'ly** *adv.* —**un·fair'ness** *n.*

un·faith·ful (un·fāth'fəl) *adj.* **1** Manifesting lack or absence of faith; unworthy of trust; perfidious; faithless; not true to marriage vows: an *unfaithful* husband. **2** Not true to a standard or to an original; not accurate or exact: an *unfaithful* description. **3** *Obs.* Not having religious faith; unbelieving; infidel. See synonyms under PERFIDIOUS. —**un·faith'·ful·ly** *adv.* —**un·faith'ful·ness** *n.*

un·fa·mil·iar (un'fə·mil'yər) *adj.* **1** Not familiarly knowing: I am *unfamiliar* with it. **2** Not familiarly known: an *unfamiliar* face. —**un'·fa·mil'i·ar'i·ty** (-mil'ē·ar'ə·tē) *n.* —**un'fa·mil'·iar·ly** *adv.*

un·fast·en (un·fas'ən, -fäs'-) *v.t.* To untie; loosen; open. —*v.i.* To become untied.

un·fa·thered (un·fä'thərd) *adj.* **1** Having no acknowledged father; hence, illegitimate. **2** Unauthenticated.

un·fa·vor·a·ble (un·fā'vər·ə·bəl) *adj.* Not favorable; unpropitious; adverse. Also *Brit.* **un·fa'vour·a·ble.** —**un·fa'vor·a·ble·ness** *n.* —**un·fa'vor·a·bly** *adv.*

Unfederated Malay States Former collective name for the states of Perlis, Kedah, Kelanton, Trengganu, and Johore, now States of Malaya in Malaysia.

un·feel·ing (un·fē'ling) *adj.* **1** Not sympathetic; hard; cruel. **2** *Obs.* Destitute of feeling or sensation. See synonyms under HARD. —**un·feel'ing·ly** *adv.* —**un·feel'ing·ness** *n.*

un·feigned (un·fānd') *adj.* Not feigned; not pretended; sincere; genuine.

un·fel·lowed (un·fel'ōd) *adj.* **1** Unequaled; unmatchable. **2** Alone; without a companion.

un·fit (un·fit') *v.t.* ·fit·ted or ·fit, ·fit·ting To deprive of requisite fitness, skill, etc.; disqualify. —*adj.* **1** Having no fitness; unsuitable. **2** Not appropriate; improper. **3** Not completely trained; not in best condition: said of race horses. —**un·fit'ly** *adv.* —**un·fit'ness** *n.*

un·fix (un·fiks') *v.t.* **1** To unfasten; loosen; detach. **2** To unsettle.

un·flap·pa·ble (un·flap'ə·bəl) *adj.* Characterized by unshakable composure; imperturbable. —**un·flap'pa·bil·i·ty** *n.*

un·fledged (un·flejd') *adj.* **1** Not yet fledged; immature, as a young bird. **2** Inexperienced: an *unfledged* orator.

un·flesh·ly (un·flesh'lē) *adj.* Not corporeal, worldly, or sensual; ethereal; spiritual.

un·flinch·ing (un·flin'ching) *adj.* Done without shrinking; steadfast; brave. —**un·flinch'ing·ly** *adv.* —**un·flinch'ing·ness** *n.*

un·fold[1] (un·fōld') *v.t.* **1** To open or spread out (something folded). **2** To lay open to view. **3** To make clear by detailed explanation; explain: to *unfold* a plan. **4** To develop. —*v.i.* **5** To become opened; expand. **6** To become manifest. See synonyms under AMPLIFY, INTERPRET, SOLVE. [OE *unfealdan*]

un·fold[2] (un·fōld') *v.t.* To free or let loose from a fold or pen.

un·for·get·ta·ble (un'fər·get'ə·bəl) *adj.* Not forgettable; memorable. —**un'for·get'ta·bly** *adv.*

un·formed (un·fôrmd') *adj.* **1** Devoid of shape or form; not fully developed in character; crude. **2** Unorganized.

un·for·tu·nate (un·fôr'chə·nit) *adj.* **1** Having ill fortune; not prosperous; unsuccessful.

2 Causing or attended by ill fortune; disastrous. See synonyms under BAD. —*n.* **1** One who is unfortunate. **2** Specifically, one who has lapsed from virtue; a prostitute. —**un·for'·tu·nate·ly** *adv.* —**un·for'tu·nate·ness** *n.*

un·found·ed (un·foun'did) *adj.* **1** Resting on no solid foundation; groundless; baseless. **2** Not founded or established. —**un·found'·ed·ly** *adv.*

un·fre·quent·ed (un'fri·kwen'tid) *adj.* Rarely or never visited or frequented.

un·friend·ed (un·fren'did) *adj.* Without friends. —**un·friend'ed·ness** *n.*

un·friend·ly (un·frend'lē) *adj.* **1** Unkindly disposed; inimical; hostile. **2** Not favorable or propitious. See synonyms under INIMICAL. —*adv.* In an unfriendly manner. —**un·friend'·li·ness** *n.*

un·frock (un·frok') *v.t.* **1** To divest of a frock or gown. **2** To depose, as a monk or priest, from ecclesiastical rank.

un·fruit·ful (un·frōōt'fəl) *adj.* **1** Bearing no fruit; having no offspring; barren. **2** Having no useful results; fruitless: an *unfruitful* line of thought. —**un·fruit'ful·ly** *adv.* —**un·fruit'·ful·ness** *n.*

un·fumed (un·fyōomd') *adj.* **1** Not fumigated. **2** *Obs.* Undistilled.

un·fund·ed (un·fun'did) *adj.* Not funded: said of a debt.

un·furl (un·fûrl') *v.t. & v.i.* **1** To unroll, as a flag; spread out; expand. **2** To unfold. —**un·furled'** *adj.*

un·gain·ly (un·gān'lē) *adj.* Lacking grace or ease; clumsy. See synonyms under AWKWARD. —*adv.* In an awkward manner. —**un·gain'·li·ness** *n.*

Un·ga·va (ung·gä'və, -gā'və) A district of northern Quebec province, extending south of Ungava Bay, and including part of Labrador; 239,780 square miles: also *New Quebec.*

Ungava Bay An inlet of Hudson Strait in northern Quebec province; 200 miles long, 160 miles wide at the mouth.

Ungava Peninsula A peninsula of northern Quebec province between Ungava Bay and Hudson Bay; 400 miles long, 350 miles wide.

un·gen·er·ous (un·jen'ər·əs) *adj.* **1** Not generous; illiberal; niggardly; unkind or harsh in judging others. —**un·gen'er·ous·ly** *adv.*

un·gift·ed (un·gif'tid) *adj.* **1** Not gifted or endowed with talent. **2** Not having received gifts.

un·god·ly (un·god'lē) *adj.* **1** Having no reverence for God; impious; wicked. **2** Unholy; sinful. **3** *Colloq.* Outrageous. —*adv.* In an ungodly manner. —**un·god'li·ness** *n.*

un·got·ten (un·got'n) *adj.* **1** Not begotten. **2** Not obtained; not acquired.

un·gov·ern·a·ble (un·guv'ər·nə·bəl) *adj.* That cannot be governed; refractory; unruly. See synonyms under PERVERSE, REBELLIOUS, VIOLENT. —**un·gov'ern·a·ble·ness** *n.* —**un·gov'·ern·a·bly** *adv.*

un·gra·cious (un·grā'shəs) *adj.* **1** Lacking in graciousness of manner; unmannerly. **2** Not pleasing; offensive; unacceptable. **3** *Obs.* Odious. —**un·gra'cious·ly** *adv.* —**un·gra'cious·ness** *n.*

un·grate·ful (un·grāt'fəl) *adj.* **1** Feeling or showing a lack of gratitude; not thankful. **2** Not pleasant; disagreeable. **3** Unrewarding; yielding no return. —**un·grate'ful·ly** *adv.* —**un·grate'ful·ness** *n.*

un·gual (ung'gwəl) *adj.* Having, resembling, or pertaining to a hoof, claw, or nail. [<L *unguis* hoof, claw, nail]

un·guard (un·gärd') *v.t.* To deprive of a guard; expose.

un·guard·ed (un·gär'did) *adj.* **1** Having no guard; being without protection. **2** Done

or spoken without proper caution; careless: *unguarded* speech. —**un·guard'ed·ly** *adv.* —**un·guard'ed·ness** *n.*

un·guent (ung'gwənt) *n.* Any ointment for local application; a salve or cerate. [<L *unguentum* <*unguere* anoint]

un·guen·tar·y (ung'gwən·ter'ē) *adj.* Of, for, like, or pertaining to unguents.

un·guic·u·late (ung·gwik'yə·lit, -lāt) *adj.* **1** *Zool.* Having claws, as a carnivorous mammal. **2** *Bot.* Having a stalklike or clawlike base, as the petals of pinks. —*n.* A mammal having claws, as distinguished from an ungulate or cetacean. [<NL *unguiculatus* <L *unguiculus* fingernail, dim. of *unguis* nail]

un·gui·form (ung'gwi·fôrm) *adj.* Claw-shaped; hooked; unciform. [<L *unguis* nail + -FORM]

un·gui·nous (ung'gwi·nəs) *adj.* Resembling, containing, or consisting of oil or fat; unctuous. [<L *unguinosus* <*unguen*, -*inis* ointment]

un·guis (ung'gwis) *n.* *pl.* ·gues (-gwēz) **1** A nail, claw, hoof, or talon. **2** A structure resembling a nail. **3** *Bot.* A claw or lower contracted part of a petal. [<L, nail]

un·gu·la (ung'gyə·lə) *n.* *pl.* ·lae (-lē) **1** *Zool.* A hoof, claw, nail, or talon. **2** *Surg.* An instrument for removing a dead fetus from the womb. **3** *Geom.* That which is left of a cone or cylinder when the top is cut off by a plane oblique to the base: so called from its resemblance to a horse's hoof. **4** *Bot.* An unguis. [<L, hoof <*unguis* nail]

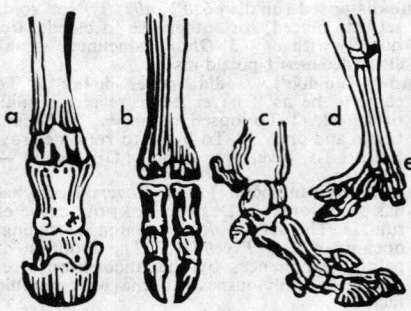

UNGULATE FEET
a. Hind foot of horse.
b. Foot of a stag.
c. Forefoot of Indian rhinoceros.
d. Side view of stag foot, showing false hoof at *e.*

un·gu·lar (ung'gyə·lər) *adj.* Of, pertaining to, or bearing a nail, hoof, or claw; ungual.

un·gu·late (ung'gyə·lit, -lāt) *adj.* **1** Having hoofs; hoof-shaped. **2** Designating, pertaining to, or belonging to a large division (*Ungulata*) of hoofed, herbivorous mammals, including the elephant, rhinoceros, horse, cony, hog, and all the ruminants. —*n.* A hoofed mammal. [<LL *ungulatus* <L *ungula* hoof]

un·gu·li·grade (ung'gyə·lə·grād') *adj.* Walking on hoofs, as a horse or cow. [<L *ungula* hoof + -GRADE]

un·hair (un·hâr') *v.t. & v.i.* To free or become free of hair, as hides by soaking and scraping.

un·hal·low (un·hal'ō) *v.t.* To profane; desecrate.

un·hal·lowed (un·hal'ōd) *adj.* **1** Left secular. **2** Not sacred. **3** Unholy; wicked.

un·halsed (un·hôlst') *adj.* *Scot.* Not saluted or greeted.

un·hand (un·hand') *v.t.* To remove one's hand from; release from the hand or hands; let go.

un·hand·y (un·han'dē) *adj.* **1** Inconvenient;

unhomogeneous	unidentified	unimportance	uninfested	uninstructive	uninterpolated	unjaded
unhonored	unidiomatic	unimportant	uninflammable	uninsurable	uninterpreted	unjoined
unhood	unilluminated	unimposing	uninflected	uninsured	uninterrupted	unjointed
un–Horatian	unillumined	unimpressed	uninfluenced	unintellectual	unintimidated	unjoyful
unhostile	unillustrated	unimpressible	uninfluential	unintelligibility	unintoxicated	unjudged
unhoused	unimaginable	unimpressionable	uninformed	unintelligible	uninvaded	unjustifiable
unhuman	unimaginably	unimpressive	uninfringed	unintelligibly	uninvented	unjustifiably
unhumanize	unimaginative	uninaugurated	uninhabitable	unintended	uninventive	unkept
unhung	unimagined	uninclosed	uninhabited	unintentional	uninverted	unkindled
unhurt	unimbued	unincorporated	uninhibited	unintentionally	uninvested	unkindliness
unhurtful	unimitated	unincumbered	uninitiated	uninteresting	uninvited	unkingly
unhygienic	unimpaired	unindemnified	uninjured	uninterestingly	uninviting	unkissed
unhyphenated	unimpassioned	unindicated	uninspired	unintermitted	uninvoked	unknelled
unhyphened	unimpeded	unindorsed	uninspiring	unintermittent	uninvolved	unknightly
unideal	unimplored	uninfected	uninstructed	unintermitting	unissued	unknit

hard to handle. **2** Clumsy; lacking in manual skill. — **un·hand′i·ly** *adv.*

un·hap·py (un-hap′ē) *adj.* **·pi·er, ·pi·est** **1** Subject to conditions that prevent or destroy happiness; sad; depressed. **2** Causing or constituting misery, unrest, or dissatisfaction: *unhappy* circumstances. **3** Characterized by or exhibiting ill fortune; unfortunate; unpropitious. **4** Exhibiting lack of tact or judgment; inappropriate; inopportune. **5** *Obs.* Evil. See synonyms under BAD, SAD. — **un·hap′pi·ly** *adv.* — **un·hap′pi·ness** *n.*

un·har·bored (un-här′bərd) *adj.* **1** Having no harbor, shelter, or cover. **2** *Obs.* Not affording shelter. Also *Brit.* **un·har′boured.**

un·har·ness (un-här′nis) *v.t.* **1** To remove the harness from; unyoke; release. **2** To remove the armor from.

un·hat (un-hat′) *v.* **·hat·ted, ·hat·ting** *v.i.* To take off one's hat, especially to show respect or in worship. — *v.t.* To remove the hat from.

un·health·y (un-hel′thē) *adj.* **·health·i·er, ·health·i·est** **1** Lacking health, vigor, or wholesomeness; sickly; unsound: *unhealthy* animals or plants; also, indicating such a condition: *unhealthy* signs. **2** Loosely, insalubrious; injurious to health. **3** Morally or spiritually unsound, defective, or pernicious: *unhealthy* fiction. — **un·health′i·ly** *adv.* — **un·health′i·ness** *n.*

un·heard (un-hûrd′) *adj.* **1** Not perceived by the ear. **2** Not granted a hearing. **3** Obscure; unknown.

un·heard-of (un-hûrd′uv′, -ov′) *adj.* Not known of before; unknown or unprecedented.

un·helm (un-helm′) *v.t.* To remove the helmet or helm of. — *v.i.* To remove one's helmet.

un·hinge (un-hinj′) *v.t.* **·hinged, ·hing·ing** **1** To take from the hinges. **2** To remove the hinges of. **3** To detach; dislodge. **4** To throw into confusion; disorder. **5** To make unstable; unsettle, as the mind.

un·hitch (un-hich′) *v.t.* To unfasten.

un·ho·ly (un-hō′lē) *adj.* **·ho·li·er, ·ho·li·est** **1** Not hallowed. **2** Lacking purity; wicked; sinful. See synonyms under PROFANE, SINFUL. [OE *unhālig*] — **un·ho′li·ly** *adv.* — **un·ho′li·ness** *n.*

un·hook (un-hŏŏk′) *v.t.* **1** To remove from a hook. **2** To unfasten the hook or hooks of. — *v.i.* **3** To become unhooked.

un·hoped (un-hōpt′) *adj.* Not hoped (for); unexpected; exceeding hope: chiefly in the compound **un·hoped′-for′.**

un·horse (un-hôrs′) *v.t.* **·horsed, ·hors·ing** **1** To throw from a horse. **2** To dislodge; overthrow. **3** To remove a horse or horses from: to *unhorse* a vehicle.

un·hou·seled (un-hou′zəld) *adj. Obs.* Not having received the last sacraments. [<UN-[1] + HOUSEL + -ED[2]]

un·hur·ried (un-hûr′ēd) *adj.* Leisurely; not hurried.

un·husk (un-husk′) *v.t.* **1** To strip the husk from. **2** To expose; lay open.

uni- *combining form* One; single; one only: *unifoliate.* [<L *unus* one]

U·ni·at (yōō′nē-at) *n.* A member of any community of Eastern Christians that acknowledges the supremacy of the pope at Rome, but retains its own liturgy, ceremonies, and rites: also called *United Armenian, United Greek.* Compare LATIN CHURCH. — *adj.* Of the Uniats or their faith. Also **U′ni·ate** (-it, -āt). [<Russian *uniyat* < *uniya* union <L *unus* one; from being in union with the Roman Catholic Church]

u·ni·ax·i·al (yōō′nē-ak′sē-əl) *adj.* **1** Having one axis. **2** Doubly refracting and having only a single optical axis, as crystals of the tetragonal and hexagonal systems. **3** *Bot.* Unbranched, as a primary stem terminating in a flower.

u·ni·cam·er·al (yōō′nə-kam′ər-əl) *adj.* Consisting of but one chamber, as a legislature.

u·ni·cel·lu·lar (yōō′nə-sel′yə-lər) *adj. Biol.* Consisting of a single cell, as a protozoan; one-celled.

u·ni·col·or (yōō′nə-kul′ər) *adj.* Of one color.

u·ni·corn (yōō′nə-kôrn) *n.* **1** A fabulous horselike animal with one horn. **2** A two-horned animal, identified with the urus, so called in the early English versions of the Bible to render the Latin and Greek mistranslations of the Hebrew *re' ēm:* translated as *wild ox* in the Revised Version. *Deut.* xxxiii 17. [<OF *unicorne* <L *unicornis* one-horned < *unus* one + *cornu* a horn]

UNICORN

u·ni·cos·tate (yōō′nə-kos′tāt) *adj.* **1** Having a single principal costa, rib, or nervure. **2** *Bot.* Having a midrib, as a leaf.

u·ni·cy·cle (yōō′nə-sī′kəl) *n.* A cycle or velocipede having a single wheel propelled by pedals.

un·i·de·aed (un′ī-dē′əd) *adj.* Not having ideas; frivolous.

u·ni·di·rec·tion·al (yōō′nə-di-rek′shən-əl, -dī-) *adj.* **1** Moving in the same direction. **2** Designed or equipped to operate best in only one direction, as a radio antenna. **3** *Electr.* Of or pertaining to a direct current.

u·ni·fi·a·ble (yōō′nə-fī′ə-bəl) *adj.* That can be unified.

u·nif·ic (yōō-nif′ik) *adj.* Unifying.

unified field theory *Physics* **1** Any mathematically rigorous generalization which will combine two or more physical theories in a form permitting accurate inclusive predictions not deducible from one theory alone, as the electromagnetic theory of Maxwell. **2** Such a generalization, as tentatively formulated by Einstein, to unify the theories of electromagnetism, gravitation, and relativity.

u·ni·fi·lar (yōō′nə-fī′lər) *adj.* **1** Possessing but a single thread. **2** Utilizing only one suspending thread.

u·ni·flo·rous (yōō′nə-flôr′əs, -flō′rəs) *adj. Bot.* One-flowered.

u·ni·fo·li·ate (yōō′nə-fō′lē-it, -āt) *adj. Bot.* Having one leaf.

u·ni·fo·li·o·late (yōō′nə-fō′lē-ə-lit, -lāt) *adj. Bot.* Having a single leaflet, as the compound leaves of the orange.

u·ni·form (yōō′nə-fôrm) *adj.* **1** Being the same or alike, as in form, appearance, quantity, quality, degree, or character; not varying: *uniform* temperature. **2** Agreeing with each other; harmonious; accordant; consonant: *uniform* tastes. See synonyms under ALIKE. — *n.* A dress or suit of uniform style and appearance worn by members of the same organization, service, etc., as soldiers, sailors, postmen, etc. See synonyms under DRESS. — **dress uniform** A military or naval uniform worn at social or ceremonial events. — *v.t.*

To put into or clothe with a uniform. [<F *uniforme* <L *uniformis* <*unus* one + *forma* form] — **u′ni·form·ness** *n.* — **u′ni·form·ly** *adv.*

u·ni·for·mal·ize (yōō′nə-fôr′məl-īz) *v.t.* **·ized, ·iz·ing** To bring into a uniform system; render uniform.

Uniform Code of Military Justice The code of laws and related procedures enacted in 1951 by the U. S. Congress for the government of the personnel of the armed services: supersedes the former Army *Articles of War* and the *Articles for the Government of the Navy.*

u·ni·formed (yōō′nə-fôrmd) *adj.* Dressed in uniform.

u·ni·form·i·tar·i·an·ism (yōō′nə-fôr′mə-târ′ē-ən-iz′əm) *n. Geol.* The doctrine that essential uniformity in causes and effects, forces and phenomena, has prevailed in all ages of the world's physical history, and that the activities of the past were similar in mode and intensity to those of the present: opposed to *catastrophism.* — **u′ni·form′i·tar′i·an** *adj. & n.*

u·ni·form·i·ty (yōō′nə-fôr′mə-tē) *n. pl.* **·ties** **1** The state or quality of being uniform, or an instance of it; consistency throughout; lack of diversity. **2** Conformity or compliance, as in opinions or religion. **3** Monotony; sameness.

u·ni·fy (yōō′nə-fī) *v.t.* **·fied, ·fy·ing** To cause to be a unit; make uniform; unite; cause to be one. [<F *unifier* <LL *unificare* <L *unus* one + *facere* make] — **u′ni·fi·ca′tion** (-fə-kā′shən) *n.* — **u′ni·fi′er** *n.*

u·ni·gen·i·ture (yōō′nə-jen′ə-chər) *n.* The state of being an only child, or, in theology, of being the only begotten Son.

u·nij·u·gate (yōō-nij′ŏŏ-gāt, yōō′nə-jŏŏ′git, -gāt) *adj. Bot.* Having one pair, as of leaflets: said especially of a pinnate leaf. [<UNI- + JUGATE]

u·ni·lat·er·al (yōō′nə-lat′ər-əl) *adj.* **1** One-sided; relating to one side only; made, undertaken, done, or signed by only one of two or more people or parties. **2** *Law* Binding or obligatory on one party only. **3** Arranged or growing on one side only, as a plant or animal organ. **4** *Med.* Affecting but one side of the body. **5** Relating to or tracing ancestry on one side only.

u·ni·lit·er·al (yōō′nə-lit′ər-əl) *adj.* Comprising but one letter.

u·ni·loc·u·lar (yōō′nə-lok′yə-lər) *adj. Biol.* Having or consisting of one cell or chamber, as an anther, ovary, etc.

U·ni·mak Island (yōō′nə-mak) The most northeasterly of the Fox Islands in the NE Aleutian Islands; 70 miles long.

un·im·peach·a·ble (un′im-pē′chə-bəl) *adj.* Not to be called in question as regards truth, honesty, etc.; faultless; blameless. — **un′im·peach′a·bly** *adv.*

un·im·proved (un′im-prōōvd′) *adj.* **1** Not improved; not bettered or advanced: *unimproved* health. **2** Having no improvements; not cleared, cultivated, or built upon: *unimproved* land. **3** Not made anything of; unused: *unimproved* opportunities. **4** *Obs.* Not proved or tried.

un·in·gen·ious (un′in-jēn′yəs) *adj.* **1** Lacking ingenuity; not possessed of inventiveness. **2** *Obs.* Uningenuous.

un·in·gen·u·ous (un′in-jen′yŏŏ-əs) *adj.* Not ingenuous; sly or designing.

un·in·tel·li·gent (un′in-tel′ə-jənt) *adj.* **1** Not intelligent; characterized by lack of intelligence. **2** Unwise; ignorant. — **un′in·tel′li·gence** *n.*

un·in·ter·est·ed (un·in′tər·is·tid, -tris-) *adj.* **1** Having no interest in, as in property.

unknowable	unlevel	unlocated	unmangled	unmaternal	unmentionability	unmodified
unknowing	unlevied	unlocked	unmanifested	unmatted	unmentioned	unmodish
unlabeled,	unlibidinous	unlovable	unmanipulated	unmatured	unmercenary	unmoistened
unlabelled	unlicensed	unloved	unmannered	unmeant	unmerchantable	unmold
unladylike	unlifelike	unloveliness	unmannish	unmeasurable	unmerited	unmolested
unlamented	unlighted	unloverlike	unmannishly	unmeasured	unmethodical	unmolified
unlash	unlikable,	unloving	unmanufacturable	unmechanical	unmilitary	unmolten
unlashed	unlikeable	unlubricated	unmanufactured	unmedicated	unmilled	unmortgaged
unlaundered	unlined	unlying	unmarketable	unmeditated	unmingle	unmotivated
unleased	unlink	unmagnified	unmarred	unmelodious	unmingled	unmounted
unled	unliquefiable	unmaidenly	unmarriageable	unmelted	unmirthful	unmourned
unlessened	unliquefied	unmailable	unmarried	unmenaced	unmistaken	unmovable
unlessoned	unlit	unmalleable	unmastered	unmendable	unmitigable	unmoved
unlet	unliveliness	unmanageable	unmatched	unmended	unmixed,	unmown
unletted	unlively	unmanful	unmated	unmensurable	unmixt	unmurmuring

add, āce, câre, pälm; end, ēven; it, īce; odd, ōpen, ôrder; tŏŏk, pōōl; up, bûrn; ə = a in *above*, e in *sicken*, i in *clarity*, o in *melon*, u in *focus*; yōō = u in *fuse*; oi, oil; ou, pout; ch, check; g, go; ng, ring; th, thin; ŧħ, this; zh, vision. Foreign sounds á, œ, ü, kh, ṅ; and ✦: see page xx. < from; + plus; ? possibly.

2 Taking no interest in; indifferent; unconcerned.

un·ion (yōōn′yən) *n.* **1** The act of uniting, or the state of being united; a joining; coalescence; junction. **2** That which is constituted as one by the combination of elements previously separate; a coalition; confederation; league. **3** A combination of co-laborers for the joint and mutual protection of their common interests. See TRADE UNION. **4** *Brit.*

PIPE UNION

An amalgamation of parishes for administration of poor relief; also, a workhouse administered by such a union. **5** Agreement in sentiment or action; harmony; concord; unanimity. **6** The joining of two persons in marriage, or the resulting state of wedlock. **7** A device emblematic of union borne in the canton of a flag, as the three crosses in a British ensign; the canton itself containing such device, sometimes used separately as a flag, as the blue canton with white stars in the flag of the United States, and the Union Jack of Great Britain. **8** A coupling or connection for pipes or rods. **9** A fabric made of two or more materials, as cotton and wool. **10** *Obs.* A pearl of extraordinary worth. — *adj.* Of, pertaining to, or adhering to a union, particularly a political or trade union. [<F <LL *unio, -onis* <L *unus* one. Doublet of ONION.]

Synonyms (noun): coalition, combination, conjunction, junction, juncture, oneness, unification, unity. *Unity* is *oneness,* the state of existing as essentially one, especially of that which never has been divided or of that which cannot be conceived of as resolved into parts; as, the *unity* of the human soul. *Union* is a bringing together of things that have been distinct, so that they combine or coalesce to form a new whole, or the state or condition of things thus brought together; in a *union* the separate individuality of the things united is never lost sight of; we speak of the *union* of the parts of a fractured bone. See ALLIANCE, ASSOCIATION, ATTACHMENT, HARMONY, MARRIAGE. *Antonyms:* analysis, contrariety, decomposition, disconnection, disjunction, dissociation, disunion, division, divorce, separation, severance.

Un·ion (yōōn′yən) *n.* **1** The United States regarded as a national unit: with *the.* **2** The Union of South Africa. — *adj.* Of, pertaining to, or loyal to the United States, especially the Federal government during the Civil War: a *Union* soldier; He was *Union* to the core.

union card **1** A card certifying that the person named belongs to a certain labor union. **2** A card certifying that the shop named hires only union labor.

union catalog A library catalog combining the catalogs of more than one library, usually in a single alphabetical list.

union down Reversed, as a flag, so as to have the union or canton at the lower edge: a signal of distress.

Union Islands See TOKELAU ISLANDS.

un·ion·ism (yōōn′yən·iz′əm) *n.* **1** The principle of combination for unity of purpose and action. **2** Trade-unionism. **3** Adherence to or advocacy of political union between states, as opposed to secession. — **un′ion·is′tic** *adj.*

un·ion·ist (yōōn′yən·ist) *n.* **1** An advocate of union or unionism. **2** A member of a trade union.

Un·ion·ist (yōōn′yən·ist) *n.* **1** One who before and during the Civil War in the United States supported the Union cause and opposed secession; a Union man. **2** One of those opposed to loosening the formal ties between Great Britain and Ireland, whether belonging to the Conservatives or the branch of the Liberals (**Liberal Unionists**) that separated from their party in 1886 in opposition to the advocates of Home Rule for Ireland. From this time the term *Unionists* began to come into use, at first to signify both the Conservative and the Liberal Unionist parties, and later, as the distinction between the two wings gradually grew smaller, the Conservative Party.

un·ion·ize (yōōn′yən·īz) *v.* **·ized, ·iz·ing** *v.t.* To cause to join, or to organize into a union, especially a trade union. — *v.i.* To become a member of or organize a trade union. — **un′·ion·i·za′tion** *n.*

union jack A flag consisting of the union or canton only.

Union Jack The British national flag. It is a combination of the flags of England, Scotland, and Ireland.

Union of South Africa Former name of the Republic of South Africa.

Union of Soviet Socialist Republics The former federal union of 26 constituent republics of eastern Europe and northern Asia, extending from the Arctic Ocean to the Black Sea and east to the Pacific, dissolved into independent nations in 1991–1993; formerly Soviet **Russia, Soviet Union.** — Abbr. **U.S.S.R., USSR.**

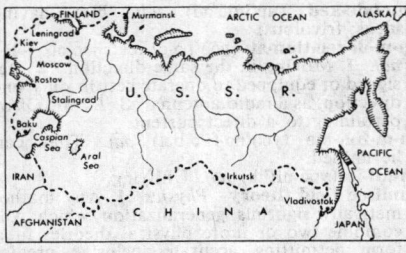

union shop An industrial establishment in which only members of a trade union are employed.

union station A railroad station or depot used by two or more railroad lines.

union suit A one-piece undergarment consisting of shirt and drawers.

Union Territory In India, under the provisions of the States Reorganization Act, which came into effect November 1, 1956, a division of India administered by the central government, rather than governing itself as a State. The six Union Territories of India are the Andaman and Nicobar Islands, Delhi, Himachal Pradesh, the Laccadive Islands, Manipura, and Tripura; Pondicherry is also temporarily administered as a Union Territory.

u·ni·pa·ren·tal (yōō′nə·pə·ren′təl) *adj.* Having or produced by one parent only; asexual.

u·nip·a·rous (yōō·nip′ər·əs) *adj.* **1** *Bot.* Having but one axis or stem. **2** Bringing forth but one offspring at a time, or not having borne more than one. [<UNI- + -PAROUS]

u·ni·per·son·al (yōō′nə·pûr′sən·əl) *adj.* **1** Manifested or existing in but one person. **2** *Gram.* Used in only one person, especially the third person singular; impersonal.

u·ni·pet·al·ous (yōō′nə·pet′l·əs) *adj. Bot.* Having only one petal.

u·ni·pla·nar (yōō′nə·plā′nər) *adj.* Lying or taking place in one plane.

u·ni·po·lar (yōō′nə·pō′lər) *adj.* **1** *Physics* Showing only one kind of polarity. **2** *Anat.* Having, or operating by means of, one pole: said especially of nerve cells having only one process.

u·nique (yōō·nēk′) *adj.* **1** Being the only one of its kind; being without equal; singular; uncommon; rare. **2** Not complicated with other things. **3** Sole. See synonyms under ODD, QUEER, RARE. [<F <L *unicus* <*unus* one] — **u·nique′ly** *adv.* — **u·nique′ness** *n.*

u·ni·sep·tate (yōō′nə·sep′tāt) *adj.* Having a single septum or partition.

u·ni·sex (yōō′nə·seks′) *Colloq. adj.* For, appropriate to, or having characteristics of both sexes: *unisex* fashions. — *n.* The embodiment or integration of qualities, characteristics, etc., of both sexes, as in appearance, clothes, or activities.

u·ni·sex·u·al (yōō′nə·sek′shōō·əl) *adj.* **1** Of one sex: specifically said of flowers and animals having one kind of sexual organs only. **2** *Colloq.* Of or having to do with unisex.

u·ni·son (yōō′nə·sən, -zən) *n.* **1** A condition of perfect agreement and accord; harmony. **2** *Colloq.* Of or having to do with unisex. or voices perform the same part; unity of pitch; also, the interval of one or more octaves. See synonyms under HARMONY, MELODY. [<L *unisonus* having a single sound <*uni-* one + *sonus* a sound]

u·nis·o·nal (yōō·nis′ə·nəl) *adj.* Being in unison. Also **u·nis′o·nant.** — **u·nis′o·nal·ly** *adv.*

u·nit (yōō′nit) *n.* **1** A single person or thing regarded as an individual but belonging to an entire group. **2** A body or group considered as a single whole among a plurality of similars. **3** A standard quantity with which others of the same kind are compared for purposes of measurement and in terms of which their magnitude is stated. **4** *Math.* A quantity whose measure is represented by the number 1; a least whole number; specifically, in arithmetic, the number 1 itself; unity. **5** *Med.* The quantity of a drug, vaccine, serum, or antigen required to produce a given effect. **6** A fundamental quantity used in calculating how much scholastic work a student has finished. [Short for UNITY]

unit angle A radian.

u·ni·tar·i·an (yōō′nə·târ′ē·ən) *n.* One who rejects the doctrine of the Trinity; a non-Trinitarian monotheist. — *adj.* Pertaining to a unit. [<NL *unitarius* unitary]

U·ni·tar·i·an (yōō′nə·târ′ē·ən) *n.* A member of a Protestant denomination which rejects the doctrine of the Trinity, but accepts the ethical teachings of Jesus and emphasizes complete freedom of religious opinion, the importance of personal character, and the independence of each local congregation. — *adj.* Pertaining to the Unitarians, or to their teachings. — **U′ni·tar′i·an·ism** *n.*

u·ni·tar·i·an·ism (yōō′nə·târ′ē·ən·iz′əm) *n.* Any unitary system.

u·ni·tar·y (yōō′nə·ter′ē) *adj.* **1** Pertaining to a unit; characterized by, based on, or pertaining to unity. **2** Having the nature of a unit; whole.

unit cell *Crystall.* Cell (def. 6).

unit character *Genetics* One of two or more contrasting characters which is transmitted as a unit and without modification.

u·nite (yōō·nīt′) *v.* **u·nit·ed, u·nit·ing** *v.t.* **1** To join together so as to form a whole; combine; compound. **2** To bring into close connection, as by legal, physical, marital, social, or other tie; join in action, interest, etc. **3** To attach permanently or solidly; cause to

unmusical	unnoted	unobtruding	unornamental	unparental	unperceivable	unphonetic
unmuzzle	unnoticeable	unobtrusive	unornate	unparted	unperceived	unpicked
unmuzzled	unnoticed	unobtrusiveness	unorthodox	unpartisan,	unperceiving	unpicturesque
unmystified	unnurtured	unoccasioned	unorthodoxy	unpartizan	unperfected	unpierced
unnail	unobjectionable	unoffended	unostentatious	unpasteurized	unperformed	unpile
unnamable,	unobliged	unoffending	unowned	unpatched	unperplexed	unpitying
unnameable	unobliging	unoffensive	unoxidized	unpatented	unpersuadable	unplaced
unnamed	unobnoxious	unoffered	unpacified	unpatriotic	unpersuaded	unplagued
unnaturalized	unobscured	unofficious	unpacker	unpaved	unpersuasive	unplait
unnavigable	unobservant	unoiled	unpainful	unpeaceable	unperturbed	unplanned
unnavigated	unobserved	unopen	unpalatable	unpeaceful	unperused	unplanted
unneeded	unobserving	unopened	unpalatably	unpedigreed	unphilanthropic	unplayed
unneedful	unobstructed	unopposed	unpardonable	unpen	unphilological	unpleasing
unnegotiable	unobtainable	unoppressed	unpardonably	unpenetrated	unphilosophic	unpledged
unneighborly	unobtained	unordained	unpardoned	unpensioned	unphilosophical	unpliable

adhere; combine. —*v.i.* **4** To become or be merged into one; be consolidated; combine. **5** To join together for action; act in conjunction; concur. [< LL *unitus*, pp. of *unire* make one < L *unus* one]
   Synonyms: amalgamate, blend, cement, cohere, combine, compound, conjoin, connect, consolidate, fuse, join, link, merge. See MIX. Compare ADD, COMPLEX. *Antonyms:* disconnect, disjoin, disrupt, dissociate, dissolve, divide, separate, sever.

u·nit·ed (yōō·nī′tid) *adj.* Incorporated into one; allied; combined; harmonious. —**u·nit′·ed·ly** *adv.* —**u·nit′ed·ness** *n.*

United Arab Republic A former republic formed in 1958 by the merger of the republics of Egypt and Syria; after the withdrawal of Syria in 1961, the official name for EGYPT.

United Armenian A Uniat.

United Church of Christ A Protestant denomination formed in 1957 by a union of the Congregational Christian Churches and the Evangelical and Reformed Church.

United Greek A Uniat.

United Kingdom 1 The kingdom of the British Isles, comprising Great Britain, Northern Ireland, the Isle of Man, and the Channel Islands; 94,284 square miles; capital, London: officially **United Kingdom of Great Britain and Northern Ireland. 2** Formerly, Great Britain and Ireland (1801–1922).

United Nations 1 A coalition to resist the military aggression of the Axis Powers in World War II, formed of 26 national states in January, 1942. **2** An international organization of sovereign states (originally called the **United Nations Organization**) created by the United Nations Charter drafted in September–October, 1944, at Dumbarton Oaks and adopted at San Francisco in May and June, 1945: the 26 states of the United Nations coalition and 25 others form the original membership.
   Membership (1945): Argentina, Australia, Belgium, Belorussian S.S.R., Bolivia, Brazil, Canada, Chile, China (Taiwan), Colombia, Costa Rica, Cuba, Czechoslovakia, Denmark, Dominican Republic, Ecuador, Egypt, El Salvador, Ethiopia, France, Greece, Guatemala, Haiti, Honduras, India, Iran, Iraq, Lebanon, Liberia, Luxembourg, Mexico, Netherlands, New Zealand, Nicaragua, Norway, Panama, Paraguay, Peru, Philippines, Poland, Saudi Arabia, South Africa (Union of South Africa), Syria, Turkey, Ukrainian S.S.R., United Kingdom, United States, Uruguay, U.S.S.R., Venezuela, Yugoslavia; (1946) Afghanistan, Iceland, Sweden, Thailand; (1947) Pakistan, Yemen; (1948) Myanmar (Burma); (1949) Israel; (1950) Indonesia; (1955) Albania, Austria, Bulgaria, Finland, Hungary, Ireland, Italy, Jordan, Kampuchea (Cambodia), Laos, Libya, Nepal, Portugal, Romania, Spain, Sri Lanka (Ceylon); (1956) Japan, Morocco, Sudan, Tunisia; (1957) Ghana, Malaysia (Malaya); (1958) Guinea; (1960) Benin (Dahomey), Burkina Faso (Upper Volta), Cameroon, Central African Republic, Chad, Congo, Côte d'Ivoire (Ivory Coast), Cyprus, Gabon, Madagascar, Mali, Niger, Nigeria, Senegal, Somalia, Togo, Zaire (Belgian Congo); (1961) Mauritania, Mongolia, Sierra Leone, Tanzania (Tanganyika, merged in 1964 with Zanzibar, member 1963); (1962) Algeria, Burundi, Jamaica, Rwanda, Trinidad and Tobago, Uganda; (1963) Kenya, Kuwait; (1964) Malawi, Malta, Zambia; (1965) Gambia, Mal-

dives, Singapore; (1966) Barbados, Botswana, Guyana, Lesotho; (1967) Democratic Yemen; (1968) Equatorial Guinea, Mauritius, Swaziland; (1970) Fiji; (1971) Bahrain, Bhutan, China (People's Republic, replaced Taiwan), Oman, Qatar, United Arab Emirates; (1973) Bahamas, Germany (German Democratic Republic and Federal Republic of); (1974) Bangladesh, Grenada, Guinea-Bissau; (1975) Cape Verde, Comoros, Mozambique, Papua New Guinea, São Tome and Príncipe; Suriname; (1976) Angola, Samoa, Seychelles; (1977) Djibouti, Vietnam; (1978) Dominica, Solomon Islands; (1979) St. Lucia; (1980) St. Vincent and the Grenadines, Zimbabwe; (1981) Antigua and Barbuda, Belize, Vanuatu; (1983) St. Kitts and Nevis; (1984) Brunei. Also called *UN*.

United Nations Trust Territory See TRUST TERRITORY.

United Presbyterian Church in the United States of America The largest U.S. Presbyterian body, formed in 1958 by the merger of two separate churches.

United Press A news-collecting and -distributing organization, merged in 1958 with the International News Service to form the **United Press International.**

United Society of Believers in Christ's Second Appearing See SHAKER.

United States The United States of America.

United States Army, Navy, Air Force, etc. See under ARMY, NAVY, AIR FORCE, etc.

United States of America A federal republic of North America, including 50 states, and the District of Columbia, the Canal Zone, Puerto Rico, the Virgin Islands of the United States, American Samoa, Guam, Wake, and several other scattered islands of the Pacific; total area, about 3,720,407 square miles; capital, Washington, in the District of Columbia. —**conterminous United States** The 48 contiguous States and the District of Columbia. —**continental United States** The District of Columbia and the 49 States on the continent of North America. Also *America, the States, United States:* abbr. *U.S.A., U.S., US.*

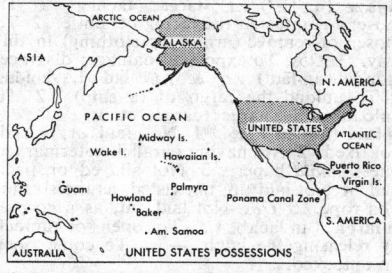

unit factor *Biol.* A gene controlling the inheritance of a unit character.

unit fraction See under FRACTION.

u·ni·tive (yōō′nə·tiv) *adj.* Productive of or promoting union; having power to unite; characterized by union.

u·ni·tize (yōō′nə·tīz) *v.t.* **·tized, ·tiz·ing** To form into a whole; unify.

unit modifier A conventional or improvised compound used adjectively before a substantive. Examples: *blue-green* algae, *bitter-sweet* chocolate, *suit-coat* pattern, *situation-comdey* plot, *storm-window* installation, *contour-plowing*

method, *most-favored-nation* clause. ◆The use of the hyphen in the unit modifier is to avoid ambiguity in a word sequence where the relationship is not immediately apparent from context: The house had faded red-brick walls (faded walls of red brick, *not* faded red walls of brick). The hyphen here is to be considered a nonce use and not as a spelling form or variant.

Unit rule *U.S.* A rule in a national convention of the Democratic party, requiring that, if so instructed by a State party convention, the vote of an entire delegation shall be determined by a majority of its members.

u·ni·ty (yōō′nə·tē) *n. pl.* **·ties 1** The state, property, or product of being united, physically, socially, or morally; oneness: opposed to *division, plurality.* **2** Union, as of constituent parts or elements: national *unity.* **3** Agreement of parts; harmonious adjustment of constituent elements; sameness of character: the *unity* of two writings. **4** The fact of something's being a whole that is more than or different from its parts or their sum. **5** Singleness of purpose or action. **6** A state of general good feeling; mutual understanding; concord: brethren dwelling together in *unity.* **7** *Math.* **a** The number one; the ratio of two equal quantities. **b** The element of a number system that leaves any number unchanged under multiplication, that is, a number e such that $ex = xe = x$ for all x. **8** In literature and the arts, combination into a homogeneous artistic whole, exhibiting oneness of purpose, thought, spirit, and style, with subordination of all parts to the general effect. **9** In the drama, observance, complete or partial, of the law of dramatic unities. **10** Identity. See synonyms under HARMONY, UNION. —**the law of dramatic unities** The law of Aristole that in a drama there must be unity of action, unity of time, and unity of place. These unities were strictly observed by the French classical dramatists of the 17th century, but were violated by Shakespeare and certain of the German playwrights. [< F *unité* < L *unitas* < *unus* one]

U·ni·ty (yōō′nə·tē) *n.* A religious philosophy, based on the teachings of Jesus Christ, stating that man is inseparable from the spirit of God within him, and that through prayerful realization of this spirit he can obtain healing of all life's inharmonies in mind, body, etc.: founded in 1889.

Unity of the Brethren See MORAVIAN.

u·ni·va·lent (yōō′nə·vā′lent) *adj.* **1** *Chem.* Having a valence or combining value of one; monovalent. **2** *Biol.* Pertaining to or designating a single unpaired chromosome. —**u·ni·va′lence, u′ni·va′len·cy** *n.*

u·ni·valve (yōō′nə·valv′) *adj.* Having only one valve, as a mollusk. Also **u′ni·val′vate, u′ni·valved′.** —*n.* **1** A mollusk having a univalve shell; a gastropod. **2** A shell of a single piece. —**u′ni·val′vu·lar** (-val′vyə·lər) *adj.*

u·ni·ver·sal (yōō′nə·vûr′səl) *adj.* **1** Prevalent or common everywhere or among all things or persons specified or implied: a *universal* belief; *universal* suffrage; a *universal* language. **2** Of or including everyone: a *universal* church. **3** Applicable to all cases: a *universal* law; a *universal* cure. **4** Accomplished or interested in a vast variety of subjects or activities: Leonardo da Vinci was a *universal* genius. **5** Of, pertaining to, or occuring throughout the universe: a *universal* being. **6** *Mech.* Adapted or adaptable to a great variety of uses, shapes, etc., as certain machines or machine parts. **7** *Logic* **a** Including all the

unpliant	unposted	unprimed	unpropitiable	unpunctual	unquenched	unreasoningly
unplighted	unpractical	unprincely	unpropitiated	unpunishable	unquestioning	unrebukable
unplowed	unpredictable	unprinted	unpropitious	unpunished	unquotable	unrebuked
unploughed	unpredictably	unprivileged	unproportionate	unpurchasable	unraised	unreceipted
unplucked	unpreoccupied	unprized	unproportioned	unpure	unransomed	unreceivable
unplugged	unprepossessing	unprobed	unproposed	unpurged	unrated	unreceived
unpoetic	unprescribed	unprocessed	unprosperous	unpurified	unratified	unreceptive
unpoetical	unpresentable	unprocurable	unprotected	unpurposed	unravaged	unreciprocated
unpointed	unpreserved	unprofaned	unproved	unpursuing	unrazored	unreclaimable
unpolarized	unpressed	unprofited	unproven	unpuzzle	unreachable	unreclaimed
unpolished	unpresumptuous	unprogressive	unprovoked	unquaffed	unreached	unrecognizable
unpolitical	unpretending	unprohibited	unprovoking	unqualifying	unreadable	unrecognized
unpolluted	unpretentious	unpromising	unpruned	unquelled	unrealizable	unrecommended
unpondered	unprevailing	unprompted	unpublished	unquenchable	unrealized	unrecompensed
unpopulated	unpreventable	unpronounced	unpucker		unreasoned	unreconcilable

add,āce,câre,pälm; end,ēven; it,īce; odd,ōpen,ôrder; tŏŏk,pōōl; up,bûrn; ə=a in *above*, e in *sicken*, i in *clarity*, o in *melon*, u in *focus*; yōō=u in *fuse*; oi,oil; ou,pout; ch,check; g,go; ng,ring; th,thin; ħ,this; zh,vision. Foreign sounds à,œ,ü,kh,ṅ; and ◆: see page xx. < from; + plus; ? possibly.

individuals of a class or genus; generic. **b** In a proposition, predicable of all the individuals denoted by the subject: opposed to particular: "All men are mortal" is a *universal* proposition. See synonyms under COMMON, GENERAL. —*n.* **1** *Logic* **a** A universal proposition. **b** One of the five predicables, that is, genus, species, difference, property, and accident, known collectively as the *universals.* **c** A general or abstract concept considered as having absolute reality or mental or nominal existence. **2** Any general or universal notion or idea. **3** A metaphysical being which preserves its identity in spite of the changes through which it passes, as the ego. [<OF <L *universalis* <*universus.* See UNIVERSE.] —**u'ni·ver'sal·ly** *adv.* —**u'ni·ver'sal·ness** *n.*

universal developer *Phot.* A developer adapted for use with various types of films, plates, or papers.

universal donor One whose blood belongs to group O and may be transfused with little or no danger of agglutination into a person belonging to any of the four blood groups.

U·ni·ver·sal·ism (yo͞o'nə·vûr'səl·iz'əm) *n. Theol.* The doctrine that all souls will finally be saved and that good will triumph universally.

U·ni·ver·sal·ist (yo͞o'nə·vûr'səl·ist) *adj.* Pertaining to Universalism or Universalists. —*n.* A believer in the doctrines of Universalism, or a member of the Universalist denomination.

u·ni·ver·sal·i·ty (yo͞o'nə·vər·sal'ə·tē) *n.* **1** The state of being all-embracing. **2** Unrestricted fitness or adaptability.

u·ni·ver·sal·ize (yo͞o'nə·vûr'səl·īz) *v.t.* **·ized, ·iz·ing** To make universal.

universal joint *Mech.* A joint that permits both connected parts of a machine to be turned in any direction within definite limits; specifically, a coupling for connecting two shafts, etc., so as to permit angular motion in all directions. Also **universal coupling.**

UNIVERSAL JOINT

u·ni·verse (yo͞o'nə·vûrs) *n.* **1** The aggregate of all existing things; the whole creation embracing all celestial bodies and all of space; the cosmos. **2** In restricted sense, the earth. **3** Human beings collectively; mankind. **4** *Logic* All objects, collectively, that are the subjects of consideration at once: also **universe of discourse. 5** *Stat.* All the instances in a given class: contrasted with *sample.* [<F *univers* <L *universum,* neut. of *universus* turned, combined into one, all collectively <*unus* one + *versus,* pp. of *vertere* turn]

u·ni·ver·si·ty (yo͞o'nə·vûr'sə·tē) *n. pl.* **·ties 1** An educational institution for higher instruction or for the examination of students already instructed. Universities arose in Europe in the Middle Ages and were first essentially ecclesiastic. Their functions gradually became specialized, some dividing into several *faculties,* each of which took charge of some one great branch of instruction, or into *colleges,* as now in the older English universities, where the relation of the university to the college is similar to that of a federal government to its component states. In the United States the word has been used loosely, chiefly to mean a collection of educational associations including a college (which offers degrees in general subjects) and several more advanced and specialized faculties, either professional, as law, medicine, etc., or academic, as history or mathematics. **2** All the students of such an institution. **3** *Brit. Colloq.* A university team or crew.

u·ni·ver·son (yo͞o'nə·vûr'son) *n. Physics* A hypothetical primordial entity originally containing the entire mass of the universe and whose splitting simultaneously gave rise to the cosmos and to its balanced opposite, the anticosmos. [<UNIVERSE]

u·niv·o·cal (yo͞o·niv'ə·kəl) *adj.* Having but one proper sense or meaning. —*n.* A word that has but one meaning. [<LL *univocus* <L *unus* one + *vox* voice]

un·just (un·just') *adj.* **1** Not legitimate, fair, or just; wrongful. **2** Unrighteous; acting contrary to right and justice. **3** *Archaic* Faithless. **4** *Archaic* Dishonest. —**un·just'ly** *adv.* —**un·just'ness** *n.*

un·kempt (un·kempt') *adj.* **1** Not combed; neglected; untidy. **2** Without polish; rough. [<UN-[1] + *kempt* combed, pp. of dial. *kemb,* var. of COMB] —**un·kempt'ness** *n.*

un·kenned (un·kend') *adj. Scot.* & *Brit. Dial.* Unknown. Also **un·kend', un·kent'** (-kent').

un·ken·nel (un·ken'əl) *v.t.* **1** To drive or release from a kennel or lair. **2** To bring to light; disclose.

un·kind (un·kīnd') *adj.* Showing lack of kindness; unsympathetic; harsh; cruel. [OE *uncynde* strange, unnatural] —**un·kind'ly** *adv.* —**un·kind'ness** *n.*

un·known (un·nōn') *adj.* **1** Not known; not apprehended mentally; not recognized, as a fact or person. **2** Not ascertained; incalculable. See synonyms under MYSTERIOUS, SECRET. —*n.* An unknown person or quantity. —**the Great Unknown** Life after death; future life.

Unknown Soldier One of the unidentified dead of World War I who is honored as a symbol of all his compatriots who died in action; extended to include unknown dead of World War II and the Korean conflict.

un·la·bored (un·lā'bərd) *adj.* **1** Produced without strain or effort; seemingly free and easy; natural. **2** Uncultivated by labor; unworked; untilled. Also *Brit.* **un·la'boured.**

un·lace (un·lās') *v.t.* **·laced, ·lac·ing 1** To loosen or unfasten the lacing of; untie. **2** To loosen or remove (armor or clothing) in this way. **3** *Obs.* To expose to damage; disgrace.

un·lade (un·lād') *v.t.* & *v.i.* **·lad·ed, ·lad·ing 1** To unload the cargo of (a ship). **2** To unload or discharge (cargo, etc.).

un·laid (un·lād') *adj.* **1** Not laid or placed; not fixed. **2** Not having parallel watermarked lines: *unlaid* paper. **3** Not allayed or pacified. **4** Not laid up; untwisted, as the strands of a rope. **5** *Obs.* Not laid out, as a corpse.

un·latch (un·lach') *v.t.* To open or unlock by releasing the latch. —*v.i.* To come open or unlocked.

un·law·ful (un·lô'fəl) *adj.* Contrary to or in violation of law; illegal; illicit; also, illegitimate. See synonyms under CRIMINAL. —**un·law'ful·ly** *adv.* —**un·law'ful·ness** *n.*

un·lay (un·lā') *v.t.* & *v.i.* **·laid, ·lay·ing** To untwist: said specifically of the strands of a rope. [<UN-[2] + LAY[1] (def. 21)]

un·lead (un·led') *v.t.* **1** To strip of lead. **2** *Printing* To remove the leads from between (lines of type matter).

un·lead·ed (un·led'id) *adj.* **1** Not supplied or weighted with lead. **2** *Printing* Having no leads between the lines; not spaced with leads.

un·learn (un·lûrn') *v.t.* **·learned** or **·learnt, ·learn·ing** To dismiss from the mind (something learned); forget.

un·learn·ed (un·lûr'nid) *adj.* **1** Not learned; not possessed of or characterized by learning; illiterate; ignorant; untaught. **2** Unworthy or unsuggestive of a scholar; not like the production of a learned man. **3** (un·lûrnd') Not acquired by learning or study. See synonyms under IGNORANT.

un·leash (un·lēsh') *v.t.* To set free from or as from a leash.

un·leav·ened (un·lev'ənd) *adj.* Not leavened: said specifically of the bread used at the feast of the Passover.

un·less (un·les') *conj.* **1** If it be not a fact that; supposing that . . . not; except that: *Unless* we persevere, we shall lose. **2** *Obs.* For fear that; lest. —*prep.* Save; except; excepting: with an implied verb: *Unless* a miracle, he'll not be back in time. See synonyms under BUT. [Earlier *onlesse (that)* in a less case <ON + LESS]

un·let·tered (un·let'ərd) *adj.* Not educated; not lettered; illiterate.

un·like (un·līk') *adj.* Having little or no resemblance; different. See synonyms under ALIEN, CONTRARY, HETEROGENEOUS. —*adv.* In another manner: with *to* expressed or implied. By the ellipsis of *to* it approaches prepositional use. [ME *unliche*] —**un·like'·ness** *n.*

un·like·ly (un·līk'lē) *adj.* **1** Improbable. **2** Not inviting or promising success. —*adv.* Improbably. —**un·like'li·ness, un·like'li·hood** *n.*

un·lim·ber (un·lim'bər) *v.t.* & *v.i.* To disconnect (a gun or caisson) from its limber; prepare for action.

un·lim·it·ed (un·lim'it·id) *adj.* **1** Having no limits in space, number, or time; unbounded; endless; unnumbered. **2** Not limited by restrictions; unconfined: *unlimited* authority. **3** Not limited by exceptions or qualifications; undefined. —**un·lim'it·ed·ly** *adv.* —**un·lim'it·ed·ness** *n.*

un·liq·ui·dat·ed (un·lik'wə·dā'tid) *adj.* **1** *Law* Unascertained as to amount; undetermined or not settled: *unliquidated* damages. **2** Not yet eliminated from the living: said of the survivors of attempted genocide.

un·list·ed (un·lis'tid) *adj.* Not listed; specifically, noting stocks quoted in the unlisted department of a stock exchange, but not admitted to dealings on the floor of the New York Stock Exchange.

un·live (un·liv') *v.t.* **·lived, ·liv·ing** To live so as to wipe out the effects of (a former period of life); undo by living; live down.

un·load (un·lōd') *v.t.* **1** To remove the load or cargo from. **2** To take off or discharge (cargo, etc.). **3** To relieve of something burdensome or oppressive. **4** To withdraw the charge of ammunition from. **5** *Colloq.* To dispose of, especially by selling in large quantities. —*v.i.* **6** To discharge freight, cargo, or other burden.

un·load·er (un·lō'dər) *n.* One who or that which unloads; specifically, a contrivance for unloading something, as hay or coal.

un·lock (un·lok') *v.t.* **1** To unfasten (something locked). **2** To open or undo; release. **3** To lay open; reveal or disclose. —*v.i.* **4** To become unlocked.

un·looked-for (un·lo͝okt'fôr') *adj.* Not anticipated; unexpected.

un·loose (un·lo͞os') *v.t.* **·loosed, ·loos·ing** To release from fastenings; set loose or free. See synonyms under RELEASE.

un·loos·en (un·lo͞o'sən) *v.t.* To loose; unloose.

un·love·ly (un·luv'lē) *adj.* Unattractive; disagreeable; ugly.

un·luck·y (un·luk'ē) *adj.* **·luck·i·er, ·luck·i·est 1** Not favored by luck; unfortunate. **2** Resulting in or attended by ill luck; causing misfortune; disastrous. **3** Ill-omened; inauspicious: an *unlucky* day. See synonyms under

unreconciled	**unrefreshed**	**unremedied**	**unrepaid**	**unreprieved**	**unrestrainable**	**unrhymed**
unrecorded	**unrefreshing**	**unremembered**	**unrepairable**	**unreprovable**	**unrestraint**	**unrhythmic**
unrecounted	**unregarded**	**unremittable**	**unrepaired**	**unrequested**	**unrestricted**	**unrhythmical**
unrecoverable	**unregistered**	**unremitted**	**unrepealed**	**unrequited**	**unretarded**	**unrighted**
unrecruited	**unregretted**	**unremorseful**	**unrepentant**	**unresented**	**unretentive**	**unrightful**
unrectified	**unregulated**	**unremovable**	**unrepented**	**unresigned**	**unretracted**	**unrimed**
unredeemed	**unrehearsed**	**unremoved**	**unrepenting**	**unresistant**	**unretrieved**	**unripened**
unredressed	**unrelated**	**unremunerated**	**unrepining**	**unresisted**	**unreturned**	**unrisen**
unreelable	**unrelatedness**	**unremunerative**	**unreplaced**	**unresisting**	**unrevealed**	**unroasted**
unrefined	**unrelaxed**	**unrendered**	**unreplenished**	**unresistingly**	**unrevenged**	**unrobe**
unreflected	**unrelaxing**	**unrenewed**	**unreported**	**unresolved**	**unreversed**	**unromantic**
unreflecting	**unrelievable**	**unrenounced**	**unrepresentative**	**unrespectable**	**unrevised**	**unromantically**
unreformable	**unrelieved**	**unrenowned**	**unrepresented**	**unrespectful**	**unrevoked**	**unroof**
unreformed	**unrelished**	**unrent**	**unrepressed**	**unrested**	**unrewarded**	**unrough**
unreformedness	**unremarked**	**unrented**	**unreprievable**	**unresting**	**unrhetorical**	**unruled**

BAD. **—un·luck′i·ly** adv. **—un·luck′i·ness** n.
un·make (un·māk′) v.t. **·made**, **·mak·ing** **1** To reverse the making of; reduce to the original condition or form. **2** To ruin; destroy. **3** To depose, as from a position of authority.
un·man (un·man′) v.t. **·manned**, **·man·ning** **1** To cause to lose courage or fortitude; dishearten. **2** To render unmanly or effeminate. **3** To deprive of virility; emasculate; castrate. **4** To remove the men from, as a ship or fortress.
un·man·ly (un·man′lē) adj. **1** Not masculine; effeminate; not virile; not courageous. **2** Not gentlemanly; not honorable. **—un·man′li·ness** n.
un·manned (un·mand′) adj. **1** Not manned. **2** Deprived of virility or manhood. **3** Obs. Unaccustomed to men; untamed: said of hawks. **4** Uninhabited.
un·man·ner·ly (un·man′ər·lē) adj. Lacking manners; rude. **—** adv. Impolitely. **—un·man′ner·li·ness** n.
un·marked (un·märkt′) adj. **1** Bearing no mark; having no distinctive mark. **2** Electr. Denoting that pole of a magnet which points south. **3** Not noticed. **4** Not examined; hence, uncorrected; ungraded: unmarked test papers.
un·mask (un·mask′, ·mäsk′) v.t. **1** To remove a mask from. **2** To reveal; disclose. **—** v.i. **3** To remove one's mask or disguise.
un·mean·ing (un·mē′ning) adj. **1** Having no meaning: an unmeaning speech or look. **2** Having no expression; not displaying intelligence. **—un·mean′ing·ly** adv. **—un·mean′ing·ness** n.
un·meet (un·mēt′) adj. Not meet, adapted, or suitable; not proper or fit; unbecoming. [OE unmǣte] **—un·meet′ly** adv. **—un·meet′·ness** n.
un·men·tion·a·ble (un·men′shən·ə·bəl) adj. Not proper to be mentioned or discussed; embarrassing; shameful; disgraceful. **—un·men′tion·a·ble·ness** n. **—un·men′tion·a·bly** adv.
un·men·tion·a·bles (un·men′shən·ə·bəlz) n. pl. Things or articles not ordinarily discussed or mentioned; usually, undergarments; formerly, trousers; pants.
un·mer·ci·ful (un·mûr′sə·fəl) adj. **1** Showing no mercy; cruel; pitiless; unconscionable. **2** Extreme; exorbitant. **—un·mer′ci·ful·ly** adv. **—un·mer′ci·ful·ness** n.
un·mew (un·myoo′) v.t. To release from confinement; set free.
un·mind·ful (un·mīnd′fəl) adj. Not keeping in mind; neglectful; inattentive. **—un·mind′ful·ly** adv. **—un·mind′ful·ness** n.
un·mis·tak·a·ble (un′mis·tā′kə·bəl) adj. That cannot be mistaken for something else; evident; clear; obvious. See synonyms under CLEAR, EVIDENT, MANIFEST. **—un′mis·tak′a·bly** adv.
un·mi·ter (un·mī′tər) v.t. To divest of a miter; deprive of the office of bishop. Also **un·mi′tre.**
un·mit·i·gat·ed (un·mit′ə·gā′tid) adj. **1** Not mitigated or lightened in effect; unabated; unassuaged: unmitigated sorrow. **2** As bad as can be; unconscionable: an unmitigated rogue. **—un·mit′i·gat′ed·ly** adv.
un·mod·u·lat·ed (un·moj′oo·lā′tid) adj. **1** Without modulation. **2** Telecom. Denoting a carrier wave of constant amplitude, as during a pause in broadcasting.
un·moor (un·moor′) Naut. v.t. **1** To loose the moorings of; release from moorings: to unmoor a ship. **2** To release all but one anchor of (a vessel formerly moored by two or more). **—** v.i. **3** To cast off moorings.

un·mor·al (un·môr′əl, ·mor′-) adj. Having no moral sense or relation; not pertaining to morality: distinguished from amoral and immoral. **—un·mo·ral·i·ty** (un′mə·ral′ə·tē) n.
un·mor·tise (un·môr′tis) v.t. **·tised**, **·tis·ing** **1** To loosen; loosen the mortised joints of. **2** To separate.
un·muf·fle (un·muf′əl) v. **·fled**, **·fling** v.t. **1** To take the covering from. **2** To remove the muffling of (a drum, oar, etc.). **—** v.i. **3** To remove that which muffles.
un·nat·u·ral (un·nach′ər·əl) adj. **1** Contrary to the laws of nature; opposed to what is natural. **2** Contrary to the common laws of morality or decency; monstrous; inhuman: unnatural crimes. **3** Destitute of natural feeling. **4** Not consistent with nature; artificial: unnatural acting. See synonyms under FACTITIOUS, IRREGULAR. **—un·nat′u·ral·ly** adv. **—un·nat′u·ral·ness** n.
un·nec·es·sary (un·nes′ə·ser′ē) adj. Not required; not necessary. **—un·nec′es·sar′i·ly** adv. **—un·nec′es·sar′i·ness** n.
un·nerve (un·nûrv′) v.t. **·nerved**, **·nerv·ing** To deprive of strength, firmness, self-control, or courage; unman. See synonyms under WEAKEN.
un·num·bered (un·num′bərd) adj. **1** Not counted. **2** Innumerable. **3** Not assigned a number; not marked with a number.
u·no an·i·mo (yoo′nō an′ə·mō) Latin With one mind; unanimously; in agreement.
un·oc·cu·pied (un·ok′yə·pīd) adj. **1** Empty; not dwelt in; uninhabited: an unoccupied house. **2** Idle; unemployed; not put to use: an unoccupied day.
un·of·fi·cial (un′ə·fish′əl) adj. **1** Not of an official character. **2** Not in an official capacity. **3** Not in the regular list of the pharmacopoeia.
un·or·gan·ized (un·ôr′gən·īzd) adj. **1** Not organized. **2** Not living; inorganic; structureless. **3** Not unionized. Also Brit. **un·or′gan·ised.**
un·o·rig·i·nal (un′ə·rij′ə·nəl) adj. Not original.
un·pack (un·pak′) v.t. **1** To open and take out the contents of. **2** To take out of the container, as something packed. **3** To remove a load or pack from; unload. **—** v.i. **4** To unpack a trunk, goods, etc.
un·paid (un·pād′) adj. **1** Not met or discharged, as a debt. **2** Not receiving pay; serving without pay. **3** Having wages remaining due.
un·paired (un·pârd′) adj. **1** Not paired; not forming one of a pair; not matched. **2** Anat. **a** Having no corresponding part in the opposite half of the body. **b** Situated in the median plane of the body.
un·par·al·leled (un·par′ə·leld) adj. Without parallel; unmatched; unprecedented.
un·par·lia·men·ta·ry (un′pär·lə·men′tər·ē) adj. Not parliamentary; contrary to the rules that govern deliberative or legislative bodies. **—un′par·lia·men′ta·ri·ly** adv. **—un′par·lia·men′ta·ri·ness** n.
un·peg (un·peg′) v.t. **·pegged**, **·peg·ging** To remove the peg or pegs from; unfasten.
un·peo·ple (un·pē′pəl) v.t. **·pled**, **·pling** To depopulate.
un·peo·pled (un·pē′pəld) adj. **1** Uninhabited. **2** Depopulated.
un·per·fo·rat·ed (un·pûr′fə·rā′tid) adj. **1** Not perforated. **2** In philately, imperforate.
un peu (œṅ pœ′) French A little; somewhat.
un·pick (un·pik′) v.t. **1** To undo by removing the stitches; also, to remove (stitches). **2** To open with a pick or picklock.

un·pin (un·pin′) v.t. **·pinned**, **·pin·ning** **1** To remove the pins from. **2** To unfasten by removing pins.
un·pleas·ant (un·plez′ənt) adj. Disagreeable; objectionable; not pleasing. **—un·pleas′ant·ly** adv.
un·pleas·ant·ness (un·plez′ənt·nis) n. **1** The quality, character, or condition of being unpleasant or disagreeable. **2** Any disagreeable experience or event; a disagreement or quarrel. **— the late unpleasantness** The American Civil War: now chiefly humorous; by extension, any recent war.
un·plumbed (un·plumd′) adj. **1** Not sounded; not explored fully; unfathomed. **2** Not furnished with plumbing.
un·poised (un·poizd′) adj. Not poised or balanced.
un·pol·i·cied (un·pol′ə·sēd) adj. **1** Having no established system of civil polity. **2** Obs. Unguided by reason or prudence; impolitic.
un·pol·i·tic (un·pol′ə·tik) adj. Impolitic.
un·polled (un·pōld′) adj. Not registered: an unpolled vote or voter; not having voted at an election.
un·pop·u·lar (un·pop′yə·lər) adj. Having no popularity; generally disliked or condemned. **—un·pop′u·lar·ly** adv. **—un·pop′u·lar′i·ty** (-lar′ə·tē) n.
un·prac·ticed (un·prak′tist) adj. **1** Being without practice; inexperienced. **2** Not carried out in practice; not used. **3** Not yet tried.
un·prec·e·dent·ed (un·pres′ə·den′tid) adj. Being without precedent; preceded by no similar case; unexampled. See synonyms under EXTRAORDINARY. **—un·prec′e·dent′ed·ly** adv.
un·prej·u·diced (un·prej′oo·dist) adj. **1** Free from prejudice or bias; impartial. **2** Not impaired, as a right. See synonyms under CANDID.
un·pre·med·i·tat·ed (un′pri·med′ə·tā′tid) adj. **1** Not planned beforehand; undesigned: unpremeditated assault. **2** Not previously considered or thought of. **—un′pre·med′i·tat′ed·ly** adv. **— un′pre·med′i·ta′tion** n.
un·pre·pared (un′pri·pârd′) adj. **1** Having made no preparations: an unprepared student. **2** Not brought into a state of preparation; not yet ready: Dinner is still unprepared. **3** Done or carried out without preparation; impromptu: an unprepared speech. **—un·pre·par′ed·ly** (un′pri·pâr′id·lē) adv. **—un′pre·par′ed·ness** n.
un·priced (un·prīst′) adj. **1** Having no fixed price. **2** Priceless.
un·prin·ci·pled (un·prin′sə·pəld) adj. Destitute of conscientious scruples; unscrupulous; wicked. See synonyms under BAD, IMMORAL. **—un·prin′ci·pled·ness** n.
un·print·a·ble (un·prin′tə·bəl) adj. Not fit to be printed.
un·priz·a·ble (un·prī′zə·bəl) adj. Obs. **1** Of worth beyond estimation; invaluable. **2** Not prized; valueless.
un·pro·duc·tive (un′prə·duk′tiv) adj. **1** Producing little or nothing; barren, literally or figuratively. **2** Econ. Not adding to exchangeable value: unproductive labor. **—un′pro·duc′tive·ly** adv. **—un′pro·duc′tive·ness** n.
un·pro·fes·sion·al (un′prə·fesh′ən·əl) adj. **1** Having no profession; also, lay; amateur. **2** Violating the rules or ethical code of a profession; not up to the standard of a profession: unprofessional work. **—un′pro·fes′sion·al·ly** adv.
un·prof·it·a·ble (un·prof′it·ə·bəl) adj. Productive of no profit; serving no desirable purpose; fruitless; futile: unprofitable conversation; an

unsafe	unsatiating	unscholarlike	unseconded	unsew	unshorn	unsized
unsafely	unsatisfactory	unscholarly	unsectarian	unsewn	unshrinkable	unskeptical
unsaintly	unsatisfied	unschooled	unsecured	unsexual	unshrinking	unslacked
unsalability,	unsatisfying	unscientific	unseeing	unshaded	unshriven	unslaked
unsaleability	unsaved	unscorched	unsegmented	unshakable	unshrouded	unsleeping
unsalable,	unsawed	unscorned	unselected	unshaken	unshrunk	unslumbering
unsaleable	unsawn	unscoured	unselective	unshamed	unshunned	unsmiling
unsalaried	unsayable	unscourged	unselfish	unshapely	unshut	unsmirched
unsalted	unscabbarded	unscratched	unselfishly	unshared	unsifted	unsmoked
unsanctified	unscaled	unscreened	unsent	unshaved	unsigned	unsoaked
unsanctioned	unscanned	unscriptural	unsentimental	unshaven	unsilenced	unsober
unsanitary	unscarred	unsculptured	unserved	unshed	unsimilar	unsocial
unsated	unscented	unsealed	unserviceable	unshelled	unsingable	unsoiled
unsatiable	unsceptical	unseaworthiness	unserviceably	unsheltered	unsinkable	unsold
unsatiated	unscheduled	unseaworthy	unset	unshod	unsisterly	unsoldierlike

add,āce,câre,pälm; end,ēven; it,īce; odd,ōpen,ôrder; took,pool; up,bûrn; ə = a in above, e in sicken, i in clarity, o in melon, u in focus; yoo = u in fuse; oi,oil; ou,pout; ch,check; g,go; ng,ring; th,thin; ŧħ,this; zh,vision. Foreign sounds á,œ,ü,kh,ṅ; and ◆: see page xx. < from; + plus; ? possibly.

unprofitable transaction. — **un·prof'it·a·ble·ness** *n.* — **un·prof'it·a·bly** *adv.*

un·pro·nounce·a·ble (un'prə-noun'sə-bəl) *adj.* 1 Not easy to pronounce, especially properly. 2 Not fit to be mentioned.

un·pro·vid·ed (un'prə-vī'did) *adj.* 1 Not furnished or provided: with *with*, formerly with *of*: to be *unprovided* with suitable raiment. 2 Not fittingly prepared; not ready: *unprovided* for a sudden change. — **un·pro·vid'ed·ly** *adv.*

un·qual·i·fied (un-kwol'ə-fīd) *adj.* 1 Being without the proper qualifications; unfit. 2 Having failed to qualify; lacking legal power or authority. 3 Without limitation or restrictions; absolute; entire: *unqualified* approval. — **un·qual'i·fied'ly** *adv.* — **un·qual'i·fied'ness** *n.*

un·ques·tion·a·ble (un-kwes'chən·ə-bəl) *adj.* Too certain or sure to admit of question; being beyond a doubt; indisputable. See synonyms under INCONTESTABLE, NOTORIOUS. — **un·ques'tion·a·bly** *adv.*

un·ques·tioned (un-kwes'chənd) *adj.* 1 Not called in question; undoubted. 2 Not to be frustrated or opposed; indisputable. 3 Not interrogated.

un·qui·et (un-kwī'ət) *adj.* 1 Not at rest; disturbed; restless, in mind or physically. 2 Causing unrest or discomfort. — **un·qui'et·ly** *adv.* — **un·qui'et·ness** *n.*

un·quote (un-kwōt') *v.t.* & *v.i.* ·quot·ed, ·quot·ing To close (a quotation).

un·rav·el (un-rav'əl) *v.* ·eled or ·elled, ·el·ing or ·el·ling *v.t.* 1 To separate the threads of, as a tangled skein or knitted article. 2 To free from entanglement; unfold; explain, as a mystery or a plot. — *v.i.* 3 To become unraveled. See synonyms under INTERPRET.

un·read (un-red') *adj.* 1 Not informed by reading; ignorant. 2 Not yet perused.

un·read·y (un-red'ē) *adj.* 1 Being without readiness or alertness; not apt or quick to see or appreciate. 2 Not in a condition to act effectively; unprepared. — **un·read'i·ly** *adv.* — **un·read'i·ness** *n.*

un·re·al (un-rē'əl, -rēl') *adj.* Having no reality, actual existence, or substance; having no genuineness; insincere; artificial; also, fanciful; visionary. — **un·re·al·i·ty** (un'rē-al'ə·tē) *n.* — **un·re'al·ly** *adv.*

un·rea·son (un-rē'zən) *n.* Lack or absence of reason; irrationality; also, absurdity; nonsense.

un·rea·son·a·ble (un-rē'zən·ə-bəl) *adj.* 1 Acting without or contrary to reason. 2 Not according to reason; irrational. 3 Exceeding what is reasonable; immoderate; exorbitant. See synonyms under ABSURD, IMMODERATE. — **un·rea'son·a·ble·ness** *n.* — **un·rea'son·a·bly** *adv.*

un·rea·son·ing (un-rē'zən·ing) *adj.* So intolerant, or so unaccompanied by reason or control, as to be obstinate, blind, or wild.

un·reck·on·a·ble (un-rek'ən·ə-bəl) *adj.* That cannot be reckoned or computed; unlimited.

un·reel (un-rēl') *v.t.* & *v.i.* To unwind, as from a reel.

un·reeve (un-rēv') *v.* ·reeved or ·rove (*for pp. also* ·rov·en), ·reev·ing *Naut. v.t.* 1 To take out or withdraw (a rope) from a block, thimble, deadeye, etc. — *v.i.* 2 To become unreeved. 3 To unreeve a rope.

un·re·flec·tive (un'ri·flek'tiv) *adj.* Not given to reflection; not thoughtful.

un·re·gen·er·ate (un'ri·jen'ər·it) *adj.* Not having been changed spiritually by regeneration; remaining unreconciled to God; loosely, sinful. Also **un're·gen'er·at'ed** (-ā'tid). — **un're·gen'er·a·cy** (-ə·sē) *n.* — **un're·gen'er·ate·ly** *adv.*

un·re·lent·ing (un'ri·len'ting) *adj.* 1 Continuing to be severe; pitiless; inexorable. 2 Not diminishing, or not changing, in pace, effort, speed, etc. — **un're·lent'ing·ly** *adv.*

un·re·li·a·ble (un'ri·lī'ə-bəl) *adj.* That cannot be relied upon; not dependable. — **un're·li'·a·bil'i·ty, un're·li·a·ble·ness** *n.* — **un're·li'a·bly** *adv.*

un·re·lig·ious (un'ri·lij'əs) *adj.* 1 Irreligious; hostile to religion. 2 Having no religion; not connected with religion.

un·re·mit·ting (un'ri·mit'ing) *adj.* Incessant; not relaxing. — **un're·mit'ting·ly** *adv.* — **un're·mit'ting·ness** *n.*

un·re·proved (un'ri·prōōvd') *adj.* 1 Not censured or blamed; not reproved. 2 Not liable to reproof; above reproach.

un·re·serve (un'ri·zûrv') *n.* Absence of reserve; freedom of style or manner.

un·re·served (un'ri·zûrvd') *adj.* 1 Given or done without reserve. 2 Having no reserve of manner; informal; open; frank. See synonyms under CANDID, IMPLICIT. — **un're·serv·ed·ly** (un'ri·zûr'vid·lē) *adv.* — **un're·serv'ed·ness** *n.*

un·re·spec·tive (un'ri·spek'tiv) *adj. Obs.* 1 Undiscriminating. 2 Inattentive; heedless. 3 Common; not restricted.

un·res·pit·ed (un-res'pit·id) *adj.* 1 Not postponed; not respited, as from a sentence of the law. 2 *Obs.* Having no intermission.

un·re·spon·sive (un'ri·spon'siv) *adj.* Showing no reaction or response; unsympathetic. — **un're·spon'sive·ly** *adv.* — **un're·spon'sive·ness** *n.*

un·rest (un-rest') *n.* 1 Restlessness, especially of the mind. 2 Trouble; turmoil: used with regard to public or political conditions and suggesting premonitions of revolt.

un·re·strained (un'ri·strānd') *adj.* Not restrained; free; not controlled. — **un·re·strain·ed·ly** (un'ri·strā'nid·lē) *adv.*

un·rid·dle (un-rid'l) *v.t.* ·dled, ·dling To solve, as a mystery.

un·ri·fled[1] (un·rī'fəld) *adj.* Smooth-bored, as a gun.

un·ri·fled[2] (un·rī'fəld) *adj.* Not rifled, seized, or plundered.

un·rig (un-rig') *v.t.* ·rigged, ·rig·ging *Naut.* To strip of rigging.

un·right·eous (un·rī'chəs) *adj.* 1 Not righteous; wicked; sinful. 2 Contrary to the law of right; unjust. See synonyms under SINFUL. — **un·right'eous·ly** *adv.* — **un·right'eous·ness** *n.*

un·rip (un-rip') *v.t.* ·ripped, ·rip·ping To separate by ripping; rip or cut open.

un·ripe (un-rīp') *adj.* 1 Not arrived at maturity; not ripe; immature. 2 Premature. 3 Not ready; not prepared. [OE, *untimely*] — **un·ripe'ness** *n.*

un·ri·valed (un·rī'vəld) *adj.* Having no rival or competitor; unequaled; matchless. Also **un·ri'valled.**

un·roll (un-rōl') *v.t.* 1 To spread or open (something rolled up). 2 To exhibit to view. 3 *Rare* To remove from a roll or register. — *v.i.* 4 To become unrolled.

un·root (un-rōōt', -rŏŏt') *v.t.* To uproot.

un·ruf·fled (un-ruf'əld) *adj.* 1 Not disturbed or agitated emotionally; calm. 2 Not ruffled or made rough physically.

un·ru·ly (un-rōō'lē) *adj.* Disposed to resist rule or discipline; intractable; ungovernable. See synonyms under RESTIVE. — **un·ru'li·ness** *n.*

un·sad·dle (un-sad'l) *v.t.* ·dled, ·dling 1 To remove a saddle from. 2 To remove from the saddle; unhorse.

un·said (un-sed') *adj.* Not said; not spoken.

un·sat·u·rat·ed (un-sach'ə-rā'tid) *adj.* 1 Falling short of saturation, as a solution. 2 *Chem.* Not combined to the greatest possible extent; capable of uniting with certain other elements or compounds to form additional compounds.

un·sa·vor·y (un-sā'vər·ē) *adj.* 1 Having a disagreeable taste or odor. 2 Suggesting something disagreeable, offensive, or unclean;

also, morally bad: an *unsavory* reputation. 3 *Obs.* Having no savor; tasteless; odorless. Also *Brit.* **un·sa'vour·y.** — **un·sa'vor·i·ly** *adv.* — **un·sa'vor·i·ness** *n.*

un·say (un-sā') *v.t.* ·said, ·say·ing To retract (something said).

un·scathed (un-skāthd') *adj.* Uninjured.

un·scram·ble (un-skram'bəl) *v.t.* ·bled, ·bling *Colloq.* To resolve the confused, scrambled, or disordered condition of.

un·screw (un-skrōō') *v.t.* 1 To remove the screw or screws from. 2 To remove or detach by withdrawing screws, or by turning. — *v.i.* 3 To permit of being unscrewed.

un·scru·pu·lous (un-skrōō'pyə-ləs) *adj.* Not scrupulous; having no scruples; unprincipled. — **un·scru'pu·lous·ly** *adv.* — **un·scru'pu·lous·ness** *n.*

un·seal (un-sēl') *v.t.* 1 To break or remove the seal of. 2 To open (that which has been sealed or closed).

un·seam (un-sēm') *v.t.* To open the seam or seams of.

un·search·a·ble (un-sûr'chə-bəl) *adj.* That cannot be searched or explored; hidden; mysterious. — **un·search'a·bly** *adv.*

un·sea·son·a·ble (un-sē'zən·ə-bəl) *adj.* Not being in the proper season or not being in time; inappropriate; ill-timed. — **un·sea'son·a·ble·ness** *n.* — **un·sea'son·a·bly** *adv.*

un·sea·soned (un-sē'zənd) *adj.* 1 Not seasoned; not flavored. 2 Immature; unripe; not properly aged. 3 Not habituated. — **un·sea'soned·ness** *n.*

un·seat (un-sēt') *v.t.* 1 To remove from a seat or fixed position. 2 To unhorse. 3 To deprive of office or rank; depose.

un·seem·ly (un-sēm'lē) *adj.* ·li·er, ·li·est Unbecoming; indecent; not handsome. — *adv.* In an unseemly fashion. — **un·seem'li·ness** *n.*

un·seen (un-sēn') *adj.* Not seen; not evident; invisible; not previously seen or prepared, as a passage for translation.

un·set·tle (un-set'l) *v.* ·tled, ·tling *v.t.* 1 To move from a fixed or settled condition. 2 To confuse; disturb. — *v.i.* 3 To become unsteady or unfixed. See synonyms under DISPLACE.

un·sex (un-seks') *v.t.* 1 To deprive of the distinctive qualities of a sex; especially, to render unfeminine or unwomanly. 2 To castrate.

un·shack·le (un-shak'əl) *v.t.* ·led, ·ling To unfetter; free from shackles. — **un·shack'led** *adj.*

un·shap·en (un-shā'pən) *adj.* Not shaped; imperfectly or badly shaped. Also **un·shaped'.**

un·sheathe (un-shēth') *v.t.* ·sheathed, ·sheath·ing To take from or as from a scabbard or sheath; bare.

un·ship (un-ship') *v.t.* ·shipped, ·ship·ping 1 To unload from a ship or other vessel; also, to dismiss from a ship. 2 To remove from the place where it is fixed or fitted, as a rudder or oar.

un·sick·er (un-sik'ər) *adj. Scot.* Insecure; unreliable; undependable. — **un·sick'er·ly** *adv.* — **un·sick'er·ness** *n.*

un·sight·ed (un-sī'tid) *adj.* 1 Not sighted; not in view. 2 Having no sight, as a cannon. 3 Not aimed with the assistance of a sight, as a shot.

un·sight·ly (un-sīt'lē) *adj.* ·li·er, ·li·est Offensive to the sight; ugly. — **un·sight'li·ness** *n.*

unsight unseen Sight unseen: former usage.

un·skaithed (un-skāthd') *adj. Scot.* Unscathed.

un·skil·ful (un-skil'fəl) *adj.* 1 Lacking or not evincing skilfulness; awkward. 2 *Obs.* Lacking in discernment; ignorant. Also **un·skill'ful.** — **un·skil'ful·ly** *adv.* — **un·skil'ful·ness** *n.*

unsoldierly	unspeculative	unsquandered	unsterilized	unsuggestive	unsustained	untalented
unsolicited	unspelled	unsquared	unstick	unsuited	unswayed	untalked-of
unsolicitous	unspent	unstack	unstigmatized	unsullied	unsweetened	untamable,
unsolid	unspilled	unstainable	unstinted	unsunk	unswept	untameable
unsoluble	unspilt	unstained	unstitched	unsunned	unswerving	untame
unsolvable	unspiritual	unstamped	unstrained	unsupportable	unsworn	untamed
unsolved	unspirituality	unstandardized	unstressed	unsupported	unsymmetrical	untangled
unsophistication	unspiritually	unstarched	unstripped	unsupportedly	unsympathetic	untanned
unsorted	unspiritualness	unstarred	unstuffed	unsuppressed	unsympathizing	untapped
unsought	unspoiled	unstatesmanlike	unstung	unsure	unsystematic	untarnished
unsounded	unspoilt	unsteadfast	unsubdued	unsurmountable	unsystematized	untasted
unsoured	unspoken	unsteadily	unsubmissive	unsurpassable	untack	untaxable
unsowed	unsportsmanlike	unsteadiness	unsubscribed	unsurpassed	untactful	untaxed
unsown	unsprinkled	unsteady	unsubstantiated	unsusceptible	untainted	unteachable
unspecified	unsprung	unstemmed	unsuccess	unsuspicious	untaken	untechnical

un·skilled (un·skild′) *adj.* **1** Destitute of skill or dexterity in artisan's work; good only for common labor: an *unskilled* workman. **2** Produced without or not requiring special skill or training; untrained. **3** Destitute of practical knowledge; unskilful.

un·sling (un·sling′) *v.t.* **·slung, ·sling·ing** **1** To remove, as a rifle, from a slung position. **2** *Naut.* To take the slings from.

un·snap (un·snap′) *v.t.* **·snapped, ·snap·ping** To undo the snap or snaps of; unfasten.

un·snarl (un·snärl′) *v.t.* To disentangle.

un·so·cia·ble (un·sō′shə·bəl) *adj.* **1** Not sociable; not inclined to seek the society of others. **2** Not congenial or in accord: an *unsociable* group. **3** Not encouraging social intercourse. **— un·so′cia·bil′i·ty, un·so′cia·ble·ness** *n.* **— un·so′cia·bly** *adv.*

un·sol·der (un·sod′ər) *v.t.* **1** To disunite or take apart (something soldered). **2** To separate; sunder.

un·son·sie (un·son′sē) *adj. Scot.* Unlucky; disagreeable. Also **un·son′cy, un·son′sy.**

un·so·phis·ti·cat·ed (un′sə·fis′tə·kā′tid) *adj.* **1** Not sophisticated; showing inexperience or naiveté; artless; simple. **2** Free from adulteration; genuine; pure. See synonyms under CANDID, RUSTIC. **— un′so·phis′ti·cat′ed·ly** *adv.* **— un′so·phis′ti·cat′ed·ness** *n.*

un·sound (un·sound′) *adj.* **1** Lacking in soundness; not having material strength and solidity; weak; rotten. **2** Not sound in health; diseased. **3** Not logically valid; erroneous; in religion, heterodox. **4** Disturbed; not profound: said of sleep. **— un·sound′ly** *adv.* **— un·sound′ness** *n.*

un·spar·ing (un·spâr′ing) *adj.* **1** Not sparing or saving; lavish; liberal. **2** Showing no mercy. **— un·spar′ing·ly** *adv.* **— un·spar′ing·ness** *n.*

un·speak (un·spēk′) *v.t.* **·spoke, ·spo·ken, ·speak·ing** To retract (something said); take back.

un·speak·a·ble (un·spē′kə·bəl) *adj.* **1** That cannot be expressed; unutterable: *unspeakable* joy. **2** Extremely bad or objectionable: an *unspeakable* crime. **3** Mute. **— un·speak′a·ble·ness** *n.* **— un·speak′a·bly** *adv.*

un·spe·cial·ized (un·spesh′əl·īzd) *adj.* **1** Not specialized. **2** *Biol.* Not set apart for a special function or purpose; generalized. Also *Brit.* **un·spe′cial·ised.**

un·sphere (un·sfir′) *v.t.* **·sphered, ·spher·ing** To take out of its sphere or place.

un·spot·ted (un·spot′id) *adj.* **1** Not marked or marred with spots. **2** Not morally tainted; immaculate; free from blemishes; perfect. **3** Ceremonially clean. See synonyms under PURE. **— un·spot′ted·ness** *n.*

un·sprung weight (un·sprung′) In automobiles, the weight of components not supported by the suspension, as the wheel assemblies: opposed to *sprung weight.*

un·sta·ble (un·stā′bəl) *adj.* **1** Lacking in stability or firmness; not stable. **2** Having no fixed purposes; easily influenced; inconstant: an *unstable* character. **3** *Chem.* Readily decomposable, as certain compounds. **4** Subject to a radical change by the application of a slight force: *unstable* equilibrium. See FICKLE, PRECARIOUS. **— un·sta′ble·ness** *n.* **— un·sta′bly** *adv.*

un·state (un·stāt′) *v.t.* **·stat·ed, ·stat·ing** **1** To divest of statehood. **2** To deprive of dignity, rank, or office.

un·steel (un·stēl′) *v.t.* To deprive of steel–like quality; disarm; soften.

un·step (un·step′) *v.t.* **·stepped, ·step·ping** To take out of a step or socket: to *unstep* a mast.

un·stop (un·stop′) *v.t.* **·stopped, ·stop·ping** **1** To remove a stop or stopper from. **2** To open by removing obstructions; clear. **3** To open the stops of (an organ).

un·stopped (un·stopt′) *adj.* **1** Not stopped; unobstructed. **2** *Phonet.* Of consonants, not stopped; capable of being prolonged: said of the continuants, as (z) and (l).

un·stowed (un·stōd′) *adj.* **1** Not stowed or filled, as a ship, with cargo. **2** Lying loose in the hold or on deck, as cargo

un·strap (un·strap′) *v.t.* **·strapped, ·strap·ping** To unfasten or loosen the strap or straps of.

un·strat·i·fied (un·strat′ə·fīd) *adj. Geol.* Not deposited in beds or strata, as igneous rocks.

un·stri·at·ed (un·strī′ā·tid) *adj.* Without striations; smooth–textured, as certain muscles.

un·string (un·string′) *v.t.* **·strung, ·string·ing** **1** To remove from a string, as pearls. **2** To take the string or strings from. **3** To loosen the string or strings of, as a bow or guitar. **4** To relax, as if by loosening; weaken: usually in the passive: Her nerves were *unstrung.*

un·striped (un·strīpt′) *adj.* **1** Not striped; unstriated. **2** *Anat.* Denoting certain muscles that act independently of the will, as the heart muscles. See under MUSCLE.

un·strung (un·strung′) *adj.* **1** Having the strings removed or relaxed. **2** Unnerved; emotionally upset; weakened; relaxed.

un·stud·ied (un·stud′ēd) *adj.* **1** Not planned; unpremeditated. **2** Not stiff or artificial; natural. **3** Not acquainted through study; unversed: with *in.* See synonyms under SIMPLE.

un·sub·stan·tial (un′səb·stan′shəl) *adj.* **1** Lacking solidity, strength, or weight. **2** Having no valid basis. **3** Having no bodily existence; fanciful. **— un′sub·stan′tial·ly** *adv.* **— un′sub·stan′ti·al′i·ty** (-shē·al′ə·tē) *n.*

un·suc·cess·ful (un′sək·ses′fəl) *adj.* Having or meeting with no success: said of persons or their acts: *unsuccessful* in business, an *unsuccessful* attempt. **— un′suc·cess′ful·ly** *adv.* **— un′suc·cess′ful·ness** *n.*

un·suit·a·ble (un·sōō′tə·bəl) *adj.* Not suitable; unfitting. **— un·suit·a·bil·i·ty** (un′sōō·tə·bil′ə·tē), **un·suit′a·ble·ness** *n.* **— un·suit′a·bly** *adv.*

un·sung (un·sung′) *adj.* **1** Not celebrated in song or poetry; obscure. **2** Not yet sung, as a song.

un·sus·pect·ed (un′sə·spek′tid) *adj.* **1** Not suspected, as of evil; not under suspicion. **2** Not imagined or known to exist.

un·sus·pect·ing (un′sə·spek′ting) *adj.* Having no suspicion; trusting.

un·swathe (un·swāth′) *v.t.* **·swathed, ·swath·ing** To remove swathings from; free from swathings.

un·swear (un·swâr′) *v.t.* **·swore, ·sworn, ·swear·ing** To revoke (an oath); retract; abjure.

un·tan·gle (un·tang′gəl) *v.t.* **·gled, ·gling** To free from entanglement or embarrassment; resolve.

un·taught (un·tôt′) *adj.* Not having been instructed; ignorant.

un·teach (un·tēch′) *v.t.* **·taught, ·teach·ing** **1** To cause to forget or to disbelieve what has been taught. **2** To cause to be forgotten or disbelieved.

un·ten·a·ble (un·ten′ə·bəl) *adj.* **1** That cannot be maintained: *untenable* theories. **2** Incapable of being defended or held, as a fortress. **— un·ten′a·ble·ness** *n.*

un·tent·ed (un·ten′tid) *adj.* **1** Having no tents. **2** *Obs.* Not kept open or dressed, as a wound.

Un·ter den Lin·den (ōōn′tər den lin′dən) A famous avenue in East Berlin; literally, under the lindens.

Un·ter·wal·den (ōōn′tər·väl′dən) A canton of central Switzerland; 296 square miles.

un·thanked (un·thangkt′) *adj.* **1** Not thanked. **2** *Obs.* Not received with thankfulness.

un·thank·ful (un·thangk′fəl) *adj.* **1** Not grateful. **2** Not received with thanks; unwelcome. **— un·thank′ful·ly** *adv.* **— un·thank′ful·ness** *n.*

un·think (un·thingk′) *v.t.* **·thought, ·think·ing** To retract in thought; change the mind concerning.

un·think·ing (un·thingk′ing) *adj.* **1** Not having the power of thought. **2** Lacking thoughtfulness, care, or attention; heedless; inconsiderate. See synonyms under IMPRUDENT. **— un·think′ing·ly** *adv.* **— un·think′ing·ness** *n.*

un·thread (un·thred′) *v.t.* **1** To remove the thread from, as a needle. **2** To find one's way out of, as a maze.

un·ti·dy (un·tī′dē) *adj.* **·di·er, ·di·est** Showing or characterized by lack of tidiness. [ME *untidi*] **— un·ti′di·ly** *adv.* **— un·ti′di·ness** *n.*

un·tie (un·tī′) *v.* **·tied, ·ty·ing** *v.t.* **1** To loosen or undo, as a knot or knotted rope. **2** To free from that which binds or restrains. *— v.i.* **3** To become untied. See synonyms under RELEASE. [OE *untīgan*] **— un·tied′** *adj.*

un·til (un·til′) *prep.* **1** Up to the time of; till: We will wait *until* midnight. **2** Before: used with a negative: The music doesn't begin *until* nine. **3** *Scot.* & *Brit. Dial.* Unto. *— conj.* **1** To the time when: *until* I die. **2** To the place or degree that: Walk east *until* you reach the river. **3** Before: with a negative: He couldn't leave *until* the car came for him. [ME *untill* < *und-* up to, as far as + TILL]

un·time·ly (un·tīm′lē) *adj.* Coming before time or not in proper time; unseasonable; ill–timed: also *Scot.* **un·time′ous.** *— adv.* Before the proper time; inopportunely.

un·ti·tled (un·tīt′ld) *adj.* **1** Having no right (to a throne). **2** Having no title, as a book. **3** Having no title of distinction: *untitled* nobility.

un·to (un′tōō) *prep.* **1** *Poetic* & *Archaic* To: used in all senses except to indicate the infinitive. **2** *Archaic* Until. *— conj. Obs.* Up to the extent or time that; until. [ME *un-, und-* up to, as far as + TO, on analogy with *until*]

un·told (un·tōld′) *adj.* **1** That cannot be told, revealed, or described; inexpressible: *untold* misery. **2** That cannot be numbered or estimated; hence, of great number or extent: *untold* numbers; *untold* treasure. **3** Not told.

un·touch·a·bil·i·ty (un′tuch·ə·bil′ə·tē) *n.* The character or state of being untouchable.

un·touch·a·ble (un·tuch′ə·bəl) *adj.* **1** Inaccessible to the touch; out of reach; intangible; unrivaled; unapproachable. **2** Forbidden to the touch. **3** Unpleasant, disgusting, vile, or dangerous to touch; that should not be touched. *— n.* In India, a member of the lowest caste; one whose touch was formerly counted as pollution by Hindus of higher station.

un·to·ward (un·tôrd′, -tōrd′) *adj.* **1** Causing annoyance or hindrance; vexatious. **2** Not yielding readily; refractory; perverse. **3** *Obs.* Uncouth; ungraceful. See synonyms under PERVERSE. **— un·to′ward·ly** *adv.* **— un·to′ward·ness** *n.*

un·trav·eled (un·trav′əld) *adj.* **1** Not passed over, as a road. **2** Not having traveled; hence, narrow in ideas; provincial. Also **un·trav′elled.**

un·tread (un·tred′) *v.t.* **·trod, ·trod·den** or **·trod, ·tread·ing** To retrace.

un·tried (un·trīd′) *adj.* **1** Not tried or tested. **2** Not tried in court.

un·trimmed (un·trimd′) *adj.* **1** Not adorned

untempered
untenanted
untended
unterrified
untested
untether
unthatched
untheatrical
unthinkable
unthoughtful
unthought–of
unthrift
unthriftiness
unthrifty
unthrone
untillable
untilled
untinged
untired
untiring
untouched
untraceable
untraced
untracked
untractable
untrained
untrammeled,
untrammelled
untransferable
untransferred
untranslatable
untranslated
untransmitted
untrapped
untraversable
untraversed
untreasured
untrim
untroubled
untrustiness
untrusty
untuck
untufted
untunable
untuned
untuneful
unturned
untwilled
untwisted
untypical
un–uniformed
un–uniformly
un–united
unurged
unusable
unutilizable
unutilized
unuttered
unvaccinated
unvacillating
unvail
unvalidated
unvanquished
unvaried
unvarying
unveiled
unventilated
unveracious
unverifiable
unverified
unversed
unvexed
unvext
unvisited
unvitiated
unvitrified
unvocal
unvolatilized
unvulcanized
unwakened
unwalled
unwanted
unwarlike
unwarmed
unwarned
unwashed
unwasted
unwasting
unwatched
unwavering
unweakened
unweaned
unwearable
unweary
unwearying
unweathered
unweave
unwed
unwedded
unweeded
unwelded
unwetted
unwhetted
unwhipped
unwhipt

add,āce,câre,pälm; end, ēven; it,īce; odd,ōpen,ôrder; tŏŏk,pōōl; up,bûrn; ə = a in *above,* e in *sicken,* i in *clarity,* o in *melon,* u in *focus*; yōō = u in *fuse*; oi,oil; ou,pout; ch,check; g,go; ng,ring; th,thin; t͟h,this; zh,vision. Foreign sounds á,œ,ü,kh,ṅ; and ◆: see page xx. < from; + plus; ? possibly.

with trimmings: an *untrimmed* hat. **2** Not made trim or orderly; not clipped or pruned: an *untrimmed* tree. **3** *Obs.* Virgin.

un·trod·den (un·trod′n) *adj.* Not having been trodden upon; hence, unfrequented. Also **un·trod′.**

un·true (un·trōō′) *adj.* **1** Lacking truth; not true; not corresponding with fact. **2** Not conforming to rule or standard. **3** Not adhering to faith, pledge, or duty; disloyal. See synonyms under BAD, PERFIDIOUS. **— un·tru′ly** *adv.*

un·truss (un·trus′) *v.t.* **1** To loosen or free from or as from a truss; unfasten; undo. **2** *Obs.* To take off (breeches); undress.

un·trust·ful (un·trust′fəl) *adj.* **1** Not trusting or trustful. **2** Not to be trusted; untrustworthy.

un·trust·wor·thy (un·trust′wûr′thē) *adj.* Worthy of no trust; unreliable. See synonyms under BAD, PERFIDIOUS. **— un·trust′wor′thi·ness** *n.* **— un·trust′wor′thi·ly** *adv.*

un·truth (un·trōōth′) *n. pl.* **·truths** (-trōōths′, -trōōthz′) **1** The quality or character of being untrue; want of veracity. **2** *Obs.* Lack of fidelity; disloyalty. **3** Something that is not true; a falsehood; lie. See synonyms under DECEPTION, LIE. [OE *untrēowth*]

un·truth·ful (un·trōōth′fəl) *adj.* Not truthful; untrue; not veracious. **— un·truth′ful·ly** *adv.* **— un·truth′ful·ness** *n.*

un·tu·tored (un·tōō′tərd, -tyōō′-) *adj.* Having had no tutor or teacher; hence, uninstructed; raw. See synonyms under IGNORANT.

un·twine (un·twīn′) *v.* **·twined, ·twin·ing** *v.t.* To undo (something twined); unwind by disentangling. **—** *v.i.* To become untwined.

un·twist (un·twist′) *v.t.* & *v.i.* To separate or open by a movement the reverse of twisting; unwind or untwine.

U·nun·gun (ōō·nŏŏng′gōōn) *n. pl.* Literally, people: the collective name for two Eskimo tribes, the Unalaskans and the Atkans, inhabiting the Aleutian Islands; the Aleuts.

un·used (un·yōōzd′) *adj.* **1** Not made use of; disused; also, never having been used. **2** Not accustomed or wont: with *to.*

un·u·su·al (un·yōō′zhōō·əl) *adj.* Of a character, kind, number, or size not usually met with. See synonyms under EXTRAORDINARY, ODD, RARE. **— un·u′su·al·ly** *adv.* **— un·u′su·al·ness** *n.*

un·ut·ter·a·ble (un·ut′ər·ə·bəl) *adj.* **1** That cannot be uttered; too great or deep for verbal expression; ineffable: *unutterable* bliss. **2** Unpronounceable. **— un·ut′ter·a·ble·ness** *n.* **— un·ut′ter·a·bly** *adv.*

un·val·ued (un·val′yōōd) *adj.* **1** Not valued; neglected; unappreciated. **2** Not having a fixed value; not appraised. **3** *Obs.* Inestimable.

un·var·nished (un·vär′nisht) *adj.* **1** Having no covering of varnish. **2** Having no embellishment; plain: the *unvarnished* truth.

un·veil (un·vāl′) *v.t.* To remove the veil or covering from; disclose to view; reveal. **—** *v.i.* To remove one's veil; reveal oneself.

un·voice (un·vois′) *v.t.* **·voiced, ·voic·ing** *Phonet.* To pronounce (a voiced sound) without vibration of the vocal cords; devocalize.

un·voiced (un·voist′) *adj.* **1** Not expressed. **2** *Phonet.* Not voiced; rendered voiceless: The final (v) in "have" is often heard *unvoiced* in "have to": also *devoiced.*

un·voic·ing (un·voi′sing) *n. Phonet.* The change of a voiced consonant to its unvoiced counterpart, as of (b) to (p).

un·war·rant·a·ble (un·wôr′ən·tə·bəl, -wor′-) *adj.* That cannot be warranted; unjustifiable; indefensible. **— un·war′rant·a·bly** *adv.*

un·war·rant·ed (un·wôr′ən·tid, -wor′-) *adj.* **1** Having no warrant; unwarrantable; unjustifiable. **2** Being without warranty or guarantee.

un·war·y (un·wâr′ē) *adj.* Taking no precautions against accident or danger; especially, not realizing the necessity of such precautions; incautious. **— un·war′i·ly** *adv.* **— un·war′i·ness** *n.*

un·wea·ried (un·wir′ēd) *adj.* **1** Not tired. **2** Indefatigable.

un·wel·come (un·wel′kəm) *adj.* **1** Not welcome; not desired: an *unwelcome* guest. **2** Causing no satisfaction: *unwelcome* news. **— un·wel′come·ly** *adv.* **— un·wel′come·ness** *n.*

un·well (un·wel′) *adj.* **1** Somewhat ill; ailing. **2** Menstruating; indisposed by reason of menstruation: a euphemism. See synonyms under SICKLY. **— un·well′ness** *n.*

un·wept (un·wept′) *adj.* **1** Not lamented or wept for, as a deceased person. **2** Not shed, as tears.

un·whole·some (un·hōl′səm) *adj.* **1** Deleterious to physical or mental health. **2** Unsound in quality or condition; diseased or decayed: *unwholesome* provisions. **3** Impaired in health; sickly in appearance: an *unwholesome* look. **4** Not contributing to moral health; pernicious: *unwholesome* literature. See synonyms under BAD, NOISOME. **— un·whole′some·ly** *adv.* **— un·whole′some·ness** *n.*

un·wield·y (un·wēl′dē) *adj.* Moved or managed with difficulty, as from great size or awkward shape; bulky; clumsy. **— un·wield′i·ly** *adv.* **— un·wield′i·ness** *n.*

un·willed (un·wild′) *adj.* **1** Not willed or intended; spontaneous. **2** Being without, or deprived of, purpose or will.

un·will·ing (un·wil′ing) *adj.* **1** Not willing; reluctant; loath. **2** Done with reluctance. **3** *Obs.* Not intended; involuntary. See synonyms under RELUCTANT. **— un·will′ing·ly** *adv.* **— un·will′ing·ness** *n.*

un·wind (un·wīnd′) *v.* **·wound, ·wind·ing** *v.t.* **1** To reverse the winding of; untwist or wind off; uncoil. **2** To disentangle. **—** *v.i.* **3** To become unwound.

un·wise (un·wīz′) *adj.* Acting with, or showing, lack of wisdom; injudicious; foolish. [OE *unwīs*] **— un·wise′ly** *adv.* **— un·wis′dom** (-wiz′·dəm) *n.*

un·wish (un·wish′) *v.t.* **1** To retract (something wished); stop wishing. **2** To wish (something) not to be. **3** *Obs.* To destroy or do away with by wishing.

un·wished (un·wisht′) *adj.* **1** Not desired or wished. **2** Unwelcome.

un·wit·ting (un·wit′ing) *adj.* **1** Having no knowledge or consciousness of the thing in question; unknowing or unconscious. **2** Unintentional. [OE *unwitende*] **— un·wit′ting·ly** *adv.*

un·wont·ed (un·wun′tid, -won′-) *adj.* **1** Not according to wont or custom; unusual; uncommon. **2** *Obs.* Not accustomed; unfamiliar. See synonyms under EXTRAORDINARY. **— un·wont′ed·ly** *adv.* **— un·wont′ed·ness** *n.*

un·world·ly (un·wûrld′lē) *adj.* **1** Not motivated by worldly values or interests; spiritually minded. **2** Unearthly; spiritual; not belonging to this world. **— un·world′li·ness** *n.*

un·wor·thy (un·wûr′thē) *adj.* **1** Not worthy or deserving of something specified: usually with *of.* **2** Not befitting or becoming: often with *of*; wrong; improper: conduct *unworthy* of a gentleman. **3** Lacking worth or merit; unfit; wrong; contemptible. See synonyms under BAD, SINFUL. **— un·wor′thi·ly** *adv.* **— un·wor′thi·ness** *n.*

un·wrap (un·rap′) *v.* **·wrapped, ·wrap·ping** *v.t.* To take the wrapping from; open; undo. **—** *v.i.* To become unwrapped.

un·wrin·kle (un·ring′kəl) *v.t.* **·kled, ·kling** To free from wrinkles; smooth.

un·writ·ten (un·rit′n) *adj.* **1** Not reduced to writing; not written down; oral; traditional. **2** Having no writing upon it; blank.

unwritten law **1** A rule or custom established by general usage: an *unwritten law* of gentlemanly decorum. **2** Law which rests on custom and judicial decision, and not on a written command, decree, or statute. See COMMON LAW under LAW. **3** A custom in some communities granting a measure of immunity to those who commit criminal acts of revenge in support of personal or family honor, especially in cases of seduction, adultery, etc.

un·yoke (un·yōk′) *v.* **·yoked, ·yok·ing** *v.t.* **1** To release from a yoke. **2** To separate; part. **—** *v.i.* **3** To become unyoked. **4** To stop work; cease. [OE *ungeocian*]

un·yoked (un·yōkt′) *adj.* **1** Not subjected to or not wearing a yoke. **2** Freed from a yoke. **3** *Obs.* Unrestrained; licentious.

up (up) *adv.* **1** Toward a higher place or level: opposed to *down.* **2** In or on a higher place; above the horizon. **3** Toward that which is figuratively or conventionally higher: **a** To or at a higher price: Barley is *up.* **b** To or at a higher rank: people who have come *up* in the world. **c** To or at a greater size or larger amount: to swell *up.* **d** To or at a higher musical pitch. **e** To or at a place that is locally or arbitrarily regarded as higher: *up* north. **4** To a vertical position; standing; on one's feet. **5** Risen from bed. **6** So as to be level (to) or even (with) in space, time, degree, or amount: *up* to date; *up* to the brim. **7** In or into commotion or activity; in progress: They were stirred *up* to mutiny; to be *up* in arms. **8** Into existence: to draw *up* a document; to turn *up.* **9** In or into prominence; under consideration: The question was *up* for debate. **10** Into or in a place of safekeeping; aside: Fruits are put *up* in glass jars. **11** At an end or close: Your time is *up.* **12** Completely; wholly: Houses were burned *up*; The brooks dried *up.* **13** In baseball and cricket, at bat: He made but one hit in three times *up.* **14** In tennis and other sports: **a** In the lead; ahead: said of a player or team. **b** Apiece; alike: said of a score. **15** Bound for: said of a ship: *up* for Panama. **16** Running for as a candidate: Jones is *up* for mayor. **17** On trial before a magistrate: *up* for manslaughter. **18** *Naut.* Shifted to windward, as a tiller. **— all up with** At an end for; no further hope for. **— to be up against** *Colloq.* To meet with; be face to face with. **— to be up against it** *Colloq.* To be in difficulty; have financial trouble. **— to be up to** **1** *Colloq.* To be doing or plotting; be about to do: What is he *up to*? **2** To be equal to; to be capable of: I'm not *up to* moving all this furniture today. **3** To be incumbent upon; be dependent upon: It's *up to* him to save us. **—** *adj.* **1** Moving, sloping, or directed upward or in a direction arbitrarily regarded as upward. **2** At stake, as in gambling: to have money *up* on a horse race. **3** *Colloq.* Going on; taking place: What's *up*? **4** *Colloq.* In a state acquainted (with), equal (to), or a match (for); of a kind or character capable (of): He is *up* in that subject. **5** In golf: **a** In advance of the opponent or opponents: with a number indicating the extent (in holes) of such advance: three *up* and four to play: opposed to *down.* **b** Struck so as to travel as far as or beyond the hole: said of the ball. **6** Rising, risen, overflowing, or at flood: The moon is *up*; The river is *up.* **— up and around** *Colloq.* Sufficiently recovered to walk, as following an illness or injury; on one's feet again; convalescent and ambulatory. **— up to no good** Engaged in or contemplating some mischief or improper act. **—** *prep.* **1** From a lower to a higher point or place of, on, or along; toward a higher condition or rank on or in: *up* the social ladder. **2** To or at a point farther above or along: The farm is *up* the road. **3** From the coast toward the interior of (a country, as being higher); from the mouth toward the source of (a river): to sail *up* a river. **4** At, on, or near the height or top of: said of position or situation. **—** *n.* One who or that which is up, as elevated ground, an ascent or upward movement, state of prosperity, etc.: usually plural. **— ups and downs** Changes of fortune or circumstance. **—** *v.* **upped, up·ping** *Colloq.* *v.t.* **1** To increase; make larger; cause to rise. **2** To put or take up. **—** *v.i.* **3** To rise. [OE]

up– *combining form* As an element in solidemes *up* has adverbial force with various meanings, as in the following examples:

1 To a higher place or level:

upbear	**upflow**	**upsend**
upbearer	**upgaze**	**upshoot**
upborne	**upgoing**	**upsoar**
upbuilder	**upgrow**	**upstare**
upbuilding	**upheap**	**upstep**
upclimb	**upleap**	**upsurge**
upcoil	**uppile**	**upswell**
upcurl	**upraiser**	**uptilt**
upcurve	**upreach**	**uptoss**
updart	**upreaching**	**upvomit**
updive	**uprise**	**upwaft**
upfling	**uprush**	**upwreathe**

unwifelike	**unwinning**	**unwomanlike**	**unwooed**	**unworn**	**unwounded**	**unwrung**
unwifely	**unwithered**	**unwomanly**	**unworkable**	**unworshiped,**	**unwoven**	**unyielding**
unwincing	**unwithering**	**unwon**	**unworked**	**unworshipped**	**unwreathe**	**unyouthful**
unwinking	**unwitnessed**	**unwooded**	**unworkmanlike**	**unwound**	**unwrought**	**unzealous**

2 To a greater size or larger amount:

upbulging **upflashing** **uplight**
upflaring **upflooding** **upswell**

3 To a vertical position:

upprop **upstand** **upsticking**

4 In or into commotion or activity:

upboil **upbubbling** **upstir**

5 Completely; wholly:

upbind **upfold** **upgird**
updry **upgather** **uphoard**

up-and-coming (up′ənd·kum′ing) *adj.* Enterprising; energetic; promising.

U·pan·i·shad (o͞o·pan′ə·shad, -pä′nə·shäd) *n.* *Sanskrit* Literally, a philosophical treatise; one of the treatises forming the third division of the Vedas, dealing with the nature of man and the universe.

u·par·na (o͞o·pär′nə) *n.* A silk or muslin scarf, interwoven with gold or silver threads, worn as a shawl by men and as a shawl or veil by women in India. [<Hind.]

u·pas (yo͞o′pəs) *n.* **1** A tall evergreen moraceous tree *(Antiaris toxicaria)* of the island of Java, with an acrid, milky, poisonous juice. **2** The poisonous sap of this tree, used by natives in the manufacture of arrow poison; also, a similar poison from the **upas-tieute,** a climbing shrub (genus *Strychnos*) of the family *Loganiaceae.* **3** Hence, something morally deadly. [<Malay *(pohon) upas* poison (tree)]

up·beat (up′bēt′) *n. Music* An unaccented beat; the beat at which the hand is raised. —*adj.* Optimistic; confident.

up-bow (up′bō′) *n.* An upward stroke of the violin bow, indicated in score by the symbol **V**: opposed to *down-bow.*

up·braid (up·brād′) *v.t.* To reproach for some wrongdoing; scold or reprove. —*v.i.* To utter reproaches. See synonyms under REPROVE, REVILE. [OE *upbregdan* <*up-* up + *bregdan* weave, twist] —**up·braid′er** *adj.* —**up·braid′ing** *n.* —**up·braid′ing·ly** *adv.*

up·bring·ing (up′bring′ing) *n.* Rearing and training received by a person during childhood.

up·bye (up′bī) *adv. Scot.* A little farther on; up the way. Also **up′by.**

up·cast (up′kast′, -käst′) *adj.* Cast, turned, or directed upward. —*n.* **1** A casting or throwing upward; that which is so cast. **2** An airshaft in a mine. **3** An upward current of air, as in a mine shaft. **4** *Scot.* An upset, or a reproach.

up·chuck (up′chuk′) *Colloq. v.t.* & *v.i.* To vomit. —*n.* Vomit.

up·com·ing (up′kum′ing) *adj.* Forthcoming; coming soon.

up·coun·try (up′kun′trē) *Colloq. n.* Country somewhat distant from the seashore or from lowlands; inland country. —*adj.* Living in, from, or characteristic of inland places. —*adv.* (up′kun′trē) In, into, or toward the interior: to move *up-country.*

up·date (up·dāt′) *v.t.* **·dat·ed, ·dat·ing** To bring up to date; to revise, with corrections, additions, etc., as a textbook or manual: to *update* an encyclopedia.

up·end (up′end′) *v.t.* & *v.i.* To set or stand on end.

up·front (up′frunt′) *adj. Colloq.* Out in the open; unconcealed.

up·grade (up′grād′) *n.* An upward incline or slope. —*v.t.* (up·grād′) **·grad·ed, ·grad·ing** **1** To improve the breed of (animals) by the introduction of a higher strain. **2** To raise to a higher grade, rank, or responsibility, as an employee.

up·growth (up′grōth′) *n.* **1** The process of growing up. **2** That which grows or has grown up.

up·heav·al (up·hē′vəl) *n.* **1** The act of upheaving, or the state of being upheaved. **2** *Geol.* An elevation of the earth's surface due to a warping of large rock masses. **3** Overthrow or violent disturbance of the established social order.

up·heave (up·hēv′) *v.* **·heaved** or **·hove, ·heav·ing** *v.t.* To heave or raise up. —*v.i.* To be raised or lifted.

up·held (up·held′) Past tense and past participle of UPHOLD.

up·hill (up′hil′) *adv.* Up or as up a hill or an ascent; against difficulties. —*adj.* **1** Going up a hill or an ascent; sloping upward. **2** Attended with difficulty or exertion. —*n.* (up′hil′) An upward slope; rising ground.

up·hold (up·hōld′) *v.t.* **·held, ·hold·ing** **1** To hold up; raise. **2** To keep from falling or sinking. **3** To give aid or support to; encourage. **4** To regard with approval. See synonyms under ABET, AID, ASSENT, CONFIRM, HELP, JUSTIFY, PRESERVE, SUPPORT. —**up·hold′er** *n.*

up·hol·ster (up·hōl′stər) *v.t.* **1** To fit, as furniture, with coverings, cushioning, etc. **2** To provide or adorn with hangings, curtains, etc., as an apartment. **3** To furnish with a covering of any kind. [Back formation <UPHOLSTERER]

up·hol·ster·er (up·hōl′stər·ər) *n.* One who furnishes upholstery; one who upholsters. [<obs. *upholster,* alter. of ME *upholder* a tradesman + -ER[1]]

up·hol·ster·y (up·hōl′stər·ē, -strē) *n. pl.* **·ster·ies** **1** Goods used in upholstering. **2** Textile decoration of an apartment. **3** The act, art, or business of upholstering.

u·phroe (yo͞o′frō, yo͞o′v′rō) See EUPHROE.

up·keep (up′kēp′) *n.* The act or state of maintenance; also, means or cost of maintenance.

up·land (up′lənd, -land′) *n.* **1** The higher portions of a region, district, farm, etc. **2** The country in the interior. —*adj.* **1** Pertaining to an upland; higher in situation. **2** Pertaining to or situated in inland districts.

upland plover See under PLOVER.

up·lift (up·lift′) *v.t.* **1** To lift up, or raise aloft; elevate. **2** To raise the tone of; put on a higher plane, mentally or morally. See synonyms under HEIGHTEN, RAISE. —*adj.* (up′lift′) Uplifted: a rare form. —*n.* (up′lift′) **1** The act of raising; the fact of being raised. **2** A movement upward. **3** *Geol.* An upheaval. **4** Mental or spiritual stimulation or elevation. **5** A social movement aiming to improve, morally or esthetically, the condition of the underprivileged. **6** A brassière designed to lift and support the breasts. —**up·lift′er** *n.*

up·most (up′mōst′) *adj.* Uppermost.

up·on (ə·pon′, ə·pôn′) *prep.* **1** On, in all its meanings. **2** On, in an elevated position: *upon* the throne. **3** On, by motion upward: to get *upon* a roof. —*adv.* On: completing a verbal idea: The paper has been written *upon.* Also *Scot.* **up·o′.** See synonyms under ABOVE. [ME]

◆ *Upon* now differs little in use from *on,* the former being sometimes used for reasons of euphony and also preferably when motion into position is involved, the latter when merely rest or support is to be indicated. When *upon* has its original meaning of *up* and *on,* it is written as two words, *up* having its adverbial force: Let us go *up on* the roof.

up·per (up′ər) *adj.* **1** Higher than something else; being above. **2** Higher in place: opposed to *lower.* **3** Higher in station or dignity; superior: opposed to *inferior:* the *upper* house. —**to get the upper hand** To get the advantage. —*n.* **1** That part of a boot or shoe above the sole: the vamp. **2** *pl.* Cloth gaiters. **3** *Slang* Any of various drugs that stimulate the central nervous system, as amphetamines. —**on one's uppers** *Colloq.* **1** Having worn out the soles of one's shoes. **2** At the end of one's resources. [ME, orig. compar. of UP]

Up·per (up′ər) *adj. Geol.* Designating a later period or a later formation of a specified period: the *Upper* Cambrian.

Upper Austria A province of northern Austria; 4,624 square miles; capital, Linz. *German* **O·ber·ös·ter·reich** (ō′bər·œs′tə·rīkh).

Upper Bavaria An administrative division of southern Bavaria, West Germany; 6,308 square miles; capital, Munich. *German* **O·ber·bay·ern** (ō′bər·bī′ərn).

upper berth The top berth in a ship, railroad sleeping-car, cabin, etc., where two bunks or beds are built one above the other.

Upper Burma See BURMA, UNION OF.

Upper Canada A former British province (1791 to 1840) in the southern part of Ontario province, Canada.

upper case **1** Case[2] (def. 3). **2** Capital letters.

upper class The socially or economically superior group in society. —**up′per-class′** (-klas′, -kläs′) *adj.*

upper classman A junior or senior in a school or college.

upper crust *Colloq.* That portion of society assuming or thought of as having more social standing by reason of wealth or ancestry.

up·per·cut (up′ər·kut′) *n.* In boxing, a blow upward from the waist or hip, delivered under or inside the opponent's guard. —*v.t.* & *v.i.* **·cut, ·cut·ting** To strike with an uppercut.

Upper Egypt See under EGYPT.

Upper Franconia An administrative division of NE Bavaria, Germany; 2,897 square miles; capital, Bayreuth. *German* **O·ber·fran·ken** (ō′bər·fräng′kən).

upper hand The advantage.

Upper House The branch, in a bicameral legislature, where membership is more restricted, as the U.S. Senate and the English House of Lords. Also **upper house.**

up·per·most (up′ər·mōst′) *adj.* **1** Highest in place, rank, authority, or vantage ground. **2** First to come into the mind: one's *uppermost* thoughts. Also *upmost.* —*adv.* In the highest place; also, first, as in time.

Upper New York Bay An arm of the Atlantic at the junction of the Hudson and the East River, joined to Newark Bay and Long Island Sound.

Upper Peninsula The northern part of Michigan, between Lake Superior and Lake Michigan; 16,538 square miles; 320 miles long, 125 miles wide.

Upper Silesia A former province of eastern Germany, now in western Poland.

Upper Vol·ta (vol′tə), **Republic of the** An independent republic of the French Community in western Africa; 105,900 square miles; capital, Ouagadougou; formerly the French overseas territory of Upper Volta.

up·pish (up′ish) *adj. Colloq.* Inclined to be self-assertive; assuming; pretentious; snobbish. Also **up′pi·ty.** —**up′pish·ly** *adv.* —**up′pish·ness** *n.*

up·raise (up·rāz′) *v.t.* **·raised, ·rais·ing** To lift up; elevate. Also **up·rear′** (-rir′).

up·right (up′rīt′) *adj.* **1** Being in a vertical position; erect. **2** Morally correct; especially, just and honest. See synonyms under GOOD, HONEST, INNOCENT, JUST, MORAL, PURE, VIRTUOUS. —*n.* **1** Something having a vertical position, as an upright timber or piano. **2** The state of being upright: a post out of *upright.* **3** In football, one of the goal posts. —*adv.* Vertically; honestly; sincerely; justly. [OE *upriht* <*up-* up + *riht* right] —**up′right′ly** *adv.* —**up′right′ness** *n.*

upright piano See under PIANO.

up·rise (up·rīz′) *v.i.* **·rose, ·ris·en, ·ris·ing** **1** To get up; rise, as from a seat or from sleep. **2** To be or become erect. **3** To go upward; ascend. **4** To increase; swell. **5** To rise into view. **6** To rise in revolt. —*n.* (up′rīz′) **1** The act of rising; ascent. **2** An upward slope; upgrade.

up·ris·ing (up·rī′zing, up′rī′zing) *n.* **1** The act of rising. **2** Revolt; insurrection. **3** An ascent; a slope; acclivity.

up·riv·er (up′riv′ər) *adj.* & *adv.* On or toward the upper part of a river. —*n.* A region located up-river.

up·roar (up′rôr′, -rōr′) *n.* Violent disturbance and noise; tumult. See synonyms under NOISE, TUMULT. —*v.* (up·rôr′, -rōr′) *Obs. v.i.* To make an uproar. —*v.t.* To throw into uproar or confusion. [<Du. *oproer* <*op-* up + *roeren* stir]

up·roar·i·ous (up·rôr′ē·əs, -rō′rē-) *adj.* Accompanied by or making uproar. See synonyms under NOISY. —**up·roar′i·ous·ly** *adv.* —**up·roar′i·ous·ness** *n.*

up·root (up·ro͞ot′, -ro͝ot′) *v.t.* To tear up by the roots; eradicate; destroy utterly. See synonyms under EXTERMINATE. —**up·root′al** *n.* —**up·root′er** *n.*

up·rouse (up·rouz′) *v.t.* **·roused, ·rous·ing** To rouse up, as from sleep.

Up·sa·la (up·sä′lə, *Sw.* o͞op′sä·lä) A city in eastern Sweden; site of Upsala University, founded 1477, one of world's oldest universities. Also **Upp·sa′la.**

up·scale (up′skāl′) *adj.* Higher than average in income and cultural appreciation: *upscale* attitudes.

up·set (up·set′) *v.* **·set, ·set·ting** *v.t.* **1** To overturn. **2** To throw into confusion or disorder. **3** To disconcert; derange or disquiet. **4** To defeat, especially unexpectedly: Navy

upset Army. **5** To shorten and thicken (metal) by hammering or by pressure: to *upset* a bolt to form a head or to *upset* the metal tire of a wheel. **6** To swage (the ends of the teeth of a saw). —*v.i.* **7** To become overturned. —*adj.* (*also* up′set′) Set up; required: in the phrase **upset price,** a price at which property is offered for sale, as by an auctioneer, as the lowest selling price. —*n.* (up′set′) The act of upsetting, or the state of being upset. **—up·set′ter** *n.*

up·shot (up′shot′) *n.* The final outcome. See synonyms under CONSEQUENCE.

up·side (up′sīd′) *n.* The upper side or part.

up·side-down (up′sīd′doun′) *adj.* Having the upper side down; in disorder. —*adv.* With the upper side down; in disorder. [Alter. of ME *up so down* up as if down]

up·si·lon (yo͞op′sə·lon, *Brit.* yo͞op·sī′lən) *n.* The twentieth letter and sixth vowel in the Greek alphabet (Υ, υ): having the sound of French *u,* Latin and Old English *y.* It is transliterated in English as *u* or *y.* See Y. [< Gk. *ypsilon* smooth y]

up·spring (up′spring′) *n.* **1** A leap up into the air. **2** *Obs.* An upstart. —*v.i.* **·sprang** or **·sprung, ·sprung, ·spring·ing** To spring up.

up·stage (up′stāj′) *n.* The half of a stage, from left to right, extending from the center to the backdrop. —*adj.* **1** Pertaining to the back half of a stage. **2** *Colloq.* Conceited; haughty; stuck-up; supercilious. —*adv.* Toward or on the back half of a stage. —*v.t.* **·staged, ·stag·ing** To steal a scene from (another actor).

up·stairs (up′stârz′) *adj.* Pertaining to an upper story. —*n.* The upper story; the part of a building above the ground floor. —*adv.* In, to, or toward an upper story. **—to kick upstairs** To promote so as to get out of the way.

up·stand·ing (up·stan′ding) *adj.* Standing up; erect; hence, honest; upright; straightforward.

up·start (up·stärt′) *v.i.* To start or spring up suddenly. —*adj.* (up′stärt′) **1** Suddenly raised to prominence, wealth, or power. **2** Characteristic of a parvenu; vulgar. —*n.* (up′stärt′) One who has suddenly risen from a humble position to consequence; a parvenu.

up·state (up′stāt′) *U.S. adj.* Of, from, or designating that part of a State lying outside, usually north, of the principal city. —*n.* The outlying, usually northern, sections of a State. —*adv.* In or toward the outlying or northern sections of a State. **—up′stat′er** *n.*

up·stream (up′strēm′) *adv.* Toward the upper part of a stream; against the current; toward or at a place nearer the source.

up·stroke (up′strōk′) *n.* An upward stroke.

up·sweep (up′swēp′) *n.* **1** A sweeping up or upward. **2** The upturning of the lower jaw, as in the bulldog. —*v.t.* & *v.i.* (up·swēp′) **·swept, ·sweep·ing** To brush or sweep upward.

up·swept (up′swept′) *adj.* Of or pertaining to a style of hairdressing in which the hair is swept upward smoothly in the back and piled high on the top of the head.

up·swing (up′swing′) *n.* **1** A swinging upward. **2** An improvement. —*v.i.* (up·swing′) **·swung, ·swing·ing** To swing upward; improve.

up·take (up′tāk′) n. **1** The act of lifting or taking up. **2** A boiler flue that unites the combustion gases and carries them toward the smokestack. **3** An upward ventilating shaft in a mine. **4** Mental comprehension; understanding.

up·throw (up′thrō′) *n.* **1** A throwing upward; an upheaval. **2** *Geol.* An upward displacement of the rock on one side of a fault.

up·thrust (up′thrust′) *n.* **1** An upward thrust. **2** *Geol.* An upheaval (usually violent) of rocks in the earth's crust.

up·tight (up′tīt′) *adj. U.S. Slang* Uneasy, anxious, or tense; nervous. Also **up′-tight′, up tight. —up′tight′ness** *n.*

up to See under UP.

up-to-date (up′tə·dāt′) *adj.* Having the latest information, fashion, manner, or improvement: an *up-to-date* dictionary.

up to date To the present time.

up·town (up′toun′) *adv.* In or toward the upper part of a town. —*adj.* Pertaining to or resident in the upper part of a town or city, or that part which is conventionally regarded as the upper part, usually the residence section.

up·turn (up·tûrn′) *v.t.* To turn up or over, as sod with the plow; hence, to overturn; upset. —*n.* (up′tûrn′) A turning upward; an increase.

up·ward (up′wərd) *adv.* **1** In or toward a higher place; in an ascending course or direction; toward the source: to look *upward*; to trace a stream *upward.* **2** With increase or advancement; toward a higher price: Prices tended *upward.* **3** In excess; more: children five years old and *upward.* **4** Toward that which is better, nobler, or holier. **5** In the upper parts. Also **up′wards. —upward of** or **upwards of** Higher than or in excess of. —*adj.* Turned or directed toward a higher place. [OE *upweard* < *up-* up + *-weard* -WARD] **—up′ward·ly** *adv.*

Ur (ûr) An ancient city of Sumer, southern Mesopotamia, the site of which is on the Euphrates in SE Iraq. Old Testament **Ur of the Chal·dees** (kal·dēz′, kal′dēz).

ur-[1] Var. of URO-[1].

ur-[2] Var. of URO-[2].

u·ra·chus (yo͝or′ə·kəs) *n. Anat.* A canal connecting the bladder of the fetus with the allantois. [< NL < Gk. *ourachos* urinary canal of a fetus < *ouron* urine + *echein* hold]

u·rae·mi·a (yo͞o·rē′mē·ə), **u·rae·mic** (yo͞o·rē′·mik) See UREMIA, etc.

u·rae·us (yo͞o·rē′əs) *n.* The emblem of the sacred serpent (haje) in the headdress of Egyptian divinities and kings: a symbol of sovereignty. [< NL < Gk. *ouraios* of a tail < *oura* tail]

URAEUS

U·ral (yo͝or′əl, *Russian* o͞o·räl′) A river in Russia and Kazakhstan, considered as forming part of the traditional boundary between Asia and Europe and flowing 1,574 miles south and west from the Ural Mountains to the Caspian Sea.

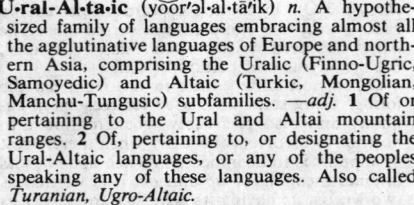

U·ral-Al·ta·ic (yo͝or′əl·al·tā′ik) *n.* A hypothesized family of languages embracing almost all the agglutinative languages of Europe and northern Asia, comprising the Uralic (Finno-Ugric, Samoyedic) and Altaic (Turkic, Mongolian, Manchu-Tungusic) subfamilies. —*adj.* **1** Of or pertaining to the Ural and Altai mountain ranges. **2** Of, pertaining to, or designating the Ural-Altaic languages, or any of the peoples speaking any of these languages. Also called *Turanian, Ugro-Altaic.*

U·ral·ic (yo͞o·ral′ik) *n.* A family of agglutinative languages comprising the Finno-Ugric and Samoyedic subfamilies: by some classified with Altaic in one great Ural-Altaic family. —*adj.* Of or pertaining to this linguistic family. Also **U·ra·li·an** (yo͞o·rā′lē·ən).

u·ral·ite (yo͝or′əl·īt) *n.* A pyroxene altered to amphibole. [from *Ural* Mountains] **—u′ral·it′ic** (-it′ik) *adj.*

U·ral Mountains (yo͝or′əl, *Russian* o͞o·räl′) the traditional boundary between Asia and Europe; 1,300 miles long, from the Artic Ocean to the Kazakhstan border; highest peak, 6,217 feet, in Russia.

U·ralsk (o͞o·rälsk′) A city on the Ural river in NW Kazakhstan .

u·ra·nal·y·sis (yo͝or′ə·nal′ə·sis) See URINALYSIS.

U·ra·ni·a (yo͞o·rā′nē·ə) **1** The Muse of astronomy. **2** The heavenly one: an epithet of Aphrodite. [< L < Gk. *Ourania* < *ouranios* heavenly < *ouranos* heaven] **—U·ra′ni·an** *adj.*

u·ran·ic (yo͞o·ran′ik) *adj. Chem.* Pertaining to or derived from uranium, especially in its higher valence. [< Gk. *ouranos* heaven]

u·ran·i·nite (yo͞o·ran′ə·nīt) *n.* A greenish-black, opaque uranium mineral containing also lead, nitrogen, helium, thorium, radium, and certain rare earths, occurring in octohedral crystals. In the massive form it is called *pitchblende.* [< URANIUM]

u·ran·ism (yo͝or′ən·iz′əm) *n.* Homosexuality: opposed to *dionism.* [< Gk. *Ourania* URANIA (def. 2)]

u·ra·nite (yo͝or′ə·nīt) *n.* Any of several uranium minerals, especially uranium phosphates, torbernite or copper uranite, autunite or lime uranite. **—u′ra·nit′ic** (-nit′ik) *adj.*

u·ra·ni·um (yo͞o·rā′nē·əm) *n.* A heavy, toxic, silvery-white, radioactive metallic element (symbol U, atomic number 92) occurring in various minerals in equilibrium with a variety of disintegration products, and in certain of its isotopes constituting the fuel for nuclear reactors. See PERIODIC TABLE. [< URANUS]

uranium series *Physics* A series of radioactive elements beginning with uranium of mass 238 and a half-life of 4.5×10^{10} years and continuing through successive disintegrations to the stable isotope of lead of mass 206.

urano- *combining form Astron.* The heavens; of or pertaining to the heavens, or to celestial bodies: *uranography.* Also, before vowels, **uran-.** [< Gk. *ouranos* heaven]

u·ra·nog·ra·phy (yo͝or′ə·nog′rə·fē) *n.* Scientific description of the celestial bodies; the making of celestial globes and maps: also spelled *ouranography.* **—u′ra·nog′ra·pher** or **·phist** *n.* **—u′ra·no·graph′ic** (-nō·graf′ik) or **·i·cal** *adj.*

u·ra·nous (yo͝or′ə·nəs) *adj. Chem.* Of or pertaining to uranium, especially in its lower valence.

U·ra·nus (yo͝or′ə·nəs) **1** In Greek mythology, the son and husband of Gaea (Earth) and father of the Titans, Furies, and Cyclopes: overthrown by his son Kronos: also spelled *Ouranos.* **2** *Astron.* A planet of the solar system; seventh in distance from the sun. Its mean distance from the sun is 1,781 millions of miles, its sidereal period about 84 terrestrial years, and its diameter about 29,600 miles. It has four satellites. See PLANET. [< L < Gk. *Ouranos* < *ouranos* heaven]

u·ra·nyl (yo͝or′ə·nil) *n. Chem.* The bivalent radical UO_2, found in many uranium compounds. [< URANIUM + -YL]

u·ra·re (yo͞o·rä′rē) *n.* Curare: also called *oorali.* Also **u·ra′ri.**

U·ra·ri·coe·ra (o͞o·rä·rē·kwā′rə) A river in northern Brazil, flowing 300 miles east from the Venezuela border to the Río Branco.

u·rase (yo͝or′ās) See UREASE.

u·rate (yo͝or′āt) *n. Chem.* A salt of uric acid.

U·ra·wa (o͞o·rä·wä) A city of central Honshu island, Japan.

ur·ban (ûr′bən) *adj.* Pertaining to, characteristic of, including, or constituting a city; situated or dwelling in a city. [< L *urbanus.* See URBANE]

Ur·ban (ûr′bən) Name of eight popes.
—Urban II, 1042?–99, pope 1088–99; preached the First Crusade.

urban district A subdivision, for administrative purposes, of a shire of England, Wales, or Northern Ireland.

ur·bane (ûr·bān′) *adj.* **1** Characterized by or having refinement, especially in manner; polite; courteous; suave: opposed to *rustic.* **2** *Obs.* Urban. See synonyms under POLITE. [< L *urbanus* of a city < *urbs, urbis* a city] **—ur·bane′ly** *adv.* **—ur·bane′ness** *n.*

ur·ban·ism (ûr′bən·iz′əm) *n.* **1** Life in the cities; the manner of life of urban dwellers. **2** The study of urban life, often with special attention to the physical environment. **3** The advocacy of living in a city. **—ur′ban·ist** *n.* **—ur·ban·is·tic** (ûr′bən·is′tik) *adj.*

ur·ban·ite (ûr′bən·īt) *n.* A city-dweller.

ur·ban·i·ty (ûr·ban′ə·tē) *n. pl.* **·ties** **1** The character or quality of being urbane; refined or elegant courtesy; strictly, the city quality, from the assumption that life in the city results in superior refinement. **2** *Obs.* Polished humor or wit. [< L *urbanitas, -tatis* < *urbs, urbis* a city]

ur·ban·i·za·tion (ûr′bə·nə·zā′shən) *n.* **1** The act or process of urbanizing an area or a rural group of people. **2** The quality or state of being urbanized. Also *Brit.* **ur′ban·i·sa′tion** *n.*

ur·ban·ize (ûr′bən·īz) *v.t.* **·ized, ·iz·ing** **1** To cause (an area) to assume the characteristics of a city: to *urbanize* a suburb. **2** To cause (people) to adopt an urban life style. Also *Brit.* **ur′ban·ise.**

ur·ban·ol·o·gy (ûr′bə·nol′ə·jē) *n.* The study of problems peculiar to cities. **—ur·ban·ol′o·gist** *n.*

urban renewal The planned upgrading of a deteriorating urban area, usually using public funds and coordinated by a local government.

urban sprawl The uncontrolled spread of urban housing, shopping centers, etc., into rural or undeveloped areas close to a city.

ur·bi·cul·ture (ûr′bə·kul′chər) *n.* The study of the proper development, planning, and use of cities, especially in relation to the needs of

their inhabitants. [<L *urbs, urbis* a city + CULTURE]

ur·bi et or·bi (ûr′bī et ôr′bī) *Latin* To the city (Rome) and to the world: used in official announcements, as papal bulls.

Urbs Ve·tus (ûrbz vē′təs) The ancient Latin name for ORVIETO.

ur·ce·o·late (ûr′sē·ə·lit, -lāt′) *adj. Bot.* Pitcher– or urn–shaped, as a corolla. [<L *urceolus,* dim. of *urceus* pitcher]

ur·chin (ûr′chin) *n.* **1** A roguish, mischievous boy. **2** A cylinder in a carding machine. **3** A hedgehog. **4** A sea urchin. **5** *Obs.* An elf, as often assuming the form of a hedgehog. — *adj. Obs.* Elfish; mischievous. [ME *irchoun* <OF *irechon, ireçon* <L *ericius* hedgehog < *er* hedgehog]

Ur·du (ŏŏr′dōō, ŏŏr·dōō′, ûr′dōō) *n.* A variety of Hindustani used by the Moslems, containing many Arabic and Persian elements and written in the Arabic alphabet: the official language of Pakistan. Also spelled *Oordoo.* [<Hind. *urdū,* short for *(zaban–i–) urdū* (language of the) camp <Turkish *ordū* camp <Persian *urdū.* Related to HORDE.]

–ure *suffix of nouns* **1** The act, process, or result of: *pressure.* **2** The function, rank, or office of: *prefecture.* **3** The means or instrument of: *ligature.* [<F <L *-ura*]

u·re·a (yōō·rē′ə) *n. Biochem.* A very soluble colorless crystalline compound, $CO(NH_2)_2$, formed by the oxidation of nitrogenous compounds in the body, and also made synthetically: used in medicine and in the making of plastics. Also called *carbamide.* [<NL <F *urée* <Gk. *ouron*] — **u·re′al** *adj.*

urea resin Any of a class of thermosetting resins obtained by the reaction of urea and formaldehyde in the presence of certain modifying agents.

u·re·ase (yŏŏr′ē·ās, -āz) *n. Biochem.* An enzyme which promotes the hydrolysis of urea, with the formation of ammonium carbonate. [<UREA + -ASE]

U·red·i·na·les (yōō·red′ə·nā′lēz) *n. pl.* An order of fungi characterized by a branched, septate mycelium and the formation of reddish or yellow spores; the rust fungi. [<NL <L *uredo, -inis* blast, blight < *urere* burn]

u·re·din·i·um (yŏŏr′ə·din′ē·əm) *n. Bot.* The spore fruit of a rust fungus which produces the uredospores. Also **u·re·di·um** (yōō·rē′dē·əm), **u′re·do·so′rus** (-dō·sôr′əs, -sō′rəs). [<NL <L *uredo, -inis* blight. See UREDO.]

u·re·do (yōō·rē′dō) *n.* **1** The uredo stage. **2** Urticaria. [<L, blight < *urere* burn]

u·re·do·spore (yōō·rē′də·spôr, -spōr) *n. Bot.* A unicellular thin–walled spore produced as a repeating generation in summer as part of the life cycle of a rust fungus. Also **u·re·din·i·o·spore** (yŏŏr′ə·din′ē·ə·spôr′, -spōr′).

uredo stage *Bot.* The stage in the life history of certain rust fungi during which uredospores are produced.

u·re·ide (yŏŏr′ē·īd, -id) *n. Chem.* Any of several nitrogenous compounds derived from urea and an acid or aldehyde by the removal of water.

u·re·mi·a (yōō·rē′mē·ə) *n. Pathol.* An abnormal condition of the blood due to the presence of urea with other urinary constituents ordinarily excreted by the kidneys. Also *uraemia, urinemia.* [<NL <UR-[1] + -EMIA] — **u·re′mic** *adj.*

–uret *suffix Chem.* Used to denote a compound: now replaced by *–ide.* [<F < *-ure* -URE]

u·re·ter (yōō·rē′tər) *n. Anat.* The duct by which urine passes from the kidney to the bladder or the cloaca. [<NL <Gk. *ourētēr* < *ourein* urinate] — **u·re′ter·al, u·re·ter·ic** (yŏŏr′ə·ter′ik) *adj.*

u·re·ter·ec·to·my (yōō·rē′tə·rek′tə·mē) *n. Surg.* Excision of all or part of the ureter. [<URETER(O)- + -ECTOMY]

uretero– *combining form Med.* A ureter; of or related to a ureter. Also, before vowels, **ureter–.** [<Gk. *ourētēr* < *ourein* urinate]

u·re·than (yŏŏr′ə·than′, yōō·reth′ən) *n. Chem.* **1** A white crystalline compound, $C_3H_7NO_2$, derived from carbamic acid by substituting ethyl for the hydrogen of the hydroxyl group: some of its derivatives are used as hypnotics and sedatives: also called *ethylurethane.* **2** Any ester of carbamic acid. Also **u·re·thane** (yŏŏr′ə·thān′, yōō·reth′ān). [<UR(EA) + ETHAN(E)]

u·re·thra (yōō·rē′thrə) *n. Anat.* The duct by which urine is discharged from the bladder of most mammals, and which, in males, carries the seminal discharge. [<LL <Gk. *ourēthra* < *ouron* urine] — **u·re′thral** *adj.*

u·re·thri·tis (yŏŏr′ə·thrī′tis) *n. Pathol.* Inflammation of the urethra. [<NL] — **u′re·thrit′ic** (-thrit′ik) *adj.*

urethro– *combining form Med.* The urethra; of or pertaining to the urethra: *urethroscope.* Also, before vowels, **urethr–.** [<Gk. *ourēthra* the urethra]

u·re·thro·scope (yōō·rē′thrə·skōp) *n. Med.* An instrument for examining the urethra. — **u·re′thro·scop′ic** (-skop′ik) *adj.* — **u·re·thros·co·py** (yŏŏr′ə·thros′kə·pē) *n.*

u·ret·ic (yōō·ret′ik) *adj. Med.* **1** Diuretic. **2** Of or pertaining to the urine; urinary. [<LL *ureticus* <Gk. *ourētikos* < *ouron* urine]

U·rey (yŏŏr′ē), **Harold Clayton,** born 1893, U. S. chemist.

Ur·fa (ŏŏr·fä′) A city in southern Turkey in Asia, near the Syrian border: ancient *Edessa.*

Ur·fé (dür·fā′), **Honoré d′,** 1568–1625, French novelist.

Ur·ga (ŏŏr′gä) The former name for ULAN BATOR.

urge (ûrj) *v.* **urged, urg·ing** *v.t.* **1** To drive or force forward; impel; push. **2** To plead with or entreat earnestly, as with arguments or explanations: He *urged* them to accept the plan. **3** To press or argue the doing, consideration, or acceptance of; advocate earnestly. **4** To move or force to some course or action; constrain. **5** To stimulate or excite; incite; intensify. **6** To ply or use vigorously, as oars. — *v.i.* **7** To present or press arguments, claims, etc. **8** To exert an impelling or prompting force. See synonyms under ACTUATE, PERSUADE, PIQUE, PLEAD, PUSH, QUICKEN. — *n.* **1** A strong impulse to perform a certain act. **2** The act of urging; the state of being urged. [<L *urgere* drive, urge]

Ur·gel (ŏŏr·hel′) A city in Lérida, NE Spain, in the Pyrenees SW of Andorra; seat of a bishop who is joint suzerain of Andorra.

ur·gen·cy (ûr′jən·sē) *n. pl.* **·cies** **1** The quality of being urgent. **2** Pressure by entreaty; pressure of necessity. **3** The act of urging. **4** Something urgent. See synonyms under NECESSITY.

ur·gent (ûr′jənt) *adj.* **1** Characterized by urging or importunity; requiring prompt attention; pressing; imperative. **2** Eagerly importunate or insistent. [<F <L *urgens, -entis,* ppr. of *urgere* drive] — **ur′gent·ly** *adv.*

Synonyms: importunate, pertinacious, pressing, solicitous.

–urgy *combining form* Development of or work with a (specified) material or product: *metallurgy, chemurgy, zymurgy.* [<Gk. *-ourgia* < *ergon* work]

U·ri (ŏŏr′ē) A canton in central Switzerland; 415 square miles; capital, Altdorf.

–uria *combining form Pathol.* A (specified) condition of the urine: usually used to indicate disease or abnormality: *hematuria, dysuria.* [<NL <Gk. *-ouria* < *ouron* urine]

U·ri·ah (yōō·rī′ə) A masculine personal name. Also *Ital.* **U·ri·a** (ōō·rē′ä), **U·ri·as** (*Ger.* ōō·rē′äs, *Lat.* yə·rī′əs), *Fr.* **U·rie** (ü·rē′). [<Hebrew, God is light]

— **Uriah** A Hittite captain in the Israelite army, husband of Bathsheba, treacherously sent to his death by David. II *Sam.* xi 15–17.

Uriah Heep An unctuous, fawning, scheming character in Dickens's *David Copperfield;* hence, an odious hypocrite.

u·ric (yŏŏr′ik) *adj.* Of, pertaining to, or derived from urine. [<F *urique*]

uric acid *Biochem.* A white, almost insoluble dibasic acid, $C_5H_4N_4O_3$, of varying crystalline forms, found in small quantity in human urine. It is a product of the incomplete oxidation of animal tissue and animal diet, and forms the nucleus of most urinary and renal calculi.

urico– *combining form* Uric acid; of or related to uric acid: *uricolysis,* the splitting up of uric acid. Also, before vowels, **uric–.** [<URIC]

U·ri·el (yŏŏr′ē·əl) A masculine personal name. [<Hebrew, light of God]

— **Uriel** One of the seven archangels of Christian legend: in Milton's *Paradise Lost,* represented as "regent of the sun."

U·rim (yŏŏr′im) *n. pl.* **1** Objects mentioned in the Old Testament (*Ex.* xxviii 30, etc.) in connection with the breastplate of the high priest: generally in the phrase **Urim and Thummim,** supposed to have been precious stones used in casting lots, one signifying an affirmative and the other a negative answer. **2** In Mormon theology, with the Thummim, the sacred objects used by seers under divine direction, especially those used by Joseph Smith in translating the *Book of Mormon.* [<Hebrew *ūrīm* fires < *ūr* shine]

u·ri·nal (yŏŏr′ə·nəl) *n.* **1** A toilet or closet convenience or fixture for men's use in urination; also, a private place containing such conveniences for public use, as in a park. **2** A receptacle for urine; a glass receptacle, as a bottle, used in the inspection of urine. [<OF <Med. L *urinale,* orig. neut. of L *urinalis* pertaining to urine < *urina* urine]

u·ri·nal·y·sis (yŏŏr′ə·nal′ə·sis) *n. pl.* **·ses** (-sēz) Chemical analysis of the urine: also spelled *uranalysis.* [<NL <URIN(O)- + (AN)ALYSIS]

u·ri·nar·y (yŏŏr′ə·ner′ē) *adj.* Of, pertaining to, or concerned in the production and excretion of urine: the *urinary* organs. — *n. pl.* **·nar·ies** **1** A reservoir for storing urine, etc., for use as manure. **2** A urinal.

urinary calculus *Pathol.* A concretion formed in the urinary passages; the stone.

u·ri·nate (yŏŏr′ə·nāt) *v.i.* **·nat·ed, ·nat·ing** To void or pass urine. [<Med. L *urinatus,* pp. of *urinare* pass urine < *urina* urine] — **u′ri·na′tion** *n.*

u·rine (yŏŏr′in) *n.* A pale–yellow fluid secreted from the blood of mammals by the kidneys, stored in the bladder, and voided through the urethra: the principal vehicle by which nitrogenous and saline matters are removed from the system. [<F <L *urina*]

u·ri·ne·mi·a (yŏŏr′ə·nē′mē·ə) *n.* Uremia. Also **u′ri·nae′mi·a.** [<URIN(O)- + -EMIA] — **u′ri·ne′mic** or **·nae′mic** *adj.*

u·ri·nif·er·ous (yŏŏr′ə·nif′ər·əs) *adj.* Concerned in the conveyance of urine.

urino– *combining form* Urine. Also, before vowels, **urin–,** as in *urinalysis.* [<L *urina* urine]

u·ri·no·gen·i·tal (yŏŏr′ə·nō·jen′ə·təl) *adj.* Urogenital.

u·ri·nos·co·py (yŏŏr′ə·nos′kə·pē) *n. pl.* **·pies** Uroscopy.

u·ri·nous (yŏŏr′ə·nəs) *adj.* Of, pertaining to, containing, or resembling urine. Also **u′ri·nose** (-nōs).

Ur·mi·a (ŏŏr′mē·ə), **Lake** The largest lake of Iran, between Tabriz and the Turkish border; in summer, 1,500 square miles; in winter, 2,300 square miles; 90 miles long, 30 miles wide: also *Rizaiyeh. Persian* **U·ru·mi·yeh** (ōō·rōō·mē·ye′)

urn (ûrn) *n.* **1** A rounded or angular vase having a foot, variously used in antiquity as a receptacle for the ashes of the dead, a water vessel, measure, etc. **2** A vessel for preserving the ashes of the dead; a grave. **3** In ancient Rome, a receptacle used to hold lots drawn in voting. **4** A vase–shaped receptacle having a faucet, and designed for keeping tea, coffee, etc., hot, as by means of a spirit lamp. ◆ Homophones: *earn, erne.* [<F *urne* <L *urna*]

URN
In park at Versailles.

uro–[1] *combining form* Urine; pertaining to urine or to the urinary tract: *urology.* Also, before vowels, *ur–.* [<Gk. *ouron* urine]

uro–[2] *combining form* A tail; of or related to the tail; caudal: *uropod.* Also, before vowels, *ur–.* [<Gk. *oura* a tail]

u·ro·bil·in (yŏŏr′ə·bil′in, -bī′lin) *n. Biochem.* A brownish, resinous bile pigment, found in urine and sometimes in the blood. [<URO-[1] + BILE + -IN]

add, āce, câre, pälm; end, ēven; it, īce; odd, ōpen, ôrder; tŏŏk, pōōl; up, bûrn; ə = a in *above,* e in *sicken,* i in *clarity,* o in *melon,* u in *focus;* yōō = u in *fuse;* oi, oil; ou, pout; ch, check; g, go; ng, ring; th, thin; t͟h, this; zh, vision. Foreign sounds à, œ, ü, kh, ń; and ◆: see page xx. < from; + plus; ? possibly.

u·ro·chord (yŏŏr'ə-kôrd) *n. Zool.* The notochord or central axis of larval ascidians and certain adult tunicates. [<URO-² + CHORD²] —**u'ro·chor'dal** *adj.*

U·ro·chor·da·ta (yŏŏr'ō-kôr-dā'tə) *n. pl.* The tunicates. [<NL <URO-² + CHORDATA]

u·ro·chrome (yŏŏr'ə-krōm) *n. Biochem.* The yellow pigment which gives to urine its characteristic color.

u·rochs (yŏŏr'oks) *n.* The urus. [<G]

U·ro·de·la (yŏŏr'ə-dē'lə) *n. pl.* Caudata. [<NL <URO-² + Gk. *dēlos* visible]

u·ro·gen·i·tal (yŏŏr'ō-jen'ə-təl) *adj.* Of or pertaining to the urinary and genital organs and their functions.

u·ro·gen·i·tals (yŏŏr'ō-jen'ə-təlz) *n. pl.* The urogenital organs.

u·rog·e·nous (yŏŏ-roj'ə-nəs) *adj.* Producing or promotive of the urinary secretion. [<URO-¹ + -GENOUS]

u·ro·lith (yŏŏr'ə-lith) *n. Pathol.* A urinary calculus. [<URO-¹ + -LITH¹] —**u'ro·lith'ic** *adj.*

u·ro·li·thi·a·sis (yŏŏr'ō-li-thī'ə-sis) *n. Pathol.* Any diseased condition due to the formation of urinary calculi. [<NL <URO-¹ + LITHIASIS]

u·rol·o·gy (yŏŏ-rol'ə-jē) *n.* The branch of medical science that relates to the urine and to the genitourinary tract in health and in disease. —**u·ro·log·ic** (yŏŏr'ə-loj'ik) or **·i·cal** *adj.* —**u·rol'o·gist** *n.*

u·ro·pod (yŏŏr'ə-pod) *n. Zool.* An abdominal or caudal limb or appendage of an arthropod, especially one of the posterior pairs of pleopods in a crustacean. [<URO-¹ + -POD] —**u·rop·o·dal** (yŏŏ-rop'ə-dəl), **u·rop'o·dous** *adj.*

u·ro·pyg·i·al (yŏŏr'ə-pij'ē-əl) *adj.* Of or pertaining to the uropygium.

uropygial gland *Ornithol.* The gland at the base of a bird's tail, secreting an oily substance used to preen the feathers.

u·ro·pyg·i·um (yŏŏr'ə-pij'ē-əm) *n. Ornithol.* The terminal part of the body supporting the tail feathers of a bird; rump. [<NL <Gk. *ouropygion*, alter. (after *oura* tail) of *orrhopygion* < *orrhos* end of the os sacrum + *pygē* rump]

u·ros·co·py (yŏŏ-ros'kə-pē) *n. Med.* Diagnosis by examination of the urine. [<URO-¹ + -SCOPY] —**u·ro·scop·ic** (yŏŏr'ə-skop'ik) *adj.* —**u·ros'co·pist** *n.*

U·ro·tro·pin (yŏŏr'ə-trō'pin) *n.* Proprietary name for a brand of methenamine.

u·ro·xan·thin (yŏŏr'ə-zan'thin) *n.* Indican (def. 2). [<URO-¹ + XANTHIN]

Ur·quhart (ûr'kərt), **Sir Thomas**, 1611–60, Scottish author; translator of Rabelais.

ur·sa (ûr'sə) *n. Latin* A she–bear: used in the phrases *Ursa Major* and *Ursa Minor.*

Ursa Major *Astron.* The Great Bear, a large northern constellation containing the seven conspicuous stars called the Septentriones, including the two Pointers, Dubhe and Merak, which point to the polestar: also called *Big Dipper, the Dipper, Charles's Wain.* See CONSTELLATION.

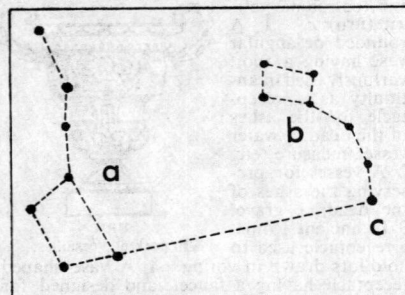

URSA MAJOR AND URSA MINOR
a. Ursa Major. *b.* Ursa Minor. *c.* Polestar.

Ursa Minor *Astron.* The Little Bear, a northern constellation including the polestar: also called *Little Dipper, Dog's Tail.* See CONSTELLATION.

ur·si·form (ûr'sə-fôrm) *adj.* Having the form of a bear. [<L *ursus* bear + -FORM]

ur·sine (ûr'sīn, -sin) *adj.* 1 Pertaining to or like a bear. 2 Clothed with dense bristles, as certain caterpillars. [<L *ursinus* < *ursus* bear]

ursine howler See HOWLER (def. 3).

Ur·spra·che (ŏŏr'shprä'khə) *n. German* A

primitive, original, or parent language; particularly, a hypothetical primitive Indo-European language.

Ur·su·la (ûr'syə-lə, -sə-, *Du.* ŏŏr'sŏŏ-lä) A feminine personal name. Also *Fr.* **Ur·sule** (ür·sül'), *Ger., Sw.* **Ur·sel** (ŏŏr'səl), *Sp.* **Ur·so·la** (ŏŏr'sō-lä). [<L, little she–bear] —**Ursula, Saint** A Cornish princess of the fourth or fifth century, martyred, according to legend, with eleven thousand virgins at Cologne by the Huns.

Ur·su·line (ûr'syə-lin, -sə-, -līn) *adj.* Pertaining to St. Ursula or to an order of nuns founded in 1537 by St. Angela Merici: they are engaged chiefly in the education of girls. —*n.* An Ursuline nun.

Ur·text (ŏŏr'tekst) *n. German* Earliest or primary form of a written text.

ur·ti·ca·ceous (ûr'tə-kā'shəs) *adj. Bot.* Belonging to a widely distributed family (*Urticaceae*) of trees, shrubs, or herbs, the nettle family, some of which are provided with sharp, stinging hairs. [<NL <L *urtica* nettle]

ur·ti·car·i·a (ûr'tə-kâr'ē-ə) *n. Pathol.* A disease of the skin, variously caused, characterized by evanescent, rounded elevations resembling wheals raised by a whip, and attended with intense itching; nettle rash; hives. [<NL <L *urtica* nettle] —**ur'ti·car'·i·al** or **·i·ous** *adj.*

ur·ti·cate (ûr'tə-kāt) *v.t. & v.i.* **·cat·ed**, **·cat·ing** To sting, as with nettles. [<Med. L *urticatus*, pp. of *urticare* sting < *urtica* nettle]

ur·ti·ca·tion (ûr'tə-kā'shən) *n. Med.* 1 Formerly, the act, process, or effect of whipping with nettles as a stimulant, as in paralysis. 2 A tingling or burning sensation. 3 The development of urticaria.

U·ru·bam·ba (ŏŏ'rŏŏ-väm'bä) A river in southern Peru, flowing about 450 miles NW and north from the Andes of SE Peru to the Ucayali in central Peru.

U·ru·guay (yŏŏr'ə-gwā, *Sp.* ŏŏ'rŏŏ-gwī) 1 A republic of SE South America, on the Atlantic; 72,172 square miles; capital, Montevideo. 2 A river in SE South America, flowing 1,000 miles SW to the Río de la Plata. —**U'ru·guay'an** *adj. & n.*

U·rum·chi (ŏŏ'rŏŏm'chē') The capital of the Sinkiang–Uigur Autonomous Region, NW China. Also **U'rum'tsi'.**

U·run·di (ŏŏ-rŏŏn'dē) A former district of German East Africa; since 1923, the southern county of Ruanda–Urundi; 10,658 square miles.

u·rus (yŏŏr'əs) *n.* An extinct, long–horned, wild ox of Germany (*Bos primigenius*), so named by Julius Caesar: also called *aurochs, urochs.* [<L <Gmc. Cf. OHG *ur.*]

u·ru·shi·ol (ŏŏr'ŏŏ-shē-ōl', -ol') *n.* A poisonous, irritant liquid, the active principle of poison ivy and the Japanese lac tree. [<Japanese *urushi* lacquer + -OL²]

us (us) *pron.* The objective case of WE. [OE *ūs*]

us·a·ble (yŏŏ'zə-bəl) *adj.* 1 Capable of being used. 2 That can be used conveniently. Also **use'a·ble.** —**us'a·ble·ness** *n.* —**us'a·bly** *adv.*

us·age (yŏŏ'sij, -zij) *n.* 1 The manner of using or treating a person or thing; treatment; also, the act of using. 2 Customary or habitual practice, or something permitted by it or done in accordance with it; custom or a custom: an act permitted by *usage*; ancient *usages.* 3 *Law* Uniform practice. 4 The way of using words, speech patterns, etc., that is general and established among the majority of the native speakers and writers of a language. 5 *Obs.* Conduct; behavior. See synonyms under HABIT. —**nonjurors' usages** In English and Scottish history, certain ceremonies, including mixing wine with water, prayer for the dead, trine immersion at baptism, the chrism at confirmation, anointing of the sick, etc., adopted by the nonjurors. [<OF <Med. L *usaticum* <L *usus.* See USE.]

us·ance (yŏŏ'zəns) *n.* 1 A period of time, variable as between various countries, which, by commercial usage, is allowed, exclusive of days of grace, for payment of bills of exchange, especially foreign. 2 *Econ.* An income derived from the possession of wealth in any way it may be invested. 3 *Obs.* Employment; use. 4 *Obs.* Interest on money. 5 *Obs.* Custom. Also *Obs.* **us'aunce.** [<OF <*us* <L *usus.* See USE.]

use (yŏŏz) *v.* **used, us·ing** *v.t.* 1 To employ for the accomplishment of a purpose; make use of. 2 To put into practice or employ habitually; make a practice of: to *use* diligence in business. 3 To expend the whole of; consume: often with *up.* 4 To conduct oneself toward; treat: to *use* one badly. 5 To make familiar by habit or practice; accustom; inure: usually in the past participle: He is *used* to exposure. 6 To partake of; smoke or chew: He does not *use* tobacco. —*v.i.* 7 To do something customarily or habitually; be accustomed or wont: now only in the past tense as an auxiliary to form a phrase equivalent to a frequentative past tense: I *used* to go there. See synonyms under EMPLOY, OCCUPY. —*n.* (yŏŏs) 1 The act of using; application or employment to an end, particularly a good or useful end; the fact or condition of being employed. 2 Suitableness or adaptability to an end; serviceableness: the *uses* of adversity. 3 Way or manner of using. 4 Occasion or need to employ; necessity: I have no *use* for it; purpose; function. 5 Habitual practice or employment; the fact of being habitually used; custom; usage. 6 Any special form, ceremony, or ritual of public worship, or any individual service that arose in or was perpetuated by a church, diocese, or branch of a church: Sarum *use*, Roman *use*, York *use.* Compare LITURGY. 7 *Law* The permanent equitable right that a beneficiary has to the enjoyment of the rents and profits of lands and tenements of which the legal title and possession are vested in another in trust for the beneficiary. 8 *Obs.* Ordinary experience or occurrence. 9 Usury. See synonyms under CUSTOM, HABIT, OCCUPATION, SERVICE, UTILITY. [<OF *user* <L *usus*, pp. of *uti* use]

use·ful (yŏŏs'fəl) *adj.* Serviceable; serving a use or purpose, especially a valuable one; productive of good; beneficial. —**use'ful·ly** *adv.* —**use'ful·ness** *n.*

Synonyms: adapted, advantageous, available, beneficial, conducive, convenient, favorable, good, helpful, profitable, salutary, serviceable, suitable, suited. See CONVENIENT, EXPEDIENT, GOOD. Compare UTILITY. *Antonyms:* see synonyms for USELESS.

use·less (yŏŏs'lis) *adj.* Unserviceable; being of no use; not serving, or not capable of serving, any beneficial purpose. —**use'less·ly** *adv.* —**use'less·ness** *n.*

Synonyms: abortive, bootless, fruitless, futile, ineffectual, nugatory, null, profitless, unavailing, unprofitable, unserviceable, vain, valueless, worthless. That which is *bootless, fruitless*, or *profitless* fails to accomplish any valuable result; that which is *abortive, ineffectual*, or *unavailing* fails to accomplish a result that it was, or was supposed to be, adapted to accomplish. That which is *useless, futile*, or *vain* is inherently incapable of accomplishing a specified result. *Useless* in the widest sense signifies not of use for any valuable purpose, and is thus closely similar to *valueless* and *worthless. Fruitless* is more final than *ineffectual*, as applying to the sum or harvest of endeavor. That which is *useless* lacks fitness for a purpose; that which is *vain* lacks imaginable fitness. See VAIN, WASTE. *Antonyms:* see synonyms for USEFUL.

us·er (yŏŏ'zər) *n.* 1 One who or that which uses. 2 *Law* The exercise or enjoyment of a right.

Ush·ant (ush'ənt) An island off NW France, comprising the westernmost point of France; 5 miles long, 2 miles wide: French *Île d'Ouessant.*

U·shas (ŏŏ'shəs, ŏŏ·shäs') In Hindu mythology, the goddess of the dawn.

ush·er (ush'ər) *n.* 1 One who acts as doorkeeper, as of a court or other assemblyroom. 2 An officer whose duty it is to introduce strangers or walk before a person of rank. 3 One who conducts persons to seats, as in a church or theater. 4 *Brit.* An under-teacher. —*v.t.* 1 To act as an usher to; escort; conduct. 2 To precede as a harbinger; be a forerunner of. [<OF *uissier* <L *ostiarius* doorkeeper < *ostium* door]

ush·er·ette (ush'ə-ret') *n.* A female usher, as in a theater.

Usk (usk) A river in SW England and SE

Wales, flowing 60 miles east, SE, and south from the eastern border of Carmarthenshire to the Bristol Channel at Newport.

Üs·küb (üs·küp′) The Turkish name for SKOPLJE.

Us·ku·da·ma (ōōs′kōō·dä′mə) An ancient name for ADRIANOPLE.

Üs·kü·dar (üs′kü·där′) A Turkish city on the Asian side of the Bosporus opposite Istanbul: also *Scutari*.

Us·nach (ōōsh′nə) In old Irish legend, a famous warrior, father of three even more famous sons.

Us·pal·la·ta (ōōs′pä·yä′tä) A pass over the Andes between Santiago, Chile, and Mendoza, Argentina: elevation, 12,650 feet: also *La Cumbre*.

us·que·baugh (us′kwə·bô) n. A distilled spirit, as whisky: so called in Ireland and Scotland. Also **us′qua·bae, us′que, us′que·bae.** [<Irish and Scottish Gaelic *uisge–beatha* <*uisge* water + *beatha* life]

Ussh·er (ush′ər), **James**, 1581–1656, Irish bishop and theologian.

Us·su·ri (ōō·sōō′rē) A river forming part of the boundary between northeasternmost China and southeasternmost U.S.S.R., and flowing 365 miles north from the SW Sikhote–Alin Range to the Amur at Khabarovsk.

U·sta·si (ōō·stä′shē) A Croat fascist party in World War II supported by the German and Italian governments. Also **U·sta′chi.**

Us·ti·la·go (us′tə·lā′gō) n. A genus of smut fungi (order *Ustilaginales*) which attack the tissues of many plants, especially cereals, as *U. zeae*, destructive of corn, *U. tritici*, parasitic on wheat, etc. [<NL <LL <L *ustulatus* scorched. See USTULATE.]

Us·ti nad La·bem A city on the Elbe in NW Bohemia, the Czech Republic. German *Aussig*.

us·tion (us′chən) n. **1** The act of burning, or the state of being burnt. **2** *Med.* Cauterization by burning. [<L *ustio, -onis* <*ustus*, pp. of *urere* burn]

us·tu·late (us′chōō·lit, -lāt) adj. Scorched, burned, or colored as if by burning or scorching. [<L *ustulatus*, pp. of *ustulare* scorch, freq. of *urere* burn]

us·tu·la·tion (us′chōō·lā′shən) n. **1** The act of burning or searing. **2** In pharmacy, the drying of substances by heat preparatory to pulverization. **3** The burning of wine.

u·su·al (yōō′zhōō·əl) adj. Such as occurs in the ordinary course of events; frequent; common. [<OF <LL *usualis* <L *usus* use. See USE.] —**u′su·al·ly** adv. —**u′su·al·ness** n.

Synonyms: accustomed, common, customary, everyday, familiar, frequent, general, habitual, normal, ordinary, prevailing, prevalent, regular, wonted. In strictness, *common* and *general* apply to the greater number of individuals in a class; but both words are in good use as applying to the greater number of instances in a series, so that it is possible to speak of one person's *common* practice or *general* custom, but *ordinary* or *usual* would in such case be preferable. See COMMON, FREQUENT, GENERAL, HABITUAL, NORMAL. *Antonyms:* exceptional, extraordinary, infrequent, out–of–the–way, rare, singular, strange, uncommon, unusual.

u·su·fruct (yōō′zyōō·frukt, yōō′syōō–) n. *Law* The right of using the property of another and of drawing the profits it produces without wasting its substance. [<LL *usufructus* <L *ususfructus* <*usus et fructus* use and fruit]

u·su·fruc·tu·ar·y (yōō′zyōō·fruk′chōō·er′ē, yōō′syōō–) n. pl. **·ar·ies** One who holds property for use by usufruct, as a tenant. —adj. Of, pertaining to, or having the nature of a usufruct. [<LL *usufructuarius* <*ususfructus*. See USUFRUCT.]

u·su·rer (yōō′zhər·ər) n. **1** One who practices usury; one who lends money, especially at an exorbitant or illegal rate. **2** *Obs.* One who lends money on interest; any money–lender. [<OF *usurier* <Med. L *usurarius* <L *usura* use, usury. See USURY.]

u·su·ri·ous (yōō·zhŏŏr′ē·əs) adj. Practicing usury; having the nature of usury. —**u·su′ri·ous·ly** adv. —**u·su′ri·ous·ness** n.

u·surp (yōō·zûrp′, -sûrp′) v.t. **1** To seize and hold (the office, rights, or powers of another)

without right or legal authority; take possession of by force. **2** To take arrogantly, as if by right. —v.i. **3** To practice usurpation; encroach: with *on* or *upon*. See synonyms under ASSUME. [<OF *usurper* <L *usurpare* make use of, usurp, ? <O *usususe* + *rapere* seize] —**u·surp′er** n. —**u·surp′ing·ly** adv.

u·sur·pa·tion (yōō′zər·pā′shən, -sər-) n. **1** The act of usurping: said especially of unlawful or forcible seizure of kingly power. **2** *Law* The wrongful intrusion into or unjust exercise of the privileges of any office, franchise, or right of another.

u·su·ry (yōō′zhər·ē) n. pl. **·ries 1** The act or practice of exacting a rate of interest beyond what is allowed by law. **2** *Obs.* The lending of money at interest; interest in general. **3** *Law* A premium paid for the use of money beyond the rate of interest established by law. [<OF *usure* <L *usura* <*usus*, pp. of *uti* use]

u·sus lo·quen·di (yōō′səs lō·kwen′dī) *Latin* Usage in speaking.

ut (ōōt) n. The first note in the Guido scale: now commonly *do*. [See GAMUT]

U·tah (yōō′tô, -tä) A State of the western United States; 84,916 square miles; capital, Salt Lake City; entered the Union Jan. 4, 1896; nickname, *Beehive State*: abbr. UT — **U′tah·an** adj. & n.

U·ta·ma·ro (ōō·tä·mä·rō), **Kitagama**, 1754?–1806, Japanese engraver and designer of color prints.

ut dic·tum (ut dik′təm) *Latin* As said or directed.

Ute (yōōt, yōō′tē) n. One of a group of tribes of North American Indians of Shoshonean stock, including the Uncompahgre, Kaviawach, and Uinta, formerly living in Utah, Colorado, and New Mexico: now on reservations in Colorado and Utah.

u·ten·sil (yōō·ten′səl) n. A vessel, tool, implement, etc., serving a useful purpose, especially for domestic or farming use. See synonyms under TOOL. [<OF *utensile* <L *utensilis* fit for use <*utens*, ppr. of *uti* use]

u·ter·ine (yōō′tər·in, -īn) adj. **1** Pertaining to the uterus. **2** Born of the same mother, but having a different father. [<LL *uterinus* born of the same mother]

u·ter·i·tis (yōō′tə·rī′tis) n. *Pathol.* Metritis. [<NL]

utero– *combining form* The uterus; of or pertaining to the uterus. Also, before vowels, **uter–**, as in *uteritis*. [<L *uterus* the uterus]

u·ter·us (yōō′tər·əs) n. pl. **u·ter·i** (yōō′tər·ī) **1** *Anat.* The organ of a female mammal in which the young are protected and developed before birth; the womb. In the higher mammals the uterus is single, but in the lower, as marsupials and monotremes, it is double. **2** *Zool.* Any differentiated portion of an oviduct found in various animals, other than mammals, serving as a repository for the development and nourishment of the eggs or the young during the embryonic stage. [<L]

Ut·gard (ōōt′gärd) In Norse mythology, the abode of Utgard–Loki.

Ut·gard–Lo·ki (ōōt′gärd·lō′kē) In Norse mythology, an invulnerable giant.

U·ther (yōō′thər) A legendary king of Britain; father of Arthur. See ARTHUR, KING; IGRAINE; PENDRAGON.

U·ti·ca (yōō′tə·kə) **1** An ancient city, 20 miles NW of Carthage in northern Africa; site 18 miles north of modern Tunis. **2** A city of central New York, on the Mohawk River.

u·tile (yōō′til) adj. Useful: now rare. [<L *utilis* <*uti* use]

u·til·i·tar·i·an (yōō·til′ə·târ′ē·ən) adj. **1** Relating to utility; especially, placing utility above beauty or the amenities of life. **2** Pertaining to or advocating utilitarianism. —n. **1** An advocate of utilitarianism. **2** One devoted to mere material utility.

u·til·i·tar·i·an·ism (yōō·til′ə·târ′ē·ən·iz′əm) n. **1** *Philos.* A system that holds usefulness to be the end and criterion of action; specifically, the ethical doctrine that actions derive their moral quality from their usefulness as means to some end, especially as means productive of happiness or unhappiness. Jeremy

Bentham, James Mill, and John Stuart Mill (who coined the word *utilitarianism*), understood by it the ethical theory which makes the pleasure or happiness of the individual or of mankind the end and criterion of the morally good and right. **2** The doctrine, in civics and politics, that the greatest happiness of the greatest number should be the sole end and criterion of all public action. **3** Devotion to mere material interests and aims.

u·til·i·ty (yōō·til′ə·tē) n. pl. **·ties 1** Fitness for some desirable, practical purpose; serviceableness; also, that which is necessary. **2** Fitness to supply the natural needs of man. **3** In philosophy, the happiness of mankind; the greatest happiness of the greatest number; the utilitarianism expounded by J. S. Mill. **4** *Obs.* Use; profit. **5** A public service, as gas, water, or other service. **6** pl. Shares of utility company stocks. [<F *utilité* <L *utilitas* <*utilis* useful <*uti* use]

Synonyms: advantage, advantageousness, avail, benefit, expediency, policy, profit, serviceableness, use, usefulness. *Utility* is somewhat more abstract and philosophical than *usefulness* or *use*, and is often employed to denote adaptation to produce a valuable result, while *usefulness* denotes the actual production of such result. We contrast beauty and *utility*. We say of an invention its *utility* is questionable, or, on the other hand, its *usefulness* has been proved by ample trial, or, I have found it of *use*. *Expediency* (literally, the getting the foot out) refers primarily to escape from or avoidance of some difficulty or trouble. *Policy* is often used in a kindred sense, more positive than *expediency*, but narrower than *utility*, as in the proverb "Honesty is the best *policy*." See PROFIT, SERVICE. *Antonyms:* disadvantage, folly, futility, impolicy, inadequacy, inexpediency, inutility, unprofitableness, worthlessness.

utility man 1 A regular member of a theatrical company who must be prepared, on short notice, to go on in any of the less important parts. **2** In baseball, a member of a team who acts as a substitute.

u·til·ize (yōō′təl·īz) v.t. **·ized, ·iz·ing** To make useful or serviceable; turn to practical account; make use of. Also *Brit.* **u′til·ise.** —**u′til·iz′a·ble** adj. —**u′til·i·za′tion** n. —**u′til·iz′er** n.

ut in·fra (ut in′frə) *Latin* As below.

u·ti pos·si·de·tis (yōō′tī pos′ə·dē′təs) *Latin* In international law, the principle that the parties to a war retain what they possessed at its close, unless otherwise provided by treaty; literally, as you possess.

ut·most (ut′mōst) adj. **1** Of the highest degree or the largest amount or number; greatest; uttermost. **2** Being at the farthest limit or most distant point; most remote; last. —n. The greatest possible extent; the most possible. See synonyms under END. [OE *ūtmest*]

U·to–Az·tec·an (yōō′tō·az′tek·ən) n. One of the chief linguistic stocks of North American Indians, formerly occupying two large regions of the NW and SW United States, comprising three branches (Shoshonean, Piman, and Nahuatlan) and embracing about fifty tribes: still surviving in the United States and Mexico. —adj. Of or pertaining to this linguistic stock.

u·to·pi·a (yōō·tō′pē·ə) n. **1** Any state, condition, or place of ideal perfection. **2** A visionary, impractical scheme for social improvement. [from *Utopia*]

U·to·pi·a (yōō·tō′pē·ə) An imaginary island described as the seat of a perfect social and political life in a romance by Sir Thomas More, published in 1516. [<NL <Gk. *ou* not + *topos* place]

u·to·pi·an (yōō·tō′pē·ən) adj. Excellent, but existing only in fancy or theory; ideal. See synonyms under IMAGINARY. —n. One who advocates impractical reforms; a visionary.

U·to·pi·an (yōō·tō′pē·ən) adj. Pertaining to or like Utopia. —n. A dweller in Utopia.

u·to·pi·an·ism (yōō·tō′pē·ən·iz′əm) n. Highly idealistic and impractical views, especially about social problems.

U·trecht (yōō′trekt, *Du.* ü′trekht) **1** A province of central Netherlands; 511 square miles. **2** Its capital, scene of the signing of a treaty (1713) ending the War of the Spanish Succession.

u·tri·cle (yōō′tri·kəl) *n.* **1** *Anat.* A small saclike cavity, especially the larger of two found in the bony vestibule of the inner ear. **2** *Bot.* **a** A small fruit having an inflated pericarp, as in the pigweed. **b** An air cell, as in certain aquatic plants. [<L *utriculus,* dim. of *uter* skin bag]

u·tric·u·lar (yōō·trik′yə·lər) *adj.* **1** Resembling a utricle or small sac. **2** Bladderlike; bearing or provided with utricles. Also **u·tric′u·late** (-lit, -lāt)

u·tric·u·li·tis (yōō·trik′yə·lī′tis) *n. Pathol.* Inflammation of a utricle, as of the inner ear. [<NL]

u·tric·u·lus (yōō·trik′yə·ləs) *n. pl.* **·li** (-lī) Utricle. [<L]

U·tril·lo (ōō·trē′lyō, ōō·tril′ō; *Fr.* ü·trē·lō′), **Maurice**, 1883–1955, French painter.

ut su·pra (ut sōō′prə) *Latin* As above: abbreviated *ut sup.*

Ut·tar Pra·desh (ōōt′ər prə·dāsh′) A constituent State of northern India, formed in 1950; 113,409 square miles; capital, Lucknow: formerly *United Provinces of Agra and Oudh.*

ut·ter¹ (ut′ər) *v.t.* **1** To give out or send forth with audible sound; express; say. **2** *Law* To put in circulation; now, especially, to deliver or offer (something forged or counterfeit) to another. **3** *Obs.* To give vent to in any way; give forth; emit. **4** *Obs.* To issue or deliver, as merchandise, in the course of trade. See synonyms under SPEAK. [ME *outre,* freq. of obs. *out* say, speak out] — **ut′ter·a·ble** *adj.* — **ut′ter·er** *n.*

ut·ter² (ut′ər) *adj.* **1** Realized or developed to the last degree; absolute; total: *utter* misery. **2** Being or done without conditions or qualifications; unqualified; final; peremptory; absolute: *utter* denial. **3** *Obs.* Outer; remote. [OE *ūttra,* orig. compar. of *ūt* out]

ut·ter·ance¹ (ut′ər·əns) *n.* **1** The act of uttering; vocal expression; manner of speaking; also, the power of speech. **2** A thing uttered or expressed. See synonyms under REMARK.

ut·ter·ance² (ut′ər·əns) *n. Obs.* The bitter end; the uttermost; the last extremity; death: in the phrase **to the utterance.** [Var. of OUTRANCE]

ut·ter·ly (ut′ər·lē) *adv.* In a complete manner; entirely; thoroughly.

ut·ter·most (ut′ər·mōst′) *adj. & n.* Utmost.

U–tube (yōō′tōōb′, -tyōōb′) *n.* A tube bent into U form, especially such a tube made of glass for laboratory use.

U–turn (yōō′tûrn′) *n. Colloq.* A continuous turn which reverses the direction of a vehicle on a road.

u·va (yōō′və) *n. Bot.* A succulent fruit having a central placenta, as a grape. [<L, grape]

u·var·o·vite (ōō·vär′ōf·it) *n.* An emerald-green calcium-chromium garnet. [after Count S. *Uvarov,* 1785–1855, Russian nobleman]

u·va·ur·si (yōō′və·ûr′sī) *n.* A trailing plant, the bearberry (def. 1). [<L, bear's grape]

u·ve·a (yōō′vē·ə) *n. Anat.* **1** The inner, colored layer of the iris. **2** The iris, ciliary muscle, and choroid coat. [<Med. L <L *uva* grape] — **u′ve·al** *adj.*

U·vé·a (ōō·vā′ä) The largest island of the Wallis archipelago, capital of the protectorate; 7 miles long, 4 miles wide.

u·ve·i·tis (yōō′vē·ī′tis) *n. Pathol.* Inflammation of the uvea or iris. [<NL <UVEA] — **u′·ve·it′ic** (-it′ik) *adj.*

u·ve·ous (yōō′vē·əs) *adj.* **1** Resembling a grape or a cluster of grapes. **2** Uveal. [<L *uva* grape]

u·vu·la (yōō′vyə·lə) *n. pl.* **·las** or **·lae** (-lē) *Anat.* **1** The pendent fleshy portion of the soft palate. **2** Either of two other similar processes, one at the neck of the bladder and the other on the under side of the cerebellum. [<LL, dim. of *uva* grape]

u·vu·lar (yōō′vyə·lər) *adj.* **1** Pertaining to or of the uvula. **2** *Phonet.* Produced by vibration of, or with the back of the tongue near or against, the uvula. — *n. Phonet.* A uvular sound.

u·vu·li·tis (yōō′vyə·lī′tis) *n. Pathol.* Inflammation of the uvula. [<NL]

Ux·bridge (uks′brij) An urban district of Middlesex, England, NW of London.

Ux·mal (ōōz·mäl′, ōōsh-, ōōs-) An ancient Mayan city of Yucatán, SE Mexico; site, 40 miles south of Mérida.

ux·or (uk′sôr) *n. Latin* Wife: abbreviated *ux.*

ux·o·ri·al (uk·sôr′ē·əl, -sō′rē-, ug·zôr′ē·əl, -zō′rē-) *adj.* **1** Of, pertaining to, characteristic of, or becoming to a wife. **2** Uxorious. [<L *uxorius* < *uxor* wife]

ux·o·ri·cide (uk·sôr′ə·sīd, -sō′rə-, ug·zôr′ə-, -zō′rə-) *n.* **1** The act of murdering or killing one's wife; wife-murder. **2** One who murders his wife. [<L *uxor* wife + -CIDE] — **ux·or′i·ci′dal** (-sīd′l) *adj.*

ux·o·ri·ous (uk·sôr′ē·əs, -sō′rē-, ug·zôr′ē-, -zō′rē-) *adj.* Fatuously or foolishly devoted to one's wife; showing extreme or foolish fondness for one's wife. [<L *uxorius* < *uxor* wife] — **ux·o′ri·ous·ly** *adv.* — **ux·o′ri·ous·ness** *n.*

Uz·bek 1 A member of a Turkic people dominant in Uzbekistan: a native or inhabitant of Uzbekistan. **2** The Turkic language of Uzbeks; the national language of Uzbekistan.

Uz·bek·i·stan A republic in Asia, 172,000 square miles; pop. 21,000,000; capital, Tashkent.

Uz·bek Soviet Socialist Republic A former republic of the U.S.S.R. in Central Asia.

U·zhok A pass of the Carpathian Mountains in SW Ukraine. *Polish* **U·zok.** *Hungarian* **U·zsok.**

V

v, V (vē) *n. pl.* **v's** or **V's, vs** or **Vs, vees** (vēz) **1** The twenty-second letter of the English alphabet; ultimately from Phoenician *vau,* vocalized by the Greeks into *upsilon,* and used by the Romans in the form V with the value of a semivowel (w) and, later, a consonant (v). In English it was used interchangeably with the character *u* until fairly modern times. Compare U, W. **2** The sound of the letter *v,* the voiced, labiodental fricative. See ALPHABET. — *n.* **1** A V-shaped piece, or two pieces at an acute angle, as part of a construction: also **vee.** **2** *Colloq.* A five-dollar bill. — *symbol* **1** The Roman numeral five. See under NUMERAL. **2** *Chem.* Vanadium (symbol V). **3** *Electr.* Volt. **4** Anything shaped like a V.

V–1 (vē′wun′) *n.* The robot bomb used against England by the Germans in World War II. See ROBOT BOMB under BOMB. [<G *vergeltungswaffe eins* retaliation weapon 1]

V–2 (vē′tōō′) *n.* A rocket bomb carrying a bomb load of one ton or more, and able to travel about 200 miles from its launching site: used against England by the Germans in World War II. [<G *vergeltungswaffe zwei* retaliation weapon 2]

Vaal (väl) A river of the Republic of South Africa, forming part of the boundary between the Orange Free State and the Transvaal and flowing 750 miles SW and west, from near the Swaziland border in SE Transvaal, to the Orange River near Kimberley.

Vaa·sa (vä′sä) A port of western Finland on the Gulf of Bothnia. *Swedish* **Va′sa.**

va·can·cy (vā′kən·sē). *n. pl.* **·cies 1** The state of being vacant; vacuity; emptiness; specifically, emptiness of mind. **2** That which is vacant, empty, or unoccupied; empty space. **3** An interruption of continuity of thought or space; a gap; chasm. **4** An unoccupied post, place, or office; a place destitute of an incumbent. **5** *Rare* Unoccupied time; leisure.

va·cant (vā′kənt) *adj.* **1** Containing or holding nothing; being without contents or occupants; especially, devoid of occupants; empty. **2** Occupied with nothing; unemployed; unencumbered; free. **3** Being or appearing without intelligence; inane. **4** Having no incumbent; unfilled: a *vacant* office. **5** *Law* Unoccupied or unused, as land; also, abandoned; having neither claimant nor heir, as an estate. **6** Free from cares. **7** Devoid of thought; unreflecting. [<F <L *vacans, -antis,* ppr. of *vacare* be empty] — **va′cant·ly** *adv.*

Synonyms: blank, empty, unemployed, unfilled, unoccupied, vacuous, void, waste. That is *empty* which contains nothing; that is *vacant* which is without that which has filled or might be expected to fill it; *vacant* has extensive reference to rights or possibilities of occupancy. A *vacant* room may not be *empty,* and an *empty* house may not be *vacant. Void* and *devoid* are rarely used in the literal sense, but are for the most part confined to abstract relations, *devoid* being followed by *of,* and having with that addition the effect of a prepositional phrase: The article is *devoid of* sense; The contract is *void* for want of consideration. *Waste,* in this connection, applies to that which is made so by devastation or ruin, or gives an impression of desolation, especially as combined with vastness, probably from association of the words *waste* and *vast; waste* is applied also to uncultivated or unproductive land, if of considerable extent; we speak of a *waste* tract or region. *Vacuous* refers to the condition of being *empty* or *vacant,* regarded as continuous or characteristic. See BLANK, IDLE. *Antonyms:* brimful, brimmed, brimming, busy, crammed, crowded, full, gorged, inhabited, jammed, occupied, overflowing, packed, replete.

va·can·ti·a bo·na (vā·kan′shē·ə bō′nə) *Latin* Goods without an owner; escheated goods.

va·cate (vā′kāt) *v.* **·cat·ed, ·cat·ing** *v.t.* **1** To make vacant; surrender possession of by removal. **2** To set aside; annul. **3** To give up (a position or office); quit. — *v.i.* **4** To leave an office, position, place, etc. **5** *Colloq.* To go away; leave. See synonyms under CANCEL. [<L *vacatus,* pp. of *vacare* be empty]

va·ca·tion (vā·kā′shən) *n.* **1** An intermission of activity, employment, or stated exercises, as for recreation or rest; a holiday. **2** *Law* The period of time intervening between stated terms of court. **3** The intermission of the course of studies and exercises in an educational institution. **4** The act of vacating. **5** *Obs.* The time during which an office is vacant. — *v.i.* To take a vacation. [<F <L *vacatio, -onis* freedom from duty < *vacatus.* See VACATE.] — **va·ca′tion·er** *n.*

va·ca·tion·ist (vā·kā′shən·ist) *n.* One who is taking a vacation or staying at a resort; a tourist.

vac·ci·nal (vak′sə·nəl) *adj.* Of the nature of or relating to vaccine or vaccination.

vac·ci·nate (vak′sə·nāt) *v.* **·nat·ed, ·nat·ing** *Med. v.t.* To inoculate with a vaccine as a preventive or therapeutic measure; especially, to inoculate against smallpox. — *v.i.* To perform the act of vaccination. [<VACCINE) + -ATE²]

vac·ci·na·tion (vak′sə·nā′shən) *n. Med.* The act or process of vaccinating, especially against smallpox.

vac·ci·na·tion·ist (vak′sə·nā′shən·ist) *n. Med.* An advocate of vaccination.

vac·ci·na·tor (vak′sə·nā′tər) *n. Med.* **1** One who vaccinates. **2** An instrument used for vaccination.

vac·cine (vak′sēn, -sin) *n.* **1** The virus of cowpox, as prepared for or introduced by vaccination: usually lymph, dried or fluid, or part of the crust from a pustule. **2** Any in-

oculable immunizing agent; a preparation containing bacteria so treated as to give immunity from specific diseases when injected into the subject. — *adj.* **1** Pertaining to or derived from cows. **2** Pertaining to cowpox or vaccination. [<L *vaccinus* pertaining to a cow <*vacca* cow]

vaccine point *Med.* A sharp-pointed piece of bone, ivory, or the like, coated with vaccine for inoculation purposes.

vac·cin·i·a (vak·sin′ē·ə) *n. Pathol.* Cowpox. Also **vac·ci·na** (vak·sī′nə). [<NL <L *vacci·us.* See VACCINE.]

vac·cin·i·a·ceous (vak·sin′ē·ā′shəs) *adj. Bot.* Pertaining or belonging to a genus (*Vaccinium*; family *Ericaceae* or *Vacciniaceae*) of shrubs with cylindrical or globular flowers and small blue, black, or red berries, including the blueberry, huckleberry, and cranberry. [<NL <L *vaccinium* blueberry]

vac·ci·ni·za·tion (vak′sə·nə·zā′shən, -nī·zā′-) *n. Med.* Repeated inoculation with a vaccine.

vac·cin·o·ther·a·py (vak′sən·ō·ther′ə·pē) *n. Med.* Treatment by bacterial vaccines.

vac·il·late (vas′ə·lāt) *v.i.* **·lat·ed, ·lat·ing** **1** To sway one way and the other; totter; waver. **2** To fluctuate. **3** To waver in mind; be irresolute. See synonyms under FLUCTUATE. [<L *vacillatus,* pp. of *vacillare* waver] — **vac′il·la′tion** *n.*

vac·il·lat·ing (vas′ə·lā′ting) *adj.* Inclined to waver; uncertain; wavering. Also **vac′il·lant, vac′il·la·to′ry** (-lə·tôr′ē, -tō′rē). — **vac′il·lat′·ing·ly** *adv.*

vac·u·a (vak′yōō·ə) Plural of VACUUM.

va·cu·i·ty (va·kyōō′ə·tē) *n.* *pl.* **·ties** **1** The state of being a vacuum; emptiness. **2** Vacant space; a void. **3** Freedom from mental exertion; idleness. **4** Lack of intelligence; stupidity. **5** Nothingness. **6** An inane or idle thing or statement: His speech was weakened by *vacuities.* [<F *vacuité* <L *vacuitas, -tatis* <*vacuus* empty]

vac·u·o·lat·ed (vak′yōō·ə·lā′tid) *adj. Biol.* Having one or more vacuoles. — **vac′u·o·la′tion** *n.*

vac·u·ole (vak′yōō·ōl) *n. Biol.* A minute cavity containing air, a watery fluid, or a chemical secretion of the protoplasm, found in an organ, tissue, or cell. [<F <L *vacuum,* neut. of *vacuus* empty]

vac·u·ous (vak′yōō·əs) *adj.* **1** Having no contents; containing no matter; empty. **2** Lacking intelligence; blank. **3** Idle; unoccupied. See synonyms under VACANT. [<L *vacuus*] — **vac′u·ous·ly** *adv.* — **vac′u·ous·ness** *n.*

vac·u·um (vak′yōō·əm, -yōōm) *n.* *pl.* **·u·ums** or **·u·a** (-yōō·ə) **1** *Physics* **a** A space absolutely devoid of matter. **b** A space from which air or other gas has been exhausted to a very high degree. **2** A partial diminution of the normal atmospheric pressure. **3** A void; an empty feeling. — *adj.* **1** Of, or used in the production of, a vacuum. **2** Exhausted or partly exhausted of gas, air, or vapor. **3** Operated by suction to produce a vacuum. — *v.t.* & *v.i. Colloq.* To clean with a vacuum cleaner. [<L, neut. of *vacuus* empty]

vacuum bottle A bottle having a double wall separated by a vacuum which permits the contents to be kept cold or hot for an appreciable period. Also **vacuum flask.**

vacuum cleaner A machine for cleaning floors, carpets, furnishings, etc., by the suction of an air current.

vacuum fan A fan producing suction or an incomplete vacuum.

vacuum gage A gage containing mercury for testing the pressure consequent on producing a vacuum, as in a condenser. Also **vacuum gauge.**

vacuum pump A pulsometer.

vacuum tube *Electronics* **1** A sealed glass tube exhausted of air to a high degree and containing electrodes between which electric discharges may be passed. **2** An electron tube.

vacuum valve *Brit.* A vacuum tube.

va·de in pa·ce (vā′dē in pā′sē) *Latin* Go in peace.

va·de me·cum (vā′dē mē′kəm) *Latin* Go with me; hence, anything carried for constant use, as a guidebook, manual, or bag. Also **va′de·me′cum, va′de–me′cum.**

Va·duz (fä·dōōts′) The capital of the principality of Liechtenstein, near the Rhine, SE of St. Gall, Switzerland.

vae vic·tis (vē vik′təs) *Latin* Woe to the vanquished.

vag·a·bond (vag′ə·bond) *n.* **1** One who wanders from place to place without visible means of support; a tramp. **2** One without a settled home; a wanderer; nomad. **3** A worthless fellow; rascal. — *adj.* **1** Pertaining to a vagabond; nomadic. **2** Having no definite residence; wandering; irresponsible. **3** Driven to and fro; aimless. [<F <L *vagabundus* <*vagus* wandering] — **vag′a·bond′age** *n.* — **vag′a·bond′ish** *adj.* — **vag′a·bond′ism** *n.*

vagabond neurosis Dromomania.

va·gar·y (və·gâr′ē) *n.* *pl.* **·gar·ies** A wild fancy; extravagant notion. See synonyms under FANCY, WHIM. [<obs. *vagary, v.,* wander <L *vagari*]

va·gi·na (və·jī′nə) *n.* *pl.* **·nas** or **·nae** (-nē) **1** *Anat.* **a** A sheath or sheathlike covering. **b** The canal leading from the external genital orifice in female mammals to the uterus. **2** *Zool.* The terminal portion of the oviduct of various invertebrates. **3** *Bot.* A tubular part surrounding another, as the basal portion of a leaf around a stem. [<L, a sheath]

vag·i·nal (vaj′ə·nəl, və·jī′-) *adj.* **1** Pertaining to or like a sheath; thecal. **2** Pertaining to the vagina.

vag·i·nate (vaj′ə·nit, -nāt) *adj.* **1** Having a sheath. **2** Formed into a sheath; tubular. Also **vag′i·nat′ed.** [<NL *vaginatus* <L *vagina* sheath]

vag·i·nec·to·my (vaj′ə·nek′tə·mē) *n. Surg.* **1** Removal or obliteration of the vaginal canal. **2** Resection of the serous membrane of the testis: also **vag′i·na·lec′to·my** (-nə·lek′tə·mē). [<VAGIN(O)- + -ECTOMY]

vag·i·nis·mus (vaj′ə·niz′məs, -nis′-) *n. Pathol.* Spasm of the sphincter muscle of the vagina with extreme sensitivity of the adjacent parts. [<NL]

vag·i·ni·tis (vaj′ə·nī′tis) *n. Pathol.* Inflammation of the vagina. [<NL]

vagino– *combining form Med.* The vagina; of or pertaining to the vagina. Also, before vowels, **vagin–,** as in *vaginectomy.* [<L *vagina* a sheath, the vagina]

va·gi·tus (və·jī′təs) *n.* The first cry of the newborn infant. [<L, pp. of *vagire* cry, squall]

va·go·to·ni·a (vā′gə·tō′nē·ə) *n. Pathol.* Excessive or morbid excitability of the vagus nerve, characterized by vasomotor instability, involuntary spasms, sweating, and constipation. [<NL <*vagus* the vagus nerve + Gk. *tonos* tone, tension] — **va′go·ton′ic** (-ton′ik) *adj.*

va·gran·cy (vā′grən·sē) *n.* *pl.* **·cies** The state, condition, or action of a vagrant. Also **va′·grant·ness.**

va·grant (vā′grənt) *n.* **1** A person without a settled home; an idle wanderer; vagabond; tramp. **2** A roving person; wanderer. — *adj.* **1** Wandering about as a vagrant. **2** Pertaining to one who or that which wanders; nomadic. **3** Having a wandering course; capricious; wayward. [ME *vagaraunt,* alter. of AF *wakerant* <OF *wacrant,* ppr. of *wacrer* walk, wander <Gmc.; infl. in form by L *vagari* wander] — **va′grant·ly** *adv.*

va·grom (vā′grəm) *adj. Obs.* Vagrant. [Alter. of VAGRANT; used by Dogberry in Shakespeare's *Much Ado About Nothing*]

vague (vāg) *adj.* **1** Lacking definiteness or precision. **2** Of uncertain source or authority: a *vague* rumor. **3** Not clearly recognized, understood, stated, or felt. **4** *Obs.* Roving; vagrant. **5** Shadowy; hazy. [<F <L *vagus* wandering] — **vague′ly** *adv.* — **vague′ness** *n.*

Synonyms: ambiguous, doubtful, dreamy, indefinite, indeterminate, indistinct, lax, loose, obscure, uncertain, undetermined, unsettled.

va·gus (vā′gəs) *n.* *pl.* **·gi** (-jī) *Anat.* Either of the tenth pair of cranial nerves originating in the medulla oblongata and sending branches to the lungs, heart, stomach, and most of the abdominal viscera; the pneumogastric nerve. Also **vagus nerve.** [<L, wandering]

Váh (väkh) A river in western Slovakia, Czechoslovakia, flowing 245 miles SW to the Danube: German *Waag.*

vail[1] (vāl) *n.* & *v.t. Obs.* Veil.

vail[2] (vāl) *Obs. v.i.* To be of use; avail. — *n.* **1** *Usually pl.* A gratuity or tip; a perquisite, often corrupt. **2** A windfall; find. **3** Advantage; proceeds; profit. ◆ Homophones: *vale, veil.* [Aphetic var. of AVAIL] — **vail′a·ble** *adj.*

vail[3] (vāl) *v.t. Archaic* **1** To let fall; lower, as the topsail, in salute or submission. **2** To take off (the hat, etc.) in respect or submission. ◆ Homophones: *vale, veil.* [Aphetic form of obs. *avale* <F *avaler* lower <*à val* down <L *ad vallem,* lit., to the valley]

vain (vān) *adj.* **1** Elated with self-admiration; greedy of applause. **2** Characterized by frivolity. **3** Ostentatious; showy: said of things. **4** Unproductive; worthless; fruitless; useless. **5** Without any substantial foundation; empty; unreal. — **in vain** **1** To no purpose; without effect. **2** In an irreverent or disrespectful manner: to take the Lord's name *in vain.* ◆ Homophones: *vane, vein.* [<F <L *vanus* empty] — **vain′ly** *adv.* — **vain′ness** *n.*

Synonyms: abortive, baseless, delusive, empty, fruitless, futile, idle, ineffectual, profitless, shadowy, trifling, trivial, unavailing, useless, vapid, worthless. *Vain* keeps the etymological idea through all changes of meaning; a *vain* endeavor is *empty* of result, or of adequate power to produce a result, a *vain* pretension is *empty* or destitute of support, a *vain* person has a conceit that is *empty* or destitute of adequate cause or reason. See USELESS. *Antonyms*: effective, efficient, firm, potent, powerful, real, solid, sound, substantial, valid, valuable, worthy.

vain·glo·ry (vān·glôr′ē, -glō′rē) *n.* Excessive or groundless vanity; also, vain pomp; boastfulness. See synonyms under PRIDE. [<OF *vaine gloire* <Med. L *vana gloria* empty pomp, show] — **vain·glo′ri·ous** *adj.* — **vain·glo′ri·ous·ly** *adv.* — **vain·glo′ri·ous·ness** *n.*

vair (vâr) *n.* **1** *Her.* One of the furs represented by rows of small shield-shaped figures. **2** *Obs.* A fur used for the garments of the nobility (14th century). [<F <LL *varius* ermine <L *varius* parti-colored, various]

Va·lais (và·le′) A canton in southern Switzerland, in the upper Rhône valley; 2,021 square miles; capital, Sion: German *Wallis.*

val·ance (val′əns, vā′ləns) *n.* **1** A drapery hanging from the tester of a bedstead. **2** A short, full drapery across the top of a window. **3** A damask used for upholstering. — *v.t.* **·anced, ·anc·ing** To furnish with or as with drapery, or a valance. [Prob. <OF *avalant,* ppr. of *avaler* descend] — **val′anced** *adj.*

Val·dai Hills (väl·dī′) A low plateau and group of hills in western European Russian S.F.S.R.; maximum height, 1,053 feet.

Val·de·mar (väl′də·mär) See WALDEMAR.

Val d'A·os·ta (väl dä·ôs′tä) An autonomous region of NW Italy bordering on France and Switzerland; 1,260 square miles; capital, Aosta.

Val·di·via (val·div′ē·ə, *Sp.* bäl·dē′vyä), **Pedro de,** 1500?–54, Spanish conqueror of Chile.

vale[1] (vāl) *n.* **1** A valley; a low-lying tract of land: now chiefly poetic. **2** A trough or channel. See synonyms under VALLEY. ◆ Homophones: *vail, veil.* [<OF *val* <L *vallis*]

va·le[2] (vā′lē) *interj. Latin* Farewell; literally, be in good health.

val·e·dic·tion (val′ə·dik′shən) *n.* A bidding farewell. See synonyms under FAREWELL. [<L *valedictus,* pp. of *valedicere* say farewell <*vale* farewell, orig. imperative of *valere* be well + *dicere* say]

val·e·dic·to·ri·an (val′ə·dik·tôr′ē·ən, -tō′rē-) *n.* One who delivers a valedictory; specifically, a student who delivers a valedictory at the graduating exercises of an educational institution: usually the member of the graduating class whose rank in scholarship is highest.

val·e·dic·to·ry (val′ə·dik′tər·ē) *adj.* Pertaining to a leave-taking. — *n.* *pl.* **·ries** A parting address, as by a member (ordinarily the first in rank) of a graduating class. See synonyms under FAREWELL.

va·lence (vā′ləns) *n. Chem.* **1** The property possessed by an element or radical of combining with or replacing other elements or radicals in definite and constant proportion. **2** The number of atoms of hydrogen (or its equivalent), taken as unity, with which an atom or radical can combine, or which it can

replace. It varies with different elements, and with certain elements in different compounds. **3** *Med.* The combining power of certain substances or bodies, as serums, chromosomes, and the like. Also **va′len·cy.** [< LL *valentia* strength, orig. neut. pl. of L *valens, -entis,* ppr. of *valere* be well, be strong]

valence electron *Chem.* One of the electrons in the outermost shell of an atom, regarded as being responsible for the chemical reaction of an element.

va·len·ci·a (və·len′shē·ə, -shə) *n.* A woven fabric with wool weft and silk or cotton warp. [from VALENCIA]

Va·len·ci·a (və·len′shē·ə, -shə; *Sp.* bä·len′thyä) **1** A region and former Moorish kingdom of eastern Spain on the Mediterranean; 8,996 square miles. **2** A province of eastern Spain, center of the Valencia region; 4,155 square miles. **3** A port of eastern Spain, the chief city of Valencia region and capital of Valencia province. **4** A city of north central Venezuela.

Va·len·ci·ennes (və·len′sē·enz′, *Fr.* vá·läṅ·syen′) *n.* A kind of bobbin lace with a floral pattern, originally made at Valenciennes. Also **Valenciennes lace, Val lace.**

Va·len·ciennes (vá·läṅ·syen′) A city of northern France on the Escaut in Nord department.

Va·lens (vā′lenz), 328?–378, Roman emperor of the East 364–378.

val·en·tine (val′ən·tīn) *n.* **1** A letter or token of affection sent, often anonymously, to a person of the opposite sex on St. Valentine's Day (Feb. 14), the anniversary of the beheading of this martyr by the Romans. **2** A sweetheart. [< OF]

Val·en·tine (val′ən·tīn) A masculine personal name. Also **Va·len·tin** (*Russian* vä·lyen·tyin′; *Ger.* vä′len·tēn; *Sw.* vä′len·tēn′; *Fr.* vá·läṅ·tań′), *Sp.* **Va·len·tín** (bä′len·tēn′), *Pg.* **Va·len·tim** (vä′leṅ·tēṅ′), *Ital.* **Va·len·ti·no** (vä′len·tē′nō), *Lat.* **Va·len·ti·nus** (val′ən·tī′nəs), *Du.* **Va·len·tijn** (vä′len·tīn). [< L, well, healthy]
—**Valentine, Saint,** Christian martyr of the third century A.D.

Val·en·tin·i·an (val′ən·tin′ē·ən) Name of three Roman emperors.
—**Valentinian I,** 321–375, reigned 364–375.
—**Valentinian II,** 372?–392, reigned 375–392.
—**Valentinian III,** 419–455, reigned 425–455: full name *Flavius Placidus Valentianus.*

Va·le·ra (və·ler′ə), **Éamon de** See under DE VALERA.

val·er·ate (val′ə·rāt) *n. Chem.* A salt of valeric acid. Also **va·le·ri·an·ate** (və·lir′ē·ən·āt′).

Va·le·ri·a (və·lir′ē·ə, *Ital.* vä·ler′yä) A feminine personal name. Also *Fr.* **Va·lé·rie** (vá·lā·rē′), *Ger.* **Va·le·ri·e** (vä·lā′rē·ə). [< L, strong]

va·le·ri·an (və·lir′ē·ən) *n.* **1** Any of a genus (*Valeriana*) of perennial herbs having flowers in cymes and roots often strong-smelling, especially the garden heliotrope. **2** The dried root of the garden heliotrope, which has been used as a sedative and carminative. [< OF *valeriane* < Med. L *valeriana,* appar. ult. < *Valerius* a personal name]

Va·le·ri·an (və·lir′ē·ən) Anglicized name of *Publius Licinius Valerianus,* 193?–260?, Roman emperor 254?–260?.

va·le·ri·a·na·ceous (və·lir′ē·ə·nā′shəs) *adj. Bot.* Pertaining to a family (*Valerianaceae*) of herbs, including valerian. [< NL < Med. L *valeriana* VALERIAN]

va·ler·ic (və·ler′ik, -lir′-) *adj.* **1** Of, pertaining to, or derived from valerian. **2** *Chem.* Pertaining to or designating one of four isomeric acids, $C_5H_{10}O_2$, of which two are found in valerian: all are made synthetically. Also **va·le·ri·an·ic** (və·lir′ē·an′ik).

Va·lé·ry (vá·lā·rē′), **Paul Ambroise,** 1871–1945, French poet and philosopher.

val·et (val′it, val′ā; *Fr.* vá·le′) *n.* **1** A gentleman's personal servant. **2** A man servant in a hotel who performs personal services for patrons. —*v.t.* & *v.i.* To serve or act as a valet. [< F, a groom < OF *vaslet, varlet,* dim. of *vasal* vassal. Doublet of VARLET.]

va·let de cham·bre (vá·le′ də shäṅ′br′) *pl.* **va·lets de cham·bre** (vá·le′) *French* A valet.

Va·let·ta (və·let′ə) See VALLETTA.

val·e·tu·di·nar·i·an (val′ə·to͞o′də·nâr′ē·ən, -tyo͞o′-) *n.* A chronic invalid; one unduly solicitous about his health. —*adj.* Seeking to recover health; infirm. Also **val′e·tu′di·nar′y.** [< L *valetudinarius* infirm < *valetudo, -inis* health, ill health < *valere* be well] —**val′e·tu′di·nar′i·an·ism** *n.*

val·gus (val′gəs) *adj.* Knock-kneed or bowlegged. —*n. Pathol.* An abnormal eversion of the foot, as by a depression of the arch. [< L, bowlegged]

Val·hal·la (val·hal′ə) **1** In Norse mythology, the great hall into which the souls of heroes fallen bravely in battle were borne by the valkyries and received and feasted by Odin. **2** An edifice wherein the remains or memorials of deceased heroes of a nation are placed. Also **Val·hall** (val·hal′): also spelled *Walhalla.* [< NL < ON *valhöll,* genitive of *valhallar* hall of the slain < *valr* the slain + *höll* hall]

val·iant (val′yənt) *adj.* **1** Strong and intrepid; powerful and courageous. **2** Performed with valor; bravely conducted; heroic. See synonyms under BRAVE. [< OF *vailant,* ppr. of *valoir* be strong < L *valere*] —**val′iant·ly** *adv.* —**val′iant·ness, val′iance, val′ian·cy** *n.*

val·id (val′id) *adj.* **1** Based on evidence that can be supported; sound; just; sufficient and effective in law. **2** *Obs.* Strong. **3** *Stat.* Having a high degree of correlation with its criterion: distinguished from *reliable.* [< F *valide* < L *validus* powerful < *valere* be strong] —**val′id·ly** *adv.* —**val′id·ness** *n.*

Synonyms: cogent, conclusive, convincing, efficacious, efficient, good, incontestable, irrefragable, irrefutable, just, logical, solid, sound, substantial, sufficient, undeniable, weighty. See POWERFUL. *Antonyms*: see synonyms for VAIN.

val·i·date (val′ə·dāt) *v.t.* **·dat·ed, ·dat·ing 1** To make valid; ratify and confirm. **2** To declare legally valid; legalize. See synonyms under RATIFY. —**val′i·da′tion** *n.*

va·lid·i·ty (və·lid′ə·tē) *n.* **1** The state or quality of being valid; soundness, as in law or reasoning; efficacy. **2** *Archaic* Health; strength. **3** *Obs.* Worth.

val·ine (val′ēn) *n. Biochem.* An essential amino acid, $C_5H_{11}O_2N$, occurring in most proteins. [< VAL(ERIC) + -INE[2]]

va·lise (və·lēs′) *n.* A portable receptacle for clothes and toilet articles; traveling bag. [< F < Ital. *valigia;* ult. origin uncertain]

val·kyr·ie (val·kir′ē, val′kir·ē) *n.* In Norse mythology, one of the maidens who ride through the air and choose heroes from among those slain in battle, and carry them to Valhalla. Also **val′kyr, Val·kyr′ie.** [< ON *valkyrja,* lit., chooser of the slain < *valr* the slain + stem of *kjōsa* choose, select] —**val·kyr′i·an** *adj.*

Val·la·do·lid (val′ə·dō′lid, *Sp.* bä′lyä·thō′lēth) **1** A province of north central Spain; 3,221 square miles. **2** A city of central Spain, former capital of Castile and capital of Valladolid province.

val·la·tion (və·lā′shən) *n.* **1** The art of planning or erecting fortifications. **2** A rampart. [< LL *vallatio, -onis* < L *vallare* protect with a wall < *vallum* a wall] —**val·la·to·ry** (val′ə·tôr′ē, -tō′rē) *adj.*

val·lec·u·la (və·lek′yə·lə) *n. pl.* **·lae** (-lē) **1** A furrow or depression. **2** *Anat.* A deep sulcus (**vallecula cerebelli**) enclosing the median lobe on the inferior surface of the cerebellum; also, a depression on the back of the tongue on either side of the epiglottis. **3** *Bot.* A groove or furrow, as those between the ridges on the fruit of plants of the parsley family. [< NL, var. of L *vallicula,* dim. of *vallis* a valley] —**val·lec′u·lar, val·lec′u·late** (-lit, -lāt) *adj.*

Val·let·ta (və·let′ə) The capital of Malta, a port on the SE coast; site of a major British naval base: also *Valetta.*

val·ley (val′ē) *n.* **1** A depression of the earth's surface, as one through which a stream flows; level or low land between mountains, hills, or high lands; also, the people who inhabit a valley. **2** *Archit.* **a** The gutter or angle formed by the meeting of the two roof slopes. **b** An interval in a vault, or the space between vault ridges as seen from above. **3** A vallecula. [< OF *valee* < *val* < L *vallis* a valley]

Synonyms: canyon, dale, dell, dingle, glen, gorge, gulch, gully, ravine, vale.

Valley Forge A village in SE Pennsylvania, scene of Washington's winter encampment, 1777–78, in the American Revolution.

Valley of Ten Thousand Smokes A region in Katmai National Monument, southern Alaska, punctuated by thousands of small volcanoes; 72 square miles.

Val·lom·bro·sa (väl′lôm·brō′zä) A resort town near Florence, Italy, in the Apennines.

Val·my (vál·mē′) A village in NE France, near Reims; scene of a French victory over the Prussians, 1792.

Va·lois (vá·lwá′) A medieval county and former duchy of northern France.

Va·lois (vá·lwá′) A French dynasty; began 1328 with Philip VI of Valois, ended with Henry III, 1589.

Va·lo·na (vä·lô′nä) An ancient port on the **Bay of Valona,** an inlet of the Strait of Otranto in SW Albania (15 miles long, 3 miles wide): formerly *Avlona*: Albanian *Vlona.*

va·lo·ni·a (və·lō′nē·ə) *n.* The dried acorn cups of the Old World **valonia oak** (*Quercus macrolepis*), used as a tanning material. [< Ital. *vallonea* < Modern Gk. *balania* an evergreen oak, pl. of *balani* an acorn < Gk. *balanos*]

val·or (val′ər) *n.* Intrepid courage, especially in warfare; personal bravery. Also *Brit.* **val′our.** See synonyms under PROWESS. [< OF *valour* < LL *valor* worth < *valere* be strong]

val·or·i·za·tion (val′ər·ə·zā′shən, -ī·zā′-) *n.* The maintenance by governmental action of an artificial price for any product. [< Pg. *valorização* < *valor* value < LL. See VALOR.]

val·or·ize (val′ə·rīz) *v.t.* **·ized, ·iz·ing** To subject to valorization. Also *Brit.* **val′or·ise.**

val·or·ous (val′ər·əs) *adj.* Courageous; valiant. —**val′or·ous·ly** *adv.* —**val′or·ous·ness** *n.*

Val·pa·rai·so (val′pə·rā′zō, -sō, -rī′-) A port of central Chile; the most important port on the west coast of South America. *Spanish* **Val·pa·ra·í·so** (bäl′pä·rä·ē′sō).

val·u·a·ble (val′yo͞o·ə·bəl, val′yə·bəl) *adj.* **1** Having financial worth, price, or value; costly. **2** Of a nature or character capable of being valued or estimated: These goods are *valuable* by money. **3** Having moral worth, value, or importance; very serviceable; worthy; estimable: a *valuable* friend. See synonyms under EXCELLENT, GOOD, IMPORTANT. —*n. Usually pl.* An article of value, as a piece of jewelry. —**val′u·a·ble·ness** *n.* —**val′u·a·bly** *adv.*

val·u·a·tion (val′yo͞o·ā′shən) *n.* **1** The act of valuing. **2** Estimated worth or value; appraisement; price. **3** Personal estimation; judgment of merit or character: to set a high *valuation* on one's skill or power.

val·u·a·tor (val′yo͞o·ā′tər) *n.* One who makes appraisals; an appraiser.

val·ue (val′yo͞o) *n.* **1** The desirability or worth of a thing; intrinsic worth; utility. **2** *Often pl.* Something regarded as desirable, worthy, or right, as a belief, standard, or precept: the *values* of a democratic society. **3** The rate at which a commodity is potentially exchangeable for others; a fair return in service, goods, etc.; worth in money; market price; also the ratio of utility to price; a bargain. **4** Attributed or assumed valuation; esteem or regard. **5** Exact meaning; signification; import: the *value* of the words "will" and "shall." **6** *Music* The relative length of a tone as signified by a note. **7** *Math.* The quantity, magnitude, or number an algebraic symbol or expression is supposed to denote. **8** Rank in a system of classification. **9** In the graphic arts, the relation of the elements of a picture, as light and shade, to one another, especially with reference to their distribution and interdependence, apart from the idea of hue. **10** *Phonet.* The special quality of the sound represented by a written character: the *values* of the letter *e.* See synonyms under PRICE, PROFIT. —**book value** The value of property or stock as shown by the books of the company that owns it; the value of stock of a corporation based on the profit or loss shown by its books, and distinguished from the face, market, or artificially created value. —**face value 1** The value stated on the face of a bond, coin, note, etc. **2** Seeming or apparent value: a promise taken at its *face value.* —**par value** The nominal value, or value printed on a security or stock: not necessarily the market value of the shares. —*v.t.* **·ued, ·u·ing 1** To estimate the value or worth of; assess; appraise. **2** To regard highly; esteem; prize. **3** To place a relative estimate of value or desirability upon:to *value* honor more than life. See synonyms under APPRECIATE, CHERISH. [< OF *valu,* pp. of *valoir* be worth < L *valere*] —**val′ue·less** *adj.* —**val′u·er** *n.*

val·ue-add·ed tax (val′yo͞o·ad′id) A tax levied on each stage of a product's manufacture

and marketing, from the raw material to the final retailer, the ultimate burden being placed on the consumer in the form of higher prices.

val·ued (val′yo̅o̅d) *adj.* **1** Regarded or estimated; hence, much or highly esteemed: a *valued* friend. **2** Having a value: a many-*valued* function.

valued policy An insurance policy in which the value of property or cargo is agreed on and inserted as the amount of damages in case of total loss.

val·val (val′vəl) *adj.* Of or pertaining to a valve. Also **val′var** (-vər).

val·vate (val′vāt) *adj.* **1** Serving as or like a valve; having a valve; valvular. **2** *Bot.* Touching by contiguous edges but not overlapping: applied to most dehiscent capsules in which the component parts separate like valves, to certain anthers, and to the petals or sepals of many flowers in estivation. [< L *valvatus* with folding doors < *valva.* See VALVE.]

valve (valv) *n.* **1** *Mech.* Any contrivance or arrangement that permits the flow of a liquid, gas, vapor, or loose material in either of two directions, and closes against its return. **2** *Obs.* One of a pair of folding doors. **3** *Anat.* A structure formed by one or more loose folds of the lining membrane of a vessel or other organ, preventing or retarding the flow of a fluid in one direction and allowing it in another. **4** *Zool.* One of the parts of a shell, as of a mollusk. **b** A covering plate or one of two or more external pieces forming a sheath, as for an ovipositor. **5** *Bot.* **a** One of the parts into which a capsule splits in dehiscence. **b** One of the halves of an anther after its opening. **6** *Electr.* A device for controlling the direction of flow of a current, as an electrolytic cell, or a vacuum tube. **7** *Brit.* A radio tube. **8** A device in certain brass-wind instruments for lengthening the air column and lowering the pitch of the instrument's scale, by turning the air current from the main tube into an additional side tube. —*v.t.* **valved, valv·ing** To furnish with valves; control the flow of by a valve. [< L *valva* leaf of a door] —**valve′less** *adj.*

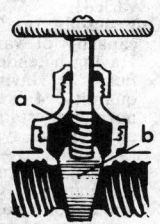

GATE VALVE
Cross-section.
a. Screw.
b. Gate closed.

valve-in-head engine (valv′in-hed′) An internal-combustion engine having overhead valves; an overhead-valve engine. See OVERHEAD VALVE.

valve·let (valv′lit) *n.* A little valve; a valvule, as of a pericarp.

val·vu·lar (val′vyə-lər) *adj.* **1** Pertaining to or of the nature of a valve, as of the heart. **2** Having valves; acting as a valve.

val·vule (val′vyo̅o̅l) *n.* A small valve; a structure like a small valve. Also **val′vu·la** (-vyə-lə). [< F < Med. L *valvula,* dim. of L *valva* a door]

val·vu·li·tis (val′vyə-lī′tis) *n. Pathol.* Inflammation of any membrane that serves as a valve in the organs or channels of circulation. [< NL < Med. L *valvula* VALVULE + -ITIS]

vam·brace (vam′brās) *n.* Armor for the forearm from the elbow to the wrist: also, *Obs., vantbrace.* [Var. of *vantbrace* < AF *vantbras,* OF *avant-bras* < *avant* in front of + *bras* arm] —**vam′braced** *adj.*

va·moose (va-mo̅o̅s′) *v.t.* & *v.i.* **·moosed, ·moos·ing** *U.S. Slang* To leave hastily or hurriedly; quit. Also **va·mose′** (-mōs′). [< Sp. *vamos* let us go]

vamp[1] (vamp) *n.* **1** The piece of leather forming the upper front part of a boot or shoe. **2** Something added to give an old thing a new appearance. **3** *Music* A simple improvised accompaniment. —*v.t.* **1** To provide with a vamp. **2** To repair or patch. **3** *Music* To improvise an accompaniment to. —*v.i.* **4** *Music* To improvise accompaniments. [< OF *avampie* forepart of the foot < *avant* before + *pied* foot] —**vamp′er** *n.*

vamp[2] (vamp) *Slang v.t.* To seduce or prey upon (a man) by utilizing one's feminine charms. —*v.i.* To play the vamp. —*n.* An unscrupulous

flirt or coquette. See VAMPIRE (def. 2). [Short for VAMPIRE]

vam·pire (vam′pīr) *n.* **1** A living corpse that rises from its grave at night to feed upon the living, usually by sucking the blood: a widespread folk belief originating in primitive cannibalism but developed primarily in Slavic folklore. It is not a demon or a ghost, but the physical body of one who has died; it cannot be exorcised, but must be disinterred and either burned or fastened in the grave with a stake through its heart. Belief in vampires still exists in Slavic Europe, Hungary, Greece, and Iceland. Bram Stoker's *Dracula* is a famous treatment of the subject. **2** A man or woman who preys upon persons of the opposite sex; especially, a woman who brings her lover to a state of poverty or degradation. **3** A large bat (genera *Desmodus* and *Diphylla*) of South or Central America, which drinks the blood of horses, cattle, and, sometimes, men: more fully **true vampire. 4** An insectivorous or frugivorous bat (genera *Phyllostomus* and *Vampyrum*) formerly supposed to suck blood: a **false vampire.** [< F < G *vampir* < Slavic] —**vam·pir′ic** (-pir′ik), **vam·pir′ish** (-pīr′ish) *adj.*

ALBINO VAMPIRE
(Bats vary from 2 to 28 inches in body length)

vam·pir·ism (vam′pī·riz′əm, -pə-) *n.* **1** Belief in vampires. See VAMPIRE (def. 1). **2** The act or practice of a vampire; bloodsucking. **3** The practice of extortion or of preying upon others.

van[1] (van) *n.* **1** A large covered wagon or vehicle, for removing furniture, household goods, etc.; a caravan. **2** *Brit.* A closed railway car for luggage, etc.; also, a vehicle, open or covered, used for carrying light goods. [Short for CARAVAN]

van[2] (van) *n.* **1** An advance guard, as of an army, or foremost division of a fleet. **2** The leaders of a movement; those at the front of any line or unit. [Short for VANGUARD]

van[3] (van) *n.* A fan or winnowing machine; hence, a wing. [Dial. var. of FAN[1]]

van[4] (vän) *prep. Dutch* Of; from: used with Dutch family names, originally designating where the family came from or received its name.

Van (vän) Singular of VANIR.

Van (vän) A town on the eastern shore of **Lake Van** (1,453 square miles) in eastern Turkey in Asia.

van·a·date (van′ə-dāt) *n. Chem.* A salt or ester of vanadic acid. Also **va·na·di·ate** (və-nā′dē-āt).

va·nad·ic (və-nad′ik) *adj. Chem.* Of, pertaining to, or derived from vanadium, especially in its higher valence.

vanadic acid *Chem.* Any of several acids known only in their salts, as *meta*-vanadic acid, a yellow compound, HVO_3, used as a pigment and a substitute for gold bronze.

va·nad·i·nite (və-nad′ə-nīt) *n.* A native vanadate and chloride of lead, found in opaque prismatic crystals of red and yellow color. [< VANAD(IUM) + -IN + -ITE[1]]

va·na·di·um (və-nā′dē-əm) *n.* A soft, ductile, toxic, lustrous metallic element (symbol V, atomic number 23) difficult to separate from its compounds, used in alloys. See PERIODIC TABLE. [< NL < ON *Vanadis,* a name of the Norse goddess Freya]

vanadium steel Steel containing from .1 to .25 percent of vanadium to increase its tensile strength.

van·a·dous (van′ə-dəs) *adj. Chem.* Of, pertaining to, or derived from vanadium, especially in its lower valence. Also **va·na·di·ous.**

Van Allen radiation A high-intensity radiation consisting of charged atomic particles circling the earth in an inner and outer belt conforming to the earth's magnetic field.

Van·brugh (van·bro̅o̅′, van′brə), **Sir John,** 1664–1726, English playwright and architect.

Van Bu·ren (van byo̅o̅r′ən), **Martin,** 1782–1862, eighth president of the United States 1837–41.

Van·cou·ver (van-ko̅o̅′vər) **1** A port of SW British Columbia opposite **Vancouver Island,** the largest island off the western coast of North America, comprising part of British Columbia; 12,408 square miles. **2** A city of SW Washington on the Columbia River.

Van·cou·ver (van-ko̅o̅′vər), **George,** 1758?–1798, English navigator.

Vancouver, Mount A peak on the Yukon-Alaska border in the St. Elias Mountains; 15,700 feet.

van·dal (van′dəl) *n.* A ruthless plunderer; wilful destroyer of what is beautiful or artistic. —*adj.* Being a vandal; barbarous. [< VANDAL] —**van·dal·ic** (van·dal′ik) *adj.*

Van·dal (van′dəl) *n.* One of a Germanic people from a region between the Vistula and Oder rivers, south of the Baltic, who invaded the western Roman Empire in the fourth century. At the beginning of the fifth century, they ravaged Gaul and overran Spain and North Africa. In 455 they pillaged the city of Rome, destroying many artistic and literary treasures. Their kingdom, established in North Africa with Carthage as its capital, was overthrown in 534 by the Byzantines under Belisarius. —**Van·dal·ic** (van·dal′ik) *adj.* —**Van′dal·ism** *n.*

van·dal·ism (van′dəl·iz′əm) *n.* Hostility to or wilful destruction of artistic works, or of property in general.

Van·den·berg (van′dən·bûrg), **Arthur Hendrick,** 1884–1951, U.S. statesman. —**Hoyt,** 1899–1954, U.S. Air Force general.

Van·der·bilt (van′dər·bilt), **Cornelius,** 1794–1877, U.S. capitalist: called "Commodore Vanderbilt."

Van Die·men Gulf (van dē′mən) An arm of the Timor Sea between Northern Territory and Melville Island, Australia; 90 miles long, 50 miles wide. [after Anthony *Van Diemen,* 1593–1645, Dutch admiral]

Van Die·men's Land (van dē′mənz) The former name for TASMANIA.

Van Do·ren (van dôr′ən, dō′rən), **Carl,** 1885–1950, U.S. writer and editor. —**Mark,** 1894–1972, U.S. poet, writer, and critic; brother of preceding.

Van Dyck (van dīk′), **Anthony,** 1599–1641, Flemish painter. Also **Van·dyke′.**

Van·dyke (van·dīk′) *adj.* Of or pertaining to Anthony Van Dyck (or Vandyke), or to his style; also, of or pertaining to the dress or fashions represented in the paintings of Van Dyck. —*n.* **1** A painting by Van Dyck. **2** A Vandyke cape, collar, or beard.

Van Dyke (van dīk′), **Henry,** 1852–1933, U.S. clergyman, educator, and author.

Vandyke beard A peaked or pointed beard resembling those depicted in Van Dyck's paintings.

Vandyke brown A deep-brown pigment, a king of bog-earth or peat color used by the painter Van Dyck; any of the various brown pigments, as those resembling burnt umber.

Vandyke collar A broad, deep collar or cape of fine linen and lace resembling those represented in portraits by Van Dyck. Also **Vandyke cape.**

vane (vān) *n.* **1** A thin plate, pivoted out of center, on a vertical rod, to indicate the direction of the wind; a weathercock: also **wind vane. 2** A slender flag or streamer used for the same purpose. **3** An arm or blade, as of a windmill, propeller, projectile, etc. **4** *Ornithol.* The web of a feather. **5** The target on a leveling rod. **6** The sight on a quadrant, compass, or similar instrument, by which the direction of the object viewed is determined. **7** One of the plates or strips of metal fixed in the tail of a bomb, guided missile, or the like, to provide stability or guidance. **8** *Obs.* A flag; pennon. ◆ Homophones: *vain, vein.* [Dial. var. of *fane* a small flag, OE *fana* a flag] —**vaned** *adj.*

WINDMILL VANES

Vane (vān), **Sir Henry,** 1613–62, English

Puritan statesman; executed on charge of treason.

Vä·ner (vā'nər), **Lake** See VENER, LAKE.

van Eyck (van īk') See EYCK, VAN.

vang (vang) *n. Naut.* One of two guy ropes from the end of a gaff to the deck: used to steady the gaff. [<Du., a catch < *vangen* catch]

van Gogh (van gō', gôkh'; *Du.* vän khokh'), **Vincent,** 1853–90, Dutch painter.

van·guard (van'gärd) *n.* 1 The advance guard of an army; the van. 2 Hence, one who or that which is foremost. [<OF *avangarde,* var. of *avantgarde* < *avant* before + *garde* guard]

Vanguard *n.* The second U. S. artificial satellite, launched from Cape Canaveral, Fla., on March 17, 1958, to a maximum altitude of 2,513 miles: diameter, 6.4 inches; weight, 3.25 pounds; equipment, two radio transmitters.

va·nil·la (və·nil'ə) *n.* 1 Any of a genus *(Vanilla)* of tall climbing orchids of tropical America. 2 The long dehiscent capsule of one species *(V. planifolia)* of this genus. 3 A flavoring extract made from these capsules. [<NL <Sp. *vainilla,* dim. of *vaina* sheath, pod <L *vagina* sheath; so called from the little pods that contain its seeds]

vanilla plant An erect perennial herb *(Trilisa odoratissima)* of the composite family growing in SE United States: the leaves have a vanilla odor when bruised: also called *hound's-tongue.*

va·nil·lic (və·nil'ik) *adj.* Of, pertaining to, or derived from vanilla or vanillin.

va·nil·lin (və·nil'in) *n. Chem.* A colorless crystalline compound, $C_8H_8O_3$, contained in vanilla, of which it is the odoriferous principle: also made synthetically. Also **va·nil'·line** (-in, -ēn).

Va·nir (vä'nir) *sing.* **Van** (vän) In Norse mythology, an early race of fertility deities, of whom the names Njord, Frey, and Freya survive: later combined with the Aesir.

van·ish (van'ish) *v.i.* 1 To disappear from sight; fade away; depart. 2 To pass out of existence; be annihilated. 3 *Math.* To become equal to zero. —*n. Phonet.* The slight terminal sound of certain vowels, as the faint (o͝o) heard after the (ō) in *go.* [Aphetic var. of OF *esvanniss-,* stem of *esvanir* <L *evanescere* fade away. See EVANESCE.] —**van'ish·er** *n.*

van·i·tas van·i·ta·tum (van'ə·tas van'ə·tā'təm) *Latin* Vanity of vanities.

van·i·ty (van'ə·tē) *n. pl.* **·ties** 1 The condition or character of being vain; a feeling of shallow pride; conceit; ambitious display; ostentation; show. 2 The quality or state of being vain or empty, or destitute of reality, etc. 3 That which is vain or unsubstantial. 4 A vanity bag or box. 5 A dressing-table. See synonyms under ARROGANCE, EGOTISM, LEVITY, PRIDE. [<OF *vanité* <L *vanitas, -tatis* < *vanus* empty, vain]

vanity bag or **box** A bag or box containing face powder, rouge, puff, mirror, etc. Also *vanity.*

Vanity Fair 1 In Bunyan's *Pilgrim's Progress,* a fair depicting the world as a scene of vanity and folly. 2 A novel by W. M. Thackeray, satirizing the weaknesses and follies of human nature. 3 The world of fashion and frivolity.

Van Loon (van lōn), **Hendrik Willem,** 1882–1944, U. S. author and lecturer born in Holland.

van·ner (van'ər) *n. Brit.* A truck driver; one who drives a van.

van·quish (vang'kwish, van'-) *v.t.* 1 To defeat in battle; overcome; conquer. 2 To suppress or overcome (a feeling or emotion): to *vanquish* lust. 3 To defeat, as in argument; confute. See synonyms under BEAT, CONQUER, SUBDUE. [<OF *veinquiss-,* stem of *veinquir* conquer <L *vincere*] —**van'quish·a·ble** *adj.* —**van'quish·er** *n.*

Van Rens·se·laer (van ren'sə·lər, -lir), **Stephen,** 1764–1839, U. S. general and politician.

Van·sit·tart (van·sit'ərt), **Robert Gilbert,** 1881–1957, first Baron Vansittart, British diplomat.

van·tage (van'tij) *n.* 1 Superiority over a competitor, as in means of attack; advantage. 2 In lawn tennis, the state of the game when either player has scored a point after deuce. 3 An opportunity; chance. [Aphetic var. of OF *avantage* ADVANTAGE] —**van'tage·less** *adj.*

vantage ground A position or condition which gives one an advantage.

vantage point A strategic position affording perspective; point of view.

vant·brace (vant'brās) See VAMBRACE.

van't Hoff (vänt hôf), **Jacobus Henricus,** 1852–1911, Dutch physical chemist.

van't Hoff's law *Chem.* A statement that the osmotic pressure of a substance in solution approximately equals the pressure it would have in a gaseous state at the same temperature and volume as the solution. [after J. H. *van't Hoff*]

Va·nu·a Le·vu (vä'no͞o·ä lā'vo͞o) Second largest of the Fiji Islands; 2,137 square miles.

van·ward (van'wərd) *adj.* Pertaining to or situated in the van or front: *vanward* regiments.

Van·zet·ti (van·zet'ē), **Bartolomeo,** 1888–1927, Italian anarchist active in the United States. See SACCO, NIKOLA.

vap·id (vap'id) *adj.* 1 Having lost sparkling quality and flavor. 2 Flat; dull; insipid. See synonyms under FLAT, VAIN. [<L *vapidus* insipid] —**va·pid·i·ty** (və·pid'ə·tē), **vap'id·ness** *n.* —**vap'id·ly** *adv.*

va·por (vā'pər) *n.* 1 Moisture in the air; especially, visible floating moisture, as light mist. 2 Any light, cloudy substance in the air, as smoke or fumes. 3 Any substance in the gaseous state, which, under ordinary conditions, is usually a liquid or solid. 4 A gas below its critical temperature. 5 That which is fleeting and unsubstantial. 6 A remedial agent applied by inhalation; also, a substance vaporized for use in industries. 7 Boastful swagger; vaporing. 8 *pl.* Depression of spirits; hypochondria. —*v.t.* 1 To vaporize. —*v.i.* 2 To emit vapor. 3 To evaporate. 4 To make idle boasts; brag. Also *Brit.* **va'pour.** [<AF *vapour,* OF *vapeur* <L *vapor* steam] —**va'por·a·bil'i·ty** *n.* —**va'por·a·ble** *adj.* —**va'por·er** *n.*

vapor density *Physics* 1 The density of a substance in the state of vapor, reaching its maximum before the substance passes into the liquid state. 2 The density of a gas or vapor as compared with that of hydrogen at the same temperature and pressure.

va·por·es·cence (vā'pə·res'əns) *n.* The process of forming mist or vapor. —**va'por·es'cent** *adj.*

vapori– *combining form* Vapor; of or related to vapor, steam, etc.: *vaporimeter.* Also, before vowels, **vapor–.** [<L *vapor* steam]

va·por·if·ic (vā'pə·rif'ik) *adj.* Producing vapors. [<NL *vaporificus* <L *vapor, -oris* steam + *facere* make]

va·por·im·e·ter (vā'pə·rim'ə·tər) *n.* An instrument for determining vapor pressure.

va·por·ing (vā'pər·ing) *adj.* Boasting; swaggering. —*n.* The act of boasting or talking pretentiously. —**va'por·ing·ly** *adv.*

va·por·ish (vā'pər·ish) *adj.* 1 Somewhat like vapor. 2 Somewhat hypochondriac.

va·por·i·za·tion (vā'pər·ə·zā'shən, -ī·zā'-) *n.* 1 The act or process of vaporizing, or the state of being vaporized. 2 *Med.* Treatment with vapors.

va·por·ize (vā'pə·rīz) *v.t.* & *v.i.* **·ized, ·iz·ing** To convert or be converted into vapor. —**va'·por·iz'a·ble** *adj.*

va·por·iz·er (vā'pə·rī'zər) *n.* 1 One who or that which vaporizes. 2 An atomizer.

va·por·ous (vā'pər·əs) *adj.* 1 Of or like vapor; foggy; misty; ethereal. 2 Full of vapors; hypochondriac; also, producing vapors; flatulent. 3 Vainly imaginative; whimsical. Also **va'por·y.** —**va·por·os·i·ty** (vā'pə·ros'ə·tē) *n.* —**va'por·ous·ly** *adv.* —**va'por·ous·ness** *n.*

vapor pressure *Physics* The pressure of a confined vapor when it is in equilibrium with its liquid at any specific temperature. Also **vapor tension.**

va·que·ro (vä·kā'rō) *n. pl.* **·ros** (-rōz, *Sp.* -rōs) A herdsman; cowboy. [<Sp. < *vaca* cow <L *vacca*]

var (vär) *n. Electr.* The reactive volt-ampere. [<V(OLT) + A(MPERE) + R(EACTIVE)]

va·ra (vä'rä) *n.* A Spanish and Portuguese measure of length, varying from 2.7 to 3.6 feet. —**square vara** A varying measure of surface. [<Sp. and Pg., lit., a rod <L, a forked pole < *varus* bent]

Va·rang·er Fjord (vä·rang'ər) An inlet of the Barents Sea in NE Norway; 60 miles long, 3 to 35 miles wide.

Va·ran·gi·an (və·ran'jē·ən) *n.* A Norse rover; one of a group of predatory Scandinavian seamen who, in the ninth century, sailed down the Volga into the Caspian Sea and established a dynasty in Caucasia. [<Med. L *Varangus* <Med. Gk. *Barangos* <Slavic, ult. <ON *Væringi* an ally < *vārar* pledges]

va·ra·ni·an (və·rā'nē·ən) *n.* One of a family of lizards *(Varanidae)* with tongue sheathed at the root and forked at the tip; a monitor: also **var·a·nid** (var'ə·nid) —*adj.* Of or pertaining to the *Varanidae.* [<NL *Varanus* < Arabic *waran* a monitor lizard]

Var·dar (vär'där) A river of southern Yugoslavia and NE Greece, flowing 230 miles NE and SE to the Gulf of Salonika near Salonika: Greek *Axios.*

va·reuse (vä·rœz') *n. French* A loose, woolen jacket, similar to a peajacket.

Var·gas (vär'gəs), **Getulio,** 1883–1954, provisional president of Brazil 1930–34; president 1934–45 and 1951–54; forced out of office.

vari– *combining form* Various; different: *variform, varicolored.* Also *vario–.* [<L *varius* varied]

var·i·a·ble (vâr'ē·ə·bəl) *adj.* 1 Having the capacity of varying; alterable; mutable. 2 Having a tendency to change; not constant; fickle. 3 Having no definite value as regards quantity. 4 *Biol.* Prone to variation from a normal or established type: said of plants and animals. See synonyms under FICKLE, IRREGULAR, MOBILE[1]. —*n.* 1 That which is liable to change. 2 *Math.* **a** A quantity susceptible of fluctuating in value or magnitude under different conditions. **b** A symbol representing one of a group of objects. 3 *Meteorol.* A shifting wind or winds; also, in the plural, places where such winds are common. [<OF <L *variabilis* < *variare* VARY] —**var'i·a·bil'·i·ty, var'i·a·ble·ness** *n.* —**var'i·a·bly** *adv.*

variable star See under STAR.

variable zone A temperate zone.

var·i·ance (vâr'ē·əns) *n.* 1 The act of varying, or the state of being variant; difference; discrepancy; hence, dissension; discord. 2 *Law* **a** A disagreement between the allegations in the pleadings and the proof in an essential matter. **b** A material disagreement between the writ beginning an action and the declaration or complaint. 3 *Stat.* The square of the standard deviation. 4 *Chem.* Degree of freedom. See synonyms under QUARREL[1].

var·i·ant (vâr'ē·ənt) *adj.* 1 Having or showing variation; varying; differing. 2 Tending to vary; variable; changing. 3 Restless; fickle; inconstant. 4 Differing from a standard or type; discrepant. See synonyms under HETEROGENEOUS. —*n.* 1 A thing that differs from another in form only; especially, a different spelling, pronunciation, or form of the same word. 2 A variate. [<OF <L *varians, -antis,* ppr. of *variare* VARY]

var·i·ate (vâr'ē·āt) *v.t.* & *v.i. Obs.* To vary. —*n.* 1 That which varies; a variable. 2 *Stat.* The magnitude or value of a variable. [<L *variatus,* pp. of *variare* VARY]

var·i·a·tion (vâr'ē·ā'shən) *n.* 1 The act, process, state, or result of varying; modification; diversity. 2 The extent to which a thing varies. 3 Inflection, as of declensions or conjugations; also, change in certain vowel sounds. 4 A repetition of the essential features of a musical theme or melody with fanciful embellishments. 5 *Astron.* **a** An inequality in the moon's motion. **b** Any change in the elements of an orbit. 6 *Biol.* Deviation in structure or function from the type or parent form of an organism, as by heredity or in response to conditions of environment. 7 *Stat.* Dispersion. See synonyms under CHANGE, DIFFERENCE. [<F] —**var'i·a'tion·al** *adj.*

var·i·cel·la (var'ə·sel'ə) *n. Pathol.* Chicken pox. [<NL, dim. of *variola.* See VARIOLA.]

var·i·cel·late (var'ə·sel'it, -āt) *adj. Zool.* Marked with small varices, as certain shells. [<NL *varicella,* dim. of L *varix* a varicose vein]

var·i·cel·loid (var'ə·sel'oid) *adj.* Resembling varicella: *varicelloid* smallpox.

varico– *combining form Med.* A vein; of or related to veins, especially to varicose veins: *varicotomy.* Also, before vowels, **varic–.** [<L *varix, varicis* a varicose vein]

var·i·ces (var'ə·sēz) Plural of VARIX.

var·i·co·cele (var'ə·kō·sēl') *n. Pathol.* A tumor formed by varicose veins of the spermatic cord. [<NL <L *varix, -icis* a varicose vein + Gk. *kēlē* a tumor]

var·i·col·ored (vâr′i·kul′ərd) *adj.* Variegated in color; parti–colored; diversified; of various colors. Also *Brit.* **var′i·col′oured.**

var·i·cose (var′ə·kōs) *adj. Pathol.* Abnormally dilated or contorted, as veins. [<L *varicosus* < *varix, -icis* a varicose vein]

var·i·co·sis (var′ə·kō′sis) *n. Pathol.* A condition in which there are varicose veins; varicosity. [<NL]

var·i·cos·i·ty (var′ə·kos′ə·tē) *n. pl.* **·ties** *Pathol.* 1 The condition of being varicose. 2 A varix.

var·i·cot·o·my (var′ə·kot′ə·mē) *n. Surg.* Excision of a varix or of a varicose vein. [< VARICO- + -TOMY]

var·ied (vâr′ēd) *adj.* 1 Partially or repeatedly altered. 2 Consisting of diverse sorts. 3 Differing from one another. 4 Varicolored. See VARY. — **var′ied·ly** *adv.*

varied thrush A robinlike bird of the western United States *(Ixoreus naevius)* with a plump, rust–colored body, black or gray wings, and a dark band across the breast.

var·i·e·gate (vâr′ē·ə·gāt′) *v.t.* **·gat·ed, ·gat·ing** 1 To mark with different colors or tints; dapple; spot; streak. 2 To make varied; diversify. — *adj.* Variegated. [<LL *variegatus,* pp. of *variegare* variegate < *varius* various + *agere* drive, do]

var·i·e·gat·ed (vâr′ē·ə·gā′tid) *adj.* 1 Having diverse colors; varied in color, as with streaks or blotches. 2 Having or exhibiting different forms, styles, or varieties. 3 *Bot.* Designating a type of inflorescence: see illustration under INFLORESCENCE.

var·i·e·ga·tion (vâr′ē·ə·gā′shən) *n.* 1 The act of variegating, or the state of being variegated. 2 Diversity of colors.

va·ri·e·tal (və·rī′ə·təl) *adj. Biol.* Of, pertaining to, or of the nature of a distinct variety: opposed to *specific* or *generic.* — **va·ri′e·tal·ly** *adv.*

va·ri·e·ty (və·rī′ə·tē) *n. pl.* **·ties** 1 The state or character of being various or varied; diversity. 2 A collection of diverse things; an assortment of unlike objects. 3 The possession of different characteristics by one individual. 4 A limited class of things that differ in certain common peculiarities from a larger class to which they belong; sometimes, an example of such a sort or kind. 5 *Biol.* An individual, or a group of individuals of a species, that differs from the type in certain characters capable of perpetuation, and that is usually fertile with any other member of the species; a subdivision of a species; subspecies. See synonyms under CHANGE. [<MF *variété* <L *varietas* < *varius* various]

variety shop 1 A store having a great variety of merchandise for sale, as hardware, dry–goods, notions, toys, and other small wares. 2 A general store. Also **variety store.**

variety show A theatrical show consisting of a series of short acts or numbers, including songs, dances, dramatic sketches, acrobatic feats, animal acts, etc.; a vaudeville show.

var·i·form (vâr′ə·fôrm) *adj.* Of diverse form; having different shapes.

vario– Var. of VARI–.

var·i·o–coup·ler (vâr′ē·ə·kup′lər) *n. Electr.* A tuning coil in which the secondary winding is mounted to rotate within the primary winding. It resembles the variometer.

va·ri·o·la (və·rī′ə·lə) *n. Pathol.* Smallpox. [< Med. L, a pustule <L *varius* speckled] — **va·ri′o·lar, va·ri′o·lous** *adj.*

var·i·o·late (vâr′ē·ə·lāt′) *v.t.* **·lat·ed, ·lat·ing** To vaccinate with smallpox virus. — **var′i·o·la′tion, var′i·o·li·za′tion** *n.*

var·i·ole (vâr′ē·ōl) *n.* 1 A foveola. 2 A spherulite or variolite. [<F <Med. L *variola.* See VARIOLA.]

var·i·o·lite (vâr′ē·ə·līt′) *n.* A dense, finely crystalline variety of basalt, characterized by whitish spheroid granules. [<G *variolit* < Med. L *variola.* See VARIOLA.]

var·i·o·lit·ic (vâr′ē·ə·lit′ik) *adj.* 1 Of, pertaining to, or containing variolite. 2 Spotted.

var·i·o·loid (vâr′ē·ə·loid′) *Pathol. n.* A mild form of smallpox, occurring after vaccination or in persons who have had smallpox. — *adj.* 1 Resembling smallpox. 2 Pertaining to varioloid.

var·i·om·e·ter (vâr′ē·om′ə·tər) *n. Electr.* 1 An instrument used to determine the variation of magnetic force at different times or at different places, usually by means of a needle suspended within the magnetic field. 2 A variable inductance device composed of two coils connected in series, one of which revolves within the other, and capable of controlling the strength of a current. [<VARIO- + -METER]

var·i·o·rum (vâr′ē·ôr′əm, -ō′rəm) *adj.* Having notes or comments by different critics or editors. — *n.* 1 An edition containing various versions of a text, usually with notes and commentary. 2 A text or edition, especially the complete works of a classical author, containing various notes and comments: also **variorum edition.** [<L *(cum notis) variorum* (with the notes) of various persons]

var·i·ous (vâr′ē·əs) *adj.* 1 Characteristically different from one another; diverse. 2 Being more than one and easily distinguishable; several. 3 Many–sided; variform. 4 Having a changeable or inconstant nature; unfixed. 5 Having a diversity of appearance; variegated. See synonyms under HETEROGENEOUS, MANY. [<L *varius*] — **var′i·ous·ly** *adv.* — **var′i·ous·ness** *n.*

Var·i–Typ·er (vâr′i·tī′pər) *n.* A compact, electrically operated, self–justifying composing machine for the rapid preparation of copy for all kinds of printing reproduction: a trade name.

var·ix (vâr′iks) *n. pl.* **var·i·ces** (vâr′ə·sēz) 1 *Pathol.* **a** Permanent dilatation of a vein or other vessel of circulation. **b** A vessel thus distorted, as a varicose vein. 2 *Zool.* A ridge marking the former position of the outer lip of certain univalve shells. [<L, a varicose vein]

var·let (vär′lit) *n.* 1 *Archaic* A low menial or subordinate; formerly, a page. 2 A knave or scoundrel. [<OF, a groom. Doublet of VALET.]

var·let·ry (vär′lit·rē) *n.* The rabble; the mob.

var·mint (vär′mənt) *n. Dial.* Any person or animal considered as troublesome; vermin. [Alter. of VERMIN] — **var′mint·ry** *n.*

Var·na (vär′nä) A major seaport on the Black Sea in eastern Bulgaria: formerly (1949–58) called *Stalin.*

var·nish (vär′nish) *n.* 1 A solution of certain gums or resins in alcohol, linseed oil, etc., used to produce a shining, transparent coat on a surface. 2 Any natural or artificial product resembling varnish. 3 Outward show, or any superficial polish, as of politeness. — *v.t.* 1 To cover with varnish. 2 To give a smooth or glossy appearance to. 3 To improve the appearance of; polish. 4 To hide by a deceptive covering or appearance; gloss over. [<OF *vernis* <Med. L *vernicium* sandarac <Med. Gk. *berniké*, prob. from Gk. *Bereniké*, a city in Cyrenaica] — **var′nish·a·ble** *adj.* — **var′nish·er** *n.* — **var′nish·ing** *n.*

varnish tree 1 A tree of China and Japan *(Toxicodendron vernicifluum)* yielding a milky juice suitable for making varnish. 2 The candlenut tree.

Var·ro (var′ō), **Marcus Terentius,** 116–27? B.C., Roman scholar and author.

var·si·ty (vär′sə·tē) *n. pl.* **·ties** *Colloq.* 1 *Brit.* University. 2 The team that represents a university, college, or school in any activity, as in football, debating, etc. [Aphetic alter. of UNIVERSITY]

Var·u·na (var′ŏŏ·nə, vûr′-) In the earliest (Vedic) Hindu mythology, the god of the sky, creator and supreme god of the universe; later, in the Puranas, the god of the waters.

var·us (vâr′əs) *n. Pathol.* A malformation in which a bone or joint is turned away from its normal position. [<NL <L, growing inward, bandy–legged]

Var·us (vâr′əs), **Publius Quintilius,** died A.D. 9, Roman general, commander in Germany; defeated by Arminius.

varve (värv) *n.* One of a series of finely stratified seasonal deposits, as of clay or shale: often useful in determining the age of geological formations. [<Sw. *varv* a layer]

var·y (vâr′ē) *v.* **var·ied, var·y·ing** *v.t.* 1 To change the form, nature, substance, etc., of; modify. 2 To cause to be different from one another. 3 To impart variety to; diversify. 4 *Music* To embellish (a melody) by changes of rhythm, harmony, etc. — *v.i.* 5 To become changed in form, nature, substance, etc. 6 To be diverse or different; differ. 7 To deviate; depart: with *from.* 8 To change in succession; alternate. 9 *Math.* To be subject to continual change. 10 *Biol.* To undergo variation. See synonyms under CHANGE, FLUCTUATE. [<OF *varier* <L *variare* < *varius* various, diverse] — **var′i·er** *n.*

varying hare Any of certain hares whose coats turn white in the winter, specifically the American *Lepus americanus.*

vas (vas) *n. pl.* **va·sa** (vā′sə) *Biol.* A vessel or duct. [<L, vessel, dish]

vas– Var. of VASO–.

Va·sa·ri (vä·zä′rē), **Giorgio,** 1511–74, Italian painter, architect, and biographer of artists.

vas·cu·lar (vas′kyə·lər) *adj. Biol.* 1 Of, pertaining to, consisting of, or containing vessels or ducts, as blood vessels, etc. 2 Having vessels. 3 Richly supplied with blood vessels. Also **vas′cu·lose** (-lōs), **vas′cu·lous** (-ləs). [<L *vasculum*, dim. of *vas* vessel] — **vas′cu·lar′i·ty** (-lar′ə·tē) *n.* — **vas′cu·lar·ly** *adv.*

vascular bundle Bundle (def. 4).

vascular tissue *Bot.* Plant tissue made up of vessels or ducts through which the sap is conveyed.

vas·cu·lum (vas′kyə·ləm) *n. pl.* **·la** (-lə) 1 A small box used in plant collecting. 2 *Bot.* An ascidium. [<L, little vessel]

vas def·er·ens (vas def′ər·ənz) *Anat.* The duct by which semen is conveyed from the epididymis to the seminal vesicles. [<NL <L *vas* vessel + *deferens* leading down]

vase (vās, vāz, väz) *n.* An urnlike vessel, usually rounded and generally of greater height than width, ordinarily used as an ornament or for holding flowers. [<F <L *vas* vessel]

va·sec·to·my (və·sek′tə·mē) *n. Surg.* Removal of a portion of the vas deferens. [<VAS- + -ECTOMY]

Vas·e·line (vas′ə·lēn, -lin) *n.* Proprietary name for various semisolid hydrocarbons derived from petroleum: a brand of petrolatum.

Vash·ti (vash′tī) In the Bible, the queen of Ahasuerus, of Persia, whom he divorced because she refused to come to a royal banquet as commanded. *Esther* i 10–21.

Va·si·lev·ski (vä′sē·lyef′skē), **Alexander Mikhailovich,** born 1901, Russian marshal and chief of general staff in World War II.

vaso– *combining form* 1 *Physiol.* A vessel, especially a blood vessel: *vasomotor.* 2 *Med.* The vas deferens: *vasosection,* the severing of the vas deferens. Also, before vowels, *vas–.* [<L *vas* a vessel]

vas·o·con·stric·tor (vas′ō·kən·strik′tər) *adj. Physiol.* Causing constriction of a blood vessel when stimulated. — *n.* A nerve or drug causing such constriction.

vas·o·den·tine (vas′ō·den′tēn, -tin) *n.* Dentine in which the capillaries have remained wide enough to give passage to the blood.

vas·o·di·la·tor (vas′ō·dī·lā′tər) *adj. Physiol.* Causing dilatation of a blood vessel, as certain nerves or drugs.

vas·o·mo·tor (vas′ō·mō′tər) *adj. Physiol.* Producing movement, either of contraction or dilatation, in the walls of vessels.

vas·sal (vas′əl) *n.* 1 One who held land of a superior lord by a feudal tenure; a liegeman or feudal tenant. 2 A dependent, retainer, or servant of any kind; a slave or bondman. — *adj.* Having the character of or pertaining to a vassal; tributary; hence, servile. [<OF <Med. L *vassallus* <LL *vassus* a servant <Celtic]

vas·sal·age (vas′əl·ij) *n.* 1 The condition, duties, and obligations of a vassal; also, the feudal system. 2 Servitude in general. 3 Lands held by feudal tenure; a fief. 4 Vassals collectively.

vas·sal·ize (vas′əl·īz) *v.t.* **·ized, ·iz·ing** To reduce to vassalage; use as a vassal.

vast (vast, väst) *adj.* 1 Of great extent; immense; enormous; huge; also, very spacious. 2 Very great in number, quantity, or amount. 3 Very great in degree, intensity, or importance. 4 *Obs.* Wide and waste; desolate; desert. See synonyms under IMMENSE, LARGE. — *n.* 1 A boundless space; immensity. 2 *Brit. Dial.* A great quantity. [<L, waste, empty, vast. Related to WASTE.] — **vast′ly** *adv.*

—**vast′ness, vas·ti·tude** (vas′tə·tōōd, -tyōōd, väs′-) *n.*

vas·ta·tion (vas·tā′shən) *n.* **1** Purification by the spiritual burning away of evil. **2** *Obs.* Devastation. [< L *vastatio, -onis* < *vastare* lay waste < *vastus* waste, empty]

Väs·ter·ås (ves·tər·ōs′) A city of east central Sweden; an industrial center: formerly *Vesterås.*

vas·ti·ty (vas′tə·tē, väs′-) *n. pl.* **·ties** Vastness; immensity. [< F *vastité* < *vaste* large]

vast·y (vas′tē, väs′-) *adj. Poetic* Vast. [< VAST]

vat (vat) *n.* A large vessel, tub, or cistern, especially for holding liquids and dyeing materials. —*v.t.* **vat·ted, vat·ting** To put into a vat; treat in a vat. [OE *fæt*]

vat dye *Chem.* A dye produced by oxidation, and resistant to sunlight and washing.

Va·té (vä′tē) See EFATE.

vat·ic (vat′ik) *adj.* Pertaining to or proceeding from a prophet or seer; oracular; prophetic; inspired: *vatic* dicta, *vatic* lips. Also **vat′i·cal.** [< L *vates* prophet]

Vat·i·can (vat′ə·kən) *n.* **1** The papal palace in Vatican City, Rome. **2** The papal government, as distinguished from the Quirinal, or Italian civil government. —**Council of the Vatican** An ecumenical council, 1869–70, at the Vatican which declared the pope's infallibility, when speaking *ex cathedra,* to be a dogma of the church. [from L *Vaticanus* Vatican Hill in Rome]

Vatican City A sovereign papal state within the city of Rome, established June 10, 1929; 108.7 acres, including the Vatican and St. Peter's Church, along with the square in front of it; twelve buildings outside this area, both in and outside Rome, enjoy extraterritorial rights: Italian *Città del Vaticano.*

Vat·i·can·ism (vat′ə·kən·iz′əm) *n.* The ecclesiastical system and the tenet based on the supremacy and infallibility of the pope.

vat·i·cide (vat′ə·sīd) *n.* The killing of a prophet; also, a prophet-slayer. [< L *vates* prophet +-CIDE]

va·tic·i·nal (və·tis′ə·nəl) *adj.* Prophetic.

va·tic·i·nate (və·tis′ə·nāt) *v.t. & v.i.* **·nat·ed, ·nat·ing** To prophesy; foretell. [< L *vaticinatus,* pp. of *vaticinari* prophesy < *vates* prophet]—**va·tic′i·na′tion** *n.* —**va·tic′i·na′tor** *n.* —**va·tic′i·na·to′ry** (-nə·tôr′ē, -tō′rē) *adj.*

Vät·ter (vet′ər), **Lake** The second largest lake in Sweden, in the south central part; 733 square miles: formerly *Vetter. Swedish* **Vät·tern** (vet′ərn).

Va·tu·tin (vä·tōō′tin), **Nikolai,** 1901?–44, Russian general in World War II.

vau (väv) See VAV.

Vau·ban (vō·bän′), **Marquis de,** 1633–1707, Sébastien le Prestre, French military engineer.

vau·che·ri·a·ceous (vō·kir′ē·ā′shəs) *adj. Bot.* Belonging or pertaining to a genus *(Vaucheria)* of green algae consisting of long and usually branched filaments which grow in feltlike masses in shallow water and on muddy banks: often called *green felt.* [< NL, after Jean Pierre *Vaucher,* 1763–1841, Swiss botanist]

Vau·cluse (vō·klüz′) A department in Provence, SE France; 1,381 square miles; capital, Avignon.

Vaud (vō) A canton in west central Switzerland; 1,239 square miles; capital, Lausanne: German *Waadt.*

vau·de·ville (vōd′də·vil, vōd′vil) *n.* **1** A miscellaneous theatrical entertainment consisting of a slight dramatic sketch or pantomime interspersed with songs and dances; a series of short sketches, songs, dances, acrobatic feats, etc., having no dramatic connection; a variety show; also, a theater presenting such shows. **2** A street ballad; originally, a satirical or topical popular song. [< F, alter. of *(chanson de) Vau de Vire* (song of) the valley of the Vire river (in Normandy), where Basselin, the best-known composer of such songs, lived]

Vau·dois (vō·dwä′) *n. pl.* **·dois** (-dwä′) **1** An inhabitant, or the inhabitants collectively, of the Swiss canton of Vaud. **2** The dialect of this canton.

Vau·dois (vō·dwä′) *n. pl.* The Waldenses.

Vaughan (vôn), **Henry,** 1622–95, English poet.

Vaughan Williams, Ralph, 1872–1958, English composer.

vault¹ (vôlt) *n.* **1** An arched apartment or chamber; also, any subterranean compartment; cellar. **2** An arched structure; arched ceiling or roof. **3** Any vaultlike covering; the sky. **4** An arched roof of a cavity. **5** An underground room or compartment for storing wine, valuables, etc. **6** A burial chamber. —*v.t.* **1** To form with a vaulted roof; cover with or as with a vault. **2** To construct in the form of a vault. [< OF *volte, vaute,* ult. < L *volutus,* pp. of *volvere* turn about, roll] —**vault′ed** *adj.*

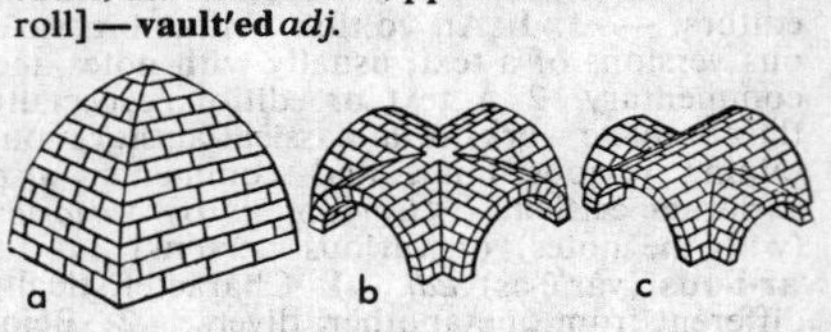

TYPES OF VAULTS
a. Cloister or cove. *b.* Groin.
c. Welsh or underpitch.

vault² (vôlt) *v.t.* **1** To leap over, especially with the aid of a pole or with the hands resting on something. **2** To mount with a leap, as a horse. —*v.i.* **3** To leap; spring. **4** To do a curvet. See synonyms under LEAP. —*n.* **1** A leap or bound; a springing leap, as one made with the aid of a pole. **2** The curvet of a horse. [< OF *volter* leap, gambol, ? ult. < L *volutus,* pp. of *volvere* turn about, roll] —**vault′er** *n.*

vault·ing¹ (vôl′ting) *n.* **1** Vaulted work, or vaults collectively. **2** The work or art of building a vault.

vault·ing² (vôl′ting) *adj.* **1** That overleaps; hence, unduly confident or presumptuous: *vaulting* ambition. **2** That can be used in vaulting, as in gymnastics.

vaunt (vônt, vänt) *v.i.* To speak boastfully. —*v.t.* To boast of. See synonyms under FLAUNT. —*n.* Boastful assertion or ostentatious display. See synonyms under OSTENTATION. [< OF *vanter* < LL *vanitare* brag < L *vanus* empty, vain]—**vaunt′er** *n.* —**vaunt′ing** *n.* —**vaunt′ing·ly** *adv.*

vaunt-cour·i·er (vänt′kōōr′ē·ər, vônt′-) *n.* **1** *Archaic* A horseman or soldier sent in advance of an army. **2** A forerunner; precursor; herald. [< F *avant-coureur*]

vaunt·ie (vôn′tē) *adj. Scot.* Boastful. Also **vaunt′y, vawnt′ie.**

Vaux (vō) A village west of Château-Thierry in north central France; point of furthest German advance on the road to Paris in World War I, 1918.

vav (väv) *n.* The sixth Hebrew letter: also spelled *vau.* Also **vaw.** See ALPHABET.

vav·a·sor (vav′ə·sôr, -sōr) *n.* **1** The rank of a principal vassal next below a baron. **2** A vassal holding lands from a great vassal, and having other vassals under him. Also **vav′a·sour** (-sōōr). [< OF *vavassour* < LL *vassus vassorum* vassal of vassals]

va·ward (vä′wərd) *adj. Obs.* Vanward. [Alter. of obs. *avantward* < AF *avantwarde,* OF *avantgarde* vanguard]

VCR A videocassette recorder.

V-day (vē′dā′) *n.* A day of victory; in World War II, **V-E Day** (vē′ē′dā′) (officially May 8, 1945), the date of victory of the United Nations in Europe, and **V-J Day** (vē′jā′dā′) (officially Sept. 2, 1945, Tokyo time), the date of their victory in the Pacific.

Ve·a·dar (vē′ä·där, vā′-) A Hebrew month. See CALENDAR (Hebrew).

veal (vēl) *n.* **1** The flesh of a calf considered as food. **2** *Obs.* A calf. —**bob veal** The flesh of a calf so young as to be unfit for food. [< OF *viel* calf < L *vitellus,* dim. of *vitulus* calf]

Veb·len (veb′lən), **Thorstein Bunde,** 1857–1929, U.S. economist and sociologist.

vec·tion (vek′shən) *n. Med.* The carrying of a disease organism from an infected to a well person. [< L *vectio, -onis* a conveyance, carrying < *vehere* carry]

vec·tor (vek′tər) *n.* **1** *Math.* **a** A line representing a physical quantity that has magnitude and direction in space, as velocity, acceleration or force: distinguished from *scalar.* **b** A radius vector. **2** *Med.* A carrier of pathogenic micro-organisms from one host to another: The anopheles mosquito is a *vector* of the malaria parasite. [< L, carrier < *vehere* carry]—**vec·to·ri·al** (vek·tôr′ē·əl, -tō′rē-) *adj.*

vectorial angle *Math.* A polar angle.

vec·tur·ism (vek′chə·riz′əm) *n. U.S.* The hobby of collecting old transportation tokens from bus and trolley lines. [< L *vecturus* fare, passage money < *vehere* carry]—**vec′tur·ist** *n.*

Ve·da (vā′də, vē′-) *n.* The body of ancient Indian sacred writings, dating from the second millennium B.C., which form the Hindu scriptures; specifically, the four major collections included in this literature: **Rigveda,** containing sacrificial hymns addressed to the gods; **Yajurveda,** containing liturgical formulas; **Samaveda,** a group of hymns chiefly in honor of Indra; and **Aharvaveda,** a large collection of charms and incantations. [< Skt., knowledge]—**Ve·da·ic** (vi·dā′ik) *adj.* —**Ve·da·ism** (vā′də·iz′əm, vē′-) *n.*

Ve·dan·ta (vi·dän′tə, -dan′-) *n.* Any of several schools of Hindu religious philosophy based on the Upanishads; especially, the monistic system of Shankara which teaches the worship of Brahma as the creator and soul of the universe. [< Skt. < *Veda* Veda + *anta* end]—**Ve·dan′tic** *adj.* —**Ve·dan′tism** *n.* —**Ve·dan′tist** *n.*

Ved·da (ved′ə) *n.* One of a primitive people of Ceylon of doubtful classification, slender, dark, small, with heavy, wavy hair, having both Caucasoid and Australoid traits, but not typically either: by some anthropologists thought to be remnants of an original Indo-Australoid race. Also **Ved′dah.** [< Singhalese, hunter]

Ved·der (ved′ər), **Elihu,** 1836–1923, U.S. painter and illustrator.

ve·dette (vi·det′) *n.* **1** A mounted sentinel placed in advance of an outpost. **2** A small vessel used to watch the movements of the enemy: also **vedette boat. 3** *Colloq.* In France, a female movie star. Also spelled *vidette.* [< F < Ital. *vedetta,* alter. (after *vedere* see) of *veletta,* dim. of Sp. *vela* vigil < L *vigilare* watch]

Ve·dic (vā′dik, vē′-) *adj.* Of or pertaining to the Vedas or the language in which they were written. —*n.* Vedic Sanskrit.

Vedic Sanskrit See under SANSKRIT.

vee (vē) *n.* **1** The sound or the shape of the letter V. **2** Anything shaped like the letter V. **3** *U.S. Slang* A five-dollar bill. —*adj.* V-shaped.

veep (vēp) *n. Slang* A vice president; specifically, the vice president of the United States. [< *V.P.,* abbr. of vice president]

veer¹ (vir) *v.i.* **1** *Naut.* To turn to another course; wear ship. **2** To change direction by a clockwise motion, as the wind. **3** To shift from one position to another; be variable or fickle. —*v.t.* **4** To change the direction of. See synonyms under CHANGE, FLUCTUATE, WANDER. —*n.* A change in direction; a swerve. [< F *virer* turn]

veer² (vir) *v.t. & v.i. Naut.* To let out or allow (a rope, anchor chain, etc.) to run out to a certain length. [< MDu. *vieren* slacken]

veer·y (vir′ē) *n. pl.* **veer·ies** A melodious tawny thrush *(Hylocichla fuscescens)* of eastern North America: also called *Wilson's thrush.* [Prob. imit.]

Ve·ga (vē′gə, vā′-) A star, Alpha in the constellation Lyra; 0.14 magnitude. [< Med. L < Arabic *(al-Nasr) al-Waqi* the falling (vulture)]

Ve·ga (vā′gə, *Sp.* bā′gä), **Lope de,** 1562–1635, Spanish dramatist and poet: full name Lope Felix de Vega Carpio.

veg·e·ta·ble (vej′ə·tə·bəl, vej′tə-) *n.* **1** The edible part of any herbaceous plant, raw or cooked, chiefly when served with an entree, or before the dessert. **2** Any member of the vegetable kingdom; a plant. **3** *Colloq.* A person who is mindless, apathetic, or passive. See synonyms under FRUIT. —*adj.* **1** Pertaining to plants, especially garden or farm vegetables. **2** Derived from, of the nature of, or resembling plants. **3** Made from or consisting of vegetables. **4** *Colloq.* Showing little mental activity; vacant. [< OF < LL *vegetabilis* full of life < L *vegetare* animate < *vegetus* vigorous, lively < *vegere* be lively]

vegetable butter See BUTTER¹ (def. 2).

vegetable fibers Textile fibers such as cotton, flax, kapok, jute, ramie, etc.

vegetable ivory Ivory nut.

vegetable kingdom The domain of nature that includes all organisms classified as plants. Compare ANIMAL KINGDOM, MINERAL KINGDOM.

vegetable marrow **1** A plant of the gourd family *(Cucurbita pepo),* having a tender,

edible fruit. 2 The fruit, esteemed as a vegetable: also called *marrow squash.*

vegetable oyster The salsify.

vegetable silk A cottonlike material obtained from the seed pods of a Brazilian tree (*Chorisia speciosa)* and used for stuffing cushions, etc.

vegetable sponge A luffa.

vegetable tallow Any of several fatty vegetable substances, variously derived, resembling tallow, and used locally for making candles, soap, etc.

vegetable wax Any wax derived from a plant.

veg·e·tal (vej′ə·təl) *adj.* 1 Of or pertaining to plants or vegetables; vegetative. 2 Characterizing those vital processes which are common to plants and animals, especially as distinguished from sensation and volition. [<L *vegetus* lively, vigorous. See VEGETABLE.]

veg·e·tant (vej′ə·tənt) *adj.* 1 Invigorating; vivifying; stimulating growth. 2 Vegetating; plantlike. [<L *vegetans, -antis,* ppr. of *vegere* be active, lively]

veg·e·tar·i·an (vej′ə·târ′ē·ən) *adj.* 1 Pertaining to or advocating the eating of only vegetable foods. 2 Exclusively vegetable, as a diet. — *n.* One who holds or practices vegetarianism: also **veg·e·tist** (vej′ə·tist).

veg·e·tar·i·an·ism (vej′ə·târ′ē·ən·iz′əm) *n.* The theory or practice of eating only vegetables and fruits. Also **veg′e·tism.**

veg·e·tate (vej′ə·tāt) *v.i.* **·tat·ed, ·tat·ing** 1 To grow, as a plant. 2 To live in a monotonous, passive way. 3 *Pathol.* To increase in size. [<L *vegetatus,* pp. of *vegetare* animate. See VEGETABLE.]

veg·e·ta·tion (vej′ə·tā′shən) *n.* 1 The process of vegetating. 2 Plant life in the aggregate. 3 *Pathol.* An excrescence on the body; an abnormal or fibrous growth. 4 A plantlike growth. — **veg′e·ta′tion·al** *adj.*

veg·e·ta·tive (vej′ə·tā′tiv) *adj.* 1 Of, pertaining to, or exhibiting the processes of plant life. 2 Growing or capable of growing as plants; productive. 3 Having a mere physical existence; showing but little mental activity. 4 Asexual. 5 Concerned with growth and nutrition. 6 Functioning involuntarily or unconsciously: a *vegetative* process. Also **veg·e·tive** (vej′ə·tiv). — **veg′e·ta′tive·ly** *adv.* — **veg′e·ta′tive·ness** *n.*

Ve·glia (ve′lyä) The Italian name for KRK.

ve·he·ment (vē′ə·mənt) *adj.* 1 Arising from or marked by impetuosity of feeling or passion; ardent. 2 Acting with great force or energy; energetic; violent; furious. See synonyms under ARDENT, EAGER[1], HOT, VIOLENT. [<OF <L *vehemens, -entis* impetuous, rash; ult. origin uncertain] — **ve′he·mence, ve′he·men·cy** *n.* — **ve′he·ment·ly** *adv.*

ve·hi·cle (vē′ə·kəl) *n.* 1 That in or on which anything is carried; especially, a contrivance fitted with wheels or runners for carrying something; a conveyance, as a car or sled. 2 *Med.* A medium, as a liquid, with which is mixed some other substance that it may be applied or administered more easily; an excipient. 3 The medium with which pigments are mixed in painting. 4 Anything by means of which something else, as power, thought, etc., is transmitted or communicated; a device used to transmit an effect. [<F *véhicule* <L *vehiculum* < *vehere* carry, ride] — **ve·hic·u·lar** (vi·hik′yə·lər) *adj.*

Vehm·ge·richt (fām′gə·rikht) *n. pl.* **·rich·te** (-rikh′tə) An institution peculiar to Germany, especially Westphalia, from about 1150 to 1568, consisting of irregular tribunals. Civil cases were tried openly, but serious crimes, such as heresy, witchcraft, murder, etc., were tried by night in secret session. [<G < *fehm* judgment, punishment + *gericht* law, court]

Ve·ii (vē′yī) An ancient Etruscan city in central Italy, destroyed by Romans, 396 B.C.; site, 10 miles NW of Rome.

veil (vāl) *n.* 1 A piece of thin and light fabric, worn over the face or head for concealment, protection, or ornament. 2 Any piece of fabric used to conceal an object; a screen; curtain; mask. 3 Figuratively, that which conceals from inspection; a disguise; pretext. 4 A velum. 5 A caul. 6 The life of a nun; vows made by a nun. — **to take the veil** To become a nun. — *v.t.* 1 To cover with a veil. 2 To hide; disguise. See synonyms under HIDE[1], MASK[1], PALLIATE. Also, *Obs., vail.* ◆ Homophones: *vail, vale.* [<OF *veile* <L *velum* piece of cloth, sail] — **veiled** *adj.* — **veil′er** *n.*

veil·ing (vā′ling) *n.* 1 The act of covering with a veil. 2 Material for veils. 3 A veil.

vein (vān) *n.* 1 *Anat.* One of the muscular tubular vessels that convey blood to the heart; loosely, any blood vessel. ◆ Collateral adjective: *venal.* 2 *Entomol.* One of the radiating supports of an insect's wing; a rib or nerve. 3 *Bot.* One of the slender vascular bundles that form the framework of a leaf. 4 *Geol.* The filling of a fissure or fault in a rock, particularly if deposited by aqueous solutions. 5 A lode. 6 A bed or shoot of ore parallel with the fault. 7 A long, irregular, colored streak, as in wood, marble, etc. 8 A distinctive trait; a specific tendency or disposition. 9 A temporary state of mind; humor; mood. 10 A cavity; cleft; fissure. 11 A crevice or natural channel through which water trickles. — *v.t.* 1 To furnish or fill with veins. 2 To streak or ornament with veins. 3 To extend over or throughout as veins. ◆ Homophones: *vain, vane.* [<OF *veine* <L *vena* blood vessel] — **vein′less** *adj.* — **vein′y** *adj.*

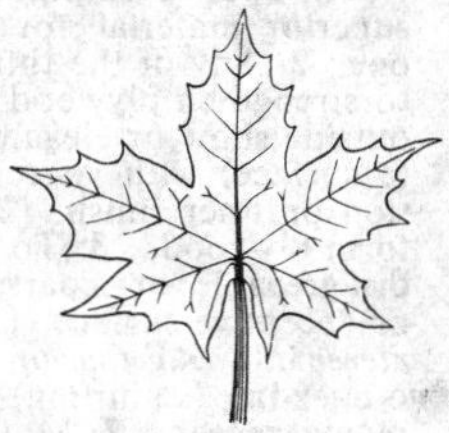

VEINING OF SILVER MAPLE LEAF

veined (vānd) *adj.* 1 Having veins. 2 Marked with or abounding in veins. 3 Marked with streaks of another color.

vein·ing (vā′ning) *n.* 1 A vein or network of veins. 2 A streaked or veined surface.

vein·let (vān′lit) *n.* A small vein.

vein·stone (vān′stōn′) *n.* Gangue.

Ve·la (vē′lə) A southern constellation, formerly part of the larger one, Argo Navis. [<L, veil]

ve·la·men (və·lā′mən) *n. pl.* **·lam·i·na** (-lam′ə·nə) 1 *Anat.* Any membrane, covering, or integument. 2 *Bot.* An envelope consisting of several layers of empty cells, forming the outer covering of the aerial roots of certain orchids and arums. Also **vel·a·men·tum** (vel′ə·men′təm). [<L, covering < *velare* veil]

ve·lar (vē′lər) *adj.* 1 Of or pertaining to a velum, especially the soft palate. 2 *Phonet.* Formed with the back of the tongue touching or near the soft palate, as (k) in *cool,* (g) in *go.* — *n. Phonet.* A velar sound. [<L *velaris* < *velum* sail, curtain]

ve·lar·ize (vē′lə·rīz) *v.* **·ized, ·iz·ing** *Phonet. v.t.* To modify (a sound) by raising the back of the tongue toward the soft palate. — *v.i.* To be modified to a velar sound.

ve·lar·i·um (və·lâr′ē·əm) *n. pl.* **·lar·i·a** (-lâr′ē·ə) *Latin* The awning spread over the seats in ancient Roman theaters or amphitheaters.

Ve·lás·quez (və·las′kwiz, *Sp.* bā·läs′kāth), **Diego Rodriguez de Silva y,** 1599–1660, Spanish painter. Also **Ve·láz·quez** (bā·läth′·kāth).

ve·late (vē′lāt, -lit) *adj. Biol.* Having a velum or veil. [<L *velatus,* pp. of *velare* veil]

ve·la·tion (vē·lā′shən) *n.* 1 The forming of a velum. 2 The act of veiling, or the state of being veiled; hence, concealment; mystery.

veldt (velt, felt) *n.* In South Africa, open country or pasture land; grassland having few shrubs or trees. Low-lying wooded land is known as **bush veldt,** and the high treeless plains as **high veldt.** Also **veld.** [<Afrikaans *veld* <Du., field]

vel·i·ger (vel′ə·jər) *n. Zool.* The larva of a mollusk at the stage succeeding the trochophore and when it has a ciliated swimming membrane or membranes. [<LL *veliger* sail-bearing <L *velum* sail + *gerere* bear]

ve·lig·er·ous (və·lij′ər·əs) *adj.* Bearing a velum or membranous partition.

Ve·li·ki Kvar·ner (ve′li·kē kvär′nər) An arm of the Adriatic Sea, SE of Istria, in NW Croatia, Yugoslavia: also *Gulf of Quarnero. Italian* **Gol·fo di Quar·ne·ro** (gôl′fō dē kwär·nā′rō).

vel·i·ta·tion (vel′ə·tā′shən) *n.* A petty skirmish; a wordy controversy. [<L *velitatio, -onis* < *velitatus,* pp. of *velitari* skirmish < *veles, velitis* a foot soldier]

ve·li·tes (vē′lə·tēz) *n. pl.* Light-armed Roman soldiers used as skirmishers in ancient legions. [<L, pl. of *veles* foot soldier]

vel·le·i·ty (ve·lē′ə·tē) *n. pl.* **·ties** A very low degree of desire or volition, not leading to action; a mere wish. [<Med. L *velleitas, -tatis* <L *velle* wish]

vel·li·cate (vel′ə·kāt) *v.t.* & *v.i.* **·cat·ed, ·cat·ing** To twitch or pluck. [<L *vellicatus,* pp. of *vellicare* twitch, freq. of *vellere* pluck] — **vel′li·ca′tion** *n.* — **vel′li·ca′tive** *adj.*

vel·lum (vel′əm) *n.* 1 Fine parchment made from the skins of calves: used for expensive binding, printing, etc. 2 A manuscript written on such parchment. 3 Paper made to resemble parchment. [<OF *velin, vellin* < *veel, viel* calf. See VEAL.]

ve·lo·ce (vā·lō′chā) *adv. Music* Rapidly; in quick tempo; swiftly. [<Ital., swift]

ve·loc·i·pede (və·los′ə·pēd) *n.* 1 An early form of bicycle or tricycle; also, a child's tricycle. 2 A light handcar or vehicle propelled by hands or feet and used along railroad tracks. [<L *velox, velocis* swift + -PEDE]

ve·loc·i·ty (və·los′ə·tē) *n. pl.* **·ties** 1 The state of moving swiftly; rapid motion; celerity; speed. 2 *Physics* **a** The rate of change of position in a moving object. **b** The rate of motion in a stated direction: a vector quantity: distinguished from *speed.* [<L *velocitas, -tatis* < *velox* swift]

velocity of escape *Physics* The minimum velocity at which any particle or object would permanently escape the gravitational field of a body of stated mass: on the earth this velocity is approximately 7 miles per second. See table under PLANET.

ve·lo·drome (vē′lə·drōm) *n.* A racecourse, as for bicycles. [<L *velox* speedy + -DROME]

ve·lours (və·lo͝or′) *n. pl.* **·lours** A soft, velvetlike, closely woven cotton or wool fabric having a short, thick pile. Also **ve·lour′.** [<F. See VELURE.]

ve·lou·té (və·lo͞o·tā′) *n. French* A rich white sauce made by thickening chicken or veal stock with flour and butter. Also **sauce velouté.**

ve·lum (vē′ləm) *n. pl.* **·la** (-lə) 1 *Biol.* A thin membranous covering or partition, as in certain jellyfishes, and in mushrooms. 2 *Anat.* The soft palate. See PALATE. [<L]

ve·lure (və·lo͝or′) *n.* 1 Velvet, or a fabric resembling velvet; specifically, a heavy fabric of linen, silk, or jute, used for hangings, table covers, and the like. 2 A velvet or silk pad for smoothing a silk hat. — *v.t.* **·lured, ·lur·ing** To smooth with a soft pad, as a hat. [<F *velours* <L *villosus* shaggy < *villus* shaggy hair]

ve·lu·ti·nous (və·lo͞o′tə·nəs) *adj. Bot.* Covered with close, soft hairs, like the pile of velvet; velvety. [<NL *velutinus* <Med. L *velutum,* var. of *velvetum.* See VELVET.]

vel·ver·et (vel′və·ret′) *n.* A velvet fabric with cotton backing.

vel·vet (vel′vit) *n.* 1 A fabric, properly of silk, now sometimes made of cotton or one of the synthetics, closely woven and having on one side a thick, short, smooth pile: called **pile velvet** when the pile is formed of loops, and **cut velvet** when the pile is of single threads. 2 The furry skin covering a growing antler. — **chiffon velvet** A very soft, lightweight velvet having the pile pressed flat. — *adj.* 1 Made of velvet. 2 Smooth and soft to the touch; velvety. [<Med. L *velvetum,* ult. <L *villus* shaggy hair]

velvet carpet A carpet having a pile longer than a Brussels carpet but cut in the manner of a Wilton carpet: also **tapestry velvet carpet.**

vel·vet·een (vel′və·tēn′) *n.* 1 A cotton fabric, with a short, close pile like velvet. 2 *pl.* Clothes, especially trousers, made of this material. [<VELVET] — **vel′vet·eened′** *adj.*

vel·vet·leaf (vel′vit·lēf′) *n.* 1 Any one of several plants, especially the Indian mallow. 2 A tropical climbing shrub (*Cissampelos pareira)* of the moonseed family, the bark of which yields a variety of pareira brava.

vel·vet·y (vel′vit·ē) *adj.* 1 Like velvet; smooth and soft to appearance or touch. 2

Mild and smooth to the taste: *velvety* liqueur.
ve·na (vē′nə) *n.* *pl.* **·nae** (-nē) *Anat.* A vein. [<L]
ve·na ca·va (vē′nə kā′və) *n.* *pl.* **ve·nae ca·vae** (vē′nē kā′vē) *Anat.* Either of the two great venous trunks (called *superior* and *inferior*) emptying into the right auricle of the heart. See illustration under HEART. [<L, hollow vein]
ve·nal[1] (vē′nəl) *adj.* **1** Ready to sell honor or principle, or to accept a bribe; mercenary; purchasable: said of persons. **2** Subject to sordid bargaining or to corrupt influences; salable. **3** Characterized by corruption and venality. [<L *venalis* < *venum* sale] **—ve′nal·ly** *adv.*
Synonyms: hireling, mercenary, purchasable, salable. *Mercenary* has especial application to character or disposition; as, a *mercenary* spirit; *mercenary* motives—that is, a spirit or motives to which money is the chief consideration or the moving principle. Thus, etymologically, the *mercenary* can be hired, while the *venal* are openly or actually for sale; *hireling* signifies serving for hire or pay, or having the spirit or character of one who works or of that which is done directly for hire or pay. The *hireling*, the *mercenary*, and the *venal* are alike in making principle, conscience, and honor of less account than gold or sordid considerations; but the *mercenary* and *venal* may be simply open to the bargain and sale which the *hireling* has already consummated. A public officer who makes his office tributary to private speculation is *mercenary*; if he receives a stipulated recompense for administering his office at the behest of some leader, faction, corporation, or the like, he is both *hireling* and *venal*; if he sells essential advantages, without subjecting himself to any direct domination, his course is *venal*, but not *hireling*. *Antonyms*: disinterested, honest, honorable, incorruptible, patriotic, unpurchasable.
ve·nal[2] (vē′nəl) *adj.* Of or pertaining to the veins; venous. [<L *vena* vein]
ve·nal·i·ty (vē·nal′ə·tē) *n.* *pl.* **·ties** The state or character of being basely or improperly influenced by sordid considerations; prostitution, as of talents, office, etc., for gain or reward; willingness to accept bribes. [<L *venalitas, -tatis*]
ve·nat·ic (vē·nat′ik) *adj.* **1** Of, used in, or pertaining to hunting. **2** Living by or fond of hunting. Also **ven·a·to·ri·al** (ven′ə·tôr′ē·əl, -tō′rē-). [<L *venaticus* < *venatus,* pp. of *venari* hunt] **—ve·nat′i·cal** *adj.* **—ve·nat′i·cal·ly** *adv.*
ve·na·tion (vē·nā′shən) *n.* *Biol.* **1** The particular arrangement of veins, as in a leaf. **2** The distribution of veins in an organism or part, as an insect wing, etc. [<L *vena* a vein]
vend (vend) *v.t.* **1** To sell. **2** To utter (an opinion); publish. **—*v.i.*** **3** To be a vender. **4** To be sold. [<F *vendre* <L *vendere* < *venum* sale + *dare* give] **—ven·di·tion** (ven·dish′ən) *n.*
ven·dace (ven′dis) *n.* A small whitefish *(Coregonus vandesius)* of some British lakes. Also **ven′dis.** [<F *vandoise* dace]
ven·dee (ven·dē′) *n.* The person or party to whom something, especially land, is sold.
Ven·dée (vän·dā′) A region and department in western France on the Bay of Biscay; scene of a royalist revolt, 1793–95; 2,708 square miles. **—Ven·de·an** (ven·dē′ən) *adj.* & *n.*
Ven·dé·miaire (vän·dā·myâr′) See under CALENDAR (Republican).
vend·er (ven′dər) *n.* One who sells; a peddler or hawker; vendor.
ven·det·ta (ven·det′ə) *n.* Private warfare or feud, as in revenge for a murder, injury, etc.; a blood feud in which the relatives of the killed or injured person take vengeance on the offender or his relatives. It is still prevalent in Sicily, Corsica, and Montenegro, and, to some extent, in certain other districts. [<Ital. <L *vindicta* vengeance]
vend·i·ble (ven′də·bəl) *adj.* Capable of being vended or sold; marketable. **—*n.*** A thing exposed for sale. [<L *vendibilis* < *vendere* sell] **—vend′i·bil′i·ty, vend′i·ble·ness** *n.* **—vend′i·bly** *adv.*
Ven·dôme (vän·dôm′) A town and former duchy in north central France.
ven·dor (ven′dər) The common legal spelling of VENDER.
ven·due (ven·dōō′, -dyōō′) *n.* A public sale or auction. [<F, orig. fem. pp. of *vendre* sell]
ve·neer (və·nir′) *n.* **1** A thin layer, as of choice wood, upon a commoner surface; a layer of superior material for overlaying a cheaper one. **2** Any of the thin layers glued together to strengthen plywood. **3** Figuratively, mere outside show or elegance. **—*v.t.*** **1** To cover (a surface) with veneers; overlay for decoration or finer finish. **2** To glue together to form plywood. **3** To conceal, as something disagreeable or coarse, with an attractive or deceptive surface. [Earlier *fineer* <G *furnieren* inlay <F *fournir* furnish] **—ve·neer′er** *n.*
ve·neer·ing (və·nir′ing) *n.* **1** The art of applying veneer. **2** Material used for veneers. **3** A facing or surface of veneer.
ven·e·punc·ture (ven′ə·pungk′chər) See VENIPUNCTURE.
Ve·ner (ve′nər), **Lake** The largest lake of Sweden, in the SW part; 2,141 square miles; 90 miles long, 5 to 46 miles wide: also *Vaner.* *Swedish* **Vä·nern** (ve′nərn).
ven·er·a·ble (ven′ər·ə·bəl) *adj.* **1** Meriting or commanding veneration; worthy of reverence: now usually implying age. **2** Exciting reverential feelings because of sacred or elevated associations. **3** Revered: used as a title for an archdeacon in Anglican churches, and for those beatified in the Roman Catholic Church. See synonyms under ANCIENT[1]. [<OF <L *venerabilis* < *venerari* revere] **—ven′er·a·ble·ness, ven′er·a·bil′i·ty** *n.* **—ven′er·a·bly** *adv.*
ven·er·ate (ven′ə·rāt) *v.t.* **·at·ed, ·at·ing** To look upon or regard with respect and deference; revere. [<L *veneratus,* pp. of *venerari* revere]
Synonyms: adore, honor, respect, revere, reverence. In the highest sense, to *revere* or *reverence* is to hold in mingled love and honor with something of sacred fear; to *revere* is a wholly spiritual act; to *reverence* is often, but not necessarily, to give outward expression to the reverential feeling; we *revere* or *reverence* the divine majesty. *Revere* is a stronger word than *reverence* or *venerate.* To *venerate* is to hold in exalted honor without fear, and is applied to objects less removed from ourselves than those we *revere,* being said especially of aged persons, of places or objects having sacred associations, and of abstractions; we *venerate* an aged friend or some great cause, as that of civil or religious liberty; we do not *venerate* God, but *revere* or *reverence* him. We *adore* with a humble yet free outflowing of soul. See ADMIRE, DEFER. *Antonyms*: contemn, despise, disdain, dishonor, disregard, scorn, slight, spurn.
ven·er·a·tion (ven′ə·rā′shən) *n.* **1** The act of venerating; reverence; profound respect combined with awe, evoked by the high character or wisdom of a person. **2** The act of worshiping; worship.
Synonyms: adoration, awe, dread, reverence. *Awe* is inspired by that in which there is sublimity or majesty so overwhelming as to awaken a feeling akin to fear; in *awe,* considered by itself, there is no element of esteem or affection, but a sense of the vastness, power, or grandeur of the object. *Dread* is a shrinking apprehension or expectation of possible harm awakened by any one of many objects or causes; in its higher uses *dread* approaches the meaning of *awe,* but with more of chilliness and cowering, and without that subjection of soul to the grandeur and worthiness of the object that is involved in *awe. Reverence* and *veneration* are less overwhelming than *awe* or *dread,* and suggest something of esteem, affection, and personal nearness. We may feel *awe* of that which we cannot reverence, as a grandly terrible ocean storm; *awe* of the divine presence is more distant and less trustful than *reverence. Veneration* is commonly applied to things which are not subjects of *awe. Adoration,* in its full sense, is loftier than *veneration,* less restrained and awed than *reverence,* and with more of the spirit of direct, active, and joyful worship. See REVERENCE. Compare VENERATE. *Antonyms*: contempt, disdain, dishonor, disregard, scorn.
ve·ne·re·al (və·nir′ē·əl) *adj.* **1** Pertaining to or proceeding from sexual intercourse. **2** Communicated by sexual relations with an infected person: a *venereal* disease. **3** Pertaining to or curative of diseases so communicated. **4** Infected with venereal disease. [<L *venereus* <*Venus, -eris,* the goddess of love]
venereal disease *Pathol.* One of several diseases propagated directly or indirectly by sexual intercourse, as syphilis, gonorrhea, and chancroid.
ve·ne·re·ol·o·gy (və·nir′ē·ol′ə·jē) *n.* The study and treatment of venereal diseases. **—ve·ne′re·ol′o·gist** *n.*
ven·er·y[1] (ven′ər·ē) *n.* Sexual indulgence, especially when excessive. [<L *Venus, -eris,* the goddess of love]
ven·er·y[2] (ven′ər·ē) *n.* *pl.* **·er·ies** The hunting of game; the sport of hunting; the chase. [<F *venerie* < *vener* hunt <L *venari* hunt]
ven·e·sec·tion (ven′ə·sek′shən) *n.* *Surg.* Phlebotomy. [<Med. L *venae sectio* cutting of a vein]
Ve·ne·ti·a (və·nē′shē·ə, -shə) **1** An ancient division of the Roman Empire comprising that part of Italy between the Po river and the Alps. **2** Venezia. **3** Veneto.
Ve·ne·tian (və·nē′shən) *adj.* Pertaining to Venice, or to the medieval school of architecture developed there. **—*n.*** **1** A native of Venice. **2** *Colloq.* A Venetian blind. **3** A heavy braid or tape used on Venetian blinds.
Venetian blind A flexible window screen that may be raised or lowered, having overlapping horizontal slats so fastened on webbing or tape as to regulate, exclude, or admit light.
Venetian carpet A worsted carpet for stairs and hallways, commonly of a simple striped pattern.
Venetian glass A delicate and fine glassware originally made at or near Venice.
Venetian red Red ocher. See under OCHER.
Venetian school **1** A school of painting originating in and near Venice in the 15th century and distinguished by richness of coloring, as in the work of Titian, Tintoretto, Giorgione, etc. **2** A school of Italian architecture.
Ve·net·ic (və·net′ik) *n.* **1** A member of an ancient people of NE Italy. **2** Their Indo-European language, possibly related to Illyrian and Messapian. **—*adj.*** Of or pertaining to these people or their language.
Ve·ne·to (vā′nā·tō) A region of northern and NE Italy; 7,093 square miles; capital, Venice.
Ve·ne·zia (vā·nā′tsyä) **1** The Italian name for VENICE. **2** A province in Veneto, northern Italy; 949 square miles; capital, Venice.
Venezia Giu·lia (jōō′lyä) A former region of NE Italy including Trieste, Rijeka, and Istria; 3,370 square miles; divided 1947 between Italy (180 square miles), Yugoslavia (2,891 square miles), and the Free Territory of Trieste (298 square miles, later also divided).
Ven·e·zue·la (ven′ə·zwē′lə, -zōō·ā′lə; *Sp.* bā′·nā·swā′lä) A republic in northern South America; 352,143 square miles; capital, Caracas. **—Ven′e·zue′lan** *adj.* & *n.*
Venezuela, Gulf of See under MARACAIBO.
ven·geance (ven′jəns) *n.* **1** The infliction of a deserved penalty; retributive punishment. **2** In a bad sense, wrathful avenging of a wrong; revenge. **3** *Obs.* Mischief; evil. See synonyms under REVENGE. **—with a vengeance** With great force or violence; extremely; to an unusual extent. [<AF <OF *venger* avenge <L *vindicare* defend, avenge < *vindex, vindicis* claimant, protector]
venge·ful (venj′fəl) *adj.* Prone to inflict vengeance; vindictive. **—venge′ful·ly** *adv.* **—venge′ful·ness** *n.*
ve·ni·al (vē′nē·əl, vēn′yəl) *adj.* That may be pardoned or overlooked; excusable. [<OF <L *venialis* < *venia* forgiveness, mercy] **—ve′·ni·al′i·ty** (-al′ə·tē), **ve′ni·al·ness** *n.* **—ve′ni·al·ly** *adv.*
Synonyms: excusable, pardonable, slight, trivial. Aside from its technical ecclesiastical use, *venial* is always understood as marking some fault comparatively *slight* or *trivial.* A *venial* offense is one readily overlooked; a *pardonable* offense requires more serious consideration, but on deliberation is found to be susceptible of pardon. *Excusable* is scarcely applied to offenses, but to matters open to doubt or criticism rather than direct censure; so used, it often falls little short of justifiable; as, I suppose, under those circumstances, his

action was *excusable*. *Antonyms*: inexcusable, mortal, unpardonable.

venial sin *Theol.* A pardonable offense, or an unpremeditated one: opposed to *mortal* or *deadly* sin.

Ven·ice (ven′is) A port in NE Italy, built on 118 islands in the **Lagoon of Venice**, the NW part of the **Gulf of Venice**, the northern sector of the Adriatic between Istria and the Po river delta: Italian *Venezia*.

Ve·ni Cre·a·tor (vē′nī krē·ā′tər) *Latin* A hymn to the Holy Ghost: so called from its beginning, *Veni Creator Spiritus* (Come, Creator Spirit).

ven·i·punc·ture (ven′ə·pungk′chər) *n. Surg.* The operation of puncturing a vein: also spelled *venepuncture*. [<L *vena* vein + PUNCTURE]

ve·ni·re (vi·nī′rē) *n. Law* A writ issued to the sheriff for summoning persons to serve as a jury in court: from its phrase *venire facias* (that you cause to come). [<L]

ve·ni·re-man (vi·nī′rē·mən) *n. pl.* **·men** (-mən) A juryman; one summoned to be on a jury.

ven·i·son (ven′ə·zən, -sən; *Brit.* ven′zən) *n.* **1** Deer flesh used for food. **2** *Obs.* The flesh of any edible game. [<F *venaison* <L *venatio, -onis* hunting < *venatus*, pp. of *venari* hunt]

venison bird *Canadian* The Canada jay.

Ve·ni·te (vi·nī′tē) *n.* The 95th psalm, used as a canticle in various liturgies: from its first word. [<L, come, imperative of *venire* come]

ve·ni, vi·di, vi·ci (vē′nī, vī′dī, vī′sī; wā′nē, wē′dē, wē′kē) *Latin* I came, I saw, I conquered: words used by Julius Caesar to report his victory over Pharnaces, king of Pontus, to the Roman Senate.

Ve·ni·ze·los (ve′nē·ze′lôs), **Eleftherios**, 1864–1936, Greek statesman; premier 1917–20 and 1928–32.

ven·om (ven′əm) *n.* **1** The poisonous fluid that certain animals, as serpents and scorpions, secrete, and which produces toxic effects when introduced into the system by a bite or sting. **2** Something harmful; hence, malignity; spite. **3** Any poison. — *v.t.* To imbue with poison; envenom. [<OF *venim* <L *venenum* poison] — **ven′om·er** *n.*

ven·om·ous (ven′əm·əs) *adj.* **1** Having glands secreting venom. **2** Able to give a poisonous sting; virulent; noxious. **3** Working harm; baneful. **4** Malignant; spiteful. See synonyms under MALICIOUS. — **ven′om·ous·ly** *adv.* — **ven′om·ous·ness** *n.*

ve·nose (vē′nōs) *adj.* **1** Having numerous or prominent veins, as a leaf; veiny. **2** Venous. [<L *venosus*]

ve·nos·i·ty (vi·nos′ə·tē) *n.* **1** An excess of venous blood in a part. **2** A plentiful supply of blood vessels.

ve·nous (vē′nəs) *adj. Physiol.* **1** Of, pertaining to, contained, or carried in a vein or veins. **2** Designating the blood carried by the veins and distinguished from arterial blood by its darker color, absence of oxygen, and presence of carbon dioxide. **3** Marked with or having veins. [<L *venosus* < *vena* vein] — **ve′nous·ly** *adv.* — **ve′nous·ness** *n.*

vent (vent) *n.* **1** An opening, commonly small, for the passage of fluids, gases, etc.; hence, an outlet of any kind: also **vent hole**. **2** The act of giving utterance, as to passion; expression; escape; passage: now usually in the phrase **to give vent to.** **3** *Zool.* The external opening of the alimentary canal, especially of animals below mammals; the anus. **4** A touchhole of a gun. — *v.t.* **1** To give expression to: to *vent* one's rage. **2** To relieve, as by giving vent to emotion. **3** To permit to escape at a vent, as a gas. **4** To make a vent in, as a mold. [ME *fent* <OF *fente* cleft < *fendre* cleave <L *findere* split]

vent·age (ven′tij) *n.* **1** A small opening. **2** A finger hole in a musical instrument. [<VENT]

ven·tail (ven′tāl) *n.* The adjustable front of a helmet, permitting complete defense of the face in combat. [<OF *ventaile* < *vent* wind]

vent·er[1] (ven′tər) *n.* One who vents.

ven·ter[2] (ven′tər) *n.* **1** The belly or stomach. **2** Any protuberant part. **3** The womb. **4** A hollowed part, as of a bone. [<L, stomach]

ven·ti·duct (ven′tə·dukt) *n.* An air passage, especially a subterranean ventilating passage. [<L *ventus* wind + DUCT]

ven·ti·late (ven′tə·lāt) *v.t.* **·lat·ed, ·lat·ing** **1** To produce a free circulation of air in, as by means of open shafts, windows, doors, etc.; admit fresh air into. **2** To provide with a vent. **3** To make widely known; expose to examination and discussion. **4** To oxygenate, as blood. **5** *Obs.* To winnow; fan, as wheat. [<L *ventilatus*, pp. of *ventilare* fan < *ventus* wind] — **ven′ti·lat′ing, ven′ti·la′tion** *n.* — **ven′ti·la′tive** *adj.*

ven·ti·la·tor (ven′tə·lā′tər) *n.* **1** One who or that which ventilates. **2** A device or arrangement for supplying fresh air. — **ven′·ti·la·to′ry** (-lə·tôr′ē, -tō′rē) *adj.*

Ven·ti·mi·glia (ven′tē·mē′lyä) An Italian port on the Gulf of Genoa NE of Nice; an important international railroad station.

Ven·tôse (väṅ·tōz′) See under CALENDAR (Republican).

ven·trad (ven′trad) *adv. Biol.* Toward the belly or undersurface. [<L *venter* belly]

ven·tral (ven′trəl) *adj.* **1** *Biol.* **a** Of, pertaining to, or situated on or near the abdomen or abdominal surface of an animal. **b** On or toward the lower surface of the body: the *ventral* plates of a serpent: opposed to *dorsal*. **2** *Bot.* Pertaining to the surface of a petal, carpel, etc., that faces the center of a flower. — *n.* One of the paired fins on the underside of fishes, homologous with the hind limb of higher vertebrates: in full, **ventral fin.** [<L *ventralis* < *venter, ventris* belly] — **ven′tral·ly** *adv.*

ven·tri·cle (ven′trə·kəl) *n. Anat.* **1** Any of various cavities in the body, as of the brain, the spinal cord, or between the true and false vocal cords in the larynx. **2** One of the two lower chambers of the heart, from which blood received from the atria is forced into the arteries. [<L *ventriculus*, dim. of *venter, ventris* belly]

ven·tri·cose (ven′trə·kōs) *adj.* **1** Having a protruding belly. **2** Swelling out or inflated on one side or in the middle; bellied; distended. Also **ven′tri·cous** (-kəs). [<NL *ventricosus* <L *venter, ventris* belly] — **ven′tri·cos′i·ty** (-kos′ə·tē) *n.*

ven·tric·u·lar (ven·trik′yə·lər) *adj.* **1** Of, pertaining to, or of the nature of a ventricle. **2** Swollen and distended; ventricose.

ven·tric·u·lose (ven·trik′yə·lōs) *adj.* Slightly ventricose. [<L *ventriculosus* < *ventriculus*. See VENTRICLE.]

ven·tri·lo·qui·al (ven′trə·lō′kwē·əl) *adj.* Pertaining to, resembling, or practicing ventriloquism. Also **ven·tril·o·qual** (ven·tril′ə·kwəl), **ven·tril′o·quous.** — **ven′tri·lo′qui·al·ly** *adv.*

ven·tril·o·quism (ven·tril′ə·kwiz′əm) *n.* The art or practice of speaking in such a manner that the sounds seem to come from some source other than the person speaking. Also **ven·tril′o·quy** (-kwē). [<L *venter* belly + *loqui* speak] — **ven·tril′o·quist** *n.* — **ven·tril′o·quis′tic** *adj.*

ven·tril·o·quize (ven·tril′ə·kwīz) *v.t.* & *v.i.* **·quized, ·quiz·ing** To speak as a ventriloquist. Also *Brit.* **ven·tril′o·quise.**

ventro- *combining form Anat.* The abdomen; related to or near the abdomen; ventral. [<L *venter, ventris* the belly, abdomen]

Vents·pils (vents′pils) A port on the Baltic Sea in NW Latvia: German *Windau*.

ven·ture (ven′chər) *v.* **·tured, ·tur·ing** *v.t.* **1** To expose to chance or risk; hazard; stake. **2** To run the risk of; brave. **3** To express at the risk of denial or refutation: to *venture* a suggestion. **4** To place or send on a chance, as in a speculative business enterprise. **5** *Obs.* To trust as an agent or doer; rely on. — *v.i.* **6** To take a risk; dare. — *n.* **1** The staking of a thing upon a contingency; a risk; hazard. **2** An undertaking attended with risk; a business speculation. **3** That which is ventured; especially, property risk. **4** That which is unforeseen and hazardous; chance; fortune: a rare usage. See synonyms under HAZARD. — **at a venture** At hazard; at random; without aim or thought. [Aphetic form of ADVENTURE] — **ven′tur·er** *n.*

ven·ture·some (ven′chər·səm) *adj.* **1** Bold; daring. **2** Involving hazard; risky. See synonyms under BRAVE, IMPRUDENT. — **ven′ture·some·ly** *adv.* — **ven′ture·some·ness** *n.*

ven·tur·ous (ven′chər·əs) *adj.* **1** Adventurous; willing to take risks and brave dangers; bold. **2** Hazardous; risky; dangerous. See synonyms under IMPRUDENT. — **ven′tur·ous·ly** *adv.* — **ven′tur·ous·ness** *n.*

ven·ue (ven′yōō) *n. Law* **1** The place or neighborhood where a crime is committed or a cause of action arises; the county or political division from which the jury must be summoned and in which the trial must be held. **2** The clause, usually at the beginning of a declaration or indictment, indicating the county in which the proceeding is pending. **3** A clause in an affidavit, stating where it was made and sworn to. — **change of venue** The change of the place of trial, for good cause shown, from one county to another. [<OF, orig. fem. pp. of *venir* come <L *venire*]

ven·ule (ven′yōōl) *n.* A small vein; veinlet, as of an insect. [<L *venula*, dim. of *vena* vein] — **ven′u·lar** (-yə·lər) *adj.*

ven·u·lose (ven′yə·lōs) *adj.* Having numerous veinlets, as a leaf. Also **ven′u·lous** (-ləs). [<VENULE]

ve·nus (vē′nəs) *n.* A bivalve having three hinge teeth in each valve, as the quahaug. [<VENUS; from the resemblance of the lunula of the closed valve to the vulva]

Ve·nus (vē′nəs) **1** In Roman mythology, the goddess of spring, bloom, and beauty: identified with the Greek *Aphrodite*. **2** A statue or painting of Venus. **3** A lovely woman. **4** *Astron.* The second planet from the sun, the most brilliant object in the heavens except the sun and the moon. It moves in an orbit between those of Mercury and Earth at a mean distance from the sun of about 67,000,000 miles, completing a revolution in 224.7 days. Its diameter is about 7,700 miles and it has no satellites. **5** *Obs.* In alchemy, the metal copper. [<L]

Ve·nus·berg (vē′nəs·bûrg, *Ger.* vā′nōōs·berkh) In medieval German legend, a mountain in the dark recesses of which Venus lured men to sensuous pleasures. See TANNHÄUSER.

Venus flytrap A plant (*Dionaea muscipula*), with clustered leaves the blades of which instantly close upon insects or other objects lighting upon them: found native chiefly in the sandy bogs of eastern North and South Carolina. Also **Ve·nus's-fly·trap** (vē′nəs·iz·flī′trap′).

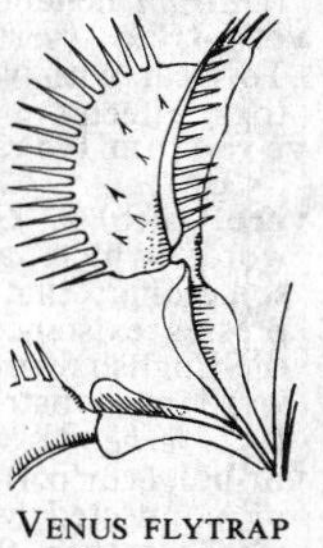

VENUS FLYTRAP
(From 4 to 14 inches tall)

Venus of Mi·lo (mē′lō) A marble statue of Venus, nude above the thighs and with the arms missing, discovered in 1820 on the island of Milo: now in the Louvre. Also **Venus de Milo.**

Ve·nus's-comb (vē′nəs·iz·kōm′) *n.* A European plant (*Scandix pecten-veneris*) with white flowers in numerous umbels, and lobed leaves suggestive of a comb: often called *shepherd's-needle, devil's-darning-needle.*

Ve·nus's-gir·dle (vē′nəs·iz·gûr′dəl) *n.* A ctenophore of warm seas, having a transparent body that shimmers with blue, green, or violet colors.

Ve·nus's-hair (vē′nəs·iz·hâr′) *n.* A maidenhair fern (*Adiantum capillus-veneris*) having a black stipe and branches.

ver·a (ver′ə, var′ə) *adj.* & *adv. Scot.* Very.

Ve·ra (vir′ə) A feminine personal name. [<Slavic, faith]

ve·ra·cious (və·rā′shəs) *adj.* **1** Habitually disposed to speak the truth; truthful. **2** Conforming to or expressing truth; true; accurate. [<L *verax, veracis* < *verus* true] — **ve·ra′·cious·ly** *adv.* — **ve·ra′cious·ness** *n.*

ve·rac·i·ty (və·ras′ə·tē) *n. pl.* **·ties** **1** The habitual regard for truth; truthfulness; honesty. **2** Agreement with truth; accuracy, or fact; trueness. **3** That which is true; truth. [<F *véracité* <L *verax*. See VERACIOUS.]

Synonyms: candor, fact, frankness, honesty, ingenuousness, reality, truth, truthfulness, verity. *Truth* is primarily and *verity* is always a quality of thought or speech, especially of speech, as in exact conformity to *fact*. *Veracity* is properly a quality of a person, the habit of speaking and the disposition to

speak the *truth*. *Truthfulness* is a quality that may inhere either in a person or in his statements or beliefs. *Candor, frankness, honesty*, and *ingenuousness* are closely allied with *veracity*, and *fact, reality*, and *verity* with *truth*, while *truthfulness* may accord with either. *Truth* in a secondary sense may be applied to intellectual action or moral character, in the former case becoming a close synonym of *veracity*: She knows him to be a man of *truth*. *Antonyms*: deceit, deception, delusion, duplicity, error, fabrication, fallacy, falsehood, falsity, fiction, guile, imposture, lie, untruth.

Ve·ra·cruz (ver'ə·kro͞oz', *Sp.* bä'rä·kro͞os', -kro͞oth') **1** A coast state in eastern Mexico; 27,752 square miles; capital, Jalapa. **2** Its chief city, a port on the Gulf of Mexico: officially **Veracruz Lla·ve** (yä'vä).

ve·ran·da (və·ran'də) *n.* An open portico, gallery, or balcony, usually roofed, along the outside of a building; a porch or stoop. Compare LOGGIA. Also **ve·ran'dah.** [<Hind. *varandā* <Pg. *varanda* railing, balustrade, prob. < *vara* rod, pole <L *vara* forked pole]

ve·ra·no (və·rä'nō) *n.* The dry midwinter season in tropical America. [<Sp., lit., summer]

ve·rat·ric acid (və·rat'rik) *Chem.* A colorless crystalline acid, $C_9H_{10}O_4$, contained in sabadilla seeds and also made synthetically. [<L *veratrum* hellebore]

ve·rat·ri·dine (və·rat'rə·dēn, -din) *n. Chem.* A yellowish, amorphous alkaloid, $C_{36}H_{51}O_{11}N$, contained in sabadilla seeds. Also **ve·rat'ri·din** (-din). [<L *veratrum* hellebore + -ID(E) + -INE[2]]

ver·a·trine (ver'ə·trēn, -trin) *n. Chem.* A white or grayish-white, amorphous (rarely crystalline), extremely poisonous mixture of alkaloids, contained in sabadilla seeds: used in medicine as an analgesic in neuralgia and rheumatism. Also **ve·ra·tri·a** (və·rā'trē·ə), **ver'a·trin** (-trin), **ver'a·tri'na** (-trī'nə). [<L *veratrum* hellebore + INE[2]]

ver·a·trize (ver'ə·trīz) *v.t.* **·trized, ·triz·ing** To treat with veratrine so as to produce its toxic effects.

ve·ra·trum (və·rā'trəm) *n.* Hellebore (def. 2). [<L]

verb (vûrb) *n. Gram.* **1** One of a class of words which assert, declare, or predicate something; that part of speech which expresses existence, action, or occurrence, as the English words *be, collide, think*. **2** Any word or construction functioning similarly. [<F *verbe* <L *verbum* word. Akin to WORD.]

ver·bal (vûr'bəl) *adj.* **1** Of, pertaining to, or connected with words; concerned with words rather than the ideas they convey: *verbal* distinctions. **2** Uttered by the mouth; expressed in words orally; not written: a *verbal* communication; a *verbal* contract or agreement. **3** Having word corresponding with word; literal: a *verbal* translation. **4** *Gram.* **a** Partaking of the nature of or derived from a verb: a *verbal* noun. **b** Used to form verbs: a *verbal* prefix. — *n. Gram.* A noun directly derived from a verb, in English often having the form of the present participle, and signifying the act or process of what is expressed in the verb root; as, there shall be *weeping* and *wailing* and *gnashing* of teeth; also, an infinitive used as a noun; as, *to err* is human: also **verbal noun.** Compare GERUND. [<F <LL *verbalis* <L *verbum* word] — **ver'bal·ly** *adv.*

Synonyms (adj.): literal, oral, vocal. These words, whose etymology would make them similar in meaning, are differentiated in usage by their applications. *Oral* (L *os* the mouth) signifies uttered through the mouth or (in common phrase) by word of mouth; *vocal* (L *vox* the voice) signifies of or pertaining to the voice, uttered or modulated by the voice, and especially uttered with or sounding with full, resonant voice; *literal* (L *litera* a letter) signifies consisting of or expressed by letters, or according to the letter in the broader sense of the exact meaning or requirement of the words used; what is called "the letter of the law" is its *literal* meaning without going behind what is expressed by the letters on the page. Thus *oral* applies to that which is given by spoken words in distinction from that which is written or printed; as, *oral* tradition; an *oral* examination. By this rule we should in strictness speak of an *oral* contract or an *oral* message, but *verbal* contract and *verbal* message, as indicating that which is spoken rather than by written word, have become fixed in the language. A *verbal* translation may be *oral* or written, so that it is word for word; a *literal* translation follows the construction and idiom of the original as well as the words; thus a *literal* translation is more than one that is merely *verbal*; both *verbal* and *literal* are opposed to *free*. In the same sense, of attending to words only, we speak of *verbal* criticism, a *verbal* change. *Vocal* has primary reference to the human voice; as, *vocal* sounds, *vocal* music; *vocal* may be applied within certain limits to inarticulate sounds given forth by other animals than man; as, The woods were *vocal* with the songs of birds; *oral* is never so applied.

ver·bal·ism (vûr'bəl·iz'əm) *n.* A verbal remark or expression; sometimes, a meaningless form of words; wordiness.

ver·bal·ist (vûr'bəl·ist) *n.* One who deals with words or is skilled in the use and meanings of words; a critic of words.

ver·bal·ize (vûr'bəl·īz) *v.* **·ized ·iz·ing** *v.t.* **1** *Gram.* To make a verb of; change into a verb. **2** To express in words. — *v.i.* **3** To speak or write verbosely. — **ver'bal·i·za'tion** *n.* — **ver'bal·iz'er** *n.*

ver·ba·tim (vər·bā'tim) *adv.* In the exact words; word for word. [<LL <L *verbum* word]

ver·ba·tim et lit·er·a·tim (vər·bā'tim et lit'ə·rā'tim) *Latin* Word for word and letter for letter.

ver·be·na (vər·bē'nə) *n.* Any of a genus (*Verbena*) of American garden plants having dense terminal spikes of showy, often fragrant flowers. [<L, foliage, vervain. Doublet of VERVAIN.]

ver·be·na·ceous (vûr'bə·nā'shəs) *adj.* Belonging to a family (*Verbenaceae*) of herbs, shrubs, and trees, the verbena family, having opposite or whorled leaves and more or less two-lipped or irregular corollas. [<NL, family name <L *verbena* vervain]

ver·bi·age (vûr'bē·ij) *n.* Use of many words without necessity; wordiness; verbosity. See synonyms under CIRCUMLOCUTION, DICTION. [<F < *verbier* gabble < *verbe*. See VERB.]

verb·i·fy (vûr'bə·fī) *v.t.* **·fied, ·fy·ing** To form into or use as a verb.

ver·big·er·ate (vər·bij'ə·rāt) *v.i.* **·at·ed, ·at·ing** *Psychiatry* To repeat meaningless words, phrases, or sentences over and over, as in certain forms of schizophrenia. [<L *verbigerare* chatter, babble < *verbum* word + *gerere* carry on, conduct] — **ver·big'er·a'tion** *n.*

ver·bose (vər·bōs') *adj.* Using or containing a wearisome and unnecessary number of words; wordy. See synonyms under GARRULOUS. [<L *verbosus* < *verbum* word] — **ver·bose'ly** *adv.* — **ver·bose'ness** *n.*

ver·bos·i·ty (vər·bos'ə·tē) *n. pl.* **·ties** The state or quality of being verbose; wordiness.

ver·bo·ten (fər·bōt'n) *adj. German* Forbidden; authoritatively prohibited.

ver·bum sat sa·pi·en·ti (vûr'bəm sat sā'pē·en'·tī) *Latin* A word to the wise is sufficient: abbr. *verbum sap.*

Ver·cin·get·o·rix (vûr'sin·jet'ər·iks) Gallic chieftain, leader of rebellion against Julius Caesar, who put him to death in 45 B.C.

Ver·dan·di (vər·dän'dē) One of the Norns.

ver·dant (vûr'dənt) *adj.* **1** Green with vegetation; covered with grass or green leaves; fresh. **2** Immature in experience; unsophisticated. See synonyms under FRESH, RUSTIC. [<F *verdoyant*, ppr. of *verdoyer* grow green, ult. <L *viridis* green] — **ver'dan·cy** *n.* — **ver'·dant·ly** *adv.*

verd antique (vûrd) **1** A variety of serpentine. **2** Dark-green andesite porphyry containing crystals of feldspar: also **Oriental verd antique.** **3** A green coating that forms on ancient bronzes. [<OF *verd antique* ancient green]

Verde (vûrd), **Cape** The westernmost point of Africa, in Senegal, a peninsula about 20 miles long, up to 7 miles wide: also *Cape Vert.*

ver·der·er (vûr'dər·ər) *n.* An officer in charge of the royal forests in early England. Also **ver'der·or.** [<AF *verder*, OF *verdier* <Med. L *viridarius* <L *viridis* green]

Ver·di (ver'dē), **Giuseppe,** 1813–1901, Italian composer.

ver·dict (vûr'dikt) *n.* **1** The decision of a jury in an action. **2** A conclusion expressed; an opinion. [<AF *verdit*, OF *voirdit* <L *vere dictum* truly said < *verus* true + *dictum*, pp. of *dicere* say; later refashioned after L]

ver·di·gris (vûr'də·grēs, -gris) *n.* **1** *Chem.* A green basic acetate of copper obtained by treating copper with acetic acid: used as a pigment, for dyeing and calico printing, in medicine, and in the preparation of other copper pigments. **2** The green or bluish patina formed on copper, bronze, or brass surfaces after long exposure to the air. [<OF *verd de Grice, vert de Grece*, lit., green of Greece]

ver·din (vûr'din) *n.* A small, brightly-colored titmouse (*Auriparus flaviceps*) with a yellow head, of the southwestern United States and northern Mexico. [<F, yellowhammer]

ver·di·ter (vûr'də·tər) *n.* **1** A pigment made by grinding a basic copper carbonate; bice: azurite yields **blue verditer,** malachite yields **green verditer.** **2** Verdigris. [<OF *verd de terre*, lit., green of earth]

Ver·dun (vâr·dun', *Fr.* ver·dœṅ') A town on the Meuse in NE France; scene of heroic French resistance to German attack during several battles of World War I, 1916. Also **Verdun-sur-Meuse** (-sür·mœz').

ver·dure (vûr'jər) *n.* **1** The fresh greenness of growing vegetation, or such vegetation itself. **2** A tapestry representing trees and other vegetation. [<F < *verd* green <L *viridis*] — **ver'dure·less** *adj.*

ver·dur·ous (vûr'jər·əs) *adj.* Covered with verdure; verdant. — **ver'dur·ous·ness** *n.*

ver·e·cund (ver'ə·kund) *adj. Rare* Modest; bashful; coy; shy. [<L *verecundus*]

Ve·ree·ni·ging (fə·rē'nə·khing) A city in the southern Transvaal, Republic of South Africa, on the Vaal: site of the signing of the treaty concluding the Boer War, 1902.

Ver·ein (fer·īn') *n. German* A society; association: often compounded, as in *Turnverein.*

Ve·re·shcha·gin (vyi·ryish·chä'gin), **Vasili Vasilevich,** 1842–1904, Russian genre painter.

verge[1] (vûrj) *n.* **1** The extreme edge of something having defined limits; brink; margin. **2** A bounding or enclosing line; a circlet; ring; also, the space enclosed. **3** A stick or rod, or something having this shape; a wand or staff as a symbol of authority or emblem of office. **4** *Obs.* In England, a stick or wand which tenants held in the hand while swearing fealty to their lord. **5** The spindle of a balance wheel, especially in an old-fashioned vertical escapement. **6** *Archit.* **a** A column shaft. **b** The projecting edge of the tiling on a gable. **7** In old English law, the area over which the authority of an official extended. See synonyms under BOUNDARY, MARGIN. — *v.i.* **verged, verg·ing** **1** To be contiguous or adjacent. **2** To form the limit or verge. [<F, rod, stick <L *virga* twig]

verge[2] (vûrj) *v.i.* **verged, verg·ing** **1** To come near; approach; border: often with *on*: His speech *verges* on the chaotic. **2** To tend; slope; incline. [<L *vergere* bend, turn]

verg·er (vûr'jər) *n.* **1** An official who carries a verge before a scholastic, legal, or ecclesiastical dignitary; specifically, in English cathedrals and collegiate churches, one who carries the mace before the dean or canons. **2** *Brit.* One in charge of the interior of a cathedral or church; usher. **3** *Obs.* A master of ceremonies. [<F < *verge* rod]

Ver·gil (vûr'jil) Anglicized name of *Publius Vergilius Maro*, 70–19 B.C., Roman epic poet. Also spelled *Virgil.*

Ver·gil·i·an (vər·jil'ē·ən) *adj.* Pertaining to or in the style of Vergil: also spelled *Virgilian.*

ver·glas (vər·gläs') *n. French* A thin, slippery coating of ice on rock: a mountaineering term.

ve·rid·i·cal (və·rid'i·kəl) *adj.* Telling or expressing the truth; truthful; accurate. Also **ve·rid'ic.** [<L *veridicus* speaking the truth < *verus* true + *dicere* say] — **ve·rid'i·cal'i·ty** (-kal'ə·tē) *n.* — **ve·rid'i·cal·ly** *adv.*

ver·i·fi·ca·tion (ver'ə·fə·kā'shən) *n.* **1** The act of verifying, or the state of being verified. **2** *Law* An oath appended to an account, petition, or plea, as to the truth of the facts stated in it; also, at common law, the formal statement at the end of a plea, "and this he is ready to verify."

ver·i·fi·ca·tive (ver'ə·fə·kā'tiv) *adj.* Aiding or resulting in verification.

ver·i·fy (ver′ə·fī) *v.t.* **·fied, ·fy·ing 1** To prove to be true or accurate; substantiate; confirm. **2** To test or ascertain the accuracy or truth of. **3** *Law* **a** To affirm under oath. **b** To add a confirmation to. [<OF *verifier* <Med. L *verificare* make true <*verus* true + *facere* make] —**ver′i·fi′a·ble** *adj.* —**ver′i·fi′er** *n.*

ver·i·ly (ver′ə·lē) *adv.* **1** In truth; assuredly; certainly. **2** Sincerely and truly; really; confidently. [<VERY]

ver·i·sim·i·lar (ver′ə·sim′ə·lər) *adj.* Appearing or seeming to be true; likely; probable. [<L *verisimilis* <*verus* true + *similis* like] —**ver′i·sim′i·lar·ly** *adv.*

ver·i·si·mil·i·tude (ver′ə·si·mil′ə·tōōd, -tyōōd) *n.* **1** Appearance of truth; likelihood. **2** That which resembles truth. See synonyms under PROBABILITY. [<L *verisimilitudo* < *verisimilis.* See VERISIMILAR.]

ver·ism (ver′iz·əm) *n.* A style in art and literature that follows the theory that reality should be rigidly represented, even when it is ugly or vulgar. [<L *verus* true] —**ver′ist** *n.* & *adj.* —**ve·ris·tic** (və·ris′tik) *adj.*

ver·i·ta·ble (ver′ə·tə·bəl) *adj.* Conforming to truth or fact; genuine; true; real. See synonyms under AUTHENTIC. [<F <*vérité.* See VERITY.] —**ver′i·ta·ble·ness** *n.* —**ver′i·ta·bly** *adv.*

ver·i·tas (ver′ə·tas) *n. Latin* Truth.

ver·i·ty (ver′ə·tē) *n. pl.* **·ties 1** The quality of being correct or true as a statement or representation of reality. **2** A true statement; a fact; truth. See synonyms under VERACITY. [<F *vérité* <L *veritas* truth <*verus* true]

ver·juice (vûr′jōōs) *n.* **1** The sour juice of green fruit, as of unripe grapes. **2** Sharpness or sourness of disposition or manner; acidity. [<OF *verjus* <*vert* green + *jus* juice]

Ver·kho·yansk Range (vir·khō·yänsk′) A mountain system in northern Yakut Autonomous S.S.R. north of the Arctic Circle; highest point, 8,000 feet.

Ver·laine (ver·len′), **Paul,** 1844–96, French poet.

Ver·meer (vər·mâr′), **Jan,** 1632–75, Dutch painter.

ver·meil (vûr′mil) *n.* **1** Silver or bronze gilt. **2** A transparent water varnish. **3** An orange-red garnet. **4** *Poetic* Vermilion, or the color of vermilion. —*adj.* Of a bright-red color. [<OF <L *vermiculus,* dim. of *vermis* worm, the cochineal insect]

vermi– *combining form* A worm; of or related to a worm, or to worms: *vermiform.* [<L *vermis* a worm]

ver·mi·cel·li (vûr′mə·sel′ē, *Ital.* ver′mē·chel′lē) *n.* A food paste made into slender wormlike cords thinner than spaghetti or macaroni. [< Ital., lit., little worms, pl. of *vermicello* <L *vermiculus.* See VERMEIL.]

ver·mi·ci·dal (vûr′mə·sīd′l) *adj.* Destructive of intestinal worms; anthelmintic.

ver·mi·cide (vûr′mə·sīd) *n.* Any substance that kills worms; specifically, any medicine or drug destructive of intestinal worms. [<VERMI- + -CIDE]

ver·mic·u·lar (vər·mik′yə·lər) *adj.* **1** Pertaining to a worm; having the form or motion of a worm. **2** Like the tracks of a worm. [<L *vermicularis* <*vermiculus,* dim. of *vermis* worm] —**ver·mic′u·lar·ly** *adv.*

vermicular work 1 A form of rusticated masonry simulating worm tracks. **2** Ornamental work consisting of winding tracks in mosaic work. Also **vermiculated work.**

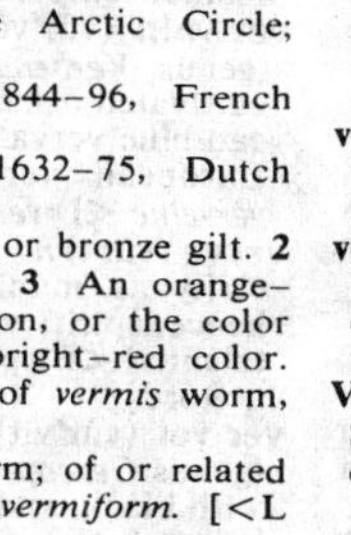

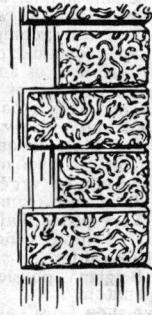

VERMICULAR WORK

ver·mic·u·late (vər·mik′yə·lāt) *v.t.* **·lat·ed, ·lat·ing 1** To adorn with tracery simulating the tracks of worms. **2** To make worm-eaten; infest with worms. —*adj.* **1** Wormlike or covered with wormlike markings. **2** Having the motions of a worm; insinuating; wavy. **3** Worm-eaten. [<L *vermiculatus,* pp. of *vermiculari* be worm-eaten <*vermiculus,* dim. of *vermis* a worm]

ver·mic·u·la·tion (vər·mik′yə·lā′shən) *n.* **1** Wormlike motion, as of the intestines. **2** Vermicular ornamentation. **3** The state of being wormy. **4** A track left by worms. **5** A fine wavy color marking, as on a bird.

ver·mic·u·lite (vər·mik′yə·līt) *n.* A laminated hydrous silicate, derived chiefly as an alteration product of biotite, phlogopite, and other micaceous minerals. [<L *vermiculus,* dim. of *vermis* worm + -ITE[1]]

ver·mic·u·lose (vər·mik′yə·lōs) *adj.* **1** Worm-eaten; wormy. **2** Worm-shaped; wormlike. Also **ver·mic′u·lous** (-ləs). [<LL *vermiculosus* <L *vermiculus,* dim. of *vermis*]

ver·mi·form (vûr′mə·fôrm) *adj.* Like a worm in shape. [<Med. L *vermiformis* <L *vermis* a worm + *forma* a form]

vermiform appendix *Anat.* A slender, wormlike diverticulum, 3 to 6 inches long, protruding from the end of the cecum in man and certain other mammals.

vermiform process *Anat.* **1** Either surface of the median lobe of the cerebellum. **2** The vermiform appendix.

ver·mi·fuge (vûr′mə·fyōōj) *n.* Any remedy that destroys intestinal worms. —*adj.* Anthelmintic. [<F <L *vermis* a worm + *fugare* expel]

ver·mil·ion (vər·mil′yən) *n.* **1** A brilliant, durable red pigment consisting of mercuric sulfide, obtained native by grinding the mineral cinnabar to a fine powder, or artificially, as by treating a mixture of mercury and sulfur with potassium hydroxide. **2** The color of the pigment, an intense orange red. —*adj.* Of a bright-red color. —*v.t.* To color with vermilion; dye bright red. [<OF *vermeilon, vermillon* <*vermeil* VERMEIL]

ver·min (vûr′min) *n. pl.* **·min 1** Noxious small animals or parasitic insects, as lice, fleas, worms, rats, mice, etc. **2** *Brit.* Certain animals injurious to game, as weasels, owls, etc. **3** A repulsive or noxious human being, or such persons collectively. [<OF <L *vermis* a worm]

ver·mi·nate (vûr′mə·nāt) *v.i.* **·nat·ed, ·nat·ing** To produce or breed vermin, especially parasitic vermin. —**ver′mi·na′tion** *n.*

ver·mi·nous (vûr′mə·nəs) *adj.* **1** Infested with vermin. **2** Affected with intestinal worms, or caused, as a disease, by vermin. **3** Of the nature of vermin.

Ver·mont (vər·mont′) A State in NE United States; 9,609 square miles; capital, Montpelier; entered the Union March 4, 1791; nickname, *Green Mountain State*: abbr. VT —**Ver·mont′er** *n.*

ver·mou·lu (ver·mōō·lü′) *adj. French* Worm-eaten.

ver·mouth (vûr′mōōth, vər·mōōth′) *n.* A liqueur made from white wine flavored with aromatic herbs. Also **ver′muth.** [<F *vermout* < G *wermuth* wormwood]

ver·nac·u·lar (vər·nak′yə·lər) *n.* **1** The native language of a locality. **2** The common daily speech of the people, as opposed to the literary language. **3** The vocabulary or jargon of a particular profession or trade: to speak the medical *vernacular.* **4** An idiomatic word or phrase. **5** The common name of a plant or animal as distinguished from its scientific designation. See synonyms under LANGUAGE. —*adj.* **1** Originating in or belonging to one's native land; indigenous: said of a language, idiom, etc. **2** Using the colloquial native tongue, rather than the literary language: *vernacular* poets. **3** Written in the language indigenous to a country or people: a *vernacular* translation of the Bible. **4** Characteristic of a specific locality or country; local: *vernacular* arts. **5** *Rare* Peculiar to a particular region; endemic: a *vernacular* disease. **6** Designating the common name of a plant or animal. [<L *vernaculus* domestic, native <*verna* a home-born slave, a native] —**ver·nac′u·lar·ly** *adv.*

ver·nac·u·lar·ism (vər·nak′yə·lə·riz′əm) *n.* **1** A vernacular term or idiom. **2** The use of the vernacular as opposed to classic or literary language.

ver·nal (vûr′nəl) *adj.* **1** Belonging to, appearing in, or appropriate to spring. **2** Pertaining to youth; having a springlike freshness. [<L *vernalis* <*vernus* belonging to spring <*ver* spring] —**ver′nal·ly** *adv.*

vernal equinox See under EQUINOX.

ver·nal·ize (vûr′nəl·īz) *v.t.* **·ized, ·iz·ing** To accelerate the growth of (a plant) by subjecting the seeds to artificial treatment, as by moistening at a low temperature. —**ver′nal·i·za′tion** *n.*

vernal point The vernal equinox. See under EQUINOX.

ver·na·tion (vər·nā′shən) *n. Bot.* The disposition of leaves within the leaf bud, as regards their folding, coiling, etc. [<NL *vernatio, -onis* <*vernare* flourish <*ver* spring]

Verne (vûrn, *Fr.* vern), **Jules,** 1828–1905, French writer of science fiction.

Ver·ner (vûr′nər), **Karl Adolph,** 1846–96, Danish philologist.

Verner's Law A law regarding certain consonant changes in Germanic languages, set forth by Karl Verner in 1876, stating that certain exceptions to Grimm's Law are due to a still wider law, namely, the position of the primary accent in the parent language. It shows that original Indo-European voiceless plosives *p, t, k,* which, according to Grimm's Law became in Germanic the voiceless fricatives *f, th* (as in *thin*), *h,* became, instead, except in specific combinations, the corresponding voiced fricatives and, ultimately, the voiced plosives, *b, d, g,* if the original Indo-European tonic stress was not on the immediately preceding syllable. This statement can be illustrated in English by the distinction in final consonant between *death* and *dead.* The same process operated for the Indo-European *s,* which became *z,* and finally *r,* as can be seen in English *was* and *were, raise* and *rear.*

ver·ni·cose (vûr′nə·kōs) *adj. Bot.* Appearing as if varnished, as some leaves. [<NL *vernicosus* <Med. L *vernicium* VARNISH]

ver·ni·er (vûr′nē·ər) *n.* **1** The small, movable, auxiliary scale for obtaining fractional parts of the subdivisions of a fixed scale on a theodolite, barometer, sextant, gage, or other measuring instrument. **2** *Mech.* An auxiliary device to insure fine adjustments in precision instruments. [after Pierre *Vernier*]

Ver·nier (ver·nyā′), **Pierre,** 1580?–1637, French mathematician.

ver·nis·sage (ver′nē·säzh′) *n.* The opening day of an exhibition of oil paintings to which critics are often invited: also called *varnishing day.* [<F <*vernir* varnish; because the painters varnish their works on this day]

Ver·no·le·ninsk (vyer′nə·lyā′nyinsk) A former name for NIKOLAEV.

Ver·non (vûr′nən), **Edward,** 1684–1757, English admiral.

Ver·nyi (vyer′nē) A former name for ALMA-ATA.

Ve·ro·na (və·rō′nə, *Ital.* vā·rō′nä) A city in Veneto, NE Italy. —**Ve·ro·nese** (ver′ə·nēz′, -nēs′) *adj.* & *n.*

Ver·o·nal (ver′ə·nəl) *n.* Proprietary name for a brand of barbital.

Ve·ro·ne·se (vā′rō·nā′zā), **Paolo,** 1528–88, Venetian painter; real name *Cagliari.*

ve·ron·i·ca[1] (və·ron′i·kə) *n.* The speedwell. [< Med. L, appar. after St. *Veronica*]

ve·ron·i·ca[2] (və·ron′i·kə) *n.* A cloth said to have been miraculously impressed with the face of Christ on his way to Calvary, handed to him by a woman named Veronica to wipe the perspiration from his face; also, the representation of the face on this handkerchief; hence, a cloth or handkerchief having on it a representation of Christ's face. See SUDARIUM. [<Med. L <LL *veraiconica,* prob. <L *verus* true + Gk. *eikōn* an image, likeness]

ve·ron·i·ca[3] (və·ron′i·kə, *Sp.* bā·rō′nē·kä) *n.* In bullfighting, a maneuver in which the torero faces the bull and holds the cape directly in front of himself. [<Sp.]

Ve·ron·i·ca (və·ron′i·kə, *Ital.* vā′rō·nē′kä) A feminine personal name. Also *Fr.* **Vé·ro·nique** (vā·rō·nēk′). [See VERONICA[2]]

—**Veronica, Saint** A legendary follower of Christ, upon whose handkerchief a picture of Christ's features is said to have appeared.

Ver·ra·za·no (ver′rä·tsä′nō), **Giovanni da,** 1480?–1528?, Italian navigator.

Ver·roc·chio (ver·rôk′kyō), **Andrea del,** 1435–88, Florentine sculptor and painter.

ver·ru·ca (ve·rōō′kə) *n. pl.* **·cae** (-sē) **1** *Med.*

A wart. 2 *Biol.* A wart or wartlike elevation on animals or plants. [<L, a wart, orig. a steep place]

ver·ru·ca·no (ver′ə·kä′nō) *n.* A hard conglomerate of quartz cemented by various siliceous materials, usually colored. [<Ital., from Mount *Verruca* near Pisa]

ver·ru·cose (ver′ə·kōs) *adj.* Abounding in wartlike elevations; warty. Also **ver′ru·cous** (-kəs). [<L *verrucosus* <*verruca* a wart] — **ver′ru·cos′i·ty** (-kos′ə·tē) *n.*

Ver·sailles (vər·sī′, -sālz′; *Fr.* ver·sä′y′) A city of north central France, 11 miles SW of Paris; site of the palace of Louis XIV; scene of the signing of a treaty (1919) between the Allies and Germany after World War I.

ver·sant (vûr′sənt) *n. Geog.* **1** An entire area having a general slope in one direction. **2** The general aspect or slope of any portion of country; inclination. [<F, ppr. of *verser* overturn, pour <L *versare,* freq. of *vertere* turn]

ver·sa·tile (vûr′sə·til) *adj.* **1** Having an aptitude for new tasks or occupations; many-sided. **2** Subject to change; inconstant; variable. **3** Freely swinging or turning: said of an anther part so slightly attached to its support that it readily swings to and fro. **4** Capable of being turned forward or backward, as the toe of a bird; movable in every direction, as insect antennae. [<F <L *versatilis* <*versare,* freq. of *vertere* turn] — **ver′sa·tile·ly** *adv.* — **ver′sa·til′i·ty, ver′sa·tile·ness** *n.*

vers de so·cié·té (ver′ də sō·syā·tā′) *French* A form of light verse characterized by grace, elegance, and wit.

verse (vûrs) *n.* **1** A single metrical or rhythmical line made up of a number of feet, arranged according to a specific rule. **2** A group of metrical lines; a stanza. **3** Metrical composition as distinguished from prose; poetry. **4 a** Composition in meter; versification. **b** A specified type of metrical composition; type of meter or metrical structure: iambic *verse.* **5** One of the short divisions of a chapter of the Bible; also, a short division of any composition. **6** The solo part of a song, anthem, or other piece. See synonyms under METER[2], POETRY. — *v.t. & v.i.* **versed, vers·ing** *Rare* To versify. [Fusion of OE *fers* and OF *vers,* both <L *versus* a turning, a verse <*vertere* turn]

versed (vûrst) *adj.* **1** Thoroughly acquainted; having ready skill; proficient. **2** Turned about; reversed. [<L *versatus,* pp. of *versari* occupy oneself]

versed sine, ver·sine (vûr′sīn) See under SINE[1]. [<NL *sinus versus* <*sinus* a sine + L *versus,* pp. of *vertere* turn]

verse·mon·ger (vûrs′mung′gər, -mong′-) *n.* A writer of inferior verses; poetaster.

ver·si·cle (vûr′si·kəl) *n.* **1** A little verse. **2** One of a series of lines said or sung alternately by minister and people. [<L *versiculus,* dim. of *versus* VERSE]

ver·si·col·or (vûr′si·kul′ər) *adj.* **1** Showing a variety of colors; variegated. **2** Changing from one color to another in different lights; iridescent. Also *Brit.* **ver′si·col′our.** [<L <*versus,* pp. of *vertere* turn + *color* color]

ver·sic·u·lar (vər·sik′yə·lər) *adj.* Relating to verses, especially Biblical verses; marking the division into verses. [<L *versiculus* VERSICLE]

ver·sie·ra (ver·syā′rä) *n. Math.* The witch of Agnesi. See WITCH OF AGNESI. [<Ital., a ghost, hobgoblin]

ver·si·fy (vûr′sə·fī) *v.* **·fied, ·fy·ing** *v.t.* **1** To change from prose into verse. **2** To narrate or treat in verse. — *v.i.* **3** To write poetry; make verses. [<OF *vercifier, versifier* <L *versificare* <*versus* VERSE + *facere* make] — **ver′si·fi·ca′tion** (-fə·kā′shən) *n.* — **ver′si·fi′er** *n.*

ver·sion (vûr′zhən, -shən) *n.* **1** That which is translated or rendered from one language into another; a translation; a translation of the original Hebrew and Greek of the Old and New Testaments, or any part of them, into some other tongue. **2** A description of something as modified by the relator. **3** *Med.* **a** The manual turning of a fetus in the womb so as to secure proper delivery. **b** Displacement of the uterus in which the organ is deflected without bending upon itself. **4** *Obs.* A transformation; conversion. [<MF <Med. L *versio, -onis* a turning <L *vertere* turn] — **ver′sion·al** *adj.*

vers li·bre (ver lē′br′) *French* Free verse.

ver·so (vûr′sō) *n. pl.* **·sos 1** A left-hand page of a book, piece of music, or sheet of folded paper: also called *reverso.* Compare RECTO. **2** The reverse of a coin or medal. Compare OBVERSE. [<L *verso (folio)* a turned (leaf), ablative neut. sing. pp. of *vertere* turn]

verst (vûrst) *n.* A Russian measure of distance: about two thirds of a mile, or 1.067 kilometers. [<F *verste* and G *werst* <Russian *versta,* orig. a line]

ver·sus (vûr′səs) *prep.* **1** Against: used in naming or entitling actions in courts: plaintiff *versus* defendant; in contests: Dempsey *versus* Tunney: usually contracted to *v.* or *vs.* **2** Considered as the alternative of: free trade *versus* high tariffs. [<L, toward, turned toward, orig. pp. of *vertere* turn]

vert (vûrt) *n.* **1** In English forest law, anything that grows and bears green leaves within a forest, especially thick coverts; also, the right to cut green or growing wood in a forest. **2** *Her.* The color or tincture green. [<MF *vert, verd* <L *viridis* green]

Vert (ver), **Cape** See VERDE, CAPE.

ver·te·bra (vûr′tə·brə) *n. pl.* **·brae** (-brē) or **·bras** *Anat.* One of the segmented bones of the spinal column. In man and the higher vertebrates, each vertebra, with its semicylindrical central body and attached processes, articulates with those on either side by means of elastic fibrous pads. [<L, a joint, a vertebra <*vertere* turn]

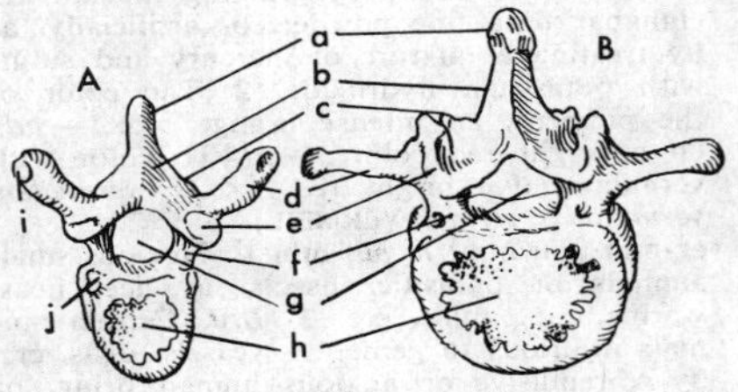

HUMAN VERTEBRAE

A. Sixth thoracic vertebra.

B. Third lumbar vertebra.

a. Spinous process. *f.* Pedicle.
b. Lamina. *g.* Vertebral foramen.
c. Inferior articular process. *h.* Body.
d. Transverse process. *i.* Facet for rib.
e. Superior articular process. *j.* Demi-facet for rib.

ver·te·bral (vûr′tə·brəl) *adj.* **1** Pertaining to or of the nature of a vertebra. **2** Having, or composed of, vertebrae.

vertebral column The spinal column; the backbone.

ver·te·brate (vûr′tə·brāt, -brit) *adj.* **1** Having a backbone or spinal column. **2** Pertaining to or characteristic of vertebrates. **3** Vertebral. — *n.* Any of a primary division or subphylum (*Vertebrata*) of animals, of the phylum *Chordata,* characterized by a spinal column, as fishes, birds, mammals, and a few primitive forms in which a notochord represents the backbone. [<L *vertebratus* jointed <*vertebra* VERTEBRA]

ver·te·bra·tion (vûr′tə·brā′shən) *n.* **1** The formation of vertebrae. **2** Segmentation like that of the spinal column.

ver·tex (vûr′teks) *n. pl.* **·tex·es** or **·ti·ces** (-tə·sēz) **1** The highest point or summit of anything; apex; top. **2** *Astron.* **a** The zenith. **b** The point in the sky toward or from which a group of stars appears to be moving. **3** The top of the head; also, in craniometry, the top of the arch of the skull. **4** *Math.* **a** The point of intersection of the sides of an angle. **b** The point opposite to, and farthest from, the base. **c** The intersection of three or more edges of a polyhedron. [<L, the top <*vertere* turn]

ver·ti·cal (vûr′ti·kəl) *adj.* **1** Of or pertaining to the vertex. **2** Occupying a position directly above or overhead; being at the highest point. **3** Directed perpendicularly to the plane of the horizon; upright; plumb. **4** Of or pertaining to the crown of the head. **5** *Bot.* **a** Perpendicular to the surface or to the axis of support. **b** In the direction of the axis of growth; lengthwise. **6** *Econ.* Of or pertaining to a business concern that undertakes a process from raw material to consumer: a *vertical* trust. — *n.* **1** A vertical line, plane, or circle. **2** An upright beam or rod in a truss. [<MF <L *verticalis* <*vertex, -icis* VERTEX] — **ver′ti·cal′i·ty** (-kal′ə·tē), **ver′ti·cal·ness** *n.* — **ver′ti·cal·ly** *adv.*

vertical circle *Astron.* A great circle perpendicular to the plane of the horizon.

ver·ti·ces (vûr′tə·sēz) Plural of VERTEX.

ver·ti·cil (vûr′tə·sil) *n. Biol.* A set of organs, as leaves or tentacles, disposed in a circle around an axis; whorl; a volution of a spiral shell. [<L *verticillus* a whorl, dim. of *vertex, -icis* VERTEX]

ver·ti·cil·las·ter (vûr′tə·si·las′tər) *n. Bot.* An inflorescence or flower cluster with the flowers seemingly in a whorl, but composed of a pair of dense sessile cymes in the axils of opposite leaves, as in most mints. [<NL <L *verticillus* VERTICIL + -ASTER]

ver·tic·il·late (vər·tis′ə·lit, -lāt, vûr′tə·sil′it, -āt) *adj.* **1** Arranged in a verticil or whorl. **2** Having parts so arranged; whorled. Also **ver·tic′il·lat′ed.** [<NL *verticillatus* <L *verticillus* VERTICIL] — **ver·tic′il·late·ly** *adv.*

ver·tic·i·ty (vər·tis′ə·tē) *n.* Tendency to move toward the north, as manifested by a magnetic needle. [<NL *verticitas, -tatis* <L *vertex, -icis* VERTEX]

ver·tig·i·nous (vər·tij′ə·nəs) *adj.* **1** Affected by vertigo; dizzy. **2** Turning round; whirling; revolving. **3** Liable to cause giddiness. [<L *vertiginosus* <*vertigo, -inis* VERTIGO] — **ver·tig′i·nous·ly** *adv.* — **ver·tig′i·nous·ness** *n.*

ver·ti·go (vûr′tə·gō) *n. pl.* **·goes** or **ver·tig·i·nes** (vər·tij′ə·nēz) *Pathol.* Any of a group of disorders, variously caused, in which a person feels as if he or his surroundings are whirling around; dizziness. [<L, lit., a turning around <*vertere* turn]

Ver·tum·nus (vər·tum′nəs) In Roman mythology, the god of the changing seasons and growing plants; husband of Pomona: also *Vortumnus.*

Ver·u·la·mi·um (ver′yŏŏ·lā′mē·əm) The ancient Roman name for ST. ALBANS.

Ve·rus (vir′əs), **Lucius Aurelius,** 130–169, Roman emperor 161–169.

ver·vain (vûr′vān) *n.* Any of various plants (genus *Verbena*), congeners of the common cultivated ornamental verbenas, as the American blue vervain *(V. hastata),* or the common European vervain *(V. officinalis).* [<OF *verveine* <L *verbena.* Doublet of VERBENA.]

verve (vûrv) *n.* **1** Enthusiasm or energy, especially as manifested in artistic production; hence, spirit; vigor. **2** *Rare* Special bent or talent. [<F, prob. <L *verba,* pl. of *verbum* a word]

ver·vet (vûr′vit) *n.* A South African monkey (genus *Cercopithecus*), grayish-green speckled with black, and with reddish-white cheeks and belly. [<F <*ver(t)* green (<L *viridis*) + *(gri)vet* a grivet; so called because of its color]

ver·y (ver′ē) *adv.* **1** In a high degree; in large measure; extremely: *very* generous. **2** Exactly: the *very* same thought. ◆ Some grammarians feel that *very* may properly be used before a participle only when the latter precedes the noun it modifies, as in *a very agitated speech*; when the participle is used after some form of the verb *to be,* another adverb is interposed, as in *He was very much* (or *greatly*) *agitated.* However, the construction without the adverb is now widely accepted with participles of emotion or feeling, and is often found, as well, with some participles describing physical condition, as in *They were very disturbed*; *His face is very changed in aspect.* — *adj.* **ver·i·er, ver·i·est 1** Absolute; actual; simple; utter: said of truth. **2** Suitable; right: the *very* tool we need. **3** Unqualified; utter; complete: a *very* rogue. **4** Selfsame; identical: my *very* words. **5** The (thing) itself: used as an intensive equivalent to *even*: The *very* stones cry out. **6** *Obs.* True: *very* God; also, truthful; veracious. [<AF *verrai,* OF *verai* <L *verus* true]

very high frequency Any wave frequency from 30 to 300 megahertz. Abbr. *vhf, VHF.*

Ver·y light (ver′ē, vir′ē) A brilliant signal flare discharged from a special type of pistol, the **Very pistol.** [after E. W. *Very,* 1847–1910, U.S. naval officer and inventor]

Ve·sa·li·us (vi·sā′lē·əs), **Andreas,** 1514–64, Belgian physician; founder of modern anatomy.

ve·si·ca (vi·sī′kə) *n. pl.* **·cae** (-sē) A bladder. [<L]

ves·i·cal (ves′i·kəl) *adj.* Of, pertaining to, supplying, or affecting the bladder.

ves·i·cant (ves′i·kənt) *adj.* Blister-producing. — *n.* **1** That which produces blisters; a

blister. 2 A chemical warfare agent which attacks the skin, as mustard gas or lewisite: also called *blister gas.* [<NL *vesicans, -antis,* ppr. of *vesicare* raise blisters <L *vesica* a blister, bladder]

ve·si·ca pis·cis (vi·sī′kə pis′is, pīsis) The pointed oval aureole used by medieval sculptors and painters to enclose the figure of Christ, the Virgin Mary, or an apostle.

ves·i·cate (ves′i·kāt) *v.* **·cat·ed, ·cat·ing** *v.t.* To raise blisters on. — *v.i.* To become blistered; blister, as the skin. [<NL *vesicatus,* pp. of *vesicare.* See VESICANT.] — **ves′i·ca′tion** *n.*

ves·i·ca·to·ry (ves′i·kə·tôr′ē, və·sik′ə·tôr′ē, -tō′rē) *adj.* Capable of producing blisters; vesicant. — *n. pl.* **·ries** Any substance, as an ointment or plaster, that causes a blister.

ves·i·cle (ves′i·kəl) *n.* 1 Any small bladderlike cavity, cell, or cyst. 2 A small sac, containing gas or fluid. 3 *Pathol.* Any small rounded elevation of the cuticle containing a clear liquid; a blister. 4 *Bot.* A small bladderlike cavity filled with air. 5 *Geol.* A small spherical cavity found commonly in volcanic rocks. [<L *vesicula,* dim. of *vesica* a bladder]

vesico– *combining form Med.* The urinary bladder; of or pertaining to the urinary bladder: *vesicotomy,* a cutting into the bladder. Also, before vowels, **vesic–.** [<L *vesica* a bladder]

ve·sic·u·la (və·sik′yə·lə) *n. pl.* **·lae** (-lē) A little bladder; vesicle. [<L, VESICLE]

ve·sic·u·lar (və·sik′yə·lər) *adj.* 1 Of, pertaining to, composed of, or resembling vesicles. 2 Bearing or containing vesicles or air bladders. [<L *vesicula* VESICLE] — **ve·sic′u·lar·ly** *adv.*

ve·sic·u·late (və·sik′yə·lāt) *v.t. & v.i.* **·lat·ed, ·lat·ing** To make or become vesicular or vesiculate. — *adj.* (-lit, -lāt) Full of or having vesicles; also, vesicular. [Back formation < *vesiculated* <NL *vesiculatus* <L *vesicula* VESICLE] — **ve·sic′u·la′tion** *n.*

Vesle (vel) A river in NE France, flowing 90 miles NW from the badlands of Champagne, NE of Châlons–sur–Marne, through Reims to the Aisne east of Soissons.

Ve·son·ti·o (və·son′shē·ō) The ancient name for BESANÇON.

Ve·soul (və·zo͞ol′) A city in eastern France, capital of Haute–Saône department.

Ves·pa·sian (ves·pā′zhən) Anglicized name of *Titus Flavius Vespasianus,* A.D. 9–79, Roman emperor 69–79.

ves·per (ves′pər) *n.* 1 A bell that calls to vespers: also **vesper bell.** 2 An evening service, prayer, or song. 3 *Obs.* Evening. — *adj.* Pertaining to or suitable for evening or vespers. [<L, the evening star]

Ves·per (ves′pər) The evening star; Hesperus; the planet Venus when an evening star. [<L]

ves·per·al (ves′pər·əl) *adj.* Pertaining to evening or the service of vespers. — *n.* 1 A book of the music and office of vespers. 2 A cover for an altar cloth.

ves·pers (ves′pərz) *n. pl. Often cap.* 1 *Eccl.* The sixth in order of the canonical hours. 2 *Eccl.* A service of worship in the late afternoon or evening; specifically, in the Anglican church, Evening Prayer; in the Roman Catholic Church, a public service on Sundays or holy days at which the office of vespers is said or sung. 3 The hour of vespers, usually about sunset. [<OF *vespres* <Med. L *vesperae* <L *vespera* evening]

vesper sparrow An American sparrow (*Pooecetes gramineus*) distinguished by the partial whiteness of its outer tail feathers: so called from its evening song.

ves·per·til·i·o·nine (ves′pər·til′ē·ə·nīn′, -nin) *adj.* Belonging to a family (*Vespertilionidae*) of insectivorous bats. [<L *vespertilio, -onis* a bat + -INE[1]] — **ves′per·til′i·o·nid** *adj. & n.*

ves·per·tine (ves′pər·tin, -tīn) *adj.* 1 Pertaining to or occurring in the evening. 2 Flying, opening, etc., in the evening, as a bat, flower, etc. 3 Descending toward the horizon at the sunset hour. Also **ves′per·ti′nal** (-tī′nəl). [<L *vespertinus* < *vesper* VESPER]

ves·pi·ar·y (ves′pē·er′ē) *n. pl.* **·ar·ies** A nest of social wasps or its colony. [<L *vespa* a wasp + (AP)IARY]

ves·pid (ves′pid) *n.* Any of a large family (*Vespidae*) of hymenopterous insects, including social wasps and hornets. — *adj.* Of or pertaining to the *Vespidae.* [<NL <L *vespa* a wasp] — **ves′pi·form** (-pə·fôrm) *adj.*

ves·pine (ves′pīn, -pin) *adj.* Of or pertaining to wasps. [<L *vespa* a wasp + -INE[1]]

Ves·puc·ci (ves·po͞ot′chē), **Amerigo,** 1451–1512, Italian navigator for whom America was named.

ves·sel (ves′əl) *n.* 1 A hollow receptacle of any form or material, especially one capable of holding a liquid. 2 A ship or craft designed to float on the water: usually one larger than a rowboat; also, an airship. 3 *Biol.* A duct or canal for containing or transporting a body fluid, as an artery, vein, etc. 4 *Bot.* A water–conducting tube in plants. 5 Figuratively, a person viewed as having capacity or fitness to receive or contain something; one who receives: chiefly in religious use: a *vessel* of mercy or of wrath. [<OF <L *vascellum,* dim. of *vas* a vessel]

vest (vest) *n.* 1 A short sleeveless jacket worn by men and sometimes by women under the coat; waistcoat; originally, a kind of cassock: in England chiefly a trade term. 2 A close jacket formerly worn by women; now, an extra piece of trimming on the front of the body or waist of a woman's dress, usually V–shaped. 3 An undervest or undershirt. 4 Clothing of any kind; vesture; array; dress. 5 *Obs.* An ecclesiastical vestment. — *v.t.* 1 To confer (ownership, authority, etc.) upon some person or persons: usually with *in.* 2 To place ownership, control, or authority with (a person or persons). 3 To clothe or robe, as with vestments. — *v.i.* 4 To clothe oneself, as in vestments. 5 To be or become vested; devolve. [<F *veste* <Ital. <L *vestis* clothing, a garment]

ves·ta (ves′tə) *n.* A friction match of wax; a short wax taper; a wooden match. [after *Vesta*]

Ves·ta (ves′tə) 1 In Roman mythology, the goddess of the hearth and the hearth fire, protectress of the state and custodian of the sacred fire tended by the vestals: identified with the Greek *Hestia.* 2 A minor planet.

ves·tal (ves′təl) *n.* 1 One of the virgin priestesses of Vesta: also **vestal virgin.** 2 A woman of pure character; a virgin; nun. — *adj.* 1 Pertaining to Vesta. 2 Suitable for a vestal or a nun; hence; chaste. [<L *vestalis* <*Vesta* Vesta]

vest·ed (ves′tid) *adj.* 1 Having vestments; robed. 2 *Law* Held by a tenure subject to no contingency; complete; established by law as a permanent right: *vested* interests.

vest·ee (ves·tē′) *n.* 1 An imitation blouse–front worn in the front of a suit or dress. 2 A broadcloth garment without sleeves worn with a formal riding habit. [Dim. of VEST]

Ves·ter·å·len (ves′tər·ô′lən) A Norwegian archipelago in the Norwegian Sea north of the Lofoten Islands; total, about 1,200 square miles. Also **Ves′ter·aa′len.**

ves·ti·ar·y (ves′tē·er′ē) *adj.* Pertaining to clothes. — *n. pl.* **·ar·ies** *Obs.* A vestry; robing–room. [<OF *vestiairie* <Med. L *vestiarium.* See VESTRY.]

ves·tib·u·lar (ves·tib′yə·lər) *adj.* Pertaining to or like a vestibule. Also **ves·tib′u·late** (-lit, -lāt).

ves·ti·bule (ves′tə·byo͞ol) *n.* 1 A small antechamber between the outer door of a building and an interior one; an entrance hall; lobby. 2 An enclosed passage from one railway passenger car to another. 3 Formerly, a walled place before the entrance to a Roman or Greek house; later, a porch. 4 *Anat.* Any one of several chambers or channels adjoining or communicating with others: the *vestibule* of the ear. — *v.t.* **·buled, ·bul·ing** 1 To provide with a vestibule or vestibules. 2 To couple (railroad cars) and connect by vestibules. [<L *vestibulum* an entrance hall] — **ves′ti·buled** *adj.*

vestibule train A passenger train with enclosed platforms connected by flexible walls and roof, forming a weatherproof passageway between connected cars, called **vestibule cars.**

ves·tige (ves′tij) *n.* 1 A visible trace, impression, or a sensible evidence or sign, of something absent, lost, or gone; trace; originally, a footprint; track. 2 *Biol.* A part or organ, small or degenerate, but well developed and functional in ancestral forms of organisms. See synonyms under MARK[1], TRACE[1]. [<F <L *vestigium* a footprint]

ves·tig·i·al (ves·tij′ē·əl) *adj.* Of, or of the nature of a vestige; surviving in small or degenerate form. — **ves·tig′i·al·ly** *adv.*

ves·tig·i·um (ves·tij′ē·əm) *n. pl.* **·tig·i·a** (-tij′ē·ə) A vestigial part; vestige. [<L, a footprint]

vest·ment (vest′mənt) *n.* 1 An article of dress; clothing or covering; particularly, a garment or robe of state or office. 2 *Eccl.* **a** One of the ritual garments of the clergy, especially one worn at the Eucharist. **b** A chasuble. See synonyms under DRESS. [<OF *vestement* <L *vestimentum* clothes < *vestire* clothe] — **vest′ment·al** *adj.*

vest–pock·et (vest′pok′it) *adj.* 1 Small enough to fit in a vest pocket; very small; diminutive: a *vest–pocket* edition. 2 Much smaller than standard or usual size: a *vest–pocket* battleship.

vest–pock·et park A small urban park, often on a vacant lot.

ves·try (ves′trē) *n. pl.* **·tries** 1 A room where vestments are put on or kept. 2 A room for altar linens, sacred vessels, etc., attached to a church and often called a *sacristy.* 3 A room in a church used for Sunday school, meetings, as a chapel, etc. 4 In the Anglican church: **a** A body administering the affairs of a parish or congregation; also, a meeting of such a body. **b** In English parishes, a business meeting of all the parishioners or their representatives. 5 A place of meeting for the parish vestry; a vestry hall. [<AF *vestrie,* OF *vestiarie* <Med. L *vestiarium* a wardrobe <L *vestis* a garment]

ves·try·man (ves′trē·mən) *n. pl.* **·men** (-mən) A member of a vestry.

ves·ture (ves′chər) *n.* 1 Something that covers; garments; clothing; a robe. 2 *Law* All that covers land, except trees. 3 A covering or envelope. See synonyms under DRESS. — *v.t.* **·tured, ·tur·ing** To cover or clothe with vesture; vest; robe; envelop: usually in the past participle. [<OF <*vestir* cloth <L *vestire* clothe]

ve·su·vi·an (və·so͞o′vē·ən) *n.* 1 Vesuvianite. 2 A kind of match or fusee which burns with a spluttering flame: used for lighting cigars, etc. [from *Vesuvius*]

ve·su·vi·an·ite (və·so͞o′vē·ən·īt′) *n.* A vitreous, brown to green, translucent hydrous silicate of calcium and aluminum, with traces of iron and magnesium: also called *idocrase.*

Ve·su·vi·us (və·so͞o′vē·əs) The only active volcano on the European mainland, on the Bay of Naples, Italy; 3,891 feet. *Italian* **Ve·su·vio** (vā·zo͞o′vyō). — **Ve·su′vi·an** *adj.*

vet (vet) *Colloq. n.* A veterinary surgeon. — *v.* **vet·ted, vet·ting** *v.t.* 1 To treat as a veterinarian does. 2 *U.S. Slang* To criticize or emend: to *vet* a manuscript. — *v.i.* 3 To treat animals medically. [Short for VETERINARIAN]

vetch (vech) *n.* 1 Any of a genus (*Vicia*) of climbing herbaceous vines of the bean family, especially the common broadbean, grown for fodder. 2 A leguminous European plant (*Lathyrus sativus*) yielding edible seeds. — **bitter vetch** A species of vetch (*V. ervilia*) of which the seeds contain a bitter, poisonous alkaloid: also called *ers.* [<AF *veche, vecce* <L *vicia*]

vetch·ling (vech′ling) *n.* A plant (genus *Lathyrus*), nearly allied to the vetches; especially, a European species (*L. pratensis*), naturalized in the United States. [Dim. of VETCH]

vet·er·an (vet′ər·ən, vet′rən) *n.* 1 One who is much experienced in any service, especially a soldier or an ex–soldier. 2 A member of the armed forces who has been in active service. — *adj.* 1 Having had long experience or practice; old in service. 2 Belonging to or suggestive of a veteran. 3 Long continued; extending over a long period. [<MF <L *veteranus* < *vetus, veteris* old]

Veterans Administration An agency of the U. S. government which administers all federal laws relating to the relief of former members of the military and naval services.

Veterans Day A U. S. national holiday honoring veterans of the armed forces, held on November 11, the anniversary of the date in 1918 when the Allies granted an armistice

to the Central Powers in World War I. Formerly called *Armistice Day.*

Veterans of Foreign Wars A society of ex-servicemen who have served in the United States Army, Navy, or Marine Corps in a war with and in a foreign country: founded 1899.

vet·er·i·nar·i·an (vet′ər·ə·nâr′ē·ən, vet′rə-) *n.* A practitioner of veterinary medicine or surgery. [<L *veterinarius* VETERINARY]

vet·er·i·nar·y (vet′ər·ə·ner′ē, vet′rə-) *adj.* Pertaining to the diseases or injuries of animals, and to their treatment by medical or surgical means. —*n. pl.* **·nar·ies** A veterinarian; a veterinary surgeon. [<L *veterinarius* pertaining to beasts of burden <*veterinus* <*veterina* beasts of burden, ult. <*vehere* carry]

vet·i·ver (vet′ə·vər) *n.* **1** An Asian grass *(Vetiveria zizanioides)* grown in Florida and the SE United States. **2** Its aromatic roots, used for weaving mats, fans, etc., and as a source of **vetiver oil,** an ingredient of perfumes. [<F *vétyver* <Tamil *vețțivēru,* lit., a root that is dug up <*vēr* a root]

Vet·lu·ga (vet·lōō′gə) A river in central European Russian S.F.S.R., flowing 500 miles west, north, and south to the Volga.

ve·to (vē′tō) *v.t.* **·toed, ·to·ing 1** To refuse executive approval of (a bill passed by a legislative body). **2** To forbid or prohibit authoritatively; refuse consent to. —*n. pl.* **·toes 1** The prerogative in a chief executive of refusing to approve a legislative enactment by withholding his signature. **2** The act of vetoing; also, the official communication containing a refusal to approve a bill. **3** Any authoritative prohibition. [<L, I forbid] —**ve′to·er** *n.*

veto message A message giving the reasons of the chief executive for refusing his approval of a proposed law.

veto power 1 The right or power possessed by a branch of the government to forbid or refuse approval of projects proposed by another department. **2** A power vested in the chief executive to prevent the enactment of bills passed by the legislature.

Vet·ter (vet′ər), **Lake** A former spelling for VÄTTER, LAKE.

vex (veks) *v.t.* **1** To provoke to anger or displeasure by small irritations; irritate; annoy. **2** To trouble or afflict. **3** To throw into commotion; agitate. **4** To make a subject of dispute: a *vexed* question. See synonyms under PIQUE[1]. [<OF *vexer* <L *vexare* shake]

vex·a·tion (vek·sā′shən) *n.* **1** The act of vexing, or the state of being vexed; irritation. **2** That which vexes; annoyance; affliction; cause of trouble or distress. See synonyms under CHAGRIN, IMPATIENCE.

vex·a·tious (vek·sā′shəs) *adj.* **1** Being a source of vexation. **2** Full of vexation; harassing; annoying. See synonyms under TROUBLESOME, WEARISOME. —**vex·a′tious·ly** *adv.* —**vex·a′tious·ness** *n.*

vexed (vekst) *adj.* **1** Harassed; troubled; irritated; agitated; disturbed. **2** Much debated; contested: a *vexed* question. —**vex·ed·ly** (vek′sid·lē) *adv.* —**vex′ed·ness** *n.*

vex·il (vek′sil) *n.* A vexillum (def. 2). [Short for VEXILLUM]

vex·il·lar·y (vek′sə·ler′ē) *n. pl.* **·lar·ies** A standard-bearer. —*adj.* **1** Of or pertaining to a vexillum: also **vex′il·lar** (-lər). **2** Of or pertaining to a standard or ensign. [<L *vexillarius* a standard-bearer <*vexillum* VEXILLUM]

vex·il·late (vek′sə·lit, -lāt) *adj.* Having a vexillum or vexilla.

vex·il·lol·o·gy (veks′ə·lol′ə·jē) *n.* The study of flags. [<L *vexillum* flag, standard + -LOGY] —**vex′il·lo·log′ic** or **·i·cal** *adj.* —**vex′il·lol′o·gist** *n.*

vex·il·lum (vek·sil′əm) *n. pl.* **vex·il·la** (vek·sil′ə) **1** In Roman antiquity, a square flag, or standard; hence, a company or troop of soldiers serving under a separate standard. **2** *Bot.* The large upper petal of a papilionaceous flower. **3** *Ornithol.* The web of a feather. [<L <*vehere* carry]

vi·a (vī′ə, vē′ə) *prep.* By way of; by a road passing through: He went to Boston *via* New Haven. [<L, ablative sing. of *via* a way]

Vi·a Ap·pi·a (vī′ə ap′ē·ə) The ancient Latin name for the APPIAN WAY.

vi·a·ble (vī′ə·bəl) *adj.* Capable of living and developing normally, as a newborn infant, a seed, etc. [<F <*vie* life <L *vita*] —**vi′a·bil′i·ty** *n.*

Vi·a Do·lo·ro·sa (vī′ə dol′ō·rō′sə) *Latin* The road traveled by Jesus to Golgotha; literally, the sorrowful way.

vi·a·duct (vī′ə·dukt) *n.* A bridgelike structure, especially a large one of arched masonry, to carry a roadway or the like over a valley or ravine. Compare AQUEDUCT. [<L *via* a way + (AQUE)DUCT]

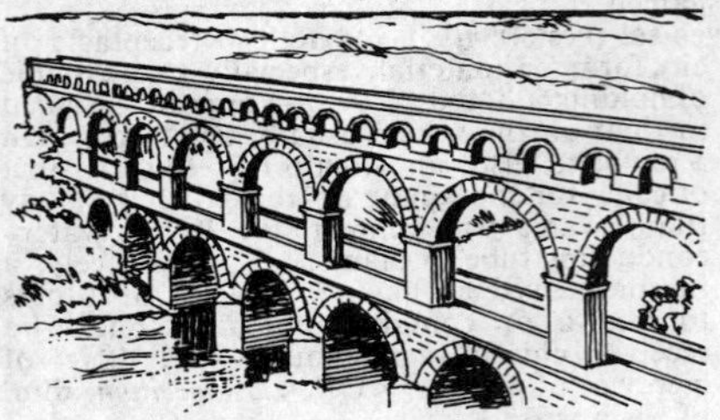

VIADUCT
Roman aqueduct, Nimes, France.

Vi·a Fla·min·i·a (vī′ə flə·min′ē·ə) The Latin name for the FLAMINIAN WAY.

vi·al (vī′əl) *n.* A small bottle for liquids, commonly cylindrical; also, more widely, any bottle: also spelled *phial.* —**to pour out the vials of wrath upon** To inflict retribution or vengeance on. See *Rev.* xvi. —*v.t.* **·aled** or **·alled, ·al·ing** or **·al·ling** To put or keep in or as in a vial. [<OF *viole* <L *phiala* a saucer <Gk. *phialē* a shallow cup]

vi·a me·di·a (vī′ə mē′dē·ə) *Latin* A middle way.

vi·and (vī′ənd) *n.* **1** An article of food, especially meat. **2** *pl.* Victuals; provisions; food. See synonyms under FOOD. [<AF *viaunde,* OF *viande,* ult. <L *vivenda,* neut. pl. gerundive of *vivere* live]

vi·at·ic (vī·at′ik) *adj.* Of or pertaining to a journey or to traveling. Also **vi·at′i·cal.** [<L *viaticus* <*via* a way]

vi·at·i·cum (vī·at′ə·kəm) *n. pl.* **·ca** (-kə) or **·cums 1** *Eccl.* The Eucharist, as given on the verge of death. **2** In ancient Rome, the provision of necessaries for an official journey of a magistrate; later, provisions for any journey. [<L, traveling money, neut. sing. of *viaticus* <*via* a way. Doublet of VOYAGE.]

vi·a·tor (vī·ā′tər) *n. pl.* **vi·a·to·res** (vī′ə·tôr′ēz, -tō′rēz) A traveler; wayfarer. [<L <*via* a way]

vibes (vībz) *n.pl.* (*usu. construed as sing. for def. 2*) *Slang* **1** Vibrations. See VIBRATION (def. 3). **2** A vibraphone.

Vi·borg (vē′bôr·y′) The Swedish name for VYBORG.

vi·brac·u·lum (vī·brak′yə·ləm) *n. pl.* **·la** (-lə) *Zool.* One of the slender, whiplike defensive organs of the cells of many polyzoans. [<NL <L *vibrare* shake] —**vi·brac′u·lar** *adj.* —**vi·brac′u·loid** *adj.*

vi·bran·cy (vī′brən·sē) *n. pl.* **·cies** The state or character of being vibrant; resonance.

vi·brant (vī′brənt) *adj.* **1** Having, showing, or resulting from vibration; vibrating; resonant. **2** Throbbing; pulsing: a nation *vibrant* with enthusiasm. **3** Energetic; vigorous. **4** *Phonet.* Produced with vibration of the vocal cords; voiced. —*n. Phonet.* A speech sound made with vibration of the vocal cords; a voiced sound. [<L *vibrans, -antis,* ppr. of *vibrare* shake] —**vi′brant·ly** *adv.*

vi·bra·phone (vī′brə·fōn) *n.* A type of marimba in which a pulsating sound is produced by motor-driven valves in the resonators. Also **vi′bra-harp′** (-härp′). [<VIBRA(TO) + -PHONE]

vi·brate (vī′brāt) *v.* **·brat·ed, ·brat·ing** *v.i.* **1** To move or swing back and forth, as a pendulum. **2** To move back and forth rapidly; quiver. **3** To sound: The note *vibrates* on the ear. **4** To be emotionally moved; thrill. **5** To vacillate; waver, as between choices. —*v.t.* **6** To cause to move or swing back and forth. **7** To cause to quiver or tremble. **8** To send forth (sound, etc.) by vibration. **9** To measure by each vibration: a pendulum *vibrating* seconds. See synonyms under QUAKE, SHAKE. [<L *vibratus* <*vibrare* shake]

vi·bra·tile (vī′brə·til, -tīl) *adj.* **1** Adapted to, having, or used in vibratory motion. **2** Pertaining to or resembling vibration.

vi·bra·til·i·ty (vī′brə·til′ə·tē) *n.* Capability, or quality, of being vibratile.

vi·bra·tion (vī·brā′shən) *n.* **1** The act of vibrating; oscillation. **2** *Physics* **a** A periodic, usually rapid back-and-forth motion of a particle, as of electrons in an atom, or the parts of an elastic or rigid body suddenly released from tension. **b** Any physical process characterized by cyclic variations in amplitude, intensity, or the like, as wave motion or an electric field. **c** A single complete oscillation. **3** *pl. Slang* One's emotional response to an aura felt to surround a person or thing, especially when considered in or out of harmony with oneself: good *vibrations.* —**vi·bra′tion·al** *adj.*

vi·bra·to (vē·brä′tō) *n. Music* A trembling or pulsating effect, not confined to vocal music, caused by rapid variation of emphasis on the same tone: properly distinguished from *tremolo,* where there is an alternation of tones. [<Ital., pp. of *vibrare* vibrate <L, shake]

vi·bra·tor (vī′brā·tər) *n.* **1** One who or that which vibrates. **2** An electrically operated massaging apparatus. **3** *Electronics* **a** An electromagnetic switch mechanism for converting direct into alternating current by continuously vibrating impulses. **b** An oscillator (def. 3).

vi·bra·to·ry (vī′brə·tôr′ē, -tō′rē) *adj.* Pertaining to, causing, or characterized by vibration. Also **vi′bra·tive** (-tiv).

vib·ri·o (vib′rē·ō) *n.* Any of a genus *(Vibrio)* of motile, rodlike bacteria in which the cells are but slightly sinuous and have one or more flagellae at each end; especially, the Gram-negative **comma vibrio** *(V. comma),* found in the intestines of cholera victims. [<NL <L *vibrare* shake]

vib·ri·oid (vib′rē·oid) *adj.* Resembling a vibrio. —*n.* A vibrioid body. [<VIBRI(O) + -OID]

vi·bris·sa (vī·bris′ə) *n. pl.* **·bris·sae** (-bris′ē) *Biol.* **1** One of the stiff, coarse hairs found in the nostrils of man and about the mouth of many other mammals, as the cat: they often function as tactile organs. **2** One of the vaneless, hairlike rictal feathers of many insectivorous birds, especially flycatchers. [<L *vibrissae* hairs in a man's nostrils <*vibrare* shake]

vi·bro·scope (vī′brə·skōp) *n.* A device for observing and recording vibrations, especially those of harmonic character.

vi·bro·tro·pism (vī′brə·trō′piz·əm) *n. Biol.* The involuntary response of an organism to a vibratory stimulus. [<*vibro-* (<VIBRATE) + -TROPISM] —**vi′bro·trop′ic** (-trop′ik) *adj.*

vi·bur·num (vī·bûr′nəm) *n.* Any of a large and widely distributed genus *(Viburnum)* of shrubs or small trees of the honeysuckle family, bearing small flowers and berrylike fruit; especially, the dockmackie, the sheepberry, and the hobble-bush. [<L, the wayfaring tree]

vic·ar (vik′ər) *n.* **1** In general, one who is authorized to perform functions, especially religious ones, in the stead of another; a substitute in office. **2** Hence, an agent; deputy. **3** *Brit.* The priest of a parish of which the main revenues are appropriated or impropriated by a layman, the priest himself receiving but a stipend; any incumbent of a parish who is not a rector. **4** In the Roman Catholic Church, a substitute or representative of an ecclesiastical person; in a strict sense, one whose jurisdiction is confined to the external forum. **5** In some parishes of the Protestant Episcopal Church, the clergyman who is the head of a chapel; also, a clergyman having charge of a church or mission as the bishop's deputy. [<AF *vikere, vicare,* OF *vicaire* <L *vicarius* a substitute <*vicis* a change]

vic·ar·age (vik′ər·ij) *n.* **1** The benefice, office, or duties of a vicar. **2** A vicar's residence or household.

vicar apostolic In the Roman Catholic Church, formerly, a bishop or archbishop appointed by the pope to act in his stead in a given district; more recently, a titular bishop exercising episcopal jurisdiction where there is no see canonically.

vicar fo·rane (fô·rān′, fō-) In the Roman Catholic Church, a clergyman appointed by a bishop, having a limited jurisdiction over the inferior clergy in the parishes constituting the deanery; a rural dean. [<VICAR + Med. L *foraneus* outside the episcopal city, rural <L *foras* out of doors]

vicar general 1 In the Roman Catholic Church, a functionary appointed by the bishop as assistant or representative in certain

matters of jurisdiction, but without power to perform the specific function of the episcopal order. 2 In the Church of England, an official assisting the bishop or archbishop in ecclesiastical causes. 3 In English history, the ecclesiastical vicegerent of the king: a title bestowed on Thomas Cromwell by Henry VIII.

vi·car·i·al (vī·kâr′ē·əl, vi-) *adj.* 1 Vicarious; delegated. 2 Belonging to, relating to, or acting as a vicar.

vi·car·i·ate (vī·kâr′ē·it, -āt, vi-) *n.* A delegated office or power; specifically, the office or authority of a vicar. Also **vic·ar·ate** (vik′ər·it).

vi·car·i·ous (vī·kâr′ē·əs, vi-) *adj.* 1 Made or performed by substitution; suffered or done in place of another; substitutionary: a *vicarious* sacrifice; also, enjoyed or felt by a person as a result of his imagined participation in an experience that is not his own: *vicarious* gratification. 2 Filling the office of or acting for another. 3 Of, pertaining to, or belonging to a vicar or deputy; deputed; delegated. 4 *Med.* Performing, as an organ, the functions of another; substitutive; also, occurring in an abnormal situation: *vicarious* menstruation. [<L *vicarius*. See VICAR.] —**vi·car′i·ous·ly** *adv.* —**vi·car′i·ous·ness** *n.*

vic·ar·ly (vik′ər·lē) *adj.* Resembling or pertaining to a vicar.

vicar of Christ The pope, regarded as Christ's representative on earth.

vic·ar·ship (vik′ər·ship) *n.* The office or position of a vicar.

vice[1] (vīs) *n.* 1 A moral blemish or taint; an immoral habit or trait: the *vice* of intemperance. 2 Habitual indulgence in degrading or harmful appetites; deviation from moral rectitude; depravity. 3 Something that mars; a defect; blemish. 4 A physical deformity, taint, or imperfection. 5 A bad trick, as of a horse. See synonyms under SIN[1]. —**inherent vice** In insurance, a hazard arising from a preexistent condition not manifest when the commodity was insured and therefore not covered by the insurance policy: Eggs of worms were the *inherent vice* that ruined the cargo of hides. ◆ Homophone: *vise.* [<OF <L *vitium* a fault]

vice[2] (vīs) See VISE.

vice[3] (vīs) *adj.* Acting in the place of; substitute; deputy: *vice* president. —*n.* One who acts in the place of another; a substitute; deputy.
—**vi·ce** (vī′sē) *prep.* Instead of; in the place of. [<L, ablative of *vicis* change]

Vice may appear as a combining form in hyphemes or as the first element in two-word phrases:

vice-chair	**vice-ministry**
vice chairman	**vice principal**
vice-chairmanship	**vice-principalship**
vice dean	**vice rector**
vice-government	**vice-rectorship**
vice governor	**vice-reign**
vice-governorship	**vice-wardenship**

vice admiral A commissioned officer in the Navy or Coast Guard who ranks next above a rear admiral and next below an admiral. [<AF *visadmirail*, OF *visamiral* < *vis-* in place (<L *vice*) + *admirail, amiral* an admiral]

vice-ad·mir·al·ty (vīs′ad′mər·əl·tē) *n.* The area under or office of a vice admiral.

vice chancellor 1 *Law* A judge in equity courts subordinate to the chancellor. 2 A deputy chancellor in a university. [<OF *vichancelier* <Med. L *vicecancellarius* <L *vice* in place + LL *cancellarius* a chancellor] —**vice′-chan′cel·lor·ship′** *n.*

vice consul One who exercises consular authority, either as the substitute or as the subordinate of a consul. —**vice-con·su·lar** (vīs′kon′sə·lər) *adj.* —**vice-con·su·late** (vīs′·kon′sə·lit) *n.* —**vice′-con′sul·ship** *n.*

vice·ge·ren·cy (vīs·jir′ən·sē) *n. pl.* **·cies** 1 The office or authority of a vicegerent; the fact of ruling as a vicegerent or deputy. 2 A district ruled by a vicegerent.

vice·ge·rent (vīs·jir′ənt) *n.* One duly authorized to exercise the powers of another; a deputy; vicar. —*adj.* Acting in the place of another, usually in the place of a superior. [<Med. L *vicegerens, -entis* <L *vice* in place + *gerens, -entis*, ppr. of *gerere* carry, manage] —**vice·ge′ral** *adj.*

vic·e·nar·y (vis′ə·ner′ē) *adj.* 1 Consisting of or pertaining to twenty. 2 Relating to a system of notation based upon twenty. [<L *vicenarius* < *viceni* twenty each < *viginti* twenty]

vi·cen·ni·al (vī·sen′ē·əl) *adj.* Occurring once in twenty years; also, lasting or existing twenty years. [<L *vicennium* a twenty-year period < *vicies* twenty times + *annus* a year]

Vi·cen·te (*Pg.* vē·sen′tə, *Sp.* bē·then′tā) Portuguese and Spanish form of VINCENT.

Vi·cen·za (vē·chen′tsä) 1 A province in Veneto, northern Italy; 1,051 square miles. 2 A city in NE Italy, capital of Vicenza province: ancient **Vi·cen·ti·a** (vi·sen′shē·ə).

vice president An officer ranking next below a president, and acting, on occasion, in his place. The vice president of the United States is elected at the same time and in the same manner as the president, and is designated by the Constitution to be president of the Senate and to succeed the president in case of that officer's death, resignation, removal, or inability. —**vice-pres·i·den·cy** (vīs′prez′ə·dən·sē) *n.* —**vice′-pres′i·den′tial** (-prez′ə·den′shəl) *adj.*

vice·re·gal (vīs·rē′gəl) *adj.* Of or relating to a viceroy, his office, or his jurisdiction. Also **vice·roy′al** (-roi′əl). —**vice·re′gal·ly** *adv.*

vice regent A deputy regent. —**vice′-re′gent** (-rē′jənt) *adj.*

vice·roy (vīs′roi) *n.* 1 One who rules a country, colony, or province by the authority of his sovereign or king. 2 A North American nymphalid butterfly (*Basilarchia archippus*), orange-red with black markings and a row of white marginal spots. The larva feeds on the willow, poplar, and certain other trees. [<MF *viceroy, visroy* < *vice-, vis-* in place (<L *vice*) + *roy* a king, ult. <L *rex, regis*]

vice·roy·al·ty (vīs·roi′əl·tē) *n.* 1 The office or authority of a viceroy. 2 The term of office of a viceroy. 3 A district ruled or governed by a viceroy. Also **vice′roy·ship.**

vice squad A police division charged with combating illegal prostitution, perversion, gambling, and other vices.

vi·ce ver·sa (vī′sē vûr′sə, vīs′) The order being changed; the relation of terms being reversed; conversely. [<L]

Vi·cha·da (bē·chä′thä) A river in eastern Colombia, flowing 400 miles east to the Orinoco at the Venezuela border.

Vi·chy (vē·shē′) A resort city in central France; provisional capital of France during German occupation, World War II.

vi·chy·ssoise (vē′shē·swäz′) *n.* A potato cream soup flavored with leeks, celery, etc., usually served cold with a sprinkling of chives. [<F, of Vichy <*Vichy* Vichy]

Vi·chy water (vish′ē) The effervescent mineral water from the springs at Vichy, France; any mineral water resembling it. Also **Vi′chy, vi′chy.**

vic·i·nage (vis′ə·nij) *n.* 1 Neighboring places collectively; vicinity. 2 The state of being a neighbor or neighbors. See synonyms under NEIGHBORHOOD. [<OF *visenage, vicenage* <L *vicinus* nearby]

vic·i·nal (vis′ə·nəl) *adj.* 1 Neighboring; adjoining; near. 2 *Mineral.* Designating a crystal form closely approximating one of the fundamental forms. 3 *Chem.* Designating a benzene derivative in which the substituted elements or radicals are in consecutive order on the benzene ring. [<L *vicinalis* < *vicinus* a neighbor, orig. nearby]

vicinal planes In crystallography, crystal planes which may approximate or take the place of the fundamental planes.

vicinal road A local road, as distinguished from one between towns.

vic·i·nism (vis′ə·niz′əm) *n. Ecol.* Plant variation resulting from the proximity of other plants.

vi·cin·i·ty (vi·sin′ə·tē) *n. pl.* **·ties** 1 Nearness in space or relationship; proximity. 2 A region adjacent or near; neighborhood; vicinage. See synonyms under NEIGHBORHOOD. [<L *vicinitas, -tatis* < *vicinus* nearby]

vi·cious (vish′əs) *adj.* 1 Addicted to vice; corrupt in conduct or habits; wicked; depraved. 2 Partaking of what is base, low, and vile; morally injurious; evil. 3 Unruly or dangerous; refractory, as an animal. 4 Defective or faulty: *vicious* arguments. 5 Impure or incorrect; corrupted, as a text, manuscript, etc. 6 Noxious; poisonous; foul, as water, air, etc. 7 *Colloq.* Marked by malice or spite; malignant: a *vicious* lie. See synonyms under CRIMINAL, IMMORAL, IRREGULAR, RESTIVE. [<OF <L *vitiosus* < *vitium* a fault] —**vi′cious·ly** *adv.* —**vi′cious·ness** *n.*

vicious circle 1 The process or predicament that arises when the solution of a problem creates a new problem and each successive solution adds another problem. 2 *Logic* Argument in a circle. See under CIRCLE. 3 *Med.* The accelerating effect of one disease upon another when the two are coexistent.

vi·cis·si·tude (vi·sis′ə·to͞od, -tyo͞od) *n.* 1 *pl.* Irregular changes or variations, as of conditions or fortune: the *vicissitudes* of life. 2 A change; especially, a complete change; mutation or mutability. 3 Alternating change or succession, as of the seasons. See synonyms under CHANGE. [<MF <L *vicissitudo* < *vicis* a turn, change]

vi·cis·si·tu·di·nar·y (vi·sis′ə·to͞o′də·ner′ē, -tyo͞o′-) *adj.* Marked by or subject to change or alternation. Also **vi·cis′si·tu′di·nous.**

Vicks·burg (viks′bûrg) A city in western Mississippi on the Mississippi River; besieged and taken by the Union army in the Civil War, 1863.

vi·con·ti·el (vī·kon′tē·əl) *adj. Obs.* Of or pertaining to a viscount or sheriff. [<AF, OF *viscontal* < *viconte* a viscount]

vic·tim (vik′tim) *n.* 1 A living creature sacrificed to some deity or as a religious rite. 2 A person sacrificed in the pursuit of some object; one who is injured or killed, as by misfortune or calamity. 3 A sufferer from any diseased condition or morbid feeling. 4 One who is swindled; a dupe. [<L *victima* a beast for sacrifice]

vic·tim·ize (vik′tim·īz) *v.t.* **·ized, ·iz·ing** To make a victim of, especially by defrauding or swindling; dupe; cheat. See synonyms under ABUSE. —**vic′tim·i·za′tion** *n.* —**vic′tim·iz′er** *n.*

vic·tor (vik′tər) *n.* One who vanquishes an enemy; one who is successful in any struggle or contest; winner; conqueror. —*adj.* Pertaining to a victor; victorious; triumphant: the *victor* nation. [<AF *victor, victour*, OF *victeur* <L *victus*, pp. of *vincere* conquer]

Synonyms (noun): conqueror, master, vanquisher, winner. A *victor* wins in a single battle or contest; a *conqueror* wins by subjugating his opponents in many battles or campaigns.

Vic·tor (vik′tər, *Fr.* vēk·tôr′) A masculine personal name. [<L, a conqueror]

Vic·tor Em·man·u·el (vik′tər i·man′yo͞o·əl) Name of three Italian kings.
—**Victor Emmanuel I,** 1759–1824, king of Sardinia 1820–21.
—**Victor Emmanuel II,** 1820–78, king of Sardinia 1849–61, and first king of Italy 1861–78.
—**Victor Emmanuel III,** 1869–1947, king of Italy 1900–46.

vic·to·ri·a (vik·tôr′·ē·ə, -tō′rē·ə) *n.* 1 A low, light, four-wheeled carriage, with a calash top, a seat for two persons over the rear axle, and a raised driver's seat. 2 A passenger automobile with a calash top which usually covers the rear seat only. [after Queen *Victoria*]

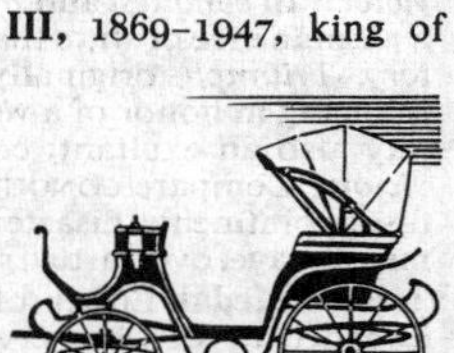

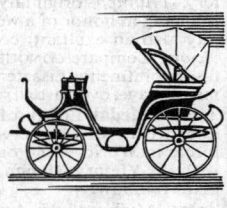

VICTORIA

Vic·to·ri·a (vik·tôr′ē·ə, -tō′rē·ə) A feminine personal name.
—**Victoria,** 1819–1901, queen of Great Britain 1837–1901.

Victoria 1 A state of SE Australia; 87,884 square miles; capital, Melbourne. 2 The capital of British Columbia, a port at the southern extremity of Vancouver Island. 3 A port on Hong Kong Island, capital of Hong Kong colony, China. 4 A province of SE Southern Rhodesia; 21,028 square miles.

Victoria, Lake The largest lake in Africa

and the second largest fresh-water body in the world, situated between Kenya, Uganda and Tanzania; 26,828 square miles. Also *Victoria Nyanza.*

Victoria, Mount 1 The highest peak of the Owen Stanley Range, SE New Guinea; 13,240 feet. **2** The highest peak of the Chin Hills, Upper Burma; 10,018 feet.

Victoria Cross See under CROSS.

Victoria Desert The southern belt of the Western Australian desert, south of the Gibson Desert: also *Great Victoria Desert.*

Victoria Falls A cataract on the Zambesi River between Zambia and Zimbabwe; 343 ft. high; over a mile wide; discovered by Livingstone in 1855.

Victoria Island An island in SW Franklin district, Northwest Territories, Canada; 80,340 square miles.

Victoria Land A part of Antarctica south of New Zealand, east of the Ross Sea, and west of Wilkes Land, consisting of a series of snow-covered mountains; highest point, 13,350 feet.

Vic·to·ri·an (vik·tôr′ē·ən, -tō′rē-) *adj.* **1** Of or relating to Queen Victoria, or to her reign. **2** Pertaining to or characteristic of the ideals and standards of morality and taste prevalent during the reign of Queen Victoria; prudish; conventional; narrow. **3** Of or pertaining to Victoria, Australia. —*n.* **1** Anyone, especially an author, contemporary with Queen Victoria. **2** An article of furniture, dress, or the like, identified with or dating from the Victorian age.

Victoria Nile See under NILE.

Vic·to·ri·an·ism (vik·tôr′ē·ən·iz′əm, -tō′rē-) *n.* The state or quality of being Victorian, as in style or moral outlook.

Victoria Ny·an·za (nī·an′zə, nyän′zä) See VICTORIA, LAKE.

Victoria River A river in western Northern Territory, Australia, flowing 350 miles NE, north, and west to the Timor Sea.

Victoria waterlily Any of a genus *(Victoria)* of very large tropical American waterlilies, having leaves often five feet in diameter, and huge, showy, crimson-and-white flowers.

vic·to·ri·ous (vik·tôr′ē·əs, -tō′rē-) *adj.* **1** Having won victory; conquering; triumphant. **2** Bringing victory: distinguished by victory; instrumental in bringing victory. **3** Relating to victory. —**vic·to′ri·ous·ly** *adv.* —**vic·to′ri·ous·ness** *n.*

vic·to·ry (vik′tər·ē) *n. pl.* **·ries 1** The state of being a victor. **2** The overcoming of an enemy or of any difficulty. [< OF *victorie, victoire* < L *victoria* < *victor* VICTOR]

Synonyms: achievement, advantage, conquest, mastery, success, supremacy, triumph. *Victory* is the state resulting from the overcoming of an opponent or opponents in any contest, or from the overcoming of difficulties, obstacles, evils, etc., considered as opponents or enemies. In the latter sense any hard-won *achievement, advantage,* or *success* may be termed a *victory.* In *conquest* and *mastery* there is implied a permanence of state that is not implied in *victory. Triumph,* originally denoting the public rejoicing in honor of a *victory,* has come to signify also an exultant, complete, and glorious *victory.* Compare CONQUER. *Antonyms*: defeat, disappointment, disaster, failure, frustration, miscarriage, overthrow, retreat, rout.

Victory Medal Either of two bronze medals awarded to all who served in the U.S. armed forces in World War I or World War II, worn with the **Victory Ribbon,** combining six colors of the rainbow.

Vic·tro·la (vik·trō′lə) *n.* A make of phonograph: a trade name.

vict·ual (vit′l) *n.* **1** *pl.* Food for human beings, as prepared for eating: except in dialect, seldom used in any but a humorous or depreciatory sense: also spelled *vittles.* **2** *Obs.* Provisions of any kind. See synonyms under FOOD. —*v.* **·ualed** or **·ualled, ·ual·ing** or **·ual·ling** *v.t.* **1** To furnish with victuals. —*v.i.* **2** To lay in supplies of food. **3** *Rare* To eat; feed. [< OF *vitaile* < LL *victualia* provisions, neut. pl. of L *victualis* of food < *victus* food]

vict·ual·age (vit′l·ij) *n. Rare* Victuals; victualing.

vict·ual·er (vit′l·ər) *n.* **1** One who supplies or sells victuals; specifically, one engaged in supplying an army, navy, or ship with provisions; a commissary; sutler. **2** An innkeeper. **3** A victualing ship. Also **vict′ual·ler.**

vi·cu·ña (vi·kōōn′yə, -kyōō′nə, vī-) *n.* **1** A small ruminant *(Lama vicugna)* of the high Andes related to the llama and alpaca, having fine and valuable wool. **2** A fiber and textile made from this wool, or some substitute. Also **vi·cu′gna,** [< Sp. < Quechua]

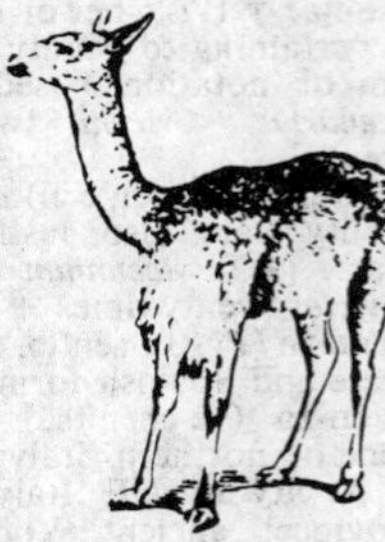

VICUÑA
(Up to 3 feet high at the shoulder)

vicuña cloth Soft cloth made of vicuña wool.

vi·de (vī′dē) See: used to make a reference or direct attention to: *vide* p. 36. [< L, imperative sing. of *videre* see]

vi·de an·te (vī′dē an′tē) *Latin* See before.

vi·de in·fra (vī′dē in′frə) *Latin* See below.

Vi·de·la (bē·thā′lä), **Gabriel González** See GONZÁLEZ-VIDELA.

vi·de·li·cet (vi·del′ə·sit) *adv.* To wit; that is to say; namely: abbr. *viz.* [< L < *videre licet* it is permitted to see]

vid·e·o (vid′ē·ō) *adj.* **1** Of or, pertaining to television, especially to the picture portion of a program. Compare AUDIO. **2** Producing a signal convertible into a television picture: a *video* cassette. —*n.* A television image or the electric signal corresponding to it. [< L, I see]

vid·e·o·cas·sette (vid′ē·ō·kə·set′) *n.* A cassette for use in a television set that contains film or videotape.

videocassette recorder An electronic device for recording and playing back of the images and sounds on a videocassette.

vid·e·o·disc (vid′ē·o·disk) *n.* A disc for recording both image and sound to be replaced through a television set.

vid·e·o·gen·ic (vid′ē·ō·jen′ik) *adj.* Having such characteristics, as coloration, form, etc., as appear effectively in television: also *telegenic.*

vid·e·o·tape (vid′ē·ō·tāp′) *n.* A recording of a television program on magnetic tape. —*v.t.* **·taped, ·tap·ing** To make such a recording.

vi·de post (vī′dē pōst′) *Latin* See after; see what follows.

vi·de su·pra (vī′dē sōō′prə) *Latin* See above.

vi·dette (vi·det′) See VEDETTE.

vi·de ut su·pra (vī′dē ut sōō′prə) *Latin* See what is written above.

vie (vī) *v.* **vied, vy·ing** *v.i.* **1** To strive for superiority; put forth effort to excel or outdo others, as in a race: with *with* or *for.* —*v.t.* **2** *Obs.* To wager; bet. [< MF *envier* invite, challenge < L *invitare* invite]

Vied·ma (vyed′mä, *Sp.* byeth′mä) The capital of Río Negro province, in SE central Argentina near the Atlantic.

Vi·en·na (vē·en′ə) A city on the Danube, capital of Austria, in the NE part: German *Wien.*

Vienne (vyen) **1** A city in SE France, on the Rhône. **2** A river of west central France, flowing 230 miles west and north to the Loire. **3** A department of west central France; 2,719 square miles; capital, Poitiers.

Vi·en·nese (vē′ə·nēz′, -nēs′) *adj.* Belonging or relating to Vienna, or to its inhabitants. —*n. pl.* **·nese** A native or citizen of Vienna.

Vien·nois (vye·nwá′) An ancient county of SE France.

Vien·tiane (vyaṅ·tyán′) A city on the Mekong river, the administrative capital of Laos, in the NW central part on the Thailand border.

Vie·ques Island (byā′kās) An island belonging to and east of Puerto Rico; 52 square miles.

Vier·wald·stät·ter See (fir′vält·shtet′ər zā) The German name for the LAKE OF LUCERNE.

vi et ar·mis (vī et är′mis) *Latin.* With force and arms.

Vi·et·cong (vē·et′kông′, vē′et-; vē·et·kong′, vē′et-) *n.* **1** The Communist guerrilla force in South Vietnam during the Vietnamese war. **2** A member of this force. —*adj.* Of or having to do with the Vietcong. Also **Viet Cong.**

Vi·et·minh (vē·et·min′, vē′et·min′) *n.* **1** The Communist party in Vietnam. **2** A member of this party. Also **Viet Minh.**

Vi·et·nam (vē·et·näm′) A country in Indochina, comprising the former **Democratic Republic of Vietnam (North Vietnam)** and the **Republic of Vietnam (South Vietnam)**; united under North Vietnamese leadership in 1975; 129,623 sq. mi.; capital Hanoi.

Vi·et·nam·ese (vē·et′nä·mēz′, -mēs′) *adj.* Of or pertaining to Vietnam. —*n.* **1** A person born or living in Vietnam. **2** The Austro-Asiatic language spoken in Vietnam.

view (vyōō) *n.* **1** The act of seeing; survey; inspection. **2** Mental examination or inspection. **3** Power of seeing, or range of vision; reach of perception or insight; range or scope of thought. **4** That which is seen; a spectacle; prospect. **5** A representation of a scene; especially, a landscape; also, a sketch; design; plan. **6** Reference to something regarded as the object of action; intention; purpose. **7** Manner of looking at things; opinion; judgment; belief: What are your *views* on this subject? **8** *Obs.* Appearance; aspect; show. See synonyms under PURPOSE, SCENE, THOUGHT¹. —**in view of** In consideration of. —**on view** Open to the public; set up for public inspection. —**with a view to** With the aim or purpose of. —*v.t.* **1** To look at; see; behold. **2** To look at carefully; scrutinize; examine. **3** To survey mentally; consider. See synonyms under EXAMINE, LOOK. [< OF *veue,* orig. pp. of *veoir* see < L *videre*] —**view′er** *n.*

view-hal·loo (vyōō′hə·lōō′) *n.* A shout uttered by a huntsman when a fox breaks cover. Also **view′-hal·lo′** (-lō′), **view′-hal·loa′.**

view·less (vyōō′lis) *adj.* **1** Devoid of a view; that cannot be viewed. **2** Having no views or opinions. **3** Invisible; unseen.

view·point (vyōō′point′) *n.* Point of view.

view·y (vyōō′ē) *adj.* **1** *Colloq.* Having visionary ideas or peculiar views; visionary. **2** Appearing good at first sight; showy.

Vi·gée-Le·brun (vē·zhā′lə·brœṅ′), **Marie Anne,** 1755–1842, French painter.

vi·ges·i·mal (vī·jes′ə·məl) *adj.* **1** Twentieth. **2** Of or pertaining to twenty; proceeding by twenties. [< L *vigesimus,* var. of *vicesimus* < *viceni.* See VICENARY.]

vig·il (vij′əl) *n.* **1** The act or state of keeping awake; a nightlong watch; watchfulness. **2** *Eccl.* **a** The eve of a holy day, especially the eve of a fast day. **b** *pl.* Religious devotions on such an eve. **3** *Usually pl.* Any nocturnal devotions. [< AF *vigile* < L *vigilia* < *vigil* awake]

vig·il·am·bu·lism (vij′əl·am′byə·liz′əm) *n. Psychol.* A state in which a person, while, awake, is unconscious of his surroundings: a condition resembling somnambulism. [< L *vigil* awake + *ambulare* walk]

vig·i·lance (vij′ə·ləns) *n.* **1** The quality of being vigilant; alertness; watchfulness in guarding against danger or providing for safety. **2** A morbid watchfulness; insomnia. See synonyms under CARE.

vigilance committee 1 A body of men self-organized for the maintenance of order and the administration of summary justice in communities where regular authority is lacking or inefficient, especially in lawless sections of the western United States. **2** Formerly, in the southern United States, a group of white citizens organized to terrify and control Negroes and abolitionists.

vig·i·lant (vij′ə·lənt) *adj.* Characterized by vigilance; being on the alert; watchful; heedful; wary. [< MF < L *vigilans, -antis,* ppr. of *vigilare* keep awake < *vigil* awake] —**vig′i·lant·ly** *adv.* —**vig′i·lant·ness** *n.*

Synonyms: active, alert, awake, careful, cautious, circumspect, heedful, mindful, sleepless, wakeful, wary, watchful, wide-awake. *Vigilant* implies more sustained activity and more intelligent volition than *alert.* One is *vigilant* against danger; he may be *alert* or *watchful* for good as well as against evil; he is *wary* in view of suspected stratagem, trickery, or treachery. A person may be *wakeful* because of some merely physical excitement or excitability, as through insomnia; yet he may be utterly careless and negligent in his wakefulness, the reverse of *watchful*; a person who is truly *watchful* must keep himself *wakeful* while on watch, in which case *wakeful* has something of mental quality. *Watchful,* from the English, and *vigilant,* from the Latin, are almost exact equivalents; but *vigilant* has a

somewhat sharper definiteness and somewhat more of a suggestion of volition; one may be habitually *watchful*; one is *vigilant* of set purpose and for direct cause. See ALERT. *Antonyms*: careless, drowsy, dull, heedless, inattentive, incautious, inconsiderate, neglectful, negligent, oblivious, thoughtless, unwary.

vig·i·lan·te (vij′ə·lan′tē) *n.* One who belongs to a vigilance committee. Also **vigilance man.** [<Sp., vigilant <L *vigilans* VIGILANT]

vi·gnette (vin·yet′) *n.* **1** Originally, a running ornament of leaves and tendrils, as in Gothic architecture. **2** A decorative or illustrative design placed on or before the title page of a book, at the end or beginning of a chapter, etc.; also, in medieval manuscript, an ornamented capital letter. **3** An engraving, photograph, or the like, having a background that shades off gradually. **4** A word-picture which delineates something subtly and delicately. — *v.t.* **·gnet·ted, ·gnet·ting 1** To make with a gradually shaded background or border, as a photograph. **2** To ornament with vignettes. [<F, dim. of *vigne* a vine]

vi·gnet·ter (vin·yet′ər) *n.* **1** A device, as a shaded paper with an oval hole in the center, used by photographers in printing vignettes. **2** One who makes vignettes: also **vi·gnet′tist.**

Vi·gno·la (vē·nyō′lä), **Giacomo da** See BAROZZI.

Vi·gny (vē·nyē′), **Comte Alfred Victor de,** 1799–1863, French poet, dramatist, and novelist.

Vi·go (vē′gō, *Sp.* bē′gō) A port of Pontevedra province, on **Vigo Bay,** an inlet of the Atlantic in NW Spain (18 miles long, 1/2 to 10 miles wide).

vig·or (vig′ər) *n.* **1** Active strength or force, physical or mental. **2** Vital or natural power, as in a healthy animal or plant. **3** Forcible exertion of strength; energy; intensity. **4** Legal force; validity. Also *Brit.* **vig′our.** — **in vigor** *Law* In operation; effective. [<AF *vigur, vigour,* OF *vigor* <L < *vigere* be lively, thrive]

vi·go·ro·so (vē′gō·rō′sō) *adj. Music* Vigorous; energetic: a direction. [<Ital.]

vig·or·ous (vig′ər·əs) *adj.* **1** Full of physical or mental vigor; robust. **2** Marked by or accompanied by vigor; performed or done with vigor; showing vigor; energetic. See synonyms under ACTIVE, FRESH, HEALTHY, POWERFUL, STRONG, VIVID. — **vig′or·ous·ly** *adv.* — **vig′or·ous·ness** *n.*

Vii·pu·ri (vē′pōō·rē) The Finnish name for VYBORG.

Vi·ja·ya·na·gar (vij′ə·yə·nug′ər) **1** A former princely state in the Rajputana States, India; since 1949 a part of Bombay State; 135 square miles. **2** A village of northern Bombay State, India, formerly capital of Vijayanagar state.

vi·king (vī′king) *n.* One of the Scandinavian warriors who harried the coasts of Europe from the eighth to the tenth centuries; a pirate; sea rover. Also **Vi′king.** [<ON *vīkingr* a pirate, ? <OE and Frisian *wicing* < *wīc* a camp <L *vicus* a village]

Vi·la (vē′lə) The capital of the New Hebrides condominium, on Efate.

vi·la·yet (vē′lä·yet′) *n.* An administrative division of Turkey. [<Turkish *vilāyet* <Arabic *wilāyat* < *wāli* a governor]

vile (vīl) *adj.* **vil·er, vil·est 1** Morally base, despicable, or loathsome; shamefully wicked; sinful; corrupt; filthy; disgusting. **2** Of little worth or account; mean. **3** Objectionable in any way; disagreeable: a general term of derogation. See synonyms under BAD[1], BASE[2], BRUTISH, COMMON, CRIMINAL, IMMORAL, INFAMOUS, SINFUL, VULGAR. [<AF, OF, fem. of *vil* <L *vilis* cheap] — **vile′ly** *adv.* — **vile′ness** *n.*

vil·i·a·co (vil′ē·ä′kō) *n. Obs.* A villain; scoundrel. [<Ital., ult. <L *vilis* cheap]

vil·i·fy (vil′ə·fī) *v.t.* **·fied, ·fy·ing 1** To speak of as vile; defame; slander; traduce. **2** To make base or vile; degrade. [<LL *vilificare* <L *vilis* cheap + *facere* make] — **vil′i·fi·ca′tion** (-fə·kā′shən) *n.* — **vil′i·fi′er** *n.*

vil·i·pend (vil′ə·pend) *v.t.* **1** To think or speak of disparagingly; depreciate. **2** To vilify; defame. [<OF *vilipender* <L *vilipendere* < *vilis* cheap + *pendere* weight]

vill (vil) *n.* In old English law, a village; hamlet; township; also, a manor. [<AF *vill,* OF *vile, ville* a country house, village <L *villa.* See VILLA.]

vil·la (vil′ə) *n.* Originally, a country house with some suggestion of opulence; now, a suburban or rural residence. See synonyms under HOUSE. [<Ital. <L, a country house, farm, dim. of *vicus* a village]

Vil·la (vē′yä, *Sp.* bē′yä), **Francisco,** 1877–1923, Mexican revolutionary leader called "Pancho": real name *Doroteo Arango.*

Vil·la Bens (bē′lyä bāns) Capital of the Southern Protectorate of Morocco, Spanish West Africa, on the SW coast; until 1940, capital of Spanish Sahara: formerly *Cabo Jubi.*

Vil·la Cis·ne·ros (bē′lyä thēs·nā′rōs) The capital of Río de Oro, Spanish West Africa, on the central western coast near the tropic of Cancer.

vil·la·dom (vil′ə·dəm) *n. Brit.* Villas collectively; also, their occupants; the world of suburban villas.

vil·lage (vil′ij) *n.* **1** A collection of houses in a rural district, smaller than a town but larger than a hamlet, and usually arranged according to a regular plan. Villages may or may not be incorporated. **2** In some States, a municipality smaller than a city. Compare TOWNSHIP. **3** A collection of habitations of animals: a gopher *village.* **4** The inhabitants of a village, collectively; the villagers. **5** An encampment or community of North American Indians or Eskimos: permanent, or sometimes temporary, during a migration or for a season. — *adj.* Of, pertaining to, or characteristic of a village. [<OF <L *villaticum,* neut. sing. of *villaticus* pertaining to a villa < *villa* a villa]

village community An agricultural community with a simple organization, such as was found in early England, Germany, Russia, India, etc.; specifically, a free, self-dependent, communal group, regarded by many writers as the political unit out of which the modern state developed.

vil·lag·er (vil′ij·ər) *n.* One who lives in a village.

vil·lage·ry (vil′ij·rē) *n. Obs.* A collection of villages.

Vil·la·her·mo·sa (bē′yä·er·mō′sä) The capital of Tabasco state, SE Mexico.

vil·lain (vil′ən) *n.* **1** One who has committed or is disposed to commit any flagitious or disgraceful crime or series of crimes; a scoundrel; rogue: often used jocosely: He's a little *villain.* **2** A character in a novel, play, etc., who represents such a person and is the opponent of the hero or protagonist; also, an actor who regularly portrays such a character. **3** A villein. **4** *Obs.* A countryman; boor; clown; rustic. — *adj.* **1** Base; vile. **2** Of low birth; occupying a low station in life. ◆ Homophone: *villein.* [<AF, OF *vilein, vilain* a farm servant <LL *villanus* <L *villa* a villa]

vil·lain·age (vil′ən·ij) See VILLEINAGE.

vil·lain·ess (vil′ən·is) *n.* A female villain.

vil·lain·ous (vil′ən·əs) *adj.* **1** Having the nature of a villain. **2** Marked by extreme depravity. **3** *Colloq.* Very bad; disgusting; abominable: said of things: *villainous* words. See synonyms under BAD[1], INFAMOUS. — **vil′lain·ous·ly** *adv.* — **vil′lain·ous·ness** *n.*

vil·lain·y (vil′ən·ē) *n. pl.* **·lain·ies 1** The quality or condition of being villainous; moral depravity. **2** Conduct befitting a villain; a villainous act; a crime. **3** *Obs.* Villeinage; servitude. **4** *Obs.* A low or miserable condition or state. See synonyms under ABOMINATION.

Vil·la-Lo·bos (vē′lə·lō′bōōsh, -bōōs), **Heitor,** 1887–1959, Brazilian composer and conductor.

vil·lan·age (vil′ən·ij) *n.* **1** Villeinage. **2** *Obs.* Villainy. [Var. of VILLEINAGE]

vil·la·nel·la (vil′ə·nel′ə, *Ital.* vēl′lä·nel′lä) *n. pl.* **·nel·le** (-nel′ē, *Ital.* -nel′lā) **1** A light, rustic part song, or dance accompanying it. **2** An early form of madrigal, popular in Naples during the sixteenth century. [<Ital., fem. dim. of *villano* <LL *villanus.* See VILLAIN.]

vil·la·nelle (vil′ə·nel′) *n.* A verse form, originally French, in 19 lines and 2 rimes, arranged in five tercets and a concluding quatrain. [<F <Ital. *villanella* a villanella]

Vil·lard (vi·lärd′), **Oswald Garrison,** 1872–1949, U. S. journalist.

Vil·lars (vē·lȧr′), **Duc Claude Louis Hector de,** 1653–1734, French marshal.

vil·lat·ic (vi·lat′ik) *adj.* Of or pertaining to a villa, farm, or village; rural. [<L *villaticus.* See VILLAGE.]

vil·lein (vil′ən) *n.* In the manorial system of feudal times, a member of any of the classes of freemen ranking below the thanes; more specifically, a free peasant ranking below a socman but above a cotter. By the 13th century the term *villein* was applied to a class of serfs who were regarded as freemen in respect to their legal relations with all persons except their lord, whose slaves they were. — *adj. Obs.* Relating to villeins; low-born. ◆ Homophone: *villain.* [<AF, OF *vilein, vilain.* See VILLAIN.]

vil·lein·age (vil′ən·ij) *n.* In feudal law, the tenure by which villeins held land; also, the status or condition of a villein: also spelled *villanage.* Also **vil′len·age.**

Ville·neuve (vēl·nœv′), **Pierre Charles Jean Baptiste Silvestre de,** 1763–1806, French admiral.

Vil·liers (vil′ərz), **George** See BUCKINGHAM.

vil·li·form (vil′ə·fôrm) *adj.* **1** Having the form of a villus. **2** Resembling nap, as of plush, as the teeth of fishes when numerous, small, and close together in velvety bands. [<NL *villiformis* <L *villus* tuft of hair + *forma* form]

Vil·lon (vē·yôṅ′), **François,** 1431–85?, French poet: real name *François de Montcorbier.*

vil·los·i·ty (vi·los′ə·tē) *n. pl.* **·ties 1** The state or condition of being villous. **2** A villous surface or coating. **3** A villus.

vil·lous (vil′əs) *adj.* **1** Covered with short, soft hairs; nappy. **2** Covered with or having villi. Also **vil′lose** (-ōs). [<L *villosus* < *villus* tuft of hair] — **vil′lous·ly** *adv.*

vil·lus (vil′əs) *n. pl.* **vil·li** (vil′ī) **1** *Anat.* One of the short, hairlike processes found on certain membranes, as of the small intestine, where they aid in the digestive process. **2** *Bot.* One of the long, close, rather soft hairs on the surface of certain plants. [<L, a tuft of hair, shaggy hair, var. of *vellus* a fleece, wool]

Vil·na (vil′nə, *Russian* vēl′nä) The capital of Lithuania, in the SE part: Polish *Wilno.* Also **Vil·ni·us** (vil′nē·əs), **Vil·nyus** (vil′nyəs).

Vi·lyui (vyē·lyōō′ē) A river in western Yakut Autonomous S.S.R., flowing 1,512 miles east to the Lena.

vim (vim) *n.* Force or vigor; energy; spirit. [<L, accusative of *vis* power]

vi·men (vī′mən) *n. pl.* **vim·i·na** (vim′ə·nə) *Bot.* A long, flexible shoot or branch. [<L *vimen, -inis* a twig < *viere* bend together, plait]

vim·i·nal (vim′ə·nəl) *adj. Rare* Pertaining to twigs; made of or producing twigs. [<L *vimen, -inis.* See VIMEN.]

Vim·i·nal (vim′ə·nəl) One of the seven hills on which ancient Rome was built.

vi·min·e·ous (vī·min′ē·əs) *adj.* **1** Having or resembling long, flexible shoots or branches. **2** Composed of twigs. [<L *vimineus* < *vimen, -inis.* See VIMEN.]

Vi·my (vē·mē′) A town in Pas-de-Calais department, northern France, near **Vimy Ridge,** scene of fierce fighting in World War I, 1915–1917.

vin (vaṅ) *n. French* Wine.

vin- Var. of VINI-.

vi·na (vē′nä) *n.* An East Indian musical instrument with seven steel strings stretched on a long, fretted fingerboard over two gourds. [<Hind. *vīṇā* <Skt.]

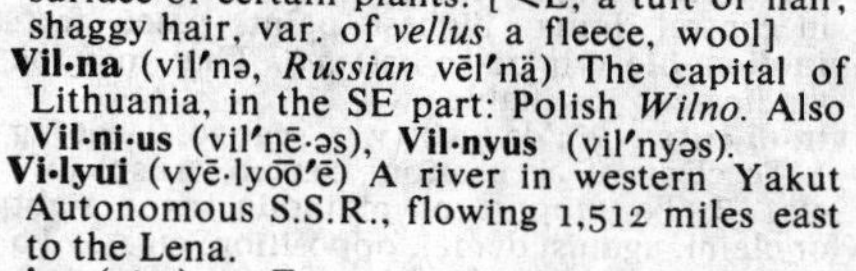

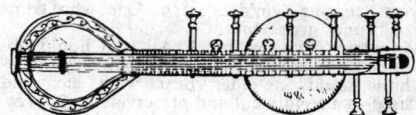

VINA OF BENARES

vi·na·ceous (vī·nā′shəs) *adj.* **1** Of or pertaining to wine or grapes. **2** Of the color of red wine. [<L *vinaceus* < *vinum* wine]

Vi·ña del Mar (bē′nyä thel mär′) A city on the Pacific in central Chile; a beach resort and industrial and agricultural center.

vin·ai·grette (vin′ə·gret′) *n.* **1** An ornamental

box or bottle, with a perforated top, for holding vinegar, smelling salts, or a pungent drug: also *vinegarette*. **2** Vinaigrette sauce. [<F, dim. of *vinaigre* vinegar]

vinaigrette sauce A vinegar and savory herb sauce served with fish and cold meats.

vi·nasse (vi·nas′) *n.* A residual product containing potassium salts, obtained from the winepress or from beets after the sugar has been extracted. [<F]

Vin·cennes (vin·senz′, *Fr.* vaṅ·sen′) **1** A city on the Wabash River in SW Indiana; site of French mission established in 1702. **2** A city just east of Paris, France.

Vin·cent (vin′sənt, *Fr.* vaṅ·säṅ′) A masculine personal name. Also *Ger.* **Vin·cenz** (vin′sents), *Ital.* **Vin·cen·zo** (vin·chen′tsō). [<L, conquering]

— **Vincent de Paul, Saint,** 1574?–1660, French Roman Catholic priest, founder of several charitable organizations.

Vin·cen·tian (vin·sen′shən) *n.* A member of a Roman Catholic order founded in 1625 by St. Vincent de Paul. See LAZARIST.

Vincent's infection *Pathol.* Trench mouth. Also **Vincent's angina, Vincent's disease.** [after J. H. *Vincent,* 1862–1950, French physician]

Vin·ci (vēn′chē), **Leonardo da** See LEONARDO DA VINCI.

vin·ci·ble (vin′sə·bəl) *adj.* That may be conquered or overcome; conquerable. [<L *vincibilis* < *vincere* conquer] — **vin′ci·bil′i·ty, vin′·ci·ble·ness** *n.*

vin·cu·lum (vingk′yə·ləm) *n. pl.* **·la** (-lə) **1** A bond of union. **2** *Anat.* A confining band of fascia. **3** *Math.* A straight line drawn over several algebraic terms, or a brace uniting them to show that all are to be operated on together. [<L < *vincire* bind]

Vin·dhya Pra·desh (vind′hyə prə·dāsh′) A former State of central India, incorporated in Madhya Pradesh State, 1956; 24,600 square miles; capital, Rewa.

Vin·dhya Range (vind′hyə) A chain of hills in central India; highest point, 3,400 feet.

vin·di·ca·ble (vin′də·kə·bəl) *adj.* That may be vindicated; justifiable.

vin·di·cate (vin′də·kāt) *v.t.* **·cat·ed, ·cat·ing** **1** To clear of accusation, censure, suspicion, etc. **2** To support or maintain, as a right or claim, against denial, opposition, etc. **3** To serve to justify. **4** *Rare* To lay claim to. **5** *Obs.* To avenge; punish. **6** *Obs.* To set free; rescue. See synonyms under AVENGE, JUSTIFY. [<L *vindicatus,* pp. of *vindicare* avenge, claim] — **vin′di·ca′tor** *n.*

vin·di·ca·tion (vin′də·kā′shən) *n.* The act of vindicating, or the state of being vindicated; justification; defense. See synonyms under APOLOGY, DEFENSE.

vin·di·ca·tive (vin′də·kā′tiv) *adj.* That contributes to vindication; that vindicates or serves to vindicate.

vin·di·ca·to·ry (vin′də·kə·tôr′ē, -tō′rē) *adj.* **1** Bringing to vindication; justificatory. **2** Punitive; avenging.

vin·dic·tive (vin·dik′tiv) *adj.* **1** Having a revengeful spirit; of a revengeful character. **2** *Obs.* Punitive. [<L *vindicta* a revenge] — **vin·dic′tive·ly** *adv.* — **vin·dic′tive·ness** *n.*

vine (vīn) *n.* **1** Any of a large and widely distributed group of plants having a slender, weak stem that may clasp or twine about a support by means of tendrils, leaf petioles, etc. **2** The stem itself. **3** A grapevine. [<OF *vigne, vine* <L *vinea* vineyard < *vinum* wine]

vine·dress·er (vīn′dres′ər) *n.* One who trims or prunes grapevines.

vin·e·gar (vin′ə·gər) *n.* **1** An acid liquid obtained by the acetous fermentation of alcoholic liquids, as cider, beer, wine, etc., and used as a condiment and preservative. **2** *Med.* A preparation of dilute acetic acid. **3** Anything metaphorically sour or soured, as a face; acerbity, as of speech. [<OF *vyn egre, vinaigre* < *vin* wine (<L *vinum*) + *aigre, egre* sour <L *acer* sharp] — **vin′e·gar·ish** *adj.*

vinegar eel A small nematode worm *(Anguillula aceti)* common in vinegar, sour paste, and similar fermenting liquids. Also **vinegar worm.**

vin·e·gar·ette (vin′ə·gə·ret′) See VINAIGRETTE (def. 1).

vinegar fly A fruit fly (def. 2).

vin·e·gar·roon (vin′ə·gə·rōōn′) *n.* The whip-tailed scorpion *(Mastigoproctus giganteus)* of the SW United States and Mexico, so called from its odor when alarmed: erroneously supposed to be venomous. Also **vin′e·ge·rone′** (-rōn′). [<Sp. *vinagre* vinegar < *vino* wine (<L *vinum*) + *agrio* sour <L *acer* sharp]

vin·e·gar·y (vin′ə·gər·ē) *adj.* **1** Being like or suggestive of vinegar; sour; acid. **2** Crabbed; of a sour disposition.

Vine·land (vīn′lənd) See VINLAND.

vin·er·y (vī′nər·ē) *n. pl.* **·er·ies** **1** A greenhouse for grapes; grapery. **2** Vines in general.

vine·yard (vin′yərd) *n.* **1** A large collection of cultivated grapevines. **2** Figuratively, a field for labor, especially spiritual culture or labor. [Earlier *wineyard,* OE *wīngeard*; infl. in form by VINE]

vine·yard·ist (vin′yər·dist) *n.* One who grows or cultivates grapevines.

vingt–et–un (vaṅ·tā·œṅ′) *n.* A game of cards played with a full pack, the object being to draw cards on which the aggregate number of spots shall reach as near as possible to but not exceed 21. Also called *twenty-one, blackjack.* [<F, twenty-one]

vini– *combining form* Wine; of or pertaining to wine or to wine grapes: *viniculture, viniferous*: also, before vowels, *vin–*. Also **vino–**. [<L *vinum* wine]

vi·nic (vī′nik, vin′ik) *adj.* Of, pertaining to, or derived from wine: *vinic* alcohol. [<L *vinum* wine]

vin·i·cul·ture (vin′ə·kul′chər) *n.* The cultivation of grapes for winemaking. — **vin′i·cul′tur·al** *adj.*

vin·i·cul·tur·ist (vin′ə·kul′chər·ist) *n.* One engaged in viniculture.

vi·nif·er·ous (vī·nif′ər·əs) *adj.* Producing wine. [<VINI- + -FEROUS]

vin·i·fi·ca·tor (vin′ə·fə·kā′tər) *n.* An apparatus for receiving and condensing the vapor of alcohol that rises from the fermenting must during the making of wine. [<VINI- + L *-ficator* a maker < *facere* make]

Vin·land (vin′lənd) A name given to part of the coast of North America by Norse voyagers: also *Vineland.*

Vin·ni·tsa (vin′it·sə, *Russian* vyēn′nyē·tsə) A city on the Bug river in SW central Ukrainian S.S.R.

Vi·no·gra·doff (vē′nə·grä′dôf), **Sir Paul Gavrilovich,** 1854–1925, Russian jurist and medieval historian, active in England.

vi·nom·e·ter (vi·nom′ə·tər, vī-) *n.* A hydrometer for measuring the percentage of alcohol in wine. [<VINO- + -METER]

vin or·di·naire (vaṅ ôr·dē·nâr′) *French* A cheap wine; literally, ordinary wine.

vi·nos·i·ty (vī·nos′ə·tē) *n.* **1** The state or quality of being vinous. **2** The general character of a wine, including the bouquet, flavor, body, etc. **3** Addiction to or fondness for wine. [<LL *vinositas, -tatis* <L *vinosus* VINOUS]

vi·nous (vī′nəs) *adj.* **1** Pertaining to, characteristic of, or having the qualities of wine. **2** Caused by, affected by, or addicted to wine. **3** Wine-colored. [<L *vinosus* <*vinum* wine]

Vin·son (vin′sən), **Fred M.,** 1890–1953, U. S. administrator and jurist; chief justice of the United States 1946–53.

vin·tage (vin′tij) *n.* **1** The yield of a vineyard or wine-growing district for one season. **2** The visible fruit of vineyards. **3** The harvesting of a vineyard and the first steps in the making of wine. **4** Wine, especially wine of high quality. **5** The year or the region in which a particular wine is produced. **6** *Colloq.* The type or kind current or appropriate at a particular time or in a particular season of the past: a joke of ancient *vintage.* [<AF *vintage,* alter. of *vindage, vendage,* OF *vendage* <L *vindemia* < *vinum* wine + *demere* remove < *de-* off + *emere* take; infl. in form by *vintner*]

vin·tag·er (vin′tij·ər) *n.* A harvester of grapes.

vintage wine Wine of an exceptionally good year, especially a dated champagne or port.

vint·ner (vint′nər) *n.* A wine merchant, especially at wholesale. [<OF *vinetier, vinotier* < *vinot,* dim. of *vin* wine <L *vinum*]

vin·y (vī′nē) *adj.* Pertaining to, like, of, full of, or yielding vines.

vi·nyl (vī′nəl) *n. Chem.* The univalent radical, CH_2:CH, derived from ethylene, especially when used in organic synthesis. [<L *vinum* wine + -YL]

vinyl acetate *Chem.* A colorless liquid, $C_4H_6O_2$, used as a starting point in the synthesis of various resins and plastics.

vinyl alcohol *Chem.* A hypothetical unstable alcohol, C_2H_4O, derived from acetylene.

vinyl chloride *Chem.* A compound of vinyl and chlorine, C_2H_3Cl, used in the production of synthetic fibers.

vinyl polymer *Chem.* Any of a class of organic compounds obtained by the polymerization of vinyl compounds.

vi·ol (vī′əl) *n.* **1** Any member of a family of stringed musical instruments, predecessors of the violin family, originating in the later Middle Ages and passing out of use in the 18th century, having usually six strings, and played with a bow. **2** A stringed instrument of the violin class. See BASS VIOL. [Earlier *vielle* <AF, OF <Med. L *vidula, vitula* <Gmc.; infl. in form by OF *viole*]

vi·o·la (vē·ō′lə, vī-; *Ital.* vyō′lä) *n.* **1** A four-stringed musical instrument of the violin family, somewhat larger than the violin, and tuned a fifth lower, with a graver and less brilliant tone. Its four strings are tuned in fifths. **2** A medieval viol. **3** An organ stop of eight-foot length and tone, producing stringlike tones. [<Ital., orig. a viol <Med. L *vidula* <Gmc.]

Vi·o·la (vī′ō·lə, vē′-, vī·ō′lə) A feminine personal name. Also **Vi·o·lan·te** (*Pg.* vē′ō·läṅ′tə, *Sp.* bē′ō·läṅ′tā), *Ger.* **Vi·o·le** (vē·ō′lə). [<L, a violet]

— **Viola** The heroine in Shakespeare's *Twelfth Night.*

vi·o·la·ble (vī′ə·lə·bəl) *adj.* That may be violated. [<L *violabilis* < *violare* VIOLATE] — **vi′o·la·ble·ness, vi′o·la·bil′i·ty** *n.* — **vi′o·la·bly** *adv.*

vi·o·la·ceous (vī′ə·lā′shəs) *adj.* **1** Having a violet hue. **2** *Bot.* Of or pertaining to the violet or the violet family *(Violaceae)* of herbs, shrubs, and trees. [<L *violaceus* < *viola* a violet]

vio·la da gam·ba (vyō′lä dä gäm′bä) **1** The bass of the viol family, held between the legs, and having a range and tone similar to those of the violoncello: also *bass viol.* **2** An organ stop producing tones akin to those of the viola da gamba and usually having an eight-foot length and tone. [<Ital., viola of the leg]

vi·o·late (vī′ə·lāt) *v.t.* **·lat·ed, ·lat·ing** **1** To break or infringe, as a law, oath, agreement, etc. **2** To treat irreverently; profane, as a holy place. **3** To break in upon; disturb. **4** To ravish; rape. **5** To do violence to; offend grossly; outrage. **6** *Obs.* To treat roughly; abuse. [<L *violatus,* pp. of *violare* use violence < *vis* force] — **vi′o·la′tor** *n.*

Synonyms: abuse, debauch, defile, deflower, desecrate, hurt, injure, outrage, pollute, profane, rape, ravish. See ABUSE, POLLUTE.

vi·o·la·tion (vī′ə·lā′shən) *n.* The act of violating, or the state of being violated.

vi·o·la·tive (vī′ə·lā′tiv) *adj.* Having a tendency to violate; violating; involving violation.

vi·o·lence (vī′ə·ləns) *n.* **1** The quality or state of being violent; intensity; fury; also, an instance of violent action. **2** Violent or unjust exercise of power; injury; outrage; desecration; profanation. **3** *Law* Physical force unlawfully exercised; an act tending to intimidate or overawe by causing apprehension of bodily injury. **4** The perversion or distortion of the meaning of a text, word, or the like; unjustified alteration of wording. [<AF, OF <L *violentia* < *violentus* violent]

Synonyms: acuteness, boisterousness, eagerness, fierceness, force, fury, impetuosity, injury, intensity, outrage, passion, poignancy, rage, severity, sharpness, vehemence, violation, wildness, wrath. See OUTRAGE. *Antonyms*: calmness, feebleness, forbearance, gentleness, meekness, mildness, patience, self-command, self-control, self-restraint.

vi·o·lent (vī′ə·lənt) *adj.* **1** Proceeding from or marked by great physical force or roughness; sudden; forcible. **2** Caused by or exhibiting intense emotional or mental excitement; passionate; impetuous; fierce. **3** Characterized by intensity of any kind; extreme: *violent* heat. **4** Marked by unjust exercise of force; harsh; severe: to take *violent* measures. **5** Resulting from external force or injury; not in the ordinary course of nature: a *violent* death. **6** Tending to

pervert the meaning or sense: a *violent* construction. [<OF <L *violentus* <*vis* force] — **vi′o·lent·ly** *adv.*

  Synonyms: acute, boisterous, fierce, forceful, frantic, frenzied, fuming, furious, immoderate, impetuous, intense, irate, mad, maniacal, outrageous, passionate, poignant, raging, raving, severe, sharp, tumultuous, turbulent, uncontrollable, ungovernable, vehement, wild. See FIERCE, HOT, IMMODERATE, TURBULENT.

violent presumption *Law* An inference based on evidence that is so strong as to be almost conclusive.

vi·o·les·cent (vī′ə·les′ənt) *adj.* Having a tinge of violet color. [<L *viola* a violet + -ESCENT]

vi·o·let (vī′ə·lit) *n.* **1** Any of a widely distributed genus (*Viola*) of herbaceous perennial herbs, bearing flowers typically of a purplish–blue color; especially, the common **garden violet** (*V. odorata*). The violet is the State flower of Illinois, New Jersey, Rhode Island, and Wisconsin. **2** Any of several similar plants: the dog's–tooth *violet*. **3** A color seen at the end of the spectrum, opposite the red and beyond the blue; also, a pigment of this color. —*adj.* Of the color of violet. [<OF *violette*, dim. of *viole* <L *viola* a violet]

violet rays High–frequency radiation from the violet end of the visible spectrum: distinguished from *ultraviolet*.

vi·o·lin (vī′ə·lin′) *n.*
1 A musical instrument having four strings and a sounding box of seasoned wood, and played by means of a bow; a fiddle. It is the treble member of the **violin family**, which includes the viola, violoncello, and double–bass, and is distinguished in its modern form by its fully molded belly and back. **2** A violinist, especially He is second *violin*. [< Ital. *violino*, dim. of *viola* a viola]

vi·o·lin·ist (vī′ə·lin′ist) *n.* One who plays the violin.

vi·ol·ist (vī′əl·ist) *n.* One who plays the viol or viola.

Viol·let–le–Duc (vyô.le′lə·dük′), **Eugène Emmanuel,** 1814–79, French architect and archeologist.

vi·o·lon·cel·list (vē′ə·lən·chel′ist) *n.* One who plays the violoncello: usually abbreviated to *cellist* or *'cellist*.

vi·o·lon·cel·lo (vē′ə·lən·chel′ō) *n. pl.* **·los** A bass instrument of the violin family, having four strings tuned an octave lower than the viola, and held between the performer's knees when played: commonly called *cello* or *'cello*. [<Ital., dim. of *violone* a bass viol, aug. of *viola*. See VIOLA.]

vio·lo·ne (vyō·lō′na) *n.* **1** The double–bass of the viol family, playing an octave lower than the viola da gamba: the immediate ancestor of the modern double–bass, which replaces the true double–bass of the violin family. **2** An organ stop with stringlike tone quality, having a 16–foot length and tone. **3** A small–scaled organ stop of eight–foot length and tone. [<Ital., aug. of *viola* a viol. See VIOLA.]

vi·os·ter·ol (vī·os′tər·ôl, -ol) *n.* Irradiated ergosterol, a vitamin D preparation variously used in medicine. [<(ULTRA)VIO(LET) + (ERGO)STEROL]

vi·per (vī′pər) *n.* **1** Any of a family (*Viperidae*) of venomous Old World snakes, especially the common European viper or adder (*Vipera berus*), about two feet long and variously colored; also, the African puff adder, and the horned viper. **2** One of a family (*Crotalidae*)

---

of typically American poisonous snakes, the **pit vipers,** including the rattlesnake, copperhead, and fer–de–lance, which are characterized by a small depression between the nostril and the eye. **3** Any poisonous or allegedly poisonous snake. **4** A venomous, malicious, treacherous, or spiteful person. **5** *U.S. Slang* A marihuana smoker. [<OF *vipere, vipre* < L *vipera*, contraction of *vivipara* <*vivus* living + *parere* bring forth] —**vi′per·ine** (vī′pər·in, -pə·rin) *adj.* —**vi′per·ish** *adj.*

vi·per·ous (vī′pər·əs) *adj.* **1** Snakelike; viperine. **2** Venomous. —**vi′per·ous·ly** *adv.*

vi·per's–bu·gloss (vī′pərz·byōō′glôs, -glos) *n.* Blueweed.

vir·a·gin·i·ty (vir′ə·jin′ə·tē) *n. Psychiatry* The assumption by a woman of male characteristics and reactions. [<L *virago, -inis* VIRAGO]

vi·ra·go (vi·rä′gō, vi-) *n. pl.* **·goes** or **·gos 1** A turbulent woman; vixen. **2** *Obs.* A woman of extraordinary size and courage; a female warrior; Amazon. [<L, manlike woman <*vir* a man]

vi·ral (vī′rəl) *adj. Med.* Of, pertaining to, caused by, or resembling a virus.

Vir·chow (vir′khō), **Rudolf,** 1821–1902, German pathologist.

vir·e·lay (vir′ə·lā) *n.* A form of old French verse, arranged in any of various arbitrary orders; especially, a verse form having only two rimes throughout; also, a form in which each stanza has two rimes, one repeated from the preceding stanza and a new one that will be repeated in the next. Also *French* **vire·lai** (vēr·le′). [<OF *virelai*, prob. alter. of *vireli, virli* a refrain of old dance songs]

vir·e·o (vir′ē·ō) *n. pl.* **·os** Any of various small, insectivorous birds (family *Vireonidae*), predominantly dull–green and grayish, which make slight, cup–shaped, pensile nests; a greenlet. The **red–eyed vireo** (*Vireo olivaceus*), the **yellow–throated vireo** (*V. flavifrons*), the **white–eyed vireo** (*V. griseus*), the **blue–headed** or **solitary vireo** (*V. solitarius*) and the **warbling vireo** (*V. gilvus*) are common in the United States. Many of the species are noted for their song. [< L, a kind of small bird, ? the greenfinch]

vir·e·o·nine (vir′ē·ə·nīn′, -nin) *adj.* Characteristic of or pertaining to a vireo and related birds. —*n.* A vireo or related bird. [<L *vireo, -onis*. See VIREO.]

vi·res·cence (vī·res′əns) *n.* **1** The state or condition of becoming green. **2** *Bot.* Abnormal assumption of green by the usually bright–colored organs of plants, as when petals become green like ordinary leaves.

vi·res·cent (vī·res′ənt) *adj.* Greenish or becoming green. [<L *virescens, -entis,* ppr. of *virescere* grow green <*vir* be green]

vir et ux·or (vir et uk′sôr) *Latin* Husband and wife.

vir·ga (vûr′gə) *n. Meteorol.* Drooping streamers or wisps of precipitation from clouds, usually of the altocumulus and altostratus types. [< L, twig, streak in the sky]

vir·gate (vûr′git, -gāt) *adj.* **1** Long, straight, and slender like a wand. **2** *Bot.* Bearing or producing many small twigs. [<L *virga* a twig, rod]

vir·gate[2] (vûr′git, -gāt) *n.* An early English measure of land, varying greatly (15, 20, 24, 30, and sometimes 40 acres) in different parts of England. [<Med. L *virgata (terrae)* a virgate (of land) <L *virga* a rod]

Vir·gil (vûr′jəl), **Vir·gil·i·an** (vər·jil′ē·ən) See VERGIL, etc.

vir·gin (vûr′jin) *n.* **1** A person, especially a young woman, who has never had sexual intercourse; a maiden. **2** A chaste young girl or unmarried woman; a spinster. **3** *Eccl.* **a** A member of a religious community who has taken a vow of chastity; a nun. **b** A chaste, unmarried woman honored for her piety or virtue: used as an epithet of saints: St. Cecilia, *virgin* and martyr. **4** Any female animal before its first copulation. **5** *Entomol.* A female insect producing fertile eggs by parthenogenesis. —*adj.* **1** Being a virgin. **2** Consisting of virgins: a *virgin* band. **3** Pertaining or suited to a virgin; chaste; maidenly. **4** Uncorrupte*pure*; undefiled: *virgin* whiteness. **5** Not hitherto used, touched, tilled, or worked upon by man: *virgin* soil; *virgin* forest. **6** Not

---

previously processed, manufactured, or acted upon; new: *virgin* rubber; *virgin* wool. **7** Obtained from the first pressing (of olives, nuts, etc.) without the use of heat: said of an oil. **8** *Metall.* Produced directly from ore, or at the primary smelting: *virgin* silver. **9** *Mining* Occurring, in native form; unalloyed; unmixed: *virgin* gold. **10** First: a ship's *virgin* voyage. **1** Untrained; lacking experience or contact with: waters *virgin* of ships. **12** *Zool.* Parthenogenetic. [<OF *virgine* <L *virgo, -inis* a maiden]

Vir·gin (vûr′jin) **1** Mary, the mother of Jesus: usually with *the*; also, **the Virgin Mary, the Blessed Virgin. 2** The constellation Virgo. See CONSTELLATION.

vir·gin·al[1] (vûr′jin·əl) *adj.* Related to, like, or suited to a virgin; pure; modest; maidenly. [< OF <L *virginalis* <*virgo, -inis* a virgin]

VIRGINAL – LATE 16TH CENTURY

vir·gin·al[2] (vûr′jin·əl) *n.* A legless keyboard musical instrument of the 16th and 17th centuries, predecessor of the harpsichord: often in the plural, sometimes called a **pair of virginals.** [<OF, VIRGINAL[1]; ? so called from its use by young men and girls]

virgin birth 1 *Zool.* Parthenogenesis. **2** *Usually cap. Theol.* The doctrine that Jesus Christ was conceived by divine agency and born without impairment of the virginity of his mother Mary.

vir·gin·hood (vûr′jin·hŏŏd) *n.* Virginity.

Vir·gin·ia (vər·jin′yə) A middle Atlantic State of the United States; 40,815 square miles; capital, Richmond; entered the Union June 25, 1788, one of the original thirteen States; nickname, *Old Dominion*: abbr. VA Original name: *Commonwealth of Virginia.*

Virginia cowslip A smooth perennial herb (*Mertensia virginica*) of the eastern United States, with clusters of blue or purple tubular flowers. Also **Virginia bluebell.**

Virginia creeper A common American climbing vine (*Parthenocissus* or *Ampelopsis quinquefolia*) of the grape family, with compound toothed leaves, small green flowers, and inedible blue berries: also called *American ivy, woodbine.*

Virginia deer A large, graceful, white–tailed deer (*Odocoileus virginianus*), native in the eastern United States and as far west as the Great Plains.

Virginia dogwood The flowering dogwood: State flower of Virginia. See under DOGWOOD.

Virginia Key Northernmost of the Florida Keys, one mile south of Miami Beach; about 2 miles long.

Vir·gin·ian (vər·jin′yən) *adj.* **1** Of, pertaining to, or from Virginia. **2** Of, pertaining to, or designating the language of certain Algonquian North American Indians of eastern Virginia, North Carolina, and Maryland, especially of the Powhatan confederacy, formerly dwelling on the James River, Virginia. —*n.* A native or citizen of Virginia.

Virginia nightingale The cardinal bird.

Virginia rail fence A worm fence; a stake–and–rider.

Virginia reel A country dance in which the performers stand in two parallel lines facing one another and perform various figures, usually at the direction of a caller.

Virginia truffle Tuckahoe.

Virginia trumpet flower The trumpet creeper.

Virgin Islands A group of islands in the West Indies, east of Puerto Rico; divided into the **Virgin Islands of the United States,** an unincorporated territory comprising the

---

VIOLIN

a.	Scroll.
b.	Peg box.
c.	Peg.
d.	Nut.
e.	Fingerboard.
f.	Neck plate.
g.	Sound holes.
h.	Bridge.
i.	Tailpiece.
j.	Chin rest.
k.	Button.

islands of St. Thomas, St. John, and St. Croix, and adjacent islets, purchased from Denmark in 1917; 133 square miles; capital, Charlotte Amalie, on St. Thomas: formerly *Danish West Indies*; and the BRITISH VIRGIN ISLANDS; total area, 200 square miles.

vir·gin·i·ty (vər·jin′ə·tē) *n.* *pl.* **·ties** **1** The state of being a virgin; maidenhood; virginal chastity. **2** The state of being unsullied or unused.

vir·gin·i·um (vər·jin′ē·əm) *n.* Former name of an element now identified as francium. [from the State of Virginia]

Virgin Mary Mary, the mother of Jesus.

Virgin River A river in Utah, Arizona, and Nevada, flowing 200 miles SW to Lake Mead.

vir·gin's–bow·er (vûr′jinz·bou′ər) *n.* A species of clematis (*Clematis virginiana*) bearing white flowers in leafy panicles.

Vir·go (vûr′gō) **1** A zodiacal constellation south of Ursa Major and Boötes; the Virgin. See CONSTELLATION. **2** The sixth sign of the zodiac. See illustration under ZODIAC. [<L, a virgin]

vir·gu·late (vûr′gyə·lit, -lāt) *adj.* Diminutively virgate; like a small rod. [<L *virgula*. See VIRGULE.]

vir·gule (vûr′gyo͞ol) *n.* A slanting line (/) used to indicate a choice between two alternatives, as in the phrase *and/or*. See SOLIDUS. [<L *virgula*, dim. of *virga* a rod]

vir·i·des·cent (vir′ə·des′ənt) *adj.* Greenish, or becoming slightly green. [<LL *viridescens*, *-entis*, ppr. of *viridescere* become green < *viridis* green] **— vir′i·des′cence** *n.*

vi·rid·i·an (və·rid′ē·ən) *n.* A durable bluish-green pigment consisting of hydrated chromic oxide. [<L *viridis* green]

vi·rid·i·ty (və·rid′ə·tē) *n.* Fresh greenness, as of vegetation; verdure. [<L *viriditas*, *-tatis* greenness, verdure < *viridis* green]

vir·ile (vir′əl) *adj.* **1** Having the characteristics of manhood. **2** Having the vigor or strength of manhood; sturdy, intrepid, and forceful; masculine. **3** Capable of procreation. See synonyms under MASCULINE. [<OF <L *virilis* < *vir* a man]

vir·il·ism (vir′əl·iz′əm) *n.* **1** The appearance in a woman of secondary male sexual and physical characteristics. **2** Female hermaphroditism.

vi·ril·i·ty (və·ril′ə·tē) *n.* *pl.* **·ties** The state, character, or quality of being virile.

vi·rip·o·tent (və·rip′ə·tənt) *adj.* **1** Sexually mature. **2** Nubile. [<LL *viripotens*, *-entis* <L *vir*, *viri* a man + *potens*, *-entis* able, powerful]

virl (vûrl) *n.* *Scot.* A ring around a column; a band; a ferrule.

vi·rol·o·gy (və·rol′ə·jē, vī-) *n.* The study of viruses, especially in their relation to disease. [< *viro-* (<VIRUS) + -LOGY] **— vi·rol′o·gist** *n.*

Vir·ta·nen (vir′tä·nen), **Artturi Ilmari,** 1895–1973, Finnish biochemist.

vir·tu (vər·to͞o′, vûr′to͞o) *n.* **1** Rare, curious, or beautiful quality: generally in the phrase **objects** or **articles of virtu.** **2** A taste for such objects. **3** Such objects collectively. [<Ital. *virtù* <L *virtus*. See VIRTUE.]

vir·tu·al (vûr′cho͞o·əl) *adj.* **1** Being in effect, but not in form or appearance; having potency, validity, or essential qualities: opposed to *apparent* or *nominal*. **2** *Obs.* Potent; effective; energizing. [<Med. L *virtualis* <L *virtus*. See VIRTUE.] **— vir′tu·al′i·ty** (-al′ə·tē) *n.* **— vir′tu·al·ly** *adv.*

virtual focus See under FOCUS.

virtual image See under IMAGE.

vir·tue (vûr′cho͞o) *n.* **1** The disposition to conform to the law of right; moral excellence; rectitude. **2** The practice of moral duties and the abstinence from immorality and vice: a life devoted to *virtue*. **3** Sexual purity; chastity, especially in women. **4** A particular moral excellence, especially one of those considered to be of special importance and classified by Plato as the four **cardinal virtues** (justice, temperance, prudence, and fortitude), to which the Christian scholastic moralists added the three **theological virtues** (faith, hope, and charity or love). The latter are sometimes called the **supernatural** or **Christian virtues** and the former the **natural virtues,** and all seven are opposed to the Seven Deadly Sins. **5** Any admirable quality, merit, or accomplishment: Patience is a *virtue*. **6** Active quality; power; efficacy; especially, medical efficacy; potency. **7** The quality of manliness; strength; valor. **8** *pl.* The fifth of the nine orders of angels in the celestial hierarchy. **— by** (or **in**) **virtue of** By or through the fact, quality, force, or authority of. [<OF *vertu* <L *virtus* strength, bravery < *vir* man]

Synonyms: chastity, duty, excellence, faithfulness, goodness, honesty, honor, integrity, justice, morality, probity, purity, rectitude, righteousness, rightness, truth, uprightness, virtuousness, worth, worthiness. *Virtue* is *goodness* that is victorious through trial, perhaps through temptation and conflict. *Goodness* may be much less than *virtue*, as lacking the strength that comes from trial and conflict, or it may be more than *virtue*, as rising above the possibility of temptation and conflict. *Virtue* is human; we do not predicate it of God. *Morality* is conformity to the moral law in action, whether in matters concerning ourselves or others, whether with or without right principle. *Honesty* and *probity* are used especially of one's relations to his fellow men, *probity* being to *honesty* much what *virtue* is to *goodness*; *probity* is *honesty* tried and proved, especially in those things that are beyond the reach of legal requirement; above the commercial sense, *honesty* may be applied to the highest truthfulness of the soul to and with itself. *Integrity*, in the full sense, is moral wholeness; when used of contracts and dealings, it has reference to inherent character and principle, and denotes more than conventional *honesty*. *Purity* is freedom from all admixture, especially of that which debases. *Duty*, the rendering of what is due to any person or in any relation, is the fulfilment of moral obligation. *Rectitude* and *righteousness* denote conformity to the standard of right; *righteousness* is used especially in the religious sense. *Uprightness* refers especially to conduct. Compare INNOCENCE, JUSTICE, RELIGION. *Antonyms*: evil, vice, viciousness, wrong. See synonyms for SIN.

vir·tu·os·i·ty (vûr′cho͞o·os′ə·tē) *n.* *pl.* **·ties** **1** The state of being a virtuoso; the technical mastery of an art, as music. **2** A taste for the fine arts, especially the taste of a dilettante. **3** Virtuosi collectively.

vir·tu·o·so (vûr′cho͞o·ō′sō) *n.* *pl.* **·si** (-sē) or **·sos** **1** A master of technique, as a skilled musician; one who displays virtuosity. **2** A connoisseur; a collector or lover of curios or works of art. **3** *Obs.* A savant; a scientist; learned person. [<Ital., skilled, learned <LL *virtuosus* full of excellence <L *virtus*. See VIRTUE.]

vir·tu·ous (vûr′cho͞o·əs) *adj.* **1** Characterized by, exhibiting, or having the nature of virtue; morally pure and good; chaste: now said especially of women. **2** Potent; efficacious. **— vir′tu·ous·ly** *adv.* **— vir′tu·ous·ness** *n.*

Synonyms: blameless, chaste, correct, dutiful, equitable, estimable, excellent, exemplary, good, honest, just, pure, right, righteous, upright, worthy. See GOOD, INNOCENT, JUST, MODEST, MORAL, PURE. *Antonyms*: see synonyms for CRIMINAL, SINFUL.

vir·tu·te of·fi·ci·i (vər·to͞o′tē ə·fish′ē·ī, vər·tyo͞o′tē) *Latin* By virtue of office.

vir·u·lence (vir′yə·ləns, vir′ə-) *n.* **1** The quality of being virulent. **2** Extreme bitterness or malignity. **3** The power of bacteria and other micro-organisms to overcome the resistance of the host.

vir·u·lent (vir′yə·lənt, vir′ə-) *adj.* **1** Manifesting or partaking of the nature of virus; exceedingly noxious. **2** Very bitter in enmity. **3** *Med.* Actively poisonous or infective; malignant. **4** Having or exhibiting virulence. See synonyms under BITTER[1], MALICIOUS. [<L *virulentus* full of poison < *virus* a poison] **— vir′u·lent·ly** *adv.*

vi·rus (vī′rəs) *n.* **1** Venom; snake poison. **2** Any virulent substance developed by morbid processes within an animal body, and capable of transmitting a specific disease, as smallpox: when inoculated in an attenuated form it is called a *vaccine*. **3** Any of a class of filter-passing, pathogenic agents, chiefly protein in composition but often reducible to crystalline form, and typically inert except when in contact with certain living cells: also **filtrable virus.** **4** An illness caused by such an agent. **5** Figuratively, a moral taint; a corrupting influence. **6** Bitterness of mind; acrimony; malice. [<L, poison, slime]

vis (vis) *n.* *pl.* **vi·res** (vī′rēz) *Latin* Force; potency.

vi·sa (vē′zə) *n.* **1** An official endorsement, as on a passport, certifying that it has been found correct and that the bearer may proceed. **2** A signature of approval, as by an authorized inspecting officer. **—** *v.t.* **·saed, ·sa·ing** **1** To put a visa on. **2** To give a visa to. Also spelled *visé*. [<F <L, fem. sing. pp. of *videre* see]

vis·age (viz′ij) *n.* The face or look of a person, or of an animal; distinctive aspect. [<OF < *vis* a face <L *visus* a look < *videre* see]

vis·aged (viz′ijd) *adj.* Having a visage of some character indicated.

vis·ard (viz′ərd) See VIZARD.

vis–à–vis (vē′zə·vē′, *Fr.* vē·zà·vē′) *n.* **1** One of two persons or things that face each other, as in dancing. **2** A seat having an S-shaped back so arranged that two persons can sit side by side, but facing in opposite directions. **—** *adj.* & *adv.* Face to face. [<F, face to face]

Vi·sa·yan (vē·sä′yən) *n.* **1** One of the native people of the Philippines, occupying the Visayan Islands and northern Mindanao. **2** The language of these people, belonging to the Indonesian subfamily of Austronesian languages. **—** *adj.* Of or pertaining to the Visayans or their language. Also spelled *Bisayan*.

Vi·sa·yan Islands (vē·sä′yən) A group of the central Philippines, comprising Bohol, Cebu, Leyte, Masbate, Negros, Panay, Samar, Romblon, and the islets adjacent to them; total 23,621 square miles: also *Bisayan Islands*. Also **Vi·sa′yas** (-yəs).

Visayan Sea A part of the Pacific in the central Philippines, bounded by the Visayan Islands.

Vis·by (vēs′bü) A port on western Gotland island, SE Sweden: German *Wisby*.

vis·ca·cha (vis·kä′chə) *n.* **1** A large burrowing rodent (*Lagostomus maximus*) of the South American pampas, related to the chinchilla, with three-toed hind feet. **2** An allied genus (*Lagidium*) of the Andes, resembling the gray squirrel but with large rabbitlike ears. [<Sp. <Quechuan *uiscacha*]

vis·cer·a (vis′ər·ə) *n. pl.* *sing.* **vis·cus** (vis′kəs) **1** *Anat.* The internal organs, especially those of the great cavities of the body, as the stomach, lungs, heart, etc. ◆ Collateral adjective: *splanchnic*. **2** Commonly, the intestines. [<L, pl. of *viscus*, *visceris* an internal organ]

vis·cer·al (vis′ər·əl) *adj.* **1** Pertaining to the viscera. **2** Abdominal.

Visch·er (fish′ər), **Peter,** 1455?–1529, German sculptor.

vis·cid (vis′id) *adj.* Sticky or adhesive; mucilaginous; viscous. See synonyms under ADHESIVE. [<LL *viscidus* <L *viscum* birdlime, mistletoe] **— vis′cid·ly** *adv.* **— vis′cid·ness** *n.*

vis·cid·i·ty (vi·sid′ə·tē) *n.* The quality or state of being viscid.

vis·coi·dal (vis·koid′l) *adj.* Somewhat viscid.

Vis·con·ti (vēs·kôn′tē) A Lombard family which ruled Milan from 1277 to 1447.

vis·cose (vis′kōs) *n.* A thick, honeylike substance produced by the action of caustic soda and carbon disulfide upon cellulose: an important source of rayon. **—** *adj.* **1** Viscous. **2** Of, pertaining to, containing, or made from viscose. [<LL *viscosus* VISCOUS]

viscose rayon Rayon formed from fibers composed of regenerated cotton or wood-pulp cellulose which has been coagulated or solidified from a solution of cellulose xanthate.

vis·co·sim·e·ter (vis′kə·sim′ə·tər) *n.* An apparatus for determining the viscosity of liquids. Also **vis·com·e·ter** (vis·kom′ə·tər). [<VISCOSI(TY) + -METER]

vis·cos·i·ty (vis·kos′ə·tē) *n.* *pl.* **·ties** **1** The state, quality, property, or degree of being viscous. **2** *Physics* That property of fluids by virtue of which they offer resistance to flow or to any change in the arrangement of their molecules. Compare POISE[2].

vis·count (vī′kount) *n.* **1** In England, a title of nobility between earl and baron. **2** In continental Europe, a title next below that of count; also, the son or younger brother of a count. **3** Formerly, a representative

or deputy of a count or earl in the government of a district; specifically, in English use, a sheriff. [<AF *viscounte*, OF *visconte* < *vis-* in place (<L *vice*) + *counte*, *conte* COUNT²]

vis·count·cy (vī′kount·sē) *n. pl.* **·cies** The rank, title, or dignity of a viscount. Also **vis′count·ship**, **vis′count·y.**

vis·count·ess (vī′koun·tis) *n.* The wife of a viscount, or a peeress holding the title in her own right.

vis·cous (vis′kəs) *adj.* **1** Glutinous; semifluid; sticky. **2** Imperfectly fluid, as warm tar. See synonyms under ADHESIVE. [<LL *viscosus* <L *viscum* birdlime, mistletoe] — **vis′cous·ly** *adv.* — **vis′cous·ness** *n.*

vis·cus (vis′kəs) Singular of VISCERA.

vise (vīs) *n.* A clamping device, usually of two jaws made to be closed together with a screw, lever, or the like, for grasping and holding a piece of work. — *v.t.* **vised**, **vis·ing** To hold, force, or squeeze in or as in a vise. ◆ Homophone *vice.* Also spelled *vice.* [<OF *vis* a screw <L *vitis* vine; with ref. to the spiral growth of vine tendrils]

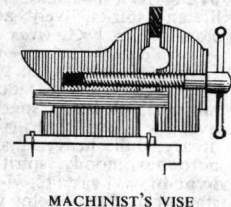
MACHINIST'S VISE
Cross-section.

vi·sé (vē′zā) See VISA.

Vish·nu (vish′nōō) In Hindu theology, the second god of the trinity (Brahma, Vishnu, and Siva), known as "the Preserver"; of his many incarnations the most famous is as Krishna.

vis·i·bil·i·ty (viz′ə·bil′ə·tē) *n. pl.* **·ties** **1** Condition, capability or degree of being seen. **2** *Meteorol.* The condition of the atmosphere as affecting the distance at which objects can be seen and identified. **3** *Physics* The ratio of the luminous flux of a given wavelength to the radiant energy producing it.

VISHNU

vis·i·ble (viz′ə·bəl) *adj.* **1** Perceivable by the eye; capable of being seen. **2** Apparent at sight; evident. **3** At hand; available; manifest. See VISIBLE SUPPLY. **4** Accessible to visitors; prepared or disposed to be seen or visited. **5** Constructed so that certain parts can be seen by the operator: a *visible* typewriter. See synonyms under EVIDENT, MANIFEST. [<OF <L *visibilis* <*visus*, pp. of *videre* see] — **vis′i·ble·ness** *n.* — **vis′i·bly** *adv.*

visible speech Phonetic symbols devised by Alexander Melville Bell to represent every possible utterance of the organs of speech.

visible supply The total of the known available supply of any commodity, as wheat in elevators and in shipment.

Vis·i·goth (viz′ə·goth) *n.* One of the western Goths, a Teutonic people that invaded the Roman Empire in the third and fourth centuries and settled in France and Spain. See OSTROGOTH. [<LL *Visigothus* <Gmc.; ? lit., the western Goths] — **Vis′i·goth′ic** *adj.*

vi·sion (vizh′ən) *n.* **1** The faculty or sense of sight, localized in the eye, which, with its receptors and associated organs, is normally adapted to receive the stimulus of radiant energy within a certain range of wavelengths. **2** That which is or has been seen; also, something or someone beautiful or delightful: She is a *vision* of loveliness. **3** A mental representation of or as of external objects or scenes, as in sleep; an apparition; dream; fantasy; specifically, an inspired revelation. **4** Some product of the fancy or imagination; an imaginary or unreal thing: *visions* of sugarplums. **5** The ability to anticipate and make provision for future events; foresight. **6** Insight; imagination. See synonyms under DREAM. — *v.t.* To see in or as in a vision. [<OF <L *visio, -onis* <*visus*, pp. of *videre* see]

vi·sion·al (vizh′ən·əl) *adj.* Of, pertaining to, or consisting of vision or a vision. — **vi′sion·al·ly** *adv.*

vi·sion·ar·y (vizh′ən·er′ē) *adj.* **1** Not founded on fact; imaginary; impracticable. **2** Affected by fantasies; dreamy; impractical. **3** Associated with apparitions, dreams, etc. See synonyms under FANCIFUL, IDEAL, IMAGINARY, ROMANTIC. — *n. pl.* **·ar·ies** **1** One who has visions. **2** A dreamer; an impractical schemer. — **vi′sion·ar′i·ness** *n.*

vis·it (viz′it) *v.t.* **1** To go or come to see (a person) from friendship, courtesy, on business, etc.; make a call on. **2** To go or come to (a place, etc.), as for transacting business or for touring: to *visit* the Louvre. **3** To be a guest of; stay with temporarily: I *visited* them for several days. **4** To go or come to so as to make official inspection or inquiry: to *visit* a military school. **5** To come upon or afflict. **6** To inflict punishment upon or for. **7** To comfort or bless: The Lord hath *visited* His people. — *v.i.* **8** To make a visit; pay a call or calls. **9** To inflict punishment or vengeance. See synonyms under AVENGE. — *n.* **1** The act of going or coming to see a person or thing, especially with some formality and with the intention of staying some time; a sojourn in a place or with a person; a call or stay. **2** *Colloq.* A talk or friendly chat. **3** An authoritative personal call for inspection and examination or discharge of an official or professional duty. — **right of visit** See RIGHT OF SEARCH. [<OF *visiter* <L *visitare* go to see, freq. of *visare* < *visus*, pp. of *videre* see]

vis·it·a·ble (viz′it·ə·bəl) *adj.* **1** Subject to visitation or punishment. **2** Agreeable to visitors, as a country or region. **3** Having a social position.

vis·i·tant (viz′ə·tənt) *n.* **1** A visitor; that which comes and goes or makes a transient appearance. **2** A migratory animal or bird at a particular region. **3** A visitor as if from another sphere; a supernatural being. — *adj.* Acting as a visitor; paying visits. [<MF <L *visitans, -antis*, ppr. of *visitare* VISIT]

vis·i·ta·tion (viz′ə·tā′shən) *n.* **1** The act or fact of visiting; a visit; also, the state or circumstance of being visited. **2** The visit of a bishop to his diocese; an official or authoritative inspection and examination of a foundation, institution, or establishment to set affairs to rights, correct abuses, enforce laws or rules, etc. **3** In Biblical and religious use, a visit of blessing or affliction: a blessed *visitation* from on high; a dreadful *visitation* of famine. **4** *Obs.* The purpose or object of a visit. **5** The resorting of birds or animals to unusual places. See synonyms under MISFORTUNE. — **vis′i·ta′tion·al** *adj.*

Vis·i·ta·tion (viz′ə·tā′shən) *n.* A religious festival held on July 2 in honor of the visit of the Virgin Mary to Elizabeth. *Luke* i 40.

vis·i·ta·to·ri·al (viz′ə·tə·tôr′ē·əl, -tō′rē-) *adj.* Of or pertaining to visitation; done under an official right of visitation. Also **vis′i·to′·ri·al.**

visiting card A calling card.

vis·i·tor (viz′ə·tər) *n.* One who visits. Also **vis′it·er.**

Vis·la (vēs′lä) The Russian name for the VISTULA.

vis ma·jor (vis mā′jər) *Latin* **1** Irresistible or uncontrollable force; inevitable accident. **2** *Law* An unavoidable accident: in civil law, nearly the same as, but broader than, an act of God.

vis med·i·ca·trix na·tu·rae (vis med′ə·kā′triks nə·choor′ē) *Latin* The curative power of nature.

vi·sor (vī′zər, viz′ər) *n.* **1** A projecting piece on a cap shielding the eyes. **2** In ancient armor, the front piece of a helmet which protected the upper part of the face and could be raised. — *v.t.* To mask; cover with a visor. Also spelled *vizor.* [<AF *viser*, OF *visiere* < *vis* face. See VISAGE.]

vis·ta (vis′tə) *n.* **1** A view or prospect, as along an avenue; an outlook. **2** A mental view embracing a series of events. [<Ital. <L *visus*, pp. of *videre* see]

Vis·tu·la (vis′chōō·lə) The longest river in Poland, flowing 678 miles north from the Carpathian Mountains to the **Vistula Lagoon** (German *Frisches Haff*), a coastal inlet (332 square miles; about 60 miles long, 7 to 11 miles wide) of the Gulf of Danzig: German *Weichsel*, Russian *Visla.*

vis·u·al (vizh′ōō·əl) *adj.* **1** Pertaining to, resulting from, or serving the sense of sight; ocular. **2** Perceptible by sight; visible. **3** Optical: the *visual* focus of a lens. **4** Produced or induced by mental images: a *visual* conception. [<MF <LL *visualis* <L *visus* a sight < *videre* see]

visual field The total area visible to the unmoving eye or eyes at any given moment.

vis·u·al·i·ty (vizh′ōō·al′ə·tē) *n. pl.* **·ties** **1** The quality or condition of being visual; mental visibility. **2** That which is or may be perceived by or as by vision.

vis·u·al·ize (vizh′ōō·əl·īz′) *v.* **·ized**, **·iz·ing** *v.t.* To form a mental image of; picture in the mind. — *v.i.* To form mental images. Also *Brit.* **vis′u·al·ise′.** — **vis′u·al·ism** *n.* — **vis′u·al·i·za′tion** *n.*

vis·u·al·iz·er (vizh′ōō·əl·ī′zər) *n.* **1** One who visualizes. **2** One whose mental images are formed chiefly by visualization: also **vis′u·al·ist** (-ist).

visual purple *Biochem.* A complex reddish-purple protein present in the rods of the vertebrate retina: it is an important factor in the process of vision, especially at night: also called *rhodopsin.*

visual yellow *Biochem.* The pigmented protein into which visual purple is changed by the action of light: heat acts upon it to produce vitamin A: also called *retinene.*

vis vi·tae (vis vī′tē) *Latin* The force of life; vitality. Also **vis vi·ta·lis** (vī·tā′lis).

vi·ta·ceous (vī·tā′shəs) *adj. Bot.* Designating or belonging to a family (*Vitaceae*) of mostly woody and climbing vines, the grape family, having alternate leaves, inconspicuous greenish flowers in clusters, and berrylike fruit. [<NL, family name <L *vitis* a vine]

vi·tal (vīt′l) *adj.* **1** Pertaining to life. **2** Essential to or supporting life. **3** Affecting life; fatal to life: a *vital* error or wound. **4** Necessary to existence or continuance; necessary; essential; life-sustaining. **5** Relating to the facts of life, as births, deaths, etc.: *vital* statistics. [<OF <L *vitalis* <*vita* life] — **vi′tal·ly** *adv.*

vital force A form of energy regarded as acting independently of all physical and chemical forces in the causation of life and in the development of living phenomena. Also **vital principle.**

vi·tal·ism (vīt′l·iz′əm) *n.* **1** The doctrine that life had its origin and support in some principle that is neither material nor organic. **2** *Philos.* A movement represented by Henri Bergson, which upholds the principles of freedom and self-determination and the creative power of the human consciousness. It places intuition above intellect, and considers the universe as living and self-evolving without predestined development or end. Compare BERGSONISM, ÉLAN VITAL. **3** *Biol.* The theory that organic growth is due to forces that operate only in living organisms and differ in kind from the chemical and physical forces at work in the inorganic world: opposed to *mechanism.* — **vi′tal·ist** *n.* — **vi′tal·is′tic** *adj.*

vi·tal·i·ty (vī·tal′ə·tē) *n.* **1** The state of being vital; vital force; the principle of life; animation; life. **2** Power of continuing in force or effect. See synonyms under LIFE.

vi·tal·ize (vīt′l·īz) *v.t.* **·ized**, **·iz·ing** To make vital; endow with life or energy; animate. — **vi′tal·i·za′tion** *n.* — **vi′tal·iz′er** *n.*

vi·tals (vīt′lz) *n. pl.* **1** The parts necessary to life, as the heart and brain: used also figuratively. **2** The parts essential to the health, maintenance, etc., of anything.

vital statistics Quantitative data relating to certain aspects and conditions of human life, especially in relation to large population groups.

vi·ta·mer (vī′tə·mər) *n. Biochem.* Any dietary factor or other substance that possesses the activity of a given vitamin or acts to counteract a vitamin deficiency, as carotenoid in human subjects. [<VITA(MIN) + Gk. *meros* a part]

vi·ta·min (vī′tə·min) *n. Biochem.* Any of a group of complex organic substances found in minute quantities in most natural foodstuffs, and closely associated with the maintenance of normal physiological functions in man and animals. Numerous forms have been isolated and described under special names. Also **vi′ta·mine** (-mēn, -min). [<L *vita* life + AMINE] **— vi′ta·min′ic** *adj.*

vitamin A The fat-soluble vitamin occurring in green and yellow vegetables, dairy products, liver oil, and fish oil: it prevents atrophy of epithelial tissue and protects against night blindness.

vitamin B complex A group of water-soluble vitamins widely distributed in plants and animals, most members of which have special names.

vitamin B_1 Thiamine.

vitamin B_2 Riboflavin.

vitamin B_6 Pyridoxine.

vitamin B_{12} A vitamin extracted from liver and believed to be protective against pernicious anemia.

vitamin C Ascorbic acid.

vitamin D The anti-rachitic vitamin occurring chiefly in fish-liver oils. Many closely related forms are known.

vitamin D_1 An impure mixture of calciferol and lumisterol.

vitamin D_2 Calciferol.

vitamin D_3 A form of vitamin D_2 found principally in fish-liver oils.

vitamin E The anti-sterility vitamin, found in whole grain cereals, seeds of legumes, corn and cottonseed oils, egg yolks, meat, and milk: known to be a mixture of alpha-, beta-, and gamma-tocopherols.

vitamin G Riboflavin.

vitamin H Biotin.

vitamin K_1 A vitamin, found in green leafy vegetables, which promotes the clotting of blood: also called *phylloquinone.*

vitamin K_2 A form of vitamin K_1 prepared from fishmeal.

vi·ta·min·ol·o·gy (vī′tə·min·ol′ə·jē) *n.* The scientific study of vitamins. [<VITAMIN + -(O)LOGY]

vitamin P The factor present in citrus juices along with vitamin C; citrin. It promotes the normal permeability of capillary walls.

vi·ta·scope (vī′tə·skōp) *n.* A device by which pictures taken by the kinetoscope are enlarged and exhibited on a screen. [<L *vita* life + -SCOPE]

Vi·tebsk (vē′tepsk) A city on the Western Dvina river in NE Belorussian S.S.R.

vi·tel·lin (vi·tel′in, vī-) *n. Biochem.* A phosphoprotein occurring in the yolk of eggs. [<VITELL(US) + -IN]

vi·tel·line (vi·tel′in, vī-) *adj.* **1** Of or pertaining to the food yolk of an egg. **2** Of a dull yellow, approaching red; of the color of the yolk of eggs. **—** *n.* The yolk of an egg. [<Med. L *vitellinus* <L *vitellus* VITELLUS]

vi·tel·lus (vi·tel′əs, vī-) *n.* The egg yolk. [<L, orig. dim. of *vitulus* a calf]

vi·tesse (vē·tes′) *n. French* Speed: used especially in the phrases **grande vitesse** (gräṅd), fast express, and **pe·tite vitesse** (pə·tēt′), ordinary express, or freight, etc.

vi·ti·ate (vish′ē·āt) *v.t.* **·at·ed, ·at·ing 1** To impair the use or value of; spoil. **2** To debase or corrupt. **3** To render legally ineffective: Fraud *vitiates* a contract. See synonyms under CORRUPT, DEFILE[1], POLLUTE. [<L *vitiatus*, pp. of *vitiare* < *vitium* a fault] **— vi·ti·a·ble** (vish′ē·ə·bəl) *adj.* **— vi′ti·a′tion** *n.* **— vi′ti·a′tor** *n.*

vi·ti·at·ed (vish′ē·ā′tid) *adj.* Contaminated; rendered defective; invalidated.

vit·i·cul·ture (vit′ə·kul′chər, vī′tə-) *n.* **1** The science and art of grape-growing. **2** The culture of the vine. [<L *vitis* a vine + CULTURE] **— vit′i·cul′tur·al** *adj.* **— vit′i·cul′tur·er, vit′i·cul′·tur·ist** *n.*

Vi·ti Le·vu (vē′tē lā′vōō) The largest of the Fiji Islands; 4,010 square miles; capital, Suva.

vit·i·li·go (vit′ə·lī′gō) *n. Pathol.* A skin disease characterized by a partial privation of color in spots, with a tendency to increase in size; piebald skin; leukoderma. [<L *vitiligo* tetter < *vitium* a fault]

Vi·tim (vi·tēm′, *Russian* vē·tyēm′) A river in NE Buryat-Mongol Autonomous S.S.R., flowing 1,132 miles to the Lena.

Vi·to·ri·a (vē·tôr′ē·ə, *Sp.* bē·tō′ryä) A city in north central Spain, capital of a Basque province.

Vi·tó·ria (vē·tô′ryə) The capital of Espírito Santo state, SE central Brazil; a port on the Altantic coast.

vit·rain (vit′rān) *n.* A variety of bituminous coal having a vitreous appearance and a structure characterized by narrow, compact, crystalline bands. [<L *vitrum* glass, on analogy with *fusain* (def. 2)]

vit·re·ous (vit′rē·əs) *adj.* **1** Pertaining to glass; glassy. **2** Obtained from glass. **3** Resembling glass in some property or properties; vitriform. **4** Pertaining to the vitreous humor. [<L *vitreus* < *vitrum* glass] **— vit′re·os′i·ty** (-os′ə·tē), **vit′re·ous·ness** *n.*

vitreous electricity Electricity generated by rubbing glass with silk: regarded as positive.

vitreous humor *Anat.* The transparent jellylike tissue that fills the ball of the eye and is enclosed by the hyaloid membrane. Also **vitreous body.**

vi·tres·cence (vi·tres′əns) *n.* The state of becoming vitreous.

vi·tres·cent (vi·tres′ənt) *adj.* **1** Capable of being turned into glass. **2** Tending to become glass. [<L *vitrum* glass + -ESCENT]

vi·tres·ci·ble (vi·tres′ə·bəl) *adj.* Capable of forming a viscous, glasslike layer under the action of great heat, as certain crushed minerals. [<VITRESC(ENT) + -IBLE]

vitri- *combining form* Glass; of or pertaining to glass; crystalline: *vitriform.* Also, before vowels, **vitr-.** [<L *vitrum* glass]

vit·ric (vit′rik) *adj.* Pertaining to or like glass.

vit·ri·fac·ture (vit′rə·fak′chər) *n.* The manufacture of vitreous or vitrified wares, as glass. [<VITRI- + (MANU)FACTURE]

vit·ri·fi·ca·tion (vit′rə·fə·kā′shən) *n.* **1** The process of vitrifying. **2** The state of being vitrified. **3** A vitrified object. Also **vit′ri·fac′tion** (-fak′shən).

vit·ri·form (vit′rə·fôrm) *adj.* Having a glassy appearance; glasslike.

vit·ri·fy (vit′rə·fī) *v.t. & v.i.* **·fied, ·fy·ing** To change into glass or a vitreous substance; make or become vitreous. [<MF *vitrifier* <L *vitrum* glass + *facere* make] **— vit′ri·fi′a·ble** *adj.*

vit·rine (vit′rin) *n.* A glass showcase for art objects. [<F < *vitre* glass <L *vitrum*]

vit·ri·ol (vit′rē·ōl, -əl) *n.* **1** *Chem.* **a** Sulfuric acid, originally made from green vitriol: more commonly called **oil of vitriol. b** Any sulfate of a heavy metal, as **green vitriol,** from iron; **blue vitriol,** from copper; **white vitriol,** from zinc. **2** Anything sharp or caustic, as sarcasm. **—** *v.t.* **·oled** or **·olled, ·ol·ing** or **·ol·ling 1** To injure (a person) with vitriol. **2** To subject (anything) to the agency of vitriol. [<OF <Med. L *vitriolum* <L *vitrum* glass; so called because of its glassy appearance]

vit·ri·ol·ic (vit′rē·ol′ik) *adj.* **1** Derived from a vitriol. **2** Corrosive, burning, or caustic.

vit·ri·ol·ize (vit′rē·əl·īz′) *v.t.* **·ized, ·iz·ing 1** To corrode, injure, or burn with sulfuric acid. **2** To convert into or impregnate with vitriol. **— vit′ri·ol·i·za′tion** *n.*

Vi·tru·vi·us (vi·trōō′vē·əs) Roman architect, military engineer, and writer of the first century B.C.; full name, *Marcus Vitruvius Pollio.* **— Vi·tru′vi·an** *adj.*

vit·ta (vit′ə) *n. pl.* **vit·tae** (vit′ē) **1** A fillet or band for the head; specifically, a sacred or sacrificial headband or chaplet worn by brides, vestals, priests, poets, and sacrificial victims. **2** *Bot.* An oil tube; a tube or canal in the fruit of plants of the parsley family, containing an aromatic oil. **3** *Zool.* A band or stripe, as of color. [<L < *viere* plait]

vit·tate (vit′āt) *adj.* **1** Having or bearing vittae or a vitta. **2** Striped.

vit·tles (vit′lz) See VICTUAL.

Vit·to·rio (vit·tô′ryō) Italian form of VICTOR.

Vit·to·rio E·ma·nue·le (vit·tô′ryō ā·mä·nwā′lā) See VICTOR EMMANUEL.

Vit·to·rio Ve·ne·to (vit·tô′ryō ve′nā·tō) A city in NE Italy: scene of an Italian victory and armistice in World War I, November 3, 1918.

vit·u·line (vich′ōō·līn, -lin) *adj.* Pertaining to, of, or like a calf or veal. [<L *vitulinus* < *vitulus* a calf]

vi·tu·per·ate (vī·tōō′pə·rāt, -tyōō′-, vi-) *v.t.* **·at·ed, ·at·ing** To find fault with abusively; rail at; berate; scold. See synonyms under ABUSE. [<L *vituperatus*, pp. of *vituperare* blame, scold < *vitium* a fault + *parare* prepare] **— vi·tu′per·a′tion** *n.* **— vi·tu′per·a′tive** *adj.* **— vi·tu′per·a′tive·ly** *adv.* **— vi·tu′per·a′·tor** *n.*

vi·va (vē′vä) *interj.* Live! Long live!: a shout of applause; an acclamation or salute. [<Ital., 3rd person sing. present subjunctive of *vivere* live <L]

vi·va·ce (vē·vä′chā) *adv. Music* Lively; quickly; briskly. Also **vi·va′ce·men′te** (-mān′tā). [<Ital. <L *vivax.* See VIVACIOUS.]

vi·va·cious (vi·vā′shəs, vī-) *adj.* **1** Full of life and spirits; lively; active. **2** *Obs.* Tenacious of life. [<L *vivax, vivacis* < *vivere* live] **— vi·va′cious·ly** *adv.* **— vi·va′cious·ness** *n.*

Synonyms: animated, brisk, cheerful, frolicsome, gay, jocose, jocund, lively, merry, mirthful, pleasant, sparkling, spirited, sportive. See ALIVE, SPRIGHTLY. *Antonyms*: dead, dreary, dull, heavy, inanimate, lifeless, monotonous, moody, spiritless, stolid, stupid.

vi·vac·i·ty (vi·vas′ə·tē, vī-) *n. pl.* **·ties 1** The state or quality of being vivacious. **2** Sprightliness, as of temper or behavior; liveliness. **3** A vivacious act, expression, etc.

Vi·val·di (vē·väl′dē), **Antonio,** 1675?-1743, Italian violinist and composer.

vi·van·dière (vē·väṅ·dyâr′) *n.* Formerly, a woman who supplied provisions and liquors to troops in the field, as in the French army. [<F, fem. of *vivandier* a sutler, ult. <L *vivenda.* See VIAND.]

vi·var·i·um (vī·vâr′ē·əm) *n. pl.* **·var·i·a** (-vâr′·ē·ə) or **·var·i·ums** A place for keeping or raising live animals, fish, or plants, as a park, pond, aquarium, cage, etc. Also **viv·a·ry** (viv′·ər·ē). [<L, orig. neut. of *vivarius* concerning live things < *vivus* alive < *vivere* live]

vi·va vo·ce (vī′və vō′sē) *Latin* By spoken word; orally: used both as an adverb and adjective.

vive (vēv) *French interj.* Live! Long live!: used in acclamation: opposed to *à bas.*

vive la ré·pu·blique (vēv lȧ rā·pü·blēk′) *French* Long live the republic!

vive le roi (vēv lə rwȧ′) *French* Long live the king!

vi·ver·rine (vī·ver′in, -in, vi-) *adj.* Belonging or pertaining to a family *(Viverridae)* of small carnivores including civets and mongooses. **—** *n.* A civet. [<NL *viverrinus* <L *viverra* a ferret]

vi·vers (vī′vərz) *n. pl. Scot.* Food; provisions.

vives (vīvz) *n. pl.* A morbid enlargement of the submaxillary glands of the horse: also called *fives.* [Earlier *avives* <OF <Sp. *avivas* <Arabic *addhība* < *al* the + *dhība* a she-wolf]

Viv·i·an (viv′ē·ən, *Ger.* vē′vē·än) A personal name. Also **Viv·i·en** (viv′ē·ən, *Fr.* vē·vyaṅ′), *Fr. fem.* **Vi·vienne** (vē·vyen′), *Ital. fem.* **Vi·via·na** (vē·vyä′nä). [<L, lively]

— Vivian In Arthurian romance, the wily mistress of Merlin, who imprisons him by his own magic: also known as *the Lady of the Lake, Nimue.* Also **Vivien, Viviane.**

viv·id (viv′id) *adj.* **1** Having an appearance of vigorous life; intense: said of colors having intense luminosity. **2** Producing or fitted to evoke lifelike imagery or suggestion. **3** Acting or exercised with lively interest; keen; clearly felt; strongly expressed. [<L *vividus* lively < *vivere* live] **— viv′id·ly** *adv.* **— viv′id·ness** *n.*

Synonyms: animated, bright, brilliant, clear, graphic, intense, keen, lively, luminous, quick, sprightly, stirring, telling, vigorous. See GRAPHIC. *Antonyms*: dim, dreary, dull, gloomy, heavy, lifeless, prosy, spiritless, stupid.

viv·i·fy (viv′ə·fī) *v.t.* **·fied, ·fy·ing 1** To give life to; animate; vitalize. **2** To make more vivid or striking. [<OF *vivifier* <LL *vivificare* <L *vivus* alive + *facere* make] **— viv′i·fi·ca′tion** (-fə·kā′shən) *n.* **— viv′i·fi′er** *n.*

vi·vip·a·rous (vī·vip′ər·əs) *adj.* **1** *Zool.* Bringing forth living young, as most mammals: contrasted with *oviparous.* **2** *Bot.* Producing bulbs or seeds that germinate while still attached to the parent plant; proliferous. [<L *viviparus* < *vivus* alive + *parere* bring forth] **— vi·vip′a·rous·ly** *adv.* **— vi·vip′a·rous·ness, viv·i·par·i·ty** (viv′ə·par′ə·tē) *n.*

viv·i·sect (viv′ə·sekt) *v.t.* To dissect or operate upon (a living animal), with a view to exposing its physiological processes. — *v.i.* To practice vivisection. [Back formation <VIVISECTION] — **viv′i·sec′tor** *n.*

viv·i·sec·tion (viv′ə·sek′shən) *n.* **1** The dissection of a living animal. **2** Experimentation on living animals by means of operations designed to promote knowledge of physiological and pathological processes. [<L *vivus* living, alive + *sectio, -onis* a cutting. See SECTION.] — **viv′i·sec′tion·al** *adj.* — **viv′i·sec′tion·ist** *n.* & *adj.*

vix·en (vik′sən) *n.* **1** A turbulent, quarrelsome woman; shrew. **2** A female fox. [ME *fixen* a she–fox, fem. of OE *fox*] — **vix′en·ish** *adj.* — **vix′en·ly** *adj.* & *adv.*

viz·ard (viz′ərd) *n.* A mask; visor: also spelled *visard.* [Alter. of VISOR]

viz·ard·ed (viz′ərd·id) *adj.* Masked; disguised or protected by a vizard.

Viz·ca·ya (vēs·kä′yä, *Sp.* bēth·kä′yä) The Spanish name for BISCAY.

Viz·e·tel·ly (viz′ə·tel′ē), **Frank Horace,** 1864–1938, U. S. lexicographer and encyclopedist born in England.

vi·zier (vi·zir′, viz′yər) *n.* A high official of a Moslem country, especially of the old Turkish Empire; a minister of state. Also **vi·zir′.** — **grand vizier** The highest dignitary in Moslem countries; the prime minister. [<Turkish *vezīr* <Arabic *wazīr* a counselor, orig. a porter < *wazara* carry]

vi·zier·ate (vi·zir′it, -āt, viz′yər·it, -yə·rāt) *n.* The office or dignity of a vizier. Also **vi·zier′·al·ty, vi·zier′ship, vi·zir′ate, vi·zir′ship.**

vi·zor (vī′zər, viz′ər) *n.* The movable upper front piece of a helmet protecting the eyes. See VISOR.

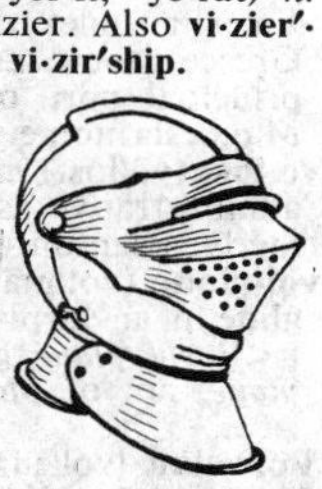

VIZOR 15th century.

Vlad·i·mir (vlad′ə·mir, *Russian* vlä·dyē′mir), 956?–1015, first Christian Russian ruler.

Vlad·i·mir (vlad′ə·mir, *Russian* vlä·dyē′mir) A city in central European Russian S.F.S.R., NE of Moscow.

Vla·di·vos·tok (vlad′ə·vos·tok′, -vos′tok; *Russian* vlä′·dyē·vos·tôk′) A port on the Sea of Japan in extreme SE Asiatic Russian S.F.S.R.

Vla·minck (vlä·mañk′), **Maurice de,** 1876–1958, French painter.

Vlis·sing·en (vlis′ing·ən) The Dutch name for FLUSHING.

Vlo·na (vlō′nä) The Albanian name for VALONA.

Vl·ta·va (vul′tä·vä) A river in central Bohemia, Czechoslovakia, flowing 267 miles north from the Bohemian Forest, through Prague, to the Elbe: German *Moldau.*

V–mail (vē′māl′) *n.* Mail written on special forms, transmitted overseas in World War II on microfilm, and enlarged at point of reception for final delivery. [<V(ICTORY) + MAIL[1]]

vo·ca·ble (vō′kə·bəl) *n.* **1** A word, chiefly as regarded in relation to its sound or combination of sounds instead of its meaning. **2** A vocal sound. — *adj.* Utterable. [<F <L *vocabulum* a name < *vocare* call < *vox* voice]

vo·cab·u·lar·y (vō·kab′yə·ler′ē) *n. pl.* **·lar·ies** **1** A list of words or of words and phrases, especially one arranged in alphabetical order and defined or translated; a lexicon; glossary. **2** All the words of a language. **3** A sum or aggregate of the words used or understood by a particular person, class, etc., or employed in some specialized field of knowledge. **4** The range of expression at a person's disposal, especially in art. [<LL *vocabularius* <L *vocabulum.* See VOCABLE.]

vocabulary entry **1** A word or term given in a vocabulary. **2** A word, term, or phrase entered in a dictionary, in some readily distinguishable type, for purposes of definition or identification. Vocabulary entries may be listed in alphabetical place (main entries), run in within a main entry (additional parts of speech, inflected forms, idioms, etc.), run on at the end of an entry (derivatives and related words), listed under a word, prefix, or combining form (self–explanatory compounds and two–word phrases), or entered in a special section of the book. In this dictionary, all vocabulary entries are shown in boldface type or preceded by a boldface em–dash.

vo·cal (vō′kəl) *adj.* **1** Of or pertaining to the voice; uttered by the voice; oral: *vocal* protests. **2** Having voice; endowed with the power of utterance: *vocal* creatures. **3** Composed for or performed by the voice: a *vocal* score. **4** Concerned in the production of voice: the *vocal* organs. **5** Full of voices or sounds; resounding: The air was *vocal* with their cries. **6** Eloquent without need of speech: the *vocal* beauty of the Parthenon. **7** Freely expressing oneself in speech; readily given to voicing opinions: the *vocal* segment of the populace. **8** *Phonet.* **a** Voiced; sonant, as *b, d, g,* distinguished from *p, t, k.* **b** Pertaining to or like a vowel; vocalic. See synonyms under VERBAL. — *n. Phonet.* **1** A vowel. **2** A voiced consonant. [<L *vocalis* speaking, sounding < *vox, vocis* a voice. Doublet of VOWEL.] — **vo′cal·ly** *adv.*

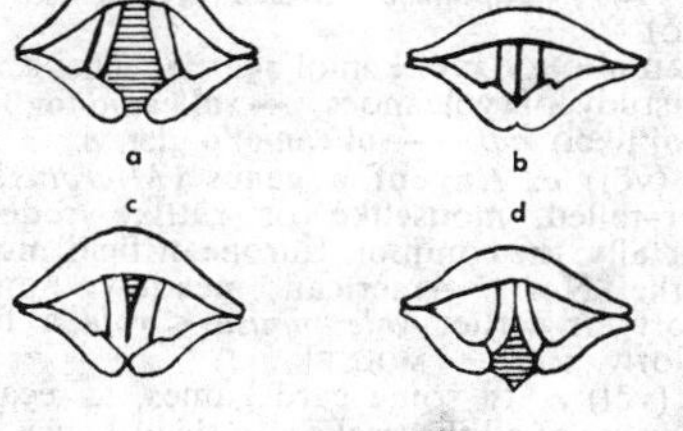

VOCAL CORDS
a. Open. *b.* Closed. *c.* Voice. *d.* Whisper.

vocal cords Two membranous bands extending from the thyroid cartilage of the larynx. The edges of these bands, when drawn tense, are caused to vibrate by the passage of air from the lungs, thereby producing voice; the degree of tension of the cords controls the pitch of the voice.

vo·cal·ic (vō·kal′ik) *adj.* Consisting of, like, or relating to vowel sounds.

vo·ca·lise (vō·kä·lēz′) *n. Music* A practice exercise for singers designed to develop flexibility and control of pitch and tonal beauty, usually employing vowels or Italian syllables. [<F]

vo·cal·ism (vō′kəl·iz′əm) *n.* **1** Vocalization. **2** A vocalic sound; also, a vowel system. **3** Singing; also, the technique of singing.

vo·cal·ist (vō′kəl·ist) *n.* A singer, especially one who has a cultivated voice.

vo·cal·ize (vō′kəl·īz) *v.* **·ized, ·iz·ing** *v.t.* **1** To make vocal; utter, say, or sing; make sonant. **2** To provide a voice for; render articulate. **3** To mark with vowel points, as a Hebrew text. **4** *Phonet.* **a** To change to or use as a vowel: to *vocalize* y. **b** To voice. — *v.i.* **5** To produce sounds with the voice, as in speaking or singing. **6** *Phonet.* To be changed to a vowel. — **vo′cal·i·za′tion** *n.* — **vo′cal·iz′er** *n.*

vo·ca·tion (vō·kā′shən) *n.* **1** A stated or regular occupation; a calling. **2** A call to, or fitness for, a certain career, especially a religious position. **3** The work or profession for which one has a sense of special fitness. See synonyms under BUSINESS. [<L *vocatio, -onis* < *vocatus,* pp. of *vocare* call] — **vo·ca′·tion·al** *adj.* — **vo·ca′tion·al·ly** *adv.*

vocational adviser One who diagnoses the personal characteristics of people with the view of suggesting suitable vocations for them; a specialist in vocational guidance. Also **vocational expert.**

vocational school See under SCHOOL.

voc·a·tive (vok′ə·tiv) *adj.* **1** Pertaining to or used in the act of calling. **2** *Gram.* In some inflected languages, denoting the case of a noun, pronoun, or adjective used in direct address: The name "Brutus" is in the *vocative* case in "Et tu, Brute." — *n. Gram.* **1** The vocative case. **2** A word in this case. [<F, fem. of *vocatif* <L *vocativus* < *vocare* call]

vo·ces (vō′sēz) Plural of VOX.

vo·cif·er·ant (vō·sif′ər·ənt) *adj.* Vociferous; clamorous; uttering loud cries. — *n.* A vociferous person. [<L *vociferans, -antis,* ppr. of *vociferari.* See VOCIFERATE.] — **vo·cif′er·ance** *n.*

vo·cif·er·ate (vō·sif′ə·rāt) *v.t.* & *v.i.* **·at·ed, ·at·ing** To cry out with a loud voice; exclaim noisily; shout; bawl. See synonyms under CALL. [<L *vociferatus,* pp. of *vociferari* cry out < *vox, vocis* a voice + *ferre* carry] — **vo·cif′er·a′tion** *n.* — **vo·cif′er·a′tor** *n.*

vo·cif·er·ous (vō·sif′ər·əs) *adj.* Making a loud outcry; clamorous. See synonyms under NOISY. — **vo·cif′er·ous·ly** *adv.* — **vo·cif′er·ous·ness** *n.*

vod·ka (vod′kə, *Russian* vôd′kä) *n.* A colorless alcoholic liquor, originally made in Poland and Russia, usually made from fermented wheat mash. [<Russian, dim. of *voda* water]

voe (vō) *n. Scot.* A small bay, creek, or inlet.

Vo·gel·kop (vō′gəl·kôp′) A peninsula of NW Netherlands New Guinea, connected to the mainland by an isthmus 20 miles wide; about 225 miles east to west, about 135 miles north to south.

vogue (vōg) *n.* **1** The prevalent way or fashion; popular temporary usage: often preceded by *in.* **2** Popular favor; popularity. [<F, fashion, orig. rowing < *voguer* row <Ital. *vogare* <MHG *wogen* sail < *woge* a wave]

Vo·gul (vō′gŏŏl) *n.* **1** One of a Finno–Ugric people of the Ural Mountains. **2** The Ugric language of these people.

voice (vois) *n.* **1** The sound produced by the vocal organs of a person or animal; also, the quality or character of such sound: a melodious *voice.* **2** The power or faculty of vocal utterance; speech. **3** A sound suggesting vocal utterance or speech: the *voice* of the wind. **4** Opinion or choice expressed; also, the right of expressing a preference or judgment: to have a *voice* in the affair. **5** Instruction; admonition; teaching: the *voice* of nature. **6** A speaker; also, a person or agency by which the thought, wish, or purpose of another is expressed: This journal is the *voice* of the teaching profession. **7** Expression of thought, opinion, feeling, etc.: to give *voice* to one's ideals. **8** *Phonet.* The sound produced by vibration of the vocal cords, as heard in the utterance of vowels and certain consonants, as (g), (m),(v): distinguished from *whisper,* and also from *breath,* as heard in (k), (sh), (f). **9** Musical tone produced by vibration of the vocal cords and resonating in the cavities of the throat and head; also, the ability to sing, or the state of the vocal organs with regard to this ability: to be in poor *voice.* **10** *Gram.* The relation of the action expressed by the verb to the subject, or the form of the verb indicating this relationship. In English, as in most Indo–European languages, a distinction between an *active* and a *passive* voice is made, indicating, respectively, that the subject of the sentence is either performing the action or is being acted upon. (Active: *He wrote the letter.* Passive: *The letter was written by him.*) In Greek and Sanskrit verbs, there is, in addition, a *middle* voice, representing the subject as acting upon himself directly, or in his own interest. **11** *Obs.* Report; rumor; fame. — **with one voice** With one accord; unitedly; unanimously. — *v.t.* **voiced, voic·ing** **1** To put into speech; give expression to; utter. **2** *Music* To regulate the tones of; tune, as the pipes of an organ. **3** *Phonet.* To utter with voice or sonance. [<OF *vois* <L *vox, vocis*]

voiced (voist) *adj.* **1** Having a voice; expressed by voice. **2** *Phonet.* Uttered with vibration of the vocal cords, as (b), (d), (z); sonant: opposed to *surd, voiceless.*

voice·ful (vois′fəl) *adj.* Having vocal quality.

voice·less (vois′lis) *adj.* **1** Having no voice, speech, or suffrage. **2** *Phonet.* Produced without voiced breath, as (p), (t), (s): surd: opposed to *sonant, voiced.* — **voice′less·ly** *adv.*

voice–o·ver (vois′ō′vər) *n.* In motion pictures and television programs, the voice of a narrator or announcer speaking off camera.

voice part A single part, as a melody written for the voice and either sung, or played by a solo instrument, in a concerted composition.

voice·print (vois′print′) *n.* A record of a speech sound, consisting of a complex pattern of wavy lines corresponding to the various pitches used in the utterance.

void (void) *adj.* **1** Not occupied by matter or by visible matter; empty. **2** Destitute; clear or free: with *of*: *void* of reason, *void* of offense.

3 Unoccupied, as a house or room; having no incumbent. 4 Having no legal force or validity; incapable of confirmation or ratification; invalid; null. 5 Producing no effect; useless. See synonyms under VACANT. — *n.* 1 An empty space; a vacuum. 2 A breach of surface or matter; a disconnecting space. 3 Empty condition or feeling; a blank. — *v.t.* 1 To make void or of no effect; annul. 2 To empty or remove (contents); evacuate, as urine. 3 *Archaic* To leave empty or vacant. [<OF *voide,* fem. of *voit,* ult. <LL *vocuus* empty <L *vacuus*] — **void′er** *n.*

void·a·ble (voi′də·bəl) *adj.* 1 Capable of being made void: A *voidable* contract is valid unless annulled. 2 That may be evacuated. — **void′· a·ble·ness** *n.*

void·ance (void′ns) *n.* 1 The act of voiding, evacuating, ejecting, or emptying. 2 The state or condition of being void; vacancy: *voidance* of a benefice. [<AF *voidaunce,* OF *vuidance* < *voider* empty < *voit* VOID]

void·ed (voi′did) *adj.* 1 Made empty or void; cleared of contents; having a vacant space. 2 *Her.* Having the central area removed, so as to leave only an outline through which the field is visible: said of a charge, as a cross.

voi·là (vwà·là′) *interj. French* There! behold! literally, see there.

voi·là tout (vwà·là tōō′) *French* That is all; there is the whole matter.

voile (voil, *Fr.* vwàl) *n.* A fine, sheer cotton, silk, wool, or rayon fabric like heavy veiling: used for summer dresses and curtains. [<F, a veil <OF *veile* VEIL]

voir dire (vwâr dēr′) *Law* A legal oath administered to a witness to be examined, to make true answers to the questions to be asked him regarding his competency. [<OF *voir* truth + *dire* say]

voix (vwä) *n. French* The voice.

voix cé·leste (vwä sā·lest′) *French* An organ stop consisting of two ranks of soft flue stops which produce a waving effect; literally, heavenly voice.

Voj·vo·di·na (voi′vō·di·nä) An autonomous province of NE Yugoslavia, included in Serbia as its northern part and bordering on Hungary and Rumania; 8,683 square miles; capital, Novi Sad. Also **Voy′vo·di·na, Vol′vo·di·na.**

vo·lant (vō′lənt) *adj.* 1 Passing through the air; flying, or able to fly. 2 Characterized by lightness and quickness; nimble. 3 *Her.* Flying, as a bird or bee. [<OF, ppr. of *voler* fly <L *volare*]

vo·lan·te (vō·län′tā) *adj. Music* Swift and light. [<Ital., ppr. of *volare* fly <L]

Vo·la·pük (vō′lə·pük′) *n.* A proposed universal language, invented in 1879 by Johann M. Schleyer, a German priest. [<Volapük *vol* world + *pük* speech] — **Vo′la·pük′ist** *n.*

vo·lar¹ (vō′lər) *adj.* Used in flying; pertaining to flight. [<L *volare* fly]

vo·lar² (vō′lər) *adj.* Pertaining to the sole of the foot or palm of the hand. [<L *vola* sole, palm]

vol·a·tile (vol′ə·til) *adj.* 1 Evaporating rapidly at ordinary temperatures on exposure to the air; capable of being vaporized. 2 Easily influenced; fickle; changeable. 3 Transient; fleeting; ephemeral. 4 *Obs.* Flying, or able to fly. See synonyms under MOBILE¹. [<OF *volatil* <L *volatilis* <*volare* fly]

volatile oil Any oil that may be readily vaporized, especially one distilled from plants: distinguished from *fixed oil.*

volatile salts Salts that volatilize without residue; sal volatile.

vol·a·til·i·ty (vol′ə·til′ə·tē) *n.* 1 The state or quality of being volatile. 2 The property of being freely or rapidly diffused in the atmosphere. Also **vol′a·tile·ness.**

vol·a·til·ize (vol′ə·til·īz′) *v.t. & v.i.* ·ized, ·iz·ing 1 To make or become volatile. 2 To pass off or cause to pass off in vapor; evaporate. — **vol′a·til·iz′a·ble** *adj.* — **vol′a·til·i·za′tion** *n.* — **vol′a·til·iz′er** *n.*

vol-au-vent (vôl·ō·väń′) *n. French* A patty shell of light puff paste filled with a ragout of meat, fowl, or fish.

vol·can·ic (vol·kan′ik) *adj.* 1 Of, pertaining to, or characteristic of a volcano or volcanoes. 2 Produced by a volcano or by igneous action: distinguished from *plutonic.* — **vol·can·ic·i·ty** (vol′kə·nis′ə·tē) *n.* — **vol·can′·i·cal·ly** *adv.*

volcanic glass An igneous rock of volcanic origin and glassy texture having cooled too quickly to crystallize, as obsidian.

volcanic rocks Rocks formed by the consolidation of lava from volcanoes.

vol·can·ism (vol′kən·iz′əm) *n.* The conditions, phenomena, or science of volcanoes or volcanic action.

vol·can·ist (vol′kən·ist) *n.* One who studies, or is expert on volcanoes; a volcanologist.

vol·can·ize (vol′kən·īz) *v.t.* ·ized, ·iz·ing To subject to the action and effects of volcanic heat. — **vol′can·i·za′tion** *n.*

vol·ca·no (vol·kā′nō) *n. pl.* ·noes or ·nos *Geol.* An opening in the earth's surface surrounded by an accumulation of ejected material, forming a hill or mountain, from which heated matter is or has been ejected: known in the former case as *active,* and in the latter as *dormant* or *extinct.* [<Ital. <L *Volcanus, Vulcanus* Vulcan]

Volcano Islands Three small islands, including Iwo Jima, in the western Pacific south of the Bonin Islands, administered by the United States; total, 11 square miles; held by Japan, 1887–1945. *Japanese* **Ka·zan Ret·to** (kä·zän ret·tō).

vol·can·ol·o·gy (vol′kən·ol′ə·jē) *n.* The scientific study of volcanoes. — **vol′can·o·log′i·cal** (-ə·loj′i·kəl) *adj.* — **vol′can·ol′o·gist** *n.*

vole¹ (vōl) *n.* Any of a genus (*Microtus*) of short–tailed, mouselike or ratlike rodents; especially, the common European field mouse or the North American meadow mouse. [Short for earlier *vole mouse* <*vole* a field (<Norw. *voll*) + MOUSE]

vole² (vōl) *n.* In some card games, as écarté, a winning of all the tricks in a deal; hence, the entire range; a slam. — **to go the vole** To risk all for great gains. [<F, appar. <*voler* fly <L *volare*]

vol·er·y (vōl′ər·ē) *n. pl.* ·er·ies A large bird cage; aviary; also, the birds in·it. [<F *volerie* a flying <*voler.* See VOLE².]

Vol·ga The longest river in Europe, in central European Russia, flowing 2,290 miles east and south from the Valdai Hills to its delta, the Volga Basin (approximately 2,500 square miles), on the Caspian Sea.

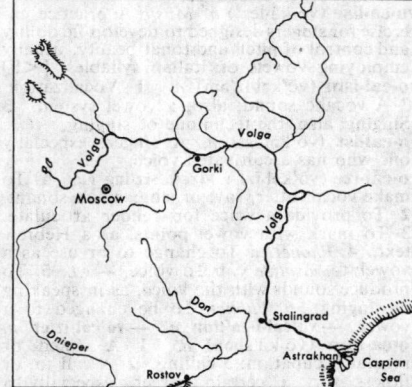

Vol·go·grad 1 A city in southern Russia, on the Volga river, pop. 1,000,000. Formerly **Stalingrad.** 2 A region (oblast) in southern Russia.

Vol·hyn·i·a A historical region, formerly in Poland, in NW Ukraine: about 27,230 square miles. *Russian* **Vo·lyn,** *Polish* **Wo·lyn** — *adj.* **Vol·hyn′· ian.**

vol·i·tant (vol′ə·tənt) *adj.* Flying, or having power to fly; volant. [<L *volitans, -antis,* ppr. of *volitare,* freq. of *volare* fly]

vol·i·ta·tion (vol′ə·tā′shən) *n.* The act or power of flying; flight. [<L *volitatus,* pp. of *volitare.* See VOLITANT.] — **vol′i·ta′tion·al** *adj.*

vo·li·tient (və·lish′ənt) *adj.* Exercising the will, or having freedom of will; willing; voluntary. [<VOLITI(ON) + -ENT] — **vo·li′tien·cy** *n.*

vo·li·tion (və·lish′ən) *n.* 1 The act or faculty of willing; exercise of the will; especially, the termination of a process of deliberation or vacillation of purpose by a decision or choice. 2 The faculty of will by which the powers are directed toward the attainment of a chosen end; willpower. 3 That which is specifically willed or determined upon. [<F <Med. L *volitio, -onis* <L *vol-,* stem of *velle* will] — **vo·li′tion·al** *adj.* — **vo·li′tion·al·ly** *adv.*

vol·i·tive (vol′ə·tiv) *adj.* 1 Of, pertaining to,

or originating in the will. 2 Expressing a wish or permission.

Vol·khov 1 A river of NW European Russia, flowing 140 miles NE from Lake Ilmen, through Novgorod, to Lake Ladoga. 2 A town on the Volkhov river in Russia. Also **Vol′khof.**

Volks·lied (fôlks′lēt′) *n. pl.* **·lied·er** (-lē′dər) *German* A folk song; popular song.

vol·ley (vol′ē) *n.* 1 A simultaneous discharge of many missiles; also, the missiles so discharged. 2 Any discharge of many things at once: a *volley* of oaths. 3 In tennis, a return of the ball before it touches the ground. 4 In soccer, a kick given the ball before its rebound. 5 In cricket, a ball bowled so that it strikes the head of the wicket before it touches the ground. — *v.t. & v.i.* ·leyed, ·ley·ing 1 To discharge or be discharged in a volley; let fly together. 2 In tennis, to return (the ball) without allowing it to touch the ground. 3 In soccer, to kick (the ball) before its rebound; in cricket, to bowl (a ball) full pitch. [<MF *volée,* pp. fem. of *voler* fly <L *volare*]

volley ball A game in which a number of players on both sides of a high net endeavor to keep a large ball in motion with the hands from side to side without letting it drop; also, the ball used. Also **vol·ley·ball** (vol′ē·bôl′).

Vo·log·da 1 A city in northwest Russia: an industrial and dairy center; capital of a 15th century principality 2 A region (oblast) in northwest Russia.

Vo·los (vō′los) A port city on the **Gulf of Volos,** an inlet of the Aegean in SE Thessaly, Greece (about 20 miles long and wide); the principal port of Thessaly and capital of Magnesia nome.

vo·lost (vō′lost) *n.* A district having one joint administrative assembly; a rural soviet; formerly, a canton. [<Russian *volost′*]

vol·plane (vol′plān) *v.i.* ·planed, ·plan·ing To glide in an airplane. — *n.* An airplane glide. [<F *vol plané* gliding flight <*vol* flight + *plané,* pp. of *planer* glide, soar] — **vol′plan·ist** *n.*

Vol·scian (vol′shən) *adj.* Of or pertaining to the **Vol·sci** (vol′sī), a warlike people of ancient Italy, subdued by the Romans about 350 B.C. — *n.* 1 One of the Volsci. 2 Their language, belonging to the Sabellian branch of the Italic languages.

Vol·stead Act (vol′sted) An act to enforce the Eighteenth (Prohibition) Amendment to the Constitution of the United States, and defining intoxicating liquors as those containing more than one half of one percent of alcohol by volume: effective 1920–33. [after Representative Andrew J. *Volstead,* 1860–1947, of Minnesota] — **Vol′stead·ism** *n.*

Vol·sun·ga Sa·ga (vol′sŏong·ä sä′gə) A prose version of the Icelandic legends of the dwarf race, the Nibelungs, and Sigurd, the grandson of Volsung. See NIBELUNGENLIED. [<ON *Völsunga saga,* lit., saga of the Volsungs]

volt¹ (vōlt) *n.* The unit of electromotive force, or that difference of potential which, when steadily applied to a conductor whose resistance is one ohm, will produce a current of one ampere. Abbr. *v., V.* [after Alessandro *Volta*]

volt² (vōlt) *n.* 1 In horse–training, a gait in which the horse moves partially sidewise round a center with the head turned out; a circular tread. 2 In fencing, a sudden leap to avoid a thrust. [<F *volte* a turn <Ital. *volta,* orig. pp. fem. of *volvere* turn <L]

vol·ta (vōl′tə, *Ital.* vôl′tä) *n. pl.* ·te (-tä) *Music* A turning; a time: used mainly in phrases. — **prima volta** First time. — **seconda volta** Second time. — **una volta** Once. [<Ital. See VOLT².]

Vol·ta (vol′tä) The principal river of Ghana, formed by the confluence, in north central Ghana, of the **Black Volta** and **White Volta,** and flowing 300 miles (with Black Volta, about 800 miles) SE to the Bight of Benin.

Vol·ta (vôl′tä), **Count Alessandro,** 1745–1827, Italian physicist and pioneer in electricity.

volt·age (vōl′tij) *n.* Electromotive force expressed in volts: the *voltage* of a current.

vol·ta·ic (vol·tā′ik) *adj.* 1 Pertaining to electricity developed through chemical action or contact; galvanic: a *voltaic* battery; *voltaic* cell. 2 Of or pertaining to Alessandro Volta. [after Alessandro *Volta*]

voltaic battery An assembly of voltaic cells which operate as a unit in generating an electric current.

voltaic cell Cell (def. 5).

voltaic couple A pair of dissimilar, usually metallic, substances which will produce an electric current when immersed in an electrolyte.

voltaic pile An arrangement of dissimilar metal disks, placed alternately and having between them paper moistened with acids for the generation of an electric current. Also *galvanic pile.*

Vol·taire (vol·târ′, *Fr.* vôl·târ′), **François Marie Arouet de,** 1694–1778, French author and philosopher.

vol·ta·ism (vol′tə·iz′əm) *n.* The act of producing an electric current by the chemical action of a liquid on dissimilar metals; galvanism. [after Alessandro *Volta*]

volt·am·e·ter (vol·tam′ə·tər) *n.* A coulometer. [< VOLTA(IC) + -METER]

volt·am·me·ter (vōlt′am′mē′tər) *n.* A wattmeter. [< VOLT(AGE) + AM(PERAGE) + -METER]

volt–am·pere (vōlt′am′pir) *n.* A watt: so called because it is the rate of working in an electric circuit when the current is one ampere and the potential one volt.

volte–face (volt·fäs′, *Fr.* vôlt·fàs′) *n.* **1** A turning about so as to face in the opposite direction. **2** A complete change of attitude or reversal of opinion. [<F <Ital. *volta faccia* < *volta* a turning + *faccia* a face <L *facies*]

vol·ti (vôl′tē) *interj. Music* Turn; specifically, a direction to turn the leaf. [<Ital., imperative sing. of *voltare* turn < *volta.* See VOLT[2].]

vol·ti·geur (vôl·tē·zhœr′) *n.* One who vaults; a tumbler; formerly, in the French army, a skirmisher in a light infantry regiment. [<F < *voltiger* hover, vault <Ital. *volteggiare* < *volta.* See VOLT[2].]

volt·me·ter (vōlt′mē′tər) *n.* An instrument for determining the voltage or potential difference existing between any two points, generally consisting of a calibrated galvanometer wound with a coil of high resistance.

Vol·tur·no (vôl·tōōr′nō) The chief river of southern Italy, arising in the Apennines and flowing 109 miles to the Tyrrhenian Sea NW of Naples.

vol·u·ble (vol′yə·bəl) *adj.* **1** Having a flow of words or fluency in speaking; talkative; garrulous. **2** Turning readily or easily; revolving; apt or formed to roll. **3** Twining, as a plant. [<MF <L *volubilis* easily turned < *volutus,* pp. of *volvere* turn] — **vol′u·bil′i·ty, vol′u·ble·ness** *n.* — **vol′u·bly** *adv.*

vol·ume (vol′yōōm, -yəm) *n.* **1** A collection of sheets of paper bound together; a book; a separately bound part of a work; anciently, a written roll, a scroll, as of papyrus or vellum. **2** Sufficient matter to fill a volume. **3** Something of a swelling form; coil; fold or turn. **4** A large quantity; a considerable amount. **5** Space occupied, as measured by cubic units, that is, cubic centimeters, cubic feet, etc. **6** The amount of space included by the bounding surfaces of a solid. **7** *Music* Fullness or quantity of sound or tone. — **to speak volumes** To be full of meaning; express a great deal. [<OF *volum* <L *volumen* a roll, scroll < *volutus.* See VOLUBLE.]

vol·umed (vol′yōōmd, -yəmd) *adj.* **1** Rounded or swelling in form: *volumed* mists. **2** Having bulk or quantity. **3** Being in one or more volumes: a two–*volumed* history.

vo·lu·me·ter (və·lōō′mə·tər) *n.* An instrument for measuring the volume of a gas by the amount of liquid displaced by it in a graduated vessel, under known conditions of pressure and temperature. [<VOLU(ME) + -METER]

vol·u·met·ric (vol′yə·met′rik) *adj. Chem.* Of or pertaining to measurement of substances by comparison of volumes or by volumetric analysis. Also **vol′u·met′ri·cal.** — **vol′u·met′ri·cal·ly** *adv.* — **vo·lu·me·try** (və·lōō′mə·trē) *n.*◆

volumetric analysis *Chem.* The quantitative analysis of a substance by determining the amount of a standard solution required to effect a reaction in a known quantity of the substance.

vo·lu·mi·nos·i·ty (və·lōō′mə·nos′ə·tē) *n.* The state or quality of being voluminous; especially, copiousness or prolixity.

vo·lu·mi·nous (və·lōō′mə·nəs) *adj.* **1** Consisting of many volumes; capable of filling several volumes; also, of great bulk. **2** Writing or having written much; productive. **3** Having coils, folds, convolutions, or windings. [<LL *voluminosus* <L *volumen, -inis* a roll] — **vo·lu′mi·nous·ly** *adv.* — **vo·lu′mi·nous·ness** *n.*

vol·un·ta·rism (vol′ən·tə·riz′əm) *n.* **1** The theory that will is the ultimate principle or constituent of reality, both in experience and development of the individual, and in the constitution and evolution of the universe. **2** The theory that will is the fundamental psychic factor. Compare VITALISM. — **vol′un·ta·rist** *n.* — **vol′un·ta·ris′tic** *adj.*

vol·un·tar·y (vol′ən·ter′ē) *adj.* **1** Proceeding from the will or from one's own free choice: *voluntary* murder; specifically, unconstrained; intentional; volitional. **2** Endowed with, possessing, or exercising will or free choice: a *voluntary* donor. **3** Effected by choice or volition; acting without constraint. **4** Subject to or directed by the will, as a muscle or movement. **5** Of or relating to voluntaryism. **6** *Law* Unconstrained of will; done without compulsion; performed without legal obligation; also, done without valuable consideration; gratuitous. See synonyms under SPONTANEOUS. — *n. pl.* **·tar·ies** **1** Any work or performance not compelled or imposed by another. **2** *Music* **a** An organ solo, often improvised, played before, during, or after a service. **b** *Rare* A piece of music, usually spontaneous, played or sung as a prelude. **3** *Obs.* A volunteer. [<OF *voluntaire* <L *voluntarius* < *voluntas* will] — **vol′un·tar′i·ly** *adv.* — **vol′un·tar′i·ness** *n.*

vol·un·tar·y·ism (vol′ən·ter′ē·iz′əm) *n.* The principle that religious and educational institutions should be supported by voluntary contributions. — **vol′un·tar′y·ist** *n.*

voluntary system A system of freely given support in distinction from state support of religious or educational institutions.

vol·un·teer (vol′ən·tir′) *n.* **1** One who enters into any service of his own free will. **2** One who voluntarily enters military service, but is then subject to the same regulations and discipline as other soldiers: opposed to *conscript.* **3** *Law* One who takes title under a deed made without valuable consideration; also, a voluntary agent or actor in a transaction. — *adj.* **1** Pertaining to or composed of volunteers; voluntary. **2** Springing up naturally or spontaneously, as from fallen or self–sown seed: a *volunteer* growth. — *v.t.* To offer to give or do. — *v.i.* To enter or offer to enter into some service or undertaking of one's free will; enlist. [< obs. F *voluntaire* <OF, VOLUNTARY]

Volunteers of America A religious and philanthropical organization founded in the United States in 1896 by Commander and Mrs. Ballington Booth, who resigned from the Salvation Army for that purpose.

Volunteer State Nickname of TENNESSEE.

vo·lup·tu·ar·y (və·lup′chōō·er′ē) *adj.* Pertaining to or promoting sensual indulgence and luxurious pleasures. — *n. pl.* **·ar·ies** One addicted to sensual pleasures; a sensualist. [<L *voluptuarius* < *voluptas* pleasure]

vo·lup·tu·ous (və·lup′chōō·əs) *adj.* **1** Belonging to, producing, exciting, or yielding sensuous gratification. **2** Pertaining to or devoted to the enjoyment of pleasures or luxuries; luxurious; sensual. **3** Having a full and beautiful form, as a woman. [<OF *voluptueux* <L *voluptuosus* full of pleasure < *voluptas* pleasure] — **vo·lup′tu·ous·ly** *adv.* — **vo·lup′tu·ous·ness** *n.*

vo·lute (və·lōōt′) *n.* **1** *Archit.* A spiral scroll–like ornament, as in Ionic capitals; a scroll. **2** *Zool.* One of the whorls or turns of a spiral shell. — *adj.* **1** Rolled up; forming spiral curves. **2** Having a spiral form, as a machine part. [<F <L *voluta* a scroll, orig. fem. pp. of *volvere* turn]

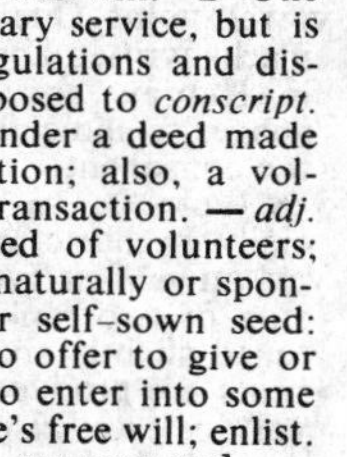

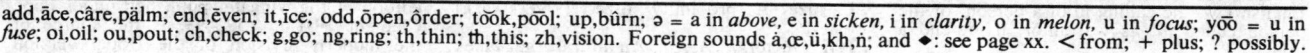

VOLUTE

vo·lut·ed (və·lōō′tid) *adj.* Having a volute or flat spiral scroll.

volute spring *Mech.* A flat metallic spring coiled in a spiral conical form.

vo·lu·tion (və·lōō′shən) *n.* **1** A spiral turn or twist; convolution. **2** A whorl of a spiral shell. **3** A revolving movement.

vol·va (vol′və) *n. Bot.* That part of the sheath enclosing certain young mushrooms which, on being ruptured in the course of growth, forms a cuplike appendage at the base of the stem. [<L < *volvere* wrap, turn]

vol·vu·lus (vol′vyə·ləs) *n. pl.* **·li** (-lī) *Pathol.* Obstruction of the intestines caused by twisting. [<NL <L *volvere* turn]

vo·mer (vō′mər) *n. Anat.* **1** A bone of the face situated between the nasal passages on the median line in vertebrates above fishes. **2** A bone of the roof of the mouth in fishes, behind the premaxillaries. [<NL <L *vomer* a plow] — **vo·mer·ine** (vō′mər·in, vom′ər-) *adj.*

vom·i·ca (vom′i·kə) *n. pl.* **·cae** (-sē) *Pathol.* **1** A collection of purulent matter within an organ. **2** An ulcerous cavity, especially in the lungs. **3** Expectoration of putrid matter. [<L, a boil, ulcer < *vomere* vomit]

vom·it (vom′it) *v.i.* **1** To throw up or eject the contents of the stomach through the mouth. **2** To issue with violence from any hollow place; be ejected. — *v.t.* **3** To throw up or eject from the stomach, as food. **4** To discharge or send forth copiously or forcibly: The volcano *vomited* smoke. — *n.* **1** Matter that is ejected, as from the stomach in vomiting. **2** A sickness which is characterized by vomiting. **3** An emetic. **4** The act of vomiting. [<L *vomitare,* freq. of *vomere* vomit] — **vom′it·er** *n.*

vomiting gas Chlorpicrin.

vom·i·tive (vom′ə·tiv) *adj.* Causing vomiting. — *n.* An emetic.

vom·i·to (vom′ə·tō, *Sp.* vō′mē·tō) *n. Pathol.* Yellow fever; black vomit. Also **vomito ne·gro** (nē′grō, *Sp.* nā′grō). [<Sp. *vómito* <L *vomitus,* pp. of *vomere* vomit]

vom·i·to·ry (vom′ə·tôr′ē, -tō′rē) *adj.* Efficacious in producing vomiting. — *n. pl.* **·ries** **1** An emetic. **2** An opening or vent through which matter is discharged. **3** In a Roman amphitheater, one of the entrances from the encircling arcades to the passages leading to the seats.

vom·i·tu·ri·tion (vom′ə·chōō·rish′ən) *n. Pathol.* **1** Violent vomiting with the ejection of but little matter; retching. **2** Vomiting with but small effort; repeated vomiting. [<F <L *vomitus* a vomiting < *vomere* vomit]

von (von, *Ger.* fôn, *unstressed* fən) *prep. German* Of; from: used in German and Austrian family names as an attribute of nobility, corresponding to the French *de.*

voo·doo (vōō′dōō) *n.* **1** A primitive religion of West African origin, found among Haitian and West Indian Negroes and the Negroes of the southern United States, characterized by belief in sorcery and the use of charms, fetishes, witchcraft, etc. **2** A witch doctor; a Negro conjurer who practices voodoo. **3** A voodoo charm or fetish. — *adj.* Of or pertaining to the beliefs, ceremonies, or practices of voodoo. — *v.t.* To put a spell upon after the manner of a voodoo; bewitch. [<Creole *voudou* <Ewe *vodu*]

voo·doo·ism (vōō′dōō·iz′əm) *n.* **1** The religion of voodoo. **2** Belief in or practice of this religion. — **voo′doo·ist** *n.* — **voo′doo·is′tic** *adj.*

-vora *combining form Zool.* Used to denote orders or genera when classified according to their food: *Carnivora.* An individual member of such an order or genus is denoted by –vore. [<NL <L *-vorus.* See –VOROUS.]

vo·ra·cious (vô·rā′shəs, vō-, və-) *adj.* **1** Eating with greediness; ravenous. **2** Greedy; rapacious. **3** Ready to swallow up or engulf. **4** Insatiable; immoderate. See synonyms under GREEDY. [<L *vorax, -acis* < *vorare* devour] — **vo·ra′cious·ly** *adv.* — **vo·rac·i·ty** (vô·ras′ə·tē, vō-, və-), **vo·ra′cious·ness** *n.*

Vor·arl·berg (fōr′ärl·berkh) An autonomous province of western Austria, bordering on Germany, Switzerland, and Liechtenstein; 1,004 square miles; capital, Bregenz.

Vor·i·ai Spor·a·des (vô′rē·e spô·rä′thes) The Greek name for the NORTHERN SPORADES. See under SPORADES.

vor·la·ge (fōr′lä·gə) *n.* In skiing, a posture in which the body leans forward, beyond the perpendicular to the incline. [<G, lit., a lying

forward <*vorlagern* extend forward <*vor-* forward + *lagern* lie, lay]

Vo·ro·nezh (vo·rô′nesh) A city in SW European Russian S.F.S.R.; a major industrial center.

Vo·ro·shi·lov (vo′ro·shē′lôf), **Klement Efremovich,** 1881–1969, Russian politician; marshall in World War II.

Vo·ro·shi·lov·grad (vo′ro·shē′lôf·grät) See LUGANSK.

-vorous *combining form* Consuming; eating or feeding upon: *omnivorous, carnivorous.* [<L -vorus <*vorare* devour]

vor·tex (vôr′teks) *n. pl.* **·tex·es** or **·ti·ces** (-tə·sēz) **1** A mass of rotating or whirling fluid, especially when sucked spirally toward the center; a whirlpool; an eddy. **2** A portion of fluid whose particles have rotary motion. [<L, var. of *vertex* top, point]

vor·ti·cal (vôr′ti·kəl) *adj.* Of, like, or causing a vortex. [<L *vortex, -icis* a vortex] **—vor′·ti·cal·ly** *adv.*

vor·ti·cose (vôr′tə·kōs) *adj.* Rotating rapidly; whirling; vortical. [<L *vorticosus* <*vortex, -icis* a vortex].

vor·tig·i·nous (vôr·tij′ə·nəs) *adj.* Moving as in a vortex. [<L *vortigo, inis,* var. of *vertigo* a spinning]

Vor·tum·nus (vôr·tum′nəs) See VERTUMNUS.

Vosges Mountains (vōzh) A mountain chain in eastern France; highest peak, 4,672 feet.

Vos·toch·no–Si·bir·sko·ye Mo·re (vos·toch′nô·sē·bir′skô·yə mô′rə) See SIBERIAN SEA, EAST.

vo·ta·ry (vō′tər·ē) *n. pl.* **·ries** **1** One devoted to some particular worship, pursuit, study, etc. **2** A worshiper, as of an idol. Also **vo′ta·rist.** *—adj.* Consecrated by a vow or promise; votive. [<L *votus,* pp. of *vovere* vow] **—vo′ta·ress, vo′tress** *n. fem.*

vote (vōt) *n.* **1** A formal expression of will or opinion in regard to some question submitted for decision, as in electing officers, passing resolutions, etc. **2** That by which such choice is expressed, as a show of hands, or ballot. **3** The result of an election; also, votes in the aggregate: the foreign *vote.* **4** The right to vote. **5** A voter. **6** *Obs.* A wish, vow, or prayer. **—casting vote** A deciding vote given by the chairman of an assembly in cases where the votes of the members tie. *—v.* **vot·ed, vot·ing** *v.t.* **1** To enact or determine by vote. **2** To cast one's vote for: to *vote* a straight ticket. **3** To elect or defeat by vote. **4** *Colloq.* To declare by general agreement: to *vote* a concert a success. *—v.i.* **5** To cast one's vote; express opinion or preference by or as by a vote. **—to vote down** To defeat or suppress by voting against. **—to vote in** To elect. [<L *votum* a vow, wish, orig. pp.neut. of *vovere* vow. Doublet of VOW.] **—vot′er** *n.*

vote-get·ter (vōt′get′ər) *n.* **1** A person with ability to win votes. **2** A campaign slogan, platform, etc., that draws votes. **—vote′-get′ting** *n.* & *adj.*

voting precinct An election district.

vo·tive (vō′tiv) *adj.* Dedicated by a vow; performed in fullfilment of a vow. [<L *votivus* <*votum.* See VOTE.] **—vo′tive·ly** *adv.* **—vo′·tive·ness** *n.*

votive mass A mass not rubrically assigned to a particular day, but said at the choice of the priest.

vouch (vouch) *v.i.* **1** To give one's own assurance or guarantee; bear witness: with *for:* I will *vouch* for their honesty. **2** To serve as assurance or proof: with *for:* The evidence *vouches* for his innocence. *—v.t.* **3** To bear witness to; attest or affirm. **4** To cite as support or justification, as a precedent, authority, etc. **5** To uphold by satisfactory proof or evidence; substantiate. **6** *Law* To call upon or summon (a person) to defend a title. **7** *Obs* To call to witness. *—n.* A declaration that attests; an assertion. [<OF *vocher, voucher* <L *vocare* call <*vox, vocis* a voice]

vouch·ee (vou·chē′) *n. Law* A person who is called into an action to warrant or defend a title.

vouch·er (vou′·chər) *n.* **1** Any material thing (as a writing) that serves to vouch for the truth of something, or attest an alleged act, especially the receipt of money. **2** One who vouches for another; a witness. **3** In early English law, the calling in of a person, or the person called in, as warrantor, to defend a title.

vouch·safe (vouch′·sāf′) *v.* **·safed, ·saf·ing** *v.t.* **1** To grant, as with condescension; permit; deign. **2** *Obs.* To assure or guarantee. *—v.i.* **3** To condescend; deign. [<VOUCH + SAFE] **—vouch′safe′ment** *n.*

vous·soir (vo͞o·swär′) *n. Archit.* A stone in an arch shaped to fit its curve. [<OF *vausoir, volsoir* curvature of a vault, ult. <L *volutus.* See VOLUBLE.]

vow (vou) *n.* **1** A solemn promise to God or to a deity or saint to perform some act or make some gift or sacrifice: generally made in a time of peril or need, and on the condition of the fulfillment of some petition or in return for special divine favor: the *vow* of Jephthah. **2** A solemn engagement to adopt a certain course of life, pursue some end, observe some moral precept, or surrender oneself to a higher life of holiness; also, a pledge of faithfulness: marriage *vows.* **3** A solemn and emphatic affirmation. See synonyms under OATH. **—to take vows** To enter a religious order. *—v.t.* **1** To promise solemnly; especially, to promise to God or to some deity. **2** To declare with assurance or solemnity. **3** To make a solemn promise or threat to do, inflict, etc. *—v.i.* **4** To make a vow. [<AF *vu,* OF *vo, vou* <L *votum.* Doublet of VOTE.] **—vow′er** *n.*

vow·el (vou′əl) *n.* **1** *Phonet.* A voiced speech sound produced by the relatively unimpeded passage of air through the mouth, altering in quality according to the shape of the resonance cavity: distinguished from *consonant.* Vowels may be characterized by the height of the tongue (high, mid, low), the place of articulation (front, central, back), the tension of the tongue muscles (tense, lax), and the presence of lip rounding; as, (ōo) is a high, back, tense, rounded vowel. **2** A letter indicating such a sound, as *a, e, i, o,* or *u.* *—adj.* Of or pertaining to a vowel; vocal. [<OF *vouele* <L *vocalis (littera)* vocal (letter) <*vox, vocis* a voice, sound. Doublet of VOCAL.]

vow·el·ize (vou′əl·īz) *v.t.* **·ized, ·iz·ing** To supply with vowel points or signs: to *vowelize* a Hebrew text. **—vow′el·i·za′tion** *n.*

vowel point One of a system of diacritical marks written above or below the consonants in Hebrew and certain other Semitic languages to indicate the vowel sound following the consonant.

vox (voks) *n. pl.* **vo·ces** (vō′sēz) Voice; especially, in music, a voice part. [<L]

vox an·gel·i·ca (voks an·jel′i·kə) **1** An organ stop of two ranks of pipes, one of which is tuned slightly sharper than the other, so that beats are produced giving a tremulous effect; voix céleste: also **vox cae·les·tis** (si·les′tis). **2** A single-rank stop of soft, sweet quality. [<L, an angelic voice]

vox clan·des·ti·na (voks klan′des·tī′nə) *Latin* A secret voice; a whisper.

vox hu·ma·na (voks hyo͞o·mā′nə) A reed stop with very short pipes useed for clarinet tones in an organ. [<L, a human voice]

vox po·pu·li (voks pop′yə·lī) *Latin* The voice of the people; public sentiment.

voy·age (voi′ij) *n.* **1** A journey by water, especially by sea: commonly used of a somewhat extended journey by water; formerly, any journey: a *voyage* across the sea. **2** A journey in an airship. **3** A book describing a voyage or voyaging: Hakluyt's *Voyages* **4** Any enterprise or project; also, course. See synonyms JOURNEY. *—v.* **·aged, ·ag·ing** *v.i.* To make a voyage: journey by water. *—v.t.* To travel over. [<OF *veiage, voiage* <L *viaticum.* Doublet of VIATICUM.] **—voy′ag·er** *n.*

voy·age·a·ble (voi′ij·ə·bəl) *adj.* Navigable.

vo·ya·geur (vwä·yȧ·zhœr′) *n. pl.* **·geurs** (-zhœr′) *French* An employee of Hudson's Bay Company, engaged in carrying men, supplies, etc., between remote trading posts; also, a Canadian boatman or fur trader.

vo·yeur (vwä·yûr′) *n.* One who is sexually gratified by looking at sexual objects or acts. [<F <*voir* see] **—vo·yeur′ism** *n.*

V-par·ti·cle (vē′pär′ti·kəl) *n. Physics* A hyperon.

vrai·sem·blance (vre·säṅ·bläṅs′) *n. French* A show or appearance of truth; verisimilitude. [<F <*vrai* true + *semblance* appearance]

Vry·burg (frī′bûrg) A town in northern Republic of South Africa.

VT fuze A proximity fuze. [<V(ARIABLE) T(IME)]

VTOL (vē′tôl) *n. Aeron.* An aircraft that takes off and lands vertically.

Vuel·ta A·ba·jo (vwel′tä ä·bä′hō) A region including all Cuba west of Havana.

vug (vug, vo͝og) *n. Mining* An opening in a mineral vein into which crystals often project. Also **vugg, vugh.** [<Cornish *vooga* a cave] **—vug′gy** *adj.*

Vuil·lard (vwē·yȧr′), **Jean Édouard,** 1868–1940, French painter.

Vul·can (vul′kən) In Roman mythology, the god of fire and of metallurgy: identified with the Greek *Hephaestus.*

vul·ca·ni·an (vul·kā′nē·ən) *adj.* **1** Volcanic: also **vul·can·ic** (vul·kan′ik). **2** Of or pertaining to Plutonism; plutonic. [<L *Vulcanius* pertaining to Vulcan <*Vulcanus* Vulcan]

Vul·ca·ni·an (vul·kā′nē·ən) *adj.* **1** Relating to Vulcan or to the art of working in metals. **2** Wrought by Vulcan or by Vulcan's art. Also **Vul·can·ic** (vul·kan′ik).

vul·can·ite (vul′kən·īt) *n.* A dark-colored hard variety of India rubber that has been subjected to vulcanization; also called *hard rubber.* *—adj.* Made of vulcanite. [after *Vulcan*]

vul·can·i·za·tion (vul′kən·ə·zā′shən, -ī·zā′-) *n.* **1** The process of treating crude India rubber with sulfur or sulfur compounds in varying proportions and at different temperatures, thereby increasing its strength and elasticity, yielding either soft rubber or vulcanite. **2** A similar process applied to other substances.

vul·can·ize (vul′kən·īz) *v.t.* & *v.i.* **·ized, ·iz·ing** To subject to or undergo the process of vulcanization. [after *Vulcan*] **—vul′can·iz′·a·ble** *adj.* **—vul′can·iz′er** *n.*

vulcanized fiber A cellulose material made from cotton and linen rags passed through a solution of zinc chloride, or sometimes of sulfuric acid.

vul·can·ol·o·gy (vul′kən·ol′ə·jē) *n.* Volcanology. [<L *Vulcanus* of Vulcan + -(O)LOGY] **—vul′can·o·log′i·cal** (-ə·loj′i·kəl) *adj.* **—vul′can·ol′·o·gist** *n.*

vul·gar (vul′gər) *adj.* **1** Pertaining to the common people; plebeian; general; popular. **2** Pertaining to or characteristic of the people at large, as distinguished from the privileged or educated classes; coarse; boorish; offensive to good taste or sensitive feelings; low. **3** Written in or translated into the common language or dialect; vernacular. *—n. Obs.* **1** The common people. **2** The vernacular tongue. [<L *vulgaris* <*vulgus* the common people] **—vul′gar·ly** *adv.*

Synonyms (adj.): base, broad, coarse, gross, ignoble, inelegant, inferior, loose, low, mean, obscene, obscure, offensive, rude, unauthorized, underbred, vile. See COMMON. *Antonyms:* aristocratic, chaste, choice, cultivated, cultured, dainty, elegant, high-bred, learned, literary, lofty, polite, refined, select, stylish.

vulgar fraction A common fraction.See under FRACTION.

vul·gar·i·an (vul·gâr′ē·ən) *n.* A person of vulgar tastes or manners; especially, a wealthy person with coarse ideas or low standards.

vul·gar·ism (vul′gə·riz′əm) *n.* **1** Vulgarity. **2** A word, phrase, or expression that is in common colloquial or unrefined usage, though not necessarily coarse or gross; distinguished from those in literary or standard usage.

vul·gar·i·ty (vul·gar′ə·tē) *n. pl.* **·ties** **1** The quality or character of being vulgar; low condition in life; commonness. **2** Lack of refinement in conduct or speech, or an instance of it; coarseness. Also **vul′gar·ness.**

vul·gar·ize (vul′gə·rīz) *v.t.* **·ized, ·iz·ing** To make vulgar. Also *Brit.* **vul′gar·ise.** **—vul′gar·i·za′tion** *n.* **—vul′gar·iz′er** *n.*

Vulgar Latin See under LATIN.

vul·gate (vul′gāt) *adj.* Common; popular; usual; generally accepted; in common use. *—n.* **1** The vulgar tongue; colloquial everyday speech. **2** Any commonly accepted text. [<L *vulgatus* common, orig. pp. of *vulgare* make common <*vulgus* the common people]

Vul·gate (vul′gāt) *n.* **1** St. Jerome's Latin version of the Bible, now revised and used as the authorized version by the Roman Catholics. Jerome translated the Gospels into Latin, then the vernacular or vulgar tongue, about A.D. 383, the remaining New Testament somewhat later, and the Old Testament from the Hebrew between 390 and 405. The Sistine edition of the Vulgate, published under Pope Clement VIII in 1592–93, is the source of the modern revision of the Douai version ordered by Pius X in 1908. *—adj.* Belonging

or relating to the Vulgate. [<Med. L *vulgata* (*editio*) the popular (edition), fem. of L *vulgatus* common]

vul·go (vul′gō) *adv. Latin* Commonly; popularly.

vul·ner·a·ble (vul′nər·ə·bəl) *adj.* **1** That may be wounded; capable of receiving injuries. **2** Liable to attack; assailable. **3** In contract bridge, having won one game of a rubber, and hence subject to doubled penalties if contract is not fulfilled. [<LL *vulnerabilis* wounding <L *vulnerare* wound <*vulnus, -eris* a wound] — **vul′ner·a·bil′i·ty, vul′ner·a·ble·ness** *n.* — **vul′·ner·a·bly** *adv.*

vul·ner·ar·y (vul′nə·rer′ē) *adj.* Tending to cure wounds. — *n. pl.* **·ries** A healing application for wounds, as a preparation of medicinal plants. [<L *vulnerarius* <*vulnus, -eris* a wound]

Vul·pec·u·la (vul·pek′yə·lə) A small northern constellation lying between Cygnus and Aquila; the Fox: sometimes called **Vulpecula cum An·se·re** (kum an′sə·rē) (*The Little Fox with the Goose*). See CONSTELLATION. [<L, dim. of *vulpes* a fox]

vul·pec·u·lar (vul·pek′yə·lər) *adj.* Of or pertaining to a fox, especially a young one; vulpine.

vul·pi·cide (vul′pə·sīd) *n.* **1** One who kills a fox otherwise than by hunting. **2** The act of killing a fox when not hunting it with hounds. [<L *vulpes, -is* a fox + -CIDE] — **vul′pi·ci′dal** (-sīd′l) *adj.*

vul·pine (vul′pin, -pīn) *adj.* **1** Pertaining to a fox; resembling foxes. **2** Like a fox; sly; crafty; cunning. [<L *vulpinus* <*vulpes* a fox]

vul·pi·nite (vul′pə·nīt) *n.* A scaly variety of anhydrite from Vulpino, Italy.

vul·ture (vul′chər) *n.*

1 Any of various large birds of prey (family *Cathartidae* or *Vulturidae*) related to the eagles, hawks, and falcons, having the head and neck naked or partly naked, and feeding mostly on carrion; especially, the common **turkey vulture**, or buzzard, and the tropical° American **king vulture** (*Gypagus papa*), strikingly colored, with black wings and tail. **2** Some-

VULTURE
(From 30 to 55 inches;
wingspread from 7 to
11 feet)

thing or someone that preys upon a person in the manner of a vulture. [<AF *vultur*, OF *voltour* <L *vultur, vulturius*] — **vul·tur·ine** (vul′chə·rīn, -chər·in), **vul′tur·ous** *adj.*

vul·va (vul′və) *n. pl.* **·vae** (-vē) *Anat.* The external genital parts of the female, including the labia majora and minora, the clitoris, and the area between the clitoris and the labia minora. [<L, a covering, womb] — **vul′val, vul′var** *adj.* — **vul′vi·form** (-və·fôrm) *adj.*

Vyat·ka (vyät′kə) **1** A former name for KIROV. **2** A river in east central European Russian S.F.S.R., flowing 849 miles north, SW, and SE from the central Ural foothills to the Kama.

Vy·borg (vē′bôrg, *Russian* vī′berk) A port on the Gulf of Finland in NW Russian S.F.S.R. near the Finnish border. Swedish *Viborg*, Finnish *Viipuri*.

Vy·cheg·da (vī′chəg·də) A river in northern European Russian S.F.S.R., flowing 700 miles south and west to the Northern Dvina.

vy·ing (vī′ing) *adj.* That vies or contends. — **vy′ing·ly** *adv.*

Vy·shin·ski (vi·shin′skē), **Andrei**, 1883–1954, U.S.S.R. lawyer and politician: also *Vishinski*.

W

w, W (dub′əl·yoo, -yoo) *n. pl.* **w's, W's** or **ws, Ws** or **doub·le·yous** **1** The 23rd letter of the English alphabet; double u: a ligature of vv or uu. It first came into English writing as a substitution by Norman scribes of the 11th century for the Old English rune *wen*, which later dropped completely out of use. **2** The sound of the letter *w*, a voiced bilabial velar semivowel before vowels (*we, wage, worry*), and a *u*-glide in diphthongs (*how, allow, dew, review*). It is silent before *r* (*wrist, write, wrong*), and is often lost internally (*two, sword, answer*). ◆ The combination *wh-* (in Old English spelled *hw-*) is pronounced in this dictionary as (hw); many educated speakers of English, however, use simple (w) instead, and this pronunciation should be inferred as an acceptable variant in every case. Some speakers normally use still a third sound here, a voiceless allophone of (w) heard also after voiceless consonants, as in *sweet, twin, etc.* See ALPHABET. — *symbol* **1** *Chem.* Tungsten (symbol W, for *wolfram*). **2** *Electr.* Watt.

wa′ (wä) *n. Scot.* Wall.

Waadt (vät) The German name for VAUD.

Waag (väkh) The German name for the VAH.

Waal (väl) The southern branch of the Rhine in the Netherlands, flowing 52 miles west from the Rhine proper to the Maas.

Waals (väls), **Johannes Diderik van der**, 1837–1923, Dutch physicist.

wab (wäb) *n. Scot.* A web.

Wa·bash (wô′bash) A river in western Ohio and north and central western Indiana, forming part of the boundary between Indiana and Illinois and flowing 475 miles NW, west, SW, and south from western Ohio to the Ohio River at the SW corner of Indiana.

wab·ble (wob′əl) *n., v.t. & v.i.* Wobble. [Var. of WOBBLE] — **wab′bler** *n.* — **wab′bly** *adj.*

WAC (wak) *n.* A member of the Women's Army Corps. [<W(OMEN'S) A(RMY) C(ORPS)]

Wace (wäs, wās), 1100?–75, Anglo-Norman poet.

wack·e (wak′ə) *n.* A brown earthy or clayey variety of basaltic rock. [<G <MHG, a large stone <OHG *waggo* a pebble]

wack·y (wak′ē) *adj.* **wack·i·er, wack·i·est** *Slang* Extremely irrational or impractical; erratic; screwy. [Prob. <WHACK; with ref. to the mental impairment caused by repeated blows on the head]

Wa·co (wā′kō) A manufacturing city in central Texas.

wad¹ (wod) *n.* **1** A small compact mass of any soft or flexible substance, especially as used for stuffing, packing, or lining; also, a lump; mass: a *wad* of hair; also, a chew of tobacco, or a portion the right size for chewing. **2** A piece of paper, cloth, or leather used to hold in a charge of powder in a muzzleloading gun; also, a pasteboard or paper disk to hold powder and shot in place in a shotgun shell. **3** Fibrous material for stopping up breaks, leakages, etc.; wadding. **4** *Colloq.* A large amount. **5** *Colloq.* A roll of banknotes; hence, money; wealth. **6** A hydrated oxide of manganese and other metals. — *v.* **wad·ded, wad·ding** *v.t.* **1** To press (fibrous substances, as cotton) into a mass or wad. **2** To roll or fold into a tight wad, as paper. **3** To pack with wadding for protection, as valuables, or to stuff or line with wadding. **4** To place a wad in, as a gun; hold in place with a wad. — *v.i.* **5** To form into a wad. [Cf. Sw. *vadd* a wad] — **wad′dy** *adj.*

wad² (wod) *n. Scot.* A pledge; wager.

wad³ (wod) *v.t. & v.i. Scot.* To wed.

wad⁴ (wäd, wod) *v. Scot.* Would.

Wa·dai (wä·dī′) A former independent sultanate of north central Africa; now part of central and eastern Chad; 94,225 square miles: French *Ouadï*.

wad·ding (wod′ing) *n.* **1** Wads collectively. **2** Any substance, as carded cotton, used as material for wads. **3** The act of applying a wad or wads.

Wad·ding·ton (wod′ing·tən), **Mount** The highest mountain in British Columbia, in the SW part; 13,260 feet.

wad·dle (wod′l) *v.i.* **·dled, ·dling** **1** To walk with short steps, swaying from side to side. **2** To move clumsily; totter. — *n.* The act of waddling; a clumsy rocking walk, like that of a duck. [Freq. of WADE] — **wad′dler** *n.* — **wad′dly** *adj.*

wad·dy (wod′ē) *n. pl.* **·dies** *Austral.* **1** A thick war club used by the aborigines. **2** A walking stick; piece of wood. — *v.t.* **·died, ·dy·ing** To strike with a waddy. [<native Australian pronunciation of *wood*]

wade (wād) *v.* **wad·ed, wad·ing** *v.i.* **1** To walk through water or, by extension, any substance more resistant than air, as mud, sand, etc. **2** To proceed slowly or laboriously: to *wade* through a lengthy book. **3** *Obs.* To go; proceed. — *v.t.* **4** To pass or cross, as a river, by walking on the bottom; walk through; ford. — **to wade in** (or **into**) *Colloq.* To attack or begin energetically or vigorously. — *n.* **1** The

act of wading. **2** A ford. [OE *wadan* go]

wad·er (wā′dər) *n.* **1** One who wades. **2** A long-legged wading bird, as a snipe, plover, or stork. **3** *pl.* High waterproof boots, worn especially by anglers.

wa·di (wä′dē) *n. pl.* **·dies** **1** In Arabia and northern Africa, a river or valley; a ravine containing the bed of a watercourse, usually dry except in the rainy season. **2** An oasis. Also **wa′dy**. [<Arabic *wādī*]

Wa·di Hal·fa (wä′dē häl′fə) A city on the Nile in the northern Sudan near the Egyptian border; the northern gateway to the Sudan.

Wad·jak (wä′jək) A village in central Java.

Wadjak man A hominid (*Homo wadjakensis*), probably of the third interglacial period, and represented solely by two skulls found near Wadjak, Java, in 1891: of larger cranial capacity than earlier types but otherwise controversial because of the crushed condition of the remains and inadequate investigation at the site.

wad·mal (wod′məl) *n. Obs.* A thick, coarse, hairy, durable woolen cloth, used by the poor of northern Europe for garments. Also **wad′maal, wad′mol**. [<ON *vathmál* woolen fabric]

wad·na (wod′nə) *Scot.* Would not.

wad·set (wod′set′) *n.* In Scots law, a pledge, as of land, as security for a debt. — *v.t.* **·set·ted, ·set·ting** In Scots law, to mortgage.

wad·set·ter (wod′set′ər) *n. Scot.* One receiving a wadset.

wae (wā) *n. Scot.* Woe. — **wae′ness** *n.*

wae·ful (wā′fool) *adj. Scot.* Woeful; sad. Also **wae′fu** (-foo).

wae·sucks (wā′suks) *interj. Scot.* Alas! Also **wae′suck**. [<WAE + alter. of SAKE]

WAF (waf, wäf) *n.* A member of the Women in the Air Force. [<W(OMEN IN THE) A(IR) F(ORCE)]

Wafd (woft) *n.* A nationalist party in Egypt founded about 1919. [<Arabic, a deputation] — **Wafd′ist** *n. & adj.*

wa·fer (wā′fər) *n.* **1** A very thin crisp biscuit, cooky, or cracker; also, a small disk of candy. **2** *Eccl.* A small flat disk of unleavened bread stamped with a cross or the letters IHS, and used in the Eucharist in some churches; the sacred host. **3** A thin hardened disk of gelatin, flour, isinglass, or other suitable substance, used for sealing letters, attaching papers, or receiving the impression of a seal. **4** *Med.* **a** A thin double layer of dried paste enclosing a pill or capsule. **b** A suppository. **5** A disk of priming material used in early

artillery. —*v.t.* To attach, seal, or fasten with a wafer. [<AF *wafre* <MLG *wafel.* Akin to WAFFLE.]

waff[1] (waf, wäf) *Scot. & Brit. Dial. v.t. & v.i.* To wave. —*n.* **1** The act of waving. **2** A light ailment. **3** A gust; puff. **4** A glimpse; sight. **5** A spirit or ghost. [Var. of WAVE]

waff[2] (waf, wäf) *Scot. adj.* **1** Low-born; worthless; inferior. **2** Strayed; solitary. —*n.* A tramp; vagrant.

waff·ie (wä'fē) *n. Scot.* A tramp.

waf·fle[1] (wof'əl, wô'fəl) *n.* A batter cake, crisper than a pancake, baked in a waffle iron marked with regular indentations. [< Du. *wafel* a wafer. Akin to WAFER.]

waf·fle[2] (wof'əl, wô'fəl) *v.i.* **·fled, ·fling** *Colloq.* **1** *Chiefly Brit.* To speak or write nonsense. **2** To avoid giving a direct answer. —*n. Chiefly Brit.* Nonsense; twaddle. [<obs. *woff, waff* to yelp]

waffle iron A type of utensil for cooking waffles, consisting of two metal griddles, hinged together, and usually marked with indentations so as to give a large heating surface when closed on each other: now usually made of aluminum and heated electrically.

waft[1] (waft, wäft) *v.t.* **1** To carry or bear gently or lightly over air or water; float. **2** To convey as if on air or water. —*v.i.* **3** To float, as on the wind. —*n.* **1** The act of one who or that which wafts. **2** A breath or current of air; also, a passing odor. [Back formation < *wafter,* in obs. sense, "an escort ship" <Du. *wachter* a guard < *wachten* guard]

waft[2] (waft, wäft) *n.* **1** A signal flag or pennant, sometimes used to indicate the direction of the wind to a ship's helmsman. **2** A signal made with a flag or pennant. —*v.t. Obs.* **1** To signal or beckon to with the hand. **2** To turn; direct, as a glance. [Alter. of dial. E *waff,* var. of WAVE]

waft[3] (waft, wäft) *n. Scot.* Woof; weft.

waft·age (waf'tij, wäf'-) *n.* Conveyance by wafting.

waft·er (waf'tər, wäf'-) *n.* **1** One who or that which wafts. **2** A form of fan or revolving disk used in a blower.

waf·ture (waf'chər, wäf'-) *n.* **1** A wafting or waving motion. **2** Conveyance by wafting. **3** That which is wafted, as an odor.

wag[1] (wag) *v.* **wagged, wag·ging** *v.t.* **1** To cause to move lightly and quickly from side to side or up and down; oscillate; swing: The dog *wags* its tail. **2** To move (the tongue) in talking. —*v.i.* **3** To move lightly and quickly from side to side or up and down. **4** To move busily in animated talk or gossip: said of the tongue. **5** To proceed at a regular pace: Life *wags* on. **6** To waddle. **7** *Brit. Slang* To play truant. —*n.* The act or motion of wagging: a *wag* of the head. [ME *waggen,* prob. <Scand. Cf. Sw. *vagga* rock a cradle. Akin to OE *wagian* oscillate.]

wag[2] (wag) *n.* A droll or humorous fellow; a wit; joker. [Short for obs. *waghalter* <WAG[1] + HALTER[1]]

wage (wāj) *v.t.* **waged, wag·ing** **1** To engage in and maintain vigorously; carry on: to *wage* war. **2** *Obs.* To pledge; put down as security; hence, to wager; bet. **3** *Obs.* To attempt; risk. **4** *Brit. Dial.* To pay a salary to; hire; employ. —*n.* **1** Payment for service rendered, especially the pay of artisans or laborers receiving a fixed sum by the day, week, or month, or for a certain amount of work; hire. **2** *pl.* The remuneration received by labor as distinguished from that received by capital, including the expenses incurred for superintendence and management, called respectively **wages of superintendence** and **wages of management.** **3** Figuratively, produce; yield. **4** *Obs.* A pledge; gage; also, the state of being pledged: to lay one's fortune in *wage.* See synonyms under SALARY. See LIVING WAGE, MINIMUM WAGE. [<AF *wagier,* OF *guagier* pledge < *gage* a pledge. Doublet of GAGE[2].] ◆ The plural of **wage** is sometimes construed as a singular: The *wages* of sin *is* death.

Wage may appear as a combining form in hyphemes or solidemes, or as the first element in two-word phrases:

wage board	**wage floor**
wage ceiling	**wage–freeze**
wage–control	**wage–labor**
wage differential	**wage law**
wage–driver	**wage level**
wage–incentive	**wage–slave**
wage–increase	**wage–slavery**
wage–paying	**wage structure**
wage rate	**wagework**

wage–earn·er (wāj'ûr'nər) *n.* One who works for wages.

wa·ger (wā'jər) *v.t. & v.i.* To stake (something) on an uncertain event; bet. —*n.* **1** An agreement between persons that something, as money, shall be delivered over to one of them on the happening or not happening of an uncertain event; a bet. **2** The thing so pledged. **3** The act of giving a pledge. [<AF *wageure* < *wagier.* See WAGE.] —**wa'ger·er** *n.*

wager of law Anciently, a mode of trial whereby a defendant acquitted himself of a debt by taking his oath that he owed the plaintiff nothing, and having eleven compurgators present to swear that they believed his oath to be true.

wage scale **1** A scale or series of amounts of wages paid for similar duties. **2** The scale of wages paid by a single employer.

wage·worker (wāj'wûr'kər) *n.* An employee receiving wages.

wag·ger·y (wag'ər·ē) *n. pl.* **·ger·ies** **1** Mischievous jocularity; drollery. **2** A jest; joke. See synonyms under WIT[1]. [<WAG[2] + -ERY]

wag·gish (wag'ish) *adj.* **1** Being or acting like a wag. **2** Said or done in waggery. See synonyms under JOCOSE. —**wag'gish·ly** *adv.* —**wag'gish·ness** *n.*

wag·gle (wag'əl) *v.* **·gled, ·gling** *v.t.* To cause to move with rapid to-and-fro motions; wag; swing: The duck *waggles* its tail. —*v.i.* To totter; wobble. —*n.* The act of waggling or wagging. [Freq. of WAG[1]] —**wag'gling·ly** *adv.* —**wag'gly** *adj.*

Wag·ner (väg'nər), **(Wilhelm) Richard,** 1813–83, German composer, poet, and critical writer.

Wag·ner·esque (väg'nə·resk') *adj.* Similar to or suggestive of the works or style of Richard Wagner.

Wag·ne·ri·an (väg·nir'ē·ən) *adj.* Relating to Richard Wagner or to his style, theory, or works. —*n.* One who advocates or accepts the theories of Richard Wagner; also, one who admires his works.

Wag·ner·ism (väg'nə·riz'əm) *n.* The theory of Richard Wagner regarding music drama, as exemplified in the construction and rendition of his own works. Its chief point, especially that in which it differs from the method of the old Italian composers of opera, is its abundant use of the leitmotif for cumulative dramatic effect and its insistence on the equal participation of music, both vocal and orchestral, poetry, scenic effect, and dramatic action, no one of these being subordinate.

Wag·ner–Jau·regg (väg'nər·you'rek), **Julius,** 1857–1940, Austrian neurologist and psychiatrist. Also **Wag'ner von Jau'regg.**

wag·on (wag'ən) *n.* **1** A strong four-wheeled vehicle used to carry heavy loads of freight. Compare DRAY, WAIN. **2** An open four-wheeled vehicle for carrying hay, corn, etc.: a farm *wagon.* **3** A light four-wheeled vehicle used for various business purposes, as a grocer's *wagon.* **4** *Brit.* A railway freight car. **5** A covered four-wheeled vehicle used as living quarters by gipsies, traveling showmen, etc. **6** *Obs.* A chariot. **7** *Colloq.* A patrol wagon. **8** A station wagon. **9** *Slang* An automobile. **10** A child's four-wheeled toy cart. **11** *Astron.* Charles's Wain. **12** A stand on wheels or casters for serving food or drink: a tea *wagon.* —**on the (water) wagon** *Colloq.* Abstaining from alcoholic beverages. —**to fix (someone's) wagon** *Slang* To even scores with; obtain revenge on: I'll *fix your wagon*! —*v.t.* To carry or transport in a wagon. Also *Brit.* **wag'gon.** [<Du. *wagen.* Akin to WAIN.]

wag·on·age (wag'ən·ij) *n.* **1** The amount paid for conveyance in a wagon. **2** Wagons collectively. Also *Brit.* **wag'gon·age.**

wagon bed The body of a wagon.

wag·on·er (wag'ən·ər) *n.* **1** One whose business is driving wagons. **2** *Obs.* A charioteer. Also *Brit.* **wag'gon·er.**

Wag·on·er (wag'ən·ər) **1** Charles's Wain. See under WAIN. **2** The constellation Auriga.

wag·on·ette (wag'ən·et') *n.* A light wagon, with or without a cover, with lengthwise seats facing inward and a crosswise seat in front for the driver. Also **wag'on·et.** [Dim. of WAGON]

wag·on–head·ed (wag'ən·hed'id) *adj. Archit.* Having a semicylindrical head or top, resembling the top of a covered wagon; having a round-arched roof.

wa·gon–lit (vá·gôṅ·lē') *n. pl.* **–lits** (-lē') *French* A sleeping-car on a French railway.

wag·on·load (wag'ən·lōd') *n.* The amount that a wagon can carry.

wagon train **1** A train or line of wagons. **2** A group of wagons and families typical of those which formerly traveled together to settle new regions, especially in the western United States. **3** The equipment of a military force for the carriage of ammunition, provisions, etc.

Wa·gram (vä'gräm) A village NE of Vienna, Austria; scene of Napoleon's victory over the Austrians, 1809.

wag·some (wag'səm) *adj. Rare* Waggish.

wag·tail (wag'tāl') *n.* **1** Any of several small singing birds (genus *Motacilla*), named from their habit of jerking the tail; especially, the **yellow wagtail** (*M. flava*) of Asia and eastern Alaska. **2** Any of certain American birds that wag the tail when walking on the ground, especially the ovenbird and the water thrush.

Wa·ha·bi (wä·hä'bē) *n.* A believer in Wahabiism. Also **Wa·ha'bee, Wah·ha'bi.**

Wa·ha·bi·ism (wä·hä'bē·iz'əm) *n.* A puristically orthodox Moslem sect of Arabia, related to the Sunnites, founded by Abdul-Wahhab; the religion of the ruling family of Saudi Arabia.

wah·con·da (wä·kon'dä) See WAKANDA.

wa·hoo[1] (wä·hōō', wä'hōō) *n.* A deciduous North American shrub or small tree (*Euonymus atropurpureus*) with finely toothed leaves, purple flowers, and scarlet fruit: also called *burningbush.* [<Siouan (Dakota) *wanhu,* lit., arrowwood]

wa·hoo[2] (wä·hōō', wä'hōō) *n.* **1** The American winged elm (*Ulmus alata*). **2** The white basswood (*Tilia heterophylla*). **3** The cascara buckthorn. [<Muskhogean (Creek) *uhawhu* the winged elm]

Wai·chow (wī'jō') A former name for WAIYEUNG.

waif (wāf) *n.* **1** A homeless, neglected wanderer; a stray. **2** *Law* Something stolen and then abandoned by the thief in his flight to avoid arrest. **3** Anything found and unclaimed, the owner being unknown. **4** A nautical signal; a waft. —*v.t.* To throw away; cast off, as a waif. —*adj.* Stray; wandering; homeless. [<AF *waif,* OF *gaif,* prob. <Scand. Cf. ON *veif* something flapping < *veifa* wave.]

Wai·ki·ki (wī'kē·kē, wī'kē·kē') A section of Honolulu; site of a resort beach on Honolulu harbor, SE Oahu, Hawaii.

wail (wāl) *v.t. & v.i.* To grieve with mournful cries; lament; cry out in sorrow. —*n.* A prolonged, high-pitched sound of lamentation; a shrill moan of grief; also, any mournful sound, as of the wind. ◆ Homophone: *wale.* [<ON *vǣla* wail < *vǣ, vei* woe] —**wail'er** *n.*

wail·ful (wāl'fəl) *adj.* **1** Deeply sorrowing; mournful. **2** Making a mournful sound.

Wailing Wall A wall on the western side of the traditional site of Solomon's temple in Jerusalem, reputedly containing fragments of Herod's temple (20 B.C.), a place of prayer, formerly of lamentation, for Jews: also *Western Wall.*

wain (wān) *n.* An open, four-wheeled wagon for hauling heavy loads. —**Charles's Wain** Seven bright stars in Ursa Major; the Dipper: also **the Wain**: sometimes called the *Wagoner.* ◆ Homophone: *wane.* [OE *wægn, wǣn.* Akin to WAGON.]

wain·scot (wān'skət, -skot) *n.* **1** A facing for inner walls, usually of wood, but sometimes of marble or other material: usually paneled and of elaborate workmanship. **2** *Brit.* A superior quality of imported oak used for paneling; also, a piece of such wood. **3** The lower part of an inner wall, when finished with material different from the rest of the wall. —*v.t.* **·scot·ed** or **·scot·ted, ·scot·ing** or **·scot·ting** To face or panel with wainscot. [<MLG *wagenschot* < *wagen* a wagon + *schot* a wooden partition]

wain·scot·ing (wān'skət·ing, -skot-) *n.* Material

for a wainscot; a wainscot; wainscots collectively. Also **wain'scot·ting.**

wain·wright (wān'rīt) *n.* A maker of wagons.

Wain·wright (wān'rīt), **Jonathan,** 1883–1953, U. S. general.

Wai·pa·hu (wī·pä'hōō) A city of southern Oahu, Hawaii, on Pearl Harbor, NW of Honolulu.

wair (wâr) See WARE[3].

waist (wāst) *n.* **1** The narrow part of the body between the chest and the hips. **2** The middle part or section of any object, especially if of less diameter than the ends: the *waist* of a violin. **3** *Naut.* That section of a ship between the quarter-deck and the forecastle. **4** The central section of an airplane. **5** That part of a woman's dress or other garment covering the body from the waistline to the neck or shoulders; a bodice; also, an undergarment for children, to which other garments may be buttoned. **6** A waistband. ◆ Homophone: *waste.* [ME *wast.* Akin to OE *wæstm* growth.]

waist·band (wāst'band', -bənd) *n.* A band encircling the waist, especially a band inside the top of a skirt or the upper part of trousers.

waist·cloth (wāst'klôth', -kloth') See LOINCLOTH.

waist·coat (wāst'kōt', wes'kit) *n.* **1** A man's garment, now commonly sleeveless, buttoning in front and extending just below the waistline; a vest. **2** A similar garment worn by women. **3** A long vest formerly worn with trunk and hose under a slip doublet.

waist·coat·ing (wāst'kō'ting, wes'kit·ing) *n.* A textile fabric specially designed for men's waistcoats.

waist·er (wās'tər) *n. Rare* An apprentice or new hand on a whaling vessel, placed at work in the ship's waist to learn his duties.

waist·ing (wās'ting) *n.* Any material suitable for making waists.

waist·line (wāst'līn') *n.* The line of the waist, between the ribs and the hips; in dressmaking, the line at which the skirt of a dress meets the waist.

wait (wāt) *v.i.* **1** To stay or remain in expectation, as of an anticipated action or event: with *for, until,* etc. **2** To be or remain in readiness. **3** To remain temporarily neglected or undone. **4** To perform duties of personal service or attendance; especially, to act as a waiter or waitress: She *waits* at table. — *v.t.* **5** To stay or remain in expectation of: to *wait* one's turn. **6** *Colloq.* To put off or postpone; defer; delay: Don't *wait* breakfast for me. **7** *Obs.* To attend; escort. **8** *Obs.* To attend as a result or consequence. See synonyms under ABIDE, LINGER. — **to wait on** (or **upon**) **1** To act as a servant or attendant to. **2** To go to see; call upon; visit. **3** To attend as a result or consequence. — **to wait up** To delay going to bed in anticipation of the arrival of someone. — *n.* **1** The act of waiting, or the time spent in waiting; delay. **2** An ambush or trap; snare: to lie in *wait* for a victim. **3** A member of a musical band organized to play and sing in the streets, at night or dawn: now applied only to those who sing carols in the streets at Christmastime. **4** *Obs.* A watchman or guard. [<AF *waitier,* OF *guaitier* <OHG *wahtēn* watch <*wahta* a guard]

wait-a-bit (wāt'ə·bit') *n.* Any one of various plants with sharp or hooked thorns that catch and tear the clothing, and thus detain those who would pass through them, as the greenbrier or the prickly ash. [Trans. of Afrikaans *wacht-een-beetje*]

Waite (wāt), **Morrison Remick,** 1816–88, U.S. jurist; chief justice of the Supreme Court 1874–88.

wait·er (wā'tər) *n.* **1** One who waits upon others, as in a restaurant. **2** One who awaits something. **3** A tray for dishes, etc. **4** *Obs.* A watchman or keeper.

wait·ing (wā'ting) *n.* The act or business of a waiter; attendance. — **in waiting** In attendance, especially at court. — *adj.* That waits; expecting.

waiting list A list of people waiting to be admitted to some institution, as a school or club, or to some privilege or opportunity.

waiting room A room for the use of persons waiting, as for a railroad train, a doctor, dentist, or the like.

wait·ress (wā'tris) *n.* A woman or girl employed to wait on guests at table, as in a restaurant.

waive (wāv) *v.t.* **waived, waiv·ing 1** To give up or relinquish a claim to. **2** To refrain from insisting upon or taking advantage of; forgo. **3** To put off; postpone; delay. **4** *Law* To surrender, abandon, or relinquish voluntarily, either expressly or by implication, as a claim, privilege, or right. **5** *Obs.* To reject; cast off; abandon; desert. ◆ Homophone: *wave.* [<AF *weyver,* OF *gaiver* abandon <AF *weyf, waif* WAIF]

waiv·er (wā'vər) *n. Law* The voluntary relinquishment of a right, privilege, or advantage; also, the instrument which evidences such relinquishment. [<AF, var. of *weyver* abandon. See WAIF.]

Wai·yeung (wī'yüng') A city in eastern Kwangtung province, China; a river port on the Tung, east of Canton: formerly *Waichow.*

wa·kan·da (wä·kän'dä) *n.* Among the Sioux, the great power or supreme being behind the world: identical with Algonquian *manito*: also spelled *wahconda.* [<Siouan]

Wa·ka·ya·ma (wä·kä·yä·mä) A port of southern Honshu island, Japan.

wake[1] (wāk) *v.* **woke** or **waked, waked** (*Dial.* **wok·en**), **wak·ing** *v.i.* **1** To be roused from sleep or slumber. **2** To be or remain awake. **3** To become active or alert after being inactive or dormant. **4** *Dial.* To keep watch or guard at night; especially, to hold a wake (def. 1). **5** *Obs.* To feast or revel late into the night. — *v.t.* **6** To rouse from sleep or slumber; awake. **7** To rouse or stir up; excite: to *wake* evil passions. **8** *Dial.* To keep a vigil over; especially, to hold a wake over. See synonyms under STIR[1]. — *n.* **1** A watch over the body of a dead person through the night, just before the burial, by the relatives and friends: common among the Irish, and often accompanied by conviviality. **2** Formerly, in the Anglican Church, a dedication festival or anniversary celebration of a parish church, preceded by a night vigil in the church. **3** The act of refraining from sleep, especially on a festive or solemn occasion. **4** *Obs.* The act of waking, or the state of being awake; vigil. [Fusion of OE *wacan* awake and *wacian* be awake. Akin to WATCH.]

◆ **awake, awaken, wake, waken** These four verbs, so similar in basic meaning, offer a confusing variety of choices in actual use. In the imperative, *Wake up!* is the familiar and homely form; the other three would be felt as poetic. *Awake* and *wake* have checkered form-histories. In the King James Bible, Shakespeare, and Milton, only the inflected forms in *-ed* are found. But *awake* and *wake* each had a strong verb as well as a weak one in its ancestry, and in the late seventeenth century the alternative inflected forms *awoke, awoken,* and *woke, woken* emerged, reinforced by analogy with *break, broke, broken,* etc. These alternative forms have led to uncertainty and confusion in usage. For the past tense of *awake, awoke* is usual; *awaked* tends to be felt as Biblical. *Awoke* as the past participle is rare, and *awaked* seems awkward to some; what happens in practice is a borrowing of the past participle from *awaken.* For *wake,* the more usual past is *woke* (or *woke up*); *waked* in the intransitive is also standard, but in the transitive sense it is dialectal, referring to holding a vigil or wake: They *waked* old Tim on Thursday night. Real uncertainty arises over the form to choose for the past participle of *wake.* In British (or dialectal American) usage, *woken,* or, for the phrasal verb, *woken up* is used: He had *woken* (or *woken up*) early. American usage here employs *waked (up),* or if this is felt as awkward, particularly in the passive, the past participle is borrowed from *waken* or *awaken*: What *woke* her? She was *awakened* (or *wakened*) by the noise of the crash.

wake[2] (wāk) *n.* **1** The track left by a vessel passing through the water. **2** Any course passed over. — **in the wake of 1** Following close behind. **2** In consequence of. [<ON *vök* an opening in ice]

Wake·field (wāk'fēld) **1** A county borough in southern Yorkshire, England; scene of Lancastrian victory in the Wars of the Roses, 1460. **2** The birthplace of George Washington, an estate in SE Virginia.

wake·ful (wāk'fəl) *adj.* **1** Remaining awake, especially at the ordinary time of sleep; not sleeping or sleepy. **2** Watchful; alert. **3** Unable to sleep; restless; suffering from insomnia. **4** Arousing from or as from sleep. See synonyms under VIGILANT. — **wake'ful·ly** *adv.* — **wake'ful·ness** *n.*

Wake Island (wāk) A U. S. naval and air base, comprising a coral atoll and three islands in the North Pacific, acquired by the United States in 1898; 4 square miles; about 4 1/2 miles long, 2 1/4 miles wide; occupied by Japanese forces, 1941–45.

wake·less (wāk'lis) *adj.* Uninterrupted; unbroken: a *wakeless* sleep.

wak·en (wā'kən) *v.t.* **1** To rouse from sleep; awake. **2** To rouse to alertness or activity. — *v.i.* **3** To cease sleeping; wake up. **4** *Obs.* To keep awake; also, to keep watch. [OE *waecnan, wacnian*]

wak·en·er (wā'kən·ər) *n. Archaic* One who or that which awakens.

wake·rife (wāk'rīf) *adj. Scot.* or *Obs.* Wakeful; alert. — **wake'rife·ness** *n.*

wake·rob·in (wāk'rob'in) *n.* **1** The cuckoo pint. **2** Any species of trillium; the mooseflower. **3** The jack-in-the-pulpit.

wakf (wukf) *n.* In Moslem law, the inalienable dedication of property in trust for the service of God or charitable uses; also, the property so dedicated. [<Arabic *waqf*]

wa·kif (wu'kif) *n.* One who makes a wakf.

wa·ki·ki (wä'ki·kē) *n.* Shell money of the South Sea Islands. [<Melanesian]

Waks·man (waks'mən), **Selman Abraham,** 1888–1973, U.S. microbiologist; discovered streptomycin.

Wa·la·chi·a (wo·lā'kē·ə) See WALLACHIA.

Wał·brzych (vä'ōō·bzhikh) A city in SW Poland, in former Lower Silesia; a coal-mining and manufacturing center. *German* **Wal·den·burg** (väl'dən·bŏŏrkh).

Wal·che·ren (väl'khə·rən) An island at the mouth of the Scheldt river in SW Netherlands; the westernmost island of Zeeland province; 80 square miles.

Wal·deck (väl'dek) An administrative district of Hesse; 420 square miles; formerly a principality of western Germany, a state of the German Republic (1918–29), and a Prussian province (1929–45).

Wal·de·mar (väl'də·mär) Name of four kings of Denmark: also *Valdemar.*
— **Waldemar I,** 1131–82, king 1157–82: called "Waldemar the Great."
— **Waldemar II,** 1170–1241, king 1202–41; greatly extended Danish territory: called "Waldemar the Victorious."

Wal·den·ses (wol·den'sēz) *n. pl.* A sect of religious dissenters founded about 1170 by Peter Waldo or Valdo, a rich merchant of Lyons, France. Waldo and his disciples sought to restore the church to its early purity and poverty, but were excommunicated by Pope Alexander III, and severely persecuted. [<Med. L *Waldenses* of (Peter) *Waldo*] — **Wal·den'si·an** *adj.* & *n.*

wald·grave (wôld'grāv) *n.* **1** An old German title of nobility. **2** Originally, the lord or intendant of a forest. Compare LANDGRAVE, MARGRAVE. [<G *waldgraf* < *wald* a wood + *graf* a count]

Wald·heim (vält'hīm'), **Kurt,** born 1918, Austrian statesman; secretary general of the United Nations 1972–.

Wal·do (wôl'dō), **Peter** Late 12th century French religious reformer: also *Valdo, Valdez.* See WALDENSES.

Wal·dorf salad (wôl'dôrf) A salad made of chopped celery, apples, and walnuts, and garnished with lettuce and mayonnaise. [from the first *Waldorf*-Astoria Hotel, New York City]

Wald·stät·ter, Die Vier (dē fēr vält'shtet'ər) Lucerne, Schwyz, Unterwalden and Uri, the forest cantons of Switzerland: the original cantons of the Swiss federation.

Wald·teu·fel (väl'toi·fəl), **Émile,** 1837–1915, French composer born in Alsace.

add,āce,câre,pälm; end,ēven; it,īce; odd,ōpen,ôrder; tŏŏk,pōōl; up,bûrn; ə = a in *above,* e in *sicken,* i in *clarity,* o in *melon,* u in *focus;* yōō = u in *fuse;* oi,oil; ou,pout; ch,check; g,go; ng,ring; th,thin; th,this; zh,vision. Foreign sounds à,œ,ü,kh,ṅ; and ◆: see page xx. < from; + plus; ? possibly.

wale[1] (wāl) *n.* **1** A stripe or ridge made on living flesh by a rod, whip, or stick; a wheal. **2** *Naut.* One of certain strakes of outer planking running fore and aft on a vessel: the channel *wales.* **3** A ridge or rib on the surface of cloth; hence texture; grain. — *v.t.* **waled, wal·ing 1** To raise wales or stripes on by striking, as with a lash; flog; beat. **2** To manufacture, as cloth, with a ridge or rib. **3** To weave, as wickerwork, with several rods together. **4** To protect, fasten, or hold with wales. ◆ Homophone: *wail.* [OE *walu*]

wale[2] (wāl) *Dial.* & *Scot. n.* A choice or preference of one thing from among others; also, the best; the cream. — *adj.* Well-selected; choice. — *v.t.* **waled, wal·ing** To choose; select; hence, to woo. ◆ Homophone: *wail.* [<ON *val* choice]

wal·er (wā′lər) *n. Anglo-Indian* A horse imported to India from New South Wales, Australia, for cavalry service; also, any horse from Australia.

Wales (wālz) A peninsula of SW Britain, comprising a principality of England, with which it has been politically united since 1536; 8,016 square miles.

Wal·fish Bay (wôl′fish) See WALVIS BAY.

Wal·hal·la (wal·hal′ə, -hä′lä, val-) See VALHALLA.

walk (wôk) *v.i.* **1** To advance on foot in such a manner that one part of a foot is always on the ground; of quadrupeds, to advance in such a manner that two or more feet are always on the ground. **2** To move or go on foot for exercise or amusement. **3** To proceed or advance slowly. **4** To move in a manner suggestive of walking, as a piece of masonry subjected to wind pressure. **5** To act or live in some manner: to *walk* in peace. **6** To return to earth and appear, as a ghost. **7** In baseball, to advance to first base on balls. **8** In basketball, to take more than two steps while holding the ball. **9** *Obs.* To be in continual motion. — *v.t.* **10** To pass through, over, or across at a walk: to *walk* the floor. **11** To cause to go at a walk; lead, ride, or drive at a walk: to *walk* a horse. **12** To force or help to walk. **13** To accompany on a walk. **14** To bring to a specified condition by walking. **15** To measure or survey by traversing on foot: to *walk* a boundary. **16** To cause to move with a motion resembling a walk: to *walk* a trunk on its corners. **17** In baseball, to allow to advance to first base on balls. **18** In basketball, to take more than two steps while holding (the ball). — **to walk off 1** To depart, especially abruptly or without warning. **2** To get rid of (fat, drunkenness, etc.) by walking. — **to walk off with 1** To win. **2** To steal. — **to walk out** *Colloq.* **1** To go out on strike. **2** To keep company: with *with* or *together.* — **to walk out on** *Colloq.* To forsake; desert. — **to walk over 1** In certain sports, to walk over the course without a competitor so as to perform the technicality of winning; hence, to gain an easy victory. **2** To defeat easily; overwhelm. — *n.* **1** The act of walking, as for enjoyment or recreation; a stroll. **2** Manner of walking; gait; specifically, the gait of a horse in which two or more feet are always on the ground. **3** Method or way of living; behavior. **4** Chosen profession or habitual sphere of action: the different *walks* of life. **5** Distance as measured by the time taken by one who walks: It's an hour's *walk* to my house. **6** A place laid out or set apart for walking or resorted to by those who walk; a path, avenue, promenade, or sidewalk for pedestrians. **7** A ropewalk. **8** The formation of, or space between, two lines or rows of plants or trees, as in a coffee plantation. **9** A piece of ground set apart for the feeding and exercise of domestic animals; range; pasture: a *sheepwalk.* **10** A hawker's or vender's district or route; a beat. **11** A contest of speed in walking. **12** In baseball slang, a base on balls. [OE *wealcan* roll, toss] — **walk′ing** *adj.* & *n.*

walk·a·bout (wôk′ə·bout′) *n. Austral.* A wandering, apparently aimless journey over long distances. — **to go walkabout** To wander.

walk–a·round (wôk′ə·round′) *n.* **1** A rhythmic Negro dance performed by a group walking around in a large circle; also, the music composed for this dance. **2** A dance of this kind performed on the stage; also, the music for it.

walk–a·way (wôk′ə·wā′) *n.* A contest won without serious opposition.

walk·er (wôk′ər) *n.* **1** One who or that which walks. **2** A shoe used for walking.

Walk·er (wô′kər), **John,** 1732–1807, English lexicographer and actor. — **William,** 1824–60, U. S. filibuster in Lower California and Nicaragua.

walk·ie–talk·ie (wô′kē·tô′kē) *n. Telecom.* A portable radio set, equipped for both sending and receiving, and light enough to be carried by one man. Also spelled *walky-talky.*

walking bass An insistently reiterated bass figure, usually in eighth notes, used in boogie-woogie music.

WALKING BEAM

walking beam *Mech.* In a vertical engine, a horizontal beam that transmits power to the crankshaft through the connecting rod.

walking delegate See under DELEGATE.

walking fern A tufted evergreen fern (*Camptosorus rhizophyllus*) with fronds ending in long tapering tips which take root and thus give rise to new plants. Also **walking leaf.**

walking papers Notice of dismissal from employment, office, position, etc.

walking stick 1 A staff or cane carried in the hand. **2** Any of a family (*Phasmidae*) of insects having legs, body, and wings resembling one of the twigs among which it lives.

walk–on (wôk′on′, -ôn′) *n.* An actor who plays a bit part or merely walks on the stage; also, the part.

walk–out (wôk′out′) *n. Colloq.* **1** The act of walking out. **2** A workmen's strike.

walk–o·ver (wôk′ō′vər) *n.* **1** A horse race in which there is only one horse entered, and which can thus be won by going over the course at a mere walk. **2** An easy or unopposed success.

walk–up (wôk′up′) *Colloq. n.* An apartment house having no elevator. — *adj.* Having no elevator.

Wal·kü·re (väl·kü′rə), **Die** *German* The second music drama in Richard Wagner's tetralogy, *Der Ring des Nibelungen.* See RING OF THE NIBELUNG, VALKYRIE.

walk·way (wôk′wā′) *n.* A sidewalk; a passage; a garden path.

wal·kyr·ie (wal·kir′ē, val-) *n.* A valkyrie. [OE *wælcyrie,* lit., a chooser of the slain]

walk·y–talk·y (wô′kē·tô′kē) See WALKIE-TALKIE.

wall (wôl) *n.* **1** A continuous structure, as of stone or brick, designed to enclose an area, to provide defense or security, or to be the surrounding exterior of a house or a partition between rooms or halls; also, a fence of stone or brickwork, surrounding or separating yards, fields, etc. ◆ Collateral adjective: *mural.* **2** A barrier or rampart constructed for defense; in the plural, fortifications. **3** A sea wall; levee. **4** The side of any cavity, vessel, or receptacle; a parietal surface: the *walls* of the abdomen. **5** Something suggestive of a wall or barrier: a *wall* of bayonets. See synonyms under RAMPART. — **to drive, push,** or **thrust to the wall** To force (one) to an extremity; crush. — **to go to the wall** To be pressed or driven to an extremity; be forced to yield. — **to take the wall** To take the inner side of the walk; hence, to take a rude advantage. — *v.t.* **1** To provide, surround, protect, etc., with or as with a wall or walls. **2** To fill or block with a wall: often with *up.* — *adj.* Of or pertaining to a wall; hanging or growing on a wall [OE *weall, wall* <L *vallum* a rampart < *vallus* a stake, palisade]

Wall may appear as the first element in two-word phrases:

wall arcade	**wall bracket**	**wall crane**
wall arch	**wall case**	**wall engine**
wall berry	**wall casing**	**wall face**
wall border	**wall clock**	**wall garden**
wall box	**wall coping**	**wall map**
wall mosaic	**wall plant**	**wall tower**
wall moss	**wall plug**	**wall tree**
wall nook	**wall top**	**wall vase**

wal·la·by (wol′ə·bē) *n. pl.* **·bies** Any of various medium-sized to small kangaroos of Australia and New Guinea, ranging from the **rock wallaby** (genus *Petrogale*), to the **pademelon wallaby,** about the size of a rabbit. [<Australian *wolaba*]

Wal·lace (wol′is), **Alfred Russel,** 1823–1913, English naturalist. — **(Richard Horatio) Edgar,** 1875–1932, English novelist. — **Henry Agard,** 1888–1965, U.S. vice president 1941–1944; agriculturist, editor, and politician. — **Lewis,** 1827–1905, U. S. general, administrator, and author: known as *Lew Wallace.* — **Sir William,** 1272?–1305, Scottish national hero; executed by the English.

Wal·lach (väl′äkh), **Otto,** 1847–1931, German chemist.

Wal·la·chi·a (wo·lā′kē·ə) A historic region and former principality in southern and SE Rumania; 29,575 square miles; chief city, Bucharest: also *Walachia.* — **Wal·la′chi·an** *adj.* & *n.*

wal·lah (wä′lä) *n. Anglo-Indian* A person engaged in a specified occupation or activity, as a merchant, vender, agent, worker, or servant; popularly and somewhat contemptuously, a man or fellow. Also **wal′la.** — **punka-wallah** The servant whose job it is to keep the punka in motion. [<Hind. *-vālā,* suffix indicating a personal agent]

wal·la·roo (wol′ə·rōō′) *n.* A species of large kangaroo (*Macropus robustus*). Also **wallaroo kangaroo.** [<Australian *wolarū*]

Wal·la·sey (wol′ə·sē) A county borough in NW Cheshire, England, on the Mersey river opposite, and forming part of the port of, Liverpool.

Wal·la·wal·la (wol′ə·wol′ə) *n.* One of a small tribe of North American Indians of Shahaptian linguistic stock of the NW Pacific coast: now on a reservation in Oregon.

Wal·la Wal·la (wol′ə wol′ə) A city in SE Washington near the Oregon border on the Walla Walla River.

Walla Walla River A river in NE Oregon and SW Washington, flowing 60 miles NW to the Columbia River.

wall·board (wôl′bôrd′, -bōrd′) *n.* A material composed of several layers of compressed wood chips and pulp, molded and sized for use as a substitute for wooden boards and plaster.

wall·creep·er (wôl′krē′pər) *n.* A small, brilliantly colored Old World bird (*Tichodroma muraria*) that obtains its insect prey by creeping on cliffs and walls.

Wal·len·stein (wol′ən·stīn, *Ger.* vol′ən·shtīn), **Albrecht Wenzel Eusebius von,** 1583–1634, Duke of Friedland; Austrian general in the Thirty Years' War.

Wal·ler (wol′ər), **Edmund,** 1606–87, English poet.

wal·let (wol′it) *n.* **1** A pocketbook, usually of leather, for holding unfolded banknotes, personal papers, etc.; a billfold. **2** A leather or canvas bag for tools, etc. **3** A knapsack. **4** *Obs.* Any baggy protuberance hanging loosely. [ME *walet,* ? metathetic var. of *watel* a bag, basket <OE *watul* a wattle]

wall·eye (wôl′ī′) *n.* **1** An eye in which the iris is light-colored or white. **2** An eye in which the cornea is opaque and whitish; also, leukoma of the cornea. **3** A large staring eye, usually one showing much white, because of divergent strabismus. **4** Any of several walleyed fishes, as the walleyed pike or perch, the alewife, or the walleyed pollack. [Back formation <WALLEYED]

wall·eyed (wôl′īd′) *adj.* **1** Affected with divergent strabismus. **2** Having a whitish or grayish eye; also, affected with leukoma of the cornea. **3** Squinting. **4** Having large, staring eyes, as a fish. **5** *Slang* Drunk. [<ON *valdeygthr,* alter. of *vagl eygr* <*vagl* a film on the eye + *eygr* having eyes < *auga* eye]

walleyed pike An American fresh-water percoid fish (genus *Stizostedion*) of the Great Lakes, having large eyes, esteemed as a game fish. Also **walleyed perch.**

walleyed pollack A coal-black North American pollack (*Pollachius fucensis*) of Pacific waters.

walleyed surf fish A sooty fish (*Hyperprosopon argenteus*) common in California waters.

wall fern The common polypody.

wall·flow·er (wôl′flou′ər) *n.* **1** Any of a genus (*Cheiranthus*) of European herbs of the mustard family, in particular the popular garden perennial *C. cheiri*, having fragrant yellow, orange, or red flowers. **2** An Australian desert shrub (genus *Gastrolobium*). **3** *Colloq.* A man or woman at a party who remains sitting or standing for want of a dancing partner.

WALL-FLOWER (Varies from 1 to 3 feet high)

wall fruit Fruit grown and ripened close to a wall or fence.

wal·lie (wol′ē) *n. Scot.* A valet.

Wal·lis and Fu·tu·na Islands (wol′is, foō·tōō′nə) Two closely connected protectorates NE of Fiji Islands, both dependencies of New Caledonia, including the chief islands of Uvéa, Futuna, and Alofi; total, 75 square miles.

wall lizard A gecko.

Wal·lo·ni·an (wo·lō′nē·ən) *adj.* Of or pertaining to the Walloons or the dialect spoken by them. — *n.* **1** A Walloon. **2** The French dialect of the Walloons.

Wal·loon (wo·loōn′) *n.* **1** One of a people inhabiting southern and southeastern Belgium and the adjoining regions of France, originally descended from the ancient Belgae. **2** Their language, a dialect of French. **3** One of the Huguenot colonists who came to the United States from Artois, France. — *adj.* Of or pertaining to the Walloons or their dialect.

wal·lop (wol′əp) *v.t. Colloq.* **1** To beat soundly; thrash. **2** To hit with a hard blow. **3** To defeat soundly. — *v.i. Dial.* or *Colloq.* **4** To move quickly and strenuously; gallop. **5** To move in an awkward, floundering manner; waddle. — *n.* **1** *Brit. Dial. & Scot.* A lively rolling motion; a gallop. **2** *Colloq.* A severe blow. [<AF *waloper*, OF *galoper*. Doublet of GALLOP.]

wal·lop·er (wol′əp·ər) *n. Colloq.* **1** One who wallops. **2** Something astounding or amazing; an extraordinary statement or act; a whopper.

wal·lop·ing (wol′əp·ing) *Colloq. adj.* Extraordinarily large; whopping: a *walloping* lie. — *n.* A beating; whipping.

wal·low (wol′ō) *v.i.* **1** To roll about, as in mud, snow, etc.; flounder: The hippopotamus *wallows* in the mud. **2** To move with a heavy, rolling motion, as a ship in a storm. **3** To live or indulge complacently or wantonly: to *wallow* in sensuality or wealth. — *n.* **1** The act of wallowing. **2** A pool, mudhole, or slough in which animals wallow; also, any depression or hollow made by or suggesting such use. [OE *wealwian*] — **wal′low·er** *n.*

wall·pa·per (wôl′pā′pər) *n.* Paper specially prepared and printed in colors and designs, for covering walls and ceilings of rooms. — *v.t.* To cover or provide with wallpaper.

wall pellitory See PELLITORY.

wall plate 1 A horizontal timber on a wall, for bearing the ends of joists, girders, etc. **2** *Mech.* A plate for attaching a bearing or the like to a wall.

wall rock *Mining* The non-metalliferous rock between two lodes.

wall rocket A British perennial (*Diplotaxis tenuifolia*) of the mustard family, with large yellow flowers.

wall rue A small delicate spleenwort (*Asplenium ruta-muraria*) growing on walls and cliffs.

Walls·end (wôlz′end) *n.* A size or grade of coal for household purposes. [from *Wallsend*, England]

Walls·end (wôlz′end) A municipal borough in SE Northumberland, England, on the Tyne just NE of Newcastle-on-Tyne.

Wall Street 1 A street in lower Manhattan, New York City: the financial center of the United States. **2** American financiers collectively, their interests, power, etc., or the American financial world.

wall tent A tent having vertical sides and peaked top.

wal·ly (wä′lē, wol′ē) See WALY¹.

wal·ly-drai·gle (wä′lē·drā′gəl, wol′ē-) *n. Scot.* **1** The youngest in a family; also, a young bird in the nest. **2** Any feeble or ill-grown creature. Also **wal′ly·drag′** (-drag′, -dräg′).

wal·nut (wôl′nut′, -nət) *n.* **1** Any of various deciduous, typically European and Asian trees (genus *Juglans*), cultivated as ornamental shade trees and valued for their timber and their edible nuts; especially, the **black walnut** (*J. nigra*) of the eastern United States, and the **English, Persian, Circassian,** or **Caucasian walnut** (*J. regia*). **2** The wood or nut of any of these trees. **3** The shagbark hickory, or its nut. **4** The color of the wood of any of these trees, especially of the black walnut, a very dark brown; also, the color of the shell of the English walnut, a dull, medium yellowish brown: also called **walnut brown.** [OE *walhhnutu, wealh hnutu* < *wealh* foreign + *hnutu* a nut]

BLACK WALNUT
a. Catkin.
b. Shuck, nut inside.
c. Nut, shuck removed.

Wal·pole (wôl′pōl, wol′-), **Horace,** 1717–97, fourth earl of Orford; English author and wit; son of Sir Robert Walpole. — **Sir Hugh Seymour,** 1884–1941, English novelist. — **Sir Robert,** 1676–1745, first earl of Orford; English statesman.

Wal·pur·gis Night (väl·poōr′gis) The night before May 1, originally dedicated to St. Walpurga, an English nun of the eighth century who founded religious houses in Germany: associated in German folklore with a witches' Sabbath on the Brocken. Also *German* **Wal·pur′gis·nacht′** (-näkht′). [<G *Walpurgisnacht*]

wal·rus (wôl′rəs, wol′-) *n.* A large, marine, seal-like mammal (family *Odobenidae*) of arctic seas, with flexible hind limbs, tusklike canines in the upper jaw, and a thick, heavy neck; especially, the common Atlantic walrus (*Odobenus rosmarus*). — *adj.* **1** Belonging to or pertaining to a walrus. **2** Designating a type of mustache suggestive of the coarse bristles on the muzzle of a walrus. [<Du. *walrus* <Scand. Cf. Dan. *hvalros,* ? <ON *hrosshvalr,* lit., a horse whale.]

WALRUS
(Body to 10 feet;
weight to 3,000 pounds)

Wal·sall (wôl′sôl) A county borough in southern Staffordshire, England.

Wal·sing·ham (wôl′sing·əm), **Sir Francis,** 1530?–90, English statesman.

Wal·ter (wôl′tər, *Ger., Sw.* väl′tər) A masculine personal name. Also *Ger., Sw.* **Wal·ther** (väl′tər). [<Gmc., ruler of the army]

Wal·ter (väl′tər), **Bruno,** 1876–1962, German orchestra conductor active in the United States: real name *Bruno Schlesinger*.

Wal·ter (wôl′tər), **John,** 1739–1812, English journalist; founder of the London *Times*.

Wal·tham (wôl′thəm) An industrial city in eastern Massachusetts on the Charles River west of Boston.

Wal·tham·stow (wôl′thəm·stō, -təm-) A municipal borough of SW Essex, England, NE of London.

Wal·ther von der Vo·gel·wei·de (väl′ter fôn der fō′gəl·vī′də), 1170?–1230?, German minnesinger.

Wal·ton (wôl′tən), **Izaak,** 1593–1683, English author. — **William Turner,** born 1902, English composer.

waltz (wôlts) *n.* **1** A round dance executed to music in triple time. **2** The music for such a dance, or any composition written in the triple time characteristic of the waltz. — *v.i.* **1** To dance a waltz. **2** To move quickly: He *waltzed* out of the room. — *v.t.* **3** To cause to waltz. — *adj.* Pertaining to, or typical of, the waltz: *waltz* time. [<G *walzer* < *walzen* waltz, roll] — **waltz′er** *n.*

Wal·vis Bay (wôl′vis) *n.* **1** An inlet of the Atlantic in South-West Africa. **2** An enclave in South-West Africa, administered by that territory, but an integral part of the Cape of Good Hope Province, Union of South Africa; on Walvis Bay; 374 square miles. **3** A port in this enclave: also *Walfish Bay. Afrikaans* **Wal·vis·baai** (wôl′vis·bī′).

wa·ly¹ (wä′lē, wol′ē) *Scot. adj.* **1** Beautiful; pleasing; excellent. **2** Strong; robust; vigorous. — *n. pl.* **·lies 1** Something pleasing to the eye; a toy; ornament. **2** Good luck. **3** *pl.* Finery. Also spelled *wally*.

wa·ly² (wä′lē) *interj. Dial. & Scot.* Alas!: an expression of sorrow or lament.

wam·ble (wom′əl, wam′-) *Dial. v.i.* **·bled, ·bling 1** To move unsteadily; roll. **2** To twist or turn; writhe. **3** *Obs.* To feel nausea; be giddy or faint. — *n.* **1** A rolling gait. **2** A rolling or upheaving of the stomach; nausea. [ME *wamlen.* Cf. Dan. *vamle* feel nausea, Norw. *vamla* stagger.] — **wam′bly** *adj.*

wame (wām) *n. Scot.* The abdomen; belly; womb.

wame·fou (wām′foō) *n. Scot.* A bellyful. Also **wame′fu′, wame′ful** (-foōl).

wamp·ish (wom′pish) *v.t. Scot.* To toss or throw about; wave; brandish.

wam·pum (wom′pəm, wôm′-) *n.* **1** Beads made of the interior parts of shells, formerly used as currency among North American Indians and between the Indians and white settlers: used loose, strung on strings, and also made into belts, scarfs, etc. The strings were often worn as ornaments, necklaces, bracelets, etc. The belts, woven with symbolic designs, were used in rituals, official communications, proposals, ratification of treaties, alliances, etc. The beads were either black, dark-purple, or white, the last being specifically **wam′pum·peag** (-pēg). The dark beads were double the value of the white. See SEAWAN. **2** *Colloq.* Money. [<Algonquian *wampum(peage)*, lit., a white (string of beads)]

WAMPUM
The historic Pennwampum — Iroquois Indian.

wampum snake The hoop snake: so called from its coloring.

wa·mus (wô′məs, wom′əs) *n.* A cardigan; a heavy outer jacket of strong, coarse cloth, worn in the United States. Also **wam′mus, wam′pus** (-pəs). [<Du. *wammes,* short for *wambuis* <OF *wambois* a leather doublet <OHG *wamba* the belly]

wan¹ (won) *adj.* **1** Pale, as from sickness or anxiety; pallid; livid; careworn; of a sickly hue. **2** Having a gloomy aspect; dismal; dark: said of scenes or landscapes. **3** *Obs.* Sad; mournful. **4** Faint; feeble: a *wan* smile. See synonyms under GHASTLY, PALE². — *v.t. & v.i.* **wanned, wan·ning** To make or become wan. — *n. Rare* The quality of being wan; paleness. [OE *wann* dark, gloomy] — **wan′ly** *adv.* — **wan′ness** *n.*

wan² (won) Obsolete past tense of WIN.

Wan·a·mak·er (won′ə·mā′kər), **John,** 1838–1922, U.S. merchant.

wand (wond) *n.* **1** A slender, flexible rod waved by a magician, conjurer, or legerdemain artist; also, any rod indicating an office or function of the bearer, as a scepter. **2** A musician's baton. **3** A thin, flexible stick or twig; also, a willow shoot; osier. **4** In archery, a slat used as a mark and placed at varying distances for men and women.

See synonyms under STICK. [<ON *vöndr.* Akin to WIND².]

wan·der (won′dər) *v.i.* **1** To move or travel about without destination or purpose; roam; rove. **2** To go casually or by an indirect route; idle; stroll. **3** To extend in an irregular course; twist or meander. **4** To turn from a true or direct course; stray. **5** To deviate in conduct or opinion; go astray. **6** To think or speak deliriously or irrationally. — *v.t.* **7** *Poetic* To wander through or across. — *n.* The act of wandering; a ramble. [OE *wandrian*] — **wan′der·er** *n.* — **wan′der·ing** *adj.* **wan′der·ing·ly** *adv.*

Synonyms (verb): deviate, digress, diverge, err, ramble, range, roam, rove, stray, swerve, veer. To *wander* is to move in an indefinite or indeterminate way which may or may not be a departure from a prescribed way; to *deviate* is to turn from a prescribed or right way, physically, mentally, or morally, usually in an unfavorable sense; to *diverge* is to turn from a course previously followed or that something else follows, and has no unfavorable implication; to *digress* is used only with reference to speaking or writing; to *err* is used of intellectual or moral action. To *swerve* or *veer* is to turn suddenly from a prescribed or previous course, and often but momentarily; *veer* is more capricious and repetitious; the horse *swerves* at the flash of a sword; the wind *veers*; the ship *veers* with the wind. To *stray* is to go in a somewhat purposeless way aside from the regular path or usual limits or abode, usually with unfavorable implication; cattle *stray* from their pastures; an author *strays* from his subject. *Stray* is in most uses a lighter word than *wander. Ramble* in its literal use is always a word of pleasant suggestion, but in its figurative use somewhat contemptuous; as, *rambling* talk. See RAMBLE.

wandering albatross A large, whitish, black-winged, web-footed sea bird (*Diomedea exulans*), having extraordinary powers of flight.

wandering jew 1 A perennial trailing herb (*Tradescantia fluminensis*) of the spiderwort family, with hairy white flowers and vivid green leaves sometimes striped with yellow. **2** A related plant (*Zebrina pendula*) with red or white flowers and striped leaves.

Wandering Jew See under JEW.

wandering kidney A floating kidney.

wan·der·lust (won′dər·lust′, *Ger.* vän′dər·lōōst) *n.* An impulse to travel; restlessness combined with a sense of adventure. [<G <*wandern* travel + *lust* joy]

wan·der·oo (won′də·rōō′) *n.* **1** A large black monkey (*Macaca silenus*) of western India, having a heavy whitish mane. **2** A Ceylonese langur (*Presbytis cephalopterus*). [<Singhalese *vanduru,* pl. of *vandurā* the Ceylonese langur <Skt. *vānara* a monkey]

wan·dle (won′dəl, -əl) *adj. Dial.* Supple; nimble. [Back formation <OE *wandlung* changeableness]

Wands·worth (wondz′wûrth) A metropolitan borough in SW London, England.

wane (wān) *v.i.* **waned, wan·ing 1** To diminish in size and brilliance: opposed to *wax.* **2** To decline or decrease gradually; draw to an end. — *n.* **1** Decrease, as of power, prosperity, or reputation. **2** The decrease of the moon's visible illuminated surface; also, the period of such decrease. **3** The beveled edge of a board sawn from a log; also, the bark or defective portion on the edge or corner of a board. ◆ Homophone: *wain.* [OE *wanian* lessen]

wane·y (wā′nē) *adj.* Having a beveled edge, as the wane of a plank: also spelled *wany.* [<WANE, *n.* (def. 3)]

Wang·a·nu·i (wông′ə·nōō′ē) A port of southern North Island, New Zealand.

wan·gle (wang′gəl) *v.* **·gled, ·gling** *Colloq. v.t.* **1** To obtain or make by indirect or irregular methods; contrive: to *wangle* an introduction to a celebrity. **2** To manipulate or adjust, especially dishonestly. **3** To wriggle or wag. — *v.i.* **4** To resort to indirect, irregular, or dishonest methods. **5** To wriggle. [? Alter. of WAGGLE] — **wan′gler** *n.*

Wan·hsien (wän′shyen′) A city on the Yangtze River, eastern Szechwan province, central China; a major commercial port NE of Chungking.

wan·i·gan (won′ə·gən) *n.* In American logging

---

camps: **1** A storage chest for clothing, etc. **2** A shanty fitted with sleeping and cooking accommodations. Also **wan′gan,** **wan′gun, wan′ni·gan.** [Earlier *wangan* <Algonquian *atawangan* < *atawan* buy, sell]

wan·ion (won′yən) *n. Archaic* Disaster, or bad luck; a curse: used only in the phrases **in a wanion, with a wanion,** etc. [Alter of dial. ME (Northern) *waniand,* ppr. of *wanien* wane]

Wan·kel engine (väng′kəl, wäng′-) A light, compact type of internal-combustion engine having combustion chambers bounded by the wall of a shallow cylinder and the sides of a triangular piston that rotates in one direction inside it. Also **Wan′kel.** [<F. *Wankel,* 1902-, German inventor]

Wan·ne-Eick·el (vän′ə·i′kəl) A city in west central North Rhine-Westphalia NW of Bochum, West Germany.

Wan·stead and Wood·ford (won′sted, -stid, wŏŏd′fərd) A municipal borough in Essex, England, NE of London.

want (wont, wônt) *v.t.* **1** To feel a desire or wish for. **2** To wish; desire: used with the infinitive: Your friends *want* to help you. **3** To be deficient in; lack; be without. **4** To be lacking to the extent of: He *wants* three inches of six feet. **5** *Brit.* To need; require. — *v.i.* **6** To have need: usually with *for.* **7** To be needy or destitute. **8** *Rare* To be lacking or absent. — *n.* **1** Lack or absence of something; scarcity; shortage. **2** Privation; destitution; need. **3** Something that is lacking or needed; a need. **4** A conscious or felt need of something; a craving. [Prob. <ON *vanta* be lacking] — **want′er** *n.*

Synonyms (noun): absence, dearth, default, defect, deficiency, lack, necessity, need, privation, scantiness, scarceness, scarcity. See NECESSITY, POVERTY. *Antonyms:* abundance, affluence, fullness, luxury, plenty, wealth.

wa′n't (wont, wônt) Was not: a dialectal contraction.

want ad *Colloq.* An advertisement in a newspaper for something wanted, as hired help, a job, a lodging, etc.

want·age (won′tij, wôn′-) *n.* Whatever is lacking; deficiency.

want column A column of want ads in a newspaper or other periodical.

want·ing (won′ting, wôn′-) *adj.* **1** Not at hand; missing; lacking: One juror is still *wanting.* **2** Marked by lack or deficiency; not coming up to need or expectation: He was found *wanting.* **3** *Colloq.* Deficient in intellect; feeble-minded. — **wanting in** Deficient in. — *prep.* With the exception of; less; save; minus.

wan·ton (won′tən) *adj.* **1** Dissolute; unchaste; licentious; lewd; lustful. **2** Recklessly inconsiderate, heartless, or unjust; evincing a malicious nature: *wanton* savagery; also, unprovoked: a *wanton* murder. **3** Of vigorous and abundant growth; rank. **4** Extravagant; running to excess; unrestrained: *wanton* speech. **5** Not bound or tied; loose: *wanton* curls; also, frolicsome; prankish. **6** *Obs.* Refractory; rebellious. — *v.i.* **1** To act wantonly or playfully; revel or sport. **2** To grow luxuriantly. — *v.t.* **3** To waste wantonly. — *n.* **1** A lewd or licentious person, especially a woman. **2** A playful or frolicsome person or animal. **3** A trifler; dallier. **4** *Obs.* A person who has been much indulged; a pet. [ME *wantoun* <OE *wan* deficient + ME *towen,* OE *togen,* pp. of *téon* bring up, educate] — **wan′ton·ly** *adv.* — **wan′ton·ness** *n.*

Synonyms (adj.): airy, free, frisky, frolicsome, gay, loose, merry, playful, reckless, sportive, unbridled, uncurbed, unrestrained, wandering, wild. See IMMODEST. *Antonyms:* austere, demure, discreet, reserved, sedate, thoughtful.

wan·y (wā′nē) See WANEY.

wap¹ (wop, wap) *Dial.* or *Archaic v.t.* & *v.i.* **wapped, wap·ping 1** To whip; beat; strike. **2** To flutter or flap, as wings. — *n.* **1** A stroke; blow. **2** A quarrel; fight. **3** A storm. [Prob. var. of WHOP.]

wap² (wop, wop) *Dial. v.t.* **wapped, wap·ping** To wrap; tie; bind. — *n.* A wrapping. [? Alter. of WARP]

wap·en·shaw (wop′ən·shô, wap′-) *n. Scot.* A show of weapons; review of weapons. Also **wap′in·schaw, wap′pen·schaw′ing.**

wap·en·take (wop′ən·tāk, wap′-) *n.* An old administrative and judicial subdivision of some English counties, equivalent to the

---

hundred of most counties. [OE *wæpengetæc* <ON *vápnatak* a (symbolical) flourish of weapons denoting confirmation of the decisions of an assembly < *vápna,* genitive pl. of *vápn* a weapon + *tak* a taking]

wap·i·ti (wop′ə·tē) *n.* A large North American deer (*Cervus canadensis*): usually *elk.* [<Algonquian. Cf. Shawnee *wapiti* pale, white.]

wap·per-jawed (wop′ər·jôd′) *adj. U.S. Dial.* **1** Having a wry or undershot jaw. **2** Out of true; askew.

war¹ (wôr) *n.* **1** A contest between or among nations or states, or between different parties in the same state, carried on by force and with arms. **2** Any act or state of hostility; enmity; strife; also, a contest or conflict. **3** *Poetic* **a** A battle. **b** The supplies and paraphernalia of war. **c** Armed troops; an army. See table MAJOR WARS OF HISTORY on page 1417. **4** The science or art of military operations; strategy. — *v.i.* **warred, war·ring 1** To wage war; fight or take part in a war. **2** To be in any state of active opposition; contend; strive. — *adj.* Of or pertaining to, used in, or resulting from war. [OE *wyrre, werre* <AF *werre* <OHG *werra* strife, confusion]

WAPITI
(About 5 feet high at the shoulders; antler spread to 3 feet)

War may appear as a combining form in hyphemes or solidemes, or as the first element in two-word phrases:

war-blasted	war-making
war-born	war march
war-breeder	war-marked
war-breeding	war neurosis
war bride	war office
war-broken	war party
war budget	war prisoner
war chant	war-production
war chief	war-proof
war cloud	war-ridden
war code	war-risk
warcraft	war service
war-debt	war-shaken
war-disabled	war song
war dog	war-stirring
war drum	war-swept
war-famed	war talk
war-footing	war tax
war gains	wartime
war-god	war-torn
war-goddess	war-tossed
war-hardened	war traitor
war-impoverished	war vessel
war insurance	war-wasted
war law	war-wearied
war leader	war-weary
war loan	war-work
war-loving	war-worker
war-machine	war-worn
war-made	warworthy
war-maimed	war-wounded
war-maker	war zone

war² (wär) *Dial. v.t.* To guard against; ware. — *adj.* Cautious; wary. [Var. of WARE²]

war³ (wär) *adj. & adv. Scot. & Brit. Dial.* Worse.

War·beck (wôr′bek), **Perkin,** 1474-99, Walloon impostor and pretender to the English throne; hanged.

war belt Among certain North American Indians, a belt of wampum bearing symbolic figures or designs, sent by one tribe to another or passed from tribe to tribe, as a message declaring war, summoning a group of tribes to war, invoking aid in war, etc.

War between the States The United States Civil War: used especially in the former Confederate States.

war bird Among certain North American Indians, the golden eagle: so called because its feathers were worn in the war bonnet.

war·ble¹ (wôr′bəl) *v.* **·bled, ·bling** *v.t.* **1** To sing with trills and runs, or with tremulous vibrations. **2** To celebrate in song. — *v.i.* **3** To sing with trills, etc. **4** To make a liquid

MAJOR WARS OF HISTORY

NAME	CONTESTANTS (victor shown first)	NOTABLE BATTLES	TREATIES
Greco-Persian Wars 499–478 B.C.	Greek states—Persia	Marathon, 490; Thermopylae, Salamis, 480; Plataea, 479	
Peloponnesian War 431–404 B.C.	Sparta—Athens	Syracuse, 415; Cyzicus, 410; Aegospotami, 405	Peace of Nicias, 421
First Punic War 264–241 B.C.; **Second Punic War** 218–201 B.C.; **Third Punic War** 149–146 B.C.	Rome—Carthage	Drepanum, 249; Aegates, 241 Lake Trasimene, 217, Cannae, 216; Zama, 202	
Islamic Invasion of Europe 630–19th century	Christianity—Islam	Constantinople, 717–718; Tours, 732; Manzikert, 1071; Hattin, 187; Lepanto, 1571; Vienna, 1524, 1683; Zenta, 1697	Pruth, 1711; Kutchuk—Kanardjii, 1774; Sistova, 1791
Norman Conquest 1066	Normandy—England	Hastings, 1066	
Crusades 1096–1291	Christianity—Islam *(indecisive)*	Jerusalem, 1099; Acre, 1191	
Hundred Years' War 1338–1453	England—France	Crécy, 1346; Poitiers, 1356; Agincourt, 1415; Siege of Orléans, 1428–39	
Wars of the Roses 1455–85	Lancaster—York *(indecisive)*	St. Albans, 1455	
Thirty Years' War 1618–48	Catholics—Protestants	Leipzig, Breitenfeld, 1631; Lützen, 1632	Westphalia, 1648
Civil War (English) 1642–46	Roundheads—Cavaliers	Marston Moor, 1643; Naseby, 1645	
War of the Spanish Succession 1701–14	England, Austria, Prussia, Netherlands—France, Spain	Blenheim, 1704	Utrecht, 1713
War of the Austrian Succession 1740–48	France, Prussia, Sardinia, Spain—Austria, England	Dettingen, 1743; Fontenoy, 1745	Aix-la-Chapelle, 1748
French & Indian War 1755–63	England—France	Plains of Abraham, 1759; Montreal, 1760	
Seven Years' War 1756–63	Prussia—Austria, France, Russia	Rossbach, Leuthen, 1757	Hubertusberg, 63
Revolutionary War 1775–83	American Colonies—England	Lexington, Concord, Bunker Hill, 1775; Saratoga, 1777; Yorktown, 1781	Paris, 1783
Napoleonic Wars 1796–1815	England, Austria, Russia, Prussia, etc.—France	Nile, 1798; Trafalgar, 1805; Jena, Auerstädt, 1806; Leipzig, 1813 Waterloo, 1815	Campoformio, 1797; Tilsit, 1807; Schönbrunn, 1809; Paris, 1814–15; Vienna, 1815
War of 1812 1812–15	Unites States—England	Lake Erie, 1813; New Orleans, 1815	Ghent, 1814
War of Independence (Greek) 1821–29	Greece, England, Sweden, Russia—Turkey	Navarino, 1827	London, 1827
Mexican War 1846–48	United States—Mexico	Resaca de la Palma, 1846; Chapultepec, 1847	Guadalupe Hidalgo, 1848
Crimean War 1854–56	Turkey, England, France, Sardinia—Russia	Sevastopol, 1854	Paris, 1856
Civil War (United States) 1861–65	Union (North)—Confederate States (South)	Bull Run, 1861; Antietam, 1862; Chancellorsville, Gettysburg, Vicksburg, Chattanooga, 1863; Wilderness, 1864	
Franco-Prussian War 1870–71	Prussia—France	Sedan, 1870	Versailles, 1871
Spanish-American War 1898	United States—Spain	Manila Bay, Santiago, 1898	Paris, 1898
Boer War 1899–1902	England—Transvaal Republic & Orange Free State	Ladysmith, 1899	Vereeniging, 1902
Russo-Japanese War 1904–1905	Japan—Russia	Port Arthur, Mukden, Tsushima, 1905	Portsmouth, 1905
First Balkan War 1912–13; **Second Balkan War** 1913	Bulgaria, Serbia, Greece, Montenegro—Turkey	Scutari, 1912; Salonika, 1912; Adrianople, 1912	London, 1913; Bucharest, 1913
World War I 1914–18	Allies—Central Powers	Dardanelles, 1915; Verdun, Somme, Jutland, 1916; Caporetto, 1917; Vittorio Veneto, Amiens, Marne, Ypres, 1918	Versailles, Saint-Germain, Neuilly, 1919; Trianon, Sèvres, 1920; Lausanne, 1923
Civil War (Spanish) 1936–39	Insurgents—Loyalists	Teruel, 1937; Ebro River, 1938	
World War II 1939–45	Allies—Axis 1939–45	Dunkirk 1940; Crete, 1941; El Alamein, 1942; Tunis, 1943; Stalingrad, 1942–43; Kharkov, 1943; Cassino, 1943–44; Saint-Lô, 1944; Rhine, Ruhr, Berlin, 1945	Potsdam, 1945
	Allies—Japan 1941–45	Pearl Harbor, 1941; Bataan, 1941–42; Singapore, Coral Sea, Midway Island, Guadalcanal, 1942; Bismarck Sea, Tarawa, 1943; Leyte Gulf, 1944; Philippines, 1944–45; Okinawa, 1945	San Francisco, 1951
Korean War 1950–52	United Nations—North Korea	Inchon, Pyongyang, 1950; Seoul, 1951	Panmunjom, 1953
Vietnam War 1957–75	North Vietnam—South Vietnam, United States	Tet Offensive, Saigon, 1968	Paris, 1973

---

add,āce,câre,pälm; end,ēven; it,īce; odd,ōpen,ôrder; tŏŏk,pōōl; up,bûrn; ə = a in *above*, e in *sicken*, i in *clarity*, o in *melon*, u in *focus*; yōō = u in *fuse*, oi,oil; ou,pout; ch,check; g,go; ng,ring; th,thin; th,this; zh,vision. Foreign sounds à,œ,ü,kh,ṅ; and ◆: see page xx. <from; + plus; ? possibly.

murmuring sound, as a stream. **5** *U.S.* To yodel. See synonyms under SING. — *n.* The act of warbling; a carol; song. [<AF *werbler,* OF *guerbler* < *werble* a warble <OHG *werbel* something that revolves. Akin to WHIRL.]

war·ble[2] (wôr′bəl) *n.* **1** A hard swelling on the back of a horse, caused by the chafing of the saddle. **2** A boil or swelling under the hide of a horse, cow, deer, or the like, caused by the maggot of a botfly or warblefly. **3** A warblefly. [Cf. obs. Sw. *varbulde* < *var* pus + *bulde* a tumor] — **war′bled** *adj.*

war·ble·fly (wôr′bəl·flī′) *n. pl.* **·flies** Any of a family *(Hypodermatidae)* of dipterous insects resembling the botflies, whose larvae produce swellings under the hides of cattle, horses, etc. [<WARBLE[2] + FLY[2]]

war·bler (wôr′blər) *n.* **1** One who or that which warbles; a songster. **2** Any of a family *(Sylviidae)* of plain-colored, mostly Old World birds allied to the kinglets and noted for their song, as the whitethroat. **3** Any of a large and varied family *(Compsothlypidae)* of small American insectivorous birds, usually brilliantly colored and with little powers of song, as the **summer** or **yellow warbler** *(Dendroica aestiva),* the redstart, ovenbird, and water thrush. Also **wood warbler.**

war bonnet The ceremonial head dress of the North American Plains Indians, consisting of a rawhide cap fitting the head and extending down the back to the heels, the crown and the extension being decorated with feathers of the golden eagle.

War·burg (vär′bŏŏrkh), **Otto Heinrich,** born 1883, German physiologist and chemist.

War College One of four colleges in the United States giving advanced instruction to experienced military, naval, and air officers; specifically, the **Army War College,** Carlisle Barracks, Pennsylvania, under the Department of the Army; the **Naval War College,** Newport, Rhode Island, under the Navy Department; and the **Air War College,** near Montgomery, Alabama, under the Department of the Air Force. The **National War College,** Washington, D.C., operating under the Joint Chiefs of Staff, prepares officers of the armed services, the State Department, and other executive departments for duties concerned with national security.

war correspondent A newspaper reporter or representative of some other periodical engaged to write up the scenes of combat from direct observation.

war cry A rallying cry used by combatants in a war, or by participants in any contest.

ward (wôrd) *n.* **1** The act of guarding; protection. **2** The state of being under a guard or guardian; custody; confinement; also, guardianship; control. **3** A guarded or protected place; a prison; jail; also, a division or subdivision of a jail or hospital: the maternity *ward.* **4** A territorial division of a city, made for convenience of government; also, in certain northern counties of England, a division equivalent to a hundred or wapentake. **5** A person who is in the charge or under the protection of a guardian. **6** An instrument or means of defense; a protection. **7** A defensive attitude or movement, as in fencing; guard. **8** A projection inside a lock, designed to obstruct the turning of any key other than the proper one; also, a corresponding notch in the bit of a key. **9** In feudal law, a minor under the care or protection of a guardian. **10** A warden; overseer. **11** A local congregation within the Mormon Church. **12** *Obs.* A company of men detailed to defend or guard; a garrison; watch. See synonyms under SHELTER. — *v.t.* **1** To repel or turn aside, as a thrust or blow: usually with *off.* **2** To put in a ward; keep in safety. **3** *Archaic* To guard; protect. [OE *weard* a watching < *weardian* watch, guard; infl. in some senses by AF *warde,* OF *garde* <Gmc.]

-ward *suffix* Toward; in the direction of: *upward, homeward.* Also **-wards.** [OE *-weard, -weardes* at, toward]

Ward (wôrd), **Artemas,** 1727–1800, American Revolutionary general. — **Artemus** Pseudonym of Charles Farrar Browne, 1834–67, U.S. humorist. — **Mary Augusta,** 1851–1920, *née* Arnold, English novelist: known as *Mrs. Humphrey Ward.*

war dance A dance of savage tribes before going to war or in celebration of a victory.

war·den[1] (wôr′dən) *n.* **1** One who keeps ward; a warder or gatekeeper. **2** A chief officer, as in a prison. **3** In England, the head of certain colleges. **4** In Connecticut, the chief executive of a borough. **5** A churchwarden. See synonyms under SUPERINTENDENT. [<AF *wardein,* OF *gardein, guarden* <Gmc. Doublet of GUARDIAN.]

war·den[2] (wôr′dən) *n.* A variety of pear used chiefly for cooking. Also **War′den.** [ME *wardon,* prob. <AF *warder,* OF *garder* keep <Gmc.]

war·den·ry (wôr′dən·rē) *n. pl.* **·ries** The office, functions, or jurisdiction of a warden. Also **war′den·ship** (-ship).

War Department A former executive department of the U. S. government (1789–1947) in charge of matters relating to the Army and (later) the Army Air Force: now absorbed into the Department of Defense.

ward·er (wôr′dər) *n.* **1** A keeper; guard; sentinel; watchman. **2** An official staff or baton; a truncheon. **3** A prison official; warden. [<AF *wardere* < *warder,* var. of OF *guarder* guard, keep]

ward-heel·er (wôrd′hē′lər) *n. U.S. Slang* A hanger-on of a political boss, who does minor tasks, canvasses votes, etc. [<WARD (def. 4) + HEELER (def. 1)]

ward-hold·ing (wôrd′hōl′ding) *n.* The holding of lands by military tenure: distinguished from *feu.*

ward·ress (wôr′dris) *n.* A female warden.

ward·robe (wôrd′rōb′) *n.* **1** A large upright cabinet for wearing apparel; formerly, a large clothes closet or room, where clothes were also made and repaired. **2** All the garments of any one person. **3** In a noble or royal household, the department responsible for clothing, jewelry, etc. **4** The costumes of a theater or theatrical troupe. **5** The styles of a particular season taken collectively: the spring *wardrobe.* [<AF *warderobe,* OF *garderobe* < *warder* keep + *robe* a robe, dress]

ward·room (wôrd′rōōm′, -rŏŏm′) *n.* On a warship, the quarters allotted to the commissioned officers above the rank of ensign, excepting the commander, who has his own quarters; especially, the dining-room of these officers; also, these officers regarded as a group.

ward·ship (wôrd′ship) *n.* **1** The state of a ward; pupilage. **2** In feudal law, the right by which the lord had the custody of the bodies, and the custody and profits of the lands, of minor heirs of a deceased tenant.

ware[1] (wâr) *n.* **1** Articles of the same class; especially, manufactured articles: used collectively, often in composition: *tableware, glassware.* **2** *pl.* Articles of commerce; goods; merchandise; products. **3** Pottery; ceramic articles; earthenware. ◆ Homophone: *wear.* [OE *waru*]

ware[2] (wâr) *v.t.* **wared, war·ing** To beware of: used mainly in the imperative: *Ware* the dog. — *adj. Obs.* Conscious; aware; hence, on one's guard; cautious. ◆ Homophone: *wear.* [Fusion of OE *warian* beware and AF *warer,* OF *garer* <Gmc. Akin to WARN.]

ware[3] (wâr) *v.t. Scot.* To expend; lay out; also, to lavish; squander: also spelled *wair.* ◆ Homophone: *wear.*

ware·house (wâr′hous′) *n.* **1** A storehouse for goods or merchandise. **2** *Brit.* A large wholesale shop. — *v.t.* **·housed** (-houzd′), **·hous·ing** (-hou′zing) To place or store in a warehouse, especially in a bonded warehouse.

ware·house·man (wâr′hous′mən) *n. pl.* **·men** (-mən) One who makes a business of storing goods.

ware·room (wâr′rōōm′, -rŏŏm′) *n.* A room for the storage, exhibition, or sale of goods or wares.

war·fare (wôr′fâr′) *n.* **1** The waging or carrying on of war; conflict with arms; war. **2** Struggle; strife.

War·field (wôr′fēld), **David,** 1866–1951, U. S. actor.

War for Southern Independence See CIVIL WAR (AMERICAN) in table under WAR.

war game **1** Kriegspiel. **2** *pl.* Practice maneuvers imitating the conditions of actual warfare.

war hawk One who advocates war; a jingo.

war·head (wôr′hed′) *n. Mil.* **1** An ogive-shaped chamber in the nose of a torpedo, containing the charge of high explosive. **2** A similar chamber in a bomb, guided missile, or the like.

war horse **1** A heavy horse used in warfare; a charger. **2** *Colloq.* A veteran; especially, an aggressive or veteran politician.

war·i·son (war′ə·sən) *n.* **1** A signal for assault: an erroneous use. **2** Reward; healing. [<AF *warison,* OF *garison* wealth, possession]

wark[1] (wärk) *n. Scot.* Work.

wark[2] (wärk) *Scot. & Brit. Dial. n.* Ache; pain. — *v.i.* To suffer pain; ache; throb.

war·like (wôr′līk′) *adj.* **1** Disposed to engage in war; belligerent. **2** Relating to, used in, or suggesting war. **3** Threatening war; belligerent; hostile.

Synonyms: martial, military, soldierlike, soldierly. *Antonyms*: civil, effeminate, meek, pacific, peaceful, unmilitary, unsoldierlike, unsoldierly, unwarlike.

war·lock[1] (wôr′lok′) *n.* A wizard; sorcerer; also, a demon. [OE *wǣrloga* a traitor, foe, devil < *wǣr* a covenant + *lēogen* lie, deny]

war·lock[2] (wôr′lok′) *n.* A scalp lock worn by the warriors of certain North American Indian tribes. [<WAR + LOCK[2]]

war·lord (wôr′lôrd′) *n.* **1** A leader or high-ranking officer in a militaristic nation. **2** The warlike ruler or leader of a local region or group of bandits, especially in the Orient.

warm (wôrm) *adj.* **1** Moderately hot; having, or characterized by, heat somewhat greater than temperate: *warm* water; a *warm* climate. **2** Imparting heat: a *warm* fire. **3** Imparting, promoting, or preserving warmth; preventing loss of bodily heat: a *warm* coat. **4** Having a feeling of heat somewhat greater than ordinary: *warm* from exertion. **5** Possessing or marked by ardor, zeal, liveliness, enthusiasm, or cordiality: a *warm* argument; *warm* wishes. **6** Excited; agitated; also, vehement; passionate: a *warm* temper. **7** United by ardent affection: *warm* friends; also, amorous; loving. **8** Having predominating tones of red or yellow: opposed to *cool.* **9** Recently made; fresh: a *warm* trail; hence, near a hidden object, as in certain games of children. **10** *Colloq.* Uncomfortable by reason of annoyances or danger: They made the town *warm* for him. **11** Characterized by brisk activity: a *warm* skirmish. **12** *Colloq.* Rich; wealthy. — *v.t.* **1** To make warm; heat slightly: often with *up.* **2** To make ardent or enthusiastic; interest. **3** To fill with kindly feeling: The sight *warms* my heart. — *v.i.* **4** To become warm. **5** To become ardent or enthusiastic: often with *up* or *to.* **6** To become kindly disposed or friendly: with *to* or *toward.* — *n. Colloq.* The state or sensation of being or becoming warm; warmth; a heating. [OE *wearm*] — **warm′ly** *adv.* — **warm′ness** *n.*

warm-blood·ed (wôrm′blud′id) *adj.* **1** Having warm blood: said of animals, as mammals and birds, that preserve a nearly uniform and high body temperature, whatever the surrounding medium; homoiothermal. **2** Enthusiastic; ardent; passionate.

warm·er (wôr′mər) *n.* One who or that which warms.

warm front *Meteorol.* The irregular boundary line between an advancing mass of warm air and the underlying colder air mass.

warm-heart·ed (wôrm′här′tid) *adj.* Kind; affectionate.

warming pan A closed metal pan with a long handle, containing live coals or hot water, for warming a bed.

warm·ish (wôr′mish) *adj.* Rather warm.

war·mon·ger (wôr′mung′gər, -mong′-) *n.* One who propagates warlike ideas; a jingo. — **war′·mon′ger·ing** *adj. & n.*

Warm Springs A resort town in western Georgia; site of an institution for the study and treatment of poliomyelitis; here Franklin D. Roosevelt died, 1945.

warmth (wôrmth) *n.* **1** The state, quality, or sensation of being warm. **2** Ardor or fervidness of disposition or feeling; excitement of temper or mind. **3** The effect produced by warm colors. [ME *wermthe,* ult. <OE *wærm* warm]

Synonyms: animation, ardor, cordiality, eagerness, earnestness, emotion, energy, enthusiasm, excitement, fervidness, fervor, geniality, glow, heat, intensity, irascibility, life, passion, vehemence, zeal. Compare ENTHUSIASM. *Antonyms*: coldness, coolness, frigidity, iciness, indifference, insensibility, torpor.

warm-up (wôrm′up′) *n. Colloq.* The act of exercising or limbering up just before a game, contest, etc.

warn (wôrn) *v.t.* **1** To make aware of impending or possible harm; put on guard; caution. **2** To advise; admonish; counsel. **3** To inform; give notice in advance. **4** To notify (a person) to stay, go, or keep: with *off*, *away*, etc. See synonyms under ADMONISH. [OE *warenian, wearnian.* Akin to WARE².] — **warn′er** *n.*

warn·ing (wôr′ning) *n.* **1** The act of one who warns, or that which he communicates; notice of danger. **2** That which warns or admonishes. See synonyms under COUNSEL, EXAMPLE. — *adj.* Serving as a warning. — **warn′ing·ly** *adv.*

war nose The end of a projectile or shell which carries the detonating device.

War of American Independence *Brit.* The American Revolution.

War of Independence The American Revolution.

War of Secession The Civil War in the United States.

War of the Rebellion The Civil War in the United States: used especially in the States that adhered to the Union.

War of the Spanish Succession See table under WAR.

War of 1812 See table under WAR.

warp (wôrp) *v.t.* **1** To turn or twist out of shape, as by shrinkage or heat. **2** To turn from a correct or proper course; give a twist or bias to; corrupt; pervert. **3** To stretch or arrange (yarn) so as to form a warp. **4** *Naut.* To move (a vessel) by hauling on a rope or cable, which is usually fastened to something stationary, as a pier or anchor. **5** *Aeron.* To change the curvature of (an airfoil or wing) by twisting, so as to bring the airplane into balance. — *v.i.* **6** To become turned or twisted out of shape, as wood in drying. **7** To turn or deviate from a correct or proper course; go astray. **8** *Naut.* To move by means of ropes fastened to a pier, anchor, etc. See synonyms under BEND¹. — *n.* **1** The state of being warped or twisted out of shape; a twist or distortion, especially in a piece of wood. **2** A mental or moral deviation or aberration; bias. **3** The threads that run the long way of a fabric, crossing the woof. **4** The heavy cords forming the carcass of a pneumatic tire. **5** *Naut.* A light cable used for warping a ship or boat; a towline or towrope. **6** A length of rope yarn or rope. [OE *weorpan* throw] — **warp′er** *n.*

war paint 1 Paint applied to faces and bodies by North American Indians and other primitive peoples in token of going to war. **2** Hence, any preparation for battle. **3** *Colloq.* Any front assumed to intimidate an adversary or increase self-confidence. **4** *Colloq.* Rouge and other cosmetics applied to the person; hence, full dress and personal adornment; finery; also, official garb or regalia.

war·path (wôr′path′, -päth′) *n.* The route taken by an attacking party of American Indians; the state of war; also, a war expedition. — **on the warpath 1** On a warlike expedition; at war. **2** Ready for a fight; thoroughly angry; ready to begin hostilities.

warp beam The roller or beam in a loom on which the warp is wound.

war·plane (wôr′plān′) *n.* An airplane equipped for fighting.

war·pow·er (wôr′pou′ər) *n.* The armed potential of a country; capacity of a nation's manpower and resources for waging war.

war powers Certain powers granted under the Constitution of the United States to the national government or to the chief executive in time of war, to prosecute war and act in all contingent emergencies.

war·rant (wôr′ənt, wor′-) *n.* **1** *Law* A judicial writ or order authorizing arrest, search, seizure, or any other designated act in aid of the administration of justice. **2** Something which assures or attests; a voucher; evidence; guarantee. **3** That which gives authority for some course or act; sanction; justification: What *warrant* have you for that statement? **4** A certificate of appointment given to army and navy officers of rank lower than commissioned officers. See under OFFICER. **5** A document giving a certain authority; specifically, a document authorizing receipt or pay-

ment of money: a dividend *warrant*. See synonyms under PRECEDENT. — *v.t.* **1** To assure or guarantee the quality, accuracy, certainty, or sufficiency of: to *warrant* a title to property. **2** To assure or guarantee the character or fidelity of; pledge oneself for. **3** To guarantee against injury, loss, etc. **4** To be sufficient grounds for; justify: The facts did not *warrant* your action. **5** To give legal authority or power to, so as to secure against harm; empower; authorize. **6** *Colloq.* To say confidently; feel sure. See synonyms under JUSTIFY. [< AF *warant,* OF *guarant* < Gmc.] — **war′rant·a·ble** *adj.* — **war′rant·a·bly** *adv.* — **war′rant·er** *n.*

war·ran·tee (wôr′ən·tē′, wor′-) *n. Law* The person to whom a warranty is given.

warrant officer See under OFFICER.

war·rant·or (wôr′ən·tôr, wor′-) *n. Law* One who makes or gives a warranty to another.

war·ran·ty (wôr′ən·tē, wor′-) *n. pl.* **·ties 1** *Law* An assurance or undertaking by the seller of property, express or implied, that the property is or shall be as it is represented or promised to be. **2** In conveyancing, a covenant in a deed whereby the grantor binds himself and his heirs to secure to the grantee the estate conveyed to him. **3** In insurance law, a stipulation or engagement on the part of the insured that the facts in relation to the risk are as stated by him. **4** Authorization; warrant. **5** *Dial.* Security; guaranty. [< AF *warantie,* OF *guarantie* < OF *guarant* a warrant. Doublet of GUARANTY.]

War·re·go River (wor′i·gō) A river in east central Australia, flowing 495 miles SW to the Darling River.

war·ren (wôr′ən, wor′-) *n.* **1** A place where rabbits live and breed in communities. **2** An enclosure for keeping small game; also, a place for keeping fish in a river. **3** An obscure crowded place of habitation. **4** In English law, a franchise, either by prescription or royal grant, to keep in an enclosure "beasts and fowls of warren," that is, animals that are by nature wild. See also FREEWARREN. [< AF *warenne* a game park, a rabbit warren < *warir* preserve < Gmc.]

War·ren (wôr′ən, wor′-), **Earl,** 1891–1974, U. S. administrator; chief justice of the U. S. Supreme Court 1953–1969. — **Joseph,** 1741–75, American physician and general. — **Robert Penn,** born 1905, U. S. poet, novelist, and educator.

war·ren·er (wôr′ən·ər, wor′-) *n.* The keeper of a warren.

Warren hoe A pointed garden hoe: used to make furrows for seeds: a trade name. See illustration under HOE.

war·ri·gal (wär′ə·gəl) *n. Austral.* **1** One who or that which is considered wild or uncivilized. **2** The dingo. Also **war′ra·gal.** [< native Australian *warregal* dog, savage]

War·ring·ton (wôr′ing·tən, wor′-) A county borough in southern Lancashire, England, on the Mersey east of Liverpool.

war·ri·or (wôr′ē·ər, -yər, wor′-) *n.* A man engaged in or experienced in warfare; one devoted to a military life. — *adj.* Military; martial. [< AF *werreieor* < *werreier* make war < *werre* WAR]

war–risk insurance (wôr′risk′) Insurance written by the government of the United States for military and naval personnel.

war·saw (wôr′sô) *n.* **1** A fish, the black grouper (*Garrupa nigrita*) of the South Atlantic and Gulf of Mexico. **2** A jewfish (*Promicrops guttatus*) of tropical American waters. [Alter. of Sp. *guasa;* prob. infl. in form by *Warsaw*]

War·saw (wôr′sô) The capital of Poland, on the Vistula, in the east central part of the country. *Polish* **War·sza·wa** (vär·shä′vä).

war·ship (wôr′ship′) *n.* Any vessel used in naval combat; especially, an armored vessel.

war·sle (wär′səl) *n., v.t. & v.i. Scot.* Wrestle. Also **war′stle.** — **war′sler** *n.*

Wars of the Roses See table under WAR.

wart (wôrt) *n.* **1** A small, usually hard and non-malignant excrescence formed on and rooted in the skin. **2** A spongy excrescence found on the pasterns of a horse. **3** A hard glandular protuberance on a plant. [OE *wearte*]

War·ta (vär′tä) A river in NW Poland, flowing 492 miles north and west to the Oder. *German* **War·the** (vär′tə).

Wart·burg (värt′boŏrkh) A castle in the former state of Thuringia, SW of Eisenach, SW East Germany, where Luther translated the New Testament (1521–22).

wart·hog (wôrt′hôg′, -hog′) *n.* An African veldt wild hog (*Phacochoerus aethiopicus*) having warty excrescences on the face and large tusks in both jaws.

WARTHOG
(From 2 to 2 1/2 feet at the shoulder)

War·ton (wôr′tən), **Thomas,** 1728–90, English literary historian, critic, and poet laureate.

wart·y (wôr′tē) *adj.* **wart·i·er, wart·i·est 1** Characterized by having warts: *warty*-flowered panic grass. **2** Of the nature of warts.

war whoop A yell made by American Indians, as a signal for attack or to terrify their opponents in battle.

War·wick (wôr′ik, wor′-) **1** A county of central England; 983 square miles. Also **War′wick·shire** (-shir). **2** A municipal borough of central Warwick on the Avon; county town of Warwick.

War·wick (wôr′ik, wor′-), **Earl of,** 1428–71, Richard Neville, Earl of Salisbury, English statesman and soldier: called the "Kingmaker."

war·y (wâr′ē) *adj.* **war·i·er, war·i·est 1** Carefully watching and guarding. **2** Shrewd; wily. See synonyms under POLITIC, VIGILANT. [< WARE², *adj.*] — **war′i·ly** *adv.* — **war′i·ness** *n.*

was (woz, wuz, *unstressed* wəz) First and third person singular, past indicative of BE. [OE *wæs,* first and third person sing. of *wesan* be]

Wa·satch Plateau (wô′sach) A high tableland of central Utah at the southern end of the Wasatch Range; highest point 12,300 feet.

Wasatch Range A section of the Rocky Mountains in SE Idaho and northern Utah; highest point, 12,008 feet.

wase (wāz) *n. Obs.* or *Dial.* A wisp or bundle of hay, straw, or the like; especially, a cushion of such material for use between the head and a load borne thereon.

wash (wosh, wôsh) *v.t.* **1** To cleanse by immersing in or applying water or other liquid, often with rubbing or scrubbing. **2** To purify from pollution, defilement, or guilt. **3** To wet or cover with water or other liquid. **4** To flow against or over; lave: a beach *washed* by the ocean. **5** To carry away or remove by the action of water: with *away, off, out,* etc. **6** To form or wear by erosion: The storm *washed* gulleys in the hillside. **7** To purify, as gas, by passing through a liquid. **8** To coat with a thin or watery layer of color. **9** To cover with a thin coat of metal. **10** *Mining* **a** To subject (gravel, earth, etc.) to the action of water so as to separate the ore, etc. **b** To separate (ore, etc.) thus. **11** *Aeron.* To warp. — *v.i.* **12** To wash oneself. **13** To wash clothes, etc., in water or other liquid. **14** To withstand the effects of washing: That calico will *wash.* **15** *Brit. Colloq.* To undergo testing successfully: That story won't *wash.* **16** To flow with a lapping sound, as waves. **17** To be carried away or removed by the action of water: with *away, off, out,* etc. **18** To be eroded by the action of water. See synonyms under CLEANSE, PURIFY. — **to wash out** *Slang* **1** To fail and be dropped from a course, especially in military flight training. **2** To damage (an aircraft) irreparably, especially in landing. — *n.* **1** The act or process of washing; cleansing; ablution. **2** A number of articles, as of clothing, set apart for washing or being washed at one time; a washing; laundry. **3** Liquid or semi-liquid refuse; especially, waste food from the kitchen; swill. **4** A preparation used in washing or coating; specifically, a liquid cosmetic or a mouthwash; also, a water-color or India-ink pigment for spreading lightly and evenly on a drawing or picture. **5** The breaking of a body of water

upon the shore, or the sound made by waves breaking or surging against a surface; swash. 6 Erosion of soil or earth by the action of rain or running water. 7 Backwash. 8 *Aeron.* Local air currents set up by the passing of an airplane. 9 An area washed by a sea or river; also, the shallow part of a river or an arm of the sea; a marsh; bog. 10 Material collected and deposited by water, as in the bed of a river or along its banks. 11 *U. S.* The dry bed of a stream; an arroyo. 12 Fermented liquor ready for the distillery. — *adj.* Washable; that may be washed without injury: *wash* fabrics. [OE *wæscan, wascan*]

Wash (wosh, wôsh), **The** An inlet of the North Sea on the eastern coast of England between Norfolk and Lincolnshire; 20 miles long, 15 miles wide.

wash·a·ble (wosh′ə·bəl, wôsh′-) *adj.* That may be washed without fading or injury.

wash-and-wear (wosh′ən·wâr′, wôsh′-) *adj.* Designating or pertaining to a garment or fabric so treated as to require little or no ironing after washing.

wash·board (wosh′bôrd′, -bōrd′, wôsh′-) *n.* 1 A board or frame having a corrugated surface on which to rub clothes while washing them. 2 *Naut.* A thin plank adjusted to turn the wash of the sea from a deck or port of a ship.

wash bowl A basin or bowl, either portable or stationary, used for washing the hands and face. Also **wash basin.**

wash·cloth (wosh′klôth′, -kloth′, wôsh′-) *n.* A small cloth used for washing the body.

wash·day (wosh′dā′, wôsh′-) *n.* A day of the week set aside for doing household washing.

washed-out (wosht′out′, wôsht′-) *adj.* 1 Faded; colorless; pale. 2 *Colloq.* Exhausted; worn-out; tired.

washed-up (wosht′up′, wôsht′-) *adj. Slang* Finished; done with; through.

wash·er (wosh′ər, wô′shər) *n.* 1 One who washes. 2 *Mech.* A small, flat, perforated disk of metal, leather, or wood, used for placing beneath a nut or at an axle bearing or joint, to serve as a cushion, to relieve friction, etc. 3 A machine for washing (ore or clothes). 4 A device for purifying gases; a scrubber.

wash·er·man (wosh′ər·mən, wô′shər-) *n. pl.* **·men** (-mən) A laundryman.

wash·er·wom·an (wosh′ər·wŏŏm′ən, wô′shər-) *n. pl.* **·wom·en** (-wim′in) A laundress.

wash·ing (wosh′ing, wô′shing) *n.* 1 The act of one who washes. 2 Things (as clothing) washed on one occasion, or collected during a certain time. 3 That which is retained after being washed: a *washing* of ore. 4 A thin coating of metal: The forks had received only one *washing* of silver. 5 The sale of stock or other securities at a stock exchange between parties of one interest, in order to create a fictitious activity. — *adj.* Used in or intended for washing.

washing soda Sodium carbonate.

Wash·ing·ton (wosh′ing·tən, wô′shing-) 1 A State in NW United States, adjoining Canada; 68,192 square miles; capital, Olympia; entered the Union Nov. 11, 1889; nickname, *Evergreen State*: abbr. *Wash.* 2 A city coextensive with the District of Columbia and capital of the United States. — **Wash′ing·to′·ni·an** (-tō′nē·ən) *adj. & n.*

Wash·ing·ton (wosh′ing·tən, wô′shing-), **Booker Taliaferro,** 1856–1915, U. S. Negro educator. — **George,** 1732–99, American patriot, soldier, and statesman; first president of the United States 1789–97. — **Martha,** 1731–1802, *née* Dandridge (Mrs. Daniel Parke Custis 1749–57), wife of George Washington.

Washington, Lake A lake in west central Washington, near Seattle; 20 miles long.

Washington, Mount The highest peak of the White Mountains of New Hampshire; 6,288 feet.

Washington palm The fan palm (*Washingtonia filifera*) of California and the Colorado desert.

Washington pie A layer cake with a filling of cream or jam.

Washington's Birthday The anniversary of George Washington's birth, February 22: a legal holiday in most States of the United States.

Wash·i·ta River (wosh′ə·tô, wô′shə-) 1 See OUACHITA RIVER. 2 A river in Texas and Oklahoma, flowing 450 miles SE and east from the Texas Panhandle near the Oklahoma border to Lake Texoma; formerly flowed 40 miles further to the Red River.

wash·out (wosh′out′, wôsh′-) *n.* 1 A considerable erosion of earth by the action of water; also, the excavation thus made; a gully or gulch. 2 *Aeron.* A decrease in the angle of incidence of an airplane wing toward the tip. 3 *Slang* A hopeless or total failure.

wash·rag (wosh′rag′, wôsh′-) *n.* A washcloth.

wash·room (wosh′rŏŏm′, -rŏŏm′, wôsh′-) *n.* A lavatory.

wash sale On a stock exchange, the buying of stock by the seller's agents, to mislead as to the real demand.

wash·stand (wosh′stand′, wôsh′-) *n.* A piece of furniture used for holding the utensils for ablutions; a stand for wash bowl, pitcher, etc.

wash·tub (wosh′tub′, wôsh′-) *n.* A tub used for washing.

wash·wom·an (wosh′wŏŏm′ən, wôsh′-) *n. pl.* **·wom·en** (-wim′in) A washerwoman.

wash·y (wosh′ē, wô′shē) *adj.* **wash·i·er, wash·i·est** 1 Overly wet; sodden; water-logged. 2 Bringing rain: said of weather or wind. 3 Wanting in substance, solidity, stamina, or force; wishy-washy; feeble. 4 Sweating: said of horses. — **wash′i·ness** *n.*

was·n't (woz′ənt, wuz′-) Was not.

wasp (wosp, wôsp) *n.* Any of numerous hymenopterous insects, chiefly of the superfamilies *Sphecoidea* and *Vespoidea*, of which the workers and females are provided with effective stings. The typical social wasps construct papery nests of masticated vegetable material; they feed on fruits, the nectar of flowers, and on insects. The solitary wasps construct nests of mud or sand. ◆ Collateral adjective: *vespine*. [OE *wæsp*]

WASP (wosp, wôsp) *n. Slang* A white Protestant American. [From the initial letters of the words "white Anglo-Saxon Protestant"]

wasp·ish (wos′pish, wôs′-) *adj.* 1 Having a nature like a wasp; irritable; irascible. 2 Having a wasplike form or slender waist. See synonyms under FRETFUL. — **wasp′ish·ly** *adv.* — **wasp′ish·ness** *n.*

wasp waist A person's waist, so slender as to suggest that of a wasp. — **wasp-waist·ed** (wosp′wās′tid, wôsp′-) *adj.*

wasp·y (wos′pē, wôs′-) *adj.* **wasp·i·er, wasp·i·est** Like a wasp; waspish.

was·sail (wos′əl, was′-, wo·sāl′) *n.* 1 An ancient salutation or toast; an expression of good will in festivities, especially when pledging someone's health. See DRINK-HAIL. 2 The liquor prepared for a wassail; especially, a mixture of ale and wine with sugar, roasted apples, spices, etc. 3 A festivity at which healths are drunk; a carousal. 4 *Brit.* A convivial song. — *v.i.* To take part in a wassail; carouse. — *v.t.* To drink the health of; toast. [ME *wæs hæil* <ON *ves heill* be whole (*i.e.*, in good health)] — **was′sail·er** *n.*

Was·ser·mann (väs′ər·män), **August von,** 1866–1925, German physician and bacteriologist. — **Jakob,** 1873–1934, German novelist.

Wasserman reaction A diagnostic test for syphilis, based on testing the serum of the blood for syphilitic antibodies. Also **Wassermann test.** [after August von *Wasserman*]

wast[1] (wost, *unstressed* wəst) Archaic second person singular, past indicative of BE: used with *thou.*

wast[2] (wast) *adj. Scot.* West.

wast·age (wās′tij) *n.* That which is lost by leakage, wear, waste, etc.

waste (wāst) *adj.* 1 Cast aside as worthless or of no practical value; used; worn out; discarded. 2 Excreted; cast out of an animal body, as food, etc. 3 Not under cultivation; untilled; hence, unproductive; unoccupied. 4 Made desolate; ruined; dismal; gloomy. 5 Containing or conveying waste products. 6 Produced in excess of consumption; superfluous: *waste* energy. 7 *Obs.* Wasteful; lavish. — **to lay waste** To destroy utterly. — *v.* **wast·ed, wast·ing** *v.t.* 1 To use or expend thoughtlessly, uselessly, or without return; be prodigal or extravagant of; squander. 2 To cause to lose strength, vigor, or bulk; make weak or feeble. 3 To use up; exhaust; consume. 4 To fail to use or take advantage of, as an opportunity. 5 To lay waste; desolate; devastate. — *v.i.* 6 To lose strength, vigor, or bulk; become weak or feeble: often with *away*. 7 To diminish or dwindle gradually. 8 To pass gradually: said of time. See synonyms under SQUANDER, WEAR[1]. — *n.* 1 The act of wasting or squandering, or the state of being wasted; useless or unnecessary expenditure. 2 A place or a region that is devastated or made desolate; wilderness; desert. 3 A continuous, gradual diminishing of strength, vigor, or substance by use or wear. 4 The act of laying waste or devastating; ravage: the *waste* of war. 5 Something rejected as worthless or unneeded; specifically, tangled spun cotton thread, the refuse of a textile factory; also, steam or other fluid that escapes without being used. 6 Garbage; rubbish; trash. 7 The waste products of the soil due to erosion by chemical or human action and carried out to sea by running water. 8 A wasting disease; specifically, consumption. ◆ Homophone: *waist*. [<AF *waster*, ult. <L *vastare* lay waste < *vastus* desert, desolate. Related to VAST.]

Synonyms (adj.): excess, extra, redundant, refuse, superfluous, useless, valueless, worthless. See BLEAK, VACANT. *Antonyms*: choice, good, precious, useful, valuable.

Synonyms (noun): chaff, debris, dregs, dross, leavings, offal, offscouring, refuse, remains, scum, sediment. See EXCESS, LOSS.

Waste may appear as a combining form in hyphemes or solidemes, or as the first element in two-word phrases, with the meaning: containing or conveying refuse or waste; as in:

waste bin	**waste sluice**
waste-collector	**waste trap**
waste gate	**waste-water**
waste heap	**wasteway**
waste pit	**wasteyard**

waste·bas·ket (wāst′bas′kit, -bäs′-) *n.* A basket for paper scraps and other waste.

waste·ful (wāst′fəl) *adj.* 1 Prone to waste; extravagant. 2 Causing waste; ruinous. — **waste′ful·ly** *adv.* — **waste′ful·ness** *n.*

waste·land (wāst′land′) *n.* A barren or desolate land.

waste paper Paper thrown away as worthless. Also **waste·pa·per** (wāst′pā′pər). — **waste′-pa′per** *adj.*

waste-paper basket A wastebasket.

waste pipe A pipe for carrying off waste-water, etc.

wast·er (wās′tər) *n.* One who wastes; a wastrel.

wast·ing (wās′ting) *adj.* 1 Producing emaciation; sapping the strength; enfeebling: a *wasting* fever. 2 Laying waste; devastating.

wast·rel (wās′trəl) *n.* 1 An abandoned child; a waif. 2 A waster; a profligate; spendthrift. [Dim. of WASTER]

wast·ry (wās′trē) *Scot.* or *Obs. adj.* Wasteful. — *n.* Wastefulness: also **waste′rie, wast′·rie, wast′rife.**

wat[1] (wat) *adj. Scot.* 1 Intemperate. 2 Wet.

wat[2] (wot) *n.* A hare. [Prob. from *Wat*, nickname for WALTER]

wa·tap (wä·täp′) *n.* Roots of the spruce, cedar, pine, etc., used by North American Indians to sew bark for canoes and other objects. Also **wa·ta·pe** (wä·tä′pe). [<Algonquian (Narraganset) *wattap* a root of a tree]

watch (woch) *v.i.* 1 To be constantly on the alert; give earnest heed; be observant, vigilant, or attentive. 2 To look attentively; observe. 3 To wait expectantly for something; be in a state of expectation: with *for*. 4 To do duty as a guard or sentinel; serve as a watchman. 5 To have in one's care or keeping; guard; tend. 6 To be awake; go without sleep; keep vigil. — *v.t.* 7 To keep under observation; look at steadily and attentively; observe. 8 To follow the course of mentally; keep informed concerning. 9 To be alert for; wait for expectantly: to *watch* one's opportunity. 10 To keep watch over; guard. See synonyms under ABIDE, LOOK. — *n.* 1 The act of watching; wakefulness with close and continuous attention; careful observation; vigil. 2 One of the divisions of the night made in ancient times: with the Hebrews, one third; with the Romans, one fourth; hence, any indefinite waking period which marks the passage of the night. 3 Position or

service as a guard or sentry. **4** *Obs.* Vigilance; a vigil; wake. **5** One or more persons set to watch; a watchman or set of watchmen; sentinel; guard. **6** The place occupied by or assigned to a guard. **7** The period of time during which a guard is on duty. **8** *Naut.* **a** One of the two divisions of a ship's officers and crew, performing duty in alternation. **b** The period of time during which each division is on duty: four hours, except the dog-watches, from 4 to 6 and from 6 to 8 p.m., which are interposed daily to shift night duty from one watch to the other alternately. **9** A small, portable timepiece, actuated by a coiled spring, for keeping and indicating time. **10** *Obs.* A candle marked into equal sections, each of which burns a known length of time. **11** *Obs.* The cry of a watchman. **12** *Obs.* Wakefulness; the state of staying or being awake. See synonyms under OVERSIGHT. [OE *waeccan.* Akin to WAKE[1].]

watch cap In the U. S. Navy, a small, knitted woolen cap of navy blue worn by enlisted men during cold weather.

watch·case (woch′kās′) *n.* **1** The protecting case of a watch: usually of gold or silver. **2** *Obs.* A sentry box.

watch·cry (woch′krī) *n.* *pl.* **·cries** A slogan; a watchword.

watch·dog (woch′dôg′, -dog′) *n.* A dog kept to guard a building or other property.

watch·er (woch′ər) *n.* **1** One who watches; especially, one who watches by a sickbed, deathbed, or corpse. **2** One who watches the voting at the polls on election day to detect dishonest practices.

watch·ful (woch′fəl) *adj.* **1** Vigilant. **2** *Obs.* Wakeful. See synonyms under ALERT, VIGILANT. — **watch′ful·ly** *adv.* — **watch′ful·ness** *n.*

watch·guard (woch′gärd′) *n.* A chain, cord, or ribbon attached to a watch and fastened to the clothing.

watch·mak·er (woch′mā′kər) *n.* One who makes or repairs watches.

watch·man (woch′mən) *n.* *pl.* **·men** (-mən) **1** Formerly, one of a group of men appointed to keep watch or patrol the streets of a town or village at night. **2** Anyone who keeps watch or guard; especially, a man employed to guard a building, etc., at night.

watch night New Year's Eve.

watch·tow·er (woch′tou′ər) *n.* A tower upon which a sentinel is stationed.

watch·word (woch′wûrd′) *n.* **1** A secret password. **2** A rallying cry or maxim.

Wa·ten·stedt–Salz·git·ter (vä′tən·shtet·zälts′git·ər) A city in SE Lower Saxony, north central West Germany.

wa·ter (wô′tər, wot′ər) *n.* **1** A colorless limpid liquid compound of hydrogen and oxygen, H_2O, in the proportion of two volumes of hydrogen to one of oxygen, or by weight of approximately 2 parts of hydrogen to 16 of oxygen. Water has its maximum density at 4° C. or 39° F., one cubic centimeter weighing a gram. It freezes at 0° C. or 32° F., and boils at 100° C. or 212° F. **2** Any body of water, as a lake, river, or a sea; in Scotland, a small river. **3** Any one of the aqueous or liquid secretions of animals; also, perspiration, tears, urine, etc. **4** Any preparation of water holding a gaseous or volatile substance in solution. **5** The transparency or luster of a precious stone or a pearl; hence, excellence; purity. **6** An undulating sheen given to certain fabrics, as silk, etc. **7** In commerce and finance, stock issued without increase of paid-in capital to represent it. — **above water** Out of danger; secure. — **hard water** Water containing in solution salts of calcium and magnesium, especially the sulfates or bicarbonates of these elements: so called because of the difficulty of obtaining a soap lather with such water. — **soft water** Water free from the salts of calcium and magnesium, as rain water and water found in sandstone districts. — *v.t.* **1** To pour water upon; irrigate. **2** To provide with water for drinking; give water to. **3** To dilute or weaken with water: often with *down.* **4** To give an undulating sheen to the surface of (silk, linen, etc.) by uneven pressure after

damping and heating. **5** To enlarge the number of shares of (a stock company) without increasing the paid-in capital in proportion. **6** To provide with streams: used in the passive participle. — *v.i.* **7** To secrete or discharge water, tears, etc. **8** To fill with saliva, as the mouth, from desire for food. **9** To drink water. **10** To take in water, as a locomotive. [OE *wæter.* Akin to OTTER.]

Water may appear as a combining form in hyphemes or solidemes, or as the first element in two-word phrases:

water-analysis	water-laden
water barge	water-locked
water-bearing	water pail
water bottle	waterplane
water-bound	water plant
water bucket	water police
water-carrier	water problem
water-carrying	water project
water cask	water pump
water channel	water-quenched
water content	water-resistant
water-deposited	water resources
water diver	water-rolling
water-drain	water-rot
water-drawer	water-rotted
water-drinker	water-route
water-drinking	water-scarcity
water flow	water-sealed
water-flushed	water service
water fountain	water-soaked
waterfree	water-sodden
water-girt	water source
water-gray	water tap
water-green	water trough
water heater	water turbine
waterhole	water-walled
water insect	water-washed
water jar	water-wasting

water adder 1 The water moccasin. **2** The water snake.

wa·ter·age (wô′tər·ij, wot′ər-) *n.* *Brit.* Conveyance of merchandise by water; also, the fee paid for such transportation.

wa·ter·back (wô′tər·bak′, wot′ər-) *n.* A coil or chamber for heating water in the back of a range or other stove.

water balance *Biol.* The preservation of a nearly uniform water content in an organism, especially a plant.

water bear See under TARDIGRADE.

Wa·ter·bear·er (wô′tər·bâr′ər, wot′ər-) The constellation Aquarius.

water bearing *Mech.* A journal bearing in which water under pressure does the work of a lubricant.

wa·ter·bed (wô′tər·bed′, wot′ər-) *n.* A bed with a water-filled container serving as a mattress, adjustable in firmness and often heated.

water beetle Any of several aquatic beetles (especially the families *Dytiscidae, Hydrophilidae* or *Gyrinidae*), having legs flattened and fringed with hairs for swimming.

water bird Any bird living on or near water.

water biscuit A plain cracker or biscuit of flour, shortening, and water.

water blink In arctic regions, a cloud or spot on the horizon arising from and indicating the presence of open water: a sign of the breaking up of winter.

water blister A blister containing limpid watery matter.

wa·ter·bloom (wô′tər·bloom′, wot′ər-) *n.* The sudden appearance of large masses of blue-green algae in bodies of fresh water.

wa·ter·borne (wô′tər·bôrn′, -bōrn′, wot′ər-) *adj.* **1** Floating on water. **2** Transported or carried by water: *water-borne* commerce.

wa·ter·brain (wô′tər·brān′, wot′ər-) *n.* A disease of sheep characterized by staggering as from giddiness; gid.

water brake *Mech.* A brake, formerly used on steam locomotives, formed by using water pressure to provide a braking effect.

wa·ter·brash (wô′tər·brash′, wot′ər-) *n. Pathol.* Pyrosis; heartburn.

wa·ter·buck (wô′tər·buk′, wot′ər-) *n.* **1** Either of two large African antelopes (genus *Kobus*), frequenting the neighborhood of rivers and swimming with ease; especially, *K. ellipsiprymnus* of south central Africa. **2** Any

of several similar antelopes. [<Du. *waterbok*]

water buffalo 1 A buffalo (*Bubalus bubalus*) of India, the largest of wild cattle, attaining a height of 6 feet at the withers and a very wide spread of horns. When domesticated it becomes a useful draft animal. **2** The carabao. Also called *Indian buffalo.*

WATER BUFFALO
(Spread of horns
up to 9 feet)

water bug 1 The Croton bug. **2** Any of various hemipterous bugs (family *Belostomatidae*) which live in the water, especially the large species (*Lethocerus americanus*) common in North America. **3** The water scorpion.

Wa·ter·bu·ry (wô′tər·ber′ē, wot′ər-) A city in SW Connecticut; an industrial center, especially of the brass industry.

water chestnut 1 The hard horned edible fruit of an aquatic plant (*Trapa natans*). **2** The plant itself: also **water caltrop, wa′ter·nut′.**

water chinkapin 1 The American or yellow lotus (*Nelumbium pentapetalum*). **2** One of its edible nutlike seeds. Also **water chinkapin.**

WATER CHINKAPIN
a. Flower. *b.* Leaf.
c. Fruit.

wa·ter·clock (wô′tər·klok′, wot′ər-) *n.* Any device, as a clepsydra, for measuring time by the fall or flow of water.

wa·ter·clos·et (wô′tər·kloz′it, wot′ər-) *n.* A room or closet having a hopper flushed and discharged by means of water, used as a privy; also, the hopper and its trap.

wa·ter·col·or (wô′tər·kul′ər, wot′ər-) *adj.* Of, pertaining to, used with, or executed in water colors.

water color 1 A color prepared for painting with water as the medium, as distinguished from one to be used with oil, tempera, etc., as the medium, and characterized by the fact that the result may be either transparent or opaque. **2** That branch of painting in which water colors are used, or the method of using them. **3** A picture or painting done in water colors.

wa·ter·cool (wô′tər·kool′, wot′ər-) *v.t.* To cool by means of water, as by using a water jacket on an internal-combustion engine. — **wa′ter·cooled′** *adj.* — **wa′ter·cool′ing** *adj.* & *n.*

water cooler A vessel or apparatus for cooling and dispensing drinking water: often operated electrically.

wa·ter·course (wô′tər·kôrs′, -kōrs′, wot′ər-) *n.* **1** A stream of water; river; brook; a stream having a bed and banks. **2** The course or channel of a stream of water; a canal. See synonyms under STREAM.

wa·ter·craft (wô′tər·kraft′, -kräft′, wot′ər-) *n.* **1** Skill in sailing boats or in aquatic sports. **2** Any boat or ship; also, sailing vessels collectively.

water crake 1 The spotted crake. **2** The water ouzel. See under OUZEL.

wa·ter·cress (wô′tər·kres′, wot′ər-) *n.* A creeping perennial herb (*Rorippa nasturtium-aquaticum*) of the mustard family, having pinnate leaves and white flowers. It grows in springs and clear cool streams and is cultivated for use as salad.

water culture Hydroponics.

water cure 1 *Med.* Hydropathy. **2** *Colloq.* A kind of torture in which large quantities of water are put forcibly down the victim's throat.

water cushion A pool of water maintained to absorb the impact of water, as from the spillway of a dam.

water dog 1 A dog that takes readily to the water, as the water spaniel. **2** A dog trained to retrieve water fowl. **3** *Colloq.* An old sailor.

Wa·ter·ee (wô′tə·rē′) The lower course of the

CATAWBA RIVER, flowing about 75 miles from north central South Carolina to a junction with the Congaree, forming the Santee.

water elm The planer tree.

wa·ter·er (wô′tər·ər, wot′ər-) *n.* **1** One who waters, in any sense. **2** Any contrivance used for watering.

wa·ter·fall (wô′tər·fôl′, wot′ər-) *n.* **1** A cataract; cascade. **2** *Colloq.* A chignon suggesting a cascade. [OE *wætergefeall*]

water fence A fence built into or across a stream, or one extending into the water on the shore of a lake or the sea, to prevent cattle, horses, etc., from passing around it.

wa·ter–find·er (wô′tər·fin′dər, wot′ər-) *n.* A dowser who tries to locate underground water with a divining rod. See RHABDOMANCY.

wa·ter·flea (wô′tər·flē′, wot′ər-) *n.* Any of numerous minute, fresh–water crustaceans (family *Daphniidae*), about the size of a flea, which swim with a jumping motion.

Wa·ter·ford (wô′tər·fərd, wot′ər-) **1** A maritime county in eastern Munster province, Ireland; 710 square miles. **2** Its county town, a port on **Waterford Harbor**, an inlet of the Atlantic in southern Ireland; 15 miles long.

water fowl **1** A bird that lives on or about the water, especially a swimming game bird. **2** Such birds collectively.

wa·ter·front (wô′tər·frunt′, wot′ər-) *n.* **1** Real property abutting on or overlooking a natural body of water. **2** That part of a town which fronts on a body of water. **3** A coil or chamber for heating water in the front of a range or other stove.

water gage A gage indicating the level of water in a boiler, etc. Also **water gauge.**

water gall **1** A hollow in the earth made by a flood, etc.; a washout. **2** A partial rainbow: also, *Scot., weather gall.* [<WATER + GALL[2]]

water gap A deep ravine in a mountain ridge giving passage to a stream.

water gas A highly poisonous mixture of hydrogen and carbon monoxide produced by forcing steam over white–hot carbon (as coal or coke): used for cooking and heating, and when carbureted, as an illuminant. — **wa·ter–gas** (wô′tər·gas′, wot′ər-) *adj.*

wa·ter·gate (wô′tər·gāt′, wot′ər-) *n.* Floodgate (def. 1).

wa·ter·glass (wô′tər·glas′, -gläs′, wot′ər-) *n.* **1** A waterclock; clepsydra. **2** A glass–bottomed tube or box for examining objects lying or moving under water. **3** A substance composed of sodium silicate, potassium silicate, or both, soluble in hot water: used in preserving eggs, as a facing for walls, etc. **4** A water gage on a steam boiler, etc. **5** A vessel for holding water; a drinking glass.

wa·ter·gum (wô′tər·gum′, wot′ər-) *n.* **1** The American sourgum or tupelo tree. **2** Any of several trees of the myrtle family, especially a tall, slender, ornamental shrub *(Tristania laurina)* native to Australia, with opposite leaves and yellow flowers.

water hammer **1** The concussion of confined water when its flow is suddenly arrested, as when a faucet is suddenly closed. **2** The hammering sound caused in pipes containing water when live steam is admitted. **3** A sealed tube void of air but containing water which strikes against the ends of the tube with a sharp knocking sound when shaken: used to demonstrate the equal rate of fall of solids and liquids in a vacuum.

water haul **1** In fishing, an empty haul of the net. **2** Any fruitless attempt or effort.

water hemlock Any of a genus *(Cicuta)* of poisonous, typically North American flowering herbs of the carrot family; especially, the **spotted water hemlock** *(C. maculata)* of the United States, highly injurious to livestock, and the Old World species *(C. virosa).*

water hen **1** Any of several coots or gallinules that frequent ponds and streams; especially, the moorhen. **2** The American coot *(Fulica americana).*

water hyacinth An aquatic herb of tropical America *(Eichornia crassipes)* with pendulous branched roots and a whorl of floating glossy leaves containing a cluster of bluish–purple to lilac and white flowers.

water ice **1** An ice made with water, sugar, and fruit juice. **2** Ice formed by the freezing of water as distinguished from that formed by the packing together of snow.

wa·ter–inch (wô′tər·inch′, wot′ər-) *n.* An old unit of hydraulic measure based on the discharge of water from a round hole with a diameter of one inch: reckoned at fourteen pints a minute.

wa·ter·ing (wô′tər·ing, wot′ər-) *n.* **1** The act of one who waters. **2** The process of producing a wavy ornamental effect. — *adj.* **1** Sprinkling; irrigating; that waters. **2** Situated near the shore or near mineral springs: a *watering* place.

watering cart A cart carrying a barrel or large tank of water: used for sprinkling streets.

watering place **1** A place where water can be obtained, as a spring; also, a place by a road where horses can be watered. **2** A health resort having mineral springs; also, a pleasure resort near the water.

watering pot A tin can having a spout fitted with a perforated nozzle: used for watering flowers, etc.

wa·ter·ish (wô′tər·ish, wot′ər-) *adj.* Resembling water; watery; hence, weak.

wa·ter–jack·et (wô′tər·jak′it, wot′ər-) *v.t.* To encase in or fit with a water jacket.

water jacket A casing containing water and surrounding a cylinder or mechanism, especially the cylinder block of an internal–combustion engine, for keeping it cool.

water jump A water barrier, as a pool, stream, or ditch, to be jumped over by the horses in a steeplechase.

water leaf Any of a genus *(Hydrophyllum)* of delicate biennial or perennial herbs with white or blue flowers, growing in the woods of North America.

wa·ter·less (wô′tər·lis, wot′ər-) *adj.* Without water; arid; dry.

wa·ter–lev·el (wô′tər·lev′əl, wot′ər-) *adj.* Following the course of a river: a *water–level* route.

water level **1** The level of still water in the sea or in any other body of water. **2** A water table. **3** *Naut.* A ship's water line. **4** A leveling instrument in which water serves to determine the horizontal line.

wa·ter·lift (wô′tər·lift′, wot′ər-) *n.* The transportation of personnel, equipment, and supplies by water, with special reference to the 1950 military campaign in Korea.

wa·ter·lil·y (wô′tər·lil′ē, wot′ər-) *n. pl.* **·lil·ies** **1** Any plant of a genus *(Nymphaea)* of showy aquatic herbs of temperate and tropical regions, with large floating leaves and flowers; especially, the fragrant **white waterlily** *(N. odorata)* of the eastern United States. **2** The yellow pondlily *(Nuphar luteum)* of the same family. **3** The Victoria waterlily.

water line **1** *Naut.* That part of the hull of a ship which corresponds with the water level at various loads. **2** Water level. **3** A river or system of waterways affording transportation.

water locust A small species of the American honey locust *(Gleditsia aquatica)* growing in southern swamps and boglands: also called *swamp locust.*

wa·ter–logged (wô′tər·lôgd′, -logd′, wot′ər-) *adj.* **1** Heavy and unmanageable on account of the leakage of water into the hold, as a ship. **2** Water–soaked; saturated with water. [<WATER + LOG *v.*, in obs. sense of "to reduce to the condition of a log"]

Wa·ter·loo (wô′tər·lo͞o, wô′tər·lo͞o′) A village in central Belgium; scene of Napoleon's final defeat by Wellington and Blücher, June 18, 1815; hence, final and decisive defeat; a complete reverse.

water lot **1** A building lot fronting on a body of water, as a river, harbor, etc. **2** A lot or piece of ground wholly or partially covered by water, or a piece of marsh or swamp land designated to be filled in for use.

water main A large conduit for carrying water, especially one laid underground.

wa·ter·man (wô′tər·mən, wot′ər-) *n. pl.* **·men** (-mən) A man who plies for hire with a boat or small vessel on the water; a boatman. — **wa′ter·man·ship′** *n.*

water marigold An aquatic plant *(Bidens becki)* with terminal heads of yellow flowers.

wa·ter·mark (wô′tər·märk′, wot′ər-) *n.* **1** A mark showing the extent to which water rises; especially, the line marking the limit of the ebb and flow of the tide. **2** A series of translucent lines, letters, or designs made in paper by shaping the wires of the dandy rolls over which the paper passes while still in a pulpous state; also, the metal pattern which produces these markings. — *v.t.* **1** To impress (paper) with a watermark. **2** To impress as a watermark.

wa·ter·mel·on (wô′tər·mel′ən, wot′ər-) *n.* **1** The large edible fruit of a trailing plant *(Citrullus vulgaris)* of the gourd family, containing a many–seeded red or pink pulp and a refreshing sweet, watery juice. **2** The plant on which this fruit grows.

water meter An instrument for registering the amount of water flowing through a pipe, etc.

water milfoil Any of a genus *(Myriophyllum)* of aquatic herbs with graceful, feathery leaves.

water mill A mill operated by waterpower.

water moccasin The cottonmouth.

water motor **1** A turbine operated by waterpower. **2** A water wheel.

water nymph In classical mythology, any nymph or goddess living in or guarding a body of water; a naiad, Nereid, Oceanid, etc.

water oak A species of oak *(Quercus nigra)* growing near swamps and streams in the eastern United States.

water of Ayr See AYR STONE.

water of crystallization *Chem.* Water forming part of crystallized salts, from which it may be eliminated by heat, often with loss of crystalline structure. Also **water of hydration.**

water of life A rare and mysterious water that restores the dead to life. The human hope and belief that death can be overcome is expressed in the water–of–life motif in the peasant folklore of every European country, in the myths of the ancient Persians, Greeks, Romans, Hebrews, Hindus, in Japanese mythology, and in the folk tales of all primitive peoples, as the Polynesians, North and South American Indians, etc.

water ouzel See under OUZEL.

water ox A water buffalo.

wa·ter–part·ing (wô′tər·pär′ting, wot′ər-) *n.* A watershed.

wa·ter·pep·per (wô′tər·pep′ər, wot′ər-) *n.* Any of several species of knotweed, especially the common smartweed.

water pimpernel **1** The brookweed. **2** The common pimpernel.

water plantain Any of a genus *(Alsima)* of common, smooth, aquatic herbs with leaves like those of the plantain, especially the North American species *(A. plantago–aquatica).*

water polo A game played in a swimming pool by two teams of seven swimmers each, who push or throw a round, buoyant ball toward opposite goals.

wa·ter·pow·er (wô′tər·pou′ər, wot′ər-) *n.* **1** The power of water derived from its gravity or its momentum as applied to the driving of machinery. **2** A descent or fall in a stream from which motive power may be obtained.

water pox *Pathol.* Varicella.

wa·ter·proof (wô′tər·pro͞of′, wot′ər-) *adj.* **1** Proof against water. **2** Impervious to water. **3** Coated with some substance, as rubber, which resists the passage of water. — *n.* **1** Material or fabric rendered impervious to water. **2** *Brit.* A raincoat or other garment made of such fabric. — *v.t.* To render waterproof.

water purslane **1** An herb *(Isnardia* or *Ludwigia palustris)* of the evening–primrose family, procumbent and creeping in muddy places and floating in water. **2** An aquatic plant *(Didiplis* or *Peplis diandra)* growing in swampy ground in the U. S.

water ram A hydraulic ram.

water rat **1** The American muskrat. **2** The European water vole *(Microtus amphibius).* **3** Any of a subfamily *(Hydromyinae)* of aquatic rodents of New Guinea, Australia, and the Philippines. **4** *Slang* A thief or tough who frequents the waterfront.

water repellent *Chem.* Any of various chemicals, as an emulsion of aluminum acetate, used to make textiles, leather, and other porous materials resistant to wetting by water but which does not waterproof them or impair their desirable properties. — **wa·ter–re·pel·lent** (wô′tər·ri·pel′ənt, wot′ər-) *adj.*

wa·ter·right (wô′tər·rīt′, wot′ər-) *n.* **1** The right to draw upon a water supply. **2** The

right to use or navigate a particular body of water. Also **water right.**

water sapphire A rich blue variety of iolite often worn as an ornament. [Trans. of F *saphir d'eau*]

wa·ter·scape (wô′tər·skāp, wot′ər-) *n.* A sea or other water view, as distinguished from a landscape. [< WATER + (LAND)SCAPE]

water scorpion Any of numerous hemipterous insects of aquatic habits (family *Nepidae*), having raptorial front legs and a long breathing tube at the end of the abdomen.

wa·ter·shed (wô′tər·shed′, wot′ər-) *n.* **1** The line of separation between two contiguous drainage valleys. **2** The whole region from which a river receives its supply of water. **3** A decisive turning point profoundly affecting or altering what follows it.

wa·ter·shield (wô′tər·shēld′, wot′ər-) *n.* **1** An aquatic American herb (*Brasenia schreberi*) of the waterlily family, with the stems and the under sides of the leaves covered with a viscid jelly. **2** Any plant of a kindred genus (*Cabomba*), especially the fanwort.

wa·ter·sick (wô′tər·sik′, wot′ər-) *adj.* Unproductive because of excessive irrigation: said of land.

wa·ter·side (wô′tər·sīd′, wot′ər-) *n.* The shore of a body of water; the water's edge. —*adj.* **1** Of, pertaining to, or living or growing by the water's edge. **2** Working by the waterside, as a stevedore.

wa·ter·ski (wô′tər·skē′, wot′ər-) *v.i.* **-skied**, **-ski·ing** To glide over water on water-skis, while being towed by a motorboat. —*n.* A broad, ski-like runner with a fitting to hold the foot: worn in the sport of water-skiing. —**wa′ter-ski′er** *n.* —**wa′ter-ski′ing** *n.*

water snake 1 A serpent of aquatic habits. **2** Any of a genus (*Natrix*) of harmless North American snakes that live chiefly in water.

wa·ter·soak (wô′tər·sōk′, wot′ər-) *v.t.* To fill the pores or crevices of with water; soak in water.

wa·ter·sol·u·ble (wô′tər·sol′yə·bəl, wot′ər-) *adj. Biochem.* Soluble in water: said especially of certain organic compounds.

water spaniel The Irish water spaniel. See under SPANIEL.

water speedwell A common plant (*Veronica anagallis-aquatica*) of the composite family, growing in damp places.

wa·ter·spout (wô′tər·spout′, wot′ər-) *n.* **1** A moving, whirling column of spray and mist, with masses of water in the lower parts, accumulated because of a tornado at sea or on other large bodies of water. **2** A pipe for the free discharge of water, especially one connecting with the gutters of a roof: also called *rainspout*.

water sprite A water nymph.

water starwort Any of a widely distributed genus (*Callitriche*) of herbaceous aquatic plants, especially *C. autumnalis*, common in the United States.

water station A place beside a railroad where there is a water tank for supplying locomotives with water.

water strider Any of a family (*Gerridae*) of hemipterous insects with elongate middle and hind legs adapted for darting over the surface of water.

water supply 1 The water available for the use of a community or region. **2** The means for supplying it, as reservoirs, lakes, etc. —**wa·ter·sup·ply** (wô′tər·sə·plī′, wot′ər-) *adj.*

water system 1 A river with all its tributaries, considered as a hydrologic unit. **2** Water supply.

water table 1 *Archit.* A projecting ledge, molding, or string-course, running along the sides of a building to shed the rain. **2** The surface marking the upper level of a water-saturated zone extending beneath the ground to depths determined by the thickness of the permeable strata.

water tank A large cistern of wood or metal, as upon an engine or building, for storing or supplying water.

water thrush 1 Any of certain American warblers (genus *Seiurus*) frequenting swamps and streams; especially, the common or **northern water thrush** (*S. noveboracensis*), olive-brown above, yellowish beneath, with dusky streaks and a buffy superciliary line, and the **Louisiana water thrush** (*S. motacilla*), with a pure-white superciliary line. **2** The water ouzel.

water tiger The larva of the diving beetle.

wa·ter·tight (wô′tər·tīt′, wot′ər-) *adj.* **1** So closely made that water cannot enter or leak through. **2** Constructed so as to be impermeable; without loopholes: a *watertight* legal document.

Wa·ter·ton Lakes National Park (wô′tər·tən) A national park in SW Alberta, Canada; 204 square miles; adjoining Glacier National Park, Montana, forming with it the **Waterton-Glacier International Peace Park**; total area, 1,800 square miles; highest U.S. point, 10,448 feet; highest Canadian point, 9,600 feet; established 1932.

water tower 1 A standpipe or tower, often of considerable height, used as a reservoir for a system of water distribution. **2** A vehicular tower-like structure having an extensible vertical pipe from which water can be played on a burning building from a great height.

wa·ter·tube boiler (wô′tər·tōōb′, -tyōōb′, wot′ər-) A type of boiler in which continuously heated water circulates through a series of tubes communicating with a steam chamber.

water turkey The snakebird.

water vapor The vapor of water, especially when found below the boiling point, as in the atmosphere. Compare STEAM.

wa·ter·vas·cu·lar system (wô′tər·vas′kyə·lər, wot′ər) A closed system unique in echinoderms consisting of water-filled canals and reservoirs which serve in locomotion and also in some species in respiration, excretion, and sensory reception.

water wave 1 An undulating effect of the hair, artificially produced when the hair is wet, and usually set by drying with heat. **2** A wave of water; a billow.

wa·ter·way (wô′tər·wā′, wot′ər-) *n.* A river, channel, or other stream of water as a means of communication; water route.

wa·ter·weed (wô′tər·wēd′, wot′ər-) *n.* **1** A submerged aquatic perennial (*Anacharis canadensis*), having whitish flowers. **2** Any of various other aquatic plants, as the pondweed.

water wheel 1 A wheel so equipped with floats, buckets, etc., that it may be turned by flowing water. See OVERSHOT WHEEL. **2** A noria.

water wings A waterproof, wing-shaped fabric device that may be inflated with air and used as a support for the body while swimming or learning to swim.

water witch 1 One who claims to discover underground springs with the use of a divining rod or hazel wand. **2** Any of various quick-diving water birds, as certain grebes.

water witching The use of a divining rod to discover water; rhabdomancy.

wa·ter·works (wô′tər·wûrks′, wot′ər-) *n. pl.* **1** A display or pageant presented on floats; a display of fountains in operation. **2** A system of machines, buildings, and appliances for furnishing a water supply, especially for a city; also, any mill or factory run by waterpower. **3** *Slang* **a** Tears: usually in the phrase *to turn on the waterworks.* **b** Rain.

wa·ter·worn (wô′tər·wôrn′, -wōrn′, wot′ər-) *adj.* Worn smooth by running or falling water.

wa·ter·y (wô′tər·ē, wot′ər-ē) *adj.* **1** Containing or discharging water; brimming; tearful; soft and flabby. **2** Resembling water; thin or liquid. **3** Consisting of or pertaining to water. —**wa′ter·i·ness** *n.*

Wat·ford (wot′fərd) A municipal borough in Hertford, England, NW of London.

Wat·ling Island (wot′ling) See SAN SALVADOR. Also **Wat′lings Island.**

Wat·son (wot′sən), **John**, 1850–1907, Scottish minister and author: pseudonym, *Ian Maclaren.* —**John Broadus**, 1878–1958, U.S. psychologist. —**Sir William**, 1858–1935, English poet.

Wat·son-Watt (wot′sən·wot′), **Sir Robert Alexander**, born 1892, Scottish physicist.

watt (wot) *n.* The practical unit of electric power, activity, or rate of work: equivalent to 10^7 ergs or one joule per second, or approximately.1/746 of a horsepower; a volt-ampere. [after James *Watt*]

Watt (wot), **James**, 1736–1819, Scottish inventor and engineer.

wat·tage (wot′ij) *n.* **1** Amount of electric power in terms of watts. **2** The total number of watts needed to operate an appliance.

Wat·teau (wä·tō′, wot′ō) *adj.* Of or pertaining to Antoine Watteau, or the costumes shown in his pictures.

Wat·teau (wä·tō′, *Fr.* và·tō′), **Jean Antoine**, 1684–1721, French painter.

Watteau back A style of women's dress in which the fullness of the back is confined at the neck in plaits or gathers, and falls from there to the waistline.

Wat·ten·scheid (vät′ən·shīt′) A city of east central North Rhine-Westphalia, central West Germany; a coal-mining and manufacturing center in the Ruhr.

Wat·ter·son (wot′ər·sən), **Henry**, 1840-1921, U.S. editor and journalist.

watt·hour (wot′our′) *n.* Electrical energy equivalent to that represented by one watt acting for one hour.

wat·tle (wot′l) *n* **1** A frame of rods or twigs woven together; a hurdle or other wickerwork. **2** A twig or withe, especially as used for interweaving with others; also, collectively, material for fences, hurdles, roofs, etc. **3** A naked, fleshy process, often wrinkled and brightly colored, hanging from the throat of a bird or snake. **4** A pendent fold of skin on the throat or neck of some domestic swine. **5** A barbel of a fish. **6** Any one of various acacias of Australia, Tasmania, and South Africa: so called by the early colonists, who used the branches to make hurdles. **7** *pl.* Rods for supporting thatch on a roof. —*v.t.* **·tled**, **·tling 1** To weave or twist, as twigs, into a network. **2** To form, as baskets, by intertwining flexible twigs. **3** To bind together with wattles. —*adj.* Made of or covered with wattles; formed by wattling. [OE *watul*]

wat·tle·bird (wot′l·bûrd′) *n.* Any of several large Australian honey-eaters (genus *Anthochaera*), having conspicuous wattles about the head and face.

wat·tled (wot′ld) *adj.* **1** Made with wattles. **2** Having a wattle, as a bird. **3** *Her.* Having wattles, comb, or gills of a tincture different from that of the body.

watt·less (wot′lis) *adj. Electr.* Denoting an alternating current, or the component of such a current, which is neutralized by the originating electromotive force and which for that reason does not produce any power.

watt·me·ter (wot′mētər) *n.* An instrument for measuring in watts the rate of doing electrical work: also called *voltammeter.*

Watts (wots), **George Frederick**, 1817–1904, English painter and sculptor. —**Isaac**, 1674–1748, English theologian and hymn writer.

Watts-Dun·ton (wots′dun′tən). **Theodore**, 1832—1914, English critic and poet.

Wa·tu·si (wä·tōō′sē) *n. pl.* **-si** One of a pastoral, Bantu-speaking people of east central Africa.

Wau (wou) A town in the Territory of New Guinea, NE New Guinea, a gold-mining center reached only by air.

Waugh (wô), **Alec**, born 1898, English novelist and travel writer. —**Evelyn**, 1903–1966, English novelist and critic; brother of preceding.

wauk[1] (wôk) *v.i. Scot.* To full cloth.

wauk[2] (wôk) *v.t. Scot.* To wake; watch over.

waul (wôl) *v.i.* To give a prolonged, plaintive cry like that of a cat: also spelled *wawl.* [Imit.]

waur (wôr) *adj. Scot.* Worse.

wave (wāv) *v.* **waved**, **wav·ing** *v.i.* **1** To move freely back and forth or up and down, as a flag in the wind; undulate or fluctuate. **2** To be moved back and forth or up and down as a signal; also, to make a signal by moving something thus. **3** To have an undulating shape or form; be sinuous: Her hair *waves.* —*v.t.* **4** To cause to move back and forth or up and down: to *wave* a banner. **5** To form with an undulating surface, edge, or outline. **6** To give a wavy appearance to; water, as silk. **7** To form into waves or undulations: to *wave* one's hair. **8** To signal by waving something: He *waved* me aside. **9** To express by waving something: to *wave* farewell. See

synonyms under FLAUNT, SHAKE. — *n.* **1** A ridge or undulation moving on the surface of a liquid, the particles composing it having an oscillatory motion usually in the form of closed or nearly closed curves in a plane at right angles to the direction of movement of the ridge itself. **2** *Physics* One of the complete vibratory impulses set up by a disturbance propagated through the particles of a body or elastic medium, as a rope, air, or water. Each impulse, as in the transmission of light or sound, has characteristics of length, frequency, duration, etc., determined by the nature of the disturbance in the medium involved. **3** One of the rising curves on an undulatory edge or surface; one of a series of curves: amber *waves* of grain. **4** Something that comes, like a wave, with great volume or power; a flood; a period of marked activity or excitement: a *wave* of enthusiasm. **5** A wavelike stripe or undulation impressed on a surface, as on watered silk; also, a wavelike tress or curl of hair. **6** *Poetic* Any body of water; the sea. **7** The act of waving; a sweeping or undulating motion, as with the hand or a flag. **8** One of a series, as of groups or events, occurring or moving with wavelike fluctuations: He went ashore with the first *wave* of Marines. **9** A progressive change in temperature or in barometrical condition passing over a large area: a heat *wave.* ◆ Homophone: *waive.* [OE *wafian*] — **wav′er** *n.*

Synonyms (noun): billow, breaker, ripple, surge, swell, undulation, vibration.

Wave (wāv) *n.* A member of the WAVES. [Back formation from WAVES (taken as a pl.)]

wave cloud *Meteorol.* A cloud consisting of parallel bands or ridges, separated by strips of clear sky, due to air currents occurring at the bounding plane between two strata of the atmosphere.

wave front The leading surface of a wave as it advances through a medium.

wave–guide (wāv′gīd′) *n.* **1** Any system of material boundaries by which the direction of waves may be controlled. **2** *Electronics* A device, typically an arrangement of hollow metal pipes of varying size and cross–section, through which high–frequency electromagnetic waves may be guided as required.

wave·length (wāv′length′) *n. Physics* The distance, measured along the line of propagation, between two points representing similar phases of two consecutive waves. It is a fundamental unit in the study of radiant energy.

wave·less (wāv′lis) *adj.* Having no waves; tranquil. See synonyms under PACIFIC.

wave·let (wāv′lit) *n.* A little wave.

Wa·vell (wā′vəl), **Sir Archibald Percival,** 1883–1950, first Earl Wavell, Viscount Wavell of Cyrenaica and Tripolitania, British field marshal and administrator in World War II.

wa·vel·lite (wā′və·līt) *n.* A vitreous, translucent, hydrous aluminum phosphate, crystallizing in the orthorhombic system. [after Dr. William *Wavell,* died 1829, English physician, its discoverer]

wave mechanics The branch of physics which investigates the wave characteristics ascribed to the atom and its associated particles, and seeks to explain physical processes in terms of these characteristics as revealed by the quantum theory of atomic structure.

wave·me·ter (wāv′mē′tər) *n.* An apparatus for determining wavelengths and wave frequencies, as in a radio circuit.

wave number *Physics* The number of electromagnetic waves in a space of 1 centimeter, equal to the frequency of the wave divided by the velocity of light: it is the reciprocal of the wavelength.

wave·off (wāv′ôf′, -of′) *n. Aeron.* The act of denying landing privileges to an approaching aircraft, usually an aircraft making a faulty approach for landing on an aircraft carrier.

wa·ver (wā′vər) *v.i.* **1** To move one way and the other; sway; flutter. **2** To be uncertain or undecided; show irresolution; vacillate. **3** To show signs of falling back or giving way; reel; falter. **4** To flicker; gleam. **5** To quaver; tremble. See synonyms under FLUCTUATE, QUAKE, SHAKE. — *n.* A wavering. ◆ Homophone: *waiver.* [<ME *waveren,* freq. of OE *wafian* wave] — **wa′ver·er** *n.* — **wa′ver·ing** *adj.* — **wa′ver·ing·ly** *adv.*

Wa·ver·ley Novels (wā′vər·lē) A series of historical novels by Sir Walter Scott, published 1814–1831.

WAVES (wāvz) *n.* A corps of women in the U. S. Navy, which includes all women except nurses; officially, *Women in the United States Navy* (1946). [<*W(omen) A(ppointed for) V(oluntary) E(mergency) S(ervice),* an earlier name]

wave train A series of waves sent out at regular intervals from a vibrating body.

wave trap **1** *Telecom.* A device, usually connected with the antenna, for improving the selectivity of a radio receiver by cutting out undesired wave frequencies. **2** A widening inward of the distance between the sides of adjoining piers to allow for the spreading of storm waves.

wa·vey (wā′vē) *n.* The snow goose. [Var. of WAVY; so called because faintly streaked on head, neck, and back with darker plumage]

wav·y (wā′vē) *adj.* **wav·i·er, wav·i·est** **1** Full of waves; ruffled by or raised into waves. **2** Undulatory; waving. **3** Unstable; wavering. — **wav′i·ly** *adv.* — **wav′i·ness** *n.*

wawl (wôl) See WAUL.

wax[1] (waks) *n.* **1** A yellow fatty solid excreted from the abdominal rings of bees and used by them to build honeycombs; beeswax. It has a honeylike odor and a balsamic taste; becomes plastic with the heat of the hand; is insoluble in water, but is almost completely dissolved by boiling alcohol. **2** Any of a class of plant and animal substances consisting of the esters of fatty acids and alcohols other than glycerol, and including spermaceti and carnauba wax; specifically, a substance derived from the fruit of the wax myrtle or bayberry. **3** A solid mineral substance resembling wax, as ozocerite or paraffin. **4** A substance used for joining surfaces, sealing documents, etc.; sealing wax. **5** A mixture of pitch and tallow or some resinous composition used by shoemakers to wax their thread. **6** Earwax; cerumen. **7** *U. S.* The sap of the sugar maple after being boiled down and cooled. **8** A substance resembling beeswax secreted by certain scale insects. — *v.t.* To coat or treat with wax. — *adj.* Made of or pertaining to wax. [OE *weax*]

wax[2] (waks) *v.i.* **waxed, waxed** (*Poetic* **wax·en**), **wax·ing** **1** To become larger gradually; increase in size or numbers; grow: said specifically of the moon as it approaches fullness: opposed to *wane.* **2** To become as specified: to *wax* angry. [OE *weaxan* grow]

wax[3] (waks) *v.t. Colloq.* To record phonographically: to *wax* a folk song. [<WAX[1]; so called because wax was formerly used in making phonograph records]

wax[4] (waks) *n. Colloq.* A tantrum; fit of bad temper. [? <phrase *wax angry*]

wax bean A variety of string bean (*Phaseolus vulgaris*) cultivated in the United States: also called *butter bean.*

wax·ber·ry (waks′ber′ē) *n. pl.* **·ries** **1** The wax myrtle, or bayberry. **2** Its wax–covered fruit. **3** The snowberry.

wax·bill (waks′bil′) *n.* **1** Any of various small Old World seed–eating birds of the weaverbird family (genus *Estrilda*), having beaks resembling sealing wax. **2** The Java sparrow.

wax·en (wak′sən) *adj.* **1** Resembling wax. **2** Consisting wholly or in part of wax; covered with wax. **3** Pale; pallid: a *waxen* complexion; also, pliable or impressible as wax.

wax end A stout thread, or the end of a thread, made stiff and pointed with shoemakers' wax, or waxed and twisted with a bristle, as for the purpose of sewing shoes. Also **waxed end.**

wax myrtle Any of a genus (*Myrica*) of North American shrubs or small trees, especially *M. cerifera,* having fragrant leaves and small berries covered with white wax, often used in making candles: also called *bayberry, candleberry.*

wax palm **1** A South American palm (*Ceroxylon andicola*) with pinnate leaves, having a lofty straight trunk covered with a waxy, whitish, resinous substance. **2** A Brazilian palm (*Copernicia cerifera*) whose young leaves yield the carnauba wax of commerce.

wax paper Paper coated or treated with wax and used to protect against moisture. Also **waxed paper.**

wax plant The Indian pipe.

wax·weed (waks′wēd′) *n.* An annual, clammy, hairy herb (*Cuphea petiolata*) of the loosestrife family with irregular purplish axillary flowers.

wax·wing (waks′wing′) *n.* Any of various crested passerine birds (family *Bombycillidae*) of America and Asia, having soft, mainly brown plumage, and the tips of the secondary wing feathers tipped with horny appendages resembling red or yellow sealing wax; especially, the two best–known North American species, the **cedar waxwing** (*Bombycilla cedrorum*), and the larger **Bohemian waxwing** (*B. garrula pallidiceps*).

CEDAR WAXWING
(About 7 inches long)

wax·work (waks′wûrk′) *n.* **1** Work produced in wax; particularly, ornaments or life–size figures of wax. **2** *pl.* A collection of such figures.

wax·work·er (waks′wûr′kər) *n.* One who works in wax; one who makes waxwork.

wax·worm (waks′wûrm′) A honeycomb moth.

wax·y (wak′sē) *adj.* **wax·i·er, wax·i·est** **1** Resembling wax in appearance, consistency, or adhesive qualities; waxen; pliable; impressionable. **2** Having the dull whitish or yellowish color of wax; pale; pallid; bloodless. **3** Made of or abounding in wax; rubbed with wax; waxed. **4** *Pathol.* Characterized by the formation of an insoluble, waxlike protein in certain organs of the body, as the kidney; amyloid. — **wax′i·ness** *n.*

way (wā) *n.* **1** Direction; turn; route; line of motion or progress: Which *way* is the city? **2** A path, course, or track leading from one place to another or along which one goes; a road, street, highway, lane, path, or the like. **3** Space or room to advance or work: Make *way* for the king. **4** Length of space passed over; hence, distance in general: a little *way* off: often, popularly or dialectally, *ways* **5** Passage from one place to another; hence, onward movement; headway; progress. **6** A customary or habitual manner or style; a manner peculiar to an individual, class, or people: the British *way* of doing things. **7** A chosen line or plan of action; a procedure; method: In what *way* will you accomplish this? **8** A point of relation; particular: He erred in two *ways.* **9** A course of life or experience: the *way* of sin. **10** *Colloq.* Vocation; line of business; profession. **11** *Colloq.* State of health: to be in a bad *way.* **12** A course wished for or resolved upon; something which one resolves to do: Have it your *way.* **13** The range of one's notice or observation: An accident threw it in his *way.* **14** *Naut.* **a** The movement of a vessel through the water; forward motion; headway. **b** *pl.* A tilted framework of timbers upon which a ship slides when launched. **15** The direction of the weave in textile goods. **16** *Law* A right of way. **17** *Mech.* A longitudinal guide for material being worked upon, or for a moving table bearing the work. **18** *Colloq.* Neighborhood, or route taken to go home: He lives out of my *way.* — **by the way** In passing; incidentally. — **by way of** **1** With the object or purpose of; to serve as: *by way of* introduction. **2** Through; via: We went home *by way of* Main Street. — **out of the way** **1** Removed, as an obstruction; unable to hinder or impede. **2** Out of the proper course; hence, remarkable; unusual; also, improper; wrong: Has he done anything *out of the way*? **3** Out of place; lost; mislaid; remote. — **under way** In motion; well along; making progress. — *adv. Colloq.* Away; very far; all the great distance: He went *way* to Denver. ◆ Homophone: *weigh.* [OE *weg*]

Synonyms (noun): alley, avenue, bridlepath, channel, course, driveway, highroad, highway, lane, pass, passage, path, pathway, road, route, street, thoroughfare, track. Wherever there is room for an object to proceed, there is a *way.* A *road* (originally a ride*way*) is a prepared way for traveling with horses or vehicles, a *way* suitable to be traversed only by foot–passengers or by animals being called a *path, bridlepath,* or *track*; as, The *roads* in that country are mere *bridlepaths.* A *road* may be private: a *highway* or *highroad* is public,

highway being a specific name for a *road* legally set apart for the use of the public forever; a *highway* may be over water as well as over land. A *route* is a line of travel, and may be over many *roads.* A *street* is in some center of habitation, as a city, town, or village; when it passes between rows of dwellings, the country *road* becomes the village *street.* An *avenue* is a long, broad, and imposing or principal *street. Track* is a word of wide signification; we speak of a goat-*track* on a mountainside, a railroad *track,* a *racetrack,* the *track* of a comet; on a traveled *road* the line worn by regular passing of hoofs and wheels is called the *track.* A *passage* is between any two objects or lines of enclosure, a *pass* commonly between mountains. A *driveway* is within enclosed grounds, as of a private residence. A *channel* is a *waterway.* A *thoroughfare* is a *way* through. See AIR[1], DIRECTION, ROAD.

way back *Colloq.* Long ago. [Short for AWAY BACK]

way·bill (wā′bil′) *n.* A list describing or identifying goods or naming passengers carried by a common carrier, as a railroad, train, steamer, or other public vehicle.

way·far·er (wā′fâr′ər) *n.* One who journeys along a way on foot.

way·far·ing (wā′fâr′ing) *adj.* & *n.* Journeying; being on the road.

way freight Freight taken on or put off at way stations; also, a freight train stopping at way stations and handling such goods: distinguished from *through freight.*

way·go·ing (wā′gō′ing) *adj.* Pertaining to one's going away; going away; departing.

way-going crop *Law* A crop sown by a tenant during his term, but ripening after its expiration. [Short for *away-going crop*]

Way·land (wā′lənd) In Teutonic and English mythology, an invisible blacksmith with magical powers: in German folklore spelled *Wieland.* Also **Wayland (the) Smith.**

way·lay (wā′lā′) *v.t.* **·laid, ·lay·ing 1** To lie in ambush for and attack, as in order to rob. **2** To accost on the way. [< WAY + LAY[1], on analogy with MHG *wegelagen* < *wegelage* an ambush] — **way′lay′er** *n.*

Wayne (wān), **Anthony,** 1745–96, American Revolutionary general: called "Mad Anthony" Wayne.

way passenger A passenger getting on or off a public conveyance, as a train, steamship, bus, etc., at a way station; a local passenger.

-ways *suffix of adverbs* In a (specified) manner, direction, or position: *noways, sideways:* often equivalent to -WISE. Also **-way.** [< WAY + -S[3]]

ways and means Means or methods of accomplishing an end or defraying expenses; specifically, in legislation, methods of raising funds for the use of the government.

way·side (wā′sīd′) *adj.* Pertaining to the side of a road; growing or being near the wayside. — *n.* The side or edge of the road or highway.

way station Any station between principal stations, especially on a railroad; a local station.

way train A train stopping at way stations; a local train.

way·ward (wā′wərd) *adj.* **1** Wandering away; wilful; froward. **2** Without definite way or course; unsteady; vacillating; capricious. **3** Unexpected or unwished for: a *wayward* fortune. See synonyms under PERVERSE. [ME *weiward,* short for *aweiward* < *awei* away + -WARD] — **way′ward·ly** *adv.* — **way′ward·ness** *n.*

way·worn (wā′wôrn′, -wōrn′) *adj.* Fatigued by travel.

Wa·zir·i·stan (wä·zir′i·stän′) A tribal region in NW central Pakistan on the Afghanistan border; 5,214 square miles.

we (wē) *pron.* **1** The persons speaking or writing as they denote themselves, or a single person writing or speaking when referring to himself and one or more others: the nominative case. **2** A single person denoting himself, as a sovereign, editor, writer, or speaker, when wishing to give his words an impersonal character. [OE]

weak (wēk) *adj.* **1** Lacking in physical strength; wanting in energy, activity, or vigor; feeble; debilitated. **2** Insufficiently resisting stress; incapable of supporting weight: a *weak* link or bridge. **3** Lacking in strength of will or stability of character; yielding easily to temptation; pliable. **4** Ineffectual, as from deficient supply: *weak* artillery support. **5** Lacking in power or sonorousness: a *weak* voice. **6** Lacking a specified component or components in the usual or proper amount; of less than customary strength or potency: *weak* tea, a *weak* tincture. **7** Lacking the power or ability to perform properly its function: a *weak* heart. **8** Lacking in mental or moral strength; liable to err or fail through feebleness of conception or vacillation of judgment. **9** Showing or resulting from poor judgment or a want of discretion or firmness: a *weak* plan; unable to persuade or convince: a *weak* argument. **10** Lacking in influence or authority: a *weak* state. **11** Deficient in strength, durability, skill, experience, or the like. **12** *Gram.* In Germanic languages: **a** Of verbs, forming the past tense and past participle by the addition of a dental suffix to the present stem; as, English *ask, asked; sight, sighted;* German *leben, lebte, gelebt.* Some weak verbs in English show vowel change in the stem (as in *leave, left*), but in such cases the change is due to factors other than ablaut. Also called *regular.* **b** Of nouns and adjectives (in German and Old English), inflected in the less full manner originally restricted to stems ending in *-n.* Weak nouns and adjectives in Old English characteristically terminate in *-a* in the masculine singular (*nama* name) and *-e* in the feminine singular (*tunge* tongue). In German, a descriptive adjective appears in the weak form when preceded by a limiting word, such as the definite article, having strong inflection (*der gute Mann*). Compare STRONG (def. 28). **13** *Phonet.* Unstressed; unaccented, as a syllable or sound. **14** *Phot.* Thin; wanting in contrast: a *weak* negative. **15** In prosody, indicating a verse ending in which the accent falls on a word or syllable otherwise without stress. **16** Declining in price; without an active market: The wheat market is *weak.* **17** Wanting in impressiveness or interest: a *weak* play or book. See synonyms under FAINT, FRAGILE, PUSILLANIMOUS, SICKLY. ◆ Homophone: *week.* [<ON *veikr.* Akin to OE *wac.*] — **weak′ly** *adv.* — **weak′ness** *n.*

Weak may appear as a combining form in hyphemes or as the first element in two-word phrases; as in:

weak-backed	**weak-nerved**
weak-bodied	**weak point**
weak-built	**weak side**
weak-eyed	**weak-sighted**
weak-growing	**weak-spirited**
weak-handed	**weak-stemmed**
weak-headed	**weak-throated**
weak-headedness	**weak-toned**
weak-hearted	**weak-voiced**
weak-limbed	**weak-walled**
weak-looking	**weak-willed**
weak-made	**weak-winged**
weak-mindedness	**weak-witted**

weak·en (wē′kən) *v.t.* & *v.i.* To make or become weak or weaker. — **weak′en·er** *n.*

Synonyms: debilitate, depress, enervate, enfeeble, impair, invalidate, lower, paralyze, reduce, relax, sap, undermine, unnerve. See IMPAIR.

weak·fish (wēk′fish′) *n. pl.* **·fish** or **·fish·es** Any of various American marine food fishes (genus *Cynoscion*), especially the common variety (*C. regalis*), frequenting coastal waters of the eastern United States.

weak-kneed (wēk′nēd′) *adj.* Weak in the knees; hence, without resolution, strong purpose, or energy; spineless.

weak·ling (wēk′ling) *n.* A feeble person or animal. — *adj.* Having no natural strength or vigor.

weak·ly (wēk′lē) *adj.* **·li·er, ·li·est** Sickly; feeble; weak. See synonyms under SICKLY.

weak-mind·ed (wēk′mīn′did) *adj.* **1** Indecisive; unable to say no. **2** Feeble-minded.

weak·ness (wēk′nis) *n.* **1** The state, condition, or quality of being weak. **2** A characteristic indicating feebleness. **3** A slight failing; a fault.

weak sister *Colloq.* **1** The weakling in any group; specifically, one who cannot be depended on to stand firm against opposition. **2** Any ineffectual person.

weak spot 1 Any spot having less strength than the contiguous area, as in a fabric, fence, etc. **2** The most vulnerable part of an argument, proposition, etc. **3** The weakest or least dependable person on a team, in a group, etc.

weal[1] (wēl) *n.* **1** A sound or healthy state, either of persons or things; prosperity; welfare. **2** *Obs.* The body politic, state, or nation: now only in the phrase, *public weal.* **3** *Obs.* Wealth; worldly store. [OE *wela.* Akin to WELL.]

weal[2] (wēl) *n.* A discolored ridge or stripe on the skin, as from the blow of a whip; a wheal. [Var. of WALE[1]; infl. in form by obs. *wheal* a pustule]

weald (wēld) *n.* An exposed forest area; waste woodland; also, an open region; down. [OE, a forest]

Weald (wēld), **The** A district of SE England between the North and South Downs in Kent, Surrey and Sussex counties; formerly forested, now primarily agricultural.

wealth (welth) *n.* **1** A large aggregate of real and personal property; an abundance of those material or worldly things that men desire to possess; riches; also, the state of being rich. **2** *Econ.* All material objects which have economic utility; also, in the private sense, all property possessing a monetary value. **3** Great abundance of anything: a *wealth* of learning. **4** *Obs.* Weal; well-being. — **personal wealth** Those faculties, energies, and habits which contribute to personal industrial efficiency. [ME *welthe* < *wele* weal, on analogy with *health*]

Synonyms: abundance, affluence, comfort, competence, competency, fortune, funds, goods, independence, lucre, mammon, money, opulence, pelf, plenty, possession, produce, property, riches, substance, treasure. See PROPERTY. *Antonyms:* see synonyms for POVERTY.

wealth·y (wel′thē) *adj.* **wealth·i·er, wealth·i·est 1** Possessing wealth; affluent. **2** More than sufficient; abounding. — **wealth′i·ly** *adv.* — **wealth′i·ness** *n.*

wean[1] (wēn) *v.t.* **1** To transfer (the young of any animal) from dependence on its mother's milk to another form of nourishment. **2** To estrange from former habits or associations; alienate the affections of: usually with *from.* [OE *wenian* accustom]

wean[2] (wēn) *n. Scot.* A baby; infant.

wean·er (wē′nər) *n.* **1** One who weans. **2** A muzzle used in weaning a calf.

wean·ling (wēn′ling) *adj.* Freshly weaned. — *n.* A child or animal newly weaned.

weap·on (wep′ən) *n.* **1** Any implement of war or combat, as a sword, gun, etc. **2** Figuratively, any means that may be used against an adversary. **3** *pl.* The thorns or prickles of plants, or the stings, claws, etc., of animals. See synonyms under ARMS. [OE *wǣpen*] — **weap′on·less** *adj.*

weap·oned (wep′ənd) *adj.* Furnished with weapons; bearing arms.

weap·on·eer (wep′ən·ir′) *n.* A person concerned with the design, improvement, production, and use of weapons, especially of the atomic and thermonuclear type.

wear[1] (wâr) *v.* **wore, worn, wear·ing** *v.t.* **1** To carry or have on the person as a garment, ornament, etc. **2** To have or bear on the person habitually or as a practice: He *wears* a derby. **3** To have in one's appearance or aspect; exhibit: He *wears* a scowl. **4** To bear habitually in a specified manner; carry: He *wears* his age well; She *wears* her hair in a chignon. **5** To display or fly: A ship *wears* its colors. **6** To impair, waste, or consume by use or constant action. **7** To cause or produce by scraping, rubbing, etc.: to *wear* a hole in a coat. **8** To bring to a specified condition by wear: to *wear* a sleeve to tatters. **9** To exhaust the strength or patience of; weary. — *v.i.* **10** To be impaired or diminished gradually by use, rubbing, etc. **11** To withstand the effects of use, wear, etc., as specified: The vest *wears* well. **12** To become as specified from use or attrition: His patience is *wearing* thin. **13** To pass gradually or

tediously: with *on* or *away*. The day *wears* on. — **to wear out** **1** To make or become worthless by use: The cloak is *worn out*. **2** To waste gradually; use up: He *wears out* patience. **3** To tire or exhaust. — *n.* **1** The act of wearing, or the state of being worn: the worse for *wear*. **2** The material or articles of dress worn or made to be worn; a fashion: silk for summer *wear*; also in compounds: *footwear, underwear*. **3** The destructive effect of use or work; impairment from use or time. **4** Capacity for resistance to use or impairment; endurance; lasting quality; durability. ◆ Homophone: *ware*. [OE *werian*] — **wear′a·ble** *adj.* — **wear′er** *n.*

Synonyms (verb): abrade, chafe, consume, deteriorate, diminish, fret, fritter, impair, rub, tire, waste.

wear² (wâr) *v.* **wore, worn, wear·ing** *Naut. v.t.* To change the course of (a vessel), so as to bring the wind to the other side, by turning it through an arc in which its head points momentarily directly to leeward. — *v.i.* To go about with the wind astern. Compare TACK¹. ◆ Homophone: *ware*. [Prob. alter. of VEER¹; infl. in form by *wear¹*]

wear·a·ble (wâr′ə·bəl) *adj.* That can be worn. — *n. pl.* Garments.

wear and tear Loss by the service, exposure, decay, or injury incident to ordinary use.

wea·ri·ful (wir′i·fəl) *adj.* Tiresome; wearisome. — **wea′ri·ful·ly** *adv.* — **wea′ri·ful·ness** *n.*

wea·ri·less (wir′i·lis) *adj.* Unwearying; untiring.

wear·ing (wâr′ing) *adj.* **1** Fatiguing; exhausting; wasting: *wearing* trials. **2** Capable of being, or designed to be, worn. — **wear′ing·ly** *adv.*

wearing apparel Clothing; garments.

wear·ish (wâr′ish) *adj. Obs. or Dial.* **1** Insipid; watery. **2** Wizened; shrunk; withered. [ME *werische*; origin uncertain] — **wear′ish·ly** *adv.* — **wear′ish·ness** *n.*

wea·ri·some (wir′i·səm) *adj.* Causing fatigue; tiresome. — **wea′ri·some·ly** *adv.* — **wea′ri·some·ness** *n.*

Synonyms: annoying, fatiguing, irksome, laborious, tedious, tiresome, vexatious, wearing, weary. See TEDIOUS, TROUBLESOME. *Antonyms*: cheering, enlivening, inspiring, inspiriting, restful, reviving, rousing, soothing, stirring, thrilling.

wea·ry (wir′ē) *adj.* **·ri·er, ·ri·est** **1** Worn with exertion, vexation, or suffering; tired; fatigued. **2** Discontented or vexed by continued endurance, or by something disagreeable: usually with *of: weary* of life. **3** Indicating or characteristic of fatigue: a *weary* sigh. **4** Causing weariness; wearisome. — *v.t. & v.i.* **·ried, ·ry·ing** To make or become weary; tire. See synonyms under TIRE¹. [OE *wērig*] — **wea′ri·ly** *adv.* — **wea′ri·ness** *n.*

wea·sand (wē′zənd) *n. Archaic* The windpipe; in general, the throat: often spelled *wizen*. Also *Scot.* **wea′son**. [OE *wǣsend*]

wea·sel (wē′zəl) *n.* Any of certain small, slender, reddish-brown, carnivorous mammals (genus *Mustela*) that prey on smaller mammals and birds. In northern regions their fur turns white in winter. [OE *wesle*]

weasel word A word that weakens a statement by rendering it ambiguous or equivocal: term popularized by Theodore Roosevelt.

weath·er (weth′ər) *n.* **1** The general atmospheric condition, as regards temperature, moisture, winds, or other meteorological phenomena. **2** The common phenomena of wind, rain, cold, heat, cloudiness, or storm. **3** Bad weather; storm. — **to keep one's weather eye open** *Colloq.* To be alert. — **under the weather** *Colloq.* **1** Ailing; ill. **2** Somewhat intoxicated. — *v.t.* **1** To expose to the action of the weather. **2** To discolor, crumble, or otherwise affect by action of the weather. **3** To pass through and survive, as a crisis. **4** To slope, as a roof,

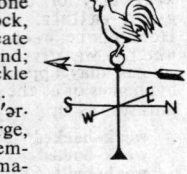

WEASEL
(Head and body from 6 to 7 inches)

so as to shed water. **5** *Naut.* To pass to windward of: to *weather* Cape Fear. — *v.i.* **6** To undergo changes resulting from exposure to the weather. **7** To resist the action of the weather. — *adj.* Facing the wind; windward: opposed to *lee*. ◆ Homophone: *wether*. [OE *weder*]

Weather may appear as a combining form in hyphemes or solidemes, or as the first element in two-word phrases:

weather-bitten	weather report
weather-bleached	weather-reporter
weather-blown	weather-reporting
weather-burnt	weather-rotted
weather-driven	weather-scarred
weather-eaten	weathersick
weather forecast	weather-tanned
weather-hardened	weathertight
weather-observer	weather-tough
weather-observing	weather-withstanding

weath·er·beat·en (weth′ər·bēt′n) *adj.* Bearing the effects of exposure to weather.

weath·er·board (weth′ər·bôrd′, -bōrd′) *n.* **1** A board for the outside covering of wooden buildings, usually feather-edged and nailed so as to form lap joints with the boards above and below and thus shed rain; a clapboard. **2** *Naut.* The windward side of a vessel. — *v.t.* To fasten weatherboards on.

weath·er·board·ing (weth′ər·bôr′ding, -bōr′-) *n.* **1** Weatherboards collectively, or material for making them. **2** The outer wooden covering of the walls and roof of a building.

weath·er·bound (weth′ər·bound′) *adj.* Detained by unfavorable weather, as a vessel in port.

Weather Bureau A bureau of the Department of Commerce in Washington, D.C., for meteorological observation, the diffusion of information concerning the weather, etc.

weath·er·cast (weth′ər·kast′, -käst′) *n.* A radio or television broadcast reporting on weather conditions. [<WEATHER + (BROAD)CAST] — **weath′er·cast′er** *n.*

weath·er·cock (weth′ər·kok′) *n.* **1** A vane, properly one in the semblance of a cock, which turns to indicate the direction of the wind; a weathervane. **2** A fickle person or variable thing.

weath·er·drome (weth′ər·drōm′) *n. Meteorol.* A large, floating structure resembling an airdrome, permanently anchored in offshore waters to serve as a weather station.

WEATHERCOCK

weath·ered (weth′ərd) *adj.* **1** Affected by exposure to the atmosphere; seasoned. **2** *Archit.* Sloped to prevent water lodging on the surface, as woodwork or stonework. **3** Worn, shaped, or stained by exposure in the atmosphere: said of rocks. **4** Denoting wood that has been artificially colored to represent weathering.

weather gage **1** *Naut.* The advantage to a ship or yacht of receiving the wind first; a position to the windward. **2** Any advantage gained.

weath·er·glass (weth′ər·glas′, -gläs′) *n.* A meteorological instrument for indicating the state of the weather; especially, a common barometer.

weath·er·ize (weth′ə·rīz′) *v.t.* **·ized, ·iz·ing** To process (fabrics, leather, etc.) chemically or otherwise, so as to make impervious or highly resistant to moisture or other effects of severe weather.

weath·er·ly (weth′ər·lē) *adj. Naut.* Capable of keeping close into the wind without drifting to leeward.

weath·er·man (weth′ər·man′) *n.* *pl.* **·men** (-men′) *n. Colloq.* A meteorologist, especially one concerned with daily weather conditions and reports.

weather map *Meteorol.* A map or chart compiled periodically from official sources and indicating, for a given region and specified time, various components of the weather, as temperature, atmospheric pressure, wind velocity, rain, snow, cloud formations, etc.

weath·er·proof (weth′ər·prōōf′) *adj.* Capable of withstanding rough weather without appreciable deterioration. — *v.t.* To make weatherproof.

weather station A station or office where meteorological observations are taken and recorded.

weath·er·strip (weth′ər·strip′) *n.* A narrow strip of material to be placed over or in crevices, as at doors and windows, to exclude drafts, rain, etc.: also **weath′er·strip′ping**. — *v.t.* **·stripped, ·strip·ping** To equip or fit with weather-strips.

weath·er·vane (weth′ər·vān′) *n.* A vane; weathercock.

weath·er·vi·sion (weth′ər·vizh′ən) *n.* A system which combines television and radar in the rapid dissemination of weather data to aircraft. [<WEATHER + (TELE)VISION]

weath·er·wise (weth′ər·wīz′) *adj.* Experienced in observing or predicting the weather.

weath·er·worn (weth′ər·wôrn′, -wōrn′) *adj.* Worn by exposure to the weather.

weave (wēv) *v.* **wove** or (*esp. for defs. 7 and 10*) **weaved, wo·ven** or (*less frequently*) **wove, weav·ing** *v.t.* **1** To form, produce, or manufacture a textile, by interlacing threads or yarns; especially, to make by interlacing woof threads among warp threads in a loom. **2** To form by interlacing strands, strips, twigs, etc.: to *weave* a basket. **3** To produce by combining details or elements: to *weave* a story. **4** To bring together so as to form a whole: to *weave* fancies into theories. **5** To twist or introduce into, about, or through something else: to *weave* ribbons through one's hair. **6** To spin (a web). **7** To make or effect by side-to-side movements: to *weave* one's way. — *v.i.* **8** To make cloth, etc., by weaving. **9** To become woven or interlaced. **10** To move with a side-to-side motion. — *n.* A particular method or style of weaving. — **plain** or **taffeta weave** A weave in which each filling yarn passes successively over and under each warp yarn, forming an even surface. — **satin weave** An irregular weave in which the warp or filling yarns pass over a number of yarns of the other set before interweaving, thus forming a smooth, unbroken, lustrous surface. — **twill weave** A strong weave having a distinct diagonal line or rib, caused by the passage of the filling yarns over one warp yarn and under two or more. [OE *wefan*. Akin to WEB, WEFT.]

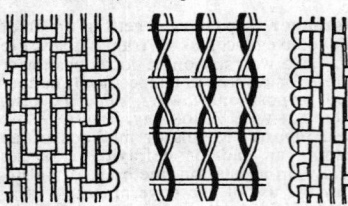

WEAVES
Simple figured.   Leno.   Five-shaft satin.

weav·er (wē′vər) *n.* **1** One who weaves. **2** A weaverbird.

weav·er·bird (wē′vər·bûrd′) *n.* Any of various finchlike birds (family *Ploceidae*) of the warmer parts of Asia, Africa, and Australia, that construct intricately woven nests.

weaver's bottom *Pathol.* An inflamed condition of the tissue over the ischium, or seat bone, arising from long sitting.

weaver's hitch A sheet bend. Also WEAVER'S KNOT.

web (web) *n.* **1** Textile fabric, especially as in the piece or as being woven in a loom. **2** A long sheet or roll of material formed like a web of cloth; especially, a roll of paper as it comes from the mill. **3** The network of delicate threads spun by a spider to entrap its prey; a cobweb. **4** Any complex network: a *web* of highways; anything artfully contrived or elaborated into a trap or snare: a *web* of espionage. **5** *Zool.* A membrane or fold of skin connecting the digits of an animal, as in aquatic birds, otters, bats, frogs, etc. **6** *Ornithol.* The series of barbs on either side of the shaft of a feather; the vane. **7** *Mech.* A plate or sheet, as of metal, connecting the heavier sections, ribs, frames, etc., of any tool or mechanical element. **8** The plate between the flange and head of a railroad rail. **9** *Archit.* The part of a ribbed vault between the ribs. **10** *Anat.* A membrane; tissue; tela. **11** A thin metal plate, as the blade of

a saw or sword, or the bit of a key. — **pin and web** A darkening speck on the cornea, with a film spreading fanwise from the cornea. — *v.t.* **webbed, web·bing 1** To provide with a web. **2** To cover or surround with a web; entangle. [OE. Akin to WEAVE, WEFT.]

Webb (web), **Beatrice,** 1858–1943, *née* Potter, English economist and sociologist; wife of Sidney James Webb. — **Mary,** 1881–1927, *née* Meredith, English novelist. — **Sidney James,** 1859–1947, Baron Passfield, English economist and sociologist.

webbed (webd) *adj.* **1** Having a web. **2** Having the digits united by a membrane.

web·bing (web′ing) *n.* **1** A woven strip of strong fiber, as for girths, seat bottoms, etc. **2** Any woven texture; the structure of a web.

web·by (web′ē) *adj.* **·bi·er, ·bi·est 1** Relating to or consisting of a web or membrane. **2** Palmate.

we·ber (vā′bər, wē′bər) *n. Physics* **1** The mks unit of magnetic flux, equal to 100,000,000 maxwells. **2** *Obs.* Coulomb. **3** *Obs.* Ampere. [after Wilhelm Eduard *Weber*]

We·ber (vā′bər), **Ernst Heinrich,** 1795–1878, German physiologist. — **Baron Karl Friedrich Ernst von,** 1786–1826, German composer. — **Wilhelm Eduard,** 1804–91, German physicist; brother of Ernst Heinrich Weber.

web·foot (web′fŏŏt′) *n.* **1** A foot with webbed toes. **2** A web-footed bird or animal. **3** The condition of being web-footed.

web-foot·ed (web′fŏŏt′id) *adj.* Having the toes connected by a membrane, as many aquatic animals and birds.

web press A printing press which is fed from a continuous roll of paper instead of sheets.

web·ster (web′stər) *n. Obs.* A weaver. [OE *webbestre,* fem. of *webba* a weaver]

Web·ster (web′stər), **Daniel,** 1782–1852, U.S. statesman. — **John,** 1580?–1625, English dramatist. — **Noah,** 1758–1843, U.S. lexicographer.

Web·ste·ri·an (web-stir′ē-ən) *adj.* Of or pertaining to Daniel or Noah Webster.

web·worm (web′wûrm) *n.* Any of various caterpillars, usually gregarious and very destructive of foliage, which build large silken webs or tents for shelter; especially, the common **garden webworm** (*Loxostege similalis*).

wecht (wekht) *n. Scot.* Weight.

wed (wed) *v.* **wed·ded, wed·ded** or **wed, wed·ding** *v.t.* **1** To take as one's husband or wife; marry. **2** To unite or give in matrimony; join in wedlock. **3** To attach as if in marriage; join securely: chiefly in the past participle, with *to: wedded* to his job. — *v.i.* **4** To take a husband or wife; marry. [OE *weddian* pledge]

we'd (wēd) **1** We had. **2** We would.

Wed·dell Sea (wed′l) An embayment of the South Atlantic in Antarctica, SE of the Palmer Peninsula and of South America.

wed·ding (wed′ing) *n.* **1** The ceremony of a marriage with the attendant nuptial festivities; also, the ceremony alone; originally, a betrothal. **2** The anniversary or celebration of a marriage. Such weddings are named from the character of the presents regarded as appropriate: golden *wedding* (50th); for list, see under ANNIVERSARY. See synonyms under MARRIAGE. [OE *wedding* < *weddian* pledge]

wedding cake A very rich fruit or pound cake served at a wedding reception, and also often divided among absent friends.

We·de·kind (vā′də-kint), **(Benjamin) Frank·lin,** 1864–1918, German poet and playwright.

wedge (wej) *n.* **1** One of the so-called mechanical powers, consisting of a double inclined plane; specifically, a V-shaped piece of metal, wood, etc., used for splitting substances, raising weights, and the like. **2** Anything in the form of a wedge, as a piece of pie; specifically, a formation, as of soldiers or football players, arranged like a wedge. **3** A right triangular prism, having one very acute angle. **4** Any one of the triangular characters used in cuneiform writing. **5** *Meteorol.* **a** A wedge-shaped area of high barometric pressure as shown on a weather map. **b** An air mass advancing in the form of a wedge. **6** Any action or procedure which facilitates a change in policy, entrance, intrusion, etc.: also **entering**

wedge. — *v.* **wedged, wedg·ing** *v.t.* **1** To force apart or split with or as with a wedge; rend; rive. **2** To compress or fix in place with a wedge. **3** To crowd or squeeze (something). — *v.i.* **4** To force oneself or itself in like a wedge. [OE *wecg*]

wedg·ie (wej′ē) *n. Colloq.* A kind of shoe worn by women, having a wedge-shaped piece making a solid sole, flat on the ground from heel to toe.

Wedg·wood (wej′wŏŏd′) *n.* Any of various fine, hard earthenwares invented by Josiah Wedgwood, characterized by an unglazed, tinted clay background bearing small, finely detailed, classical figures in cameo relief applied in white paste. It is typically tinted either light or dark blue, but **Wedgwood bamboo ware** (yellow), **Wedgwood basalt** (black), and **Wedgwood queen's** (cream-colored) are also famous. Also **Wedgwood ware.**

Wedg·wood (wej′wŏŏd), **Josiah,** 1730–95, English potter; inventor of the ware bearing his name. — **Josiah Clement,** 1872–1943, first Baron Wedgwood of Barlaston, English naval architect and statesman; great-great-grandson of the preceding: called the "Father of the Labour Party."

Wedgwood blue Either of two shades of blue, a light grayish blue and a dark reddish blue: the typical blues of the Wedgwood wares.

wedg·y (wej′ē) *adj.* Having the form or uses of a wedge; cuneal.

wed·lock (wed′lok) *n.* The ceremony of marriage, or the state of being married; matrimony. See synonyms under MARRIAGE. [OE *wedlāc* < *wed* a pledge + -*lāc,* suffix of nouns of action]

Wednes·day (wenz′dē, -dā) *n.* The fourth day of the week. [OE *Wōdnes dæg* day of Woden, trans. of LL *Mercurii dies* day of Mercury]

wee (wē) *adj.* **we·er, we·est** Very small; tiny. — *n. Scot.* A short time or space; a bit: bide a *wee.* [ME *wei,* OE *wēg, wēge* a quantity]

weed[1] (wēd) *n.* **1** Any unsightly or troublesome plant that grows in abundance; especially, any coarse, herbaceous plant growing to injurious excess on cultivated or fallow ground where it is not wanted, as dock, ragweed, etc. **2** *Colloq.* Tobacco: usually with *the;* also, a cigarette or cigar. **3** Any worthless animal or thing; specifically, a horse that is unfit for racing or breeding. **4** The stem and leaves of any useful plant as distinguished from its flower and fruit: The plant runs to *weed.* **5** *Obs.* Thick, luxuriant growth, as of underbrush or shrubs. — *v.t.* **1** To pull up and remove weeds from: to *weed* a garden. **2** To remove (a weed): often with *out.* **3** To remove (anything regarded as harmful or undesirable): with *out.* **4** To rid of anything harmful or undesirable. — *v.i.* **5** To remove weeds, etc. [OE *wēod*] — **weed′less** *adj.*

weed[2] (wēd) *n.* **1** A token of mourning, as a band of crape, worn as part of the dress: He wore a *weed* on his hat; especially in the plural, a widow's mourning garb. **2** *Obs.* Any article of clothing. [OE *wǣd, wǣde* a garment]

Weed (wēd), **Thurlow,** 1797–1882, U.S. journalist and politician.

weed·er (wē′dər) *n.* **1** One who weeds. **2** An implement for removing weeds.

weeding hoe A narrow-bladed hoe for weeding: usually with prongs on the end opposite the blade. See illustration under HOE.

weed·y (wē′dē) *adj.* **weed·i·er, weed·i·est 1** Having or containing a growth of weeds; abounding in weeds. **2** Of or pertaining to a weed or weeds. **3** Resembling a weed; weedlike, as in rapid, ready growth. **4** *Colloq.* Gawky; awkward; ungainly: *weedy* youths. — **weed′i·ly** *adv.* — **weed′i·ness** *n.*

wee folk The fairies, elves, etc.

Wee·haw·ken (wē′hô·kən) A township in NE New Jersey opposite the Hudson River from New York City; scene of the fatal wounding of Alexander Hamilton in a duel with Aaron Burr, 1804.

week (wēk) *n.* **1** A period of seven successive days; especially, such a period beginning with Sunday. **2** The period of time within a week devoted to work: The office has a 35-hour *week.* **3** A period of seven days preceding or following any given day or date: a *week* from

Tuesday. ◆ Homophone: *weak.* [OE *wicu, wice*]

week·day (wēk′dā′) *n.* Any day of the week except Sunday.

week-end (wēk′end′) *n.* The end of the week; specifically, the time from Friday evening or Saturday noon to the following Monday morning. — *v.i.* To pass the week-end: We *week-ended* in the country.

week-end·er (wēk′en′dər) *n.* One who goes on week-end vacation trips.

Week·ley (wēk′lē), **Ernest,** 1865–1954, English lexicographer and etymologist.

week·ly (wēk′lē) *adv.* Once a week; especially, at regular seven-day intervals. — *adj.* **1** Of or pertaining to a week or to weekdays. **2** Done or occurring once a week; also, reckoned by the week; hebdomadal. — *n. pl.* **·lies** A publication issued once a week.

weel (wēl) *adj., adv., & interj. Scot.* Well.

Weems (wēmz), **Mason Locke,** 1759–1825, American clergyman and biographer: known as *Parson Weems.*

ween (wēn) *v.t. & v.i. Archaic* To suppose; guess; fancy. [OE *wēnan* think]

ween·di·go (wēn′də·jō) See WINDIGO.

ween·ie (wē′nē) *n. Colloq.* A wiener.

weep[1] (wēp) *v.* **wept, weep·ing** *v.i.* **1** To manifest grief or other strong emotion by shedding tears: to *weep* for joy. **2** To mourn; lament: with *for.* **3** To give out or shed water or other liquid in drops, as the stems of some plants under pressure; bleed. — *v.t.* **4** To weep for; mourn or bewail. **5** To shed (tears, or drops of other liquid). **6** To bring to a specified condition by weeping: to *weep* oneself to sleep. — *n.* The act of weeping, or a fit of tears. [OE *wēpan*]

weep[2] (wēp) *n.* A lapwing; pewit. [Imit.]

weep·er (wē′pər) *n.* **1** One who weeps, as a hired mourner. **2** A long piece of black crape worn as a sign of mourning, customarily hanging down from the hat. **3** A pendant of moss, as from a branch. **4** A hole through which water may drip.

weep·ing (wē′ping) *adj.* **1** That weeps; crying; tearful. **2** Having slim, pendulous branches: the *weeping* ash.

weeping ash A variety of the common European ash (*Fraxinus excelsior pendula*) with drooping branches.

WEEPING WILLOW
a. Leaves. *b.* Catkin. *c.* Tree.

weeping willow An Old World willow (*Salix babylonica*), remarkable for its long, slender, pendulous branches.

weet (wēt) *n.* **1** The imitation of the call of various birds. **2** The peetweet, or common European sandpiper. [Imit.]

wee·ver (wē′vər) *n.* Any of various edible marine fishes (genus *Trachinus*), having upward-looking eyes and sharp dorsal and opercular spines, with which they can inflict serious wounds. [<AF *wivre,* OF *guivre,* orig. a serpent, dragon <L *vipera* a viper]

wee·vil (wē′vəl) *n.* **1** Any of numerous small beetles (family *Curculionidae*) with elongated snoutlike heads which bear the mouth parts at the end and the antennae along the sides: also called *curculio.* Weevil larvae feed on plants and plant products, especially flowers, fruits, and trees; many are serious pests. **2** Any insect injurious to stored grain. [OE *wifel* a beetle] — **wee′vil·y, wee′vil·ly** *adj.*

weft (weft) *n.* **1** The cross-threads in a web

of cloth; woof. **2** A woven fabric; web. [OE. Akin to WEAVE, WEB.]

Wehr·macht (vâr′mäkht) *n. German* The armed forces, collectively, of Germany: literally, defense force.

Wei (wā) A river in NW central China, flowing 540 miles east from SE Kansu province to the Yellow River.

Weich·sel (vīkh′səl) The German name for the Vistula.

wei·ge·la (wī·gē′lə, -jē′-, wī′jə·lə) *n.* Any of a large genus (*Weigela*) of deciduous Asian shrubs of the honeysuckle family; especially, *W. florida,* cultivated extensively in the United States for its profusion of dark rose-purple flowers. [<NL, after Dr. C. E. *Weigel,* 1748–1831, German physician]

weigh¹ (wā) *v.t.* **1** To determine the weight of, as by measuring on a scale or balance. **2** To balance or hold in the hand so as to estimate weight or heaviness. **3** To measure (a quantity or quantities of something) according to weight: with *out.* **4** To consider carefully; estimate the worth or advantages of: to *weigh* a proposal. **5** To press or force down by weight or heaviness; burden or oppress: with *down.* **6** To raise or hoist: now only in the phrase *to weigh anchor.* **7** *Obs.* To think well of; esteem; regard. — *v.i.* **8** To have weight; be heavy to a specified degree: She *weighs* ninety pounds. **9** To have influence or importance: The girl's testimony *weighed* heavily with the jury. **10** To be burdensome or oppressive: with *on* or *upon*: What *weighs* on your mind? **11** *Naut.* **a** To raise anchor. **b** To begin to sail. See synonyms under CONSIDER, DELIBERATE, EXAMINE. — **to weigh in 1** Of a prize fighter or other contestant, to be weighed before a contest. **2** In racing, to be weighed, as a jockey, after a race. — **to weigh one's words** To consider one's words carefully before speaking them. — **to weigh out** In racing, to be weighed, as a jockey, before a race. ♦ Homophone: *way.* [OE *wegan* weight, carry, lift] — **weigh′er** *n.*

weigh² (wā) *n.* Way: used in the phrase *under weigh* by mistaken analogy with *aweigh.* See AWEIGH. ♦ Homophone: *way.* [Var. of WAY; infl. in form by *weigh¹,* in phrase "weigh anchor"]

weight (wāt) *n.* **1** The measure of the force with which bodies tend toward the earth's center, or the quality thus measured. The weight of a body is a product of its mass and the acceleration due to gravity. **2** Any object or mass which weighs a definite or specific amount. **3** A definite mass of brass, iron, or other metal, used in weighing machines as a standard; any unit of heaviness, as a pound, ounce, etc. **4** Any mass used as a counterpoise or to exert pressure by force of gravity: a *paperweight.* **5** Burden; pressure; oppressiveness: the *weight* of care; the *weight* of an attack. **6** Any quantity of heaviness, expressed indefinitely or in terms of standard units. **7** The relative tendency of any mass toward a center of superior mass: the *weight* of a planet. **8** A scale or graduated system of standard units of weight: avoirdupois *weight.* See tables below; see also under METRIC SYSTEM. **9** Influence; importance; consequence: a man of *weight.* **10** The comparative heaviness of clothes, as appropriate to the season: summer *weight.* **11** *Stat.* **a** The relative value of an item in a statistical compilation. **b** The frequency of its occurrence among related items, or the number used to express such frequency. — *v.t.* **1** To add weight to; make heavy. **2** To oppress or burden. **3** To adulterate or treat (fabrics or other merchandise) with cheap foreign substances. **4** *Stat.* To give weight to. [OE *wiht, gewiht*]

Synonyms (noun): burden, gravity, heaviness, import, load, moment. See LOAD.

AVOIRDUPOIS WEIGHT

27.34+ grains (gr.)	= 1 dram (dr. av.)
16 drams av.	= 1 ounce (oz. av.)
16 ounces av.	= 1 pound (lb., lbs. av.)
2000 pounds av.	= 1 short ton (sh. tn.)
2240 pounds av.	= 1 long ton (l. tn.)

TROY WEIGHT

24 grains	= 1 pennyweight (dwt.)
20 pennyweight	= 1 ounce (oz. t.)
12 ounces	= 1 pound (lb., lbs. t.)

weight·less (wāt′lis) *adj.* **1** Having little or no heaviness. **2** Subject to little or no gravitational force. — **weight′less·ly** *adv.* — **weight′less·ness** *n.*

weight·y (wā′tē) *adj.* **weight·i·er, weight·i·est 1** Having great weight; ponderous. **2** Having power to move the mind; cogent. **3** Of great importance. **4** Influential, as in public affairs. **5** Burdensome. See synonyms under HEAVY, IMPORTANT. — **weight′i·ly** *adv.* — **weight′i·ness** *n.*

Wei·hai (wā′hī′) A port and naval base in NE Shantung province, NE China; leased with the surrounding area (285 square miles) to Great Britain, 1898–1930. Formerly **Wei·hai·wei** (wā′hī′wā′).

Wei·mar (vī′mär) A city in SW East Germany, formerly capital of Thuringia.

Wei·mar·an·er (vī′mər·ä′nər) *n.* A breed of dog of the hound type, blue- or amber-eyed, gray in color, used for hunting and as a watchdog. [from *Weimar,* Germany, where the breed originated]

weir (wir) *n.* **1** An obstruction placed in a stream to raise the water, divert it into a millrace or irrigation ditches, or form a fish pond; a dam. **2** A series of wattled enclosures in a stream, to catch fish. [OE *wer* < *werian* dam up]

Weir (wir), **Robert Walter,** 1803–89, and his sons, **John Ferguson,** 1841–1926, and **Julian Alden,** 1852–1919, U.S. painters.

weird (wird) *adj.* **1** Concerned with the unnatural or with witchcraft; unearthly; uncanny. **2** Pertaining to or having to do with fate or the Fates. — **the Weird Sisters 1** The Fates. **2** The three witches in Shakespeare's *Macbeth.* — *n. Scot.* **1** One's allotted fate; fortune. **2** Destiny; fate. **3** One of the Fates. **4** A prophecy; prediction. **5** A spell; enchantment. [OE *wyrd* fate]

weird·o (wir′dō) *n. pl.* **·os** *Slang* A person who is strange or eccentric. Also **weird′ie, weird′y** (-dē).

Weis·mann (vīs′män), **August,** 1834–1914, German biologist. — **Weis·man·ni·an** (vīs·män′ē·ən) *adj. & n.*

Weis·mann·ism (vīs′män·iz′əm) *n.* The theory of evolution, as propounded by August Weismann, which asserts the continuity of the germ plasm within but in isolation from the soma, and denies the heritability by offspring of characters acquired by the parents during their lifetime.

weiss beer (vīs) A light, whitish beer, brewed usually from wheat. [<G *weissbier* pale Berlin beer, lit., white beer]

Weis·sen·fels (vī′sən·fels) A city in south central East Germany.

Weiss·horn (vīs′hôrn) A peak in southern Switzerland; 14,804 feet.

Weiz·mann (wīts′mən, vīts′män), **Chaim,** 1874–1952, Israeli chemist and Zionist leader; first president of Israel 1948–52; born in Russian Poland.

we·jack (wē′jak) *n.* The fisher or pekan. [<Algonquian. Cf. Cree *otchek.*]

we·ka (wē′kə, wā′-) *n.* A wingless rail (genus *Ocydroma*) of New Zealand, now nearly extinct: also called *woodhen.* [<Maori]

welch (welch, welsh) See WELSH.

Welch (welch, welsh) See WELSH.

Welch (welch), **William Henry,** 1850–1934, U.S. pathologist and sanitarian.

wel·come (wel′kəm) *adj.* **1** Admitted gladly to a place or festivity; received cordially: a *welcome* guest. **2** Producing satisfaction or pleasure; pleasing: *welcome* tidings. **3** Made free to use or enjoy: She is *welcome* to my purse. See synonyms under AGREEABLE, DELIGHTFUL. — *n.* The act of bidding or making welcome; a hearty greeting given or cordial reception accorded to a guest or visitor. — **to wear out one's welcome** To come so often or to linger so long as no longer to be welcome. — *v.t.* **·comed, ·coming 1** To give a welcome to; greet gladly or hospitably. **2** To receive with pleasure: to *welcome* constructive advice. [OE *wilcuma* < *will-* will, pleasure + *cuma* a guest; infl. in form by WELL² and COME, on analogy with OF *bien venu*] — **wel′come·ly** *adv.* — **wel′come·ness** *n.* — **wel′com·er** *n.*

weld¹ (weld) *v.t.* **1** To unite, as two pieces of metal, with or without pressure, by the application of heat along the area of contact. **2** To bring into close association or

connection. — *v.i.* **3** To admit of being welded. — *n.* The consolidation of pieces of metal by welding; also, the closed joint so formed. [Alter of WELL¹, *v.*] — **weld′a·bil′i·ty** *n.* — **weld′a·ble** *adj.* — **weld′er** *n.*

weld² (weld) *n.* **1** An erect Old World annual (*Reseda luteola*), formerly cultivated for dyers' use: also called *yellowweed.* **2** The yellow pigment obtained from it: also spelled *woald.* [ME *welde.* Cf. MLG *walde,* MDu. *woude.*]

wel·fare (wel′fâr) *n.* **1** The condition of faring well; exemption from pain or discomfort; prosperity; also, condition, as regards well-being: Inquire concerning thy brethren's *welfare.* **2** Organized efforts by a community or organization to improve the social and economic condition of a group or class: also **welfare work. 3** Money, food, clothing, etc., given to those in need; relief. — **on welfare** Receiving money, food, clothing, etc., from a local or other government because of need. [ME *wel fare* < *wel* well + *fare* a going <OE *faran* go]

Welfare Island An island in the East River, New York City; 139 acres; site of two municipal hospitals; formerly *Blackwell's Island.*

welfare state A state or polity in which the government assumes a large measure of responsibility for the social welfare of its members, as through unemployment and health insurance, etc.

wel·kin (wel′kin) *n. Archaic* or *Poetic* **1** The vault of the sky; the heavens. **2** The air. [OE *wolcn, wolcen* a cloud]

well¹ (wel) *n.* **1** A hole or shaft sunk into the earth to obtain a fluid, as water, oil, brine, or natural gas. **2** A spring of water; a place where water issues from the ground; a fountain. **3** A source of continued supply, or that which issues forth continuously; a wellspring: a *well* of learning. **4** A depression, cavity, or vessel resembling a well: an *inkwell.* **5** A cavity in the lower part of some sorts of furnaces to receive falling metal. **6** In an English law court, the railed-in space between the bench and the bar, reserved for solicitors. **7** *Archit.* **a** The vertical opening contained within a winding staircase. **b** A similar opening descending through floors, or a deep enclosed space in a building for light or ventilation: an air *well*; an elevator *well.* **8** *Naut.* The boxed-in space in a vessel's hold, enclosing the pumps. **9** A compartment admitting water, in which fish are preserved alive. — *v.i.* To pour forth or flow up, as water in a spring. — *v.t.* To gush: Her eyes *welled* tears. [OE *wielle* < *weallan* boil, bubble up]

well² (wel) *adv.* **bet·ter, best 1** Satisfactorily; favorably; according to one's wishes: Everything goes *well.* **2** In a good or correct manner; properly; excellently; expertly: to dance or speak *well.* **3** Suitably; befittingly; with reason or propriety: I cannot *well* remain here. **4** In a successful manner; prosperously; also, agreeably or luxuriously: He lives *well.* **5** Intimately: How *well* do you know him? **6** To a large or proper extent or degree; plentifully: a *well*-stocked larder. **7** Completely; wholly. **8** Far; at some distance: He lagged *well* behind us. — **as well 1** Also; in addition. **2** With equal effect or consequence: He might just as *well* have sold it. — **as well as 1** As satisfactorily as. **2** To the same degree as. **3** In addition to. — *adj.* **1** Satisfactory; rightly done or arranged; fortunate; suitable; gratifying: always in the predicate position: It is *well.* **2** Having physical health; free from ailment of mind or body. **3** Prosperous; comfortable. — *interj.* An exclamation used to express surprise, expectation, resignation, doubt, indignation, etc., or merely to preface a remark. [OE *wel.* Akin to WEAL.]

Synonyms (adj.): advantageous, beneficial, convenient, desirable, excellent, expedient, favorable, fortunate, good, happy, lucky, prosperous. See HEALTHY. *Antonyms:* see synonyms for BAD.

Well may appear as a combining form in hyphenes when joined to participles to form unit modifiers; thus, predicatively, His words were *well* chosen; but attributively, his *well*-chosen words. The following examples are self-explanatory:

well-accepted	well-acquainted
well-accustomed	well-acted
well-acknowledged	well-adjusted

well-administered	well-knit
well-aimed	well-liked
well-aired	well-looking
well-armed	well-loved
well-armored	well-made
well-arranged	well-managed
well-assorted	well-mannered
well-assured	well-measured
well-attested	well-ordered
well-attired	well-paid
well-authenticated	well-phrased
well-behaved	well-placed
well-beloved	well-planned
well-built	well-pleased
well-chaperoned	well-pleasing
well-chosen	well-poised
well-considered	well-prepared
well-contented	well-preserved
well-covered	well-proportioned
well-cultivated	well-recognized
well-defended	well-regulated
well-defined	well-remembered
well-deserving	well-rooted
well-digested	well-seasoned
well-disciplined	well-selected
well-done	well-skilled
well-dressed	well-spent
well-earned	well-stocked
well-educated	well-swept
well-established	well-timed
well-financed	well-trained
well-fitted	well-trimmed
well-formed	well-understood
well-fortified	well-used
well-fought	well-versed
well-furnished	well-wooded
well-governed	well-worded
well-handled	well-worn
well-informed	well-woven
well-judged	well-written
well-kept	well-wrought

we'll (wēl) We shall; we will: a contraction.

Wel·land (wel'ənd) A city in southern Ontario, on the **Welland Ship Canal**, a waterway (28 miles long) connecting Lake Ontario with Lake Erie.

well-ap·point·ed (wel'ə-poin'tid) adj. Properly equipped; excellently furnished.

well·a·way (wel'ə-wā') interj. Obs. Woe is me! alas! Also **well'a·day'**. [OE wei lā wei, alter. of wā lā wā woe! lo! woe!; infl. in form by ON vei woe]

well-bal·anced (wel'bal'ənst) adj. Evenly balanced; adjusted with reference to welfare.

well-be·ing (wel'bē'ing) n. A condition of happiness or prosperity; welfare.

well-born (wel'bôrn') adj. Of good lineage.

well-bred (wel'bred') adj. 1 Well brought up; polite. 2 Of good ancestry; of good or pure stock.

well-curb (wel'kûrb') n. The frame or stone ring around the mouth of a well.

well-dis·posed (wel'dis-pōzd') adj. Favorably inclined.

well-do·er (wel'dōō'ər) n. 1 A performer of moral and social duties. 2 Scot. & Brit. Dial. One who is prosperous or well-to-do. — **well'-do'ing** adj. & n.

Wel·le (we'lā) See UELE.

well enough Tolerably good or satisfactory. — **to let well enough alone** To leave things as they are lest the result of interference be worse.

Welles (welz), **Gideon,** 1802-78, U.S. politician and writer. — **(George) Orson,** born 1915, U.S. actor and producer. — **Sumner,** 1892-1961, U.S. diplomat.

Welles·ley (welz'lē), **Richard Colley,** 1760-1842, first Marquis of Wellesley, British statesman; brother of the Duke of Wellington.

well-fa·vored (wel'fā'vərd) adj. Of attractive appearance; comely; handsome. Also Brit. **well'-fa'voured.**

well-fed (wel'fed') adj. Plump; fat; sleek.

well-fixed (wel'fikst') adj. Colloq. Affluent; well-to-do.

well-found (wel'found') adj. 1 Found to meet expectations. 2 Well equipped.

well-found·ed (wel'foun'did) adj. Based on fact: well-founded suspicions.

well-groomed (wel'grōōmd') adj. 1 Carefully curried, as a horse. 2 Carefully dressed and scrupulously neat; having a fashionable, sleek appearance.

well-ground·ed (wel'groun'did) adj. 1 Ade-

quately schooled in the elements of a subject. 2 Well-founded.

well-head (wel'hed') n. A natural source supplying water to a spring or well.

well-heeled (wel'hēld') adj. Slang Plentifully supplied with money. [<WELL[2] + HEEL[1], v. (def. 6)]

Wel·ling·ton (wel'ing-tən) The capital of New Zealand, a port on southern North Island.

Wel·ling·ton (wel'ing-tən), **Duke of,** 1769-1852, Arthur Wellesley, British general; defeated Napoleon at Waterloo; prime minister; born in Ireland.

Wellington boot A high boot covering the leg as far as the knee in front but cut away behind.

well-in·ten·tioned (wel'in-ten'shənd) adj. Having good intentions; well-meant: often with connotation of failure or of clumsy or harmful execution.

well-known (wel'nōn') adj. Widely known; famous.

well-mean·ing (wel'mē'ning) adj. Having good intentions. — **well'-meant'** (-ment') adj.

well met Welcome.

well-nigh (wel'nī') adv. Very nearly; almost.

well-off (wel'ôf', -of') adj. In comfortable circumstances; wealthy; fortunate.

well-read (wel'red') adj. Having a wide knowledge of literature or books; having read much: usually with in.

Wells (welz) A municipal borough in east central Somerset, England; noted for its 12th century cathedral.

Wells (welz), **Henry,** 1805-78, U.S. express operator; organized Wells, Fargo & Co. in 1852. — **H(erbert) G(eorge),** 1866-1946, English author.

wells·ite (welz'īt) n. A vitreous hydrated silicate of barium, calcium, potassium, and aluminum, crystallizing in the monoclinic system. [after H. L. Wells, 1855-1924, U.S. chemist]

well-spo·ken (wel'spō'kən) adj. 1 Fitly or excellently said. 2 Of gentle speech and manners.

well-spring (wel'spring') n. 1 An inexhaustible fountain. 2 A source of continual supply.

well sweep A long tapering pole swung on a pivot attached to a high post, and having the bucket suspended from one end, for use in drawing water.

well-thought-of (wel'thôt'uv', -ov') adj. In good repute; esteemed; respected.

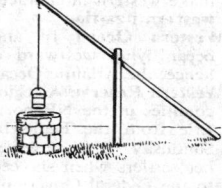

WELL SWEEP

well-to-do (wel'tə-dōō') adj. In prosperous circumstances; evincing a state of comfort or wealth.

well-wish·er (wel'wish'ər) n. One who wishes well, as to another. — **well'-wish'ing** adj. & n.

Wels·bach (welz'bak, Ger. vels'bäkh), **Baron Carl Auer von,** 1858-1929, Austrian chemist and inventor.

Welsbach burner A burner of the Bunsen type, having a cotton-gauze mantle impregnated with thoria and ceria, so arranged that upon ignition of a mixture of gases the mantle becomes incandescent. [after Baron Carl A. von Welsbach]

welsh (welsh, welch) v.t. & v.i. Slang 1 To cheat by failing to pay a bet or debt. 2 To avoid fulfilling (an obligation). Also spelled welch. [? Back formation < welsher, prob. <Welsher a Welshman, with ref. to supposed national traits]

Welsh (welsh, welch) adj. Pertaining to Wales, its people, or their language. — n. 1 The natives of Wales, a people of Celtic stock: with the: also called Cymry. 2 The language of Wales, belonging to the Brythonic or Cymric group of the Celtic subfamily of Indo-European languages: also called Cymric. Also spelled Welch. [OE Wēlisc < wealh a foreigner (one not of Saxon origin)] — **Welsh'·man** n.

Welsh cor·gi (kôr'gē) n. Either of two ancient breeds of a Welsh working dog, characterized by a long body, short legs, and erect ears:

the **Cardigan Welsh corgi** has a long tail, the **Pembroke Welsh corgi** a short tail. [< Welsh < corr dwarf + ci dog]

Welsh rabbit A concoction of melted cheese cooked in cream or milk, often with ale or beer added, and served hot on toast or crackers. ◆ The form rarebit was a later development and is the result of mistaken etymology.

welt (welt) n. 1 A strip of material, covered cord, etc., applied to a seam to cover or strengthen it. 2 In shoemaking, a strip of leather set into the seam between the edges of the upper and the outer sole. 3 In carpentry, a batten or strip made fast over a flush seam. 4 A wale or stripe raised on the skin by a blow. — v.t. 1 To sew a welt on or in; decorate with a welt. 2 Colloq. To flog severely, so as to raise welts or wales. [ME welte, walt. Cf. OE weltan roll.]

Welt·an·schau·ung (velt'än-shou'ŏong) n. German Literally, world viewing; philosophy of life: a comprehensive philosophy regarding the cosmos; ideology.

Welt·an·sicht (velt'än-zikht') n. German Literally, world view; a special view or interpretation of reality, seen as a whole.

wel·ter[1] (wel'tər) v.i. 1 To roll about; wallow. 2 To lie or be soaked in some fluid, as blood. 3 To surge or move tumultuously, as the sea. — n. 1 A rolling movement, as of waves; hence, commotion. 2 That in which weltering is done; a wallow. [<MDu. welteren]

wel·ter[2] (wel'tər) adj. Designating or pertaining to a horse race in which welterweights are carried. [< welter a heavyweight (horseman), ? <WELT, v. (def. 2)]

welter race A horse race in which heavy weights are imposed on the horses, in order to permit amateur jockeys to ride.

wel·ter·weight (wel'tər·wāt') n. 1 The weight (regularly 28, sometimes 40 pounds, in addition to weight for age) borne by a horse running in a welter race; hence, loosely, a heavyweight. 2 A boxer whose fighting weight is between 135 and 147 pounds. [< welter a heavyweight + WEIGHT]

Welt·lit·e·ra·tur (velt'lit'ə·rä·tōōr') n. German World literature.

Welt·po·li·tik (velt'pō·li·tēk') n. German International politics; world policy.

Welt·schmerz (velt'shmerts) n. German World-weariness; melancholy pessimism over the state of the world; romantic discontent.

Wem·bley (wem'blē) A municipal borough of Middlesex, England, 8 miles NW of London.

Wemyss (wēmz) A parish on the Firth of Forth, central Fifeshire, Scotland.

wen[1] (wen) n. 1 Pathol. Any encysted tumor containing a suetlike substance, occurring commonly on the scalp. 2 Any protuberance. [OE wenn, wænn] — **wen'nish, wen'ny** adj.

wen[2] (wen) n. The old English rune ᚹ, replaced by modern English w. [OE, var. of wynn joy]

Wen·ces·laus (wen'səs·lôs), 1361-1419, Holy Roman Emperor 1378-1400; king of Bohemia 1378-1419. Also **Wen'ces·las** (-läs), Ger. **Wenzel** (ven'tsəl), **Wen·zes·laus** (ven'tsəs·lous).

wench (wench) n. 1 A young peasant woman; also, a female servant; maid. 2 Any young woman; girl; maiden. 3 Archaic A prostitute; strumpet. — v.i. To keep company with strumpets. [ME wenche, short for wenchel <OE wencel a child, servant]

Wen·chow (wen'chou', Chinese wun'jō') A port on the Wu (def. 2) and chief city of SE Chekiang province, central eastern China.

wend (wend) v.t. & v.i. To direct (one's course); go. [OE wendan]

Wend (wend) n. One of a Slavic people now occupying the region between the Elbe and Oder rivers in Saxony and Prussia; a Sorb. [<G Wende, Winde]

Wen·dat (wen'dat) See WYANDOT.

Wen·dell (wen'dəl), **Barrett,** 1855-1921, U.S. scholar.

Wend·ish (wen'dish) adj. Of or pertaining to the Wends or their language; Sorbian. — n. The West Slavic language of the Wends; Sorbian. Also **Wend'ic.**

went (went) An obsolete past tense and past participle of wend, now used as past tense of GO.

wen·tle·trap (wen'təl·trap') n. Any of a genus (*Epitonium*) or family (*Epitoniidae*) of mollusks, having a white, turreted, many–whorled shell. [< Du. *wenteltrap* a spiral staircase or shell]

wept (wept) Past tense and past participle of WEEP.

were (wûr, *unstressed* wər) Plural and second person singular past indicative, and past subjunctive singular and plural of BE. [OE *wære, wæron*, pt. forms of *wesan* be]

we're (wir) We are: a contraction.

wer·en't (wûr'ənt) Were not: a contraction.

were·wolf (wir'wŏŏlf', wûr'-) n. pl. **·wolves** (-wŏŏlvz') In European folklore, a human being transformed into a wolf by bewitchment, or one having power to assume wolf form at will. Also **wer'wolf**. [OE *werwulf* man–wolf < *wer* a man + *wulf* a wolf]

Wer·fel (ver'fəl), **Franz**, 1890–1945, German novelist, poet, and dramatist.

wer·geld (wûr'geld) n. In Anglo–Saxon and Teutonic law, a fine or pecuniary compensation for crime against the person, especially for homicide, paid by the kindred of the slayer to those of the slain. Also **were'gild** (-gild), **wer'gelt** (-gelt). [OE, lit., man–yield, *i.e.*, man–price < *wer* a man + *geld, gield* yield]

Wer·ner (ver'nər), **Alfred**, 1866–1919, Swiss chemist.

wer·ner·ite (wûr'nər·īt) n. Scapolite. [after A. G. *Werner*, 1750–1817, German mineralogist]

wert (wûrt, *unstressed* wərt) Archaic second person singular, past tense of both indicative and subjunctive of BE: used with *thou*.

Wes·cott (wes'kot), **Glenway**, born 1901, U.S. novelist and poet.

we'se (wēz) 1 *Dial.* We is: a mistake for *we are; We'se* going. 2 *Scot.* We shall.

We·ser (vā'zər) A river in east and north central West Germany, flowing 300 miles north to the North Sea.

Wes·ley (wes'lē, *Brit.* wez'lē), **Charles**, 1707?–1788, English clergyman and hymn writer; brother of John Wesley. —**John**, 1703–91, English clergyman; founder of Methodism.

Wes·ley·an (wes'lē·ən, *Brit.* wez'lē·ən) adj. Of or pertaining to the Wesleys, especially John Wesley, as the founder of Methodism. —n. A disciple of John Wesley; a Methodist. —**Wes'·ley·an·ism** n.

Wes·sex (wes'iks) The ancient kingdom of the West Saxons, including modern Berkshire, Dorset, Hampshire, Somerset, and Wiltshire in southern England.

west (west) n. 1 The point of the compass at which the sun sets at the equinox, directly opposite *east*. See COMPASS CARD. 2 Any direction, region, or part of the horizon near that point. —**the West 1** The countries lying west of Asia and Turkey; the Occident. 2 The western hemisphere, discovered by explorers sailing westward from Europe. 3 The Western Roman Empire. 4 In the United States: **a** Formerly, the region west of the Allegheny Mountains. **b** The region west of the Mississippi, especially the northwestern part of this region. —adj. 1 To, toward, facing, or placed in the west; western. 2 Coming from the west: the *west* wind. 3 Designating or located in that part of a church directly opposite the altar. —adv. In or toward the west; in a westerly direction. —**go West, young man** Go settle in the unsettled western regions of the United States, a land of little competition and unusual opportunity: advice usually attributed to Horace Greeley. [OE]

West (west), **Benjamin**, 1738–1820, American painter. —**Rebecca** Pseudonym of Cicily Isabel Fairfield, born 1892, English novelist and critic.

West Bengal See under BENGAL.

west·bound (west'bound') adj. Going westward. Also **west'bound'**.

West Brom·wich (brum'ich, -ij) A county borough in southern Stafford, England, just NW of Birmingham.

west by north One point north of west on the mariner's compass. See COMPASS CARD.

west by south One point south of west on the mariner's compass. See COMPASS CARD.

West·cott (west'kot), **Edward Noyes**, 1846–1898, U.S. banker and novelist.

West End The western part of London, England; includes parks and a fashionable shop-

ping district and notable residential section.

west·er (wes'tər) v.i. To turn, trend, or shift to the west. —n. A wind, especially a storm, blowing from the west. [< WEST + -ER[5]]

west·er·ing (wes'tər·ing) adj. Moving or turning westward: the *westering* sun. —n. Movement or declension toward the west.

west·er·ly (wes'tər·lē) adj. 1 In, toward, or of the west. 2 From the west: a *westerly* wind. —n. pl. **·lies** A wind blowing from the west. —adv. 1 From the west. 2 Toward the west. —**west'er·li·ness** n.

Wes·ter·marck (ves'tər·märk), **Edward Alexander**, 1862–1939, Finnish anthropologist.

west·ern (wes'tərn) adj. 1 Being in the west; of, pertaining to, or directed toward the west. 2 Coming from the west: the *western* winds. —n. 1 A westerner. 2 A type of fiction or motion picture using cowboy and pioneer life in the western United States as its material.

West·ern (wes'tərn) adj. 1 Proceeding from or characteristic of the West; Occidental. 2 Belonging or pertaining to the Western Church: *Western* ritual. 3 Of or pertaining to the western part of the United States of America. —n. A person identified with or belonging to the Western Church.

Western Australia The largest state of the Commonwealth of Australia, including all of the Australian continent west of 129° E.; about 975,920 square miles; capital, Perth.

Western Church The medieval church of the Western Roman Empire, now the Roman Catholic Church: distinguished from the church of the Eastern Empire, now the Greek or Eastern Church.

Western Dvina See DVINA (def. 2).

west·ern·er (wes'tər·nər) n. One who dwells in a western region, especially in the western United States.

western frontier Formerly, that part of the United States bordering on the west in still unsettled regions.

western hemisphere See under HEMISPHERE.

Western Islands The Hebrides.

west·ern·ism (wes'tər·niz'əm) n. An expression or practice peculiar to the West, especially the western United States.

west·ern·ize (wes'tər·nīz) v.t. **·ized, ·iz·ing** To make western in characteristics, habits, etc. —**west'ern·i·za·tion** n.

Western Ocean In ancient geography, the ocean lying westward of the known world; hence, the Atlantic Ocean.

Western Reserve A region now comprising ten counties in the NE portion of Ohio, on Lake Erie from the Pennsylvania border to near Sandusky, Ohio, reserved by Connecticut for her settlers when she ceded her western lands to the Federal Government in 1786, but relinquished in 1800.

Western (Roman) Empire The part of the Roman Empire west of the Adriatic, which existed as a separate empire from 395 A.D. until the fall of Rome in 476 A.D.

Western Samoa See SAMOA.

Western Turkestan See under TURKESTAN.

Western Wall Wailing Wall.

West Flanders A province of western Belgium; 1,249 square miles; capital, Bruges.

West Germanic See under GERMANIC.

West Germany See under GERMANY.

West Ham A county borough in Essex, England; a NE suburb of London.

West Har·tle·pool (här'təl·pōōl) A county borough on the North Sea in SE Durham, England.

West Indies A series of island groups separating the North Atlantic from the Caribbean, between North and South America, divided into the *Bahamas*, the *Greater Antilles*, and the *Lesser Antilles*. —**West Indian**

West Indies, The A former federation of British colonies in the Caribbean, including Antigua, Barbados, Dominica, Grenada, Jamaica, Montserrat, St. Lucia, St. Vincent, Trinidad and Tobago, and St. Christopher, Nevis and Anguilla; formed January, 1958; dissolved May 31, 1962.

west·ing (wes'ting) n. 1 Distance accomplished toward the west. 2 *Naut.* The amount by which a ship has increased her west longitude from a specified meridian.

West·ing·house (wes'ting·hous), **George**, 1846–1914, U.S. inventor.

West Ir·i·an (ir'ē·ən) A province of Indonesia comprising the western part of New Guinea and several adjacent islands, the former *Netherlands New Guinea;* capital, Kotabaru: also **West New Guinea.**

West Lo·thi·an (lō'thē·ən) A county in SE Scotland on the Firth of Forth; 120 square miles; county town, Linlithgow: formerly *Linlithgowshire.*

West·meath (west'mēth) An inland county of Leinster province, Ireland; 681 square miles; county town, ingar.

West·min·ster (west'min·stər) A city and borough in the county of London, England, on the north bank of the Thames; London's largest borough; site of the Houses of Parliament and Buckingham Palace.

Westminster Abbey A Gothic church in Westminster, London, begun in A.D. 1050; burial place of English kings and notables.

West·mor·land (west'môr·lənd, -mər-; *Brit.* west'mər·lənd) A county in the Lake District, NW England; 789 square miles; county town, Appleby.

west–north·west (west'nôrth'west', *in nautical usage* west'nôr·west') adj., adv., & n. Midway between west and northwest. See COMPASS CARD.

Wes·ton su·per Ma·re (wes'tən sōō'pər mā'rē, mâr') A resort and municipal borough on Bristol Channel, in NE Somerset, England.

West Pakistan 1 A province of Pakistan comprising all of Pakistan west of the Republic of India with the exception of the **Federal District of Pakistan** around and including Karachi (812 square miles); formed in 1955 by the merger of the former provinces of Baluchistan, North–West Frontier Province, Punjab and Sind, along with Bahawalpur, Khairpur, and the other princely states in the area; 309,424 square miles; capital, Lahore. 2 Formerly, the region comprising all of the western portion of Pakistan, including the four former provinces, the princely states, and the present federal district; 310,236 square miles.

West·pha·li·a (west·fā'lē·ə) A former province of Prussia, since 1945 a part of North Rhine–Westphalia, West Germany; scene of the signing of a treaty by France, Sweden, and the Holy Roman Empire at the end of the Thirty Years' War, 1648; 7,806 square miles; capital, Münster. *German* **West·fa·len** (vest·fä'lən). —**West·pha'li·an** adj. & n.

West Point A U.S. military reservation on the Hudson River in SE New York; seat of the United States Military Academy.

West Prussia A former province of Prussia; since 1945 under Polish administration; capital, Danzig. *German* **West·preus·sen** (vest'·proi'sən).

West Quod·dy Head (kwod'ē) The eastern-most point of continental United States, a promontory on the Atlantic coast of Maine near the Canadian border.

Wes·tra·li·a (wes·trā'lē·ə, -trāl'yə) A contraction of WESTERN AUSTRALIA. —**Wes·tra'li·an** adj. & n.

West Riding An administrative division of SW York, England; 2,936 square miles; capital, Wakefield.

West River The chief river of southern China, flowing 1,250 miles east from eastern Yünnan province (900 miles as the Hungshui to its confluence with the Yü) to the South China Sea: Chinese *Si Kiang.*

West Saxon The dialect of Old English spoken in Wessex: preserved in most of the literature of the period.

west–south·west (west'south'west', *in nautical usage* west'sou·west') adj., adv., & n. Midway between west and southwest. See COMPASS CARD.

West Spitsbergen The largest island of the Spitsbergen group, NW Svalbard; about 15,000 square miles.

West Virginia A State of the east central United States; 24,181 square miles; capital, Charleston; entered the Union June 20, 1863; nickname, *Panhandle State:* abbr. WV. —**West Virginian**

west·wall (west'wôl) See LIMES (def. 2).

west·ward (west'wərd) adj. Tending, moving, lying, or facing toward the west. —adv. Toward the west: also **west'wards.** [OE *westweard* < *west* the west] —**west'ward·ly** adv.

wet (wet) adj. **wet·ter, wet·test 1** Moistened

or saturated with water or other liquid; consisting of or covered with moisture. **2** Marked by showers or by heavy rainfall; rainy: the *wet* season. **3** Not dry: *wet* varnish. **4** *Colloq.* Favoring or not prohibiting the manufacture and sale of alcoholic beverages: a *wet* State; also, opposed to prohibition. **5** Preserved in liquid; also, bottled in alcohol, as laboratory specimens. **6** *Chem.* Treated or separated by means of liquid reagents. — **all wet** *Slang* Quite wrong; crazy; mistaken: He's *all wet.* — *n.* **1** Water; moisture; wetness. **2** Showery or rainy weather; rain. **3** *Colloq.* One opposed to prohibition. — *v.t.* & *v.i.* **wet** or **wet·ted, wet·ting** To make or become wet. — **to wet one's whistle** *Colloq.* To take a drink. [OE *wǣt*] — **wet′ly** *adv.* — **wet′ness** *n.* — **wet′ta·ble** *adj.* — **wet′ter** *n.*

We·tar (wē′tär) One of the southern Molucca Islands, Indonesia, north of Portuguese Timor; 1,400 square miles.

wet·back (wet′bak′) *n. U.S. Colloq.* A Mexican laborer who enters the United States illegally. [So called from those who swim or wade across the Rio Grande]

wet–blank·et (wet′blang′kit) *v.t.* To discourage; depress.

wet blanket A discouragement, or one who discourages any proceedings.

weth·er (weth′ər) *n.* A castrated ram. ◆ Homophone: *weather.* [OE]

wet–nurse (wet′nûrs′) *n.* A woman who is hired to suckle the child of another woman.

wet pack *Med.* A method of reducing fever or of relieving a disturbed neurotic condition by wrapping the patient in wet sheets.

wet suit A skin–tight rubber garment worn by divers, surfers, etc., to retain body warmth in cold waters.

Wet·ter·horn (vet′ər·hôrn) A mountain of three peaks in the Bernese Alps, Switzerland; 12,153 feet.

wet·ting agent (wet′ing) *Chem.* Any of a class of substances that, by reducing surface tension, enable a liquid to spread more readily over a solid surface to which it is applied: a form of detergent.

we've (wēv) We have: a contraction.

Wex·ford (weks′fərd) **1** A maritime county of SE Leinster province, Ireland; 908 square miles. **2** Its county town, a port on **Wexford Harbor,** an inlet of St. George's Channel in SE Ireland.

Wey·den (wī′dən), **Roger van der,** 1399?–1464, Flemish painter.

Wey·gand (ve·gän′), **Maxime,** 1867–1965, French general in World Wars I and II.

Wey·man (wā′mən), **Stanley,** 1855–1928, English novelist.

Wey·mouth (wā′məth) A port in southern Dorset, England; the old part of the present municipal borough of **Weymouth and Melcombe Regis.**

wha (hwä) *pron. Scot.* Who.

whack (hwak) *v.t.* & *v.i.* **1** *Colloq.* To strike sharply; beat; hit. **2** *Slang* To share: often with *up.* **3** *Colloq.* To drive (mules or oxen). — *n.* **1** *Colloq.* A sharp, resounding stroke or blow. **2** The noise made by such a blow. **3** *Slang* A share; portion. **3** *Slang* A turn; a chance; a try. — **to have a whack at** *Slang* **1** To give a blow to. **2** To have a chance or turn at; to have a chance to try. — **out of whack** *Slang* Out of order. [? Var. of THWACK]

whack·er (hwak′ər) *n.* **1** One who whacks. **2** The driver of a mule team. **3** *Colloq.* A whopper.

whack·ing (hwak′ing) *Colloq. adj.* Strikingly large; whopping. — *adv.* Very; extremely.

whai·sle (hwā′zəl) *v.i. Scot.* To breathe hard or roughly; wheeze. Also **whai′zle.**

whale[1] (hwāl) *n.* **1** A cetaceous mammal of fishlike form, especially one of the larger pelagic species, as distinguished from dolphins and porpoises. Whales have the fore limbs developed as broad flattened paddles, the hind limbs absent, and a thick layer of fat or blubber immediately beneath the skin. The principal types are the toothless or whalebone whales (suborder *Mysticeti*), and the toothed whales (suborder *Odontoceti*). **2** *Colloq.* Something extremely good or large: a *whale* of a party. — *v.i.* **whaled, whal·ing**

To engage in the hunting of whales. [OE *hwæl*]

whale[2] (hwāl) *v.t.* **whaled, whal·ing** *Colloq.* To strike as if to produce wales or stripes; flog; wale. [Var. of WALE[1], *v.*]

whale·back (hwāl′bak′) *n.* A steamship having a convex main deck, used on the Great Lakes in passenger and freight traffic.

whale·boat (hwāl′bōt′) *n.* A long, deep rowboat, sharp at both ends, often steered with an oar: so called because first used in whaling, now carried on steamers as lifeboats.

WHALEBOAT

whale·bone (hwāl′bōn′) *n.* **1** The horny substance developed in plates from the palate of the whalebone whales; baleen. **2** A strip of whalebone, used in stiffening dress bodies, corsets, etc.

whale iron A harpoon.

whale·man (hwāl′mən) *n. pl.* **·men** (-mən) One who hunts whales; a whaler.

whal·er (hwā′lər) *n.* **1** A person or a vessel engaged in whaling. **2** A whaleboat.

Whales (hwālz), **Bay of** An inlet of the Antarctic Ocean in Ross Shelf Ice just north of Little America.

whale shark A very large pelagic shark (*Rhineodon typus*) somewhat resembling the basking shark in its habits but often reaching a length of 50 feet: it has a spotted body and very small teeth adapted for feeding on plankton.

whal·ing (hwā′ling) *n.* The industry of capturing whales. — *adj. Slang* Huge; whopping.

whaling station A place on shore to which whales are taken to be flensed and the oil tried out.

wham·my (hwam′ē) *n. pl.* **·mies** *U.S. Slang* **1** A gesture made by extending in parallel the index and little finger from the closed fist and pointing toward the person or object intended: an ancient form of hexing (*mano cornuta*, sign of the horns). If the fingers of both hands are used, the fists being in contact, it is a *double whammy.* **2** A jinx; hex: to put the *whammy* on someone. [<*wham,* colloq. interjection imit. of the sound of a hard blow]

Wham·po·a (hwäm′pō′ä′) The deep–water port for Canton in southern Kwangtung province, China, on an island in the Canton River.

whang[1] (hwang) *v.t.* & *v.i. Colloq.* To beat or sound with a resounding noise. — *n. Colloq.* A beating or banging; heavy blow; whack. [Imit.]

whang[2] (hwang) *n.* **1** A buckskin thong or one made of a deer sinew. **2** Whang leather. **3** *Scot.* A big slice, as of bread or cheese; a chunk. — *v.t.* **1** To beat as with a thong; lash. **2** To beat or strike violently. **3** *Scot. & Dial.* To fling; throw violently; hurl. **4** *Scot.* To slice, usually in large pieces. [Var. of OE *thwang* a thong]

whang·ee (hwang·ē′) *n.* **1** Any of a genus (*Phyllostachys*) of tall woody Asian grasses related to the bamboo. **2** A cane or stick made of the stalk of one of these plants. [<Chinese *huang* bamboo sprout]

whang leather A leather, usually of deerskin, made for lacings, thongs, etc. [<WHANG[2] + LEATHER]

Whang·poo (hwang′pōō′) See HWANGPOO.

whap (hwap), **whap·per** (hwap′ər), etc. See WHOP, etc.

wharf (hwôrf) *n. pl.* **wharves** (hwôrvz) or **wharfs 1** A structure of masonry or timber erected on the shore of a harbor, river, or the like, alongside which vessels may lie to load or unload cargo, passengers, etc.; also, any landing place for vessels, as a pier or quay. **2** *Obs.* A river bank; also, the seashore.

— *v.t.* **1** To moor to a wharf. **2** To provide or protect with a wharf or wharves. **3** To deposit or store on a wharf. [OE *hwearf, hwerf* a dam]

wharf·age (hwôr′fij) *n.* **1** Charge for the use of a wharf. **2** Wharf accommodations for shipping.

wharf boat A barge or float with a platform used as a landing stage for men and freight on rivers where the water level is changeful: usually connected with the shore or levee by a bridge.

wharf·in·ger (hwôr′fin·jər) *n.* One who keeps a wharf for landing goods and collects wharfage fees. [Earlier *wharfager* + intrusive *n*]

wharf rat 1 A rat that inhabits wharves; especially, the brown or Norway rat. **2** *U.S. Slang* A man or boy who loiters habitually about wharves, especially with thievish or other criminal intent.

Whar·ton (hwôr′tən), **Edith Newbold,** 1862–1937, *née* Jones, U. S. novelist.

wharve (hwôrv) See WHERVE.

wha's (hwäz), **whase** (hwäz) *pron. Scot.* Whose.

what (hwot, hwut) *adj.* **1** In interrogative construction, asking for information that will specify the person or thing qualified by it: Of *what* person do you speak? **2** How surprising, ridiculous, great, or the like: used in exclamation to express excess or something exceptional in the person or thing qualified: commendatory or the reverse according to circumstances: *What* genius! *What* a noise that boy is making! **3** How much: an ambiguous use: *What* cash has he? — *pron.* **1** Which circumstance, event, relation, or the like: asking for some specification concerning persons or things referred to: an interrogative pronoun used in absolute interrogation: Who and *what* is he? When used of persons, it ordinarily implies some shade of contempt. In this sense *what* is used elliptically for "What did you say?" or in surprise or indignation: *What!* did he really say that? Formerly it was used as a common introductory expletive like *well,* especially in a summons, as in the phrase *what ho!* **2** That which: a double relative, equivalent to a demonstrative followed by a simple relative: Tell me *what* it is; *What* followed occupied little time. **3** *Dial.* or *Illit.* That or which: a simple relative: a donkey *what* wouldn't go. — **what for 1** Why: *What* did you do that *for?* **2** *Slang* Physical punishment or verbal rebuke: He took the bully outside and gave him the *what for.* — *adv.* **1** In what respect; to what extent: *What* are you profited? **2** In some measure; partly: usually followed by *with: What* with the heat, and *what* with the noise, it is distracting. **3** For what reason; why. **4** How extraordinarily! how!: an exclamatory or intensive use. — *conj.* **1** So far as; as well as: He did *what* he could at the time. **2** That: especially in the phrase *but what.* [OE *hwæt,* neut. of *hwā* who]

what–all (hwot′ôl′, hwut′-) *pron. Colloq.* Whatever; everything.

Whate·ly (hwāt′lē), **Richard,** 1787–1863, English prelate and logician.

what·ev·er (hwot·ev′ər, hwut′-) *pron.* **1** As a compound relative, the whole that; anything that; no matter what: often added for emphasis to a negative assertion: *whatever* makes life dear; I do not want anything *whatever.* **2** *Colloq.* What: usually interrogative: *What·ever* were you saying? Also *Poetic* **what'e·er′** (-âr′).

what–not (hwot′not′, hwut′-) *n.* **1** An ornamental set of shelves for holding bric–à–brac, etc. **2** Anything you please; something or other.

what·so·ev·er (hwot′sō·ev′ər, hwut′-) *adj.* & *pron.* Whatever: a slightly more formal usage. Also *Poetic* **what'so·e'er′** (-âr′).

whaup[1] (hwäp, hwôp) *n. Scot. & Brit. Dial.* A curlew. [Imit.]

whaup[2] (hwäp, hwôp) *Scot. v.i.* **1** To fuss about noisily. **2** To whine; whistle. — *n.* **1** A whistle or cry. **2** A pod; capsule. **3** A clumsy lout; also, a scamp. **4** An outcry; a fuss.

wheal (hwēl) *n.* A discolored ridge on the skin, as from hives or the stroke of a whip;

also, a whelk. ◆Homophone: *wheel*. [Alter. of WALE¹]

wheat (hwēt) *n.* **1** A grain yielding an edible flour, the annual product of a cereal grass (genus *Triticum*): the most important of the cereals, it is excelled only by rice in the number of people by whom it is used as a staple food. **2** The plant that produces this grain, especially *Triticum aestivum* and varieties, a tall, slender annual or biennial of cosmopolitan distribution, bearing at its summit an imbricated spike of usually four-flowered spikelets called the ear or head. **3** A wheatfield; a crop of wheat. [OE *hwÆte*]

wheat·ear (hwēt'ir) *n.* A thrushlike bird (*Oenanthe oeonanthe*) of the northern parts of the northern hemisphere, related to the whinchat, ash-gray above and white below, with the wings, sides of head, and tip of tail black. [Earlier *wheatears* < WHITE + *ers, eeres* rump]

WHEAT
a. Ear of bearded wheat.
b. Ear of beardless wheat.
c, d. Grain: front and back of b.

wheat·en (hwēt'n) *adj.* Belonging to or made of Wwheat.

Wheat·ley (hwēt'lē), **Phillis,** 1753?–84, American Negro poet born in Africa.

Wheat·stone (hwēt'stōn), **Sir Charles,** 1802–1875, English physicist.

Wheatstone bridge (hwēt'stōn) *Electr.* An instrument for the measurement of differential resistance in an electric current. Also **Wheatstone's bridge.** [after Sir Charles *Wheatstone*]

wheat·worm (hwēt'wûrm') *n.* A threadworm (*Tylenchus tritici*) destructive of wheat. Also **wheat eelworm.**

WHEATSTONE BRIDGE
a. Galvanometer.
b. Battery.
c, d. Bridge.
R¹, R² Resistances to be compared.
R³, R⁴ Known resistances which can be varied. When galvanometer shows no current, R¹R⁴ = R²R³.

whee·dle (hwēd'l) *v.* **·dled, ·dling** *v.t.* **1** To persuade or try to persuade by flattery, cajolery, etc.; coax. **2** To obtain by cajoling or coaxing. —*v.i.* **3** To use flattery or cajolery. [? OE *wædlian* beg, be poor <*wædl* poverty] —**whee'dler** *n.* —**whee'dling·ly** *adv.*

wheel (hwēl) *n.* **1** A circular rim and hub connected by spokes or rays in one structure, or a disk, capable of rotating on a central axis and used to reduce friction and facilitate movement or transportation, as in vehicles, or to act with a rotary motion, as in machines. **2** Anything resembling or suggestive of a wheel; a disk or a circle, or any circular object or formation. **3** An instrument or device having a wheel or wheels as its distinctive characteristic, as a bicycle, a steering wheel or steering gear, or the like. **4** An old instrument of torture or execution, consisting of a wheel to which the limbs of the victim were tied and then broken with an iron bar; also, the death so inflicted. **5** The wheel with which the goddess of fortune is represented, symbolizing the vicissitudes and uncertainty of human fate. **6** A turning; revolution; rotation. **7** Figuratively, that which imparts or directs motion or controls activity; the moving force: the *wheels* of democracy. **8** A turning of a body of troops or a swinging of a line of ships in which a change of direction is accomplished while the different units keep in alinement. **9** A rotating firework; a pinwheel or catherine wheel. **10** A refrain of a song. **11** The rotating disk used in various gambling games, especially roulette; hence, roulette. —**Pelton wheel** A device consisting of a wheel

which carries on it a succession of cupshaped buckets, and is made to rotate by the impingement of high-pressure jets of water on the buckets, the form of which is such as to prevent the accumulation of dead water. —*v.t.* **1** To move or convey on wheels. **2** To cause to turn on or as on an axis; pivot or revolve. **3** To perform with a circular movement. **4** To provide with a wheel or wheels. —*v.i.* **5** To turn on or as on an axis; pivot; rotate or revolve. **6** To take a new direction or course of action; change attitudes, opinions, etc.: often with *about*. **7** To move in a circular or spiral course. **8** To roll or move on wheels. —**to wheel and deal** *Slang* To act freely, aggressively, and often unscrupulously, as in the arrangement of a business or political deal. —*adj.* **1** Pertaining to or shaped like a wheel. **2** Harnessed to a vehicle directly in front of the wheels: said of a draft animal when there is a leader or leaders in front. ◆Homophone: *wheal.* [OE *hwēol*]

wheel and axle *Mech.* A wheel or drum mounted on an axle with a rope wound about the drum so that a slight pull on one end of the rope will raise a disproportionately heavy weight attached to the other: one of the so-called simple machines.

wheel animalcule A rotifer.

wheel·bar·row (hwēl'bar'ō) *n.* A boxlike vehicle ordinarily with one wheel and two handles, for moving small loads. —*v.t.* To convey in a wheelbarrow.

wheel·base (hwēl'bās') *n.* The distance from the center of the back axle to the center of the front axle, as in an automobile.

wheel·bug (hwēl'bug') *n.* A large hemipterous insect (*Arilus cristatus*) of the southern United States, which preys upon caterpillars and other soft-bodied insects: so called from a semicircular crest on the thorax resembling a cogwheel.

wheel·chair (hwēl'châr') *n.* A mobile chair mounted between large wheels, for the use of invalids. Also **wheel chair.**

wheeled (hwēld) *adj.* **1** Having wheels; furnished with a wheel or wheels: often in compounds: a two-*wheeled* cart. **2** Effected or borne by wheels: *wheeled* transportation.

wheel·er (hwē'lər) *n.* **1** One who wheels. **2** A wheelhorse or other draft animal working next the wheel. **3** Something furnished with a wheel or wheels: a side-*wheeler*.

Wheel·er (hwē'lər), **Joseph,** 1836–1906, American Confederate general.

wheel·er-deal·er (hwē'lər-dē'lər) *n. Slang* One who wheels and deals.

wheel·horse (hwēl'hôrs') *n.* **1** A horse harnessed to the pole or shafts when there is a leader or leaders in front; hence, one who does the heaviest work. **2** In politics, a person bearing great responsibility, or one to be greatly depended upon.

wheel·house (hwēl'hous') *n.* **1** A small house on the deck of a vessel in which the steering wheel is located; a pilothouse. **2** A paddle box.

wheel·ing (hwē'ling) *n.* **1** The act of one who wheels, especially of one riding a bicycle. **2** The condition of the roads, as regards traveling on wheels. **3** A rotating movement; a turning.

Wheel·ing (hwē'ling) A port on the Ohio River in NW West Virginia; an industrial center.

wheel lock 1 An old form of lock for small arms, in which a small steel wheel, actuated by a spring and released by a trigger, produced sparks by rotating against a flint. **2** A lock or catch for stopping a vehicle wheel.

wheel·man (hwēl'mən) *n. pl.* **·men** (-mən) **1** The man who steers a vessel. **2** A bicyclist. Also **wheel'man.**

Whee·lock (hwē'lok), **Eleazar,** 1711–79, U.S. clergyman and educator.

wheel window See ROSE WINDOW.

wheel·work (hwēl'wûrk') *n. Mech.* The gearing and arrangement of wheels in a machine or mechanical device.

wheel·wright (hwēl'rīt') *n.* A man whose business is making or repairing wheels and wheeled vehicles.

wheen (hwēn) *n. Scot. & Dial.* A few.

wheeze (hwēz) *v.t. & v.i.* **wheezed, wheez·ing**

To breathe or utter with a husky, whistling sound. —*n.* **1** A wheezing sound. **2** A whispering sound so exaggerated as to give rise to the sound popularly called a "stage whisper." **3** *Colloq.* A popular tale, saying, or trick, especially an ancient one. [Prob. <ON *hvæsa* hiss] —**wheez'er** *n.* —**wheez'ing·ly** *adv.*

wheez·y (hwē'zē) *adj.* **wheez·i·er, wheez·i·est** Subject to wheezing, or making a wheezing sound. —**wheez'i·ly** *adv.* —**wheez'i·ness** *n.*

whelk¹ (hwelk) *n.* Any of several large marine snails found in temperate waters, having whorled shells and preying on other mollusks or scavenging; a popular food in Europe. [OE *weoloc*]

whelk² (hwelk) *n.* A swelling protuberance, or pustule; wheal; especially, a pimple or eruption of pimples on the face. [OE *hwylca* a pustule <*hwelian* suppurate]

whelk·y¹ (hwel'kē) *adj.* **whelk·i·er, whelk·i·est 1** Protuberant; rounded. **2** Shelly. Also spelled *welky.* [<WHELK¹]

COMMON WHELK
(About 4 inches)

whelk·y² (hwel'kē) *adj.* **whelk·i·er, whelk·i·est** Marked with pustules or whelks. [<WHELK²]

whelm (hwelm) *v.t.* **1** To cover with water or other fluid; submerge; engulf. **2** To overpower; overwhelm. —*v.i.* **3** To roll with engulfing force. [Prob. blend of OE *helmian* cover and *gehwelfan* bend over]

whelp (hwelp) *n.* **1** One of the young of a dog, wolf, lion, or other beast of prey; sometimes, a dog of any age. **2** A worthless young fellow; a cub; puppy: used contemptuously. **3** *Mech.* **a** One of series of longitudinal ridges on a windlass or capstan. **b** One of the teeth of a sprocket wheel. —*v.t. & v.i.* To give birth (to): said of dogs, lions, etc. [OE *hwelp*]

when (hwen) *adv.* **1** Interrogatively, at what or which time: *When* did you arrive? **2** Conjunctively: **a** At which: the time *when* we went on the picnic. **b** At which or what time: They watched till midnight *when* they fell asleep. **c** As soon as: He laughed *when* he heard it; You may play *when* you finish work. **d** Although: He walks *when* he might ride. **e** At the time that; while: *when* you were in church; *when* we were young. **f** If; considering that: *When* in doubt, ask; How can I buy it *when* I have no money? **g** After which; then: We had just awakened *when* you called. —*pron.* What or which time: since *when*; till *when*. —*n.* The time; date: I don't know the *when* or the circumstances. [OE *hwanne, hwænne*]

when·as (hwen'az') *conj. Obs.* **1** Whereas; while. **2** When. Also **when that.**

whence (hwens) *adv.* **1** Interrogatively, from what place or source; of what origin: *Whence* and what art thou? *Whence* is the correlative of *thence.* **2** Conjunctively: **a** From what or which place, source, or cause; from which: the place *whence* these sounds arise. **b** To which place; where: Return *whence* you came. **c** For which reason; wherefore. [ME *whannes, whennes,* adverbial genitive of *whanne,* OE *hwanne* when]

whence·so·ev·er (hwens'sō·ev'ər) *adv. & conj.* From whatever place, cause, or source.

when·e'er (hwen·âr') *adv. & conj. Poetic* Whenever.

when·ev·er (hwen·ev'ər) *adv. & conj.* At whatever time.

when·so·ev·er (hwen'sō·ev'ər) *adv. & conj.* At what time soever; whenever.

where (hwâr) *adv.* **1** Interrogatively: **a** At or in what place, relation, or situation: *Where* is my book? **b** To what place or end; whither: *Where* are you going? **c** From what place; whence: *Where* did you get that hat? **2** Conjunctively: **a** At or in which or what place; at the place in which: *where* men gather. **b** To a place or situation in or to which; whither: Let us go *where* the mountains and the trees are. ◆*Where* is the correlative of *there.* In composition with a preposition, *where*

has sometimes the force of an interrogative pronoun and sometimes that of a relative: *Wherein* was he wrong? *Wherein* he was much deceived. — *pron.* The place in which: The accident occurred 100 yards from *where* we stood. — *n.* Place; locality. [OE *hwǣr*]

where·a·bouts (hwâr′ə·bouts′) *adv.* **1** Near or at what place; about where. **2** *Obs.* About which; concerning which. Also *Rare* **where′·a·bout′.** — *n.* The place in or near which a person or thing is.

where·as (hwâr′az′) *conj.* **1** Since the facts are such as they are; seeing that: often used in the preamble of a resolution, etc. **2** The fact of the matter being that; when in truth: implying opposition to a previous statement. — *n. pl.* **·as·es** A clause or item beginning with the word "whereas."

where·at (hwâr′at′) *adv.* **1** Interrogatively, at what: *Whereat* are you angry? **2** Conjunctively, at which; for which reason; whereupon: He won the race, *whereat* we were delighted.

where·by (hwâr′bī′) *adv.* **1** Interrogatively, by what; how. **2** Conjunctively, by, near, or through which.

wher·e′er (hwâr′âr′) *adv. Poetic* Wherever.

where·fore (hwâr′fôr′, -fōr′) *adv.* **1** Interrogatively, for what reason; what for; to what end; why: *Wherefore* didst thou doubt? **2** Conjunctively, for which reason. See synonyms under THEREFORE. — *n.* The cause; reason: the whys and *wherefores.* [<WHERE + FOR]

where·from (hwâr′frum′, -from′) *conj.* From which; whence.

where·in (hwâr′in′) *adv.* **1** Interrogatively, in what; in what particular or regard: *Wherein* is the error? **2** Conjunctively, in which thing, place, circumstance, etc.: a state *wherein* there is discord.

where·in·to (hwâr′in·to͞o′) *adv.* **1** Interrogatively, into what. **2** Conjunctively, into which: the gulf *whereinto* he sailed.

where·of (hwâr′uv′, -ov′) *adv.* **1** Interrogatively, of or from what: *Whereof* did you partake? **2** Conjunctively, of which or whom: the house *whereof* he is the head.

where·on (hwâr′on′, -ôn′) *adv.* **1** Interrogatively, on what or whom. **2** Conjunctively, on which: a rock *whereon* to build.

where·so·ev·er (hwâr′sō·ev′ər) *adv.* & *conj.* **1** In or to whatever place; wherever. **2** Whithersoever. **3** Whencesoever.

where·som·ev·er (hwâr′səm·ev′ər) *adv.* & *conj. Dial.* Wherever; wheresoever. [<WHERE + SOMEVER < *som* ever, just (<Scand.) + EVER]

where·through (hwâr′thro͞o′) *adv.* & *conj.* Through which.

where·to (hwâr′to͞o′) *adv.* **1** Interrogatively, to what place or end: *Whereto* serves avarice? **2** Conjunctively, to which or to whom; whither: the grave *whereto* we haste. Also *Archaic* **where′un·to′.**

where·up·on (hwâr′ə·pon′, -ə·pôn′) *adv.* **1** Interrogatively, upon what; whereon. **2** Conjunctively, upon which or whom; in consequence of which; after which: *whereupon* they took in sail.

wher·ev·er (hwâr′ev′ər) *adv.* & *conj.* In, at, or to whatever place; wheresoever.

where·with (hwâr′with′, -with′) *adv.* **1** Interrogatively, with what: *Wherewith* shall I do it? **2** Conjunctively, with which; by means of which: *wherewith* we abated hunger. — *pron.* That with or by which: with the infinitive: I have not *wherewith* to do it. — *n.* The requisites; wherewithal.

where·with·al (hwâr′with·ôl′) *n.* The necessary means or resources; especially, the necessary money: with the definite article. — *adv.* & *pron.* (hwâr′with·ôl′) Wherewith.

wher·ry (hwer′ē) *n. pl.* **·ries 1** A light, fast rowboat used on inland waters. **2** *Brit.* A decked fishing vessel with two sails. **3** An open rowboat for racing or exercise, built for one person. **4** *Brit.* A very broad, light barge. — *v.t.* & *v.i.* **·ried, ·ry·ing** To transport in or use a wherry. [? <WHIR; with ref. to rapid movement]

wherve (hwûrv) *n.* In spinning, a pulley on the spindle: also spelled *wharve.* [OE *hweorfa*]

whet (hwet) *v.t.* **whet·ted, whet·ting 1** To sharpen, as a knife, by friction. **2** To make more keen or eager; excite; stimulate, as the appetite. — *n.* **1** The act of whetting. **2** Something that whets. [OE *hwettan*] — **whet′ter** *n.*

wheth·er (hweth′ər) *conj.* As the first alternative; in case; if: introducing an alternative clause, followed by a correlative *or,* or *or whether*; sometimes also introducing a single alternative, the other, usually a negative, being implied: Tell us *whether* you are going (or not). — *pron.* Which: properly of two, less exactly of more than two: an archaism used interrogatively and relatively. — **whether or no** Regardless; in any case. [OE *hwæther, hwether*]

whet·slate (hwet′slāt′) *n.* A hard, fine-grained siliceous rock used for whetstones.

whet·stone (hwet′stōn′) *n.* A fine-grained stone for whetting knives, axes, etc. [OE *hwetstān* < *hwettan* whet + *stān* a stone]

whew (hwyo͞o) *interj.* An exclamatory sound, expressive usually of amazement, dismay, relief, admiration (real or feigned), or discomfort (from the heat). [Imit. of whistling]

Whew·ell (hyo͞o′əl), **William,** 1794–1866, English scientist and philosopher.

whey (hwā) *n.* A clear, straw-colored liquid that separates from the curd when milk is curdled, as in making cheese. [OE *hwæg, hweg*] — **whey′ey, whey′ish** *adj.*

whey-face (hwā′fās′) *n.* Formerly, a face or person pale as if from fear; now, one of pale, sallow complexion. — **whey′-faced′** *adj.*

which (hwich) *pron.* & *adj.* **1** Interrogatively, what individual person or thing, or group of persons or things collectively, of a certain number or class: asking for the indication or definite description. In this sense *which* is used both substantively and adjectively, singular and plural: *Which* shall I take? *Which* apple do you want? *Which* mammals are carnivorous? **2** As a relative pronoun, that particular one or ones of a certain number or class of impersonal beings or things: pointing out or definitely fixing upon that which is designated in the antecedent word, phrase, or clause to which it is related: now generally as a substantive, but sometimes as an adjective: He raised his hand, *which* gesture attracted my attention. *Which* as a relative now refers only to animals, without distinction of masculine or feminine, or to things without life; it was formerly used for persons, even in the most exalted sense, as "Our Father, *which* art in heaven." **3** Also relatively, the one that: often equivalent to the use of the interrogative in a dependent question: used substantively or adjectivally: Tell me *which* (or *which* apple) you prefer. [OE *hwelc, hwilc*]

which·ev·er (hwich′ev′ər) *pron.* & *adj.* Whether one or another (of two or of several); no matter which. Also **which′so·ev′er.**

whick·er (hwik′ər) *v.i.* & *n.* Whinny. [Imit.]

whid[1] (hwid) *Scot. n.* A brisk, nimble, scurrying movement. — *v.i.* **whid·ded, whid·ding** To move nimbly: said of small animals.

whid[2] (hwid) *Scot. n.* **1** A fib; lie. **2** A quarrel. **3** A word. — *v.i.* **whid·ded, whid·ding** To tell a lie; fib.

whid·ah bird (hwid′ə) An African weaverbird (subfamily *Viduinae*), the male of which has the tail greatly lengthened in the breeding season: formerly called *widow bird.* Also **whid′ah, whidah finch**: also spelled *whydah.* [Alter. of *widow bird*; infl. in form by *Whidah* former name of Ouidah, a seaport in French West Africa, near which this bird is commonly found]

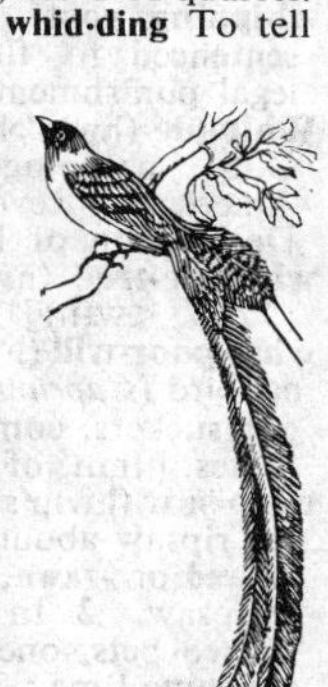

WHIDAH BIRD
(From 12 to 14 inches over all)

whiff (hwif) *n.* **1** Any sudden or slight gust or puff of air. **2** A gust or puff of odor: a *whiff* of onions. **3** A sudden expulsion of breath or smoke from the mouth; a puff. **4** An inhalation, as of smoke. — *v.t.* **1** To drive or blow with a whiff or puff. **2** To exhale or inhale in whiffs. **3** To smoke, as a pipe. — *v.i.* **4** To blow or move in whiffs or puffs. **5** To exhale or inhale whiffs. [Alter. of ME *weffe* an offensive odor; imit.] — **whiff′er** *n.*

whif·fet (hwif′it) *n. Colloq.* **1** A trifling, useless person; whippersnapper: in slight contempt. **2** A small, snappish dog. **3** A little whiff. [? Dim. of WHIFF]

whif·fle (hwif′əl) *v.* **·fled, ·fling** *v.i.* **1** To blow with puffs or gusts; shift about, as the wind. **2** To vacillate; veer. — *v.t.* **3** To blow or dissipate with or as with a puff. [Freq. of WHIFF]

whif·fler (hwif′lər) *n.* **1** One who fluctuates or shuffles in argument; a trifler. **2** One who whiffs tobacco. **3** A piper; fifer. — **whif′·fler·y** *n.*

whif·fle·tree (hwif′əl·trē′) *n.* A swingletree: also called *whippletree.* [Var. of WHIPPLETREE]

whig[1] (hwig) *v.i. Scot.* To drive onward; move along easily; jog.

whig[2] (hwig) *n. Dial.* **1** Sour whey. **2** Buttermilk. [Var. of OE *hweg* whey]

Whig (hwig) *n.* **1** An American colonist who supported the Revolutionary War in the 18th century: opposed to *Tory*; later, a member of a party opposed to the Democratic and succeeded by the Republican party in 1856. **2** A member of the Liberal party in England in the 18th and 19th centuries, as opposed to a *Tory* or *Conservative.* **3** In earlier usage, a Presbyterian rebel of the west of Scotland in the 17th century: thus named in derision; also, after the Restoration (1660), a Roundhead, as opposed to a Cavalier. — *adj.* Consisting of or supported by Whigs. [Prob. short for WHIGGAMORE] — **Whig′gish** *adj.* — **Whig′gish·ly** *adv.* — **Whig′gish·ness** *n.*

Whig·ga·more (hwig′ə·môr, -mōr) *n.* **1** A member of a body of insurgents who in 1648 marched on Edinburgh and opposed the compromise with Charles I. **2** In the later 17th century, a Scotch Presbyterian; a Whig (def. 3). Also **Whig′a·more.** [Prob. <dial. E (Scottish) *whiggamaire* < *whig* a cry to urge on a horse + *mere* a horse]

Whig·ger·y (hwig′ər·ē) *n. pl.* **·ger·ies** The doctrines of Whigs. Also **Whig′gism.**

whig·ma·lee·rie (hwig′mə·lir′ē) *n. Scot.* A small or useless ornament; gewgaw; also, a whim. Also **whig′ma·lee′ry, whig′me·lee′rie.**

while (hwīl) *n.* **1** A short time; also, a period of time, or time in general: Stay and rest a *while.* **2** Time or pains expended on a thing; trouble; labor: only in the phrase *worth while* or *worth one's while.* — **between whiles** From time to time. — **the while** At the same time: He went about his work and sang *the while.* — *conj.* **1** During the time that; as long as. **2** At the same time that; although: *While* he found fault, he also praised. **3** *Colloq.* Whereas: This man is short, *while* that one is tall. **4** *Brit. Dial.* Until; till. — *v.t.* **whiled, whil·ing** To cause to pass lightly and pleasantly; spend; pass: usually with *away*: to *while* away the time. [OE *hwīl*]

whiles (hwīlz) *Archaic* or *Dial. adv.* Occasionally; at intervals. — *conj.* While; during the time that.

whi·lom (hwī′ləm) *Archaic adj.* Being once upon a time; former. — *adv.* **1** Formerly; at one time. **2** At times. [OE *hwīlum* at times, dative pl. of *hwīl* a while]

whilst (hwīlst) *conj.* While: an old form still widely used, especially in England. [ME *whilest* < *whiles,* genitive of WHILE + *-t*]

whim (hwim) *n.* **1** A sudden, unexpected, and unreasonable deviation of the mind from its usual or natural course; caprice; freak. **2** An old form of mine hoist, run by horsepower. [Short for earlier *whim-wham* a trifle, ? < Scand. Cf. ON *hvima* wander with the eyes.]

Synonyms: caprice, crotchet, fancy, freak, humor, kink, quirk, vagary, whimsy, wrinkle. See FANCY.

whim·brel (hwim′brəl) *n.* A small northern curlew with a white rump, especially a species (*Numenius phaeopus*) of northern portions of the eastern hemisphere. [? <obs. *whimp* whimper, prob. imit. of its cry]

whim·per (hwim′pər) *v.i.* To cry or whine with plaintive broken sounds. — *v.t.* To utter with a whimper. — *n.* A low, broken, whining cry; whine. [Imit.] — **whim′per·er** *n.* — **whim′per·ing** *n.* — **whim′per·ing·ly** *adv.*

whim·si·cal (hwim′zi·kəl) *adj.* 1 Having eccentric ideas; capricious. 2 Oddly constituted; fantastic; quaint. See synonyms under FICKLE, ODD, QUEER. — **whim′si·cal·ly** *adv.* — **whim′·si·cal·ness** *n.*

whim·si·cal·i·ty (hwim′zi·kal′ə·tē) *n. pl.* **·ties** 1 Whimsicalness. 2 A singularity. 3 A quaint, fanciful, or odd idea or its expression.

whim·sy (hwim′zē) *n. pl.* **·sies** 1 A whim; caprice; freak. 2 Tenuously fanciful humor. Also **whim′sey.** See synonyms under WHIM. [Prob. related to WHIM]

whin[1] (hwin) *n.* Furze; gorse. [Prob. <Scand. Cf. Dan. & Norw. *hvine* a kind of grass.]

whin[2] (hwin) *n.* Whinstone. [< dial. E (Scottish) *quin*; ult. origin uncertain]

whin·chat (hwin′chat) *n.* A small, Old World, thrushlike singing bird *(Saxicola rubetra)*, streaked with brown above and rufous below. [<WHIN[1] + CHAT[1]]

whine (hwīn) *v.* **whined, whin·ing** *v.i.* 1 To utter a low, plaintive, nasal sound expressive of grief or distress. 2 To complain in a mean or childish way. — *v.t.* 3 To utter with a whine. — *n.* The act or sound of whining; any peevish complaint. [OE *hwīnan* whiz] — **whin′er** *n.* — **whin′ing·ly** *adv.* — **whin′y** *adj.*

whinge (hwinj) *v.i.* **whinged, whinge·ing** *Austral. Slang* To complain; whine.

whing·er (hwing′ər) *n. Brit. Dial.* A dirk, used at meals or as a weapon; a hanger. See HANGER. Also **whing′ar.** [Prob. var. of WHINYARD]

whin·ny[1] (hwin′ē) *v.* **·nied, ·ny·ing** *v.i.* To neigh, especially in a low or gentle way. — *v.t.* To express with a whinny. — *n. pl.* **·nies** The cry or call of a horse; a neigh. [<WHINE]

whin·ny[2] (hwin′ē) *adj.* **·ni·er, ·ni·est** Abounding in whin or furze. [<WHIN[1]]

whin·stone (hwin′stōn′) *n.* Any very hard, dark-colored rock, as basalt or chert. [<WHIN[2] + STONE]

whin·yard (hwin′yərd) *n. Dial.* 1 One of certain ducks, especially the pochard. 2 A hanger or sword. [Earlier *whyneherd,* ? <OE *hwīnan* whiz; the duck is so called because of the swordlike shape of its bill]

whip (hwip) *v.* **whipped** or **whipt, whip·ping** *v.t.* 1 To strike with a lash, rod, strap, etc. 2 To punish by striking thus; flog. 3 To drive or urge with lashes or blows: with *on, up, off,* etc. 4 To strike in the manner of a whip: The wind *whipped* the trees. 5 To attack with scathing criticism; berate; flay. 6 To beat, as eggs or cream, to a froth. 7 To seize, move, jerk, throw, etc., with a sudden motion: with *away, in, off, out,* etc. 8 In fishing, to make repeated casts upon the surface of (a stream, etc.). 9 To wrap (rope, cable, etc.) with light line so as to prevent chafing or wear; serve. 10 To wrap or bind about something. 11 To form, as a flat seam, by laying two selvages of a fabric together and sewing with a loose overcast or overhand stitch. 12 *U.S. Colloq.* To defeat; overcome, as in a contest. 13 *Naut.* To hoist by means of a whip (def. 5). — *v.i.* 14 To go, come, move, or turn suddenly and quickly: with *away, in, off, out,* etc. 15 To thrash about in a manner suggestive of a whip: pennants *whipping* in the wind. 16 In fishing, to make repeated casts with rod and line. — **to whip in** 1 To keep from scattering, as hounds in a hunt. 2 To keep together or united, as a political party. — **to whip up** 1 To excite; arouse. 2 *Colloq.* To prepare quickly, as a meal. — *n.* 1 An instrument consisting of a lash attached to a handle, used for driving draft animals or for administering punishment. 2 One who handles a whip expertly; a driver. 3 A stroke, blow, or cut with a whip. 4 A member of a legislative body appointed unofficially to enforce the discipline and look after the interests of his party: often called **party whip;** also, a call made upon members of a legislature by such a person to bring or keep them in their places at a given time, as when a vote or division may be expected. 5 *Mech.* A simple form of hoisting apparatus, consisting of a rope passing over an elevated single pulley, and used for lifting light objects. 6 One who operates such an apparatus. 7 A huntsman who whips in the hounds to control them; a whipper-in. 8 *Electr.* A vibrating spring that whips back and forth, closing different circuits in electrical apparatus. 9 A dish or dessert containing cream or eggs whipped to a froth: prune *whip.* 10 A thrashing motion, as of a rope or wire suddenly broken. 11 Flexibility in the shaft of a golf club. 12 An arm of a windmill. 13 *Obs.* or *Scot.* An attack of illness; also, a sudden movement; a single swift attack or blow. [ME *wippen, hwippen.* Cf. MDu. *wippen* swing, leap, dance.]

whip·cord (hwip′kôrd′) *n.* 1 A strong, hard-twisted, sometimes braided hempen cord, used in making whiplashes. 2 A cord of catgut. 3 A twill-weave fabric, similar to gabardine, but with a more pronounced diagonal rib on the right side: used for riding habits and other outdoor garments.

whip·graft (hwip′graft′, -gräft′) *v.t. Bot.* To graft by fitting a tongue cut on the cion to a slit cut slopingly in the stock. — **whip′graft′·age, whip′graft′ing** *n.*

whip·hand (hwip′hand′) *n.* 1 The hand that wields the whip; in riding or driving, the right hand. 2 An instrument or means of mastery; advantage: She, not he, has the *whiphand.*

whip·lash (hwip′lash′) *n.* The flexible striking part of a whip.

whiplash injury An injury to the upper spine or base of the brain caused by a sudden jolting of the neck, as in an automobile collision.

whip·per (hwip′ər) *n.* One who whips.

whip·per-in (hwip′ər·in′) *n.* 1 In hunting, one employed to assist the huntsman and to enforce obedience among the hounds. 2 A political or parliamentary whip.

whip·per·snap·per (hwip′ər·snap′ər) *n.* A pretentious but insignificant person. [? Extension of *whipsnapper* a cracker of whips]

whip·pet (hwip′it) *n.* 1 A swift dog resembling an English greyhound in miniature, characterized by a long, narrow head, long arched back, smooth, close coat, and a long, tapering tail. 2 A small, light, speedy tank used in World War I: also **whippet tank.** 3 Anything suggestive of a whippet, as in size, speed, etc. [Dim. of WHIP; so called with ref. to its rapid movement]

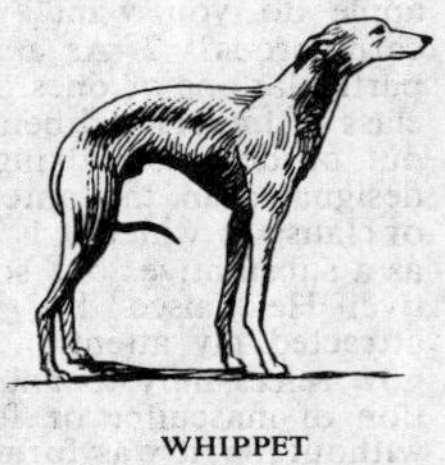

WHIPPET
(From 23 to 28 inches high at the shoulder)

whip·ping (hwip′ing) *n.* 1 The act of one who whips; castigation; state or fact of being flogged or defeated. 2 Material used to bind the head of a rope, or to bind the head to the shaft of a golf club.

whipping boy Formerly, a boy brought up as companion to a prince or other noble youth, and punished in his stead for all misdeeds; now, anyone who receives punishment deserved by another.

whipping post The fixture to which those sentenced to flogging are secured; hence, legal punishment by flogging.

Whip·ple (hwip′əl), **George Hoyt,** born 1878, U.S. pathologist. — **William,** 1730–85, American Revolutionary general; signed Declaration of Independence.

whip·ple·tree (hwip′əl·trē′) *n.* A swingletree. [Prob. <WHIP]

whip·poor·will (hwip′ər·wil) *n.* A small nocturnal bird *(Caprimulgus vociferus),* allied to the goatsuckers, common in the eastern United States. [Imit. of its reiterated cry]

whip·saw (hwip′sô′) *n.* A thin, narrow, tapering ripsaw about six feet long. — *v.t.* **·sawed, ·sawed** or **·sawn, ·saw·ing** 1 To saw with a whipsaw. 2 In faro, to beat (an opponent) in two bets, one to win and one to lose, at the same time. 3 To get the best of (an opponent) in spite of every effort he makes.

whip scorpion Any of various scorpionlike arachnids (family *Thelyphonidae*) having an abdomen terminating in a slender appendage like a whiplash, and lacking a sting; especially, the vinegarroon.

whip·stall (hwip′stôl′) *Aeron. n.* The stalled condition of a sharply climbing airplane in which the nose whips violently downward. — *v.i.* To bring about or go into a whipstall.

whip·stitch (hwip′stich′) *v.t.* To sew or gather with overcast stitches, as the turned edge of a ruffle; overcast. — *n.* 1 An overcast stitch in whipping an edge or seam. 2 A tailor.

whip·stock (hwip′stok′) *n.* That part of a whip to which the lash is attached; a whip handle.

whipt (hwipt) Alternative past tense and past participle of WHIP.

whip·worm (hwip′wûrm′) *n.* A nematode *(Trichuris trichiura),* with the posterior part of the body thickened: found in the human cecum.

whir (hwûr) *v.t.* & *v.i.* **whirred, whir·ring** To fly, move, or whirl with a buzzing sound. — *n.* 1 A whizzing, swishing sound, as that caused by the sudden rising of birds. 2 Confusion; bustle. Also **whirr.** [Prob. <Scand. Cf. Dan. *hvivre.* Akin to WHIRL.]

whirl (hwûrl) *v.i.* 1 To turn or revolve rapidly, as about a center. 2 To turn away or aside quickly. 3 To move or go swiftly. 4 To have a sensation of spinning: My head *whirls.* — *v.t.* 5 To cause to turn or revolve rapidly. 6 To carry or bear along with a revolving motion: The wind *whirled* the dust into the air. 7 *Obs.* To hurl. — *n.* 1 A swift rotating or revolving motion. 2 Something whirling, as a cloud of dust. 3 Confusion; turmoil. [Prob. <ON *hvirfla* revolve. Akin to WARBLE[1].]

whirl-a·bout (hwûrl′ə·bout′) *n.* Anything that turns swiftly around or about; a whirligig.

whirl·er (hwûr′lər) *n.* 1 One who or that which whirls. 2 A rotating hook or reel used in ropemaking.

whirl·i·gig (hwûr′lə·gig′) *n.* 1 Any toy or small device that revolves rapidly on an axis. 2 A merry-go-round. 3 Anything that performs quick revolutions or moves in a cycle: the *whirligig* of time. 4 Any of a family *(Gyrinidae)* of water beetles that frequent the surface of smooth water and move in swift circles: also **whirligig beetle.** 5 A trifling ornament, as one used by printers; also, a fanciful notion. [< *whirly* (<WHIRL) + GIG[1] (def. 4)]

whirl·pool (hwûrl′pōol′) *n.* 1 An eddy or vortex where water moves with a gyrating sweep, as from the meeting of two currents. 2 Any disturbance from such causes, whether accompanied by vortical motion or not.

whirl·wind (hwûrl′wind′) *n.* 1 A moving atmospheric vortex; a funnel-shaped column of air, with a rapid circular and upward spiral motion around a vertical or inclined axis, causing waterspouts, sand pillars, and dust whirls. 2 Any violent rushing or rotatory movement. See synonyms under CYCLONE. — *adj.* Extremely swift or impetuous: a *whirlwind* courtship.

whirl·y·bird (hwûr′lē·bûrd′) *n. Colloq.* A helicopter. [< *whirly* (<WHIRL) + BIRD]

whir·ry (hwûr′ē) *v.t.* & *v.i.* **·ried, ·ry·ing** *Scot.* To hurry.

whish[1] (hwish) *v.i.* To move with a sibilant, whistling sound. — *n.* A swishing sound like that made by cutting the air with a pliant rod. [Imit.]

whish[2] (hwish) *interj.* Hush! silence! Also **whisht** (hwisht). [Alter. of HUSH; infl. in form by WHISHT]

whisht (hwisht, hwist, wisht; *Scot.* hwusht) *Scot. v.t.* To hush. — *v.i.* To be silent. — *n.* The slightest sound; a whisper. — **to hold one's whisht** To be or remain silent.

whisk (hwisk) *v.t.* 1 To bear along or sweep with light movements, as of a small broom or a fan: often with *away* or *off:* to *whisk* flies away. 2 To cause to move with a quick sweeping motion. 3 To beat or mix with a quick movement, as eggs, cream, etc. — *v.i.* 4 To move quickly and lightly. — *n.* 1 A light stroke; a sudden, sweeping movement. 2 A little broom or brush. 3 A little bunch, as of straw, feathers, etc.; wisp. 4 A small culinary instrument for rapidly whipping (cream, etc.) to a froth. 5 A neckerchief of lawn or lace formerly worn by women. [Prob. <Scand. Cf. Dan. *viske* wipe, rub.]

whisk·broom (hwisk′brōom′, -brŏom′) *n.* A small, short-handled broom for brushing clothing, etc.

whisk·er (hwis′kər) *n.* 1 *pl.* The hair that grows on the sides of a man's face, as distinguished from that on his lips, chin, and throat; loosely, the beard or any part of the beard; also, formerly, a mustache. 2 A hair from the whiskers or beard. 3 One of the long, bristly hairs on the sides of the mouth of some

animals, as the cat, or a similar formation of bristles, as about the mouth of a bird; a vibrissa. **4** One who or that which whisks; formerly, a switch. **5** One of two small projecting spars or booms on the side of a bowsprit, to extend the jib or flying-jib guys: also **whisker boom.** —**whisk′ered, whisk′er·y** *adj.* —**whisk′er·less** *adj.*

whisk grass Zacatón.

whis·ky (hwis′kē) *n. pl.* **·kies 1** An alcoholic liquor obtained by the distillation of a fermented starchy compound, usually a grain. Whisky is often named (sometimes improperly) from the substance from which it is made, as **corn whisky, rye whisky,** etc.; or from the place or country of production, as **Bourbon whisky, Irish whisky,** etc. **2** A drink or portion of whisky. Compare USQUEBAUGH. —*adj.* Pertaining to or made of whisky. Also **whis′key.** [Short for *usquebaugh* <Irish *uisgebeatha,* lit., water of life <*uisge* water + *beatha* life]

whis·ky-jack (hwis′kē·jak′) *n.* The gray or Canada jay *(Perisoreus canadensis),* common in the northern forests of North America, about lumber camps, etc. [Alter. of earlier *whisky-john,* alter. of Algonquian (Cree) *wiskatjan*]

whis·per (hwis′pər) *n.* **1** A low, soft, sibilant voice; articulated but not sonant breath; also, a low, rustling sound, as of waves or leaves. See VOICE. **2** A whispered utterance; secret communication; hint; insinuation. —*v.i.* **1** To speak in a whisper. **2** To talk cautiously or furtively; plot or gossip. **3** To make a low, rustling sound, as leaves. —*v.t.* **4** To utter in a whisper. **5** To speak to in a whisper. [OE *hwisprian*] —**whis′per·er** *n.* —**whis′per·ing** *n. & adj.* —**whis′per·ing·ly** *adv.* —**whis′per·y** *adj.*

whist[1] (hwist) *n.* A game of cards played by four persons with a full pack of 52 cards, opposite players being partners: all the cards are played in each hand, the highest card of the suit led played in each of the 13 tricks, or a card of the trump suit, or the highest trump played, winning such trick. Every trick above the sixth counts one point. See CONTRACT BRIDGE under BRIDGE[2]. [Alter. of earlier *whisk*; ult. origin unknown]

whist[2] (hwist) *interj.* Hush! be still! —*adj.* Silent or quiet; mute. See also WHISHT. [Prob. imit.]

whis·tle (hwis′əl) *n.* **1** A device for producing a shrill, musical sound, operated on the principle of forcing a current of air, steam, or the like, through a pipe or tube of narrowed aperture or against a thin edge. **2** A musical sound, more or less shrill, made without the use of the vocal cords, by sending the breath through a small orifice formed by contracting the lips; also, the act of making this sound. **3** The sound produced by a whistle, or any sound suggestive of it, as the sound of wind rushing by an object, or of a flying missile, or the shrill cry of some birds. **4** A summons or call made by a whistle: The dog comes at his master's *whistle.* **5** *Slang* The mouth and throat: to wet one's *whistle.* **6** The short, loud cry of a male moose or elk. —*v.* **·tled, ·tling** *v.i.* **1** To make a sound or series of sounds like a whistle. **2** To cause a sharp, shrill sound by swift passage through the air, or by passage past an edge or through an orifice: The bullets *whistled* over our heads. **3** To blow or sound a whistle. —*v.t.* **4** To produce, as a tune or melody, by whistling. **5** To call, manage, or direct by whistling. **6** To send with a whistling sound. —**to whistle for** To go without; fail to get. [OE *hwistle* a shrill pipe]

whis·tler (hwis′lər) *n.* **1** One who or that which whistles. **2** A large gray marmot *(Marmota caligata)* of NW North America. **3** One of various birds, as the American goldeneye or the English widgeon: so called from the noise of their wings in flight.

Whis·tler (hwis′lər), **James Abbott McNeill,** 1834–1903, U.S. artist and etcher. —**Whis·tle·ri·an** (hwis·lir′ē·ən) *adj.*

whistle stop *U.S. Colloq.* A small town, where a train stops only on signal. —**whis·tle-stop** (hwis′əl·stop′) *adj.*

whistling swan See under SWAN.

whit (hwit) *n.* The smallest particle; speck: usually with a negative: not a *whit* abashed. See synonyms under PARTICLE. [Var. of WIGHT[1], as used in phrases *any wight, no wight,* OE *ænig wiht, nān wiht* a little amount]

Whit·by (hwit′bē) A port on the North Sea in the North Riding, NE York, England.

white (hwīt) *adj.* **whit·er, whit·est 1** Having the color produced by reflection of all the rays of the solar spectrum, as from a finely powdered surface; having the color of new snow: opposed to *black.* **2** Light or comparatively light in color; specifically, light-colored as opposed to *red: white* wine. **3** Bloodless; ashen: *white* with rage. **4** Very fair; blond. **5** Silvery, hoary, or gray, as with age. **6** Covered with snow; snowy. **7** Made of silver; also unburnished, as silverwork. **8** Habited in white clothing: *white* nuns. **9** Not intentionally wicked or evil; not malicious or harmful: a *white* lie. **10** Figuratively, free from spot or stain; innocent: a *white* soul. **11** Incandescent; being at white heat. **12** Blank; unmarked by ink: said of a space in an advertisement or the like. **13** Belonging to a racial group characterized by light-colored skin; especially, Caucasian. **14** Of, pertaining to, or controlled by white men: the *white* power structure. **15** *Colloq.* Fair and honorable; straightforward; honest. **16** Propitious; auspicious: a rare meaning. **17** In certain European countries, constitutional; conservative, as a party; opposed to the radicals or revolutionaries. See synonyms under PALE[2]. —*n.* **1** That color seen when sunlight is reflected without sensible absorption of any of the visible rays of the spectrum; the color in the scale of grays which is entirely without hue and is the opposite of *black.* **2** The state or condition of being white; whiteness; figuratively, innocence; truth. **3** The white or light-colored part of something; specifically, the albumen of an egg, or the white part of the eyeball. **4** Anything that is white or nearly white, as cloth or garments; in the plural, a white uniform or outfit: The sailor wore his summer *whites.* **5** White wine. **6** A white paint or pigment; hence, by comparison, a color approaching pure white in its effect. **7** In chess or checkers, the white or light men, or the player who has them. **8** *pl.* Flour made from the finest and whitest part of the wheat. **9** *pl. Printing* Blank spaces in a picture, plate, mold, etc. **10** In archery, the outermost ring of a target; also, a hit on that ring, scoring one point. **11** A member of the so-called white race. **12** In some European countries, a member of a party opposed to the radicals or revolutionaries; a conservative. **13** *pl. Pathol.* Leukorrhea. **14** A breed of animal, especially a swine, that is white in color. —*v.t.* **whit·ed, whit·ing 1** To make white; whiten; bleach. **2** *Printing* To make or leave blank spaces in, as between lines or about an illustration: often with *out:* to *white* out a column. [OE *hwīt*]

White (hwīt), **Andrew,** 1832–1918, U.S. educator, historian, and diplomat. —**Byron Raymond,** born 1917, U.S. lawyer; associate justice of the Supreme Court 1962–. —**E(lwyn) B(rooks),** born 1899, U.S. writer and editor. —**Gilbert,** 1720–93, English naturalist and antiquary. —**Peregrine,** 1620–1704, first child of English parentage born in New England. —**Stanford,** 1853–1906, U.S. architect. —**William Allen,** 1868–1944, U.S. editor.

white alkali 1 The product obtained from soda ash during the manufacture of carbonate of soda, dissolved in water, clarified, and freed from moisture by evaporation. **2** Pure soda ash.

white ant A small, whitish, isopterous insect, the termite, closely resembling the true ant in general appearance and social habits: it exists in tropical and warmer temperate regions, and does much damage to wooden structures, furniture, etc., by boring. For illustration see INSECTS (injurious) —**to white ant** *Austral.* To undermine or sabotage.

white-ant·er (hwīt′ant′ər) *n. Austral.* One who undermines or sabotages.

white·bait (hwīt′bāt′) *n.* **1** The young of various clupeoid fishes, especially of sprat and herring, served as a delicacy. **2** One of various species of silversides of fresh and salt waters of the United States.

white bear The polar bear.

white birch 1 The North American birch *(Betula papyrifera)* with thin, white bark resembling paper. **2** The common European birch *(Betula pendula, B. pubescens),* having an ash-colored bark; also, a related Asian species *(B. platyphylla).*

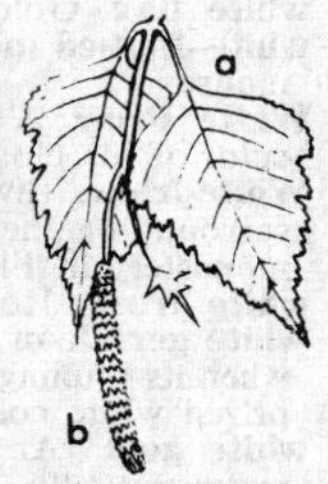

WHITE BIRCH
a. Leaf. *b.* Fruit.
(Tree 20 to 30 feet tall, rarely 40)

white blood cell Leukocyte.

white book In some European countries and in Japan, a formal report issued by a government on some special subject; in England an alternate of the bluebook: so called from the colors of the bookbinding.

white brant The snow goose.

white bryony A species of bryony *(Bryonia alba)* common in Europe.

white·cap (hwīt′kap′) *n.* **1** A foam-crested wave. **2** One of several birds having white about the head.

White·cap (hwīt′kap′) *n.* Formerly, in the Middle West and southward, one of a lawless, secret organization of men, who, under the pretense of regulating public morals, imposed lynch-law rule upon individuals who incurred their ill will: so named from their white caps or hoods.

white cedar 1 An evergreen tree *(Chamaecyparis thyoides)* of the cypress family, growing in moist places along the Atlantic coast. **2** Its soft, easily worked wood. **3** The arborvitae.

White·chap·el (hwīt′chap·əl) A district in Stepney borough, eastern London, England; the older Jewish quarter.

white clover A common variety *(Trifolium repens)* of clover, with white flowers.

white coal Water considered as a source of power.

white-col·lar (hwīt′kol′ər) *adj.* Pertaining to or designating salaried workers in occupations which demand a well-dressed appearance.

white comb A contagious disease of poultry, caused by a fungus *(Lophophyton gallinae),* and marked by the formation of grayish patches on the comb and a breaking off of the feathers.

white corpuscle Leukocyte.

white crane The whooping crane *(Grus americana)* of North America, which is pure white when adult.

white curlew The white ibis *(Guara alba)* of the southern United States.

whit·ed sepulcher (hwī′tid) A hypocrite; a person with a pleasing outward aspect, but corrupted thoughts. Matt. xxiii 27.

white elephant 1 A rare pale-gray variety of Asian elephant held sacred by the Burmese and Siamese. **2** Anything rare, expensive, and difficult to keep; a burdensome possession.

white-eye (hwīt′ī′) *n.* **1** The white-eyed vireo *(Vireo griseus)* of North America. **2** Any of numerous small singing birds (*Zosterops* and related genera), mostly of the Old World tropics: named from the circle of white feathers around the eye.

white-eyed (hwīt′īd′) *adj.* Having the iris of the eye white or colorless, as an albino.

white-faced (hwīt′fāst′) *adj.* **1** Pallid in countenance; pale. **2** Having a white mark or spot on the face or front of the head: the *white-faced* hornet. **3** Having a white facing or exposed surface, as a skirt.

white feather A mark of cowardice, full-blooded gamecocks being said to have no white feathers.

White·field (hwit′fēld), **George,** 1714–70, English preacher; a founder of Methodism.

white·fish (hwīt′fish′) *n. pl.* **·fish** or **·fish·es 1** A salmonoid food fish (genus *Coregonus*) of North America, living mostly in lakes and having teeth minute or absent. **2** One of various other species of fish, as the menhaden, the European whiting, or the silver salmon *(Oncorhynchus kisutch).* **3** A tropical marine food fish of California *(Caulolatilus princeps).* **4** The young of the bluefish. **5** The beluga.

white flag 1 A flag of truce. **2** A signal of surrender when hoisted over a fortified position or a body of men.

white flax Gold-of-pleasure.

white-foot·ed mouse (hwīt'fŏŏt'id) The deer mouse.

White Friar A Carmelite: so called from the color of his cloak.

White·fri·ars (hwīt'frī'ərz) The neighborhood surrounding the site of a former Carmelite monastery in Fleet Street, London.

white frost Hoar frost.

white gerfalcon The gerfalcon in the phase when its plumage is of a conspicuous, highly prized white color.

white gold An alloy of gold with a white metal, usually nickel and zinc, sometimes palladium.

white-gum (hwīt'gum') n.   1 An Australian eucalyptus with a white bark. 2 The American sweetgum.

White·hall (hwīt'hôl) 1 A former royal palace near Westminster Abbey. 2 A street in Westminster, London, where a number of government offices are located. 3 The British government.

White·head (hwīt'hed), **Alfred North,** 1861–1947, English mathematician and philosopher, active in the United States.

white heat 1 The temperature at which a body becomes incandescent. 2 A condition of extreme anger or emotional strain.

White·horse (hwīt'hôrs) The capital of Yukon Territory on the upper Yukon River. Also **White Horse.**

white-hors·es (hwīt'hôr'siz) n. pl. Foam-crested waves; white caps (def. 1).

white-hot (hwīt'hot') adj. 1 Exhibiting the condition of white heat. 2 Colloq. Extremely angry.

White House, The 1 The official residence of the president of the United States, at Washington, D.C.: a white building in American colonial style, officially called the Executive Mansion. 2 The executive branch of the United States government.

white lead 1 A poisonous white pigment composed of lead carbonate and hydrated lead oxide and prepared by several processes: also called ceruse. 2 Native carbonate of lead; cerusite. See LEAD.

white leather Whiteleather.

white lie See under LIE.

white-liv·ered (hwīt'liv'ərd) adj. 1 Having a pale and feeble look. 2 Base; cowardly; envious.

white lupine A white-flowered variety (Lupinus albus) of lupine, grown in Europe for forage.

white·ly (hwīt'lē) adv. With a pale appearance; so as to look white.

white mahogany Primavera.

white man 1 A person belonging to a racial group characterized by light-colored skin: territory first settled by white men in 1740. 2 A male member of the so-called white race.

white man's burden The alleged duty of the white peoples to spread culture among the so-called backward peoples of the world: phrase originated by Rudyard Kipling.

white maple Any of certain maples having a whitish bark, as the silver maple (Acer saccharinum) and red maple (A. rubrum), both of North America.

white matter Anat. That portion of the brain and spinal cord that is composed mainly of medullated nerve fibers, giving it a white appearance: contrasted with gray matter.

white meat 1 The light-colored meat or flesh of animals, as veal or the breast of turkey. 2 Obs. Food made from milk, butter, cheese, eggs, and other animal products.

white metal See under METAL.

White Mountains 1 A range of the Appalachians in north central New Hampshire; highest peak, 6,288 feet. 2 A range of mountains in eastern Arizona; highest point, 11,590 feet. 3 A range of mountains in eastern California and SW Nevada; highest point, 14,242 feet.

whit·en (hwīt'n) v.t. & v.i. To make or become white; blanch; bleach. See synonyms under BLEACH. — **whit'en·er** n.

white·ness (hwīt'nis) n. 1 The state of being white; freedom from stains or darkness of surface. 2 Pallor from emotion or from illness. 3 Cleanness or pureness of heart; innocence.

White Nile See NILE.

white oak 1 A North American oak (Quercus alba) of the eastern United States, with long leaves having from five to nine entire, rounded lobes. 2 Either of two related species, the **swamp white oak** (Q. bicolor) and the **Oregon white oak** (Q. garryana). 3 The British oak (Q. petraea). 4 The wood of any species of white oak.

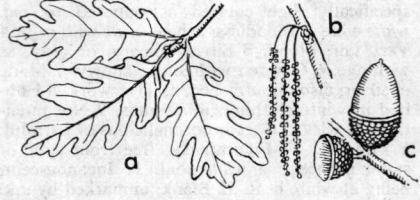

WHITE OAK
a. Leaf. b. Blossom. c. Acorn.

white of egg Egg white.

white-out (hwīt'out') n. Meteorol. An atmospheric condition in arctic regions in which a blending of clouds and snow cover produces a uniform milky whiteness characterized by the absence of shadow and the invisibility of all but very dark objects.

white paper A government publication on some subject of less importance than that treated in a white book or a bluebook. See WHITE BOOK, BLUEBOOK.

White Pass A pass in the Coast Mountains, on the border between SE Alaska and NW British Columbia; elevation 2,888 feet.

white pepper See under PEPPER.

white perch A small food fish (Morone americana) related to the sea basses, found in Atlantic coastal waters and sometimes landlocked in streams of the eastern United States.

white pine 1 A pine (Pinus strobus) widely distributed in eastern North America, with soft, bluish-green leaves in clusters of five. The cone and tassel of this tree are the State emblem of Maine. 2 The light, soft wood of this tree. 3 Any of several varieties of this pine.

white-pine weevil (hwīt'pīn') A weevil (Pissodes strobi) of NE North America which feeds on the leading shoots of white pine and other conifers. For illustration see INSECTS (injurious).

white plague Pathol. Tuberculosis, especially of the lungs.

white poplar 1 A large, rapidly growing Old World tree (Populus alba), often planted in the United States for shade or for its ornamental leaves, which are green above and clothed with a silvery-white down beneath; the silver poplar. 2 The aspen.

white potato The common potato.

white rabbit The varying hare.

white race The Caucasoid ethnic division of mankind.

white rat 1 Any albino rat. 2 One of a special breed of albino Norway rats much used in biological and medical experimentation.

White River 1 A river in northern and eastern Arkansas and SW Missouri, flowing 690 miles to the Mississippi. 2 A river in Nebraska and southern South Dakota, flowing 507 miles NE to the Missouri.

White Russian See under RUSSIAN.

White Russian S.S.R. See BELORUSSIAN SOVIET SOCIALIST REPUBLIC. Also **White Russia.**

White Sands National Monument A government reservation in southern New Mexico; 219 square miles; established 1933.

white sapphire A variety of translucent, colorless corundum.

White Sea An inlet of the Barents Sea in NW European U.S.S.R.; 36,680 square miles. Russian **Be·lo·e Mo·re** (bye'lə-yə mô'ryə).

white slave A girl forced into or held in prostitution. — **white-slave** (hwīt'slāv') adj.

White-slave Act The Mann Act.

white-slav·er (hwīt'slā'vər) n. One who procures for or engages in white-slavery.

white-slav·er·y (hwīt'slā'vər-ē) n. The business or practice of forced prostitution.

white-smith (hwīt'smith') n. 1 A worker in white metals, as a tinsmith. 2 A finisher,

polisher, or galvanizer of iron. Compare BLACKSMITH.

white spruce A spruce (Picus glauca) of Canada and the northern United States.

white squall Meteorol. A small whirlwind occurring in the tropics, having no accompanying cloud and often making ocean waters foam-white.

white-tail (hwīt'tāl') n. 1 The white-tailed deer. 2 The wheatear.

white-tailed deer (hwīt'tāld') The common North American deer (Odocoileus virginianus), having a moderately long tail white on the underside: also called Virginia deer.

white-throat (hwīt'thrōt') n. One of various Old World warblers, especially the common or **greater whitethroat** (Sylvia cinerea), with gray head, white throat, and rufous wings.

white-throat·ed sparrow (hwīt'thrō'tid) A common North American sparrow (Zonotrichia albicollis), with a prominent white patch on the throat.

white tie 1 A white bow tie, worn with a swallowtail coat. 2 A swallowtail coat and its correct accessories: the phrase is used on invitations, etc., to indicate formal attire.

white trash Poor whites: an offensive term.

white turnip The common turnip (Brassica rapa).

white vitriol Hydrated zinc sulfate, $ZnSo_4 \cdot 7H_2O$, widely used in medicine as an emetic, astringent, and antiseptic.

white-wash (hwīt'wosh', -wôsh') n. 1 A mixture of slaked lime and water, sometimes with salt, whiting, and glue added, used for whitening walls, etc. 2 A toilet preparation for whitening the skin. 3 Figuratively, a report falsely ascribing virtues, suppressing adverse evidence, etc. 4 A failure to score in a game. — v.t. 1 To coat with whitewash. 2 To gloss over; hide. 3 Colloq. In sports, to defeat without allowing the losing side to score. See synonyms under BLEACH. — **white'wash'er** n.

white wax Paraffin.

white-weed (hwīt'wēd') n. The oxeye daisy.

white whale The beluga.

white-wing (hwīt'wing') n. 1 One of the members of the Department of Sanitation of New York City: so called because they formerly wore white uniforms. 2 Any person who wears a white uniform. 3 The surf duck.

white-winged dove (hwīt'wingd') A dove (Melopelia asiatica) of the SW United States with a conspicuous white patch on the wings.

white·wood (hwīt'wŏŏd') n. 1 Any of various trees yielding a whitish timber, as the basswood, the tuliptree, the cottonwood, the wild cinnamon, etc. 2 The wood of these trees.

Whi·tey (hwī'tē, wī'-) n. pl. -teys U.S. Slang 1 The white man, especially when considered as the oppressor or enemy of the Negro. 2 A white man: an offensive term. Also **whi'tey.**

whith·er (hwith'ər) adv. 1 As a relative, to which or what: approaching a conjunctive use: the village whither we went. 2 As an interrogative, to which or to what place. 3 Wheresoever; whithersoever. 4 To what degree or extent. [OE hwider]

whith·er·so·ev·er (hwith'ər·sō·ev'ər) adv. To whatever place.

whit·ing[1] (hwī'ting) n. A pure white chalk, levigated and washed for use in making putty and whitewash, as a pigment, and for polishing.

whit·ing[2] (hwī'ting) n. 1 A small European gadoid food fish (Merlangus merlangus) without a barbel. 2 The hake (def. 1). 3 Any of several silvery sciaenoid fishes (genus Menticirrhus), especially the **Carolina whiting** (M. americanus), common on the coast of the southern United States. 4 The menhaden. [< MDu. wijting < wit white]

whit·ish (hwī'tish) adj. Somewhat white or, especially, very light gray. — **whit'ish·ness** n.

whit·leath·er (hwīt'leth'ər) n. Leather tawed with alum to render it pliable; white leather. [< WHITE + LEATHER]

whit·low (hwīt'lō) n. Pathol. An inflammatory tumor, especially on the terminal phalanx of a finger, seated between the epidermis and true skin; a felon. [ME whitflaw, appar. < WHITE + FLAW[1]]

Whit·man (hwit'mən), **Marcus,** 1802–47, U.S. missionary massacred by Indians in Oregon. — **Walt,** 1819–92, U.S. poet.

Whit–Mon·day (hwit′mun′dē, -dā) *n.* The Monday next following Whitsunday: observed in England as a holiday. Also **Whit′mon′day, Whit′sun–Mon′day.** [On analogy with WHITSUNDAY]

Whit·ney (hwit′nē), **Eli,** 1765–1825, American inventor. — **Gertrude,** 1877?–1942, *née* Vanderbilt, U. S. sculptress. — **Josiah Dwight,** 1819–96, U. S. geologist. — **William Dwight,** 1827–94, U. S. philologist; brother of Josiah Dwight.

Whit·ney (hwit′nē), **Mount** A peak of the southern Sierra Nevada Range in eastern California; 14,496 feet; highest point in the United States.

whit·rack (hwit′rak) *n. Dial. & Scot.* A weasel. [ME *whitratt* <WHITE + RAT]

Whit·sun (hwit′sən) *n.* Whitsunday: frequently used in composition: *Whitsun*-ale, *Whitsun*-week. [ME *witsonen, whitsone* < *whitsondei* WHITSUNDAY]

Whit·sun·day (hwit′sun′dē, -dā) *n.* The seventh Sunday after Easter: a church festival commemorating Pentecost. [OE *Hwīta Sunnandæg,* lit., white Sunday; so called from the white robes worn by recently baptized persons on that day]

Whit·sun–week (hwit′sən·wēk′) *n.* The week that begins with Whitsunday. Also **Whit′·sun·tide′** (-tīd′).

Whit·ta·ker (hwit′ə·kər), **Charles E(vans),** born 1901, U. S. jurist; associate justice of the U. S. Supreme Court 1957–1962.

whit·ter (hwit′ər) *n. Scot.* **1** A copious draft of liquor, etc. **2** Anything weak. **3** Chatter; loquacity. **4** A token; sign.

Whit·ti·er (hwit′ē·ər) A port of southern Alaska on Prince William Sound.

Whit·ti·er (hwit′ē·ər), **John Greenleaf,** 1807–1892, U. S. poet.

Whit·ting·ton (hwit′ing·tən), **Richard,** 1358?–1423, English tradesman; lord mayor of London, 1397, 1406, and 1419.

whit·tle[1] (hwit′l) *v.* **·tled, ·tling** *v.t.* **1** To cut or shave bits from (wood, a stick, etc.). **2** To make or shape by carving or whittling. **3** To reduce or wear away by paring a little at a time: with *down, off, away,* etc.: to *whittle* down costs. — *v.i.* **4** To whittle wood, usually as an aimless diversion. See synonyms under CUT. [<*n.*] — *n. Dial. & Scot.* A knife; especially, a sheath knife worn at the belt, or any large knife. [Alter. of ME *thwitel* <OE *thwitan* cut] — **whit′tler** *n.*

whit·tle[2] (hwit′l) *n. Dial.* **1** A blanket. **2** A shaggy mantle formerly worn by country-women. Also **whittle shawl.** [OE *hwītel* < *hwīt* white]

whit·tlings (hwit′lingz) *n. pl.* The fine chips and shavings made with a whittle or by a whittler.

Whit–Tues·day (hwit′tōōz′dē, -dā, -tyōōz′-) *n.* The day after Whit–Monday. Also **Whit′sun–Tues′day.** [On analogy with WHITSUNDAY]

whiz (hwiz) *v.* **whizzed, whiz·zing** *v.i.* **1** To make a hissing and humming sound while passing rapidly through the air. **2** To move or pass with such a sound. — *v.t.* **3** To cause to whiz. — *n.* **1** A sibilant sound with some sonant character, such as is produced by a missile passing through the air. **2** *Slang* Any person or thing of extraordinary excellence or ability. **3** *Slang* A bargain. **4** *Slang* A celebration; a spree. Also **whizz.** [Imit.]

whiz–bang (hwiz′bang′) *n. Slang* A high-explosive shell; also, a firecracker that explodes with a loud noise. Also **whizz′–bang′.**

who (hōō) *pron. possessive case* **whose;** *objective case* **whom** **1** As an interrogative, which or what person or persons. **2** As a relative, that: pointing out or fixing upon a particular person or persons, and identifying the subject or object in a relative clause with that of the principal clause. **3** As a compound relative, he, she, or they that: *Who* steals my purse steals trash. — **as who should say** As one who should say; as if one should say. [OE *hwā, hwā*]

◆ In modern usage, *who* as a relative is applied only to persons, *which* only to animals or to inanimate objects, *that* to persons or things indifferently. *Whose* is correctly used as the possessive of *which,* as well as of *who,* especially where the phrase *of which* would seem awkward: the man *whose* house was sold; a peak *whose* (*of which* the) summit seeks the sky. The use of *whom* as an interrogative pronoun in initial position, as in *Whom* did you see?, is supported by some grammarians, but the more natural *Who* did you see? *Who* did you give the book to? are in wider use and are now considered acceptable. However, when used after a verb or preposition, *whom* is still required, as in To *whom* did you give it? You saw *whom*? See also usage note under THAT (pronoun).

whoa (hwō) *interj.* Stop! stand still! [Var. of HO]

who·dun·it (hōō·dun′it) *n. Colloq.* A type of mystery fiction or dramatic production which challenges the reader or auditor to detect the perpetrator of a crime. [<WHO + DONE + IT; coined by Donald Gordon in 1930 in *American News of Books*]

who·ev·er (hōō·ev′ər) *pron.* Any one without exception; any person who.

whole (hōl) *adj.* **1** Containing all the parts necessary to make up a total; undivided and undiminished; entire; complete. **2** Having all the essential or original parts in their proper constitution; unbroken and uninjured; sound; intact. **3** Specifically, in or having regained sound health; hale. **4** Having the same parents; full, as opposed to *half–*: a *whole* brother. **5** *Colloq.* Each one of (something); all: He ate the *whole* batch of cookies. **6** *Math.* Integral. — **on the whole** Taking one thing with another. — **out of whole cloth** Fabricated; made up, without foundation in truth or fact, as a story or lie. — *n.* **1** All the parts or elements entering into and making up a thing. **2** An organization of parts making a unity or system; an organism. See synonyms under AGGREGATE, MASS[1]. ◆ Homophone: *hole.* [OE (Northumbrian) *hol,* var. of *hāl.* Related to HALE[2].]

whole blood **1** Full blood. **2** Blood as taken direct from the body, especially that used in transfusions.

whole brother See under BROTHER.

whole gale *Meteorol.* A gale of force 10 on the Beaufort scale.

whole·heart·ed (hōl′här′tid) *adj.* Done or experienced with all earnestness; characteristically sincere, sound, generous, or kind. — **whole′heart′ed·ly** *adv.* — **whole′heart′ed·ness** *n.*

whole–hog (hōl′hôg′, -hog′) *adj. Colloq.* Thoroughgoing.

whole hog *Colloq.* **1** The whole of anything: to believe in the *whole hog,* accept the *whole hog.* **2** Reliance or approval; trust: We don't put the *whole hog* on them. — **to go the whole hog** *Colloq.* To do something thoroughly; become involved without reservation.

whole milk Milk containing all its constituents: distinguished from *skim milk.*

whole·ness (hōl′nis) *n.* Entireness; completeness.

whole note *Music* A semibreve. See NOTE *n.* (def. 12).

whole number *Math.* A unit or a number composed of units; an integral number or integer: distinguished from *fraction* and *mixed number.*

whole·sale (hōl′sāl′) *n.* The sale of goods by the piece or in large bulk or quantity: opposed to *retail.* — *adj.* **1** Selling in quantity, not at retail: a *wholesale* druggist. **2** Done in buying and selling in quantity: the *wholesale* trade. **3** Pertaining to wholesale trade: the *wholesale* price. **4** Hence, made or done on a large scale; made or done indiscriminately: *wholesale* murder. — *adv.* In bulk or quantity; hence, indiscriminately: to berate the medical profession *wholesale.* — *v.t.* & *v.i.* **·saled, ·saling** To sell at wholesale. [ME *holesale* < *by hole sale* in large quantities] — **whole′sal′er** *n.*

whole sister See under SISTER.

whole snipe See under SNIPE.

whole·some (hōl′səm) *adj.* **1** Tending to promote health; salubrious; healthful: *wholesome* air or food. **2** Favorable to virtue and well–being; salutary; sound; beneficial. **3** Healthy; physically, mentally, and morally sound: a *wholesome* girl. **4** Indicative or characteristic of health: *wholesome* red cheeks. **5** Safe; free from danger or risk: This is not a *wholesome* situation. **6** *Obs.* Auspicious; favorable. See synonyms under HEALTHY. [ME *holsum* < *hol* WHOLE + OE *-sum* -SOME[1]] — **whole′some·ly** *adv.* — **whole′some·ness** *n.*

whole–souled (hōl′sōld′) *adj.* Feeling or acting with one's whole heart; devoted; generous.

whole–wheat (hōl′hwēt′) *adj.* Made from wheat grain and bran.

who'll (hōōl) Who will; who shall: a contraction.

whol·ly (hō′lē, hōl′lē) *adv.* **1** Completely; totally. **2** Exclusively; only.

whom (hōōm) *pron.* The objective case of WHO. [OE *hwam,* dative of *hwā* who]

whom·ev·er (hōōm′ev′ər), **whom·so** (hōōm′·sō′), **whom·so·ev·er** (hōōm′sō·ev′ər) Objective cases of WHOEVER, WHOSO, etc.

whoop (hōōp, hwōōp, hwŏŏp) *v.i.* **1** To utter loud cries, as of excitement, rage, or exultation. **2** To hoot, as an owl. **3** To make a loud, gasping inspiration, as after a paroxysm of coughing. — *v.t.* **4** To utter with a whoop or whoops. **5** To call, urge, chase, etc., with whoops; hoot. — **to whoop up** **1** To arouse enthusiasm in or for; ballyhoo. **2** To raise, as a price, or sum of money. — **to whoop it** (or **things**) **up** **1** *Slang* To make noisy revelry. **2** To arouse enthusiasm. — *n.* **1** A shout of excitement, encouragement, or exultation; also, a hoot of derision. **2** A signal halloo or a guiding call, as to incite dogs or men in the chase. **3** A loud, convulsive inspiration after a paroxysm of coughing in whooping cough; a sonorous indrawing of breath. **4** An owl's hoot. — *interj.* Hurrah! halloo! [Imit.]

whoop·ee (hwōō′pē, hwŏŏp′ē) *Slang interj.* An exclamation of joy, excitement, etc. — *n.* A hilarious, festive time. — **to make whoopee** To have a noisy, festive time. [<WHOOP]

whoop·er (hōō′pər, hwōō′pər, hwŏŏp′ər) *n.* **1** One who or that which whoops. **2** A large Old World swan (*Cygnus cygnus*). **3** The white crane: so called from its loud cry.

whoop·ing cough (hōō′ping, hŏŏp′ing) *Pathol.* A contagious respiratory disease of bacterial origin chiefly affecting children, marked in its final stage by recurrent paroxysms of violent coughing, ending with a whoop; pertussis.

whooping crane See under CRANE.

whop (hwop) *Colloq. n.* A blow or fall, or the resulting noise. — *v.* **whopped, whop·ping** *v.t.* **1** To strike or beat. **2** To defeat convincingly. — *v.i.* **3** To drop or fall suddenly; flop. Also spelled *whap.* [Var. of WAP[1]]

whop·per (hwop′ər) *n. Colloq.* **1** One who whops. **2** Something large or remarkable, especially a surprising falsehood. Also spelled *whapper.*

whop·ping (hwop′ing) *adj.* Unusually large; excessively exaggerated.

whore (hôr, hōr) *n.* A prostitute. — *v.* **whored, whor·ing** *v.i.* **1** To have illicit sexual intercourse, especially with a prostitute. **2** To be a whore. — *v.t.* **3** To make a whore of; corrupt; debauch. ◆ Homophone: *hoar.* [OE *hōre,* prob. <ON *hōra*]

whore·dom (hôr′dəm, hōr′-) *n.* **1** The practice of illicit sexual intercourse. **2** Whores collectively. **3** In the Bible, idolatry. [Prob. <ON *hōrdōmr*]

whore·house (hôr′hous′, hōr′-) *n.* A house of prostitution.

whore·mas·ter (hôr′mas′tər, -mäs′-, hōr′-) *n.* **1** A procurer; pander. **2** A whoremonger.

whore·mon·ger (hôr′mung′gər, -mong′-, hōr′-) *n.* **1** A man who has intercourse with whores. **2** A pander.

whore·son (hôr′sən, hōr′-) *n. Obs.* The son of a whore: commonly, a term of contempt. [ME *hores son,* trans. of AF *fiz a putain*]

whor·ish (hôr′ish, hōr′ish) *adj.* Addicted to unlawful sexual indulgences; unchaste; lewd. — **whor′ish·ly** *adv.* — **whor′ish·ness** *n.*

whorl (hwûrl, hwôrl) *n.* **1** The flywheel of a spindle; wherve. **2** *Bot.* A set of leaves, etc., on the same plane with one another; distributed in a circle; a verticil. **3** *Zool.* A turn or volution, as of a spiral shell. **4** Any of the convoluted ridges of a fingerprint. [ME *wharwyl,*

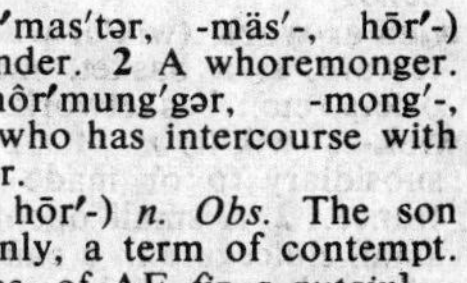

WHORL (*def. 2*)

whorwhil, appar. vars. of WHIRL; infl. in form by *wharve*]

whorled (hwûrld, hwôrld) *adj.* Furnished with or arranged in whorls.

whort (hwûrt) *n.* The whortleberry, or its fruit. Also **whor·tle** (hwûr′təl). [OE *horta* a whortle-berry]

whor·tle·ber·ry (hwûr′təl·ber′ē) *n. pl.* **·ries** 1 A European variety of blueberry (*Vaccinium myrtillus*); the bilberry. 2 Its blue-black fruit. 3 The huckleberry. [Dial. var. of HURTLE-BERRY]

whose (hōōz) The possessive case of WHO and often of WHICH. See under WHO. [OE *hwæs*, genitive of *hwā* who]

whose·so·ev·er (hōōz′sō·ev′ər) Possessive case of WHOSOEVER.

who·so (hōō′sō) *pron.* Whoever; any person who. [Reduced form of OE *swā hwā swā*, generalized form of *hwā* who]

who·so·ev·er (hōō′sō·ev′ər) *pron.* Any person whatever; who; whoever.

why (hwī) *adv.* 1 For what cause, purpose, or reason; wherefore: used interrogatively: *Why* did you go? 2 Because of which; for which; the reason or cause for which: used relatively: I don't know *why* he went; I know no reason *why* he went. — *n. pl.* **whys** 1 An explanatory cause; reason; cause. 2 A puzzling problem; riddle; enigma. — *interj.* An introductory expletive, sometimes denoting surprise. [OE *hwī, hwȳ*, instrumental case of *hwæt* what]

why·dah (hwid′ə), **whydah bird** See WHIDAH BIRD.

wi' (wi) *prep. Scot.* With.

wich (wich) See WITCH².

Wich·i·ta (wich′ə·tô) *n.* A member of a North American Indian confederacy of Caddoan linguistic stock, formerly inhabiting Oklahoma and Texas.

Wich·i·ta (wich′ə·tô) A city on the Arkansas River in south central Kansas; a center of the food and oil industries.

Wichita River A river in Texas, flowing 250 miles NE to the Red River.

wick¹ (wik) *n.* A band of loosely twisted or woven fibers, as in a candle or lamp, acting by capillary attraction to convey oil or other illuminant to a flame. [OE *wēoca*] — **wick′-ing** *n.*

wick² (wik) *Scot. v.t.* In curling, to strike (a stone) obliquely. — *n.* 1 In curling, an opening surrounded by stones already played. 2 A creek; inlet.

wick³ (wik) *n.* A village or town: now mostly in composition, often as **-wich**: *Woolwich*. [OE *wīc*, appar. <L *vicus*]

wick·ed (wik′id) *adj.* 1 Evil in principle and practice; vicious; sinful; depraved. 2 Mischievous; roguish. 3 Noxious; pernicious. 4 Troublesome; painful. See synonyms under BAD, CRIMINAL, IMMORAL, INFAMOUS, PROFANE, SINFUL. [ME < *wikke, wicke*, appar. <OE *wicca* a wizard] — **wick′ed·ly** *adv.*

wick·ed·ness (wik′id·nis) *n.* 1 The quality of being wicked; moral depravity; sin; vice; crime: opposed to *goodness*. 2 A wicked thing or act; wicked conduct: to work *wickedness*.

wick·er (wik′ər) *adj.* Made of twigs, osiers, etc. — *n.* 1 A pliant young shoot or rod; twig; osier. 2 Ware made of such shoots. [Prob. <Scand. Cf. dial. Sw. *viker* <*vika* bend.]

wick·er·work (wik′ər·wûrk′) *n.* A fabric or texture, as a basket, made of woven twigs, osiers, etc.; basketwork.

wick·et (wik′it) *n.* 1 A small door or gate subsidiary to or made within a larger entrance. 2 A small opening in a door. 3 A small sluicegate in a canal lock or at the end of a millrace. 4 In cricket, an arrangement of three upright rods called *stumps* set near together, with two crosspieces called *bails* laid over the top; also, the place at which the wicket is set up; the right or turn of each batsman at the wicket; the playing pitch between the wickets: a fast *wicket*; an inning that is not finished or not begun: The eleven won by three *wickets*, that is, the two men at bat and one yet to go in. 5 In croquet, an arch, usually of wire. [<AF *wiket*, OF *guichet*, prob. <Gmc.]

wick·et-keep·er (wik′it-kē′pər) *n.* In cricket, the fielder stationed immediately behind the wicket which is being bowled at.

wick·i·up (wik′ē·up) *n.* A loosely constructed hut of certain North American Indian tribes: distinguished from *tepee* or *wigwam*: also spelled *wikiup*. [<Algonquian. Cf. Sac and Fox *wikiyap* a lodge.]

Wick·liffe (wik′lif), **Wic·lif, Wic·liff·ite**, etc. See WYCLIF, etc.

Wick·low (wik′lō) A maritime county of eastern Leinster province, Ireland; 782 square miles; county town, Wicklow.

wic·o·py (wik′ə·pē) *n. pl.* **·pies** 1 The leather-wood. 2 The basswood. 3 Any of several species of willow herb. [<Algonquian. Cf. Cree *wikupiy*.]

wid·der·shins (wid′ər·shinz) See WITHERSHINS.

wid·dle (wid′l) *v.t. & n. Dial. & Scot.* Wriggle; struggle; waddle.

wid·dy¹ (wid′ē) *n. pl.* **·dies** *Scot.* A halter of withes; withy; hangman's noose; hence, the gallows. Also **wid′die**.

wid·dy² (wid′ē) *n. pl.* **·dies** *Dial.* Widow. [Var. of WITHY]

wide (wīd) *adj.* **wid·er, wid·est** 1 Having relatively great extent between sides; broad, as opposed to *narrow*. 2 Extended far in every direction; ample; spacious: a *wide* expanse. 3 Having a specified degree of width or breadth: an inch *wide*. 4 Distant from the desired or proper point by a great extent of space; remote; wild: *wide* of the mark. 5 Figuratively, having intellectual breadth; considering questions from all points of view; liberal: a man of *wide* views. 6 Fully open; expanded or extended: *wide* eyes. 7 *Phonet.* Lax. 8 Comprehensive; inclusive: *wide* learning. 9 Loose; ample; roomy: *wide* breeches. 10 In the stock exchange, exhibiting a considerable range between high and low, or bid and offered prices: a *wide* opening. See synonyms under LARGE. — *n.* 1 In cricket, a ball bowled too far over or on either side of the wicket to be within the batsman's reach. 2 Breadth of extent; also, a broad, open space. — *adv.* 1 To a great distance; extensively. 2 Far from the mark. 3 To the greatest extent; fully open. [OE *wīd*] — **wide′ly** *adv.* — **wide′ness** *n.*

◆ Various self-explaining compounds where *wide* as their first element: **wide′-arched′, wide′-branched′, wide′-brimmed′**, etc.

wide-an·gle lens (wīd′ang′gəl) *Phot.* A type of camera lens designed and ground to permit an angle of view wider than that of the ordinary lens, or more than 50 degrees.

wide-a·wake (wīd′ə·wāk′) *adj.* Marked by vigilance and alertness; keen. See synonyms under ALERT, VIGILANT. — *n.* A soft, broad-brimmed felt hat: also **wide′-a·wake′ hat**.

wide-eyed (wīd′īd′) *adj.* 1 With the eyes wide open, as if gazing intently in wonder or surprise. 2 Marked by an innocent readiness to believe or admire; uninformed or unsophisticated: *wide-eyed* trust of any stranger she happened to meet.

wid·en (wīd′n) *v.t. & v.i.* To make or become wide or wider. See synonyms under AMPLIFY. — **wid′en·er** *n.*

wide-o·pen (wīd′ō′pən) *adj.* 1 Opened wide: The gates are *wide-open*. 2 *Colloq.* Remiss in the enforcement of laws which regulate various forms of vice, as gambling, prostitution, etc.: a *wide-open* city.

wide-spread (wīd′spred′) *adj.* Extending over a large space or territory; general: a *widespread* belief. Also **wide′spread′**.

widge·on (wij′ən) *n.* Any of a genus (*Mareca*) of river ducks with short bill and wedge-shaped tail; especially, the **American widgeon**, or baldpate (*M. americana*), esteemed as a game bird: also spelled *wigeon*. [Cf. MF *vigeon* a wild duck]

Wi·dor (vē·dôr′), **Charles Marie**, 1845–1937, French organist and composer.

wid·ow (wid′ō) *n.* 1 A woman who has lost her husband by death and has not remarried. 2 In some card games, an additional hand dealt to the table; also, a kitty. 3 *Printing* An incomplete line of type ending a paragraph; especially, a single line or less at the top of a page or column. — *v.t.* 1 To make a widow of; deprive of a husband: usually in the past participle: a woman *widowed* by war. 2 To deprive of something desirable; bereave. 3 *Rare* To survive as the widow of. 4 *Rare* To recognize as a widow; give the rights of

a widow to. — *adj.* Widowed. [OE *widewe, wuduwe*]

widow bird A whidah bird. [<NL *Vidua*, genus name, trans. of Pg. *viuva*, lit., a widow]

wid·ow·er (wid′ō·ər) *n.* A man whose wife is dead, and who has not married again. [ME *widwer* < *widwe*, OE *widewe* a widow]

wid·ow·hood (wid′ō·hŏŏd) *n.* The state or condition of being a widow, or, rarely, of being a widower; also, the period during which one is a widow.

widow's cruse An endless or inexhaustible supply: in allusion to the stories in I *Kings* xvii 10–16, and II *Kings* iv 1–7.

widow's mite See MITE².

widow's peak See PEAK¹.

width (width) *n.* 1 Dimension or measurement of an object taken from side to side, or at right angles to the length. 2 Wideness; the state or fact of being wide. 3 Something that has width; specifically, in dressmaking, one of the several pieces of material used in making a garment. [<WIDE, on analogy with *breadth*]

width·wise (width′wīz′) *adv.* In the direction of the width; from side to side. Also **width′-way′** (-wā′), **width′ways′**.

Wi·du·kind (vē′dŏŏ·kint) See WITTEKIND.

wiel (wēl) *n. Scot.* An eddy; pool.

Wie·land (vē′länt), **Christoph Martin**, 1733–1813, German poet, novelist, and translator. — **Heinrich**, 1877–1957, German chemist.

wield (wēld) *v.t.* 1 To use or handle, as a weapon or instrument, especially with full command and effect. 2 To exercise (authority, power, influence, etc.). 3 *Obs.* To exercise authority over; command. [Fusion of OE *wealdan* cause and OE *wildan* rule] — **wield′-a·ble** *adj.* — **wield′er** *n.*

wield·y (wēl′dē) *adj.* **wield·i·er, wield·i·est** Easily handled; wieldable: opposed to *un-wieldy*.

Wie·licz·ka (vye·lech′kä) A town 7 miles SE of Cracow, Poland; a salt-mining center since the 11th century.

Wien (vēn) The German name for VIENNA.

Wien (vēn), **Wilhelm**, 1864–1928, German physicist.

wie·ner (wē′nər) *n. U.S.* A kind of sausage, often shorter than a frankfurter, made of beef and pork: often called *weenie*. Also **wie·ner·wurst** (wē′nər·wûrst′), *Ger.* vē′nər·vŏŏrst′). [Short for G *wiener-(wurst)* Vienna (sausage)]

Wie·ner schnit·zel (vē′nər shnit′səl) A breaded veal cutlet, seasoned or garnished in any of several ways, as with capers, anchovies, a fried egg, or the like. [<G *Wiener* Viennese + *schnitzel* a cutlet, dim. of *schnitz* a slice < *schneiden* cut]

Wieprz (vyepsh) A river in central Poland, flowing 194 miles NW to the Vistula.

Wies·ba·den (vēs′bä·dən) The capital of Hesse, West Germany, on the Rhine west of Frankfurt: site of a famous spa.

wife (wīf) *n. pl.* **wives** (wīvz) 1 A woman joined to a man in lawful wedlock; a spouse: the correlative of *husband*. ◆ Collateral adjective: *uxorial*. 2 A grown woman; adult female: usually in composition or in certain phrases: *housewife*, old *wives'* tales. — **to take (a woman) to wife** To marry (a woman). [OE *wīf*] — **wife′dom, wife′hood** *n.* — **wife′less** *adj.* — **wife′ly** *adj.*

wife-carl (wīf′kärl) *n. Scot.* A man who meddles with household affairs, especially such as belong naturally to women.

wig (wig) *n.* An artificial covering of hair for the head, so constructed as to form an imitation of the natural growth or to act as a coiffure. — *v.t.* **wigged, wig·ging** 1 To furnish with a wig or wigs. 2 *Brit. Colloq.* To censure severely; berate or scold, especially in public. [Short for PERIWIG]

wig·an (wig′ən) *n.* A stiff, canvaslike fabric used for stiffening the borders of garments. [from *Wigan*, where originally made]

BARRISTER'S WIG

Wig·an (wig′ən) A county borough in south central Lancashire, England.

wig·eon (wij′ən) See WIDGEON.

wigged (wigd) *adj.* Furnished with or wearing a wig.

wig·ger·y (wig′ər·ē) *n. pl.* **·ger·ies** 1 A peruke;

wig; also, wigs collectively. 2 Excessive formality; red-tapism. 3 The material of a wig; false hair.

Wig·gin (wig′in), **Kate Douglas,** *née* Smith, 1856–1923, U. S. educator and novelist.

wig·ging (wig′ing) *n. Brit. Colloq.* A rebuke; a scolding.

wig·gle (wig′əl) *v.t. & v.i.* **·gled, ·gling** To move or cause to move quickly and irregularly from side to side; squirm; wriggle. — *n.* The act of wiggling. [? <MLG *wiggelen*] —**wig′gly** *adj.*

wig·gler (wig′lər) *n.* 1 One who or that which wiggles. 2 The larva of a mosquito; a wiggletail.

Wig·gles·worth (wig′əlz·wûrth), **Michael,** 1631–1705, American divine and poet.

wig·gle·tail (wig′əl·tāl′) *n.* 1 The larva of a mosquito. 2 A tadpole.

wight[1] (wīt) *n.* A person; creature: usually an archaic or humorous term. [OE *wiht* a creature]

wight[2] (wīt) *adj. Obs.* Full of prowess; strong and valiant; active; swift. [<ON *vigt,* neut. of *vigr* able to fight]

Wight (wīt), **Isle of** An island in the English Channel just off the southern coast of England, comprising an administrative county of Hampshire; 147 square miles.

Wig·man (vikh′män), **Mary,** born 1886, German dancer; leading pioneer of modern dance.

Wig·ner (wig′nər), **Eugene Paul,** born 1902, U.S. physicist born in Hungary.

Wig·town (wig′tən) A county in SW Scotland; 487 square miles; county town, Wigtown. Also **Wig′town·shire** (-shir).

wig·wag (wig′wag′) *v.t. & v.i.* **·wagged, ·wag·ging** 1 To move briskly to and fro; wag. 2 To send (a message) by hand flags, torches, etc. — *n.* The act or art of signaling with such flags, etc., or the message so sent. [< dial. E *wig* wiggle + WAG[1]] —**wig′wag′·ger** *n.*

wig·wam (wig′wom, -wôm) *n.* 1 A dwelling or lodge of the North American Indians of Algonquian stock, used in the area from Canada to North Carolina and in the Great Lakes regions: commonly an arbor-shaped or conical framework of poles covered with bark, rush matting, or hides. 2 By extension, a family of Indians. 3 A dwelling or lodge of North American Indians of other than Algonquian stock: a misuse by early travelers. 4 *Slang* A public building used for political gatherings, mass meetings, etc. —**the Wigwam** Tammany Hall. [<Algonquian (Ojibwa) *wigwaum,* lit., their dwelling]

WIGWAM
Eastern North American Indian.

wik·i·up (wik′ē·up) See WICKIUP.

Wil·ber·force (wil′bər·fôrs, -fōrs), **William,** 1759–1833, English abolitionist and philanthropist.

Wil·bur (wil′bər) A masculine personal name. [<Gmc., ? resolute protection]

Wil·cox (wil′koks), **Ella,** *née* Wheeler, 1855?–1919, U. S. poet and author.

wild (wīld) *adj.* 1 Inhabiting the forest or open field; not domesticated or tamed; living in a state of nature: a *wild* horse; shy and easily startled: The deer are *wild.* 2 Growing or produced without care or culture; not cultivated: *wild* flowers. 3 Being in the natural state: being without civilized inhabitants or cultivation; desert; waste: *wild* prairies. 4 Living without any civilization and in a rude, savage way; uncivilized: the *wild* men of Borneo. 5 Boisterous; in a bad sense, dissolute; prodigal; in a milder sense, frolicsome and gay. 6 Affected with or originating violent disturbances, as of the elements or of human passions; stormy; turbulent: a *wild* night, a *wild* crowd. 7 Showing reckless want of judgment; rashly imprudent; extravagant: a *wild* speculation. 8 Fantastically irregular or disordered; odd in arrangement or effect; strange or weird: a *wild* imagination, *wild* dress. 9 Eager and excited, as by reason of joy, fear, desire, etc.: She was *wild* with delight. 10 Excited to frenzy or distraction; roused to fury or desperation; crazed or crazy: The mosquitoes are driving me *wild.* 11 Being or going far from the proper course or from the mark aimed at; erratic; wide of the mark: a *wild* ball, a *wild* guess. 12 In some card games, having its value arbitrarily determined by the dealer or holder: to play poker with fours *wild.* 13 *Slang* a Terrific; great: a *wild* party. b Showy; jazzy: a *wild* necktie. See synonyms under ABSURD, BLEAK[1], FIERCE, INSANE, ROMANTIC, TURBULENT, VIOLENT, WANTON. — *n.* An uninhabited or uncultivated place; a waste; wilderness. —**the wild** The wilderness; also, the free, natural, wild life: the call of *the wild.* — *adv.* 1 Wildly. 2 Without control; unrestrainedly: The locomotive is running *wild.* [OE *wilde*] —**wild′ly** *adv.* —**wild′ness** *n.*

wild allspice The spicebush.

wild boar The native hog (*Sus scrofa*) of continental Europe, southern Asia, and North Africa, and formerly of Great Britain.

wild brier 1 Any species of rose in the wild state. 2 The dog rose. 3 The sweetbrier.

wild carrot An umbelliferous herb (*Daucus carota*) from which the cultivated carrot is derived; Queen Anne's lace.

wild·cat (wīld′kat′) *n.* 1 A small, undomesticated feline carnivore (*Felis sylvestris*) of Europe, resembling the domestic cat, but larger and stronger. 2 The North American bobcat (genus *Lynx*). 3 One of several other small felines, as the ocelot and serval. 4 Figuratively, an aggressive, quick-tempered person. 5 An unattached locomotive and its tender, used on special work, as when sent out to haul a train, etc. 6 A successful oil well drilled in an area previously unproductive. 7 A tricky or unsound business venture; specifically, a worthless mine. Also **wild cat.** — *adj.* 1 Unsound; risky; especially, financially unsound or risky: a *wildcat* venture. 2 Illegal; made, produced, or carried on without official sanction or authorization. 3 Not running on schedule time; also, running wild or without control, as a railroad train or engine. — *v.t. & v.i.* **·cat·ted, ·cat·ting** To drill for oil in (an area not known to be productive). —**wild′cat′ting** *n. & adj.*

wildcat bank Prior to the passage of the National Bank Act of 1863–64, a bank operating with insufficient capital to redeem its circulating notes.

wildcat bill A note of a wildcat bank.

wildcat mine A worthless mine; especially, one represented to possible investors as being profitably productive.

wildcat strike A strike unauthorized by regular union procedure.

wild·cat·ter (wīld′kat′ər) *n.* 1 A promoter of mines of doubtful value. 2 One who develops oil wells in unproved territory. 3 One who manufactures illicit whisky.

wild cherry Any of certain species of cherry found growing wild; especially, the **wild black cherry** (*Prunus serotina*) and the chokecherry.

Wilde (wīld), **Oscar Fingall O'Flahertie Wills,** 1856–1900, Irish poet and playwright.

wilde·beest (wīld′bēst, wil′də-; *Du.* vil′də·bāst) *n.* A gnu. [<Afrikaans <Du. *wild* wild + *beeste* a beast]

wil·der (wil′dər) *Poetic v.t.* 1 To bewilder. 2 To lead astray; mislead. — *v.i.* 3 To be bewildered. 4 To wander; stray. [Prob. back formation <WILDERNESS] —**wil′der·ment** *n.*

Wil·der (wīl′dər), **Thornton Niven,** 1897–1975, U.S. novelist and playwright.

wil·der·ness (wil′dər·nis) *n.* 1 An uncultivated, uninhabited, or barren region. 2 A waste, as of an ocean. 3 A multitudinous and confusing collection: a *wilderness* of curiosities. 4 *Obs.* Wildness. [OE *wilder* a wild beast (< *wilde* wild + *deor* an animal, deer) + -NESS]

Wil·der·ness (wil′dər·nis), **The** A region in NE Virginia; scene of a Civil War battle, 1864.

wild·fire (wīld′fīr′) *n.* 1 A raging, destructive fire: now generally in phrases like *to spread like wildfire.* 2 A composition of inflammable materials, or the flame produced by it, very hard to put out; Greek fire. 3 A phosphorescent luminousness; ignis fatuus. 4 *Obs.* A spreading inflammation of the skin; erysipelas. 5 A skin disease of sheep with inflammation.

wild flax 1 Toadflax. 2 Gold-of-pleasure.

wild·flow·er (wīld′flou′ər) *n.* 1 Any uncultivated flower. 2 The plant growing it. Also **wild flower.**

wild·fowl (wīld′foul′) *n.* Wild game birds, especially wild ducks and geese. Also **wild fowl.**

wild gean (gēn) 1 A European wild cherry (*Prunus avium*), yielding a fine cabinet wood. 2 Its small dark fruit, the mazzard cherry. [<WILD + dial. E *gean* the wild cherry <OF *guine,* prob. <Gmc.]

wild goose An undomesticated goose, as the English graylag, or the Canada goose.

wild-goose chase (wīld′gōōs′) Pursuit of the unknown or unattainable; a bootless enterprise.

wild honeysuckle The pinkster flower.

wild hyacinth 1 The eastern camas (*Camassia scilloides*) of the United States. 2 The wood hyacinth.

wild indigo Any of a genus (*Baptisia*) of perennial North American herbs, especially one (*B. tinctoria*) having yellow flowers and a root which yields a purgative glycoside.

wild·ing (wīl′ding) *adj.* Growing wild; uncultivated; undomesticated. — *n.* 1 An uncultivated plant; a fruit tree on its own roots growing among grafted trees. 2 A cultivated plant that has sprung up spontaneously; an escape (def. 4). 3 A creature not conforming to type.

wild lettuce 1 A tall, yellow-flowered herb (*Lactuca virosa*) found in the northern United States. 2 The round-leaved wintergreen (*Pyrola rotundifolia*). 3 The prickly lettuce (*Lactuca serriola*).

wild·life (wīld′līf′) *n.* Wild animals, trees, and plants collectively, especially as objects of government conservation. — *adj.* Pertaining to wild animals, trees, and plants collectively.

wild·ling (wīld′ling) *n.* An uncultivated plant or flower; a wild animal. [<WILD + -LING[1]]

wild madder 1 Madder (def. 1). 2 Either of two herbs (genus *Galium*) of the madder family, the white bedstraw (*G. mollugo*) and the dye bedstraw (*G. tinctorium*).

wild mandrake The May apple.

wild mare 1 A nightmare. 2 A see-saw.

wild mustard An annual herb (*Brassica kaber*) of the mustard family, frequently growing as a weed, whose seeds are sometimes used as a substitute for mustard and its leaves cooked as greens: also called *charlock.*

wild oat 1 An uncultivated grass (genus *Avena*); especially, the common European meadow weed (*A. fatua*). 2 *pl.* Indiscretions of youth.

wild olive Any of various trees resembling the olive or bearing an olivelike fruit.

wild pansy The European heartsease (*Viola tricolor*), from which the common garden pansy is derived.

wild parsley 1 Any of a genus (*Lomatium*) of perennial herbs of the carrot family, especially the nine-leaf species (*L. simplex*), valued as a forage plant in the western United States: also called *biscuitroot.* 2 Lovage.

wild parsnip 1 The parsnip in its uncultivated, weedlike form. 2 A perennial herb (*Angelica lyalli*) of the carrot family, resembling the water hemlock but non-poisonous and useful as a forage plant.

wild pink An American catchfly (*Silene caroliniana*) with white or rose-colored flowers and long spatulate or lanceolate flowers.

wild rice 1 A tall aquatic grass of North America (*Zizania aquatica*). 2 The grain of this plant: formerly used as food by North American Indians, now esteemed as a table delicacy: also called *Indian rice.*

wild rose Any of various uncultivated roses of the north temperate zone, as the sweetbrier.

wild rubber Rubber as extracted from the rubber tree (genus *Hevea*) in its wild state.

wild rye A tall perennial grass (genus *Elymus*), widely distributed in temperate regions.

wild sage 1 The sagebrush of the western United States. 2 The Old World vervain sage (*Salvia verbeneca*) known as wild clary.

wild spinach 1 A goosefoot sometimes used as a substitute for spinach. 2 One of several other spinaceous plants.

wild turkey A large North American turkey

(Meleagris gallopavo silvestris) formerly ranging east of the Rocky Mountains from southern Canada to Florida and Mexico, and first domesticated in Mexico.

wild vanilla A smooth, erect, perennial herb *(Trilisa odoratissima)* of the composite family, found in the SE United States. Its leaves give off an odor of vanilla.

wild wall A soundproof movable wall used on motion-picture sets: also called *jockey wall.*

Wild West The western United States, especially in its early period of Indian fighting, pioneer conditions, and lawlessness.

Wild West show A circus or a feature of a circus presenting feats of Indian and cowboy horsemanship; also, a rodeo.

wild·wood (wild′wŏŏd′) *n.* Natural forest land.

wild yam An uncultivated species of yam *(Dioscorea villosa)* of the eastern United States; the colic root.

wile (wīl) *n.* **1** An act or a means of cunning deception; also, any beguiling trick or artifice. **2** Craftiness; cunning. See synonyms under ARTIFICE. — *v.t.* **wiled, wil·ing 1** To lure, beguile, or mislead. **2** To pass divertingly, as time: usually with *away*: by confusion with *while.* [OE *wīl,* prob. <Scand. Cf. ON *vēl* an artifice.]

Wi·ley (wī′lē), **Harvey Washington,** 1844–1930, U. S. chemist.

Wil·fred (wil′frid) A masculine personal name. Also **Wil′frid.** [<Gmc., willing peace]

wil·ful (wil′fəl) *adj.* **1** Bent on having one's own way; headstrong; self-willed. **2** Resulting from the exercise of one's own will; voluntary; intentional. Also spelled *willful.* See synonyms under PERVERSE. — **wil′ful·ly** *adv.* — **wil′ful·ness** *n.*

Wil·helm (vil′helm) German form of WILLIAM. — **Wilhelm I,** 1797–1888, king of Prussia 1861–88 and emperor of Germany 1871–88. — **Wilhelm II,** 1859–1941, emperor of Germany 1888–1918.

Wil·hel·mi·na (wil′hel·mē′nə) A feminine personal name. Also **Wil·hel·mine** (wil′hel·mēn, *Fr.* vē·lel·mēn′, *Ger.* vil′hel·mē′nə). [Fem. of WILHELM]

— **Wilhelmina,** 1880–1962, queen of the Netherlands 1890–1948; abdicated in favor of her daughter Juliana: full name *Wilhelmina Helena Pauline Maria of Orange-Nassau.*

Wil·helms·ha·ven (vil′helms·hä′fən) A port on the North Sea in former Oldenburg state, Lower Saxony, NW West Germany.

Wil·helm·stras·se (vil′helm·shträ′sə) **1** A street in Berlin on which the German foreign office and government offices were formerly located. **2** Formerly, the German government, especially its foreign policies.

Wilkes (wilks), **Charles,** 1798–1877, U.S. admiral and Antarctic explorer. — **John,** 1727–97, English politician.

Wilkes-Bar·re (wilks′bar·ē) A city on the Susquehanna River in NE Pennsylvania, an industrial and coal-mining center.

Wilkes Land (wilks) Part of Antarctica on the Indian Ocean south of Australia, between Queen Mary Coast and George V Coast; site of the south magnetic pole in its eastern part.

Wil·kins (wil′kinz), **Sir George Hubert,** 1888–1958, Australian aviator and explorer. — **Mary Eleanor** See FREEMAN, MARY E. WILKINS. — **Roy,** born 1901, U. S. civil rights leader for Negroes.

Wil·kin·son (wil′kən·sən), **James,** 1757–1825, American Revolutionary general and politician.

will¹ (wil) *n.* **1** The power of conscious, deliberate action; the faculty by which the rational mind makes choice of its ends of action, and directs the energies in carrying out its determinations; in popular usage, choice, purpose, or directive effort. **2** The act or experience of exercising this faculty; a volition or a choice. **3** Strong determination; practical enthusiasm; energy of character: He works with a *will*; also, self-control. **4** That which has been resolved or determined upon; a purpose. **5** Power to dispose of a matter arbitrarily; discretion. **6** *Law* The legal declaration of a man's intentions as to his estate after his death; the written instrument by which someone declares his desires for the distribution of his property. **7** A conscious inclination toward any end or course; a wish. **8** A request or command. — **at will** As one pleases. — *v.* **willed, will·ing;** third person singular, present indicative **wills** *v.t.* **1** To decide upon; choose. **2** To resolve upon as an action or course; determine to do. **3** To give, devise, or bequeath by a will. **4** To control, as a hypnotized person, by the exercise of will. **5** *Archaic* To have a wish for; desire. — *v.i.* **6** To exercise the will. [OE *willa*] — **will′a·ble** *adj.*

Synonyms (noun): decision, desire, disposition, inclination, resolution, volition, wish. *Will* is a word of wide range of meaning, and both as faculty and act has been the subject of many and various theories; in popular language *will* is often equivalent to *desire* or *inclination,* as when we speak of doing something against our *will. Volition* is a word of scientific precision, denoting the determinative element of *will.*

will² (wil) *v.* Present *sing.* & *pl.*: **will** (*Archaic* **thou wilt**); past: **would** (*Archaic* **thou would·est** or **wouldst**) As an auxiliary verb *will* is used with the infinitive without *to,* or elliptically without the infinitive, to express: **1** Futurity: They *will* arrive by dark. ◆ See usage note under SHALL. **2** Willingness or disposition: Why *will* you not tell the truth? **3** Capability or capacity: The ship *will* survive any storm. **4** Custom or habit: He *will* sit for hours and brood. **5** *Colloq.* Probability or inference: I expect this *will* be the main street. — *v.t.* & *v.i.* To wish or have a wish; desire: What *wilt* thou? As you *will.* [OE *willan*]

Wil·lam·ette River (wi·lam′it) A river in NW Oregon, flowing 190 miles north to the Columbia River.

Wil·lard (wil′ərd), **Emma,** 1787–1870, *née* Hart, U. S. pioneer in education for women. — **Frances Elizabeth Caroline,** 1839–98, U. S. temperance advocate.

Will·cocks (wil′koks), **Sir William,** 1852–1932, English engineer.

willed (wild) *adj.* Having a will, especially one of a given character: mostly in composition: self-*willed.*

wil·lem·ite (wil′əm·īt) *n.* A vitreous or resinous orthosilicate of zinc, crystallizing in the hexagonal system and occurring in many colors. [<Du. *willemit,* after *Willem I* William of Orange]

Wil·lem·stad (wil′əm·stät, vil′-) A town on Curacao, capital of Netherlands Antilles.

will·er (wil′ər) *n.* One who wills.

Willes·den (wilz′dən) A municipal borough in Middlesex, England, NW of London.

wil·let (wil′it) *n.* A large, light-colored shore bird *(Catoptrophorus semipalmatus)* of North America, related to the snipes. [Short for *pill-will-willet,* imit. of the cry of the bird]

will·ful (wil′fəl), **will·ful·ly, will·ful·ness** See WILFUL. etc.

will I, nill I or **will he, nill he** or **will ye, nill ye** Willingly or unwillingly; without choice. See WILLY-NILLY.

Wil·liam (wil′yəm) A masculine personal name. Also *Du.* **Wil·lem** (vil′əm). See also WILHELM. [<Gmc., resolute protection]

— **William I,** 1027–87, invaded England, 1066; king of England 1066–87: known as *William the Conqueror.*

— **William II,** 1056–1100, king of England 1087–1100: known as *William Rufus.*

— **William III,** 1650–1702, stadholder of Holland 1672–1702; invited to England; ruled 1689–1702 jointly with his wife Mary.

— **William IV,** 1765–1837, king of England 1830–37.

— **William of Malmesbury,** 1095?–1143? English historian.

— **William of Orange,** 1533–84, founded the Dutch republic; stadholder 1579–84: called "William the Silent."

Wil·liams (wil′yəms), **Roger,** 1603?–85, English clergyman; founded Rhode Island. — **Roger John,** born 1893, U. S. biochemist. — **Tennessee,** born 1914, U. S. playwright: original name *Thomas Lanier Williams.* — **William Carlos,** 1883–1963, U. S. poet, novelist, playwright, and physician.

Wil·liams·burg (wil′yəmz·bûrg) A town in eastern Virginia; founded in 1693; capital of Virginia (1699–1779); restored to condition of the colonial period.

wil·lies (wil′ēz) *n. pl. Slang* Nervousness; jitters; the creeps: with *the.* [? <WILLY-NILLY; with ref. to a state of indecision]

will·ie·waught (wil′ē·wäkht) *n. Scot.* A draft of liquor. Also **will′ie·waucht.**

will·ing (wil′ing) *adj.* **1** Having the mind favorably inclined or disposed. **2** Answering to demand or requirement; compliant. **3** Gladly proffered or done; hearty. **4** Of or pertaining to the faculty or power of choice; volitional. See synonyms under SPONTANEOUS. — **will′ing·ly** *adv.* — **will′ing·ness** *n.*

Wil·lis (wil′is), **Nathaniel Parker,** 1806–67, U. S. writer and editor.

wil·li·waw (wil′ē·wô) *n.* A sudden, violent blast of wind moving seaward down the slope of a mountainous coast, especially in the Strait of Magellan. [Origin unknown]

Will·kie (wil′kē), **Wendell Lewis,** 1892–1944, U. S. lawyer and political leader.

will-o′-the-wisp (wil′ə·thə·wisp′) *n.* **1** Ignis fatuus. **2** Any elusive or deceptive object. — *adj.* Deceptive; fleeting; misleading. [Earlier *Will with the wisp*]

wil·low (wil′ō) *n.* **1** Any of a large genus *(Salix)* of shrubs and trees related to the poplars, having generally smooth branches and often long, slender, pliant, and sometimes pendent branchlets. **2** The soft white wood of the willow. **3** *Colloq.* Something made of willow wood, especially a baseball or cricket bat. **4** A machine for giving a preliminary cleaning to cotton, flax, hemp, wool, etc., by means of long spikes projecting from a revolving cone or cylinder. — *v.t.* To clean, as cotton, wool, etc., with a willow. — *adj.* Of or pertaining to the willow; made of willow wood. [OE *wilige, welig*] — **wil′low·ish** *adj.*

wil·low·er (wil′ō·ər) *n.* One who or that which willows.

willow herb **1** Any of a genus *(Epilobium)* of perennial herbs of the evening-primrose family, especially the fireweed (*E. angustifolium*), having scattered, willowlike leaves and large, pink flowers. **2** The purple loosestrife *(Lythrum salicaria).*

willow oak **1** An oak *(Quercus phellos)* of the eastern United States, having long, slender, entire leaves resembling willow leaves. **2** The laurel oak *(Q. laurifolia).*

willow pattern A decorative design introduced on household china in England in 1780 and since extremely popular: so called from the willow tree, usually blue on a white background, which appears in the design.

wil·low·ware (wil′ō·wâr′) *n.* China decorated with the willow pattern.

wil·low·y (wil′ō·ē) *adj.* **1** Abounding in willows. **2** Having supple grace of form or carriage. See synonyms under SUPPLE.

will·pow·er (wil′pou′ər) *n.* Ability to control oneself; determination; firmness of mind.

Will·stät·ter (vil′shtet·ər), **Richard,** 1872–1942, German organic chemist.

will·y¹ (wil′ē) *adj. Obs.* Willing; also, propitious. [Cf. ON *viljugr*]

wil·ly² (wil′ē) *v.t.* **·lied, ·ly·ing** To willow, as cotton, flax, hemp, etc.

will·yard (wil′yərd) *adj. Scot.* Wilful; also, abashed; bewildered. Also **will′yart** (-yərt).

wil·ly-nil·ly (wil′ē·nil′ē) *adj.* Having no decisiveness; uncertain; irresolute. — *adv.* Willingly or unwillingly. [Earlier *will I, nill I* whether I will or not]

willy willy *Austral.* **1** A violent storm of wind and rain on the NW coast of Australia: also called *cockeye bob.* **2** A brief but violent duststorm.

Wil·ming·ton (wil′ming·tən) **1** A port of entry on the Delaware River in northern Delaware. **2** A port of entry in SE North Carolina.

Wil·no (vil′nô) The Polish name for VILNA.

Wil·son (wil′sən), **Alexander,** 1766–1813, American ornithologist born in Scotland. — **Charles Thomson Rees,** 1869–1959, Scottish physicist. — **Edmund,** 1895–1972, U. S. critic, author, and dramatist. — **Henry,** 1812–75 U. S. statesman. — **James,** 1742–98, American patriot, signed Declaration of Independence. — **John,** 1785–1854, Scottish poet: pseudonym *Christopher North.* — **(Thomas) Woodrow,** 1856–1924, U. S. educator and statesman; president of the United States 1913–21.

Wil·son (wil′sən), **Mount** A peak in SW California, near Pasadena; 5,710 feet; site of a famous observatory.

Wilson Dam A power dam in the Tennessee River at Muscle Shoals, NW Alabama; 137 feet high, 4,862 feet long; forms **Lake Wilson** (25 square miles; 15 1/2 miles long, 1 1/2 miles wide) over Muscle Shoals.

Wilson's petrel The storm petrel. [after Alexander *Wilson*]
Wilson's phalarope A shore bird *(Steganopus tricolor)* which breeds in northern North America and winters as far south as the Falkland Islands. [after Alexander *Wilson*]
Wilson's plover The ring plover *(Charadrius wilsonia)* of the southern United States and South America. [after Alexander *Wilson*]
Wilson's snipe Snipe (def. 1). [after Alexander *Wilson*]
Wilson's thrush The veery. [after Alexander *Wilson*]
Wilson's warbler A small, very active flycatcher *(Wilsonia pusilla)* of eastern North America, black-crowned with a yellow and olive-green body. [after Alexander *Wilson*]
wilt[1] (wilt) *v.i.* **1** To lose freshness; droop or become limp, as a flower that has been cut or that has not been watered. **2** To lose energy and vitality; become faint or languid: We *wilted* under the hot sun. **3** To lose courage or spirit; subside suddenly. — *v.t.* **4** To cause to droop or wither. **5** To cause to lose vitality and energy. — *n.* **1** The act of wilting; also, languor; faintness. **2** An infectious and virulent disease sometimes epidemic among certain caterpillars and insect larvae, which are reduced to a liquefied mass by its ravages: also **wilt disease.** [Prob. dial. var. of obs. *welk* wither. Cf. MDu. *welken* wither.]
wilt[2] (wilt) Archaic second person singular, present tense of WILL[2], used with *thou.*
Wil·ton (wil′tən) *n.* A kind of carpet resembling the Brussels carpet, but having the loops of the pile cut, thus giving it a velvety texture: originally made at Wilton, England. Also **Wilton carpet, Wilton rug.**
Wilt·shire (wilt′shir) *n.* One of a breed of long-horned sheep raised in Wiltshire, England.
Wilt·shire (wilt′shir) A county in southern England; 1,345 square miles; county town, Salisbury. Shortened form **Wilts.**
Wiltshire cheese A variety of Cheddar cheese.
wi·ly (wī′lē) *adj.* **·li·er, ·li·est** Full of or characterized by wiles; sly; cunning. See synonyms under INSIDIOUS, POLITIC. — **wi′li·ly** *adv.* — **wi′li·ness** *n.*
wim·ble (wim′bəl) *n.* Anything that bores a hole, especially if turned by hand, as a gimlet, auger, brace and bit, or the like. — *v.t.* **·bled, ·bling** To bore or pierce, as with a wimble. [<AF, OF *guimbel* <MLG *wiemel.* Akin to GIMLET.]
Wim·ble·don (wim′bəl·dən) A town and municipal borough SW of London in NE Surrey, England; scene of international tennis matches.
wim·ple (wim′pəl) *n.* **1** A cloth, as of linen or silk, wrapped in folds around the neck close under the chin and over the head, exposing only the face: formerly worn as a protection by women outdoors, and still by nuns. **2** *Scot.* A fold; plait; also, a curve; a winding turn, as in a river or road. — *v.* **·pled, ·pling** *v.t.* **1** To cover or clothe with a wimple; veil. **2** To make or fold into plaits, as a veil. **3** To cause to move with slight undulations; ripple. **4** *Obs.* To deceive; hoodwink. — *v.i.* **5** To lie in plaits or folds. **6** To ripple. [OE *wimpel*]

WIMPLE 14th century.

Wims·hurst machine (wimz′hûrst) A machine for the generation of static electricity by means of two insulated rotating disks carrying a number of equally spaced strips of conducting material which, by friction, build up an electrostatic charge. [after James *Wimshurst,* 1832–1903, English engineer, its inventor]
win[1] (win) *v.* **won** (*Obs.* **wan**), **won, win·ning** *v.i.* **1** To gain a victory; be victorious; prevail, as in a contest: May the best man *win.* **2** To succeed in an effort or endeavor. **3** To succeed in reaching or attaining a specified end or condition; get: often with *across, over, through,* etc.: The fleet *won* through the storm. **4** *Obs.* To fight; struggle. — *v.t.* **5** To be successful in; gain victory in: to *win* a game; to *win* an argument. **6** To gain in competition or contest: to *win* the blue ribbon. **7** To gain by effort, persistence, etc.: to *win* fame or fortune. **8** To influence so as to obtain the good will or favor of: often with *over*: His eloquence *won* the audience; We *won* him over to our side. **9** To secure the love of; gain in marriage: He wooed and *won* her. **10** To succeed in reaching; attain: to *win* the harbor. **11** To make (one's way), especially with effort. **12** To capture; take possession of. **13** To earn or procure, as a living: to *win* support from poor soil. **14** *Mining* **a** To extract, as ore or coal, or metal from ore. **b** To reach and open (a deposit, vein, etc.); prepare for mining. See synonyms under ALLURE, CONQUER, GAIN[1], GET, OBTAIN, PERSUADE, SUCCEED. — **to win out** *Colloq.* To succeed to the fullest extent or expectation. — *n.* **1** A victory; success. **2** Profit; winnings. [OE *winnan* contend, labor]
win[2] (win) *v.t. Scot. & Irish* **1** To winnow. **2** To cure, as hay.
win[3] (win) *n. Scot.* Wind.
win·cey (win′sē) *n.* A fabric woven with cotton or linen warp and woolen filling. [Short for *wincey-woolsey,* alter. of LINSEY-WOOLSEY]
wince[1] (wins) *v.i.* **winced, winc·ing** To shrink back or start aside, as from a blow or pain; flinch. — *n.* The act of wincing. [<AF *wenchier* (assumed), var. of OF *quenchier* avoid <Gmc.] — **winc′er** *n.*
wince[2] (wins) *n.* A dyer's winch or windlass. [Var. of WINCH[1]]
winch[1] (winch) *n.* **1** A windlass, particularly one used for hoisting, as on a truck or the mast of a crane, derrick, etc., having usually one or more hand cranks geared to a drum around which the rope or chain winds. **2** A crank with a handle, used to impart motion to a grindstone or the like. — *v.t.* To move, hoist, or haul with or as with a winch. [OE *wince*] — **winch′er** *n.*

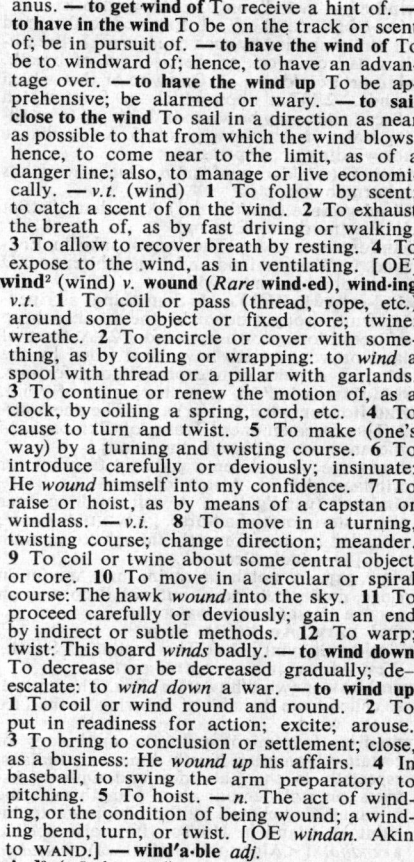

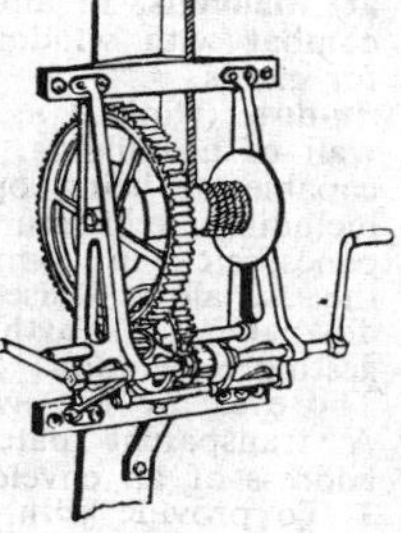
WINCH

winch[2] (winch) *v.i. Obs.* To wince; flinch. [See WINCE[1].]
Win·ches·ter (win′ches·tər) **1** The county town of Hampshire, England; known for its 11th century cathedral. **2** A city of northern Virginia near eastern West Virginia; scene of several Civil War battles, 1862 and 1864.
Winchester rifle A breechloading, lever-action, repeating rifle with a tubular magazine under the barrel, first produced in 1866: a trade name. Also **Winchester.** [after Oliver F. *Winchester,* 1810–80, U. S. industrialist]
Winck·el·mann (vingk′əl·män), **Johann Joachim,** 1717–68, German archeologist and art critic.
wind[1] (wind, *Poetic* wīnd) *n.* **1** Any movement of air, especially a natural horizontal movement; air in motion naturally. See BEAUFORT SCALE. **2** Any powerful or destructive wind; a tornado; hurricane. **3** The direction from which a wind blows; one of the cardinal points of the compass: They gathered from the four *winds.* **4** Air in motion by artificial means: the *wind* of a bullet, *wind* from a bellows. **5** Air pervaded by a scent: The deer got *wind* of the hunter; hence, figuratively, a suggestion or intimation: to get *wind* of a plot. **6** The power of breathing or respiring; breath: He lost his *wind* in the race. **7** Breath as expended in words, especially as having more sound than sense; idle chatter; also, vanity; conceit. **8** *pl.* The wind instruments of an orchestra; also, the players of these instruments. See WIND INSTRUMENT. **9** The gaseous product of indigestion; flatulence. **10** In pugilism, the pit of the stomach where a blow may cause temporary stoppage of breath: He was hit in the *wind.* — **in the wind** **1** Impending; astir; afoot. **2** Inebriated; drunk. — **in the wind's eye** Directly opposed to the point from which the wind blows. — **to break wind** To expel gas through the anus. — **to get wind of** To receive a hint of. — **to have in the wind** To be on the track or scent of; be in pursuit of. — **to have the wind of** To be to windward of; hence, to have an advantage over. — **to have the wind up** To be apprehensive; be alarmed or wary. — **to sail close to the wind** To sail in a direction as near as possible to that from which the wind blows; hence, to come near to the limit, as of a danger line; also, to manage or live economically. — *v.t.* (wind) **1** To follow by scent; to catch a scent of on the wind. **2** To exhaust the breath of, as by fast driving or walking. **3** To allow to recover breath by resting. **4** To expose to the wind, as in ventilating. [OE]
wind[2] (wīnd) *v.* **wound** (*Rare* **wind·ed**), **wind·ing** *v.t.* **1** To coil or pass (thread, rope, etc.) around some object or fixed core; twine; wreathe. **2** To encircle or cover with something, as by coiling or wrapping: to *wind* a spool with thread or a pillar with garlands. **3** To continue or renew the motion of, as a clock, by coiling a spring, cord, etc. **4** To cause to turn and twist. **5** To make (one's way) by a turning and twisting course. **6** To introduce carefully or deviously; insinuate: He *wound* himself into my confidence. **7** To raise or hoist, as by means of a capstan or windlass. — *v.i.* **8** To move in a turning, twisting course; change direction; meander. **9** To coil or twine about some central object or core. **10** To move in a circular or spiral course: The hawk *wound* into the sky. **11** To proceed carefully or deviously; gain an end by indirect or subtle methods. **12** To warp; twist: This board *winds* badly. — **to wind down** To decrease or be decreased gradually; de-escalate: to *wind down* a war. — **to wind up** **1** To coil or wind round and round. **2** To put in readiness for action; excite; arouse. **3** To bring to conclusion or settlement; close, as a business: He *wound up* his affairs. **4** In baseball, to swing the arm preparatory to pitching. **5** To hoist. — *n.* The act of winding, or the condition of being wound; a winding bend, turn, or twist. [OE *windan.* Akin to WAND.] — **wind′a·ble** *adj.*
wind[3] (wīnd, wind) *v.t.* **wind·ed** (*erroneously* **wound**), **wind·ing** **1** To blow, as a horn; sound. **2** To give (a call or signal), as with a horn. [<WIND[1]; infl. by *wind*[2]]
wind·age (win′dij) *n.* **1** The rush of air caused by the rapid passage of an object, as a projectile or a railway train. **2** Deflection of an object, as a bullet, from its natural course due to wind pressure. **3** In a muzzleloading rifled gun, the difference between the diameter of a projectile and the bore through which it is discharged; also, in a smoothbore gun, the space between the surface of the bore and the projectile. **4** *Mech.* The free air space between any moving piece and the socket or bore in which it travels. **5** A contusion caused by sudden compression of air due to the passing of gunshot nearby. **6** *Naut.* The surface offered to the wind by a vessel.
Win·dau (vin′dou) The German name for VENTSPILS.
wind·bag (wind′bag′) *n.* **1** A wordy talker. **2** A bellows. **3** *Slang* The chest.
wind-blown (wind′blōn′) *adj.* **1** Tossed or blown by the wind. **2** Having a permanent direction of growth as determined by prevailing winds: said of plants and trees. **3** Pertaining to an irregular hair arrangement causing the hair in front to appear as if blown forward by the wind.
wind-borne (wind′bôrn′, -bōrn′) *adj.* Carried or transported by the wind.
wind-bound (wind′bound′) *adj.* Delayed by contrary winds.
wind·break (wind′brāk′) *n.* Anything, as a hedge, fence, etc., that protects from or breaks the force of the wind.
wind·break·er (wind′brā′kər) *n.* A sports jacket for outer wear, having a close-fitting or elastic waistband and cuffs. [<*Windbreaker,* a trade name]
wind-bro·ken (wind′brō′kən) *adj.* Asthmatic; broken-winded: said of a horse.
Wind Cave National Park (wind) A region containing a large limestone cavern in the Black Hills in SW South Dakota; 41 square miles; established 1903.

wind·cone (wind′kōn′) *n.* A windsock.

wind·ed (win′did) *adj.* 1 Exposed to the wind or air, or spoiled by such exposure. 2 Breathless, as from work or exercise; out of breath.

wind·er[1] (wīn′dər) *n.* 1 One who or that which winds. 2 That upon which or from which thread, etc., may be wound. 3 A step in winding stairs. 4 A twining plant. 5 An appliance for winding up a spring.

wind·er[2] (wīn′dər, win′dər) *n.* One who winds a horn, bugle, etc.

Win·der·mere (win′dər·mir) An urban district in Westmorland, England.

Windermere, Lake The largest lake in England, in Westmorland and Lancashire; 10 1/2 miles long by 1 mile wide.

wind·fall (wind′fôl′) *n.* 1 Something, as ripening fruit, brought down by the wind; a heap of trees blown down by wind. 2 A tract of land on which trees have been felled by the wind. 3 A piece of unexpected good fortune.

wind·flaw (wind′flô) *n.* A sharp gust of wind.

wind·flow·er (wind′flou′ər) *n.* 1 The anemone. 2 The rue anemone. [Trans. of Gk. *anemōnē* the anemone < *anemos* the wind]

wind gage A scale on a gunsight to allow for windage (def. 2). Also **wind gauge.**

wind·gall (wind′gôl′) *n.* A soft swelling near the pastern joint of a horse. [< WIND + GALL[2]; so called because formerly thought to contain wind] — **wind′galled′** *adj.*

wind gap A notch or ravine in a mountain ridge, moderately deep, but not deep enough to give passage to a watercourse.

wind harp An Eolian harp.

Wind·hoek (vint′hŏŏk) The capital of South-West Africa, in the central part.

wind·hov·er (wind′huv′ər) *n. Brit.* The kestrel: so called from its habit of hovering in the face of the wind.

win·di·go (win′di·gō) *n.* In the mythology of certain Algonquian North American Indians, especially in the Labrador and Ojibwa districts, an evil demon; also, a mythical tribe of cannibals believed by the Chippewa to inhabit an island in Hudson Bay: also spelled *weendijo.* [< Algonquian (Ojibwa) *weendigo* a cannibal]

wind·ing[1] (wīn′ding) *n.* 1 The act or condition of one who or that which winds; a spiral turning or coiling. 2 A bend or turn, or a series of them. 3 A warp or twist from a plane surface. 4 *Electr.* The manner in which the wire is wound in a coil, as on the armature of a dynamo. 5 A defective gait of horses in which one leg seems to wind around the other. — *adj.* 1 Turning spirally about an axis or core. 2 Having bends or lateral turns. 3 Twisting from a plane.

wind·ing[2] (wīn′ding) *n.* A boatswain's signal.

winding frame A device or machine for winding, as a reel.

wind·ing·ly (wīn′ding·lē) *adv.* In a winding manner.

winding sheet (wīn′ding) The sheet that wraps a corpse.

wind instrument (wind) A musical instrument whose sounds are produced by vibrations of air injected by the lungs or by mechanical bellows. Those blown by air from the lungs are known as **wood-wind instruments** or **woodwinds**, consisting of the flutes, oboes, clarinets, etc., and the **brass-wind instruments** or **brasses**, consisting of the horns, trumpets, trombones, tubas, etc. Those in which the vibration of the air column is induced by bellows are the various types of organ, accordion, etc.

wind·jam·mer (wind′jam′ər) *n.* 1 *Naut.* A merchant sailing vessel, as distinguished from a steamship. 2 A member of its crew. 3 *Slang* A chatterbox; a loquacious person.

wind·lass (wind′ləs) *n.* Any of several devices for hauling or lifting, especially that form familiar in well curbs, consisting of a drum or barrel on which the hoisting rope winds, and turned by means of cranking. — **Chinese** or **differential windlass** A horizontal wheel and axle having two drums of different di-

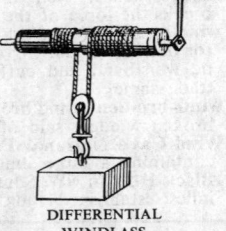

DIFFERENTIAL WINDLASS

ameters on the same axis, one of which pays out as the other winds up, the power being increased in inverse proportion to the difference between the diameters. — *v.t. & v.i.* To raise or haul with a windlass. [Alter. of ME *windas* <ON *vindass* < *vinda* wind + *ass* a beam; infl. in form by WINDLE[2]]

win·dle[1] (win′dəl) *n.* A basket. [OE *windel* a basket < *windan* plait, twist]

win·dle[2] (win′dəl) *Scot. & Brit. Dial. v.t. & v.i.* To wind. — *n.* Something used for winding or turning. [Freq. of WIND[2]]

wind·less (wind′lis) *adj.* 1 Without wind; breezeless; calm. 2 Being out of breath.

win·dle-straw (win′dəl·strô′) *n. Scot. & Brit. Dial.* 1 A withered stalk of any one of several grasses, used in plaiting or ropemaking. 2 A feeble, unhealthy person. 3 The white-throat warbler. Also **win′dle-strae′** (-strā′). [OE *windelstrēaw,* ? < *windel* basket + *strēaw* straw]

wind·ling (wind′ling) *n.* 1 *Dial.* That which is torn off by the wind, as a branch of a tree. 2 *Scot.* A bottle of straw. [< WIND[1] + -LING[1]]

wind·mill (wind′mil′) *n.* 1 A mill consisting of a tower within which is a shaft having at the top a horizontal axis which bears a rudder at one end and at the other a system of adjustable slats, wings, or sails which, in revolving, transmit motion to a pump, millstone, or the like. 2 Anything resembling a windmill. 3 An imaginary wrong, evil, or foe: usually in the phrase, **to fight** (or **tilt at**) **windmills,** in allusion to Don Quixote's combat with windmills, which he mistook for giants.

win·dow (win′dō) *n.* 1 An opening in the wall of a building, to admit light or air, capable of being opened and closed, and including, architecturally, the casement, sash, panes, etc.; in common usage, sometimes, the sash alone: Raise the *window.* 2 A windowpane. 3 Anything resembling or suggesting a window; a windowlike aperture: The eyes are the *windows* of the soul. 4 A transparent patch through which the address of an envelope can be read. — *v.t.* 1 To provide with a window or windows. 2 To fill with holes resembling windows. [< ON *vindauga* < *vindr* wind + *auga* an eye]

window box 1 One of the grooves along the sides of a window frame for the weights that counterbalance a lifting sash. 2 A box, generally long and narrow, along a window ledge or sill, for growing plants.

win·dow-dress·ing (win′dō-dres′ing) *n.* 1 The act or the art of arranging merchandise attractively in shop and store windows; also, the goods so displayed; hence, anything superficially attractive. 2 A business report that unduly stresses favorable conditions. 3 Anything added or done to make something else more attractive: The prosecution of the thieves was mere *window-dressing* for his campaign for governor. — **win′dow-dress′er** *n.*

win·dow·pane (win′dō·pān′) *n.* A single sheet of glass for a window. Also **window pane.**

window seat A seat in the recess of a window.

window shade A flexible fabric shade, usually mounted on a spring roller, used to regulate light at a window.

win·dow-shop (win′dō·shop′) *v.i.* **-shopped, -shop·ping** To look at goods shown in store windows without buying them. — **win′dow-shop′per** *n.* — **win′dow-shop′ping** *n. & adj.*

wind·pipe (wind′pīp′) *n.* The duct by which the breath is carried to and from the lungs; the trachea.

Wind River Range A range of the Rocky Mountains in west central Wyoming; highest point, 13,787 feet, highest point in Wyoming.

wind rose *Meteorol.* A diagram indicating the direction and relative velocities of the wind in a given locality by means of lines of varying length radiating from a common center.

wind·row (wind′rō′) *n.* 1 A long ridge or pile of hay or grain raked together preparatory to building into cocks. 2 A row of Indian corn made by setting two rows together. 3 A wind-swept line of dust, surf,

leaves, etc. 4 A deep furrow made for planting. 5 Land on which the trees have been felled by the wind; sometimes, a tornado track: also **wind slash.** — *v.t.* To rake or shape into a windrow. — **wind′row′er** *n.*

wind sail 1 *Naut.* A canvas tube or funnel with a spreading opening at one side of the top that may be stayed to face the wind: used to conduct fresh air below decks. 2 A sail on the arm of a windmill.

wind scale See BEAUFORT SCALE.

wind-shake (wind′shāk′) *n.* A defect in wood; anemosis.

wind-shield (wind′shēld′) *n.* 1 Any arrangement for breaking the force of the wind against an object. 2 A transparent screen of glass or similar material, attached in front of the occupants of an automobile, airplane, etc., as protection against wind and weather. 3 A covering for a chimney.

wind·sock (wind′sok′) *n. Meteorol.* A large, conical bag, open at both ends, mounted on a pivot, and used to indicate the direction of the wind by the current of air which blows through it; a drogue: also called *windcone.*

Wind·sor (win′zər) Name of the royal family of Great Britain since July 27, 1917, when it was officially changed from *Saxe-Coburg-Gotha.*

Wind·sor (win′zər) 1 A municipal borough in eastern Berkshire, England; site of **Windsor Castle,** a residence of the English sovereigns since the time of William the Conqueror. Officially **New Windsor.** 2 A city on the Detroit River in SE Ontario, Canada, opposite Detroit, Michigan.

Wind·sor (win′zər), **Duke of** See EDWARD VIII.

Windsor chair A wooden chair, with or without arms, common in England and America in the 18th century, typically with a spindle back, turned, slanting legs, and a flat or saddle seat.

Windsor tie A wide, soft necktie knotted loosely in a double bow, usually of black silk cut on the bias.

COMB-BACKED WINDSOR CHAIR

wind·storm (wind′stôrm′) *n.* A violent wind, usually with little or no precipitation.

wind·suck·er (wind′suk′ər) *n.* A horse that cribs. — **wind′suck′ing** *n. & adj.*

wind tee (wind) A T-shaped weathervane, especially one located on or near an aircraft landing field.

wind tunnel *Aeron.* A tunnel-like structure in which the effects of artificially produced winds may be investigated, as on airplane wings and other surfaces.

wind-up (wīnd′up′) *n.* 1 The act of concluding or closing. 2 A conclusion; a final act or part. 3 In baseball, the swing of the arm preparatory to pitching the ball.

wind·ward (wind′wərd) *adj.* Being on the side exposed to the wind. — *n.* The direction from which the wind blows. — **to windward of** Advantageously placed with respect to. — *adv.* In the direction from which the wind blows; opposed to *leeward.*

Wind·ward Islands (wind′wərd) A West Indies island group north of Trinidad, comprising four British colonies, all federating units of The West Indies, on the islands of Dominica, Grenada, St. Lucia, and St. Vincent, together with the Grenadines; 820 square miles; capital, St. George's, on Grenada. The French island of Martinique; Barbados, a British colony; and three islands of the Netherlands Antilles, Aruba, Bonaire, and Curaçao, are also sometimes included in this group.

Windward Passage The strait between Cuba and Hispaniola in the West Indies; 50 miles wide.

wind·y (win′dē) *adj.* **wind·i·er, wind·i·est** 1 Pertaining to, consisting of, or abounding in wind; stormy; tempestuous: *windy* weather. 2 Exposed to the wind; wind-swept: high on a *windy* hill. 3 Suggestive of wind; boisterous;

swift: *windy* emotions. **4** Producing, due to, or troubled with gas in the stomach or intestines; producing or affected with flatulence; flatulent: *windy* food. **5** Given to or expressed in bombast; pompous, loquacious, or bragging: *windy* talk, a *windy* orator. See synonyms under BLEAK[1]. —**wind′i·ly** *adv.* —**wind′i·ness** *n.*

Windy City A nickname for CHICAGO.

wine (wīn) *n.* **1** The fermented juice of the grape, containing various percentages of alcohol by volume, commonly used as a beverage and in cooking. Wines are often classified as dry or sweet, red or white, still or sparkling. Fortified wines have brandy added, and contain alcohol of from 16 to 23 percent. **2** By extension, the fermented juice of some fruit other than the grape: elderberry *wine;* sometimes, a fermented vegetable juice: dandelion *wine.* **3** The effects of drinking too much wine; intoxication. **4** A convivial gathering at which wine and other liquors are served; a wine party. **5** A medicinal preparation in which wine is used as the menstruum: *wine* of opium. **6** Any color resembling the color of wine, especially of a red wine, usually a dark, purplish red. —**Adam's wine** Water. —**new wine in old bottles** Any dynamic new thing, as a doctrine, theory, etc., which cannot be restricted by older forms or customs: with reference to *Matt.* ix 17. —*v.* **wined, win·ing** *v.t.* To entertain or treat with wine. —*v.i.* To drink wine. [OE *wīn* < L *vinum*]

wine·bib·bing (wīn′bib′ing) *adj.* Addicted to excessive drinking of wine. —*n.* The habitual, excessive drinking of wine. —**wine′bib′ber** *n.*

wine card The list of alcoholic drinks for sale at a hotel or restaurant.

wine cellar A storage space for wines; also, the wines stored.

wine-col·ored (wīn′kul′ərd) *adj.* Having the color of red wine.

wine fly Any fly (as of the genus *Piophila*) whose larva lives in wine or other fermented liquor.

wine gallon See under GALLON.

wine·glass (wīn′glas′, -gläs′) *n.* A small goblet from which to drink wine.

wine·glass·ful (wīn′glas·fŏŏl′, -gläs-) *n. pl.* **·fuls** The amount a wineglass will hold, approximately equivalent to two fluid ounces or four tablespoonfuls.

wine·grow·er (wīn′grō′ər) *n.* One who cultivates a vineyard and makes wine; a viticulturist. —**wine′grow′ing** *adj. & n.*

wine measure A system of liquid measures formerly used for wines and spirits in which the gallon was equal to the present U.S. gallon.

wine palm Any palm from which palm wine is obtained.

wine·press (wīn′pres′) *n.* An apparatus or a place where the juice of grapes is expressed. —**wine′press′er** *n.*

wine purple A hue of purple consisting of 50 percent red, 33 percent black, and 17 percent blue.

win·er·y (wī′nər·ē) *n. pl.* **·er·ies 1** An establishment for making wine. **2** A room for fining and storing wines.

Wine·sap (wīn′sap) *n.* An American variety of red winter apple.

wine·skin (wīn′skin′) *n.* The skin of some domestic quadruped kept as entire as possible and made into a tight bag for containing wine: much used in the Orient.

wine·sop (wīn′sop′) *n.* Any farinaceous foodstuff steeped or sopped in wine, as bread or cake.

wine steward An attendant in a restaurant or hotel who takes orders for wines, and who is in charge of the wine cellar.

wine·tast·er (wīn′tās′tər) *n.* A person who tastes wine to judge its quality.

wine vinegar A vinegar made from wine.

wine whey *Brit.* A beverage made of wine and curdled milk.

Win·fre·da (win·frā′də) Latin form of WINIFRED. Also *Du.* **Win·fried** (vin′frēt), *Sw.* **Winfrid** (vin′frid).

wing (wing) *n.* **1** An organ of flight; specifically, one of the anterior movable pair of appendages of a bird or bat, homologous with the forelimbs of vertebrates but adapted for flight. **2** An analogous organ in insects and some other animals. **3** One of the pectoral fins of a flying fish. **4** *Slang* An arm; specifically, in baseball, the arm used for throwing or pitching. **5** Something regarded as conferring the power of swift motion or performing some function of a wing: on *wings* of song. **6** Flight or passage by or as by wings; also, the means or act of flying: to take *wing.* **7** Anything resembling or suggestive of a wing in form, function, or appearance; specifically, one of a pair of pneumatic devices for aid in swimming; a shoulder ornament. **8** The flare of a moldboard plowshare; also, the curved mudguard or fender of an automobile. **9** Something moved by or moving in the wind, as the vane of a windmill or a winnowing fan. **10** *Mil.* Either division of a military force on either side of the center. **11** An analogous formation in certain outdoor games, as hockey or football. **12** Either of two extremist groups or factions in a political or other organization: the left *wing.* **13** *Archit.* A part attached to a side; especially, a projection or extension of a building on the side of the main portion. **14** A sidepiece at the top of an armchair. **15** A side section of something that shuts or folds, as a double door, a screen, etc. **16** In fortifications, one of the sides connecting an outwork with the main fort. **17** *Anat.* An ala: a *wing* of the nose. **18** *Bot.* Any thin membranous or foliaceous expansion of an organ, as of certain stems, seeds, samaras, etc. **19** *Zool.* One of the lateral finlike expansions of the foot of a pteropod. **20** One of the sides of a stage; a small platform at either side of the stage; also, a piece of scenery for the side. **21** *Aeron.* One of the sustaining surfaces of an airplane. **22** A tactical and administrative unit of the U.S. Air Force, under the direction of a wing commander, larger than a group and smaller than a command. **23** A shore dam or jetty for narrowing a channel; also, an extension of a dam at either end, usually built at an angle. —**on** (or **upon**) **the wing** In flight; as, a bird *on the wing;* hence, just about to go; departing; also, journeying. —**to take wing** To fly away. —**under one's wing** Under one's protection. —*v.t.* **1** To pass over or through in flight. **2** To accomplish by flying: the eagle *winged* its way. **3** To enable to fly. **4** To cause to go swiftly; speed: Hope *winged* his steps. **5** To transport by flight. **6** To provide with wings for flight; also, to feather (an arrow). **7** To supply with a side body or part: The house was *winged* on both sides. **8** To wound (a bird) in a wing; hence, to disable by a minor wound: I *winged* him in the arm. —*v.i.* **9** To fly; soar. [< ON *vængr*]

wing and wing *Naut.* With sails spread or boomed out on each side like wings: said of a fore-and-aft vessel running downwind.

wing·back (wing′bak′) *n.* In football, the position taken by one **(single wingback)** or two **(double wingback)** of the backs behind or beyond the ends; also, the back so posted.

wing·bow (wing′bō′) *n.* A distinctive mark of color on the bend of the wing in a domestic fowl.

wing chair A large armchair, upholstered throughout, with high back and side pieces designed as protection from drafts.

WING CHAIR

wing cover The elytron of an insect. Also **wing case.**

wing covert *Ornithol.* One of the small close feathers clothing the bend of a bird's wing and covering the insertion of the flight feathers. Those of the lining of the wing are called *undercoverts.*

winged (wingd, *Poetic* wing′id) *adj.* **1** Having wings. **2** Passing swiftly; soaring; lofty; rapt. **3** Alive with creatures having wings. **4** (wingd) *Colloq.* Wounded or disabled in or as in the wing.

winged bean A tropical leguminous plant *(Psophocarpus tetragonolobus)* having a pod with a wing along four edges, cultivated for the nutrients provided by the foliage, roots, and fruit.

winged wolf A harpy (def. 2).

wing flap *Aeron.* A control surface hinged to an airplane wing, used primarily to increase lift and to retard the speed.

wing-foot·ed (wing′fŏŏt′id) *adj.* Rapid; swift.

wing·less (wing′lis) *adj.* Having no wings, or having aborted wings.

wing·let (wing′lit) *n.* An alula.

wing loading *Aeron.* The over-all weight of a fully loaded airplane divided by the area of the supporting surface, exclusive of the stabilizer and elevators. Also **wing load.**

wing-nut (wing′nut′) *n.* A thumbnut.

wing·o·ver (wing′ō′vər) *n. Aeron.* A flight maneuver in which an airplane at the top of a climbing turn and just before stalling is put into a dive before resuming normal flight in the direction from which it started.

wing rail A guardrail, as at a railway switch.

wing skid *Aeron.* A device set beneath the wing tip of an airplane to guard the tip against contact with the ground.

wing·spread (wing′spred′) *n.* The distance between the tips of the fully extended wings of a bird, insect, or airplane.

wing walk *Aeron.* A reinforced section of an airplane wing, used as a walking strip.

Win·i·fred (win′ə·frid) A feminine personal name. Also **Win′e·fred, Win′i·frid.** [< Welsh *Gwenfrewi* a white wave]

wink (wingk) *v.i.* **1** To close and open the eye or eyelids quickly. **2** To draw the eyelids of one eye together, as in conveying a hint or making a sign. **3** To shut one's eyes, especially in ignoring; pretend not to see: usually with *at.* **4** To emit fitful gleams; twinkle. —*v.t.* **5** To close and open (the eye or eyelids) quickly. **6** To move, force, etc., by winking: with *away, off,* etc. **7** To signify or express by winking. —*n.* **1** The act of winking. **2** The time necessary for a wink. **3** A twinkle. **4** A hint conveyed by winking. **5** A short nap: especially in the phrase **forty winks.** [OE *wincian* close the eyes]

Win·kel·ried (ving′kəl·rēt), **Arnold von** A 14th century Swiss patriot.

wink·er (wing′kər) *n.* **1** One who winks. **2** A blinder for a horse. **3** *Slang* An eyelash. **4** A small secondary bellows for use with an organ. **5** The nictitating membrane, as of a bird. **6** The muscle by which winking is done. **7** *pl. Slang* Spectacles.

win·kle (wing′kəl) *n.* A periwinkle[1]. [Short for PERIWINKLE[1]]

win·na (win′ə) *Scot.* Will not.

Win·ne·ba·go (win′ə·bā′gō) *n. pl.* **·gos** or **·goes** One of a tribe of North American Indians of Siouan linguistic stock, formerly occupying what is now eastern Wisconsin, south of Green Bay, where many still survive.

Win·ne·ba·go (win′ə·bā′gō), **Lake** The largest lake in Wisconsin, in the eastern part; 215 square miles; 30 miles long.

Win·ne·pe·sau·kee (win′ə·pə·sô′kē), **Lake** The largest lake in New Hampshire, in the east central part; 25 miles long, 12 miles wide. Also **Win′ni·pe·sau′kee.**

win·ner (win′ər) *n.* One who or that which wins.

win·ning (win′ing) *adj.* **1** Successful in achievement, especially in competition. **2** Capable of winning or charming; attractive; winsome. —*n.* **1** The act of one who wins. **2** That which is won: usually in the plural. **3** A new opening in a mine; also, a section of a mine prepared for working. —**win′ning·ly** *adv.* —**win′ning·ness** *n.*

winning gallery In court tennis, the grille or square opening in the penthouse in the rear of the hazard court: so named because a ball played into it counts as a win.

winning hazard See HAZARD *n.* (def. 6).

winning post The post or goal at the end of a racecourse.

Win·ni·peg (win′ə·peg) The capital of Manitoba, Canada, on the Red River in the SE part.

Winnipeg, Lake A lake in south central Manitoba, Canada; 240 miles long, 55 miles wide; 9,398 square miles.

Winnipeg goldeye *Canadian* The goldeye.

Win·ni·pe·go·sis (win′ə·pə·gō′sis), **Lake** A lake in western Manitoba, Canada, west of Lake Winnipeg; 125 miles long, 25 miles wide; 2,086 square miles.

Winnipeg River A river in NW Ontario and

add,āce,câre,pälm; end,ēven; it,īce; odd,ōpen,ôrder; tŏŏk,pōōl; up,bûrn; ə = a in *above,* e in *sicken,* i in *clarity,* o in *melon,* u in *focus* ; yōō = u in *fuse,* oi,oil; ou,pout; ch,check; g,go; ng,ring; th,thin; th,this; zh,vision. Foreign sounds à,œ,ü,kh,ṅ; and ◆: see page xx. < from; + plus; ? possibly.

SE Manitoba, flowing 200 miles NW from Lake of the Woods to Lake Winnipeg.

win·nock (win′ək) *n. Scot.* A window.

win·now (win′ō) *v.t.* **1** To separate (grain, etc.) from the chaff by means of wind or a current of air. **2** To blow away (the chaff) thus. **3** To examine so as to separate good from bad; analyze minutely; sift. **4** To separate (what is valuable) from what is valueless, or to eliminate (what is valueless) from what is valuable; distinguish, sort: often with *out.* **5** To blow upon; cause to flutter. **6** To beat or fan (the air) with the wings. **7** To scatter by blowing; disperse. **8** *Rare* To proceed along (a course) by flapping the wings. —*v.i.* **9** To separate grain from chaff. **10** To fly; flap. —*n.* **1** Any device used in winnowing grain. **2** The act of winnowing; also, a vibrating motion caused by a current of air. [OE *windwian* < *wind* the wind] —**win′now·er** *n.*

win·o (wī′nō) *n. pl.* **·noes** or **·nos** *U.S. Slang* A drunkard who habitually drinks sweet, fortified wines. [< WINE]

Wins·low (winz′lō), **Edward,** 1595–1655, English Puritan, governor of Plymouth Colony.

win·some (win′səm) *adj.* Having a winning appearance or manner; pleasing; attractive; rarely, joyous. See synonyms under AMIABLE, LOVELY. [OE *wynsum* < *wyn* joy] —**win′some·ly** *adv.* — **win′some·ness** *n.*

Win·sor (win′zər), **Justin,** 1831–97, U.S. historian and librarian.

Win·ston (win′stən) A masculine personal name. [Orig. from *Winston,* a hamlet near Cirencester, England]

Win·ston-Sa·lem (win′stən·sā′ləm) A city in NW central North Carolina; one of the world's chief tobacco centers.

win·ter (win′tər) *n.* **1** The coldest season of the year, extending from the end of autumn to the beginning of spring: in the northern hemisphere, astronomically from the winter solstice, December 21, to the vernal equinox, March 21, but popularly regarded as including December, January, and February. ◆ Collateral adjectives: *hibernal, hiemal.* **2** Any time compared to winter, as being marked by lack of life, warmth, and cheer. **3** A year as including the winter season: used in reckoning the age of elderly persons: a man of ninety *winters.* —*v.i.* To pass the winter: We *wintered* in Bermuda. —*v.t.* To care for, feed, or protect during the winter: to *winter* animals or plants. —*adj.* **1** Pertaining to or taking place in winter; hibernal. **2** Suitable to or characteristic of winter. [OE] —**win′ter·er** *n.* —**win′terish** *adj.* — **win′ter·less** *adj.*

winter aconite A European tuberous-rooted, hardy, flowering garden herb *(Eranthis hyemalis)* of the crowfoot family, 5 to 8 inches high, with bright-yellow sessile flowers and oblong anthers.

win·ter·ber·ry (win′tər·ber′ē) *n. pl.* **·ries** Any of several North American shrubs (genus *Ilex*) of the holly family, bearing bright-red berrylike drupes about the size of a pea; especially, the smooth winterberry *(I. laevigata)* of the eastern United States.

win·ter·bourne (win′tər·bôrn′, -bōrn′, -bo͞orn′) *n.* A stream flowing only during excessive rain fall, as in winter, when water at the source rises above a certain level. [OE *winter burna* < *winter* + *burna* a stream]

win·ter-feed (win′tər·fēd′) *v.t.* **-fed, -feed·ing** To feed (stock) during the time when grazing is impossible.

win·ter·green (win′tər·grēn) *n.* **1** A small evergreen plant *(Gaultheria procumbens)* of eastern North America, bearing a cluster of aromatic oval leaves and white, bell-shaped flowers surrounded by red berries (often called *teaberries* or *checkerberries*). **2** Oil of wintergreen: a colorless, volatile oil extracted from the leaves of the true wintergreen, used as a flavor and in medicine: often called *Gaultheria oil.* **3** Any of various English low evergreen herbs (genus *Pyrola*). In the United States they are sometimes called *shinleaf* or **English** or **false wintergreen.** [On analogy with Du. *wintergroen;* so called because it is an evergreen]

winter itch Frost itch.

win·ter·ize (win′tə·rīz) *v.t.* **·ized, ·iz·ing** To prepare or equip for winter.

win·ter·kill (win′tər·kil′) *v.t.* & *v.i.* To die or kill by exposure to extreme cold: said of plants and grains. —**win′ter·kill′ing** *adj.* & *n.*

win·ter·ly (win′tər·lē) *adj.* Wintry; cheerless.

winter melon A hardy, cold-resistant muskmelon *(Cucumis melo,* variety *inodorus).*

winter squash Any of various varieties of squash having a tough rind that is resistant to spoilage.

Win·ter·thur (vin′tər·to͞or) A city of northern Switzerland NE of Zurich; a rail and industrial center.

win·ter·tide (win′tər·tīd′) *n. Poetic* Winter. Also **win′ter·time′** (-tīm′).

winter wheat Wheat planted before snowfall and harvested the following summer.

Win·throp (win′thrəp), **John,** 1588–1649, English Puritan; governor of Massachusetts Colony. —**John,** 1606–76, governor of Connecticut Colony; son of the preceding.

win·try (win′trē) *adj.* **·tri·er, ·tri·est** Belonging to winter; cold; frosty; brumal. Also **win′ter·y** (-tər·ē). —**win′tri·ly** *adv.* —**win′tri·ness** *n.*

win·y (wī′nē) *adj.* **win·i·er, win·i·est** Having the taste or qualities of wine.

winze[1] (winz) *n. Mining* A small inclined shaft from one level of a mine to another. [Earlier *winds,* ? < obs. *wind* a windlass, fusion of MDu. *winde* a windlass and WIND[2]]

winze[2] (winz) *n. Scot.* An oath.

wipe (wīp) *v.t.* **wiped, wip·ing 1** To subject to slight friction or rubbing, usually with some soft, absorbent material. **2** To remove by rubbing lightly; brush: usually with *away* or *off.* **3** To move, apply, or draw for the purpose of wiping: He *wiped* his hand across his brow. **4** To apply solder to with a piece of greased cloth or leather; solder with a wiper or pad: to *wipe* a joint. See synonyms under CLEANSE. —**to wipe out** To remove or destroy utterly; annihilate. —*n.* **1** The act of wiping or rubbing. **2** *Slang* A sweeping blow or stroke; a swipe. **3** *Mech.* A wiper or cam. **4** *Slang* A handkerchief. **5** *Slang* A jeer; jibe. [OE *wīpian.* Akin to WISP.]

wip·er (wī′pər) *n.* **1** One who wipes. **2** An article designed or used for wiping. **3** *Mech.* A cam having one or more slightly curved projections serving, when mounted on a rock shaft or rotating shaft, to give a reciprocating (usually vertical) motion to another part. **4** *Electr.* A moving member of an electrical device which makes contact with the terminals. **5** One who cleans locomotives in a roundhouse.

wire (wīr) *n.* **1** A slender rod, strand, or thread of ductile metal, usually formed by drawing through dies or holes. **2** Something made of wire, as a fence, a bar of a cage, or a snare made for catching small animals. **3** A telegraph cable. **4** The telegraph system as a means of communication. **5** A telegram. **6** The screen of a papermaking machine. **7** A fine metallic thread, a cobweb, or one of a set of ruled lines, in the focus of a telescope. **8** *Ornithol.* A long slender filament of the plumage of various birds. **9** *pl.* A secret means of exerting influence: to pull the *wires:* from the analogy with the system of hidden wires by which puppets are operated. **10** An imaginary line marking the finish of a racecourse. —**to lay wires for** To prepare for. —**under wire** Fenced. —*v.* **wired, wir·ing** *v.t.* **1** To fasten with wire. **2** To furnish or equip with wiring: The studio was *wired* for sound. **3** In croquet, to place (a ball) so that the wire of an arch will be between it and another ball. **4** To catch, as a rabbit, with a snare of wire. **5** *Colloq.* To transmit or send by electric telegraph: to *wire* an order. **6** *Colloq.* To send a telegram to: Will you *wire* John? **7** To place on wire, as beads. —*v.i.* **8** *Colloq.* To telegraph. [OE *wīr*]

wire cloth A fabric of woven wire, as for strainers, window screens, etc.

wire coat An outer coat, as of some dogs, of dense stiff hair.

wire-danc·er (wīr′dan′sər, -dän′-) *n.* One who performs feats of balancing, etc., upon a wire stretched in mid-air: also called *wirewalker.* — **wire′-danc′ing** *n.*

wire-draw (wīr′drô′) *v.t.* **-drew, -drawn, -draw·ing 1** To draw, as a metal rod, through a series of holes of diminishing diameter to produce a wire. **2** To treat (a subject) with excessive subtlety or overrefinement. —**wire′-draw′er** *n.* — **wire′-draw′ing** *n.*

wire gage 1 A gage for measuring the diameter of round wire, usually a round plate with slots on its periphery numbered according to an arbitrary standard, or a long graduated plate with a slot of diminishing width. **2** A standard system of sizes for wire. Also **wire gauge.**

wire gauze A material of a gauzelike structure made of interwoven strands of wire.

wire glass See under GLASS.

wire·grass (wīr′gras′, -gräs′) *n.* **1** A European grass *(Poa compressa)* having slender, compressed stems, cultivated in the United States and Canada: also called *Canada bluegrass.* **2** Any one of several similar grasses.

wire-haired griffon (wīr′hârd′) A griffon (def. 2).

wire·less (wīr′lis) *adj.* **1** Without wire or wires; having no wires. **2** *Brit.* Radio. —*n.* **1** The wireless telegraph or telephone system, or a message transmitted by either. **2** *Brit.* Radio. —*v.t.* & *v.i. Brit.* To communicate (with) by wireless telegraphy; radio.

wireless telegraphy or **telephony** Telegraphy or telephony without wires connecting the points of transmission and reception, the message being transmitted through space by electromagnetic waves; radio communication.

wire·man (wīr′mən) *n. pl.* **·men** (-mən) **1** A man who has to do with wire. **2** One who handles wire for telegraph lines, etc.; a wirer.

wire mark The faint impression left on paper by the wires of the mold during manufacture.

wire netting Netting made of wire, as window screens, fences, etc.

Wire·pho·to (wīr′fō′tō) *n. pl.* **·tos** An apparatus and method for transmitting and receiving photographs by wire: a trade name.

wire·pull·er (wīr′po͝ol′ər) *n.* One who pulls wires, as of a puppet; hence, one who uses secret means to control others or gain his own ends; an intriguer.

wire·pull·ing (wīr′po͝ol′ing) *n.* **1** The pulling of wires, as in a puppet show. **2** The use of secret influence to obtain an end.

wir·er (wīr′ər) *n.* **1** A trapper who snares with wire contrivances. **2** A wireman.

wire recorder A device for recording sounds on an uncoiling fine wire by magnetic registration of variations in the flow of electrical current from a microphone: these sounds are reproduced as the magnetized wire is passed back between the poles of the electromagnet.

wire rope A rope of wires firmly wound together.

wire·sonde (wīr′sond′) *n. Meteorol.* A type of radiosonde for use at low altitudes, the required data being transmitted by wire to ground stations. [< WIRE + (RADIO)SONDE]

wire-spun (wīr′spun′) *adj.* Wire-drawn; spun or drawn out too fine; overrefined.

wire·tap (wīr′tap′) *n.* **1** A device used to make a connection with a telephone or telegraph wire to listen to or record the message transmitted. **2** The act of wiretapping. —*v.t.* **·tapped, ·tap·ping 1** To connect a wiretap to. **2** To monitor by the use of a wiretap. —**wire′tap′per** *n.*

wire·walk·er (wīr′wô′kər) *n.* A wire-dancer.

wire wheel In automobiles, a wheel in which slender metal spokes, usually in a criss-cross pattern, connect the hub and rim.

wire·work (wīr′wûrk′) *n.* **1** Small articles made of wire cloth. **2** Wire fabrics in general. — **wire′work′er** *n.*

wire·works (wīr′wûrks′) *n. pl.* **·works 1** A factory where wire or articles of wire are made. **2** A shop where wire is woven and manufactured into protective screens, filters, or the like.

wire·worm (wīr′wûrm′) *n.* **1** The cylindrical brown to whitish larva of a click beetle, with a stiff, wiry texture: some species are common in fields, where they damage the roots of plants. For illustration see INSECTS (injurious). **2** A millipede.

wire-wove (wīr′wōv′) *adj.* **1** Denoting a high grade of paper with a smooth writing surface. **2** Woven of wire.

wir·ing (wīr′ing) *n.* An entire system of wire installed for the distribution of electric power, as for lighting, heating, radio, engine ignition, or the like.

wir·ra (wir′ə) *interj.* An exclamation of sorrow or despair. [Earlier O *wirra,* partial trans. of Irish *a Muire* O Mary]

wir·y (wir′ē) *adj.* **wir·i·er, wir·i·est 1** Having great resisting power; thin, but tough and sinewy: said of persons. **2** Like wire; stiff. —**wir′i·ly** *adv.* —**wir′i·ness** *n.*

wis (wis) *v.t. Obs.* To suppose; think. [<IWIS]

Wis·by (wiz′bē, *Ger.* viz′bē) The German name for VISBY.

Wis·con·sin (wis·kon′sən) A State of the Great Lakes region of the United States; 56,154 square miles; capital, Madison; entered the Union May 29, 1848; nickname, *Badger State*: abbr. WI —**Wis·con′sin·ite** (-īt) *n.*

Wisconsin River A river in central Wisconsin, flowing 430 miles south and SW to the Mississippi.

wis·dom (wiz′dəm) *n.* **1** The power of true and right discernment; conformity to the course of action dictated by such discernment. **2** Good practical judgment; common sense. **3** A high degree of knowledge; learning. **4** A wise saying. [OE *wīsdōm* < *wīs* wise]

Synonyms: attainment, depth, discernment, discretion, enlightenment, erudition, foresight, information, insight, judgment, judiciousness, knowledge, learning, lore, prescience, profoundity, prudence, reason, reasonableness, sagacity, sense, skill, understanding. *Enlightenment, erudition, information, knowledge, learning,* and *skill* are acquired, as by study or practice. *Insight, judgment, profundity* or *depth, reason, sagacity, sense,* and *understanding* are native qualities of mind, but are capable of increase by cultivation. *Wisdom* is mental power acting upon the materials that fullest *knowledge* gives in the most effective way. There may be what is termed "practical *wisdom*" that looks only to material results; but in its full sense *wisdom* implies the highest exercise of all the faculties. *Prudence* is a more negative form of the same virtue and largely with a view of avoiding loss and injury. *Judgment,* the power of forming decisions, is broader and more positive than *prudence,* leading one to do, as readily as to refrain from doing; but *judgment* is more limited in range and less exalted in character than *wisdom. Skill* is far inferior to *wisdom,* consisting largely in the practical application of acquired *knowledge,* power, and habitual processes, or in the ingenious contrivance that makes such application possible. In the making of something perfectly useless there may be great *skill,* but no *wisdom.* Compare KNOWLEDGE, PRUDENCE. *Antonyms*: absurdity, error, fatuity, folly, foolishness, idiocy, imbecility, imprudence, indiscretion, miscalculation, misjudgment, nonsense, shallowness, silliness, stupidity.

wisdom literature The didactic books of the Old Testament, comprising Proverbs and Ecclesiastes, and the book of Wisdom and Ecclesiasticus in the Apocrypha.

Wisdom of Jesus, the Son of Si·rach (sī′rak) Ecclesiasticus.

Wisdom of Solomon A book of the Old Testament Apocrypha, consisting of a hymn in praise of wisdom: ascribed by tradition to Solomon, but probably dating from the first or second century B.C.

wisdom tooth The last molar tooth on either side of the upper and lower jaws in man, appearing between the 17th and 22d year. —**to cut one's wisdom teeth** To acquire mature judgment by age and experience.

wise[1] (wīz) *adj.* **wis·er, wis·est 1** Possessed of wisdom; seeing clearly what is right and just; having sound judgment concerning one's highest interests, and in one's own conduct choosing the best end and the best means for reaching that end; in a lower sense, sagacious; also, shrewd or calculating. **2** Marked by wisdom; prudent; sensible. **3** Having great learning; erudite. **4** Suited to a man of wisdom; sage. **5** Having practical knowledge of the arts or sciences. **6** Versed in mysterious things. **7** *Colloq.* Aware of; onto: *wise* to his motives. —**to get wise** *Slang* To know the true facts. —*v.t. Slang* To make cognizant of; inform. —**to wise up** *Slang* To make or become aware, informed, or sophisticated. [OE *wīs*] —**wise′ly** *adv.* —**wise′ness** *n.*

Synonyms: deep, discerning, enlightened, erudite, intellectual, intelligent, judicious, knowing, profound, rational, reasonable, sagacious, sage, sapient, solid, sound, thoughtful. See EXPEDIENT, POLITIC, SAGACIOUS. *Antonyms*: see synonyms for ABSURD, IGNORANT.

wise[2] (wīz) *n.* Way of doing; manner; method: chiefly in phrases: **in any wise, in no wise,** etc. [OE *wīse* manner. Akin to GUISE.]

wise[3] (wīz) *v.t. & v.i. Dial. & Scot.* or *Obs.* To incline; turn. [OE *wīsian*]

-wise *suffix of adverbs & nouns* **1** In a (specified) way or manner: *no wise, likewise.* **2** In a (specified) direction or position: *lengthwise, clockwise*: often equivalent to *-ways.* **3** *Colloq.* With reference to: *Moneywise,* the job is worth considering. [OE *wīse* manner, fashion]

Wise (wīz), **Stephen Samuel,** 1872–1949, U.S. rabbi born in Hungary.

wise·a·cre (wīz′ā′kər) *n.* **1** One who affects great wisdom. **2** A wise man; sage. [< MDu. *wijsseggher* a soothsayer; infl. in form by ACRE]

wise·crack (wīz′krak′) *Slang n.* A smart or supercilious remark. —*v.i.* To utter a smart remark. —**wise′crack′er** *n.* —**wise′crack′ing** *adj. & n.*

wise·ling (wīz′ling) *n. Rare* One who pretends to or affects wisdom.

Wise·man (wīz′mən), **Nicholas Patrick Stephen,** 1802–65, English cardinal and author born in Spain.

wis·er·ite (wis′ər·īt) *n. Mineral.* A hydrous carbonate of manganese, yellowish-white to gray in color, found in Switzerland. [after D. F. *Wiser,* 19th c. Swiss mineralogist]

wise woman A woman skilled in magic; a soothsayer; sorceress; a witch, usually benevolent, who deals in charms against disease, misfortune, etc.

wish (wish) *n.* **1** A desire or longing, usually for some definite thing. **2** An expression of such a desire; petition. **3** Something wished for. **4** *Psychoanal.* An impulse, tendency, or striving toward the satisfaction of some need, especially when originating in or generated by the unconscious. See synonyms under WILL[1]. [< *v.*] —*v.t.* **1** To have a desire or longing for; crave; want: usually with a clause or infinitive as object: We *wish* to be sure. **2** To desire a specified condition or state for (a person or thing): I *wish* this day were over. **3** To invoke upon or for someone: I *wished* him good luck. **4** To bid: to *wish* someone good morning. **5** To request or entreat: I *wish* you would tell me what you are whispering about; also, to command. —*v.i.* **6** To have or feel a desire; yearn; long: usually with *for*: to *wish* for a friend's return. **7** To make or express a wish. —**to wish on** To impose (something or someone) on a person. [OE *wȳscan*]

wish·bone (wish′bōn′) *n.* The forked bone formed by the united clavicles of a carinate bird; the furcula: so called from the old belief that when pulled apart by two persons, each making a wish, the one who gets the longer part will have his wish fulfilled. See MERRYTHOUGHT.

wish·ful (wish′fəl) *adj.* Having a wish or desire; full of longing. —**wish′ful·ly** *adv.* —**wish′·ful·ness** *n.*

wish fulfilment 1 The satisfaction of a wish. **2** *Psychoanal.* The illusory realization of a strongly motivated, often unconscious and repressed aim by mental processes divorced from or not in accord with reality.

wish·ton·wish (wish′tən·wish) *n.* **1** The prairie dog. **2** The whippoorwill: incorrect use by James Fenimore Cooper. [<Caddoan; orig. prob. imit.]

wish-wash (wish′wosh′, -wôsh′) *n.* Any thin, weak, insipid drink; slops. [Varied reduplication of WASH]

wish·y-wash·y (wish′ē·wosh′ē, -wôsh′ē) *adj. Colloq.* **1** Thin; diluted, as liquor. **2** Lacking in solidity, consistence, or vigor; unsubstantial.

Wis·mar (vis′mär) A port on the Baltic in NW East Germany, in the former state of Mecklenburg.

wisp (wisp) *n.* **1** A small bunch, as of hay, straw, or hair. **2** A small bit; a mere indication: a *wisp* of vapor. **3** A whiskbroom. **4** A will-o'-the-wisp. —*v.t.* **1** To dress, brush, or groom with a wisp or whisk. **2** To fold and lightly twist into a wisp or wisplike form; rumple; crumple. [ME *wisp, wips.* Akin to WIPE.] —**wisp′y** *adj.*

wisp·ish (wis′pish) *adj.* Like or having the nature of a wisp.

wist (wist) Past tense and past participle of WIT[2].

wis·tar·i·a (wis·târ′ē·ə) *n.* **1** Any of a genus (*Wistaria*) of woody twining shrubs of the bean family, with pinnate leaves, elongated pods, and handsome clusters of blue, purple, or white flowers. The two best-known species are the **Chinese wistaria** (*W. sinensis*) and the later blossoming **Japanese wistaria** (*W. floribunda*). The common spelling **wis·te·ri·a** (wis·tir′ē·ə, -târ′-) was the one originally given by the botanist Nuttall. **2** A shade of dull, purplish blue. [after Caspar *Wistar,* 1761–1818, U.S. anatomist]

WISTARIA

Wis·ter (wis′tər), **Owen,** 1860–1938, U.S. novelist.

wist·ful (wist′fəl) *adj.* **1** Wishful; longing. **2** Musing; pensive. [Appar. <obs. *wistly* intently; infl. in form by *wishful*] —**wist′ful·ly** *adv.* —**wist′ful·ness** *n.*

wist·less (wist′lis) *adj. Obs.* Inattentive; unobservant.

wit[1] (wit) *n.* **1** The power of knowing or perceiving; intelligence; ingenuity; sagacity; keen or good sense. **2** The power or faculty of rapid and accurate observation; the power of comprehending and judging. **3** *pl.* The mental faculties, as of perception and understanding: to use one's *wits*; also, the mental faculties with regard to their state of balance: out of her *wits.* **4** The ready perception and happy expression of unexpected or amusing analogies or other relations between apparently incongruous ideas; sudden and ingenious association of ideas or words causing delight and surprise; loosely, any form of humor which expresses irony or satire by a happy association of words. **5** One who has a keen perception of the incongruous or ludicrous and makes skilful use of it in writing or speaking; also, a clever conversationalist; one gifted in repartee or clever sayings. **6** Significance; meaning; import. **7** *Obs.* Mental activity. —**at one's wits' end** At the limit of one's devices and resources; not knowing what to do. —**to live by one's wits** To make a living by using one's practical intelligence and resourcefulness, often in unscrupulous or fraudulent ways. [OE]

Synonyms: banter, drollery, facetiousness, fun, humor, jest, jocularity, joke, playfulness, pleasantry, raillery, waggery, waggishness. *Wit* is the quick perception of unusual or commonly unperceived analogies or relations between things apparently unrelated; it depends on the production of a diverting, entertaining, or merrymaking surprise. The analogies with which *wit* plays are often superficial or artificial; *humor* deals with real analogies of an amusing or entertaining kind, or with traits of character that are seen to have a comical side. *Wit* is keen, sudden, brief, and sometimes severe; *humor* is deep, thoughtful, sustained, and kindly. *Pleasantry* is lighter and less vivid than *wit. Fun* denotes the merry results produced by any fortuitous occasion of mirth, and is pronounced and often hilarious. *Antonyms*: gravity, seriousness, sobriety, solemnity, stolidity.

wit[2] (wit) *v.t. & v.i.* Present indicative: **I wot,** thou **wost,** he **wot,** *pl.* **wite(n)**; *pt.* and *pp.* **wist**; *ppr.* **wit·ting** *Archaic* To be or become aware (of); learn; know. —**to wit** That is to say; namely; scilicet: used, especially in legal documents, to introduce a detailed statement or an explanation. [OE *witan* know]

wit·an (wit′ən) *n. pl.* **1** Members of the national council in Saxon England. **2** The council itself. [OE, councilors, pl. of *wita* a wise man, witness]

witch[1] (wich) *n.* **1** A person who practices

sorcery; a sorcerer or sorceress; one having supernatural powers in the natural world, especially to work evil, and usually by association with evil spirits or the devil: formerly applied to men, women, and children, now generally restricted to women. **2** An ugly, malignant old woman; a hag. **3** A bewitching or fascinating woman or girl. — *v.t.* **1** To overcome by witchcraft; work an evil spell upon. **2** To effect by witchcraft or sorcery. **3** To fascinate or bewitch; enchant. [OE *wicce* a witch, fem. of *wicca* a wizard < *wiccian* bewitch]

witch² (wich) *n.* The wych-elm: also spelled *wich, wych.* [OE *wice* < *wican* bend]

witch alder A shrub *(Fothergilla gardeni)* resembling the witch hazel in its fruit and the alder in its leaves. It is found along shady swamps from Virginia to Florida. [< WITCH² + ALDER]

witch broom Leaf curl. [< WITCH¹ + BROOM]

witch·craft (wich′kraft′, -kräft′) *n.* **1** The practices or powers of witches or wizards, especially when regarded as due to dealings with evil spirits or the devil; black magic; sorcery; also, an instance of such practices. **2** Extraordinary influence or fascination; witchery. See synonyms under SORCERY.

witch doctor **1** Among certain primitive peoples of Africa, especially the Kaffirs, a medicine man skilled in detecting witches and counteracting evil spells; hence, any medicine man or magician. **2** One who professes to heal or cure by sorcery; a hex.

witch·dom (wich′dəm) *n.* *Rare* Witchcraft.

witch–elm (wich′elm′) *n.* The wych-elm. [< WITCH² + ELM]

witch·er·y (wich′ər·ē) *n. pl.* **·er·ies** **1** Witchcraft. **2** Power to charm; fascination.

witch·es′–broom (wich′iz·bro͞om′, -bro͝om′) *n.* A compact broomlike growth of portions of various trees and shrubs, characterized by excessive multiplication of branches, and due in some cases to the presence of parasitic fungi: also called *hexenbesen.* Also **witch′·broom′.**

witches′ Sabbath In medieval folklore, a midnight orgy of demons and witches, which in German folklore is believed to occur on May Day eve or Walpurgis Night: also called *sabbat.*

witch·et·ty (wich′it·ē) *n.* The grub of a longicorn beetle, living in the roots of shrubs, in decayed timber, or in the earth, which is roasted and eaten by Australian aborigines. [< Australian]

witch–find·er (wich′fīn′dər) *n.* Formerly, one employed to seek and obtain information against witches.

witch·grass (wich′gras′, -gräs′) *n.* **1** The panic grass, common in sandy soils and cultivated fields, with a very loose, pyramidal, compound hairy panicle. **2** The couchgrass. [Alter. of QUITCHGRASS]

witch hazel **1** A shrub *(Hamamelis virginiana)* of the United States and Canada, with several branching crooked trunks and small yellow flowers. **2** An ointment and fluid extract used as a remedy for bruises, sprains, etc., derived from the bark and dried leaves of this shrub. **3** The wych-elm. Also *wych-hazel.* [< WITCH² + HAZEL]

witch hunt An investigation of persons ostensibly to uncover subversive activities, but intended for ulterior motives, such as harassing political opposition.

witch·ing (wich′ing) *adj.* Having power to enchant; weird; fascinating. — *n.* Witchcraft; sorcery. — **witch′ing·ly** *adv.*

witch·mon·ger (wich′mung′gər, -mong′-) *n.* One who deals with witches or believes in witchcraft.

witch moth Any of several moths (family *Noctuidae*) of nocturnal habits and typically somber appearance; especially, the large black witch moth *(Erebus odora)* of South and North America.

witch of A·gne·si (ä·nyā′zē) *Math.* The plane curve of the equation $x^2y = 4a^2(2a-y)$: it is symmetric with respect to the y-axis and asymptotic to the x-axis. Also called the *versiera.* [after Donna Maria Gaetani *Agnesi,* 1718–1799, Italian mathematician]

wite (wīt) *n. Scot. & Brit. Dial.* **1** A penalty; fine. **2** A reproach; blame. **3** A guilty action; fault. [OE *wīte*]

wit·e·na·ge·mot (wit′ə·nə·gə·mōt′) *n.* The assembly of the witan. [OE *witena gemōt* councilors' assembly]

with (with, with) *prep.* **1** In the company of; as a member or associate of. **2** Next to; beside: Walk *with* me. **3** Having; bearing: a hat *with* a feather. **4** Characterized or marked by; characteristically possessed of: the house *with* green shutters; a man *with* brains. **5** In a manner characterized by; exhibiting: to dance *with* grace. **6** Among: counted *with* the others. **7** During; in the course of: We forget *with* time. **8** From; so as to be separated from: to part *with* the past; to dispense *with* luxury. **9** Against: to struggle *with* an adversary. **10** In the opinion of: That is all right *with* me. **11** Because of; as a consequence of: faint *with* hunger. **12** In charge of; in possession of: Leave the key *with* the janitor; I have my fiddle *with* me. **13** Using; by means or aid of: to write *with* a pencil. **14** By adding or having as a material or quality: trimmed *with* lace; endowed *with* beauty. **15** Under the influence of: confused *with* drink. **16** In spite of: *With* all his money, he could not buy health. **17** At the same time as: to go to bed *with* the chickens. **18** In the same direction as: to drift *with* the crowd. **19** In regard to; in the case of: Be gentle *with* the horse; I am angry *with* them. **20** Onto; to: Join this tube *with* that one. **21** In proportion to: His fame grew *with* his achievements. **22** In support of: He voted *with* the Left. **23** Of the same opinion as: I'm *with* you there! **24** Compared to; contrasted to: Consider this picture *with* that one. **25** Immediately after; following: *With* that, he slammed the door. **26** Having received or been granted: *With* your consent I'll go now. [OE]

with– *prefix* **1** Against: *withstand.* **2** Back; away: *withhold.* [OE *with-* < *with* against]

with·al (with·ôl′, with-) *Archaic adv.* With the rest; in addition. — *prep.* With: intensive form used after its object and at the end of the clause: a bow to shoot *withal.* [ME *with alle* < *with* + *alle* all]

with·draw (with·drô′, with-) *v.* **·drew, ·drawn, ·draw·ing** *v.t.* **1** To draw or take away; remove. **2** To take back, as an assertion or a promise; recall. **3** To keep or abstract from use. — *v.i.* **4** To draw back; retire. See synonyms under ABSTRACT, SEPARATE. [< WITH- + DRAW] — **with·draw′al, with·draw′ment** *n.*

with·draw·ing (with·drô′ing, with-) *adj.* Stretching back or away; receding.

withdrawing room **1** A room behind another room for retirement. **2** A drawing room.

withe (with, with, wīth) *n.* **1** A willowy, supple twig. **2** A band made of twisted flexible shoots, straw, or the like. **3** An elastic handle for a tool. — *v.t.* **withed, with·ing** To bind with withes. [OE *withthe*]

with·er (with′ər) *v.i.* **1** To become limp or dry, as a plant when cut down or deprived of moisture. **2** To waste, as flesh. **3** To droop or languish. — *v.t.* **4** To cause to become limp or dry. **5** To abash, as by a scornful glance. [Appar. var. of WEATHER, *v.*]

Synonyms: blast, blight, collapse, droop, shrink, shrivel. See DIE¹. *Antonyms*: bloom, develop, expand, flourish, freshen, grow, luxuriate, swell.

With·er (with′ər), **George,** 1588–1667, English poet. Also **With′ers.**

with·er·ite (with′ə·rīt) *n.* A white, translucent barium carbonate, $BaCO_3$, occurring massive or in orthorhombic crystals. [after Dr. Wm. *Withering,* 1741–99, English physician, who first described and analyzed it]

withe rod A shrub *(Viburnum cassinoides)* of the honeysuckle family, growing in swamps from Newfoundland to New Jersey and Minnesota.

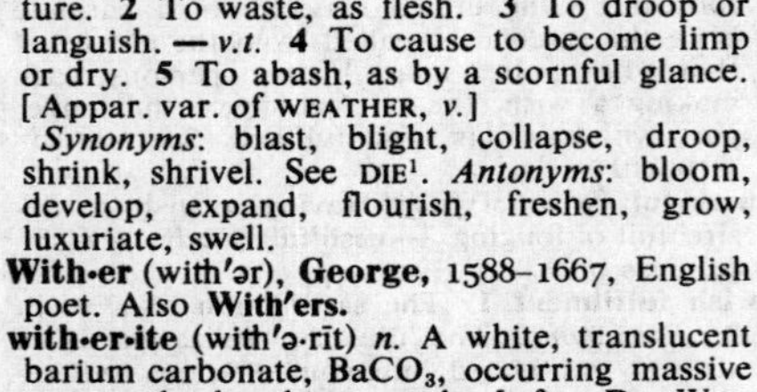

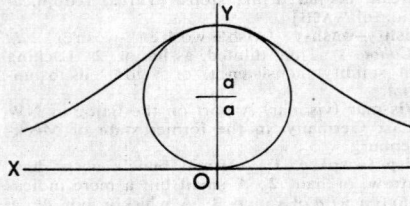

WITCH OF AGNESI

with·ers (with′ərz) *n. pl.* **1** The highest part of the back of the horse between the shoulder blades. **2** The similar part in some other animals, as the deer and ox. [OE *withre* resistance < *wither* against; so called because the horse opposes this part against the load he pulls]

with·er·shins (with′ər·shinz) *adv. Scot.* In the opposite direction; in a reversed way. Also spelled *widdershins, widershins.*

With·er·spoon (with′ər·spo͞on), **John,** 1722–94, American educator born in Scotland; signed Declaration of Independence.

with·hold (with·hōld′, with-) *v.* **·held, ·hold·ing** *v.t.* **1** To hold back; restrain. **2** To keep back; decline to grant. — *v.i.* **3** To refrain; forbear. See synonyms under KEEP, RETAIN, SUSPEND. [< WITH- + HOLD] — **with·hold′er** *n.*

withholding tax That part of an employee's wages or salary which is deducted as an instalment on his income tax.

with·in (with·in′, with-) *adv.* **1** In the inner part; interiorly. **2** Inside the body, heart, or mind. **3** Indoors. — *prep.* **1** In the inner or interior part or parts of; inside: *within* the house. **2** In the limits, range, or compass of (a specified time, space, or distance): *within* a mile of here; *within* ten minutes' walk. **3** Not exceeding (a specified quantity): Live *within* your means. **4** In the reach, limit, or scope of: *within* my power. See synonyms under AT. [OE *withinnan* < *with* with + *innan* in]

with·in·doors (with·in′dôrz′, -dōrz′, with-) *adv.* Inside a building.

with–it (with′it) *adj. Slang* **1** In touch with modern habits, fashions, trends, etc.; up-to-date; hip. **2** Lively and modern; swinging. Also **with it.**

with·out (with·out′, with-) *prep.* **1** Not having, as the result of loss, privation, negation, etc.; lacking: *without* money; *without* a home. **2** In the absence of: We must manage *without* help. **3** Free from: *without* fear. **4** At, on, or to the outside of. **5** Outside of or beyond the limits of: living *without* the pale of civilization. **6** With avoidance of: He listened *without* paying attention. **7** *Obs.* Besides. — *adv.* **1** In or on the outer part; externally. **2** Out of doors. — *conj. Dial.* Unless; except. [OE *withūtan* < *with* with + *ūtan* out]

without day Sine die.

with·out·doors (with·out′dôrz′, -dōrz′, with-) *adv.* Out of doors; outside.

with·stand (with·stand′, with-) *v.* **·stood, ·stand·ing** *v.t.* To oppose with any force; resist successfully. — *v.i.* To make resistance; endure. See synonyms under OPPOSE. [OE *withstandan* < *with-* against + *standan* stand] — **with·stand′er** *n.*

with·y (with′ē, with′ē) *adj.* Made of withes; flexible and tough. — *n. pl.* **with·ies** **1** A rope made of withes. **2** A withe. [< WITHE]

wit·less (wit′lis) *adj.* Lacking in wit; foolish. — **wit′less·ly** *adv.* — **wit′less·ness** *n.*

wit·ling (wit′ling) *n.* A person who has little wit or understanding. [< WIT¹ + -LING¹]

wit·ness (wit′nis) *n.* **1** An act or fact of attestation to a fact or an event; testimony; evidence. **2** A person who has seen or knows something, and is therefore competent to give evidence concerning it; a spectator. **3** That which serves as or furnishes evidence or proof. **4** *Law* One who has knowledge of facts relating to a given cause and is subpoenaed to testify; also, a person who has signed his name to an instrument executed by another in order that he may testify to the genuineness of the maker's signature. See synonyms under SPECTATOR, TESTIMONY. — *v.t.* **1** To see or know by personal experience. **2** To furnish or serve as evidence of. **3** To give testimony to. **4** To be the site or scene of: This spot has *witnessed* many heinous crimes. **5** *Law* To see the execution of (an instrument) and subscribe to it for the purpose of establishing its authenticity. — *v.i.* **6** To give evidence; testify. See synonyms under AVOW. [OE *witnes* knowledge, testimony] — **wit′ness·er** *n.*

witness stand The platform in a courtroom from which a witness gives evidence.

wit·ney (wit′nē) *n.* A heavy woolen fabric, preshrunk and napped, used for blankets and coats. [from *Witney,* England, where it was first manufactured]

Wit·te (vit′ə), **Count Sergei Yulievitch,** 1849–1915, Russian statesman, diplomat, and financier.

wit·ted (wit'id) *adj.* Having wit: used principally in compounds with the meaning having (a specified kind of) wit: quick-*witted*, half-*witted*.

Wit·te·kind (vit'ə·kint), died in battle 807?, leader of the Saxons against Charlemagne. Also spelled *Widukind*.

Wit·ten (vit'n) A city on the Ruhr in North Rhine–Westphalia, Germany.

Wit·ten·berg (wit'n·bûrg, *Ger.* vit'n·berkh) A city on the Elbe river in central East Germany, in the former state of Saxony-Anhalt; the Protestant Reformation originated here, 1517.

Witt·gen·stein (vit'gən·shtīn), **Ludwig**, 1889–1951, Austrian philosopher active in England.

Witt·gen·stein Island (vit'gən·shtīn) A former name for FAKARAVA.

wit·ti·cism (wit'ə·siz'əm) *n.* A witty saying. [<WITTY, on analogy with *criticism*; coined by Dryden]

wit·ting[1] (wit'ing) *adj.* Aware; done consciously, with knowledge and responsibility. [<WIT[2]]

wit·ting[2] (wit'ing) *n. Obs.* Knowledge; information. [<ON *vitand* consciousness < *vita* know]

wit·ting·ly (wit'ing·lē) *adv.* With knowledge and by design; knowingly and designedly.

wit·tol (wit'l) *n. Obs.* A contented cuckold; a husband who is aware of, but indifferent to, his wife's infidelity. [ME *wetewold* < *wete* know + (*coke*)*wold* cuckold]

wit·ty (wit'ē) *adj.* **·ti·er**, **·ti·est** **1** Given to making original or clever speeches; quick at repartee; humorous. **2** Displaying or full of wit. See synonyms under HUMOROUS. [OE *wittig* wise] — **wit'ti·ly** *adv.* — **wit'ti·ness** *n.*

Wit·wa·ters·rand (wit·wä'tərs·ränt, -rand) A region of southern Transvaal on a rocky ridge near Johannesburg; 1,000 square miles; site of the world's richest gold fields: also *The Rand*.

witz·chour·a (wits·chŏŏr'ə) *n.* A mantle with large sleeves and a wide collar, worn in the early 19th century. [<F *vitchoura* <Polish *wilczura* a wolf-skin coat < *wilk* a wolf]

wive (wīv) *v.* **wived, wiv·ing** *v.t.* **1** To furnish with a wife. **2** To marry. — *v.i.* **3** To marry a woman. [OE *wīfian* < *wīf* a wife, woman]

wi·vern (wī'vərn) *n. Her.* A two-legged, winged dragon, with barbed and knotted tail: often spelled *wyvern*. Also **wi'ver**. [<AF *wivre*, OF *guivre* a dragon, serpent, var. of *vivre* <L *vipera*]

wives (wīvz) Plural of WIFE.

wiz (wiz) *n. Slang* A wizard (def. 2). [Short for WIZARD]

wiz·ard (wiz'ərd) *n.* **1** One supposed to be in league with the devil; a male witch; sorcerer. **2** *Colloq.* A very skilful or clever person: He's a *wizard* with machinery. **3** *Obs.* A wise man; sage. — *adj.* **1** Having magical powers. **2** Fascinating; enchanting. [ME *wysard* < *wys*, OE *wīs* wise]

wiz·ard·ry (wiz'ərd·rē) *n.* The practice or methods of a wizard.

wiz·en[1] (wiz'ən) *v.t.* & *v.i.* To become or cause to become withered; shrivel. — *adj.* Wizened; shrunken; shriveled. [OE *wisnian* dry up, wither]

wiz·en[2] (wiz'ən) *n. Dial.* or *Obs.* The weasand. Also **wiz'zen.**

wiz·ened (wiz'ənd) *adj.* Shrunken; withered; dried up.

Wło·cła·wek (vwô·tswä'vek) A city on the Vistula in central Poland; a manufacturing center. *Russian* **Vlo·tslavsk** (vlo·tsläfsk').

woad (wōd) *n.* **1** An Old World herb (*Isatis tinctoria*) of the mustard family; dyer's-weed. **2** The blue dyestuff obtained from its leaves. [OE *wād*] — **woad'ed** *adj.*

woad·wax·en (wōd'wak'sən) *n.* Dyer's-broom: also spelled *woodwaxen*.

woald (wōld) See WELD[2].

wob·ble (wob'əl) *v.* **·bled, ·bling** *v.i.* **1** To move or sway unsteadily, as a top while rotating at a low speed. **2** To show indecision or unsteadiness; waver; vacillate. — *v.t.* **3** To cause to wobble. — *n.* An unsteady motion, as that of unevenly balanced rotating bodies. Also spelled *wabble*. [? <LG *wabbeln*] —

wob'bler *n.* — **wob'bling** *adj.* — **wob'bling·ly** *adv.* — **wob'bly** *adj.*

wobble pump A hand pump.

wob·bly (wob'lē) *n. pl.* **·blies** *U.S. Slang* A member of the Industrial Workers of the World (I.W.W.). [Appar. mispronunciation of *w* in I.W.W.]

Wode·house (wŏŏd'hous, wōd'-), **Sir P(elham) G(renville)**, 1881–1975, English humorous novelist.

Wo·den (wōd'n) The Old English name for Odin, the chief Norse god. Wednesday is named for Woden. Also **Wo'dan.**

woe (wō) *n.* **1** Overwhelming sorrow; grief. **2** Heavy affliction or calamity; disaster: His *woes* are many. — *interj.* Alas! used to proclaim disaster or to express sorrow, to denounce, or invoke censure. Also **wo.** [OE *wa* misery]

woe·be·gone (wō'bi·gôn', -gon') *adj.* Overcome with woe; mournful; sorrowful. Also **wo'be·gone'.** See synonyms under SAD.

woe·ful (wō'fəl) *adj.* **1** Accompanied by or causing woe; direful. **2** Expressive of sorrow; doleful. **3** Deserving condemnation; paltry; miserable; mean. Also **woe'some, wo'ful.** See synonyms under PITIFUL, SAD. — **woe'ful·ly** *adv.* — **woe'ful·ness** *n.*

Wo·ë·vre (vō·e'vr') A tableland in NE France, near Verdun; scene of severe fighting in World War I, 1915 and 1918.

Wof·fing·ton (wof'ing·tən), **Margaret**, 1714?–1760; English actress born in Dublin: commonly called "Peg Woffington."

Wöh·ler (vœ'lər), **Friedrich**, 1800–82, German chemist.

wok (wok) *n.* A Chinese cooking pan, as of iron, aluminum, or copper, with handles and a rounded bottom, usually equipped with a separate metal ring to prevent tipping. [< Chinese]

wo·kas (wō'kəs) *n.* A yellow waterlily (*Nuphar polysepalum*) of western North America, having small seeds formerly roasted and eaten by the Klamath Indians. [<Klamath]

woke (wōk) Past tense of WAKE[1].

wok·en (wō'kən) Dialectal past participle of WAKE[1].

Wol·cott (wŏŏl'kət), **Oliver**, 1726–97, American statesman; signed Declaration of Independence.

wold (wōld) *n.* An undulating tract of open upland; down or moor. [OE *wald* a forest]

Wolds (wōldz), **the** A range of hills in Lincolnshire and Yorkshire, England, parallel to the coast, north and south of the Humber; highest point, 800 feet.

wolf (wŏŏlf) *n. pl.* **wolves** (wŏŏlvz) **1** Any of a genus (*Canis*) of large carnivorous mammals related to the dog, especially the common European species (*C. lupus*) or the timber wolf of North America. ◆ Collateral adjective: *lupine*. **2** Any ravenous, cruel, or rapacious person or thing; hence, popularly, a philanderer. **3** *Entomol.* The destructive larva of various beetles and moths. **4** The harsh, dissonant sound of certain chords on a keyed instrument, as an organ or piano, when tuned by a system of unequal temperament; in bowed instruments, a harsh, discordant sound caused by defective vibration of one or more notes of a scale. — **to cry wolf** To give a false alarm. — **to keep the wolf from the door** To avert want or starvation. — *v.t.* To devour ravenously; gulp down: He *wolfed* his food. [OE *wulf*]

Wolf (wŏŏlf) The constellation Lupus.

Wolf (vôlf), **Friedrich August**, 1759–1824, German classical scholar. — **Hugo**, 1860–1903, Austrian composer.

wolf·ber·ry (wŏŏlf'ber'ē) *n. pl.* **·ries** A shrub (*Symphoricarpos occidentalis*) of the honeysuckle family, with pinkish, bell-shaped flowers and white berries in spikes, growing in the western United States.

Wolf Cub A member of the division of Boy Scouts for boys between 8 and 11 years of age.

wolf dog **1** A large dog for hunting wolves. **2** A cross between a wolf and a dog.

Wolfe (wŏŏlf), **Charles**, 1791–1823, Irish poet. — **James**, 1727–59, English general; defeated the French under Montcalm at Quebec; both he and Montcalm were killed. — **Thomas Clayton**, 1900–38, U.S. novelist.

Wolff (vôlf), **Christian von**, 1679–1754, German philosopher. — **Kaspar Friedrich**, 1733–1794, German anatomist.

Wolf–Fer·ra·ri (vôlf'fer·rä'rē), **Ermanno**, 1876–1948, Italian composer.

Wolff·i·an (wŏŏl'fē·ən) *adj.* Pertaining to or named after the German anatomist Kaspar F. Wolff.

Wolffian body *Anat.* The mesonephros.

wolf fish A large fish (*Anarhichas lupus*) of the North Atlantic, with powerful teeth adapted for crushing shellfish.

Wolf·gang (vôlf'gäng) *German* A masculine personal name. [<G, a wolf's progress]

wolf·hound (wŏŏlf'hound') *n.* Either of two breeds of large dogs, the **Russian wolfhound** or *borzoi* and the **Irish wolfhound**, a dog resembling the Great Dane, trained, or originally intended, to catch and kill wolves.

wolf·ish (wŏŏl'fish) *adj.* **1** Having the qualities of a wolf; rapacious; savage. **2** *Colloq.* Ravenously hungry. — **wolf'ish·ly** *adv.* — **wolf'ish·ness** *n.*

wolf pack A number of submarines which cooperate in making concerted attacks on enemy ships or convoys.

wolf·ram (wŏŏl'frəm) *n.* **1** Wolframite. **2** Tungsten. [<G, prob. < *wolf* a wolf + *rahm* cream, soot]

wolf·ram·ite (wŏŏl'frəm·īt) *n.* A submetallic, grayish-black or brown tungstate of iron and manganese, crystallizing in the monoclinic system. It is important commercially as a source of tungsten and its compounds. [<G *wolframit* < *wolfram* tungsten]

Wol·fram von Esch·en·bach (vôl'främ fôn esh'ən-bäkh), 1165?–1220?, German poet.

wolf's–bane (wŏŏlfs'bān') *n.* **1** A species of aconite; monkshood. **2** A species of European arnica (*Arnica montana*), used as a lotion for bruises. **3** The silk vine. [Trans. of NL *lycoctonum* <Gk. *lykoktonon*, lit., a wolf-slayer < *lykos* a wolf + *kteinein* kill]

Wol·las·ton (wŏŏl'əs·tən), **William Hyde**, 1766–1828, English chemist and physicist.

wol·las·ton·ite (wŏŏl'əs·tən·īt') *n.* A vitreous, white, translucent calcium silicate, crystallizing in the monoclinic system. [after Dr. W. H. *Wollaston*]

Wolse·ley (wŏŏlz'lē), **Garnet Joseph**, 1833–1913, first Viscount Wolseley, British general.

Wol·sey (wŏŏl'zē), **Thomas**, 1475?–1530, English cardinal and statesman.

wolv·er (wŏŏl'vər) *n.* One who hunts wolves.

Wol·ver·hamp·ton (wŏŏl'vər·hamp'tən) A county borough and industrial center in southern Stafford, England.

wol·ver·ine (wŏŏl'və·rēn') *n.* A rapacious and cunning carnivore (genus *Gulo*) of northern forests, with stout body and limbs and bushy tail. Also **wol'ver·ene'.** [Dim. of WOLF]

WOLVERINE (Body to 3 feet long; tail, 1 1/2 feet)

Wolverine State Nickname of MICHIGAN.

wolves (wŏŏlvz) Plural of WOLF.

wom·an (wŏŏm'ən) *n. pl.* **wom·en** (wim'in) **1** An adult human female. **2** The female part of the human race; women collectively. **3** Womanly character; femininity: usually with *the*. **4** As applied to a man, one who is effeminate, timid, or weak. **5** A female attendant or servant. **6** A paramour or kept mistress. **7** *Colloq.* A wife. — *adj.* **1** Feminine; characteristic of women. **2** Female: when used with a plural noun, usually *women*: *women* students. **3** Affecting or pertaining to women. — *v.t. Obs.* To play the part of a woman in or in reference to. [OE *wifmann* < *wif* a wife + *mann* a human being]

wom·an·hood (wŏŏm'ən·hŏŏd) *n.* **1** The state of a woman or of womankind. **2** Women collectively.

wom·an·ish (wŏŏm'ən·ish) *adj.* Characteristic of a woman; effeminate. See synonyms under FEMININE. — **wom'an·ish·ly** *adv.* — **wom'an·ish·ness** *n.*

wom·an·ize (wŏŏm'ən·īz) *v.* **·ized, ·iz·ing** *v.t.*

To make effeminate or womanish. —*v.i. Colloq.* To consort with women illicitly.

wom·an·kind (woõm′ən·kīnd′) *n.* Women collectively.

wom·an·ly (woõm′ən·lē) *adj.* Having the qualities natural, suited, or becoming to a woman; feminine. —*adv.* In a feminine manner; like a woman. —**wom′an·li·ness** *n.*

woman suffrage See under SUFFRAGE. — **wom′an·suf′fra·gist** *n.*

womb (woõm) *n.* **1** The organ in which the young of higher mammals are developed; the uterus. **2** The place where anything is engendered or brought into life. **3** A cavity viewed as enclosing something. **4** *Obs.* The belly or stomach. [OE *wamb, womb* the belly]

wom·bat (wom′bat) *n.* An Australian nocturnal marsupial (family *Vombatidae*) resembling a small bear. [< Australian]

wombed (woõmd) *adj.* Having a womb; hence, hollow; capacious; cavernous. Also **womb′y.**

wom·en (wim′in) Plural of WOMAN.

wom·en·folk (wim′in·fōk′) *n. pl.* Women collectively. Also **wom′en·folks′.**

Women in the Air Force A corps of women in the U.S. Air Force, including all women except nurses and medical specialists. Abbr. *WAF* or *W.A.F.*

Women's Army Corps A corps of women in the U.S. Army, composed of all women except nurses and medical specialists. Abbr. *WAC* or *W.A.C.*

women's rights The rights of women to enjoy equal legal rights and privileges with men, as of suffrage, property, and education.

wom·er·a (wom′ər·ə) *n.* A stick used by Australian aborigines for throwing javelins, spears, etc.: also **woomera.** [< Australian]

won (wun) Past tense and past participle of WIN.

won·der (wun′dər) *n.* **1** A feeling of mingled surprise and curiosity; astonishment. **2** That which causes wonder; a prodigy; a strange thing; a miracle. See synonyms under PRODIGY. —**nine days' wonder** Something that excites public wonder for a short time. —*v.t.* **1** To have a feeling of doubt and strong curiosity in regard to. —*v.i.* **2** To be affected or filled with wonder; marvel. **3** To be doubtful; query mentally. —*adj.* Spectacularly successful: a *wonder* drug. [OE *wundor*] — **won′der·er** *n.* —**won′der·ing** *adj.* **won′der·ing·ly** *adv.*

won·der·ful (wun′dər·fəl) *adj.* Of a nature to excite wonder; marvelous. —**won′der·ful·ly** *adv.* — **won′der·ful·ness** *n.*

won·der·land (wun′dər·land′) *n.* A realm of fairy romance or wonders.

won·der·ment (wun′dər·mənt) *n.* **1** The emotion of wonder; surprise. **2** Something wonderful; a marvel.

Wonder State Nickname for ARKANSAS.

won·der·strick·en (wun′dər·strik′ən) *adj.* Suddenly smitten with wonder or admiration. Also **won′der·struck′** (-struk′).

won·der·work (wun′dər·wûrk′) *n.* A work inspiring wonder; miracle. —**won′der·work′er** *n.* **won′der·work′ing** *adj.*

won·drous (wun′drəs) *adj.* Commanding wonder; wonderful; marvelous. —*adv.* Surprisingly. [Alter. of ME *wonders,* genitive of WONDER] — **won′drous·ly** *adv.* —**won′drous·ness** *n.*

won·ky (wong′kē) *adj. Brit. Slang* Unsteady; liable to break down; shaky; feeble. [Prob. OE *wancol* shaky]

Won·san (wœn·sän) A port in eastern Korea: Japanese *Gensan.*

wont (wunt, wōnt) *v.* **wont, wont** or **wont·ed, wont·ing** *v.t.* **1** To accustom or habituate: used reflexively. —*v.i.* **2** To be accustomed; be used. **3** *Obs.* To dwell. [< *adj.*] —*adj.* Doing habitually; accustomed; used. —*n.* Ordinary manner of doing or acting; habit. See synonyms under

HABIT. [OE *gewunod,* pp. of *gewunian* be accustomed]

won't (wōnt) Will not: a contraction of Middle English *woll not.* Also *Scot.* **won·na** (wun′nə).

wont·ed (wun′tid, wōn′-) *adj.* **1** Commonly used or done; habitual. **2** Habituated; accustomed; at ease; at home. See synonyms under HABITUAL, USUAL. —**wont′ed·ness** *n.*

woo¹ (woõ) *v.t.* **1** To make love to, especially so as to marry; court. **2** To entreat earnestly; beg. **3** To invite; solicit; seek. —*v.i.* **4** To pay court; make love. See synonyms under ADDRESS. [OE *wōgian*]

woo² (woõ) *n. Scot.* Wool.

wood¹ (woõd) *n.* **1** A large and compact collection of trees; a forest; grove: also **woods. 2** The tough, fibrous material, composed mainly of cellulose and lignin, which forms the xylem of trees and shrubs and constitutes the bulk of their stems and branches under the bark. **3** The hard substance of a tree or shrub, whether as growing or as cut for use, for building, fuel, etc.; lumber; timber. **4** Something made of wood. **5** *pl.* A rural district; backwoods. —**to knock wood** To tap on a piece of wood or a wooden object as a charm against bad luck, especially while making an optimistic statement. —*adj.* **1** Made of wood; wooden. **2** Made for using or holding wood: a *wood* stove. **3** Living or growing in woods: the *wood* anemone. —*v.t.* **1** To furnish with wood for fuel. **2** To convert into a forest; plant with trees. —*v.i.* **3** To take on a supply of wood. [OE *widu, wiodu*]

wood² (woõd) *Obs. v.i.* To act like a maniac; rave. —*adj.* Furious; frantic; raging; mad. [OE *wōd* insane]

Wood (woõd), **Grant,** 1892–1942, U.S. painter. —**Leonard,** 1860–1927, U.S. physician, army officer, and colonial administrator.

wood alcohol Methanol, especially if produced by the destructive distillation of wood.

wood anemone Any of several small plants (genus *Anemone*), growing in woodlands and blooming in the early spring, especially the common American species (*A. quinquefolia*), and the common European species (*A. nemorosa*).

wood betony 1 The common lousewort (*Pedicularis canadensis*) of the eastern United States, with yellow or reddish flowers. **2** The common betony (*Stachys officinalis*).

wood·bin (woõd′bin′) *n.* A box or crib for holding firewood.

wood·bine (woõd′bīn′) *n.* **1** The common European honeysuckle. **2** The Virginia creeper. [OE *wudubinde* < *wudu* wood + *bindan* bind]

wood·block (woõd′blok′) *n.* **1** A block of wood prepared for engraving. **2** A woodcut.

wood block 1 A block of wood for paving, etc. **2** *Music* A percussion instrument consisting of a hollow block of wood struck with a drumstick.

wood·bor·er (woõd′bôr′ər, -bō′rər) *n.* Any of a large family (*Buprestidae*) of brilliantly colored beetles whose larvae are very destructive of trees. For illustration see INSECTS (injurious).

wood·carv·ing (woõd′kär′ving) *n.* **1** The art of carving wood, especially for decoration. **2** A carving in wood. —**wood′carv′er** *n.*

wood·chat (woõd′chat) *n.* **1** A European butcherbird (*Lanius collorio*) with reddish plumage and a notched beak. **2** Any of several Asian birds (genera *Ianthia* and *Larvivora*) of the thrush family. [Prob. partial trans. of G *waldkatze* the butcherbird, lit., wood cat]

wood·chuck (woõd′chuk) *n.* A marmot (*Marmota monax*) of eastern North America; a ground hog. [Prob. alter. of WEJACK; infl. in form by WOOD¹ and CHUCK¹]

wood coal 1 Charcoal made from wood: also **wood charcoal. 2** Lignite.

wood·cock (woõd′kok′) *n.* **1** A small European game bird (*Scolopax rusticola*), having the thighs entirely feathered. **2** A related North American bird (*Philohela minor*). **3** *Obs.* A dolt; fool.

wood·craft (woõd′kraft′, -kräft′) *n.* **1** Skill in such things as belong to woodland life, such as hunting or trapping; the faculty of finding

WOODCHUCK
(Head and body to 14 inches; tail, 5 inches)

one's way, and living comfortably in the wilderness. **2** Skill in woodwork or in constructing articles of wood. —**wood′crafts′man** (-krafts′mən, -kräfts′-) *n.*

wood·cut (woõd′kut′) *n.* **1** An engraving on wood. **2** A print from such a block.

wood·cut·ter (woõd′kut′ər) *n.* One who cuts or chops wood. —**wood′cut′ting** *n.*

wood·ed (woõd′id) *adj.* Having a supply of wood; abounding with trees.

wood·en (woõd′n) *adj.* **1** Made of wood: *wooden* tools. **2** Like a block of wood; stupid; mechanical; stiff; awkward. **3** Dull; spiritless. —**wood′en·ly** *adv.* —**wood′en·ness** *n.*

wood engraving 1 The art of cutting designs on wood for printing; the making of woodcuts. **2** A block thus engraved or a print therefrom. — **wood engraver**

wood·en·head (woõd′n·hed′) *n. Colloq.* A stupid person; blockhead. —**wood′en·head′ed** *adj.*

wooden horse See TROJAN HORSE (def. 1).

wooden Indian 1 A carved and painted wooden figure of a North American Indian, usually in a standing position, formerly placed in front of cigar stores as an advertisement. **2** An inarticulate, sluggish, or dull person.

wooden nutmeg 1 An imitation nutmeg: proverbially used by New England (especially Connecticut) traders. **2** Any deceptive device.

wood·en·shoe dance (woõd′n·shoō′) The trasko.

wood·en·ware (woõd′n·wâr′) *n.* Dishes, vessels, bowls, etc., made of wood: said especially of household utensils.

wood grouse The capercaillie.

wood·hen (woõd′hen′) *n.* A weka.

wood·hoo·poe (woõd′hoō′pō) *n.* Any of a genus (*Phoeniculus*) of gregarious, insect-eating birds with metallic green, blue, or purple plumage, related to the hoopoes in the family Upupidae but lacking a crest and restricted to African forests.

wood·house (woõd′hous′) *n.* A house or shed for storing firewood. Also called *woodshed.*

wood hyacinth A small European squill (*Scilla nonscripta*), with clusters of bell-shaped blue, white, or pink flowers.

wood ibis A very large storklike bird (*Mycteria americana*) with a white body, glossy black tail, and naked head, common in wooded swamps of South America and the southern United States.

wood·ie (woõd′ē) *n. Scot.* The gallows; a hangman's rope: used humorously.

wood·land (woõd′lənd, -land′) *n.* Land occupied by or covered with wood or trees; timberland. —*adj.* (-lənd) Belonging to or dwelling in the woods. —**wood′land′er** *n.*

woodland caribou See under CARIBOU.

wood·lark (woõd′lärk′) *n.* A European passerine bird (*Lullula arborea*) resembling the skylark but with a sweeter note.

wood lot A plot of land devoted to the growing of forest trees or consisting of woodland.

wood louse Any of numerous small terrestrial flat-bodied crustaceans (genera *Oniscus, Porcellion,* and others) commonly found under old logs; a sow bug or pill bug.

wood·man (woõd′mən) *n. pl.* **·men** (-mən) **1** A woodcutter; lumberman. **2** A forester; also, a dweller in forests. **3** A hunter of forest game. Also *woodsman.*

wood·note (woõd′nōt′) *n.* A simple, artless, or natural song, as of a wild bird.

wood nymph 1 A goddess or nymph of the forest; a dryad. **2** Any of several South American hummingbirds (genus *Thalurania*). **3** A butterfly of the family *Satyridae,* including species usually brown in color and with eyelike spots on the wings. They occur in woods and are not attracted to flowers.

wood·peck·er (woõd′pek′ər) *n.* Any of a large family (*Picidae*) of birds related to the flickers, having stiff tail feathers to aid in climbing, strong claws, and a sharp, chisel-like bill for drilling holes in wood in search of insects; especially, **thered-headed woodpecker** (*Melanerpes erythrocephalus*) of North America, which has the head

RED–HEADED WOODPECKER
(9 to 9 1/2 inches long)

and upper breast deep red and the tail black, tipped with white; and the **pileated woodpecker** of North America *(Ceophloeus pileatus)* with a scarlet crest, white throat, white wing markings, and a large yellowish bill.

wood pewee Pewee (def. 1).

wood pigeon 1 The cushat. 2 The wild band-tailed pigeon *(Columba fasciata)* of the western United States.

wood·pile (wood′pīl′) *n.* A pile of wood, especially of wood cut or split in sizes for burning in a fireplace or stove.

wood pitch The final residuum of wood tar.

wood·print (wood′print′) *n.* A woodcut.

wood pulp Wood reduced to a pulp, as by grinding to a powder and digesting with chemicals: used for making paper.

wood pussy *Colloq.* A skunk.

wood rat A pack rat.

wood·ruff (wood′ruf′) *n.* Any of several common European woodland herbs (genus *Asperula*) of the madder family, especially the **sweet-scented woodruff** *(A. odorata),* used to flavor wine and in perfumery. [OE *wudurofe < wudu* wood]

woods (woodz) *n. pl.* A forest or wooded area.

Woods, Lake of the See LAKE OF THE WOODS.

wood-screw (wood′skroo′) *n.* A screw with a thread of coarse pitch, used for fastening pieces against wood. See illustration under SCREW.

wood·shed (wood′shed′) *n.* A woodhouse.

woods·i·a (wood′zē·ə) *n.* Any of a genus *(Woodsia)* of small tufted ferns, found in rocky places. [after Joseph *Woods,* 1776–1864, English botanist]

woods·man (woodz′mən) *n. pl.* **·men** (-mən) 1 A woodman. 2 A man skilled in woodcraft.

wood sorrel Oxalis.

wood spirit Wood alcohol or methanol.

Wood·stock (wood′stok′) A municipal borough of central Oxfordshire, England.

wood sugar Xylose.

woods·y (wood′zē) *adj. Colloq.* Of, pertaining to, or dwelling in the woods; suggesting the woods: a *woodsy* fragrance.

wood tar A tar produced by the dry distillation of wood: it contains turpentine, resins, oils, creosote, and other hydrocarbons, and yields pyroligneous acid.

wood thrush 1 A large, common woodland thrush of North America *(Hylocichla mustelina),* noted for the vigor and sweetness of its song. 2 The missel thrush.

wood tick Any of certain ticks found in the woods, especially *Dermacentor variabilis* which transfers itself from underbrush to passing animals or human beings.

wood·turn·ing (wood′tûr′ning) *n.* The process or art of shaping blocks of wood into various forms by means of a lathe. —**wood′turn′er** *n.*

wood vinegar 1 Impure acetic acid from the distillation of wood. 2 Pyroligneous acid.

wood violet The bird's-foot violet.

wood·wax·en (wood′wak′sən) See WOAD-WAXEN.

wood·wind (wood′wind′) *n.* A musical wind instrument made of wood. See WIND INSTRUMENT. —*adj.* Pertaining to or characteristic of a wooden wind instrument.

wood·work (wood′wûrk′) *n.* 1 The wooden parts of any structure, especially interior wooden parts, as moldings or doors. 2 Work made of wood. —**wood′work′er** *n.* —**wood′work′ing** *n.*

wood·worm (wood′wûrm′) *n.* A worm or larva dwelling in or that bores in wood.

wood·y (wood′ē) *adj.* **wood·i·er, wood·i·est** 1 Of the nature of wood; containing wood; ligneous. 2 Pertaining to wood; resembling wood. 3 Wooded; abounding with woods; sylvan. —**wood′i·ness** *n.*

woo·er (woo′ər) *n.* One who woos; a lover.

woof¹ (woof) *n.* 1 The weft of a woven fabric; the threads that are carried back and forth across the fixed threads of the warp in a loom. 2 The texture of a fabric. [OE *ōwef*]

woof² woof) *n.* A sound made in imitation of the growl or low suppressed bark of a dog or bear. [Imit.]

woof·er (woof′ər) *n. Electronics* A loudspeaker used to reproduce the bass register in high-fidelity sound equipment, generally in connection with a tweeter. [< WOOF²]

wool (wool) *n.* 1 The soft, curly or crisped hair obtained from the fleece of sheep and some allied animals, especially that from domesticated sheep, noted for its felting properties and which provides the widest range of fibers for yarns and textiles. 2 The under-fur of a fur-bearing animal. 3 Short kinky or crisp human hair. 4 Material or garments made of wool. 5 Something resembling or likened to wool. —**all wool and a yard wide** Perfect in quality and quantity; hence, one hundred percent genuine. —**to pull the wool over one's eyes** To delude or deceive one. —*adj.* Made of or pertaining to wool or woolen material. [OE *wull*]

wool-clip (wool′klip′) *n.* The amount of wool clipped from the sheep in one year.

wool-dyed (wool′dīd′) *adj.* Dyed before the wool has been spun into yarn: said of fabrics.

wool·en (wool′ən) *adj.* 1 Consisting wholly or in part of wool; like wool. 2 Pertaining to wool or its manufacture. —*n.* Cloth or clothing made of wool: especially in the plural. Also **wool′len.**

Woolf (woolf), **(Adeline) Virginia,** 1882–1941, *née* Stephen, English novelist and essayist.

wool fat Lanolin. Also **wool grease.**

wool-fell (wool′fel′) *n.* The pelt of a sheep or other wool-bearing animal with the wool still on it. [< WOOL + FELL⁴]

wool-gath·er·ing (wool′gath′ər·ing) *n.* Any trivial or purposeless employment; especially, idle reverie: from gathering wool caught on bushes, which required much wandering to collect even a little. —*adj.* Idly indulging in fancies. —**wool′gath′er·er** *n.*

wool-grow·er (wool′grō′ər) *n.* A person who raises sheep for the production of wool. —**wool′grow′ing** *adj.*

Wooll·cott (wool′kət), **Alexander,** 1887–1943, U.S. journalist and critic.

Wool·ley (wool′ē), **Sir (Charles) Leonard,** 1880–1960, English archeologist.

wool·ly (wool′ē) *adj.* **·li·er, ·li·est** 1 Consisting of, covered with, or resembling wool; wool-bearing. 2 Soft and vaporous; lacking clearness; not sharply detailed; fuzzy; blurry. 3 Having a rounded and somewhat fleecy appearance, as clouds. 4 Having a growth of wool-like hairs. 5 Resembling the roughness and excitement of the West: usually in the phrase *wild and woolly.* —*n. pl.* **·lies** A garment made of wool; especially, woolen underwear. Also **wool′y.** —**wool′li·ness, wool′i·ness** *n.*

woolly bear The larva of any of several tiger moths: so called because covered with long dense hairs.

wool-pack (wool′pak′) *n.* 1 A bag or wrapper of canvas, cotton, etc., for packing a bale of wool. 2 A bale or bundle of wool. 3 *Meteorol.* A cumulus cloud.

wool-sack (wool′sak′) *n.* 1 A sack of wool. 2 The seat of the lord chancellor in the English House of Lords, a cushion stuffed with wool. 3 The office of lord high chancellor.

wool-sta·pler (wool′stā′plər) *n.* A dealer in or sorter of wool. —**wool′-sta′pling** *adj. & n.*

Wool·wich (wool′ich, -ij) A metropolitan borough of London on the south bank of the Thames.

Wool·worth (wool′wûrth), **Frank Winfield,** 1852–1919, U.S. merchant; developed the five-and-ten-cent store.

woom·e·ra (woo′mər·ə) *n.* A womera.

Woon·sock·et (woon·sok′it) A city in NE Rhode Island on the Blackstone River.

woo·ra·li (woo·rä′lē) *n.* Curare. Also **woo·ra′ri** (-rē). [Var. of CURARE]

Woo·sung (woo′soong′) The outer port of Shanghai, China, at the mouth of the Hwang-poo, north of Shanghai.

wooz·y (woo′zē) *adj. Slang* 1 Befuddled, especially with drink. 2 Fuzzy. [Prob. < *wooze,* var. of OOZE] —**wooz′i·ly** *adv.* —**wooz′i·ness** *n.*

wop (wop) *n. Slang* An Italian: a derogatory term. [? < dial. Ital. (Sicilian) *guapo* a dandy < Sp.]

Worces·ter (woos′tər) 1 A midland county in England; 699 square miles. Also **Worces′ter·shire** (-shir). 2 Its county town, famous for its 14th century cathedral. 3 A city in central Massachusetts, second largest in the State; an industrial, rail, and university center.

Worces·ter (woos′tər), **Joseph Emerson,** 1784–1865, U.S. lexicographer.

Worcester china A very fine china or porcelain made in Worcester, England, from 1751: also **Worcester porcelain,** and called **Royal Worcester** by royal warrant.

Worcestershire sauce A piquant sauce made originally in Worcester, England, from vinegar and many other ingredients. Also **Worcester sauce.**

word (wûrd) *n.* 1 A speech sound or combination of sounds which has come to signify and communicate a particular idea or thought, and which functions as the smallest meaningful unit of a language when used in isolation. There are **basic** or **radical words** as *master, man,* **derivative words** as *masterful, manly,* **inflectional words** as *masters, men,* and **compound words** as *masterpiece, manpower,* etc. In terms of modern linguistics, a word may be a single morpheme (a free form, as *master*) or a union of morphemes (free and bound forms, as *masters, masterful, masterpiece).* 2 The letters or characters that stand for a significant vowel sound. 3 A vocable considered only as a sound: ideas rather than *words.* 4 *Usually pl.* Conversation; talk: a man of few *words.* 5 A brief remark; hence, a short and pithy saying. 6 A communication or message: Send him *word.* 7 A command, signal, or direction: Give the *word* to start. 8 A promise; hence, good faith: a man of his *word.* 9 A party cry; watchword. 10 *pl.* Language used in anger, rebuke, or otherwise emotionally: They had *words.* See synonyms under TERM. —*v.t.* To express in a word or words, especially in selected words; phrase. [OE. Akin to VERB.]

Word (wûrd) *n.* 1 The Logos; the Son of God. 2 Divine Wisdom, as in *John* i. 3 The Scriptures as an embodiment of divine revelation.

word·age (wûr′dij) *n.* Words collectively.

word blind·ness *n.* Alexia.

word·book (wûrd′book′) *n.* 1 A collection of words; vocabulary; lexicon; dictionary. 2 An opera libretto.

word deafness Inability to understand speech, resulting from disease of the cortical center: a form of aphasia.

word for word In the exact words; literally; verbatim.

word·i·ly (wûr′də·lē) *adv.* In a wordy manner; verbosely. —**word′i·ness, word′ish·ness** *n.*

word·ing (wûr′ding) *n.* The act or style of expressing in words; phraseology; also, words used; expression. See synonyms under DICTION.

word·less (wûrd′lis) *adj.* Having no words; dumb; silent.

word play 1 Repartee; fencing with words. 2 Subtle discussion on words and their meaning. 3 Play on words.

word processing The production of typewritten documents through the use of computer tapes and other automated equipment.

word square An arrangement of a set of words in rectangular form, so that they can be read in either horizontal or vertical lines, as in the accompanying example.

```
FRET
REAR
EASE
TREE
```

Words·worth (wûrdz′wûrth), **William,** 1770–1850, English poet; laureate 1843–50.

word·watch·er (wûrd′woch′ər) *n.* A close observer of words and their ways.

word·y (wûr′dē) *adj.* **word·i·er, word·i·est** 1 Of the nature of words; verbal. 2 Expressed in many words. 3 Given to the use of words; verbose; prolix.

wore (wôr, wōr) Past tense of WEAR¹ & WEAR².

work (wûrk) *n.* 1 Continued exertion or activity directed to some purpose or end; especially, manual labor; hence, opportunity for labor; occupation. 2 That upon which labor is expended; an undertaking; task. 3 That which is produced by or as by labor; specifically, an engineering structure; fortification; a design produced with a needle; also, a product of mental labor, as a book or opera. 4 A manufacturing or other industrial establishment: usually in the plural. 5 *pl.* Running gear or machinery, as of a watch. 6

Manner of working, or style of treatment; management; workmanship. 7 *pl.* Moral duties considered as external acts, especially as meritorious. 8 A froth or foam produced by fermentation in making vinegar, etc. 9 A feat or deed. 10 *Physics* A transference of energy from one body to another, resulting in the motion or displacement of the body acted upon, in the direction of the acting force: it is expressed as the product of the force and the amount of displacement in the line of its action. —*v.* **worked** (*Archaic* **wrought**), **work·ing** *v.i.* 1 To perform work; labor; toil. 2 To be employed in some trade or business. 3 To perform a function; operate: The machine *works* well. 4 To prove effective or influential; succeed: His stratagem *worked.* 5 To move or progress gradually or with difficulty: He *worked* up in his profession. 6 To become as specified, as by gradual motion: The bolts *worked* loose. 7 To have some slight improper motion in functioning: The wheel *works* on the shaft. 8 To move from nervousness or agitation: His features *worked* with passion. 9 To undergo kneading, hammering, etc.; be shaped: Copper *works* easily. 10 To ferment. 11 *Naut.* To labor in a heavy sea so as to loosen seams and fastenings: said of a ship. —*v.t.* 12 To cause or bring about; effect; accomplish: to *work* a miracle. 13 To cause to function; direct the operation of: to *work* a machine. 14 To make or shape by toil or skill. 15 To prepare, as by manipulating, hammering, etc.: to *work* dough. 16 To decorate, as with embroidery or inlaid work. 17 To cause to be productive, as by toil: to *work* a mine. 18 To cause to do work: He *works* his employees too hard. 19 To cause to be as specified, usually with effort: We *worked* the timber into position. 20 To make or achieve by effort: He *worked* his way to the top of his profession; to *work* one's passage on a ship. 21 To carry on some activity in (an area, etc.); cover: to *work* a stream for trout. 22 To solve, as a problem in arithmetic. 23 To cause to move from nervousness or excitement: to *work* one's jaws. 24 To excite; provoke: He *worked* himself into a passion. 25 To influence or manage, as by insidious means; lead. 26 To cause to ferment. 27 *Colloq.* To practice trickery upon; cheat; swindle. 28 *Colloq.* To make use of for one's own purposes; use. **—to work in** To put in; insert or be inserted. **—to work off** To get rid of, as extra flesh by exercise. **—to work on (or upon)** 1 To try to influence or persuade. 2 To influence or affect. **—to work out** 1 To make its way out or through. 2 To effect by work or effort; accomplish. 3 To exhaust, as a mineral vein or a subject of inquiry. 4 To discharge, as a debt, by labor rather than by payment of money. 5 To develop; form, as a plan. 6 To solve. 7 **a** To prove effective or successful. **b** To result as specified. **—to work up** 1 To excite; rouse, as rage or a person to rage. 2 To form or shape by working; develop. 3 To make one's or its way. [OE *weorc*]

Synonyms (noun): achievement, action, business, deed, doing, drudgery, employment, exertion, labor, occupation, performance, product, production, toil. *Work* is the generic term for any continuous application of energy toward an end; *work* may be hard or easy. *Labor* is hard and wearying *work*; *toil* is straining and exhausting *work. Work* is also used for any result or working, physical or mental; as, a *work* of art; a *work* of genius. In this connection, *work* has special uses, which *labor* and *toil* do not share. *Drudgery* is plodding, irksome, and often menial *work.* See ACT, BUSINESS, PRODUCTION, TASK, TOIL[1]. *Antonyms*: ease, idleness, leisure, recreation, relaxation, repose, rest, vacation.

-work *combining form* 1 A product made from a (specified) material: *paperwork, brickwork.* 2 Work of a (given) kind: *piecework.* 3 Work performed in a (specified) place: *housework.* [<WORK]

work·a·ble (wûr′kə·bəl) *adj.* 1 Of a nature to be operated, as a machine. 2 Practicable, as a plan. 3 That can be developed, as a mine. 4 Able to work. 5 That can be worked upon or influenced. **—work′a·bil′i·ty, work′a·ble·ness** *n.*

work·a·day (wûrk′ə·dā′) *adj.* 1 Of, pertaining to, or suitable for working days; everyday. 2 Commonplace; prosaic. [Alter. of ME *werkeday* < *werke,* OE *weorca* work + DAY; infl. in form by NOWADAYS]

work·a·hol·ic (wûrk′ə·hol′ik, -hôl′ik) *n.* A person who works to excess.

work·bag (wûrk′bag′) *n.* A bag for holding tools or materials, as for needlework.

work·bench (wûrk′bench′) *n.* A bench for work, as that of a carpenter, machinist, etc.

work·book (wûrk′bo͝ok′) *n.* 1 A booklet based on a course of study and containing problems and exercises which a student works out directly on the pages. 2 A manual containing operating instructions. 3 A book for recording work performed or planned.

work·box (wûrk′boks′) *n.* A small bag or box for needlework, etc.

work·day (wûrk′dā′) *n.* 1 Any day not a Sunday or holiday; a working day. 2 The part of the day or number of hours of one day spent in work. —*adj.* Workaday.

work·er (wûrk′kər) *n.* 1 One who or that which performs work; specifically, a laborer as distinguished from a *capitalist.* 2 An individual female of an insect colony, as a true ant, a bee, or a white ant, with undeveloped sexual organs.

work·fare (wûrk′fâr′) *n.* Welfare that is conditional upon assigned work or training by those receiving payments.

work·fel·low (wûrk′fel′ō) *n.* A companion in work.

work·folk (wûrk′fōk′) *n. pl.* Manual laborers.

work·house (wûrk′hous′) *n.* 1 *Brit.* A house for paupers able to work; an almshouse. 2 An industrial prison for petty offenders.

work·ing (wûr′king) *adj.* 1 Engaged actively in some employment. 2 That works, or performs its function: This is a *working* model. 3 Sufficient for use or action: They formed a *working* agreement. 4 Relating to or occupied by work: a *working* day. 5 Throbbing with pain; also, twitching: said especially of the face muscles. 6 Fermenting, as wine. —*n.* 1 The act or operation of any person or thing that works, in any sense. 2 That part of a mine or quarry where excavation is going on or has gone on.

working capital 1 That part of the finances of a business available for its operation. 2 The amount of quick assets which exceed current liabilities.

working day A workday.

working drawing In engineering, etc., a drawing made to scale, as of a part of a machine or building, for the direction of workmen, contractors, etc.

work·ing·man (wûr′king·man′) *n. pl.* **·men** (-men′) A male worker; laborer.

working papers An age certificate and other official papers certifying that a minor may be legally employed.

working substance *Mech.* The fluid, as steam, or gasoline vapor, under pressure, that serves to operate a prime mover. Also **working fluid.**

work·ing·wom·an (wûr′king·wo͝om′ən) *n. pl.* **·wom·en** (-wim′in) A female worker; laborer.

work·less (wûrk′lis) *adj.* Jobless; unemployed.

work·load (wûrk′lōd′) *n.* The amount of work apportioned to a person, machine, or department over a given period.

work·man (wûrk′mən) *n. pl.* **·men** (-mən) One who earns his bread by manual labor; an artisan; mechanic; workingman. **—work′man·ly** *adj.*

work·man·like (wûrk′mən·līk) *adj.* Like or befitting a skilled workman; skilfully done. —**work′man·ly** *adv.*

work·man·ship (wûrk′mən·ship) *n.* 1 The art or skill of a workman, or the quality of work. 2 The work or result produced by a worker.

work of art A product of the fine arts, especially painting and sculpture, but including artistic, literary, and musical productions.

work·out (wûrk′out′) *n.* A test, trial, practice performance, etc., to discover, maintain, or increase ability for some work or competition, as a practice boxing bout, a fast turn around a track by a horse, runner, etc.

work·peo·ple (wûrk′pē′pəl) *n. pl.* People employed in work, especially in manual labor; working people.

work·place (wûrk′plās′) *n.* A place where a person works.

work·room (wûrk′ro͞om′, -ro͝om′) *n.* A room where work is performed.

works (wûrks) *n.* 1 A manufacturing establishment including buildings and equipment: a gas *works.* 2 *Slang* The whole of anything; the kit and caboodle; everything: the whole *works.* **—to give (someone) the works** *Slang* To maul; kill by shooting. **—to shoot the works** *Slang* To make a supreme effort; risk one's all in one single attempt.

works council A committee of employed workers organized by an employer to discuss company and industrial problems and relations; a company union or similar group.

work·sheet (wûrk′shēt) *n.* 1 A sheet of paper on which practice work or rough drafts of problems are written. 2 A sheet of paper used to record work schedules and operations.

work·shop (wûrk′shop′) *n.* 1 A building or room where any work is carried on; workroom. 2 A seminar or single session for training, discussion, etc., in a specialized field: a writer's *workshop.*

work·ta·ble (wûrk′tā′bəl) *n.* A table with drawers and other conveniences for use while working, especially while sewing.

work·up (wûrk′up′) *n.* A thorough study of a sick person's symptoms and bodily condition.

work·week (wûrk′wēk′) *n.* The total number of hours worked in a week; also, the number of working hours in a week.

world (wûrld) *n.* 1 The earth; the terraqueous globe; the universe (of which the earth was once supposed to be the center); any similar orb; a part of the earth: the Old *World.* 2 A division of existing or created things belonging to the earth; natural grand division: the mineral, vegetable, or animal *world.* 3 The human inhabitants of the earth; mankind. 4 A definite class of people having certain interests or activities in common: the scientific *world*; a sphere or domain: the *world* of letters. 5 Man regarded socially; the public; hence, public or social life and intercourse. 6 The practices, usages, and ways of men: He knows the *world.* 7 A total of things as pertaining to or affecting an individual man; a career among men; one's experience in life: to begin the *world* anew. 8 The course of events as affecting one personally; individual condition or circumstances: How goes the *world* with you? Your *world* is changed then. 9 A scene of existence or of affairs regarded from a moral or religious point of view; secular affairs; worldly aims, pleasures, or people collectively; earthly existence; mortal life. 10 Figuratively, great quantity, number, or size: a *world* of trouble. **—for all the world** In every respect. **—on top of the world** *Colloq.* Elated. **—to bring into the world** To give birth to. [OE *weorold*]

World may appear as a combining form in hyphemes or as the first element in two-word phrases; as in:

world affairs	**world love**
world battle	**world-old**
world builder	**world order**
world-changing	**world peace**
world citizen	**world politics**
world commerce	**world price**
world conflict	**world problem**
world-conquering	**world-rejoicing**
world destroyer	**world-renowned**
world-domination	**world report**
world dominion	**world revolution**
world empire	**world sadness**
world-encircling	**world-shaking**
world-famed	**world state**
world-famous	**world struggle**
world hero	**world trade**
world history	**world-wandering**
world leader	**world-winning**

World Court See PERMANENT COURT OF INTERNATIONAL JUSTICE under COURT.

world·ling (wûrld′ling) *n.* One who lives merely for this world; a worldly-minded person.

world·ly (wûrld′lē) *adj.* **·li·er, ·li·est** 1 Pertaining to the world; mundane; earthly; not spiritual. 2 Devoted to temporal things; secular. 3 Sophisticated; worldly-wise. 4 *Obs.* Lay, as opposed to clerical. —*adv.* In a worldly manner. See synonyms under PROFANE. **—world′li·ness** *n.*

world·ly-mind·ed (wurld′lē-mīn′did) *adj.* Absorbed in the things of this world. **—world′ly-mind′ed·ly** *adv.* **—world′ly-mind′ed·ness** *n.*

world·ly-wise (wûrld′lē·wīz′) *adj.* Wise in the

ways and affairs of the world; sophisticated.

world power A state or organization whose policy and action are of world-wide influence.

world series In baseball, the games played at the finish of the regular schedule between the champion teams of the American and National Leagues, the first team to win four games being adjudged world's champions. Also **world's series.**

world's fair An international exhibit of the folk crafts and arts, agricultural and industrial products, and scientific progress of various countries.

world soul 1 The hypothetical soul of the world; the All-Soul, conceived of after the analogy of the indwelling soul of man. 2 The principle that animates and informs the physical world. Also **world spirit.**

world's people Worldly people; those not belonging to some specific religious sect or group: a term used especially by the Friends.

World War See table under WAR.

world-wea·ry (wûrld′wir′ē) adj. ·ri·er, ·ri·est Dissatisfied with life and its conditions; weary and tired of this life.

world-wide (wûrld′wīd′) adj. Extended throughout the world.

world without end Forever.

worm (wûrm) n. 1 A small, legless, invertebrate crawling animal, with an elongated, soft, and usually naked body, as a flatworm, roundworm, or annelid. ◆ Collateral adjective: *vermicular.* 2 A small creeping animal with short or undeveloped feet, as an insect larva, a grub, angleworm, etc. 3 Figuratively, that which suggests the action or habit of a worm as eating away or as an agent of decay or destruction, as remorse, death, etc. 4 A despicable or despised person; also, a feeble mortal. 5 Something conceived to be like a worm. 6 A screw thread. 7 A worm screw. 8 The spiral part of a corkscrew. 9 A spiral part in a still. 10 An organ or part that resembles a worm in shape, as the lytta of the dog or the vermiform process. 11 *pl.* An intestinal disorder due to the presence of parasitic worms. 12 The windings of a log road made to lessen the steepness of a grade. 13 The zigzag course of a log fence or a rail fence. — *v.t.* 1 To insinuate (oneself or itself) in a wormlike manner; effect as by crawling: with *in* or *into*: to *worm* one's way. 2 To draw forth by artful means, as a secret: with *out.* 3 To remove worms from. 4 To wind yarn, etc., along (a rope) so as to fill up the grooves between the strands. 5 To remove the lytta or worm from, as a dog. — *v.i.* 6 To move or progress slowly and stealthily. [OE *wyrm*] — **worm′er** n.

Worm (vōōrm), **Olaus,** 1588–1654, Danish anatomist and physician.

worm-eat·en (wûrm′ēt′n) adj. Eaten or bored through by worms.

worm fence See under FENCE.

worm gear 1 *Mech.* A worm wheel having teeth shaped so as to mesh with a worm screw. 2 A worm wheel.

worm-hole (wûrm′hōl′) n. The hole made by a worm or a wormlike animal, as in plants, earth, or stone. — **worm′holed′** adj.

Wor·mi·an (wôr′mē·ən) adj. Relating to or discovered by Olaus Worm.

Wormian bones *Anat.* Small bones occasionally lying along the lines of the cranial sutures.

wor·mil (wûr′məl) n. A warblefly or botfly larva. [Var. of dial. *warnel,* OE *wernægel*]

worm-root (wûrm′rōōt′, -rŏŏt′) n. Pinkroot.

Worms (wûrmz, *Ger.* vôrms) A city on the Rhine in Rhenish Hesse, SW West Germany; scene of the Diet of Worms (1521) by which Martin Luther was pronounced a heretic.

worm screw *Mech.* A short threaded portion of a shaft constituting an endless screw formed to mesh with a worm wheel.

worm-seed (wûrm′sēd′) n. 1 The seeds of any of various plants used as a vermifuge. 2 The

plants themselves; especially, santonica, and a species of goosefoot *(Chenopodium ambrosioides).*

worm wheel *Mech.* A toothed wheel gearing with a worm screw.

worm-wood (wûrm′wŏŏd′) n. 1 Any of a genus *(Artemisia)* of European herbs or small shrubs related to the sagebrush, especially a common species *(A. absinthium),* aromatic, tonic, bitter, and used in making absinthe. 2 That which embitters or makes bitter; bitterness. [Alter. of obs. *wermod* <OE; infl. in form by *worm* and *wood*[1]]

worm·y (wûr′mē) adj. worm·i·er, worm·i·est 1 Infested with or injured by worms. 2 Of or pertaining to worms; resembling a worm. 3 Earthy; groveling. — **worm′i·ness** n.

worn (wôrn, wōrn) Past participle of WEAR. — adj. 1 Affected by attrition or any similar continuous action. 2 Used, as a garment; showing the effects of anxiety, etc., as the mind; hackneyed, as phrases. 3 Exhausted or spent; used up.

worn-out (wôrn′out′, wōrn′-) adj. 1 Used until without value for its purpose. 2 Thoroughly tired; exhausted.

wor·ri·cow (wûr′ē·kou′) n. *Scot.* A hobgoblin; the devil; any hideous object or person; bugbear; a scarecrow.

wor·ri·some (wûr′i·səm) adj. Causing worry or anxiety.

wor·rit (wûr′it) n. *Colloq.* Worry; vexation. [Appar. alter. of WORRY]

wor·ry (wûr′ē) v. ·ried, ·ry·ing v.i. 1 To be uneasy in the mind; feel anxiety about something; fret. 2 To pull or tear at something with the teeth: with *at.* 3 *Colloq.* To advance or manage despite trials or difficulties: with *along* or *through.* — v.t. 4 To cause to feel uneasy in the mind; trouble. 5 To bother; pester. 6 To mangle or kill by biting, shaking, or tearing with the teeth. 7 *Scot.* or *Obs.* To strangle; choke. See synonyms under PERSECUTE. — n. pl. ·ries A state of anxiety; vexation. See synonyms under ANXIETY, CARE. [OE *wyrgan* strangle] — **wor′ri·er** n. — **wor′ri·ment** n.

worse (wûrs) Used as comparative of *bad, ill, evil,* and the like. — adj. 1 Bad or ill in a greater degree; more evil, unworthy, etc. 2 Physically in a greater degree. 3 Less favorably situated as to means and circumstances. — n. Something worse; disadvantage; loss. — adv. 1 In a manner more evil or ill. 2 With greater intensity, severity, etc. 3 Decreasingly; less. [OE *wyrsa*]

wors·en (wûr′sən) v.t. & v.i. To make or become worse.

wors·er (wûr′sər) adj. & adv. Worse: a former redundant form of the comparative, on the analogy of *lesser*: now regarded as a vulgarism.

wors·et (wûr′sit) adj. & n. *Scot.* Worsted.

wor·ship (wûr′ship) n. 1 The act or feeling of adoration or homage; the paying of religious reverence, as in prayer, praise, etc. 2 The act or feeling of deference, respect, or honor toward virtue, power, or the like. 3 Excessive or ardent admiration; also, the object of such love or admiration. 4 A title of honor in addressing persons of station. See synonyms under RELIGION, REVERENCE. — v. ·shiped or ·shipped, ·ship·ing or ·ship·ping v.t. 1 To pay an act of worship to; venerate; adore. 2 To treat with intense or exaggerated admiration or affection. 3 *Obs.* To honor. — v.i. 4 To perform acts or have sentiments of worship. [OE *weorthscipe* < *weorth* worthy] — **wor′ship·er, wor′ship·per** n.

Synonyms (verb): adore, deify, exalt, honor, idolize, revere, reverence. See PRAISE. *Antonyms:* abhor, abjure, abominate, blaspheme, curse, denounce, detest, renounce, revile, scoff, scorn.

wor·ship·ful (wûr′ship·fəl) adj. 1 Worthy of honor; entitled to respect by reason of character or position: applied to dignitaries, as magistrates, etc. In Freemasonry, it is part of a specific official title, as of masters. 2 Esteemed; distinguished; honorable. 3 Giving reverence; adoring. — **wor′ship·ful·ly** adv. — **wor′ship·ful·ness** n.

worst (wûrst) Used as the superlative of *bad, ill,* or *evil.* — adj. Bad, ill, or evil in the

highest degree. — **in the worst way** *Slang* Very much. — n. The most evil state or result. — **at worst** On the most pessimistic estimate. — **to get the worst of it** To be defeated or put at a disadvantage. — adv. In the worst or most extreme manner or degree. — v.t. To get the advantage over; defeat; vanquish. See synonyms under BEAT, CONQUER. [OE *wyrsta*]

wors·ted (wŏŏs′tid, wûr′stid) n. 1 Woolen yarn spun from long staple, with fibers combed parallel and twisted hard. 2 A lightly twisted woolen yarn. 3 A tightly woven or smooth fabric made from worsted yarns, as gabardine or serge. — adj. Consisting of or made from this yarn. [from *Worsted,* former name of a parish in Norfolk, north of Norwich, England]

wort (wûrt) n. 1 A plant or herb: usually in combination: *liverwort, navelwort.* 2 The sweet, unfermented infusion of malt that becomes beer when fermented. [OE *wyrt* a root, a plant]

worth[1] (wûrth) n. 1 That quality which renders a thing useful or desirable; value or excellence of any kind; hence, market value. 2 That quality or combination of qualities that makes one deserving of esteem; mental and moral excellence. 3 Wealth. — adj. 1 Having value; equal in value (to); exchangeable (for). 2 Deserving (of): in either a good or bad sense. 3 Having possessions to the value of: He is *worth* a million. — **for all it is worth** To the utmost. — **for all one is worth** With every effort possible; to the utmost of one's capacity. [OE *weorth*]

Synonyms (noun): character, desert, excellence, integrity, merit, preciousness, value. See PRICE, VIRTUE.

worth[2] (wûrth) v.i. To betide or befall: now only in phrases, as **woe worth the day,** etc. [OE *weorthan* come to be]

-worth *combining form* Of the value of: *pennyworth.* [OE *weorth* worth]

Wor·thing (wûr′thing) A municipal borough on the coast of southern Sussex, southern England, west of Brighton.

worth·less (wûrth′lis) adj. Having no worth; having no utility or value; destitute of dignity, virtue, or standing. See synonyms under BAD[1], BASE[2], USELESS, VAIN, WASTE. — **worth′less·ly** adv. — **worth′less·ness** n.

worth·while (wûrth′hwīl′) adj. Sufficiently important to occupy the time; of enough value to repay the effort. ◆ This compound originated from the phrase *worth the while* and it is firmly established as a solideme in American usage. In British usage it is usually a hypheme: **worth-while.** — **worth′while′ness** n.

wor·thy (wûr′thē) adj. ·thi·er, ·thi·est 1 Possessing worth; deserving of respect or honor; having valuable or useful qualities. 2 Having such qualities as to be deserving of or adapted to some specified thing; fit; suitable: followed by *of* (rarely *for*), sometimes by an infinitive and rarely by the object directly. 3 *Obs.* Well deserved; fitting. See synonyms under BECOMING, EXCELLENT, GOOD, MORAL, VIRTUOUS. — n. pl. ·thies 1 A person of eminent worth. 2 Humorously, a person of local note; a character. [ME *wurthi, worthi*] — **wor′thi·ly** adv. — **wor′thi·ness** n.

-worthy *combining form* 1 Meriting or deserving: *trustworthy.* 2 Valuable as; having worth as: *newsworthy.* 3 Fit for: *seaworthy.* [OE *wyrthe* worthy]

wot (wot) Present tense, first and third person singular, of WIT[2].

Wot·ton (wot′n), **Sir Henry,** 1568–1639, English diplomat and poet.

would (wŏŏd) Past tense of WILL, expressing desire, condition, or what might be expected: used also to express determination: He *would* go, I couldn't stop him. [OE *wolde,* pt. of *willan* will]

◆ **would & should** Anybody dealing in ifs, as-ifs, promises, threats, hopes, wishes, or similar feelings and attitudes about the real or imagined future, will find himself making plentiful use of *would* and/or *should,* which do duty to express the vestigial and fast vanishing subjunctive mood. As to which one to use, the distinctions are subtle and fine-drawn and at several points British usage calls for *should* where American practice is

---

to use *would,* although *would* has not here displaced *should* to the extent that *shall* has given way to *will* (see usage note under SHALL vs. WILL). (1) In simple factual conditions, for example, British usage calls for *should* in the first person in the conclusion: If he failed, I *should* (U.S. *would*) still support him. (2) When one of these modal auxiliaries is to be used in the first person preceding such verbs as *like, prefer, care, be glad,* etc., British usage holds firmly to *should*; but American, Scottish, and Irish usage calls for *would:* We *would* (Brit. & formal U.S. *should*) like to have you come to dinner next Tuesday. *Would* in this example represents true present time. (3) *Would* is the true past expressing an act of will mostly in negations or expressions of indifference: They asked him to wait, but he *would* not (was unwilling to comply). (4) *Would* can also convey customary or habitual action in the past: He *would* take her gifts every time he called. Except for these rare instances in which *would* is used as a true past, it is usually confined to the purposes of the subjunctive. (5) It may express an act of will under projected or imagined conditions: (I, You, He) *wouldn't* tolerate that insult even if it were offered with smiling politeness. (6) When no condition is expressed, *would* in the second and third person often lacks even a vestigial trace of any act of will: She *would* be no more than second choice in the matrimonial sweepstakes. (7) When *would* is stressed with the voice it may indicate (a) an element of malign fate or misfortune: She *would* be the one to lose her take–home fare; or (b) the notion of persistent contrariness: You *would* insist on bumping your head against a stone wall twice! (8) In conditions contrary to fact, *would* is used in conclusion without any feeling of volition involved: Had he left sooner he *would* have heard less to his discredit. If I had been able to dodge the small souls around the commission, I *would* (Brit. *should*) have got a third share in the radio station. (9) *Would* may also express probability in cases where some contingency or hypothesis is unexpressed: "He was very boastful." "He *would* be." (10) Finally, there is the matter of the idiomatic use of *would* and *should* in indirect or reported discourse. In most cases, if the direct utterance used *shall,* the reported discourse employs *should.* Similarly, if it was *will* in the direct utterance, *would* is used in the indirect discourse. If obligation is involved, *should* must be used. Except in this area of obligation, *would* is the more common form in American usage.

would–be (wŏŏd′bē′) *adj.* Desiring or professing to be: a *would-be* poet.

would·n't (wŏŏd′nt) Would not: a contraction.

wound[1] (wōōnd, *Poetic* wound) *n.* **1** A hurt or injury caused by violence; especially, a cut, bruise, stab, etc.; a trauma. **2** A breach or cut of the bark or substance of a tree or plant. **3** Hence, any injury or cause of pain or grief, as to the feelings, honor, etc. — *v.t. & v.i.* To inflict a wound or wounds (upon); cause injury or grief (to); hurt. See synonyms under AFFRONT, HURT, PIQUE[1]. [OE *wund*] — **wound′ed** *adj.* — **wound′less** *adj.*

wound[2] (wound) Past tense and past participle of WIND[2].

Wou·ter (wou′tər) Dutch form of WALTER.

wove (wōv) Past tense and alternative past participle of WEAVE.

wo·ven (wō′vən) Past participle of WEAVE.

wove paper Paper carrying the marks of the wire gauze on which it was laid during finishing.

wow (wou) *interj.* An exclamation of wonder, surprise, pleasure, or pain. — *n. Slang* An extraordinary success. — *v.t. Slang* To be extraordinarily successful with.

wow·ser (wou′zər) *n. Australian Slang* One who is opposed to Sunday amusements, sports, etc.; a hypocritical censor of the lesser vices; a meddlesome puritan or sanctimonious reformer. [Origin unknown]

wrack[1] (rak) *n.* **1** Marine vegetation and floating material cast ashore by the sea, as seaweed or eelgrass; kelp. **2** The state of being wrecked; ruin; destruction: chiefly in the phrase **wrack and ruin. 3** Shipwreck; a wrecked vessel; wreckage. **4** *Scot. & Brit. Dial.* Weeds. — *v.t. & v.i.* To wreck or be wrecked. ◆ Homophone: *rack.* [Fusion of

OE *wræc* punishment, revenge and MDu. *wrak* a wreck]

wrack[2] (rak) *n.* A rack of clouds; any floating vapor. Compare RACK[3]. [Var. of RACK[3]]

wraith (rāth) *n.* **1** An apparition of a person thought to be alive, seen shortly before or shortly after his death. **2** Any specter, ghost, or apparition. [< dial. E (Scottish), alter. of *warth* <ON *vörthr* a guardian < *vartha* guard]

wrang (rang) *adj. & n. Scot.* Wrong.

Wran·gel (vrän′gil), **Ferdinand Petrovich von,** 1794?–1870, Russian explorer. Also **Wran′gell.**

Wran·gell (rang′gəl), **Mount** An active volcano (14,005 feet) in the western **Wrangell Mountains,** a range in SE Alaska; highest peak, 16,208 feet.

Wran·gell Island (rang′gəl) **1** An island of the Alexander Archipelago, SE Alaska; 30 miles long, 5 to 14 miles wide. **2** An island in the western Chukchi Sea off NE Siberia; part of Khabarovsk territory, Asiatic Russian S.F.S.R.; 75 miles long, 45 miles wide; 1,740 square miles. Also **Wran′gel Island.** *Russian* **O·strov Vran·ge·ly** (ô′strôf vrän′gi·lyə).

wran·gle (rang′gəl) *v.* **·gled, ·gling** *v.i.* **1** To argue or dispute noisily and angrily; brawl. — *v.t.* **2** To argue; debate. **3** To herd or round up, as livestock on a range. See synonyms under CONTEND. — *n.* An angry or noisy dispute; a quarrel. See synonyms under ALTERCATION, DISPUTE, QUARREL[1]. [Cf. LG *wrangeln* quarrel, freq. of *wrangen* struggle]

wran·gler (rang′glər) *n.* **1** One who wrangles. **2** At Cambridge University, England, one who has taken the highest mathematical honors. **3** A herdsman on a range.

wrap (rap) *v.* **wrapped** or **wrapt, wrap·ping** *v.t.* **1** To surround and cover by something folded or wound about; swathe; enwrap. **2** To cover with paper, etc., folded about and secured. **3** To wind or fold (a covering) about something. **4** To surround so as to obscure; blot out or conceal; envelop. **5** To fold, wind, or draw together. — *v.i.* **6** To be or become twined or coiled: with *about, around,* etc. — *n.* **1** An article of dress drawn or folded about a person; a wrapper. **2** *pl.* Outer garments collectively, as cloaks, scarfs, etc. **3** A blanket. [ME *wrappen*; origin uncertain]

wrap·a·round windshield (rap′ə·round) In automobiles, a windshield curving back into the sides of the body, thus providing a greater field of vision.

wrap·per (rap′ər) *n.* **1** A paper enclosing a newspaper, magazine, or similar packet for mailing or otherwise. **2** A detachable paper cover to protect the binding of a book. **3** A loose flowing outer garment; a dressing gown. **4** A tobacco leaf of high quality enclosing a cigar or plug of tobacco. **5** One who wraps articles.

wrap·ping (rap′ing) *n.* A covering; something in which an object is wrapped.

wrap·ras·cal (rap′ras′kəl) *n.* A long loose overcoat fashionable during the 18th century.

wrapt (rapt) Erroneous spelling of RAPT.

wrasse (ras) *n.* Any of a group of spiny–finned food fishes (family *Labridae*) of warm tropical seas, often highly colored; especially, the tautog. [<Cornish *wrach* < *gwrach,* orig., an old woman]

wrath (rath, räth; *Brit.* rôth) *n.* **1** Determined and lasting anger; extreme or violent rage; fury; vehement indignation. **2** An act done in violent rage. See synonyms under ANGER, VIOLENCE. — *v.t. & v.i. Obs.* To make or become angry. — *adj. Obs.* Wroth; angry. [OE *wræththu* < *wrath* wroth]

Wrath (rath, räth), **Cape** A promontory at the NW extremity of Scotland in NW Sutherland.

wrath·ful (rath′fəl, räth′-) *adj.* **1** Full of wrath; extremely angry. **2** Springing from or expressing wrath. — **wrath′ful·ly** *adv.* — **wrath′ful·ness** *n.*

wrath·y (rath′ē, räth′ē) *adj.* **wrath·i·er, wrath·i·est 1** Disposed to wrath. **2** *Colloq.* Wroth. — **wrath′i·ly** *adv.* — **wrath′i·ness** *n.*

wreak (rēk) *v.t.* **1** To inflict or exact, as vengeance. **2** To satiate; give free expression to, as a feeling or passion. ◆ Homophone: *reek.* [OE *wrecan* drive, avenge]

wreath (rēth) *n.* **1** A twisted band, as of flowers, commonly circular, as for a crown or chaplet. **2** Any curled band of circular

or spiral shape, as of smoke or snow. [OE *writha* <*wrīthan* writhe] — **wreath′y** *n.*

Wreath (rēth) See CORONA AUSTRALIS.

wreathe (rēth) *v.* **wreathed, wreath·ing** *v.t.* **1** To form into a wreath, as by twisting or twining. **2** To adorn or encircle with or as with wreaths. **3** To envelop; cover: His face was *wreathed* in smiles. — *v.i.* **4** To take the form of a wreath. **5** To twist, turn, or coil, as masses of cloud. See synonyms under TWIST. [Earlier *wrethe,* back formation <ME *wrethen,* var. of *writhen,* pp. of *writhen* writhe; infl. by *wreath*]

wreck (rek) *v.t.* **1** To cause the destruction or wreck of, as a vessel; shipwreck. **2** To bring ruin, damage, or destruction upon. **3** To tear down, as a building; dismantle. — *v.i.* **4** To suffer wreck; be ruined. **5** To engage in wrecking, as for plunder or salvage. See synonyms under RUIN. [< *n.*] — *n.* **1** The act of wrecking, or the state of being wrecked; the ruin of anything, especially if effected violently. **2** That which has been wrecked or ruined, as a vessel or an army; hence, an emaciated person. **3** Wreckage; shipwreck. **4** *Law* Property cast upon land by the sea, either broken portions of a wrecked vessel or cargo from it. ◆ Homophone: *reck.* [<AF *wrec, wrech,* OF *warec* <ON (assumed) *wrek* < *wrekan* drive]

wreck·age (rek′ij) *n.* **1** The act of wrecking, or the state of being wrecked; wrecked material. **2** Broken or disordered remnants or fragments from a wreck.

wreck·er (rek′ər) *n.* **1** One who causes wreck, destruction, or frustration of any sort. **2** One employed in tearing down and removing old buildings. **3** A person, train, car, or machine that clears away wrecks. **4** One employed to recover disabled vessels or wrecked cargoes for the owners; also, a vessel employed in this service; a salvager. **5** One who lures ships to destruction by false lights on the shore in order to plunder the wreck. **6** One who ruins something valuable, as a bank or a railroad, especially for his own profit.

wreck·ful (rek′fəl) *adj. Poetic* Causing wreck; involving ruin.

wrecking company 1 A business organization that salvages wrecked ships. **2** A business organization that tears down and removes old buildings.

wren (ren) *n.* **1** Any of numerous small passerine birds (family *Troglodytidae*) having short rounded wings and a short tail, including the common **house wren** (*Troglodytes aëdon*), the **Carolina wren** (*Thryothorus ludovicianus*), **Bewick's wren** (*Thryomanes bewicki*) of North America, and the European wren (*Nannus troglodytes*). **2** Any one of numerous similar birds. [OE *wrenna*]

Wren (ren), **Sir Christopher,** 1632–1723, English architect. — **Percival Christopher,** 1885–1941, English novelist.

wrench (rench) *n.* **1** A violent twist; hence, a twist causing pain or injury; sprain. **2** Any strain or sudden and violent tension; sudden and violent emotion. **3** Any perversion or distortion of an original meaning. **4** A tool for twisting or turning bolts, nuts, pipe, etc.

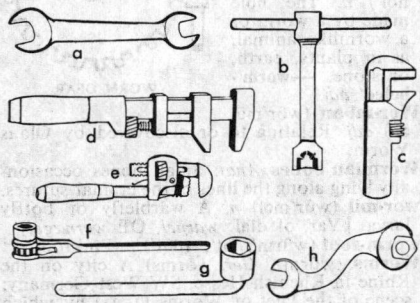

TYPES OF WRENCHES
a. Engineer's wrench.   *e.* Pipe wrench.
b. Socket wrench.   *f.* Ratchet wrench.
c. Bicycle wrench.   *g.* Offset wrench.
d. Monkey wrench.   *h.* S–wrench.

— *v.t.* **1** To twist violently; turn suddenly by force; wrest. **2** To twist forcibly so as to

cause strain or injury; sprain. 3 To twist from the proper meaning, intent, or use. —*v.i.* 4 To give a twist or wrench. [OE *wrenc* a trick. Akin to WRINKLE[1].]
Wrens (renz) *n. pl. Brit. Colloq.* Women's Royal Naval Service, an organization to relieve men of certain shore duties connected with the Royal Navy: so called from the initial letters *W,R,N,S,* plus *E.*
wrest (rest) *v.t.* 1 To pull or force away by violent twisting or wringing; wrench. 2 To turn from the true meaning, character, intent, or application; distort; pervert. 3 To seize forcibly by violence, extortion, or usurpation. —*n.* 1 An act of wresting; a violent twist. 2 A misapplication or perversion. 3 A crooked act; wile. 4 A key for tuning a stringed instrument, as a harp. ◆ Homophone: *rest.* [OE *wrǣstan*] —**wrest′er** *n.*
wres·tle (res′əl) *v.* **·tled, ·tling** *v.i.* 1 To engage in wrestling. 2 To struggle, as for mastery; contend. —*v.t.* 3 To engage in (a wrestling match), or wrestle with. 4 To throw (a calf) and hold it down for branding. —*n.* A wrestling match; a hard struggle. [OE *wrǣstlian,* freq. of *wrǣsten* wrest]
wres·tler (res′lər) *n.* One who wrestles; especially, a person who competes in wrestling matches.
wres·tling (res′ling) *n.* A sport or exercise in which each of two unarmed contestants endeavors to throw the other to the ground or force him into a certain fallen position.
wretch (rech) *n.* 1 A base, vile, or contemptible person; despicable character. 2 A miserable or unhappy person; also, sometimes, any person or creature viewed with pity. ◆ Homophone: *retch.* [OE *wrecca* an outcast < *wrecan* drive]
wretch·ed (rech′id) *adj.* 1 Sunk in dejection; profoundly unhappy. 2 Causing misery or grief. 3 Mean; paltry; worthless; unsatisfactory in ability or quality. 4 Despicable; contemptible. See synonyms under BAD[1], BASE[2], PITIFUL. —**wretch′ed·ly** *adv.* —**wretch′ed·ness** *n.*
wrig·gle (rig′əl) *v.* **·gled, ·gling** *v.i.* 1 To twist in a sinuous manner; squirm; writhe. 2 To proceed as by twisting or crawling. 3 To make one's way by evasive or indirect means. —*v.t.* 4 To cause to wriggle. —*n.* The motion of one who or that which wriggles; a squirm. [<MLG *wriggeln,* freq. of *wriggen* twist] —**wrig′gly** *adj.*
wrig·gler (rig′lər) *n.* 1 Someone or something that wriggles. 2 A mosquito larva.
wright (rīt) *n.* 1 One who does mechanical or constructive work. 2 An artificer or workman: used chiefly in compounds: *shipwright.* ◆ Homophones: *right, rite, write.* [OE *wyrhta*]
Wright (rit), **Frank Lloyd,** 1867–1959, U.S. architect. —**Harold Bell,** 1872–1944, U.S. novelist. —**Joseph,** 1855–1930, English philologist and lexicographer. —**Orville,** 1871–1948, U.S. pioneer in aviation, with his brother **Wilbur,** 1867–1912. —**Richard,** 1908–1960, U.S. novelist. —**Willard Huntington,** 1888–1939, U.S. writer and art critic: pseudonym *S. S. Van Dine.*
wring (ring) *v.* **wrung** (*Rare* **wringed**), **wring·ing** *v.t.* 1 To squeeze or compress by twisting; turn and strain with force; pass (clothes) through a wringer. 2 To squeeze or press out, as water, by twisting. 3 To extort; acquire by extortion. 4 To distress; torment. 5 To twist or wrest violently out of shape or place: to *wring* his neck. 6 *Obs.* To pervert; distort. —*v.i.* 7 To writhe or squirm, as with anguish. 8 To perform the action of wringing. ◆ Homophone: *ring.* [OE *wringan*]
wring·bolt (ring′bōlt′) A ring bolt. [Earlier *wrainbolt,* var. of *ring bolt*]
wring·er (ring′ər) *n.* 1 One who or that which wrings. 2 A contrivance used to press water out of fabrics after washing; also, the operator of such a machine.
wrin·kle[1] (ring′kəl) *n.* 1 A small ridge or prominence, as on a smooth surface; a crease; fold. 2 Specifically, a small fold or crease in the skin, usually produced by age or by excessive exposure to the elements. 3 A ripple; little wave. —*v.t. & v.i.* **·kled, ·kling** To contract or be contracted into wrinkles or ridges; pucker. [OE *wrincle.* Akin to WRENCH.] —**wrin′kly** *adj.*
wrin·kle[2] (ring′kəl) *n. Colloq.* A curious or ingenious notion or device; happy thought; a novelty, as in dress. See synonyms under WHIM. [Prob. dim. of OE *wrenc* a trick]
wrist (rist) *n.* 1 The part of the arm immediately adjoining the hand; the carpus. ◆ Collateral adjective: *carpal.* 2 The part of a glove or garment that covers the wrist. 3 A wrist pin. [OE, prob. < *wrīthan* writhe]
wrist·band (rist′band′, -bənd, riz′-) *n.* The band of a sleeve that covers the wrist or ends a shirt sleeve.
wrist-drop (rist′drop′) *n. Pathol.* Paralysis of the forearm, usually due to lead poisoning.
wrist·let (rist′lit) *n.* 1 A flexible band worn on the wrist for ornament or warmth. 2 A bracelet. 3 *Slang* A handcuff.
wrist·lock (rist′lok′) *n.* In wrestling, a hold whereby an opponent is made helpless by twisting his arm with a grip at the wrist.
wrist pin *Mech.* 1 A pin holding together the piston and connecting rod of a steam engine. 2 A similar pin in the cross-head of an internal-combustion engine.
wrist watch A watch set in a leather or metal wristlet and worn at the wrist.
writ[1] (rit) *n.* 1 *Law* A written order, under seal, issued by a court, and commanding the person to whom it is addressed to do or not to do some act. 2 That which is written: now chiefly in the phrase **Holy Writ,** meaning the Bible. [OE, a writing < *wrītan* write]
writ[2] (rit) Archaic or dialectal past tense and past participle of WRITE.
write (rīt) *v.* **wrote** (*Archaic* or *Dial.* **writ**), **writ·ten** (*Archaic* or *Dial.* **writ**), **writ·ing** *v.t.* 1 To trace or inscribe (letters, words, numbers, symbols, etc.) on a surface with pen or pencil, or by other means. 2 To describe in writing: to *write* one's impressions of a journey. 3 To communicate by letter: Be sure to *write* all the news; He *writes* that he will be home soon. 4 To communicate with by letter: He *writes* her every day. 5 To produce by writing; be the author or composer of. 6 To draw up; draft: to *write* one's will; to *write* a check. 7 To cover or fill with writing: to *write* two full pages. 8 To leave marks or evidence of: Anxiety is *written* on his face. 9 To spell or inscribe as specified: He *writes* his name with two *n's.* 10 To entitle or designate in writing: He *writes* himself "General." 11 To underwrite: to *write* an insurance policy. —*v.i.* 12 To trace or inscribe letters, etc., on a surface, as of paper. 13 To write a letter or letters; communicate in writing. 14 To be engaged in the occupation of a writer or author. 15 To produce a specified quality of writing. See synonyms under INSCRIBE. —**to write down** 1 To put into writing. 2 To injure or depreciate in writing. —**to write in** 1 To insert in writing, as in a document. 2 To cast (a vote) for one not listed on a ballot by inserting his name in writing. —**to write off** 1 To cancel or remove (claims, debts, etc.) from an open account. 2 To acknowledge the loss or failure of. —**to write out** 1 To put into writing. 2 To write in full or complete form. —**to write up** 1 To describe fully in writing; put in written form: to *write up* a report. 2 To praise fully or too fully in writing. 3 In accounting, to put an unusually high value upon. ◆ Homophones: *right, rite, wright.* [OE *wrītan*]
◆ *Writ,* the archaic or dialectal past participle of *write,* is now used chiefly in the phrase **writ large,** written or shown on a grand scale: *a name writ large in history.*
write-off (rīt′ôf′, -of′) *n.* 1 A cancellation. 2 An amount canceled or noted as a loss.
writ·er (rī′tər) *n.* 1 One who writes. 2 One who engages in literary composition. 3 That which writes or assists in writing: used in composition: *typewriter.*
writer's cramp *Pathol.* Spasmodic contraction of the muscles of the fingers and hand, caused by excessive writing. Also **writer's palsy** or **spasm.**
write-up (rīt′up′) *n. Colloq.* A written description, record, or account, usually laudatory, as of a person, theatrical performance, etc.
writhe (rīth) *v.t. & v.i.* **writhed, writh·ing** To twist with violence; wrench; distort, as the body, face, or limbs in pain. —*n.* An act of writhing; a contortion. See synonyms under STRUGGLE. [OE *wrīthan*] —**writh′er** *n.*
writh·en (rith′ən) Obsolete past participle of WRITHE. —*adj. Poetic* Twisted; distorted.
writ·ing (rī′ting) *n.* 1 The act of one who writes. 2 The characters so made; chirography; handwriting. 3 Anything written or expressed in letters, especially a literary production. 4 *Law* A written instrument: words, or characters that stand for words or ideas, traced on some substance, as paper, wood, or stone, with an implement, as a pen, pencil, or brush, or by some other device, as stamping, printing, or engraving. 5 The profession or occupation of a writer. 6 The practice, art, form, or style of literary composition.
writing machine A typewriter.
writ·ing-mas·ter (rī′ting·mas′tər, -mäs′-) *n.* A teacher of penmanship.
writing paper Paper prepared to receive ink in writing.
writ of error *Law* A commission by which the judges of one court are authorized to examine a record upon which a judgment was given in another court, and to affirm or reverse the judgment according to law.
writ of prohibition *Law* A writ issued by a superior court to an inferior court, commanding it to desist from proceeding in a matter not within its jurisdiction.
writ of right *Law* 1 Formerly, in England, a writ in an action for the purpose of establishing a title to real estate. 2 A similar common-law writ.
writ of summons *Law* The writ by which, in modern practice, a civil action is commenced; a written order to an authorized officer to notify a person to appear in court to answer a complaint.
writ·ten (rit′n) Past participle of WRITE.
Wro·cław (vrô′tswäf) A city in SW Poland, on the Oder; a German city from the 13th century; part of Prussia 1741–1945; a major industrial center: German *Breslau.*
wrong (rông, rong) *adj.* 1 Deviating from moral rectitude as prescribed by civil or divine law or by conscience; immoral. 2 Not just, proper, or equitable according to a standard, code, or convention; incongruous; improper. 3 Deviating from fact and truth; not according to reality; erroneous; mistaken: a *wrong* estimate. 4 Not in accordance with rule or appropriateness; improper; incorrect: to enter the *wrong* store. 5 Deviating from the proper design, intention, or requirement; unsuitable: the *wrong* side of cloth; the *wrong* letter in a word. 6 Unsatisfactory: a *wrong* reply. —**to go wrong** 1 To lapse from the strict path of rectitude. 2 To turn out badly; go astray. —**on the wrong side of (30, 40,** etc.) Older than (30, etc.). See synonyms under IMMORAL, SINFUL. —*adv.* In a wrong direction, place, or manner; awry or amiss; erroneously. —*n.* 1 That which is contrary to justice or rectitude; an injury; mischief. 2 Hence, some particular form of disobedience or non-conformity to lawful authority, human or divine. 3 *Law* An invasion or violation of one's legal rights; specifically, a crime; a tort. See synonyms under INJURY, INJUSTICE, SIN[1]. —*v.t.* 1 To violate the rights of; inflict injury or injustice upon. 2 To impute evil to unjustly; misrepresent: If you think so, you *wrong* him. 3 To seduce (a woman). 4 To treat dishonorably; malign. 5 *Scot.* To injure. See synonyms under ABUSE. [OE *wrang* twisted <ON *rangr* awry, unjust] —**wrong′ness** *n.*
wrong·do·er (rông′dōō′ər, rong′-) *n.* One who commits a fault or crime. —**wrong′do′ing** *n.*
wrong·er (rông′ər, rong′-) *n.* One who commits an offense, injury, or trespass.
wrong font *Printing* The wrong font or type face: indicated by the abbreviation *w.f.* in marking printers' proofs.
wrong·ful (rông′fəl, rong′-) *adj.* 1 Characterized by wrong or injustice; injurious; unjust. 2 Unlawful; illegal. —**wrong′ful·ly** *adv.* —**wrong′ful·ness** *n.*
wrong-head·ed (rông′hed′id, rong′-) *adj.* Having perverted judgment; perverse; obstinate.

—**wrong'·head'ed·ly** *adv.* —**wrong'·head'ed·ness** *n.*

wrong·ly (rông'lē, rong'-) *adv.* In a wrong manner; erroneously; falsely.

wrote (rōt) Past tense of WRITE.

wroth (rôth) *adj.* Filled with anger; angry. —*n. Obs.* Anger. [OE *wrāth*]

wrought (rôt) Archaic past tense and past participle of WORK. —*adj.* **1** Beaten or hammered into shape by tools: *wrought* gold. **2** Worked; molded. **3** Made with delicacy; elaborated carefully. **4** Made; fashioned; formed: The cathedral was *wrought* by skilled hands. [ME *wrogt*, var. of *worht*, pp. of *wirchen* work]

wrought iron Commercially pure iron, prepared from pig iron and easily forged and welded into various shapes.

wrought up Excited.

wrung (rung) Past tense and past participle of WRING.

wry (rī) *adj.* **wri·er, wri·est 1** Bent to one side or out of position; contorted; askew; also, made by twisting or distorting the features: a *wry* smile. **2** Hence, deviating from that which is right or proper; perverted, as a course or an interpretation; warped. —*v.t.* **wried, wry·ing** To twist; contort. ◆ Homophone: *rye.* [ME *wrye* < OE *wrigian* move, tend] —**wry'ly** *adv.* —**wry'ness** *n.*

Wry may appear as a combining form in hyphemes, with the meaning of adjective definition 1:

wry–eyed	**wry–looking**	**wry–set**
wry–faced	**wry–mouthed**	**wry–toothed**

wry·neck (rī'nek') *n.* **1** A bird (genus *Jynx*) resembling and allied to the woodpeckers, with the habit of twisting its head and neck. **2** A rheumatic affection in the muscles of the neck; torticollis. **3** One having a twisted neck; a person afflicted with torticollis.

Wu (wōō) The chief river of Kweichow province, south central China, comprising the upper course of the Kien and flowing over 5000 miles NE, north, and NW into the Kien proper in SE Szechwan province.

Wu (wōō), **C. C.**, 1886–1934, Chinese statesman and diplomat: full name *Wu Ch'ao–ch'u.*

Wu·chang (wōō'chäng') A formerly independent city and former capital of Hupeh province, China, on the Yangtze river, now part of Wuhan.

Wuch·er·e·ri·a (vukh'ə·rer'ē·ə) *n.* A genus of parasitic nematode worms, especially *W. bancrofti*, the causative agent of elephantiasis. [after Otto *Wucherer*, 1820–73, German physician]

wud (wud) *adj. Scot.* Mad; insane.

Wu·han (wōō'hän') A city comprising the three formerly independent cities of Hankow, Hanyang, and Wuchang on the Yangtze river, capital of Hupeh province, east central China: also *Han Cities.*

Wu·hu (wōō'hōō') A port on the Yangtze river in central Anhwei province, central eastern China.

wul·fen·ite (wŏŏl'fən·īt) *n.* A resinous or hard, yellow, brown, or red molybdate of lead, PbMoO₄, usually occurring in tabular crystals. [after F. X. von *Wulfen*, 1728–1805, Austrian mineralogist]

Wul·fi·la (wŏŏl'fə·lə) See ULFILAS.

wun (wun) *Scot.* Won. —*v.t. & v.i.* To win. —*n.* Wind.

Wundt (vŏŏnt), **Wilhelm Max**, 1832–1920, German psychologist and physiologist. —**Wundt'i·an** *adj.*

wun·na (wun'nə) *Scot.* Will not.

Wup·per·tal (vŏŏp'ər·täl) A city in SW central North Rhine–Westphalia, west central West Germany, formed by the union of the cities of Barmen and Elberfeld.

Würm (vürm) See GLACIAL EPOCH.

Würm·see (vürm'zā) See STARNBERGERSEE.

Würt·tem·berg (wûr'təm·bûrg, *Ger.* vür'təm·berkh) A former state of SW Germany; 7,532 square miles; capital, Stuttgart; divided after 1945 into Württemberg–Baden and Württemberg–Hohenzollern, which merged in 1951, along with Baden, to form the state of Baden–Württemberg.

Würt·tem·berg–Ba·den (wûr'təm·bûrg·bäd'. *Ger.* vür'təm·berkh·bä'den) A former state of SW Germany in the Federal Republic (1949) formed in 1945 by the union of northern Württemberg and northern Baden; 6,062 square miles; capital, Stuttgart; in 1951 the states Baden, Württemberg–Baden and Württemberg–Hohenzollern merged to form the state of Baden–Württemberg; 13,800 square miles; capital, Stuttgart.

Würt·tem·berg–Ho·hen·zol·lern (wûr'təm·bûrg·hō'ən·zol'ərn, *Ger.* vür'təm·berkh·hō'·ən·tsôl'ərn) A state of SW Germany in the Federal Republic (1949); formed in 1945 by the union of southern Württemberg and the former Prussian province of Hohenzollern; 4,018 square miles; capital, Tübingen; merged into the state of Baden–Württemberg in 1951.

Würz·burg (würts'bûrg, *Ger.* vürts'bŏŏrkh) A city in Lower Franconia, NW Bavaria, SW central West Germany.

Wu·sih (wōō'shē') A city of southern Kiangsu province, central eastern China.

Wu T'ing–fang (wōō' ting'fäng'), 1841–1922, Chinese reformer and diplomat; father of C. C. Wu.

Wu·wei (wōō'wā') A city in central Kansu province, north central China.

Wy·an·dot (wī'ən·dot) *n.* One of a tribe of North American Indians of Iroquoian stock, formerly very powerful in the Ohio valley and lake regions: descendants of a group of fugitive Hurons who called themselves *Wendat*: presently settled in Oklahoma. Also **Wy'an·dotte.**

Wy·an·dotte (wī'ən·dot) *n.* One of an American breed of domestic fowls. [after the *Wyandot* Indians]

Wy·att (wī'ət), **Sir Thomas**, 1503–42, English poet and diplomat.

wych (wich) See WITCH².

wych–elm (wich'elm') *n.* **1** A wide–spreading elm (*Ulmus glabra*), with large, dull–green leaves, common in England, Ireland, and Scotland: also called *Scotch elm.* **2** Witch hazel. Also **witch.** [< *wych*, var. of WITCH² +ELM]

Wych·er·ley (wich'ər·lē), **William**, 1640?–1716, English dramatist and poet.

wych–ha·zel (wich'hā'zəl) *n.* **1** Witch hazel. **2** Wych–elm. [Var. of WITCH HAZEL]

Wyc·lif (wik'lif), **John**, 1324?–84, English reformer; first translator, with assistants, of the entire Bible into English. Also spelled *Wiclif, Wickliffe, Wycliffe.* —**Wyc'lif·ite** *adj. & n.*

wye (wī) *n.* The letter Y, or something Y–shaped.

Wye (wī) A river of SE Wales and SW England, flowing 130 miles SE from SW Montgomery to the Severn estuary.

Wyld (wīld), **Henry Cecil Kennedy**, 1870–1945, English philologist and lexicographer.

wyle (wīl) *v.t. Scot.* or *Obs.* To beguile; wile.

Wy·lie (wī'lē), **Elinor Morton**, 1885–1928, *née* Hoyt, U.S. poet and novelist: married name *Mrs. William Rose Benét.* —**Philip Gordon**, 1902–1971, U.S. author.

wy·lie–coat (wī'lē·kōt', wīl'ē-, wul'ē-) *n. Scot.* A boy's flannel underdress; also, a flannel petticoat.

Wy·o·ming (wī·ō'ming) A State in the NW United States; 97,914 square miles; capital, Cheyenne; entered the Union July 10, 1890; nickname, *Equality State*: abbr. WY —**Wy. o'ming·ite** *n.*

Wyoming Valley A valley along the north branch of the Susquehanna River in NE Pennsylvania; scene of a massacre of settlers by Indians and Tories, 1778; chief city, Wilkes-Barre.

Wythe (with), **George**, 1726–1806, American jurist; signer of the Declaration of Independence.

wy·vern (wī'vərn) See WIVERN.

X

x, X (eks) *n. pl.* **x's** or **X's, xs** or **Xs, ex·es** (ek'siz) **1** The 24th letter of the English alphabet: from the ancient western Greek alphabets of Chalcis, Boeotia, and Elis, and Roman *X.* **2** The sound of the letter *x*: in English variously sounded as (ks), as in *axle, box, next*; (gz), as in *executive, exert*; (ksh), as in *noxious*; (gzh), as in *luxurious*; and initially, always (z) as in *xenophobe, xylophone, Xanthippe.* See ALPHABET. —*symbol* **1** The Roman numeral ten. See under NUMERAL. **2** *Math.* The principal unknown quantity; hence, anything unknown. **3** A mark shaped like an X, representing the signature of one who cannot write. **4** A mark used in diagrams, maps, etc., to place some event or substance, or to point out something to be emphasized. **5** A symbol used to indicate a kiss. **6** Anything shaped like an X. —**X marks the spot** *Colloq.* "Here": used in diagrams, maps, or the like, to indicate a specific locality.

xan·thate (zan'thāt) *n. Chem.* A salt or ester of xanthic acid. [< XANTH(IC) + -ATE³]

xan·the·in (zan'thē·in) *n. Biochem.* A water-soluble yellow coloring matter found in the cell sap of some plants. [< F *xanthéine* < Gk. *xanthos* yellow]

xan·the·las·ma (zan'thə·laz'mə) *n. Pathol.* A form of xanthoma marked by the appearance of small yellowish disks on the eyelids. [< NL < Gk. *xanthos* yellow + *elasmos* a metal plate]

Xan·thi·an (zan'thē·ən) *adj.* Relating to Xanthus.

xan·thic (zan'thik) *adj.* **1** Having a yellow or yellowish color. **2** *Chem.* Of or pertaining to xanthin or xanthine. [< F *xanthique* < Gk. *xanthos* yellow]

xanthic acid *Chem.* Any of a group of unstable, colorless, liquid thio compounds made by decomposing a xanthate with a dilute acid.

xan·thin (zan'thin) *n. Biochem.* An insoluble yellow pigment found in yellow flowers. [< G < Gk. *xanthos* yellow]

xan·thine (zan'thēn, -thin) *n. Biochem.* A white, crystalline, nitrogenous compound. C₅H₄N₄O₂, contained in blood, urine, and other animal secretions, and in some plants. It leaves a yellow residue when evaporated with nitric acid. [< F < Gk. *xanthos* yellow]

Xan·thip·pe (zan·tip'ē) The wife of Socrates; renowned as a shrew. Also **Xan·tip'pe.**

xantho– *combining form* Yellow: *xanthophyll.* Also, before vowels, **xanth–.** [< Gk. *xanthos* yellow]

xan·tho·car·pous (zan·thō·kär'pəs) *adj. Bot.* Yellow–fruited.

xan·tho·chroid (zan'thə·kroid) *Anthropol. adj.* Characterized by a light–colored or fair complexion. —*n.* One who exhibits xanthochroid characteristics. [< XANTHO- + Gk. *chroa* color + -OID]

xan·tho·ma (zan·thō'mə) *n. Pathol.* A skin disease marked by the presence of small yellowish disks formed by the deposit of lipoids. [< XANTH- + -OMA]

xan·tho·phyll (zan'thə·fil) *n. Biochem.* A yellow pigment, C₄₀H₅₆O₂, contained in plants and related to carotene. Also **xan'tho·phyl.** [< F *xanthophylle* < Gk. *xanthos* yellow + *phyllon* a leaf]

xan·thop·si·a (zan·thop'sē·ə) *n. Pathol.* A disorder of vision in which all objects appear yellow. [< NL < Gk. *xanthos* yellow + *opsis* a sight]

xan·thous (zan'thəs) *adj.* **1** Yellow. **2** *Anthropol.* **a** Of or pertaining to the yellow–skinned or Mongoloid type of mankind. **b** Of or re-

lating to that variety of mankind that has yellowish, brown, or auburn hair, including the Teutons and Scandinavians; blond. Opposed to *melanous*. [<XANTH(O)- + OUS]

Xan·thus (zan′thəs) An ancient ruined city of Lycia, SW Turkey in Asia, near the Mediterranean.

Xa·vi·er (zā′vē·ər, zav′ē-; *Sp.* hä·vyer′), **Saint Francis,** 1506–52, Spanish Jesuit missionary in the Orient; founder, with Ignatius Loyola, of the Society of Jesus: called "the Apostle of the Indies." — **Xa·ve·ri·an** (zā·vir′ē·ən) *adj. & n.*

X-chro·mo·some (eks′krō′mə·sōm) *n.* A sex chromosome.

Xe *Chem.* Xenon (symbol Xe).

xe·bec (zē′bek) *n.* A small, three-masted Mediterranean vessel, with both square and lateen sails: formerly used by Algerine pirates: also spelled *zebec.* [Earlier *chebec* <F <Sp. *jabeque, xabeque* <Arabic *shabbāk*]

xe·ni·a (zē′nē·ə) *n. Bot.* The influence of the pollen of one species upon the maternal tissues of another species after hybrid fertilization: a phenomenon observed particularly in maize, which often shows blue kernels in a yellow-seeded variety pollinated by a blue-seeded one. [<NL <Gk. *xenia* hospitality <*xenos* a guest]

xe·ni·al (zē′nē·əl) *adj.* Of or pertaining to hospitality. [<Gk. *xenia.* See XENIA.]

xeno- combining form Strange; foreign; different: *xenophobia.* Also, before vowels, **xen-.** [<Gk. *xenos* a stranger]

Xe·noc·ra·tes (zi·nok′rə·tēz), 396?–314 B.C., Greek philosopher.

xe·nog·a·my (zi·nog′ə·mē) *n. Biol.* Cross-fertilization. — **xe·nog′a·mous** *adj.*

xen·o·gen·e·sis (zen′ə·jen′ə·sis) *n. Biol.* 1 Abiogenesis. 2 Metagenesis. 3 The fancied production of an organism unlike either of its parents. Also **xe·nog·e·ny** (zi·noj′ə·nē). — **xen′o·ge·net′ic** (-jə·net′ik), **xen′o·gen′ic** *adj.*

xe·no·gloss·i·a (zē′nə·glô′sē·ə, -glos′ē·ə) *n.* In psychic research, the alleged power of a person to communicate with others in a language which he has never learned. [<NL <Gk. *xenos* strange + *glōssa* a tongue]

xen·o·lith (zen′ə·lith) *n. Geol.* A rock fragment enclosed in a larger mass of igneous rock.

xen·o·mor·phic (zen′ə·môr′fik) *adj. Mineral.* Not having its own characteristic form, but having an irregular shape that is imposed by the interference of surrounding minerals: said of the constituents of a crystalline rock.

xe·non (zē′non) *n.* A colorless, odorless, almost inert gaseous element (symbol Xe, atomic number 54) occurring in small traces in the atmosphere. See PERIODIC TABLE. [<Gk., neut. of *xenos* strange]

Xe·noph·a·nes (zi·nof′ə·nēz) Sixth century B.C. Greek philosopher and poet.

xen·o·phobe (zen′ə·fōb) *n.* A person who hates or distrusts strangers or foreigners.

xen·o·pho·bi·a (zen′ə·fō ′bē·ə) *n.* Dislike of strangers or foreigners.

Xen·o·phon (zen′ə·fən), 435?–355? B.C., Greek historian and soldier.

Xe·res (hā′rās, *older* shā′rās, sher′es) The former name for JEREZ.

Xé·rez (hā′rās, -räth), **Francisco de,** 1504–1547?, Spanish historian of the conquest of Peru.

xer·ic (zer′ik, zir′ik) *adj.* Of, pertaining to, or characterized by extreme dryness; arid.

xero- combining form Dry; dryness: *xerophyte.* Also, before vowels, **xer-.** [<Gk. *xēros* dry]

xe·ro·chore (zir′ə·kôr, -kōr) *n. Ecol.* A region of extreme dryness; the desert areas of the earth, collectively. — **xe′ro·chor′ic** (-kôr′ik, -kor′ik) *adj.*

xe·ro·der·ma (zir′ō·dûr′mə) *n. Pathol.* Roughness and dryness of the skin, with scaly desquamation. [<NL <Gk. *xēros* dry + *derma* skin] — **xe′ro·der·mat′ic** (-dər·mat′ik), **xe′ro·der′ma·tous** (-dûr′mə·təs) *adj.*

Xe·ro·form (zir′ə·fôrm) *n.* Proprietary name for a yellow powder containing bismuth and tribromphenol in equal quantities: used as an intestinal and surgical antiseptic.

xe·rog·ra·phy (zi·rog′rə·fē) *n.* A method of printing by electrostatic attraction in which a negatively charged ink powder is sprayed

upon the positively charged copy area of a metal plate, whence it is transferred to the positively charged printing surface. — **xe·ro·graph·ic** (zir′ō·graf′ik) *adj.* — **xe·rog′raph·er** *n.*

xe·ro·mor·phy (zir′ō·môr′fē) *n. Bot.* The form or structure of the plant by which it is protected from desiccation. [<XERO- + Gk. *morphē*form] — **xe′ro·mor′phic** *adj.*

xe·roph·i·lous (zi·rof′ə·ləs) *adj. Bot.* Growing in or adapted to drought: said of plants living in dry, hot climates, as the cactus.

xe·roph·thal·mi·a (zir′əf·thal′mē·ə) *n. Pathol.* Inflammation with thickening of the lining membrane of the eye, but without liquid discharge: associated with conjunctivitis and a lack of vitamin A. [<NL <Gk. *xēros* dry + *ophthalmos* an eye]

xe·ro·phyte (zir′ə·fīt) *n. Bot.* A plant adapted to dry conditions of air and soil. — **xe′ro·phyt′ic** (-fit′ik) *adj.*

xe·ro·print·ing (zir′ō·prin′ting) *n.* A simplified variation of xerography which uses a suitably prepared plate on a rotating cylinder.

xe·ro·esere (zir′ə·sir) *n. Ecol.* The series of changes in the succession of the plant formation found upon dry soil. [<XERO- + SERE²]

xe·ro·sis (zi·rō′sis) *n. Pathol.* A condition of abnormal dryness of a part; specifically, a dry, thickened, and scaly condition of the skin or mucous membrane of a part. [<NL <Gk. *xēros* dry] — **xe·rot′ic** (-rot′ik) *adj.*

xe·ro·tro·pism (zir′ō·tr + 340 ′piz·əm) *n. Bot.* The tendency of plants, or plant parts, to alter their position so as to protect themselves from desiccation. — **xe′ro·trop′ic** *adj.*

Xer·ox (zir′oks) *n.* A xerographic process for producing copies of printed or pictorial matter: a trade name. — *v.t.* To make or reproduce by Xerox. Also **xer′ox.**

Xerx·es (zûrk′sēz), 519?–465? B.C., Persian king 486?–465; invaded Greece, but was defeated at Salamis 480 B.C.

Xho·sa (kō′sä) *n.* 1 Member of a Bantu-speaking people of the Republic of South Africa. 2 Bantu language of the Xhosa people. Also spelled *Xosa.*

xi (zī, sī; *Gk.* ksē) *n.* The fourteenth letter in the Greek alphabet (Ξ, ξ): equivalent to English *x* or *z.* [<Gk.]

Xin·gú (shing·gōō′) A river in northern and central Brazil, flowing 1,230 miles north from central Mato Grosso to the Amazon at the head of its delta.

-xion Var. of -TION.

xiphi- combining form A sword; of or pertaining to a sword: *xiphisternum.* Also, before vowels, **xiph-.** [<Gk. *xiphos* a sword]

xiph·i·ster·num (zif′ə·stûr′nəm) *n. pl.* **·na** (-nə) *Anat.* The lower segment or ensiform process of the sternum. Also *xiphoid.* [<NL <Gk. *xiphos* a sword + *sternon* the breastbone]

xiph·oid (zif′oid) *adj.* Shaped like a sword: the *xiphoid* cartilage at the lower end of the breastbone. —*n.* The xiphisternum.

xiph·o·su·ran (zif′ə·sŏor′ən) *n.* Any of an order (*Xiphosura*) of primitive arachnids having a horseshoe-shaped carapace and a long swordlike tail; a king crab. —*adj.* Of or pertaining to the Xiphosura. [<NL <Gk. *xiphos* a sword + *oura* a tail]

Xmas Christmas: popular abbreviation. [< *X,* abbr. for *Christ* <Gk. *X,* chi, the first letter of *Christos* Christ + -MAS]

Xo·chi·mil·co (sō′chi·mēl′kō) A resort city south of Mexico City in Federal District, central Mexico; famous for its "floating gardens."

Xo·sa (kō′sä) See XHOSA.

XP Chi and rho: The first two letters of ΧΡΙΣΤΟΣ, the Greek word for Christ: introduced by Constantine the Great as an emblem of Christ.

X-ray (eks′rā′) *v.t.* To examine, diagnose, or treat with X-rays. —*n.* A picture made with X-rays; roentgenogram: also **X-ray photograph.**

X-rays (eks′rāz′) *n. pl.* Electromagnetic radiations of extremely short wavelength, emitted from a substance when it is bombarded by a stream of electrons moving at a sufficiently high velocity, as in a Coolidge tube. Their great penetrating power, ionizing effect, and property of acting on photographic plates have many useful applications, especially in

the detection, diagnosis, and treatment of certain organic disorders, chiefly internal. Also called *Roentgen rays.* [Trans. of G *X-strahlen,* name coined by Roentgen, their discoverer, because their nature was unknown]

X-ray therapy Medical treatment by the use of X-rays.

Xu·thus (zōō′thəs) In Greek legend, son of Hellen and ancestor of the Ionians.

xy·lan (zī′lan) *n. Biochem.* A yellow, gummuy hemicellulose found in straw, oat hulls, peanut shells, and other plant wastes: it yields xylose on hydrolysis. [<Gk. *xylon* wood]

xy·lem (zī′ləm) *n.* The chief fluid-transporting and supportive tissue in vascular plants, made up of various arrangements of tracheids, parenchyma, fibers, and associated cells. [<G <Gk. *xylon* wood]

xy·lene (zī′lēn) *n. Chem.* Any one of three isomeric colorless hydrocarbons, $C_6H_4(CH_3)_2$, contained in coal tar and wood tar. A mixture of the three yields a colorless, inflammable liquid used as a solvent and in medicine as an antiseptic. Also **xy′lol** (-lōl, -lol). [<Gk. *xylon* wood + -ENE]

xy·lic (zī′lik) *adj.* Of, pertaining to, or derived from xylene. [<XYL (ENE) + -IC]

xylic acid *Chem.* One of six isomeric crystalline carboxyl derivatives of xylene, C_8H_9 COOH.

xy·li·dine (zī′lə·dēn, -din, zil′ə-) *n. Chem.* Any of six isomeric amino derivatives of xylene, $C_8H_{11}N$: they are homologs of aniline, and are used in the synthesis of certain dyes. Also **xy′li·din** (-din). [<XYL (ENE) + -ID(E) + -INE²]

xylo- combining form Wood; of or pertaining to wood; woody: *xylocarpous.* Also, before vowels, **cxyl-.** [<Gk. *xylon* wood]

xy·lo·car·pous (zī′lō·kär′pəs) *adj. Bot.* Having a hard, woody fruit.

xy·lo·graph (zī′lə·graf, -gräf) *n.* 1 An engraving on wood, or a print from such engraving. 2 An impression obtained from the grain of wood, as used for surface decoration. — **xy′lo·graph′ic** or **·i·cal** *adj.* — **xy·log·ra·pher** (zī·log′rə·fər) *n.*

xy·log·ra·phy (t)zī·log′rə ·fē) *n.* 1 Wood engraving, especially of the 15th century. 2 Printing with wood engravings. 3 Painting or printing on wood for decorative purposes. 4 The making of prints or impressions showing the grain of wood.

xy·loid (zī′loid) *adj.* Of, pertaining to, or resembling wood.

xy·loph·a·gous (zī·lof′ə·gəs) *adj.* Feeding on or boring in wood, as insect larvae. [<XYLO- + -PHAGOUS] — **xy·lo·phage** (zī′lə·fāj) *n.*

xy·lo·phone (zī′lə·fōn) *n.* A musical instrument consisting of a row of parallel wooden bars graduated in length to form a musical scale and struck by small mallets or sounded by rubbing. [<XYLO- + -PHONE] — **xy·loph·o·nist** (zī·lof′ə·nist) *n.*

XYLOPHONE

xy·lose (zī′lōs) *n. Chem.* A pentose, $C_5H_{10}O_5$, obtained by treating xylan with sulfuric acid; wood sugar: the levorotatory form is used in the synthesis of vitamin C. [<XYL(AN) + -OSE²]

xy·lot·o·mous (zī·lot′ə·məs) *adj.* Adapted to cutting or boring wood, as an insect. [<XYLO- + Gk. *tomē* a cutting <*temnein* cut]

xy·lot·o·my (zī·lot′ə·mē) *n.* The preparation of wood for examination by microscope, as for scientific purposes. [<XYLO- + -TOMY] — **xy·lot′o·mist** *n.*

xy·lyl (zī′lil) *n. Chem.* The univalent radical, $(CH_3)_2C_6H_3$, derived from xylene. [<XYL(ENE) + -YL]

xy·ly·lene (zī′lə·lēn) *n. Chem.* The bivalent radical, C_8H_8, contained in xylene. [<XYLYL + -ENE]

xyst (zist) *n.* **1** In classical antiquity, a hall or covered portico used by athletes for their exercises: chiefly for use in stormy weather.

2 A garden walk or terrace. [< L *xystus* < Gk. *xystos,* orig. scraped, polished < *xyein* scrape, polish]

xys·ter (zis′tər) *n.* A surgical instrument for scraping bones. [< NL < Gk. *xystēr* a scraper, < *xyein* scrape]

Y

y, Y (wī) *n. pl.* **y's, Y's,** or **ys, Ys** or **wyes** (wīz) **1** The 25th letter of the English alphabet: ultimately from Phoenician *vau,* Greek *upsilon.* The Romans took it from the Greek alphabet sometime in the first century B.C. and used it as a vowel. **2** The sound of the letter *y.* Initial *y* (introducing either a vowel or a syllable) is a voiced palatal semivowel, as in *yet, you, yonder, beyond.* Final *y* is either a vowel, pronounced (ē), as in *honey, pretty, steady;* a diphthong, pronounced (ī), as in *fly, my;* or the final glide of a diphthong, as in *gray, obey, annoy.* Internal *y* is pronounced as a vowel (i), as in *lyric, myth, syllable;* a diphthong (ī), as in *lyre, type, psychic;* an *r*-colored central vowel (ûr) or (ər), as in *myrtle, martyr.* See ALPHABET.

Y (wī) *n.* **1** Something similar to a Y in shape. **2** A branch pipe, forked pipe, or coupling in the shape of the letter Y. **3** A forked piece, often with the branches curved, usually one of a pair, serving as a rest or support, as for some part of a sighting instrument.
—*symbol Chem.* Yttrium (symbol Y).

y- *prefix* Used in Middle English as a sign of the past participle, as an intensive, or without perceptible force: *yclad, yclept.* It survives (as *a-*) in such words as *alike, aware,* etc. Also spelled *i-,* as in *iwis.* [OE *ge-*]

-y¹ *suffix of adjectives* Being, possessing, or resembling what is expressed in the main element: *stony, rainy.* Also *-ey,* when added to words ending in *y,* as in *clayey, skyey.* [OE *-ig*]

-y² *suffix* The quality or state of being: *victory:* often used in abstract nouns formed from adjectives in *-ous* and *-ic.* [< F *-ie* < L *-ia;* also < Gk. *-ia, -eia*]

-y³ *suffix* Little; small: *kitty:* often used in nicknames or to express endearment, as in *Tommy.* [Prob. < dial. E (Scottish) < OF *-i, -e,* dim. suffixes]

Ya·an (yä′än′) A city in west central Szechwan province, western China.

yab·ber (yab′ər) *n. Austral. Colloq.* Speech; talk; jabber. [< Australian *yabba* < *ya* speak]

Ya·blo·noi Range (yi·blə·noi′) Part of the watershed between the Arctic and Pacific drainage areas, in SE Asiatic Russian S.F.S.R.; highest peak, 5,280 feet. Also **Ya·blo·no·vy** (yi′blə·nô′vē).

yacht (yot) *n.* A relatively small vessel specially built or fitted for private pleasure excursions, as distinguished from war or commerce. —*v.i.* To cruise, race, or sail in a yacht. [< Du. *jaghte,* short for *jaghtschip* a pursuit ship < *jaght* hunting (< *jagen* hunt) + *schip* a ship]

yacht club A club of yachtsmen.

yacht·ing (yot′ing) *n.* The act, practice, or pastime of sailing in or managing a yacht.

yachts·man (yots′mən) *n. pl.* **·men** (-mən) One who owns or sails a yacht; a devotee of yachting. Also **yacht′er, yacht′man.** —**yachts′wom·an** (-woom′ən) *n. fem.*

yachts·man·ship (yots′mən·ship) *n.* The art of managing a yacht; skill in yachting. Also **yacht′man·ship.**

yack·er (yak′ər) *n. Austral. Slang* Work, especially hard work: also spelled *yakker.*

Yad·kin River (yad′kin) The upper course of the Pee Dee River, flowing 204 miles NE and SE from NW to south central North Carolina.

yaff (yaf) *v.i. Brit. Dial.* To bark like a dog when excited; hence, to speak sharply; scold.

yaf·fle (yaf′əl) *n.* The green woodpecker. [Imit. of its cry]

yag·ger (yag′ər) *n. Scot.* An itinerant peddler; wanderer; ranger.

ya·gua·run·di (yä·gwə·run′dē) See JAGUARONDI.

yah¹ (yä, ya) *interj.* An exclamation of disgust; bah.

yah² (yä, yâ) *interj. Colloq.* Yes. [Alter. of YES; infl. in form by G *ja* yes]

Ya·ha·ta (yä·hä·tä) See YAWATA.

ya·hoo (yä′hōō, yä′-, yä·hōō′) *n.* **1** Any person of low or vicious instincts. **2** An awkward fellow; a bumpkin. [< YAHOO]

Ya·hoo (yä′hōō, yä′-, yä·hōō′) *n.* One of an imaginary race of brutes possessing human form and vices, described by Swift in *Gulliver's Travels.* See HOUYHNHNM.

Yah·weh (yä′we) In the Old Testament, the national god of Israel; God: a modern transliteration of the Tetragrammaton. See JEHOVAH. Also spelled *Jahveh, Jahwe.* Also **Yah·veh** (yä′ve). [< Hebrew *YHWH*]

Yah·wism (yä′wiz·əm) *n.* **1** The ancient Hebrew religion centered on the monotheistic worship of Yahweh. **2** The use of the name Yahweh for God. Also spelled *Jahvism, Jahwism.* Also **Yah′vism** (-viz·əm).

Yah·wist (yä′wist) *n.* In Biblical criticism, the writer supposed to have written those parts of the Hexateuch in which God is mentioned as Yahweh (erroneously Jehovah). Compare ELOHIST. Also spelled *Jahvist, Jahwist.* Also **Yah′vist** (-vist).

Yah·wis·tic (yä·wis′tik) *adj.* **1** Of or relating to Yahwist or Yadwism. **2** Characterized by the use of the name Yahweh (or Jehovah) for God. Compare ELOHISTIC. Also spelled *Jahvistic, Jahwistic.* Also **Yah·vis′tic** (-vis′-).

yaird (yârd) *n. Scot.* **1** A yard (36 inches). **2** A garden; courtyard; churchyard.

yak (yak) *n.* A large bovine ruminant *(Bos grunniens)* of the higher regions of central Asia: it has long hair fringing the shoulders, sides, and tail, and is often domesticated. [< Tibetan *gyag*]

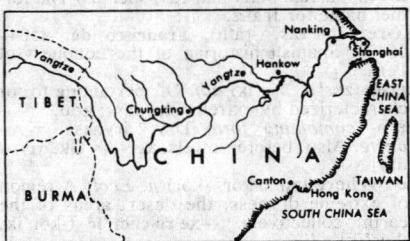

YAK
(From 5 to 5 1/2 feet high at the shoulder)

Yak·i·ma (yak′ə·mə) A city on the Yakima River in southern Washington.

Yakima River A river in central and southern Washington, flowing 203 miles SE from the Cascade Range to the Columbia River.

yak·ker (yak′ker) *n.* Yacker.

Ya·ko (yä′kōō) See JACO.

Ya·kof (yä′kôf) Russian form of JAMES.

Ya·kut (yä·kōōt′) *n.* **1** One of a people living in the Yakut Autonomous S.S.R. **2** The Turkic language of these people.

Ya·kut Autonomous Soviet Socialist Republic (yä·kōōt′) An administrative division of NE Asiatic Russian S.F.S.R.; 1,181,971 square miles; capital, Yakutsk.

Ya·kutsk (yä·kōōtsk′) A city on the Lena river; capital of Yakut Autonomous S.S.R.

yald¹ (yäd, yôd) See YELD.

yald² (yäd, yôd) *adj. Scot.* Athletic; supple; active: also spelled *yauld.*

Yale (yāl), **Elihu,** 1649–1721, English merchant; benefactor of Yale College (now Yale University); born in America. —**Linus,** 1821–68, U.S. locksmith.

Yal·ta (yäl′tə, yôl′-) A port on the Black Sea in the southern Crimea, U.S.S.R.; scene of a conference of Roosevelt, Churchill, and Stalin in February, 1945.

Ya·lu (yä′lōō′) A river forming part of the boundary between Manchuria, NE China, and Korea, and flowing 500 miles SW to the Yellow Sea: Japanese *Oryokko.*

Ya·lung (yä′lōōng′) A river in Szechwan province, China, flowing 800 miles south from SE Tsinghai province to the Yangtze, on the border of Yünnan province.

yam (yam) *n.* **1** The fleshy, edible, tuberous root of any of a genus *(Dioscorea)* of climbing tropical plants. **2** Any of the plants growing this root. **3** A large variety of the sweet potato. **4** *Scot.* A potato. [< Pg. *inhame* < Senegal *nyami* eat]

Ya·ma·ga·ta (yä·mä·gä·tä), **Prince Aritomo,** 1838–1922, Japanese general.

Ya·mal Peninsula (ye·mäl′) A peninsula of Asiatic Russian S.F.S.R. between the Kara Sea and Ob Gulf, about 400 miles long, up to 140 miles wide.

Ya·ma·mo·to (yä·mä·mō·tō), **Isoroku,** 1884–1943, Japanese admiral.

Ya·ma·shi·ta (yä·mä·shē·tä), **Tomoyuki,** 1885–1946, Japanese general; captured Singapore (February) and Philippines (May) 1942; executed as war criminal; called "the Tiger of Malaya."

Yam·bol (yäm′bôl) A city of east central Bulgaria: also *Jambol.* Turkish **Yam·bo·li** (yäm′bô·lē′).

yam·mer (yam′ər) *v.i. Colloq.* **1** To complain peevishly; whine, whimper. **2** To howl; roar; shout. —*v.t.* **3** To utter peevishly; complain. [OE *geōmrian* lament < *geōmor* sorrowful; infl. in form by MDu. *jammeren* complain]

ya·men (yä′mən) *n. Chinese* The office or official residence of a public functionary, as a mandarin; also, any department of the public service: the *yamen* of public justice. Also **ya′mun.**

Ya·nam (yə·num′) A city and former French settlement in NE Andhra Pradesh State, SE India. French **Ya·na·on** (yä·nȧ·ôn′).

yang (yang) *n.* In Chinese philosophy and art, the male element, source of life and heat, represented symbolically by a circular diagram bisected by an S-curve, one half red *(yang),* the other half black *(yin):* originated during the Han Dynasty: opposed to *yin.* Also **Yang.** [< Chinese]

Yang (yang), **C(hen) N(ing),** born 1922, U.S. physicist born in China.

Yang·chow (yäng′jō′) A city in central Kiangsu province, eastern China.

Yang·tze (yang′tsĕ′, Chinese yäng′tse′) The longest river of Asia and China, flowing 3,430 miles from the Tibetan highlands to the East China Sea near Shanghai; forms border between Tibetan Autonomous Region and Szechwan province. Also **Yang′tze-Ki·ang′** (-kē·ang′, Chinese jē·äng′), **Yangtse-Kiang.**

Ya·ni·na (yä′nē·nä) See IOANNINA.

yank (yangk) *v.t.* **1** To jerk or pull suddenly. —*v.i.* **2** To give a pull or jerk. **3** *Brit.* To be vigorously active. **4** *Brit.* To jabber; scold. —*n.* **1** *Colloq.* A sudden sharp pull; jerk. **2** *Scot.* A sharp blow or slap; buffet. [? < dial. E (Scottish) *yank* a sharp sudden blow]

Yank (yangk) *n. & adj. Colloq.* Yankee. [Short for YANKEE]

Yan·kee (yang′kē) *n.* **1** Originally, a native or inhabitant of New England. **2** A Northerner; especially, a Federal soldier during the Civil War: so called in the South. **3** Any

citizen of the United States; an American: a foreign, chiefly British, usage. —*adj.* **1** Of or pertaining to the Yankees. **2** *Brit.* American. [Prob. back formation < *Jan Kees* (taken as a plural), John Cheese, orig. a nickname for a Hollander; later applied by Dutch colonists in New York to English settlers in Connecticut]

Yan·kee·dom (yang′kē·dəm) *n.* **1** New England or the northern States as opposed to southern. **2** The United States as a whole. **3** Yankees collectively or as a class.

Yankee Doodle A song, of many humorous verses, popular in pre-Revolutionary times and one of the national airs of the United States.

Yan·kee·ism (yang′kē·iz′əm) *n.* **1** Yankee characteristics collectively. **2** A Yankee word, trait, or idiom, especially as restricted to New England.

Yan·kee·land (yang′kē·land′) *n. Colloq.* **1** The United States. **2** New England or the northern States as opposed to the southern.

yank·ing (yang′king) *adj.* **1** Inclined to jerk or pull sharply, as a horse. **2** *Scot.* Active; enterprising.

Yan·tra (yän′trä) A river in northern Bulgaria, flowing 168 miles NE to the Danube.

Ya·oun·dé (yä·ōōn·dā′) The capital of French Cameroons, central western Africa; a trading, manufacturing, and educational center.

yap (yap) *n.* **1** *Slang.* Talk; jabber. **2** *Slang* A rowdy or bumpkin. **3** A bark or yelp. **4** A worthless dog. —*v.i.* **yapped, yap·ping 1** *Slang* To prate; jabber. **2** *Colloq.* To bark or yelp, as a cur. [Imit. of a dog's bark]

Yap (yäp, yap) An island group in the western Carolines; 80 square miles: formerly *Guap.*

ya·pon (yä′pon) See YAUPON.

Ya·qui (yä′kē) *n.* **1** One of a tribe of North American Indians belonging to the Piman branch of the Uto-Aztecan linguistic stock, now living in southern Sonora, Mexico.

Ya·qui (yä′kē) A river in NW Mexico, flowing 420 miles SW and south from the Sierra Madre Occidental to the Gulf of California; the largest river of Sonora state.

Yar·bor·ough (yär′bûr·ō, *Brit.* yär′bər·ə) *n.* A whist or bridge hand with no card above a nine. [after an earl of *Yarborough,* who bet against the occurrence of such a hand]

yard[1] (yärd) *n.* **1** The standard English and American measure of length: 3 feet, or 36 inches, or 0.914 meter. **2** A yardstick. **3** *Naut.* A long, slender, tapering spar set crosswise on a mast and used to support sails. [OE *gyrd* a rod, a measure of length]

yard[2] (yärd) *n.* **1** A tract of ground enclosed or set apart. **2** An enclosure, usually small and near a residence or other building; by extension, the grounds near a house, college, or university, whether enclosed or not. **3** An enclosure used for some specific work: often in composition: a *brickyard, shipyard.* **4** An enclosure or piece of ground adjacent to a railroad station, used for making up trains and for storing the rolling stock. **5** The winter pasturing ground of deer and moose: a moose *yard.* **6** An enclosure for animals, poultry, etc. —*v.t.* To put or collect into or as into a yard. —*v.i.* To gather into an enclosure or yard. [OE *geard* an enclosure]

yard·age[1] (yär′dij) *n.* The amount or length of something in yards, as of silk. [< YARD[1]]

yard·age[2] (yär′dij) *n.* The use or charge for a yard in handling cattle as they are moved to and from railway cars. [< YARD[2]]

yard·arm (yärd′ärm′) *n. Naut.* Either end of a yard of square sail.

yard·grass (yärd′gras′, -gräs′) *n.* A coarse, widely distributed, annual grass (*Eleusine indica);* goosegrass.

yard·man[1] (yärd′mən) *n. pl.* **·men** (-mən) *Naut.* A sailor who works on the yards.

yard·man[2] (yärd′mən) *n. pl.* **·men** (-mən) A man employed in a yard, especially on a railroad.

yard·mas·ter (yärd′mas′tər, -mäs′-) *n.* A railroad official having charge of a yard.

yard·stick (yärd′stik′) *n.* **1** A graduated measuring stick a yard in length. **2** A measure or standard of comparision. Also **yard′wand′** (-wond′).

---

yare (yâr) *adj. Archaic & Dial.* **1** Responding quickly to the helm; manageable: said of a ship. **2** Brisk; prompt. **3** Prepared; ready. —*adv. Obs.* With dispatch; quickly; soon. [OE *gearu* ready] —**yare′ly** *adv.*

Yar·kand (yär·kand′) **1** A town and oasis of SW Sinkiang-Uigur Autonomous Region, NW China: Chinese *Soche.* **2** A river of SW Sinkiang-Uigur Autonomous Region, NW China, flowing 500 miles NE from the Karakoram range to the Tarim.

Yar·mouth (yär′məth) **1** A port at the entrance to the Bay of Fundy in SW Nova Scotia, Canada. **2** See GREAT YARMOUTH, England.

yarn (yärn) *n.* **1** Any spun material, natural or synthetic, prepared for use in weaving, knitting, or crotcheting. **2** Continous strands of spun fiber, as wool, cotton, linen, silk, jute, or rayon. **3** A quantity of such spun material. **4** *Colloq.* A long, exciting story of adventure, often of doubtful truth: a sailor spinning a *yarn.* —*v.i. Colloq.* To tell a yarn or yarns. [OE *gearn*]

Ya·ro·slavl (yä′rō·släv′əl) A city on the Volga in north central European Russian S.F.S.R.

yar·row (yar′ō) *n.* A genus (*Achillea*) of perennial carduaceous herbs of Europe and North America; especially, the common yarrow or milfoil, with small white flowers and a pungent odor and taste. [OE *gearwe*]

yar·rup (yar′əp) *n.* Flicker[2]. [Imit. of its song]

yash·mak (yäsh·mäk′, yäsh′mak) *n.* The double veil or covering for the face worn by Moslem women when in public. Also **yash·mac′, yas·mak′.** [< Arabic *yashmaq*]

yat·a·ghan (yat′ə·gan, -gən; *Turkish* yä′tä·gän′) *n.* A Turkish sword or scimitar with a double-curved blade and a handle without a guard: often called *ataghan.* Also **yat′a·gan.** [< Turkish *yātāghan*]

TURKISH YATAGHAN

yaud (yäd, yôd) *n. Scot.* An old mare. See JADE.

yauld[1] (yôd, yäd, yäld) See YALD[2].

yauld[2] (yäld) See YELD.

yaup (yôp) See YAWP.

yau·pon (yô′pən) *n.* A bushy evergreen shrub (*Ilex vomitoria*) of the holly family, found in the southern United States, where its leaves were used for tea and by the North Carolina Indians for their celebrated *black drink:* also spelled *yapon, youpon, yupon.* [< Siouan (Catawba) *yopún,* dim. of *yop* a bush]

Ya·va·ri (yä′vä·rē′) See JAVARI. Also **Ya′va·ry′.**

yaw (yô) *v.i.* **1** *Naut.* To steer wildly or out of its course, as a ship when struck by a heavy sea. **2** To move unsteadily or irregularly. **3** *Aeron.* To deviate from the flight path by angular displacement about the vertical axis; fishtail. —*v.t.* **4** To cause to yaw. —*n.* **1** A movement of a ship or aircraft by which it temporarily alters its course. **2** Irregular, unsteady, or deviating motion. [Cf. ON *jaga* move to and fro]

Ya·wa·ta (yä·wä·tä) A city of northern Kyushu island, Japan: also *Yahata.*

yawl[1] (yôl) See YOWL.

yawl[2] (yôl) *n.* **1** A fore-and-aft rigged two-masted vessel similar to a ketch but having the mizzen- or jiggermast aft of the rudder post. **2** A ship's small boat; jollyboat. **3** A small fishing boat. [Appar. < Du. *jol,* orig. a boat used in Jutland]

yawl-rigged (yôl′rigd′) *adj. Naut.* Having two masts, the after one very small and stepped astern of the rudder post, and both rigged with fore-and-aft sails.

yaw-me·ter (yô′mē′tər) *n. Aeron.* An instrument for measuring the angle of yaw in an aircraft.

GAFF-RIGGED YAWL

---

yawn (yôn) *v.i.* **1** To open the mouth wide, either voluntarily, as an animal seeking its prey, or involuntarily, with a long, full inspiration of the breath, usually as the result of drowsiness, fatigue, or boredom. **2** To be or stand wide open, especially as ready to engulf or receive something: A chasm *yawned* below. —*v.t.* **3** To express or utter with a yawn. —*n.* **1** A wide opening of the mouth, especially as from weariness. **2** The act of opening wide. [Prob. fusion of OE *geonian* yawn and *gānian* gape] —**yawn′er** *n.*

yawp (yôp) *v.i.* **1** To bark or yelp. **2** *Colloq.* To gape; yawn audibly. **3** *Brit. Colloq.* To shout; bawl; talk loudly. —*n.* **1** A bark or yelp. **2** A shout; noise; noisy talking; also, a loud, uncouth outcry. **3** *Scot.* The scream of a bird, especially when in distress. **4** *Scot.* A cough. Also spelled *yaup.* [Imit.] —**yawp′er** *n.*

yaws (yôz) *n. pl.* (also construed as *sing.*) A contagious tropical disease caused by a spirochete (*Treponema pertenue*) and superficially resembling syphilis in first appearing as a skin eruption. Also called *frambesia.* [< Cariban *yáya*]

yay (yā) *U.S. Dial. adj.* **1** This many; this much. **2** Ever so many: for *yay* years. —*adv.* **1** To this extent. **2** Ever so: *yay* big. [Cf. G *je* ever]

Yazd (yezd) See YEZD.

Yaz·oo River (yaz′ōō) A river in west central Mississippi, flowing 189 miles SW to the Mississippi at Vicksburg.

Yb *Chem.* Ytterbium (symbol Yb).

Y-car·ti·lage (wī′kär′tə·lij) *n. Anat.* A piece of cartilage shaped like the letter Y, situated at the bottom of the socket of the hip joint.

Y-chro·mo·some (wī′krō′mə·sōm) *n.* A sex chromosome.

y-clept (i-klept′) *adj. Archaic* Called; named: now a humorous term. Also **y-cleped′.** [OE *geclypod,* pp. of *clypian* call]

ye[1] (thē) The: an archaic contraction in which the *y* represents the thorn (*ρ*) of the Old and Middle English alphabet. Often printed y[e].

ye[2] (yē) *pron. Archaic* The persons addressed: now confined almost exclusively to poetic or formal pulpit style. Historically *ye* is only a nominative form: "Blessed are *ye* when men shall revile *you.*" Matt. v 11. [OE *ge,* nominative pl.]

yea (yā) *adv.* **1** Yes: used to express affirmation or assent: in this sense now superseded by *yes.* **2** Not only so, but more so: to intensify or amplify a meaning: fifty, *yea,* a hundred: an archaic term. **3** In reality; verily: a form of introduction in a sentence. **4** So as to be realized: All the promises of God in him are *yea* and Amen; truly; really: a use of the Authorized Version of the Bible. —*n.* An expression of affirmation; an affirmative vote; by extension, one who casts such a vote. [OE *gēa*]

ye·ah (ye′ə) *adv. Slang* Yes. [< YES]

yeal·ing (yē′ling) *n. Scot.* A contemporary; an equal in age: also spelled *yeelin.*

yean (yēn) *v.t. & v.i.* To bring forth (young), as a goat or sheep. [OE (assumed) *geēanian*]

yean·ling (yēn′ling) *n.* The young of a goat or sheep. —*adj.* Young; newly born.

year (yir) *n.* **1** The period of time in which the earth completes a revolution around the sun: about 365 days, used as a unit of time, and divided into 12 months. It is now reckoned as beginning January 1 and ending December 31. **2** Any period of 12 months. **3** The period of time during which a planet revolves around the sun. **4** *pl.* Length or time of life; age; sometimes, old age: active for his *years.* —**astronomical year** The period between two passages of the sun through the same equinox, which determines the changing seasons. Its length is 365 days, 5 hours, 48 minutes, 46 seconds. Also **equinoctial, natural, solar,** or **tropical year.** —**calendar, civil,** or **legal year** The period of time from midnight of December 31 to the same hour twelve months thereafter. Formerly, in England, the legal year began with March 25, but historic years were counted from January 1. In 1751 the English Parliament prescribed that the legal year should begin with the

first of January, 1752. — **common year** That of 365 days, approaching most nearly in the number of days to the astronomical year. The leap year has 366 days. — **fiscal year** A financial year of a national treasury or of a business at the end of which accounts are balanced; any twelve-month period used as a basis of business reckoning. — **lunar year** That of thirteen months, one month being added at intervals to make the mean length of the astronomical year, as in the Hebrew calendar. — **sidereal year** The period of 365 days, 6 hours, 9 minutes, 9 seconds, in which the sun apparently returns to the same position among the stars. It is longer than the astronomical year, owing to the precession of the equinoxes. — **Sothic year** The fixed solar year of the Egyptians, consisting of 365 days and 6 hours: so called because determined by the heliacal rising of the Dog Star (Sothis). [OE *gēar*]

year·book (yir′bŏŏk′) *n.* A book published annually, presenting information about the previous year.

year·ling (yir′ling) *n.* A young animal past its first year and not yet two years old; specifically, a colt or filly a year old dating from January 1 of the year of foaling. — *adj.* Being a year old.

year·long (yir′lông′, -long′) *adj.* Continuing through a year.

year·ly (yir′lē) *adj.* 1 Included within a year's time. 2 Occurring once a year; annual. 3 Continuing or lasting for a year: a *yearly* subscription. — *adv.* Once a year; annually.

yearn (yûrn) *v.i.* 1 To desire something earnestly; long: with *for*. 2 To be deeply moved; feel sympathy. [OE *giernan, geornan.* Akin to OE *georn* eager.]

yearn·ing (yûr′ning) *n.* A strong emotion of longing or desire, especially with tenderness. — **yearn′ing·ly** *adv.*

yeast (yēst) *n.* 1 A substance consisting of minute cells of ascomycetous fungi (genus *Saccharomyces*) that clump together, forming a yellow, frothy, viscous growth which, in contact with saccharine liquids, develops or increases by germination, producing fermentation by means of enzymes, in which process alcohol and carbon dioxide are produced, as in the brewing of beer and the raising of bread. 2 Such a substance mixed with flour or meal, and sold commercially. 3 Any of a family (*Saccharomycetaceae*) of yeast-forming fungi. 4 Froth or spume. 5 Figuratively, mental or moral ferment: the *yeast* of youth. — *v.i.* To foam; froth. [OE *gist*]

yeast cake A mixture of living yeast cells and starch in compressed form suitable for use in baking or brewing.

yeast powder Dried and powdered yeast used as a leavening agent.

yeast·y (yēs′tē) *adj.* 1 Of, pertaining to, or resembling yeast. 2 Causing or characterized by fermentation. 3 Restless; unsettled; frivolous. 4 Covered with or consisting mainly of froth or foam. 5 Light or unsubstantial. — **yeast′i·ness** *n.*

Yeats (yāts), **William Butler**, 1865–1939, Irish poet, dramatist, and essayist.

Ye·do (ye·dō) A former name for TOKYO.

yeel·in (yē′lin) See YEALING.

yegg (yeg) *n. Slang* An itinerant burglar; a criminal tramp; a safe-cracker; loosely, any burglar. Also **yegg′man.** [Prob. < earlier *yekkman* a beggar in San Francisco's Chinatown < dial. Chinese *yekk* a beggar]

Ye·gor·yevsk (yə·gôr′yəfsk) A city in west central European Russian S.F.S.R.; a cotton milling center: also *Egorevsk.*

Ye·hsien (ye′shyen′) A city of NE Shantung province, NE China, near the Gulf of Chihli.

yeld (yeld) *adj. Scot.* Not giving milk; barren: also spelled *yald, yauld.* Also **yell.**

Yel·ga·va (yel′gə·və) See JELGAVA.

yelk (yelk) *n. Dial.* Yolk.

yell (yel) *v.t. & v.i.* To shout; scream; roar; also, to cheer. See synonyms under CALL, ROAR. — *n.* 1 A sharp, loud, inarticulate cry, as of pain, terror, anger, etc. 2 A rhythmic cheer composed of a prearranged set of words and shouted by a group in unison. [OE *gellan, giellan*] — **yell′er** *n.*

yell·och (yel′əkh) *v.i. & n. Scot.* Yell; scream.

yel·low (yel′ō) *adj.* 1 Having the color of ripe lemons, or sunflowers. 2 Changed to a sal-

low color by age, sickness, or the like: a paper *yellow* with age. 3 Having a sallow complexion, as a member of the Mongoloid ethnic group. 4 Jaundiced; hence, melancholy; jealous. 5 Sensational, especially offensively so: said of newspapers: *yellow* journalism. 6 *Colloq.* Cowardly; mean; dishonorable. — *n.* 1 The color of the spectrum between green and orange, including wavelengths centering at about 5,890 angstroms; the color of ripe lemons. 2 Any pigment or dyestuff having such a color. 3 The yolk of an egg. 4 *pl.* Any of various unrelated plant diseases in which there is stunting of growth and yellowing of the foliage; especially, an infectious virus disease of peach, nectarine, apricot, and almond trees. 5 *pl.* Jaundice, especially a variety that affects domestic animals. 6 *pl. Obs.* Jealousy; hence, a jealous frame of mind. — *v.t. & v.i.* To make or become yellow. [OE *geolu*] — **yel′low·ly** *adv.* — **yel′low·ness** *n.*

yel·low·bark (yel′ō·bärk′) *n.* Calisaya.

yel·low-bel·lied (yel′ō-bel′ēd) *adj.* 1 *Slang* Cowardly; yellow. 2 Having a yellow underside: *yellow-bellied* sapsucker.

yellow-bellied glider The fluffy glider.

yel·low·bird (yel′ō·bûrd′) *n.* 1 The goldfinch (def. 2). 2 The yellow warbler.

yellow daisy The black-eyed Susan.

yel·low-dog contract (yel′ō-dôg′, -dog′) A contract with an employer in which an employee agrees not to join a labor union.

yellow fever *Pathol.* An acute, infectious intestinal disease of tropical and semitropical regions, caused by a filtrable virus transmitted by the bite of a mosquito (genus *Aëdes*). It is characterized by hemorrhages, jaundice, vomiting, and fatty degeneration of the liver. Also *yellow jack.*

yel·low-ham·mer (yel′ō-ham′ər) *n.* 1 An Old World bunting (*Emberiza citrinella*) with the sides of the head, neck, and breast bright yellow, the back yellow and black, and the top of the head and tail feathers blackish. 2 The flicker or golden-winged woodpecker. [Alter. of earlier *yelambre,* prob. <OE *geolo* yellow + *amore,* a kind of bird]

yel·low·ish (yel′ō-ish) *adj.* Somewhat yellow. — **yel′low·ish·ness** *n.*

yellow jack 1 A carangoid fish (*Caranx bartholomaei*) of the West Indies and Florida. 2 The flag of the quarantine service. 3 Yellow fever.

yellow jacket Any of various social wasps (genus *Vespa*) with bright-yellow markings.

yellow jasmine or **jessamine** A smooth twining shrub (*Gelsemium sempervirens*) with bright-yellow flowers.

yellow journal A cheaply sensational newspaper or other publication. [So called from the use of yellow ink in printing a cartoon strip, "The Yellow Kid," in the *New York Journal,* commencing Oct. 18, 1896]

yellow lead ore Wulfenite.

yel·low·legs (yel′ō·legz′) *n.* 1 Either of two North American sandpipers (genus *Totanus*) with long yellow legs: the **greater,** or **winter, yellowlegs** (*T. melanoleucus*), or the **lesser yellowlegs** (*T. flavipes*). 2 *U.S. Colloq.* Formerly, in the U.S. Army, a cavalry soldier.

yellow metal 1 A brass consisting of 60 parts copper and 40 parts zinc. 2 Gold.

yellow perch Perch² (def. 1).

yellow peril The political power of the peoples of eastern Asia, conceived of as threatening white supremacy.

yellow pine 1 Any of various American pines, as the Georgia or loblolly pine. 2 Their tough, yellowish wood.

yellow poplar The tuliptree.

yellow race The Mongoloid ethnic division of mankind.

Yellow River See HWANG HO.

yel·lows (yel′ōz) See YELLOW (*n.* defs. 4 and 5).

Yellow Sea An arm of the Pacific between Korea and the eastern coast of China; 400 miles long, 400 miles wide: Chinese *Hwang Hai.*

yellow spot *Anat.* A small yellowish spot in the retina, the region of most acute vision.

Yellowstone Falls Two waterfalls of the Yellowstone River in Yellowstone National Park: **Upper Yellowstone Falls,** 109 feet; **Lower Yellowstone Falls,** 308 feet.

Yellowstone National Park The largest and ·oldest of the United States national parks,

at the junction of Wyoming, Montana, and Idaho, largely in NW Wyoming; 3,458 square miles; established, 1872.

Yel·low·stone River (yel′ō-stōn) A river in NW Wyoming, SE Montana, and NW North Dakota, flowing 671 miles NW to the Missouri River and passing through Yellowstone National Park where it forms **Yellowstone Lake,** 20 miles long, 14 miles wide; 140 square miles.

yellow streak A personality trait combining cowardice, treachery, and meanness.

yel·low·tail (yel′ō-tāl′) *n.* 1 Any of various fishes having a yellowish tail. 2 A carangoid fish (genus *Seriola*), especially the **California yellowtail** (*S. dorsalis*). 3 A California rockfish (*Sebastodes flavidus*). 4 The menhaden.

yel·low·throat (yel′ō-thrōt′) *n.* Any of various American warblers (genus *Geothlypis*), especially the **Maryland yellowthroat** (*G. trichas*), olive-green, with yellow throat and breast.

yel·low-throat·ed warbler (yel′ō-thrō′tid) A warbler (*Dendroica petechia*) of wooded regions of the southern United States.

yellow waterlily A yellow variety of pondlily (genus *Nuphar*).

yel·low·weed (yel′ō-wēd′) *n.* 1 Any of various goldenrods; especially, the Canada goldenrod (*Solidago canadensis*). 2 The bulbous crowfoot (*Ranunculus bulbosus*). 3 The European ragwort (*Senecio jacobaea*). 4 Weld² (def. 1).

yel·low·wood (yel′ō-wŏŏd′) *n.* 1 The yellowish wood of a tree (*Cladrastis lutea*) of the southern United States, with smooth bark and showy white flowers; gopherwood. The wood yields a yellow dye. 2 The tree. 3 Any one of several other trees with yellowish wood, as the Osage orange, buckthorn, smoketree, or the like.

yel·low·y (yel′ō-ē) *adj.* Yellowish.

yellow yel·dring (yel′drin) *Dial.* The yellowhammer. [<YELLOW + var. of dial. E *yowlring* < *yowlo* yellow + RING]

yelp (yelp) *v.i.* To utter a sharp or shrill cry; give a yelp. — *v.t.* To express by a yelp or yelps. — *n.* 1 A sharp, shrill cry; a sharp, crying bark, as of a dog in distress. 2 The sharp, staccato cry of the turkey hen. [OE *gielpan* boast] — **yelp′er** *n.*

yelp·ing (yel′ping) *n.* The act of one who yelps; utterance of quick, sharp cries or barks, as of a dog; also, the sounds so uttered.

Yem·en (yem′ən) A kingdom of the SW Arabian peninsula; 75,000 square miles; capitals, Sana and Ta'iz; joined United Arab States, 1958. — **Yem·e·ni** (yem′ə·nē), **Yem·e·nite** (yem′ə·nīt) *adj. & n.*

yen¹ (yen) *Slang n.* An ardent longing or desire; an intense want; an infatuation. — *v.i.* **yenned, yen·ning** To yearn; long. [<Chinese, opium, smoke]

yen² (yen) *n.* The monetary unit of the Japanese, containing 100 sen. [<Japanese <Chinese *yüan* round, a dollar]

Ye·nan (ye′nän′) A city in northern Shensi province, north central China; a commercial center; headquarters of the Chinese Communist party, 1937–47: formerly (1913–1948) *Fushih.*

Yen-geese (yeng′gēz) *n. pl.* White people; specifically, English settlers in New England. [Appar. N. Am. Ind. alter. of ENGLISH]

Yen·i·sei (yen′ə·sā′) A river in central Asiatic Russian S.F.S.R., flowing 2,364 miles NW through **Yenisei Bay** to **Yenisei Gulf** (90 miles wide), its estuary in the Arctic Ocean: also *Enisei.*

Yen·i·seisk (yen′ə·sāsk′) A city on the Yenisei river in central Krasnoyarsk territory, central Asiatic Russian S.F.S.R.

yen·ta (yen′tə) *n.* A female gossip or meddler. Also **yen′teh.** [<Yiddish]

Yen·tai (yen′tī′) A port on the Yellow Sea in NE Shantung province, NE China, on the northern coast of the Shantung peninsula: formerly *Chefoo.*

yeo·man (yō′mən) *n. pl.* **·men** (-mən) 1 *Brit.* A freeholder next under the rank of gentleman; in early times, one who owned a small landed estate; in modern usage, a farmer, especially one who cultivates his own farm; loosely, a man of the common people. 2 A petty officer in the U.S. Navy, Coast Guard, or Army Transport Service, who performs clerical duties. 3 *Brit.* One of the higher-class attendants in the service of a nobleman

or of royalty: *a yeoman of the crown*; sometimes, a servitor of lower rank: *a yeoman of the chamber, the buttery,* etc. **4** *Brit.* A member of the yeomanry cavalry; also, a Yeoman of the (Royal) Guard. **5** *Obs.* One who acts as an assistant in a subordinate capacity; a helper; journeyman. [ME *yeman, yoman,* prob. contraction of *yengman* a young man < OE *geong* young + *mann* a man]

yeo·man·ly (yō′mən·lē) *adj.* Pertaining to or resembling a yeoman; of yeoman's rank; brave; rugged; staunch. —*adv.* Like a yeoman; bravely; staunchly.

Yeoman of the (Royal) Guard A member of the special bodyguard of the English royal household, consisting of one hundred yeomen chosen from the best rank below the gentry, and first appointed by Henry VII. See BEEFEATER.

yeo·man·ry (yō′mən·rē) *n.* **1** The collective body of yeomen; freemen; farmers. **2** *Brit.* A home guard of volunteer cavalry, created in 1761, consisting of gentlemen and gentlemen farmers, known since 1901 as the **Imperial yeomanry.** In 1907 it became a part of the Territorial Army.

yeoman's service Faithful and useful support or service; loyal assistance in need. Also **yeoman service.**

yep (yep) *adv. Colloq.* Yes. [Alter. of YES]

-yer Var. of -IER.

yer·ba (yâr′bə, yûr′-) *n.* Maté (def. 1). [< Sp. *yerba (maté)* the herb (maté)]

Yer·ba Bue·na Island (yâr′bə bwā′nə, yûr′-) An island of 300 acres in San Francisco Bay, California; mid-point of the San Francisco-Oakland Bay Bridge.

yerb tea (yûrb, yärb) *Dial.* Herb tea. [< *yerb,* dial. var. of HERB + TEA]

Ye·re·men·ko (yi·ryi·myen′kə), **Andrei Ivanovich,** born 1892, Russian general; broke the siege of Stalingrad in World War II.

Ye·re·van (ye·re·vän′) The Armenian name for ERIVAN.

yerk (yûrk) *Obs.* or *Dial. v.t. & v.i.* **1** To tie with a jerk; bind tightly. **2** To crack, as a whip. **3** To beat; lash; excite. **4** To jerk; to kick, as a horse. —*n.* A jerk; a smart blow.

Yer·kes (yûr′kēz), **Charles Tyson,** 1837–1905, U.S. financier. —**Robert Mearns,** 1876–1956, U.S. psychobiologist.

yes (yes) *adv.* As you say; truly; just so: a reply of affirmation or consent: opposed to *no,* and equivalent to a repetition of the words of a question or command in the form of an assertion. The word is sometimes used to enforce by repetition or addition something that precedes. —*n. pl.* **yes·es** or **yes·ses** A reply in the affirmative. —*v.t. & v.i.* **yessed, yes·sing** To say "yes" (to). [OE *gēse,* prob. < *gēa* yea + *si,* third person sing. present subj. of *bēon* be]

ye'se (yēs) *Scot.* You shall; ye shall.

Ye·sil Ir·mak (ye·shēl′ ir·mäk′) A river in northern Turkey in Asia, flowing 260 miles NW to the Black Sea: ancient *Iris.*

Ye·sil·köy (ye′shēl·kœē′) The Turkish name for SAN STEFANO.

yes man *Colloq.* One who agrees without criticism; a servile, acquiescent assistant or subordinate; a toady.

yester- *prefix* Pertaining to the day before the present; by extension of the preceding, used of longer periods than a day: *yesteryear.* [< YESTER(DAY)]

yes·ter·day (yes′tər·dē, -dā) *n.* **1** The day preceding today. **2** Loosely, the near past. —*adv.* **1** On the day last past. **2** At a recent time. [OE *geostran dæg* < *geostran* yesterday + *dæg* day]

yes·ter·eve·ning (yes′tər·ēv′ning) *n.* The evening of yesterday. Also **yes′ter·eve′, yes′ter·e′ven** (-ē′vən), **yes·treen** (yes·trēn′).

yes·ter·morn·ing (yes·tər·môr′ning) *n.* The morning of yesterday. Also **yes′ter·morn′.**

yes·tern (yes′tərn) *adj. Archaic* Of or pertaining to yesterday. [< YESTER(DAY), on analogy with *eastern, western,* etc.]

yes·ter·night (yes′tər·nīt′) *n. Archaic & Poetic* The night last past. —*adv.* In or during the night last past. [OE *geostran* yesterday + *niht* night]

yes·ter·noon (yes′tər·nōōn′) *n.* The noon of yesterday.

yes·ter·week (yes′tər·wēk′) *n.* Last week.

yes·ter·year (yes′tər·yir′) *n.* Last year. [Trans. of F *antan*; coined by D. G. Rossetti]

yet (yet) *adv.* **1** In addition; besides; further: often with a comparative. **2** Before or at some future time; eventually: He will *yet* succeed. **3** In continuance of a previous state or condition; still: I can hear him *yet.* **4** At the present time; now: Don't go *yet.* **5** After all the time that has or had elapsed: Are you not ready *yet?* **6** Up to the present time; heretofore: commonly with a negative: He has never *yet* lied to me. **7** Than that which has been previously affirmed: with a comparative: It was hot yesterday; today it is hotter *yet.* **8** As much as; even: He did not believe the reports, nor *yet* the evidence. —**as yet** Up to now. —*conj.* **1** Nevertheless; notwithstanding: I speak to you peaceably, *yet* you will not listen. **2** But: He is willing, *yet* unable. **3** Although: active, *yet* ill. See synonyms under BUT[1], NOTWITHSTANDING. [OE *gīet, gīeta*]

Synonyms (adverb): besides, further, hitherto, now, still. *Yet* and *still* have many closely related senses, and, with verbs of past time, are often interchangeable; we may say "while he was *still* a child." *Yet,* like *still,* often applies to past action or state extending to and including the present time, especially when joined with *as;* we can say "He is feeble *as yet,*" or "He is *still* feeble," with scarcely appreciable difference of meaning, except that the former statement implies somewhat more of expectation than the latter. *Yet* with a negative applies to completed action, often replacing a positive statement with *still:* "He has not gone *yet*" is nearly the same as "He is here *still.*" *Yet* has a reference to the future which *still* does not share; "We may be succesful *still*" implies that we may continue to enjoy in the future such success as we are winning now.

yet·i (yet′ē) *n.* The abominable snowman. [< Tibetan]

yett (yet) *n. Scot.* A gate.

yew (yōō) *n.* **1** Any one of several evergreen trees or shrubs (genus *Taxus*), with flat, lanceolate, dark-green leaves and a red berrylike fruit; especially, the **European** or **English yew** (*T. baccata*), a medium-sized coniferous tree of slow growth and long life, with spreading horizontal branches and dense darkgreen foliage. **2** The hard, fine-grained, durable wood of the common yew, of a purplish or deep-brown color. **3** A bow made from the wood of the yew tree. ◆ Homophones: *ewe, you.* [OE *ēow, īw*]

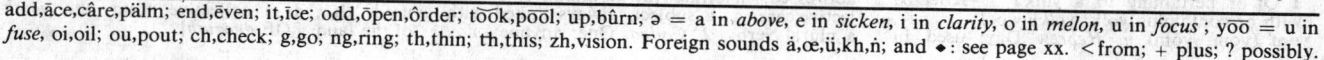

YEW

Yezd (yezd) A city in central Iran: also *Yazd.*

Ye·zo (ye·zō) The former name for HOKKAIDO.

Yg·dra·sil (ig′drə·sil) In Norse mythology, the huge ash tree whose roots and branches bind together heaven, earth, and hell: also spelled *Igdrasil.* Also **Yg′dra·sill, Ygg′dra·sill.**

Y·gerne (i·gûrn′) See IGRAINE.

Y·gun (wī′gun′) *n. Mil.* A gun having two barrels set at an angle, used for discharging depth bombs against enemy submarines, and mounted aft, usually on a destroyer. [So called because shaped like a Y]

YHWH Yahweh. See JEHOVAH.

Yid·dish (yid′ish) *n.* A Germanic language derived from the Middle High German spoken in the Rhineland in the thirteenth and fourteenth centuries, now spoken primarily by Jews in Poland, Lithuania, the Ukraine, and Rumania, and by Jewish immigrants from those regions in other parts of the world. It contains elements of Hebrew and the Slavic languages, and is written in slightly modified Hebrew characters. —*adj.* **1** Of or pertaining to Yiddish; written or spoken in Yiddish. **2** *Slang* Jewish. [< G *jüdisch* Jewish]

yield (yēld) *v.t.* **1** To give forth by a natural proc-

ess, or as a result of labor or cultivation: The field will *yield* a good crop. **2** To give in return, as for investment; furnish: The bonds *yield* five percent interest. **3** To give up, as to superior power; surrender; relinquish: often with *up*: to *yield* a fortress; to *yield* oneself up to one's enemies. **4** To concede or grant: to *yield* precedence; to *yield* consent. **5** *Obs.* To pay, repay, or reward. —*v.i.* **6** To provide a return; produce; bear. **7** To give up; submit; surrender. **8** To give way, as to pressure or force; bend, collapse, etc. **9** To assent or comply, as under compulsion; consent: We *yielded* to their persuasion. **10** To give place, as through inferiority or weakness: with *to:* We will *yield* to them in nothing. See synonyms under ALLOW, BEND[1], DEFER[2], OBEY, PRODUCE, SURRENDER. —*n.* **1** The amount yielded; product; result, as of cultivation or mining. **2** The profit derived from invested capital. **3** The proceeds of a tax after the expenses of collection and administration have been deducted. **4** *Mil.* The explosive force of an atomic or thermonuclear bomb as expressed in kilotons or megatons. See synonyms under HARVEST, PRODUCT. [OE *gieldan, geldan* pay] —**yield′er** *n.*

yield·ing (yēl′ding) *adj.* Disposed to yield; flexible; obedient. See synonyms under DOCILE, SUPPLE. —**yield′ing·ly** *adv.* —**yield′ing·ness** *n.*

yield point *Physics* The amount of stress, measured in unit area, under which a given material, as a rod of metal, will exhibit permanent deformation; the point at which a stress or strain just exceeds the elastic strength of the material. Also **yield strength.**

yill (yil) *n. Scot.* Ale.

yin[1] (yin) *n. Scot.* One.

yin[2] (yin) *n.* In Chinese philosophy and art, the female element, which stands for darkness, cold, and death. Compare YANG. Also **Yin.** [< Chinese]

yince (yins) *adv. Scot.* Once.

Yin·chwan (yin′chwän′) A city of NE Kansu province, NW central China; capital (1928–1954) of former Ningsia province: formerly (until 1945) *Ningsia.*

Ying·kow (ying′kō′) A port on the Gulf of Liaotung in SW Lianoing province, NE China.

yip (yip) *n.* A yelp, as of a dog. —*v.i.* **yipped, yip·ping** To yelp. [Imit.]

yird (yûrd) *n. Scot.* Earth. Also **yirth** (yûrth).

yirr (yûr) *v.i. Scot.* To snarl; yell; growl, as a dog.

yit (yit) *adv. & conj. Dial. & Obs.* Yet. [Var. of YET]

-yl *suffix Chem.* Used to denote a radical, especially a univalent one: *ethyl, butyl.* [< Gk. *hylē* wood, matter]

y·lang-y·lang (ē′läng·ē′läng) *n.* **1** A tree (*Cananga odorata*) of Malaysia; the Malayan custard apple. **2** A perfume derived from the greenish-yellow flowers of this tree. Also spelled *ilang-ilang.* [< Tagalog *álang-ílang* flowers of flowers]

Y-lev·el (wī′lev′əl) *n.* A combined telescope and spirit level on a Y-shaped mounting which may be rotated: used in surveying, etc.

Y·mir (ē′mir, ü′mir) In Norse mythology, the progenitor of the giants, formed of frost and fire, out of whose body the gods created the world. Also **Y′mer.**

y·nogh (i·nuf′) *adj. & adv. Obs.* Enough. Also **y·nough′, y·now** (i·nou′, i·nō′). [ME, enough, OE *genōg*]

yod (yōd, *Hebrew* yōōd) *n.* The tenth Hebrew letter. Also **yodh.** See ALPHABET. [< Hebrew *yōdh,* lit., a hand]

yo·del (yōd′l) *n.* A melody or refrain sung to meaningless syllables, with abrupt changes from chest to head tones and the reverse: common among Swiss and Tirolese mountaineers. —*v.t. & v.i.* **·deled** or **·delled, ·del·ing** or **·del·ling** To sing with a yodel, changing the voice quickly from its natural tone to a falsetto and back. Also **yo′dle.** [< G *jodeln,* lit., utter the syllable *jo*] —**yo′del·er, yo′del·ler, yo′dler** *n.*

yo·ga (yō′gə) *n.* A Hindu system of mystical and ascetic philosophy which involves withdrawal from the world and abstract meditation upon any object, as the Supreme Spirit,

with the purpose of identifying one's consciousness with the object. [<Hind. <Skt., lit., union] — **yo'gic** *adj.*

yogh (yōkh) *n.* A Middle English letter which represented a voiced or voiceless palatal fricative, or a voiced velar fricative. It is variously spelled in Modern English as *y,* as in *lay, w,* as in *law,* and *gh,* as in *daughter* and *enough.*

yo·gi (yō'gē) *n.* A follower of the yoga philosophy; an ascetic or adept, supposed to possess magical powers. Also **yo'gee, yo'·gin.** [<Hind. *yogī* <Skt. *yogin* < *yoga* yoga]

yo·gurt (yō'gŏŏrt) *n.* A thick, curdled milk treated with cultures of bacteria regarded as beneficial to the intestines: also called *matzoon.* Also **yo'ghurt, yo'ghourt.** [<Turkish *yōghurt*]

yoicks (yoiks) *interj.* A cry formerly used in foxhunting to urge on the hounds: also *hoicks.* [Earlier *hoik,* var. of *hike*; prob. imit.]

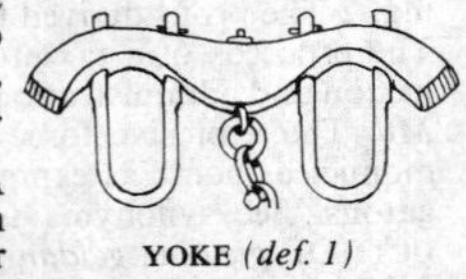

YOKE *(def. 1)*

yoke (yōk) *n.* **1** A curved timber with attachments used for coupling draft animals, as oxen, usually having a bow at each end to receive the neck of the animal. **2** Any of many similar contrivances, as a frame fitted for a person's shoulders from the ends of which are suspended burdens intended to balance, as pails of milk. **3** *Naut.* A crosspiece on a rudder head, carrying yoke lines for steering. **4** *Mech.* A strap, clamp, clip, slotted piece, or the like, serving to confine, guide, or guard the movement of a part of a machine or mechanism. **5** A crossbar suspended from the collars in double harness for supporting the tongue or pole. **6** A part of a garment designed to support a plaited or gathered part, as at the hips or shoulders, giving shape to the garment. **7** That which binds or connects; a bond: the *yoke* of love. **8** In ancient Rome, a device consisting of two upright spears with a third laid transversely across them, under which a conquered army was made to march. **9** Servitude, or some visible mark of it; bondage. **10** *sing. & pl.* A couple; pair; team: a *yoke* of oxen. **11** *Obs.* The amount of land a yoke of oxen can plow in a day. **12** *Scot.* The time required for a yoke of oxen to accomplish a specified amount of work; hence, a part of the day. — *v.* **yoked, yok·ing** *v.t.* **1** To attach by means of a yoke, as draft animals; put a yoke upon. **2** To join with or as with a yoke; couple or link. **3** To join in marriage. **4** *Rare* To bring into bondage; enslave. — *v.i.* **5** To be joined or linked; unite. [OE *geoc*]

yoke·fel·low (yōk'fel'ō) *n.* A mate or companion in labor. Also **yoke'mate'** (-māt').

yo·kel (yō'kəl) *n.* A countryman; country bumpkin: a contemptuous term. [? < dial. E, a green woodpecker, a yellowhammer] — **yo'·kel·ish** *adj.*

yok·ing (yō'king) *n.* **1** The act of one who yokes. **2** *Scot.* As much work as is done by a yoke of draft animals at a time.

Yok·kai·chi (yōk·kī·chē) A city of central southern Honshu island, Japan, on Ise Bay.

Yo·ko·ha·ma (yō'kə·hä'mə) A port on Tokyo Bay in central Honshu island, Japan.

Yo·ko·su·ka (yō'kə·sōō'kə) A port at the entrance to Tokyo Bay, central Honshu island, Japan.

yol·dring (yōl'drin) *n. Scot. & Brit. Dial.* A species of bunting; the yellowhammer (def. 1). Also **yol'ding** (-ding), **yol'drin.** [Var. of earlier *yowlring* <ME *yowlow* yellow + RING]

yolk (yōk, yōlk) *n.* **1** The yellow portion of an egg. **2** *Biol.* That portion of the contents or substance of the ovum which is used for the nourishment and formation of the embryo, consisting of fat or oil drops, etc., as distinguished from the albumen or white of an egg. ◆ Collateral adjective: *vitelline.* **3** A fine yellow soapy exudation in sheep's wool. [OE *geol(o)ca,* lit., (the) yellow part < *geolu* yellow]

yolk·y (yō'kē, yōl'kē) *adj.* **yolk·i·er, yolk·i·est** **1** Of or pertaining to a yolk. **2** Affected with or containing yolk: *yolky* wool.

yom (yom, yōm) *n. Hebrew* Day: used in designating days of feast or fasting: *Yom Kippur.*

Yom Kip·pur (yom kip'ər, *Hebrew* yōm kip'·ōōr) The Jewish Day of Atonement: the 10th of Tishri (September–October). It is marked by continuous prayer and fasting for 24 hours from sundown on the evening previous. [<Hebrew *yōm kipūr* day of atonement]

yon (yon) *adj. & adv. Archaic, Dial. & Poetic* Yonder; that or those over there: *yon* fine house. [OE *geon*]

yond (yond) *adj. & adv. Archaic & Dial.* Yonder. [OE *geond* across; infl. in meaning by *yon*]

yon·der (yon'dər) *adj.* Being at a distance indicated. — *adv.* In that place; there: Do you see that tree *yonder*? [ME, prob. extension of *yone,* OE *geon* yon]

yo·ni (yō'nē) *n.* The female organ of generation: the symbol under which Shakti is worshiped in India. [<Skt.]

yon·ker (yong'kər) See YOUNKER.

yont (yont) *prep. Scot.* Beyond.

yore (yôr, yōr) *n.* Old time; time long past: in days of *yore.* — *adv. Obs.* Long ago; in olden times. [OE *geara* formerly, prob. orig. genitive pl. of *gear* year]

Yor·ick (yôr'ik, yor'-) A court jester to the king of Denmark, mentioned in Shakespeare's *Hamlet.*

York (yôrk) A royal house of England that reigned from 1461–85; a branch of the Plantagenet line.

York (yôrk) **1** A maritime county in NE England; the largest county in England; 6,080 square miles; divided into East, West, and North Riding: also *Yorkshire.* **2** Its county town, a city on the Ouse, famous for its Norman cathedral: capital of Roman Britain as *Eboracum.*

York (yôrk), **Alvin Cullum,** 1887–1964, U. S. soldier and hero in World War I.

York (yôrk), **Cape** **1** The northernmost point of Australia, in Queensland on Torres Strait. **2** A promontory of NW Greenland on Baffin Bay at the western end of Melville Bay; site of major meteorites, discovered by Peary.

York boat *Canadian* A type of heavy cargo canoe used by the Hudson's Bay Company. [after *York* factory on Hudson Bay]

Yorke Peninsula (yôrk) A promontory of southern South Australia; 160 miles long, 35 miles wide. Also **Yorke's Peninsula.**

York·ist (yôr'kist) *n.* An adherent of the house of York.

York River An estuary in SE Virginia, flowing into Chesapeake Bay; 40 miles long, 1 to 2 1/2 miles wide.

York·shire (yôrk'shir, -shər) See YORK (def. 1).

York·shire pudding (york'shir, -shər) A batter pudding baked in the drippings of roasting meat, often in the same pan.

York·town (yôrk'toun) A town in SE Virginia on the York River; scene of Cornwallis's surrender to Washington in 1781.

Yo·ru·ba (yō'rōō·bä) *n.* **1** A Negro belonging to an extensive linguistic family of the African Slave Coast between the lower Niger and Dahomey rivers. Many North American Negroes are of Yoruba descent. **2** The language of the Yoruba, one of the dominant tongues of the Sudanic family. — **Yo'ru·ban** *adj.*

Yo·ru·ba (yō'rōō·bä) A former native state in SW Nigeria.

Yo·sem·i·te National Park (yō·sem'ə·tē) A government reservation in east central California noted for its scenic grandeur; 1,183 square miles; highest point, 13,095 feet; established in 1890.

Yosemite Valley A gorge in the western Sierra Nevada mountains in Yosemite National Park in east central California; 7 miles long, 1 mile wide; including **Yosemite Falls,** a triple cataract (Upper Fall, 1,430 feet; Lower Fall, 320 feet; total drop, with intermediate cascades, 2,425 feet).

Yo·shi·hi·to (yō·shē·hē·tō), 1879–1926, emperor of Japan 1912–26.

Yo·su (yō·sōō) A port of southern South Korea. *Japanese* **Rei·sui** (rā·syē).

you (yōō) *pron.* **1** The person or persons, animal or animals, personified thing or things addressed, in either the nominative or objective case: as a subject, always linked with a plural verb. **2** *Colloq.* One; anyone: *You* learn by trying. [OE *ēow,* dative and accusative pl. of *ge* ye]

you'd (yōōd) You had; you would: a contraction.

you'll (yōōl) You will: a contraction.

young (yung) *adj.* **young·er** (yung'gər), **young·est** (yung'gist) **1** Being in the early period of life or growth; having existed a short or comparatively short time; not old. **2** Not having progressed far; newly formed: The day was *young.* **3** Pertaining to youth or early life. **4** Full of vigor or freshness. **5** Being without experience; immature. **6** Denoting the younger of two persons having the same name or title; junior. **7** *Geol.* Having the characteristics of an early stage in the geological cycle: said of a river or of certain land forms. **8** Radical or progressive in social or political aims: used with proper names: the *Young* Turks, *Young* Italy. See synonyms under FRESH, NEW, YOUTHFUL. — *n.* **1** Young persons as a group; youth collectively. **2** Offspring, especially of animals. — **with young** With child; pregnant. [OE *geong*]

Young (yung), **Arthur Henry,** 1866–1943, U. S. cartoonist. — **Brigham,** 1801–77, U. S. Mormon leader. — **Edward,** 1683–1765, English poet. — **Francis Brett,** 1884–1954, English novelist. — **Mahonri Mackintosh,** 1877–1957, U. S. sculptor. — **Owen D.,** 1874–1962, U. S. lawyer and industrialist. — **Thomas,** 1773–1829, English physicist. — **Whitney Moore, Jr.,** 1921–1971, U. S. civil rights leader for Negroes.

young·ber·ry (yung'ber'ē) *n. pl.* **·ries** A type of large dark-red berry, hybridized from a trailing blackberry and a dewberry, found in the western United States. [after B. M. *Young,* U. S. horticulturist]

young blood Youth; young people.

younger hand In card games, the hand next to the leader: also called *pone*: opposed to *eldest hand.*

young-eyed (yung'īd') *adj.* Having youthful eyes or fresh vision; bright-eyed.

young·ish (yung'ish) *adj.* Rather young.

young·ling (yung'ling) *n.* **1** A young person, animal, or plant. **2** An inexperienced person. — *adj.* Young. [OE *geongling*]

Young Plan The plan, adopted in 1929, whereby the amount of German reparations for World War I was finally determined. [after Owen D. *Young*]

Young Pretender See STUART, CHARLES EDWARD.

young·ster (yung'stər) *n.* **1** A young person; a child; youth; sometimes, also, a colt or other young animal. **2** *Colloq.* A junior military officer. [<YOUNG + -STER, infl. by *younker*]

Youngs·town (yungz'toun) A city in NE Ohio; a major steelmaking center.

youn·ker (yung'kər) *n.* **1** A German squire. **2** *Colloq.* A youngster. **3** A young gentleman; knight. Also spelled *yonker.* [<MDu. *jonckher* a young gentleman < *jonc* young + *here* a lord, master]

you·pon (yōō'pən) See YAUPON.

your (yôr, yŏŏr) *pronominal adj.* The possessive case of the pronoun *you* employed attributively; belonging or pertaining to you: *your* fate. [OE *ēower,* genitive of *gē* ye]

you're (yŏŏr, yôr) You are: a contraction.

yours (yôrz, yŏŏrz) *pron.* **1** The possessive case of *you* used predicatively; belonging or pertaining to you: This room is *yours.* **2** The things or persons belonging or pertaining to you: a home as quiet as *yours*; God bless you and *yours.* — **of yours** Belonging or relating to you; your: the double possessive. [ME *youres*]

your·self (yôr·self', yŏŏr-) *pron. pl.* **·selves** (-selvz') A reflexive and often emphatic form of the pronoun of the second person. *Yourself* is employed as a simple objective: This rests with *yourself,* or in apposition with *you*: You did it *yourself.* Its use as a subject nominative is obsolete. *Yourself* is also used reflexively: You've cut *yourself,* and, rarely, as a substantive: You're not *yourself* today. Also *Scot.* **your·sel'.**

youth (yōōth) *n. pl.* **youths** (yōōths, yōōthz) **1** The state or condition of being young. **2** The period when one is young; that part of life between childhood and manhood; adolescence. **3** The early period of being or development, as of a movement. **4** A young man: in this sense with plural: several *youths*: used, also, as a collective noun: the *youth* of the land. [OE *geoguth*]

youth·ful (yōōth'fəl) *adj.* **1** Pertaining to youth; characteristic of youth; hence, buoyant; vigorous. **2** Having youth; being still young; immature. **3** Not far advanced; early; new. **4** *Geol.* Young. —**youth'ful·ly** *adv.* —**youth'ful·ness** *n.*
   Synonyms: boyish, childish, childlike, girlish, juvenile, puerile, young. *Boyish, childish,* and *girlish* are used in a good sense of those to whom they properly belong, but in a bad sense of those from whom more maturity is to be expected; *childish* eagerness or glee is pleasing in a child, but unbecoming in a man; *puerile* in modern use is distinctly contemptuous. *Juvenile* and *youthful* are commonly used in a favorable and kindly sense in their application to those still *young; youthful* may have a favorable import as applied to any age, as when we say the old man still retains his *youthful* ardor, vigor, or hopefulness: *juvenile* in such use would belittle the statement. See FRESH, NEW.

you've (yōōv) You have: a contraction.

yow (you) See YOWL.

yowe (yō) *n. Obs. & Dial.* A ewe. Also **yow** (yō). [Dial. var. of EWE]

yow·ie (yō'ē) *n. Scot.* A small ewe. [Dim. of YOWE]

yowl (youl) *v.i.* To utter a yowl; howl; yell. —*n.* A loud, prolonged, wailing cry; a howl. Also spelled *yawl, yow.* [Cf. ON *gaula* howl, yell]

yo-yo (yō'yō) *n. pl.* **-yos** A wheel-like toy with a deep central groove around which is looped a string connecting the toy with the operator's finger. As the toy spins up and down the string it may be put through a variety of movements by manipulation of the string. **2** *Slang* A compromising person; one whose political ideas and opinions change as necessary for personal advantage. [Origin unknown]

Y·pres (ē'pr') A town in NW Belgium; site of three major battles of World War I, 1914, 1915, 1917. Flemish **Ie·per** (yā'pər); popularly spelled **Wi·pers** (wī'pərz) by British soldiers in World War I.

Yp·si·lan·ti (ip'sə·lan'tē, *Gk.* ēp'sē·län'tē), **Alexander,** 1792–1828, Greek patriot. —**Demetrios,** 1793–1832, Greek patriot; brother of the preceding.

Yp·si·lan·ti (ip'sə·lan'tē) a city in southeastern Michigan; pop. 30,000.

Y·quem (ē·kem') *n.* A highly esteemed Sauterne wine. [from Château *Yquem,* an estate in SW France]

Y·sa·bel (ē·sä·bel') See SANTA ISABEL.

Y·ser (ē·zer') A river in northern France and western Belgium, flowing 48 miles NE from near St. Omer through Nord department and West Flanders to the North Sea at Nieuport.

Y·seult (i·sōōlt') See ISEULT.

Ys·sel (ī'səl) See IJSSEL.

Ys·trad·y·fod·wg (üs'träd·i·vod'ōog) See RHONDDA.

Y-track (wī'trak') *n.* A track at approximately right angles to a line of railroad, and connected with it by two switches: used in place of a turntable.

yt·ter·bi·a (i·tûr'bē·ə) *n. Chem.* White ytterbium oxide, Yb₂O₃.

yt·ter·bi·um (i·tûr'bē·əm) *n.* A metallic element (symbol Yb, atomic number 70) occurring in minute amounts in ores containing other rare-earth elements. See PERIODIC TABLE. [< NL, from *Ytterby,* a town in Sweden where gadolinite was first found] —**yt·ter'bic** *adj.*

yt·tri·a (it're·ə) *n. Chem.* A white insoluble earth, yttrium sesquioxide, Y₂O₃. [< NL, from *Ytterby.* See YTTERBIUM.]

yt·tric (it'rik) *adj. Chem.* Of, pertaining to, or derived from yttrium, especially in its higher valence. [< YTTR(IUM) + -IC]

yt·trif·er·ous (i·trif'ər·əs) *adj.* Yielding or containing yttrium. [< YTTR(IUM) + -FEROUS]

yt·tri·um (it'rē·əm) *n.* A metallic element (symbol Y, atomic number 39) found in association with rare-earth elements. See PERIODIC TABLE. [< NL < YTTRIA]

Yü (yü) A river of southern China, flowing 500 miles east from eastern Yünnan through southern Kwangsi to a confluence with the Hungshui, forming the West River proper: also *Siang.*

yu·an (yōō·än', *Chinese* yü·än') *n.* The monetary unit of China. Also **yuan dollar.** Also called *Taiwan dollar.* [< Chinese *yüan,* lit., a circle]

Yü·an (yü'än') A river in NW Hunan province, SE central China, flowing 540 miles NE and east from western Kweichow province to Tungting Lake. Also **Yü·en** (yü'en').

Yü·an Shih-k'ai (yü·än' shē'kī'), 1859–1916, Chinese general; president of the Chinese Republic 1912–1916.

Yu·bi (yōō'bē), **Cape** See JUBY, CAPE.

Yu·ca·tán (yōō'kə·tan', *Sp.* yōō'kä·tän') **1** A peninsula of SE Mexico and NE Central America (including British Honduras and part of Guatemala); 70,000 square miles; separated from Cuba by **Yucatán Channel,** a strait between Yucatán and Cuba, connecting the Gulf of Mexico with the Caribbean; 135 miles wide. **2** A state in SE Mexico at the NW end of the peninsula; 13,706 square miles; capital, Mérida.

yuc·ca (yuk'ə) *n.* **1** Any of a large genus (*Yucca*) of liliaceous plants of the southern United States, Mexico, and Central America, generally found in dry, sandy places, having a woody stem, usually very short, but sometimes arborescent, which bears a large panicle of white, bell-shaped, drooping flowers emerging from a crown of sword-shaped leaves. **2** The flower of this plant, the State flower of New Mexico. [< NL < Sp. *yuca* < Taino]

yucca moth A moth (*Tegeticula* or *Pronuba yuccasella*) whose larvae feed on yucca seed pods.

Yu·chi (yōō'chē) *n.* One of a tribe of North American Indians, the one tribe comprising the Uchean linguistic stock, formerly dwelling along the Savannah River in eastern Georgia. In 1836 they migrated with the Creeks to what is now Oklahoma.

YUCCA
(Plant from 2 to
10 feet tall)

Yu·ga (yōō'gə) *n.* An age; cycle; a period of long duration according to Hindu thought. Each **Mahâ-yuga** or great age of the world, consisting of 4,320,000 years, is subdivided into four *Yugas* or ages: **Krita-yuga** (1,728,000 years), **Treta-yuga** (1,296,000 years), **Dvâpara-yuga** (864,000 years), and **Kali-yuga** (432,000 years), which began in 3094 B.C. These ages decrease successively in excellence; the life of man is supposed to last for 400 years in the first, 300 years in the second, 200 years in the third, and 100 years in the present or Kali age. Also **Yug** (yōōg). [< Skt., an age, yoke]

Yu·go·sla·vi·a (yōō'gō·slä'vē·ə) A state of SE Europe on the Adriatic; the largest country of the Balkans; 98,538 square miles; capital, Belgrade; 1918–1929, the *Kingdom of the Serbs, Croats, and Slovenes,* formed by the union of Serbia and Montenegro with former Austro-Hungarian provinces; 1929–41 the *Kingdom of Yugoslavia;* 1941–45 occupied by Axis Powers; the present federal republic comprises six "people's republics": Bosnia and Herzegovina, Croatia, Macedonia, Montenegro, Serbia, and Slovenia: also *Jugoslavia.* —**Yu'go·slav** (-släv, -slav), **Yu'go·sla'vi·an** *adj. & n.* —**Yu·go·slav'ic** (-slä'vik, -slav'ik) *adj.*

Yu·it (yōō'it) *n.* One of the Eskimos inhabiting northeastern Siberia. Compare INNUIT. [< Eskimo, men]

Yu·ka·wa (yōō·kä·wä), **Hideki,** born 1907, Japanese physicist.

Yu·kon (yōō'kon) A territory in NW Canada between Alaska and the Northwest Territories; 207,076 square miles; capital, Whitehorse.

Yu·kon River (yōō'kon) A river in NW Canada and central Alaska, flowing 1,979 miles to the Bering Sea.

Yule (yōōl) *n.* Christmas time, or the feast celebrating it. [OE *geōl(a)* Christmas day, Christmastide]

yule candle A large candle formerly used to light Christmas festivities.

Yule Day *Dial.* or *Scot.* Christmas Day.

yule log A large log or block of wood, brought in with much ceremony, and made the foundation of the Christmas Eve fire. Also **yule block, yule clog.**

Yule·tide (yōōl'tīd') *n.* Christmas time.

Yu·ma (yōō'mə) *n.* One of a tribe of North American Indians, the dominant tribe of the Yuman linguistic stock, formerly living along the Gila and Colorado rivers in northern Mexico and Arizona and in SE California: now on a reservation in California.

Yu·man (yōō'mən) *n.* A North American Indian linguistic stock of the SW United States and NW Mexico, including the Mohave and Yuma tribes.

Yün·nan (yōō'nän', *Chinese* yün'nän') A province of SW China; 154,014 square miles; capital, Kunming.

yu·pon (yōō'pən) See YAUPON.

Yup·pie (yup'ē) *n. pl.* **·pies** *Slang* A member of the young, professional segment of the population. [< Y(OUNG) U(RBAN) P(ROFESSIONAL) + -IE]

Yur·ev (yōōr'yəf) The Russian name for TARTU.

Yu·zov·ka (yōō'zəf·kə) The former name for STALINO.

Z

z, Z (zē, *Brit.* zed) *n. pl.* **z's, Z's** or **zs, Zs** or **zees** (zēz) **1** The 26th letter of the English alphabet: from Phoenician *zayin,* Greek *zeta,* Roman Z. It was not used by the Romans until about the first century B.C. **2** The sound of the letter z, a voiced alveolar fricative corresponding to the voiceless s. See ALPHABET.

Z (zē) *n.* Something resembling a letter Z in shape: sometimes written *zee.*

Za·brze (zäb'zhe) A city in southern Poland, formerly (1742–1945) in Upper Silesia: German *Hindenburg.*

Za·ca·te·cas (sä'kä·tā'käs) A state in central Mexico; 28,117 square miles; capital, Zacatecas.

za·ca·tón (sä'kä·tōn', *Sp.* thä'kä·tōn') *n.* A species of muhly grass (*Muhlenbergia macroura*) found in Mexico, the roots of which are often used in making brushes: also called *Mexican broomroot, whisk grass.* [< Sp. < *zacate* forage, grass, hay < Nahuatl *zacatl*]

Zac·chae·us (za·kē'əs) A masculine personal name. Also **Zac·che·us** (za·kē'əs), *Fr.* **Za·chée** (zà·shā'), *Ital.* **Za·che·o** (dzä·kā'ō). [< Hebrew, remembrance of the Lord] —**Zacchaeus** A wealthy publican at whose house Jesus dined in Jericho. *Luke* xix 2.

Zach (zak) Diminutive of ZACHARIAH, ZACHARIAS.

Zach·a·ri·ah (zak'ə·rī'ə) A masculine personal

name. Also **Zach·a·ry** (zak′ər·ē), *Dan., Du., Sw.* **Zach·a·ri·as** (zä′kä·rē′äs), *Fr.* **Za·cha·rie** (zä·shä·rē′), *Ital.* **Zac·ca·ri·a** (dzäk′ kä·rē′ä), *Lat.* **Zach·a·ri·as** (zak′ə·rī′əs), *Sp.* **Za·ca·ri·as** (thä′kä·rē′äs). [<Hebrew, remembrance of the Lord]
— **Zachariah** The last king of Israel of Jehu's race. II *Kings* xiv 29.
— **Zacharias** The father of John the Baptist. *Luke* i 5.
Za·cyn·thus (zə·sin′thəs) The ancient name for ZANTE.
Za·dar (zä′där) A port of western Croatia, Yugoslavia, on the Adriatic; formerly (1918–1947) in Venezia Giulia, Italy: Italian *Zara*.
Za·dok (zä′dok) A masculine personal name. Also *Fr.* **Za·doc** (zä·dôk′), *Lat.* **Za·do·cus** (zə·dō′kəs). [<Hebrew, the just]
zaf·fer (zaf′ər) *n.* A blue pigment made by roasting cobalt ores to yield an impure cobalt oxide: used for enamel and for painting on glass. Also **zaf′far, zaf′fir, zaf′fre**. [<Ital. *zaffera*, prob. <Arabic *sufr* copper]
zaf·tig (zäf′tik) *adj. U.S. Slang* Curvaceous.
Zag·a·zig (zag′ə·zig, zä·gä·zēg′) A city of SE Lower Egypt.
Za·greb (zä′greb) The capital of Croatia, in NW Yugoslavia; a major industrial center and the second largest city of Yugoslavia: German *Agram*.
Za·gre·us (zä′grē·əs, -grōōs) In Greek mythology, a son of Zeus and Persephone, slain by the Titans and revived as Dionysus. See ORPHIC MYSTERIES.
Zag·ros Mountains (zag′rəs) The chief mountain system of Iran, extending from Azerbaijan to Iranian Baluchistan; highest point, over 14,900 feet.
Za·ha·roff (zä·hä′rəf), **Sir Basil**, 1850?–1936, international financier and armament manufacturer born in Turkey of Greek and Russian parents.
Zah·ran (zä′rän) See DHAHRAN.
zai·bat·su (zī′bät·sōō) *n. Japanese* The wealthy clique of Japan, representing four or five dominant families.
Zaire Republic (zär) An independent republic in central Africa; 904,754 square miles; capital, Kinshasa: formerly *Belgian Congo, Democratic Republic of the Congo.*
Za·les·ki (zä·les′kē), **August**, 1883–1972, Polish statesman.
Za·ma (zä′mə) An ancient town in Numidia, northern Africa, SW of Carthage: scene of Hannibal's defeat by Scipio Africanus, 202 B.C., ending the strength of Carthage; site of a modern village of north central Tunisian.
za·mar·ra (zə·mär′ə, -mär′ə) *n.* A sheepskin coat worn by Spanish shepherds. Also **za·mar′ro** (-mär′ō, -mär′ō). [<Sp.]
Zam·be·zi (zam·bē′zē) One of the largest rivers in Africa, flowing SE 1,650 miles from Eastern Angola and western Zambia to the Indian Ocean in Mozambique; forms an international boundary between Zambia and Zimbabwe, Botswana, and Namibia. Also **Zam·be′si**. *Portuguese* **Zam·be·ze** (zäm·bā′zə).
Zam·bi·a (zam′bē·ə) An independent member of the Commonwealth of Nations in south central Africa; 288,130 square miles; capital, Lusaka: formerly *Northern Rhodesia.*
Zam·bo·an·ga (säm′bō·äng′gä) A port of SW Mindanao, Philippines.
za·mi·a (zä′mē·ə) *n.* Any of a genus (*Zamia*) of palmlike trees and low shrubs of the cycad family, having unbranched stems terminating in a tuft of thick, pinnate, often spiny-edged leaves. [<NL <LL *zamiae*, misreading of L (*nuces*) *azaniae* pine (nuts)]
za·min·dar (zə·mēn′där) See ZEMINDAR.
Za·mo·ra (thä·môr′ä) 1 An ancient city of NW Spain; capital of Zamora province. 2 A province of NW Spain, bordering on Portugal; 4,081 square miles.
Za·mo·ra y Tor·res (thä·môr′ä ē tôr′räs), **Niceto Alcalá**, 1877–1949, Spanish politician; president of Spain 1931–36.
za·na·na (zə·nä′nə) See ZENANA.
Zang·will (zang′wil), **Israel**, 1864–1926, English novelist and dramatist.
Zan·te (zan′tē, *Ital.* dzä n′tä) 1 The southernmost main island of the Ionian Islands, Greece; 157 square miles: ancient *Zacynthus. Greek* **Za·kyn·thos** (zə·kin′ thəs). 2 Its capital, a port on the SE coast.
Zan·thox·y·lum (zan·thok′sə·ləm) *n.* A genus of trees of the rue family with prickly stems,

of which some species have medicinal properties. [<NL <Gk. *xanthos* yellow + *xylon* wood]
za·ny (zä′nē) *adj.* **·ni·er, ·ni·est** Absurdly funny; ludicrous. —*n. pl.* **·nies** 1 In old comic plays, a clown who imitates the other performers with ludicrous failure. 2 A simpleton; buffoon; fool. [<F *zani* < Ital. *zanni* servants who act as clowns in early Italian comedy <dial. Ital. *Zanni*, var. of *Guiovanni* John]
— **za′ni·ly** *adv.* — **za′ni·ness** *n.*
Zan·zi·bar (zan′zə·bär, zan′zə·bär′) A region of Tanzania consisting of the islands of **Zanzibar** (640 square miles) and Pemba; capital, Zanzibar.
zap (zap) *Slang. v.t.* **zapped, zap·ping** 1 To kill. 2 To attack; hit; clobber. 3 To confront or impress suddenly and forcefully; astound; overwhelm. —*n.* 1 Vigorous effort; punch. 2 An attack or confrontation.
Za·pa·ta (sä·pä′tä), **Emiliano**, 1877?–1919, Mexican revolutionary leader 1911–1916.
za·pa·te·o (thä′pä·tä′ō) *n.* A Spanish folk dance. [<Sp. < *zapato* a shoe, clog]
Za·po·rozh·e (zə·pə·rôzh′yə) A city on the Dnieper in southern Ukrainian S.S.R.: formerly *Aleksandrovsk, Alexandrovsk.*
Za·ra (zä′rä, *Ital.* dzä ′rä) The Italian name for ZADAR.
Za·ra·go·za (thä′rä·gō′thä) The Spanish name for SARAGOSSA.
za·ra·pe (sä·rä′pä) See SERAPE.
Za·ra·thus·tra (zä′rä·thōōs′trä, zar′ə·thōōs′ trə) See ZOROASTER.
za·ra·tite (zä′rə·tīt) *n.* A massive, vitreous nickel carbonate found usually as an emerald-green incrustation: also called *emerald nickel*. [<Sp. *zaratita*, after a Señor *Zarate* of Spain]
za·re·ba (zə·rē′bə) *n.* 1 In the Sudan, a stockade, thorn hedge, or other palisaded enclosure for protecting a village or camp: used also as a means of military defense. 2 A village or camp so protected; by extension, any village. Also **za·ree′ba**. [<Arabic *zarībah* a pen for cattle <*zarb* a sheepfold]
zarf (zärf) *n.* A metal cup-shaped holder, of open or ornamental filigree, for a hot coffee cup, used in the Levant. [<Arabic *zarf* a vessel, sheath]
zar·zue·la (thär·thwä′lä) *n. Spanish* A form of lyrical theater in which song is intermingled with spoken dialog; operetta.
za·stru·ga (zä·strōō′gə) *n. pl.* **·gi** (-jē) *Meteorol.* One of a series of long parallel snow ridges formed by the wind on the open plains of Russia; also spelled *sastruga*. [<Russian]
za·yin (zä′yin) *n.* The seventh Hebrew letter. See ALPHABET. [<Hebrew *zāyin*]
Z-bar (zē′bär′), **Z-beam** (zē′bēm′) *n.* A Z-iron.
Ze·a (zē′ə) *n.* A genus of tall annual cereal grasses which includes corn or maize. *Zea mays,* Indian corn, is the only species. [<NL < LL, *spelt* <Gk. *zeia* one-seeded wheat]
Ze·a (zē′ə) The medieval name for KEOS.
zeal (zēl) *n.* Ardor for a cause, or, less often, for a person; enthusiastic devotion; fervor. See synonyms under ENTHUSIASM, WARMTH. [<OF *zele* <L *zelus* <Gk. *zēlos* < *zēein* boil]
Zea·land (zē′lənd) A Danish island between the Kattegat and the Baltic Sea, on which Copenhagen is located; the largest island of Denmark, separated from Sweden by the Oresund; 2,709 square miles: German *Seeland, Danish Sjaelland.*
zeal·ot (zel′ət) *n.* One who is overzealous; a fanatic; immoderate partisan. [<LL *zelotes* <Gk. *zēlōtēs* <*zēloein* be zealous <*zēlos* zeal]
Zeal·ot (zel′ət) *n.* A member of a fanatical Jewish party (A.D. 6–70) in almost continual revolt against the Romans.
zeal·ot·ry (zel′ət·rē) *n.* The conduct or disposition of a zealot.
zeal·ous (zel′əs) *adj.* Filled with or incited by zeal; enthusiastic. See synonyms under EAGER. — **zeal′ous·ly** *adv.* — **zeal′ ous·ness** *n.*
ze·a·xan·thin (zē′ə·zan′thin) *n. Biochem.* A yellow pigment, $C_{40}H_{56}O_{20}$, related to carotene and obtained in the form of golden-orange leaflets from yellow corn, egg yolk, and green leaves. [<ZEA + XANTH- + -IN]
Zeb·a·di·ah (zeb′ə·dī′ə) A masculine personal name. [<Hebrew, God has bestowed]
ze·bec (zē′bek), **ze·beck** See XEBEC.
Zeb·e·dee (zeb′ə·dē) A masculine personal name. [Contraction of ZEBADIAH]

— **Zebedee** The father of James and John, disciples of Christ. *Matt.* iv. 21.
ze·bra (zē′brə) *n.*

ZEBRA
(From 10½ to 13 hands high at the withers)

Any of various African equine mammals resembling the ass, having a white or yellowish-brown body fully marked with variously patterned, dark-brown or blackish bands; especially, the true or **mountain zebra** (*Equus zebra*) of the Cape of Good Hope Province and Grevy's zebra. (*E. grevyi*) of Abyssinia and northeast Africa. [<Pg. < Bantu (Congo)]
— **ze′brine** (-brēn, -brin), **ze′broid** (-broid) *adj.*
zebra wolf The thylacine.
ze·bra·wood (zē′brə·wŏŏd′) *n.* 1 The wood of a large tree (*Connarus guianensis*) of Guiana, light brown in color with dark stripes, used in making furniture. 2 The tree. 3 The striped or banded wood of various other trees.
ze·bu (zē′byōō) *n.*

ZEBU
(From 3 to 4½ feet high at the shoulder)

The domesticated ox (*Bosindicus*) of India, China, and East Africa, having a hump on the withers, a large dewlap, and short curved horns: there are many breeds, varying in color, some being reared for milk and flesh, and others for riding and draft. [<F *zébu* <Tibetan]
Zeb·u·lon (zeb′yə·lən) A son of Jacob and ancestor of the tribe of Israel bearing that name. *Gen.* xxx 20. Also **Zeb′u·lun.**
zec·chi·no (tsek·kē′nō) *n. pl.* **·ni** (-nē) A gold coin of the republic of Venice; the sequin. Also **zec·chin** (zek′in), **zech′in.** [<Ital. See SEQUIN.]
Zech·a·ri·ah (zek′ə·rī′ə) A masculine personal name. [Var. of ZACHARIAH]
— **Zechariah** Hebrew prophet of the sixth century B.C., who promoted the rebuilding of the Temple; also, the Old Testament book bearing his name. Also *Zacharias.*
zed (zed) *n. Brit.* The letter z: generally called *zee* in the United States. [<F *zède* <L *zeta* <Gk. *zēta*]
Zed·e·ki·ah (zed′pwə·kī′ə) A masculine personal name. [<Hebrew, justice of the Lord]
— **Zedekiah** The last king of Judah, 597–586 B.C.; son of Josiah. II *Kings* xxiv 17.
zed·o·ar·y (zed′ō·er′ē) *n.* The root of a species of turmeric (*Curcuma zedoaria*), used in medicine as a stomachic and as a carminative. [<Med. L *zedoarium* <Arabic *zedwār*]
zee¹ (zē, *Du.* zā) *n. Dutch* Sea: used in geographic names: Zuyder *Zee*, Tappan *Zee.*
zee² (zē) *n.* The letter Z, z.
Zee·brug·ge (zē′brŏŏg·ə, *Flemish* zä′brœkh·ə) A port of NW Belgium on the North Sea in West Flanders province.
Zee·land (zē′lənd, *Du.* zā ′länt) A province of SE Netherlands bordering on Belgium and including Walcheren and other islands; 650 square miles.
Zee·man (zä′män), **Pieter**, 1865–1943, Dutch physicist.
Zeeman effect *Physics* The splitting of spectral lines when the source emitting them is placed in a strong magnetic field. [after Pieter *Zeeman*]
ze·in (zē′in) *n. Biochem.* A simple protein derived from corn: it is insoluble in water but soluble in 70 to 80 percent alcohol. [<ZEA + -IN]
Zeit·geist (tsīt′gīst) *n. German* The spirit of the time; the intellectual and moral tendencies that characterize any age or epoch. [<G < *zeit* time + *geist* spirit]
Zeke (zēk) Diminutive of EZEKIEL.
Ze·lin·ski (zyi·lyēn′skē), **Nikolai**, 1861–1953, Russian chemist.

ze·min·dar (zə·mēn′där′) *n.* In India, a tax farmer, required, under the Mogul rule, to pay a fixed sum for the tract of land assigned him; hence, later, especially in Bengal, a native landlord required to pay a certain land tax to the English government; an owner of the soil: also spelled *zamindar.* [< Hind. < Persian *zamīndār* < *zamīn* earth + *dār* a holder]

Zem·po·al·te·pec (sām′pō-äl′tä-pek′) A peak in Oaxaca, Mexico; 11,142 feet. Also **Zem·po·al·té·petl** (sām′pō-äl′tä′petl).

zemst·vo (zem′stvō, *Russian* zyem′stfô) *n.* A Russian elective district and provincial representative assembly; replaced in 1917 by the soviet system. [< Russian *zemlya* land]

Ze·mun (ze′mōōn) The port section of Belgrade, Yugoslavia, on the Danube; formerly a separate city: German *Semlin.*

ze·na·na (zə·nä′nə) *n.* In India, the women's apartments; the East Indian harem: also spelled *zanana.* [< Hind. *zenāna* belonging to women < Persian *zanāna* < *zan* woman]

Zen Buddhism (zen) A form of meditative Buddhism whose adherents believe in and work toward abrupt enlightenment; much emphasis is placed on the identity of nirvana and samsara, and on direct transmission of the enlightened state from master to pupil, with a minimum of words; scriptures and ritual forms are minimized, while continual meditation and practical physical labor are stressed. It originated in China when late northern Indian Buddhism came into contact with Taoism around A.D. 500, whence it acquired many Taoist features; it then spread to Japan, where it greatly influenced Japanese culture in all areas, especially in the age of the Samurai, whose feudal code, bushido, derived from Zen, as did judo and jiujitsu. [< Japanese *zen* meditation < Chinese *chan* < Skt. *dhyana*]

Zend (zend) *n.* **1** The ancient translation and commentary, in a literary form of Middle Persian (Pahlavi), of the Avesta, the sacred writings of the Zoroastrian religion. **2** Erroneously, the language of the Avesta; Avestan. [< F < Persian, interpretation] —**Zend′ic** *adj.*

Zend-A·ves·ta (zend′ə-ves′tə) *n.* The Avesta, including the later translation and commentary called the Zend. [Alter. of Persian *Avestā-va-Zend* the Avesta with its interpretation < Avestan *Avestā* a sacred text + Persian *zend* interpretation] —**Zend′-A·ves·ta′ic** (-ə·ves·tā′ik) *adj.*

zen·dik (zen·dēk′) *adj.* In Eastern countries, an atheist or heretic; one who practices black magic. [< Arabic *zindīq* an atheist < Persian *zandīq* a fire worshiper]

Zeng·er (zeng′ər), **John Peter**, 1697–1746, American printer and publisher.

ze·nith (zē′nith) *n.* **1** The point in the celestial sphere that is exactly overhead: opposed to *na·dir.* **2** The culminating point of prosperity, greatness, etc.; summit. [< OF *cenit* < Arabic *samt* (*ar-rās*) the path (over the head)]

Ze·no (zē′nō) Either of two ancient Greek philosophers:
—**Zeno of Elea**, 490?–430? B.C., early Greek philosopher, noted for his arguments (paradoxes) against motion and multiplicity.
—**Zeno the Stoic**, 342?–270? B.C., Greek philosopher; founder of the Stoic school.

Ze·no·bi·a (zi·nō′bē-ə) Queen of Palmyra in the third century; conquered and captured by the Roman emperor Aurelian.

ze·o·lite (zē′ə-līt) *n.* A secondary mineral occurring in cavities and veins in eruptive rocks, usually a hydrous silicate of aluminum and sodium: various forms are used as water softeners. [< Sw. *zeolit* < Gk. *zeēin* boil + *lithos* stone] —**ze′o·lit′ic** (-lit′ik) *adj.*

Zeph·a·ni·ah (zef′ə·nī′ə) A masculine personal name. [< Hebrew, the Lord has hidden]
—**Zephaniah** Hebrew prophet of the seventh century B.C.; also, the book of the Old Testament bearing his name. Also *Sophonias.*

zeph·yr (zef′ər) *n.* **1** The west wind; poetically, any soft, gentle wind. **2** Worsted or woolen yarn of very light weight used for embroidery, shawls, etc.: also **zephyr worsted.** **3** Figuratively, anything very light and airy. [< L *zephyrus* < Gk. *zephyros*]

zephyr cloth Thin, fine cashmere used for women's clothing.

Zeph·y·rus (zef′ər-əs) In Greek mythology, the west wind: regarded as the mildest and gentlest of all sylvan deities.

Zep·pe·lin (zep′ə-lin, *Ger.* tsep′ə·lēn′) *n.* A large dirigible having a rigid, cigar-shaped body, as originally designed and constructed by Count Ferdinand von Zeppelin.

Zep·pe·lin (zep′ə-lin, *Ger.* tsep′ə·lēn′), **Count Ferdinand von**, 1838–1917, German general; aeronaut and airship builder.

Zer·matt (tser·mät′) A resort village of SE Valais canton, SW Switzerland; elevation, 5,315 feet.

ze·ro (zir′ō, zē′rō) *n.* *pl.* **ze·ros** or **ze·roes 1** The numeral or symbol o; a cipher. ♦ In nontechnical speech, this symbol is often pronounced (ō). **2** *Math.* The element of a number system that leaves any element unchanged under addition, in particular, a real number 0 such that $a + 0 = 0 + a = a$ for any real number a. **3** The point on a scale, as of a thermometer, from which measures are counted. **4** *Mil.* A setting for a gunsight which adjusts both for elevation and wind. **5** The lowest point in any standard of comparison; nullity. —*v.t.* **ze·roed, ze·ro·ing** To adjust (instruments) to an arbitrary zero point for synchronized readings. —**to zero in 1** To bring an aircraft into a desired position, as for bombing or landing. **2** To adjust the sight of (a gun) by calibrated results of firings. —**to zero in on 1** To direct gunfire, bombs, etc., toward (a specific target). **2** To concentrate or focus one's energy, attention, etc., on. —*adj.* Without value or appreciable change. [< F *zéro* < Ital. *zero* < Arabic *sifr.* Doublet of CIPHER.]

ze·ro-beat (zir′ō-bēt′) *adj. Electronics* Homodyne.

zero hour 1 The time set for attack or other military operations: also called *H-hour.* **2** Any critical moment.

zest (zest) *n.* **1** Agreeable excitement and keen enjoyment of the mind accompanying exercise, mental or physical. **2** That which imparts such excitement and relish. **3** Specifically, an agreeable and piquant flavor in anything tasted, especially if added to the usual flavor, as that imparted to soups or wines by the essential oil of lemon peel, or by spice; figuratively, increase of enjoyment produced by the addition of any agreeable stimulant. **4** A piece of orange or lemon peel used to flavor anything, or the aromatic oil squeezed from it: a rare usage. See synonyms under APPETITE, RELISH. —*v.t.* To give zest or relish to; make piquant. [< F *zeste* lemon peel (for flavoring)] —**zest′ful** *adj.*

ze·ta (zāt′ə, zē′-) *n.* The sixth letter (Z,ζ) in the Greek alphabet, corresponding to English *z,* in ancient Greek sounded *zd* or *dz,* in modern Greek *z.*

Ze·thus (zē′thəs) In Greek mythology, Amphion's twin brother. Also **Ze′thos.** See AMPHION.

Zet·land (zet′lənd) See SHETLAND.

zeug·ma (zōōg′mə) *n.* A rhetorical figure in which an adjective is made to modify, or a verb to govern, two nouns, while applying properly only to one: *She was* remembered but *they* forgotten. Compare SYLLEPSIS. [< NL < Gk., a yoking < *zeugnymi* yoke]

Zeus (zōōs) In Greek mythology, the supreme deity, ruler of the celestial realm, son of Kronos and Rhea and husband of Hera: identified with the Roman *Jupiter.*

Zeus-Am·mon (zōōs′am′ən) See AMMON.

Zeux·is (zōōk′sis) Greek painter of the late fifth century B.C.

Zhda·nov (zhdä′nôf) A port on the Sea of AZOV, SE Ukrainian S.S.R.: formerly *Mariupol.*

Zhda·nov (zhdä′nôf), **Andrei**, 1896–1948, U.S.S.R. politician and general.

Zhi·to·mir (zhi·tô′mir) A city in west central Ukrainian S.S.R.

Zhu·kov (zhōō′kôf), **Georgi**, 1895–1974, U.S.S.R. marshal and statesman.

zib·e·line (zib′ə·lin, -lin) *adj.* Pertaining to the sable; made of sable fur. —*n.* The fur of the sable. Also **zib′el·line.** [< F < OF *sebelin,* ult. < Slavic. Akin to SABLE.]

zib·et (zib′it) *n.* A carnivore, the Asian or Indian civet (*Viverra zibetha*), with the black

markings less distinct and the tail more ringed than the common civet. It is often domesticated. Also **zib′eth.** [< Med. L *zibethum* < Arabic *zabād* a civet]

Zieg·feld (zēg′feld, zig′-), **Florenz**, 1869–1932, U.S. theatrical producer.

zig·gu·rat (zig′ŏŏ-rat)*n.* Among the Assyrians and Babylonians, a terraced temple tower pyramidal in form, each successive story being smaller than the one below, leaving a terrace around each of the floors. Also **zik′ku·rat** (zik′-).

ZIGGURAT

[< Assyrian *ziqqur-atu,* orig. a mountain top]

zig·zag (zig′zag) *n.* A series of short, sharp turns or angles from one side to the other in succession, or something, as a path or pattern, characterized by such angles. —*adj.* Having a series of short alternating turns or angles from side to side: a *zigzag* pattern. —*adv.* In a zigzag manner. —*v.t. & v.i.* **·zagged, ·zag·ging** To form or move in zigzags. [< F < G *zickzack,* prob. reduplication of *zacke* a sharp point]

zig·zag·ger (zig′zag-ər) *n.* **1** One who or that which zigzags. **2** A sewing-machine attachment for stitching appliqué, joining lace and insertion to fabric, etc.

zilch (zilch) *n. Slang* Nothing; naught. [Origin unknown]

zil·lah (zil′ə) *n. Anglo-Indian* A provincial governmental district in India.

zil·lion (zil′yən) *n. Colloq.* A very large, indeterminate number: She said she had a *zillion* things to do before the plane left. [Imit. of *million, trillion,* etc.] —**zil′lionth** *adj.*

Zil·pah (zil′pə) The mother of Gad. *Gen.* xxx 10.

Zim·ba·bwe (zim-bä′bwä) **1** An independent republic in south central Africa, formed in 1980 from the British colony of Southern Rhodesia; 150,699 sq. mi.; capital Harare (Salisbury). See RHODESIA. **2** The site of a ruined city (probably of a Bantu people, dating from the 15th century) of SE Zimbabwe; discovered about 1870.

Zim·ba·list (zim′bə-list, *Russian* zim′bə-lyēst′), **Efrem**, born 1889, U.S. violinist born in Russia.

zinc (zingk) *n.* A bluish-white, lustrous metallic element (symbol Zn, atomic number 30) occurring in various ores and essential in traces for the activity of many plant and animal enzymes. See PERIODIC TABLE. —*v.t.* **zinced** or **zincked, zinc·ing** or **zinck·ing** To coat or cover with zinc; galvanize. [< G *zink;* ult. origin unknown] —**zinc′ic** *adj.* —**zinck′y, zinc′y, zink′y** *adj.*

zinc·al·ism (zingk′əl-iz′əm) *n. Pathol.* Chronic zinc poisoning.

zinc·ate (zingk′āt) *n. Chem.* A salt derived from zinc hydroxide by substitution of a metal for the hydrogen. [< ZINC + -ATE³]

zinc blende Sphalerite.

zinc chloride *Chem.* A white deliquescent compound, $ZnCl_2$, extensively used in medicine, industry, and the arts.

zinc·if·er·ous (zingk·if′ər-əs, zin·sif′ər-əs) *adj.* Yielding zinc, as ore. Also **zink·if′er·ous.** [< ZINC + -(I)FEROUS]

zinc·i·fy (zingk′ə-fī) *v.t.* **·fied, ·fy·ing** To apply zinc to, as by coating or impregnating. [< ZINC + -(I)FY] —**zinc′i·fi·ca′tion** (-fə·kā′shən) *n.*

zinc·ite (zingk′īt) *n.* A deep-red, translucent to subtranslucent zinc oxide, ZnO, crystallizing in the hexagonal system; zinc ore. [< ZINC + -ITE²]

zin·co·graph (zingk′ə-graf, -gräf) *n.* An etching on zinc; a picture obtained by zincography. Also **zin′co·type** (-tīp). [< ZINC + -(O)GRAPH] —**zin·cog·ra·pher** (zing·kog′rə-fər) *n.*

zin·cog·ra·phy (zing·kog′rə-fē) *n.* The art of etching on zinc to produce plates for printing. [< ZINC + -(O)GRAPHY] —**zinc·o·graph·ic** (zingk′ə-graf′ik) or **·i·cal** *adj.*

zinc ointment A medicated ointment containing zinc oxide.

zinc·ous (zingk'əs) *adj. Chem.* Pertaining to or derived from zinc; zincic.

zinc oxide *Chem.* White pulverulent oxide, ZnO, made by burning zinc in air. It is used as a pigment, chiefly as a substitute for white lead, and in medicine as a mild antiseptic.

zinc sulfate *Chem.* A crystalline compound, $ZnSO_4 \cdot 7H_2O$, obtained by the action of sulfuric acid on zinc; white vitriol.

zinc white Zinc oxide used as a pigment.

zin·fan·del (zin'fən·del) *n.* A dry, red or white, claret-type wine made in California. [? from a European place name]

zing (zing) *Colloq. n.* 1 A high-pitched buzzing or humming sound. 2 Energy; vitality. —*v.i.* To make a shrill, humming sound.

zin·ga·ro (tsĕng'gä·rō) *n. pl.* **·ri** (-rē) *Italian* A gipsy. Also **zin'ga·no** (-nō). —**zin'ga·ra** (-rä) *n. fem.*

zin·gi·ber·a·ceous (zin'jə·bə·rā'shəs) *adj. Bot.* Of or pertaining to a family (*Zingiberaceae*) of monocotyledonous tropical plants, the ginger family, having aromatic rootstocks and including cardamon. Also **zin'zi·ber·a'ceous** (zin'zə-). [< NL, family name < LL *zingiber* GINGER]

Zin·jan·thro·pus (zin·jan'thrə·pəs) *n.* Scientific name of a supposed forerunner of modern man, the evidence consisting of the remains of a skull found in East Africa and thought to be nearly two million years old. [< NL < Arabic *Zinj* eastern Africa + Gk. *anthrōpos* man]

zink·en·ite (zingk'ən·īt) *n.* A metallic steel-gray mineral, $PbSb_2S_4$, crystallizing in the orthorhombic system. Also **zinck'en·ite.** [< G *zinkenit,* after J. K. L. Zinken, 1798–1862, German mine director]

zin·ni·a (zin'ē-ə) *n.* Any of a genus (*Zinnia*) of American, chiefly Mexican, herbs of the composite family, having opposite entire leaves and showy flowers; especially, the common zinnia (*Z. elegans*), the State flower of Indiana. [< NL, after J. G. Zinn, 1727–59, German professor of medicine]

Zi·nov·iev (zē·nôv'yif), **Grigori,** 1883–1936, U.S.S.R. political leader.

Zins·ser (zin'sər), **Hans,** 1878–1940, U.S. bacteriologist.

Zin·zen·dorf (tsin'tsən·dôrf), **Count Nicholas Ludwig von,** 1700–60, German theologian.

Zi·on (zī'ən) *n.* 1 A hill in Jerusalem, the site of the Temple and the royal residence of David and his successors: regarded by the Jews as a symbol for the center of Jewish national culture, government, and religion. 2 The Jewish people. 3 Any place or community considered to be especially under God's rule, as ancient Israel or the Christian church. 4 The heavenly Jerusalem; heaven. Also spelled *Sion.* [OE *Sion* < LL < Gk. *Seōn,* *Seiōn* < Hebrew *tsiyōn* a hill]

Zi·on·ism (zī'ən·iz'əm) *n.* A movement for a resettlement of the Jews in Palestine. The form which lays stress upon the political questions involved is sometimes called **political Zionism,** and the term **religious Zionism** is used by those Zionists who lay a special stress upon the regeneration of the Holy Land as a center of social and religious influence for Judaism. Also **Zion movement.** —**Zi'on·ist** *adj. & n.* —**Zi'on·is'tic** *adj.* —**Zi'on·ite** *n.*

Zion National Park A government reservation in SW Utah; 147 square miles; established in 1919; contains **Zion Canyon,** a gorge ½ mile deep, about 15 miles long.

Zi·on·ward (zī'ən·wərd) *adv.* Toward Zion; Godward; heavenward.

zip (zip) *n.* 1 A sharp, hissing sound, as of a bullet passing through the air. 2 *Colloq.* Energy; vitality; vim. —*v.* **zipped, zip·ping** *v.t.* 1 To fasten with a sliding fastener. —*v.i.* 2 *Colloq.* To be very energetic. 3 To move or fly with a zip. [Imit.]

Zi·pan·gu (zi·pang'gōō) Japan: name used by Marco Polo.

ZIP Code (zip) A numerical code devised by the U.S. Post Office to aid in the distribution of domestic mail. Also **Zip Code.** [< z(ONE) I(MPROVEMENT) P(LAN)]

zip gun A home-made pistol consisting of a small pipe or other tube fastened to a block of wood and equipped with a firing pin actuated by a spring or rubber band.

zip·per (zip'ər) *n.* A slide fastener.

Zip·per (zip'ər) *n.* An overshoe or boot secured with a slide fastener: a trade name.

zip·py (zip'ē) *adj.* **·pi·er, ·pi·est** *Colloq.* Brisk; energetic; lively; snappy.

zir·con (zûr'kon) *n.* 1 An adamantine, variously colored zirconium silicate, $ZrSiO_4$. The transparent reddish variety, called *hyacinth,* is used as a gem, as are also the leaf-green, yellowish, colorless, or smoky varieties called *jargon.* 2 A variety of this mineral having an artificially produced steely-blue color of high brilliance and luster: esteemed as a gem. [< F *zircone* < Arabic *zarqūn* cinnabar < Persian *zargūn* golden < *zar* gold + *gūn* color]

zir·con·ate (zûr'kən·āt) *n. Chem.* A salt formed by replacing hydrogen in zirconium hydroxide with a metal. [< ZIRCON(IUM) + -ATE³]

zir·co·ni·a (zûr·kō'nē·ə) *n. Chem.* A white pulverulent zirconium dioxide, ZrO_2, obtained by heating zirconium to redness in contact with air: when strongly heated it becomes luminous, and it is hence used in certain forms of incandescent burners. [< NL < ZIRCON]

zir·co·ni·um (zûr·kō'nē·əm) *n.* A corrosion-resistant metallic element (symbol Zr, atomic number 40), having five naturally occurring isotopes, of which one is weakly radioactive. See PERIODIC TABLE. [< NL < ZIRCON] —**zir·con'ic** (zûr·kon'ik) *adj.*

Z-i·ron (zē'ī'ərn) *n.* An angle iron of Z form: also called *Z-bar, Z-beam.*

Zis·ka (tsis'kä), **John,** 1360?–1424, Bohemian general; leader of the Hussites. Also **Žiž·ka** (zhizh'kä).

zith·er (zith'ər) *n.* A simple form of stringed instrument, having a flat sounding board and from thirty to forty strings that are played by plucking with a plectrum. Also **zith'ern** (-ərn). [< G < L *cithara* < Gk. *kithara.* Doublet of CITHARA and GUITAR.]

zit·tern (zit'ərn) See CITHERN.

zi·zith (tsē·tsēt', tsi'tsis) *n.* The fringe or tassel formerly worn by Jews on the outer garment (*Num.* xv 38), but now worn on the tallith during prayer. [< Hebrew *tsitsith*]

ziz·zle (ziz'əl) *v.i.* **·zled, ·zling** *Brit. Dial.* To make a sputtering or hissing sound, as meat when cooking; sizzle. [Imit.]

Zla·to·ust (zlä'tə·ōōst') A city of SW Asiatic Russian S.F.S.R. in the southern Urals.

zlo·ty (zlô'tē) *n. pl.* **·tys** or **·ty** The monetary unit of Poland. [< Polish, lit., golden]

Zn *Chem.* Zinc (symbol Zn).

zo- Var. of ZOO-.

-zoa *combining form Zool.* Used to denote the names of groups: *Protozoa, Hydrozoa.* An individual in such a group is denoted by **-zoan.** [< NL < Gk. *zōion* an animal]

Zo·an (zō'an) The Old Testament name for TANIS.

zo·an·thro·py (zō·an'thrə·pē) *n.* The obsessive delusion that one has become a beast; lycanthropy. [< NL *zoanthropia* < Gk. *zōion* an animal + *anthrōpos* a man] —**zo·an·throp·ic** (zō'ən·throp'ik) *adj.*

SIGNS OF THE ZODIAC
Reading clockwise:
A. Vernal equinox: Aries, Taurus, Gemini.
B. Summer solstice: Cancer, Leo, Virgo.
C. Autumnal equinox: Libra, Scorpio, Sagittarius.
D. Winter solstice: Capricorn, Aquarius, Pisces.

zo·di·ac (zō'dē·ak) *n.* 1 An imaginary belt encircling the heavens and extending about 8° on each side of the ecliptic, within which are the orbits of the moon, sun, and larger planets. It is divided into twelve parts, called **signs of the zodiac,** which formerly corresponded to twelve constellations bearing the same names. Now, owing to the precession of the equinoxes, each constellation is in the sign that has the name next following its own. 2 Figuratively, a complete circuit; round. 3 *Rare* A circle or halo; also, a girdle. [< OF *zodiaque* < L *zodiacus* < Gk. *(kyklos) zōdiakos* (circle) of animals < *zōdion* a sculptured animal, dim. of *zōion* an animal] —**zo·di·a·cal** (zō·dī'ə·kəl) *adj.*

zodiacal light *Astron.* A cone-shaped tract of faint light lying near the plane of the ecliptic: it may be seen in the west after twilight in winter and spring, or in the east before daybreak from September till January. It is attributed to the reflection of sunlight from a cloud of fine meteoric dust.

Zo·e (zō'ē) A feminine personal name. [< Gk., life]

zo·e·trope (zō'ə·trōp) *n.* A toy having a revolving cylinder with slits through which a series of pictures inside are seen in apparent motion. Compare PHENAKISTOSCOPE. [< Gk. *zōē* life + -TROPE] —**zo·e·trop·ic** (-trop'ik) *adj.*

zo·ic (zō'ik) *adj.* Pertaining to or characterized by animals or animal life. [< Gk. *zōikos* < *zōion* an animal]

zois·ite (zoi'sīt) *n.* A vitreous, transparent to subtranslucent silicate of aluminum and calcium, in which iron sometimes replaces the aluminum. [< G *zoisit,* after Baron *Zois* von Edelstein, 1747–1819, its discoverer]

Zo·la (zō'lə, zō·lä'; *Fr.* zō·lá'), **Émile,** 1840–1902, French writer. —**Zo'la·esque'** (-esk') *adj.*

zoll·ver·ein (tsôl'fer·īn) *n.* 1 A former trade league constituted by twenty-six German states. 2 Hence, a union of states for tariff purposes. [< G *zoll* a tax, custom + *verein* a union]

Zom·ba (zom'bə) The capital of Nyasaland, Federation of Rhodesia and Nyasaland, in the SE part.

zom·bi (zom'bē) *n.* 1 In West African voodoo cults, the python deity; also, the snake deity of the voodoo cults of Haiti and of the southern United States. 2 The supernatural power by which a dead body is believed to be reanimated; specifically, a corpse reactivated by sorcery, but still dead. 3 Loosely, a ghost. Also **zom'bie.** [< West African. Cf. Bantu (Congo) *zumbi* fetish.] —**zom'bi·ism** *n.*

Zom·bie (zom'bē) *n.* A large, strong cocktail made from several kinds of rum, fruit juices, and liqueur. [< ZOMBI]

zo·nal (zō'nəl) *adj.* Of, pertaining to, exhibiting, or marked by a zone or zones; having the form of a zone. Also **zo'na·ry** (-nər·ē).

zo·nate (zō'nāt) *adj.* 1 Marked with zones or concentric colored bands. 2 *Bot.* Disposed in a single row, as certain tetraspores. Also **zo'nat·ed.** [< ZON(E) + -ATE¹] —**zo·na·tion** (zō·nā'shən) *n.*

zone (zōn) *n.* 1 One of five divisions of the earth's surface, enclosed between two parallels of latitude and named for the prevailing climate. These are the **torrid zone,** extending on each side of the equator 23° 27'; the **temperate** or **variable zones,** included between the parallels 23° 27' and 66° 33' on both sides of the equator; and the **frigid zones,** within the parallels 66° 33' and the poles. 2 In war, a region proscribed for neutrals as being within the range of military or naval operations: a defense *zone,* combat *zone*; also, any region neutralized by agreement of combatants: a demilitarized *zone.* 3 *Ecol.* A belt or area delimited from others by the character of its plant or animal life, its climate, geological formations, etc. 4 A region of land distinguished or set off by some special characteristic: a canal zone. 5 *Anat.* A beltlike area distinguished from its surroundings either by structure or appearance.

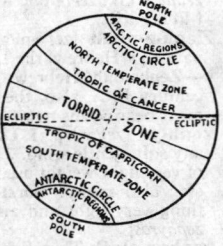

TERRESTRIAL ZONES

6 *Mineral.* Any series of faces upon a crystal whose planes form a prismatic surface. 7 A belt, stripe, etc., distinguished by color or

the like, encircling an object. **8** *Geom.* A portion of the surface of a sphere enclosed between two parallel planes. **9** Originally (now chiefly in poetry), a belt or girdle. **10** The total number of railroad stations situated in a certain area measured from a place whence traffic is shipped; also, a circular area within which a uniform fare is charged by the transportation companies. **11** In the United States parcel post system, any one of the concentric areas within each of which a uniform rate is charged. **12** A postal district in a city. —*v.t.* **zoned, zon·ing 1** To divide into zones; especially, to divide (a city, etc.) into zones which are restricted as to types of construction and activity, as residential, industrial, etc. **2** To encircle with a zone or belt. **3** To mark with or as with zones or stripes. [< MF < L *zona* < Gk. *zōnē* a girdle] **—zoned** *adj.*

zone axis *Mineral.* The imaginary line through a crystal, to which all the faces in a given zone, and the mutual intersections of those faces, are parallel.

zone·less (zōn′lis) *adj.* Having no zone or belt.

zone time See under TIME.

Zon·gul·dak (zông′gōōl·däk′) **1** A port on the Black Sea in NW Turkey in Asia, capital of Zonguldak province; a coal-shipping center. **2** A province of NW Turkey in Asia, bordering on the Black Sea; 2,876 square miles.

zo·nule (zōn′yōōl) *n.* A small zone, belt, or ring. Also **zo′nu·la.** [< NL *zonula*, dim. of L *zona* ZONE]

zoo (zōō) *n.* A menagerie. [Short for ZOOLOGICAL GARDEN]

zoo- *combining form* Animal; of or related to animals, or to animal forms: *zoology, zoophyte.* Also, before vowels, *zo-*. [< Gk. *zōion* an animal]

zo·o·chem·is·try (zō′ə·kem′is·trē) *n.* Animal chemistry; specifically, the chemistry of the solids and fluids contained in the animal organism. **—zo′o·chem′i·cal** (-kem′i·kəl) *adj.*

zo·o·ge·o·graph·ic (zō′ə·jē′ə·graf′ik) *adj.* Of, pertaining to, or engaged in zoogeography. Also **zo′o·ge′o·graph′i·cal. —zo′o·ge′o·graph′i·cal·ly** *adv.*

zoogeographic realm One of a series of major geographic areas characterized by the dominance of certain animal groups. The principal realms in the classification of A. R. Wallace are: the Palearctic, Nearctic, Neotropical, Ethiopian, Oriental, and Australian. The first two are often considered together as the Holarctic realm.

zo·o·ge·og·ra·phy (zō′ə·jē·og′rə·fē) *n.* **1** The systematic study of the distribution of animals and of the factors controlling it. **2** The study of the relations between special animal groups and the land or aquatic areas in which they predominate. **—zo′o·ge·og′ra·pher** *n.*

zo·o·gloe·a (zō′ə·glē′ə) *n. pl.* **·gloe·ae** (-glē′ē) A colony of bacteria forming a jellylike mass held together by a viscid sheath secreted by themselves. [< NL < Gk. *zōion* an animal + *gloios* sticky stuff]

zo·og·ra·phy (zō·og′rə·fē) *n.* The branch of zoology that describes animals; descriptive zoology. **—zo·og′ra·pher** or **·phist** *n.* **—zo·o·graph·ic** (zō′ə·graf′ik) or **·i·cal** *adj.*

zo·oid (zō′oid) *n.* **1** *Biol.* Any organism, usually very small, capable of spontaneous movement and independent existence, as a spermatozoon. **2** *Zool.* **a** One of the distinct members of a compound or colonial organism, as in a bryozoan. **b** A free-swimming organism produced as a stage in the life cycle of a jellyfish. —*adj.* Having essentially the nature of an animal: also **zo·oi·dal** (zō·oid′l). [< ZO- + -OID]

zo·ol·a·try (zō·ol′ə·trē) *n.* Animal-worship. [< ZOO- + -LATRY] **—zo·ol′at·er** *n.* **—zo·ol′a·trous** *adj.*

zo·o·log·i·cal (zō′ə·loj′i·kəl) *adj.* **1** Of, pertaining to, or occupied with zoology. **2** Relating to or characteristic of animals. Also **zo′o·log′ic. —zo′o·log′i·cal·ly** *adv.*

zoological garden A park or garden in which wild animals are kept for exhibition.

zo·ol·o·gy (zō·ol′ə·jē) *n.* **1** The science that treats of animals with reference to their structure, functions, development, nomenclature, and classification. **2** The animal kingdom, or local examples of it, regarded biologically. **3** A scientific treatise on animals. [< NL *zoologia* < Gk. *zōion* an animal + *logos* a word, discourse] **—zo·ol′o·gist** *n.*

zoom (zōōm) *v.i.* **1** To make a low-pitched but loud humming or buzzing sound. **2** To climb sharply in an airplane, using the energy of momentum. **3** To move a motion picture or TV camera rapidly or adjust the focus, as with a zoom lens, to make an object in view appear to come very close or become much more distant. —*v.t.* **4** To cause to zoom. —*n.* The act of zooming. [Imit.]

zo·om·e·try (zō·om′ə·trē) *n.* Measurement of the parts of animals and determination of their relative magnitude. [< ZOO- + -METRY] **—zo·o·met·ric** (zō′ə·met′rik) *adj.*

zoom lens *Photog.* A lens, used chiefly on television and motion picture cameras, that permits the size of the image to be varied continuously without loss of focus.

zo·o·mor·phism (zō′ə·môr′fiz·əm) *n.* **1** The conception, symbolization, or representation of a man or a god in the form of an animal; also, the attribution of divine or human qualities to animals. **2** The representation of animals or animal forms in art or symbolism. **3** Transformation into animals. In this sense compare BEAST MARRIAGE, SWAN MAIDEN. See also CIRCE. Also **zo′o·mor′phy. —zo′o·mor′·phic** *adj.*

zo·on (zō′on) *n. pl.* **zo·ons** or **zo·a** (zō′ə) *Biol.* A developed individual of a compound animal or of a simple egg. [< NL < Gk. *zōion* an animal] **—zo·on·al** (zō·on′əl) *adj.*

zo·oph·a·gous (zō·of′ə·gəs) *adj.* Feeding on animals. [< ZOO- + -PHAGOUS]

zo·o·phile (zō′ə·fil, -fīl) *n.* **1** A zoophilous plant. **2** A lover of animals; specifically, one who objects to vivisection; also, one addicted to zoophilism: also **zo·oph·i·list** (zō·of′ə·list). [< ZOO- + -PHILE] **—zo′o·phil′ic** (-fil′ik) *adj.*

zo·oph·i·lism (zō·of′ə·liz′əm) *n.* **1** Fondness for animals. **2** The obtaining of sexual gratification by the fondling of animals. Also **zo·o·phil·i·a** (zō′ə·fil′ē·ə).

zo·oph·i·lous (zō·of′ə·ləs) *adj.* **1** Animal-loving. **2** Adapted for pollination by animals, as certain plants. [< ZOO- + -PHILOUS]

zo·o·pho·bi·a (zō′ə·fō′bē·ə) *n.* A morbid fear of animals. [< ZOO- + -PHOBIA] **—zo′o·pho′·bic** *adj.*

zo·o·phyte (zō′ə·fīt) *n.* An invertebrate animal resembling a plant, as a coral or sea anemone. [< ZOO- + -PHYTE] **—zo′o·phyt′ic** (-fit′ik) or **·i·cal** *adj.*

zo·o·plas·ty (zō′ə·plas′tē) *n. Surg.* That operation by which a part of an animal body is grafted on some part of the human body. **—zo′o·plas′tic** *adj.*

zo·o·sperm (zō′ə·spûrm) *n.* **1** A zoospore. **2** A spermatozoon. **—zo′o·sper·mat′ic** (-spər·mat′ik) *adj.*

zo·o·spo·ran·gi·um (zō′ə·spə·ran′jē·əm) *n. pl.* **·gi·a** (-jē·ə) *Bot.* A sporangium producing zoospores. [< NL < Gk. *zōion* an animal + *spora* a seed + *angeion* a vessel]

zo·o·spore (zō′ə·spôr, -spōr) *n.* **1** *Bot.* A motile spore destitute of any cell wall, produced particularly among some algae and fungi: they move sometimes in an ameboid manner, but more frequently they are provided with cilia, by the lashing of which the spore is propelled through the water. **2** *Zool.* A flagellate or ameboid motile cell in certain protozoa. [< ZOO- + SPORE] **—zo′o·spor′ic** (-spôr′ik, -spor′ik), **zo·os·po·rous** (zō·os′pər·əs) *adj.*

zo·ot·o·my (zō·ot′ə·mē) *n.* The anatomy or dissection of animals; comparative anatomy. [< NL *zootomia* < Gk. *zōion* an animal + *tomē* a cutting < *temnein* cut] **—zo·o·tom·ic** (zō′ə·tom′ik) or **·i·cal** *adj.* **—zo′o·tom′i·cal·ly** *adv.* **—zo·ot′o·mist** *n.*

zo·o·tox·in (zō′ə·tok′sin) *n.* A toxin derived from animals, as snake venom, the poison of bee stings, etc.

zoot suit (zōōt) *Slang* A suit having an extra-long coat and baggy trousers narrowing at the ankle. [Origin uncertain]

zo·ri (zō′rē) *n.* A flat, thonged sandal of straw or rubber. [< Japanese]

zor·il (zôr′il, zor′-) *n.* An African musteline carnivore *(Ictonyx striata)* which can emit a noxious odor; the Cape polecat. Also **zo·ril·la.** (zə·ril′ə). [< F *zorille* < Sp. *zorrilla* a polecat, dim. of *zorra* a fox]

Zorn (sôrn), **Anders Leonhard,** 1860–1920, Swedish painter, etcher, and sculptor.

Zo·ro·as·ter (zō′rō·as′tər) The traditional founder of the ancient Persian religion, believed to have lived about 600 B.C.: also called *Zarathustra.* **—Zo′ro·as′tri·an** *adj.* & *n.*

Zo·ro·as·tri·an·ism (zō′rō·as′trē·ən·iz′əm) *n.* The religious system founded by Zoroaster on the old Aryan folk religion and taught in the Zend-Avesta. It recognizes two creative powers, one good and the other evil, includes the belief in life after death, and teaches the final triumph of good over evil. See AHRIMAN, ORMUZD. Also **Zo′ro·as′trism.**

Zor·ril·la y Mo·ral (thôr·rē′lyä ē mō·räl′), **José,** 1817–93, Spanish poet and dramatist.

Zos·i·mus (zos′ə·məs, zō′sə-) Greek historian of the fifth century A.D.

zos·ter (zos′tər) *n.* **1** An ancient Greek belt or girdle worn especially by men. **2** *Pathol.* Shingles; herpes zoster. [< L < Gk. *zōstēr* a girdle < *zōnynai* gird]

Zou·ave (zōō·äv′, zwäv) *n.* **1** A light-armed French infantryman wearing a brillant Oriental uniform, originally an Algerian recruit. **2** In the Civil War, a member of a volunteer regiment assuming the name and part of the dress of the French Zouaves. **3** A woman's short, gaily embroidered jacket: also **Zouave jacket.** [< F < Arabic *Zouaoua*, a Kabyle tribe; so called because orig. recruited from this tribe]

zounds (zoundz) *interj.* An exclamation denoting astonishment: also spelled *swounds.* [Short for *God's wounds*]

zoy·sia (zoi′shə, zoi′sē·ə) *n.* Any grass of a genus *(Zoysia)*, used esp. on lawns in warm, dry regions.

Zr *Chem.* Zirconium (symbol Zr).

Zsig·mon·dy (zhig′môn·dē), **Richard,** 1865–1929, German chemist born in Austria.

zuc·chet·to (tsōōk·ket′tō) *n.* A skullcap worn by ecclesiastics in the Roman Catholic Church: black for a priest, purple for a bishop, red for a cardinal, and white for the pope. Also **zuc·chet′ta.** [Var. of Ital. *zucchetta*, orig. a small gourd, dim. of *zucca* a gourd]

zuc·chi·ni (zōō·kē′nē, *Ital.* dzōōk·kē′nē) *n.* A type of green summer squash (evolved from *Cucurbita pepo*) of a small cylindrical shape. Also called *Italian squash.* [< Ital., pl. of *zucchino*, dim. of *zucca* a gourd, squash]

Zug (tsōōkh) **1** The smallest canton of Switzerland; 92 square miles. **2** Its capital, a town on the **Lake of Zug** (15 square miles; about 9 miles long), in the north central part of the country. *French* **Zoug** (zōōg).

Zug·spit·ze (tsōōk′shpit·sə) The highest mountain in Germany, in the Bavarian Alps on the Austrian border; 9,722 feet.

Zu·lu (zōō′lōō) *n. pl.* **Zu·lus** or **Zu·lu 1** One of a Bantu nation of Natal, South Africa, sometimes included with the Kaffirs. **2** The language of the Zulus, belonging to the Bantu family of agglutinative languages. —*adj.* Of, pertaining to, or characteristic of the Zulus or their language.

Zu·lu·land (zōō′lōō·land′) A district of NE Natal, Union of South Africa, formerly a native kingdom; 10,362 square miles.

zum Bei·spiel (tsōōm bī′shpēl) *German* For example: abbreviated *z.B.*

Zu·ñi (zōō′nyē) *n.* **1** One of a tribe of North American Indians of pueblo culture but comprising a distinct linguistic stock; still occupying the big Zuñi pueblo in New Mexico, which is now a reservation. **2** The language of this tribe. **—Zu′ñi·an** *adj.* & *n.*

Zur·ba·rán (thōōr′bä·rän′), **Francisco de,** 1598–1662, Spanish painter.

Zu·rich (zōōr′ik) **1** A canton of NE Switzerland on the border of Baden-Württemberg, West Germany; 667 square miles. **2** Its capital, a city on the northern shore of the **Lake of Zurich** (35 square miles; 25 miles long) in NE Switzerland. *German* **Zü·rich** (tsü′rikh).

Zuy·der Zee (zī′dər zē, *Du.* zœi′dər zā) A former shallow inlet of the North Sea in NW Netherlands; 80 by 34 miles; enclosed by a dike; drainage projects have reclaimed much

add,āce,câre,pälm; end,ēven; it,īce; odd,ōpen,ôrder; tŏŏk,pōōl; up,bûrn; ə = a in *above*, e in *sicken*, i in *clarity*, o in *melon*, u in *focus*; yōō = u in *fuse*, oi,oil; ou,pout; ch,check; g,go; ng,ring; th,thin; th,this; zh,vision. Foreign sounds à,œ,ü,kh,ń; and ♦: see page xx. < from; + plus; ? possibly.

of the land and formed Lake Ijssel. Also **Zui′-der Zee.**

Zweig (tsvīg, tsvīkh), **Arnold,** 1887–1968, German novelist. — **Stefan,** 1881–1942, Austrian dramatist and novelist.

Zwick·au (tsvik′ou) A city in the former state of Saxony, central southern East Germany.

zwie·back (zwī′bak, zwē′-, swī′-, swē′-, -bäk; *Ger.* tsvē′bäk) *n.* A biscuit of wheaten bread or rusk baked yellow in the loaf and later sliced and toasted. [<G, twice baked < *zwie·twice* (< *zwei* two) + *backen* bake]

Zwing·li (tsving′lē), **Ulrich,** 1484–1531, Swiss Protestant reformer. Also *Huldreich Zwingli.*

Zwing·li·an (zwing′lē·ən, tsving′-) *adj.* Of or pertaining to the doctrines taught by Zwingli, especially to the doctrine that the Eucharist is simply a memorial or a symbolic commemoration of the death of Christ. — *n.* A follower of Zwingli. — **Zwing′li·an·ism** *n.*

zwit·ter·i·on (tsvit′ər·ī′ən) *n. Physics* An ion which carries both a negative and a positive charge, as in certain amino acids. [<G *zwitter* hybrid, hermaphrodite, mongrel + ION] — **zwit′ter·i·on′ic** (-ī·on′ik) *adj.*

Zwol·le (zvôl′ə) The capital of Overijssel province, north central Netherlands; a manufacturing and dairy center; site of many 15th century buildings.

Zwor·y·kin (zwôr′i·kin), **Vladimir Kosma,** born 1889, U.S. research engineer in electronics; born in Russia.

zyg·a·poph·y·sis (zig′ə·pof′ə·sis) *n.* *pl.* **·ses** (-sēz) *Anat.* One of the processes, usually disposed in pairs, by which a vertebra articulates with another; an articular process. [<NL <Gk. *zygon* a yoke + *apophysis* a branch. See APOPHYSIS.] — **zyg′a·po·phys′e·al** (-pō·fiz′ē·əl) or **·i·al** *adj.*

zygo- *combining form* Yoke; pair; resembling a yoke, especially in shape: *zygospore.* Also, before vowels, **zyg-.** [<Gk. *zygon* a yoke]

zy·go·dac·tyl (zī′gō·dak′til) *Zool. adj.* Having paired toes, one pair directed forward and the other pair backward, as in parrots and woodpeckers. — *n.* A zygodactyl bird. [<ZYGO- + Gk. *daktylos* a finger]

zy·go·ma (zī gō′mə) *n.* *pl.* **·ma·ta** (-mə·tə) *Anat.* 1 The long arch that joins the temporal and malar bones on the side of the skull. 2 The zygomatic bone. 3 The zygomatic process. [<NL <Gk. *zygōma* < *zygon* a yoke] — **zy·go·mat·ic** (zī′gō·mat′ik) *adj.*

zygomatic arch *Anat.* The zygoma.

zygomatic bone *Anat.* The malar bone or cheek bone.

zygomatic process *Anat.* That process of the temporal bone which helps to form the zygomatic arch.

zy·go·mor·phic (zī′gō·môr′fik) *adj. Biol.* Bilaterally symmetrical: said of organisms or parts of organisms divisible into similar halves in only one plane. Also **zy′go·mor′-phous.** [<ZYGO- + -MORPHIC] — **zy′go·mor′-phism** *n.*

zy·go·phyl·la·ceous (zī′gō·fi·lā′shəs) *adj. Bot.* Designating or pertaining to a family (*Zygophyllaceae*) of herbs and shrubs, the caltrop family, having jointed branches, two-foliolate or pinnate stipulate leaves, and axillary white, red, or yellow flowers: mainly tropical in distribution. [<NL <Gk. *zygon* a yoke + *phyllon* a leaf]

zy·go·phyte (zī′gō·fīt) *n. Bot.* A plant in which reproduction is by means of zygospores. [< ZYGO- + -PHYTE]

zy·go·sis (zī·gō′sis) *n. Biol.* The union of gametes or cells; conjugation. [<NL <Gk. *zygōsis* a joining < *zygon* a yoke]

zy·go·spore (zī′gō·spôr, -spōr) *n. Bot.* A spore formed by the conjugation of two similar gametes, as in algae and fungi. Also **zy′go·sperm** (-spûrm). [<ZYGO- + SPORE]

zy·gote (zī′gōt, zig′ōt) *n. Biol.* 1 The product of the union of two gametes. 2 An individual developed from such a union. [<Gk. *zygōtos* yoked < *zygoein* yoke < *zygon* a yoke] — **zy·got·ic** (zī·got′ik) *adj.*

zy·mase (zī′mās) *n. Biochem.* An enzyme, obtained principally from yeast, which induces fermentation by breaking down glucose and related carbohydrates into alcohol and carbon dioxide. [<F <Gk. *zymē* leaven]

zyme (zīm) *n.* 1 A ferment. 2 A disease germ or virus supposed to be the specific cause of a zymotic disease. [<Gk. *zymē* leaven]

zy·mic (zī′mik) *adj.* Relating to or produced by fermentation.

zymo- *combining form* Fermentation; of or related to fermentation: *zymology.* Also, before vowels, **zym-.** [<Gk. *zymē* leaven]

zy·mo·gen (zī′mə·jən) *n.* 1 *Biochem.* A substance that develops into an enzyme when suitably activated, as in the stomach or pancreas. 2 *Biol.* A bacterial organism which produces enzymes or fermentation. Compare PATHOGEN. Also **zy′mo·gene** (-jēn). [<ZYMO- + -GEN]

zy·mo·gen·e·sis (zī′mō·jen′ə·sis) *n. Biochem.* The transformation of a zymogen into an enzyme.

zy·mo·gen·ic (zī′mō·jen′ik) *adj.* 1 Of, pertaining to, or relating to zymogen. 2 Capable of producing a ferment, as yeast. Also **zy·mog·e·nous** (zī·moj′ə·nəs).

zymogenic organism Any micro-organism which causes fermentation, as yeast.

zy·mol·o·gy (zī·mol′ə·jē) *n.* The study of the principles of fermentation and the action of enzymes. [<ZYMO- + -LOGY] — **zy·mo·log·ic** (zī′mə·loj′ik) or **·i·cal** *adj.* — **zy·mol′o·gist** *n.*

zy·mol·y·sis (zī·mol′ə·sis) *n.* Fermentation or the action of enzymes. [<ZYMO- + -LYSIS] — **zy·mo·lyt·ic** (zī′mə·lit′ik) *adj.*

zy·mom·e·ter (zī·mom′ə·tər) *n.* An instrument for measuring the degree of fermentation. [<ZYMO- + -METER]

zy·mo·sis (zī·mō′sis) *n.* 1 Any form of fermentation. 2 *Med.* a A fermentation giving rise to a morbid or diseased condition, as by the action of bacteria. b Any contagious or infectious disease produced by morbific fermentation; a zymotic disease. [<NL <Gk. *zymōsis* < *zymoein* leaven, ferment < *zymē* leaven]

zy·mot·ic (zī·mot′ik) *adj.* Relating to or produced by or from fermentation, as certain epidemic or contagious diseases. [<Gk. *zymōtikos* < *zymoein.* See ZYMOSIS.]

zy·mur·gy (zī′mûr·jē) *n.* A branch of chemistry treating of processes in which fermentation is the principal feature, as brewing, making of yeast, and winemaking. [<ZYM(O)- + -URGY]

Zy·ri·an Autonomous Region (zir′ē·ən) A former name for the KOMI AUTONOMOUS S.S.R.

Zyr·ya·novsk (zir·yä′nôfsk) A city of NE Kazakh S.S.R. near the Russian S.F.S.R. border.

ENCYCLOPEDIC SUPPLEMENTS

TABLE OF CONTENTS

Abbreviations	1469
Gazetteer	1488
Grammar and Usage Handbook	1515
The Library Research Paper	1529
Greek and Latin Elements in English	1542
Foreign Words and Phrases	1557
Given Names	1573
Business Law	1585
Business Math	1594
Business Letter Writing	1617
Wills and Estate Planning	1650
Where To Write for Vital Records	1656
Perpetual Calendar	1670
Glossary of Computer Terms	1673
Word Processing Glossary	1678
Spanish Glossary	1684
German Glossary	1694
Glossary of Biological Terms	1703
Glossary of Physics Terms	1708
African American History	1713
African American Biographies	1725
Chemical Elements	1731
Periodic Table of Elements	1734
Metrics Glossary	
Units of Measurement—Conversion Factors	1738
Tables of Weights and Measures	1743
Special Signs and Symbols	1746
Medical Glossary	1750
Generic Drugs	1785
Biographies	1794
Quotations Dictionary	1846
Spelling Dictionary	1896

ENCYCLOPEDIC SUPPLEMENTS

TABLE OF CONTENTS

Abbreviations	1505
Grammar and Usage Handbook	
The Library Research Paper	
Greek and Latin Elements in English	
Foreign Words and Phrases	
Given Names	
Business Law	
Business Math	
Business Letter Writing	
Wills and Estate Planning	
Where To Write for Vital Records	
Perpetual Calendar	
Glossary of Computer Terms	
Word Processing Glossary	
Spanish Glossary	
German Glossary	
Glossary of Biological Terms	
Glossary of Physics Terms	
African American History	
African American Biographies	
Chemical Elements	
Periodic Table of Elements	
Metric Glossary	
Units of Measurement—Conversion Factors	1745
Tables of Weights and Measures	
Special Signs and Symbols	
Medical Glossary	
Generic Drugs	
Biographies	
Onomastic Dictionary	
Spelling Dictionary	1900

Abbreviations

This list of abbreviations and meanings is a selection of those commonly in use in printed works. There are many forms of abbreviations—capital letters or lower-case letters, periods or no periods, spaces between letters or no spaces, and so on. In this list abbreviations are given without periods. Most are given without spaces and the majority are in lower-case letters unless usage dictates otherwise.

Most of the words that the abbreviations represent are spelled here in lower-case letters, although they may appear elsewhere with initial capital letters. Abbreviations such as *mt* for *mount* usually begin with a capital letter when used with proper nouns—as in *Mt Shasta*.

In abbreviations of foreign words or phrases, such as those from French or Latin, the English meaning always appears first, followed by the word or phrase in the language of origin.

A

a abbreviation, about, acre, alto, ampere, are (measure), argent, assists (baseball), before (Lat. *ante*), year (Lat. *anno*)

A absolute (temperature), angstrom (unit), argon

AA Alcoholics Anonymous, antiaircraft, author's alteration

AAA American Automobile Association

AAAL American Academy of Arts and Letters

AAAS American Academy of Arts and Sciences, American Association for the Advancement of Science

AAE American Association of Engineers

AAF Army Air Forces

A and M Agricultural and Mechanical (College)

Aar Aaron

AARP American Association of Retired Persons

AAU Amateur Athletic Union

ab able-bodied (seaman), (times) at bat

Ab alabamine

AB adapter booster, airborne, Bachelor of Arts (Lat. *Artium Baccalaureus*)

ABA American Bar Association, American Booksellers Association

a&b assault and battery

abbr, abbrev abbreviation

ABC the alphabet, American Broadcasting Company, Audit Bureau of Circulation, Australian Broadcasting Commission

ab ex from without (Lat. *ab extra*)

ab init from the beginning (Lat. *ab initio*)

abl ablative

ABM antiballistic missile

abp archbishop, arterial blood pressure

abr abridged, abridgment

abs absent, absolute (temperature), absolutely, abstract

abstr abstract, abstracted

ac before meals (Lat. *ante cibum*)

a/c account, account current, air conditioning

Ac actinium

AC after Christ, Air Corps, alternating current

acad academic, academy

acc acceptance, accompanied, account, accountant

acc, accus accusative

ACC Air Coordinating Committee

accel accelerando, accelerate

acct account, accountant

ack acknowledge, acknowledgment

ACLU American Civil Liberties Union

ACP American College of Physicians

acpt acceptance

ACS American Chemical Society

A/cs Pay accounts payable

A/cs Rec accounts receivable

act active

ACT American College Test

actg acting

ACTH adrenocorticotropic hormone

ad advertisement, before the day (Lat. *ante diem*)

AD year of our Lord (Lat. *anno domini*)

ADA American Dental Association, Americans for Democratic Action

adc aide-de-camp

ADC aid to families with dependent children

add addenda, addendum, addition, additional, address

ad fin at the end, to one end (Lat. *ad finem*)

ad inf to infinity (Lat. *ad infinitum*)

adj adjacent, adjective, adjourned, adjunct, adjustment

Adj, Adjt adjutant

ad lib to the amount desired (Lat. *ad libitum*)

adm administrative, administrator, admitted

Adm admiral, Admiralty

adv adverb, adverbial, advertisement

ad val according to value (Lat. *ad valorem*)

advt advertisement

ae, aet, aetat of age (Lat. *aetatis*)

AEA Actors' Equity Association

AE and P ambassador extraordinary and plenipotentiary

AEC Atomic Energy Commission

AEF American Expeditionary Force

aeron aeronautics

af audio frequency

Af Africa, African

AF Air Force

AFAM, AF & AM Ancient Free and Accepted Masons

AFB Air Force Base

AFC American Football Conference, automatic frequency control

AFDC aid to families with dependent children

Afg, Afgh Afghanistan

AFL, AF of L American Federation of Labor

AFL-CIO American Federation of Labor–Congress of Industrial Organizations

AFM American Federation of Musicians

Afr Africa, African

AFT American Federation of Teachers

AFTRA American Federation of Television and Radio Artists

Ag August, silver (Lat. *argentum*)

AG adjutant general, attorney general, corporation (Ger. *aktiengesellschaft*)

agcy agency

agr, agri, agric agricultural, agriculture, agriculturist

agt agent, agreement

AHQ Army Headquarters

AI artificial intelligence, in the year of the discovery (Lat. *anno inventionis*)

AIDS acquired immuno-deficiency syndrome

AIM American Indian Movement

AK Alaska

aka also known as

AKC American Kennel Club

al other things (persons) (Lat. *alia, alii*)

Al aluminum

AL Alabama, aviation electronicsman

Ala Alabama

ALA American Library Association

Alas Alaska

Alb Albania, Albanian, Albany, Alberta

Alba Alberta

Ald, Aldm alderman

alg algebra

Alg Algeria, Algerian

ALP American Labor Party, Australian Labor Party

alt alteration, alternate, altitude, alto

Alta Alberta

alum aluminum

am ammeter, before noon (Lat. *ante meridiem*)

Am alabamine, America, American, americium

AM air mail, amplitude modulation, in the year of the world (Lat. *anno mundi*), Master of Arts (Lat. *Artium Magister*)

AMA American Management Association, American Medical Association

Amb ambassador

AMDG to the greater glory of God (Lat. *ad majorem Dei gloriam*)

AME African Methodist Episcopal

Amer America, American

AMG Allied Military Government (of Occupied Territory)

Am Ind American Indian
amp ampere, amperage
amp-hr ampere-hour
amt amount
amu atomic mass unit
AMVETS American Veterans (of World War II and the Korean War)
an anonymous, before (Lat. *ante*)
anal analogous, analogy, analysis, analytic(al)
anat anatomical, anatomy
anc ancient, anciently
and moderately slow (It. *andante*)
And Andorra
Ang Anglican, Angola
Angl Anglican, Anglicized
anim animated (It. *animato*)
ann annals, annual, annuities, annuity, years (Lat. *anni*)
anon anonymous
ans answer, answered
ant antenna, antiquarian, antiquity, antonym
Ant Antarctic, Antarctica
anthrop, anthropol anthropological, anthropology
antilog antilogarithm
antiq antiquarian, antiquities
A/O account of
AOL absent over leave
ap apothecary
Ap apostle, April
AP Associated Press, antipersonnel
APB all points bulletin
apmt appointment
APO Army Post Office
Apoc Apocalypse, Apocrypha, Apocryphal
app apparatus, apparent, appended, appendix, apprentice
appar apparatus, apparent
approx approximate, approximately
Apr April
APR annual percentage rate
APS Army Postal Service
apt apartment
aq aqueous, water (Lat. *aqua*)
AQ Achievement Quotient
ar argent, aromatic, arrival, arrive, in the year of the reign (Lat. *anno regni*)
Ar argon, silver (Lat. *argentum*)
Ar, Arab Arabia, Arabian, Arabic
AR Arkansas
Aram Aramaic
ARC American Red Cross, AIDS-related complex
arch archaic, archaism, archery, archipelago, architect
Arch, Archbp archbishop
archaeol archaeology
Archd archdeacon, archduke
archeol archeology

archit architecture
archt architect
arg argent, silver (Lat. *argentum*)
Arg Argentina, Argyll
arith arithmetic, arithmetical
Ariz Arizona
Ark Arkansas
Arm Armenia, Armenian
ArM Master of Architecture (Lat. *Architecturae Magister*)
ARM adjustable-rate mortgage
arr arrange, arranged, arrangements, arrival, arrive, arrived
art article, artificial, artist
ARV American Revised (Standard) Version (of the Bible)
as, asym asymmetric
As arsenic
AS Anglo-Saxon, antisubmarine
ASA American Standards Association
asb asbestos
ASCAP American Society of Composers, Authors and Publishers
ASCII American Standard Code for Information Interchange
ASE American Stock Exchange
ASEAN Association of South-East Asian Nations
asgd assigned
ASPCA American Society for the Prevention of Cruelty to Animals
assd assigned
assn association
assoc associate, association
asst assistant
Assyr Assyria, Assyrian
astr, astron astronomer, astronomical, astronomy
astrol astrologer, astrological, astrology
ASVAB Armed Services Vocational Apptitude Battery
at atmosphere, atomic
At astatine
AT antitank
ATC Air Transport Command
athl athlete, athletic, athletics
Atl Atlantic
atm atmosphere, atmospheric
at no atomic number
ATS Army Transport Service, Auxiliary Territorial Service
att, attn, atten attention
att, atty attorney
Atty Gen attorney general
ATV all-terrain vehicle
at wt atomic weight
au angstrom unit
Au gold (Lat. *aurum*)
AUC from (the year of) the building of the city (of

Rome) (Lat. *ab urbe condita*)
aud audible, audit, auditor
Aug August, Augustan, Augustus
Aus, Aust Austria
Aus, Austl Australia
AUS Army of the United States
auth authentic, author, authority, authorized
Auth Ver Authorized Version (of the Bible)
auto automatic, automotive
aux, auxil auxiliary
av according to value (Lat. *ad valorem*)
av, avdp avoirdupois
av, avg average
Av avenue
AV Authorized Version (of the Bible)
avc automatic volume control
Ave avenue
avg average
avn aviation
avoir avoirdupois
A/W actual weight, all water
AWL absent with leave
AWOL absent without leave
AWVS American Women's Volunteer Services
ax axiom, axis
az azimuth, azure
AZ Arizona

B

b bachelor, balboa (coin), base, base hit, baseman, bass, basso, bat, battery, bay, bench, bicuspid, bolívar (coin), boliviano (coin), book, born, brass, breadth, brother
B bacillus, Bible, bishop (chess), boron, British, brotherhood
B/- bag, bale
Ba barium
BA Bachelor of Arts (Lat. *Baccalaureus Artium*), British Academy
bach bachelor
bact, bacteriol bacteriological, bacteriologist, bacteriology
BAE Bachelor of Aeronautical Engineering, Bachelor of Arts in Education
BAg, BAgr Bachelor of Agriculture
BAgSci Bachelor of Agricultural Science
bal balance, balancing
Balt Baltic
Bap, Bapt Baptist
bapt baptized
bar barometer, barometric, barrel, barrister
BAR Browning automatic rifle
BAr, BArch Bachelor of Architecture

barit baritone
Bart baronet
BAS, BASc Bachelor of Agricultural Science, Bachelor of Applied Science
BASIC Beginner's All-purpose Symbolic Instruction Code
bat, batt battalion, battery
bb base(s) on balls
BBA, BBusAd Bachelor of Business Administration
BBB Better Business Bureau
BBC British Broadcasting Corporation
bbl barrel
BC Bachelor of Chemistry, Bachelor of Commerce, before Christ, British Columbia
BCD binary coded decimal
BCE Bachelor of Chemical Engineering, Bachelor of Civil Engineering, before Christian era
bch bunch
BCL Bachelor of Civil Law
BCP Book of Common Prayer
BCS Bachelor of Chemical Science
bd board, bond, bound, bundle
BD Bachelor of Divinity
B/D bank draft, bills discounted, brought down
bd ft board foot
bdg binding
bdl, bdle bundle
bds bundles, (bound in) boards
BDS Bachelor of Dental Surgery
Be beryllium
BE Bachelor of Education, Bachelor of Engineering, Bank of England, Board of Education
B/E bills of exchange
BEE Bachelor of Electrical Engineering
bef before
BEF British Expeditionary Force(s)
Bel, Belg Belgian, Belgium
Beng Bengal, Bengali
B ès L Bachelor of Letters (Fr. *Bachelier ès Lettres*)
B ès S Bachelor of Sciences (Fr. *Bachelier ès Sciences*)
bet, betw between
bev billion electron volts
bf bold face
BF Bachelor of Finance, Bachelor of Forestry
B/F brought forward
BFA Bachelor of Fine Arts
bg bag
BG brigadier general
BHE Bureau of Higher Education
bhp brake horsepower
Bi bismuth

Bib Bible, Biblical
bibl biblical, bibliographical
bibliog bibliography
bicarb bicarbonate of soda
b i d twice a day (Lat. *bis in die*)
biochem biochemistry
biog biographer, biographical, biography
biol biological, biologist, biology
BIOS basic input-output system
BIS British Information Services
BJ Bachelor of Journalism
bk bank, block, book
Bk berkelium
bkg banking
bkkpg bookkeeping
bklr black letter
bkpt bankrupt
bks barracks, books
bkt basket, bracket
bl bale, barrel, black, blue
BL, BLL Bachelor of Laws
B/L bill of lading
BLA Bachelor of Liberal Arts
bld bold face
bldg, blg building
BLE Brotherhood of Locomotive Engineers
B Lit, B Litt Bachelor of Letters, Bachelor of Literature (Lat. *Baccallaureus Litterarum*)
blk black, block
bln balloon
bls bales, barrels
BLS Bachelor of Library Science, Bachelor of Library Service, Bureau of Labor Statistics
blvd boulevard
bm board measure
BM Bachelor of Medicine (Lat. *Baccalaureus Medicinae*), Bachelor of Music (Lat. *Baccalaureus Musicae*), Bureau of Mines
BME Bachelor of Mechanical Engineering, Bachelor of Mining Engineering
BMechE Bachelor of Mechanical Engineering
BMEWS Ballistic Missile Early Warning System
BMR basal metabolic rate
BMus Bachelor of Music
Bn battalion
BN bank note
BNA Basel Anatomical Nomenclature (Lat. *Basle Nomina Anatomica*), British North America Act
bo back order, body odor, box office, branch office, broker's order, buyer's option
BO Board of Ordnance
B/O brought over
Boh Bohemia, Bohemian

Bol Bolivia, Bolivian
bor borough
bot botanical, botanist, botany, bottle
BOT Board of Trade
bp below proof, birthplace, bishop, blood pressure, boiling point
BP Bachelor of Pharmacy
BP, BPh, BPhil Bachelor of Philosophy (Lat. *Baccalaureus Philosophiae*)
B/P bill of parcels, bills payable
BPd, BPe Bachelor of Pedagogy
BPE Bachelor of Physical Education
BPH Bachelor of Public Health
BPI Bureau of Public Inquiries
BPOE Benevolent and Protective Order of Elks
br branch, brand, bridge, brief, brig, bronze, brother
Br Breton, Britain, British, bromine
BR Bill of Rights
B/R bills receivable
Braz Brazil, Brazilian
Brazil Brazilian
BRCS British Red Cross Society
B Rec bills receivable
brev brevet, brevetted
Br Hond British Honduras
Brig brigade, brigadier
Brig Gen brigadier general
Brit Britain, Britannia, Britannica, British
bro brother
bros brothers
bs balance sheet
BS Bachelor of Surgery
B/S bags, bales, bill of sale
BS, BSc Bachelor of Science (Lat. *Baccalaureus Scientiae*)
BSA Bachelor of Scientific Agriculture, Bibliographical Society of America, Boy Scouts of America
BSEd Bachelor of Science in Education
bsh bushel
BSS, BSSc, BS in SS Bachelor of (Science in) Social Sciences
Bt baronet
BT, BTh Bachelor of Theology
BTU, Bthu, btu British thermal unit
Btry battery
bu bureau, bushel, bushels
buck buckram
bul, bull bulletin
Bulg Bulgaria, Bulgarian
BV Blessed Virgin (Lat. *Beata Virgo*), farewell (Lat. *bene vale*)

BVM Blessed Virgin Mary (Lat. *Beata Virgo Maria*)
bvt brevet, brevetted
bx box
Bz benzine

C

c about (Lat. *circa*), candle, capacity (electrical), carton, case, catcher (baseball), cathode, Celsius, cent, centigrade, centime, centimeter, chapter, chief, child, cost, cubic
C calends, capacity (electrical), cape, carbon, cathode, Catholic, Celtic, century, Chancellor, chapter, church, Congress, Conservative, constant, copyright, Court, current, Roman numeral for 100
ca about (Lat. *circa*), cathode, centiare, chief accountant, claim agent, commercial agent, consular agent, controller of accounts
Ca calcium
CA California, Catholic Action, Central America, chronological age, Coast Artillery, Confederate Army
C/A commercial account, credit account, current account
CAA Civil Aeronautics Administration
CAB Civil Aeronautics Board
CAD computer-aided design, computer-aided drafting
CAF cost and freight; cost, assurance, and freight
CAI computer-aided instruction
cal calendar, calends, caliber, calomel, small calorie
Cal caliber, large calorie
Cal, Calif California
Cam camouflage
CAM computer-aided manufacturing
can canon, canto
Can Canada, Canadian
Canad Canadian
canc cancel, cancellation, cancelled
cant canton, cantonment
Cant Canterbury, Canticles, Cantonese
Cantab Cambridge (Lat. *Cantabrigia*)
cap capital, capitalize, chapter (Lat. *caput*)
CAP Civil Air Patrol
caps capital letters
Capt Captain
car carat
CAR Civil Air Regulations
Card Cardinal
CARE Cooperative for American Remittances Everywhere

cat catalog, catechism
CAT computerized axial tomography
cath cathedral
Cath Catholic
CATV community antenna television
cav cavalier, cavalry
CAVU ceiling and visibility unlimited
cb center of buoyancy, confined to barracks
Cb columbium, cumulonimbus
CB citizens band (radio), Construction Battalion, Bachelor of Surgery (Lat. *Baccalaureus Chiurgiae*)
CBC Canadian Broadcasting Corporation
CBD cash before delivery
CBOE Chicago Board Options Exchange
CBOT Chicago Board of Trade
CBS Columbia Broadcasting System
cc carbon copy, cash credit, cashier's check, chapters, chief clerk, circuit court, city council, city councilor, civil court, common councilman, company clerk, company commander, consular clerk, contra credit, copy, county clerk, county commissioner, county council, county court, cubic centimeter, current account (Fr. *compte courant*)
Cc cirrocumulus
CC cyanogen chloride (poison gas)
CCA Chief Clerk of the Admiralty, circuit court of appeals
CCC Civilian Conservation Corps; Commodity Credit Corporation
CCF Cooperative Commonwealth Federation (of Canada)
CCS Combined Chiefs of Staff
cd candela, cash discount, cord
Cd cadmium
CD certificate of deposit, civil defense, compact disc
C/D carried down
cd ft cord foot (feet)
CDR, Cdr commander
CDT central daylight time
Ce cerium
CE chemical engineer, chief engineer, Church of England, civil engineer, Council of Europe, Corps of Engineers
CEA Council of Economic Advisers
CEEB College Entrance Examination Board
Celt Celtic

cen, cent central, century

cent centered, centigrade, centimeter, one hundred (Lat. *centum*)

CERN European Council for Nuclear Research (Fr. *Centre Européen des Recherches Nucléaires*)

cert certificate, certify

certif certificate, certificated

cet par other things being equal (Lat. *ceteris paribus*)

Cey Ceylon

cf center field, center fielder, compare (Lat. *confer*)

Cf californium

CF cost and freight

C/F carried forward

CFI cost, freight, and insurance

cfm cubic feet per minute

CFR Code of Federal Regulations

cfs cubic feet per second

cg center of gravity, consul general

cg, cgm centigram

CG Coast Guard, commanding general

CGH Cape of Good Hope

cgs centimeter-gram-second

ch chain, champion, chargé d'affaires, check (chess), chestnut, chevronets, chief, child, children, chirurgeon, church, clearinghouse, courthouse, customhouse, of surgery (Lat. *chiurgiae*)

c-h, c-hr candle-hour

ch chaplain, chapter

Ch Chaldean, Chaldee, China, Chinese

CH Companion of Honor

Chanc chancelor, chancery

chap chaplain, chapter

char character, charter

ChB Bachelor of Surgery (Lat. *Chiurgiae Baccalaureus*)

ChE, CheE chemical engineer

chem chemical, chemist, chemistry

chg charge

chgd charged

Chin Chinese

ChJ chief justice

ChM Master of Surgery (Lat. *Chiurgiae Magister*)

chm checkmate

chm, chmn chairman

Chr Christ, Christian

chron, chronol chronological, chronology

Chron Chronicles

chs chapters

Ci cirrus

Cia company (Sp. *Compania*)

CIA Central Intelligence Agency

CIC Counter-Intelligence Corps

CID Criminal Investigation Division (Brit.)

Cie company (Fr. *compagnie*)

CIF cost, insurance, and freight

C in C, CINC, Cinc commander in chief

CIP cataloging in publication

CIO Congress of Industrial Organizations

cir, circ about (Lat. *circa, circiter, circum*), circular, circulation, circumference

cit citation, cited, citizen

civ civil, civilian

CJ body of law (Lat. *corpus juris*), chief judge, chief justice

ck cask, check, cook

cl carload, carload lots, center line, centiliter, civil law, claim, class, classification, clause, clearance, clergyman, clerk, cloth, craft loss (insurance)

Cl chlorine

clar clarinet

class classic, classical, classification, classified, classify

cler clerical

climatol climatological, climatology

clin clinic, clinical

clk clerk, clock

clm column

CLU chartered life underwriter

cm church missionary, circular mil, common meter, corresponding member

cm centimeter

Cm curium

CM court martial, Master of Surgery (Lat. *Chiurgiae Magister*)

Cmdr commander

CMG Companion (of the Order) of St. Michael and St. George

cml commercial

CMTC Citizens' Military Training Camp

Cn cumulonimbus

C/N circular note, credit note

CNN Cable News Network

CNO chief of naval operations

CNS central nervous system

c/o care of, carried over, cash order

Co cobalt, company, county

CO Colorado, commanding officer, conscientious objector

coad coadjutor

COBOL common business-oriented language

Cod codex

COD cash on delivery, collect on delivery

Codd codices

coef coefficient

C of C chamber of commerce

C of S chief of staff

cog, cogn cognate

col collected, collector, college, colonial, colony, color, colored, column

Col Colombia, colonel, Colorado, Colossians, Columbia

coll colleague, collect, collection, collective, collector, college, colloquial

collab collaborated, collaboration, collaborator

collat collateral

colloq colloquial, colloquialism, colloquially

Colo, Col Colorado

colog cologarithm

Coloss Colossians

com comedy, comic, comma, commentary, commerce, common, commonly, commune, communication, community

Com commission, commissioner, committee, commodore, communist

Com, Comdr commander, commodore

Com, Como commodore

comb combination

comdg commanding

Comdt Commandant

Com in Ch, Cominch Commander in Chief

coml commercial

comm commander, commentary, commerce, commercial, commissary, commission, committee, commonwealth, commutator

Como Commodore

comp companion, compare, compilation, compiled, complete, composition, compositor, compound, comprising

compar comparative

compt compartment, comptometer

Comr Commissioner

Com Ver Common Version (of the Bible)

con against (Lat. *contra*), concerto, conclusion, condense, conduct, connection, consols, consolidate, continued, wife (Lat. *conjunx*)

Con Conformist, Consul

conc concentrate, concentrated, concentration, concerning

Confed Confederate, Confederation

cong gallon (Lat. *congius*)

Cong Congregational, Congress, Congressional

conj conjugation, conjunction, conjunctive

Conn Connecticut

cons consecrated, conserve, consigned, consignment, consolidated, consonant, constable, constitution,

constitutional, construction, consul, consulting

consol consolidated

const constable, constant, constitution

constr construction, construed

cont containing, contents, continent, continue, contract, contraction, contrary, control

Cont Continental

contd continued

contemp contemporary

contg containing

contin continued, let it be continued (Lat. *continuetur*)

contr contract, contralto, control

contrib contribution, contributor

CONUS Continental United States

coop, co-op cooperative

cop copper, copyright, copyrighted

Cop Copernican, Coptic

cor corner, cornet, coroner, corpus, correct, corrected, correction, correlative, correspondence, correspondent, corresponding, corrupt

Cor Corinthians

corol, coroll corollary

corp, corpn corporation

Corp Corporal

corr correct, corrected, correspond, correspondence, correspondent, corresponding, corrupt, corrupted, corruption

correl correlative

corresp correspondence

cos companies, cosine, counties

COS cash on shipment

cosec cosecant

cosh hyperbolic cosine

cot cotangent

coth hyperbolic cotangent

covers coversed sine

cp candlepower, chemically pure, compare, court of probate

CP Canadian Press, Cape Province, center of pressure, Chief Patriarch, command post, Common Prayer, Communist Party

CPA certified public accountant

cpd compound

CPH Certificate in Public Health

Cpl corporal

cpm characters per minute, cost per million, cycles per minute

CPO chief petty officer

CPR cardiopulmonary resuscitation

cps characters per second, cycles per second

cpt counterpoint

CQ charge of quarters

cr created, credit, creditor, crescendo, creek, crown

Cr chromium

CR carriage return, Costa Rica

craniol craniological, craniology

craniom craniometry

cres, cresc crescendo

crim con criminal conversation

crit critic, critical, criticism

CRLF carriage return and line feed

crs credits, creditors

CRT cathode-ray tube

cryst crystalline, crystallography, crystals

cs capital stock, civil service

Cs cesium, cirrostratus

CS Christian Science, Christian Scientist, Confederate States

C/S case

CSA Confederate States of America

csc cosecant

CSC Civil Service Commission, Conspicuous Service Cross

csch hyperbolic cosecant

CSigO chief signal officer

CSIRO Commonwealth Scientific and Industrial Research Organization (Australia)

CSO chief staff officer

CSS Commodity Stabilization Service

CST central standard time

ct cent, certificate, county, court

Ct Connecticut, Count

CT central time, communications technician, computed tomography, Connecticut

CTC Citizens' Training Camp

ctg cartridge

ctn carton, cotangent

ctnh hyperbolic cotangent

ctr center

cts centimes, cents, certificates

cu cubic

Cu copper (Lat. *cuprum*), cumulus

cu cm cubic centimeter

cu ft cubic foot

cu in cubic inch

cur currency, current

cu yd cubic yard

cv, cvt convertible

CV Common Version (of the Bible)

cw continuous wave

CWO cash with order, chief warrant officer, commissioned warrant officer

CWS Chemical Warfare Service

cwt hundredweight (Lat. *centum* weight)

cy capacity, currency, cycles

cyc cyclopedia, cyclopedic

cyl cylinder

CYO Catholic Youth Organization

CZ Canal Zone

D

d date, daughter, day, dead, decree, degree, delete, democrat, democratic, deputy, diameter, died, director, dividend, dollar, door, dose, dyne, give (Lat. *da*), penny, pence (Lat. *denarius, denarii*)

D December, department, deuterium, Dutch, God (Lat. *Deus*), Lord (Lat. *Dominus*), Roman numeral for 500

da daughter, day

DA delayed action, dental apprentice, district attorney

DAB Dictionary of American Biography

DAE Dictionary of American English

DAH Dictionary of American History

Dak Dakota

Dan Daniel, Danish

Danl Daniel

DAR Daughters of the American Revolution

DARE Dictionary of American Regional English

dat dative

DAT Dental Apptitude Test

dau daughter

Dav David

DAV Disabled American Veterans

db daybook

db,dB decibel, decibels

DB Domesday Book

dba doing business as

DBE Dame (Commander of the Order) of the British Empire

dbh diameter at breast height (forestry)

DBib Douai Bible

dbl double

DC Dental Corps, direct current, Disarmament Commission, District of Columbia, Doctor of Chiropractic, from the beginning (Ital. *da capo*)

DCL Doctor of Canon Law, Doctor of Civil Law

DCM Distinguished Conduct Medal (Brit.)

DCS deputy clerk of sessions, Doctor of Christian Science, Doctor of Commercial Science

dd days after date, days' date, delivered, demand draft

DD Department of Defense, developmentally disabled, Doctor of Divinity (Lat. *Divinitatis Doctor*)

DDS Doctor of Dental Science, Doctor of Dental Surgery

DDSc Doctor of Dental Science

DE Delaware, destroyer escort, Doctor of Engineering, Doctor of Entomology

deb, deben debenture

Deb Deborah

dec deceased, declaration, declension, declination, decrease, decrescendo

dec, decim decimeter

Dec December

decd deceased

decl declension

decoct decoction

decresc decrescendo

ded, dedic dedication

def defective, defendant, defense, deferred, defined, definite, definition

deg degree

del delegate, delete, deliver, he or she drew it (Lat. *delineavit*)

Del Delaware

deliq deliquescent

Dem Democrat, Democratic

demon demonstrative

Den Denmark

denom denomination

dent dental, dentist, dentistry

dep departs, departure, deposed, deposit, depot

dep, dept department, deponent, deputy

Dep dependency

der, deriv derivation, derivative, derive, derived

dermatol dermatological, dermatologist, dermatology

desc descendant

descr descriptive, description

D ès L Doctor of Letters (Fr. *Docteur ès Lettres*)

D ès S Doctor of Sciences (Fr. *Docteur ès Sciences*)

det detach, detachment, detail

Deu, Deut Deuteronomy

devel development

DF dean of the faculty, defender of the faith (Lat. *Defensor Fidei*), direction finding, Federal District (Port. *Districto Federal*; Sp. *Distrito Federal*)

DFC Distinguished Flying Cross

dg decigram

DG by the grace of God (Lat. *Dei gratia*)

dh deadhead, designated hitter (baseball), that is to say (Ger. *das heisst*)

DHQ division headquarters

di, dia diameter

Di didymium

diag, diagr diagram

dial dialect, dialectic, dialectical

diam diameter

dict dictation, dictator, dictionary

diet dietetics

diff difference, different, differential

dil dilute

dim dimension

dim, dimin diminuendo, diminutive

din dinar

dioc diocesan, diocese

dipl diplomat, diplomatic

dir director

dis distance, distant

disc discount, discover, discovered

disch discharged

diss dissertations

dist discount, distance, distant, distinguish, distinguished, district

Dist Atty district attorney

distr distribute, distributed, distribution, distributive, distributor

div divergence, diversion, divide, divided, dividend, divine, division, divisor, divorced

Div divinity

dk deck, dock

DK disbursing clerk

dkg dekagram

dkl dekaliter

dkm dekameter

dks dekastere

dl deciliter

D/L demand loan

D Lit, D Litt Doctor of Letters, Doctor of Literature (Lat. *Doctor Litterarum*)

dlr dealer

DLS Doctor of Library Science

dm decameter, decimeter

Dm Deutschmark

DM deputy master, draftsman

DMB defense mobilization board

DMD Doctor of Dental Medicine (Lat. *Dentariae Medicinae Doctor*)

D Mus Doctor of Music

DN our Lord (Lat. *Dominus noster*)

DNA deoxyribonucleic acid

DNB Dictionary of National Biography (Brit.)

do ditto

DO Doctor of Osteopathy

DOA dead on arrival

doc document

DOD Department of Defence

DOE Department of Education, Department of Energy

dol dolce, dollar

dols dollars

dom domestic, dominion

E

Dom Dominica, Dominican
Dor Dorian, Doric
DOS disk operating system
DOT Department of Transportation
dow dowager
doz dozen
DP data processing, degree of polymerization, diametrical pitch, displaced person
DPH Doctor of Public Health
DPHy Doctor of Public Hygiene
DPh, DPhil Doctor of Philosophy
dpt department, deponent
DPW Department of Public Works
dr debtor, dram
Dr doctor, drive
DR dead reckoning, deposit receipt
dram pers dramatis personae
ds daylight saving, days after sight, decistere, document signed, (repeat) from this sign (It. *dal segno*)
Ds dysprosium
DS, DSc Doctor of Science
DSC Distinguished Service Cross
DSIR Department of Scientific and Industrial Research
DSM Distinguished Service Medal
DSO Distinguished Service Order (Brit.), district staff officer
dsp died without issue (Lat. *decessit sine prole*)
DSRD Department of Scientific Research and Development
DST daylight saving time, Doctor of Sacred Theology
dt delerium tremens, double time
DT dental technician
DT, DTh, DTheol Doctor of Theology
dts delerium tremens
Du duke, Dutch
dup, dupl duplicate
Dv, DV God willing (Lat. *Deo volente*)
DV Douai Version (of the Bible)
DVM Doctor of Veterinary Medicine
DVMS Doctor of Veterinary Medicine and Surgery
D/W dock warrant
DWI driving while intoxicated, Dutch West Indies
DWS Department of Water Supply
dwt dead weight tons, pennyweight (Lat. *denarius* weight)
DX distance, distant
Dy dysprosium
dyn, dynam dynamics
dz dozen

e east, eastern, erg, error
E earl, Earth, east, eastern, English
ea each
e and o e errors and omissions excepted
Eb erbium
EBCDIC Extended Binary Coded Decimal Interchange Code
EbN east by north
EbS east by south
EC Engineering Corps, Established Church, European Community
ECA Economic Cooperation Administration
ECAFE Economic Commission for Asia and the Far East
eccl, eccles ecclesiastical
Ecc, Eccl, Eccles Ecclesiastes
Ecclus Ecclesiasticus
ECE Economic Commission for Europe
ECG electrocardiogram
ECLA Economic Commission for Latin America
ECME Economic Commission for the Middle East
ecol ecological, ecology
econ economic, economics, economy
ECOSOC Economic and Social Council (of the United Nations)
ECSC European Coal and Steel Community
Ecua Ecuador, Ecuadorian
ed edited, edition, editor
EdB Bachelor of Education
EdD Doctor of Education
edit edited, edition, editor
EdM Master of Education
EDT eastern daylight time
educ education, educational
ee errors excepted
EE Early English, electrical engineer, electrical engineering, envoy extraordinary
EEC European Economic Community
EE&MP envoy extraordinary and minister plenipotentiary
EEG electroencephalogram
EEOC Equal Employment Opportunity Commission
EER energy efficiency rating
eff efficiency
efflor efflorescent
EFTA European Free Trade Association
EFTS electronic funds transfer system
eg for example (Lat. *exempli gratia*)
Eg Egypt, Egyptian
Egyptol Egyptology
EHF extremely high frequency

EHFA electric home and farm authority
EHV extra high voltage
EI, EInd East Indian, East Indies
EKG electrocardiogram
el elevated, elevation
ELD electroluminescent display
elec, elect electric, electrical, electrician
elem elementary, elements
elev elevation
ellipt elliptical
e long east longitude
elong elongation
Em, eman emanation (chemistry)
EM electrician's mate, engineer of mines, enlisted man
emb, embryol embryology
emf electromotive force
EMH educable mentally handicapped
Emp emperor, empire, empress
emph emphasis, emphatic
EMT emergency medical technician
emu electromagnetic units
emul emulsion
enc, encl enclosed, enclosure
ency, encyc, encycl encyclopedia
ENE east-northeast
eng engine, engineer, engineering, engraved, engraver, engraving
Eng England, English
EngD Doctor of Engineering
engin engineering
engr engineer, engraved, engraver, engraving
enl enlarged, enlisted
Ens ensign
ENT ear, nose, throat (physician)
entom, entomol entomological, entomology
env envelope
eo from office (Lat. *ex officio*)
EOM end of month
ep en passant (chess)
Ep, Epis, Epist Epistle, Epistles
EP extended play
EPA Environmental Protection Agency
Eph, Ephes Ephesians
Epis Episcopal
epil epilogue
EPU European Payments Union
eq equal, equalizer, equation, equator, equivalent
EQ educational quotient
equiv equivalent
er earned run
Er erbium
ER emergency room, King Edward (Lat. *Eduardus*

Rex), Queen Elizabeth (Lat. *Elizabeth Regina*)
ERA earned run average, Educational Research Association, Emergency Relief Administration, Equal Rights Amendment
ERIC Educational Resources Information Center
ERISA Employee Retirement Income Security Act
ERP European Recovery Program
erron erroneous, erroneously
ERV English Revised Version (of the Bible)
Es einsteinium
ESA Economic Stabilization Administration
ESC Economic and Social Council (of the United Nations)
eschat eschatology
Esd Esdras
ESE east-southeast
Esk Eskimo
ESL English as a second language
ESOP employee stock option plan
esp especially
ESP extrasensory perception
espec especially
Esq, Esqr esquire
est estate, estimated, estuary
Est Estonia
EST eastern standard time
estab established
Esth Esther
esu electrostatic unit
ET electronics technician, extraterrestrial
eta estimated time of arrival
et al and others (Lat. *et alii*), and elsewhere (Lat. *et alibi*)
etc and so forth, and others (Lat. *et ceteri, ceterae,* or *cetera*)
eth ether, ethical, ethics
Eth Ethiopia, Ethiopian, Ethiopic
ethnog ethnographical, ethnography
ethnol ethnological, ethnology
ETO European Theater of Operations
et seq and the following, and what follows (Lat. *et sequens, sequentes,* or *sequentia*)
ety, etym, etymol etymological, etymology
Eu europium
euphem euphemism, euphemistic
Eur Europe, European
ev electron volt
EV English Version (of the Bible)
EVA extra-vehicular activity (in space)

evac evacuation

evan, evang evangelical, evangelist

Evang Evangelical

evap evaporation

ex examination, examine, examined, example, except, excepted, exception, exchange, excursion, executed, executive

Ex, Exod Exodus

exam examination, examined, examinee, examinor

exc excellent, except, excepted, exception, excursion

Exc excellency

exch exchange, exchequer

excl exclusive

excl, exclam exclamation

exec executive, executor

Ex-Im Export-Import Bank

ex int without interest

ex lib from the library (of) (Lat. *ex libris*)

ex off from office (Lat. *ex officio*)

exp expenses, expiration, expired, export, exportation, exported, exporter, express

exper experimental

expt experiment

exptl experimental

exr executor

ext extension, external, extinct, extra, extract

Ez, Ezr Ezra

Eze, Ezek Ezekiel

F

f activity coefficient, farad, farthing, fathom, feet, female, feminine, fine, fluid (ounce), folio, following, foot, formed, forte, foul, franc, frequency, from, function (of), let it be made (Lat. *fiat*), strong (Lat. *forte*)

f/ f number (photography)

F Fahrenheit, February, fellow, fluorine, France, French, Friday, son (Lat. *filius*)

fa fire alarm, freight agent

FA field artillery, fine arts, food administration

FAA Federal Aviation Administration

FAAAS Fellow of the American Association for the Advancement of Science

fac facsimile, factor, factory

FACD Fellow of the American College of Dentists

FACP Fellow of the American College of Physicians

FACS Fellow of the American College of Surgeons

FAF financial aid form

Fah, Fahr Fahrenheit

FAIA Fellow of the American Institute of Architects

fam familiar, family

FAM, F&AM Free and Accepted Masons

FAO Food and Agriculture Organization (of the United Nations)

fas free alongside ship

FASA Fellow of the Acoustical Society of America

fasc a bundle (Lat. *fasiculus*)

fath fathom

fb freight bill, fullback

FBA Fellow of the British Academy

FBI Federal Bureau of Investigation

fbm feet board measure (board feet)

fc follow copy (printing)

Fc fractocumulus

FCA Farm Credit Administration

FCC Federal Communications Commission, Federal Council of Churches, first class certificate, Food Control Committee

FCDA Federal Civil Defense Administration

FCIC Federal Crop Insurance Corporation

fcp foolscap

FD defender of the faith (Lat. *Fidei Defensor*), fire department

FDA Food and Drug Administration, Food Distribution Administration

FDIC Federal Deposit Insurance Corporation

Fe iron (Lat. *ferrum*)

Feb, Febr February

FEB Fair Employment Board

fec he or she made it (Lat. *fecit*)

fed federal, federated, federation

fem female, feminine

FEPC Fair Employment Practices Commission

FERA Federal Emergency Relief Administration

feud feudal, feudalism

ff fixed focus, folios, following, fortissimo

ffa free foreign agent, free from alongside

FFA Future Farmers of America

FFS family financial statement

FFV First Families of Virginia

fg field goal

FGSA Fellow of the Geological Society of America

FHA Federal Housing Administration

FHLBB Federal Home Loan Bank Board

fhp friction horsepower

FICA Federal Insurance Contributions Act

fid fidelity, fiduciary

FIFO first in, first out

fig figuratively, figure

FIL Fellow of the Institute of Linguists

FILO first in, last out

fin finance, financial, finished

Fin Finland, Finnish

FIPS federal information processing standards

fl floor, florin, flower, fluid, flute

Fl Flanders, Flemish, fluorine

FL, Fla Florida

FLB Federal Land Bank

fl dr fluid dram

Flem Flemish

flex flexible

fl oz fluid ounce

fm fathom, from

Fm fermium

FM field manual, field marshal, frequency modulation

FMCS Federal Mediation and Conciliation Service

FmHA Farmers Home Administration

FNMA Federal National Mortgage Association ("Fannie Mae")

FO field officer, Foreign Office

fob free on board

FOE Fraternal Order of Eagles

fol folio, following

foll following

FOP Fraternal Order of Police

for foreign, forestry, free on rails

fort fortification, fortified

FORTRAN formula translator

fp fireplug, fire policy, floating policy, foolscap, footpound, forte piano (Ital.), forward pass, freezing point, fully paid

FPC Federal Power Commission

FPHA Federal Public Housing Administration

fpm feet per minute

FPO fleet post office

fps feet per second, footpound-second (system)

fr fragment, franc, from, right-hand page (Lat. *folio recto*)

Fr brother (Lat. *Frater*), father, France, francium, French, Friday, wife (Ger. *Frau*)

FRB Federal Reserve Bank, Federal Reserve Board

FRC Federal Radio Commission, Federal Relief Commission

FRCP Fellow of the Royal College of Physicians

FRCS Fellow of the Royal College of Surgeons

freq frequency, frequently, frequentitive

FRGS Fellow of the Royal Geographical Society

Fr Gui French Guiana

Fri Friday

Frl Miss (Ger. *Fräulein*)

FRS Federal Reserve System, Fellow of the Royal Society

FRSA Fellow of the Royal Society of Arts

frt freight

fs foot-second

Fs fractostratus

FS field service, fleet surgeon

FSA Farm Security Administration, Federal Security Agency

FSCC Federal Surplus Commodities Corporation

FSH follicle-stimulating hormone

FSLIC Federal Saving and Loan Insurance Corporation

FSP Food Stamp Program

FSR Field Service Regulations

ft feet, foot, fort, fortification, fortified

FT fire control technician

ft-c foot-candle

FTC Federal Trade Commission

FTE full-time equivalent

fth, fthm fathom

ft-l foot-lambert

ft-lb foot-pound

fur furlong

furl furlough

furn furnished, furniture

fut future

fv on the back of the page (Lat. *folio verso*)

FWA Federal Works Agency

fwd forward, front wheel drive

fwy freeway

FY fiscal year

FYI for your information

FZS Fellow of the Zoological Society

G

g conductance, gauge, gender, general, general intelligence, genitive, goal, goalie, goalkeeper, gold, gourde, grain, gram, grand, (specific) gravity, guide, guilder, guinea, gulf

G German, Germany, gram, (specific) gravity, gun

ga general average

Ga gallium, Georgia

GA Gamblers Anonymous, general agent, General Assembly, Georgia

Gael Gaelic

gal, gall gallon

Gal Galatians, Galen

galv galvanic, galvanism, galvanized

GAO General Accounting Office

GAR Grand Army of the Republic

GATT General Agreement on Tariffs and Trade

GAW guaranteed annual wage

gaz gazette, gazetteer

GB Great Britain

GBE (Knight or Dame) Grand (Cross) of the (Order of the) British Empire

GCA ground control approach (radar)

g-cal gram calorie

GCB (Knight) Grand Cross of the (Order of the) Bath

gcd greatest common divisor

gcf greatest common factor

GCI ground controlled interception (aircraft)

GCLH Grand Cross of the Legion of Honor

gcm greatest common measure

GCM general court martial

GCT Greenwich civil time

GCVO (Knight) Grand Cross of the (Royal) Victorian Order

Gd gadolinium

GD grand duchess, grand duchy, grand duke

gds goods

Ge germanium

geb born (Ger. *geboren*)

GED general equivalency diploma

gen gender, genera, general, generally, generator, generic, genitive, genus

Gen general, Genesis, Geneva, Genevan

geneal genealogical, genealogy

genit genitive

genl general

gent gentleman, gentlemen

geod geodesy, geodetic

geog geographer, geographic, geographical, geography

geol geologic, geological, geologist, geology

geom geometer, geometric, geometrical, geometry

ger gerund

Ger, Germ German, Germany

gest died (Ger. *gestorben*)

GFTU General Federation of Trade Unions

ggr great gross

GHA Greenwich hour angle

GHQ general headquarters

gi gastrointestinal, gill

GI general issue, government issue

Gib Gibraltar

Gk Greek

gl glass, gloss

gld guilder

gloss glossary

gm gram

GM general manager, grand master, gunner's mate

Gmat Greenwich mean astronomical time

GmbH limited company (Ger. *Gesell-schaft mit beschränkter Haftung*)

Gmc Germanic

GMT Greenwich mean time

GNMA Government National Mortgage Association ("Ginnie Mae")

GNP gross national product

GO general orders

GOP Grand Old Party (Republican Party)

Goth gothic, Gothic

gov, govt government

Gov governor

GP general practitioner, Graduate in Pharmacy, general paresis

GPA grade point average

gpm gallons per minute

GPO General Post Office, Government Printing Office

gps gallons per second

GQ general quarters

gr grade, grain, gram, grammar, great, gross, group

Gr Grecian, Greece, Greek

GR King George (Lat. *Georgius Rex*)

grad graduate, graduated

gram grammar, grammarian, grammatical

GrBr, GrBrit Great Britain

GRE graduate record examination

gro gross

gr wt gross weight

GS general secretary, general staff, German silver, Girl Scouts

GSA General Services Administration, Girst Scouts of America

GSC General Staff Corps

GSO general staff officer

gt gilt, great

gtc good till canceled

gtd guaranteed

gtt a drop (Lat. *gutta*)

gu genitourinary

guar guaranteed

Guat Guatemala, Guatemalan

Guin Guinea

gun gunnery

guttat by drops (Lat. *guttatim*)

gv gravimetric volume

gym gymnasium, gymnastics

gyn, gynecol gynecological, gynecology

H

h harbor, hard, hardness, heavy sea, height, hence, high, hit, horns (music), hour, hundred, husband

h, hy henry (electricity)

H hydrogen, intensity of magnetic field

ha hectare, this year (Lat. *hoc anno*)

Hab Habakkuk

hab corp have the body (Lat. *habeas corpus*)

Hag Haggai

Hal halogen

hb halfback

Hb hemoglobin

HBM his or her Britannic majesty

HC House of Commons

hcap, hcp handicap

hcf highest common factor

HCL high cost of living

hd hand, head

hdbk handbook

hdkf handkerchief

hdqrs headquarters

He helium

HE high explosive, his eminence, his or her excellency

Heb, Hebr Hebrew

her heraldic, heraldry

herp, herpetol herpetology

HEW (Department of) Health, Education, and Welfare

hex hexachord, hexagon, hexagonal

hf half

Hf hafnium

HF high frequency

hfbd half-bound (bookbinding)

hfmor half-morocco (bookbinding)

hg hectogram, heliogram

Hg mercury (Lat. *hydrargyrum*)

HG High German, his or her grace, Home Guard

hgt height

HH his or her highness, his holiness

hhd hogshead

HHFA Housing and Home Finance Agency

HHS (Department of) Health and Human Services

HI Hawaii

HIH his or her imperial highenss

HIM his or her imperial majesty

Hind Hindi, Hindu, Hindustan, Hindustani

hist histology, historian, historical, history

HJ here lies (Lat. *hic jacet*)

HJS here lies buried (Lat. *hic jacet sepultus*)

hkf handkerchief

hl hectoliter

HL House of Lords, mustard-lewisite (poison gas)

HLBB Home Loan Bank Board

hm hectometer, in this month (Lat. *hoc menses*)

HM his or her majesty

HMO health maintenance organization

HMS his or her majesty's service (or ship or steamer)

HN nitrogen mustard gas

ho house

Ho holmium

HO head office, Home Office

HOLC Home Owners' Loan Corporation

hon honorably, honorary

Hon honorable

Hond Honduras

hor horizon, horizontal

horol horology

hort, hortic horticultural, horticulture

Hos Hosea

hosp hospital

hp high pressure, horsepower

HP high power

hp-hr horsepower-hour

hq look for this (Lat. *hoc quaere*)

HQ headquarters

hr home run, hour

HR mister (Ger. *Herr*)

HR home rule, House of Representatives

HRE Holy Roman Empire

HRH his or her royal highness

HRIP here rest in peace (Lat. *hic requiescat in pace*)

hrs hours

HS here is buried (Lat. *hic sepultus*), here lies (Lat. *hic situ*), high school, Home Secretary (Brit.), in this sense (Lat. *hoc sensu*)

HSH his or her serene highness

HSM his or her serene majesty

ht at this time (Lat. *hoc tempore*), heat, height, in or under this title (Lat. *hoc titulo*)

Hts heights

HUD (Department of) Housing and Urban Development

Hun, Hung Hungarian, Hungary

HV high voltage

HVAC heating, ventilation, and air conditioning

hw high water

hwm high water mark

hwy highway

hyd, hydros hydrostatics

hydraul hydraulic, hydraulics

hyg hygiene, hygroscopic

hyp, hypoth hypotenuse, hypothesis, hypothetical

I

i incisor, interest, intransitive, island

I iodine, island or islands, isle or isles, Roman numeral for 1

Ia, IA Iowa

IADB Inter-American Defense Board

IAEA International Atomic Energy Agency (of the United Nations)

ib, ibid in the same place (Lat. *ibidem*)

IBEW International Brotherhood of Electrical Workers

IBRD International Bank for Reconstruction and Development

IBT International Brotherhood of Teamsters (Chauffeurs, Warehousemen, and Helpers of America)

ICA International Cooperation Administration

ICAO International Civil Aviation Organization (of the United Nations)

ICBM intercontinental ballistic missile

ICC Indian Claims Commission, Interstate Commerce Commission

Ice, Icel Iceland, Icelandic

ICES International Council for the Exploration of the Sea

ICFTU International Confederation of Free Trade Unions

icth icthyology

ICJ International Court of Justice (of the United Nations)

ICNAF International Commission for Northwest Atlantic Fisheries

ICU intensive care unit

icw interrupted continuous wave

id the same (Lat. *idem*)

ID Idaho, identification, infantry division, intelligence department, inside diameter

Ida Idaho

ie that is (Lat. *id est*)

IE Indo-European

IEP individualized education program

if intermediate frequency

IFCTU International Federation of Christian Trade Unions

IFF identification friend or foe (British radar device)

IFO identified flying object

IG amalgamation (Ger. *Interessengemeinschaft*), Indo-Germanic, inspector general

ign ignites, ignition, unknown (Lat. *ignotus*)

ihp indicated horsepower

IHS Jesus. Often taken to mean Jesus Savior of Mankind (Lat. *Iesus hominum salvator*) or in this sign (Lat. *in hoc signo*).

Il illinium

IL Illinois

ILA International Longshoremen's Association

ILGWU International Ladies' Garment Workers' Union

ill, illus, illust illustrate, illustrated, illustration, illustrator

Ill Illinois

illit illiterate

ILO International Labor Organization (of the United Nations)

ILS instrument landing system

IMCO Intergovernmental Maritime Consultative Organization (of the United Nations)

IMF International Monetary Fund (of the United Nations)

imit imitation, imitative

immun immunology

imp imperative, imperfect, imperial, impersonal, import, important, imported, importer, imprimatur, improper

Imp emperor (Lat. *imperator*)

imper imperative

imperf imperfect, imperforate

impers impersonal

impf imperfect

imp gal imperial gallon

impv imperative

in inch

IN Indiana

inbd inboard, inbound

inc inclosure, including, inclusive, income, incorporated, increase

inch, incho inchoative

incl inclosure, including

incog incognito

incorp incorporated

incorr incorrect

incr increased, increasing

ind independence, independent, index, indicated, indicative, indigo, indirect, industrial

Ind India, Indian, Indiana, Indies

IND in the name of God (Lat. *in nomine Dei*)

indecl indeclinable

indef indefinite

inden, indent indention

indic indicating, indicative, indicator

individ individual

induc induction

ined unpublished

in ex at length (Lat. *in extenso*)

in f at the end (Lat. *in fine*)

inf below (Lat. *infra*), inferior, infinitive, information

Inf infantry

infin infinitive

infl influence, influenced

init initial, in the beginning (Lat. *initio*)

inj injection

in-lb inch-pound

in lim at the outset (on the threshold) (Lat. *in limine*)

in loc in its place (Lat. *in loco*)

in loc cit in the place cited (Lat. *in loco citato*)

inorg inorganic

INRI Jesus of Nazareth, King of the Jews (Lat. *Iesus Nazarenus Rex Iudaeorum*)

ins inches, inspector, insular, insulated, insulation, insurance

INS International News Service

insc, inscr inscribe, inscribed, inscription

insep inseparable

insol insoluble

insp inspected, inspector

inst instant, instantaneous, instrument

Inst institute, institution

instr instruction, instructor, instrument

insur insurance

int intelligence, interest, interior, interjection, internal, interval, intransitive

intens insensitive

inter intermediate

interj interjection

internat international

interp interpreted, interpreter

Interpol International Police Organization

interrog interrogative

intr, intrans intransitive

in trans on the way (Lat. *in transitu*)

Int Rev Internal Revenue

introd introduction, introductory

inv invented, invention, inventor, invitation, invoice

invert invertebrate

invt inventory

Io ionium

IOBB Independent Order of B'nai B'rith

IOOF Independent Order of Odd Fellows

IOU I owe you

ip in passing (chess), innings pitched (baseball)

IPA International Phonetic Alphabet (association)

IPI International Press Institute

IPPC International Penal and Penitentiary Commission

IPR Institute of Pacific Relations

ips inches per second

iq the same as (Lat. *idem quod*)

IQ intelligence quotient

iqed what was to be proved (Lat. *id quod erat demonstrandum*)

Ir Ireland, iridium, Irish

IRA individual retirement account, Irish Republican Army

Iran Iranian, Iranic

IRBM intermediate range ballistic missile

Ire Ireland

IRO International Refugee Organization (of the United Nations)

irreg irregular, irregularly

IRS Internal Revenue Service

is island or islands, isle or isles

Is, Isa Isaiah

ISBN international standard book number

isl island, islands

iso isotropic

isom isometric

isoth isothermal

Isr Israel

ISSN international standard serial number

isth isthmus

it, ital italic, italics

It, Ital Italian, Italy

ITA Initial Teaching Alphabet

itin itinerant, itinerary

ITO International Trade Organization

ITU International Telecommunication Union, International Typographical Union

IU international unit

IWW Industrial Workers of the World

J

J joule (physics), judge, justice

ja joint account

Ja January

JA judge advocate

JAG judge advocate general

Jam Jamaica, Jamaican

Jan January

Jap Japan, Japanese

Jas James

JCAH Joint Commission on Accreditation of Hospitals

JCD Doctor of Canon Law (Lat. *Juris Canonici Doctor*), Doctor of Civil Law (Lat. *Juris Civilis Doctor*)

JCS joint chiefs of staff

jct, jctn junction

JD Doctor of Laws (Lat. *Jurum Doctor*)

Je June

Jer Jeremiah

jg junior grade

Jl July

Jn John

Jon Jonah

Jos Joseph, Joshua, Josiah

jour journal, journalist, journeyman

JP jet propulsion, justice of the peace

jr junior

Ju Judges

JUD Doctor of Civil and Canon Law (Lat. *Juris Utriusque Doctor*)

Judg Judges

Jul July

jun junior

Jun June

junc, junct junction

JurD Doctor of Law (Lat. *Juris Doctor*)

jursp jurisprudence

jus, just justice

juv juvenile

jv junior varsity

jwlr jeweler

Jy July

K

k calends (Lat. *kalendae*), capacity, carat, constant, kilo, kilogram, king, king (chess), knot (naut.), kopeck (coin), koruna (coin), krone (coin)

K potassium (Lat. *kalium*), strikeout

ka kathode (cathode)

kal kalends (calends)

Kan, Kans, Kas Kansas

KB king's bench, king's bishop (chess), knight bachelor

KBP king's bishop's pawn (chess)

kc kilocycle

KC king's counsel, knight commander, Knights of Columbus

kcal kilocalorie

KCB Knight Commander of the (Order of the) Bath

KCVO Knight Commander of the (Royal) Victorian Order

Ken Kentucky

kg keg, kilogram

KG Knight of the (Order of the) Garter

KGB Commission of State Security (Russ. *Komitet Godsudarvstvennoi Bezopasnost'i*)

Ki Kings (book of the Bible)

kilo kilogram, kilometer

kilog kilogram

kilol kiloliter

kilom kilometer

kingd kingdom

KKK Ku Klux Klan

kl kiloliter

km kilometer

kn kronen (coin)

KN king's knight (chess)

KNP king's knight's pawn (chess)

ko knockout

K of C Knights of Columbus

K of P Knights of Pythias

kop kopeck (coin)

KP king's pawn (chess), kitchen police, Knight (of the Order of St.) Patrick, Knight of Pythias

kr krona (coin), krone (coin)

Kr krypton

KR king's rook (chess)

KRP king's rook's pawn (chess)

KS Kansas

kt karat (carat), knight

KT Knights Templar

kv kilovolt

kva kilovolt-ampere

kvar reactive kilovolt-ampere

kw kilowatt

kwh kilowatt-hour

Ky, KY Kentucky

L

l book (Lat. *liber*), (games) lost, lake, land, lat, latitude, law, leaf, league, left, lempira, length, leu, lev, lex, line, link, lira, lire, lit, liter, low, place (Lat. *locus*)

L coefficient of inductance, Latin, length, lewisite, licentiate, Linnaeus, longitude

La lanthanum, Louisiana

LA Legislative Assembly, Library Association, local agent, Los Angeles, Louisiana

lab laboratory

lam laminated

Lam Lamentations

LAM Master of Liberal Arts (Lat. *Liberalium Artium Magister*)

LAN local area network

lang language

laryngol laryngological, laryngology

lat latitude

Lat Latin, Latvia

Latv Latvia

lb pound (Lat. *libra*)

LB Bachelor of Letters (Lat. *Litterarum Baccalaureus*), local board

lb ap apothecary pound

lb av avoirdupois pound

LBO leveraged buyout

lbs pounds

lb t troy pound

lc in the place cited (Lat. *loco citato*), left center, lower case

l/c letter of credit

LC Library of Congress

LCD liquid crystal display, lowest common denominator

lcl less than carload lot

lcm least common multiple, lowest common multiple

ld lead (printing)

Ld lord

LD Low Dutch

ldg landing, leading, loading

LDiv Licentiate in Divinity

ld lmt load limit

ldry laundry

LDS Latter-day Saints, Latter Day Saints, Licentiate in Dental Surgery

le left end

lea league, leather, leave

led ledger

LED light-emitting diode

leg legal, legate, legato, legislation

legis legislation, legislative, legislature

LEM lunar excursion module

L ès S Licentiate in Sciences (Fr. *Licencié ès Sciences*)

Lev, Levit Leviticus

lex lexicon

lf left field, left fielder, left forward, lightface (printing), low frequency

lg left guard

LG Low German

lg, lge large

LGk Late Greek

lgth length

lh left halfback, left hand

LH luteinizing hormone

LHA local hour angle

LHD Doctor of Humanities (Lat. *Litterarum Humaniorum Doctor*)

Li lithium

LI lithographer, Long Island

lib book (Lat. *liber*), librarian, library

Lib Liberal, Liberia

Lieut lieutenant

LIFO last in, first out

LILO last in, last out

lin lineal, linear

ling linguistics

linim liniment

Linn Linnaeus, Linnean

lino linotype

liq liquid, liquor

li qts liquid quarts

lit liter, literal, literally, literary, literature

LitB, LittB Bachelor of Letters or Bachelor of Literature (Lat. *Litterarum Baccalaureus*)

LitD, LittD Doctor of Letters or Doctor of Literature (Lat. *Litterarum Doctor*)

lith, litho, lithog lithograph, lithography

Lith Lithuania, Lithuanian

Lk Luke

ll leaves, lines

LL Late Latin, Legal Latin, Low Latin, lower left

LLB Bachelor of Laws (Lat. *Legum Baccalaureus*)

LLD Doctor of Laws (Lat. *Legum Doctor*)

LLM Master of Laws (Lat. *Legum Magister*)

LM Legion of Merit, Licentiate in Medicine, Licentiate in Midwifery, lunar (excursion) module

LMT local mean time

ln lane

LNG liquefied natural gas

loc local, location

local localism

loc cit in the place cited (Lat. *loco citato*)

log logarithm

long longitude

loq he, she, or it speaks (Lat. *loquitur*)

lox liquid oxygen

lp large paper, long playing, long primer, low pressure

LPG liquified petroleum gas

LPS Lord Privy Seal

LR living room, long run, lower right

LS left side, library science, Licentiate in Surgery, place of the seal (Lat. *locus sigilli*), long shot

lsc in the place cited above (Lat. *loco supra citato*)

LSCA Library Services and Construction Act

LSD landing ship, dock; lysergic acid diethylamide

LSS lifesaving service

LST landing ship, tank

lt left tackle

lt long ton

Lt Lieutenant

LTA Lawn Tennis Association

ltd limited

ltn long ton

LTh Licentiate in Theology

LtInf light infantry

Ltjg lieutenant, junior grade

LTL less than truckload lot

LTS launch telemetry station, launch tracking system

Lu lutetium

lubric lubricate, lubrication

Luth Lutheran

Lux Luxemburg

lv leave, leaves

lw low water

Lw Lawrencium

lwl load waterline

lwm low water mark

LXX Septuagint

lyr lyric, lyrical

M

m majesty, male, manual, mark, married, masculine, mass, measure, medicine, medium, member, meridian, meter, mile, mill, minim, minute, month, moon, morning, mountain, noon (Lat. *meridies*)

M handful (Lat. *manipulus*), master, medieval, middle, monsieur, of medicine (Lat.

medicinae), Roman numeral for 1,000

Ma masurium

MA machine accountant, Maritime Administration, Massachusetts, Master of Arts (Lat. *Magister Artium*), mental age, military academy

Mac, Macc Maccabees

MAC mean aerodynamic chord

Maced Macedonia, Macedonian

mach machine, machinery, machinist

Mad Madam

MADD Mothers Against Drunk Driving

Madm Madam

mag magazine, magnet, magnetism, magnitude

MAgr, MAgric Master of Agriculture

maj majority

Maj major

Mal Malachi, Malay, Malayan, Malta

malac malacology

Man manila (paper), Manitoba

Manch Manchukuo, Manchuria, Manchurian

manuf manufacture, manufactured, manufacturer, manufacturing

mar marine, maritime, married

Mar March

March marchioness

marg margarine, margin, marginal

Marq marquess, marquis

mas, masc masculine

MASH mobile Army surgical hospital

Mass Massachusetts

mat matinee, matins, maturity

MAT Master of Arts in Teaching, Miller Analogy Test

MATS Military Air Transport Service

math mathematical, mathematician, mathematics

matr, matric matriculate, matriculation

Matt Matthew

max maximum

Max Maximilian

MB Bachelor of Medicine (Lat. *Medicinae Baccalaureus*)

MBA Master of Business Administration

MBS Mutual Broadcasting System

mc megacycle, millicurie

MC Maritime Commission, master commandant, master of ceremonies, Medical Corps, member of Congress

MCAT Medical College Admission Test

MCh Master of Surgery (Lat. *Magister Chiurgiae*)

MCL Master of Civil Law

m/d memorandum of deposit, months' date

Md Maryland, mendelevium

MD Doctor of Medicine (Lat. *Medicinae Doctor*), Maryland, medical department, mentally deficient, Middle Dutch

MDS Master of Dental Surgery

mdse merchandise

MDT Mountain Daylight Time

MDu Middle Dutch

me marbled edged (bookbinding)

Me Maine, methyl

ME Maine, mechanical engineer, Methodist Episcopal, Middle English, military engineer, mining engineer

meas measurable, measure

mech, mechan mechanical, mechanics, mechanism

med medical, medicine, medieval, medium

MEd Master of Education

MedGk Medieval Greek

Medit Mediterranean

MedL Medieval Latin

meg megabyte, megacycle, megohm

megs megabytes

mem member, memoir, memorandum, memorial

memo memorandum

mensur mensuration

mep mean effective pressure

mer meridian, meridional

merc mercantile, mercurial, mercury

Messrs messieurs

met metaphor, metaphysics, meteorological, metronome, metropolitan

metal, metall metallurgical, metallurgy

metaph metaphor, metaphorical, metaphysics

metath metathesis, metathetical

meteor, meteorol meteorological, meteorology

meth method, methylated

Meth Methodist

meton metonymy

metrol metrological, metrology

metrop metropolitan

mev million electron volts

Mex Mexican, Mexico

mf fairly loud (It. *mezzoforte*), millifarad

mf, mfd microfarad

MF medium frequency, Middle French

mfg manufacturing

MFlem Middle Flemish

mfr manufacture, manufacturer

mg milligram

Mg magnesium

MG military government

Mgr manager, monseigneur, monsignor

mgt management

mh millihenry

MH Medal of Honor

MHG Middle High German

mi mile

MI Michigan

Mic Micah

Mich Michigan

micro microcomputer

micros microscope, microscopic, microscopy

MICU mobile intensive care unit

mid middle, midshipman

MidDan Middle Danish

MidSw Middle Swedish

mil mileage, military, militia, million

milit military

mimeo mimeograph, mimeographed

min mineralogical, mineralogy, minim, minimum, mining, minor, minute

mineral mineralogy

Minn Minnesota

mip marine insurance policy, mean indicated pressure

MIPS million instructions per second

MIr Middle Irish

MIRV multiple independently targetable reentry vehicle

misc miscellaneous, miscellany

MISL Major Indoor Soccer League

Miss Mississippi

mkk mark, markka

Mk mark

mkd marked

MKS meter-kilogram-second (system)

mkt market

ml milliliter

ML Medieval Latin, Middle Latin, molder

MLA member of the Legislative Assembly, Modern Language Association

MLD minimum lethal dose

MLG Middle Low German

Mlle Mademoiselle (Fr.)

Mlles Mesdemoiselles (Fr.)

MLS Master of Library Science

mm milimeter, thousands (Lat. *millia*), with the necessary changes (Lat. *mutatis mutandis*)

MM machinist's mate, messieurs (Fr.)

Mme Madame (Fr.)

Mmes Mesdames (Fr.)

mmf magnetomotive force

mmfd micromicrofarad

mn the name being changed (Lat. *mutato nomine*)

Mn manganese

MN Minnesota

mo month, monthly

Mo Missouri, molybdenum, Monday

MO mail order, medical officer, Missouri, money order

mod moderate, moderato, modern

ModGr Modern Greek

ModL Modern Latin

Moham Mohammedan

MOI Ministry of Information

mol molecular, molecule

mol wt molecular weight

mon monastery, monetary

Mon Monday, monsignor

Mong Mongolia, Mongolian

monocl monoclinic

monog, monogr monograph

Mons monsieur

Monsig monsignor

Mont Montana

mor morocco (bookbinding)

Mor Moroccan, Morocco

MOR middle of the road

morn morning

morph morpheme, morphological, morphology

mort mortuary

mos months

MOS military occupational specialty

mot motor, motorized

mp melting point, moderately soft (It. *mezzo piano*)

MP Member of Parliament, military police

MPd Master of Pedagogy

MPE Master of Physical Education

mpg miles per gallon

mph miles per hour

MPPDA Motion Picture Producers and Distributors of America (Inc.)

Mr Mister

MR machinery repairman, mentally retarded, motivational research

MRA Moral Re-Armament

MRI magentic resonance imaging

Mrs Mistress

ms manuscript, months after sight

MS Master of Science (Lat. *Magister Scientiae*), minesweeper, Mississippi, multiple sclerosis, sacred to the memory of (Lat. *memoriae sacrum*)

MSA Mutual Security Agency

MSc Master of Science

msg message

MSG master sergeant, monosodium glutamate

Msgr monsignor

MSgt master sergeant
msl mean sea level
mss manuscripts
MST Mountain Standard Time
mt mean time, metric ton, motor transport, mount, mountain, mountain time
Mt Matthew
MT Montana
mtg meeting, mortgage
mtge mortgage
mtl material, mean tidal level
mtn mountain
MTO Mediterranean Theater of Operations
Mt Rev most reverend
mts mountains
MU musician
mun municipal, municipality
mus museum, music, musician
MusB Bachelor of Music (Lat. *Musicae Baccalaureus*)
MusD Doctor of Music (Lat. *Musicae Doctor*)
MusM Master of Music (Lat. *Musicae Magister*)
mut mutilated, mutual
mv millivolt, softly (It. *mezzo voce*)
Mv mendelevium
MVA Missouri Valley Authority
MVD Ministry of Internal Affairs (Rus. *Ministerstvo Vnutrennik Del*)
MVP most valuable player
MW most worshipful, most worthy
MY May
mya myriare
mycol mycological, micology
myg myriagram
myl myrialiter
mym myriameter
myth, mythol mythological, mythology

N

n born (Lat. *natus*), name, net, neuter, neutron, new, nominative, noon, normal, note, noun, number, our (Lat. *noster*)
N knight (chess), nationalist, navy, nitrogen, Norse, north, northern, November
Na sodium (Lat. *natrium*)
NA national army, North America
NAACP National Association for the Advancement of Colored People
NAB New American Bible
NAD National Academy of Design
Nah Nahum
NAm North American
NAM National Association of Manufacturers

NAS National Academy of Sciences, naval air station
NASA National Aeronautics and Space Administration
NASCAR National Association of Stock Car Auto Racing
NASL North American Soccer League
nat national, native, natural, naturalist
nathist natural history
natl national
NATO North Atlantic Treaty Organization
NATS National Air Transport Service
naut nautical
nav naval, navigable, navigation
navig nagivation, navigator
nb note well (Lat. *nota bene*)
Nb niobium
NB New Brunswick
NBA National Basketball Association, National Boxing Association
NBC Natinal Broadcasting Company
NbE north by east
NBS National Bureau of Standards
NbW north by west
nc nitrocellulose
NC no charge, no credit, North Carolina, nurse corps
NCAA National Collegiate Athletic Association
NCar North Carolina
NCE New Catholic Edition (of the Bible)
NCO noncommissioned officer
nd no date
Nd neodymium
ND, NDak North Dakota
Ne neon
NE Nebraska, New England, northeast, northeastern
NEA National Education Association
NEB New English Bible
Neb, Nebr Nebraska
nec not elsewhere classified
NEC National Electrical Code
NED New English Dictionary (Oxford English Dictionary)
neg negative, negatively
Neh Nehemiah
nei not elsewhere indicated
neol neologism
NEP New Economic Policy
nes not elsewhere specified, not elsewhere stated
Neth Netherlands
neur, neurol neurological, neurologic
neut neuter, neutral
Nev Nevada
Newf Newfoundland
NewTest New Testament
nf noun feminine

NF National Formulary, Newfoundland, no funds, Norman French
NFC National Football Conference
NFL National Football League
ng no good
NG national guard, New Guinea
NGk New Greek
NH New Hampshire
NHG New High German
nhp nominal horsepower
NHS National Health Service (Brit.)
Ni nickel
NI Northern Ireland
Nic, Nicar Nicaragua, Nicaraguan
Nig Nigeria, Nigerian
NIH National Institutes of Health
NIMH National Institute of Mental Health
NIRA National Industrial Recovery Act
NIre Northern Ireland
NJ New Jersey
NKVD People's Commissariat of Internal Affairs (Rus. *Narodnyi Komissariat Vnutrennikh Del*)
nl new line (printing), north latitude, not clear (Lat. *non liquet*), not far (Lat. *non longe*), not lawful (Lat. *non licet*)
NL New Latin
Nlat north latitude
NLRB National Labor Relations Board
nm nautical mile, noun masculine
NM, NMex New Mexico
NMR nuclear magnetic resonance
NMSQT National Merit Scholarship Qualifying Test
NMU National Maritime Union
NNE north-northeast
NNW north-northwest
no north, northern, number
No nobelium
NOAA National Oceanic and Atmospheric Administration
nob for our part or on our part (Lat. *nobis*)
nol pros unwilling to prosecute (Lat. *nolle prosequi*)
nom nomenclature, nominal, nominative
nomin nominative
noncom noncommissioned (officer)
non cul not guilty (Lat. *non culpabilis*)
non dest notwithstanding (Lat. *non destante*)
non obs, non obst notwithstanding (Lat. *non obstante*)

non pros he or she does not prosecute (Lat. *non prosequitur*)
non seq it does not follow (Lat. *non sequitur*)
nor north, northern
Nor Norman, Norway, Norwegian
NORAD North American Air Defense Command
norm normal
Norw Norway, Norwegian
nos numbers
nov novelist
Nov November
NOW National Organization for Women, negotiable order of withdrawal
np net proceeds, new paragraph, no paging, no place (of publication)
Np neptunium
NP knight's pawn, neuropsychiatrist, no protest, notary public, unless before (Lat. *nisi prius*)
NPN nonprotein nitrogen
np or d no place or date
NPR National Public Radio
npt normal pressure and temperature
nr near
NRA National Recovery Administration, National Rifle Association
NRC National Research Council, Nuclear Regulatory Commission
ns near side (shipping), new series, new style, not specified
Ns nimbostratus
NS new style, Nova Scotia
NSC National Security Council
NSF National Science Foundation, not sufficient funds
NSPCA National Society for the Prevention of Cruelty to Animals
NSPCC National Society for the Prevention of Cruelty to Children
NSW New South Wales
nt net
NT New Testament, Northern Territory (Australia)
ntp normal temperature and pressure
NTSB National Transportation Safety Board
nt wt net weight
num number, numeral
Num, Numb Numbers
numis numismatic, numismatics
ny nonvoting (stock)
NV Nevada
NW northwest, northwestern
NWT Northwest Territories (Canada)
NY New York
NYC New York City

NYSE New York Stock Exchange

NZ New Zealand

O

o octavo, off, ohm, old, only, order, pint (Lat. *octavius*)

o- ortho-

O ocean, October, Ohio, old, Ontario, Oregon, oxygen

OAPC Office of Alien Property Custodian

OAr Old Arabic

OAS Organization of American States

OAU Organization of African Unity

ob he or she died (Lat. *obit*), in passing (Lat. *obiter*), obstetrical, obstetrics

Ob, Obad Obadiah

obb obbligato

obdt obedient

OBE Officer of the (Order of the) British Empire

ob-gyn obstetrician gynecologist, obstetrics gynecology

obit obituary

obj object, objection, objective

obl oblique, oblong

obs obscure, observation, observatory, obsolete, obsolescence

obsol obsolescent

ob s p died without issue (Lat. *obit sine prole*)

obstet obstetrical, obstetrics

obt obedient

obv obverse

oc in the work cited (Lat. *opere citato*)

o/c old charter, overcharge

Oc ocean

OC office of censorship, officer commanding, original cover

OCAS Organization of Central American States

occ occasion, occasionally, occident, occidental

occult occultism

OCD Office of Civilian Defense

oceanog oceanography

OCR optical character reading, optical character recognition

OCS office of contract settlement, officer candidate school

oct octavo

Oct October

octupl octuplicate

od olive drab, on demand, outside diameter

OD Doctor of Optometry, officer of the day, Old Dutch, Ordnance Department, overdraft, overdrawn

ODan Old Danish

ODu Old Dutch

OE Old English

OECD Organization for Economic Cooperation and Development

OED Oxford English Dictionary

OEEC Organization for European Economic Cooperation

OEM original equipment manufacture

OES office of economic stabilization, Order of the Eastern Star

OF Old French

off offered, office, official, officinal

OFM Order of Friars Minor

OG officer of the guard, original gum (philately)

OH Ohio

OHG Old High German

OHMS on his or her majesty's service

OIAA office of inter-American affairs

OIC office of information and culture (of the State Department)

OIr Old Irish

OIT office of international trade

OK, Okla Oklahoma

OL Old Latin

Old Test Old Testament

oleo oleomargarine

OM Order of Merit (Brit.)

OMB Office of Management and Budget

ON Old Norse

ONI Office of Naval Intelligence

ONormFr Old Norman French

onomat onomatopoeia, onomatopoeic

ONR Office of Naval Research

Ont Ontario

OOD officer of the day, officer of the deck

op operation, opposite, out of print, overprint, overproof, work (Lat. *opus*), works (Lat. *opera*)

OP observation post, Order of Preachers

OPA office of price administration

op cit in the work cited (Lat. *opere citato*)

OPEC Organization of Petroleum Exporting Countries

OPer Old Persian

ophthal ophthalmology

opp oppose, opposed, opposite

opt optative, optical, optics

OR operating room, Oregon

orat oratorical, oratory

orch orchestra, orchestral

ord ordained, order, ordinal, ordinance, ordinary, ordnance

ordn ordnance

Ore, Oreg Oregon

org organic, organism, organized

orig origin, original, originally

Ork Orkney (Islands)

ornith, ornithol ornithological, ornithologist, ornithology

orth orthopedic, orthopedics

Orth orthodox

Os osmium

OS Old Saxon, old style, ordinary seaman

OSA Order of Saint Augustine

OSB Order of Saint Benedict

osc oscillating, oscillator

OSerb Old Serbian

OSF Order of Saint Francis

OSHA Occupational Safety and Health Administration

OSl Old Slavic

OSp Old Spanish

OSRD Office of Scientific Research and Development

OSS Office of Strategic Services

osteo osteopath, osteopathy

OT Old Testament, on truck, overtime

OTC Officer's Training Corps

otol otology

OTS Officer Training School

ott octave (It. *ottava*)

OW one-way

OWI Office of War Information

Oxon Oxford (Lat. *Oxonia*)

oz ounce

oz ap apothecary ounce

oz av avoirdupois ounce

ozs ounces

oz t troy ounce

P

p after (Lat. *post*), by (Lat. *per*), by weight (Lat. *pondere*), first (Lat. *primus*), for (Lat. *pro*), in part (Lat. *partim*), page, part, participle, past, penny, perch (measure), period, perishable, peseta, peso, pint, pipe, pitcher, pole (measure), population, post, power, pressure, softly (It. *piano*)

p- para- (chemistry)

P bishop (Lat. *pontifex*), father (Fr. *père*, Lat. *pater*), parental, pastor, pawn (chess), pengö, people (Lat. *populus*), peso, phosphorus, piaster, pope (Lat. *papa*), president, pressure, priest, prince, prisoner, prompter (theater)

P- pursuit (military)

pa for the year (Lat. *pro anno*), paper, participial adjective, particular average (insurance), public address, yearly (Lat. *per annum*)

Pa Pennsylvania, protactinium

PA passenger agent, Pennsylvania, personal assistant, physician's assistant, power of attorney, press agent, private account, public address (system), purchasing agent

PABA para-aminobenzoic acid

Pac, Pacif Pacific

PAC Pan-American Congress, political action committee

p ae equal parts (Lat. *partes aequales*)

Pal Palestine

paleob paleobotany

paleog paleography

paleontol paleontology

palm palmistry

pam, pamph pamphlet

Pan Panama

p and h postage and handling

P and L profit and loss

pap paper

par paragraph, parallel, parenthesis

Par, Para Paraguay

paren parenthesis

parens parentheses

parl parliamentary

part participle, particular

pass everywhere (Lat. *passim*), passage, passenger, passive

pat patent, patented, patrol, pattern

PAT point after touchdown

patd patented

path, pathol pathology

Pat Off Patent Office

pat pend patent pending

PAU Pan American Union

PAYE pay as you earn, pay as you enter

payt payment

PB Pharmacopoeia Britannica, prayer book

PBA Public Buildings Administration

PBS Public Broadcasting Service, Public Buildings Service

PBX private branch (telephone) exchange

pc after meals (Lat. *post cibos*), percent, percentage, piece, postcard, price

p/c petty cash, price current

PC personal computer, police constable, post commander, Privy Council, professional corporation

PCA Progressive Citizens of America

PCB polychlorinated biphenyl

Pcs preconscious

pct percent

pd by the day (Lat. *per diem*), paid, potential difference

Pd palladium

PD per diem, phenyl dichloride, police department, postal district

PdB Bachelor of Pedagogy (Lat. *Pedagogiae Baccalaureus*)

PdD Doctor of Pedagogy (Lat. *Pedagogiae Doctor*)

PdM Master of Pedagogy (Lat. *Pedagogiae Magister*)

PDT Pacific Daylight Time

p/e price-earnings ratio

PE petroleum engineer, presiding elder, printer's error, probable error, Protestant Episcopal

ped pedal, pedestal, pedestrian

PEI Prince Edward Island

pen peninsula, penitent, penitentiary

PEN (International Association of) Poets, Playwrights, Editors, Essayists, and Novelists

Penn, Penna Pennsylvania

penol penology

per period, person

per an, per ann by the year (Lat. *per annum*)

perd, perden dying away (It. *perdendo*)

perf perfect, perforated, performer

perh perhaps

perm permanent

perp perpendicular, perpetual

pers person, personal

Pers Persia, Persian

persp perspective

pert pertaining

Peru, Peruv Peruvian

pet petroleum

petn petition

petrog petrography

petrol petrology

pf louder (It. *più forte*), pfennig (coin), power factor

pg page

PFC private first class

pfd preferred

pfg pfennig (coin)

Pg Portugal, Portuguese

PG past grand (master), paying guest, postgraduate

PGA Professional Golfers' Association

ph phrase

Ph phenyl

PH Purple Heart

phar, pharm pharmaceutical, pharmacist, pharmacy

PharB Bachelor of Pharmacy (Lat. *Pharmaciae Baccalaureus*)

PharD Doctor of Pharmacy (Lat. *Pharmaciae Doctor*)

PharM Master of Pharmacy (Lat. *Pharmaciae Magister*)

pharmacol pharmacology

PhB Bachelor of Philosophy (Lat. *Philosophiae Baccalaureus*)

PhC pharmaceutical chemist

PhD Doctor of Philosophy (Lat. *Philosophiae Doctor*)

phil philosopher, philosophical, philosophy

Phil Philippians, Philippines

Phila Philadelphia

philol philology

philos philosopher, philosophical, philosophy

phon phonetic, phonetics, phonology

phonet phonetic, phonetics

phot, photo, photog photograph, photographer, photographic, photography

photom photometrical, photometry

phr phrase

phren, phrenol phrenological, phrenology

PHS Public Health Service

phys physical, physician, physicist, physics

physiol physiological, physiology

Pi, pias piaster

pict pictorial, picture

pil pill (Lat. *pilla*)

pinx he or she painted (Lat. *pinxit*)

PIO public information officer

pizz plucked (music) (It. *pizzicato*)

pk pack, park, peak, peck

pkg package

pkt packet

PKU phenylketonuria

pl place, plate, plural

plat plateau, platform, platoon

plen plenipotentiary

plf, plff plaintiff

plu plural

plup, plupf pluperfect

plur plural, plurality

pm after death (Lat. *post mortem*), afternoon (Lat. *post meridiem*), postmortem

Pm promethium

PM pacific mail, past master, paymaster, police magistrate, postmaster, prime minister, provost marshall

pmk postmark

pmkd postmarked

pn promissory note

pneum pneumatic, pneumatics

png a person who is not acceptable (Lat. *persona non grata*)

PNG Papua New Guinea

pnxt he or she painted (Lat. *pinxit*)

po personnel officer, petty officer, postal order, post office, put-out

Po polonium

PO post office

POC port of call

pod pay on delivery

PoD Doctor of Podiatry

POD Post Office Department

POE port of embarkation, port of entry

poet poetic, poetical, poetry

pol, polit political, politics

Pol Poland, Polish

pol econ, polit econ political economy

pop popular, population

POP point of purchase

por pay on return

port portrait

Port Portugal, Portuguese

pos, posit position, positive

poss possession, possessive, possible, possibly

post postal

pot potential

POW prisoner of war

pp pages, parcel post, parish priest, past participle, postpaid, privately printed, very softly (It. *pianissimo*)

PP pellagra preventive (factor)

ppc to take leave (Fr. *pour prendre congé*)

ppd postpaid, prepaid

pph pamphlet

ppi policy proof of interest

PPI plan position indicator (radar)

ppl participle, past participle

ppm parts per million

ppp pianissimo

ppr present participle

pps additional postscript (Lat. *post postscriptum*), Parliamentary private secretary

ppv pay per view (television)

pq previous questions

PQ Province of Quebec

pr pair, pairs, paper, power, preferred, preposition, present, price, priest, prince, printing, pronoun

Pr praesodymium

PR proportional representation, public relations, Puerto Rico

preb prebend, prebendary

prec preceding

pred predicate, predication, predicative, prediction

pref preface, prefatory, preference, preferred, prefix

prelim preliminary

prem premium

prep preparation, preparatory, prepare, preposition

pres present, presidency, president, presumptive

Presb, Presbyt presbyter, Presbyterian

pret preterit

prev previous, previously

prim primary, primitive

prin principal, principally, principle

print printer, printing

priv private, privately, privative

prn whenever necessary (Lat. *pro re nata*)

pro professional

PRO Professional Review Organization, public relations officer

prob probable, probably, problem

proc proceedings, process, proclamation

prod produce, produced, product

prof professor

prog program, progress, progressive

prom promenade, promontory

pron pronoun, pronounced, pronunciation

pronom pronominal

prop proper, properly, property, proposition, proprietary, proprietor

propr proprietary, proprietor

pros prosody

Prot protectorate, Protestant

pro tem for the time being (Lat. *pro tempore*)

prov proverbial, providence, provident, province, provincial, provision, provost

Prov Proverbs

prox next (month) (Lat. *proximo*)

prs pairs

prtd printed

prtg printing

Prus, Pruss Prussia, Prussian

prv to return a call (Fr. *pour rendre visite*)

ps passenger steamer, permanent secretary, pieces, postscript, private secretary, prompt side (theater), pseudonym, public sale

Ps Psalms

PS police sergeant, Privy Seal, public school

PSAT Preliminary Scholastic Aptitude Test

pseud pseudonym

psf pounds per square foot

psi pounds per square inch

PSRO Professional Standards Review Organization

pss postscripts

PSS Psalms

PST Pacific Standard Time

psych, psychol psychological, psychologist, psychology

psychoanal psychoanalysis

pt for the time being (Lat. *pro tempore*), part, part time, payment, pint, point, port, post town, postal telegraph, preterit

Pt platinum

PT part time, physical training

pta peseta

PTA Parent-Teachers' Association

ptbl portable

ptg printing

pts parts, payments, pints

PTSA Parent-Teacher-Student Association

pty proprietary

Pu plutonium

pub public, publication, published, publisher

publ publication, published, publisher

pulv pulverized

punct punctuation

pur, purch purchaser, purchasing

pv par value, post village, priest vicar

PVC polyvinyl chloride

Pvt private

PW prisoner of war

PWA Public Works Administration

PWP Parents Without Partners

pwr power

pwt pennyweight

PX post exchange

pymt payment

Q

q quart, quarter, quarterly, quarto, query, question, queen

Q quarto, Quebec, queen (chess)

qb quarterback

QB Queen's Bench, queen's bishop (chess)

QBP queen's bishop's pawn (chess)

QC Quartermaster Corps, Queen's Counsel

qd as if he or she had said (Lat. *quasi dixisset*), as if one should say (Lat. *quasi dicat*), as if said (Lat. *quasi dictum*)

qe which is (Lat. *quod est*)

QED which was to be demonstrated (Lat. *quod erat demonstrandum*)

QEF which was to be done (Lat. *quod erat faciendum*)

QEI which was to be found out (Lat. *quod erat inveniendum*)

QID four times a day (Lat. *quater in die*)

ql as much as you please (Lat. *quantum libet*), quintal

Qld Queensland

qlty quality

QM quartermaster

QMC Quartermaster Corps

QMG quartermaster general

qn question

QN queen's knight (chess)

QNP queen's knight's pawn (chess)

QP queen's pawn (chess)

q pl, QP as much as you wish (Lat. *quantum placeat*)

Qq quartos

qqv which see (plural) (Lat. *quos vide*)

qr quarter, quarterly, quire

QR queen's rook (chess)

QRP queen's rook's pawn (chess)

qrs farthings (Lat. *quadrantes*), quarters, quires

qrtly quarterly

qs as much as suffices (Lat. *quantum sufficit*), quarter section

qt quantity, quart, quiet

qto quarto

qts quarts

qu quart, queen, query, question

quad quadrangle, quadrant, quadrat, quadrilateral, quadruple, quadruplet

quar, quart quarter, quarterly

Que Quebec

ques question

quin, quint quintuple, quintuplet

quor quorum

quot quotation, quoted

qv as much as you will (Lat. *quantum vis*), which see (Lat. *quod vide*)

qy query

R

r range, rare, received, recipe, residence, resides, retired, right, right-hand page (Lat. *recto*), rises, river, road, rod, roentgen, royal, rubber, ruble, run

R commonwealth (Lat. *res publica*), gas constant (chemistry), king (Lat. *rex*), queen (Lat. *regina*), rabbi, radical (chemistry), radius, railroad, railway, ratio, Réaumur, rector, redactor, Republican, resistance (electrical), respond or response (ecclesiastical), ring (chemistry), rook (chess), ruble, rupee, take (Lat. *recipe*)

Ra radium

RA rear admiral, regular army, right ascension, Royal Academy

rad radical, radio, radius, root (Lat. *radix*)

RAF Royal Air Force

ral, rall gradually slower (It. *rallentando*)

RAM random-access memory

R&D research and development

RAR radio acoustic ranging

Rb rubidium

rbi run batted in

RC Red Cross, reserve corps, Roman Catholic

RCAF Royal Canadian Air Force

RCCh Roman Catholic Church

rcd received

RCMP Royal Canadian Mounted Police

RCP Royal College of Physicians

rcpt receipt

RCS Royal College of Surgeons

Rct recruit

rd reduce, rix-dollar, road, rod, round

Rd Radium, road

RD research and development, rural delivery

re right end

Re rhenium, rupee

RE real estate, Reformed Episcopal, right excellent, Royal Engineers

REA Rural Electrification Administration

react reactance (electricity)

rec receipt, received, recipe, record, recorded, recorder, recording

recd received

recip reciprocal, reciprocity

recit recitative

rec sec recording secretary

rect receipt, rectified, rector, rectory

red reduced, reduction

redisc rediscount

redup, redupl reduplicated, reduplication

ref referee, reference, referred, refining, reformation, reformed

Ref Ch Reformed Church

refl reflection, reflective, reflectively, reflex, reflexive

refrig refrigeration

reg regent, regiment, region, register, registered, registrar, registry, regular, regularly, regulation, regulator

Reg queen (Lat. *regina*)

regt regent, regiment

REIT real estate investment trust

rel relating, relative, relatively, released, religion, religious

rel pron relative pronoun

rem remittance

REM rapid eye movement

rep repair, repeat, report, reporter, representative, reprint, republic

Rep representative, republic, Republican

repr representing, reprinted

Repub Republican

req required, requisition

res research, reserve, residence, resides, residue, resigned, resistance, resistor, resolution

resp respective, respiration, respondent

rest restaurant

Resurr Resurrection

ret retain, retired, returned

retd retained, returned

retrog retrogressive

rev revenue, reverse, reversed, review, revise, revised, revision, revolution, revolving

Rev Revelation, reverend

Rev Ver Revised Version (of the Bible)

rf radio frequency, range finder, rapid fire, right field, right fielder, right forward

RFA Royal Field Artillery

RFC Reconstruction Finance Corporation, Royal Flying Corps

RFD rural free delivery

rg right guard

RGB red-blue-green television tube

rh relative humidity, right halfback, right hand

Rh Rhesus (blood factor), rhodium

RH Royal highness

rhap rhapsody

rhbdr rhombohedral

rhet rhetoric, rhetorical

rhin, rhinol rhinology

rhomb rhombic

rhp rated horsepower

RI king and emperor (Lat. *rex et imperator*), queen and empress (Lat. *regina et imperatrix*), Rhode Island

rip supplementary (music) (It. *ripieno*)

RIP may he, she, or they rest in peace (Lat. *requiescat* or *requiescant in pace*)

RISC reduced instruction set computer

rit slow (It. *ritardando*)

riv river

rkva reactive kilovolt-ampere

rm ream, room

Rm Reichsmark

rms reams, rooms, root mean square

Rn radon

RN Royal Navy

RNA ribonucleic acid

RNR Royal Naval Reserve

RNWMP Royal Northwest Mounted Police

ro recto, rood

ROK Republic of Korea

rom roman (type)

Rom Roman, Romance, Romania, Romanian, Romans

ROM read-only memory

ROP record of production, run of press

rot rotating, rotation

ROTC Reserve Officers' Training Corps

roul roulette (philately)

roy royal

RP Reformed Presbyterian, Regius Professor

RPD Doctor of Political Science (Lat. *Rerum Politicarum Doctor*)

rpm revolutions per minute

RPO railway post office

rps revolutions per second

rpt report

rr very rarely (Lat. *rarissime*)

RR railroad, right reverend

RRB Railroad Retirement Board

rs reis, rupees

RS recording secretary, reformed spelling, revised statutes

RSFSR Russian Soviet Federated Socialist Republic

RSV Revised Standard Version (of the Bible)

rsvp please reply (Fr. *répondez s'il vous plaît*)

RSVP Retired Seniors Volunteer Program

rt right, right tackle

Rt Hon right honorable

Rt Rev right reverend

Rts rights

Ru Ruth, ruthenium

rub ruble

Rus, Russ Russia, Russian

RV recreational vehicle, Revised Version (of the Bible)

rva reactive volt-ampere

RW right worshipful, right worthy

ry railway

S

s buried (Lat. *sepultus*), fellow (Lat. *socius* or *sodalis*), lies (Lat. *situs*), sacral, saint, school, scribe, second, secondary, section, see, semi-, senate, series, set, shilling (Lat. *solidus*), sign, signed, silver, singular, sire, socialist, society, solo, son, soprano, southern, steel, stem, stere, stock, substantive, sun, surplus

s- symmetrical (chemistry)

S knight (chess) (Ger. *Springer*), sabbath, Saturday, Saxon, seaman, Senate, September, signature, Signor, south, southern, sulfur, Sunday

Sa samarium, Samuel

SA corporation (Fr. *société anonyme*), Salvation Army, seaman apprentice, sex appeal, South Africa, South America, South Australia

Sab sabbath

SAC Strategic Air Command

SADD Students Against Driving Drunk

SAE Society of Automotive Engineers

SAfr South Africa, South African

SALT strategic arms limitation talks

SAm, SAmer South America, South American

SAM surface-to-air missile

Sans, Sansk Sanskrit

S ap apothecary's scruple

SAR Sons of the American Revolution

Sask Saskatchewan

sat saturated, saturation

Sat Saturday, Saturn

SAT Scholastic Aptitude Test

sav savings

sb stolen base, substantive

Sb antimony (Lat. *stibium*)

SB Bachelor of Science (Lat. *Scientiae Baccalaureus*)

SBA Small Business Administration

SbE south by east

SbW south by west

sc he or she carved or engraved it (Lat. *sculpsit*), namely (Lat. *scilicet*), salvage charges, scale, scene, science, screw, scruple (weight), sized and calendered, small capitals (printing), supercalendered

Sc scandium, stratocumulus

SC Security Council (of the United Nations), Signal Corps, South Carolina, Supreme Court

Scan, Scand Scandinavia, Scandinavian

s caps small capitals (printing)

ScB Bachelor of Science (Lat. *Scientiae Baccalaureus*)

ScD Doctor of Science (Lat. *Scientiae Doctor*)

sch school, schooner

sched schedule

schol scholar, scholastic

sci science, scientific

sci fa show cause (Lat. *scire facias*)

scil namely (Lat. *scilicet*)

ScM Master of Science (Lat. *Scientiae Magister*)

Scot Scotland, Scots, Scottish

scr scrip, script, scruple (weight)

Script scriptural, scriptures

sculpt he or she carved it (Lat. *sculpsit*), sculptor

sd indefinitely (without date) (Lat. *sine die*), standard deviation

SD Doctor of Science (Lat. *Scientiae Doctor*), South Dakota, steward

SDR special drawing rights

SDS Students for a Democratic Society

Se selenium

SE southeast, southeastern

SEATO Southest Asia Treaty Organization

sec according to (Lat. *secundum*), secant, second, secondary, secretary, section, sector

SEC Securities and Exchange Commission

sec-ft second-foot

sech hyperbolic secant

sec leg according to law (Lat. *secundum legem*)

sec reg according to rule (Lat. *secundum regulam*)

secs seconds, sections

sect section, sectional

secy secretary

seg segment

seismol seismology

sel selected, selection

Sem seminary, Semitic

sen senate, senator, senior

sent sentence

sep sepal, separate

Sep, Sept September, Septuagint

seq sequel

seq, seqq the following (Lat. *sequens, sequentia*)

ser serial, series, sermon

serv servant, service

sess session

sf, sforz with emphasis (It. *sforzando, sforzato*)

SFSR Soviet Federated Socialist Republic

sfz with emphasis (It. *sforzando, sforzato*)

sg senior grade, specific gravity

sgd signed

Sgt sergeant

sh share, sheet, shilling, shunt

SHAEF Supreme Headquarters, Allied Expeditionary Forces

Shak Shakespeare

SHAPE Supreme Headquarters Allied Powers (Europe)

SHF super-high frequency

shipt, shpt shipment

shtg shortage

sh tn short ton

Si silicon

SI international system of weights and measures (Fr. *Système International*), Staten Island

Sib Siberia, Siberian

SIDS sudden infant death syndrome

sig signal, signature, signor, signore, signori

sigill seal (Lat. *sigillum*)

sim simile

sin sine

sing singular

sinh hyperbolic sine

SIPC Securities Investment Protection Corporation

sist sister

sj under consideration (Lat. *sub judice*)

SJ Society of Jesus (Lat. *Societas Jesu*)

SJD Doctor of Juridicial Science (Lat. *Scientiae Juridicae Doctor*)

sk sack

Skr, Skt Sanskrit

sl without place (Lat. *sine loco*)

slan without place, date, or name (Lat. *sine loco, anno, vel nomine*)

S lat south latitude

Slav Slavic, Slavonian

sld sailed, sealed

slp without lawful issue (Lat. *sine legitima prole*)

SLR single-lens reflex (camera)

sm small

Sm samarium

SM Master of Science (Lat. *Scientiae Magister*), sergeant major, state militia

sm c, sm caps small capitals

smorz dying away (It. *smorzando*)

smp without male issue (Lat. *sine mascula prole*)

SMSA standard metropolitan statistical area

sn without name (Lat. *sine nomine*)

Sn tin (Lat. *stannum*)

so seller's option, strike out

So south, southern

soc socialist, society

sociol sociologist, sociology

sol solicitor, soluble, solution

Sol Solomon

soln solution

Som Somalia

son sonata

sop soprano

SOP standard operating procedure

SOPA senior officer present afloat

sos, sost, sosten sustained (It. *sostenuto*)

sp single phase, single pole, special, species, specific, specimen, spelling, spirit, without issue (Lat. *sine prole*)

Sp Spain, Spaniard, Spanish

SP shore patrol, shore police

SPAS Fellow of the American Philosophical Society (Lat. *Societatis Philosophiae Americanae Socius*)

SPCA Society for the Prevention of Cruelty to Animals

SPCC Society for the Prevention of Cruelty to Children

spec special, specification, speculation

specif specifically

spg spring

sp gr specific gravity

sp ht specific heat

sph spherical

spp species (plural)

SPQR government and people of Rome (Lat. *Senatus populusque Romanus*)

SPR Society for Psychical Research

spt seaport

sq sequence, square, the following (Lat. *sequentia*)

Sq squadron, Square (street)

sq ft square foot

sq in square inch

sq mi square mile

sq rd square rod

sq yd square yard

sr steradian

Sr senior, señor, sir, sister, strontium

Sra señora

SRO standing room only

Srta señorita

ss namely (in law) (Lat. *scilicet*), shortstop

SS saints, Silver Star, steamship, storm troopers (Ger. *Schutz-staffeln*), Sunday school, written above (Lat. *supra scriptum*)

SSA Social Security Act (Administration)

SSB Social Security Board

SSE south-southeast

SSgt staff sergeant

SSR Soviet Socialist Republic

SSS Selective Service System

SST supersonic transport

SSW south-southwest

st short ton, stand, stanza, statute, stet, stitch, stone (weight), street, strophe

St saint, straight, strait, stratus, street

sta station, stationary, stator

Sta saint (Sp. *Santa*), station

stac, stacc staccato

stan stanchion

Staph staphylococcus

stat immediately (Lat. *statim*), static, stationary, statistics, statuary, statute

STB Bachelor of Sacred Theology (Lat. *Sacrae Theologiae Baccalaureus*)

stbd starboard

std standard

STD Doctor of Sacred Theology (Lat. *Sacrae Theologiae Doctor*), sexually transmitted disease

Ste saint (Fr. *Sainte*)

steno, stenog stenographer, stenography

ster, stg sterling

St Ex stock exchange

stge storage

stip stipend, stipendiary, stipulation

Stir Stirling, Stirlingshire

stk stock

STOL short take-off and landing

stor storage

stp stamped

STP standard temperature and pressure

str steamer, strait, string

Strep streptococcus

stud student

sub subaltern, submarine, subscription, substitute, suburb, suburban, understand (or supply) (Lat. *subaudi*)

subd subdivision

subj subject, subjective, subjunctive

subs subscription, subsidiary

subseq subsequent, subsequently

subst substantive, substitute

succ successor

suf, suff suffix

sug, sugg suggested, suggestion

Sun, Sund Sunday

sup above (Lat. *supra*), superfine, superior, superlative, supplement, supplementary, supply, supreme

super superfine, superintendent, superior, supernumerary

superl superlative

supp, suppl supplement, supplementary

supr supreme

supt superintendent

sur surcharged, surplus

surg surgeon, surgery, surgical

surr surrender, surrendered

surv survey, surveying, surveyor, surviving

susp suspended

sv sailing vessle, under this word (Lat. *sub verbo*)

SV Holy Virgin (Lat. *Sancta Virgo*)

SW southwest, southwestern

Sw Sweden, Swedish

SWA, SWAfr South-West Africa

SWAT special weapons and tactics (team)

Swe, Swed Sweden, Swedish

Swit, Switz, Swtz Switzerland

syl, syll syllable

sym symbol, symmetrical, symphony

syn synchronize, synonym, synonymous, synonymy

syr syrup (pharmacy)

Syr Syria, Syriac, Syrian

syst system, systematic

T

t in the time of (Lat. *tempore*), tare, target, tea-

spoon, telephone, temperature, tempo, tenor, tense (grammar), terminal, territory, time, tome, ton, town, township, transit, transitive, troy (weight), volume (Lat. *tomus*)

T tablespoon, tantalum, technician, temperature (absolute), tension (surface), testament, time, trinity, Tuesday, Turkish

Ta tantalum

tab table, tablet

TAC Tactical Air Command, Technical Assistance Committee

tal qual as they come (or average quality) (Lat. *talis qualis*)

tan tangent

tanh hyperbolic tangent

TAP Technical Assistance Program

tart tartaric

taut tautological, tautology

tb trial balance

Tb terbium

TB tubercle bacillus, tuberculosis

tba to be announced

tbs, tbsp tablespoon, tablespoonful

tc tierce

Tc technetium

TC Trusteeship Council (of the United Nations)

tchr teacher

td touchdown

TD tank destroyer, tradesman, traffic director, Treasury Department

tdn total digestible nutrients

Te tellurium

tech technical, technological, techonology

technol technology

TEFL teaching English as a foreign language

tel telegram, telegraph, telegraphic, telephone

telecom telecommunication

teleg telegram, telegraph, telegraphic, telegraphy

temp in the time of (Lat. *tempore*), temperature, temporary

ten hold (It. *tenuto*), tenement, tenor

Tenn Tennessee

terr terrace, territorial, territory

term terminal, termination, terminology

test testamentary, testator

Test testament

tetr, tetrag tetragonal

Teut Teuton, Teutonic

Tex Texas, Texan

tfr transfer

tg type genus

TGIF thank God it's Friday

tgt target

Th thorium

Th Thursday

ThB Bachelor of Theology (Lat. *Theologiae Baccalaureus*)

ThD Doctor of Theology (Lat. *Theologiae Doctor*)

Th-Em thoron (thorium emanation)

theol theologian, theological, theology

theor theorem

theos theosophical, theosophist, theosophy

therm thermometer

thermochem thermochemical, thermochemistry

thermodynam thermodynamics

Thess Thessalonians, Thessaly

THI temperature-humidity index

Thu, Thurs Thursday

Ti titanium

t i d three times daily (Lat. *ter in die*)

tinct tincture

tit title

Tit Titus

tk truck

TKO technical knock-out

Tl thallium

TL trade last

T/L time loan

TLC tender loving care

tm true mean

Tm thulium

TMH trainable mentally handicapped

tn ton, train

Tn thoron

TN Tennessee

tng training

TNT trinitrotoluene, trinitrotoluol

to turn over, turnover

tonn tonnage

top, topog topographical, topography

tp title page, township, troop

tpke turnpike

tpr temperature, pulse, respiration

tps townships

tr tare, tincture, trace, train, transitive, translated, translation, translator, transpose, treasurer, trust

Tr terbium, troop

trag tragedy, tragic

trans transactions, transfer, transferred, transitive, translated, translation, translator, transportation, transpose, transverse

transf transfer, transference, transferred

transl translated, translation

transp transparent, transportation

trav traveler, travels

treas treasurer, treasury

trf transfer, tuned radio frequency

trfd transferred

tricl triclinic (crystal)

trig trigonometric, trigonomy

trim trimetric (crystal)

triple triplicate

trit triturate

trl trail

trop tropic, tropical, tropics

ts tensile strength

TSgt technical sergeant

tsp teaspoon, teaspoonful

Tu thulium

Tu Tuesday

TU trade union, training unit

TUC Trades Union Congress (Brit.)

Tue, Tues Tuesday

Turk Turkey, Turkish

TV television, terminal velocity

TVA Tennessee Valley Authority

twp township

TX Texas

Ty territory

typ, typo, typog typographer, typographic, typographer

typo typographic error

typw typewriter, typewritten

U

u and (Ger. *und*), uncle, university, upper

U uranium

UAW United Automobile (Aircraft, and Agricultural Implement) Workers (of America)

uc upper case (printing)

UCMJ Uniform Code of Military Justice

UFO unidentified flying object

UHF ultra-high frequency

UJD Doctor of Civil and Canon Law (Lat. *Utriusque Juris Doctor*)

UK United Kingdom

Ukr Ukraine

ult ultimate, ultimately

ult, ulto last month (Lat. *ultimo*)

UMT universal military training

UMW United Mine Workers

UN United Nations

unabr unabridged

unb, unbd unbound (bookbinding)

undsgd undersigned

undtkr undertaker

UNEDA United Nations Economic Development Administration

Unesco, UNESCO United Nations Educational, Scientific, and Cultural Organization

ung ointment (Lat. *unguentum*)

UNICEF United Nations Children's Fund (originally United Nations International Children's Emergency Fund)

Unit Unitarian, Unitarianism

univ universal, universally, university

Univ Universalist

unl unlimited

unm unmarried

unof unofficial

unp unpaged

unpub unpublished

UNREF United Nations Refugee Emergency Fund

UNRRA United Nations Relief and Rehabilitation Administration

UNRWA United Nations Relief and Works Agency

UNSCOB United Nations Special Committee on the Balkans

UP Union Pacific (railroad), United Press

UPC universal product code

UPI United Press International

UPS United Parcel Service

UPU Universal Postal Union (of the United Nations)

Ur uranium

urol urology

Uru Uruguay, Uruguayan

us as above (Lat. *ut supra*), in the place mentioned above (Lat. *ubi supra*)

US United States

USA United States Army, United States of America

USAF United States Air Force

USC&GS United States Coast and Geodetic Survey

USCG United States Coast Guard

USDA United States Department of Agriculture

USES United States Employment Service

USIA United States Information Agency

USM United States Mail, United States Marines, United States Mint

USMA United States Military Academy

USMC United States Marine Corps, United States Maritime Commission

USN United States Navy

USNA United States Naval Academy

USNG United States National Guard

USNR United States Naval Reserve

USO United Service Organizations

USOE United States Office of Education

USP United States patent, United States Pharmacopoeia

US Pharm United States Pharmacopoeia

USPHS United States Public Health Service

USPS United States Postal Service

USS United States Senate, United States Ship

USSCt United States Supreme Court

USSR Union of Soviet Socialist Republics

usu usual, usually

usw and so forth (Ger. *und so weiter*)

USW United Steel Workers

ut universal time, utility

Ut, UT Utah

UTC universal time coordinate

ut dict as directed (Lat. *ut dictum*)

ut sup as above (Lat. *ut supra*)

UTWA United Textile Workers of America

ux wife (Lat. *uxor*)

V

v against (Lat. *versus*), of (Ger. *von*), see (Lat. *vide*), valve, ventral, verb, verse, version, versus, vicar, vice-, village, vision, vocative, voice, volt, voltage, volume, volunteer, von

V vanadium, vector, velocity, venerable, victory, viscount, volume

va active verb, verbal adjective, volt-ampere

Va Virginia

VA Veterans Administration, Vicar apostolic, vice admiral, (Order of) Victoria and Albert, Virginia

vac vacuum

val valentine, valuation, value

var reactive volt-ampere, variant, variation, variety, various

Vat Vatican

VAT value-added tax

v aux auxiliary verb

vb verb, verbal

vb n verbal noun

VC Veterinary Corps, vice chairman, vice chancellor, vice consul, Victoria Cross

vd vapor density, various dates

Vd vanadium

VD venereal disease

VDT video display terminal

VDU video display unit

veg vegetable, vegetation

vel vellum (bookbinding)

Ven venerable, Venice, Venus

Venez Venezuela, Venezualan

vent ventilating, ventilation, ventilator

ver verse, version

vers versed sine, versine

vert vertebra, vertebrate, vertical

ves vessel, vestry, vesicle, vesicular

vet veteran, veterinarian, veterinary

veter veterinary

VFD volunteer fire department

VFR visual flight rules

VFW Veterans of Foreign Wars (of the United States)

vg for example (Lat. *verbi gratia*)

VG vicar general

VHF very high frequency

vi see below (Lat. *vide infra*), intransitive verb

Vi virginium

VI Virgin Islands

vic vicar, vicarage

Vic, Vict Victoria, Victorian

vil village

v imp impersonal verb

VIP very important person

v irr irregular verb

vis visibility, visual

Vis, Visc, Visct viscount, viscountess

VISTA Volunteers in Service to America

viv lively (music) (Lat. *vivace*)

viz namely (Lat. *videlicet*)

VL Vulgar Latin

VLF very low frequency

vm voltmeter

VMD Doctor of Veterinary Medicine (Lat. *Veterinariae Medicinae Doctor*)

vn, v neut neuter verb

vo verso

vocab vocabulary

vol volcano, volume, volunteer

volc volcanic, volcano

vols volumes

vox pop voice of the people (Lat. *vox populi*)

voy voyage

vp passive verb, various pagings, various places, voting pool (stocks)

VP vice president

vr reflexive verb

VR Queen Victoria (Lat. *Victoria Regina*)

V Rev very reverend

vs see above (Lat. *vide supra*), versus, vibration seconds (sound), volumetric solution

VS veterinary surgeon

VSS versions

vt transitive verb

Vt, VT Vermont

VTOL vertical take-off and landing

Vul, Vulg Vulgate
vulg vulgar, vulgarity
vv verses, vice versa, violins

W

w wanting, warden, warehousing, watt, week, weight, west, western, wide, width, wife, with, won, word, work
W tungsten (Ger. *wolfram*), Wales, Washington, watt, Wednesday, Welsh, west, western
WA Washington (state)
WAC Women's Army Corps
wae when actually employed
WAF Women in the Air Force
war warrant
WASP Women's Air Force Service Pilots
watt-hr watt-hour
WAVES Women Appointed for Voluntary Emergency Service
wb warehouse book, water ballast, westbound
W/B waybill
WbN west by north
WbS west by south
wc water closet, without charge
WCTU Women's Christian Temperance Union
Wed Wednesday
wf wrong font (printing)
WFlem West Flemish

WFTU World Federation of Trade Unions
WGmc, WGer West Germanic
wh, whr watt-hour
whf wharf
WHO World Health Organization (of the United Nations)
wi when issued (stocks), wrought iron
WI West Indies, West Indian, Wisconsin
WInd West Indies
Wis, Wisc Wisconsin
wk weak, week, work
wkly weekly
wks weeks, works
wl water line, wavelength
wldr welder
W long west longitude
wm wattmeter
wmk watermark
WMO World Meteorological Organization (of the United Nations)
WNW west-northwest
WO wait order, warrant officer
wp weather permitting, wire payment, word processing
WPA Work Projects Administration, Works Progress Administration
wpm words per minute
WRAC Women's Royal Army Corps
WRAF Women's Royal Air Force

WREN, WRNS Women's Royal Naval Service
wrnt warrant
WSW west-southwest
wt weight
WV, WVa West Virginia
WVS Women's Volunteer Service
WY, Wyo Wyoming

X

x symbol for an unknown quantity
X Christ, Christian, a ten-dollar bill, xenon
xc ex-coupon
xd unlisted (ex-directory), ex-dividend
Xe xenon
x-int ex-interest
Xmas Christmas
Xn Christian
Xnt Christianity
x ref cross-reference
x-rts ex-rights
Xtian Christian
Xty Christianity
xyl xylograph

Y

y yard, year, younger, youngest
Y Young Men's Christian Association, Young Men's Hebrew Association, Young Women's Christian Associ-

ation, Young Women's Hebrew Association, yttrium
Yb ytterbium
yd yard
yds yards
Yid Yiddish
YM, YMCA Young Men's Christian Association
YM, YMHA Young Men's Hebrew Association
YPSCE Young People's Society of Christian Endeavor
yr year, younger, your
yrs years, yours
YSL Young Socialists' League
Yt yttrium
YT Yukon Territory
YW Young Women's Christian Association, Young Women's Hebrew Association
YWCA Young Women's Christian Association
YWHA Young Women's Hebrew Association

Z

z zone
Z zenith distance, zone
Zec, Zech Zechariah
Zep, Zeph Zephaniah
Z/F zone of fire
Zn zinc
zool zoological, zoologist, zoology
ZPG zero population growth
Zr zirconium

Gazetteer

This section lists all of the more important political divisions and geographical features of the world, and all the urban localities in the United States and Canada having a population of 15,000 or more. The population figures given for places in the United States are from the census of 1980; those for Canada are from the census of 1976. All other population figures are from the latest available official censuses or official estimates, usually 1990. Maps of virtually all countries and of other important geographical features may be found in the main section of this dictionary at the appropriate alphabetic place of entry.

Postal ZIP codes are included for places in the United States. These were not, however, available in all cases. The asterisk (*) following some ZIP codes indicates that the city is further divided into postal zones and that the number given does not adequately identify a post office. In such cases further information is available from local postal authorities.

In the table below the authorized post office abbreviations of U.S. states are listed.

Alabama	AL	Kentucky	KY	Ohio	OH
Alaska	AK	Louisiana	LA	Oklahoma	OK
Arizona	AZ	Maine	ME	Oregon	OR
Arkansas	AR	Maryland	MD	Pennsylvania	PA
California	CA	Massachusetts	MA	Puerto Rico	PR
Colorado	CO	Michigan	MI	Rhode Island	RI
Connecticut	CT	Minnesota	MN	South Carolina	SC
Delaware	DE	Mississippi	MS	South Dakota	SD
District of		Missouri	MO	Tennessee	TN
Columbia	DC	Montana	MT	Texas	TX
Florida	FL	Nebraska	NE	Utah	UT
Georgia	GA	Nevada	NV	Vermont	VA
Hawaii	HI	New Hampshire	NH	Virginia	VA
Idaho	ID	New Jersey	NJ	Virgin Islands	VI
Illinois	IL	New Mexico	NM	Washington	WA
Indiana	IN	New York	NY	West Virginia	WV
Iowa	IA	North Carolina	NC	Wisconsin	WI
Kansas	KS	North Dakota	ND	Wyoming	WY

The following abbreviations have been used throughout this section:

ab.	about	pop.	population
adm.	administrative	poss.	possession
ASSR	Autonomous Soviet	prot.	protectorate
	Socialist Republic	prov.	province
betw.	between	reg.	region
boro.	borough	RSFSR	Russian Soviet
caps(s).	capital(s)		Federated Social-
CEN.	central		ist Republic
co.	county	s	south(ern)
col.	colony	SE	southeast(ern)
ctr.	center	sq. mi.	square mile(s)
dept.	department	SSR	Soviet Socialist
dist.	district		Republic
div.	division	sw	southwest(ern)
E	east(ern)	terr.	territory
ft.	feet	twp.	township
isl(s).	island(s)	uninc.	unincorporated
mi.	mile(s)	urb.	urban
mtn(s).	mountain(s)	USSR	Union of Soviet So-
N	north(ern)		cialist Republics
NE	northeaster(ern)	vill.	village
NW	northwest(ern)	w	west(ern)
penin.	Peninsula		

Aachen city, w West Germany; pop. 242,971.
Aarhus co., E Denmark; 310 sq. mi.; pop. 534,000.
— city, E Aarhus co.; cap.; pop. 244,839.
Aberdeen co., NE Scotland; 1,972 sq. mi.; pop. 324,574.
— city, SE Aberdeen co.; cap.; pop. 209,189.
— city, NE South Dakota 57401*; pop. 25,851.
— city, w Washington 98520; pop. 18,739.
Abidjan city, SE Ivory Coast; cap.; pop. 1,100,000.
Abilene city, CEN. Texas 79604*; pop. 98,315.
Acapulco city, sw Mexico; pop. 421,100.
Accra city, s Ghana; cap.; pop. 633,880.
Achaea dept., N Peloponessus, Greece; 1,146 sq. mi.; pop. 229,000; cap. Patras.
Aconcagua extinct volcano, CEN. Argentina; 22,831 ft.
Acre city, NE Israel; pop. 37,900.
Addis Ababa city, CEN. Ethiopia; cap.; pop. 1,125,340.
Addison vill. NE Illinois 60101; pop. 29,826.
Adelaide city, SE South Australia; cap.; pop. 933,350.
Aden former British col.; now part of Yemen.
— city, Yemen; pop. 318,000.
Aden, Gulf of inlet of Arabian Sea betw. People's Democratic Republic of Yemen and Somalia.
Aden Protectorate former group of Arab tribal districts comprising a British protectorate; now part of Yemen.
Adirondack Mountains mtn. range, NE New York.
Adrian city, SE Michigan 49221; pop. 21,276.
Adriatic Sea inlet of the Mediterranean Sea, E of Italy.
Aegean Sea inlet of the Mediterranean Sea betw. Greece and Asia Minor.
Afghanistan republic, sw Asia; 251,825 sq. mi.; pop. 15,592,000; cap. Kabul.
Africa second largest continent, s of Europe and w of Asia; 11,710,000 sq. mi.
Affton uninc. place, NE Missouri 63123; pop. 23,181.
Agaña city, w Guam 96910; cap.; pop. 896.
Agawam town, w Massachusetts 01001; pop. 26,271.
Agra city, N India; site of Taj Mahal; pop. 591,917.
Aguadilla town, NW Puerto Rico 00603*; pop. 20,879.
Aguascalientes state, CEN. Mexico; 2,499 sq. mi.; pop. 430,000.
— city, CEN. Aguascalientes state; cap.; pop. 247,800.
Agulhas, Cape cape, s South Africa; southernmost point of Africa.
Ahmedabad city, w India; former cap. of Gujarat; pop. 1,585,544.
Aisne river, N France; 175 mi. long.
Ajaccio city, w Corsica; cap.; birthplace of Napoleon; pop. 41,000.
Akron city, NE Ohio 44309*; pop. 237,177.
Alabama state, SE United States; 51,609 sq. mi.; pop. 3,893,978; cap. Montgomery.
Alameda city, w California 94501*; pop. 63,852.
Alamogordo town, s New Mexico 88310; site of the first atom bomb test; pop. 24,024.
Alaska state of the United States, NW North America; 586,412 sq. mi.; pop. 401,851; cap. Juneau.
Alaska, Gulf of inlet of the Pacific on the s coast of Alaska.
Alaska Highway road joining Dawson Creek, British Columbia and Fairbanks, Alaska; 1,527 mi.
Alaska Peninsula promontory of sw Alaska; ab. 400 mi. long.
Alaska Range mtn. range, CEN. Alaska.
Albania Balkan republic s of Yugoslavia; 11,100 sq. mi.; pop. 3,262,000; cap. Tirana.
Albany city sw Georgia 31701*; pop. 83,245.
— city, E New York 12207*; cap.; pop. 101,727.
— city, w Oregon 97321; pop. 28,062.

Albemarle Sound inlet of the Atlantic, NE North Carolina.

Alberta prov., W Canada; 255,290 sq. mi.; pop. 1,838,037; cap. Edmonton.

Albert Lea city, S Minnesota 56007; pop. 19,200.

Albuquerque city, NW New Mexico 87101*; pop. 332,336.

Alcan Highway *unofficial name of* Alaska Highway.

Alderney island, N Channel Islands; 3 sq. mi.

Aleppo city, NE Syria; pop. 878,000.

Aleutian Islands isl. group, SW of Alaska Peninsula.

Alexandria N Egypt; summer cap., pop. 2,409,000.

— city, CEN. Louisiana 71301*; pop. 51.565.

— city, NE Virginia 22313*; pop. 103,217.

Algeria republic, NW Africa; 919,595 sq. mi.; pop. 23,039,000; cap. Algiers.

Algiers city, N Algeria; cap.; pop. 1,507,241.

Alhambra city, SW California 91802*; pop. 82,106.

Alicante prov., E Spain; 2,264 sq. mi.; pop. 920,000.

— city, E Alicante prov.; cap.; pop. 235,868.

Alice city, S Texas, 78332; pop. 20,961.

Aliquippa boro., W Pennsylvania 15001; pop. 17,094.

Allahabad city N India; pop. 490,622.

Allegheny Mountains mtn. range of Appalachian system; extends from Pennsylvania through Virginia.

Allegheny River river, W New York and Pennsylvania; 325 mi. long.

Allen Park vill., SE Michigan 48101; pop. 34,196.

Allentown city, E Pennsylvania 18101*; pop. 103,758.

Alliance city, NE Ohio 44601; pop. 24,315.

Alma city, S Quebec, Canada; pop. 25,638.

Alma-Ata city, SE Kazakh SSR; cap.; pop. 928,000.

Alps mtn. system, S Europe; extends from S coast of France to W coast of Yugoslavia.

Alsace reg. and former prov., NE France.

Alsace-Lorraine oft-disputed border reg., NE France; adjoins SW Germany

Altadena uninc. place, SW California 91001; pop. 40,983.

Altai Mountains mtn. system, CEN. Asia.

Altamont uninc. place, S Oregon 97601; pop. 19,805.

Alton city, SW Illinois 62002; pop. 34,171.

Altoona city, CEN. Pennsylvania 16603*; pop. 57,078.

Altus city, SW Oklahoma 73521*; pop. 23,101.

Alum Rock uninc. place, SW California 95116; pop. 16,890.

Amarillo city, NW Texas 79105*; pop. 149,230.

Amazon river, N South America; 3,910 mi. long; carries the largest volume of water of all rivers.

America 1 The United States of America. 2 North and South America; the western Hemisphere.

American Samoa See **Samoa.**

Americus city, CEN. Georgia 31709; pop. 16,120.

Ames city, CEN. Iowa 50010*; pop. 45,775.

Amherst uninc. place, CEN. Massachusetts 01002*; pop. 33,229.

Amiens city, N France; pop. 131,476.

Amman city, CEN. Jordan; cap.; pop. 648,587.

Amoy isl. of China, Formosa Strait.

— city, Amoy isl.; pop. 224,000.

Amritsar city, W Punjab, India; pop. 407,628.

Amsterdam city, W Netherlands; cap.; pop. 694,680.

— city, CEN. New York 12010; pop. 21,872.

Amur river, E Asia; 2,700 mi. long.

Anaheim city, SW California 92803*; pop. 219,494.

Anatolia penin. at W end of Asia; comprises most of Turkey.

Anchorage city, S Alaska 99510*; pop. 174,431.

Andalusia reg., S Spain.

Anderson city, CEN. Indiana 46011*; pop. 64,695.

— city, NW South Carolina 29621*; pop. 27,546.

Andes mtn. range, W South America; connects with the Rockies; more than 4,000 mi. long.

Andorra Co-principality betw. France and Spain; 181 sq. mi.; pop. 51,000.

— city, CEN. Andorra; cap.; pop. 2,000.

Andover town, NE Massachusetts 01810; pop. 26,370.

Angel Falls waterfall, SE Venezuela; more than 3,300 ft.

Angola republic, W Africa; 481,354; sq. mi.; pop. 10,002,000; cap. Luanda.

Anjou town, S Quebec, Canada; pop. 36,596.

Ankara city, CEN. Turkey; cap.; pop. 2,553,209.

Annandale uninc. place, NE Virginia 22003; pop. 49,524.

Annapolis city, CEN. Maryland 21401*; cap.; site of U.S. Naval Academy; pop. 31,740.

Ann Arbor city, SE Michigan 48106*; pop. 107,969.

Anniston city, NE Alabama 36201*; pop. 29,523.

Ansonia city, SW Connecticut 06401; pop. 19,039.

Antarctica continent surrounding the South Pole; 5,405,000 sq. mi. Also **Antarctic Continent.**

Antarctic Circle parallel of latitude at 66° 33′ S; the boundary of the South Frigid Zone.

Antarctic Ocean parts of Atlantic, Pacific, and Indian oceans bordering on Antarctica.

Antarctic Zone region enclosed by the Antarctic Circle.

Antiqua and Barbuda monarchy, island group of the West Indies; 171 sq. mi.; pop. 80,600; cap. St. John's.

Antilles islands of the West Indies excluding the Bahamas; comprises Greater Antilles: Cuba, Hispaniola, Jamaica, and Puerto Rico; and Lesser Antilles: Trinidad, the Windward Islands, the Leeward Islands, and other small islands.

Antioch city, S Turkey; pop. 91,511.

— city, W California 94509; pop. 42,683.

Antwerp city, N Belgium; pop. 1,105,000.

Apennines mtn. range of Italy S of Po valley.

Appalachian Mountains E North America.

Appleton city, E Wisconsin 54911*; pop. 58,913.

Aquitaine reg., SW France.

Arabia penin., SW Asia, betw. the Red Sea and Persian Gulf.

Arabian Gulf See **Persian Gulf.**

Arabian Sea part of the Indian Ocean betw. Arabia and India.

Arab Republic of Egypt See **Egypt.**

Aragon reg., NE Spain.

Aral Sea salt inland sea, CEN. **USSR.**

Ararat, Mount mtn., E Turkey; 17,011 ft.; traditional landing place of Noah's ark.

Arcadia dept., CEN. Peloponnesus, Greece; 1,168 sq. mi.; pop. 112,000; cap. Tripolis.

— city, SW California 91006*; pop. 45,993.

Arctic Circle parallel of latitude at 66° 33′ N; the boundary of the North Frigid Zone.

Arctic Ocean sea, N of Arctic Circle, surrounding North Pole.

Arden-Arcade uninc. place, CEN. California 95825; pop. 89,600.

Ardmore city, S Oklahoma 73401; pop. 23,689.

Arecibo town, N Puerto Rico 00612*; pop. 48,586.

Argentina republic, S South America; 1,073,399 sq. mi.; pop. 23,364,431; cap. Buenos Aires.

Argonne ridge, N France; site of battles in World Wars I and II.

Arizona state, SW United States; 113,909 sq. mi.; pop. 2,718,425; cap. Phoenix.

Arkansas state, CEN. United States; 53,104 sq. mi.; pop. 2,286,419; cap. Little Rock.

Arkhangelsk city, NW RSFSR; pop. 387,000.

Arlington town, E Massachusetts 02174; pop. 48,219;

— city, N Texas 76010*; pop. 160,113.

— uninc. place, NE Virginia 22210*; pop. 152,599.

— urb. co., NE Virginia; site of **Arlington National Cemetery,** containing tomb of the Unknown Soldier.

Arlington Heights vill., NE Illinois 60004*; pop. 66,116.

Armenia 1 former country, SW Asia. 2 the Armenian SSR.

Armenian SSR republic, S USSR; 11,500 sq. mi.; pop. 3,074,000, cap. Yerevan.

Arnhem city, E Netherlands; pop. 127,846.

Aruba island member of the Netherlands, N of Venezuala; 75 sq. mi.; pop. 62,900; cap. Oranjestad.

Arvada town, CEN. Colorado 80001*; pop. 84,576.

Arvida city, CEN. Quebec, Canada; pop. 18,448.

Asbury Park city, E New Jersey 07712; pop. 17,015.

Ascension isl. poss. of Great Britain, South Atlantic; 34 sq. mi.; pop. 750.

Asheville city, W North Carolina 28801*; pop. 53,583.

Ashland city, NE Kentucky 41101; pop. 27,064.

— city, CEN. Ohio 44805; pop. 20,326.

Ashtabula city, NE Ohio 44004; pop. 23,449.

Asia, E part of Eurasian land mass; largest of the continents; 17,240,000 sq. mi.

Asia Minor penin. of extreme W Asia, comprising most of Turkey.

Aspen Hill uninc. place, NW Maryland 20906; pop. 47,455.

Astrakhan city, SE RSFSR; pop. 465,000.
Asunción city, SW Paraguay; cap.; pop. 607,706.
Aswan city, S Egypt; site of **Aswan Dam,** 1¼ mi. long; pop. 144, 377.
Athens city, SE Greece; cap.; pop. 2,885,737.
— city, CEN. Georgia, 30603*; pop. 42,549.
— city, SE Ohio 45701; pop. 19,743.
Atlanta city, CEN. Georgia 30301*; cap.; pop. 425,022.
Atlantic City city, SE New Jersey 08401*; pop. 40,199.
Atlantic Ocean ocean, extending from the Arctic to the Antarctic between the Americas and Europe and Africa.
Atlas Mountains mtn. range, NW Africa.
Attleboro city, SE Massachusetts 02703; pop. 34,196.
Auburn city, CEN. Alabama 36830*; pop. 28,471.
— city, SW Maine 04210; pop. 23,128.
— town, CEN. Massachusetts 01501; pop. 14,845.
— city, CEN. New York 13021; pop. 32,548.
— city, CEN. Washington, 98002*; pop. 26,417.
Auckland city, N North Island, New Zealand; pop. 775,000.
Augsburg city, S Germany; pop. 245,940.
Augusta city, E Georgia 30901*; pop. 47,532.
— city, S Maine 04330; cap.; pop. 21,819.
Aurora city, CEN. Colorado 80010*; pop. 158,588.
— city, NE Illinois 60507*; pop. 81,293.
Auschwitz, German name for Ošwiecim, city, SW Poland; site of Nazi extermination camp in World War II; pop. 44,200.
Austin city, SE Minnesota 55912; pop. 23,020.
— city, CEN. Texas 78710*; cap.; pop. 345,890.
Austintown uninc. place, NE Ohio 44515; pop. 33,636.
Australasia isls. of the South Pacific, including Australia, New Zealand, and New Guinea.
Australia federal state, situated on an isl. continent in South Pacific; 2,966,200 sq. mi.; pop. 17,073,000; cap. Canberra.
Australia Capital Territory reg., SE Australia; 900 sq. mi.; contains Canberra, the capital; pop. 241.500.
Austria republic, CEN. Europe; 32,376 sq. mi.; pop. 7,623,000.
Austronesia isls. of the South Pacific, including Indonesia, Melanesia, Micronesia, and Polynesia.
Avignon city, SE France; pop. 90,786.
Avon river, CEN. England; 96 mi. long.
Azerbaijan prov., NW Iran: **Eastern Azerbaijan:** 25,908 sq. mi.; pop. 4,097,000; cap. Tabriz; **Western Azerbaijan:** 15,000 sq. mi.; pop. 1,915,000; cap. Orumiyeh.
Azerbaijan SSR republic, SW USSR; 33,400 sq. mi.; pop. 6,112,000; cap. Baku.
Azores three isl. groups of Portugal, E Atlantic; 922 sq mi.; pop. 335,000.
Azov, Sea of inlet of the Black Sea, S USSR.
Azusa city, S California 91702; pop. 29,380.
Baden-Baden city, SW Germany; site of famous mineral springs; pop. 49,399.
Bad Lands arid plateau, South Dakota and Nebraska. also **Badlands.**
Baghdad city, CEN. Iraq; cap.; pop. 5,348,117.
Baguio city, Luzon, N Philippines; pop. 97,449.
Bahamas isl. republic SE of Florida; 5,382 sq. mi.; pop. 253,000; cap. Nassau.
Bahrain isl. monarchy, Persian Gulf near Saudi Arabia; 267 sq. mi.; pop. 503,000; cap. Manama.
Baikal freshwater lake, S USSR; 12,150 sq. mi.
Baker, Mount mtn., Cascade range, N Washington; 10,750 ft.
Bakersfield city, S California 93302*; pop. 105,735.
Baku city, SE Azerbaijan SRR; cap.; pop. 1,800,000.
Balboa Heights adm. ctr. of Canal Zone, near Balboa; pop. 232.
Baldwin uninc. place, SE New York 11510; pop. 31,630.
— boro., SW Pennsylvania 15234; pop. 24,714.
Baldwin Park city, SW California 91706; pop. 50,554.
Balearic Islands isl. group, W Mediterranean; prov. of Spain; 1,936 sq. mi.; pop. 642,702; cap. Palma.
Bali isl. of Indonesia, E of Java; 2,243 sq. mi.
Balkan Mountains, mtn. range, Balkan penin.
Balkan Peninsula large penin. of SE Europe.
Balkan States countries of Balkan penin.: Albania, Bulgaria, Greece, Rumania, Yugoslavia, and part of Turkey.
Baltic Sea inlet of the Atlantic in NW Europe.
Baltimore city, N Maryland 21233*; pop. 786,741.
Bamako city, CEN. Mali; cap.; pop. 646,163.

Banaras Hindu sacred city, NE India; pop. 553,000. Also **Benares.**
Bandar Seri Begawan city, N Brunei; cap.; pop. 37,000.
Bandung city, W Java, Indonesia; pop. 1,201,730.
Bangalore city, E Mysore, India; cap.; pop. 1,540,741.
Bangkok city, SW Thailand; cap.; pop. 3,133,834.
Bangladesh republic, S Asia; 55,598 sq. mi.; pop. 113,005,000; cap. Dacca.
Bangor city, CEN. Maine 04401; pop. 31,643.
Bangui city, SW Central African Republic; cap.; pop. 596,776.
Banjul city, W Gambia; cap.; pop. 45,600.
Barbados isl. monarchy, E Caribbean; 166 sq. mi.; pop. 267,000; cap. Bridgetown.
Barberton city, NE Ohio 44203; pop. 29,751.
Barcelona prov., NE Spain; 2,985 sq. mi.; pop. 3,975,000.
— city, S Barcelona prov.; cap.; pop. 1,902,713.
Barnstable town, SE Massachusetts 02630; pop. 30,898.
Barranquilla city, N Colombia; pop. 859,000.
Barrie city, S Ontario, Canada; pop. 34,389.
Barrington town, E Rhode Island 02806; pop. 16,174.
Barrow, Point extreme N point of Alaska.
Barstow city, E California 92311; pop. 17,690.
Bartlesville city, NE Oklahoma 74003*; pop. 34,568.
Basel city, N Switzerland; pop. 180,900.
Bataan prov. S Luzon, Philippines; 517 sq. mi.; pop. 116,000; cap. Balanga; occupies **Bataan Peninsula,** scene of World War II surrender of U.S. forces to the Japanese.
Batavia city, W New York 14020; pop. 16,703.
Bath co. boro., SW England; pop. 83,900.
Bathurst town, NE New Brunswick, Canada; pop. 16,301.
— Banjul; *the former name of.*
Baton Rouge city, CEN. Louisiana 70821*; cap.; pop. 238,876.
Battle Creek city, S Michigan 49016*; pop. 56,339.
Bavaria state, SE Germany; 27,241 sq. mi.; pop. 10,870,968; cap. Munich.
Bayamon town, N Puerto Rico 00619; pop. 184,854.
Bay City city, CEN. Michigan 48706*; pop. 41,593.
Bayonne city, NE New Jersey 07002; pop. 65,047.
Baytown city, S Texas 77520*; pop. 56,923.
Bay Village city, NE Ohio 44140; pop. 17,846.
Beaconsfield town, S Quebec, Canada; pop. 20,417.
Beaumont city, SE Texas 77701*; pop. 118,102.
Beaverton city, NW Oregon 97005*; pop. 31,926.
Beckley city, S West Virginia 25801*; pop. 20,492.
Bedford city, NE Ohio 44146; pop. 15,056.
Beijing. See **Peking.**
Beirut city, W Lebanon; cap.; pop. 200,000.
Belém city, N Brazil; pop. 565,097.
Belfast co. boro., and port, SE N. Ireland; cap.; pop. 354,400.
Belgium monarchy, NW Europe; 11,783 sq. mi.; pop. 9,958,000; cap. Brussels.
Belgrade city E Yugoslavia; cap.; pop. 770,140.
Belize monarchy, NE Central America; 8,867 sq. mi.; pop. 189,000; cap. Belmopan.
Bell city, S California 90201; pop. 25,450.
Bellaire city, S Texas 77401; pop. 14,950.
Belle Glade city, SE Florida 33430; pop. 16,535.
Belleville city, SW Illinois 62220*; pop. 41,580.
— town, NE New Jersey 07109; pop. 35,367.
— city, SE Ontario, Canada; pop. 35,311.
Bellevue city, E Nebraska 68005; pop. 21,813.
— city, CEN. Washington 98009*; pop. 73,903.
Bellflower city, SW California 90706; pop. 53,441.
Bell Gardens city, SW California 90201; pop. 34,117.
Bellingham city, NW Washington 98225*; pop. 45,794.
Bellmawr boro., SW New Jersey 08031; pop. 13,721.
Bellmore uninc. place, SE New York 11710; pop. 18,106.
Bellwood vill., NE Illinois 60104; pop. 19,811.
Belmont city, CEN. California 94002; pop. 24,505.
— town, E Massachusetts 02178; pop. 26,100.
Beloit city, S Wisconsin 53511; pop. 35,207.
Bengal former prov., NE British India; divided (1947) into; East Bengal, now part of Bangladesh, and **West Bengal,** a state of India; 34,200 sq. mi.; pop. 49,788,000; cap. Calcutta.
Benghazi city, N Libya; pop. 170,000.
Benin republic, W Africa; 43,450 sq. mi.; pop. 4,741,000.
Benton city, CEN. Arkansas 72015; pop. 17,717.
Benton Harbor city, SW Michigan 49022; pop. 14,707.

Berea city, NE Ohio 44017; pop. 19,567.

Bergen city, SW Norway; pop. 209,000.

Bergenfield boro., NE New Jersey 07621; pop. 25,568.

Bering Sea part of the North Pacific betw. Alaska and the USSR, joined to the Arctic by **Bering Strait.**

Berkeley city, W California 94701*; pop. 103,328.

— city, CEN. Missouri 63134; pop. 15,922.

Berkley city, SE Michigan 48072; pop. 18,637.

Berlin city, CEN. Germany; cap. prior to 1945 when divided into the British, French, Soviet, and US sectors. In 1949 the Soviet sector, **East Berlin,** was designated capital of East Germany. The remaining sectors formed **West Berlin,** associated with West Germany; when Germany was reunited in 1990, Berlin became the capital again in 1991; pop. 3,352,848.

— city, N New Hampshire 03570; pop. 13,084.

Bermuda isl. group, W Atlantic; British col.; 21 sq. mi. pop. 59,330, cap. Hamilton.

Bern city, CEN. Switzerland; cap.; pop. 141,300. Also **Berne.**

Berwyn city, NE Illinois 60402; pop. 46,849.

Bessemer city, CEN. Alabama 35020*; pop. 31,729.

Bethany city, CEN. Oklahoma 73008; pop. 22,038.

Bethel Park boro., SW Pennsylvania 15102; pop. 34,755.

Bethesda uninc. area, W Maryland 20814*; pop. 63,022.

Bethlehem ancient town, W Jordan; birthplace of Jesus; pop. 25,000.

— city, E Pennsylvania 18016*; pop. 70,419.

Bettendorf city, CEN. Iowa 52722; pop. 27,381.

Beverly city, NE Massachusetts 01915; pop. 37,655.

Beverly Hills city, SW California, 90210*; pop. 32,646.

Bhutan monarchy, S Asia, between NE India and Tibet; 18,150 sq. mi.; pop. 1,442,000; cap. Thimphu.

Biddeford city, SW Maine 04005; pop. 19,638.

Big Spring city, W Texas 79720*; pop. 24,804.

Bikini atoll, Marshall Islands; 2 sq. mi.; site of US nuclear tests, July 1946.

Billerica town, NE Massachusetts 01821; pop. 36,727.

Billings city, CEN. Montana 59011*; pop. 66,824.

Biloxi city, SE Mississippi 39530*; pop. 49,311.

Binghamton city, CEN. New York 13902*; pop. 55,860.

Birkenhead co. boro., NW England; pop. 342,300.

Birmingham co. boro., CEN. England; pop. 1,033,900.

— city, CEN. Alabama 35203*; pop. 286,799.

— city, SE Michigan 48012*; pop. 21,689.

Biscay, Bay of inlet, of the Atlantic betw. W and SW France and N and NW Spain.

Bismarck city, CEN. North Dakota 58501*; cap.; pop. 44,485.

Bismarck Archipelago isl. group, Trust Territory of New Guinea; 19,200 sq. mi.

Bizerte city, N Tunisia; pop. 62,856.

Black Forest wooded mtn. reg., SW Germany.

Black Hills mtn. reg., SW South Dakota and NE Wyoming.

Black Sea inland sea betw. Europe and Asia, connects with the Aegean via the Bosporus, the Sea of Marmara, and the Dardanelles.

Blaine vill., E Minnesota 55433; pop. 28,558.

Bloomfield town, CEN. Connecticut 06002; pop. 18,608.

— city, NE New Jersey 07003; pop. 47,792.

Bloomington city, CEN. Illinois 61701; pop. 44,189.

— city, CEN. Indiana 47401*; pop. 52,044.

— city, E Minnesota 55420; pop. 81,831.

Bluefield city, S West Virginia 24701; pop. 16,060.

Blue Island city, NE Illinois 60406; pop. 21,855.

Blue Ridge Mountains, SW part of the Appalachians.

Blytheville city, NE Arkansas 72315*; pop. 23,844.

Boardman uninc. place, NE Ohio 44512; pop. 39,161.

Boca Raton city, SE Florida 33432*; pop. 49,447.

Bogalusa city, SE Louisiana 70427; pop. 16,976.

Bogotá city, CEN. Colombia; cap.; pop. 4,067,000.

Bohemia former prov., W Czechoslovakia.

Boise city, SW Idaho 83707*; cap.; pop. 102,160.

Bolivia republic, CEN. South America; 424,164 sq. mi.; pop. 7,332,000; caps. Sucre (judicial), La Paz (admin).

Bologna prov., CEN. Italy; 1,429 sq. mi.; pop. 925,113.

— city, cap. of Bologna prov.; pop. 422,204.

Bombay city, W India; pop. 5,970,575.

Bonn city, W Germany; was cap. of West Germany; pop. 286,184.

Bordeaux city, SW France; pop. 201,000.

Borneo (Kalimantan) isl., betw. Java and South China seas; comprising North Borneo, Sarawak, Brunei, and Indonesian Borneo; 286,969 sq. mi.

Bosnia and Herzegovina constituent republic, CEN. Yugoslavia; 19,741 sq. mi.; pop. 4,029,000; cap. Sarajevo.

Bosporus strait, betw. the Black Sea and the Sea of Marmara.

Bossier City city, NW Louisiana 71111*; pop. 50,817.

Boston city, E Massachusetts 02205*; cap.; pop. 562,994.

Botany Bay inlet of the Pacific, S of Sydney, Australia.

Botswana republic, S Africa; 224,607 sq. mi.; pop. 1,295,000; cap. Gaborone.

Boucherville town, S Quebec, Canada; pop. 25,530.

Boulder city, CEN. Colorado 80302*; pop. 76,685.

Boulder Dam *the former name of* Hoover Dam.

Bountiful city, CEN. Utah 84010; pop. 32,877.

Bowie city, CEN. Maryland 20715; pop. 33,695.

Bowling Green city, S Kentucky 42101*; pop. 40,450.

— city, NW Ohio 43402*; pop. 25,728.

Boynton Beach city, SE Florida 33435*; pop. 35,624.

Bozeman city, SW Montana 59715*; pop. 21,645.

Bradenton city, W Florida 33506*; pop. 30,228.

Braintree town, E Massachusetts 02184; pop. 36,337.

Brampton town, SE Ontario, Canada; pop. 103,459.

Brandon city, SW Manitoba, Canada; pop. 34,901.

Branford town, CEN. Connecticut 06405; pop. 23,363.

Brantford city, SE Ontario, Canada; pop. 66,950.

Brasilia city, CEN. Brazil; cap.; pop. 750,000.

Brazil republic, NE and CEN. South America; 3,286,500 sq. mi.; pop. 150,368,000; cap. Brasilia.

Brazzaville city, SE Congo; cap.; pop. 596,200.

Brea city, SW California 92621; pop. 27,913.

Breed's Hill hill, near Bunker Hill. See **Bunker Hill.**

Bremen state, NW Germany, 156 sq. mi.; pop. 695,115;

— city, cap. of Bremen state; pop. 556,128.

Bremerhaven city, part of Bremen state, NW Germany; pop. 138,987.

Bremerton city, W Washington 98310*; pop. 36,208.

Brenner Pass Alpine pass, Austrian–Italian border.

Brentwood uninc. place, SE New York 11717; pop. 48,800.

Breslau Wroclaw: German name of city in Poland.

Brest city, NW France; pop. 166,826.

— city, SW Byelorussian SSR; pop. 186,000.

Bridgeport city, SW Connecticut 06601*; pop. 142,546.

Bridgeton town, E Missouri 63044; pop. 18,445.

— city, SW New Jersey 08302; pop. 18,795.

Brighton co. boro. and resort, SW England; pop. 166,000.

Brisbane city, SE Queensland, Australia; cap.; pop. 1,240,300.

Bristol co. boro., SW England; pop. 408,000.

— city, CEN. Connecticut 06010; pop. 57,370.

— urb. twp., SE Pennsylvania 19007; pop. 10,867.

— town, E Rhode Island 02809; pop. 20,128.

— city, NE Tennessee 37620*; pop. 23,986.

Bristol Channel inlet of the Atlantic betw. Wales and SW England.

Britain see **Great Britain.**

British Columbia prov., W Canada; 358,971 sq. mi.; pop. 2,466,608; cap. Victoria.

British Guiana former British col., NE South America. See **Guyana.**

British Virgin Islands British col., E Greater Antilles; 59 sq. mi.; pop. 10,484; cap. Road Town.

British West Indies See **West Indies.**

Brittany reg., W France; former prov.

Brno city, CEN. Czechoslovakia; pop. 372,793.

Brockton city, E Massachusetts 02403*; pop. 95,172.

Brockville town, SE Ontario, Canada; pop. 19,903.

Bronx boro., N New York City 10451*; pop. 1,169,115. Also **the Bronx.**

Brookfield vill., NE Illinois 60513; pop. 19,395.

— city, SE Wisconsin 53005; pop. 34,035.

Brookline town, E Massachusetts 02146; pop. 55,062.

Brooklyn boro. SE New York City 11201*; pop. 2,250,000.

Brooklyn Center vill., SE Minnesota 55429; pop. 31,230.

Brooklyn Park vill., SE Minnesota 55007; pop. 43,332.

Brook Park vill., N Ohio 44142; pop. 26,195.

Brossard city, S Quebec, Canada; pop. 37,641.

Browardale uninc. place, SE Florida 33311; pop. 7,409.

Browns Village uninc place, SE Florida 33142; pop. 23,442.

Brownsville uninc. place, NW Florida 33142; pop. 18,058.
— city, s Texas 78520*; pop. 84,997.
Brownwood city, CEN. Texas 76801*; pop. 19,396.
Brunei sultanate, NW Borneo; 2,226 sq. mi.; pop. 259,000; cap. Bandar Sari Begawan.
Brunswick city, NE Germany; pop. 261,669.
— city, SE Georgia 31520*; pop. 17,605.
— uninc. place, s Maine 04011; pop. 17,366.
— vill., N Ohio 44212; pop. 28,104.
Brussels city, CEN. Belgium; cap.; pop. 2,400,000.
Bryan city, CEN. Texas 77801*; pop. 45,917.
Bucharest city, s Rumania; cap.; pop. 1,858,418.
Budapest city, CEN. Hungary; cap.; pop. 2,060,000.
Buena Park city, sw California 90622*; pop. 64,165.
Buenos Aires city, E Argentina; cap.; pop. 10,300,000.
Buffalo city, w New York 14240*; pop. 357,870.
Bulgaria republic, SE Europe; 42,855 sq. mi.; pop. 8,997,400; cap. Sofia.
Bull Run small stream, NE Virginia; site of Union defeats in the Civil War, 1861 and 1862.
Bunker Hill hill, Charlestown, Massachusetts, near which (on Breed's Hill) occurred the first organized engagement of the American Revolution, June 17, 1775.
Burbank city, sw California 91505*; pop. 84,625.
Burgundy reg., CEN. France.
Burkina Faso republic, w Africa; 105,869 sq. mi.; pop. 9,012,000; cap. Ouagadougou.
Burlingame city, CEN. California 94010*; pop. 26,173.
Burlington city, SE Iowa 52601*; pop. 29,529.
— town, NE Massachusetts 01803; pop. 23,486.
— city, CEN. North Carolina 27215*; pop. 37,266.
— city, NW Vermont 05401*; pop. 37,712.
— town, SE Ontario, Canada; pop. 104,314.
Burma See **Myanmar.**
Burma Road road betw. N Burma and sw China; a World War II supply route.
Burnsville city, SE Minnesota 55337; pop. 35,674.
Burundi military régime, CEN. Africa; *formerly part of* Ruanda-Urundi; 10,747 sq. mi.; pop. 5,451,000; cap. Bujumbura.
Butler city, w Pennsylvania 16001*; pop. 17,026.
Butte city, sw Montana 59701*; pop. 37,205.
Byelorussian SSR constituent republic, USSR; 80,200 sq. mi.; pop. 9,611,000; cap. Minsk.
Cádiz city, sw Spain; pop. 156,328.
Caguas town, CEN. Puerto Rico 00625*; pop. 87,218.
Cahokia vill. sw Illinois 62206; pop. 18,904.
Cairo city, NE Egypt; cap.; pop. 6,052,836.
Calais city, N France; pop. 78,820.
Calcutta city, NE India; pop. 3,148,746.
Calgary city, s Alberta, Canada; pop. 469,917.
Caticut *an alternate name of* Kozhikode.
California state, w United States; 158,693 sq. mi.; pop. 23,667,837; cap. Sacramento.
California, Gulf of inlet of the Pacific, w Mexico, betw. Lower California and the rest of Mexico.
Calumet City city, NE Illinois 60409; pop. 39,697.
Camarillo city, sw California 93010; pop. 37,797.
Cambodia (State of Kampuchia), republic, 70,238 sq. mi.; pop. 8,592,000; cap. Phnom Penh.
Cambridge city, SE England; site of Cambridge University; pop. 101,600.
— city, E Massachusetts 02138*; pop. 95,322.
Camden city, s Arkansas 71701; pop. 15,356.
— city, sw New Jersey 08101*; pop. 84,910.
Cameroon republic, w equatorial Africa; 179,714 sq. mi.; pop. 7,663,246; cap. Yaounde. Also **Cameroun.**
Campbell city, w California 95008; pop. 31,039.
Camp Le Jeune uninc. place, SE North Carolina 28542; pop. 30,764.
Camp Springs uninc. place, sw Maryland 20748; pop. 16,118.
Canada independent member of the Commonwealth of Nations, N North America; 3,849,675 sq. mi.; pop. 22,992,604; cap. Ottawa.
Canal Zone US leased terr., CEN. Panama; extending five miles on either side of the Panama Canal.
Canary Islands isl. group of Spain near NW coast of Africa; 2,796 sq. mi.; pop. 1,410,655.
Canaveral, Cape, cape, E Florida 32920; pop. 5,733; site of the

John F. Kennedy Space Center, a space research and missiles installation.
Canberra city, SE Australia; cap.; pop. 277,300.
Canea city, NW Crete; pop. 40,564. Also **Khania.**
Cannes city, SE France; pop. 70,527.
Canterbury co. boro., SE England; site of famous cathedral; pop. 34,512.
Canton city, s China; pop. 1,296,000.
— town, E Massachusetts 02021; pop. 18,182.
— city, NE Ohio 44701*; pop. 93,077.
Cap-de-la-Madeleine city, s Quebec, Canada; pop. 31,126.
Cape Girardeau city, SE Missouri 63701; pop. 34,361.
Cape Town city, s South Africa; legislative cap.; pop. 776,617. Also **Capetown.**
Cape Verde Islands republic in the CEN. Atlantic Ocean, w of Cape Verde; 1,557 sq. mi.; pop. 339,000; cap. Praia.
Capri isl. near the w coast of Italy; 4 sq. mi.
Caracas city, N Venezuela; cap.; pop. 1,658,500.
Carbondale city, s Illinois 62901; pop. 26,414.
Cardiff co. boro., SE Wales; pop. 282,000.
Caribbean Sea part of the Atlantic betw. the West Indies and Central and South America.
Carlisle boro., s Pennsylvania 17013; pop. 18,314.
Carlsbad city, SE New Mexico 88220; pop. 25,496.
Carlsbad Caverns National Park area, SE New Mexico; contains **Carlsbad Caverns,** a series of limestone caves.
Carmichael uninc. place, CEN. California 95608; pop. 43,108.
Carnegie boro., sw Pennsylvania 15106; pop. 10,099.
Carol City uninc place, SE Florida, 33055; pop. 47,349.
Caroline Islands isl. group in the Pacific, E of the Philippines; 463 sq. mi.
Carpathian Mountains mtn. range, CEN. and E Europe.
Carpentersville vill., NE Illinois 60110; pop. 23,272.
Carrara city, CEN. Italy; site of white marble quarries; pop. 70,227.
Carson city, sw California 90744; pop. 81,221.
Carson City city, w Nevada 89701*; cap.; pop. 32,022.
Carteret boro, NE New Jersey 07009; pop. 20,598.
Casablanca city, NW Morocco; pop. 1,506,373.
Cascade Range mtn. range in Oregon, Washington, and British Columbia.
Cashmere See **Kashmir.**
Casper city, CEN. Wyoming 82601*; pop. 51,016.
Caspian Sea saltwater lake in the s USSR and N Iran; 163,800 sq. mi.
Castile reg., N and CEN. Spain.
Castro Valley uninc. place, w California 94546; pop. 44,010.
Catalina Island *an alternate name of* Santa Catalina.
Catalonia reg. NE Spain.
Catania prov., E Sicily; 1,371 sq. mi.; pop. 1,029,515.
— city, Catania prov.; cap.; pop. 370,679.
Cataño town, N Puerto Rico 00638; pop. 26,318.
Catonsville uninc. place, CEN. Maryland 21228; pop. 33,208.
Catskill Mountains range of the Appalachians in SE New York.
Caucasus mtn. range betw. the Black and Caspian Seas.
— reg., sw USSR, betw. the Black and Caspian Seas. Also **Caucasia.**
Cayey town, CEN. Puerto Rico 00633; pop. 40,927.
Cedar Falls city, CEN. Iowa 50613; pop. 36,322.
Cedar Grove twp., NE New Jersey 07009; pop. 12,600.
Cedar Rapids city, E Iowa 52401; pop. 110,243.
Celebes *the former name of* Sulawesi.
Center Point uninc. place, CEN. Alabama 35215; pop. 23,317.
Central African Republic , republic, CEN. Africa; 240,324 sq. mi.; pop. 2,875,000; cap. Bangui.
Central America s part of North America, betw. Mexico and Colombia.
Central Falls city, NE Rhode Island 02863; pop. 16,995.
Centralia city, s Illinois 62801*; pop. 15,126.
Central Islip uninc. place, SE New York 11722; pop. 26,000.
Cerritos city, s California 90701; pop. 53,020.
Ceylon See **Sri Lanka.**
Chad, Lake lake, CEN. Africa; 8,000 sq. mi.
Chad, Republic of republic, CEN. Africa; 495,752 sq. mi.; pop. 5,678,000; cap. N'Djamena.
Chambersburg boro., s Pennsylvania 17201; pop. 16,174.
Champaign city, CEN. Illinois 61820; pop. 58,267.
Champlain, Lake lake, betw. New York and Vermont, extending into Canada; 600 sq. mi.

Changchun city, NE China; pop. 1,309,000.
Channel Islands British isl. group, English Channel near Normandy; includes Jersey, Guernsey, Alderney, and Sark; 75 sq. mi.
Chapel Hill town, CEN. North Carolina 27514*; pop. 32,421.
Charlesbourg city, s Quebec, Canada; pop. 63,147.
Charleston city, E Illinois 61920; pop. 19,355.
— city, SE South Carolina 29401*; pop. 69,855.
— city, CEN. West Virginia 25301*; cap.; pop. 63,968.
Charlotte city, CEN. North Carolina 28202*; pop. 315,473.
Charlotte Amalie city, s St. Thomas, U.S. Virgin Islands 00801*; cap.; pop. 12,220.
Charlottesville city, CEN. Virginia 22906*; pop. 39,916.
Charlottetown city, CEN. Prince Edward Island, Canada; cap.; pop. 17,063.
Chateauguay town, s Quebec, Canada; pop. 36,329.
Chatham city, s Ontario, Canada; pop. 38,685.
Chattanooga city, SE Tennessee 37401*; pop. 169,728.
Cheektowaga uninc. place, w New York 14225; pop. 92,145.
Chelmsford town, NE Massachusetts 01824; pop. 31,174.
Chelsea metropolitan boro., sw London, England; pop. 47,000.
— city, E Massachusetts 02150; pop. 25,431.
Cheltenham urb. twp., SE Pennsylvania 19012; pop. 35,509.
Cherbourg city, N France; pop. 32,536.
Chesapeake city, SE Virginia 23320*; pop. 114,486.
Chesapeake Bay inlet of the Atlantic in Virginia and Maryland.
Cheshire town, CEN. Connecticut 06410; pop. 21,788.
Chester co. boro., w Cheshire, England; cap.; pop. 61,370.
— city, SE Pennsylvania 19013*; pop. 45,794.
Cheviot Hills mtn. range, on the border betw. England and Scotland.
Cheyenne city, SE Wyoming 82001*; cap.; pop. 47,716.
Chicago city, NE Illinois 60607*; third largest city in the United States; pop. 3,005,072.
Chicago Heights city, NE Illinois 60411; pop. 37,026.
Chico city, CEN. California 95926*; pop. 26,716.
Chicopee city, sw Massachusetts 01021*; pop. 55,112.
Chicoutimi city, s Quebec, Canada; pop. 57,737.
Chihuahua state, N Mexico; 94,830 sq. mi.; pop. 2,000,000.
Chihuahua city, Chihuahua state, Mexico; cap.; pop. 369,500.
Chile republic, w South America; 292,153 sq. mi.; pop. 13,173,000; cap. Santiago.
Chillicothe city, CEN. Ohio 45601; pop. 23,420.
Chillum uninc. place, sw Maryland 20783; pop. 14,900.
China, People's Republic of republic, E and CEN. Asia; 3,696,100 sq. mi.; pop. 1,133,683,000; cap. Peking (Beijing).
China, Republic of (Taiwan) republic on Taiwan and several smaller isls.; 13,900 sq. mi.; pop. 20,221,000; cap. Taipei.
China Sea part of the Pacific bordering on China. See **East China Sea, South China Sea.**
Chino city, sw California 91710; pop. 40,165.
Chula Vista city, sw California 92010*; pop. 83,927.
Chungking city, CEN. China; cap. during World War II; pop. 1,900,000.
Cicero city, NE Illinois 60650; pop. 61,232.
Cincinnati city, sw Ohio 45234*; pop. 385,457.
Circassia reg., NW Caucasus, RSFSR.
Citrus Heights uninc. place, NE California 95610; pop. 85,911.
Clairton city, sw Pennsylvania 15025; pop. 12,188.
Claremont city, sw California 91711*; pop. 31,028.
Clark twp., NE New Jersey 07066; pop. 16,699.
Clarksburg city, N West Virginia 26301*; pop. 22,371.
Clarksdale city, NW Mississippi 38614; pop. 22,384.
Clarksville city, N Tennessee 37041*; pop. 54,777.
Clawson city, SE Michigan 48017; pop. 15,103.
Clayton city, E Missouri 63105; pop. 14,273.
Clearwater city, w Florida 33515*; pop. 85,528.
Cleburne city, CEN. Texas 76031; pop. 19,218.
Cleveland city, N Ohio 44101*; pop. 573,822.
— city, SE Tennessee 37311*; pop. 26,415.
Cleveland Heights city, N Ohio 44118; pop. 56,438.
Clifton city, NE New Jersey 07015*; pop. 74,388.
Clinton city, E Iowa 52732; pop. 32,828.
Clovis city, E New Mexico 88101; pop. 31,194.
Cocoa city, E Florida 32922*; pop. 16,096.
Cod, Cape penin., SE Massachusetts.
Coeur d'Alene city, N Idaho 83814; pop. 21,177.
Coffeyville city, SE Kansas 67337; pop. 15,185.

Cohoes city, E New York 12047; pop. 18,144.
College Park city, w Georgia 30337; pop. 24,632.
— city, w Maryland 20740*; pop. 23,614.
College Station city, CEN. Texas 77840*; pop. 37,272.
Collingswood boro., w New Jersey 08108; pop. 15,838.
Collinsville city, sw Illinois 62234; pop. 19,613.
Cologne city, w Germany; pop. 976,136.
Colombia republic, NW South America; 440,831 sq. mi.; pop. 32,978,000; cap. Bogotá.
Colombo city, w Sri Lanka; cap.; pop. 609,000.
Colón city, Caribbean end of the Canal Zone; an enclave of Panama; pop. 73,600.
Colonial Heights city, CEN. Virginia, 23834; pop. 16,509.
Colorado state, CEN. United States; 104,247 sq. mi.; pop. 2,889,735; cap. Denver.
Colorado River river flowing through Colorado, Utah, Arizona, California, and Mexico to the Gulf of California; length ab. 1,400 mi.
Colorado Springs city, CEN. Colorado 80901*; site of U.S. Air Force Academy; pop. 214,821.
Colton city, s California, 92324; pop. 15,201.
Columbia city, CEN. Missouri 65201*; pop. 62,061.
— city, CEN. South Carolina 29201*; cap.; pop. 101,229.
— city, CEN. Tennessee 38401*; pop. 26,571.
Columbia Heights city, E Minnesota 55421; pop. 20,029.
Columbia River river, sw Canada and NW United States; 1,200 mi. long.
Columbus, city, w Georgia 31902*; pop. 169,441.
— city, CEN. Indiana 47201*; pop. 30,614.
— city, E Mississippi 39701*; pop. 27,503.
— city, E Nebraska 68601; pop. 18,057.
— city, CEN. Ohio 43216*; cap.; pop. 565,032.
Commerce City town, CEN. Colorado 80022; pop. 16,234.
Comoros Islands isl. republic in the Indian Ocean, NW of Madagascar; 719 sq. mi.; pop. 463,000; cap. Moroni.
Compton city, sw California 90220*; pop. 81,230.
Conakry city, w Guinea; cap.; pop. 197,267.
Concord city, w California 94520*; pop. 103,763.
— town, NE Massachusetts 01742; pop. 16,293.
— uninc. place, NE Missouri 63128; pop. 20,896.
— city, CEN. New Hampshire 03301*; cap.; pop. 30,400.
— city, CEN. North Carolina 28025; pop. 16,942.
Congo republic, CEN. Africa; 132,047 sq. mi.; pop. 2,326,000; cap. Brazzaville.
Congo River river, CEN. Africa; 2,720 mi. long.
Connecticut state, NE United States; 5,009 sq. mi.; pop. 3,107,576; cap. Hartford.
Connersville city, E Indiana 47331; pop. 17,023.
Continental Divide ridge of the Rockies separating westflowing and east-flowing streams in North America.
Conway city, CEN. Arkansas 72032; pop. 20,375.
Coon Rapids vill., E Minnesota 55433; pop. 35,826.
Copenhagen city, E Denmark; cap.; pop. 1,343,916.
Copiague uninc. place, SE New York 11726; pop. 20,132.
Coral Gables city, SE Florida 33134; pop. 43,241.
Coral Sea part of the Pacific, E of Australia and New Guinea.
Cork co., sw Ireland; 2,880 sq. mi.; pop. 402,465.
— co. boro., CEN. Cork co.; cap.; pop. 138,267.
Corner Brook city, w Newfoundland, Canada; pop. 25,198.
Corning city, w New York 14830; pop. 12,953.
Cornwall city, sw Ontario, Canada; pop. 46,121.
Corona city, s California 91720; pop. 37,791.
Coronado city, s California 92118; pop. 18,790.
Corpus Christi city, s Texas 78408*; pop. 231,134.
Corsica isl., N Mediterranean; a dept. of France; 3,352. sq. mi.; pop. 244,600; cap. Ajaccio.
Corsicana city, CEN. Texas 75110; pop. 21,712.
Cortland city, CEN. New York 13045; pop. 20,138.
Corvallis city, w Oregon 97333*; pop. 40,960.
Costa Mesa city, sw California 92626*; pop. 82,562.
Costa Rica republic, Central America; 19,730 sq. mi.; pop. 3,015,000; cap. San José.
Côte d'Ivoire See **Ivory Coast.**
Côte-St.-Luc city, s Quebec, Canada; pop. 25,721.
Council Bluffs city, sw Iowa 51501*; pop. 56,449.

Coventry   city and co. boro., CEN. England; pop. 339,300.
— town, CEN. Rhode Island 02816; pop. 27,065.
Covina   city, SW California 91722*; pop. 38,743.
Covington   city, N Kentucky 41011*; pop. 49,567.
Cranford   urb. twp., E New Jersey 07106. pop. 24,573.
Cranston   city, E Rhode Island 02910; pop. 71,992.
Crestwood   city, E Missouri 63126; pop. 12,815.
Crete   isl., E Mediterranean; adm. div. of Greece; 3,219 sq. mi.; pop. 502,165.
Crimea   penin., SE Ukrainian SSR.
Croatia   constituent republic, W Yugoslavia; 21,829 sq. mi.; pop. 4,648,000; cap. Zagreb.
Crowley   city, S Louisiana 70526; pop. 16,036.
Crystal   vill., SE Minnesota 55428; pop. 25,543.
Cuba   isl. republic, Caribbean Sea; 42,804 sq. mi. (with the Isle of Pines); pop. 10,603,000; cap. Havana.
Cudahy   city, SW California 90201; pop. 18,275.
— city, SE Wisconsin 53110; pop. 19,547.
Culver City   city, SW California 90230*; pop. 38,139.
Cumberland   city, NW Maryland 21502*; pop. 25,933.
— town, NE Rhode Island 02864; pop. 27,069.
Cumberland Gap.   passage through Cumberland Mountains, betw. Tennessee and Virginia.
Cumberland River   river, Kentucky and Tennessee; flows to Ohio River.
Cupertino   city, W California 95014; pop. 37,037.
Curaçao   isl., W Netherlands Antilles; 171 sq. mi.; pop. 147,388; cap. Willemstad.
Cutler Ridge   uninc. place, SE Florida 33157; pop. 20,886.
Cuyahoga Falls   city, NE Ohio 44222*; pop. 43,890.
Cyclades   isl. group, S Aegean; a dept. of Greece; 1,023 sq. mi.; pop. 86,000; cap. Hermoupolis.
Cypress   city, SW California 90630; pop. 40,391.
Cyprus   isl. republic, E Mediterranean; 2,276 sq. mi.; pop. 568,000; cap. Nicosia.
Czechoslovakia   republic, CEN. Europe; 49,381 sq. mi.; pop. 15,664,000; cap. Prague.
Dacca   city, CEN. Bangladesh; cap.; pop. 5,300,000.
Dachau   town, SE Germany; site of a Nazi concentration camp; pop. 34,162.
Dakar   city, W Senegal; cap.; pop. 1,382,000.
Dallas   city, N Texas 75260*; pop. 904,078.
Dalmatia   reg., Croatia, W Yugoslavia; 4,954 sq. mi. pop. 750,000; cap. Split.
Dalton   city, NW Georgia 30720; pop. 20,548.
Daly City   city, W California 94017*; pop. 78,427.
Damascus   city, SW Syria; cap.; pop. 1,156,000.
Danbury   city, SW Connecticut 06810*; pop. 60,470.
Danube   river, CEN. and E Europe; 1,770 mi. long.
Danvers   town, NE Massachusetts 01923; pop. 24,100.
Danville   city, E Illinois 61832; pop. 38,985.
— city, S Virginia 24541*; pop. 45,642.
Danzig   the former name of Gdańsk.
Dardanelles   strait, NW Turkey; connects Sea of Marmara with the Aegean.
Darien   town, SW Connecticut 06820; pop. 18,892.
Darien, Gulf of   inlet of the Caribbean, E coast of Panama.
Dartmouth   town, SE Massachusetts 02714; pop. 23,966.
— city, S Nova Scotia, Canada; pop. 65,341.
Davenport   city, E Iowa 52802*; pop. 103,264.
Davis   city, CEN. California 95616; pop. 36,640.
Dayton   city, SW Ohio 45401*; pop. 193,536.
Daytona Beach   city, E Florida 32015*; pop. 54,176.
Dead Sea   large salt lake on Israel–Jordan border; 1,292 ft. below sea level.
Dearborn   city, SE Michigan 48120*; pop. 90,660.
Dearborn Heights   city, SE Michigan 48127; pop. 67,706.
Death Valley   desert basin, SE California; maximum depth 280 ft. below sea level.
Decatur   city, N Alabama 35601*; pop. 42,002.
— city, CEN. Georgia 30030*; pop. 18,404.
— city, CEN. Illinois 62521*; pop. 93,896.
Deccan Plateau   triangular tableland covering most of the penin. of India.
Dedham   town, E Massachusetts 02026; pop. 25,298.
Deerfield   vill., NE Illinois 60015; pop. 17,430.
Deerfield Beach   town, SE Florida 33441; pop. 39,193.
Deer Park   uninc. place, SE New York 11729; pop. 30,394.

Defiance   city, NW Ohio 43512; pop. 16,810.
De Kalb   city, N Illinois 60115; pop. 33,157.
Delaware   state, E United States; 1,982 sq. mi.; pop. 594,317; cap. Dover.
— city, CEN. Ohio 43015; pop. 18,780.
Delaware River   river separating Pennsylvania and Delaware from New York and New Jersey; 315 mi. long.
Del City   city, CEN. Oklahoma 73115; pop. 28,523.
Delhi   terr., CEN. India; 573 sq. mi.; pop. 5,116,000; contains New Delhi.
— city; Delhi terr.; cap.; pop. 3,706,558.
Delray Beach   city, SE Florida 33444; pop. 34,468.
Del Rio   city, SW Texas 78840; pop. 30,034.
Denison   city, N Texas 75020; pop. 23,884.
Denmark   monarchy, NW Europe; 16,633 sq. mi.; pop. 5,139,000; cap. Copenhagen.
Denton   city, N Texas 76201; pop. 48,063.
Denver   city, CEN. Colorado 80202*; cap.; pop. 492,365.
Depew   vill., W New York 14043; pop. 19,819.
Des Moines   city, CEN. Iowa 50318*; cap.; pop. 191,003.
Des Plaines   city, NE Illinois 60016*; pop. 55,374.
Detroit   city, SE Michigan 48233*; pop. 1,202,463.
Devil's Island   rocky isl. off the coast of French Guiana; formerly a penal colony.
District of Columbia   federal dist., E United States; coextensive with Washington, the capital; pop. 638,432.
Dixon   city, N Illinois 61021; pop. 15,710.
Djibouti   republic, E Africa; 8,950 sq. mi.; pop. 530,000; cap. Djibouti.
Dnepropetrovsk   city, SW Ukrainian SSR; pop. 1,083,000. Also **Dniepropetrovsk.**
Dnieper   river, SW USSR; 1,420 mi. long. Also **Dnepr.**
Dneister   river, SW USSR; 876 mi. long. Also **Dnestr.**
Dodecanese   isl. group, Aegean Sea; a dept. of Greece; 1,036 sq. mi.; pop. 120,000; cap. Rhodes.
Dolomite Alps   E div. of the Alps, N Italy.
Dolton   vill., NE Illinois 60419; pop. 24,766.
Dominican Republic   republic, E Hispaniola; 18,704 sq. mi.; pop. 7,170,000; cap. Santo Domingo.
Don   river, SW RSFSR; 1,222 mi. long.
Donets   river SW USSR; 631 mi. long.
Dorval   city, S Quebec, Canada; pop. 19,131.
Dothan   city, SE Alabama 36301*; 48,750.
Douai   town, N France; pop. 45,239.
Dover   municipal boro., SE England; pop. 34,160.
— city, CEN. Delaware 19901; cap.; pop. 23,507.
— city, SE New Hampshire 03820; pop. 22,377.
Dover, Strait of   strait at the E end of the English Channel; 21 mi. wide.
Downers Grove   vill., NE Illinois 60515; pop. 42,691.
Downey   city, SW California 90241*; pop. 82,602.
Dracut   town, NE Massachusetts 01826; pop. 21,249.
Drayton Plains   city, SE Michigan 48020; pop. 18,000.
Dresden   city, S Germany; pop. 514,508.
Drummondville   city, S Quebec, Canada; pop. 29,286.
Dublin   city, E Ireland; cap.; pop. 544,586.
— city, CEN. Georgia 31021; pop. 16,083.
Dubuque   city, E Iowa 52001*; pop. 62,321.
Duisburg   city, W Germany; pop. 559,066.
Duluth   city, NE Minnesota 55806*; pop. 92,811.
Dumont   boro., NE New Jersey 07628; pop. 18,334.
Duncan   city, S Oklahoma 73533; pop. 22,517.
Dundalk   uninc. place, CEN. Maryland 21222; pop. 71,293.
Dundas   town, S Ontario, Canada; pop. 19,179.
Dundee   burgh, E Scotland; pop. 190,793.
Dunedin   city, W Florida 33528; pop. 30,203.
Dunkerque   town, N France; scene of evacuation of British forces in World War II, May–June 1940; pop. 83,163.
Dunkirk   city, W New York 14048; pop. 15,310.
Dunmore   boro., NE Pennsylvania 18512; pop. 16,781.
Durban   city, SE South Africa; pop. 634,301.
Durham   city, CEN. North Carolina 27701*; pop. 100,538.
Düsseldorf   city, W West Germany; pop. 594,770.
Dutch Guiana   See **Surinam.**
Eagle Pass   city, SW Texas 78852; pop. 21,407.
East Berlin   See **Berlin.**
Eastchester   uninc. place, SE New York 10709; pop. 20,305.
East Chicago   city, NW Indiana 46312*; pop. 39,786.

East China Sea NE part of the China Sea.

East Cleveland city, NE Ohio 44112; pop. 36,957.

East Detroit city, SE Michigan 48021; pop. 38,280.

Easter Island isl. of Chile, South Pacific; known for stone monuments found there; 45 sq. mi.

East Germany See **Germany.**

East Hartford town, CEN. Connecticut 06108; pop. 52,563.

East Haven town, S Connecticut 06512; pop. 25,036.

East Indies 1 The isls. of the Malay Archipelago. 2 SE Asia. 3 Formerly, India. Also **East India.**

Eastlake city, NE Ohio 44094; pop. 22,104.

East Lansing city, CEN. Michigan 48823*; pop. 51,329.

East Liverpool city, E Ohio 43920; pop. 16,687.

East Los Angeles uninc. place, SW California 90022; pop. 110,017.

East Massapequa uninc. place, SE New York; pop. 13,987.

East Meadow uninc. place, SE New York 11554; pop. 39,317.

East Millcreek uninc. place, NE Utah 84101; pop. 24,150.

East Moline city, NW Illinois 61244; pop. 20,907.

Easton city, S Pennsylvania 18042; pop. 26,027.

East Orange city, NE New Jersey 07019*; pop. 77,878.

East Peoria city, CEN. Illinois 61611; pop. 22,385.

East Point city, CEN. Georgia 30044; pop. 37,486.

East Providence town, E Rhode Island 02914; pop. 50,980.

East Prussia former prov. of Prussia, NE Germany.

East Ridge town, SE Tennessee 37412; pop. 21,236.

East Saint Louis city, SW Illinois 62201*; pop. 55,200.

Eau Claire city, CEN. Wisconsin 54703*; pop. 78,805.

Ecuador republic, NW South America; 103,930 sq. mi.; pop. 10,782,000; cap. Quito.

Eden city, CEN. North Carolina 27288; pop. 15,672.

Edina city, SE Minnesota 55424; pop. 46,073.

Edinburg city, S Texas 78539; pop. 26,103.

Edinburgh city, E Scotland; cap.; pop. 420,169.

Edmond city, CEN. Oklahoma 73034; pop. 34,637.

Edmonds city, NW Washington 98020; pop. 27,679.

Edmonton city, CEN. Alberta, Canada; cap.; pop. 573,982.

Egypt republic, NE Africa; 385,229 sq. mi.; pop. 53,170,000; cap. Cairo: official name **Arab Republic of Egypt.**

Eire the Irish Gaelic name of Ireland.

Elba isl. betw. Italy and Corsica; sovereign under the exiled Napolean Bonaparte, 1814–15.

Elbe river, CEN. Europe; 725 mi. long.

Elbrus, Mount mtn., NW Georgian SSR; 18,603 ft.

Elburz Mountains mtn. range N Iran.

El Cajon city, SW California 92020*; pop. 73,892.

El Centro city, S California 92243*; pop. 23,996.

El Cerrito city, W California 94530; pop. 22,731.

El Dorado city, S Arkansas 71730; pop. 25,270.

Elgin city, NE Illinois 60120; pop. 63,668.

Elizabeth city, NE New Jersey 07201*; pop. 106,201.

Elk Grove Village vill., NE Illinois 60007; pop. 28,679.

Elkhart city, N Indiana 46515*; pop. 41,305.

Ellis Island isl., upper New York Bay; former site of US immigration station, now a museum about immigration.

Elmhurst city, NE Illinois 60126; pop. 44,276.

Elmira city, S New York 14901*; pop. 35,327.

Elmont uninc. place, SE New York 11003; pop. 27,529.

El Monte city, SW California 91734*; pop. 79,494.

Elmwood Park vill., NE Illinois 60635; pop. 24,016.

El Paso city, W Texas 79940*; pop. 425,259.

El Salvador republic, W Central America; 8,124 sq. mi.; pop. 5,221,000; cap. San Salvador.

Elyria city, N Ohio 44035*; pop. 57,538.

Emporia city, CEN. Kansas 66801; pop. 25,287.

Enfield town, N Connecticut 06082; pop. 42,695.

England S part and largest political division of Great Britain; 50,363 sq. mi.; pop. 47,536,300; cap. London.

Englewood city, CEN. Colorado 80110; pop. 30,021.

— city, NE New Jersey 07631*; pop. 23,701.

English Channel strait, betw. England and France; 20–100 mi. wide.

Enid city, N Oklahoma 73701*; pop. 50,363.

Eniwetok atoll, Marshall Islands; U.S. nuclear weapons testing area.

Enterprise city, SE Alabama 36330*; pop. 18,033.

Epsom town, SE England; site of famous racecourse; pop. 72,000.

Equatorial Guinea republic, W Africa; 10,831 sq. mi.; pop. 350,000; cap. Malabo.

Erie city, NW Pennsylvania 16501*; pop. 119,123.

Erie, Lake southernmost of the Great Lakes; 9,940 sq. mi.

Erie Canal waterway betw. Albany and Buffalo, New York; integrated with New York State Barge Canal.

Eritrea state E Africa; federated with Ethiopia; 45,300 sq. mi.; pop. 2,704,000; cap. Asmara.

Erivan see YEREVAN.

Escondido city, SW California 92025*; pop. 64,355.

Essen city, W Germany; pop. 652,501.

Essex uninc. place, N Maryland 21221; pop. 39,614.

Estonian SSR constituent republic, W USSR; 17,400 sq. mi.; pop. 1,519,000; cap. Tallinn. Also **Estonia.**

Ethiopia republic, E Africa; 472,400 sq. mi.; pop. 50,341,000; cap. Addis Ababa.

Etna, Mount volcano, E Sicily, Italy; 10,868 ft.

Euboea isl. of Greece in the Aegean; 1,457 sq. mi.

Euclid city, NE Ohio 44117; pop. 59,999.

Eugene city, W Oregon 97401*; pop. 105,664.

Euphrates river, SW Asia; 1,740 mi. long.

Eurasia large land mass comprising Europe and Asia.

Eureka city, NW California 95501*; pop. 24,153.

Europe continent comprising the W part of the Eurasian land mass; about 4,063,000 sq. mi.

Evanston city, NE Illinois 60204*; pop. 73,706.

Evansville city, SW Indiana 47708*; pop. 130,496.

Everest mtn., E Nepal; highest point of the earth's surface; 29,028 ft.

Everett city, E Massachusetts 02149; pop. 37,195.

— city, W Washington 98201*; pop. 54,413.

Everglades large swampy reg., S Florida.

Evergreen Park vill., NE Illinois 60642; pop. 22,260.

Exeter co. boro., CEN. Devonshire, England; cap; pop. 95,600.

Faeroe Islands isl. group of Denmark, North Atlantic; 540 sq. mi.; pop. 48,400; cap. Tórshavn.

Fairborn city, SW Ohio 45324; pop. 29,702.

Fairfax town, N Virginia 22030; pop. 20,537.

Fairfield city, CEN. California 94533; pop. 58,099.

— town, SW Connecticut 06430; pop. 54,849.

Fairhaven town, SE Massachusetts 02719; pop. 15,759.

Fair Lawn boro., NE New Jersey 07410; pop. 32,229.

— city, N West Virginia 26554*; pop. 23,863.

Fairview Park city, NE Ohio 44126; pop. 19,311.

Falkland Islands British col., South Atlantic; 4,618 sq. mi.; pop. 1,081; cap. Stanley.

Fall River city, SE Massachusetts 02722*; pop. 92,574.

Falls urb. twp., NE Pennsylvania 18615; pop. 36,083.

Falmouth town, E Massachusetts 02540; pop. 23,640.

Fargo city, SE North Dakota 58102*; pop. 61,383.

Faribault city, SE Minnesota 55021; pop. 16,241.

Farmers Branch city, N Texas 75234; pop. 24,863.

Farmington town, NW New Mexico 87401; pop. 31,222.

Fayetteville city, NW Arkansas 72701*; pop. 36,608.

— city, CEN. North Carolina 28302*; pop. 59,507.

Federal Republic of Germany See **Germany.**

Ferguson city, E Missouri 63135; pop. 24,549.

Ferndale city, SE Michigan 48220; pop. 26,227.

Fiji republic, South Pacific; comprises **Fiji Islands** (7,039 sq. mi.) and **Rotuma** (18 sq. mi.); pop. 740,000; cap. Suva.

Findlay city, CEN. Ohio 45840*; pop. 35,594.

Finland republic, N Europe; 130,559 sq. mi.; pop. 4,978,000; cap. Helsinki.

Finland, Gulf of part of the Baltic Sea betw. Finland and the USSR.

Fitchburg city, N Massachusetts 01420*; pop. 39,580.

Flagstaff city, CEN. Arizona 86001*; pop. 34,743.

Flanders reg., N France and S Belgium.

Flint city, CEN. Michigan 48502*; pop. 159,611.

Floral Park vill., SE New York 11001*; pop. 16,805.

Florence city, CEN. Tuscany, Italy; cap.; pop. 417,487.

— city, NW Alabama 35630*; pop. 37,029.

— city, E South Carolina 29501; pop. 29,842.

Florence-Graham uninc. place, SW California 90001; pop. 48,662.

Florida state, SE United States; 58,560 sq. mi.; pop. 9,746,412; cap. Tallahassee.

Florida Keys isl. group SW of Florida.

Florissant city, E Missouri 63033*; pop. 55,372.

Fond du Lac town, N Wisconsin 54935; pop. 35,863.

Fontainebleau town, N France; site of a former royal residence; pop. 16,778.

Fontana city, CEN. California 92335; pop. 39,713.

Forest Park town, CEN. Georgia 30050; pop. 18,782.

— vill., NE Illinois 60130; pop. 15,177.

— city, SW Ohio 45405; pop. 18,675.

Forestville uninc. place, SW Maryland 20747; pop. 16,401.

Formosa *a former name of* Taiwan.

Fort Benning South uninc. place, W Georgia 31905; pop. 15,074.

Fort Bragg uninc. place, CEN. North Carolina 28307; pop. 37,834.

Fort Carson uninc. place, CEN. Colorado 80913; pop. 13,219.

Fort Collins city, N Colorado 80521*; pop. 64,632.

Fort Dix uninc. place, CEN. New Jersey 08460; pop. 14,297.

Fort Dodge city, CEN. Iowa 50501; pop. 29,423.

Forth, Firth of estuary of the Forth River; 51 mi. long.

Fort Hood uninc. place, CEN. Texas 76544; pop. 31,250.

Forth River river, SE Scotland; 65 mi. long.

Fort Knox military reservation, N Kentucky 40120*; site of the Federal gold bullion depository.

Fort-Lamy *the former name of* N'Djamena.

Fort Lauderdale city, SE Florida 33301*; pop. 153,256.

Fort Lee boro., NE New Jersey 07024; pop. 32,449.

Fort Leonard Wood uninc. place, SE Missouri 65473; pop. 21,262.

Fort Lewis uninc. place, CEN. Washington 98433; pop. 23,761.

Fort Myers city, SW Florida 33920*; pop. 36,638.

Fort Pierce city, E Florida 33454*; pop. 33,802.

Fort Sill uninc. place, SW Oklahoma 73503; pop. 15,924.

Fort Smith city, W Arkansas 72901*; pop. 71,384.

Fort Thomas city, N Kentucky 41075; pop. 16,012.

Fort Walton Beach city, NW Florida 32548; pop. 20,829.

Fort Wayne city, NE Indiana 46802*; pop. 172,391.

Fort Worth city, N Texas 76101*; pop. 385,141.

Fostoria city, N Ohio 44830; pop. 15,743.

Fountain Valley city, SW California 92708; pop. 55,080.

Framingham town, E Massachusetts 01701; pop. 65,113.

France republic, W Europe; 210,026 sq. mi.; pop. 56,647,000; cap. Paris.

Frankfort city, CEN. Kentucky 40601; cap.; pop. 25,973.

Frankfurt am Main city, CEN. Germany; pop. 628,203.

Frankfurt an der Oder city, E Germany; pop. 77,175.

Franklin town, E Massachusetts 02038; pop. 18,217.

Franklin Park vill., NE Illinois 60131; pop. 17,507.

Franklin Square uninc. place, SE New York 11010; pop. 29,051.

Frederick city, NW Maryland 21701; pop. 27,557.

Fredericton city, CEN. New Brunswick, Canada; pop. 45,248.

Freeport city, NW Bahamas, on Grand Bahama Island; pop. 25,423.

— city, N Illinois 61032; pop. 26,406.

— vill., SE New York 11520; pop. 40,347.

Fremont city, N California 94536; pop. 131,945.

— city, E Nebraska 68025; pop. 23,979.

— city, N Ohio 43420; pop. 17,834.

French Guiana French overseas dept. NE South America; 33,399 sq. mi.; pop. 117,000; cap. Cayenne.

French Polynesia French overseas terr., South Pacific; comprises the Society, Marquesas, Gambier, and other islands; 1,550 sq. mi.; pop. 197,000; cap. Papeete.

French West Indies isls. comprising Guadaloupe and Martinique.

Fresno city, CEN. California 93706*; pop. 217,491.

Fridley city, E Minnesota 55421; pop. 30,228.

Friesland prov., N Netherlands; 1,295 sq. mi.; pop. 597,600; cap. Leeuwarden.

Frigid Zone See **North Frigid Zone, South Frigid Zone.**

Frisian Islands isl. group, North Sea near Germany, Denmark, and the Netherlands.

Fuji extinct volcano, Honshu, Japan; 12,389 ft.

Fullerton city, SW California 92631*; pop. 102,246.

Fundy, Bay of inlet of the Atlantic betw. Nova Scotia and New Brunswick and NE Maine.

Fuzhou city, SE China; pop. 710,000.

Gabon republic, W equatorial Africa; 103,347 sq. mi.; pop. 1,171,000; cap. Libreville.

Gadsden city, NE Alabama 35901*; pop. 47,565.

Gainesville city, N Florida 32601*; pop. 81,371.

— city, CEN. Georgia 30501*; pop. 15,280.

Galápagos Islands isl. group of Ecuador, South Pacific.

Galesburg city, W Illinois 61401; pop. 35,305.

Galicia reg., SE Poland and NW Ukrainian SSR.

— reg., NW Spain.

Galilee reg., N Israel.

Galilee, Sea of freshwater lake; betw. NE Israel, SW Syria, and NW Jordan; 64 sq. mi.

Gallipoli Peninsula penin., NW Turkey.

Galveston city, SE Texas 77550*; pop. 61,902.

Gambia, Republic of the, republic, W Africa; 4,127 sq. mi.; pop. 860,000; cap. Banjul.

Ganges river, N India and Bangladesh, sacred to Hindus; 1,560 mi. long.

Gardena city, SW California 90247*; pop. 45,165.

Garden City city, SE Michigan 48135; pop. 35,640.

— vill., SE New York 11530; pop. 22,927.

Garden Grove city, SW California 92640*; pop. 123,351.

Gardner city, N Massachusetts 01440; pop. 17,900.

Garfield city, NE New Jersey 07026; pop. 26,803.

Garfield Heights city, NE Ohio 44125; pop. 33,380.

Garland city, N Texas 75040*; pop. 138,857.

Gary city, NW Indiana 46401*; pop. 151,968.

Gascony reg., SW France.

Gastonia city, SW North Carolina 28052*; pop. 47,333.

Gatineau town, SW Quebec, Canada; pop. 73,479.

Gaza city, SW Palestine; adm. by the United Arab Republic with the **Gaza Strip,** the surrounding area; pop. 356,261.

Gdańsk port city, N Poland: formerly, as **Danzig,** cap. of the territory of the Free City of Danzig; pop. 449,200.

Gdynia city, NW Poland; pop. 232,500.

Geneva city, SW Switzerland; pop. 389,000.

— city, CEN. New York 14456; pop. 15,133.

Geneva, Lake of lake, SW Switzerland; 224 sq. mi.

Genoa city, NW Italy; pop. 714,641.

Georgetown city, N Guyana; cap.; pop. 187,056.

Georgia state, SE United States; 58,876 sq. mi.; pop. 5,463,087.

Georgian SSR constituent republic, SW USSR; 26,900 sq. mi.; pop. 5,171,000; cap. Tbilisi.

German Democratic Republic See **Germany.**

Germany republic, CEN. Europe; divided 1949–90, into the **Federal Republic of Germany** (West Germany), cap. Bonn; and the **German Democratic Republic** (East Germany), cap. East Berlin. 137,820 sq. mi.; pop. 79,082,000; cap. Berlin.

Ghana republic W Africa; 92,098 sq. mi.; pop. 12,815,000; cap. Accra.

Ghent city, NW Belgium; pop. 241,695.

Gibraltar British col. on the Rock of Gilbraltar; 2.25 sq. mi.; pop. 29,760.

Gibraltar, Rock of penin., S Spain; dominates the Strait of Gibraltar.

Gibraltar, Strait of strait, betw. Spain and Africa, W Mediterranean.

Gilbert Islands See **Kiribati.**

Glace Bay town, NE Nova Scotia, Canada; pop. 21,836.

Gladstone city, W Missouri 64118; pop. 24,990.

Glasgow burgh, SW Scotland; pop. 794,316.

Glastonbury city, CEN. Connecticut 06033; pop. 24,327.

Glen Burnie uninc. place, NE Maryland 21061; pop. 37,263.

Glen Cove city, SE New York 11542; pop. 24,618.

Glendale city, CEN. Arizona 85301*; pop. 96,988.

— city, SW California 91209*; pop. 139,060.

Glendora city, SW California 91740; pop. 38,500.

Glen Ellyn vill., NE Illinois 60137*; pop. 23,649.

Glens Falls city, E New York 12801; pop. 15,897.

Glenview vill., NE Illinois 60025; pop. 30,842.

Gloucester co. boro., CEN. Gloucestershire, England; cap.; pop. 91,300.

— city, NE Massachusetts 01930*; pop. 27,768.

Gloversville city, CEN. New York 12078; pop. 17,836.

Goa former Portuguese terr., W India; annexed by India in 1961; 1,394 sq. mi., pop. 954,000; cap. New Goa.

Gobi Desert desert, CEN. Asia; 500,000 sq. mi.

Golden Gate strait betw. San Francisco Bay and the Pacific.

Golden Valley vill., SE Minnesota 55427; pop. 22,775.
Goldsboro city, CEN. North Carolina 27530; pop. 31,871.
Good Hope, Cape of promontory, SW South Africa.
Gorki city, CEN. RSFSR; pop. 1,358,000. Also **Gorkiy, Gorky.**
Goshen city, N Indiana 46526; pop. 19,665.
Göteborg city, SW Sweden; pop. 434,699.
Gotland isl. of SE Sweden, Baltic Sea; 1,167 sq. mi.
Granada city, S Spain; pop. 229,108.
Granby city, S Quebec, Canada; pop. 37,132.
Grand Banks submarine shoal, North Atlantic; near Newfoundland.
Grand Canyon gorge of the Colorado River, NW Arizona; ab. 250 mi. long.
Grand Forks uninc. place, E North Dakota 58201*; pop. 43,765.
Grand Island city, CEN. Nebraska 68801; pop. 33,180.
Grand Junction city, W Colorado; 81501*; pop. 27,956.
Grand' Mère city, CEN. Quebec, Canada; pop. 15,999.
Grand Prairie city, N Texas 75051*; pop. 71,462.
Grand Rapids city, W Michigan 49501*; pop. 181,843.
Grandview city, W Missouri 64030; pop. 24,561.
Granite City city, SW Illinois 62040; pop. 36,815.
Great Barrier Reef coral reef off the coast of Queensland, Australia.
Great Bend city, CEN. Kansas 67530; pop. 16,608.
Great Britain principal isl. of the United Kingdom; comprises England, Scotland, and Wales; 94,248 sq. mi.; pop. 56,518,000; cap. London.
Great Divide See **Continental Divide.**
Greater Antilles See **Antilles.**
Great Falls city, CEN. Montana 59401*; pop. 56,725.
Great Lakes chain of five lakes, CEN. North America; on Canada–United States border; comprises Lakes Superior, Michigan, Huron, Ontario, and Erie; total 94,710 sq. mi.
Great Plains plateau, W North America; E of the Rockies.
Great Russia CEN. and NW reg. of the USSR.
Great Salt Lake salt lake, NW Utah; ab. 2,000 sq. mi.
Great Slave Lake lake, S Northwest Territories, Canada; 11,170 sq. mi.
Great Smoky Mountains mtn. range, North Carolina and Tennessee.
Greece republic, SE Europe; 50,949 sq. mi.; pop. 10,038,000; cap. Athens.
Greeley city, N Colorado 80631*; pop. 53,006.
Green Bay city, E Wisconsin 54305*; pop. 87,899.
Greenbelt city, CEN. Maryland 20770; pop. 16,000.
Greendale vill., SE Wisconsin 53129; pop. 16,928.
Greenfield uninc. place, NW Massachusetts 01301*; pop. 18,436.
— town, SE Wisconsin 53220; pop. 31,353.
Greenfield Park town, S Quebec, Canada; pop. 18,430.
Greenland isl. territory of Denmark near NE North America; 840,000 sq. mi.; pop. 55,900.
Green Mountains mtn. range, CEN. Vermont.
Greensboro city, CEN. North Carolina 27420*; pop. 155,642.
Greensburg city, SW Pennsylvania 15601*; pop. 17,558.
Greenville city, W Mississippi 38701*; pop. 40,613.
— city, E North Carolina 27834*; pop. 35,740.
— city, NW South Carolina 29602*; pop. 58,242.
— city, NE Texas 75401; pop. 22,161.
Greenwich boro., SE London; former site of the Royal Observatory; location of prime meridian; pop. 218,000.
— town, SW Connecticut 06830*; pop. 59,578.
Greenwood city, CEN. Mississippi 38930; pop. 20,115.
— city, W South Carolina 29646*; pop. 21,613.
Grenada republic in the West Indies; 133 sq. mi.; pop. 101,000; cap. St. George's.
Gretna city, SE Louisiana 70053; pop. 20,615.
Griffin city, CEN. Georgia 30223; pop. 20.728.
Griffith town, NW Indiana 46319; pop. 17,026.
Grimsby town, S Ontario, Canada; pop. 15,567.
Grosse Pointe city, SE Michigan 48236; pop. 18,886.
Groves city, SE Texas 77619; pop. 17,090.
Guadalajara city, CEN. Mexico; pop. 1,813,100.
Guadalcanal isl., British Solomons; scene of an Allied invasion in World War II, 1943.
Guadeloupe French overseas dept., Lesser Antilles; 687 sq. mi.; pop. 380,000; cap. Basse-Terre.

Guam uninc. terr. of the United States, an isl. in the Marianas; 209 sq. mi. pop. 134,000; cap. Agaña.
Guantánamo city, SE Cuba, near, **Guantánamo Bay;** pop. 155,217.
Guatemala republic, N Central America; 42,042 sq. mi.; pop. 9,197,000.
— City, CEN. Guatemala; cap. pop. 1,057,210.
Guayama town, SE Puerto Rico 00654; pop. 21,044.
Guayaquil city, W Ecuador; pop. 1,022,010.
Guelph city, S Ontario, Canada; pop. 67,538.
Guernica town, N Spain; object of a German bombing, 1937; pop. 11,704.
Guernsey one of the Channel Islands; 25 sq. mi.
Guiana coastal reg., NE South America. See **British Guiana, French Guiana, Guyana, Surinam.**
Guinea republic, W Africa; 94,900 sq. mi.; pop. 5,429,000; cap. Conakry.
Guinea, Gulf of large bay of the Atlantic off W Africa.
Guinea-Bissau republic, W Africa; 13,948 sq. mi.; pop. 973,000; cap. Bissau.
Gulfport city, SE Mississippi 39501*; pop. 39,676.
Gulf Stream A warm ocean current flowing from the Gulf of Mexico northeastward toward Europe.
Guyana republic, NE South America, 83,044 sq. mi.; pop. 756,000; cap. Georgetown.
Harlem city, wNetherlands; pop. 158,291.
Hacienda Heights city, S California 91745; pop. 49,422.
Hackensack city, NE New Jersey 07602*; pop. 36,039.
Haddon urb. twp., SW New Jersey 08108; pop. 15,875.
Hagerstown city, W Maryland 21740; pop. 34,132.
Hague, The city, W Netherlands; seat of government; pop. 443,845. Also **s'Gravenhage.**
Haifa city, NW Israel; pop. 229,300.
Haiti republic, W Hispaniola; 10,579 sq. mi.; pop. 5,862,000; cap. Port-au-Prince.
Halifax city, S Nova Scotia; Canada; cap.; pop. 117,882.
Hallandale city, SE Florida 33009; pop. 36,517.
Halle city, SW Germany; pop. 232,543.
Haltom City vill., N Texas 76117; pop. 29,014.
Hamburg state and city, N Germany; 288 sq. mi.; pop. 1,653,043.
Hamden town, S Connecticut 06514; pop. 51,071.
Hamilton city, CEN. Bermuda; cap.; pop. 2,060.
— city, SW Ohio 45012*; pop. 63,189.
— city, S Ontario, Canada; pop. 312,003.
Hammond city, NW Indiana 46320*; pop. 93,714.
Hampton city, SE Virginia 23660*; pop. 122,617.
Hampton Roads channel, SE Virginia; connects several rivers with Chesapeake Bay; scene of the engagement of the ''Monitor'' and the ''Merrimack,'' 1862.
Hamtramck city, SE Michigan 48212; pop. 21,300.
Hanford city, CEN. California 93230*; pop. 20,958.
Hangzhou city, E China; pop. 933,000.
Hannibal city, NE Missouri 63401*; pop. 18,811.
Hannover city, CEN. Germany; pop. 535,834.
Hanoi city, CEN. Vietnam; cap; pop. 1,600,000.
Harbin city, NE China; pop. 2,094,000.
Harlingen city, S Texas 78551*; pop. 43,543.
Harper Woods city, SE Michigan 48236; pop. 16,361.
Harrisburg city, CEN. Pennsylvania 17105*; cap; pop. 53,264.
Hartford city, CEN. Connecticut 06101*; cap.; pop. 136,392.
Harvey city, NE Illinois 60426; pop. 35,810.
Hastings city, S Nebraska 68901; pop. 23,045.
Hattiesburg city, SE Mississippi 39401*; pop. 40,829.
Havana city, W Cuba; cap.; pop. 1,961,674.
Haverford urb. twp., SE Pennsylvania 19083; pop. 52,349.
Haverhill city, NE Massachusetts 01831*; pop. 46,865.
Hawaii state of the United States, North Pacific; coextensive with the Hawaiian Islands; 6,450 sq. mi.; pop. 965,691; cap. Honolulu.
— largest of the Hawaiian Islands; 4,020 sq. mi.
Hawthorne city, SW California 90250; pop. 56,437.
— boro., NE New Jersey 07007; pop. 19,173.
Hays city, CEN. Kansas 67601; pop. 16,301.
Hayward city, W California 94544*; pop. 93,585.
Hazel Park city, SE Michigan 48030; pop. 20,914.
Hazleton city, E Pennsylvania 18201; pop. 27,318.

Hebrides isl. group off w coast of Scotland, ab. 3,000 sq. mi.

Heidelberg city, sw Germany; pop. 128,773.

Hejaz div., w Saudi Arabia; 150,000 sq. mi.; pop. 1,754,000; cap. Mecca.

Helena city, CEN. Montana 59601*; cap.; pop. 23,938.

Helicon mtn. range, CEN. Greece.

Helsinki city, s Finland; cap.; pop. 490,693.

Hempstead vill., SE New York 11551*; pop. 40,404.

Henderson city, NW Kentucky 42420; pop. 24,834.

— city, s Nevada 89015; pop. 24,363.

Hermosa Beach city, sw California 90254; pop. 18,070.

Herzegovina See **Bosnia and Herzegovina.**

Hesse state, w Germany; 8,152 sq. mi.; pop. 5,576,085; cap. Wiesbaden.

Hialeah city, SE Florida 33010*; site of a famous racetrack; pop. 145,254.

Hibbing vill., NE Minnesota 55746; pop. 21,193.

Hickory city, CEN. North Carolina 28601*; pop. 20,757.

Hicksville uninc. place, SE New York 11802*; pop. 43,245.

Highland town, NW Indiana 46322; pop. 25,935.

Highland Park city, NE Illinois 60035*; pop. 30,599.

— city, SE Michigan 48203; pop. 27,909.

High Point city, CEN. North Carolina 27260*; pop. 63,479.

Hillcrest Heights city, s Maryland; pop. 17,021.

Hillside urb. twp., NE New Jersey 07205; pop. 21,440.

Hilo city, E Hawaii island, Hawaii 96720; pop. 37,017.

Himalayas mtn. range. CEN. Asia.

Hindustan **1** loosely, the reg. of the Ganges where Hindi is spoken. **2** loosely, India.

Hingham town, E Massachusetts 02043; pop. 20,339.

Hinsdale vill., NE Illinois 60521*; pop. 16,726.

Hiroshima city, sw Honshu isl., Japan; devastated by the first atom bomb used in war, Aug. 6, 1945; pop. 899,394.

Hispaniola isl., West Indies; ab. 30,000 sq. mi.; divided into Haiti and the Dominican Republic.

Hobart city, SE Tasmania, Australia; cap; pop. 170,200.

— city, NW Indiana 46342; pop. 22,987.

Hobbs city, SE New Mexico 88240; pop. 28,794.

Hoboken city, NE New Jersey 07030; pop. 42,460.

Ho Chi Minh City See **Saigon.**

Hoffman Estates city, NE Illinois 60172; pop. 38,258.

Hokkaido isl. of N Japan; ab. 29,000 sq. mi.

Holladay uninc. place, NW Utah 84117; pop. 22,189.

Holland See **Netherlands.**

— city, sw Michigan 49423*; pop. 26,281.

Hollywood area, NW Los Angeles, California; ctr. of US motion-picture industry.

— city, SE Florida 33022*; pop. 117,188.

Holyoke city, CEN. Massachusetts 01040*; pop. 44,678.

Homewood city, CEN. Alabama 35209; pop. 21,271.

— vill., NE Illinois 60430; pop. 19,724.

Honduras republic, NE Central America; 43,277 sq. mi.; pop. 4,674,000; cap. Tegucigalpa.

Hong Kong British col., SE China; includes **Hong Kong Island**; 415 sq. mi.; pop. 5,841,000; cap. Victoria.

Honolulu city, SE Oahu, Hawaii 96815*; cap.; pop. 365,048.

Honshu isl. of GEN. Japan; 88,745 sq. mi.

Hood, Mount volcanic peak, Cascade Range, NW Oregon 11,245 ft.

Hoover Dam dam, Colorado River at the Arizona–Nevada border; 727 ft. high; 1,282 ft. long.

Hopewell city, SE Virginia 23860; pop. 23,397.

Hopkinsville city, sw Kentucky 42240; pop. 27,318.

Horn, Cape s extremity of South America.

Hot Springs city, CEN. Arkansas 71901; pop. 35,166.

Houma city, SE Louisiana 70360*; pop. 32,602.

Houston city, SE Texas 77013*; pop. 1,594,086.

Huber Heights city, sw Ohio 45424; pop. 31,731.

Hudson Center uninc. place, CEN. Massachusetts 01749; pop. 14,156.

Hudson Bay inland sea, N Canada; connected with the Atlantic by **Hudson Strait**; ab. 475,000 sq. mi.

Hudson River river, E New York; 306 mi. long.

Hull city, sw Quebec, Canada; pop. 61,039.

Hungary republic, CEN. Europe; 35,920 sq. mi.; pop. 10,437,000; cap. Budapest.

Huntington city, NE Indiana 46750; pop. 16,202.

— city, w West Virginia 25701*; pop. 63,684.

Huntington Beach city, sw California 92647*; pop. 170,505.

Huntington Park city, sw California 90255*; pop. 45,932.

Huntington Station uninc. place, SE New York 11746*; pop. 28,769.

Huntsville city, N Alabama 35804*; pop. 142,513.

— city, E Texas 77340*; pop. 23,936.

Huron, Lake one of the Great Lakes; betw. Michigan and Ontario; 23,010 sq. mi.

Hurst city, N Texas 76053; pop. 31,420.

Hutchinson city, CEN. Kansas 67501; pop. 40,284.

Hwang Ho river, N China; 2,900 mi. long.

Hyde Park public park, London, England.

Hyderabad city, CEN. India; pop. 1,607,396.

— city, SE Pakistan; pop. 600,796.

Iberia part of sw Europe containing Spain and Portugal.

Iceland isl. republic, North Atlantic; 39,699 sq. mi.; pop. 256,000; cap. Reykjavik.

Idaho state, NW United States; 83,557 sq. mi.; pop. 944,038; cap. Boise.

Idaho Falls city, SE Idaho 83402*; pop. 39,734.

Ijssel, Lake freshwater lake, CEN. Netherlands.

Illinois state, CEN. United States; 56,400 sq. mi.; pop. 11,427,414; cap. Springfield.

Imperial Beach city, sw California 92032; pop. 22,689.

Imperial Valley argricultural reg., SE California.

Independence city, w Missouri 64051*; pop. 111,797.

India republic, s Asia; 1,222,559 sq. mi.; pop. 853,373,000; cap. New Delhi.

Indiana state, CEN. United States; 36,291 sq. mi.; pop. 5,490,260; cap. Indianapolis.

— boro., CEN. Pennsylvania 15701; pop. 16,051.

Indianapolis city, CEN. Indiana 46206*; cap.; pop. 700,807.

Indian Ocean ocean betw. Africa, Asia, Australia, and Antarctica.

Indies See **East Indies, West Indies.**

Indochina **1** SE penin. of Asia. **2** Cambodia, Laos, Vietnam.

Indonesia republic, SE Asia; comprises over 100 isls. of the Malay Archipelago; 752,409 sq. mi.; pop. 180,763,000; cap. Jakarta.

Indus river, Tibet, Kashmir, and Pakistan; 1,800 mi. long.

Inglewood city, sw California 90306*; pop. 94,162.

Inkster vill. SE Michigan 48141; pop. 35,190.

Ionian Sea part of the Mediterranean betw. Greece and Sicily.

Iowa state, CEN. United States; 56,290 sq. mi.; pop. 2,913,808; cap. Des. Moines.

Iowa City city, E Iowa 52240*; pop. 50,508.

Iraklion city, N CEN. Crete; pop. 78,000. Also **Candia, Heraklion.**

Iran republic, sw Asia; ab. 636,372 sq. mi.; pop. 56,293,000; cap. Tehran.

Iraq republic, sw Asia; 169,975 sq. mi.; pop. 17,754,000; cap. Baghdad.

Ireland westernmost of the British Isles; 31,838 sq. mi.

— republic, s Ireland; 27,137 sq. mi.; pop. 3,614,000; cap. Dublin. See also **Northern Ireland.**

Irish Sea part of the Atlantic betw. Great Britain and Ireland.

Irkutsk city, s USSR; pop. 561,000.

Irondequoit uninc. place, w New York 14617; pop. 57,648.

Irrawaddy river, Tibet and Myanmar; 1,200 mi. long.

Irving city, N Texas 75061*; pop. 109,943.

Irvington town, NE New Jersey 07111; pop. 61,493.

Islamabad city, NE Pakistan; cap.; pop. 204,364.

Israel republic, E end of the Mediterranean; 7,992 sq. mi.; pop. 4,666,000; cap. Jerusalem.

Istanbul city, NE Turkey; pop. 6,748,435.

Italy republic, s Europe; 116,324 sq. mi.; pop. 57,512,000; cap. Rome.

Ithaca isl. of Greece, Ionian Sea; 36 sq. mi.

— city, CEN. New York 14850; pop. 28,732.

Ivory Coast (Côte d'Ivoire) republic, w Africa; 123,847 sq. mi.; pop. 12,657,000; cap. Abidjan.

Izmir city, w Turkey; pop. 1,762,849. Also **Smyrna.**

Jackson city, s Michigan 49201*; pop. 39,739.

— city, CEN. Mississippi 39205*; cap.; pop. 202,895.

— city, w Tennessee 38301*; pop. 49,258.

Jacksonville city, CEN. Arkansas 72076*; pop. 27,589.

— city, NE Florida 32201*; pop. 540,898.

— city, CEN. Illinois 62650*; pop. 20,284.

— city, E North Carolina 28540*; pop. 18,237.

Jakarta city, NW Java; cap. of Indonesia; pop. 7,829,000.
Jamaica isl. monarchy of the Greater Antilles; 4,244 sq. mi.; pop. 2,391,000; cap. Kingston.
Jamestown town, NW St. Helena; cap.; pop. 1,516.
— city, SW New York 14701; pop. 35,775.
— city, CEN. North Dakota 58401; pop. 16,280.
— restored vill., E Virginia 23081; site of the first English settlement in the present limits of the United States, 1607.
Jammu and Kashmir state, N India; subject of a territorial dispute with Pakistan; 85,806 sq. mi.; pop. 5,120,000; caps. Sringar and Jammu.
Janesville city, S Wisconsin 53545*; pop. 51,071.
Japan constitutional monarchy; E Asia; situated on a chain of isls.; 145,862 sq. mi.; pop. 123,692,000; cap. Tokyo.
Japan, Sea of part of the Pacific betw. Japan and the Asian mainland.
Java isl. of Indonesia; SE of Sumatra; 48,842 sq. mi.
Jefferson uninc. place, NE Virginia 22042; pop. 24,342.
Jefferson City city, CEN. Missouri 65101*; cap.; pop. 33,619.
Jefferson uninc. place, SE Louisiana 70121; pop. 15,550.
Jeffersonville city, SE Indiana 47130*; pop. 21,220.
Jennings city, E Missouri 63136; pop. 16,934.
Jericho vill., W Jordan; on the site of the ancient city.
Jersey one of the Channel Islands; 45 sq. mi.
Jersey City city, NE New Jersey 07303*; pop. 223,532.
Jerusalem city, E Israel; cap.; pop. 493,500.
Jidda city, W Saudi Arabia; pop. 561,104.
Johannesburg city, NE South Africa; cap.; pop. 632,369.
Johnson City vill., S New York 13790; pop. 17,126.
— city, NE Tennessee 37601; pop. 39,753.
Johnston town, NE Rhode Island 02919; pop. 24,907.
Johnstown city, CEN. Pennsylvania 15901*; pop. 35,496.
Joliet city, NE Illinois 60431*; pop. 77,956.
Joliette city, S Quebec, Canada; pop. 18,118.
Jonesboro city, NE Arkansas 72401; pop. 31,530.
Jonquière city, CEN. Quebec, Canada; pop. 60,691,
Joplin city, SW Missouri 64801*; pop. 39,023.
Jordan constitutional monarchy, W Asia; 34,443 sq. mi.; pop. 3,169,000; cap. Amman.
Jordan River river, CEN. Palestine; more than 200 mi. long.
Junction City city, CEN. Kansas 66441; pop. 19,305.
Juneau city, SE Alaska 99801; cap.; pop. 19,528.
Jungfrau mtn. peak, CEN. Switzerland; 13,653 ft.
Jura Mountains mtn. range, E France and W Switzerland.
Jutland penin., N Europe; comprises continental Denmark and part of Germany.
Kabul city, CEN. Afghanistan; cap.; pop. 1,424,400.
Kailua-Lanikai uninc. place, E Oahu, Hawaii 96734*; pop. 35,812.
Kalamazoo city, SW Michigan 49001*; pop. 79,722.
Kalimantan *the Indonesian name of* Borneo.
Kaliningrad city, extreme W USSR; pop. 361,000.
Kamchatka penin, E USSR, betw. The Bering and Okhotsk Seas.
Kampuchea, Roat (Cambodia) republic, SW Indochina peninsula, formerly **Khmer Republic**; 69,698 sq. mi.; pop. 8,592,000; cap. Phnom Penh.
Kaneohe uninc. place, E Oahu, Hawaii 96744; pop. 29,919.
Kankakee city, NE Illinois 60901; pop. 29,633.
Kannapolis uninc. place, CEN. North Carolina 28081; pop. 34,564.
Kansas state, CEN. United States; 82,276 sq. mi.; pop. 2,364,236; cap. Topeka.
Kansas City city, N Kansas 66110*; pop. 161,148.
— city, W Missouri 64108*; pop. 448,028.
Karachi city, S Pakistan; former cap.; pop. 5,208,132.
Karelian ASSR adm. div., NW RSFSR; 66,560 sq. mi.; pop. 711,000; cap. Petrozavodsk.
Karnak vill., S Egypt; near the site of ancient Thebes.
Kashmir See **Jammu and Kashmir.**
Kathmandu city, CEN. Nepal; cap.; pop. 150,402.
Kauai one of the Hawaiian Islands; 551 sq. mi.
Kaunas city, CEN. Lithuanian SSR; pop. 377,000.
Kazakh SSR constituent republic, CEN. USSR; 1,049,200 sq. mi.; pop. 15,654,000; cap. Alma-Ata.
Kazan city, NW Tatar ASSR; cap.; pop. 1,002,000.
Kearney city, CEN. Nebraska 68847; pop. 21,158.
Kearns uninc. place, N Utah 84118; pop. 21,353.

Kearny town, NE New Jersey 07032; pop. 35,735.
Keene city, SW New Hampshire 03431; pop. 21,449.
Kelowna city, S British Columbia, Canada; pop. 51,955.
Kendall uninc. place, SE Florida 33156; pop. 73,758.
Kenmore vill., W New York 14217; pop. 18,474.
Kennedy, Cape *the former name of* Cape Canaveral.
Kenner city, SE Louisiana 70062; pop. 66,382.
Kennewick city, S Washington 99336; pop. 34,397.
Kenosha city, SE Wisconsin 53141*; pop. 77,685.
Kent city, NE Ohio 44240*; pop. 26,164.
— city, CEN. Washington 98031; pop. 22,961.
Kentucky state, CEN. United States; 40,409 sq. mi.; pop. 3,660,257; cap. Frankfort.
Kentucky River river, N Kentucky; 259 mi. long.
Kentwood city, SW Michigan 49508; pop. 30,438.
Kenya republic, E Africa; 224,961 sq. mi.; pop. 24,872,000; cap. Nairobi.
Kenya, Mount extinct volcano, CEN. Kenya; 17,058 ft.
Kettering city, SW Ohio 45429; pop. 61,186.
Key West southwesternmost of the Florida Keys.
— city, Key West Island, Florida 33040; pop. 24,292.
Kharkov city, NE Ukrainian SSR; pop. 1,464,000.
Khartoum city, CEN. Sudan; cap.; pop. 790,000.
Khmer Republic *the former name of* Cambodia.
Khyber Pass mtn. pass betw. Afghanistan and Pakistan; ab. 30 mi. long.
Kiel city, N Germany; pop. 250,750.
Kiel Canal ship canal betw. Kiel and the mouth of the Elbe; ab. 61 mi. long.
Kiev city, CEN. Ukrainian SSR; cap.; pop. 2,192,000.
Kilauea active crater, Mauna Loa volcano, Hawaii.
Kilimanjaro, Mount mtn., NE Tanzania; highest in Africa; 19,565 ft.
Killeen city, CEN. Texas 76540*; pop. 46,296.
Kimberley city, CEN. South Africa; pop. 105,258.
Kingsport city, NE Tennessee 37662*; pop. 32,027.
Kingston city, SE Jamaica; cap.; pop. 524,638.
— city, SE New York 12401; pop. 24,481.
— boro., CEN. Pennsylvania 18704; pop. 15,681.
— city, SE Ontario, Canada; pop. 56,032.
Kingsville city, S Texas 78363*; pop. 28,808.
Kinshasa city, W Zaire; cap.; pop. 3,562,122.
Kinston city, CEN. North Carolina 28501; pop. 25,234.
Kirghiz SSR constituent republic, S USSR; 76,600; sq. mi.; pop. 3,875,000; cap. Frunze.
Kiribati, republic including 3 isl. groups SW Pacific, comprising the Gilbert, Line, Phoenix Islands, and Banaba Island; 328 sq. mi.; pop. 71,000; cap. Bairiki.
Kirkland city, CEN. Washington 98033; pop. 18,785.
Kirksville city, N Missouri 63501; pop. 17,167.
Kirkwood city, E Missouri 63122; pop. 27,987.
Kitchener city, S Ontario, Canada; pop. 131,870.
Kitty Hawk vill., NE North Carolina; site of the first sustained airplane flight, by Wilbur and Orville Wright, 1903.
Klamath Falls city, S Oregon 97601*; pop. 16,661.
Klondike reg., NW Canada in the basin of the **Klondike River.**
Knoxville city, E Tennessee 37901*; pop. 175,045.
Kobe city, S Japan; pop. 1,367,392.
Kodiak Island isl., S Alaska.
Kokomo city, CEN. Indiana 46902*; pop. 47,808.
Kolonia city, cap. Micronesia; pop. 6,000.
Königsberg *the former German name of* Kaliningrad.
Korea penin., E Asia; 85,509 sq. mi.; divided into the **Democratic People's Republic of Korea** (North Korea) single-party republic; 47,250 sq. mi.; pop. 22,937,000; cap. Pyongyang; and the **Republic of Korea** (South Korea) multi-party republic; 38,259 sq. mi.; pop. 42,793,000; cap. Seoul.
Korea Strait strait, betw. the Sea of Japan and the East China Sea.
Kozhikode city, S India; pop. 333,979. Also **Calicut.**
Krakatoa isl. volcano betw. Sumatra and Java, Indonesia; site of most violent volcanic eruption of modern times, 1883.
Kraków city, S Poland; pop. 743,700.
Krasnodar city, SW USSR; pop. 620,000.
Kronshtadt city, W USSR; pop. 39,477.
Kuala Lumpur city, CEN. Malaysia; cap.; pop. 1,103,200.
Kunming city, SW China; pop. 1,085,100.

Kurdistan reg., NW Iran, NE Iraq, and SE Turkey; peopled largely by Kurds.

Kure city, SW Japan; pop. 234,550.

Kurile Island isl. group, SE USSR; 5,700 sq. mi.

Kuwait monarchy, NE Arabia; 6,880 sq. mi.; pop. 2,143,000.
— **City**, E Kuwait; cap.; pop. 44,224.

Kyoto city, SW Japan; pop. 1,470,564.

Kyushu isl., S Japan; 16,247 sq. mi.; pop. 1,034,328.

Labrador terr., Newfoundland, Canada; ab. 110,000 sq. mi.; pop. 21,157.
— the penin. of North America betw. the St. Lawrence River and Hudson Bay.

La Canada-Flintridge uninc. place, SW California 91011; pop. 20,153.

Lachine city, S Quebec, Canada; pop. 41,503.

Lackawanna city, W New York 14218; pop. 22,701.

La Crosse city, W Wisconsin 54601*; pop. 48,347.

Ladoga, Lake lake, NW RSFSR; 7,100 sq. mi.

Lafayette uninc. place, W California 94549; pop. 20,837.
— city, CEN. Indiana 47901*; pop. 43,011.
— city, S Louisiana 70509*; pop. 80,584.

Lagos city, SW Nigeria; cap.; pop. 1,274,000.

La Grange city, W Georgia 30240; pop. 24,204.
— vill., NE Illinois 60525; pop. 15,693.

La Habra city, SW California 90631*; pop. 45,232.

Lahore city, E Pakistan; pop. 2,952,689.

Lake Charles city, SW Louisiana 70601*; pop. 75,051.

Lake District reg., NW England; contains 15 lakes.

Lake Forest city, NE Illinois 60045; pop. 15,245.

Lakeland city, CEN. Florida 33082*; pop. 47,406.

Lakes District uninc. place, CEN. Washington 98499; pop. 54,533.

Lakewood city, SW California 90714*; pop. 74,654.
— city, CEN. Colorado 80215; pop. 113,808.
— uninc. place, E New Jersey 08701; pop. 22,863.
— city, N Ohio 44107, pop. 61,963.

Lake Worth city, SE Florida 33460; pop. 27,048.

La Marque city, SE Texas 77568; pop. 15,372.

La Mesa city, SW California 92041*; pop. 50,342.

La Mirada city, SW California 90638; pop. 40,986.

Lancaster city, SW California 93534*; pop. 48,027.
— city, CEN. Ohio 43130; pop. 34,953.
— city, SE Pennsylvania 17604*; pop. 54,725.

Lanzhou city, NW China; pop. 1,151,700.

Lansdale boro., SE Pennsylvania 19446; pop. 16,526.

Lansdowne–Baltimore Highlands uninc. place, CEN. Maryland 21227; pop. 16,759.

Lansing vill., NE Illinois 60438; pop. 29,039.
— city, CEN. Michigan 48924*; cap.; pop. 130,414.

Laos republic, SE Indochina; 91,430 sq. mi.; pop. 4,024,000.

La Paz city, W Bolivia; admin. cap.; pop. 1,049,800.

Lapland reg., N Norway, Sweden, and Finland, and the NE USSR; inhabited by Lapps.

La Plata city, E Argentina; pop. 454,884.

La Porte city, NW Indiana 46350; pop. 21,796.

La Puente city, SW California 91747*; pop. 30,882.

Laramie city, SE Wyoming 82070; pop. 24,410.

Laredo city, S Texas 78040*; pop. 91,449.

Largo city, W Florida 33540*; pop. 58,977.

La Salle city, S Quebec, Canada; pop. 76,713.

Las Cruces city, S New Mexico 88001*; pop. 45,086.

Las Vegas city, SE Nevada 89114*; pop. 164,674.

Latvian SSR constituent republic, NE USSR; 24,600 sq. mi.; pop. 2,680,000; cap. Riga. Also **Latvia.**

Laurel city, SE Mississippi 39440*; pop. 21,897.

Lurentian Mountains mtn. range, E Canada.

Lausanne city, W Switzerland; pop. 128,800.

Laval town, S Quebec, Canada; pop. 284,164.

Lawndale city, SW California 90260; pop. 23,460.

Lawrence town, CEN. Indiana 46226; pop. 25,591.
— city, E Kansas 66044*; pop. 52,738.
— city, NE Massachusetts 08142*; pop. 63,175.

Lawton city, SW Oklahoma 73501*; pop. 80,054.

Leavenworth city, NE Kansas 66048; pop. 33,656.

Lebanon republic, SW Asia; 3,950 sq. mi.; pop. 2,965,000; cap. Beirut.
— city, SE Pennsylvania 17042; pop. 25,711.

Leeds city and co. boro., CEN. England; pop. 451,845.

Lees Summit city, W Missouri 64063; pop. 28,741.

Leeward Islands N isl. group, Lesser Antilles.

Leghorn city, NW Italy; pop. 176,757. Also **Livorno.**

Le Havre city, N France; pop. 196,000.

Leicester co. boro., CEN. England; pop. 328,835.

Leiden city, W Netherlands; pop. 109,254.

Leipzig city, CEN. Germany; pop. 545,307.

Lemay uninc. place, NE Missouri 63125; pop. 35,424.

Lemon Grove city, SW California 92045; pop. 20,780.

Leningrad city, NW RSFSR; pop. 4,456,000; *formerly called* St. Petersburg, Petrograd.

Leominster city, CEN. Massachusetts 01453; pop. 34,508.

Leopoldville *the former name of* Kinshasa.

Lesbos isl. of Greece off NW Turkey; 623 sq. mi.

Lesotho independent member of the Commonwealth of Nations; enclave in E South Africa; 11,720 sq. mi.; pop. 1,760,000; cap. Maseru.

Lesser Antilles See **Antilles.**

Lethbridge city, S Alberta, Canada; pop. 46,752.

Lévis city, S Quebec, Canada; pop. 17,819.

Levittown uninc. place, SE New York 11756; pop. 57,045.

Lewiston city, W Idaho 83501; pop. 27,986.
— city, SW Maine 04240; pop. 40,481.

Lewiston W Idaho 83501; pop. 27,986.

Lexington city, CEN. Kentucky 40511*; pop. 204,165.
— town, NE Massachusetts 02173; pop. 29,479.
— city, CEN. North Carolina 27292; pop. 15,711.

Leyden See **Leiden.**

Leyte isl., E Philippines, 2,875 sq. mi.

Lhasa city, S Tibet, cap.; pop. 80,000.

Liberia republic, W Africa; 38,250 sq. mi.; pop. 2,595,000; cap. Monrovia.

Libreville city, W Gabon; cap.; pop. 352,000.

Libya socialist state, N Africa; 685,524 sq. mi.; pop. 4,206,000; cap. Tripoli.

Liechtenstein monarchy, CEN. Europe; 62 sq. mi.; pop. 28,000; cap. Vaduz.

Liège city, E Belgium pop. 196,825.

Lille city, N France; pop. 167,791.

Lilongwe city, CEN. Malawi; cap.; pop. 220,300.

Lima city, W Peru; cap.; pop. 5,659,200.
— city, W Ohio; 45802*; pop. 47,827.

Limerick co. boro., W Ireland; pop. 60,665.

Limoges city, CEN. France; pop. 133,000.

Lincoln city, CEN. Illinois 62656; pop. 16,327.
— city, SE Nebraska 68501*; cap.; pop. 171,932.
— town, NE Rhode Island 02865; pop. 16,949.

Lincoln Park city, SE Michigan 48146; pop. 45,105.

Linden city, NE New Jersey 07036; pop. 37,836.

Lindenhurst vill., SE New York 11757; pop. 26,919.

Lisbon city, W Portugal; cap; pop. 829,600.

Lithuanian SSR constituent republic, NW USSR; 25,200 sq. mi.; pop. 3,690,000; cap. Vilnius. Also **Lithuania.**

Little Rock city, CEN. Arkansas 72201*; cap.; pop. 158,915.

Littleton town, CEN. Colorado 80120*; pop. 28,631.

Livermore city, W California 94550*; pop. 48,349.

Liverpool co. boro., W England; pop. 544,861.

Livingston urb. twp., NE New Jersey 07039; pop. 28,040.

Livonia city, SE Michigan 48150*; pop. 104,814.

Lockport city, NW New York 14094; pop. 24,844.

Lodi city, CEN. California 95240*; pop. 35,221.
— boro., NE New Jersey 07644; pop. 23,956.

Lódz city, CEN. Poland; pop. 851,500.

Logan city, N Utah 84321; pop. 26,844.

Logan, Mount peak, SW Yukon Territory, Canada; 19,850 ft.

Logansport city, CEN. Indiana 46947; pop. 17,731.

Loire river, SE France; 620 mi. long.

Lombard vill., NE Illinois 60148; pop. 36,879.

Lomé city, S Togo; cap.; pop. 366,476.

Lomita city, SW California 90717; pop. 17,191.

Lompoc city, SW California 93436*; pop. 26,267.

London city and co., SE England; cap.; 1 sq. mil.; pop. 5,000 (the city proper): 117 sq. mi.; pop. 3,195,000 (the co.): 610 sq. mi.; pop. 6,677,928 (Greater London).
— city, Ontario, Canada; pop. 240,392.

Long Beach city, SW California 90801*; pop. 361,355.
— city, SE New York 11561*; pop. 34,073.

Long Branch city, E New Jersey 07740*; pop. 29,819.

Long Island isl., SE New York; 1,723 sq. mi.
Long Island Sound inlet of the Atlantic betw. Long Island and Connecticut.
Longmeadow town, S Massachusetts 01106; pop. 16,301.
Longmont city, N Colorado 80501; pop. 42,942.
Loungueuil city, SW Quebec, Canada; pop. 122,429.
Longview city, NE Texas 75601*; pop. 62,762.
— city, SW Washington 98632; pop. 31,052.
Lorain city, N Ohio 44052*; pop. 75,416.
Lorraine reg., E France.
Los Alamos uninc. place, CEN. New Mexico 87544; site of the development of the atom bomb; pop. 11,039.
Los Altos city, W California 94022; pop. 25,769.
Los Angeles city, SW California 90052*; pop. 2,968,579.
Los Gatos city, W California 95030*; pop. 26,593.
Louisiana state, S United States; 48,523 sq. mi.; pop. 4,206,098; cap. Baton Rouge.
Louisville city, N Kentucky 40201*; pop. 298,694.
Lourdes town, SW France; famous shrine; pop. 17,870.
Loveland city, N Colorado 80537; pop. 30,215.
Lowell city, NE Massachusetts 01853*; pop. 92,418.
Lower California penin., NW Mexico; betw. the Gulf of California and the Pacific. Also **Baja California.**
Lower Merion uninc. urb. twp., SE Pennsylvania 19003; pop. 59,651.
Lowlands areas of low elevation, E and S Scotland.
Luanda city, NW Angola; cap.; pop. 475,328.
Lubbock city, NW Texas 79408*; pop. 173,979.
Lübeck city, NE Germany; pop. 210,681.
Lucerne, Lake of lake, CEN. Switzerland; 44 sq. mi.
Lucknow city, CEN. Uttar Predesh, India; cap.; pop. 895,721.
Lüda city, NE China; pop. 1,185,000.
Ludlow town, S Massachusetts 01056; pop. 18,150.
Lufkin city, E Texas 75901*; pop. 28,562.
Lumberton city, S North Carolina 28358; pop. 18,340.
Lusaka city, CEN. Zambia; cap.; pop. 870,030.
Lutherville-Timonium uninc. place, NE Maryland 21093; pop. 17,854.
Luxembourg, Grand Duchy of, monarchy; betw. Belgium, France, and Germany; 999 sq. mi.; pop. 379,000.
— city, CEN. Luxembourg; cap.; pop. 76,640. Also **Luxemburg.**
Luxor city, E Egypt; near the site of ancient Thebes; pop. 30,000.
Luzon isl., N Philippines; 40,420 sq. mi.
Lvov city, W Ukrainian SSR; pop. 790,000.
Lynbrook vill., SE New York 11563; pop. 20,424.
Lynchburg city, CEN. Virginia 24505*; pop. 66,743.
Lyndhurst urb. twp., NE New Jersey 07071; pop. 20,326.
— city, N Ohio 44124; pop. 18,092.
Lynn city, NE Massachusetts 01901*; pop. 78,471.
Lynnwood city, CEN. Washington 98036; pop. 21,937.
Lynwood city, SW California 90262*; pop. 48,409.
Lyon city, CEN. France; pop. 415,000.
Macao isl., Canton river delta, China.
— Portuguese special terr. comprising a penin. of Macao isl. and two small isls.; 6 sq. mi.; pop. 461,000.
— city; cap of Macao; pop. 461,000.
Macedonia reg., SE Europe; divided among Bulgaria, Greece, and Yugoslavia; 25,636 sq. mi.
Mackenzie river, NW Canada; 2,640 mi. long.
Mackinac, Straits of channel betw. Lakes Michigan and Huron; ab. 5 mi. wide and 40 mi. long.
Mackinac Island isl., Straits of Mackinac.
Macomb city, W Illinois 61455; pop. 19,682.
Macon city, CEN. Georgia 31201*; pop. 116,860.
Madagascar isl. republic, Indian Ocean off SE Africa; 226,662 sq. mi.; pop. 11,980,000; cap. Antananarivo: also called **Malagasy Republic.**
Madeira isl. group W of Morocco; an adm. dist. of Portugal; 306 sq. mi.; pop. 264,787; cap. Funchal.
Madera city, CEN. California 93637; pop. 21,732.
Madison boro., N New Jersey 07940; pop. 15,357.
— city, CEN. Wisconsin 53701*; cap.; pop. 170,616.
Madison Heights city, SE Michigan 48071; pop. 35,375.
Madisonville city, W Kentucky 42431; pop. 16,979.
Madras city, S India; pop. 3,276,622.
Madrid city, CEN. Spain; cap.; pop. 3,100,507.

Madura isl. of Indonesia E of Java; 1,762 sq. mi.
Magdeburg city, CEN. Germany; pop. 290,579.
Magellan, Strait of channel betw. the Atlantic and Pacific, separating the South American mainland from Tierra del Fuego.
Magnitogorsk city, S RSFSR; pop. 410,000.
Maine state, NE United States; 33,215 sq. mi.; pop. 1,125,030; cap. Augusta.
Main River river, CEN. Germany; 305 mi. long.
Majorca largest of the Balearic Islands; 1,405 sq. mi.
Malabar coastal reg., SW India. Also **Malabar Coast.**
Malacca city, W Malaysia; pop. 86,357.
Malacca, Strait of strait betw. Sumatra and the Malay Peninsula.
Málaga city, S Spain; pop. 566,330.
Malagasy Republic See **Madagascar.**
Malawi republic, SE Africa; 45,747 sq. mi.; pop. 8,831,000; cap. Lilongwe.
Malay Archipelago isl. group off SE Asia; includes isls. of Indonesia, Malaysia, and the Philippines.
Malay Peninsula S penin. of Asia; includes Malaya, Singapore, and part of Thailand.
Malaysia island monarchy including Malaya, Sarawak, and Sabah (North Borneo); 127,581 sq. mi.; pop. 17,886,000; cap. Kuala Lumpur.
Malden city, NE Massachusetts 02148; pop. 53,386.
Maldives isl. republic, Indian Ocean S of India; 115 sq. mi.; pop. 214,000; cap. Male.
Mali republic, W Africa; 478,841 sq. mi.; pop. 8,151,000; cap. Bamako.
Mallorca the Spanish name of Majorca.
Malta republic, CEN. Mediterranean; comprises the islands of Malta, Gozo, Comino, and two islets; 122 sq. mi.; pop. 353,000; cap. Valletta.
Mamaroneck vill., SE New York 10543; pop. 17,616.
Man, Isle of one of the British Isles, CEN. Irish Sea; 227 sq. mi.; pop. 61,723; cap. Douglas.
Managua city, SW Nicaragua; cap.; pop. 552,900.
Managua, Lake lake, SW Nicaragua; 390 sq. mi.
Manchester co. boro. and city, SE Lancashire, England; pop. 448,604.
— town, N Connecticut 06040*; pop. 49,061.
— city, S New Hampshire 03101*; pop. 90,936.
Manchuria former div., NE China.
Mandalay city, CEN. Myanmar; pop. 533,000.
Manhattan city, NE Kansas 66502*; pop. 32,644.
— boro., New York 10001*; pop. 1,428,285.
Manhattan Beach city, SW California 90266; pop. 31,542.
Manila city, W Luzon, Philippines; pop. 1,879,000.
Manitoba prov., CEN. Canada; 246,512 sq. mi.; pop. 1,021,506; cap. Winnipeg.
Manitoba, Lake lake, SW Manitoba; 1,817 sq. mi.
Manitowoc city, E Wisconsin 54220*; pop. 32,547.
Mankato city, S Minnesota 56001*; pop. 28,646.
Mansfield city, NE Connecticut 06250; pop. 20,634.
— city, CEN. Ohio 44901*; pop. 53,927.
Maple Heights city, NE Ohio 44137; pop. 29,735.
Maple Shade urb. twp., SW New Jersey 08052; pop. 20,525.
Maplewood vill., E Minnesota 55109; pop. 26,990.
— urb. twp. NE New Jersey 07040; pop. 22,950.
Maracaibo city, NW Venezuela; pop. 1,206,726.
Maracaibo, Lake lake, NW Venezuela; ab. 5,000 sq. mi.
Marblehead town, NE Massachusetts 01945*; pop. 20,126.
Marietta city, NW Georgia; 30060*; pop. 30,821.
— city, SE Ohio 45750; pop. 16,467.
Marion city, CEN. Indiana 46952*; pop. 35,874.
— city, E Iowa 52302; pop. 19,474.
— city, CEN Ohio 43302; pop. 37,040.
Markham vill., NE Illinois 60426; pop. 15,172.
Marlborough city, CEN. Massachusetts 01752; pop. 30,617.
Marmara, Sea of sea betw. Europe and Asia, connecting the Bosporus and the Dardanelles. Also **Marmora.**
Marne river, NE France; 325 mi. long.
Marquesas Islands isl. group, French Polynesia; 492 sq. mi.
Marquette city, NW Michigan 49855; pop. 21,967.
Marrakech city, SW Morocco; provincial cap.; pop. 1,455,000.
Marrero uninc. place; SW Louisiana 70072; pop. 36,548.
Marseille city, SE France; pop. 801,000. Also **Marseilles.**
Marshall city, NE Texas 75670*; pop. 24,921.

Marshall Islands isl. group in Pacific; an adm. dist. of the Trust Terr. of the Pacific Islands; 66 sq. mi.; pop. 25,000; cap. Jaluit.

Marshalltown city, CEN. Iowa 50158; pop. 26,938.

Marshfield city, E Massachusetts 02050; pop. 20,916.

Marshfield city, CEN. Wisconsin 54449; pop. 18,290.

Martinez city, W California 94553*; pop. 22,582.

Martinique isl. Lesser Antilles; French overseas dept.; 421 sq. mi.; pop. 360,000; cap. Fort-de-France.

Martinsville city, S Virginia 24112*; pop. 18,149.

Maryland state, E United States; 10,577 sq. mi.; pop. 4,216,941; cap. Annapolis.

Mason City city, N Iowa 50401*; pop. 30,144.

Mason-Dixon Line boundary betw. Pennsylvania and Maryland, surveyed by Charles Mason and Jeremiah Dixon in 1763; regarded as the division line for the North and the South, United States.

Massachusetts state, NE United States; 8,257 sq. mi.; pop. 5,737,081; cap. Boston.

Massapequa uninc. place, SE New York; 11758*; pop. 24,454.

Massapequa Park vill., SE New York 11762; pop. 19,779.

Massillon city, NE Ohio 44646; pop. 30,557.

Matsu isl. of the Republic of China, Formosa Strait; 4 sq. mi.

Matterhorn mtn. in the Alps on the Swiss-Italian border; 14,701 ft.

Mattoon city, CEN. Illinois 61938; pop. 19,293.

Maui isl. of the Hawaiian Islands; 728 sq. mi.

Maumee city, NW Ohio 43537; pop. 15,747.

Mauna Loa active volcano, CEN. Hawaii (isl.); 13,675 ft.

Mauritania, Islamic Republic of republic, W Africa; 397,700 sq. mi.; pop. 2,000,000; cap. Nouakchott.

Mauritius island monarchy in the Indian Ocean, 788 sq. mi., pop. 1,080,000; cap. Port Louis.

Mayagüez city, W Puerto Rico 00708; pop. 82,703.

Mayfield Heights city, N Ohio 44124; pop. 21,550.

Mayotte dependency of France, isl. in the Mozambique Channel, off Madagascar, 144 sq. mi.; pop. 82,300; cap. Dzaoudzi.

Maywood city, SW California 90270; pop. 16,996.

— vill., NE Illinois 60153*; pop. 27,998.

McAlester city, CEN. Oklahoma 74501*; pop. 17,255.

McAllen city, S Texas 78501*; pop. 67,042.

McKeesport city, SW Pennsylvania 15134*; pop. 31.012.

McKinley, Mount peak, CEN. Alaska, highest in North America; 20,300 ft.

McKinney city N Texas 75069; pop. 16,249.

McLean uninc. place, NE Virginia 22101; pop. 35,664.

Mead, Lake reservoir formed by Hoover Dam in the Colorado River, Arizona and Nevada; 246 sq. mi.

Meadville city, NW Pennsylvania 16335; pop. 15,544.

Mecca city, W Saudi Arabia; birthplace of Mohammed and holy city to which Muslims make pilgrimages; pop. 550,000.

Medford city, NE Massachusetts 02155; pop. 58,076.

— city, SW Oregon 97501*; pop. 39,603.

Medicine Hat city, SE Alberta, Canada; pop. 32,811.

Medina city, W Saudi Arabia; a Muslim holy city and site of Mohammed's tomb; pop. 90,000.

Mediterranean Sea sea betw. Europe, Asia, and Africa; 965,000 sq. mi.

Mekong river, SE Asia; 2,500 mi. long.

Melanesia isls. of the W Pacific S of the Equator; ab. 60,000 sq. mi.

Melbourne city, S Victoria, Australia; cap.; pop. 3,002,300.

— city, E Florida 32901*; pop. 46,536.

Melrose city, NE Massachusetts 02176; pop. 30,055.

Melrose Park vill., NE Illinois 60160*; pop. 20,735.

Memphis city, SW Tennessee 38101*; pop. 646,174.

— ancient city, cap. of Egypt during the Old Kingdom, S of the Nile Delta.

Menlo Park city, W California 94025*; pop. 26,438.

Menomonee Falls vill., SE Wisconsin 53051*; pop. 27,845.

Mentor city, NE Ohio 44060; pop. 42,065.

Merced city, CEN. California 95340*; pop. 36,423.

Mercerville-Hamilton Square uninc. place, CEN. New Jersey 08619*; pop. 25,446.

Meriden city, CEN. Connecticut 06450; pop. 57,118.

Meridian city, E Mississippi 39301*; pop. 46,577.

Merrick uninc. place, SE New York 11566; pop. 24,478.

Merrillville city, NW Indiana 46410; pop. 27,677.

Merritt Island uninc. place, CEN. Florida 32952; pop. 30,708.

Mesa city, CEN. Arizona 85201*; pop. 152,453.

Mesabi Range range of hills, NE Minnesota; site of iron ore deposits.

Mesquite city, N Texas 75149; pop. 67,053.

Messina city, NE Sicily; pop. 272,119.

Metairie city, SW Louisiana 70004*; pop. 164,160.

Methuen city, NE Massachusetts 01844; pop. 36,701.

Meuse river, W Europe; 580 mi. long.

Mexico republic S North America; 756,066 sq. mi., pop. 81,883,000.

— **City**, CEN Mexico; cap.; pop. 8,236,960.

Mexico, Gulf of inlet of the Atlantic, among the United States, Mexico, and Cuba; 700,000 sq mi

Miami city, SE Florida 33152*; pop. 346,931.

Miami Beach city SE Florida 33139; pop. 96,298.

Michigan state, N United States; 58,216 sq. mi.; pop. 9,262.070; cap. Lansing.

Michigan, Lake one of the Great Lakes; betw. Michigan and Wisconsin; 22,400 sq. mi.

Michigan City city, N Indiana 46360; pop. 36,850.

Micronesia, Federated States of, isl. republic of the W Pacific, N of the equator; 271 sq. mi.; pop. 108,000; cap. Kolonia.

Middle River uninc. place, N Maryland 21220; pop. 26,756.

Middletown city, CEN Connecticut; 06457; pop. 39,040.

— urb. twp., E New Jersey 07748; pop. 61,615.

— city, SE New York 10940; pop. 21,454.

— city, SW Ohio 45042; pop. 43,719.

— town, SE Rhode Island 02840; pop. 17,216.

Midi S reg. of France.

Midland city, CEN. Michigan 48640*; pop. 37,269.

— city, W Texas 79701*; pop. 70,525.

Midlands counties of CEN. England.

Midway Islands 2 isls. NW of Honolulu, under control of the U.S. Navy; 2 sq. mi.; scene of an important battle of World War II, June 1942.

Midwest City city, CEN. Oklahoma 73110; pop. 49,559.

Milan city, N Italy; pop. 1,464,127.

Milford city, SW Connecticut 06460; pop. 50,898.

— uninc. place, CEN. Massachusetts 01757; pop. 23,390.

Millbrae city, W California 94030; pop. 20,058.

Millburn urb. twp., NE New Jersey 07041; pop. 19,543.

Millcreek boro., CEN. Pennsylvania 17060, pop. 44,303.

Millington town, SW Tennessee 38053; pop. 20,236.

Millville city, S New Jersey 08332; pop. 24,815.

Milpitas city, W California 95035; pop. 37,820.

Milton town, E Massachusetts 02186; pop. 25,860.

Milwaukee city, SE Wisconsin 53203*; pop. 636,297.

Milwaukie city, NW Oregon 97222; pop. 17,931.

Mindanao isl. S Philippines; 36,537 sq. mi.

Mindoro isl., CEN. Philippines; 3,759 sq. mi.

Mineola vill., SE New York 11501*; pop. 20,757.

Minneapolis city, E Minnesota 55401*; pop. 370,951.

Minnesota state, N United States; 84,068 sq. mi.; pop. 4,075,970; cap. St. Paul.

Minnetonka vill., E Minnesota 55343; pop. 38,683.

Minorca one of the Balearic islands; 271 sq. mi.

Minot city, N North Dakota 58701*; pop. 32,843.

Minsk city, CEN. Byelorussian SSR; cap.; pop. 1,295,000.

Miramar city, SE Florida 33023; pop. 32,813.

Mishawaka city, N Indiana 46544; pop. 40,224.

Mississippi state S United States; 47,716 sq. mi.; pop. 2,520,631; cap. Jackson.

Mississippi River river, CEN. United States; 2,350 mi. long.

Missoula city, W Montana 59801; pop. 33,351.

Missouri state, CEN. United States; 69,686 sq. mi.; pop. 4,916,759; cap. Jefferson City.

Missouri River river, CEN. United States; 2,470 mi. long.

Mobile city, SW Alabama 36601*; pop. 200,452.

Mobile Bay inlet of the Gulf of Mexico, SW Alabama.

Modesto city, CEN. California 95350*; pop. 106,963.

Mojave Desert arid reg. S California; ab. 15,000 sq. mi.

Moldavian SSR constituent republic, SW USSR; 13,000 sq. mi.; pop. 4,338,000; cap. Kishinev. Also **Moldavia.**

Moline city, NW Illinois 61265; pop. 46,407.

Molokai isl., CEN. Hawaiian Islands; 259 sq. mi.

Molucca Islands isl. group of Indonesia, betw. Sulawesi and New Guines; 33,315 sq. mi.

Monaco monarchy, SE France; 368 acres: pop. 29,000.

Moncton city, SE New Brunswick, Canada; pop. 55,934.

Mongolia republic (**Mongolian People's Republic,** *formerly* **Outer Mongolia**). CEN Asia; 604,000 sq. mi.; pop. 2,116,000; cap. Ulan Bator

— **Inner Mongolia** reg. N China, 454,600 sq. mi.; pop. 21,456,798; cap. Hohhot.

Monongahela River river, West Virginia and W Pennsylvania; 128 mi. long.

Monroe city, N Louisiana 71201*; pop. 57,597.

— city, SE Michigan 48161; pop. 23,531.

Monroeville boro., SW Pennsylvania 15145; pop. 30,977.

Monrovia city, E Liberia; cap.; pop. 421,000.

— city, SW California 91016; pop. 30,531.

Montana state, NW United States; 147,138 sq. mi.; pop. 786,690; cap. Helena.

Mont Blanc highest mountain of the Alps, on the French-Italian border; 15,781 ft.; site of tunnel, 7½ mi. long, connecting France and Italy.

Montclair city, SW California 91763; pop. 22,628.

— town, NE New Jersey 07042*; pop. 38,321.

Montebello city, SW California 90640; pop. 52,929.

Monte Carlo city, Monaco; pop. 10,000.

Montenegro constituent republic, S Yugoslavia; 5333 sq. mi.; pop. 633,000; cap. Titograd.

Monterey city, W California 93940*; pop. 27,558.

Monterey Park city, SW California 91754; pop. 54,338.

Monterrey city, NE Mexico; pop. 1,090,000.

Montevideo city, S Uruguay; cap.; pop. 1,311,976.

Montgomery city, CEN. Alabama 36104*; cap.; pop. 178,157.

Monticello estate and residence of Thomas Jefferson, near Charlottesville, Virginia.

Montmartre dist., N Paris; former artists' quarter.

Montpelier city, CEN. Vermont 05602*; cap.; pop. 8,241.

Montreal city, S Quebec, Canada; pop. 1,080,546.

Montreal-Nord city, S Quebec, Canada; pop. 97,250. Also **Montreal-North.**

Mont-Royal town, S Quebec, Canada; pop. 20,514.

Mont Saint Michel isl. off NW France; site of an ancient fortress and abbey.

Montville city, SE Connecticut 06353; pop. 16,455.

Moorehead city, CEN. Oklahoma 73852; pop. 18,761.

Moorhead city, W Minnesota 56560; pop. 29,998.

Moose Jaw city, S Saskatchewan, Canada; pop. 32,581.

Moravia reg., CEN. Czechoslovakia.

Morgan City city, S Louisiana 70380; pop. 16,114.

Morgantown city, N West Virginia 26505*; pop. 27,605.

Morocco monarchy, NW Africa; ab. 177,117 sq. mi.; pop. 25,113,000; cap. Rabat.

Morristown town, CEN. New Jersey 07960; pop. 16,614.

— city, NE Tennessee 37814*; pop. 19,570.

Morton Grove vill., NE Illinois 60053; pop. 23,747.

Moscow city, W USSR; cap. USSR and RSFSR; pop. 7,915,000.

Moselle river, NE France, Luxembourg, and W Germany; 320 mi. long.

Moss Point city, SE Mississippi 39563; pop. 18,998.

Mosul city, N Iraq; pop. 293,100.

Mountain Brook city, CEN. Alabama 35223; pop. 17,400.

Mountain View city, W California 94042*; pop. 58,655.

Mount Clemens city, SE Michigan 48046*; pop. 18,991.

Mountlake Terrace city, CEN. Washington 98043; pop. 16,534.

Mount Lebanon uninc. urb. twp., SW Pennsylvania 15228; pop. 34,414.

Mount Pleasant city, CEN. Michigan 48858; pop. 23,746.

Mount Prospect vill., NE Illinois 60056*; pop. 52,634.

Mount Vernon home and burial place of George Washington, near Washington, D.C.

— city, S Illinois 62864; pop. 16,995.

— city, SE New York 10551*; pop. 66,713.

Mozambique republic SE Africa; 313,661 sq. mi.; pop. 15,696,000; cap. Maputo.

Muncie city, E Indiana 47302; pop. 77,216.

Mundelein vill., NE Illinois 60060; pop. 17,053.

Munich city, SE Germany; pop. 1,211,617.

Munster town, NW Indiana 46321; pop. 20,671.

Murfreesboro city, CEN. Tennessee; 37130*; pop. 32,845.

Murmansk city, NW USSR; pop. 388,000.

Murray city, CEN. Utah 84107; pop. 25,750.

Murray River river, SE Australia; 1,600 mi. long.

Muscat and Oman: *the former name of* Oman.

Muscatine city, E Iowa 52761; pop. 22,405.

Muskegon city, W Michigan 49440*; pop. 40,823.

Muskogee city, E Oklahoma 74401*; pop. 40,011.

Myanmar military govt., *formerly* **Burma,** SE Asia; 261,228 sq. mi.; pop. 41,675,000; cap. Yangôn (Rangoon).

Mysore city, S India; pop. 355,685.

Nacogdoches city E Texas 75961*; pop. 27,149.

Nagasaki city, NW Kyushu island, Japan; largely destroyed by a U.S. atomic bomb, Aug. 9, 1945; pop. 445,854.

Nagoya city, CEN. Honshu isl., Japan; pop. 2,149,517.

Nagpur city, CEN. India; pop. 1,219,461.

Nairobi city, SW Kenya; cap.; pop. 1,103,600.

Namibia republic, SW Africa; 317,818 sq. mi.; pop. 1,302,000; cap. Windhoek.

Nampa city, SW Idaho 83651; pop. 25,112.

Nanjing city, E China; cap. 1928–37; pop. 2,022,500.

Nantes city, W France; pop. 245,000.

Nantucket isl. off SE Massachusetts; 57 sq. mi.

Napa city, W California 94558*; pop. 50,879.

Naperville city, NE Illinois 60540; pop. 42,601.

Naples city, SW Italy; pop. 1,202,582.

Narragansett Bay inlet of the Atlantic, SE Rhode Island.

Nashua city, S New Hampshire 03060; pop. 67,865.

Nashville city, CEN. Tennessee 37202*; cap.; pop. 455,651.

Nassau city, New Providence, Bahamas Islands; cap.; pop. 101,503.

Natal prov., E South Africa; 21,344 sq. mi.; pop. 2,145,018; cap. Pietermaritzburg.

Natchez city, SW Mississippi 39120*; pop. 22,209.

Natchitoches city, CEN. Louisiana 71457; pop. 16,664.

Natick town, NE Massachusetts 01760*; pop. 29,461.

National City city, SW California 92050; pop. 48,772.

Naugatuck town, CEN. Connecticut 06770; pop. 26,456.

Nauru Republic isl. W-CENT. Pacific just south of Equator (Oceania); 8 sq. mi., pop. 9,000; cap. Yaren.

Navarre reg. and former kingdom, N Spain and SW France.

Nazareth town, N Israel; scene of Christ's childhood; pop. 40,400.

Nebraska state, CEN. United States; 77,227 sq. mi.; pop. 1,569,825; cap. Lincoln.

Nederland city, SE Texas 77627; pop. 16,855.

Needham town, NE Massachusetts 02192; pop. 29,748.

Neenah city, CEN. Wisconsin 54956; pop. 23,272.

Negev desert reg., S Israel; 4,700 sq. mi. Also **Negeb.**

Nejd prov., CEN. Saudi Arabia; ab. 450,000 sq. mi.; cap. Riyadh.

Nepal monarchy betw. Tibet and India; 56,827 sq. mi.; pop. 19,000,000; cap. Kathmandu.

Neptune urb. twp., E New Jersey 07753; pop. 28,366.

Netherlands monarchy, NW Europe; 16,026 sq. mi.; pop. 14,472,000; cap. Amsterdam; seat of government, The Hague.

Netherlands Antilles 3 isls. N of Venezuela and 3 in the Leeward Islands group; 308 sq. mi.; pop. 196,000; cap. Willemstad.

Netherlands Guiana See **Suriname.**

Nevada state, W United States; 110,540 sq. mi.; pop. 800,493; cap. Carson city.

New Albany city, S Indiana 47150; pop. 37,103.

Newark city, W California 94560; pop. 32,126.

— city, NW Delaware 19715*; pop. 25,247.

— city, NE New Jersey 07102*; pop. 329,248.

— city, CEN. Ohio 43055*; pop. 41,200.

New Bedford city, SE Massachusetts 02741*; pop. 98,478.

New Berlin city, SE Wisconsin 53151; pop. 30,529.

New Braunfels city, CEN. Texas 78130*; pop. 22,402.

New Brighton vill., E Minnesota 55112; pop. 23,269.

New Britain city, CEN. Connecticut 06050*; pop. 73,840.

New Brunswick city, CEN. New Jersey 08901*; pop. 41,442.

— prov., SE Canada; 27,834 sq. mi.; pop. 718,400; cap. Fredericton.

Newburgh city, SE New York 12550*; pop. 23,438.

Newburyport city, NE Massachusetts 01950; pop. 15,900.

New Caledonia isl. E of Australia; comprising with adjacent isls. a French overseas terr.; 7,233 sq. mi.; pop. 168,000; cap. Nouméa.

New Canaan city, SW Connecticut 06840; pop. 17,931.
New Castle city, E Indiana 47362; pop. 20,056.
— city, W Pennsylvania 16101*; pop. 33,621.
Newcastle upon Tyne city, NE England; pop. 203,591. Also Newcastle, Newcastle on Tyne.
New City uninc. place, SE New York, 10956; pop. 35,859.
New Delhi city, Delhi terr., India; cap. of India; pop. 273,036.
New England NE section of the United States, including Maine, New Hampshire, Vermont, Massachusetts, Rhode Island, and Connecticut.
Newfoundland prov., E Canada; comprising the island of Newfoundland (43,359 sq. mi.) and Labrador on the mainland; 143,510 sq. mi.; pop. 579,700; cap. St. John's.
New Georgia isl. group, British Solomon Islands; ab. 2,000 sq. mi.
New Guinea isl., N of Australia; 304,200 sq. mi. See Papua New Guinea, West New Guinea.
New Hampshire state, NE United States; 9,304 sq. mi.; pop. 920,610; cap. Concord.
New Haven city, S Connecticut 06510*; pop. 126,089.
New Hebride See Vanuatu.
New Hope city, SE Minnesota 55428; pop. 23,087.
New Iberia city, S Louisiana 70560*; pop. 32,766.
New Ireland volcanic isl. of the Bismarck Archipelago, S Pacific; 3,700 sq. mi.; pop. 70,800; part of Papua New Guinea.
Newington city, CEN. Connecticut 06111; pop. 28,841.
New Jersey state, E United States; 7,836 sq. mi.; pop. 7,365,011; cap. Trenton.
New Kensington city, W Pennsylvania 15068*; pop. 17,660.
New London city, SE Connecticut 06320; pop. 28,842.
Newmarket town S Ontario, Canada; pop. 24,795.
New Mexico state, SW United States; 121,666 sq. mi.; pop. 1,303,445; cap. Santa Fé.
New Milford boro., NE New Jersey 07646; pop. 16,876.
New Orleans city, SE Louisiana 70113*; pop. 557,927.
New Philadelphia city, CEN. Ohio 44663; pop. 16,883.
Newport city, N Kentucky 41071*; pop. 21,587.
— city, SE Rhode Island 02840*; pop. 29,259.
Newport Beach city, SW California 92660*; pop. 63,475.
Newport News city, SE Virginia 23607*; pop. 144,903.
New Rochelle city, SE New York 10802*; pop. 70,794.
New South Wales state, SE Australia; 309,500 sq. mi.; pop. 5,771,900; cap. Sydney.
Newton city, CEN. Iowa 50208; pop. 15,292.
— city, CEN. Kansas 67114; pop. 16,332.
— city, E Massachusetts 02158; pop. 83,622.
Newtown city, SW Connecticut 06470; pop. 19,107.
New Westminster city, SW British Columbia, Canada; pop. 36,393.
New York state, NE United States; 49,576 sq. mi.; pop. 17,558,072; cap. Albany.
— city, SE New York 10001*; divided into the five boroughs of the Bronx, Brooklyn, Manhattan, Queens, and Richmond (Staten Island); 365 sq. mi.; pop. 7,071,639.
New York State Barge Canal waterway system, New York; connects the Hudson River with Lakes Erie, Champlain, and Ontario, 525 mi. long.
New Zealand monarchy, comprising a group of isle SE of Australia; 104,454 sq. mi.; pop. 3,389,000; cap. Wellington.
Niagara Falls city, W New York 14302*; pop. 71,384.
— city, S Ontario, Canada; pop. 69,423.
Niagara River river betw. Ontario, Canada, and New York State, connecting Lakes Erie and Ontario; in its course occurs Niagara Falls, a cataract divided by Goat Island into the American Falls, ab. 167 ft. high and 1,000 ft. wide, and Horseshoe Falls on the Canadian side, ab. 160 ft. high and 2,500 ft. wide.
Nicaragua republic, Central America; 49,291 sq. mi.; pop. 3,871,000; cap. Managua.
Nicaragua, Lake lake, SW Nicaragua; 3,100 sq. mi.
Nice city, SE France; pop. 342,000.
Nicobar Islands isl. terr. of India; 19 isls. in the Bay of Bengal; 754 sq. mi.; pop. 22,000.
Nicosia city, CEN. Cyprus; cap.; pop. 166,900.
Niger river, W Africa; ab. 2,600 mi. long.
Niger, Republic of republic, CEN. Africa, 458,074 sq. mi.; pop. 7,800,000; cap. Niamey.
Nigeria, Federation of republic, W Africa; 356,669 sq. mi.; pop. 119,812,000; cap. Lagos.

Nile river, E Africa; 4,130 mi. long; the longest river in the world.
Niles vill., NE Illinois 60648; pop. 30,363.
— city, NE Ohio 44446; pop. 23,088.
Norfolk city, NE Nebraska 68701; pop. 19,449.
— city, SE Virginia 23501*; pop. 266,979.
Normal town, CEN. Illinois 61761; pop. 35,672.
Norman city, CEN. Oklahoma 73070*; pop. 68,020.
Normandy reg. and former prov., NW France.
Norridge vill., NE Illinois 606556; pop. 16,880.
Norristown boro., SE Pennsylvania 19401*; pop. 34,684.
North Adams city, NW Massachusetts 01247*; pop. 18,063.
North America N continent of the Western Hemisphere; 9,410,000 sq. mi. (including adjacent islands).
Northampton city, W Massachusetts 01060*; pop. 29,286.
North Andover town, NE Massachusetts 01845; pop. 20,129.
North Arlington boro., NE New Jersey 07032; pop. 16,587.
North Atlanta uninc. place, CEN. Georgia 30319; pop. 30,521.
North Attleborough town, E Massachusetts 02760*; pop. 21,095.
North Babylon uninc. place, SE New York 11703; pop. 19,019.
North Bay city, CEN. Ontario, Canada; pop. 51,639.
North Bellmore uninc. place, SE New York 11710; pop. 20,630.
North Bergen urb. twp., NE New Jersey 07047; pop. 47,019.
North Borneo See Sabah.
Northbrook vill., NE Illinois 60062; pop. 30,735.
North Cape promontory, N Norway.
North Carolina state, SE United States; 52,586 sq. mi.; pop. 5,881,385; cap. Raleigh.
North Chicago city, NE Illinois 60064; pop. 38,774.
North Dakota state, N United States; 70,665 sq. mi.; pop. 652,717; cap. Bismarck.
Northern Ireland part of the United Kingdom in N reg. of Ireland; 5,452 sq. mi.; pop. 1,578,100; cap. Belfast.
Northern Territory reg., N Australia; 519,800 sq. mi.; pop. 156,500; cap. Darwin.
Northglenn city, CEN. Colorado 80233; pop. 29,847.
North Haven city, S Connecticut 06473; pop. 22,080.
North Highlands uninc. place, CEN. California 95660; pop. 37,825.
North Island isl., N New Zealand; 44,281 sq. mi.
North Kingston town, S Rhode Island 02852; pop. 21,938.
North Korea See Korea.
North Las Vegas city, SE Nevada 89030; pop. 42,739.
North Little Rock city, CEN. Arkansas 72114*; pop. 64,388.
North Massapequa uninc. place, SE New York 11758; pop. 21,385.
North Miami city, SE Florida 33161; pop. 42,566.
North Miami Beach city, SE Florida 33160; pop. 36,481.
North Olmsted city, N Ohio 44070; pop. 36,486.
North Park uninc. place, NE Illinois 61111; pop. 15,806.
North Plainfield boro., NE New Jersey 07060; pop. 19,108.
North Platte city, CEN. Nebraska 69101*; pop. 24,509.
North Pole N extremity of the earth's axis.
North Providence town, NE Rhode Island 02908; pop. 24,188.
North Richland Hills town, N Texas 76118; pop. 30,592.
North Sea part of the Atlantic betw. Great Britain and Europe.
North Tonawanda city, SW New York 14120; pop. 35,760.
North Vancouver city, SW British Columbia, Canada; pop. 31,934.
Northwest Territories adm. div., N Canada; 1,271,442 sq. mi.; pop. 42,609.
Northwest Territory reg. awarded to the United States by Britain in 1783, extending from the Great Lakes S to the Ohio River and from Pennsylvania W to the Mississippi.
Norton Shores city, SW Michigan 49441; pop. 22,025.
Norwalk city, SW California 90650; pop. 84,901.
— city, SW Connecticut 06856*; pop. 77,767.
Norway monarchy, N Europe; 125,050 sq. mi.; pop. 4,246,000; cap. Oslo.
Norwich co. boro., E England; pop. 119,300.
— city, SE Connecticut 06360; pop. 38,074.
Nottingham co. boro., CEN. England; pop. 278,600.
Nova Scotia prov., E Canada; 20,402 sq. mi.; pop. 828,571; cap. Halifax.

Novato city, w California 94947; pop. 43,916.
Novaya Zemlya two isls., Arctic Ocean, NE RSFSR; ab. 35,000 sq. mi.
Novosibirsk city, sw Asian Russian SFSR, ab. 1,700 mi. E of Moscow; pop. 1,328,000.
Nürnberg city, CEN. Germany; pop. 484,184.
Nutley town, NE New Jersey 07110; pop. 28,998.
Oahu isl., CEN. Hawaiian Islands; 589 sq. mi.
Oak Forest city, NE Illinois 60452; pop. 26,096.
Oakland city, w California 94615*; pop. 339,288.
Oakland Park city, SE Florida 33308; pop. 22,944.
Oak Lawn vill., NE Illinois 60454*; pop. 60,590.
Oak Park vill., NE Illinois 60301*; pop. 54,887.
— city, SE Michigan 48237; pop. 31,537.
Oak Ridge city, E Tennessee 37830*; pop. 27,662.
Oakville town, s Ontario, Canada; pop. 68,950.
Ocala city, CEN. Florida 32670; pop. 37,170.
Oceania isls. of Melanesia, Micronesia, and Polynesia, and sometimes the Malay Archipelago and Australasia.
Oceanside city, sw California 92054*; pop. 76,698.
— uninc. place, SE New York 11572; pop. 33,639.
Oder river, CEN. Europe; 563 mi. long.
Odessa city, s Ukrainian SSR; pop. 1,115,000.
— city, w Texas 79760*; pop. 90,027.
Ogden city, N Utah 84401*; pop. 64,407.
Ohio state, CEN. United States; 41,222 sq. mi.; pop. 10,797,624; cap. Columbus.
Ohio River river, CEN. United States; 981 mi. long.
Oildale uninc. place, CEN. California 93308; pop. 23,382.
Okhotsk, Sea of inlet of the Pacific w of Kamchatka and the Kurile Islands.
Okinawa Japanese isl., largest of the Ryukyu Islands; 870 sq. mi.; pop. 1,161,000; cap. Naha.
Oklahoma state, CEN. United States; 69,919 sq. mi.; pop. 3,025,495; cap. Oklahoma City.
Oklahoma City city, CEN. Oklahoma 73100*; cap.; pop. 403,213.
Okmulgee city, CEN. Oklahoma 74447; pop. 16,263.
Okolona uninc. place, NW Kentucky 40219; pop. 20,039.
Olathe city, E Kansas 66061; pop. 37,258.
Old Bridge city, CEN. New Jersey 08857; pop. 21,815.
Olean city, sw New York 14760; pop. 18,207.
Olympia city, w Washington 98501*; cap.; pop. 27,447.
Olympus, Mount mtn., N Greece; regarded in Greek mythology as the home of the gods; 9,570 ft.
Omaha city, E Nebraska 68108; pop. 313,939.
Oman independent sultanate, SE Arabia; 120,000 sq. mi.; pop. 1,400,000; cap. Muscat.
Omsk city, s RSFSR; pop. 1,028,000.
Ontario city, sw California 91760*; pop. 88,820.
— prov., SE Canada; 344,090 sq. mi.; pop. 8,264,465; cap. Toronto.
Ontario, Lake easternmost of the Great Lakes; 7,540 sq. mi.
Opelika city, E Alabama 36801; pop. 21,896.
Opelousas city, CEN. Louisiana 70570; pop. 18,903.
Oporto city, w Portugal; pop. 335,700.
Opportunity uninc. place, E Washington 99214; pop. 21,241.
Orange former principality, now part of SE France.
— city, sw California 92667*; pop. 91,450.
— city, NE New Jersey 07050*; pop. 31,136.
— city, E Texas 77630*; pop. 23,628.
Orange River river, s Africa; 1,300 mi. long.
Orangevale uninc. place, CEN. California 95662; pop. 20,585.
Oregon state, NW United States; 96,981 sq. mi.; pop. 2,663,149; cap. Salem.
— city, N Ohio 43616; pop. 18,675.
Orem city, CEN. Utah 84057; pop. 52,399.
Orillia town, s Ontario, Canada; pop. 24,412.
Orinoco river, Venezuela; ab. 1,700 mi. long.
Orkney Islands isl. group, N of Scotland, comprising **Orkney**, a co. of Scotland; 376 sq. mi.; pop. 18,134; cap. Kirkwall.
Orlando city, CEN. Florida 32802*; pop. 128,394.
Orléans city, CEN. France; pop. 106,246.
Osaka city, s Honshu, Japan; pop. 2,635,156.
Oshawa city, s Ontario, Canada; pop. 107,023.
Oshkosh city, E Wisconsin 54901*; pop. 49,678.
Oslo city, SE Norway; cap.; pop. 457,819.
Ossa mtn., E Greece; 6,490 ft. See **Pelion.**

Ossining vill., SE New York 10562; pop. 120,196.
Ostend city, NW Belgium; pop. 70,125.
Oswego city, N New York 13126; pop. 19,793.
Otranto, Strait of strait betw. the Adriatic and Ionian seas; ab. 43 mi. wide.
Ottawa city, N Illinois 61350; pop. 18,166.
— city, SE Ontario, Canada; cap. of Canada; pop. 304,462.
Ottumwa city, SE Iowa 52501; pop. 27,381.
Ouagadougou city, CEN. Burkina Faso; cap.; pop. 441,500.
Outremont city, s Quebec, Canada; pop. 27,089.
Overland city, E Missouri 63114; pop. 19,620.
Overland Park uninc. place, NE Kansas 66204; pop. 81,784.
Owatonna city, s Minnesota 55060; pop. 18,632.
Owensboro city, NW Kentucky 42301*; pop. 54,450.
Owen Sound city, s Ontario, Canada; pop. 19,525.
Owosso city, CEN. Michigan 48867; pop. 16,455.
Oxford co. boro., CEN. England; pop. 119,909.
— city, sw Ohio 45056; pop. 17,655.
Oxnard city, sw California 93030*; pop. 108,195.
Ozark Mountains hilly uplands, sw Missouri, NW Arkansas, and NE Oklahoma.
Pacifica city, w California 94044; pop. 36,866.
Pacific Ocean ocean betw. the American continents and Asia and Australia; extending betw. the Arctic and Antarctic regions; ab. 70 million sq. mi.
Padua city, NE Italy; pop. 222,163.
Paducah city, w Kentucky 42001*; pop. 29,315.
Pago Pago town, SE Tutuila, American Samoa 96920; pop. 2,450.
Painesville city, NE Ohio 44077; pop. 16,341.
Pakistan republic, s Asia; 307,374 sq. mi.; pop. 122,666,000; cap. Islamabad.
Palatine vill., NE Illinois 60067; pop. 32,176.
Palau Islands isl. group, w Caroline Island; 188 sq. mi.
Palermo city, NW Sicily, Italy; cap.; pop. 731,483.
Palestine terr., E Mediterranean; 10,434 sq. mi.; cap. Jerusalem; divided (1947) by the United Nations into Israel and a terr. that became part of Jordan.
Palma city, w Majorca; cap. of the Balearic Islands, pop. 287,389.
Palm Springs city, s California 92263*; pop. 32,350.
Palo Alto city, w California 94303*; pop. 55,225.
Palomar, Mount mtn., s California; 6,126 ft.; site of **Mount Palomar Observatory.**
Pampa city, N Texas 79065; pop. 21,396.
Panama republic, Central America; 29,157 sq. mi. (excluding Canal Zone); pop. 2,418,000.
— **City,** near the Pacific end of the Panama Canal; cap of Panama; pop. 411,500.
Panama, Isthmus of isthmus connecting North and South America.
Panama Canal ship canal connecting the Atlantic and the Pacific across Panama; completed (1914) by the United States on the leased Canal Zone; 40 mi. long.
Panama Canal Zone See **Canal Zone.**
Panama City city, NW Florida 32401*; pop. 33,346.
Panay isl., CEN. Philippines; 4,446 sq. mi.
Papal States region in CEN. and NE Italy over which the Roman Catholic Church formerly had temporal power.
Papua New Guinea independent monarchy in the Commonwealth of Nations, s Pacific, consisting of the E half of New Guinea; the isls. of the Bismarck Archipelago; Bougainville and Buka in the Solomon Isls.; and a number of smaller isls.; 178,704 sq. mi.; pop. 3,671,000; cap. Port Moresby.
Paradise uninc. place, SE Nevada 89109; pop. 84,818.
Paraguay republic, CEN. South America; 157,048 sq. mi.; pop. 4,279,000; cap. Asunción.
Paraguay River river, CEN. South America; ab. 1,300 mi. long.
Paramaribo city, N Surinam; cap.; pop. 175,000.
Paramount city, sw California 90723; pop. 36,407.
Paramus boro., NE New Jersey 07652; pop. 26,474.
Paraná river, CEN. South America; ab. 1,827 mi. long.
Paris city, N France; cap.; pop. 2,150,500.
— city, NE Texas 75460; pop. 25,498.
Parkersburg city, w West Virginia 26101*; pop. 39,941.
Park Forest vill., NE Illinois 60466; pop. 26,222.
Parkland uninc. place, CEN. Washington 98444; pop. 23,355.
Park Ridge city, NE Illinois 60068; pop. 38,704.

Parkville-Carney uninc. place N Maryland 21234; pop. 35,159.
Parma city, CEN. Italy; pop. 174,827.
— city, N Ohio 44129; pop. 92,548.
Parma Heights city, NE Ohio 44130; pop. 23,112.
Parnassus, Mount mtn., CEN. Greece; anciently regarded as sacred to Apollo and the Muses; 8,062 ft.
Parsippany urb. twp., N New Jersey 07054; pop. 49,868.
Pasadena city, SW California 91109*; pop. 118,072.
— city, SE Texas 77501*; pop. 112,560.
Pascagoula city, SE Mississippi 39567; pop. 29,318.
Passaic city, NE New Jersey 07055*; pop. 52,463.
Patagonia reg. at the S tip of South America.
Paterson city, NE New Jersey 07510*; pop. 137,970.
Pawtucket city, NE Rhode Island 02860*; pop. 71,204.
Peabody city, NE Massachusetts 01960*; pop. 45,976.
Pearl City city, S Oahu, Hawaii 96782; pop. 33,000.
Pearl Harbor inlet, S Oahu, Hawaii; site of a U.S. naval base, bombed by Japanese, December 7, 1941.
Pearl River uninc. place, SE New York 10965; pop. 15,893.
Peekskill city, SE New York 10566; pop. 18,236.
Pekin city, CEN. Illinois 61554*; pop. 33,967.
Peking city, N China; cap.; pop. 9,540,000; Also **Beijing.**
Pelion mtn. range, SE Thessaly, Greece, In Greek mythology, the Titans attempted to reach heaven by piling Pelion on Ossa and both on Olympus.
Peloponnesus penin. betw. Aegean and Ionian Seas; one of the main divisions of S Greece; 8,603 sq. mi.; pop. 986,000.
Pembroke town, SE Ontario, Canada; pop. 14,927.
Pembroke Pines city, SE Florida 33023; pop. 35,776.
Penn Hills uninc. place; sw Pennsylvania 15235; pop. 57,632.
Pennine Alps sw div. of the Alps on the Swiss–Italian border.
Pennsauken urb. twp., w New Jersey 08110; pop. 33,775.
Pennsylvania state, E United States, 45,333 sp. mi.; pop. 11,864,751; cap. Harrisburg.
Pensacola city, NW Florida 32502*; pop. 57,619.
Penticton city, S British Columbia, Canada; pop. 21,344.
Peoria city, CEN. Illinois 61601*; pop. 124,160.
Persia *the former name of* Iran.
Persian Gulf inlet of the Arabian Sea betw. Iran and Arabia; also the **Arabian Gulf.**
Perth city, sw Western Australia; cap. pop. 1,118,800.
Perth Amboy city, E New Jersey 08861*; pop. 38,951.
Peru republic, W South America; 496,225 sq. mi.; pop. 22,332,000; cap. Lima.
Petaluma city, W California 94952*; pop. 33,834.
Peterborough city, S Ontario, Canada; pop. 59,683.
Petersburg city, SE Virginia 23803*; pop. 41,055.
Pharr city, S Texas 78577; pop. 21,381.
Phenix City city, E Alabama 36867; pop. 26,928.
Philadelphia city, SE Pennsylvania 19104*; pop. 1,688,210.
Philippines, Republic of the republic occupying the **Philippine Islands,** a Pacific archipelago SE of China; 115,800 sq. mi.; pop. 61,480,000; cap. Manila.
Phillipsburg city, W New Jersey 08865*; pop. 16,645.
Phnom Penh city, S CEN. Cambodia; cap.; pop. 564,000.
Phoenix city CEN. Arizona 85026*; cap.; pop. 764,911.
Picardy reg. and former prov., N France.
Pico Rivera city, sw California 90660; pop. 53,387.
Piedmont reg., E United States; extends from New Jersey to Alabama E of the Appalachians; ab. 80,000 sq. mi.
Pierre city, CEN. South Dakota 57501; cap.; pop. 11,973.
Pierrefonds town, S Quebec, Canada; pop. 35,402.
Pike's Peak mtn., CEN. Colorado; 14,110 ft.
Pikesville uninc. place, CEN. Maryland 21208; pop. 22,555.
Pine Bluff city, CEN. Arkansas 71601*; pop. 56,576.
Pinellas Park city, W Florida 33565; pop. 32,811.
Piqua city, W Ohio 45356; pop. 20,480.
Piraeus city, S Greece; pop. 187,362.
Pisa city, NW Italy; noted for its leaning tower; pop. 102,908.
Pittsburg city, W California 94565; pop. 33,465.
— city, SE Kansas 66762; pop. 18,770.
Pittsburgh city, sw Pennsylvania 15200*; pop. 423,938.
Pittsfield city, W Massachusetts 01201; pop. 51,974.
Placentia city, sw California 92670; pop. 35,041.
Plainfield city, NE New Jersey 07061*; pop. 45,555.
Plainview uninc. place, SE New York 11803; pop. 28,037.
— city, NW Texas 79072*; pop. 19,096.

Plainville city, CEN. Connecticut 06062; pop. 16,401.
Plano city, CEN. Texas 75074*; pop. 72,331.
Plantation city, NE Florida 33314; pop. 48,653.
Plant City city W Florida 33566; pop. 17,064.
Platte River river, S Nebraska; 310 mi. long.
Plattsburgh city, NE New York 12901; pop. 21,057.
Pleasant Hill uninc. place, W California 94523; pop. 28,547.
Pleasanton city, W California 94566; pop. 35,160.
Pleasure Ridge Park uninc. place, N Kentucky 40258; pop. 27,332.
Plum boro., sw Pennsylvania 15239; pop. 25,390.
Plymouth co. boro. and port, sw England; pop. 255,500.
Plymouth town, E Massachusetts 02360*; site of the first settlement in New England; pop. 35,913.
— vill., E Minnesota 55427; pop. 31,615.
Plymouth Colony colony of the shore of Massachusetts Bay founded by the Pilgrim Fathers in 1620.
Plymouth Rock rock at Plymouth, Massachusetts, on which the Pilgrim Fathers are said to have landed in 1620.
Pocatello city, Idaho 83201*; pop. 46,340.
Pointe-aux-Trembles city, S Quebec, Canada; pop. 55,618.
Pointe-Claire city, S Quebec, Canada; pop. 25,917.
Point Pleasant boro., E New Jersey 08742; pop. 17,747.
Poland republic, CEN. Europe; 120,727 sq. mi.; pop. 38,064,000; cap. Warsaw.
Polynesia isls. of Oceania, CEN. and SE Pacific; E of Melanesia and Micronesia.
Pomerania former province of Prussia, N Germany; now divided between Germany and Poland.
Pomona city, sw California 91766*; pop. 92,742.
Pompano Beach city, SE Florida 33060*; pop. 52,618.
Pompeii ancient city, S Italy; buried in the eruption of Mount Vesuvius, A.D. 79, now excavated.
Ponca City city N Oklahoma 74601*; pop. 26,238.
Ponce city, S Puerto Rico 00731; pop. 161,260.
Pontiac city, SE Michigan 48053*; pop. 76,715.
Poona city, W India; pop. 356,105.
Poplar Bluff city, SE Missouri 63901; pop. 17,139.
Popocatepetl dormant volcano, CEN. Mexico; 17,887 ft.
Po River river, N Italy; 405 mi. long.
Portage town, NW Indiana 46368; pop. 27,409.
— city, sw Michigan 49081; pop. 38,157.
Port Angeles city, NW Washington 98362; pop. 17,311.
Port Arthur city, SE Texas 77640*; pop. 61,195.
Port-au-Prince city, S Haiti; cap.; pop. 514,438.
Port Chester vill., SE New York 10573*; pop. 23,565.
Port Colborne town, S Ontario, Canada; pop. 20,536.
Port Huron city, E Michigan 48060*; pop. 33,981.
Portland city, sw Maine 04101*; pop. 61,572.
— city, NW Oregon 97208*; pop. 368,148.
Port-of-Spain city, NW Trinidad; cap. of Trinidad and Tobago; pop. 58,300. Also **Port of Spain.**
Porto-Novo city, SE Benin; cap.; pop. 104,000.
Port Said city, N Egypt; at the Mediterranean end of the Suez Canal; pop. 400,000.
Portsmouth co. boro., S England; site of the chief British naval station; pop. 191,000.
— city, SE New Hampshire 03801*; pop. 26,254.
— city, S Ohio 45662; pop. 25,943.
— city, SE Virginia 23705*; pop. 104,577.
Portugal republic, sw Europe; 35,672 sq. mi.; pop. 10,388,000; cap. Lisbon.
Potomac River river through Maryland, West Virginia, and Virginia; 287 mi. long.
Potsdam city, CEN. Germany; scene of meeting of Allied leaders, 1945; pop. 126,262.
Pottstown boro., SE Pennsylvania 19464; pop. 22,729.
Pottsville city, CEN. Pennsylvania 17901; pop. 18,195.
Poughkeepsie city, SE New York 12601*; pop. 29,757.
Poznan city, W Poland; pop. 586,600.
Prague city, W Czechoslovakia; cap.; pop. 1,213,792.
Prairie Village city, NE Kansas 66208; pop. 24,657.
Pretoria city, CEN. South Africa; adm. cap.; pop. 443,059.
Prichard city, sw Alabama 36610; pop. 39,541.
Prince Albert city, CEN. Saskatchewan, Canada; pop. 28,631.
Prince Edward Island prov., NE Canada; 2,185 sq. mi.; pop. 118,229; cap. Charlottestown.
Prince George city, CEN. British Columbia, Canada; pop. 59,929.

Prince Rupert city, w British Columbia, Canada; pop. 14,754.
Provence reg. and former prov., SE France.
Providence city, NE Rhode Island 02904*; cap.; pop. 156,804.
Provo city, CEN. Utah 84601; pop. 74,111.
Prussia former state, N Germany; dissolved 1947.
Pueblo city, CEN. Colorado 81003*; pop. 101,686.
Puerto Rico isl., Greater Antilles; a Commonwealth of the United States 3,515 sq. mi.; pop. 3,187,570; cap. San Juan.
Puget Sound inlet of the Pacific, NW Washington.
Pullman city, SE Washington 99163*; pop. 23,579.
Punjab reg., NW India and E Pakistan.
P'yongyang city, W North Korea; cap.; pop. 2,000,000.
Pyrenees mtn. chain betw. France and Spain.
Qatar monarchy, E Arabia, w coast of the Persian Gulf; 4,400 sq. mi.; pop. 444,000; cap. Doha.
Quebec prov., E Canada; 523,859 sq. mi.; pop. 6,572,300.
— city, S Quebec prov., cap.; pop. 164,580.
Queens boro., E New York; pop. 1,891,325.
Queensland state, NE Australia; 666,900 sq. mi.; pop. 2,505,100; cap. Brisbane.
Quemoy Islands 2 isls. of the Republic of China in Formosa Strait; 54 sq. mi.
Quezon City city, CEN. Philippines; cap.; pop. 1,587,140.
Quincy city, W Illinois 62301*; pop. 42,352.
— city, E Massachusetts 02169; pop. 84,743.
Quito city, CEN. Ecuador; cap.; pop. 1,233,865.
Rabat city, N Morocco; cap.; pop. 518,616.
Racine city, SE Wisconsin 53401*; pop. 85,725.
Radnor urb. twp. SE Pennsylvania 19087; pop. 27,676.
Rahway city, NE New Jersey 07065*; pop. 26,723.
Rainier, Mount extinct volcano, Cascade Range, SW Washington; 14,408 ft.
Raleigh city, CEN. North Carolina 27611*; cap.; pop. 149,771.
Rancho Cordova uninc. place, CEN. California 95670; pop. 42,881.
Randallstown uninc. place, NE Maryland 21133; pop. 25,927.
Randolph town, E Massachusetts 02368; pop. 28,218.
Rangoon (Yangôn) city, S Myanmar; cap.; pop. 2,500,000.
Rantoul vill., CEN. Illinois 61866; pop. 20,161.
Rapid City city, SW South Dakota 57701*; pop. 46,492.
Ravenna city, N Italy, famous for its art treasures and architecture; pop. 136,306.
Rawalpindi city, N Pakistan; pop. 794,843.
Raytown city, W Missouri 64133; pop. 31,831.
Reading town, NE Massachusetts 01867; pop. 22,678.
— city, SE Pennsylvania 19603*; pop. 78,686.
Recife city, NE Brazil; pop. 1,184,215.
Red Deer city, CEN. Alberta, Canada; pop. 32,184.
Redding city, N California 96001*; pop. 42,103.
Redlands city, SW California 92373*; pop. 43,619.
Redondo Beach city, SW California 90277*; pop. 57,102.
Red River river in Texas, Arkansas, and Louisiana; ab. 1,300 mi. long.
— river in N United States and S Canada; 540 mi. long.
Red Sea sea betw. Egypt and Arabia; 1,450 mi. long; ab. 170,000 sq. mi.
Redwood City city, W California 94064*; pop. 54,965.
Regina city, S Saskatchewan, Canada; cap.; pop. 149,593.
Reims city, NE France; site of a famous cathedral; pop. 181,000.
Reno city, W Nevada 89501*; pop. 100,756.
Renton city, CEN. Washington 98055; pop. 31,031.
Repentigny town, S Quebec, Canada; pop. 26,698.
Réunion French overseas dept.; isl. E of Madagascar; 970 sq. mi.; pop. 600,000; cap. Saint-Denis.
Revere city, E Massachusetts 02151; pop. 42,423.
Reykjavik city, SW Iceland; cap.; pop. 96,708.
Rheims an alternate name of Reims.
Rhine river, CEN. Europe; 810 mi. long.
Rhode Island state, NE United States; 1,214 sq. mi.; pop. 947,154; cap. Providence.
Rhodes isl. of the Dodecanese groups; 545 sq. mi.
Rhodesia See **Zimbabwe.**
Rhône river, Switzerland and SE France; 504 mi. long. Also **Rhone.**
Rialto city, S California 92376; pop. 37,862.
Richardson city, N Texas 75080*; pop. 72,496.
Richfield vill., E Minnesota 55423; pop. 37,851.

Richland city, S Washington 99352; pop. 33,578.
Richmond city, W California 94802*; pop. 74,676.
— city, E Indiana 47374; pop. 41,349.
— city, CEN. Kentucky 40475; pop. 16,861.
— boro, SW New York City; pop. 295,443.
— city, CEN. Virginia 23232*; cap.; cap. of the Confederacy 1861–65; pop. 219,214.
Richmond Hill town, S Ontario, Canada; pop. 34,716.
Ridgewood urb. twp., NE New Jersey 07451*; pop. 25,208.
Ridley urb. twp., SE Pennsylvania 19303; pop. 33,371.
Rif mtn. range, N Morocco. Also **Riff.**
Riga city, CEN. Latvian SSR; cap.; pop. 915,000.
Rijeka City, NW Yugoslavia; including its SE suburb and officially called **Rijeka-Susak;** pop. 132,933.
Rimouski town, E Quebec, Canada; pop. 27,897.
Rio de Janeiro city, SE Brazil; former cap.; pop. 5,603,388. Also **Rio.**
Rio de la Plata estuary of the Paraná and Uruguay rivers betw. Argentina and Uruguay; 170 mi. long.
Rio Grande river betw. Texas and Mexico; 1,890 mi. long.
Riverside city, SW California 92502*; pop. 170,591.
Riviera coastal strip on the Mediterranean from Hyeres, France to La Spezia, Italy.
Riviera Beach town, SE Florida 33404; pop. 26,596.
Roanoke city, W Virginia 24001*; pop. 100,427.
Roanoke Island isl. off North Carolina; 12 mi. long, 3 mi. wide.
Rochester city, SE Minnesota 55901; pop. 57,906.
— city, SE New Hampshire 03867; pop. 21,560.
— city, W New York 14603*; pop. 241,741.
Rockford city, N Illinois 61125*; pop. 139,712.
Rock Hill city, N South Carolina 29730*; pop. 35,327.
Rock Island city, NW Illinois 61201*; pop. 46,321.
Rockland town, E Massachusetts 02370; pop. 15,695.
Rockville city, CEN. Maryland 20850*; pop. 43,811.
Rockville Centre vill., SE New York 11570*; pop. 25,412.
Rocky Mount city, CEN. North Carolina 27801*; pop. 41,526.
Rocky Mountains mtn. system, W North America; extends from the Arctic to Mexico.
Rocky River city, N Ohio 44116; pop. 21,084.
Rolling Meadows city, NE Illinois 60008; pop. 20,167.
Romania an alternate form of Rumania.
Rome city, W Italy; cap.; site of the Vatican City; cap. of the former Roman republic, the Roman Empire, and the States of the Church; pop. 2,816,474.
— city, NW Georgia 30161*; pop. 29,654.
— city, CEN. New York 13440*; pop. 43,826.
Rosario city, CEN. Argentina; pop. 810,000.
Rosedale uninc. place, NW Maryland 21237; pop. 19,956.
Roselle boro., NE New Jersey 07203 pop. 20,641.
Rosemead city, SW California 91770; pop. 42,604.
Roseville city, CEN. California 95678; pop. 24,347.
— city SE Michigan 48066; pop. 54,311.
— vill., SE Minnesota 55113; pop. 35,820.
Ross urb twp., SW Pennsylvania 15237; pop. 35,102.
Rostov-on-Don city, SW RSFSR; pop. 934,000.
Roswell city, SE New Mexico 88201*; pop. 39,676.
Rotterdam city, W Netherlands; pop. 1,576,232.
— uninc. place E New York 12303; pop. 22,933.
Rouen city, N France; site of a famous cathedral; scene of the burning of Joan of Arc; pop. 114,927.
Roumania an alternate form of Rumania.
Rouyn city, W Quebec, Canada; pop. 17,678.
Royal Oak city, SE Michigan 48068*; pop. 70,893.
Rugby municipal boro., CEN. England; site of a boys' school; pop. 60,380.
Ruhr river, W Germany; 142 mi. long.
— reg. S of the Ruhr, an industrial and coal-mining district. 1,770 sq. mi.
Rumania republic, SE Europe; 91,700 sq. mi.; pop. 22,265,000; cap. Bucharest.
Russia before 1917, an empire, E Europe and N Asia; cap. Saint Petersburg (Petrograd); now part of the Union of Soviet Socialist Republics.
Russian Soviet Federated Socialist Republic constituent republic, N USSR; 6,592,800 sq. mi.; pop. 147,400,000; cap. Moscow.

Ruston city, N Louisiana 71270*; pop. 20,585.
Rutherford boro., NE New Jersey 07070*; pop. 19,068.
Rutland city, CEN. Vermont 05701; pop. 18,436.
Rwanda republic, CEN. Africa; 10,169 sq. mi.; pop. 7,232,000; cap. Kigali.
Rye city, SE New York, 10580; pop. 15,083.
Ryukyu Islands isl. group betw. Kyushu and Taiwan; 870 sq. mi.; pop. 1,161,000; chief isl. Okinawa; adm. by Japan.
Saar river, NE France and Germany; 152 mi. long.
Saar, The state, W Germany; 993 sq. mi.; pop. 1,051,000; cap. Saarbrücken.
Sabah part of Malaysia in N Borneo; 28,460 sq. mi.; pop. 1,176,400; cap. Kota Kinabalu.
Sacramento city, CEN. California; 95813*; cap.; pop. 275,741.
Sacramento River river, CEN. California; 382 mi. long.
Saginaw city, CEN. Michigan 48605*; pop. 77,508.
Sahara desert area, N Africa; ab. 3 million sq. mi. Also **Sahara Desert.**
Saigon city, S Vietnam; formerly cap. of South Vietnam; pop. 3,169,135; also called **Ho Chi Minh City.**
Saipan one of the Mariana isls.; 47 sq. mi.; captured from Japan by U.S. forces in World War II, 1944.
Saint, Sainte See entries beginning ST., STE.
Sakhalin isl. SE RSFSR; 29,700 sq. mi.; pop. 649,000; adm. ctr. Yuzhno-Sakhalinsk.
Salem city, NE Massachusetts 01970*; pop. 38,276.
— city, SE New Hampshire 03079; pop. 24,124.
— city, NW Oregon 97301*; cap.; pop. 89,233.
— town, CEN. Virginia 24153; pop. 23,958.
Salerno city, SW Italy; scene of a battle in World War II betw. Germans and Allied landing forces, 1943; pop. 153,091.
Salina city, CEN Kansas 67401*; pop. 41,843.
Salinas city, W California 93901*; pop. 80,479.
Salisbury city, SE Maryland 21801; pop. 16,429.
— city, CEN. North Carolina 28144; pop. 22,677.
— city, N Zimbabwe; cap.; pop. 633,000: Now called **Harare.**
Salonika city, NE Greece; pop. 345,799.
Salt Lake City city, CEN. Utah 84101*; cap.; pop. 163,034.
Salvador city, E Brazil; pop. 1,506,602.
— See **El Salvador.**
Salzburg city, W Austria; birthplace of Mozart; pop. 139,000.
Samar one of the Visayan isls., Philippines; 5,050 sq. mi.
Samarkand city, E Uzbek SSR; pop. 481,000.
Samoa isl. group, SW Pacific; 1,173 sq. mi.; divided into **American** (or **Eastern**) **Samoa,** an uninc. terr. of the United States; 76 sq. mi.; pop. 27,159; cap. Pago Pago; and **Western Samoa,** an independent monarchy; 1,093 sq. mi.; pop. 165,000; cap. Apia.
Samos isl. of Greece, E Aegean; 184 sq. mi.
Samothrace isl. of Greece, NE Aegean; 71 sq. mi.
San Angelo city, CEN. Texas 76902*; pop. 73,240.
San Antonio city, CEN. Texas 78284*; site of the Alamo; pop. 785,940.
San Benito city, S Texas 78586; pop. 17,988.
San Bernardino city, SW California 92403*; pop. 118,794.
San Bruno city, W California 94066; pop. 35,417.
San Carlos city, W California 94070; pop. 24,710.
San Clemente city, S California 92672; pop. 27,325.
San Diego city, SW California 92109*; pop. 875,504.
San Dimas city, SW California 91773; pop. 24,014.
Sandusky city, N Ohio 44870*; pop. 31,360.
San Fernando city, SW California 91340*; pop. 17,731.
Sanford city, CEN. Florida 32771; pop. 23,176.
— city, SW Maine 04073; pop. 18,020.
San Francisco city, W California 94101*; pop. 678,974.
San Francisco Bay inlet of the Pacific, W California.
San Gabriel city, SW California 91776*; pop. 30,072.
San Joaquin River river, CEN. California; 317 mi. long.
San José city, CEN. Costa Rica; cap.; pop. 239,800.
San Jose city, W California 95101*; pop. 629,400.
San Juan city, NE Puerto Rico 00936*; cap.; pop. 431,227.
San Leandro city, W California 94577*; pop. 63,952.
San Lorenzo uninc. place, W California 94580; pop. 20,545.
San Luis Obispo city, W California 93401*; pop. 34,252.
San Marcos city, CEN. Texas 78666; pop. 23,420.
San Marino republic, an enclave in NE Italy; 24 sq. mi.; pop. 23,000.
— city, San Marino; cap.; pop. 2,343.

San Mateo city, W California 94402*; pop. 77,640.
San Pablo city, W California 94806; pop. 19,750.
San Rafael city, W California 94901*; pop. 44,700.
San Salvador city, S El Salvador; cap.; pop. 459,902.
— isl. CEN. Bahamas; site of Columbus' first landing in the western hemisphere, 1492.
Santa Ana city, SW California 92711*; pop. 204,023.
Santa Barbara city, SW California 93102*; pop. 74,542.
Santa Catalina isl. off SW California; 70 sq. mi.
Santa Clara city, W California 95050*; pop. 87,700.
Santa Cruz city, W California 95060*; pop. 41,483.
Santa Fe city, N New Mexico 87501*; cap.; pop. 49,160.
Santa Fe Trail trade route, important from 1821–80, betw. Independence, Missouri, and Santa Fe, New Mexico.
Santa Maria city, SW California 93454*; pop. 39,685.
Santa Monica city, SW California 90406*; pop. 88,314.
Santa Paula city, SW California 93060; pop. 18,001.
Santa Rosa city, W California 95402*; pop. 83,205.
Santee uninc. place, SW California 92071; pop. 47,080.
Santiago city, CEN. Chile; cap.; pop. 5,133,700. Also **Santiago de Chile.**
Santo Domingo city, S Dominican Republic; cap.; pop. 1,600,000.
São Paulo city, SE Brazil; pop. 10,063,000.
São Tomé and Principe republic, isls. off W Africa; 366 sq. mi.; pop. 121,000; cap. São Tomé.
— **São Tomé** city; cap. São Tomé isl.; 34,997.
Sapulpa city, CEN. Oklahoma 74066; pop. 15,853.
Sarajevo city, CEN. Yugoslavia; scene of the assassination of Archduke Franz Ferdinand, June 28, 1914; pop. 244,045.
Sarasota city SW Florida 33578*; pop. 48,868.
Saratoga city, W California 95070; pop. 29,261.
Saratoga Springs city, CEN. New York 12866; pop. 23,906.
Sarawak part of Malaysia on NW Borneo; 48,050 sq. mi.; pop. 1,591,100; cap. Kuching.
Sardinia isl., CEN. Mediterranean; with adjacent isls. a reg. of Italy; 9,301 sq. mi.; pop. 1,617,215; cap. Cagliari.
Sarnia city, S Ontario, Canada; pop. 55,576.
Saskatchewan prov., CEN. Canada; 251,866 sq. mi.; pop. 1,000,300; cap. Regina.
Saskatoon city, CEN. Saskatchewan, Canada; pop. 177,641.
Saudi Arabia monarchy, N and CEN. Arabia; 865,000 sq. mi.; pop. 14,131,000; cap. Riyadh.
Saugus town, NE Massachusetts 01906; pop. 24,746.
Sault Ste. Marie city, CEN. Ontario, Canada; pop. 81,044.
Sault Sainte Marie Canals 3 canals that circumvent the rapids in the St. Marys River betw. Lakes Superior and Huron.
Savannah city, E Georgia 31401*; pop. 141,654.
Saxony reg. and former duchy, electorate, kingdom, and prov., CEN. Germany.
Sayreville boro., E New Jersey 08872; pop. 29,969.
Scandinavia reg. NW Europe; includes Sweden, Norway, and Denmark and sometimes Finland, Iceland, and the Faeroe Islands.
Scapa Flow sea basin and British naval base in the Orkney Islands, Scotland; 50 sq. mi.
Scarsdale town, SE New York 10583; pop. 17,650.
Schaumburg city, NE Illinois 60172; pop. 53,355.
Scheldt river, N France, Belgium and the Netherlands; 270 mi. long.
Schenectady city, E New York 12301*; pop. 67,972.
Schleswig-Holstein state, NE Germany; 6,069 sq. mi.; pop. 2,614,000; cap. Kiel.
Schuylkill River river, SE Pennsylvania; 130 mi. long.
Scituate city, NE Massachusetts 02066; pop. 17,317.
Scotch Plains urb. twp., NE New Jersey 07076; pop. 20,774.
Scotland a political div. and the N part of Great Britain; a separate kingdom until 1707; 30,418 sq. mi.; pop. 5,094,000; cap. Edinburgh.
Scott urb. twp., SW Pennsylvania 15106; pop. 20,413.
Scottsdale city, CEN. Arizona 85251*; pop. 88,622.
Scranton city, NE Pennsylvania 18503*; pop. 88,117.
Seaford uninc. place, SE New York 11783; pop. 16,117.
Seal Beach city, SW California 90740; pop. 25,975.
Seaside city, W California 93955; pop. 36,567.
Seattle city, CEN. Washington 98109*; pop. 493,846.
Sebastopol See **Sevastopol.**
Security unic. place, CEN. Colorado 80911; pop. 18,786.

Sedalia city, CEN. Missouri 65301*; pop. 20,927.

Seguin city, CEN. Texas 78155; pop. 17,854.

Seine river, NE France; 482 mi. long.

Selma city, CEN. Alabama 36701*; pop. 26,684.

Semarang city, N Java, Indonesia; pop. 646,590.

Senegal river, NW Africa; ab. 1,000 mi. long.

Senegal, Republic of republic, NW Africa; 75,955 sq. mi.; pop. 7,277,000; cap. Dakar.

Seoul city, NW South Korea; cap.; pop. 8,114,000.

Sept-Iles city, E Quebec, Canada; pop. 30,617.

Serbia constituent republic, E Yugoslavia; 21,609 sq. mi.; pop. 5,627,000; cap. Belgrade.

Sevastopol city, S Crimea, USSR; pop. 308,000.

Severn river, N Wales and W England; 210 mi. long.

Severna Park city, NE Maryland 21146; pop. 21,253.

Seville city, SW Spain; pop. 655,435.

Sèvres city, N France; pop. 21,149.

Seychelles isl. republic off E Africa; 175 sq. mi.; pop. 68,700; cap. Victoria.

Shaker Heights city, N Ohio 44120; pop. 32,487.

Shaler urb. twp., SW Pennsylvania 15116; pop. 33,712.

Shanghai city, E China; pop. 7,228,600.

Shannon river, CEN. Ireland; 224 mi. long.

Sharon city, W Pennsylvania 16146; pop. 19,057.

Shasta, Mount extinct volcano, Cascade Range, N California; 14,162 ft.

Shawinigan city, S Quebec, Canada; pop. 24,921.

Shawnee city, NE Kansas 66203*; pop. 29,653.

— city, CEN. Oklahoma 74801*; pop. 26,506.

Sheboygan city, E Wisconsin 53081; pop. 48,085.

Sheffield co. boro., CEN. England; pop. 544,200.

Shelby city, SW North Carolina 28150; pop. 15,310.

Shelton city, SW Connecticut 06484; pop. 31,314.

Shenandoah river, N Virginia and NE West Virginia; 170 mi. long.

Shenyang city, NE China; pop. 3,700,000; formerly called Mukden.

Sherbrooke city, S Quebec, Canada; pop. 76,804.

Sherman city, N Texas 75090; pop. 30,413.

Sherrelwood uninc. place, CEN. Colorado 80221; pop. 17,621.

Shetland Islands isl. group NE of the Orkney Islands, comprising **Shetland,** a co. of Scotland; 551 mi.; pop. 17,000; cap. Lerwick.

Shikoku isl., SW Japan; 7,248 sq. mi.

Shiloh national military park, SW Tennessee; scene of a Union victory in the Civil War, 1862; 6 sq. mi.

Shively city, N Kentucky 40216; pop. 16,645.

Shreveport city, NW Louisiana 71102*; pop. 205,815.

Shrewsbury city, CEN. Massachusetts 01545; pop. 22,674.

Siam the former name of Thailand.

Siam, Gulf of part of the South China Sea betw. the Malay Peninsula and Indochina.

Siberia reg., E RSFSR; ab. 5 million sq. mi.

Sicily isl. of Italy, CEN. Mediterranean; comprises with neighboring islands a reg. of 9,926 sq. mi.; pop. 5,006,684; cap. Palermo.

Sidney city, W Ohio 45365; pop. 17,657.

Sierra Leone republic, W Africa; 27,699 sq. mi.; pop. 4,151,000; cap. Freetown.

Sierra Nevada mtn. range, E California.

Silesia reg., CEN. Europe; divided betw. Czechoslovakia and Poland.

Silver Spring uninc. place, W Maryland 20907*; pop. 72,893.

Simi Valley city, SW California 93065; pop. 77,500.

Simla city, N India; pop. 55,368.

Simsbury city, CEN. Connecticut 06070; pop. 21,161.

Sinai penin., E Egypt, betw. the Mediterranean and the Red Sea.

Singapore isl. republic off the tip of the Malay Peninsula; 239 sq. mi.; pop. 2,718,000.

— city, S Singapore; cap.; pop. 2,390,800.

Sinkiang-Uigur Autonomous Region div. W China; 635,900 sq. mi.; pop. ab. 15,155,000; cap. Urumchi (Tihwa). Also formerly **Sinkiang.**

Sioux City city, W Iowa 51101*; pop. 82.003.

Sioux Falls city, SE South Dakota 57101*; pop. 81,343.

Skokie vill., NE Illinois 60076*; pop. 60,278.

Slidell town, SE Louisiana 70458; pop. 26,718.

Slovakia reg. and former prov., E Czechoslovakia.

Slovenia constituent republic, NW Yugoslavia; 7,819 sq. mi.; pop. 1,866,000; cap. Ljubljana.

Smyrna town, CEN. Georgia 30080; pop. 20,312.

— an alternate name of Izmir, Turkey.

Society Islands isl. group, French Polynesia; ab. 650 sq. mi.

Sofia city, W Bulgaria; cap.; pop. 1,047,920.

Solomon Islands isl. monarchy, SW Pacific; ab. 10,954 sq. mi.; pop. 319,000; cap. Honiara.

Somalia republic, E Africa; 246,000 sq. mi.; pop. 7,555,000; cap. Mogadishu. Also **Somali Democratic Republic.**

Somerset town, SE Massachusetts 02725; pop. 18,813.

Somerville city, E Massachusetts 02143, pop. 77,372.

Somme river, N France; 150 mi. long.

Soo Canals informal name of Sault Sainte Marie Canals.

Sorel city, S Quebec, Canada; pop. 19,666.

South Africa, Republic of republic, S Africa; 433,680 sq. mi.; pop. 30,797,000; seat of government Pretoria; seat of legislature Cape Town.

South America S continent of the Western Hemisphere; ab. 6,860,000 sq. mi.

Southampton co. boro., S England; pop. 207,800.

South Australia state, S Australia; 379,900 sq. mi.; pop. 1,425,000; cap. Adelaide.

South Bend city, N Indiana 46624*; pop. 109,727.

Southbridge uninc. place S Massachusetts 01550*; pop. 16,665.

South Carolina state, SE United States; 31,055 sq. mi.; pop. 3,122,814; cap. Columbia.

South Charleston city, CEN. West Virginia 25303; pop. 15,968.

South China Sea part of the Pacific betw. SE Asia and the Malay Archipelago.

South Dakota state, CEN. United States; 77,047 sq. mi.; pop. 690,768; cap. Pierre.

Southern Yemen See Yemen.

South Euclid city, NE Ohio 44121; pop. 25,713.

South Farmingdale uninc. place, SE New York 11735; pop. 16,493.

Southfield city, SE Michigan 48075*; pop. 75,568.

Southgate city, SE Michigan 48198; pop. 32,058.

South Gate city, SW California 90280; pop. 66,784.

South Hadley town, CEN. Massachusetts 01075; pop. 16,399.

South Holland vill, SE Illinois 60473; pop. 24,977.

Southington city, CEN. Connecticut 06489; pop. 36,879.

South Island one of the two main isls. of New Zealand; 58,093 sq. mi.

South Kingston town, S Rhode Island 02879; pop. 20,414.

South Korea See Korea.

South Milwaukee city SE Wisconsin 53172; pop. 21,069.

South Orange vill., NE New Jersey 07079; pop. 15,864.

South Pasadena city, SW California 91030; pop. 22,681.

South Plainfield boro., NE New Jersey 07080; pop. 20,521.

South Pole S extremity of the earth's axis.

South Portland city, SW Maine 04106; pop. 22,712.

South St. Paul city, E Minnesota 55075; pop. 21,235.

South San Francisco city, W California 94080*; pop. 49,393.

South Sea Islands isls. of the South Pacific.

South Seas waters of the Southern Hemisphere, esp. the **South Pacific Ocean.**

South Valley city, CEN. New Mexico 87105; pop. 29,389.

South-West Africa formerly mandated terr., SW Africa; administered by the Republic of South Africa; now **Namibia.**

South Whittier uninc. place, SW California 90605; pop. 43,815.

South Windsor city, CEN. Connecticut 06074; pop. 17,184.

Soviet Russia 1 Russian Soviet Federated Socialist Republic. 2 Union of Soviet Socialist Republics.

Soviet Union an alternate name of Union of Soviet Socialist Republics.

Spain monarchy, SW Europe; 194,885 sq. mi.; pop. 39,618,000; cap. Madrid.

Spanish America parts of the W hemisphere where Spanish is the predominant language.

Spanish Lake uninc. place, NE Missouri 63138; pop. 20,632.

Sparks city, W Nevada 89431; pop. 40,780.

Sparta city-state of ancient Greece, famous for its military power: sometimes called **Lacedaemon.**

Spartanburg city, NW South Carolina 29301*; pop. 43,826.

Spitsbergen See **Svalbard.**

Spokane city E Washington 99210*; pop. 171,300.

Springdale city, NW Arkansas 72764; pop. 23,458.

Springfield city, CEN. Illinois 62703*; cap.; pop. 100,054.

— city, SW Massachusetts 01101*; pop. 152,319.

— city, SW Missouri 63801*; pop. 133,116.

— city, CEN. Ohio 45501*; pop. 72,563.

— city, W Oregon 97477; pop. 41,621.

— uninc. place, SE Pennsylvania 19064; pop. 25,326.

Springfield urb. twp., SE Pennsylvania 19118; pop. 20,344.

Spring Valley uninc. place, SE California 92077*; pop. 40,191.

— vill., SE New York 10977; pop. 20,537.

Sri Lanka isl. republic S of India, formerly called Ceylon; 25,332 sq. mi.; pop. 16,109,000; cap. Colombo.

Stalingrad *the former name of* Volgograd.

Stamford city, SW Connecticut 06904*; pop. 102,466.

St. Ann city, E Missouri 63074; pop. 15,523.

Stanton city, SW California 90680; pop. 21,144.

State College boro., CEN. Pennsylvania 16801*; pop. 36,130.

Staten Island isl., SE New York, at the entrance to New York Habor; coextensive with Richmond boro. 10314*; pop. 352,121.

Statesville city, CEN North Carolina 28677; pop. 18,622.

Staunton city, CEN. Virginia 24401; pop. 21,857.

St.-Bruno-de-Montarville town, CEN. Quebec, Canada; pop. 21,272.

St. Catharines city, S Ontario, Canada; pop. 123,351.

St. Charles city, E Missouri 63301*; pop. 37,379.

St. Clair, Lake lake betw. S Ontario and SE Michigan; 460 sq. mi.

St. Clair Shores vill., SE Michigan 48083*; pop. 76,210.

St. Cloud city, CEN. Minnesota 56301*; pop. 42,566.

St. Croix one of the Virgin Islands of the United States; 82 sq. mi.

Ste.-Foy city, S Quebec, Canada; pop. 71,237.

Sterling city, NW Illinois 61081; pop. 16,273.

Sterling Heights city, SE Michigan 48078*; pop. 108,999.

Ste.-Thérèse city, S Quebec, Canada; pop. 17,479.

Stettin *the German name for* Szczecin.

Steubenville city, E Ohio 43952; pop. 26,400.

Stevens Point city, CEN. Wisconsin 54481; pop. 22,970.

St. Helena isl., South Atlantic; British colony with Ascension Island and the Tristan da Cunha group as dependencies; 133 sq. mi.; pop. 5,147; cap. Jamestown; site of Napoleon's exile, 1815 to 21.

St. Hubert town, S Quebec, Canada; pop. 49,706.

St. Hyacinthe city, S Quebec, Canada; pop. 37,500.

Stillwater city, CEN. Oklahoma 74074*; pop. 38,268.

St. Jean city, S Quebec, Canada; pop. 34,363.

St. Jérôme city, S Quebec, Canada; pop. 25,175.

St. John one of the Virgin Islands of the United States; 19 sq. mi.

— city, S New Brunswick, Canada; pop. 85,976.

St. John's city, SE Newfoundland, Canada; cap.; pop. 86,576.

St. Joseph city, NW Missouri 64501*; pop. 76,691.

St. Kitts and Nevis monarchy isls. in the Lesser Antilles; 104 sq. mi.; pop. 44,100; cap. Basseterre.

St. Lambert city, S Quebec, Canada; pop. 20,318.

St. Laurent city, S Quebec, Canada; pop. 64,404.

St. Lawrence, Gulf of inlet of the Atlantic E Canada.

St. Lawrence River river, SE Canada; the outlet of the Great Lakes system; 1,900 mi. long.

St. Lawrence Seaway system of ship canals extending 114 miles along the St. Lawrence River from Montreal to Lake Ontario.

St. Leonard city, CEN. Quebec, Canada; pop. 78,452.

St. Louis city, E Missouri 63155*; pop. 452,801.

St. Louis Park vill., E Minnesota 55426; pop. 42,931.

Stockholm city, SE Sweden; cap.; pop. 1,629,631.

Stockton city, CEN. California 95204*; pop. 149,779.

Stoneham town, NE Massachusetts 02180; pop. 21,424.

Stonington city, NE Connecticut 06378; pop. 16,220.

Stoughton town, E Massachusetts 02072; pop. 26,710.

Stow vill., CEN. Ohio 44224; pop. 25,303.

St. Paul city, SE Minnesota 55101*; cap.; pop. 270,230.

St. Petersburg city, W Florida 33730*; pop. 236,893.

— *the former name of* Leningrad.

Strasbourg city, NE France; pop. 253,834.

Stratford town, SE Connecticut 06497; pop. 50,541.

— city, S Ontario, Canada; pop. 25,657.

Stratford-on-Avon town, CEN. England; birthplace and burial place of Shakespeare; pop. 20,080.

Streamwood city, NE Illinois 60103; pop. 23,450.

Strongsville vill., N Ohio 44136; pop. 28,577.

St. Thomas one of the Virgin Islands of the United States; 28 sq. mi.; pop. 16,201.

— city, S Ontario, Canada; pop. 27,206.

Stuttgart city, SW Germany; pop. 581,989.

St. Vincent and the Grenadines monarchy isls. in the Windward Islands; 150 sq. mi.; pop. 115,000; cap. Kingstown.

Sucre city, CEN. Bolivia; judicial cap.; pop. 105,800.

Sudan reg., N Africa S of the Sahara.

Sudan, Republic of the republic, NE Africa; 966,757 sq. mi.; pop. 28,311,000; cap. Khartoum.

Sudbury city, CEN. Ontario, Canada; pop. 97,604.

Sudetenland border dists., W Czechoslovakia.

Suez city, NE Egypt; pop. 204,000.

Suez, Gulf of inlet of the Red Sea, NE Egypt.

Suez, Isthmus of strip of land joining Asia and Africa, betw. the Gulf of Suez and the Mediterranean.

Suez Canal ship canal across the Isthmus of Suez; 107 mi.

Suitland-Silver Hills uninc. place, CEN. Maryland 20023; pop. 32,164.

Sulawesi isl. of Indonesia, E of Borneo; 73,057 sq. mi.; pop. 11,341,000.

Sulu Archipelago isl. group, SW Philippines; 1,086 sq. mi.

Sumatra isl. of Indonesia S of the Malay Peninsula; 208,948 sq. mi.; pop. 22,934,000.

Summit city, NE New Jersey 07901; pop. 21,071.

Sumter city, CEN. South Carolina 29150*; pop. 24,921.

Sunnyvale city, W California 94086*; pop. 106,618.

Superior city, NW Wisconsin 54880*; pop. 29,571.

Superior, Lake largest of the Great Lakes; 31,820 sq. mi.

Surabaya city, NE Java, Indonesia; pop. 2,027,913.

Suriname republic, former Dutch colony NE coast of S. America; 63,251 sq. mi.; pop. 411,000; cap. Paramaribo.

Susquehanna river, New York, Pennsylvania, and Maryland; 444 mi. long.

Suwannee River river, Georgia and Florida; 250 mi. long.

Svalbard isl. group of Norway, Arctic Ocean; 23,958 sq. mi.; sometimes called **Spitsbergen.**

Swaziland republic, SE Africa; 6,704 sq. mi.; pop. 770,000; caps. Mbabane (admin.) and Lobamba (legislat.).

Sweden monarchy, NW Europe; 173,732 sq. mi.; pop. 8,529,000; cap. Stockholm.

Sweetwater Creek city, NW Florida 33601; pop. 19,433.

Swift Current city, SW Saskatchewan, Canada; pop. 14,264.

Switzerland federal state, CEN. Europe; 15,943 sq. mi.; pop. 6,756,000; cap. Bern.

Sydney city, NE Nova Scotia, Canada; pop. 30,645.

— city, E New South Wales, Australia; cap.; pop. 3,596,000.

Syracuse city, CEN. New York 13201*; pop. 170,105.

Syria republic, SW Asia; 71,498 sq. mi.; pop. 12,116,000; cap. Damascus.

Szczecin city, NW Poland; pop. 409,500. German name **Stettin.**

Tabriz city, NW Iran; pop. 971,482.

Tacoma city, W Washington 98402*; pop. 158,501.

Tadzhik SSR constituent republic, S USSR; 55,300 sq. mi.; pop. 5,109,000; cap. Dushanbe.

Tahiti isl., Society group; 402 sq. mi.; pop. 85,000.

Tahoe, Lake lake E California and W Nevada; ab. 195 sq. mi.

Taipei city, N Taiwan; cap.; pop. 2,681,857.

Taiwan isl. off SE China; comprises with the Pescadores, the Republic of China; 13,900 sq. mi.; pop. 20,221,000; cap. Taipei; *formerly called* **Formosa.**

Takoma Park city W Maryland 20912; pop. 16,231.

Talledaga city, CEN. Alabama 35160; pop. 19,128.

Tallahassee city, N Florida 32303*; pop. 81,548.

Tallinn city, N Estonian SSR; cap.; pop. 436,000.

Tallmadge city, NE Ohio 44278; pop. 15,269.

Tampa city, W Florida 33602*; pop. 271,577.

Tampico city, E Mexico; pop. 240,000.

Tanganyika, Lake lake, CEN. Africa; 12,700 sq. mi.

Tangier city, N Morocco; pop. 187,894.

Tanzania republic, E Africa, includes **Tanganyika** and **Zanzibar**; 364,217 sq. mi.; pop. 24,403,000; cap. Dar es Salaam.

Taranto city, SE Italy; pop. 247,681.

Tashkent city, E Uzbek SSR; cap.; pop. 1,816,000.

Tasmania isl., SE Australia; comprises a state; 26,200 sq. mi.; pop. 437,300; cap. Hobart.

Taunton city, SE Massachusetts 02780*; pop. 45,001.

Taylor city, SE Michigan 48180; pop. 77,568.

Tbilisi city, SE Georgian SSR; cap.; pop. 1,260,000.

Teaneck urb. twp., NE New Jersey 07666; pop. 39,007.

Tegucigalpa city, CEN. Honduras; cap.; pop. 551,606.

Tehran city, CEN. Iran; cap.; pop. 6,042,584.

Tel Aviv city, W Israel; includes Jaffa; pop. 317,800.

Tempe city, CEN. Arizona 85282*; pop. 106,919.

Temple CEN. Texas 76501; pop. 42,354.

Tennessee state, CEN. United States; 42,244 sq. mi.; pop. 4,591,120; cap. Nashville.

Tennessee River river, flowing through E Tennessee, N Alabama, W Tennessee, and SW Kentucky; 652 mi. long.

Terre Haute city, W Indiana 47808*; pop. 61,125.

Tewksbury city, NE Massachusetts 01876; pop. 24,635.

Texarkana city, SW Arkansas at the Arkansas-Texas line 75501; pop. 21,459.

— city, NE Texas; adjacent to and integrated with Texarkana, Arkansas 75501*; pop. 31,271.

Texas N state S United States; 267,338 sq. mi.; pop. 14,227,574; cap. Austin.

Texas City city, SE Texas 77590*; pop. 41,201.

Thailand monarchy, SE Asia; 198,115 sq. mi.; pop. 56,217,000; cap. Bangkok: *formerly called* Siam.

Thames river, S England; 209 mi. long.

Thessaly div., CEN. Greece; 5,399 sq. mi.

Thetford Mines city S Quebec, Canada; pop. 20,784.

Thomasville city, S Georgia 31792; pop. 18,463.

Thorold town, S Ontario, Canada; pop. 14,944.

Thousand Islands group of ab. 1,500 isls. in the St. Lawrence River.

Thousand Oaks city, SE California 91360*; pop. 77,797.

Thrace reg., E Balkan Peninsula.

Thunder Bay city, W Ontario, Canada; pop. 111,476.

Tiber river, CEN. Italy; 245 mi. long.

Tibet adm. div., W China; 471,700 sq. mi.; pop. 1,930,000; cap. Lhasa; formerly independent.

Tientsin city, NE China; pop. 4,300,000.

Tierra del Fuego isl. group, S South America, included in Chile and Argentina; 7,996 sq. mi. (Argentina), 19,480 sq. mi. (Chile).

Tiffin city, CEN. Ohio 44883; pop. 19,599.

Tigris river, SW Asia, ab. 1,150 mi. long.

Tijuana city, NW Lower California, Mexico; pop. 535,000.

Timbuktu town, CEN. Mali; pop. 11,900.

Timmins town, CEN. Ontario, Canada; pop. 44,747.

Timonium-Lutherville uninc. place, CEN. Maryland 21093; pop. 17,845.

Timor isl., SE Malay Archipelago; 11,965 sq. mi.; pop. 1,356,000; W Timor has been part of Indonesia since 1949; E Timor, formerly a Portuguese overseas province, was annexed by Indonesia in 1976.

Tirana city, CEN. Albania; cap.; pop. 238,100.

Tirol See Tyrol.

Titicaca, Lake lake betw. SE Peru and W Bolivia; 3,200 sq. mi.; elevation 12,500 ft.

Titusville city, E Florida 32870; pop. 31,910.

Tobago See **Trinidad and Tobago.**

Togo republic, W Africa; 21,925 sq. mi.; pop. 3,764,000; cap. Lomé.

Tokyo city, E Japan; cap.; pop. 8,278,116.

Toledo city, CEN. Spain; pop. 56,414.

— city, NW Ohio 43601*; pop. 354,635.

Tomsk city, S RSFSR; pop. 431,000.

Tonawanda city, W New York 14150*; pop. 18,693.

Tonga monarchy; isl. group, SE of Fiji; 301 sq. mi.; pop. 96,300; cap. Nuku'alofa.

Topeka city, NE Kansas 66603*; cap.; pop. 118,690.

Toronto city, S Ontario, Canada; pop. 633,318.

Torrance city, SW California 90510*; pop. 131,497.

Torrington city, SW Connecticut 06790*; pop. 30,987.

Toulon city, S France; pop. 168,000.

Toulouse city, S France; pop. 359,000.

Towson uninc. place, CEN. Maryland 21204; pop. 51,083.

Trafalgar, Cape headland, SW Spain; scene of a naval victory of Nelson over the French and Spanish, 1805.

Transcaucasia reg., SE USSR; betw. the Caucasus mountains and Iran and Turkey.

Transvaal province, NE South Africa; 101,352 sq. mi.; pop. 8,950,000; cap. Pretoria.

Traverse City city, NW Michigan 49684; pop. 15,516.

Trenton city, SE Michigan 48183; pop. 22,762.

— city, W New Jersey 08608*; cap.; pop. 92,124.

Trieste city, NE Italy; pop. 235,014.

Trinidad and Tobago isl republic off N Venezuela; comprises isls. of **Trinidad**; 1,864 sq. mi., and **Tobago**; 116 sq. mi.; pop. 1,233,000; cap. Port-of-Spain.

Tripoli city, NW Lebanon; pop. 500,000.

— city, NW Libya; cap.; pop. 591,062.

Trois-Rivieres city, S Quebec, Canada; pop. 52,518.

Troy city, SE Michigan 48084; pop. 67,102.

— city, E New York 12180*; pop. 56,638.

— city, W Ohio 45373; pop. 19,086.

Trumbull city, SE Connecticut 06611; pop. 32,989.

Tucson city, SE Arizona 85726*; pop. 330,537.

Tulare city, CEN. California 93274; pop. 22,530.

Tullahoma city, CEN. Tennessee 37388; pop. 15,800.

Tulsa city, NE Oklahoma 74101*; pop. 360,919.

Tunis city, NE Tunisia; cap.; pop. 596,654.

Tunisia republic, N Africa; 59,664 sq. mi.; pop. 8,182,000; cap. Tunis.

Tupelo city, NE Mississippi 38801*; pop. 23,905.

Turin city, NW Italy; pop. 1,160,162.

Turkestan reg., CEN. Asia; extends from the Caspian Sea to the Gobi Desert.

Turkey republic, SW Asia; 300,948 sq. mi.; pop. 56,941,000; cap. Ankara. See **Anatolia.**

Turkmen SSR constituent republic, S USSR; 188,500 sq. mi.; pop. 3,534,000; cap. Ashkhabad.

Tuscaloosa city, CEN. Alabama 35403*; pop. 75,143.

Tustin city, SW California 92680; pop. 32,248.

Tustin-Foothills uninc. place, SW California 92705; pop. 26,174.

Tutuila chief isl., American Samoa; 53 sq. mi.

Twin Falls city, S Idaho 83301*; pop. 26,209.

Tyler city, E Texas 75702*; pop. 70,508.

Tyrol reg., W Austria and N Italy.

Ubangi river, CEN. Africa; 1,400 mi. long.

Uganda military republic, CEN. Africa; 93,100 sq. mi.; pop. 16,928,000; cap. Kampala.

Ukrainian SSR constituent republic SW USSR; 233,100 sq. mi.; pop. 51,707,000; cap. Kiev. Also **Ukraine.**

Ulan Bator city, CEN. Mongolia; cap.; pop. 548,400.

Ulster former prov., N Ireland, of which the N part became Northern Ireland, 1925.

— prov., N Republic of Ireland; comprises the part of Ulster that remained after 1925; 3,093 sq. mi.; pop. 230,159.

Union urb. twp., NE New Jersey 07083*; pop. 50,184.

Union City city, NE New Jersey 07087; pop. 55,593.

Uniondale uninc. place, SE New York 11553; pop. 20,016.

Union of Soviet Socialist Republics federal union of 15 constituent republics occupying most of N Eurasia; 8,649,800 sq. mi.; pop. 290,122,000; cap. Moscow.

United Arab Emirates monarchy, E Arabia, composed of 7 emirates (*formerly* **Trucial States**); 30,000 sq. mi.; pop. 1,903,000; cap. Abu Dhabi.

United Arab Republic *the former name of* Egypt.

United Kingdom constitutional monarchy comprising Great Britain, Northern Ireland, the Isle of Man, and the Channel Islands; 94,248 sq. mi.; pop. 57,384,000; cap. London: officially **United Kingdom of Great Britain and Northern Ireland.**

United States of America federal republic, including 50 states (49 in North America, and Hawaii, an archipelago in the Pacific Ocean), and the District of Columbia (3,679,192 sq. mi.; pop. 251,394,000), and the Canal Zone, Puerto Rico, the Virgin Islands of the United States, American Samoa, and Guam, Wake, and other Pacific isls.; cap. Washington, coextensive with the District of Columbia.

University City city, E Missouri 63130; pop. 42,690.

University Heights city, N Ohio 44118; pop. 15,401.

University Park city, N Texas 76308; pop. 22,254.

Upland city, SW California 91786; pop. 47,647.

Upper Arlington city, CEN. Ohio 43221; pop. 35,648.

Upper Darby uninc. place, SE Pennsylvania 19082; pop. 84,054.

Upper Moreland uninc. place, SE Pennsylvania 19090; pop. 25,874.

Upper Volta *the former name of* Burkina Faso.

Ural Mountains mtn. system in the RSFSR, extending from the Arctic Ocean to the Kasakh SSR.

Ural River river S RSFSR and W Kazakh SSR; 1,574 mi. long.

Urbana city, E Illinois 61801*; pop. 35,978.

Uruguay republic, E South America; 68,037 sq. mi.; pop. 3,033,000; cap. Montevideo.

Uruguay River river, SE South America; 1,000 mi. long.

Utah state, CEN. United States; 84,916 sq. mi.; pop. 1,461,037; cap. Salt Lake City.

Utica city, CEN. New York 13503*; pop. 75,632.

Utrecht city, CEN. Netherlands; pop. 230,634.

Uzbek SSR constituent republic S USSR; 172,700 sq. mi.; pop. 19,905,000; cap. Tashkent.

Vacaville city, CEN. California 95688; pop. 43,367.

Val-d'Or town, W Quebec, Canada; pop. 19,915.

Valdosta city, S Georgia 31603*; pop. 37,596.

Valencia city, E Spain; pop. 732,491.

Valinda uninc. place, SE California 91744; pop. 18,700.

Vallejo city, W California 94590*; pop. 80,188.

Valleyfield city, S Quebec, Canada; pop. 29,716. Also **Salaberry de Valleyfield.**

Valley Forge locality, SE Pennsylvania, scene of Washington's winter encampment 1777–78.

Valley Station uninc. place, N Kentucky 40272; pop. 24,474.

Valley Stream vill., SE New York 11580*; pop. 35,769.

Valparaiso city, CEN. Chile; pop. 288,294.

— city, NW Indiana 46383; pop. 22,247.

Vancouver city, SW Washington 98660*; pop. 42,834.

— city, SW British Columbia, Canada; pop. 431,137.

Vancouver Island isl., off SW British Columbia, Canada; 12,408 sq. mi.

Vanuatu republic, isl. group member of the Commonwealth, SW Pacific, formerly **New Hebrides;** 4,707 sq. mi.; pop. 147,000; cap. Vila.

Vatican City sovereign papal state within Rome; includes the Vatican and St. Peter's Church; established June 10, 1929; 108.7 acres; pop. 1,000.

Venezuela republic, N South America; 352,144 sq. mi.; pop. 19,735,000; cap. Caracas.

Venice city, NE Italy; pop. 324,294.

Venice, Gulf of N part of the Adriatic.

Ventura city, S California 93002*; pop. 73,774.

Veracruz state, SE Mexico; 27,683 sq. mi.; pop. 6,171,000; cap. Jalapa; largest city Veracruz.

Verde, Cape westernmost point of Africa; a penin.; ab. 20 mi. long.

Verdun town, NE France; scene of several battles of World War I; pop. 23,621.

— city, S Quebec, Canada; pop. 68,013.

Vermont state, NE United States; 9,609 sq. mi.; pop. 511,456; cap. Montpelier.

Vernon city, NE Connecticut 06060; pop. 27,974.

Verona city, NE Italy; pop. 258,724.

Versailles city, N France; site of the palace of Louis XIV; scene of the signing of a treaty (1919) betw. the Allies and Germany after World War I; pop. 94,145.

Vesuvius active volcano, W Italy; 3,891 ft.

Vichy city, CEN. France; provisional cap. during German occupation, World War II; pop. 32,117.

Vicksburg city, W Mississippi 39180; pop. 25,434; besieged and taken by the Union Army in the Civil War, 1863.

Victoria state, SE Australia; 87,900 sq. mi.; pop. 4,321,500; cap. Melbourne.

— city, SW British Columbia; cap.; pop. 62,551.

— city, S Texas 77901*; pop. 50,695.

Victoria, Lake lake betw. Uganda, Tanganyika, and Kenya; 26,828 sq. mi. Also **Victoria Nyanza.**

Victoria Falls cataract on the Zambesi River betw. Northern and Southern Rhodesia; 343 ft. high; over a mile wide.

Victoriaville town, S Quebec, Canada; pop. 21,825.

Vienna city, NE Austria; cap.; pop. 1,482,825.

— town, NE Virginia 22180; pop. 15,469.

Vientiane city, CEN. Laos; adm cap.; pop. 377,409.

Vietnam republic, SW Indochina; 127,246 sq. mi.; pop. 66,128,000; cap. Hanoi; from 1954 to 1976 divided into **North Vietnam** and **South Vietnam,** with caps. at Hanoi and Saigon, respectively.

Villa Park vill., NE Illinois 60181; pop. 23,156.

Vilnius city, SE Lithuanian SSR; cap.; pop. 582,000. Also **Vilna, Vilnyus.**

Vincennes city, SW Indiana 47591; pop. 20,857.

Vineland boro., S New Jersey 08360; pop. 53,753.

Virginia state, E United States; 40,817 sq. mi.; pop. 5,346,797; cap. Richmond.

Virginia Beach city, SE Virginia 23458*; pop. 262,199.

Virgin Islands isl. group, West Indies E of Puerto Rico. See **British Virgin Islands.**

Virgin Islands of the United States uninc. terr., Virgin Islands; 136 sq. mi.; pop. 107,000; cap. Charlotte Amalie.

Visalia city, CEN. California 93279*; pop. 49,729.

Visayan Islands isl. group, CEN. Philippines; 23,621 sq. mi.

Vista city, SW California 92083; pop. 35,834.

Vistula river, CEN. and N Poland; 678 mi. long.

Vladivostok city, SE RSFSR; pop. 558,000.

Volga river, W RSFSR; 2,290 mi. long.

Volgograd city, W RSFSR; scene of a Russian victory over German forces in World War II, Sept. 1942 to Jan. 1943; pop. 999,000: from 1925–61 **Stalingrad.**

Volta river, E Ghana; 800 mi. long.

Vosges Mountains mtn., chain, E France.

Wabash river, W Ohio and Indiana; 475 mi. long.

Waco city, CEN. Texas 76701*; pop. 101,261.

Wade-Hampton uninc. place, NW South Carolina 29607; pop. 20,180.

Wahiawa city, CEN. Oahu, Hawaii 96786; pop. 41,562.

Waikiki beach on Honolulu harbor, SE Oahu, Hawaii.

Waipio city, Oahu, Hawaii 96786; pop. 29,139.

Wakefield town, E Massachusetts 01880*; pop. 24,895.

Wake Island coral atoll in the North Pacific; 4 sq. mi.; site of a U.S. naval and air base.

Wales penin., SW Britain; a principality of England; 8,019 sq. mi.; pop. 2,857,000.

Walla Walla city, SE Washington 99362; pop. 25,618.

Wallingford town, CEN. Connecticut 06492; pop. 37,274.

Walnut Creek city, W California 94596*; pop. 54,410.

Walpole town, E Massachusetts 02081; pop. 18,859.

Waltham city, E Massachusetts 02154; pop. 58,200.

Wantagh uninc. place, SE New York 11793; pop. 19,817.

Warminster uninc. place, SE Pennsylvania 18974; pop. 35,543.

Warner Robins city, CEN. Georgia 31093*; pop. 39,893.

Warren city, SE Michigan 48089*; pop. 161,134.

— city, NE Ohio 44481*; pop. 56,629.

Warrensville Heights vill., N Ohio 44122; pop. 16,565.

Warrington uninc. place, NW Florida 32507; pop. 15,792.

Warsaw city, CEN. Poland; cap.; pop. 1,651,200.

Warwick city, CEN. Rhode Island 02887*; pop. 87,123.

Washington state, NW United States; 68,192 sq. mi.; pop. 4,132,204; cap. Olympia.

— city, E United States; coextensive with the District of Columbia 20013*; pop. 638,432.

— city, SW Pennsylvania 15301; pop. 18,363.

Waterbury city, W Connecticut 06701*; pop. 103,266.

Waterford city, NE Connecticut 06385; pop. 17,843.

Waterloo vill., CEN. Belgium; scene of Napoleon's final defeat, June 18, 1815; pop. 24,536.

— city, CEN. Iowa 50701*; pop. 75,985.

— city, S Ontario, Canada; pop. 46,623.

Watertown city, SW Connecticut 06795; pop. 19,489.

— town, E Massachusetts 02172; pop. 34,384.

— city, N New York 13601; pop. 27,861.

— city, SE Wisconsin 53094; pop. 18,113.

Waterville city, CEN. Maine 04901*; pop. 17,779.

Waukegan city, NE Illinois 60085*; pop. 67,653.

Waukesha city, SE Wisconsin 53186*; pop. 50,365.

Wausau city, CEN. Wisconsin 54401*; pop. 32,426.

Wauwatosa city, SE Wisconsin 53213; pop. 51,308.

Waycross city, SE Georgia 31501; pop. 19,371.

Wayne vill., SE Michigan 48184; pop. 21,159.

— urb. twp., N New Jersey 07470*; pop. 46,474.

Waynesboro city, CEN. Virginia 22980; pop. 15,329.
Webster Groves city, E Missouri 63119; pop. 23,097.
Weimar city, SW Germany; pop. 62,803.
Weirton city, NW West Virginia 26062; pop. 25,371.
Welland city, S Ontario, Canada; pop. 45,047.
Welland Canal waterway betw. Lakes Erie and Ontario.
Wellesley town. E Massachusetts 02181; pop. 27,209.
Wellington city, CEN. New Zealand; cap.; pop. 135,400.
Wenatchee city, CEN. Washington 98801; pop. 17,257.
Weslaco city, S Texas 78596; pop. 19,331.
West Allis city, SE Wisconsin 53214; pop. 63,982.
West Bend city, SE Wisconsin 53095; pop. 21,484.
West Berlin See **Berlin.**
West Carson uninc. place, SE California 90502; pop. 17,997.
Westchester vill., NE Illinois 60153; pop. 17,730.
West Chester boro., SE Pennsylvania 19380; pop. 17,453.
West Covina city, SW California 91793*; pop. 80,292.
West Des Moines city, CEN. Iowa 50265; pop. 21,894.
Westerly city, SW Rhode Island 02891; pop. 18,580.
Western Australia state, W Australia; 975,100 sq. mi.; pop. 1,549,700; cap. Perth.
Western Sahara area on the W coast of Africa, claimed by Mauritania and Morocco; 102,703 sq. mi.; pop. 152,000.
Western Samoa See **Samoa.**
Westfield city, SW Massachusetts 01085; pop. 36,465.
— town, E New Jersey 07091*; pop. 30,447.
West Germany See **Germany.**
West Hartford town, CEN. Connecticut 06107; pop. 61,301.
West Haven town, S Connecticut 06516; pop. 53,184.
West Hempstead-Lakeview uninc. place, SE New York 11552; pop. 18,536.
West Hollywood city, SW California 90069; pop. 35,703.
West Indies series of isl. groups separating the North Atlantic from the Caribbean, including Cuba, Jamaica, Hispaniola, Puerto Rico, the Bahamas, Trinidad and Tobago, and the Leeward and Windward Islands.
West Indies, the group of British cols. in the Caribbean, including the Leeward Islands (Antigua, St. Kitts-Nevis-Anguilla, Montserrat, and the British Virgin Islands) and the Windward Islands (St. Vincent, St. Lucia and Dominica).
West Islip uninc. place, SE New York 11795; pop. 29,533.
West Lafayette city, CEN. Indiana 47906; pop. 21,247.
Westlake city, N Ohio 44145; pop. 19,483.
Westland city, SE Michigan 48185; pop. 84,603.
West Memphis city, E Arkansas 72301; pop. 28,138.
West Mifflin boro., SW Pennsylvania 15122; pop. 26,322.
Westminster city and metropolitan boro., London, England; site of the Houses of Parliament and Buckingham Palace; pop. 85,000.
— city, SW California 92863; pop. 71,133.
— city, CEN. Colorado 80030; pop. 50,211.
Westmont city, SE California 90047; pop. 27,916.
Westmount city, S Quebec, Canada; pop. 22,153.
West New York town, NE New Jersey 07093; pop. 39,194.
West Orange town, NE New Jersey 07052; pop. 39,510.
West Palm Beach city, SE Florida 33401*; pop. 62,530.
West Pensacola uninc. place, SW Florida 32505; pop. 24,371.
West Point U.S. military reservation, SE New York 10996; seat of the U.S. Military Academy.
Westport city, SW Connecticut 06880; pop. 25,290.
West Puente Valley uninc. place, SE California 91746; pop. 20,445.
West Saint Paul city, E Minnesota 55118; pop. 18,527.
West Seneca uninc. place, W New York 14224; pop. 51,210.
West Springfield town, S Massachusetts 01089; pop. 27,042.
West Virginia state, E United States; 24,181 sq. mi.; pop. 1,950,258; cap. Charleston.
West Warwick town, CEN. Rhode Island 02893; pop. 27,026.
West Whittier-Los Nietos uninc. place, SE California 90606*; pop. 20,962.
Wethersfield town, CEN. Connecticut 06109; pop. 26,013.
Weymouth town, E Massachusetts 02188; pop. 55,601.
Wheaton city, NE Illinois 60187*; pop. 43,043.
Wheaton Glenmont uninc. place, CEN. Maryland 20902; pop. 48,598.
Wheat Ridge uninc. place, CEN. Colorado 80033; pop. 30,293.
Wheeling city, NW West Virginia 26003*; pop. 43,070.
Whitby Whitby town, S Ontario, Canada; pop. 28,173.

White Bear Lake city, E Minnesota 55110; pop. 22,538.
Whitehall city, CEN. Ohio 43213; pop. 21,299.
— boro, SW Pennsylvania 18052; pop. 15,143.
White Mountains range of the Appalachians, CEN. New Hampshire.
White Plains city, SE New York 10602*; pop. 46,999.
Whitney, Mount peak, E California; 14,496 ft.
Whittier city, SW California 90605*; pop. 68,558.
Wichita city CEN. Kansas 67202*; pop. 279,835.
Wichita Falls city, N Texas 76307*; pop. 94,201.
Wickliffe city, NE Ohio 44092; pop. 16,790.
Wight, Isle of isl. off the S coast of England; 147 sq. mi.
Wilkes-Barre city, NE Pennsylvania 18701*; pop. 51,551.
Wilkinsburg boro., SW Pennsylvania 15221; pop. 23,669.
Williamsburg city, E Virginia 23185; capital of Virginia (1699–1779); restored to colonial condition; pop. 9,870.
Williamsport city, CEN. Pennsylvania 17701; pop. 33,401.
Willoughby city, NE Ohio 44094; pop. 19,329.
Willowbrook uninc. place, SE California 90222; pop. 30,845.
Willowick city, NE Ohio 44094; pop. 17,834.
Wilmette vill., NE Illinois 60091; pop. 28,221.
Wilmington city, N Delaware; 19899*; pop. 70,195.
— city, NE Massachusetts 01887; pop. 17,471.
— city, SE North Carolina 28401*; pop. 44,000.
Wilson town, CEN. North Carolina 27893; pop. 34,424.
Wilson, Mount peak, SW California; 5,710 ft; site of a famous observatory.
Wilson Dam power dam in the Tennessee River at Muscle Shoals, NW Alabama; 137 ft. high, 4,862 ft. long.
Wimbledon town and municipal boro., S England; scene of international tennis matches; pop. 20,000.
Winchester town, E Massachusetts 01890; pop. 20,701.
Windham city, NE Connecticut 06280; pop. 21,062.
Windhoek city, CEN. Namibia; cap.; pop. 114,000.
Windsor municipal boro., S England; site of **Windsor Castle,** a residence of the English sovereigns; pop. 29,660: officially **New Windsor.**
— city, SE Ontario, Canada; pop. 196,526.
Windward Islands isl. group, S Lesser Antilles.
Winnipeg city, SE Manitoba, Canada; cap.; pop. 560,874.
Winnipeg, Lake lake, S Manitoba, Canada; 9,398 sq. mi.
Winona city, SE Minnesota 55987*; pop. 25,075.
Winston-Salem city, CEN. North Carolina 27102*; pop. 131,885.
Winter Haven city, CEN. Florida 33880*; pop. 21,119.
Winter Park city, CEN. Florida 32708; pop. 22,314.
Winthrop town, E Massachusetts 02152; pop. 19,294.
Wisconsin state, N United States; 56,154 sq. mi.; pop. 4,705,642.
Wisconsin Rapids city, CEN. Wisconsin 54494; pop. 17,995.
Woburn city, E Massachusetts 01808*; pop. 36,626.
Woodbridge urb. twp., NE New Jersey 07095; pop. 90,074.
Woodbridge-Marumso city, NE Virginia 22191; pop. 24,004.
Woodland city, CEN. California 95695*; pop. 30,235.
Woodmere uninc. place, SE New York 11598; pop. 17,205.
Woodstock city, S Ontario, Canada; pop. 26,779.
Woonsocket city, NE Rhode Island 02895; pop. 45,914.
Wooster city, CEN. Ohio 44691*; pop. 19,289.
Worcester city, CEN. Massachusetts 01613*; pop. 161,799.
Worms city, SW Germany; pop. 73,505.
Worthington city, CEN. Ohio 43085; pop. 15,016.
Wroclaw city, SW Poland; pop. 637,400: *formerly called* **Breslau.**
Wuhan collective name for the cities of Hankow, Hanyang, and Wuchang, CEN. China; pop. 4,250,000.
Wuppertal city, W Germany; pop. 371,283.
Würzburg city, CEN. Germany; pop. 125,589.
Wyandotte city, SE Michigan 48192*; pop. 34,006.
Wyckoff urb. twp., NE New Jersey 07481; pop. 15,500.
Wyoming state, NW United States; 97,914 sq. mi.; pop. 469,557; cap. Cheyenne.
— city, W Michigan 49509; pop. 59,616.
Xenia city, CEN. Ohio 45385; pop. 24,653.
Yakima city, S Washington 98901*; pop. 49,826.
Yalta city, S Crimea; scene of a conference of Roosevelt, Churchill, and Stalin in February, 1945; pop. 81,000.
Yalu river forming part of the boundary betw. NE China and Korea; 500 mi. long.

Yangôn See **Rangoon.**
Yangtze river flowing from Tibet to the East China Sea; 3,600 mi. long.
Yellow River *an alternate name of* Hwang Ho.
Yellow Sea inlet of the Pacific betw. Korea and China; 400 mi. long, 400 mi. wide.
Yellowstone Falls 2 waterfalls of the Yellowstone River in Yellowstone National Park: **Upper Yellowstone Falls,** 109 ft.; **Lower Yellowstone Falls,** 308 ft.
Yellowstone National Park largest and oldest of the US national parks, largely in NW Wyoming; 3,458 sq. mi.; established 1872.
Yellowstone River river, NW Wyoming, SE Montana, and NW North Dakota; 671 mi. long.
Yemen, Republic of, republic, SW Arabia, formed by the joining of the former **People's Democratic Republic of Yemen (South Yemen)** and **The Yemen Arab Republic (North Yemen)** on May 22, 1990; 531,869 sq. mi.; pop. 11,546,000; cap. San'a.
Yerevan city, W Armenian SSR; cap.; pop. 1,199,000.
Yokohama city, CEN. Honshu, Japan; pop. 2,773,322.
Yonkers city, SE New York 10701*; pop. 195,351.
York co. boro., CEN. Yorkshire, England; cap.; pop. 126,377.
— city, S Pennsylvania 17405*; pop. 44,619.
Yosemite Valley gorge in **Yosemite National Park** (1,183 sq. mi., established 1890), CEN. California; 7 mi. long, 1 mi. wide; traversed by the Merced River that forms **Yosemite Falls:** Upper Fall, 1,430 ft.; Lower Fall, 320 ft.; with intermediate cascades, 2,425 ft.
Youngstown city, NE Ohio 44501*; pop. 115,511.
Ypres town, NW Belgium; site of three major battles of World War I, 1914, 1915, 1917; pop. 21,000.
Ypsilanti city, SE Michigan 48197; pop. 24,031.

Yucaipa uninc. place, SW California 92399; pop. 23,345.
Yucatán penin., SE Mexico and NE Central America; 70,000 sq. mi.
Yugoslavia, Socialist Federal Republic of republic, SE Europe; 98,766 sq. mi.; pop. 23,861,000; cap. Belgrade.
Yukon terr., NW Canada; 186,661 sq. mi.; pop. 26,000; cap. Whitehorse.
Yukon River river, NW Canada and CEN. Alaska; 1,770 mi. long.
Yuma city, SW Arizona 85364; pop. 42,481.
Zagreb city, CEN. Croatia, Yugoslavia; cap.; pop. 649,586.
Zaire republic, CEN. Africa; 905,446 sq. mi.; pop. 34,138,000; cap Kinshasa.
Zambezi river, S Africa; 1,700 mi. long.
Zambia republic, CEN. Africa; 290,586 sq. mi.; pop. 8,456,000; cap. Lusaka.
Zanesville city, CEN. Ohio 43701*; pop. 28,655.
Zanzibar reg. of Tanzaniatoff the coast of E Africa; comprises isls. of Zanzibar (640 sq. mi.) and **Pemba** (380 sq. mi.); pop. 354,000.
— city, W Zanzibar; cap.; pop.110,506.
Zealand isl. of Denmark betw. the Kattegat and the Baltic Sea; 2,709 sq. mi.
Zimbabwe republic, S Africa; 150,873 sq. mi.; pop. 9,369,000; cap. Harare.
Zion city, NE Illinois 60099; pop. 17,865.
Zululand dist., NE Natal, South Africa; formerly a native monarchy; 10,362 sq. mi.; pop. 570,000.
Zurich city, NE Switzerland; pop. 345,159.
Zuyder Zee former shallow inlet of the North Sea, NW Netherlands; drainage projects have reclaimed much of the land and formed Lake Ijssel. Also **Zuider Zee.**

Grammar and Usage Handbook

Word Usage and Word Relationships

Agreement of Subject and Verb

It may seem needless to say that a singular subject takes a singular verb, while a plural subject takes a plural verb; however, when phrases or other elements come between the subject and the verb, the agreement may not be clear.

The small table around which the children play *was* in the hall.

The small tables owned by the church *were* in the hall.

The men, as well as the policeman, *were* aghast at the sight.

The following words are generally considered singular and take singular verbs: *each, either, neither, one, someone, anyone, everybody, nobody, somebody, much, anybody, everyone.*

The following words are plural and take plural verbs: *both, few, many, several.*

The following pronouns may be singular or plural depending on the meaning intended: *all, most, some, every, none, any, half, more.*

When one is referring to two or more persons who are of different sexes, or to a group of people whose gender one has no way of determining, the pronouns *they, them,* and *their* are often used to refer to *anyone, each, everybody,* etc., in order to avoid the awkward *he or she, him or her, his or her.*

Either—Or; Neither—Nor

Neither always takes *nor; either* takes *or.*

When a subject is compounded with *neither . . . nor* or *either . . . or,* the verb is normally singular if the nouns joined are singular, and plural if they are plural. If, however, one noun is singular and one plural, the verb agrees with the second or nearer subject.

Either Bill or Ralph *is* lying.

Neither she nor her sisters *skate* well.

Collective Nouns

A collective noun, such as *class, company, club, crew, jury, committee,* takes a singular verb when the whole is considered as a unit, and a plural verb when members of the whole are being considered separately.

The jury *has* deliberated for six hours.

The crew *were* near exhaustion after their many hours of exposure.

Some collective nouns, as *police* and *cattle,* are used only in the plural form; others, as *mankind* and *wildlife,* are generally used in the singular form.

The cattle *were* almost destroyed by the severe storm.

The New England wildlife *has* been protected.

Agreement of Pronoun with Its Antecedent

If the antecedent is singular, the pronoun is singular, if the antecedent is plural, the pronoun is likewise plural.

The *boy* did *his* best in the contest.

The *boys* in the school did *their* best.

The *boy and* the *girl* did *their* best.

Neither one of the boys did *his* best.

Capitalization

Conventions governing the use of capital letters are quite clear.

Capitalize the first word of every sentence.

The first person singular pronoun *I* and the vocative *O* are generally capitalized.

Unless style requires a different form, *a.m.* and *p.m.* are set in small letters without a space between them. Capital letters are used for B.C. and A.D. but, again, there is no space between them.

9:30 a.m.   10:30 p.m.

A.D. 1760 *or* 1760 A.D.

76 B.C.

Note: Although A.D. should technically precede the number of the year, popular usage permits it to follow the date. In printed matter B.C., A.D., a.m., and p.m. usually appear in small capitals (B.C., A.D., A.M., P.M.).

The first letter of a line of conventional poetry is capitalized. Much modern poetry, however, ignores this convention.

Hickory, dickory, dock
The mouse ran up the clock.

The first word after a colon should be capitalized only when it begins a complete sentence.

The candidate made only one promise: If elected, he would fight for better conditions.

The list contained these items: five pounds of flour, two dozen eggs, and a pound of butter.

Every direct quotation should begin with a capital,

except where the quoted passage is grammatically woven into the text preceding it.

> The announcer shouted, "There it goes, over the back wall for a home run!"

> The announcer shouted that the ball was going "over the back wall for a home run."

Capitalize the first letters of all important words in the titles of books, newspapers, magazines, chapters, poems, articles. Short conjunctions and prepositions are generally not capitalized.

> How to Win Friends and Influence People

Geographical divisions and regions require capitals.

Arctic Circle	the Atlantic Seaboard
the Orient	the Great Plains

Compass points are capitalized when they are part of a generally accepted name, but not when they denote direction or locality.

Middle East	eastern New York
Old South	Head west for twenty-five miles.

Capitalize names of streets, parks, buildings, but not the general categories into which they fall.

> Fifth Avenue

> Which avenue is widest?

> General Post Office

> We went to the post office.

Religions, religious leaders, the various appellations for God and the Christian Trinity require capitalization, as do all names for the Bible and its parts.

> the Father, the Son, and the Holy Ghost

> Virgin Mary, the Immaculate Virgin

> Yahweh, Jehovah, Saviour, Messiah

> Buddhism, Shintoism, Taoism

> New Testament

> Exodus

> Sermon on the Mount

> Ten Commandments

Capitalize the names of political parties, classes, clubs, organizations, movements, and their adherents. Use small letters for the terms that refer generally to ideology (bolshevism, fascism, socialism).

> Democratic Party

> the Right Wing

> Farm bloc

> Boy Scouts of America

Political Divisions are capitalized.

Holy Roman Empire	the Colonies
French Republic	Suffolk County
the Dominion	Eighth Election District

Government bodies, departments, bureaus, and courts are capitalized.

the Supreme Court	the Cabinet
House of Representatives	Census Bureau
Department of Labor	British Parliament

Capitalize the titles of all high-ranking government officials, and all appellations of the President of the United States. Many publishers, it should be pointed out, prefer small letters for titles that are not accompanied by the name of the official.

President	Commander-in-Chief
Secretary of State	Chief Justice
Undersecretary	Prime Minister
Ambassador to India	Minister of War

Capitalize the names of treaties, documents, and important events.

Second World War	Declaration of Independence
Treaty of Versailles	Boston Tea Party

Family designations, when used without a possessive pronoun, take a capital letter.

> I sent Mother home by taxi.

> I sent my mother home by taxi.

Capitalize seasons only when they are personified. All personifications require capitals.

> The frosty breath of Winter settled on the land.

> The voice of Envy whispered in her ear.

> Necessity is the mother of Invention.

> When Headquarters commands, we jump.

> He saw Mother Nature's grim visage.

Names and epithets of peoples, races, and tribes are capitalized.

Caucasian	Sioux
Negro	Cliff Dwellers

Articles and prepositions are generally capitalized in the names of Englishmen and Americans, and are not capitalized in French, Italian, Spanish, German, and Dutch names, unless otherwise specified by family usage.

Thomas De Quincey	Ludwig van Beethoven
Martin Van Buren	Leonardo da Vinci
Fiorello La Guardia	San Juan de la Cruz

Capitalize the names of holidays and festivals.

Christmas	Shrove Tuesday
Yom Kippur	New Year's Day

Capitalize such parts of a book as Glossary, Contents, Index, and Preface.

Capitalize the first and last words in the salutation in business letters, and all titles.

My dear Sir	Dear Doctor Brown
My dear Reverend Lothrop	Dear Reverend Father

Capitalize only the first word of the complimentary close of a letter.

Very truly yours   Sincerely yours

Spelling

General Suggestions

When in doubt as to the correct spelling of a word, consult the dictionary; do not take anything for granted.

Keep a list of your spelling errors and study them.

Learn the most commonly misspelled words in the lists below.

Learn to spell by syllables, carefully pronouncing each syllable. Faulty spelling is often due to faulty pronunciation.

Use newly acquired words and make them part of your oral and written vocabulary.

Do not use the simplified or modern forms of spelling in business correspondence, as *thru* for *through*.

Learn some basic spelling rules such as the following.

cede, ceed, and sede endings According to the Government Style Manual, there is only one word which ends in *sede—supersede,* and three that end in *ceed—proceed, exceed, succeed.* All other words having this sound end in *cede—precede, secede, recede,* etc.

ie and ei a. After *c,* when the sound is long *e* (ē), the *e* usually precedes the *i:* rec*ei*ve, dec*ei*ve, c*ei*ling, rec*ei*pt.

b. After most other letters, the *i* precedes the *e:* th*ie*f, gr*ie*f, bel*ie*ve, ach*ie*ve, l*ie*n.

c. When the sound is *not* long *e* (ē); and especially if the sound is long *a* (ā), the *e* precedes the *i:* sl*ei*gh, v*ei*l.

The exceptions must be learned, since they follow no rule: n*ei*ther, l*ei*sure, w*ei*rd, s*ei*ze.

Beginnings and Endings of Words (Prefixes and Suffixes)

a. As a general rule, drop the final *e* in the base word when a suffix beginning with a vowel is added.

decide—deciding; write—writing; type—typist

b. As a rule, retain the final *e* in the base word when a suffix beginning with a consonant is added.

remote—remotely; care—carefully; infringe—infringement

c. In applying the rule for adding *ed* or *ing,* the accent (or lack of it) may serve as a guide. Words of one syllable (and most words of more than one syllable) that end in a single consonant (except *f, h,* or *x*), preceded by a single vowel, double the final consonant *if the accent falls on the last syllable.*

plan—planned, planning; whet—whetted, whetting

transfer—transferred, transferring; control—controlled, controlling

When the word is *not* accented on the last syllable, the consonant is usually not doubled.

travel—traveled, traveler; profit—profited, profiteer

d. When the endings *ness* and *ly* are added to a word not ending in *y,* the base word rarely changes. In most words ending in *y,* the *y* changes to *i* when *ly* is added.

natural—naturally; similar—similarly; genuine—genuineness; blessed—blessedness; hazy—hazily; body—bodily

If the base word ends in *n* and the suffix *ness* is added, the *n* is doubled.

sudden—suddenness; mean—meanness; vain—vainness

e. In regard to the word endings *ise, ize, yze,* the most common form is *ize,* but here the dictionary should be consulted if there is doubt.

legalize, fraternize, criticize, jeopardize

advertise, merchandise, surmise, enterprise

paralyze, analyze

In British English *ise* is sometimes used for *ize,* as *realise* for *realize.*

f. When adding the suffix *ful,* the *l* is single except when *ly* is also added (*fully*).

care—careful—carefully; hope—hopeful—hopefully

g. When the word beginnings (prefixes) *in, en, im, em, un, dis, mis, be, de, re, il,* and *over* are added to a word, the spelling of the word is not changed.

inactive, enjoy, impending, embrace, uneasy, dismiss, mistrust, beguile, degrade, retreat, illegal, overhaul

Forming the Plurals of Nouns

a. Most nouns form the plural by simply adding *s.*

table—tables; house—houses

b. Some nouns, especially those ending in *s,* form the plural by adding *es.*

class—classes; fox—foxes

c. Words ending in *y* preceded by a consonant form the plural by changing the *y* to *i* and adding *es.*

candy—candies; study—studies; secretary—secretaries

d. Words ending in *y* preceded by a vowel form the plural by adding *s* but without any other change in the word.

key—keys; boy—boys

e. Nouns ending in *o* preceded by a vowel form the plural by adding *s.*

rodeo—rodeos; radio—radios

When the *o* is preceded by a consonant, the plural is formed by adding *es.*

hero—heroes; torpedo—torpedoes

f. Nouns referring to music which end in *o* preceded by a consonant form the plural by simply adding *s*.

piano—pianos; oratorio—oratorios; contralto—contraltos; soprano—sopranos

g. Some few nouns follow none of the above rules but form the plural in an unusual way.

child—children; tooth—teeth; mouse—mice; ox—oxen

h. Compound nouns (more than one word) form the plural from the main word.

trade union—trade unions; father-in-law—fathers-in-law

i. When a solid compound ends in *ful,* the plural is formed at the end of the solid compound and not within the word.

basketful—basketfuls; pocketful—pocketfuls

j. When the words in compounds are of almost equal importance, both parts of the compound are pluralized.

head of department—heads of departments; woman operator—women operators

k. Words taken from another language sometimes form the plural as they would in the original language.

stratum—strata; addendum—addenda; datum—data

Summary of Spelling Rules

Problem	Rule	Examples	Exceptions

IE and **EI**	I before E, except after C.	ach*ie*ve, but c*ei*ling	1. Use *EI* when:
			  a. Sounded as *ā*: n*ei*ghbor, w*ei*gh
			  b. Sounded as *ī*: counterf*ei*t
			  c. Sounded as *ĭ*: h*ei*ght
			2. Use *IE* for almost all other sounds: friend, lieutenant.
			3. If *i* and *e* do not form a digraph, rules do not apply: f*ie*ry, d*ei*ty.

Final Silent **E**	1. **Drop** before suffix beginning with a vowel. 2. **Retain** before suffix beginning with a consonant.	grieve—grievance absolute—absolutely	1. Retain *e* after soft *c* and soft *g* before suffixes beginning with *a* or *o*: peacable, manageable.
Final **Y**	1. **Change** final *y* to *i* if *y* is **preceded** by a **consonant** and **followed** by any **suffix** except one beginning with *i*. 2. **Retain** final *y* if it is **preceded** by a **vowel.**	beauty—beautiful BUT carry—carrying boy—boys; valley—valleys	dry—dryness; sly—slyness. day—daily; pay—paid
Final Consonants	**Double** final consonants when: 1. Preceded by a single vowel 2. Followed by a suffix beginning with a vowel. 3. The consonant terminates a monosyllabic word. 4. The consonant terminates a polysyllabic word accented on the last syllable.	1. drop—dropped; beg—beggar 2. quit—quitting; swim—swimmer 3. hit—hitter; run—running 4. omit—omitted; transfer—transferred	Final consonant is not doubled if: 1. Accent shifts to preceding syllable when suffix is added: confer′—confer′ring BUT con′ference. 2. Final consonant is preceded by a consonant: start—started. 3. Final consonant is preceded by two vowels: beat—beating; boil—boiling.
k added to words ending in **c**	**Add** *k* to words ending in *c* before a suffix beginning with *e, i, y.*	frolic—frolicking—frolicked; picnic—picnicking—picnicked	
-cede **-ceed** **-sede**	Except for super*sede*, ex*ceed*, pro*ceed*, suc*ceed*, all words having this sound end in -*cede*.	accede, precede, recede, concede	

Plurals	1. Regular noun plurals add -*s* to the singular.
	2. Irregular plurals:
	  a. Add -*es* if noun ends in *o* preceded by consonant.
	  b. Change *y* to *i* and add -*es* if noun ends in *y* preceded by consonant.
	  c. Add -*s* if noun ends in *y* preceded by vowel.
		boy—boys; book—books
		
		a. echo—echoes; Negro— Negroes
		b. sky—skies; enemy—enemies
		c. play—plays; day— days
			a. piano—pianos; zero—zeros; solo—solos.

Possessives	1. Don't confuse contractions with possessive pronouns.
	
	2. Use no apostrophes with possessive or relative pronouns.
	3. If singular or plural noun **does not** end in *s*, add **apostrophe** and *s*.
	4. If singular or plural noun **does** end in *s*, add **apostrophe**
		Contraction Possessive
		1. it's (it is) its
		  they're their
		  (they are)
		2. *his, hers, ours, yours, theirs, whose*
		3. child's (Sing.), children's (Plur.)
		4. hostess' (Sing.), hostesses' (Plur.), princes' (Plur.)	

Spelling Lists

List of Words Most Frequently Misspelled by High School Seniors

The list of words below* contains 149 words most frequently misspelled by high school seniors. These words and word-groups (those which are variants of the same word, as *acquaint* and *acquaintance*), were compiled by Dean Thomas Clark Pollock of New York University from 14,651 examples of misspelling submitted by 297 teachers in the United States, Canada and Hawaii. Each of the words represented was misspelled twenty times or more, and yet these words, comprising fewer than three per cent of the original list of 3,811 words, account for thirty per cent of the total misspellings.

NOTE: The trouble spots in each word are italicized. Numbers beside the words indicate how frequently each word is misspelled.

accom*m*odate	25	together	23	me*a*nt	21
excel*l*ent	25	de*s*cend	13	*wh*ere	21
op*por*tunity	25	de*s*cendant	9	chie*f*	20
marry	4	d*u*ring	22	he*r*o	10
marries	6	f*or*ty	22	hero*es*	9
marriage	15	wom*a*n	22	hero*i*ne	1
		cert*ain*	21		
				lon*e*ly	20
chara*c*ter	24	commi*t*	4	opin*i*on	20
comple*te*	24	com*m*it*t*ed	12	parl*i*ament	20
fr*ie*nd	24	com*m*it*t*ing	5	pos*s*es*s*	20
tru*ly*	24	criti*c*ism	21	profes*s*or	20
accident*al*ly	23	di*s*ap*p*ear	21	resta*u*rant	20
do*esn't*	23	*exagg*erate	21	villa*in*	20

th*eir*	179	al*l r*ight	91	*its*	52
rec*ei*ve	163	sep*a*rate	91	*it's*	22
too	152	unt*il*	88		
		privi*le*ge	82	*occur*	9
writer	11	defin*i*te	78	*occurred*	52
writing	81	th*ere*	78	*occurrence*	10
written	13	bel*ie*ve	77	*occurring*	2
describe	28	*study*	1	prob*ably*	33
description	38	*studied*	3	spe*e*ch	33
		studies	3	argum*e*nt	32
trage*dy*	64	*studying*	34		
decide	48	*convenience*	5	*image*	3
decision	15	*convenient*	33	*imagine*	7
				imaginary	5
occa*s*ion	54	*difference*	15	*imagination*	17
occa*s*ion*ally*	8	*different*	23		
				qui*et*	32
succeed	25	th*an*	38	th*en*	32
success	22	a*th*letic	37		
successful	12	*to*	37	preju*d*ice	30
		business	36	*sense*	30
inter*est*	56			sim*i*lar	30
begin*n*ing	55	*equipped*	21		
		equipment	14	*your*	2
immediate	3			*you're*	28
immediately	51	princip*al*	18		
		princi*ple*	18	ap*pear*ance	29
com*i*ng	53			cons*cious*	29
embar*rass*	48	*prophecy*	35	pleas*ant*	29
gramm*ar*	47	*prophesy*	35		
		benefit	16	*stop*	1
hum*or*	2	*beneficial*	5	*stopped*	24
hum*or*ous	45	*benefited*	11	*stopping*	4
		benefiting	1		
exist	3			sur*prise*	29
existence	43	devel*op*	34		
		environ*ment*	34	*excite*	1
lose	28	re*comm*end	34	*excited*	7
losing	15	fa*s*cinate	33	*excitement*	13
		fin*ally*	33	*exciting*	7
di*s*appoint	42				
rhythm	41	*necessary*	24	experi*e*nce	28
		necessity	9	govern*m*ent	27
acquaint	17			labor*at*ory	27
acquaintance	9	*foreign*	14	tr*ied*	27
		foreigners	9		
aff*ect*	26			famil*i*ar	21
ac*c*ept	25	per*formance*	23	e*s*cape	21

List of 100 Words Most Frequently Misspelled by College Freshmen

absence	effect	o'clock
accidentally	eighth	omitted
across	embarrassed	parallel
aggravate	environment	perhaps
all right	exercise	principal
amateur	February	principles
argument	forth	privilege
around	forty	proceed
athletic	fourth	pronunciation
believed	friend	quiet
benefited	government	quite
business	grammar	received
busy	grievance	recommend
capital	hadn't	referred
cemetery	height	relieve
choose	indispensable	rhythm
chosen	interested	schedule
coming	its	seize
committee	it's	separate
competition	knowledge	shining
conscientious	laboratory	stationery
conscious	latter	strength
coolly	literature	succeed
council	loose	superintendent
counsel	lose	supersede
criticism	losing	tragedy
deceive	maintenance	tries
definite	marriage	truly
desert	mischievous	villain
dessert	noticeable	Wednesday
dining	occasion	weird
disappointed	occurred	whether
doesn't	occurrence	woman
don't		

List of Words Frequently Misspelled on Civil Service Examinations

accident	municipal	society
all right	principal	simplified
auxiliary	principle	technicality
athletic	promotional	tendency
buoyant	president	their
catalogue		thousandth
career	precede	transferred

* The list compiled by Dr. Pollock appears in the *Teachers' Service Bulletin in English* (Macmillan, November, 1952).

comptroller	proceed	transient
criticise	promissory	truly
dividend	recommend	villain
	personnel	
embarrass	purchasable	Wednesday
expedient	responsibility	writ
government	received	whether
inveigle	regrettable	yield
monetary	supersede	

Confusing Words

accept See EXCEPT.

addition, edition *Addition* means the process of joining together or finding the sum of. *Edition* refers to the form in which a book, magazine, or other literary work is published: first *edition*.

advice, advise *Advice* is the noun: to give *advice*. *Advise* is the verb: to *advise* a person.

affect *See* EFFECT.

all ready See ALREADY.

all right, alright *All right* is the only spelling to be used: It is *all right* to do so. The spelling *alright* is not yet considered acceptable and should not be used.

allude, elude *Allude* means to make indirect or casual reference: He *alluded* to one of Shakespeare's sonnets. *Elude* means to avoid or escape: The meaning *eludes* me.

already, all ready *Already* means before or by this time or the time mentioned: The group has *already* gone. *All ready* (two words) means that everyone is ready to do a given thing. We are *all ready* to go.

among, between. *Among* is used when referring to more than two persons or things. *Between* is usually preferable when referring to only two persons or things.

appraise, apprise *Appraise* means to make an official valuation of. *Apprise* means to notify or inform.

ascent, assent *Ascent* means rising, soaring, or climbing: the *ascent* of the mountain. *Assent* means agreement, consent, sanction: *assent* to a course of action.

between *See* AMONG.

can *See* MAY.

capital, capitol *Capital* means a city that is important in some special way: Albany is the *capital* of New York. *Capitol* means a building in which a State legislature meets: The *capitol* is on Chamber Street.

censor, censure *Censor* means (*n.*) an official examiner of manuscripts, plays, etc.; (*v.*) to act as a censor; delete; suppress. *Censure* means (*v.*) to express disapproval of; (*n.*) the expression of disapproval or blame.

census *See* SENSES.

cite, sight, site *Cite* means to mention or bring forward: to *cite* an incident. *Sight* (*n.*) means a view, a vision: a beautiful *sight*. *Site* means a place or location: the *site* of the church.

compliment, complement *Compliment* (*n.*) means praise or congratulation. *Complement* (*n.*) means one of two parts that mutually complete each other.

consul *See* COUNCIL.

council, counsel, consul *Council* (*n.*) means an assembly convened for consultation. *Counsel* (*n.*) means guidance, advice; also, a lawyer. *Consul* (*n.*) means an officer residing in a foreign country to protect his own country's interests.

creditable, credible *Creditable* means deserving credit or esteem; praiseworthy: a *creditable* project for reducing poverty. *Credible* means capable of being believed; reliable: a *credible* alibi.

decent, descent, dissent *Decent* means proper; respectable. *Descent* means the act of descending or going downward. *Dissent* means (*v.*) to disagree; (*n.*) a disagreement.

devise, device *Devise* (*v.*) means to invent, contrive, or plan. *Device* (*n.*) is something devised; invention; contrivance.

dissent See DECENT.

edition See ADDITION.

effect, affect *Effect,* common as both a noun and a verb, means (*v.*) to bring about; to cause or achieve: The treatments will *effect* an early cure; and (*n.*) result, outcome. *Affect,* in common use a verb only, means to influence or act upon: Fear *affects* the mind.

effective, effectual *Effective* means producing a desired result: *Effective* action averted the strike. *Effectual* means having the power to produce a desired result: *effectual* legal steps.

elicit, illicit *Elicit* means to bring to light: to *elicit* the truth. *Illicit* means unlawful or unauthorized.

elude See ALLUDE.

eminent, imminent *Eminent* means high in station; distinguished; prominent: an *eminent* statesman. *Imminent* means about to happen (said especially of danger): an *imminent* calamity.

except, accept *Except* (*v.*) means to take or leave out: to *except* no one from the restrictions. *Accept* means to receive or agree to; acknowledge: to *accept* an invitation.

formerly, formally *Formerly* means some time ago; once: He was *formerly* a judge. *Formally* means with formality or with regard to form: *formally* dressed.

illicit See ELICIT.

imminent See EMINENT.

lay, lie See not under LAY[1] in the body of this dictionary.

learn See TEACH.

lesson, lessen *Lesson* refers to instructive or corrective example. *Lessen* means to make less; decrease.

loose, lose *Loose* means not fastened or attached. *Lose* means to mislay or be deprived of.

may, can *May* expresses permission: The child *may* play in the yard. *Can* expresses ability to do: The child *can* do better than he is doing at present.

past, passed *Past* means (*adj.*) ended or finished: His hopes are *past;* and (*n.*) time gone by: He dreams of the *past. Passed,* the past tense and past particle of *pass,* means went (or gone) beyond or farther than: The car, which was going at high speed, *passed* him easily.

persecute, prosecute *Persecute* means to maltreat or oppress; to harass. *Prosecute,* generally used in a legal sense, means to bring suit against.

personal, personnel *Personal* pertains to a person: *personal* matters, *personal* opinions. *Personnel* pertains to a body or group of persons: *personnel* problem, *personnel* department.

practical, practicable *Practical* pertains to actual use and experience. *Practicable* means feasible or usable.

prosecute See PERSECUTE.

senses, census *Senses,* the plural of *sense,* refers to awareness and rationality or to the faculty of sensation: to come to one's *senses;* Her *senses* were dulled by the accident. *Census* refers to an official count of the people of a country or district, etc.

shall, will See note under SHALL in the body of this dictionary.

sight See CITE.

site See CITE.

stationery, stationary *Stationery* refers to writing supplies. *Stationary* means remaining in one place.

sweet, suite *Sweet* means having a taste like sugar. *Suite* refers to a set or series of things intended to be used together: *suite* of rooms, *suite* of furniture.

teach, learn *Teach* means to impart knowledge; *learn* means to acquire knowledge. The teacher *teaches;* the student *learns.*

will, shall See note under SHALL in the body of this dictionary.

Sample Business Letters

Letterhead

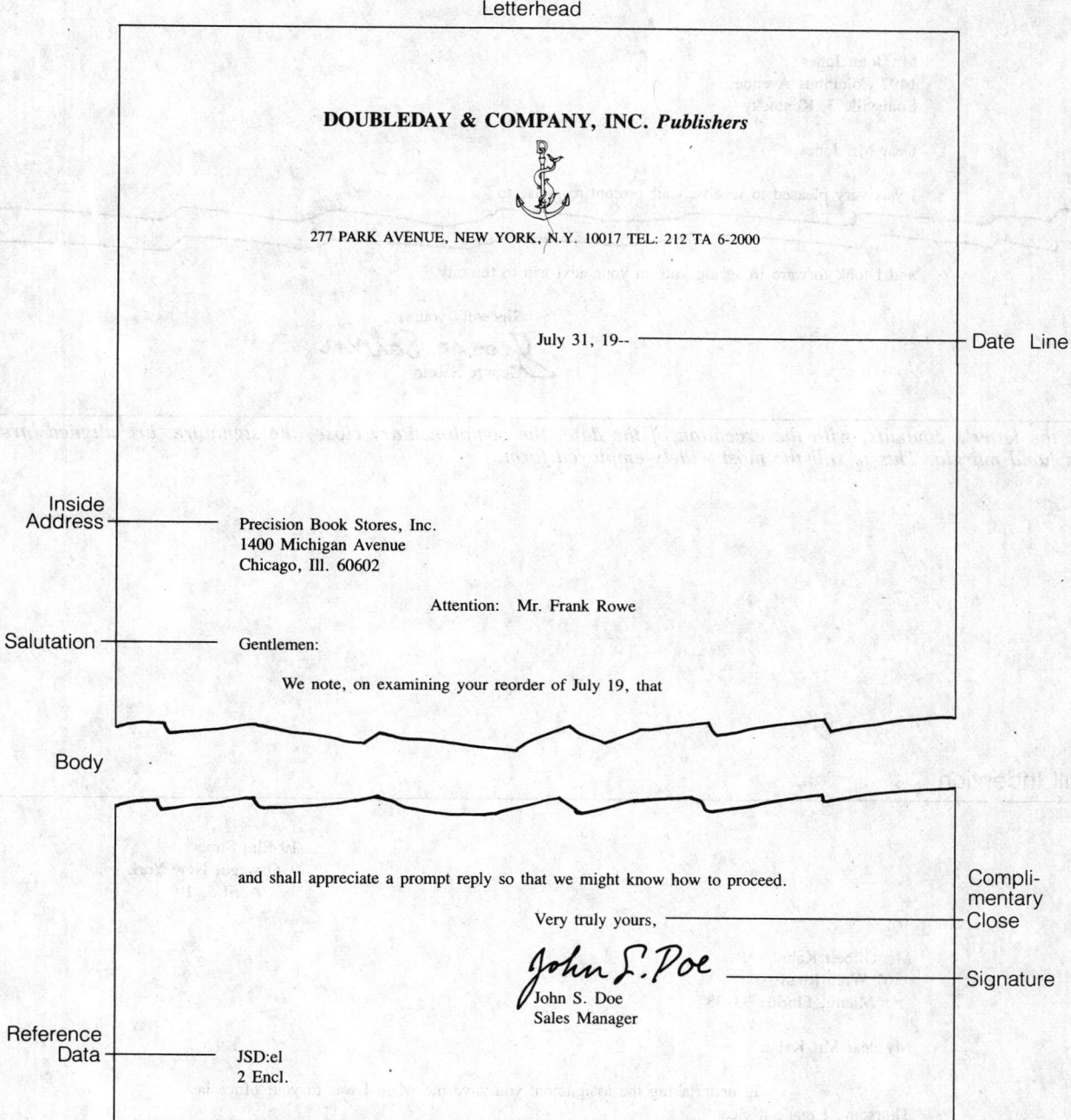

DOUBLEDAY & COMPANY, INC. *Publishers*

277 PARK AVENUE, NEW YORK, N.Y. 10017 TEL: 212 TA 6-2000

July 31, 19-- —————————————— Date Line

Inside
Address —————— Precision Book Stores, Inc.
1400 Michigan Avenue
Chicago, Ill. 60602

Attention: Mr. Frank Rowe

Salutation ———————— Gentlemen:

We note, on examining your reorder of July 19, that

Body

and shall appreciate a prompt reply so that we might know how to proceed.

Very truly yours, ——————————— Complimentary
Close

John S. Doe ————————— Signature

John S. Doe
Sales Manager

Reference
Data ———— JSD:el
2 Encl.

This model letter includes in standard form all *the elements normally employed in the business letter.*

From *Business Letter Writing Made Simple,* revised ed., by Irving Rosenthal and Harry W. Rudman, Copyright © 1955, 1968 by Doubleday & Co., Inc.

The "Modified Block" Form

February 28, 19

Mr. John Jones
1492 Columbus Avenue
Louisville 3, Kentucky

Dear Mr. Jones:

I was very pleased to receive your prompt response to

and I look forward to seeing you on your next trip to the city.

Sincerely yours,

George Sabrin
George Sabrin

All the letter's contents, with the exception of the date, the complimentary close, the signature, are aligned on the left hand margin. This is still the most widely employed form.

Full Indention

19 Elm Street
Oswego, New York
April 5, 19

Mr. Gilbert Kahn
67 Wren Road
Miami, Florida 33138

My dear Mr. Kahn:

In undertaking the assignment you gave me when I was in your office last
Thursday, I made it clear

nevertheless intend to do the best job I can.

Sincerely yours,

Lucille Graham
Lucille Graham

This form is all but obsolete, and there seems little doubt that in time it will cease entirely to be used.

Additional Sheets

Mr. John Jones—page 2—January 14, 19

therefore feel that we cannot accept the return of the merchandise at this late date. We like to cooperate

with all our accounts. . . .

It was necessary, because of its length, to continue this letter on an additional sheet. The additional sheet is headed by the addressee's name, the page number, and the date. There is the requisite minimum of three lines of text, in addition to complimentary close and signature.

The "Full Block" Form

February 28, 19

Mr. John Jones
1492 Columbus Avenue
Louisville 3, Kentucky

Dear Mr. Jones:

I was very pleased to receive your prompt response to my

and I look forward to seeing you on your next trip to the city.

Sincerely yours,

George Sabrin
George Sabrin

In the "full block" form all the letter's contents are aligned on the left hand margin.

Forms of Address

President of the United States

Address: Business: The President
The White House
Washington, D.C.
Social: The President
and Mrs. Roberts
The White House
Washington, D.C.
Salutation: Formal: Mr. President:
Informal: Dear Mr. President:
Closing: Formal: Most respectfully yours,
Informal: Sincerely yours,
In Conversation: Mr. President *or* Sir
Title of Introduction: The President *or* Mr. Roberts

Vice President of the United States

Address: Business: The Vice President
United States Senate
Washington, D.C.
Social: The Vice President
and Mrs. Hope
Home Address
Salutation: Formal: Mr. Vice President:
Informal: Dear Mr. Vice President:
Closing: Formal: Very truly yours,
Informal: Sincerely yours,
In Conversation: Mr. Vice President *or* Sir
Title of Introduction: The Vice President *or* Mr. Hope

Chief Justice of the United States

Address: Business: The Chief Justice
The Supreme Court
Washington, D.C.
Social: The Chief Justice
and Mrs. Page
Home Address
Salutation: Formal: Sir:
Informal: Dear Mr. Chief Justice:
Closing: Formal: Very truly yours,
Informal: Sincerely yours,
In Conversation: Mr. Chief Justice *or* Sir
Title of Introduction: The Chief Justice

Associate Justice of the Supreme Court

Address: Business: Mr. Justice Katsaros
The Supreme Court
Washington, D.C.
Social: Mr. Justice Katsaros
and Mrs. Katsaros
Home Address
Salutation: Formal: Sir:
Informal: Dear Mr. Justice Katsaros:
Closing: Formal: Very truly yours,
Informal: Sincerely yours,
In Conversation: Mr. Justice *or* Mr. Justice
Katsaros *or* Sir
Title of Introduction: Mr. Justice Katsaros

Cabinet Officer

Address: Business: The Honorable Gary George
Gussin
Secretary of the Treasury *or*
Attorney General of the United
States
Washington, D.C.

Social: The Secretary of the Treasury
and Mrs. Gussin
Home Address
or (for a woman cabinet member)
The Honorable Beatrice Schwartz
or (if she is married)
Mr. and Mrs. Henry Leo Woods
Salutation: Formal: Sir: *or* Dear Sir: *or* Madam:
Informal: Dear Mr. Secretary: *or*
Dear Madam Secretary:
Closing: Formal: Very truly yours,
Informal: Sincerely yours,
In Conversation: Mr. Secretary *or* Madam Secretary
or Mr. Attorney General *or*
Mr. (*or* Miss *or* Mrs.) Smith
Title of Introduction: The Secretary of the Treasury,
Mr. Smith *or*
The Attorney General of the
United States, Mr. Smith

Former President

Address: Business: The Honorable Alfred Edward
Work
Office Address
Social: The Honorable and Mrs. Alfred
Edward Work
Home Address
Salutation: Formal: Sir:
Informal: Dear Mr. Work:
Closing: Formal: Very truly yours,
Informal: Sincerely yours,
In Conversation: Mr. Work *or* Sir
Title of Introduction: The Honorable Alfred Edward
Work

United States Senator

Address: Business: The Honorable John Wandzilak
United States Senate
Washington, D.C.
Social: The Honorable and Mrs. John
Wandzilak
Home Address
or (for a woman senator)
The Honorable Marguerite
Sanders
or (if she is married)
Mr. and Mrs. John Row Doe
Salutation: Formal: Sir: *or* Madam:
Informal: Dear Senator Wandzilak:
Closing: Formal: Very truly yours,
Informal: Sincerely yours,
In Conversation: Senator *or* Senator Wandzilak *or*
Sir
Title of Introduction: Senator Wandzilak

Speaker of the House of Representatives

Address: Business: The Honorable Walter Fry
The Speaker of the House of
Representatives
Washington, D.C.
Social: The Speaker of the House of
Representatives and Mrs. Fry
Home Address
Salutation: Formal: Sir:
Informal: Dear Mr. Speaker:
Closing: Formal: Very truly yours,

Informal: Sincerely yours,
In Conversation: Mr. Speaker *or* Sir
Title of Introduction: The Speaker of the House of
Representatives *or*
The Speaker, Mr. Fry

Member of the House of Representatives

Address: Business: The Honorable Henry Cobb
Wellcome
United States House of
Representatives
Washington, D.C.
Social: The Honorable and Mrs. Henry
Cobb Wellcome
Home Address
or (for a woman member)
The Honorable Ann Davenport
or (if she is married)
Mr. and Mrs. John Knox Jones
Salutation: Formal: Sir: *or* Madam:
Informal: Dear Mr. Wellcome:
Closing: Formal: Very truly yours,
Informal: Sincerely yours,
In Conversation: Mr. Wellcome *or* Miss Davenport *or*
Mrs. Jones *or* Sir *or* Madam
Title of Introduction: Representative Wellcome

Ambassador of the United States

Address: Business: The Honorable John Wilson
Smith
The Ambassador of the United
States
American Embassy
London, England
Social: The Honorable and Mrs. John
Wilson Smith
Home Address
or (for a woman ambassador)
The Honorable Janet Lund
or (if she is married)
Mr. and Mrs. Joseph Leeds
Walker
Salutation: Formal: Sir: *or* Madam:
Informal: Dear Mr. Ambassador: *or* Dear
Madam Ambassador:
Closing: Formal: Very truly yours,
Informal: Sincerely yours,
In Conversation: Mr. Ambassador *or* Madam
Ambassador *or* Sir *or* Madam
Title of Introduction: The American Ambassador *or*
The Ambassador of the
United States

Minister Plenipotentiary of the United States

Address: Business: The Honorable James Lee Row
The Minister of the United States
American Legation
Oslo, Norway
Social: The Honorable and Mrs. James
Lee Row
Home Address
or (for a woman minister)
The Honorable Eugenia Carlucci
or (if she is married)
Mr. and Mrs. Arthur Johnson
Salutation: Formal: Sir: *or* Madam:

Informal: Dear Mr. Minister *or* Dear
Madam Minister:
Closing: Formal: Very truly yours,
Informal: Sincerely yours,
In Conversation: Mr. Row *or* Miss Carlucci *or*
Mrs. Johnson
Title of Introduction: Mr. Row, the American
Minister

Consul of the United States

Address: Business: Mr. John Smith
American Consul
Rue de Quelque Chose
Paris, France
Social: Mr. and Mrs. John Smith
Home Address
Salutation: Formal: Sir: *or* Dear Sir:
Informal: Dear Mr. Smith:
Closing: Formal: Very truly yours,
Informal: Sincerely yours,
In Conversation: Mr. Smith
Title of Introduction: Mr. Smith

Ambassador of a Foreign Country

Address: Business: His Excellency, Juan Luis Ortega
The Ambassador of Mexico
Washington, D.C.
Social: His Excellency
The Ambassador of Mexico and
Señora Ortega
Home Address
Salutation: Formal: Excellency:
Informal: Dear Mr. Ambassador:
Closing: Formal: Very truly yours,
Informal: Sincerely yours,
In Conversation: Mr. Ambassador *or* Sir
Title of Introduction: The Ambassador of Mexico

Minister of a Foreign Country

Address: Business: The Honorable
Carluh Matti
The Minister of Kezeah
Washington, D.C.
Social: The Honorable and Mrs. Carluh
Matti
Home Address
Salutation: Formal: Sir:
Informal: Dear Mr. Minister:
Closing: Formal: Very truly yours,
Informal: Sincerely yours,
In Conversation: Mr. Minister *or* Sir
Title of Introduction: The Minister of Kezeah

Governor of a State

Address: Business: The Honorable Joseph L. Marvin
Governor of Idaho
Boise, Idaho
Social: The Honorable and Mrs. Joseph L.
Marvin
Home Address
or (for a woman governor)
The Honorable Katherine Marvin
or (if she is married)
Mr. and Mrs. Walter O'Reilly
Salutation: Formal: Sir:
Informal: Dear Governor Marvin:

Closing: Formal: Very truly yours,
      Informal: Sincerely yours,
In Conversation: Governor Marvin *or* Sir *or* Madam
Title of Introduction: The Governor *or* The
              Governor of Idaho

State Senators and Representatives are addressed
in the same manner as U.S. Senators and Representatives.

Mayor

Address: Business: Honorable Roger Shute
              Mayor of Easton
              City Hall
              Easton, Maryland
      Social: The Honorable
              and Mrs. Roger Shute
              Home Address
              or (for a woman mayor)
              The Honorable Martha Wayne
              or (if she is married)
              Mr. and Mrs. Walter Snow
Salutation: Formal: Sir: *or* Madam:
      Informal: Dear Mayor Shute:
Closing: Formal: Very truly yours,
      Informal: Sincerely yours,
In Conversation: Mr. Mayor *or* Madam Mayor
Title of Introduction: Mayor Shute

Judge

Address: Business: The Honorable Carson Little
              Justice, Appellate Division
              Supreme Court of the State of
                New York
              Albany, New York
      Social: The Honorable and Mrs. Carson
              Little
              Home Address
              or (for a woman judge)
              The Honorable Josefina Gonzalez
              or (if she is married)
              Mr. and Mrs. Rafael Montoya
Salutation: Formal: Sir:
      Informal: Dear Judge Little:
Closing: Formal: Very truly yours,
      Informal: Sincerely yours,
In Conversation: Mr. Justice *or* Madam Justice
Title of Introduction: Justice Little

Protestant Bishop

Address: Business: The Right Reverend John S.
                Bowman
              Bishop of Rhode Island
              Providence, Rhode Island
      Social: The Right Reverend and
              Mrs. John S. Bowman
Salutation: Formal: Right Reverend Sir:
      Informal: Dear Bishop Bowman:
Closing: Formal: Respectfully yours,
      Informal: Sincerely yours,
In Conversation: Bishop Bowman
Title of Introduction: Bishop Bowman

Protestant Clergyman

Address: Business: The Reverend David Dekker
              or (if he holds the degree)
              The Reverend David Dekker,
                D.D.
              Address of his church
      Social: The Reverend and Mrs. David
              Dekker
              Home Address
Salutation: Formal: Dear Sir:
      Informal: Dear Mr. (*or* Dr.) Dekker:
Closing: Formal: Sincerely yours,
      Informal: Sincerely yours,
In Conversation: Mr. (*or* Dr.) Dekker
Title of Introduction: Mr. (*or* Dr.) Dekker

Rabbi

Address: Business: Rabbi Paul Aaron Fine
              or (if he holds the degree)
              Dr. Paul Aaron Fine, D.D.
              Address of his synagogue
      Social: Rabbi (*or* Dr.) and Mrs. Paul
              Aaron Fine
              Home Address
Salutation: Formal: Dear Sir:
      Informal: Dear Rabbi (*or* Dr.) Fine:
Closing: Formal: Sincerely yours,
      Informal: Sincerely yours,
In Conversation: Rabbi (*or* Dr.) Fine
Title of Introduction: Rabbi (*or* Dr.) Fine

The Pope

Address: His Holiness Pope Paul VI
      or His Holiness the Pope
      Vatican City
Salutation: Your Holiness:
Closing: Your Holiness' most humble servant,
In Conversation: Your Holiness
Title of Introduction: *One is presented to:* His
              Holiness *or* The Holy Father

Cardinal

Address: His Eminence Alberto Cardinal Vezzetti
      Archbishop of Baltimore
      Baltimore, Maryland
Salutation: Formal: Your Eminence:
      Informal: Dear Cardinal Vezzetti:
Closing: Your Eminence's humble servant,
In Conversation: Your Eminence
Title of Introduction: *One is presented to:* His
              Eminence, Cardinal Vezzetti

Roman Catholic Archbishop

Address: The Most Reverend Preston Lowen
      Archbishop of Philadelphia
      Philadelphia, Pennsylvania
Salutation: Formal: Your Excellency: *or* Most
              Reverend Sir:
      Informal: Dear Archbishop Lowen:
Closing: Your Excellency's humble servant,
In Conversation: Your Excellency
Title of Introduction: *One is presented to:* The Most
              Reverend
              The Archbishop of Philadelphia

Roman Catholic Bishop

Address: The Most Reverend Matthew S. Borden
    Address of his church
Salutation: Formal: Your Excellency: or Most
        Reverend Sir:
    Informal: Dear Bishop Borden:
Closing: Formal: Your obedient servant,
    Informal: Sincerely yours,
In Conversation: Your Excellency
Title of Introduction: Bishop Borden

Monsignor

Address: The Right Reverend Monsignor Ryan
    Address of his church
Salutation: Formal: Right Reverend Monsignor:
    Informal: Dear Monsignor Ryan:
Closing: Formal: I remain, Right Reverend
        Monsignor, yours faithfully,
    Informal: Faithfully yours,
In Conversation: Monsignor Ryan
Title of Introduction: Monsignor Ryan

Priest

Address: The Reverend John Matthews (and the
        initials of his order)
    Address of his church
Salutation: Formal: Reverend Father:
    Informal: Dear Father Matthews:
Closing: Formal: I remain, Reverend Father, yours
        faithfully,
    Informal: Faithfully yours,
In Conversation: Father or Father Matthews
Title of Introduction: The Reverend Father
        Matthews

Member of Religious Order

Address: Sister Angelica (and initials of order) or
    Brother James (and initials)
    Address
Salutation: Formal: Dear Sister: or Dear Brother:
    Informal: Dear Sister Angelica: or Dear
        Brother James
Closing: Formal: Respectfully yours,
    Informal: Faithfully yours,
In Conversation: Sister Angelica or Brother James
Title of Introduction: Sister Angelica or Brother
        James

University Professor

Address: Business: Professor Robert Knowles
        Office Address
    Social: Professor or Mr.
        or (if he holds the degree)
        Dr. and Mrs. Robert Knowles
        Home Address
        or (for a woman professor)
        Professor or Miss (or Dr.)
            Catherine Stone
        or (if she is married)
        Mr. and Mrs. Wallace Bryant
Salutation: Formal: Dear Professor (or Dr.) Knowles:
    Informal: Dear Mr. (or Miss or Mrs. or
        Ms.) Knowles:
Closing: Formal: Very truly yours,

Informal: Sincerely yours,
In Conversation: Professor (or Dr. or Mr. or Miss
        or Mrs.) Knowles
Title of Introduction: Professor (or Dr.) Knowles

Physician

Address: Business: William L. Barnes, M.D. or
        Dr. William L. Barnes
        Office Address
    Social: Dr. and Mrs. William L. Barnes
        Home Address
Salutation: Dear Dr. Barnes:
Closing: Formal: Very truly yours,
    Informal: Sincerely yours,
In Conversation: Dr. Barnes
Title of Introduction: Dr. Barnes

Canada

Prime Minister

Address: Business: The Right Hon. John Smith,
        P.C., M.P.
        Prime Minister of Canada
        Parliament Building
        Ottawa, Ontario
    Social: The Hon. and Mrs. John Smith
        Home Address
Salutation: Formal: Sir: or Dear Sir:
    Informal: Dear Mr. Prime Minister: or
        Dear Mr. Smith:
Closing: Formal: Yours very truly,
    Informal: Yours very sincerely,
In Conversation: Mr. Prime Minister or Mr. Smith
        or Sir

Governor General—The Commonwealth

Address: Business: His Excellency
        John Smith (or his personal title)
        Government House
        Ottawa, Ontario
    Social: Their Excellencies
        The Governor General and
            Mrs. John Smith
        Home Address
Salutation: Formal: Sir: or Dear Sir:
    Informal: Dear Mr. Smith:
Closing: Formal: Your Excellency's obedient servant,
    Informal: Yours very sincerely,
In Conversation: Your Excellency

Former Prime Minister

Address: The Honourable (or Right Honourable)
        John Smith
        Home Address (or Office Address)

Cabinet Officer

Address: Business: The Hon. John Smith, P.C., M.P.
        Minister of Forestry
        Ottawa, Ontario
    Social: The Hon. and Mrs. John Smith
        Home Address
        or (for a woman cabinet member)
        The Hon. Mary Jones
        (or, if she is married)
        Mr. and Mrs. John Smith

Salutation: Formal: Sir: *or* Dear Sir: *or* Madam:
                        or Dear Madam:
        Informal: Dear Mr. Smith; *or* Dear
                        Mrs. Smith:
Closing: Formal: Yours very truly,
        Informal: Yours very sincerely,
In Conversation: Sir *or* Madam (*formally*); Mr. *or*
                        Mrs. Smith *or* Mr. Minister
                        (*informally*)

Judges

Judges of the following federal and provincial courts have the title The Honourable.

Supreme Court of Canada, Exchequer Court of Canada, Courts of appeal of the provinces of British Columbia, Manitoba, and Saskatchewan, Court of Chancery of the province of Prince Edward Island, Courts of Queen's Bench of the Provinces of Manitoba, Quebec, and Saskatchewan, Superior Court of the province of Quebec, Supreme courts of the provinces of Alberta, British Columbia, New Brunswick, Nova Scotia, Ontario, Prince Edward Island, and Newfoundland; and the territorial courts.

Address: Business: The Hon. Mr. Justice John Smith
        Social: The Hon. Mr. Justice John Smith
                and Mrs. Smith
Salutation: Formal: Sir:

Informal: Dear Mr. Justice Smith:
Closing: Formal: Yours very truly,
        Informal: Yours very sincerely,
In Conversation: Sir (*formally*); Mr. Justice
                        (*informally*)

Mayor

Address: His Worship
        The Mayor of St. Lazare
Salutation: Formal: Dear Sir:
        Informal: Dear Mr. Mayor:
Closing: Formal: Yours very truly,
        Informal: Yours very sincerely,
In Conversation: Sir (*formally*): Mr. Mayor
                        (*informally*)

Member of Parliament

Address: John Smith, Esq., M.P.
        House of Commons
        Ottawa, Ontario
Salutation: Formal: Dear Sir: *or* Dear Madam:
        Informal: Dear Mr. (*or* Miss *or* Mrs.) Smith
Closing: Formal: Yours very truly,
        Informal: Yours very sincerely,
In Conversation: Sir *or* Madam (*formally*): Mr. (*or*
                        Miss *or* Mrs.) Smith (*informally*)

The Library Research Paper

by William W. Watt

What is research? In recent years the word has filtered out of the ivory tower and spread like an epidemic in the marketplace. Loose popular usage has worn the sharp edges from its meaning and threatened to deface its value. To many people *research* refers loosely to the act of looking up or checking up on anything, anywhere, in any way. Political polls, television ratings, the detection of factual errors in unpublished magazine articles, traffic counts at intersections, questionnaires on consumer habits, comparison shopping to price silk stockings—all are called *research*. The transitive verb ("I'll research it for you") appears to be catching up with the noun in popularity, and the well-drilled team is crowding out the lonely adventurer.

Though the weakening of a noble word may be disturbing, it is a useful reminder that the natural human passion for discovering, recording, and evaluating data is not—and never was—the special province of the academic expert in the library, laboratory, museum, geological quarry, or archaeological digging. The scholar's methods may be more systematic and his conclusions more profound. He may have a more sincere faith in the freedom that lies in the pursuit of truth for its own sake—in "pure" research. But he has no monopoly on the activity of research.

Of the infinite varieties, none is more generally useful than the experience that begins as a hunting expedition in a library and ends when the last period is typed on the finished paper. The library research paper is an inevitable academic assignment. Commonly known as the *term paper,* it regularly serves as a sort of commencement exercise at the end of the course or year. For the secondary school student who goes on to college, or for the college undergraduate who proceeds to graduate professional school, there is always another commencement, another beginning of a new research paper. But though the project may become increasingly ambitious and the process more complex, the essential discipline does not change with academic advancement. The basic rules remain the same. The student who forms scholarly habits of research in school will find them invaluable later, whether under the discipline of further formal education or the self-discipline of his vocation, his avocation, or a civic activity. Because the responsible adult is a student all his life, the word *student* will have no chronological limits in this article.

The experience of writing even a single research paper pays educational dividends to any serious student. It encourages him to develop a personal interest in a subject of his own choice. It offers an opportunity for genuine independent study. It introduces him to the resources of whatever library he is privileged to use. It shows him the excitement of tracking down knowledge that is not neatly packaged in a textbook or on a blackboard. It offers him the satisfaction of completing a task more thorough than any routine writing assignment. (The word *re-search* suggests thoroughness: a *searching again,* checking *and* double-checking.)

The task demands discriminating reading at various speeds and levels, accurate note-taking, intelligent summarizing, honest and systematic acknowledgement of intellectual indebtedness, and a more intricate organization than is ever required on a short composition. The process of separating truth from error and facts from judgments, of compiling and selecting evidence to support a credible conclusion, is a general application of *scientific* method; the problem of organizing the results on paper so that they will instruct and even intrigue a reader belongs to the province of *art*. In first-rate research the "two cultures" meet.

Ideally, then, the library research paper is the product of both critical thinking and creative writing. It should reflect the enthusiasm of an alert mind, not the methodological digging of a reluctant mole. But the most talented and enthusiastic student cannot even approach the ideal unless he is aware from the start that rigorous scholarly method (not pedantic methodology) is the foundation of success. To present an elementary understanding of that method is the purpose of this article.

Finding and Limiting a Subject

Unless the student has a specific assignment thrust upon him by a teacher, his first problem is to choose a subject for investigation. (He is luckier, of course, if the subject has chosen him.) Selecting a suitable subject should not be a haphazard process like rolling dice at random until the right combination pays off. As soon as the writer knows that he is faced with a research deadline—usually a comfortable number of weeks away—he should do some preliminary prowling in the library, along the open stacks if that is permitted, to see what, if anything, it contains within his spheres of general interest. If a teacher has restricted the choice to the limits of a single course, he should be on the alert for clues in the unfinished business of the required reading or class discussion. A good discussion in class is full of loose ends that need to be tied together or of questions that require more time and information to answer. A good teacher will always start more game than he can bring to earth; few mortals irritate him more than the student who, after weeks of classroom suggestions, both explicit and implicit ("This would make a good subject for a research paper") comes staggering toward the deadline still fumbling around for "something to write about."

The first rule for finding a subject is hallowed by age. Two thousand years ago the Roman poet Horace put it this way: "Choose a subject, ye who write, suited to your strength." This does not mean that a student should regard a research assignment only as another chance to ride a familiar hobby. It means that the beginner's reach should not so far exceed his grasp that he will quickly become bogged down in learned technicalities that defy translation.

The second rule is that even a subject well suited to the writer's taste and talent should be strictly limited in accordance with the proposed or required length of the paper. Overly ambitious intentions usually lead to unsuccessful research papers because the student cannot possibly treat his subject adequately within the allotted space and time.

The tentative choice of a subject may be nothing more than a general idea of the territory to be explored, but before the student has ventured far he should become aware of the boundaries so that he won't waste precious hours wandering off limits. Sometimes during the early stages of research a large, nebulous subject will rapdily assume a clearly defined shape, if only because of the limitations of a particular library. More often the reverse is true: a general topic divides and subdivides and the student, who thought he had focused on a subject, finds himself helplessly confused. It is best to limit the subject in advance and avoid this predicament, especially when there is a deadline to meet.

The problem of limiting a subject for research is no different in kind from the routine dilemma of channeling an ambitious idea into a short composition. The same writer who struggles to capture the significance of "Love" or "Ambition" or "The Beat Generation" in 500 words is just as likely to propose a research paper of 3,000 on "The Poetry of Robert Browning" or "The History of Television." Certainly "Browning's Dramatic Monologues" or "Educational Television" would be preferable. Making the necessary allowances for the experience of the writer and the resources of the library, "Browning's Dramatic Monologues on Renaissance Painters" or "Closed Circuit Television in the High School Science Class" would be even better. Nothing more quickly betrays the limitations of a writer's knowledge than his inability to limit his subject.

A more specific way of limiting is to begin with a definite *thesis*—a proposition to prove, perhaps even a side to defend in a hypothetical pro and con debate: to presume to show, for example, that Browning's failure to achieve success in the theater was largely the fault of the Victorian audience, or that classroom television costs more money than it's worth. Such a proposition gives direction to the research and provides a convenient mold for the paper. But the pre-fabricated thesis has caused many dangerous detours from the truth. When a writer has flown effortlessly to a conclusion, it is hard for him to persuade himself that he ought to go back and trudge over the land on foot. It is a human weakness, even among scholars, to warp the truth to accommodate a foregone conclusion, casually ignoring the stubborn facts that won't conform. Moreover, many useful subjects for research do not lend themselves to a thesis statement: they involve explanation, narrative, analysis, or revelation—but not necessarily proof. On the whole, unless a writer is already something of an expert on his subject at the start, he should postpone the choice of a thesis until he has done most of the digging.

He might, like a scientist, begin with a *working hypothesis,* a tentative proposition to serve as a guidepost. But he should always be careful not to mistake a hunch for a fact, or a prejudice for an opinion. Objectivity is at the heart of genuine scholarship. Any researcher would do well to remember Thomas Henry Huxley's definition of a tragedy: "the slaying of a beautiful hypothesis by an ugly fact."

Whatever the subject, there should be no misconceptions about the requirements of the job. Though no two subjects require identical treatment, *the final paper should make it clear that the writer has reflected on the material and marshaled it as evidence to support one or more convincing conclusions*. Many beginners honestly believe that research is only an exercise in genteel plagiarism: tracking down information and transferring it—in great chunks or little snippets—from print to typescript by way of hastily jotted notes—producing a result that could have been achieved more efficiently with a Gillette blade and a roll of Scotch tape. Many failing papers are little more than anthologies of unfamiliar quotations or patchwork quilts of paraphrase. To be sure, the novice is not required to aim at the goal of the ideal Ph.D. dissertation: "an original contribution to knowledge." He is not expected to be an authority on his subject and should not presume to be. Most of his material will have been carefully sifted by more experienced hands, but this does not exempt him from the duty of critical thinking. If he understands this from the start, he will not arbitrarily divide his labor into a physical act of compilation and a mental act of composition. From the first visit to the library he will be reflecting carefully upon the material, not just thoughtlessly jotting down notes. The final product will be a transfusion, not a series of transplants.

Using the Library

Because no two libraries are identical, no general instruction on "how to use the library" is custom-tailored to the individual in Azusa or Zanesville. The best way for a reader to get familiar with the machinery of a particular library is to make himself at home there. He should not stride directly to the delivery desk and say to whoever is in charge: "Do you have any books on closed circuit television?" Though the librarian—especially a trained reference librarian—may provide indispensable help at a later stage of the investigation, the student should begin with a declaration of independence. Given the run of the stacks in a small or middle-sized library, he can get off to a good start by going at once to the general territory of his subject (he can find *English Literature* or *American History* on a chart without memorizing the Dewey Decimal System). Wandering up and down the aisles from A to Z, he can get a preliminary view of the land by merely scanning the backbones of books.

But such freedom is not usually permitted in a large library, where the student may have to spend many minutes at the delivery desk waiting to receive the books he has requested. Moreover, a good research paper is not the end-product of aimless browsing. The student will save both himself and the librarian time and trouble by learning the names of the standard reference guides, where to find them, and how to use them. To do this is to practice one of the fundamental principles of research: *Always take pains in the present to avoid panic in the future.*

Regardless of the subject, three reference guides will probably prove indispensable: (1) the card catalogue; (2) a comprehensive encyclopedia: and (3) the *Reader's Guide to Periodical Literature*.

The Card Catalogue

The proper use of a card catalogue requires both imagination and persistence. (Serendipity—the ability to discover treasures that you are not looking for—is probably more of a reward for alertness and patience than a native gift.) In a complete catalogue any book in the library may be listed alphabetically on at least three cards:

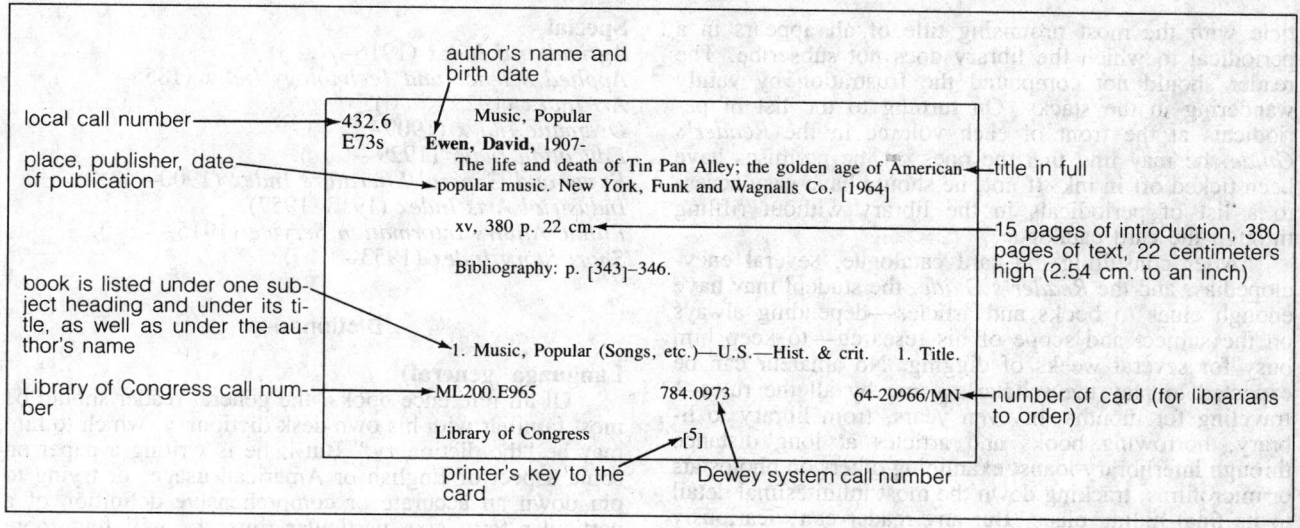

local call number —

place, publisher, date of publication —

book is listed under one subject heading and under its title, as well as under the author's name

Library of Congress call number

author's name and birth date

432.6
E73s

Music, Popular
Ewen, David, 1907-
    The life and death of Tin Pan Alley; the golden age of American — title in full
popular music. New York, Funk and Wagnalls Co. [1964]

    xv, 380 p. 22 cm. — 15 pages of introduction, 380 pages of text, 22 centimeters high (2.54 cm. to an inch)

    Bibliography: p. [343]-346.

    1. Music, Popular (Songs, etc.)—U.S.—Hist. & crit.   1. Title.

ML200.E965   784.0973   64-20966/MN — number of card (for librarians to order)

Library of Congress   [5]

printer's key to the card

Dewey system call number

---

by subject, author (last name first), and title. Other cards serve as cross-references.

For example, a student planning a paper on "Closed Circuit Television in the High School Science Class" might begin by looking up "Television." He should find a number of subject cards with this label at the top (probably typed in red), each alphabetically arranged by author. As he shuffles further, he should find other cards with more specific subject labels. "Television—apparatus and supplies" may interest him; "Television—law and legislation" may not. A group of books catalogued under "Television in education" certainly will. The student is on his way.

A single card, like a single dictionary entry, contains a wealth of information, some of which is essential for a bibliography. Consider the scope of the data on a typical subject card of the kind disseminated throughout the country by the Library of Congress (*above*).

A Comprehensive Encyclopedia

The reader digging for a research paper should ordinarily regard a complete encyclopedia as an indispensable guide, not an ultimate goal. The writer whose footnotes and bibliography show that he has quarried his material from a half dozen competing encyclopedias—however reputable—is easily identified as an explorer who has never left his safe home in the reference room.

For the conscientious student a good encyclopedia article has two main virtues: (1) it provides an authoritative and comprehensive view of a general subject, probably one in which he has staked out a more restricted claim; (2) it supplies bibliographical references which the student may not have discovered in the card catalogue. Let us take one possible example. The 1963 printing of the *Encyclopaedia Britannica* has an article on "Television" that runs to 19 large double-column pages, complete with photographs and diagrams. As the key to the contributors' initials reveals in the index volume, it is an authoritative article written by the Director of the Research Division of the Philco Corporation. But less than half a column is devoted to the applications of closed circuit TV in education. On the other hand, the article is followed by a list of six more extensive treatments of the general subject, any one of which might find a place in the student's final bibliography. Moreover, if the reader turns to "television" in the index volume, he will find

other references to "educational television" that do not appear in the general entry. By consulting several good encyclopedias on a subject the student may choose one which he feels will best help him construct a firm foundation for a research paper.

The *Reader's Guide*

Neither the card catalogue nor the most complete encyclopedia can pretend to give a comprehensive listing of magazine articles that have not been corralled in a book. Even in these days of prolific publishing, many interesting subjects of limited appeal have never been fully treated in book form. New developments, especially in science, are arriving and changing with such speed that even an encyclopedia publishing an annual supplement can never be completely up-to-date. On almost any subject of general interest the first place to hunt for magazine articles is the *Reader's Guide to Periodical Literature*.

The *Reader's Guide* has been indexing current contributions to the best-known American magazines since 1901 and now includes references to more than 125 publications. The semi-monthly issues (monthly in July and August) are conveniently bound in volumes that cover periods of one to four years. Articles are listed by author and subject. If a student's chosen subject relates to a specific event since 1901 ("The Hamlet of John Barrymore," "The Attack on Pearl Harbor"), he can begin at that date and work toward the present. If not, especially if he has no clues to authors, he should start with the subject entries in the most recent issues and hunt backward through the bound volumes. On looking up "Television," for example, in the volume for March 1963–February 1964, he would find three articles listed under "TELEVISION, Closed circuit" and twenty-one under "TELEVISION in education." (Any abbreviations in the entries can be understood easily by referring to a key at the front of the volume.) And these would be only a selection of the articles for one year in popular magazines: a glance at the *Education Index* (see below) would uncover many more in professional journals. It is no wonder that teachers turn gray when students report that they "can't find any material" on an obvious subject in an adequate library.

The reader with limited time and facilities cannot expect to locate every one of these articles. It is one of the inevitable frustrations of research to find that the ar-

ticle with the most promising title of all appears in a periodical to which the library does not subscribe. The reader should not compound the frustration by vainly wandering in the stacks. On turning to the list of periodicals at the front of each volume in the *Reader's Guide*, he may find that the ones on the premises have been ticked off in ink. If not, he should have easy access to a list of periodicals in the library without riffling through the card catalogue.

After consulting the card catalogue, several encyclopedias, and the *Reader's Guide*, the student may have enough clues to books and articles—depending always on the subject and scope of his research—to keep him busy for several weeks of digging. No amateur can be expected to play the scholar's game by all the rules— traveling for months, or even years, from library to library, borrowing books and articles at long distance through interlibrary loans, examining others on photostats or microfilms, tracking down the most infinitesimal detail to its final hiding place. But any reader can vicariously experience the excitement of such sleuthing on a smaller scale. Even the beginner should be familiar with more than three guides to research. Some of these tools can prove indispensable to him for detecting clues to possible sources of information on his topic.

Of the unnumerable research tools in a great library—including reference guides to reference books and bibliographies of bibliography—the following list contains only a generous sample.

Catalogues and Bibliographies

Books in Print (1948–   ). An annual author and title index to the *Publisher's Trade List Annual*. Lists the books still available from more than 1,100 American publishers. *Subject Guide to Books in Print* (1957–   ) lists them annually by subject.

Library of Congress Catalog (1942–   ). A complete catalogue by authors, showing facsimiles of the cards in the great library in Washington, D.C. A similar catalogue arranges books by subject.

Periodical Indexes

General

Book Review Digest (1905–   ). A monthly collection of excerpts from current book reviews indexed by author, subject, and title. It helps the reader to get a quick general picture of whether the first greetings were favorable, unfavorable, or lukewarm. More important, it directs him to reviews that he may want to read *in toto*.

International Index to Periodicals (1907–   ). A key to articles in scholarly journals that are not indexed in the *Reader's Guide*, which is limited to more popular magazines.

New York Times Index (1913–   ). A detailed index (now published twice a month) to a distinguished newspaper. Indispensable for a writer whose subject is related to any newsworthy event since the year before World War I. Even if the library does not have the complete file of the *Times* (now available in microfilm), he can make extensive use of the index to pin down exact dates, establish the chronological order of events, and find leads to news in any paper that may be available.

Poole's Index to Periodical Literature (1802–1906). Though much less thorough than the *Reader's Guide*, this annual subject index is a useful key to articles in English and American magazines in the nineteenth century.

Special

Agricultural Index (1916–   ).
Applied Science and Technology Index (1858–   ).
Art Index (1929–   ).
Dramatic Index (1909–   ).
Education Index (1929–   ).
Essay and General Literature Index (1900–   ).
Industrial Arts Index (1913–1957).
Public Affairs Information Service (1915–   ).
Short Story Index (1953–   ).

Dictionaries

Language (general)

Of all reference books, the general reader should be most familiar with his own desk dictionary, which to him may be "the dictionary." But if he is writing a paper on some aspect of English or American usage, or trying to pin down an accurate or comprehensive definition of a particular term at a particular time, he will find more complete or specialized information in the following works:

Dictionary of American English on Historical Principles. 4 vols. Chicago, 1936–1944. Supplemented by *A Dictionary of Americanisms*, 1951.

New "Standard" Dictionary. rev. ed. New York, 1959. A revision of an unabridged dictionary published by Funk and Wagnalls since 1913.

Oxford English Dictionary. 12 vols. and supplement. London and New York, 1933. When a writer is summoning up remembrance of things past, few records are more suggestive than the changing history of a word's meaning through the years. The great OED supplies such a record by citing the use of words in passages of prose and poetry, arranged in chronological order from the earliest occurrences. Once published as the *New English Dictionary* (NED).

Webster's Third New International Dictionary. Springfield, Mass., 1961. "Webster's Third" contains many new words and meanings not included in the second edition of the 1934 and illustrates them profusely in actual contexts. Based on recent linguistic theory, it records—often without restrictive labels— many usages that are widely frowned on.

Language (special)

Evans, Bergen and Cornelia. *A Dictionary of Contemporary American Usage*. New York, 1957.

Fowler, H. W. *A Dictionary of Modern English Usage*. London, 1926.

Nicholson, Margaret. *A Dictionary of American-English Usage*. New York, 1957. Based on Fowler.

Roget's International Thesaurus. 3rd ed., New York, 1962.

Webster's Dictionary of Synonyms. Springfield, Mass., 1942.

Biography

Dictionary of American Biography. 20 vols. and supplements. New York, 1928–   . The DAB contains lives of dead Americans.

Dictionary of National Biography. 22 vols. and supplements. London, 1885–   . The DNB has lives of dead Britons.

International Who's Who. London, 1936–   . Annual.

Kunitz, Stanley J. and Howard Haycraft. *Twentieth Century Authors*. New York, 1942. Supplement, 1945.

Webster's Biographical Dictionary. Springfield, Mass., 1943.

Who's Who. London, 1849–   . An annual dictionary of living Britons.

Who's Who in America. Chicago, 1899–   . A biennial dictionary of living Americans.

Encyclopedias and Surveys

General

There are many good, comprehensive encyclopedias which are following an editorial program of constant revision. Any good library should have several such encyclopedias of recent copyright. These encyclopedia publishers also supply yearbooks or supplemental material to make the most recent information promptly available to the researcher.

Special

Bailey, Liberty Hyde, ed. *Cyclopedia of American Agriculture.* 4 vols. New York, 1908–1909.

Baldwin, James M., and B. Rand, eds. *Dictionary of Philosophy and Psychology.* new ed. 3 vols. New York, 1949.

Bartlett's Familiar Quotations. 13th ed. Boston, 1955.

Blom, Eric., ed. *Grove's Dictionary of Music and Musicians.* 5th ed. 10 vols. London, 1954. Supplement, 1961.

Cambridge Ancient History. 17 vols., including plates. Cambridge, 1928–1939.

Cambridge Medieval History. 16 vols., including maps and plates. Cambridge, 1911–1936.

Cambridge Modern History. 2nd ed. 13 vols. and atlas. Cambridge, 1902–1926.

Cambridge Bibliography of English Literature. 5 vols. Cambridge, 1941. Supplement 1957.

Cambridge History of American Literature. 4 vols. New York, 1917–1921.

Cambridge History of English Literature. 15 vols. Cambridge, 1907–1927.

Catholic Encyclopedia. rev. ed. 17 vols. New York, 1936–   .

Dictionary of American History. rev. ed. 5 vols. and index. New York, 1946.

Encyclopedia of World Art. New York, 1958–   . In progress.

Feather, Leonard. *Encyclopedia of Jazz.* rev. ed. New York, 1960.

Fletcher, Sir Banister. *A History of Architecture.* 17th ed. New York, 1961.

Good, C. V. *Dictionary of Education.* 2nd ed. New York, 1959.

Harper's Encyclopedia of Art. 2 vols. New York, 1937. Re-issued as *New Standard Encyclopedia of Art,* 1939.

Hart, James D. *Oxford Companion to American Literature.* 3rd ed. New York, 1956.

Harvey, Sir Paul, ed. *Oxford Companion to Classical Literature.* 3rd ed. New York, 1956. *Oxford Companion to English Literature.* 3rd ed. New York, 1946.

Hastings, James, ed. *Encyclopedia of Religion and Ethics.* new ed. 13 vols. New York, 1951.

Kirk, Raymond E., and Donald F. Othmer. *Encyclopedia of Chemical Technology.* 15 vols. and supplements. New York, 1947–   .

Langer, William L., ed. *Encyclopedia of World History.* rev. ed. Boston, 1952.

McGraw-Hill Encyclopedia of Science and Technology. 15 vols. New York, 1960.

McLaughlin, Andrew C., and A. B. Hart, eds. *Cyclopedia of American Government.* 3 vols. New York, 1914.

Monroe, Walter S., ed. *Encyclopedia of Educational Research.* 3rd ed. by Chester Harris, New York, 1960.

Munn, Glenn G. *Encyclopedia of Banking and Finance.* rev. ed. L. Garcia. Boston, 1962.

Oxford History of English Literature. 12 vols. projected. Oxford, 1947–

Sarton, George. *Introduction to the History of Science.* 3 vols. Baltimore, 1927–1948.

Seligman, Edwin R. A., and A. Johnson, eds. *Encyclopedia of the Social Sciences.* 15 vols. New York, 1930–1935. Reissued in 8 vols., 1948.

Singer, Charles, ed. *History of Technology.* 5 vols. New York, 1956–1958.

Smith, Horatio, ed. *Columbia Dictionary of Modern European Literature.* New York, 1947.

Spiller, Robert E., ed. *A Literary History of the United States.* 3 vols. New York, 1948. rev. ed. 1 vol. 1953. Supplement by R. M. Ludwig, 1959.

Stevenson, Burton. *The Home Book of Quotations.* 9th ed. New York, 1959. Organized by subjects.

Thompson, Oscar, and N. Slonimsky, eds. *International Cyclopedia of Music and Musicians.* new ed. 3 vols. New York, 1940.

Tweney, C. F., and L. E. C. Hughes, eds. *Chamber's Technical Dictionary.* 3rd rev. ed. New York, 1958.

Universal Jewish Encyclopedia. 10 vols. and index. New York, 1939–1944.

Van Nostrand's Scientific Encyclopedia. 3rd ed. New York, 1958.

Yearbooks

In addition to the yearbooks made available by encyclopedia publishers, the following may be found useful.

American Year Book (1910–   ).
The New International Year Book (1907–   ).
Statesman's Year Book (1864–   ).
World Almanac and Book of Facts (1868–   ).

The Working Bibliography

At the very beginning of his search for materials the reader should be armed with a dependable pen and a supply of 3 x 5 index cards. (Pencils may smudge and encourage illegible scribbling; items jotted in notebooks or on miscellaneous scraps of paper are harder to organize and easier to overlook.) Though the search through the reference guides will turn up some material that will later prove unavailable or useless, it will pay at this stage to make a written record of every title that may conceivably bear on the chosen subject. When arranged in alphabetical form—with no more than one title on a card—these entries will form a tentative list of sources: a working bibliography. When the actual reading of sources begins, some of the cards will be jettisoned, and—as new references turn up in the reading—others will be added. The final bibliography, compiled after the paper is written, may have only a general family resemblance to its pioneering ancestor. But it is far less trouble to tear up a card that has not proved useful than to remember an unrecorded title or to return repeatedly to the reference guides.

To avoid trouble later on, the student should write down *the same facts in the same form* that will be required in the final bibliography. Authorities differ about the formal details, but if every researcher were permitted to follow his own fancy, whether through careless indif-

ference or conscious resistance to tradition, the useful shorthand of scholarship would soon degenerate into chaos. The forms illustrated here for both bibliography and footnotes (pp. 1024–1026) are those recommended in *The MLA Style Sheet* (revised edition), compiled by William Riley Parker for the Modern Language Association after consulting with the editors of 109 journals and 34 university presses. No prudent beginner would ignore such an expert jury to accommodate his own whims. Accurate scholarly form demands *the right facts in the right order with the right punctuation.* Though the standard may seem pedantic to the novice, even the substitution of a semicolon for a colon is not acceptable.

Here are some sample entries for bibliography cards.

For a book with one author:

Galbraith, John K. *The Affluent Society.* Boston, 1958.

Notice that the entry contains four parts in the following order: (1) Author's name, last name first—for alphabetizing; (2) full title—underlined (italicized); (3) place of publication; (4) date of publication. Periods separate the parts except for the comma between place and date. A period also comes at the end of the entry. Unless a different form of an author's name is well known (Eliot T. S. or Maugham, W. Somerset), give the first name and any initials. Nobody wants to search through a large catalogue for Brown, J.

Some authorities insist on including the name of the publisher. It comes after the place of publication and is preceded by a colon and followed by a comma:

Galbraith, John K. *The Affluent Society.* Boston: Houghton Mifflin, 1958.

For a book with more than one author:

Sledd, James H., and Gwin J. Kolb. *Dr. Johnson's Dictionary.* Chicago, 1955.

Because the second name does not determine the alphabetical placing of the entry, it follows the normal order. If a book has more than two authors, it is sufficient to give the name of the first and add "and others."

For a periodical article:

Lippmann, Walter. "Cuba and the Nuclear Risk," *Atlantic,* CCXI (February 1963), 55–58.

The standard form has five parts in this order: (1) Author's name, last name first (the title comes first if the author is not known); (2) full title of article—in quotes; (3) name of periodical—underlined (italicized); (4) volume—in Roman numerals—and date—in parentheses; (5) page numbers. Except for the period after the author's name, the parts are separated by commas. Notice that this form differs from that of the *Reader's Guide,* where the entry reads:

Cuba and the nuclear risk. Atlan 211:55–8 F '63.

Such an abbreviated form should not be copied onto bibliography cards.

For a newspaper article:

New York *Times,* December 28, 1964, p. 6.

The place of publication is not ordinarily underlined, and the page number is preceded by the standard abbre-

viation for *page* (lower case p.). If a newspaper has two or more sections with separate paging, the section number is included after the date:

New York *Times,* January 3, 1965, sec. 4, p. 7.

For an encyclopedia article:

Fink, Donald G. "Television," *Encyclopaedia Britannica* (1963), XXI, 910A–913.

In addition to this minimum of information, the student should allow room in the upper left-hand corner of the card for the call number. This will save unnecessary trips to the card catalogue. If the library is large and unfamiliar and the stacks are open, it is helpful to add a further note about the location:

613.84   Neuberger, Maurine B. *Smoke Screen:*
N478s   *Tobacco and the Public Welfare.* En-
(2nd floor,   glewood Cliffs, N.J., 1963.
north stack)

Evaluating Sources

As soon as the student turns from the cards of his working bibliography to the actual pages of the sources, he can begin to evaluate the material. Often a quick glance at a book or article will assure him that it is not appropriate; the card, in this case, may be torn up at once. Though other sources will require more careful attention, the researcher should always be ready to change his reading pace, slowing down when the material is complicated or difficult, and speeding up when it is readily comprehensible. The independent reading for research will give him an incomparable opportunity to practice whatever he knows about the difference between skimming and thorough reading. Bacon's proverbial wisdom will become a practical reality: "Some books are to be tasted, others to be swallowed, and some few to be chewed and digested. . . ." "A man," said Samuel Johnson, "will turn over half a library to make one book." But not, the Doctor might have added, if the man plods through all the reading at the same unchanging pace.

Only a seasoned expert in a field can know for certain what authors to respect as authorities or disregard as quacks. But even the beginner can show some intelligent discrimination. The inexperienced reader can learn to evaluate sources just as the scholar does, by asking a few questions based on *external* and *internal evidence.* For example:

External Evidence

Who wrote the book or article? What's in a name? To a conscientious scholar, a great deal. If a name turns up again and again during the investigation—especially if others explicitly refer to the owner as an authority—it is a reasonable, though not a foolproof, assumption that he is more dependable than an obscure author. If the author has a pedigree in one or more standard biographical dictionaries, so much the better, though it must not be forgotten that the elect compile their own pedigrees. A Civil War historian in a great university probably knows more about the battle of Gettysburg than a feature writer commemorating the anniversary for a small town newspaper. A professional folklorist should have a more accurate knowledge of the history of the popular ballad than an itinerant guitar strummer.

Who published it? Though it is risky to make odious comparisons in the mushrooming world of publishing, a reader with some experience will be safer in trusting a reputable imprint of long standing than a new and untested brand name. A scholarly book published by a university press is probably a safer, if duller, guide to a specialized subject than a popular best-seller concocted for the trade. A sober account in the New York *Times* should be fitter to quote than a sensational exposé in a cheap tabloid.

When was it written? Is the material first-hand, second or third? A newspaper extra printed on December 8, 1941 might capture the confused excitement of the attack on Pearl Harbor, but an unbiased study published ten years later would probably be a more reliable source for the facts. An estimate of Winston Churchill published in 1919 would lack the perspective of a book written after the Battle of Britain. A student writing on a subject that is changing as swiftly as "Space Travel" or "Jet Propulsion" will naturally look for the latest word; a scholar delving into the past will be eager to uncover the earliest. The investigator with limited time and experience will lack the scholar's opportunities for tracking down a subject to its *primary sources*—burrowing beyond the printed page to the original manuscript. But he can share the scholar's desire for getting as near as possible to the first-hand truth of an event, the actual wording of a text or document. If he is writing about Shakespeare's treatment of the theme of mercy, he doesn't have to summarize a paraphrase of Portia's speech from a student cram book when a reputable text of *The Merchant of Venice* is close at hand. Nor should he quote a critic from the *Book Review Digest* when the original review is on a nearby shelf.

Internal Evidence

What does the actual text of the book or article reveal about the reliability of the author? The experienced reader will find it easier to answer such a question than the novices but it does not take much sophistication to distinguish between critical thinking and slanted writing (is the author's manner analytical or emotional, are the words neutral or loaded?); or between a distinterested search on all sides of the truth and an argument that is mere propaganda; or between a thorough investigation leading to conclusions founded on facts and a superficial survey resulting in unsupported conjectures.

Considering the amount of piffle on paper, no experienced reader has an ingenuous faith in the sanctity of print for its own sake. But many a reader who ought to know better, eager to accumulate evidence to support a thesis, will gather material at random without the slightest attention to the quality or reliability of his sources. The true scholar does not snap up ill-considered trifles; he is a discriminating reader and a natural skeptic. He not only wants to be shown, he insists on being convinced.

Taking Notes

It is sometimes convenient to jot down a general note about a book or article on one of the 3 x 5 bibliography cards. "A comprehensive survey with no recent evidence on the subject." "A jazzy sketch to amuse the reader, not inform him." But more specific or extensive notes should be on separate cards. Because they will not be shuffled in the same deck with the bibliography, these note cards need not be of the same size. Most scholars recommend 4 x 6 note cards (or slips of paper); some prefer half sheets (5½ x 8). Here convenience is more important than tradition. Note cards should be small enough to sort handily, large enough to allow room for legible notes, but not so large as to invite wholesale transcribing.

Note taking is a useful art, whether in routine reading, lectures, class discussions, or meetings of clubs and

---

II. 2. a   "Social Balance"   Galbraith, 251-269

We ignore need for balance between private production and public services. Inadequate services in cities, blighted and polluted countryside, neglected education and recreation inadequate housing -- vs. more and more cars, T.V. sets, comic books, switchblade knives, gimmicks and gadgets. "Social balance," which would bring greater enjoyment to life, hindered by power of private advertising, "the truce on inequality," tendency to inflation.

[This published in 1958. How much progress since?]

committees. In research it assumes some of the dimensions of an exact science. The individual may eventually derive a personal method that suits him best. The following are some hints and warnings:

Do not take too many notes. Note-taking should be an aid to discriminating reading, not an opportunity for voluminous writing. The reader who postpones all his mental sorting until he begins to go through his note cards to write the paper is making his task unnecessarily difficult.

Restrict each note to one point on one side of the card. The definition of *point* is always arbitrary. It may be a sharp point like a brief direct quotation or a broad point like a short summary of a paragraph or a whole article. But do not clutter up a note with a miscellaneous scattering of quotations and reactions scribbled at random on both sides. The careful assignment of points to cards is another step in the winnowing process that accompanies research from start to finish. Organizing a research paper is not unlike playing a hand of bridge. If aces could not be quickly distinguished from deuces, or face-up cards from face-down, the game would be impossible.

Identify each card accurately at the top with a brief caption for the note and a key to the source, including the exact page number or numbers. If the complete information on that source appears as it should, on a bibliography card, all that is necessary on a note card is the author's name and the page—or, if he is responsible for more than one source, a short title: Muir, p. 61 or *The Present Age,* pp. 158–159. If a direct quotation extends from one page to another, carefully indicate the division with a slant line (/) at the appropriate point.

Taking notes with meticulous care. Note-taking is not jotting. Even when reading rapidly, come to a full stop at any important intersection. If necessary, look back and ahead to avoid the common distortion that comes from ripping a passage hastily out of its context. Remember that a careless glance may change *psychology* to *physiology,* and a single illegible word in a key quotation may later require an emergency trip to the library to revisit a book that somebody else has since withdrawn. Get it right the first time.

Take pains to distinguish between direct quotations and paraphrase and between the author's ideas and your own reactions to them. (The word *paraphrase* is used here in its general sense to mean any rewriting of another's material in your own words, whether it expands, contracts (summarizes), or keeps to the scale of the original.)

Nothing is more confusing and annoying to the reader of a research paper than the writer's failure to make these distinctions clear. Wholesale transgressions of this kind may represent conscious plagiarism. More often they result from ignorance of the meaning of research or of the rules of literary ethics. Because the problem sometimes arises at the writing stage, it is discussed in more detail on page 1024. But often a bad research paper—like a failing examination—can be traced back to poor or carelessly taken notes. Any passage taken word-for-word from the text, even a clause or unusual phrase, should appear in the notes in bold quotation marks. The student who "forgot to put in the quotes" is either dishonest, naive, or inexcusably careless. If the note-taker temporarily abandons direct quotations for paraphrase, he should carefully close the quotes and open them again when the paraphrase is finished. If he makes an independent comment of his own in the middle of a quotation or paraphrase, he should enclose it in square brackets [thus], not parentheses (thus). He might even go so far as to identify it with his own initials.

Take particular pains to copy quotations precisely.

Any scholar will quote much more than he finally uses, but even at the note-taking stage, it is wise to limit direct quotations to short passages *precisely* transcribed. Precisely means word for word, spelling for spelling (except for obvious typographical errors), punctuation mark for punctuation mark. Any omission from a quotation should be carefully identified with three spaced periods (. . .) followed by the period at the end of the sentence where appropriate. Every theater-lover is familiar with the way a press agent can play fast and loose with a critic's review. The reviewer may write: "My final judgment is that, except for the acting, the play is brilliant." With the dots carefully omitted, the advertisement reads: "My final judgment is that the play is brilliant." The scholar's rule is not pedantry, but simple honesty.

Examine each of the sample note cards carefully. The first note, conceivably for a paper on "The Economics of American Poverty," presents a brief summary of an entire chapter in John Kenneth Galbraith's *The Affluent Society.* (The code number in the upper left-hand corner has presumably been supplied later when the cards were organized to match an outline for the paper.) Because the phrases "Social Balance" and "the truce on inequality" are, at least in this context, Galbraith's own, they are put in quotation marks. The reader's reaction is carefully segregated in square brackets.

A passage of direct quotation has been sandwiched between two short pieces of paraphrase in the second note. Notice the slant line marking the transition from page 258 to 259, the parentheses (Galbraith's, not the note-taker's), the line under *minimum* to represent Galbraith's italics, and the three spaced periods to mark an omission from the quotation. Were the omission at the end of a sentence, a fourth spaced period would follow (. . . .).

The Outline

When a student has made the last of his notes and carefully read them all through to get a bird's eye view of the land, he is finally ready to plan the actual writing of the paper. Teachers of writing differ about the value of a formal outline for a short composition, but for a research paper of 2,000 words or more, some sort of blueprint is indispensable. Even the liveliest argument can't move ahead in a straight line without a well-articulated skeleton.

Though the traditional outline form can at times become a strait jacket for a writer, it has a number of virtues: (1) It tells the writer where he has been, where he is, and where he is going; (2) It reminds the writer that the reader demands the same information, suggesting the need for topic sentences (expressed or implied) and adequate transitions; (3) It avoids unnecessary repetition; (4) It emphasizes the importance of symmetry and proportion; (5) It requires the writer to coordinate his main points, subordinate his subpoints, and relegate trivia to limbo.

A formal outline should follow the accepted method of subordination:

I.
   A.
      1.
      2.
         a.
         b.
   B.

> 11. 3. 4 *Services* *Galbraith, pp. 258-259*
>
> *Residential housing can't be limited to private sector. "It is improbable that the housing industry is greatly more incompetent or inefficient in the United States than in those countries--(Scandinavia, Holland, or (for the most part) England-- where slums have been largely eliminated and where <u>minimum</u> standards of cleanliness and comfort are well above our own. As the experience of these countries shows ... the housing industry functions well only in combination with a large, complex, and costly array of public services." Land purchase, clearance, city planning, zoning, research and architectural services, public assistance for poor.*

The writer should use either a *topic outline* (limited to words or phrases) or a *sentence outline* (with complete sentences). According to strict rule, the two types should not be mixed. The sentence outline has the advantage of requiring specific assertions (which may turn into topic sentences) instead of ambiguous catchall topics. But with many kinds of material, sustaining a sentence outline is an artificial struggle.

Common errors in outlining should be strictly avoided; examples of these are given below.

The meaningless category

"Introduction," "Body," and "Conclusion," for example, are often too general to be useful. Oftentimes a writer can do better by ignoring the introduction entirely and plunging his pen right into the body.

Illogical coordination

I. Athletics
   A. Football
   B. Baseball
   C. Basketball
   D. Team sports

Improper subordination

Placing a topic under the wrong heading:

I. Athletics
   A. Football
   B. Baseball
      1. Good sportsmanship

Or putting a main point in a subordinate position:

I. School life
   A. Athletics

   1. Major sports
   2. Minor sports
B. Classroom activities
   1. Discussion
   2. Learning

Single subdivision

If *I* is divided at all, it should have at least two subheads, A and B. If A is divided, it should have at least two subheads, 1 and 2. And so forth. The temptation to use a single subhead can be resisted by following a heading with a colon and a qualifying phrase. A. Athletics: a cause of student failure.

Here is a topic outline displaying the organization of this article: (Because details can be tucked in place as the writing progresses, a practical working outline might be simpler than this. The small bones are supplied here to help the reader in studying and reviewing the article.)

The Library Research Paper

I. The meaning of research
   A. A fashionable word
   B. A popular human activity
   C. The value of the research paper

II. Choosing and limiting a subject
   A. How and where to look
   B. Over-sized subjects
   C. Ways of reducing
      1. From general to specific
      2. The thesis: use and abuse
      3. The working hypothesis
   D. Keeping the end in view

III. Using the library
   A. Browsing in the stacks
   B. Consulting reference works

1. Three indispensable guides
   a. The card catalogue
   b. A comprehensive encyclopedia
   c. The *Reader's Guide*
2. Other research tools
   a. Catalogues and bibliographies
   b. Periodical indexes
   c. Dictionaries
   d. Encyclopedias and surveys
   e. Yearbooks

IV. The working bibliography
   A. The value of cards and completeness
   B. The proper forms
      1. For a book
      2. For a periodical article
      3. For a newspaper article
      4. For an encyclopedia article
   C. Evaluating sources
      1. Shifting reading speed
      2. External evidence
         a. Who wrote it?
         b. Who published it?
         c. When was it written?
      3. Internal evidence: the necessity for skepticism

V. Taking notes
   A. Hints and warnings
      1. Taking too many
      2. One to a card
      3. Identifying cards
      4. Meticulous care
      5. Quotation, paraphrase, comment
      6. Precise copying
   B. Samples

VI. The outline
   A. The uses of outlining
   B. The accepted form
      1. Proper subordination
      2. Topic and sentence outlines
   C. Common errors
      1. The meaningless category
      2. Illogical coordination
      3. Improper subordination
      4. Single subdivision
   D. A sample

VII. Writing the paper
   A. Style: English vs. Academese
   B. Tone
   C. Quotation and paraphrase revisited
      1. Short quotation
      2. Long quotation
      3. Partial paraphrase
      4. Complete paraphrase
      5. Half-baked paraphrase
   D. Footnotes
      1. For a book
      2. For a periodical article
      3. For a newspaper article
      4. For an encyclopedia article
      5. Shortened footnotes
   E. Abbreviations
   F. The final bibliography
   G. The final draft

Writing the Paper

Except for the greater complexity of organization and the special problems of quotation, paraphrase, and proper acknowledgment, "writing up" the results of research is not essentially different from writing any other kind of paper. Whatever laws govern grammar and diction, spelling and punctuation, sentence and paragraph structure, none of them is suspended for research. The freedom to experiment with language may be more limited; the premium on clarity and accuracy is even higher. There is less room for the infinite riches of rhetoric: the drama and poetry of narrative and description are usually replaced by the humbler virtues of clear exposition. But good writing is good writing regardless of its habitat.

Illusions about research die hard. Even students who are convinced that the paper should be composed, not compiled, often assume that the art of composition requires a special style—freighted with *Academese*—and a special tone—impersonal, stuffy, and deadly dull.

Academese is only one kind of jargon. There is also *Pedagese,* the jargon of educationists, and *Scientese,* the jargon of would-be scientists, *Legalese, Commercialese,* and *Officialese.* All these dialects share the traits of jargon: involved sentence structure; unnecessary repetition and interminable circumlocution; a pseudotechnical vocabulary. Such writing has been called *gobbledygook* or—suggesting that it is often contrived to impress or even confuse—*bafflegab.* It might be better to revive the old-fashioned word *crabbed*—pronounced slowly with two syllables. A crabbed style suggests an animal that can move its imposing armaments forward only by slow, sideways slithering.

An expert talking to other experts will inevitably use the technical terms of his trade. Nobody writing on a technical subject, whether the propulsion of a rocket or the scansion of a poem, can entirely avoid technical language. But the problem is to explain it, not exploit it, to understand it, not merely parrot it. Genuine technical language is concise, concrete, and clear; it serves to identify and limit a phenomenon—a *paramecium,* not a *wiggly beasty, iambic pentameter,* not *words with a regular beat.* Pseudotechnical language is pulpy, abstract, and cryptic—*the intellectual confrontation in an interpersonal situation* instead of *the meeting of human minds.* The proliferation of such jargon by scholars does not make it scholarly.

The style and tone appropriate to a research paper will vary, of course, with the subject, the writer, and the intended reader. A style can be formal without being involved, or informal without being casual and careless. For the general writer who does not pretend to expert knowledge, the best advice on style is simply this: Relax but don't be lax; say simple things simply in your own language; do not write anything, even a quotation or a borrowed idea, in words that you do not understand yourself; be as concrete as possible; remember that, of all the virtues of good writing, the greatest is *clarity.*

The tone of a research paper can be serious without solemnity, dignified without stuffiness. The goal is not a charming personal essay; the reader is presumably interested in the subject, not the personality of the middle man. But the studied effort to be impersonal—and therefore ostensibly disinterested—often results in writing without either personality or interest. Though practice varies, it is better for a writer to use the first person, *I,* than to get tangled in the circumlocutions—the passive voice, for example—of the impersonal manner. Humor and irony may be useful if they grow naturally out of the subject instead of being thrust upon it. Irrelevant wisecracking is taboo. Jokes will not improve stale prose. The essential rule for tone is that all good writing more nearly reflects the living sound of a human voice, than the metallic chatter of a computer.

Quotation and Paraphrase Revisited

One special writing problem—anticipated in the discussion of note-taking—requires expansion here: the proper use of quotation and paraphrase. Make a careful comparison of the following samples:

(1) Short quotation

Leo Stein once said this about composition: "Every personal letter one writes, every personal statement one makes, may be creative writing if one's interest is to make it such."

(A short quotation in a research paper, as in any other paper, is introduced by a colon, or a comma, and carefully enclosed in quotation marks.)

(2) Long quotation

Talking about how to teach the proper use of language, Leo Stein said:

There is no difficulty in teaching them the routine of expression . . . but it is good to make them realize that there is no essential difference between them and those who write, except interest, use and purpose—that creativity in writing means nothing more than fitting words accurately and specifically to what one specifically and accurately intends. Shakespeare certainly intended more than most and had exceptional gifts, but anyone who has anything to say and wants to interest the receiver has a like object. Every personal letter one writes, every personal statement one makes, may be creative writing if one's interest is to make it such. Most people do not have this interest; what they write in ordinary communications is as dull as they can make it. They have never been taught to think of all writing as in its degree *writing* and all speaking *speaking,* and so they write in rubber stamps [clichés] and speak in the current routine of slang, as though writing and speaking were something reserved for the elect.

(Because the quotation is long—meaning, according to a common rule, five lines or more of typescript—it is set off in a separate paragraph, indented, and typed single-space without quotation marks. The student has represented Stein's italics (*writing, speaking*) by underlining. The three spaced periods in the first sentence stand for a deletion by the writer of the paper, and the bracketed word [clichés] in his addition.)

(3) Partial paraphase

Leo Stein maintains that creative writing is "nothing more than fitting words accurately and specifically to what one specifically and accurately intends." That Shakespeare had greater intentions and gifts does not, he insists, alter the rule. "Every personal letter one writers, every personal statement one makes, may be creative writing if one's interest is to make it such." A person who has no interest in writing or speaking, who mistakenly assumes that they are "reserved for the elect," will inevitably settle for dullness couched in clichés.

(To compress Stein's passage while preserving some of the original flavor, the writer of the paper uses an acceptable blend of paraphrase and direct quotation. Restricting the paraphrase to his own words and carefully setting off Stein's exact words in quotation marks, he weaves the two into a single tapestry.)

(4) Complete paraphrase

Leo Stein argues that creativity is not a special gift awarded to writers and speakers and denied to ordinary mortals. If he has something to say and is interested in saying it well, anyone, even in a personal letter, can be a creative writer.

(The summary, entirely in the student's own words, reproduces Stein's essential meaning but loses some of the flavor. It has the advantage of brevity.)

All four techniques are acceptable, depending on the purpose and scope of the paper. One *unacceptable* technique is far too common: a confusing mixture of the words of the source and the words of the student without proper distinction between them. It has been called *half-baked paraphrase.*

(5) Half-baked paraphrase

Stein says that students ought to be taught that people in general just don't bother to take advantage of their creativity, which only means in writing fitting words accurately and specifically to what one specifically and accurately intends. Shakespeare intended more than most and had exceptional gifts, but anyone who has anything to say and wants to interest the receiver has a like object. People in general are dull with words because they couldn't care less. They don't bother to think of all writing as in its degree writing and all speaking speaking, and so they use rubber stamps and slang.

(Though they are mixed clumsily with some comment of his own, the student has appropriated appreciable amounts of Stein's own wording without identifying it in quotation marks. A footnote or a bibliographical entry does not excuse this common practice. Whether it results from carelessness, laziness, or dishonesty, it is plagiarism.)

To quote or not to quote? No sacred formula answers the question. A historian working with original documents will resort to frequent quotation. A literary scholar cannot adequately analyze the work of a poet without reproducing excerpts from the poems, line by line, exactly as they appear in the original. But many inexperienced students quote too much: their research papers are merely collections of quotes loosely tethered by incidental interruptions. Generally speaking, direct quotation is useful to clinch an important point, to preserve some of the authentic flavor of the source, or to reproduce a passage that is particularly well written or peculiarly inept. A student should never quote at length unless the passage is especially important for his purpose.

Footnotes

Footnotes should be carefully supplied during the writing process, not superimposed later as an afterthought. In the first draft they can be included temporarily in the text itself. Even in the final draft, short notes may be conveniently inserted in the text in parentheses (*Hamlet* III, ii. 61–64) if the source is clearly identified and they do not clutter up the page with too many interruptions. Otherwise, footnotes are usually placed at the bottom of the page, not at the end of the paper. They are keyed to the text with Arabic numerals—not asterisks or other symbols—and should be numbered consecutively throughout the paper. The number in the text should be raised slightly above the line, and placed after any mark of punctuation and at the end—not the beginning—of any quotation, long or short. The number should not be enclosed in parentheses or followed by a period, either in the text or at the bottom of the page. At the foot of the page each note should begin with a capital letter on a new line—with the number raised and indented—and end with a period.

Occasionally a footnote is useful to supply an interesting detail or incidental comment that does not fit conveniently into the text. But in a research paper most footnotes are supplied to acknowledge specific borrowings from sources. Unlike the bibliography, which is a general listing of sources, they usually provide exact page references. With that exception, a complete footnote furnishes the same essential information as a bibliographical entry, but with a different system of punctuation and in a slightly different order.

A footnote is always used to acknowledge a direct quotation unless its exact source is made clear in the text or is familiar (like the Gettysburg Address) to any educated reader. But in spite of a common illusion, the student's responsibility does not end there. He should also use a footnote (1) to acknowledge the use of another writer's idea or opinion *even if it is completely paraphrased*, and (2) as a receipt for the loan of any facts, statistics, or other illustrative material that he has not acquired by original observation.

Here is a representative group of complete footnotes: (Compare them with the bibliographical entries on page 7, observing the differences in punctuation and order of their parts.)

For a book with one author:

¹John K. Galbraith, *The Affluent Society* (Boston, 1958), p. 23.

For a book with more than one author:

²James H. Sledd and Gwin J. Kolb, *Dr. Johnson's Dictionary* (Chicago, 1955), pp. 49–50.

For a periodical article:

³Walter Lippman, "Cuba and the Nuclear Risk," *Atlantic*, CCXI (February 1963), 57.

For a newspaper article:

⁴New York *Times*, December 28, 1964, p. 6.

⁴New York *Times*, January 3, 1965, sec. 4, p. 7.

For an encyclopedia article:

⁵Donald G. Fink, "Television," *Encyclopaedia Britannica* (1963), XXI, 912.

Whenever a source is used for the first time, the student should give a complete footnote even though most of the information will be repeated in the bibliography. If, however, some of the details appear in the text—the author's name, for example, or the title—it is unnecessary to repeat them at the foot of the page. After the first footnote, an abbreviated form may be used if the complete note is not buried too far back. The easiest short form is the author's last name:

⁶Galbraith, p. 29.

If previous notes refer to more than one work by the same author, a shortened title should be added:

⁷Galbraith, *Affluent Society*, p. 29.

The popularity of the following Latin abbreviations is on the wane, partly because they have led to widespread misunderstanding. Though the writer may never

be required to use them, he should understand their meaning in the footnotes of others: (They are sometimes italicized because of their foreign origin.)

Ibid.	short for *ibidem*, meaning "in the same place." Refers to the same page of the same source cited in the footnote *immediately preceding*.
Ibid., p. 57.	another page of the same source cited in the footnote *immediately preceding*.
Galbraith, *op. cit.*, p. 59.	short for *opere citato*, meaning "in the work cited." Refers here to page 59 of the opus by Galbraith cited in a recent footnote. Obviously has no advantage over the use of the author's name alone or author and short title.
Op. cit., p. 59.	may be used if the author's name is made clear in the text.
Loc. cit.	short for *loco citato*, meaning "in the place cited"—that is, the same passage as in a recent footnote. Never used with a page number. Not used at all by many modern scholars.

Because documentation is intended to help the reader, not impress or confuse him, discretion is the better part of valor. If, for example, a number of short quotations from the same source appear in one paragraph of the paper, or if the writer is indebted to one authority for a tissue of small facts, it is unnecessary to present the reader with a whole flock of ibids. On occasion a single covering note may be sufficient:

¹My main authority for the facts about the charge of the Light Brigade is Cecil Woodham-Smith, *The Reason Why* (New York, 1953), pp. 207–257.

As Frank Sullivan once observed, if you give a footnote an inch it will take a foot.

The student may find the following abbreviations useful in either footnotes or bibliography:

Abbreviations Commonly Used in Footnotes and Bibliographies

anon.—anonymous

c. or ca.—from Latin *circa*, meaning "about." Used with approximate dates (c. 1340).

cf.—compare (cf. p. 47). Should not be used interchangeably with *see* (see p. 79).

ch., chs., chap., chaps.—chapter(s)

col., cols.—column(s)

ed., eds.—editor(s), edition(s)

f., ff.—and the following page(s) or line(s). 76f. or 76ff. 76–78 and 76–87 are more exact.

l., ll.—line(s)

n., nn.—note(s). For example, p. 69, n. 3 refers to the third footnote on page 69. Also p. 69n (italicized without the period).

n.d.—no date. Inserted in square brackets when date of publication is not given.

no., nos.—number(s)

par., pars.—paragraph(s)

passim—here and there throughout the work

pseud.—pseudonym

rev.—review, reviewed (by), revised (by), revision

sc.—scene in a play. Unnecessary in short notes if acts are put in large Roman numerals, scenes in small Roman numerals, lines in Arabic (IV.iii.27–46).

sic—Latin for "thus" or "so." Inserted in square brackets to make a succinct comment on something in a quotation such as an error in logic or spelling [sic].

vol., vols.—volume(s)

The Final Bibliography

If exact indebtedness to sources is carefully acknowledged throughout the footnotes, a final bibliography may not be required. In scholarly publishing, a full-length book is usually supplied with one, an article is not. A teacher will often insist on a bibliography as an exercise in formal acknowledgment and a convenient map of the ground actually covered in preparing the paper. Ordinarily it should be no more than a *selected bibliography*. A complete inventory of all the discoverable sources may be useful to a specialist, but only an ingenuous student would expect extra credit for his ability to transcribe the card catalogue and the *Reader's Guide*. A selected bibliography contains only those items on the bibliography cards that have proved useful in writing the paper. The length of the list is roughly proportionate to the paper's scope. In a long list it may be convenient to have two or more groupings, separating books from articles, or sources of special importance from sources of general interest. For most research papers a single alphabetical listing is sufficient. Note that each entry in the following specimen contains the same information in the same order as on a bibliography card. If a book or article does not have an author, it is usually listed alphabetically under the first important word of the title.

Selected Bibliography

Ashworth, John. "Olivier, Freud, and Hamlet," *Atlantic*, CLXXXIII (May 1949), 30–33.

Brown, John R., "Theatrical Research and the Criticism of Shakespeare and His Contemporaries," *Shakespeare Quarterly*, XIII (1962), 451–461.

Hankins, John E. "Caliban the Bestial Man," PMLA, LXII (September 1947), 793–801.

Knight, G. Wilson. "The Embassy of Death: An Essay on Hamlet," *The Wheel of Fire* (London, 1949), 17–30.

Littleton, Taylor, and Robert R. Rea, eds. *To Prove a Villain: The Case of King Richard III*. New York, 1964.

Raysor, Thomas M., ed. *Coleridge's Shakespearean Criticism*. 2 vols. Cambridge, Mass. 1930.

"Shakespeare at 400," *Life*, LVI (April 24, 1964), 58–99.

Shakespeare, William. *The Complete Works*, ed. George Lyman Kittredge. Boston, 1936.

Tillyard, E. M. W. *The Elizabethan World Picture*. London, 1943.

Traversi, D. A. *An Approach to Shakespeare*, 2nd rev. ed. New York, 1956.

The Final Draft

The final draft of the research paper should be typed—double-spaced—on one side of heavy white paper (not onion skin) 8½ x 11 inches and unlined. Footnotes and long indented quotations should be single-spaced. Two spaces should appear between footnotes and three between the text and the first note. The pages should be numbered with Arabic numerals, either centered at the top or in the upper right-hand corner. Whether held in a binder or merely with a paper clip, the pages should be kept flat, not folded as in a shorter composition. Margins should be at least an inch wide all around. The title should appear on both the first page (about two inches from the top) and on a separate title page, which should also include the author's name, the date, and the name of the course, if any. Corrections in the final draft should be strictly limited, preferably made by neat erasing and retyping. A sloppy paper inevitably suggests a sloppy mind. Besides, it is absurd for the writer to stumble in haste over the final barrier after he has taken so long to come so far.

Greek and Latin
Elements in English

Combining Forms

Greek/Latin	English	Example(s)
acantho-, Gk	spiny	acanthoid
acid-, acri-, acer-, acu-, L	keen, sharp, point	acrid, acerbic, acute
acme, Gk	culmination	acme
acous-, Gk	to hear	acoustic
acro-, Gk	tip, top	acrophobia
act-, -action, L	lead, drive, carry	interaction
actino-, Gk	light ray, radiate	actinoid
adeno-, Gk	gland	adenoid
adip-, L	fat	adipose
aeri-, L	air	aerie
aero-, Gk	air, aircraft, gas	aerobic, aerodrome
agit-, ag-, ig-, -act, L	to drive	agitate, agent, exigency, counteract
-agog, -agogue, Gk	leading	demagog, pedagogue
agon-, -agonist, Gk	contest, struggle	agony, antagonist
agri-, agro-, Gk	agriculture, field	agriculture, agronomy
alb-, L	white	albino, albumin
-algia, Gk	pain	neuralgia
alien-, alia-, alter-, L	foreign, strange, other	alienation, alternative
allo-, Gk	other	allotropy
alti, alto-, L	high, height	altimeter
amat-, ami-, amo-, -amour, L	love	amatory, amicable, paramour
ambi-, L	both	ambiguous
ambul-, L	to walk	ambulatory
amphi-, Gk	both	amphibian
amylo-, Gk	starch	amylopectin
andro-, -androus, anthropo-, Gk	man	android, polyandrous, anthropology
anemo-, Gk	wind	anemometer
angi-, angu- anx-, L	choking	angina, anguish, anxiety
angio-, Gk	vessel	angiosperm
Anglo-, L	English	Anglo-American
anima, L	breath, mind	animal, animate
ankylo-, Gk	bent	ankylosis
ann-, L	year	annual
antho-, Gk	flower	anthophore, anthology
aqua-, aque-, L	water	aquatic, aqueous
arbor-, L	tree, beam	arboretum
arch-, archi-, Gk	chief, primitive	architect
archeo-, Gk	ancient	archeology
-archy, Gk	govern	monarchy
arterio-, Gk	artery	arteriosclerosis
arthro-, arthri-, Gk	joint	arthropod, arthritis
articul-, L	joint	articulate

Greek/Latin	English	Example(s)
asco-, Gk	bag	ascospore
atmo-, Gk	air, breath, wind	atmosphere
audio-, L	hear	audiovisual
aug-, L	increase	augment
auto-, Gk	self	automatic
auro-, auriculo-, L	ear	auroventricular, auricle
aux-, Gk	strengthen	auxiliary
avi-, L	bird	aviation
bacci-, L	berry	baccivorous
bacteri-, Gk & L	bacterium	bacteriophage
ball-, Gk	to throw	ballistic
barb-, barbar-, L	beard	barber, barbarian
baro-, bari-, Gk	atmospheric pressure, weight	barometer, bariatrics
-base, bass-, L	low	abase, bassoon
basis, basi-, Gk	a step, foot	basic, basidium
bat-, L	to beat	battle
batho-, bathy-, Gk	deep, depth	bathos, bathysphere
bi-, bin-, L	two, double	bisect, binary
bibl-, biblio-, Gk	book	bible, bibliography
bio-, -biosis, Gk	life	biography, symbiosis
blasto-, -blast, Gk	bud, shoot	blastocele
blephar-, blepharo-, Gk	eyelid	blepharitis
bovi-, L	cattle	bovine
brachio-, -brace, Gk	arm	brachial
brachy-, Gk	short	brachycephaly
brady-, Gk	slow	bradycardia
branch-, Gk	fin, paw, limb	branching
branchio-, -branch, Gk	gills	branchiopod
brevi-, L	short	brevity
bronch-, broncho-, Gk	windpipe	bronchoscopy
bull-, L	bubble	bullet, ebullient
burs-, L	purse	bursar, bursitis
caco-, Gk	bad	cacophany
cad-, cid-, L	case, casualty, to fall	decadent, incident
cal-, chal-, L	to be hot	calorie, chaldron
calcul-, L	pebble, stone	calculate
calli-, Gk	fair, beautiful	calligraphy
camer-, L	chamber	bicameral
camp-, champ-, L	a plain	campus, champion
canal-, channel-, L	canal	canalization
cani-, L	dog	canine
cap-, capt-, cept-, L	to seize, take hold of	capable, capture, concept
capit-, cipit-, L	head	capital, occipital
carbo-, carboni-, -carbon, L	carbon	carboniferous, fluorocarbon
cardio-, Gk	heart	cardiovascular, cardiac
carn-, L	flesh	carnivorous
carpo-, -carpous, Gk	fruit	carpogonium, syncarpous
caus-, cus-, L	cause	causation, excuse
-cele, Gk	cavity, tumor, hernia, swelling	blastocele
-cene, Gk	recent	eocene
ceno-, Gk	common	cenocyte
centi-, cent-, L	hundred	centimeter, century
centr-, Gk & L	center	central
cephalo-, -cephalic, -cephalous, Gk	head, brain	microcephalic

Greek/Latin	English	Example(s)
cer-, cero-, Gk & L	wax	cerumin
cerebro-, L	brain	cerebrospinal
cervic-, cervico-, L	neck	cervical
chalc-, chalco-, Gk	copper	chalcedony
chemo-, Gk	chemical	chemotherapy
chilo-, Gk	lip	chiloplasty
chiro-, Gk	hand	chiropody
chloro-, Gk	green, chlorine	chlorophyll, chloromethane
chole-, cholo-, Gk	bile	cholesterol
chondro-, Gk	cartilage	chondritis
choreo-, choro-, Gk	dance	choreography, chorus
chromato-, chromo-, -chrome, Gk	color	chromatography
chron-, chrono-, Gk	time	chroni, chronograph
chryso-, Gk	gold	chrysolite
-cidal, -cide, L	to kill	suicidal, genocide
cine-, Gk	motion pictures	cinema
circ-, L	ring	circle, circus
cirri-, cirro-, L	curly	cirrostratus
cit-, L	incite	cite, solicit
clar-, L	clear	clarify, declare
claud-, claus-, clud-, clus-, L	to shut	claustrophobia, occlude
climato-, Gk	climate	climatology
clino, -cline, Gk & L	slope	clinometer, incline
cocci-, -coccus, Gk & L	berry-shaped, bacterium	streptococci
col-, cult-, L	to till	colony, culture
colo-, Gk	colon	colorectal
colori-, L	color	colorimeter
cono-, Gk	cone	conoid
contra-, counter-, L	against	contrast
copro-, Gk	dung	coprophagous
corn-, cornu-, L	horn	cornea, cornucopia
cosmo-, Gk	world, universe	cosmology
cost-, costo-, L	rib	costal
-cracy, -crat, Gk	govern	democracy
cred-, L	believe	credible, credit
cruci-, L	cross	crucial
cryo-, Gk	cold	cryogenic
crypto-, Gk	hidden	cryptogram
crystallo-, Gk	crystal	crystallography
cteno-, Gk	comb	ctenoid
cupri-, cupro-, L	copper	cupric, cuprous
curr-, curs-, cour-, L	to run	current, excursion, course
curvi-, curva-, L	curved	curvilinear, curvaceous
cyano-, cyani-, Gk	bluish, cyanogen	cyanotic, cyanide
cyclo-, -cyclic, -cycle, Gk	circle	cyclopentane, tricycle
cymo-, Gk	wave	cymoscope
cyst-, cysto-, Gk	bladder, cyst	cystic, cystotomy
cyto-, Gk	cell	cytoplasm
dactylo-, -dactyl, Gk	finger	pterodactyl
deca-, Gk	ten	decameron
deci-, L	a tenth	decile
demi-, L	half	demimonde

Greek/Latin	English	Example(s)
demn-, dam-, L	loss	condemn, indemnity, damn
demo-, Gk	people	democrat
dendro-, -dendron, Gk	tree	rhododendron
denti-, L	tooth	dentition
dermato-, derm-, dermo-, Gk	skin	dermatologist
deuter-, deutero-, Gk	second (adj.)	deuterium
dextro-, L	right	ambidextrous
di-, Gk	double	dimer
di-, dis-, L	apart	digress
digit-, digiti-, digito-, L	finger	digitigrade
dino-, Gk	terrible	dinosaur
diplo-, Gk	double	diploma, diplomacy
dodeca-, Gk	twelve	dodecahedron
dors-, dorsi-, dorso-, L	back	dorsoventral
-drome, -dromous, Gk	run	hippodrome
duo-, du-, L	two	dualism
duoden-, duodeno-, L	duodenum	duodenal
dyna-, dynamo-, Gk	power	dynamic, dynamometer
dys-, Gk	bad, difficult	dyslexia
echino-, Gk	spiny	echinoderm
ecto-, exo-, Gk	external, outside	ectomorphy, exogenous
electro-, Gk & L	electric	electromechanical
embryo-, Gk	embryo	embryology
-emia, Gk	blood condition or disease	septicemia
endo-, ento-, Gk	interior	endogenous
ennea-, Gk	nine	ennead
enter-, entero-, Gk	intestine	enteritis
eo-, Gk	early, earliest	eocene
equ-, equi-, L	equal, like, same	equate
erg-, Gk	work	ergon
erythro-, Gk	red	erythrocyte
ethn-, ethno-, Gk	nation	ethnocentric
eu-, Gk	good	euphoria
eury-, Gk	broad	eurycephalic
extra-, extro-, L	external	extraneous, extrovert
fac-, fec-, fic-, fact-, fect-, fict-, L	to do	fact, perfect, deficit
febri-, L	fever	febrile
-fend, -fense, L	to strike	defend
-fer, -ferous, L	bearing	transfer
ferro-, ferri-, L	iron	ferric
fibro-, L	fibrous	fibroid
fid-, L	faith	confidence
fin-, L	end	final, finance
fissi-, -fid, L	split	fission
-fix, L	to fix	prefix
flagr-, L	to burn	conflagration
flexi-, L	bent	flexible
flig-, -flict, L	to strike	profligate, inflict
fluo-, fluoro-, fluor-, L	fluorescence, fluorine	fluoride
flor-, flour-, L	flower	florist, flourish

Greek/Latin	English	Example(s)
fluv-, fluvi-, fluvio-, L	river	fluvial
foli-, folia-, folio-, L	leaf, leafy	foliation
form-, -form, L	form	formal, conform
fort-, forti-, L	strong	fortify
fract-, frang-, frag-, L	to break	fraction, frangible, fragment
fru-, fruit-, L	to enjoy	fruition
fug-, fuge-, -fugal, L	to flee	refugee, centrifugal
fund-, found-, L	bottom	fundament, profound
fungi-, L	fungus	fungicide
galacto-, Gk	milk	galactose
Gallo-, Gall-, L	French	Gallic
gameto-, Gk	gamete	gametophyte
gamo-, -gamy, Gk	union, sexual union	gamogenesis, oogamy
ganglio-, gangli-, Gk	ganglion	gangliated
gastro-, gastero-, Gk	stomach, abdomen	gastroenterology
gemm-, L	bud	gemmule
gen-, L	kin	genus
-gen, -genous, -geny, -gony, Gk	producing	oxygen, cosmogony
genito-, L	genital	genitourinary
geo-, Gk	earth	geography
geri-, geronto-, Gk	old age	geriatric, gerontology
-gerous, L	bearing	crystalligerous
giganto-, Gk	gigantic	gigantomachy
glauco-, Gk	light or blue-gray	glaucoma
glosso-, gloss-, Gk	tongue	glossary
glyco-, Gk	sweet	glycolysis
glypto-, -glyph, Gk	carved, carving	glyptodont, hieroglyphics
gnatho-, -gnathous, Gk	jaw	prognathous
-gon, gonio-, Gk	angle	polygon, goniometer
-gonium, Gk	seed	syngonium
gono-, Gk	reproduction	gonorrhea
-grade, -gress, L	walking, step	plantigrade, congress
grani-, L	grain	graniform
grapho-, -graph, -graphy, -gram, Gk	to write	polygraph
grat-, grate-, grati-, L	pleasing	gratitude
Greco-, L	Greek	Greco-Roman
greg-, L	a flock	aggregate, gregarious
gust-, gusta-, L	a tasting	disgust, gustatory
gymno-, gymn-, Gk	naked	gymnosophist, gymnast
gyneco-, gyneo- gyno-, Gk	woman, ovary	gynecology
gyro-, gyr-, Gk	circle	gyrate
hab-, hib-, L	to have	habit, inhibit
hagio-, hagi, Gk	sacred	hagiography
halo-, Gk	salt, sea	halogen, halophyte
haplo-, Gk	simple, single	haploid
hect-, hecto-, Gk	hundred	hectare
-hedral, -hedron, Gk	side	polyhedron
heli-, helico-, Gk	spiral	helicopter
helio-, Gk	sun	heliocentric
hema-, hemato-, hemo-, Gk	blood	hematocrit

Greek/Latin	English	Example(s)
hemi-, Gk	half	hemisphere
hepa-, hepat-, hepato-, Gk	liver	heparin
hepta-, Gk	seven	heptad
her-, L	heir	heredity
hernio-, L	hernia	herniotomy
hetero-, Gk	different	heteronym
hexa-, Gk	six	hexagon
hiero-, Gk	sacred	hieroglyph
hippo-, Gk	horse	hippocampus
histo-, Gk	tissue	histopathology
holo-, hol-, Gk	whole	hologram, holism
homo-, homeo-, homoio-, Gk	like, same	homoiothermy
horr-, -hor, L	to bristle	horrible, abhor
hum-, L	the ground	humus, humble
hyalo-, Gk	glass, glassy	hyaloid
hydro-, Gk	water	hydrotherapy
hygro-, Gk	wet	hygrometer
hylo-, Gk	matter, material	hylozoism
hymeno-, Gk	membrane	hymenopterous
hypno-, Gk	sleep	hypnosis
hystero-, hyster-, Gk	hysteria, uterus	hysterotomy, hysterical
i-, -it, L	to go	exit, itinerary
-iasis, Gk	disease	schistosomiasis
iatro-, -iatrics, -iatry, Gk	medicine	iatrogenic, psychiatry
ichth-, ichthyo-, Gk	fish	ichthyosaur
icono-, Gk	image	iconoclast
ideo-, Gk	idea	ideology
idio-, Gk	individual	idiosyncrasy
igni-, L	fire	ignition
ileo-, -ileac, L	ileum (small intestine)	ileocecal
ilio-, -iliac, L	ilium	sacroiliac
inguin-, inguino-, L	groin	inguinal
int-, L	within	intestine, internal
intra-, intro-, L	interior, inward	introduce
iodo-, Gk	iodine	iodoform
iso-, Gk	equal, like, same	isometric
-itis, Gk	inflammation	chondritis
jac-, -ject, L	to throw	adjacent, eject
jug-, junct-, -join, L	to join, yoke	conjugal, conjunction
jur-, jus-, L	to swear	jury, justify
juxta-, L	near	juxtaposition
kerato-, Gk	cornea, horn	keratin
kinesi-, kineto-, -kinesis, Gk	movement	psychokinesis
labi-, labio-, L	lip	labium
labor-, L	labor	elaborate
lac-, lec-, lic-, L	to entice	delectable
lacto-, L	milk	lactose
laryngo-, Gk	larynx	laryngoscope
lati-, L	broad	latitude
leg-, lect-, L	to collect, read	legible, recollect
lepid-, lepido-, Gk	scale, scaly	lepidopterous
-lepsy, -leptic, Gk	seizure	epilepsy

Greek/Latin	English	Example(s)
lept-, lepto-, Gk	small, think	leptophyllous
leuko-, Gk	white	leukocyte
levo-, L	left, left-sided	levotartaric
liber-, L	free	liberty
lig-, L	to bind	ligament, oblige
ligni-, lign-, L	wood	lignite
lin-, L	a line	delineate
lip-, lipo-, Gk	fat	lipoma
litera-, L	a letter	literature
litho-, -lith, Gk	stone	monolith
loc-, L	a place	local, locomotion
logo-, log-, Gk	speech, word	logic
-logy, -logical, Gk	science of	ecology
longi-, L	long	longitude
luci-, L	light	lucid
lumin-, lumini-, L	light	illuminate
lun-, luni-, L	moon	lunar
lympho-, lymphat-, lymphato-, L	lymph	lymphoma
lyo-, -lysis, -lyte, Gk	dissolving	electrolyte
-machy, Gk	fight	tauromachy
macro-, Gk	large	macrocosm
magneto-, L	magnet	magnetosphere
magni-, L	great, large	magnificent
mal-, L	bad	maladjustment
man-, main-, L	hand	manner, maintain
-mancy, -mantic, Gk	divining	chiromancy
-mania, -maniac, Gk	craving	monomania
mast-, masto-, Gk	breast	mastectomy
matri-, L	mother	matrilineal
medi-, medio-, L	middle	mediocre
medico-, L	medicine	medicolegal
mega-, megalo-, Gk	great	megalomania
melan-, melano-, Gk	black, dark	melanin
mem-, L	remembering	memoir
ment-, mon-, L	mind	mental, demonstrate
mero-, -mere, -merous, Gk	part, of parts	blastomere, trimerous
meso-, mes-, Gk	middle	mesozoic
metro-, -meter, -metry, Gk	measure	metrology, centimeter, telemetry
micro-, Gk	small	micron
milli-, L	thousand, thousandth	millipede
mir-, mar-, L	wonderful	miracle, marvel
miso-, mis-, Gk	hate	misanthrope
-mit, -miss, L	to send	emit, mission
mod-, L	manner	model, modify
mono-, Gk	one	monocle
mor-, mori-, mort-, L	to die	morgue, mortal
-morph, morpho-, -morphic, -morphous, Gk	form	endomorph, amorphous
mot-, mov-, L	to move	emotion, remove
moun-, L	hill	mound, mountain
muco-, muci-, L	mucus, slimy	mucilage
multi-, L	many	multifaceted
myco-, -mycete, Gk	fungus	ascomycete

Greek/Latin	English	Example(s)
myel-, myelo-, Gk	spinal cord	myelin
myo-, Gk	muscle	myocardial
myria-, Gk	very many	myriad
mytho-, Gk	myth	mythology
myxo-, Gk	slime	myxophobia
narco-, Gk	torpor	narcolepsy
nas-, naso-, L	nose	nasal
nati-, L	birth	nativity
necro-, Gk	corpse	necromancy
-nect, -nex, L	to bind	connect, annex
nemato-, Gk	thread	nematode
neo-, Gk	new	neo-Freudian
nephro-, Gk	kidney	nephron
neuro-, Gk	nerve	neuroanatomy
nitro-, nitr-, L	nitrogen	nitrate
noct-, nocti-, L	night	nocturnal
nomen-, nomin-, -noun, L	name	nomenclature, pronoun
nomo-, Gk	custom, law	nomothetic
noso-, -nose, -nosis, Gk	disease	diagnosis
not-, nit-, nis-, L	to get to know	notice, cognition
nota-, L	a mark	notary, notation
noto-, Gk	a back	notochord
nucleo-, L	nucleus	nucleotide
nudi-, L	bare	nudity
numer-, L	number	enumerate
nutr-, nur-, L	to nourish	nutrition, nurse
nycti-, nycto-, nyct-, Gk	night	nyctalopic
octa-, octo-, Gk & L	eight	octopus
oculo-, ocul-, L	eye	oculist
odonto-, -odont, Gk	tooth	odontology
odyno-, -odynia, Gk	pain	odynometer
-oid, -ode, Gk	like	spheroid
oleo-, L	oil	oleomargarine
oligo-, olig-, Gk	few	oligarchy
-oma, Gk	tumor	lymphoma
omni-, L	all	omnipotent
oneiro-, Gk	dream	oneiromancy
onto-, Gk	existence	ontology
oo-, Gk	egg	oogonium
ophio-, Gk	snake	ophiophobia
ophthalmo-, Gk	eye	ophthalmologist
-opia, Gk	vision defect	myopia
-opsis, Gk	appearance, sight	synopsis
orb-, L	a circle	orbit
orchido-, Gk	orchid	orchid
orchio-, orchi-, Gk	testicle	orchialgia
ord-, ordin-, L	order	ordain, subordinate
organo-, Gk	organ, organic	organometallic
ornitho-, Gk	bird	ornithology
oro-, L	mouth	oronasal
ortho-, Gk	correct, upright	orthopedic
-osis, Gk	disease	neurosis
ossi-, L	bone	ossify
oste-, osteo-, Gk	bone	osteoarthritis

Greek/Latin	English	Example(s)
oto-, Gk	ear	otology
ovi-, ovo-, ov-, L	egg	ovate
oxy-, Gk	oxygen; sharp	oxyacid; oxytone
pachy-, Gk	thick	pachyderm
paleo-, Gk	ancient	paleolithic
palmi-, palm-, L	palm	palmitic
pan-, panto-, Gk	all	pandemic, pantothenic
par-, per-, L	to prepare	apparatus, imperative
para-, Gk	near	paragraph
pari-, L	equal, like	par, disparity
-parous, L	bearing	viviparous
part-, -part, L	part	depart, partake
-pathy, patho-, Gk	disease, suffering	neuropathy, pathos
patri-, L	father	patrician
-ped, -pede, pedi-, L	foot	impede
peda-, pedo-, Gk	child	pedagogue
-pel, L	to drive	compel
pelvi-, L	pelvis	pelvic
-pend, -pond, L	to weigh	depend, ponder
penta-, Gk	five	pentagon
petro-, Gk	stone	petroglyph
-phage, phago-, -phagous, -phagy, Gk	eat	phagocyte
pharmaco-, Gk	drug	pharmacology
pharyngo-, Gk	pharynx	pharyngoscope
-phasia, Gk	speech defect	aphasia
pheno-, phanero-, -phany, Gk	visible	phenomenon
-philia, -phily, Gk	morbid love	pedophilia
philo-, -phile, Gk	love	philosophy, bibliophile
phleb-, phlebo-, Gk	vein	phlebitis
-phobia, Gk	fear	agoraphobia
-phone, phono-, -phony, Gk	sound	phonograph
photo-, Gk	light	photograph
phren-, phreno-, Gk	brain, mind	schizophrenic, phrenology
phyl-, phylo-, Gk	species	phylum, phylogeny
phyllo-, -phyllous, -phyll, Gk	leaf, leafy	chlorophyll
physio-, Gk	nature	physiocrat
-phyte, phyto-, Gk	plant (bot.)	phytoplankton
picr-, picro-, Gk	bitter	picric
piezo-, Gk	pressure	piezochemistry
pinna-, pinni-, L	fin, web, leaf	pinnate, pinniped
pisci-, L	fish	pisciculture
plano-, L	flat	planoconvex
-plasia, -plasis, Gk	growth	hyperplasia
-plasm, Gk	material, matter	cytoplasm
-plast, Gk	cell	chloroplast
-plastic, -plasty, Gk	making, forming	rhinoplasty
platy-, Gk	flat	platypus
-plegia, Gk	paralysis	quadriplegia
plen-, L	to fill	plenty
pleur-, pleuro-, Gk	pleura, side	pleurisy
plic-, -plex, L	to fold	implicate, complex
plumb-, plumbo-, L	lead (metal)	plumbing

Greek/Latin	English	Example(s)
pneumat-, pneumato-, Gk	breath	pneumatic
pneumo-, Gk	lung	pneumothorax
-pod, -podous, Gk	foot	arthropod
-poietic, Gk	making	hematopoietic
polio-, Gk	gray matter	poliomyelitis
poly-, Gk	many	polygyny
pon-, pos-, L	to place	opponent, position
popul-, pub-, L	people	popular, public
port-, L	to carry	portable
-prehend, L	to seize	apprehend
primi-, prim-, L	first	prime
procto-, Gk	rectum	proctoscope
proto-, Gk	first	prototype
pseudo-, Gk	false	pseudonym
psycho-, psych-, Gk	mind; spirit	psychology; psychic
psychro-, Gk	cold	psychrometer
ptero-, -pterous, -pter, Gk	wing	pterodactyl, helicopter
pulmo-, L	lung	pulmonary
punct-, pung-, L	to prick	puncture, pungent
pur-, L	pure	purity, puritan
-pute, L	clear	compute
py-, pye-, Gk	pus	pyorrhea
pyelo, Gk	pelvis	pyelogram
pyro-, pyr-, Gk	fire	pyromania, pyre
quadri-, quadru-, L	four	quadrilateral
quasi-, L	like, as if	quasi-serious
-quer, -quire, -quest, L	to seek	conquer, acquire, inquest
quin-, quinque-, quinqua-, L	five	quintuplet
radic-, L	root	radical
radio-, L	radiant energy, radio, radioactive	radioactivity, radioisotope
rat-, rati-, L	to suppose	ratio, ratify
recti-, L	straight	rectitude
recto-, L	rectum	rectoabdominal
reg-, res-, L	to rule	regal, resource
ren-, reni-, L	kidney	renal, reniform
rheo-, Gk	current	rheostat
rhino-, Gk	nose	rhinoceros
rhizo-, Gk	root	rhizome
rot-, rotat-, L	a wheel	rotor, rotate
-rrhea, -rrhagia, -rrhagic, -rrhage, Gk	flow	hemorrhage
-rupt, L	to break	interrupt
racchar-, saccharo-, Gk	sugar	saccharin
sacro-, L	sacrum	sacroiliac
sangui-, L	blood	sanguine
sapro-, Gk	decompose	saprophyte
sarco-, Gk	flesh	sarcophagus
scato-, Gk	dung	scatological
-scend, L	to climb	condescend
schisto-, Gk	to divide	schistosome
schizo-, Gk	to split	schizophrenia
sclero-, Gk	hard	sclerosis
-scope, -scopy, Gk	observation	microscope

Greek/Latin	English	Example(s)
scoto-, Gk	darkness	scotoma
-scribe, scrip-, L	to write	describe, scripture
scyph-, Gk & L	cup	scyphiform
seb-, sebi-, sebo-, L	fat, fatty	sebaceous
-sect, -section, L	cut	bisect
sed-, sid-, -sess, siz-, L	to sit	sediment, residue, possess, size
seismo-, Gk	earthquake	seismograph
semi-, L	half	semiconductor
-sent, sent-, L	to feel	assent, sentiment
sept-, septi-, L	seven	septet
sequ-, sec-, L	to follow	sequence, second
sero-, L	serum	serous
serv-, -serve, L	a slave	servant, conserve
sex-, L	six	sexagenarian
sider-, sidero-, Gk	star	sidereal
-sign, L	a sign	assign, signal
silico-, L	silicon	silicosis
simil-, sem-, L	same	similar, resemble
simplici-, L	simple	simplicity
Sino-, L	Chinese	Sino-Soviet
sito-, -site, Gk	food, eat	parasite
socio-, L	society	socioeconomic
sol-, solit-, L	alone	sole, solitary
solu-, -solve, L	to loosen	solution, resolve
somato-, -soma, -some, Gk	body	chromosome
somn-, somni-, L	sleep	insomnia
-son, son-, L	sound	sonata
-sophy, -sopher, Gk	knowledge of	philosopher
spec-, -spect, L	to look	specimen, inspect
spectro-, L	spectrum	spectrogram
speleo-, spel-, Gk & L	cave	spelunker
spermo-, spermato-, -spermous, Gk	seed, spermatozoa	spermatozoid
-sphere, Gk	sphere	hemisphere
sphygmo-, Gk	pulse	sphygmomanometer
spiro-, spir-, Gk	spiral	spirogyra, spiral
spiro-, -spire, spir-, L	breath	spirometer, inspire, spirit
-stant, -sist, -stitute, -stance, L	to stand	constant, desist, institute, substance
-stat, Gk	to stop	thermostat, static
stato-, stat-, Gk	position	status
stell-, stelli-, L	star	stellar
steno-, Gk	narrow	stenosis
stereo-, Gk	solid	stereophonic
stetho-, Gk	chest	stethoscope
-stomy, Gk	surgical opening	ileostomy
-strict, -strain, L	to draw tight	constrict, restrain
-struct, L	to build	construct
sulfa-, sulfo-, L	sulfur	sulfonamide
sup-, sum-, L	above	superior, summit
tachy-, Gk	swift	tachyon
-tain, tang-, L	to touch	attain, tangible
tauro-, Gk	cattle	tauromachy
tauto-, Gk	same	tautology

Greek/Latin	English	Example(s)
taxo-, -taxis, -taxy, Gk	order	taxonomy
techno-, Gk	art, technical	technology
teg-, -tect, L	to cover	tegument, detect
tele-, teleo-, telo-, Gk	far, final	television, teleology
temp-, L	time	temporary
ten-, -tain, L	to hold	tenacity, contain
ter-, tre-, tri-, L	three	tercentenary
terato-, Gk	monster	teratology
termin-, L	end	exterminator
terr-, -ter, L	to scare	terror, deter
terri-, L	earth	territory
test-, -test, L	witness	testament, contest
tetra-, Gk	four	tetrad
-text, text-, L	to weave	context, textile
thanato-, Gk	death	thanatology
theo-, Gk	god	theology
thermo-, Gk	heat	thermometer
thio-, Gk	sulfur	Thiokol
thorac-, thoraco-, Gk	thorax	thoracic
thyro-, Gk	thyroid	thyroxin
tom-, -tome, tomo-, Gk	knife, cutting	tome, epitome, tomograph
tono-, Gk	tone	tonometer
topo-, Gk	place	topology
tot-, toti-, L	whole	totalitarian
toxico-, Gk	poison	toxicology
tracheo-, Gk	trachea	tracheotomy
-tract, treat-, L	to draw	extract, treatise
trib-, L	tribe	contribute
tricho-, Gk	hair	trichomonad
trop-, -troupous, -tropy, Gk	turned	tropism
tropho-, -trophy, Gk	nourishment	dystrophy
typhlo-, Gk	blind	typhlosis
typo-, Gk	type	typology
ultima-, ultra-, L	beyond	ultimate
uni-, L	one	unite
urethr-, urethro-, Gk	urethra	urethral
urin-, urino-, L	urine	urinary
uro-, -uria, Gk	urine	glycosuria
uter-, utero-, L	uterus	uterology
vagin-, vagino-, L	vagina	vaginectomy
val-, -vail, L	to be strong	valid, prevail
vari-, vario-, L	different	various
vaso-, L	vessel	vasodilation
vei-, -vey, veh-, L	to carry	vein, convey, vehicle
ven-, veni-, L	vein	venous
ven-, -vent, -vene, L	to turn	avenue, adventure, convene
ventr-, ventro-, L	abdomen	ventral
ver-, verit-, L	true	verdict, very, verity
vermi-, L	worm	vermiculite
-verse, -vert, vert-, L	to turn	adverse, revert, vertigo
via-, vio-, -vey, -voy, L	way	viaduct, obvious, convey, convoy

Greek/Latin	English	Example(s)
vic-, -vid, vis-, -view, -vise, L	to see	evident, visage, review, supervise
vice-, L	substitute	vice-president
vin-, vini-, L	wine, grapes	vineyard, viniculture
-vince, -vict, L	to conquer	convince, evict
vitr-, vitri-, L	glass	vitreous, vitriform
viv-, -vive, L	to live	vivacity, survive
voc-, -voke, L	voice	vocal, evoke
-volve, -volt, L	to roll	evolve, revolt
vor-, -vorous, L	eat	voracious, omnivorous
xeno-, Gk	foreign	xenophobia
xero-, Gk	dry	xerography
xylo-, Gk	wood	xylophone
zoo-, Gk	animal	zoology
zygo-, Gk	pair, yoke	zygote
-zyme, zymo-, Gk	fermentation	enzyme

Prefixes

Greek/Latin	English	Example(s)
a-, an-, Gk	not	amoral, anesthesia
ab-, a-, abs-, L	from, away, off, away from, down	abject, absent
ad-, a-, ac-, af-, ag-, al-, an-, ap-, ar-, as-, at-, L	to, toward	admit, align, accept, affinity, aggregate, alleviate, annex, appear, arrest, assimilate, attend
ana-, Gk	again	anadiplosis
ana-, Gk	according to, similar to	analog
ana-, Gk	thoroughly	anaphylaxis
ana-, Gk	up	analysis, anabolism
ana-, Gk	upon	anaclitic
ante-, Gk & L	before	antediluvian
anti-, Gk	against	antiaircraft
apo-, Gk	away from, off	apogee
cata-, cath-, cat-, Gk	down, away, in accordance with, against, very, completely	catacomb, catalog, catharsis, catabolism
cis-, L	on this side of	cisalpine
com-, co-, col-, con-, cor-, L	with, together, very, thoroughly	combat, collect, connect, correspond
contra-, L	against	contradict
de-, L	not	decentralize
de-, L	down	decline
dia-, Gk	through	diameter
dis-, di-, L	apart, not	disperse, disapprove, digress
en-, el-, em-, L	in, into	encounter, embed
endo-, Gk	within	endogenous
epi-, eph-, Gk	on, beside, among, outside, over, before	epilog, epitome, epiphenomenon
ex-, e-, ec-, ef-, Gk & L	out, off, from, beyond, not, thoroughly	exhale, exclude, exceed, efface
exo-, Gk	outside	exogenous
extra-, L	outside	extracurricular
hyper-, Gk	over, above, beyond	hyperactive
hypo-, Gk	under, beneath, less than	hypokinesis
in-, il-, im-, ir-, L	in, into, on	invade, induce
in-, il-, im-, ir-, L	not, against	inimical
inter-, L	between, among, together, mutual	intermix, interdependent
intra-, L	within	intramural
juxta-, L	next to	juxtapose

Greek/Latin	English	Example(s)
mal-, L	badly, evil	malcontent, maltreat
meta-, met-, Gk	after, beyond, changed, along with	metaphysics, metamorphosis
mis-, L	badly	misadventure
non-, L	not	nonchalant
ob-, oc-, of-, op-, L	against	obverse, oppress
para-, Gk	beside, beyond	parallel
per-, L	through, very, thoroughly	percussion
peri-, Gk	around, about, round, near	perimeter, perigee
post-, L	after	postpartum, postwar
pre-, L	before	premarital
preter-, L	beyond	preternatural
pro-, Gk	before	progestin
pro-, L	for	proslavery
pro-, Gk & L	forward	progress
pro-, L	substitute	pronoun
re-, L	again, back	rerun, return
retro-, L	back, backward	retrograde
sub-, suc-, suf-, sug-, sum-, sup-, sur-, sus-, L	under, less, subordinate, division	substance, subcategory, suffer
subter-, L	under, beneath, less than	subterfuge
super-, supra-, L	over, above, exceeding	superpose, suprarational
sym-, sy-, syl-, syn-, Gk	with, associated, simultaneous	symmetry, syllogism, synthesis
trans-, L	on that side of, across	transpose
ultra-, L	beyond, exceeding	ultraconservative

Suffixes of Adjectives

Greek/Latin	English	Example(s)
-able, -ive, L	tending to	irritable, restive
-able, -ile, -il, L	able to, able to be	teachable, ductile
-ac, L & Gk	affected by	maniac
-ac, -ic, Gk & L	pertaining to	iliac, manic
-aceous, -al, -ar, -ary, -ile, -il, -ine, -ory, Gk & L	pertaining to	curvaceous, dorsal, temporary, puerile, promissory
-al, -ate, -id, L	characterized by	jovial, ornate, flaccid
-an, L	coming from, originating in	European
-an, L	adhering to or following	Republican
-an, L	belonging to (in biology)	crustacean
-ant, -ent, L	doing, agency	errant, decadent
-escent, L	beginning to	obsolescent
-fic, -ficent, L	causing, making	terrific, magnificent
-ine, -in, -ing, -ive, -ory, L	like, of the nature of	bovine, charming, desultory
-ose, -ous, L	full of	verbose, aqueous

Suffixes of Nouns

Greek/Latin	English	Example(s)
-al, L	instance, nouns formed from adjs.	oval, signal
-al, L	act, action	recital
-ana, L	collection	Americana
-ance, -ence, -ancy, -ency, L	act, condition, concrete thing	assistance, violence, eminence

Greek/Latin	English	Example(s)
-arium, -ary, -orium, -ory, L	place	aquarium, apiary, auditorium, dormitory
-ary, L	practitioner	notary
-ate, L	office	episcopate
-ate, L	result	mandate
-cion, -sion, -ion, -tion, L	action, result, condition	ascension, demolition, condition
-ese, -ic, -ics, Gk	native art, system	Chinese, chiropractic, phonics
-ist, L	practitioner	psychiatrist
-ist, -ite, Gk	advocate, adherent	separatist, Jacobite
-ite, Gk	descendent of	Israelite
-ite, Gk	native	Canaanite
-ity, L	condition	acidity
-ium, L	chemical element	uranium
-ment, L	act, condition, instrument, result	movement, predicament, instrument
-mony, L	result	alimony
-or, L	practitioner	elector
-ory, L	instrument	depilatory
-trix, L	female practitioner	aviatrix
-tude, L	condition	negritude
-ure, L	action, office, result, instrument	divestiture, suture

Suffixes of Verbs

Greek/Latin	English	Example(s)
-ate, L	combine, combine with, treat with	associate, medicate
-esce, L	begin	coalesce
-fy, L	become, make	solidify, codify
-ize, Gk	become, make, practice, treat with	realize, canonize, idolize, simonize

Foreign Words and Phrases

A

à bas [Fr.], down, down with.

à beau jeu, beau retour [Fr.], one good turn deserves another; tit for tat.

ab extra [L.], from without.

ab imo pectore [L.], from the bottom of the heart.

ab incunabulis [L.], from the cradle.

ab initio [L.], from the beginning.

ab intra [L.], from within.

a bisogni si conoscono gli amici [It.], a friend in need is a friend indeed.

à bon chat, bon rat [Fr.], to a good cat, a good rat; tit for tat.

à bon marché [Fr.], cheap; a good bargain.

ab origine [L.], from the origin.

ab ovo [L.], from the egg; from the beginning.

ab ovo usque ad mala [L.], from the egg to the apples (as in Roman banquets); from beginning to end.

à bras ouverts [Fr.], with open arms.

abrégé [Fr.], an abridgment.

absens hæres non erit [L.], the absent one will not be heir; out of sight, out of mind.

absente reo [L.], the accused being absent.

absit invidia [L.], let there be no ill-will; envy apart.

absit omen [L.], may this not prove of (evil) omen.

ab uno disce omnes [L.], from one specimen judge of all the rest.

a buon vino non bisogna frasca [It.], good wine needs no bush.

ab urbe condita [L.], from the founding of the city, i.e. Rome (753 B.C.).

a capite ad calcem [L.], from head to heel.

à chaque saint sa chandelle [Fr.], to each saint his candle; honor to whom honor is due.

à cheval [Fr.], on horseback.

a che vuole, non mancano modi [It.], where there's a will there's a way.

à compte [Fr.], on account.

à corps perdu [Fr.], with breakneck speed.

à coup sûr [Fr.], of a certainty; without fail.

à couvert [Fr.], under cover.

a cruce salus [L.], salvation by the cross.

actionnaire [Fr.], shareholder in a company.

ad aperturam (libri) [L.], at the opening of the book; wherever the book opens.

ad arbitrium [L.], at will.

ad astra per aspera [L.], to the stars through hardship.

ad calendas Græcas [L.], at the Greek calends; i.e. never, as the Greeks had no calends in their mode of reckoning.

ad captandum vulgus [L.], to attract or please the rabble.

a Deo et rege [L.], from God and the king.

à dessein [Fr.], on purpose; intentionally.

à deux mains [Fr.], for two hands; two-handed; having a double office.

ad extremum [L.], to the last, or extremity.

ad finem [L.], to the end; at or near the end.

ad gustum [L.], to one's taste.

ad hominem [L.], to the man; to an individual's interests or passions.

adhuc sub judice lis est [L.], the case is still before the judge; the controversy is not yet settled.

a die [L.], from that day.

ad infinitum [L.], to infinity.

ad instar [L.], after the fashion of.

ad interim [L.], in the meanwhile.

ad internecionem [L.], to extermination.

à discrétion [Fr.], at discretion; without restriction.

ad libitum [L.], at pleasure.

ad majorem Dei gloriam [L.], for the greater glory of God.

ad modum [L.], in the manner of.

ad multos annos [L.], for many years.

ad nauseam [L.], to disgust or satiety.

adorer le veau d'or [Fr.], to worship the golden calf.

ad patres [L.], gathered to his fathers.

ad referendum [L.], for further consideration.

ad rem [L.], to the purpose; to the point.

à droite [Fr.], to the right.

adscriptus glebæ [L.], attached to the soil.

adsum [L.], I am present; here!

ad summum [L.], to the highest point.

ad unguem [L.], to the nail; to a nicety; exactly; perfectly.

ad unum omnes [L.], all to a man.

ad utrumque paratus [L.], prepared for either case or alternative.

ad valorem [L.], according to the value.

ad vitam aut culpam [L.], for life or fault; i.e. till some misconduct be proved.

ad vivum [L.], to the life; portrayed in a lifelike manner.

ægrescit medendo [L.], he becomes worse by the remedies used.

æquabiliter et diligenter [L.], equably and diligently.

æquo animo [L.], with an equal mind; with equanimity.

ære perennius [L.], more lasting than brass.

æs triplex [L.], triple brass; armor of adamant.

ætatis suæ [L.], of his (or her) age.

affaire d'amour [Fr.], a love affair.

affaire d'honneur [Fr.], an affair of honor; a duel.

affaire du cœur [Fr.], an affair of the heart.

affreux [Fr.], frightful; shocking.

à fleur d'eau [Fr.], on a level with the water.

à fond [Fr.], to the bottom; thoroughly; heartily.

a fortiori [L.], with stronger reason. See in Dict.

à gauche [Fr.], to the left.

à genoux [Fr.], on the knees.

age quod agis [L.], attend to what you are about.

à grands frais [Fr.], at great expense.

à haute voix [Fr.], aloud.

à huis clos [Fr.], with closed doors; secretly.

aide toi, et le ciel t'aidera [Fr.], help yourself, and Heaven will help you.

à la belle étoile [Fr.], under the stars; in the open air.

à la bonne heure [Fr.], in good time; very well, all right, as you please.

à l'abri [Fr.], under shelter.

à la campagne [Fr.], in the country.

à la carte [Fr.], according to the bill of fare at table.

à la dérobée [Fr.], by stealth.

à la française [Fr.], after the French mode.

à la mode [Fr.], according to the custom or fashion.

à la Tartuffe [Fr.], like Tartuffe, i.e. hypocritically.

al bisogno si conoscono gli amici [It.], friends are known in time of need.

à l'envi [Fr.], emulously; so as to vie.

alere flammam [L.], to feed the flame.

al fresco [It.], in the open air; cool.

alieni appetens, sui profusus [L.], greedy of other people's possessions, lavish of his own.

à l'improviste [Fr.], on the sudden.

alla vostra salute [It.], to your health.

allez-vous-en! [Fr.], away with you!

allons [Fr.], let us go; come on; come.

al piu [It.], at most.

alter ego [L.], another self.

alter idem [L.], another exactly similar.

alter ipse amicus [L.], a friend is the counterpart of oneself.

alterum tantum [L.], as much more.

à main armée [Fr.], by force of arms.

amantium iræ amoris integratio [L.], the quarrels of lovers are the renewal of love.

à ma puissance [Fr.], to the best of my power.

amar y saber no puede ser [Sp.], no one can love and also be wise.

a maximis ad minima [L.], from the greatest to the least.

âme de boue [Fr.], a soul of mud.

amende honorable [Fr.], satisfactory apology; reparation.

à merveille [Fr.], to a wonder; marvellously.

amici probantur rebus adversis [L.], friends are tested in adversity.

amicus humani generis [L.], a friend of the human race.

amicus Plato, sed magis amica veritas [L.], Plato is my friend, but truth is still more a friend to me.

amicus usque ad aras [L.], a friend even to the sacrificial altar, i.e. to the utmost extremity.

ami de cour [Fr.], a court friend; a false or unreliable friend.

à mon avis [Fr.], in my opinion.

amor patriæ [L.], love of country.

amour propre [Fr.], self-love; vanity.

ancient régime [Fr.], the ancient or former order of things.

anglicé [Fr.], in English; in the English language.

anguis in herba [L.], a snake in the grass; an unsuspected danger; a false friend.

animo et fide [L.], with courage and confidence.

anno ætatis suæ [L.], in the year of his or her age.

anno Christi [L.], in the year of Christ.

anno Domini [L.], in the year of our Lord.

anno humanæ salutis [L.], in the year of man's redemption.

anno mundi [L.], in the year of the world.

anno urbis conditæ [L.], in the year from the time the city (Rome) was founded (753 B.C.).

annuit cœptis [L.], He (God) has smiled on our

undertakings: motto, adapted from Virgil, on the reverse of the great seal of the United States.

annus mirabilis [L.], year of wonders; especially used in reference to the year 1666, in which occurred the great plague, and the great fire of London.

ante lucem [L.], before the dawn.

ante meridiem [L.], before noon.

à outrance [Fr.], to extremities.

à pas de géant [Fr.], with a giant's stride; with gigantic steps.

à peindre [Fr.], to be painted; worthy of the painter's art.

aperçu [Fr.], a general sketch or survey.

à perte de vue [Fr.], till beyond one's view.

à peu près [Fr.], nearly.

à pied [Fr.], on foot.

à point [Fr.], to a point; just in time; perfectly right.

a posse ad esse [L.], from possibility to reality.

appartement [Fr.], set of rooms on the same floor.

aprés moi le déluge [Fr.], after me the deluge.

a prima vista [It.], at first sight.

à propos de bottes [Fr.], apropos of boots; in an irrelevant manner; without rhyme or reason.

à propos de rien [Fr.], apropos of nothing; without reference to anything in particular; without a motive.

aquila non capit muscas [L.], an eagle does not catch flies.

arbiter bibendi [L.], ruler of the symposium; toastmaster.

arbiter elegantiarum [L.], a judge or supreme authority in matters of taste.

arcades ambo [L.], Arcadians both; fellows of the same stamp.

arcana cælestia [L.], celestial mysteries.

arcana imperii [L.], state secrets.

ardentia verba [L.], glowing language.

argent comptant [Fr.], ready money.

argumentum ad crumenam [L.], an argument to the purse, i.e. to one's interests.

argumentum ad hominem [L.], an argument to the individual man, i.e. to his interests and prejudices.

argumentum ad ignorantiam [L.], an argument intended to work on a person's ignorance.

argumentum ad judicium [L.], argument appealing to the judgment.

argumentum ad verecundiam [L.], argument appealing to modesty.

argumentum baculinum [L.], the argument of the cudgel; brute force.

ariston metron [Gr.], moderation is best.

arrectis auribus [L.], with ears pricked up; all attention.

arrière pensée [Fr.], mental reservation.

ars est celare artem [L.], it is true art to conceal art.

ars longa, vita brevis [L.], art is long, life is short.

Artium Magister [L.], Master of Arts.

asinus ad lyram [L.], an ass at the lyre; a stupid awkward fellow.

Athanasius contra mundum [L.], Athanasius against the world.

à tort et à travers [Fr.], at random; without consideration.

à toute force [Fr.], with all one's might.

à tout hasard [Fr.], at all hazards.

à tout prix [Fr.], at any price; at all costs.

at spes non fracta [L.], but hope is not crushed.

au bout de son Latin [L.], at the end of his Latin, at his wit's end; in a fix or quandary.

au contraire [Fr.], on the contrary.

au courant [Fr.], fully acquainted with matters; up to date.

audaces (or **audentes**) **fortuna juvat** [L.], fortune aids the bold.

au désespoir [Fr.], in despair.

audi alteram partem [L.], hear the other side.

audiatur et altera pars [L.], let the other side also be heard.

au fait [Fr.], well acquainted with; expert.

au fond [Fr.], at bottom; in reality.

auf Wiedersehen [G.], till we meet again; **au revoir.**

au grand sérieux [Fr.], in all seriousness.

au jour le jour [Fr.], from day to day; without thought of tomorrow; from hand to mouth.

au naturel [Fr.], in the natural state.

au pis aller [Fr.], at the worst.

aurea mediocritas [L.], the golden or happy mean.

au reste [Fr.], as for the rest.

au revoir [Fr.], adieu; until we meet again.

auri sacra fames [L.], the accursed craving for gold.

au sérieux [Fr.], seriously.

auspicium melioris ævi [L.], an auspice (or augury) of a better age (to come).

aussitôt dit, aussitôt fait [Fr.], no sooner said than done.

autant d'hommes, autant d'avis [Fr.], so many men, so many minds.

aut Cæsar aut nullus [L.], either Cæsar or nobody.

aut inveniam viam aut faciam [L.], I shall either find a way or make one.

autrefois acquit [Fr.], formerly acquitted; previously tried for the same offense and acquitted.

autre temps, autres mœurs [Fr.], other times, other manners.

au troisième [Fr.], on the third story.

aut vincere aut mori [L.], either to conquer or to die; victory or death.

aux armes! [Fr.], to arms!

auxilium ab alto [L.], help from on high.

avant-propos [Fr.], preliminary matter; preface.

avec permission [Fr.], with permission.

ave, Imperator! morituri te salutant [L.], hail, Emperor! those about to die (gladiators) salute thee.

a verbis ad verbera [L.], from words to blows.

avito viret honore [L.], flourishes on his ancestral honors.

à volonté [Fr.], at pleasure.

à vostra salute [It.]
à votre santé [Fr.] } to your health.
a vuestra salud [Sp.]

B

badaud [Fr.], a lounger in the streets; an idler.

badinage [Fr.], jocularity; chaff.

ballon d'essai [Fr.], a balloon sent up to ascertain the direction of the air-currents; hence, a device to test public opinion on any subject.

bas bleu [Fr.], a blue-stocking; a literary woman.

beatæ memoriæ [L.], of blessed memory.

beau idéal [Fr.], the ideal of perfection.

beauté du diable [Fr.], the dévil's good looks; youthful freshness.

beaux esprits [Fr.], men of wit.

beaux yeux [Fr.], fine eyes; good looks.

bel esprit [Fr.], a person of wit or genius; a brilliant mind.

bella! horrida bella! [L.], wars! horrid wars!

bella matribus detestata [L.], wars hated by mothers.

bellum internecinum [L.], a war of extermination.

benedetto è quel male che vien solo [It.], blessed the misfortune that comes singly.

bene orasse est bene studuisse [L.], to have prayed well is to have striven well.

ben trovato [It.], well invented; cleverly fabricated or concocted.

bête noire [Fr.], a black beast; a bugbear.

bêtise [Fr.], a piece of stupidity; stupidity.

billet d'amour [Fr.], a love-letter.

bis dat qui cito dat [L.], he gives twice who gives quickly.

bis peccare in bello non licet [L.], it is not permissible to blunder twice in war.

bis pueri sens [L.], old men are twice boys.

bona fide [L.], in good faith.

bona fides [L.], good faith.

bon ami [Fr.], good friend.

bon avocat, mauvais voisin [Fr.], a good lawyer is a bad neighbor.

bon diable [Fr.], a good-natured fellow.

bon gré, mal gré [Fr.], with good or ill grace; willing or unwilling.

bon jour [Fr.], good day; good morning.

bon jour, bonne œuvre [Fr.], a good day, a good work; i.e. the better the day, the better the deed.

bonne bouche [Fr.], a delicate morsel, titbit.

bonne et belle [Fr.], good and handsome.

bonne foi [Fr.], good faith.

bon soir [Fr.], good evening.

bon vivant [Fr.], one fond of luxury and good living; a gourmet.

bon voyage! [Fr.], a good voyage (or journey) to you!

Borgen macht Sorgen [G.], borrowing makes sorrowing; who goes a-borrowing goes a-sorrowing.

breveté [Fr.], patented.

brevi manu [L.], with a short hand; extemporaneously.

brevis esse laboro obscurus fio [L.], if I labor to be brief, I become obscure.

brutum fulmen [L.], a senseless thunderbolt; striking blindly.

C

cadit quæstio [L.], the question falls; there is no further discussion.

cæca est invidia [L.], envy is blind.

cælum non animum mutant qui trans mare currunt [L.], they who cross the sea change their sky but not their feelings.

cætera desunt [L.], the rest is wanting.

cæteris paribus [L.], other things being equal.

campo santo [It.], a burying-ground—lit. "holy field."

candida Pax [L.], white-robed Peace.

cantabit vacuus coram latrone viator [L.], the penniless traveler will sing in the presence of the highwayman; i.e. a penniless man has nothing to lose.

cantate Domino [L.], sing unto the Lord.

cap à pié [Fr.], from head to foot.

caput mortuum [L.], lit. "dead head"; worthless residue.

cara sposa [It.], dear wife.

carent quia vate sacro [L.], because they have no sacred bard (to celebrate their praise).

carpe diem [L.], enjoy the present day; improve the time.

castello che dà orecchia si vuol rendere [It.], the fortress that parleys speedily surrenders.

casus belli [L.], that which causes or justifies war.

catalogue raisonné [Fr.], a catalogue arranged according to the subjects.

causa sine qua non [L.], an indispensable cause or condition.

cause célèbre [Fr.], a celebrated law case or trial.

caveat emptor [L.], let the buyer beware.

cave canem [L.], beware of the dog.

cavendo tutus [L.], safe by using caution.

cedant arma togæ [L.], let arms yield to the gown, that is, military authority to the civil power.

cela va sans dire [Fr.], that goes without saying; needless to say; that is a matter of course.

cela viendra [Fr.], that will come.

ce n'est pas être bien aise que de rire [Fr.], laughing is not always a sign that the mind is at ease.

ce n'est que le premier pas qui coute [Fr.], it is only the first step that is difficult.

censor morum [L.], a censor of morals.

c'est à dire [Fr.], that is to say.

c'est le commencement de la fin [Fr.], it is the beginning of the end.

c'est magnifique, mais ce n'est pas la guerre [Fr.], it is magnificent, but it is not war; said by a French officer as he watched the Charge of the Light Brigade at Balaklava.

c'est selon [Fr.], that is according to circumstances; that is as may be.

c'est un autre chose [Fr.], that's quite another thing.

cetera desunt [L.], the rest is wanting; here there is a break.

ceteris paribus [L.], see cæteris.

chacun à son goût [Fr.], every one to his taste.

chacun tire de son coté [Fr.], every one inclines to his own side.

chapeau bras [Fr.], a cocked hat.

chapelle ardente [Fr.], the chamber in which a dead body lies in state.

chemin de fer [Fr.], iron road; a railway.

cherchez la femme [Fr.], look for the woman (to find where she has had a hand in the matter).

chère amie [Fr.], a dear (female) friend.

che sarà, sarà [It.], what will be, will be.

cheval de bataille [Fr.], a war-horse; what one chiefly relies on.

chevalier d'industrie [Fr.], lit. a knight of industry; a swindling or cheating rogue; one who lives by his wits.

chi tace confessa [It.], he who keeps silence confesses.

ci git [Fr.], here lies.

clarior e tenebris [L.], brighter from darkness or obscurity.

clarum et venerabile nomen [L.], an illustrious and venerable name.

cogito, ergo sum [L.], I think, therefore I exist.

comitas inter gentes [L.], politeness between nations.

comme il faut [Fr.], as it should be.

commune bonum [L.], a common good.

commune periculum concordiam parit [L.], common danger begets concord.

communibus annis [L.], on the annual average.

communi consensu [L.], by common consent.

compagnon de voyage [Fr.], a traveling companion.

componere lites [L.], to settle disputes.

compos voti [L.], having obtained one's wish.

compte rendu [Fr.], an account rendered; a report.

con amore [It.], with love; very earnestly.

conciergerie [Fr.], a doorkeeper's lodge; also name of an ancient prison at Paris.

concio ad clerum [L.], a discourse to the clergy.

concordia discors [L.], discordant concord.

concours [Fr.], a competition, as for a prize.

con diligenza [It.], with diligence.

conditio sine qua non [L.], a necessary condition.

con dolore [It.], with grief; sorrowfully.

confido et conquiesco [L.], I trust and am at peace.

conjunctis viribus [L.], with united powers.

conseil d'état [Fr.], a council of state; a privy-council.

consensus facit legem [L.], consent makes the law.

consilio et animis [L.], by wisdom and courage.

consilio et prudentia [L.], by wisdom and prudence.

constantia et virtute [L.], by constancy and virtue (or bravery).

consuetudo pro lege servatur [L.], custom or usage is held as law.

consule Planco [L.], when Plancus was consul; when I was a young fellow.

contra bonos mores [L.], against good manners or morals.

copia verborum [L.], rich supply of words.

coram nobis [L.], before us; in our presence.

coram non judice [L.], before one who is not a proper judge.

coram populo [L.], in presence of the people.

cordon bleu [Fr.], blue-ribbon; a cook of the highest excellence.

cordon sanitaire [Fr.], a line of guards to prevent the spreading of contagion or pestilence; a quarantine.

corps d'armée [Fr.], the body of an army; an army corps.

corps de garde [Fr.], a body of men in a guardroom; the room itself.

corps diplomatique [Fr.], a diplomatic body; a body of ambassadors and similar representatives.

corrigenda [L.], things to be corrected; a list of errors or imperfections.

corruptio optimi pessima [L.], a corruption of what is best is worst.

cos ingeniorum [L.], a whetstone for wits.

couleur de rose [Fr.], rose-color; an alluring aspect of circumstances.

coup [Fr.], a stroke.

coup de grâce [Fr.], a finishing stroke.

coup de main [Fr.], a sudden attack of enterprise.

coup de maître [Fr.], a master stroke.

coup de pied [Fr.], a kick.

coup de soleil [Fr.], sunstroke.

coup d'essai [Fr.], a first attempt.

coup d'état [Fr.], a sudden decisive blow in politics; a stroke of policy.

coup de théâtre [Fr.], a theatrical effect.

coup d'œil [Fr.], a rapid glance of the eye.

courage sans peur [Fr.], fearless courage.

coûte que coûte [Fr.], cost what it may.

crambe repetita [L.], cabbage warmed up a second time; i.e. the repetition of an old joke, a truism, etc.

credat Judæus Apella [L.], let Apella, the superstitious Jew, believe it, I won't; "tell that to the marines."

crede quod habes, et habes [L.], believe that you have it, and you have it.

credo quia absurdum [L.], I believe because it is absurd.

credo quia impossibele est [L.], I believe it because it is impossible.

crême de la crême [Fr.], cream of the cream; the very best or most select.

crescit amor nummi, quantum ipsa pecunia crescit [L.], the love of money increases as wealth grows.

crescit eundo [L.], it increases as it goes.

crescit sub pondere virtus [L.], virtue increases beneath oppression.

crimen falsi [L.], the crime of perjury.

crimen læsæ majestatis [L.], the crime of high treason; lese-majesty.

Croix rouge [Fr.], Red Cross.

crux [L.], a cross; puzzle; difficulty.

crux criticorum [L.], the puzzle of critics.

crux medicorum [L.], the puzzle of the doctors.

cucullus non facit monachum [L.], the cowl does not make the friar; i.e. don't trust to appearances.

cui bono? [L.], for whose advantage? to what end?

cui Fortuna ipsa cedit [L.], to whom Fortune herself yields.

cuilibet in arte sua credendum est [L.], everyone is to be trusted in his own special art.

culpam pœna premit comes [L.], punishment follows hard on crime.

cum bona venia [L.], with your good leave.

cum grano salis [L.], with a grain of salt; with some allowance.

cum multis aliis [L.], with many others.

cum notis variorum [L.], with the notes of various commentators.

cum privilegio [L.], with privilege or license from the authorities.

curiosa felicitas [L.], nice felicity of expression.

currente calamo [L.], with a running or rapid pen.

custus morum [L.], guardian of manners (or morals).

D

d'accord [Fr.], in agreement.

da locum melioribus [L.], give place to your betters.

dame d'honneur [Fr.], matron of honor.

dames de la halle [Fr.], women who sell articles in a market; market-women.

damnant quod non intelligunt [L.], they condemn what they do not understand.

dare pondus fumo [L.], to give weight to smoke; i.e. attach importance to matters of no consequence.

das Beste ist gut genug [G.], the best is good enough.

das Ewig-Weibliche zieht uns hinan [G.], the eternal-feminine draws us upwards.

data et accepta [L.], expenses and receipts.

data obolum Belisario [L.], give an obolus to Belisarius (a general of Justinian, said to have been neglected in his old age by that emperor and compelled to beg).

Davus sum non Œdipus [L.], I am Davus not Œdipus (who solved the riddle of the Sphinx); I am a bad hand at riddles.

de bon augure [Fr.], of good augury or omen.

de bonne grâce [Fr.], with good grace; willingly.

deceptio visus [L.], an optical illusion.

decet verecundum esse adolescentem [L.], it becomes a young man to be modest.

decies repetita placebit [L.], when ten times repeated it will still please.

decipimur specie recti [L.], we are deceived by the show of rectitude.

decori decus addit avito [L.], he adds distinction to his ancestral honors.

de die in diem [L.], from day to day.

de facto [L.], in point of fact; actual; actually.

dégagé [Fr.], free; easy; unconstrained.

de gustibus non est disputandum [L.], there is no disputing about tastes.

de haut en bas [Fr.], in a contemptuous or supercilious manner.

dei gratia [L.], by the grace of God.

de integro [L.], anew; over again from beginning to end.

déjeuner à la fourchette [Fr.], breakfast with a fork; a breakfast or luncheon with meat.

de jure [L.], from the law; by right.

de l'audace, encore de l'audace, et toujours de l'audace [Fr.], audacity, more audacity, and always audacity.

delenda est Carthago [L.], Carthage must be blotted out, or destroyed.

de luxe [Fr.], of luxury; made with unusual elegance.

de mal en pis [Fr.], from bad to worse.

de minimis non curat lex [L.], the law does not concern itself with trifles.

de mortuis nil nisi bonum [L.], (say) nothing but good of the dead.

de nihilo nihil fit [L.], from nothing nothing is made.

dénouement [Fr.], issue; solution.

de novo [L.], anew.

Deo adjuvante [L.], God assisting.

Deo duce [L.], God being the leader.

Deo favente [L.], God favoring.

Deo gratias [L.], thanks to God.

Deo juvante [L.], with God's help.

de omnibus rebus et quibusdam aliis [L.], concerning all things and certain others.

Deo non fortuna [L.], from God, not by chance.

Deo volente [L.], God willing.

de pis en pis [Fr.], from worse to worse.

de profundis [L.], out of the depths.

de retour [Fr.], having come back; returned.

de rigueur [Fr.], imperatively necessary; not to be dispensed with.

dernier ressort [Fr.], a last resource.

désagrément [Fr.], something disagreeable.

desipere in loco [L.], to jest or be jolly at the proper time.

désorienté [Fr.], having lost one's way; not knowing where to turn.

desunt cætera [L.], the remainder is wanting.

de trop [Fr.], too much; more than is wanted.

detur digniori [L.], let it be given to the more worthy.

detur pulchriori [L.], let it be given to the more (or most) beautiful.

Deus avertat! [L.], God forbid!

deus ex machina [L.], a god out of the machine; a deity introduced to bring about the dénouement of a drama; referring to the machinery and practice of the Greek and Roman stage.

Deus vobiscum! [L.], God be with you!

Deus vult [L.], God wills it.

di buona volontà sta pieno l'inferno [It.], hell is full of good intentions.

Dichtung und Wahrheit [G.], fiction and fact; poetry and truth.

dictum factum [L.], no sooner said than done.

dies non [L.], a day on which a law-court is not held.

Dieu est toujours pour les plus gros bataillons [Fr.], God is always on the side of the largest battalions; the leader with the largest army has the best chance of victory.

Dieu et mon droit [Fr.], God and my right.

Dieu vous garde [Fr.], God protect you.

digito monstrari [L.], to be pointed out with the finger (as a person of note).

dignus vindice nodus [L.], a difficulty worthy of powerful intervention.

dii majorum gentium [L.], gods of the superior class; the twelve higher gods of the Romans.

dii penates [L.], household gods.

diis aliter visum [L.], the gods decided otherwise; fate willed differently.

Dios me libre de hombre de un libro [Sp.], God deliver me from a man of one book.

di salto [It.], by leaps.

diseur de bons mots [Fr.], a sayer of good things; one noted for witty sayings.

disjecta membra [L.], scattered remains.

divide et impera [L.], divide and rule.

docendo discimus [L.], we learn by teaching.

dolce far niente [It.], sweet doing-nothing; sweet idleness.

Dominus vobiscum [L.], the Lord be with you.

domus et placens uxor [L.], home and a pleasing wife.

dorer la pilule [Fr.], to gild the pill.

double entendre [Fr.], incorrect for next.

double entente [Fr.], a double or equivocal meaning; a play on words.

do ut des [L.], I give that you may give; reciprocity.

doux yeux [Fr.], soft glances.

dramatis personæ [L.], the characters in the play.

droit au travail [Fr.], the right to live by labor.

droit des gens [Fr.], the law of nations.

drôle [Fr.], funny; a comic actor.

ducit amor patriæ [L.], love of country draws me.

dulce domum [L.], sweet home (or rather homeward).

dulce est desipere in loco [L.], it is pleasant to play the fool at times.

dulce et decorum est pro patria mori [L.], it is sweet and glorious to die for one's country.

dum spiro, spero [L.], while I breathe, I hope.

dum vivimus, vivamus [L.], while we live, let us live.

duomo [It.], a cathedral.

durante bene placito [L.], during good pleasure.

durante vita [L.], during life.

E

eau sucrée [Fr.], sweetened water: a French beverage.

ébauche [Fr.], a preliminary sketch; a rough outline.

ecce homo! [L.], behold the man!

ecce signum! [L.], behold the sign!

école [Fr.], a school.

e contra [L.], on the other hand.

édition de luxe [Fr.], a splendid and expensive edition of a book.

editio princeps [L.], the first printed edition of a book.

égarement [Fr.], bewilderment, mental confusion.

ego et rex meus [L.], I and my king.

eheu! fugaces labuntur anni [L.], alas! the fleeting years glide by.

elapso tempore [L.], the time having elapsed.

élève [Fr.], a pupil or student.

embarras de richesses [Fr.], an embarrassment of riches; an over-supply.

emeritus [L.], retired or superannuated after long service.

empressement [Fr.], promptitude; eagerness.

en ami [Fr.], as a friend.

en arrière [Fr.], in the rear; behind; back.

en attendant [Fr.], in the meantime.

en avant [Fr.], forward.

en badinant [Fr.], in sport; jestingly.

en cueros [Sp.], naked; unclothed.

en déshabillé [Fr.], in undress.

en Dieu est ma fiance [Fr.], my trust is in God.

en Dieu est tout [Fr.], in God are all things.

en effet [Fr.], in effect; substantially; really.

en famille [Fr.], with one's family; in a domestic state.

enfant gâté [Fr.], a spoiled child.

enfants perdus [Fr.], lost children; the soldiers forming a forlorn hope.

enfant terrible [Fr.], a terrible child, or one that makes disconcerting remarks.

enfant trouvé [Fr.], a foundling.

enfin [Fr.], in short; at last; finally.

en grand seigneur [Fr.], like a grandee or magnate.

en grande tenue [Fr.], in full dress, either official or evening.

en masse [Fr.], in a mass.

en passant [Fr.], in passing.

en pension [Fr.], in a boarding-house.

en plein jour [Fr.], in broad day.

en queue [Fr.], standing one behind another.

en rapport [Fr.], in harmony; in agreement.

en règle [Fr.], according to rules; in order.

en revanche [Fr.], in requital; in return.

en route [Fr.], on the way.

en suite [Fr.], in company; in a set.

entente cordiale [Fr.], cordial understanding, especially between two states.

entêté [Fr.], obstinate; self-willed.

entourage [Fr.], surroundings; adjuncts.

entr'acte [Fr.], the interval between the acts of a play.

entre deux feux [Fr.], between two fires.

entre deux vins [Fr.], between two wines; half-drunk.

entremets [Fr.], side dishes of dainties to be eaten between the serving of the joints.

entre nous [Fr.], between ourselves.

en vérité [Fr.], in truth; verily.

en vieillissant on devient plus fou et plus sage [Fr.], in growing old, men become more foolish and more wise.

eo animo [L.], with that mind or design.

eo nomine [L.], by that name.

epea pteroenta [Gr.], winged words.

Epicuri de grege porcus [L.], a swine from the herd of Epicurus; an Epicurean.

e pluribus unum [L.], one out of many; one composed of many.

epulis accumbere divum [L.], to sit down at the banquets of the gods.

e re nata [L.], according to the exigency.

errare humanum est [L.], to err is human.

esprit borné [Fr.], a narrow or contracted spirit.

esprit de corps [Fr.], the animating spirit of a collective body, as a regiment.

essayez [Fr.], try; make the attempt.

esse quam videri [L.], to be, rather than to seem.

est modus in rebus [L.], there is a method in all things.

esto quod esse videris [L.], be what you seem to be.

et cætera (or **et cetera**) [L.], and the rest.

et hoc genus omne [L.], and everything of the sort.

et id genus omne [L.], and everything of the kind.

et sequentes or **et sequentia** [L.], and those that follow.

et sic de cæteris [L.], and so of the rest.

et sic de similibus [L.], and so of the like.

et tu, Brute! [L.], thou also, Brutus!

eureka [Gr.], I have found it.

événement [Fr.], an event.

eventus stultorum magister [L.], fools must be taught by the result.

Ewigkeit [G.], eternity.

ex abrupto [L.], suddenly.

ex abundantia [L.], out of the abundance.

ex adverso [L.], on the opposite side; over against.

exæquo et bono [L.], agreeably to what is good and right.

ex animo [L.], heartily; sincerely.

ex auctoritate mihi commissa [L.], by virtue of the authority intrusted to me.

ex capite [L.], from the head; from memory.

ex cathedra [L.], from the chair or seat of authority; with high authority.

excelsior [L.], higher; that is, loftier or taller; not correctly used as an adverb.

exceptio probat regulam [L.], the exception proves (or tests) the rule.

exceptis excipiendis [L.], the due exceptions being made.

excerpta [L.], extracts.

ex concesso [L.], from what has been conceded or granted in argument.

ex curia [L.], out of court.

ex delicto [L.], from the crime.

ex dono [L.], by the gift.

exegi monumentum ære perennius [L.], I have reared a monument more lasting than brass.

exempla sunt odiosa [L.], examples are offensive.

exempli gratia [L.], by way of example.

ex facto jus oritur [L.], the law springs from the fact.

excitus acta probat [L.], the event justifies the deed.

ex mera gratia [L.], through mere favor.

ex mero motu [L.], from his own impulse; from his own free-will.

ex more [L.], according to custom.

ex necessitate rei [L.], from the necessity of the case.

ex nihilo nihil fit [L.], from, or out of, nothing, nothing comes; nothing produces nothing.

ex officio [L.], by virtue of office.

ex opere operato [L.], by outward acts.

ex pede Herculem [L.], from the foot (we recognize) a Hercules; we judge of the whole from the specimen.

experientia docet stultos [L.], experience instructs fools.

experimentum crucis [L.], the trial or experiment of the cross; an experiment of a most searching nature.

experto crede [L.], trust one who has had experience.

expertus metuit [L.], having experience, he fears it.

exposé [Fr.], statement; showing up.

ex post facto [L.], after the deed is done; retrospective.

expressis verbis [L.], in express terms.

ex professo [L.], professedly.

ex propriis [L.], from one's own resources.

ex quocunque capite [L.], for whatever reason.

ex tacito [L.], tacitly.

extinctus amabitur idem [L.], the same man when dead will be loved.

extrait [Fr.], extract.

extra muros [L.], beyond the walls.

ex ungue leonem [L.], from a claw (we may know) the lion.

ex uno disce omnes [L.], from one learn all; from this specimen judge of the rest.

ex usu [L.], by use.

ex vi termini [L.], by the force or meaning of the term or word.

ex voto [L.], according to one's prayer or vow.

F

faber suæ fortunæ [L.], the architect of his own fortune, a self-made man.

fâcheux [Fr.], vexatious; annoying; troublesome.

facies non omnibus una [L.], all have not the same face or features.

facile est inventis addere [L.], it is easy to add to things already invented.

facile princeps [L.], easily preëminent; indisputably the first; the admitted chief.

facilis descensus Averni [L.], the descent to the lower world is easy; the road to evil is easy.

facit indignatio versum [L.], indignation instigates the verse.

façon [Fr.], manner, style.

façon de parler [Fr.], manner of speaking.

facta non verba [L.], deeds not words.

fade [Fr.], insipid; tasteless.

fænum habet in cornu, longe fuge [L.], he has hay upon his horn (of old the sign of a dangerous bull), beware of him.

fæx populi [L.], the dregs of the people.

faire bonne mine [Fr.], to put a good face upon the matter.

faire l'homme d'importance [Fr.], to assume an air of importance.

faire mon devoir [Fr.], to do my duty.

faire sans dire [Fr.], to do, not to say; to act without ostentation.

fait accompli [Fr.], a thing already done.

falsi crimen [L.], the crime of forgery.

falsus in uno, falsus in omnibus [L.], false in one thing, false in all.

fama clamosa [L.], a current scandal; a prevailing report.

fama nihil est celerius [L.], nothing travels swifter than scandal.

fama semper vivat [L.], may his fame endure forever.

far niente [It.], the doing of nothing.

fas est et ab hoste doceri [L.], it is right to be taught even by an enemy.

Fata obstant [L.], the Fates oppose it.

Fata viam invenient [L.], the Fates will find a way.

faux pas [Fr.], a false step; a slip in behavior; a lapse from virtue.

fax mentis incendium gloriæ [L.], the passion for glory is the torch of the mind.

felicitas multos habet amicos [L.], prosperity has many friends.

femme couverte [Fr.], a married woman.

femme de chambre [Fr.], a chambermaid.

femme galante [Fr.], a gay woman; a courtesan.

femme seule (as a law term, **femme sole**) [Fr.], an unmarried woman.

fendre un cheveu en quatre [Fr.], to split a hair in four; to make a very subtle distinction.

festina lente [L.], hasten slowly.

fête champêtre [Fr.], an open-air festival or entertainment; a rural festival.

feu de joie [Fr.], a fire of joy; a bonfire; a fusillade as a sign of rejoicing.

feuilleton [Fr.], a fly-sheet; a novel or a story appearing in a newspaper.

fiat experimentum in corpore vili [L.], let the trial (or experiment) be made on a worthless subject.

fiat justitia, ruat cælum [L.], let justice be done though the heavens should fall.

fiat lux [L.], let there be light.

fide et amore [L.], by faith and love.

fide et fiducia [L.], by fidelity and confidence.

fide et fortitudine [L.], with faith and fortitude.

fidei coticula crux [L.], the cross is the touchstone of faith.

fidei defensor [L.], defender of the faith.

fideli certa merces [L.], to the faithful one reward is certain.

fide non armis [L.], by faith, not by arms.

fide, sed cui vide [L.], trust, but see whom.

fides et justitia [L.], fidelity and justice.

fides Punica [L.], Punic faith; treachery.

fidus Achates [L.], faithful Achates; i.e. a true friend.

fidus et audax [L.], faithful and bold.

filius nullius [L.], a son of nobody.

filius populi [L.], a son of the people.

filius terræ [L], a son of the earth; one of low birth.

fille de chambre [Fr.], a chambermaid.

fille de joie [Fr.], a woman of licentious pleasure; a prostitute.

fille d'honneur [Fr.], a maid of honor.

fin de siècle [Fr.], end of the (nineteenth) century.

finem respice [L.], look to the end.

finis coronat opus [L.], the end crowns the work.

flagrante bello [L.], during hostilities.

flagrante delicto [L.], in the actual commission of the crime.

flamma fumo est proxima [L.], flame is akin to smoke; where there is smoke there is fire.

flâneur [Fr.], a lounger.

flecti, non frangi [L.], to be bent, not broken.

flosculi sententiarum [L.], flowers of fine thoughts.

flux de bouche [Fr.], an inordinate flow of words; garrulity.

foi en tout [Fr.], faith in everything.

foi pour devoir [Fr.], faith for duty.

fons et origo [L.], the source and origin.

forensis strepitus [L.], the clamor of the forum.

forte scutum salus ducum [L.], a strong shield is the safety of leaders.

fortes fortuna juvat [L.], fortune helps the brave.

forti et fideli nihil difficile [L.], nothing is difficult to the brave and faithful.

fortiter et recte [L.], with fortitude and rectitude.

fortiter, fideliter, feliciter [L.], boldly, faithfully, successfully.

fortiter in re [L.], with firmness or resolution in acting.

fortunæ filius [L.], a spoiled child of fortune.

fortuna favet fortibus [L.], fortune favors the bold.

frangas, non flectes [L.], you may break but not bend (me).

fraus pia [L.], a pious fraud.

fripon [Fr.], a rogue; a knave; a cheat.

froides mains, chaud amour [Fr.], cold hands, warm heart.

front à front [Fr.], face to face.

fronti nulla fides [L.], there is no trusting to appearances.

fruges consumere nati [L.], born to consume fruits; born only to eat.

fugit irreparabile tempus [L.], irrecoverable time flies on.

fuimus Troes [L.], we were once Trojans (but Troy has been overthrown).

fuit Ilium [L.], Troy has been (but is now no more).

fulmen brutum [L.], a senseless thunderbolt; striking blindly.

fumum et opes, strepitumque Romæ [L.], the smoke, the show, and the noise of Rome.

functus officio [L.], having performed one's office or duty; hence, out of office.

furor arma ministrat [L.], rage provides arms.

furor loquendi [L.], a rage for speaking.

furor poeticus [L.], poetic fire.

furor scribendi [L.], a rage for writing.

fuyez les dangers de loisir [Fr.], avoid the dangers of leisure.

G

gage d'amour [Fr.], a pledge of love.

gaieté de cœur [Fr.], gaiety of heart.

Gallice [L.], in French.

garçon [Fr.], a boy; a waiter.

garde à cheval [Fr.], a mounted guard.

garde du corps [Fr.], a body-guard.

garde mobile [Fr.], a guard liable to general service.

gardez [Fr.], be on your guard; take care.

gardez bien [Fr.], take good care.

garde la foi [Fr.], keep the faith.

gaudeamus igitur [L.], therefore let us be joyful.

gaudet tentamine virtus [L.], virtue rejoices in temptation.

gaudium certaminis [L.], the joy of conflict.

genius loci [L.], the presiding spirit or genius of the place.

gens d'armes [Fr.], men at arms.

gens de condition [Fr.], people of standing.

gens d'église [Fr.], churchmen.

gens de guerre [Fr.], military men.

gens de lettres [Fr.], literary men.

gens de loi [Fr.], lawyers.

gens de même famille [Fr.], persons of the same family; birds of a feather.

gens de peu [Fr.], the meaner class of people.

gens togata [L.], civilians.

gentilhomme [Fr.], a gentleman.

genus irritabile vatum [L.], the irritable race of poets.

Germanice [L.], in German.

gibier de potence [Fr.], a gallowsbird.

giovine santo, diavolo vecchio [It.], a young saint, an old devil.

gitano [Sp.], a gypsy.

gli assenti hanno torto [It.], the absent are in the wrong.

gloria in excelsis [L.], glory to God in the highest.

gloria Patri [L.], glory be to the Father.

glückliche Reise! [G.], a pleasant journey!

gnothi seauton [Gr.], know thyself.

gobe-mouche [Fr.], a person who has no ideas of his own; a ninny; a trifler.

goût [Fr.], taste; relish.

goutte à goutte [Fr.], drop by drop.

grâce à Dieu [Fr.], thanks to God.

gradu diverso, via una [L.], the same road by different steps.

gradus ad Parnassum [L.], a step to Parnassus; aid in writing Greek or Latin verse.

grande chère et beau feu [Fr.], good cheer and a good fire; comfortable quarters.

grande fortune, grande servitude [Fr.], a great fortune is a great slavery.

grande parure } [Fr.], full
grande toilette } dress.

grand merci [Fr.], many thanks.

gratia placendi [L.], the delight of pleasing.

gratis dictum [L.], mere assertion.

graviora manent [L.], greater afflictions await us, more serious matters remain.

graviora quædam sunt remedia periculis [L.], some remedies are worse than the disease.

grex venalium [L.], a venal rabble.

grosse tête et peu de sens [Fr.], a large head and little sense.

grossièreté [Fr.], coarseness; vulgarity in conversation.

guerra al cuchillo [Sp.], war to the knife.

guerra cominciata, inferno scatenato [It.], war begun, hell unchained.

guerre à mort [Fr.], war to the death.

guerre à outrance [Fr.], war to the uttermost.

gutta cavat lapidem non vi, sed sæpe cadendo [L.], the drop hollows the stone by frequent falling, not by force.

H

habitué [Fr.], one who is in the habit of frequenting a place.

hac lege [L.], on this condition; with this restriction.

hæc olim meminisse juvabit [L.], it will delight us to remember this some day.

Hannibal ad portas [L.], Hannibal before the gates; the enemy close at hand.

hapax legomenon [Gr.], a word or expression occurring once only.

hardi comme un coq sur son fumier [Fr.], bold as a cock on his own dunghill.

haud longis intervallis [L.], at intervals of no great length.

haud passibus æquis [L.], not with equal steps.

haut goût [Fr.], high flavor; elegant taste.

helluo librorum [L.], a devourer of books; a bookworm.

heu pietas! heu prisca fides! [L.], alas for piety! alas for the ancient faith!

hiatus valde deflendus [L.], a hiatus or deficiency much to be regretted.

hic et nunc [L.], here and now.

hic et ubique [L.], here and everywhere.

hic jacet [L.], here lies.

hic labor, hoc opus est [L.], this is a laborious task; this is a toil.

hic sepultus [L.], here buried.

hinc illæ lacrimæ [L.], hence these tears.

hoc opus, hic labor est [L.], same as **hic labor, hoc opus est.**

hodie mihi, cras tibi [L.], mine today, yours tomorrow.

hoi polloi [Gr.], the many; the vulgar; the rabble.

hombre de un libro [Sp.], a man of one book.

hominis est errare [L.], to err is human.

homme d'affaires [Fr.], a businessman.

homme de bien [Fr.], a good man.

homme de lettres [Fr.], a man of letters.

homme d'épée [Fr.], a man of the sword; a soldier.

homme de robe [Fr.], a man in civil office; magistrate.

homme d'esprit [Fr.], a man of wit or genius.

homme d'état [Fr.], a statesman.

homo factus ad unguem [L.], a highly polished man; one finished to the highest degree.

homo homini lupus [L.], man is a wolf to man.

homo multarum litterarum [L.], a man of great learning.

homo sui juris [L.], a man who is his own master.

homo sum; humani nihil a me alienum puto [L.], I am a man; I count nothing that is human indifferent to me.

honi soit qui mal y pense [O. Fr.], shame to him who thinks evil of it; evil to him who evil thinks.

honores mutant mores [L.], honors change men's manners or characters.

honos habet onus [L.], honor brings responsibility.

horæ canonicæ [L.], prescribed hours for prayer; canonical hours.

horas non numero nisi serenas [L.], I number only hours of sunshine. (Motto for a sun dial.)

horresco referens [L.], I shudder as I relate.

horribile dictu [L.], horrible to relate.

hors de combat [Fr.], rendered unable any longer to fight.

hors de concours [Fr.], out of the competition.

hors de la loi [Fr.], in the condition of an outlaw.

hors de propos [Fr.], not to the point or purpose.

hors de saison [Fr.], out of season.

hors d'œuvre [Fr.], out of course; out of order.

hos ego versiculos feci, tulit alter honores [L.], I wrote these lines, another has borne away the honor.

hôtel de ville [Fr.], a townhall; municipal building of a town.

hôtel Dieu [Fr.], a hospital.

hôtel garni [Fr.], a furnished lodging.

humanum est errare [L.], to err is human.

hunc tu Romane caveto [L.], Roman, beware of that man.

hurtar para dar por Dios [Sp.], to steal for the purpose of giving to God (in alms).

I

ich dien [G.], I serve.

ici on parle Français [Fr.], French is spoken here.

idée fixe [Fr.], a fixed idea.

id genus omne [L.], all of that sort or description.

ignorantia legis neminem excusat [L.], ignorance of the law excuses no one.

ignorantio elenchi [L.], ignorance of the point in question; the logical fallacy of arguing to the wrong point.

ignoscito sæpe alteri, nunquam tibi [L.], forgive others often, yourself never.

ignoti nulla cupido [L.], no desire is felt for a thing unknown.

ignotum per ignotius [L.], the unknown (explained) by the still more unknown.

i gran dolori sono muti [It.], great griefs are silent.

il aboie après tout le monde [Fr.], he snarls at everybody.

il a la mer à boire [Fr.], he has the sea to drink up; i.e. all his powers will be taxed to succeed.

il a le diable au corps [Fr.], the devil is in him.

il conduit bien sa barque [Fr.], he steers his boat well; he knows how to get on.

il est plus aisé d'être sage pour les autres, que pour soi-même [Fr.], it is easier to be wise for others than for oneself.

il est plus honteux de se défier de ses amis, que d'en être trompé [Fr.], it is more disgraceful to suspect one's friends than to be deceived by them.

il faut attendre le boiteux [Fr.], it is necessary to wait for the lame man; we must wait for the truth.

il faut de l'argent [Fr.], money is needful.

Ilias malorum [L.], an Iliad of ills; a host of evils.

il n'a ni bouche ni éperon [Fr.], he has neither mouth nor spur; neither wit nor courage.

il n'appartient qu'aux grands hommes d'avoir de grands défauts [Fr.], only great men may have great faults.

il ne faut jamais défier un fou [Fr.], never defy a fool.

il ne faut pas éveiller le chat qui dort [Fr.], it is not wise to awake the cat that sleeps; let sleeping dogs lie.

il n'y a pas de héros pour son valet de chambre [Fr.], no man is a hero in the eyes of his valet.

il penseroso [It.], the pensive man.

il rit bien qui rit le dernier [Fr.], he laughs best who laughs last.

il sent le fagot [Fr.], he smells of the faggot; he is suspected of heresy.

il vaut mieux tâcher d'oublier ses malheurs, que d'en parler [Fr.], it is better to try to forget one's misfortunes, than to talk of them.

imitatores, servum pecus [L.], imitators, a servile herd.

immedicabile vulnus [L.], an incurable wound; irreparable injury.

imo pectore [L.], from the bottom of the breast.

impari Marte [L.], with unequal military strength.

impedimenta [L.], travelers' luggage; the baggage of an army.

imperium in imperio [L.], a state within a state, a government within another.

implicite [Fr.], by implication.

impos animi [L.], of weak mind.

in actu [L.], in act or reality.

in æternum [L.], forever.

in ambiguo [L.], in doubt.

in articulo mortis [L.], at the point of death; in the last struggle.

in bianco [It.], in blank; in white.

in camera [L.], in the chamber of the judge; in secret.

in capite [L.], in chief.

in cælo quies [L.], there is rest in heaven.

incredulus odi [L.], being incredulous I cannot endure it.

in curia [L.], in court.

inde iræ [L.], hence these resentments.

Index Expurgatorius [L.], a list of expurgated books (compiled by the Roman Catholic authorities).

Index Prohibitorius [L.], a list of prohibited books (prohibited to Roman Catholics).

in dubio [L.], in doubt.

in equilibrio [L.], in equilibrium; equally balanced.

in esse [L.], in being; in actuality.

in extenso [L.], at full length.

in extremis [L.], at the point of death.

infandum renovare dolorem [L.], to revive unspeakable grief.

in forma pauperis [L.], as a poor man or pauper.

in foro conscientiæ [L.], before the tribunal of conscience.

infra dignitatem [L.], below one's dignity.

in futuro [L.], in future; henceforth.

in hoc signo spes mea [L.], in this sign is my hope.

in hoc signo vinces [L.], under this sign or standard thou shalt conquer.

in limine [L.], at the threshold.

in loco [L.], in the place; in the passage mentioned; in the natural or proper place.

in loco parentis [L.], in the place of a parent.

in medias res [L.], into the midst of things.

in medio tutissimus ibis [L.], you will go safest in a middle course.

in memoriam [L.], to the memory of; in memory.

in necessariis unitas, in dubiis libertas, in omnibus caritas [L.], in things essential unity, in things doubtful liberty, in all things charity.

in nomine [L.], in the name of.

in nubibus [L.], in the clouds.

in nuce [L.], in a nutshell.

in omnia paratus [L.], prepared for all things.

inopem copia fecit [L.], abundance made him poor.

in ovo [L.], in the egg.

in pace [L.], in peace.

in partibus infidelium [L.], in parts belonging to infidels, or countries not adhering to the Roman Catholic faith.

in perpetuam rei memoriam [L.], in perpetual memory of the thing.

in perpetuum [L.], forever.

in petto [It.], within the breast; in reserve.

in pleno [L.], in full.

in posse [L.], in possible existence; in possibility.

in præsenti [L.], at the present moment.

in propria persona [L.], in one's own person.

in puris naturalibus [L.], purely in a state of nature; quite naked.

in re [L.], in the matter of.

in rerum natura [L.], in the nature of things.

in sæcula sæculorum [L.], for ages on ages.

in sano sensu [L.], in a proper sense.

in situ [L.], in its original situation.

in solo Deo salus [L.], in God alone is safety.

insouciance [Fr.], unconcern; careless indifference.

insouciant [Fr.], unconcerned; indifferent.

instar omnium [L.], equivalent to them all.

in statu quo [L.], in the former state; in the same state as before (some event).

in te, Domine, speravi [L.], in thee, Lord, have I put my trust.

inter alia [L.], among other things.

inter arma silent leges [L.], laws are silent in the midst of arms.

inter canem et lupum [L.], between dog and wolf; at twilight.

interdum vulgus rectum videt [L.], the rabble sometimes see what is right.

inter nos [L.], between ourselves.

inter pocula [L.], at one's cups.

in terrorem [L.], as a means of terrifying; by way of warning.

inter se [L.], among themselves.

inter spem et metum [L.], between hope and fear.

in totidem verbis [L.], in so many words.

in toto [L.], in whole; entirely.

intra muros [L.], within the walls.

in transitu [L.], in course of transit or passage.

intra parietes [L.], within walls; in private.

in usum Delphini [L.], for the use of the Dauphin; applied to editions of the classical authors.

in utramque fortunam paratus [L.], prepared for either fortune (or result).

in utroque fidelis [L.], faithful in both or each (of two).

in vacuo [L.], in empty space; in a vacuum.

inverso ordine [L.], in an inverse order.

in vino veritas [L.], there is truth in wine; truth is told under the influence of intoxicants.

invita Minerva [L.], against the will of Minerva; at variance with one's mental capacity; without genius.

ipse dixit [L.], he himself said it; a dogmatic saying or assertion.

ipsissima verba [L.], the very words.

ipso facto [L.], by the fact itself.

ipso jure [L.], by the law itself.

ira furor brevis est [L.], anger is a short madness.

ir por lana y volver trasquilado [Sp.], to go for wool, and come back shorn.

ita est [L.], it is so.

ita lex scripta [L.], thus the law stands written.

Italice [L.], in the Italian language.

J–K

Jacquerie [Fr.], French peasantry; a revolt of peasants.

jacta est alea [L.], the die is cast.

j'ai bonne cause [Fr.], I have a good cause.

jamais arrière [Fr.], never behind.

jamais bon coureur ne fut pris [Fr.], a good runner is never caught; an old bird is not to be caught with chaff.

januis clausis [L.], with closed doors.

je maintiendrai le droit [Fr.], I will maintain the right.

je me fie en Dieu [Fr.], I trust in God.

je ne sais quoi [Fr.], I know not what; a something or other.

je n'oublierai jamais [Fr.], I shall never forget.

je suis prêt [Fr.], I am ready.

jet d'eau [Fr.], a jet of water; a fountain.

jeu de main [Fr.], horseplay, practical joke.

jeu de mots [Fr.], a play on words; a pun.

jeu d'esprit [Fr.], a display of wit; a witticism.

jeu de théâtre [Fr.], stage-trick; clap-trap.

jeunesse dorée [Fr.], gilded youth; rich young fellows.

je vis en espoir [Fr.], I live in hope.

joci causa [L.], for the sake of a joke.

joli [Fr.], pretty; fine.

jour de fête [Fr.], a feast day.

jour de l'an [Fr.], New Year's day.

jubilate Deo [L.], rejoice in God; be joyful in the Lord.

jucundi acti labores [L.], accomplished labors are pleasant.

judex damnatur cum nocens absolvitur [L.], the judge is condemned when the offender is acquitted.

judicium Dei [L.], the judgment of God.

judicium parium, aut leges terræ [L.], the judgment of our peers or the laws of the land.

juge de paix [Fr.], a justice of peace.

juniores ad labores [L.], the younger men (are fittest) for labors.

jurare in verba magistri [L.], to swear to the words of a master.

jure divino [L.], by divine law.

jure humano [L.], by human law.

juris peritus [L.], skilled in the law; one who is learned in the law.

juris utriusque doctor [L.], doctor of both the civil and canon law.

jus canonicum [L.], the canon law.

jus civile [L.], the civil law.

jus divinum [L.], the divine law.

jus et norma loquendi [L.], the law and rule of speech.

jus gentium [L.], the law of nations.

jus gladii [L.], the right of the sword.

jus possessionis [L.], right of possession.

jus proprietatis [L.], the right of property.

jus summum sæpe summa malitia est [L.], law carried to extremes is often extreme wrong.

juste milieu [Fr.], the golden mean.

justum et tenacem propositi virum [L.], a man upright and tenacious of purpose.

kein Kreuzer, kein Schweizer [G.], no money no Swiss; a proverb of the time when the Swiss were common as mercenaries.

ktema es aei [Gr.], a possession for all time.

L

la beauté sans vertu est une fleur sans parfum [Fr.], beauty without virtue is like a flower without perfume.

labitur et labetur in omne volubilis ævum [L.], it glides on, and will glide on forever. See Rusticus expectat.

laborare est orare [L.], to work is to pray.

labore et honore [L.], by labor and honor.

labor ipse voluptas [L.], labor itself is a pleasure.

labor omnia vincit [L.], labor conquers everything.

laborum dulce lenimen [L.], the sweet solace of our labors.

la bride sur le cou [Fr.], with rein on neck; at full speed.

la critique est aisée, et l'art est difficile [Fr.], criticism is easy, and art is difficult.

l'affaire s'achemine [Fr.], the business is progressing.

la fortune passe partout [Fr.], fortune passes everywhere; all suffer change or vicissitude.

l'allegro [It.], the merry man.

l'amour et la fumée ne peuvent se cacher [Fr.], love and smoke cannot conceal themselves.

lana caprina [L.], goat's wool; hence, a thing of little worth.

langage des halles [Fr.], the language of the markets, profane or foul.

la patience est amère, mais son fruit est doux [Fr.], patience is bitter, but its fruit is sweet.

lapis philosophorum [L.], the philosophers' stone.

la poverta è la madre di tutte le arti [It.], poverty is the mother of all the arts.

la propriété c'est le vol [Fr.], property is robbery.

lapsus calami [L.], a slip of the pen.

lapsus linguæ [L.], a slip of the tongue.

lapsus memoriæ [L.], a slip of the memory.

lares et penates [L.], household gods.

la reyne (or le roy) le veult [Norm. Fr.], the queen (or the king) wills it; the formula expressing the sovereign's assent to a bill.

l'argent [Fr.], money.

lasciate ogni speranza, voi ch'entrate [It.], abandon hope all ye who enter here.

lateat scintilla forsan [L.], perhaps a small spark may lie hid.

latet anguis in herba [L.], a snake lies hid in the grass.

Latine dictum [L.], spoken in Latin.

lauda la moglie e tienti donzello [It.], praise a wife and remain a bachelor.

laudari a viro laudato [L.], praised by one who is himself praised.

laudationes eorum qui sunt ab Homero laudati [L.], praises from those who were themselves praised by Homer.

laudator temporis acti [L.], one who praises time past.

laudum immensa cupido [L.], insatiable desire for praise.

laus Deo [L.], praise to God.

l'avenir [Fr.], the future.

la vertu est la seule noblesse [Fr.], virtue is the only nobility.

le beau monde [Fr.], the fashionable world.

le bon temps viendra [Fr.], the good time will come.

le coût ôte le goût [Fr.], the cost takes away the taste.

lector benevole [L.], kind or gentle reader.

le dessous des cartes [Fr.], the underside of the cards.

le diable boiteux [Fr.], the devil on two sticks or with crutches.

legalis homo [L.], a lawful person, i.e. one not outlawed, infamous, or excommunicated.

legatus a latere [L.], a papal ambassador.

le génie c'est la patience [Fr.], genius is patience.

le grand monarque [Fr.], the great monarch; a name applied to Louis XIV of France.

le grand œuvre [Fr.], the great work; the philosophers' stone.

le jeu ne vaut pas la chandelle [Fr.], the game is not worth the candle; the object is not worth the trouble.

le jour viendra [Fr.], the day will come.

le mieux est l'ennemi du bien [Fr.], the better is the enemy of the good.

le monde est le livre des femmes [Fr.], the world is woman's book.

le monde savant [Fr.], the learned world.

le mot de l'énigme [Fr.], the key to the mystery.

l'empire des lettres [Fr.], the republic (lit. empire) of letters.

leonina societas [L.], partnership with a lion.

le pas [Fr.], precedence in place or rank.

le point du jour [Fr.], daybreak.

le roi est mort, vive le roi! [Fr.], the king is dead, long live the king (his successor)!

le roi et l'état [Fr.], the king and the state.

le roi le veut [Fr.], the king wills it.

le roi s'avisera [Fr.], the king will consider or deliberate.

les absents ont toujours tort [Fr.], the absent are always in the wrong.

les affaires font les hommes [Fr.], business makes men.

les bras croisés [Fr.], with folded arms; idle.

les doux yeux [Fr.], tender glances.

lèse majesté [Fr.], high treason.

les extrêmes se touchent [Fr.], extremes meet.

les murailles ont des oreilles [Fr.], walls have ears.

les plus sages ne le sont pas toujours [Fr.], the wisest are not so always.

le style, c'est l'homme [Fr.], the style is the man.

l'état, c'est moi [Fr.], it is I who am the state.

l'étoile du nord [Fr.], the star of the north.

le tout ensemble [Fr.], the whole together.

lettre de cachet [Fr.], a sealed letter containing private orders; a royal warrant.

lettre de change [Fr.], bill of exchange.

lettre de créance [Fr.], letter of credit.

lettre de marque [Fr.], a letter of marque or reprisal.

levamen probationis [L.], relief from proving.

leve fit quod bene fertur onus [L.], the burden which is well borne becomes light.

le vrai n'est pas toujours vraisemblable [Fr.], the truth is not always probable; truth is stranger than fiction.

lex loci [L.], the law or custom of the place.

lex non scripta [L.], unwritten law; common law.

lex scripta [L.], statute (or written) law.

lex talionis [L.], the law of retaliation.

lex terræ [L.], the law of the land.

l'homme propose, et Dieu dispose [Fr.], man proposes, and God disposes.

libertas et natale solum [L.], liberty and one's native land.

liberum arbitrium [L.], free will.

libraire [Fr.], a bookseller.

licentia vatum [L.], the license of the poets; poetic license.

limæ labor et mora [L.], the labor and delay of the file; the slow and laborious polishing of a literary composition.

l'inconnu [Fr.], the unknown.

l'incroyable [Fr.], the incredible.

lingua franca [It.], the mixed language used between Europeans and Orientals in the Levant.

lis litem generat [L.], strife begets strife.

lit de justice [Fr.], a bed of justice; the throne of the king in the parliament of Paris; the sitting of that parliament when the king was present.

litem lite resolvere [L.], to settle strife by strife, to remove one difficulty by introducing another.

lite pendente [L.], during the trial.

littera scripta manet [L.], the written letter remains.

l'occasion fait le larron [Fr.], opportunity makes the thief.

loci communes [L.], common places.

loco citato [L.], in the place or passage cited.

locos y niños dicen la verdad [Sp.], fools and children speak the truth.

locum tenens [L.], one occupying the place of another; a substitute.

locus classicus [L.], a classical passage.

locus criminis [L.], place of the crime.

locus in quo [L.], the place in which.

locus pænitentiæ [L.], place for repentance.

locus sigilli [L.], the place of the seal on a document.

longe aberrat scopo [L.], he goes far from the mark.

longo intervallo [L.], by or with a long interval.

loyal devoir [L.], loyal duty.

loyal en tout [L.], loyal in everything.

loyauté m'oblige [Fr.], loyalty binds me.

loyauté n'a honte [Fr.], loyalty has no shame.

lucidus ordo [L.], a lucid arrangement.

lucri causa [L.], for the sake of gain.

lucus a non lucendo [L.], used as typical of an absurd derivation or explanation— **lucus**, meaning *grove*, is wrongly implied to be another form of **lucere**, meaning to *shine*.

ludere cum sacris [L.], to trifle with sacred things.

lupum auribus teneo [L.], I hold a wolf by the ears, i.e. I have caught a tartar.

lupus in fabula [L.], the wolf in the fable.

lupus pilum mutat, non mentem [L.], the wolf changes his coat, not his disposition.

lusus naturæ [L.], a sport or freak of nature.

M

ma chère [Fr.], my dear (fem.).

macte virtute [L.], go on or persevere in virtue.

ma foi [Fr.], upon my faith.

maggiore fretta, minore atto [It.], the more haste the less speed.

magister cæremoniarum [L.], master of the ceremonies.

magna civitas, magna solitudo [L.], a great city is a great solitude.

magnæ spes altera Romæ [L.], another hope of great Rome.

magna est veritas et prevalebit [L.], truth is mighty and will prevail.

magna est vis consuetudinis [L.], great is the force of habit.

magnanimiter crucem sustine [L.], bear the cross nobly.

magnas inter opes inops [L.], poor in the midst of great wealth.

magni nominis umbra [L.], the shadow of a great name.

magnum bonum [L.], a great good.

magnum vectigal est parsimonia [L.], economy is itself a great income.

magnum opus [L.], a great work.

magnus Apollo [L.], great Apollo, i.e. one of great authority.

maigre [Fr.], fasting. See in Dict.

main de justice [Fr.], the hand of justice; the sceptre.

maintien le droit [Fr.], maintain the right.

maison de campagne [Fr.], a country house.

maison de santé [Fr.], a private asylum or hospital.

maison de ville [Fr.], a town-house.

maître des basses œuvres [Fr.], literally, "master of low works"; i.e. a sewer-cleaner.

maître des hautes œuvres [Fr.], an executioner; a hangman.

maître d'hôtel [Fr.], a house-steward.

maladie du pays [Fr.], home-sickness.

mala fide [Fr.], with bad faith; treacherously.

mal à propos [Fr.], ill-timed. See in Dict.

mal de dents [Fr.], toothache.

mal de mer [Fr.], sea-sickness.

mal de tête [Fr.], headache.

malentendu [Fr.], a misunderstanding; a mistake.

male parta, male dilabuntur [L.], things ill gotten are consumed without doing any good.

malgré nous [Fr.], in spite of us.

malgré soi [Fr.], in spite of himself.

malheur ne vient jamais seul [Fr.], misfortunes never come singly.

mali exempli [L.], of a bad example.

mali principii malus finis [L.], bad beginnings have bad endings.

malis avibus [L.], with unlucky birds; with bad omens.

malo modo [L.], in a bad manner.

malo mori quam fœdari [L.], I would rather die than be debased.

malpropre [Fr.], slovenly; not neat and clean.

malum in se [L.], evil or an evil in itself.

malum prohibitum [L.], an evil prohibited; evil because prohibited.

malus pudor [L.], false shame.

manet alta mente repostum [L.], it remains deeply fixed in the mind.

manibus pedibusque [L.], with hands and feet.

manu forti [L.], with a strong hand.

manu propria [L.], with one's own hand.

Mardi gras [Fr.], Shrove Tuesday.

mare clausum [L.], a closed sea; a bay.

mariage de conscience [Fr.], a private marriage.

mariage de convenance [Fr.], marriage from motives of material interest rather than of love.

mariage de la main gauche [Fr.], left-handed marriage; a morganatic marriage.

Mars gravior sub pace latet [L.], a severer war lies hidden under peace.

más vale saber que haber [Sp.], better to be wise than to be rich.

más vale ser necio que porfiado [Sp.], better to be a fool than obstinate.

más vale tarde que nunca [Sp.], better late than never.

materfamilias [L.], the mother of a family.

materiam superabit opus [L.], the workmanship will prove superior to the material.

matre pulchra filia pulchrior [L.], a daughter more beautiful than her beautiful mother.

mauvaise honte [Fr.], false modesty.

mauvais goût [Fr.], bad taste.

mauvais sujet [Fr.], a bad subject; a worthless scamp.

maxima debetur puero reverentia [L.], the greatest reverence is due to a boy.

maximus in minimis [L.], very great in trifles.

mea culpa [L.], by my fault.

médecin, guéris-toi toi-même [Fr.], physician, heal thyself.

mediocria firma [L.], moderate or middle things are surest.

medio tutissimus ibis [L.], in a medium course you will be safest.

medium tenuere beati [L.], happy are they who have held the middle course.

mega biblion, mega kakon [Gr.], a great book is a great evil.

me judice [L.], I being judge; in my opinion.

memento mori [L.], remember death.

memor et fidelis [L.], mindful and faithful.

memoria in æterna [L.], in eternal remembrance.

mendacem memorem esse oportet [L.], a liar should have a good memory.

mens agitat molem [L.], mind moves matter.

mens legis [L.], the spirit of the law.

mens sana in corpore sano [L.], a sound mind in a sound body.

mens sibi conscia recti [L.], a mind conscious of its own rectitude.

meo periculo [L.], at my own risk.

meo voto [L.], according to my wish.

merum sal [L.], pure or genuine wit.

mésalliance [Fr.], marriage with one of a lower rank.

meum et tuum [L.], mine and thine.

mihi cura futuri [L.], my care is for the future.

mirabile dictu [L.], wonderful to relate.

mirabile visu [L.], wonderful to see.

mirabilia [L.], wonders.

mirum in modum [L.], in a wonderful manner.

mise en scène [Fr.], the getting up for the stage, or the putting on the stage.

miserabile vulgus [L.], a wretched crew.

miseris succurrere disco [L.], I learn to succor the wretched.

mittimus [L.], we send; name of a writ in law. See in Dict.

mobile perpetuum [L.], perpetual motion.

modo et forma [L.], in manner and form.

modus operandi [L.], manner of working.

mole ruit sua [L.], it falls in ruins by its own weight.

mollia tempora fandi [L.], times favorable for speaking.

mon ami [Fr.], my friend.

mon cher [Fr.], my dear (masc.).

montani semper liberi [L.], mountaineers are always free men.

monumentum ære perennius [L.], a monument more lasting than brass.

more Hibernico [L.], after the Irish fashion.

more majorum [L.], after the manner of our ancestors.

more suo [L.], in his own way.

mors janua vitæ [L.], death is the gate of eternal life.

mors omnibus communis [L.], death is common to all.

mos pro lege [L.], custom or usage for law.

mot du guet [Fr.], a watchword.

mots d'usage [Fr.], words in common use.

motu proprio [L.], of his own accord.

mucho en el suelo, poco en el cielo [Sp.], much on earth, little in heaven.

muet comme un poisson [Fr.], dumb as a fish.

multa gemens [L.], with many a groan.

multum in parvo [L.], much in little.

mundus vult decipi [L.], the world wishes to be deceived.

munus Apolline dignum [L.], a gift worthy of Apollo.

muraglia bianca, carta di matto [It.], a white wall is the fool's paper.

murus æneus conscientia sana [L.], a clear conscience is a firm wall.

mutare vel timere sperno [L.], I scorn to change or to fear.

mutatis mutandis [L.], with the necessary changes.

mutato nomine de te fabula narratur [L.], the name being changed the story is true of yourself.

muta est pictura poema [L.], a picture is a silent poem.

mutuus consensus [L.], mutual consent.

N

naissance [Fr.], birth.

natale solum [L.], native soil.

natura lo fece, e poi ruppe la stampa [It.], nature made him, and then broke the mould.

naturam expellas furca tamen usque recurret [L.], though you drive out Nature with a pitchfork, yet will she ever return.

natura non facit saltum [L.], nature does not make a leap; i.e. nature proceeds slowly.

naviget Anticyram [L.], let him sail to Anticyra (where he will get hellebore to cure him of madness).

nec cupias, nec metuas [L.], neither desire nor fear.

ne cede malis [L.], yield not to misfortune.

necessitas non habet legem [L.], necessity has no law.

nec mora, nec requies [L.], neither delay nor repose.

nec pluribus impar [L.], not an unequal match for numbers.

nec prece, nec pretio [L.], neither by entreaty nor by bribe.

nec quærere, nec spernere honorem [L.], neither to seek nor to contemn honors.

nec scire fas est omnia [L.], it is not permitted to know all things.

nec temere, nec timide [L.], neither rashly nor timidly.

née [Fr.], born; having as her maiden name.

nefasti dies [L.], days on which judgment could not be pronounced, nor assemblies of the people be held; hence, unlucky days.

ne fronti crede [L.], trust not to appearances.

négligé [Fr.], morning dress; an easy loose dress.

ne Jupiter quidem omnibus placet [L.], not even Jupiter pleases everybody.

nel bisogno si conoscono gli amici [It.], a friend in need is a friend indeed.

nemine contradicente [L.], no one speaking in opposition; without opposition.

nemine dissentiente [L.], no one dissenting; without a dissenting voice.

nemo bis punitur pro eodem delicto [L.], no one is twice punished for the same offence.

nemo me impune lacessit [L.], no one assails me with impunity.

nemo mortalium omnibus horis sapit [L.], no one is wise at all times.

nemo repente fuit turpissimus [L.], no one ever became a villain in an instant.

nemo solus sapit [L.], no one is wise alone (with no person to consult).

ne nimium [L.], avoid excess.

ne plus ultra [L.], nothing further; the uttermost point, perfection.

ne puero gladium [L.], intrust not a boy with a sword.

ne quid detrimenti respublica capiat [L.], lest the state receive any detriment.

ne quid nimis [L.], in nothing go too far.

nervi belli pecunia [L.], money is the sinews of war.

nervus probandi [L.], the sinews of the argument.

n'est-ce pas? [Fr.], is it not so?

ne sutor supra crepidam [L.], let not the shoemaker go beyond his last (properly sandal); let no one meddle with what lies beyond his range.

ne tentes, aut perfice [L.], either attempt it not or succeed.

netteté [Fr.], neatness.

ne vile fano [L.], let nothing vile be in the temple.

niaiserie [Fr.], silliness; simplicity.

nicht wahr? [G.], is it not so? am I not right?

ni firmes carta que no leas, ni bebas agua que no veas [Sp.], never sign a paper you have not read, nor drink water you have not examined.

nihil ad rem [L.], nothing to the point.

nihil (properly **nullum**) **quod tetigit non ornavit** [L.], he touched nothing without embellishing it.

nil admirari [L.], to be astonished at nothing.

nil conscire sibi nulla pallescere culpa [L.], to be conscious of no fault, and to turn pale at no accusation.

nil desperandum [L.], there is no reason for despair.

nil nisi cruce [L.], no dependence but on the cross.

ni l'un ni l'autre [Fr.], neither the one nor the other.

nimium ne crede colori [L.], trust not too much to looks (or externals).

n'importe [Fr.], it matters not.

nisi Dominus frustra [L.], unless God be with us all is in vain.

nitor in adversum [L.], I strive against opposition.

nobilitas sola est atque unica virtus [L.], virtue is the true and only nobility.

noblesse oblige [Fr.], rank imposes obligations; much is expected from one in good position.

no es oro todo lo quo reluce [Sp.], all is not gold that glistens.

no hay cerradura si es de oro la ganzúa [Sp.], there is no lock that a golden key will not open.

nolens volens [L.], willing or unwilling.

noli irritare leones [L.], do not irritate lions.

noli me tangere [L.], touch me not.

nolle prosequi [L.], to be unwilling to proceed. See in Dict.

nolo episcopari [L.], I do not wish to be made a bishop.

nom de guerre [Fr.], a war name; an assumed traveling name; pen name.

nom de plume [Fr.], an assumed name of a writer: an English expression formed from the French.

nomina stultorum parietibus hærent [L.], fools' names are stuck upon the walls.

non compos mentis [L.], not of sound mind.

non cuivis homini contingit adire Corinthum [L.], every man has not the fortune to go to Corinth.

non datur tertium [L.], there is not given a third one or a third chance.

non deficiente crumena [L.], the purse not failing; if the money holds out.

non est [L.], it is not; it is wanting or absent.

non est inventus [L.], he has not been found.

non est vivere sed valere vita [L.], life is not merely to live, but to be strong.

non far mai il medico tuo erede [It.], never make your physician your heir.

non ignara mali, miseris succurrere disco [L.], not unacquainted with misfortune I learn to succor the wretched.

non libet [L.], it does not please me.

non liquet [L.], the case is not clear or proved.

non mi ricordo [It.], I do not remember.

non multa, sed multum [L.], not many things but much.

non nobis solum [L.], not to ourselves alone.

non nostrum est tantas componere lites [L.], it is not for us to settle such weighty disputes.

nonobstant clameur de haro [Fr.], notwithstanding the hue and cry.

non ogni fiore fa buon odore [It.], not every flower has a sweet perfume.

non omne licitum honestum [L.], not every lawful thing is honorable.

non omnia possumus omnes [L.], we cannot, all of us, do everything.

non omnis moriar [L.], I shall not wholly die.

non quis, sed quid [L.], not who but what, not the person but the deed.

non quo, sed quomodo [L.], not by whom, but in what manner.

non sequitur [L.], it does not follow.

non sibi, sed omnibus [L.], not for self, but for all.

non sibi, sed patriæ [L.], not for himself but for his country.

non sine numine [L.], not without divine aid.

non sum qualis eram [L.], I am not what I once was.

non tali auxilio [L.], not with such aid or help.

nonum prematur in annum [L.], let it be kept back (from publication) till the ninth year.

nosce te ipsum [L.], know thyself.

noscitur a (or e) sociis [L.], he is known by his companions.

nostro periculo [L.], at our risk.

nota bene [L.], mark well.

Notre Dame [Fr.], Our Lady.

n'oubliez pas [Fr.], don't forget.

nous avons changé tout cela [Fr.], we have changed all that.

nous verrons [Fr.], we shall see.

novus homo [L.], a new man; one who has raised himself from obscurity.

nuance [Fr.], shade; subtle variation.

nudis verbis [L.], in plain words.

nudum pactum [L.], a mere agreement, unconfirmed by writing.

nugæ canoræ [L.], melodious trifles.

nul bien sans peine [Fr.], no pains, no gains.

nulla dies sine linea [L.], not a day without a line; no day without something done.

nulla nuova, buona nuova [It.], no news is good news.

nulli secundus [L.], second to none.

nullius addictus jurare in verba magistri [L.], not bound to swear to the opinions of any master.

nullius filius [L.], a son of nobody; an illegitimate son.

nunc aut nunquam [L.], now or never.

nunquam minus solus, quam cum solus [L.], never less alone than when alone.

nunquam non paratus [L.], never unprepared; always ready.

nuptiæ [L.], nuptials; wedding.

O

obiit [L.], he, or she, died.

obiter dictum [L.], a thing said by the way.

obra de común, obra de ningún [Sp.], everybody's business is nobody's business.

obscurum per obscurius [L.], explaining an obscurity by something more obscure still.

observanda [L.], things to be observed.

obsta principiis [L.], resist the beginnings.

obstupui steteruntque comæ [L.], I was astonished and my hair stood on end.

occasio facit furem [L.], opportunity makes the thief.

occurrent nubes [L.], clouds will intervene.

oderint dum metuant [L.], let them hate provided they fear.

odi profanum vulgus [L.], I loathe the profane rabble.

odium medicum [L.], the hatred of physicians.

odium in longum jacens [L.], hatred long cherished.

odium theologicum [L.], the hatred of theologians.

œil de bœuf [Fr.], a bull's-eye.

œuvres [Fr.], works.

officina gentium [L.], the workshop of the world.

O fortunatos nimium sua si bona norint agricolas [L.], O too happy husbandmen if only they knew their own blessings.

ofrecer mucho especie es de negar [Sp.], to offer much is a kind of denial.

ogni bottega ha la sua malizia [It.], every shop has its tricks; tricks in all trades.

ogni medaglia ha il suo riverso [It.], every medal has its reverse side.

ogniuno per se, e Dio per tutti [It.], every one for himself, and God for all.

ohe! jam satis [L.], hold! enough.

ohne Hast, aber ohne Rast [G.], without haste, but without rest.

olet lucernam [L.], it smells of the lamp ("the midnight oil"); it is a labored production.

omen faustum [L.], a favorable omen.

omne ignotum pro magnifico [L.], whatever is unknown is held to be magnificent.

omnem movere lapidem [L.], to turn every stone; to leave no stone unturned; to make every exertion.

omne solum forti patria [L.], every soil is a brave man's country.

omne trinum perfectum [L.], every perfect thing is threefold.

omne tulit punctum qui miscuit utile dulci [L.], he gains the approval of all who mixes the useful with the agreeable.

omne vivum ex ovo [L.], every living thing comes from an egg (or germ).

omnia ad Dei gloriam [L.], all things for the glory of God.

omnia bona bonis [L.], all things are good to the good.

omnia mutantur, nos et mutamur in illis [L.], all things change, and we change with them.

omnia vincit amor [L.], love conquers all things.

omnia vincit labor [L.], labor overcomes all things.

omnis amans amens [L.], every lover is demented.

on commence par être dupe, on finit par être fripon [Fr.], one begins by being a fool, and ends in becoming a knave.

on connait l'ami au besoin [Fr.], a friend is known in time of need.

operæ pretium est [L.], it is worthwhile.

opprobrium medicorum [L.], the reproach of the doctors.

optimates [L.], men of the first rank. See in Dict.

opus operatum [L.], an effective work or operation. See **Opus**, in Dict.

ora et labora [L.], pray and work.

ora pro nobis [L.], pray for us.

orator fit, poeta nascitur [L.], an orator is made, a poet is born.

ore rotundo [L.], with round full voice.

ore tenus [L.], from the mouth merely.

origo mali [L.], origin of the evil.

oro è che oro vale [It.], that is gold that is worth gold; all is not gold that glitters.

O! si sic omnia [L.], O! if all things were so; O! if he had always so spoken or acted.

O tempora! O mores! [L.], O the times! O the manners!

otia dant vitia [L.], idleness occasions vice.

otiosa sedulitas [L.], idle industry; laborious trifling.

otium cum dignitate [L.], ease with dignity; dignified leisure.

otium sine litteris est mors [L.], leisure without literature is death.

oublier je ne puis [Fr.], I can never forget.

ouï-dire [Fr.], hearsay.

ou la chèvre est attachée, il faut qu'elle broute [Fr.], where the goat is tethered, there it must browse.

ouvrage de longue haleine [Fr.], a work of long breath; a work long in being accomplished; a long-winded or tedious business.

ouvrier [Fr.], a workman; an operative.

P

pabulum Acherontis [L.], food for Acheron, or the tomb.

pace [L.], by leave of; not to give offence to.

pace tua [L.], by your leave; with your consent.

pacta conventa [L.], the conditions agreed on.

pactum illicitum [L.], an illegal agreement.

padrone [It.], a master; a landlord.

pallida mors [L.], pale death.

palmam qui meruit ferat [L.], let him who has won the palm wear it.

palma non sine pulvere [L.], the palm is not won without dust; i.e. no success without exertion.

par accès [Fr.], by fits and starts.

par accident [Fr.], by accident or chance.

par accord [Fr.], by agreement; in harmony.

par avion [Fr], by airplane: French label for air mail.

par ci par là [Fr.], here and there.

par complaisance [Fr.], by complaisance.

par dépit [Fr.], out of spite.

pardonnez-moi [Fr.], pardon me; excuse me.

parem non fert [L.], he suffers no equal.

par excellence [Fr.], by way of eminence.

par exemple [Fr.], by example; for instance.

parfaitement bien [Fr.], perfectly well.

par faveur [Fr.], by favor; with the countenance of.

par force [Fr.], by force.

par hasard [Fr.], by chance.

pari passu [L.], with equal step; together.

paritur pax bello [L.], peace is produced by war.

par le droit du plus fort [Fr.], by the right of the strongest.

par les mêmes voies on ne va pas toujours aux mêmes fins [Fr.], by the same methods we do not always attain the same ends.

parlez du loup, et vous en verrez sa queue [Fr.], speak of the wolf, and you will see his tail; talk of the devil and he will appear.

parlez peu et bien si vous voulez qu'on vous regarde comme un homme de mérite [Fr.], speak little and well if you would be esteemed as a man of merit.

par manière d'acquit [Fr.], by way of acquittal; for form's sake.

par negotiis, neque supra [L.], neither above nor below his business.

par nobile fratrum [L.], a noble pair of brothers; two just alike; the one as good or as bad as the other.

parole d'honneur [Fr.], word of honor.

par oneri [L.], equal to the burden.

par parenthèse [Fr.], by way of parenthesis.

par pari refero [L.], I return like for like; tit for tat.

par précaution [Fr.], by way of precaution.

par privilège [Fr.], by privilege; license.

par rapport [Fr.], by reason of.

pars adversa [L.], the opposite party.

par signe de mépris [Fr.], as a token of contempt.

pars pro toto [L.], part for the whole.

parti [Fr.], a party; person.

particeps criminis [L.], an accomplice in a crime.

particulier [Fr.], a private person.—**en particulier,** in private.

partout [Fr.], everywhere; in all directions.

parturiunt montes, nascetur ridiculus mus [L.], the

mountains are in travail, a ridiculous mouse will be brought forth.

parva componere magnis [L.], to compare small things with great.

parva leves capiunt animas [L.], trifles captivate small minds.

parvenu [Fr.], a person of low origin who has risen suddenly to wealth or position.

parvum parva decent [L.], trifles become a little person.

pas [Fr.], a step.

pas à pas on va bien loin [Fr.], step by step one goes a long way.

passé [Fr.], past; out of date.

passe-partout [Fr.], a master-key, passport.

pas seul [Fr.], a dance performed by one person.

passim [L.], everywhere; throughout the book or writing referred to.

pasticcio [It.], patchwork.

paté de foie gras [Fr.], goose-liver paste.

pater patriæ [L.], father of his country.

patience passe science [Fr.], patience surpasses knowledge.

pâtisserie [Fr.], pastry; pastry shop.

patois [Fr.], a provincial dialect; the language of the lower classes.

patres conscripti [L.], the conscript fathers; Roman senators.

patriis virtutibus [L.], by ancestral virtues.

paucis verbis [L.], in a few words.

paulo majora canamus [L.], let us sing of somewhat higher themes.

pax in bello [L.], peace in war.

pax vobiscum [L.], peace be with you.

peccavi [L.], I have sinned.

peine forte et dure [Fr.], strong and severe punishment; a kind of judicial torture.

penchant [Fr.], a strong liking.

pensée [Fr.], a thought.

penetralia [L.], secret or inmost recesses.

per [L.], by; by means of; through.

per [It.], for; through; by.

per ambages [L.], by circuitous ways; hence, by allegory; figuratively; metaphorically.

per angusta ad augusta [L.], through trials to triumphs.

per annum [L.], by the year; annually.

per aspera ad astra [L.], through rough ways to the stars; through suffering to renown.

per baroniam [L.], by right of barony.

per capita [L.], by the head or poll.

per centum [L.], by the hundred.

per contante [It.], for cash.

per conto [It.], upon account.

per contra [L.], contrariwise.

per curiam [L.], by the court.

per diem [L.], by the day; daily.

perdu [Fr.], lost.

pereant qui ante nos nostra dixerunt [L.], deuce take those who said our good things before us.

père de famille [Fr.], the father of a family.

pereunt et imputantur [L.], they (the hours) pass away and are laid to our charge.

per fas et nefas [L.], through right and wrong.

perfervidum ingenium Scotorum [L.], the intense earnestness of Scotsmen.

per gradus [L.], step by step.

periculum in mora [L.], there is danger in delay.

per interim [L.], in the meantime.

perjuria ridet amantium Jupiter [L.], at lovers' perjuries Jove laughs.

per mare per terras [L.], through sea and land.

per mese [It.], by the month.

permitte divis cetera [L.], leave the rest to the gods.

per pares [L.], by one's peers.

per più strade si va a Roma [It.], there are many roads to Rome.

per saltum [L.], by a leap or jump.

per se [L.], by, or in, itself.

per stirpes [L.], by stocks.

per troppo dibatter la verità si perde [It.], truth is lost by too much controversy.

per viam [L.], by the way of.

petit chaudron, grandes oreilles [Fr.], little pitchers (have) big ears.

petitio principii [L.], a begging of the question.

petit-maître [Fr.], a fop.

peu-à-peu [Fr.], little by little; by degrees.

peu de chose [Fr.], a little thing; a trifle.

peu de gens savent être vieux [Fr.], few people know how to be old.

pezzo [It.], a piece; an Italian coin.

piccolo [It.], small.

pièce de résistance [Fr.], the chief dish of a meal; something substantial by way of entertainment; a substantial joint of meat.

pied-à-terre [Fr.], a resting-place; a temporary lodging.

pietra mossa non fa muschio [It.], a rolling stone gathers no moss.

pinxit [L.], he, or she, painted it.

pis aller [Fr.], the worst or last shift.

piuttosto mendicante che ignorante [It.], better be a beggar than be ignorant.

place aux dames [Fr.], make way for the ladies.

plebs [L.], common people; the multitude.

plein de soi-même [Fr.], full of himself.

plein pouvoir [Fr.], full power or authority.

pleno jure [L.], with full power or authority.

plus aloes quam mellis habet [L.], he has more gall than honey; sarcastic wit.

plus on est de fous, plus on rit [Fr.], the more fools, the more fun.

plus sage que les sages [Fr.], wiser than the wise.

poca barba, poca verguenza [Sp.], little beard, little shame.

poca roba, poco pensiero [It.], little wealth, little care.

poco a poco [It.], little by little.

poeta nascitur, non fit [L.], the poet is born, not made; nature, not study, must form the poet.

point d'appui [Fr.], point of support; prop.

poisson d'avril [Fr.], April fool (lit. April fish).

pondere, non numero [L.], by weight not by number.

pons asinorum [L.], an ass's bridge; a name given to the fifth proposition of the first book of Euclid.

populus vult decipi [L.], the populace wishes to be deceived.

possunt quia posse videntur [L.], they are able because they think they are.

post bellum auxilium [L.], aid after the war.

post cineres gloria venit [L.], after death comes glory.

post equitem sedet atra cura [L.], behind the rider sits black care.

poste restante [Fr.], to be left at the post office till called for: applied to letters.

post hoc ergo propter hoc [L.], after this, therefore on account of this; a non sequitur in argument.

post nubila jubila [L.], after sorrow joy.

post nubila Phœbus [L.], after clouds comes Phœbus, or the sun.

post obitum [L.], after death.

pour acquit [Fr.], received payment; paid; written at the bottom of a discharged account.

pour comble de bonheur [Fr.], as the height of happiness.

pour couper court [Fr.], to cut the matter short.

pour encourager les autres [Fr.], to encourage the others.

pour faire rire [Fr.], to excite laughter.

pour faire visite [Fr.], to pay a visit.

pour passer le temps [Fr.], to pass away the time.

pour prende congé [Fr.], to take leave: often abbreviated p.p.c. on visiting-cards.

pour se faire valoir [Fr.], to make himself of value.

pour tout potage [Fr.], all that one gets; all that a person is allotted.

pour y parvenir [Fr.], to attain the object.

præcognita [L.], things previously known.

præmonitus, præmunitus [L.], forewarned, forearmed.

præscriptum [L.], a thing prescribed.

prendre la balle au bond [Fr.], to catch the ball as it bounds.

prendre la lune avec les dents [Fr.], to take the moon by the teeth; to aim at impossibilities.

prends moi tel que je suis [Fr.], take me just as I am.

prenez garde [Fr.], beware; look out.

presto maturo, presto marcio [It.], soon ripe, soon rotten.

prêt d'accomplir [Fr.], ready to accomplish.

prêt pour mon pays [Fr.], ready for my country.

preux chevalier [Fr.], a brave knight.

prima donna [It.], the chief female vocalist. See in Dict.

primæ viæ [L.], the first passages; the chief canals of the body.

prima facie [L.], on first sight. See in Dict.

primo [L.], in the first place.

primo uomo [It.], the chief actor or vocalist.

primum mobile [L.], the souce of motion, the mainspring.

primus inter pares [L.], first among his peers.

principia, non homines [L.], principles, not men.

principiis obsta [L.], resist the beginnings.

prior tempore, prior jure [L.], first in time, first by right; first come, first served.

pro aris et focis [L.], for our altars and our hearths; for civil and religious liberty.

probatum est [L.], it is proved.

probitas laudatur, et alget [L.], honesty is praised, and is left to starve.

pro bono publico [L.], for the good of the public.

pro confesso [L.], as if conceded.

procul, O procul este, profani [L.], far, far hence, O ye profane!

pro Deo et ecclesia [L.], for God and the church.

pro et contra [L.], for and against.

profanum vulgus [L.], the profane rabble.

pro forma [L.], for the sake of form.

pro hac vice [L.], for this occasion.

proh pudor! [L.], for shame!

projet de loi [Fr.], a legislative bill.

prolétaire [Fr.], member of the lower classes; workingman.

pro memoria [L.], for a memorial.

pro nunc [L.], for the present.

propaganda [L.], the propagation of principles or views. See in Dict.

pro patria [L.], for our country.

propria quæ maribus [L.], things appropriate to males, men, or husbands (a fragment of a rule in old Latin grammars).

propriétaire [Fr.], an owner or proprietor.

pro rata [L.], according to rate or proportion.

pro rege, lege, et grege [L.], for the king, the law, and the people.

pro re nata [L.], for a particular emergency arising.

pro salute animæ [L.], for the health of the soul.

prosit! [L.], a health to you!

pro tanto [L.], for so much; for as far as it goes.

protégé [Fr.], one under the protection of another.

pro virili parte [L.], according to one's power; with all one's might.

prudens futuri [L.], thoughtful of the future.

publice [L.], publicly.

publiciste [Fr.], one who writes on national laws and customs; a publicist.

pugnis et calcibus [L.], with fists and heels; with all one's might.

punctum saliens [L.], a salient or prominent point.

Punica fides [L.], Punic or Carthaginian faith; treachery.

Q

quæ fuerunt vitia, mores sunt [L.], what were once vices are now customs.

quæ nocent, docent [L.], things which injure, instruct; we learn by what we suffer.

qualis ab incepto [L.], the same as at the beginning.

qualis rex, talis grez [L.], like king, like people.

qualis vita, finis ita [L.], as life is, so is its end.

quam diu se bene gesserit [L.], during good behavior.

quand même [Fr.], even though; nevertheless.

quand on ne trouve pas son repos en soi-même, il est inutile de le chercher ailleurs [Fr.], when a man finds no repose in himself, it is futile for him to seek it elsewhere.

quand on voit la chose, on la croit [Fr.], that which one sees he gives credit to.

quandoque bonus dormitat Homerus [L.], even good Homer sometimes nods; the wisest make mistakes.

quanti est sapere [L.], how desirable is wisdom or knowledge.

quantum libet [L.], as much as you please.

quantum meruit [L.], as much as he deserved.

quantum mutatus ab illo! [L.], how changed from what he once was!

quantum suffit [L.], as much as suffices; a sufficient quantity.

quantum vis [L.], as much as you wish.

que la nuit parait longue à la douleur qui veille! [Fr.], to sleepless grief how long must night appear.

quelque chose [Fr.], something; a trifle.

quelqu'un [Fr.], somebody.

quem deus vult perdere prius dementat [L.], whom a god would destroy he first drives mad.

quem di diligunt adolescens moritur [L.], he whom the gods love dies young.

querelle d'Allemand [Fr.], a German quarrel; a drunken affray.

qui a bu boira [Fr.], the tippler will go on tippling.

quid faciendum? [L.], what is to be done?

qui docet discit [L.], he who teaches learns.

quid pro quo [L.], one thing for another; tit for tat; value received.

quid rides? [L.], why do you laugh?

quién sabe? [Sp.] who knows?

quieta non movere [L.], not to disturb things at rest.

qui facit per alium facit per se [L.], he who acts by another acts by himself.

qu'il soit comme il est desiré [Fr.], let it be as desired.

qui m'aime, aime mon chien [Fr.], love me, love my dog.

qui n'a point de sens à trente ans, n'en aura jamais [Fr.], he who has no sense when thirty years old, will never have any.

qui n'a santé n'a rien [Fr.], he who lacks health lacks everything.

qui nimium probat, nihil probat [L.], he proves nothing who proves too much.

qui non proficit, deficit [L.], he who does not advance goes backward.

qui perd, péche [Fr.], he who loses, offends; an unsuccessful man is always deemed to be wrong.

quis custodiet ipsos custodes? [L.], who shall keep the keepers themselves?

qui s'excuse s'accuse [Fr.], he who excuses himself accuses himself.

qui tacet consentit [L.], he who is silent gives consent.

qui timide rogat, docet negare [L.], he who asks timidly invites denial.

qui transtulit sustinet [L.], he who transports, supports.

qui va là? [Fr.], who goes there?

qui vive? [Fr.], a challenge: "Who goes there?"

quoad hoc [L.], to this extent.

quo animo? [L.], with what intention?

quocunque jeceris stabit [L.], where-ever you throw it, it will stand.

quocunque modo [L.], in whatever manner.

quocunque nomine [L.], under whatever name.

quod avertat Deus! [L.], which may God avert!

quod bene notandum [L.], which may be especially noticed.

quod bonum, felix, faustumque sit! [L.], and may it be advantageous, fortunate, and favorable!

quod erat demonstrandum [L.], which was to be proved or demonstrated.

quod erat faciendum [L.], which was to be done.

quod non opus est, asse carum est [L.], what is not wanted (or is of no use to a person) is dear at a copper.

quod semper, quod ubique, quod ab omnibus [L.], what (has been believed) always, everywhere, by all.

quod vide [L.], which see; see that reference.

quo Fata vocant [L.], whither the Fates call.

quo jure [L.], by what right?

quo pax et gloria ducunt [L.], where peace and glory lead.

quorum pars magna fui [L.], of whom, or which, I was an important part.

quot homines, tot sententiæ [L.], many men, many minds.

R

raconteur [Fr.], a teller of stories.

railleur [Fr.], a jester; one addicted to raillery.

raison d'état [Fr.], a reason of state.

raison d'être [Fr.], the reason for a thing's existence.

rappel [Fr.], a recall.

rapprochement [Fr.], the act of bringing together.

rara avis in terris, nigroque simillima cygno [L.], a rare bird on earth, and very like a black swan (formerly believed to be nonexistent).

rari nantes in gurgite vasto [L.], swimming here and there on the vast sea.

Rathaus [G.], a townhall.

ratione soli [L.], as regards the soil.

re [L.], in the matter of; in reference to the question of.

Realschule [G.], a real school; a secondary German school giving an education more in modern subjects than in classics.

réchauffé [Fr.], lit. something warmed up; hence old literary material worked up into a new form.

recoje tu heno mientras que el sol luziere [Sp.], make hay while the sun shines.

reconnaissance [Fr.], survey. See Dict.

recte et suaviter [L.], justly and agreeably.

rectus in curia [L.], upright in court; with clean hands.

reçu [Fr.], received; a receipt.

recueil [Fr.], a collection.

reculer pour mieux sauter [Fr.], to go back in order to leap the better.

rédacteur [Fr.], an editor; one who edits or gives literary form to something.

redolet lucerna [L.], it smells of the lamp; it is a labored production.

reductio ad absurdum [L.], the reducing of a supposition or hypothesis to an absurdity.

regium donum [L.], a royal gift; the former annual grant of public money to the Presbyterian ministers of Ireland. See in Dict.

re infecta [L.], the business being unfinished.

relâche [Fr.], intermission; relaxation; respite.

relata refero [L.], I repeat the story as it was given me.

religieux [Fr.], a monk or friar. See in Dict.

religio loci [L.], the religious spirit of the place.

rem acu tetigisti [L.], you have touched the matter with a needle; you have hit the thing exactly.

rem facias, rem; recte si possis, si non quocumque modo rem [L.], make money, money; honestly if you can, if not, make it anyhow.

remisso animo [L.], with mind remiss or listless.

remis velisque [L.], with oars and sails; using every endeavor.

remuda de pasturaje haze bizerros gordos [Sp.], change of pasture makes fat calves.

renascentur [L.], they will be born again.

rencontre [Fr.], an encounter; a hostile meeting.

renommée [Fr.], renown; celebrity.

renovate animos [L.], renew your courage.

renovato nomine [L.], by a revived name.

rentes [Fr.], funds; stocks.

répertoire [Fr.], a list; a stock of songs, dramas, etc., already prepared. See in Dict.

répondez s'il vous plait [Fr.], send an answer if you please.

répondre en Normand [Fr.], to give an evasive answer.

requiescat in pace [L.], may he (or she) rest in peace; **requiescant,** may they.

rerum primordia [L.], the first elements of things.

res angusta domi [L.], narrow circumstances at home.

res est sacra miser [L.], a sufferer is a sacred thing.

res gestæ [L.], things done; exploits.

res judicata [L.], a case or suit already settled.

respice finem [L.], look to the end.

respublica [L.], the commonwealth.

résumé [Fr.], a summary or abstract. See in Dict.

resurgam [L.], I shall rise again.

revanche [Fr.], revenge.

revenons à nos moutons [Fr.], let us return to our sheep; let us return to our subject.

re vera [L.], in truth; in actual fact.

revoir [Fr.], a meeting again; **au revoir,** good-bye until we meet again.

rez-de-chaussée [Fr.], the ground-floor.

rideau d'entr'acte [Fr.], the scene let down between the acts of a play.

ridere in stomacho [L.], to laugh secretly; to laugh in one's sleeve.

ride si sapis [L.], laugh, if you are wise.

rien n'arrive pour rien [Fr.], nothing comes for nothing.

rien n'est beau que le vrai [Fr.], there is nothing beautiful except the truth.

rifacimento [It.], a remaking. See Dict.

rigueur [Fr.], strictness; strict etiquette.

rira bien, qui rira le dernier [Fr.], he laughs well who laughs last.

rire entre cuir et chair [Fr.]
rire sous cape [Fr.] } to laugh in one's sleeve.

risum teneatis, amici? [L.], could you keep from laughing, friends?

rixatur de lana caprina [L.], he contends about goat's wool; he quarrels about trifles.

robe de chambre [Fr.], a morning-gown or dressing-gown.

robe de nuit [Fr.], a nightgown.

rôle [Fr.], a character represented on the stage. See in Dict.

rôle d'équipage [Fr.], the list of a ship's crew.

roué [Fr.], a man of fashion devoted to sensual pleasure. See in Dict.

rouge et noir [Fr.], red and black, a game of chance. See in Dict.

ruat cælum [L.], let the heavens fall.

rudis indigestaque moles [L.], a rude and undigested mass.

ruit mole sua [L.], it falls to ruin by its own weight.

ruse contre ruse [Fr.], trick against trick; diamond cut diamond.

ruse de guerre [Fr.], a stratagem of war.

rus in urbe [L.], the country in town.

rusticus expectat dum defluat amnis at ille labitur et labetur in omne volubilis ævum [L.], the rustic waits till the river flows past (and ceases to flow), but it glides on and will glide for all time.

S

sa boule est demeurée [Fr.], his bowl has stopped short of the mark; he has failed in his object.

sabreur [Fr.], a brave soldier distinguished for his use of his sabre.

sæpe stylum vertas [L.], often turn the style or pen (and make erasures with the blunt end on the waxen tablets); correct freely (if you wish to produce good literature).

saggio fanciullo è chi conosce il suo vero padre [It.], he is a wise child who knows his own father.

sal Atticum [L.], Attic salt; i.e. wit.

salle [Fr.], a hall; **salle à manger**, a dining-room; **salle de batailles**, a gallery or room decorated with pictures of martial subjects; **salle de réception**, a room in which visitors are received.

salon [Fr.], a saloon or drawing-room; a picture gallery.

salus populi suprema lex est [L.], the welfare of the people is the supreme law.

salve! [L.], hail!

salvo jure [L.], the right being safe; without prejudice to one's rights.

salvo pudore [L.], without offence to modesty.

salvo sensu [L.], the sense being preserved.

sang-froid [Fr.], coolness; indifference. See in Dict.

sang pur [Fr.], pure blood; of aristocratic birth.

sans cérémonie [Fr.], without ceremony or formality.

sans-culotte [Fr.], without breeches. See in Dict.

sans Dieu rien [Fr.], nothing without God.

sans façon [Fr.], without ceremony.

sans pain, sans vin, amour n'est rien [Fr.], without bread, without wine, love is naught.

sans pareil [Fr.], without equal.

sans peine [Fr.], without difficulty.

sans peur et sans reproche [Fr.], without fear and without reproach.

sans rime et sans raison [Fr.], without rhyme or reason.

sans souci [Fr.], without care.

sans tache [Fr.], without spot, stainless.

santé [Fr.], health; **en bonne santé**, in good health; **maison de santé**, a private hospital.

sapere aude [L.], dare to be wise.

sartor resartus [L.], the botcher repatched; the tailor re-tailored or mended.

sat cito, si sat bene [L.], soon enough done, if well enough done.

satis dotata si bene morata [L.], well enough dowered, if well principled.

satis eloquentiæ, sapientiæ parum [L.], eloquence enough, but little wisdom.

satis superque [L.], enough, and more than enough.

satis verborum [L.], enough of words; no more need be said.

sat pulchra, si sat bona [L.], she is handsome enough, if good enough.

sauce piquante [Fr.], a pungent sauce; a relish.

sauf et sain [Fr.], safe and sound.

sauve qui peut [Fr.], let him save himself who can.

savoir faire [Fr.], the knowing how to act; tact.

savoir vivre [Fr.], good-breeding; refined manners.

scandalum magnatum [L.], speech or writing defamatory to dignitaries.

scire facias [L.], cause it to be known. See in Dict.

scribendi recte sapere est et principium et fons [L.], the principle and source of good writing is to possess good sense.

scribimus indocti doctique [L.], learned and unlearned, we all write.

sdegno d'amante poco dura [It.], a lover's anger is short-lived.

séance [Fr.], See in Dict.

secrétaire [Fr.], a secretary; **secrétaire d'état**, a secretary of state.

secret et hardi [Fr.], secret and bold.

secundum artem [L.], according to art or rule; scientifically.

secundum naturam [L.], according to nature.

secundum ordinem [L.], in due order.

secundum usum [L.], according to practice.

sed hæc hactenus [L.], but so far, this will suffice.

seigneur [Fr.], a lord, nobleman; a seignior (which see in Dict.).

se jeter dans l'eau de peur de la pluie [Fr.], to cast oneself into the water out of fear of rain.

selon les règles [Fr.], according to rule.

selon lui [Fr.], according to him.

semel abbas, semper abbas [L.], once an abbot, always an abbot.

semel et simul [L.], once and together.

semel insanivimus omnes [L.], we have all, at some time, been mad.

semel pro semper [L.], once for all.

semper avarus eget [L.], the avaricious is always in want.

semper fidelis [L.], always faithful.

semper idem [L.], always the same.

semper paratus [L.], always ready.

semper timidum scelus [L.], guilt is always timid.

semper vivit in armis [L.], he lives always in arms.

sempre il mal non vien per nuocere [It.], misfortune does not always come to injure.

senatus consultum [L.], a decree of the senate.

senex bis puer [L.], the old man is twice a child.

se non è vero, è ben trovato [It.], if not true, it is cleverly invented (or fabricated).

sensu bono [L.], in a good sense.

sensu malo [L.], in a bad sense.

sequiturque patrem non passibus æquis [L.], he follows his father, but not with equal steps.

sero sed serio [L.], late, but seriously.

sero venientibus ossa [L.], those who come late shall have the bones.

serus in cælum redeas [L.], late may you return to heaven; may you live long.

servabo fidem [L.], I will keep faith.

servare modum [L.], to keep within bounds.

servus servorum Dei [L.], a servant of the servants of God.

sesquipedalia verba [L.], words a foot and a half long.

sic eunt fata hominum [L.], thus go the fates of men.

sic itur ad astra [L.], such is the way to the stars, or to immortality.

sic passim [L.], so here and there throughout; so everywhere.

sic semper tyrannis [L.], ever so to tyrants.

sic transit gloria mundi [L.], thus passes away the glory of this world.

sicut ante [L.], as before.

sicut patribus, sit Deus nobis [L.], as with our fathers, so may God be with us.

sic volo sic jubeo; stat pro ratione voluntas [L.], thus I will, thus I command; let my will stand for a reason.

sic vos non vobis [L.], thus you labor but not for yourselves.

si Deus nobiscum, quis contra nos? [L.], if God be with us, who shall stand against us?

si Dieu n'existait pas, il faudrait l'inventer [Fr.], if God did not exist, it would be necessary to invent him.

si diis placet [L.], if it pleases the gods.

siècle [Fr.], an age; **siècle d'or**, the golden age; **siècles des ténèbres**, the dark ages.

siesta [Sp.], a short nap during the heat of the day.

sile et philosophus esto [L.], be silent and pass for a philosopher.

silentium altum [L.], deep silence.

silent leges inter arma [L.], amidst arms, or in war, laws are silent, or disregarded.

similia similibus curantur [L.], like things are cured by like.

similis simili gaudet [L.], like is pleased with like.

si monumentum quæris circumspice [L.], if you seek his monument, look around you.

simplex munditiis [L.], elegant in simplicity.

sine cura [L.], without charge or care.

sine die [L.], without a day being appointed.

sine dubio [L.], without doubt.

sine mora [L.], without delay.

sine præjudicio [L.], without prejudice.

sine qua non [L.], without which, not.

si nous n'avions point de défauts, nous ne prendrions pas tant de plaisir à en remarquer dans les autres [Fr.], if we had no faults we should not take so much pleasure in remarking those of others.

si parva licet componere magnis [L.], if small things may be compared with great.

siste viator [L.], stop, traveler!

sit tibi terra levis [L.], light lie the earth upon thee.

sit ut est aut non sit [L.], let it be as it is, or not at all.

sit venia verbis [L.], may the words be excused.

si vis pacem, para bellum [L.], if you wish for peace, prepare for war.

sobriquet [Fr.], a nickname. See in Dict.

sœurs de charité [Fr.], sisters of charity.

soi-disant [Fr.], self-styled.

soi-même [Fr.], oneself.

sola nobilitas virtus [L.], virtue the only nobility.

solitudinem faciunt, pacem appellant [L.], they make a wilderness and call it peace.

sottise [Fr.], absurdity; foolishness.

sotto voce [It.], in an undertone.

soubrette [Fr.], a waiting-maid; an actress who plays the part of a waiting-maid, etc.

souffler le chaud et le froid [Fr.], to blow hot and cold.

sous tous les rapports [Fr.], in all respects or relations.

soyez ferme [Fr.], be firm; persevere.

spero meliora [L.], I hope for better things.

spes sibi quisque [L.], let every one hope in himself.

spirituel [Fr.], intellectual; witty.

splendide mendax [L.], nobly untruthful; untrue for a good object.

spolia optima [L.], the choicest of the spoils.

sponte sua [L.], of one's (or its) own accord.

spretæ injuria formæ [L.], the insult of despising her beauty.

stat magni nominis umbra [L.], he stands in the shadow of a mighty name.

stat pro ratione voluntas [L.], will stands in place of reason.

statu quo ante bellum [L.], in the state in which things were before the war.

status quo [L.], the state in which.

sta viator, heroem calcas [L.], halt, traveler, thou standest on a hero's dust.

stemmata quid faciunt? [L.], of what value are pedigrees?

sternitur alieno vulnere [L.], he is slain by a blow aimed at another.

stratum super stratum [L.], layer above layer.

studium immane loquendi [L.], an insatiable desire for talking.

Sturm und Drang [G.], storm and stress.

sua cuique voluptas [L.], every man has his own pleasures.

suaviter in modo, fortiter in re [L.], gentle in manner, resolute in execution (or action).

sub colore juris [L.], under color of law.

sub hoc signo vinces [L.], under this standard you will conquer.

sub judice [L.], still before the judge; under consideration.

sublata causa, tollitur effectus [L.], the cause being removed, the effect ceases.

sub pœna [L.], under a penalty.

sub prætexto juris [L.], under the pretext of justice.

sub rosa [L.], under the rose; secretly.

sub silentio [L.], in silence.

sub specie [L.], under the appearance of.

sub voce [L.], under such or such a word.

succès d'estime [Fr.], success of esteem; success with more prestige than profit.

sufre por saber y trabaja por tener [Sp.], suffer in order to be wise, and labor in order to have.

suggestio falsi [L.], suggestion of falsehood.

sui generis [L.], of its own or of a peculiar kind.

suivez raison [Fr.], follow reason.

summa summarum [L.], the sum total.

summum bonum [L.], the chief good.

summum jus, summa injuria [L.], the rigor of the law is the height of oppression.

sumptibus publicis [L.], at the public expense.

sum quod eris; fui quod es [L.], I am what you will be (dead), I was what you are (alive): inscription on tombstones.

sunt lacrimæ rerum [L.], there are tears for misfortune.

suo Marte [L.], by his own prowess.

suppressio veri, suggestio falsi [L.], a suppression of the truth

is the suggestion of a falsehood.

surgit amari aliquid [L.], something bitter arises.

sursum corda! [L.], lift up your hearts!

surtout pas de zèle! [Fr.], above all, no zeal!

suum cuique [L.], to each his own.

suus cuique mos [L.], every one has his particular habit.

T

tabagie [Fr.], a smoking-room.

table à manger [Fr.], a dining-table.

tableau vivant [Fr.], a living picture; the representation of some scene by groups of persons.

table d'hôte [Fr.], a public dinner at a hotel; a meal at a fixed price.

tabula rasa [L.], a smooth or blank tablet.

tâche sans tache [Fr.], a work (or task) without a stain.

tædium vitæ [L.], weariness of life.

taisez-vous [Fr.], be quiet; hold your tongue.

tam Marte quam Minerva [L.], as much by Mars as by Minerva; as much by courage as by skill.

tangere vulnus [L.], to touch the wound.

tantæne animis cælestibus iræ? [L.], can such anger dwell in heavenly minds?

tant mieux [Fr.], so much the better.

tanto buon che val niente [It.], so good as to be good for nothing.

tant pis [Fr.], so much the worse.

tant s'en faut [Fr.], far from it.

tantum vidit Virgilium [L.], he merely saw Virgil; he only looked on the great man.

Te, Deum, laudamus [L.], we praise Thee, O God (or rather, as God).

te judice [L.], you being the judge.

tel brille au second rang qui s'éclipse au premier [Fr.], a man may shine in the second rank, who would be eclipsed in the first.

tel est notre plaisir [Fr.], such is our pleasure.

tel maître, tel valet [Fr.], like master, like man.

tel père, tel fils [Fr.], like father, like son.

telum imbelle, sine ictu [L.], a feeble weapon thrown without effect.

tempora mutantur, nos et mutamur in illis [L.], the times are changing and we with them.

tempori parendum [L.], we must yield to the times.

tempus edax rerum [L.], time the devourer of all things.

tempus fugit [L.], time flies.

tempus ludendi [L.], the time for play.

tempus omnia revelat [L.], time reveals all things.

tenax propositi [L.], tenacious of his purpose.

tenez [Fr.], take it; hold; hark; look here.

tentanda via est [L.], a way must be attempted.

teres atque rotundus [L.], smooth and round; polished and complete.

terminus ad quem [L.], the term or limit to which.

terminus a quo [L.], the term or limit from which.

terræ filius [L.], a son of the earth.

terra firma [L.], solid earth; a secure foothold.

terra incognita [L.], an unknown or unexplored region.

tertium quid [L.], a third something; a nondescript.

tête de famille [Fr.], the head of the house; paterfamilias.

tête de fou ne blanchit jamais [Fr.], the head of a fool never becomes white.

tibi seris, tibi metis [L.], you sow for yourself, you reap for yourself.

tiens à la vérité [Fr.], maintain the truth.

tiens ta foi [Fr.], keep thy faith.

tiers-état [Fr.], the third estate. See in Dict.

timeo Danaos et dona ferentes [L.], I fear the Greeks even when they bring gifts.

tirailleur [Fr.], a sharpshooter; skirmisher. See in Dict.

toga virilis [L.], the manly toga; the dress of manhood.

to kalon [Gr.], the beautiful; the chief good.

tomava la por rosa mas devenia cardo [Sp.], I took her for a rose but she proved to be a thistle.

tombé des nues [Fr.], fallen from the clouds.

ton [Fr.], taste; fashion; high life.

to prepon [Gr.], the becoming (or proper).

tôt gagné, tôt gaspillé [Fr.], soon gained, soon spent.

tot homines, quot sententiæ [L.], so many men, so many opinions.

totidem verbis [L.], in just so many words.

toties quoties [L.], as often as.

totis viribus [L.], with all his might.

toto cælo [L.], by the whole heavens; diametrically opposite.

tôt ou tard [Fr.], sooner or later.

totus, teres, atque rotundus [L.], complete, polished, and rounded.

toujours perdrix [Fr.], always partridges; always the same thing over again.

toujours prêt [Fr.], always ready.

tour de force [Fr.], a feat of strength or skill.

tourner casaque [Fr.], to turn one's coat; to change sides.

tous frais faits [Fr.], all expenses paid.

tout-à-fait [Fr.], wholly; entirely.

tout-à-l'heure [Fr.], instantly.

tout au contraire [Fr.], on the contrary.

tout à vous [Fr.], wholly yours.

tout bien ou rien [Fr.], the whole or nothing.

tout comprendre est tout pardonner [Fr.], to understand all is to forgive all.

tout court [Fr.], quite short; abruptly.

tout de même [Fr.], quite the same.

tout de suite [Fr.], immediately.

tout ensemble [Fr.], the whole together. See in Dict.

tout frais fait [Fr.], all expenses paid.

tout le monde est sage aprés le coup [Fr.], everybody is wise after the event.

tout mon possible [Fr.], everything in my power.

tout vient de Dieu [Fr.], all things come from God.

traducteur [Fr.], a translator.

traduction [Fr.], a translation.

traduttori traditori [It.], translators are traitors.

trahit sua quemque voluptas [L.], every one is attracted by his own liking.

transeat in exemplum [L.], may it pass into an example or precedent.

travaux forcés [Fr.], hard labor.

tria juncta in uno [L.], three joined in one.

tristesse [Fr.], depression of spirits.

Troja fuit [L.], Troy was; Troy is no more.

Tros Tyriusque mihi nullo discrimine agetur [L.], Trojan and Tyrian—there shall be no distinction so far as I am concerned.

trottoir [Fr.], the pavement; the footway on the side of a street or road.

trouvaille [Fr.], sudden good fortune; a godsend.

truditur dies die [L.], one day is pressed onward by another.

tu ne cede malis [L.], do not thou yield to evils.

tu quoque [L.], thou also; you're another.

tu quoque, Brute! [L.], thou also, Brutus!

tutor et ultor [L.], protector and avenger.

tutte le strade conducono a Roma [It.], all roads lead to Rome.

tuum est [L.], it is your own.

U

uberrima fides [L.], superabounding faith.

ubi bene, ibi patria [L.], where it is well, there is one's country.

ubi jus incertum, ibi jus nullum [L.], where the law is uncertain, there is no law.

ubi lapsus? [L.], where have I fallen?

ubi libertas, ibi patria [L.], where liberty is, there is my country.

ubi mel, ibi apes [L.], where honey is, there are the bees.

ubique [L.], everywhere.

ubique patriam reminisci [L.], to remember our country everywhere.

ubi supra [L.], where above mentioned.

Übung macht den Meister [G.], practice makes the master; practice makes perfect.

ultima ratio regum [L.], the last argument of kings; war.

ultima Thule [L.], remotest Thule; some far distant region.

ultimus Romanorum [L.], the last of the Romans.

ultra licitum [L.], beyond what is allowable.

ultra vires [L.], transcending authority.

una scopa nuova spazza bene [It.], a new broom sweeps clean.

una voce [L.], with one voice, unanimously.

una volta furfante e sempre furfante [It.], once a knave, always a knave.

un bienfait n'est jamais perdu [Fr.], an act of kindness is never lost.

un cabello hace sombra [Sp.], a single hair makes a shadow.

und so weiter [G.], and so forth.

une affaire flambée [Fr.], a gone case.

une fois n'est pas coutume [Fr.], one act does not constitute a habit.

un fait accompli [Fr.], an accomplished fact.

unguibus et rostro [L.], with claws and beak; tooth and nail.

unguis in ulcere [L.], a claw in the wound.

un je servirai [Fr.], one I will serve.

uno animo [L.], with one mind; unanimously.

un sot à triple étage [Fr.], an egregious fool.

un sot trouve toujours un plus sot qui l'admire [Fr.], a fool always finds a greater fool to admire him.

unter vier Augen [G.], under four eyes; between ourselves.

urbem lateritiam invenit, marmoream reliquit [L.], he (Augustus) found the city (Rome) brick, and left it marble.

urbi et orbi [L.], to the city (Rome) and the world.

usque ad aras [L.], to the very altars; to the last extremity.

usque ad nauseam [L.], so as to induce disgust.

usus loquendi [L.], usage in speaking.

ut ameris, amabilis esto [L.], that you may be loved, be lovable.

ut apes geometriam [L.], as bees practice geometry.

utcunque placuerit Deo [L.], as it shall please God.

utile dulci [L.], the useful with the pleasant.

utinam noster esset [L.], would that he were of our party.

ut infra [L.], as below.

uti possidetis [L.], as you now possess; each retaining what he at present holds.

ut pignus amicitiæ [L.], as a pledge of friendship.

ut prosim [L.], that I may do good.

ut quocunque paratus [L.], prepared for every event.

ut supra [L.], as above stated.

V—W—Z

vacuus cantat coram latrone viator [L.], the traveler with an empty purse sings in presence of the highwayman.

vade in pace [L.], go in peace.

væ victis [L.], woe to the vanquished.

vale (sing), **valete** (pl.) [L.], farewell.

valeat quantum valere potest [L.], let it pass for what it is worth.

valet anchora virtus [L.], virtue serves as an anchor.

valet de chambre [Fr.], a personal attendant; a body-servant.

valet de place [Fr.], a guide for visitors to a place.

valete et plaudite [L.], good-by and applaud us; said by Roman actors at the end of a piece.

variæ lectiones [L.], various readings.

variorum notæ [L.], the notes of various commentators.

varium et mutabile semper femina [L.], woman is ever a changeful and capricious thing.

vaudeville [Fr.], a ballad; a comic opera. See in Dict.

vaurien [Fr.], a worthless fellow.

vedi Napoli e poi muori [It.], see Naples and then die.

vehimur in altum [L.], we are carried out into the deep.

velis et remis [L.], with sails and oars; by every possible means.

vel prece, vel pretio [L.], with either entreaty or payment; for love or money.

veluti in speculum [L.], even as in a mirror.

venalis populus, venalis curia patrum [L.], the people are venal, and the senate is equally venal.

venenum in auro bibitur [L.], poison is drunk from golden vessels.

venia necessitati datur [L.], indulgence is granted to necessity; necessity has no law.

venienti occurrite morbo [L.], meet the coming of the disease; prevention is better than cure.

venit summa dies et ineluctabile tempus [L.], the last day has come, and the inevitable doom.

veni, vidi, vici [L.], I came, I saw, I conquered.

ventis secundis [L.], with favoring winds.

ventre à terre [Fr.], with belly to the ground; at full speed.

vera incessu patuit dea [L.], the real goddess was made manifest by her walk.

vera pro gratiis [L.], truth before favor.

vera prosperità è non necessità [It.], it is true prosperity to have no want.

verbatim et litteratim [L.], word for word and letter for letter.

verbum sat sapienti [L.], a word is enough for a wise man.

verdad es verde [Sp.], truth is green.

veritas odium parit [L.], truth begets hatred.

veritas prevalebit [L.], truth will prevail.

veritas vincit [L.], truth conquers.

veritatis simplex oratio est [L.], the language of truth is simple.

vérité sans peur [Fr.], truth without fear.

ver non semper viret [L.], spring is not always green; as a punning motto of the Vernons, Vernon always flourishes.

vestigia nulla retrorsum [L.], no returning footsteps; no traces backward.

vexata quæstio [L.], a disputed question.

via [L.], by way of. See in Dict.

via crucis, via lucis [L.], the way of the cross, the way of light.

via media [L.], a middle course.

via militaris [L.], a military road.

via trita, via tuta [L.], the beaten path is the safe path.

vice [L.], in the place of. **Vice versa.** See in Dict.

vide et crede [L.], see and believe.

videlicet [L.], namely.

video meliora proboque deteriora sequor [L.], I see and approve the better things, I follow the worse.

videtur [L.], it appears.

vide ut supra [L.], see what is stated above.

vidi tantum [L.], I merely saw him.

vi et armis [L.], by force and arms; by main force; by violence.

vigilate et orate [L.], watch and pray.

vigueur de dessus [Fr.], strength from on high.

vilius argentum est auro, virtutibus aurum [L.], silver is less valuable than gold, and gold than virtue.

vincit amor patriæ [L.], the love of our country prevails.

vincit omnia veritas [L.], truth conquers all things.

vincit qui patitur [L.], he who endures conquers.

vincit qui se vincit [L.], he conquers who conquers himself.

vinculum matrimonii [L.], the bond of marriage.

vindex injuriæ [L.], an avenger of injury.

vino dentro, senno fuori [It.], when the wine is in, the wit is out.

vin ordinaire [Fr.], a cheap wine commonly used in wine-growing countries.

vires acquirit eundo [L.], as it goes it acquires strength (originally said of rumor).

Virgilium vidi tantum [L.], Virgil (or some great man) I merely saw.

virginibus puerisque [L.], for girls and boys.

vir sapit qui pauca loquitor [L.], he is a wise man who says but little.

virtus in actione consistit [L.], virtue consists in action.

virtus in arduis [L.], virtue or courage in difficulties.

virtus incendit vires [L.], virtue kindles strength.

virtus laudatur, et alget [L.], virtue is praised, and suffers from cold.

virtus millia scuta [L.], virtue (or valor) is a thousand shields.

virtus semper viridis [L.], virtue is always green.

virtus sola nobilitat [L.], virtue alone ennobles.

virtus vincit invidiam [L.], virtue overcomes envy or hatred.

virtute et fide [L.], by or with virtue and faith.

virtute et labore [L.], by or with virtue and labor.

virtute non astutia [L.], by virtue (or valor), not by craft.

virtute non verbis [L.], by virtue, not by words.

virtute officii [L.], by virtue of office.

virtute quies [L.], rest or quietude in virtue.

virtute securus [L.], secure through virtue.

virtuti, non armis, fido [L.], I trust to virtue, not to weapons.

virtutis amore [L.], from love of virtue.

virtutis fortuna comes [L.], fortune is the companion of valor or virtue.

virum volitare per ora [L.], to hover on men's lips; to be in everybody's mouth.

vis-à-vis [Fr.], opposite; face to face.

vis comica [L.], comic power or talent.

vis conservatrix naturæ [L.], the preservative power of nature.

vis consili expers mole rui sua [L.], strength without judgment falls by its own might.

vis inertiæ [L.], the power of inertia; dead resistance to force applied.

vis medicatrix naturæ [L.], the healing power of nature.

vis unita fortior [L.], united power is stronger.

vis vitæ [L.], the vigor of life.

vita brevis, ars longa [L.], life is short, art is long.

vitæ via virtus [L.], virtue, the way of life.

vitam impendere vero [L.], to stake one's life for the truth.

vita sine litteris mors est [L.], life without literature is death.

vivat regina! [L.], long live the queen!

vivat respublica! [L.], long live the republic!

vivat rex! [L.], long live the king!

viva voce [L.], by the living voice; orally.

vive la bagatelle! [Fr.], long live folly!

vive le roi! [Fr.], long live the king!

vive memor leti [L.], live ever mindful of death.

vivere est cogitare [L.], to live is to think.

vive ut vivas [L.], live that you may live.

vive, vale [L.], farewell, be happy.

vivida vis animi [L.], the living force of the mind.

vivit post funera virtus [L.], virtue survives the grave.

vivre ce n'est pas respirer, c'est agir [Fr.], life consists not in breathing, but in doing.

vix ea nostra voco [L.], I scarcely call these things our own.

vixere fortes ante Agamemnona [L.], brave men lived before Agamemnon; great men lived in previous ages.

vogue la galère! [Fr.], let come what may!

voilà! [Fr.], behold! there is; there are.

voilà tout [Fr.], that's all.

voilà une autre chose [Fr.], that's another thing; that is quite a different matter.

voir le dessous des cartes [Fr.], to see the under side of the cards; to be in the secret.

volens et potens [L.], willing and able.

volenti non fit injuria [L.], no injustice is done to the consenting person.

volo, non valeo [L.], I am willing, but unable.

volventibus annis [L.], as the years roll by.

vota vita mea [L.], my life is devoted.

vous y perdrez vos pas [Fr.], you will there lose your steps or labor.

vox et præterea nihil [L.], a voice and nothing more; sound but no sense.

vox faucibus hæsit [L.], his voice, or words, stuck in his throat; he was dumb from astonishment.

vox populi, vox Dei [L.], the voice of the people is the voice of God.

vraisemblance [Fr.], probability; apparent truth.

vulgo [L.], commonly.

vulnus immedicabile [L.], an irreparable injury.

vultus animi janua et tabula [L.], the countenance is the portal and picture of the mind.

vultus est index animi [L.], the countenance is the index of the mind.

Wahrheit gegen Freund und Feind [G.], truth in spite of friend and foe.

Wahrheit und Dichtung. See **Dichtung.**

Zeitgeist [G.], the spirit of the age.

zonam perdidit [L.], he has lost his purse; he is in straitened circumstances.

zum Beispiel [G.], for example.

Given Names

Masculine Names

Aar·on (âr′ən, ar′ən) ? Enlightener. [< Hebrew]

A·bel (ā′bəl) Breath. [< Hebrew]

A·bi·el ā′bē·el, ə·bī′əl) Strong father. [< Hebrew]

Ab·ner (ab′nər) Father of light. [< Hebrew]

A·bra·ham (ā′brə·ham; *Fr.* à·brà·àm′; *Ger.* ä′brä·häm) Exalted father of multitudes. [< Hebrew] Also *Sp.* **A·bra·hán** (ä′brä·än′). Dims. **Abe, A′bie.**

A·bram (ā′brəm; *Fr.* à·brän′; *Sp.* ä· bräm′) Exalted Father. [< Hebrew]

Ab·sa·lom (ab′sə·ləm) The father is peace. [< Hebrew]

Ad·am (ad′əm) Red; man of red earth. [< Hebrew]

Ad·el·bert (ad′l·bûrt, ə·del′bûrt) Var. of ALBERT.

Ad·olph (ad′olf, ā′dolf) Noble wolf. [< Gmc.] Also *Dan., Du., Ger.* **A·dolf** (ä′dôlf); *Fr.* **A·dolphe** (à·dôlf′); *Ital., Sp.* **A·dol·fo** (*Ital.* ä·dôl′fō; *Sp.* ä·thôl′fō), *Lat.* **A·dol·phus** (ə·dol′fəs), *Pg.* **A·dol·pho** (ə·thôl′foo).

A·dri·an (ā′drē·ən) Of Adria: from the name of two Italian cities, or the Adriatic Sea. [< L] Also *Fr.* **A·dri·en** (à·drē·àn′), *Ital.* **A·dri·a·no** (ä′drē·ä′nō), *Lat.* **A·dri·a·nus** (ä′drē·ä′nəs).

Af·fon·so (ə·fôn′soo) Pg. form of ALPHONSO.

Al·an (al′ən) Handsome [< Celtic] Also **Al′lan, Al′len.** Dim. **Al.**

Al·a·ric (al′ə·rik) All-ruler. [< Gmc.]

Al·as·tair (al′əs·tər) Scot. contr. of ALEXANDER. Also **Al′is·ter.**

Al·ban (ôl′bən, al′-) White; of Alba: from the name of several Italian cities. [< L] Also **Al′bin.**

Al·bert (al′bûrt; *Fr.* àl·bâr′; *Ger., Sw.* äl′bert) Nobly bright. [< F < Gmc.] Also *Ital., Sp.* **Al·ber·to** (äl·ber′tō), *Lat.* **Al·ber·tus** (al·bûr′təs). Dims. **Al, Alb, Bert.**

Al·den (ôl′dən) Old friend. [OE]

Al·do (al′dō) Meaning uncertain. [< Gmc. or Hebrew]

Al·dous (ôl′dəs, al′-) From the old place. [OE] Also **Al′·dis, Al′dus.**

Al·ex·an·der (al′ig·zan′dər, -zän′-; *Du., Ger.* ä′lek·sän′dər) **Defender of men.** [< Gk.] Also *Fr.* **A·lex·an·dre** (à·lek·sän′dr′), *Modern Gk.* **A·le·xan·dros** (ä·lâ′ksän·drôs), *Ital.* **A·les·san·dro** (ä′läs·sän′drō), *Pg.* **A·le·xan·dre** (ə·lē·shann′·drə), *Russ.* **A·le·ksandr** (ə·lyi·ksän′dər), *Sp.* **A·le·jan·dro** (ä′lā·hän′drō). Dims. **Al′ec, Al′eck, Al′ex, San′der, San′dy.**

A·lex·is (ə·lek′sis) Defender. [< Gk.]

Al·fon·so (äl·fôn′sō) Ital. and Sp. form of ALPHONSO. Also *Dan., Ger.* **Al·fons** (äl′fôns).

Al·fred (al′frid; *Ger.* äl′frät; *Fr.* àl·fred′) Elf counselor; hence, wise. [OE] Also *Ital., Sp.* **Al·fre·do** (*Ital.* äl·frä′dō; *Sp.* äl·frä′thō), *Lat.* **Al·fre·dus** (al·frē′dəs) or **Al·u·re·dus** (al′yoo·rē′dəs). Dims **Al, Alf, Fred.**

Al·ger (al′jər) Noble spear. [< Gmc.]

Al·ger·non (al′jər·nən) Mustached. [< OF] Dims. **Al′gie, Al′gy** (al′jē).

Al·len (al′ən) Var. of ALAN. Also **Al′lan.**

A·lon·zo (ə·lon′zō) Var. of ALPHONSO. Also *Ital., Sp.* **A·lon·so** (ä·lôn′sō).

Al·o·y·sius (al′ō·ish′əs) Lat. form of LOUIS. Also **A·lois** (ə·lois′).

Al·phon·so (al·fon′zō, -sō) Nobly ready. [< Sp. < Gmc.] Also *Fr.* **Al·phonse** (àl·fôns′). Dims. **Al, Alph, Al′phy.**

Al·va (al′və; *Sp.* äl′vä) White. [< L]

Al·vin (al′vin) Noble friend. [< Gmc.] Also **Al·win** (al′·win; *Ger.* äl′vēn), **Al′van,** *Fr.* **A·luin** (à·lwaṅ′), *Ital.* **Al·vi·no** (äl·vē′nō), *Sp.* **A·lui·no** (ä·lwē′nō).

Am·brose (am′brōz) Divine; immortal. [< Gk.] Also *Fr.* **Am·broise** (äṅ·brwàz′), *Lat.* **Am·bro·si·us** (am·brō′zhē·əs, -zē·əs).

A·me·ri·go (ä′mä·rē′gō) Ital. form of EMERY.

A·mos (ā′məs) Burden. [< Hebrew]

An·a·tole (an′ə·tōl; *Fr.* à·nà·tôl′) Sunrise. [< Gk.]

An·drew (an′droo) Manly. [< Gk.] Also **An·dre·as** (an′·drē·əs, an·drē′əs; *Dan.* än·dres′; *Du., Ger.* än·drä′äs; *Lat.* an′drē·əs), *Fr.* **An·dré** (äṅ·drä′), *Ital.* **An·dre·a** (än·drâ′ä), *Russ.* **An·drei** (än·drā′), *Sp.* **An·drés** (än·drās′). Dims. **An′·dy, Drew.**

An·gus (ang′gəs) Singular. [< Celtic]

An·selm (an′selm; *Ger.* än′zelm) Divine helmet. [< Gmc.] Also **An·sel** (an′səl), *Fr.* **An·selme** (äṅ·selm′), *Ital., Sp.* **An·sel·mo** (än·sel′mō), *Lat.* **An·sel·mus** (än·sel′məs).

An·tho·ny (an′thə·nē,-tə-) Inestimable: from the name of a Roman clan. Also **An·to·ny** (an′tə·nē). *Fr.* **An·toine** (äṅ·twàn′) *Ger., Lat.* **An·to·ni·us** (*Ger.* än·tō′nē·ŏōs; *Lat.* an·tō′·nē·əs), *Ital., Sp.* **An·to·nio** (än·tô′nyō). Dim. **To′ny.**

An·ton (än′tōn) Dan., Du., Ger. and Sw. form of ANTHONY.

Ar·chi·bald (är′chə·bôld) Nobly bold. [< Gmc.] Dims. **Ar′chie, Ar′chy.**

Ar·mand (är′mänd; *Fr.* àr·män′) Fr. form of HERMAN.

Ar·min·i·us (är·min′ē·əs) Lat. form of HERMAN.

Ar·nold (är′nəld; *Ger.* är′nôlt) Eagle power. [< Gmc.] Also *Fr.* **Ar·naud** (àr·nō′), *Ital.* **Ar·nol·do** (är·nôl′dō), *Sp.* **Ar·nal·do** (är·näl′tho). Dims. **Arn, Ar′nie.**

Ae·te·mas (är′tə·məs) He of Artemis. [< Gk.] Also **Ar′·te·mus.**

Ar·thur (är′thər; *Fr.* àr·tōōr′) He-bear; from a totemic or royal title suggesting valor, strength, and nobility. [< Celtic] Also *Ital.* **Ar·tu·ro** (är·tōō′rō). Dims. **Art, Art′ie.**

A·sa (ā′sə) Healer. [< Hebrew]

Ash·ley (ash′lē) Dweller among ash trees: from a surname. [< Gmc.]

Ath·el·stan (ath′əl·stan) Noble stone or jewel. [OE] Also **Ath′el·stane** (-stān).

Au·brey (ô′brē) Elf ruler. [< F < Gmc.]

Au·gus·tine (ô′gəs·tēn, ô·gus′tin) Dim. of AUGUSTUS. Also **Au·gus·tin** (ô·gus′tən; *Fr.* ō·güs·taṅ′; *Ger.* ou′gŏōs·tēn′), *Ital.* **A·go·sti·no** (ä′gō·stē′nō), *Lat.* **Au·gus·ti·nus** (ô′gəs·tī′nəs), *Pg.* **A·gos·ti·nho** (ə·gōōsh·tē′nyōō), *Sp.* **A·gus·tin** (ä′gōōs·tēn′).

Au·gus·tus (ô·gus′təs) Venerable. [< L] Also **Au·gust** (ô′gəst; *Ger.* ou′gōost), *Fr.* **Au·guste** (ō·güst′).

Au·re·li·us (ô·rē′lē·əs, ô·rēl′yəs) The golden one. [< L]

Aus·tin (ôs′tən) Contr. of AUGUSTINE.

A·ver·y (ā′vər·ē, ā′vrē) Courageous. [< Gmc.] Also **A·ver·il, A·ver·ill** (ā′vər·əl, ā′vrəl).

Bald·win (bôld′win) Bold friend. [< Gmc.] Also *Fr.* **Bau·doin** (bō·dwaṅ′).

Bal·tha·zar (bäl·thā′zər, -thaz′ər) Bel's or Baal's prince [< Chaldean], or splendid prince [< Persian]. Also **Bal·tha′sar** (-zər).

Bap·tist (bap′tist) Baptizer. [< Gk.] Also *Fr.* **Bap·tiste** (bà·tēst′).

Bar·na·bas (bär′nə·bəs) Son of consolation [< Hebrew], or prophetic son [< Aramaic]. Also **Bar·na·by** (bär′nə·bē). Dim. **Bar′ney.**

Bar·nard (bär′nərd) Var. of BERNARD.

Bar·ney (bär′nē) Dim. of BARNABAS or BERNARD.

Bar·ry (bar′ē) Spear; hence, straightforward. [< Celtic]

Bar·thol·o·mew (bär·thol′ə·myōō)   Son of furrows. [< Hebrew] Also *Fr.* **Bar·thé·le·my** (bȧr·tāl·mē′), *Ger.* **Bar·tho·lo·mä·us** (bär′tō·lō·mä′ŏŏs), *Ital.* **Bar·to·lo·me·o** (bär·tō′lō·mâ′ō), *Lat.* **Bar·thol·o·mae·us** (bär·tol′ə·mē′əs), *Sp.* **Bar·to·lo·mé** (bär·tō′lō·mā′). Dims. **Bart, Bat.**

Bas·il (baz′əl, bā′zəl)   Kingly. [< Gk.]

Bax·ter (bak′stər)   Baker. [< Gmc.]

Bay·ard (bā′ərd, bī′-, -ärd)   From a surname. [< OF]

Ben·e·dict (ben′ə·dikt)   Blessed. [< L] Also **Ben′e·dick,** *Fr.* **Be·noît** (bə·nwä′), *Ger.* **Be·ne·dikt** (bā′nä·dikt), *Ital.* **Be·ne·det·to** (bā′nä·dāt′tō) or **Be·ni·to** (bā·nē′tō), *Lat.* **Ben·e·dic·tus** (ben′ə·dik′təs), *Sp.* **Be·ni·to** (bā·nē′tō).

Ben·ja·min (ben′jə·mən; *Fr.* bań·zhȧ·man′; *Ger.* ben′yä·mēn)   Son of the right hand; hence, favorite son. [< Hebrew] Also *Ital.* **Ben·ia·mi·no** (ben′yä·mē′nō), *Sp.* **Ben·ja·mín** (ben′hä·mēn′). Dims. **Ben, Ben′jy, Ben′ny.**

Ben·net (ben′it)   Var. of BENEDICT. Also **Ben′nett.**

Ber·nard (bûr′nərd, bər·närd′; *Fr.* ber·nȧr′)   Bear-brave: probably from a totemic title. [< Gmc.] Also *Ger.* **Bern·hard** (bern′härt), *Ital., Sp.* **Ber·nar·do** (*Ital.* bär·när′dō; *Sp.* (ber·när′thō), *Lat.* **Ber·nar·dus** (bər·när′dəs). Dims. **Bar′ney, Ber′ney, Ber′nie.**

Bert (bûrt)   Dim. of ALBERT, BERTRAM, GILBERT, HERBERT, and HUBERT. Also **Ber·tie** (bûr′tē).

Ber·tram (bûr′trəm)   Bright raven. [< Gmc.] Also **Ber·trand** (bûr′trənd; *Fr.* ber·trän′). Dim. **Bert.**

Bill (bil)   Dim. of WILLIAM. Also **Bil′ly.**

Bob (bob)   Dim. of ROBERT. Also **Bob′bie, Bob′by.**

Bo·ris (bôr′is, bō′ris; *Russ.* bə·ryēs′)   Warrior. [< Russ.]

Boyd (boid)   Yellow-haired. [< Celtic]

Bri·an (brī′ən)   Strong. [< Celtic] Also **Bry′an, Bry·ant** (brī′ənt).

Brice (brīs)   Meaning uncertain. [? < Celtic] Also **Bryce.**

Bruce (brōōs)   From a Norman Fr. surname; orig. a place name.

Bru·no (brōō′nō)   The brown one. [< Gmc.]

Bur·gess (bûr′jis)   Citizen. [< Gmc.]

By·ron (bī′rən)   From a Fr. surname; orig. a place name. Also **Bi′ron.**

Cad·wal·la·der (kad·wol′ə·dər)   Battle arranger. [< Welsh] Also **Cad·wal′a·der.**

Cae·sar (sē′zər)   Long-haired: ? symbolic title suggesting royalty or holiness. [< L] Also **Ce′sar,** *Fr.* **Cé·sar** (sā·zȧr′), *Ital.* **Ce·sa·re** (chā′zä·rā).

Ca·leb (kā′ləb)   Dog; hence, loyal. [< Hebrew]

Cal·vin (kal′vin)   Bald: from a Roman name. [< L] Dim. **Cal.**

Carl (kärl)   English form of KARL.

Car·ol (kar′əl)   English form of CAROLUS.

Car·o·lus (kar′ə·ləs)   Lat. form of CHARLES.

Car·y (kâr′ē)   ? Dim. of CAROL. Also **Car′ey.**

Cas·per (kas′pər)   English form of KASPAR. Also **Cas′par** (-pər).

Ce·cil (sē′səl, ses′əl)   Blind: from the name of a Roman clan.

Ced·ric (sed′rik, sē′drik)   War chief. [< Celtic]

Charles (chärlz; *Fr.* shȧrl)   Manly. [< F < Gmc.] Also *Ital.* **Car·lo** (kär′lō), *Lat.* **Car·o·lus** (kar′ə·ləs), *Sp.* **Car·los** (kär′lōs). Dims. **Char′ley, Char′lie, Chuck.**

Chaun·cey (chôn′sē, chän′-)   Chancellor. [< OF]

Ches·ter (ches′tər)   Dweller in camp; hence, soldier: from a surname. [< L] Dims. **Ches, Chet.**

Chris·tian (kris′chən; *Ger.* kris′tē·än)   Christian. [< L < Gk.] Also *Fr.* **Chré·tien** (krā·tyaṅ′). Dim. **Chris.**

Chris·to·pher (kris′tə·fər)   Bearer of Christ. [< Gk.] Also *Fr.* **Chris·tophe** (krēs·tôf′), *Ger.* **Chris·toph** (kris′tōf), *Ital.* **Chri·sto·fo·ro** (krēs·tô′fō·rō), *Sp.* **Cris·tó·bal** (krēs·tō′·väl). Dims. **Chris, Kit.**

Clar·ence (klar′əns)   From the name of an English dukedom.

Claude (klôd; *Fr.* klôd)   Lame: from the name of a Roman clan. Also *Ital., Sp.* **Clau·di·o** (*Ital.* klou′dyō; *Sp.* klou′·thyō), *Lat.* **Clau·di·us** (klô′dē·əs).

Clay·ton (klā′tən)   From an English surname; orig. a place name.

Clem·ent (klem′ənt)   Merciful. [< L] Dim. **Clem.**

Clif·ford (klif′ərd)   From an English surname; orig. a place name. Dim. **Cliff.**

Clif·ton (klif′tən)   From an English surname; orig. a place name.

Clin·ton (klin′tən)   From an English surname; orig. a place name. Dim. **Clint.**

Clive (klīv)   Cliff; cliff-dweller: from an English surname.

Clyde (klīd)   From a Scot. surname; orig. the river *Clyde.*

Col·in (kol′ən, kō′lən)   Dove. [< Scot. < L]

Con·rad (kon′rad)   Bold counsel. [< Gmc.]

Con·stant (kon′stənt; *Fr.* kôṅ·stäṅ′)   Var. of CONSTANTINE.

Con·stan·tine (kon′stən·tīn, -tēn)   Constant; firm. [< L]

Cor·nel·ius (kôr·nēl′yəs; *Ger.* kôr·nä′lē·ŏŏs)   ? Horn: from the name of a Roman clan. Dims. **Con, Con′nie, Neil.**

Craig (krāg)   Crag; crag-dweller: from a Scot. surname.

Cris·pin (kris′pin)   Curly-headed. [< L] Also *Lat.* **Cris·pi·nus** (kris·pī′nəs) or **Cris·pus** (kris′pəs).

Cur·tis (kûr′tis)   Courteous. [< OF]

Cuth·bert (kuth′bərt)   Notably brilliant. [OE]

Cyr·il (sir′əl)   Lordly [< Gk.]

Cy·rus (sī′rəs)   The sun. [< Persian] Dim. **Cy.**

Dan (dan)   Judge. [< Hebrew]

Dan·iel (dan′yəl; *Fr.* dȧ·nyel′; *Ger.* dä′nē·el)   God is my judge. [< Hebrew] Dims. **Dan, Dan′ny.**

Da·ri·us (də·rī′əs)   Wealthy. [< Persian]

Da·vid (dā′vid; *Fr.* dȧ·vēd′; *Ger.* dä′vēt)   Beloved. [< Hebrew] Dims. **Dave, Da′vey, Da′vie, Da′vy.**

Dean (dēn)   From an ancient religious or military title. [< OF < LL] Also **Deane.**

De·me·tri·us (di·mē′trē·əs)   He of Demeter. [< Gk.] Also *Russ.* **Dmi·tri** (dmyē′trē).

Den·nis (den′is)   Var. of DIONYSIUS. Also **Den′is,** *Fr.* **De·nis** or **De·nys** (də·nē′). Dim. **Den′ny.**

Der·ek (der′ik)   Du. dim. of THEODORIC. Also **Der′rick, Dirck** (dûrk; *Du.* dirk), **Dirk.**

DeWitt (də·wit′)   From a surname. Also **De Witt.**

Dex·ter (dek′stər)   Right; right-handed; hence, fortunate or skillful. [< L]

Dick (dik)   Dim. of RICHARD.

Dolph (dolf)   Dim. of ADOLPH or RUDOLPH. Also **Dolf.**

Dom·i·nic (dom′ə·nik)   Of the Lord. [< L] Also **Dom′i·nick.** Dim. **Dom.**

Don·ald (don′əld)   World chief. [< Celtic] Dims. **Don, Don′nie.**

Doug·las (dug′ləs)   Dark. [< Celtic] Dims. **Doug, Doug′ie.**

Drew (drōō)   Skilled one [< Gmc.], or dim. of ANDREW.

Duane (dwān, dōō·än′)   Poem. [< Celtic]

Dud·ley (dud′lē)   From an English surname; orig. a place name.

Duke (dōōk, dyōōk)   From the title. [< OF]

Dun·can (dung′kən)   Brown warrior. [< Celtic]

Dun·stan (dun′stən)   From an English place name.

Dwight (dwīt)   Meaning uncertain. [< Gmc.]

Earl (ûrl)   From the title. [OE] Also **Earle.**

Eb·en·e·zer (eb′ə·nē′zər)   Stone of help. [< Hebrew] Dim. **Eb·en** (eb′ən).

Ed·gar (ed′gər)   Rich spear; hence, fortunate warrior. [OE] Dims. **Ed, Ed′die, Ned.**

Ed·mund (ed′mənd; *Ger.* et′mōōnt)   Rich protector. [OE] Also **Ed·mond** (ed′mənd; *Fr.* ed·môṅ′). Dims. **Ed, Ed′die, Ned.**

Ed·ward (ed′wərd)   Rich guardian. [OE] Also *Fr.* **É·dou·ard** (ā·dwȧr′), *Ger.* **E·du·ard** (ā′dōō·ärt), *Sp.* **E·duar·do** (ā·thwär′thō). Dims. **Ed, Ed′die, Ned, Ted, Ted′dy.**

Ed·win (ed′win)   Rich friend. [OE] Dims. **Ed, Ed′die.**

Eg·bert (eg′bərt)   Bright sword; hence, skilled swordsman. [OE] Dims. **Bert, Bert′ie.**

El·bert (el′bərt)   Var. of ALBERT.

El·dred (el′drid)   Mature counsel. [OE]

El·e·a·zar (el′ē·ā′zər)   God has helped. [< Hebrew] Also **El′e·a′zer.**

E·li (ē′lī)   The highest one. [< Hebrew]

E·li·as (i·lī′əs)   Var. of ELIJAH.

El·i·hu (el′ə·hyōō)   Var. of ELIJAH.

E·li·jah (i·lī′jə)   Jehovah is God. [< Hebrew]

El·i·ot (el'ē·ət)   God's gift.   [< Hebrew]   Also **El'li·ot, El'li·ott.**

E·li·sha (i·lī'shə)   God is salvation.   [< Hebrew]

El·lis (el'is)   Var. of ELIAS.

El·mer (el'mər)   Nobly famous.   [OE]

El·ton (el'tən)   From an English surname; orig. a place name.

El·vin (el'vin)   Of the elves.   [OE]   Also **El·win** (el'win).

E·man·u·el (i·man'yōō·əl)   Var. of IMMANUEL.   Also **Em·man'u·el.**

Em·er·y (em'ər·ē)   Work ruler.   [< Gmc.]   Also **Em·er·ic** (em'ər·ik), **Em'o·ry.**

E·mile (ā·mēl')   From the name of a Roman clan.   Also *Fr.* Émile (ā·mēl'), *Ger.* **E·mil** (ā'mēl), *Ital.* **E·mi·lio** (ā·mē'lyō).

Em·mett (em'it)   Ant; hence, industrious.   [OE]   Also **Em'met.**

E·ne·as (i·nē'əs)   Praiseworthy.   [< Gk.]

E·noch (ē'nək)   Dedicated.   [< Hebrew]

E·nos (ē'nəs)   Man.   [< Hebrew]

En·ri·co (än·rē'kō)   Ital. form of HENRY.

E·phra·im (ē'frē·əm, ē'frəm)   Doubly fruitful.   [< Hebrew]

E·ras·mus (i·raz'məs)   Lovable.   [< Gk.]

E·ras·tus (i·ras'təs)   Lovable.   [< Gk.]   Dim. **Ras·tus** (ras'·təs).

Er·ic (er'ik)   Honorable king.   [< Scand.]   Also **Er'ich, Er'ik.**

Er·man·no (er·män'nō)   Ital. form of HERMAN.

Er·nest (ûr'nist)   Earnest.   [< Gmc.]   Also *Ger.* **Ernst** (ernst).   Dims. **Ern, Er'nie.**

Er·win (ûr'win)   Var. of IRVING.

Es·te·ban (ās·tā'bän)   Sp. form of STEPHEN.

E·than (ē'thən)   Firmness.   [< Hebrew]

Eth·el·bert (eth'əl·bûrt)   Nobly bright.   [OE]

Eth·el·red (eth'əl·red)   Noble council.   [< Gmc.]

É·tienne (ā·tyen')   Fr. form of STEPHEN.

Eu·gene (yōō·jēn')   Well-born.   [< Gk.]   dim. **Gene.**

Eus·tace (yōōs'tis)   Good harvest.   [< Gk]

Ev·an (eva'n)   Welsh form of JOHN.

Ev·e·lyn (ēv'lin, ev'ə·lin)   Ancestor.   [< OF < Gmc]

Ev·er·ard (ev'ər·ärd)   Strong as a boar.   [< Gmc.]   Also **Ev·er·art** (ev'ər·ärt).

Ev·er·ett (ev'ər·it)   Var. of EVERARD.   Also **Ev'er·et.**

E·ze·ki·el (i·zē'kē·əl, -kyəl)   God gives strength.   [< Hebrew]   Dim. **Zeke** (zēk).

Ez·ra (ez'rə)   Helper.   [< Hebrew]

Fë·dor (fyô'dər)   Russ. form of THEODORE.   Also **Fe·o·dor** (fyi·ô'dər).

Fe·li·pe (fā·lē'pā)   Sp. form of PHILIP.

Fe·lix (fē'liks)   Happy; fortunate.   [< L]

Fer·di·nand (fûr'də·nand; *Fr.* fer·dē·nän'; *Ger.* fer'dē·nänt)   Peaceful courage.   [< Gmc.]   Also *Sp.* **Fer·nan·do** (fer·nän'dō), **Her·nan·do** (her·nän'dō).   Dim. **Fer'die.**

Floyd (floid)   Var. of LLOYD.

Fran·cis (fran'sis, frän'-)   Free.   [< Gmc.]   Also *Fr.* **Fran·çois** (frän·swä'), *Ger.* **Franz** (fränts), *Ital.* **Fran·ce·sco** (frän·chā'skō), *Sp.* **Fran·cis·co** (frän·thes'kō).   Dim. **Frank, Frank'ie.**

Frank (frangk)   Dim. of FRANCIS or FRANKLIN.   Also **Frank'ie.**

Frank·lin (frangk'lin)   Freeman.   [ME]   Dims. **Frank, Frank'ie.**

Fred (fred)   Dim. of ALFRED, FREDERICK, or WILFRED.   Also **Fred'die, Fred'dy.**

Fred·er·ick (fred'ər·ik, fred'rik)   Peace ruler.   [< Gmc.]   Also **Fred'er·ic, Fred'ric, Fred'rick,** *Fr.* **Fré·dé·ric** (frā·dā·rēk'), *Ger.* **Frie·drich** (frē'driҟh), *Sp.* **Fe·de·ri·co** (fā'dā·rē'·kō).   Dims. **Fred, Fred'die, Fred'dy, Fritz.**

Fritz (frits)   Ger. dim. of FREDERICK.

Ga·bri·el (gā'brē·əl; *Fr.* gȧ·brē·el'; *Ger.* gä'brē·el)   Man of God.   [< Hebrew]   Dim. **Gabe** (gāb).

Ga·ma·li·el (gə·mā'lē·əl, -mäl'yəl)   Reward of God.   [< Hebrew]

Gar·di·ner (gärd'nər, gär'də·nər)   From an English surname.   Also **Gar'de·ner, Gard'ner.**

Gar·ret (gar'it)   Var. of GERARD.   Also **Gar'rett.**

Gar·y (gâr'ē)   Dim. of GARRET.

Gas·par (gas'pər)   Var. of CASPER.   Also *Fr.* **Gas·pard** (gȧs·pär').

Gas·ton (gas'tən; *Fr.* gȧs·tôn')   Meaning uncertain.

Gau·tier (gō·tyā')   Fr. form of WALTER.

Gene (jēn)   Dim. of EUGENE.

Geof·frey (jef'rē)   English form of Fr. *Geoffroi;* var. of GODFREY.   Dim. **Jeff.**

George (jôrj)   Earthworker; farmer.   [< Gk.]   Also *Fr.* **Georges** (zhôrzh), *Ger.* **Ge·org** (gā·ôrkh'), *Ital.* **Gior·gio** (jôr'·jō), *Russ.* **Ge·or·gi** (gyi·ôr'gyi).   Dim. **Georg'ie, Geor'die.**

Ger·ald (jer'əld)   Spear ruler.   [< Gmc.]   Also *Fr.* Gé·raud (zhā·rō') or **Gi·raud** (zhē·rō').   Dims. **Ger'ry, Jer'ry.**

Ge·rard (ji·rärd'; *Brit.* jer'ärd)   Hard spear.   [< Gmc.]   Also *Fr.* Gé·rard (zhā·rär'), *Ger.* **Ger·hard** (gär'härt).   Dims. **Ger'ry, Jer'ry.**

Ge·ro·ni·mo (jä·rô'nē·mō)   Ital. form of JEROME.

Gia·co·mo (jä'kō·mō)   Ital. form of JAMES.

Gid·e·on (gid'ē·ən)   Hewer.   [< Hebrew]

Gi·e·ron·y·mus (jē'ə·ron'i·məs)   Lat. form of JEROME.

Gif·ford (gif'ərd, jif'-)   Meaning uncertain.   [< Gmc.]

Gil·bert (gil'bərt; *Fr.* zhēl·bâr')   Bright wish.   [< Gmc.]   Dims. **Bert, Gil.**

Giles (jīlz)   From the name of the goddess Athena's shield; hence, shield or protection.   [< OF < Gk.]

Gio·van·ni (jō·vän'nē)   Ital. form of JOHN.

Giu·lio (jōō'lyō)   Ital. form of JULIUS.

Giu·sep·pe (jōō·zep'pā)   Ital. form of JOSEPH.

Glenn (glen)   From a Celtic surname; orig. a place name.   Also **Glen.**

God·dard (god'ərd)   Divine resoluteness.   [< Gmc.]

God·frey (god'frē)   Peace of God.   [< Gmc.]   Also *Ger.* **Gott·fried** (gôt'frēt).

God·win (god'win)   Friend of God.   [OE]

Gor·don (gôr'dən)   From a Scot. surname.

Gra·ham (grā'əm)   From an English surname; orig. a place name.

Grant (grant)   From a Norman Fr. surname.

Greg·o·ry (greg'ər·ē)   Vigilant.   [< Gk.]   Dim. **Greg.**

Grif·fin (grif'in)   Var. of GRIFFITH.

Grif·fith (grif'ith)   Red-haired.   [< Celtic]

Gro·ver (grō'vər)   Grove-dweller.   [< Gmc.]

Gual·te·ri·o (gwäl·tā'rē·ō)   Sp. form of WALTER.

Gu·gliel·mo (gōō·lyel'mō)   Ital. form of WILLIAM.

Guil·laume (gē·yōm')   Fr. form of WILLIAM.

Guil·ler·mo (gē·lyer'mō, gē·yer'mō)   Sp. form of WILLIAM.

Gus (gus)   Dim. of AUGUSTUS or GUSTAVUS.

Guy (gī; *Fr.* gē)   Leader   [< F < Gmc.]   Also *Ital.* **Gui·do** (gwē'dō).

Hal (hal)   Dim. of HAROLD or HENRY.

Ham·il·ton (ham'əl·tən)   From a surname.

Hank (hangk)   Dim. of HENRY.

Han·ni·bal (han'ə·bəl)   Grace of Baal.   [< Phoenician]

Hans (häns)   Ger. dim. of JOHANNES.   See JOHN.

Har·ley (här'lē)   From an English surname; orig. a place name.

Har·old (har'əld)   Chief of the army.   [OE < Scand.]   Dim. **Hal.**

Har·ry (har'ē)   Dim. of HAROLD or var. of HENRY.

Har·vey (här'vē)   Army battle.   [< F < Gmc.]

Hec·tor (hek'tər)   He who holds fast; defender.   [< Gk.]

Hen·ry (hen'rē)   Home ruler.   [< F < Gmc.]   Also *Du.* **Hen·drick** (hen'drik), *Fr.* **Hen·ri** (än·rē'), *Ger.* **Hein·rich** (hīn'riҟh).   Dims. **Hal, Hank, Har'ry, Hen.**

Her·bert (hûr'bərt)   Glory of the army.   [OE]   Dims. **Bert, Bert'ie, Herb.**

Her·man (hûr'mən)   Man of the army.   [< Gmc.]   Also *Ger.* **Her·mann** (her'män).

Her·mes (hûr'mēz)   Of the earth.   [< Gk.]

Her·nan·do (er·nän'dō)   Sp. form of FERDINAND.

Hez·e·ki·ah (hez'ə·kī'ə)   God strengthens.   [< Hebrew]

Hil·a·ry (hil'ər·ē)   Joyful.   [< L]   Also *Fr.* **Hi·laire** (ē·lâr').

Hi·ram (hī'rəm)   Honored brother.   [< Hebrew]   Dims. **Hi, Hy.**

Ho·bart (hō'bərt, -bärt)   Var. of HUBERT.

Hodge (hoj) Dim. of ROGER. Also **Hodg′kin.**

Ho·mer (hō′mər) Pledge, or blind one. [< Gk.]

Ho·no·ré (ô·nô·rā′) Honored. [< F < L]

Hor·ace (hôr′is, hor′-) Var. of HORATIO.

Ho·ra·ti·o (hə·rā′shē·ō) From the name of a Roman clan.

Ho·se·a (hō·zē′ə, -zā′ə) Salvation. [< Hebrew]

How·ard (hou′ərd) From an English surname. Dim. **How′ie.**

Hu·bert (hyōō′bərt) Bright spirit or mind. [< F < Gmc.]

Hugh (hyōō) Mind; intelligence. [< OF < Gmc.] Also **Hu·go** (hyōō′gō), *Fr.* **Hugues** (üg). Dim. **Hugh′ie.**

Hum·bert (hum′bərt) Bright support. [< OF < Gmc.]

Hum·phrey (hum′frē) Peaceful stake or support. [< OF < Gmc.] Also **Hum′frey, Hum′phry.**

I·an (ē′ən, ī′ən) Scot. form of JOHN.

Ich·a·bod (ik′ə·bod) ? Inglorious. [< Hebrew]

Ig·na·ti·us (ig·nā′shē·əs, -shəs) Fiery. [< Gk.] Also *Fr.* **I·gnace** (ē·nyàs′), *Ger.* **Ig·naz** (ig′näts), *Ital.* **I·gna·zio** (ē·nyä′tsyō).

Im·man·u·el (i·man′yōō·əl) God with us. [< Hebrew]

I·ra (ī′rə) Vigilant. [< Hebrew]

Ir·ving (ûr′ving) From a Scot. surname; orig. a place name. Also **Ir·vin** (ûr′vin).

Ir·win (ûr′win) Var. of IRVING.

I·saac (ī′zək) Laughter. [< Hebrew] Dim. **Ike** (īk).

I·sa·iah (ī·zā′ə, ī·zī′ə) Salvation of God. [< Hebrew]

Is·i·dore (iz′ə·dôr, -dōr) Gift of Isis. [< Gk.] Also **Is′a·dore, Is′a·dor, Is′i·dor.** Dim. **Iz·zy** (iz′ē).

Is·ra·el (iz′rē·əl) Contender with God. [< Hebrew]

I·van (ī′vən; *Russ.* i·vän′) Russ. form of JOHN.

Ja·bez (jā′biz) Sorrow. [< Hebrew]

Jack (jak) English form of Fr. **Jacques;** dim. of JOHN.

Ja·cob (jā′kəb) He who seizes by the heel; hence, successor. [< LL < Hebrew] Also *Ger.* **Ja·kob** (yä′kôb). Dims. **Jack, Jake** (jāk), **Jock** (jok).

Jacques (zhàk) Fr. form of JACOB. [< OF < LL]

James (jāmz) English form of Sp. *Jaime;* var. of JACOB. [< Sp. < LL] Also *Sp.* **Jai·me** (hī′mä). Dims. **Jam·ie** (jā′mē), **Jem, Jem′my, Jim, Jim′mie, Jim′my.**

Jan (yän)Du., Ger., and Pol. form of JOHN.

Já·nos (yä′nōsh) Hung. form of JOHN.

Ja·pheth (jā′fith) Enlarged; hence, powerful or honored. [< Hebrew] Also **Ja′phet** (-fit).

Jar·ed (jâr′id) Descent. [< Hebrew]

Jar·vis (jär′vis) From a Norman Fr. surname. Also **Jer·vis** (jûr′vis; *Brit.* Jär′vis).

Ja·son (jā′sən) Healer. [< Gk.]

Jas·per (jas′pər) Treasury lord [< OF, ? < Persian], or from the name of the jewel.

Jay (jā) ? Jay bird. [? < OF]

Jean (jēn; *Fr.* zhäń) French form of JOHN.

Jef·frey (jef′rē) Var. of GEOFFREY. Dim. **Jeff.**

Je·hu (jē′hyōō) Jehovah is he. [< Hebrew]

Jeph·thah (jef′thə) Opposer. [< Hebrew]

Jer·e·mi·ah (jer′ə·mī′ə) God's chosen. [< Hebrew] Also **Jer·e·my** (jer′ə·mē). Dim. **Jer′ry.**

Je·rome (jə·rōm′; *Brit.* jer′əm) Holy name. [< Gk.] Also *Fr.* **Jé·rôme** (zhā·rôm′), *Sp.* **Je·ró·ni·mo** (hā·rō′nē·mō).

Jer·ry (jer′ē) Dim. of GERALD, GERARD, JEREMIAH, or JEROME.

Jes·se (jes′ē) Meaning uncertain. [< Hebrew] Also **Jess.**

Je·sus (jē′zəs) English form of Lat. *Josua;* var. of JOSHUA.

Jeth·ro (jeth′rō) Abundant or excellent. [< Hebrew]

Jim (jim) Dim. of JAMES. Also **Jim′mie, Jim′my.**

Jo·ab (jō′ab) Jehovah is father. [< Hebrew]

Jo·a·chim (jō′ə·kim) Jehovah will judge. [< Hebrew] Also *Sp.* **Joa·quín** (hwä·kēn′)

João (hwouń) Pg. form of JOHN.

Job (jōb) Persecuted. [< Hebrew]

Jock (jok) Scot. form of JACK.

Joe (jō) Dim. of JOSEPH. Also **Jo′ey.**

Jo·el (jō′əl) Jehovah is God. [< Hebrew]

John (jon) God is good. [< Hebrew] Also *Ger.* **Jo·hann** (yō′hän) or **Jo·han·nes** (yō·hän′əs). Dims. **Jack, Jack′ie, Jack′y, Jock, John′nie, John′ny.**

Jon (jon) Var. of JOHN, or dim. of JONATHAN.

Jo·nah (jō′nə) Dove. [< Hebrew] Also **Jo·nas** (jō′nəs).

Jon·a·than (jon′ə·thən) God has given. [< Hebrew] Dims. **Jon, Jon′nie, Jon′ny.**

Jor·ge (*Pg.* zhôr′zhə; *Sp.* hôr′hä) Pg. and Sp. form of GEORGE.

Jo·seph (jōzəf; *Fr.* zhō·zef′; *Ger.* yō′zef) God shall give (a son). [< Hebrew] Also *Lat.* **Jo·se·phus** (jō·sē′fəs), *Pg., Sp.* **Jo·sé** (*Pg.* zhōō·ze′; *Sp.* hō·sā′). Dims. **Jo, Joe, Jo′ey.**

Josh·u·a (josh′ōō·ə) God is salvation. [< Hebrew] Also *Fr.* **Jo·sué** (zhō·zwä′), *Lat.* **Jos·u·a** (jos′ōō·ə). Dim. **Josh.**

Jo·si·ah (jō·sī′ə) God supports. [< Hebrew] Also *Lat.* **Jo·si·as** (jō·sī′əs).

Jo·tham (jō′thəm) God is perfection. [< Hebrew]

Juan (hwän) Sp. form of JOHN.

Ju·dah (jōō′də) Praised. [< Hebrew] Also **Jude** (jōōd; *Fr.* zhüd), *Lat.* **Ju·das** (jōō′dəs).

Jules (jōōlz; *Fr.* zhül) Fr. form of JULIUS.

Jul·ian (jōōl′yən) Var. of JULIUS.

Jul·ius (jōōl′yəs) Downy-beared; youthful: from the name of a Roman clan. Also *Sp.* **Ju·lio** (hōō′lyō). Dims. **Jule** (jōōl), **Jul·ie** (jōō′lē).

Jun·ius (jōōn′yəs, jōō′nē·əs) Youthful: from the name of a Roman clan.

Jus·tin (jus′tin) Just. [< L] Also **Jus·tus** (jus′təs).

Karl (kärl) Ger. form of CHARLES.

Kas·par (käs′pär) Ger. form of JASPER.

Keith (kēth) From a Scot. surname; orig. a place name.

Kel·vin (kel′vin) From a Celtic surname.

Ken·neth (ken′ith) Handsome. [< Celtic] Dims. **Ken, Ken′nie, Ken′ny.**

Kent (kent) From an English surname; orig. a place name.

Kev·in (kev′ən) Handsome birth. [< Celtic]

Kit (kit) Dim. of CHRISTOPHER.

Kon′rad (kôn′rät) Ger. form of CONRAD.

La·ban (lā′bən) White. [< Hebrew]

La·fay·ette (lä′fē·et′, laf′ē·et′; *Fr.* à·fà·yet′) From a Fr. surname. Dim. **Lafe** (läf).

Lam·bert (lam′bərt) The land's brightness. [< F < Gmc.]

Lance (lans, läns) Of the land. [< Gmc.]

Lan·ce·lot (lan′sə·lot, län′-; *Fr.* läṅ·slō′) Fr. dim. of LANCE. Also **Laun·ce·lot** (lôn′sə·lot, lan′-, län′-).

Lars (lärz; *Sw.* lärs) Sw. form of LAURENCE.

Lau·rence (lôr′əns, lor′-) Laureled; hence, prophetic or poetic. [< L] Also **Law′rence,** *Fr.* **Lau·rent** (lō·räṅ′), *Ger.* **Lo·renz** (lō′rents). Dims. **Lar·ry** (lar′ē), **Lau·rie** or **Law·rie** (lôr′ē).

Laz·a·rus (laz′ə·rəs) God has helped. [< Hebrew] Also *Fr.* **La·zare** (là·zàr′), *Ital.* **Laz·za·ro** (läd′dzä·rō).

Le·an·der (lē·an′dər) Lion man. [< Gk.]

Lee (lē) From an English surname.

Leif (lēf) Loved one. [< Scand.]

Leigh (lē) From an English surname.

Lem·u·el (lem′yōō·əl) Belonging to God. [< Hebrew] Dim. **Lem.**

Le·o (lē′ō) Lion. [< L < Gk.]

Le·on (lē′on, -ən) Lion. [< L < Gk.] Also *Fr.* **Lé·on** (lā·ôṅ′)

Leon·ard (len′ərd) Lion-strong. [< Gmc.] Also *Fr.* **Lé·o·nard** (lā·ō·nàr′), *Ger.* **Le·on·hard** (lā′ōn·härt), *Ital.* **Le·o·nar·do** (lā′ō·när′dō). Dims. **Len, Len′ny.**

Le·on·i·das (lē·on′ə·dəs) Lionlike. [< Gk.]

Le·o·pold (lē′ə·pōld; *Ger.* lā′ō·pōlt) The people's strong one. [< Gmc.]

Le·roy (lə·roi′, lē′roi) Royal. [< OF]

Les·lie (les′lē, lez′-) From an English surname. Dim. **Les.**

Les·ter (les′tər) From an English surname; orig. the place name *Leicester.* Dim. **Les.**

Le·vi (lē′vī) He who unites. [< Hebrew]

Lew·is (lōō′is) Var. of LOUIS. Dims. **Lew, Lew′ie.**

Lin·coln (ling′kən) From an English surname.

Li·nus (lī′nəs) Meaning uncertain. [< Gk]

Li·o·nel (lī′ə·nəl, -nel) Young lion. [< F < L]

Lisle (līl) Var. of LYLE.

Llew·el·lyn (lōō·el′ən) Meaning uncertain. [< Welsh]

Lloyd (loid) Gray. [< Welsh]

Lo·ren·zo (lə·ren′zō; *Ital.* lō·ren′tsō; *Sp.* lō·rän′thō) Var. of LAURENCE.

Lot (lot) Veiled. [< Hebrew] Also **Lott.**

Lou·is (lo͞o′is, lo͞o′ē; *Fr.* lwē) War famous. [< OF < Gmc.] Also **Lew′is,** *Du.* **Lo·de·wijk** (lō′də·vīk), *Ger.* **Lud·wig** (lo͞ot′vikh), *Ital.* **Lu·i·gi** (lo͞o·ē′jē), or **Lo·do·vi·co** (lō′dō·vē′kō), *Pg.* **Lu·iz** (lo͞o·ēsh′), *Sp.* **Lu·is** (lo͞o·ēs′). Dims. **Lew, Lou.**

Low·ell (lō′əl) Beloved. [OE] Also **Lov·ell** (luv′əl).

Lu·cas (lo͞o′kəs) Light. [< L]

Lu·cian (lo͞o′shən) Var. of LUCIUS. [< L *Lucianus*] Also **Lu·cien** (lo͞o′shən; *Fr.* lü·syań′).

Lu·ci·fer (lo͞o′sə·fər) Light-bearer. [< L]

Lu·cius (lo͞o′shəs) Light. [< L]

Lu·cre·tius (lo͞o·krē′shəs, -shē·əs) Shining or wealthy. [< L]

Luke (lo͞ok) English form of LUCAS.

Lu·ther (lo͞o′thər) Famous warrior. [< Gmc.] Also *Fr.* **Lo·thaire** (lô·târ′), *Ital.* **Lo·ta·rio** (lo·tä′ryō).

Mac (mak) Son. [< Celtic] Also **Mack.**

Mal·a·chi (mal′ə·kī) Messenger. [< Hebrew]

Mal·colm (mal′kəm) Servant of (St.) Columba. [< Celtic]

Ma·nu·el (mä·nwel′) Sp. form of IMMANUEL.

Mar·cel·lus (mär·sel′əs) Dim. of MARCUS. Also *Fr.* **Mar·cel** (mår·sel′), *Ital.* **Mar·cel·lo** (mär·chel′lō).

Mar·cus (mär′kəs) Of Mars. [< L]

Mar·i·on (mar′ē·ən, mâr′-) Of Mary. [< F]

Mark (märk) English form of MARCUS. Also *Fr.* **Marc** (märk), *Ital.* **Mar·co** (mär′kō).

Mar·ma·duke (mär′mə·do͞ok, -dyo͞ok) Meaning uncertain. [? < Celtic]

Mar·shal (mär′shəl) From the title. [< Gmc.] Also **Mar′shall.**

Mar·tin (mär′tən; *Fr.* mår·tań′; *Ger.* mär′tēn) Of Mars. [< L] Dims. **Mart, Mar′ty.**

Mar·vin (mär′vin) Sea friend. [< Gmc.]

Ma·son (mä′sən) Stoneworker. [< Gmc.]

Mat·thew (mat′yo͞o) Gift of God. [< Hebrew] *Fr.* **Ma·thieu** (må·tyœ′), *Ital.* **Mat·te·o** (mät·tā′ō), *Sp.* **Ma·te·o** (mä·tā′ō). Dims. **Mat, Matt.**

Mat·thi·as (mə·thī′əs) Var. of MATTHEW. [< Gk.]

Mau·rice (mə·rēs′, môr′is, mor′is; *Fr.* mô·rēs′) Moorish; dark. [< F < L]

Max (maks; *Ger.* mäks) Dim. of MAXIMILIAN.

Max·i·mil·ian (mak′sə·mil′yən; *Ger.* mäk′sē·mē′lē·än) Prob. coined by Frederick III from the Roman names *Maximus* and *Aemilianus*. Dim. **Max.**

May·nard (mā′nərd, -närd) Powerful strength. [< Gmc.]

Mel·vin (mel′vin) High protector. [OE] Dim. **Mel.**

Mer·e·dith (mer′ə·dith) Sea protector. [< Welsh]

Mer·vin (mû′vin) Var. of MARVIN.

Mi·cah (mī′kə) Who is like God? [< Hebrew]

Mi·chael (mī′kəl; *Ger.* mi′khä·el) Who is like God? [< Hebrew] Also *Fr.* **Mi·chel** (mē·shel′), *Ital.* **Mi·che·le** (mē·kâ′·lā), *Sp., Pg.* **Mi·guel** (mē·gel′). Dims. **Mike** (mīk), **Mick·ey** or **Mick·y** (mik′ē), **Mik·ey** (mī′kē).

Mi·klós (mi′klōsh) Hung. form of NICHOLAS.

Miles (mīlz) Meaning uncertain. [< Gmc.] Also **Myles.**

Mi·lo (mī′lō; *Ital.* mē′lō) Ital. var. of MILES.

Mil·ton (mil′tən) From an English surname; orig. a place name. [< Gmc.] Dim. **Milt.**

Mitch·ell (mich′əl) Var. of MICHAEL. Dim. **Mitch.**

Mon·roe (mən·rō′, *Brit.* mun′rō) From a Celtic surname; orig. a place name.

Mon·ta·gue (mon′tə·gyo͞o) From a Norman Fr. surname; orig. a place name. Dim. **Mon′ty.**

Mont·gom·er·y (mont·gum′ər·ē) From a Norman Fr. surname; orig. a place name. Dim. **Mon′ty.**

Mor·gan (môr′gən) Sea-dweller. [< Welsh]

Mor·ris (môr′is, mor′-) Var. of MAURICE.

Mor·ti·mer (môr′tə·mər) From a Norman Fr. surname; orig. a place name. Dims. **Mort, Mor′ty.**

Mor·ton (môr′tən) From an English surname; orig. a place name. Dim. **Mort, Mor′ty.**

Mo·ses (mō′zis, -ziz) ? Son. [< Hebrew, ? < Egyptian] Dim. **Moe** (mō), **Moi·she** (moi′shə), **Mose** (mōz).

Moss (môs, mos) Var. of MOSES.

Mur·dock (mûr′dok) Seaman. [< Celtic] Also **Mur′doch.**

Mur·ray (mûr′ē) From a Scot. surname, or var. of MAURICE.

Myles (Mīlz) Var. of MILES.

Na·hum (nā′əm) Consolation. [< Hebrew]

Na·po·le·on (nə·pō′lē·ən) Of the new city. [< F < Gk.] Also *Fr.* **Na·po·lé·on** (nà·pô·lā·ôn′), *Ital.* **Na·po·le·o·ne** (nä·pō′lā·ō′nä).

Na·than (nā′thən) Gift. [< Hebrew] Dims. **Nat.** (nat), **Nate** (nāt).

Na·than·iel (nə·than′yəl) Gift of God. [< Hebrew] Also **Na·than′a·el.** Dims. **Nat, Nate.**

Ned (ned) Dim. of EDGAR, EDMUND, or EDWARD. Also **Ned′dy.**

Ne·he·mi·ah (nē′hə·mī′ə) Comfort of God. [< Hebrew]

Neil (nēl) Champion. [< Celtic] Also **Neal.**

Nel·son (nel′sən) Neal's son: from an English surname.

Ne·ro (nir′ō) Strong: from the name of a Roman clan.

Nev·ille (nev′il, -əl) From a Norman Fr. surname; orig. a place name. Also **Nev′il, Nev′ile, Nev′ill.**

New·ton (no͞ot′n, nyo͞ot′n) From an English surname; orig. a place name.

Nich·o·las (nik′ə·ləs) The people's victory. [< Gk.] Also **Nic′o·las,** *Fr.* **Ni·co·las** (nē·kô·lä′), *Ital.* **Nic·co·lò** (nēk′kō·lô′), *Lat.* **Ni·co·la·us** (nik′ō·lā′əs), *Russ.* **Ni·ko·lai** (nyi·kə·lī′), *Sp.* **ni·co·lás** (nē′kō·läs′). Dims. **Nick, Nick′y.**

Ni·gel (nī′jəl) Noble. [< Celtic]

No·ah (nō′ə) Comfort. [< Hebrew]

No·el (nō′əl) Christmas. [< OF < L] Also *Fr.* **No·ël** (nō·el′).

Nor·bert (nôr′bərt) Brightness of Njord. [< Gmc.]

Nor·man (nôr′mən) Northman. [< Scand.] Dim. **Norm.**

O·ba·di·ah (ō′bə·dī′ə) Servant of God. [< Hebrew]

Oc·ta·vi·us (ok·tā′vē·əs) The eighth (born). [< L]

O·laf (ō′ləf; *Dan., Norw.* ō′läf; *Sw.* o͞o′läf) Ancestor's heirloom. Also **O′lav** [< Scand.]

Ol·i·ver (ol′ə·vər) Of the olive tree. [< F < L] Dims. **Ol′lie, Ol′ly.**

Or·lan·do (ôr·lan′dō; *Ital.* ôr·län′dō) Ital. form of ROLAND.

Os·bert (ôz′bərt) Divine brilliance. [OE]

Os·car (os′kər) Divine spear. [OE]

Os·wald (oz′wəld, -wôld) Divine power. [OE] Also **Os′wold.**

Ot·to (ot′ō; *Ger.* ôt′ō) Rich. [< Gmc.]

O·wen (ō′ən) Young warrior [< Welsh]

Pat·rick (pat′rik) Patrician; aristocratic. [< L] Dims. **Pad′dy, Pat, Patsy.**

Paul (pôl; *Fr.* pôl; *Ger.* poul) Little: from a given name of the Aemiliani, a Roman clan. Also *Ital.* **Pa·o·lo** (pä′ō·lō), *Lat.* **Pau·li·nus** (pô·lī′nəs) or **Pau·lus** (pô′ləs), *Pg.* **Pau·lo** (pou′lo͞o), *Sp.* **Pa·blo** (pä′vlō).

Per·ci·val (pûr′sə·vəl) Meaning uncertain. [< OF] Also **Per′ce·val.**

Per·cy (pûr′sē) From a Norman Fr. surname; orig. a place name.

Per·ry (per′ē) Of the pear tree: from an English surname.

Pe·ter (pē′tər; *Du., Ger., Norw., Sw.* pā′tər) A rock. [< Gk.] Also *Dan.* **Pe·der** (pā′thər), *Du.* **Pie·ter** (pē′tər), *Fr.* **Pierre** (pyâr), *Modern Gk.* **Pe·tros** (pâ′trôs), *Ital.* **Pie·tro** (pyâ′trō), *Pg., Sp.* **Pe·dro** (*Pg.* pā′thro͞o; *Sp.* pā′thrō), *Russ.* **Pëtr** (pyô′tər). Dim. **Pete.**

Phi·lan·der (fi·lan′dər) Lover of men. [< Gk.]

Phi·le·mon (fi·lē′mən) Loving. [< Gk.]

Phil·ip (fil′ip) Lover of horses. [< Gk.] Also *Fr.* **Phi·lippe** (fē·lēp′), *Ger.* **Phi·lipp** (fē′lip). Dims. **Phil, Pip.**

Phin·e·as (fin′ē·əs) Mouth of brass: prob. an oracular priest's title. [< Hebrew]

Quen·tin (kwen′tin) The fifth (born). [< L] Also **Quin·tin** (kwin′tən).

Quin·cy (kwin′sē) ? var. of QUENTIN. [< OF]

Ralph (ralf; *Brit.* rāf) Wolf-wise. [< Gmc.] *Fr.* **Ra·oul** (rà·o͞ol′).

Ran·dal (ran′dəl) Shield wolf. [OE] Also **Ran′dall.**

Ran·dolph (ran′dolf) Shield wolf. [OE] Dim. **Ran′dy.**

Ra·pha·el (rā′fē·əl, raf′ē·əl) God has healed. [< Hebrew]

Ray (rā) Dim. of RAYMOND.

Ray·mond (rā′mənd; *Fr.* rā·môǹ′) Wise protection. [< Gmc.] Also **Ray′mund,** *Sp.* **Rai·mun·do** (rī·mōōn′dō) or **Ra·món** (rä·mōn′). Dim. **Ray.**

Reg·i·nald (rej′ə·nəld) Judicial ruler. [< Gmc.] Also *Fr.* **Re·gnault** (rə·nyō′) or **Re·naud** (rə·nō′), *Ital.* **Ri·nal·do** (rē·näl′dō), *Sp.* **Rey·nal·do** (rā·näl′thō). Dims. **Reg** (rej), **Reg′gie, Rex.**

Re·né (rə·nā′) Reborn. [< F < L]

Reu·ben (rōō′bin) Behold, a son! [< Hebrew] Dim. **Rube.**

Rex (reks) King [< L], or dim. of REGINALD.

Rey·nard (rā′nərd, ren′ərd) Brave judgment. [< Gmc.]

Reyn·old (ren′əld) Var. of REGINALD. [< OF]

Rich·ard (rich′ərd; *Fr.* rē·shàr′; *Ger.* riḥ′ärt) Strong king. [< OF < Gmc.] Also *Ital.* **Ric·car·do** (rēk·kär′dō), *Sp.* **Ri·car·do** (rē·kär′thō). Dims. **Dick, Dick′ie, Dick′y, Rich, Rich′ie, Rick, Rick′y.**

Ro·ald (rō′äl) Famous power. [< Norw. < Gmc.]

Rob·ert (rob′ərt; *Fr.* rô·bâr′) Bright fame. [< Gmc.] Also *Ital., Sp.* **Ro·ber·to** (rō·ber′tō). Dims. **Bob, Bob′by, Dob, Dob′bin, Rob, Rob′bie, Rob′in.**

Rod·er·ick (rod′ər·ik) Famous king. [< Gmc.] Also **Rod′·er·ic, Rod·rick** (rod′rik), *Fr.* **Ro·drigue** (rô·drēg′), *Ital., Sp.* **Ro·dri·go** (*Ital.* rō·drē′gō; *Sp.* rō·thrē′gō). Dims. **Rod, Rod′dy.**

Rod·ney (rod′nē) From an English surname; orig. a place name. Dim. **Rod.**

Ro·dolph (rō′dolf) Var. of RUDOLPH. Also **Ro·dol·phus** (rō·dol′fəs)

Rog·er (roj′ər; *Fr.* rô·zhā′) Famous spear. [< OF < Gmc.] Dims. **Hodge, Hodg′kin, Rodge.**

Ro·land (rō′lənd; *Fr.* rô·läṅ′) Country's fame. [< Celtic < Gmc.] Also **Row′land.**

Rolf (rolf) Dim. of RUDOLPH. Also **Rolph.**

Rol·lo (rol′ō) Dim. of RUDOLPH.

Ron·ald (ron′əld; *Norw.* rō·näl′) Old Norse form of REGINALD.

Ro·ry (rôr′ē, rō′rē) Red. [< Celtic]

Ros·coe (ros′kō) From an English surname; orig. a place name.

Ross (rôs) From an English surname; orig. a place name.

Roy (roi) King. [< OF]

Ru·dolph (rōō′dolf) Famous wolf. [< Gmc.] Also **Ru′·dolf, Ru·dol·phus** (rōō·dol′fəs). *Fr.* **Ro·dolphe** (rô·dôlf′), *Ital.* **Ro·dol·pho** (rō·dôl′fō), *Sp.* **Ro·dol·fo** (rō·thôl′fō). Dims. **Rol′lo, Ru′dy.**

Ru·fus (rōō′fəs) Red-haired. [< L] Dim. **Rufe.**

Ru·pert (rōō′pərt) Var. of ROBERT. [< G] Also *Ger.* **Ru·precht** (rōō′preḥt).

Rus·sell (rus′əl) Red: from an English surname. [OE < OF] Dim. **Russ.**

Sal·o·mon (sal′ə·mən) Var. of SOLOMON.

Sam·son (sam′sən) The sun. [< Hebrew] Also **Samp′·son** (samp′sən, sam′-).

Sam·u·el (sam′yōō·əl) Name of God. [< Hebrew] Dims. **Sam, Sam′my.**

San·dy (san′dē) Dim. of ALEXANDER. Also **San·der** (san′·dər, sän′-).

Saul (sôl) Asked (of God). [< Hebrew]

Schuy·ler (skī′lər) Shelter. [< Du.]

Scott (skot) The Scot: from an English surname.

Seam·us (shā′məs) Irish form of JAMES.

Sean (shôn, shan) Irish form of JOHN.

Se·bas·tian (si·bas′chən) Venerable. [< Gk.]

Seth (seth) Appointed. [< Hebrew]

Sew·ard (sōō′ərd) ? Sow-herder: from an English surname.

Sey·mour (sē′môr, -mōr) From an English surname; orig. a place name. Dims. **Cy, Sy.**

Shawn (shôn) Irish form of JOHN. Also **Shaun.**

Shel·don (shel′dən) From an English surname; orig. a place name.

Shir·ley (shûr′lē) From an English surname; orig. a place name.

Sid·ney (sid′nē) St. Denis: from an English surname. Dim. **Sid.**

Sieg·fried (sēg′frēd; *Ger.* zēk′frēt) Victorious peace. [< Gmc.]

Sig·is·mund (sij′ə s mənd, sig′-) Victorious protection. [< Gmc.]

Sig·mund (sig′mənd; *Ger.* zeḥ′mōōnt) Var. of SIGISMUND.

Si·las (sī′ləs) Meaning uncertain. [< Gk.] Dim. **Si** (sī).

Sil·va·nus (sil·vā′nəs) From the name of the Roman god of woods and crops.

Sil·ves·ter (sil·ves′tər) Of the woods; rustic. [< L]

Sim·e·on (sim′ē·ən) He who is heard (widely); hence, famous. [< Hebrew] Dim. **Sim** (sim).

Si·mon (sī′mən) Var. of SIMEON.

Sin·clair (sin·klâr′, sin′klâr) St. Clair: from a Norman Fr. surname.

Sol·o·mon (sol′ə·mən) Peaceful. [< Hebrew] Dim. **Sol.**

Stan·ley (stan′lē) From an English surname; orig. a place name. Dim. **Stan.**

Ste·phen (stē′vən) Crown. [< Gk.] Also **Ste′ven,** *Ger.* **Ste·phan** or **Ste·fan** (shte′fän), *Ital.* **Ste·fa·no** (stā′fä·nō), *Russ.* **Ste·pan** (styi·pän′). Dims. **Steve, Ste′vie.**

Stew·art (stooərt, styōō′-) Steward: from an English surname. Also **Stu′art.** Dims. **Stew, Stu.**

Sum·ner (sum′nər) Summoner: from an English surname.

Syd·ney (sid′nē) Var. of SIDNEY.

Syl·va·nus (sil·vā′nəs) Var. of SILVANUS.

Syl·ves·ter (sil·ves′tər) Var. of SILVESTER.

Taf·fy (taf′ē) Welsh dim. of DAVID.

Tad (tad) Dim. of THEODORE or THADDEUS.

Ted (ted) Dim. of EDWARD or THEODORE. Also **Ted′dy.**

Ter·ence (ter′əns) From the name of a Roman clan. Also **Ter′rence.** Dim. **Ter′ry.**

Thad·de·us (thad′ē·əs) Praised. [< Aramaic] Dims. **Tad, Thad, Tha′dy, Thad′dy.**

The·o·bald (thē′ə·bôld, tib′əld) The people's brave one. [< Gmc.]

The·o·dore (thē′ə·dôr, -dōr) Gift of God. [< Gk.] Also *Fr.* **Thé·o·dore** (tā·ô·dôr′), *Ger.* **The·o·dor** (tā′ō·dôr), *Modern Gk.* **The·o·do·ros** (thâ·ô′ḥô·rôs), *Ital., Sp.* **Te·o·do·ro** (*Ital.* tā′ō·dô′rō; *Sp.* tā′ō·thô′rō). Dims. **Tad, Ted, Ted′dy, Dode** (dōd).

Thom·as (tom′əs; *Fr.* tô·mä′; *Ger.* tō′mäs) Twin. [< Aramaic] Also *Ital.* **Tom·ma·so** (tōm·mä′zō), *Sp.* **To·más** (tō·mäs′). Dims. **Tom, Tom′my.**

Thurs·ton (thûrs′tən) Thor's stone. [< Scand.]

Tim·o·thy (tim′ə·thē) Honor of God. [< Gk.] Also *Fr.* **Ti·mo·thée** (tē·mô·tā′), *Ital.* **Tim·mo·te·o** (tē·mô′tā·ō). Dims. **Tim, Tim′my.**

Ti·tus (tī′təs) Meaning uncertain. [< L]

To·bi·as (tō·bī′əs) God is good. [< Hebrew] Also **To·bi·ah** (tō·bī′ə). Dim. **To·by** (tō′bē).

Tod (tod) Fox: from an English surname. Also **Todd.**

To·ny (tō′nē) Dim. of ANTHONY.

Tris·tan (tris′tän; -tən) Confusion. [< Celtic] Also **Tris·tram** (tris′trəm). Dim. **Tris.**

Tyb·alt (tib′əlt) Var. of THEOBALD.

U·lys·ses (yōō·lis′ēz) ? Hater: Lat. form of Gk. *Odysseus.*

Um·ber·to (ōōm·ber′tō) Ital. form of HUMBERT.

Ur·ban (ûr′bən) Of the city. [< L]

U·ri·ah (yōō·rī′ə) God is light. [< Hebrew] Also **U·ri·as** (yōō·rī′əs).

U·ri·el (yōōr′ē·əl) Light of God. [< Hebrew]

Val·en·tine (val′ən·tīn) Strong; healthy. [< L] Dim. **Val.**

Van (van) From an English surname, or from the Ger. or Du. name element *von, van,* indicating residence or origin.

Va·si·li (və·syē′lyē) Russ. var. of BASIL.

Ver·gil (vûr′jəl) Var. of VIRGIL.

Ver·non (vûr′nən) Meaning uncertain. [< L or F] Dim. **Vern.**

Vic·tor (vik′tər; *Fr.* vēk·tôr′) Conqueror. [< L] Also *Ital.* **Vit·to·rio** (vit·tô′ryō). Dims. **Vic, Vick.**

Vin·cent (vin′sənt; *Fr.* vaṅ·säṅ′) Conquering. [< L] Also *Ger.* **Vin·cenz** (vin′tsents), *Ital.* **Vin·cen·zo** (vēn·chen′tsō), *Sp.* **Vi·cen·te** (vē·thän′tā). Dims. **Vin, Vince, Vin′ny.**

Vir·gil (vûr′jəl) Flourishing: from the name of a Roman clan. Also **Ver′gil.** Dims. **Virge, Vir′gie.**

Viv·i·an (viv′ē·ən, viv′yən) Lively. [< F] Also **Viv·i·en** (viv′ē·ən; *Fr.* vē·vyäṅ′).

Wal·do (wôl′dō, wol′-) Ruler. [< Gmc.]

Wal·lace (wol′is) Welsh(man): from a Scot. surname. Also **Wal′lis.** Dim. **Wal′ly.**

Wal·ter (wôl′tər; *Ger.* väl′tər) Ruler of the Army. [< Gmc.] Also *Ger.* **Wal·ther** (väl′tər). Dims. **Walt, Wal′ly.**

Ward (wôrd) Guard: from an English surname.

War·ren (wôr′ən, wor′-) From an English surname.

Wayne (wān) From an English surname. [? < Celtic]

Wes·ley (wes′lē; *Brit.* wez′lē) From an English surname; orig. a place name. Dim. **Wes.**

Wil·bur (wil′bər) Bright will. [< Gmc.] Also **Wil′ber.**

Wil·fred (wil′frid) Resolute peace. [< Gmc.] Also **Wil′·frid.** Dim. **Fred.**

Wil·lard (wil′ərd) From an English surname.

Wil·liam (wil′yəm) Resolute protection. [< Gmc.] Also *Du.* **Wil·lem** (vil′əm), *Ger.* **Wil·helm** (vil′helm). Dims. **Bill, Bil′ly, Will, Wil′lie, Wil′ly.**

Wil·lis (wil′is) Willie's son: from an English surname.

Win·fred (win′frid) Friend of peace. [OE] Also **Win′frid.** Dims. **Win, Win′nie.**

Win·ston (win′stən) From an English surname; orig. a place name.

Wy·att (wī′ət) Dim. of GUY. [< OF]

Wys·tan (wis′tən) Battle stone. [OE]

Zach·a·riah (zak′ə·rī′ə) Remembrance of God. [< Hebrew] Also **Zach·a·ri·as** (zak′ə·rī′əs). Dims. **Zach** (zak), **Zack.**

Zach·a·ry (zak′ər·ē) Var. of ZACHARIAH.

Zeb·a·di·ah (zeb′ə·dī′ə) Gift of God. [< Hebrew]

Zeb·e·dee (zeb′ə·dē) Contr. of ZEBADIAH.

Zech·a·ri·ah (Zek′ə·rī′ə) Var. of ZACHARIAH.

Zeke (zēk) Dim. of EZEKIEL.

Zeph·a·ni·ah (zef′ə·nī′ə) Protected by God. [< Hebrew] Dim. **Zeph.**

Feminine Names

Ab·i·gail (ab′ə·gāl) Father's joy. [< Hebrew] Dims. **Ab′·by, Ab′bie.**

A·da (ā′də) Joyful; flourishing. [< Gmc.]

A·dah (ā′də) Beauty. [< Hebrew] Also **A′da.**

Ad·e·la (ad′ə·lə; *Sp.* ä·thä′lä) Noble. [< Gmc.] Also **A·dele** (ə·del′). *Fr.* **A·dèle** (à·del′), *Ger.* **A·de·le** (ä·dā′lə).

Ad·e·laide (ad′ə·lād) Nobility. [< Gmc.] Also *Fr.* **A·dé·la·ide** (à·dā·là·ēd′), *Ger.* **A·del·heid** (ä′dəl·hīt), *Ital.* **A·de·la·i·de** (ä′d·lä′ē·dä). Dims. **Ad′die, Ad′dy.**

Ad·e·line (ad′ə·līn; *Fr.* àd·lēn′) Of noble birth. [< Gmc.] Also **Ad′a·line, Ad·e·li·cia** (ad′ə·lish′ə), **Ad·e·li·na** (ad′ə·lī′nə). Dims. **Ad′die, Ad′dy.**

A·dri·enne (ā′drē·en; *Fr.* à·drē·en′) Fem. of ADRIAN. [< F]

Ag·a·tha (ag′ə·thə) Good; kind. [< Gk.] Also *Fr.* **A·gathe** (à·gàt′), *Ger.* **A·ga·the** (ä·gä′tə). Dim. **Ag′gie.**

Ag·nes (ag′nis; *Ger.* äg′nes) Pure; sacred. [< Gk.] Also *Fr.* **A·gnès** (à·nyâs′). Dim. **Ag′gie.**

A·i·da (ä·ē′d, ä′dä) From the heroine of Verdi's opera.

Ai·leen (ā·lēn′; *Irish* ī·lēn′) Var. of EILEEN.

Ai·mée (ā·mā′) French form of AMY.

Al·ber·ta (al·bûr′tə) Fem. of ALBERT. Also **Al·ber·ti·na** (al′bər·tē′nə), **Al·ber·tine** (al′bər·tēn).

Al·e·the·a (al′ə·thē′ə, ə·lē′thē·ə) Truth. [< Gk.]

Al·ex·an·dra (al′ig·zan′drə, -zän′-) Fem. of ALEXANDER. Also **Al·ex·an·dri·na** (al′ig·zan·drē′nə, -zän-), *Fr.* **A·lex·an·drine** (à·lek·sän·drēn′), *Ital.* **A·les·san·dra** (ä′läs·sän′drä), *Sp.* **A·le·jan·dra** (ä′lā·hän′drä) or **A·le·jan·dri·na** (ä′lā·hän·drē′nä). Dims. **A·lex·a** (ə·lek′sə), **Al·ex·in·a** (al′ig·zē′nə), **Al·ix** (al′iks), **San·dra** (san′drə).

A·lex·is (ə·lek′sis) Fem. of ALEX. Also **A·lex·i·a** (ə·lek′sē·ə).

Al·fre·da (al·frē′də) Fem. of ALFRED.

Al·ice (al′is; *Fr.* à·lēs′; *Ger.* ä·lē′sə; *Ital.* ä·lē′chä) Truth. [< OF < Gmc.] Also **Al′lis, Al′yce, Al′ys.** Dim. **Al′lie.**

A·li·cia (ə·lish′ə, ə·lish′ē·ə) Var. of ALICE. [< L]

A·line (ə·lēn′, al′ēn) Var. of ADELINE.

Al·i·son (al′ə·sən) Of sacred memory. [< Gmc.] Also **Al′li·son.**

Al·ix (al′iks) Dim. of ALEXANDRIA.

Al·le·gra (ə·lā′grə) Spirited. [< Ital. < L]

Al·ma (al′mə) Providing; gracious. [< L]

Al·mi·ra (al·mī′rə) Lofty; princess. [< Arabic]

Al·the·a (al·thē′ə) Healer. [< Gk.]

Al·vi·na (al·vī′nə, al·vē′nə) Fem. of ALVIN.

Am·a·bel (am′ə·bel) Lovable. [< L] also **Am′a·belle.** Dim. **Mab** (mab).

A·man·da (ə·man′də) Lovable. [< L] Also *Fr.* **A·man·dine** (à·män·dēn′). Dim. **Man′dy.**

Am·a·ran·tha (am′ə·ran′thə) Immortal. [< Gk.]

Am·a·ryl·lis (am′ə·ril′əs) Country sweetheart. [< L]

A·mel·ia (ə·mēl′yə, ə·mē′lē·ə; *Ital.* ä·mâ′lyä; *Sp.* ä·mä′lyä) Industrious. [< Gmc.] Also *Fr.* **A·mé·lie** (à·mā·lē′). Dim. **Mil′lie, Mil′ly.**

Am·i·ty (am′ə·tē) From the abstract noun.

A·my (ā′mē) Beloved. [< L]

An·as·ta·sia (an′ə·stā′zhə, -shə) Able to live again. [< L]

An·dre·a (an′drē·ə; *Ital.* än·drä′ä) Fem. of ANDREW.

An·ge·la (an′jə·lə) Angel. [< Gk.] Also **An·ge·li·na** (an′·jə·lē′nə, -lī′-), *Fr.* **An·gèle** (äṅ·zhel′).

An·gel·i·ca (an·jel′i·kə; *Ital.* än·jâ′lē·kä) Angelic. [< Gk.] Also *Fr.* **An·gé·lique** (äṅ·zhā·lēk′).

A·ni·ta (ə·nē′tə) Dim. of ANNA. [< Sp.] Also **A·ni·tra** (ə·nē′trə).

Ann (an) Grace. [< Hebrew] Also *Sp.* **A·na** (ä′nä). Dims. **An′nie, Nan, Nan′cy, Ni′na.**

An·na (an′ə; *Ger.* ä′nä) Var. of HANNAH. Dim. **An′nie.**

An·na·bel (an′ə·bel) Gracefully fair. [< Hebrew] Also **An·na·bel·la** (an′ə·bel′ə), **An′na·belle.**

Anne (an) Var. of ANN.

An·nette (ə·net′; *Fr.* à·net′) Dim. of ANNE. [< F]

An·the·a (an·thē′ə) Flowery. [< Gk.]

An·toi·nette (an′twə·net′; *Fr.* äṅ·twà·net′) Fr. form of ANTONIA. Also *Ital.* **An·to·niet·ta** (än′tō·nyet′tä). Dims. **Net′tie, Net′ty, To′ni.**

An·to·ni·a (an·tō′nē·ə, an·tō′·nē′ə) Fem. of ANTHONY. [< L] Also *Ital.*, *Sp.* **An·to·ni·na** (än′tō·nē′nä).

A·pril (ā′prəl) From the name of the month.

Ar·i·ad·ne (ar′ē·ad′nē) Most pure. [< Gk.]

Ar·lene (är′lēn) Meaning and origin uncertain. Also **Ar·leen** (är·lēn′), **Ar·line** (är·lēn′).

As·pa·sia (as·pā′zhə, -zhē·ə) Welcome. [< L < Gk.]

As·trid (as′trid) God's power. (< Scand.]

A·the·na (ə·thē′nə) From the name of the greek goddess of wisdom. Also **A·the·ne** (ə·thē·nē).

Au·drey (ô′drē) Noble might. [< OF < Gmc.]

Au·gus·ta (ô·gus′tə; *Ger.* ou·gōos′tä; *Ital.* ou·gōos′tä) Fem. of AUGUSTUS. Also **Au·gus·ti·na** (ô′gəs·tē′nə), **Au·gus·tine** (ô′gəs·tēn). Dims. **Gus′sie, Gus′ta.**

Au·re·lia (ô·rēl′yə) Golden. [< L]

Au·ro·ra (ô·rôr′ə, ô·rō′rə) From the name of the Roman goddess of the dawn.

A·va (ā′və) Meaning and origin uncertain.

Av·e·line (av′ə·lēn, -līn) Hazel. [< F]

A·vis (ā′vis) Bird. [< L]

Ba·bette (bä·bet′) Fr. dim. of ELIZABETH.

Bap·tis·ta (bap·tis′tə) Fem of BAPTIST. Also *Ital.* **Bat·tis·ta** (bät·tēs′tä).

Bar·ba·ra (bär′bər·ə, -brə) Foreign; strange. [< Gk.] Dims. **Bab, Bab′bie, Babs, Barb, Bar′bie, Bob′bie.**

Bath·she·ba (bath·shē′bə, bath′shi·bə) Daughter of the promise. [< Hebrew]

Be·a·ta (bē·ä′tə) Blessed. [< L]

Be·a·trice (bē′ə·tris; *Ital.* bä′ä·trē′chä) She who makes happy. [< L] Also **Be·a·trix** (bē′ə·triks; *Ger.* bä·ä′triks), *Fr.* **Bé·a·trice** or **Bé·a·trix** (bā·à·trēs′). Dims. **Bea, Bee, Trix, Trix′ie, Trix′y.**

Beck·y (bek′ē) Dim. of REBECCA.

Be·lin·da (bə·lin′də) Serpent: title of an oracular priestess. [< Gmc.] Dim. **Lin′da.**

Bel·la (bel′ə) Dim. of ARABELLA or ISABELLA. Also **Bell.**

Belle (bel) Beautiful. [< F]

Ben·e·dic·ta (ben′ə·dik′tə) Fem. of BENEDICT. Also *Ital.* **Be·ne·det·ta** (bā′nā·dāt′tä), *Sp.* **Be·ni·ta** (bā·nē′tä).

Ber·e·ni·ce (ber′ə·nī′sē) Victorious. [< Gk.]

Ber·na·dette (bûr′nə·det′, *Fr.* ber·nà·det′) Fem. of BERNARD. [< F]

Ber·nar·dine (bûr′nər·dēn) Fem. of BERNARD. [< F] Also **Ber·nar·di·na** (bûr′nər·dē′nə).

Ber·nice (bər·nēs′, bûr′nis) Var. of BERENICE.

Ber·tha (bûr′thə; *Du., Ger., Sw.* ber′tä) Bright; famous. [< Gmc.] Also *Fr.* **Berthe** (bert), *Ital., Sp.* **Ber·ta** (ber·tä). Dims. **Ber′tie, Ber′ty.**

Ber·yl (ber′əl) From the name of the jewel.

Bess (bes) Dim. of ELIZABETH. Also **Bes′sie, Bes′sy.**

Beth (beth) Dim. of ELIZABETH.

Beth·el (beth′əl) House of God. [< Hebrew]

Bet·sy (bet′sē) Dim. of ELIZABETH.

Bet·ti·na (bə·tē′nə) Dim. of ELIZABETH. [< Ital.]

Bet·ty (bet′ē) Dim. of ELIZABETH. Also **Bet′te** (bet′ē, bet).

Beu·lah (byoo′lə) Married. [< Hebrew] Also **Beu′la.**

Bev·er·ly (bev′er·lē) From an English surname; orig. a place name. Also **Bev′er·ley.** Dim. **Bev.**

Bid·dy (bid′ē) Dim. of BRIDGET.

Blanche (blanch, blänch; *Fr.* blänsh) White; shining. [< F < Gmc.] Also **Blanch,** *Ital.* **Bian·ca** (byäng′kä), *Sp.* **Blan·ca** (bläng′kä).

Bon·ny (bon′ē) Good. [< F] Also **Bon′nie.**

Bren·da (bren′də) Sword or torch. [< Gmc.]

Bridg·et (brij′it) High; august. [< Celtic] Also **Brig·id** (brij′id, brē′id). Dims. **Bid′dy, Bri·die** (brī′dē).

Ca·mel·lia (kə·mēl′yə) From the name of the flower.

Ca·mil·ia (kə·mil′ə; *Ital.* kä·mēl′lä) Attendant at a sacrifice. [< L] Also *Fr.* **Ca·mille** (kà·mēl′), *Sp.* **Ca·mi·la** (kä·mē′lä).

Can·dice (kan′dis) Radiant. [< L] Also **Can·da·ce** (kan′·də·sē, kan′dā′sē).

Can·di·da (kan′di·də) White; pure. [< L]

Ca·ra (kär′ə) Loved one. [< L]

Car·la (kär′lə) Fem. of CARLO.

Car·lot·ta (kär·lot′ə; *Ital.* kär·lôt′tä) Ital. form of CHARLOTTE. Also *Sp.* **Car·lo·ta** (kär·lō′tä). Dims. **Lot′ta, Lot′·tie, Lot′ty.**

Car·mel (kär′məl) Garden. [< Hebrew] Also **Car·mel·a** (kär·mel′ə). Dim. **Car·me·li·ta** (kär′mə·lē′tə).

Car·men (kär′mən) Song. [< L]

Car·ol (kar′əl) From CAROL, masc., var. of CHARLES. Also **Car·o·la** (kar′ə·lə), **Car′ole, Kar′ol.**

Car·o·line (kar′ə·līn, -lin; *Fr.* kà·rô·lēn′) Fem. of CHARLES. Also **Car·o·lyn,** (kar′ə·lin), **Car·o·li·na** (kar′ə·lī′nə; *Ital., Sp.* kä′rō·lē′nä). Dim. **Car′rie.**

Cas·san·dra (kə·san′drə) From the name of the Trojan prophetess in the *Iliad.* [< Gk.] Dims. **Cass, Cas′sie.**

Cath·er·ine (kath′ər·in, kàth′rin, *Fr.* kà·trēn′) Purity. [< L] Also **Kath′er·ine, Cath′a·rine, Cath·a·ri·na** (kath′ə·rē′nə), *Ital., Sp.* **Ca·ta·ri·na** (kä′tä·rē′nä), or **Ca·te·ri·na** (kä′·tä·rē′nä). Dims. **Cath′y, Kate, Kath′y, Kath′ie, Ka′tie, Kay, Kit, Kit′ty.**

Cath·leen (kath′lēn, kath·lēn′) Var. of KATHLEEN.

Ce·cil·ia (si·sil′yə, -sēl′yə) Fem. of CECIL. Also **Ce·cel′ia, Ce·cile** (si·sēl′), *Fr.* **Cé·cile** (sā·sēl′). Dims. **Cis, Cis′sie, Cis′sy.**

Ce·leste (si·lest′) Heavenly. [< F < L] Also **Ce·les·tine** (si·les′tin, sel′is·tīn), *Fr.* **Cé·les·tine** (sā·les·tēn′).

Cel·ia (sēl′yə, sē′lē·ə; *Ital.* chä′lyä) From the name of a Roman clan. Also *Fr.* **Cé·lie** (sā·lē′).

Cha·ris·sa (kə·ris′ə) Love; grace. [< Gk.]

Char·i·ty (char′ə·tē) From the abstract noun. Dim. **Cher′ry.**

Char·lene (shär·lēn′) Fem. of CHARLES.

Char·lotte (shär·lət; *Fr.* shàr·lôt′; *Ger.* shär·lôt′ə) Fem. of CHARLES. [< F] Dims. **Car′ry, Lot′ta, Lot′tie, Lot′ty.**

Cher·yl (cher′əl) Meaning and origin uncertain.

Chlo·e (klō′ē) Bud; sprout. [< Gk.]

Chris·ta·bel (kris′tə·bel) The fair anointed. [< L] Also **Chris′ta·bel′la, Chris′ta·belle.**

Chris·ti·an·a (kris′tē·an′ə) Fem. of CHRISTIAN. Also *Ger.* **Chri·sti·a·ne** (kris′tē·ä′nə)

Chris·ti·na (kris·tē′nə) Var. of CHRISTIANA. Also **Chris·tine** (kris·tēn′; *Fr.* krēs·tēn′; *Ger.* kris·tē′nə). Dims. **Chris, Chris′sie, Chris′ta, Chris′tie, Ti′na.**

Cic·e·ly (sis′ə·lē) Var. of CECILIA.

Cin·dy (sin′dē) Dim. of LUCINDA.

Claire (klâr) Var. of CLARA. [< F] Also **Clare.**

Clar·a (klar′ə, klâr′ə; *Ger., Sp.* klä′rä) Bright; illustrious. [< L]

Clar·i·bel (klar′ə·bel) Brightly fair. [< L] Also **Clar′a·belle.**

Cla·rice (klə·rēs′, klar′is) Derived from CLARA. Also **Cla·ris·sa** (klə·ris′ə), **Cla·risse** (klə·rēs′).

Cla·rin·da (klə·rin′də) Derived from CLARA.

Clau·dette (klô·det′; *Fr.* klō·det′) Fem. of CLAUDE. [< F]

Clau·di·a (klô′dē·ə) Fem. of *Claudius,* Lat. form of CLAUDE.

Clem·en·tine (klem′ən·tēn, -tīn) Fem. of CLEMENT. [< F]

Cle·o·pat·ra (klē′·ə·pat′rə, -pā′trə, -pä′trə) Celebrated of her country. [< Gk.] Dim. **Cle·o** (klē′ō).

Cli·o (klī′ō, klē′ō) From the name of the Greek muse of history.

Clo·til·da (klō·til′də) Famous in war. [< Gmc.] Also **Clo·thil′da, Clo·thil′de,** *Fr.* **Clo·tilde** (klô·tēld′).

Co·lette (kō·let′; *Fr.* kô·let′) Fem. dim. of NICHOLAS. [< F]

Col·leen (kol′ēn, ko·lēn′) Girl. [< Irish]

Con·stance (kon′stəns, *Fr.* kôn′·stäns′) Constant; firm. [< L] Dims. **Con′nie, Con′ny.**

Con·sue·lo (kən·swā′lō; *Sp.* kōn·swä′lō) Consolation. [< Sp.]

Co·ra (kôr′ə, kō′rə) Maiden. [< Gk.]

Cor·del·ia (kôr·dēl′yə, -dē′lē·ə) Meaning uncertain. [< L]

Co·rin·na (kə·rin′ə) Maiden. [< Gk.] Also **Co·rinne** (kə·rin′, -rēn′; *Fr.* kô·rēn′).

Cor·nel·ia (kôr·nēl′yə, -nē′lē·ə) Fem. of CORNELIUS. [< L]

Cris·ti·na (krēs·tē′nä) Ital. and Sp. form of CHRISTINA.

Crys·tal (kris′təl) From the common noun.

Cyn·thi·a (sin′thē·ə) Of Mount Cynthius: an epithet of the Greek goddess Artemis; poetically ,the moon.

Dag·mar (dag′mär) Bright day. [< Dan.]

Dai·sy (dā′zē) From the name of the flower.

Dale (dāl) From the common noun.

Daph·ne (daf′nē) Laurel. [< Gk.]

Dar·leen (därl·lēn′) Beloved. [OE] Also **Dar·lene′, Dar·line′.**

Dawn (dôn) From the common noun.

Deb·o·rah (deb′ər·ə, deb′rə) Queen bee. [< Hebrew] Dims. **Deb, Deb′by.**

Deir·dre (dir′drə) From the name of a heroine of Irish myth.

Del·ia (dēl′yə) Of Delos: an epithet of the Greek goddess Artemis. [< Gk.]

De·li·lah (di·lī′lə) Delicate; languid. [< Hebrew]

Del·la (del′ə) Var. of ADELA.

Del·phin·i·a (del·fin′ē·ə) Of Delphi. [< Gk.] Also *Fr.* **Del·phine** (del·fēn′).

De·nise (də·nēz′, -nēs′) Fem. of *Denis.* Fr. form of DENNIS.

Des·i·ree (dez′ə·rē) Desired. [< F] Also *Fr.* **Dé·si·rée** (dā·zē·rā′).

Di·an·a (dī·an′ə) From the name of the Roman goddess of the moon. Also **Di·ane** (dī·an′; *Fr.* dyàn). Dim. **Di** (dī).

Di·nah (dī′nə) Judged. [< Hebrew]

Do·lo·res (də·lôr′is, -lō′ris; *Sp.* dō·lō′räs) Our Lady of

Sorrows: a title of the Virgin Mary. [< Sp.] Dim. **Lo·la** (lō′lə).

Dom·i·nique (dom′ə·nēk; *Fr.* dô·mē·nēk′) Fr. fem. of DOMINIC. Also **Dom·i·ni·ca** (dom′ə·nē′kə, də·min′ə·kə).

Don·na (don′ə) Lady. [< Ital.]

Do·ra (dôr′ə, dō′rə) Dim. of DOROTHY, EUDORA, or THEODORA.

Dor·cas (dôr′kəs) Gazelle. [< Gk.]

Do·reen (dô·rēn′, dôr′ēn, dō-) Irish dim. of DORA.

Do·rin·da (də·rin′də) Gift. [< Gk.]

Do·ris (dôr′is, dor′-) Dorian woman. [< Gk.]

Dor·o·thy (dôr′ə·thē, dor′-) Gift of God. [< Gk.] Also **Dor·o·the·a** (dôr′ə·thē′ə, dor′-; *Ger.* dō′rō·tā′ä), *Fr.* **Do·ro·thée** (dô·rô·tā′). Dims. **Doll, Dol′lie, Dol′ly, Do′ra, Dot, Dot′ty.**

Dru·sil·la (droō·sil′ə) She who strengthens. [< L] Also **Dru·cil′la.**

E·dith (ē′dith) Prosperous in war. [OE] Also *Lat.* **Ed·i·tha** (ed′i·thə, ē′di·thə). Dim. **E·die** or **Ea·die** (ē′dē).

Ed·na (ed′nə) Rejuvenation. [< Hebrew]

Ed·wi·na (ed·wē′nə, -win′ə) Fem. of EDWIN.

Ef·fie (ef′ē) Dim. of EUPHEMIA.

Ei·leen (ī·lēn′) Irish form of HELEN.

E·ka·te·ri·na (yə·kə·tyi·ryē′nə) Russ. form of CATHERINE.

E·laine (i·lān′, ē·lān′) Var. of HELEN. [< OF] Also **E·layne′.**

El·ber·ta (el·bûr′tə) Fem. of ELBERT.

El·ea·nor (el′ə·nər, -nôr) Var. of HELEN. [< F] Also **El′i·nor, El·ea·no·ra** (el′ə·nôr′ə, -nō′rə, el′ē·ə-), **Fr. É·lé·o·nore** (ā·lā·ô·nôr′), **Ger. E·le·o·no·re** (ā′lā·ō·nō′rə), *Ital.* **E·le·o·no·ra** (ā′lā·ō·nô′rä). Dims. **El′la, El′lie, Nell, Nel′lie, Nel′ly.**

E·lec·tra (i·lek′trə) Shining; golden-haired. [< Gk.] Also **E·lek′tra.**

E·le·na (el′ə·nə, ə·lē′nə; *Ital.* â′lā·nä) Var. of HELEN. [< Ital.]

E·li·za (i·lī′zə) Dim. of ELIZABETH. Also *Fr.* **É·lise** (ā·lēz′).

E·liz·a·beth (i·liz′ə·bəth) Consecrated to God. [< Hebrew] Also **E·lis·a·beth** (i·liz′ə·bəth; *Ger.* ā·lē′zä·bet), *Fr.* **É·li·sa·beth** (ā·lē·zà·bet′), *Ital.* **E·li·sa·bet·ta** (ā·lē′zä·bāt′tä). Dims. **Bess, Bes′sie, Beth, Bet′sy, Bet′te, Bet′ty, El′sa, El′sie, Lib′by, Li′sa, Liz, Liz′beth, Liz′zie, Liz′zy.**

El·la (el′ə) Dim. of ELEANOR. Also **El′lie.**

El·len (el′ən) Var. of HELEN.

E·lo·i·sa (ā′lō·ē′zä) Ital. form of LOUISE.

El·o·ise (el′ō·ēz′, el′ō·ēz) Var. of LOUISE. [< F]

El·sa (el′sə; *Ger.* el′zä) Dim. of ELIZABETH. Also **El·sie** (el′·sē).

El·speth (el′spəth) Scot. form of ELIZABETH.

El·va (el′və) Elf. [< Gmc.]

El·vi·ra (el·vī′rä, -vir′ə) Elf ruler. [< Sp. < Gmc.]

Em·e·line (em′ə·līn, -lēn) Derived from EMILY. Also **Em′me·line.**

Em·i·ly (em′ə·lē) Fem. of EMIL. Also **Em′i·lie,** *Fr.* **É·mi·lie** (ā·mē·lē′), *Ger.* **E·mi·li·e** (e·mē′lē·ə), *Ital., Sp.* **E·mi·lia** (ā·mē′lyä). Dim. **Em.**

Em·ma (em′ə) Grandmother. [< Gmc.] Dims. **Em, Em′mie.**

E·nid (ē′nid) Chastity; purity. [< Celtic]

Er·i·ca (er′i·kə) Fem. of ERIC. Also **Er′i·ka.**

Er·ma (ûr′mə) Dim. of ERMENGARDE.

Er·men·garde (ûr′mən·gärd) Great guardian. [< Gmc.]

Er·men·trude (ûr′mən·troōd) Great strength. [< Gmc.]

Er·nes·tine (ûr′nəs·tēn) Fem. of ERNEST.

Es·me·ral·da (es′mə·ral′də) Emerald. [< Sp.]

Es·telle (es·tel′) Star. [< L] Also **Es·tel·la** (es·tel′ə).

Es·ther (es′tər) Star. [< Pers.] Dims. **Es′sie, Het′ty.**

Eth·el (eth′əl) Noble. [< Gmc.]

Et·ta (et′ə) Dim. of HENRIETTA.

Eu·do·ra (yoō·dôr′ə, -dō′rə) Good gift. [< Gk.]

Eu·ge·nia (yoō·jē′nē·ə, -jēn′yə) Fem. of EUGENE. Also **Eu·ge·nie** (yoō·jē′nē), *Fr.* **Eu·gé·nie** (œ·zhä·nē′). Dims. **Gene, Ge′nie.**

Eu·la·li·a (yoō·lā′lē·ə, -lāl′yə) Fair speech. [< Gk.] Also **Eu·la·lie** (yoō′lə·lē; *Fr.* œ·là·lē′).

Eu·nice (yoō′nis; *Lat.* yoō·nī′sē) Good victory. [< Gk.]

Eu·phe·mi·a (yoō·fē′mē·ə) Of good repute. [< Gk.] Also *Fr.* **Eu·phé·mie** (œ·fä·mē′). Dims. **Ef·fie** (ef′ē), **Phe′mie.**

E·va (ē′və; *Ger., Ital., Sp.* ä′vä) Var. of EVE. [< L]

E·van·ge·line (i·van′jə·lin, -līn, -lēn) Bearer of glad tidings. [< Gk.]

Eve (ēv; *Fr.* ev) Life. [< Hebrew]

Ev·e·lyn (ev′ə·lin; *Brit.* ēv′lin) Hazelnut. [< L] Also **Ev·e·li·na** (ev′ə·lī′nə, -lē′-).

E·vi·ta (ā·vē′tä) Sp. dim. of EVA.

Faith (fāth) From the abstract noun. Dim. **Fay.**

Fan·ny (fan′ē) Dim. of FRANCES. Also **Fan′nie.**

Faus·ti·na (fôs·tī′nə, -tē′-) Lucky. [< L] Also **Faus·tine** (fôs·tēn′; *Fr.* fôs·tēn′)

Fawn (fôn) From the name of the animal.

Fay (fā) Fairy or faith. [OF] Also **Fae, Faye.**

Fe·li·cia (fə·lish′ə, -lish′ē·ə, -lē′shə) Happy. [< L] Also **Fe·lice** (fə·lēs′), **Fe·lic′i·ty** (-lis′ə·tē)

Fern (fûrn) From the common noun.

Fer·nan·da (fer·nän′dä) Fem. of *Fernando,* Sp. form of FERDINAND.

Fi·del·ia fi·dēl′yə, -dē′lē·ə) Faithful. [< L]

Fi·o·na (fē·ō′nə) Fair or white. [< Celtic]

Fla·vi·a (flā′vē·ə) Blonde. [<]

Flo·ra (flôr′ə, flō′rə) Flower. [< L]

Flor·ence (flôr′əns, flor′-; *Fr.* flô·räns′) Blooming. [< L] Dims. **Flo** (flō), **Flor·rie** (flôr′ē, flor′ē), **Flos·sie** (flos′ē).

Fran·ces (fran′sis, frän′-) Fem. of FRANCIS. Also *Fr.* **Fran·çoise** (frän·swàz′) or **Fran·cisque** (frän·sēsk′), *Ital.* **Fran·ces·ca** (frän·chäs′kä). Dims. **Fan′nie, Fan′ny, Fran, Fran′cie, Frank, Fran′nie.**

Fran·cine (fran·sēn′) Derived from FRANCES. Also **Fran·cene′.**

Fred·er·i·ca (fred′ə·rē′kə, fred·rē′kə) Fem. of FREDERICK. Dim. **Fred′die.**

Frie·da (frē′də) Peace. [< G] Also **Fre′da.**

Ga·bri·elle (gä′brē·el′, gab′rē-; *Fr.* gà·brē·el′) Fem. of GABRIEL. Also **Ga·bri·el·la** (gä′brē·el′ə) Dim. **Ga·by** (gä·bē′).

Gail (gāl) Short for ABIGAIL. Also **Gale.**

Gay (gā) From the adjective.

Gen·e·vieve (jen′ə·vēv, jen′ə·vēv′) White wave. [< F < Celtic] Also *Fr.* **Ge·ne·viève** (zhen·vyev′).

Ge·nev·ra (ji·nev′rə) Var. of GUINEVERE. [< Ital.] Also **Ge·ne·va** (ji·nē′və).

Geor·gia (jôr′jə) Fem. of GEORGE.

Geor·gi·an·a (jôr′jē·an′ə) Fem. of GEORGE. Also **Geor·gi·na** (jôr·jē′nə), *Fr.* **Geor·gine** (zhôr·zhēn′) or **Geor·gette** (zhôr·zhet′).

Ger·al·dine (jer′əl·dēn) Fem. of GERALD. Dims. **Ger′ry, Jer′ry.**

Ger·maine (jər·mān′) German. [< F < L]

Ger·trude (gûr′troōd, *Fr.* zher·trüd′) Spear maid. [< Gmc.] Also *Ger.* **Ger·trud** (ger′troōt). Dims. **Ger′tie, Ger′·ty, Tru′da, Tru′dy.**

Gil·ber·ta (gil·bûr′tə) Fem. of GILBERT. Also **Gil·ber·tine** (gil′bər·tēn), *Fr.* **Gil·berte** (zhēl·bert′)

Gil·da (gil′də) Servant of God. [< Celtic]

Gil·li·an (jil′ēl·ən, jil′yən) Var. of JULIANA.

Gi·nev·ra (ji·nev′rə) Var. of GUINEVERE. (< Ital.]

Gin·ger (jin′jer) From the plant name.

Gio·van·na (jō·vän′nä) Fem. of *Giovanni,* Ital. form of JOHN.

Gi·sele (zhē·zel′) Pledge or hostage. (< F < Gmc.] Also **Gi·selle′.**

Giu·lia (joō′lyä) Ital. form of JULIA.

Glad·ys (glad′is) Welsh fem. form of CLAUDIUS.

Glen·na (glen′ə) Fem. of GLENN. Also **Glen·nis** (glen′is), **Gly·nis** (glin′is).

Glo·ri·a (glôr′ē·ə, glō′rē·ə) Glory. [< L]

Grace (grās) Grace; favor. [< L] Also **Gra·ci·a** or **Gra·ti·a** (grā′shē·ə, -shə).

Gret·a (gret′ə, grēt′ə; *Ger.* grā′tə) Dim. of MARGARET. [< G] Also **Gre·tel** or **Gre·thel** (grā′təl).

Gretch·en (grech′ən; *Ger.* grāt′Қhən) Dim. of MARGARET. [< G]

Gri·sel·da (gri·zel′də)   Stony or unbeatable heroine. [< Gmc.]   Also **Gris·sel** (gris′əl), **Griz·el** (griz′əl).

Gus·sie (gus′ē)   Dim. of AUGUSTA.   Also **Gus·ta** (gus′tə)

Gwen·do·lyn (gwen′də·lin)   White-browed.   [< Celtic] Also **Gwen′do·len, Gwen′do·line** (-lin, -lēn).   Dims. **Gwen, Gwenn, Wen·dy** (wen′dē).

Gwen·eth (gwen′ith)   Fair or blessed.   [< Celtic]   Also **Gwen′ith, Gwyn·eth** (gwin′ith), **Gyn·eth** (gin′ith).

Gwyn (gwin)   Fair or White.   [< Celtic]   Also **Gwynne.**

Han·nah (han′ə)   Grace.   [< Hebrew]   Also **Han′na.**

Har·ri·et (har′ē·ət)   Fem. of HARRY.   Dims. **Hat′tie, Hat′ty.**

Ha·zel (hā′zəl)   From the plant name.

Heath·er (heth′ər)   From the plant name.

Hed·da (hed′ə)   War.   [< Gmc.]

Hed·wig (hed′wig)   War.   [< Gmc.]

Hel·en (hel′ən)   Light; a torch.   [< Gk.]   Also *Fr.* **Hé·lène** (ā·len′).   Dims. **Nell, Nel′lie, Nel′ly.**

Hel·e·na (hel′ə·nə)   Var. of HELEN.   Dim. **Le·na** (lē′nə).

Hel·ga (hel′gə)   Holy.   [< Gmc.]

Hé·lo·ïse (ā·lō·ēz′)   Fr. form of ELOISE.

Hen·ri·et·ta (hen′rē·et′ə)   Fem. of HENRY.   Also *Fr.* **Hen·ri·ette** (än·ryet′).   Dims. **Et′ta, Et′tie, Hat′tie, Hat′ty, Het′·ty, Net′tie, Ret′ta.**

Heph·zi·bah (hep′zə·bə)   She who is my delight.   [< Hebrew].

Her·mi·o·ne (hər·mī′ə·nē)   Fem. of HERMES.

Hes·ter (hes′tər)   Var. of ESTHER.   Also **Hes′ther.**   Dim. **Het′ty.**

Het·ty (het′ē)   Dim. of ESTHER, HENRIETTA, or HESTER.

Hil·a·ry (hil′ər·ē)   Joyful.   [< L]

Hil·da (hil′də)   Battle maiden.   [OE]

Hil·de·garde (hil′də·gärd)   Guardian battle maiden.   [< Gmc.]   Also **Hil′de·gard.**

Hol·ly (hol′ē)   From the plant name.

Ho·no·ra (hō·nôr′ə, -nō′rə)   Honor.   [< L]   Also **Ho·no·ri·a** (hō·nôr′ē·ə, -nō′rē·ə)   Dims. **No′ra, No′rah.**

Hope (hōp)   From the abstract noun.

Hor·tense (hôr′tens; *Fr.* ôr·täns′)   Gardener: from the name of a Roman clan.   [< F < L]   Also *Lat.* **Hor·ten·si·a** (hôr·ten′shē·ə).

I·da (ī′də)   Happy; godlike.   [< Gmc.]

I·lo·na (i·lō′nə)   Radiantly beautiful.   [< Hung. < Gk.]

Il·se (il′sə; *Ger.* il′zə)   Dim. of ELIZABETH.   [< G]

Im·o·gene (im′ə·jēn)   Meaning and origin uncertain.   Also **Im·o·gen** (im′ə·jən).

I·na (ī′nə)   From the Lat. suffix for fem. names.

I·nez (ī′nez, ē′nez; *Sp.* ē·nāth′)   Var. of AGNES.   [< Sp. & Pg.]

In·grid (ing′grid)   Daughter of Ing (a god in Gmc. mythology).   [< Gmc.]   Also **In·ga** (ing′gə).

I·rene (ī·rēn′)   Peace.   [< Gk.]

I·ris (ī′ris)   Rainbow.   [< Gk.],   or from the name of the flower.

Ir·ma (ûr′mə)   Var. of ERMA.

Is·a·bel (iz′ə·bel; *Sp.* ē′sä·bel′)   Oath of Baal.   [< Hebrew]   Also **Is·a·bel·la** (iz′ə·bel′ə; *Ital.* ē′zä·bel′lä), **Is·a·belle** (iz′ə·bel; *Fr.* ē·zà·bel′), **Is′o·bel,** *Fr.* **I·sa·beau** (ē·zà·bō′).   Dims. **Bell, Bel′la, Belle.**

Is·a·do·ra (iz′ə·dôr′ə, -dō′rə)   Fem. of ISIDORE.

I·vy (ī′vē)   From the plant name.

Jac·que·line (jak′wə·lin, -lēn, jak′ə-; *Fr.* zhä·klēn′)   Fem. of *Jacques,* Fr. form of JACOB.   Dim. **Jac′kie.**

Jane (jān)   Var. of JOAN.   [< OF]

Jan·et (jan′it, jə·net′)   Dim. of JANE.

Jan·ice (jan′is)   Var. of JANE.

Jas·mine (jaz′min, jas′-)   From the name of the flower.

Jean (jēn)   Var. of JOAN.   [< F]

Jeanne (jēn, *Fr.* zhän)   Fr. form of JOAN.

Jean·nette (jə·net′)   Dim. of JEANNE.

Je·mi·ma (jə·mī′mə)   Dove.   [< Hebrew]

Jen·ni·fer (jen′ə·fər)   Var. of GUINEVERE.   Dims. **Jen′ny, Jin′ny.**

Jer·ry (jer′ē)   Dim. of GERALDINE.

Jes·si·ca (jes′i·kə)   Fem. of JESSE.   Dims. **Jess, Jes′sie, Jes′sy.**

Jew·el (jōō′əl)   From the common noun.

Jill (jil)   Short for JULIA.

Jo (jō)   Dim. of JOSEPHINE.

Joan (jōn, jō·an′)   Fem. of JOHN.   Also **Jo·an·na** (jō·an′ə), **Jo·anne** (jō·an′)

Joc·e·lyn (jos′ə·lin)   Playful; merry.   [< L]   Also **Joc′e·lin, Joc′e·line** (-lin).

Jo·han·na (jō·han′ə; *Ger.* yō·hän′ä)   Ger. form of JOAN.

Jo·se·pha (jō·sē′fə)   Var. of JOSEPHINE.

Jo·se·phine (jō′sə·fēn, -zə-)   Fem. of JOSEPH.   [< F]   Dims. **Jo, Jo′sie, Jo′zy.**

Joy (joi)   From the abstract noun.

Joyce (jois)   Joyful.   [< L]

Jua·na (wä′nə; *Sp.* hwä′nä)   Fem. of *Juan,* Sp. form of JOHN.

Jua·ni·ta (wä·nē′tə; *Sp.* hwä·nē′tä)   Sp. dim. of JUANA.

Ju·dith (jōō′dith)   Praised.   [< Hebrew]   Dim. **Ju′dy.**

Jul·ia (jōōl′yə)   Fem. of JULIUS.   Also **Ju·lie** (jōō′lē; *Fr.* zhü·lē′).

Ju·li·an·a (jōō′lē·an′ə, -ä′nə)   Fem. of JULIAN.   Also *Fr.* **Ju·li·enne** (zhü·lyen′).

Ju·li·et (jōō′lē·et, jōō′lē·et′)   Dim. of JULIA.

June (jōōn)   From the name of the mouth.

Jus·ti·na (jus·tī′nə, -tē′-)   Fem. of JUSTIN.   Also **Jus·tine** (jus·tēn′; *Fr.* zhüs·tēn′).

Kar·en (kâr′ən; *Dan., Norw.* kä′rən)   Var. of CATHERINE.   [< Dan. & Norw.]

Kate (kāt)   Dim. of CATHERINE.   Also **Ka′tie.**

Kath·a·rine (kath′ə·rin, kath′rin)   Var. of CATHERINE.   Also **Kath′er·ine, Kath′ryn.**

Kath·leen (kath′lēn, kath·lēn′)   Irish form of CATHERINE.

Kath·y (kath′ē)   Dim. of CATHERINE.

Ka·tri·na (kə·trē′nə)   Var. of CATHERINE.   Also **Kat·rine** (kat′rin, -rēn).   Dim. **Tri·na** (trē′nə).

Kay (kā)   Dim. of CATHERINE.

Kir·sten (kûr′stən; *Norw.* khish′tən, khir′stən)   Norw. form of CHRISTINE.

Kit·ty (kit′ē)   Dim. of CATHERINE.   Also **Kit.**

Kla·ra (klä′rä)   Ger. form of CLARA.

Lau·ra (lôr′ə)   Laurel.   [< L]   Also *Fr.* **Laure** (lôr).   Dims. **Lau′rie, Lol′ly.**

Lau·ret·ta (lô·ret′ə)   Dim. of LAURA.   Also **Lau·rette′.**

Lau·rin·da (lô·rin′də)   Derived from LAURA.

La·verne (lə·vûrn′)   From the name of the Roman goddess of spring and grain.

La·vin·i·a (lə·vin′ē·ə)   Purified.   [< L]

Le·ah (lē′ə)   Gazelle.   [< Hebrew]   Also **Le′a.**

Lei·la (lē′lä)   Dark night or dark beauty.   [< Arabic]

Le·na (lē′nə)   Dim. of HELENA or MAGDALENE.

Le·no·ra (lə·nôr′ə, -nō′rə)   Var. of ELEANOR.   Also **Le·nore** (lə·nôr′).

Le·o·na (lē·ō′nə)   Fem. of LEO and LEON.   Also *Fr.* **Lé·o·nie** (lā·ô·nē′).

Le·or·a (lē·ôr′ə, -ō′rə)   Var. of LEONORA.

Les·lie (les′lē, les′-)   From LESLIE. masc.   Also **Les′ley.**

Le·ti·tia (li·tish′ə)   Joy.   [< L]   Dim. **Let′ty** (let′ē).

Lib·by (lib′ē)   Dim. of ELIZABETH.

Li·la (lī′lə, lē′-)   Var. of LILLIAN.

Lil·i·an (lil′ē·ən, lil′yən)   Lily.   [< L]   Also **Lil′li·an.**   Dims. **Lil, Lil′ly, Lil′y.**

Lil·y (lil′ē)   From the name of the flower; also, dim. of LILIAN.

Lin·da (lin′də)   Pretty   [< Sp.],   or short for BELINDA or MELINDA.

Li·sa (lī′zə, lē′)   Dim. of ELIZABETH.   Also **Li′za,** *Ger.* **Li·se** (lē′zə).

Li·sette (lē·zet′)   Fr. dim. of ELIZABETH.   Also **Li·zette′.**

Liz·beth (liz′bəth)   Dim. of ELIZABETH.

Liz′zie (liz′ē)   Dim. of ELIZABETH.   Also **Liz′zy, Liz. Lo·is** (lō′is)   Desirable.   [< Gk.]

Lo·la (lō′lə; *Sp.* lō′lä)   Dim. of DOLORES.   [< Sp.]   Dim. **Lo·li·ta** (lō·lē′tə; *Sp.* lōl·lē′tä).

Lor·ene (lô·rēn′)   Var. of LAURA.   Also **Laur·een′, Laur·ene′, Lor·een′.**

Lor·et·ta (lô·ret′ə, lō-) Dim. of LAURA. Also **Lor·ette** (lô·ret′).

Lo·rin·da (lô·rin′də, lə-) Var. of LAURINDA.

Lor·na (lôr′nə) Lost. [OE]

Lor·raine (lə·rān′) Var. of LAURA.

Lot·tie (lot′ē) Dim. of CHARLOTTE. Also **Lot′ta, Lot′ty.**

Lou·el·la (lōō·el′ə) Var. of LUELLA.

Lou·ise (lōō·ēz′) Fem. of LOUIS. [< F] Also **Lou·i·sa** (lōō·ē′zə). Dims. **Lou, Lou′ie, Lu, Lu′lu.**

Lu·cia (lōō′shə; *Ital.* lōō·chē′ä) Fem. of LUCIUS.

Lu·cille (lōō·sēl′) Var. of LUCIA. [< F] Also **Lu·cile′.**

Lu·cin·da (lōō·sin′də) Derived from LUCY. Dim. **Cin·dy** (sin′dē).

Lu·cre·tia (lōō·krē′shə, -shē·ə) Fem. of LUCRETIUS. Also *Fr.* **Lu·crèce** (lü·kres′), *Ital.* **Lu·cre·zia** (lōō·krā′tsyä).

Lu·cy (lōō′sē) Var. of LUCIA. Also *Fr.* **Lu·cie** (lü·sē′).

Lu·el·la (lōō·el′ə) Meaning and origin uncertain. Also **Lou·el′la.**

Lu·i·sa (lōō·ē′zä) Ital. form of LOUISA. Also *Ger.* **Lu·i·se** (lōō·ē′zə).

Lu·lu (lōō′lōō) Dim. of LOUISE.

Lyd·i·a (lid′ē·ə) She of Lydia. [< Gk.]

Ma·bel (mā′bəl) Short for AMABEL. Dim. **Mab** (mab).

Mad·e·leine (mad′ə·lin, -lān, *Fr.* mà·dlen′) Var. of MAGDALENE. [< F] Also **Mad·e·line** (mad′ə·lin, -līn).

Madge (madj) Dim. of MARGARET.

Mae (mā) Var. of MAY.

Mag (mag) Dim. of MARGARET. Also **Mag′gie.**

Mag·da·lene (mag′də·lēn, mag′də·lē′nē) Woman of Magdala. [< Hebrew] Also **Mag·da·len** (mag′də·lən), **Mag·da·le·na** (mag′də·lē′nə; *Sp.* mäg′thä·lā′nä). Dims. **Le·na** (lē′nə), **Mag·da** (mag′də).

Mai·sie (mā′zē) Dim. of MARGARET. [< Scot.]

Mal·vi·na (mal·vī′nə, -vē′-) Meaning and origin uncertain.

Ma·mie (mā′mē) Dim. of MARGARET.

Man·dy (man′dē) Dim. of AMANDA.

Mar·cel·la (mär·sel′ə) Fem. of MARCELLUS. Also *Fr.* **Mar·celle** (mär·sel′).

Mar·cia (mär′shə) Fem. of *Marcius,* var. of MARCUS.

Mar·ga·ret (mär′gə·rit, mär′grit) Pearl. [< Gk.] Also *Ger.* **Mar·ga·re·te** (mär′gä·rā′tə), *Ital.* **Mar·ghe·ri·ta** (mär′·gä·rē′tä), *Ital., Sp.* **Mar·ga·ri·ta** (mär′gä·rē′tä). Dims. **Gret′a, Gretch′en, Madge, Mag, Mag′gie, Ma′mie, Meg, Me′ta, Peg, Peg′gy, Ri′ta.**

Marge (märj) Dim. of MARJORIE. Also **Mar′gie, Marj.**

Mar·ger·y (mär′jər·ē) Var. of MARGARET.

Mar·got (mär′gō; *Fr.* mar·gō′) Var. of MARGARET. [< F] Also **Mar′go.**

Mar·gue·rite (mär′gə·rēt′; *Fr.* mar·gə·rēt′) Var. of MARGARET. [< F]

Ma·ri·a (mə·rī′ə, -rē′ə; *Ger., Ital.* mä·rē′ä) Var. of MARY. [< L] Also *Sp.* **Ma·rí·a** (mä·rē′ä).

Mar·i·an (mar′ē·ən, mâr′-) Var. of MARION.

Mar·i·anne (mâr′ē·an′) From MARY and ANNE. Also **Mar·i·an·na** (mâr′ē·an′ə).

Ma·rie (mə·rē′; *Fr.* mà·rē′) Var. of MARY. [< F]

Mar·i·et·ta (mâr′ē·et′ə, mar′-) Dim. of MARIA.

Mar·i·gold (mar′ə·gōld, mâr′-) From the name of the flower.

Mar·i·lyn (mar′ə·lin, mâr′-) Var. of MARY.

Mar·i·on (mar′ē·ən, mâr′-) Var. of MARY.

Mar·jo·rie (mär′jər·ē) Var. of MARGARET. Also **Mar′jo·ry.** Dims. **Marge, Mar′gie, Marj.**

Mar·lene (mär·lēn′; *Ger.* mär·lā′nə) Var. of MAGDALENE.

Mar·sha (mär′shə) Var. of MARCIA.

Mar·tha (mär′thə) Lady. [< Aramaic] Also *Fr.* **Marthe** (màrt), *Ital., Sp.* **Mar·ta** (mär′tä). Dims. **Mar′ty, Mat′tie, Mat′ty.**

Mar·y (mâr′ē) Meaning uncertain. [< Hebrew] Dims. **May, Min′nie, Mol′ly, Pol′ly.**

Ma·til·da (mə·til′də) Mighty battle maiden. [< Gmc.] Also **Ma·thil·da** (mə·til′də), *Ger.* **Ma·thil·de** (mä·til′də). Dims. **Mat′tie, Mat′ty, Pat′ty, Til′da, Til′lie, Til′ly.**

Maud (môd) Contr. of MAGDALENE. Also **Maude.**

Mau·ra (môr′ə) Irish form of MARY. Also **Maur·ya** (môr′·yə).

Mau·reen (mô·rēn′) Dim. of MAURA.

Ma·vis (mā′vis) From the name of the bird, or the Irish fairy queen Maeve or Mab.

Max·ine (mak·sēn′, mak′sēn) Fem. of MAX. [< F]

May (mā) Dim. of MARY.

Meg (meg) Dim. of MARGARET.

Mel·a·nie (mel′ə·nē) Black. [< Gk.]

Me·lin·da (mə·lin′də) Var. of BELINDA.

Me·lis·sa (mə·lis′ə) Bee. [< Gk.]

Mer·ce·des (mər·sā′dēz, -sē′-, mûr′sə·dēz; *Sp.* mer·thä′thäs) Mercies. [< Sp.]

Mer·cy (mûr′sē) From the abstract noun.

Me·ta (mā′tə, mē′-) Dim. of MARGARET. [< G]

Mi·gnon (min′yon, *Fr.* mē·nyôn′) Dainty. [< F]

Mil·dred (mil′drid) Moderate power. [OE] Dims. **Mil′·lie, Mil′ly.**

Mil·li·cent (mil′ə·sənt) Power to work. [< Gmc.] Also **Mil′i·cent.**

Mi·mi (mē′mē) Fr. dim. of WILHELMINA.

Mi·na (mē′nə) Dim. of WILHELMINA.

Mi·ner·va (mi·nûr′və) From the name of the Roman goddess of wisdom.

Min·na (min′ə) Dim. of WILHELMINA.

Min·nie (min′ē) Memory or love [< Gmc.]; also, dim. of MARY.

Mi·ran·da (mi·ran′də) Admirable. [< L]

Mir·i·am (mir′ē·əm) Var. of MARY. [< Hebrew]

Moi·ra (moi′rə) Var. of MAURA.

Mol·ly (mol′ē) Dim. of MARY. Also **Moll.**

Mo·na (mō′nə) Noble. [< Irish]

Mon·i·ca (mon′ə·kə) Adviser. [< L]

Mu·ri·el (myŏŏr′ē·əl) Myrrh. [< Gk.]

Myr·na (mûr′nə) Meaning and origin uncertain.

Myr·tle (mûrt′l) From the plant name.

Na·dine (nā·dēn′, nə-; *Fr.* nà·dēn′) Hope. [< F < Russ.]

Nan (nan) Dim. of ANN.

Nan·cy (nan′sē) Dim. of ANN.

Nan·nette (na·net′) Dim. of ANN. [< F] Also **Na·nette′.**

Na·o·mi (nā·ō′mē, nā′ō·mē) Pleasant. [< Hebrew]

Nat·a·lie (nat′ə·lē) Christmas child. [< L] Also *Russ.* **Nat·ta·sha** (nä·tä′shə).

Nell (nel) Dim. of ELEANOR, ELLEN, or HELEN. Also **Nel′·lie, Nel′ly.**

Net·tie (net′ē) Dim. of ANTOINETTE, HENRIETTA, or JEANNETTE. Also **Net′ty.**

Ni·cole (ni·kōl′; *Fr.* nē·kôl′) Fem. of *Nicolas,* Fr. form of NICHOLAS.

Ni·na (nī′nə, nē′-) Dim. of ANN. [< Russ.]

Ni·ta (nē′tə; *Sp.* nē′tä) Dim. of JUANITA. [< Sp]

No·na (nō′nə) Ninth. [< L]

No·ra (nôr′ə, nō′rə) Dim. of ELEANOR, HONORA, LEONORA. Also **No′rah.**

No·reen (nôr′ēn, nô·rēn′) Irish dim. of NORA.

Nor·ma (nôr′mə) Pattern. [< L]

Oc·ta·vi·a (ok·tā′vē·ə) Fem. of OCTAVIUS.

Ol·ga (ol′gə) Holy. [< Russ. < Scand.]

O·live (ol′iv) Var. of OLIVIA.

O·liv·i·a (ō·liv′ē·ə) She of the olive tree: prob. an epithet of the goddess Athena. [< L] Dims. **Liv′i·a, Liv′ie.**

O·lym·pi·a (ō·lim′pē·ə) She of Olympus. [< L < Gk.]

O·pal (ō′pəl) From the name of the gem.

O·phel·ia (ō·fēl′yə) Help. [< Gk.]

Ot·ti·lie (ot′ə·lē) Fem. of OTTO. [< Ger.]

Pam·e·la (pam′ə·lə) ? Invented by Sir Philip Sidney. Dim. **Pam.**

Pan·sy (pan′zē) From the name of the flower.

Pa·tience (pā′shəns) From the abstract noun.

Pa·tri·cia (pə·trish′ə) Fem. of PATRICK. Dims. **Pat, Pat′sy, Pat′ty.**

Paul·a (pô′lə) Fem. of PAUL.

Pau·lette (pô·let′) Fr. fem. dim. of PAUL.

Pau·line (pô·lēn′) Fem. of PAUL. [< F] Also *Lat.* **Pau·li·na** (pô·lī′nə).

Pearl (pûrl) From the name of the jewel.

Peg (peg) Dim. of MARGARET. Also **Peg′gy.**

Pe·nel·o·pe (pə·nel′ə·pē) Weaver. [< Gk.] Dim. **Pen′ny.**

Per·sis (pûr′sis) She of Persia. [< Gk.]

Phi·lip·pa (fi·lip′ə, fil′ə·pə) Fem. of PHILIP.

Phoe·be (fē′bē) Bright; shining: an epithet of Artemis. [< Gk.] Also **Phe′be.**

Phyl·lis (fil′is) Green bough or leaf. [< Gk.] Also **Phil′·lis.**

Pol·ly (pol′ē) Dim. of MARY.

Pop·py (pop′ē) From the name of the flower.

Por·tia (pôr′shə, pōr′-) Fem. of *Porcius*, name of a Roman clan. [< L]

Pris·cil·la (pri·sil′ə) Ancient. [< L]

Pru·dence (prōōd′ns) From the abstract noun. Dim. **Prue.**

Queen·ie (kwē′nē) Derived from QUEEN, used as dim. of REGINA.

Ra·chel (rā′chəl; *Fr.* rà·shel′) Ewe or lamb. [< Hebrew] Dims. **Rae, Ray.**

Ra·mo·na (rə·mō′nə) Fem. of *Ramón*, Sp. form of RAYMOND.

Re·ba (rē′bə) Short for REBECCA.

Re·bec·ca (ri·bek′ə) Ensnarer. [< Hebrew] Dim. **Beck′y.**

Re·gi·na (ri·jē′nə, -jī′-) Queen. [< L]

Re·née (rə·nā′, rä′nē, rē′nē) Reborn. [< F]

Rhe·a (rē′ə) From the name of the Greek goddess.

Rho·da (rō′də) Rose. [< Gk.]

Ri·ta (rē′tə) Dim. of *Margarita,* Ital. and Sp. form of MARGARET.

Ro·ber·ta (rə·bûr′tə) Fem. of ROBERT. Dims. **Bert, Bob′·bie, Bob′by.**

Rob·in (rob′in) From the name of the bird, or from the masc. name.

Ro·chelle (rə·shel′) Stone or small rock. [< F]

Ron·ny (ron′ē) Dim. of VERONICA. Also **Ron′nie.**

Ro·sa (rō′zə) Var. of ROSE. [< L]

Ro·sa·bel (rō′zə·bel) Beautiful rose. [< L]

Ro·sa·lie (rō′zə·lē) Little rose. [< L] Also **Ro·sal·ia** (rō·zāl′yə, -zā′lē·ə).

Ros·a·lind (roz′ə·lind) Fair rose. [< Sp.] Also **Ros·a·lin·da** (roz′ə·lin′də).

Ros·a·line (roz′ə·lin, -līn, -lēn, rō′zə-) Var. of ROSALIND. Also **Ros′a·lyn** (-lin).

Ros·a·mond (roz′ə·mənd, rō′zə-) Famous protector. [< Gmc.] **Also Ros′a·mund, Ro·sa·mun·da** (rō′zə·mun′də).

Ros·anne (rōz·an′) From ROSE and ANNE. Also **Ros·an·na** (rōz·an′ə), **Rose·anne′, Rose·an′na.**

Rose (rōz) From the name of the flower. Also **Ro·sa** (rō′zə; *Fr.* rō·zà′; *Ger.* rō′zä; *Ital.* rô′zä; *Sp.* rō′sä).

Rose·mar·y (rōz′mâr′ē, -mə·rē) From the plant name. Also **Rose·ma·rie** (rōz′mə·rē).

Row·e·na (rō·ē′nə) ? From the name of an ancient Celtic goddess.

Rox·an·a (rok·san′ə) Dawn of day. [< Persian] Also **Rox·an′na, *Fr.* Rox·ane** (rôk·saň′). Dim. **Rox′y.**

Ru·by (rōō′bē) From the name of the jewel.

Ruth (rōōth) Companion. [< Hebrew]

Sa·bi·na (sə·bī′nə) A Sabine woman. [< L]

Sa·die (sā′dē) Dim. of SARAH.

Sal·ly (sal′ē) Dim. of SARAH.

Sa·lo·me (sə·lō′mē) Peace. [< Hebrew]

San·dra (san′drə, sän′-) Dim. of ALEXANDRA.

Sar·ah (sâr′ə) Princess. [< Hebrew] Also **Sar·a** (sâr′ə). Dims. **Sa′die, Sal′ly.**

Sel·ma (sel′mə) Fair [< Celtic], or a fem. dim. of ANSELM.

Se·re·na (sə·rē′nə) Serene. [< L]

Shar·on (shar′ən, shâr′-) Of Sharon. [< Hebrew]

Shei·la (shē′lə) Irish form of CECILIA.

Shir·ley (shûr′lē) From an English surname; orig. a place name.

Sib·yl (sib′əl) Prophetess. [< Gk.] Also **Syb′il.**

Sid·ney (sid′nē) From an English surname. Also **Syd′ney.**

Sig·rid (sig′rid; *Ger.* zē′grit; *Norw.* sē′grē) Conquering counsel. [< Gmc.]

Sil·vi·a (sil′vē·ə) Var. of SYLVIA.

Si·mone (sē·mōn′) Fr. fem. of SIMON.

So·fi·a (sō·fē′ä) Ger., Ital., and Sw. form of SOPHIA.

Son·ia (sōn′yə) Russ. dim. of SOPHIA. Also **Son′ya.**

So·phi·a (sō·fī′ə, -fē′ə) Wise. [< Gk.] Also **So·phie** (sō′·fē; *Fr.* sô·fē′) Dims. **So′phie, So′phy.**

So·phro·ni·a (sə·frō′nē·ə) Prudent. [< Gk.]

Sta·cie (stā′sē) Orig. dim. of ANASTÁSIA. Also **Sta′cy.**

Stel·la (stel′ə) Star. [< L]

Steph·a·nie (stef′ə·nē) Fem. of STEPHEN. Also **Steph·a·na** (stef′ə·nə), *Fr.* **Sté·pha·nie** (stā·fà·nē′).

Su·san (sōō′zən) Var. of SUSANNAH. Dims. **Sue, Su′sie, Su′zy.**

Su·san·nah (sōō·zan′ə) Lily. [< Hebrew] Also **Su·san′na, Su·zanne** (sōō·zan′; *Fr.* sü·zaň′). Dims. **Sue, Su·ky** (sōō′kē), **Su′sie, Su′zy.**

Syb·il (sib′əl) Var. of SYBIL.

Syl·vi·a (sil′vē·ə) Of the forest. [< L] Also **Sil′vi·a.**

Tab·i·tha (tab′ə·thə) Gazelle. [< Aramaic]

Te·re·sa (tə·rē′sə, -zə); *Ital.* tā·rā′zä; *Sp.* tā·rā′sä) Var. of THERESA. [< Ital. & Sp.] Dims. **Ter′ry, Tess, Tes′sie.**

Thal·ia (thāl′yə, thal′-) Flourishing; blooming. [< Gk.]

The·a (thē′ə) Goddess. [< Gk.]

Thel·ma (thel′mə) ? Var. of SELMA.

The·o·do·ra (thē′ə·dôr′ə, -dō′rə) Fem. of THEODORE. Dims. **Do′ra, The′da, The′o.**

The·o·do·sia (thē′ə·dō′shə) Gift of God. [< Gk.]

The·re·sa (tə·rē′sə, -zə) She who reaps. [< Gk.] Also *Fr.* **Thé·rèse** (tā·râz′) Dims. **Ter′ry, Tess, Tes′sie.**

Til·da (til′də) Dim. of MATILDA.

Til·ly (til′ē) Dim. of MATILDA. Also **Til′lie.**

Ti·na (tē′nə) Dim. of CHRISTINA.

Tri·na (trē′nə) Dim. of KATRINA.

Trix·ie (trik′sē) Dim. of BEATRICE or BEATRIX. Also **Trix, Trix′y.**

Tru·dy (trōō′dē) Dim. of GERTRUDE.

U·na (yōō′nə) One. [< L]

Un·dine (un·dēn′, un′dēn) She of the waves. [< L]

U·ra·ni·a (yōō·rā′nē·ə) From the name of the Greek goddess of heaven, the muse of astronomy.

Ur·su·la (ûr′syə·lə, -sə-) Little she-bear. [< L]

Va·le·ri·a (və·lir′ē·ə) Fem. of *Valerius,* name of a Roman clan. Also **Val·er·ie** or **Val·er·y** (val′ər·ē), *Fr.* **Va·lé·rie** (và·lā·rē′) Dim. **Val.**

Va·nes·sa (və·nes′ə) Butterfly. [< Gk.]

Ve·ra (vir′ə) Faith [< Slavic], or truth [< L].

Ver·na (vûr′nə) Short for *Laverna,* var. of LAVERNE.

Ve·ron·i·ca (və·ron′i·kə) True image. [< LL] Also *Fr.* **Vé·ro·nique** (vā·rô·nēk′). Dim. **Ron′nie, Ron′ny.**

Vic·to·ri·a (vik·tôr′ē·ə, -tō′rē·ə) Victory. [< L] Also *Fr.* **Vic·toire** (vēk·twàr′). Dim. **Vick′y.**

Vi·o·la (vī′ō·lə, vī·ō′lə, vē-) Violet. [< L]

Vi·o·let (vī′ə·lit) From the name of the flower.

Vir·gin·ia (vər·jin′yə) Fem. of *Virginius,* name of a Roman clan. Also *Fr.* **Vir·gi·nie** (vēr·zhē·nē′). Dim. **Gin′ny.**

Viv·i·an (viv′ē·ən, viv′yən) Lively. [< L] also **Viv′i·en,** *Fr.* **Vi·vienne** (vē·vyen′).

Wan·da (wän′də) Shepherdess or roamer. [< Gmc.]

Wen·dy (wen′dē) Dim. of GWENDOLYN.

Wil·hel·mi·na (wil′hel·mē′nə, wil′ə-; *Ger.* vil′hel·mē′nä) Fem. of *Wilhelm,* Ger. form of WILLIAM. Dims. **Mi′na, Min′na, Wil′la, Wil′ma.**

Wil·la (wil′ə) Dim. of WILHELMINA.

Wil·ma (wil′mə) Dim. of WILHELMINA.

Win·i·fred (win′ə·frid, -fred) White wave or stream. [< Welsh] Dim. **Win′nie.**

Yo·lan·a (yō·lan′də) Meaning uncertain. [? < OF] Also **Yo·lan′de** (-də).

Y·vonne (i·von′, ē-) Meaning uncertain. [< F]

Ze·no·bi·a (zi·nō′bē·ə) She who was given life by Zeus. [< Gk.]

Zo·e (zō′ē) Life. [< Gk.]

Business Law

Business law deals with legal rules and principles of primary interest to the business community. Because of the complexity of modern business, the laws affecting businesses necessarily reach into diverse areas. Many of the laws are difficult and technical. Nevertheless, the person going into business or already in business should gain at least some familiarity with basic regulations and principles.

Although not a substitute for legal advice, such basic knowledge of the law allows the business person to make intelligent decisions and to foresee problems that may actually require legal advice or assistance. The following material provides an introduction to key concepts of business law.

Establishing a Business: Formats

Typically, the person going into business wants to be the sole owner of a particular enterprise. The simplicity of sole ownership, or *sole proprietorship,* is attractive. Whether the owner plans to add partners or employees later, it is usually possible simply to "set up shop."

The two main alternatives to sole proprietorship are the *partnership* and the *corporation.* In the former, two or more persons work together in a business enterprise, often on the basis of a partnership agreement. With a corporation (a separate legal entity) one or more persons can conduct business operations without taking responsibility for the debts of the business. Both the partnership and the corporation can take variant forms while maintaining a basic organizational pattern.

The Sole Proprietorship

The person operating a sole proprietorship owns the business in his or her own name. But the business can operate under the owner's name or a trade or business name: for example, "Mary Jones DBA ("doing business as") Jones Dress Shoppe."

Many states require that the person going into business as a sole proprietor register an assumed or fictitious business name under state and county laws. Typically, such a law is called an Assumed Names Act. Specific information is usually required, including the business name and the names and addresses of all persons who have an interest in the business.

There are many advantages to creating a sole proprietorship. The owner can keep track of the business' progress from month to month or year to year. He or she can control operating costs and can often avoid much of the paperwork required by other business arrangements. The sole proprietor remains the boss. If the business stays small, fulltime employees may not be needed.

Partnerships

A partnership is somewhat more complicated than the sole proprietorship but is less complex than the corporation. Formed, by two or more persons, the partnership is considered a business entity but not a tax entity. In other words, each partner must pay taxes on all partnership income.

Some other factors identify the partnership. Each partner, for example, is responsible for the debts and credit arrangements contracted by any other partner. Thus, any member of the partnership can bind the business and all its partners to business contracts and transactions. Professional partnerships were once common, but today, because most state laws allow doctors, lawyers, accountants, and other professional people to incorporate, the professional corporation has become a more standard form of business association. All members of such corporations share in the tax benefits.

The partnership agreement is sometimes informal—even oral. But ideally, partners should decide the terms of their agreement with the aid of a lawyer (see below).

A partnership has many of the advantages of a sole proprietorship but may also face similar strictures or regulations. An assumed or fictitious name must be registered. Generally, the various states levy no taxes on the right to function as a partnership or franchise. In addition, the partnership does not have to keep the general records required of a corporation. Unlike a corporation, which can stay in business indefinitely, a partnership usually dissolves on the death, retirement, or withdrawal of a partner.

The four main types of partnerships, each of which is used in specific circumstances, are the limited partnership, the joint venture, syndication, and the joint stock company.

Limited Partnership

In a limited partnership some or most of the partners can avoid the unlimited liability that characterizes the general partnership. Usually, the limited partnership has one general partner and a number of limited partners. The general partner is liable for the debts of the partnership and often for supervising all operations; the limited partners are liable only to the extent that they have invested in the partnership.

In those states that have Uniform Limited Partnership acts, the persons establishing a limited partnership must file a certificate of registration, usually with the secretary of state. The certificate gives the name of the business, its location, the names of the limited partners, and the partners' liabilities, powers, privileges, and duties.

A typical limited partnership may buy, manage, and sell apartment houses, hotels, and other kinds of real estate. The partners invest capital in the business and receive shares of the profits according to the amounts invested. A hybrid between the general partnership and the corporation, the limited partnership does not have to file articles of incorporation. Nor is it required to keep min-

utes or other records of operations. The limited partnership must, however, file partnership tax returns.

The Joint Venture

When two or more persons agree to join in a single transaction or project their partnership is called a joint venture. The partners in a joint venture agree to control and manage the business together. They must also agree to share profits and losses, usually on the basis of each partner's ownership interest in the property or project.

Thus, for example, should two or more persons jointly buy and own property but for some reason do not share its profits or losses, this would not be considered a joint venture. A joint venture occurs only when the parties intend to do business as a *partnership*.

Syndication

A joint venture that involves a large number of individuals is usually known as a *syndicate*. As with all true joint ventures, syndication requires tax filing as a partnership.

A public offering to sell a syndicate share or interest in a property or business requires special legal handling. The Securities and Exchange Commission (SEC) has ruled that such sales to the public fall under securities laws.

Joint Stock Company or Association

Some partnerships operate under articles of association that provide for the issuance of a share of stock or certificate to each partner. The certificates represent each partner's interest. In such a joint stock company or association, the articles of association also provide that a group of partners, called the board of directors, will control the business. Individual partners cannot bind the other partners by entering into separate transactions in the name of the company or association. But participants in the association are responsible for all the legal debts and obligations incurred by the association as a whole.

Federal and state securities laws apply to sales of joint stock company shares or certificates. But, under the typical articles of association, individual partners can transfer their certificates without the consent of other participants. The articles normally specify how long the association will exist and provide that the death or withdrawal of any member will not affect the association.

The Corporation

Many consider the corporation the ideal way to organize a business. By law, the person or persons who own and operate the corporation are separate from it.

The corporation may be small or large. A small corporation is usually referred to as a *close*, or *closely held*, *corporation*. An individual may own all the stock in such a corporation and manage it alone or jointly with a few others.

But many corporations have hundreds or thousands of shareholders or stockholders. In either case the corporation files its own tax returns and pays its own taxes. Corporate meetings must be held and minutes kept for each meeting. To do business under an assumed name, the corporation—like the sole proprietorship or the partnership—must register according to state law.

The corporation, as a flexible form of business organization, generally has the following advantages:

• The persons who invest in the corporation have no liability for corporate debts or obligations beyond the amounts each has invested.

• By selling stock and securities the corporation can raise substantial sums to finance business programs and projects.

• By corporate charter, the corporation can exist "in perpetuity"—in effect, forever.

• Because the typical corporation of any size has a manager or board of directors who run day-to-day operations, the individual shareholders need not bother with the details of such operations.

The corporate format does have some disadvantages. For example, the corporation must pay taxes on its earnings. Later, when these earnings are distributed to shareholders as *dividends*, the shareholders must claim them in their own tax returns and pay additional taxes on them. Careful planning, however, can reduce or eliminate the hazards of such "double taxation." And many corporations find ways to enjoy other major tax advantages.

Another disadvantage of the corporation is that, as a separate legal entity, it must operate in accordance with specific laws and keep certain records. Some expense is involved in incorporating, and an application for a corporate charter must be accompanied by initial tax statements and other documentation in addition to the necessary filing fees.

Two other kinds of corporations or corporation-like business structures should be noted: the Subchapter S corporation and the business trust.

Subchapter S Corporations

The unique advantage of the Subchapter S structure is that such a business may operate as a corporation while following partnership tax regulations. This type of business organization, permitted under federal and most state laws, thus avoids corporate taxes while operating in corporate form.

All the income or losses of a Subchapter S corporation are taxed individually according to the amount invested by each shareholder. The shareholders have immunity from personal liability for the debts and obligations of the firm. At the same time they avoid double taxation. But a "Sub-S" corporation can have no more than 35 shareholders.

The Business Trust

The business trust is taxed as a corporation and enjoys many of the advantages of a corporation. It can be formed and operated under federal and most state tax laws. The death or withdrawal of a shareholder does not terminate the trust, nor do the shareholders have personal liability for the trust's debts and obligations.

Also known as a Massachusetts business trust or a common trust, the business trust has been defined as an unincorporated business organization. The trust document specifies that property is to be held and managed by the trustee for the benefit of beneficiaries who hold transferable certificates. The beneficiaries receive the profits from management of the property. The states that provide for the legal creation of business trusts generally require that a declaration of trust be filed before beneficiaries' shares can be sold or distributed. Transfers or sales of trust shares must take place in accordance with the securities laws of the various states.

Launching a Business: Documents and Procedures

"I'm forming a partnership with a close friend. Do I need an agreement in writing?"

This is a question that lawyers hear frequently. In nearly all cases the answer is Yes, definitely. Prospective partners may be members of the same family, old friends, or business associates, but the written agreement is nonetheless appropriate.

The reasons for drawing up such a partnership agreement are much the same as for preparation of a preincorporation agreement. Both help to build a foundation for the enterprise and to reduce the possibility of later misunderstandings and disagreements.

The Partnership Agreement

Most states have adopted what is called the Uniform Partnership Act to guide partners as they set up and conduct their businesses. Such an act has some commonsense provisions. For example, it may provide that if *no* partnership agreement exists, the partners will share equally in the business' profits. The law may also specify that each partner will, in the absence of an agreement, have an equal voice in the operation of the business.

An agreement in writing takes precedence over such legal provisions. The partners may specify in the agreement the percentage of profits each will receive or who will supervise which aspects of the business. For instance, Partner A may receive 60% of the profits and Partner B may supervise the business' sales force. Someone who brings special knowledge or expertise to the business, or who will have to work unusually long hours, may receive advance recognition. The agreement might also specify special compensation arrangements.

Other Terms of the Agreement

In general, the terms of a partnership should deal with basics as well as with the finer points of the business relationship. The basics include the name chosen for the business, the rights and duties of each partner, and the objectives of the business. The agreement can also make note of the investments or other assets contributed by each partner, such as real estate, vehicles, or office equipment.

The business name deserves some thought. Do not choose a name that could be confused with another company name already in use. It is important to select a name that will characterize the business, give it stature, or make it sound attractive or impressive. Some partnerships have names formed from partners' initials or names.

The agreement should typically indicate how long the partnership will last. If all partners feel it is appropriate, the partnership may be of indefinite duration. In such a case, the partnership will continue until it is dissolved by one or more of the partners or until one of them dies or withdraws.

Many partnership agreements state that the partnership will continue for five or ten years. At the end of the specified period the agreement can be renewed if desired.

Other clauses typically appear in partnership agreements. For example, the agreement gives the starting and ending dates of the partnership's fiscal year. Specific provisions may indicate how any partner can exercise the right to examine the partnership's books, make specific banking arrangements, and lay out procedures for hiring employees, with special attention in many cases to employment contracts.

Contribution of Capital

It is important that the partnership agreement indicate how much capital or other assets each partner has contributed. Insofar as possible, all such assets should be listed. They can include not only those items mentioned but leases, patent rights, and special equipment of one kind or another. All such items rank as *capital*.

In any partnership one partner may contribute one kind of capital whereas another may contribute another kind. The agreement should specify clearly what is being contributed and what its value is. Some evaluations may have to be made by rough estimate; in other cases an appraiser should be hired to place a value on a partner's noncash contribution.

The terms of the agreement should spell out, with dates or target times if possible, when partners' contributions are due. One partner may invest cash at the time the partnership comes into being; another may contribute funds a year later; a third may make working premises available from the time the partnership goes into business. A partner may agree to invest in the business the first $10,000 of his share of the partnership's profits. Another may loan money to the partnership under specified conditions of repayment. The conditions should include the interest rate to be charged.

Partners' Responsibilities and Powers

In most partnerships, the various partners perform different but complementary jobs. The roles to be played by the partners should be described in the agreement as clearly as possible.

Making such terms clear beyond the possibility of misunderstanding may be impossible. But the effort should be made. The management responsibilities and the amount of time to be devoted to each can obviously vary widely. Insofar as a determination of such details can be made, it should be.

Court cases involving partners frequently hinge on the question of whether one partner is devoting enough time and effort to the business. That fact alone suggests the importance of the advance thinking put into this part of the agreement. A number of related questions should receive attention. Is each partner to be allowed to engage in other business activities while also working for the partnership? To what extent? What other business activities? Will the partners be allowed to take part only in other activities that are completely different from the partnership business?

The answers to such questions may call for thought—in particular where the question of partners' participation in other businesses is concerned. Will a partner investing in and operating a business identical to that of the partnership be in competition with his or her partners? Such questions lie at the heart of many court decisions.

Profits and Losses

The most basic method of providing for equitable distribution of profits and losses is simple. The partners simply agree to distribute profits according to the investment of each partner in the business. A partner who contributes 25% of the funding for the partnership, receives 25% of the profits. He or she also bears 25% of the losses, if any.

That formula need not control in any given case. For any group of partners, another approach may be more appropriate. The important thing is that the partners work the formula out in advance and include it in the agreement. A special formula may work best. In one case three partners establishing a real estate management business agreed that in the first year Partner A would receive half of the first $50,000 in profits while partners B and C would receive $12,500 each. From that point on the partners would divide the profits equally.

Among other important financial questions, salaries and expense accounts rank high. Unless the agreement contains provisions on salaries, for example, no partner would be entitled to anything more than a share of the profits. Yet a salary might be appropriate if one partner is to spend more time on partnership business than the others. As for expense accounts, is any partner to have unlimited privileges? Will any partner receive advances from company funds to cover business travel and entertainment?

Dissolution of the Partnership

The terms of the partnership agreement should specify under what conditions dissolution may take place. Some examples suggest possibilities. In one case a partnership agreement provided that the business would continue if any of the four partners died or had to withdraw for health or other reasons. Thus, the agreement, in effect, ensured that a new partnership would take the place of the original one. The agreement also specified how the partner leaving the business, or that partner's family, would be compensated in case of death or withdrawal. The partnership share could, of course, have substantial value.

In another case a partnership agreement contained a buy–sell clause. That provision, common to most partnership agreements, specified the conditions under which the remaining partners could buy the share of a partner who was withdrawing for any reason. A method of establishing the value of a partnership share was also specified; an arbitrator familiar with business appraisals would be named to conduct an evaluation.

Such terms, in a sense, help to resolve legal problems in advance. They can, however, be even more specific. Some buy–sell provisions provide for a departing partner's right to select an arbitrator. The remaining partner or partners have the same right. After the two arbitrators have selected a third person to assist in the arbitration, the three jointly decide on the value of a partnership share. The decision is then final and binding.

A recommended way to make sure that surviving partners will be able to buy the share of a deceased or ailing partner is to buy life insurance on the lives of all the partners. The insurance provides the cash needed for the surviving partners to buy the deceased's share.

Corporate Agreements

Three friends have decided to go into business and incorporate. What now?

First, remember that state law controls the establishment of corporations. But different laws refer to the basic documents of incorporation in different ways. The *articles of incorporation* may, for example, be called the *articles of agreement* or *charter,* or the *certificate of incorporation.*

Second, in forming their corporation they will be making decisions regarding the ownership of the business, issuance of stock shares, contributions of the various owners, and other matters. As in the case of partnership agreements, the more thorough the answers to such questions are, the better the chance that the business will succeed.

There will be four directors. Because the state in which this corporation is formed requires a minimum of three directors, they have fulfilled a basic requirement. Many other states, as noted, would allow an individual to incorporate alone. But either way, as a group or singly, the procedures are essentially the same from state to state,

with one exception. An individual incorporating as a one-person firm would not prepare a preincorporation agreement, but for four persons incorporating together, such an agreement is a good idea even though it is not required by law.

The Preincorporation Agreement

The agreement serves as an opportunity for each of the associates to make all the key decisions in advance. They can focus on areas of agreement and areas of potential disagreement and can make sure they are thinking alike. In this way they build for future business success.

The preincorporation agreement contains much that can be found in the typical partnership agreement: the corporate name, the purposes of the business, and so on. But the preincorporation agreement should address other questions as well, such as the stock to be issued, the number of shares to be authorized, the price per share, and the number of shares each associate will buy. The agreement should also specify any restrictions on transfers of shares and the procedures under which the corporation would buy the shares of an associate who dies or decides to sell out.

If such procedures are listed, the method of funding the purchases of associates' shares should be noted. Life insurance offers one effective method of funding in case of death.

Information as to how the corporation will be managed and controlled should appear in the agreement. It is important to specify the number of directors, to agree on what work each associate will perform in the corporation, and to establish salary schedules.

The name of the corporation has legal status. Most states require that the name be different enough from others already in use to avoid confusion. Because a name that is identical or very similar to any existing one may be rejected by state authorities, it is advisable to check with the governmental agency responsible for the registry of names to make sure the desired choice is available. If the name is already being used, it may nevertheless be possible to use it or a variation of it anyway, by obtaining permission from the owner of the name. Such permission should be in writing.

Most states require that the business name include a word or abbreviation indicating that the business is incorporated. The words that appear most often are *Incorporated, Corporation, Company, Limited,* or their abbreviated forms: *Inc., Corp., Co.,* and *Ltd.*

The Articles of Incorporation

With the preincorporation agreement on paper, the articles of incorporation can follow. This is the document that actually establishes the corporation: the corporate charter, filed with a state agency and usually in a standard form according to instructions issued by the agency itself. The agency may be the office of the secretary of state. In some states the articles of incorporation have to be filed with the local county clerk as well.

Other information in the articles of incorporation parallels that of the preincorporation agreement to some extent. The corporate name appears, followed by a statement of corporate purposes. Whereas some states require only a statement that the new firm will engage exclusively in lawful activities, others need specific information. The statement should be worded broadly so that the corporation has reasonable latitude in its later selection of business activities.

The business purposes of many young corporations change with time. In such cases the corporations simply

file an amendment to the articles of incorporation to broaden the range of corporate purposes.

The articles of incorporation state how many shares of stock will be issued, where the firm's main office will be, and who in the corporation can be served with lawsuit papers. Most states do not require that all the shares of stock be issued at once. For that reason many corporations issue only enough shares to cover immediate and foreseeable needs. In some states lawsuit papers have to be filed with the secretary of state, who then serves the corporate officer designated in the articles of incorporation.

Finally, the articles of incorporation should note the names and addresses of the incorporators. The period for which the corporation is formed should be given if it is not perpetual. The state collects a filing fee when the incorporators register the articles.

Normally, the beginning corporation faces five other basic challenges.

1. To draw up bylaws. Much more complete than the articles of incorporation, the bylaws detail the rights and powers of the corporate officers, shareholders, and directors. The bylaws also give a time and place for the annual meetings, specify how notices of meetings will be sent out, indicate what constitutes a quorum, make provision for special meetings, and state how shareholders can act without formal meetings.

The bylaws touch on other subjects as well. They note how many directors the corporation has—usually a president, secretary, and treasurer; who the directors are and how they are elected; and what their powers and responsibilities are. In other provisions the bylaws describe the stock certificates, name the person or persons authorized to sign contracts and insert the corporate books and records, and specify how the bylaws can be amended.

2. To adopt the bylaws and elect the first board of directors. This task falls to the shareholders of the new corporation, the persons holding ultimate power. In a meeting held after the state has approved the articles of incorporation, the shareholders adopt the bylaws and elect the corporation's first board of directors.

In a small corporation, the same people may be officers, directors, and shareholders. When they set the ground-rules under which the business will operate, they are in effect making rules for themselves. In a larger corporation, the shareholders set policy but do not take part in day-to-day operations. They meet at least annually—and more frequently if the need arises. The annual meetings provide opportunities to review the corporation's annual report, elect new directors or reelect incumbents, and vote on policy changes.

3. To hold the first directors' meeting. The directors of the new corporation usually meet for the first time after the incorporators' meeting. Among other items of business, the directors elect the corporate officers, consider and ratify contracts, and approve all management plans. The board of directors may also confirm corporate banking arrangements and authorize the issuance of stock.

4. To issue corporate stock. Once the stock has been paid for, the corporation issues certificates that show the name of the corporation, the number of shares that each certificate represents, the type of share, and the name of the individual shareholder. Usually, the corporate president and secretary sign the certificates. If the stock sale is restricted, this information generally appears on the back of each certificate.

5. To make a Subchapter S election. In this step the business founders decide whether they want to be treated, for federal tax purposes, as a Subchapter S corporation. To be eligible to make such an election, the firm cannot have more than 35 shareholders. It must also have only one class of stock. The election must be made during the first 75 days of the tax year. All the shareholders must agree that the election of Subchapter S status should be made.

The Factor of Control

Whether a new business starts as a partnership or corporation, the founders should carefully consider the question of control: of ways and means of maintaining the authority of the founders and protecting their interests in the business.

A number of considerations are involved, such as those framed in the following questions: Who will be allowed to buy, inherit, or otherwise gain ownership of partners' or other shares? How do the controlling parties ensure that they retain management and supervisory responsibility? Who might be admitted to the inner circle in the future?

Retention of control involves complex legal questions. These reinforce the contention that a lawyer should help prepare all the basic business documents. The type of business, the methods by which interests may be transferred to others, possible restrictions on such transfers, employment contracts—all are important. Particular questions may hinge on interpretations of state laws dealing with restrictions on transfers of shares, on transfers of business control, and on other questions.

Some widely used methods of retaining control include the following:

1. Restrictions on transfers of interest. In general, the law frowns on restraints on sales or on assignments of business or property rights. But shareholders in a corporation can, for example, agree on a stock transfer restriction. Under such an agreement, the other partners or shareholders have the right of first refusal before a business share or stock can be sold to a third party outside the business. Where multiple shares are for sale, the other shareholders can usually buy in proportion to the total number of shares each owns.

Stock transfer restrictions generally appear in corporate bylaws. They are also printed on share certificates. The printed restriction puts a prospective purchaser on legal notice that resale restrictions exist.

2. Employment Contracts. An employment contract, or a series of them, between a partnership and its partners or between a corporation and its officers ranks as another way to retain control of a business. The contract spells out the rights, duties, and obligations of both parties—company and individual. The contract may restrict the individuals' ownership rights.

An employment contract may have other purposes. It may, for example, help the owner of a business protect patents or inventions with which the employee becomes acquainted. The contract may also provide details on a complicated compensation plan, or protect against competition from the employee should he or she leave the firm's employment.

3. Voting Rights. As businesses grow and add employees, shareholders, and others, voting rights become extremely important. A majority of shareholders might, in a given case, try to assume control by changing the business' purpose, design, or basic direction. Various kinds of voting restrictions can be used to protect the business operation, among them these:

• A corporation may provide for voting and nonvoting stock, for voting rules that ensure that the minority

group is represented on the board of directors, and for elections of different directors in specified years.

• Shareholder agreements may require that shareholders vote their stock in a certain way. Shareholders might, for example, be able to vote only for other shareholders for the board of directors. "Outsiders" would be excluded. It should be noted, however, that such restrictions on voting or transfers of shares could inhibit many investors from buying the company's stock.

• Using a voting trust agreement, a number of shareholders may join together to give a lesser number, called the trustees, the right to vote on all the shares. The trustees themselves can agree on how the votes will be cast.

• Where state laws permit, the charter and bylaws of a corporation may provide for special requirements on quorums and shareholder votes. For example, a two-thirds majority might be needed to change the business' bylaws.

• A corporation's bylaws, a partnership agreement, or a shareholder agreement might make arbitration an alternative where disagreements arise. The arbitration option would be invoked in case of a voting deadlock.

4. <u>Buy–Sell Agreements.</u> A buy–sell agreement among the shareholders of a corporation ensures that the corporation can buy the stock of a deceased stockholder. The estate of the deceased has to sell the stock; the corporation has an obligation to buy. To ensure the corporation's ability to repurchase such shares, the firm must have a *stock retirement program*. Under an alternative program, called a *cross-purchase plan,* other stockholders can buy the shares of the deceased.

Establishing a price for stock to be purchased from the estate of a deceased shareholder may or may not be a problem. If the shares are traded on a regional or national stock exchange, the price quotation for a given day determines the price. In a close corporation, however, the problem of evaluation becomes critical. A mandatory buy–sell agreement always outlines an effective method of determining the price of a share of stock. The methods include the appraisal, the book value, and various other methods.

5. <u>Partnership Buy–Sell Agreement.</u> Under a partnership buy–sell agreement, the estate of a deceased partner has an obligation to offer the decedent's partnership interest for sale to the surviving partner or partners. The agreement should specify the terms of the sale. Both the partners and their spouses should sign the agreement. In many cases, life insurance offers the best method of purchasing the partnership interest of a deceased partner.

Business Contracts

You decide to have your office painted. You sit down with Tom Johnson, a painter, to discuss cost. Tom says he can do the job for $550. He would have the work completed in exactly two weeks. You say, "It's a deal." With those words you have a legally binding contract. All the necessary elements are present:

• Parties competent to contract.

• An offer (Tom's indication that he can do the work at a certain price by a certain date).

• Acceptance (your agreement to pay the $550).

• Consideration. The two of you are exchanging things of value. You have promised to pay $550 and Tom has promised to paint your office.

The Four Elements

Obviously, business contracts are rarely as simple and straightforward as the above example. But all contracts have to share the basic elements or they will not be regarded as contracts under the law.

The requirement that the parties to the contract be competent has special meaning. The contracting parties cannot be minors, for example, under the laws of the state in which the contract is made. Also, the parties must be sane. They must be capable of handling their own affairs.

At the offer stage of contract formulation, the law presumes that one party to the arrangement can provide something of value. In the example, Tom the painter *offered* to paint your office. He told you what the work would cost. He did not say he could *probably* do the work for $550, or that he would need half of that sum down, with the rest to follow on completion of the job; he stated his price.

Your acceptance followed when you said, "It's a deal." Where the second element involves *mutuality of obligation,* the acceptance phase involves *legal consideration:* in this case, what you agree to pay. The legal consideration can be many things besides money or property. An exchange can involve services.

Another type of consideration is known as *detrimental reliance*. You would have created the possibility of such a consideration if you had said to five painters, "I will pay $500 if one of you will paint my office." A painter relies on your promise, paints your office, and can sue you for breach of contract if you do not pay the $500.

Legality of purpose has equally broad legal meanings. No contract is enforceable if its purpose is illegal. But what does illegal mean? If the contract calls for the performance of an immoral or statutorily illegal act, it is unenforceable. The same applies if it goes contrary to a state's public policy. Examples of the latter include contracts to restrain trade, to evade or oppose revenue laws, and to corrupt legislative or judicial bodies.

Breach of Contract

Whether written or oral, a contract that has the four basic elements is enforceable at law. Enforcement becomes an alternative in the case of a *breach of contract* by one party or the other. A lawsuit in such a case seeks to recover whatever damages are suffered because of the breach.

The Uniform Commercial Code (UCC), valid in all states except Louisiana, sets the standards of some key aspects of contract law. The UCC, for example, provides that a written agreement be produced in a breach-of-contract case involving the sale of goods for $500 or more. The agreement need not be extremely detailed. It has only to indicate that the parties agreed on the sale and that such-and-such a quantity was involved. The UCC requires inclusion of such other factors as price, time and place of delivery, and quality of the goods.

Article Two of the UCC deals with the sale or transfer of goods or personal property. It specifies that a "merchant" (a person with special knowledge, skills, and familiarity with a business) has special rights and obligations. He or she has a kind of professional status. Three principal rules apply:

• Between merchants, the law usually requires a written contract where goods valued at more than $500 are sold.

• A merchant's offer to buy or sell goods, made in

writing and signed by the merchant, must be held open for a "reasonable" or specified length of time—and is not revocable during that time.

• A definite, written, and timely expression of acceptance creates a contract between merchants.

Violation of any of the stated UCC rules creates a cause of action—a reason to sue. A successful plaintiff generally receives *compensatory damages*. Insofar as possible, these compensate the plaintiff for damages ensuing from the broken contract. But there are other kinds of damages:

• *Consequential damages,* awarded where a plaintiff proves that a breach of contract had secondary negative effects.

• *Liquidated damages,* awarded when, for example, delay in the delivery of services or goods resulted in day-by-day losses for a plaintiff.

• *Equitable relief* may be invoked by a court to compel a delinquent defendant to deliver on a promise in a contract. A defendant may be required to deliver, for example, a work of art or an item of jewelry as promised in a legal contract.

Required Written Contracts

Under the statutes of frauds enacted by all states, some contracts have to be in writing. Typically, a statute of frauds would require that contracts be written when:

• the ownership of real estate is changing hands;
• real estate is being leased for more than a year;
• someone promises to pay the debt of someone else;
• performance under the contract will take more than a year;
• someone is agreeing to pay a commission for the sale of real estate; or
• a sale of goods, or tangible personal property, is being transacted.

Ordinarily, a contract need not be a formal legal document. A memorandum may be enough. But it should give the names of the parties, information on the subject matter, and the important terms and conditions. The signatures of the contracting parties should appear on the memorandum even though both may not be required legally.

What happens when a statute of frauds states that a contract is required but the parties have proceeded under an oral agreement? A lawsuit may be possible anyway. A suit may be justified, for example, where the oral agreement has been partially performed.

Defenses in a Breach-of-Contract Suit

A defendant in a breach-of-contract suit can utilize any of a variety of defenses. He or she may, depending on the circumstances, claim any of the following:

• That no breach took place.
• That the plaintiff suffered no damages.
• That the contract is invalid because a basic element is missing.
• That the statute of frauds requires a written contract and none exists.
• That the contract is illegal or against public policy and is therefore illegal.
• That the other contracting party misrepresented the facts to induce the defendant to sign the contract.
• That the contracting parties made a mutual mistake that resulted in a misunderstanding of what was to be sold or done.

The Business and the Consumer

Currently, the consumer protection movement is gathering momentum. Based on the concept that the consumer needs the protection of the law, the movement tries to prevent companies from exerting pressure on the consumer, or from taking advantage of him or her. Because the consumer is in fact vulnerable when buying goods, borrowing funds, or investing for financial gain, a business owner should know some basics of consumer law.

Consumers have protection today in a number of areas, including the following:

• methods by which goods are presented, including during sales and in advertising;
• packaging and labeling of goods;
• methods used in selling goods;
• credit sales; and
• protection of consumer defenses.

Many more such areas could be listed. But these are among the most important. Each can be discussed separately.

Deceptive Practices in Sales

Various government agencies have passed statutes, rules, and regulations that forbid or restrict deceptive practices in the sale of consumer goods. Endorsements by persons with high public exposure, for example, may not be false or misleading. In a typical case an athlete or movie star will state publicly (perhaps on television or radio) that a specific product is safe or of outstanding quality. If the product does not meet the described standards, the endorser has taken part in deception. A lawsuit may be the consumer's best remedy.

Even if not intended to do so, a company's advertising may in effect deceive potential buyers. The deception need not involve an intentionally fraudulent act; the only test today is whether the buyer was misled.

The Federal Trade Commission (FTC) repeatedly challenges advertisers regarding misleading or deceptive advertising. The FTC also tries to protect consumers in other ways. The Public Health Cigarette Smoking Act, for example, requires that a health warning appear on each package of cigarettes sold. Radio and TV can no longer carry cigarette advertising. Other forms of cigarette advertising have to display the health warning prominently.

In advertising goods for sale at retail, store owners and others once used various forms of deception. One, called the "bait and switch," involved ads for "specials" that were not in stock in sufficient quantity to meet anticipated demand—or that were not in stock at all. The advertiser counted on "baiting" the customer into the shop or store and then selling him or her some other item or items, usually at higher prices.

The laws of many states outlaw such practices. Such laws may also prohibit "going out of business" advertising when the business is not really being discontinued, "fire sales" when there has been no fire, or "lost our lease" sales when no lease has been lost.

Packaging and Labeling

Many federal laws have dealt in recent years with deception in labeling and packaging. Among the laws are the Fair Packaging and Labeling Act; the Fair Products

Labeling Act; and the Food, Drug, and Cosmetics Act. In addition, various state and federal laws have outlawed the use of such terms as "full," "jumbo size," and "giant size."

Legislation in existence also requires specifics on labels. Under the Fair Products Labeling Act, a product label must identify the type of product, the name and place of business of the manufacturer, the packer or distributor, the net quantity of all the contents, and the net quantity of one serving if the label also gives the number of servings. Both the FTC and the U.S. Department of Health and Human Services have authority to require additional information or disclosures on a label.

Other legislation establishes standards and protects consumers in various ways. Food, drugs, and cosmetics receive special attention. The federal Food and Drug Administration (FDA) regulates labeling and packaging of all such items. The FDA also has authority to prevent "quackery" in medicine and drugs and to investigate "miracle drug" claims.

Approval and Testing of Goods

Many products are sold with a guarantee, tag, or other indication that the products have been tested and approved by some agency or organization. The "seal of approval" or tag means that the product has been tested and approved for normal consumer use. The seller has violated a warranty made to the consumer and may be liable for fraud if the product has not actually been tested and approved.

Tests and approvals, or tests alone, may precede the sale of some products. Products involving fire and electrical safety features may undergo tests by manufacturers' associations or testing companies for insurance purposes. Successful testing means a product meets industry safety standards. Some private and industry testing agencies, including consumer organizations that publish test results in their own magazines, simply report what their tests have revealed. No conclusions are drawn.

Some magazines also accept product advertising that includes "money back" guarantees. The guarantee requires only that the price of a product be refunded or that it be replaced if the product is defective. If a consumer is injured by the defective item, the magazine or organization giving its approval may be liable under the expanding concept of *product liability*.

Controls on Methods of Selling Goods

Many laws today regulate the ways in which merchants can sell their goods. The goal is always the same: to prevent violations of consumer rights. But some laws also provide for means of punishing the fraudulent or unlawful merchant. In two areas in particular, fair disclosure of contract terms and sales by mail, legislative action has created a network of protections for buyers or consumers.

Fair Disclosure of Contract Terms

The Consumer Credit Protection Act, better known as the "Truth in Lending Act," was designed to let the consumer know exactly what the credit offered by a lender will cost. Knowing what one lender's rates are, the consumer can "comparison shop" for a better "deal." This is true whether the individual is taking out a mortgage loan to buy a house, buying furniture or an auto-

mobile, paying for home improvements on the installment plan, or charging meals, gasoline, or repair costs.

The Truth in Lending Act does not apply if no interest or other charges are added to the basic cost of a given item. The Act does ensure the availability of information on the two key factors in the cost of credit— the finance charge, or the amount paid to obtain credit, and the annual percentage rate (APR), the percentage of interest paid over a year's time. The finance charge includes not only the interest to be paid but also any service, carrying, or other charges. The APR must be computed for the consumer on the total cost of credit.

The Truth in Lending Act deals also with advertising. Where an ad mentions one feature of credit, such as the amount of the down payment, it must also mention all the other important terms.

Mail-Order Sales

More and more businesses are offering goods and services through the mail. Federal laws protect the consumer from mail fraud. State statutes may also prohibit mail-order fraud or deceit. Because most mail-order sales involve small amounts, the consumer may find it difficult or impossible to recover losses.

In mail-order sales the consumer has the following rights:

• to know when shipment of the merchandise can be expected;

• to have the merchandise shipped within 30 days;

• to cancel an order when merchandise is not shipped within 30 days;

• to be notified of delays and to have a free means of replying, such as a postage-free postcard;

• to agree to a new shipping date; and

• to have any payment returned if 30 days elapse and the merchandise is not shipped.

Where a person receives free samples or items mailed by charitable organizations seeking contributions, the recipient can, as he or she wishes, regard the merchandise as a gift.

Control of Methods of Payment

Protective laws regulate the methods by which payments may be made or demanded by a creditor on a consumer sale. Some state laws provide that if a creditor accepts payment in a form other than cash or check, the creditor takes a chance. State laws may also provide that installment payments have to be applied to the oldest unpaid portions of a debt. The payment sent by a debtor who is three months delinquent on an open credit account must go toward payment of the oldest monthly charge.

Both federal and state laws regulate accelerated and "balloon" final payments. At one time unscrupulous creditors or lenders could make the last payment in a monthly series larger than the debtor could pay. The lender could then repossess the merchandise when the debtor defaulted. Most laws now specify that if the final payment is double the average of the earlier scheduled payments, the debtor has the right to refinance the final payment on terms similar to those of the original transaction.

Other Financial Areas

In many other money areas the laws protect the consumer without prejudicing the rights of the businessperson. Credit cards, for example, the symbols of the so-called "cashless society," can no longer be issued to per-

sons who have not applied for them. Also, in case of loss of a credit card, the owner cannot be held liable for more than $50 for purchases made illegally by the finder. But such purchases must have been made before the owner has notified the company issuing the card. If they are made after that time, the card holder cannot be held liable at all.

In contract sales, the "fine print" on the reverse sides of some agreements once provided that the buyer waived some legal protections. Under some recent consumer statutes, however, the buyer cannot inadvertently waive all such defenses. Where a household appliance is defective, for example, under the consumer protection statutes of many states the buyer has the right to withdraw from the contract.

Wages and salaries make up another sensitive area.

In general, the laws provide that the right to earn a living and support one's family takes precedence over any right to garnish or attach a person's earnings.

Federal and state laws contain many other provisions designed to protect the consumer. For example, the methods by which debts may be collected are strictly controlled. Credit reporting, which affects the individual's credit rating and, often, his or her ability to get a job and to purchase needed items, falls under the provisions of the Fair Credit Reporting Act of 1970. The Act applies only to personal, household, and family credit, and not to business or commercial credit. Very importantly, the Act gives the person whose credit-worthiness is in question the right to find out the name and address of the reporting agency. The individual then has the right to have any errors in the report corrected.

Business Math

Business Math is, as the term implies, the math that meets the needs of business. It differs from the math used in our daily lives only in the respect that its methods have been adapted to the special requirements of business. The businessman wants to know at what price to sell an article in order to make a certain profit, how much he may deduct from a bill if he pays for an order in cash, whether it is to his advantage to invest his money in one kind of stock or another. These and other practical problems that the businessman faces constitute the bulk of our Business Math section. In addition, we present at the outset some helpful hints that will save time in performing the mathematical computation that is required in solving the business problems later in the section.

It is suggested that the steps given here in solving problems be followed exactly, and that all information required be written down and clearly labeled. Only later, when the methods of solution can be readily applied, should short cuts be taken and steps be performed without indicating them on paper.

Easy Methods of Calculation

Short Cuts in Addition

In adding a column of figures, speed and rapidity will be attained by following these suggestions:

1. Take a combination of numbers which adds to 10 and add them as 10.

Example

Add:

$$\begin{array}{ccc} 8 & 7 & 5 \\ 2 & 8 & 6 \\ 2 & 8 & 4 \\ 2 & 8 & 3 \\ 2 & 2 & 2 \\ 8 & 9 & 5 \\ \hline 2 \; 8 & 4 & 5 \end{array}$$

Add the right-hand column from the top down as follows: 5, 15, 25, carry 2.

Add the second column from the top down as follows: 2, 9, 17, 25, 35, 44, carry 4.

Add the third column from the top down as follows: 4, 14, 16, 18, 28.

2. Take any combination of numbers which total 10 or less and add them as that total. For example, add 2, 3, 4 as 9; add 2, 2, 3 as 7; add 1, 2, 3 as 6; add 2, 4, 2 as 8.

3. Add 9 as 10 and then subtract 1. For example, $65 + 9 = 75 - 1 = 74$.

Short Cuts in Multiplication

1. To multiply an integer (whole number) by 10 or a power of 10. **Rule:** Add one zero to the number to be multiplied for each zero in the multiplier.

Example

65 × 10	= 650	Add 1 zero.
301 × 100	= 30,100	Add 2 zeros.
750 × 1000	= 750,000	Add 3 zeros.
236 × 10,000	= 2,360,000	Add 4 zeros.
185 × 100,000	= 18,500,000	Add 5 zeros.

2. To multiply an integer by 5. **Rule:** Multiply by 10; take ½ of the answer.

Example

$$650 \times 5$$
$$650 \times 10 = 6500$$
$$\tfrac{1}{2} \text{ of } 6500 = 3250, \; Answer$$

3. To multiply an integer by 15. **Rule:** Multiply by 10: take ½ the answer and add both.

Example

$$786 \times 15$$
$$786 \times 10 = \quad 7860$$
$$\tfrac{1}{2} \text{ of } 7860 = \underline{\quad 3930}$$
$$11,790, \; Answer$$

4. To multiply an integer by 11. **Rule:** Multiply by 10; add the original number.

Example

$$295 \times 11$$
$$295 \times 10 = 2950$$
$$295$$
$$\text{(original number)} \quad \underline{\quad 295}$$
$$3245, \; Answer$$

5. To multiply an integer by 9. **Rule:** Multiply by 10; subtract the original number.

Example

293×9
$293 \times 10 = 2930$
293
(original
number) $- \underline{293}$
$\underline{2637}$, *Answer*

6. To multiply an integer by 50, 25, 12½. **Rule:** Multiply by 100; then multiply the answer by ½, ¼, or ⅛ as the case may be because 50, 25, and 12½ are ½, ¼, and ⅛ of 100 respectively.

Example 1

275×50
$275 \times 100 = 27,500$
½ of $27,500 = 13,750$, *Answer*

Example 2

326×25
$326 \times 100 = 32,600$
¼ of $32,600 = 8150$, *Answer*

Short Cuts in Division

1. To divide an integer by 10 or a power of 10. **Rule:** Move the decimal point in the number to be divided as many places to the left as there are zeros in the divisor.

Example 1

$875 \div 10$
$875 \div 10 = 87.50$, *Answer*

Example 2

$\$975.85 \div 1000$
$\$975.85 \div 1000 = \$.97585$, *Answer*

Exercise

1. $800 \times 10 =$
2. $900 \times 50 =$
3. $1756 \times 100 =$
4. $288 \times 25 =$
5. $300 \times 15 =$
6. $756 \div 10 =$
7. $97.8 \div 100 =$
8. $42.6 \div 1000 =$
9. $285 \times 5 =$
10. $88 \times 11 =$
11. $99 \times 9 =$
12. $1725 \times 15 =$
13. $836 \times 1000 =$
14. $19.5 \div 10 =$
15. $28.65 \div 100 =$

Answers:
1. 8000
2. 45,000
3. 175,600
4. 7200
5. 4500
6. 75.6
7. .978
8. .0426
9. 1425
10. 968
11. 891
12. 25,875
13. 836,000
14. 1.95
15. .2865

Devices for Checking the Four Fundamental Operations

Addition

Add the column from top to bottom. Write the answer. Check by adding the column from bottom to top.

Subtraction

Add the answer or remainder to the subtrahend. The result should equal the minuend.

Operation	Check
86 minuend	68 remainder
− 18 subtrahend	+ 18 subtrahend
68 remainder	86 minuend

Multiplication

Multiply the multiplicand by the multiplier. Then make the multiplicand the multiplier and the multiplier the multiplicand, and multiply.

Operation	Check
85 multiplicand	15 multiplicand
× 15 multiplier	× 85 multiplier
425	75
85	120
1275 product	1275 product

A second check is to divide the product by the multiplier. The answer should be the multiplicand. Or divide the product by the multiplicand and the answer should be the multiplier.

Check

$$\text{multiplier } 15 \overline{)\ 1275} \quad \begin{array}{l} 85 \text{ multiplicand} \\ \text{ product} \end{array}$$
$$\underline{120}$$
$$75$$

$$\text{multiplicand } 85 \overline{)\ 1275} \quad \begin{array}{l} 15 \text{ multiplier} \\ \text{ product} \end{array}$$
$$\underline{85}$$
$$425$$
$$425$$

Division

Multiply the answer or quotient by the divisor. The product should equal the dividend.

Operation

$$\text{divisor } 18 \overline{)\ 7500} \quad \begin{array}{l} 416⅔ \text{ quotient} \\ \text{ dividend} \end{array}$$
$$\underline{72}$$
$$30$$
$$\underline{18}$$
$$120$$
$$\underline{108}$$
$$\underline{12}$$
$$18 \quad = ⅔$$

Check

$$\begin{array}{l} 416⅔ \text{ quotient} \\ \underline{18} \text{ divisor} \end{array}$$
$$3 \overline{)\ 36}$$
$$12$$
$$3328$$
$$\underline{416}$$
$$7500 \quad \text{dividend}$$

Percentage

The term "per cent" is derived from the Latin. It means "by the hundred." To illustrate, take the number 1 and divide it into 100 parts. Each part is $\frac{1}{100}$ of 1 and may be expressed in three ways, as follows:

1. Common fraction—$\frac{1}{100}$.
2. Decimal fraction—.01.
3. Per cent—1%.

The value of percentage lies in its use as a basis of comparison in various business transactions. It acts as a common denominator to which everything may be reduced, thus enabling the comparison to be made.

Per Cent, Fractions, and Decimals

1. To change a decimal to per cent. **Rule:** Move the decimal point two places to the right and then write a per cent sign.

Example 1

Change .15 to per cent.
.15 = 15%

Example 2

Change .075 to per cent.
.075 = 7.5%

Example 3

Change 6 to per cent.
6.00 = 600%

2. To change a common fraction to per cent. **Rule:** Change the common fraction to a decimal; then change the decimal to a per cent.

Example 1

Change $\frac{3}{8}$ to a per cent.
$$\frac{3}{8} = 8 \overline{)3.000}$$
$$.375$$
.375 = 37.5% or 37½%

Example 2

Change $\frac{17}{19}$ to a per cent.
$$\frac{17}{19} = 19 \overline{)17.00} \quad .89\frac{9}{19}$$
$$15\ 2$$
$$18\ 0$$
$$17\ 1$$
$$\frac{9}{19}$$
$.89\frac{9}{19} = 89\frac{9}{19}\%$

Exercise

Express the following as per cent:

1. ½
2. ⁴⁄₃
3. ⁵⁄₆
4. ¹¹⁄₂₀
5. .08

6. .0075
7. .02½
8. .3
9. ¹⁵⁄₂₈
10. .006

Answers:
1. 50%
2. 133⅓%
3. 83⅓%
4. 55%
5. 8%

6. .75% or ¾%
7. 2½%
8. ³⁄₁₀% or 30%
9. 53⁴⁄₇%
10. ³⁄₅% or .6%

3. To change a per cent to a decimal. **Rule:** Move the decimal point two places to the left and take away the per cent sign.

Example 1

Express 17% as a decimal.
17% = .17

Example 2

Express 8.5% as a decimal.
08.5% = .085

Example 3

Express 525% as a decimal.
525% = 5.25

Example 4

Express .75% as a decimal.
75% = .0075

Exercise

Express the following per cents as decimals:

1. 2½%
2. 37½%
3. 650%
4. 7.5%
5. 18.8%

6. .5%
7. .05%
8. .25%
9. 16.75%
10. 123%

Answers:
1. .025
2. .375
3. 6.50
4. .075
5. .188

6. .005
7. .0005
8. .0025
9. .1675
10. 1.23

4. To change a per cent to a common fraction. **Rule:** Change the common fraction to a decimal; then to a per cent.

Example 1

Change 25% to a common fraction.
$$25\% = .25$$
$$.25 = \frac{25}{100} = \frac{1}{4}, \ Answer$$

Example 2

Change 150% to a common fraction.
$$150\% = 1.50$$
$$1.50 = 1½ \ or \ \frac{3}{2}, \ Answer$$

Exercise

Change the following to common fractions:

1. 50%
2. 20%
3. 40%
4. 33⅓%
5. 16⅔%

6. 75%
7. 80%
8. 62½%
9. 87½%
10. 12½%

Answers:
1. ½
2. ⅕
3. ⅖
4. ⅓
5. ⅙

6. ¾
7. ⅘
8. ⅝
9. ⅞
10. ⅛

Problems in Percentage

In computing a problem in percentage, the number or quantity upon which the per cent is to be computed is called the *base*, the per cent is called the *rate*, and the product of the base and the rate is called the *percentage*. All problems in percentage fall into three groups or cases.

Case I. Given the base and the rate, to find the percentage. **Rule:** Base × Rate = Percentage.

Example 1

Find 25% of 7800.

Change 25% to .25; then multiply:
7800 × .25 = 1950, *Answer*

Example 2

Find 250% of 19,600.
19,600 × 2½ = 49,000, *Answer*

Exercise

Find the percentage:

1. 15% of 980
2. 12½% of 640
3. 33⅓% of 999
4. 125% of 260
5. 18% of 480

6. ¾% of 1200
7. .75% of 1600
8. 2½% of 1640
9. 10% of 968
10. 19% of 200

Answers:

1. 147
2. 80
3. 333
4. 325
5. 86.4

6. 9
7. 12
8. 41
9. 96.8
10. 38

Case II. Given the base and the percentage, to find the rate. **Rule:** Divide the percentage by the base.

Example

17 is what per cent of 29?
$^{17}/_{29} = .58^{18}/_{29} = 58^{18}/_{29}\%$

Exercise

1. 25 is what per cent of 800?
2. 16 is what per cent of 280?
3. 180 is what per cent of 36,000?
4. 17.5 is what per cent of 85.6?
5. 18.4 is what per cent of 2.86?

Answers:

1. 3⅛%
2. 5⁵⁄₇%

3. ½% or .5%
4. 20⁹⁵⁄₂₁₄%

5. 643⁵¹⁄₁₄₃%

Case III. Given the percentage and rate, to find the base. This is called the indirect case. **Rule:** Percentage divided by rate equals the base.

Example

18 is 3% of what number?
18 ÷ .03 = 600, *Answer*

Exercise

1. 25 is 20% of what number?
2. 180 is 50% of what number?
3. 27 is 75% of what number?
4. 260 is 80% of what number?
5. 1704 is 12% of what number?

Answers:

1. 125
2. 360

3. 36
4. 325

5. 14,200

Aliquot Parts

Arithmetical calculations may be made much easier if the aliquot parts of 100% are used. By an aliquot part is

meant a number which can be divided into another number so that the answer will be a whole number. Thus 25% is an aliquot part of 100% because 100% divided by 25% equals 4. It would be well to memorize the aliquot parts of 100%, and multiples of these aliquot parts for greater ease and speed in performing problems.

Aliquot Parts of 100%

50%	= ½	87½%	= ⅞	70%	= ⁷⁄₁₀
25%	= ¼	1%	= ¹⁄₁₀₀	80%	= ⅘
75%	= ¾	10%	= ¹⁄₁₀	33⅓%	= ⅓
6¼%	= ¹⁄₁₆	20%	= ⅕	66⅔%	= ⅔
12½%	= ⅛	30%	= ³⁄₁₀	16⅔%	= ⅙
37½%	= ⅜	40%	= ⅖	8⅓%	= ¹⁄₁₂
62½%	= ⅝	60%	= ⅗	83⅓%	= ⅚

Example

Find 37½% of 800.
⅜ of 800 = 300, *Answer*

Exercise

Compute the following, using aliquot parts:

1. 20% of 850
2. 87½% of 864
3. 12½% of 960
4. 75% of 1200
5. 33⅓% of 963
6. 10% of 786
7. 16⅔% of 282
8. 66⅔% of 1296

9. 80% of 9000
10. 8⅓% of 2460
11. 83⅓% of 288
12. 62½% of 1200
13. 6¼% of 3200
14. 5% of 870
15. 50% of 1900

Answers:

1. 170
2. 756
3. 120
4. 900
5. 321
6. 78.6
7. 47
8. 864

9. 7200
10. 205
11. 240
12. 750
13. 200
14. 43½
15. 950

Aliquot Parts of $1.00

It will be noticed that the aliquot parts of $1.00 are the same as those of 100%. Therefore the same fractional equivalents may be used at all times.

Example

Find cost of 840 yards of silks @ 62½¢ per yd.
62½ = ⅝
⅝ of 840 = 525, *Answer*

Exercise

Compute the following, using aliquot parts:

1. 160 yds. @ 50¢
2. 980 yds. @ 10¢
3. 750 yds. @ 40¢
4. 138 lbs. @ 33⅓¢
5. 280 lbs. @ 62½¢
6. 1780 lbs. @ 60¢
7. 66⅔ lbs. @ 90¢
8. 16⅔ lbs. @ 48¢

9. 75 yds. @ 88¢
10. 40 yds. @ $2.50
11. 270 lbs. @ 66⅔¢
12. 726 ft. @ 16⅔¢
13. 6480 yds. @ 62½¢
14. 22½ lbs. @ 40¢
15. 256 ft. @ 6¼¢

In problems 7 to 10, the base and the rate may be interchanged so that problem 7 will read 90 lbs. @ 66⅔¢ and will be done in the same manner as problems 1 to 6.

Answers:

1. $80	**9.** $66		**5.** $175	**13.** $4050	
2. $98	**10.** $100		**6.** $1068	**14.** $9	
3. $300	**11.** $180		**7.** $60	**15.** $16	
4. $46	**12.** $121		**8.** $8		

Business Uses of Math

Discounts on Invoices

Invoices and Terms

After a sale is made, the seller sends an *invoice* to the buyer. On it is listed the date, terms, goods and quantity sold, the price of each item, the extensions, and the total. The terms are most important because they are the conditions of payment. Some examples of terms are:

C.O.D.—Collect or cash on delivery.
Cash—Cash is to be paid on the date of the sale.
On account—Payment to be made within a reasonable time after the end of the month.
E.O.M.—End of the month.
n/30—Net 30 days after the date of the invoice (net means no discounts).
2/10 n/30—2% discount if paid within 10 days after the date of the invoice, net after 10 days and within 30 days.
2/5 1/15 n/30—2% discount if paid within 5 days, 1% discount if paid after 5 days but within 15 days; net if paid after 15 days and within 30 days.

Trade and Cash Discounts

Discounts on invoices are of two kinds, cash discounts and trade discounts. Cash discounts are those mentioned under terms, an inducement to the customer to pay his bill ahead of time. The customer is the one who decides whether he will take advantage of the discount. Trade discounts differ from cash discounts because they are deducted, not by the customer, but by the seller.

Manufacturers and wholesalers print catalogues once or twice a year. They are expensive. In order to bring the catalogue price down to the market price, they send their customers discount sheets, on which they list discounts given on the catalogue price to bring it down to the market price. If the price drops, two or more trade discounts may be given.

Problem 1: The Rowe Co. offers to sell a dining room suite for $250 less 20%, 10%, and 10%. The Wilson Co. offers a similar suite for $260 less 40%. Which is the better offer and by how much?

Rowe Co.

$250	List Price or Catalogue Price
50	Trade Discount 20%
$200	Balance
20	Trade Discount 10%
$180	Balance
18	Trade Discount 10%
$162	Net Cost

Wilson Co.

$260	List Price
140	Trade Discount 40%
$156	Net Cost
$162	Net Cost—Rowe Co.
156	Net Cost—Wilson Co.
$6	Wilson Co. offer better.

Problem 2: The Domestic Rug Co. received an invoice on November 10 amounting to $1280 less 20%, and 5%, terms 3/10 n/60. The invoice was paid November 20. Find the amount of the payment.

$1280.00	List Price
256.00	Trade Discount 20%
$1024.00	Balance
51.20	Trade Discount 5% (½ of 10%)
$ 972.80	Balance
29.18	Cash Discount 3%
$ 943.62	Net Cost

Problem 3: A dealer purchased a bicycle for $32.40 less 33⅓%, terms 2/10 n/30, plus a freight charge of 90¢. The invoice was dated March 15 and paid March 25. Find the amount of the payment.

$32.40	List Price
10.80	Trade Discount 33⅓%
$21.60	Balance
.43	Cash Discount 2%
$21.17	Net Cost
.90	Freight Charge
$22.07	Total Cost

Note: The discounts are taken only on the invoice; they cannot be taken on the freight charge or any other buying expense.

Exercise

1. Find net cost of invoice of $1375 less 20% and 10%.
2. Find total cost of invoice of $45 less 20% and buying expense of $2.10.
3. Find net cost of invoice dated April 16, terms 2/10 n/30, amounting to $1500 less 20% and 10% and paid on April 26.
4. A dealer offeres a rug for $60 less 30% and 10%. Another offers the same quality for $60 less 40%. Which offer is better and how much?

Answers:

1. $990		**3.** $1058.40	
2. $38.10		**4.** Second offer by $1.80	

Single Discount Equivalent to a Series of Trade Discounts

For ease in computation and for purposes of comparison, it is often desirable to find one discount that is equivalent to a series. The procedure is as follows: Consider the catalogue price as 100%. Multiply this by the first discount and subtract from 100%. Multiply this difference or balance by the second discount and subtract the answer from the balance. Continue this multiplication and subtraction until all the discounts have been taken. The answer will be the net cost. To find the single discount, subtract the net cost from 100%.

Problem: Find one discount equivalent to a series of 30%, 20% and 10%.

100%	List Price
30	Trade Discount 30%
70%	Balance
14	Trade Discount 20% (20% of 70%)
56.0%	Balance
5.6	Trade Discount 10% (10% of 56%)
50.4	Net Cost

100% List Price − 50.4% Net Cost = 49.6%, *Ans.*
Proof: 30% + 14% + 5.6% = 49.6%, *Answer*

Exercise

Find one discount equivalent to the following series:

1. 20% and 10%
2. 30% and 10%
3. 50% and 20%
4. 25% and 20%
5. 37½% and 24%
6. 20%, 10%, and 5%
7. 20%, 10%, and 10%
8. 50%, 25%, and 20%
9. 40%, 30%, 20%, and 10%
10. 50%, 25%, and 10%

Answers:
1. 28%
2. 37%
3. 60%
4. 40%
5. 52½%
6. 31.6%
7. 35.2%
8. 70%
9. 69.76%
10. 66.25%

Commissions

Salesmen are usually paid a percentage of their sales as compensation for their work. This percentage is called *commission*. Commissions are generally paid on the amount of the sales, although in some cases they are calculated on the quantity of merchandise sold. When a salesman is paid commission only, he is on a straight commission basis. If he receives a drawing account, the amount of the drawings is deducted from his total commission at the end of the accounting period, and the balance paid him at that time.

To encourage salesmen to greater efforts, commission may be paid on a graduated basis; that is for example, 10% commission on the first $20,000 of sales and 15% on all sales over $20,000. Inside salesmen are usually paid on a commission and salary basis. Very often, no commission is paid until a stated amount or quota has been sold; commission is then paid on sales over the

quota. The problems that follow deal with each of these phases of selling.

Straight Commission

Problem 1: A salesman sells 2500 yards of silk at $2 per yard. His rate of commission is 2½%. Find his commission.

2500 × $2 = $5000, Sales
2½% of $5000 = $125, Commission

Problem 2: A salesman sells 2500 yards of silk at $2 per yard. His rate of commission is 5¢ per yard. Find his commission.

2500 yards × 5¢ = $125, Commission

Note that in the first problem the commission was based on price whereas in the second problem it was based on quantity.

Salary and Commission

Problem: A salesman is offered a salary of $50 per week and a commission of 5% on all sales. His sales for the year are $36,000. Find his yearly earnings.

Time	Sales	5% Commission	Salary	Total
1 year	$36,000	$1800	$2600 (52 × $50)	$4400 *Answer*

Salary, Commission, and Quota

Problem: A salesman is offered a salary of $110 per month and a 6% commission on all sales over $2000 per month. In April, his sales were $1950; in May, $3250; in June, $3375. Find his total earnings.

Time	Salary	Sales	Quota Over $2000	6% Commission	Totals
April	$110	$1950	$ 0	$ 0	$110.00
May	110	3250	1250	75.00	185.00
June	110	3375	1375	82.50	192.50
Totals	$330	$8575	$2625	$157.50	$487.50 *Answer*

To check the answer, add the vertical totals, then the horizontal totals. The grand total must be the same.
Thus, vertically, 110 + 185 + 192.50 = 487.50
horizontally, 330 + 157.50 = 487.50

Salary, Graduated Commission, and Quota

Problem: Noll, a salesman, receives a salary of $200 per month, 1% commission on all sales, and 2% commission on all monthly sales over $3000. In January his sales were $6000; in February, $4500; in March, $7400. Find his total income for the three months.

Salary, Graduated Commission, and Quota Problem Table

Time	Salary	Sales	On All Sales Com. 1%	Quota Over $3000	Over $3000 Com. 2%	Totals
January	$200	$ 6000	$ 60	$3000	$ 60	$320
February	200	4500	45	1500	30	275
March	200	7400	74	4400	88	362
Totals	$600	$17,900	$179	$8900	$178	$957 *Answer*

To check the answer of the problem just solved, add the horizontal totals:

$$600 + 179 + 178 = 957.$$

Exercise

In doing these problems use the diagram method of the previous problems. The headings can be found very easily by reading the problem carefully and then heading each column as the problem indicates.

1. Find the commission a salesman receives if his sales are $6500 and the commission is 7%.
2. John Miller, a salesman, receives a monthly salary of $90 and 5% commission on all sales. In addition, he receives 2% on sales over $3000 in any single month. His sales in April were $3850 and in May $2700. Find his total earnings.
3. A salesman has offers of employment from two firms. Kolapep offers him a salary of $100 per month, a commission of 5% in total monthly sales and 2% additional commission on monthly sales in excess of $2000. Cocapep offers him a commission of 8% on the first $1000 of monthly sales, 10% on the next $1000 of monthly sales and 12% on all monthly sales in excess of $2000. If his average sales are $3500 a month, where would he earn more and how much more?
4. The Electric Supply Co. has an agency for the sale of vacuum cleaners. Their commission is $12.50 each for the first 50 cleaners; $15 each for the second 50 cleaners or part thereof; $17.50 each for all over 100 cleaners sold each month. In May, they sold 76 cleaners; in June, they sold 105 cleaners. Find their commission.

Answers:
1. $455
2. $524.50
3. Cocapep is better by $55
4. $2477.50

Commission Merchants

For those people who cannot do their own buying or selling, agents known as commission merchants will attend to all such transactions. They charge a commission for their services, in the same manner as do salesmen. After selling the merchandise, they submit a statement called an *account sales*. After buying the merchandise, they submit a statement called an *account purchase*.

Problem 1: Williams has 860 bushels of potatoes to sell. He can sell them at $2.10 a bushel, with no expense. However, he sends them to a commission merchant who sells 450 bushels at $2.60 and the remainder at $2.25 a bushel. The merchant charges 3¢ a bushel for storage, $36.80 for freight, 1% for insurance, and 3% commission.

A. Find the amount of the net proceeds remitted to Williams.

B. How much does Williams gain or lose by having the merchant sell the potatoes?

A. Income

450 bu. @ $2.60	$1170.00
410 bu. @ $2.25	922.50
Total Proceeds	$2092.50

Charges

Storage (3¢ per bu., 860 bu.) ..	$25.80
Freight	36.80
Insurance (1% of $2092.50)	20.93
Commission (3% of $2092.50) .	62.78
Total Charges	$ 146.31
Net Proceeds	$1946.19

B.   860 bu. @ $2.10 = $1806, Total Proceeds

$1946.19, Net Proceeds—Commission Merchant
1806.00, Total Proceeds
$ 140.19, Gain by sending to commission merchant

Note: All charges or expenses must be subtracted on a sale.

Problem 2: Benton, a sugar broker, purchases 35,000 pounds of sugar for a candy manufacturer at 5.5¢ per pound. Benton's expenses and charges are: handling $23.40, freight 36¢ per hundredweight, commission 5%. Find the total cost of the sugar to the candy manufacturer.

35,000 lbs. sugar @ 5.5¢ per lb. = $1925, Cost

Charges

Handling	$ 23.40
Freight (36¢ per cwt.—35,000 lbs.	126.00
Commission (5% of $1925)	96.25
Total Charges	$ 245.65
Total Cost	$2170.65

Note: All charges and expenses must be added on a purchase.

Exercise

1. Wilson, a commission merchant, receives 1500 bushels of potatoes to sell. He sold 635 bushels at $1.50; 475 bushels at $1.40; and the remainder at $1.30 a bushel. He charged a commission of 5%. His expenses were: freight charges $84.50, sorting and weighing $38.40, and storage charges of 3¢ per bushel. Find the net proceeds.
2. Harris purchased 50,000 feet of lumber for a builder at $60 per 1000 feet. Freight charges were $150, insurance 1%, trucking $75 and commission 4%. Find the total cost of the lumber to the builder.

3. A fruit farm shipped 100 crates (32 boxes per crate) of strawberries to a commission merchant. He sold 1280 boxes at $.20, 960 boxes at $.15 and the remainder at $.12 per box. Freight charges were $24, storage $22.66, cartage $15.60, commission 5%. Find the net proceeds.

Answers:
1. $1850.37   **2.** $3375   **3.** $427.18

Payrolls

Time Basis

Employees other than salesmen are usually paid on a time basis. So-called white-collar workers such as clerks, bookkeepers, and the like are paid on an annual, monthly, or weekly salary basis. Other workers, especially those who do manual labor, are paid on an hourly basis, with forty hours per week generally regarded as regular time, and everything over forty hours as overtime. In many organizations each employee has a time card on which an accurate record of his time may be kept.

Problem 1: Below is the time card of a worker showing the time he has worked for one week. His regular wage is $1.10 per hour for a 40 hour week.

Day	In	Out	In	Out
Monday	7:00	12:00	1:00	4:00
Tuesday	7:00	12:00	1:00	4:00
Wednesday	7:00	12:00	1:00	4:00
Thursday	7:00	12:00	1:00	4:00
Friday	7:00	12:00	1:00	4:00

A. Find his total wages for the week.
B. His employer deducts 3% for social security and $6.38 for withholding tax. What is his take-home pay?

A.

Day	Hours
Monday	8
Tuesday	8
Wednesday	8
Thursday	8
Friday	8
Total	40
	× 1.10
	$44.00, Total Wages

B. Total wages $44.00

Deductions
Social Security (3%) $1.32
Withholding Tax 6.38
                                  7.70
   Take-home pay $36.30

Problem 2: A mechanic is working in a factory where his regular time is 40 hours a week. He is paid time and a half (1½ times) for overtime. His regular wages are $1.50 per hour. Deductions are 3% for social security and $14.25 for withholding tax. Last week he worked 57 hours.

A. Find his total earnings.
B. Find his take-home pay.

A.

Total Time (Hours)	Regular Time (Hours)	1½ Over-Time (Hours)*
57	40	17
		× 1½
		8½
		17
		25½

*(One hour of overtime equals 1½ hours of regular time. Convert overtime to regular time by multiplying by the overtime rate.)

          40   Regular Allowance
        25½   Overtime Allowance
        65½   Total Hours
    × $1.50   Rate
     $98.25,   Total Wages

B. Total wages $98.25
Deductions
Social Security (3%) .... $ 2.95
Withholding Tax 14.25
                             17.20
   Take-home pay $81.05

Exercise

1. William Randall, a machinist, worked last week as follows: Monday 8 hours, Tuesday 10 hours, Wednesday 11 hours, Thursday 9 hours, Friday 10 hours and Saturday 5 hours. His regular time is 40 hours per week, with time and a half for overtime. His hourly rate is $1.60 per hour. Deductions of 3% for social security taxes and $13.81 for withholding taxes are made.
   a. Find his total wages.
   b. Find his take-home pay.
2. Hawkins, a mechanic, worked 47 hours last week. His regular time is 40 hours with time and a half for overtime. His hourly rate is $1.40 per hour. Social security tax deduction was 3% and withholding tax was $11.67.
   a. Find his total wages.
   b. Find his take-home pay.

Answers:
1. *a.* $95.20   **2.** *a.* $70.70
   b. $78.53   *b.* $56.91

Piecework Wages

Another method of compensation depends not on the time worked but on the quantity or pieces which the worker produces. The wage is computed by multiplying the number of pieces by the rate per piece.

Problem: Harris, a dress operator, produces 108 pieces of work during the week. His rate per piece is 35¢. Find his total wages.

   108 × .35 = $37.80, Total Wages

Deductions for social security and withholding tax are computed in the same manner as in time wages.

Averages

By an average is meant a figure which is typical of a group of numbers. Averages are useful in comparing groups of numbers. To find an average, add all the items and divide the total by the number of items.

Problem 1: A salesman's sales per week are $1500, $2000, $3000, $6000, and $2500. Find his average sales for the five weeks.

$$\begin{array}{r} \$1500 \\ 2000 \\ 3000 \\ 6000 \\ 2500 \\ \hline \$15,000 \end{array}$$

$15,000 ÷ 5 = $3000, Average Sales per Week

Problem 2: Clark's average sales for the last 8 weeks of the year were $362.15 a week. For the first 3 weeks of the new year, his sales per week were $415.16, $523.25, and $392.35. Find his average sales per week for the 11 weeks.

$362.15 × 8 = $2897.20, Total sales for 8 weeks

$$\begin{array}{r} 415.16 \\ 523.25 \\ 392.35 \\ \hline \$4227.96, \text{ Total sales for 11 weeks} \end{array}$$

$4227.96 ÷ 11 = $384.36, Average sales per week
for 11 weeks

Exercise

1. The Acme Sales Co. had a contest for its salesmen. Potter's average sales for the last 8 weeks of the year were $340. For the first 4 weeks of the new year, his weekly sales were $376, $625, $429, and $374. Find his average weekly sales for the 12 weeks.
2. In the same contest, Wolcott's sales for the last 6 weeks averaged $425. For the first 4 weeks of the new year, his weekly sales were $500, $735, $658, and $695. Find his average weekly sales for the 10 weeks.

Answers:
1. $377   **2.** $513.80

Simple Interest

Basic Method of Calculation

Interest is the charge made for the use of money for a specified time. The money used is called the *principal*. The per cent is called the *rate*. The rule for calculating interest is:

Principal × Rate × Time = Interest

Problem 1: Find the interest on $600 for 1 year at 6%.

$600 × $\frac{6}{100}$ × 1 = $36, Interest

Problem 2: Find the interest on $1200 for 90 days at 4%.

$1200 × $\frac{4}{100}$ × $\frac{90}{360}$ = $12, Interest

Note that for purposes of easier and faster computation the year is considered to have 360 days, and each month, regardless of how many days it actually has, is considered to have only 30 days.

Exercise

Find the interest:

	Principal	Time	Rate %	Rate %	Rate %
1.	$1600	6 months	6	4	3
2.	1200	3 months	6	3	2
3.	2400	2 months	6	5	3
4.	720	60 days	6	1	4
5.	840	80 days	6	1	2
6.	480	40 days	6	5	4
7.	220	120 days	6	3	2
8.	180	9 months	6	8	4½
9.	2800	8 months	6	2	3
10.	960	30 days	6	4	3

Answers:

1.	$ 48	$32	$24
2.	18	9	6
3.	24	20	12
4.	7.20	1.20	4.80
5.	11.20	1.87	3.73
6.	3.20	2.67	2.13
7.	4.40	2.20	1.47
8.	8.10	10.80	6.08
9.	112	37.33	56
10.	4.80	3.20	2.40

The Sixty-Day Method

To find interest on sums of money when the time is less than a year, the *sixty-day method* is used. This method is based upon the fact that 60 days (2 months) are ⅙ of one year. Therefore, if the annual interest rate is 6%, the interest charge for 60 days is ⅙ of 6% or 1%. **Rule:** To find the interest on any sum of money for 60 days (2 months) take 1% of that amount.

Problem 1: Find the interest on $1200 for 60 days at 6%.

1% of $1200 = $12.00, Interest for 60 days
Proof: $1200 × $\frac{6}{100}$ × $\frac{60}{360}$ = $12.

Finding the interest for 60 days is the basis for computing interest for other periods of time. For example, the interest for 30 days is half of that for 60 days; for 15 days, a quarter; for 10 days, a sixth, etc.

Problem 2: Find the interest on $1200 at 6% for the days shown below:

Interest on $1200 for 60 days at 6%	=	$12.00
Interest for 30 days (½ of 60)	=	6.00
Interest for 20 days (⅓ of 60)	=	4.00
Interest for 15 days (¼ of 60)	=	3.00
Interest for 12 days (⅕ of 60)	=	2.40
Interest for 10 days (⅙ of 60)	=	2.00
Interest for 6 days (⅒ of 60)	=	1.20

From this point, it is easy to find the interest for any number of days. Always find the interest for 60 days first. That is the base. Then, break up the days for which the interest is to be calculated into aliquot parts of 60 and add the interest for those days. The following illustrations will show just what is to be done:

Problem 3: Find the interest on $1800 for 90 days at 6%. 90 = 60 + 30.

Interest on $1800 for 60 days at 6% =	$18
Interest on $1800 for 30 days at 6% =	9
Interest on $1800 for 90 days at 6% =	$27

Problem 4: Find the interest on $1500 for 47 days at 6%.

  A. 47 = 20 + 20 + 6 + 1
    or
  B. 47 = 30 + 15 + 2.

A.

Interest on $1500 for 60 days at 6% = $15.00
Interest on $1500 for 20 days at 6% = $5.00
Interest on $1500 for 20 days at 6% =   5.00
Interest on $1500 for 6 days at 6% =   1.50
Interest on $1500 for 1 day at 6% =   .25
Interest on $1500 for 47 days at 6% = $11.75

B.

Interest on $1500 for 60 days at 6% = $15.00
Interest on $1500 for 30 days at 6% = $7.50
Interest on $1500 for 15 days at 6% =   3.75
Interest on $1500 for 2 days at 6% =   .50
Interest on $1500 for 47 days at 6% = $11.75

Problem 5: Find the interest on $270 for 56 days at 6%.

  A. 56 = 30 + 20 + 6.
    or
  B. 56 = 20 + 20 + 12 + 4.
    or
  C. 56 = 60 − 4.

A.

Interest on $270 for 60 days at 6% = $2.70
Interest on $270 for 30 days at 6% = $1.35
Interest on $270 for 20 days at 6% =   .90
Interest on $270 for 6 days at 6% =   .27
Interest on $270 for 56 days at 6% = $2.52

B.

Interest on $270 for 60 days at 6% = $2.70
Interest on $270 for 20 days at 6% = $ .90
Interest on $270 for 20 days at 6% =   .90
Interest on $270 for 12 days at 6% =   .54
Interest on $270 for 4 days at 6% =   .18
Interest on $270 for 56 days at 6% = $2.52

C.

Interest on $270 for 60 days at 6% = $2.70
Interest on $270 for 4 days at 6% =   .18
Interest on $270 for 56 days at 6% = $2.52

Note that it is also possible to use aliquot parts of the other numbers besides 60 as well. Thus in Problem 4a, 1 day is ⅙ of 6 days. Therefore ⅙ of $1.50 = $.25. In Problem 5b, 4 days are ⅕ of 20 days or ⅓ of 12 days. The interest can be computed by taking ⅕ of $.90 or ⅓ of $.54, the answer in each case being $.18.

Exercise

Find the interest:

	Principal	Time	Rate %
1.	$1600	80 days	6
2.	1800	3 months	6
3.	1200	75 days	6
4.	4000	46 days	6
5.	280	23 days	6
6.	970	38 days	6
7.	250.68	14 days	6
8.	168.95	4 months	6
9.	1280	53 days	6
10.	560.80	44 days	6

Answers:

1.	$21.33	5.	$1.07	9.	$11.31
2.	27.00	6.	6.14	10.	4.11
3.	15.00	7.	.58		
4.	30.67	8.	3.38		

To Find the Interest at 6% for Any Time in Days

Frequently the number of days in an interest problem cannot easily be divided into aliquot parts of 60, such as 29 days, 71 days, etc. In such cases another method may be used, as follows:

Rule:
1. Divide the principal by 1000.
2. Multiply the result by the number of days.
3. Divide the product by 6.

Problem: Find the interest on $150 for 29 days at 6%.

$$\frac{\$150}{1000} = \$.150$$

$$
\begin{array}{r}
\$.150 \\
29 \\
\hline
1350 \\
300 \\
\hline
6\,)\,4350 \\
\hline
.725 \ Answer
\end{array}
$$

The answer arrived at by this method may be checked by the first method:

Interest on $150 for 60 days at 6% = $1.50
Interest on $150 for 30 days at 6% = $.75
Interest on $150 for 1 day at 6% = $.025
Interest on $150 for 31 days at 6% =   .775
Interest on $150 for 29 days at 6% = $ .725 or $.73

Exercise

Do the examples in the preceding exercise, but use the above method.

To Find the Interest at Rates Other Than 6%

Rule:
1. Find the interest at 6%.
2. Multiply the answer by the desired rate.
3. Divide by 6.

Problem: Find the interest on $800 for 37 days at 4½%.

A.

Interest on $800 for 60 days at 6% = $8.00
Interest on $800 for 30 days at 6% = $4.00
Interest on $800 for 6 days at 6% =   .80
Interest on $800 for 1 day at 6% =   .133
Interest on $800 for 37 days at 6% = $4.933

B.

$$
\begin{array}{r}
\$4.933 \\
4\frac{1}{2} \\
\hline
\$22.1985
\end{array}
$$

C.

$$
\begin{array}{r}
6\,)\,22.1985 \\
\hline
3.6997\frac{1}{2} \ or \ \$3.70, \ Answer
\end{array}
$$

Another method may also be used. For 5% take ⅚ of the answer; for 4%, ⅔ (or ⁴⁄₆); for 3%, ½ (or ³⁄₆); for 2%, ⅓ (or ²⁄₆) and for 1%, ⅙. Whichever method is used is a matter of one's own preference.

Exercise

Find the interest.

	Principal	Time	Rate %	Rate %	Rate %
1.	$1836	60 days	5	4	3
2.	680	26 days	4	3	2
3.	275	3 months	3	2	1
4.	368	6 months	2	1	5
5.	212.50	72 days	1	5	4
6.	505.80	90 days	5	4	3
7.	906	36 days	4	3	2
8.	412.76	45 days	3	2	1
9.	1300	18 days	2	1	5
10.	1560	52 days	1	5	4

Answers:

1.	$15.30	$12.24	$9.18
2.	1.97	1.48	.98
3.	2.06	1.38	.69
4.	3.68	1.84	9.20
5.	.43	2.13	1.70
6.	6.32	5.06	3.79
7.	3.62	2.72	1.81
8.	1.55	1.03	.52
9.	1.30	.65	3.25
10.	2.25	11.27	9.01

Bank Discount

Discounting One's Own Notes

When a businessman needs money, he borrows it at the bank. In return he will give the bank his written promise to repay the money at a certain time. This written promise is called a *promissory note*. The bank will charge interest on the loan which it will deduct in advance, giving the borrower the difference between the value of the note at maturity and the interest. This difference is called the *net proceeds*. When interest is deducted in advance, it is called *bank discount*, and the rate is called the *rate of bank discount*.

In order to find how much a borrower will actually receive on a loan, calculate the interest and subtract the amount from the principal.

Problem: A businessman borrows $1500 from a bank on his 60-day note at a discount rate of 6%. Find the net proceeds.

Interest on $1500
for 60 days at 6% = $15, Bank Discount

$1500 Maturity Value
  15 Bank Discount
$1485 Net Proceeds

Exercise

Find the net proceeds of the following notes:

	Note	Time of Discount	Rate of Discount %
1.	$1200	90 days	6
2.	680	45 days	6
3.	420	120 days	6
4.	1100	60 days	6
5.	975	30 days	6

Answers:

1.	$1182		3.	$ 411.60	5. $970.12
2.	674.90		4.	1089	

Discounting Others' Notes

Frequently, a businessman who is in need of money has customers' notes and acceptances on hand. He may borrow on these.

Problem 1: Harry Williams has received a note of $600 from a customer. It is dated April 15 and runs for 90 days. On May 12, he needs money. He sells it to the bank or, to use the correct business term, he *discounts* the note. What are the net proceeds?

To do this problem, four steps must be performed.

1. Find the day the note is due (date of maturity).
2. Find how long the bank must wait for payment (term of discount).
3. Find the bank discount.
4. Find the net proceeds.

Date of Maturity

Apr. 30
    − 15
Apr. 15
May   31
June 30
July 14 Date of Maturity
      90 days

Term of Discount

May   31
    − 12
May   19
June 30
July 14
      63 days, Term of Discount

Bank Discount

$6.30 for 63 days (By previously indicated method)

Net Proceeds

$600.00 Maturity Value
   6.30 Bank Discount
$593.70 Net Proceeds

Note that in finding the date of maturity and the term of discount, the actual number of days is used.

Explanation of the Solution:

1. *Date of Maturity.* The date of maturity is 90 days from April 15. There are 30 days in April; 15 days have already passed, so we have 15 days left in April. In May there are 31, in June, 30 days. This gives us 76 days, leaving 14 more to make up the 90. We reach, then, July 14.
2. *Term of Discount.* Counting from the date the note was discounted, May 12, to the date of maturity, July 14, there are 63 days.
3. *Bank Discount.* The bank discount is found by finding the interest for the term of discount, 63 days.
4. *Net Proceeds.* Net proceeds are found by deducting the bank discount from the value at maturity.

When the time of the note is not in days, but in months, the date of maturity is found by counting months, and not days.

Problem 2: Find the net proceeds of a note of $1500, dated July 16, time 3 months, and discounted August 31.

Date of Maturity

July 16
Aug.
Sept.
Oct. 16 Date of Maturity
3 months

Term of Discount

Aug. 31
−31
Aug. 0
Sept. 30
Oct. 16
46 days, Term of Discount

Bank Discount

$11.50, for 46 days (By previously indicated method)

Net Proceeds

$1500.00 Maturity Value
11.50 Bank Discount
$1488.50 Net Proceeds

Exercise

Find the net proceeds:

	Face Value	Date	Time	Rate %	Date of Discount
1.	$1200	Mar. 2	60 days	6	Apr. 7
2.	1800	Apr. 30	90 days	6	June 3
3.	240	Sept. 16	30 days	6	Sept. 25
4.	550	Jan. 20	1 mo.	6	Jan. 31
5.	728	Feb. 17	3 mo.	6	Apr. 12
6.	2800	May 4	2 mo.	6	June 6

Answers:
1. $1195.20   3. $239.16   5. $ 723.75
2. 1783.20   4. 548.17   6. 2786.93

Discounting Interest-Bearing Notes

The face value and the maturity value of a non-interest-bearing note are the same. In the case of an interest-bearing note, the face value and maturity value differ, because the interest must be added to the face value to arrive at the maturity value.

Problem 1: Find the maturity value of a 60-day note of $800 bearing interest at 3%.

Interest = $4

$800 Face Value
4 Interest
$804 Maturity Value

To discount an interest-bearing note, the maturity value must be found, because the bank discount is computed on the maturity value, not the face value.

Problem 2: Find the net proceeds of a 60-day note of $1200, bearing interest at 4%, dated January 18 and discounted February 13.

Date of Maturity

Jan. 31
−18
Jan. 13
Feb. 28
Mar. 19, Date of Maturity
60 days

Term of Discount

Feb. 28
−13
Feb. 15
Mar. 19
34 days, Time of Discount

Interest and Maturity Value

$1200.00 Face
9.00 Interest
$1209.00 Maturity Value

Bank Discount

$6.85 for 34 days (By previously indicated method)

Net Proceeds

$1209.00 Maturity Value
6.85 Bank Discount
$1202.15 Net Proceeds

Note that there is a new step in this solution; namely, finding the maturity value. Otherwise the solution is the same as in the non-interest-bearing notes.

Exercise

Find the net proceeds:

	Face Value	Date	Time	Interest Rate %	Rate of Discount %	Date of Discount
1.	$ 900	Mar. 12	60 da.	6	6	Mar. 30
2.	1200	Dec. 28	3 mo.	6	6	Feb. 6
3.	2600	July 6	1 mo.	3	6	July 25
4.	750	Nov. 19	90 da.	4	6	Jan. 20
5.	960	Aug. 27	120 da.	2	6	Oct. 14

Answers:
1. $ 902.64   3. $2601.29   5. $954.80
2. 1207.85   4. 753.96

Borrowing Money to Pay a Bill

A firm may buy goods and the discount for cash may be so great that it will be worthwhile borrowing the money to be able to take advantage of the discount. It is important, then, to be able to figure out how much can be gained by borrowing to pay for cash, and, also, whether it is actually worthwhile to do so.

Problem: On April 3, F. B. Clark bought goods for $1500, terms 2/10, n/30. He did not have the money to pay the invoice on April 13, so that he could take advantage of the discount. He therefore borrowed sufficient money to pay the bill on his 20-day interest-bearing note. Did he gain or lose and how much?

$1500 Amount of Invoice
30 Cash discount 2%
$1470 Net Cost
Interest on $1470 for 20 days
at 6% = $4.90

$30.00 Cash Discount
4.90 Interest
$25.10 Gain by borrowing

Note that he must borrow the amount of the *net cost*.

Exercise

1. A merchant bought goods for $3640, terms 3/10, n/90. To take advantage of the cash discount, he borrowed the money for 80 days at 6% and paid the bill. How much was gained by borrowing the money?
2. A merchant purchased goods for $1500 less 20% and 10%, terms 2/10, n/30. To take advantage of the cash discount, he borrowed the money for 20 days at 6% and paid the bill. How much was gained by borrowing?
3. The Hudson Co. bought goods for $2480 less 25%, terms 2/10, n/60. To take advantage of the cash discount, they borrowed the money at 6% for 50 days. How much was gained by borrowing?

Answers:
1. $62.12   **2.** $18.07   **3.** $22.01

Borrowing Money for Loan Companies

Small-loan companies are permitted by law to lend money, usually up to $300, and charge a stated rate per cent of interest on the unpaid balance. Payments on such loans are generally made in monthly installments.

Problem: A man borrows $300 from a finance company. The company charges 2% interest per month on the unpaid balance. Payments of $50 are to be made monthly. The loan is for 6 months. Find the total amount of interest paid.

Interest Period	Unpaid Balance	Interest at 2%	Payment
End of first month	$300	$6.00	$50
End of second month	250	5.00	50
End of third month	200	4.00	50
End of fourth month	150	3.00	50
End of fifth month	100	2.00	50
End of sixth month	50	1.00	50
Total Interest		$21.00	

Note that the interest is computed on the amount due at the end of each month. The unpaid balance at the end of the first month is $300 so the interest at 2% of $300 is $6. At the end of the next month the unpaid balance, reduced by $50, is $250, and the interest is $5, etc.

Problem: A man borrows $200 for 4 months. The interest charges are 2½% on the first $100, 2% on the balance. Find the interest charges.

Interest Period	Unpaid Balance	Interest Charges	Payment
End of first month	$200	$4.50	$50
End of second month	150	3.50	50
End of third month	100	2.50	50
End of fourth month	50	1.25	50
Total Interest		$11.75	

Computation:
2½% of $100 = $2.50; 2% of $100 = $2.00; Total $4.50
2½% of $100 = $2.50; 2% of $ 50 = $1.00; Total $3.50
2½% of $100 = $2.50
2½% of $50 = $1.25

Exercise

1. Gates borrows $240 from a credit union for 5 months. He repays the loan in five monthly installments of $48 each, plus interest charges of ¾% per month on the unpaid balance. Find the interest charges.
2. Brown borrows $150 from a finance company and will repay it in 5 monthly installments of $30 each. The company charges 2½% on the first $100, 2% on the balance. Find the interest charges.
3. Aarons borrows $150 from a finance company and will repay it in 6 monthly installments of $25 each. The company charges 2% on the unpaid balance. Find the interest charges.

Answers:
1. $5.40   **2.** $10.90   **3.** $10.50

Compound Interest

Compound interest is interest which has been added to the principal, to form a part of the new principal. For example, if Brown deposits $100 in a savings bank and at the end of the year he is credited with 2% interest, his new principal is $102. At the end of the next year, the bank will compute the interest upon $102. If this is done each year, the interest is compounded annually. Banks add interest at stated periods, such as at the end of a month, quarter year, half year, or year, and interest is said to be compounded monthly, quarterly, semi-annually, or annually. Banks use compound-interest tables to compute the compound interest. Below, it will be computed arithmetically. Interest is not computed on cents, but on dollars only.

Problem: On January 2, 1943, Clark deposited $500 in a savings bank. Interest at the rate of 2% per annum was compounded semi-annually. On January 2, 1944, Clark deposited an additional $400. Find how much he had on deposit July 1, 1944.

$500.00	Principal Jan. 2, 1943
5.00	Interest July 1, 1943 (2% per year, 1% for ½ year)
$505.00	Principal July 1, 1943
5.05	Interest Jan. 2, 1944
$510.05	Principal Jan. 2, 1944
400.00	Deposit Jan. 2, 1944
$910.05	Principal Jan. 2, 1944
9.10	Interest July 1, 1944
$919.15	Principal July 1, 1944

Note that interest is computed and added before deposits are added or withdrawals deducted.

Exercise

1. A savings bank pays 2% interest on its deposits and adds the interest on June 1 and December 1 of each year. On June 1, 1944 H. Williams deposits $600. If he makes no deposits or withdrawals, how much will he have on deposit December 1, 1945?
2. A savings bank pays 1½% interest on its deposits and adds the interest on January 2 and July 1 of each year. On January 2, 1943 W. Harris deposits $600. He deposits $400 on July 1, 1943 and withdraws $100 on January 2, 1944. How much will he have on deposit July 1, 1944?

Answers:
1. $618.18   **2.** $918.87

Profits and Pricing

Per Cent of Profit

Businessmen, in order to stay in business, must operate at a profit. To do so, it is imperative that they have certain information on their operations. This information will be considered here.

Per Cent of Profit on Cost

The selling price of goods less the cost of goods is the entire or gross profit. The gross profit less the overhead is the net profit. By overhead is meant the expenses or cost of doing business, such as rent, salaries, supplies, etc. What the businessman wants to know very often is whether he is making a big enough profit in comparison to his cost.

Problem: Goods costing $500 are sold for $800. The overhead is $100. Find *A*. rate of gross profit on cost; *B*. rate of net profit on cost.

$800 Selling Price
500 Cost
$300 Gross Profit
100 Overhead
$200 Net Profit

A. $300/500 = 60\%$, Rate of Gross Profit on Cost
B. $200/500 = 40\%$, Rate of Net Profit on Cost

Per Cent of Profit on Sales

Many businessmen prefer to base their profit on sales and not on cost. The reasons are that the sales price is known at once whereas the cost must be looked up and because expenses and profits are compared with sales.

Problem: Goods costing $500 are sold for $800. The overhead is $100. Find *A*. rate of gross profit on sales; *B*. rate of net profit on sales.

$800 Selling Price
500 Cost
$300 Gross Profit
100 Overhead
$200 Net Profit

A. $300/800 = 37\frac{1}{2}\%$, Rate of Gross Profit on Sales
B. $200/800 = 25\%$, Rate of Net Profit on Sales

Exercise

	Selling Price	Cost	Gain	Rate of Gain on Cost	Rate of Gain on Sales
1.	$ 75	$ 60			
2.	48	32			
3.	25	15			
4.	60	30			
5.	150	100			

Answers:

	Gain	Rate of Gain on Cost %	Rate of Gain on Sales %
1.	$15	25	20
2.	16	50	33⅓
3.	10	66⅔	40
4.	30	100	50
5.	50	50	33⅓

Selling Prices

Find the Selling Price, Given the Cost and Percent of Profit on Cost

Having determined the rate of gain on cost, it will be easy to compute the selling price of similar articles with the same rate of profit or mark-up.

Problem: Goods cost $50. The rate of profit on cost is 20%. Find the sales price.

$50 Cost
10 20% Rate of Profit on Cost 20%
$60 Sales Price

Exercise

Find the sales price.

	Cost	Rate of Gross Profit on Cost %
1.	$120	50
2.	264	16⅔
3.	180	33⅓
4.	290	40
5.	175	100

Answers:
1. $180   3. $240   5. $350
2. 308   4. 406

Finding the Selling Price, Given the Cost and Per Cent of Profit on Sales

Here the rate of profit is figured on sales and not on cost. The procedure in finding the sales price differs because an indirect method is used.

Problem: A refrigerator is billed to a dealer at $75 less 20% and 10%. At what price should he sell the refrigerator to gain 20% of the sales price?

$75 List Price
15 Trade Discount 20%
$60 Balance
6 Trade Discount 10%
$54 Net Cost

Sales Price	100%	
Profit	20%	
Cost		$54

Sales Price	100%	$67.50
Profit	20%	$13.50
Cost	80%	$54.00

$54 \div .8 = \$67.50$ or $54 \div \frac{4}{5} =$
$\$54 \times \frac{5}{4} = \$67.50$, *Answer*

To prove, take 20% of the sales, $67.50. The profit is $13.50. Sales, $67.50, minus Profit, $13.50, equal $54, Cost.

In this type of problem, the unknown is the sales price. This is 100%. The profit on sales is known to be 20% of 100%, or 20%. The cost is known to be $54. Now, subtract 20% from 100% to get the cost: 80%. The cost also equals $54. The problem now is: $54 is 80% of what number? As done in Percentage, Percentage ÷ Rate = Base or $54 \div .8$.

Finding the Selling Price, Given the Cost, the Per Cent of Profit and Overhead Based on Selling Price

Problem: A refrigerator is billed to a dealer at \$75 less 20% and 10%. At what price should he sell the refrigerator to gain 20% on sales, if he gives his salesman a commission of 8% on sales and his overhead is 12% of sales?

\$75 List Price
15 Trade Discount 20%
\$60 Balance
6 Trade Discount 10%
\$54 Net Cost

Sales Price		100%	
Commission	8%		
Overhead	12%		
Profit	20%	40%	
Cost			\$54

Sales Price		100%	\$90
Commission	8%		
Overhead	12%		
Profit	20%	40%	\$36
Cost		60%	\$54

$\$54 \div .6 = 90$ or
$\$54 \div 3/5 = 54 \times 5/3 = \$90$, *Answer*

The procedure followed is as in the previous problem. Everything based on sales is placed in the middle of the diagram, totaled, and subtracted from the sales, 100%. The difference is the cost. The problem is the same as before: the net cost is a certain percentage of what number? Prove as before.

Exercise

1. A merchant bought rugs at \$27 less 25%. At what price must he sell them to make a profit of 16⅔% on sales?
2. A druggist buys face powder at 50¢ per box. The wholesaler offers the druggist a discount of 10% and 5%, if he will buy a carton (36 boxes). The druggist accepts. At what price must he mark each box to make a profit of 33⅓% on cost?
3. A dealer buys radios at \$150 less 20% and 10%. He has an expense of \$6 per radio for delivery and installation. (This is a selling expense and must be added to sales price to get total sales price.)
   a. At what price must he sell each radio to gain 25% on the purchase price?
   b. At what price must he sell each radio to gain 25% on the sales price?
4. A dealer buys fountain pens at \$36 per dozen less 25% and 20%. The overhead is 25% of sales. At what price must he sell each pen to gain 15% on the sales price?
5. In 1944 the Brown Rug Co. determined its sales price by basing the gross profit of 40% on cost. In 1945, the company decided to base the 40% gross profit on sales price.
   a. If a rug cost \$6, what was the sales price in 1944?
   b. If the cost of the rug was \$6 in 1945, what was the sales price in 1945?
   c. By what per cent was the gross profit decreased or increased in 1945 as compared with 1944.
6. A dealer ordered 24 thermometers at \$45 a dozen, less 20%. He found 6 defective items and returned them. The buying expenses on the purchase were \$2.16. (Add buying expenses to find total cost.) If he wished to make a profit of 30% on sales, and if the overhead was 10%, at what price was each thermometer sold?
7. A dealer purchased bicycles at \$32.50 less 20% and 5%, plus a freight charge of 90¢ on each bicycle. If his overhead is 24% of sales, at what price must he sell each bicycle to make a profit of 12% of the sales price?

Answers:

1. \$24.30	4. \$3	6. \$ 5.20
2. 57	5. *a.* 8.40	7. 40
3. *a.* 141	*b.* 10	
b. 150	*c.* 19 1/21% Increase	

Find the List or Marked Price, Given the Selling Price and the Trade Discount

Wholesalers who sell their goods subject to a trade discount must be able to compute the list or catalogue price so that they will receive the market price they desire. The procedure is the same as in the preceding problem.

Problem: A radio cost \$150 and it is to be sold at a profit of 33⅓% on cost. At what price should it be listed in the catalogue, if there is a trade discount of 60% to be given?

First Step.—To Find the Sales Price:
\$150 Cost
50 Profit 33⅓% on cost
\$200 Selling Price

Second Step.—To Find the List Price:

List Price	100%	\$500
Trade Discount	60%	\$300
Selling Price	40%	\$200

$\$200 \div .40 = \$500$, List Price or
$\$200 \div 2/5 = \$200 \times 5/2 = \$500$, List Price

Problem: A shoe store owner buys shoes at \$7 a pair. He wants to make a profit of 20% on the sales price, after offering a discount of 12½% on the marked or list price. Find the marked price.

First Step–To Find the Sales Price:

Sales Price	100%	\$8.75
Profit	20%	\$1.75
Cost	80%	\$7.00

$\$7 \div .80 = \$8.75$, Sales Price or
$\$7 \div 4/5 = \$7 \times 5/4 = 35/4 = \$8.75$, Sales Price

Second Step–To Find the List Price:

List Price	100%	\$10.00
Trade Discount	12½%	\$1.25
Sales Price	87½%	\$8.75

$\$8.75 \div .875 = \$10$, List Price or
$\$8.75 \div 7/8 = \$8.75 \times 8/7 = \$10$, List Price

Exercise

1. A haberdasher buys hats at $40 per dozen less 25% and 20%. He wants to make a profit of 25% on the cost and to offer a trade discount of 16⅔% off the list price. Find the marked or list price.
2. A merchant buys gloves at $18 per dozen pairs. He wants to make a profit of 33⅓% on cost and offer a trade discount of 20% off the list price. Find the list price.
3. A dealer pays $60 less 30%, and 10% for a rug. Selling expenses are 7½% of the selling price. He sells the rug to gain 25% on the sales price, after allowing a trade discount of 20% off the marked price. Find the marked price.
4. It cost a manufacturer $17 to make a rug. At what price should he list the rug in his catalogue to make a profit of 15% on the sales price after allowing a trade discount of 33⅓% on the catalogue price?
5. A merchant buy rugs at $28 less 25%. What is the marked price if he wishes to make a profit of 20% on the selling price after allowing a discount of 40% on the marked price?
6. A merchant buys a desk for $80. He wants to make a profit of 25% on cost. At what price must he mark it to allow a discount of 20% off the marked price?
7. A dealer buys suits at $40 less 10%. He wants to make a profit of 25% on the selling price and allow a special discount of 16⅔% off the marked price. Find the marked price.
8. A merchant buys stoves for $40 less 20% and 10%. He wants to make a profit on 33⅓% on the selling price after allowing a 10% discount on the marked price. Find the marked price.

Answers:
1. $36   4. $ 30   7. $57.60
2. 30   5. 43.75   8. 48
3. 70   6. 125

Comparison of Profits

Very often a merchant will have a special sale on certain goods. He then wishes to make a comparison between the profit realized on the goods sold at the old price and the profit at the sale price.

Problem: During November a hardware dealer sold 24 coal stoves at $125 each. The net cost of each stove was $87.50. The overhead expense was $17.50 per stove. In December, he ran a special sale and reduced the sales price to $117.50 per stove, and sold 32 stoves. The overhead in December was $17.25 per stove.

A. How much profit did the dealer make in November?
B. How much profit did he make in December?
C. What was the rate of increase or decrease?

This problem may be calculated by two methods: on the basis of one stove or the total number of stoves.

Calculation on 1 Stove

A.   November

1 stove @ $125.00 each = $125.00 Sales Price
1 stove @ $ 87.50 each =   87.50 Cost
                        $ 37.50 Gross Profit
                          17.50 Overhead
                        $ 20.00 Net Profit
24 stoves @ $20.00 profit on ea. = $480, Total Profit
                                            Answer

B.   December

1 stove @ $117.50 each = $117.50 Sales Price
1 stove @ $ 87.50 each =   87.50 Cost
                        $ 30.00 Gross Profit
                          17.25 Overhead
                        $ 12.75 Net Profit
32 stoves @ $12.75 profit on ea. = $408, Total Profit
                                            Answer

C. $480 Net Profit, November
        408 Net Profit, December
       $ 72 Decrease in Profit

       $ 72 Decrease
       $480 Net Profit, November $= \dfrac{72}{480} =$

       15% Rate of Decrease, _Answer_

Calculation on Total Number of Stoves

A.   November

24 stoves @ $125.00 each = $3000 Sales Price
24 stoves @ $ 87.50 each = 2100 Cost
                          $ 900 Gross Profit
24 stoves @ $ 17.50 each =   420 Overhead
                          $ 480 Net Profit,
                                      Answer

B.   December

32 stoves @ $117.50 each = $3760 Sales Price
32 stoves @ $ 87.50 each = 2800 Cost
                          $ 960 Gross Profit
32 stoves @ $ 17.25 each =   552 Overhead
                          $ 408 Net Profit,
                                      Answer

C. $480 Net Profit, November
        408 Net Profit, December
       $ 72 Decrease in Profit

       $ 72 Decrease
       $480 Net Profit, November $= \dfrac{72}{480} =$

       15% Decrease, _Answer_

Exercise

1. A merchant bought chairs at $15 each. He sold them at $25 each. During October his sales were 150 chairs. In November, he ran a special sale, reducing the sales price to $20 per chair. The sales increased to 400 chairs.
   a. How much was the profit in October?
   b. How much was the profit in November?
   c. What was the rate of increase or decrease in the profit?
2. The Home Appliance Co. bought washing machines at $130 less 30% each. During April, 15 machines were sold at $129 each. During May, each machine was sold at $117.50 each. As a result 30 machines were sold.
   a. During which month did the company make more profit and how much?
   b. What was the rate of increase or decrease in the profit?

Distribution of Partnership Profits

Profits are distributed among partners according to the arrangements set forth in the partnership contract. If no mention is made, the profits or losses are distributed equally.

There are three usual methods of division of profits. They are:

1. According to an agreed-upon ratio.
2. According to partnership investment ratio.
3. Allowing interest on investment, and then dividing the balance equally.

Problem: Vincent, Dugan, and Carver have invested $6000, $8000, and 12,000 respectively in their wholesale business. The first year their profit was $7800.

A. How much will each receive if they agree to divide their profits equally?
B. How much will each receive if they agree to divide their profits in proportion to their investments (capital ratio)?
C. How much will they receive if each partner is allowed 6% on his investment, and then the remaining profit is divided equally?

A. There are three partners.
⅓ of $7800 = $2600, each partner's share

B.

Partner	Invest-ment	Share according to Capital Ratio	Computation of Share	Share
Vincent	$ 6000	6000/2600	³⁄₁₃ of $7800	$1800
Dugan	8000	8000/26000	⁴⁄₁₃ of $7800	2400
Carver	12000	12000/26000	⁶⁄₁₃ of $7800	3600
Totals	$26000	26000/26000	¹³⁄₁₃ of $7800	$7800

C.

Partner	Invest-ment	6% Interest on Capital	⅓ of Remaining Profit	Share
Vincent	$6000	$360	$2080	$2440
Dugan	8000	480	2080	2560
Carver	12000	720	2080	2800
Totals	$26000	$1560	$6240	$7800 Total Profit

$7800 Total Profit
1560 Interest
3) 6240
$2080

Exercise

1. Todd invested $12,000 and Olsen $15,000 in their business. They agreed to allow interest on their investments of 8% and divide the remaining profit equally.
   a. How much must the business earn in one year to cover the 8% interest?
   b. If the profit at the end of the year was $5380, how much did each receive?
2. Abbot invested $12,000, Johnson $16,000, and Moore his services. Out of the first year's profit of $9675, Abbot and Johnson were allowed 12½% interest on their investments, and Moore $1600 as salary. The remaining profit was divided equally. Find each partner's income for the year.
3. Davis and Lee invested $8000 and $4000 respectively in their business. At the end of the year their sales were $18,525, cost of goods sold was $12,200 and overhead expenses were $1522. If the profit was to be divided according to their capital ratio, find each partner's share of the profit.
4. Young and Harrington invested $6000 and $12,000 respectively in their business. The sales for the year 1944 were $28,440; cost of goods sold, $15,460; overhead, $3200.
   a. Find the net profit.
   b. The profits are to be shared in capital ratio. Find each partner's share.
   c. If each partner is allowed 6% on his investment and the profit which remains is to be shared equally, how much will each partner receive?

Answers:
1. *a.* $2160
   b. Todd $2570
      Olsen $2810
2. Abbot $3025
   Johnson $3525
   Moore $3125
3. Davis $3202
   Lee $1601
4. *a.* $9780
   b. Young $3260
      Harrington $6520

Corporation Stock

Definitions and Terms

Corporations issue stock as evidence of ownership in the corporation. When a corporation makes a profit, its directors distribute a part or all of this profit among the stockholders. This distribution of profit is called a *dividend*. All undistributed profit is called *surplus*.

The value imprinted on the face of the stock certificate is called its par value. The par value of the stock is usually $100, although stock may be issued at other par values, such as $50 or $25. Some corporations issue stock with no par value. The market price of stock is the price at which the stock is sold in the various stock markets.

In this section we take up some of the problems of computing dividends and buying and selling stock.

Computing Dividends on Stock

Problem: A corporation has a capital stock of $500,000, each share having a par value of $100. It declares a dividend of 9%. If the net profits for the year are $75,000, find the amount of the dividend and how much is left in surplus.

$500,000 \div $100 = 5000$ shares
9% of $100 = $9, Dividend on 1 share
5000 shares $\times$ $9 = $45,000, Dividend declared
$75,000 - $45,000 = $30,000, Amount left in surplus

Problem: A corporation has a capital stock of $400,000 each share having par value of $100. Its net profit for the year is $60,000. The directors declare a dividend of 4%. Find *A.* the amount of the dividend; *B.* the amount added to surplus; *C.* the dividend received by a stockholder who owns 60 shares of stock.

A. $400,000 \div 100$ = 4000 shares
   4% of 100 = $4, dividend on 1 share
   4000×4 = $16,000, amount of dividend

B. $60,000 - $16,000 = $44,000 amount added to surplus

C. 60 shares @ $4 per share = $240, dividend received by stockholder

Exercise

(Where no par value is stated, assume it is $100.)

1. A corporation declares a semi-annual dividend of 5%. Find Mr. Jones' dividend if he owns 100 shares.
2. A corporation's capital stock is $600,000. It declares a dividend of 5%. Find the amount of the dividend declared.
3. The Lincoln Radio Co. has capital stock of $500,000. Its profit is $80,000. Its directors declare an annual dividend of 6%.
   a. What does the total annual dividend amount to?
   b. How much will go to surplus?
   c. If Harry Wells has 75 shares, how much dividend will he receive?
4. The Ocean Hardware Corp. has a capital stock of $200,000. It declares semi-annual dividends of 3%.
   a. Find the total annual dividend.
   b. Find how much Max Morse, who owns 50 shares, will receive annually.
5. Anthony Lamb has 50 shares of common stock and 12 shares of 8% preferred stock in a certain corporation. A quarterly dividend of 60¢ per share is paid on the common stock and the regular 8% dividend on the preferred. How much income annually will Mr. Lamb receive from his stock holdings?

Answers:
1. $500
2. $30,000
3. *a.* $30,000
   b. $50,000
   c. $450
4. *a.* $12,000
   b. $300
5. $216

Finding the Rate of Dividend

Problem: A corporation which has a capital stock of $400,000 has a net profit of $80,000 for the year. It decides to keep $20,000 in surplus and distribute the rest of the profits as dividends. Find the annual rate of dividend.

$80,000 Total Profit
 20,000 Surplus
$60,000 Dividend declared

$\dfrac{60,000 \text{ Dividend declared}}{400,000 \text{ Capital stock}}$ = 15%, Rate of dividend, *Answer*

Exercise

1. A corporation with capital stock of $300,000 has a net profit of $50,000. The directors declare a dividend of $30,000. Find the rate of dividend.
2. A corporation is capitalized at $200,000. It makes a profit of $45,000. If $15,000 is set aside for surplus, what will be the rate of dividend?
3. The Borax Corp, is capitalized at $500,000. At the end of the year it will pay $60,000 in dividends.
   a. Find the annual dividend rate.
   b. Find how much a person who has 50 shares will receive in dividends.
4. The Lastelle Corp., with capital stock of $1,000,000, earns $180,000 for the year. The directors declare a dividend of $120,000.
   a. Find the amount left in surplus.
   b. Find the annual rate of dividend on the stock.
   c. Find how much a stockholder who has 100 shares receives.

Answers:
1. 10%
2. 15%
3. *a.* 12%
   b. $600
4. *a.* $60,000
   b. 12%
   c. $1200

Buying and Selling Stock

Stock may be bought and sold at any stock exchange through the medium of a broker who is a member of that exchange. The broker charges a fee, called *brokerage,* for his services. In addition a state and a federal tax must be paid on all stock sold.

Problem: Harry Wilson bought 300 shares of stock at 56½ (i.e., $56.50) and sold it at 65. Brokerage each way was 25¢ a share and the total taxes were 4¢ per share. Find his net profit on the transaction.

Sale
300 shares @ $65 each = $19,500 Sales Price
300 shares
  @ 25¢ each = $75 brokerage
300 shares
  @ 4¢ each = $12 tax   87
                         $19,413 Net Proceeds

Purchase
300 shares @ $56.50 each = $16,950 Cost
300 shares @ 25¢ each =   75 Brokerage
                        $17,025 Total Cost

$19,413 Net Proceeds of Sale
 17,025 Total Cost
$ 2,388 Net Profit

Exercise

1. Stock costing $50 per share was sold for $58 per share. Brokerage each way was 24¢ per share and the taxes on the sale amounted to 4¢ per share. Find the net profit.
2. Warren bought 100 shares of stock at 90 and sold them for 105. Brokerage each way was 24¢ per share and the taxes on the sale were 4½¢ per share. Find the net profit.

3. Harris bought 300 shares of stock at 98½¢ and sold them at 112½. If brokerage is 25¢ per share each way and the taxes on the sale were 4¢ per share, find the amount of the net profit.

Answers:
1. $7.48   2. $1447.50   3. $4038

Finding Profit on Sale of Stock, Dividends Having Been Received

Problem: Morris bought 300 shares of stock at 98 and sold them at 110, after holding them a year. During this time, he received 2 semi-annual dividends of 4%. Brokerage was 25¢ per share each way and taxes on the sale were 4¢. Find his total profit.

Sale

300 shares @ $110 each	= $33,000 Sales Price
300 shares @ 25¢ each	= $75 brokerage
300 shares @ 4¢ each	= $12 tax 87
	$32,913 Net Proceeds

Purchase

300 shares @ $98 each =	$29,400 Cost
300 shares @ 25¢ each =	75 Brokerage
	$29,475 Total Cost

$32,913 Net Proceeds of Sale
28,475 Total Cost
$ 3,438 Net Profit on Sale

Dividends

4% of 100	=	$4 per share, dividend for ½ year
300 shares @ $4	=	1200, Dividend for ½ year
1200 × 2	=	2400, Dividend for 1 year

$ 3,438 Net Profit on Sale
2,400 Dividends
$ 5,838 Total Profit, *Answer*

Exercise

1. Harvey bought 50 shares of stock at 32, brokerage 24¢ per share. The stock pays a quarterly dividend of 1%. At the end of a year, he sold the stock at 40, brokerage 25¢ per share, tax 4¢ per share. Find his total profit on the transaction.
2. On February 1, M. King bought 70 shares of stock at 98½, brokerage 22¢ a share. On April 1 and again on October 1, he received a cash dividend of $2.50 a share. On November 1 he sold the stock at 112, brokerage 24¢ a share, tax 4¢ a share. What was King's profit?
3. Mr. Carson bought 10 shares of 7% preferred stock at $140 a share. He received dividends for one year and then sold the stock at $142 per share. Brokerage was 26¢ per share on the purchase, 27¢ per share on the sale, and there was a tax of 10¢ per share on the sale. Find his total gain on the transaction.

Answers:
1. $573.50   2. $1260   3. $83.70

Finding the Rate of Return on Investment

Problem: A share of stock, par value $100, is bought for $81. A dividend of 9% is declared on the stock. Find the rate of return.

9% of $100 = $9, Dividend on 1 share

$$\frac{\$9 \text{ Dividend}}{\$81 \text{ Cost of Stock}} = \frac{1}{9} = 11\frac{1}{9}\%, \text{ Rate of return}$$

Exercise

1. On January 2, 1945 J. Martin invested $3400 in aircraft stock at 42½ (including brokerage). During 1945 he received 4 quarterly dividends of 60¢ each on each share of stock. (To find the number of shares, divide the investment by the cost of 1 share.) Find the rate of return on his investment.
2. An industrial stock, which yields an annual dividend of 3%, sells at $60. A public utility stock is quoted at 90 and yields a dividend of 5%. (No brokerage charges).
   a. Find the rate of return on each.
   b. Which is the better investment and by how much?
3. H. G. Lee purchases 50 shares of American Telephone & Telegraph at 190, paying a dividend of 9% per year. (Disregard brokerage.) Find the rate of return.

Answers:
1. $5\frac{11}{17}\%$
2. *a.* Industrial 5%, utility $5\frac{5}{9}\%$
   b. Utility by $\frac{5}{9}\%$
3. $4\frac{14}{19}\%$

Bonds
Definitions and Interest

A bond is an indebtedness of a corporation. As a rule, the par value of bonds is $1000, unless otherwise stated. Bonds with a par value of less than $1000 are called baby bonds. Since bonds are evidence of debt, the corporation which issues the bonds pays interest on the bonds, usually semi-annually. The interest is called the *income* or *yield*.

Bonds are bought and sold through brokers on the stock exchanges. The price of bonds is shown in two figures, for example, 98½; however the price actually represents three figures, namely $985. Brokers charge a commission on the purchase and sale of each bond.

Bond problems, as a rule, follow the procedures set forth in the solution of stock problems, with one exception which will be shown below.

Purchase of Bonds with Accrued Interest

Since interest on bonds is usually paid semi-annually, it follows that when bonds are bought on a day which is not a day on which interest is due and payable, the buyer will have to refund to the seller the interest which has accumulated or accrued up to the date of the purchase.

Problem: Find the cost of 10 bonds, par value $1000, bought at 96 on February 1. The interest rate is 6%. Interest is payable on January 1 and July 1. Brokerage, $2.50 per bond.

Accrued interest on $1000 for 31 days from January 1 to February 1 at 6%	$ 5.17
Brokerage	2.50
Price of 1 bond	960.00
Cost of 1 bond	$ 967.67
Cost of 10 bonds—$967.67 × 10	$9676.70, *Answer*

Exercise

1. Find the cost of 4 bonds, par value $1000, bought at 110 on March 28, interest rate 4%, interest due March 1 and September 1, brokerage $2.50 per bond.
2. Find the cost of 20 bonds, par value $1000, bought at 98 on February 18, interest rate 6%, interest due January 1 and July 1, brokerage $2.50 per bond.

Answers:
1. $4422   2. $19,810

Sale of Bonds with Accrued Interest

The procedure in the sale of bonds is the opposite of that in computing the purchase of bonds. The accrued interest is given to the seller because it is his. Therefore, the accrued interest is added on to the selling price and the commission deducted.

Problem: A man sold 10 bonds, par value $1000, for 98 on November 30. Interest on the bonds was at the rate of 6%; the interest was due on April 1 and October 1. Brokerage was $2.50 per bond.

Accrued interest on $1000 at 6% from
  October 1 to November 30; 60
  days ....$ 10.00
Price of 1 bond 980.00
Gross Proceeds ....$ 990.00
Brokerage, $2.50 ....   2.50
Net Proceeds for 1 bond ....$ 987.50
Net Proceeds for 10 bonds—
  $987.50 × 10 ....$9875.00, *Answer*

Exercise

1. Find the net proceeds of 5 bonds, par value $1000, sold for 105 on September 19. Interest at the rate of 6% is due on January 1 and July 1. Brokerage $2.50 per bond.
2. Find the net proceeds of 15 bonds, par value $1000, sold for 97½ on October 30. Interest at the rate of 4%, payable on February 1 and August 1. Brokerage is $2.50 per bond.

Answers:
1. $5304.15   2. $14,737.50

Fire Insurance

Computation of Premiums

Insurance is the protection of the insured against any money loss arising from destruction or damage to the insured property.

Problem: Conroy's place of business, valued at $7500, was insured for 60% of its value for one year. The 1-year rate was 15¢ per C (per hundred dollars). Find the amount of the premium.

60% of $7500   = $4500, Value of Policy
$4500 @ 15¢ per C = $6.75, Premium for 1 year

Suppose that in the above problem the insurance company offers Conroy a 3-year rate which is 2½ times the annual rate. Find the premium for the 3 years and the average annual premium on a 3-year policy.

$6.75, Premium for 1 year
$6.75 × 2½ = $16.88, Premium for 3 years
$1688 ÷ 3 = $5.62⅔ or $5.63, Average annual
              premium

Exercise

1. George Allen owns a building valued at $18,000. He insures it for 80% of its value at $1.65 per $100 for 3 years. He has a stock of goods worth $5250. He insures the stock at its inventory value at $1.20 per $100 for 1 year.
   a. Find the premium on the building.
   b. Find the premium on the stock.
   c. Find the total yearly cost of insurance.
2. Personal property valued at $5000 was insured for 80% of its value at the 3-year rate of $5.00 per M ($1000). Find the average yearly cost of insurance.
3. On January 1 a man received a bill for insurance as follows: car insurance for 1 year, $48.50; fire insurance for $6000 on his home at a 3-year rate of $8 per M, and insurance for $3000 on the contents at the 3-year rate of 50¢ per C.
   a. Find the total cost of the premiums to be paid.
   b. Find the average yearly cost of the insurance.

Answers:
1. a. $237.60   2. $6.66⅔ or $6.67
   b. $ 63.00   3. a. $111.50
   c. $142.20   b. $ 69.50

Eighty Per Cent Co-Insurance Clause

Experience has shown that a fire will seldom destroy a piece of property completely. Consequently, many people insure themselves only for a fraction of the value of the property. To encourage people to take greater precautions, the insurance companies have a clause in the policy which states that the insured will not be paid in full for a fire loss, unless he has insured himself for at least 80% of the value of the property. If he has insured himself for less than the stipulated 80%, he becomes a co-insurer with the insurance company and bears part of the loss.

Problem: A factory building valued at $24,000 was insured for $12,800 under an 80% co-insurance clause. A fire caused a loss of $6600. How much did the insurance company pay and how much of the loss did the insured bear?

The formula for determining the loss is:

$$\frac{\text{Policy}}{80\% \text{ of value of property}} \times \text{Loss}$$

Substituting:

$$\frac{\$12,800}{80\% \text{ of } \$24,000} = \frac{\$12,800}{\$19,200} = \frac{2}{3} \times \$6600$$

$$= \$4400 \text{ Company pays}$$

$6600 Loss
 4400 Company pays
$2200 Loss suffered by insured

Exercise

1. A house valued at $7500 was insured for $5000. The policy contained an 80% co-insurance clause. A fire caused a loss of $4200.
   a. How much did the insurance company pay?
   b. How much loss did the insured suffer?

2. Martin's house is valued at $6000. He insures it for $4800 under a policy containing an 80% co-insurance clause. A fire caused a loss of $3000.
   a. How much did Martin receive under his policy?
   b. How much loss did he suffer?
3. A residence valued at $9000 was insured for $6000 under a policy containing an 80% clause. A fire caused a loss of $3600.
   a. How much did the insurance company pay?
   b. What per cent of the fire loss was borne by the owner?

Answers:
1. a. $3500   2. a. $3000   3. a. $3000
   b. $700   b. 0   b. 16⅔%

Reinsurance and Contributing Insurance

If a policy calls for a very large amount, the insurance company may share the risk with other companies by reinsuring the property with other companies. Thus, if a policy of $600,000 is issued, the company will reinsure the property with other companies for, say, $500,000. Thus, by reinsuring the company assumes a risk of only $100,000. Another method of sharing the risk is to have the owner of the property take policies with a number of companies. Then, when a loss occurs, each company will pay a pro-rata share.

Problem: A building is insured for $50,000 as follows: Phoenix Insurance Co., $10,000; Globe Insurance Co., $20,000; World Insurance Co., $20,000. There is a loss of $20,000. How much will each company pay?

Company	Policy	Pro-rata Share	Calculation of Share	Share
Phoenix	$10,000	$\frac{10,000}{50,000} = \frac{1}{5}$	⅕ of $20,000	$ 4000
Globe	20,000	$\frac{20,000}{50,000} = \frac{2}{5}$	⅖ of 20,000	8000
World	20,000	$\frac{20,000}{50,000} = \frac{2}{5}$	⅖ of 20,000	8000
Total	$50,000	$\frac{50,000}{50,000} = \frac{5}{5}$	⅗ of $20,000	$20,000

Note that this problem is solved in the same way as the partnership problem which involved pro-rata share of profits according to capital ratio.

Exercise

1. The Atlas Co. insured its building for $10,000 in three companies as follows: Star Insurance Co., $4500; Western Insurance Co., $3500, and United Insurance Co., $2000. A fire caused a partial loss of $2000. For how much is each company liable?
2. A building was insured in three companies as follows: National Co., $8000; Standard Co., $9000; Mutual Co., $3000. If a loss of $1620 occurred, for how much is each company liable?
3. A factory valued at $20,000 was insured in two companies, each policy having an 80% co-insurance clause. The policy in the Arrow Co. was for $4000 and in the Bow Co. for $10,000. There is a fire loss of $3200. How much must each company pay? (Note: The first step is to find the loss under the 80% clause; then distribute the loss between the two companies.)

Answers:
1. Star $900   3. Arrow $800
   Western $700   Bow $2000
   United $400
2. National $648
   Standard $729
   Mutual $243

Real Estate

Rent

People who wish to buy real estate are confronted by a number of problems. Among them are:

1. Is it cheaper to rent or to buy?
2. If the house is rented to a tenant, what will be the per cent of return on the investment?
3. If the house is rented to a tenant, how much rent should be charged?

Renting vs. Buying

Problem: Henry Clark is paying $35 a month rent for a cottage. He can buy it for $4900 by paying 10% of the purchase price in cash and giving a mortgage bearing 5% interest on the balance. His estimated annual expenses are: taxes $125, water charges $25, repairs $50, and insurance $2. If he can earn 2% interest on his cash investment in the bank, will it be cheaper to rent or to buy?

Rental

12 months @ $35 per mo. = $420 Rental per year

Purchase

$4900 Cost of House
 490 Cash Payment 10%
$4410 Mortgage

Expenses

Interest on mortgage (5% of $4410)	$220.50
Taxes	125.00
Water charges	25.00
Repairs	50.00
Insurance	2.00
Interest on investment (2% of $490)	9.80
Total Expense	$432.30

$432.30 Total Expense
 420.00 Rental
$ 12.30 Cheaper to Rent

Rate of Return on Investment

Problem: Vinson bought a house for $6700, giving $1200 cash as a down payment and a 5% mortgage for the balance. In addition to the mortgage interest, other annual expenses were: taxes $143, insurance $9, repairs $75, depreciation 2% of cost of house. He rented the house to a tenant for $60 per month. Find the rate of return on his cash investment.

Rental to Tenant

12 months @ $60 per mo. = $720, Rental

Annual Expense

$6700 Cost of House
 1200 Cash Payment
$5500 Mortgage

Expenses

Interest on mortgage (5% of $5500)	$275.00
Taxes	143.00
Insurance	9.00
Repairs	75.00
Depreciation (2% of $6700)	134.00
Total Expenses	$636.00

$720 Rental
636 Expenses
$ 84 Net Income

$$\frac{84}{1200} = 7\% \text{ Return, } Answer$$

Note that the actual cash investment is the down payment of $1200.

How Much Rent to Charge a Tenant

Problem: Harris owns a house that cost $8500. His yearly taxes are $225, repairs $100, insurance $26, and water bill $20. What monthly rental, to the nearest dollar, must he charge to realize 6% on his investment?

Desired Income

6% of $8500 = $510 Desired Annual Income

Expenses

Taxes	$225
Repairs	100
Insurance	26
Water bill	20
Total expenses	$371

$510 Desired Income
371 Expenses
$881 Annual Rent to be charged

$881 ÷ 12 = $73.41⅔ or $74.00
per month (to the nearest dollar)

Since the expenses must be borne by the tenant, they are added to the desired income to calculate the rental to be paid by the tenant.

Exercise

1. Brown buys a house for $5500, paying $1000 cash and giving a 5% mortgage for the balance. He insures the house for $4500 at the rate 50¢ per C. Taxes amount to $85 and depreciation and repairs are estimated at 3% of the cost. Brown desires a 6% return on his cash investment. What monthly rent, to the nearest dollar, must he charge a tenant?
2. Bernard bought a house for $10,000, paying $3500 cash and giving a 5% mortgage for the balance. Besides the interest on the mortgage, his annual expenses were: Taxes $300, water $80, oil $250, insurance $110, depreciation $490. He rented the house to a tenant for $150 per month. Find the rate of return on his cash investment.
3. Altman is paying $4800 a year rent for the first floor of a building. He can buy the building for $60,000. He would then receive $3000 yearly in rent from the other two floors. His annual expenses would amount to: taxes $950, insurance $240, repairs and janitor service $1700. If money is worth 6% to him in his business (6% of $60,000 would be lost and therefore is considered an expense), how much would he gain or lose by buying the building?

Answers:
1. $47   2. 7%   3. $1310 saved

Real Estate Taxes

Finding the Tax Rate

A government, to maintain itself, must impose taxes. Chief among taxes are those imposed on real estate. To levy the tax equitably and fairly, a value is given each piece of real estate. This value is called the *assessed value* and the tax is levied on the *assessed valuation*. To find out the tax rate the rule to follow is:

$$\frac{\text{Money Needed or Expenses}}{\text{Assessed Valuation}} = \text{Tax Rate}$$

The tax rate may be expressed as a per cent, or mills per dollar (a mill is .001 cent) or dollars per C ($100) or M ($1000).

Problem: Property in the city of Newcastle is assessed at $9,850,000. The expenses for the year are estimated to be: street improvements, $18,600; salaries, $46,300; schools, $102,500; sewers, $7250; buildings, $13,750; interest on bonded debt, $1300. It is estimated that $1500 will be received from special licenses and $5000 from the state as aid for schools.

A. Find the tax rate correct to the nearest hundred thousandth (5 places).
B. Express this rate per $1000.

A. **Money Needed or Expenses**

$ 18,600	Street improvements
46,300	Salaries
102,500	Schools
7,250	Sewers
13,750	Buildings
1,300	Interest on debt
$189,700	Total expense
6,500	Total income
$183,200	Net expense to be raised by taxes

Income

$1500	Special licenses
5000	State school aid
$6500	Total income

$189,700	Total expense
6,500	Total income
$183,200	Net expense to be raised by taxes

$$\frac{\$183,200}{\$9,850,000} = \$.01859 \text{ per dollar, } Answer$$

B. $.01859 × 1000 = $18.59 per M ($1000), *Answer*

Finding the Tax Rate

When an owner of real estate knows his assessed valuation and the tax rate, he can find how much tax he must pay by multiplying the assessed valuation by the tax rate.

Problem: In the above problem, how much will Jones pay if his house, worth $10,000, is assessed at 80% of its value?

80% of $10,000 = $8000, Assessed valuation
$8000 × .01859 (tax rate) or
$8000 × 18.59 per M ($1000) = $148.72 Tax

Exercise

1. Taxable property in a certain town is assessed at $4,540,000. It is estimated that $2500 will be received from special licenses and $75,300 in state aid for schools. The estimated yearly expenses are: wages, $55,000; schools, $52,800; buildings, $20,000; improvements, $8000; interest on bonds, $12,000.
   a. Find the tax rate (correct to 5 places) to yield income to pay the budget (expenses).
   b. Express this rate as a tax per M ($1000).
   c. Mr. Johnson's property is valued at $7500 and is assessed at 80% of its value. How much tax will Mr. Johnson pay?
2. The assessed valuation of taxable property in a school district is $9,450,000. The gross cost of operating the schools is $300,669.21. Income from state aid and non-resident tuition fees is $126,623.97.
   a. Find the tax rate (carry the decimal to five places).
   b. Express this rate as tax rate per M ($1000).
   c. John Sperry's house is valued at $12,000 and assessed for 75% of its value. Find the amount of Mr. Sperry's school tax.
3. In a certain city, the assessed valuation of taxable property is $63,143,000. The city's total budget to meet expenses is $1,896,190. Receipts from other sources will amount to $736,240.
   a. Find the tax rate (carry the decimal to five places).
   b. Express the rate as a tax rate per M ($1000).
   c. H. Groves' property, valued at $16,000, is assessed at 75% of its value. Find the amount of his tax.

Answers:
1. a. .01541   2. a. .01841   3. a. .01837
   b. $15.41   b. $18.41   b. $18.37
   c. $92.46   c. $165.69   c. $220.44

Business Letter Writing

by Irving Rosenthal
and Harry W. Rudman

Appearance and Structure
of the Business Letter

In your letters, just as in your clothes, a good appearance is vital to making a favorable first impression. And the first is usually the lasting impression. Therefore it pays to take pains with the looks of your business letters. Use good paper; see that the typing is neat, well spaced and free from erasures; and let no error slip through that you can possibly catch.

Paper

Use good stationery. A secretary, sorting her employer's mail, may put your letter into the heap for "second" instead of "first reading" if it is on recognizably cheap paper. Why run that risk?

Showy, expensive stationery should also be avoided. Certainly the reader may take notice of parchment textures, deckle edges, and other ostentation; but it may not be with the reactions you desire. Such paper may arouse suspicion or contempt. A paper stock suitable for diplomatic correspondence, ceremonial invitations, or graduation certificates is obviously out of place in business correspondence.

Moreover, the most expensive paper is not always the best for correspondence. It may take ink poorly and prevent even and legible typing.

Sizes

Use standard 8½ by 11 inch sheets for longer letters and half sheets, 5½ by 8½ inches, for shorter letters. A brief message on a half sheet will look better than the same message lost on a full-size sheet.

Sometimes the so-called "Baronial" size, 10½ by 7¼ inches, is used. But this is generally reserved for correspondence by executives, with their names and titles engraved and embossed on the letterheads.

Color

White will probably remain the favored color of business letters. But the trend to other colors, especially in sales correspondence, has been increasing. It has been found that the bright colors, such as yellow and red, are "attention getters." These are being used increasingly for just that purpose. Color may also be used for associative value. An air travel company may select sky blue for its stationery; a vacation resort, green.

The Letterhead

Your letterhead has two purposes. Because it is your identification, you want it to be attractive and impressive.

And because it supplies the reader with essential information about your company—name, address, telephone number, etc., you want it to be clear and readable.

Fussy lettering and fancy symbols, mistakenly intended to impress the reader, unfortunately produce a different effect. Like pretentiously expensive stationery they may evoke annoyance and ill will instead. In any case, if they serve to a make a letterhead hard to read at first glance, they may be considered unsatisfactory.

Below are some letterheads showing attractive lettering and symbols that are impressive and in good taste without sacrifice of clarity.

Bottom and
Side-Margin Messages

Business stationery sometimes carries printed matter at the foot of the sheet or down the side margins. The foot-line (it is seldom longer than a line) is usually the motto or slogan of the firm or a special sales message. Such messages may also be printed on the side margins, usually the left-hand margin. Most marginal matter, however, consists of lists of officers, sponsors, or branches of the organization.

Additional Sheets

Whenever a letter is longer than one page, the extra sheets should be of the same paper stock but without the letterhead imprint. A continuation line carrying the name of the addressee (the person to whom the letter is addressed), the page number, and the date should be typed at the top of each additional page. See that a minimum of three lines of text, besides the complimentary close and the signature, appear on the final page of the letter. For the sake of appearance it will be worth retyping the preceding page, if necessary, to make that possible.

Framing

Good typography requires proper placement of type on the page so that it sits in its margins like a well-framed picture. Since typewriting is a form of typography, accordingly it follows the same rules. The typewriting on a letter should be so arranged that, within its margins, in the spacing of dateline, salutation, and closing lines, and in its paragraphing, it resembles a well-composed and well-framed picture.

To achieve this pleasing effect the typist does not have to be an artist. She need only follow her own orderly habits of care in her margins (which should be larger in a brief letter), in her paragraph spacing, and in her indentations.

From *Business Letter Writing Made Simple*, revised ed., by Irving Rosenthal and Harry W. Rudman, Copyright © 1955, 1968 by Doubleday & Co., Inc.

Indentations

When letters were hand-written, paragraph indentations were necessary for visual clarity. The universal use of the typewriter has tended to make indentations encumbrances instead of conveniences. Many business letters, today, dispense with them. It is becoming general practice to use line space separations instead. This device speeds up stenographic work and improves the appearance as well. But whichever practice is used, it should be employed uniformly throughout the letter.

Nevertheless, the change from indentations to line spaces for paragraph indications and other purposes has not been complete. Today four forms are in use: The "full block" form; a kind of transitional form called "modified block"; the old "full indentation" form; and a type used for special effects, called "hanging indentation."

Additional Sheets

Mr. John Jones—page 2—January 14, 19

therefore feel that we cannot accept the return of the

merchandise at this late date. We like to cooperate

with all our accounts. . . .

It was necessary, because of its length, to continue this letter on an additional sheet. The additional sheet is headed by the addressee's name, the page number, and the date. There is the requisite minimum of three lines of text, in addition to complimentary close and signature.

The "Full Block" Form

February 28, 19

Mr. John Jones
1492 Columbus Avenue
Louisville 3, Kentucky

Dear Mr. Jones:

I was very pleased to receive your prompt response to my

and I look forward to seeing you on your next trip to the city.

Sincerely yours,

George Sabrin
George Sabrin

In the "full block" form all the letter's contents are aligned on the left hand margin.

The "Modified Block" Form

February 28, 19

Mr. John Jones
1492 Columbus Avenue
Louisville 3, Kentucky

Dear Mr. Jones:

I was very pleased to receive your prompt response to

and I look forward to seeing you on your next trip to the city.

Sincerely yours,

George Sabrin
George Sabrin

All the letter's contents, with the exception of the date, the complimentary close, and the signature are aligned on the left hand margin. This is still the most widely employed form.

Full Indention

19 Elm Street
Oswego, New York
April 5, 19

Mr. Gilber Kahn
67 Wren Road
Miami, Florida 33138

My dear Mr. Kahn:

In undertaking the assignment you gave me when I was in your office last
Thursday, I made it clear

nevertheless intend to do the best job I can.

Sincerely yours,

Lucille Graham
Lucille Graham

This form is all but obsolete, and there seems little doubt that in time it will cease entirely to be used.

The "Full Block" Form

The "full block" form is gaining in usage because of its simplicity. In the full block form everything under the letterhead—dateline, inside address, salutation, body of the letter, complimentary close and signature—is aligned along the left-hand margin.

The "Modified Block" Form

The "modified block" form is the style in widest use. Here certain parts of the letter, such as the date line, the complimentary close, and the signature, are aligned to the right to help balance the rest of the letter, which has a left-hand alignment.

Some companies use the full block form for short letters (where it makes a better appearance) and the modified block form for longer letters.

Full Indentation

As mentioned before, the fully indented letter is a survival of the period when letters were hand-written. The typewriter has rendered this form obsolete. Today only a small proportion of business correspondence is typed in the full indentation form.

In the full indentation form not only paragraphs are indented but also the separate lines in the inside address and other sequences of lines in salutations and complimentary closings.

Hanging Indentation

"Hanging indentation" is seldom seen in business correspondence other than sales-promotion letters. There, it is used to focus attention or attain a repetitive, "hammering-home" effect.

Punctuation and Abbreviations

Along with the dropping of indentations there has been a tendency to do without unessential punctuation and to avoid abbreviations, especially in the inside address where these would necessitate punctuation. This economy is for improvement of appearance—lines without terminal punctuation marks look less fussy—and for speed and convenience. The typist, freed of the bother of punctuating and figuring out abbreviations, can turn out more letters a day.

A stark, attractive simplicity, characteristic of the full block form of business letter, is increasingly to be noticed in the modified block letter as well. Periods are being omitted from the end of the dateline and after ordinal numbers such as 43rd and 44th; and commas, from the ends of the inside address lines. It is now also allowable to omit the colon from the salutation and the comma from the complimentary close. Most letters, however, still retain these marks of punctuation.

Abbreviations of cities and states are being avoided. Such abbreviations as Mr. or initials for first names are being retained and are followed by periods.

The new, unpunctuated form, where all punctuation is omitted, is called "open punctuation." The practice of using some punctuation is termed "mixed punctuation." The old form is called "closed punctuation." See the examples below:

Open Punctuation
Mr. Ferdinand L. Shorey
12 West 44 Street
New York, N.Y. 10036
Dear Mr. Shorey
      Yours sincerely

Mixed Punctuation
Mr. Ferdinand L. Shorey,
12 West 44 Street,
New York, N.Y. 10036.
Dear Mr. Shorey:
      Yours sincerely,

Closed Punctuation
Mr. Ferdinand L. Shorey
12 West 44 Street
New York, N.Y. 10036
Dear Mr. Shorey:
      Yours sincerely,

Hanging Indention

Dear Sir:

If you've been reading COSMOS for years, I hope you'll forgive me for sending you a letter

you don't need—But you'll understand why I jumped at the chance to write a special

letter to a list (on which your name appears) of successful executives who have been

appointed to even more responsible posts.

For readers of COSMOS know that the busier a man is the more rewarding COSMOS can be.

And if you haven't yet discovered the added advantage of reading COSMOS for every

week's news, then I hope you'll look into it now.

It's a quick, reliable short-cut to information you'll use a dozen times a day. A readable, reli-

able report on the

It is to be noted that this form is not appropriate for normal business correspondence, but is widely used in the sales letter for the apparent reason that it readily strikes the eye, arrests attention.

Even in the past the use in the salutation of the semi-colon or the colon and dash was incorrect. Such practices today are grossly illiterate. Do not use **Dear Mr. Shorey;** or **Dear Mr. Shorey:—**

Elements of the Letter

Business letters should have at least the following elements: the letterhead, dateline, inside address, salutation, body, complimentary close, two signatures (the name of the company typed out and the written signature of the writer), and the dictator's and typist's initials, the former, usually in capitals and the latter in small letters. In addition, depending upon the operating procedure of the writer's company, there may be a file number, an order number, or a subject line for the purpose of future reference; an "attention" line where the letter is directed to a particular person or department; notice of an enclosure; and a postscript.

The Dateline

Usually the dateline is typed at the right. In full block letters it may be typed flush with the left margin. Sometimes it is centered under the letterhead.

The customary sequence is month, day, and year: as April 5, 1971. Some logical persons have been advocating a usage, now standard in Great Britain and in our armed forces, of a progressive time-interval sequence—the shortest interval, the day, first, followed by the month, and then the year: as 5 April 1971. Although not common, this form is acceptable.

The Inside Address

Inside addresses are included in business letters for several practical purposes. The inside address serves as a ready identification since envelopes are usually thrown away; it helps in filing correspondence; and it can be used with window envelopes. It is also useful to the post office when checking misdirected letters or letters with no return address on the envelope.

The inside address usually consists of three lines: the name of the person or the firm, the street address, and the line carrying city, state, and zip code. In foreign mail a fourth line carries the name of the country. If the addressee is associated with a company, its name may appear under his as the second line.

Examples: Mr. Thomas Smith
            24 West 98 Street
            New York, N.Y. 10025

            Mr. Alan May
            16 Charing Cross
            London, N.W. (Zone No.)
            England

            Mr. Thomas Smith
            West Side Riding Academy
            24 West 98 Street
            New York, N.Y. 10025

The Salutation

Present-day usage for the normal salutation is the word **Dear** and the title and the name of the addressee: as **Dear Mr. Doe** or **Dear Mr. Roe**. In personal friendships between businessmen it is permissible for them to use first names or nicknames in salutations: as **Dear John**

or **Dear Hank.** In formal address the expression, **My Dear Mr. Doe,** is often used.

Sales letters addressed to regular patrons may use terms like **Dear Customer, Dear Madam, Dear Subscriber,** etc. In mass mailings any general terms such as **Dear Sir, Dear Madam, Dear Friend, Dear Fellow Citizen, Dear Reader** or any other salutation considered appropriate may be used—or none at all.

Whenever open punctuation is used, the colon may be omitted after the salutation. But, as we have mentioned before, it is more customary to retain it. The colon-dash and the semicolon, however, are never correct.

There are special forms of address for persons of high rank in government, the armed forces, the church, and the professions. These will be found in Appendix D.

Body

The body of the letter is, of course, its most important part. In appearance it should be clearly typed, neatly spaced, and uniform in typographical construction.

Long paragraphs should be avoided. The paragraphs should not be so short, however, as to give any impression of talking down to the addressee. But in sales letters short paragraphs are almost always the rule, in order to sustain interest.

Underlining to indicate italics or to give emphasis is being displaced by capitalizing. Capitals are regarded as more readable, more emphatic, and more pleasing in appearance. Moreover, capitalizing makes for easier and more rapid typing. Titles of books and names of periodicals, however, should continue to be underlined or placed in quotation marks.

The contents of the body will be dealt with at greater length in the separate sections discussing the different types of business letters. Here we may generalize as follows:

The opening paragraph should be short and, unless there is a compelling negative reason, it should immediately introduce the subject of the letter or connect it with a previous development in the correspondence. The middle paragraphs should do the main job of the letter—expand on the subject in such a way as to persuade the addressee to act upon it in the manner you desire. Let it convince him that it will be proper for or advantageous to him to conclude the purchase or the agreement, or to make the postponement, the payment, or the adjustment you are seeking.

The closing paragraph should summarize your message and make clear the action you desire. Avoid wavering words like **hoping, wishing, trusting,** etc. Be positive. Say something like "We feel certain that you will agree that this is the most satisfactory solution." Avoid dangling participial endings, such as "Hoping we hear from you."

The Complimentary Close

Just as you open your letter with a word of friendly greeting, so you close it with a cordial expression—what is called the complimentary close. Some people propose dispensing with both, and recommended plunging into the letter without salutation and closing abruptly with the signature. But the convention is so firmly entrenched as to render it unlikely that this suggested procedure will take hold.

The customary forms are "Yours truly," "Yours sincerely," or "Yours very truly" where the relationship is formal. The terms "Yours sincerely," "Sincerely yours," "Faithfully yours," and "Cordially yours" express rising

degrees of intimacy. "Respectfully yours" has gone out of fashion and is now generally restricted to correspondence with dignitaries or official superiors in formal situations.

The Signature

It is considered a discourtesy not to sign a letter personally. If this becomes an impossibility and a rubber stamp has to be used, it should be inked and imprinted in such a way as to resemble the true signature as closely as possible. If the writer's secretary signs for him, she should put her initials under the signature to make that fact clear.

New attitudes regarding the position of women do not seem to have penetrated into business correspondence, at least as regards their marital status. That has to be indicated in the signature. A married woman who wishes to use her maiden name in business should add her married name (Mrs._____) in parentheses. A widow retains her married name unless she takes legal steps to resume her maiden name. A divorcee retains her former husband's surname but may not use his initials or his first name.

Where the company name is included in the signature, it is typed one or two lines below the complimentary close. Four spaces should be left for the writer's signature, and his name and company position should follow:

Yours sincerely,

Thomas Smith

THE JOHN JONES COMPANY
Sales Manager

To make sure that the signature is not misread, the name is often typed above or below it.

Yours sincerely,
THE JOHN JONES COMPANY

Thomas Smith

Thomas Smith
Sales Manager

Special Parts of the Business
Letter: File Numbers

In addition to the standard parts of the letter special requirements may call for additional lines or items. On traffic or mail order correspondence file or other reference numbers may appear, usually at the left of the dateline or under it.

Attention Line

When a letter is addressed to an individual in a firm but is not intended for him exclusively, or if it is intended to be routed to a certain department, a line is added to that effect. Letters are often addressed to the **attention** of an individual instead of to him directly so that, if he should be away, the letter will not be held up but will be acted upon by the person temporarily taking his place.

The attention line is usually put between the inside address and the salutation, and may be placed either at the left, as in the example below, or in the center of the line.

The John Jones Company
710 West 10 Street
New York, N.Y. 10011

Attention Mr. Thomas Smith, Sales Manager

Gentlemen:

Note that where the attention line is used, the salutation is **Gentlemen,** not **Dear Mr. Smith.**

Enclosure Line

The enclosure line in the letter is not for the addressee, who will be informed about the enclosure in the text of the letter. It is for the mailing clerk or the stenographer herself as a reminder to include the enclosure in the mailing. It should therefore be in an inconspicuous position. It is usually typed under the stenographer's initials, as an abbreviation: Encl.

Postscripts

Postscripts in business letters differ from those in personal letters, which are afterthoughts set down after the letters have been finished. In business correspondence, postscripts have a definite, planned function. They may emphasize a point made elsewhere in the letter, or they may make a special offer. They are more customary in sales letters than in other business correspondence, and are designed to draw special attention. Examples will be found in the section on sales letters.

Envelopes

As much care should be observed with the envelope as with the letter itself. It is the first part of the letter to be seen, and, as we have already observed, the first impression is important. It should, of course, be of the same paper stock as the letter. The address should be typed in such a way as to be in pleasing balance with the imprint on the top left-hand corner, if there is such an imprint; or it should be well framed on the front of the envelope if the return address is imprinted on the flap in back.

The two standard envelope sizes are the number 6¾ and the number 10. The latter is also called the "official size" envelope. It is long enough to hold the full standard letterhead width of 8½ inches. The number 6¾ size averages that number of inches in width. Envelopes used for Baronial size stationery average 7½ inches in width, enough to permit enclosure folded the full width of the sheet.

Folding the Letter and
Inserting Enclosures

Part of the appearance of the letter depends, of course, on the way it is folded and placed in the envelope. Here the convenience of the addressee also receives consideration. The letter should be folded so that he can open it with ease and read it with comfort.

For the number 10 or the long "official size" envelope, the letter should be folded from the bottom to a little over a third of the page. Crease the fold down firmly. Then fold the top third down over the bottom fold and crease firmly again. Then slip the folded letter into the envelope.

For the number 6¾ envelope, fold the letter from

Sample Business Letter

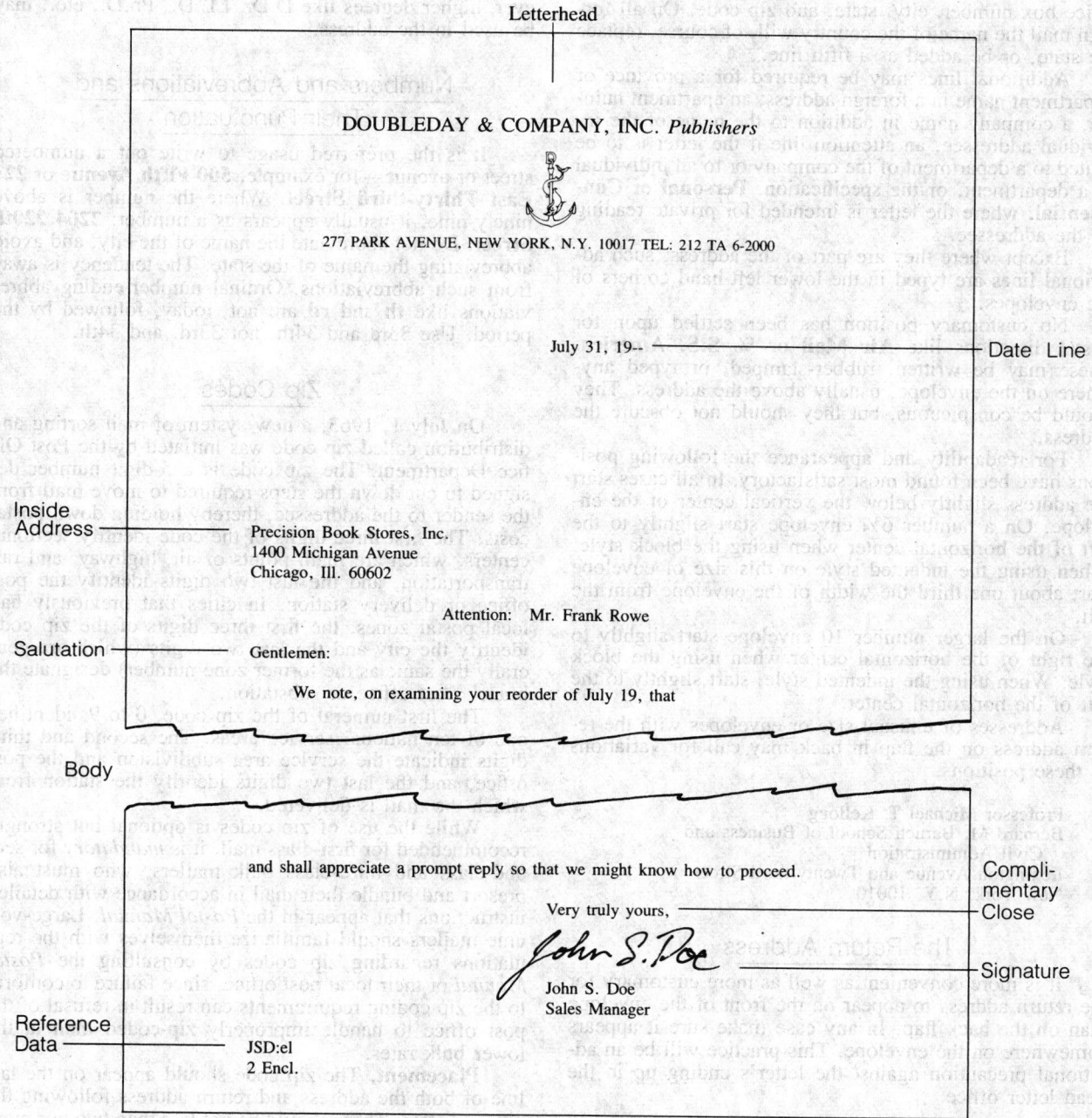

Letterhead

DOUBLEDAY & COMPANY, INC. *Publishers*

277 PARK AVENUE, NEW YORK, N.Y. 10017 TEL: 212 TA 6-2000

July 31, 19-- ——————————————— Date Line

Inside
Address ——— Precision Book Stores, Inc.
1400 Michigan Avenue
Chicago, Ill. 60602

Attention: Mr. Frank Rowe

Salutation ——— Gentlemen:

We note, on examining your reorder of July 19, that

Body

and shall appreciate a prompt reply so that we might know how to proceed.

Very truly yours, ——————————— Complimentary
Close

John S. Doe ——————————— Signature

John S. Doe
Sales Manager

Reference
Data ——— JSD:el
2 Encl.

This model letter includes in standard form all *the elements normally employed in the business letter.*

the bottom to about a quarter of an inch from the top. See that the sides are even when creasing. Now fold from the sides, first from right to left about a third of the way and then from left to right, creasing firmly after each of the two folds. Then enclose the letter with the last fold toward you. This will insure that when it is received the letter can be removed with the open end on top.

Checks, receipts, or other small enclosures should be placed inside the folds. If placed outside the folds, in the envelope, such vital items may be torn or cut when the envelope is opened; or they may be overlooked by

the recipient and thrown away with the discarded envelope.

Letters mailed in window envelopes must be folded in a special way.

The Outside Address

Each year, according to post office records, some thirty million pieces of mail end up in the dead letter office. The chief reason is careless addressing.

The customary address form consists of four lines: the name and title of the addressee, street address or post office box number, city, state, and zip code. On all foreign mail the name of the country will, of course, replace the state, or be added as a fifth line.

Additional lines may be required for a province or department name in a foreign address, an apartment number, a company name in addition to the name of the individual addressee, an attention line if the letter is to be routed to a department of the company or to an individual in a department, or the specification, **Personal** or **Confidential,** where the letter is intended for private reading by the addressee.

Except where they are part of the address, such additional lines are typed in the lower left-hand corners of the envelopes.

No customary position has been settled upon for postal directions like **Air Mail** or **% S.S. America.** These may be written, rubber-stamped, or typed anywhere on the envelope, usually above the address. They should be conspicuous, but they should not obscure the address.

For readability and appearance the following positions have been found most satisfactory. In all cases start the address slightly below the vertical center of the envelope. On a number 6¾ envelope start slightly to the left of the horizontal center when using the block style. When using the indented style on this size of envelope start about one third the width of the envelope from the left.

On the larger number 10 envelope start slightly to the right of the horizontal center when using the block style. When using the indented style, start slightly to the left of the horizontal center.

Addresses of unusual size or envelopes with the return address on the flap in back may call for variations of these positions.

> Professor Michael T. Kellogg
> Bernard M. Baruch School of Business and
>   Civil Administration
> Lexington Avenue and Twenty-third Street
> New York, N.Y. 10010

The Return Address

It is more convenient as well as more customary for the return address to appear on the front of the envelope than on the back flap. In any case make sure it appears somewhere on the envelope. This practice will be an additional precaution against the letter's ending up in the dead letter office.

Titles of Respect

It is customary to include certain titles of respect in the address. This courtesy extends to physicians after whose name M.D. usually appears, and to engineers (C.E., M.E., or E.E.). These abbreviations are professional as well as academic designations. Purely scholastic

titles like M.A. or non-professional titles like B.S. or Ph.B., etc., are omitted. In formal correspondence, however, higher degrees like D.D., LL.D., Ph.D., etc., may be used in the address.

Numbers and Abbreviations and Their Punctuation

It is the preferred usage to write out a numbered street or avenue—for example, **500 Fifth Avenue** or **223 East Thirty-third Street.** Where the number is above ninety-nine, it usually appears as a number: **2204 220th Street.** Do not abbreviate the name of the city, and avoid abbreviating the name of the state. The tendency is away from such abbreviations. Ordinal number-ending abbreviations like **th** and **rd** are not, today, followed by the period. Use 33rd and 34th, not 33rd. and 34th.

Zip Codes

On July 1, 1963, a new system of mail sorting and distribution called zip code was initiated by the Post Office Department. The zip code is a 5-digit number designed to cut down the steps required to move mail from the sender to the addressee, thereby holding down postal costs. The first three digits of the code identify sectional centers, which are main points of air, highway, and rail transportation, and the last two digits identify the post office or delivery station. In cities that previously had local postal zones, the first three digits of the zip code identify the city and the last two digits (which are generally the same as the former zone number) designate the branch post office or substation.

The first numeral of the zip code, 0 to 9, identifies one of ten national service areas. The second and third digits indicate the service area subdivision and the post office, and the last two digits identify the station from which the mail is delivered.

While the use of zip codes is optional but strongly recommended for first-class mail, it is *mandatory* for second-class and third-class bulk mailers, who must also presort and bundle their mail in accordance with detailed instructions that appear in the *Postal Manual.* Large-volume mailers should familiarize themselves with the regulations regarding zip codes by consulting the *Postal Manual* or their local post office, since failure to conform to the zip coding requirements can result in refusal of the post office to handle improperly zip-coded mail at the lower bulk rates.

Placement. The zip code should appear on the last line of both the address and return address following the city and state. There should be not less than two nor more than six spaces between the last letter of the state and the zip code, and no characters of any kind should follow the zip code:

> Mr. Harold Jones
> 3025 Theresa Street
> Arlington, Va.   22207

The Sales Letter

The concern of all business is to sell goods or services. Consequently all business letters are, directly or indirectly, sales letters.

Your best collection letter, for example, is one that does more than induce a delinquent customer to pay up.

It is the one that leaves him convinced, after the payment, that he has been dealing with a fair and considerate house with which he is glad to continue doing business.

Sales letters, as such, are distinguished from other business letters by the fact that their sales objective is

not indirect but direct and, more or less, immediate. The qualifying phrase, "more or less," is used because some varieties of sales letters are not intended to make an immediate sale but rather to lead **gradually** to sales. And others are intended to pave the way for sales by other means.

Certain sales letters, for example, may be written to help a salesman make the sale. Others may be written to bring customers for your products to one of your dealers.

The most common and largest variety of sales letter is used in direct mail selling. Devices employed in that type of sales letter are presented in a later section; here we shall deal with the more general aspects of sales letters, and take up types of sales correspondence that are part of regular business operations.

Your Satisfied Customer

No selling job is ever over. The alert businessman keeps analyzing his accounts. Can A's volume be increased? B's orders show a slight decline over last year's; does that mean a decline in his business? Or is he sampling the ware of a competitor? Whatever his conclusion, the alert businessman sends off the appropriate letter.

In An Effort to Increase
Sales

Dear Mr. Martin:

I have been very pleased to note the steady increase in the frequency and size of your orders since we started doing business together. It is gratifying to know that our product is being well received in your area and that you are making money with it.

My reason for writing is twofold—to thank you for your patronage and to offer our cooperation in any way that will build your sales of our product even further. Under separate cover I am sending you some advertising aids that can be used in window and counter displays; mats for newspaper ads; and suggested spot announcements for your local radio station. Frank Moss, our representative in your territory, will drop in on you next Thursday to help you set up these displays and to offer his assitance in every way. If there is anything special you may need, don't hesitate to get in touch with me.

I look forward to the continuance of our pleasant, and I hope, mutually profitable relationship. With all good wishes, I am,

Sincerely yours,
Robert Johns

In An Effort to Retain
Good Will

Dear Mr. Burke:

Somewhere or other we read: "There are many good excuses for losing an order—but no excuse whatever for losing good will!"

That's why we're writing to you—not to ask why you preferred to place your recent order with somebody else, but to make sure it wasn't because of something which has lost us your good will as well.

If it was the latter, we'd be most grateful if you'd write us about it.

But regardless, we sincerely hope your new equipment gives you the kind of performance you expect of it—and that you won't hesitate to make use of
our nationwide service facilities should the need arise.

Next time, perhaps, it will be our good fortune to take care of your requirements.

Sincerely,
William H. Wolcott

The alert businessman never feels smug about his satisfied customers. He does not leave the initiative to them, content merely to take orders. He bears in mind those two business adages: "It costs less to keep a customer than to get one," and "Your customer is your competitor's prospect."

If he starts a new line, if he makes an improvement in one of his staples, if he has a plan for reducing the price to a customer by quantity shipping of combined orders, the alert businessman lets his satisfied customer know about it. He does not wait for the word to get around; he sees to it that it gets around. Keeping the satisfied customer posted is a good way of keeping them satisfied.

Dear Larry:

I hope this finds you well and your business booming. I think I have something that you ought to be able to go to town on.

I've just picked up a special lot of piece goods off-price that I'm going to cut tomorrow in Style 637, with which you have done so well. I plan to bring out the number at two dollars less than you have been paying, and I know it will fit in well with your January sale.

I can get a limited number of garments out of the lot, so I'd like to know how many you can use before I offer it to anyone else. We'll be able to ship within ten days.

All good wishes.

Sincerely yours,
Phil Nelson

Dear Mr. Forman:

When you were in the city several weeks ago, you mentioned the difficulties you were having in getting fast deliveries of merchandise shipped to you by us and by other manufacturers. I think I've come across something that can help you.

I have just had a conversation with Jack Bell of Vanguard Trucking, 247 Terhune Place, Jersey City, N.J., who runs a fleet of trucks through your territory. He told me that if you can work out an arrangement with a few other merchants near you to consolidate shipments, he will be glad to set aside one of his trucks to serve your group. If the amount of freight warrants it, he can provide daily overnight deliveries, and is confident he can cut your present transportation costs by forty per cent. I think its worth looking into, and I suggest you get in touch with Mr. Bell for more particulars.

Sincerely yours,
Robert Glass

Frequent Communication

Keep the contacts with your customers unbroken and, so far as you can, make the contacts personal. Some firms regard communication with their customers, once a month, a minimum requirement for good customer relations. They do not limit the correspondence to invoices and routine acknowledgments of orders and payments. To the routine mail they add interesting enclosures. And they take advantage of every suitable occasion to extend the contact. They avoid formalities and try to set up a personal relationship. For signatures they do not use only the firm name but rather the name of an officer of the firm, the head of a department, or a salesman.

Some concerns go about unobtrusively getting personal items about their customers and keep the data cur-

rent. Birthdays are remembered. If a buyer gets married or has an addition to the family, the event is observed.

Many service firms such as laundries and cleaning establishments find it profitable to send their customers and prospective customers blotters bearing calenders and reminders of seasonal cleaning needs.

Department stores keep in touch with their charge-customers by sending them advance notices of sales, seasonal announcements, and letters about special services. Whatever your business is, there are sure to be occasions for getting in touch with your customers other than through routine notices and acknowledgments.

Special Customers

In every business there are customers who rate or demand special attention. Some should get it merely because the large volume of their business calls for every possible special and even personal consideration. Special and personal letters, if feasible, will be in order.

Others may have special needs. For example, dealers located in hot, moist regions may require special packaging or other measures to keep the wares they receive in good condition. Letters dealing with such special needs are in order.

Others may be merely fussy or eccentric. These may be hard to do business with and require special sales correspondence. If you decide that the volume of their business justifies it, carry on that additional correspondence with good grace.

Letters to Help
Your Salesmen

The salesman may be assisted, through letters, in two general ways. One type of letter prepares the ground for him—introduces him, mentions the new line he will demonstrate, some special offer he will explain in detail, etc.

Such help to a salesman may be needed for several reasons. One is the lingering effect of the fictional presentation of the salesman as an intrusive, high-pressure man with his toes wedged in the door sill, launched on a non-stop spiel. Even dealers who have good relations with salesmen and have found them helpful may think of those they know as exceptions and look for the obnoxious type in a new man. A letter can help the new man by presenting him in a friendly light, stressing the useful service he is to perform—the demonstration he will make or the plan he will explain, etc.

In such letters, however, take care not to tell the customer too much. Remember that the purpose is to introduce the salesman, not to substitute for his call. The letter should stimulate the customer's curiosity and leave it to the salesman to satisfy it. Similar letters can serve to bring customers to your show rooms, to exhibition booths, to dealers handling your products or services.

Letters sent between sales calls can strengthen the salesman-customer relationship. The seasonal nature of certain kinds of merchandise or the fact that salesmen will make only a few trips a year in the ordinary course, gives rise to considerable correspondence about reorders, substitutions, cancellations, returns, complaints, and the acknowledgments and adjustments these call for. As much of this correspondence as is practical should go out under the salesman's signature.

In addition it is frequently advisable to send out, also under the salesman's signature, letters advising the customer of new developments, new lines, new policies, etc.

Even in business the strongest bonds are personal, and a good salesman-customer relationship means a good relationship with the customer for the firm.

Testimonials

When enough time has elapsed for a new account to have tested your products and your business procedures, it is a good plan to write to the customer and ask whether he is satisfied and whether he has any suggestions or comments to make. This kind of inquiry should be the first step in the continuous keeping-your-customer-sold campaign that was mentioned earlier.

Such letters may evoke testimonials that will prove valuable in your promotion. And the letters will probably have the additional value of providing a running check on your business methods by revealing from time to time the need for changes.

Build up a testimonial file from the favorable letters your inquiries bring you. You can draw upon such a file when approaching prospects in the same area or in the same general line as the writers of the testimonials. The signer of the testimonial can say more for you than almost anything you can say for yourself.

Dear Mr. Seaman:

It is now eight months since we first started doing business together, and I note with satisfaction that the volume each month has been increasing nicely. At first, we were skeptical about the possibility of developing sales in your territory, because our product has been sold mainly in colder sections of the country. Your experience, therefore, has been gratifying.

My purpose in writing is to find out whether you have any thoughts about how we can increase our volume to mutual advantage even further. As you can see, we're trying to work with you the best way we know how, and we'd appreciate hearing from you with any comments you may wish to make about our service and product. We like to receive brickbats as well as pats on the back. We can correct our faults—to the advantage of all concerned—only when they're pointed out.

Sincerely yours,
John Thomas

The Inquiry Letter

Answers to inquiries are a major part of business correspondence, and can be the most important type of sales letter. Those that are part of a direct-mail sales campaign will be dealt with in the next section. Here we touch upon the type of inquiry that originates in other ways.

Someone in the market for your sort of goods or services has looked up your firm in a trade directory; or has had it recommended to him by one of your customers with whom he is acquainted; or has heard of you in some other way. He writes to you for information. His inquiry to you may be the only one he is making. But the chances are that he is simultaneously asking for similar information from your competitors.

It is wise to assume that that is the case, and that your answer must stand the test of competition. Do your best to make your reply a sales letter that wins the inquirer's business.

Promptness is of the first importance. Your prospect will be quite as much sold by evidence of your alertness and efficiency as by what you may say.

Directness is also important. Give specific answers to the questions. If the questions are vague, don't follow that bad example; be specific about what you have to sell

and thus you will probably answer effectively the questions your prospect has not been able to express.

Being specific does not mean being detailed. Leave the details to the catalogue or the other enclosures you send. A good sales letter is organized to have a certain impact. It cannot have that impact if it interrupts itself to go into minutiae.

Enclosures

Your postage outlay pays for an ounce per unit of reading matter. That ounce gives you leeway for several sheets besides your letter which—barring necessary exceptions—will usually be less than a page in length. Businessmen have found it profitable to take advantage of the full permissible weight by adding enclosures that reinforce the sales punch.

The enclosures can be particularly useful in supplying details which, if put into the body of the letter, might blunt its impact. If the prospect had to pause, while reading the letter, to take in details of measurement, construction, delivery schedules, etc., his interest would be too diffused for him to react as you would like him to.

Your letter should do two things. It should put the prospect into the buying mood and whet his interest so that he will want to look up the details. These can be furnished in an effective enclosure.

However, avoid a clutter of accompanying "literature." Some mailers believe in the more-the-better principle. But experience has shown that beyond a certain point **more** can become **too much.** Then, no matter how colorful and clever the enclosures are, they begin to clash with one another. They distract attention from the letter. They even become a nuisance to the recipient—and the letter may lose its effectiveness.

Moreover, the enclosures should not overshadow the letter. The letter itself should be attractive to look at, but above all its copy should be so carefully, sensibly, and effectively prepared that it produces the results desired.

It is generally advisable, when dealing with a smaller enclosure, to fold it into the letter so that it comes out along with the letter when the envelope is opened.

Dear Mr. Merton:

I am going to make this letter brief. I feel the enclosed brochure speaks for itself. But I am writing merely to let you know that the sales potential of the lamp described has been tested carefully in thirty selected stores similar to yours. Every one of them has come back with quick reorders. So we know WE HAVE SOMETHING YOU CAN DO WELL WITH.

We developed this item with a view to shooting for volume. We've brought it out at the lowest price possible, and we have complete confidence in its sales potential.

We all get a steady stream of mail across our desks, but I hope you will take a few minutes to study the brochure carefully, and to try out a sample order of the lamp. We'll let the selling talk for itself.

Sincerely yours,

Ivan Hubbell

Form Letters

Whatever the special function of the sales letter you write, make it personal if possible. If the volume of the correspondence makes this impractical, use forms and methods that will make it appear like a personal letter.

There are two main kinds of form letters—**complete** and **paragraph.** The complete form, even when it is individually typed and signed, is prepared in advance to cover certain standard needs.

Usually **complete form letters** are produced on a word processor or xeroxed, depending on the purpose they serve. Word processing is useful in letters where spaces can be provided to fill in dates, individual salutations, addresses, etc. In virtually all cases, the name of an individual, even in rubber stamp or stencil reproductions, is preferable in the signature to simply the name of the firm.

Complete form letters are usually identified by some combination of letters or initials under which they can be filed. Thus there may be a series of form letters with which catalogues are to be enclosed. These are keyed with the letter C and their numbers in the series. Then the secretary can be instructed to send out Form Letter C-4.

The greater flexibility of the **paragraph form letter** makes it possible to meet a larger number of calculable special situations. Such a letter is assembled from designated prepared passages kept on file in a "paragraph book." Some firms have several paragraph books with hundreds of paragraphs in each.

For illustration let us take a paragraph book containing ninety passages. Of these, one to ten may be devoted to letter openings; eleven to forty may consist of second paragraphs; forty-one to seventy may consist of third paragraphs; and the remaining twenty entries may be closings. Thus a typist may be instructed to use 7: 24: 51: 82, and will construct the letter from corresponding paragraphs in the paragraph book.

Structure of the Sales Letter

In **sales letters** the same general principles of structure apply as in all business letters. But greater latitude is allowed in sales letters, just as greater latitude is allowed in the sales approach in general. You can be more unconventional and use more color and typographic tricks; and you will be pardoned a certain amount of puffing. Of course, if any one of these is carried to excess, it will prove self-defeating.

The salutation: One of the liberties that may be taken is with the salutation. In mass-mailings, where fill-in salutations and inside addresses are impossible, anonymous salutations such as **Dear Friend, Dear Sir** or **Dear Madame** may be used; or, if the list is a selected one permitting such specifications, **Dear Doctor, Dear Business Executive, Dear Fellow-Angler,** etc.

In some cases the salutation may be dispensed with and a flattering introductory phrase substituted for it, such as "To a Forward-Looking and Ambitious Young Businessman" or "To a Young Lady Who Keeps in Step with the Times." Or just a catchy headline like "Play Ball!" may be employed. However, these devices should be shunned in ordinary correspondence, and might be resorted to only where the multitude of identical letters is so great that individual salutations are impractical.

The opening: The opening is more crucial in a sales letter than in any other business correspondence. It is the sender's bid for attention; if it fails, the whole effort is wasted.

Some firms go to considerable trouble and expense in striving for attention-getting openings. In a conspicuous position on the letter they may have—stapled, glued on, or affixed in some other way—a small metal, cloth, or plastic object that pictorially symbolizes the opening line.

For example, one firm used a cord lasso, fastened to an upper corner of a letter so that the rope end touched

the first line, to give animation to this opening: "Yes, we want to rope you in—and you'll be glad of it. . . ." Similarly a small aluminum bat glued to another letter helped to fix attention on this opening: "This is the season to go to bat for . . ."

Devices like these must be used with care for they are novelties that may appeal to some readers and by their "cuteness" irritate others. You may not be able to afford such expensive attention-getters; but still less can you afford a dull or lifeless opening. You can always attract attention with an imaginative thought and vivid words.

The question opening: One sure method is to put your opening in the form of a question. In that way you can take advantage of a quirk of human nature. We always react to a question as a challenge, and it is a rare person who does not feel the compulsion to make some response.

Of course the question should be provocative and relevant personally to the prospect, and should bring in the article or service being promoted.

This question opening was used by a home development company: "Are you over thirty, married, and a churchgoer?" Since the mailing list had been selected to concentrate on mature, married, churchgoing people, the reader was bound to answer "yes" and was thereby put in a receptive frame of mind to the rest of the proposition.

The striking statement: Another good type of opening is the **striking statement.** A good example is the one used, some twenty-five years ago, by the New York *Daily News* when it introduced itself and tabloid journalism to the metropolis. To its advertising prospects it sent a letter advising them to "Tell it to the Sweeneys" (through its pages) because "the Vanderbilts don't care." This was followed of course, with interesting material on the advantages of the mass market and its lower sales resistance.

Another example of the striking statement as an opening was the following, used in a letter to advertisers by a large woman's magazine: "Yes, men still carry on most of the nation's business—but their wives do still more of the buying!"

A proverb, too, can provide a good opening, especially when it is given an arresting new twist: "The early bird catches the worm—but was it wise for the worm to be early?"

Body of the letter: Having gained attention by your opening, you must next sustain interest while making sales points in the body of the letter.

The anecdote: Some writers have recourse to a story or anecdote for this purpose. An organization arranging outdoor exercise and entertainment for businessmen used this anecdote in a sales letter to its prospects:

"A vigorous man in his nineties was asked the secret of his longevity. 'Wal,' he replied, 'when my wife and I got married we agreed to do something to spare our nerves. If I was the grumpy one she'd go into the other room and take up her knittin'. And if she started to pick on me I'd put on my hat and go out for a walk. . . . So you see I been outdoors most of my life.'

"Being outdoors, that tried and true recipe for a long life and a healthy one, can be made easy for you by joining the _____ Outdoors Club. (And equally easy for your wife as well, who won't be so inclined to pick on you if you include her.) Drive out in your own car or one of the Club's limousines will pick you up outside your office and bring you to the club grounds. Then you can swim, golf, swing a racket, walk or do anything else you like in clear sunlight and unpolluted country air."

Enclosures gave further details.

Facts and figures: Other writers rely on facts and figures. They support tempting descriptions of the article or service they are marketing with data giving the results of laboratory tests, consumption statistics, testimonials, guarantees, and other inducements.

Incidentally, experienced sales-letter writers advise that the core of the sales message should appear about two-fifths of the way down the letter.

The closing: In earlier business correspondence, in the days when businessmen dressed in frock coats and striped trousers like diplomats, it was considered proper to close sales letters with polite wishes like "hoping" or "trusting we shall hear from you." Such expressions tend to linger on. Usually they are left in mid-air as dangling participles. If you find them in your correspondence, pull out the blue pencil!

Sales letters now end with forceful suggestions for immediate action. They ask for the order; and they enforce it with all sorts of inducements, bargain offers, samples, free examination privileges, and a wide variety of other appeals.

Here is an example of the appeal of **exclusiveness:**

"There are many more than three thousand discriminating readers who will want this book, but only three thousand copies were printed. As this letter is being mailed, the day's orders reduce the number still available to 422. Better make sure of getting **your** free-examination copy by filling out and mailing the enclosed card **today.**"

The "You" Attitude again: Among the numerous factors that contribute to effective correspondence, the "you" attitude, referred to earlier, is paramount. The seller takes care not to show his anxiety to make a sale. What he stresses is the buyer's interests. The buyer will get a bargain; he will be guaranteed against dissatisfaction by the privilege of returning the merchandise; payment will be made easy for him by special terms, etc. In sales letters as much as in any other form of business correspondence be sure to consider the reader at all times.

The postscript: In that same frock-coat-and-striped-pants business era alluded to above, the postscript was frowned upon. It was considered unkempt—allowable, perhaps, in private correspondence, but distinctly incorrect in well-dressed business correspondence.

Today, however, few sales letters are without postscripts. As a typographical device, the postscript has won general adoption because of the special services it can perform. It can remove from the body of the letter, whose unity it might impair, some special matter which should be brought to the reader's attention. Or it can give a needed emphasis to something as no other method can.

"P.S. Special discount terms can be arranged" stands out in a postscript, yet does not interfere with other persuasions as it might if set in the body of the letter. And if you have already mentioned your booth at a convention, a postscript reminder can do a lot to draw visits there: for example, "P.S. We're looking forward to seeing you at booth 16. Ask for Mr. Elkin."

"Letters You Don't Have To Write"

A recent speech by Maxwell C. Ross, a well known sales promotion expert, listed **sixteen** ways letters can be used to create good will—and, eventually, sales. "There's just one prerequisite," he said; "the person using them has to be a nice guy, courteous, friendly, and above all, sincere."

Each is simply a friendly, personal letter that you send on some occasion when nobody would have thought

very much about it if you hadn't sent the letter at all. They don't *have* to be written, but they create a tremendously favorable impression because they *are* written.

1. *You can use a letter to follow up a salesman's call.* You don't need to, for it isn't expected, but you'll be surprised at the reception it gets. You could start something like this: "John Smith told me today of the pleasant visit he had with you about your insurance program. I know that John will do a fine job for you." Then finish off in your own words.

2. *You can use letters to make appointments.* You say, "It's about time for me to sit down with you, Jim, and go over your insurance in the light of the new tax changes. I want to do this when you have the time for it, but it should be soon. I suggest that we get together late Friday afternoon. How would 4 o'clock be?" You don't need to say much more, but you'll be surprised at the nice reception you get.

3. *Whenever a customer or client has been promoted or changed jobs,* it's a nice gesture to send a letter like this—"Congratulations on your appointment to District Sales Manager. This is fine news, and I know you'll do a great job. If I can ever be of any help to you, please let me know."

4. *When a customer is ill,* there's no more appreciated time to get mail. All you need to say is—"I'm certainly sorry to hear that you are laid up for an operation. I hope it won't be many days before you're back at your desk." Add to that a book, or the loan of one, a magazine, or a box of candy, and the good will you build is far above the effort you take in doing it.

5. *When there is a death in the family.* If it's tactfully done a short message of sympathy can mean much.

6. *When a daughter or son gets married,* or *a new baby arrives.* These letters make no tangible effort to sell; they're simply good-will builders—the kind that some day will bring something nice to you because you went out of your way to do something nice for somebody else.

7. *When people buy a home,* write to them. You letter doesn't need to be long or fancy. Perhaps: "I hope you are enjoying your new home, and that you have recovered from the trials of moving." If you have somethinag to sell, go ahead and mention it. Tell these folks you'd appreciate a chance to call when things are squared away. In some cases, an inexpensive gift like a small rosebush or a young tree creates far more good will than the cost.

8. *When a customer has a birthday.* Quite a few successful salesmen make a practice of keeping birthday lists and sending cards or letters. A personal letter is best, but if you use a card, write something in longhand on it.

9. *When people move to your town* a letter of welcome is an excellent source of new business. They don't know where to go for dry cleaning, laundry, milk—what service station to trade with, where to do their banking, or the nicer places to eat. So you write: "Welcome to Omaha. We know you'll like it here. If there is any way we can help you get settled, please let us know."

10. *When people move from your town,* it may seem a futile gesture to seem sorry—but the intangible good will you create may come back to you in unsuspected ways. And sometimes people *do* return. So you write: "I am sorry you are moving away from Lincoln. We will miss you as a customer, but should you ever return we'll be waiting to serve you again."

11. *When you read about a customer in the newspaper,* send him a letter. Clip the article, send it to him, and say: "I don't know whether your children keep a scrapbook of the nice things that happen to you, but just in case they do, here's an extra copy I clipped for you to give them." And if congratulations are deserved, give them!

12. *When a customer is elected to some office,* or honored in any other way, perhaps you would say: "I've heard some nice things about the work you've done for the Chamber of Commerce, so I was not surprised to see that you have been elected vice president for the coming year."

13. *When someone has done you a favor* he will appreciate a note from you. "Those two extra tickets got me off a rough spot. I hope I can repay the favor soon."

14. *When some product or service pleases you,* take time to write about it. "Quite often people write to you only with their complaints, but I wanted you to know how pleased I am with our new floor furnace, and with the courteous and efficient way your men installed it."

15. *When a serviceman comes home write to him* or to his parents if he lives at home. That's a small way to show your appreciation for all he has done for you and his country. Never again in his life will he so much *want* to be welcomed back; or want to feel that all he went through was not in vain.

16. *You can use letters to thank new and old customers for their orders.* Perhaps you do, but many don't. In Des Moines, a filling station operator sends a post card to new customers. All the card says is, "It was nice of you to stop at our station. I hope you'll come back often." That's all it needs to say.

Talent scout, G. L. Fultz, St. Louis' best dressed credit man, and staunch enemy of Whiskers and Goozle, says of the following assembled hogwash: "I know you will want to read this letter, for it's a dandy."

"Thank you very kindly (who was kind?) for your letter of November 12th, just received. I am sorry that our bookkeeping department (mass production) erroneously (new spelling) billed you for storage on the car that we handled for you. I am attaching corrected bill for which (?) I am sure you will find in order. Thanking you very kindly, we remain, very truly yours."

Miscellaneous Business Letters

Inquiries and Replies; Orders and Acknowledgments; Introduction and Recommendation;
Social Correspondence in Business, Inter-Office; Good Will; Payments By Mail.

Routine Letters

In terms of quantity the largest part of business correspondence consists of routine letters—inquiries, replies to inquiries, orders and remittances, acknowledgments, bills, etc. In these letters the writer needs little art; the basic requirements are to be clear and accurate.

Inquiry Letters

Inquiry letters and replies to inquiries should be concise, simple, and direct, except in cases that call for sensitivity, judgment, or tact. An inquiry about the price of an article need do no more than ask the price. But an inquiry about credit standing or about a job opportunity, and the answers to such inquiries, require care and tact. Similarly answers to inquiries in mail-order campaigns, where the objective is to produce sales, call for thought and skill.

In ordinary inquiries, however, the important thing, on the part of the inquirer, is to phrase his question simply, precisely, and inclusively so that he can be told just what he wants to know, without extraneous matter; and also all that he wants to know so that he does not have to send further letters to fill out details. Similarly, the important thing on the part of the correspondent in answering such inquiries is to make the reply full and precise so that the inquirer does not have to come back to him to have matters cleared up or filled out.

If the information sought is adequately covered in a catalogue or booklet, enclose it in your reply and use the letter to refer to the paragraphs or pages dealing explicitly with the matter inquired about.

To facilitate quick comprehension both of the inquiry and the reply it is advisable to present them as separate items, allowing an individual paragraph for each.

If either the question or the answer is to be kept confidential, do not rely on the other person to guess it. Say so. Examles:

Gentlemen:

We are organizing a summer camp for boys and are in the market for 24 two-occupant portable tents for camping out. We are undecided whether to use conventional canvas tents, with which we are familiar, or your new nylon tents. Would you be good enough:

To send us whatever literature you have available on the construction of your nylon tents, accessory equipment, etc.

To inform us of their suitability to the summer climate of the Catskill Mountains, where the camp is located.

To furnish comparative weights and costs between canvas and nylon.

To give us an idea of the durability of your product with estimates of how many years of service may be expected in ordinary use.

We shall appreciate your referring us to customers who have had experience with your tents in conditions approximating those of the boys' camp in the Catskills.

Sincerely yours,
Arthur Ives

Gentlemen:

We are in the market for a line of work pants.
We should like to know—
What fabrics you make up.
What colors.
Minimum orders accepted per size.
Terms (including discount for cash).
Please send us a swatch catalogue with your reply.

Sincerely yours,
Bruce Samuelson

Gentlemen:

My wife and I will be in New York for the Christmas week vacation. We are people of modest means—I am an associate professor at the University here. We should like good (not lavish) hotel accommodations in Manhattan, but a little out of the immediate railroad-terminal district. We would like to take in the theater (dramas, not musicals). We enjoy good cooking, preferably without noisy entertainment.

Would your bureau book reservations such as we describe and provide information about restaurants?

Could you send us a selected list of hotels that would come within our description, listing locations and price ranges for rooms for two?

Could you list the well-reviewed plays and the price range for seats in medium locations. Fortunately our vision and hearing are good.

If you can provide such services, we will send you, by return mail, our first and alternate choices of hotel and theater reservations and a check for whatever sum you may require for deposit.

Sincerely yours,
Howard Carver

Answers to Inquiries

Dear Mr. Alexander:

We thank you for your letter of August 16 about our line of women's belts.

We wish to call your attention to the perforated pages in the back of the enclosed catalogue containing information on terms and convenient order forms.

Ours is a quality line. It is used for accessories by manufacturers serving exclusive shops, and is stocked by the New York Fifth Avenue stores.

We hope to have the pleasure of serving you.

Sincerely yours,
A. S. Cantor

Dear Mr. Jones:

Because of the decline in demand we have discontinued manufacture of the "union suit" type of men's underwear.

As the enclosed catalogue illustrates, we carry a full line of the currently popular types of men's underwear in a wide range of styles, colors, and prices.

We will be happy to serve you.

Sincerely yours,
V. A. Miles

Dear Mr. Hector:

Since your letter does not make clear what your speech defect is, we are unable to furnish a specific answer.

Our public speaking course has been designed to help shy people who are not sure of themselves to speak readily and effectively in public. If your defect

is among those associated with shyness, we are confident that the course will help you overcome it.

But if the defect is organic, that may require surgical treatment. If it is a long-standing problem, such as chronic stuttering, that may call for pyschiatric treatment. We recommend that you try to determine the cause with the aid of a physician or professionally qualified person.

But common difficulties in speaking—such as inability to face an audience, lack of practice of organizing a speech, unfamiliarity with the techniques of preparing material, groping for words, difficulties over parliamentary rules, etc.,—can be overcome by our course of study.

If you do not find the answer you require, please try us again with the questions put in more specific terms.

Sincerely yours,
Marc Rafferty

A final note: Though answers to inquiries need not be elaborate, they should avoid stuffy over-formality. For example, instead of "Acknowledging yours of the 20th requesting a copy of our booklet, *Paint It Yourself,* we wish to advise you that the booklet is being mailed to you forthwith," write something like: "We are pleased to send you our booklet, *Paint It Yourself,* which you requested on May 20. Its suggestions have been useful to people of good taste who must keep within a modest budget." Or, instead of "Yours of September 10 received and contents noted. Be advised that the matter has been put into the hands of our Sales Department from whom you should hear shortly," write something like, "Our Sales Department has your inquiry of September 10 and is assembling material which should be helpful in answering your questions."

Orders

Many firms use printed order forms. If for some reason a letter is needed to accompany or precede the order to add some specific instructions about the order, make the letter concise and unmistakably clear.

Where the letter itself constitutes the order, care should be taken to make it direct, clear, and accurate. To facilitate this it is advisable to arrange the items in tabular form, giving a separate line to each. Details of color, size, material, price, identifying mark or number, etc., should be precisely stated. Manner of shipment should be specified—whether by mail, express, freight, etc.

If the goods are needed by a certain date, if method of payment is, in any way, to differ from the customary procedure, if delivery is to be made to an address other than the regular mailing address, anything requiring specific instructions should be made clear, and should be given a separate paragraph to prevent its being misunderstood or ignored.

Where remittance is enclosed, attention should be drawn to it and its nature specified—whether it is by check, money-order, express-order, draft, cash, or stamps.

Even in letters transmitting orders for goods, ordinary courtesy and tact should be observed. In his book *"Effective Letters in Business,"* Robert L. Shurter gives an example of a tactless order letter that drew a deservedly caustic reply: The letter—"Gents. Please send me one of them gasoline engines you show on page 785 and if it's any good I'll send you a check for it."

The reply—"Dear Mr. . . . Please send us the check and if it's any good we'll send you the engine."

Variations from ordinary punctuation are frequently used in orders. To compress items into single lines or a

minimum number of lines, customary punctuation may be omitted and every possible abbreviation used. Names of separate articles are capitalized and also words that help to distinguish them from other kinds of goods of the same order. Thus Red will be capitalized to distinguish it from other colors an article may be manufactured in; or Wool to distinguish a garment in that fabric from garments in other fabrics. The objectives are conciseness and clarity and any typographic or grammatical means that promote these ends is justified.

Order Letters— Some Examples

Gentlemen:

Please rush to us to reach our stockroom next Thursday: 10 doz. Yo-yos, 50 checker sets, 50 anagram sets. This is for a special sales week which is going well. Our stock on these items is running out.

Our regular purchase order is being made out in the routine way and should reach you in a day or two; but please do not hold up delivery of this special order. A delay of even a few hours may mean lost sales.

Sincerely yours,
Kenneth Miller

Dear Mr. Bates:

The enclosed purchase order is in confirmation of the order we placed with you over the phone this morning. The order was phoned in to avoid delays. I must emphasize again that the shipment must reach us before October 4, when our sales will start.

Sincerely yours,
Seth Bellows

Gentlemen:

Please send us, for earliest possible delivery, the following goods selected from your latest catalogue. Charge my account.

3	doz.	Men's Nylon Hose, Black, asst. sizes @ $4.00	$12.00
3	doz.	Men's Nylon Hose, Blue, asst. sizes @ $4.00	12.00
3	doz.	Men's Nylon Hose, Brown, asst. sizes @ $4.00	12.00
1½	doz.	Men's Nylon Hose, Green, asst. sizes @ $4.00	6.00
4	doz.	Men's Cotton Hose, Black, Triangle Clocks @ $4.50	18.00
2	doz.	#61 Work Shirts, asst. sizes @ $9.00	18.00
2	doz.	Men's White Broadcloth Cotton Shirts, asst. sizes @ $16.00	32.00
			$110.00

Ship freight.

Sincerely yours,
Charles Bloom

Acknowledgments

Dear Mr. Thayer:

Thank you for your order of October 5. As you instructed, it will be shipped freight, via the D & W. The order is being made up today and will be at the yards tomorrow. It should reach you well within the time you specified.

Sincerely yours,
J. H. Hudson

Dear Mr. Jones:

We have just telegraphed you the following: "Cannot ship your order May 10. Goods not available." The telegram was sent to minimize any incon-

venience this may cause you. We can supply the cheaper grade, #43, on the date required. The earliest we can supply the #41 grade specified in your order would be June 11. If the #43 grade is all right, please wire collect and we will ship immediately.

Sincerely yours,
Adam Pierce

Dear Mr. Poynter:

Thank you for your order of August 14.

Unfortunately your letter did not specify which color or colors, and which weight or weights, you wish. In our Queen's Taste stationery line the colors are Rose, Fern, Mauve, Beige, Robin's Egg, Canary, Russet, Shell White, and Alpine Snow. The weights are Tissue, Regular and Baronial. Probably our catalogue was not at hand when you made out your order. We are enclosing another giving samples of each color and weight.

A prompt reply will be to our mutual advantage.

Yours sincerely,
Eric Hunter

Dear Mr. Magnes:

Thank you for your order for Clover Danish Blue Cheese. It is being shipped out to you today.

We enclose a catalogue of our other products. Please note that with orders of $10.00 or more, customers may receive, free, their choice of a jar of Lingonberry or Currant preserves.

Yours sincerely,
Einar Toksvig

Follow-Ups on Orders

Sometimes orders are poorly attended to and it is necessary, strange as it may seem, to jog the attention of the supplier. Here, again, as emphasized in the section on **Complaints and Adjustments,** an irritable tone is inadvisable, even where loss or inconvenience has been caused by the delay. A calm letter will get quicker and more favorable attention and will enhance the writer's status as a considerate customer whose patronage is worth retaining. It is seldom necessary to write more than one reminder; but when that becomes necessary, a sharper tone is not always politic, especially where the writer has reasons of his own for maintaining business relations with the ineffecient firm. Examples:

Gentlemen:

Although our order #216 was acknowledged on June 2, and it is now near the end of the month, the air conditioners have not yet arrived. We have already undergone a hot spell and soon July will be upon us. I cannot understand the delay or your leaving us without an explanation for your delay in delivery of such a seasonal article. Up to now your deliveries have been prompt; and expecting delivery any day, I did not write to you. There is no question now that I shall lose some sales and I expect you to make up for the lost time, not to speak of the lost business, by shipping the goods by express at your expense. Please wire what you plan to do in the matter.

Sincerely yours,
Edward Hines

Answers to follow-ups on orders should be prompt, and they should be tactful even where the tone of the complaining letter is disagreeable. Give the reason for the delay, assure the customer that care will taken to avoid such delays in the future, and specify the date and the manner of the planned shipment.

Dear Mr. Osgood:

We regret the delay in shippping out your order #644, dated February 10.

You probably have read of the recent labor troubles in the lumber industry. These made it difficult for us to secure proper crating materials for the goods. Rather than risk damage in transit we held up the shipment until satisfactory crates were available. We have now managed to get some from another source of supply. Even though our shipping costs have risen, we feel the added expense, like the delay, is preferable to having the machinery arrive in poor condition.

Your order was shipped out today, express. We hope it reaches you in good time as, we are confident now, it will reach you in good order.

Sincerely yours,
Mark Lyons

Letters with Enclosures

When remittance such as checks, etc., or when invoices or special notices are enclosed, the number of enclosures should be stated in the letter. This is customarily done in a separate line, at the left margin, under the signature.

Gentlemen:

The enclosed check for $146.00 is in settlement of our account to date. We also enclose your bill. Please receipt and return it.

Sincerely yours,
Joseph Evans

2 enclosures

Gentlemen:

Thank you for your order #324 for a dozen Pop-Up Toasters. They were shipped today. The invoice is enclosed. We also enclose the catalogue on waffle irons requested in your letter.

Sincerely yours
Morton James

2 enclosures

Letters of Introduction

Letters of introduction should not be given thoughtlessly. Avoid them unless you can feel that it would actually be in the interest of both parties to get acquainted. Good-natured people often do harm when they mean to do good, by writing letters of introduction indiscriminately. The tenth "promising" young chap sent to glean advice in the field of his ambition from a busy executive is likely to get a discouraging brushoff.

Therefore, the first consideration in writing a letter of introduction is whether to write it at all. Having decided that the letter should be written, you might well consider several other elements. Since the best way to present letters of introduction is in person, the envelope containing the introduction should be unsealed and should bear the name of the person to whom it is addressed and, in the lower left-hand corner, the line "Introducing Mr. . . ." This enables the recipient to welcome the caller by name and facilitates the relationship.

The letter should be brief and restrained. A long letter might impose an embarrassingly long wait on the caller while the letter is read. And extravagant statements about the caller, if they do not predispose the reader to skepticism, may evoke embarrassing comments of other sorts.

Sometimes there is a reason to mail the letter to the person addressed; for example, to allow him to appoint a time for the meeting. In that case a copy should be sent to the person being introduced so that he will be familiar with what has been said about him. Examples:

Dear Mr. Clements:

I hope you will have the time to see Mr. Wilbur, who was a student in my class this semester. You have several times expressed an interest in seeing "the cream of the crop" in each graduating class. It is because I can unreservedly place Mr. Wilbur in that category that I have suggested that he call on you.

Yours sincerely,
Roger Hessian

Dear Mr. Canning:

It gives me great pleasure to introduce to you Mr. Harvey Wright, who operates a large bottling plant in our city.

Mr. Wright is contemplating opening a branch in your city, and I could think of no one better for him to see than you for a quick survey of local conditions and prospects. My business association with Mr. Wright is now in its twelfth year and has led to a friendship which has enabled me to discover and appreciate his personal qualities.

I feel certain that any association this introduction may result in will be valued on both sides.

Yours sincerely,
Hiram Godkin

Letters of Recommendation

There are two main types of recommendation—the general recommendation "to whom it may concern," and the individual recommendation addressed to a specific person. The latter obviously is preferable, since the writer's personal acquaintance with the person addressed generally means that the letter will be given more attention than might otherwise be the case.

The best kind of recommendation is the one that performs a mutual service to the recommended person and the one to whom he is sent. So far as possible, therefore, it is well to find out beforehand whether and how the person about whom you are writing can be of service to the individual you are addressing.

Vital to any letter of recommendation is truthfulness and restraint. False statements are almost inevitably found out. In time they create handicaps that outweigh any temporary advantage that they gain for the person recommended. And exaggerated claims usually predispose the reader to skepticism and suspicion, and thus are often more injurious than helpful. Examples:

To Whom It May Concern:

Mr. Clarence Loman has been on our sales staff for the past eight years and has compiled an excellent sales record. He is a friendly person by nature and has won the friendship as well as the business patronage of his customers. We have convincing evidence of that from the letters we have received in response to the announcement of his retirement from traveling.

For reasons of health he cannot continue traveling, but he can serve in an inside position. We regret there is nothing of this kind available in our organization. He would make a crackerjack inside salesman and we can unreservedly recommend him to anyone in need of a person with real selling talents. It would take him no time to get a feeling of your stock and your methods; and to establish really friendly relations with customers. We are confident that he would be an asset to any firm that can use his services.

Very truly yours,
Martin Ullmann

Dear Mr. Carter:

I am taking the liberty of writing to you because

I know that you sometimes give out manuscripts for first readings, and accepted manuscripts for preparations for the printer, to qualified young people, on a free-lance basis. I have heard that you do this, as a means of testing or training candidates for anticipated future openings in your editorial staff.

If that is the case, I feel that you will appreciate my sending Miss Ethel Willison to you. You have already become acquainted with her work and have even complimented her, without knowing it, when you complimented me on the excellent shape of the manuscript I turned in, and again, when I sent back corrected proofs. Miss Willison assisted me through all the stages of my book, and it is to her that I owe the smoothness and ease with which it went through all its stages.

Miss Willison has taken all the courses given here in preparation for a career in publishing and has applied what she learned, first on the college paper and, later, in helping other faculty members, as she has helped me, in preparing articles and books.

I am confident that she is just the kind of person you will look for when you are considering taking on a new editorial assistant. I take great pleasure in recommending her to you.

Sincerely yours,
David Proctor

Social Correspondence
in Business

Though the phrase "strictly business" symbolizes freedom from emotional involvements in or out of business, the words connote an attitude or a goal, rather than the reality of business itself. It would be unnatural to expect that human beings, who spend most of their waking hours in business, would not form personal relationships of varying degrees of closeness in the course of their business. The truth is that most of the friendships men form in their mature years arise out of business contacts. And friendly qualities are recognized as assets in business.

This is so generally understood that trade associations of businessmen have the fostering of friendly cooperation as their major aim. Generally, too, a business relationship would hardly be accounted good or secure if it failed to develop some measure of personal regard between heads or representatives of the two firms.

Consequently, there are many occassions for letters that should not be "strictly business," although they are essential to the conduct of business. Examples are given in the following pages:

Letters of Congratulations

Dear Mr. Leonard:

What a pleasure it was to see the item in *The Times* business section this morning about your promotion to the position of Sales-Manager. Actually I think I ought to write to the President of your concern, Mr. Tate, to congratulate him. He had the good sense to recognize a good man. From what I know about people in the field he couldn't have picked a better man. Congratulations on a well-deserved promotion.

Dear Mr. Slocum:

I don't know how others are reacting to the news in this morning's real-estate section, but I want to congratulate you on taking such a far-sighted and enterprising step. I have already heard some say that the site is too remote for such a development, but I put them with those who once thought Forty-second Street was too far outside the city. I think you have judged

correctly that the site is directly in the path of the city's future growth.

Again, my congratulations and my best wishes for the success of a project which should serve the community as well as bring you well-deserved returns.

Admiringly yours,
Edmund Gates

Letters of Sympathy and Condolence

Dear Walter:

When your secretary called this morning to tell me that you wouldn't be able to keep our appointment because of your sudden illness, I was deeply disturbed. She told me that you were to spend some days in the hospital, under observation, to determine whether an operation will be necessary. I hope the tests indicate no such necessity and that you will be back in your office very soon and in condition to renew our postponed engagement.

Cordially yours,
Arthur Reinhardt

Dear Mrs. Rodd:

It was a hard blow to us, too, to hear of your husband's death. We missed him here, very much, two years ago, when he retired. During our association with him over the twelve years that he was with us, all of us developed the highest regard for his wonderful qualities. We can fully understand how deeply you must feel his loss. But it must be a consolation to you that his last years were serene. We and his other friends feel grateful to you for having contributed so much to making him so happy.

Sincerely yours,
Charles U. Clifford

Dear George:

I was very sorry to receive the sad news of your great loss. I know that nothing anyone may say at a time like this can assuage your deep grief, but I hope that you will soon find abiding comfort in the high regard everyone had for your father's accomplishments, and in the good health, happiness, and achievements of those dear to you. I hope you will have no more sorrow for many years to come.

Sincerely yours,
Frank

Dear Mr. Cass:

I have just learned of the emergency appendicitis operation you have had to undergo. I had Miss Hale phone the hospital immediately and was reassured to hear that there were no complications and that you are getting along nicely.

That's fine and we want to keep it so. Therefore, I want it understood that no matter how good your recovery is, you are not to come back to the office until the doctor, on his most conservative estimate, tells you you may. And don't think of the office. This is an order!

In the meanwhile, to help you pass the time, there will be a package of books at the hospital. The well-read Miss Hale did the choosing and I think she has a good idea of your taste.

With all best wishes,
Robert E. Griffin

Accepting Invitations

Dear Mr. Canby:

It will be a pleasure to see you when I visit New York next month. Thank you for suggesting it. Indeed one of the prospects that made the trip so pleasing to me was the opportunity it might give me to become acquainted with you personally.

Sincerely yours,
Elmer Robinson

Dear Sir:

I consider it a great honor to be asked to speak at the Credit Men's Luncheon next month. Thank you very much.

I hope the enclosed data are what you need for the newspaper release. And I will be on hand an hour before the start of the luncheon, as you suggest, to talk over the details of the program.

Yours very truly,
Leon Hart

Declining Invitations

Dear Mr. Hopkins:

Unfortunately I will be out of town during the week of March 10 and will not be able, therefore, to be present at the reception celebrating the opening of your new store. Since I will not be there to offer my congratulations to you in person, permit me to do so here. And I wish to add my sincere best wishes for the success of the new store and the continued growth of your business.

Sincerely yours,
Anthony Asch

Dear Mr. Mann:

It is with deep regret that I must decline the great honor of organizing and heading the committee to arrange a reception for the Vice-President, who is to be one of the speakers at our coming convention. As you may have heard, Mr. Bixby, head of our Foreign Department, died suddenly last week. I have had to take over his duties temporarily, which for the present rules out any other activities for me. I will let you know as soon as I am free again for any service to the organization.

Sincerely yours,
Horace Seton

Resignations

Dear Sir:

I have just been appointed Coordinator of Sales for our firm. This will mean extensive traveling in order to keep in continual contact with our stores throughout the country. It will, therefore, be impossible for me to continue to serve as secretary of the club. And, so, with deep regret, I must tender my resignation from that office.

It has been a pleasure to serve the club during the past four years, and I have enjoyed and profited from the association with its able officers and members. Needless to say, I will be on hand for every get-together my new duties will permit.

Sincerely yours,
Edwin Robbins

Dear Sir:

I have agreed to serve on the Mayor's Committee for Emergency Housing. Since it may prejudice the value of the work I can do for the committee, if I continue as a member of the firm, I am submitting my resignation to take effect immediately.

This is a step I take not without regret, for the years I have been privileged to spend with the firm have been happy ones. But I feel that the opportunity afforded me by the Mayor to serve the community in so important a sphere of activity is one that I cannot pass up.

Sincerely yours,
Alan W. Furness

Inter-Office Correspondence

In concerns of any size a good many memos pass between departments, between the management and the staff, between individuals in different departments, etc. Thus the Stock Department may inform the Sales Department of the arrival of certain needed goods; or the management will send memoranda to department heads about certain changes of policy; or it may send a memo to the entire staff about price changes, the announcement of a special holiday, etc.; or a salesman may send a note to Shipping giving special instructions regarding the shipment of an order; or Promotion may send a memo to Sales and other departments concerned, reminding them of the start of a national advertising campaign so that they can prepare for the anticipated inquiries and orders.

Most firms provide printed forms and restrict inter-office correspondence to one subject only in order to encourage conciseness and clarity and to facilitate filing and reference. The printed forms also assure that the date, the department, the person, and the subject are clearly indicated. This makes salutations and signatures superfluous and they are omitted except in memoranda with a deliberately personal touch.

Although such notes are "stripped for action," the tone should nevertheless always be courteous. Inter-departmental feuds have often begun over tactless expression in such memoranda. And office morale has sometimes been damaged by an unintended curt note by management. Certain indispensible formalities of respect should be observed in inter-office correspondence as in other forms. Examples:

Form G-14	One Subject Only
Inter-Office Memo-	Made Simple Books
randum	Inc.
To:	From:
Department:	Department:
Subject:	Date:

To: Staffs	From: J. B. Wolcott
Department: Sales,	Department: Man-
Correspondence	agement
Subject: New Price	Date: April 10, 1954
List	

On May 1, our new price-list goes into effect. Copies should be in the hands of all our salesmen before the end of the week and in the hands of our dealers by April 28. Copies can be obtained from Miss Andrews.

To: Staffs	From: G. E. Ander-
Department: All	son
departments	Department: Per-
Subject: July 4	sonnel
Holiday	Date: July 1, 1954

Since July 4, this year, falls on a Sunday, the office will be closed Monday, July 5, to allow a full holiday weekend.

To: Mr. Taylor, Mr.	From: Edward
Green, Mr. Johns,	Earnshaw
Mr. Maxfield	Department: Promo-
Department: Sales,	tion
Shipping, Personnel,	Date: February 10,
Accounting	1954
Subject: Advertising	
campaign	

This weekend our special advertising campaign on our new Infra-Red cooker opens with full pages in the magazine supplements of metropolitan newspapers. There will be page ads in leading national magazines, along with other promotion: Most of the advertising will carry keyed coupons. Your departments should be prepared for the special load of mail that will come in. Just a reminder.

To: E. Dirksen	From: J. Meyers
Department:	Department: Sales
Shipping	Date: January 11,
Subject: Johnson	1954
Brothers order	

Dear Ed:

When Billing sends down the Johnson Brothers' order, please put a note on it to double wrap the shipment. Old Mr. Johnson complains that our wrapping paper isn't thick enough. The trouble is in his storeroom, which is a filthy damp place. So it'll be best to double wrap his stuff, or he'll come back at us with claims for spoilage. Hope it's not too much bother. Thanks.

Joe

Other types of memo forms frequently used are:

From the Desk of Frank Gannon

To:_____ Date:_____

To:_____ Date:_____

From:_____

It might be noted, in passing, that in large corporations or organizations, intra-company mail is frequently placed in heavy-stock envelopes that can be used over and over again. These envelopes have ruled lines on the outside, and the sender need merely place on the first free line the name and department of the person to whom the communication is addressed. That person in turn can use the same envelope by doing similarly the next time he wishes to dispatch a memo or some papers to another person in the organization.

Good-Will Letters

It should be enough, of course, to service customers promptly and efficiently. Yet it is human for them to want to be appreciated as well and to be given personal attention. If thanking a customer for his order has been overlooked, write him a special note of appreciation for his business.

Letting customers feel that they are "in" on your operations is another way of building their good will. If you are expanding your business, or promoting a man on your staff with whom your customers may have had occasion to become acquainted, or if you are making any operational change of interest to them, let your customers know about it.

If you are making gifts—calendars, personal memopads, initialed pencils, etc.,—to new customers, don't leave the old customers out. Give it to them, also.

There are also occasions and circumstances that might be used for the promotion of good will by drawing attention to them. We have already mentioned letters of congratulation and letters of sympathy and condolence. Watch significant dates in the lives or careers of customers, when it is possible or advisable—anniversaries of the concern, birthdays of the officers, marriages in their families, and send congratulations and appropriate gifts.

Send Christmas greetings to all customers, and mail them well in advance of the rush period, so that they don't come so late as to seem like afterthoughts.

Unusual occurrences may be made the occasion for a good-will note. Thus when Lever Brothers were constructing their striking New York building, they sent letters to all in the neighborhood within range of the sounds of construction, private families in nearby residential blocks as well as business neighbors, apologizing for the noise. They gave assurance that everything was being done to finish the building as soon as possible and that all avoidable construction sounds were being eliminated.

During the recent period of rapid and successive price boosts some firms notified their customers that they were not raising their prices though raw-material costs had risen; and others explained what they were doing to absorb part of the necessary price advances in operational economies.

Good will within an organization is as important as the good will of outside customers and neighbors. Well run concerns make use of their inter-office correspondence to keep up office morale through informational memoranda that make the staff feel they are part of what is happening: through announcements that will please the staff; and through personal notes of congratulation from management on pleasant occasions, such as the birth of children, the graduation of sons, etc.; and condolences in bereavements. Examples:

Dear Mr. Smythe:

The enclosed is the latest issue of our house organ, *Cuttings*. I am sure you will be interested in the piece on page twelve, on the old Smythe Tool Works which, I believe, were founded by your great-grandfather.

Would you like to get *Cuttings* regularly? I'd have it sent without asking if it weren't for my own experience. I groan at the amount of unsolicited mail I get from people who send it with the best of intentions; there aren't enough hours in the day to read everything that comes through the mail. So for that reason I have made it a policy to send *Cuttings* only if customers let us know that they want it. Incidentally, I shall be happy to send you as many copies of this issue as you may require.

Sincerely yours,
Gabriel Harcourt

Dear Mr. Connor:

It occurred to me, recently, that it was just about ten years ago that I entered your first order with our company in our order book. I was not then sales manager, of course—that came as the result of the good orders you and other friendly customers favored me with.

To make sure, I had my secretary look it up, and it turned out, sure enough, that our business connections did begin ten years ago, this month! That first order, incidentally, was for an assortment of our fans. Your latest order is for air conditioners! Time does move.

If we could get together, we'd be celebrating the glad occasion properly at Ludlow's or Keen's. But since that's not possible, here's the next best thing. Please join me in a glass of champagne of a kind I've found particularly palatable. A case of it should be in your office this morning if American Express is on its toes.

Your health and best wishes for ten more good years of business together.

Cordially,
Ed Schacht

Dear Mr. Alter:

We prepared a map for use by our office staff of the new city postal zones. It proved to be such a convenience that we decided to print up copies for our customers. Here's your copy and we hope you'll find it useful.

Sincerely yours,
Conrad Dietrichstein

Dear Mr. Freud:

As a customer of the Hooker Hat Company you will be interested to know that we have just completed negotiations which bring this fine firm into our organization. It was our desire to fill out our line of men's furnishings with a quality hat line, and Hooker was our choice.

We were glad, of course, that with so fine a product we could make the acquaintance of new customers appreciative of fine quality apparel for men.

We want to assure you that you will continue to receive the efficient service you have become accustomed to from the Hooker staff (which is being preserved intact), plus, we venture to add, special services made possible by the facilities of our larger organization.

On his next call your Hooker salesman will have our other lines of quality goods to offer you. We are mailing you our catalogue so that you may become acquainted with them. Any orders you wish to place from the catalogue will be credited to the salesman's account, and you will be billed on the same terms as in your account with Hooker.

Please let us know if there is any way that we can be of service to you. I look forward to the continuance of what I hope will be a pleasant and profitable relationship for us both.

Sincerely yours,
A. E. Handley

Dear Mr. Gates:

Thank you for your order number 112, which arrived this morning. It will be shipped today; the invoice is enclosed.

The same company is making a new line of waffle irons, and the introductory offer is so attractive we decided to call it to the attention of all our customers. We have tested the device and found it sturdy and efficient. We are enclosing a circular giving the details. Perhaps you'll want to take advantage of this offer.

Sincerely yours,
Morton James

2 enclosures

Dear Mr. Magnus:

Thank you for your order of Clover Danish Blue Cheese. It is being shipped to you today.

I think you will be interested in seeing a copy of a periodical we issue, *Good Cheer*, which contains recipes and notes about new European delicacies being introduced to American lovers of good foods. If you would like to receive it regularly, we shall be glad to put you on our mailing list.

Sincerely yours,
Gail Longinetti

1 enclosure

Requests for Charity

Although the solicitation of contributions for charity is a highly specialized, professional activity these days, businessmen frequently have occasion to sell theater tickets or to ask for donations for a pet organization. In such cases make your letter brief; leave the "selling" to the professional fund-raiser. You will get a check because the person you are writing to knows you, and values your friendship or patronage. Some examples:

Dear Mr. Adams:

I am taking the liberty of sending you the enclosed advertising blank in behalf of the United Orphans League. I am very much interested in the organization and know of its good work and great need. I shall appreciate your check to the best of your ability. With many thanks and good wishes, I am,

Sincerely yours,
Sam Laury

Dear Ben:

Enclosed are a couple of tickets for "Ah, Take the Cash." The seats are not so good, and I don't know anything about the show, but the cause is good. So I'd appreciate your taking the tickets and letting me have your check for $20 made out to the Community Chest. I hope you will enjoy the show and have the double satisfaction of knowing you've aided a worthy cause.

Sincerely yours,
Norman Rich

Although it is desirable to keep letters of this type short, they can vary in tone, length, and appeal if in the judgement of the writer, the nature of his relationship with the person to whom he is writing requires more than the semi-formal approach illustrated above.

Example of an Acceptance Letter

Dear Mr. Bingham:

I am happy to send you the enclosed check for the theater tickets you sent me. I know the cause is a good one, and I hope the project is a success. Keep up the good work.

Sincerely yours,
David K. Nelson

Words and Expressions to Avoid

Superfluous, Overformal, Flabby, Tactless, Hackneyed Language

According to our records—Often superfluous and can be omitted.

Acknowledge receipt of your letter—Overformal. Better, **We thank you for your letter.**

(Please) advise—Better **inform** or **tell** unless actually soliciting advice.

Agreeable to your letter—Old fashioned.

Along these lines—Better, **the gist of his remarks** or simply **like.**

Amount of, preceded by **in the, to the, for the**—Better say **check** or **remittance** for $_____.

(Please) arrange to return—Sufficient to say, **please return.**

As per your letter—**As per** is a legal term, therefore out of place in an ordinary letter. Better, **according to** or **as mentioned in.**

As stated above—Better to repeat what you stated, or **as I have mentioned.**

As yet—For **yet.**

Assuring you of—Old fashioned.

As to—Awkward.

At all times, at this time—Usually superfluous.

At hand—Usually superfluous.

Attached you will find—Overformal. Better, **we are attaching** or **we are enclosing.**

At the present time—**Now** is preferable.

At this writing—Formal. Better **now.**

At your earliest convenience, at an early date, at the earliest possible moment—Overformal. Better say **soon.**

Awaiting your favor—Better, **please let us hear from you soon.**

Beg—Relic of old-fashioned courtesy, now abandoned in business correspondence.

Claim—Avoid in the sense of **to assert** or **assertion;** might antagonize.

Communication—Formal. Better, **message, letter, report, inquiry,** etc.

Complaint—Aggressive sound. Usually better to say **request for adjustment.**

In compliance with your request—Overformal.

Contents noted—Superfluous.

(To) date—Overformal. "To date we have not received"—better, **we have not yet received.**

Deal—Improperly used for **transaction.**

It is desired that we receive—Inactive, weak, and long-winded. Better, **we want to receive** or **we'd appreciate receiving.**

We have duly investigated—**Duly** is superfluous.

Each and every—**Each** or **every** is sufficient by itself.

Early date—May mean two or three days or two or three weeks. Better be specific.

Enclosed please find—Better **here is** or **I enclose.**

Esteemed—Old-fashioned.

Even date—(meaning today). Better be specific. Say **your letter of this morning** or **of December _____ 19 _____.**

Event—Avoid "in the event that." **If** is preferable.

Favor—In sense of letter—old-fashioned, better say **your letter of _____.** Only proper, nowadays, when referring to a specific act of kindness.

For the reason that—**Because** is preferable.

Forward—**Send** or **ship** are preferable.

For your information—Superfluous. Omit.

Hand you—**Send out check** or **enclose our check** preferable.

Have for acknowledgement—Simpler to say "thanks."

Herewith—Superfluous.

Hoping—Weak and usually superfluous. Avoid, especially as dangling particple before complimentary close of letter.

Inasmuch as—Just say, **because.**

(We are) in receipt of—Overformal. Better, **we have received** or **thank you for.**

In order to—Just say **to.**

In reference to—Overformal, avoid. Better, **about.**

In regard to—Just say **about.**

In reply would wish to—Overformal, avoid.

Instant—Abbreviated as Inst., meaning the current month. A legal term, out of place in ordinary correspondence. Better name the month—instead of "the 5th Inst." say **October 5.**

In the nature of—Long-winded. Just say **like.**

It is the hope of the undersigned—for **I hope.**

Kindly let us know—Kindly is old fashioned. **Please let us know** is preferable.

Liberty (May we take the liberty to . . .)—Usually no

liberty involved. Preferable to be direct and say **may we.**

Line—Sometimes inaccurately used in sense of a business.

(To) lineup—Vague. Better say **try to interest, try to sell,** etc.

Lot—Often inaccurately used to indicate quantity. Watch it.

Miss—Avoid using alone. Always use with a name.

Must say—Avoid. Just say it.

Oblige—Antiquated.

Our Mr. . . .—Pretentious. If name does not sufficiently identify him, describe him as **Mr. . . . , our representative,** or **our Chicago manager,** etc.

Passive constructions—Avoid them. Recast when convenient into active construction. Instead of **The goods ordered by you have been shipped,** say **We have shipped the goods you ordered.**

Permit me to say—No permission needed; just say it.

Pertaining to—**About** is better.

Pleasure (We take pleasure in)—Overformal. Better, **We are sending** or **are glad to send.**

Posted—In sense of informed, is a poor usage. Better say **informed** or **well informed.**

Prior to—**Before** is better.

Pronoun—Should not be omitted because of risk of sounding curt. Avoid, "Goods received. Sending check today." Better say, "We have received the goods and are sending you our check today."

Proposition—Avoid using the term in the sense of task. "To ship this order during the Christmas rush will be a difficult proposition" is not as good as "To ship this order during the Christmas rush will be difficult."

Proximo—(Abbreviated as prox.) Meaning next month. Legal term, out of place in ordinary business correspondence. Say **next month.**

Pursuant to your order—Overformal. Better say **following your directions.**

Recent date—your letter of—Preferable, **your letter** or **your order of . . .** (give date).

Regret—When used the following way: **we regret very deeply,** or **most sincerely,** overformal. Better, **I'm sorry,** or **I regret.**

Replying, Regarding, Referring—Weak. Avoid hanging participles. The simple straight statement is usually more direct and forceful.

Return mail—Shopworn. Better, **this week.**

Same—Stilted. Instead of "We received the goods and found same satisfactory," "We received the goods and found them satisfactory."

State—Not as good as simple word **say** or some other expression. For example: Instead of as **stated above,** use **as we have said** or merely repeat the statement.

Thanking you in advance—A trite device; may antagonize as unwarranted.

Thank you again—Once is enough.

Trust—**Hope, believe, think,** etc. preferable.

Ultimo—(Abbreviation ult.) Meaning last month. A legal term, out of place in business correspondence. Better say, **last month.**

Under separate cover—Use sparingly. Better specify means of shipment, **we are sending you by parcel post.**

(The) Undersigned—Overformal. Preferable to say **I.**

Valued—Formal word. Avoid expressions like **your valued patronage.**

We—In place of **I,** is right only when emphasis is on action by the firm. Otherwise it is preferable to say **I.**

Wish to say—Say it.

Would say—Say it.

(The) Writer—Overformal. Don't hesitate to say **I.**

Glossary of Terms Commonly
Used in Business and Formal
Correspondence

Abstract of Title—Record summarizing deeds, mortgages, and other documents and transactions affecting title to a piece of real estate.

Accessory after the Fact—One who knowingly aids the criminal after a criminal act.

Accessory before the Fact—One who instigates or aids in a crime but takes no part in its commission.

Accommodation Paper—Negotiable paper bearing the endorsement of a person who thereby lends his credit to the maker of the paper.

Account—Right to transact business in a bank by depositing money or its equivalent therein; a salesman's customers; business transacted with a firm or an individual; right to conduct business with a firm by establishing credit; record of business transactions with a firm or an individual.

Accountant—One skilled in keeping the accounts of a firm and responsible for their accuracy. Certified Public Accountants (abbrev. CPA), corresponding to a Chartered Accountant in England, is one who has qualified for a certificate from the state and is consequently engaged to check on and certify the accuracy of a firm's books.

Account Sales—Record delivered by a broker or commission merchant to the owner of a consignment of goods, showing the amount and sale prices of goods sold and deductions for commissions and freight and other expenses.

Actuary—One whose profession is to calculate insurance risks and premiums.

Adjust (in insurance)—To determine the sum to be paid in settlement of a loss covered by a policy. **Adjustor, Adjuster**—one who makes the settlement in claims arising out of losses or complaints with the purpose of avoiding possible litigation.

Administrator, Administratrix—A person appointed by a court to settle an estate.

Advertising—Promotion of business through notices in the public prints, on posters, by radio, television, or other media. **Classified Advertising**—small advertisements listed alphabetically. **Display Advertising**—large advertisements usually using illustrations and type arrangements for effect. **Poster Advertising**—advertising on large cards posted in public places. **Outdoor Advertising**—very large advertising posted on roadside structures, on top of buildings, on sides of wall, etc. **Car Card Advertising**—small poster inserted in panels on cars, buses, railroad cars, etc. **Radio Advertising**—advertising over the radio with an "advertiser" paying the cost of programs as "sponsor." **Television Advertising**—advertising over television with an "advertiser" paying the cost of programs as "sponsor." **Mail Order Advertising**—advertising by mail or periodical advertisements, leading to purchases transacted by mail.

Affiant—A signer of an affidavit.

Affidavit—An attestation of the truth of a written statement.

Affiliate—A company in financial association with another.

Agent—Person or company acting for another person or company.

Agreement—Mutual consent to terms of trade or employment, usually in written form.

Allocation—Apportionment of goods in short supply so that all companies, when the government is the allocator, or all customers, when a company is the allocator, may secure a share assigned according to their regular consumption or their comparative immediate needs.

Allowance—A customary deduction from the gross weight of goods; in law, a sum in addition to regular taxable costs awarded by the court; a reduction in cost allowed the purchaser by the seller.

Amortization—Gradual liquidation of a mortgage or other debt by periodic payments in addition to interest.

Announcer—A person hired by a radio station or commercial sponsor to introduce radio programs and performers.

Annuity (in insurance)—Annual or periodic income to the insured for life or for a specified long term.

Appeal—Resort to a higher court for review of a lower court's decision in the hope of having it reversed, or the case retried.

Appraise—To set a value on goods, land, the estate of a deceased person; to estimate loss as by fire, etc.; **Appraisal**—act of appraising or the stated result of appraising; **Appraiser**—one designated by court or appointed by agreement to set a value on property.

Appreciate—To increase in value; **Appreciation**—a rise in value.

Arbitrage—Purchase of stock in one market for profitable resale in another.

Arbitration—Submission of a dispute to judgment by a third party agreed on by both parties to the dispute.

Arraignment—Formal summoning of accused into court where indictment is read to him and he is called upon to plead "guilty" or "not guilty."

Arrival Notice—Announcement by transportation company to consignee when shipment reaches destination.

Arson—Deliberate burning of a house (in some states, of any property); a statutory crime.

Assess—To set a value for taxation; to impose a fine; to impose a contribution as a "lodge assessment." **Assessment**—a valuation of property; a fine; an imposed contribution; **Assessor**—one appointed or elected to value property for taxation.

Asset Currency (in banking)—Currency secured exclusively by the general assets of the issuing bank as distinguished from that secured by special deposit of government bonds, commercial paper, etc.

Assets (Property)—In accounting, items on balance sheet of business showing book values of its resources as at a given date; **Fixed or Permanent Assets**—land, building, machinery, capital stock of another company which can be used repeatedly; **Current, Liquid or Floating Assets**—cash or materials which can be used only at one time; **Quick Assets**—cash or goods which can be immediately disposed of without loss.

Association—Organization of a large number of people

to transact business; if not incorporated, members are liable for its debts as in a partnership.

Attachment—Court order authorizing seizure of property, usually pending outcome of trial.

Auction—Public sale of property by competitive bidding of prospective buyers.

Auctioneer—A person whose job it is to conduct auction sales.

Audit—A verification of accounts; to make an audit.

Auditor—A person authorized to examine accounts.

Backlog—Amount of orders remaining to be filled.

Balance (in bookkeeping)—To prepare an accounting of assets and liabilities; the money in a bank account left after current withdrawals.

Balance Sheet—Statement of financial condition showing current assets and liabilities.

Bank—Institution where money or other property is deposited **A National Bank** is one organized under the National Bank Act; it functions as a commercial bank but may have trust and savings departments, depending on the laws of the state in which it operates. **A State Bank** is organized under state laws; it operates as a commercial bank, but may have trust and savings departments. **A Commercial Bank** does business primarily in short-term and seasonal loans to business organizations. **A Savings Bank** does business primarily in savings and their investment, but may also do commercial banking where state law permits. **A Trust Company** acts as fiduciary agent for trust funds of individuals or corporations; if part of commercial bank, trust funds are separate from bank funds. The **Federal Reserve Bank** is a banker's bank acting under the Federal Reserve Act as agent for the government in relations with other banks. The **Land Bank** lends money on real estate mortgages under terms of the Federal Farm Loan Act.

Bank Discount—Interest deducted in advance.

Banker—Officer of a bank. **Investment Banker** is one who supplies capital in securities, and finances transactions or advises on investments. **Private Banker** generally lends money to finance international projects, may also engage in commercial banking.

Bankruptcy—Condition of a company unable to meet its debts. In **Voluntary Bankruptcy,** the company petitions to be declared bankrupt; in **Involuntary Bankruptcy,** a creditor or group of creditors is the petitioner.

Bargain—Agreement or terms of a sale; purchase of material at an advantage.

Barter—Direct exchange of commodities without use of money.

Bear—One with a pessimistic attitude toward business; one who anticipates downswings in the market, as opposed to Bull.

Beneficiary—One in whose benefit a gift, trust fund income, or insurance money, is drawn.

Bequeath—To will personal property (property other than realty).

Bid—A possible offer at which goods will be supplied or work performed.

Big Board—A term for the New York Stock Exchange.

Bill—Account of or invoice for goods sold or work done. Abbreviations for "bill or exhcange," now chiefly designating piece of paper money.

Bill of Lading—Certificate drawn up and signed by transportation company, enumerating articles being shipped; acts as contract and receipt for shipment.

Binder—A sum of money or other valuable consideration binding parties to a contract.

Black Market—Trading that violates legal restrictions such as price ceilings, etc.

Blanket—Covering everything, rather than a specified item, such as blanket insurance, etc.

Block (in currency)—Legal prohibition or restriction of foreign credit, currency, securities or other property, usually during war; e.g., blocked currency.

Blue Chip—A stock regarded as an especially good investment.

Board of Directors—Group of persons directing affairs of a company, corporation, or association.

Board Room—Room in which Board of Directors meets; room in brokerage office containing board on which is posted records of transactions, prices, etc.

Board of Trade—Organization for advancement of business, usually of an industry or geographical area such as a town or state.

Bourse—The Paris Stock Exchange

Bond—An interest-bearing certificate of indebtedness; a bond differs from stock in not representing ownership. In actuality, bonds are long-term interest-bearing notes representing loans; or goods being manufactured, stored, or transported under care of bonded agencies.

Bonded Debt—Bond issue representing indebtedness.

Bonus—Extra goods shipped without charge on an order; sum given to employee in addition to contracted wages or salary.

Bookkeeper—One who keeps "books" or accounts of a company; generally distinguished from an accountant in having less formal training and lower status.

Book Value—Value given to assets on the books of owner, may be above or below current market value.

Boycott—Organized effort to prevent purchases of goods produced by a certain firm or industry and usually arising out of labor trouble.

Brand Name—Name of manufactured article registered to prevent copying.

Breach of Contract—Refusal to carry out terms of a contract in whole or in part.

Brief—Lawyer's statement of his client's case, containing legal citations supporting it.

Broker—Agent; one who buys or sells for another on commission.

Bucket Shop—A dishonest brokerage house where the customer's money is gambled with, against the customer's interest.

Budget—Plan for the expenditure of income.

Building and Loan Association—Association of investors whose savings are used to finance home construction and make loans on improved real estate.

Bull—One with optimistic attitude toward business; one who anticipates upswings in the market; opposite of Bear.

Bullion—Bars of gold and silver intended for coinage.

Business—Commercial transaction; organization conducting commercial transactions.

Business cycle—Recurrent succession of business fluctuations loosely divided into prosperity, crisis, liquidation, depression, recovery.

Call—Purchased rights to demand a certain amount of goods at a fixed price or within a fixed time; demand for payment of money as on a stock-holder, member of a mutual insurance company, etc., to pay installment of subscription to capital, or a contribution to meet losses.

Call Loan—One which may be terminated by either party at any time.

Call Money—Money that must be returned when demanded.

Cancel—To annul an order for goods or services.

Capacity—Calculated space of any form of container from warehouse or ship to carton.

Capital—A stock of accumulated wealth; amount of property and funds as distinguished from income.

Capitalism—An economic system in which capital plays a leading part in production and distribution.

Capitalist—One who uses capital for investment.

Capital Stock—Shares of a corporation considered as an aggregate.

Capital Surplus—Profits, such as from sale of stock above par value, other than earned surplus.

Carrier—A company transporting passengers or freight, e.g., railroad, airlines, bus or trucking company, etc.

Cartel—International combination allocating markets and supplies, and fixing prices in order to eliminate competitive buying and selling.

Catalogue—A list, usually with illustrations and textual description, of items for sale at announced prices.

Ceiling—Maximum wage, rent, etc., fixed by the government.

Certified Check—Bearing the signature or stamp of the cashier of the bank on which it is drawn. Its significance is that the sum has been withdrawn from the account of the drawer and the bank assumes responsibility for payment.

Chain Store—Branch of a large system of stores belonging to a single ownership.

Chamber of Commerce—A board of trade; an association to promote the commerce of a community, state or nation.

Charter—Certificate from the state approving the organization of a company and authorizing it to do business in the approved form.

Check—A standard form of written order to a bank to make a designated payment out of a depositor's balance.

Circulation—In a periodical, the number of purchasers by subscription or individual sales; in a store, movement of customers in and out.

Clearing House—Organization maintained by a banking group to exchange checks and adjust accounts among its members.

Closed Corporation—One in which all stock is privately held in a few hands; it usually may not be disposed of by holders without the consent of the other holders.

C.O.D.—Abbreviation for "cash on delivery." In C.O.D. transactions, goods must be paid for at the time of delivery.

Code—An arrangement of words, letters or other symbols to achieve secrecy or brevity in communication; a set of rules governing the conduct of a business.

Codicil—Addition to a will, modifying some provision in it.

Collateral—Property used as security for a loan.

Collective Bargaining—Negotiations between employers and a committee of their workers and/or representatives of the union.

Co-Maker—One who shares obligations of another by endorsing a contract.

Commercial Paper—Promissory notes of a large, reputable firm; dealt in by note brokers and sold to banks which discount them and, in that way, realize interest on them.

Commission—Percentage or allowance made to broker or agent for transacting business for another, e.g., salesman's commission.

Company—Association of persons for carrying on commercial or industrial enterprise; may be partnership, corporation or other joint enterprise.

Complaint (in law)—Statement of the cause of an action; the person initiating the complaint is called the complainant. In commerce, customer's charge of faulty goods, delivery or other service.

Comptroller—Auditor with the rank of executive.

Consign—To send or address goods by bill of lading, etc., to an agent in another place to be stored, sold or otherwise cared for.

Consignee—One to whom goods are shipped.

Consignment—Transaction in which purchase is not final; unsold goods may be returned to consignor.

Consumer—Ultimate purchaser or user of merchandise.

Contingent Order (in advertising)—Space in small circulation media to be paid for by returns from the advertisement.

Contract—Witnessed agreement, usually in writing, the terms of which are legally enforceable.

Contractor—One who specializes in a certain type of work; e.g., building contractor. **Sub-contractor**—one who performs part of a piece of work; e.g., plumbing sub-contractor.

Convenience Merchandise—Goods kept in a store for the convenience of certain customers.

Cooperative—A business enterprise or association with the object of producing, purchasing, selling, or occupying quarters at common savings to members by eliminating middle-man fees and profits.

Copy—Text of advertising; duplicate of an original letter or of an article of commerce. Ordinarily, carbon copy duplication for typing.

Copyright—Exclusive publication rights, now extended to cover plays, movie scenarios and movie films and radio and television scripts; other pieces of creative work are copyrighted **after** publication. Application must be made to Register of Copyrights, Library of Congress, Washington, D.C.

Corner—To secure such control of stock or commodities as to be able to dictate quotation prices.

Corporation—A business association operating on a state franchise and with liability limited to the amount of the investment.

Co-Sign—To assume joint responsibility in indebtedness by adding one's signature to the note of another.

Cottage Industry—One where operations are performed by workers at home.

Countermand—To reverse a personal order.

Courts—Where cases involving offenses against the law or claims protected by the law are tried. Courts where large claim cases are tried include Superior, Circuit, certain District, Chancery or County courts. Courts where small claim cases are tried are Justice courts, presided over by a Justice of the peace, and include Magistrate's court and certain District courts.

Covenant—Promise of some future action, made in contracts and other legal papers.

Coverage—The amount and type of protection against risks agreed on in an insurance policy.

Credit—Financial standing influencing sales to a concern on deferred payment; permission to defer payment for a certain period.

Creditor—One who extends credit; lender.

Credit Line—Amount of credit extended; e.g., "X's credit line is $2,000." Also, reproduction of signature, symbol or other acknowledgment in print to signify the originator or owner of writing, photographs or illustrations.

Credit Rating—Summary of credit line as published in Dun & Bradstreet or other credit house ratings and reports.

Cum Div—With dividend declared or pending.

Curb Market—The usual reference is to the American

Stock Exchange (formerly New York Curb Exchange), formerly conducted out-of-doors but now housed in a building of its own; it is the second largest stock market in the United States.

Custom—Generally accepted practice, company practice; customer's account.

Customer—Person or concern purchasing goods.

Cut—In printing, zinc etching, or copper or zinc halftone, usually reproducing a picture or hand-lettering.

Cutback—Reduction in production schedule; reduction in salary or other compensation.

Damage—Loss in merchandise, machinery, service, productive capacity or trade standing. Compensation for such damage may be claimed depending on the circumstances, in a court of law.

Dead Spot—Store location at point of little traffic.

Dead Stock—Unsaleable merchandise.

Debenture—Synonym for debt; documentary evidence of debt.

Debit and Credit Memoranda—Issued by companies to effect necessary adjustments in the course of business transactions.

Decontrol—Removal of government restrictions on prices, rents, etc.

Deduction—Sum or money subtracted from amount to be paid for goods or services.

Deed—Contract by which real estate is conveyed by one party to another; **Warranty Deed** contains a guarantee to clear title ownership; **Quick Claim Deed** relinquishes rights of former owner without guaranteeing clear title to purchaser; **Joint Tenancy Deed** transfers property to two or more owners with the provision that the survivor will own the entire property; **Trust Deed** is given as security for a debt and is a form of mortgage; **Tax Deed** is received by purchaser at a tax sale.

Defalcation—Misappropriation of money placed in trust; the sum misappropriated.

Default—To fail in fulfilling a contract or other financial obligation.

Deficit—Amount by which expenses exceed income, liabilities exceed assets, production falls below expectation.

Deflation—Decline in prices, volume of production, etc., usually accompanied by unemployment.

Delaware Corporation—A corporation chartered in Delaware to take advantage of low incorporation fees and tax rates.

Demand—Desire to purchase commodity together with capacity to pay for it.

Demand Bill or Draft—A bill payable at sight, or on demand.

Demand Item—Article in constant demand, which must be carried in stock constantly.

Demand Loan—Loan payable on demand.

Demand Note—Note payable on demand.

Demurrage—Charge by transportation company for detention of carriers beyond allotted time.

Deposit—Money or equivalent entrusted for safe-keeping with another, as in a bank; money given as partial payment in a transaction or as a binder in a contract.

Deposition—Testimony given by witness unable to appear in court.

Depreciation—Decline in value, usually as a result of loss through wear, neglect, exposure, etc. Machinery is usually calculated to suffer an annual depreciation of 10% in value through wear.

Depression—Deep and prolonged deline of industrial and general business activity.

Deteriorate—To spoil or lose quality with time, e.g.,

food and certain manufactured articles such as photographic film.

Detriment—Damage by intangible cause, such as injury to a firm's reputation through rumors.

Devise—To will property in real estate.

Director—Person entrusted with determining policies and decisions of a firm.

Disbursements—Payments to meet bills.

Discount—Allowance for cash or quick payment; **Trade Discounts** are discounts from wholesale prices allowed to customers and scaled according to amount of purchases and other considerations.

Distributor—Person or company through whom goods reach the consuming public; **Wholesale Distributors** supply **Retail Distributors** who serve the public directly.

Dividend—Money paid to shareholders or depositors as share of profits.

Dock Receipt—Signed by steamship company for freight delivered to dock.

Draft—Papers by which one party, usually the seller, orders another party, usually the buyer, to deliver to a third party, usually a bank, a sum to be credited to the account of the first party. Used to assure payment and to secure settlement of unpaid accounts, since rejection of a draft when presented by the bank is recorded and affects credit standing.

Drawee—Bank on which check or draft is drawn.

Drawer—Person who draws money from his bank account by check.

Dry Goods—Commodities made from fabrics.

Due Bill—In brokerage business, a type of IOU by broker, promising to deliver certain stocks not available at time of sale; also used for promised future delivery of dividends, etc.

Dummy—Sample of proposed book, magazine, or booklet to show size, format, and sample pages.

Dummy Corporation—One organized solely for intermediate purposes, and not for open business activity.

Duplicate—Copy or identical likeness, e.g., duplicate of bill.

Duty—Payment imposed by the government on goods imported, exported, or consumed, such as customs duties, excises, etc.

Earned Income—Income derived from wages, salary, or fees in return for labor, advice or management services.

Earned Surplus—Balance of profits and income remaining after deducting losses, dividends, and transfers to capital stock, etc.

Earnest Money—Deposit or binder; a sum of money paid to seal a bargain and to be deducted from purchase payment.

Economy—Organization of the production, distribution, and consumption of goods in a community.

Efficiency Engineer—A person whose profession it is to plan or change production methods to secure greater economy and efficiency.

Embezzle—To fraudulently appropriate to one's own use property entrusted to him.

Endorse (also Indorse)—To sign one's name as a payee or to indicate co-responsibility for payment on a check, bill, note, or other document.

Enterprise—In association with the word "free" or "private" has come to replace "capitalism" to differentiate the non-socialist from the socialist type of economy.

Entrepreneur—One who takes commercial risks; enterpriser.

Entry—Item in a business record.

Equity—In real estate, difference between value of prop-

erty and owner's debt on it. In margin buying difference between market value of a stock and customer's indebtedness for its purchase.

Escrow—Papers or money in keeping of responsible third party such as a bank, held until certain conditions are fulfilled.

Estate—Property in lands or tenements, sometimes inaccurately used for property other than lands or tenements; total property left by a deceased person.

Estimate—Statement of amount of goods to be produced or stored or of sum for which certain work will be done.

Ex-Bonus
Ex-Coupon
Ex-Dividend } Earnings or privileges not included in the purchase of particular shares.
Ex-Interest
Ex-Privileges
Ex-Rights

Exchange—Transfer of goods; place where business interests of a certain sort meet for transaction, e.g., stock exchange, cotton exchange, etc.

Executor (Executrix)—One designated to carry out terms of a will.

Execution—Carrying out a term of a will or a court order.

Expedite—To accelerate production or distribution of goods or rendering of service.

Expediter—One whose job it is to expedite or facilitate business and other transactions.

Export-Import Bank of Washington—Organized by the government in 1934 to facilitate foreign trade.

Express—Shipment by fast or unobstructed transportation; via Railway Express Agency.

Facsimile—Exact copy not necessarily of same size; photostat can serve as satisfactory facsimile.

Factor—Commercial agent who sells or buys goods for others on commission; commission agent.

Factor—Building where manufacture of goods is carried on.

Fail—To become insolvent.

Fee—Compensation for professional or special services; fixed charge for services of a public officer, e.g., sheriff's fee.

Feeder—Branch line in railroad, bus, or air transport that connects with trunkline.

Fee Simple—Unrestricted title to property.

Felony—Crime whose penalty is death or prison sentence.

Fiduciary—In trust; a fiduciary is a trustee.

Finance—Management of money matters.

Financial Rating—Financial information carried in directory such as *Moody's Manual*.

Firm—Correct meaning is partnership; in common usage, any business organization.

Fiscal—Relating to finance, e.g., U.S. fiscal year, period in which annual taxes are collected.

Fixtures—Fixed equipment in business or professional premises.

Foreclosure—Transfer of property to mortgagee when mortgagor defaults on interest payment.

Franchise—Special commercial rights granted by a city to operator of a public conveyance, e.g., a bus line; special rights granted by a manufacturer to a dealer.

Freight Bill—Prepared by transportation company and rendered to receiver or sender, depending on who is paying the freight charges.

Freight Claim—Also called "Loss and Damage Claim" or "Overcharge Claim," claim on transportation company for loss, damage or overcharge.

Fund—Cash or specified assets set aside for a specific purpose.

Funded Debt—Fund set up for payment of long-term indebtedness.

Funded Reserve—A reserve for which a fund has been invested to earn income.

Futures—In commodity exchange, contracts for subsequent delivery, as of a crop not yet harvested.

Garnishee—To take over property or money to satisfy a debt or a claim. A claimant may "garnishee" a defendant's wages.

Gold Standard—Rating of currency in terms of supposed value in gold.

Good will—Intangible asset resting on a special earning power gained through advertising, reputation, good business methods, favorable location, business standing, etc.

Gray Market—Trading by undercover methods, in between black market and regular market methods.

Gross—As a number, 12 dozen or 144; as an adjective, indicating a complete sum before deductions have been made, e.g., gross income before deductions of taxes, expenses, etc.

Handbill—Printed announcement handed out to passers-by.

Handicrafts—Goods produced by hand, e.g., certain pottery, woven goods, embroidery, basket work, etc.

Hedging—Stock trading in which sales or purchases are made to offset or "hedge" against possible loss in other transactions. "Puts and calls" are a form of hedging.

Heir—Person entitled by law or terms of a will to an inheritance.

High Pressure—To make sales of goods not actually needed or desired.

Holding Company—One organized to buy and hold stock of another company.

Holographic Will—One entirely in the handwriting of the testator, not valid in some states.

Huckster—One who prepares radio or television advertising, usually with methods of exaggerated showmanship.

Hypothecation—Pledging of collateral. Governments may "hypothecate" tax revenues as security for a loan. Property may be "hypothecated" for payment of a debt. Its earnings may be so used and the property remain with the debtor; but if payment is defaulted, the creditor may demand sale of the property to secure payment of the debt.

Identification—Driver's license, social security card or other document required as identification in check payments at stores, hotels, or other public places.

Implement—To find means to carry out an agreement.

Impulse Item—Something marketed to appeal to spontaneous decision of customer, usually novelties and luxuries as opposed to staples or necessities.

Income Group—Classification of people according to earnings.

Incorporate—To secure a charter of incorporation from a state, and to organize operations under its provisions.

Indemnify—To make secure against loss or damage; to make good a loss or damage.

Indenture—Sealed agreement of which each party concerned holds a signed copy.

Index—Stock market term referring to listed price quotations of securities traded on the market and analyzed for trends.

Indictment—Formal grand jury charge against a person accused of a major crime.

Industry—Collectively, manufacturing as contrasted to

agriculture; any branch of production, e.g., shoe industry, paper industry, etc.

Inflation—Rise in prices where income advance fails to keep up with prices.

Injunction—Court order restraining certain action.

Insert—Something added in a document; an enclosure in a mailing.

Insolvency—Inability to meet current financial obligations.

Installment—Periodic payment on a time-payment purchase. The British equivalent is "hire-purchase."

Institutional Advertising—Directed not at immediate sales but at increasing prestige leading to consideration of a company as an established institution.

Instrument—Person or document useful in accomplishing a stated purpose.

Interest—Payment by borrower for use of borrowed money measured in percentages and units of time; **simple** interest is payment on principal alone; **compound** interest is payment of accrued interest added to capital; **penal** interest is payment of special interest by defaulting debtor.

Interstate Commerce—Commerce across state boundaries.

Intestate—Descriptive of a property holder who dies without leaving a will. Division of property will then be made according to state inheritance laws.

Intrastate Commerce—Commerce within a state.

Inventory—Record of merchandise on hand and in stock rooms; **perpetual** inventory is one maintained by recording every sale and receipt of goods on an inventory card. Usually inventories are made at periodic intervals.

Investment—Money or other property risked with expectations of profit.

Investment Trust—Company whose business is investment in securities and bond issue, and which markets its own securities on the basis of these investments.

Invoice—A bill itemizing goods shipped and their prices.

IOU—Document bearing the letters "IOU" and a notation of a sum of money. If signed, an IOU has legal status as a debit account.

Island Counter—Table displaying or carrying goods for sale in such a position in a store that customers may walk around it.

Joint Stock Company—Large partnership with some of the features of a corporation.

Journal—Bookkeeping record in which transactions are first entered.

Judgment—Court decision; in a civil trial for damages, the sum awarded to the plaintiff.

Jury—Of two kinds. The **grand** jury consists of 12 to 23 persons who serve as an investigating body and dismiss or indict a suspect, depending on the evidence at hearings. Functions only in cases involving major crimes. **Petit** jury, an ordinary jury, usually consisting of 12 persons who hear civil suits and cases of minor law-breaking.

Kickback—Unauthorized payment out of wages, prices, or fees as extortion or bribery.

Know-How—Technical skill gained through training and experience.

Kraft—Strong brown paper used in packing for shipping.

Landlord—Owner of real estate; usually reference is to owner of specified building.

Layout—Sketch of a proposed advertisement, booklet, etc., in store merchandising, arrangement of merchandise.

Lease—A contract for the temporary conveyance of property, usually in consideration of rent.

Ledger—Account book. In larger sense, accounting in general.

Legacy—Inheritance through a will.

Legal Standard—Measure of value in gold or silver established by a government for the rating of its currency.

Legal Tender—Money that may lawfully be used in settlement of debts.

Lessee—Tenant under a lease.

Lessor—One who grants a lease.

Letters Patent—Document transferring title to public lands or rights to inventions (see Patent).

Liability—Indebtedness; **current** liabilities are short term debts such as taxes, accounts payable, etc., to be met within the year; **fixed** liabilities are long term debts such as mortgages, bonds, etc.; **deferred** liabilities are advance payments such as rent or interest before they come due.

Libel—Written statement held to be damaging to person or business about which it is made. To be distinguished from **slander,** which is a damaging statement made orally.

License—Legal permission to sell certain goods, e.g., a liquor license; or to practice a profession; or to sell goods on the street, e.g., a peddler's license, etc.

Lien—Legal right to property in payment of debt; usually has priority over other claims, e.g., tax lien, mechanics lien, etc.

Limit Order—Order to buy or sell stock at or above or below a specified price.

Line—Type of merchandise offered for sale, e.g., line of pearl buttons.

Liquid—Convertible into cash, e.g., liquid assets.

Liquidate—To convert assets into cash, generally in reference to business in financial difficulty and in need of ready cash.

List Price—Selling price as listed in catalogue.

Loan—Money lent on interest.

Lockout—Shutting out of employees during a labor dispute. Now illegal.

Logotype—Trademark or symbol used by a firm in its advertising.

Long and Short—To be **long** is to hold stock in expectation of a rise; to be **short** is to sell stocks one does not own, in a falling market, in expectation of buying them in at a still lower quotation and profiting from the difference.

Lots—In real estate, specified arrangement of ground; in the stock market, number of shares traded in. **Round** lots are those taken in round numbers, such as 100 shares; **odd** lots are transactions in lots under 100.

Maintenance of Membership—Clause in labor contract making it obligatory upon workers to keep in good standing in the union in order to retain jobs.

Malfeasance—Wrongful action: To be distinguished from **nonfeasance,** failure to perform an action agreed upon; and **misfeasance,** performance of an agreed action in such a way as to violate the rights of others.

Malice Aforethought—Intentional or planned injury.

Manifest—Invoice of a ship's cargo, for evidence at customs house.

Manufacture—Conversion of raw materials into a finished product, e.g., converting iron ore into steel plate.

Margin—Money deposited with a broker as security on stock purchases; thus margin may be forfeited if stock quotations take an adverse turn.

Markdown—Lowering of prices, usually to make sales for slow-moving goods.

Market—In general, the range for buying and selling; in particular, the range for buying and selling in a par-

ticular field, e.g., the stock market, the cotton market, etc.

Market Order—Order to sell at the market price of the day on which the order is issued.

Mark-Up—Amount added, in selling price, to wholesale price to cover overhead and profit.

Marshall Plan—Plan to extend economic aid abroad, initiated by George C. Marshall as United States Secretary of State in 1947.

Mass Market—The general public considered as potential consumers.

Mass Production—Large scale, mechanized production designed to lower production costs to permit purchase by the majority of potential consumers.

Maximum Hours—Limit of time workers may be employed without overtime payment.

Mediation—Resort to third party in disputes between employer and worker; not as conclusive as arbitration.

Melon—Extra dividend on stock, distributing surplus earnings or profits.

Merger—Consolidation of two or more companies into one.

Metes and Bounds—Dimensions and boundaries of a parcel of real estate.

Mill—A machine for grinding, pressing, stamping, or almost every repetitive process; a building or group of buildings containing manufacturing machinery.

Minimum Wage—Lowest limit of wages that may be paid to workers.

Minor—Person under legal age to assume certain responsibilities. The age varies—it is different for marriage, for business transaction, or for liability to criminal charges.

Model Change-Over—Reorganization of manufacturing process for the manufacture of a new model (sometimes called **mark**) of an article.

Monopoly—Exclusive control of an industry or some form of trade.

Morris Plan Company—Makes small personal loans for repayment in installments.

Mortgage—Transfer of rights in property as security for a loan or for other considerations. **Real estate** mortgages are on land and improvements upon it; **chattel** mortgages cover other forms of property; **crop** mortgage is a chattel mortgage on crops; a **first** mortgage is one which has priority in any claims on the property over subsequent mortgages (**second** and **third** mortgages, etc.)

Mortgage Certificates—Certificates for small shares of large first mortgages or first mortgage bonds. Issued by mortgage customers to investors.

National Advertising—Advertising in periodicals or over radio and television, nationwide in scope.

Negotiable—Salable or transferable as payment for debts.

Net—Sum, after deductions have been made, e.g., net income after expenses, taxes, etc. have been taken out.

Nonfeasance—see Malfeasance.

Notary Public—A person authorized by state law to witness and certify to the authenticity of signatures affixed to documents or statements in his presence.

Number—Item of manufacture; usually refers to item in a catalogue.

O.K.—With signature, constitutes endorsement or approval of something presented in writing. According to popular belief, from Old Kinderhook, birthplace of Martin van Buren, and used by his supporters in his campaign for the presidency.

Omnibus Clause—Section in a contract covering several items not specifically covered elsewhere in the document.

One Day Order—Order for stock transaction on a certain day, and cancelled if not executed on that day.

Open Order—Order for a stock transaction to be executed at any time and to hold good until notice of withdrawal is received. Also called GTC (Good till cancelled) order.

Option—First choice or right to obtain goods or services without competition for a specified period, e.g., ten days' option.

Order—Customer's itemized descripton of goods desired for purchase.

Overhead—Fixed expenses, such as rent, salaries, maintenance costs, etc.

Overstock—Goods in excess of current demand.

Over-the-Counter Trading—Trading by private dealers in securities not listed on the stock exchange.

Package—Combined merchandise and/or services, offered as a unit, in a "package deal," e.g., radio or television program in which script, actors, announcer, etc., are all provided as a unit in a "package program."

Pamphlet—Paper-covered booklet used as advertising or to convey information about a business.

Panic—Sudden widespread fright over financial situation causing artifical depression through sales of securities and other property.

Paper—Documents of any sort, negotiable notes, bills, etc.

Par—Normal or face value of securities.

Parcel—Package of goods; piece of property; to apportion merchandise in small lots to provide some supply to all accounts.

Parity—Rate of exchange at which different currencies acquire equal purchasing power.

Partnership—Defined in Uniform Partnership Act: "An association of two or more persons to carry on as co-owners of a business for profit"; except in "limited partnership" in which liability of certain partners is restricted to the amount of capital contributed, partners are individually liable for debts contracted by the business.

Passbook—A book borne by customer, containing records of credit purchases; also bankbook.

Passing a Dividend—Failure to declare an expected dividend.

Patent—Right granted by the government for a term of seventeen years, for the exclusive production of an invented article or for an improvement of an article, not renewable.

Patent Attorney—One specializing in the preparation of patent applications and in the search to determine that the invention is new and does not infringe on previous patents.

Patent Office—Government bureau that registers patent applications and issues "letters patent," granting patent rights.

Patron—Customer.

Patronage—Business given by a customer.

Pattern (in industry)—A model made for duplication as in metal casting, dress manufacture, etc.

Pattern-Maker—One who makes patterns needed in industry.

Pay—to make an acceptable return, usually in money, for property delivered, or services rendered; remuneration such as wages or salaries.

Payee—Person to whom money has been, or is to be, paid.

Paymaster—One under whose management wage or salary payments are made.

Payroll—Paymaster's list of those entitled to wages or salary.

Peculation—Embezzlement.

Peg—To hold market prices at a set value by manipulating purchases or sales.

Pension—Payment made through grant, insurance, or other arrangement to person retired from employment, business, or public office.

"Percents"—Investments such as bonds or other securities, described by their interest rate, e.g., 3%.

Perpetual Trust—Trust estate with no prescribed duration.

Personal Property or Personal Estate—Property other than real estate.

Personnel—Employed staff.

Petition—Written application to a court instituting an action or requesting action upon a matter before it.

Petition in Bankruptcy—Written application by a debtor or his creditors that he be declared bankrupt.

Petty Cash—Cash fund used to make small payments.

Photo Engraving—Process of reproducing pictures through photography, where printing surface is in relief in contrast to lithography or gravure.

Photostat—Photographic process for reproducing documents, drawings, etc.; a document or drawing so reproduced.

Pica—12-point type, usually used on typewriters and in other print where readability is desired.

Picket—Person, during a strike, standing or walking back and forth before entrance of business to discourage non-striking employees or customers from entering.

Piece-Goods—Fabrics sold by pieces or fixed lengths.

Pilot Plant—A business operated to determine rates to be charged in its industry.

Pipeline—Piping over long distances used in the transportation of oil or gas.

Piracy—Infringement on copyrighted or patent property rights.

Pit—Section of Chicago Board of Trade where a specific commodity is traded; e.g., wheat pit.

Pivotal—A stock whose quotations influence the course of the market.

Planned Economy—Economical organization, usually of a state, in which production is arranged to prevent or reduce fluctuation and waste.

Plant—The building, machinery, etc., taken together that are used in a unit of industrial production.

Plantation—Large scale farming operation, carried on by hired labor; e.g., rubber plantation.

Plastics (in industry)—Synthetic materials mainly produced by molding process.

Pledge—Piece of property given as security for a loan.

Point—Unit used in quoting prices on stocks. In the United States, one point usually stands for $1 a share.

Point System—Method of wage payment by time units of work performed. Also called the "Bedaux System," from its originator.

Policy—Contract of insurance; guiding principles of a concern, usually determined or governed by a Board of Directors.

Pool—Merger of property or financial interests of a group, usually with the expectation of manipulating the market in its favor.

Portal-to-Portal Pay—Payment for time spent, as in mines, in passing to and from the entrance of the actual place of work.

Position—On produce exchanges, undertaking to make delivery in a given month; e.g., October position.

Possession—Such control of property as to give exclusive legal enjoyment of it.

Posthumous—Taking effect after death.

Power of Attorney—Legal authority to act for another, not as a lawyer, but to carry out transactions.

Practice—Professional service; e.g., legal practice; customary procedure of a firm.

Pre-Fab—A prefabricated article, usually a house or small industrial building, to facilitate speedy erection.

Preference Shop—One where, by agreement between union and management, preference is given to union members in employment, promotion, and tenure, but management may employ non-union workers if union cannot supply qualified personnel.

Preferred Stock—Issue which receives preference over common stock in dividends or distribution of assets.

Premium (in insurance)—Money or other consideration paid by the insured according to terms of contract. (In economics)—Greater value of one currency over another; additional payment for loan of money. (On the stock market)—Amount above par that securities are being quoted at; sum paid for an option.

Prepaid—Paid in advance.

Price—Value at which goods are exchanged or services rendered.

Pricing—Setting a price on goods.

Primary Markets—Markets in farm produce such as foods or fibers.

Principal—Actual party to transaction as distinguished from agent; money or other property on which interest is earned.

Priority—Precedence as in transportation, goods production, delivery of order, etc.

Privilege—Option on the sale or purchase of securities on specified items.

Probate—Proof established by legal procedures; e.g., probate of a will.

Process—A method of manufacture or of rendering services.

Production—Creation of goods having value to purchasers; e.g., agricultural production, industrial production.

Profit—What remains after production and sales costs have been deducted.

Profit and Loss—Accounting, after a given period, to determine condition of a business.

Promissory Note—Note undertaking payment of a debt at a specified time or occasion.

Promoter—One who initiates organization of a company, floating of securities, or other business undertaking.

Property—Things owned; real property is property in real estate, while personal property or personal estate refers to all other possessions of value.

Proprietor—Owner; one with legal right to possession.

Proxy—To act for another; one whose voting rights are entrusted to another, the usual reference being to voting of stock holders.

Public Domain—The field of property rights belonging to the public at large, such as manufacturing processes or literary properties not, or no longer, covered by patents and copyrights.

Public Utility—Company servicing the general public, such as a railroad, supplier of electricity, etc.

Put and Call—To "put" is to deliver, according to agreement, specified stock at a specified price to a buyer

who receives a payment for this service. The privilege of "putting" may be sold to a third party. To "call" is to receive on demand specified stock at a specified price from a seller who is paid for this service. The privilege of "calling" may be sold to a third party.

Pyramid—To engage in transactions in banking or stock market, using gains as "margin" for further purchases or sales, in order to take continuous advantage of a market trend.

Qualified—Fit to do required work.

Quantity—Used relatively, usually in reference to goods in bulk, e.g., "These castings can be supplied in any reasonable quantity."

Quantity Theory of Money—Economic theory that changes in quantity of money in circulation affect price levels and currency values.

Query—To recheck a shipment, a shipper or an account; may refer to goods, invoices, personnel, etc. e.g., "Please query Hobson, rubber tape shipment overdue at warehouse."

Quit Claim—Document in legal form relinquishing some property right.

Quotations—Statements, oral or written, of market prices of stocks, bonds or commodities.

Quotation Board—Board in brokerage office on which market quotations are displayed.

Rebate—Repayment of a percentage of sum received in payment for goods or services. Rebate may be allowed for damage, delay, or savings in shipping costs, etc.

Receipt—Signed paper in evidence that goods or money has been received.

Receipts—Earnings of a business for a given period; e.g., "today's receipts."

Receiver—Person, firm, or bank appointed by courts to conduct a business declared bankrupt.

Recession—Decline in industrial activity, not so drastic as a depression.

Redemption—Payment of outstanding loans; e.g., redemption of a bond issue.

Referee—Appointed by court to hear evidence and render decision in business disputes.

Refund—Return of entire amount paid for goods or services, usually because of their unsatisfactory nature.

Reimburse—Repay money expended by another. An agent will be reimbursed for costs incurred during his operation.

Reorganization—Reestablishment of insolvent business with the consent of creditors and under court supervision, with the aim of avoiding receivership costs and forced sale losses.

Requisition—Order for supplies, materials, etc.

Rescued—Withdrawal of order or instructions.

Restrictive—Limiting. A restrictive covenant is a clause in a document setting certain conditions, as in real estate contracts restricting residence to certain races.

Retail Trade—Trade with consumers.

Retirement—Withdrawal from circulation, e.g., retirement of a currency.

Revenue—Source of income, usually referring to government income from taxation.

Revenue Bond—Short-term issue in anticipation of revenue payments.

Rigged Market—Subject to manipulation so that it does not reflect real values.

Rollback—Price reduction to previous levels, usually by government action.

Royalty—Share of profits paid by manufacturer to inventor (or owner of an invention), author, etc. or to his heirs.

Runaway—Removal of business to a region of low labor costs as an employer measure in labor trouble.

Sabotage—Obstruction, malicious waste of materials, or spoilage of product by workers during labor trouble.

Sales Engineering—Computing and adjusting installation and production costs from plans, as a means of promoting sales of equipment and machinery to a specific industry or factory.

Salvage—Goods rescued from shipwreck or other disaster.

Sample—A representative piece of an article offered for sale; e.g., swatch of cloth.

Scab—Opprobrious term, used in labor relations for person employed in place of strikers or refusing to strike with his fellow workers.

Schedule—Systematic listing of time for production or other performance in manufacturing, transportation, distribution, etc.

Search—To verify status of a property; e.g., mortgage title search, patent search, etc.

Seat—Membership in the Stock Exchange entitling one to share in its assets and privilege of trading there.

Security—(Chiefly used in the plural.) Stock certificates, bonds, or other documentary evidence of indebtedness giving the possessor the right to claim property secured by the document; **listed** security is one which, by meeting certain requirements, is listed for trading on the Stock Exchange.

Self-Mailer—Advertising message that can be sent by mail without enclosure in an envelope. A sticker or stamp is affixed to hold pages or folded edges together.

Shakeout—Minor decline in industrial activity in course of adjustment after inflation.

Shape-up—Hiring of dockworkers by selection of applicants at piers, usually arbitrarily, at the discretion of labor supervisor.

Shortage—Something missing from inventory or from cash, due to theft, loss, or error.

Silver Standard—Rating of currency in terms of a specified value in silver.

Sinking Fund—Fund continually added to and invested toward the payment of bonds or other maturing debts.

Sitdown Strike—One where striking employees stay in or at their places of work to prevent operation of machinery by others.

Slander—Oral statement held to be damaging to person or business about whom it is made. To be distinguished from libel, which is a damaging written statement.

Sleeper—Film, book, novel, or other property or article of trade that gains unexpected commercial success, doing better business than other items for which greater sales were anticipated.

Slowdown—Slowing down of work operations without actual walkout, as a worker tactic in labor dispute.

Smog—Saturation of air with smoke or other industrial exhausts leading to fog conditions.

Social Security—System and fund set up, under the Social Security Act, to insure security in old age. The fund is made up of compulsory contributions by employers and employees

Solicit—To seek business accounts.

Solvency—Capacity to meet financial obligations.

Specie—Metal (hard) money as distinguished from paper currency.

Specimen—Sample of minerals, ores, plants, or other things that are complete units of their kind.

Speculation—Buying or selling with chance of high profits and risk of considerable loss.

Spot Announcement (in radio advertising)—A commercial not part of a sponsored program.

Spot Delivery—In stock market, immediate delivery of stock.

Staple—An established product; e.g., oil is a staple of Texas.

Statement—List of unpaid items in a business account; a financial statement is a listing of assets and liabilities.

Statute of Limitations—Law setting time limit for legal action.

Stipulation—Condition specified in agreement or contract, usually something undertaken by buyer to bolster his credit.

Stock—Share of ownership in an incorporated business; supply of merchandise for sale; **common** stock is ordinary stock as distinguished from **preferred** stock, which takes precedence over it in distribution of assets or dividends; **guaranteed** stock is one whose dividends are guaranteed by another company.

Stockpile—Reserve supply of essential material.

Strike—Refusal by employees to work unless demands, generally for pay increases, vacations, and other benefits are met. Usually accompanied by picketing of the premises of the business affected.

Strike-Breaking—Coercive action with the intention of defeating strike action.

Sublease—To lease all or part of premises one has leased.

Sublet—To rent all or part of premises one has rented.

Subpoena—Court order served on witnesses summoning them to give testimony.

Subsidiary—A company, control of whose stock is held by another company.

Subsidy—Agreed sum paid, over and above market charges, to assure supply or service that would otherwise be unavailable because of lack of profit.

Substandard—Below standard quality.

Supermarket—Departmentalized branch in chain store system, where some departments may be rented as concessions, and doing a gross annual business of a specified figure, usually $100,000.

Supply—Amount of goods for sale at a given price.

Surplus—Oversupply; amount by which assets exceed liabilities and capital; amount of goods on hand above current demand.

Swindle—To defraud; dishonest business transaction.

Swindler—One who defrauds.

Swindle Sheet—Expense account, when padding or the possibility of padding is implied.

Syndicate—Group organized for special financing, such as purchase and resale of certain securities or underwriting of a stock issue, purchasing it at a discount.

Take-Home Pay—What is left of earnings after withholding tax and other deductions have been made.

Tariff—Schedule of duties imposed on importers and exporters.

Tax—To exact payment, usually payment exacted by government to provide revenue for its operations.

Tax Sale—Sale of a property to recover unpaid taxes.

Technological—Referring to technical processes or changes in industry; e.g., technological unemployment.

Tenant—Occupant of premises, generally one who pays rent for the occupancy.

Tenders—Sealed bids or offers for securities.

Terms—Terms of payment; prearranged conditions for payment of a debt; e.g., cash in 30 days, $5 down and $1 a week, etc.

Testator—One who makes a will.

Ticker—Machine in which messages are stamped on paper tape, used in reporting market quotations.

Tie-in Sale—Where additional product must be purchased to effect purchase of a certain article.

Title—All factors combined which accord right to exclusive possession of property.

Tool Engineering—New branch of engineering concerned with perfecting new machinery processes, equipment and use of raw material in preparation for production of a new product or a new model.

Tracer—Investigation designed to trace article undelivered by post office or transportation company; one who makes such an investigation.

Trade Acceptance—Bill of exchange governing purchase price, drawn by seller upon buyer whose endorsement constitutes "acceptance."

Trade Agreement—Agreement between employer and union, fixing wages, hours, working conditions.

Trade Edition or Trade Book—Edition designed for general public as distinguished from educational and professional use.

Trademark—Coined name, monogram, logotype, signature, picture, distinctively designed words or name, symbol, emblem or device, which may be registered in the Government Patent Office for exclusive use by the applicant. Registration term is 20 years and may be renewed.

Trade Name—Name or other symbol under which a firm does business and protected by common law against attempt to deceive customers by use of a similar name by a competing firm.

Trade Paper—Endorsed notes (two or more names) given in payment for merchandise; a periodical published in the interest of a certain branch of business.

Transcript—Letter-perfect copy of a document, which does not seek to reproduce exact appearance of original.

Travelers Checks—Issued by banks, travel agencies, American Express, and Western Union for the convenience of travelers.

Treasury Bills—Short-term government offerings, bearing no interest, but sold at a discount to buyers.

Treasury Certificates—Interest-bearing certificates of indebtedness issued in place of short-term bonds.

Trust—Holding of property by a responsible person or bank (trustee) for the good of another person (beneficiary).

Turnover—Number of times, within a specified period such as a year, in which a given commodity is sold out.

Upgrade—To advance an employee, a work process or a product in rank, earnings, price or quality.

Venue—Place where case is tried. **A change of venue** may be granted with the object of securing a fairer trial.

Volume—Amount of business done.

Voucher—A receipt or other proof of money paid, vouches for the accuracy of the terms of a transaction.

Wages—Payment for labor.

Waive—To voluntarily forego a right.

Warrant—Order for the payment of money or delivery of goods or documents; in banking, primarily written order for the payment of money.

Wash Sale—Fictitious trading to give an appearance of activity to inactive stocks.

Wharfage—Fee for use of piers.

Wholesale—Sale of goods to dealers for resale to retail merchants.

Will—Testament of a property-holder directing the distribution of his property after his death.

Window Dressing—Manipulations in financial statement to give it a more favorable appearance than is due.

Withholding Tax—Income tax payment deducted at source, as from wages, dividends, etc.

Without Prejudice—A contract term signifying that the agreement will not injure any prior or subsequent rights.

Zoning—Laws governing real estate, setting off special areas for special types of occupation; e.g., residence, business, hospitals, etc.

Wills and Estate Planning

Everyone should have an up-to-date will that reflects an estate plan adapted to individual needs and circumstances. The estate plan is a thoughtfully designed arrangement for the distribution of one's assets in such a way as to achieve maximum realization of the planner's objectives. These can include keeping taxes at a minimum; providing financial management for the benefit of a surviving widow and children; selection of a trusted relative, friend, or advisor as executor or guardian; and so on. An estate plan can be simple and inexpensive to draw up; for a larger estate or one with special problems the plan may be extremely complex.

Most persons or couples of reasonable means should have an estate plan—and a will or wills as integral parts of that plan. But whether it is part of an estate plan or not the will is ordinarily a written document that takes effect on the death of the testator, the legal term for the person making out a will. The will's purpose is to distribute one's worldly assets to those whom the testator desires or "wills" to have them.

The estate plan may deal with broader categories of assets than the will. The estate plan may, for example, have provisions covering gifts, insurance, and annuities, special types of contracts such as those providing for the purchase of a business by surviving associates, trusteeship arrangements, and other devices designed to accomplish the testator's purposes. The estate plan may also provide for changes in the estate to be made before the planner's death. The will generally takes effect only on the testator's death.

Estate Planning: Four Main Tools

You can make a beginning toward estate planning by considering the four main tools a planner can use. The four are trusts, lifetime gifts, joint ownership, and wills. Other tools are, of course, available, and each has a valid purpose. Under specific arrangements, for example, death benefits may be paid to named beneficiaries under pension plans, profit-sharing programs, IRAs, tax-sheltered annuities, and deferred compensation arrangements. Some estates use irrevocable living trusts or buy-sell agreements dealing with businesses.

Adding It Up. In general, property is anything you can own. Everything you own belongs in your estate. That includes both real property, or real estate, meaning both land and all the things that are permanently attached to the land, and personal property. The latter includes tangibles, those items that have bulk or substance, and intangibles, things without physical substance. Among common tangibles are furniture, an automobile, cameras, clothing, a boat, and so on. Intangibles are such items as stocks, bonds, life insurance policies, and bank deposits.

A first step in estate planning involves inventorying all your property of whatever kind. With each item you should note the value or estimated value. You should also indicate how the property is owned—outright, in joint tenancy, or otherwise.

Objectives. What do you want to accomplish when you plan your estate? Your objectives should be clear; they often determine what methods you will use to transfer your property, or specific parts of it, to your spouse, relatives, friends, charities, or other beneficiaries. At the least you will want to know who your heirs will be and what each heir will receive.

Some specific objectives help to shape estate plans. A property owner may want to provide financial support for dependents, including both money to live on and funds that would be available in emergencies. Nearly all estate planners hope to reduce such estate transfer costs as federal estate and state inheritance taxes, the expenses of administering the estate, and others. Very basically, a valid objective is to ensure that the estate will have sufficient assets to meet its obligations.

Other objectives may seem obvious. As noted, you will want to name the person or persons who will administer or settle your estate after your death—and under what terms. The disposition of closely held business interests should be provided for. Finally, property distribution should make up parts of the estate plan.

Tool 1: Trusts

As one of the key tools of estate planning, trusts play unique roles. Whatever the type of trust, and there are many kinds for persons in many economic categories, the typical trust instrument places *legal* title in one person, called the *trustee*, and *equitable* title in another person, the *beneficiary*. In each case the "person" may be an individual, a corporation, group, or organization. The *grantor* (or creator or settlor) who establishes the trust gives the trustee the right to hold and administer the trust *corpus*, or principle, for the benefit of the other person or entity.

Three main kinds of trusts are used by the estate planner: living, or *inter vivos* ("between the living"), trusts; testamentary trusts established by will; and insurance trusts. Living trusts are set up while the grantor is alive, and take effect at once. Testamentary trusts take effect on the grantor's death. The corpus of the insurance trust consists of funds from an insurance policy—or funds to be paid out under an insurance policy or policies—and, possibly, other property as well.

Why a trust? To some extent the reasons parallel those that justify estate planning itself. Among the reasons:

• To protect spendthrift heirs or other beneficiaries who may be mentally, physically, or emotionally unable to manage property. The trustee can have total management responsibility.

• To enable the trustee to use discretion and, often, expert knowledge in managing trust property for the benefit of heirs, the grantor, and family members or others.

• To have a device for giving or leaving property to minors with the assurance that the trustee will manage the property until the beneficiaries are old enough to handle the property themselves.

• To take all or part of your estate property out of probate and in that way to save your heirs the costs and delays of going through the probate process.

• To set up a useful tax-saving plan.

Tax Savings

Depending on your financial status and the complexity of the trust you want to set up, you could pay from $100 to $10,000 or more to an attorney to prepare your trust agreement. On average, you would pay about $300 to $500.

Such an expense could definitely be worth it. Remember that the federal government has provided that estates of $500,000 or less were to escape estate taxes in 1986. That figure was to rise to $600,000 in 1987 and subsequent years. In one case a couple had property worth $800,000, all in the husband's name. Assuming that the husband dies first, in 1987 or later, the entire estate passes to the wife. The so-called *marital deduction* allows whole estates of whatever kind to pass to a surviving spouse tax-free. But when the wife dies a different rule applies.

On the wife's death in 1987 or later, the federal exemption would apply only to the first $600,000 of the $800,000 estate. At rates in effect in 1986 the couple's heirs would pay $52,000 in estate taxes on the remaining $200,000.

This couple could have saved all $52,000 in federal taxes by establishing a trust. The couple would have had several choices, including these:

• A *bypass trust* that would set aside $600,000 of the husband's estate as the trust principle, with income from the trust and part of its principle going to the wife during her lifetime. The other $200,000 in the husband's estate would go directly, on his death, to the wife for her unrestricted use. On the wife's death the trust would dissolve and the entire estate would be distributed to the beneficiaries free of federal taxes.

• A *marital deduction trust,* with either of two kinds available: a general power of appointment trust or a so-called QTIP (qualified terminable interest property) trust. Again the couple's beneficiaries would pay no federal estate taxes on the death of the second spouse.

Under the general power of appointment trust, your spouse can decide after you die who will receive the trust's assets after he or she dies. The QTIP, by contrast, makes it possible for you to select the ultimate trust beneficiaries. With the QTIP you can make sure, if desired, that your spouse will not cut off your children by an earlier marriage. Otherwise the general power of appointment and the QTIP trust are virtually identical. Both, for example, qualify for the marital deduction and are included in the surviving spouse's estate. Both also produce income that must go to the surviving spouse.

• A *generation-skipping trust,* under which trust income goes to a grantor's children rather than to the wife and the principle goes to the grantor's grandchildren.

In many cases a grantor can use an *irrevocable life insurance trust* under which the proceeds from insurance policies are removed from the grantor's estate, to be distributed after the second spouse's death to the named beneficiaries. The spouse receives income from the trust until he or she dies.

Selecting the Trustee

The problem of selecting a trustee usually resolves into a choice between an individual and a corporation. The individual, whether the creator of the trust or someone else, might be closer to the trust beneficiaries than a corporate trustee—and might therefore be more responsive to the beneficiaries' needs. The individual might not even charge a fee. Under any circumstances, the person or persons serving as trustees could, as needed, obtain legal, investment, accounting, and other advice from experts.

The corporate trustee could offer different advantages. Such trustees are professional money and property managers. Unlike the individual trustee, they do not, usually, die or become incapacitated; personnel changes do not interrupt their services. Beyond that, they remain unbiased, independent of family pressures, and able to answer to charges of mismanagement. By comparison with the individual trustee who is also a trust beneficiary, the corporate trustee cannot incur personal income tax liabilities in administering trust property. A corporate trustee can, of course, act as cotrustee with an individual or individuals.

Tool 2: Gifts

Lifetime gifts function much like trusts. Essentially, they reduce the value of your estate and thus help to avoid estate taxes. An important difference, however, is that your surviving spouse has no access to the money you have given away. Thus most persons make certain that the surviving spouse will have enough income to live on after the first spouse's death.

In the 1980s the federal government liberalized the laws regulating gifts of property or money. In 1986 individuals could give up to $10,000 each to as many persons as they chose. For couples, the law allowed joint gifts of as much as $20,000 each to any number of donees. You need not report gifts of less than $10,000 to the Internal Revenue Service, but must (whether individual or couple) report all gifts exceeding that sum. After your death, the IRS will add up all the taxable gifts—those exceeding $10,000 per year per person—that you made during your lifetime and (if applicable) subtract the total from your $600,000 (1987) estate tax exemption.

Kinds of Gifts

You can give gifts in many different ways. A *charitable remainder trust* is actually a way to give assets to a charity while ensuring that you or your beneficiaries will receive the income from the gift property for a specified period. At the end of the period the trust dissolves and the charity receives the principle. Very wealthy persons may use a *GRIT* (grantor retained income trust) that sets aside part of the grantor's estate as a gift to a family member or friend. The grantor receives the income from the gift property for a specified period, whereupon it passes out of his or her estate and into the ownership of the beneficiary.

A third method of giving away assets operates on a principle opposite to that of the remainder trust. This *charitable lead trust* provides that a charity will receive the income from the specified property—but not the principle. When the trust ends, your heirs receive the principle. You arrange for a charitable lead trust in your will. Often, your estate enjoys even larger tax deductions than it would under a remainder trust.

Tool 3: Joint Ownership

Joint ownership of property offers both advantages and disadvantages that should be considered in estate

planning. Joint ownership (a legal device that exists when two or more persons have ownership rights in property) allows that property to pass automatically to the other joint owner or owners *outside the probate estate* of the first owner to die. The device thus saves the time and expenses often involved in the probate process.

Other advantages may be noted. Some states levy lower inheritance taxes, or no taxes, where property is held jointly. Usually, too, the survivor receives jointly held property free of the claims of the creditors of a deceased joint owner.

Joint, Outright, and Community Property Ownership

Joint ownership is one of four basic ways in which real or personal property may be owned. The other three are outright ownership, community property ownership or rights, and tenancy in common. The three types of joint ownership or tenancy include:

Joint Tenancy with Right of Survivorship. Under joint tenancy with right of survivorship (WROS), the property interest of a descendant passes with his or her death to the surviving joint owner or owners. A married couple typically own their home jointly. When one dies, the property interest of that deceased passes to the survivor, who then owns the property outright in his or her own name.

A joint tenant can destroy the survivorship aspect of a joint tenancy. For example, if one joint tenant sells his or her share in property to a third party, that person and the remaining joint tenant own the property as tenants in common (see below).

Tenancy by the Entirety. A second form of joint tenancy is tenancy by the entirety. Some states provide for this special kind of joint ownership when a wife and husband own property jointly and exclusively. Tenancy by the entirety differs from joint tenancy with right of survivorship in three key ways: the former can only exist between husband and wife; in many states the survivorship rights can be terminated only with the consent of both parties; and, again depending on the laws of the particular state, the husband may have control over the property (and the right to any income from it) during their lifetimes.

Other Joint Interests. Where joint bank accounts or jointly owned government savings bonds are concerned, the owners may again have rights of survivorship. Thus family members commonly hold both types of property under this joint ownership arrangement. With a bank account, either party can make deposits or withdraw funds. On the death of one, the survivor becomes sole owner of the account by operation of law.

With savings bonds, a similar rule applies. Both joint owners have survivorship rights even though the bonds may be registered in co-ownership form and held in the name of "A" or "B." Either A or B could cash the bonds during the lifetime of the other.

Tenancy in Common

Under tenancy in common arrangements, no co-owner has survivorship rights: none acquires the interest of another in case of the other's death. Rather, the interest of a decedent goes to the decedent's heirs as if the interest had been owned outright. The survivor retains his or her share. Tenants in common can own proportionate interests in property—for example, 75 percent and 25 percent respectively.

In outright ownership, one person owns property exclusively in his or her name. Community property is discussed below.

Not a Will

Despite some advantages, joint ownership does not take the place of a will. In cases on record, couples owning property jointly, but having no wills, were involved in serious accidents. One spouse died instantly. The other survived by a few hours or days. The survivor could not make out a will. By law, the property passed to the surviving spouse on the death of the other. On the death of the second spouse, the property typically passed entirely to the second spouse's relatives.

Joint ownership may also produce results contrary to those intended, may save few or no taxes and other expenses, and may even increase taxes dramatically. The effects depend on state laws. But in many states lawyers cannot say for certain what the effects of joint tenancy may be. It may nonetheless be advisable to hold checking accounts and small savings accounts in joint ownership to provide the survivor with ready cash on the death of one joint owner; even if the account is frozen for a time it will normally become available well before the assets of the deceased's estate.

For sentimental or other reasons, a husband and wife usually own the family home jointly. Ownership of other assets should be based on sound legal advice—which also applies to the overall estate plan, including the will.

Joint Ownership—How Much?

No simple rules are available to indicate how much property should be held in joint tenancy. If the federal estate tax is not an important factor, a couple may hold all property jointly. But even if the couple's estate is large enough to be federally taxable, some joint ownership may be appropriate for the reasons noted.

The Economic Recovery Tax Act (ERTA) of 1981 produced some new rules on joint tenancies held by married couples. In particular, the act provided that only one-half of the value of the property held in a taxable joint tenancy is includable in the gross estate of the first spouse to die. This "fractional interest" applies regardless of whether the surviving spouse contributed to the purchase of the property.

As a caveat, joint ownership may actually result in a gift. This occurs where one joint owner has contributed all or a disproportionate share of the cost of purchasing property. If Mrs. Jones, for example, uses her own funds to buy corporate stock in her own and Daughter Joanne's name, and if the ownership is irrevocable, Mrs. Jones has made a gift, for federal tax purposes, to her daughter of one-half the value of the stocks. Her daughter has also gained some control over the stocks.

Different from Community Property

Property owned jointly should not be confused with community property. The latter exists in some western and southwestern states that follow Roman law rather than the English common law where property relationships between husbands and wives are concerned. In common-law states marriage gives husbands and wives certain rights in each other's property that often cannot be changed by a will. This is also true in community property states, but the rights are somewhat different.

In these states one-half the income earned during the marriage by either spouse belongs to the other. All property owned by the couple is presumably community property, of which each owns half. But property owned by either spouse before marriage and kept separate, with the income from such property also kept separate, and property acquired by one spouse individually, without contributions from the other spouse—for example, by gift

or inheritance—are the separate properties of each spouse owning it.

In community property states married couples' wills cannot touch the separate property of either spouse or either spouse's share of the community property. But a couple can by contract agree on what is community property and what is the separate property of either. Such contracts take effect when written and signed. They are an essential tool of estate planning in community property states. But they do not obviate the need for a will any more than joint tenancy does.

The nine community property states are Arizona, California, Idaho, Louisiana, Nevada, New Mexico, Texas, Washington, and Wisconsin. In these states estate planners should be wary of making a person other than the spouse a joint owner of community property. As a rule, half the wife's or husband's share of the community property passes to the surviving spouse and the other half goes to the heirs named in the descedant's will. The surviving spouse may or may not be named as an heir.

Tool 4: Wills

As the fourth and most important tool used in estate planning, wills need always to be individualized to the creator's (or testator's) situation, estate, and desires. The written will is signed by the testator in the presence of witnesses; it operates at his or her death to distribute property according to specifications in the document itself. The law imposes certain obligations, including the primary duty to pay tax liabilities, debts, funeral expenses, and the costs of administration. The law also provides for a surviving spouse's legal rights in a decedent's estate and refuses to recognize, on public policy grounds, provisions discouraging marriage, wasting assets, or tying up wealth for unreasonable periods of time.

Wills may be short and simple or long and complex. But in all cases certain essential requirements must be met. The will must, for example, be signed and witnessed to be valid. For his or her own peace of mind, a testator should have a lawyer prepare the "last will and testament." "Do-it-yourself" wills, and wills written on standard forms, are generally inadvisable, largely because so many of them lead to legal problems later.

Advantages

A will allows you to dispose of your property to the persons you select, at the time you choose, in the amounts and proportions you specify. You can also indicate how your property will be protected and who will be responsible for its protection. Anyone who is 21 years of age and mentally capable of understanding the nature of a will can have one drawn up. In some states or under some conditions the age requirement is reduced or waived.

The cases of husbands and wives who sustained fatal injuries in a common disaster point up the importance of wills. Usually, the husband and wife have left their estates to each other. The deaths of both in the same accident could create difficulty, especially where the order in which the two died cannot be determined. For that reason most wills contain a common diasaster clause providing for the distribution of family assets in the event of simultaneous deaths or deaths resulting from the same accident.

Selecting an Executor

Selecting the person who will oversee the distribution of your estate according to your will is as important as choosing a trustee. Many of the same principles apply.

The loyalty and ability of the executor may be the single most critical factor in ensuring effective and fair administration of your assets after your death: particularly in preventing losses and protecting the property you have left under your will.

Subject to the supervision of an appropriate court, the executor takes possession of the assets specified in the will, manages the estate as the deceased would have, pays debts, taxes, and expenses, retains legal counsel as required, and through counsel handles all the legal obligations and procedures incident to the "execution" of the will. The executor also accounts to the court and heirs for his or her stewardship and distributes the estate's assets according to the provisions of the will and applicable legal strictures. Business skill and judgment, diligence, and the capacity to attend to details and maintain proper records are essential qualities of the good executor.

As a testator, you can nominate the executor of your choice, and can also name alternates if desired. Often a testator appoints a surviving widow or trusted friend or relative. Testators often name their legal counsel as executor or co-executor. At your discretion as testator, you can name a corporate executor or trustee—usually the trust department of a bank. Such a selection means that your executor will have complete institutional facilities available, will enjoy permanence and freedom from personal and business distractions, and will be able to call on the staff and professional skills necessary to do the work properly. The widow, a relative, or a lawyer may be named coexecutor as a means of combining the close personal relationship of a trusted individual with the skills and facilities of the corporate executor.

Obviously, where a will establishes a trust, the bank trust officer or some equally qualified person is a logical choice as executor/trustee. The executor or trustee must be compensated for his or her services—except in the case of a relative or friend who serves out of a sense of duty or because he or she is a principal heir. Executors' fees are based on the size of the estate, but typically range from 1 or 1.5 percent to about 2.5 percent of the gross estate.

Preparation and Execution

Some statutory formalities govern the preparation of all wills. For example, as noted, wills must be in writing, must demonstrate the testator's intent to pass property to heirs, and may as a rule incorporate another document or other documents if the other documents exist when the will is drawn and if the will adequately identifies the additions. The only exceptions to the rule that wills must be written are *nuncupative*, or oral, wills. All wills have also to be signed, or given some visible mark intended as a signature—at the end of the will in some states and in other places in other jurisdictions.

Most states require that two witnesses *attest to,* or witness, the will's signature; some others require three witnesses. Where statutes require it, wills have to be published, with the testator stating that the will is his or her own. Witnesses generally sign in the presence of the testator and each other. No witness should be a beneficiary under the will. An attestation clause appearing before the witnesses' signatures states that all formalities have been complied with, but is not mandatory; the clause merely serves as evidence of proper execution.

Alteration, Revocation

A will can be either changed or revoked. But alteration or revocation has to take place before the death of the testator. The latter must sign any amendment, or cod-

icil, in the presence of witnesses—exactly as when the original was executed.

Revocation may take place in a number of ways. Marking with intent to revoke, tearing up, or burning, or otherwise destroying a will effects revocation; so may the operation of law in given cases, or the testator's preparation and execution of a new will containing a specific clause of revocation or provisions that nullify or clash with provisions in an earlier document. Legal invalidation of a will may take place when a testator remarries, obtains a divorce along with agreement to a property settlement, or becomes a parent. State laws generally govern such invalidations.

Depending on the jurisdiction, destruction or revocation of a later will may revive an earlier one. But some states recognize revival only through republication—unless the intent appears otherwise.

Instructions and Disposition

A letter of instructions may provide a lawyer or executor with essential information and simplify the task of carrying out a testator's desires. Such a letter is not part of the will, and need not comply with any formal requirements. Its purpose is to furnish a detailed inventory of the estate's assets, give instructions regarding the locations of all needed documents—including birth, marriage, and military discharge records; social security card; insurance policies; a list of bank accounts and safe deposit boxes; title deeds; pension papers; and so on—and summarize instructions regarding liquidation of business affairs.

Other portions of the letter may indicate where the will is kept, detail funeral instructions, and state the testator's wishes concerning investment of the proceeds of the estate, the education of children or grandchildren, future plans for the widow or widower, and similar subjects. The will becomes a public record; the letter remains private, and can thus express hopes or suggestions on very private, personal matters.

Where to keep the will? The safe deposit box is the most appropriate place if it can be opened without undue delay after the testator's death. Alternatively, the will may be delivered to the executor or to the testator's lawyer, or kept in a safe place with personal papers at home. In no event should it be accessible to a "disappointed heir."

Intestacy

The person who dies *intestate*—without having made out a will—already has a kind of will: state laws governing intestacy. These laws comprise a "standard" will reflecting the legislature's conception of the deceased's probable objectives. Under intestacy laws, property left by a decedent passes to survivors according to rules fixed by the deceased's state of residence.

Such rules never operate as would an individual will made out according to a person's wishes. The rules frequently lead to serious shrinkage of the estate—and often to a distribution of assets quite different from what the deceased probably wanted. If the estate is large, long and costly litigation may follow the person's death. If the estate is small, it may be divided among various survivors in portions too small to help anyone. If the deceased leaves minor children, they will inherit part of the estate along with his widow.

The laws of intestacy provide in other ways for minor children. A guardian is usually appointed for the children, a process that involves expensive and time-consuming court proceedings. The guardian has to post a bond, renewable annually at a substantial premium. The guard-

ian is supervised by the court and must account to it annually, resulting in more expense and loss of time. All of these procedures are designed to protect the children—and none takes into consideration the fact that the guardian may be the children's mother and the deceased's widow.

Intestacy laws have other effects. They make it impossible for all assets to go to the widow if there are children too. Nor do the laws consider the needs of the deceased's parents if a widow or child survives. Children are treated equally even though their needs may be quite unequal. Under the laws, faithful, loving spouses and mere legal mates are treated exactly alike; so are helpless widows and surviving spouses who are capable in business affairs.

In brief, the time and expense involved in making out a will is infinitesimal in comparison with the problems that may come with intestacy. The "will you already have" is always inferior to the will you ought to have—even though the laws represent the state's best efforts to protect and provide for survivors.

Common Provisions

Intestacy laws work in parallel ways in specific situations. For example, where a husband leaves a widow but no children or parents, the widow inherits the entire estate—after deductions for various expenses that a proper will could have avoided. Where only the decedent's parents survive, the parents usually receive the whole estate—though in some states brothers and sisters also receive shares. As indicated, where a deceased leaves as survivors both wife and parents, the wife usually receives everything even if she is financially independent and the parents are aged and destitute. In a few states, however, the parents receive up to half of their son's estate regardless of the widow's needs.

If the wife and one child survive, each, usually, takes half the estate—but in some jurisdictions the child may take two-thirds or even virtually the entire estate under certain circumstances. Where the wife and two or more children survive, one-third of the estate generally goes to the wife and the remaining two-thirds are divided equally among the children.

The various state laws may, obviously, work great hardship or injustice. Further, the laws are subject to change without notification. A will, by contrast, can be changed only by the person making it out or under the circumstances already noted. A will should be reviewed from time to time, for example when a testator moves to another state; but the will remains the best available means of disposing of property after death.

What Law Governs?

The laws of the testator's state of legal residence determine the validity (or nonvalidity) of a will where personal property is involved. But because each state reserves the right to fix title to land situated within its boundaries, the law of the state where real property is located governs the validity and effect of the will respect to real estate.

All of this may affect the estate plan. A sound plan may call for avoidance of unnecessary ownership of real estate in states where the testator is a nonresident, particularly if there is any possibility that two or more states may claim a descendant as a resident and try to tax the entire estate rather than just the local real property. Most states, and indeed most countries of the world, cooperate with one another by recognizing as valid a will that is valid in the jurisdiction in which the will was made, the jurisdiction in which the testator was a resident, or—as

regards real estate—the jurisdiction in which the property is located.

The extent of this cooperation may vary in given situations. The protocols governing such cooperation may, also, change. Thus it is desirable that the will be consistent with the requirements of the state of residence. Some unusual types of wills are recognized in only a few states; but a proper will drawn by legal counsel will be prepared in such a way as to meet the requirements of most if not all states.

Where To Write for Vital Records

Introduction

An official certificate of every birth, death, marriage, and divorce should be on file in the locality where the event occurred. The federal government does not maintain files or indexes of these records. These records are filed permanently either in a state vital statistics office or in a city, county, or other local office.

To obtain a certified copy of any of the certificates, write or go to the vital statistics office in the state or area where the event occurred. Addresses and fees are given for each event in the state or area concerned.

To ensure that you receive an accurate record for your request and that your request be filled with all due speed, please follow the steps outlined below for the event in which you are interested:

• Write to the appropriate office to have your request filled.

• For all certificates send a money order or certified check because the office cannot refund cash lost in transit. All fees are subject to change.

• Type or print all names and addresses in the letter.

• Give the following facts when writing for **Birth or Death Records:**

1. Full name of person whose record is being requested.
2. Sex and race.
3. Parents' names, including maiden name of mother.
4. Month, day, and year of birth or death.

5. Place of birth or death (city or town, county, and State; and name of hospital, if any).
6. Purpose for which copy is needed.
7. Relationship to person whose record is being requested.

• Give the following facts when writing for **Marriage Records:**

1. Full names of bride and groom (including nicknames).
2. Residence addresses at time of marriage.
3. Ages at time of marriage (or dates of birth).
4. Month, day, and year of marriage.
5. Place of marriage (city or town, county, and State).
6. Purpose for which copy is needed.
7. Relationship to persons whose record is being requested.

• Give the following facts when writing for **Divorce Records:**

1. Full names of husband and wife (including nicknames).
2. Present residence address.
3. Former addresses (as in court records).
4. Ages at time of divorce (or dates of birth).
5. Date of divorce or annulment.
6. Place of divorce or annulment.
7. Type of final decree.
8. Purpose for which copy is needed.
9. Relationship to persons whose record is being requested.

Place of event	Cost of copy	Address	Remarks
Alabama			
Birth or Death	$5.00	Bureau of Vital Statistics State Department of Public Health Montgomery, AL 36130	State office has had records since January 1908. Additional copies at same time are $2.00 each. Fee for special searches is $5.00 per hour.
Marriage	$5.00	Same as Birth or Death	State office has had records since August 1936.
	Varies	See remarks	Probate Judge in county where license was issued.
Divorce	$5.00	Same as Birth or Death	State office has had records since January 1950.
	Varies	See remarks	Clerk or Register of Court of Equity in county where divorce was granted.
Alaska			
Birth or Death	$3.00	Department of Health and Social Services Bureau of Vital Statistics Pouch H-02G Juneau, AK 99811	State office has had records since 1913.
Marriage	$3.00	Same as Birth or Death	Records since 1913.
Divorce	$3.00	Same as Birth or Death	Records since 1950.
	Varies	See remarks	Clerk of the Superior Court in judicial district where divorce was granted. Juneau and Ketchikan (First District), Nome (Second District), Anchorage (Third District), Fairbanks (Fourth District).

Place of event	Cost of copy	Address	Remarks
American Samoa			
Birth or Death	$2.00	Registrar of Vital Statistics Vital Statistics Section Government of American Samoa Pago Pago, AS 96799	Registrar has had records since 1900.
Marriage	$2.00	Same as Birth or Death	
Divorce	$1.00	High Court of American Samoa Tutuila, American Samoa 96799	
Arizona			
Birth (Long form) Birth (Short form) Birth Registration card Death	$5.00 $3.00 $5.00 $3.00	Vital Records Section Arizona Department of Health Services P.O. Box 3887 Phoenix, AZ 85030	State office has had records since July 1909 and abstracts of records filed in counties before then.
Marriage	Varies	See remarks	Clerk of Superior Court in county where license was issued.
Divorce	Varies	See remarks	Clerk of Superior Court in county where divorce was granted.
Arkansas			
Birth Death	$2.00 $3.00	Division of Vital Records Arkansas Department of Health 4815 West Markham Street Little Rock, AR 72201	State office has had records since February 1914 and some original Little Rock and Fort Smith records from 1881.
Marriage	$2.00	Same as Birth or Death	Records since 1917.
	$2.00	See remarks	Full certified copy may be obtained from County Clerk in county where license was issued.
Divorce	$2.00	Same as Birth or Death	Coupons since 1923.
	Varies	See remarks	Full certified copy may be obtained from Circuit or Chancery Clerk in county where divorce was granted.
California			
Birth Death	$8.00 $4.00	Vital Statistics Section Department of Health Services 410 N Street Sacramento, CA 95814	State office has had records since July 1905. For earlier records, write to County Recorder in county where event occurred.
Marriage	$4.00	Same as Birth or Death	State office has had records since July 1905. For earlier records, write to County Recorder in county where event occurred.
Divorce	$4.00	Same as Birth or Death	Fee is for search and identification of county where certified copy can be obtained. Certified copies are not available from State Health Department.
	Varies	See remarks	Clerk of Superior Court in county where divorce was granted.
Canal Zone			
Birth or Death	$2.00	Panama Canal Commission Vital Statistics Clerk APO Miami 34011	Records available from May 1904 to September 1979.
Marriage	$1.00	Same as Birth or Death	Records available from May 1904 to September 1979.
Divorce	$0.50	Same as Birth or Death	Records available from May 1904 to September 1979.
Colorado			
Birth or Death	$6.00 Regular Service $10.00 Same Day Service	Vital Records Section Colorado Department of Health 4210 East 11th Avenue Denver, CO 80220	State office has had death records since 1900 and birth records since 1910. State office also has birth records for some counties for years before 1910.
Marriage	See remarks	Same as Birth or Death	Statewide index of records for all years except 1940–75. Inquiries will be forwarded to appropriate office. Fee for verification is $2.00. Certified copies are not available from State Health Department.
	Varies	See remarks.	County Clerk in county where license was issued.
Divorce	See remarks	Same as Birth or Death	Statewide index of records for all years except 1940–67. Inquiries will be forwarded to appropriate office. Fee for verification is $2.00. Certified copies are not available from State Health Department.
	Varies	See remarks.	Clerk of District Court in county where divorce was granted.

Place of event	Cost of copy	Address	Remarks
Connecticut			
Birth or Death (Short form)	$3.00 $2.00	Department of Health Services Vital Records Section Division of Health Statistics State Department of Health Services 150 Washington Street Hartford, CT 06106	State office has had records since July 1897. For earlier records, write to Registrar of Vital Statistics in town or city where event occurred.
Marriage	$3.00 $3.00	Same as Birth or Death See remarks	Records since July 1897. Registrar of Vital Statistics in town where license was issued.
Divorce	See remarks $3.00	Same as Birth or Death See remarks	Index of records since 1947. Inquiries will be forwarded to appropriate office. Certified copies are not available from State office. Clerk of Superior Court in county where divorce was granted.
Delaware			
Birth or Death	$2.50	Bureau of Vital Statistics Division of Public Health Jesse S. Cooper Building Dover, DE 19901	State office has records for 1861 to 1863 and since 1881 but no records for 1864 to 1880.
Marriage	$2.50	Same as Birth or Death	Records since 1847.
Divorce	See remarks $2.00	Same as Birth or Death See remarks	Records since 1935. Inquiries will be forwarded to appropriate office. Fee for search and verification of essential facts of divorce, $2.50. Certified copies are not available from State office. Prothonotary in county where divorce was granted up to 1975. For divorces granted after 1975 the parties concerned should contact Family Court in the county where the divorce was granted.
District of Columbia			
Birth or Death	$3.00	Vital Records Branch 425 I Street N.W., Room 3009 Washington, D.C. 20001	Office has had death records since 1855 and birth records since 1874 but no death records were filed during the Civil War.
Marriage	$3.00 $5.00	Same as Birth or Death Marriage Bureau 515 5th Street, NW Washington, D.C. 20001	Records since January 1, 1982. Fee for proof of marriage, $2.50; proof of age, $2.50.
Divorce	$3.00 Varies Varies	Same as Birth or Death Clerk, Superior Court for the District of Columbia, Family Division 500 Indiana Avenue, NW Washington, D.C. 20001 Clerk, U.S. District Court for the District of Columbia Washington, D.C. 20001	Records since January 1, 1982. Records since September 16, 1956. Records before September 16, 1956.
Florida			
Birth or Death	$2.50	Department of Health and Rehabilitative Services Office of Vital Statistics P.O. Box 210 Jacksonville, FL 32231	State office has had some birth records since April 1865 and some death records since August 1877. The majority of records date from January 1917. (If the exact date is unknown, the fee is $2.50 for the first year searched and $1.00 for each additional year up to a maximum of $25.00. Fee includes one copy of record if found.)
Marriage	$2.50	Same as Birth or Death	Records since June 6, 1927. (If the exact date is unknown, the fee is $2.50 for the first year searched and $1.00 for each additional year up to a maximum of $25.00. Fee includes one copy of record if found.)
Divorce	$2.50	Same as Birth or Death	Records since June 6, 1927. (If exact date is unknown, the fee is $2.50 for the first year searched and $1.00 for each additional year up to a maximum of $25.00. Fee includes one copy of record if found.)
Georgia			
Birth or Death	$3.00	Georgia Department of Human Resources Vital Records Unit Room 217-H 47 Trinity Avenue, SW Atlanta, GA 30334	State office has had records since January 1919. For earlier records in Atlanta or Savannah, write to County Health Department in county where event occurred. Additional copies of same record ordered at same time are $1.00 each. Birth cards are $2.00 each.
Marriage	See remarks $3.00	Same as Birth or Death See remarks	Centralized State records since June 9, 1952. Certified copies are not issued at State office. Inquiries will be forwarded to appropriate office. Probate Judge in county where license was issued.

Place of event	Cost of copy	Address	Remarks
Divorce	See remarks	Same as Birth or Death	Centralized State records since June 9, 1952. Certified copies are not issued at State office. Inquiries will be forwarded to appropriate office.
	Varies	See remarks	Clerk of Superior Court in county where divorce was granted.
Guam			
Birth or Death	$2.00	Office of Vital Statistics Department of Public Health and Social Services Government of Guam P.O. Box 2816 Agana, GU, M.I. 96910	Office has had records since October 26, 1901.
Marriage	$2.00	Same as Birth or Death	
Divorce	Varies	See remarks	Clerk, Superior Court of Guam, Agana, GU, M.I. 96910.
Hawaii			
Birth or Death	$2.00	Research and Statistics Office State Department of Health P.O. Box 3378 Honolulu, HI 96801	State office has had records since 1853.
Marriage	$2.00	Same as Birth or Death	
Divorce	$2.00	Same as Birth or Death	Records since July 1951.
	Varies	See remarks	Circuit Court in county where divorce was granted.
Idaho			
Birth or Death	$6.00	Bureau of Vital Statistics, Standards, and Local Health Services State Department of Health and Welfare Statehouse Boise, ID 83720	State office has had records since 1911. For records from 1907 to 1911, write to County Recorder in county where event occurred.
Marriage	$6.00	Same as Birth or Death	Records since 1947.
	Varies	See remarks	County Recorder in county where license was issued.
Divorce	$6.00	Same as Birth or Death	Records since January 1947.
	Varies	See remarks	County Recorder in county where divorce was granted.
Illinois			
Birth or Death	$10.00 Certified Copy $5.00 Certification	Office of Vital Records State Department of Public Health 535 West Jefferson Street Springfield, IL 62761	State office has had records since January 1916. For earlier records and for copies of State records since January 1916, write to County Clerk in county where event occurred. (The fee for a search of the files is $5.00. If the record is found, one CERTIFICATION is issued at no additional charge. Additional certifications of the same record ordered at the same time are $2.00 each. The fee for a full CERTIFIED COPY is $10.00. Additional certified copies of the same record ordered at the same time are $2.00 each.)
Marriage	See remarks	Same as Birth or Death	Records since January 1962. All items may be verified (fee $5.00). Inquiries will be forwarded to appropriate office. Certified copies are not available from State office.
	$3.00	See remarks	County Clerk in county where license was issued.
Divorce	See remarks	Same as Birth or Death	Records since January 1962. Some items may be verified (fee $5.00). Certified copies are not available from State office.
	Varies	See remarks	Clerk of Circuit Court in county where divorce was granted.
Indiana			
Birth or Death	$4.00	Division of Vital Records State Board of Health 1330 West Michigan Street P.O. Box 1964 Indianapolis, IN 46206–1964	State office has had birth records since October 1907 and death records since 1900. Additional copies of same record ordered at same time are $1.00 each. For earlier records, write to Health Officer in city or county where event occurred.
Marriage	See remarks	Same as Birth or Death	Marriage Index since 1958. Certified copies are not available from State Health Department.
	Varies	See remarks	Clerk of Circuit Court or Clerk of Superior Court in county where license was issued.
Divorce	Varies	See remarks	County Clerk in county where divorce was granted.

Place of event	Cost of copy	Address	Remarks
Iowa			
Birth or Death	$6.00	Iowa State Department of Health Vital Records Section Lucas State Office Building Des Moines, IA 50319	State office has had records since July 1880.
Marriage	$6.00	Same as Birth or Death	State Office has had records since July 1880.
Divorce	See remarks	Same as Birth or Death	Brief statistical record only since 1906. Inquiries will be forwarded to appropriate office. Certified copies are not available from State Health Department.
	$6.00	See remarks	Clerk of District Court in county where divorce was granted.
Kansas			
Birth or Death	$6.00	Office of Vital Statistics Kansas State Department of Health and Environment Forbes Field Building 740 Topeka, KS 66620	State office has had records since July 1911. For earlier records, write to County Clerk in county where event occurred. Additional copies of same record ordered at same time are $3.00 each.
Marriage	$6.00	Same as Birth or Death	Records since May 1913.
	Varies	See remarks	Probate Judge in county where license was issued.
Divorce	$36.00	Same as Birth or Death	Records since July 1951.
	Varies	See remarks	Clerk of District Court in county where divorce was granted.
Kentucky			
Birth Death	$5.00 $4.00	Office of Vital Statistics Department for Human Resources 275 East Main Street Frankfort, KY 40621	State office has had records since January 1911 and some records for the cities of Louisville, Lexington, Covington, and Newport before then.
Marriage	$4.00	Same as Birth or Death	Records since June 1958.
	Varies	See remarks	Clerk of County Court in county where license was issued.
Divorce	$4.00	Same as Birth or Death	Records since June 1958.
	Varies	See remarks	Clerk of Circuit Court in county where decree was issued.
Louisiana			
Birth (Long form) Birth (Short form) Death	$6.00 $3.00 $5.00	Division of Vital Records Office of Health Services and Environmental Quality P.O. Box 60630 New Orleans, LA 70160	State office has had records since July 1914. Birth records for City of New Orleans are available from 1790, and death records from 1803.
Marriage Orleans Parish	$3.00	Same as Birth or Death	
Other Parishes	Varies	See remarks	Certified copies are issued by Clerk of Court in parish where license was issued.
Divorce	Varies	See remarks	Clerk of Court in parish where divorce was granted. For Orleans Parish, copies may be obtained from State office for $2.00.
Maine			
Birth or Death	$3.00	Office of Vital Records Human Services Building Station 11 State House Augusta, ME 04333	State office has had records since 1892. For earlier records, write to the municipality where event occurred.
Marriage	$3.00	Same as Birth or Death	
	$2.00	See remarks	Town Clerk in town where license was issued.
Divorce	$3.00	Same as Birth or Death	Records since January 1892.
	$5.00	See remarks	Clerk of District Court in judicial division where divorce was granted.
Maryland			
Birth or Death	$2.00	Division of Vital Records State Department of Health and Mental Hygiene State Office Building P.O. Box 13146 201 West Preston Street Baltimore, MD 21203	State office has had records since August 1898. Records for City of Baltimore are available from January 1875.
Marriage	$2.00	Same as Birth or Death	Records since June 1951.
	See remarks	See remarks	Clerk of Circuit Court in county where license was issued or Clerk of Court of Common Pleas of Baltimore City (for licenses issued in City of Baltimore).

Place of event	Cost of copy	Address	Remarks
Divorce	See remarks	Same as Birth or Death	Records since January 1961. Certified copies are not available from State office. Some items may be verified. Inquiries will be forwarded to appropriate office.
	Varies	See remarks	Clerk of Circuit Court in county where divorce was granted.
Massachusetts			
Birth or Death	$3.00	Registry of Vital Records and Statistics 150 Tremont Street, Room B-3 Boston, MA 02111	State office has records, since 1891. For earlier records, write to the State Archives, State House, Boston, MA.
Marriage	$3.00	Same as Birth or Death	Records since 1891.
Divorce	See remarks	Same as Birth or Death	Index only since 1952. Inquirer will be directed where to send request. Certified copies are not available from State office.
	$3.00	See remarks	Registrar of Probate Court in county where divorce was granted.
Michigan			
Birth or Death	$10.00	Office of The State Registrar and Center for Health Statistics Michigan Department of Public Health 3500 North Logan Street Lansing, MI 48909	State office has had records since 1867. Copies of records since 1867 may also be obtained from County Clerk in county where event occurred. Fees vary from County to County. Detroit records may be obtained from the City of Detroit Health Department for births occurring since 1893 and for deaths since 1897.
Marriage	$10.00	Same as Birth or Death	Records since April 1867.
	Varies	See remarks	County Clerk in county where license was issued.
Divorce	$10.00	Same as Birth or Death	Records since 1897.
	Varies	See remarks	County Clerk in county where divorce was granted.
Minnesota			
Birth or Death	$5.00	Minnesota Department of Health Section of Vital Statistics 717 Delaware Street SE P.O. Box 9441 Minneapolis, MN 55440	State office has had records since January 1908. Copies of earlier records may be obtained from Clerk of District Court in county where event occurred or from the Minneapolis or St. Paul City Health Department if the event occurred in either city.
Marriage	See remarks	Same as Birth or Death	Statewide index since January 1958. Inquiries will be forwarded to appropriate office. Certified copies are not available from State Health Department.
	$5.00	See remarks	Clerk of District Court in county where license was issued.
Divorce	See remarks	Same as Birth or Death	Index since January 1970. Certified copies are not available from State office.
	$5.00	See remarks	Clerk of District Court in county where divorce was granted.
Mississippi			
Birth (Long form) Birth (Short form) Death	$10.00 $5.00 $5.00	Vital Records State Board of Health P.O. Box 1700 Jackson, MS 39215–1700	State office has had records since 1912. Full copies of birth certificates obtained within 1 year after the event are $5.00. Additional copies of same record ordered at same time are $1.00 each.
Marriage	$5.00	Same as Birth or Death	Statistical records only from January 1926 to July 1, 1938, and since January 1942.
	$3.00	See remarks	Circuit Clerk in county where license was issued.
Divorce	See remarks $0.50 per page plus $1.00 for Certification	Same as Birth or Death	Records since January 1926. Certified copies are not available from State office. Inquiries will be forwarded to appropriate office.
		See remarks	Chancery Clerk in county where divorce was granted.
Missouri			
Birth or Death	$4.00	Division of Health Bureau of Vital Records P.O. Box 570 Jefferson City, MO 65102	State office has had records since January 1910. If event occurred in St. Louis (city), St. Louis County, or Kansas City before 1910, write to the City or County Health Department. Copies of these records are $3.00 each in St. Louis City and County. In Kansas City, $6.00 for first copy and $3.00 for each additional copy ordered at same time.
Marriage	No fee	Same as Birth or Death	Indexes since July 1948. Correspondent will be referred to appropriate Recorder of Deeds in county where license was issued.
	Varies	See remarks	Recorder of Deeds in county where license was issued.

Place of event	Cost of copy	Address	Remarks
Divorce	See remarks	Same as Birth or Death	Indexes since July 1948. Certified copies are not available from State Health Department. Inquiries will be forwarded to appropriate office.
	Varies	See remarks	Clerk of Circuit Court in county where divorce was granted.
Montana			
Birth or Death	$5.00	Bureau of Records and Statistics State Department of Health and Environmental Sciences Helena, MT 59620	State office has had records since late 1907.
Marriage	See remarks	Same as Birth or Death	Records since July 1943. Some items may be verified. Inquiries will be forwarded to appropriate office. Apply to county where license was issued if known. Certified copies are not available from State office.
	Varies	See remarks	Clerk of District Court in county where license was issued.
Divorce	See remarks	Same as Birth or Death	Records since July 1943. Some items may be verified. Inquiries will be forwarded to appropriate office. Apply to county where license was issued if known. Certified copies are not available from State office.
	Varies	See remarks	Clerk of District Court in county where divorce was granted.
Nebraska			
Birth or Death	$5.00	Bureau of Vital Statistics State Department of Health 301 Centennial Mall South P.O. Box 95007 Lincoln, NE 68509	State office has had records since late 1904. If birth occurred before then, write the State office for information.
Marriage	$5.00	Same as Birth or Death	Records since January 1909.
	Varies	See remarks	County Court in county where license was issued.
Divorce	$5.00	Same as Birth or Death	Records since January 1909.
	Varies	See remarks	Clerk of District Court in county where divorce was granted.
Nevada			
Birth or Death	$4.00	Division of Health - Vital Statistics Capitol Complex Carson City, NV 89710	State office has had records since July 1911. For earlier records, write to County Recorder in county where event occurred. Additional copies of Death Records ordered at the same time are $4.00 for second and third copies, $3.00 each for the next three copies, and $2.00 each for any additional copies.
Marriage	See remarks	Same as Birth or Death	Indexes since January 1968. Certified copies are not available from State Health Department. Inquiries will be forwarded to the appropriate office.
	Varies	See remarks	County Recorder in county where license was issued.
Divorce	See remarks	Same as Birth or Death	Indexes since 1968. Certified copies are not available from State Health Department. Inquiries will be forwarded to appropriate office.
	Varies	See remarks	County Clerk in county where divorce was granted.
New Hampshire			
Birth or Death	$3.00	Bureau of Vital Records Health and Welfare Building Hazen Drive Concord, NH 03301	State office has had some records since 1640. Copies of records may be obtained from State office or from City or Town Clerk in place where event occurred.
Marriage	$3.00	Same as Birth or Death	Records since 1640.
	$3.00	See remarks	Town Clerk in town where license was issued.
Divorce	$3.00	Same as Birth or Death	Records since 1808. Fee includes search and one copy if found.
	$3.00	See remarks	Clerk of Superior Court where divorce was granted.
New Jersey			
Birth or Death	$4.00	State Department of Health Bureau of Vital Statistics CN 360 Trenton, NJ 08625	State office has had records since June 1878. Additional copies of same record ordered at same time are $2.00 each. If the exact date is unknown, the fee is an additional $0.50 per year searched.
		Archives and History Bureau State Library Division State Department of Education Trenton, NJ 08625	For records from May 1848 to May 1878.
Marriage	$4.00	Same as Birth or Death	If the exact date is unknown, the fee is an additional $1.00 per year searched.

Place of event	Cost of copy	Address	Remarks
Marriage	No fee	Archives and History Bureau State Library Division State Department of Education Trenton, NJ 08625	Records from May 1848 to May 1878.
Divorce	$2.00	Superior Court, Chancery Division State House Annex, Room 320 CN 971 Trenton, NJ 08625	The fee is for the first four pages. Additional pages cost $0.50 each.
New Mexico			
Birth or Death	$4.00	Vital Statistics Bureau New Mexico Health Services Division P.O. Box 968 Santa Fe, NM 87504–0968	State office has had records since 1920 and delayed records since 1880.
Marriage	Varies	See remarks	County Clerk in county where license was issued.
Divorce	Varies	See remarks	Clerk of District Court in county where divorce was granted.
New York (Except New York City)			
Birth or Death	$5.00	Bureau of Vital Records State Department of Health Empire State Plaza Tower Building Albany, NY 12237	State office has had records since 1880. For records before 1914 in Albany, Buffalo, and Yonkers or before 1880 in any other city, write to Registrar of Vital Statistics in city where event occurred. For the rest of the State, except New York City, write to State office.
Marriage	$5.00	Same as Birth or Death	Records from 1880 to present.
	$5.00	See remarks	Records from 1880–1907 and license issued in the cities of Albany, Buffalo, or Yonkers apply to: Albany: City Clerk, City Hall, Albany, NY 12207; Buffalo: City Clerk, City Hall, Buffalo, NY 14202; Yonkers: Registrar of Vital Statistics, Health Center Building, Yonkers, NY 10701.
Divorce	$5.00	Same as Birth or Death	Records since January 1963.
	Varies	See remarks	County Clerk in county where divorce was granted.
New York City			
Birth or Death	$4.00	Bureau of Vital Records Department of Health of New York City 125 Worth Street New York, NY 10013	Office has had birth records since 1898 and death records since 1920. For Old City of New York (Manhattan and part of the Bronx) birth records for 1865–1897 and death records for 1865–1919 write to Municipal Archives and Records Retention, 52 Chambers St., New York, NY 10038.
Marriage	$10.00	See remarks	Records from 1847 to 1865. Municipal Archives and Records Retention Center, 52 Chambers St., New York, NY 10038, except Brooklyn records for this period which are filed with County Clerk's Office, Kings County, Supreme Court Building, Brooklyn, NY 11201. Additional copies of the same record ordered at the same time are $5.00 each.
	$10.00	See remarks	Records from 1866 to 1907. City Clerk's Office in borough where marriage was peformed.
	$10.00	See remarks	Records from 1908 to May 12, 1943. New York City residents write to City Clerk's Office borough of bride's residence; nonresidents write to City Clerk's Office in borough where license was obtained.
	$10.00	See remarks	Records since May 13, 1943. City Clerk's Office in borough where license was issued.
Bronx Borough	$10.00	Marriage License Bureau 1780 Grand Concourse Bronx, NY 10457	
Brooklyn Borough	$10.00	Marriage License Bureau Municipal Building Brooklyn Borough Hall Brooklyn, NY 11201	
Manhattan Borough	$10.00	Marriage License Bureau No. 1 Center Street Municipal Building New York, NY 10007	
Queens Borough	$10.00	Marriage License Bureau Queens Borough Hall 120–55 Queens Boulevard Kew Gardens, NY 11424	
Staten Island Borough (no longer called Richmond)	$10.00	Marriage License Bureau Staten Island Borough Hall St. George Staten Island, NY 11201	
Divorce			See New York State

Place of event	Cost of copy	Address	Remarks
North Carolina			
Birth or Death	$3.00	Department of Human Resources Division of Health Services Vital Records Branch P.O. Box 2091 Raleigh, NC 27602	State office has had birth records since October 1913 and death records since January 1, 1930. Death records from 1913 through 1929 are available from Archives and Records Section, State Records Center, 215 North Blount Street, Raleigh, NC 27602.
Marriage	$3.00	Same as Birth or Death	Records since January 1962.
	$3.00	See remarks	Registrar of Deeds in county where marriage was performed.
Divorce	$3.00	Same as Birth or Death	Records since January 1958.
	Varies	See remarks	Clerk of Superior Court where divorce was granted.
North Dakota			
Birth or Death	$5.00	Division of Vital Records State Department of Health Office of Statistical Services Bismarck, ND 58505	State office has had some records since July 1893. Years from 1894 to 1920 are incomplete.
Marriage	$5.00	Same as Birth or Death	Records since July 1925. Requests for earlier records will be forwarded to appropriate office.
	Varies	See remarks	County Judge in county where license was issued.
Divorce	See remarks	Same as Birth or Death	Index of records since July 1949. Some items may be verified. Certified copies are not available from State Health Department. Inquiries will be forwarded to appropriate office.
	Varies	See remarks	Clerk of District Court in county where divorce was granted.
Ohio			
Birth or Death	$3.00	Division of Vital Statistics Ohio Department of Health G-20 Ohio Departments Building 65 South Front Street Columbus, OH 43215	State office has had records since December 20, 1908. For earlier records, write to Probate Court in county where event occurred.
Marriage	See remarks	Same as Birth or Death	Records since September 1949. All items may be verified. Certified copies are not available from State Health Department. Inquiries will be referred to appropriate office.
	Varies	See remarks	Probate Judge in county where license was issued.
Divorce	See remarks	Same as Birth or Death	Records since September 1949. All items may be verified. Certified copies are not available from State Health Department. Inquiries will be referred to appropriate office.
	Varies	See remarks	Clerk of Court of Common Pleas in county where divorce was granted.
Oklahoma			
Birth or Death	$2.00	Vital Records Section State Department of Health Northeast 10th Street & Stonewall P.O. Box 53551 Oklahoma City, OK 73152	State office has had records since October 1908.
Marriage	Varies	See remarks	Clerk of Court in county where license was issued.
Divorce	Varies	See remarks	Clerk of Court in county where divorce was granted.
Oregon			
Birth or Death	$5.00	Oregon State Health Division Vital Statistics Section P.O. Box 116 Portland, OR 97207	State office has had records since January 1903. Some earlier records for the City of Portland since approximately 1880 are available from the Oregon State Archives, 1005 Broadway, N.E., Salem, OR 97310.
Marriage	$5.00	Same as Birth or Death	Records since January 1906.
	Varies	See remarks	County Clerk in county where license was issued. County Clerks also have some records before 1906.
Divorce	$5.00	Same as Birth or Death	Records since 1925.
	Varies	See remarks	County Clerk in county where divorce was granted. County Clerks also have some records before 1925.

Place of event	Cost of copy	Address	Remarks
Pennsylvania			
Birth (Long Form) Birth (Short Form) Death	$4.00 $5.00 $3.00	Division of Vital Statistics State Department of Health Central Building 101 South Mercer Street P.O. Box 1528 New Castle, PA 16103	State office has had records since January 1906. For earlier records, write to Register of Wills, Orphans Court, in county seat where event occurred. Persons born in Pittsburgh from 1870 to 1905 or in Allegheny City, now part of Pittsburgh, from 1882 to 1905 should write to Office of Biostatistics, Pittsburgh Health Department, City-County Building, Pittsburgh, PA 15219. For events occurring in City of Philadelphia from 1860 to 1915, write to Vital Statistics, Philadelphia Department of Public Health, City Hall Annex, Philadelphia, PA 19107.
Marriage	See remarks	Same as Birth or Death	Records since January 1941. Certified copies are not available from State Health Department. Inquiries will be forwarded to appropriate office.
	Varies	See remarks	Marriage License Clerks, County Court House, in county seat where license was issued.
Divorce	Varies	Same as Birth or Death	Records since January 1946. Certified copies are not available from State Health Department. Inquiries will be forwarded to appropriate office.
	Varies	See remarks	Prothonotary, Court House, in county seat where divorce was granted.
Puerto Rico			
Birth or Death	$2.00	Division of Demographic Registry and Vital Statistics Department of Health San Juan, PR 00908	Central office has had records since July 22, 1931. Copies of earlier records may be obtained by writing to local Registrar (Registrador Demografico) in municipality where event occurred or by writing to central office for information.
Marriage	$2.00	Same as Birth or Death	
Divorce	$0.60	See remarks	Superior Court where divorce was granted.
Rhode Island			
Birth or Death	$5.00	Division of Vital Statistics State Department of Health Room 101, Cannon Building 75 Davis Street Providence, RI 02908	State office has had records since 1853. For earlier records, write to Town Clerk in town where event occurred. Additional copies of the same record ordered at the same time are $3.00 each.
Marriage	$5.00	Same as Birth or Death	Records since January 1853. Additional copies of the same record ordered at the same time are $3.00 each.
Divorce	$1.00	Clerk of Family Court 1 Dorrance Plaza Providence, RI 02903	
South Carolina			
Birth or Death	$5.00	Office of Vital Records and Public Health Statistics S.C. Department of Health and Environmental Control 2600 Bull Street Columbia, SC 29201	State office has had records since January 1915. City of Charleston births from 1877 and deaths from 1821 are on file at Charleston County Health Department. Ledger entries of Florence City births and deaths from 1895 to 1914 are on file at Florence County Health Department. Ledger entries of Newberry City births and deaths from late 1800's are on file at Newberry County Health Department. These are the only early records obtainable.
Marriage	$5.00	Same as Birth or Death	Records since July 1950.
	Varies	See remarks	Records since July 1911. Probate Judge in county where license was issued.
Divorce	$5.00	Same as Birth or Death	Records since July 1962.
	Varies	See remarks	Records since April 1949. Clerk of county where petition was filed.
South Dakota			
Birth or Death	$5.00	State Department of Health Health Statistics Program Joe Foss Office Building Pierre, SD 57501	State office has had records since July 1905 and access to other records for some events that occurred before then.
Marriage	$5.00	Same as Birth or Death	Records since July 1905.
	$5.00	See remarks	County Treasurer in county where license was issued.
Divorce	$5.00	Same as Birth or Death	Records since July 1905.
	Varies	See remarks	Clerk of Court in county where divorce was granted.

Place of event	Cost of copy	Address	Remarks
Tennessee			
Birth (Long form) Birth (Short form) Death	$6.00 $4.00 $4.00	Tennessee Vital Records Department of Health and Environment Cordell Hull Building Nashville, TN 37219–2505	State office has had birth records for entire State since January 1914, for Nashville since June 1881, for Knoxville since July 1881, and for Chattanooga since January 1882. State office has had death records for entire State since January 1914, for Nashville since July 1874, for Knoxville since July 1887, and for Chattanooga since March 6, 1872. Birth and death enumeration records by school district are available for July 1908 through June 1912. For Memphis birth records from April 1874 through December 1887 and November 1898 to January 1, 1914, and for Memphis death records from May 1848 to January 1, 1914, write to Memphis-Shelby County Health Department, Division of Vital Records, Memphis, TN 38105.
Marriage	$4.00	Same as Birth or Death	Records since July 1945.
	Varies	See remarks	County Court Clerk in county where license was issued.
Divorce	$4.00	Same as Birth or Death	Records since July 1945.
	Varies	See remarks	Clerk of Court in county where divorce was granted.
Texas			
Birth or Death	$5.00	Bureau of Vital Statistics Texas Department of Health 1100 West 49th Street Austin, TX 78756	State office has had records since 1903. Additional copies of same death record ordered at same time are $2.00 each.
Marriage	See remarks	Same as Birth or Death	Records since January 1966. Certified copies are not available from State office. Fee for search and verification of essential facts of marriage is $2.00
	Varies	See remarks	County Clerk in county where license was issued.
Divorce	See remarks	Same as Birth or Death	Records since January 1968. Certified copies are not available from State office. Fee for search and verification of essential facts of divorce is $2.00
	Varies	See remarks	Clerk of District Court in county where divorce was granted.
Trust Territory of the Pacific Islands			
Birth or Death Commonwealth of Northern Mariana Islands	$1.50	Commonwealth Courts Commonwealth Governments Saipan, CM 96950	Courts have had records since November 21, 1952. Beginning in 1950, a few records have been filed with the Hawaii Bureau of Vital Statistics. If not sure of the area in which the event occurred, write to the Director of Health Services, Trust Territory of the Pacific Islands, Saipan, Northern Mariana Islands, 96950 to have the inquiry referred to the correct area.
Republic of the Marshall Islands	$0.25 plus $0.10 per 100 words	Chief Clerk of Supreme Courts Republic of the Marshall Islands Majuro, Marshall Islands 96960	
Republic of Palau	$0.25 plus $0.10 per 100 words	Chief Clerk of Supreme Courts Republic of Palau Koror, Palau, W.C.I. 96940	
Federated States of Micronesia	$0.25 plus $0.10 per 100 words	Clerk of Courts State of Truk, FSM Moen, Truk, E.C.I. 96942	
		Clerk of Courts State of Ponape, FSM Kolonia, Ponape, E.C.I. 96941	
		Clerk of Courts State of Kosrae, FSM Lelu, Kosrae, E.C.I. 96944	
		Clerk of Courts State of Yap, FSM Colonia, Yap, W.C.I. 96943	
Marriage	Varies	See remarks	Clerk of Court in district where marriage was performed.
Divorce	Varies	See remarks	Clerk of Court in district where divorce was granted.

Place of event	Cost of copy	Address	Remarks
Utah			
Birth or Death	$5.00	Bureau of Health Statistics Utah Department of Health 150 West North Temple P.O. Box 2500 Salt Lake City, UT 84110	State office has had records since 1905. If event occurred from 1890 to 1904 in Salt Lake City or Ogden, write to City Board of Health. For records elsewhere in the State from 1898 to 1904, write to County Clerk in county where event occurred.
Marriage	$5.00	Same as Birth or Death	State office has had records since 1978. Only short form certified copies are available.
	Varies	See remarks	County Clerk in county where license was issued.
Divorce	$5.00	Same as Birth or Death	State office has had records since 1978. Only short form certified copies are available.
	Varies	See remarks	County Clerk in county where divorce was granted.
Vermont			
Birth or Death	$3.00	Vermont Department of Health Vital Records Section Box 70 60 Main Street Burlington, VT 05402	Town or City Clerk of town where birth or death occurred.
Marriage	$3.00	Same as Birth or Death	
	$3.00	See remarks	Town Clerk in town where license was issued.
Divorce	$3.00	Same as Birth or Death	
Virginia			
Birth or Death	$5.00	Bureau of Vital Records State Department of Health P.O. Box 1000 Richmond, VA 23208–1000	State office has had records from January 1853 to December 1896 and since June 14, 1912. For records between those dates, write to the Health Department in the city where event occurred.
Marriage	$5.00	Same as Birth or Death	Records since January 1853.
	Varies	See remarks	Clerk of Court in county or city where license was issued.
Divorce	$5.00	Same as Birth or Death	Records since January 1918.
	Varies	See remarks	Clerk of Court in county or city where divorce was granted.
Virgin Islands (U.S.)			
Birth or Death St. Croix	$5.00	Registrar of Vital Statistics Charles Harwood Memorial Hospital St. Croix, VI 00820	Registrar has had birth and death records on file since 1840.
St. Thomas and St. John	$5.00	Registrar of Vital Statistics Charlotte Amalie St. Thomas, VI 00802	Registrar has had birth records on file since July 1906 and death records since January 1906.
Marriage	See remarks	Bureau of Vital Records and Statistical Services Virgin Islands Department of Health Charlotte Amalie St. Thomas, VI 00801	Certified copies are not available. Inquiries will be forwarded to appropriate office.
St. Croix	$2.00	Chief Deputy Clerk Territorial Court of the Virgin Islands P.O. Box 929 Christiansted St. Croix, VI 00820	
St. Thomas and St. John	$2.00	Clerk of the Territorial Court of the Virgin Islands P.O. Box 70 Charlotte Amalie St. Thomas, VI 00801	
Divorce	See remarks	Same as Marriage	Certified copies are not available. Inquiries will be forwarded to appropriate office.
St. Croix	$2.00	Same as Marriage	
St. Thomas and St. John	$2.00	Same as Marriage	
Washington			
Birth or Death	$6.00	Vital Records P.O. Box 9709, ET-11 Olympia, WA 98504	State office has had records since July 1907. For King, Pierce, and Spokane counties copies may also be obtained from county health departments. County Auditor of county of birth has registered births prior to July 1907.
Marriage	$6.00	Same as Birth or Death	State office has had records since January 1968.
	$2.00	See remarks	County Auditor in county where license was issued.
Divorce	$6.00	Same as Birth or Death	State office has had records since January 1968.

Place of event	Cost of copy	Address	Remarks
Divorce	Varies	See remarks	County Clerk in county where divorce was granted.
West Virginia			
Birth or Death	$5.00	Division of Vital Statistics State Department of Health State Office Building No. 3 Charleston, WV 25305	State office has had records since January 1917. For earlier records, write to Clerk of County Court in county where event occurred.
Marriage	$5.00	Same as Birth or Death	Records since 1921. Certified copies available from 1964.
	Varies	See remarks	County Clerk in county where license was issued.
Divorce	See remarks	Same as Birth or Death	Index since 1968. Some items may be verified (fee $5.00). Certified copies are not available from State Office.
	Varies	See remarks	Clerk of Circuit Court, Chancery Side, in county where divorce was granted.
Wisconsin			
Birth Death	$7.00 $5.00	Bureau of Health Statistics Wisconsin Division of Health P.O. Box 309 Madison, WI 53701	State office has scattered records earlier than 1857. Records before October 1, 1907, are very incomplete. Additional copies of the same record ordered at the same time are $2.00 each.
Marriage	$5.00	Same as Birth or Death	Records since April 1836. Records before October 1, 1907, are incomplete. Additional copies of the same record ordered at the same time are $2.00 each.
Divorce	$5.00	Same as Birth or Death	Records since October 1907. Additional copies of the same record ordered at the same time are $2.00 each.
Wyoming			
Birth or Death	$2.00	Vital Records Services Division of Health and Medical Services Hathaway Building Cheyenne, WY 82002	State office has had records since July 1909.
Marriage	$2.00	Same as Birth or Death	Records since May 1941.
	Varies	See remarks	County Clerk in county where license was issued.
Divorce	$2.00	Same as Birth or Death	Records since May 1941.
	Varies	See remarks	Clerk of District Court where divorce took place.

Where To Write for Birth and Death Records of U.S. Citizens Who Were Born or Died Outside of the United States and Birth Certifications For Alien Children Adopted by U.S. Citizens

Birth Records of Persons Born in Foreign Countries Who Are U.S. Citizens at Birth

Births of U.S. citizens in foreign countries should be reported to the nearest American consular office as soon after the birth as possible on the Consular Report of Birth (Form FS-240). This report should be prepared and filed by one of the parents. However, the physician or midwife attending the birth or any other person having knowledge of the facts can prepare the report.

Documentary evidence is required to establish citizenship. Consular offices provide complete information on what evidence is needed. The Consular Report of Birth is a sworn statement of facts of birth. When approved, it establishes in documentary form the child's acquisition of U.S. citizenship. It has the same value as proof of citizenship as the Certificate of Citizenship issued by the Immigration and Naturalization Service. Filing a Consular Report of Birth is not authorized for children 5 years of age or older.

A $13.00 fee is charged for reporting the birth. The original document is filed in the Passport Services, Correspondence Branch, U.S. Department of State, Washington, D.C. 20524. The parents are given a certified copy of the Consular Report of Birth (Form FS-240) and a short form, Certification of Birth (Form DS-1350 or Form FS-545).

To obtain a copy of a report of the birth in a foreign country of a U.S. citizen, write to Passport Services, Correspondence Branch, U.S. Department of State, Washington, D.C. 20524. State the full name of the child at birth, date of birth, place of birth, and names of parents. Also include any information about the U.S. passport on which the child's name was first included. Sign the request and state the relationship to the person whose record is being requested and the reason for the request.

The fee for each copy is $4.00. Enclose a check or money order made payable to the U.S. Department of State.

The Department of State issues two types of copies from the Consular Report of Birth (Form FS-240):

• A full copy of Form FS-240 as it was filed.

- A short form, Certification of Birth (Form DS-1350), which shows only the name and sex of child and the date and place of birth.

The information in both forms is valid. The Certification of Birth may be obtained in a name subsequently acquired by adoption or legitimation after proof is submitted to establish that such an action legally took place.

Birth Records of Alien Children
Adopted by U.S. Citizens

Birth certifications for alien children adopted by U.S. citizens and lawfully admitted to the United States may be obtained from the Immigration and Naturalization Service (INS), U.S. Department of Justice, Washington, D.C. 20536, if the birth information is on file.

Certification may be issued for children under 21 years of age who were born in a foreign country. Requests must be submitted on INS Form G-641, which can be obtained from any INS office. (Address can be found in a telephone directory.) For Certification of Birth Data (INS Form G-350), a $5.00 search fee, paid by check or money order, should accompany INS Form G-641.

Certification can be issued in the new name of an adopted or legitimated child after proof of an adoption or legitimation is submitted to INS. Because it may be issued for a child who has not yet become a U.S. citizen, this certification (Form G-350) is not proof of U.S. nationality.

Certificate of Citizenship

U.S. citizens who were born abroad and later naturalized or who were born in a foreign country to a U.S. citizen (parent or parents) may apply for a certificate of citizenship pursuant to the provisions of Section 341 of the Immigration and Nationality Act. Application can be made for this document in the United States at the nearest office of the Immigration and Naturalization Service (INS). The INS will issue a certificate of citizenship for the person if proof of citizenship is submitted and the person is within the United States. The decision whether to apply for a certificate of citizenship is optional; its possession is not mandatory.

Death Records of U.S. Citizens
Who Die in Foreign Countries

The death of a U.S. citizen in a foreign country is normally reported to the nearest U.S. consular office. The consul prepares the official "Report of the Death of an American Citizen Abroad" (form OF-180), and a copy of the Report of Death is filed permanently in the U.S. Department of State (see exception below).

To obtain a copy of a report, write to Passport Serv-ices, Correspondence Branch, U.S. Department of State, Washington, D.C. 20524. The fee for a copy is $4.00.

Exception:

Reports of deaths of members of the Armed Forces of the United States are made only to the branch of the service to which the person was attached at the time of death—Army, Navy, Air Force, or Coast Guard. In these cases, requests for copies of records should be directed as follows.

For members of the Army, Navy, or Air Force:
Secretary of Defense
Washington, D.C. 20301

For members of the Coast Guard:
Commandant, P.S.
U.S. Coast Guard
Washington, D.C. 20226

Records of Births and Deaths
Occurring on Vessels or Aircraft
on the High Seas

When a birth or death occurs on the high seas, whether in an aircraft or on a vessel, the determination of where the record is filed is decided by the direction in which the vessel or aircraft was headed at the time the event occurred.

a. If the vessel or aircraft was outbound or docked or landed at a foreign port, requests for copies of the record should be made to the U.S. Department of State, Washington, D.C. 20520.

b. If the vessel or aircraft was inbound and the first port of entry was in the United States, write to the registration authority in the city where the vessel or aircraft docked or landed in the United States.

c. If the vessel was of U.S. registry, contact the U.S. Coast Guard facility at the port of entry.

Records Maintained by
Foreign Countries

Most, but not all, foreign countries record births and deaths. It is not feasible to list all foreign vital records offices, the charges they make for copies of records, or the information they may require to locate a record. However, most foreign countries will provide certifications of births and deaths occurring within their boundaries.

U.S. citizens who need a copy of a foreign birth or death record may obtain assistance by writing to the Office of Overseas Citizens Services, U.S. Department of State, Washington, D.C. 20520.

Aliens residing in the United States who seek records of these events should contact their nearest consular office.

Perpetual Calendar

Directions: Choose year you want in key below. Number opposite year is number of calendar to use for that year.

1776...9	1793...3	1810...2	1827...2	1844...9	1861...3	1878...3	1895...3	1912...9	1929...3	1946...3	1963...3	1980...10	1997...4
1777...4	1794...4	1811...3	1828...10	1845...4	1862...4	1879...4	1896...11	1913...4	1930...4	1947...4	1964...11	1981...5	1998...5
1778...5	1795...5	1812...11	1829...5	1846...5	1863...5	1880...12	1897...6	1914...5	1931...5	1948...12	1965...6	1982...6	1999...6
1779...6	1796...13	1813...6	1830...6	1847...6	1864...13	1881...7	1898...7	1915...6	1932...13	1949...7	1966...7	1983...7	2000...14
1780...14	1797...1	1814...7	1831...7	1848...14	1865...1	1882...1	1899...1	1916...14	1933...1	1950...1	1967...1	1984...8	2001...2
1781...2	1798...2	1815...1	1832...8	1849...2	1866...2	1883...2	1900...2	1917...2	1934...2	1951...2	1968...9	1985...3	2002...3
1782...3	1799...3	1816...9	1833...3	1850...3	1867...3	1884...10	1901...3	1918...3	1935...3	1952...10	1969...4	1986...4	2003...4
1783...4	1800...4	1817...4	1834...4	1851...4	1868...11	1885...5	1902...4	1919...4	1936...11	1953...5	1970...5	1987...5	2004...12
1784...12	1801...5	1818...5	1835...5	1852...12	1869...6	1886...6	1903...5	1920...12	1937...6	1954...6	1971...6	1988...13	2005...7
1785...7	1802...6	1819...6	1836...13	1853...7	1870...7	1887...7	1904...13	1921...7	1938...7	1955...7	1972...14	1989...1	2006...1
1786...1	1803...7	1820...14	1837...1	1854...1	1871...1	1888...8	1905...1	1922...1	1939...1	1956...8	1973...2	1990...3	2007...2
1787...2	1804...8	1821...2	1838...2	1855...2	1872...9	1889...3	1906...2	1923...2	1940...9	1957...3	1974...3	1991...3	2008...10
1788...10	1805...3	1822...3	1839...3	1856...10	1873...4	1890...4	1907...3	1924...10	1941...4	1958...4	1975...4	1992...11	2009...5
1789...5	1806...4	1823...4	1840...11	1857...5	1874...5	1891...5	1908...11	1925...5	1942...5	1959...5	1976...12	1993...6	2010...6
1790...6	1807...5	1824...12	1841...6	1858...6	1875...6	1892...13	1909...6	1926...6	1943...6	1960...13	1977...7	1994...7	2011...7
1791...7	1808...13	1825...7	1842...7	1859...7	1876...14	1893...1	1910...7	1927...7	1944...14	1961...1	1978...1	1995...1	2012...8
1792...8	1809...1	1826...1	1843...1	1860...8	1877...2	1894...2	1911...1	1928...8	1945...2	1962...2	1979...2	1996...9	2013...3

1 — 1989

JANUARY · FEBRUARY · MARCH · APRIL · MAY · JUNE · JULY · AUGUST · SEPTEMBER · OCTOBER · NOVEMBER · DECEMBER

2 — 1990

JANUARY · FEBRUARY · MARCH · APRIL · MAY · JUNE · JULY · AUGUST · SEPTEMBER · OCTOBER · NOVEMBER · DECEMBER

3 — 1985

JANUARY · FEBRUARY · MARCH · APRIL · MAY · JUNE · JULY · AUGUST · SEPTEMBER · OCTOBER · NOVEMBER · DECEMBER

4 — 1986

JANUARY · FEBRUARY · MARCH · APRIL · MAY · JUNE · JULY · AUGUST · SEPTEMBER · OCTOBER · NOVEMBER · DECEMBER

5 1987

JANUARY

S	M	T	W	T	F	S
				1	2	3
4	5	6	7	8	9	10
11	12	13	14	15	16	17
18	19	20	21	22	23	24
25	26	27	28	29	30	31

FEBRUARY

S	M	T	W	T	F	S
1	2	3	4	5	6	7
8	9	10	11	12	13	14
15	16	17	18	19	20	21
22	23	24	25	26	27	28

MARCH

S	M	T	W	T	F	S
1	2	3	4	5	6	7
8	9	10	11	12	13	14
15	16	17	18	19	20	21
22	23	24	25	26	27	28
29	30	31				

APRIL

S	M	T	W	T	F	S
			1	2	3	4
5	6	7	8	9	10	11
12	13	14	15	16	17	18
19	20	21	22	23	24	25
26	27	28	29	30		

MAY

S	M	T	W	T	F	S
					1	2
3	4	5	6	7	8	9
10	11	12	13	14	15	16
17	18	19	20	21	22	23
24	25	26	27	28	29	30
31						

JUNE

S	M	T	W	T	F	S
	1	2	3	4	5	6
7	8	9	10	11	12	13
14	15	16	17	18	19	20
21	22	23	24	25	26	27
28	29	30				

JULY

S	M	T	W	T	F	S
			1	2	3	4
5	6	7	8	9	10	11
12	13	14	15	16	17	18
19	20	21	22	23	24	25
26	27	28	29	30	31	

AUGUST

S	M	T	W	T	F	S
						1
2	3	4	5	6	7	8
9	10	11	12	13	14	15
16	17	18	19	20	21	22
23	24	25	26	27	28	29
30	31					

SEPTEMBER

S	M	T	W	T	F	S
		1	2	3	4	5
6	7	8	9	10	11	12
13	14	15	16	17	18	19
20	21	22	23	24	25	26
27	28	29	30			

OCTOBER

S	M	T	W	T	F	S
				1	2	3
4	5	6	7	8	9	10
11	12	13	14	15	16	17
18	19	20	21	22	23	24
25	26	27	28	29	30	31

NOVEMBER

S	M	T	W	T	F	S
1	2	3	4	5	6	7
8	9	10	11	12	13	14
15	16	17	18	19	20	21
22	23	24	25	26	27	28
29	30					

DECEMBER

S	M	T	W	T	F	S
		1	2	3	4	5
6	7	8	9	10	11	12
13	14	15	16	17	18	19
20	21	22	23	24	25	26
27	28	29	30	31		

6 1982

JANUARY

S	M	T	W	T	F	S
					1	2
3	4	5	6	7	8	9
10	11	12	13	14	15	16
17	18	19	20	21	22	23
24	25	26	27	28	29	30
31						

FEBRUARY

S	M	T	W	T	F	S
	1	2	3	4	5	6
7	8	9	10	11	12	13
14	15	16	17	18	19	20
21	22	23	24	25	26	27
28						

MARCH

S	M	T	W	T	F	S
	1	2	3	4	5	6
7	8	9	10	11	12	13
14	15	16	17	18	19	20
21	22	23	24	25	26	27
28	29	30	31			

APRIL

S	M	T	W	T	F	S
				1	2	3
4	5	6	7	8	9	10
11	12	13	14	15	16	17
18	19	20	21	22	23	24
25	26	27	28	29	30	

MAY

S	M	T	W	T	F	S
						1
2	3	4	5	6	7	8
9	10	11	12	13	14	15
16	17	18	19	20	21	22
23	24	25	26	27	28	29
30	31					

JUNE

S	M	T	W	T	F	S
		1	2	3	4	5
6	7	8	9	10	11	12
13	14	15	16	17	18	19
20	21	22	23	24	25	26
27	28	29	30			

JULY

S	M	T	W	T	F	S
				1	2	3
4	5	6	7	8	9	10
11	12	13	14	15	16	17
18	19	20	21	22	23	24
25	26	27	28	29	30	31

AUGUST

S	M	T	W	T	F	S
1	2	3	4	5	6	7
8	9	10	11	12	13	14
15	16	17	18	19	20	21
22	23	24	25	26	27	28
29	30	31				

SEPTEMBER

S	M	T	W	T	F	S
			1	2	3	4
5	6	7	8	9	10	11
12	13	14	15	16	17	18
19	20	21	22	23	24	25
26	27	28	29	30		

OCTOBER

S	M	T	W	T	F	S
					1	2
3	4	5	6	7	8	9
10	11	12	13	14	15	16
17	18	19	20	21	22	23
24	25	26	27	28	29	30
31						

NOVEMBER

S	M	T	W	T	F	S
	1	2	3	4	5	6
7	8	9	10	11	12	13
14	15	16	17	18	19	20
21	22	23	24	25	26	27
28	29	30				

DECEMBER

S	M	T	W	T	F	S
			1	2	3	4
5	6	7	8	9	10	11
12	13	14	15	16	17	18
19	20	21	22	23	24	25
26	27	28	29	30	31	

7 1983

JANUARY

S	M	T	W	T	F	S
						1
2	3	4	5	6	7	8
9	10	11	12	13	14	15
16	17	18	19	20	21	22
23	24	25	26	27	28	29
30	31					

FEBRUARY

S	M	T	W	T	F	S
		1	2	3	4	5
6	7	8	9	10	11	12
13	14	15	16	17	18	19
20	21	22	23	24	25	26
27	28					

MARCH

S	M	T	W	T	F	S
		1	2	3	4	5
6	7	8	9	10	11	12
13	14	15	16	17	18	19
20	21	22	23	24	25	26
27	28	29	30	31		

APRIL

S	M	T	W	T	F	S
					1	2
3	4	5	6	7	8	9
10	11	12	13	14	15	16
17	18	19	20	21	22	23
24	25	26	27	28	29	30

MAY

S	M	T	W	T	F	S
1	2	3	4	5	6	7
8	9	10	11	12	13	14
15	16	17	18	19	20	21
22	23	24	25	26	27	28
29	30	31				

JUNE

S	M	T	W	T	F	S
			1	2	3	4
5	6	7	8	9	10	11
12	13	14	15	16	17	18
19	20	21	22	23	24	25
26	27	28	29	30		

JULY

S	M	T	W	T	F	S
					1	2
3	4	5	6	7	8	9
10	11	12	13	14	15	16
17	18	19	20	21	22	23
24	25	26	27	28	29	30
31						

AUGUST

S	M	T	W	T	F	S
	1	2	3	4	5	6
7	8	9	10	11	12	13
14	15	16	17	18	19	20
21	22	23	24	25	26	27
28	29	30	31			

SEPTEMBER

S	M	T	W	T	F	S
				1	2	3
4	5	6	7	8	9	10
11	12	13	14	15	16	17
18	19	20	21	22	23	24
25	26	27	28	29	30	

OCTOBER

S	M	T	W	T	F	S
						1
2	3	4	5	6	7	8
9	10	11	12	13	14	15
16	17	18	19	20	21	22
23	24	25	26	27	28	29
30	31					

NOVEMBER

S	M	T	W	T	F	S
		1	2	3	4	5
6	7	8	9	10	11	12
13	14	15	16	17	18	19
20	21	22	23	24	25	26
27	28	29	30			

DECEMBER

S	M	T	W	T	F	S
				1	2	3
4	5	6	7	8	9	10
11	12	13	14	15	16	17
18	19	20	21	22	23	24
25	26	27	28	29	30	31

8 (Leap Year) 1984

JANUARY

S	M	T	W	T	F	S
1	2	3	4	5	6	7
8	9	10	11	12	13	14
15	16	17	18	19	20	21
22	23	24	25	26	27	28
29	30	31				

FEBRUARY

S	M	T	W	T	F	S
			1	2	3	4
5	6	7	8	9	10	11
12	13	14	15	16	17	18
19	20	21	22	23	24	25
26	27	28	29			

MARCH

S	M	T	W	T	F	S
				1	2	3
4	5	6	7	8	9	10
11	12	13	14	15	16	17
18	19	20	21	22	23	24
25	26	27	28	29	30	31

APRIL

S	M	T	W	T	F	S
1	2	3	4	5	6	7
8	9	10	11	12	13	14
15	16	17	18	19	20	21
22	23	24	25	26	27	28
29	30					

MAY

S	M	T	W	T	F	S
		1	2	3	4	5
6	7	8	9	10	11	12
13	14	15	16	17	18	19
20	21	22	23	24	25	26
27	28	29	30	31		

JUNE

S	M	T	W	T	F	S
					1	2
3	4	5	6	7	8	9
10	11	12	13	14	15	16
17	18	19	20	21	22	23
24	25	26	27	28	29	30

JULY

S	M	T	W	T	F	S
1	2	3	4	5	6	7
8	9	10	11	12	13	14
15	16	17	18	19	20	21
22	23	24	25	26	27	28
29	30	31				

AUGUST

S	M	T	W	T	F	S
			1	2	3	4
5	6	7	8	9	10	11
12	13	14	15	16	17	18
19	20	21	22	23	24	25
26	27	28	29	30	31	

SEPTEMBER

S	M	T	W	T	F	S
						1
2	3	4	5	6	7	8
9	10	11	12	13	14	15
16	17	18	19	20	21	22
23	24	25	26	27	28	29
30						

OCTOBER

S	M	T	W	T	F	S
	1	2	3	4	5	6
7	8	9	10	11	12	13
14	15	16	17	18	19	20
21	22	23	24	25	26	27
28	29	30	31			

NOVEMBER

S	M	T	W	T	F	S
				1	2	3
4	5	6	7	8	9	10
11	12	13	14	15	16	17
18	19	20	21	22	23	24
25	26	27	28	29	30	

DECEMBER

S	M	T	W	T	F	S
						1
2	3	4	5	6	7	8
9	10	11	12	13	14	15
16	17	18	19	20	21	22
23	24	25	26	27	28	29
30	31					

9 (Leap Year)

JANUARY

S	M	T	W	T	F	S
	1	2	3	4	5	6
7	8	9	10	11	12	13
14	15	16	17	18	19	20
21	22	23	24	25	26	27
28	29	30	31			

FEBRUARY

S	M	T	W	T	F	S
				1	2	3
4	5	6	7	8	9	10
11	12	13	14	15	16	17
18	19	20	21	22	23	24
25	26	27	28	29		

MARCH

S	M	T	W	T	F	S
					1	2
3	4	5	6	7	8	9
10	11	12	13	14	15	16
17	18	19	20	21	22	23
24	25	26	27	28	29	30
31						

APRIL

S	M	T	W	T	F	S
	1	2	3	4	5	6
7	8	9	10	11	12	13
14	15	16	17	18	19	20
21	22	23	24	25	26	27
28	29	30				

MAY

S	M	T	W	T	F	S
			1	2	3	4
5	6	7	8	9	10	11
12	13	14	15	16	17	18
19	20	21	22	23	24	25
26	27	28	29	30	31	

JUNE

S	M	T	W	T	F	S
						1
2	3	4	5	6	7	8
9	10	11	12	13	14	15
16	17	18	19	20	21	22
23	24	25	26	27	28	29
30						

JULY

S	M	T	W	T	F	S
	1	2	3	4	5	6
7	8	9	10	11	12	13
14	15	16	17	18	19	20
21	22	23	24	25	26	27
28	29	30	31			

AUGUST

S	M	T	W	T	F	S
				1	2	3
4	5	6	7	8	9	10
11	12	13	14	15	16	17
18	19	20	21	22	23	24
25	26	27	28	29	30	31

SEPTEMBER

S	M	T	W	T	F	S
1	2	3	4	5	6	7
8	9	10	11	12	13	14
15	16	17	18	19	20	21
22	23	24	25	26	27	28
29	30					

OCTOBER

S	M	T	W	T	F	S
		1	2	3	4	5
6	7	8	9	10	11	12
13	14	15	16	17	18	19
20	21	22	23	24	25	26
27	28	29	30	31		

NOVEMBER

S	M	T	W	T	F	S
					1	2
3	4	5	6	7	8	9
10	11	12	13	14	15	16
17	18	19	20	21	22	23
24	25	26	27	28	29	30

DECEMBER

S	M	T	W	T	F	S
1	2	3	4	5	6	7
8	9	10	11	12	13	14
15	16	17	18	19	20	21
22	23	24	25	26	27	28
29	30	31				

10 (Leap Year)

JANUARY

S	M	T	W	T	F	S
		1	2	3	4	5
6	7	8	9	10	11	12
13	14	15	16	17	18	19
20	21	22	23	24	25	26
27	28	29	30	31		

FEBRUARY

S	M	T	W	T	F	S
					1	2
3	4	5	6	7	8	9
10	11	12	13	14	15	16
17	18	19	20	21	22	23
24	25	26	27	28	29	

MARCH

S	M	T	W	T	F	S
						1
2	3	4	5	6	7	8
9	10	11	12	13	14	15
16	17	18	19	20	21	22
23	24	25	26	27	28	29
30	31					

APRIL

S	M	T	W	T	F	S
		1	2	3	4	5
6	7	8	9	10	11	12
13	14	15	16	17	18	19
20	21	22	23	24	25	26
27	28	29	30			

MAY

S	M	T	W	T	F	S
				1	2	3
4	5	6	7	8	9	10
11	12	13	14	15	16	17
18	19	20	21	22	23	24
25	26	27	28	29	30	31

JUNE

S	M	T	W	T	F	S
1	2	3	4	5	6	7
8	9	10	11	12	13	14
15	16	17	18	19	20	21
22	23	24	25	26	27	28
29	30					

JULY

S	M	T	W	T	F	S
		1	2	3	4	5
6	7	8	9	10	11	12
13	14	15	16	17	18	19
20	21	22	23	24	25	26
27	28	29	30	31		

AUGUST

S	M	T	W	T	F	S
					1	2
3	4	5	6	7	8	9
10	11	12	13	14	15	16
17	18	19	20	21	22	23
24	25	26	27	28	29	30
31						

SEPTEMBER

S	M	T	W	T	F	S
	1	2	3	4	5	6
7	8	9	10	11	12	13
14	15	16	17	18	19	20
21	22	23	24	25	26	27
28	29	30				

OCTOBER

S	M	T	W	T	F	S
			1	2	3	4
5	6	7	8	9	10	11
12	13	14	15	16	17	18
19	20	21	22	23	24	25
26	27	28	29	30	31	

NOVEMBER

S	M	T	W	T	F	S
						1
2	3	4	5	6	7	8
9	10	11	12	13	14	15
16	17	18	19	20	21	22
23	24	25	26	27	28	29
30						

DECEMBER

S	M	T	W	T	F	S
	1	2	3	4	5	6
7	8	9	10	11	12	13
14	15	16	17	18	19	20
21	22	23	24	25	26	27
28	29	30	31			

11 (Leap Year)

JANUARY

S	M	T	W	T	F	S
			1	2	3	4
5	6	7	8	9	10	11
12	13	14	15	16	17	18
19	20	21	22	23	24	25
26	27	28	29	30	31	

FEBRUARY

S	M	T	W	T	F	S
						1
2	3	4	5	6	7	8
9	10	11	12	13	14	15
16	17	18	19	20	21	22
23	24	25	26	27	28	29

MARCH

S	M	T	W	T	F	S
1	2	3	4	5	6	7
8	9	10	11	12	13	14
15	16	17	18	19	20	21
22	23	24	25	26	27	28
29	30	31				

APRIL

S	M	T	W	T	F	S
			1	2	3	4
5	6	7	8	9	10	11
12	13	14	15	16	17	18
19	20	21	22	23	24	25
26	27	28	29	30		

MAY

S	M	T	W	T	F	S
					1	2
3	4	5	6	7	8	9
10	11	12	13	14	15	16
17	18	19	20	21	22	23
24	25	26	27	28	29	30
31						

JUNE

S	M	T	W	T	F	S
	1	2	3	4	5	6
7	8	9	10	11	12	13
14	15	16	17	18	19	20
21	22	23	24	25	26	27
28	29	30				

JULY

S	M	T	W	T	F	S
			1	2	3	4
5	6	7	8	9	10	11
12	13	14	15	16	17	18
19	20	21	22	23	24	25
26	27	28	29	30	31	

AUGUST

S	M	T	W	T	F	S
						1
2	3	4	5	6	7	8
9	10	11	12	13	14	15
16	17	18	19	20	21	22
23	24	25	26	27	28	29
30	31					

SEPTEMBER

S	M	T	W	T	F	S
		1	2	3	4	5
6	7	8	9	10	11	12
13	14	15	16	17	18	19
20	21	22	23	24	25	26
27	28	29	30			

OCTOBER

S	M	T	W	T	F	S
				1	2	3
4	5	6	7	8	9	10
11	12	13	14	15	16	17
18	19	20	21	22	23	24
25	26	27	28	29	30	31

NOVEMBER

S	M	T	W	T	F	S
1	2	3	4	5	6	7
8	9	10	11	12	13	14
15	16	17	18	19	20	21
22	23	24	25	26	27	28
29	30					

DECEMBER

S	M	T	W	T	F	S
		1	2	3	4	5
6	7	8	9	10	11	12
13	14	15	16	17	18	19
20	21	22	23	24	25	26
27	28	29	30	31		

12 (Leap Year)

JANUARY

S	M	T	W	T	F	S
				1	2	3
4	5	6	7	8	9	10
11	12	13	14	15	16	17
18	19	20	21	22	23	24
25	26	27	28	29	30	31

FEBRUARY

S	M	T	W	T	F	S
1	2	3	4	5	6	7
8	9	10	11	12	13	14
15	16	17	18	19	20	21
22	23	24	25	26	27	28
29						

MARCH

S	M	T	W	T	F	S
	1	2	3	4	5	6
7	8	9	10	11	12	13
14	15	16	17	18	19	20
21	22	23	24	25	26	27
28	29	30	31			

APRIL

S	M	T	W	T	F	S
				1	2	3
4	5	6	7	8	9	10
11	12	13	14	15	16	17
18	19	20	21	22	23	24
25	26	27	28	29	30	

MAY

S	M	T	W	T	F	S
						1
2	3	4	5	6	7	8
9	10	11	12	13	14	15
16	17	18	19	20	21	22
23	24	25	26	27	28	29
30	31					

JUNE

S	M	T	W	T	F	S
		1	2	3	4	5
6	7	8	9	10	11	12
13	14	15	16	17	18	19
20	21	22	23	24	25	26
27	28	29	30			

JULY

S	M	T	W	T	F	S
				1	2	3
4	5	6	7	8	9	10
11	12	13	14	15	16	17
18	19	20	21	22	23	24
25	26	27	28	29	30	31

AUGUST

S	M	T	W	T	F	S
1	2	3	4	5	6	7
8	9	10	11	12	13	14
15	16	17	18	19	20	21
22	23	24	25	26	27	28
29	30	31				

SEPTEMBER

S	M	T	W	T	F	S
			1	2	3	4
5	6	7	8	9	10	11
12	13	14	15	16	17	18
19	20	21	22	23	24	25
26	27	28	29	30		

OCTOBER

S	M	T	W	T	F	S
					1	2
3	4	5	6	7	8	9
10	11	12	13	14	15	16
17	18	19	20	21	22	23
24	25	26	27	28	29	30
31						

NOVEMBER

S	M	T	W	T	F	S
	1	2	3	4	5	6
7	8	9	10	11	12	13
14	15	16	17	18	19	20
21	22	23	24	25	26	27
28	29	30				

DECEMBER

S	M	T	W	T	F	S
			1	2	3	4
5	6	7	8	9	10	11
12	13	14	15	16	17	18
19	20	21	22	23	24	25
26	27	28	29	30	31	

13 (Leap Year) 1988 14 (Leap Year)

Calendar 13 — 1988 (Leap Year)

JANUARY
```
S  M  T  W  T  F  S
            1  2
3  4  5  6  7  8  9
10 11 12 13 14 15 16
17 18 19 20 21 22 23
24 25 26 27 28 29 30
31
```

FEBRUARY
```
S  M  T  W  T  F  S
   1  2  3  4  5  6
7  8  9  10 11 12 13
14 15 16 17 18 19 20
21 22 23 24 25 26 27
28 29
```

MARCH
```
S  M  T  W  T  F  S
      1  2  3  4  5
6  7  8  9  10 11 12
13 14 15 16 17 18 19
20 21 22 23 24 25 26
27 28 29 30 31
```

APRIL
```
S  M  T  W  T  F  S
                  1  2
3  4  5  6  7  8  9
10 11 12 13 14 15 16
17 18 19 20 21 22 23
24 25 26 27 28 29 30
```

MAY
```
S  M  T  W  T  F  S
1  2  3  4  5  6  7
8  9  10 11 12 13 14
15 16 17 18 19 20 21
22 23 24 25 26 27 28
29 30 31
```

JUNE
```
S  M  T  W  T  F  S
         1  2  3  4
5  6  7  8  9  10 11
12 13 14 15 16 17 18
19 20 21 22 23 24 25
26 27 28 29 30
```

JULY
```
S  M  T  W  T  F  S
            1  2
3  4  5  6  7  8  9
10 11 12 13 14 15 16
17 18 19 20 21 22 23
24 25 26 27 28 29 30
31
```

AUGUST
```
S  M  T  W  T  F  S
   1  2  3  4  5  6
7  8  9  10 11 12 13
14 15 16 17 18 19 20
21 22 23 24 25 26 27
28 29 30 31
```

SEPTEMBER
```
S  M  T  W  T  F  S
            1  2  3
4  5  6  7  8  9  10
11 12 13 14 15 16 17
18 19 20 21 22 23 24
25 26 27 28 29 30
```

OCTOBER
```
S  M  T  W  T  F  S
                  1
2  3  4  5  6  7  8
9  10 11 12 13 14 15
16 17 18 19 20 21 22
23 24 25 26 27 28 29
30 31
```

NOVEMBER
```
S  M  T  W  T  F  S
      1  2  3  4  5
6  7  8  9  10 11 12
13 14 15 16 17 18 19
20 21 22 23 24 25 26
27 28 29 30
```

DECEMBER
```
S  M  T  W  T  F  S
               1  2  3
4  5  6  7  8  9  10
11 12 13 14 15 16 17
18 19 20 21 22 23 24
25 26 27 28 29 30 31
```

Calendar 14 (Leap Year)

JANUARY
```
S  M  T  W  T  F  S
                  1
2  3  4  5  6  7  8
9  10 11 12 13 14 15
16 17 18 19 20 21 22
23 24 25 26 27 28 29
30 31
```

FEBRUARY
```
S  M  T  W  T  F  S
      1  2  3  4  5
6  7  8  9  10 11 12
13 14 15 16 17 18 19
20 21 22 23 24 25 26
27 28 29
```

MARCH
```
S  M  T  W  T  F  S
         1  2  3  4
5  6  7  8  9  10 11
12 13 14 15 16 17 18
19 20 21 22 23 24 25
26 27 28 29 30 31
```

APRIL
```
S  M  T  W  T  F  S
                  1
2  3  4  5  6  7  8
9  10 11 12 13 14 15
16 17 18 19 20 21 22
23 24 25 26 27 28 29
30
```

MAY
```
S  M  T  W  T  F  S
   1  2  3  4  5  6
7  8  9  10 11 12 13
14 15 16 17 18 19 20
21 22 23 24 25 26 27
28 29 30 31
```

JUNE
```
S  M  T  W  T  F  S
            1  2  3
4  5  6  7  8  9  10
11 12 13 14 15 16 17
18 19 20 21 22 23 24
25 26 27 28 29 30
```

JULY
```
S  M  T  W  T  F  S
                  1
2  3  4  5  6  7  8
9  10 11 12 13 14 15
16 17 18 19 20 21 22
23 24 25 26 27 28 29
30 31
```

AUGUST
```
S  M  T  W  T  F  S
      1  2  3  4  5
6  7  8  9  10 11 12
13 14 15 16 17 18 19
20 21 22 23 24 25 26
27 28 29 30 31
```

SEPTEMBER
```
S  M  T  W  T  F  S
                  1  2
3  4  5  6  7  8  9
10 11 12 13 14 15 16
17 18 19 20 21 22 23
24 25 26 27 28 29 30
```

OCTOBER
```
S  M  T  W  T  F  S
1  2  3  4  5  6  7
8  9  10 11 12 13 14
15 16 17 18 19 20 21
22 23 24 25 26 27 28
29 30 31
```

NOVEMBER
```
S  M  T  W  T  F  S
         1  2  3  4
5  6  7  8  9  10 11
12 13 14 15 16 17 18
19 20 21 22 23 24 25
26 27 28 29 30
```

DECEMBER
```
S  M  T  W  T  F  S
               1  2
3  4  5  6  7  8  9
10 11 12 13 14 15 16
17 18 19 20 21 22 23
24 25 26 27 28 29 30
31
```

Glossary of Computer Terms

Absolute address Usually associated with memory locations, absolute address means the address by which the machine will select a specific location in memory without further address modification. It is the final numeric address of a memory location as opposed to a symbolic name or a number that requires change before it is used to select a memory location.

Absolute value The value of a number without regard to its sign.

Access time Applies to storage devices, and means the interval between a request for access to a specific storage location and availability of the contents of that location.

Accumulator A central register in the arithmetic unit, usually holding one of the operands involved in arithmetic and holding the results when arithmetic is completed. The register whose contents the computer usually operates on and to which most arithmetic-class instructions apply.

Acknowledgment Any signal or message that indicates the receipt of data or commands. Usually associated with data communications where it means that the message just sent was received correctly.

Adder The portion of the arithmetic unit where the addition of binary numbers takes place, but adders also perform the logical operations as well.

Address modification Any process by which the address specified in an instruction is changed before being applied to memory. Addition of the contents of an index register to a base address specified by an instruction is an example of address modification.

Address register A register that holds a memory address before the address is forwarded to memory.

Application program The program that *applies* the computer to a specific task for which the computer is intended. A program that causes a computer to print bank statements is an application program, but a program that detects and isolates computer faults is not.

Arithmetic unit The core of the computer where most arithmetic operations, logical operations, and testing of results are done.

Array Applied to memories, array means the overall organization of memory. It might be said that a memory is an 8-bit-by-4096-location array. In general, however, array means a group of items organized into a pattern.

Assembler program The program that translates statements made in a symbolic language by a programmer into the machine-language program that the computer executes.

Asynchronous Applied to two units of the computer, asynchronous means that each is operating at its own rate and that their operations are not synchronized. An IO controller, for example, can operate asynchronously with respect to the control unit except to notify each other when certain operations are required. In data communications, asychronous operation means that the sending and receiving units do not maintain common timing. Characters are sent between units complete with information necessary to start and stop the receiving unit.

Backspace Associated with magnetic tape units, backspace means to back up one record and stop.

Backup copy A second copy of the same data in case the primary copy is destroyed. For example, important information stored on disks for daily operation may also be stored on magnetic tapes, but the tapes would be copied onto the disks only if the original information was lost.

Baud A rate of information transfer over communication lines, roughly equivalent to bits per second but with minor differences. Expressed as 1600 baud, 4800 baud, etc. Derived from *Baud*ot code.

Baudot code A standard teletypewriter code named after the French postal telegraph engineer. Five information bits make up each character.

BCD (binary coded decimal) An arrangement in which a certain number of bits are intended to be read as a group representing a single decimal digit. Most often four bits are used to represent the decimal digit.

Bi-stable Any electronic component having only two stable states but most often called a flip-flop or latch and having states called set and reset.

Bit The contraction of the words "binary digit," but is also used to mean the position that holds a binary digit, such as bit 5, which means bit *position* 5.

Block Data or storage locations handled as a group.

Bootstrap Derived from the saying "to pull himself up by his bootstraps," in computers this usually means a short program capable of loading a large program into memory in response to the operator pushing a "load" switch. Such a program is called a bootstrap loader.

Branch Instructions in a computer program are performed in sequential order unless a branch instruction causes a departure from this sequence. Equivalent to a *branch* leaving the trunk of a tree.

Buffer Most commonly used to mean a temporary storage area for data being moved between two locations. May mean a single register or a group of many registers.

Byte A group of eight bits handled as a unit is the generally accepted meaning of byte, but some also call smaller groups bytes.

Calling To select a program for execution by stating its name or symbol. The program size varies from a subroutine to a very large program.

Capstan The small cylindrical device or shaft that spins and moves the tape in a magnetic-tape unit. The capstan actually touches the tape to move it, and the supply and take-up reels move only after the capstan has moved the tape out of the storage loops.

Carry The digit that exceeds the capacity of a bit position and thus must be combined in the next higher order bit position. When the sum of the quantities in one bit position exceeds "1" in binary arithmetic, a carry of "1" must be inserted into the bit position to the left.

Character A character is one of the set of symbols handled by the computer. Each letter of the alphabet may be included in the character set, as are numerals, punctuation, and special symbols. There are also control characters included in many character sets; these cause actions and are not shown on display screens and printers. Each character in the character set is represented by a unique binary code.

Check digit A digit produced for the purposes of verifying correct storage and transfer of the number to which it is at-

tached. A parity bit is a check digit. There are several methods of arriving at a check digit but all are based upon determining the contents of the number or numbers to which the check digit is attached and assigning the value of the check digit so that it has a fixed relationship to the contents.

Check sum An expansion of the check-digit scheme, check sum is the sum of all data handled as a block, without regard to overflow. The check sum is attached to the data block when it is stored or transferred.

Clock An electronic timing circuit in a computer. A "clock" produces signals on which all computer operations are based.

Codes Within a computer, a set of binary digits organized so as to represent higher-level functions or symbols; 101111 might always be used to represent an "A," for example, and 00111010 might be the operation code for an ADD instruction.

Compiler Similar to an assembler program listed earlier, a compiler program also translates statements made by a programmer into machine language. However, a compiler is usually more powerful than an assembler in that the assembler translates on a one-for-one basis, one programmer statement for one machine instruction, but a compiler is capable of translating one programmer statement into several machine instructions. In other words, the compiler can expand the input while an assembler cannot.

Complements Simply, the complement of a number is the value which when added to the number will produce the highest symbol that can be held in each positon in the numbering system used. The complement of 44 in the decimal system is 55, resulting in 99, the highest symbols in the numbering system. In the binary system, the complement of 010 is 101, resulting in 111, the highest symbols that can be represented in this system.

Conditional jump instructions Instuctions that test for the presence of a certain condition in the computer and, upon finding it, jump to an instruction not in sequential order rather than performing the following instruction.

Control unit One of the basic units in all general-purpose computers, the control unit decodes instructions and causes them to be carried out.

Control word Usually a supplement to an instruction, a control word holds information that a unit needs to further define the operation required. A control word may also be appended to blocks of data to give important information regarding the content and handling of the data.

Conversational mode A computer operating so as to accept English or "near English" statements directly from the user, normally from a keyboard/display unit, and to provide an immediate response that has meaning to the user without translation.

Core memory Nearly obsolete as of this writing, core memory was once the primary storage device used within a computer. Tiny circles of magnetic material, organized into large arrays, each provided storage for one bit of information. When the circle, or "core," was magnetized in one direction, it held a "1," and when magnetized in the other direction, it held a "0." Core memory was so dominant that the word "core" is still often used to mean memory, although most memories are now banks of integrated circuits.

Counter (1) A computer curcuit that maintains a sequential binary count, such as the instruction address count. (2) Any temporary storage location in which a program is maintaining a count.

CRT (cathode ray tube) The display device used in most display screens. A vacuum tube that uses an electron beam to excite an interal coating that glows. A TV picture tube is a CRT.

Cursor A special indicator placed on a display screen to point out the character or position that is the subject of attention. If the display screen and keyboard are being used by the operator to enter information, the cursor points out the next entry position.

Cyclic redundacy check A checking scheme in which all the data being considered as a block are processed by a complex mathematical equation and one or two check characters formed as a result. The check characters are then attached to the data block when it is stored or transferred. The receiving unit or the unit retrieving the data block performs the same mathematical operation on the data block and compares its CRC characters with those received to check the accuracy of transmission or storage.

Data base Usually a large collection of information maintained permanently, or semipermanently, on which a computer is to operate. Examples of a data base are the payroll records of a company and a list of all the parts maintained in its inventory.

Data link A communications link over which computer data are transferred. This may range from voice-grade telephone lines that handle data transfer at low rates to radio links capable of very high rates of transfer.

Debug To remove the "bugs" from equipment or programs during the initial testing of these products. A "bug" is usually thought of as a design flaw that prevents the equipment or program from fulfilling its intended function rather than a malfunction that occurs after the system has been tested.

Decision instruction An instruction whose action depends upon the conditions it finds existing when it is executed. A Branch on 0 instruction, for example, will branch if it finds that the accumulator contents are 0 but will not branch if they are not 0.

Decrement (1) To reduce a quantity by a specific number, or (2) the number by which the quantity is reduced. When a 1 is subtracted from the contents of an index register, that register is said to have been decremented by 1.

Diagnostic program A program intended to test computer equipment and, through a logical process of testing and elimination, isolate failures to small sections of the machine.

Digital A computer in which all quantities are represented by discrete numbers rather than variations in voltage or current level. A computer that uses voltage and current levels to represent quantities in an analog computer.

Disk memory The storage area maintained on magnetic disk units.

Double precision A scheme in which the results of an arithmetic operation have twice the number of positions of the individual quantities involved so as to be more precise.

Down counter A computer circuit that is originally set to a number and then counts toward zero. A program may also establish memory location as a counter and reduce its contents, producing a down counter.

Drum memory The storage area maintained on magnetic drum units.

Dump Usually means the copying of memory contents to another storage medium or displaying or printing them for examination. Dump implies the lack of discrimination among the data transferred. In other words, copying is not selective.

Encoder a device or program that converts one form of information to another. For example, an encoder would convert an "A" to the binary representation to an "A," while a decoder would translate the binary representation and produce an "A.".

End-around-carry A carry from the most significant position of the adder that is brought back to the least significant position and added in when subtraction is done with the subrahend represented in one's complement form. Use of the 2's complement form does not eliminate the end-around-carry but allows it to be discarded rather than added in the least significant adder stage.

End of file A special mark recorded in storage media that des-

ignates the end of a group of records that is to be considered a file.

Excess 3 code A code in which the decimal value of the binary representation of a deciaml digit is three greater than the digit itself. For example, the digit 0 is represented by binary 011, read "3" in decimal, but when 011 is translated it produces a 0 on the printer and display screen.

Executable Applied to programs, executable means a program that can be performed by the computer rather than a source program that must be assembled or compiled before it can be executed. An executable program is usually called an "object" program.

Executive The name usually given to a program whose function is to control the jobs to be performed and to select the programs required to perform them. An executive would also manage the storage media as required to provide input data and to store processed data.

File A group of records organized so as to be treated as a unit. All the records in a file hold information that is of the same general type.

Fixed-point arithmetic The arithmetic operations performed in a computer in which the position of the binary point is established by the computer design and is not subject to change.

Floating-point arithmetic The arithmetic operations performed in a computer in which the position of the binary point in a number is specified by a point position indicator section attached to each number.

Flow chart A method by which certain symbols are used to show the functions that a program is to perform and the order in which these functions are to be performed. Decisions to be made, inputs required, outputs produced, and actions to be taken are among the functions shown in program flow charts.

Full adder A complete adder capable of handling a carry-in to each stage, forming the sum of two numbers, and producing a carry-out of each stage. See "adder" earlier, and "half adder" following.

Half adder The portion of an adder that handles only the two numbers being added and produces a sum and carry-out. A half adder does not handle a carry-in.

Header Identifying or labeling information that precedes the date.

Hexadecimal numbering system A system in which four binary digits are read as a decimal digit, 0 through 9, and six letters, usually A through F. Counting progresses 1, 2, 3, 4, 5, 6, 7, 8, 9, A, B, C, D, E, F. A total of sixteen combinations are used; therefore the name hexadecimal is given to this system.

Hollerith code A code used in punched cards in which one column of twelve positions each is read as a unit. The combinations of punches in these twelve positions is Hollerith code. Named for Dr. Herman Hollerith.

Increment (1) To increase a quantity by a specific number, or (2) the number by which the quantity is increased. When a 1 is added to the contents of an index register, for example, that register is said to have been incremented by 1.

Index register A register, usually in the arithmetic unit, that holds a count. The most common use of this count is to modify memory addresses so that the same operations can be performed repeatedly but with a different memory address each time.

Indexing Generally means the modification of a memory address by the contents of an index register. Can also mean a system of electronic record-keeping in which an index of the contents of a file is maintained.

Indirect addressing Normally, the address portion of an instruction is the address of the data to be operated on. However, indirect addressing is a method by which the address portion of an instruction directs the control unit to a memory location in which the address of the data to be opearated on is held. In other words: "Go to this address to get your final address."

Instruction register Always part of the control unit, the instruction register holds each instruction after it is read from memory and while it is being decoded and executed.

Instruction word This means an instruction consisting of an operation code, specifying what is to be done, and an operand, which is a quantity to be used in the execution of the instruction.

Integrated circuit Circuits formed so that their components cannot be separated. Usually called "chips" because they are very small and are composed of materials such as silicon.

Interrupt A signal used by other computer units to gain the attention of the control unit. Usually produced in response to important external conditions, an interrupt signal produces a break in the flow of activities. Action taken in response to the interrupt varies according to the programs being executed, but the immediate needs of the external device are normally met before the control unit returns to the point at which it was interruped.

Keypunch (1) The equipment used to translate data into coded form acceptable to a computer or (2) the action of operating the equipment to accomplish the translation. Older systems used equipment that actually punched the data into cards as an operator read the data from input sheets and typed the data at a keyboard. However, modern systems convert the keyboard input directly to electronic form.

Lateral parity Usually means the individual parity bit assigned to a single byte or character.

Logic diagram The method of representing the circuits that make up a computer by symbols that illustrate the function of each circuit.

Longitudinal parity A parity character formed at the end of a block of data. Each bit in the parity character represents the total parity of all preceding bits of the same level. For example, bit 1 of the parity character is the parity bit for bit 1 of all preceding characters.

Longitudinal redundancy check character (LRCC) Usually associated with magnetic-tape units, LRCC means the longitudinal parity characters recorded at the end of a block a data, normally at the end of a file.

Loops Applies to programs, and means a group of instructions that return to the starting point and repeat themselves, usually until a certain event takes place to break the loop.

Machine code The binary numbers used within the computer to represent instructions, addresses, numbers, and other characters. Most often, however, machine code is more narrowly defined to mean the binary representation of the operation code portion of an instruction.

Macro instruction (1) A source statement that causes at least several instructions to be generated. (2) A "large" instruction that may call for routines or programs to be executed.

Matrix An array of elements in a rectangle, such as the printing pattern of a matrix printer. Also an array of numbers.

Memory The storage device immediately accessible to the control and arithmetic units of a computer, where the current instructions and operating data are stored.

Memory-address register The register, usually in the memory unit, that holds the address applied to the memory array.

Memory cycle The functions performed by a memory unit in response to a read or a write command.

Micro operations Most often used to mean the individual steps necessary to carry out an instruction. Sometimes associated with micro programming, which means to select the steps and processes to be performed within an instruction.

Microsecond One one-millionth of a second.

Millisecond One one-thousandth of a second.

MODEM An abbreviation for *Mod*ulator-*Dem*odulator, a device used to convert data from a computer to a form suitable for transmission and back again to computer form. A MODEM, for example, is used at both ends of a voice-grade telephone line when two computers are exchanging data over that line.

Multiple address Applies to a computer whose instruction word holds more than one address section. Such a computer is called a multiple-address machine, as opposed to a single-address machine.

Multiplex To place information from several different sources on a single channel, usually separating them by choosing one source at a time for connection to the channel.

Nanosecond One one-billionth of a second.

Nondestructive readout The process by which data can be read from a storage device without affecting the stored information. This term is usually applied to memory units rather than other storage devices because older memories destroyed the contents of each location read and required that they be restored.

Nonexecutable Applied to statements entered by a programmer, this means that that statement is not converted to a machine instruction and executed. An example of a nonexecutable statement is "enter remarks."

Nonreturn-to-zero recording In magnetic recording devices, the practice of not returning the magnetic field to zero at the end of a bit position.

Object program A program that is in machine language and is executed by the computer. It is the "object" of entering and assembling source statements and represents the final results of the process.

Off-line operations An operation that is not in the primary flow of computer activities. For example, data from a magnetic tape may be printed out while a computer is not engaged in or available for its primary task. In this case, the computer is doing off-line printing. Can also mean an operation such as a direct connection between the tape and printer, which bypasses the computer completely and is not under computer control. A peripheral unit that is said to be off line is one that is not immediately accessible to the computer.

On-line operation The opposite of the off-line operation above, an on-line operation *is in the primary flow* of the computer activities. When applied to the status of a peripheral unit, it means that that unit is *immediately accessible* to the computer.

Operand Usually considered to be one of two major parts of an instruction, the operation code being the other. An operand is an item to be operated upon or is somehow involved in the operation specified by the operation code. An operand may be a memory address, a number to be added, a parameter of some type, etc.

Operation code A portion of an instruction or control word that specifies the function that the computer is to perform. Eventually translated into binary-form machine language, the operation code may be any one of several high-level forms, including a symbolic form, when entered by the programmer.

Overflow The condition resulting from an operation in which the result exceeds the capacity of the computer's basic unit of information to represent it. A decimal 15 could be represented by four bit positons, for example, but if the results of an addition were 16, an overflow would have occurred and the result is meaningless because it has exceeded the capacity of the basic unit of information.

Parallel The organization of a unit so that all parts of an element are available at the same time. Usually used to describe the way in which bytes and words are available and operated on. When all eight bits of a byte are made available simultaneously, that is said to be parallel; if they are available only one at a time, that is said to be serial. The word "parallel" also applies to high-level operations, but always has the same basic meaning: simultaneous availability or operation.

Parity checking As defined in the dictionary, "parity" has to do with maintaining equality. Applied to computer use, it means adding a bit to a unit of information so as to maintain the total number of 1s in that unit always odd or always even, depending upon which method is chosen. The bit added is called the parity bit, and it is a way of checking the accuracy of storage or transfer.

Polling A scheme in which a central unit chooses one remote unit after another and exchanges data with each remote unit that has information ready. Usually associated with a central computer and many remote terminals.

Positional notation The assignment of different weights to the positions that a digit in any numbering system occupies, such as the units, tens, and hundreds positions in the decimal system. The weight of a specific character depends upon the position that it occupies. Contrast this with the confusing positions used by the Roman numeral system.

Program (1) A collection of computer instructions arranged so as to cause the computer to perform a specific task. (2) The act of selecting and placing in the proper order the instructions required.

Protocol Most often associated with the exchange of data between two systems separated by considerable distance, protocol means the rules and conventions that will be followed by each system during the exchange.

Pseudo instruction An instruction issued as a source statement by the programmer but that is not executed by the computer directly on a one-machine instruction for one psuedo-instruction basis. An example of a pseudo instruction might be "title the page, TTP," which would be converted to many machine instructions in order to carry out that act.

Queue Usually a number of inputs placed in order to be processed in sequence, but can also apply to a number of units awaiting output. The first group would be called the "input queue" and the latter the "output queue." It should be noted that the elements placed in a queue are usually large—messages between computer sites, for example—rather than just a few bytes to be processed one after another.

Radix The quantity of characters in a numbering system. The radix of the binary system is 2; two characters, 1 and 0, make up the system. The radix of the decimal system is 10, the ten characters being 0 through 9.

Random access The ability to gain access to any one storage location among many in an equal amount of time and effort and not depending upon any previous action. Tape units, for example, are serial access rather than random access. Usually only the memory within the computer is thought of as being a random-access storage unit.

Reading The retrieval of information from some form of storage.

Read-only memory A storage unit whose contents cannot be changed during normal operation. In other words, data cannot be written into this memory by the computer; it was placed there in advance by a special means, and the computer can only read the memory contents. Read-only memories have the advantage of being very small and requiring a minimum of supporting circuits.

Read/write head A small unit capable of both producing and sensing magnetic fields. Used to record and play back information on magnetic tapes, disks, drums, and any other magnetic recording device.

Real-time processing The processing of data from an event when the event is actually occurring rather than storing the data for processing later. An example of realtime processing would be a machine tool being operated by a computer in which the progress of the tool was sensed by the computer, and directions given by the computer were based on the tool's progress.

Record A group of bytes, characters, or words organized and handled as a unit is the narrow definition of "record" used in the computer industry. "Record" is usually applied to the organization of data on magnetic tapes and disks.

Register A group of bi-stable devices used to hold a unit of information handled by a computer. Most often associated with the groups of bi-stables in the control, arithmetic, and input-output units, but the locations in storage (particularly memory) are called registers by some.

"Scratch pad" storage A very small memory maintained in the arithmetic or control units for the purpose of temporarily storing certain information without using the main memory. This information may be the interim results of calculations or the information required to return from an interrupt.

Serial The organization of a unit so that only one part of an element is available at a time. (See Parallel.) Used to describe the way in which data are transferred or processed, such as only one bit of a byte being available at a time. To handle or process in sequence rather than simultaneously.

Serial access The ability to reach information in storage only sequentially. Tape units are serial-access storage units in that the tape must be moved past the read/write head until the desired location is reached.

Shift register A register in which the information can be moved laterally—that is, the register contents can be shifted so that a bit moves to the adjacent position.

Software Very commonly used to mean programs, while hardware means the equipment, but originally meant the programs, programming aids, and the documentation associated with programs.

Source program The statements originally entered by the programmer before they are assembled or compiled. The program written in the source language that is converted to machine code and the object program by an assembler or compiler.

Subroutine A small group of instructions intended to perform one specific function. Whenever this function is required by a program, the subroutine is called and executed. This allows several different programs to use the same subroutine and avoids the need to include these instructions in every program.

Synchronous Applied to data communications, synchronous means that the sending and receiving units use a common timing signal to remain "in step" while data are being transferred, and the data stream is continuous. When applied to computers it means that the computer units are related by a common timing cycle and that their operations have a fixed timing relationship to one another.

Time-out (1) A specific interval in which an event must occur or the operation is considered in error or ended is called a "time-out." (2) The act of allowing this interval to elapse is called a "time-out."

Time sharing Generally thought of as the sharing of a large central computer by several parties, usually from remote locations, on the basis of having certain intervals assigned to each party. Sometimes the access is based on demand, and in other cases it is based upon time assignments made in advance.

Trace routine A program intended to assist programmers in locating flaws during the program-testing process. A trace routine allows the programmer to execute one instruction at a time in order to examine the results of that instruction, the inputs provided, and the contents of the most significant registers involved. Large-scale computers with elaborate control panels do not require the use of trace routines because the controls and displays available to the programmer enable him to accomplish the same thing. Trace routines are most often used in small computers where the controls and displays available are limited.

Translation The conversion of one form of code to another. For example, source statements are "translated" to machine language by assemblers and compilers, operation codes are translated into commands by decoders in the control units, and a code such as EBCDIC held in storage is translated to ASCII for transmission to another system.

Transparent To "see through" predetermined character assignments and view only the binary representation. An example of this is "transparent mode" of data communications. Until this mode is chosen, the bit patterns are interpreted in a preassigned way, an "END" command might be represented by 10101111, for example, and whenever 10101111 was received the computer would recognize it as the END command. In the transparent mode, the computer receiving 10101111 would simply process it as a number and not interpret it as an END command, thus "seeing through" the preassigned meaning.

User program An application program operated by the computer user.

Volume A large collection of files, usually a large physical division such as a reel of magnetic tape.

Word One of the basic units of information processed by the computer. Most often, a word is considerably larger than a byte. A computer may use a sixteen-bit, thirty-two-bit, or forty-eight-bit word as its basic unit of information.

Writing The process of placing information in a storage medium.

Word Processing Glossary

abbreviation document A document on which words or phrases are stored; each one is identified by a short code or abbreviation and can be called out and inserted into your main document by using that code or abbreviation only, rather than having to re-enter the entire word or phrase. For complicated words that are used often, use of an abbreviation document saves both time and typographical errors.

access To make something available to use; to access a document means to call it out for revision or printing.

application A specific task that your system can perform; you can "apply" the software/hardware parts of your system to achieve a desired result. Copying a document from one disk to another is a concrete application of one of your system's many possibilities.

automatic A function your system will perform repeatedly for you without specific prompting each time. An "automatic sheet feeder" feeds a new sheet of paper for each new page without your having to put the sheet into the system manually; "automatic page numbering" prints the proper page number on each sheet on a large job without your having to enter each page number separately.

automatic sheet feeder An optional piece of hardware that feeds single sheets of paper automatically to the printer. Most automatic sheet feeders have two trays and can feed the first sheet of a document from one tray, with all the rest of the sheets needed for that document being fed from the second tray. This feature permits the use of letterhead for the first page and blank sheets for all the following pages. Every automatic sheet feeder system has a manual feed option, so you can slip in a single job that bypasses the automatic feature.

backspace A key that moves the cursor backward one space at a time; in some systems the use of this key will delete the character the cursor backs over.

back up To move the cursor backward through the document without deleting copy.

backup copy A copy of an entire disk or documents on a disk that is made for safekeeping. Backup copies can also be made of program (systems or software) disks.

batch printing Lining up jobs in a queue (a waiting line) to print automatically one right after another. The creation or revision of other documents that are not in the printing queue can take place while the printing is going on.

bidirectional Pertaining to the ability to move in both directions. Most daisy wheel and thimble printwheels used on letter-quality printers and most matrix printheads move and print in both right-to-left and left-to-right directions. If your system can print superscripts and subscripts, the paper moves bidirectionally—first up and then down or first down and then up—when printing these characters.

block A storage space on a diskette that holds a certain number of characters. Each block holds the same number of characters. Your manufacturer can tell you how many characters are contained in the blocks in your system. Knowing this information is helpful in determining the total size of any document.

boilerplate Standard paragraphs used in your work. They can be filed by name or number and stored in a paragraph document to be called up for inclusion in a document whenever needed.

bold To overprint the same text with the same characters in order to make them appear slightly darker. Not all systems have the capability of printing each character twice.

breaking hyphen A hyphen that joins compound words ("long-standing") and will break if the first half of the compound word is at the end of a line ("long-"; "standing"). Entering a breaking hyphen may require a supershift, depending on the software program in your system.

brightness control The device on your system that allows you to lighten or darken the text that appears on your screen. It is especially useful if you work in a natural light setting in which the room's light varies from strong sunlight to early winter darkness.

carbon ribbon A better-quality printer ribbon. It normally is used only once, with each character striking at an unused spot on the ribbon, in contrast to a cloth ribbon that is used several times in a continuous loop. The carbon ribbon produces a darker, cleaner image.

carriage The mechanism in your printer that holds the printwheel or printhead and moves the printwheel (printhead) back and forth across the paper while printing is taking place. (Sometimes called a "carrier.")

carriage return (carrier return) *See* **return.**

center To position a word or phrase at the center of a line or centered on a tab stop. Once the centering location is determined and the centering commands are executed, the word or phrase will automatically center as it is entered.

character Any letter, number, space, command, or instruction that you enter into the system. You will normally see only the letters, punctuation marks, numbers, and spaces on the screen. If you enter a display or view mode, you will see all the other special characters you have entered that control the format of your document, such as hard returns, superscripts, tab stops, format changes, and so on. These normally invisible characters will not print out, but they do take up space on your disk.

cloth ribbon A printer ribbon that is on a continuous loop and can be reused until you decide it is printing too light to use any longer. A carbon ribbon is used only once and has to be replaced when it has run once through the printer.

code In some systems the supershift key is called "code." It needs to be pressed at the same time (or on some systems, just before) a coded character key is pressed to make the key perform its coded function. For example, the "u" key pressed alone results in a lowercase "u" being entered; shift + "u" results in an uppercase "U" being entered; and supershift (or code) + "u" results in the word last entered being underlined (if underlining a word is the function of the supershift + "u" key in your system).

column Vertically arranged blocks of text, usually found in tables or in newsletters or bulletins. Some systems will adjust the space between the columns automatically; some require you to tab to the space manually. Most systems will center columns around a center point, around a decimal, around a comma, or will print a column flush right or flush left.

communications The transferring of data to and from your word processing system to another computer system (word processor, data processor, intelligent copier, and so on) by

cable or telephone. Communications requires special hardware (cable and/or modem) and software.

composite character A character that is produced by two or more characters one on top of the other.

continuous-form paper A long piece of paper that can go continuously through your printer. The paper is perforated at regular intervals so pages can be separated. This paper is pulled through the printer by a form-feed tractor.

copy (1) The content of your document; (2) to duplicate your document or disk on another disk, or to duplicate your document elsewhere on the same disk; (3) the duplicate of your document or disk.

create To start a new document. The first step is to give this new document a name, so you can later go back to it for revision or call it up for printing, or even instruct the system to erase it.

CRT An abbreviation of "cathode ray tube," another name for your screen (sometimes more technically called "video display" or VD).

cursor The indicator that shows where the next character to be entered will enter the system (sometimes a blinking underline or rectangle, sometimes a solid highlight).

cursor keys Some systems have keys with arrows that move the cursor up or down, right or left, depending on which key is pressed. If the key is held down, the cursor will continue to move in a given direction until the key is released. Other systems have keys with names that move the cursor forward or backward by character, by word, by sentence, by paragraph, or by page. Most systems have supershift combinations that enable you to move the cursor directly to a particular page in a long document, or to the start (top) or the end (bottom) of the document. By using "find" or "search" commands, you can move the cursor to particular words in your document.

cut To remove or copy part of a document (sometimes called "move"). In some systems you have to "paste" this part of the document elsewhere in the document; in other systems you have an option of "forgetting it," and thus deleting a sizable portion of the document at once rather than word by word or line by line.

date and time A time clock in the system. It must be set with the current date and time each time the system is turned on. Some systems can print the date and time from the clock onto a document, thus providing an automatic "stamp" as to when work was begun and/or ended. A system with a date and time feature will automatically keep track of the time spent working on each document.

decimal alignment The ability of the system to line up numbers in a column on a decimal point.

default The settings that are preassigned and will format and control the system unless you specifically enter different settings. The software manufacturer initially preassigns these settings, on the basis of the most widespread expected usage. You may enter new settings for a particular document: these will thereafter apply to that document unless you change the settings later. In some systems, you can enter new settings on the program diskette—creating your own default settings to which the system will automatically revert when not specifically told otherwise.

delete To remove (erase) characters, words, pages, documents, or entire disks. Deleted parts of a document normally cannot be retrieved (only if they are placed in the system's temporary memory can they be retrieved).

directory Another name for index: the system's list of documents that are stored on a disk.

disk A thin, flexible magnetic disk, enclosed in a rather stiff protective jacket. Depending on your system, it will be 5¼ inches in diameter or 8 inches in diameter. Some newer mini-systems are appearing with disks that are 3 inches in diam-

eter. Documents and software programs are stored on disks. The amount of data that can be placed on a disk is not directly related to its diameter, but rather to the density of its formatting. (Often disks are called "diskettes.")

disk drives The recording and reading devices that are located on your screen console or in a separate disk drive unit. You place the disks into the slots in the disk drive, close the slot door or gate, and the system will automatically load the contents of the disks into the system for work. (In some systems, you need to instruct the system to load, or "boot," the program disk into the system.

disk name The name you assign a disk. It may be an actual name, an abbreviation, or an alphanumeric code. This name will thereafter be used in the system to gain access to the contents of the disk. You can change a disk name at any time.

display To show the contents of a disk on the screen. In a display mode, the hidden or invisible characters are also shown.

document A body of text of any length that you create, name, and store on a document disk.

document comment Some systems allow you to enter a comment about the document. This comment will serve as a reminder of some work function, deadline, or routing you need to remember. This comment will appear only on your screen: it will not be printed out, nor will it affect the formatting of the document. The document comment is a kind of electronic memo slip you can attach to your document, if you wish.

document name The name you give a document when you create it. That name is the means you have thereafter to gain access to the document for revision, copying, printing, or deletion.

document number Some systems will assign each document on a disk a number. That number does not change as you add or delete other documents on the disk.

double-density disk A disk that is initialized in such a way as to take considerably more data than a single-density disk. The amount varies from nearly double to over three times as much, depending on your system.

draft printer A high-speed matrix printer that prints out documents on continuous-form paper. You can use this printer for initial proofing and revision; its output is not as attractive as the output of a letter-quality printer.

duplicate To copy a document or disk elsewhere, but still leave the original intact.

edit To revise the text of a document.

edit keys The functional keys that allow you to instruct the system directly to perform functions relating to editing. Moving the cursor, going to a page or word, searching or finding, replacing, filing or ending, inserting required page ends, calling up view mode, are all typical functions performed directly by pressing edit keys.

elite Another name for a 12-pitch typeface; a 10-pitch typeface is sometimes called "pica."

end A term used in some systems for filing a document onto the document disk. Some systems require using a page end key to file each page as you proceed through the document, without having to file the entire document and then recall it again to continue work.

enter To put text and instructions into the system by pressing on keys. Some systems use the term "enter" to refer to their execute-an-instruction command.

erase To remove or delete text from a disk, making that space available for receiving new text. A system will normally have several methods of erasing text, ranging from single characters to documents to entire disks.

error message A brief message that may appear on your screen to tell you that you cannot perform a function the way you

are trying to perform it. The message will usually prompt you to help you perform the function in a way that works in the system.

execute A command to the system to perform a function. You usually need to set the function up; when you execute the command, the function occurs. Some systems have a special "execute" or "enter" key; others use the return key as the execute key.

feature A function that your system is capable of performing. A spelling-hyphenation dictionary is an example of a feature.

field A distinctly identifiable part of your document that can be recalled and used by reference to its identity. For example, a list of addresses may include the state as a separate identifiable part or field. "State" is the field name, and "Iowa" or "IA" is a part of the field. When the field name is called up for use, the system will use "Iowa" or "IA."

file To store a document on a disk for future use. Also, "file" is another name for the document itself.

file name The name or alphanumeric code you have given the system to identify a particular document.

find A term used in some systems to define the search feature.

footer Text placed automatically at the bottom of each page, such as a document name, page number, date, or author's name.

format The layout of the page, using such specific instructions as margin width, tabs, number of lines, and line spacing.

global search and replace A feature that automatically searches out every instance of a string of characters in a document and replaces them with a different string of characters. You have told the system which word or phrase to search and which word or phrase to use as the replacement. The word "global" indicates this process occurs throughout the entire document without stopping, rather than moving from one instance to the next individually on your command.

go-to A feature that enables you to move quickly to a specific page (by page number) in a document.

hard copy A printout on paper of a document from your system.

hard return A return caused by pressing the return key rather than an automatic return (soft return) created by the system when a line turns over. The hard return will function wherever it appears, even though the document rearranges itself when text is added or deleted.

hard space A space made in combination with a supershift key; this space holds letters together as though it were a character itself. It is useful in ensuring that initials that are part of a person's name do not separate over two different lines.

hardware The physical equipment parts of a word processing system. Printers and keyboards are hardware.

header Text placed automatically at the top of each page, such as a document name, page number, date, or author's name.

highlight A feature that makes some text stand out on the screen. Highlighting may be by underlining, by brighter appearance of certain characters, or by lighting up the background behind characters, words, or blocks of text.

hyphenation Use of the character - at the end of a line to divide a word into syllables or between parts of compound words. Some systems can use a hyphenation dictionary to divide words automatically (though not always correctly). All systems differentiate between a hard hypen, which always appears and holds characters on either side together; a breaking hyphen, which always appears but will allow the characters that follow it to drop down to the next line if a line turnover is required: and an invisible hyphen, which is used in word division and will appear if at the end of a line but will not be printed if the word is elsewhere in the text.

index The list of documents on a document disk. The index can be viewed on the screen and printed out on paper.

initialize To prepare a disk to receive data. The data may be a software program or documents. The preparation may be for single- or double-density use, depending on your needs and the capabilities of your system.

insert To place text into a document between characters that are already in the document. The system will rearrange existing text around the new, inserted text.

justify To print a document with even right and left margins. Some systems have a "half-justify" option that makes the right-hand margin somewhat more even than a regular ragged right but not exactly even as in a justified right-hand margin. The system will require hyphenating when printing a justified right-hand margin, since the lines will spread so open as to be unattractive if there are too few characters on a line.

keyboard The hardware part that has keys for entering characters and commands. It is either part of the terminal or is connected to the terminal by a flexible cable.

keystroke One press of any key on the keyboard, including spaces, returns, and any command keys.

keystroke save A feature on some systems that allows you to put a certain number of characters into a temporary memory and play them back on command for any number of times until you replace them with a new set of characters. On other systems, this feature can be used with the cut-and-paste feature.

left justify A tab stop on which the first character of any entry in a column always lines up; the words or figures build toward the right.

left margin The place where all left-hand lines normally start to print. The placement of your left-hand margin on the paper is related to how you set up your margins when you format the page. You should learn how far in from the edge of the paper your left-hand margin should be for letterhead correspondence and use that setting routinely for correspondence work.

letter-quality printer Often referred to as an LQP. This printer uses an impact printing method with printwheels or thimbles to produce a quality of printing equal to or better than that produced by a good typewriter.

library A feature that enables you to store words, phrases, and even paragraphs elsewhere on a disk (in a library document) and to call them up for reproduction in the document you are working on by using a shorthand code of letters or numbers.

line counter Some systems show you which line you are working on at any given time. They normally count from the top of the page, so you have to calculate the number of top margin lines to figure out how far down the page you are at any line number.

line spacing The spacing between lines of print when your document prints out. Systems vary in their capability of ranging from single-line spacing (normally six lines to an inch) to increments of a single line or triple-line spacing. Half-line spacing or less is useful in printing superscripts and subscripts: if you can control your system to produce less than half-line spacing, your superscripts will not overlap the descenders on the line above when you are printing them in a single-spaced document.

list processing The feature that allows you to combine lists with a form (or shell) document in order to produce an original, personalized document that combines the individual features in the list with the copy in the form document.

load The term used in some systems to describe the function of placing your software program into the system's computer after you have turned the machine on.

lowercase The uncapitalized form of letters. The term is taken from earlier printing times when these letters were manually taken by typesetters one by one from a large compartmentalized drawer (called a "case") in which the uncapitalized letters were stored in the compartments located at the lower two-thirds of the case.

margin The space between any of the four edges of the paper and the place where your printing begins or ends. There are top, right, left, and bottom margins to each job.

math A feature that allows you to enter numbers together with numeric commands (addition, subtraction, multiplication, division, percentage) that will function in your job. Most often this feature is used in list processing and sorting work.

matrix printer A high-speed printer that prints dots instead of entire letters. The dots fit into a matrix, or pattern, to form the general shape of a letter or number. The more dots and the tighter the matrix, the more the matrix-produced letter looks like an impact-produced letter.

menu Choices listed on the screen from which you can select on option. You need to go to the proper menu to select a particular feature you want to make happen. Your manual illustrates all the possible menus you can call up and tells you how to call them up.

merge The act of combining elements from lists with a form document when list processing.

message Information, questions, or warnings that appear on your screen as a result of some condition that calls for a response from you. This condition may be due to the fact that you have asked the machine to do something it cannot do, or do it out of its own sequence, or it may be due to the printer running out of paper or ribbon, or needing a print-wheel change.

module A piece of hardware that can be combined with other hardware pieces to form a working computer or word processing unit. Some modules are changeable; for instance, you can use more than one kind of printing module (printer) with a word processor. Or you can use more than one kind of keyboard (for instance, if you have a French-language software program, you could use a French-language keyboard without having to change any other elements in your system except to secure a French-language printwheel).

numeric keyboard Some systems use a special ten-key (0–9) section for numbers, configured in the same style as most calculators. Other systems use the 1–0 sequence of keys on an upper row in the main keyboard section.

operator A person who makes a word processing system function by entering characters and commands.

option Any one of the choices that can be selected by an operator from a menu.

originator A person who writes or dictates a document for word processing by a word processing operator.

overstrike To place a character over another character. If the same character overstrikes a character, the result is a slightly bolder appearance; if a different character overstrikes, the result is a combined character or a character with an accent mark. In legal work, many words are overstruck with a hyphen (as in "~~effective immediately~~") to show words that are proposed to be deleted from a legal document. Many word processing systems are able to actually delete those over-struck words in a revision after both parties have agreed to their deletion and the final document is being prepared.

page A section in a document marked off by a page end mark. This mark may be placed there automatically during pagination or it may be placed there manually. The system registers this area in the document as a page in its numbering system. The page may be full of type, partially full, or even completely empty.

page mark (page end mark) A character that instructs the system to end a page and to begin a new page with the next character. The page end mark may be placed automatically or manually. This mark is sometimes called a "new page" mark.

pagination The feature that divides a document into pages. You determine how many lines should be on a page when you enter the automatic pagination instructions, or you do so by entering a required page end mark at the place of your choice.

paper jam Paper has become wedged into the printer or feeder and needs to be manually removed.

paragraph Text of one or more lines that is separated from other text in the document by a paragraph marker (if your system has one and if you use it) or by two hard returns. In some systems, a number of printed paragraphs that you separate by a single hard return followed by a tab indent will be understood by the system's logic to be a single long paragraph if you try to move forward or backward by paragraphs. The system only recognizes the paragraph mark or two hard returns in sequence for its paragraph functioning.

paragraph document Copy—from a single word to an entire paragraph in length—that is stored in an alternate location, that is, not in the document you are working on, but can be inserted into your document either by a couple of manual keystrokes or by including a format command in your shell document.

paste To insert data that has been temporarily stored in a "paste" area or "keystroke save" area. The content of the data in the paste area does not change (and so can be used many times) until new data are stored in that area.

pica An often-used name for 10-pitch characters.

pitch The number of characters per horizontal inch. The pitches normally used in word processing are 10-pitch (sometimes called "pica"), 12-pitch (sometimes called "elite"), and 15-pitch. You need to instruct your system about which pitch you are using and make sure that you have the proper print-wheel in the printer for that pitch setting.

platen The cylinder against which the printhead strikes to produce an impression.

printer The hardware unit that produces a paper copy of your document.

printhead The hardware device in the printer that produces matrix characters or that strikes a printwheel to produce impact characters.

printwheel A circular printing element, sometimes called a "daisy wheel" or a "thimble," depending on its shape.

program A software set of instructions that enables your system to perform word processing functions. You load your program into the system each time you turn the system on. Your manual explains how to enter commands into the system to make it perform functions that the program enables it to do. Most word processing programs are "packaged"; that is, they are prepared by the manufacturer and are licensed property. Generally, you are not able to change the content of a word processing program.

prompt A message that appears on your screen and requires a response from you.

proportional spacing Spacing between characters that is somewhat proportional to the amount of space taken up by each character (for instance, in proportional spacing, or PS, an "m" uses more space than an "I"). To use proportional spacing, your system must be able to use a PS print setting and you must have PS printwheels that are compatible with your system.

queue A waiting line. Sometimes you can have a queue of documents to be printed one after the other automatically, while you are editing yet a different document.

ragged right An uneven right-hand margin. Unless you justify a document, it will print out as you see it on the screen.

replace A feature of putting in new characters in the place of previously entered characters that now are deleted.

return Use of the return key ends a line at that point where it is pressed. The return key is also used in many systems to execute commands.

revision The work you do to change the contents of a document or the commands that control its appearance.

ribbon A narrow strip of carbon or cloth used in the printer against which the printwheel or printhead strikes to create an impression on the paper. In word processors, ribbons come in self-contained cartridges. Some ribbons made of cloth are in continuous-loop cartridges and can be used several times over; other ribbons can be used only once.

right justify A tab setting for the rightmost character in a column. All the other characters or numbers in the column will build out toward the left from the tab setting.

right margin The setting that controls the placing of rightmost characters on the page. If your document is ragged right, no character will extend beyond the right margin setting; if it is justified, all lines will end on the right margin setting (except possibly the last line of each paragraph).

screen The video screen on which your document and various menus, messages, and other information are displayed.

scroll To move the cursor forward or backward through a document, often resulting in the text of the document moving up or down the screen.

search To instruct the system to look for (find) a particular string of characters (a word or phrase), most often with a view to replacing those characters with others.

sentence The part of a document ending with a period, a question mark, or an exclamation mark. If your system advances or backs up by sentences, it will move from period to period (or the other sentence end marks). If there are several periods after initials (as in "F.D.R."), your system will read the text between each period as a sentence.

setting A location (margin setting) or command (typeface setting) you have put into a document or a program. Settings can be changed through appropriate menus.

shadow printing Some systems have the capability of over-striking characters with the same character moved slightly to one side of the original character, giving an impression of very bold printing.

shared printer A feature whereby more than one terminal can use the same printer.

shell A form document that permits the inclusion of variables taken from a list.

single density A method of formatting a disk to receive information that permits the storage of much less information per disk than double-density formatting. Systems that have double-density capability can normally read single-density diskettes, but single-density systems can read only single-density diskettes.

software Instructions on a program disk that tell the hardware (the physical equipment) what functions to perform and lead you through a series of menus to give the appropriate commands to make the system perform the functions you want. Software that works on your system to perform a wide variety of tasks can be purchased directly from your manufacturer or from companies that write software programs for your brand of equipment.

sort A feature that enables your system to organize lists in a wide variety of alphanumeric combinations. Each alphanumeric element in your sort is organized in either an ascending or a descending order (A to Z, 1 to 10000; or reverse).

spelling A feature that loads a spelling dictionary into the sys-tem to check the spelling of words in a document. The size of these dictionaries varies from 10,000 to 150,000 words, depending on the complexity of the software and the hardware. The larger the dictionary, the larger the working memory the system requires.

store To place (file) information on a disk, where it is available for recall and adjustment later. Depending on your system, print settings, lists, rulers or margins, paragraphs, phrases, and words can be stored in various ways for recall and inclusion in the content or formatting of a document.

subscript and superscript Characters printed off the main line of the text. Subscripts are generally printed half a line below the main line (H_2); superscripts above the main line (for footnote reference[5]).

swap Some systems have a special key function that exchanges a character with the character to its right. This is useful when correcting transpositions ("teh" instead of "the").

system The entire word processing unit, including all its hardware and software parts.

system page number The page number in a document assigned by the system for a given page. Each document begins with a system number of "1." If your document is the second one of a long work that is consecutively numbered, you may instruct the system to number the pages of the document beginning with another number, such as "38." In such a case, book or report page 38 will be system page 1, 39 will be 2, and so on. Depending on your system, you will need to use the system page number to "go to" or "print" a particular page (although some systems renumber all the pages in a document based on the initial page number you enter for the document).

systems disk The disk that holds the software program.

tab To enter a tab mark or to press the tab key to move the cursor over to the next tab mark.

temporary marker Markers that are automatically erased by the system when they are no longer needed. Some are entered by the system, such as a word-wrap return—as opposed to a hard return—that the system places at the end of each line when it drops down to the text line. If you rearrange the text, old word-wrap returns will be erased automatically, and new word-wrap returns entered automatically for the new lines, if line endings have been changed. The same happens to soft page end markers when lines are added or deleted.

text The part of a document that is normally displayed on the screen and printed out as the desired output. All the commands—both hard and soft—are considered not part of the text, even though they are essential to the word processing operation. The characters that show which commands have been entered can usually be seen only on the view (display) mode.

thousands separator On some systems a comma can be used in columnar work as a point on which numbers line up. The comma, in this case, separates the thousands position from the hundreds in large numbers.

top margin The number of lines between the top of the sheet of paper and the first line of printing.

typeface or typestyle The characters of a particular design of type appearance and size. A printwheel will contain characters of a single typestyle or typeface and of a single pitch. Light Italic is an example of a typeface, as are Boldface and Prestige.

underline To print with a line under the text for emphasis or as a substitute for italics. Each system has special function keys to make underlining easy.

update To revise text and bring the information on a disk to current status. It is especially important to update backup copies of disks, so you don't inadvertently use disks that are unlike the most recently revised printout.

uppercase The capitalized form of letters. The term is taken from earlier printing times when these letters were manually taken one by one by typesetters from a large compartmentalized drawer (called a "case") in which the capitalized letters were stored in compartments located at the upper third of the case.

variable Information, usually in a list or in a stored paragraph, that can be inserted automatically into a standardized form (shell) document.

view mode A special display of the document that shows all the commands as well as the text.

word A group of characters separated from adjoining groups by space. A punctuation mark is considered by the system to be part of the word it is attached to. The space following a word is also usually read by the system as being part of that word. When deleting the characters that make up a word,

it is also necessary to delete the appropriate space, since the system does not do so automatically.

word processing The use of a computer system to create, edit, store, and print text. Dedicated word processors are computers in which many word processing functions are built into the construction of the hardware and the nature of the program in the software to perform the required tasks as rapidly and efficiently as possible.

word wrap A feature wherein a word that is entered and passes over the right-hand margin drops down to form the first word of the next line. This feature is performed automatically on word processors. Word wraps will be automatically readjusted by the system when line endings are changed due to text editing.

work station The screen/disk drive/computer/keyboard parts of your word processor considered as the place where you perform your word processing. The printer is not automatically a part of your work station, since you can share a printer with another work station.

Spanish Glossary
Spanish–English

A

a to, at
abajo under, below
abierto, -a open, opened
el abogado lawyer
el abrigo overcoat
abril (*m.*) April
abrir to open
acá here (*usually with a verb of motion*)
acabar to finish
  acaba de + *infin.* = to have just
aceptar to accept
la acera the sidewalk
acerca de about, concerning
acercarse (a) to approach
acompañar to accompany
aconsejar to advise
acordarse (ue) (de) to remember
acostarse (ue) to go to bed
acostumbrar to accustom
el acuerdo agreement
adelantar to progress
adelante straight ahead, forward
además moreover, also
adiós good-bye
admirar to admire
el adobe adobe, sun-dried brick
aereo: por correo aereo by air mail
el aeropuerto airport
el aficionado sport fan
afortunado, -a lucky
afuera outside
el agente agent
agosto (*m.*) August
agradable agreeable, pleasant
agradecido, -a thankful, grateful
el agua (*f.*) water
ahí there
ahora now
ahorita just now, in just a minute
el aire air; **al aire libre** in the open air
alegrar to gladden
  alegrarse to rejoice, to be glad
alegre lively, merry
la alfarería pottery
algo something; somewhat
el algodón cotton
alguien someone, anyone
alguno (algún), -a someone, any
el alimento food
el alma (*f.*) soul
el almacén department store
el almuerzo lunch
alquilar to rent

alrededor de around
los alrededores surrounding area
alto, -a tall, high
la altura altitude
el alumno, la alumna student
allá there (*usually with a verb of motion*)
allí there
amable kind
amar to love
amarillo, -a yellow
el amigo, la amiga friend
el amor love
anaranjado, -a orange-colored
ancho, -a wide
andar to go, to walk
animado, -a lively, animated
el ánimo soul, spirit; courage
anoche last night
de antaño ancient, of long ago
ante before, in face of
anteayer day before yesterday
antes de before (*refers to time*)
  cuanto antes as soon as possible
antiguo, -a old
anunciar to announce
el año year
  el año que viene next year
el aparador sideboard
aparecer to appear
apenas scarcely
el apetito appetite
apreciar to appreciate
aprender (a) to learn (to)
apresurarse to hurry
aprisa swiftly, quickly
apropiado appropriate
aprovecharse de to take advantage of
aquel, aquella that
aquél, aquélla that (one); the former
aquí here
  Aquí lo tiene Ud. Here it is.
el árbol tree
arreglar to arrange
arriba above, upstairs
el arroz rice
el arte (*m. and f.*) art
el artículo article
el artesano craftsman
el(la) artista artist
artístico artistic
el ascensor elevator
así thus, so

el asiento seat
asistir(a) to attend
el aspecto appearance
atento attentive
atrás backwards, behind
atravesar(ie) to cross
aun (aún) even, yet, still
aunque although
el automóvil automobile
la avenida avenue
averiguar to find out
el avión airplane
avisar to inform
¡ay! alas!
ayer yesterday
la ayuda aid
ayudar(a) to aid, help (to)
el azúcar sugar
el azucarero sugar bowl
azul blue
el azulejo tile

B

bailar to dance
el baile dance
bajar (de) to get out (of); to climb (go) down
bajo, -a low
el balcón balcony
el banco bench
bañar to bathe
el baño bath; bathtub; bathroom
barato, -a cheap
¡basta! enough!
bastante quite, enough
la batalla battle
el baúl trunk
beber to drink
la bebida drink
el béisbol baseball
bello, -a beautiful
el beso kiss
la biblioteca library
bien well
bienvenido, -a welcome
el billete bill
blanco, -a white
la blusa blouse
la boca mouth
la boletería ticket window
el boletero ticket seller
el boleto (de primera) (de segunda) (first-class) (second-class) ticket
la bolsa purse
el bolsillo pocket
la bondad kindness
bonito, -a pretty, nice
la botella bottle
el brazo arm
brillar to shine
la brisa breeze

bueno (buen), -a good; **¡bueno!** hello! (*on telephone*)
el bulto bundle
el burro donkey
buscar to look for
el buzón mailbox
  echar en el buzón to mail

C

el caballo horse
la cabeza head
cada each, every
caer to fall
el café coffee, cafe
la caja box
la cajuela trunk (of car)
el calcetín sock
caliente warm, hot
el calor heat; **hace calor** it is hot (weather)
  tener calor to be hot (for persons)
la calle street
la cama bed
cambiar to change, exchange
el cambio change
  de cambio in change
caminar to go, to travel, to walk
el camino road
el camión (*Mex.*) bus, truck
la camisa shirt
el campesino peasant
el campo country
la canasta basket
la canción song
cansado, -a tired
cansarse to grow weary, tired
cantar to sing
la cantidad quantity
la caña de azucar sugar cane
la cara face
la carga load
el cariño affection
la carne meat
la carnicería butcher shop
caro, -a expensive, dear
la carta letter
el cartel poster
el cartero postman
la casa house
  en casa at home
  volver a casa to go home
casarse con to marry
casi almost
la causa cause; **a causa de** because of
la cebolla onion
celebrar to celebrate

la cena supper
cenar to have supper
el centavo cent
el centro center
la cerámica pottery
cerca de (*prep.*) near
cercano nearby
el cerillo wax match
el cero zero
cerrado, -a closed, shut
cerrar(ie) to close, shut
el certificado certificate
la cerveza beer
la cesta basket
el cielo sky
el científico scientist
ciento (cien) one hundred
 por ciento percent
cierto certain, true
 por cierto certainly
el cigarro cigar
el cine movies
la cinta film
el cinturón belt
la cita appointment
citar to make an appointment with
la ciudad city
claro, -a clear, light
 ¡Claro que sí! Of course!
 ¡Claro que no! Of course not!
la clase class, kind
el clavel carnation
el cliente client
el clima climate
el cobre copper
cocido, -a cooked, boiled
la cocina kitchen
el coche car, automobile (*Mex.*)
coger to catch, gather, pick up
el color color
 ¿De qué color es . . . ? What color is . . . ?
el comedor dining room
comenzar(ie) to begin
comer to eat
 comerse to "eat up"
el comerciante businessman
la comida meal, food, dinner
como like, as, how;
 ¿cómo? how?
 ¿cómo no? of course, why not?
 ¿cómo se dice? how do you say?
cómodo, -a comfortable
el compañero companion
el compatriota countryman
completo, -a complete
la compra purchase
 ir de compras to go shopping
el comprador purchaser
comprar to buy
comprender to understand
común common
con with; **conmigo** with me; **con tal que** provided that
el concierto concert
condecorado, -a decorated
conducir to lead; to conduct
confesar(ie) to confess

conocer to know, meet, be acquainted with
conocido, -a well-known
conseguir(i) to get, obtain
el consejo advice
consentir(ie) to consent
consiguiente: por consiguiente consequently
consistir en to consist of
contar(ue) to count; to relate
contener to contain
contento, -a contented, happy
contestar(a) to answer
continuar to continue
contra against
conveniente convenient
conversar to converse
la copia copy
el corazón heart
la corbata necktie
coronado crowned
correcto, -a correct
corregir(i) to correct
el correo the post office, mail
 por correo aéreo by air mail
correr to run
la corrida de toros bullfight
corriente current, popular
cortar to cut
la cortesía courtesy
corto, -a short
la cosa thing
 ¡qué cosa! the idea!
la costa coast
costar(ue) to cost
la costumbre custom
es costumbre it's the custom
crecer to grow
creer to believe, "think"
 Creo que no. I think not.
 Creo que sí. I think so.
 ¡Ya lo creo! Yes indeed; I should say so!
la criada maid
el cristal glass
cruzar to cross
la cuadra block
cuadrado, -a a square
el cuadro picture
¿cuál? ¿cuáles? which (one, ones)? what?
cualquier any
cuando when; **¿cuándo?** when?
¿cuánto, -a? how much?
¿cuántos, -as? how many?
el cuarto room, quarter, fourth
cubierto de covered (with)
cubrir to cover
la cuchara spoon
la cucharita teaspoon
el cuchillo knife
la cuenta bill
el cuento story
el cuero leather
el cuerpo body
cuidar to look after: **cuidar de** to take care of
¡Cuidado! Take care!
la culpa guilt, fault
la cultura culture
el cumpleaños birthday

cumplir to fulfill
el cura priest
cuyo, -a whose

CH

el chamaco (*Mex.*) boy
charlar to chat
la chuleta chop
chico (a) small
el chico, la chica small boy (girl)

D

el danzante dancer
el daño harm
dar to give
 dar a to face (*the street, etc.*)
 dar buen viaje to wish a pleasant journey
 dar las gracias a to give thanks to
 dar un paseo to go out walking or driving
 darse la mano to shake hands
de of, from, about
debajo de under, beneath
deber ought to, be obliged to, must
débil weak
decidir to decide
décimo, -a tenth
decir to tell, say
 es decir that is to say
defender to defend
dejar to let, to leave, allow;
 dejar de to fail to (do something)
delante de in front of
demandar to demand
los demás the rest
demasiado, -a too (much)
 pl. too many
dentro (de) inside (of)
el dependiente clerk
el deporte sport
derecho, -a right
 a la derecha to the right
 derecho straight ahead
desaparecer to disappear
desayunarse to breakfast
el desayuno breakfast
descansar to rest
el descanso rest
el descendiente descendant
describir to describe
descubrir to discover
desde from, since
 desde luego of course
desear to wish, want
deseoso desirous
el desfile parade, procession
desgraciadamente unfortunately
el desierto desert
desocupado unoccupied
despacio slowly
despedirse(i) de to take leave of
despertar(ie) to wake up (*somebody*)
despertarse to wake up (*oneself*)
despierto, -a awake

después afterwards
después de after
detrás de behind
devolver(ue) to give back, return
el día day
 al día siguiente next day
 hoy día nowadays
diario, -a daily
el dibujo drawing
diciembre (*m.*) December
el diente tooth
diferente different
difícil difficult
el difunto deceased
digno worthy
diligente diligent
el dinero money
el dios god
la dirección address
dirigirse a to go to, to address (a person)
dispensar to excuse
 dispénseme excuse me
distinto, -a different
la diversión amusement
diverso, -a varied
divertido, -a amusing
divertirse(ie) to have a good time, amuse oneself
dividir to divide
el dólar dollar
el dolor de cabeza (muelas), (estómago) headache, (toothache), (stomachache)
dominar to dominate
el domingo Sunday
don (*m.*), **doña** (*f.*) title used with first name
donde where; **¿dónde?** where?
 ¿Por dónde se va a . . . ? How does one get to . . . ?
dormir(ue) to sleep
 dormirse(ue) to fall asleep
el dormitorio bedroom
el drama play
la duda doubt
 sin duda alguna without any doubt
dulce sweet
 los dulces candy
durante during
durar to last

E

echar to throw; **echarse** to stretch out
 echar de menos to miss
la edad age
efecto: en efecto in fact
elevar to raise; **elevarse** to rise
la embajada embassy
embargo: sin embargo nevertheless
emocionante touching, thrilling
empezar(ie) (a) to begin (to)
el empleado employee
emplear to use
en in, on, at
 en seguida at once

en vez de instead of
encantar to enchant, charm
la enchilada a kind of pancake with chile and meat stuffing
encima(de) on top (of)
encontrar(ue) to find; meet
enero (*m.*) January
enfermo, -a sick, ill
enfrente de opposite, facing
enorme enormous
enseñar to teach
entender(ie) to understand
entero whole
entonces then
la entrada entrance
entrar(en) to enter
entre between
entretanto meanwhile
enviar to send
el envío shipment
el equipaje baggage
equivocado, -a mistaken
la escalera stairway
escoger to choose
el escolar scholar, student
escribir to write
el escritor writer
el escritorio desk
escuchar (a) to listen (to)
la escuela school
ese, -a that
ése, -a that (one)
eso that (*referring to a statement or idea*)
  a eso de at about (*time*)
  por eso therefore
espacioso spacious
el español Spanish (*lang.*)
el español Spaniard; **la española** Spanish woman
el espectador spectator
esperar to wait (for), hope, expect
  Espero que no. I hope not.
  Espero que sí. I hope so.
el esposo husband; **la esposa** wife
la esquina corner
la estación de ferrocarril railroad station
el estado state
los Estados Unidos (*abbr.* E.U.A. *or* E.E.U.U.) the United States
el estante shelf, bookcase
estar to be (*place*)
  estar de prisa to be in a hurry
  estar en camino to be on the way
  estar para to be about to
la estatua statue
el este east
este, -a this
éste, -a this (one)
el estilo style
esto this (*referring to a statement or idea*)
estrecho, -a narrow
la estrella star
el estudiante student
el estudio study
estudiar to study
el examen examination
examinar to examine
excelente excellent

excepto except
explicar to explain
expresar to express
la expresión expression
extender(ie) to extend

F

fácil easy
facilitar to facilitate
facilmente easily
facturar to check (baggage)
la faja sash
la falda skirt
falso, -a false
la falta mistake, lack
  Me hace falta I lack, I need
faltar to be lacking, need
  me falta I need
la familia family
famoso, -a famous
la farmacia pharmacy
favor: favor de please
  Es favor que Ud. me hace You flatter me
  por favor please
febrero (*m.*) February
la fecha date
  ¿Cuál es la fecha? What is the date?
felicitar to congratulate
feliz happy
la fiesta holiday
la fila row
el fin end; **al fin** finally, at last
fino, -a fine
firmar to sign
el flan custard
la flor flower
la formalidad formality
la fortuna fortune
el fósforo match
el francés French (*lang.*), Frenchman; **la francesa** Frenchwoman
la frase sentence
la frente front; **en frente de** in front of; **frente a** opposite, facing
fresco cool
los frijoles beans
frío cold
  hacer frío to be cold (*weather*)
  tener frío to be cold (*persons*)
la fruta fruit
la fuente fountain
el fuego fire
fuera de outside of
fuerte strong
la función performance

G

la gana desire; **de buena gana** willingly
ganar to earn, to win
el garage garage
gastar to spend
generoso, -a generous
la gente people
gordo, -a fat
gozar (de) to enjoy
gracias thanks

gracioso, -a graceful, amusing
grande large, great
gris gray
gritar to shout
el grito shout, cry
grueso, -a thick
el grupo group
el guajalote turkey (*Mex.*)
el guante glove
guapo, -a neat, elegant, handsome
guardar to keep, guard
la guía guide book
gustar to be pleasing to
  me gusta I like
el gusto pleasure
  con mucho gusto with much pleasure
  el gusto es mío the pleasure is mine
  tanto gusto en conocerle very pleased to meet you

H

haber to have (*auxiliary*)
el habitante inhabitant
hablador, -a talkative
hablar to speak
hacer to do, make
  hace algún tiempo some time ago
  hace calor, frio, etc. it is hot, cold, etc. (weather)
  hacer daño a to hurt
  me hace falta I need
  hacer preguntas to ask questions
hallar to find
el hambre hunger, **tener hambre** to be hungry
hasta until, to, as far as, even
  hasta luego so long
  hasta mañana until tomorrow
  hasta la vista so long
hay there is, there are
  hay que it is necessary to, one must
  hay (sol) (viento) (polvo) (lodo) it is (sunny) (windy) (dusty) (muddy)
hecho made
  hecho a mano handmade
el helado ice cream
el hermano brother; **la hermana** sister
hermoso, -a beautiful
el héroe hero
el hierro iron
el hijo son; **la hija** daughter; **los hijos** children
la hoja leaf, sheet (of paper)
la hojalata tinplate
el hombre man
la hora hour; time
  ¿A qué hora? At what time?
el horario timetable
la hospitalidad hospitality
hoy today; **hoy día** nowadays
el huevo egg
huir to flee
húmedo, -a wet

I

el idioma language
la iglesia church
igual equal
igualmente equally, the same to you
imaginar to imagine
imitar to imitate
impaciente impatient
el impermeable raincoat
imponente imposing
el importador importer
importante important
importar to matter, to be important; to import
  no importa it does not matter
la impresión impression
indicar to point out
indígena indigenous, native
el indio, -a Indian
la industria industry
informar to inform
el informe information
  pedir informes to ask for information
el inglés English (*lang.*) Englishman; **la inglesa** Englishwoman
el iniciador founder
inmediatamente immediately
inmenso, -a immense
inteligente intelligent
el interés interest
interesar to interest
el invierno winter
invitar to invite
ir to go
  irse to go away, leave
  ir de compras to go shopping
  ir de paseo to go out walking or riding
izquierdo, -a left
  a la izquierda to the left

J

¡ja! ¡ja! ha! ha!
el jabón soap
jamás never
el jamón ham
el jardín garden
el jarro jar
el jefe chief
la joya jewel
la joyería jewelry shop, jewelry
joven young
el joven young man
el juego game, set
el jueves Thursday
el jugador player, gambler
jugar to play (*a game*)
el jugo juice
el juguete toy
julio (*m.*) July
junio (*m.*) June
juntar to join, unite
junto a near, close to
  junto con together with

K

el kilo kilogram
el kilómetro kilometer

L

el labio lip
laborado worked, tilled
la laca lacquer
el lado side; **al lado de** beside
la lámpara lamp
la lana wool
el lápiz pencil
largo, -a long
la lástima shame, pity
  ¡Qué lástima! What a pity!
la lata can
lavar to wash;
  lavarse to wash oneself
la lección lesson
la leche milk
la lechuga lettuce
leer read
la legumbre vegetable
lejano, -a far-off
lejos de far from;
  a lo lejos in the distance
lentamente slowly
levantar to raise, lift;
  levantarse to rise, get up
la libra pound
el libre taxi (*Mex.*)
la librería bookstore
el libro book
el líder leader
ligero, -a light
la lima lime
el limón lemon
limpiar to clean
la lista menu
listo, -a ready
la lotería lottery
la lucha struggle
luego then
  hasta luego so long
el lugar place
el lujo luxury
luminoso, -a bright
la luna moon
el lunes Monday
la luz light

LL

llamar to call
  llamar por teléfono to call up
llamarse to be called
  Me llamo Pablo. My name is Paul.
la llanura plain
la llegada arrival
llegar to arrive
llenar to fill
lleno, -a full
llevar to carry; to take, to wear;
  llevarse to carry (take) away
llover(ue) to rain
la lluvia rain
lluvioso, -a rainy

M

la madera wood
la madre mother
el madrugador early riser
el maestro teacher
magnífico magnificent

el maíz corn
el malestar indisposition
la maleta suitcase;
  hacer una maleta to pack a suitcase
malo, -a bad, sick
la mamá mamma
mandar to order, to send
manejar to drive
la manera manner;
  de manera que so that
  de (otra) (la misma) manera in (another) (the same) way
la mano hand
  darse la(s) mano(s) to shake hands;
  a la mano derecha on the right;
  a la mano izquierda on the left
la manta blanket
mantener to maintain
la manzana apple
mañana tomorrow
  hasta mañana till tomorrow
la mañana morning
  por la mañana in the morning
la máquina de escribir typewriter
el mar sea
el martes Tuesday
marzo (*m.*) March
más more, most;
  más o menos more or less
la máscara mask
matar to kill
las matemáticas mathematics
mayo (*m.*) May
mayor older
la mayoría majority
la media stocking
el médico doctor
la medida measure
medio, -a half (a, an)
medir(i) to measure
mejor better
  el (la) mejor best
el melocotón peach
el melón melon
la memoria memory
de memoria by heart
menor younger
  el (la) menor youngest
menos less, minus, except;
  por lo menos at least;
  echar de menos to miss
menudo: a menudo often
el mercado market
la mercancía merchandise
la merienda a light supper, "tea"
la mesa table
el mesero waiter
el mexicanismo Mexicanism
mexicano Mexican
México Mexico
mientras while
  mientras tanto meanwhile
el miércoles Wednesday
mil thousand
la milla mile
el millón million

mirar to look (at)
mismo, -a same
  él mismo be himself
  lo mismo the same thing
la mitad half
moderno, -a modern
el modismo idiom
el modo way
  de este modo in this way
  de todos modos anyway
mojado, -a soaked, wet
la moneda currency, money
la montaña mountain
el montón heap, pile
mostrar(ue) to show
el movimiento movement
el mozo waiter
el muchacho boy; **la muchacha** girl
mucho, -a much
  muchos, -as many
mudarse to move (change house)
la muerte death
el muerto corpse, dead man
la mujer woman
el mundo world
  todo el mundo everybody
el museo museum
muy very

N

nada nothing, not anything;
  de nada you're welcome
nadie no one, nobody
la naranja orange
la naturaleza nature
la Navidad Christmas
necesario, -a necessary
la necesidad necessity
necesitar to need
el negociante businessman
el negocio business
negro, -a black
la nariz nose
ni neither nor
  ni yo tampoco nor I either, neither do I
la nieve snow
ninguno, -a no, none, nobody
el niño, la niña child
no not
la noche night
  por la noche in the evening
  esta noche tonight
nombrar to name
el nombre name
el norte north
el norteamericano North American (*usually means a person from the U.S.*)
notable worthy of note
las noticias news
noviembre (*m.*) November
nuevo, -a new
el número number
nunca never

O

o or (u *before* o *or* ho)
obedecer to obey
el objeto object

observar to observe
obtener to obtain
occidental western
octubre (*m.*) October
ocupado, -a busy
el oeste west
la oficina office
ofrecer to offer
el oído ear (*hearing*)
oír to hear
el ojo eye
olvidar to forget
omitir to omit
la oportunidad opportunity
la orden order
a sus órdenes at your service
ordinario, -a ordinary
el orgullo pride
orgulloso, -a proud
el oro gold
oscuro, -a dark
el otoño autumn
otro, -a other, another

P

pacífico peaceful
el padre father
pagar to pay
el país country
la paja straw
el pájaro bird
la palabra word
el palo stick
el pan bread
el panadero baker
el panecillo roll
el panqueque pancake
la pantalla screen
el papá papa
el papel paper, role
el paquete package
  el paquete postal parcel post
el par pair
para in order to, for
  para que in order that
el paraguas umbrella
parar to stop
parecer to seem
  Le parece bien. It seems all right to him.
  parecerse a to resemble
la pared wall
el pariente relative
la parte part; **por todas partes** everywhere
la partida departure
el partidario partisan, supporter
partir to leave
el pasaje fare, passage
el pasaporte passport
pasar to pass, spend (*time*), happen;
  pasar sin to get along without
  pasar un buen rato to spend a pleasant time
  ¿Qué pasa? What is going on?
Pase Ud. Come in; Go ahead.
el pasado past
pasear to take a walk, to walk about

pasearse (en coche) (a caballo) (en barco) to go for a walk or a ride (in a car) (on horseback) (in a boat)
el paseo promenade
el paso step
la patata potato
el patio courtyard
el pato duck
pedir(i) to ask for
pedir informes to ask for information
la película motion picture
peligroso, -a dangerous
el pelo hair
pensar(ie) to think, to intend to;
pensar en to think about
peor worse
pequeño, -a small
la pera pear
perder(ie) to lose
perdonar to pardon
perezoso, -a lazy
perfectamente perfectly
el periódico newspaper
el permiso permission
con su permiso allow me
permitir to permit
pero but
la persona person
pesado, -a heavy
pesar to weigh
a pesar de in spite of
el pescado fish
pescar to fish
pescar un catarro to catch cold
el peso weight; monetary unit of Mexico
picante spicy, "hot" (*of food*)
el pico peak
el pie foot
estar de pie to stand
la piedra stone
la pierna leg
la pieza piece
pintar to paint
el pintor painter
pintoresco, -a picturesque
la pintura painting
la piña pineapple
la piñata pot full of candy and toys, broken by children at Christmas
la pirámide pyramid
el piso story (*of building*)
el placer pleasure
la plata silver
el plátano banana
el platero silversmith
platicar to chat
el platillo saucer
el plato dish
la plaza square, park
la pluma pen
la plumafuente fountain pen
pobre poor
poco, -a little
dentro de poco in a short time;
pocos, -as few
poder(ue) to be able, can, may

(no) se puede one can (not)
el policía policeman
el pollo chicken
poner to put, to place
poner la mesa to set the table;
ponerse to put on, to become
La natura se pone verde. Nature turns green.
ponerse en marcha to start
por for, in exchange for, by, through, along;
por cierto certainly;
por eso therefore;
por lo tanto therefore;
por supuesto of course;
por todas partes everywhere
¿por qué? why?
porque because
el portal arcade
el porvenir future
posible possible
postal; el paquete postal parcel post
el postre dessert
practicar to practice
el precio price
precioso, -a exquisite, beautiful
precisamente exactly
preferir(i) to prefer
la pregunta question
preguntar to ask
el premio prize
preocuparse de to worry (about)
presentar to introduce
prestar to lead
la primavera spring
primer(o), -a first
principar to begin
el principio beginning
al principio at first
prisa: de prisa fast, quickly
tener prisa to be in a hurry
probablemente probably
probar(ue) to try, to prove, to taste
el problema problem
producir to produce
el profesor professor
profundo, -a profound
el programa program
prometer to promise
pronto soon
la propina tip
propio, -a own
proponer to propose
propósito: a propósito by the way
proteger to protect
próximo, -a next (in time)
el pueblo town; people
puertorriqueño, -a Puerto Rican
la puerta door
pues well, then
el puesto stand, booth
puesto que since
el punto point, period
en punto on the dot (*time*)

Q

que who, that, which, than;
lo que that which, what
¿qué? what, which
¿Qué tal? How's everything?
quedar(se) to remain, stay
querer(ie) to wish, want;
querer a to love
¿Qué quiere decir? What does it mean?
querido, -a dear, beloved
quien, -es who
¿quién, -es? who?
¿a quién, -es? whom? to whom?
¿de quién, -es? whose?
¿quién sabe? goodness knows?
quitar to remove; **quitarse** to take off (*clothing*)

R

el radio radio (set)
la radio radio (broadcast)
la rapidez speed
rápidamente rapidly
rápido, -a rapid, swift
raro, -a strange, rare
el rato while
largo rato a long time
razón; tener razón to be right
no tener razón to be wrong
el rebozo shawl
la recámara bedroom (*Mex.*)
recibir to receive
reconocer to recognize
recordar(ue) to remember
el recuerdo souvenir
el recreo recreation
redondo round
boleto de viaje redondo round-trip ticket
el refresco soft drink
el regalo gift
regatear to bargain
regresar to return
reír(i) to laugh
reírse de(i) to laugh at
la reja grating
el reloj watch clock
reluciendo shining, glittering
repente; de repente suddenly
repetir(i) to repeat
el representante representative
requisito necessary
el resfriado cold (illness)
resistir to resist
respecto a in regard to
el respeto respect
responder to answer
la respuesta answer
el restaurant(e) restaurant
los restos remains
el retrato portrait, photograph
revisar to examine
la revista magazine
el rey king
rico, -a rich

el río river
la risa laugh
rodeado, -a surrounded
rojo, -a red
romper to break
la ropa clothing
rosado, -a pink
el ruido noise

S

el sábado Saturday
saber to know, to know how
sabroso, -a tasty, delicious
sacar to take out
la sala living room, hall
la sala de espera waiting room
salir de to leave, to go out of;
salir para to leave for
la salsa sauce
la salud health
saludar to greet
el saludo greeting
el santo saint
santo holy
el sarape blanket
satisfecho, -a satisfied
seco, -a dry
sed; tener sed to be thirsty
la seda silk
seguida; en seguida at once
seguir(i) to continue, to follow
según according to
segundo, -a second
el boleto de segunda clase second-class ticket
seguramente surely
seguro sure
de seguro surely
le semana week
semejante similar
sencillo, -a simple
sentado, -a seated, sitting down
sentarse(ie) to sit down
el sentido meaning, sense
sentir(ie) to regret, be sorry
Lo siento mucho. I am very sorry.
sentirse(ie) to feel
le señal signal
señalar to point out
el señor gentleman; Mr.
la señora lady; Mrs.
la señorita young lady; Miss
septiembre (*m.*) September
ser to be
el servicio service
el servidor servant
servir(i) to serve; **servir para** to serve as
¿En que puedo servirle? May I help you?
si if; whether
sí yes; certainly
siempre always
la sierra mountain range
la siesta afternoon nap, rest
el siglo century
significar to mean
siguiente following;
al día siguiente the following day

la silla chair
el sillón armchair
simpático, -a pleasant, nice
sin without (*prep.*); **sin que** without (*conj.*)
sino but (on the contrary)
el sistema system
el sitio place
situado, -a situated
sobre upon, over
el sol sun
solamente only
  no solamente . . . sino también not only . . . but also
sólo, -a alone, only
solo only (*adv.*)
la sombra shade
el sombrero hat
sonar(ue) to sound, ring
el sonido sound
sonreír(i) to smile
soñar(ue) to dream
la sopa soup
sorprendido surprised
subir to go up, to climb, to get into (bus, taxi, etc.)
el suburbio suburb
sucio, -a dirty
el suelo floor, ground
el sueño dream
  tener sueño to be sleepy
la suerte fate, luck
  buena suerte good luck
el suéter sweater
sumamente extremely
supuesto; por supuesto of course
el sur south
el surtido assortment

T

el tabaco tobacco
el taco a tortilla sandwich
tal such (a);
  tal vez maybe
el tamaño size
también also
tampoco neither, either;
  ni yo tampoco nor I either
tan as, so; **tan . . . como** as . . . as
el tanque tank
tanto, -a so much, (*pl.*) so many
  tanto . . .como as much . . . as, (*pl.*) as many . . . as
la taquígrafa stenographer

la taquilla ticket window
la tarde afternoon
  tarde (*adj.*) late
la tarjeta de turista (turismo) tourist card
la taza cup
el té tea
el teatro theater
el tejado roof
el tejido textile
la tela cloth
el teléfono telephone
  llamar por teléfono to call up
la televisión television
el tema theme, subject
temer to fear
la temperatura temperature
templado temperate
temprano early
el tenedor fork
tener to have
  tener calor, frío to be warm, cold (person)
  tener cuidado to be careful
  tener dolor de (cabeza) (muelas) to have a (head) (tooth) ache
  tener ganas de to have a desire to
  tener hambre, sed to be hungry, thirsty
  tener prisa to be in a hurry
  tener que to have to
  tener razón to be right
  tener sueño to be sleepy
  ¿Qué tiene Ud.? What is the matter with you?
teñido, -a dyed
tercer(o), -a third
terminar to end
la ternera veal
el tiempo weather; time
  a tiempo on time
la tienda store
la tierra land
el timbre stamp, bell
la tinta ink
el tío uncle; **la tí** aunt
típico, -a typical
tocar to play (an instrument); to ring (a bell)
el tocino bacon
todavía still, yet
  todavía no not yet
todo, -a all, every, whole, everything
  ante todo first of all
  todo el mundo everybody
  todo el año all year

todo lo posible as much as possible
  sobre todo especially
tomar to take, to eat, drink;
  tomar la cena to dine
el tomate tomato
el tópico topic
el torero bullfighter
el toro bull
la toronja grapefruit
la torta cake
la tortilla Mexican "pancake" of corn
trabajador, -a hard-working
trabajar to work
el trabajo work
traducir to translate
traer to bring
el traje suit, costume
el tranvía streetcar
tratar (de) to try (to), deal with
el trigo wheat
triste sad
el (la) turista tourist

U

u or (*before words beginning with* o *or* ho)
ultimo, -a last
unir to unite; **unirse** to join
la universidad university
usar to use
el uso use
útil useful
la uva grape

V

la vaca cow
las vacaciones vacation
vacío, -a empty
la vacuna vaccination
valer to be worth;
  no vale nada it is not worth anything
  valer la pena to be worthwhile
  más vale tarde que nunca better late than never
la valija valise
el valle valley
la variedad variety
varios, -a several
el vaso glass (*for drinking*)
la velocidad speed
  a toda velocidad at full speed
vendado, -a bandaged

el vendedor seller
vender to sell
venir to come
la ventana window
ver to see
  ¡a ver! let's see!
el verano summer
veras: ¿de veras? really?
la verdad truth
  ¿verdad? is(n't) that so?
verdaderamente truly
verde green
el vestido dress
vestir(i) to dress
  vestirse (de) to dress in
la vez, *pl.* **veces** time
  a la vez at the same time
  a veces sometimes
  de vez en cuando from time to time
  en vez de instead of
  otra vez again
  tal vez perhaps
el viaje trip
  dar buen viaje to wish a pleasant journey
la vida life
el viejito little old man
viejo, -a old
el viento wind
  hace viento it is windy
el viernes Friday
la visita visit, visitor
la vista view
  hasta la vista so long
vivir to live; **¡viva!** long live!
vivo, -a lively
volver(ue) to return
  volver a casa to go home
  volver a + *infin.* to do again
la voz voice
el vuelo flight
la vuelta turn, return; change (money)
  a la vuelta around the corner

Y

y and
ya already, now
  ¡Ya lo creo! I should say so!

Z

el zapato shoe
el zapatero shoemaker
la zapatería shoe shop

English–Spanish

A

able, to be poder(ue)
about de, acerca de
  about 2 o'clock a eso de las dos
accept, to aceptar
accompany, to acompañar
ache el dolor
  headache dolor de cabeza
  toothache dolor de muelas
according to según

accustom, to acostumbrar
address la dirección
admire, to admirar
advice el consejo
advise, to aconsejar
affection el cariño
after después de (*prep.*) después que (*conj.*)
afternoon la tarde
  in the afternoon por la tarde; **p.m.** de la tarde
again otra vez;

to do again volver a + *infin.*
against contra
ago: two years ago hace dos años
agent el agente
agreeable agradable
aid la ayuda
aid, to ayudar
air el aire
  in the open air al aire libre

airmail: by airmail por correo aéreo
airplane el avión
airport el aeropuerto
almost casi
alone solo
along por
already ya
also también
although aunque
always siempre
amusement la diversión

and y, e (*before i or hi*)
announce anunciar
another otro, -a
answer la respuesta
answer, to contestar, responder
any cualquier
anyone alguien, alguno, -a
apple la manzana
approach, to acercarse a
arm el brazo
around alrededor de
arrange, to arreglar
arrival la llegada
arrive, to llegar
art el arte (*f*) and (*m*)
article el artículo
artist el (la) artista
as as tan como
ask, to preguntar; **to ask for** pedir(i);
  to ask questions hacer preguntas
assortment el surtido
at a, en
attend, to asistir a
attention la atención
aunt la tía
automobile el automóvil
avenue la avenida
awake, to be estar despierto, -a
awaken, to (arouse) despertar(ie)

B

bacon el tocino
bad malo, -a
badly mal
baggage el equipaje
baker el panadero
banana el plátano
bargain, to regatear
basket la cesta, la canasta
bath el baño; **bathroom** el cuarto de baño
bathe, to bañar, bañarse
be, to ser, estar;
  to be in a hurry estar de prisa
  to be on the way estar en camino
  to be about to estar para
beans los frijoles
beautiful bello, -a; hermoso; -a
because porque
become, to ponerse, hacerse
  He becomes sick. Se pone enfermo.
  He is becoming rich. Se hace rico.
bed la cama
bedroom la recámara (*Mex.*), la alcoba; el dormitorio
before (*time*) antes de
  before (*place*) delante de
begin, to comenzar(ie), empezar(ie), principiar
beginning el principio
  at the beginning al principio
behind detrás de
believe, to creer
belt el cinturón

bench el banco
better mejor
between entre
big grande
bill la cuenta
bird el pájaro
birthday el cumpleaños
black negro, -a
blanket la manta, el sarape
block la cuadra
blouse la blusa
blue azul
boat el barco
body el cuerpo
boiled cocido, -a
book el libro
bookshelf el estante
bookstore la librería
bottle la botella
box la caja
boy el muchacho
bread el pan
break, to romper
breakfast el desayuno
breakfast, to have desayunarse; tomar el desayuno
bring, to traer, llevar
brother el hermano
building el edificio
bundle el bulto
bus el camión (*Mex.*), autobús
business el negocio
businessman el comerciante, el negociante
busy ocupado, -a
but pero; **but on the contrary** sino
buy, to comprar
buyer el comprador

C

cake la torta, el pastel
call, to llamar
can (be able to) poder(ue)
car el coche; **by car** en coche
care: Be careful! ¡Cuidado!
carry, to llevar; **to carry away** llevarse
catch, to coger
  to catch cold coger (atrapar) un resfriado
celebrate, to celebrar
century el siglo
certain cierto, -a
certainly por cierto
certificate el certificado
chair la silla
change el cambio; **in change** de cambio
change, to cambiar
  to change clothes cambiar de ropa
chat, to platicar, charlar
cheap barato, -a
check, to (baggage) facturar
cheese el queso
chicken el pollo
child el niño, la niña
choose, to escoger
chop la chuleta
church la iglesia
cigar el puro (*Mex.*), cigarro
city la ciudad

class la clase
clean limpio, -a
clean, to limpiar
clear claro, -a
clerk el dependiente
climate el clima
close, to cerrar(ie)
closed cerrado, -a
cloth la tela
clothing la ropa
coffee el café
cold frío, -a
  It is cold (weather). Hace frío.
  I am cold. Tengo frío.
color el color;
  What is the color of ? ¿De qué color es ?
come, to venir
comprehend, to comprender, entender(ie)
comfortable cómodo, -a
concert el concierto
confess, to confesar(ie)
congratulate, to felicitar
complete, to completar
consequently por consiguiente
contain, to contener
continue, to continuar, seguir(i)
conversation la conversación
converse, to conversar
cooked cocido, -a
cool fresco, -a
  It (weather) is cool. Hace fresco.
copper el cobre
corn el maíz
corner la esquina
correct correcto, -a
cost, to costar(ue)
costume el traje
cotton el algodón
count, to contar(ue)
course: of course por supuesto; desde luego: Creo que sí.
  Of course not. Creo que no.
country el campo, el país (*nation*)
cross, to cruzar
cousin el primo, la prima
cover, to cubrir
craftsman el artesano
cream la crema
cry el grito
cry, to (shout) gritar
current corriente
custard el flan
culture la cultura
custom la costumbre
cut, to cortar

D

daily diario, -a
dance, to bailar
dangerous peligroso, -a
dark obscuro, -a
date la fecha
  What is the date? ¿Cuál es la fecha?
daughter la hija
day el día; **nowadays** hoy día

on the following day al día siguiente
death la muerte
dear caro, -a; querido, -a (*beloved*)
decide, to decidir
decoration el adorno
defend, to defender
demand, to demandar
descend, to bajar
depart, to partir
describe, to describir
desire, to desear; tener ganas
desk el escritorio
dessert el postre
die, to morir(ue)
different diferente, distinto, -a
difficult difícil
diligent diligente
dine, to tomar la cena, comer
dining room el comedor
dinner la comida
dirty sucio, -a
discover, to discubrir
dish el plato
distant lejano, -a
divide, to dividir
do, to hacer
doctor el médico, el doctor
dollar el dólar
door la puerta
doubt la duda
  without any doubt sin duda alguna
doubt, to dudar
drawing el dibujo
dress el vestido
dress, to vestir(i); **to dress** in vestirse de
drink la bebida
drink, to beber, tomar
drive manejar
dry seco, -a
dry clean limpiar en seco
during durante

E

each cada; **each one** cada uno
ear el oído (*hearing*), la oreja
early temprano
earn, to ganar
east el este
eat, to comer
educate, to educar
egg el huevo
elevator el ascensor, el elevador
employ, to emplear
employee el empleado
empty vacío
end el fin; **finally** al fin
end, to terminar, acabar
English el inglés (*lang.*)
  Englishman el inglés;
  Englishwoman la inglesa
enjoy, to gozar de
enough basta, bastante
enter, to entrar en
entire entero, -a
entrance la entrada
equal igual

especially sobre todo
everybody todo el mundo
everywhere por (en) todas partes
examination el examen
examine, to examinar, revisar (*baggage*)
excellent excelente
except excepto, menos
excuse, to dispensar, perdonar, excusar;
excuse me dispénseme
expect, to esperar
explain, to explicar
exporter el exportador
express, to expresar
eye el ojo

F

fable la fábula
face la cara
fall, to caer
fall asleep, to dormirse(ue)
false falso, -a
family la familia
famous famoso, -a
far from lejos de
fare el pasaje
fat gordo, -a
fast rápido, -a
father el padre
favor el favor
fear, to temer, tener miedo
feel, to (well, ill) sentirse(ie)
few pocos(as)
find, to hallar; **to find out** averiguar
fine fino, -a
finish, to terminar, acabar
first primero, -a
fish el pescado
flight el vuelo
floor el suelo; el piso (story)
flower la flor
follow, to seguir(i)
following: on the following day al día siguiente
food la comida, los alimentos
foot el pie; **on foot** a pie
for por, para
forget, to olvidar
fork el tenedor
form, to formar
fountain la fuente
fountain pen la plumafuente
French (*lang.*) el francés
Frenchman el francés
Frenchwoman la francesa
friend el amigo, la amiga
from de; **from . . . to** desde . . . hasta
fruit la fruta
full lleno, -a

G

game el juego
garage el garage
garden el jardín
gentleman (Mr.) el señor
get, to obtener, conseguir
to get (become) ponerse
to get up levantarse

to get on subir a
to get off salir, bajar de
gift el regalo
give, to dar; **to give back** devolver
glad alegre
glass el vaso (*for drinking*), el vidrio, el cristal
glove el guante
go, to ir; **to go away** irse
to go shopping ir de compras
gold el oro
good bueno, -a
grandfather el abuelo
grandmother la abuela
grape la uva
grapefruit la toronja
gray gris
green verde
greet, to saludar
greeting el saludo
group el grupo
guess, to adivinar

H

hair el pelo
half la mitad; medio, -a
ham el jamón
hand la mano
handmade hecho a mano
to shake hands darse la mano
happen, to pasar
happy contento, -a; feliz
hard difícil
hat el sombrero
have, to haber (*auxiliary*); tener (*possess*)
head la cabeza
headache dolor de cabeza
healthy sano, -a
to be healthy tener salud
hear, to oír
heart el corazón
heavy pesado, -a
help la ayuda
help, to ayudar
here aquí, acá (*usually after a verb of motion*)
Here it is. Aquí lo tiene Ud.
high alto, -a
holiday la fiesta
home en casa; **to go home** ir a casa
hope, to esperar
I hope so. Espero que sí.
I hope not. Espero que no.
horse el caballo
hot caliente
It (weather) is hot. Hace calor.
I am hot. Tengo calor.
hour la hora
house la casa
how como, ¿cómo?
how much ¿cuánto, -a?
how many ¿cuántos, -as?
hungry; to be hungry tener hambre
hurry; to be in a hurry tener prisa
hurry, to apresurarse
hurt, to hacer daño a
husband el esposo

I

ice cream el helado
if si
ill enfermo, -a; malo, -a
imagine imaginar
immediately inmediatamente, en seguida
in en
inside of dentro de
Indian el indio
industry la industria
inform, to informar, avisar
inhabitant el habitante
ink la tinta
instead of en vez de
intelligent inteligente
intend, to pensar + *infinitive*
interest el interés
interest, to interesar
introduce, to presentar
invitation la invitación
invite, to invitar
iron el hierro

J

jar el jarro
jewel la joya
jewelry shop la joyería
juice el jugo

K

keep, to guardar
kill, to matar
kind amable
king el rey
kiss, to besar
kitchen la cocina
knife el cuchillo
know, to saber; **to know how** saber; **to be acquainted with** conocer

L

lady (Mrs.) la señora
lamp la lámpara
land la tierra
language la lengua, el idioma
last último, -a
last year el año pasado
laugh la risa
laugh, to reír(i)
to laugh at reírse de
lawyer el abogado
lazy perezoso, -a
leaf la hoja
learn, to aprender
leave, to (go out of) salir de
least el menos
at least por lo menos
leather el cuero
left izquierdo, -a
to the left a la izquierda
lemon el limón
lend, to prestar
less menos
let, to (permit) permitir, dejar
letter la carta
library la biblioteca
lie down, to acostarse(ue)
life la vida

light la luz
like, so gustar
I like the game. Me gusta el juego.
listen, to escuchar
little pequeño, -a; **a little** un poco
live, to vivir
lively vivo, -a
living room la sala
load la carga
long largo, -a
look at, to mirar
look for, to buscar
lose, to perder(ie)
loud alto, -a
love el amor
love, to querer(ie) a, amar a
low bajo, -a
luck la suerte
lucky afortunado, -a
lunch el almuerzo

M

magnificent magnífico, -a
magazine la revista
maid la criada
mail, to echar en el buzón, echar al correo
maintain, to mantener
make, to hacer; **to make a trip** hacer un viaje
majority la mayor parte, la mayoría
man el hombre
manner la manera; **in the same manner** de la misma manera
many muchos, -as
market el mercado
marry, to (someone) casarse con
match el cerillo, el fósforo
matter, to importar; **It doesn't matter.** No importa. **What is the matter?** ¿Que hay? **What is the matter with you?** ¿Qué tiene Ud.?
meal la comida
mean, to significar; querer(ie) decir
meanwhile entretanto
measure la medida
measure, to medir(i)
meat la carne
meet, to (make the acquaintance of) conocer a; **Glad to meet you.** Mucho gusto en conocerle.
meet, to (come together with) encontrar(ue)
melon el melón
memory la memoria
menu la lista, el menú
merchandise la mercancía
merry alegre
month el mes
Mexican mexicano, -a
Mexico México
milk la leche
mile la milla
million el millón
Miss (young lady) la señorita
miss, to echar de menos

mistake la falta
mistaken (to be) estar equivocado, -a
modern moderno, -a
money el dinero, la moneda (*currency*)
moon la luna
more más
morning la mañana; **in the morning** por la mañana; **a.m.** de la mañana
most el(la) más
mother la madre
motion picture la película
mountain la montaña
mouth la boca
move, to mover(ue)
movies el cine
much mucho, -a
music la música
must (ought to) deber; **(to have to)** tener que; **(probably)** deber de

N

name el nombre
name, to nombrar
nature la naturaleza
near cerca de (*prep.*)
necessary necesario, -a; **it is necessary** es necesario, hay que + *infinitive*
necessity la necesidad
need, to necesitar
neither tampoco; **neither nor** ni ni
never nunca, jamás
nevertheless sin embargo
new nuevo, -a
news las noticias
newspaper el periódico, el diario
next próximo, -a
nice bonito, -a, simpático, -a
night la noche; **at night** por la noche; **p.m.** de la noche
nobody nadie
noise el ruido
none, no ninguno, -a
north el norte
North American norteamericano, -a
nose la nariz
nothing nada
now ahora, ahorita
number el número

O

obey, to obedecer
object el objeto
observe, to observar
obtain, to obtener, conseguir(i)
occasion la ocasión
of de
offer, to ofrecer
office la oficina
often a menudo, muchas veces
old viejo, -a, antiguo, -a
older mayor
oldest el(la) mayor
on (top of) encima de

only sólo, solamente; **not only but also** no solamente sino también
open abierto, -a
open, to abrir
opportunity la oportunidad
opposite frente a
or o (*u before o or ho*)
orange la naranja
order, to mandar, pedir(i)
other otro, -a
over sobre
overcoat el abrigo
ought to deber
outside of fuera de
owe, to deber
own propio, -a

P

pack; to pack a suitcase hacer una maleta
package el paquete
paint, to pintar
painter el pintor
painting la pintura
pancakes los panqueques
paper el papel
parcel post el paquete postal
parents los padres
park el parque
passport el pasaporte
pass (by), to pasar
pay, to pagar
peach el melocotón
pear la pera
pen la pluma
pencil el lápiz
people la gente, las personas
perfectly perfectamente
permission el permiso
permit, to permitir, dejar
person la persona
pharmacy la farmacia
picture el cuadro
pick up, to cojer, recojer
piece la pieza
pineapple la piña
pink rosado, -a
pity la lástima **What a pity!** ¡Qué lástima!
place el sitio, el lugar
place, to poner
plane el avión
play el drama, la comedia
play, to tocar (*instrument*) jugar(ue) (*game*)
pleasant agradable
please por favor; hágame Ud. el favor de; tenga la bondad de
pleasure el placer, el gusto; **with pleasure** con mucho gusto
pocket el bolsillo
point out, to señalar, indicar, mostrar(ue)
policeman el policía
poor pobre
portrait el retrato
poster el cartel
possible posible
post office el correo
potato la patata
pottery la cerámica, la alfarería

pound la libra
pour, to echar
practice, to practicar
prefer, to preferir(ie)
prepare, to preparar
present, to presentar
pretty bonito, -a
price el precio
priest el cura
prize el premio
produce, to producir
production la producción
professor el profesor, la profesora
program el programa
progress, to adelantar
promenade el paseo
promise, to prometer
proud orgulloso, -a
purchase la compra
purse la bolsa
put, to poner; **to put on** (*clothing*) ponerse

Q

quantity la cantidad
question la pregunta
quickly de prisa, aprisa

R

radio el radio (*set*), la radio (*broadcast*)
rain la lluvia
rain, to llover(ue)
raincoat el impermeable
rainy lluvioso, -a
rapid rápido, -a
rapidly rápidamente
raise, to levantar
rare raro, -a
read, to leer
ready listo, -a
really! ¡de veras!
receive, to recibir
recognize, to reconocer
recreation el recreo
red rojo, -a
regret, to sentir(ie)
relate, to contar(ue)
relative el pariente
remain, to quedar, quedarse
remember, to recordar(ue), acordarse(ue)
rent, to alquilar
repeat, to repetir(i)
reply, to responder, contestar
representative el representante
request, to pedir(i)
resemble, to parecerse a
resist, to resistir
respect el respeto
rest el descanso
restaurant el restaurante
return, to volver(ue) (*to go back*); regresar (*to go back*); devolver (*to give back*)
rice el arroz
rich rico, -a
ride, to ir (en coche, etc.); **to go for a ride** pasearse (en coche, etc.), dar un paseo (en coche, etc.)

right; to be right tener razón
right derecho, -a
river el río
road el camino
roof el tejado
roll el panecillo
room el cuarto
round redondo, -a
round trip ticket el boleto de viaje redondo
row la fila
run, to correr

S

salt la sal
same mismo, -a **the same thing** lo mismo
sash la faja
sauce la salsa
say decir **How does one say?** ¿Cómo se dice?
scarcely apenas
school la escuela
screen la pantalla
season la estación
seat el asiento
seated sentado, -a
silk la seda
see, to ver; **Let's see.** A ver.
seek, to buscar
seem, to parecer
sell, to vender
seller el vendedor
send, to mandar, enviar
sense el sentido
sentence la frase
serve, to servir(i)
set, to poner; **to set the table** poner la mesa
shade la sombra
shawl el rebozo
shine, to brillar
shipment el envío
shirt la camisa
shoe el zapato
short corto, -a, breve
shout, to gritar
show, to (point out) mostrar(ue), enseñar
sick enfermo, -a; malo, -a
side el lado; **beside** al lado de
sidewalk la acera
sight la vista
silk la seda
silver la plata
silversmith el platero
similar semejante
simple sencillo, -a
since (because) puesto que
sing, to cantar
sister la hermana
sit down, to sentarse(ie); **to be sitting** estar sentado
size el tamaño
skirt la falda
sky el cielo
sleep, to dormir(ue)
sleepy; to be sleepy tener sueño
slowly despacio, lentamente
small pequeño, -a
smile, to sonreír(i)
snow la nieve; **it is snowing** nieva

so así; **so much** tanto, -a; **so that** para que, de modo que
some alguno, -a
someone alguien
something algo
somewhat algo
son el hijo
song la canción
soon pronto
sorry; to be sorry sentir(ie); **I am very sorry.** Lo siento mucho.
south el sur
soup la sopa
souvenir el recuerdo
Spain España
Spaniard el español, la española
Spanish (*lang.*) el español
speak, to hablar
spend, to (*time*) pasar
spend, to (*money*) gastar
spicy picante
spite; in spite of a pesar de
spoon la cucharita (**teaspoon**)
spring la primavera
square cuadrado, -a
stairway la escalera
stamp el timbre (*Mex.*), la estampilla
stand el puesto
stand up, to ponerse en pie; **to be standing** estar de pie
star la estrella
state el estado
station (railroad) la estación de ferrocarril
statue la estatua
steak (beef) el filete (*Mex.*)
stenographer la taquígrafa
step el paso
still todavía
stop, to parar
store la tienda
story el cuento
story (*of building*) el piso
straw la paja
street la calle
streetcar el tranvía
strong fuerte
student el(la) estudiante
study, to estudiar
style el estilo
subject el tema
suburb el suburbio
suit el traje
suitcase la maleta; **to pack a suitcase** hacer una maleta
summer el verano
sun el sol; **it is sunny** hay sol
supper la cena
surely de seguro
surprised sorprendido
surrounded rodeado, -a
sweater el suéter
sweet dulce; **sweets (candy)** los dulces

T

table la mesa; **to set the table** poner la mesa
tailor el sastre
take, to tomar; **to take away** llevarse
take out, to sacar
tall grande, alto, -a
tank el tanque
taste, to probar(ue)
tasty sabroso, -a
tea el té
teach, to enseñar
teacher el maestro, la maestra, el profesor, la profesora
telephone el teléfono
telephone, to llamar por teléfono, telefonear
tell, to decir
temperate templado
temperature la temperatura
textile el tejido
thankful agradecido, -a
thanks gracias
that ese, -a; aquel, aquella; que (*conj.*)
theater el teatro
then entonces
there allí, ahí, allá (*usually with a verb of motion*); **there is (are)** hay
therefore por eso, por lo tanto
these (*adj.*) estos, -as
thick grueso, -a
thing la cosa
think, to (believe) creer; **to think of** pensar en
thirsty: to be thirsty tener sed
this (*adj.*) este, -a
those (*adj.*) esos, -as; aquellos, -as
through por
thus así
ticket window la taquilla
ticket el boleto (*Mex.*); el billete
tile el azulejo
time: What time is it? ¿Qué hora es? **one time, two times** una vez, dos veces, etc.; **on time** a tiempo; **to have a good time** pasar un buen rato, divertirse(ie)
time table el horario
tinplate la hojalata
tip la propina
tire, to cansarse
tired cansado, -a
to a; **in order to** para
tobacco el tabaco
today hoy
tomato el tomate
tomorrow morning mañana por la mañana
too (also) también
too many demasiados, -as
too much demasiado, -a
tooth el diente

toothache dolor de muela
topic el tópico, el tema
tourist el(la) turista
tourist card la tarjeta de turista
towards hacia
town el pueblo, la población
toy el juguete
train el tren
travel, to viajar
traveler el viajero
tree el árbol
trip el viaje; **to take a trip** hacer un viaje
trousers los pantalones
trunk el baúl
trunk of car la cajuela
truth la verdad
try, to tratar de; **to try on** probar(ue)
turkey el guajolote (*Mex.*)
typewriter la máquina de escribir
typical típico, -a

U

umbrella el paraguas
uncle el tío
under debajo de
understand comprender, entender(ie)
unfortunately desgraciadamente
United States los Estados Unidos (*abbreviation*) E.U.A.; E.E.U.U.
university la universidad
upon sobre, encima de
use, to usar, emplear
useful útil

V

vacation las vacaciones
valise la valija
valley el valle
very muy
view la vista
visit la visita
visit, to visitar
voice la voz
voyage el viaje

W

wait for, to esperar
waiter el mozo, el mesero
waiting room la sala de espera
wake up, to (*somebody*) despertar(ie), (*oneself*) despertarse
walk, to andar, ir a pie, caminar; **to take a walk** dar un paseo, pasearse
wall la pared
want desear, querer(ie)
wash, to lavar
watch el reloj

water el agua(f)
way: by the way a propósito
weak débil
wear llevar, vestir(i) de
weather; What's the weather? ¿Qué tiempo hace?
week la semana
weigh, to pesar
well pues, bien
   All right. Está bien.
well known conocido, -a
when cuando, ¿cuándo?
where donde, ¿dónde?
where (whither) ¿a dónde?
whether si
which que, ¿qué?
which one (ones) ¿cuál (cuáles)?
while mientras
white blanco, -a
who que, quien, ¿quién?
whom que, ¿á quien?
whose cuyo, -a, ¿de quién?
why ¿por qué? ¿para qué?
wide ancho, -a
wife la esposa
win, to ganar
wind el viento
   It is windy. Hace viento.
window la ventana
winter el invierno
wise sabio, -a
wish el deseo
wish, to querer(ie), desear
with con
without sin
woman la mujer
wood la madera
wool la lana
word la palabra
work el trabajo
work, to trabajar
world el mundo
worse peor
worth, to be valer
   It is worthwhile. Vale la pena.
worthy digno, -a
worry, to preocuparse
write, to escribir
writer el escritor
wrong: to be wrong no tener razón

Y

year el año; **last year** el año pasado; **next year** el año que viene
yellow amarillo, -a
yesterday ayer
   day before yesterday anteayer
yet todavía; **not yet** todavía no
young joven
youth el joven
younger menor
youngest el menor

German Glossary
German–English

A

der **Abend, -s, -e** evening; **am Abend, abends** in the evening

das **Abendessen, -s, -** supper

aber but, however

ab-fahren, er fährt ab, fuhr ab, ist abgefahren to depart, leave, ride off

ab-holen to call for, fetch

die **Abreise, -n** departure

ab-reisen to depart, leave on a trip

abwesend absent

acht-geben (auf) er gibt acht, gab acht, hat achtgegeben to pay attention (to)

alle all, everyone; **alles** everything

allerlei all kinds of

als *sub. conj.* when, as (*in comparisons* than)

also so, thus, therefore; well

alt old; **älter** older

das **Ame′rika** America; der **Amerika′ner** American; **amerika′nisch** *adj.* American

sich **amüsie′ren** to have a good time, enjoy oneself

an *prep. w. dat. or acc.* at, on, to, up against

an-bieten, er bietet an, bot an, hat angeboten to offer

ander other; der **andere** the other; die **anderen** the others; etc.; **anders** different

der **Anfang, -s, -e** beginning; **anfangs** at first

an-fangen, er fängt an, fing an, hat angefangen to begin

an-geben, er gibt an, gab an, hat angegeben to indicate

die **Angelegenheit, -en** matter, affair

angenehm pleasant, comfortable

an-halten, er hält an, hielt an, hat angehalten to stop

an-kommen, er kommt an, kam an, ist angekommen to arrive

an-nehmen, er nimmt an, nahm an, hat angenomen to take on, accept

an-rufen, er ruft an, rief an, hat angerufen to call up, telephone

an-schauen to look at

an-sehen, er sieht an, sah an, hat angesehen to look at; **etwas ansehen** to look over, view, inspect

anstatt *prep. w. gen.* instead of

an-telephonie′ren to ring up

die **Antwort, -en** answer

antworten *w. dat.* to answer

an-ziehen, er zieht an, zog an, hat angezogen to put on, dress; **sich anziehen** to get dressed

der **Anzug, -s, -e** suit (man's)

der **Apfel, -s, -** apple

der **Apparat′, -s, -e** apparatus, appliance

der **Appetit′, -s** appetite

die **Arbeit, -en** work

arbeiten to work

das **Arbeitszimmer, -s, -** workroom, study

der **Arm, -s, -e** arm

der **Arzt, -es, -e** doctor, physician

der **Aschenbecher, -s, -** ashtray

auch also, too

auf *prep. w. dat. or acc.* on, upon

auf-bleiben, er bleibt auf, blieb auf, ist aufgeblieben to stay awake, open

der **Aufenthalt** stay, sojourn

die **Aufgabe, -n** task, assignment

aufgeregt excited

sich **auf-halten, er hält sich auf, hielt sich auf, hat sich aufgehalten** stay, sojourn

auf-hören to stop

auf-machen to open

aufmerksam attentive

der **Aufsatz, -es, -e** composition

auf-stehen, er steht auf, stand auf, ist aufgestanden to stand up, get up

auf-warten to wait on, serve

auf-suchen to look up, seek out

das **Auge, -es, -en** eye

aus *prep. w. dat.* out, out of, from

der **Ausdruck, -es, -e** expression

der **Ausflug, -s, -e** excursion

ausführlich in detail

der **Ausgang, -s, -e** exit

aus-gehen, er geht aus, ging aus, ist ausgegangen to go out

ausgezeichnet excellent

aus-kommen, er kommt aus, kam aus, ist ausgekommen to get along

die **Auskunft, -e** information

aus-nützen to make full use of

aus-packen to unpack

aus-rufen, er ruft aus, rief aus, hat ausgerufen to cry out

aus-sehen, er sieht aus, sah aus, hat ausgesehen to look, appear

ausser *prep. w. dat.* outside of, except

ausserdem besides, moreover

aussergewöhn′lich unusual

ausseror′dentlich extraordinary

aus-steigen, er steigt aus, stieg aus, ist ausgestiegen to get out, climb out (of a vehicle)

ausverkauft sold out

das **Auto, -s, -s,** das **Automobil, -s, -e** automobile, car

der **Autobus, -usses, -usse** bus

B

baden to bathe

das **Badezimmer, -s, -** bathroom

der **Bahnhof, -s, -e** railroad station

der **Bahnsteig, -s, -e** railroad platform

bald soon

der **Balkon′, -s, -e** balcony

der **Ball, -es, -e** ball

beabsichtigen to intend

der **Beamte, -n, -n** official

beantworten to answer

bedeu′ten to mean

die **Bedeu′tung** meaning

been′den to finish

sich **befin′den** to feel; **ich befinde mich wohl** I feel well

sich **befin′den** to be located; **Wo befindet sich das Hotel?** Where is the hotel?

bege′gnen *w. dat.* to meet

begin′nen, er beginnt, begann, hat begonnen to begin

beglei′ten to accompany

der **Begriff** idea, concept; **im Begriff sein** to be about to

begrüs′sen to greet

behal′ten, er behält, behielt, hat behalten to retain

behilf′lich helpful

bei *prep. w. dat.* at, with, beside, at the house of; **bei uns** at our house

beide both; **die beiden Herren** both gentlemen

das **Bein, -es, -e** leg

beina′he almost

beitragen to contribute

bekannt′ known

bekom′men, er bekommt, bekam, hat bekommen to receive

beläs′tigen to annoy

beliebt′ (bei) popular (among, with)

bemer′ken to notice

sich **bemü′hen** to try, endeavor

benei′den to envy

bequem′ comfortable

bereit′ ready; **bereits** already

berei′ten to prepare

der **Berg, -es, -e** mountain

berich′ten to report, inform

der **Beruf′, -s, -e** occupation, profession

berühmt′ famous

beschäf′tigt busy

beschrei′ben, er beschreibt, beschrieb, hat beschrieben to describe

besetzt′ occupied

besich′tigen to view

besiegen to defeat

beson′ders especially

besor′gen to take care of, to obtain

bespre′chen, er bespricht, besprach, hat besprochen to discuss

besser better; **best-, am besten** best

beste′hen, er besteht, bestand, hat bestanden to pass (an examination)

beste′hen (auf) to insist (on)

beste′hen (aus) to consist of

bestei′gen, er besteigt, bestieg, hat bestiegen to get on, mount

bestel′len to order (goods)

besu′chen to visit

betragen, beträgt, betrug, betragen to come to, to amount to

betre′ten, er betritt, betrat, hat betreten to step into (a place)

das **Bett, -es, -en** bed

bevor′ *conj.* before

bewoh′nen to occupy

bewun′dern to admire

bewun′dernswert wonderful, admirable

bezah′len to pay

bezeich′nen to denote

die **Bibliothek′, -en** library

das **Bier, -es, -e** beer

bieten, er bietet, bot, hat geboten to offer

das **Bild, -es, -er** picture

bilden to form, shape

das **Billet′, -s, -e** ticket

bis until

bisher until now

ein **bisschen** a little

bitte please; you are welcome

bitten (um), er bittet, bat, hat gebeten to ask for, to request

blau blue

bleiben, er bleibt, blieb, ist geblieben to remain, stay

der **Bleistift, -s, -e** pencil

die **Blume, -, -n** flower

die **Bluse, -, -n** blouse

das **Blut, -es** blood

böse angry

brauchen to need, use

braun brown

breit broad

der **Brief, -es, -e** letter

bringen, er bringt, brachte, hat gebracht to bring

das **Brot, -es, -e** bread

das **Brötchen, -s, -** roll

des **Bruder, -s, -** brother

das **Buch, -es, -er** book

das **Büfett, -s, -e** sideboard

das **Büro′, -s, -s** office

der **Burger, -s, -** citizen

C

der **Chef** head, manager

D

da *adv.* there, then; *conj.* since, because
dabei at the same time, in connection with that
daher' therefore
die **Dame, -n** lady
damit with it; **damit'** *sub. conj.* so that
der **Dampfer, -s, -** steamer
danach' after that
der **Dank** gratitude; **vielen Dank!** thanks a lot!
danken *w. dat.* to thank; **danke!** thank you; **danke schön!** thank you kindly!
dann then; **dann und wann** now and then
die **Darstellung, -en** performance
das the, that, that one, who, which
dass *sub. conj.* that
dasselbe the same
das **Datum, -s, die Daten** date
dauern to last
dein, deine, dein, etc. your
denken, er denkt, dachte, hat gedacht to think; **denken an** *w. acc.* to think of
denn *conj.* for, because; *adv.* then
dennoch' nevertheless
der the, that, that one, who, which
dersel'be, dieselbe, dasselbe the same
das **Dessert', -s** dessert
deshalb, deswegen therefore
das **Deutsch** German (language); **auf deutsch** in German
deutsch *adj.* German; der **Deutsche** the German (man)
das **Deutschland, -s** Germany
der **Dezem'ber, -s** December
der **Dichter, -s, -** poet, writer
die the, that, that one, who, which
der **Dienstag, -s, -e** Tuesday
das **Dienstmädchen, -s, -** maid, servant girl
dieser, diese, dieses this
diktie'ren to dictate
das **Ding, -es, e** thing
dividie'ren durch divide by
doch nevertheless
der **Doktor, -s, Dokto'ren** doctor
der **Dollar, -s, -s** dollar
der **Dom, -es, -e** cathedral
der **Donnerstag, -es, -e** Thursday
Donnerwetter! the dickens!
das **Dorf, es, ⸚er** village
dort there
das **Drama, -s, -en** drama
draussen outside
dunkel dark
dünn thin
durch *prep. w. acc.* through
durch-führen to carry on, carry out, accomplish
durch-kommen, er kommt durch, kam durch, ist durchgekommen to get along, get through
der **Durst, -es** thirst; **Ich habe Durst** I am thirsty
dürfen, er darf, durfte, hat gedurft to be permitted to, allowed to, may
das **Dutzend, -s, -e** dozen
duzen to address with **du; sich duzen** to say **du** to each other

E

eben *adv.* just, just now
ebenso just as
die **Ecke, -n** corner
die **Eile** haste
ehe *sub. conj.* before
das **Ei, -es, -er** egg
eigen own
eigentlich really, actually
eilen to hurry
ein, eine, ein *indef. art.* a, an, one
einander each other, one another
das **Einfamilienhaus, -es, ⸚er** private dwelling
der **Eingang, -s, ⸚e** entrance
einige several, some
der **Einkauf, -s, ⸚e** purchase
ein-kaufen to purchase
ein-laden, er lädt ein, lud ein, hat eingeladen to invite
die **Einladung, -en** invitation
ein'mal once; **auf einmal'** all at once
ein-schliessen, er schliesst ein, schloss ein, hat eingeschlossen include, enclose
die **Eisenbahn, -en** railroad
ein-steigen, er steigt ein, stieg ein, ist eingestiegen to get on (vehicle)
ein-treten, er tritt ein, trat ein, ist eingetreten to step into, enter
die **Eintrittskarte** entrance ticket
ein-wandern to immigrate
der **Einwohner, -s, -** inhabitant
einzig single, sole
das **Eisen, -s** iron; **eisern** *adj.* iron
die **Eltern** parents
empfeh'len, er empfiehlt, empfahl, hat empfohlen to recommend
das **Ende, -s, -n** end; **zu Ende** at an end; **endlich** finally, at last
das **Englisch** English; *adj.* **englisch** English; **auf englisch** in English
die **Entfer'nung, -en** distance
entfernt' distant
entschul'digen to excuse, pardon
entste'hen, er entsteht, entstand, ist entstanden to arise, originate
entweder . . . oder either . . . or
das **Ereig'nis, -nisses, nisse** event
erfah'ren, er erfährt, erfuhr, hat erfahren to find out
der **Erfolg', -s, -e** success
ergrei'fen, er ergreift, ergriff, hat ergriffen to seize, take
erhal'ten, er erhält, erhielt, hat erhalten to receive
erin'nern an *w. acc.* to remind (of); **sich erinnern an** *w. acc.* to remember
sich **erkäl'ten** to catch cold
erken'nen, er erkennt, erkannte, hat erkannt to recognize, know, discern
erklä'ren to state, declare
erlau'ben to permit, allow
erle'digen to settle, finish
erler'nen to learn, acquire (knowledge)
ernst earnest
errei'chen to reach
erschei'nen, er erscheint, erschien, ist erschienen to appear
erschre'cken to frighten
erst first, only, not until
erwar'ten to await, expect
erwi'dern to answer
erzäh'len to relate
die **Erzäh'lung, -en** story, tale
essen, er isst, ass, hat gegessen to eat
das **Essen, -s, -** meal
das **Esszimmer, -s, -** dining room
euer, -e, euer your
etwa approximately, about
etwas something
das **Europa** Europe; **europä'ish** European

F

die **Fabrik', -en** factory
fahren, er fährt, fuhr, ist gefahren to ride
der **Fahrer, -s, -** driver
die **Fahrkarte, -n** ticket (for vehicle)
der **Fahrplan, -s ⸚e** timetable
der **Fahrstuhl, -s, ⸚e** elevator
fallen, er fällt, fiel, ist gefallen to fall
die **Fami'lie, -n** family
die **Farbe, -n** color
fast almost, nearly
der **Februar** February
die **Feder, -n** pen
fehlen *w. dat.* to be lacking; **was fehlt dir?** what is the matter with you?
der **Fehler, -s, -** mistake
das **Feld, -(e)s, -er** field
der **Felsen, -s, -** rock, cliff
das **Fenster, -s, -** window
die **Ferien** (*pl. only*) vacation
das **Fernsehen, -s** television
fertig finished, done
fest-setzen to fix, to arrange
das **Feuer, -s, -** fire
das **Fieber, -s** fever
der **Film, -(e)s, -e** film, motion picture
finden, er findet, fand, hat gefunden to find
die **Firma, -en** firm, business
der **Fisch, -es, -e** fish
die **Flasche, -en** bottle, flask
das **Fleisch, -es** meat
fleissig diligent, industrious
fliegen, er fliegt, flog, ist geflogen to fly
fliessend fluent(ly)
der **Flughafen, -s, -** airport
das **Flugzeug, -s, -e** airplane
das **Fluss, Flusses, Flüsse** river
folgen *w. dat.* to follow
der **Fortschritt, -s, -e** progress
die **Frage, -n** question; **Fragen stellen** to ask (put) questions
fragen to ask
das **Franzö'sisch** French; **auf französisch** in French
das **Frankreich** France
die **Frau, -en** woman, wife, Mrs.
das **Fräulein, -s, -** young lady, Miss
frei free, unoccupied
der **Freitag** Friday
die **Freude, -en** joy, pleasure; **Es macht mir Freude** It gives me pleasure
freuen to please; **sich freuen über** *w. acc.* to be happy about; **sich freuen auf** *w. acc.* to look forward to
der **Freund, -es, -e** friend
frisch fresh
froh happy, glad
fröhlich cheerful, happy, gay
früh early
der **Früh'ling, -s** spring
das **Früh'stück, -s, -e** breakfast
früh'stücken to have breakfast
fühlen to feel (something)
sich **fühlen** to feel (well, sick, etc.); **Ich fühle mich wohl.** I feel well.
führen to lead, to guide
die **Füllfeder, -n** fountain pen
für *prep. w. acc.* for
der **Fuss, -es, ⸚e** foot

G

die **Gabel, -n** fork
ganz whole, quite, entire
gar nicht not at all
gar nichts nothing at all
der **Garten, -s, ⸚n** garden
der **Gast, -es, ⸚e** guest
das **Gebäu'de, -s, -** building
geben, er gibt, gab, hat gegeben to give
das **Gebir'ge, -s, -** mountain range
gebo'ren born; **ich bin geboren** I was born, **er wurde geboren** he was born (*now dead*)
der **Gebrauch, -s, ⸚e** use, custom
gebrauchen to use, make use of
die **Geburt', -en** birth
der **Geburts'tag, -s, -e** birthday
gedul'dig patient
gefal'len *w. dat.* **er gefällt, gefiel, hat gefallen** to please; **es hat mir gefallen** it pleased me, I liked it
gegen *prep. w. acc.* toward, against
die **Gegend, -en** neighborhood, region
das **Gegenteil, -s, -e** opposite
das **Geheim'nis, -nisses, -nisse** secret
gehen, er geht, ging, ist gegangen to go
gehören *w. dat.* to belong to
gelb yellow
das **Geld, -es, -er** money
der **Geldbeutel, -s, -** purse
geling'en, es gelingt, gelang, ist gelungen to be successful; **es gelang mir** I succeeded
die **Gele'genheit, -en** opportunity
das **Gemü'se, -s, -** vegetable, vegetables
gemüt'lich sociable, cozy, comfortable
die **Gemüt'lichkeit** comfort, sociability
genies'sen, er geniesst, genoss, hat genossen to enjoy
genug' enough
die **Geographie'** geography
das **Gepäck', -s** baggage
gera'de just now; straight

das **Gericht'**, -s, -e food, dish
gern gladly; **er spielt gern** he likes to play
das **Geschäft'**, -s, -e business
der **Geschäfts'mann**, -s businessman; **Geschäftsleute** businessmen
die **Geschäfts'sache**, -n business matter
gesche'hen, **es geschieht, geschah, ist geschehen** to happen
das **Geschenk'**, -s, -e gift
die **Geschich'te**, -n history, story
geschmack'voll tasty
das **Gespräch'**, -s, -e conversation
geste'hen, er gesteht, gestand, hat gestanden to confess
gestern yesterday
die **Gesund'heit** health
das **Gewicht'**, -s weight
gewin'nen, er gewinnt, gewann, hat gewonnen to win
gewiss' certain, certainly
gewöhn'lich usual, usually
giessen, er giesst, goss, hat gegossen to spill, pour
der **Gipfel**, -s, - peak
das **Glas**, -es, ⸚er glass
glauben to believe, think
glücklich happy, fortunate
glücklicherweise luckily
der **Gott**, -es, ⸚er god
das **Gras**, -es, ⸚er grass
gratulie'ren w. dat. to congratulate
grau gray
gross (grösser, am grössten) big, great
grossartig splendid
grün green
gründlich thoroughly
der **Gruss**, -es, ⸚e greeting
grüssen to greet
der **Gummischuh**, -s, -e rubber overshoe
gut (besser, am besten) good
das **Gymna'sium**, -s, -ien German secondary school

H

das **Haar**, -es, -e hair
haben, er hat, hatte, hat gehabt to have
der **Hafen**, -s, - harbor
halb half; **halb fünf (Uhr)** half past four
der **Hals**, -es, ⸚e neck; **Halsschmerzen** sore throat
das **Halstuch**, -s, ⸚er scarf, neckerchief
halten, er hält, hielt, hat gehalten to hold
halt-machen to stop
die **Hand**, ⸚e hand; **sie geben sich die Hand** they shake hands
handeln to deal
der **Handkoffer**, -s, - suitcase
der **Handschuh**, -s, -e glove
die **Handtasche**, -n handbag
hängen to hang
das **Haupt**, -es, ⸚er head, chief
die **Hauptstadt**, ⸚e capital
das **Haus**, -es, ⸚er house; **zu Hause** at home, **nach Hause** (toward) home
die **Hausaufgabe**, -n homework
die **Hausfrau**, -en housewife

das **Heft**, -es, -e notebook
die **Heimat** native place or country
heim-kommen to come home
das **Heimweh** homesickness; **er hat Heimweh** he is homesick
heissen, er heisst, hiess, hat geheissen to be called; **wie heissen Sie?** what is your name?
helfen w. dat., **er hilft, half, hat geholfen** to help
hell bright
der **Held**, -en, -en hero
das **Hemd**, -(e)s, -en shirt
her shows direction (hither)
der **Herbst** autumn
herein'-kommen to come in
der **Herr**, -n, -en gentleman, Mr., Lord
her-reisen to travel here (hither)
herrlich splendid
herun'ter-nehmen, er nimmt herunter, nahm herunter, hat heruntergenommen to take down
herzlich sincere, sincerely, hearty, cordial
heute today; **heute früh** this morning
hier here
die **Hilfe** help
der **Himmel**, -s heaven, sky
hin shows direction away; **hin und her** back and forth
hinauf-tragen, er trägt hinauf, trug hinauf, hat hinaufgetragen to carry up
hinaus-schauen to look out
sich hingeben, er gibt sich hin, gab sich hin, hat sich hingegeben to devote oneself
hinten in back
hinter prep. w. dat. or acc. behind, in back of
hinzu'-fügen to add, say further
die **Hitze** heat
hoch (hoh- before -e**) höher, am höchsten** high
hoffen to hope
hoffentlich I hope, it is to be hoped
die **Hoffnung**, -en hope
hören to hear
das **Hotel**, -s, -s hotel
hübsch pretty
der **Hunger**, -s hunger, **ich habe Hunger** I am hungry
der **Hut**, -es ⸚e hat

I

ich I
ihr pers. pron. fam. plu. you; **ihr** poss. adj. her, their; **Ihr** poss. adj. pol. form your
illustrie'ren to illustrate
der **Imbiss**, -isses, -isse lunch, snack
immer always; **immer wieder** again and again
importie'ren to import
der **Importeur'**, -s, -e importer
in prep. w. dat. or acc. in, into
indem' sub. conj. while
indes'sen adv. meanwhile
intelligent' intelligent
interessant' interesting
das **Interes'se**, -s, -en interest
interessie'ren to interest; **sich interessie'ren für** to be interested in

irgendein, irgendwelcher any (whatsoever)
das **Ita'lien** Italy
das **Italie'nisch** Italian (language)
italie'nisch adj. Italian

J

ja yes
die **Jacke**, -n jacket
das **Jahr**, -es, -e year
die **Jahreszeit**, -en season
jährlich yearly, annual
der **Januar**, -s January
jawohl' yes indeed
jeder, -e, -es that, each, every
jedermann everybody
jedesmal every time
jemand somebody
jetzt now
der **Juli** July
jung young
der **Junge**, -n, -n boy, youth
der **Juni** June

K

der **Kaffee'**, -s coffee
der **Kaiser**, -s, - emperor
der **Kalen'der**, -s, - calendar
kalt cold
die **Kälte** cold
das **Kapi'tel**, -s, - chapter
die **Karte**, -n ticket
der **Kartenschalter**, -s, - ticket office
kaufen to buy
der **Käufer**, -s, - the buyer
der **Kaufmann**, -s, pl. **Kaufleute** merchant
kaum scarcely
kein, keine, kein no, not a
keiner nobody
der **Kellner**, -s, - waiter
kennen, er kennt, kannte, hat gekannt to know, be acquainted with; **kennenlernen** to get to know, make the acquaintance of
die **Kenntnis**, -nisse knowledge, information
die **Kera'mik** ceramics
der **Kessel**, -s, - kettle
das **Kilo**, -s, -s kilogram
der **Kilome'ter**, -s, - kilometer
das **Kind**, -es, -er child
das **Kino** cinema, movies; **ins Kino gehen** to go to the movies
die **Kirche**, -n church
klar clear
die **Klasse**, -n class
das **Klavier'**, -s, -e piano
das **Kleid**, -(e)s, -er dress; pl. clothes
klein small
das **Klima**, -s, -s climate
klingeln to ring
klug clever, wise
der **Knabe**, -n, -n boy
kochen to cook
kommen, er kommt, kam, ist gekommen to come
die **Kommode**, -n dresser
komponie'ren to compose
der **König**, -s, -e king
können, er kann, konnte, hat gekonnt to be able, can; **er kann Deutsch** he knows German

das **Konzert'**, -s, -e concert; **Ins Konzert gehen** to go to the concert
der **Kopf**, -es, ⸚e head
der **Korb**, -es, ⸚e basket
kostbar dear, expensive
köstlich delicious
kräftig strong, powerful
der **Kraftwagen**, -s, - automobile
krank sick, ill
die **Krankheit**, -en sickness
die **Krawat'te**, -en necktie
der **Krieg**, -(e)s, -e war
die **Küche**, -n kitchen, cuisine
der **Kuchen**, -s, - cake
kühl cool
die **Kultur'**, -en culture
der **Kunde**, -n, -n customer
die **Kunst**, ⸚e art
der **Kursus**, des **Kursus**, die **Kurse** course
kurz short
küssen to kiss
die **Kuss, Kusses, Küsse** kiss

L

lachen to laugh
der **Laden**, -s, ⸚ shop, store
die **Lage**, -n situation, location
die **Lampe**, -n lamp
das **Land**, -es, ⸚er land, country; **auf dem Lande** in the country; **aufs Land** to the country
die **Lankarte**, -n map
die **Landschaft**, -en landscape
lang long
langsam slowly
sich langweilen to be bored
der **Larm**, -(e)s noise
lassen, er lässt, liess, hat gelassen to let, allow, have something done
der **Lanstwagen**, -s, - truck
laut loud
das **Leben**, -s, - life
leben to live, be alive
lebhaft lively
legen to put, place, lay
die **Legende**, -n legend
der **Lehnstuhl**, -(e)s, ⸚e easy chair
lehren to teach
der **Lehrer**, -s, - teacher
leicht easy, light
das **Leid** sorrow; **es tut mir leid** I am sorry
leider unfortunately
leihen, er leiht, lieh, hat geliehen to lend
leisten to perform, achieve; **Dienste leisten** to render services
die **Lektion'**, -en lesson
lernen to learn
lesen, er liest, las, hat gelesen to read
das **Lesebuch**, -(e)s, ⸚er reader, reading book
letzt last
die **Leute** people
lieb (lieber, am liebsten) dear, agreeable; **ich gehe lieber** I prefer to go; **Ich spiele am liebsten** I like best of all to play
liebenswürdig likable, charming
das **Lied**, -es, -er song
liegen, er liegt, lag, hat gelegen to lie, be situated
die **Liste**, -n list

loben to praise
der **Löffel**, -s, - spoon
die **Luft**, -e air
das **Lustspiel**, -s, -e comedy
der **Lyriker**, -s, - lyric poet

M

machen to make, do
das **Mädchen**, -s, - girl
die **Mahlzeit**, -en meal
das **Mal**, -es, -e time; **einmal, zweimal, usw.** once, twice, three times, etc.; **manchmal** sometimes; **das erste Mal** the first time
der **Mai**, -s May
malerisch picturesque
man *indef. pron.* one, people, they
mancher, -e, -es many a; *pl.* many, some
der **Mann**, es, ⸚er man, husband
der **Mantel**, -s, ⸚ coat
die **Mark** mark (unit of German currency, now about 34 cents)
der **Markt**, -es, ⸚e market
der **März** March
die **Masse**, -n mass
die **Mathematik'** mathematics
die **Medizin'** medicine
mehr more
mehrere several
die **Meile**, -n mile
mein, meine, mein my
meinen to mean, to believe
die **Meinung**, -en opinion, meaning; **meiner Meinung nach** in my opinion
meist most; **meistens** for the most part
der **Meister**, -s, - master
der **Mensch**, -en, -en human being, man
das **Messer**, -s, - knife
mieten to rent
das **Miethaus** apartment house
die **Milch** milk
mild mild
mildern to moderate, soften
die **Minute**, -n minute
mit *prep. w. dat.* with
der **Mittag**, -s, -e noon
das **Mittagessen**, -s, - noon meal
die **Mitte** middle
mit-teilen to inform, impart
der **Mittwoch** Wednesday
möbliert' furnished
modern' modern
mögen, er mag, mochte, hat gemocht to like, care to, may
möglich possible
die **Möglichkeit**, -en possibility
möglichst bald as soon as possible
der **Monat**, -s, -e month
der **Montag**, -s Monday
der **Morgen**, -s, - morning; **guten Morgen** good morning; **morgen** tomorrow; **morgen früh** tomorrow morning
müde tired
multiplizie'ren to multiply
munter cheerful
das **Museum**, -s, **Muse'en** museum
die **Musik'** music
müssen, er muss, musste, hat gemusst to have to, must
die **Mutter**, ⸚ mother

N

nach *prep. w. dat.* after, to, according to
die **Nachbarschaft**, -en neighborhood
nachdem *sub. conj.* after
nach-prüfen to check
die **Nachricht**, -en report, news
nach-schauen to look after
die **Nacht**, ⸚e night
nah (näher, nächst) near
die **Nähe** vicinity
nahrhaft nutritious
die **Nahrungsmittel** *pl.* foods, groceries
der **Name**, -ns, -n name
nämlich namely, that is
nass wet
die **Natur** nature
natür'lich naturally, of course
neben *prep. w. dat. or acc.* beside, next to
nehmen, er nimmt, nahm, hat genommen to take
nein no (opposite of **ja**)
nennen, er nennt, nannte, hat genannt to name, call
nett nice
neu new
neugierig curious
die **Neuigkeit**, -en piece of news; *pl.* news
neulich recently
nicht not; **nicht wahr?** isn't that so?
nichts nothing
nie never; **niemals** never
nieder down
niedrig low
niemand nobody
nimmer never
noch still, yet; **noch ein** one more; **noch nicht** not yet
der **Norden**, -s north
das **Notenheft**, -s, -e music book
die **Nummer**, -n number
nun well, now; **nun also** well then
nur only; **nicht nur . . . sondern auch** not only . . . but also

O

ob whether, if
obwohl' *sub. conj.* although
das **Obst**, -es fruit
oder or; **entweder . . . oder** either . . . or
offen open
öffnen to open
oft often
ohne *prep. w. acc.* without
der **Onkel**, -s, - uncle
die **Oper**, -n opera
die **Operet'te**, -n musical comedy
die **Oran'ge**, -n orange; der **Orangensaft** orange juice
der **Osten** east

P

das **Paar**, -(e)s, -e pair; **ein Paar (Schuhe)** a pair (of shoes); **ein Paar** a couple
packen to pack
das **Papier'**, -s, -e paper
der **Park**, -es, -e park
das **Parkett'**, -s, -e orchestra (part of theater)

der **Passagier'**, -s, -e passenger
die **Person'**, -en person
persön'lich personally
der **Pfennig**, -s, -e pfennig, penny
das **Pfund**, -es, -e pound
die **Photographie'**, -n photograph
plagen to pester, annoy
das **Plakat'**, -(e)s, -e placard, poster
die **Platte**, -n record, disc
der **Platz**, -es, ⸚e place, seat
plaudern to chat
plötzlich sudden(ly)
die **Polizei'wache**, -n police station
das **Porträt'**, -s, -e portrait
die **Post** mail
das **Postamt**, -s, ⸚er post office
der **Preis**, -es, -e price, prize
das **Problem'**, -s, -e problem
der **Profes'sor**, -s, **Professo'ren** professor
das **Programm'**, -s, -e program
das **Prozent'**, -s, -e percent
der **Prozent'satz** percentage
prüfen to test, examine
die **Prüfung**, -en the test, examination; **eine Prüfung bestehen** to pass an examination
das **Pult**, -(e)s, -e desk
der **Punkt**, -es, -e period; **Punkt neun Uhr** nine o'clock sharp
pünktlich punctual(ly), on time

Q

die **Qualität'**, -en quality
die **Quantität'**, -en quantity

R

das **Radio**, -s radio; **im Radio** on the radio
der **Rang**, -es ⸚e balcony (of theater)
rasch quickly
rasen to rage, rush madly, speed
raten *w. dat.,* **er rät, riet, hat geraten** to guess; **ich rate Ihnen** I advise you
der **Rauch**, -es smoke
rauchen to smoke
sich **rasie'ren** to shave oneself
rechnen to figure, reckon
die **Rechnung**, -en bill, sum
das **Recht**, -es, -e right; **mit Recht** correctly, rightly; **sie haben recht** you are right
reden to talk
die **Regel**, -n rule
der **Regen**, -s rain
der **Regenmantel**, -s, ⸚ raincoat
der **Regenschirm**, -s, -e umbrella
regnen to rain
reich rich
reichen to hand, to pass
die **Reihe**, -en row
die **Reise**, -n trip
reisen to travel
das **Reisebuch**, -(e)s, ⸚er guide book
reisefertig finished, ready to travel
der **Reisende**, -n, -n traveller
der **Reisepass**, -es, -pässe passport
das **Restaurant**, -s, -s restaurant
reservie'ren to reserve

richtig correct, right
die **Rolle**, -n role
rot red
die **Rückreise**, -n trip back
die **Rückfahrkarte**, -n return ticket
die **Rückfahrt** trip back
rufen, er ruft, rief, hat gerufen to call
ruhen to rest
die **Ruhepause**, -n rest period
ruhig quiet
rund round

S

der **Saal**, -es, **Säle** hall, large room
die **Sache**, -n thing
sagen to say, tell
der **Salat'**, -s, -e salad
die **Sammlung**, -en collection
der **Samstag** Saturday
sanft softly, gently
der **Sänger**, -s, - singer
der **Satz**, -es, ⸚e sentence
die **Schachtel**, -n box
scharf sharp
schätzen to estimate
das **Schauspiel**, -s, e play
der **Schauspieler**, -s, - actor
der **Scheck**, -s, -e check
scheinen, er scheint, schien, hat geschienen to seem, to shine
schenken to present
scherzen to joke
schicken to send
schlafen, er schläft, schlief, hat geschlafen to sleep
das **Schlafzimmer**, -s, - bedroom
schlagen, er schlägt, schlug, hat geschlagen to hit, defeat
schlecht bad(ly)
schliessen, er schliesst, schloss, hat geschlossen to close
schliesslich finally
schlimm bad
das **Schloss, Schlosses, Schlösser** castle
schmecken to taste
der **Schnee**, -s snow
schneiden, er schneidet, schnitt, hat geschnitten to cut
schnell quick(ly), fast
schneien to snow
der **Schnellzug**, -(e)s, ⸚e express
schon already
schön beautiful, fine
der **Schrank**, -es, ⸚e closet; der **Kleiderschrank** wardrobe
schrecklich terrible
schreiben, er schreibt, schrieb, hat geschrieben to write
die **Schreibmaschine**, -n typewriter
der **Schreibtisch**, -es, -e desk
der **Schuh**, -es, -e shoe
schulden to owe
die **Schule**, -n school
der **Schüler**, -s, - schoolboy, pupil
der **Schutzmann**, -s, **Schutzleute** policeman
schwach weak
schwärmen to be enthusiastic
schwarz black
schwer heavy, difficult
die **Schwester**, -n sister
schwierig difficult, hard

der **See**, -s, -n lake
die **See**, -n ocean, sea
sehen, er **sieht**, **sah**, **hat gese-hen** to see
die **Sehenswürdigkeit**, -en, sight, object of interest
sehr very
seiden adj. silk, silken
die **Seife**, -n soap
sein, er **ist**, **war**, **ist gewesen** to be
sein, -e, sein his
seit prep. w. dat. since; **seit einer Woche** for a week
seitdem sub. conj. since; adv. since then
die **Siete**, -n page
die **Sekunde**, -n second
selber self; **ich selber** I myself, etc.
selbst self; **ich selbst** I myself, etc.
selbstverständlich obviously, it goes without saying
die **Semmel**, -n roll
senden, er **sendet**, **sandte**, **hat gesandt** to send
der **September**, -s September
das **Servier'brett**, -(e)s, -er tray
setzen to place, put
sich setzen to sit down, seat oneself
sicher sure
sicherlich surely
sie she, they; **Sie** you
singen, er **singt**, **sang**, **hat gesungen** to sing
die **Sitte**, -n custom
sitzen, er **sitzt**, **sass**, **hat gesessen** to sit
so so, thus; **so gross wie** as large as
sobald sub. conj. as soon as; adv. immediately
soeben just, just now
das **Sofa**, -s, -s sofa
sofort' at once, immediately
sogar' even
sogleich' = sofort' immediately
der **Sohn**, -(e)s, -e son
solcher, -e, -es such; **solch ein** such a
sollen, er **soll**, **sollte**, **hat gesollt** shall, to be supposed to, ought to, should
der **Sommer**, -s, - summer
sondern but, but on the contrary; **nicht nur . . . sondern auch** not only . . . but also
der **Sonntag**, -s, -e Sunday
sonst otherwise
sorgen für to care for, to take care of
die **Sorte**, -n kind
sowie as well as
sowohl als as well as
das **Spanien**, -s Spain
spanisch Spanish
spät late
spazie'ren to walk, stroll
spazie'ren-gehen, er **geht spazieren**, **ging spazieren**, **ist spazierengegangen** to go for a walk
der **Spazier'gang**, -s, -e walk
die **Speise**, -n food
die **Speisekarte**, -n menu
speisen to dine
spielen to play
der **Sport**, -(e)s, -e sport
die **Sprache**, -n language, speech

sprechen, er **spricht**, **sprach**, **hat gesprochen** to speak
das **Sprichwort**, -(e)s, -er proverb
der **Staat**, -es, -en state
der **Staatsmann**, -s, -er statesman
die **Stadt**, -e city
der **Stamm**, -es, -e trunk; tribe
stark strong
die **Station'**, -en station
statt prep. w. gen. instead of
statt-finden, er **findet statt**, **fand statt**, **hat stattgefunden** to take place
stehen, er **steht**, **stand**, **hat gestanden** to stand
stellen to place, put; **Fragen stellen** to ask questions
die **Stellung**, -en position, job
sterben, er **stirbt**, **starb**, **ist gestorben** to die
stets always
still still, quiet
stimmt! that's correct
der **Stock**, -es, -e stick, story (of house)
der **Stoff**, -es, e stuff, material
stolz proud
die **Strasse**, -en street
die **Strecke**, -n stretch, distance
strecken to stretch
streiten, er **streitet**, **stritt**, **hat gestritten** to quarrel, fight
der **Strudel**, -s strudel
das **Stück**, -(e)s, -e piece
der **Student'**, -en, -en student
studie'ren to study
das **Studium**, -s, **Studien** study
der **Stuhl**, -es, -e chair
die **Stunde**, -n hour, lesson
stürmisch stormy
suchen to look for, seek
der **Süden**, -s south
die **Summe**, -n sum
die **Suppe**, -n soup

T

der **Tag**, -es, -e day
täglich daily
tanken to buy gasoline, fill up
die **Tante**, -n aunt
tanzen to dance
das **Taschentuch**, -(e)s, -er handkerchief
die **Tasse**, -n cup; **eine Tasse Kaffee** a cup of coffee
tatsäch'lich in fact
tauschen to change
das **Taxi**, -s, -s taxi
der **Tee**, -s tea
der **Teil**, -(e)s, -e part; **zum Teil** in part
teilen to divide; **geteilt durch** divided by
das **Telefon**, -s, -e telephone
telefonie'ren mit to carry on a telephone conversation with a person
telefo'nisch anrufen to telephone (someone)
der **Teller**, -s, - plate
die **Temperatur'** temperature
teuer dear, expensive
das **Thea'ter**, -s, - theater; **ins Theater gehen** to go to the theater
das **Thema**, -s, **Themen** theme, topic
die **Tinte**, -n ink
das **Tier**, -(e)s, -e animal

der **Titel**, -s, - title
die **Tochter**, - daughter
der **Tod**, -es, -e death
die **Torte**, -n tart, cake
die **Toilet'te**, -n ladies' or men's room
der **Tourist'**, -en, -en tourist
tragen, er **trägt**, **trug**, **hat getragen** to carry
traurig sad
trennen to separate
trinken, er **trinkt**, **trank**, **hat getrunken** to drink
das **Trinkgeld**, -(e)s, -er tip, gratuity
trotz prep. w. gen. in spite of
das **Tuch**, -es, -er cloth
tüchtig capable
tun, er **tut**, **tat**, **hat getan** to do
die **Tür**, -en door

U

üben to practice
über prep. w. dat. or acc. over, across, about
überall' everywhere
überhaupt' at all
übermorgen day after tomorrow
überra'schen to surprise
die **Überra'schung**, -en surprise
überset'zen to translate
die **Überset'zung**, -en translation
der **Überzieher**, -s, - overcoat
die **Übung**, -en exercise
das **Ufer**, -s, - shore
die **Uhr**, -en watch, clock; **wieviel Uhr ist es?** what time is it? **um wieviel Uhr?** at what time?
um prep. w. acc. around; **um . . . zu** in order to
die **Umge'bung**, -en surroundings
umher-reisen to travel around
sich umkleiden to change clothes
um-schauen to look around
und and; **und so weiter (usw.)** and so forth (etc.)
der **Unfall**, -s, -e mishap
ungefähr' about, approximately
die **Universität'**, -en university
unter prep. w. dat. or acc. under, among
unterhal'ten, er **unterhält**, **unterhielt**, **hat unterhalten** to entertain; **sich unterhalten (über)** to converse (about)
unterneh'men, er **unternimmt**, **unternahm**, **hat unternommen** to undertake
der **Unterricht**, -s instruction
unterrich'ten to teach, instruct
der **Unterschied**, -s, -e difference
die **Untersuch'ung**, -en inspection
die **Untertasse**, -n saucer
unterwegs' on the way

V

der **Vater**, -s, - father
die **Verab'redung**, -en appointment
das **Verb**, -(e)s, -en verb
die **Verän'derung**, -en change
verbringen, er **verbringt**, **verbrachte**, **hat verbracht** to spend (time)

verdie'nen to earn
die **Verei'nigten Staaten** United States
verges'sen, er **vergisst**, **vergass**, **hat vergessen** to forget
das **Vergnü'gen**, -s, - pleasure
vergnü'gungsvoll pleasurable
verhei'ratet married
verkau'fen to sell
verlas'sen, er **verlässt**, **verliess**, **hat verlassen** to leave, desert
verlie'ren, er **verliert**, **verlor**, **hat verloren** to lose
der **Vers**, -es, -e verse
verschie'den different, varied
verschrei'ben, er **verschreibt**, **verschrieb**, **hat verschrieben** to prescribe
versich'ern to assure, to insure
verspre'chen, er **verspricht**, **versprach**, **hat versprochen** to promise
die **Verspä'tung**, -en lateness, delay; **der Zug hat Verspä'tung** the train is late
verst'hen, er **versteht**, **verstand**, **hat verstanden** to understand; **das versteht sich** that goes without saying
versu'chen to try, taste
der **Vertre'ter**, -s, - representative, agent
der **Verwand'te**, -n, -n relative
verzei'hen, er **verzeiht**, **verzieh**, **hat verziehen** to pardon
die **Verzei'hung** pardon; **ich bitte um Verzeihung** I beg your pardon
viel (mehr, meist-) much, many
vielleicht perhaps
vielmals often, many times
voll full
vollkom'men fully, completely
von prep. w. dat. from, of
vor prep. w. dat. or acc. before, in front of; **vor einer Woche** a week ago
voraus ahead; **im voraus** in advance
vorbei'fahren, er **fährt vorbei**, **fuhr vorbei**, **ist vorbeigefahren** to ride past
sich vorbereiten (auf) w. acc. to prepare for
vorgestern day before yesterday
vorig former, last; **voriges Jahr** last year
vor-legen to place before
vorne in front
der **Vorort**, -es, -e suburb
vor-stellen to introduce
die **Vorstellung**, -en performance, introduction
vorteilhaft advantageous
vor-ziehen, er **zieht vor**, **zog vor**, **hat vorgezogen** to prefer
vorzüg'lich excellent

W

der **Wagen**, -s, - wagon, car
wählen to choose
wahr true; **nicht wahr?** isn't it true?
die **Wahrheit**, -en truth
während prep. w. gen. during; sub. conf. = **indem** while
wahrschein'lich probable, probably
der **Wald**, -es, -er forest
die **Wand**, -e wall
die **Wanduhr**, -en wall clock

wann? when?
die **Ware, -n** goods, ware
das **Warenhaus, ⸚er** department store
warm warm
sich **wärmen** to warm oneself
warten auf *w. acc.* to wait for
der **Wartesaal, -es, -säle** waiting room
warum'? why?
was what; **was für** what kind of; **was für ein Tag!** what a day!
sich **waschen, er wäscht sich, wusch sich, hat sich gewaschen** to wash (oneself); **sie waschen sich die Hände** they are washing their hands
das **Wasser, -s** water
wechseln to change; **er wechselt Dollars gegen Mark** he changes dollars into marks
weder . . . noch neither . . . nor
der **Weg, -es, -e** way; **weg** away
wegen *prep. w. gen.* on account of
weg-gehen to go away
weh-tun, es tut weh, tat weh, hat wehgetan to hurt; **es tut mir weh** it hurts me
die **Weihnachten** Christmas; **zu Weihnachten** for Christmas
weil *sub. conj.* because
die **Weile** while
der **Wein, -es, -e** wine
die **Weise** manner, way; **auf diese Weise** in this way
weiss white
weit far
weiter further, farther; **lesen Sie weiter!** read on, continue reading

weiter-fahren, er fährt weiter, fuhr weiter, ist weitergefahren to ride, drive on
weiter-sprechen, er spricht weiter, sprach weiter, hat weitergesprochen to go on speaking
welcher, -e, -es *interrog. adj. & pron.* which, what; *rel. pron.* who, which, that
die **Welt, -en** world
wenig little, few; **weniger** less, minus; **ein wenig** a little
wenigstens at least
wenn *sub. conf.* if, when, whenever
wer? who? he who
werden, er wird, wurde, ist geworden to become, get; **er wird alt** he is getting old
wert worth
wertvoll useful, worthwhile
der **Westen, -s** west
das **Wetter, -s** weather
wichtig important
wie! how? **so gross wie** as large as
wieder again
wiederho'len to repeat
Wiedersehen; auf Wiedersehen! good-by, au revoir
wiegen, er wiegt, wog, hat gewogen to weigh
wieviel'? how much? how many?
der **Wind, -es, -e** wind
winken to beckon
der **Winter, -s** winter
wir we
wirklich really
wissen, er weiss, wusste, hat gewusst to know (a fact)
die **Wissenschaft, -en** science

wo? where? (at what place?)
die **Woche, -n** week
die **Wochenschau** newsreel
woher? from where?
wohin? where? (to what place?)
wohl well, indeed (*used for emphasis:* **ich bin wohl müde** I am indeed tired)
wohnen to dwell, live
die **Wohnung, -en** dwelling, home
das **Wohnzimmer, -s, -** living room
die **Wolke, -n** cloud
der **Wolkenkratzer, -s, -** skyscraper
wolkenlos cloudless
wollen, er will, wollte, hat gewollt to want to, wish to, intend to
das **Wort, -(e)s, die Worte** (*words in phrases and sentences*), die **Wörter** (*words not connected in sense*)
das **Wörterbuch, -s, ⸚er** dictionary
wunderbar wonderful
sich **wundern (über** *w. acc.*) to be surprised (at)
wünschen to wish

Z

die **Zahl, -en** number
zahlen to pay
zählen to count
zeigen to show
die **Zeit, -en** time
zeitig early
die **Zeitschrift, -en** magazine
die **Zeitung, -en** newspaper

zerbrechen, er zerbricht, zerbrach, hat zerbrochen to break to pieces
ziehen, er zieht, zog, hat gezogen to pull
das **Ziel, -(e)s, -e** goal
ziemlich rather, fairly
die **Zigaret'te, -n** cigarette
das **Zimmer, -s, -** room
das **Zimmermädchen, -s, -** chambermaid
zitieren to cite
die **Zivilisation'** civilization
zu *prep. w. dat.* to, toward; *adv.* too
zu-bereiten to prepare
die **Zuckerdose** sugar bowl
zuerst first, at first
zufrie'den satisfied
der **Zug, -(e)s, ⸚e** train
zugleich at the same time
zu-hören to listen to
sich **zurecht'-finden, er findet sich zurecht, fand sich zurecht, hat sich zurechtgefunden** to find one's way
sich **zurück-ziehen, er zieht sich zurück, zog sich zurück, hat sich zurück gezogen** to withdraw
zurück-geben, er gibt zurück, gab zurück, hat zurückgegeben to give back, to return
zurück-legen to put back, to cover a distance
die **Zuversicht** confidence, faith
zuvor'kommend obliging
zusam'men together
zwar it is true
der **Zweifel, -s, -** doubt
zweifel'los doubtless
zwischen *prep. w. dat. or acc.* between

English–German

A

able (to be) können, er kann, konnte, hat gekonnt
actor der Schauspieler, -s, -
advantageous vorteilhaft
affair die Angelegenheit, -en
after nach *prep. w. dat.*; **nachdem** *sub. conj.*
again wieder; **again and again** immer wieder
against gegen *prep. w. dat.*
air die Luft, -, ⸚e
airport der Flughafen, -s, ⸚
all aller, -e, -es; **all kinds of** allerlei; **not at all** gar nicht
almost fast, beina'he
already schon
also auch; **not only . . . but also** nicht nur . . . sondern auch
always immer, stets
although obgleich' *sub. conj.*
and und; **and so forth, etc.** und so weiter, usw.
another (one more) noch ein
answer die Antwort, -, -en
answer (to) (*a person*) antworten *w. dat.*; (*a question*) antworten auf *w. acc.*; **or** beant'worten *w. acc.*
apartment house das Miethaus, -es, ⸚er
appetite der Appetit'; **I have an appetite** ich habe Appetit'

arm der Arm, -es, -e
arrive (to) ankommen
around um *prep. w. acc.*
art die Kunst, ⸚e
as . . . as so . . . wie; **as soon as** sobald *sub. conj.*
ashtray der Aschenbecher, -s, -
ask (to) fragen; **to ask for** bitten um; **to ask questions** Fragen stellen
assignment die Aufgabe, -en
aunt die Tante, -n
at an *prep. w. acc.*
attentive aufmerksam
automobile das Automobil', -s, -e; das Auto, -s, -s; der Kraftwagen, -s, -
autumn der Herbst, -es, -e
await (to) erwar'ten

B

bad schlecht
balcony der Rang, -es, ⸚e
basket der Korb, -es, ⸚e
bathroom das Badezimmer, -s, -
be (to) sein, er ist, war, ist gewesen; **to be located** sich befinden
beautiful schön
because weil *sub. conj.*; **denn** *coord. conj.*

become (to) werden, er wird, wurde, ist geworden
bed das Bett, -es, -en
bedroom das Schlafzimmer, -s, -
beer das Bier, -es, -e
before vor *prep. w. dat. or acc.*; **ehe (bevor)** *sub. conj.*
beginning der Anfang, -s, ⸚e
begin (to) beginnen, er beginnt, begann, hat begonnen; **an-fangen, er fängt an, fing an, hat angefangen**
behind hinter *prep. w. dat. or acc.*
believe (to) glauben (*w. dat. of persons*)
belong to (to) gehö'ren *w. dat.*
beside neben *prep. w. dat. or acc.*; **bei** *prep. w. dat.*
besides ausserdem
better besser
between zwischen *prep. w. dat. or acc.*
big gross
bill die Rechnung, -en
birthday der Geburts'tag, -es, -e
black schwarz
blue blau
book das Buch, -es, ⸚er
bored (to be) sich langweilen
both beide

bottle die Flasche, -n
boy der Knabe, -n, -n; der Junge, -n, -n
bread das Brot, -es, -e
breakfast das Frühstück, -(e)s, -e
breakfast (to) frühstücken
bring (to) bringen, er bringt, brachte, hat gebracht
bright hell
broad breit
brother der Bruder, -s ⸚
brown braun
building das Gebäude', -s, -
business das Geschäft', -es, -e
busy beschäf'tigt
but aber; **but (on the contrary)** sondern; **not only . . . but also** nicht nur . . . sondern auch
buy (to) kaufen
buyer der Käufer, -s, -

C

cake der Kuchen, -s, -
calendar der Kalen'der, -s, -
call (to) rufen, er ruft, rief, hat gerufen; **to call for** abholen; **to call up** anrufen
called (to be) heissen, er heisst, hiess, hat geheissen
capable tüchtig

capital die Hauptstadt, ⸚e
car der Wagen, -s, -; das Auto, -s, -s; **people's car** der Volkswagen
carry (to) tragen, er trägt, trug, hat getragen; **to carry up** hinauftragen
certain(ly) gewiss', sicher
chair der Stuhl, -es, ⸚
change (to) wechseln
chat (to) plaudern
cheerful munter, fröhlich
child das Kind, -es, -er
cigarette die Zigaret'te, -n
citizen der Bürger, -s, -
city die Stadt, ⸚e
class die Klasse, -n
clear klar
clever klug
climate das Klima, -s, -s
clock die Uhr, -en; **what time is it?** wieviel Uhr ist es?
close (to) schliessen, er schliesst, schloss, hat geschlossen
clothes die Kleider *pl.*
coat der Mantel, -s, ⸚
coffee der Kaffee', -s
cold kalt; **to catch cold** sich erkälten
color die Farbe, -n
come (to) kommen, er kommt, kam, ist gekommen; **to come in** herein'- kommen
comfortable angenehm, bequem
cool kühl
concert das Konzert', -s, -e; **to go to a concert** ins Konzert gehen
congratulate (to) gratulie'ren *w. dat.*
conversation das Gespräch', -s, -e
cook (to) kochen
correct richtig
cost (to) kosten
count (to) zählen
country das Land, -es, ⸚er; **to the country** aufs Land; **in the country** auf dem Lande
cup die Tasse, -, -n
curious neugierig
customer der Kunde, -n, -n
cut (to) schneiden, er schneidet, schnitt, hat geschnitten

D

daily täglich
dance (to) tanzen
dark dunkel
date das Datum, -s, Daten
daughter die Tochter, ⸚
day der Tag, -es, -e; **day after tomorrow** übermorgen; **day before yesterday** vorgestern
dear teuer **(expensive)**, lieb
depart (to) ab-reisen, abfahren
departure die Abreise, -n
describe (to) beschrei'ben, er beschreibt, beschrieb, hat beschrieben
desk der Schreibtisch, -es, -e; das Pult, -es, -e
dictionary das Wörterbuch, es, ⸚er
different anders, verschie'den
difficult schwer
diligent fleissig
dine (to) speisen
dining room das Esszimmer, -s, -

dinner *(midday)* das Mittagessen, -s, -
dish der Teller, -s, -; die Platte, -n
divide (to) dividi'eren, teilen
do (to) tun, machen
doctor der Doktor, -s, Dokto'ren; der Arzt **(physician)**, -es, ⸚e
door die Tür, -en
doubt der Zweifel, -s, -; **doubtless** zweifellos, ohne Zweifel
dozen das Dutzend, -s, -e
drama das Drama, -s, Dramen
dress das Kleid, -er, -er
dress oneself sich an-ziehen
driver der Fahrer, -s, -
drink (to) trinken, er trinkt, trank, hat getrunken
during während *prep. w. gen.*
dwell (to) wohnen

E

each jeder, -e, -es
early früh
earnest ernst
earn verdie'nen
easy leicht
eat (to) essen, er isst, ass, hat gegessen
egg dass Ei, -es, -er
either . . . or entweder . . . oder
end das Ende, -s, -en; **at an end** zu Ende
English das Englisch *noun;* englisch *adj.;* **in English** auf englisch
enjoy (to) genies'sen, er geniesst, genoss, hat genossen; **to enjoy oneself** sich amüsie'ren
enough genuq
enter (to) ein-treten
entrance der Eingang, -s, ⸚e
even sogar
evening der Abend, -s, -e; **in the evening** am Abend; **evenings** abends
event das Ereig'nis, -ses, -se
everybody jedermann
everywhere überall
examination die Prüfung, -en
excellent vorzüg'lich, ausgezeich'net
except ausser *prep. w. dat.*
excited aufgeregt
excursion der Ausflug, -s, ⸚e
exercise die Übung, -en
exit der Ausgang, es, ⸚e
expensive teuer, kostbar
explain (to) erklären
express *(train)* der Schnellzug, -s, ⸚e
extraordinary ausseror'dentlich
eye das Auge, -s, -n

F

factory die Fabrik, -en
fall (to) fallen, er fällt, fiel, ist gefallen
family die Fami'lie, -n
famous berühmt'
far weit, fern
fast schnell, rasch
father der Vater, -s, ⸚
feel (to) fühlen; **to feel well, sick, etc.** sich fühlen; **I feel well** ich fühle mich wohl

fever das Fieber, -s, -
finally schliesslich, endlich
foot der Fuss, -es, ⸚e
French das Franzö'sisch; französisch *adj.;* **in French** auf französisch
friend der Freund, -es, -e
from von *prep. w. dat.*
fruit das Obst, -es, -e; die Frucht, ⸚e
full voll
further weiter; **read further** lesen Sie weiter!

G

garden der Garten, -s, ⸚
German das Deutsch; deutsch *adj.;* **in German** auf deutsch
get (to) bekom'men, erhal'ten; **to get along** sich zurecht'- kommen; **to get on** *(mount)* bestei'gen, einsteigen; **to get out** *(of vehicle)* aus-steigen; **to get up** auf-stehen
gift das Geschenk', -s, -e
girl das Mädchen, -s, -
give (to) er gibt, gab, hat gegeben; **to give back** zurück-geben
glad froh
gladly gern; **he likes to play** er spielt gern
glass das Glas, -es, ⸚er
glove der Handschuh, -s, -e
go (to) gehen, er geht, ging, ist gegangen
goal das Ziel, -es, -e
good gut
goods die Ware, -n
gray grau
green grün
greet (to) grüssen
greeting der Gruss, -es, ⸚e
guest der Gast, -es, ⸚e

H

hand die Hand, ⸚e
hand (to) reichen
handbag die Handtasche, -n
handkerchief das Taschentuch, -s, ⸚er
hang (to) *(something)* hängen
happen (to) gesche'hen, es geschieht, geschah, ist geschehen
happy glücklich
hat der Hut, -es, ⸚e
have (to) haben; **to have to** müssen, er muss, musste, hat gemusst
head der Kopf, -es, ⸚e
hear (to) hören
heavy schwer
help die Hilfe
help (to) helfen *w. dat.*, er hilft, half, hat geholfen
here hier
high hoch; **higher** höher; **highest** der, die, das höchste
hold (to) halten, er hält, hielt, hat gehalten
home die Wohnung, -en, das Heim; **home country** die Heimat; **I am going home** ich gehe nach Hause; **I am at home** ich bin zu Hause; **home-sickness** das Heimweh; **he was homesick** er hatte Heimweh

homework die Hausaufgabe, -n
hope (to) hoffen
hot heiss
hotel das Hotel, -s, -s
hour die Stunde, -n
house das Haus, -es, ⸚er
how? wie?; **how many?** wieviel'(e); **how much?** wieviel?
human being der Mensch, -en, -en
hunger der Hunger; **I am hungry** ich habe Hunger
hurry eilen
hurt (to) weh-tun *w. dat.;* **it hurts me** es tut mir weh

I

if wenn *sub. conj.*
immediately sofort', sobald', sogleich'
import (to) importie'ren
important wichtig
in, into in *prep. w. dat. or acc.*
industrious fleissig
information die Auskunft, ⸚e
inhabitant der Einwohner, -s, -
ink die Tinte, -n
intelligent intelligent'
interested; to be interested in sich interessie'ren für
interesting interessant'
introduce vor-stellen
introduction die Vorstellung, -en
invitation die Einladung, -en
invite (to) ein-laden, er lädt ein, lud ein, hat ein-geladen

J

job die Stellung, -en
joke (to) scherzen
joy die Freude; **it gives me pleasure** es macht mir Freude
just: just now soe'ben

K

kind die Sorte, -n
kilogram das Kilogramm', -s, -e; das Kilo, -s, -s
kilometer der Kilome'ter, -s, -
kiss (to) küssen
kitchen die Küche, -n
knife das Messer, -s, -
know (to): to know facts wissen; **to know, be acquainted with** kennen; **to get to know** kennen-lernen
known bekannt'

L

lady die Dame, -n
lake der See, -s, -n
lamp die Lampe, -n
land das Land, -es, ⸚er
language die Sprache, -, -n
last letzt
last (to) dauern
late spät
laugh (to) lachen
lead (to) führen
leave (to) on a trip ab-reisen, ab-fahren; **to leave a person or place** verlassen
lend (to) leihen, er leiht, lieh, hat geliehen
less weniger

lesson die Stunde, -, die Lektion', -en; **assignment** die Aufgabe, -n
let (to) lassen, er lässt, liess, hat gelassen
letter der Brief, -es, -e
library die Bibliothek', -en
lie (to) liegen, er liegt, lag, hat gelegen
life das Leben, -s, -
like (to) mögen, er mag, mochte, hat gemocht; *verb +* gern **I like to read** ich lese gern
listen (to) zu-hören
little klein; **a little** ein wenig, ein bisschen
live (to) leben; *(dwell)* wohnen
living room das Wohnzimmer, -s, -
long lang
look sehen, er sieht, sah, hat gesehen; schauen; **to look at** an-schauen; **to look for** suchen
lose (to) verlie'ren, er verliert, verlor, hat verloren
loud laut
love (to) lieben
luckily glücklicherweise

M

magazine die Zeitschrift, -en
maid (servant) das Dienstmädchen, -s, -
mail die Post
make (to) machen
man der Mann, -es, ̈er
manager (head) der Chef, -s, -s
many viel, viele
map die Landkarte, -n
mark *(unit of German currency)* die Mark
married verhei'ratet
market der Markt, -es, ̈e
may *(to be permitted to)* dürfen, er darf, durfte, hat gedurft
meal die Mahlzeit, -en
mean (to) bedeu'ten, meinen
meat das Fleisch, -es
medicine die Medizin
meet (to) begeg'nen *w. dat.;* **to get acquainted with** kennenlernen
menu die Speisekarte, -n
merchant der Kaufmann, -s, die Kaufleute
milk die Milch
minute die Minu'te, -en
mistake der Fehler, -s, -
Miss das Fräulein, -s, -
money das Geld, -es, -er
month der Monat, -s, -e
more mehr
morning der Morgen, -s, -; **good morning!** guten Morgen; **tomorrow morning** morgen früh; **this morning** heute morgen
most der, die, das meiste; **for the most part** meistens
mother die Mutter, ̈
mount (to) *(a vehicle)* einsteigen
movies das Kino; **I am going to the movies** ich gehe ins Kino
Mr. der Herr, -n, -en
museum das Muse'um, -s, die Muse'en
music die Musik'
must müssen, er muss, musste, hat gemusst

N

name (to) nennen, er nennt, nannte, hat genannt
named (to be) heissen, hiess, hat geheissen
naturally natür'lich
near nah(e); **nearer** näher
nearly fast, beina'he
need (to) brauchen
never nie, niemals, nimmer
neither . . . nor weder . . . noch
new neu
news die Nachricht, -en
newspaper die Zeitung, -en
next der, die, das nächste
nevertheless doch
nice nett
night die Nacht, ̈e
no nein; **no, not a, not any** kein, keine, kein
nobody keiner, niemand
not nicht; **not at all** gar nicht
notebook das Heft, -es, -e
nothing nichts
now jetzt, nun
number die Zahl, -en; die Nummer, -n

O

occupation der Beruf', -s, -e
occupied besetzt'
occupy (to) bewoh'nen
of von *prep. w. dat.*
offer (to) bieten, er bietet, bot hat geboten; an-bieten
office das Büro, -s, -s
often oft, vielmals
old alt; **older** älter
on (on top of) auf *prep. w. dat. or acc.;* **on (at, up against)** an *prep. w. dat. or acc.*
one (people, they) man *indef. pron.;* **one says (people say, it is said)** man sagt
once einmal; **all at once** auf einmal
only nur
open öffnen
open (to) öffnen, auf-machen
opportunity die Gele'genheit, -en
or oder; **either . . . or** entweder . . . oder
order: in order to um . . . zu
other der, die, das andere
otherwise sonst
ought sollen, or soll, sollte, hat gesollt
out of aus *prep. w. dat.*
outside draussen
outside of ausser *prep. w. dat.*
over über *prep. w. dat. or acc.*

P

pack (to) packen
page die Seite, -n
pair das Paar, -es, -e
paper das Papier', -s, -e; **newspaper** die Zeitung, -en
pardon (to) entschul'digen *w. acc.;* verzei'hen *w. dat.,* er verzeiht, verzieh, hat verziehen
parents die Eltern
parking lot der Parkplatz, -es, ̈e
part der Teil, -es, -e; **in part** zum Teil

pass (to) *(an examination)* bestehen
passenger der Passagier', -s, -e
passport der Reisepass, -passes, -pässe
pay (to) (be)zahlen
pay attention (to) acht-geben
pen die Feder, -n
pencil der Bleistift, -s, -e
people die Leute
percent das Prozent, -s, -e
performance die Vorstellung, -en
perhaps vielleicht'
permit (to) erlau'ben
permitted (to be) dürfen, er darf, durfte, hat gedurft
person die Person', -en
photograph die Photographie', -n
piano das Klavier', -s, -e
picture das Bild, -es, -er
piece das Stück, -es, -e
place der Platz, -es, ̈e
place (to) setzen; **to place before** vor-legen
plate der Teller, -s, -
play das Schauspiel, -s, -e
play (to) spielen
pleasant angenehm
please bitte!
please (to) gefal'len *w. dat.,* er gefällt, gefiel, hat gefallen
pleasure das Vergnü'gen, -s, -
popular (with) beliebt (bei)
portrait das Porträt', -s, -e
position die Stellung, -en
possible möglich
post office das Postamt, -s, ̈er
pound das Pfund, -es, -e
practice üben
praise loben
prefer (to) vor-ziehen; lieber + *verb:* **I prefer spring** ich habe den Frühling lieber
prepare (to) berei'ten
present (to) schenken
present das Geschenk', -s, -e
pretty hübsch
price der Preis, -es, -e
probably wahrschein'lich
problem das Problem', -s, -e
profession der Beruf', -s, - e
professor der Profes'sor, -s, Professo'ren
program das Programm', -s, -e
progress der Fortschritt, -s, -e
promise (to) verspre'chen
proud (of) stolz auf *w. acc.*
pupil der Schüler, -s, -
purchase der Einkauf, -s, ̈e
purchase (to) kaufen, ein-kaufen
put (to) stellen

Q

question die Frage, -n
quickly schnell, rasch
quiet ruhig, still
quite ganz, recht

R

radio das Radio, -s; **on the radio** im Radio
rain der Regen, -s
rain (to) regnen
raincoat der Regenmantel, -s, ̈
rather ziemlich
reach (to) errei'chen

read (to) lesen, er liest, las, hat gelesen
really eigentlich, wirklich
recently neulich
receive (to) bekom'men; erhal'ten
recognize (to) erken'nen
record die Schallplatte, -n
red rot
relate (to) erzäh'len
remain (to) bleiben, er bleibt, blieb, ist geblieben
remember (to) sich erin'nern an *w. acc.*
rent (to) mieten
report (to) berich'ten
representative der Vertre'ter, -s, -
rest (to) ruhen
restaurant das Restaurant', -s, -s
rich reich
ride fahren, er fährt, fuhr, ist gefahren; **to ride past** vorbeifahren
right das Recht; **rightly** mit Recht; **you are right** Sie haben recht
ring up (to) an-rufen
role die Rolle, -, -n
room das Zimmer, -s, -
round rund
row die Reihe, -n
run (to) laufen, er läuft, lief, ist gelaufen

S

sad traurig
say (to) sagen
satisfied zufrie'den
saucer die Untertasse, -n
scarcely kaum
school die Schule, -n
sea die See, -n
season die Jahreszeit, -en
seat der Platz, -es, ̈e; der Sitz, -es, -e
see (to) sehen, er sieht, sah, hat gesehen
sell (to) verkau'fen
send (to) senden, schicken
several einige, mehrere
sharp scharf; **5 o'clock sharp** Punkt 5 Uhr
shirt das Hemd, -es, -en
shoe der Schuh, -es, -e
shop der Laden, -s, ̈
shop (to) ein-kaufen, Ein-käufe machen
short kurz
should sollen, er soll, sollte, hat gesollt
show (to) zeigen
sick krank
side die Seite, -n
since seit *prep. w. dat.;* seitdem' *sub. conj.*
sincerely herzlich
sing (to) singen, er singt, sang, hat gesungen
single *(sole)* einzig
sister die Schwester, -n
sit (to) sitzen, er sitzt, sass, hat gesessen; **to sit down** sich setzen
sleep schlafen, er schläft, schlief, hat geschlafen
slow langsem
small klein
smoke (to) rauchen
snow (to) schneien

so so, also
sofa das Sofa, -s, -s
some etwas, einige, mehrere
somebody jemand
something etwas
son der Sohn, -es, ⸗e
soon bald; **as soon as** sobald′ *sub. conj.*
sorry: I am sorry es tut mir leid
soup die Suppe, -n
speak (to) sprechen, er spricht, sprach, hat gesprochen
spend (to) *(time)* verbrin′gen; *(money)* ausgeben
spite: in spite of trotz *prep. w. gen.*
splendid herrlich, grossartig
spoon der Löffel, -s, -
spring der Frühling, -s
stand (to) stehen, er steht, stand, hat gestanden; **to stand up** auf-stehen
station die Station′, -en; der Bahnhof, -s, ⸗e
stay (to) bleiben, er bleibt, blieb, ist geblieben
steamship der Dampfer, -s, -
still ruhig, still
stop (to) halt-machen; *(cease)* auf-hören
store der Laden, -s, ⸗
story die Geschich′te, -, -n
street die Strasse, -n
student der Student′, -en, -en
study *(workroom)* das Arbeits-zimmer, -s, -
suburb der Vorort, -s, -e
succeed (to) gelin′gen *w. dat.*; es gelingt, gelang, ist gelun-gen; **I succeed** es gelingt mir
such solcher, -e, -es; **such a** solch ein
suddenly plötzlich
suit *(man's)* der Anzug, -s, ⸗e; *(woman's)* das Kostüm′, -s, -e
suitcase der Handkoffer, -s, -
sum die Summe, -n
summer der Sommer, -s
supper das Abendessen, -s, -
supposed: to be supposed to sollen, er soll, sollte, hat ge-sollt

surely sicherlich, gewiss
surprise die Überra′schung, -en

T

take (to) er nimmt, nahm, hat genommen; **to take place** statt-finden
talk (to) reden, sprechen
taste (to) *w. obj.* versu′chen; **it tastes good** es schmeckt gut
taxi das Taxi, -s, -s
tea der Tee, -s
teacher der Lehrer, -s, -
teach (to) lehren, unterich′ten
telephone das Telephon′, -s, -e
telephone (to) telepho′nisch an-rufen
television das Fernsehen; *(set)* der Fernsehapparat
test (to) prüfen
thank danken *w. dat.*; **thanks** danke!, danke schön; **many thanks** vielen Dank!
that jener, -e, -es; dass *sub. conj.*; das **(pointing out) that is a book, etc.** das ist ein Buch, usw.
theater das Thea′ter, -s, -; **to the theater** ins Theater
their ihr, ihre, ihr
then dann, denn; **now and then** dann und wann
there dort, da
therefore deshalb, deswegen, daher
thing die Sache, -n; das Ding, -es, -e
think (to) denken, er denkt, dachte, hat gedacht; **to think of** denken an *w. acc.*
thirst der Durst; **I am thirsty** ich habe Durst
through durch *prep. w. acc.*
ticket die Karte, -n; *(of admis-sion)* die Eintrittskarte, das Billet′, -s, -e; *(for vehicle)* die Fahrkarte
time die Zeit, -en; **once, twice, three times, etc.** einmal, zweimal, dreimal, usw.; **at the same time** zugleich′
tip das Trinkgeld, -s, -er

tired müde
to zu *prep. w. dat.;* **up to** bis
today heute
together zusam′men
too zu; *(also)* such
tourist der Tourist′, -en, -en
train der Zug, -es, ⸗e
travel (to) reisen
traveller der Reisende, -n, -n
trip die Reise, -n
true wahr; **isn't it true** nicht wahr?
truth die Wahrheit, -en
try (to) versu′chen
typewriter die Schreibmaschine, -n

U

uncle der Onkel, -s, -
under unter *prep. w. dat. or acc.*
understand (to) versteh′en, er versteht, verstand, hat ver-standen
unfortunately leider
university die Universität′, -en
until bis
use (to) gebrau′chen
usual gewöhn′lich

V

vacation die Ferien *(pl.)*
vegetable das Gemü′se, -s, -
very sehr
village das Dorf, -es, ⸗er
visit (to) besu′chen

W

wait (to) warten; **to wait for** warten auf *w. acc.*
waiter der Kellner, -s, -
waiting room der Wartesaal, -s, -säle
walk gehen, er geht, ging, ist gegangen; **to take a walk** spa-zie′rengehen, einen Spa-zier′gang machen
wall die Wand, ⸗e
want wollen, er will, wollte, hat gewollt

warm warm; **warmer** wärmer
wash (to) waschen, er wäscht, wusch, hat gewaschen; **to wash oneself** sich waschen
watch die Uhr, -en
water das Wasser, -s
weather das Wetter, -s
week die Woche, -n
well gut, wohl; **well-known** be-kannt
wet nass
what? was? welcher, -e, -es; **what kind of?** was für ein?
when, whenever wenn *sub. conj.;* wann *interr.*
where? wo? **(at what place?);** wohin? **(to what place?)**
whether ob *sub. conj.*
which welcher, -e, -es
while während *sub. conj.*
white weiss
who? wer?
whole ganz
why? warum?
win (to) gewin′nen, er gewinnt, gewann, hat gewonnen
window das Fenster, -s, -
wine der Wein, -es, -e
winter der Winter, -s, -
wish (to) wünschen
with mit *prep. w. dat.*
without ohne *prep. w. acc.*
woman die Frau, -en
wonderful wunderbar
word (in phrases and senten-ces) das Wort, -es, -e; **(not connected in sense)** das Wort, -es, ⸗er
work die Arbeit, -en
work (to) arbeiten
world die Welt
write schreiben, er schreibt, schrieb, hat geschrie′ben

Y

year das Jahr, -es, -e
yesterday gestern
yet noch; **not yet** noch nicht
you du, ihr, Sie; **your** dein, deine, dein; euer, euere, euer; Ihr, Ihre, Ihr
young jung

Glossary of
Biological Terms

A

abdomen, Posterior section of the body; between diaphragm and pelvis in vertebrates.

absorption, The passage of liquids through a cell membrane.

adaptation, Fitness of structure for function; fitness for environmental conditions.

ADP, adenine diphosphate, A low-energy compound produced during respiration.

adrenal, Ductless glands above the kidneys; "glands of combat."

Adrenalin, Laboratory product that has the chemical make-up of adrenin.

adrenin, A hormone secreted by the inner part of the adrenal glands.

adventitious, Appearing in an unusual place (roots above ground).

afferent, Nerves that receive stimuli and send impulses to the brain or spinal cord.

agar agar, Gelatin material obtained from seaweed; used in bacteriology.

algae, Simplest green plants.

alternation of generations, Life cycle in which an asexual generation follows a sexual generation.

altricial, Born helpless.

ameba, Simplest (one-celled) animal.

amphibian, Vertebrates that live part of their lives in water and may live part of their lives on land.

anal spot, Weak point in cell membrane for elimination of solid wastes (paramecium).

anemia, Deficiency of red blood corpuscles or hemoglobin in red blood corpuscles.

antennae (sing.: antenna), Sense organs, or "feelers," on heads of insects and related arthropods.

anther, Pollen-producing structure of the stamen of flowering plants (part of male reproductive organ).

anthropologist, One who specializes in the study or science of man and his activities as a rational animal.

antibiotic, Chemical substance produced by a living thing which can stop growth of some disease-producing bacteria, virus, or protozoa.

antibodies, Chemical substances in blood that fight against bacteria, toxins and other foreign substances.

antiseptic, A substance that prevents growth of some bacteria and destroys others.

antitoxin, A substance produced in animal bodies that counteracts harmful effects of disease-producing organisms; may provide immunity to certain diseases.

aphid, "Ant-cow"; provides nourishing fluid for ants; receives shelter and protection from ants.

appendage, A structure or organ attached to the main body.

appendix, Vestigial organ in man; part of digestive tube.

aquatic, Water-living.

arboreal, Tree-living.

Archaeopteryx, Fossil bird-form showing relationship to reptiles.

arteriosclerosis, Hardening of the arteries.

artery, Blood vessel that carries blood away from the heart to all parts of the body.

aseptic, Free of microorganisms; sterile.

asexual, Reproduction without the union of two unlike parent cells.

assimilation, Process by which digested food is changed into protoplasm.

astigmatism, Defect in the curvature of the eyes; results in indistinct vision.

atabrine, Synthetic drug used in the treatment of malaria.

atoll, Coral reef in the form of a ring.

atom, The smallest quantity of an element that enters into chemical combination.

ATP, adenine triphosphate, A high-energy compound produced during respiration.

auricle, Upper chamber of the heart which receives blood from the veins.

Australopithecus africanus, A South African man-ape genus, a meat-eater and tool-user, a member of the Australopithecine group.

Australopithecines, A group of man-apes, ancestral to man, who lived around 3 million years ago.

auxin, Plant hormone that controls plant growth.

axon, Main, long fiber or branch leading from a neuron; carries impulses away from neuron cell body.

B

bacillus, Rod-shaped bacteria.

backbone, Bony, internal vertebral or spinal column.

bêche-de-mer, Sea cucumbers, dried and used for food (related to starfish).

beriberi, Deficiency disease caused by lack of thiamin (B_1 of B complex).

binary fission, Simple splitting of a parent cell into two daughter cells.

bivalve, Mollusk having two shells (clam, oyster).

botulism, Food poisoning caused by specific bacteria.

bronchi, Bronchial tubes branching from the trachea or windpipe and leading into each lung.

budding, Form of asexual reproduction; growth from mother cell which remains attached to or separates from mother cell.

C

calcareous, Made of calcium.

calorie, A heat-measuring unit used in reference to foods.

calyx, Sum total of sepals or outermost leaflike structures of a true flower.

capillary, Smallest blood vessel in the body; between and connecting an artery and a vein; in closest contact with body cells for exchange of digested food, gases, and waste fluids.

carnivorous, Meat-eating.

cartilage, Soft, flexible, prebone tissue; "gristle."

castings, Undigested solids containing soil (excreted from the earthworm); enriches the topsoil.

catalyst, Activating agents that bring about changes but are not themselves changed during the processes.

caterpillar, Larval stage in the metamorphosis of butterfly and moth.

cattaloes, Hybrids resulting from cross-breeding of a buffalo and a cow.

cell, The unit of protoplasmic structure and function of all living things.

cellulose, Organic substance found in the cell walls of plant cells.

cerebellum, Part of the vertebrate brain behind the cerebrum; regulates muscular activity and controls body balance.

cerebrum, Largest area of brain; center of conscious mental processes and voluntary muscular activity.

chemotherapy, Branch of medical science; study of the use of drugs and other substances of chemical nature in the treatment of specific diseases.

chlorophyll, Green color pigment in plant cells; necessary for photosynthesis.

choroid coat, Membrane around the eyeball that contains blood vessels for nourishment and pigmentation for eye color.

chrysalis, Pupa stage of butterfly (similar to cocoon of moth); quiescent stage before adulthood.

cilia, Threads of protoplasm surrounding entire cell of paramecium; used for locomotion.

coccus, Round type of bacteria.

coccyx, Bone at end of spinal column consisting of four fused vertebrae; taillike vestigial structure in man.

cochlea, Snail shell-like portion of inner ear which contains nerve endings of auditory nerve.

cocoon, Pupa stage in the metamorphosis of a moth; quiescent stage.

colchicine, Plant extract (drug type) used in experiments on Jimson weeds to induce formation of mutants.

cold-blooded, Having the same body temperature as that of the immediate environment.

compound, A substance resulting from the chemical combination of one or more elements.

conditioned reflex, An acquired response; a response to a stimulus other than the usual or original one.

conjugation, Temporary union of two similar cells during which there is an exchange of nuclear material.

corm, An underground plant stem that stores food for the plant.

cornea, Transparent layer covering the front of the eyeball.

corolla, The sum total of the petals of a flower.

corpuscle, Blood cell (red or white).

cotyledon, Part of a seed that contains stored food for the embryo plant.

cretin, One who was born with a serious deficiency of the thyroid gland.

cutin, Transparent, waxy secretion that protects outer surface of some leaves.

cytoplasm, Protoplasm of the cell minus the nucleus.

D

dendrite, A branching process of a neuron which carries impulses to the cell body.

dental caries, Tooth decay.

dentine, Bony portion of the tooth beneath the enamel.

diaphragm, A layer of muscle tissue that separates the chest from the abdominal cavity in mammals; important in breathing process.

diatom, A species of algae; cell is enclosed in boxlike shell containing silica.

diffusion, Spreading of molecules of gas or liquid from an area of greatest density toward an area of lower density.

dinosaur, Extinct, prehistoric reptile.

disinfectant, A substance used to destroy harmful bacteria; usually too strong to be used on the body.

dissemination, Distribution (as of seeds).

dominant, Referring to hereditary characteristics or traits that show in a hybrid.

DNA, Deoxyribonucleic acid, The material in a cell that makes up the genes and controls the cell.

E

ecology, The study of the relationships of living things to one another and to their environment.

ectoderm, The outer layer of cells; one of the three germ layers of an embryo.

efferent, Referring to nerves that carry impulses away from the brain to glands or muscles; motor nerves.

electrocardiograph, A machine used to make a recording of electrical waves from the heart; used in diagnosis of heart conditions.

element, A substance that cannot be further simplified by chemical means.

embryo, A young plant or animal before germination or birth.

endocrine, Referring to ductless glands that secrete hormones or "body regulators."

endoderm, The inner layer of cells; an embryonic layer.

endoplasmic reticulum, The cell "skeletal system"; provides transport system between cell parts and a surface on which reactions may take place.

endoskeleton, Bony skeleton within the body of vertebrate animals.

enzymes, Chemical substances in plants and animals that induce or hasten chemical changes (as in digestion) without being, in themselves, changed.

Eohippus, Prehistoric horse.

epiglottis, A lid of tissue that covers the opening of the windpipe or trachea during the act of swallowing.

erosion, The wearing away of a substance (soil) by the action of water, wind, etc.

esophagus, The gullet, or food tube, leading from the mouth to the stomach.

estrogen, Female hormone, responsible for secondary sex characteristics.

eugenics, The study of the improvement of the human race, applying the laws of heredity.

euthenics, A science that deals with improving the race by improving the environment.

evolution, Succession of gradual changes that take place in an individual plant or animal or species of plant or animal or form of life, over a long period of time, usually from the simple toward the more complex.

excretion, The process by which waste products are eliminated from a living organism.

exoskeleton, An outer or external skeleton (shell of crayfish).

F

fauna, Animals within a given life zone or natural habitat.

feces, Indigestible, solid waste materials.

fertilized egg, Result of the union of male cell with female cell.

fetus, Unborn young of mammals, after it has assumed the appearance of the parents.

fibrinogen, A substance in the blood plasma that is changed to fibers to form a "clot" under certain conditions.

fins, Organs of locomotion, steering, and balance of fish.

flaccid, A soft or relaxed condition of a cell, usually due to lack of water within the cell.

flora, Sum total of all plants within a given life zone or natural habitat.

fossil, Petrified remains, imprints, tracks, or other markings of prehistoric plants or animals.

fraternal twins, Twins that develop from two separate eggs fertilized at approximately the same time.

frond, The leafy part of a fern.

fruit, A ripened ovary and its contents (seeds) plus any parts of the flower adhering closely to the ovary.

fry, Young fish with yolk sac still attached but almost used up.

function, The use or work of any living organism or part thereof.

fungus, Plant that lacks chlorophyll; a thallophyte (simplest group); dependent on dead or living organic food.

G

gamete, A sexual reproductive cell; a female gamete is an ovum or egg cell and a male gamete is a sperm cell.

gametogenesis, Process during which gametes, or sex cells, are formed.

ganglion, A mass of nerve cells.

gene, A unit in a chromosome that carries hereditary characteristics.

genetics, The science of heredity.

geologist, One who studies the science of geology, the study of the earth's crust, past and present.

gills, Organs of breathing of fish.

gizzard, Muscular organ of earthworms, birds, and some other animals in which food is crushed and partly digested.

glycogen, "Animal starch"; a carbohydrate stored in the liver and present in muscles.

Golgi bodies, Help to produce secretions in animal cells.

grafting, Joining a twig or scion to another plant stem called a stock.

guard cells, Cells on either side of a stoma which regulate the size of the stoma opening.

gullet, Esophagus or food tube extending from the back of the mouth to the stomach.

H

hemoglobin, Red coloring matter in red blood corpuscles of vertebrates; an organic compound that carries oxygen.

hemophilia, Hereditary disease in which the blood will not clot normally even after a slight injury.

herbivorous, Plant-eating animal.

heredity, The passing on of traits or characteristics from parent to offspring through the gametes.

hibernate, Prolonged sleeplike inactivity during a winter season (bears, frogs, etc.).

Homo erectus, Recent ancestors of man, who made tools in the Acheulian Tradition.

Homo habilis, An ape-man ancestor, the first to make tools.

Homo sapiens, Scientific name of present-day man.

hormone, Substance that is secreted by ductless or endocrine glands directly into the bloodstream; controls actions in some part of the body or some body process; "chemical messengers."

humus, Substances in soil formed by decay of plants and animals.

hybrid, A plant or animal carrying unlike genes in the same pair of chromosomes.

hybridization, Crossing individuals in breeding that carry contrasting traits.

hypocotyl, Part of a plant embryo that develops into the root of the plant.

I

identical twins, Twins that result from the fertilization of a single egg cell which splits into two like parts in early cell division.

immunity, Ability to resist a certain disease because of a previous attack or natural ability to resist it or by preventative inoculations, vaccinations, etc.

incisor, The cutting teeth with chisel-like edges; front teeth in jaws of mammals.

ingestion, Process of taking in food.

inorganic, That which is not alive, nor ever was alive, nor came from anything alive.

insectivorous, Insect-eating animal or plant.

insulin, A hormone secreted by the islands of Langerhans of the pancreas; controls oxidation of sugars.

invertebrate, An animal without a backbone.

iris, The colored part of the eye of vertebrate animals.

irradiation, Exposure of food, human skin, etc. to ultraviolet rays.

K

kelp, Brown algae seaweed; used for food in China and Japan; burned to produce iodine.

kidney, Paired organs in vertebrates that extract nitrogenous wastes from the blood for elimination.

L

Lacteal, Small lymph vessel in the center of each villus; absorbs digested fats from the small intestines.

larva, Wormlike, eating stage in the complete metamorphosis of some insects (caterpillar of moth and butterfly, maggot of fly).

larynx, Voice box ("Adam's apple") in the trachea; contains vocal cords.

lateral line, Line of nerve cells on sides of fish; indicates depth of water for the fish; helps keep balance.

legume, Plants that have pod fruits (peas, beans).

lens, A transparent body in the eye that is biconvex; light rays pass through the lens and are bent to focus on the retina.

lichen, A symbiotic relationship between a fungus plant and a green algae; common on moist rock surfaces.

ligament, A band of tissue that connects bone to bone.

linkage, Referring to the grouping together of genes (in a chromosome) that are transmitted together to the offspring.

lungs, Organs of breathing of vertebrate animals from adult amphibians through mammals.

lymph, Part of the blood serum which is outside the blood vessels; bathes the cells.

lysosomes, Contain digestive enzymes in animal cells.

M

maggot, Larval stage in the metamorphosis of the common housefly.

malaria, Disease caused by a parasitic protozoan (malarial plasmodium) which is carried by and transmitted by the anopheles mosquito; plasmodium lives in the bloodstream of man (alternate host).

mammals, Vertebrates that have hair on their bodies, breathe by means of lungs, bear their young alive, and nourish their young with milk from mammary glands.

mammary gland, Milk-secreting glands of mammals.

medulla oblongata, Posterior part of the brain connecting the spinal cord; controls respiration and heartbeat.

meiosis, Reduction division; reduction of original number of chromosomes so that each sex cell (egg or sperm) has half the original number of chromosomes characteristic of the species.

mesentery, Tissue that holds the intestine in place in the abdominal cavity.

mesoderm, The middle layer of cells formed during embryonic development.

metamorphosis, The changes in form an organism undergoes during its development from the egg to the adult stage.

mitochondria, Where food is oxidized and energy produced in a cell for the cell activities.

mitosis, Cell division during which the chromatin material (chromosomes) splits in half making like pairs.

mixture, The physical combination of two or more elements or compounds, each of which retains its original characteristics and can be separated from each other.

molecule, Smallest particle of a compound capable of having the properties of the compound.

morphology, The study of the structure of plants and animals.

mutation, A sudden appearance of a new trait or variation that is heritable.

myxedema, A disease in adults resulting from a deficiency of thyroid hormone.

N

nacre, "Mother-of-pearl"; substance that forms a pearl in the "irritated" bivalve.

neuron, A nerve cell.

nitrate, A compound containing nitrogen, oxygen, and at least one other element.

nuclear membrane, Double membrane around the nucleus of a cell that controls movement in and out of the nucleus.

nucleus, Specialized protoplasm in a cell that controls all cellular activity in general and governs heredity in reproduction in particular (contains chromatin material).

O

oogenesis, Process of sex-cell reproduction in the female.

organ, A group of different tissues working together to perform a specific function.

organic, Pertaining to something living, or which was at one time living, or which was produced by something living.

organism, Any living plant or animal.

osmosis, Diffusion through a semipermeable membrane.

ovary, Organ of the reproductive system of flowering plants and higher animals in which eggs are produced.

oxidation, The chemical combination of oxygen with another element.

P

paleontologist, One who studies fossils.

pancreas, A digestive gland that pours digestive juice into the small intestine; also a ductless gland that controls sugar oxidation.

Paranthropus (Australopithecus robustus), Vegetarian member of the Australopithecines.

parasite, An organism that takes its nourishment from another living organism without giving any benefits to its host.

parathyroid, Ductless or endocrine glands near the thyroid glands in the neck; regulates calcium assimilation in the body.

Pasteurization, Process of treating milk by heating it to 145° F. and rapidly cooling it, thereby killing most of the harmful bacteria therein.

pathogenic, Referring to disease-producing bacteria.

pellagra, Deficiency disease resulting from lack of vitamin niacin (PP of B complex).

pelvis, Broad bones that support the organs of the abdomen.

penicillin, An organic chemical product isolated from a common mold; used in treating diseases caused by certain types of bacteria; now synthesized.

pericardium, A membrane surrounding and protecting the heart.

peristalsis, Wavelike muscular motion of the food tube of higher vertebrate animals which forces food along alimentary tube.

phagocyte, White corpuscles of the blood which act as scavengers.

photosynthesis, Manufacture of carbohydrates by the green plant in the sunshine.

pineal, An endocrine or ductless gland located in the brain; active only in early childhood, regulating growth.

pistil, The female reproductive organ in the flowering plant.

pituitary, Ductless or endocrine gland; called the "master gland" because it controls all other endocrine glands.

plankton, Minute forms of plant and animal life floating near the surface in the ocean.

plasma, The liquid portion of the blood of vertebrates.

platelets, Small cells in blood that aid in clotting.

Pleistocene, Period of earth from 1,750,000 years ago to 50,000 years ago.

pleurococcus, Single-celled (algae) green plant that grows on the shady side of tree trunks; the "Indian's Friend."

plumule, Part of the plant embryo that develops into the shoot with its leaves.

pollen, Grains formed in the anther of a flower or the male cone of an evergreen; contains sperm, or male sex cells.

pollination, Transfer of pollen from the anther of a flower to the stigma.

precocial, Young born relatively independent of their parents.

primate, Order of mammals that includes monkeys, apes, etc., and man.

Proconsul (Dryopithecus africanus), Prehistoric ape.

protein, A food nutrient necessary for the building of protoplasm; contains nitrogen in addition to oxygen, hydrogen, and carbon.

protoplasm, The living substance of all plants and animals.

pseudopod, Projection of protoplasm; aids in locomotion of ameba.

ptomaine, A type of food poisoning produced by bacteria of decay.

pulp, Innermost section of a human tooth; contains blood vessels and nerves.

pulse, Rhythmic wave of motion indicating beat of the heart felt in an artery.

pupa, Quiescent stage in the complete metamorphosis of an insect; stage during which the adult develops.

pupil, Referring to the round opening in the iris of the eye through which light rays enter the eye.

Q

quinine, Drug used in the treatment of malaria.

R

Ramapithecus, Man-ape predecessor of man.

recessive, Referring to a hidden trait or characteristic in a hybrid contrasting pair.

rectum, Terminal end of large intestine; functions in the elimination of solid wastes from the body.

reduction division, See **Meiosis.**

reflex, Simple, involuntary action in response to a stimulus; no thought involved.

regeneration, The act of growing a new body part for one that has been injured or lost.

reproduction, The process by which new individuals of the same kind are produced by a plant or animal; producing offspring.

respiration, A life function in which oxygen is taken into the cells and the waste gas, carbon dioxide, is given off.

retina, Innermost layer of tissue in the eyeball; contains nerve endings (from optic nerve) that receive light stimulus.

rhizome, Underground plant stem that stores food for the plant.

ribosome, Small body in a cell, the sites of protein synthesis.

rickets, Deficiency disease resulting from an insufficiency of vitamin D in the diet or inadequate assimilation of it.

RNA, ribonucleic acid, Messenger RNA carries genetic code from nucleus to cytoplasm; transfer RNA moves about the cytoplasm picking up amino acids.

roe, Fish eggs.

root hairs, Elongated epidermal cells of a root; for absorption of soil water.

S

saliva, Digestive juice secreted by glands in the mouth.

saprophyte, Plant or animal that lives on dead organic matter (some fungi).

sclerotic coat, Tough, outer protective layer of the eye.

scurvy, Deficiency disease caused by lack of vitamin C in the diet.

scutes, Scales on the under or belly surface of snakes; aid in locomotion.

secretion, A chemical substance produced by a living cell (enzyme or hormone).

sedimentary, Referring to a type of rock that is formed by materials deposited from suspension in water.

semicircular canal, Part of the inner ear; functions as organ of balance.

Sequoia, Oldest living tree on earth; a giant redwood tree in the evergreen group.

serum, Blood plasma from which the fibrinogen has been removed.

sex-linked, Refers to a hereditary trait whose gene is in the X chromosome.

sexual, Referring to reproduction in which the new individual is a result of the union of an egg cell (female) and a sperm cell (male).

soluble, That which can be dissolved in a fluid.

spawn, To deposit eggs or roe (as fishes).

specialization, Referring to the adaptation of cells or groups of cells to perform a particular function.

sperm, The male sex cell or gamete.

spermatogenesis, Process of sex-cell production in males.

sphygmomanometer, Instrument used to measure blood pressure.

spinal cord, The main nerve cord of all vertebrates.

spiracles, Openings in the abdomen of insects through which they breathe.

spirillum, A spiral-shaped bacterium.

spirogyra, A filamentous green alga; commonly known as "pond scum."

spleen, Gland in vertebrates (except fish) that destroys used-up red blood cells; a "graveyard" of blood cells.

spore, Nonsexual reproductive body, common to fungi, bacteria, mosses, and other plants and some protozoa.

stamen, Male reproductive organ in flowering plants.

stethoscope, Instrument used to listen to heart sounds and lung sounds.

stigma, Top of a pistil of a flower, part that receives pollen.

stoma, Opening on lower surface of a green leaf through which there is an exchange of gases and water vapor.

streptomycin, An antibiotic used in the treatment and control of tuberculosis and other pulmonary diseases, infections of the urinary tract and other diseases.

symbiosis, A state in which two dissimilar organisms live together to mutual advantage (lichen).

synapse, The space over which a nerve impulse passes from the dendrites of one neuron to the dendrites of another.

system, A group of organs working together to perform a particular function (digestive system).

T

tadpole, The fishlike stage in the metamorphosis of a frog and a toad.

taxonomist, One who specializes in classification of plants and animals.

tendon, Tissue that attaches a muscle to a bone.

tentacles, Flexible armlike projections of jellyfish and related animals; used in food-getting and locomotion.

testes, The primary male sex organs.

testosterone, Male hormone responsible for secondary sex characteristics.

thorax, The middle division of an animal's body; between the head and abdomen.

thymus, An endocrine or ductless gland; controls growth.

thyroid, An endocrine or ductless gland in the neck, just below the larynx; controls rate of metabolism in the body.

tissue, A group of similar cells that performs the same function.

toxins, Poisons released by disease-producing bacteria.

trachea, Windpipe; tube that delivers air from throat to lungs in vertebrates; air passages in insects.

transpiration, Loss of water by evaporation through the stomates of the leaves of plants.

trichocysts, Dartlike substances ejected by paramecium as a means of defense.

tropism, Response of plants and simple animals to external stimuli.

U

urea, Nitrogenous waste collected and excreted by the kidneys.

univalve, Mollusk with a single shell (snail).

V

vaccine, Substance used in preventive inoculation; (virus of cowpox used in inoculation against smallpox).

vacuoles, Small spaces in cytoplasm of a cell, containing liquid or solid food or waste matter.

vein, Blood vessel in which blood returns to the heart from all over the body; liquid-conducting vessels in leaves.

venom, Poison secreted by glands of poisonous snakes, lizards, etc.

ventricle, Lower, muscular chamber of a vertebrate heart; pumps blood through arteries to the rest of the body.

vertebrae, Bones of the backbone.

vertebrates, Group of animals that has internal backbones.

vestigial, Referring to a remnant of a once useful organ or a structure formerly more complete in function.

villus, A small (microscopic) projection in the lining of the small intestine; organ of absorption of digested food.

virus, Submicroscopic substance that has characteristics both organic and inorganic; causative agent of some diseases.

W

warm-blooded, Referring to an animal that maintains a constant body temperature.

Y

yolk sac, Stored food material for embryo vertebrate.

Z

zygote, The result of the fusion of two dissimilar gametes.

Glossary of Physics Terms

Absolute Magnitude The magnitude that would be assigned to a star if it were placed at a distance of 10 parsecs from the observer. Stars closer to us than that distance would appear fainter. Stars farther from the solar system would appear brighter.

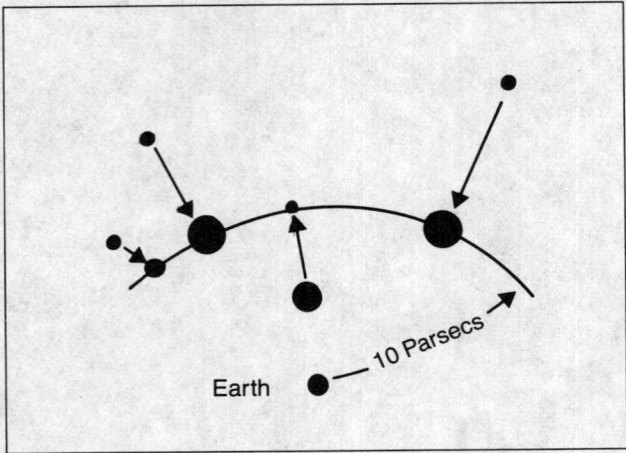

Earth — 10 Parsecs

Achromatic Lens A lens that transmits white light without dispersing it into a color spectrum. It usually consists of two component parts, cemented together to form one unit.

Albedo Percentage of light reflected by a body, such as a planet, of total amount of light falling on it.

Altitude Angular distance between the horizon and a given object, measured along a vertical circle.

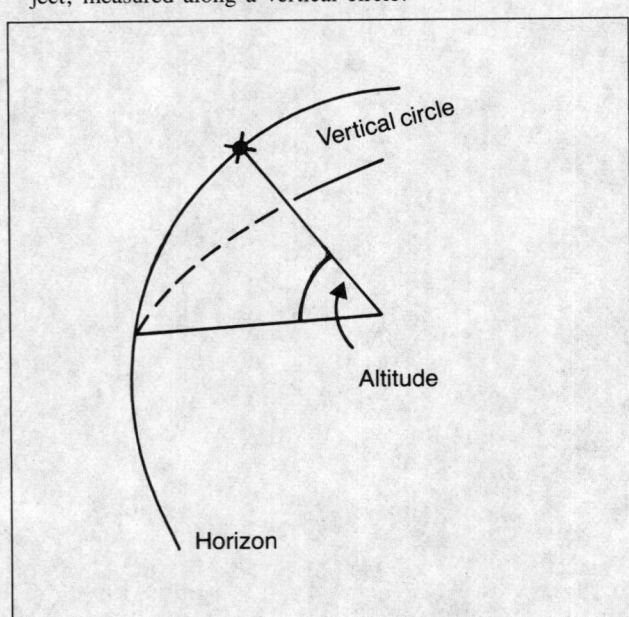

Vertical circle

Altitude

Horizon

Annular Eclipse An eclipse of the central portion of the solar disk; an outer ring shows.

Aphelion The point on planet's orbit farthest from the sun.

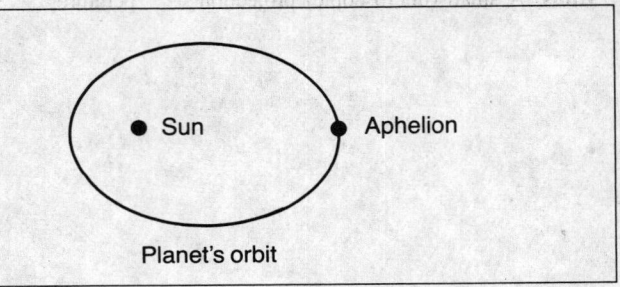

Sun • • Aphelion

Planet's orbit

Apogee Point on the moon's orbit farthest from the earth.

Apollo The name assigned to the U.S. project, whose mission was to land men on the moon. Also the name of the vehicles used. Apollo 11 landed Neil Armstrong and Edwin Aldrin on the moon on July 20, 1969.

Artificial Satellite A man-made object placed into an orbit about the earth or about another celestial body such as the sun or the moon.

Astronomical Unit The average distance between the earth and the sun 93 million miles or, more exactly, 92,955,700.

Aurora A diffused glow of light in the form of curtains, or bands, seen at high latitudes (70°N or 70°S). The glow is due to the interaction between the solar wind and particles in the earth's atmosphere. The aurora in the northern hemisphere is known as the Aurora Borealis, or northern lights; in the southern hemisphere it is known as the Aurora Australis, or southern lights.

Binary Star Two close stars held together by a gravitational force and revolving like a dumbbell about a common center of gravity. The center is closer to the more massive star.

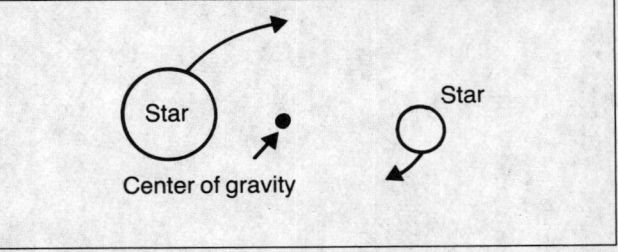

Star   Star

Center of gravity

Cassini's Division The empty space that separates the outer rings of Saturn from the bright inner rings.

Celestial Sphere An imaginary sphere of infinite radius surrounding the earth and serving as a screen against which all celestial objects are seen.

Cepheid A star the brightness of which varies periodically because of pulsations.

Chromatic Aberration (also called **Color Defect**) Blurring of image due to the separation of colors by a lens. A point of white light in the object appears as a complete spectrum of colored points in the image.

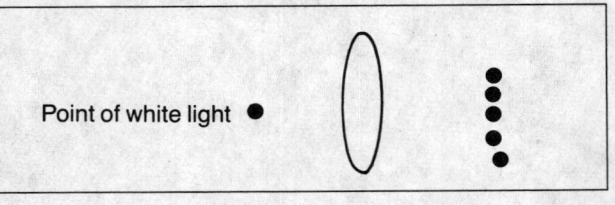

Point of white light •

Collimator (also called **Collimating Lens**) A lens whose function it is to make rays of light parallel.

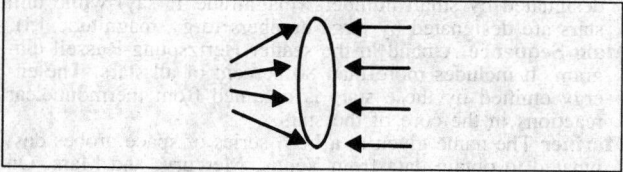

Colure, equinoctial (also called **Prime Hour Circle**) The hour circle that goes through the first point of Aries. The hour angles (same as longitude on earth) are measured from the equinoctial colure.

Conjunction Apparent line-up of sun, earth, and a planet. Inferior conjunction is when the planet is between the earth and the sun.

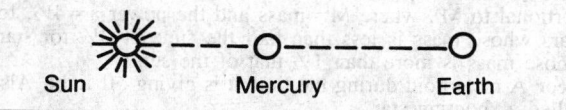

Superior conjunction is when the planet is on the opposite side of the sun.

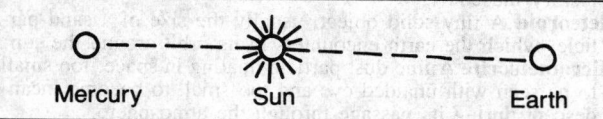

Constellation A group of stars apparently close together in the sky. Modern astronomy recognizes 88 such groups (e.g., Cassiopeia, Leo, etc.). Actually, the individual stars of a constellation may be great distances apart and moving in different directions one from the other.

Copernican System The system that assumes that the sun is at the center, and the earth and the other planets move around it.

Culmination The position of a celestial body when it is on the meridian. A star is said to be at its "upper culmination" when it has reached its highest point for the day.

Declination Angular distance of an object from the celestial equator, measured in degrees, minutes, and seconds. Analogous to latitude in geography.

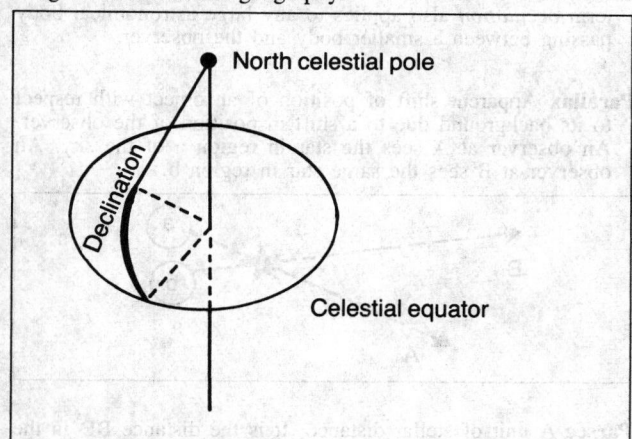

Diffraction of Light A phenomenon exhibited by light on passing through a narrow slit or a small aperture. The light is modified to form alternate dark and bright fringes.

Discrete Source A small area in the sky—almost a point—from which very intense electromagnetic waves of radio frequency reach the earth. These points were formerly called radio stars.

Doppler Effect Change in frequency of light due to relative motion between observer and source of light.

Eccentricity Eccentricity indicates the degree of flatness of an ellipse, or its departure from a circle. It is denoted by e; its value is obtained from the formula $e = \dfrac{2c}{2a}$, when 2c is the distance between the foci, and 2a is the length of the major axis. When e is small (e.g., .05), the ellipse approaches a circle in shape; when it is large (e.g., .8), the ellipse is elongated.

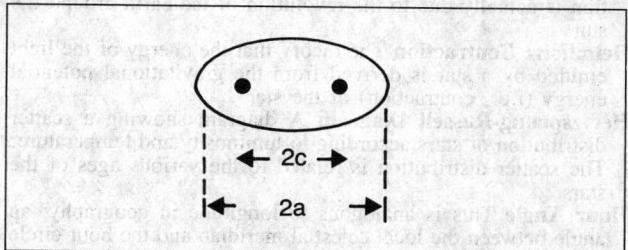

Eclipse
A. *Solar*. The sun's light is cut off by the moon's interposition between the sun and the earth.
B. *Lunar*. The moon darkens because the earth intercepts the sunlight on its way to the moon.

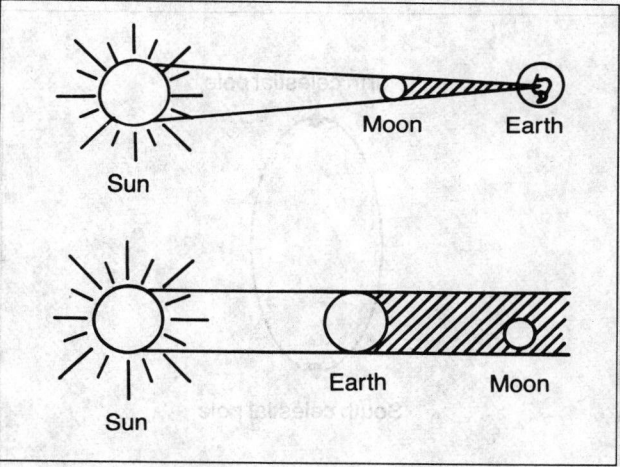

Ecliptic Two equivalent definitions are possible.
A. The great circle on the celestial sphere formed by the intersection of that sphere with the plane of the earth's orbit.
B. The path described on the celestial sphere by the sun during its apparent annual motion around the earth.

Elongation Angular distance from the sun, measured in degrees, minutes, and seconds of angle.

Ephemeris A book of tables showing computed daily positions of heavenly objects.

Equinox One of the points of intersection between the ecliptic and the celestial equator. When the sun is at one of these two points, the length of day and night are equal everywhere on the earth. The sun is at these points every year on or about March 21 (vernal) and September 23 (autumnal).

Evening Star This is not a star, but a planet, especially Mercury or Venus when seen in the western sky just after sunset.

Extragalactic Beyond our galaxy.

Faculae Areas on the surface of the sun that appear brighter by comparison to surrounding regions.

Flyby A research mission in which the satellite collects data while passing close to the object of research.

Galaxy A large community of stars in space, such as the Milky Way (our galaxy), to which the sun belongs. Galaxies contain billions of stars. Many are shaped in the form of a spiral.

Gemini The name given to the U.S. program, as well as to the vehicles, designed to prepare man for landing on the moon. Gemini 3 to Gemini 12 (1965–66) carried crews of two astronauts each. The program included space walks, rendezvous with other space craft, as well as docking techniques.

Granules The smallest visible units on the sun's surface. Granules or granulations have diameters hundreds of miles long. They change in size and in structure continuously.

Heliocentric Parallax The apparent motion of nearby stars seen against the background of far away stars. The apparent motion is actually due to the revolution of the earth around the sun.

Helmholtz Contraction The theory that the energy of the light emitted by a star is derived from the gravitational potential energy (i.e., contraction) of the star.

Hertzsprung-Russell Diagram A diagram showing a scatter distribution of stars according to luminosity and temperature. The scatter distribution is related to the various ages of the stars.

Hour Angle This is analogous to longitude in geography: an angle between the local celestial meridian and the hour circle of a given object in the sky, measured westward from the meridian. It may be given in units of time (hours, minutes and seconds); 1 hour = 15 degrees of angle. Hour angles are easily visualized as either arcs along the celestial equator, or angles at the celestial poles.

Hour Circle This is similar to meridian in geography: a great circle passing through the two celestial poles.

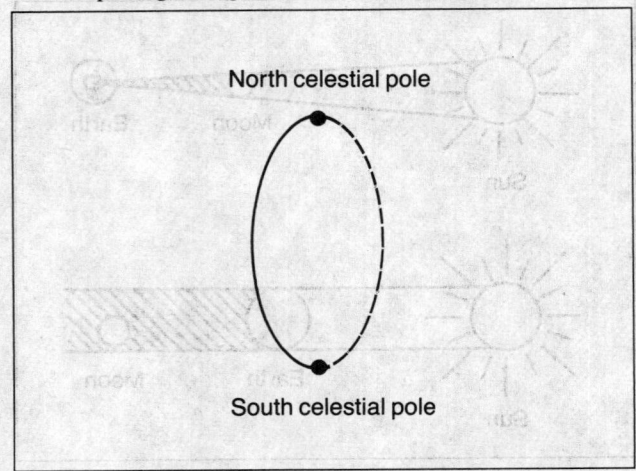

Hubble's Constant The ratio of the velocity of recession to the distance of a galaxy. This ratio is 100 km/sec for every 1 million parsecs.

Infrared Radiation Invisible radiation of wavelength slightly longer than red light.

Ionosphere Several layers of ionized air high in the atmosphere. The ionosphere plays an important part in reflecting radio waves.

Libration Apparent "rocking" or "nodding" of moon or the planet Mercury. Due to this oscillation, some of the usually hidden sides are exhibited to the terrestrial observer.

Light Year The distance that light travels in a year.

Luminosity The ratio of the total light emitted by a celestial object to the total light emitted by the sun. Also, the total energy emitted by a star, per second.

Lunar Module The term for the vehicles that carried two men, in the Apollo project, from the command modules to the surface of the moon and back.

Magellanic Clouds These are not clouds; they are galaxies. Two relatively nearby galaxies visible from the southern hemisphere, of irregular shape, named after Magellan, the Portuguese explorer who first described them.

Magnitude (also called **Apparent Magnitude**) A number indicating the apparent brightness of a star. Bright stars are designated by small numbers (magnitude 1, say) while dim stars are designated by large numbers (e.g., magnitude 15).

Main Sequence A band in the scatter Hertzspung-Russell diagram. It includes more than 80 percent of all stars. The energy emitted by these stars is obtained from thermonuclear reactions in the core of the stars.

Mariner The name given to a U.S. series of space probes designated to obtain data from Venus, Mercury, and Mars. On December 14, 1962, Mariner 2 passed within 22,000 miles of Venus. Mariner 9 (launched on May 30, 1971) came within a distance of 900 miles of Mars. It was the first spacecraft to go into orbit around a planet other than earth. Mariner 10 (launched November 3, 1973) came within 3,600 miles of Venus and 450 miles of Mercury. This was the first probe of Mercury.

Mass-Luminosity Relationship This relationship, which applies to main sequence stars, states that luminosity is proportional to M^a, where M = mass and the power a = 4½, for stars whose mass is less than half the sun; a = 3½ for stars whose mass is more than 1½ that of the sun.

Meteor A meteoroid during the time it is giving off light. Also called a shooting star.

Meteorite A meteoroid that survived, because of its size, collision with the earth's atmosphere and reached the earth's surface. Meteorites can be seen on exhibit in many natural history museums.

Meteoroid A tiny solid object, usually the size of a sand particle, which the earth encounters in its orbit around the sun.

Micrometeorite A fine dust particle floating in space, too small to be seen with unaided eye and too small to become incandescent during its passage through the atmosphere.

Milky Way A luminous band across the sky, of which our galaxy is part. The light is due to the fact that the vast majority of stars in our (disk-shaped) galaxy are located along this narrow band on the celestial sphere.

Morning Star This is not a star, but a planet, e.g., Mercury, when seen in the eastern sky just before sunrise.

Neap Tide The lowest tide of the month.

Nebula A vast cloud of gas or gas and dust in space.

Node A point of intersection of one orbit (say, the moon's) with the plane of another orbit (say, the earth's).

Nova A star that suddenly increases in brightness and later returns to its original value of brightness.

Occultation The eclipse of a star or a planet by the moon. The term *occulation* also applies to any large astronomical body passing between a smaller body and the observer.

Parallax Apparent shift of position of an object with respect to its background due to a shift in position of the observer. An observer at A sees the star in region a of the sky. An observer at B sees the same star in region b.

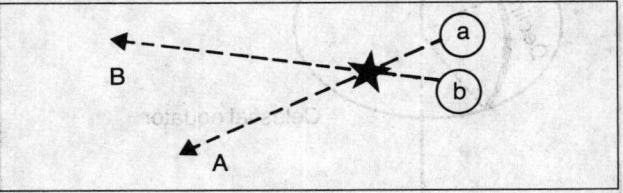

Parsec A unit of stellar distance. It is the distance BD in the triangle ABD.

One parsec is equal to 19.2 million million miles.

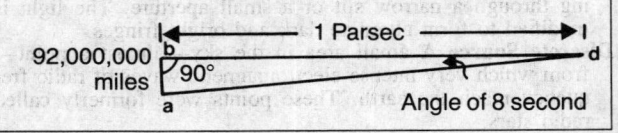

Penumbra The outer and lighter part of a shadow cast by a planet or satellite, as in regions A and B.

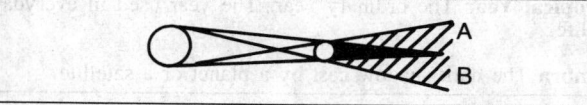

Perigee The point in orbit of, say, the moon nearest the earth (point A).

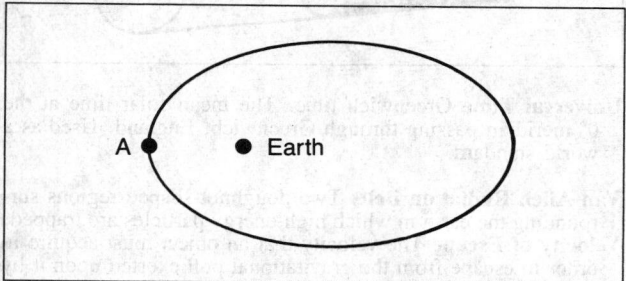

Perihelion The point in orbit of a planet or a comet nearest the sun (point A).

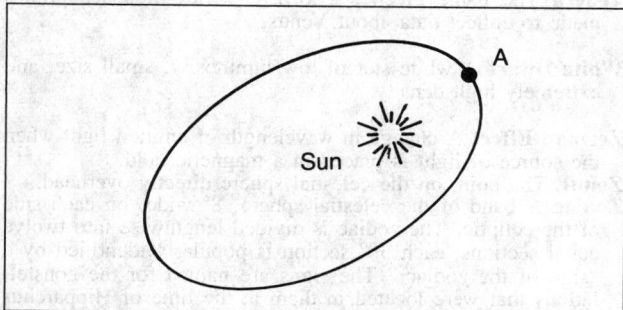

Photosphere The visible surface of the sun or star. Below it is the interior of the sun; above it, the atmosphere.

Pioneer The name given to the first series of U.S. unmanned space-probe vehicles. They were instrumental in developing launching and guiding techniques for the Mariner, Lunar Orbiter, Ranger, and Surveyor series.

Planet One of the nine bodies revolving about the sun in almost circular orbits. Planets are made visible to us by reflected sunlight. It is reasonable to assume that many stars have planets revolving about them.

Planetary Nebula A nebula resembling a planet in shape.

Planetoid (also called **Asteroid**) A small irregularly shaped solid body revolving about the sun. Also considered to be a minor planet.

Plasma An ionized gas.

Poles, Celestial Points of intersection of extensions of earth's axis and the celestial sphere.

Precession The slow change in direction of the earth's axis due to the gravitational pull of the moon on the bulge at the earth's equator. The slow change in the axis causes the westward motion of the equinoxes among the constellations.

Proper Motion of Star The angular velocity (in seconds of angle per year) of a star in a direction perpendicular to the line of sight of a terrestrial observer.

Protostar The portion of a nebula that is about to become a star.

Pulsar A neutron star emitting pulsed radio signals. The first pulsar was discovered in 1967. Its pulse lasts 1/3 of a second and repeats with great regularity every 1 1/3 second.

Pulsating Stars Stars that periodically vary in brightness because of periodic changes in volume.

Quadrature An elongation of 90° east or west of the sun.

Quasar The popular name for quasi-stellar object. These are extremely luminous objects (the most luminous known) at enormous distances (the most distant object known), which generate incredible amounts of energy. The true nature of quasars is still under study.

Radial Velocity of Star The velocity (in miles or kilometers per second) in line of sight of a terrestrial observer.

Radiant Point of Meteors A point in the sky from which meteors seem to come.

Radio Astronomy The branch of astronomy that deals with the radio waves emitted by various celestial bodies, as well as the theory of their emission.

Radio Star See **Discrete Source**.

Radio Telescope An instrument used for examination of celestial objects by means of the radio waves emitted by these objects.

Radio Window The transparency of the atmosphere to radio waves that range between .25 cm and 30 m in length.

Ranger The name given to a series of nine U.S. lunar probe vehicles, designed to transmit photographs before crashlanding on the moon. More than 17,000 photographs were obtained from the Rangers, the closest one taken .2 seconds before impact.

Red Giant A member of the giant sequence in the Hertzsprung-Russell diagram. They have radii fifteen to thirty times larger than the radius of sun and luminosities a hundred times that of the sun.

Red Shift The shift of all spectral lines toward longer wavelengths observed in all galaxies. Galactic red shift is due to the expansion of the universe. Gravitational red shift is due to the high value of the mass of the emitter.

Refraction A change in direction of light on entering a different medium (such as glass).

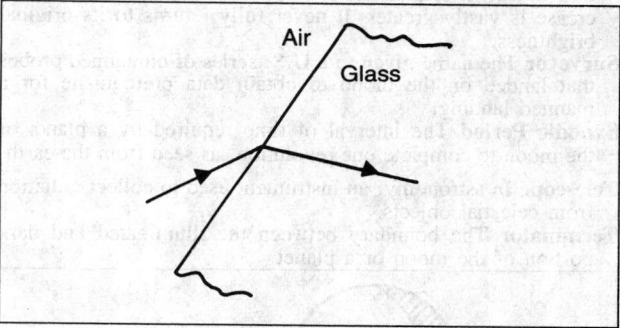

Resolving Power of Telescope The power to separate two close points into two distinct units.

Retrograde Motion Apparent backward (westward) motion of a planet, through a starfield.

Reversing Layer The lowest of the three solar atmospheric layers; it is responsible for most of the dark lines in the solar spectrum.

Right Ascension The angular distance from the prime meridian to a celestial body measured eastward along the celestial equator from 0° to 360°, or from 0 to 24 hours. Analogous to longitude in geography.

Rocket A tube designed to move through space that derives its thrust by ejecting hot, expanding gases—called a jet—that have been generated in its motor. The rocket contains within itself all the material needed for the production of the jet.

Saros The interval (about 18 1/3 years) between two successive lunar or solar eclipses of the same series.

Satellite A celestial body revolving about one of the planets; e.g., the moon. Also any small body that revolves about a larger body, man-made or otherwise.

Sedimentary Rocks Rocks formed by precipitation from water or any other solution.

Service Module That part of the vehicle in the Apollo and other programs that contains the power, supplies, and fuel.

Sidereal Period The interval of time required by a planet to make one revolution (as seen from one of the fixed stars) about the sun.

Solar Constant The quantity of radiant solar heat, 1.94 calories per minute, received per square centimeter of the earth's surface.

Solar Wind The material, mainly protons and electrons, streaming out from the sun into space. The sun loses normally millions of tons per second of its mass because of this wind.

Solstice The point of maximum declination of the earth on the ecliptic. The solstices are halfway between the equinoctial points. In the northern hemisphere, the summer solstice occurs when the sun is farthest north from the equator; the winter solstice, when the sun is farthest south.

Space Probe An unmanned vehicle that is sent into space to obtain scientific data.

Spectrograph An instrument that (A) collimates (makes parallel rays of light), then (B) disperses the light (by means of a prism or grating) into a spectrum, and, finally, (C) produces a photograph of the spectrum.

Spectroheliograph An instrument that photographs the sun in monochromatic (single color) light.

Spectroscopic Binary A system of two stars that can be detected only with the aid of a spectroscope.

Spherical Aberration A shape defect of a lens. Light passing a spherical lens near its edge is converged more than light passing the center of the same lens, which causes the image to blur.

Spiral Nebula A galaxy of stars (*not* a nebula) in the form of a spiral.

Star A large globe of intensely hot gas, shining by its own light (e.g., the sun).

Sunspots Dark (by contrast with the surroundings) patches that appear from time to time on the photosphere of the sun.

Supernova A star that quite suddenly increases, perhaps a million times, in brightness. It is similar to a nova, but its increase is vastly greater. It never fully returns to its original brightness.

Surveyor The name given to a U.S. series of unmanned probes that landed on the moon to obtain data prerequisite for a manned landing.

Synodic Period The interval of time required by a planet or the moon to complete one revolution, as seen from the earth.

Telescope In astronomy, an instrument used to collect radiation from celestial objects.

Terminator The boundary between the illuminated and dark portion of the moon or a planet.

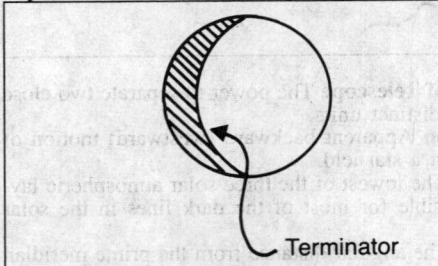

Terminator

Transit The motion of a small body (e.g., Mercury) across the face of a larger body (e.g., the sun).

Tropical Year The ordinary year. The year used in everyday life.

Umbra The dark shadow cast by a planet or a satellite.

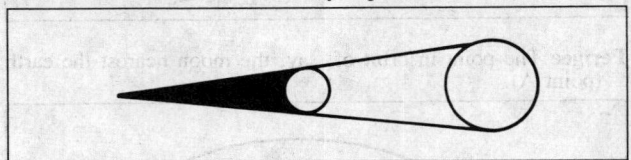

Universal Time Greenwich time. The mean solar time at the 0° meridian passing through Greenwich, England. Used as a world standard.

Van Allen Radiation Belts Two doughnut-shaped regions surrounding the earth in which high-energy particles are trapped.

Velocity of Escape The velocity that an object must acquire in order to escape from the gravitational pull exerted upon it by another body. The velocity of escape at the earth's surface is 7 miles per second. Any terrestrial body that can reach this velocity will permanently leave the earth.

Venera The name given a U.S.S.R. series of space probes made to collect data about Venus.

White Dwarf A white star of low luminosity, small size, and extremely high density.

Zeeman Effect A change in wavelength of emitted light when the source of light is placed in a magnetic field.

Zenith The point on the celestial sphere directly overhead.

Zodiac A band of the celestial sphere, 8° wide, on each side of the ecliptic. The zodiac is divided lengthwise into twelve equal sections; each 30° section is popularly identified by a "sign of the zodiac." The signs are named for the constellations that were located in them at the time of Hipparchus more than 2,000 years ago. The sun, moon, and planets appear to "travel" within this belt. The sun passes through three signs each season of the year, e.g., during spring the sun passes through Aries, Taurus, and Gemini.

African American History

The Slave Trade

1526 Spanish explorers bring the first Africans to the new territory, twenty years after Spain approves the shipment of slaves to the New World. It is believed that the first group of Africans brought over managed to escape and settle inland with Native Americans.

1619 Twenty Africans arrive in Jamestown, Virginia, on a Dutch ship. They are brought in as indentured servants, with four to seven year contracts to fulfill. At the end of the term, they are released and are entitled to own property as members of the free laboring class.

1640 Laws begin to shift in the colonies from limited indentured servitude for imported servants to life indentured slaves. The first colony, Massachusetts, formally legalizes slavery in 1641. Laws are also passed in several states, including Virginia, that punish people who harbor any escaped servant or slave.

1650 Virginia holds 300 slaves.

1652 Rhode Island passes a statute prohibiting slavery. It is unenforced and openly violated by residents.

1661 The House of Burgesses, Virginia's assembly, votes in legislation that children born in the colony will have their status determined by whether their mother is bound or free. The law formally recognizes the institution of slavery in Virginia.

1663 Maryland votes in a slave law that declares all blacks currently in or to be brought into Maryland as slaves for life.

1660– Slave codes are increasingly restrictive in the South.
1700 Regulations forbid slaves from owning property, travelling without written permission from their owners, and carrying weapons. Punishments for violation of crimes are swift and severe, including brandings, whippings, and hangings. The move toward such restriction and retribution is believed to be caused by fear of slave rebellions and uprisings.

Colonial and Revolutionary Times

1700 Ten percent of the population of the colonies, 27,000 blacks, are slaves. Ninety percent of the slaves live in the South, where tobacco, rice, and indigo are the major crops.

Judge Samuel Sewall publishes the first pamphlet, or tract, in the colonies condemning slavery. He argues in the three page document that no man has the right to own another.

1704 Elias Neau opens a religious education school for slaves at Trinity Church in New York City.

1705 Statutes are established in colonies that further limit the rights of blacks. Massachusetts forbids marriage between blacks and whites. Virginia bars blacks and Native Americans from military and civil office.

1712 In New York City there is a large rebellion by slaves. Nine whites are killed during the uprising, and the militia is called in to end the rioting. Twelve slaves are executed for charges stemming from the riots; another six commit suicide before their hanging. The religious school opened by Neau in 1704 is closed because the education of blacks is seen as dangerous.

1717 Cotton Mather opens a school for Native Americans and African Americans in Boston.

1721 Boston experiences an epidemic outbreak of smallpox. Oneissimus, a slave of Cotton Mather, explains how Africans immunize against the disease by inoculation. Mather passes the information on to Dr. Zabdiel Boylston, who inoculates Mather's son Thomas and two slaves. With their survival, Boylston inoculates 240 more, of which only six die of smallpox. The inoculation practice, despite its success, is met with widespread hostility in Boston.

1733 Spain declares that escaped slaves from the colonies will be free upon reaching Spanish territory, including Florida.

1735 John van Zandt is found innocent of murder charges that he whipped his slave to death. The ruling states that the death was caused by God's visitation.

1739 South Carolina experiences a series of slave rebellions. Revolt in Charleston leaves 21 whites and 44 blacks dead. The slave Cato leads a revolt in Stono River where 30 whites and an unknown number of blacks are killed. Berkeley county experiences the third revolt. All the rebellions are blamed on slaves attempting to get to Florida for their freedom.

1741 Twenty-nine blacks and four whites are executed for arson outbreaks in New York City. No direct proof is given for the crimes, and a prosecutor on the case later states that no conspiracy evidence linked those found guilty. Tense race relations are blamed for the atmosphere that led to the verdict that condemned the men.

1750 Crispus Attucks escapes slavery in Massachusetts.

1753 Benjamin Franklin publishes a tract that states that slavery is a bad economic system.

1761 Benjamin Banneker constructs a wooden clock that keeps precise time. The self-taught astronomer and mathematician produces a chiming clock that keeps accurate time for longer than twenty years.

1769 Thomas Jefferson proposes a law before the Virginia assembly that would emancipate slaves. It is rejected.

1770 Crispus Attucks is shot and killed, along with four white colonialists, in the Boston Massacre.

A school for blacks is established in Philadelphia by Anthony Benezet, a Quaker.

Phyllis Wheatley, an eighteen-year-old slave in Boston, has her poetry printed by The University of Cambridge in New England. Her work is lauded internationally and she tours London in 1773.

1773   Caesar Hendrick is freed by an all-white jury in Massachusetts. Suing his owner for wrongful enslavery, he is awarded freedom, financial reparations and court costs on the grounds that he was enslaved against his will.

1775   Peter Salem and Salem Poor fight at the Battle of Bunker Hill. They are later commended for their bravery and service to the army.

George Washington declares that no blacks can serve in the Continental Army. The British offer freedom to any black that serves with the Loyalist troops. Washington, after the British decision, reverses his order and allows blacks to remain in the army.

1776   With the revolution against England in full force, slaves are offered freedom if they enlist in some army companies. Maryland, in 1780, is the only southern state to enlist slaves, arming them for battle. Gradually, states award equal pay to black and white soldiers, with Connecticut the first to do so in 1777. Integration is still controversial, and two black companies are established.

The Declaration of Independence is ratified by all thirteen colonies, after Jefferson's passage condemning slavery is removed.

Ten thousand African Americans fight with colonial forces. Many are honored for valor and heroism, including Oliver Cromwell, William Flora, James Robinson, and Deborah Sampson (who fought disguised as a man).

1777   Vermont frees blacks and abolishes slavery. It is the first state to do so.

1780   Pennsylvania abolishes slavery, with a gradual system of emancipation.

1783   Massachusetts ends slavery and awards voting privileges to African Americans.

The Revolutionary War is over. The black regiments are disbanded.

James Derham purchases his freedom from his owner, a doctor with whom he apprenticed, and starts his own medical practice in New Orleans.

The Cotton Era, and Western Expansion

1784   Connecticut and Rhode Island ban slavery in their state boundaries.

1785   New York declares slavery illegal.

Lemuel Haynes becomes the first black minister to a white congregation, in Connecticut. Haynes is a veteran of the Revolutionary War, having served with distinction at Lexington.

1786   New Jersey bans slavery.

1787   The Northwest Territory is declared by Congress to be free—slavery is forbidden.

The Constitution of the United States is adopted by Congress. It sets five slaves as the equivalent of three freemen in census and electoral calculations. Importation of slaves from abroad is forbidden by law after 1808.

1789   Benjamin Banneker accurately predicts a solar eclipse.

1790   Banneker is appointed by George Washington to the Commission of the District of Columbia. He surveys the territory that becomes Washington, D.C.

Constitutional law declares that only free whites can be considered citizens of the new United States. Blacks cannot be issued passports for international travel.

Jean Baptiste Pointe du Sable, a black explorer, establishes a settlement at the southern end of Lake Michigan. The settlement becomes the city of Chicago.

1791   Benjamin Banneker publishes his own annual almanac. It remains in publication for more than a decade.

Kentucky is admitted to the union as a slave state.

Slaves on the island of Santa Domingua rise up against the French landowners and overthrow the island government. Toussaint L'Ouverture establishes a new government that rules until an attack by Napoleon I in 1799. It is estimated that there are more than 400,000 freed slaves on the island that is renamed Haiti. Slave trade between the West Indies and the United States is halted, out of fear of importing rebellion into the U.S.

The Expansion of Slavery

1793   Eli Whitney invents the cotton gin. This speeds the cleaning of cotton, and creates a boon in the profitability of cotton. The increase in cotton production makes slave labor extremely cost-effective in the southern states and establishes a strong desire on the part of plantation owners to maintain the right to own slaves.

Laws are passed in the new states that restrict the rights of African Americans. Congress declares in the Fugitive Slave Act that no one may harbor runaway slaves or prevent the capture and arrest of a runaway slave. Virginia does not allow free African Americans into the state.

1796   Tennessee enters the Union as a slave state, but gives free blacks the right to vote.

1798   The Secretary of Navy bans African Americans from serving in the navy.

Benjamin Franklin publishes an address to the public and the Congress that urges abolition of slavery. He is president of The Pennsylvania Society for Promoting the Abolition of Slavery and the Relief of Free Negroes unlawfully held in Bondage.

1799   In his will, George Washington frees his slaves, declaring that his heirs are to provide for those who are too old to take care of themselves and are to educate those young enough to work.

1800   Following a series of smaller rebellions in slave states, the biggest rebellion in the U.S. to date takes place near Richmond, Virginia. More than 1,000 slaves attempt to attack Richmond, but heavy storms destroy the uprising. Thirty-five slaves are hanged for sedition, including the leader Gabriel Prosser.

1801   Congress is petitioned by free African Americans to end slavery in the U.S. Congress votes down the petition.

1803   Louisiana and South Carolina reopen slave trade with the West Indies and Spanish territories, which had been halted following the uprising in Haiti.

Black rioting continues in the United States. African Americans riot for many days in New York following

the arrest of several blacks for arson charges. Numerous houses in New York City are burned. Twenty African Americans are convicted on related arson charges.

1804   New Jersey declares slavery abolished.

1807   In England, the Parliament abolishes the slave trade.

1808   The Act to Prohibit the Importation of Slaves of 1807 goes into effect for the entire United States and territories. The act quite specifically forbids anyone bringing people in who are held for service or labor. Despite this law, an estimated 250,000 slaves will be brought in illegally before the Civil War.

1811   On a plantation outside of New Orleans, Charles Deslands, a Haitian freedman, leads a rebellion of more than 400 slaves. The U.S. Army, assisted by local planters, suppresses the uprising. Several dozen, perhaps 100, slaves are killed during the repression of the rebellion.

1812   Louisiana is admitted as the 18th state, as a slave state. The law does recognize free blacks, and allows black men to join the army.

1812–   In the War of 1812, several African Americans serve
1814   with the armed forces. There are black Americans in all of the sea battles; several serve with distinction. Commander Isaac Chauncey fervently defends the African Americans in his forces to his subordinate Admiral Perry.

1815   Escaped slaves and Native Americans capture Fort Blount in Florida. The fort is used to house escaped slaves. Armed forces attack the fort and reclaim the building, killing several of the rebels.

1819   Alabama joins the Union as a slave state, but allots in the legal system a method to emancipate slaves if the legislature so chooses.

1820   In the Missouri Compromise, the wrangling over the number of free states versus slave states is resolved. Missouri is accepted as a slave state with Maine recognized as a free state. This raises the number of slave and free states to twelve each. From this point forward, the dividing line for slave and free territory is the 36°30′ parallel.

According to the 1820 census, there are an estimated 1,538,000 slaves in the United States and 233,524 free African Americans. The overall population of the United States is 4,896,605. Thirty-one percent of the population are slaves; 5 percent are free blacks.

The American Colonization Society, founded in 1816, sponsors a ship to carry African Americans to Africa. The goal of the ACS is to recolonize Africa with free American blacks. Eighty-six African Americans settle on the territory that becomes Liberia.

1822   Denmark Vesey, a freedman, leads a large group of slaves in an attempted rebellion in Charleston, South Carolina. The estimate is that more than 9,000 slaves are involved. A house slave leaks the information to the owner, and 139 people are arrested, including 4 whites. Vesey and 36 others are hanged for their insurrection plan. This is the largest known rebellion.

1823   The Circuit Court passes two laws affecting the status of slaves: slaves moved to a free state are free; mistreatment of slaves is a indictable offense. State laws are passed, however, that restrict black rights. Mississippi prohibits the teaching of reading and writing skills to African Americans.

1826   The first African American males to graduate from college are John Russwurm from Bowdoin College and Edward A. Jones from Amherst College.

1827   The first newspaper published by an African American is issued in New York City by John Russwurm and Samuel Cornish. The editorial page of *Freedom's Journal* is dedicated to arguing against slavery and racial discrimination.

New York abolishes slavery, and 10,000 slaves are emancipated.

1829   Cincinnati suffers a race riot where several black residents have their homes burned. More than 1,000 blacks flee the city to live in Canada. Cincinnati's remaining black citizens suffer under the continued strain of white hostility.

1831   Nat Turner, a slave and preacher, leads a band of six slaves on a violent rebellion against slavery. At the end of the three-day uprising, fifty-seven whites, including women and children, are killed. Seventy or more slaves join in the rebellion as they cover Southampton County, Virginia. On August 24 the rioters are met by the militia, and several dozen slaves are killed. Turner flees into Dismal Swamp for several weeks, but is caught and hanged with sixteen other African Americans. The southern states are thrown into panic over this uprising and restrict the movement and rights of assembly of all blacks, free and slave.

A weekly abolitionist newspaper, *The Liberator*, is published for the first time in Boston, on January 1. Founded by William Garrison, a white man, the paper continues publication until 1865. It is credited with shifting public opinion in the North to total abolition.

The first Convention of the People of Color is held at Wesleyan Church in Philadelphia. Delegates from five states set the agenda for studying various aspects of black life and conditions. They also oppose the American Colonization Society's plan for migration to Africa.

1832   The New England Anti-Slavery Society is founded in Boston by an all-white group. Several other anti-slavery societies will be established by both black and white groups in the next several years.

1833   Oberlin College is founded as an integrated institution. It is the first college in the U.S. to be established as such; other colleges and universities have changed policy to admit blacks. By 1865, the enrollment of Oberlin is 35 percent black.

1834   The British Empire frees all slaves held in its territories. Slave owners are compensated by the British government, resulting in an overall expense to the government of 20 million British pounds. The estimated number of blacks liberated is 700,000.

1836   Congress passes a resolution, supported and promoted by southern state senators, that restricts federal action on state slave laws. Nicknamed the gag rule, the only time allowed for federal control of slavery is during war.

1837   Elijah Lovejoy, publisher of abolitionist literature, is killed at his office in Alton, Illinois, after refusing to give in to a mob's demands that he cease publishing. He is shot while defending his printing press.

Canada gives blacks the right to vote.

1839   Joseph Cinque, an African slave bound for Puerto Principe from Cuba on the *Amistad*, commandeers a mutiny by the slaves held on board. All but two of the crew are killed, and the two are to sail the ship to Africa. They

sail north instead and come ashore on Long Island, NY. The fifty-three slaves are tried and found innocent in 1841 of all charges. They are defended by John Quincy Adams. Cinque returns to Africa after lecturing in the U.S. to raise funds for his passage.

1841 The ship *Creole* carrying slaves from Virginia to Louisiana is overpowered by the slaves on board, who sail the ship to the Bahamas. In the Bahamas, the slaves are granted their freedom.

Frederick Douglass begins his long and illustrious career as a public lecturer, speaking for the Massachusetts Anti-Slavery Society.

1842 Rhode Island gives African Americans the right to vote.

An escaped slave, George Latimer, is captured and held on trial for his fugitive status. This marks the beginning of several trial cases to determine the legality of returning African Americans to slavery after they reach a free state. Latimer is purchased from his master by northern abolitionists and set free.

1843 The governing bodies of the states of Massachusetts and Vermont forbid the assistance and abetment of federal officials who capture escaped slaves. This puts the states in direct defiance of the Fugitive Slave Act of 1793.

Sojourner Truth, born Isabella Van Wagener, begins lecturing on religion and emancipation. She was held as a slave for most of her life.

1844 Jim Beckwourth discovers a pass to the Pacific Ocean through the Sierra Nevada mountains. The pass is named for him: Beckwourth Pass.

1845 Texas is admitted to the Union as a slave state despite attempts by northern senators to ban slavery in the new state. The gag rule of 1836 is overturned.

1847 Dred Scott files his initial case in St. Louis for his freedom. The case will not be settled for ten years, but in 1857 the U.S. Supreme Court rules that Scott cannot be free despite his residence in a free state because blacks have no rights "which any white man was bound to respect."

The North Star begins publication. Frederick Douglass' newspaper becomes a forum for abolitionists.

1849 Harriet Tubman, a major force behind the Underground Railroad, escapes from slavery. She will return to the South nineteen times to assist others in their flight to freedom.

The Massachusetts Supreme Court declares in *Roberts* v. *the City of Boston* that Benjamin Roberts' daughter is not entitled to attend public schools for white children, despite the lack of schools for African American children. The case establishes the legislation that recognizes "separate but equal"as constitutional until *Brown* v. *the Board of Education* in 1954.

The Breakdown of Slavery and the Civil War

1850 The Compromise of 1850 establishes several regulations on slavery after the Mexican War. California becomes a free state and Washington, D.C., abolishes slavery. New Mexico and Utah are not voted either slave or free; Texas is a slave state. The most damaging element of the Compromise is the Fugitive Slave Act, which toughens the regulations freeing escaped slaves. A bounty is paid to federal officers for returned slaves.

1852 *Uncle Tom's Cabin* by Harriet Beecher Stowe is published for the first time. It sells 300,000 copies in the first year. The story is about a generous slave who is held by Simon Legree, a brutal owner who eventually flogs Tom to death. The story fuels anti-slavery sentiment.

Frederick Douglass delivers a scathing public lecture entitled "What to the Slaves is the Fourth of July?" Douglass attacks the celebration for its injustice to those held in bondage. He ends the speech by saying "for revolting barbarity and shameless hypocrisy, America reigns without a rival."

1853 Ashmond Institute in Oxford, Pennsylvania, is the first black college in the U.S. It is eventually renamed Lincoln University.

William Wells Brown, the first African American to publish a novel, has *Clotel* published in England after all American publishers reject the manuscript. Brown has a book of poetry successfully published in 1851, called *The Anti-Slavery Harp*.

1854 Escaped slave Anthony Burns is returned to his slave owners in Virginia after capture in Boston. He is paraded through the streets by federal law enforcement officials before his return. Despite attempts by abolitionists to buy his freedom, his owner refuses to relinquish custody of him.

The Kansas–Nebraska Act allows both states to enter the union without slavery restrictions, violating the Missouri Compromise of 1850. Stephen Douglas is the sponsor of the act. Abraham Lincoln denounces the act in one of his first public addresses directed beyond his home state of Illinois.

1855 Two more states, Michigan and Maine, forbid the assistance of federal officials enforcing the Fugitive Slave Act. Massachusetts also desegregates the public school system without incident.

1856 Violence erupts over abolitionist sentiment in three places. The town of Lawrence, Kansas, has five pro-slavery settlers killed by abolitionists. John Brown is blamed. Osawatomie, Kansas, is raided by 300 pro-slavery men in retaliation. Osawatomie is John Brown's home. Brown, an anti-slavery activist has moved to Kansas to protest the slavery status of the territory. In Washington, D.C., Senator Charles Sumner of Massachusetts is beaten unconscious by representative Preston Brooks of South Carolina. Brooks objected to Sumner's abolitionist views.

1857 The Dred Scott decision is issued by the U.S. Supreme Court. The decision strengthens anti-slavery sentiment in the North, when the Court declares that Congress cannot restrict slavery in the territories. Scott, who had resided in free Illinois and the free territory of Wisconsin, sued for his freedom because of his residency in a free area. The Court declares that he is property of his owner and cannot be taken away by the court. He is freed by his owner, nonetheless.

Maine and New Hampshire grant citizenship to African Americans.

1858 Lincoln and Douglas debate, following Lincoln's proclamation at his nomination that "a house divided . . . cannot stand . . . permanently half slave and half free." Lincoln does not call for the freeing of African Americans, although he does personally oppose slavery.

1859 John Brown, a folk hero to the abolitionists, attacks Harper's Ferry, West Virginia, with a band of thirteen whites and five blacks. They attempt to seize the arsenal

to gain ammunition for a black uprising. Brown is hanged for treason. He predicts on the gallows that bloodshed will resolve the slave issue.

1860   Abraham Lincoln is elected the sixteenth president of the United States. One month after the election, and three months before Lincoln's swearing-in, South Carolina secedes from the Union.

According to the 1860 census, there are 3,953,760 slaves in the U.S. They are almost evenly divided between male and female. The 488,070 free African Americans that are counted make up less than two percent of the population; slaves are 12 percent.

1861   Mississippi, Florida, and Alabama secede by January 11. Georgia, Louisiana, and Texas secede by the beginning of February. In March, President Lincoln is sworn in to office, and the South establishes the Constitution of the Confederacy. April 12 marks the official beginning of the Civil War with the attack by Confederate troops on Fort Sumter. Blacks are not accepted as enlisted men in the Union Army by most of the commanding officers.

1862   Robert Smalls sneaks aboard the Confederate gunboat, the *Planter*, and pilots it to Union officers. Smalls, his family, and the other escaped slaves who command the boat are freed for their heroism.

Congress allows black soldiers in the Union Army. Until now, they were only to be used as hired hands and paid laborers at $10 a day, minus expenses. Soldiers are paid $13 a day plus a clothing allowance. Once blacks are enlisted, though, they do not receive soldiers' pay. The Confederacy also declares that all captured soldiers will be sold as slaves or hanged; any officer commanding black troops will be executed. Through the duration of the war, no black prisoners of war are given in exchange by the South.

1863   President Lincoln declares on January 1 that all slaves in the Confederate states are hereafter free. In the Emancipation Proclamation, Lincoln does not free the slaves in territories that do not participate in the southern rebellion. The effectiveness of the proclamation depends on the Union Army winning.

The 54th Massachusetts Volunteers are the first black soldiers enlisted in the North. Frederick Douglass, Martin Delaney, and other voices of the abolition movement recruit for the 54th. The 54th fights in several battles but the most decisive in proving their honor is at Fort Wagner, South Carolina. Sergeant William Carney receives the Congressional Medal of Honor thirty-seven years after the war.

The first major battle to use black troops is at Milliken's Bend in Louisiana. The bravery of the black soldiers shifts the sentiment of some officers previously opposed to arming blacks.

1864   Thirty-eight black regiments participate in the two-month siege at Petersburg, Virginia. The disastrous attack on July 30 leaves Union troops open to attack by the Confederacy. Confederate policy is to capture white soldiers and kill all black soldiers. Hundreds of black soldiers are clubbed and bayoneted while trying to surrender.

Grant declares an end to the prisoner exchange until the South agrees to release black soldiers as well as white. The South refuses, and the lack of returned Confederate soldiers taxes southern troops, already weakened by continued losses in battle. The Confederacy prisoner-of-war camps become hellholes of overcrowded, unsanitary, disease ridden death camps.

Congress passes a bill equalizing pay, clothing supplements, and equipment for black soldiers. The Fugitive Slave Act is repealed.

1865   By the end of the Civil War 178,975 black soldiers enlist in the Union Army. More than 68,000 die, and 23 win the Congressional Medal of Honor. One hundred sixty-six regiments in the Union Army are black. Because of the lower pay, the lack of clothing money, and reticence of white doctors to treat the soldiers during most of the war, black soldiers have double the mortality rate from disease compared to the white soldiers.

Congress passes the Thirteenth Amendment, abolishing slavery in the United States. All Confederate states wishing to reenter the Union must illegalize slavery. South Carolina is the first to do so.

The Freedmen's Bureau is created by Congress to help emancipated slaves make the transition to independence and freedom. Southern states pass several laws that restrict black rights and freedom. The Ku Klux Klan is formed to promote white supremacy.

1866   The first blacks to be elected to public office in the United States are Edward Walker and Charles Mitchell, as representatives in Massachusetts.

Fisk University is founded.

The Civil Rights Act of 1866 is passed over a veto by President Johnson, nullifying southern codes and laws repressing black rights and granting citizenship to African Americans.

1867   The Reconstruction Act, overriding another presidential veto, declares that all states wishing to reenter the Union submit to military control and reorganization of the state government. The state must also pass the pending Fourteenth Amendment and grant the right to vote to all African Americans age 21 and older. Enforcement of the Reconstruction Act gives blacks the majority in several states.

1868   The Fourteenth Amendment passes Congress, defining citizenship and granting federal oversight of all state rulings involving constitutional rights of individuals. This allows federal intervention on racial issues, where black rights may be violated by state governments.

Oscar Dunn is elected Lieutenant Governor of Louisiana. Dunn is a freed slave who fought in the Union Army.

1870   The Fifteenth Amendment establishes the right to vote of all citizens, specifically banning any possible restriction of voting rights on the basis "of race, color, or previous servitude."

Hiram Revel is elected by Mississippi as the first black senator. Joseph Rainey of South Carolina and Jefferson Long of Georgia are elected as Representatives to the U.S. Congress.

1871   The terrorist tactics of the Ku Klux Klan for intimidating blacks reaches a level that Congress decides requires federal intervention. The Ku Klux Klan Act of 1871 illegalizes the activity of any organization that is deemed to deprive any citizen of his constitutional rights. It also forbids the hindrance of executing any law of the land. This is enacted to combat the Klan's attempts to prevent blacks from voting, running for office, or engaging in other legal activity.

Robert Elliot (South Carolina), Robert DeLarge (South Carolina), Benjamin Tumer (Alabama), and Josieh

Walls (Florida) are elected as Representatives to Congress.

1873   Richard Cane of South Carolina and John Lynch of Mississippi are elected to the House of Representatives. Cane will serve two non-consecutive terms; Lynch will serve three terms. James Rapier (Alabama) and Alonzo Ransier (South Carolina) are also elected as representatives.

1875   The Civil Rights Act of 1875 bans discrimination in public places and illegalizes discriminatory accommodations. This functionally bans segregated hotels, inns, theaters, and other public gathering areas.

Blanche Bruce of Mississippi is elected to the Senate. He will be the last black senator until 1967. Thirty-two representatives will serve in the House between 1870 and 1970. During that one hundred–year period, there will only be 28 scattered years that do not have at least one black voice in the Congress. The longest period without a black representative is between 1901 and 1929.

1879   A number of African Americans begin a migration to northern states. With the continued discrimination and violence against blacks in the southern states, and the lack of job opportunities, the North is seen as a better place to live. Large cities also attract African Americans because of the increased likelihood of finding work. By 1910, more than a quarter of the black population will live in cities; before 1880, 90 percent of the black population lived in rural areas.

The Stagnation of Civil Rights

1881   "Jim Crow" laws, segregating blacks and whites in public facilities and accommodations, are passed in Tennessee, violating the Civil Rights Act of 1875.

1883   The Civil Rights Act of 1875 is overturned by the Supreme Court, leaving the path open for "Jim Crow" laws to be established in state legislatures. Florida, Mississippi, Texas, and Louisiana all establish segregation laws by 1890.

1884   The first African American baseball teams are formed with the increased pressure for segregated teams. Although there are still a few black players on white professional teams until 1900, the trend is rapid to keep baseball teams exclusively white.

1885   Michigan establishes anti-segregation laws that protect integration of public establishments and accommodations. Seventeen states, mainly in the North, have similar laws established by 1910.

1887   The first baseball franchise for African Americans is founded: the Union Giants.

1889   Frederick Douglass is appointed as ambassador to Haiti.

1890   Mississippi is the first state to establish rules that restrict who can vote. The rules, instituting literacy tests and such, are designed to eliminate black voters from registration. Most of the southern states follow suit.

The boll weevil migrates to the United States from Mexico and proceeds to devastate cotton crops. With 3 million bales of cotton destroyed each year, the cotton industry is forced to respond by laying off workers. This increases African American migration to enormous levels. In 1915 alone, a quarter million blacks will relocate from the South to the North.

1896   *Plessy* v. *Ferguson* is the first Supreme Court ruling to follow the "separate but equal" doctrine that remains the rule of the land until *Brown* v. *the Board of Education* in 1954. This follows on the 1849 ruling in Massachusetts. In the dissenting opinion written by Justice Harlan, he states, "If a white man and a black man choose to occupy the same public conveyance on a public highway, it is their right to do so, and no government, proceeding alone on grounds of race, can prevent it without infringing the personal liberty of each."

1898   When some of the literacy tests designed to keep blacks from voting are found to also keep whites from voting, Louisiana enacts the Grandfather Clause. This law, used to circumvent federal law forbidding racially motivated voting rules, declares that anyone who had a father or grandfather registered to vote in 1867 can vote. Louisiana had few registered black voters in 1867, and thus 123,000 blacks lose their right to vote because of the law. Other southern states follow with similar laws.

In the Spanish-American War, 100 blacks achieve officer ranking in the U.S. military. Five receive Congressional Medals of Honor.

1901   One month after being sworn in as president, Theodore Roosevelt invites Booker T. Washington to dinner at the White House. Reaction in the South is hostile to Roosevelt because of this social association with a black man.

1907   Rioting in Brownsville, Texas, leaves one dead and several injured, as well as vast property damage. Soldiers from the 25th Infantry are believed responsible. Several black soldiers are involved, and President Roosevelt discharges 167 black soldiers and bars them from reenlistment because of the incident. The decision is reversed in 1972 when only one of the dishonorably discharged soldiers is still alive to receive compensation.

1909   The National Association for the Advancement of Colored People (NAACP) is founded in New York. It is the 100th anniversary of the birth of Abraham Lincoln. The organization works to reverse discriminatory laws and offer legal assistance to blacks unconstitutionally imprisoned.

1910   Thirty of the 48 states have laws illegalizing interracial marriage. Five states had such laws but reversed them before the turn of the century. Seven states (Colorado, Idaho, Iowa, Michigan, Minnesota, New Mexico, Rhode Island) are the only states to never have segregated schools. They all establish laws to illegalize them, nonetheless. Another seven states which do have segregated schools pass laws illegalizing segregation.

1911   The National Urban League is founded. The main purpose of the organization is to raise the educational and employment opportunities of African Americans.

1915   The NAACP sponsors lawyers to challenge the government before the Supreme Court in *Guinn* v. *United States*. The case attacked the Grandfather Clause voting laws in Oklahoma. The Supreme Court rules against the Oklahoma laws, stating that they are instituted to specifically circumvent the 15th Amendment.

1917   The NAACP sponsors a challenge to a St. Louis, Missouri, regulation that bars blacks from buying homes in predominantly white neighborhoods, and whites from buying in black neighborhoods. In *Buchanan* v. *Warley* the regulation is struck down by the Supreme Court as a violation of the 14th Amendment.

World War One begins, and 600 African Americans are commissioned as officers through a black officers' training camp. Black soldiers will make up more than 10 percent of the fighting troops. Two black battalions receive

the Croix de Guerre and two officers receive awards for bravery.

1918 The NAACP commences a strong public campaign to make lynchings illegal under federal law. They publish a booklet, *Thirty Years of Lynching in the United States, 1889–1918* with detailed case histories of 100 actual lynchings. They assemble statistics on lynchings in the U.S. and push for legislation combatting such attacks.

1919 Some states try to pass legislation that declares membership in the NAACP illegal. Rioting over racial discrimination and lynching swells to epidemic proportions throughout the U.S.

1920 The Dyer Anti-Lynching Bill is voted down in the Senate, although it is passed in the House of Representatives. No subsequent bill on anti-lynching is approved by Congress either. Several states pass or strengthen their anti-Klan and anti-lynching legislation, including Illinois, Kentucky, and Louisiana. Several Supreme Court decisions are passed during the 1920s and 30s to defend black rights in juried trials, both for treatment of the accused and the rights for blacks to sit on juries.

1924 As immigration laws tighten with the closing of Ellis Island, one of the restrictions is that no immigrants from Africa will be accepted.

The Grassroots of Civil Rights

1926 Negro History Week is declared for the first time by The Association for the Study of Negro Life and History.

1927 Following on some of the southern boycotts of segregated transportation systems, Chicago blacks and the Urban League organize a boycott of stores that hire only white employees. This leads to other cities boycotting against discriminatory practices in their towns as well.

1930 The NAACP, now with more than 100,000 members, has the political clout to prevent the confirmation of a racist nominee for the Supreme Court. It also assists in the defeat of some congressmen who voted to confirm the judge.

1933 Franklin D. Roosevelt is president, and the country is in the midst of the worst depression in U.S. history. A disproportionate number of blacks are on government assistance.

1935 The NAACP loses a major decision in the Supreme Court. In *Grovey* v. *Townsend*, the Court reverses a previous stand over the exclusion of blacks from voting in primaries. The Court finds that the Democratic Party in Texas is a voluntary political association, entitled to admit or refuse anyone they choose.

1936 Jesse Owens competes in the Olympics in Germany and wins four gold medals. This humiliates the German team and the German Chancellor, Adolph Hitler, who have sought to prove racial superiority of whites in athletic competition.

1938 Thurgood Marshall is appointed as chief counsel of the NAACP.

1939 Marion Anderson is barred from singing in Constitution Hall in Washington, D.C., by the Daughters of the American Revolution (DAR). She sings instead on the steps of the Lincoln Memorial. The president's wife, Eleanor Roosevelt, appalled by the DAR's actions, resigns from the organization.

1940 The first African American to achieve the rank of general is Benjamin Oliver Davis, awarded the post of Brigadier General. As the country prepares for war, Roosevelt allows black enlistment in the armed forces to be expanded. During the presidential campaign of 1940, both the democratic and republican platforms include promises to equalize economic standards and political involvement of blacks and whites.

1941 Roosevelt issues an executive order banning segregation in defense industries and establishing a committee on Fair Employment Practice. Roosevelt came out strongly against segregation in a memo preceding his order, declaring that we need "to strengthen our unity and morale by refuting at home the very theories which we are fighting abroad."

When the Japanese attack Pearl Harbor, Messman Dorie Miller volunteers to man a machine gun on his ship and downs four enemy planes. He is awarded the Navy Cross for valor.

1942 The Congress of Racial Equality (CORE) is founded in Chicago. The organization is dedicated to peaceful, active promotion of black rights.

1943 CORE stages a sit-in at a Chicago restaurant that does not serve blacks.

Race riots break out in major cities. In Detroit, 34 people are killed during one uprising, and federal troops have to be called in.

The 761st tank battalion fights at Omaha Beach on D-Day, along with several hundred other black regiments. The 761st is awarded for courage.

1945 One million African Americans serve with the American Armed Forces.

Morgan v. *Virginia* decides in the Supreme Court that integration of interstate busses is the only way to prevent unnecessary discriminatory practices when transport moves from largely white populations into more integrated states. Although this does not declare the concept of separate facilities illegal, it does support that accommodations must be essentially equal, and when that cannot be achieved, integrated services must be established. The NAACP's lawyer, Thurgood Marshall, argues the case before the Court.

1946 Ralph Bunche is appointed to a trusteeship in the United Nations, which he helped to organize.

1947 President Harry Truman's committee on civil rights issues their report on racial injustice, "To Secure These Rights." Truman, in speaking before the NAACP on discrimination and racism, says, "We cannot wait another decade or another generation to remedy these evils. We must work, as never before, to cure them now."

CORE sponsors the first of the "Freedom Rides" to protest segregated local transportation facilities in the south.

Jackie Robinson becomes the first black baseball player in the major leagues. He plays for the Brooklyn Dodgers. Two years later, Robinson is voted Most Valuable Player for the National League.

1948 President Truman integrates the U.S. Armed Forces. By executive order, Truman bans all forms of military segregation and assigns an advisory committee to oversee all regulations to ensure fair practice.

U.N. diplomat Ralph Bunche is appointed as mediator in the Arab-Israeli conflict.

1949 Decisions by the federal courts further erode segregation on public transportation. In *Whiteside* v. *Southern Bus Lines* and *Lee* v. *Commonwealth of Virginia* the courts declare that companies cannot impose segregated seating in states that do not have segregation laws.

In the House of Representatives, William Dawson (Illinois) becomes the first African American to chair a committee: Expenditures Committee.

Atlanta, Georgia, has the first African American–owned radio station.

1950 Ralph Bunche is the first black to be awarded the Nobel Peace Prize. Bunche is honored for his role as mediator in the Arab–Israeli War.

Gwendolyn Brooks, a poet, is awarded a Pulitzer Prize. She is the first African American honored by a Pulitzer award.

Truman's advisory committee for the armed forces integration process issues its first report. The special forces and some training programs remain segregated despite the executive order to integrate. However, the majority of the military has complied with desegregation.

1951 The National Association of Colored Graduate Nurses votes to disband after they announce they have achieved their goal of integrating the nursing profession. Mabel Keaton Staupers wins the Spingarn Award for her efforts in leading the NACGN to its goal.

One of the NAACP's district leaders, Harry Moore, is killed by a bomb at his home in Florida on Christmas night.

1952 The Tuskegee Institute, which has been filing statistics on lynching since 1881, announces that this is the first year in their history with no lynchings.

Thurgood Marshall, arguing for the NAACP, presents evidence to the Supreme Court for striking down *Plessy* v *Ferguson* and stating that separate, segregated institutions can never be equal. The District of Columbia, Delaware, Kansas, South Carolina, and Virginia all have cases before the court that challenge the "separate but equal" rule. The black schools are deemed to be relatively equal in caliber to the white schools, but still discriminatory. The Court requests further information, and a team of 100 lawyers for the NAACP proceed to gather information for two years to fulfill the request.

The March of Civil Rights

1954 Under the stewardship of Chief Justice Earl Warren, a unanimous decision is handed down by the Supreme Court on "separate but equal" educational facilities. In the case entitled *Brown* v. *the Board of Education*, the Court decides on five cases dealing with segregated schools. The Court holds that separate is inherently unequal and therefore schools have to be integrated to comply with federal law. The ruling technically only affects schools from the four states and the District of Columbia which are involved in the suits. Other schools battling integration need to be successfully sued before integration becomes a general part of the land. The White Citizens Council is formed in the South to battle against integrated schools. Some southern states pass various resolutions to circumvent integration of their public schools.

1955 Ralph Bunche is appointed undersecretary to the United Nations.

Rosa Parks refuses to move to the back of the bus in Montgomery, Alabama. She is arrested for noncompliance of the segregation laws. The Reverend Martin Luther King, Jr., uses this incident to arrange a boycott of the buses in Montgomery by African Americans and sympathetic whites.

Marion Anderson is the first African American to sing with the Metropolitan Opera Company.

1956 Eight states have completely ignored the integration laws of schools, including Alabama and Mississippi. A court order forces the University of Alabama to enroll Autherine Lucy, but she is almost immediately expelled on a technicality. Rioting accompanies her short attendance at the university.

The Supreme Court declares bus segregation unconstitutional. Buses cannot have separate seating assignments for blacks and whites. This ends the Montgomery boycott which has lasted over a year.

In several cases, the Supreme Court continues to strike down segregation laws. The cases involve segregation on beaches, in swimming pools, public parks, and recreational facilities, and in every instance the Court declares that they must, by law, be integrated facilities.

1957 President Dwight D. Eisenhower proposes and Congress passes the Civil Rights Act of 1957, the first major civil rights act of this century. The Act establishes a Commission on Civil Rights that will oversee the adherence to any and all regulations integrating facilities and schools, allowing blacks to vote, and allowing blacks on juries. It also establishes the right to fine or jail anyone who acts in contempt of these laws.

By Executive Order, President Eisenhower ends segregation at Little Rock's Central High School in Arkansas. Federal troops are assigned to line the streets to assist 18 African American high school students to attend school without being harmed.

Mississippi only has 3 percent of its black citizens registered to vote.

1958 The Youth Council of the NAACP begins a series of sit-ins at segregated restaurants and lunch counters.

1959 Prince Edward County in Virginia votes to abolish the school system rather than give in to integration.

1960 The Civil Rights Act of 1960 increases the ability of the government to punish anyone interfering with the civil rights of another or attempting to avoid prosecution. It establishes as a federal crime acts of obstructing the law, interfering with enforcement of a federal or court order, fleeing across state lines to avoid prosecution, and destroying election documents and ballots. It also places a five year prison sentence on anyone possessing explosives with intent to do personal or property damage, and a minimum sentence of ten years on anyone actually committing such an act.

Greensboro, North Carolina, has one of the most publicized sit-ins at a Woolworths' lunch counter. Four blacks sit at a whites only counter and refuse to move. Cameras film the hostilities this incident triggers. Other sit-ins follow at Nashville and Montgomery, and eventually spread to many major cities. Dozens of people are arrested at the sit-ins for violation of local segregation laws. In response to this passive resistance, several cities begin integrating facilities.

1961 CORE sponsors a freedom ride through southern states to check state compliance with desegregation orders, following the 1949 and 1956 rulings of the Supreme

Court barring segregation on public transportation. Along with finding noncompliance in many southern states, the riders are arrested in several places, and meet with violent crowds in others. The tension and violence require the federal government to send federal marshals to maintain the peace in Montgomery, Alabama. By 1963 more than 70,000 people will have participated in various freedom rides in the U.S.

President John F. Kennedy appoints several African Americans to posts in his administration. He has a greater percentage of African Americans on his staff than anyone in U.S. history. Kennedy appoints Thurgood Marshall as a U.S. Appeals Court Judge.

Several states legislate against integrated public housing.

President Kennedy issues an Executive Order that forms the Committee on Equal Employment Opportunity. Under the jurisdiction of the Department of Labor, the secretary of labor enforces the implementation of equal employment practices.

1962 President Kennedy issues an Executive Order that bars any racially motivated discrimination in public housing, housing financed by federal grants or loans, or in housing owned or operated by the government.

James Meredith is accepted to the University of Mississippi on court order, and 12,000 federal troops are assigned to the campus to maintain order during the rioting that follows. In Meredith's first attempts to register for classes, Mississippi Governor Ross Barnett personally blocks his entrance. Two people are killed during the civil disturbance of whites protesting the integration of the university.

1963 World War II veteran and NAACP regional representative Medgar Evers is shot in the back and killed at his home a few hours after President Kennedy gives a television address on the importance of civil rights. He is buried with honors at Arlington National Cemetery.

Four children, all African American, are killed by a bomb blast in a church in Birmingham, Alabama. Segregationists are believed to be responsible. Riots follow.

Martin Luther King, Jr., is arrested in Birmingham, Alabama, during one of the many confrontations between black protestors and police. Several African Americans are injured by fire hoses, attack dogs, and clubs wielded by the Birmingham police. Thousands of people participate in the protests, and thousands more watch the attack on the protestors on television. King issues a letter in response to those who accuse him of instigating violence. The letter is smuggled from the jail. He is released shortly thereafter.

The March on Washington is the largest civil rights rally in history. Two hundred fifty thousand people march to the Lincoln Memorial to hear several speakers, including the Reverend Martin Luther King, Jr. King's speech, "I Have a Dream," is a plea for equality and brotherhood between blacks and whites. It becomes one of the most quoted orations in U.S. history. The March is a culmination of CORE and NAACP efforts to publicize racism in the country.

President Kennedy is assassinated. Lyndon Johnson is sworn is as the new president.

1964 President Johnson signs the Civil Rights Act of 1964 into law. Initiated under the Kennedy Administration, the Act is the broadest legislation in support of civil rights since the Civil War. It affects legislation for voting, accommodations, schools, employment, federal aid, and treatment of civil rights cases in the courts. Southern congressmen try filibustering to avoid passing the legislation, but they are voted down by congressmen supporting the Act.

Martin Luther King, Jr., is awarded the Nobel Peace Prize for his work in civil rights in the United States.

Three civil rights workers are killed in Mississippi. Local law enforcement officials are suspected of assisting in their deaths, but charges are dismissed.

The first of the large-scale big city riots occurs in New York City, in Harlem. One person is killed and more than 100 people are injured during the melee.

In *Griffin* v. *School Board of Prince Edward County*, the Supreme Court orders the Virginia county schools to reopen their doors after closing them in 1959 to avoid integration. The court declares that as long as any public school system in Virginia remains open, Prince Edward County must also remain open. The county had been collecting funds from taxpayers to pay for private school tuition only for white children, saying that no private schools existed for black children, so payment was not necessary to blacks.

Malcolm X establishes the Organization for Afro-American Unity.

1965 Malcolm X is assassinated while speaking at a public rally.

Martin Luther King, Jr., leads a march from Selma, Alabama, to the state capital, Montgomery. The marchers first attempt the five-day walk on March 7, but they are attacked by police—under the order of Governor George Wallace—using whips, clubs, and tear gas. Almost 100 people are injured; several are hospitalized. Television captures the brutality of the police action. Another attempt is made on March 9, which is again met by force, but without violent incident. On March 21, under federal order of police protection and a court injunction against disrupting the marchers, 2,100 people set out from Selma. Three hundred marchers are allowed along the path, but 25,000 walk up to the capital building in Montgomery on March 25. One white woman is killed during the walk, by Klan members. 4,000 troops protect the marchers.

CORE sponsors a major protest at Bogalusa, Louisiana. During the several days of protest, there is considerable confrontation, and one man is shot and wounded. The local officials ignore a Justice Department order to protect the protestors, and criminal charges are filed against the Bogalusa officials.

President Johnson signs into law the 1965 Voting Rights Act. The Act responds to African American protests over voting restrictions in southern states. It bans literacy, knowledge, and character tests for voters. It eliminates poll taxes, used to keep the poor from voting. It adds federal support to protecting the Fifteenth Amendment.

The Watts district in Los Angeles suffers, during a hot August, from the most extensive racial riots to date. Several thousand people are arrested during the six-day melee, and 35 are killed. Several blocks are looted and burned in the black neighborhood, resulting in millions of dollars in losses and damage to property. President Johnson vehemently condemns the rioters.

1966 James Meredith, who broke the color barrier at the University of Mississippi in 1962, is shot in the back during a 200-mile march to promote voter registration among the African American population. He is shot in Her-

nando, Mississippi, sustaining serious injury, but survives. After the march political activist Stokely Carmichael uses the term "black power" in discussing motivation for the marchers. Carmichael is head of the Student Nonviolent Coordinating Committee and advocates a more militant role for black activists.

CORE votes to endorse and the NAACP votes to reject the concept of "Black Power."

Riots break out in Chicago, Cleveland, and other cities across the U.S. In one of the many marches in Chicago, Martin Luther King, Jr., is stoned by angry crowds objecting to integration of the white neighborhoods on the city's southwest side.

The Black Panthers are founded in California by Huey Newton and Bobby Seale. They issue the organization's ten-point Manifesto, outlining the goals of the Panthers.

Years of Turmoil

1967   Representative Adam Clayton Powell is dismissed from serving in Congress because of charges of misappropriation of public funds. He takes his case to the District Court, and wins reelection during the review process but is not allowed to take his seat in Congress. Powell has been in office since 1945.

Thurgood Marshall is appointed by President Johnson to the U.S. Supreme Court. He is the first African American to sit on the Court.

Riots occur throughout the country during the summer. Riots in Boston, Tampa, and Cincinnati during June are broken up by National Guardsmen. By the end of June major riots take place in Newark, Detroit, and Buffalo. The most violent of the race riots is in Detroit. Forty-three people are killed and several blocks in the city are completely destroyed by arson and looting. Much of the massive physical devastation to the city remains unrepaired 25 years later. The National Guards take over the streets in tanks to quell the rioting. Curfews are imposed, and President Johnson establishes the Kerner advisory commission to investigate the causes of such violent rioting.

The NAACP holds its annual convention, but the meeting is divisive. Members defending the recent outburst of militant black groups are attacked for alienating white supporters of civil rights. Several leaders of the more militant civil rights groups meet in Newark and call for a separate black nation.

The Student Nonviolent Coordinating Committee publishes an article attacking Israel, charging that Zionists are discriminating against the Arab population. Jewish supporters and members of the SNCC resign in protest.

President Johnson nominates Walter Washington to be mayor of Washington, D.C., in the reorganized city government. Washington becomes the first African American to govern a major U.S. city.

1968   The Reverend Martin Luther King, Jr., is assassinated in Memphis by a lone gunman. During the rioting that follows in most of the major cities, 38 people are killed.

The Kerner Commission issues its findings for President Johnson on the riots. It charges that racism against African Americans is the major cause of unrest and dissatisfaction among the black community. The continued pressure on the black community includes poverty and discrimination. Any effort to dispel the problems should include increased educational, employment, and housing opportunities for blacks. In response to the findings

of the commission and to the death of Reverend King, Congress passes the Civil Rights Bill of 1968. This opens up housing to complete integration.

In demonstrations designed to draw attention to the plight of the poor, a march of welfare mothers, led by Coretta Scott King, travels through 20 cities. In Washington, D.C., a shantytown is built, and 2,500 people live in the ramshackle homes on the Mall to persuade Congress to reform funding for housing and welfare programs.

Riots take place in Cleveland, where black mayor Carl Stokes holds office, and in Miami. Eleven are killed in Cleveland and 3 in Miami. In Brooklyn, white militants attack a group of blacks, reputed to be with the Black Panthers, and white supporters, in the Criminal Court building. The attackers use blackjacks to violently harm the crowd.

Huey Newton is convicted on manslaughter charges, stemming from the shooting death of an Oakland, California, police officer. The conviction is overturned on technical grounds by the California Court of Appeals. Other Black Panthers are in exile avoiding prosecution or are under arrest for violent attacks. Three Panthers are arrested for the machine gun attack on a Newark police station.

1969   James Earl Ray pleads guilty to the charge of first-degree murder of Martin Luther King, Jr. He is sentenced to life in prison.

During the Chicago trial of eight Black Panthers accused of conspiracy to incite a riot during the Democratic Convention of 1968, Bobby Seale is ordered gagged and bound by the trial judge. Seale is given four years for contempt of court after further disturbances during the trial.

Representative Powell is reinstated by the Congress to his seat. He is fined for misuse of public funds and is stripped of his seniority status.

1970   Some local public school systems decide to honor the birthday of Martin Luther King, Jr., by either closing or by holding special classes about the work of King.

Several school systems are forced by state and federal Supreme Court decisions to instigate integration into the public school system immediately. This includes school districts in Memphis, Denver, several in Louisiana, and elsewhere around the country. Many of the efforts to integrate are met with violence and property destruction by whites opposing integration and bussing. Congress passes an amendment that denies federal funds to any school district that does not comply with the integration guidelines.

Confrontational demonstrations and gatherings are becoming increasingly violent in the nation. In Augusta, Georgia, six African Americans are killed by gunfire; several are shot from behind. In a campus uprising at Jackson State College in Mississippi, two students are killed in a residence hall by police. One of the most dramatic incidents is the shooting death of a judge during a trial in San Rafael, California. Three prisoners and the escape van driver are killed by police. The guns are traced to Angela Davis, who goes into hiding after the shootout.

1971   Prisoners, mostly black, riot at Attica State Prison in New York. Conditions are cramped in the prison, and black prisoners charge that white guards are excessively abusive. The takeover lasts four days and is broken up by state troopers storming the facilities. Eleven guards and 32 prisoners are killed in the uprising.

The government Commission on Civil Rights finds in its report that the justice department is not adequately supporting the standing civil rights legislation.

1973 In a major victory for the Equal Employment Opportunity Commission (EEOC), AT&T is forced to pay $15 million in back wages to 15,000 minority men and women who are employed by AT&T. They are also charged with equalizing pay scales between black and white employees and promoting minorities to balance staff.

1977 Karen Farmer is the first African American accepted to the Daughters of the American Revolution, an organization that once forbid the performance of Marion Anderson because she was black.

1978 Benjamin Hooks becomes the new director of the NAACP, and his first action is to restructure the organization with more local chapters and more emphasis on fundraising to increase NAACP activities.

In a ruling by the Supreme Court, Alan Bakke wins his argument against the University of California, Davis, that the system of minority quotas is inherently discriminatory against individual applicants. The concept of reverse discrimination is established, where whites are discriminated against if blacks with lesser test scores or academic ability are given positions over the white applicant.

1980 Rioting results in Miami after a jury acquits four white police officers in the beating death of a black man held in custody by the police. Nine people are killed and more than 100 are injured during the uprising.

The Supreme Court rules that intentional discrimination must be proved in order to substantiate violation of the law. Any law that by design, but not by purpose, discriminates is not a legal violation. The case stems from the voting system in Mobile, Alabama, which has a voting system that dilutes the black voting power base. This is the first in a series of Supreme Court decisions that weakens the ability of minorities to sue for discrimination. In another decision, however, the Supreme Court upholds the legality of federal set-asides for minority contractors, allowing 10 percent of contracts to be restricted to minority owned companies.

The Justice Department, in enforcing the Civil Rights Act of 1964, establishes revised hiring standards to increase minority employment in the police department of Cincinnati, the fire department in Chicago, and the police department in New York City.

In one of his last actions in office, President Jimmy Carter vetos legislation that bans federal action to order busing to integrate schools. The bill, if passed, would have forbidden the government to use federal funding to prosecute or investigate noncompliance with busing for integration.

1981 President Reagan's appointment to the post of attorney general, William French Smith, declares publicly that the Justice Department will no longer involve itself in desegregation cases of public schools where busing is advised. It will also no longer pursue enforcement of racial hiring quotas and affirmative action plans. Reagan takes further action by reducing the Justice Department's ability to enforce Civil Rights legislation on discriminatory practices.

1982 Clarence Thomas is nominated for the chairmanship of the Equal Employment Opportunity Commission, after President Reagan withdraws his original nominee because of heavy protest from civil rights groups.

The Senate passes an anti-busing bill despite efforts by liberal Democrats to stall action on the bill. The Congress also passes the renewal of the Civil Rights Act of 1965, despite conservative Republican efforts to block the vote.

1983 The Supreme Court rules that discriminatory private schools cannot hold the status for tax-exemption. The Reagan Administration supported tax-exemption status for schools that do not practice integration.

A report issued by the Center for the Study of Social Policies states that African American family incomes have not improved at all since 1960 and that the gap between minority and white earnings is still great.

President Reagan reverses his initial position and signs into law the national holiday for Martin Luther King, Jr.

Jesse Jackson, founder of PUSH, declares his candidacy for the presidency.

1984 Acting independently of the Reagan Administration, Jesse Jackson obtains the release of navy officer Robert Goodman, who had been held by Syrian captors.

Jesse Jackson becomes the first black candidate in a presidential primary to win the majority vote in any state. The District of Columbia and Louisiana both turn out a record number of black voters in support of Jackson.

1986 The Supreme Court, in separate rulings, declares that affirmative action plans do not affect seniority when laying off workers, even if earlier hiring patterns were discriminatory. They also allow Norfolk, Virginia, school systems to ban busing for integration, because it is suspected that busing will only lead to whites moving away from the city. The Court does uphold the use of affirmative action plans, despite strong Reagan Administration objections to such plans.

In an incident that triggers widespread accusations of racism, Michael Griffith is beaten to death by an angry white mob in Howard Beach, Queens, New York, after his car breaks down in the white neighborhood. His companions are beaten but manage to escape.

The director of Federal Contract Compliance in the Department of Labor resigns in protest over the Reagan Administration's record of nonenforcement of affirmative action laws.

1987 In a narrow, 5–4 margin, the Supreme Court upholds hiring quotas to remedy past racially discriminatory practices. The Alabama state police are ordered to continue hiring black officers for 50 percent of the new positions. The Reagan Administration fought to reverse the hiring quota.

1988 In his second run for the Democratic nomination for the presidency, Jesse Jackson wins the majority of delegates in several states. He is in second place for the nomination halfway through the primaries and finishes a strong third at the end of the primaries, demonstrating the ability of an African American to be a major political candidate.

1989 The Supreme Court rules that minority quota set-asides that involve government contracts can only be required in response to specific previous discrimination. They cannot be used as general policy. They also rule, in separate cases, that the burden of proving racial discrimination lays on the employee, and that accidental discrimination is not ground for suit. In *Patterson* v. *McLean Credit Union*, the Supreme Court declares that racial discrimination legislation applies only to hiring, that

discrimination and harassment on the basis of race after hiring is not covered.

1990   Douglas Wilder takes office in Virginia, becoming the first black state governor in U.S. history.

1991   Thurgood Marshall announces his retirement from the Supreme Court. Citing his age and deteriorating health, Marshall removes himself amid fears that the court will now shift to a conservative majority.

President George Bush and the Congress agree on a compromise package for a 1991 Civil Rights Bill, designed to reverse several Supreme Court rulings that dis-

allow suits filed for discriminatory hiring practices. The compromise package provides the burden of proof for nondiscriminatory hiring practices to lay on the shoulders of the employer. This reverses the position of the Supreme Court decision of 1989.

During a rancorous and bitter confirmation process, Clarence Thomas is accepted to the Supreme Court to replace Thurgood Marshall. The conservative Republican served as director of the Equal Employment Opportunity Commission and is charged during the confirmation proceedings with sexually harassing a female employee while there. Thomas is confirmed by a margin of two votes in the Senate.

African American Biographies

Anderson, Marian (1902–), singer. Anderson received her first voice training in her church choir. Her family was poor, and money for private singing lessons came from church collections. In 1925 she placed first in a voice competition over 300 other singers, winning an opportunity to sing with the New York Philharmonic. With her career well underway, she toured Europe between 1925 and 1935, gaining experience and renown. The most controversial point in her career came in 1939 when she was barred by the Daughters of the American Revolution from singing at Constitution Hall because she was black. In protest of this, Eleanor Roosevelt organized another concert at Lincoln Hall, which was attended by 75,000 people. Anderson became the first African American to sing at the Metropolitan Opera in 1955. She retired in 1965. Her rich, pure contralto voice is known for its wide range and mastery of several styles. Anderson was awarded the lifetime achievement award by the National Academy of Recording Arts and Sciences in 1991.

Armstrong, Louis (1900–71), jazz musician. Armstrong learned to play the coronet while living at the New Orleans Colored Waifs' Home, to which he was sentenced for a year and a half after a boyhood prank. After his release he studied music with New Orleans jazz musician King Oliver, and in 1918 he replaced Oliver in Kid Ory's band. He eventually joined Oliver in Chicago and then went on to play the trumpet in the Fletcher Henderson band in New York. After 1925 he began making records and quickly became popular as a big band leader and soloist known for his raspy voice. Armstrong's style strongly influenced the Swing Era, but after World War II he went back to performing with informal sextets. He appeared in several movies, among them *Pennies from Heaven* (1936) and *Hello Dolly* (1969). His nickname, "Satchelmouth," was abbreviated to "Satchmo" by an English critic during his first British tour in 1932.

Attucks, Crispus (1723?–70), martyr of the American Revolution. Attucks was the first to fall in the Boston Massacre on March 5, 1770. Three were killed instantly when the British soldiers fired on the crowd assembled before their garrison, and two others were mortally wounded. Whether Attucks was an innocent victim or provoked the attack by grabbing a Redcoat's bayonet remains in dispute. His body lay in state at Faneuil Hall, and in 1888 a monument was erected in the Boston Common in his honor. Little is known of his life, although he is believed to have been a runaway slave.

Baker, Josephine (1906–75), singer, dancer. Baker began touring with a Philadelphia dance troupe when she was sixteen. After a time in Boston and then New York, Baker moved to Paris to appear in *La Revue négre* at the *Théâtre des Champs Elysées* where she introduced *le jazz hot* to France. She became a French citizen in 1937. During World War II she worked with the Red Cross and was a member of the Résistance and for this work was later awarded the Légion d'Honneur and the Croix de Guerre. On her estate in southwestern France, she raised her adopted children of all nationalities, her "experiment in brotherhood."

Baldwin, James (1924–87), writer. Baldwin's first and most famous book, the semi-autobiographical *Go Tell it on the Mountain* (1953), describes the conversion to Christianity of a young boy in desperate need of love. Baldwin grew up in poverty in Harlem, the eldest of nine children. From 14 to 16 he was a minister in a small revivalist church, and his devout Christian beliefs are central to his works. His work in the 1960s generally concentrated on civil rights themes, exploring black-white relations in *Nobody Knows My Name* (1961) and *Another Country* (1962), and examining the Black Muslims in *The Fire Next Time* (1963). His play *Blues for Mister Charlie* (1964) focuses on racist oppression. In 1948 Baldwin moved to Paris and generally spent the rest of his life abroad, returning periodically to the United States.

Banneker, Benjamin (1731–1806), mathematician, scientist. A self-educated free African American, Banneker first gained recognition in 1761 by building a completely wooden clock that kept accurate time. From 1791 to 1802 he published an almanac, the first such scientific work ever produced by an African American, which was widely circulated in the middle states. After 1790 he participated in the surveying of Washington, D.C., and in 1791 he wrote a famous letter to Secretary of State Thomas Jefferson denouncing slavery.

Bethune, Mary McLeod (1875–1955), educator. Bethune started her own school for girls in 1904 in Daytona Beach, Florida. In 1923 it merged with a boys' school to become the Bethune-Cookman College. From 1936 to 1944 she was the director of the Division of Negro Affairs of the National Youth Administration, the first African American woman to head a federal office. She also served as a special advisor to President Franklin D. Roosevelt on the problems of minorities and was a member of the unofficial "Black Cabinet" seeking integration in government. She was awarded the Spingarn Medal in 1935.

Brooks, Gwendolyn (1917–), poet. Brooks was the first African American poet to win the Pulitzer Prize (for *Annie Allen*, 1949) and in 1969 she was named the poet laureate of Illinois. After graduating from college, Brooks began writing poetry for the *Chicago Defender*, a newspaper primarily serving the black community of Chicago. Brooks's poetry explores the everyday lives of ordinary urban people. Her most noted collections include *A Street in Bronzeville* (1945), *The Bean Eaters* (1960), *Selected Poems* (1963), and *In the Mecca* (1968).

Bunche, Ralph (1904–71), diplomat. Orphaned at 11, Bunche was raised by his grandmother, a former slave. He received his education with the help of an athletic scholarship and went on to receive his Ph.D. in government from Harvard in 1934. Bunche's distinguished career as a diplomat of the United Nations included participation in the creation of the U.N. charter and service as director of the Department of Trusteeship and Non-Self-Governing Territories, undersecretary of Special Political Affairs, and undersecretary general. Throughout his career he acted as special U.N. representative to various countries; the special peace-seeking Palestine commission that he headed in 1948 helped bring about temporary peace to the Arab-Israeli conflict in 1949, earning him the Nobel Prize for peace in 1950. He was awarded the Presidential Medal of Freedom in 1963.

Carver, George Washington (1864–1943), scientist. As the head of the agricultural department and director of agricultural research at Tuskegee Institute in Alabama, Carver devoted his life to improving the lot of the African American southern farmer by introducing new, soil enriching crops (peanut, soybean), teaching new farming methods, and developing new products from common foods. (He developed

300 derivative products from the peanut alone). Born on a slave plantation and orphaned at an early age, Carver was used to making his own way from the start. Throughout his life he was known for his austere lifestyle and dedication to his work. Although he had numerous, lucrative offers from business and government, he chose to remain at Tuskegee.

Chisholm, Shirley (1924–), politician. Chisholm became the first African American woman elected to Congress in 1968. She began her career as a nursery school teacher, later serving as the director of a child-care center in New York and then as an educational consultant in the division of day care of the New York City Bureau of Child Welfare. In 1964 she was elected to the New York State legislature.

Cullen, Countée (1903–46), poet. A gifted student to whom academic honors came easily, Cullen was fortunate to be the foster son of the minister of one of Harlem's largest churches. He won a city-wide poetry contest while still in high school and went on to win several more prizes and to publish regularly in major literary magazines. His first collection of poetry, *Color* (1925), was published before he finished college. After receiving his M.A. from Harvard, Cullen spent two years in France and England on a Guggenheim Fellowship where he met many leading writers. From 1934 until his death he taught French at Frederick Douglass High School. Notable works include: *Copper Sun* (1927), *The Ballad of the Brown Girl* (1928), and *The Medea and Some Poems* (1935).

Davis, Benjamin O. (1877–1970), army officer. In 1940 Davis became the first African American in the U.S. armed forces to be promoted to the rank of brigadier general. He had begun his career as a volunteer in the army during the Spanish-American war and later went on to serve in the Philippines during World War I and to teach military science at Wilberforce University and Tuskegee Institute. In 1938 he became the commanding officer of the all-black 369th Harlem Regiment of the New York National Guard. After his promotion to brigadier general, Davis served as an advisor on the use of black troops to General Eisenhower. He retired in 1948.

Douglass, Frederick (1817–95), abolitionist, orator. Douglass was an escaped slave whose natural gift for expressing himself brought him to the forefront of the abolitionist movement. His autobiography, *Life and Times of Frederick Douglass,* continues to be a popular primary source on slavery. Douglass made enough money on a two-year speaking tour of Great Britain and Ireland to found his own antislavery newspaper, the *North Star* (later *Frederick Douglass's Paper*), which he published from 1847 to 1860. He served as a consultant to President Lincoln during the Civil War and later fought for civil rights and the women's movement. He served at various government posts, the last as U.S. minister and consul general to Haiti.

Du Bois, W(illiam) E(dward) B(urghardt) (1868–63), sociologist, protest leader. Du Bois' early studies on race relations were the first empirical inquiries into the condition of African Americans. He gradually moved away from academic inquiry, however, and became more politically outspoken. His book, *The Souls of Black Folk* (1903), made him famous as an adversary of Booker T. Washington and his philosophy of accommodation. In 1905 Du Bois helped to found the Niagara Movement, whose chief purpose was to attack the ideas of Washington, and in 1909 he also helped to found the NAACP, becoming its director of research and serving as editor of its magazine, *Crisis,* from 1910 to 1934. Du Bois believed that all people of African descent should work together for freedom (Pan-Africanism). He encouraged the development of African American literature and art, and lectured that African Americans should develop a separate "group economy" as a way to combat discrimination and poverty. Du Bois' leftist views eventually caused him to be indicted as a spy. Although acquitted, Du Bois in 1961 joined the Communist Party, moved to Ghana, and renounced his American citizenship.

Ellison, Ralph (1914–), writer. Ellison's one novel, *Invisible Man* (1952), a National Book Award winner, describes the emotional withdrawal of a man overwhelmed by the irrationality of society. The contradiction of the concept of the existence of individuality in modern society is also a theme in his collection of essays *Shadow and Act* (1964). Ellison studied at Tuskegee Institute from 1933 to 1936, then left for New York City where he worked for the Federal Writers Project. He received a Rosenwald Fellowship in 1945, which enabled him to write *Invisible Man.* After lecturing in Rome for two years, he joined the faculty of Bard College in 1958, teaching Russian and American literature until 1961. Since that time he has been a visiting professor and lecturer at numerous universities.

Garvey, Marcus (1887–1940), leader. In 1914 Garvey founded the Universal Negro Improvement Association in Jamaica, where he was born. The movement had a greater following in the U.S., however, where, by the 1920s there were almost a million members. In 1918 he founded a newspaper, *Negro World,* to laud African American heroes and to extol African culture. He believed that racial discrimination would end only with African Americans becoming economically independent within the framework of white capitalism. His steamship line, the Black Star Line, which he founded in 1919 to promote African American trade, suspended operations in 1922 when he was indicted for mail fraud. After serving two years of a subsequent five-year sentence, Garvey's sentence was commuted by President Coolidge, and he was deported to Jamaica. He died in relative obscurity.

Handy, W. C. (1873–1958), composer. Known as the "father of the blues," Handy was the son of a minister who disapproved of his son's musical bent. He had various jobs as a schoolteacher, bandleader, and cornetist. Handy was a natural entrepreneur, however, and quickly saw the commercial value in the folk music of poor southern African Americans, which he arranged to blend with the popular music of the time—ragtime. He first received attention with "Memphis Blues" (1909), which he composed as a campaign song for Memphis mayor E. H. Crump. His most famous song, "St. Louis Blues" (1914), necessitated the founding of his own publishing company, the Handy Brothers Music Co., in order to get it published.

Henson, Matthew (1866–1955), explorer. Henson was orphaned at an early age and went to sea as a cabin boy. He met Lt. Robert Peary in 1887, and Peary asked him to accompany him on a trip to survey a canal route through Nicaragua. He subsequently became Peary's attendant on his other expeditions, and in 1909 he, Peary, and four Eskimos became the first men to reach the North Pole. He published his account of the journey in *A Negro Explorer at the North Pole* in 1912.

Holiday, Billie (1915–59), singer. Although she never had any technical training as a singer, Billie Holiday is considered to be the most outstanding jazz singer of her time. She was especially known for her unique phrasing and the dramatic intensity she brought to her songs. She first encountered music through Louis Armstrong and Bessie Smith records, which she was permitted to listen to by the brothel owner for whom she ran errands as a child. She debuted in 1931 in obscure Harlem nightclubs and made her first records two years later. By 1940 she was a nightclub solo attraction. She eventually succumbed to what had been a long struggle with an addiction to heroin.

Hughes, Langston (1902–67), writer. Hughes began writing poetry when he was still in school and had his first poem published when he was 18 ("The Negro Speaks of Rivers"). By the time he graduated from college, he had won two poetry prizes and published two books, *The Weary Blues* (1926) and *Fine Clothes to the Jew* (1927). A novel, a short story anthology, and volume I of his autobiography followed. Aside from his own contributions to American culture, Hughes was an important force in promoting the contributions of other Afri-

can Americans (*The First Book of Negroes*, 1952, and *Famous American Negroes*, 1954). He was a newspaper correspondent during the Spanish Civil War and later wrote a column for which he created the character of Jesse B. Semple, later adapted into a successful Broadway play. Hughes' work remains cogent and popular because it is a true and entertaining reflection of the rhythms, idioms, and symbols of African American culture.

Hurston, Zora Neale (1903–60), writer. Part of the Harlem Renaissance of the 1920s, Hurston wrote about African American culture through the eyes of an anthropologist and ethnologist. Her novel *Their Eyes Were Watching God* (1937) was both controversial and widely acclaimed, as it neither endorsed the myth of African American inferiority, nor portrayed African Americans as victims of it. The subject of racial tension and traces of white culture are notably absent from her fiction, which liberally incorporates folklore and African American vernacular. Hurston's writing influenced such contemporary African American authors as Ralph Ellison and Toni Morrison.

Johnson, John H. (1918–), publisher. While working as a clerk and editor of the house newsletter at Supreme Life Insurance Company, a company serving primarily the black community in Chicago, it occured to Johnson that there might be a market for a digest of magazine stories, similar to *Reader's Digest*, but focusing exclusively on stories of interest to African Americans. Borrowing money on his mother's furniture, Johnson launched the risky publication, *Negro Digest*, and its first issue (1942) sold some 3,000 copies. The success of *Negro Digest* led to another black-oriented magazine, *Ebony*, which was patterned after *Life*. *Ebony* was an immediate success, quickly selling out its initial press run of 25,000 copies. Johnson went on to start other magazines, *Jet*, *Ebony Jr.*, and *Ebony Man* as well as venture into radio and television broadcasting and book publication. Johnson subsequently became one of the richest men, black or white, in the United States.

Joplin, Scott (1868–1917), composer. Joplin hoped to become a classical pianist and composer, but he is most famous as the "king of ragtime." His 1907 instruction book, *The School of Ragtime*, outlined the rudiments of his unique style, which were widely imitated and hugely popular. His final years were occupied with his three-act opera, *Treemonisha*, a synthesis of his musical ideas. The opera was not a commercial success, and its failure led Joplin to suffer a nervous breakdown for which he was subsequently institutionalized.

King, Martin Luther, Jr. (1929–68), civil rights leader. King first came to public prominence as the leader of the Montgomery bus boycott that began in 1955. A well-educated, well-respected Baptist minister, his eloquent speeches helped give the boycott credence. He went on to found the Southern Christian Leadership Conference and tour the country lecturing on civil rights and African American problems. A believer in the nonviolent philosophy of Mohandas Gandhi, King and his followers sought to confront segregation and discrimination with direct action—sit-ins, walks, and marches. The most famous example of his nonviolent confrontation was the 1963 March on Washington, where 200,000 people heard King's "I Have a Dream" speech. In town to support a strike by city sanitation workers, King was assassinated on the balcony of his Memphis hotel room on April 4, 1968. He is the first African American to be honored with a national holiday, held around his birthday on the third Monday in January.

Lawrence, Jacob (1917–), painter. Lawrence received his early training as an artist at free art classes in Harlem, and he went on to study at the Harlem Art Workshop. Working primarily in gouache and oil, Lawrence painted series on historical and social themes and on the lives of Frederick Douglass and Harriet Tubman. He was awarded the Spingarn Medal in 1970. In 1972 he was appointed head of the art department at the University of Washington.

Louis, Joe (1914–81), boxer. Louis began boxing in Detroit in 1930, winning the U.S. Amateur Athletic Union championship in 1934, after which he turned professional. As a professional he won 68 of 71 bouts, 54 of them by knockouts. Louis suffered his first defeat at the hands of Max Schmeling, former heavyweight champion, in 1936 but came back to win the title when he knocked out Jim Braddock in the eighth round. (He successfully defended his title against Schmeling in 1938.) Known as the "Brown Bomber," Louis held the world heavyweight championship title longer than any other boxer, from 1937 to 1949, when he retired. His second and third defeats came in a comeback attempt in 1950, when he lost a fifteen-round decision to Ezzard Charles; he then went on to fight eight more times, only to lose in 1951 to Rocky Marciano. He was elected to the Boxing Hall of Fame in 1954.

Malcolm X (1925–65), African American activist. In jail for burglary in 1946, Malcolm Little converted to the Black Muslim faith (Nation of Islam) and changed his name to Malcolm X. Upon his release in 1952 he met the Nation's leader, Elijah Muhammad, who sent him on speaking tours promoting the Nation's separatist views, including the use of violence for self-protection. Malcolm X's growing popularity put him at odds with Muhammad, who suspended him from the movement in 1964. Malcolm responded by founding the Organization of Afro-American Unity and making a pilgrimage to Mecca, after which he later converted to orthodox Islam and ceased to speak of whites as evil. As his following continued to grow, threats against his life increased, and he was eventually assassinated at a rally in Harlem by Black Muslims. *The Autobiography of Malcolm X*, published after his death, helped to make him a legendary figure.

Marshall, Thurgood (1908–), jurist. Marshall became the first African American member of the U.S. Supreme Court in 1967. He graduated first in his class from Howard University Law School in 1933 and went on to become chief of the legal staff for the NAACP. He was appointed a judge of the U.S. circuit court of appeals in New York in 1961 and in 1965 became the solicitor general of the United States. During his tenure at the NAACP, Marshall argued 32 cases before the Supreme Court and won 29 of them, among which was the famous *Brown* v. *the Board of Education of Topeka* (1954) in which racial segregation in public schools was declared unconstitutional. A consistent liberal on the Supreme Court, Marshall continued to champion the rights of minorities. He retired from the court in 1991.

Mitchell, Arthur (1934–), ballet dancer. Mitchell received his early training at the High School for the Performing Arts in New York City. In 1956 he became the only African American dancer in the New York City Ballet, soon becoming a principal of the company. In 1966 he formed the integrated American Dance Company, which debuted in 1971 in New York City and at the Spoleto Festival in Italy. He was also the founder of the Dance Theater of Harlem.

Motley, Archibald (1891-1981), painter. Motley painted African American people in vibrant colors, capturing them in the middle of their everyday activities, a novel idea for a time when African American themes meant pictures of mammies and still-lifes with African masks. Having grown up in an all-white neighborhood, Motley's experience with African Americans was curiously more from an outsider's point of view; he studied his subjects almost like an anthropologist. He sought to paint people honestly, neither glorifying nor detracting, in order to bring about a better understanding between blacks and whites. Motley had only one major show during his lifetime, at the New Gallery in New York City in 1928.

Muhammad, Elijah (1896–1975), religious leader. Muhammad's life changed in his early 30s when he met religious leader Wallace Fard, founder of the Nation of Islam, and became an assistant minister in the sect. Upon Fard's disappearance in 1934, Muhammad succeeded him as the head of the

movement. He and his followers were known for their extreme separatist views and hatred of whites. Later, Muhammad softened his position somewhat, advocating self-help and self-sufficiency among African Americans.

Owens, Jesse (1913–80), track-and-field athlete. Owens won four gold medals in the 1936 Olympic Games in Berlin (much to the chagrin of Adolf Hitler, who had intended the games to prove Aryan superiority). Owens' world record for the long jump (8.06 meters) stood for 25 years. He also set world records in the 200-meter run (20.7 seconds) and the 400-meter relay (39.8 seconds) and tied the Olympic record in the 100-meter run (10.3 seconds). Owens went on to work in community service with young people, promoting patriotism, clean living, and the importance of fair play.

Parks, Rosa (1913–), civil rights activist. On the evening of December 1, 1955, Rosa Parks was tired after a long day of work. So tired that, when ordered to give up her seat on the crowded bus to a white man, she refused. Her subsequent arrest became the catalyst for the Montgomery, Alabama, bus boycott, led by Martin Luther King, Jr., in which Montgomery's black residents refused to ride the segregated public buses for more than a year. Because the bus boycott brought King to public prominence and virtually launched the civil rights movement, Parks is known as the mother of the modern civil rights movement. The pressures of the situation, however, eventually forced the Parks family to leave Montgomery for Detroit, where she became involved in youth work, job guidance, and cultural and recreational planning.

Poitier, Sidney (1924–), actor. Widely recognized as the actor who broke the color barrier in the U.S. motion-picture industry, Poitier in 1963 became the first African American to win an Academy Award for best actor (in *Lilies of the Field*). Poitier grew up in the British West Indies, and when he first decided to become an actor—at the American Negro Theater in New York City—he was turned down because of his accent. He spent six months practicing enunciation and listening to the radio, and when he tried again was accepted. He first won acclaim on Broadway in 1959 as the star of *A Raisin in the Sun,* going on to star in many major motion pictures, among them *Blackboard Jungle* (1955), *The Defiant Ones* (1958), *In the Heat of the Night* (1967), and *Guess Who's Coming to Dinner* (1967).

Powell, Adam Clayton, Jr. (1908–72), political leader. Powell followed in his successful father's footsteps as he received his DD degree 1935 and became assistant pastor, then successor, to his father at the Abyssinian Baptist Church in Harlem. Powell's charismatic oratorical style and his drive to achieve, however, led him to a career in politics, where he played an active role in the growing civil rights movement, especially in organizing direct action forces to end discriminatory labor practices. In 1941 he became the first African American elected to the New York City Council, and in 1944 he was elected to the U.S. House of Representatives. Although he later came under severe criticism from Congress for alleged misuse of money, absenteeism, and failure to pay damages owed because of a 1960 libel suit, Powell's prestige as a national African American political figure had no contemporary equal.

Price, Leontyne (1929–), opera singer. Price's first singing experiences were in her church choir, but it was not until graduating from college that she decided to make a career of singing, going on to study at the Julliard School of Music. She made her singing debut in 1952 in a Broadway revival of *Four Saints in Three Acts,* which led to her being chosen to play Bess in Gershwin's revival of *Porgy and Bess.* She first sang opera on television in a 1955 production of *Tosca,* and her stage debut took place in 1957 with the San Francisco Opera, with which she sang until 1960. Although now one of the most popular opera singers in the United States and lauded in Europe, it was not until 1961 that she first sang at the Metropolitan Opera in New York, in the difficult role of

Leonora in *Il Trovatore*. After that brilliant performance she subsequently became one of the Met's leading sopranos.

Randolph, A. Philip (1889–1979), civil rights leader. In 1925 Randolph founded and became president of the first successful African American trade union, the Brotherhood of Sleeping Car Porters. A radical socialist, Randolph worked tirelessly for unionism and integration. In 1941 he threatened President Roosevelt with a march on Washington to protest racial discrimination in wartime hiring. The president's subsequent executive order made that practice illegal. Seven years later, again after pushing by Randolph, President Truman banned discrimination in the armed forces. Randolph was an obvious choice for a director of the 1963 March on Washington, and his arguments helped win the support of President Kennedy. In 1955 Randolph was made a vice president and member of the executive council of the newly combined AFL-CIO. He retired from public life in 1968.

Robeson, Paul (1898–1976), singer, actor, African American activist. Robeson's full, basso voice lent special force to African American spirituals and international folk songs, which he sang on tours throughout the world. His signature song was "Ol' Man River" from the musical *Showboat*. An all-American football player and valedictorian at Rutgers University, Robeson went on to earn a law degree from Columbia University in 1923 but abandoned a career in law for the stage. He first won acclaim for his performance in the title role in *Emperor Jones* in 1924 and went on to star in several films and plays. In the mid 1930s Robeson became increasingly involved in international movements for peace, racial equality, and better labor conditions. As a result of his activities, and for his refusal to sign an affidavit disclaiming membership in the Communist Party, the U.S. government suspended his passport, an act that effectively ended his career until the suspension was revoked in 1958 by the Supreme Court. Robeson then moved to London and resumed touring, but returned to the U.S. in 1963 when ill health forced him to retire.

Robinson, Bill (1878–1949), tap dancer. Robinson was orphaned at an early age and raised by his grandmother. As a stableboy in Washington, D.C. he began tap dancing on street corners for money. Eventually he made it to vaudeville where he became one of its biggest stars. He is most widely known for his performances in fourteen films, three of them with Shirley Temple (*The Little Colonel*, 1935; *The Littlest Rebel,* 1935; and *Rebecca of Sunnybrook Farm,* 1937) and his ingenious creation of new dance steps, among them the famous "stair dance."

Robinson, Jackie (1919–72), baseball player. Robinson was an outstanding athlete in college. After a tour in the army he played in the American Negro Baseball League for the Kansas City Monarchs. From there he was chosen by Branch Rickey, head of the Brooklyn Dodgers, to be the first official African American player in the major leagues. He was named Rookie of the Year in 1947 and went on to help to the Dodgers win six pennants and one World Series. His career batting average was .311. He was elected to the Baseball Hall of Fame in 1962. After retiring in 1957 he served as vice president of Chock Full O'Nuts, as cochairman of the Freedom National Bank of Harlem, and as an aide to New York Governor Nelson Rockefeller.

Rudolph, Wilma (1940–), track-and-field athlete. Rudolph was the first American woman to win three track-and-field gold medals in the Olympic Games (Rome, 1960). She won the 200-meter run and set world records in the 100-meter run (11.2 seconds) and the 400-meter relay (44.4 seconds). Rudolph's achievements were remarkable because, until age 11, she wore a brace on her leg, the result of the combined effects of pneumonia, scarlet fever, and polio when she was 4. Her determination to excel in sports made her a star basketball player and runner and first carried her to the Olympics at the age of 16 (Melbourne, 1956), where she won a bronze medal for the 400-meter relay. After retiring from running in

the mid 1960s, Rudolph went on to work with young people promoting sports and education.

Smalls, Robert (1839–1915), Civil War hero. On May 13, 1862, Smalls and 12 other slaves seized control of the Confederate frigate *Planter*, on which Smalls was the wheelman, and turned it over to the blockading Union naval squadron in Charleston, South Carolina. Smalls continued to serve as pilot on the ship and became its captain in 1863. After the war, Smalls went into politics, serving from 1868 to 1870 in the South Carolina House of Representatives, from 1871 to 1874 in the state Senate, from 1875 to 1879, and again from 1881 to 1887 in the U.S. Congress. Although convicted in 1877 for accepting a $5,000 bribe while in the state Senate, he was pardoned by the governor.

Smith, Bessie (1894–1937), singer. Known as the "Empress of the Blues," Smith began her singing career in the saloons and small theaters of the South. She was eventually discovered by pianist Clarence Williams of Columbia Records and made her first recording in 1923. She became a huge success and recorded with such famous performers as Louis Armstrong, Fletcher Henderson, and Benny Goodman. In 1929 she made a short motion picture, *St. Louis Blues*, which was initially banned for its realism. By the time of the Depression, however, the blues had lost its popularity, and her career was in decline. She died from injuries sustained in a car accident.

Tanner, Henry Ossawa (1859–1937), painter. After studying with Thomas Easton and teaching briefly at Clark University, Tanner went to Paris to continue his studies. His subjects were mostly biblical, which he rendered in a conservative style. Finding it difficult to work in the United States because of the racism he experienced there, he remained an expatriate in France, returning only to exhibit his works. The recipient of many awards, Tanner was made a chevalier of the Légion d'Honneur in 1923.

Truth, Sojourner (1797–1883), evangelist, reformer. Originally named Isabella, Truth was given her freedom by her last master just before New York state outlawed slavery in 1827. As Isabella Van Wagener, she went to New York City in 1829 and became involved with various religious groups, supporting herself as a servant. She left the city in 1843, changed her name to Sojourner Truth, and became a travelling preacher. She encountered the abolitionist movement in Northampton, Mass., and thereafter became one of its primary figures. Soon after she also became an advocate of women's rights, and she travelled widely in the East and Midwest lecturing on these topics. In 1864 she was received at the White House by President Lincoln and later was appointed to the National Freedmen's Relief Association, counseling ex-slaves.

Tubman, Harriet (1820–1913), abolitionist, activist. Known as the "Moses of her people," Tubman escaped slavery in Maryland to become one of the primary "conductors" on the Underground Railroad, leading two to three hundred slaves to freedom in the North. During the Civil War she served as a nurse, laundress, and spy with the Federal forces in South Carolina. She was awarded numerous honors, but did not receive a pension for her war efforts until thirty years later.

Turner, Nat (1800–31), slave rebellion leader. Inspired by religious fanaticism and a vehement hatred of slavery, Turner, on August 21, 1831, led a rebellion that began with the murder of his master's family and ended only a few miles from the county seat of Jerusalem, the intended destination. Along the way he had collected only 75 followers, most of whom were killed or captured outside of Jerusalem. Turner himself escaped but was captured six weeks later and hanged. The rebellion terrified southerners, who had always believed that slaves were too contented or too servile to rebel. As a consequence, a new wave of oppressive legislation spread throughout the South.

Walker, Alice (1944–), poet, novelist. Although Walker published her first book of poetry in 1968 (*Once*) and continued regularly to publish novels, short stories, and volumes of poetry, it was not until the publication of her third novel, *The Color Purple* in 1982, that she achieved real recognition. The novel won the American Book Award and the Pulitzer Prize in 1983, and in 1985 it was made into a successful motion picture. Walker's works primarily depict strong black women facing constant battles against sexism and racism, and they have been praised for the truth they reveal about what is mostly a neglected topic in modern American literature. Other works include: *Revolutionary Petunias & Other Poems* (1973), *In Love and Trouble: Stories of Black Women* (1973), *You Can't Keep a Good Woman Down* (1981), and *The Temple of My Familiar* (1989).

Walker, Madame C. J. (Sarah Breedlove Walker) (1867–1919), businesswoman. Regarded as the first African American woman millionaire in the United States, Walker was orphaned at 7, first married at 14, and left a widow with a young daughter at 20. She made her fortune after developing a method of straightening curly hair. She subsequently developed an entire line of beauty products, which were sold door-to-door by "Walker agents"—saleswomen dressed in white blouses and long black skirts. She also established several Walker Schools of Beauty around the country. Walker shared her wealth freely, donating large sums to such organizations as the NAACP, Bethune-Cookman College, and homes for the aged.

Washington, Booker T. (1856–1915), educator, reformer. Washington rose from slavery and poverty to become the first president of Tuskegee Institute, which he developed into a well-endowed, well-equipped, prestigious facility that annually taught trades and professions to some 1,500 students. Washington believed that the best way for African Americans to gain respect and political power from the white community was to temporarily forget about civil rights and segregation and instead focus on economic stability by acquiring a vocational education and practicing patience, enterprise, and thrift. He was most influential between 1895 and 1915. One of his most outspoken opponents was W. E. B. DuBois.

Wells-Barnett, Ida Bell (1862–1931), journalist and reformer. Wells-Barnett is best known for her writings and lectures against the practice of lynching. In 1892, after three of her friends had been lynched, she decried the act in an editorial in the *Memphis Free Speech* (of which she was part owner). As a result, the newspaper's office was burned down, and she was run out of town. In 1893 she settled in Chicago where she organized a African American women's club and the Chicago Negro Fellowship League and helped to found the National Association for the Advancement of Colored People. Her paper *The Red Record* (1895) was the first published statistical study of lynching and earned her international acclaim. She was also a strong advocate of women's rights and campaigned for women's suffrage.

Wheatley, Phillis (1753–84), poet. Wheatley was taught to read and write by understanding masters, and at the age of 14 began writing poetry. Her work, published when she was 16, was largely pious, lauding such popular figures as George Whitefield and George Washington, and she became very popular in America and Europe. Wheatley was invited to the White House to have dinner with the Washingtons after her literary tour of London at the age of 18. She eventually married a man who was unsuccessful in business, however, and died in poverty.

Wilkins, Roy (1901–81), civil rights leader. Wilkins served the NAACP for fifty years in various capacities, including editor of *The Crisis* (1934–49) and executive secretary (1955–77). He won the U.S. Medal of Freedom in 1968 and the Joseph Prize for Human Rights in 1975. He helped to organize the 1963 March on Washington. A proponent of nonviolence, he believed that the best way to combat racism and discrimination was to make their evils plain to all; good-hearted people,

then, could not fail to notice the injustices. Wilkins devoted his life to the NAACP and the civil rights movement as well and was often referred to as its senior statesman.

Wilson, August (1945–), playwright. The New York Drama Critics Circle has chosen several of Wilson's plays to receive its award for best play of the year: *Ma Rainey's Black Bottom* (1985), *Fences* (1987), *Joe Turner's Come and Gone* (1988), *The Piano Lesson* (1989), and *Two Trains Running* (1990). *Fences* won both the Tony Award for best play of 1987 and the Pulitzer Prize; Wilson received his second Pulitzer for *The Piano Lesson*. Wilson's plays chronicle the cycle of black history in the 20th century, decade by decade, and they all attempt to show the importance of reconnecting with the past, with the South, to discover the black man's relation to American society.

Wright, Richard (1908–60), novelist. Wright grew up in poverty in Mississippi and eventually moved to Chicago where he began working for the Federal Writers' Project. His leftist political views led him to join the Communist Party in 1932, but he rescinded his membership in 1944 because of personal differences. He later settled permanently in Paris. More than that of any other writer, Wright's work marks the beginning of a period of black protest in modern American literature. In his novels and stories he explored the position of the black man in a white society. His most famous work, *Native Son* (1940) describes the plight of Bigger Thomas, who accidentally kills a white girl. It was an instant best-seller and was adapted for Broadway in 1941. Wright first received attention for a volume of novellas, *Uncle Tom's Children* (1938), which was based on his boyhood experiences in Mississippi. Other works include the autobiographical *Black Boy* (1945), *The Outsider* (1953), and *Eight Men* (1961).

Vaughan, Sarah (1924–), singer. "The Divine One" began singing at an early age in her church choir. In 1943 on a dare she entered a talent contest at Harlem's Apollo Theater and not only won, but was lucky enough to be heard by singer Billy Eckstine, who then recommended her to his boss, Earl Hines. Vaughan subsequently joined Hines' band (among whom the other members were Dizzy Gillespie and Charlie Parker). When Eckstine left to form his own band, she and Gillespie and Parker joined him, and she made her first recording with them in 1944. By 1945 she was recording and performing solo, and by 1951 she was a major concert attraction in the United States and Europe. Her voice had the range of an opera star, and her virtuosity in improvisation and interpretation were famous.

Chemical Elements

Element	Symbol	Atomic Number	Discoverer	Year
actinium	Ac	89	Debierne	1899
aluminum	Al	13	Oersted	1825
americium	Am	95	Seaborg, James, Morgan, Ghiorso	1944
antimony	Sb	51	Early historic times	——
argon	Ar	18	Rayleigh and Ramsay	1894
arsenic	As	33	Albertus Magnus	1250?
astatine	At	85	Corson, Segre, Mackenzie	1940
barium	Ba	56	Davy	1808
berkelium	Bk	97	Seaborg, Thompson, Ghiorso	1949
beryllium	Be	4	Vauquelin	1798
bismuth	Bi	83	Geoffroy	1753
boron	B	5	Gay-Lussac and Thénard; Davy	1808
bromine	Br	35	Balard	1826
cadmium	Cd	48	Stromeyer	1817
calcium	Ca	20	Davy	1808
californium	Cf	98	Seaborg, Thompson, Ghiorso, Street	1950
carbon	C	6	Prehistoric	——
cerium	Ce	58	Berzelius and Hisinger; Klaproth	1803
cesium	Cs	55	Bunsen and Kirchhoff	1860
chlorine	Cl	17	Scheele	1774
chromium	Cr	24	Vauquelin	1797
cobalt	Co	27	Brandt	1735
copper	Cu	29	prehistoric	——
curium	Cm	96	Seaborg, James, Ghiorso	1944
dysprosium	Dy	66	Boisbaudran	1886
einsteinium	Es	99	Ghiorso et al.	1952
element 104	——	104	claimed by Flerov and others claimed by Ghiorso and others	1964 1968
element 105	——	105	claimed by Flerov and others claimed by Ghiorso and others	1968 1970
element 106	——	106	claimed by Flerov and others claimed by Ghiorso and others	1974 1974
element 107	——	107	claimed by Flerov, Oganessian and others claimed by Armbruster and others	1976 1981
erbium	Er	68	Mosander	1843
europium	Eu	63	Demarçay	1901
fermium	Fm	100	Ghiorso et al.	1953
fluorine	F	9	Moissan	1886

Element	Symbol	Atomic Number	Discoverer	Year
francium	Fr	87	Perey	1939
gadolinium	Gd	64	Marignac	1880
gallium	Ga	31	Boisbaudran	1875
germanium	Ge	32	Winkler	1886
gold	Au	79	prehistoric	——
hafnium	Hf	72	Coster and von Hevesy	1923
helium	He	2	Janssen	1868
holmium	Ho	67	Delafontaine and Soret	1878
hydrogen	H	1	Cavendish	1766
indium	In	49	Reich and Richter	1863
iodine	I	53	Courtois	1811
iridium	Ir	77	Tennant	1804
iron	Fe	26	prehistoric	——
krypton	Kr	36	Ramsay and Travers	1898
lanthanum	La	57	Mosander	1839
lawrencium	Lr	103	Ghiorso, Sikkeland, Larsh, Latimer	1961
lead	Pb	82	prehistoric	——
lithium	Li	3	Arfvedson	1817
lutetium	Lu	71	Urbain	1907
magnesium	Mg	12	Davy	1808
manganese	Mn	25	Gahn	1774
mendelevium	Md	101	Ghiorso, Seaborg, Harvey, Choppin, Thompson	1955
mercury	Hg	80	prehistoric	——
molybdenum	Mo	42	Scheele	1778
neodymium	Nd	60	von Welsbach	1885
neon	Ne	10	Ramsay and Travers	1898
neptunium	Np	93	McMillan and Abelson	1940
nickel	Ni	28	Cronstedt	1751
niobium (colum-bium)	Nb	41	Hatchett	1801
nitrogen	N	7	Rutherford	1772
nobelium	No	102	Ghiorso et al.	1957
osmium	Os	76	Tennant	1804
oxygen	O	8	Priestley, Scheele	1774
palladium	Pd	46	Wollaston	1803
phosphorus	P	15	Brandt	1669
platinum	Pt	78	Ulloa	1735
plutonium	Pu	94	Seaborg, McMillan, Kennedy, Wahl	1940
polonium	Po	84	P. and M. Curie	1898
potassium	K	19	Davy	1807
praseodymium	Pr	59	von Welsbach	1885
promethium	Pm	61	Marinsky, Glendenin, Coryell	1945
radium	Ra	88	P. and M. Curie	1898
radon	Rn	86	Dorn	1900

Element	Symbol	Atomic Number	Discoverer	Year
rhenium	Re	75	Noddack, Berg, Tacke	1925
rhodium	Rh	45	Wollaston	1803
rubidium	Rb	37	Bunsen, Kirchoff	1861
ruthenium	Ru	44	Klaus	1844
samarium	Sm	62	Boisbaudran	1879
scandium	Sc	21	Nilson	1879
selenium	Se	34	Berzelius	1817
silicon	Si	14	Berzelius	1823
silver	Ag	47	prehistoric	—
sodium	Na	11	Davy	1807
strontium	Sr	38	Crawford	1790
sulfur	S	16	prehistoric	—
tantalum	Ta	73	Ekeberg	1802
technetium	Tc	43	Perrier and Segrè	1937
tellurium	Te	52	von Reichenstein	1782
terbium	Tb	65	Mosander	1843
thallium	Tl	81	Crookes	1861
thorium	Th	90	Berzelius	1828
thulium	Tm	69	Cleve	1879
tin	Sn	50	prehistoric	—
titanium	Ti	22	Gregor	1791
tungsten (wolfram)	W	74	J. and F. d'Elhuyar	1783
uranium	U	92	Klaproth	1789
vanadium	V	23	Sefström	1830
xenon	Xe	54	Ramsay and Travers	1898
ytterbium	Yb	70	Marignac	1878
yttrium	Y	39	Gadolin	1794
zinc	Zn	30	prehistoric	—
zirconium	Zr	40	Klaproth	1789

Periodic Table of Elements

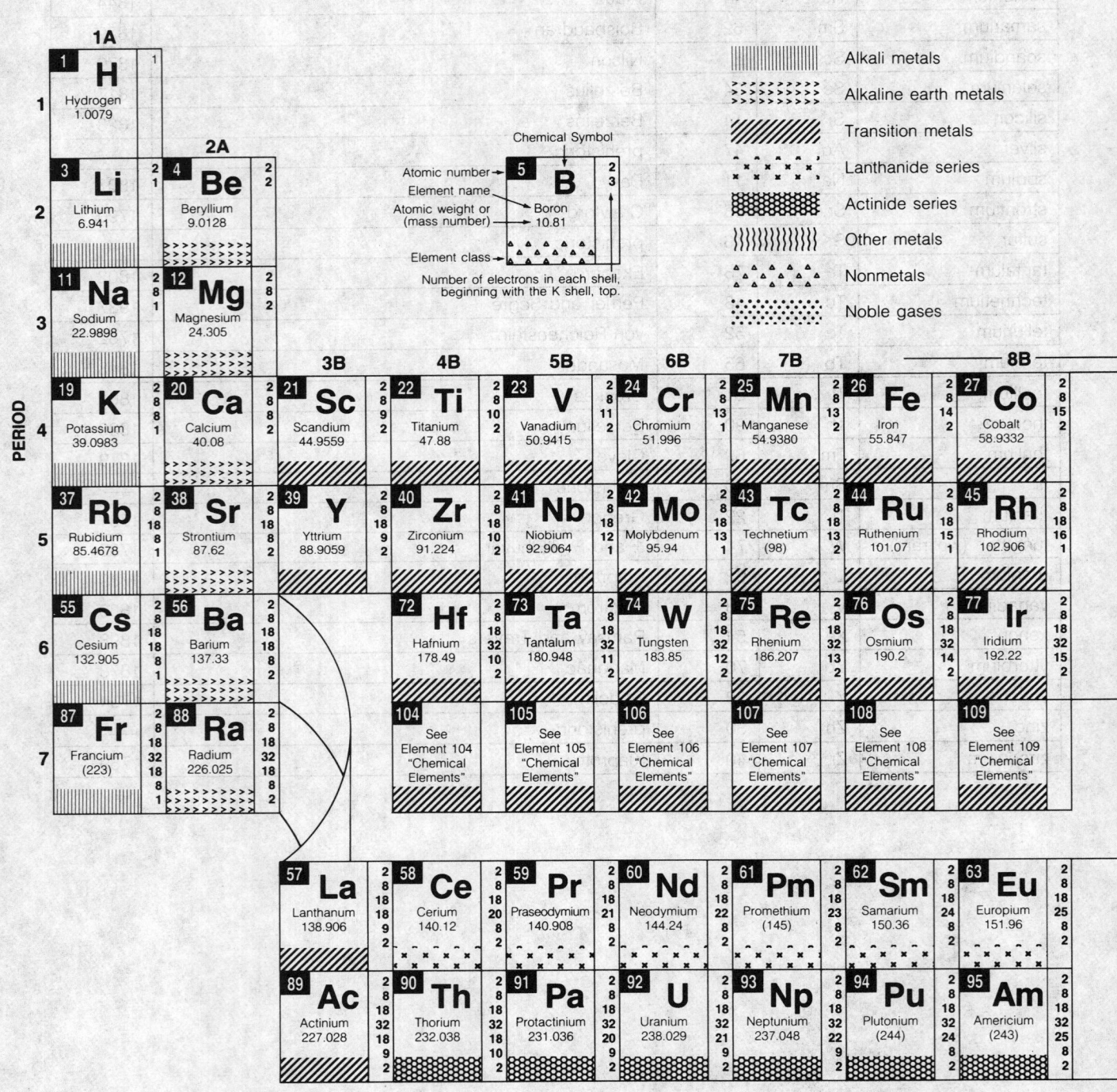

							8A
							2 **He** 2 / Helium 4.00260

3A	4A	5A	6A	7A	
5 **B** 2/3 Boron 10.81	**6** **C** 2/4 Carbon 12.011	**7** **N** 2/5 Nitrogen 14.0067	**8** **O** 2/6 Oxygen 15.9994	**9** **F** 2/7 Fluorine 18.9984	**10** **Ne** 2/8 Neon 20.179
13 **Al** 2/8/3 Aluminum 26.9815	**14** **Si** 2/8/4 Silicon 28.0855	**15** **P** 2/8/5 Phosphorus 30.9738	**16** **S** 2/8/6 Sulfur 32.06	**17** **Cl** 2/8/7 Chlorine 35.453	**18** **Ar** 2/8/8 Argon 39.948

1B	2B						
28 **Ni** 2/8/16/2 Nickel 58.69	**29** **Cu** 2/8/18/1 Copper 63.546	**30** **Zn** 2/8/18/2 Zinc 65.39	**31** **Ga** 2/8/18/3 Gallium 69.72	**32** **Ge** 2/8/18/4 Germanium 72.59	**33** **As** 2/8/18/5 Arsenic 74.9216	**34** **Se** 2/8/18/6 Selenium 78.96	**35** **Br** 2/8/18/7 Bromine 79.904	**36** **Kr** 2/8/18/8 Krypton 83.80
46 **Pd** 2/8/18/18/0 Palladium 106.42	**47** **Ag** 2/8/18/18/1 Silver 107.868	**48** **Cd** 2/8/18/18/1 Cadmium 112.41	**49** **In** 2/8/18/18/3 Indium 114.82	**50** **Sn** 2/8/18/18/4 Tin 118.71	**51** **Sb** 2/8/18/18/5 Antimony 121.75	**52** **Te** 2/8/18/18/6 Tellurium 127.60	**53** **I** 2/8/18/18/7 Iodine 126.905	**54** **Xe** 2/8/18/18/8 Xenon 131.29
78 **Pt** 2/8/18/32/17/1 Platinum 195.08	**79** **Au** 2/8/18/32/18/1 Gold 196.967	**80** **Hg** 2/8/18/32/18/2 Mercury 200.59	**81** **Tl** 2/8/18/32/18/3 Thallium 204.383	**82** **Pb** 2/8/18/32/18/4 Lead 207.2	**83** **Bi** 2/8/18/32/18/5 Bismuth 208.980	**84** **Po** 2/8/18/32/18/6 Polonium (209)	**85** **At** 2/8/18/32/18/7 Astatine (210)	**86** **Rn** 2/8/18/32/18/8 Radon (222)

64 **Gd** 2/8/18/25/9/2 Gadolinium 157.25	**65** **Tb** 2/8/18/27/8/2 Terbium 158.925	**66** **Dy** 2/8/18/28/8/2 Dysprosium 162.50	**67** **Ho** 2/8/18/29/8/2 Holmium 164.930	**68** **Er** 2/8/18/30/8/2 Erbium 167.26	**69** **Tm** 2/8/18/31/8/2 Thulium 168.934	**70** **Yb** 2/8/18/32/8/2 Ytterbium 173.04	**71** **Lu** 2/8/18/32/9/2 Lutetium 174.967
96 **Cm** 2/8/18/32/25/9/2 Curium (247)	**97** **Bk** 2/8/18/32/26/9/2 Berkelium (247)	**98** **Cf** 2/8/18/32/28/8/2 Californium (251)	**99** **Es** 2/8/18/32/29/8/2 Einsteinium (252)	**100** **Fm** 2/8/18/32/30/8/2 Fermium (257)	**101** **Md** 2/8/18/32/31/8/2 Mendelevium (258)	**102** **No** 2/8/18/32/32/8/2 Nobelium (259)	**103** **Lr** 2/8/18/32/32/9/2 Lawrencium (260)

Metrics Glossary

Ampere A unit for measuring the flow of electricity. Symbol: amp.

Area Amount of surface, measured in square units.

Are A metric surface measure, equal to 100 m². Symbol: a.

Atto- A prefix indicating one quintillionth of a given unit.

Barrel The amount contained in a barrel; especially the amount (as 31 gallons of fermented beverage or 42 gallons of petroleum) fixed for a certain commodity and used as a unit of measure for that particular commodity. Symbol: bbl.

Boardfoot A unit of quantity for lumber equal to the volume of a board 12 × 12 × 1 inches. Symbol: fbm.

Bushel A unit of dry capacity equal to 4 pecks (2150.42 in³) or 35.238 liters

Candela A unit for measuring the luminous intensity (amount) of a light produced by a light source.

Capacity See Volume.

Celsius The name of the scale for temperature commonly used in conjunction with the metric system. Also known as the Centigrade scale. In the Celsius scale, water boils at 100° C and freezes at 0° C, as opposed to 212° F and 32° F, respectively, in the Fahrenheit scale. Symbol: ° C.

Centare A metric surface measure equal to 1 m². Symbol: ca.

Centi- A prefix indicating one hundredth of a given unit.

Centigram One hundredth of a gram. Symbol: cg.

Centiliter One hundredth of a liter. Symbol: cl.

Centimeter One hundredth of a meter. One centimeter equals .3937 inch. Symbol: cm.

Chain A unit of measure equal to 66 feet (20.1168 meters). Symbol: ch.

Cubic unit symbols Examples: mm³, cm³, m³, etc., used to denote volume.

Customary unit Units of weights and measures currently in use in the United States, known also as English units. These include: inches, feet, yards, and miles for length; ounces, pounds, and tons for weight; pints, quarts, and gallons.

Deci- A prefix indicating one tenth of a given unit.

Decigram One tenth of a gram. Symbol: dg.

Deciliter One tenth of a liter. Roughly equal to .21 pint. Symbol: dl.

Decimeter Ten centimeters or one tenth of a meter. Symbol: dm.

Deka- A prefix indicating ten times a given unit.

Dekagram Ten grams. Symbol: dag.

Dekaliter Ten liters, roughly equivalent to 2.64 gallons. Symbol: dal.

Dekameter Ten meters. One dekameter roughly equals 10.91 yards. Symbol: dam.

Density The weight of any sample of a substance divided by the volume measure of that sample.

Dram A unit of avoirdupois weight equal to 27.343 grains or .0625 ounce (1.771 grams). Symbol: dr.

Fathom A unit of length equal to 6 feet (1.8288 meters) used for measuring the depth of water. Symbol: fath.

Femto- A prefix indicating one quadrillionth of a given unit.

Furlong A unit of distance equal to 220 yards (201.168 meters). No symbol.

Giga- A prefix indicating a billion times a given unit.

Gill A unit of liquid measure equal to .25 pint or 118.291 milliliters.

Grain A unit of weight equal to .002083 ounce (.0648 gram), originally based on the weight of a grain of wheat. Symbol: gr.

Gram A common metric unit of weight equal to one thousandth of a kilogram. Symbol: g.

Hectare The common unit of land measure in the metric system, equal to 100 acres or 10,000 square meters and equivalent to 2.471 acres. Symbol: ha.

Hecto- A prefix indicating one hundred times a given unit.

Hectogram One hundred grams. Symbol: hg.

Hectoliter One hundred liters. Symbol: hl.

Hectometer One hundred meters. Symbol: hm.

Hogshead A U.S. unit of capacity equal to 63 gallons (238.4809 liters). Symbol: hka.

Hundredweight A unit of weight (avoirdupois) commonly equivalent to 100 lbs. (45.359 kilograms) in the United States and 112 lbs (50.803 kilograms) in England. The former is known as the short hundredweight and the latter as the long hundredweight. Symbol: cwt.

Kelvin scale A temperature scale often used with the metric system and developed by the British physicist Lord Kelvin. The starting or zero point on the Kelvin scale is absolute zero (—273.15° C, —459.67° F)—the lowest theoretical temperature that a gas can reach. On this scale, water freezes at 273.15° K and boils at 373.15° K.

Kilo- A prefix indicating one thousand times a given unit.

Kilogram The standard unit of mass in the metric system. The kilogram is a cylinder of platinum-iridium alloy kept by the International Bureau of Weights and Measures near Paris. A duplicate kilogram is kept by the National Bureau of Standards in Washington and serves as the mass standard for the United States. One kilogram is approximately equal to 2.2 pounds. Symbol: kg.

Kiloliter One thousand liters. Symbol: kl.

Kilometer One thousand meters, equivalent to 3,280.8 feet or .621 mile. Symbol: km.

Link One of the standardized divisions of a surveyor's chain that is 7.92 inches (201.168 millimeters) long and serves as a measure of length. No symbol.

Liter The basic metric unit of liquid measure, equal to the volume of one kilogram of water at 4° C or one cubic decimeter. A liter is equivalent to 1.057 quarts. Symbol: l.

Lumen A unit for measuring the brightness of light when it reaches the surface of an object.

Mass The amount of material in an object, measured in kilograms (q.v.).

Mega- A prefix indicating one million times a given unit.

Meter The basic unit of length in the metric system. It is defined in terms of the wavelength of orange-red light emitted by a krypton-86 atom (1,650,763.73 such wavelengths to the meter). One meter equals 39.37 inches. Symbol: m.

Metric system A decimal system of weights and measures, adopted first in France and now in common use worldwide.

Metric ton One thousand kilograms, roughly equivalent to 2,200 pounds. Symbol: t.

Micron The millionth part of a meter. Symbol: μ.

Mile, International Nautical A unit of distance in sea and air navigation equal to 1.852 kilometers or 6,076.1033 feet.

Mill A unit of money (but not an actual coin) used primarily in accounting.

Milli- A prefix indicating one thousandth of a given unit.

Milligram One thousandth of a gram. Symbol: mg.
Milliliter One thousandth of a liter. Symbol: ml.
Millimeter One tenth of a centimeter or one thousandth of a meter. Symbol: mm.
Minim The smallest unit of liquid measure, the sixtieth part of a fluid dram, roughly equivalent to one drop.

Nano- A prefix indicating one billionth of a given unit.

Ounce, avoirdupois A unit of weight equal to 437.5 grains or .625 pound avoirdupois (28.349 grams). Symbol: oz. avdp.
Ounce, troy A unit of weight equal to 480 grains or .833 pound troy (31.103 grams). Symbol: oz. tr.

Peck A dry measure of 8 quarts or the fourth part of a bushel (8.89 liters).
Perimeter The measure of the distance around a figure.
Pico- A prefix indicating one trillionth of a given unit.
Pound, avoirdupois A unit of weight and mass equal to 7,000 grains (.453 kilogram) divided into 16 ounces, used for ordinary commercial purposes. Symbol: lb. avdp.
Pound, troy A unit of weight equal to 5,760 grains (.373 kilogram) divided into 12 ounces troy, used for gold, silver, and other precious metals. Symbol: lb. tr.

Radian An arc of a circle equal in length to the radius of that circle. An angle emanating from the center of a circle that subtends (cuts off) such an arc is said to measure one radian. Measuring angles in radians is preferred with the metric system.
Rod A unit of linear, 5.5 yards or 16.5 feet (5.0292 meters). A unit of surface measure 30.25 yd² (25.2901 m²). No symbol.

Second The sixtieth part of a minute of a degree, often represented by the sign ″ as in 13 15′ 45″, read as 13 degrees, 15 minutes, 45 seconds.
Specific gravity The ratio of the density of a substance to the density of water at 4° C.
Square unit symbol Example: mm², cm², m², etc.
Stere A cubic measure equivalent to 35.315 cubic feet or 1.3080 cubic yards (1.001 m³). Used to measure cordwood. No symbol.

Tera- A prefix indicating a trillion times a given unit.
Ton, metric See Metric ton.

Volume The measure in cubic units of the amount of space inside any given container; also the measure of the amount such a container will hold. The latter is known as the *capacity* of the container and can be given in either units of liquid measure (see Liter, also Milliliter) or in cubic units.

Weight The force of the earth's pull on an object. Weight, in the Metric system, is commonly measured in grams.

Units of Measurement–
Conversion Factors*

Units of Length

To Convert from Centimeters

To	Multiply by
Inches	0.393 700 8
Feet	0.032 808 40
Yards	0.010 936 13
Meters	**0.01**

To Convert from Meters

To	Multiply by
Inches	39.370 08
Feet	3.280 840
Yards	1.093 613
Miles	0.000 621 37
Millimeters	**1,000**
Centimeters	**100**
Kilometers	**0.001**

To Convert from Inches

To	Multiply by
Feet	0.083 333 33
Yards	0.027 777 78
Centimeters	**2.54**
Meters	**0.025 4**

To Convert from Feet

To	Multiply by
Inches	**12**
Yards	0.333 333 3
Miles	0.000 189 39
Centimeters	**30.48**
Meters	**0.304 8**
Kilometers	**0.000 304 8**

To Convert from Yards

To	Multiply by
Inches	**36**
Feet	**3**
Miles	0.000 568 18
Centimeters	**91.44**
Meters	**0.914 4**

To Convert from Miles

To	Multiply by
Inches	**63,360**
Feet	**5,280**
Yards	**1,760**
Centimeters	**160,934.4**
Meters	**1,609.344**
Kilometers	**1.609 344**

Units of Mass

To Convert from Grams

To	Multiply by
Grains	15.432 36
Avoirdupois drams	0.564 383 4
Avoirdupois ounces	0.035 273 96
Troy ounces	0.032 150 75
Troy pounds	0.002 679 23
Avoirdupois pounds	0.002 204 62
Milligrams	**1,000**
Kilograms	**0.001**

To Convert from Avoirdupois Pounds

To	Multiply by
Grains	**7,000**
Avoirdupois drams	**256**
Avoirdupois ounces	**16**
Troy ounces	14.583 33
Troy pounds	1.215 278
Grams	**453.592 37**
Kilograms	**0.453 592 37**
Short hundredweights	**0.01**
Short tons	**0.000 5**
Long tons	0.000 446 428 6
Metric tons	**0.000 453 592 37**

*All boldface figures are exact; the others generally are given to seven signficant figures.

In using conversion factors, it is possible to perform division as well as the multiplication process shown here. Division may be particularly advantageous where more than the significant figures published here are required. Division may be performed in lieu of multiplication by using the reciprocal of any indicated multiplier as divisor. For example, to convert from centimeters to inches by division, refer to the table headed "To Convert from *Inches*" and use the factor listed at "centimeters" (*2.54*) as divisor.

To Convert from **Kilograms**

To	Multiply by
Grains	15,432.36
Avoirdupois drams	564.383 4
Avoirdupois ounces	35.273 96
Troy ounces	32.150 75
Troy pounds	2.679 229
Avoirdupois pounds	2.204 623
Grams	1,000
Short hundredweights	0.022 046 23
Short tons	0.001 102 31
Long tons	0.000 984 2
Metric tons	0.001

To Convert from **Metric Tons**

To	Multiply by
Avoirdupois pounds	2,204.623
Short hundredweights	22.046 23
Short tons	1.102 311 3
Long tons	0.984 206 5
Kilograms	1,000

To Convert from **Grains**

To	Multiply by
Avoirdupois drams	0.036 571 43
Avoirdupois ounces	0.002 285 71
Troy ounces	0.002 083 33
Troy pounds	0.000 173 61
Avoirdupois pounds	0.000 142 86
Milligrams	64.798 91
Grams	0.064 798 91
Kilograms	0.000 064 798 91

To Convert from **Troy Ounces**

To	Multiply by
Grains	480
Avoirdupois drams	17.554 29
Avoirdupois ounces	1.097 143
Troy pounds	0.083 333 3
Avoirdupois pounds	0.068 571 43
Grams	31.103 476 8

To Convert from **Long Tons**

To	Multiply by
Avoirdupois ounces	35,840
Avoirdupois pounds	2,240
Short hundredweights	22.4
Short tons	1.12
Kilograms	1,016.046 908 8
Metric tons	1.016 046 908 8

To Convert from **Avoirdupois Ounces**

To	Multiply by
Grains	437.5
Avoirdupois drams	16
Troy ounces	0.911 458 3
Troy pounds	0.075 954 86
Avoirdupois pounds	0.062 5
Grams	28.349 523 125
Kilograms	0.028 349 523 125

To Convert from **Short Hundredweights**

To	Multiply by
Avoirdupois pounds	100
Short tons	0.05
Long tons	0.044 642 86
Kilograms	45.359 237
Metric tons	0.045 359 237

To Convert from **Short Tons**

To	Multiply by
Avoirdupois pounds	2,000
Short hundredweights	20
Long tons	0.892 857 1
Kilograms	907.184 74
Metric tons	0.907 184 74

To convert from **Troy Pounds**

To	Multiply by
Grains	5,760
Avoirdupois drams	210.651 4
Avoirdupois ounces	13.165 71
Troy ounces	12
Avoirdupois pounds	0.822 857 1
Grams	373.241 721 6

Units of Capacity, or Volume, Liquid Measure

To Convert from **Milliliters**

To	Multiply by
Minims	16.230 73
Liquid ounces	0.033 814 02
Gills	0.008 453 5
Liquid pints	0.002 113 4
Liquid quarts	0.001 056 7
Gallons	0.000 264 17
Cubic inches	0.061 023 74
Liters	**0.001**

To Convert from **Cubit Meters**

To	Multiply by
Gallons	264.172 05
Cubic inches	61,023.74
Cubic feet	35.314 67
Liters	**1,000**
Cubic yards	1.307 950 6

To Convert from **Liters**

To	Multiply by
Liquid ounces	33.814 02
Gills	8.453 506
Liquid pints	2.113 376
Liquid quarts	1.056 688
Gallons	0.264 172 05
Cubic inches	61.023 74
Cubic feet	0.035 314 67
Milliliters	**1,000**
Cubic meters	**0.001**
Cubic yards	0.001 307 95

To Convert from **Minims**

To	Multiply by
Liquid ounces	0.002 083 33
Gills	0.000 520 83
Milliliters	0.061 611 52
Cubic inches	0.003 759 77

To Convert from **Liquid Pints**

To	Multiply by
Minims	**7,680**
Liquid ounces	**16**
Gills	**4**
Liquid quarts	**0.5**
Gallons	**0.125**
Cubic inches	**28.875**
Cubic feet	0.016 710 07
Milliliters	**473.176 473**
Liters	**0.473 176 473**

To Convert from **Gills**

To	Multiply by
Minims	**1,920**
Liquid ounces	**4**
Liquid pints	**0.25**
Liquid quarts	**0.125**
Gallons	**0.031 25**
Cubic inches	**7.218 75**
Cubic feet	0.004 177 517
Milliliters	**118.294 118 25**
Liters	**0.118 294 118 25**

To Convert from **Liquid Ounces**

To	Multiply by
Minims	**480**
Gills	**0.25**
Liquid pints	**0.062 5**
Liquid quarts	**0.031 25**
Gallons	**0.007 812 5**
Cubic inches	1.804 687 5
Cubic feet	0.001 044 38
Milliliters	29.573 53
Liters	0.029 573 53

To Convert from **Cubic Inches**

To	Multiply by
Minims	265.974 0
Liquid ounces	0.554 112 6
Gills	0.138 528 1
Liquid pints	0.034 632 03
Liquid quarts	0.017 316 02
Gallons	0.004 329 0
Cubic feet	0.000 578 7
Milliliters	**16.387 064**
Liters	**0.016 387 064**
Cubic meters	**0.000 016 387 064**
Cubic yards	0.000 021 43

To Convert from **Liquid Quarts**

To	Multiply by
Minims	**15,360**
Liquid ounces	**32**
Gills	**8**
Liquid pints	**2**
Gallons	**0.25**
Cubic inches	**57.75**
Cubic feet	0.033 420 14
Milliliters	**946.352 946**
Liters	**0.946 352 946**

To Convert from **Cubic Feet**

To	Multiply by
Liquid ounces	957.506 5
Gills	239.376 6
Liquid pints	59.844 16
Liquid quarts	29.922 08
Gallons	7.480 519
Cubic inches	**1,728**
Liters	**28.316 846 592**
Cubic meters	**0.028 316 846 592**
Cubic yards	0.037 037 04

To convert from **Cubic Yards**

To	Multiply by
Callons	201.974 0
Cubic inches	**46,656**
Cubic feet	**27**
Liters	**764.554 857 984**
Cubic meters	**0.764 554 857 984**

To Convert from **Gallons**

To	Multiply by
Minims	**61,440**
Liquid ounces	**128**
Gills	**32**
Liquid pints	**8**
Liquid quarts	**4**
Cubic inches	**231**
Cubic feet	0.133 680 6
Milliliters	**3,785.411 784**
Liters	**3.785 411 784**
Cubic meters	**0.003 785 411 784**
Cubic yards	0.004 951 13

Units of Capacity, or Volume, Dry Measure

To Convert from **Liters**

To	Multiply by
Dry pints	1.816 166
Dry quarts	0.908 082 98
Pecks	0.113 510 4
Bushels	0.028 377 59
Dekaliters	**0.1**

To Convert from **Dekaliters**

To	Multiply by
Dry pints	18.161 66
Dry quarts	9.080 829 8
Pecks	1.135 104
Bushels	0.283 775 9
Cubic inches	610.237 4
Cubic feet	0.353 146 7
Liters	**10**

To Convert from **Cubic Meters**

To	Multiply by
Pecks	113.510 4
Bushels	28.377 59

To Convert from **Dry Pints**

To	Multiply by
Dry quarts	**0.5**
Pecks	**0.062 5**
Bushels	**0.015 625**
Cubic inches	**33.600 312 5**
Cubic feet	0.019 444 63
Liters	0.550 610 47
Dekaliters	0.055 061 05

To Convert from **Dry Quarts**

To	Multiply by
Dry pints	**2**
Pecks	**0.125**
Bushels	**0.031 25**
Cubic inches	**67.200 625**
Cubic feet	0.038 889 25
Liters	1.101 221
Dekaliters	0.110 122 1

To Convert from **Pecks**

To	Multiply by
Dry pints	**16**
Dry quarts	**8**
Bushels	**0.25**
Cubic inches	**537.605**
Cubic feet	0.311 114
Liters	8.809 767 5
Dekaliters	0.880 976 75
Cubic meters	0.008 809 77
Cubic yards	0.011 522 74

To Convert from **Bushels**

To	Multiply by
Dry pints	**64**
Dry quarts	**32**
Pecks	**4**
Cubic inches	**2,150.42**
Cubic feet	1.244 456
Liters	35.239 07
Dekaliters	3.523 907
Cubic meters	0.035 239 07
Cubic yards	0.046 090 96

To Convert from **Cubic Inches**

To	Multiply by
Dry pints	0.029 761 6
Dry quarts	0.014 880 8
Pecks	0.001 860 10
Bushels	0.000 465 025

To Convert from **Cubit Feet**

To	Multiply by
Dry pints	51.428 09
Dry quarts	25.714 05
Pecks	3.214 256
Bushels	0.803 563 95

To Convert from **Cubic Yards**

To	Multiply by
Pecks	86.784 91
Bushels	21.696 227

Units of Area

To Convert from **Square Centimeters**

To	Multiply by
Square inches	0.155 000 3
Square feet	0.001 076 39
Square yards	0.000 119 599
Square meters	**0.000 1**

To Convert from **Square Feet**

To	Multiply by
Square inches	**144**
Square yards	0.111 111 1
Acres	0.000 022 957
Square centimeters	**929.030 4**
Square meters	**0.092 903 04**

To Convert from **Square Meters**

To	Multiply by
Square inches	1,550.003
Square feet	10.763 91
Square yards	1.195 990
Acres	0.000 247 105
Square centimeters	**10,000**
Hectares	**0.000 1**

To Convert from **Square Yards**

To	Multiply by
Square inches	**1,296**
Square feet	**9**
Acres	0.000 206 611 6
Square miles	0.000 000 322 830 6
Square centimeters	**8,361.273 6**
Square meters	**0.836 127 36**
Hectares	**0.000 083 612 736**

To Convert from **Hectares**

To	Multiply by
Square feet	107,639.1
Square yards	11,959.90
Acres	2.471 054
Square miles	0.003 861 02
Square meters	**10,000**

To Convert from **Acres**

To	Multiply by
Square feet	**43,560**
Square yards	**4,840**
Square miles	**0.001 562 5**
Square meters	**4,046.856 422 4**
Hectares	**0.404 685 642 24**

To Convert from **Square Inches**

To	Multiply by
Square feet	0.006 944 44
Square yards	0.000 771 605
Square centimeters	**6.451 6**
Square meters	**0.000 645 16**

To Convert from **Square Miles**

To	Multiply by
Square feet	**27,878,400**
Square yards	**3,097,600**
Acres	**640**
Square meters	**2,589,988.110 336**
Hectares	**258.998 811 033 6**

Tables of
Weights and Measures

Linear Measure

Measure	Equivalents	
1 inch		2.54 centimeters
12 inches	1 foot	0.3048 meter
3 feet	1 yard	0.9144 meter
5½ yards	1 rod	
16½ feet	(or pole or perch)	5.029 meters
40 rods	1 furlong	201.17 meters
8 furlongs		
1,760 yards	1 (statute) mile	1,609.3 meters
5,280 feet		
3 miles	1 (land) league	4.83 kilometers

Square Measure

Measure	Equivalents	
1 square inch		6.452 square centimeters
144 square inches	1 square foot	929 square centimeters
9 square feet	1 square yard	0.8361 square meter
30¼ square yards	1 square rod (or square pole or square perch)	25.29 square meters
160 square rods or 4,840 square yards or 43,560 square feet	1 acre	0.4047 hectare
640 acres	1 square mile	259 hectares
		2.59 square kilometers

Cubic Measure

Measure	Equivalents	
1 cubic inch		16.387 cubic centimeters
1,728 cubic inches	1 cubic foot	0.0283 cubic meter
27 cubic feet	1 cubic yard (in units for cordwood, etc.)	0.7646 cubic meter
16 cubic feet	1 cord foot	
8 cord feet	1 cord	3.625 cubic meters

Chain Measure (for Gunter's, or surveyor's, chain)

Measure	Equivalents	
7.92 inches	1 link	20.12 centimeters
100 links	1 chain	20.12 meters
66 feet		
10 chains	1 furlong	201.17 meters
80 chains	1 mile (for engineer's chain)	1,609.3 meters
1 foot	1 link	0.3048 meter
100 feet	1 chain	30.48 meters
52.8 chains	1 mile	1,609.3 meters

Surveyor's (Square) Measure

Measure	Equivalents	
625 square links	1 square pole	25.29 square meters
16 square poles	1 square chain	404.7 square meters
10 square chains	1 acre	0.4047 hectare
640 acres	1 square mile	259 hectares
	1 section	2.59 square kilometers
36 square miles	1 township	9,324.0 hectares
		93.24 square kilometers

Nautical Measure

Measure	Equivalents	
6 feet	1 fathom	1.829 meters
100 fathoms	1 cable's length (ordinary)[1]	
10 cables' lengths	1 nautical mile	1.852 kilometers[2]
	6,076.10333 feet	
1 nautical mile	1.1508 statute miles[3]	
3 nautical miles	1 marine league	5.56 kilometers
	3.45 statute miles	
60 nautical miles	1 degree of a great circle of the earth	

Dry Measure

Measure	Equivalents		
1 pint		33.60 cubic inches	0.5505 liter
2 pints	1 quart	67.20 cubic inches	1.1012 liters
8 quarts	1 peck	537.61 cubic inches	8.8096 liters
4 pecks	1 bushel	2,150.42 cubic inches	35.2383 liters
1 British dry quart	1.032 U.S. dry quarts		

According to United States government standards, the following are the weights avoirdupois for single bushels of the specified grains: for wheat, 60 pounds; for barley, 48 pounds; for oats, 32 pounds; for rye, 56 pounds; for corn, 56 pounds. Some states have specifications varying from these.

Liquid Measure

Measure	Equivalents		
1 gill	4 fluid ounces (see next table)	7.219 cubic inches	0.1183 liter
4 gills	1 pint	28.875 cubic inches	0.4732 liter
2 pints	1 quart	57.75 cubic inches	0.9463 liter
4 quarts	1 gallon	231 cubic inches	3.7853 liters
4 British imperial quarts	1 imperial gallon	277.42 cubic inches	4.546 liters

The barrel in Great Britain equals 36 imperial gallons, in the United States, usually 31½ gallons.

Apothecaries' Fluid Measure

Measure	Equivalents		
1 minim		0.0038 cubic inch	0.0616 milliliter
60 minims	1 fluid dram	0.2256 cubic inch	3.6966 milliliters
8 fluid drams	1 fluid ounce	1.8047 cubic inches	0.0296 liter
16 fluid ounces	1 pint	28.875 cubic inches	0.4732 liter
1 British pint	20 fluid ounces		

See table immediately preceding for quart and gallon equivalents.

[1] In the U.S. Navy 120 fathoms or 720 feet equals 1 cable's length; in the British Navy, 608 feet equals 1 cable's length.

[2] By international agreement, 1954

[3] The length of a minute of longitude at the equator. Also called geographical, sea, or air mile, and, in Great Britain, Admiralty mile.

Circular (or Angular) Measure

Measure	Equivalent
60 seconds (″)	1 minute (′)
60 minutes	1 degree (°)
90 degrees	1 quadrant
	1 right angle
4 quadrants	1 circle
360 degrees	

Avoirdupois Weight

Measure	Equivalents	
1 grain		0.0648 gram[1]
1 dram		1.772 grams
27.34 grains		
16 drams	1 ounce	28.3495 grams
437.5 grains		
16 ounces	1 pound[2]	453.59 grams
7,000 grains		
100 pounds	1 hundredweight	45.36 kilograms
2,000 pounds	1 ton	907.18 kilograms

Troy Weight

Measure	Equivalents	
1 grain		0.0648 gram[1]
3.086 grains	1 carat	200 milligrams
24 grains	1 pennyweight	1.5552 grams
20 pennyweights	1 ounce	31.1035 grams
480 grains		
12 ounces	1 pound	373.24 grams
5,760 grains		

Apothecaries' Weight

Measure	Equivalents	
1 grain		0.0648 gram[1]
20 grains	1 scruple	1.296 grams
3 scruples	1 dram	3.888 grams
8 drams	1 ounce	31.1035 grams
480 grains		
12 ounces	1 pound	373.24 grams
5,760 grains		

[1]The grain is the same in all three tables of weight.
[2]In Great Britain, 14 pounds (6.35 kilograms) equals 1 stone, 112 pounds (50.80 kilograms) equals 1 hundredweight, and 2,240 pounds (1,016.05 kilograms) equal 1 long ton.

Special Signs and Symbols

Astronomy

Astronomical Bodies

Symbol(s)	Meaning(s)
⊙	the sun
	Sunday
☿	Mercury
	Wednesday
♀	Venus
	Friday
⊕ ♁ ⊖	the earth
☽, ☾, ●	the moon
	Monday
○, ☺	full moon
☽, ●, ☾, ☽,	the moon, first quarter
☾, ●, ☾, ☾,	the moon, last quarter
●	new moon
♂	Mars
	Tuesday
①, ②, ③	asteroids; in order of discovery, as ① Ceres, ② Pallas, etc.
♃	Jupiter
	Thursday
♄	Saturn
	Saturday
♅, ♅, ♅	Uranus
♆	Neptune
♇, P	Pluto
☄	comet
✳, ∗	star; fixed star
α, β, γ, etc.	stars (of a constellation): in order of brightness, the Greek letter followed by the Latin genitive of the name of the constellation, as α Centauri

Position and Notation

Symbol(s)	Meaning(s)
☌	in conjuction; having the same longitude or right ascension
✳	sextile; 60° apart in longitude or right ascension
☐	quadrature; 90° apart in longitude or right ascension
△	trine; 120° apart in longitude or right ascension
☍	opposition; 180° apart in longitude or right ascension
☊	ascending node
☋	descending node

Symbol(s)	Meaning(s)
♈	vernal equinox
≏	autumnal equinox
α	right ascension
β	celestial latitude
δ	declination
λ	celestial or geographical longitude
Δ	distance
θ	siderial time
a	mean distance
ν, ☊	longitude of ascending node
φ	angle of eccentricity
	geographical latitude

Signs of the Zodiac

Symbol	Meaning	
♈	Aries, the Ram	Spring Signs
♉	Taurus, the Bull	
♊, Ⅱ	Gemini, the Twins	
♋, ♋	Cancer, the Crab	Summer Signs
♌	Leo, the Lion	
♍	Virgo, the Virgin	
≏	Libra, the Balance	Autumn Signs
♏	Scorpio, the Scorpion	
♐ ♐	Sagittarius, the Archer	
♑, ♑	Capricorn, the Goat	Winter Signs
♒	Aquarius, the Water Bearer	
♓, ♓	Pisces, the Fishes	

Biology

Symbol(s)	Meaning(s)
○, ⊙, ①	annual plant
⊙, ⊙, ♂	biennial plant
♃	perennial herb
△	evergreen plant
⊙	monocarpic plant
|w	plant useful to wildlife
♂, ♂	male organism or cell
	staminate flower or plant
♀	female organism or cell
	pistillate plant or flower
☿	hermaphroditic or perfect plant or flower
♀	neuter organism or cell
○	individual organism, especially female

Symbol(s)	Meaning(s)
□	individual organism, especially male
∞	indefinite number
P	parental generation
F	filial generation
F_1, F_2, F_3, etc.	first, second, third, etc., filial generation

Books

Symbol(s)	Meaning
f°	folio
4mo, 4°	quarto
8vo, 8°	octavo
12mo, 12°	duodecimo
18mo, 18°	octodecimo
32mo, 32°	thirty-twomo

Chemistry

Elements
(See *Periodic Table of Elements* supplement)

Compounds
Compounds are represented by the symbols for their constituent elements, each element followed by a subscript numeral if the number of atoms of it appearing in the compound is greater than one, as $NaCl$, H_2O, H_2SO_4, etc. If a radical appears more than once in a compound, the radical is enclosed in parentheses followed by a subscript numeral, as $Ca(OCl)_2$, $Al_2(SO_4)_3$, etc. Molecules consisting entirely of one element are represented by the symbol for the element followed by a subscript numeral indicating the number of atoms in the molecule, as H_2, O_2, O_3, etc. In addition: · denotes water of crystallization or hydration, as $CaSO_4 \cdot 5H_2O$.

Symbol(s)	Meaning
α, β, γ, etc. 1, 2, 3, etc.	in names of compounds, indicates different positions of substituted atoms or radicals
+	denotes dextrorotation, as + 120°.
−	denotes levorotation, as − 113°.
[ ]	include parentheses if one radical contains another, as $Fe_3[Fe(CN)_6]_2$.
−, =, ≡, etc., ∴ ,∶ ,etc.,	in structural formulas, denotes a single, double, or triple bond, etc.
R__	in structural formulas, denotes any alkyl radical
⬡ or ⬡	in structural formulas, denotes a benzene ring

Ions
Ions are represented by the symbols for their respective elements or by the symbols for the elements composing them, followed by a superscript symbol indicating the electric charge, as H^+, Cl^-, SO_4^{--}, etc. Thus:

Symbol(s)	Meaning
−, =, ≡ etc. $_{-1}$, $_{-2}$, $_{-3}$ etc	denote a single, double, triple, etc. negative charge

Symbol(s)	Meaning
+, ++, +++ etc. $^{+1}$, $^{+2}$, $^{+3}$ etc.	denote a single, double, triple, etc. positive charge
′, ″, ‴ etc.	denote single, double, triple, etc. Valence or charge (especially negative), as S″

Chemical Reactions
Chemical reactions are written in a form resembling equations, with reactants on the left and products on the right. If more than one equivalent of a compound appears, it is preceded by a coefficient. Conditions of temperature, pressure, catalysis, etc., are indicated above the arrow that shows direction. The following symbols are used.

Symbol(s)	Meaning
→, ←	denotes "yields"; also indicates the direction of the reaction
⇌	indicates a reversible reaction
+	denotes "added to; together with."
↓	(written after a compound) denotes appearance as a precipitate
↑	(written after a compound) denotes appearance as a gas
△	denotes the presence of heat
=, ⇌	denotes equivalence of amounts in a quantitative equation

Commerce and Finance

Symbol(s)	Meaning(s)
@	at: peaches @ $.39 per pound
	to: nails per pound $.50 @ $.60
$, $	dollar(s); peso(s): $100
¢	cent(s): 37¢
₱	peso(s) Phillipines)
/	shilling(s) (British): 3/
£	pound(s) £25
d	penny, pence (British): 4d
¥, Y	yen
₨, R	rupee(s)
Rs	rupees
₱	per: 50¢ ₱ dozen
#	number: #60 thread

Mathematics

Symbol(s)	Meaning
+	plus (sign of addition); positive
−	minus (sign of subtraction); negative
±	plus or minus
×	times, multiplied by (multiplication sign)
·	multiplied by
÷	divided by (sign of division)

Symbol(s)	Meaning(s)
$\frac{2}{3}$, ⅔	divided by (2 divided by 3)
:	is to. divided by (ratio sign)
::	equals, as (in proportion)
<	less than
>	greater than
=	equals
≡	identical with
~	similar to
≅	congruent, equals approximately
≦	equal to or less than
≧	equal to or greater than
≠, ≠	not equal to
∝	varies directly as
∞	infinity
√	square root of
$\sqrt[n]{}$	nth root of
∴	therefore
∥	parallel to
⊥	perpendicular to
π	pi, ratio of circumference of circle to diameter (3.14159 +)
°	degrees
′	minutes
″	seconds
∠	angle
dx	differential of x
Δx	(delta) increment of x
∫	integral of
Σ	(sigma) summation of
f(x), F(x), φ(x)	function of x
8!, ⌐8	factorial 8

Measurements

Symbol(s)	Meaning
amp	ampere
a	are
bbl	barrel
fbm	board foot
bu	bushel
no symbol	candela
c	carat
°C	Celsius, degree
ca	centare
cg	centigram
cl	centiliter
cm	centimeter
ch	chain
cm³	cubic centimeter
dm³	cubic decimeter
dam³	cubic dekameter
hm³	cubic hectometer
km³	cubic kilometer
m³	cubic meter
mm³	cubic millimeter
dg	decigram
dl	deciliter

Symbol(s)	Meaning
dm	decimeter
dag	dekagram
dal	dekaliter
dam	dekameter
dr.avdp.	dram, avoirdupois
fath	fathom
no symbol	furlong
no symbol	grain
g	gram
ha	hectare
hg	hectogram
hl	hectoliter
hm	hectometer
cwt	hundredweight
INM	International Nautical Mile
°K	Kelvin, degree
kg	kilogram
kl	kiloliter
km	kilometer
no symbol	link
l	liter
no symbol	lumen
m	meter
μg	microgram
μl	microliter
μ	micron
mg	milligram
ml	milliliter
mm	millimeter
no symbol	minim
oz.	ounce
oz. avdp.	ounce, avoirdupois
oz. tr.	ounce, troy
no symbol	peck
lb.	pound
lb. avdp.	pound, avoirdupois
lb. tr.	pound, troy
no symbol	radian
no symbol	rod
s(″)	second
cm²	square centimeter
dm²	square decimeter
dam²	square dekameter
hm²	square hectometer
km²	square kilometer
m²	square meter
mm²	square millimeter
no symbol	stere
t	ton, metric

Miscellaneous

Symbol(s)	Meaning
&, &	and (See AMPERSAND)
&c	et cetera
7ber, 8ber, etc.	September, October, etc
†	died
%	percent
×	by: used in expressing dimensions, as a sheet of paper 8½″ × 11″

Symbol(s)	Meaning(s)
©	copyright, copyrighted
♠	spade
♥	heart
♦	diamond
♣	club

Symbol(s)	Meaning
8va	all' ottava; at the octave (raises the pitch of a staff one octave when written above it, lowers it when written below)
⌢, ⌣	hold

Music

Music is generally written on one or more staves. The pitch of each staff is indicated by a clef. The forms of the various notes and their corresponding rests indicate relative duration. In addition the following are used:

Symbol(s)	Meaning
♭	flat
♯	sharp
♭♭	double flat
✻	double sharp
♮	natural
C	common time; 4/4 meter
¢	alla breve; 2/2 or 4/2 meter
~	turn
ͻ	inverted turn
♦	mordent
~	inverted mordent
>, <, ∧	accent
.	staccato
—	tenuto
tr	trill
⌢, ⌣	slur or tie
,	phrase or breath mark
♪	grace note
◁	crescendo
▷	diminuendo; decrescendo
⊓	down-bow
V	up-bow

Physics

Symbol	Meaning
α	alpha particle
β	beta particle
c	velocity of light
g	acceleration due to gravity
h	Planck's constant
λ	wavelength
ν	frequency
j	square root of minus one
∿	cycles (of alternating current or voltage)

Religion

Symbol(s)	Meaning(s)
✠, +	a sign of the cross used by bishops before their names
	in some service books, an indication that the sign of the cross is to be made
*	in some service books, a mark used to divide psalm verses into two parts
℟	response
℣, v', v,	versicle
☧, ☧, ☧	a monogram for Christ [Gk. Χρ(ιστὸς)]

Medical Glossary

a- (*prefix*): not, as in afebrile, not feverish

abdomen: in human beings, the cavity between the diaphragm and the floor of the pelvis, in which the stomach, intestines, liver, and other organs are located

abortion: the expulsion of a nonviable fetus prior to term, either induced or involuntary (miscarriage or spontaneous abortion)

abrasion: scraped place on the skin, as from a fall

abscess(es): collection of pus in a body cavity formed by tissue disintegration, and often accompanied by painful inflammation

absorption: assimilation by means of the digestive process

accommodation: the thinning or thickening of the lens of the eye in order to adjust the focus of vision at different distances

acetabulum: the hip socket

achalasia: failure of a sphincter muscle to relax, causing, in the case of the cardiac sphincter, abnormal dilation of the esophagus

Achilles tendon: the thick tendon that connects the muscles at the back of the calf of the leg to the bone of the heel

acid: any of various chemical compounds that in water solution are sour in taste, turn blue litmus paper red, and are capable of reacting with another compound (a base) to form a salt

acidosis: chemical imbalance in the blood marked by an excess of acid, sometimes affecting diabetics and leading possibly to diabetic coma

acidotic: having or marked by acidosis

acinous cell: cell in the pancreas that secretes digestive juice, as distinguished from the cells of the islets of Langerhans

acne: common eruptive skin disorder resulting from the clogging or inflammation of the sebaceous glands

acoustic nerve: auditory nerve

acromegaly: disorder of the pituitary gland characterized by enlarged head, hands, feet, and most body organs

acrophobia: fear of heights

acupuncture: the Oriental art of traditional medicine in which needles are inserted at specific points through the skin to treat disease and induce anesthesia

acupuncturist: one skilled in acupuncture

acute: sudden and severe, as a disease

Adams-Stokes disease: temporary loss of consciousness caused by the heart's missing a beat, i.e., its failure to contract and pump blood on schedule

addiction: the compulsive habitual use of a drug for other than medical reasons

Addison's anemia: anemia, pernicious

Addison's disease: chronic hypofunction (underfunctioning) of the adrenal cortex, characterized by weakness, loss of body hair, and increased skin pigmentation

adenocarcinoma: carcinoma involving epithelial tissue of a gland

adenoid(s): enlarged lymphoid growth behind the pharynx

adenoidectomy: surgical removal of the adenoids

adenoma: benign tumor which can cause hyperfunction of the parathyroid glands

adenopathy: any glandular disease characterized by swelling of the lymph nodes

adenotonsillectomy: T and A operation

adipose: of or pertaining to fat; fatty

adolescents: age groups, teenagers

adrenal cortex: the outer part of the adrenal gland, which produces several hormones that affect metabolism of foods, secondary sex characteristics, skin pigmentation, and resistance to infection

adrenalectomy: surgical removal of an adrenal gland

adrenal gland: either of two small ductless glands situated above each kidney

adrenaline/epinephrine: adrenal hormone that acts to stimulate the heart, dilate the blood vessels, and relax bronchial smooth muscles

adrenal medulla: inner part of the adrenal gland

adrenocorticotrophic hormone/ACTH: hormone secreted by the anterior lobe of the pituitary gland which stimulates the growth and function of the adrenal cortex

aerobic: capable of living only in air or free oxygen, as certain bacteria

aerobics: exercises that involve a workout for the lungs and heart as well as the muscles

affect: emotion, as distinguished from thought or perception

afferent: applied to nerves receiving sensations; sensory

afferent nerves: nerves, sensory

aflatoxin: toxic substance produced by a fungus that develops typically in stored grains or legumes such as peanuts and that is associated with cancer of the liver

African trypanosomiasis: *see* sleeping sickness

afterbirth/the placenta: so called when expelled from the uterus after the birth of a baby

agoraphobia: fear of open spaces

agranulocytosis: acute disease characterized by almost total disappearance of neutrophils from the blood, and often following the use of certain drugs

AHF: antihemophilic factor

AIDS (acquired immune deficiency syndrome): a serious condition whose main characteristic is a deficiency in the body's natural immunity against various diseases

ailurophobia: fear of cats

airway: 1. passageway for air 2. plastic breathing tube for administering artificial respiration from rescuer's mouth to victim's mouth

albino: organism with deficient pigmentation. In human beings, skin is usually milky or translucent, hair is white, and eyes appear pink

albumin: any of a class of protein substances found in the blood

albuminuria: the presence of protein in the urine

alcohol: colorless, flammable liquid distilled from fermented grains, fruit juices, and starches

alcoholic: one suffering from alcoholism

alcoholism: disease characterized by excessive and compulsive use of alcoholic beverages

aldose: a kind of sugar

algophobia: fear of pain

alimentary tract or **canal/gastrointestinal tract** or **canal:** passageway for food utilized in the digestive process, extending from the mouth to the anus, and including the esophagus, stomach, intestines, and rectum

alkali: any of various chemical compounds that neutralize acids and turn litmus paper blue

alkaloid: organic substance containing nitrogen and having a powerful toxic effect on animals and man, as morphine or strychnine

alkalosis: chemical imbalance in the blood marked by an excessive alkali content

allergen: substance or material capable of causing an allergic reaction

allergenic: having the properties of an allergen

allergic: pertaining to or caused by allergy

allergic rhinitis/hay fever: annually recurring inflammation of the mucous membranes of the nose and eyes caused chiefly by the pollen of certain plants

allergic shock/anaphylactic shock: violent shock reaction, often accompanied by a rash, resulting from an oversensitized reaction to a foreign substance such as medication or the substance transmitted by an insect bite

allergist/allergologist: physician specializing in the diagnosis and treatment of allergies

allergology: the branch of medical science dealing with the diagnosis and treatment of allergies

allergy(ies): condition of heightened susceptibility to a substance that in similar amounts is innocuous to others

allograft: *see* homograft

alopecia: baldness

alopecia areata: baldness, patchy

alveolar bone: either of the bones of the upper and lower jaws that include sockets for the teeth

alveoli (*sing., alveolus*): air sacs situated in the lungs

Alzheimer's disease: presenile dementia

amalgam: mercury and silver compound, often used to fill teeth

amblyopia: dimness of sight not resulting from refractive error or disease

ambulation: act of walking or moving about, postoperative

ambulatory: able to walk

amenorrhea: absence or cessation of menstruation

amenorrhea, acquired: *see* amenorrhea, secondary

amenorrhea, primary: failure of menarche (the onset of menstruation) to occur

amenorrhea, secondary/acquired amenorrhea: cessation or interruption in the occurrence of menstruation

American trypanosomiasis: *see* Chagas' disease

amino acid: any of a group of compounds that form an essential part of the protein molecule

amnesia: loss or impairment of memory, sometimes temporary

amniocentesis/prenatal diagnosis: procedure for determining whether a fetus is afflicted with an inherited disorder by sampling the amniotic fluid of a pregnant woman

amnion/amniotic sac: membranous sac enclosing the embryo in mammals, birds, and reptiles

amniotic fluid/bag of waters: the fluid within a membrane surrounding an embryo in the uterus of a pregnant woman

amoebic dysentery: form of dysentery caused by an amoeba

amphetamine/Benzedrine: any of a class of drugs that stimulate the central nervous system, used medically to treat depressive mental disorders and sometimes to retard appetite, and used illicitly to induce a state of abnormal alertness and excitement

Amphotericin B: antibiotic substance used to treat histoplasmosis and other deepseated fungus infections

ampulla (*pl., ampullae*): any dilated part or sac, as the base of each of the semicircular canals of the inner ear

amputate: to remove surgically by cutting, as a gangrenous limb

anabolism: the process by which nutrients are built up into the living organism; constructive metabolism

anaerobic: capable of living without air or free oxygen, as certain bacteria

anal fissure: crack, split, or ulceration in the area of the two anal sphincters that control the release of feces

analgesia: incapacity to feel pain

analgesic: drug that lessens or eliminates the capacity to feel pain

anal sphincter: the ring of muscle fibers surrounding the anus and controlling the passage of wastes from the body

anaphylactic shock: allergic shock

androgen: any of various hormones found in males that control the appearance and development of masculine characteristics, also present although in smaller amounts in females

androsterone: an androgen secreted in the urine

anemia: deficiency in the amount or quality of red blood corpuscles or of hemoglobin in the blood

anesthesia: loss of sensation

anesthesiologist: physician specializing in the study and administration of anesthetics

anesthesiology: the branch of medical science that deals with the study and administration of anesthetics

anesthetic: drug, gas, or other substance or procedure that produces anesthesia

anesthetist: person trained to administer anesthetics

aneurysm: localized dilation of the wall of an artery, forming a pulsating sac and usually accompanied by pain resulting from abnormal pressure

angina pectoris: condition causing acute chest pain because of interference with the supply of oxygen to the heart

angiocardiography: visualization by X ray of the heart and its major blood vessels after injection of an opaque fluid

angioedema: swelling of the subcutaneous tissues

angiogram: X ray of a blood vessel obtained by the injection of an opaque liquid material into the blood vessels that supply the brain

angiography: visualization of the blood vessels

angiology: the branch of medical science dealing with the blood vessels and lymph vessels

ankylosing spondylitis: spondylitis, rheumatoid

ankylosis: the stiffening or fixation of a joint, as by disease or surgery

annular: having the shape of a ring

anorexia: loss of appetite

anorexia nervosa: emotional disturbance, especially of young women, characterized by aversion to food and resulting emaciation

anovulatory: without ovulation

anoxemia: deficiency of oxygen in the blood

anoxia: oxygen deficiency of the body tissues

antacid: any alkaline substance that can neutralize stomach acidity caused by gastric juices, often prescribed in ulcer diets

anterior: toward the front

anterior lobe hypophysis: the anterior part of the pituitary gland that produces growth hormones and hormones that stimulate other glands

anterior urethra: the meatus, or external opening, of the urethra in the penis

anthrax: malignant, infectious disease of sheep, cattle, and other animals, caused by a bacillus and sometimes transmitted to humans

anti- (*prefix*): against; opposed to; opposite to

antibiotic(s): any of a large class of substances, such as penicillin and streptomycin, produced by various microorganisms and fungi that have the power to destroy or arrest the growth of other microorganisms, including many that cause infectious diseases

antibody: substance produced by the body to counteract infection and in response to specific antigens

anticlotting compounds: anticoagulant

anticoagulant: substance that retards clotting of the blood

anticonvulsant: medicine used to control epileptic seizures

antidepressant: drug that stimulates physiological activity, thereby tending to alleviate depression

antidiuretic hormone: vasopressin

antidote: anything that neutralizes or counteracts the effects of a poison

antigen: any of several substances, including toxins, enzymes, and proteins, that cause the development of antibodies when introduced into an organism

antihelminthic: drug or remedy used to destroy intestinal worms, or helminths

antihemophilic factor/AHF: substance that causes clotting and stops bleeding in hemophiliacs

antihistamine: any of a number of drugs that counteract the nasal engorgement and vasoconstrictor action of histamine in the body, often used in the treatment of hay fever

antimetabolite: chemical that interferes with cell metabolism

antiperspirant: astringent preparation that acts to diminish or prevent perspiration

antitoxin: antibody produced in response to the presence of a specific toxin, which it neutralizes

antivenin: antitoxin to venom or serum prepared to counteract the effects of venom

anuria: inability to urinate

anus: the opening at the lower extremity of the alimentary canal

anvil/incus: the middle of the three ossicles of the middle ear, the bone between the hammer and the stirrup

anxiety reaction: neurosis characterized chiefly by anxiety unrelated to any apparent cause

aorta: the large artery originating from the left ventricle of the heart that forms the main arterial trunk from which blood is distributed to all of the body except the lungs

aortic valve: the membranous valve between the left ventricle of the heart and the aorta

Apgar system: system of rating the health of newborn babies

aphasia: partial or total loss of the power of articulate speech resulting from a disorder in the cerebrum of the brain

aplasia: arrested development or congenital absence of a part or organ of the body

aplastic: marked by aplasia; underdeveloped

apnea: cessation or interruption of breathing

apoplexy: stroke

appendectomy: surgical removal of the vermiform appendix

appendicitis: inflammation of the vermiform appendix characterized by pain in the right lower abdomen, nausea, and vomiting

appendicular skeleton: skeleton

appendix vermiformis: vermiform appendix

aqueous humor: the clear, limpid alkaline fluid that fills the anterior chamber of the eye from the cornea to the lens

arachnoid: the middle of the three membranes that envelop the brain and spinal cord

areola: the dark circular area around the nipple of a breast or around a pustule

arrest: slow or stop the progress of, as a disease

arrhythmia: variation from the normal heartbeat

arterial: having to do with or carried by the arteries

arteriogram: X-ray picture of an artery

arteriography: technique of injecting an opaque substance into the coronary arteries and observing the material by X ray as it runs its course through the heart muscle

arteriole: small artery, especially the one that leads to a capillary

arteriosclerosis: thickening and hardening of the walls of an artery, with impairment of blood circulation

arteritis: inflammation of an artery

artery: any of a large number of muscular, tubular vessels conveying blood away from the heart to all parts of the body

arthritis: inflammation of a joint, characterized by pain, swelling, and tenderness

arthropathy: any disease of the joints

articulate: form a joint, as one bone with another

artificial respiration: artificial maintenance of respiration in someone who has ceased to breathe, especially mouth-to-mouth resuscitation

ascaris: roundworms

ascorbic acid/vitamin C: white, odorless, crystalline compound found in citrus and other fresh fruits and green leafy vegetables, and also made synthetically, that prevents scurvy

asepsis: prevention of infection by the maintenance of sterile conditions

aseptic: free from disease-causing microorganisms

aseptic meningitis: *see* meningitis, aseptic

asphyxiation: loss of consciousness caused by too little oxygen in the blood, generally as a result of suffocation by drowning or the breathing in of noxious gases

aspirate: withdraw by suction

aspiration: act or process of aspirating

aspiration, vacuum: *see* vacuum aspiration

aspirin (acetylsalicylic acid): analgesic drug that has fever-reducing properties, widely used to treat symptoms of the common cold, rheumatoid arthritis, and many other conditions

assimilation: the process by which digested food is made an integral part of the solid or fluids of an organism

asthenia: lack or loss of strength; weakness

asthma: chronic respiratory disorder characterized by recurrent paroxysmal coughing caused by spasms of the bronchi or diaphragm, and resulting in many cases from an allergic reaction

astigmatism: distorted vision caused by an uneven curvature of the cornea

asymptomatic: condition in which antibodies for a disease are present in the blood but no symptoms of the disease can be observed

ataxia: absence or failure of muscular coordination

atherosclerosis: hardening of the inner walls of the arteries, resulting in a loss of elasticity, and accompanied by the deposit of fat and degenerative tissue changes

athetosis: derangement of the nervous system in which the hands and feet, especially the fingers and toes, keep moving or twitching

athlete's foot: ringworm of the foot, caused by a parasitic fungus

atrioventricular block: disruption of normal transmission of signals between the upper and lower chambers of the heart, as from scar tissue, that may affect blood flow to the brain and cause blackouts or convulsions

atrium (*pl., atria*)**/auricle:** one of the two upper chambers of the heart, which receive blood from the veins and transmit it to the ventricles

atrophy: the wasting or withering away of the body or any of its parts, as from disease or lack of use

attenuated: weakened in strength, as a microorganism for use in a vaccine

audiologist: one who specializes in the treatment of those with hearing problems

audiometer: device that measures hearing

auditory canal/auditory meatus: either of two passageways, the *external auditory canal* leading from the outer ear to the tympanic membrane or eardrum, and the *internal auditory canal* passing through the temporal bone to the brain

auditory nerve/acoustic nerve: nerve consisting of the cochlear nerve and the vestibular nerve and connecting the inner ear with the brain, conveying the sense of hearing and of equilibrium

aura: subjective, momentary sensory perception of an unusual nature that occurs just before the onset of an epileptic convulsion

Aureomycin: trade name for the antibiotic tetracycline

auricle: atrium

auscultation: diagnostic procedure of listening, as to sounds in the chest with a stethoscope

autism: mental disorder of children, marked by lack of response to external activities

autistic: suffering from or pertaining to autism

autograft: tissue graft taken from one part of a patient's body for transplanting in another part

autonomic nervous system: network of nerves originating in the spinal column, and including the sympathetic and parasympathetic nervous systems, that controls and stimulates the functions of body tissues and organs not subject to voluntary control, such as the heart or stomach

autopsy: postmortem examination of a body, as to determine the cause of death

avulsion: a tearing or wrenching away, as a structure or part of the body, as a result of an accident or by surgery

axillar: underarm

axillary: pertaining to or in the region of the armpit

axon: cylindrical fiber in neurons carrying impulses away from the cells

Babinski relex: reflex of the toes, normal in infants, in which the large toe is extended upward and the other toes splayed when the underside of the foot is stroked, an indication in adults of neurological disease

baby: *see* infant; newborn

baby teeth/deciduous teeth/milk teeth: the first temporary set of human teeth, 20 in all, which begin to appear about the age of six months are usually complete by the end of the second year

bacillary dysentery: a usually acute form of dysentery caused by bacilli

bacillus (*pl., bacilli*)**:** any of a class of straight, rod-shaped bacteria having both beneficial and disease-causing effects

backbone: *see* spinal column

bacteria (*sing., bacterium*)**:** one-celled microorganisms that come in three varieties—bacillus, coccus, and spirillum—and that range from the harmless and beneficial to the virulent and lethal

bacteriophobia: fear of germs

bag of waters: amniotic fluid

baldness/alopecia: common hereditary condition of males marked by a gradual loss of hair on the crown of the head until only a fringe remains around the sides and in the back, often called *male pattern baldness*

barber's itch: sycosis

barbiturates: any of a class of drugs derived from barbituric acid that depress the central nervous system, used medically as sedatives and sleeping pills and in the treatment of epilepsy and high blood pressure, and illicitly to counteract the effects of stimulant drugs

barium: metallic element used in compounds, especially barium sulfate, in radiography of the gastrointestinal tract because it is radiopaque—impervious to X rays

barium enema: enema in which a barium mixture is used to visualize the inner walls of the large intestine by X ray; used to detect cancer and other diseases

barium meal: liquid containing barium taken orally for the visualization of the upper gastrointestinal tract by X ray

barium sulfate: an insoluble barium compound used to facilitate X-ray pictures of the stomach and intestines

barium swallow: X-ray examination of the esophagus as the patient swallows a liquid containing barium

baroreceptors/barostats: sensitive nerve cells that respond to changes in blood pressure and may help to regulate it

Basal Body Temperature/BBT: accurate measure of body temperature taken under uniform conditions, used to determine a woman's day of ovulation

basal ganglia: group of nerve cells embedded in the cerebral hemisphere, the largest part of the human brain

basal metabolism: the minimum energy, measured in calories, that the body needs to maintain essential vital activities when it is at rest

basal thermometer: thermometer scaled in tenths of degrees instead of fifths, used by women to determine the time of ovulation

BBT: *see* Basal Body Temperature

bed-wetting: enuresis

belladonna: plant with purple-red flowers whose leaves and roots yield a number of poisonous alkaloids used in medicine

Bell's palsy: facial paralysis resulting from a lesion of the facial nerve

bends: *see* decompression sickness

benign: mild or nonmalignant, and responding to treatment

Benzedrine: amphetamine

beriberi: disease of the peripheral nerves characterized by partial paralysis and swelling of the legs, caused by the absence of B complex vitamins

bicuspid/premolar: one of the four upper or four lower cusped teeth located between the cuspids (or canine teeth) and the molars

bile: bitter, viscid alkaline fluid used in digestion, especially of fats, that is secreted by the liver and stored in the gallbladder

bilharziasis: *see* schistosomiasis

biliary tract: duct that conveys bile

bilirubin: pigment found in bile

biodegradable: capable of being broken down, as a chemical compound, by microorganisms

biodegrade: break down (a substance) chemically by the action of microorganisms

biological death: death of the brain, following clinical death

biomicroscope: slit lamp microscope

biopsy: excision of tissue or other material from a living subject for clinical and diagnostic examination

birth abnormalities: birth defects

birth canal: passageway formed by the cervix and vagina through which a fetus passes in the birth process

birth control: the regulation of conception by employing preventive methods or devices

birthmark: mark or stain existing on the body from birth

bite, improper: *see* malocclusion

black cancer: *see* melanoma

black fever: *see* kala-azar

black lung disease: form of pneumoconiosis common in coal miners and caused by constant exposure to coal dust

bladder: elastic membranous sac near the front of the pelvic cavity, used to store urine temporarily

bleb: blister formed in the epidermis

bleeder: *see* hemophiliac

blepharoplasty: surgical technique to correct congenital defects in the eyelids or to alter their size or shape

blister: small rounded sac, especially on the skin containing fluid matter, often resulting from injury, friction, or scalding

blood blister: blister containing blood from broken capillaries, often resulting from a pinch or other injury

blood count: examination of blood components, used in diagnosis. A *complete blood count* reveals the size, shape, and number of white and red cells and platelets in a cubic millimeter of blood. A *differential blood count* determines the percentage of leukocytes and other cells

blood group/blood type: classification of the blood, commonly designated AB, A, B, and O, based on the specific generic differences in the composition and chemical properties of the blood

bloodletting: *see* phlebotomy

blood poisoning/septicemia: introduction of virulent bacteria into the bloodstream, usually from a local infection such as a boil or wound and marked by chills, fever, and fatigue

blood pressure: diagnostic procedure of measuring the pressure of the blood on the walls of the arteries, varying with the resilience of the blood vessels and with the heart's contraction (*systole*) or relaxation (*diastole*), usually represented by two numbers, the systolic pressure followed by the diastolic pressure

blood serum: the watery, clear portion (*serum*) of blood

blue baby: infant born with cyanosis (imperfect oxygenation of the blood) resulting from a congenital heart defect

body scanner: *see* CT scanner

body scanning: *see* CT scanning

Boeck's sarcoid: *see* sarcoidosis

boil: abscess of the skin caused by bacterial infection of a hair follicle or sebaceous gland

bolus: lump or mass of food that has been chewed and softened with saliva

bone(s): hard tissue of which the skeleton of a vertebrate animal is largely composed

bone atrophy: decalcification

botulism: poisoning caused by eating spoiled or improperly prepared or canned food and characterized by acute gastrointestinal and nervous disorders

bowel, large: *see* intestine, large

Bowman's capsule: dilated structure surrounding a glomerulus as part of the nephron of a kidney

boy (*slang*): heroin

brain cage: cranium

brain damage: tissue destruction of the brain caused by an injury before, at, or after birth

brain death: biological death

brain scan: procedure of injecting a radioactive substance into the brain tissue or fluid and recording its movement by X rays

brain scanning: *CT scanning* of the brain

brain stem: all of the brain except the cerebellum, cerebrum, and cerebral cortex; the midbrain

brain surgeon: neurosurgeon

breastbone: *see* sternum

breathalyser: device for measuring the concentration of alcohol in the bloodstream of drivers of motor vehicles

breech presentation: birth with the baby positioned to present the buttocks first instead of the head first

bridge: a mounting for holding false teeth, attached to adjoining teeth on each side

Bright's disease: *see* nephritis

bromidrosis: perspiration odor

bronchi (*sing., bronchus*): the two forked branches of the trachea

bronchial asthma: *see* asthma

bronchial tree: the bronchi and bronchial tubes

bronchial tubes: the subdivisions of the trachea conveying air into the lungs

bronchiole: minute subdivision in a bronchial tube

bronchitis: inflammation of the bronchial tubes, characterized by coughing, chest pain, and fever

brucellosis/Malta fever/undulant fever: persistent infectious disease caused by a bacterium (*Brucella*) transmitted to humans from infected animals, as goats, cattle, or swine, and marked by recurrent fever, sweating, weakness, and generalized aches and pains

bruxism: habit of grinding the teeth during sleep or when otherwise under strain

bubo: inflammatory swelling of a lymph gland, especially in the groin or armpit

bubonic plague: form of plague characterized by buboes

buccal: pertaining to the cheek or mouth cavity

Buerger's disease: circulatory disorder associated with cigarette smoking

bulbar: pertaining to a bulb, especially the bulb of the medulla oblongata of the brain

bulimia: disorder involving overeating followed by self-induced vomiting

bunion: painful swelling of the foot, usually at the outer side of the base of the big toe

Burkitt's lymphoma: malignant lymphoma affecting the jaw, found especially among children in Africa

bursa: any of the fluid-filled sacs within the body that tend to lessen friction between movable parts

bursitis: inflammation of a bursa

byssinosis/white lung disease: lung disorder caused by inhaling cotton dust

cadaver: dead human body, especially one intended for dissection

Caesarian section: surgical delivery of a baby by cutting through the abdominal wall into the uterus

caffeine: chemical found in the leaves and berries of coffee, used as a stimulant and diuretic

caisson disease: *see* decompression sickness

calcification: the degenerative hardening of tissue because of the deposit of calcium salts

calcinosis: interstitial calcinosis

calcitonin: hormone secreted by the parathyroid glands, important in regulating the amount of calcium in the body

calculus: collection of hard material, as a deposit on the teeth

calorie(s): unit of heat used especially to express the heat- or energy-producing content of foods

calyx (*pl., calyces*): cup-shaped recess in the kidney pelvis that serves as a collecting point for urine

canalization: formation of new channels or ducts within tissues

canals of Schlemm: ringlike vein in the sclera of the eye that helps maintain a proper balance of aqueous humor

cancer: any of various diseases that probably have different causes and originate in different tissues, but which all involve neoplasms that spread by metastasis, resulting in progressive tissue degeneration

cancer-producing agents: carcinogens

candidiasis: *see* moniliasis

canine teeth: the sharp, pointed teeth, two in the upper jaw (called *eye teeth*), and two in the lower jaw, located between the incisors and the molars

canker sore: small ulcerous lesion in the mouth near the molar teeth, inside the lips or in the lining of the mouth

cannabis: hashish or marihuana

Cannabis sativa: the Indian hemp plant, from whose flowering tops are derived marihuana and hashish

cannula: narrow tube inserted into a body cavity or vessel, as to extract a substance or introduce a medication

capillary(ies): minute blood vessel

caput succedaneum: swelling under a newborn baby's scalp soon after birth, that usually dissolves in a few days

carbohydrate(s): any of a group of compounds, including sugars, starches, and cellulose, that contain carbon combined with hydrogen and oxygen, essential in the metabolism of plants and animals

carbolic acid/phenol: powerful caustic poison distilled from coal tar oil and used as a disinfectant

carbon monoxide: colorless, odorless gas that is highly poisonous when inhaled because it combines with the hemoglobin in the blood and thus excludes oxygen

carbon tetrachloride: colorless liquid that can be poisonous if inhaled over a long period, and often used as a fire extinguisher or cleaning fluid

carbuncle: painful, extensive inflammation of the skin, marked by hardness and the discharge of pus

carcinogen: cancer-producing agent

carcinogenic: causing cancer or increasing the incidence of cancer in a population

carcinoma: malignant tumor that arises in the tissue that lines body cavities and ducts (epithelial tissue)

cardia: the opening between the esophagus and the stomach

cardiac: of or relating to the heart

cardiac arrest: a stopping of the heartbeat

cardiac catheterization: the advancing of a catheter, or thin tube, through the veins to the heart chamber, in order to detect abnormalities and obtain blood samples

cardiac massage/cardiovascular pulmonary resuscitation/ CPR: emergency procedure consisting of the application of rhythmic pressure on the chest in order to compress the heart and start it beating again

cardiac muscle: the striated but involuntary muscle of which the heart is composed

cardiac sphincter: ring of muscle at the entrance of the stomach, or cardia, that opens to allow food to enter from the esophagus

cardiac X-ray series: chest X rays taken after the patient has swallowed an opaque liquid such as barium sulfate

cardiogram: 1. record produced by a cardiograph 2. electrocardiogram

cardiograph: 1. instrument for recording the force of the movements of the heart 2. electrocardiograph

cardiologist: physician specializing in the diagnosis and treatment of heart disease

cardiology: the branch of medical science dealing with the heart, its physiology, and its pathology

cardiovascular: pertaining to the heart and blood vessels

cardiovascular disease/heart disease: disorders affecting the heart and blood vessels

cardiovascular pulmonary resuscitation: *see* cardiac massage

cardiovascular specialist: physician specializing in the diagnosis and the treatment of diseases of the heart and blood vessels

caries: decay of a bone or tooth (dental caries); see tooth decay

cariogenic: causing caries, or tooth decay

carotene: orange or red crystalline pigment converted to vitamin A in animal metabolism

carotid artery: either of two major arteries of the neck supplying blood to the head

carpal(s): pertaining to the bones of the carpus, or wrist

carpus: the wrist

carrier: person who is immune from infection of specific disease-causing bacteria that his body carries and that can be transmitted to others who are not immune

cartilage: tough, elastic supporting tissue

cartilage plate/epiphysis: extremity of a long bone, originally separated from it by cartilage but later consolidated with it by ossification

cast(s): bit of tissue, often microscopic, having taken the shape of a vessel or cavity in which it was formed, that is found in excretions and may indicate the presence of disease

catabolism: the destructive aspect of metabolism, in which living matter breaks down nutrients into simpler substances

catalepsy: abnormal condition characterized by lack of response to stimuli and by muscular rigidity, often associated with a psychological disorder

catalyst: substance or agent that causes a chemical reaction while remaining stable, such as an enzyme or hormone in the human body

cataract: the gradual clouding and opacity of the lens of the eye, leading to impaired passage of light and loss of vision

catatonic schizophrenia: *see* schizophrenia, catatonic

cathartic: medicine for purging the bowels

catheter: slender tube for drawing off fluid from a body cavity, especially urine from the bladder

catheterization: the introduction of a catheter into the body

caudal: situated at the tail end or bottom; posterior

caudal anesthesia/caudal/caudal block: form of anesthesia in which the patient is injected in the region of the lower spinal cord (sacral canal) to block pain in the pelvic area

caul: membrane (*amnion*) surrounding the fetus if it is unruptured and intact about the baby's head at delivery

cautery, chemical: chemosurgery

cavities: dental caries; *see* tooth decay

CBC: complete blood count; *see* blood count

cc: cubic centimeter

cecum: blind pouch or cavity open at one end, especially the cavity below the ileocecal valve that forms the first section of the large intestine

celiac: pertaining to the abdomen

celiac disease: *see* malabsorption syndrome

cellular therapy: treatment for the process of aging in which a person is injected with cells from healthy embryonic animal organs with the idea that the animal cells from the particular organ injected will then migrate to the same organ in the aging body and reactivate it

cementum: the layer of body tissue developed over the roots of the teeth

central nervous system: the portion of the nervous system that contains the brain and spinal cord and controls voluntary action and movement

centrifuge: 1. (*n.*) rotary machine employing centrifugal force to separate substances having different densities, as the constituents of blood 2. (*v.*) subject to a whirling motion to separate component parts, as of blood, that have different densities

cephalhematoma: swelling under a newborn baby's scalp, that usually dissolves within a few weeks

cerebellum: large section of the brain located below and behind the cerebrum, consisting of a central lobe and two lateral lobes, and which coordinates voluntary muscle movements, posture, and equilibrium

cerebral arteriogram: an X-ray picture of the brain used to investigate brain damage, especially after a hemorrhage or stroke, and made by injecting opaque dye into the blood vessels serving the brain and X raying them

cerebral arteriosclerosis: degenerative changes in the arteries of the brain

cerebral cortex: the cells and fibers that look like a convoluted layer of gray matter and that cover the cerebral hemisphere of the brain

cerebral hemisphere: one of the two halves into which the brain is divided

cerebral hemorrhage: hemorrhage into the cerebrum of the brain or within the cranium

cerebral palsy: inability to control movement caused by nonprogressive brain damage resulting from a prenatal defect or birth injury

cerebrospinal fluid/CSF: the clear, colorless fluid that surrounds the brain and spinal cord

cerebrospinal meningitis: inflammation of the membranes that cover the brain and spinal cord

cerebrovascular: of or relating to the vessels supplying blood to the brain

cerebrum: the upper anterior part of the brain, consisting of two hemispherical masses that constitute the chief bulk of the brain in man and is assumed to be the seat of thought and will

cervical: 1. pertaining to the cervix of the uterus 2. pertaining to the neck or any neck-like part

cervical cap: contraceptive device made usually of soft plastic that fits over the cervix

cervical spine: cervical vertebrae

cervical vertebrae/cervical spine: the top seven vertebrae of the backbone, which are located in the neck and support the head

cervicitis: inflammation of the cervix of the uterus

cervix: neck of the uterus

cestode: tapeworm

chafing: inflammation of two opposing skin surfaces, caused by warmth, moisture, or friction

Chagas' disease/American trypanosomiasis: disease of Central and South America, a form of trypanosomiasis, caused by certain protozoa and spread by the bite of the assassin bug, characterized by fever, edema, and chronic heart disease

chancre: primary syphilitic lesion resembling a sore with a hard base

chancroid/soft chancre: venereal disease that produces a soft chancre

change of life: menopause

chapping: condition where skin is irritated, cracked, or roughened, more common in wintry weather

character disorder: *see* personality disorder

charas: resin obtained from the Cannabis sativa (marihuana) plant

chemical diabetes: *see* diabetes, chemical

chemosurgery: medical technique that utilizes chemistry, surgery, and microscopic analysis, especially used in the treatment of skin cancers

chemotherapy: medical technique used in the prevention or treatment of disease by chemical disinfection of affected organs and tissues, especially through the use of synthetic drugs whose action is specific against certain pathogenic microorganisms but nontoxic to the patient

chest cavity/thoracic cavity: body cavity corresponding to the chest, enclosed by the ribs

chest/thorax: part of body enclosed by ribs

chest X ray: X-ray photograph of the chest cavity that may reveal various abnormalities of the heart, blood vessels, or lungs

chicken pox: contagious viral disease, especially of children, marked by a rash

chilblains: localized inflammation of the skin, usually on the extremities or face, causing itching, swelling, and redness

chin, plastic surgery on: mentoplasty

chiropodist: podiatrist

chiropody: podiatry

chiropractic: method of therapy based on the theory that disease is mainly a result of nerve malfunction, which may be corrected by manipulation

chloasma: liver spots

Chloromycetin: brand name of an antibiotic used to treat typhoid

chloroquine: drug used in the treatment of gout and other conditions

cholecyst: *see* gallbladder

cholecystectomy: *see* gallbladder, removal of

cholecystitis: inflammation of the gallbladder

cholecystogram: visualization of the gallbladder by X ray

cholera: acute, infectious, chiefly epidemic bacterial disease characterized by diarrhea, vomiting, prostration, and dehydration

cholesterol: fatty crystalline alcohol derived principally from the bile and present in gallstones, the blood, and in brain and nerve tissues

chondromalacia: the softening of a cartilage, as under the kneecap

chondrosarcoma: form of cancer originating in the cartilage at the end of a bone

chorea/St. Vitus dance: disease of the nervous system characterized by involuntary muscular twitching

choroid: the middle, vascular coat of the eyeball

chromosome: one of the rod- or loop-shaped bodies, usually paired, found in the nucleus of every cell and containing genes

chronic: occurring gradually over an extended period of time, as a disease

chyme: partly digested food, in semiliquid form, as it passes from the stomach to the small intestine

cilia (*sing., cilium*): tiny hairs in the nose and breathing passages that help filter out foreign particles that enter the body

ciliary muscles: the set of muscle fibers, attached to ligaments, that support the lens of the eye

cirrhosis: condition associated with excessive drinking in which there is an abnormal formation of connective tissue and a wasting of the tissue of the liver

clap: *see* gonorrhea

claustrophobia: fear of being in an enclosed place

clavicle: the bone connecting the shoulder blade and breastbone; the collarbone

cleft lip/harelip: genetic defect in which the upper lip is not completely joined

cleft palate: genetic defect in which the hard palate is not completely joined

climacteric, female: *see* menopause

climacteric, male: in men, the psychological equivalent of the menopause, characterized by forgetfulness, depression, and declining sexual interest

clinical: pertaining to or based on the actual process or symptoms of a disease as observed, as distinguished from those described as typical from a statistical or theoretical point of view

clinical death: cessation of respiration and heartbeat

Clinoril: sulindac

clitoris: small, erectile organ of the female in the front part of the vulva

clonic: of or characteristic of clonus

clonic phase: the period during a grand mal epileptic convulsion when spasms of rigidity and relaxation (or jerking) occur in rapid succession

clonus: muscular spasm characterized by rapid alternation of contraction and relaxation

closed bite: form of malocclusion, a severe overbite in which upper teeth extend far over lower teeth when the jaws are together

closed-chest massage: *see* external cardiopulmonary resuscitation

closed fracture/simple fracture/complete fracture: fracture in which bone is completely broken, but without accompanying break in the skin

clotting-deficiency diseases: hemorrhagic diseases

coagulation: clotting, as of blood

coarctation: stricture or contraction, as of a cavity or blood vessel

coated tongue: condition in which the tongue is coated with a whitish substance, consisting of food particles and bacteria, which can indicate fever, illness, or a temporary lack of saliva

cocaine: white, bitter, crystalline alkaloid used as a local anesthetic and a narcotic

cocarcinogen: substance that is not cancer-producing but reacts with other substances to produce cancers

coccidioides fungus: fungus, the spores of which can cause coccidioidomycosis

coccidioidomycosis/desert rheumatism/valley fever: infectious disease caused by fungus spores and characterized by symptoms resembling pneumonia and tuberculosis and the formation of reddened bumps

coccyx: the tail end of the spinal cord

cochlea: spiral-shaped structure of the inner ear containing the essential organs of hearing, including the organ of Corti

cochlear nerve: the part of the auditory nerve leading from the cochlea of the inner ear to the brain, conveying the sense of hearing

codeine: white, crystalline alkaloid, derived from morphine and used in medicine as an analgesic and to suppress coughing

coitus: sexual intercourse

coitus interruptus: contraceptive method whereby the male withdraws before he ejaculates

cold, common: viral infection of the respiratory tract

cold sores: herpes simplex

colitis: inflammation of the colon

collagen: fibrous protein that forms the chief constituent of the connective tissues of the body, such as cartilage, skin, bone, and hair

collapsed lung: pneumothorax

collarbone: clavicle

colon: the part of the large intestine extending from the cecum to the rectum and divided into the ascending colon, transverse colon, descending colon, and the sigmoid

colonoscope: speculum used to examine the colon

color blindness: inherited vision defect consisting of the total or partial inability to discriminate between certain colors, usually red, green, and blue

colostomy: the formation of an artificial opening in the colon through which solid wastes can pass

colostrum: the creamy, yellowish, milklike substance rich in proteins, that is produced by a mother's breasts the first few days after having given birth

colposcopy: microscopic technique for visual examination of the cervix and vagina

coma: prolonged loss of consciousness

comminuted fracture: fracture in which bone is splintered or crushed

common bile duct: duct formed by the juncture of the hepatic and cystic ducts, and carrying digestive enzymes from the liver, pancreas, and gallbladder to the duodenum

complete fracture: *see* closed fracture

compound fracture/open fracture: fracture accompanied by an open wound, often exposing bone that is completely broken

compulsion: urgent need to perform certain ritualistic acts, often irrational, a symptom of certain neuroses

computed tomography: *see* CT scanning

conception: union of spermatozoon and ovum, first step in the birth process; fertilization

concussion: violent shock to the brain, typically caused by a blow to the head, as in a fall, that impairs the functioning of the brain, usually temporarily

condom: membranous sheath for the penis that serves as a contraceptive device

condyloma acuminatum: *see* venereal wart

cone: one of many photosensitive cone-shaped bodies in the retina of the eye, sensitive to color and daylight vision

congener: natural product of fermentation found in small amounts in all alcoholic beverages

congenital: acquired prior to or at birth, or during development as a fetus, as fetal abnormality because of the mother's contraction of rubella

congenital defects: *see* birth defects

congenital heart disease: deformity of the heart or of major blood vessels existing from birth

congestion: excessive accumulation of blood or fluid in an organ or tissues

conjunctiva: mucous membrane on the inner part of the eyelid and extending over the front of the eyeball

conjunctival sac: the small sac at the inner corner of the eye between the eyeball and the lower lid that serves as a collecting pool for tears

conjunctivitis: inflammation of the conjunctiva (pinkeye)

connective tissue: the fibrous tissue that binds together or supports the parts of the body, as cartilage, tendons, and ligaments

conscience: superego

conservative: of or involving procedures or treatment intended to preserve function of diseased or injured parts, utilizing established therapeutic methods

constipation: inactivity of the bowels resulting in difficult, infrequent, or incomplete evacuation

constrict: to become narrower, as a blood vessel

contact dermatitis: *see* dermatitis, contact

contact lens: one of a pair of glass or plastic lenses fitted directly over the cornea of each eye to correct vision defects

contagion: communication of disease by contact, direct or indirect

contagious: (of a disease) transmitted by direct or indirect contact

continuous positive airway pressure: procedure in which high-oxygen is forced into the lungs of newborns suffering from respiratory difficulty

contraception: the prevention of conception

contraceptive: device or substance designed to prevent conception

contraindication: symptom or sign that makes a particular course of treatment inadvisable

conversion hysteria: *see* conversion reaction

conversion reaction/conversion hysteria: neurosis characterized by manifestation of physical symptoms, such as blindness or deafness, without organic cause, as an expression of psychic conflict

convulsion/seizure: spontaneous violent and abnormal muscular contraction or spasm of the body

Cooley's anemia: *see* thalassemia

corium: dermis

corn(s): horny thickening of the cuticle common on the feet

cornea: the transparent lens surface of the eye

coronary: encircling or crowning, such as the two arteries branching from the aorta and encircling the heart

coronary arteries and veins: the network of arteries and veins that nourishes the muscle and tissue of the heart

coronary artery disease: fatty obstructions in the coronary vessels that nourish the heart, thus impairing adequate delivery of oxygen to heart

coronary attacks: heart attacks

coronary insufficiency: insufficient blood circulation through the coronary arteries

coronary occlusion: closure of the coronary artery resulting from buildup of fatty deposits or coronary thrombosis

coronary thrombosis: interference with the blood supply to the heart muscle because of a blood clot in the coronary artery

corpus callosum: fibrous tissue connecting the two hemispheres of the cerebrum of the brain

corpuscle: one of the cells that make up blood, either a red corpuscle (*erythrocyte*) or a white corpuscle (*leukocyte*)

corpus luteum: mass in the ovary formed by the rupture of a Graafian follicle that releases an ovum during each menstrual cycle

cortex: the outer layer or covering of an organ or part, as of the cerebrum or cerebellum of the brain (called *gray matter*), of the adrenal glands, or of the kidneys

corticoids: any of the hormones manufactured in the adrenal cortex

corticosteroid: 1. any of the steroids secreted by the cortex of the adrenal gland 2. any steroid hormone resembling in its effects the steroids secreted by the adrenal gland

corticosterone: steroid hormone of the adrenal cortex associated with blood sugar levels and other metabolic functions

Corti, organ of: *see* organ of Corti

cortisone: powerful hormone extracted from the adrenal cortex and also made synthetically

coryza: inflamed mucous membranes in the nose, with discharge of mucus characteristic of a head cold

cosmetic surgeon: physician specializing in cosmetic surgery

cosmetic surgery: plastic surgery concerned with improving the appearance of parts of the body

costal: pertaining to or near a rib or ribs

cough: to expel air or phlegm from the lungs in a noisy or spasmodic manner

cowpox: live calf lymph virus, used in smallpox vaccinations

coxa: the hip or hip joint

coxa vara: deformity of the hip joint caused by curvature of the femur toward the joint, thus shortening the affected leg and causing a limp

Coxsackie virus: any of a group of viruses causing various diseases in humans, including a form of meningitis

cradle cap: disease of the scalp, especially in babies, marked by yellowish crusts

cranial nerves: the twelve pairs of nerves that originate within the brain

cranioplasty: surgical correction of the skull, as to repair a congenital defect

craniotomy: any surgery involving an opening in the skull

cranium: the part of the human skull that encloses and protects the brain

crash: (*slang*) amphetamine

cresol: compound obtained by destructive distillation of coal, beechwood, or pinewood, used as an antiseptic and disinfectant

cretinism: stunted or impaired physical and mental development because of deficiency of thyroxin, a secretion of the thyroid gland, in infancy or during the fetal period

crib death: *see* sudden infant death syndrome

crossed eyes/crosseye: strabismus characterized by a tendency of the eyes to turn inward toward the nose

cross-match: to intermix constituents of the blood of a prospective donor with that of a prospective recipient to check blood compatibility

croup: spasm of the trachea, especially the larynx, occurring in children and marked by difficulty in breathing and a barking cough

crown: the part of a tooth exposed beyond the gum and covered with enamel

cryosurgery: type of surgery in which extremely low temperatures are employed either locally or generally to destroy tissue, as in malignant skin lesions

cryotherapy: inducement of peeling by freezing the skin with carbon dioxide to improve appearance of flat acne scars and shallow wrinkles

cryptorchidism/cryptorchism: failure of the testicles to descend normally

CSF: *see* cerebrospinal fluid

CT scanner/body scanner: computerized X-ray machine used in CT scanning

CT (computed tomography) scanning/body scanning: procedure for producing a cross-sectional, computer-generated, composite X-ray picture of the body or an organ, as the brain, by rotating about a site and taking a series of radiographs directed to it

culdoscopy: technique for examining the female reproductive organs within the abdominal cavity

culture: the development of microorganisms or living cells in a special medium, as gelatin, often as a means of analyzing a body fluid or tissue for the presence of disease

Cuprimine: penicillamine

cupula: structure within each of the semicircular canals of the inner ear, communicating changes in motion

curettage: the scraping of a cavity with a curette, as to remove morbid matter or obtain tissue for diagnosis

curette: small instrument, usually resembling a spoon or scoop with sharpened edges, used in curettage

Cushing's syndrome: excess of hormones secreted by the adrenal cortex, characterized by weakness, purple streaks in the skin, and a moon face

cusp: 1. one of the projections or points on the crown of a tooth 2. one of the triangular flaps of a heart valve

cuspid/canine tooth/eye tooth: one of the two upper or two lower sharp, pointed teeth located between the incisors and the bicuspids

cutaneous: pertaining to, affecting, or on the skin

cuticle: 1. epidermis 2. crescent of toughened skin around the base of the nail

cyanosis: disordered circulatory condition resulting from inadequate oxygen supply in the blood and causing a livid bluish color of the skin

cyanotic: bluish in color because of cyanosis

cyclamates: sodium cyclamate

cycloid: *see* cyclothymic

cyclothymic/cycloid: describing a personality disorder in which the individual is subject to sharply defined moods of elation or depression

cynophobia: fear of dogs

cyst: saclike mass containing liquid or semisolid material

cystectomy: 1. surgical removal of the gallbladder or of the urinary bladder 2. surgical removal of a cyst

cystic duct: duct that carries bile from the gallbladder to the juncture with the hepatic duct, where the common bile duct is formed

cystic fibrosis: hereditary disease of infants and young children marked by cysts, excessive fibrous tissue, and mucous secretion

cystitis: inflammation of the bladder, characterized by a burning sensation when voiding, frequent need to urinate, and sometimes blood in the urine

cystocele: hernia in which part of the bladder protrudes through the wall of the vagina

cystoscope: device used to view the interior of the bladder after being inserted in the urethra

cystoscopy: the technique of viewing the interior of the bladder by means of a cystoscope

cystostomy: the making of an artificial outlet from the urinary bladder

D and C: *see* dilation and curettage

dandruff: condition marked by itching and flaking of the skin, especially of the scalp

db: decibel

DBI/phenformin: drug that stimulates the production of insulin in the pancreas

D.D.S.: Doctor of Dental Surgery

decalcification/bone atrophy: the loss of lime or calcium salts from the bones or teeth

decibel/db: unit for measuring the intensity of sound

deciduous teeth: baby teeth

decision-maker: ego

decompression sickness/caisson disease/the bends: painful, sometimes fatal condition that results from bubbles of nitrogen formed in the blood when a rapid reduction in pressure occurs, as when a diver returns directly to the surface after a period deep under water

decongestant: agent designed to relieve congestion

defecation: the discharge of feces

defibrillation: act or process of stopping fibrillation of the heart muscle and restoring normal rhythm, as by jolting it with an electric current

defibrillator: device that sends a jolt of electricity into the heart muscle in order to stop fibrillation and get the heart back to normal rhythm

degenerative: characterized by deterioration or change from a normally active state to a lower or less active form, especially of body tissue, as in a disease process

degenerative joint disease: *see* osteoarthritis

deglutition: act of swallowing

dehydration: loss or removal of water, as from body tissues

déjà vu: distortion of memory in which a new situation or experience is regarded as having happened before

delirium tremens/DTs: violent form of delirium characterized by nausea, confusion, crawling sensation on the skin, and hallucinations caused especially by rapid lowering of blood alcohol levels in very heavy drinkers

dementia: mental deterioration resulting from an organic or functional disorder

Demerol: meperidine

demyelination: gradual loss of myelin, resulting in paralysis, numbness, or other loss of nerve function

dendrites: short, gray filaments in neurons that conduct impulses toward the cell body

dental calculus/tartar: hard deposit of minerals and other substances that collects on teeth

dental caries/cavities: ulceration and decay of teeth; *see* tooth decay

dental floss: strong, silky filament for cleaning between the teeth

dental surgeon: *see* oral surgeon

dentin: the hard calcified substance that forms the body of a tooth

dentist: one who specializes in the diagnosis, prevention, and treatment of disease affecting the teeth and their associated structures

dentistry: the branch of medical science that concerns the study, diagnosis, prevention, and treatment of diseases of the teeth, gums, and associated structures

dentition: the kind, number, and arrangement of the teeth in the mouth

denture(s): frame of plastic or other material adapted to fit the mouth and containing one, several, or a complete set of artificial teeth to replace natural teeth that have been lost

depilatory: chemical product capable of removing or loosening hair

depressant: drug or other substance that reduces or calms the physiological processes of body or mind

depression: 1. mental state marked by melancholy, pessimism, or dejection 2. psychotic condition characterized by stuporous withdrawal from reality and intense guilt feelings

depressive reaction: 1. neurosis characterized by persistent feelings of depression and pessimism unrelated to any apparent cause 2. (involutional melancholia) psychosis usually occurring in women around the time of menopause, and in men during their 50s, characterized by hopeless melancholy, anxiety, weeping, and often delusions

dermabrasion: the removal of layers of skin by planing with an abrasive tool to dispose of wrinkles or skin blemishes

dermal: of or relating to the skin

dermatitis: inflammation of the skin

dermatologist: physician specializing in the diagnosis and treatment of disorders of the skin

dermatology: the branch of medical science dealing with disorders of the skin

dermis/corium/true skin: the inner layer of the skin, which contains blood vessels, nerves, connective tissue, sweat glands, and sebaceous glands

DES: *see* diethylstilbestrol

desert rheumatism: coccidioidomycosis

Desoxyn: methamphetamine

detached retina/separated retina: eye disorder in which the membrane at the back of the eye (retina) is separated from its bed, as by being torn, thus impairing vision

developmental disability: any condition which interferes with a child's development, especially one which will constitute a handicap throughout the individual's life, such as mental retardation or cerebral palsy

Dexedrine: dextroamphetamine

dextroamphetamine (d-amphetamine)/Dexedrine: isomer of the amphetamine compound, considered to have a more stimulating effect on the central nervous system than amphetamine

dextrose: form of glucose (a sugar) found normally in animals, used in intravenous feeding because it is readily assimilated by the blood

diabetes, chemical/prediabetic condition: condition indicating predisposition to development of diabetes, when blood sugar level remains abnormally high for too long after taking a glucose tolerance test

diabetes insipidus: production of excessive amount of urine because of deficiency of antidiuretic hormone

diabetes mellitus: disease associated with inadequate production of insulin and characterized by excessive urinary secretion containing abnormal amounts of sugar, accompanied by emaciation, excessive hunger, and thirst

diabetic: one who has diabetes

diabetic acidosis: advanced stage of diabetes treated with insufficient insulin, characterized by increasing buildup of ketone bodies, drowsiness, and, if untreated, coma

diabetic coma: state of unconsciousness in a diabetic resulting from insufficient insulin, characterized by deep, labored breathing and a fruity odor to the breath

diabetic ketosis: early stage of diabetes treated with insufficient insulin, characterized by excessive urination, thirst, and hot, dry skin

diabetic retinopathy: disease of the eye associated with diabetes in which new, abnormal blood vessels form on the surface of the retina, sometimes marked by bleeding

diacetylmorphine: heroin

diagnosis: identification of a disease or disorder by its characteristic symptoms, or the conclusions reached in a particular instance

dialysis: the separating of mixed substances by means of wet membranes, as the action of the kidneys, especially applied to an artificial process to remove waste products and excess fluid from the bloodstream of a patient with defective kidneys

diaper rash: rash caused by the ammonia produced by the urine in diapers

diaphragm: 1. dome-shaped layer of muscle between the chest and abdomen whose contraction enlarges the rib cage for inflation of the lungs in breathing 2. contraceptive device of molded rubber or soft plastic material used to cover the cervix and prevent entry of spermatoza

diaphragmatic hernia: hernia, hiatus

diarrhea: frequent and fluid evacuation of feces

diastole: the instant when the heart is relaxed as the ventricles fill with blood prior to contraction and pumping (systole)

diastolic pressure: measure of blood pressure taken when the heart is resting, the lower of the two figures in a reading

diathermy: treatment by means of heat generated within the body of high-frequency radiation

diethylstilbestrol/DES/stilbestrol: synthetic hormone resembling estrogen implicated in the formation of vaginal and cervical cancers in the daughters of women who had taken the hormone during pregnancy

differential blood count: *see* blood count

digestion: process of dissolving and chemically changing food in the alimentary tract so that it can be assimilated by the blood and its nutrients can be absorbed by the body

digestive tract: *see* gastrointestinal tract

digitalis: the dried leaves of foxglove, containing several glycosides, often used as a heart tonic

dilate: to become larger, as the pupil of the eye in diminished light

dilation and curettage/D and C: enlarging the opening into the uterus and the scraping of the uterus with a curette

dimethyltryptamine: *see* DMT

diphenylhydantoin: phenytoin

diphtheria: respiratory, bacterial disease marked by the formation of a false membrane that obstructs breathing

diplopia: *see* double vision

disclosing tablets: tablets which, after being chewed, leave a temporary stain on plaque remaining on teeth after brushing

disinfectants: germicides

dislocation(s): the partial or completed displacement of one or more of the bones at a joint

displacement: transference of intense anxiety unconsciously felt about a particular conflict to a substitute, which is regarded consciously with the same intensity of anxiety, a manifestation of the phobic reaction

dissociative reaction: neurosis characterized by escape from a part of the personality by means of dream states, amnesia, forgetfulness, etc.

distal: relatively remote from the center of the body, or from a point considered as central

distal muscles: the muscles of the extremities (the hands and the feet)

distillation: separation of the more volatile parts of a substance from the less volatile by boiling and condensing the vapors into separate liquids

diuresis: excessive excretion of urine

diuretic(s): substance stimulating the secretion of urine

diverticula (*sing., diverticulum*): pouches or sacs opening off the large intestine

diverticulitis: inflammation of diverticula in the digestive tract, especially in the colon

diverticulosis: the presence of diverticula in the digestive tract

diverticulum (*pl. diverticula*): abnormal pouch or bulge protruding from an organ or part, as from the colon or the intestines

DNT/dimethyltryptamine: synthetic hallucinogen

DNA (deoxyribonucleic acid): chemical in the human cell that controls body development

Dolly (*slang*): methadone

DOM/STP: synthetic hallucinogen

dopamine: chemical compound found in the brain, needed in the synthesis of norepinephrine and epinephrine

Doriden: glutethimide

dorsal: toward, near, or in the back

double vision/diplopia: condition in which a single object is perceived as two images because of an inability to coordinate focusing of the eyes

douching: flushing of a body part or cavity, especially the vagina, with water as a means of cleansing

Down's syndrome/Mongolism: congenital mental and physical retardation resulting from a chromosomal anomaly, accompanied by variable signs, including a flat face and pronounced epicanthic folds

downs/downers/goof balls (*slang*): barbiturates or other drugs that depress the central nervous system

DPT injection: injection to provide immunity against diphtheria, pertussis (whooping cough), and tetanus

Dramamine: proprietary drug used to counteract motion sickness

dreamer (*slang*): morphine

dropsy: former term for edema, especially when caused by cardiac insufficiency

drug(s): 1. any substance other than food that changes or has an effect on the body or mind 2. narcotic drug

dry socket: painful complication of a tooth extraction in which underlying tissue of the alveolar bone is exposed to infection

DTs: delirium tremens

Duchenne's muscular dystrophy: pseudohypertrophic muscular dystrophy

duct/hepatic: either of two ducts of the liver that join to form the common hepatic duct and that carry bile

ductless glands: *see* endocrine glands

dumdum fever: *see* kala-azar

duodenal ulcer: ulcer of the duodenum of the small intestine

duodenum: the first section of the small intestine, leading from the stomach to the jejunum

dura mater: the tough, fibrous, outermost membrane of the three membranes covering the brain and spinal cord

dwarfism: disorder characterized by stunted growth

dysentery: severe inflammation of the mucous membrane of the large intestine, characterized by bloody stools, pain, cramps, and fever

dysfunction: impairment or abnormal functioning, as of an organ

dyslexia: 1. impairment or loss of the ability to read, as from a stroke 2. in children, impairment of ability to acquire language skills because of motor or perceptual disabilities

dysmenorrhea: painful menstruation

dyspareunia: painful sexual intercourse

dyspepsia: indigestion, characterized by heartburn, nausea, pain in the upper abdomen, and belching

dysphagia: difficulty in swallowing

dysphasia: disorder of the cerebral centers characterized by difficulty in understanding or using speech

dyspnea: labored, difficult breathing

dystrophy: 1. defective or faulty nutrition 2. any of various neurological or muscular disorders, as muscular dystrophy

dysuria: difficult, painful, or incomplete urination

eardrum/tympanic membrane/tympanum: drumhead membrane separating the middle ear from the external ear

earwax: waxy substance secreted by the glands lining the passages of the external ear

ECG: electrocardiogram

echocardiogram: graph recording the pattern of deflection of sound waves by the heart, used in diagnosing heart abnormalities

eclampsia: toxemia of pregnancy involving convulsions

E. coli/Escherichia coli: common bacillus found normally in the human intestines, usually harmless but having certain strains that cause urinary tract and other infections

ECPR/external cardiopulmonary resuscitation: closed-chest massage, used for those suffering cardiac arrest

ectoderm: outermost layer of tissue

ectopic/atopic: out of normal place or position

ectopic pregnancy: abortive pregnancy outside the uterus, as in the Fallopian tubes or abdominal cavity

eczema: noncontagious skin condition characterized by itching and scaling of the skin

edema: swelling of tissues because of abnormal fluid accumulation

edentulous: toothless

EEG: *see* electroencephalogram

efferent: applied to nerves, communicating impulses so that directive action can be taken

egg cell: ovum

ego: the self, considered as the seat of consciousness

ejaculation: expulsion of semen during orgasm

EKG: *see* electrocardiogram

elective surgery: surgery that is not essential for the maintenance of physical health, as cosmetic surgery

Electra complex: repressed sexual attachment of daughter to father, analogous to the Oedipal complex involving the son and mother

electric shock: the body's reactions to the passage through it of an electric current, as involuntary muscular contractions

electrocardiogram/ECG/EKG: graph recording the pattern of electric impulses produced by the heart, used in the diagnosis of heart disease

electrocardiograph: machine used to record the electric current produced by the heart muscle

electrocardiography: technique of producing electrocardiograms and interpreting them

electroencephalogram/EEG: graph recording the pattern of electric impulses produced by the brain, used in the diagnosis of neurological disorders

electroencephalograph: machine used to record the electric current produced by the brain

electroencephalography: technique of producing electroencephalograms and interpreting them

electrolysis: technique for removing unwanted hair by destroying the hair root with an electric current

electromyogram/EMG: graph recording the electrical activity of a muscle

electromyography: technique of producing electromyograms and interpreting them

electroshock: describing a form of treatment for psychological disorders in which a controlled electric current is passed through the patient's head, producing convulsions and unconsciousness, usually given in series

electrosurgery/surgical diathermy: surgical procedure utilizing electricity to destroy tissue

elephantiasis: lymphatic edema, especially of the legs and scrotum, a symptom of filariasis

embolism: the stopping up of a vein or artery, as by a blood clot, that has been brought to the point of obstruction by the bloodstream

embolus: object moving within the bloodstream, as a blood clot or air bubble, that is capable of causing an obstruction (embolism) in a smaller vessel

embryo: the rudimentary form of an organism in its development before birth, usually considered in the human species to be the first two months in utero

emetic: medicine or substance used to induce vomiting

emphysema: puffed condition of the alveoli or air sacs of the lung (or other tissues or organs) because of infiltration of air and consequent loss of tissue elasticity

enamel: the layer of hard, glossy material forming the exposed outer covering of the teeth

encephalitis: inflammation of the brain

encephalogram: X-ray picture of the brain made by encephalography

encephalography: X-ray visualization of the brain following the removal of cerebrospinal fluid and its replacement with air or other gases

endarterectomy: surgical procedure in which carbon dioxide is forced through hardened arteries to ream out fatty blockages

endemic: confined to or characteristic of a given locality, as a disease

endocarditis: inflammation of the membrane (endocardium) lining the chambers of the heart, sometimes caused by bacteria

endocardium: the delicate membrane that lines the chambers of the heart

endocrine gland: one of several ductless glands that release secretions (hormones) directly into the blood or lymph and that exert powerful influences on growth, sexual development, metabolism, and other vital body processes

endocrinologist: physician specializing in endocrinology

endocrinology: the branch of medical science dealing with the structure and function of the endocrine glands and their hormones

endoderm: innermost layer of tissue

endodontics: branch of dentistry dealing with root canal work and the dental pulp

endodontist: dentist specializing in root canal work

endogenous insulin: self-produced insulin

endolymph: fluid within the semicircular canals of the inner ear

endometrial: of or pertaining to the endometrium

endometrioma: mass of tumorlike endometrial cells as a result of endometriosis

endometriosis: condition in which tissue that lines the uterus (endometrium) grows outside the uterus in the pelvic cavity

endometrium: the lining of the uterus

endoscope: instrument for examining a hollow organ or an internal cavity, as the urinary bladder or the urethra

endoscopy: examination with an endoscope

enema: liquid injected into the rectum as a purgative or for diagnostic purposes

ENT: otolaryngology (ear, nose, and throat doctor)

enteric: pertaining to the intestines

enteric fever: *see* typhoid

enteritis: inflammation of the intestines, especially of the small intestine

enterocele: hernia in which part of the small intestine protrudes through the wall of the vagina

enuresis/bed-wetting: involuntary urination during sleep at night

enzyme(s): organic substance, usually a protein, produced by cells and having the power to initiate or accelerate specific chemical reactions in metabolism, such as digestion

eosinophil: any of a type of white blood cell that stains easily when a particular red dye (eosin) is applied

ephedrine: drug that dilates the bronchi, used to reduce nasal congestion and relieve asthma

epicanthic fold/epicanthus: vertical fold of skin at the inner corner of the eyelid, found chiefly in certain Asian peoples

epicanthus: *see* epicanthic fold

epidemic: 1. (*adj.*) affecting many in a community at once, as a disease 2. (*n.*) the temporary prevalence of a disease in a community or throughout a large area

epidemiologist: physician specializing in epidemiology

epidemiology: the branch of medical science concerned with the study and prevention of epidemic diseases

epidermis/cuticle: the outer, nonvascular layer of the skin, overlying the dermis

epididymis: portion of the seminal ducts just above the testis

epigastric: pertaining to the upper middle part of the abdomen

epigastrium: the upper middle (epigastric) part of the abdomen

epiglottis: the leaf-shaped plate of cartilage at the base of the tongue that covers the trachea during the act of swallowing

epilepsy: chronic nervous disorder characterized by sudden loss of consciousness and sometimes by convulsions

epileptic: 1. (*adj.*) pertaining to epilepsy 2. (*n.*) person who has epilepsy

epinephrine: *see* adrenaline

epiphysis: cartilage plate on the extremity of a long bone

episiotomy: incision made during labor to enlarge the vaginal area enough to permit passage of the baby

epistaxis: nosebleed

epithelial: pertaining to the epithelium

epithelium: membranous tissue that lines the canals, cavities, and ducts of the body, as well as all free surfaces exposed to the air

erection: enlarged and firm state of the penis when sexually stimulated

eruption: 1. emergence of a tooth through the gums 2. a breaking out of a rash on the skin

erysipelas: acute bacterial skin infection characterized by bright red patches

erythema: redness of the skin, a symptom occurring in various forms in different conditions having various causes, as from infection or a burn

erythremia: polycythemia vera

erythrocyte/red blood cell/red corpuscle: cell found in the bloodstream, often lacking a nucleus, the carrier of hemoglobin

erythrophobia: fear of blushing

eschar: dry crust or scab left by a burn caused by heat or corrosive chemical action

Escherichia coli: *see* E. coli

esophagoscope: device inserted into the esophagus to permit its inspection

esophagus (gullet): the tube through which food passes from the mouth to the stomach

essential: of unknown cause, as a disease or condition

essential hypertension: *see* hypertension, essential

estrogen: any of several hormones found in the ovarian fluids of the female which promote growth of secondary sex characteristics and influence cyclical changes in the female reproductive system

ethanol: ethyl alcohol

ether: colorless, volatile, flammable chemical compound used as an anesthetic

ethmoid bone: sievelike bone at the base of the skull behind the nose

ethyl alcohol/grain alcohol/ethanol: product of the distillation of fermented grains, fruit juices, and starches, used in beverages, and having intoxicating properties

etiologist: physician specializing in studying the causes of disease

etiology: 1. the cause or causes of a disease 2. the branch of medical science dealing with the causes of disease

eunuch: in males, the failure at puberty to develop secondary sex characteristics because of removal or disorder of the testicles

Eustachian tube: passage connecting the middle ear to the upper throat which equalizes air pressure on both sides of the eardrum

Ewing's sarcoma: malignant tumor of the shafts of the long bones in children

excise: cut out or remove by surgery

excision: act or procedure of cutting out or removing surgically

excrete: to eliminate, as waste matter, by normal discharge from the body

excretion: 1. the act of excreting 2. the body's waste matter, as sweat, urine, and feces

exocrine gland: any of various glands, such as mammary or sebaceous glands, having ducts that carry their secretions to specific locations

exophthalmic goiter: hyperthyroidism

expectorant: medicine that promotes the discharge of mucus from the respiratory tract

expectorate: discharge from the mouth, as saliva or phlegm

exploratory: performed for the purpose of making a diagnosis: said of a surgical operation

extension: state of being extended or straightened

extensor: muscle whose function is to extend or straighten a part of the body

external cardiac massage: cardiac massage

extraction: surgical removal of a tooth

extrinsic: originating or situated outside an organ or part

exudate: substance filtered through the walls of living cellular tissue, sometimes as a result of disease or injury, as in the case of inflammation

eyeground: the inner side of the back of the eyeball

eyestrain: disorder caused by excessive or improper use of the eyes and characterized by fatigue, tearing, redness, and a scratchy feeling in the eyelids

eye teeth: the upper canine teeth

face lift: rhytidoplasty

facial canal: Fallopian canal

facial neuralgia: *see* trigeminal neuralgia

facial plasty: rhytidoplasty

fainting: brief loss of consciousness

Fallopian canal/facial canal: bony canal in the skull

Fallopian tubes: the pair of tubes connecting the ovaries and the uterus, through which the egg must pass at the time of ovulation

family therapy: form of group therapy in which the patient group are members of the same family

farsightedness/hypermetropia/hyperopia: inability to see nearby objects clearly

fascia: fibrous tissue in the form of sheets that connect, surround, and support muscles and organs of the body

fascitis: inflammation of the fascia

fat: chemical compound forming an important food reserve and a source of hormones, vitamins, and other products essential in metabolism

fat pad: mass of fatty tissue

FDA: Food and Drug Administration

febrile: feverish

feces/stool: animal waste discharged following a bowel movement, usually containing indigestible foods, bacteria, bile, and mucus

femur: the long bone that supports the thigh; the thigh bone

fermentation: the conversion of glucose into ethyl alcohol, especially through the action of an enzyme (zymase) found in yeast

fetus: organism developing in the uterus before birth, sometimes considered in the human species to begin with the third month in utero, prior to which is called an embryo

fever/pyrexia: body temperature above the normal

fever blisters: *see* cold sores

fiberoptic: consisting of or making use of fibers of glass or plastic, as in optical instruments designed for viewing the intestines or stomach

fibrillation: irregular, uncoordinated contraction (arrhythmia) of muscle fibers of the heart

fibrin: insoluble protein that forms an interlacing network of fibers in clotting blood

fibrinogen: complex protein found in plasma which, in combination with the enzyme thrombin, forms fibrin

fibrinolysin: enzyme present in the blood that liquefies fibrin, thus dissolving blood clots

fibroid: *see* tumor, fibroid

fibroma: benign tumor composed of fibrous connective tissue

fibula: the outer of the two bones of the lower leg

field block: form of local anesthesia in which the anesthetic is injected into the tissue area in which surgery is to be performed

filariasis: tropical disease transmitted by mosquitoes and caused by a parasitic worm that invades the lymphatic system, producing edema and elephantiasis

fistula: abnormal channel leading from a hollow organ or cavity to another part or to the surface of the body

flaccidity: lack of firmness or elasticity; limpness

flatulence: accumulation of gas in the stomach and bowels

flexion: state of being bent or flexed

flexor: muscle whose function is to flex or bend a part of the body

flexure: bend or fold, as in the colon sigmoid

floss: *see* dental floss

flu: *see* influenza

fluke: *see* schistosoma

fluoridation: the addition of sodium fluoride to drinking water as a means of preventing tooth decay

fluoride: compound of fluorine, often added to public water supplies or toothpastes to retard or prevent tooth decay in children

fluoroscope: device for directly observing internal body structures by passing X rays through the patient and projecting shadows on a screen coated with a fluorescent substance

fluoroscopy: examination conducted by means of a fluoroscope

flu shots: influenza inoculation

focal convulsion: epileptic convulsion that affects only one part of the body

follicle: small cavity or saclike structure that secretes or excretes body fluids

follicle, hair: tiny sac within the dermis from which hair grows and is nourished

follicle-stimulating hormone/FSH: hormone secreted at the start of puberty by the pituitary gland, causing maturation of ovaries in girls and formation of sperm in boys

follicular cyst: *see* cyst, follicular

fontanel: either of two soft places at juncture points of the skull of a baby, the *anterior fontanel*, near the front, and the *posterior fontanel*, near the back

food chain: the relationship of organisms considered as food sources or consumers or both, as the relationship of a flowering plant to a bee or to a bird

food poisoning: digestive disorder marked by nausea and vomiting, caused by bacteria found in decaying or rancid food

food tube: esophagus

foot doctor: podiatrist

foot drop: condition in which the foot drops when extended in stepping forward, as caused by paralysis of a leg muscle

foramen: natural aperture or passage, as in a bone

forceps: two-bladed instrument for grasping and compressing or pulling, various types of which are used by dentists and surgeons

forces, balance of: *see* Yin; Yang

forensic medicine/forensic pathology: sub-specialty of pathology dealing with the various aspects of medicine and the law

forensic pathology: forensic medicine

foreskin: the loose skin (prepuce) covering the head of the penis

fossa: pit or depression in a surface

fovea: shallow rounded depression in the retina, directly in the line of vision at a point where vision is most acute

fracture: break in a bone; *see* closed fracture; complete fracture; incomplete fracture

fraternal twins: twins who are not identical, derived from separately fertilized ova

freckle: small, brownish or dark-colored spot on the skin

free association: psychoanalytic technique in which the patient talks freely about anything that comes to mind

freezing of skin: cryosurgery

Freud, Sigmund: Austrian neurologist (1856–1939) who founded psychoanalysis and shaped the course of modern psychiatry

frigidity: sexual unresponsiveness in women

Froehlich's syndrome: failure of secondary sex characteristics to develop in males because of anterior pituitary disease

frontal lobe: the front portion of each cerebral hemisphere of the brain, whose functions are uncertain

frontal lobotomy: rarely performed surgical operation of cutting into the frontal lobes of the brain to alter behavior

frostbite partial freezing of a part of the body, especially of the extremities or ears

fructose/levulose: very sweet crystalline sugar

FSH: follicle-stimulating hormone

fulguration: destruction of tissue, especially malignant growths, by electric cautery

functional: 1. able to function, especially in spite of structural defect 2. affecting performance, as in illness, but lacking any verifiable physical basis

functional hypertension: hypertension, essential

fundus: the rounded base or bottom of any hollow organ

fungus (*pl., fungi*): any of a group of plants including the mushrooms, molds, yeasts, and various microorganisms, some of which cause diseases in human beings

funnel chest/pectus excavatum: congenital deformity in which the sternum is depressed

furuncle: *see* boil

fusion of spinal joints: *see* spondylitis, rheumatoid

galactosemia: hereditary condition affecting infants who lack an enzyme that converts galactose (a sugar) into glucose in the blood

gallbladder/cholecyst: small pear-shaped pouch situated beneath the liver that serves as a reservoir for bile

gallstone(s): solid substance formed in the gall bladder that can obstruct the flow of bile and prevent the digestion of fats

gamete: either of two mature reproductive cells, an ovum or sperm cell

gamma globulin: component of blood serum which contains various antibodies

ganglion (*pl., ganglia*): 1. cluster of nerve cells outside of the central nervous system 2. cyst of a tendon, as on the wrist

gangrene: death of tissues in a part of the body, caused by lack of adequate blood supply

gastrectomy: surgical removal of all or part of the stomach

gastric analysis: extraction and study of gastric juices

gastric juice: the acid fluid secreted by the glands lining the stomach, containing several enzymes

gastric ulcer: ulcer of the mucous membrane of the stomach

gastritis: inflammation of the stomach

gastrocnemius: the large muscle at the back of the calf of the leg

gastroenteritis: inflammation of the mucous membrane that lines the stomach and intestines

gastroenterologist: physician specializing in the diagnosis and treatment of gastrointestinal disorders

gastroenterology: the branch of medical science dealing with the study of the stomach and intestines and the disorders affecting them

gastroscope: device that allows inspection of the interior of the stomach

gastroscopy: examination of the stomach with a gastroscope

GC: *see* gonorrhea

gene: hereditary unit contained within a chromosome and associated with specific physical characteristics transmitted from parents to offspring

general practitioner/GP: physician whose training is not specialized and includes some preparation in pediatrics, surgery, and obstetrics and gynecology, thus enabling him or her to care for an entire family

genetic counselor: specialist, usually a physician, who counsels couples on the probability of genetic disorders occurring in their offspring

genitalia: genitals

genitals/genitalia: the reproductive organs

genitourinary tract: urinogenital tract

genus: class or category of plants and animals ranking next above the species, as the genus *Homo* in *Homo sapiens*

geriatrics: branch of medicine dealing with diseases and physiological changes associated with aging and old people

German measles: *see* rubella

germicide: disinfectant or other agent capable of killing disease germs

gerontology: scientific study of the processes and phenomena of aging

gestation: the total period of pregnancy, from conception to birth

GI: gastrointestinal

gifted: having ability or intelligence above the normal range

gigantism/giantism: disorder resulting from oversecretion of somatotrophin by the pituitary gland and resulting in excessive growth

gingiva: mucous membrane and soft tissue of the gums surrounding the teeth

gingival: pertaining to the gums

gingivitis: inflammation of the gum tissues

gingivitis, necrotizing ulcerative: *see* trench mouth

GI series/gastrointestinal series: X rays of the esophagus, stomach, and intestines utilizing an opaque substance swallowed by the patient

glabrous: without hair

gland(s): any of various organs that secrete substances essential to the body or for the elimination of waste products

glandular fever: mononucleosis, infectious

glaucoma: disease of the eye characterized by increased pressure on the eyeball and leading to the loss of vision if untreated

glomeruli (*sing., glomerulus*): tiny tufts of capillaries in the kidneys through which the blood passes in the filtering of wastes

glomerulonephritis: inflammation of the glomeruli

glossitis: inflammation of the tongue, characterized by a bright red or glazed appearance

glossopharyngeal nerve: the nerve that supplies sensation to the throat and rear of the tongue

glottis: the passage between the vocal cords at the upper opening of the larynx

glucagon: hormone produced by the islets of Langerhans in the pancreas

glucose/blood sugar: sugar found normally in blood and abnormally in urine, as in the case of diabetes mellitus

glucose tolerance test/GTT: test that determines the rate at which glucose in the blood is reduced, or metabolized, used as an indicator of chemical diabetes or a prediabetic condition

glucosuria: condition, as diabetes mellitus, in which the urine contains glucose

gluten: protein component of wheat and rye

gluteus: any of the three muscles that form each buttock

glycerol/glycerin: sweet, oily alcohol, one of the components of natural fat

glycogen: animal starch usually stored in the liver for conversion to glucose when the body needs energy

glycosuria: glucosuria

goiter: enlargement of the thyroid gland, often because of a lack of iodine in the diet

gonad(s): male or female sex gland; ovary or testicle

gonadotrophic hormone/gonadotrophin/gonadotropin: any of three hormones that stimulate the gonads and are secreted by the anterior pituitary gland

gonioscope: specialized ophthalmoscope for examining the angle between the cornea and the iris

gonococcus: parasitic bacterium that can cause gonorrhea

gonorrhea/clap/GC: contagious venereal disease transmitted by sexual contact

goof balls (*slang*): barbiturates

gout: metabolic disease characterized by painful inflammation of a joint, as of the big toe, and an excess of uric acid in the blood

gouty arthritis, chronic: form of gout characterized by urate deposits and consequent joint stiffness

GP: general practitioner

Graafian follicles: small sacs in the ovaries that contain the developing ova

graft: piece of tissue removed from one organism and inserted in a new site in the same organism or in a different organism

grain alcohol: ethyl alcohol

grand mal: major epileptic seizure, characterized by falling, loss of consciousness, and spasmodic jerking of the arms and legs

granulation: process of forming new tissue in the healing of wounds

granulation tissue/proud flesh: new, temporary, vascular tissue formed in a wound as a stage in the healing process, usually soft and moist

granulocyte: *see* neutrophil

granulocytic leukemia: *see* leukemia, granulocytic

granuloma: small tumor composed mainly of granulation tissue

granuloma inguinale/granuloma venereum: chronic venereal disease that produces lesions in the genital or anal regions

grass (*slang*): marihuana

gravid: pregnant

Grawitz's tumor/hypernephroma: malignant tumor of the kidney, found chiefly among men

gray matter: cortex

greenstick fracture: incomplete fracture, with the bone bending on the unbroken side, more common in children than adults

grippe: influenza

groin: the fold or depressed area where the thigh joins the abdomen

group therapy/group psychotherapy: psychotherapy in which interactions within a group under the direction of a therapist are intended to provoke therapeutic insights and lead to improved social adjustment

growth hormone/growth-stimulating hormone/somatotrophin: hormone secreted by the posterior lobe of the pituitary gland that stimulates growth

GTT: glucose tolerance test

"guard hairs": vibrissae, nasal

gullet: *see* esophagus

gum disease: *see* periodontal disease

gumma: rubbery tumor that develops within organs in the late stages of syphilis

gums: *see* gingiva

gurney: stretcher mounted on wheels, commonly used to move nonambulatory patients in hospitals

gynecologist: physician specializing in gynecology, often an obstetrician as well

gynecology: the branch of medical science that deals with the care and treatment of women and their diseases, especially of the reproductive system

H (*slang*): heroin

hair transplant: the surgical grafting of hair-bearing skin from the back or sides of the scalp onto bald areas of the head

halitosis: offensive mouth odor, usually caused by poor oral hygiene

hallucinate: have hallucinations

hallucination: apparent perception without any corresponding external stimulus

hallucinogen: drug or chemical capable of inducing hallucinations

hallucinogenic: capable of producing hallucinations

halothane: a general anesthetic taken by inhalation

hammer/malleus: the outermost of the three ossicles of the middle ear, the bone between the eardrum and the anvil

hammer toe: clawlike deformity of a toe

hamstrings: any of several tendons at the back of the thigh and controlling the flexing of the knee

hangnail: piece of skin partially torn loose from the root or side of a fingernail

hangover: headache, nausea, dizziness, and other after-effects of excessive alcoholic consumption, an allergic reaction to alcohol, or emotional stress while drinking

Hansen's disease: *see* leprosy

hard palate: *see* palate, hard

hashish: hallucinogenic substance more potent than marihuana, obtained from the leaves and flowers of the Indian hemp plant

hatter's disease: chronic mercury poisoning, common among hatters in former times because of their use of mercury in preparing felt

hay fever: allergic rhinitis

headache: pain or ache across the forehead or within the head

heart: hollow muscular structure which maintains the circulation of the blood by alternate contraction and dilation

heart block: lack of coordination in the heartbeat of the atria and ventricles, often causing unconsciousness and other symptoms (Stokes-Adams syndrome)

heartburn: burning sensation in the lower esophagus caused by a flow of gastric juices from the stomach back into the esophagus

heart failure: inability of the heart to pump enough blood to maintain normal circulation

heart-lung machine: pumping machine used to divert a patient's blood from the heart during heart surgery and to keep it oxygenated and in circulation

heart murmur: abnormal sound heard in the region of the heart

heat cramps: muscle spasms resulting from loss of salt due to excessive sweating

heat exhaustion/heat prostration: weakness or fainting as a result of prolonged exposure to heat, caused by a decreased blood supply to the heart and brain and an increased supply to the skin

heat prostration: heat exhaustion

heat rash: prickly heat

heatstroke: sunstroke

hebephrenic schizophrenia: *see* schizophrenia, hebephrenic

Heimlich maneuver: emergency treatment for obstruction of the windpipe in which sharp pressure is applied just below the rib cage so that the air in the lungs ejects the obstruction

Heine-Medin disease: *see* poliomyelitis

helminth: parasitic worm that invades the intestines, most often via food or water

hemal: of or relating to blood

hemangioma: reddish, usually raised birthmark consisting of a cluster of small blood vessels near the surface of the skin

hematocrit: 1. instrument for measuring the relative amount of plasma and red corpuscles of the blood by centrifuging it (whirling it around to separate parts having different densities) 2. measurement of relative amounts of plasma and red corpuscles by a hematocrit

hematologist: physician specializing in the study of the blood and in the diagnosis and treatment of blood diseases

hematology: the branch of medical science dealing with the blood, including its formation, functions, and diseases

hematoma: blood tumor

hematoma, subdural: mass of blood clots or partially clotted blood in the space beneath the outermost (dura mater) and middle (arachnoid) membranes covering the brain

hematuria: blood in the urine

hemiplegia: paralysis of one side of the body, involving both the arm and leg

hemiplegic: one affected by hemiplegia

hemodialysis: *see* dialysis

hemoglobin: pigment of red blood corpuscles serving as the carrier of oxygen and carbon dioxide

hemophilia: inherited disorder characterized by an incapacity of the blood to clot normally, thus resulting in profuse bleeding even from slight cuts, typically affecting males only

hemophiliac/bleeder: one afflicted with hemophilia

hemorrhage: discharge of blood from a ruptured blood vessel

hemorrhoidal: 1. of or pertaining to the blood vessels in the rectal area 2. of or pertaining to hemorrhoids

hemorrhoidectomy: surgical removal of hemorrhoids

hemorrhoids/piles: swollen varicose veins in the rectal mucous membrane

hemorrhoids, prolapsed: hemorrhoids that protrude from the anus

hemotoxic: (of certain poisonous snakes) transmitting venom that is carried by the bloodstream of the toxified animal

Henle's loop: U-shaped part of a tubule of the kidney

heparin: chemical compound that prevents coagulation of the blood

hepatic: of or relating to the liver

hepaticologist: physician specializing in the diagnosis and treatment of liver diseases

hepaticology: branch of medical science concerned with the study, diagnosis, and treatment of diseases of the liver

hepatitis: inflammation of the liver

hepatitis, infectious: inflammation of the liver caused by a viral infection usually transmitted by food and water contaminated by feces from an infected person

hepatitis, serum: form of infectious hepatitis usually spread by blood transfusions or by infected hypodermic needles

hereditary: acquired through one's genetic makeup by inheritance, as physical characteristics, disease, etc.

hernia/rupture: protrusion of an organ or part, as the intestine, through the wall or body cavity that normally contains it

hernia, hiatus/diaphragmatic hernia: hernia in which the lower end of the esophagus or stomach protrudes through the diaphragm

hernia, inguinal: protuberance of part of the intestine into the inguinal region (near the groin)

hernia, strangulated: hernia that has become tightly constricted, thus cutting off blood supply

hernia, umbilical: hernia in which an abdominal part protrudes through the abdominal wall at the navel

herniate: slip away from its proper position as an organ or part to form a hernia

herniating disk: slipped disk

herniation: forming of a hernia

heroic: extraordinary or extreme, as measures undertaken when life is in immediate danger

heroin/diacetylmorphine: addictive narcotic drug derived from morphine, illegal in the United States

herpes: any of various acute viral diseases characterized by the eruption of small blisters on the skin and mucous membranes

herpes simplex: virus that causes cold sores and other skin conditions in humans

herpes simplex, Type 1/HSV-1: variety of herpes simplex that causes cold sores

herpes simplex, Type 2/HSV-2: variety of herpes simplex that often affects the genital region and can result in congenital damage to the baby of an infected mother

heterograft/xenograft: tissue graft taken for transplanting from a donor of a different species from that of the patient receiving it

hexachlorophene: antibacterial agent used in some soaps

hiatus hernia: *see* hernia

hiccup/hiccough: involuntary, spasmodic grunt caused by spasms of the diaphragm and the abrupt closure of the glottis

high (*slang*): amphetamine

high blood pressure: *see* hypertension

hip bone: ilium

hip joint: acetabulum

hirsutism: abnormal or excessive hairiness, especially in women

histamine: substance found in animal tissues that can cause allergic symptoms when allergens stimulate the body to produce it in large amounts

histoincompatibility: incompatibility between tissues, as between the tissues of a patient and the tissues of a transplanted organ or part

histoplasma: fungus that can cause histoplasmosis

histoplasmosis: chronic fungus disease of the lungs

hives/urticaria: skin condition marked by large, irregularly shaped swellings that burn and itch

Hodgkin's disease: disease of the lymph system, characterized by chronic, progressive enlargement of the lymph nodes, lymphoid tissue, and spleen

homeopathy: system of medicine in which disease is treated by administering minute doses of medicine that would in a healthy person produce the symptoms of the disease treated

homeostasis: maintenance of uniform physiological stability within an organism and between its parts

homograft/allograft: tissue graft taken for transplanting from a donor of the same species as the patient receiving it

hookworm: parasitic intestinal worm whose larvae usually enter the body by penetrating the skin of the feet of people who go barefooted

hormone: internal secretion released in minute amounts into the bloodstream by one of the endocrine glands or other tissue and stimulating a specific physiological activity

horny layer of epidermis: stratum corneum

horse (*slang*): heroin

housemaid's knee: chronic inflammation of the bursa in front of the knee resulting from pressure from constant kneeling or injury

HSV-1: *see* herpes simplex, Type 1

HSV-2: *see* herpes simplex, Type 2

HTLV-3: *see* human T-cell leukemia virus (HTLV)

Hubbard tank: large, specially designed tub in which a patient may be immersed in water for exercises as a means of physical therapy

humerus: the long bone of the arm from elbow to shoulder

humpback, hunchback: kyphosis

hyaline membrane disease/respiratory distress syndrome: disease of newborn babies characterized by severe respiratory distress caused by the presence of a membrane lining the alveoli of the lungs

hydatidiform mole: benign tumor formed from a placenta that has degenerated into a mass of grapelike cysts

hydrocele: localized accumulation of fluid, especially surrounding the testicles in the scrotum

hydrocephalus: accumulation of cerebrospinal fluid within the brain

hydrochloric acid: colorless, corrosive acid which in dilute form is present in gastric juice

hydrogenation: the subjection of a material to hydrogen, as the process by which unsaturated fats are solidified

hydronephrosis: enlargement of the kidneys with urine because of an obstruction of the ureter

hydrophilic: having an affinity for water, as the soft contact lens

hydrophilic lenses: contact lenses, soft plastic

hydrophobia: rabies

hydrotherapy: treatment of disease by the use of water

hymen: thin membrane usually partially covering the entrance of the vagina in virgins

hyperactive child: *see* hyperkinesis

hyperacusis: abnormal and sometimes painful acuteness of hearing

hyperaldosteronism: syndrome of muscle weakness, hypertension, and excessive excretion of urine, because of oversecretion of an adrenal hormone

hyperbaric: of or using pressures in excess of the usual pressure of the atmosphere, as a chamber for treating one suffering from decompression sickness

hyperfunction: disorder of an endocrine gland, characterized by excess secretion of a hormone

hyperglycemia: abnormally high amount of sugar in the blood

hyperkinesis: behavioral disorder of children marked by overactivity, excitability, and inability to concentrate

hyperkinetic: suffering from or pertaining to hyperkinesis

hypermetropia: *see* farsightedness

hypermetropic: farsighted

hypernephroma: *see* Grawitz's tumor

hyperopia: *see* farsightedness

hyperopic: farsighted

hyperplasia: excessive production of cells, resulting in enlargement of tissue or of an organ

hyperplastic: characterized by hyperplasia

hypersensitivity: unusual sensitivity or allergic response to a particular substance

hypertension/high blood pressure: excessively high blood pressure, sometimes caused by a disease (secondary hypertension) and sometimes not (essential hypertension)

hypertension, chronic: essential hypertension

hypertension, essential/chronic/functional: hypertension that is not a symptom of disease and has no known cause

hypertension, malignant: form of essential hypertension with an acute onset and rapid rise in pressure

hypertension, secondary: hypertension arising as a consequence of another known disorder

hypertensive heart disease: *see* heart disease, hypertensive

hyperthyroidism: abnormal and excess activity of the thyroid gland, resulting in oversecretion of thyroxin and an abnormally high metabolism, characterized by fatigue, weight loss, rapid pulse, intolerance to heat, and sometimes by protruding eyes (in which case the disorder is called *exophthalmic goiter*)

hypertonic: characterized by an abnormally high degree of tension, as muscle

hypertrophic: characterized by hypertrophy

hypertrophic arthritis: *see* osteoarthritis

hypertrophy: excessive development of an organ or tissue because of enlargement of the size of its constituent cells

hyperventilation: abnormally fast or deep breathing, resulting in loss of carbon dioxide from the blood and sometimes causing dizziness and muscle spasms

hypnotic: tending to produce sleep

hypoallergenic: less likely to produce an allergic reaction

hypochondria: extreme anxiety about one's health, usually associated with a particular part of the body and accompanied by imagined symptoms of illness

hypochondriac: 1. (*n.*) one suffering from hypochondria 2. (*adj.*) pertaining to the upper right or left parts of the abdomen

hypodermic: pertaining to the tissue just under the skin or to an injection made under the skin

hypofunction: disorder of an endocrine gland, characterized by too little secretion of a hormone

hypogastric: pertaining to the lower middle part of the abdomen

hypogastrium: the lower middle (hypogastric) part of the abdomen

hypoglycemia/low blood sugar: abnormally small amount of glucose in the blood, which can lead to insulin shock

hypoglycemic drug: drug intended to reduce the amount of glucose in the blood by stimulating the release of insulin from the pancreas

hypophysis: *see* pituitary gland

hypophysis cerebri: pituitary gland

hyposensitization: program for desensitizing allergy patients by injecting them with progressively larger doses of pollen or other allergens to build tolerance levels

hypotension: excessively low blood pressure

hypothalamus: region of the brain below the thalamus, important in regulating the internal organs and associated with the functioning of the pituitary gland

hypothermia: artificially low body temperature produced by gradually cooling blood, used to slow metabolism and reduce tissue oxygen need so that heart and brain can withstand short periods of interrupted blood flow during surgery

hypothyroidism: deficient functioning of the thyroid gland, resulting in undersecretion of thyroxin and an abnormally low metabolism, characterized by lack of energy, thick skin, and intolerance to cold

hypotonic: characterized by an abnormally low degree of tension, as muscle

hysterectomy: surgical procedure in which the uterus is completely removed

hysterectomy, radical: surgical removal of the uterus, cervix, ovaries, and Fallopian tubes

hysterectomy, total: surgical removal of the uterus and cervix

hysteria: neurotic condition characterized by impulsive, demonstrative, and attention-getting behavior and sometimes by symptoms of organic disorders

hysteria, conversion: *see* conversion reaction

hysterogram: X-ray examination of the uterus and surrounding areas

id: the concealed, inaccessible part of the mind, the seat of impulses that tend to fulfill instinctual needs

identical twins: twins having the same genetic makeup, derived from a single fertilized egg

identification: mental process, often unconscious, by which a person associates with himself the attributes of another with whom he has formed an emotional tie

idiopathic: (of diseases) originating spontaneously or of unknown cause

ileitis: inflammation of the ileum of the small intestine

ileocecal valve: the valve between the ileum of the small intestine and the cecum, the first section of the large intestine

ileum: the last section of the small intestine, following the jejunum and leading to the large intestine

iliac: pertaining to or near the ilium

ilium: the large upper portion of the hip bone

immune: protected from a communicable or allergic disease by the presence of antibodies in the blood

immunity: resistance to infection or lack of susceptibility of an organism to a disease or poison to which its species is usually subject, either by means of antibodies produced by the organism itself (*active immunity*) or by another and subsequently introduced into its body (*passive immunity*), as by injection

immunization: act or process of making immune, especially by inoculation

immunize: make immune, as by inoculation

immunoglobulin: any of various proteins of the body that are active as antigens or otherwise contribute to the formation of antibodies

immunologist: physician or specialist in the study of immunity

immunology: the branch of medical science concerned with the phenomena and techniques of immunity from disease

immunosuppressive: acting to suppress natural immune responses, as to foreign tissue in an organ transplant

immunotherapy: therapy to relieve allergic response consisting of a series of injections of a dilute allergen, gradually increased in strength

impacted tooth: tooth wedged between the jawbone and another tooth so as to prevent its eruption

impaction: state of being firmly packed or tightly wedged, as feces in the rectum or a tooth in the jaw; *see* impacted tooth

imperforate: lacking a normal opening

impetigo: contagious bacterial skin infection characterized by blisters that break and form yellow encrusted areas

impotence: in men, the inability to have sexual intercourse

incision: 1. cut or gash, as of a wound 2. cut or slit made in a surgical operation

incisor: one of the four upper and four lower cutting teeth near the front of the mouth

incompetence: inadequate performance, as of the heart valves

incomplete fracture: partial fracture of a bone in which continuity of the bone is not destroyed

incontinence: inability to control the flow of urine or the evacuation of the bowels

incubation period: the period between the entry of a disease-causing organism in the body and the onset of the symptoms of that disease

incus: anvil

indomethacin: analgesic and anti-inflammatory drug used for arthritic disorders, often as a substitute for aspirin

infantile paralysis: *see* poliomyelitis

infantile sexuality: the sexual interest and pleasure that infants and young children take in their genitals and other body parts

infarct: tissue rendered necrotic (dead) by an obstructed blood supply, as because of a thrombus (clot) or an embolus

infarction: death of tissue because of deprivation of blood caused by an obstruction, as in a coronary thrombosis (heart attack)

infection(s): communication of disease by entrance into the body of disease-causing organisms

infectious: (of a disease) transmitted by organisms, as bacteria

infectious mononucleosis/glandular fever/kissing disease: acute communicable disease marked by fever, malaise, and swollen lymph nodes, especially in the throat

inferior vena cava: the large vein that brings blood from the lower part of the body to the heart

infertility: inability to conceive or to produce offspring

inflammation: localized reaction to infection, injury, etc., characterized by heat, redness, swelling, and pain

inflammation of arterial walls: arteritis

inflammation of bladder: cystitis

inflammation of bone: osteomyelitis

inflammation of brain: encephalitis

inflammation of brain coverings: meningitis

inflammation of bursa: bursitis

inflammation of femoral head: Legg-Perthes' disease

inflammation of glomeruli: nephritis

inflammation of gums: gingivitis

inflammation of joints: arthritis

inflammation of larynx: laryngitis

inflammation of liver: hepatitis

inflammation of mucous membrane: laryngitis

inflammation of prostate: prostatitis

inflammation of skin: dermatitis

inflammation of spinal joints: spondylitis, rheumatoid

inflammation of stomach lining: gastritis

inflammation of tendons: tendinitis

inflammation of tendon sheath: tenosynovitis

inflammation of tongue: glossitis

inflammation of veins: phlebitis

inflammation of vertebrae: osteomyelitis, spinal

influenza/flu/grippe: acute, contagious, sometimes epidemic disease caused by a virus and characterized by inflammation of the upper respiratory tract, fever, chills, muscle ache, and fatigue

ingrown toenail: toenail that has grown into the surrounding flesh

inguinal: pertaining to or near the groin

inguinal hernia: *see* hernia

inner ear: the innermost part of the ear, containing the essential organs of hearing within the cochlea, the auditory nerve, and the semicircular canals that govern equilibrium

innervation: distribution or supply of nerves to a part

inoculate: immunize by administering a serum or vaccine to 2. introduce microorganisms into (a culture medium)

inoculation: act or process of inoculating

inoperable: characterized by a condition that excludes surgery as a course of treatment

in situ: in its original site or position

insomnia: chronic inability to sleep

insufficiency: inability to function adequately, as the heart (cardiac insufficiency)

insufflation: tubal insufflation

insulin: protein hormone secreted by the islets of Langerhans in the pancreas that checks the accumulation of glucose in the blood and promotes the utilization of sugar in the treatment of diabetes

insulin shock: condition caused by too low a level of blood sugar, and characterized by sweating, dizziness, palpitation, shallow breathing, confusion, and ultimately loss of consciousness

insulin shock therapy: former method of treating psychotic patients involving large injections of insulin, inducing coma

insult: injury to tissue caused by stress or trauma

integument: skin

intelligence quotient/IQ: a score obtained from standardized tests indicating the level of a person's intelligence

intensive care unit (ICU): section of a hospital specially equipped and staffed to monitor the vital systems of patients and provide close, round-the-clock care for a relatively brief period, as for patients just removed from surgery or for those in an unstable or critical condition

intercostal muscles: the muscles between each of the ribs that contract when air is exhaled

intercourse: sexual intercourse

intermittent claudication: vascular disease associated with aging and marked by muscle fatigue and pain, especially in the legs, due to atherosclerosis

intern: advanced medical student or graduate (M.D.) undergoing resident training in a hospital

internal medicine: the branch of medical science that deals with the study, diagnosis, and nonsurgical treatment of diseases of the internal organs

internist: physician specializing in internal medicine

interstitial calcinosis: condition characterized by deposits of calcium salts in the skin and subcutaneous tissue

intestine(s): tubular part of the alimentary canal, linking the stomach to the anus

intestine, large: the lower part of the intestine, of greater diameter than the small intestine and divided into the cecum, colon, and rectum

intestine, small: the convoluted upper and narrower part of the intestines, where most nutrients are absorbed by the bloodstream, between the pylorus and the cecum, divided into three parts, the duodenum, jejunum, and ileum

intoxicated: in legal use, having more than 0.10% alcohol in the bloodstream

intracutaneous: within the dermis

intramuscular: situated within or injected into a muscle or muscular tissue

intrauterine device/IUD: contraceptive device consisting usually of a plastic coil, spiral, or loop that is inserted and left within the uterus for as long as contraception is desired

intravenous: into or within a vein, as an injection

intrinsic: originating or situated within an organ or part, as a disease

introitus: entrance into a body cavity, especially into the vagina

intussusception: the turning inward or inversion of a portion of the intestine into an adjacent part, thus obstructing it, found especially in male infants

in utero: in the uterus, prior to birth

invasive: invading or spreading to tissues other than at the place of origin: said of malignant growths

involutional melancholia: *see* depressive reaction

IQ: intelligence quotient

iris: colored, circular, contractile membrane between the cornea and the lens of the eye, whose central perforation is occupied by the pupil

irradiation: process of exposing a part of the body to radiant energy, as X rays

irrigate: wash out or cleanse, as a body cavity or a wound, with a flow of water or other liquid

irrigation: act or process of irrigating a body cavity, wound, etc.

ischemia: localized deficiency of blood, as from a contracted blood vessel

ischium: the part of the hip bone on which the body rests when sitting

islands of Langerhans: islets of Langerhans

islets of Langerhans/islands of Langerhans: small, cellular masses in the pancreas which produce and secrete insulin

isomer: compound with the same molecular weight and formula as another, but with a different arrangement of its atoms, resulting in different properties

isometrics: means of strengthening muscles by forcefully contracting them against immovable resistance

isoniazid/INH: isonicotinic acid hydrazide, a chemical compound used in the treatment of tuberculosis

isopropyl: chemical in the family of methyl alcohol, used as a rubbing alcohol

itch, the: scabies

IUD: intrauterine device

Jacksonian epilepsy: form of epilepsy characterized by recurrent focal seizures, spasmodic movements or tingling or burning sensations, as of an arm, leg, or facial area, caused by a condition affecting a motor area of the brain

Jacksonian seizure: form of focal seizure that characterizes Jacksonian epilepsy

jaundice: yellowish tint to the skin and tissues, as the whites of the eyes, caused by excessive bile in the blood, a symptom of certain disorders

jejunum: the middle section of the small intestine, between the duodenum and the ileum

joint(s): place where two or more bones or separate parts of the skeleton meet

junk (slang): heroin

juvenile rheumatoid arthritis: *see* rheumatoid arthritis, juvenile

kala-azar/black fever/dumdum fever/visceral leishmaniasis: form of leishmaniasis that is usually fatal if not treated

keratin: horny substance that is the main constituent of nails and hair, and in nonhuman animals of claws and horns

keratosis: disease of the skin characterized by an outer layer of horny tissue

ketone bodies: organic compounds that are a by-product of fat metabolism

kidney: one of a pair of organs located at the rear of the abdomen near the base of the spine, whose function is to filter the fluid portion of the blood in regulating the composition and volume of body fluids, and to dispose of waste in the form of urine

kidney failure, acute: sudden loss of kidney function, characterized by decreased amount of urine, passage of bloody urine, edema, fatigue, and loss of appetite

kidney stone/renal calculus: mass of hard material, such as crystallized salt, that may collect within the kidney and obstruct the flow of urine

kissing disease: infectious mononucleosis

kyphosis: backward curvature of the spine characterized as a humpback or hunchback

labia: 1. *pl.* of labium 2. the folds of skin and mucous membrane of the vulva, consisting of the outer folds (*labia majora*) and the inner folds (*labia minora*)

labium: 1. *sing.* of labia 2. lip or liplike part or organ

labor: process of giving birth, during which the uterus undergoes periodic contractions in moving the fetus through the birth canal

labyrinth: the winding passages of the inner ear

labyrinthitis: inflammation of the labyrinth of the inner ear, usually disturbing the sense of equilibrium

laceration: wound made by tearing or ripping

lacrimal gland: tear-producing gland over the eye

lactation: formation or secretion of milk from the breast

lactic acid: bitter, syrupy acid found in sour milk and collected in muscle tissues during anaerobic exercise

lactogenic hormone/LTH/luteotrophic hormone/luteotrophin/luteotropin/prolactin: hormone secreted by the anterior lobe of the pituitary gland that stimulates the production of milk in the mammary glands

Lamaze, Dr. Ferdinand: French physician who pioneered in the development of a natural childbirth technique

Langerhans: islets of Langerhans

laparotomy: surgical procedure for examining or treating the female reproductive organs within the abdominal cavity

lapse attack or seizure: *see* petit mal

laryngectomy: surgical removal of all or part of the larynx

laryngitis: inflammation of the mucous membranes of the larynx, causing the voice to become hoarse or disappear altogether

laryngitis, chronic: permanently hoarse voice resulting from thickened, toughened mucous membrane in the larynx, resulting from too many attacks of laryngitis

laryngologist: physician specializing in the diagnosis and treatment of disorders of the throat

laryngology: the branch of medical science concerned with the study and treatment of the throat and related areas

laryngoscope: instrument for inspecting the larynx

larynx/voice box: the organ of voice in humans and most other vertebrates, consisting of a cartilaginous box in the upper part of the trachea across which are stretched vocal cords whose vibrations produce sound

latent: not visible or apparent, as symptoms of a disease at an early stage

lateral: 1. relating to or directed toward the side 2. more distant from the midline of the body, as compared to a nearer (medial) position

lavage: cleansing or washing out of an organ, as the stomach

laxative: substance that has the power to loosen the bowels, as milk of magnesia

L-dopa/levodopa: medicine used in treating the symptoms of Parkinson's disease

leaflet: flap of a heart valve

learning disability: condition in which a child cannot acquire certain skills or assimilate certain kinds of knowledge at or near the normal rate

Legg-Perthes' disease: inflammation of the bone and cartilage in the head of the femur (thigh bone)

leiomyoma: benign tumor consisting of smooth muscle tissue

leishmaniasis: tropical disease resembling malaria in which an animal parasite is transmitted by the sandfly

leishmaniasis, visceral: *see* kala-azar

lens: biconvex transparent body behind the iris of the eye that focuses entering light rays on the retina

lepromatous: characterized by nodular skin lesions, as a form of leprosy

leprosy/Hansen's disease: chronic bacterial disease characterized by skin lesions, nerve paralysis, and physical deformity

lesion: any abnormal change in an organ or tissue caused by disease or injury

leukemia: form of cancer involving the blood and blood-making tissues, characterized by a marked and persistent excess of leukocytes

leukemia, granulocytic: form of leukemia characterized by predominance of granulocytes (or neutrophils)

leukemia, lymphocytic: form of leukemia characterized by uncontrolled over-activity of the lymphoid tissue

leukemic: of or characteristic of leukemia

leukocyte/white blood cell/white corpuscle: white or colorless cell found in the bloodstream important in providing protection against infection

leukopenia: abnormal reduction in the number of leukocytes in the blood

leukorrhea: whitish, viscid discharge from the vagina

levodopa: medicine used in treating the symptoms of Parkinson's disease

levulose: fructose

LGV: *see* lymphogranuloma venereum

LH: luteinizing hormone

libido: the instinctual craving or drive behind all human activities, especially sexual, the repression of which leads to neurosis

Librium: chlordiazepoxide

lidocaine: chemical used as a local anesthetic

ligament(s): band of tough, fibrous connective tissue that binds together bones and provides support for organs

ligate: tie or close off with a ligature

ligation: the act of tying or binding up, as an artery

ligature: thread, wire, etc., used to close off or tie a vessel

lightening: during the last few weeks of pregnancy, a shift in fetal pressure from the upper abdomen to the pelvic region as the head of the fetus moves toward the birth canal

lipase: enzyme that breaks down fats

lipid: fatty substance essential to living cells

lipid storage disease: any of various usually fatal diseases, typically occurring in childhood, caused by the lack of a particular enzyme

lip reading/speech reading: interpretation of speech by watching the position of the lips and mouth of the speaker, practiced especially by the deaf

lithium salts: salts of lithium (a metal), used as a medication in the treatment of manic-depressive psychosis

lithotomy position: position used in gynecological examinations in which the patient lies on her back and the legs are drawn back and apart at the thighs

liver: large, glandular organ situated just under the diaphragm on the right side, that processes blood and regulates its composition, as by storing sugar and releasing it in assimilable form (glucose), and that secretes bile

liver spots/chloasma: yellowish brown patches that appear on the skin

lobe(s): rounded or protruding section or subdivision, as of an organ

lobotomy: *see* frontal lobotomy

lockjaw: *see* tetanus

locomotor ataxia: *see* tabes dorsalis

loiasis: form of filariasis transmitted by a biting fly from monkey to man or vice versa

loins: the part of the body between the lower rib and the hip bone

lordosis: abnormal inward curvature of the spine

lordotic posture: posture characteristic of some women in late pregnancy, in which the shoulders are slumped, the neck bent, and the lower spine curved forward to bear the weight of the fetus

Lou Gehrig's disease: sclerosis, amyolotrophic lateral

low blood sugar: hypoglycemia

LSD/lysergic acid diethylamide: colorless, odorless, tasteless drug produced synthetically that causes the user to experience hallucinations

LTH: lactogenic hormone

lumbago: pain in the lower back

lumbar: pertaining to or situated near the loins

lumbar puncture: *see* spinal tap

lumen: space enclosed by the walls of a blood vessel, duct, etc.

lung: either of two porous organs of respiration in the chest cavity of humans, having the function of absorbing oxygen and discharging carbon dioxide

lunula: the living part of the nail, the pale, half-moon shape at the nail base

luteinizing hormone/LH: a hormone secreted by the anterior lobe of the pituitary gland that stimulates a Graafian follicle to release an ovum during each menstrual cycle and converts the follicle into corpus luteum

luteotrophic hormone: lactogenic hormone

luteotrophin: lactogenic hormone

lymph: transparent fluid resembling blood plasma that is conveyed through vessels (lymphatic vessels) and lubricates the tissues

lymphangiogram: the visualization by X ray of lymph nodes after injection of an opaque fluid

lymphatic: pertaining to or conveying lymph

lymph gland: *see* lymph node

lymph node/lymph gland: one of the rounded bodies about the size of a pea, found in the course of the lymphatic vessels, that produces lymphocytes

lymphoblast: young cell that matures into a lymphocyte

lymphocyte: variety of leukocyte formed in the lymphoid tissue

lymphogranuloma inguinale: *see* lymphogranuloma venereum

lymphogranuloma venereum/LGV/lymphogranuloma inguinale: venereal disease affecting the lymph nodes

lymphoid: pertaining to lymph or to the tissue of lymph nodes

lymphoma: abnormal (neoplastic) growth of lymphoid tissue, symptomatic of various diseases, as lymphocytic leukemia or Hodgkin's disease

lymphosarcoma: malignant growth of the lymphatic system

lysergic acid diethylamide: LSD

lysozyme: enzyme present in tears that is destructive to bacteria

lyssophobia: fear of becoming insane

M (*slang*): morphine

macrobiotic: of or pertaining to macrobiotics

macrobiotics: the idea, Oriental in origin, that an equilibrium should be maintained between foods that make one active (Yang) and foods that make one relax (Yin)

macrocephalic: individual with macrocephaly

macrocephaly: excessive head size

macula: spot or discoloration

macula lutea: yellowish area in the retina related to color perception and marked by most acute vision

mainlining: injection of heroin directly into a vein

malabsorption syndrome/celiac disease: syndrome characterized by bulky, foul-smelling stools and other symptoms resulting from the inability of the body to absorb certain nutrients from the intestinal tract

malaise: feeling of being run-down, listless, uncomfortable, weary, and generally unwell

malaria: disease caused by certain animal parasites transmitted by the bite of the infected Anopheles mosquito, causing intermittent chills, and fever

malignancy: 1. malignant tumor 2. state of being malignant

malignant: so aggravated as to threaten life, usually resistant to treatment, and often having the property of uncontrolled growth, as a cancer

malleus: hammer

malnutrition: nutritional deficiency, as of essential proteins, vitamins, or minerals, causing impairment of health and certain specific diseases

malocclusion: faulty closure of the upper and lower teeth

Malta fever: *see* brucellosis

mammogram: X-ray picture of the breast by the technique of mammography

mammography: specialized X-ray examination of the breasts

mammoplasty: surgical procedure to augment the size of the breasts

mandible: the lower jawbone

mania: psychotic condition characterized by excessive activity, elation, extreme talkativeness, and agitation

manic-depressive reaction/affective reaction: psychosis characterized by mania or depression or by the alternation of both

marihuana: the dried leaves and flowers of the hemp plant (*Cannabis sativa*), which if smoked in cigarettes or otherwise ingested can produce distorted perception and other hallucinogenic effects

marrow: either of two types of soft, vascular tissue found in the central cavities of bones—*red marrow*, which produces red blood cells, and *yellow marrow*, composed mainly of fat cells

mastectomy: surgical removal of the breast

mastectomy, radical: surgical removal of the breast, underlying chest muscles, and lymph glands in the armpit

mastectomy, simple: surgical removal of the breast only

master gland: pituitary gland

mastitis: inflammation of the breast

mastoiditis: inflammation of the air cells in the mastoid process

mastoid process: process of the temporal bone behind the ear

mastoplasty: surgical procedure to reduce the size of the breasts

masturbation: the touching or rubbing of the genitals for sexual pleasure and usually orgasm

materia alba: white, viscous mixture of mucus, molds, tissue cells, and bacteria adhering to teeth or to the spaces between teeth and gums, a potential source of disease

maxilla: the upper jawbone

maxillary sinus: *see* paranasal sinus

MBD: *see* minimal brain dysfunction

MD: *see* muscular dystrophy

M.D.: Doctor of Medicine

measles/rubeola: contagious viral disease, especially of children, marked by rash, fever, and conjunctivitis, sometimes having severe complications

measles, German: *see* rubella

meatus: passage or canal in the human body, especially one with an external opening such as the anterior urethra of the penis

medial: 1. middle, or relatively near the middle 2. nearer to the midline of the body, as compared to a more distant (lateral) position

medical: 1. of or relating to medicine 2. of or relating to the treatment of disease by nonsurgical means

medical history: the questions asked by a doctor of a patient that are designed to give an outline of the patient's state of health

medicine: 1. the profession dealing with the maintenance of health and the treatment of physical and psychological disorders 2. the treatment of disease by nonsurgical means

medulla: 1. medulla oblongata: the lower part of the brain continuous with the spinal cord that controls certain involuntary processes such as breathing, swallowing, and blood circulation 2. the inner portion of an organ or part, as of the kidneys or the adrenal glands

melancholia, involutional: *see* depressive reaction

melanin: dark brown or black pigment of the skin

melanin cell clusters: *see* moles

melanoma/black cancer: malignant tumor formed of cells that produce melanin

menarche: the first menstrual period of a girl

Ménière's disease/Ménière's syndrome: symptoms including vertigo, ringing or buzzing sensations (tinnitus), nausea, and vomiting, associated with disease of the inner ear and often leading to progressive deafness of one ear

Ménière's syndrome: *see* Ménière's disease

meninges: the membranes that cover the brain and spinal cord

meningioma: uncontrolled new cell growth in one of the membranes (arachnoid) covering the brain and spinal cord

meningitis: inflammation of the membranes that cover the brain and spinal cord

meningitis, aseptic/viral: meningitis thought to be caused by a virus instead of a bacterium

meningococcal: pertaining to meningococcus, a bacterium

meningococcus: bacterium that causes a form of meningitis

menopausal: of or occurring during the menopause

menopause/change of life/climacteric: the cessation of menstruation and the end of a woman's capacity to bear children, normally occurring between 40–50 years of age and often marked by hot flashes, dizzy spells, and other physical and emotional symptoms

menopause, surgical: abrupt onset of menopause in women resulting from the surgical removal of the uterus and ovaries

menses: menstruation

menstrual: of or relating to menstruation

menstruation/the menses: periodic bloody discharge of the unfertilized ovum and tissue from the uterus of a female of child-bearing age

mental retardation: failure in mental development that is severe enough to prevent normal participation in everyday life

mentoplasty: plastic surgery of the chin, especially a procedure to build up an underdeveloped chin

meperidine/pethidine/Demerol: medicine used as an analgesic and sedative

meprobamate/Equanil/Miltown: tranquilizer used as a sedative and muscle relaxant

mescaline: chemical extracted from the peyote cactus that induces hallucinations in its users

mesentery: the fan-shaped fold of the membrane (peritoneum) that enfolds the small intestine and connects it with the abdominal wall

mesoderm: middle layer of tissue

metabolic: of or relating to metabolism

metabolism: aggregate of all physical and chemical processes continuously taking place in living organisms, including those which build up and break down assimilated materials

metacarpal: any of the five bones of the metacarpus

metacarpus: the five bones of the hand connecting the wrist to the fingers (phalanges)

metastasis: the transfer of a disease or its manifestations, as a malignant tumor, from one part of the body to another

metatarsalgia: painful inflammation of the nerves in the region of the metatarsus of the foot

metatarsals: the bones of the metatarsus

metatarsus: the fine bones of the foot connecting the ankle to the toes (phalanges)

methadone/Dolophine: synthetic opiate used as an analgesic and experimentally as a substitute for heroin in the treatment of addicts

methamphetamine/Methedrine/Desoxyn: chemical compound that allays hunger and has a more stimulating effect on the central nervous system than does amphetamine or dextroamphetamine

methanol: methyl alcohol

Methedrine: methamphetamine (meth-head)

methotrexate: drug used in the treatment of psoriasis and leukemia

methyl alcohol/wood alcohol/methanol: flammable liquid obtained through the distillation of wood or made synthetically, poisonous if taken internally

metorrhagia: erratic or unpredictable menstrual bleeding

microcephalic: individual with microcephaly

microcephaly: abnormal smallness of the head, with imperfect development of the cranium

micrographia: very minute handwriting, a symptom of some nervous disorders

micron: 1/1000th of a millimeter (symbol *mu*, Greek letter *mu*)

microsurgery: surgery or dissection of minute parts, as of individual cells, with the aid of a microscope and especially precise instruments

micturate: urinate

micturition: urination

middle ear: the part of the ear between the eardrum and the inner ear, including the tympanum and the ossicles—hammer, anvil, and stirrup

migraine/sick headache: recurrent severe form of headache, temporarily disabling, usually affecting one side of the head and often accompanied by nausea, dizziness, and sensitivity to light

miliaria: prickly heat

milk teeth: baby teeth

Miltown: meprobamate

mineral(s): naturally occurring, homogeneous, inorganic material, some of which, as salt and iron, are required by the body

minimal brain dysfunction/minimal brain damage: condition of children who suffer from a motor or perceptual impairment because of slight brain damage

miscarriage/spontaneous abortion: the involuntary expulsion of a nonviable fetus after the first three months of pregnancy

Miss Emma (*slang*): morphine

mitral valve: the membranous valve between the left atrium and left ventricle of the heart that prevents the backflow of blood into the atrium

mittelschmerz: pain during ovulation about midway between menstrual periods

modality: 1. method of treatment or its application, especially a physical procedure 2. any form of sensation, as touch or taste

molar: any of the three upper and three lower grinding teeth with flattened crowns at both sides of the rear of the mouth, making 12 in all

mole: permanent pigmented spot on the skin, usually brown and often raised

molluscum contagiosum: contagious viral disease marked by raised lesions containing waxy material

Mongolism: congenital disorder characterized by mental retardation

moniliasis/candidiasis: fungus infection involving the skin or mucous membranes of various parts of the body, such as the mouth, especially in babies (when it is called thrush) or the vagina

monocyte: relatively large leukocyte

mononucleosis: infectious mononucleosis

monovalent: pertaining to a form of the Sabin polio vaccine in which each dose gives protection against a different strain of polio

morning sickness: nausea and vomiting experienced by some pregnant women in the morning hours, especially in early pregnancy

morphine: addictive narcotic drug derived from opium, used medically to relieve pain

morphinism: abnormal condition of the body system caused by an excessive dose or habitual use of morphine

Morton's toe: painful inflammation of the nerves in the region of the metatarsus of the foot (metatarsalgia) between the third and fourth toes

motion sickness: nausea and sometimes vomiting caused by the effect of certain complex movements on the organ of

balance in the inner ear, typically experienced in a moving vehicle, ship, or airplane

motor nerve/efferent nerve: nerve that conveys information from the central nervous system to a muscle with a directive for action

mouth-to-mouth respiration/mouth-to-mouth resuscitation: form of artificial respiration in which the rescuer places his or her mouth over the victim's mouth and breathes rhythmically and forcefully to inflate the victim's lungs and start respiration

MS: multiple sclerosis

mu: micron

mucosa: mucous membrane

mucosal: of or pertaining to the mucous membrane

mucous: pertaining to, producing, or resembling mucus

mucous membrane/mucosa: membrane that lines many of the body's inner surfaces, kept moist by glandular secretions

mucus: viscous substance secreted by the mucous membranes

multipara: woman who has borne more than one child

multiphasic: having many phases or aspects; said especially of testing performed in the course of a comprehensive physical examination

multiple myeloma: malignant tumor of the bone marrow occurring at numerous sites

multiple sclerosis/MS: chronic disease in which patches of nerve tissue thicken (sclerose), causing failure of coordination and other nervous and mental symptoms

mumps: contagious, viral disease marked by fever and swelling of the facial glands

muscular dystrophy/MD: any of various diseases of unknown cause characterized by the progressive wasting away (atrophy) of the muscles

musculoskeletal system: the human body's network of muscles and bones

myasthenia gravis: chronic disease characterized by muscular weakness and general and progressive exhaustion

mycobacterium: kind of rod-shaped, aerobic bacterium

myelin: semisolid fatlike sheath that surrounds the axon of a neuron

myelitis: 1. inflammation of the spinal cord 2. inflammation of the bone marrow

myelogram: X ray of the spinal cord obtained by the injection of a radioopaque liquid material into the spinal cord area

myelography: technique of recording myelograms and the science of interpreting them

myeloma: malignant tumor of the bone marrow

myocardial infarction: the process of congestion and tissue death (necrosis) in the heart muscle caused by an interruption of the blood supply to the heart

myocardium: the muscular tissue of the heart

myomectomy: surgical excision of a type of uterine fibroid tumor

myopathy: any abnormality or disease of the muscles

myopia: nearsightedness

myopic: nearsighted

myotonia: disorder characterized by increased rigidity or spasms of muscle

myotonia, congenita: congenital disease characterized by temporary muscle spasms and muscle rigidity

myotonic dystrophy: chronic, progressive disease characterized by weakness and wasting of muscles, cataracts, and heart abnormality

myringotomy: surgical incision of the eardrum

mysophobia: fear of dirt and contamination

naprapathy: the treatment of disease by the manipulative correction of ligaments and connective tissues

narcolepsy: disease in which the patient is overcome by drowsiness or an uncontrollable desire for sleep

narcosis: stupor or unconsciousness produced by a narcotic drug

narcotic: 1. any of various substances, such as morphine, codeine, and opium, that in medicinal doses relieve pain, induce sleep, and in excessive or uncontrolled doses may produce convulsions, coma, and death 2. inducing sleep, in anesthesia

nares: the nasal passages or nostrils

nasopharyngeal: pertaining to the nasopharynx

nasopharynx: the upper part of the pharynx above and behind the soft palate

Natulan: procarbazine

natural foods: foods processed minimally, although not necessarily organically grown

nausea: feeling of sickness or dizziness usually accompanied by the impulse to vomit

navel/umbilicus: the depression at the middle of the abdomen where the umbilical cord of the fetus was attached

nearsightedness/myopia: inability to see distant objects clearly

neck vertebra: vertebra, cervical

necrosis: death of a group of cells, tissue, or a part of the body

necrotizing ulcerative gingivitis: *see* trench mouth

needle biopsy: the excising of a tissue sample for biopsy by means of a long needle

nematode: any of a class of roundworms, many of which, such as the hookworm or pinworm, are intestinal parasites in man and other animals

neonate: newborn baby

neoplasm: any abnormal growth of new tissue, as a tumor, which may be benign or malignant

neoplastic: of or characteristic of neoplasms

nephrectomy: surgical removal of a kidney

nephric: renal

nephritis/Bright's disease: inflammation of the kidneys

nephroblastoma: *see* Wilm's tumor

nephrologist: physician specializing in the diagnosis and treatment of diseases of the kidney

nephrology: branch of medical science dealing with the structure, function, and diseases of the kidney

nephron: one of the basic filtration units of the kidney, consisting of Bowman's capsule, a glomerulus, and tubules

nephrosis/nephrotic syndrome: disease of the kidneys characterized by degenerative lesions of the renal tubules and loss of protein (albumin) through the urine

nerve block/plexus block: form of local anesthesia in which the anesthetic is injected into nerve trunks leading to the area in which surgery is to be performed

nerve bundle, master: *see* spinal cord

nerve cell: 1. one of the cells of the nervous system 2. the cell body of a neuron

nerve, lingual: nerve beneath the floor of the mouth that conveys taste sensations to the brain motor

nerve, olfactory: the special nerve of smell

nerve, optic: the special nerve of vision connecting the retina with the occipital lobe of the brain

nerve, sensory/afferent: nerve that conveys information and stimuli from the outside world to the central nervous system

nerve, spinal: the thirty-one pairs of nerves that originate in the spinal cord

nervous breakdown: popular, nontechnical term for any debilitating or incapacitating emotional disorder

neural: of or relating to a nerve

neuralgia: acute pain along the course of a nerve

neuralgia, facial: *see* trigeminal neuralgia

neuralgia, trigeminal/facial/tic douloureux: acutely painful neuralgia of a region of the face, with paroxysmal muscular twitchings, associated with branches of the trigeminal (cranial) nerve in the affected area

neuritis: inflammation of a nerve

neuroblastoma: malignant tumor of the nerve tissue of the adrenal glands, found especially in children

neurofibroma: tumor on a nerve fiber

neurogenic shock: shock resulting from impairment of the regulatory capacity of the nervous system because of pain, fright, or other stimulus

neurologist: physician specializing in the care and treatment of the nervous system

neurology: the branch of medical science that deals with the nervous system

neuron: nerve cell with all its processes and extensions, such as the axon and dendrites

neuropathologist: physician specializing in neuropathology

neuropathology: the branch of medical science that deals with the study, diagnosis, and treatment of diseases of the nervous system

neurosis/psychoneurosis (*pl., neuroses*): mental disorder having no organic cause and less severe than psychosis

neurosurgeon: physician specializing in surgery of the nervous system

neurosurgery: the branch of medical science that deals with the treatment of disease of the nervous system by means of surgery

neurosyphilis: syphilis of the brain and spinal cord

neurotic: 1. one who has a neurosis 2. of or relating to neurosis

neurotoxic: 1. (of certain poisonous snakes) transmitting venom that directly affects the nervous system and brain of the toxified animal 2. causing destruction or damage to nerve tissue

neutrophil/granulocyte/polymorphonuclear leukocyte: granular leukocyte that can be stained with dyes that are neither acid nor alkaline (i.e., neutral)

nevus: birthmark or congenital mole junction

nicotine: poisonous chemical with acrid taste contained in tobacco leaves

night terrors: childhood nightmares which occur in deep sleep and in which the child cries out in terror

nit(s): the egg of a louse or other parasitic insect

nitrogen dioxide: suffocating gas that is poisonous when inhaled

nitroglycerin: colorless or pale yellow oily liquid used to treat angina pectoris

nocturia: frequent urination during the night

node: 1. swelling or enlargement, as in an arthritic joint, or a firm, flattened tumor on a bone or tendon 2. any knoblike part, as a lymph gland

nodule: little node

Noludar: methprylon

norepinephrine: hormone manufactured by the adrenal medulla that affects heart action and sympathetic nerve impulses

"nose brain": rhinencephalon

nostril: one of the outer openings in the nose

no-take: absence of any reaction to a vaccination, indicating that the person vaccinated has not developed an immunity and should be revaccinated

nutrient: substance that gives nourishment

nutriment: substance that nourishes or promotes development

nutrition: all of the processes by which food is consumed, digested, absorbed, and assimilated by the body

nutritionist: specialist in the study of nutrition

nyctophobia: fear of the dark

nystagmus: spasmodic, involuntary movement of the eyes, symptomatic of certain diseases, as of the inner ear

obesity: excessive accumulation of body fat

ob-gyn specialist: physician trained as an obstetrician and gynecologist

objective: (of symptoms) of a kind that can be observed or measured by the examining physician through diagnostic techniques

obsession: persistent, unwanted idea or feeling, a symptom of certain neuroses

obsessive-compulsive reaction: neurosis characterized by obsessions that are relieved temporarily by the compulsive performance of certain acts

obstetrician: physician specializing in obstetrics, often a gynecologist as well

obstetrics: the branch of medical science dealing with pregnancy and childbirth

obstructive-airway disease: condition characterized by the presence of chronic bronchitis and pulmonary emphysema, and involving damage to lung tissue and the bronchi

obturator: special device inserted into a cleft palate to close it against the flow of air

occipital: of or relating to the lower back part of the skull (occiput)

occipital lobe: the rear portion of each cerebral hemisphere which receives messages from the optic nerve

occlusion: 1. the act of closing or shutting off so as to block a passage, as a blood vessel 2. the manner of being shut, as the teeth of the upper and lower jaws

occupational disease: disease resulting from exposure in one's occupation to toxic substances or other hazards to health

ocular: of or relating to the eye

oculist: ophthalmologist

Oedipal complex: repressed sexual attachment of son to mother, analogous to the Electra complex involving the daughter and father

oil glands: glands, sebaceous

olfaction: the act, sense, or process of smelling

olfactory: pertaining to the sense of smell or the capacity to smell

olfactory lobe: the portion of each cerebral hemisphere of the brain on the underside of the frontal lobes, the centers for smelling

olfactory nerve: *see* nerve, olfactory

oliguria: decreased production of urine

onchocerciasis: form of filariasis transmitted by a blackfly and sometimes leading to blindness

oncologist: physician specializing in the diagnosis and treatment of tumors

oncology: the branch of medical science concerned with the study of tumors

Oncovin: vincristine

oophorectomy: *see* ovariectomy

open bite: form of malocclusion in which incisors of the upper and lower jaws do not meet when the jaws are together

open fracture: compound fracture

open surgery: surgery involving an incision and opening of the skin

ophthalmic: of or pertaining to the eye

ophthalmologist/oculist: physician specializing in the care and treatment of the eyes

ophthalmology: the branch of medical science dealing with the structure, function, and diseases of the eye

ophthalmoscope: optical instrument for examining the interior of the eye

opiate: drug derived from opium, as morphine

opium: narcotic drug obtained from the opium poppy from which morphine, codeine, heroin, and other drugs are derived

optic/optical: pertaining to the eye or to vision

optician: one who makes or sells eyeglasses and other optical equipment

optic nerve: special nerve of vision, conveying sensations from the retina to the brain

optometrist: one who practices optometry

optometry: profession of measuring the power of vision and prescribing corrective lenses

oral: pertaining to or situated near the mouth

oral cancer: *see* mouth

oral surgeon/dental surgeon: dentist who specializes in oral surgery

oral surgery: the diagnosis and surgical treatment of diseases, injuries, and defects of the mouth and jaw

orbit: either of the bony sockets of the eyes

orchidopexy/orchiopexy: surgical correction of an undescended testicle

orchiectomy: surgical removal of one or both testicles

orchiopexy: *see* orchidopexy

orchitis: inflammation of the testicles

organic: 1. of or pertaining to an organ of the body 2. having a physical basis, as a disorder 3. of or pertaining to animals or plants 4. pertaining to foods grown only with natural fertilizers of animal or plant origin

organic foods: foods grown with the use of organic fertilizers only, such as compost or animal (not human) manure, and without the use of pesticides or herbicides

organ of Corti: the true center of hearing within the cochlea of the inner ear, a complex spiral structure of hair cells

orgasm: the climax of the sexual act, normally marked by the male's ejaculation of semen and by relaxation of tension of both male and female

orifice: opening into a body cavity

orthodontia: orthodontics

orthodontics/orthodontia: the care and treatment of irregularities and faulty positions of the teeth, including the fitting of braces

orthodontist: dentist specializing in orthodontics

orthopedics: the branch of surgery dealing with the treatment and correction of deformities, injuries, and diseases of the skeletal system and its associated structures, as muscles and joints

orthopedic surgeon: orthopedist

orthopedist/orthopedic surgeon/orthopod: surgeon specializing in orthopedics

orthopod: orthopedist

orthoptist: medical technician trained to diagnose defects of the eye muscles and to provide corrective exercises

oscilloscope: instrument for visibly representing electrical activity on a fluorescent screen

osseous: osteal

ossicle: one of the three small connecting bones of the middle ear, the hammer (or malleus), the anvil (or incus), and the stirrup (or stapes), that transmit sound from the eardrum to the cochlea

ossification: conversion into bone

ossify: to convert or be converted into bone

osteal/osseous: of or relating to bone

osteitis: inflammation of a bone

osteitis deformans: *see* Paget's disease

osteoarthritis/degenerative joint disease/hypertrophic arthritis: chronic degenerative disease that affects the joints

osteogenesis: formation and growth of bones

osteogenesis, imperfecta: condition in which bones are abnormally brittle and liable to fracture because of a deficiency of calcium

osteogenic: pertaining to osteogenesis

osteomyelitis: inflammation of the bone tissue or marrow

osteopath: physician trained in osteopathy

osteopathy: system of healing based on a theory that most diseases are caused by structural abnormalities that may best be corrected by manipulation

osteophyte(s): abnormal bony outgrowth

osteoporosis: reduction in bone mass and increase in interior space, porosity, and fragility of bone

otitis media: inflammation of the middle ear

otitis media, nonsuppurative: inflammation of the middle ear resulting from a blocked Eustachian tube and fluid collection in the middle ear, causing hearing damage

otolaryngologist: physician specializing in the diagnosis and treatment of the ear, nose, and throat

otolaryngology: the branch of medicine dealing with the study and diseases of the ear, nose, and throat

otologist: one who specializes in the ear and its diseases

otology: the branch of medical science dealing with the functions and diseases of the ear

otoplasty: surgical technique to correct protruding or overlarge ears or to build up or replace a missing ear

otosclerosis: ear disorder resulting in hearing loss caused by the formation of spongy bone in the middle ear

otoscope: instrument used for examining the interior of the ear

outer ear: the external, fleshy part of the ear, including the auditory canal leading to the eardrum (tympanic membrane)

outpatient: patient who is not an inmate of a hospital or clinic at which treatment or diagnosis is received

ova: plural of *ovum*

ovarian: of or relating to the ovaries

ovarian dysgenesis: defective development of ovaries

ovariectomy/oophorectomy: surgical removal of an ovary

ovaries (*sing., ovary*): pair of female reproductive glands (gonads) that produce eggs (ova) and female sex hormones

overbite: extent to which upper teeth extend over lower teeth when the jaws are in closed position

overweight: *see* obesity

ovoid: egg-shaped

ovulation: the discharge of a mature egg cell (ovum) from the ovaries, occurring about once every 28 days at about the middle of the menstrual cycle

ovum/egg cell (*pl. ova*): female reproductive cell or gamete from which an embryo might develop if fertilized

oxytocin: hormone secreted by the pituitary gland to help the muscles of the uterus contract during labor

ozone: blue gas with a pungent odor that can be formed by the passage of electricity through the air

pacemaker, artificial: electrically activited, battery- or nuclear-powered device used to stimulate normal heartbeat if the natural cardiac pacemaker fails to function

pacemaker, cardiac: object or substance in the heart that regulates contraction of the heart muscle, or heartbeat

Paget's disease: 1. (osteitis deformans) chronic disease characterized by the softening and enlargement of the bones and usually the bowing of the long, weight-bearing bones 2. cancerous disease of the breast marked by the inflammation of the areola and nipple

palate: the roof of the mouth

palate, hard: the bony part of the roof of the mouth

palate, soft/velum: the soft, muscular tissue at the rear of the roof of the mouth

palpation: diagnostic procedure of feeling, pressing, or manipulating the body

palpitation: rapid or fluttering heartbeat

palsy/paralysis: Bell's palsy, cerebral palsy

PAN: peroxyacl nitrate

pancreas: large gland situated behind the stomach and containing the islets of Langerhans that produce insulin and glucagon, and secreting pancreatic juice via small ducts to the duodenum

pancreatic juice: secretion of the pancreas containing digestive enzymes

pancreatitis: inflammation of the pancreas

pandemic: epidemic occurring over a very large area or worldwide

Papanicolaou, Dr. George N.: developer of a test, called the *Pap smear* or *Pap test,* for detecting cancer of the cervix

Papanicolaou smear: Pap smear

papillae (*sing., papilla*): tiny, nipple-shaped projections that cover the inner layer (dermis) of the skin and the surface of the tongue

papillary tumor: 1. papilloma: benign tumor of the papillae of the skin, as a wart or corn 2. malignant tumor of the bladder, so called because it is nipplelike in shape (Latin *papilla* means nipple)

Pap smear/Papanicolaou smear/Pap test: method of early detection of cervical cancer consisting of painless removal of cervical cell samples, which are stained and examined

Pap test: Pap smear

papule: pimple

paralysis agitans: Parkinson's disease

paralysis, infantile: *see* poliomyelitis

paranasal sinus: air cavity in one of the cranial bones communicating with the nostrils

paranoid: describing a personality disorder in which the individual is extraordinarily sensitive to praise or criticism and subject to suspicions and feelings of persecution

paranoid reaction/paranoia: psychosis characterized by invariable delusion, usually of persecution, sometimes of grandeur

paranoid schizophrenia: *see* schizophrenia, paranoid

paraplegia: paralysis of the lower half of the body

paraplegic: one who is paralyzed in the lower half of the body, including both legs

parasite(s): animal or plant that lives in or on another organism (called the host), at whose expense it obtains nourishment

parasiticide: medication designed to destroy parasites such as body lice

parasympathetic nervous system: the part of the autonomic nervous system that controls such involuntary actions as the constriction of pupils, dilation of blood vessels and salivary glands, and slowing of heartbeat

parathormone/parathyroid hormone: hormone secreted by the parathyroid glands, important in regulating the amount of calcium in the body

parathyroid glands: four small endocrine glands near or embedded within the thyroid gland, usually two per side, that regulate blood calcium and phosphorus levels

parathyroid hormone: *see* parathormone

paresis: 1. partial paralysis 2. general paralysis (*general paresis*) caused by degeneration of the brain as a result of syphilis

parkinsonism: Parkinson's disease

Parkinson's disease/paralysis agitans/parkinsonism: chronic, progressive nervous disease characterized by muscle tremor when at rest, stiffness, and a rigid facial expression

parotid gland: either of two large salivary glands located below and in front of the ear

paroxysm: sudden onset of acute symptoms, as an attack or convulsions

parrot fever: psittacosis

particulate matter: fine particles in smoke that are dispersed by the wind and fall back to earth

parturition: act or process of giving birth

passive-dependent: describing a personality disorder in which the individual needs excessive emotional support from an authority figure

patch test: skin test for determining hypersensitivity by applying small pads of possibly allergy-producing substances to the skin's surface

patchy baldness: alopecia areata

patella: the kneecap

pathogen: disease-causing bacterium or microorganism

pathogenic: disease-causing

pathologic: caused by or relating to disease

pathologic fracture: fracture that occurs spontaneously, as because of preexisting disease, without external cause

pathologist: physician or expert specializing in pathology

pathology: the branch of medical science dealing with the causes, nature, and effects of diseases, especially disease-induced changes in organs, tissues, and body chemistry

PCBs/polychlorinated biphenyls: chemicals related to DDT and having many industrial uses, posing a potential threat to health as a water pollutant from industrial wastes

pectus carinatum: *see* pigeon breast

pectus excavatum: *see* funnel chest

pedal: of or relating to the foot

pediatric dentist: dentist specializing in the care and treatment of the teeth of children

pediatrician: physician specializing in the care and treatment of children

pediatrics: the branch of medicine dealing with the care and treatment of children and their diseases

pedodontics: branch of dentistry specializing in the care of children

pedodontist: dentist specializing in pedodontics

pellagra: disease caused by a vitamin deficiency and characterized by gastric disturbance, skin eruptions, and nervous symptoms

pelvic girdle: the part of the human skeleton to which the lower limbs are attached

pelvis: 1. the part of the skeleton that forms a bony girdle or basin joining the lower limbs to the body, and consisting of the two hip bones and the sacrum 2. the central area of the kidney from which urine drains into the ureter

penicillin: powerful antibacterial substance found in a mold fungus and prepared in several forms for the treatment of a wide variety of infections

penis: tubular male organ of sexual intercourse and excretion of urine, located at the front of the pelvis

Pentothal/sodium Pentothal/thiopental: trademark for an ultra-short-acting barbiturate used as an anesthetic, as in dentistry

pep pills: *see* amphetamines

pepsin: enzyme secreted by the gastric juices of the stomach

peptic ulcer: ulcer of the mucous membrane of the stomach (gastric ulcer) or small intestine (duodenal ulcer) caused by the action of acid juices

percussion: diagnostic procedure of striking or tapping the body with instruments or with the fingers

perianal: situated around the anus

pericarditis: inflammation of the pericardium

pericardium: the membrane that surrounds and protects the heart

peridental: periodontal

perimeter: device for determining peripheral vision

perineal: of or pertaining to the perineum

perineum: region of the body at the lower end of the trunk, between the genital organs and the anus

periodontal/peridental: situated around a tooth

periodontal membrane: membrane, periodontal

periodontia: periodontics

periodontics/periodontia: the branch of dentistry dealing with the diagnosis and treatment of periodontal (gum) diseases

periodontist: dentist who specializes in periodontics

periodontitis: inflammation of the tissues around a tooth, leading to destruction of the alveolar bone

periodontium: the supporting structures of the teeth, comprised of the gingiva, alveolar bone, and periodontal ligaments

periosteum: the tough, fibrous membrane that surrounds and nourishes bones

peripheral nervous system: the nerves and ganglia outside the brain and spinal cord

peristalsis: wavelike muscular contractions of the alimentary canal that move the contents along in the processes of digestion and excretion

peristaltic wave: the alternate contraction and relaxation of muscles in the alimentary canal in peristalsis

peritoneoscopy: technique for examining the female reproductive organs within the abdominal cavity

peritoneoscope/laparoscope: instrument used for examining the organs within the abdominal cavity, especially the female reproductive organs

peritoneum: the serous membrane that lines the abdominal cavity enclosing the abdominal organs

peritonitis: inflammation of the lining (peritoneum) of the abdominal cavity

peritonsillar abscess/quinsy: abscess in the tissues adjoining a tonsil as a complication of tonsillitis

pernicious: severe, destructive, and often fatal

pernicious anemia: severe, progressive anemia caused by lack of vitamin B_{12}, formerly fatal but now controllable

personality disorder/character disorder: any of a group of mental illnesses that apparently stem from an arrested development of the personality

perspiration: *see* sweat

pertussis: *see* whooping cough

pessary: 1. device worn inside the vagina as a contraceptive or to support uterine prolapse 2. medicated suppository for use in the vagina

petit mal: minor epileptic seizure, with very brief loss of consciousness

Peyer's patches: oval areas of lymphoid tissue in the intestine that manufacture lymphocytes

peyote: the mescal cactus of Mexico or the powerful hallucinogenic drug obtained from its dried upper part (called buttons)

phalanges (*sing., phalanx*): the bones of the fingers or toes

pharmacist: one skilled in the compounding and dispensing of medicines

pharmacologist: expert in pharmacology

pharmacology: the science of the action of medicines, their nature, preparation, administration, and effects

pharyngitis: inflammation of the pharynx, commonly called a sore throat

pharynx: the part of the alimentary canal between the palate and the esophagus, serving as a passage for air and food

phenformin: *see* DBI

phenol: *see* carbolic acid

phenylketonuria/PKU: inherited metabolic disorder that can cause mental retardation if not treated by a special diet soon after birth

phlebitis: inflammation of the inner membrane of a vein

phlebotomy/bloodletting/venesection: the opening of a vein for letting blood

phlegm: viscid, stringy mucus secreted in abnormally large amounts, as in the air passages

phobia: intense anxiety irrationally felt for any of a variety of things or situations, such as closed or open places, animals of a particular kind, heights, etc., a manifestation of the phobic reaction

phobic reaction: neurosis characterized by displacement of anxiety of a conflict to a substitute, such as a particular domestic animal, closed places, etc.

phonocardiogram: graph recording the sounds produced by the heart, used to evaluate heart murmurs and other abnormal sounds

physical dependence: accommodation of the body to continued use of a drug, such that withdrawing the drug causes pronounced physical reactions (withdrawal symptoms)

physical fitness: *see* fitness

physical medicine: branch of medicine utilizing physical procedures, such as heat, cold, massage, or mechanical devices, to diagnose disease or treat disabled patients

physical therapist: specialist in physical therapy

physical therapy/physiotherapy: the treatment of disability, injury, or disease by external physical means, such as heat, massage, planned exercises, electricity, or mechanical devices, to restore function or aid rehabilitation

physician(s): 1. any authorized practitioner of medicine 2. one trained in medicine, as distinguished from surgery

physiotherapy: *see* physical therapy

pia mater: the delicate, vascular, innermost membrane of the three membranes that envelop the brain and spinal cord

pica: appetite for substances unfit to eat

piebald skin: vitiligo

pigeon breast/pectus carinatum: congenital deformity in which the sternum protrudes

pigment: substance that imparts coloring to tissue

piles: *see* hemorrhoids

"pill, the": contraceptives, oral

pimple/papule: small, usually inflamed swelling on the skin

pineal body: *see* pineal gland

pineal gland/pineal body: small, cone-shaped body of rudimentary glandular structure located at the base of the brain and having no known function

pinkeye: acute, contagious conjunctivitis, marked by redness of the eyeball

pinworm: parasitic worm of the lower intestines and rectum, especially of children, causing intense itching in the anal area

pituitary body: *see* pituitary gland

pituitary gland/hypophysis cerebri/pituitary body: small endocrine gland situated at the base of the brain, consisting of anterior and posterior lobes whose hormonal secretions stimulate the production of hormones in other glands and regulate vital body functions such as growth and metabolism

pityriasis rosea: skin disease, especially of children, marked by a rash

PKU: *see* phenylketonuria

placebo: any harmless substance given to humor a patient or as a test in controlled experiments on the effects of drugs

placenta: the vascular structure in pregnant women that unites the fetus with the uterus, and through which the fetus is nourished via the umbilical cord, usually expelled naturally immediately following birth (when it is called the *afterbirth*)

Placidyl: ethchlorvynol

plague: 1. any epidemic disease that is contagious and often deadly 2. contagious, often fatal disease caused by a bacterium transmitted by fleas from infected rats, and characterized by fever, chills, prostration, and often by buboes (hence the name *bubonic plague*)

plantar warts: warts on the soles of the feet, caused by a virus

plaque: mucus containing bacteria that collects on teeth

plasma: the clear fluid portion of the blood

plastic surgeon: physician specializing in plastic or cosmetic surgery

plastic surgery: surgery that deals with the restoration or healing of lost, injured, or deformed parts of the body, mainly by the transfer of tissue, and with the improvement of appearance (cosmetic surgery)

platelet/thrombocyte: small, disk-shaped body found in blood that aids in clotting

play therapy: psychotherapy, especially for patients who are children, in which toys or other playthings are made available for the patient to play with in the presence of the therapist

playthings: *see* toys

pleura: serous membrane that enfolds the lungs and lines the chest cavity

pleural cavity: the space between the two pleuras lining the lungs and chest cavity

pleurisy: inflammation of the pleura, characterized by fever, chest pain, and difficulty in breathing

plexus: interlacement of cordlike body structures, such as blood vessels or nerves

plexus block: *see* nerve block

pneumococcus: bacterium that can cause pneumonia

pneumoconiosis: any of various lung disorders, such as silicosis or black lung disease, resulting from the inhalation of dust or other minute particles

pneumoencephalogram: X-ray picture of the brain taken after air or gas has been injected to partially replace the cerebrospinal fluid

pneumoencephalography: technique of producing pneumoencephalograms and interpreting them

pneumonia: inflammation of the lungs, usually bacterial in origin and acute in course, characterized by high fever, chills, breathing difficulty, and cough

pneumothorax: accumulation of air or gas in the pleural cavity, causing the lung to collapse, as from injury or disease, or by injection (artificial pneumothorax) in the treatment of tuberculosis

podiatrist/chiropodist: one who specializes in the treatment of the foot

podiatry/chiropody: the study and treatment of disorders of the feet

polio: *see* poliomyelitis

poliomyelitis/infantile paralysis/Heine-Medin disease: acute viral disease of the central nervous system characterized by fever, headache, sore throat, stiffness of the neck and back, and sometimes by paralysis and eventual atrophy of muscles

pollutant: something that pollutes the air, water, or soil

polycystic: characterized by numerous cysts

polycythemia: condition characterized by too many red blood corpuscles

polycythemia vera/erythremia: condition characterized by abnormally high number and proportion of red blood corpuscles

polymenorrhea: abnormally frequent menstruation

polymorphonuclear leukocyte: *see* neutrophil

polymyositis: inflammation of a number of muscles and connective tissue, characterized by pain, swelling, and weakness

polyp: smooth growth or tumor found in the mucous membranes, as of the nose, bladder, uterus, or rectum

polyunsaturated: (of fats) tending to lower the cholesterol content of the blood

polyuria: excessive urination

pons: mass in the brain containing fibers that connect the medulla oblongata, the cerebellum, and the cerebrum

pontic: in dentistry, a part of a bridge serving as a substitute for a missing tooth

popliteal: pertaining to the back part of the leg behind the knee

portal vein: vein that conveys blood from the intestines and stomach to the liver

"port wine stain": hemangioma

positive pressure breathing: breathing of air or other gas mixture at pressure greater than the surrounding atmospheric pressure

posterior: toward the rear

posterior lobe hypophysis: the posterior part of the pituitary gland that produces hormones regulating kidney function and other vital processes

posterior urethra: prostatic urethra

postmenopausal: being or occurring after menopause

postpartum: after childbirth

postural drainage: the loosening and draining of lung secretions by assuming a prone position with the head lower than the feet

pot (*slang*): marihuana

Pott's disease: tuberculosis or tissue destruction of the spinal vertebrae, causing angular, spinal curvature

PPD: purified protein derivative

prediabetic condition: diabetes, chemical

pre-eclampsia: disorder of late pregnancy or following childbirth

preemie/premie: premature infant

pregnancy: condition or time of being pregnant

pregnant: carrying developing offspring in the uterus

preinvasive: before spreading to other tissues: said of malignant growths

Preludin: phenmetrazine

premature: of a newborn baby, weighing less than 5 pounds

premature ejaculation: ejaculation of semen during sexual intercourse before the female has had time to respond

premenopausal: being or occurring before menopause

premolar: *see* bicuspid

prenatal: before birth

prenatal diagnosis: amniocentesis

preop: *see* preoperative

preoperative/preop: performed or occurring before a surgical operation, as shaving of the affected area, administration of certain drugs, etc.

prep: preparation of a patient for surgery, usually including cleansing and shaving of the affected area

prepuce: the loose skin covering the head of the penis or the clitoris

presbyopia: farsightedness caused by aging of the lens or the muscles that expand and contract it

pressor: tending to raise blood pressure, as certain hormones

preventive medicine: the branch of medical science concerned with preventing disease, as through immunological methods

prickly heat/heat rash/miliaria: itchy rash of small red pimples caused by excessive sweating in hot weather

primary: 1. not produced as a secondary effect or complication of another condition 2. original and not resulting from metastasis or other means of transmission, as a tumor or infection

primary teeth: *see* baby teeth

primipara: woman who is pregnant for the first time or who has borne one child

process: in anatomy, any outgrowth or projecting part of a larger structure, as the knobby portion of a vertebra

proctologist: physician specializing in proctology

proctology: the branch of medicine that deals with the diagnosis and treatment of diseases of the lower colon, rectum, and anus

proctoscope: surgical instrument for examining the interior of the rectum and part of the colon

proctoscopy: examination of the rectum and colon with the aid of a proctoscope

proctosigmoidoscopy: examination of the rectum and a portion of the colon (sigmoid) with the aid of a sigmoidoscope

prodrome: symptom resembling a premonition that signals the onset of a disease or of an epileptic seizure

profibrinolysin: the inactive precursor of fibrinolysin, an agent in the process of dissolving blood clots

progesterone: hormone of the ovary that prepares the uterus for receiving the fertilized ovum

prognathism: the condition of having a protruding jaw, especially the lower

prognosis: prediction made by a doctor as to the probable course of a disease

prolactin: lactogenic hormone

prolapse: move or slip forward or downward, as a displaced organ

prolapsed: slipped or moved from the usual place

pronate: turn, as the hand or foot, in a movement of pronation

pronation: 1. rotation of the hand or forearm so that the palm of the hand faces downward or backward 2. movement of the foot, as in improper walking, in which the sole is raised along the outer side and the toes turned out, often with an inward leaning of the ankle

prone: lying on the chest, with the face downward

proof: strength of alcohol in an alcoholic beverage, indicated by a proof number equal to twice the percentage of alcohol by volume (100 proof = 50% alcohol)

prophylactic: tending to ward off or prevent, as disease or conception

prophylaxis: treatment intended to prevent disease, as the cleaning of teeth

propranolol: drug that causes blood vessels to dilate, used in the treatment of angina pectoris

prostate: partly muscular gland in males at the base of the bladder around the urethra that releases a fluid to convey spermatozoa

prostate, enlarged benign: enlargement of the prostate gland resulting in difficulty in voiding and retention of urine in the bladder

prostate, inflammation of: prostatitis

prostatectomy: surgical removal of all or part of the prostate gland

prostatic urethra/posterior urethra: the part of the male urethra that passes across the prostate gland

prostatitis: inflammation of the prostate gland, characterized by painful and excessive urination

prostatitis, acute: severe, relatively uncommon form of prostatitis, marked by painful and excessive urination, high fever, and a discharge of pus from the penis

prosthesis (*pl., prostheses*)/**prosthetic device:** artificial substitute for a missing or amputated part, as an arm or leg

prosthetic device: prosthesis

protein(s): any of a class of highly complex organic compounds, composed principally of amino acids, that occur in all living things and form an essential part of animal food requirements

proteinuria: excretion of protein through the urine

prothrombin: the inactive precursor of thrombin, an agent in the process of forming blood clots

protozoa (*sing., protozoon*): microscopic animal organisms that exist in countless numbers, including one-celled organisms and parasitic forms that cause malaria, sleeping sickness, and other diseases

proud flesh: *see* granulation tissue

proximal: relatively near the center of the body or near a point considered as central

proximal muscles: those muscles closest to the trunk of the body, such as the shoulder-arm and hip-thigh muscles

pruritus: localized or general itching

pruritus, anal: intense itching in the area of the anus

pseudohypertrophic muscular dystrophy/Duchenne's muscular dystrophy: disease characterized by the enlargement and apparent overdevelopment (hypertrophy) of certain muscles, especially of the shoulder girdle, which subsequently atrophy

pseudoneoplasm: *see* pseudotumor

pseudotumor/pseudoneoplasm: condition that has the appearance of a tumor but is not a tumor, such as an inflammation

psilocybin: derivative of the mushroom *Psilocybe mexicana*, which produces hallucinations in the user

psittacosis/parrot fever: infectious disease of parrots and other birds that can be transmitted to humans and cause symptoms like those of influenza

psoralen: chemical derived from a plant that is used in the treatment of psoriasis

psoriasis: a noncontagious chronic condition of the skin, marked by bright red patches covered by silvery scales

psychiatrist: physician specializing in psychiatry

psychiatry: the branch of medicine that treats disorders of the mind (or psyche), including psychoses and neuroses

psychoanalysis: system of psychotherapy originated by Sigmund Freud for treating emotional disorders by bringing to the attention of the conscious mind the repressed conflicts of the unconscious

psychoanalyst: one who practices psychoanalysis

psychodrama: psychotherapy in which a patient or group of patients act out situations centered about their personal conflicts in the presence of the therapist

psychogenic: caused by or contributed to by psychological factors

psychological dependence: emotional desire or need to continue using a drug

psychologist: specialist in psychology

psychology: the science dealing with the mind, mental phenomena, consciousness, and behavior

psychomimetic: having properties capable of producing changes in behavior that mimic psychoses

psychomotor: having to do with muscular movements resulting from mental processes

psychomotor convulsion/temporal lobe convulsion: epileptic convulsion characterized by compulsive and often repetitious behavior of which the patient later has no memory

psychoneurosis: neurosis

psychopathic: *see* sociopathic

psychophysiological/psychosomatic: pertaining to a class of disorders in which psychological factors contribute substantially to the physiological condition

psychosis (*pl., psychoses*): severe mental disorder often involving disorganization of the total personality, with or without organic disease

psychosomatic: pertaining to the effects of the emotions on body processes, especially with respect to initiating or aggravating disease

psychotherapist: specialist in psychotherapy

psychotherapy: the treatment of emotional and mental disorders by psychological methods, such as psychoanalysis

psychotic: one suffering from a psychosis

psychotropic: affecting the mind: said of certain drugs

ptomaine: substance derived from decomposing or putrefying animal or vegetable protein, rarely the cause of food poisoning, which is usually caused by bacteria such as Salmonella

ptosis: dropping of the upper eyelid

ptyalin: enzyme in saliva that begins the chemical breakdown of starch

puberty: period during which a person reaches sexual maturity and becomes functionally capable of reproduction

puberty, precocious: early menarche (first occurrence of menstruation), before the age of eight or nine

pubic: in the region of the lower abdomen

pubis: the lower anterior part of the hip bone

pulmonary: of or relating to the lungs

pulmonary artery: artery, pulmonary

pulmonary emphysema: emphysema of the lungs; *see* emphysema

pulmonary tuberculosis: *see* tuberculosis

pulmonary vein: *see* vein, pulmonary

pulp: (of teeth) the soft tissue of blood vessels and nerves that fills the central cavity of a tooth

pulpotomy: surgical removal of the pulp of a tooth

pulse: rhythmic pressure in the arteries resulting from the beating of the heart

puncture wound: wound caused by an object that pierces the skin, as a nail or tack, involving increased danger of tetanus

pupil: contractile opening in the iris of the eye through which light reaches the retina

purine: one of a group of chemicals occurring naturally in certain foods and formerly implicated as a contributing cause of gout

purpura: blood disease characterized by hemorrhaging into the skin and mucous membranes

purulent: consisting of or secreting pus

pus: secretion from inflamed and healing tissues, usually viscid or creamy, and containing decaying leukocytes, bacteria, and other tissue debris

pustule: pus-filled bump on the skin, inflamed at the base

pyelitis: pyelonephritis

pyelogram: visualization of the kidney and ureter by X ray

pyelonephritis/pyelitis: infection and inflammation of the kidneys

pyloric sphincter: the ring of muscle surrounding the pylorus that acts as a valve, allowing food to pass from the stomach to the duodenum

pyloric stenosis: congenital condition in which the pylorus is too narrow to allow the stomach's contents to empty normally

pylorus: the opening between the stomach and the duodenum

pyorrhea: discharge of pus, especially when applied to the progressive inflammation of the gingival (gum) tissue, which may lead to loosening and loss of teeth

pyrexia: *see* fever

pyrogenic: causing or inducing fever

Q fever: infectious disease (rickettsial disease) transmitted by sheep and cattle and characterized by high fever, chills, and muscle pains

quadriplegia: paralysis of both arms and both legs

quadriplegic: one suffering from paralysis of both arms and both legs

quinine: bitter substance obtained from the bark of the cinchona tree, used to treat malaria and myotonia

quinsy: *see* peritonsillar abscess

rabies/hydrophobia: acute viral disease of the central nervous system transmitted to humans by the bite or saliva of an infected animal, as a dog, bat, or squirrel, invariably fatal unless treated before symptoms appear

radiation sickness: illness caused by the body's absorption of excess radiation, marked by fatigue, nausea, vomiting, and sometimes internal hemorrhage and tissue breakdown

radiation therapy/radiotherapy: treatment of disease by radiation, as by X rays or other radioactive substances

radical: of or involving procedures or treatment intended to go to the root of a disease and thereby eliminate it, as by excising an entire organ or part that is diseased

radiograph: X-ray photograph

radiography: X-ray photography

radiologist: physician specializing in radiology

radiology: the branch of medical science that deals with radiant energy, such as X rays and energy produced by radium, cobalt, and other radioactive substances, especially in the diagnosis and treatment of disease

radiopaque: impervious to X rays

radiotherapy: *see* radiation therapy

radius (*pl., radii*): the bone of the forearm on the same side as the thumb, thicker and shorter than the ulna bone

rale: abnormal sound heard in the chest with the aid of a stethoscope, indicating the presence of disease

Raynaud's disease: Raynaud's syndrome

Raynaud's syndrome/Raynaud's disease: condition characterized by spasms of small blood vessels when exposed to cold, especially the fingers and toes, which become cyanotic (bluish) and then red

RBC: red blood cell

recovery room: hospital room or section for patients immediately following surgery, where their post-operative conditions can be closely monitored

rectocele: hernia in which part of the rectum protrudes through the wall of the vagina

rectum: the terminal portion of the large intestine, extending from the sigmoid bend of the colon to the anus

red corpuscle: *see* erythroctye

red marrow: marrow

reduce: move back into proper position, as a herniating bowel or the fragments of a broken bone

reducing: *see* weight reduction

reduction: manipulation back into proper position to restore normal function, as a fracture, dislocation, or herniated part

referred pain: pain felt in one part of the body though originating in another part, as pain of the left shoulder and arm caused by a heart attack

reflex: involuntary response to a stimulus

reflux: a flowing back, as of urine from the bladder up into the ureter

refraction: the change of direction of a ray of light as it passes from one medium to another of different density

regional enteritis: enteritis in a chronic state

regurgitation: the act of rushing or surging back, as in vomiting, or the backward rush of blood in the heart because of defective valves or leaflets

Reiter's syndrome: form of arthritis characterized by occurrence of conjunctivitis of the eye and inflammation of the urethra

relaxant: drug or other agent that reduces tension, especially of the muscles

remission: period with less severe symptoms or without symptoms during the course of a disease

renal/nephric: of or relating to the kidneys

renal calculus: kidney stone

renal colic: pain that results from the passage of a kidney stone through the ureter

renal diabetes: renal glucosuria

renal glucosuria/renal diabetes: glucose in the urine in conjunction with normal blood sugar levels, due to failure of the renal tubules to reabsorb glucose

rennin: milk-curdling enzyme present in gastric juice

repression: exclusion from consciousness of painful desires, memories, etc., and consequent manifestation through the unconscious

resect: perform a resection on

resection: surgical removal of a part of a bone, organ, etc.

resectoscope: surgical instrument used especially for resection of the prostate gland by insertion into the urethra

residency: period of training in a hospital, usually in a medical specialty, for physicians preparing for private practice

resident: physician working and undergoing training (residency) in a hospital in preparation for private practice in a specialty

resorb: to reabsorb

respiration: the process by which an animal or plant takes in oxygen from the air and gives off carbon dioxide and other products of oxidation

respiratory arrest: see breathing, cessation of

respiratory distress syndrome: see hyaline membrane disease

resuscitation: mouth-to-mouth respiration

retardation, mental: see mental retardation

retention cyst: see cyst, follicular

reticulum: network of cells or cellular tissue

retina: the inner membrane at the back of the eyeball, containing light-sensitive rods and cones which receive the optical image

retinoblastoma: tumor of the eye, found especially in children

retinopathy: diseased condition of the retina of the eye

retinopathy, diabetic: see diabetic retinopathy

retinoscope: special device for examining the retina

rhesus factor: Rh factor

rheumatic fever: acute infectious disease chiefly affecting children and young adults, characterized by painful inflammation around the joints, intermittent fever, and inflammation of the pericardium and valves of the heart

rheumatic heart disease: impairment of heart function as a result of rheumatic fever

rheumatism: painful inflammation and stiffness of muscles, joints, or connective tissue

rheumatoid arthritis: chronic disease characterized by swelling and inflammation of one or more joints, often resulting in stiffness and eventual impairment of mobility

rheumatoid arthritis, juvenile/Still's disease: form of rheumatoid arthritis affecting children, often characterized by fever, rash, pleurisy, and enlargement of the spleen as well as rheumatoid joint symptoms

rheumatoid spondylitis: see spondylitis, rheumatoid

rheumatologist: physician specializing in rheumatology

rheumatology: subspecialty of internal medicine concerned with the study, diagnosis, and treatment of rheumatism and other diseases of the joints and muscles

Rh factor/rhesus factor: protein present in the blood of most people (called Rh-positive) and absent from others (called Rh-negative). Under certain conditions the blood of a pregnant Rh-negative woman may be incompatible with the blood of her fetus

rhinecephalon/"nose brain": the part of the brain controlling the sense of smell

rhinitis: inflammation of the mucous membranes of the nose

rhinoplasty: plastic surgery of the nose

Rh negative: see Rh factor

Rh positive: see Rh factor

rhythm method: birth control method whereby sexual intercourse is avoided during the period of ovulation in the menstrual cycle

rhytidoplasty/face lift/facial plasty: plastic surgery to eliminate facial wrinkles

rib(s): one of the series of curved bones attached to the spine and enclosing the chest cavity

rib cage/thoracic cage: the part of the skeleton that encloses the chest, bound by the ribs and the spinal vertebrae

riboflavin/vitamin B$_2$: member of the vitamin B complex, found in milk, green leafy vegetables, eggs and meats

rickets: early childhood disease characterized by softening of bones and consequent deformity, caused by deficiency of vitamin D

rickettsiae (sing., rickettsia): parasitic microorganisms transmitted to humans by the bites of infected ticks, lice, and fleas, and causing Rocky Mountain spotted fever, Q fever, rickettsial pox, and typhus

rickettsial: caused by or pertaining to rickettsiae

rickettsial disease: any of the diseases, as typhus or Rocky Mountain spotted fever, caused by rickettsiae

rickettsial pox: infectious disease, rickettsial disease, transmitted by mites which infest mice, and characterized by fever, chills, rash, headache, and backache

ringworm/tinea: contagious fungus disease of the skin, hair, or nails marked by ring-shaped, scaly, reddish patches of skin

Ritalin: methylphenidate

Rocky Mountain spotted fever: infectious disease (rickettsial disease) transmitted by the bite of certain ticks and characterized by fever, chills, rash, headache, and muscular pain

rod: one of many rod-shaped bodies in the retina of the eye, sensitive to faint light and peripheral objects and movements

roentgenogram: X-ray photograph

roentgenologist: physician specializing in the diagnosis and treatment of diseases with the application of X rays

roentgenology: the branch of medical science dealing with the properties and effects of X rays

root canal: the passageway of nerves and blood vessels in the root of a tooth leading into the pulp

roseola infantum: childhood illness characterized by high fever followed by a body rash

roughage: food material containing a high percentage of indigestible constituents

roundworm/ascaris: parasitic nematode worm, as the hookworm and pinworm, whose eggs hatch in the small intestines

rubella/German measles: contagious viral disease benign in children but linked to birth defects of children born of women infected in early pregnancy

rubeola: measles

Rubin's test: tubal insufflation

rupture: 1. any breaking apart, as of a blood vessel 2. hernia

Sabin vaccine: live polio vaccine taken orally to immunize against polio

sacral: pertaining to the sacrum

sacroiliac: pertaining to the sacrum or the ilium, or to the places on either side of the lower back where they are joined

sacrum: bone in the lower spine formed by the fusing of five vertebrae, constituting the rear part of the pelvis

saddle block: form of anesthesia used especially for childbirth, in which the patient is injected in the lower spinal cord while in a sitting position

safety glass: glass strengthened by any of various methods to reduce the likelihood of the glass shattering upon impact

St. Vitus dance: chorea

saline amniocentesis/salting out: technique of inducing abortion by injecting a saline solution into the amniotic fluid

saliva: fluid secreted by the salivary glands in the mouth that lubricates food and contains an enzyme (ptyalin) that begins to break down starch

salivary glands: glands located in the mouth which secrete saliva

Salk vaccine: dead polio virus taken by injection to immunize against polio

Salmonella: genus of aerobic bacteria that cause food poisoning and other diseases, including typhoid fever

Salmonella typhosa: rod-shaped bacteria that cause typhoid fever

salpingitis: 1. inflammation of a Fallopian tube, a potential cause of sterility 2. inflammation of a Eustachian tube

salt: sodium chloride

salting out: the injection of a saline solution into the amniotic fluid to induce labor and thus terminate a pregnancy

salt, table: *see* sodium chloride

saphenous vein: either of two large, superficial veins of the leg, a common site of varicosity

sarcoid: *see* sarcoidosis

sarcoidosis/Boeck's sarcoid/sarcoid: disease of unknown cause with symptoms resembling those of tuberculosis, marked by the formation of nodules, especially on the skin, lungs, and lymph nodes

sarcoma: malignant tumor that arises in the connective tissue (bones, cartilage, tendons)

saturated: (of fats) tending to increase the cholesterol content of the blood

saucerization: procedure of forming a shallow depression by scraping away tissue to assist healing

scabies/the itch: contagious inflammation of the skin caused by a mite and characterized by a rash and intense itching

scag (*slang*): heroin

scan: to measure for diagnostic purposes the concentration in a particular area of a radioactive material that has been introduced into the body

scapula: shoulder blade

scarlet fever: contagious disease caused by streptococci and characterized by a scarlet rash and high fever

schistosomiasis/bilharziasis: tropical disease caused by a fluke worm (trematode) whose larvae penetrate the skin and invade the circulatory system

schizoid: 1. describing a personality disorder in which the individual is withdrawn from and indifferent to other people 2. pertaining to or resembling schizophrenia

schizophrenia, catatonic: schizophrenia marked by motor disturbances, such as maintenance of fixed, often awkward, position with muscles rigid

schizophrenia, hebephrenic: schizophrenia marked by delusions, hallucinations, and regressed or childish behavior

schizophrenia, paranoid: schizophrenia marked by variable delusions of persecution or grandeur, often with hallucinations and behavioral deterioration

schizophrenic: of or pertaining to schizophrenia

schizophrenic reaction/schizophrenia: psychosis characterized by withdrawal from external reality and a retreat into a fantasy life, with deterioration of behavior

schoolboy (*slang*): codeine

sciatica: pain along the sciatic nerve

sciatic nerve: nerve of the lower spine that traverses the hips and runs down the back of the thigh of each leg

sclera: the firm outer coat of the eye continuous with the cornea, visible as the white of the eye

sclerose: to harden and thicken, as tissue

sclerosis: abnormal thickening and hardening of tissue, as of the lining of arteries

sclerosis, amyotrophic lateral/Lou Gehrig's disease: disease characterized by increasing muscle weakness (atrophy) or paralysis, caused by the progressive degeneration of motor nerve cells in the brain and spinal cord

scoliosis: spine, lateral curvature

scratch test: skin test for allergic response to different substances by applying suspected allergens in diluted form to scratches

scrofula: tuberculosis of the lymph nodes, especially of the neck

scrotum: pouch that contains the testicles

scrub nurse: operating room nurse authorized to handle sterilized equipment in assisting the surgeon

scurvy: disease characterized by livid spots under the skin, swollen and bleeding gums, and prostration, caused by lack of vitamin C

seasickness: motion sickness

sebaceous cyst: hard, round, movable mass contained in a sac, resulting from accumulated oil from a blocked sebaceous gland duct

sebaceous gland: gland within the dermis that secretes oil (sebum) for lubricating the skin and hair

seborrhea: abnormal increase of secretion from the sebaceous skin glands

sebum: fatty lubricating substance secreted by the sebaceous glands

secondary: produced as an effect or complication of another condition, as distinguished from *primary.*

secondary disease: disorder of a target gland caused by an excess or deficiency of a stimulating hormone supplied by the anterior pituitary gland

sedation: reduction of sensitivity to pain, stress, etc., by administering a sedative

sedative: medicine for allaying irritation or nervousness

seizure: *see* convulsion

semen: thick, whitish fluid containing spermatozoa that is ejaculated by the male at orgasm

semicircular canals: three fluid-filled tubes of the inner ear that govern the sense of balance and communicate with the vestibular nerve

seminal fluid: *see* semen

seminal vesicle: one of two small pouches on either side of the prostate gland that serve to store spermatozoa temporarily

senile macula degeneration: visual defect affecting the elderly

senile psychosis/senile dementia: mental disorder of the aged characterized by progressive deterioration of the personality, irritability, loss of memory, etc.

senile purpura: small hemorrhages in the skin of older people

senility: state of being senile

separated retina: detached retina

sepsis: infection of the blood by disease-causing microorganisms

septicemia: blood poisoning

septic shock: shock resulting from infection of the blood by disease-causing microorganisms

septum: dividing wall between two cavities, as in the nose

serous: pertaining to, producing, or resembling serum

serous membrane: membrane producing serum

serratus muscles: muscles that run vertically along the ribs

serum: the watery, clear portion of blood or lymph

serum analysis: laboratory analysis of blood serum as a diagnostic aid

serum sickness: acute illness caused by reaction to serum, such as that used in inoculations

sex act: *see* sexual intercourse

sex glands: *see* ovaries; testicles

sexual intercourse/coitus: male's ejaculation of semen into a female's vagina

sexuality: sexual interest or activity

shingles/herpes zoster: acute viral infection and inflammation of a sensory nerve, characterized by pain and small blisters on the skin along the path of the nerve

shock, allergic: allergic shock

shock, cardiac: shock resulting from diminished heart function

shock, circulatory: emergency condition in which the circulation of the blood is so disrupted that all bodily functions are affected

sick headache: *see* migraine

sickle-cell anemia: hereditary disease occurring most commonly among black men and women, in which many or a majority of the red blood cells are sickle-shaped, producing chronic anemia

sickle-cell trait/sicklemia: trait in the genetic make-up of an individual that could cause sickle-cell anemia in his or her offspring if the other parent also has the trait

sigmoid: 1. (*adj.*) shaped like the letter S 2. (*n.*) (sigmoid colon/sigmoid flexure) S-shaped fold in the colon of the large intestine just above the rectum

sigmoid colon: *see* sigmoid 2

sigmoid flexure: *see* sigmoid 2

sigmoidoscope: surgical instrument for examining the interior of the sigmoid

sign: (of disease) observable or objective manifestation, as distinguished from symptoms reported by the patient

silica: extremely hard mineral, the chief constituent of quartz and sand

silicosis: lung disorder, a form of pneumoconiosis, caused by inhaling silica dust, as of stone or sand

simple fracture: closed fracture

sinoatrial node: sinus node

sinus: opening or cavity, as in bone, or a channel or passageway, as for blood

sinusitis: inflammation of a sinus

sinus node/sinoatrial node: small mass of nerve tissue in the right atrium of the heart that triggers heart contractions and regulates heartbeat, thus serving as cardiac pacemaker

sitz bath: hot bath taken in a sitting position

skeletal muscle/voluntary muscle: striated muscle attached to bones and joints, used chiefly in voluntary action

skeleton, appendicular: the bones of the arms, hands, legs, and feet

skeleton, axial: the bones of the head and the trunk

skin/integument: the outer, membranous covering of the body, consisting of an outer layer (epidermis) and inner layer (dermis)

skin-popping (*slang*): subcutaneous injection of heroin

sleep disorders: *see* insomnia; narcolepsy

sleeping pill: sedative, especially one of the barbiturates taken to relieve insomnia

sleeping sickness/trypanosomiasis: tropical African disease caused by certain protozoa and spread by the bite of the tsetse fly, characterized by lethargy, recurrent fever, and oppressive drowsiness, often fatal

sleepwalking/somnambulism: act of walking in one's sleep

slip lamp microscope/biomicroscope: microscope for examining the eye, as the cornea, with the aid of an intense beam of light

smack (*slang*): heroin

smallpox/variola: acute, highly contagious viral disease characterized by high fever and the eruption of deep-seated pustules that leave scars upon healing

smegma: cheesy secretion that may collect under the prepuce of the uncircumcised penis or of the clitoris

smooth muscle/involuntary muscle: nonstriated muscle, used chiefly in involuntary action, such as that of the stomach and intestines

social worker(s): person trained to work in a clinical, social, or recreational service for improving community welfare or aiding the rehabilitation or emotional adjustment of individuals

sociopathic/psychopathic: describing a personality disorder in which the individual characteristically lacks a sense of personal responsibility or morality and may be disposed to aggressive and violent behavior, to self-destructive behavior, or to sexual deviation

sodium amytal: chemical used as sedative for soldiers in World War I

sodium cyclamate: *see* cyclamate

sodium Pentothal: *see* Pentothal

soft spots: fontanels

soldier's disease: morphinism

somnambulism: *see* sleepwalking

soot-wart: name for cancer of the scrotum that afflicted 18th-century chimney sweeps

sore throat: *see* pharyngitis

spasm: involuntary convulsive contraction of muscles, called *clonic* when alternately contracted and relaxed, and *tonic* when persistently contracted

spastic: of or characteristic of spasms

spasticity: the condition of having spasms

specimen: sample, as of blood, sputum, etc., for laboratory analysis

speculum: instrument that dilates a passage of the body, as for examination

speech reading: lip reading

speed (*slang*): methamphetamine

speed freak (*slang*): heavy user of methamphetamine (speed), especially by intravenous injection, to induce altered mental state

sperm: spermatozoa

spermatozoa (*sing., spermatozoon*)**/sperm/sperm cells:** male reproductive cells or gametes, one of which must fertilize an ovum to produce an embryo

sperm cell: the male reproductive cell, one of the spermatozoa

sperm cells: spermatozoa

sperm ducts: vas deferens

spermicide: contraceptive substance that destroys sperm

sphincter(s): ringlike muscles surrounding an opening or tube that serves to narrow or close it

sphygmomanometer: device for measuring arterial blood pressure

spinal: *see* spinal anesthesia

spinal anesthesia/spinal: form of anesthesia in which the patient is injected in the region of the spinal cord

spinal arthritis: arthritis of the spine, found especially in the elderly

spinal column/backbone/spine: the series of segmented bones (vertebrae) which enclose the spinal cord and provide support for the ribs

spinal cord: the part of the central nervous system within the spinal column

spinal fluid: *see* cerebrospinal fluid

spinal fluid exam: spinal tap

spinal puncture: spinal tap

spinal reflex: reaction to an outside stimulus that originates in the spinal cord and bypasses the brain

spinal tap/lumbar puncture/spinal fluid exam/spinal puncture: needle puncture and withdrawal of cerebrospinal fluid from the lower spinal column for diagnostic examination

spine: *see* spinal column

spirochete: any of various spiral-shaped bacteria, some of which cause syphilis and yaws

spleen: vascular, ductless organ located near the stomach that produces red blood cells in infancy and modifies blood composition

splint: appliance for supporting or immobilizing a part of the body, as a fractured bone

spondylitis: inflammation of the vertebrae of the spine

spondylitis, rheumatoid/ankylosing: chronic disease characterized by inflammation of the spine and resulting in the fusing (ankylosing) of the spinal joints

spondylolisthesis: forward displacement of one of the lower vertebrae over the vertebra below it or over the sacrum, causing severe pain in the lower back

spontaneous abortion: miscarriage

sporadic: characterized by scattered cases, as of a disease, rather than by concentration in one area

spore: single-celled reproductive body of a flowerless plant, capable of developing into an independent organism

sprain: the stretching or rupturing of ligaments, usually accompanied by damage to blood vessels

sputum: expectorated matter, as saliva, sometimes mixed with mucus

sputum exam: bacteriological, chemical, and microscopic testing of sputum for presence of disease

stapedius: small muscle in the tympanum of the middle ear whose function is to dampen loud sounds

stapes: stirrup

staph: *see* staphylococcus

staphylococcus (*pl., staphylococci*)**/ staph:** parasitic bacterium that can cause boils and other infections

staphylococcus aureus: bacterium that causes food poisoning

startle reflex: *see* startle response

startle response/startle reflex: complex involuntary reaction to sudden noise occurring especially in infancy, where it is marked by a sudden jerk of the arms and legs

static exercises: isometrics

status epilepticus: series of epileptic seizures, occurring virtually without interruption

stenosis: the narrowing of a duct or canal in the body

sterile: 1. being incapable of producing offspring 2. being free of germs

sterility: 1. condition of being incapable of producing offspring 2. condition of being free of germs

sterilization: the process of destroying reproductive capacity by surgical means, as by tying the Fallopian tubes of a woman (tubal ligation) or by tying the seminal duct of a man (vasectomy)

steroid(s): any of a group of organic compounds occurring naturally and produced synthetically, including the sex hormones, the bile acids, oral contraceptives, and many drugs

stethoscope: diagnostic device that conducts sounds produced within the body, as the heartbeat, to the ear of the examiner

stiff toe: pain and stiffness in the joint of the big toe

stilbestrol: *see* diethylstilbestrol

Still's disease: *see* rheumatoid arthritis, juvenile

stimulant: drug or other substance that increases or agitates the physiological processes of body or mind

stimulus (*pl., stimuli*): that which initiates an impulse or affects the activity of an organism

stirrup/stapes: the innermost of the three ossicles of the middle ear, the bone between the anvil and the cochlea

Stokes-Adams syndrome: sudden unconsciousness and sometimes convulsions caused by heart block

stoma: small opening in a surface, as in a membrane or wall of a blood vessel

stomach, ulcers of: *see* peptic ulcer

stool exam: laboratory analysis of feces, as for presence of blood or parasitic organisms

STP: DOM

strabismus/squint: disorder of the eye muscles in which one eye drifts so that its position is not parallel with the other

strain: excessive stretching of a muscle, tendon, or ligament

stratum corneum: the outermost layer of the epidermis, consisting of horny, lifeless cells

strep throat: streptococcal infection of the throat

streptococcal: of or relating to the streptococcus bacterium

streptococcus: kind of bacteria including some forms that cause diseases, as pneumonia and scarlet fever

stress fracture: tiny crack in a bone caused by repeated stress

striated: striped, as certain muscle

striated muscle: *see* skeletal muscle

striped muscle: *see* skeletal muscle

stripping: surgical removal of lengths of varicosed veins, especially one of the saphenous veins of the leg

stroke/apoplexy: attack of paralysis caused by the rupture of an artery and hemorrhage into the brain, or by an obstruction of an artery, as from a blood clot

stupor: condition in which the senses and faculties are suspended or greatly dulled, as from shock, drugs, etc.

sty: small, inflamed swelling of a sebaceous gland on the edge of the eyelid

subacute: intermediate between *acute* and *chronic:* said of a disease

subarachnoid: situated or occurring between the middle layer (arachnoid) and the innermost layer (pia mater) of the brain

subcutaneous: situated or applied beneath the skin

subcutaneous injection: an injection given in the subcutaneous tissue beneath the skin

subcutaneous tissue: layer of fatty tissue below the skin (dermis) which acts as an insulator against heat and cold and as a shock absorber against injury

subdural: situated or occurring between the outermost layer (dura mater) and the middle layer (arachnoid) of the brain

subdural hematoma: *see* hematoma, subdural

subjective: (of symptoms) of a kind that only the patient is aware of

sublingual gland: either of a pair of salivary glands located beneath the tongue

submandibular gland: submaxillary gland

submaxillary gland/submandibular gland: either of a pair of salivary glands located under each side of the lower jaw

subtotal: less than total, as a surgical procedure involving the excision of an organ or part

sudden infant death syndrome/crib death/SIDS: death of an infant, usually between one and six months of age, without any preceding sign of distress and of undetermined cause

sudoriferous glands: *see* sweat gland

sulfa drug: any of a group of organic compounds used in the treatment of a variety of bacterial infections

sulfonamide(s): any of a group of chemical compounds including the sulfa drugs, used in the treatment of bacterial infections

sulfonylurea: drug used to treat diabetes

sunstroke/heatstroke: condition marked by an acutely high fever and the cessation of perspiration, caused by prolonged exposure to heat and sometimes leading to convulsions and coma

superego/conscience: largely unconscious element of the personality, regarded as dominating the ego, for which it acts principally in the role of conscience and critic

superficial: of, situated near, or on the surface

superior vena cava: the large vein that brings blood from the upper part of the body to the heart

supination: rotation of the hand or forearm so that the palm of the hand faces upward or forward

supine: lying on the back, with the face upward

suppository: solid, usually cylindrical medicated preparation that liquefies from heat after insertion in a body cavity, as the rectum or the vagina

suppuration: the formation of pus

suppurative: characterized by the formation of pus; pussy

surgeon: physician who specializes in the diagnosis and treatment of disease by means of surgery

surgery: the branch of medicine dealing with the correction of disorders or other physical change by operation or manipulation

surgical: of or relating to surgery

surgical diathermy: electrosurgery

suture: 1. to sew together cut or separated edges, as of a wound, to promote healing 2. the thread, wire, gut, etc., used in this process

suture line: line formed by the edges of the separate bones of a baby's skull

sweat gland/sudoriferous gland: any of numerous glands that secrete sweat, found almost everywhere in the skin except for the lips and a few other areas

swimmer's itch: mild form of schistosomiasis in which parasitic fluke worm larvae invade the skin of swimmers, causing dermatitis

sycosis/barber's itch: bacterial infection of hair follicles, marked by inflammation, itching, and the formation of pus-filled pimples

sympathetic nervous system: the part of the autonomic nervous system that controls such involuntary actions as the dilation of pupils, constriction of blood vessels and salivary glands, and increase of heartbeat

symptom: change in one's normal feeling or condition of well-being, indicating the presence of disease

symptomatic: having observable symptoms of a disease or condition

symptomatology: the combined symptoms of a disease

Synanon: organized live-in community of drug addicts in which group psychotherapy is used to encourage rehabilitation

synapse: the junction point between two neurons, across which a nerve impulse passes from the axon of one neuron to the dendrite of another

syncope: temporary loss of consciousness; fainting

syndrome: set of symptoms occurring at the same period and indicating the presence or nature of a disease

synovia/synovial fluid: viscid, transparent fluid secreted as a lubricating agent in the interior of joints and elsewhere

synovial aspiration/synovial fluid exam: laboratory analysis of synovia, withdrawn from joints by needle, in order to diagnose gout or certain forms of arthritis

synovial fluid: synovia

synovial fluid exam: synovial aspiration

syphilis: contagious venereal disease transmitted by sexual contact and congenitally to offspring of infected mothers

systemic: pertaining to or affecting the body as a whole

systole: the instant of peak pumping action of the heart, when the ventricles contract and blood is impelled outward into the arteries, followed immediately by relaxation (diastole)

systolic pressure: measure of blood pressure taken when the heart is contracting; the higher of the two figures in a reading

tabes dorsalis/locomotor ataxia: form of syphilis involving demyelination of spinal nerves and other destructive changes in the spinal cord

tachycardia: abnormally rapid heartbeat

tachycardia, paroxysmal: attacks of abnormally rapid heartbeat (tachycardia) that begin and end abruptly

Tagamet: cimetidine

tampon: plug of absorbent material for insertion in a body cavity or wound to stop bleeding or absorb secretions

T and A operation: *see* adenotonsillectomy

tapeworm/cestode: any of various worms with segmented, ribbonlike bodies, often of considerable length, that are parasitic on the intestines of humans and other vertebrates

target gland: any of the endocrine glands that function when stimulated by hormones secreted by the anterior pituitary, as the thyroid adrenal cortex, testicles, or ovaries

tarsal: any of the bones of the tarsus, or ankle

tarsus: ankle

taste bud: one of the clusters of cells in the tongue that contain receptors for discriminating salt, sweet, sour, or bitter tastes

teething: process by which new teeth break (erupt) through the gums in infants and young children

tempered glass: safety glass that has high resistance to blunt objects and breaks by crumbling into small fragments instead of shattering

temporal lobe: the portion of each cerebral hemisphere of the brain in back of and partly below the frontal lobes, the centers for hearing

temporal lobe convulsions: convulsions, psychomotor

tendinitis: inflammation of a tendon

tendon: band of tough, fibrous connective tissue that binds a muscle to another part, as a bone, and by means of which muscular force can be exerted on other parts of the body

tendon sheath, inflammation of: tenosynovitis

tennis elbow: pain in the outer side of the elbow joint, usually caused by a too vigorous twisting motion of the hand that strains a tendon or inflames a bursa

tenosynovitis: inflammation of the sheath that covers a tendon

tension headache: severe headache induced by tension, which causes unconscious constriction of head and neck muscles

Terramycin: trade name for the antibiotic tetracycline

testes: testicles

testicle(s)/testis(*pl., testes*)**:** one of a pair of male reproductive glands (gonads) that produce spermatozoa and male sex hormones, situated in a pouch (scrotum) at the base of the penis

testis: *see* testicle

testosterone: male sex hormone manufactured in the testicles

tetanus/lockjaw: acute bacterial infection usually introduced through a puncture wound leading to muscle spasms, especially of the jaw muscles, and often fatal

tetany: nerve disorder characterized by muscle spasms and sometimes convulsions, caused by too little calcium in the blood

tetracycline: crystalline powder isolated from a soil bacillus that forms the base of several antibiotics, including Aureomycin and Terramycin

tetrahydrocannabinol/THC: principal compound of cannabis (hashish or marihuana), believed to be the active ingredient

thalamus: round mass of gray matter at the base of the brain that transmits sensory impulses to the cerebral cortex

thalassemia/Cooley's anemia: form of anemia caused by inherited abnormality of red blood cells, often fatal in utero

THC: tetrahydrocannabinol

therapeutic: designed or tending to heal or to cure disease

therapist: *see* psychotherapist

therapy: treatment of a disease by prescribed method or medicine

thermogram: measurement of the surface temperature of a region of the body, such as the breast, with an infrared sensing device

thermography: technique of measuring the surface temperature of a region of the body, such as the breast, with an infrared sensing device

thiamine/vitamin B₁: vitamin found in cereal grains, green peas, liver, egg yolk, and other sources, and also made synthetically, that protects against beriberi

thoracic: of or relating to the thorax, or chest cavity

thoracic cage: *see* rib cage

thoracic cavity: *see* chest cavity

thoracic spine: *see* vertebrae, thoracic

thoracic surgeon: surgeon specializing in thoracic surgery, having to do with the chest cavity

thoracic surgery: branch of surgery having to do with the chest cavity and its organs, the heart and lungs, and large blood vessels

thorax: chest

Thorazine/chlorpromazine: trademark for a commonly used tranquilizer

throat: *see* pharynx

throat, sore: *see* pharyngitis

thrombin: enzyme present in the blood that reacts with fibrinogen to form fibrin in the process of clotting

thrombocytes: platelets

thromboembolism: obstruction of a blood vessel by a blood clot (thrombus) that has broken away from the place where it was formed

thrombophlebitis: formation of a blood clot (thrombus) in the wall of an inflamed vein (phlebitis)

thromboplastin: substance found in blood platelets that helps to convert pro-thrombin into thrombin in the clotting process

thrombosis: formation of a blood clot (thrombus) in a blood vessel, resulting in the partial or complete blocking of circulation

thrombus: stationary blood clot within a blood vessel

thrush: fungus infection in the mouth, especially of infants, characterized by white patches that become sores

thymectomy: surgical removal of the thymus

thymus: glandlike, lymphoid organ located near the base of the neck, believed to play a role in the body's immunological responses

thyroid gland: endocrine gland located at the neck just below the larynx, extending around the front and to either side of the trachea (windpipe), and secreting the hormone thyroxin, which is vital to growth and metabolism

thyroid hormone: *see* thyroxin

thyroid-stimulating hormone/TSH: hormone secreted by the anterior lobe of the pituitary gland which stimulates the production of hormones in the thyroid gland

thyroxin: hormone secreted by the thyroid gland, vital to growth and metabolism

tibia: the shin bone, the inner and larger of the two bones of the lower leg

tic: involuntary, recurrent muscle twitch or spasm

tic douloureux: *see* trigeminal neuralgia

tick fever: *see* Rocky Mountain spotted fever

tinea: ringworm

tinnitus: ringing, buzzing, hissing, or clicking sound in the ears, not caused by external stimuli

tissue, death of: *see* gangrene

tolerance: the ability of the body to adjust to increasingly larger doses of a drug through habitual use

tomography: radiography of a section of the body

tomography, computerized axial: *see* CT scanning

tone/tonicity: the normal tension of muscle tissue

tonic: of or characteristic of tonus

tonicity: *see* tone

tonic phase: the period during a grand mal epileptic convulsion when the body is rigid

tonic spasm: *see* spasm

tonometer: device for measuring pressure, as of the eyeball

tonsil: either of two small round, lymphoid organs at each side of the back of the throat

tonsillectomy: surgical removal of the tonsils

tonsillitis: inflammation of the tonsils

tonus: muscular spasm characterized by persistent contraction

tophus (*pl. tophi*)**:** deposit of urate in the joints, a cause of gout

tourniquet: bandage or other material tied tightly to constrict an artery to stop bleeding

toxemia of pregnancy: metabolic disorder of pregnant women, characterized by a rise in blood pressure, swelling of tissue, weight gain, and headaches (pre-eclampsia) and sometimes by convulsions and loss of consciousness (eclampsia)

toxic: 1. caused by or having to do with a toxin or poison 2. poisonous

toxic psychosis: psychosis caused by a toxic agent, such as lead or alcohol

toxin(s): any of a group of poisonous compounds produced by animal, vegetable, or bacterial organisms

trabecula (*pl., trabeculae*): strand of connective tissue, as in a bone

trachea/windpipe: the passageway for air from the larynx to the lungs

tracheostomy/tracheotomy: emergency surgical procedure of cutting into the trachea

tracheotomy: *see* tracheostomy

traction: subjection of muscle or a fractured part to a pulling force, as by a system of weights and pulleys

tranquilizer: drug with a calming or sedative effect

transference: in psychoanalysis, the redirection of repressed childhood emotions to the analyst

transplant: tissue or organ transferred from its original site to another part of the body or to another individual

transsexual: person who is genetically and physically of one sex but who identifies psychologically with the other and may seek treatment by surgery or with hormones to bring the physical sexual characteristics into conformity with the psychological preference

transudate: fluid passing through pores or tissues, as of a membrane

transverse colon: the section of the colon leading from the ascending colon and extending horizontally across the abdomen beneath the liver and stomach

transvestism: practice of wearing the clothes of the opposite sex

transvestite: one who wears the clothes of the opposite sex

trauma: 1. any injury or wound to the body 2. severe emotional shock

trematode: any of a class of parasitic flatworms, as the flukes, causing various diseases such as schistosomiasis

tremor: any involuntary quivering or trembling, as of a muscle

trench foot: foot condition resembling frostbite resulting from exposure to continued dampness and cold

trench mouth/Vincent's angina/Vincent's disease: painful infection of the gums (called necrotizing ulcerative gingivitis) and sometimes of the pharynx and palate, characterized by the formation of ulcers and necrosis

trichina: Trichinella spiralis

Trichinella spiralis/trichina: the parasitic worm that causes trichinosis

trichinosis: disease caused by a parasitic worm (Trichinella spiralis) that enters the body via under-cooked or raw meat, especially pork, invading the intestines and muscles and provoking gastrointestinal symptoms initially and muscle stiffness and pain later

trichomonas: genus of protozoa that cause vaginal infections in women

trichomoniasis: vaginal infection by the trichomonas organism

triglyceride: glycerol compound containing one to three acids

trimester: period of three months, used to identify the progress of a pregnancy which consists of three such periods

trip (*slang*): hallucinogenic experience

trivalent: pertaining to a form of the Sabin polio vaccine in which each dose gives protection against three strains of polio

trophoblast: layer of cells developing around a fertilized ovum and contributing to the formation of the placenta

trophoblastic disease: disease of the trophoblast in a pregnant woman, marked by the degeneration of the placenta into a mass of grapelike cysts (*hydatidiform mole*)

true skin: dermis

trypanosomiasis: sleeping sickness

tropanosomiasis, African: *see* sleeping sickness

tropanosomiasis, American: *see* Chagas' disease

trypsin: enzyme in the pancreatic juice that breaks up proteins for digestion

TSH: thyroid-stimulating hormone

tubal insufflation/Rubin's test: the injection of carbon dioxide gas, or sometimes ordinary air into the uterus to check for obstructions in the Fallopian tubes

tubal ligation: the tying or binding of a tube, especially of the Fallopian tubes as a method of sterilization

tubercle: small nodule or tumor formed within an organ, as that produced by the bacillus causing tuberculosis

tubercle bacillus: rod-shaped bacterium that causes tuberculosis

tuberculin: liquid containing substances extracted from weakened (attenuated) tubercle bacilli, used as a test for tuberculosis

tuberculin test: skin test for determining whether tuberculosis bacteria are present, used especially for children

tuberculoid: of or resembling a tubercle or tuberculosis

tuberculosis: infectious, communicable disease caused by the tubercle bacillus and characterized by the formation of tubercles within some organ or tissue, often the lungs (pulmonary tuberculosis)

tubule(s): very narrow, minute tube or duct of kidney

tularemia: acute bacterial infection that can be transmitted to humans from infected rabbits, squirrels, or other animals, by the bite of certain flies, or by direct contact

tumor: mass of tissue growing independently of surrounding tissue and having no physiological function, sometimes confined to the area of origin (benign) and sometimes invading other cells and tissue and causing their degeneration (malignant)

tumor, fibroid: benign tumor composed of fibrous tissue, usually attached to the wall of the uterus

turbinate: one of the thin, curved bones on the walls of the nasal passages

tympanum: 1. the cavity in the middle ear lined with the tympanic membrane (eardrum) and containing the ossicles 2. eardrum

tympanic membrane: *see* eardrum

typhoid fever/enteric fever: acute infectious disease caused by a Salmonella bacterium and characterized by diarrhea, fever, eruption of bright red spots on the chest and abdomen, and physical prostration

typhus: acute disease caused by a rickettsial microorganism that is transmitted to humans by the bite of certain lice and fleas, and is characterized by high fever, severe headaches, and a red rash

ulcer(s): open sore with an inflamed base on an external or internal body surface

ulcer(s) of gastrointestinal tract: *see* peptic ulcers

ulcerative colitis: colitis accompanied by ulcerated lesions on the colon, characterized by bloody diarrhea and abdominal pain

ulna: the bone of the forearm on the same side as the little finger, longer and thinner than the radius bone

umbilical: pertaining to the middle part of the abdomen

umbilical cord: the ropelike tissue connecting the navel of the fetus with the placenta

umbilicus: navel

unconsciousness: loss of consciousness, having the appearance of sleep, usually caused by injury, shock, or serious physical disturbance

underskin: tissue, subcutaneous

undulant fever: *see* brucellosis

unsaturated: (of fats) not tending to increase the cholesterol content of the blood

ups/uppers/pep pills (*slang*): drugs or compounds that have a stimulating effect on the central nervous system, such as amphetamines

urate: salt of uric acid

urea: soluble compound containing nitrogen, found in urine and in small amounts in the blood

uremia: toxic condition of the blood caused by the failure of the kidneys to function normally in filtering and excreting waste products, such as urea

ureter: either of two narrow, muscular ducts which convey urine from the kidneys to the bladder

urethra: duct from the bladder by which urine is discharged and which in males carries seminal fluid

urethritis: inflammation of the urethra

urinalysis (UA): chemical and microscopic analysis of the urine to determine for diagnostic purposes whether it is normally constituted

urination: the excretion of urine

urine: waste products and excess water separated in the kidneys and stored in the bladder for eventual elimination from the body

urinogenital tract/genitourinary tract/urogenital tract: the urinary and genital systems, including the kidneys, ureters, bladder, urethra, vagina and associated parts

urogenital tract: urinogenital tract

urologist: physician specializing in urology

urology: the branch of medical science that deals with the diagnosis and treatment of diseases of the kidneys, bladder, ureters, urethra, and of the male reproductive organs

urticaria: *see* hives

uterine: of or pertaining to the uterus

uterus/womb: muscular, glandular organ in women in which the developing fetus is protected until birth

uvula: fleshy, teardrop-shaped appendage of the soft palate at the back of the mouth

vaccinate: inoculate with a vaccine as a preventive or therapeutic measure

vaccination: 1. act or process of vaccinating 2. scar produced at the site of inoculation with a vaccine

vaccine: preparation of live, attenuated, or dead microorganisms injected or administered orally to create immunity against a specific disease

vacuum aspiration: technique of inducing abortion in early pregnancy by utilizing suction to draw out embryo tissue

vagina: canal in the female leading from the external genital orifice below the pubis to the uterus

vaginal sponge: contraceptive device made of polyurethane permeated with spermicide nonoxynol-9

vaginitis: inflammation of the vagina

vagotomy: surgical procedure of cutting the vagus nerves

vagus: the tenth cranial nerve, which originates in the brain and extends branches to the lungs, heart, stomach, and intestines

Valium/diazepam: trademark for commonly used tranquilizer

Valmid: ethinamate

valve: membranous structure inside a vessel or other organ, as the heart, allowing fluid to flow in one direction only

valve, disease of: endocarditis

vaporizers: *see* steam inhalators

varicose: abnormally dilated, as veins

varicose ulcer: ulcer resulting from varicose veins, usually on the inner side of the leg above the ankle

varicose vein/varix: swollen and contorted vein, often in the leg

varicosity: 1. condition of being varicose 2. *see* varicose vein

variola: smallpox

varix (*pl., varices*): varicose vein

vascular: of, involving, or supplied with vessels, as blood vessels

vascularization: process of becoming vascular

vascular surgeon: surgeon specializing in vascular surgery, having to do with the blood vessels

vascular surgery: branch of surgery having to do with the operative treatment of diseases of the blood vessels

vas deferens: duct in males that conveys semen from the testicles to the seminal vesicles

vasectomy: surgical removal of part of the vas deferens or sperm duct of the male, thus rendering him sterile by preventing semen from reaching the seminal vesicles

vasconstrictor: medicine that causes the blood vessels to contract, thus restricting blood flow

vasodilator: medicine that causes the blood vessels to dilate, thus producing greater blood flow

vasomotor: producing contraction or dilation of the blood vessels

vasopressin: hormone secreted by the posterior lobe of the pituitary gland that raises blood pressure and increases peristalsis, known also as antidiuretic hormone because of its action on the kidneys to stimulate the reabsorption of water

VD: *see* venereal disease

vector cardiogram: graph indicating the magnitude and direction of the electrical currents of the heart

vein(s): any of a large number of muscular, tubular vessels conveying blood from all parts of the body to the heart

vein, pulmonary: vein that delivers oxygen-rich blood from the lungs to the heart

velum: soft palate

vena cava: either of two large veins that bring blood to the heart from the upper part of the body (superior vena cava) and lower part of the body (inferior vena cava)

venereal disease: any of those diseases transmitted by sexual intercourse, such as syphilis and gonorrhea

venereal wart/condyloma acuminatum: wart caused by a virus and occurring in the anal and genital areas, transmitted by sexual contact and by other means

venesection: *see* phlebotomy

venom: poison secreted by certain reptiles, insects, etc., transferred to a victim by a bite or sting

venous: having to do with or carried by the veins

ventral: toward, near, or in the abdomen

ventricle(s): any of various body cavities, as of the brain, or chambers, especially either of the two lower chambers of the heart, which receive blood from the atria and pump it into the arteries

ventriculography: technique of X raying the brain after the removal of cerebrospinal fluid and the injection of air into the ventricles

venule: small vein continuous with a capillary

vermiform appendix/appendix vermiformis: the worm-shaped appendage attached to the cecum of the large intestine

vermifuge: any drug or remedy that destroys intestinal worms

vernix caseosa: cheesy substance sometimes covering a newborn baby's skin

vertebra (*pl., vertebrae*): one of the segmented bones that make up the spinal column

vertebra, thoracic/thoracic spine: the vertebra to which the ribs are attached

vertebrate: any animal having a backbone

vertigo: disorder in which a person feels as if self or surroundings are whirling around

vesical: of or pertaining to the bladder

vesicle: small bladderlike cavity, or a small sac containing fluid

vestibular nerve: the part of the auditory nerve leading from the vestibule of the inner ear to the brain, controlling equilibrium

vestibule: space or cavity, as within the labyrinth of the inner ear

vestigial: of the nature of a remnant of an organ that is no longer functional

viable: capable of living and developing normally, as a newborn infant

vibrissae (*sing., vibrissa*): hairs that grow in the nasal cavity

villi (*sing., villus*): minute, hairlike structures on the mucous membrane of the small intestine that absorb nutrients

Vincent's angina: *see* trench mouth

Vincent's disease: *see* trench mouth

virulent: 1. severe and rapid in its progress, as a disease 2. highly infectious, as a disease-causing microorganism

virus (*pl., viruses*): any of a large group of particles too small to be seen by an ordinary microscope, that are typically inert except when in contact with certain living cells, and that can cause a variety of infectious diseases

viscera: 1. the internal organs of the body, as the stomach, lungs, heart, etc. 2. the intestines

visceral: pertaining to the viscera

viscid: sticky or adhesive

viscous: semifluid or gluelike in texture

visual purple: reddish purple protein found in the rods of the retina, especially important to night vision

visual radiations: smaller nerve bundles that split off from the optic nerve and enter the occipital lobes of the brain

vitalometer: device for measuring sensitivity of a tooth

vital signs: measurement of body temperature, pulse rate, and respiration

vitamin(s): any of a group of complex organic substances found in minute quantities in most natural foods and closely associated with the maintenance of normal physiological functions

vitamin A: vitamin found in green and yellow vegetables, dairy products, liver and fish liver oils, that prevents atrophy of epithelial tissue and protects against night blindness

vitamin B$_1$: thiamine

vitamin B$_2$: riboflavin

vitamin B$_{12}$: vitamin extracted from liver and believed to protect against pernicious anemia

vitamin B complex: group of water-soluble vitamins including thiamine and riboflavin

vitamin C: *see* ascorbic acid

vitamin D: vitamin that protects against rickets, found in fish liver oils, butter, egg yolks, and specially treated cow's milk, and also produced in the body on exposure to sunlight

vitamin E: vitamin found in whole grain cereals, legume seeds, corn oil, egg yolks, meat, and milk, sometimes called the anti-sterility vitamin because its absence in rats causes sterility

vitamin K: vitamin that promotes the clotting of blood and is found in green leafy vegetables

vitiligo/piebald skin: skin disorder characterized by a loss of pigment in sharply defined areas

vitreous humor: the transparent, jellylike tissue that fills the posterior chamber or ball of the eye and is enclosed by the hyaloid membrane

vocal cords/vocal folds: two bands of ligaments extending across the larynx which, when tense, are made to vibrate by the passage of air, thereby producing voice

vocal folds: *see* vocal cords

voice box: larynx

void: excrete waste, especially urine

voluntary muscle: *see* skeletal muscle

volvulus: obstruction of the intestines caused by twisting

vomitus: vomited substance

vulva: the external genitals of the female, located beneath the front part of the pelvis

walking pneumonia: mild viral pneumonia that does not confine the patient to bed

walleye: strabismus characterized by a tendency of the eyes to turn outward, away from the nose

wart: small, usually hard, benign growth formed on and rooted in the skin, caused by a virus

Wasserman test: blood test for the presence of the organism causing syphilis

water blister: blister beneath the epidermis that contains lymph

"water pills": diuretics

wet dream/nocturnal emission: male's involuntary expulsion of semen while asleep

wheal: raised area on the skin, as from hives or an insect bite, usually transitory and characterized by itching

whiplash: injury to neck ligaments, usually caused by a sudden jolt to the neck, as in automobile accidents

white blood cells: *see* leukocytes

white corpuscle: *see* leukocyte

white of eye: *see* sclera

white lung disease: byssinosis

WHO: World Health Organization

whooping cough/pertussis: respiratory, bacterial disease of children marked by paroxysms of coughing ending with a sharp sound (or "whoop") upon intake of breath

whooping cough/pertussis, immunization against: *see* DPT injections

Wilms' tumor/nephroblastoma: malignant tumor of the kidney, found especially in children

windpipe: *see* trachea

wisdom tooth: the last tooth, or third molar on either side of the upper and lower jaws

withdrawal symptom: any of the symptoms caused by the withdrawal of a physically addictive drug from an addict, as tremors, sweating, chills, vomiting, and diarrhea

womb: *see* uterus

wood alcohol: methyl alcohol

writer's cramp: spasmodic contraction of the muscles of the fingers and hand, caused by excessive writing

xenograft: *see* heterograft

xenophobia: fear of strangers

xerography: method of reproducing an image of electrostatic attraction, used experimentally as a diagnostic tool

xeroradiogram: picture developed by xeroradiography

xeroradiography: diagnostic procedure utilizing xerography to develop X-ray pictures

X ray: 1. to examine, diagnose, or treat with X rays 2. photograph made with X rays

X rays: electromagnetic radiations of extremely short wavelengths, used to reproduce on photosensitive film images of the internal organs and the skeleton as an aid in the detection, diagnosis, and treatment of certain disorders

Yang: in the Chinese philosophy underlying acupuncture, the masculine principle, identified with activity

yaws: infectious tropical disease that is not venereal but is caused by the syphilis bacterium (spirochete), characterized by rheumatic pains and ulcerating sores of the skin

yellow fever: acute, infectious, intestinal disease of tropical and semi-tropical regions, caused by a virus transmitted by the bite of a mosquito, and characterized by jaundice and hemorrhages

yellow marrow: marrow

Yin: in the Chinese philosophy underlying acupuncture, the female principle, identified with passivity

zymase: enzyme, obtained principally from yeast, important in fermentation

Generic Drugs

Name	Action			Prescribed for	

Trade Names (CD) = combined drug)

Acetaminophen	Believed to reduce concentration of chemicals involved in production of pain, fever, and inflammation (analgesic; antipyretic)			Relief of mild to moderate pain; reduction of fever	
Anacin-3 Bancap (CD) Capital (CD) Codalan (CD) Co-Gesic (CD) Comtrex (CD) Congesprin (CD) for children	Co-Tylenol (CD) Darvocet-N (CD) Datril Dolacet (CD) Dorcol (CD) for children Dristan (CD) Esgic (CD) Excedrin (CD)	Hycomine (CD) Hyco-Pap (CD) Lorcet (CD) Midrin (CD) Pacaps (CD) Percocet (CD) Percogesic (CD)		Penaphen (CD) Protid (CD) Repan (CD) Sinarest (CD) Sine-Aid (CD) Sinutab (CD) Talacen (CD)	Tylenol Tylenol Infant Drops Tylenol Junior Strength Tylox (CD) Unisom (CD) Vicodin (CD) Wygesic (CD)
Alprazolam	Believed to depress the central nervous system, slowing nervous response, and relieving nervousness and tension			Relief of anxiety attacks and insomnia; reduction of symptoms of chronic anxiety	
Xanax					
Amitriptyline	Believed to restore to normal levels the constituents of brain tissue that transmit nerve impulses (antidepressant)			Relief of emotional depression; gradual improvement of mood	
Elavil Endep Etrafon (CD)	Limbitral (CD) Triavil (CD)				
Ampicillin	Interferes with ability of susceptible bacteria to produce new protective cell walls as they grow and multiply (antibiotic)			Elimination of infections responsive to action of this drug	
Omnipen Polycillin	Principen Unasyn				
Antacids (Aluminum Hydroxide) (Calcium Carbonate) (Sodium Bicarbonate)	Neutralizes stomach acid; reduces action of digestive enzyme pepsin (relief from gastric hyperacidity)			Relief of heartburn, sour stomach, acid indigestion, and discomfort associated with peptic ulcer, gastritis, esophagitis, hiatal hernia	
Absorbable: Sodium bicarbonate: Alka-Seltzer	Brioschi Bromo-Seltzer	Less absorbable: Aluminum hydroxide:		Amphojel Calcium carbonate:	Alka-2 Amitone
Aspirin (Acetylsalicylic Acid)	Dilates blood vessels in skin, thus hastening loss of body heat (antipyretic); reduces tissue concentration of inflammation and pain (analgesic; antirheumatic)			Reduction of fever; relief of mild to moderate pain and inflammation; prevention of blood clots, as in phlebitis, heart attack, stroke	
Bayer Easprin Empirin St. Joseph's Children's Aspirin Alka-Seltzer (CD) Anacin (CD)	Ascriptin (CD) Axotal (CD) Buff-A Comp (CD) Bufferin (CD) Congesprin (CD) for children Darvon (CD)	Ecotrin Equagesic (CD) Excedrin (CD) 4-Way Cold Tablets (CD) Fiorinal (CD) Midol (CD) Norgesic (CD)		Percodan (CD) Robaxisal (CD) Soma Compound (CD) Supac (CD) Synalgos-DC (CD) Talwin (CD)	Zorprin
Atropine (Belladonna, Hyoscyamine)	Prevents stimulation of muscular contractions and glandular secretions in organ involved (antispasmodic [anticholinergic])			Relief of discomfort associated with excessive activity and spasm of digestive tract; irritation and spasm of lower urinary tract; painful menstruation	
Antrocol (CD) Arco-Lase Plus (CD) Donnagel-PG (CD)	Donnatal (CD) Donnatal	Donnazyme (CD) Lomotil (CD)		Ru-Tuss (CD) SK-Diphenoxylate (CD)	Urised (CD)
Bendroflumethiazide	Increases elimination of salt and water (diuretic); relaxes walls of smaller arteries, allowing them to expand; combined effect lowers blood pressure (antihypertensive)			Elimination of excessive fluid retention (edema); reduction of high blood pressure	
Naturetin	Corzide (CD)	Rauzide (CD)			
Beta-Adrenergic Blocking Agents	Decreases physical responses at beta-adrenergic receptors, slowing heart rate, dilating the vascular and bronchial systems (antihypertensive); believed to reduce cardiac output and nervous system responses in some forms of the medication			Treatment of high blood pressure; medication to reduce the incidence of another attack in heart attack patients; prevention of migraine headaches in chronic sufferers of migraines	
Blocadren Corgard	Lopressor Normodyne	Sectral Tenormin		Visken	

Name	Action	Prescribed for
Trade Names (CD = combined drug)		
Brompheniramine	Blocks action of histamine after release from sensitized tissue cells, thus reducing intensity of allergic response (antihistamine)	Relief of symptoms of hay fever (allergic rhinitis) and of allergic reactions of skin (itching, swelling, hives, rash)
Dimetane Bromfed (CD)	Dimetapp (CD) Poly-histine-DX (CD)	
Butabarbital	Believed to block transmission of nerve impulses (hypnotic; sedative)	Low dosage: relief of moderate anxiety or tension (sedative effect); higher dosage: at bedtime to induce sleep (hypnotic effect)
Butisol Pyridium Plus (CD)		
Butalbital	Affects the actions of the central nervous system, relieving anxiety (anxiolytic), and relaxing muscles (barbiturate sedative)	Relief of headaches related to tension or stress, psychic tension; relaxation of muscle strain and contraction in the head, neck, and shoulders
Esgic (CD) Fioricet (CD) Fiorinal (CD)	Medigesic (CD) Sedapap (CD) Phrenilin (CD) Repan (CD)	
Caffeine	Constricts blood vessel walls; increases energy level of chemical systems responsible for nerve tissue activity (cardiac, respiratory, psychic stimulant)	Prevention and early relief of vascular headaches such as migraine; relief of drowsiness and mental fatigue
No-Doz Anacin (CD) Cafergot (CD)	Esgic (CD) Fiorinal (CD) Excedrin Extra Strength Maximum Strength Midol (CD)	Pacaps (CD) Wigraine (CD) Vivarin
Carisoprodol	Believed to block transmission of nerve impulses and/or to produce a sedative effect (muscle relaxant)	Relief of discomfort caused by spasms of voluntary muscles
Soma (CD) Soma Compound (CD)		
Chloral Hydrate	Believed to affect wake-sleep centers of brain (hypnotic)	Low dosage: relief of mild to moderate anxiety or tension (sedative effect); higher dosage: at bedtime to relieve insomnia (hypnotic effect)
SK-Chloral Hydrate		
Chloramphenicol	Prevents growth and multiplication of susceptible bacteria by interfering with formation of their essential proteins (antibiotic)	Elimination of infections responsive to action of this drug
Chloromycetin Ophthochlor Ophthocort		
Chlordiazepoxide	Believed to reduce activity of some parts of limbic system (tranquilizer)	Relief of mild to moderate anxiety and tension without significant sedation
Libritabs Librium Librax (CD)	Limbitrol (CD) Menrium (CD)	
Chlorpheniramine	Blocks action of histamine after release from sensitized tissue cells, thus reducing intensity of allergic response (antihistamine)	Relief of symptoms of hay fever (allergic rhinitis) and of allergic reactions of skin (itching, swelling, hives, rash)

Chlor-Trimeton
Teldrin
Comtrex (CD)
Contac
Dristan (CD)
	PediaCare (CD) for
	  children
	Tylenol Cold Medication
	  (CD)	

Chlorpromazine	Believed to inhibit action of dopamine, thus correcting an imbalance of nerve impulse transmission thought to be responsible for certain mental disorders (antiemetic; tranquilizer)	Relief of severe anxiety, agitation, and psychotic behavior
Thorazine		
Chlorzoxazone	Inhibits nerve responses that trigger muscle contractions	Pain relief of muscle tension and injuries to the muscles and joints; relaxation of muscular tension for use in combination with physical therapy
Paraflex	Parafon (CD) Remular	
Codeine	Believed to affect tissue sites that react specifically with opium and its derivatives (antitussive; narcotic analgesic)	Relief of moderate pain; control of coughing
Acetaco (CD) Actifed with Codeine (CD) Ambenyl (CD) Calcidrine Syrup (CD) Codalan (CD) Codimal PH (CD) Dimetane-DC (CD)	Empirin with Codeine Nucofed (CD) (CD) Pediacof (CD) Fiorinal with Codeine (CD) Phenaphen with Codeine IoTuss (CD) (CD) Naldecon-CX (CD) Phenergan with Codeine Novahistine DK (CD) (CD)	Promethazine (CD) Tylenol with Codeine (CD) Robitussin A-C (CD) Soma Compound (CD) Triaminic with Codeine Tussar (CD)

Name	Action	Prescribed for
Trade Names (CD = combined drug)		
Dexamethasone	Believed to inhibit several tissue mechanisms that induce inflammation (adrenocortical steriod [anti-inflammatory])	Symptomatic relief of inflammation (swelling, redness, heat, pain)
Decadron Dalalone	Hexadrol Neodecadron	
Dextroamphetamine (d-Amphetamine)	Increases release of nerve impulse transmitter (central stimulant); this may also improve concentration and attention span of hyperactive child (primary calming action unknown); alters chemical control of nerve impulse transmission in appetite control center of brain (appetite suppressant [anorexiant])	Reduction or prevention of sleep epilepsy (narcolepsy); reduction of symptoms of abnormal hyperactivity (as in minimal brain dysfunction); suppression of appetite in management of weight reduction
Dexedrine	Biphetamine (CD)	
Diazepam	Believed to reduce activity of some parts of limbic system (tranquilizer)	Relief of mild to moderate anxiety and tension without significant sedation
Valium		
Dicyclomine	Believed to produce a local anesthetic action that blocks reflex activity responsible for spasm (antispasmodic)	Relief of discomfort from muscle spasm of the gastrointestinal tract
Bentyl		
Digitoxin	Increases availability of calcium within the heart muscle, thus improving conversion of chemical energy to mechanical energy; slows pacemaker and delays transmission of electrical impulses (digitalis preparations [cardiotonic])	Improvement of heart muscle contraction force (as in congestive heart failure); correction of certain heart rhythm disorders
Crystodigin		
Digoxin	Same as above	Same as above
Lanoxicaps Lanoxin		
Diphenhydramine	Blocks action of histamine after release from sensitized tissue cells, thus reducing intensity of allergic response (antihistamine)	Relief of symptoms of hay fever (allergic rhinitis) and of allergic reactions of skin (itching, swelling, hives, rash)
Ambenyl (CD) Benadryl Benadryl DM (CD) Bromanyl (CD)	Dytuss (CD) Tylenol Cold Night Time (CD) Unisom Dual Relief (CD)	
Doxylamine	Same as above	Same as above
Unisom	Cremacoat 4 (CD) Nyquil (CD)	
Ephedrine	Blocks release of certain chemicals from sensitized tissue cells undergoing allergic reaction; relaxes bronchial muscles; shrinks tissue mass (decongestion) by contracting arteriole walls in lining of respiratory passages (adrenergic [bronchodilator])	Prevention and symptomatic relief of bronchial asthma; relief of congestion of respiratory passages
Primatene Mist Bronkolixir (CD) Bronkotabs (CD)	Medicone-Derma HC (CD) Nyquil (CD) Marax (CD) Primatene (CD) Mudrane (CD) Quadrinal (CD)	Quelidrine (CD) Rynatuss (CD) Tedral (CD)
Ergotamine	Constricts blood vessel walls, thus relieving excessive dilation that causes pain of vascular headaches (migraine analgesic [vasoconstrictor])	Prevention and early relief of vascular headaches such as migraines or histamine headaches
Ergomar Ergostat	Medihaler Ergotamine Cafergot (CD) Bellergal (CD)	Wigraine (CD)
Erythromycin	Prevents growth and multiplication of susceptible bacteria by interfering with formation of their essential proteins (antibiotic)	Elimination of infections responsive to action of this drug
A/T/S E.E.S. E-Mycin ERYC	EryDerm Erythrocin Erymax Ilosone EryPed Ilotycin Ery-Tab P.C.E.	Staticin/T-Stat Wyamycin S SK-Erythromycin Pediazole (CD)
Estrogens (Estrogenic Substances) Conjugated Estrogens, Esterified Estrogens (Estrone and Equilin) Estradiol Mestranol	Prepares uterus for pregnancy or induces menstruation by cyclic increase and decrease in tissue stimulation; when taken regularly, blood and tissue levels increase to resemble those during pregnancy, thus preventing pituitary gland from producing hormones that induce ovulation; reduces frequency and intensity of menopausal symptoms (female sex hormone)	Regulation of menstrual cycle; oral birth control; prevention of pregnancy; relief of symptoms of menopause
Estratab Premarin Estratest (CD)	Mediatric (CD) Brevicon (CD) Menrium (CD) Demulen (CD) PMB (CD) Enovid (CD)	Modicon (CD) Ortho-Novum (CD) Norethin (CD) Norinyl (CD)

Name	Action	Prescribed for
Trade Names (CD = combined drug)		

Name	Action	Prescribed for
Fluoxetine	Believed to inhibit nerve uptake of serotonin to reduce depression (antidepressant, sedative)	Relief from acute depression or major depressive episodes
Prozac		
Griseofulvin	Believed to prevent growth and multiplication of susceptible fungus strains by interfering with their metabolic activities (antibiotic; antifungal)	Elimination of fungus infections responsive to actions of this drug
Fulvicin-U/F Fulvicin P/G Grifulvin V		Grisactin Gris-PEG
Guaifenesin	Loosens phlegm and mucous from the bronchial passages by reducing viscosity and adhesiveness (expectorant)	Relief of painful coughs due to colds and influenzas; usually taken in conjunction with a decongestant
Codiclear (CD) Dilaudid (CD) Guaifed (CD) Codimal (CD) Donatussin (CD) Mudrane (CD)		Naldecon (CD) Quibron (CD) Robitussin (CD) Triaminic (CD)
Hydralazine	Lowers pressure of blood in vessels by causing direct relaxation and expansion of vessel walls—mechanism unknown (antihypertensive)	Reduction of high blood pressure
Apresoline Ser-Ap-Es (CD) Apresazide (CD) Serpasil-Apresoline (CD) Apresoline-Esidrex (CD)		
Hydrochlorothiazide	Increases elimination of salt and water (diuretic); relaxes walls of smaller arteries, allowing them to expand; combined effect lowers blood pressure (antihypertensive)	Elimination of excessive fluid retention (edema); reduction of high blood pressure
Esidrix Apresoline-Esidrex (CD) Maxzide (CD) HydroDIURIL Dyazide (CD) Moduretic (CD) Oretic Esimil (CD) SK-Hydro- Aldactazide (CD) Hydropres (CD) chlorothiazide Aldoril (CD) Inderide (CD) Timolide (CD) Apresazide (CD)		
Hydrocodone	Believed to affect opiate receptors in the nervous system, reducing pain and relaxing muscles (narcotic analgesic)	Relief of moderate to severe pain; severe cough and cold symptoms
Anexsia (CD) Codimal (CD) Entuss (CD) Lortab (CD) Azdone (CD) Co-Gesic (CD) Hyco-Pap (CD) Ru-Tuss with Bancap (CD) Donatussin (CD) Hydrocet (CD) Hydrocodone (CD) Codiclear (CD) DuoCet (CD) Lorcet (CD) Triaminic (CD)		
Hydrocortisone (Cortisol)	Believed to inhibit several tissue mechanisms that induce inflammation (adrenocortical steroid [anti-inflammatory])	Symptomatic relief of inflammation (swelling, redness, heat, pain)
Aeroseb-HC Penecort Derma-Sone (CD) Otocort (CD) Carmol HC Synacort Di-Hydrotic (CD) Proctocort Cortef Vanoxide-HC Hill Cortac (CD) Proctocream (CD) Eldecort Vioform-Hydrocortisone Hysone (CD) Proctofoam (CD) F-E-P VōSoL HC Iodo-Cortifair (CD) Hydrocortone Corticaine (CD) Oticol (CD) Hytone Cortisporin (CD)		
Hydroxyzine	Believed to reduce excessive activity in areas of brain that influence emotional health (antihistamine; tranquilizer)	Relief of anxiety, tension, apprehension, and agitation
Atarax Marax (CD) Vistaril SK-Hydroxyzine		
Ibuprofen	Believed to inhibit prostaglandin sythetase production, acting as an anti-inflammatory agent; reduces fever (antipyretic), reduces inflammation and pain (antirheumatic, analgesic)	Relief of inflammation and pain from rheumatoid arthritis, osteoarthritis, and primary dysmenorrhea
Advil IBU-TAB Motrin Children's Advil Medipren Nuprin		PediaProfen for children SK-Ibuprofen Rufen
Insulin (Human, beef, pork)	Facilitates passage of sugar through cell wall to interior of cell (hypoglycemic)	Control of diabetes
Humulin Lente Insulin NPH Insulin Iletin Mixtard Regular Insulin Insulatard NPH Novolin Semilente Insulin		Ultrlente Insulin Velosulin
Isoniazid	Believed to interfere with several metabolic activities of susceptible tuberculosis organisms (antibacterial; tuberculostatic)	Prevention and treatment of tuberculosis
INH Laniazid Rifamate (CD)		
Isopropamide	Prevents stimulation of muscular contraction and glandular secretion in organ involved (antispasmodic [anticholinergic])	Relief of discomfort from excessive activity and spasm of digestive tract
Darbid		

Name	Action	Prescribed for
Trade Names (CD = combined drug)		
Isoproterenol/ Isoprenaline	Dilates bronchial tubes by stimulating sympathetic nerve terminals (Isoproterenol: adrenergic [bronchodilator]; Iso-prenaline: sympathomimetic)	Management of acute bronchial asthma, bronchitis, and emphysema
Isuprel Medihaler-Iso Norisodrine	Duo-Medihaler (CD) Isuprel Hydrochloride (CD)	
Isosorbide Dinitrate	Acts directly on muscle cells to produce relaxation which permits expansion of blood vessels, thus increasing supply of blood and oxygen to heart (coronary vasodilator)	Management of pain associated with angina pectoris (coronary insufficiency)
Dilatrate Iso-Bid Isordil Sorbitrate		
Levodopa	Believed to be converted to dopamine in brain tissue, thus correcting a dopamine deficiency and restoring more normal balance of chemicals responsible for transmission of nerve impulses (anti-Parkinsonism)	Management of Parkinson's disease
Larodopa Sinemet		
Liothyronine (T-3)	Increases rate of cellular metabolism and makes more energy available for biochemical activity (thyroid hormone)	Correction of thyroid hormone deficiency (hypothyroidism)
Cytomel Euthroid (CD) Thyrolar (CD)		
Lithium	Believed to correct chemical imbalance in certain nerve impulse transmitters that influence emotional behavior (antidepressant)	Improvement of mood and behavior in chronic manic-depression
Eskalith Cibalith-S Lithane Lithobid		
Meclizine	Blocks transmission of excessive nerve impulses to vomiting center (antiemetic)	Management of nausea, vomiting, and dizziness associated with motion sickness
Antivert Bonine Meclizine HCl		
Meperidine/Pethidine	Believed to increase chemicals that transmit nerve impulses (narcotic analgesic)	Relief of moderate to severe pain
Demerol Mepergan (CD)		
Meprobamate	Not known (tranquilizer)	Relief of mild to moderate anxiety and tension (sedative effect); relief of insomnia resulting from anxiety and tension (hypnotic effect)
Equanil Miltown	Deprol (CD) Meprospan Equagesic (CD) PMB (CD)	
Methadone	Believed to increase chemicals that transmit nerve impulses (narcotic analgesic)	Treatment of heroin addiction; sometimes for relief of moderate to severe pain
Dolophine Methadone Hydrochloride		
Methyclothiazide	Increases elimination of salt and water (diuretic); relaxes walls of smaller arteries, allowing them to expand; combined effect lowers blood pressure (antihypertensive)	Elimination of excess fluid retention (edema); reduction of high blood pressure
Aquatensen	Enduron Diutensen (CD)	Enduronyl (CD)
Methylphenidate	Believed to increase release of nerve impulse transmitter, which may also improve concentration and attention span of hyperactive child (primary action unknown) (central stimulant)	Management of fatigue and depression; reduction of symptoms of abnormal hyperactivity (as in minimal brain dysfunction)
Ritalin		
Nicotinic Acid/Niacin	Corrects a deficiency of nicotinic acid in tissues; dilation of blood vessels is believed limited to skin—increased blood flow within head has not been demonstrated; reduces initial production of cholesterol and prevents conversion of fatty tissue to cholesterol and triglycerides (vitamin B-complex component; cholesterol reducer)	Management of pellagra; treatment of vertigo, ringing in ears, premenstrual headache; reduction of blood levels of cholesterol and triglycerides
Niacor Nicobid Nicolar	Nicotinex Elixir Slo-Niacin	

Name	Action	Prescribed for
Trade Names (CD = combined drug)		
Nitrofurantoin	Believed to prevent growth and multiplication of suscepti-ble bacteria by interfering with function of their essential enzyme systems (antibacterial)	Elimination of infections responsive to action of this drug
Furacin	Macrodantin	
Nitroglycerin	Acts directly on muscle cells to produce relaxation which permits expansion of blood vessels, thus increasing sup-ply of blood and oxygen to heart (coronary vasodilator)	Management of pain associated with angina pectoris (coronary insufficiency)
Nitro-Bid Nitrodisc Nitro-Dur Nitroglyn Nitrol	Nitrong Nitrostat Transderm-Nitro Tridil	
Nystatin	Prevents gorwth and multiplication of susceptible fungus strains by attacking their walls and causing leakage of internal components (antibiotic; antifungal)	Elimination of fungus infections responsive to action of this drug
Mycostatin Nilstat Nystex	Mycolog (CD) Myco-Triacet (CD) Mytrex (CD)	
Oral Contraceptives	Suppresses the two pituitary gland hormones that pro-duce ovulation (oral contraceptives)	Prevention of pregnancy
Ovcon Brevicon Demulen Enovid-E	Loestrin LO/Ovral Micronor Medicon	Nordette Norinyl Norlestrin Ortho-Novum	Ovral Triphasil Ovrette Ovulen Tri-Norinyl
Oxycodone	Believed to affect tissue sites that react specifically with opium and its derivatives (narcotic analgesic)	Relief of moderate pain; control of coughing
Percocet (CD) Percodan (CD) SK-Oxycodone with Acetaminophen (CD)	SK-Oxycodone with Aspirin (CD) Tylox (CD) Roxicet (CD)	Roxicodone Roxiprin (CD)	
Oxytetracycline	Prevents growth and multiplication of susceptible bacteria by interfering with their formation of essential proteins (antibiotic)	Elimination of infections responsive to action of this drug
Terra-Cortril (CD)	Terramycin Urobiotic (CD)	
Papaverine	Causes direct relaxation and expansion of blood vessel walls, thus increasing volume of blood which increases oxygen and nutrients (smooth muscle relaxant; vasodila-tor)	Relief of symptoms associated with impaired circulation in extremities and within brain
SK-Papaverine Pavabid		
Paregoric (Camphorated Tincture of Opium)	Believed to affect tissue sites that react specifically with opium and its derivatives to relieve pain; its active ingre-dient, morphine, acts as a local anesthetic and blocks release of chemical that transmits nerve impulses to muscle walls of intestine (antiperistaltic)	Relief of mild to moderate pain; relief of intestinal cramp-ing and diarrhea
Donnagel-PG (CD) Parepectolin (CD)		
Penicillin G	Interferes with ability of susceptible bacteria to produce new protective cell walls as they grow and multiply (anti-biotic)	Elimination of infections responsive to action of this drug
Bicillin C-R Pentids Pfizerpen	SK-Pencillin G Wycillin	
Penicillin V	Same as above	Same as above
Betapen-VK Pen-Vee K Ledercillin	SK-Pencillin VK Veetids	
Pentobarbital	Believed to block transmission of nerve impulses (hyp-notic; sedative)	Low dosage: relief of mild to moderate anxiety or tension (sedative effect); higher dosage: at bedtime to induce sleep (hypnotic effect)
Cafergot PB (CD) Nembutal		
Phenazopyridine	Acts as local anesthetic on lining of lower urinary tract (urinary-analgesic)	Relief of pain and discomfort associated with acute irrita-tion of lower urinary tract as in cystitis, urethritis, and prostatitis
Azo Gantanol (CD) Azo-Standard Pyridium	Thiosulfil-A (CD) Urobiotic (CD)	

Name	Action	Prescribed for
Trade Names (CD = combined drug)		
Pheniramine	Blocks action of histamine after release from sensitized tissue cells, thus reducing intensity of allergic response (antihistamine)	Relief of symptoms of hay fever (allergic rhinitis) and of allergic reactions of skin (itching, swelling, hives, and rash)
Triaminic Citra Forte (CD) Dristan (CD) Fiogesic (CD)	Poly-Histine-D (CD) Robitussin AC (CD) Ru-Tuss with Hydrocodone (CD)	S-T Forte (CD) Triaminicin (CD) Tussagesic (CD)	Tussirex (CD)
Phenobarbital/ Phenobarbitone	Believed to block transmission of nerve impulses (anticonvulsant; hypnotic; sedative)	Low dosage: relief of mild to moderate anxiety or tension (sedative effect); higher dosage: at bedtime to induce sleep (hypnotic effect); continuous dosage: prevention of epileptic seizures (anticonvulsant effect)
SK-Phenobarbital Solfoton Antrocol (CD)	Bellergal-S (CD) Bronkolixir (CD) Bronkotabs (CD)	Mudrane (CD) Mudrane GG (CD) Phazyme (CD)	Primatene (CD) Quadrinal (CD) T-E-P (CD)
Phentermine	Believed to alter chemical control of nerve impulse transmitter in appetite center of brain (appetite suppressant [anorexiant])	Suppression of appetite in management of weight reduction
Adipex-P Fastin Ionamin		
Phenylbutazone	Believed to suppress formation of chemical involved in production of inflammation (analgesic; anti-inflammatory; antipyretic)	Symptomatic relief of inflammation, swelling, pain, and tenderness associated with arthritis, tendinitis, bursitis, superficial phlebitis
Butazolidin		
Phenylephrine	Shrinks tissue mass (decongestion) by contracting arteriole walls in lining of nasal passages, sinuses, and throat, thus decreasing volume of blood (decongestant [sympathomimetic])	Relief of congestion of nose, sinuses, and throat associated with allergy
Codimal (CD) Comhist (CD) Cogespirin (CD) for children Coryban-D Cough Syrup (CD) Dallergy (CD) Dimetapp (CD) Donatussin (CD) Dristan, Advanced	Formula (CD) Dura-Tap/PD (CD) Dura-Vent/PD (CD) Entex (CD) Extendryl (CD) 4-Way Nasal Spray (CD) Histor-D (CD) Hycomine (CD) Korigesic (CD) Naldecon (CD)	Neo-Synephrine (CD) P-V-Tussin (CD) Pediacof (CD) Phenergan VC (CD) Protid (CD) Quelidrine (CD) Ru-Tuss (CD) Rynatan (CD) Rynatuss (CD)	Sinarest (CD) S-T Decongest (CD) S-T Forte (CD) Tamine S.R. (CD) Tussar DM (CD) Tussirex (CD)
Phenylpropanolamine	Same as above	Same as above
Help Propagest Rhindecon Alka-Seltzer Plus (CD) Allerest (CD) Appedrine, Maximum Strength (CD) Bayer Children's Cold Tablets (CD) Bayer Cough Syrup for Children (CD) Codimal Expectorant (CD) Comtrex (CD) Conex (CD) Congesprin (CD) for children	Contac (CD) Control (CD) Coryban-D (CD) CoTylenol Children's Liquid (CD) Cremacoat 3 (CD) Dehist (CD) Dexatrim (CD) Dieutrim (CD) Dimetane (CD) Dimetapp (CD) Dura-Tapp/PD (CD) Dura-Vent (CD) Dura-Vent/A (CD) Entex (CD) 4-Way (CD)	Fiogesic (CD) Heat & Chest (CD) Histalet (CD) Hycomine (CD) Naldecon (CD) Nolamine (CD) Ornacol (CD) Ornade (CD) Poly-Histine (CD) Prolamine, Extra Strength (CD) Quadrahist (CD) Resaid (CD) Rescaps (CD) Rhinolar (CD) Ru-Tuss (CD)	S-T Decongest (CD) S-T Forte (CD) Sinubid (CD) Sinulin (CD) Sinutab (CD) Tamine S.R. (CD) Tavist-D (CD) Triaminic (CD) Triaminicin (CD) Triaminicol (CD) Tuss-Ade (CD) Tuss-Ornade (CD)
Phenytoin (formerly Diphenylhydantoin)	Believed to promote loss of sodium from nerve fibers, thus lowering their excitability and inhibiting spread of electrical impulse along nerve pathways (anticonvulsant)	Prevention of epileptic seizures
Dilantin		
Pilocarpine	Lowers internal eye pressure (antiglaucoma [miotic])	Management of glaucoma
Almocarpine	Isopto Carpine	Pilocar	
Potassium	Maintains and replenishes potassium content of cells (potassium preparations)	Management of potassium deficiency
Kaon Kay Ciel	K-Lor Kaochlor	Klorvess Pima Syrup	
Prednisolone	Believed to inhibit several mechanisms that induce inflammation (adrenocortical steroid [anti-inflammatory])	Symptomatic relief of inflammation (swelling, redness, heat, and pain)
Delta-Cortef Hydeltra-T.B.A. Metimyd Metreton Predate		

Name	Action	Prescribed for
Trade Names (CD = combined drug)		
Prednisone	Same as above	Same as above
Deltasone Liquid Pred SK-Prednisone Sterapred		
Probenecid	Reduces level of uric acid in blood and tissues; prolongs presence of penicillin in blood (antigout [uricosuric])	Management of gout
Benemid SK-Probenecid ColBENEMID (CD)	Col-Probenecid (CD) Polycillin-PRB (CD)	
Promethazine	Blocks action of histamine after release from sensitized tissue cells, thus reducing intensity of allergic response (antihistamine); blocks transmission of excessive nerve impulses to vomiting center (antiemetic); action producing sedation and sleep is unknown (sedative)	Relief of symptoms of hay fever (allergic rhinitis) and of allergic reactions of skin (itching, swelling, hives, rash); prevention and management of nausea, vomiting, and dizziness associated with motion sickness; production of mild sedation and light sleep
Phenergan	Mepergan (CD)	
Propantheline	Prevents stimulation of muscular contraction and glandular secretion within organ involved (antispasmodic [anticholinergic])	Relief of discomfort associated with excessive activity and spasm of digestive tract
Pro-Banthine	SK-Propantheline	
Propoxyphene	Increases chemicals that transmit nerve impulses, somehow contributing to the analgesic effect (analgesic)	Relief of mild to moderate pain
Darvon Darvocet-N (CD) Darvon Compound (CD) Dolene (CD)	SK-65 APAP (CD) SK-65 Compound (CD) Wygesic (CD)	
Pseudoephedrine (Isoephedrine)	Shrinks tissue mass (decongestion) by contracting arteriole walls in lining of nasal passages, sinuses, and throat, thus decreasing volume of blood (decongestant [sympathomimetic])	Relief of congestion of nose, throat, and sinuses associated with allergy
Sudafed Actifed (CD) Ambenyl-D (CD) Anafed (CD) Anamine (CD) Brexin (CD) Bromfed (CD) Chlor-Trimeton (CD) Chlorafed (CD)	Codimal-L.A. (CD) Congess (CD) CoTylenol Cold Medication (CD) Deconamine (CD) Dimacol (CD) Dorcol (CD) Extra-Strength Sine-Aid (CD)	Fedahist (CD) Gunifed (CD) Histalet (CD) Isoclor (CD) Kronofed-A (CD) Novafed (CD) Novahistine (CD) Nucofed (CD) Phenergan (CD)
		Poly-Histine-DX (CD) Respaire-SR (CD) Robitussin-DAC (CD) Sine-Aid (CD) Triafed (CD) Tussend Expectorant (CD) Zephrex (CD)
Pyrilamine/Mepyramine	Blocks action of histamine after release from sensitized tissue cells, thus reducing intensity of allergic response (antihistamine)	Relief of symptoms of hay fever (allergic rhinitis) and of allergic reactions of skin (itching, swelling, hives, and rash)
Albatussin (CD) Citra Forte (CD) Codimal (CD) 4-Way Nasal Spray (CD) Fiogesic (CD) Kronohist (CD)	Mydol PMS (CD) P-V-Tussin (CD) Poly-Histine-D (CD) Primatene-M (CD) Ru-Tuss (CD)	Triaminic (CD) Triaminicin (CD) Triaminicol (CD)
Quinidine	Slows pacemaker and delays transmission of electrical impulses (cardiac depressant)	Correction of certain heart rhythm disorders
Cardioquin Duraquin Quinaglute	Quinidex SK-Quinidine	
Reserpine	Relaxes blood vessel walls by reducing availability of norepinephrine (antihypertensive; tranquilizer)	Reduction of high blood pressure
Sandril Serpasil SK-Resperine	Demi-Regroton (CD) Diupres (CD) Diutensen-R (CD)	Hydromox R (CD) Hydropres (CD) Regrotin (CD)
		Salutensin (CD) Ser-Ap-Es (CD)
Rifampin	Prevents growth and multiplication of susceptible tuberculosis organisms by interfering with enzyme systems involved in formation of essential proteins (antibiotic; tuberculostatic)	Treatment of tuberculosis
Rifadin Rifamate Rimactane		
Secobarbital	Believed to block transmission of nerve impulses (hypnotic; sedative)	Low dosage: relief of mild to moderate anxiety or tension (sedative effect); higher dosage: at bedtime to induce sleep (hypnotic effect)
Seconal		

Name	Action	Prescribed for
Trade Names (CD = combined drug)		
Sulfamethoxazole	Prevents growth and multiplication of susceptible bacteria by interfering with their formation of folic acid (antibacterial)	Elimination of infections responsive to action of this drug
Gantanol Azo Gantanol (CD) Bactrim (CD) Septra (CD)		
Sulfisoxazole	Same as above	Same as above
Gantrisin SK-Soxazole Azo Gantrisin (CD) Pediazole (CD) for children		
Tetracycline	Prevents growth and multiplication of susceptible bacteria by interfering with their formation of essential proteins (antibiotic)	Elimination of infections responsive to action of this drug
Achromycin V Robitet SK-Tetracycline Topicycline Sumycin (CD)		
Theophylline (Aminophylline, Oxtriphylline)	Reverses constriction by increasing activity of chemical system within muscle cell that causes relaxation of bronchial tube (bronchodilator)	Symptomatic relief of bronchial asthma
Accurbron Bronkodyl Constant-T Elixicon LABID Respbid Somophyllin	Sustaire Synophylate Theobid Theoclear Theo-Dur Theolair Theon	Theo-Organidin Theophyl Aerolate (CD) Amesec (CD) Aquaphyllin (CD) Brondecon (CD) Bronkolixir (CD)	Bronkotabs (CD) Elixophyllin (CD) Marax (CD) Primatene (CD) Quadrinal (CD) Quibron (CD)	Slo-bid (CD) Slo-Phyllin (CD) T.E.H (CD) T-E-P (CD) Tedral (CD) Theozine (CD)
Thyroid Liothyronine Thyroglobulin Levothyroxine	Makes more energy available for biochemical activity and increases rate of cellular metabolism by altering pocesses of cellular chemicals that store energy (thyroid hormones)	Correction of thyroid hormone deficiency (hypothyroidism)
Armour Thyroid Cytomel Euthroid Levothroid	Proloid S-P-T Synthroid Thyrolar	Choloxin L-Thyroxine Thyrolar (CD)	
Tolbutamide	Stimulates secretion of insulin by pancreas (hypoglycemic)	Correction of insulin deficiency in adult diabetes
Orinase		
Trimethoprim	Prevents growth and multiplication of susceptible organisms by interfering with formation of proteins (antibacterial)	Elimination of infections responsive to action of this drug
Proloprim Trimpex Bactrim (CD)	Cotrim (CD) Septra (CD) Sulfatrim (CD)	
Triprolidine	Blocks action of histamine after release from sensitized tissue cells, thus reducing intensity of allergic response (antihistamine)	Relief of symptoms of hay fever (allergic rhinitis) and of allergic reacitons of skin (itching, swelling, hives, and rash)
Actidil Actifed (CD) Actifed-C (CD) Triafed (CD) Trifed (CD)		
Vitamin C (Ascorbic Acid)	Believed to be essential to enzyme activity involved in formation of collagen; increases absorption of iron from intestine and helps formation of hemoglobin and red blood cells in bone marrow; inhibits growth of certain bacteria in urinary tract; enhances effects of some antibiotics (vitamin)	Prevention and treatment of scurvy; treatment of some types of anemia; maintenance of acid urine
Cetane Cevalin Cevi-Bid Cevi-Fer (CD) Mediatric (CD)		

Biographies

Aalto, (Hugo) Alvar (Henrik), 1898–1976, Finn. architect.
Aaron, Henry, 1934–, U.S. baseball player.
Abbott, George, 1887–, U.S. theatrical director & playwright.
—Sir John Joseph Caldwell, 1821–93, Can. statesman; Can. prime minister 1891–92.
—William (Budd), 1896–1974, U.S. comedian & actor.
Abd-el-Krim, 1885?–1963, Moorish leader in Rif region of Morocco.
Abd-ul-Baha, 1844–1921, Pers. religious leader; called **Abbas Effendi.**
Abdul-Jabbar, Kareem, b. Lew Alcindor, 1947–, U.S. basketball player.
Abel, I(orwith) W(ilbur), 1908–, U.S. labor leader.
—Rudolph, 1902–72, Soviet spy.
Abélard, Peter, 1079–1142, Fr. theologian, philosopher, & teacher; also **Abailard.** See also HELOÏSE.
Abercombie, James, 1706–81, Brit. general.
Abernathy, Ralph David, 1926–90, U.S. clergyman & civil rights leader.
Abrams, Creighton W., Jr., 1914–74, U.S. general.
Abruzzi, Luigi Amedeo, Duca degli, 1873–1933, Ital. Arctic explorer.
Abzug, Bella Savitzky, 1920–, U.S. politician & women's advocate.
Ace, Goodman, 1899–1982, U.S. comic writer & radio performer.
—Jane, 1900–74, U.S. radio performer, wife of prec.
Acheampong, Ignatius Kutu, 1931–79, African military officer; president of Ghana 1972–78.
Acheson, Dean Gooderham, 1893–1971, U.S. lawyer; secretary of state 1949–53.
Acton, John Emerich Edward Dalberg, Lord, 1843–1902, Eng. historian & author.
Adam, James, 1730–94, Scot. architect & furniture designer.
—Robert, 1728–92, Scot. architect; brother of prec.
Adams, Abigail Smith, 1744–1818, U.S. writer.
—Ansel, 1902–84, U.S. photographer.
—Brooks, 1848–1927, U.S. historian.
—Charles Francis, 1807–86, U.S. lawyer & diplomat; father of prec.
—Franklin Pierce (F.P.A.), 1881–1960, U.S. journalist.
—Henry Brooks, 1838–1918, U.S. historian & philosopher.
—James Truslow, 1878–1949, U.S. historian.
—John, 1735–1826, 2nd U.S. president 1797–1801; husband of Abigail.
—John Quincy, 1767–1848, 6th U.S. president 1825–29; son of prec. & father of Charles Francis.
—Maude, 1872–1953, U.S. actress.
—Samuel, 1722–1803, Amer. revolutionary leader.
—Samuel Hopkins, 1871–1958, U.S. author.
Adamson, Joy, 1910–80, Silesian naturalist & author.
Addams, Charles Samuel, 1912–, U.S. cartoonist.
—Jane, 1860–1935, U.S. social worker.
Adderley, Julian Edwin (Cannonball), 1928–75, U.S. jazz musician.
Addinsell, Richard, 1904–77, Eng. film composer.
Addison, Joseph, 1672–1719, Eng. essayist & poet.
—Thomas, 1793–1860, Eng. physician.

Adenauer, Konrad, 1876–1967, Ger. statesman; first chancellor of W. Germany 1949–63.
Adler, Alfred, 1870–1937, Austrian psychiatrist.
—Felix, 1851–1933, U.S. educator & reformer.
—Larry, 1914–, U.S. musician.
—Luther, 1903–84, U.S. actor.
—Mortimer Jerome, 1902–, U.S. philosopher.
—Richard, 1921–, U.S. composer.
Adrian IV, b. Nicholas Breakspear, 1100?–59, pope 1154–59.
—VI, b. Adrian Florensz, 1459–1523, Du. pope 1522–23.
Adrian, Frederick 1903–59, U.S. fashion designer.
Aeschylus, 525–456 B.C., Gk. writer of tragedies.
Aesop, 6th c. B.C. Gk. writer of fables.
Aga Khan III, 1877–1957, Muslim spiritual leader.
—IV, 1936–, grandson & successor of prec.
Agassiz, Alexander, 1835–1910, U.S. zoologist.
—(Jean) Louis (Rodolphe), 1807–73, Swiss-born U.S. naturalist; father of prec.
Agee, James, 1909–55, U.S. author & critic.
Agnelli, Giovanni, 1921–, Ital. industrialist.
Agnew, Spiro Theodore, 1918–, U.S. politician; U.S. vice president 1968–73; resigned.
Agnon, Shmuel Yosef, 1888–1970, Russ.-born Israeli author; Nobel Prize winner.
Agricola, Gnaeus Julius, A.D. 37–93, Roman general.
Agrippa, Marcus Vipsanius, 63–12 B.C. Roman statesman.
Agrippina, 13 B.C.–A.D. 33, mother of Caligula: called **the Elder.**
— A.D. 15?–59, mother of Nero: called **the Younger.**
Aguinaldo, Emilio, 1869–1964, Filipino statesman & revolutionary leader.
Aiken, Conrad Potter, 1889–1973, U.S. poet & author.
—Howard H., 1900–73, U.S. mathematician.
Ailey, Alvin, 1931–89, U.S. choreographer.
Akbar, 1542–1605, Mogul emperor of Hindustan.
Akhmatova, Anna, 1888–1966, Soviet poet.
Akihito, 1933–, emperor of Japan.
Akuffo, Frederick William Kwasi, 1937–79, African military officer; president of Ghana 1978–79.
Alarón, Pedro Antonio de, 1833–91, Sp. playwright.
Alaric, 370?–410, king of the Visigoths; sacked Rome.
—II, ?–507, king of the Visigoths.
Albanese, Licia, 1913–, Ital. soprano active in U.S.
Albee, Edward, 1928–, U.S. playwright.
Albéniz, Isaac, 1860–1909, Sp. composer & pianist.
Albers, Josef, 1888–1976, Ger.-born U.S. painter.
Albert I, 1875–1934, king of Belgium 1909–34.
Albert, Prince, of Saxe-Coburg-Gotha, 1819–61, consort of Queen Victoria of England.
Albert, Carl Bert, 1908–, U.S. politician; speaker of House of Representatives 1971–77.
—Eddie, 1908–, U.S. actor.
Alberti, Leon Battista, 1404–72, Ital. architect & painter.
Albertson, Jack, 1910?–81, U.S. actor.
Albertus Magnus, Saint, 1200?–80, Ger. scholastic philosopher & theologian.
Albright, Ivan, 1897–1983, U.S. painter.
Albuquerque, Alfonso de, 1453–1515, Pg. viceroy in India.

Alcibiades, 450–404 B.C., Athenian general & politician.

Alcott, (Amos) Bronson, 1799–1888, U.S. educator.

—**Louisa May,** 1832–88, U.S. novelist; daughter of prec.

Alcuin, 735–804, Eng. theologian & scholar.

Alda, Alan, 1936–, U.S. actor.

Alden, John, 1599–1687, pilgrim at Plymouth Colony.

Aldrich, Nelson Wilmarth, 1841–1915, U.S. public official.

Aldrin, Edwin Eugene, Jr., 1930–, U.S. astronaut.

Aleichem, Sholem, pseud. of Solomon Rabinowitz, 1859–1916, Russ.-born U.S. author.

Aleixandre, Vicente, 1898–1984, Sp. poet; Nobel Prize winner.

Alemán Valdés, Miguel, 1902–83, Mexican statesman; president of Mexico 1946–52.

Alexander II, 1818–81, Russ. czar; emancipated serfs; assassinated.

Alexander III, 356–323 B.C., king of Macedonia & conqueror of Egypt & Asia Minor: called **the Great.**

Alexander VI, b. Rodrigo Lanzol y Borja, 1431–1503, pope 1492–1503.

Alexander Nevski, 1220?–63, Russ. military hero & saint.

Alexander Severus, 208?–235, Roman emperor 222–35.

Alexander, Grover Cleveland, 1887–1950, U.S. baseball player.

—**Harold Rupert Leofric George (1st Earl Alexander of Tunis),** 1891–1969, Brit. field marshal.

Alexanderson, Ernst F. W., 1878–1969, Swed.-born U.S. electrical engineer & inventor.

Alfieri, Count Vittorio, 1749–1803, Ital. playwright.

Alfonso XIII, 1886–1941, king of Spain 1902–31.

Alfred, 849–901, king of West Saxons: called **the Great.**

Alfvén, Hannes Olof Gösta, 1908–, Swed. physicist; Nobel Prize winner.

Alger, Horatio, 1832–99, U.S. author.

Algren, Nelson, 1909–81, U.S. author.

Ali, Muhammad, b. Cassius Clay, 1942–, U.S. boxer.

Alinsky, Saul David, 1909–72, U.S. social reformer.

Allen, Ethan, 1737–89, Amer. revolutionary soldier.

—**Fred,** 1894–1956, U.S. humorist & radio performer.

—**Frederick Lewis,** 1890–1954, U.S. editor & historian.

—**Gracie,** 1906–64, U.S. actress & comedienne.

—**Richard,** 1760–1831, Amer. black religious leader.

—**Stephen Valentine Patrick William (Steve),** 1921–, U.S. comedian & author.

—**Woody,** 1935–, U.S. comedian, actor, author, & film director.

Allenby, Edmund Henry, 1861–1936, Brit. field marshal.

Allende Gossens, Salvador, 1908–73, president of Chile 1970–73.

Allgood, Sara, 1883–1950, Irish-born U.S. actress.

Allison, Fran, 1924?–89, U.S. actress.

Allport, Gordon Willard, 1897–1967, U.S. psychologist & author.

Allston, Washington, 1779–1843, U.S. painter.

Allyson, June, 1923–, U.S. actress.

Alma-Tadema, Sir Lawrence, 1836–1912, Dutch-born Eng. painter.

Alonso, Alicia, 1921–, Cuban ballerina.

Alpini, Prospero, 1553–1617, Ital. physician & botanist.

Alsop, Joseph, 1910–89, U.S. journalist & author.

—**Stewart,** 1914–74, U.S. journalist & author; brother of prec.

Altgeld, John Peter, 1847–1902, Ger.-born U.S. politician.

Altman, Benjamin, 1840–1913, U.S. merchant & art collector.

—**Robert,** 1925–, U.S. film director.

Alva, Fernando Alvarez de Toledo, Duke of, 1508–82, Sp. general in the Netherlands.

Alvarado, Pedro de, 1495?–1541, Sp. soldier in the New World.

Alvarez, Luis Walter, 1911–, U.S. physicist; Nobel Prize winner.

Amado, Jorge, 1912–, Braz. author.

Amara, Lucine, 1927–, U.S. soprano.

Amati, Nicola, 1596–1684, Ital. violinmaker.

Ambler, Eric, 1909–, Eng. author.

Ambrose, Saint, 340?–397, bishop of Milan.

Ameche, Don, 1908–, U.S. actor.

Amenhotep III, 14th c. B.C. king of Egypt; reigned ca. 1411–1375 B.C..

Amherst, Lord Jeffrey, 1717–97, Brit. governor-general of North America.

Amin Dada, Idi, 1925?–, Ugandan general; president of Uganda 1971–79.

Amis, Kingsley, 1922–, Brit. novelist.

Amory, Cleveland, 1917–, U.S. author & critic.

Ampère, André Marie, 1775–1836, Fr. physicist.

Amundsen, Roald, 1872–1928, Norw. explorer.

Anacreon, 572?–488 B.C., Gk. poet.

Anaxagoras, 500–428 B.C., Gk. philosopher.

Anaximander, 610–546? B.C., Gk. philosopher & astronomer.

Andersen, Hans Christian, 1805–75, Dan. writer of fairy tales.

Anderson, Carl David, 1905–91, U.S. physicist.

—**Jack,** 1922–, U.S. journalist.

—**Dame Judith,** 1898–, Austral.-born U.S. actress.

—**Marian,** 1902–, U.S. contralto.

—**Maxwell,** 1888–1959, U.S. playwright.

—**Sherwood,** 1876–1941, U.S. author.

Andersson, Bibi, 1935–, Swed. actress.

André, John, 1751–80, Brit. major & spy in American Revolutionary War.

Andretti, Mario Gabriel, 1940–, Ital.-born U.S. auto racer.

Andrews A family of U.S. singers incl. three sisters: **La Verne,** 1916–67; **Maxine,** 1918–, & **Patty,** 1920–.

—**Julie,** 1935–, Eng. actress & singer.

—**Roy Chapman,** 1884–1960, U.S. naturalist.

Andreyev, Leonid Nikolayevich, 1871–1919, Russ. author.

Andropov, Yuri Vladimirovich, 1914–84, general secretary U.S.S.R. communist party 1982–84.

Andros, Sir Edmund, 1637–1714, Brit. governor in North America.

Angela Merici, Saint, 1474?–1540, Ital. nun & founder of Ursuline order.

Angeles, Victoria de los, b. Victoria Gamez Cima, 1924–, Sp. soprano active in U.S.

Angelico, Fra, b. Giovanni da Fiesole, 1387–1455, Ital. painter.

Anglin, Margaret Mary, 1876–1958, Canadian actress active in U.S.

Ångstrom, Anders Jonas, 1814–74, Swed. physicist.

Anne, 1665–1714, queen of Great Britain 1702–14.

Anne of Cleves, 1515–57, Ger. princess; 4th wife of King Henry VIII of England.

Ann-Margret, b. Ann-Margret Olsson, 1941–, Swed.-born U.S. singer, actress.

Anouilh, Jean, 1910–87, Fr. playwright.

Anselm, Saint, 1033–1109, archbishop of Canterbury.

Ansermet, Ernest, 1883–1969, Swiss conductor.

Antheil, George, 1900–59, U.S. composer.

Anthony, Saint, ca. 250–350, Egyptian monk.

—**of Padua, Saint,** 1195–1231, Pg.-born Ital. Franciscan monk.

Anthony, Susan B(rownell), 1820–1906, U.S. women's suffragist.

Antisthenes, 444?–371? B.C., Gk. philosopher; founder of Cynic school.

Antonescu, Ion, 1882–1946, Rumanian general & dictator; premier of Romania 1940–44.

Antoninus Pius, A.D. 86–161, Roman emperor 131–61.

Antonio (Ruiz), 1922–, Sp. dancer.

Antonioni, Michelangelo, 1912–, Ital. film director.

Antony, Marc (L. Marcus Antonius), 83–30 B.C., Roman general & politician.

Apgar, Virginia, 1909–74, U.S. physician.

Apollinaire, Guillaume, pseud. of Wilhelm Apollinaris de Kostrowitzky, 1880–1918, Ital.-born Fr. author.

Appia, Adolphe, 1862–1928, Swiss theatrical producer & pioneer in stage lighting.

Appleton, Sir Edward Victor, 1892–1965, Brit. physicist; Nobel Prize winner.

Apuleius, Lucius, 2nd c. A.D. Roman satirist.

Aquinas, Saint Thomas, 1225?–74, Ital. theologian & philosopher.

Arafat, Yasir, 1929–, Palestinian leader.

Arcaro, George Edward (Eddie), 1916–, U.S. jockey.

Archimedes, 287?–212 B.C., Gk. mathematician & inventor.

Archipenko, Alexander, 1887–1964, Russ.-born U.S. sculptor.

Arden, Elizabeth, 1884–1966, Can.-born U.S. businesswoman.

—Eve, 1912–90, U.S. actress.

Ardito Barletta Vallarina, Nicolás, 1938–, Panamanian statesman; president 1984–.

Ardrey, Robert, 1908–80, U.S. anthropologist & author.

Arendt, Hannah, 1906–75, Ger.-born U.S. political scientist & author.

Aretino, Pietro, 1492–1556, Ital. satirist.

Argentina, La, b. Antonia Mercé, 1888–1936, Argentine-born Spanish dancer.

Ariosto, Lodovico, 1474–1533, Ital. poet.

Aristarchus, 220?–150 B.C., Gk. grammarian.

—of Samos, 3rd c. B.C., Gk. astronomer.

Aristides, 530?–468 B.C., Athenian statesman & general: called **the Just.**

Aristippus, 435?–356? B.C., Gk. philosopher.

Aristophanes, 450?–380? B.C., Gk. playwright.

Aristotle, 384–322 B.C., Gk. philosopher.

Arius, 256?–336, Egyptian priest & theologian.

Arkin, Alan, 1934–, U.S. actor & director.

Arkwright, Sir Richard, 1732–92, Eng. inventor & industrialist.

Arlen, Harold, b. Hyman Arluck, 1905–86, U.S. composer.

Arletty, b. Léonie Bathiat, 1898–, Fr. actress.

Arliss, George, 1868–1946, Eng. actor active in U.S.

Armour, Philip Danforth, 1832–1901, U.S. industrialist.

Armstrong, Louis, 1900–71, U.S. jazz musician: called **Satchmo.**

—Neil Alden, 1930–, U.S. astronaut; first on the moon.

Arnaz, Desi, 1917–86, Cuban-born U.S. actor & producer.

Arno, Peter, 1904–68, U.S. cartoonist.

Arnold, Benedict, 1741–1801, Amer. revolutionary general & traitor.

—Matthew, 1822–88, Eng. poet & critic.

Aronson, Boris, 1900–80, Russ.-born stage designer & artist active in U.S.

Arp, Jean (or **Hans**), 1887–1966, Fr. sculptor & painter.

Arpad, ?–907, Hung. national hero.

Arrabal, Fernando, 1932–, Sp. playwright & author.

Arrau, Claudio, 1903–, Chilean pianist.

Arrhenius, Svante August, 1859–1927, Swed. physicist & chemist.

Arrow, Kenneth Joseph, 1921–, U.S. economist; Nobel Prize winner.

Arroyo, Martina, 1937–, U.S. soprano.

Artaud, Antonin, 1896–1948, Fr. playwright & director.

Arthur, legendary 6th c. Brit. king.

Arthur, Chester Alan, 1829–86, 21st U.S. president 1881–85.

—Jean, 1905–, U.S. actress.

Asch, Sholem, 1880–1957, Pol.-born U.S. Yiddish author.

Ashcroft, Dame Peggy, 1907–, Eng. actress.

Ashe, Arthur Robert, Jr., 1943–, U.S. tennis player.

Ashkenazy, Vladimir, 1937–, Soviet pianist active in U.S.

Ashton, Sir Frederick, 1904–88, Eng. choreographer.

Ashton-Warner, Sylvia, 1908–84, New Zealand author.

Ashurbanipal, 7th c. B.C. Assyrian king.

Asimov, Isaac, 1920–, Soviet-born U.S. biochemist & author.

Asoka, ?–232 B.C., king of Magadha, India.

Aspasia, 470?–410 B.C., Gk. hetaera; consort of Pericles.

Asquith, Herbert Henry, 1852–1928, Brit. statesman; prime minister 1908–16.

Assad, Hafiz al, 1928–, president of Syria 1971–.

Astaire, Fred, 1899–1987, U.S. dancer, singer, & actor.

Aston, Francis William, 1877–1945, Eng. chemist & physicist.

Astor, John Jacob, 1763–1848, Ger.-born U.S. financier.

Astor, Lady, b. Nancy Langhorne, 1879–1964, U.S.-born Brit. politician; first woman member of House of Commons.

—Mary, 1906–87, U.S. actress & author.

Asturias, Miguel Angel, 1899–1974, Guat. author & diplomat; Nobel Prize winner.

Atahualpa, 1500?–33, last Inca king of Peru.

Atatürk, Kemal, 1881–1938, Turk. statesman; founded modern Turkey; president 1923–38.

Athanasius, Saint, 296?–373, Alexandrian bishop & theologian.

Atkinson, (Justin) Brooks, 1894–1984, U.S. drama critic & author.

Atlas, Charles, 1894–1972, Ital.-born U.S. physical culturist.

Attenborough, Richard, 1923–, Eng. actor & director.

Attila, 406?–453, king of the Huns.

Attlee, Clement Richard, Earl, 1883–1967, Eng. statesman; prime minister 1945–51.

Attucks, Crispus, 1723–70, black patriot in the Amer. Revolution.

Atwood, Margaret, 1939–, Can. poet, novelist, & critic.

Auchincloss, Louis, 1917–, U.S. author.

Auden, W(ystan) H(ugh), 1907–73, Eng.-born U.S. poet.

Audubon, John James, 1785–1851, Haitian-born U.S. ornithologist & painter.

Auenbrugger, Leopold, 1722–1809, Austrian physician.

Auer, Leopold, 1845–1930, Hung. violinist & teacher.

Augustine, Saint, 354–430, early Christian church father; bishop of Hippo.

—Saint, ?–604, Roman monk sent to convert England to Christianity; first archbishop of Canterbury.

Augustus, b. Gaius Julius Caesar Octavianus, 63 B.C.–A.D. 14; first Roman emperor 27 B.C.–A.D. 14: also called **Octavian.**

Aug San Suu Kyi, 1945–, Burmese political leader, Nobel Prize winner.

Aurelian (L. Lucius Domitius Aurelianus), 212?–275, Roman emperor 270–75.

Auriol, Vincent, 1884–1966, Fr. statesman; president of France 1947–54.

Austen, Jane, 1775–1817, Eng. novelist.

Austin, Stephen Fuller, 1793–1836, U.S. politician & colonizer of Texas.

Autry, (Orvon) Gene, 1907–, U.S. actor, singer, & businessman.

Avedon, Richard, 1923–, U.S. photographer.

Averroes (Ar. ibn-Rushd), 1126–98, Sp.-Arab philosopher & physician.

Avicenna (Ar. ibn-Sina), 980–1037, Pers. philosopher & physician.

Ávila, Camacho, Manuel, 1897–1955, Mex. soldier, diplomat, & political leader; president 1940–46.

Avogadro, Amadeo, 1776–1856, Ital. chemist & physicist.

Axis Sally, b. Mildred Gillars, 1901–88, U.S.-born Ger. propagandist in World War II.

Ayub Khan, Mohammad, 1907–74, Pakistani politician; president of Pakistan 1958–69.

Baal Shem Tov, b. Israel Ben Eliezer, 1700?–60, Jewish religious leader in Poland; founder of Chassidism.

Babbage, Charles, 1792–1871, Eng. mathematician & inventor.

Babbitt, Irving, 1865–1933, U.S. scholar & critic.

—Milton, 1916–, U.S. composer.

Babel, Isaak Emmanuilovich, 1894–1941, Russ. author.

Baber, b. Zahir-ud-din Mohammed, 1480–1530, founder of the Mogul empire of India.

Babeuf, Francois, 1760–97, Fr. revolutionist.

Babson, Roger Ward, 1875–1967, U.S. statistician.

Bacall, Lauren, 1924–, U.S. actress.

Bach A family of Ger. composers & musicians incl **Johann Sebastian,** 1685–1750, & his sons: **Carl Philipp Emmanuel,** 1714–88; **Johann Christian,** 1735–82; & **Wilhelm Friedemann,** 1710–84.

Bacharach, Burt, 1929–, U.S. composer.

Bachauer, Gina, 1913–76, Gk. pianist.

Bache, Harold L., 1894–1968, U.S. business executive.

Backaus, Wilhelm, 1884–1969, Ger. pianist.

Bacon, Francis, 1561–1626, Eng. philosopher, essayist, & statesman.

—Francis, 1909–, Irish-born Brit. painter.

—Roger, 1214?–92?, Eng. scientist & philosopher.

Baddeley, Hermione, 1906–, Brit. actress.

Baden-Powell, Robert Stephenson Smyth, 1857–1941, Brit. general; founder of Boy Scouts.

Badoglio, Pietro, 1871–1956, Ital. general; premier of Italy 1943–44.

Baedeker, Karl, 1801–59, Ger. author & publisher.

Baekeland, Leo, 1863–1944, Belg.-born U.S. chemist & industrialist.

Baer, Karl Ernst von, 1792–1876, Russ. embryologist active in Germany.

Baeyer, Adolf von, 1835–1917, Ger. chemist, Nobel Prize winner.

Baez, Joan, 1941–, U.S. folk singer.

Baffin, William, 1584?–1622, Eng. navigator & explorer.

Bagnold, Enid, 1890–1981, U.S. author.

Bahaullah, Mirza Husayn Ali, 1817–92, Pers. religious leader.

Bailey, F. Lee, 1933–, U.S. lawyer.

—**Mildred** 1903–51, U.S. singer.

—**Pearl Mae,** 1918–90, U.S. singer.

Baird, John Logie, 1888–1946, Scot. inventor.

—**William Britton (Bil),** 1904–, U.S. puppeteer.

Bairnsfather, Bruce, 1888–1959, Eng. cartoonist.

Baker, George (Father Divine), 1877?–1965, U.S. religious leader.

—**George,** 1915–75, U.S. cartoonist.

—**Josephine,** 1906–75, U.S. entertainer.

—**Russell,** 1925–, U.S. journalist & author.

Bakr, Ahmed Hassan al-, 1914–82, Iraqi military officer; president & prime minister of Iraq 1968–79.

Bakst, Leon Nikolaevich, 1866?–1924, Russ. painter & set designer.

Bakunin, Mikhail, 1814–76, Russ. anarchist leader.

Balaguer, Joaquin, 1902–, president of Dominican Republic 1966–78, 1986–.

Balanchine, George, 1904–83, Russ.-born U.S. choreographer.

Balboa, Vasco Núñez de, 1475?–1519, Sp. explorer; discovered the Pacific Ocean.

Baldwin, James, 1924–87, U.S. author.

—**Matthias William,** 1795–1866, U.S. inventor.

—**Stanley,** 1867–1947, Eng. statesman; prime minister 1923–24, 1924–29, 1935–37.

Balenciaga, Cristobal, 1896?–1972, Sp. fashion designer active in France.

Balfour, Arthur James, Earl of, 1848–1930, Eng. statesman & philosopher; prime minister 1902–05.

Ball, Ernest, 1878–1927, U.S. composer.

—**Lucille,** 1911–89, U.S. actress & comedienne.

Ballard, Kaye, 1926–, U.S. actress.

Balmain, Pierre, 1914–82, Fr. fashion designer.

Balzac, Honoré de, 1799–1850, Fr. novelist.

Bancroft Anne, 1931–, U.S. actress.

—**George,** 1800–91, U.S. historian.

Bandaranaike, Sirimavo, 1916–, prime minister of Sri Lanka 1960–65, 1970–77.

Bankhead, Tallulah Brockman, 1903–68, U.S. actress.

Banneker, Benjamin, 1731–1806, U.S. astronomer, mathematician, & inventor.

Bannister, Sir Roger, 1929–, Eng. track runner & physician.

Banting, Sir Frederick Grant, 1891–1941, Can. physiologist.

Banton, Travis, 1874–1958, U.S. costume designer.

Banzer Suarez, Hugo, 1926–, Bolivian military officer; president of Bolivia 1971–78.

Bara, Theda, 1890–1955, U.S. actress.

Baraka, Amiri, b. (Everett) LeRoi Jones, 1934–, U.S. poet, playwright, & social activist.

Barber, Samuel, 1910–81, U.S. composer.

—**Walter Lanier (Red),** 1908–, U.S. sports announcer.

Barbirolli, Sir John, 1899–1970, Eng. conductor.

Bardeen, John, 1908–91, U.S. physicist.

Bardot, Brigitte, 1934–, Fr. actress.

Barenboim, Daniel, 1942–, Argentine-born Israeli pianist & conductor.

Barkley, Alben William, 1877–1956, U.S. lawyer & politician; U.S. vice president 1949–53.

Bar Kokba, Simon, ?–A.D. 135, Jewish leader & self-proclaimed Messiah.

Barlach, Ernst Heinrich, 1870–1938, Ger. sculptor & author.

Barnard, Christian Neethling, 1922–, South African surgeon.

—**Edward Emerson,** 1857–1923, U.S. astronomer.

—**Frederick Augustus Porter,** 1809–89, U.S. educator.

Barnes, Djuna, 1892–1982, U.S. author & artist.

Barnet, Charlie, 1913–91, U.S. band leader.

Barnhart, Clarence L., 1900–, U.S. lexicographer.

Barnum, P(hineas) T(aylor), 1810–91, U.S. showman & circus proprietor.

Baroja, Pio, 1872–1956, Sp. novelist.

Barrault, Jean-Louis, 1910–, Fr. actor & stage director.

Barrie, Sir James Matthew, 1860–1937, Scot. author & playwright.

Barron, Clarence Walker, 1855–1928, U.S. financial editor & publisher.

Barrow, Clyde, 1909–34, U.S. criminal.

Barry, Gene, 1922–, U.S. actor.

—**Philip,** 1896–1949, U.S. playwright.

Barrymore A family of U.S. actors incl. **Ethel,** 1879–1959; **John,** 1882–1942; **Lionel,** 1878–1954; & **Maurice (Herbert Blythe),** 1847–1905, father of Ethel, John, & Lionel.

Barth, John Simmons, 1930–, U.S. author.

—**Karl,** 1886–1968, Swiss theologian.

Barthelme, Donald, 1931–89, U.S. author.

Barthes, Roland, 1915–80, Fr. author & critic.

Bartholdi, Frédéric Auguste, 1834–1904, Fr. sculptor.

Bartlett, John, 1820–1905, U.S. editor & publisher.

Bartók, Béla, 1881–1945, Hung. composer.

Bartolommeo, Fra, b. Baccio della Porta, 1472–1517, Ital. painter.

Bartolozzi, Francesco, 1727?–1815, Ital. engraver.

Barton, Bruce, 1886–1967, U.S. advertising executive & author.

—**Clara,** 1821–1912, U.S. civic worker; founder of the American Red Cross.

Baruch, Bernard Mannes, 1870–1965, U.S. financier & political adviser.

Barye, Antoine Louis, 1795–1875, Fr. sculptor, painter, & water colorist.

Baryshnikov, Mikhail, 1947–, Soviet-born ballet dancer & artistic director active in U.S.

Barzini, Luigi, 1908–84, Ital. author & statesman.

Barzun, Jacques, 1907–, Fr.-born U.S. educator & author.

Basehart, Richard, 1914–84, U.S. actor.

Basho, 1648–94, Jap. poet.

Basie, William (Count), 1904–84, U.S. jazz musician.

Basil, Saint (L. Basilius), 330?–379, bishop of Caesarea.

Baskerville, John, 1706–75, Eng. typographer.

Baskin, Leonard, 1922–, U.S. painter & illustrator.

Bass, Sam, 1851–78, U.S. outlaw.

Bassey, Shirley, 1937–, Welsh-born U.S. singer.

Bates, Alan, 1934–, Eng. actor.

Bateson, William, 1861–1926, Eng. biologist.

Batista y Zaldivar, Fulgencio, 1901–73, Cuban soldier & political leader; president 1940–44, 1952–59.

Batu Khan, ?–1255, Mongol leader.

Baudelaire, Charles Pierre, 1821–67, Fr. poet.

Baudouin, 1930–, king of Belgium 1951–.

Baugh, Samuel Adrian (Sammy), 1914–, U.S. football player.

Baum, L(yman) Frank, 1856–1919, U.S. author.

—**Vicki,** 1888–1960, Austrian-born U.S. author.

Baxter, Anne, 1923–86, U.S. actress.

Baylis, Dame Lilian, 1874–1937, Eng. theater manager.

Baylor, Elgin, 1934–, U.S. basketball player.

Beadle, George Wells, 1903–89, U.S. geneticist.

Bean, Roy, 1825?–1903, U.S. frontiersman.

Beard, Charles Austin, 1874–1948, & his wife **Mary Ritter,** 1876–1958, U.S. historians.

—**Daniel Carter,** 1850–1941, U.S. author; founder of the Boy Scouts of America.

—**James,** 1903–85, U.S. culinary expert & author.

Beardsley, Aubrey Vincent, 1872–98, Eng. artist & illustrator.

Beaton, Cecil, 1904–80, Eng. photographer & theatrical designer.

Beatrix, 1938–, queen of the Netherlands 1980–.

Beatty, Clyde, 1905–65, U.S. animal trainer & circus performer.

—**Warren,** 1937–, U.S. actor, director, & screenwriter.

Beaumarchais, Pierre Augustin Caron de, 1732–99, Fr. playwright.

Beaumont, Francis, 1584–1616, Eng. playwright.

—**William,** 1785–1853, U.S. surgeon.

Beauregard, Pierre Gustave Toutant de, 1818–93, U.S. Confederate general.

Beauvoir, Simone de, 1908–86, Fr. author.

Beaverbrook, Lord, b. William Maxwell Aitken, 1879–1964, Can.-born Brit. publisher & politician.

Bechet, Sidney, 1897–1959, U.S. jazz musician.

Beck, C. C., 1910–, U.S. cartoonist.

Becket, Saint Thomas à, 1118–70, Eng. Catholic martyr; archbishop of Canterbury 1162–70.

Beckett, Samuel Barclay, 1906–89, Irish-born novelist & playwright.

Beckmann, Max, 1884–1950, Ger. painter.

Becquerel A family of Fr. physicists incl. **Alexandre Edmond,** 1820–91; **Antoine César,** 1788–1878, father of prec.; & **Antoine Henri,** 1852–1908, son of Alexandre.

Bede, Saint, 673–735, Eng. scholar, historian, & theologian; called **the Venerable Bede.**

Beebe, Charles William, 1877–1962, U.S. naturalist.

—**Lucius Morris,** 1902–66, U.S. journalist & author.

Beecham, Sir Thomas, 1879–1961, Eng. conductor.

Beecher, Henry Ward, 1813–87, U.S. clergyman & writer; brother of Harriet Beecher Stowe.

—**Lyman,** 1775–1863, U.S. clergyman; father of prec.

Beene, Geoffrey, 1927–, U.S. fashion designer.

Beerbohm, Sir Max, 1872–1956, Eng. author & caricaturist.

Beery, Noah, Jr., 1916–, U.S. actor.

—**Wallace,** 1886–1949, U.S. actor; father of prec.

Beethoven, Ludwig van, 1770–1827, Ger. composer.

Begin, Menahem, 1913–, Pol.-born Israeli statesman; prime minister of Israel, 1977–83; Nobel Prize winner.

Behan, Brendan Francis, 1923–64, Irish playwright.

Behn, Aphra, 1640–89, Brit. playwright, author, & poet.

Behrens, Peter, 1868–1940, Ger. architect.

Behring, Emil von, 1854–1917, Ger. bacteriologist.

Behrman, S(amuel) N(athaniel), 1893–1973, U.S. playwright.

Beiderbecke, Leon Bismarck (Bix), 1903–31, U.S. jazz musician.

Béjart, Maurice, 1928–, Fr. dancer, choreographer, & ballet-company director.

Belafonte, Harry, 1927–, U.S. singer.

Belasco, David, 1859–1931, U.S. theatrical producer & playwright.

Belinsky, Vissarion Grigorievich, 1811–48, Russ. critic & journalist.

Bell, Alexander Graham, 1847–1922, Scot.-born U.S. physicist; inventor of the telephone.

Bellamy, Edward, 1850–98, U.S. author.

—**Ralph,** 1904–, U.S. actor.

Bellarmine, Saint Robert Francis Romulus, 1542–1621, Ital. Jesuit theologian.

Belli, Melvin, 1907–, U.S. lawyer.

Bellinghausen, Fabian von, 1778–1852, Russ. admiral & explorer.

Bellini A family of Venetian painters incl. **Jacopo,** 1400?–70?, & his sons **Gentile,** 1429?–1507, & **Giovanni,** 1430?–1516.

—**Vincenzo,** 1801–35, Ital. operatic composer.

Belloc, Hilaire, 1870–1953, Eng. poet & author.

Bellow, Saul, 1915–, Can.-born U.S. novelist.

Bellows, George Wesley, 1882–1925, U.S. painter & lithographer.

Belmondo, Jean-Paul, 1933–, Fr. actor.

Belmont, August, 1816–90, Ger.-born U.S. financier.

Belmonte, Juan, 1892–1962, Sp. bullfighter.

Bemelmans, Ludwig, 1898–1962, Austrian-born U.S. author & illustrator.

Benavente, Jacinto, 1866–1954, Sp. playwright; Nobel Prize winner.

Ben Bella, Ahmed, 1918–, Algerian revolutionary leader; premier of Algeria 1962–65.

Benchley, Robert Charles, 1889–1945, U.S. humorist & author.

Bendix, Vincent, 1882–1945, U.S. inventor & manufacturer.

Benedict, Saint, 480–547, Ital. monk; founder of the Benedictine order.

Benedict, Ruth Fulton 1887–1948, U.S. anthropologist.

Benes, Eduard, 1884–1948, Czech statesman; president of Czechoslovakia 1935–38 & 1946–48.

Benét, Stephen Vincent, 1898–1943, U.S. poet & author.

—**William Rose,** 1886–1950, U.S. author & editor; brother of prec.

Ben-Gurion, David, 1886–1973, Russ.-born Israeli statesman; prime minister of Israel 1948–53 & 1955–63.

Benjamin, Judah Philip, 1811–84, U.S. lawyer & Confederate cabinet member.

Bennett, (Enoch) Arnold, 1867–1931, Eng. author.

—**Floyd,** 1890–1928, U.S. aviator.

—**James Gordon,** 1795–1872, Scot.-born U.S. journalist.

—**Michael,** 1943–, U.S. stage director & choreographer.

—**Richard Bedford,** 1870–1947, Can. statesman; prime minister 1930–35.

—**Robert Russell,** 1894–1981, U.S. composer.

—**Tony,** 1926–, U.S. singer.

Benny, Jack, 1894–1974, U.S. comedian.

Bentham, Jeremy, 1748–1832, Eng. jurist & philosopher.

Bentley, Eric Russell, 1916–, Eng.-born author & critic active in U.S.

Benton, Thomas Hart, 1889–1975, U.S. painter.

—**William,** 1900–73, U.S. businessman, publisher, & government official.

Berdyaev, Nikolai Alexsandrovich, 1874–1948, Russ.-born religious philosopher resident in France.

Berenson, Bernard, 1865–1959, Lithuanian-born U.S. art critic & writer.

Berg, Alban, 1885–1935, Austrian composer.

—**Gertrude,** 1899–1966, U.S. actress.

Bergen, Edgar John, 1903–78, U.S. ventriloquist & actor.

Berger, Frank M(ilan), 1913–, Czech-born U.S. pharmacologist.

—**Hans,** 1873–1941, Ger. neurologist & psychiatrist.

Bergerac, Cyrano de, 1619–55, Fr. poet & soldier.

Bergman, Ingmar, 1918–, Swed. film director.

—**Ingrid,** 1915–82, Swed.-born actress active in U.S.

Bergner, Elisabeth, 1900–, Austrian actress.

Bergson, Henri Louis, 1859–1941, Fr. philosopher.

Beria, Lavrenti Pavlovich, 1899–1953, Soviet politician.

Bering, Vitus, 1680–1741, Dan. navigator.

Berio, Luciano, 1925–, Ital.-born composer active in U.S.

Berkeley, Busby, 1895–1976, U.S. film director & choreographer.

—**George,** 1685–1753, Irish-born Eng. prelate & philosopher.

Berle, Adolf Augustus, 1895–1971, U.S. diplomat & author.

—**Milton,** 1908–, U.S. comedian.

Berlin, Irving, 1888–1989, U.S. composer.

—**Sir Isaiah,** 1909–, Latvian-born Brit. historian.

Berlioz, Hector, 1803–69, Fr. composer.

Berman, Lazar, 1930–, Soviet-born pianist active in U.S.

Bernadette, Saint, b. Bernadette Soubirous, 1844–79, Fr. nun: called **Bernadette of Lourdes.**

Bernadotte, Folke, Count of Wisborg, 1895–1948, Swed. diplomat & mediator in Palestine; assassinated.

—**Jean Baptiste Jules,** 1763?–1844, Fr. general; king of Sweden & Norway as Charles XIV 1818–44.

Bernard, Claude, 1813–78, Fr. physiologist.

Bernard of Clairvaux, Saint, 1090–1153, Fr. Cistercian monk.

Bernbach, Willian, 1911–82, U.S. advertising executive.

Bernhardt, Sarah, 1844–1923, Fr. actress.

Bernini, Gian Lorenzo, 1598–1680, Ital. sculptor & architect.

Bernoulli A family of Swiss mathematicians & scientists incl. **Daniel,** 1700–82; **Jacques,** 1654–1705; & **Jean,** 1667–1748, father of Daniel & brother of Jacques.

Bernstein, Leonard, 1918–90, U.S. conductor, composer, & pianist.

Berra, Lawrence Peter (Yogi), 1925–, U.S. baseball player & manager.

Berrigan, Daniel, 1921–, U.S. priest, poet, & political activist.

—**Philip,** 1923–, U.S. priest & political activist; brother of prec.

Berry, Charles Edward (Chuck), 1926–, U.S. musician & singer.

Berryman, John, 1914–72, U.S. poet & critic.

Bert, Paul, 1833–86, Fr. physiologist.

Bertillon, Alphonse, 1853–1914, Fr. anthropologist & criminologist.

Bertolucci, Bernardo, 1940–, Ital. film director.

Berzelius, Baron Jöns Jakob, 1779–1848, Swed. chemist.

Besant, Annie Wood, 1847–1933, Eng. theosophist.

Bessel, Friedrich Wilhelm, 1784–1846, Ger. astronomer.

Bessemer, Sir Henry, 1813–98, Eng. engineer.

Betancourt, Romulo, 1908–81, president of Venezuela 1945–48 & 1959–64.

Bethe, Hans Albrecht, 1906–, Ger.-born U.S. physicist; Nobel Prize winner.

Bethune, Mary McLeod, 1875–1955, U.S. educator.

Betjeman, Sir John, 1906–84, Eng. poet; poet laureate 1972–84.

Bettelheim, Bruno, 1903–90, Austrian-born U.S. psychologist, educator, & author.

Betti, Ugo, 1892–1953, Ital. playwright.

Betz, Pauline, 1919–, U.S. tennis player.

Bevan, Aneurin, 1897–1960, Welsh labor leader & Brit. government official.

Bevin, Ernest, 1881–1951, Eng. labor leader & statesman.

Bhave, Acharya Vinoba, 1895–1982, Indian social reformer.

Bhutto, Zulfikar Ali, 1928–79, president of Pakistan 1971–77; executed.

Bialik, Chaim Nachman, 1873–1934, Russ.-born Israeli poet.

Biddle, John, 1615–62, Eng. theologian.

—**Nicholas,** 1786–1844, U.S. financier.

Bienville, Sieur de, b. Jean Baptiste le Moyne, 1680–1768, Fr. colonial governor of Louisiana.

Bierce, Ambrose Gwinnett, 1842–1914?, U.S. author.

Bierstadt, Albert, 1830–1902, Ger.-born U.S. painter.

Biggs, E(dward George) Power, 1906–77, Eng.-born U.S. organist.

Bikila, Abebe, 1932–73, Ethiopian track runner.

Binet, Alfred, 1857–1911, Fr. psychologist.

Bing, Sir Rudolph, 1902–, Austrian-born opera manager active in U.S. & Eng.

Bingham, George Caleb, 1811–79, U.S. painter.

Birdseye, Clarence, 1886–1956, U.S. inventor & industrialist.

Birendra Bir Bikram Shah Dev, 1945–, king of Nepal 1972–.

Bishop, Elizabeth, 1911–79, U.S. poet.

—**Joey,** 1918–, U.S. entertainer.

Bismarck, Prince Otto Eduard Leopold von, 1815–98, Ger. statesman; chancellor of German empire 1871–90.

Bizet, Georges, 1838–75, Fr. composer.

Björling, Jussi, 1911–60, Swed. tenor.

Bjørnson, Bjørnstjerne, 1832–1910, Norw. poet & author; Nobel Prize winner.

Black, Hugo La Fayette, 1886–1971, U.S. jurist; justice of the U.S. Supreme Court 1937–71.

—**Shirley Temple,** 1928–, U.S. actress & diplomat.

Blackett, Patrick Maynard Stuart, 1897–1974, Eng. physicist.

Black Hawk, 1767–1838, Sac Am. Ind. chief.

Blackmun, Harry Andrew, 1908–, U.S. jurist; justice of the U.S. Supreme Court 1970–.

Blackstone, Sir William, 1723–80, Eng. jurist.

Blackwell, Elizabeth, 1821–1910, Eng.-born U.S. physician.

Blaine, James Gillespie, 1830–93, U.S. statesman.

Blake, Eugene Carson, 1906–85, U.S. clergyman & social activist.

—**James Hubert (Eubie),** 1883–1983, U.S. pianist & songwriter.

—**William,** 1757–1827, Eng. poet & painter.

Blakelock, Ralph Albert, 1847–1919, U.S. landscape painter.

Blanc, Mel(vin Jerome), 1908–89, U.S. entertainer.

Blanda, George Frederick, 1927–, U.S. football player.

Blankers-Koen, Francina Eisje (Fanny), 1918–, Du. track & field athlete.

Blasco Ibáñez, Vicente, 1867–1928, Sp. author.

Blass, Bill, 1922–, U.S. fashion designer.

Blavatsky, Elena Petrovna, 1831–91, Russ. theosophist.

Blériot, Louis, 1872–1936, Fr. engineer & pioneer aviator.

Bleuler, Eugen, 1856–1939, Swiss psychiatrist.

Bligh, William, 1754–1817, Brit. naval officer.

Blitzstein, Marc, 1905–64, U.S. composer.

Bloch, Ernest, 1880–1959, Swiss-born composer active in U.S.

—**Konrad Emil,** 1912–, Ger.-born U.S. biochemist; Nobel Prize winner.

Block, Herbert Lawrence, 1909–, U.S. political cartoonist: called **Herblock.**

Bloomer, Amelia Jenks, 1818–94, U.S. social reformer.

Bloomfield, Leonard, 1887–1949, U.S. linguist & educator.

Blücher, Gebhard Leberecht von, 1742–1819, Prussian field marshal.

Bluford, Guion S., 1942–, U.S. astronaut.

Blum, Léon, 1872–1950, Fr. politician.

Blume, Judy, 1938–, U.S. author.

Boadicea, ?–A.D. 62, queen of a tribe of Britons; defeated by the Romans.

Boas, Franz, 1858–1942, Ger.-born U.S. anthropologist.

Boccaccio, Giovanni, 1313–75, Ital. writer.

Boccherini, Luigi, 1743–1805, Ital. composer.

Boccioni, Umberto, 1882–1916, Ital. sculptor & painter.

Bock, Jerry, 1928–, U.S. composer.

Bode, Johann Elert, 1747–1826, German astronomer.

Bodenheim, Maxwell, 1893–1954, U.S. poet.

Bodoni, Giambattista, 1740–1813, Ital. printer & type designer.

Böhm, Karl, 1894–1981, Ger. conductor.

Boehme, Jakob, 1575–1624, Ger. theosophist & mystic.

Boethius, Anicius Manlius Severinus, 480?–524, Roman philosopher.

Bogarde, Dirk, 1920–, Brit. actor & director.

Bogart, Humphrey, 1899–1957, U.S. actor.

Bogdanovich, Peter, 1939–, U.S. film director.

Bohlen, Charles Eustis, 1904–74, U.S. diplomat.

Bohr, Aage Niels, 1922–, Dan. physicist; Nobel Prize winner.

—**Niels,** 1885–1962, Dan. physicist; Nobel Prize winner; father of prec.

Boileau-Despréaux, Nicolas, 1636–1711, Fr. poet & critic.

Boito, Arrigo, 1842–1918, Ital. composer & librettist.

Bok, Edward William, 1863–1930, Du.-born U.S. editor.

Bokassa, Jean-Bedel, 1922–, African general; president of Central African Republic 1972–77; as **Bokassa I,** emperor of Central African Empire 1977–79.

Bolden, Charles (Buddy), 1868?–1931, U.S. jazz musician.

Boleyn, Anne, 1507?–36, second wife of Henry VIII of England; mother of Elizabeth I.

Bolger, Ray, 1904–1987, U.S. dancer & actor.

Bolívar, Simón, 1783–1830, South American revolutionary patriot & military leader.

Böll, Heinrich Theodor, 1917–85, Ger. author; Nobel Prize winner.

Boltzmann, Ludwig Edward, 1844–1906, Austrian physicist.

Bombeck, Erma, 1927–, U.S. humorist.

Bonaparte, Napoleon, 1769–1821, Fr. general & emperor of France as Napoleon I 1805–14.

—**(Louis) Napoleon,** 1808–73, emperor of France as Napoleon III 1852–71; nephew of prec. Also **Buonaparte.**

Bonaventure, Saint, 1221–74, Ital. philosopher.

Bond, Julian, 1940–, U.S. politician & civil rights leader.

Bonheur, Rosa, 1822–99, Fr. painter.

Bonhoeffer, Dietrich, 1906–45, Ger. theologian.

Boniface VIII, b. Benedetto Gaetani, 1235?–1303, pope 1294–1303.

—**Saint,** 680?–755, Eng. missionary in Germany.

Bonnard, Pierre, 1867–1947, Fr. painter.

Bonney, William, 1859–81, U.S. outlaw: called **Billy the Kid.**

Boole, George, 1815–64, Eng. mathematician & logician.

Boone, Daniel, 1734–1820, Amer. frontiersman.

—**Pat,** 1934–, U.S. singer & actor.

Boorstin, Daniel J., 1914–, U.S. historian & author.

Booth, Edwin Thomas, 1833–93, U.S. actor.

—**John Wilkes,** 1838–65, U.S. actor; assassinated Abraham Lincoln; brother of prec.

—**Shirley,** 1907–, U.S. actress.

—**William,** 1829–1912, Eng. religious leader; founder of the Salvation Army.

Borah, William Edgar, 1865–1940, U.S. statesman.

Bordaberry, Juan Maria, 1928–, president of Uruguay 1972–76.

Borden, Gail, 1801–74, U.S. inventor.

—**Lizzie,** 1860–1927, U.S. alleged murderer.

—**Sir Robert Laird,** 1854–1937, Can. statesman; prime minister 1911–20.

Borg, Bjorn, 1956–, Swed. tennis player.

Borge, Victor, 1909–, Dan. pianist & entertainer active in U.S.

Borges, Jorge Luis, 1899–1986, Argentinian poet & author.

Borgia, Cesare, 1476–1507, Ital. military & religious leader.

—**Lucrezia,** 1480–1519, duchess of Ferrara & art patron; sister of prec.

Borglum, Gutzon, 1867–1941, U.S. sculptor.

Bori, Lucrezia, 1887–1960, Sp. soprano active in U.S.

Borlaug, Norman Ernest, 1914–, U.S. agronomist; Nobel Prize winner.

Borman, Frank, 1928–, U.S. astronaut & businessman.

Bormann, Martin Ludwig, 1900–45, Ger. Nazi politican.

Born, Max, 1882–1970, Ger. physicist; Nobel Prize winner.

Borodin, Alexander Porfirevich, 1834–87, Russ. composer.

Borromini, Francesco, 1599–1667, Ital. architect.

Bosch, Carl, 1874–1940, Ger. chemist & industrialist; Nobel Prize winner.

—**Hieronymus,** 1450?–1516, Du. painter.

Bose, Sir Jagadis Chandra, 1858–1937, Indian physicist & plant physiologist.

Boswell, James, 1740–95, Scot. author & lawyer; biographer of Samuel Johnson.

Botha, Louis, 1862–1919, Boer general; first prime minister of Union of South Africa.

—**Pieter Willem,** 1916–, South African politician; prime minister 1978–89.

Botticelli, Sandro, b. Allesandro di Mariano dei Filipepi, 1444?–1510, Florentine painter.

Botvinnik, Mikhail, 1911–, Soviet chess master.

Boucher, François, 1703–70, Fr. painter.

Boucicault, Dion, 1820?–90, Irish playwright & actor.

Bougainville, Louis Antoine de, 1729–1811, Fr. navigator.

Boulanger, Nadia Juliette, 1887–1979, Fr. composer & music teacher.

Boulez, Pierre, 1925–, Swiss-born composer & conductor active in U.S.

Boult, Sir Adrian, 1889–1983, Eng. conductor.

Boumédiene, Houari, 1927–78, Algerian army officer; president & premier of Algeria 1965–78.

Bourguiba, Habib ben Ali, 1903–, Tunisian statesman; president of Tunisia 1957–87.

Bourke-White, Margaret, 1906–72, U.S. photographer.

Bournonville, August, 1805–79, Danish dancer & choreographer.

Bouts, Dierick, 1420?–75, Du. painter.

Bovet, Daniele, 1907–, Swiss-born Ital. pharmacologist.

Bow, Clara, 1905–65, U.S. actress.

Bowditch, Nathaniel, 1773–1838, U.S. mathematician & navigator.

Bowdler, Thomas, 1754–1825, Eng. physician & editor of Shakespeare's plays.

Bowell, Sir Mackenzie, 1823–1917, Eng-born Can. statesman; prime minister 1894–96.

Bowen, Elizabeth, 1899–1973, Irish-born Brit. author.

Bowes, Edward (Major), 1874–1946, U.S. radio personality.

Bowie, David, 1947–, Eng. actor & singer.

—**James,** 1796–1836, U.S. soldier & frontiersman.

Bowker, R(ichard) R(ogers), 1848–1933, U.S. editor & publisher.

Bowles, Chester, 1901–86, U.S. business executive & diplomat.

—**Jane Sydney Auer,** 1917–73, U.S. author.

—**Paul,** 1910–, U.S. author, composer, & musicologist; husband of prec.

Boyd, William (Bill), 1898–1972, U.S. actor.

Boyd Orr, Lord, 1880–1971, Brit. nutritionist & agricultural scientist; Nobel Prize winner.

Boyer, Charles, 1899–1978, Fr. actor.

Boyle, Kay, 1903–, U.S. author.

—**Robert,** 1627–91, Irish-born Brit. chemist & physicist.

Bradbury, Ray Douglas, 1920–, U.S. author.

Braddock, Edward, 1695–1755, Brit. general in N. America.

Bradford, William, 1590–1657, Eng.-born Pilgrim father & governor of Plymouth Colony.

Bradley, Milton, 1836–1911, U.S. manufacturer of games.

—**Omar Nelson,** 1893–1981, U.S. general.

—**Thomas,** 1917–, U.S. politician.

Bradstreet, Anne Dudley, 1612–72, Eng.-born Amer. poet.

Brady, Alice, 1892–1939, U.S. actress.

—**James Buchanan (Diamond Jim),** 1856–1917, U.S. financier & philanthropist.

—**Mathew,** 1823?–96, U.S. photographer.

Bragg, Sir William Henry, 1862–1942, Eng. physicist.

—**Sir (William) Lawrence,** 1890–1971, Austral.-born Eng. physicist; son of prec.

Brahe, Tycho, 1546–1601, Dan. astronomer.

Brahms, Johannes, 1833–97, Ger. composer.

Braille, Louis, 1809–52, Fr. educator.

Brailowsky, Alexander, 1896–1976, Russ.-born pianist active in U.S.

Bramante, b. Donato d'Angelo, 1444–1514, Ital. architect.

Brancusi, Constantin, 1876–1957, Rumanian sculptor.

Brand, Max, pseud. of Frederick Schiller Faust, 1892–1944, U.S. author.

Brandeis, Louis Dembitz, 1856–1941, U.S. jurist; justice of the U.S. Supreme Court 1916–39.

Brando, Marlon, 1924–, U.S. actor.

Brandt, Willy, 1913–, Ger. statesman; chancellor of W. Germany 1969–74.

Braque, Georges, 1882–1963, Fr. painter.

Brattain, Walter Houser, 1902–87, Chin.-born U.S. physicist; Nobel Prize winner.

Braudel, Fernand, 1902–85, Fr. historian & author.

Brautigan, Richard, 1935–84, U.S. author & poet.

Bream, Julian, 1933–, Eng. guitarist & lutenist.

Breasted, James Henry, 1865–1935, U.S. archaeologist.

Brecht, Bertolt, 1898–1956, Ger. playwright & poet.

Breckinridge, John Cabell, 1821–75, U.S. statesman & Confederate general; U.S. vice president 1857–61.

Brel, Jacques, 1929–78, Belg. singer & composer.

Brennan, Walter, 1894–1974, U.S. actor.

—**William Joseph, Jr.,** 1906–, U.S. jurist; justice of the U.S. Supreme Court 1956–90.

Breslin, James (Jimmy), 1930–, U.S. journalist & author.

Bresson, Robert, 1907–, Fr. film director.

Breton, André, 1896–1966, Fr. poet & author.

Breuer, Josef, 1842–1925, Austrian physician.

—**Marcel,** 1902–81, Hung.-born architect active in U.S.

Brewster, William, 1567–1644, Eng.-born Pilgrim father.

Brezhnev, Leonid Ilyich, 1906–82, Soviet statesman; general secretary of the Communist Party of the Soviet Union 1966–82.

Brian Boru, 926–1014, king of Ireland 1002–14.

Briand, Aristide, 1862–1932, Fr. statesman & diplomat.

Brice, Fannie, 1891–1951, U.S. singer & comedienne.

Bricktop, b. Ada Beatrice Queen Victoria Louise Virginia Smith, 1894–1984, U.S. singer & entertainer.

Bridger, James, 1804–81, U.S. frontiersman & scout.

Bridges, Harry, 1901–90, Austral.-born U.S. labor leader.

—**Robert,** 1844–1930, Eng. poet.

Bridgman, Percy Williams, 1882–1961, U.S. physicist; Nobel Prize winner.

Bright, Richard, 1789–1858, Eng. physician.

Brill, A(braham) A(rden), 1874–1948, Austrian-born U.S. psychiatrist.

Brillat-Savarin, Anthelme, 1755–1828, Fr. writer on food & cooking.

Brinkley, David, 1920–, U.S. journalist & television news commentator.

Britten, (Edward) Benjamin, 1913–76, Eng. composer.

Broca, Pierre Paul, 1824–80, Fr. surgeon & anthropologist.

Brogan, Sir D(ennis) W(illiam), 1900–74, Eng. historian.

Brokaw, Tom (Thomas John), 1940–, U.S. journalist.

Bromfield, Louis, 1896–1956, U.S. author.

Bronk, Detlev W(ulf), 1897–1975, U.S. physiologist & educator.

Brontë An Eng. family incl. three sisters who were authors: **Anne,** 1820–49; **Charlotte,** 1816–55; **Emily (Jane),** 1818–48.

Bronzino, Il, b. Agnolo di Cosimo Allori, 1503?–74, Ital. painter.

Brook, Clive, 1887–1974, Eng. actor.

—**Peter,** 1925–, Eng. stage director & producer.

Brooke, Alan Francis, 1st Viscount Alanbrooke, 1883–1963, Brit. field marshal.

—**Edward William,** 1919–, U.S. senator.

—**Rupert,** 1887–1915, Eng. poet.

Brookings, Robert Somers, 1850–1932, U.S. businessman & philanthropist.

Brooks, Louise, 1905–85, U.S. actress.

—**Gwendolyn,** 1917–, U.S. poet.

—**Mel,** 1926–, U.S. author, actor, & film director.

—**Phillips,** 1835–93, U.S. bishop.

—**Van Wyck,** 1886–1963, U.S. critic & author.

Brosio, Manlio, 1897–1980, Ital. lawyer & diplomat.

Broun, (Matthew) Heywood (Campbell), 1888–1939, U.S. journalist & critic.

Browder, Earl Russell, 1891–1973, U.S. Communist Party leader.

Brown, Helen Gurley, 1922–, U.S. author & editor.

—**James,** 1933–, U.S. singer.

—**Jim,** 1936–, U.S. football player & actor.

—**Joe E.,** 1892–1973, U.S. comedian & actor.

—**John,** 1800–59, U.S. abolitionist.

—**Nacio Herb,** 1896–1964, U.S. songwriter.

—**Norman O(liver),** 1913–, Mexican-born U.S. author & educator.

Browne, Dik, 1917–, U.S. cartoonist.

—**Sir Thomas,** 1606–82, Eng. physician & author.

Browning, Elizabeth Barrett, 1806–61, Eng. poet.

—**Robert,** 1812–89, Eng. poet; husband of prec.

Brown-Sequard, Charles E., 1817–94, Fr.-born Brit. physician & physiologist.

Brubeck, David Warren (Dave), 1920–, U.S. jazz musician & composer.

Bruce, Lenny, 1926–66, U.S. comedian.

Bruch, Max, 1838–1920, Ger. composer.

Bruckner, Anton, 1824–96, Austrian composer.

Brueghel A family of Flemish painters incl. **Peter,** 1525?–69 (known as **the Elder**), & his sons, **Peter,** 1564?–1638? (**the Younger**), and **Jan,** 1568–1625.

Bruhn, Erik, 1928–, Dan. ballet dancer & choreographer.

Brumel, Valery, 1942–, Soviet track athlete.

Brummell, George Bryan (Beau), 1778–1840, Eng. man of fashion.

Brunelleschi, Filippo, 1377–1446, Florentine architect & sculptor.

Brunner, Emil, 1889–1966, Swiss theologian.

Bruno, Giordano, 1548?–1600, Ital. philosopher; burned as a heretic.

Brutus, Marcus Junius, 85–42 B.C., Roman republican leader; conspirator against Caesar.

Bryan, William Jennings, 1860–1925, U.S. statesman & orator.

Bryant, Sir Arthur Wynne Morgan, 1899–1985, Brit. historian.

—**William Cullen,** 1794–1878, U.S. poet.

Bryce, James, Viscount, 1838–1922, Eng. statesman & author.

Brynner, Yul, 1920–85, Russ.-born U.S. actor.

Brzezinski, Zbigniew, 1928–, Pol.-born U.S. educator and government official.

Buber, Martin, 1878–1965, Austrian-born Israeli Jewish philosopher & theologian.

Buchan, John, 1st Baron Tweedsmuir, 1875–1940, Scot. author & statesman; governor-general of Canada 1935–40.

Buchanan, Jack, 1891–1957, Scot.-born actor active in England & U.S.

—**James,** 1791–1868, 15th U.S. president 1857–61.

Buchman, Frank Nathan Daniel, 1878–1961, U.S. evangelist.

Buchner, Eduard, 1860–1917, Ger. organic chemist.

Buchwald, Art, 1925–, U.S. journalist & author.

Buck, Frank, 1884–1950, U.S. hunter & animal collector.

—**Pearl Sydenstricker,** 1892–1973, U.S. author.

Buckley, William Frank, Jr., 1925–, U.S. author & political commentator.

Buddha, Siddhartha Gautama, 563?–483? B.C., Indian religious teacher & philosopher; founder of Buddhism.

Budge, Donald, 1915–, U.S. tennis player.

Buffon, Comte Georges Louis Leclerc, 1707–88, Fr. naturalist.

Bujones, Fernando, 1942–, U.S. ballet dancer.

Bulfinch, Charles, 1763–1844, U.S. architect.

Bulgakov, Mikhail, 1891–1940, Russ. author & playwright.

Bulganin, Nikolai Aleksandrovich, 1895–1975, premier of the U.S.S.R. 1955–58.

Bull, Ole Bornemann, 1810–80, Norw. violinist.

Bülow, Hans von, 1830–94, Ger. conductor & pianist.

Bultmann, Rudolf Karl, 1884–1976, Ger. theologian.

Bulwer-Lytton, Edward George, 1803–73, Eng. playwright & author.

Bumbry, Grace, 1937–, U.S. mezzo-soprano.

Bunche, Ralph Johnson, 1904–71, U.S. educator & U.N. official; Nobel Prize winner.

Bundy, McGeorge, 1919–, U.S. government official & foundation executive.

Bunin, Ivan Alekseyevich, 1870–1953, Russ. poet & author; Nobel Prize winner.

Bunker, Ellsworth, 1894–1984, U.S. diplomat.

Bunsen, Robert Wilhelm, 1811–99, Ger. chemist.

Buñuel, Luis, 1900–1983, Sp. film director.

Bunyan, John, 1628–88, Eng. preacher & author.

Burbage, Richard, 1567?–1619, Eng. actor.

Burbank, Luther, 1849–1926, U.S. horticulturist.

Burchfield, Charles Ephraim, 1893–1967, U.S. painter.

—**Robert William,** 1923–, New Zealand-born Brit. lexicographer.

Burckhardt, Jacob Christoph, 1818–97, Swiss art historian.

Burger, Warren Earl, 1907–, U.S. jurist; chief justice of the U.S. Supreme Court 1969–86.

Burgess, Anthony, 1917–, Eng. author.

—**(Frank) Gelett,** 1866–1951, U.S. author & illustrator.

Burgoyne, John, 1722–92, Brit. general in American Revolutionary War; known as **Gentleman Johnny.**

Burke, Edmund, 1729–97, Irish-born Brit. orator, author, & statesman.

Burne-Jones, Sir Edward Coley, 1833–98, Eng. painter.

Burnett, Carol, 1936–, U.S. actress, singer, & comedienne.

Burney, Fanny, 1752–1840, Eng. author & diarist.

Burnham, Daniel H., 1846–1912, U.S. architect.

Burns, Arthur, 1904–, Russ.-born U.S. economist.

—**George,** 1896–, U.S. actor & comedian.

—**Robert,** 1759–96, Scot. poet.

Burnside, Ambrose Everett, 1824–81, U.S. Civil War general.

Burr, Aaron, 1756–1836, Amer. lawyer & statesman; U.S. vice president 1801–05.

Burroughs, Edgar Rice, 1875–1950, U.S. author.

—**John,** 1837–1921, U.S. naturalist & author.

—**William,** 1914–, U.S. author.

Burrows, Abe, 1910–85, U.S. author, playwright, & director.

Burton, Richard, 1925–84, Brit. actor.

—**Sir Richard Francis,** 1821–90, Eng. traveler & author.

Busch, Adolphus, 1839–1913, Ger.-born U.S. businessman & philanthropist.

Bush, George, 1924–, U.S. statesman; U.S. vice president 1981–89; 41st U.S. president 1989–.

—**Vannevar,** 1890–1974, U.S. electrical engineer.

Bushman, Francis Xavier, 1883–1966, U.S. actor.

Bushmiller, Ernie, 1905–82, U.S. cartoonist.

Busoni, Ferruccio Benvenuto, 1866–1924, Ital. composer & pianist.

Butler, Nicholas Murray, 1862–1947, U.S. educator.

—**Samuel,** 1612–80, Eng. satirical poet.

—**Samuel,** 1835–1902, Eng. author.

Button, Richard Totten (Dick), 1929–, U.S. figure skater & TV commentator.

Buxtehude, Dietrich, 1637–1707, Dan.-born Ger. organist & composer.
Byrd, Richard Evelyn, 1888–1957, U.S. explorer.
—William, 1543–1623, Brit. composer.
Byron, George Gordon, Lord, 1788–1824, Eng. poet.

Caballe, Montserrat, 1933–, Sp. soprano.
Cabell, James Branch, 1879–1958, author.
Cable, George Washington, 1844–1925, U.S. author.
Cabot, John, b. Giovanni Caboto, 1451?–98, Ital. navigator & explorer.
Cabral, Pedro Alvares, 1460?–1526, Pg. navigator.
Cabrini, Saint Frances Xavier, 1850–1917, Ital.-born. U.S. nun; canonized 1946: known as **Mother Cabrini.**
Cadillac, Sieur Antoine de la Mothe, 1658–1730, Fr. explorer in N. America.
Cadmus, Paul, 1904–, U.S. painter.
Caedmon, 7th c. Eng. poet; first to be known by name.
Caesar, Gaius Julius, 100–44 B.C., Roman general, statesman, & historian; assassinated.
—Sid, 1922–, U.S. comedian & actor.
Caetano, Marcelo, 1906–80, Pg. lawyer; premier of Portugal 1968–74.
Cage, John, 1912–, U.S. composer.
Cagliostro, Count Alessandro di, 1743–95, Ital. charlatan.
Cagney, James, 1899–1986, U.S. actor.
Cahn, Sammy, 1913–, U.S. lyricist.
Calder, Alexander, 1898–1976, U.S. sculptor.
Calderón de la Barca, Pedro, 1600–81, Sp. poet & playwright.
Caldwell, Erskine, 1903–87, U.S. author.
—(Janet) Taylor, 1900–85, Eng.-born U.S. author.
—Sarah, 1928–, U.S. opera director & conductor.
—Zoe, 1933–, Austral. actress.
Calhoun, John Caldwell, 1782–1850, U.S. lawyer & politician; U.S. vice president 1825–32.
Caligula, b. Gaius Caesar, A.D. 12–41, Roman emperor 37–41; assassinated.
Calisher, Hortense, 1911–, U.S. author.
Callaghan, James, 1912, Eng. politician; prime minister 1976–79.
—Morley, 1903–90, Can. author.
Callas, Maria Meneghini, 1923–77, U.S. soprano.
Callisthenes, 360?–328? B.C., Gk. philosopher & historian.
Calloway, Cab(ell), 1907–, U.S. singer & band leader.
Calvert, Sir George, 1580?–1632, Eng. statesman; founder of Maryland.
Calvin, John, 1509–64, Fr. Protestant reformer.
—Melvin, 1911–, U.S. chemist; Nobel Prize winner.
Cambyses, ?–522 B.C., king of Persia; son of Cyrus.
Camões, Luiz Vaz de, 1524–80, Pg. poet.
Camp, Walter Chauncey, 1859–1925, U.S. football coach.
Campbell, Mrs. Patrick b. Beatrice Stella Tanner, 1865–1940, Eng. actress.
—Thomas, 1777–1844, Eng. poet.
Campin, Robert, 1375?–1444, Flem. painter.
Campion, Thomas, 1567–1620, Eng. poet & musician.
Camus, Albert, 1913–60, Algerian-born Fr. writer.
Canaletto, b. Antonio Canale, 1697–1768, Ital. painter.
Canary, Martha Jane, 1852–1903, U.S. frontierswoman: known as **Calamity Jane.**
Canby, Henry Seidel, 1878–1961, U.S. educator.
Candler, Asa, 1851–1929, U.S. industrialist.
Candolle, Augustine Pyrame de, 1778–1841, Swiss botanist.
Caniff, Milton, 1907–88, U.S. cartoonist.
Cannon, Joseph Gurney (Uncle Joe), 1836–1926, U.S. lawyer & politician.
—Walter Bradford, 1871–1945, U.S. physiologist.
Canova, Antonio, 1757–1822, Ital. sculptor.
Cantor, Eddie, 1892–1964, U.S. singer & actor.
Canute, 994?–1035, king of England, Denmark, & Norway.
Čapek, Karel, 1890–1938, Czech author & playwright.
Capet, Hugh, 940?–996, king of France 987–996.
Capone, Al(phonse), 1898–1947, U.S. criminal.
Capote, Truman, 1924–84, U.S. author.
Capp, Al, 1909–79, U.S. cartoonist.
Capra, Frank, 1897–1991, Ital.-born U.S. film director.

Captain Kangaroo, pseud. of Robert James Keeshan, 1927–, U.S. TV personality.
Caracalla b. Marcus Aurelius Antoninus Bassianus, A.D. 188–217, Roman emperor 212–17.
Caramanlis, Constantine, 1907–, Gr. statesman; prime minister, 1955–63 & 1974–80.
Caravaggio, Michelangelo Amerighi da 1573–1610, Ital. painter.
Cárdenas, Lázaro, 1895–1970, Mexican general; president of Mexico 1934–40.
Cardin, Pierre, 1922–, Ital.-born Fr. fashion designer.
Cardozo, Benjamin Nathan, 1870–1938, U.S. jurist; justice of U.S. Supreme Court 1932–38.
Carducci, Giosuè, 1835–1907, Ital. poet; Nobel Prize winner.
Carême, Marie Antoine, 1784–1833, Fr. chef & gastronome.
Carew, Thomas, 1595?–1645?, Eng. poet.
Carl XVI Gustaf, 1946–, king of Sweden 1973–.
Carlota, 1840–1927, Austrian-born empress of Mexico 1864–67.
Carlyle, Thomas, 1795–1881, Scot. author
Carman, (William) Bliss, 1861–1929, Can. poet & journalist active in U.S.
Carmichael, Hoaglund Howard (Hoagy), 1899–1981, U.S. songwriter.
Carnap, Rudolf, 1891–1970, Ger.-born U.S. philosopher.
Carné, Marcel, 1909–, Fr. film director.
Carnegie, Andrew, 1835–1919, Scot.-born U.S. industrialist & philanthropist.
—Dale, 1888–1955, U.S. author & teacher of public speaking.
Carney, Art, 1918–, U.S. actor.
Carnot, Lazare Nicolas Marguerite, 1753–1823, Fr. revolutionary statesman & general.
—Nicolas Léonard Sadi, 1796–1832, Fr. physicist; son of prec.
Carol II, 1893–1953, king of Romania 1930–40; abdicated.
Carpaccio, Vittore, 1460?–1525?, Ital. painter.
Carracci A family of Ital. painters incl. **Lodovico,** 1555–1619, & his nephews **Agostino,** 1557–1602, & **Annibale,** 1560–1609.
Carranza, Venustiano, 1859–1920, Mexican revolutionist & statesman; president of Mexico 1915–20.
Carrel, Alexis, 1873–1944, Fr. surgeon & biologist.
Carreras, José, 1947–, Sp. tenor.
Carrington, Richard Christopher, 1826–75, Eng. astronomer.
Carroll, Charles, 1737–1832, Amer. revolutionary patriot.
—Lewis, pseud. of Charles Lutwidge Dodgson, 1832–98, Eng. mathematician & author.
Carson, Christopher (Kit), 1809–68, U.S. frontiersman.
—Johnny, 1925–, U.S. comedian & television personality.
—Rachel Louise, 1907–64, U.S. biologist & author.
Carter, Howard, 1873–1939, Eng. archaeologist.
—Elliott Cook, 1908–, U.S. composer.
—James Earl (Jimmy), 1924–, politician, 39th U.S. president 1977–81.
Cartier, Jacques, 1491–1557, Fr. explorer; discoverer of the St. Lawrence River.
Cartier-Bresson, Henri, 1908–, Fr. photographer.
Cartwright, Edmund, 1743–1823, Eng. inventor of the power loom.
Caruso, Enrico, 1873–1921, Ital. tenor.
Carver, George Washington, 1864?–1943, U.S. chemist & botanist.
—John, 1576?–1621, Eng.-born Amer. colonist; 1st governor of Plymouth colony.
—Raymond, 1938–, U.S. author.
Cary, (Arthur) Joyce (Lunel), 1888–1957, Eng. author.
Casadesus, Robert, 1899–1972, Fr. pianist.
Casals, Pablo, 1876–1973, Sp. cellist & composer.
Casanova, Giovanni Jacopo, 1725–98, Ital. adventurer; known for his *Memoirs.*
Casement, Sir Roger, 1864–1916, Irish nationalist; hanged by the British for treason in World War I.
Casey, William J., 1913–87, U.S. public official.
Cash, Johnny, 1932–, U.S. singer & songwriter.
Caslon, William, 1692–1766, Eng. typographer.
Cassatt, Mary, 1845–1926, U.S. painter.

Cassini, Giovanni Domenico, 1625–1712, Fr. astronomer.
Cassiodorus, Flavius Magnus Aurelius, ?–575, Roman statesman & author.
Cassirer, Ernst, 1874–1945, Ger. philosopher.
Cassius Longinus, Gaius, ?–42 B.C., Roman general; conspirator against Caesar.
Catagno, Andrea del, ?–1457?, Ital. painter.
Castiglione, Count Baldassare, 1478–1529, Ital. statesman & author.
Castle, Irene, 1893–1969, U.S. dancer.
—**Vernon,** 1887–1918, Eng.-born U.S. dancer & aviator; husband of prec.
Castlereagh, Robert Stewart, Viscount, 1769–1822, Brit. statesman.
Castro (Ruz), Fidel, 1926–, Cuban revolutionary leader; dictator of Cuba 1959–.
Catharine of Aragon, 1485–1536, first wife of Henry VIII of England; mother of Mary I.
Cather, Willa Sibert, 1876–1947, U.S. author.
Catherine II (Ekaterina Alekseevna), 1729–96, Ger.-born empress of Russia 1762–96: known as **Catherine the Great.**
Catiline (L. Lucius Sergius Catilina), 108?–62 B.C., Roman politician & conspirator.
Catlin, George, 1796–1872, U.S. painter & sculptor.
Cato, Marcus Porcius, 234–149 B.C., Roman statesman: known as **the Elder.**
—**Marcus Porcius,** 95–46 B.C., Roman statesman & philosopher; great-grandson of prec.: known as **the Younger.**
Catt, Carrie Chapman Lane, 1859–1947, U.S. suffragist.
Catton, (Charles) Bruce, 1899–1978, U.S. journalist & historian.
Catullus, Gaius Valerius, 84?–54 B.C., Roman poet.
Cavafy, Constantinos, 1863–1933, Gk. poet.
Cavell, Edith, 1865–1915, Eng. nurse & patriot; executed by the Germans in World War I.
Cavendish, Henry, 1731?–1810, Eng. chemist & physicist.
Cavett, Dick, 1936–, U.S. TV personality & author.
Cavour, Count Camillo Benso di, 1810–61, Ital. statesman.
Caxton, William, 1422–91, first Eng. printer.
Cayce, Edgar, 1877–1945, U.S. photographer & psychic.
Cayley, Sir George, 1773–1857, Eng. engineer & aircraft designer.
Ceausescu, Nicolae, 1918–89, president of Rumania 1967–89.
Cecchetti, Enrico, 1850–1928, Russ. ballet teacher.
Cecil, Lord (Edward Christian) David, 1902–86, Eng. author.
—**William, 1st Baron Burghley,** 1520–98, Eng. statesman.
Céline, Louis Ferdinand, 1894–1961, Fr. author.
Cellini, Benvenuto, 1500–71, Ital. sculptor & goldsmith.
Celsius, Anders, 1701–44, Swed. astronomer.
Cenci, Beatrice, 1577–99, Ital. noblewoman; executed for parricide.
Cerf, Bennett Alfred, 1895–1971, U.S. author & publisher.
Cervantes Saavedra, Miguel de, 1547–1616, Sp. novelist & playwright.
Cézanne, Paul, 1839–1906, Fr. painter.
Chabrier, Alexis Emmanuel, 1841–94, Fr. composer.
Chabrol, Claude, 1930–, Fr. film director.
Chadwick, Sir James, 1891–1974, Eng. physicist.
Chagall, Marc, 1887–1985, Russ.-born painter active in France.
Chaliapin, Feodor Ivanovich, 1873–1938, Russ. basso.
Chamberlain, (Arthur) Neville, 1869–1940, Eng. statesman; prime minister 1937–40.
—**Austen,** 1863–1937, Brit. statesman.
—**Owen,** 1920–, U.S. physicist; Nobel Prize winner.
—**Richard,** 1935–, U.S. actor.
—**Wilt(on Norman),** 1936–, U.S. basketball player.
Chambers, (Jay David) Whittaker, 1901–61, U.S. journalist.
Champion, Gower, 1921–80, U.S. dancer, choreographer, & stage director.
—**Marjorie (Marge),** 1925–, U.S. dancer.
Champlain, Samuel de, 1567?–1635, Fr. explorer in America.
Champollion, Jean François, 1790–1832, Fr. Egyptologist.
Chancellor, John, 1927–, U.S. journalist & TV commentator.
Chandler, Raymond, 1888–1959, U.S. author.
Chanel, Gabrielle (Coco), 1883?–1971, Fr. fashion designer.

Chaney, Lon, 1883–1930, U.S. actor.
Chang & Eng, 1811–74, Siamese-born conjoined twins residing in U.S.; the original "Siamese twins."
Channing, Carol, 1923–, U.S. actress.
—**Edward,** 1856–1931, U.S. historian.
—**William Ellery,** 1780–1842, U.S. clergyman & social reformer.
Chaplin, Sir Charles Spencer (Charlie), 1889–1977, Eng.-born film actor & producer active in U.S.
—**Geraldine,** 1944–, U.S. actress; daughter of prec.
Chapman, George, 1559?–1634, Eng. playwright & translator.
—**John,** 1774–1845, U.S. pioneer: called **Johnny Appleseed.**
Charcot, Jean Martin, 1825–93, Fr. neurologist.
Chardin, Jean Baptiste Siméon, 1699–1779, Fr. painter.
Chardonnet, Hilaire Bernigaud, Comte de, 1839–1924, Fr. chemist & inventor.
Charlemagne, 742–814, king of the Franks 768–814 & Holy Roman emperor 800–814: known as **Charles the Great.**
Charles I, 1600–49, king of England 1625–49; beheaded.
—**II,** 1630–85, king of England 1660–85; son of prec.
Charles V, 1337–80, king of France 1364–80: known as **Charles the Wise.**
Charles V, 1500–58, Holy Roman emperor; king of Spain as Charles I.
Charles XIV See BERNADOTTE, JEAN, BAPTISTE, JULES.
Charles Philip Arthur George, 1948–, Prince of Wales, heir apparent to the Brit. throne.
Charles, Jacques Alexandre César, 1746–1823, Fr. physicist.
Charpentier, Gustave, 1860–1956, Fr. composer.
Chase, Lucia, 1907–86, U.S. ballet dancer & ballet company director.
—**Mary Ellen,** 1887–1973, U.S. author & educator.
—**Salmon Portland,** 1808–73, U.S. statesman; chief justice of the U.S. Supreme Court.
Chateaubriand, François René, Vicomte de, 1768–1848, Fr. author & politician.
Chatterton, Ruth, 1893–1961, U.S. actress.
—**Thomas,** 1752–70, Eng. poet.
Chaucer, Geoffrey, 1340?–1400, Eng. poet.
Chávez, Carlos, 1899–1978, Mexican composer & conductor.
—**Cesar Estrada,** 1927–, U.S. labor leader.
Chayefsky, Sidney (Paddy), 1923–81, U.S. playwright.
Cheever, John, 1912–82, U.S. author.
Chekhov, Anton Pavlovich, 1860–1904, Russ. playwright & author.
Chénier, André Marie de, 1762–94, Fr. poet.
Chennault, Claire Lee, 1890–1958, U.S. Air Force general.
Cheops, Egyptian king of the 4th dynasty ca. 2650 B.C.; built the Great Pyramid at Gizeh: also known as **Khufu.**
Chernenko, Konstantin Ustinovich, 1911–85, Soviet statesman; general secretary U.S.S.R. Communist Party 1984–85.
Cherenkov, Pavel Alekseevich, 1904–90, Soviet physicist.
Chernyshevski, Nikolai Gavrilovich, 1829–89, Russ. revolutionist & author.
Cherubini, (Maria) Luigi, 1760–1842, Ital. composer.
Chessman, Caryl (Whittier), 1921–60, U.S. criminal & author; executed.
Chesterfield, Earl of, b. Philip Dormer Stanhope, 1694–1773, Eng. statesman & author.
Chesterton, Gilbert Keith, 1874–1936, Eng. author.
Chevalier, Maurice, 1888–1972, Fr. entertainer.
Chevrolet, Louis, 1878–1941, U.S. automobile manufacturer.
Chiang Ching, 1913–, Chin. government official; wife of Mao Tse-tung.
—**Kai-shek,** 1886–1975, Chin. general & statesman; president of Republic of China (Taiwan) 1948–75.
—**Madame Chiang Kai-shek** See SOONG.
Chikamatsu Monzaemon, 1653?–1724, Jap. dramatist.
Child, Francis James, 1825–96, U.S. philologist & ballad editor.
—**Julia McCormick,** 1912–, U.S. culinary expert & author.
Chippendale, Thomas, 1718–79, Eng. cabinetmaker.
Chirico, Giorgio di, 1888–1978, Ital. painter.
Chisholm, Shirley, 1924–, U.S. politician.
Chittenden, Russell Henry, 1856–1943, U.S. physiological chemist.

Chomsky, Noam, 1928–, U.S. linguist.

Chopin, Frédéric François, 1810–49, Pol. composer & pianist active in France.

—**Kate,** 1851–1904, U.S. author.

Chou En-Lai, 1898–1976, Chin. statesman.

Chrétien de Troyes, 12th c. Fr. poet.

Christensen, Lew, 1909–84, U.S. dancer, choreographer, & ballet company director.

Christians, Mady, 1900–51, Austrian actress.

Christie, Dame Agatha, 1890–1976, Eng. author.

Christoff, Boris, 1919–, Bulgarian basso.

Christophe, Henri, 1767–1820, Haitian revolutionary leader; king of Haiti 1811–20.

Christopher, Saint, 3rd c. Christian martyr.

Christy, Howard Chandler, 1873–1952, U.S. painter & illustrator.

Chrysler, Walter Percy, 1875–1940, U.S. automobile manufacturer.

Chuang-tzu, 4th c. B.C. Chin. philosopher.

Churchill, Lord Randolph, 1849–95, Eng. statesman.

—**Winston,** 1871–1947, U.S. author.

—**Sir Winston Leonard Spenser,** 1874–1965, Eng. statesman & author; prime minister 1940–45 & 1951–55; Nobel Prize winner; son of Lord Randolph.

Chu Teh, 1886–1976, Chin. military leader.

Ciano, Count Galeazzo, 1903–44, Ital. diplomat.

Ciardi, John, 1916–86, U.S. poet & critic.

Cibber, Colley, 1671–1757, Eng. actor & poet.

Cicero, Marcus Tullius, 106–43 B.C., Roman statesman, orator, & writer.

Cimabue, Giovanni, 1240–1302, Florentine painter.

Cimarosa, Domenico, 1749–1801, Ital. composer.

Cimino, Michael, 1943–, U.S. film director.

Cincinnatus, Lucius Quinctius, 5th c. B.C. Roman general & statesman.

Claiborne, Craig, 1920–, U.S. journalist, author, & critic.

Clair, René, 1898–1981, Fr. film director.

Claire, Ina, 1892–1985, U.S. actress.

Clare, Saint, 1194–1253, Ital. nun.

Clark, Bobby, 1888–1960, U.S. comedian.

—**(Charles) Joseph,** 1939–, Can. statesman; prime minister of Canada, 1979–80.

—**Dick,** 1929–, U.S. TV personality.

—**George Rogers,** 1752–1818, U.S. soldier & frontiersman.

—**James Beauchamp (Champ),** 1850–1921, U.S. politician.

—**Kenneth Bancroft,** 1914–, U.S. psychologist.

—**Sir Kenneth MacKenzie,** 1903–83, Brit. art historian.

—**Mark,** 1896–1984, U.S. general.

—**William,** 1770–1838, U.S. explorer.

—**(William) Ramsey,** 1927–, U.S. lawyer & politician.

Clarke, Arthur Charles, 1917–, Eng. author.

—**Kenny,** 1914–1985, U.S. jazz musician.

Claude, Albert, 1899–1983, Belg. biologist.

Claude (de) Lorrain, b. Claude Gellée, 1600–82, Fr. painter.

Claudel, Paul Louise Charles, 1868–1955, Fr. author & diplomat.

Claudius I, born Tiberius Claudius Drusus Nero Germanicus, 10 B.C.–A.D. 54, 4th Roman emperor 41–54.

Clausewitz, Karl von, 1780–1831, Prussian general & writer on military science.

Clausius, Rudolf Julius Emanuel, 1822–88, Ger. physicist & mathematician.

Clavell, James, 1924–, Brit. author.

Clay, Cassius Marcellus, 1810–1903, U.S. politician & abolitionist.

—**Henry,** 1777–1852, U.S. statesman & orator.

—**Lucius DuBignon,** 1897–1978, U.S. general & banker.

Cleary, Beverly, 1916–, U.S. author.

Cleaver, (Leroy) Eldridge, 1935–, U.S. author & political activist.

Clemenceau, Georges Benjamin Eugène, 1841–1929, Fr. statesman; premier of France 1906–09 & 1917–20.

Clemens, Samuel Langhorne, See TWAIN, MARK.

Clement VII, b. Guilio de' Medici, 1478–1534, pope 1523–34.

Clement of Alexandria, (L. Titus Flavius Clemens), A.D. 150?–220?, Gk. theologian.

Cleopatra, 69–30 B.C., queen of Egypt 51–30 B.C.

Cleveland, (Stephen) Grover, 1837–1908, 22nd & 24th U.S. president 1885–89 & 1893–97.

Cliburn, Harvey Lavan (Van), 1934–, U.S. pianist.

Clift, Montgomery, 1920–66, U.S. actor.

Clinton, De Witt, 1769–1828, U.S. lawyer & statesman.

Clive, Robert (Baron Clive of Plassey), 1725–74, Brit. general in India.

Clough, Arthur Hugh, 1819–61, Eng. poet.

Clovis, I, 466?–511, Frankish king.

Clurman, Harold, 1901–80, U.S. director & drama critic.

Cobb, Irvin Shrewsbury, 1876–1944, U.S. journalist & humorist.

—**Lee J.,** 1911–76, U.S. actor.

—**Ty(rus Raymond),** 1886–1961, U.S. baseball player.

Cobbett, William, 1762–1835, Eng. political economist.

Cobden, William, 1804–65, Eng. statesman & economist.

Coca, Imogene, 1908–, U.S. comedienne & actress.

Cochise, ?–1874, Apache Am. Ind. chief.

Cochran, Jacqueline, 1912?–80, U.S. businesswoman & aviatrix.

Cockcroft, Sir John Douglas, 1897–1967, Eng. nuclear physicist; Nobel Prize winner.

Cocteau, Jean, 1889–1963, Fr. author & film director.

Cody, William Frederick, 1846–1917, U.S. plainsman, army scout, & showman: known as **Buffalo Bill.**

Coe, Frederick, 1914–79, U.S. TV producer & stage & film director.

Coffin, Robert Peter Tristram, 1892–1955, U.S. poet & author.

Cohan, George Michael, 1878–1942, U.S. theatrical producer, actor, & composer.

Cohn, Ferdinand Julius, 1828–98, Ger. botanist.

—**Harry,** 1891–1958, U.S. film executive.

Cohn-Bendit, Daniel, 1945–, Ger.-born anarchist & student leader: called **Danny the Red.**

Coke, Sir Edward, 1552–1634, Eng. jurist.

Colbert, Claudette, 1905–, Fr.-born U.S. actress.

—**Jean Baptiste,** 1619–83, Fr. statesman.

Colby, William E., 1920–, U.S. government official.

Cole, Nat "King", 1919–65, U.S. singer & pianist.

—**Thomas,** 1801–48, Eng.-born U.S. painter.

Coleman, Ornette, 1930–, U.S. jazz musician & composer.

Coleridge, Samuel Taylor, 1772–1834, Eng. poet.

Colet, John, 1466?–1519, Eng. theologian & scholar.

Colette, (Sidonie-Gabrielle Claudine), 1873–1954, Fr. author.

Colfax, Schuyler, 1823–85, U.S. statesman; U.S. vice president 1869–73.

Colgate, William, 1783–1857, U.S. businessman & philanthropist.

Collins, Joan, 1933–, Eng. actress active in U.S.

—**Judy,** 1939–, U.S. singer.

—**Michael,** 1890–1922, Irish revolutionist.

—**(William) Wilkie,** 1824–89, Eng. author.

Colman, Ronald, 1891–1958, Eng. actor active in U.S.

Colt, Samuel, 1814–62, U.S. inventor & firearms manufacturer.

Coltrane, John, 1926–67, U.S. jazz musician & composer.

Colum, Padraic, 1881–1972, Irish poet & playwright.

Columbus, Christopher, 1451–1506, Ital. navigator; discovered America.

Comaneci, Nadia, 1962–, Romanian gymnast.

Comden, Betty, 1919–, U.S. lyricist.

Commager, Henry Steele, 1902–, U.S. historian.

Commoner, Barry, 1917–, U.S. biologist & educator.

Commons, John R., 1862–1945, U.S. economist & historian.

Como, Perry, 1913–, U.S. singer.

Compton, Arthur Holly, 1892–1962, U.S. physicist.

Compton-Burnett, Ivy, 1892–1969, Eng. author.

Comstock, Anthony, 1844–1915, U.S. social reformer.

Comte, Auguste, 1798–1857, Fr. philosopher.

Conant, James Bryant, 1893–1978, U.S. chemist, educator, & statesman.

Condon, Eddie, 1905–73, U.S. jazz musician.

—**Edward Uhler,** 1902–74, U.S. physicist.

Condorcet, Marie Jean Antoine Nicolas de Caritat, Marquis de, 1743–94, Fr. philosopher, mathematician, & politician.
Confucius, Latinized form of **Kung Fu-tse,** 551–478 B.C., Chin. philosopher & teacher.
Congreve, William, 1670–1729, Eng. playwright.
Connally, John Bowden, 1917–, U.S. politician.
Connelly, Marc(us Cook), 1890–1980, U.S. playwright.
Connery, Sean, 1930–, Scot.-born U.S. actor.
Connolly, Cyril, 1903–74, Eng. critic & editor.
—**Maureen,** 1934–69, U.S. tennis player.
Connors, James Scott (Jimmy), 1952–, U.S. tennis player.
Conrad, Joseph, b. Teodor Jozef Konrad Korzeniowski, 1857–1924, Pol.-born Eng. author.
—**Paul,** 1924–, U.S. political cartoonist.
Constable, John, 1776–1837, Eng. painter.
Constantine I, ?–715, pope 708–715.
Constantine I, b. Flavius Valerius Aurelius, 272–337, first Christian emperor of Rome: called **the Great.**
Constantine II, 1940–, king of Greece 1964–67.
Coogan, John Leslie, Jr., (Jackie), 1914–84, U.S. actor.
Cook, Barbara, 1927–, U.S. singer & actress.
—**James,** 1728–79, Eng. naval officer & explorer.
Cooke, (Alfred) Alistair, 1908–, Eng.-born U.S. author, journalist, & TV narrator.
—**Jay,** 1821–1905, U.S. financier.
Cooley, Denton Arthur, 1920–, U.S. surgeon.
Coolidge, (John) Calvin, 1872–1933, 30th U.S. president 1923–29.
Cooper, Gary, 1901–61, U.S. actor.
—**Gladys,** 1888–1971, Eng. actress.
—**Jackie,** 1922–, U.S. actor & director.
—**James Fenimore,** 1789–1851, U.S. novelist.
—**Peter,** 1791–1883, U.S. manufacturer, inventor, & philanthropist.
Copernicus, Nicolaus, 1473–1543, Pol. astronomer.
Copland, Aaron, 1900–90, U.S. composer.
Copley, John Singleton, 1738–1815, U.S. painter.
Coppola, Francis Ford, 1939–, U.S. film director.
Coquelin, Benoît Constant, 1841–1909, Fr. actor.
Corbett, James John, 1866–1933, U.S. boxer.
Corbusier, Le, b. Charles Edouard Jeanneret, 1887–1965, Swiss architect active in France.
Corday, Charlotte, 1768–93, Fr. patriot; assassinated Marat.
Cordobés, El, b. Manuel Benitez Perez, 1936–, Sp. bullfighter.
Corelli, Arcangelo, 1653–1713, Ital. composer & violinist.
—**Franco,** 1924–, Ital. tenor.
Cori, Carl Ferdinand, 1896–1984, & his wife **Gerty Theresa Radnitz,** 1896–1957, Czech-born U.S. biochemists; Nobel Prize winners.
Corio, Ann, 1914?–, U.S. stripteaser.
Corneille, Pierre, 1606–84, Fr. playwright.
Cornell, Ezra, 1807–74, U.S. financier & philanthropist.
—**Katherine,** 1898–1974, Ger.-born U.S. actress.
Corning, Erastus, 1794–1872, U.S. financier.
Cornwallis, Charles, Marquis, 1738–1805, Eng. general & statesman.
Coronado, Francisco Vásquez de, 1510?–54, Sp. explorer.
Corot, Jean Baptiste Camille, 1796–1875, Fr. painter.
Correggio, Antonio Allegri da, 1494–1534, Ital. painter.
Correll, Charles, 1890–1972, U.S. radio actor.
Corsaro, Frank, 1924–, U.S. opera director.
Cortázar, Julio, 1914–84, Argentine author.
Cortés, Hernando, 1485–1547, Sp. conqueror of Mexico.
Cosby, Bill, 1937–, U.S. comedian & actor.
Cosell, Howard, 1920–, U.S. TV commentator.
Costa-Gavras, Henri, 1933–, Gk. film director.
Costello, Lou, 1908–59, U.S. comedian & actor.
Cotton, John, 1584–1652, Eng.-born Puritan clergyman in America.
Coughlin, Charles Edward, 1891–1979, U.S. clergyman & political spokesman: called **Father Coughlin.**
Coulomb, Charles Augustin de, 1736–1806, Fr. physicist.
Couper, Archibald Scott, 1831–92, Scot. chemist.
Couperin, François, 1668–1733, Fr. composer.
Courbet, Gustave, 1819–77, Fr. painter.

Cournand, André Frédéric, 1895–, Fr.-born U.S. physiologist.
Courrèges, André, 1923–, Fr. fashion designer.
Court, Margaret Smith, 1942–, Austral. tennis player.
Cousin, Victor, 1792–1867, Fr. philosopher.
Cousins, Norman, 1912–90, U.S. editor & author.
Cousteau, Jacques-Yves, 1910–, Fr. naval officer, underwater explorer, & filmmaker.
Cousy, Robert Joseph (Bob), 1928–, U.S. basketball player & coach.
Coverdale, Miles, 1488–1568, Eng. translator of the Bible.
Coward, Sir Noel, 1899–1973, Eng. playwright, composer, & actor.
Cowell, Henry Dixon, 1897–1965, U.S. composer.
Cowl, Jane, 1884–1950, U.S. actress.
Cowles, Gardner, Jr., (Mike), 1903–85, U.S. publisher.
Cowley, Abraham, 1618–67, Eng. poet.
—**Malcolm,** 1898–1989, U.S. critic.
Cowper, William, 1731–1800, Eng. poet.
Coxe, George Harmon, 1901–84, U.S. author.
Cozzens, James Gould, 1903–78, U.S. author.
Crabbe, George, 1754–1832, Eng. poet.
—**Larry (Buster),** 1908–83, U.S. swimmer & actor.
Craig, (Edward) Gordon, 1872–1966, Eng. director & stage designer.
Craigavon, James Craig, 1st Viscount, 1871–1940, Irish statesman; first prime minister of N. Ireland, 1921–40.
Craigie, Sir William Alexander, 1867–1957, Scot. philologist & lexicographer.
Cram, Ralph Adams, 1863–1942, U.S. architect & author.
Cranach, Lucas, 1472–1553, Ger. painter & engraver.
—**Lucas,** 1515–86, Ger. portrait painter; son of prec.: called **the Younger.**
Crane, (Harold) Hart, 1899–1932, U.S. poet.
—**Stephen,** 1871–1900, U.S. author & poet.
Cranko, John, 1928–73, South African-born choreographer & ballet-company director active in W. Germany.
Cranmer, Thomas, 1489–1556, archbishop of Canterbury; burned at the stake.
Crashaw, Richard, 1613–49, Eng. poet.
Crassus, Marcus Licinius, 115?–53 B.C., Roman politician.
Crater, Joseph Force, 1889–1937?, U.S. jurist.
Crawford, Cheryl, 1902–, U.S. theatrical producer.
—**Joan,** 1908–77, U.S. actress.
Crazy Horse, b. Tashunca-Utico, 1849?–77, Sioux Am. Ind. chief.
Creasy, John, 1908–73, Eng. author.
Crespin, Régine, 1927–, Fr. soprano.
Crèvecoeur, Michel-Guillaume St. Jean de, 1735–1813, Fr.-born author active in America.
Crichton, James, 1560?–82, Scot. scholar & adventurer: called **the Admirable Crichton.**
—**Michael,** 1942–, U.S. physician, author, & film director.
Crick, Francis, 1916–, Eng. geneticist.
Cripps, Sir (Richard) Stafford, 1889–1952, Eng. lawyer & socialist statesman.
Crist, Judith, 1922–, U.S. film critic & journalist.
Croce, Benedetto, 1866–1952, Ital. philospher, statesman, critic, & historian.
Crockett, David (Davy), 1786–1836, U.S. frontiersman & congressman.
Croesus, 6th c. B.C. Lydian king famed for great wealth.
Cromwell, Oliver, 1599–1658, Eng. general & statesman.
—**Richard,** 1626–1712, Eng. general & statesman; son of prec.
Cronin, Archibald Joseph, 1896–1981, Eng. physician & author.
Cronkite, Walter Leland, Jr., 1916–, U.S. journalist & TV news commentator.
Cronyn, Hume, 1911–, Can.-born U.S. actor.
Crookes, Sir William, 1832–1919, Eng. physicist & chemist.
Crosby, Harry Lillis (Bing), 1904–77, U.S. singer & actor.
Cross, Milton, 1897–1975, U.S. opera commentator.
Crouse, Russel, 1893–1966, U.S. journalist & playwright.
Cruikshank, George, 1792–1878, Eng. illustrator & caricaturist.
Crumb, George, 1929–, U.S. composer.
Cukor, George, 1899–1983, U.S. film director.

Culbertson, Ely, 1893–1955, Romanian-born U.S. expert on the game of bridge.

Cullen, Countee, 1903–46, U.S. poet.

Cummings, Edward Estlin, 1894–1962, U.S. poet; usu. known as **e. e. cummings.**

Cunard, Sir Samuel, 1787–1865, Can. steamship executive.

Cunha, Tristão da, 1460?–1540, Pg. navigator & explorer.

Cunningham, Merce, 1922–, U.S. choreographer.

Cuomo, Mario, 1932–, U.S. politician.

Curie, Marie, b. Marja Sklodowska, 1867–1934, Pol.-born Fr. physicist & chemist.

—**Pierre,** 1859–1906, Fr. physicist; husband of prec.

Curley, James Michael, 1874–1958, U.S. politician.

Currier & Ives, A U.S. firm of lithographers established 1835 by **Nathaniel Currier,** 1813–88; later joined by **James Merritt Ives,** 1824–95.

Curry, John Steuart, 1897–1946, U.S. painter.

Curtis, Cyrus Hermann Kotzschmar, 1850–1933, U.S. publisher & philanthropist.

Curtiss, Glenn Hammond, 1878–1930, U.S. aviator & inventor.

Curtiz, Michael, 1888–1962, Hung.-born U.S. film director.

Curzon, Clifford, 1907–82, Brit. pianist.

Cushing, Harvey, 1869–1939, U.S. surgeon & author.

Cushman, Charlotte Saunders, 1816–76, U.S. actress.

Custer, George Armstrong, 1839–76, U.S. general.

Cuvier, Baron Georges Léopold, 1769–1832, Fr. naturalist.

Cynewulf, 8th c. Anglo-Saxon poet.

Cyril, Saint, 827–869, Gk. missionary & apostle to the Slavs.

Cyrus, ?–529 b.c., king of Persia 559–529 b.c.; founder of the Persian Empire: called **the Great.**

Czerny, Karl, 1791–1857, Austrian composer & pianist.

da Gama, Vasco, 1469?–1524, Pg. navigator.

Daguerre, Louis Jacques Mandé, 1787–1851, Fr. inventor.

Daimler, Gottlieb, 1834–1900, Ger. engineer & automobile manufacturer.

Daladier, Édouard, 1884–1970, Fr. statesman.

Daley, Richard Joseph, 1902–76, U.S. politician; mayor of Chicago 1955–76.

Dali, Salvador, 1904–89, Sp.-born painter active in U.S.

Dallapicola, Luigi, 1904–75, Ital. pianist & composer.

Dallas, George Mifflin, 1792–1864, U.S. statesman; U.S. vice president 1845–49.

Dalton, John, 1766–1844, Eng. chemist & physicist.

—**Robert,** 1867–92, U.S. outlaw.

Daly, (John) Augustin, 1838–99, U.S. playwright & theater manager.

D'Amboise, Jacques, 1934–, U.S. ballet dance & choreographer.

Damien de Veuster, Joseph, 1840–89, Belg. missionary to lepers in Hawaiian Islands: called **Father Damien.**

Damrosch, Leopold, 1832–85, violinist & conductor.

—**Walter Johannes,** 1862–1950, Ger.-born U.S. conductor; son of prec.

Dana, Charles Anderson, 1819–97, newspaper editor.

—**Richard Henry, Jr.,** 1815–82, U.S. lawyer & author.

Dane, Clemence, pseud. of Winifred Ashton, 1888–1965, Eng. author.

Daniel, Samuel, 1562?–1619, Eng. poet.

Danilova, Alexandra, 1904–, Russ.-born ballerina active in U.S.

D'Annunzio, Gabriele, 1863–1938, Ital. author & adventurer.

Dante Alighieri, 1265–1321, Ital. poet.

Danton, Georges Jacques, 1759–94, Fr. revolutionary leader.

Da Ponte, Lorenzo, 1749–1838, Ital. librettist.

Dare, Virginia, 1587–?, first child born in America of Eng. parents.

Darío, Rubén, pseud. of Félix Rubén García-Sarmiento, 1867–1916, Sp. poet.

Darius I, 558?–486 b.c., king of Persia 521–486 b.c.: called **the Great.**

Darling, Ding, 1876–1962, U.S. political cartoonist.

Darnley, Henry Stewart, Lord, 1545–67, Scot. nobleman; second husband of Mary, Queen of Scots; assassinated.

Darrow, Clarence Seward, 1857–1938, U.S. lawyer.

Darwin, Charles Robert, 1809–82, Eng. naturalist; founder of evolutionary theory of natural selection.

—**Erasmus,** 1731–1802, Eng. physiologist & poet; grandfather of prec.

Daubigny, Charles François, 1817–78, Fr. painter.

Daudet, Alphonse, 1840–97, Fr. author.

—**Léon,** 1867–1942, Fr. journalist & author; son of prec.

Daumier, Honoré, 1808–79, Fr. painter & caricaturist.

David, 1030?–960? b.c., second king of Israel.

David, Gerard, 1450?–1523, Du. painter.

—**Hal,** 1921–, U.S. lyricist.

—**Jacques-Louis,** 1748–1825, Fr. painter.

Davidson, Jo, 1883–1952, U.S. sculptor.

Davies, Marion, 1897–1961, U.S. actress.

—**Robertson,** 1913–, Can. novelist, playwright, & journalist.

Davis, Adelle, 1904–74, U.S. nutritionist & author.

—**Benjamin Oliver, Sr.,** 1877–1970, U.S. general; first black general in U.S. army.

—**Benjamin Oliver, Jr.,** 1912–, U.S. general; son of prec.

—**Elmer Holmes,** 1890–1958, U.S. radio news commentator.

—**Jefferson,** 1808–89, U.S. statesman; president of the Confederacy 1862–65.

—**Jim,** 1945–, U.S. cartoonist.

—**Miles,** 1926–91, U.S. jazz musician.

—**Richard Harding,** 1864–1916, U.S. war correspondent & author.

—**Ruth Elizabeth (Bette),** 1908–89, U.S. actress.

—**Sammy, Jr.,** 1925–90, U.S. singer & actor.

—**Stuart,** 1894–1964, U.S. painter.

Davy, Sir Humphry, 1778–1829, Eng. chemist.

Day, Clarence Sheperd, 1874–1935, U.S. author.

—**Doris,** 1924–, U.S. actress & singer.

—**Dorothy,** 1897–1980, U.S. journalist & social reformer.

Dayan, Moshe, 1915–81, Israeli soldier & statesman.

Day-Lewis, C(ecil), 1904–72, Irish-born Brit. poet & author.

Deacon, Richard, 1922–84, U.S. comic actor.

Dean, James, 1931–55, U.S. actor.

—**Jay Hanna (Dizzy),** 1911–74, U.S. baseball player.

DeBakey, Michael Ellis, 1908–, U.S. surgeon.

de Beauvoir, Simone, 1908–86, Fr. author & philosopher.

De Broca, Philippe, 1935–, Fr. film director.

de Broglie, Louis Victor, Prince, 1892–, Fr. physicist.

Debs, Eugene Victor, 1855–1926, U.S. labor leader & socialist.

Debussy, Claude Achille, 1862–1918, Fr. composer.

Debye, Peter Joseph William, 1884–1966, Du.-born U.S. physicist & chemist.

Decatur, Stephen, 1779–1820, U.S. naval officer.

Deere, John, 1804–86, U.S. inventor.

Defoe, Daniel, 1661?–1731, Eng. author.

De Forest, Lee, 1873–1961, U.S. inventor.

Degas, (Hilaire Germain) Edgar, 1834–1917, Fr. painter & sculptor.

De Gasperi, Alcide, 1881–1954, Ital. statesman; premier of Italy 1945–53.

de Gaulle, Charles André Joseph Marie, 1890–1970, Fr. general & statesman; president of France 1945–46 & 1959–69.

De Geer, Charles, 1720–78, Swed. entomologist.

de Ghelderode, Michel, 1898–1962, Belg. playwright.

de Havilland, Olivia, 1916–, U.S. actress born in Japan.

De Kalb, Johann, 1721–80, Ger. soldier; served in Amer. revolutionary army.

Dekker, Thomas, 1572?–1632?, Eng. playwright.

de Klerk Frederik Wilhelm, 1936–, president of Republic of South Africa (1989–1994).

de Kooning, Willem, 1904–, Du.-born U.S. painter.

De Kruif, Paul, 1890–1971, U.S. bacteriologist & author.

Delacroix, (Ferdinand Victor) Eugène, 1798–1863, Fr. painter.

de la Madrid Hurtado, Miguel, 1934–, president of Mexico 1982–89.

de la Mare, Walter, 1873–1956, Eng. poet & author.

de la Renta, Oscar, 1932–, Dom. Rep. fashion designer.

Delaunay, Robert, 1885–1951, Fr. painter.

de la Warr, Thomas West, Lord, 1577–1618, Eng. colonial administrator in America.

Delbrück, Max, 1906–81, Ger.-born U.S. molecular geneticist.

Delibes, (Clement Philibert) Lèo, 1836–91, Fr. composer.

Delius, Frederick, 1862–1934, Eng. composer.

Dellinger, John Howard, 1886–1962, U.S. radio engineer.

Dello Joio, Norman, 1913–, U.S. composer.

Del Monaco, Mario, 1915–82, Ital. tenor.

Delmonico, Lorenzo, 1813–81, Swiss-born U.S. restaurateur.

Delon, Alain, 1935–, Fr. actor.

Del Rio, Dolores, 1905–83, Mexican-born U.S. actress.

De Mille, Agnes George, 1908–, U.S. dancer & choreographer.

—Cecil Blount, 1881–1959, U.S. film director; uncle of prec.

Democritus, 460?–352? B.C., Gk. philosopher.

Demosthenes, 384?–322 B.C., Athenian orator & patriot.

Dempsey, William Harrison (Jack), 1895–1983, U.S. boxer.

Demuth, Charles, 1883–1935, U.S. painter.

Deneuve, Catherine, 1943–, Fr. actress.

Deng Xiaoping, 1904–, Chin. statesman; vice-premier Chin. Communist Party 1977–.

De Niro, Robert, 1945–, U.S. actor.

Denis, Saint, 3rd c., first bishop of Paris & patron saint of France.

De Quincey, Thomas, 1785–1859, Eng. author.

Derain, André, 1880–1954, Fr. painter.

Desai, Morarji, 1896–, Indian political leader; prime minister of India 1977–79.

Descartes, René, 1596–1650, Fr. mathematician & philosopher.

de Seversky, Alexander Prokofieff, 1894–1974, Russ.-born U.S. aeronautical engineer.

De Sica, Vittorio, 1902–74, Ital. film director and actor.

Desmoulins, Camille, 1760–94, Fr. revolutionist.

De Soto, Hernando, 1499?–1542, Sp. explorer.

Des Prez, Josquin, 1450?–1521, Du. composer.

Dessalines, Jean Jacques, 1758?–1806, Haitian military leader; emperor of Haiti as Jacques I.

De Sylva, Buddy, 1895–1950, U.S. lyricist.

De Valera, Éamon, 1882–1975, U.S.-born Irish statesman; president of Ireland 1959–73.

de Valois, Dame Ninette, 1898–, Irish-born ballerina, teacher, & impressario active in England.

De Voto, Bernard Augustine, 1897–1955, U.S. author & historian.

de Vries, Hugo, 1848–1935, Du. botanist.

De Vries, Peter, 1910–, U.S. author.

Dewey, George, 1837–1917, U.S. admiral.

—John, 1859–1952, U.S. philosopher, psychologist, & educator.

—Melvil, 1851–1931, U.S. librarian.

—Thomas Edmund, 1902–71, U.S. lawyer & politician.

Dewhurst, Colleen, 1924–91, U.S. actress.

Diaghilev, Sergei Pavlovich, 1872–1929, Russ. ballet producer active in Paris.

Diamond, John Thomas (Legs), 1898–1931, U.S. criminal.

Dias, Bartholomeu, 1450?–1500, Pg. navigator.

Diaz, Porfirio, 1830–1915, Mexican general & statesman; president of Mexico 1884–1911.

Dickens, Charles, 1812–70, Eng. author.

Dickey, James, 1923–, U.S. poet & author.

Dickinson, Emily Elizabeth, 1830–86, U.S. poet.

Diderot, Denis, 1713–84, Fr. critic, encyclopedist, & philosopher.

Didion, Joan, 1934–, U.S. author.

Didrikson, Babe, 1914–56, U.S. athlete.

Diefenbacker, John G., 1895–1979, Can. statesman; prime minister 1957–63.

Diem, Ngo Dinh, 1901–63, first president of S. Vietnam 1955–63; assassinated.

Dies, Martin, 1901–72, U.S. politician.

Diesel, Rudolf, 1858–1913, Ger. mech. engineer & inventor.

Dietrich, Marlene, 1901–, Ger.-born film actress active in U.S.

Dietz, Howard, 1896–1983, U.S. lyricist & film executive.

Dillard, Harrison, 1923–, U.S. track runner.

Dillinger, John, 1903–34, U.S. criminal.

Dillon, C(larence) Douglas, 1909–78, U.S. government official.

DiMaggio, Joseph Paul (Joe), 1914–, U.S. baseball player.

Dinesen, Isak, pseud. of Baroness Karen Blixen-Finecke, 1885–1962, Dan. writer.

Diocletian, (L. Gaius Aurelius Valerius Diocletianus), 245–313, Roman emperor.

Diogenes, 412?–323? B.C., Gk. philosopher.

Dionysius the Areopagite, Saint, 1st c. A.D. Gk. mystic & theologian.

Dior, Christian, 1905–57, Fr. fashion designer.

Dioscorides, Pedanius, 1st c. A.D. Gk. physician & botanist.

Dirac, Paul Adrien Maurice, 1902–84, Eng. mathematician, physicist, & Nobel Prize winner.

Dirks, Rudolph, 1877–1968, U.S. cartoonist.

Dirksen, Everett McKinley, 1896–1969, U.S. politician.

Disney, Walt(er Elias), 1901–66, U.S. producer of animated & live films.

Disraeli, Benjamin, 1804–81, Eng. statesman & author; prime minister 1868 & 1874–80.

Di Stefano, Giuseppe, 1921–, Ital. tenor.

Dix, Dorothea Lynde, 1802–87, U.S. social reformer.

—Dorothy, pseud. of Elizabeth Meriwether Gilmer, 1870–1951, U.S. journalist.

Dixon, Jeremiah, ?–1777, Eng. astronomer & surveyor; with Charles Mason, established the Mason-Dixon line.

Djilas, Milovan, 1911–, Yugoslav author.

Dobrynin, Anatoly, 1919–, Soviet diplomat.

Dobzhansky, Theodosius, 1900–75, Russ.-born U.S. geneticist.

Doctorow, E(dgar) L(aurence), 1931–, U.S. author.

Dodd, Frank Howard, 1844–1916, U.S. publisher.

Dodgson, Charles Lutwidge, See CARROLL, LEWIS.

Dohnányi, Ernst von, 1877–1960, Hung. composer.

Dolin, Sir Anton, 1904–83, Eng. ballet dancer & choreographer.

Dollfuss, Engelbert, 1892–1934, Austrian statesman; chancellor of Austria 1932–34; assassinated.

Dolly, Jenny, 1892–1941, & her sister **Rosie,** 1892–1970, Hung.-born vaudeville performers active in U.S.

Domenichino II, b. Domenico Zampieri, 1581–1641, Ital. painter.

Domingo, Placido, 1941–, Sp. tenor.

Dominguín, Luis Miguel, 1926–, Sp. bullfighter.

Dominic, Saint, 1170–1221, Sp. friar; founded the Dominican Order.

Donahue, Phil, 1935–, U.S. TV personality.

Donat, Robert, 1905–59, Eng. actor.

Donatello, b. Donato di Niccolò di Betto Bardi, 1386–1466, Ital. sculptor.

Donen, Stanley, 1924–, U.S. film director & producer.

Dönitz, Karl, 1891–1980, Ger. admiral.

Donizetti, Gaetano, 1797–1848, Ital. composer.

Donne, John, 1573?–1631, Eng. poet & clergyman.

Donovan, William Joseph (Wild Bill), 1883–1959, U.S. lawyer & military intelligence officer.

Dooley, Thomas Anthony, 1927–61, U.S. physician in Indochina.

Doolittle, Hilda (H.D.), 1886–1961, U.S. poet. active in Europe.

—James Harold, 1896–, U.S. aviator & Air Force general.

Doppler, Christian Johann, 1803–53, Austrian physicist & mathematician.

Dorati, Antal, 1906–, Hung.-born U.S. conductor.

Doré, (Paul) Gustave, 1832–83, Fr. painter & engraver.

Dors, Diana, 1931–84, Brit. actress.

Doria, Andrea, 1466–1560, Ital. admiral & statesman.

Dorsey, James Francis (Jimmy), 1904–57, U.S. clarinetist & band leader.

—Thomas Francis (Tommy), 1905–56, U.S. trombonist & band leader; brother of prec.

Dos Passos, John, 1896–1970, U.S. author.

Dostoevski Fyodor Mikhailovich, 1821–81, Russ. author.

Dou, Gerard, 1613–75, Du. painter.

Doubleday, Abner, 1819–93, U.S. military officer; reputed inventor of baseball.

—Frank Nelson, 1862–1934, U.S. publisher.

Douglas, Aaron, 1900–79, U.S. painter.
—**Helen Gahagan,** 1900–80, U.S. actress, author, & politician.
—**Kirk,** 1918–, U.S. actor.
—**Melvyn,** 1901–81, U.S. actor; husband of Helen Gahagan.
—**Michael,** 1944–, U.S. actor, director, & producer; son of Kirk.
—**Norman,** 1868–1952, Eng. author.
—**Stephen Arnold,** 1813–61, U.S. senator; opposed Lincoln in campaign debates.
—**William Orville,** 1898–1980, U.S. jurist; justice of the U.S. Supreme Court 1939–75.
Douglass, Frederick, 1817–95, U.S. black leader & statesman.
Dove, Arthur Garfield, 1880–1946, U.S. painter.
Dow, Charles Henry, 1851–1902, U.S. economist & editor.
—**Herbert H.,** 1866–1930, Can.-born U.S. industrialist.
Dowland, John, 1563–1626, Eng. musician & composer.
Downes, (Edwin) Olin, 1886–1955, U.S. music critic.
Downing, Andrew Jackson, 1815–52, U.S. architect & landscape designer.
Doxiadis, Constantinos Apostolos, 1913–75, Gk. architect & urban planner.
Doyle, Sir Arthur Conan, 1859–1930, Eng. physician & author; creator of Sherlock Holmes.
D'Oyly Carte, Richard, 1844–1901, Eng. operatic producer.
Drabble, Margaret, 1939–, Eng. author.
Draco, 7th c. B.C. Gk. lawgiver & statesman.
Drake, Alfred, 1914–, U.S. singer & actor.
—**Edwin Laurentine,** 1819–80, U.S. military officer & petroleum entrepreneur.
—**Sir Francis,** 1540–96, Eng. admiral & circumnavigator of the globe.
Draper, Henry, 1837–82, U.S. astronomer.
—**Ruth,** 1884–1956, U.S. monologuist.
Drayton, Michael, 1563–1631, Eng. poet.
Dreiser, Theodore, 1871–1945, U.S. author.
Dreisner, Samuel P., 1933–, U.S. chemist.
Dressler, Marie, 1869–1934, U.S. actress & comedienne.
Drew, John, 1826–62, Irish-born U.S. actor & his son **John,** 1853–1927, U.S. actor.
Dreyer, Carl Theodore, 1889–1968, Dan. film director.
Dreyfus, Alfred, 1859–1935, Fr. army officer.
Dreyfuss, Richard, 1947–, U.S. actor.
Driesch, Hans Adolf Eduard, 1867–1941, Ger. biologist & philosopher.
Drury, Allen, 1918–, U.S. author.
Dryden, John, 1631–1700, Eng. poet & playwright.
Duarte, José Napoleón, 1926–90, El Salvadoran politician; president 1984–89.
du Barry, Comtesse Marie Jeanne, 1746–93, mistress of Louis XV.
Dubček, Alexander, 1921–, Czech politician; first secretary of the communist party of Czechoslovakia 1968–69.
Dubin, Al, 1891–1945, U.S. lyricist.
Dubinsky, David, 1892–1982, Russ.-born U.S. labor leader.
Dubois, William Edward Burghardt, 1868–1963, U.S. historian, black leader, & educator.
Du Bois-Reymond, Emil, 1818–96, Ger. physiologist.
Dubos, René, 1906–82, Fr. biologist.
Dubuffet, Jean, 1901–85, Fr. painter & sculptor.
Duccio di Buoninsegna, 1255?–1319, Ital. painter.
Duchamp, Marcel, 1887–1968, Fr. painter.
Duchin, Edwin Frank (Eddy), 1909–51, U.S. pianist & band leader.
Dufy, Raoul, 1877–1953, Fr. painter.
Dujardin, Felix, 1801–60, Fr. biologist.
Dukas, Paul, 1865–1935, Fr. composer.
Duke, Benjamin Newton, 1855–1929, & his brother **James Buchanan Duke,** 1856–1925, U.S. tobacco industrialists.
—**Vernon,** 1903–69, Russ.-born U.S. composer.
Dulles, Allen Welsh, 1893–1969, U.S. government official.
—**John Foster,** 1888–1959, U.S. statesman; secretary of state 1953–59; brother of prec.
Dumas, Alexandre (père), 1802–70, Fr. author & playwright.
—**Alexandre (fils),** 1824–95, Fr. author & playwright; son of prec.

Du Maurier, Daphne, 1907–89, Eng. author.
—**George Louis,** 1834–96, Fr.-born Eng. author & illustrator; grandfather of prec.
Dunant, Jean Henri, 1828–1910, Swiss philanthropist & founder of the Red Cross.
Dunbar, Paul Laurence, 1872–1906, U.S. poet.
Duncan, David Douglas, 1916–, U.S. photographer & author.
—**Isadora,** 1878–1927, U.S. dancer.
Dunham, Katherine, 1910–, U.S. dancer & choreographer.
Dunne, Irene, 1904–90, U.S. actress.
—**John Gregory,** 1932–, U.S. author & screenwriter.
Dunois, Comte Jean de, 1403?–68, Fr. general & companion of Joan of Arc; called the **Bastard of Orleans.**
Dunsany, Edward John Plunkett, Lord, 1878–1957, Irish poet & playwright.
Duns Scotus, Johannes, 1265–1308, Scot. monk & philosopher.
du Pont de Nemours, Pierre, 1739–1817, Fr.-born U.S. economist.
—**Eleuthère Irénée,** 1771–1834, Fr.-born U.S. industrialist; son of prec.
Du Pré, Jacqueline, 1945–87, Eng. cellist.
Dupré, Marcel, 1886–1971, Fr. organist.
Durand, Asher Brown, 1796–1886, U.S. painter.
Durant, William, 1861–1947, U.S. industrialist.
—**Will(iam James),** 1885–1981, U.S. historian & his wife **Ariel,** b. Ida Kaufman, 1898–1981, Russ.-born U.S. historian.
Durante, James Francis (Jimmy), 1893–1980, U.S. comedian & actor.
Duras, Marguerite, 1914–, Fr. author.
Durbin, Deanna, 1921–, Can.-born U.S. actress.
Dürer, Albrecht, 1471–1528, Ger. painter & engraver.
Durkheim, Émile, 1858–1917, Fr. sociologist.
Durocher, Leo Ernest, 1906–, U.S. baseball player & manager.
Durrell, Gerald Malcolm, 1925–, Eng. zoologist & author.
—**Lawrence George,** 1912–90, Indian-born Eng. author & poet; brother of prec.
Dürrenmatt, Friedrich, 1921–90, Swiss playwright.
du Sable, Jean Baptiste Point, 1745–1818, U.S. pioneer trader & first settler of Chicago.
Duse, Eleanora, 1859–1924, Ital. actress.
Dutrochet, René, 1776–1847, Fr. biologist.
Dutton, Edward, 1831–1923, U.S. publisher.
Duvalier, François (Papa Doc), 1907–71, Haitian president 1957–71.
—**Jean-Claude,** 1951–, president of Haiti 1971–86; son of prec.
Duvall, Robert, 1931–, U.S. actor.
Duvivier, Julien, 1896–1967, Fr. film director.
Dvořák, Antonin, 1841–1904, Czech composer.
Dylan, Bob, 1941–, U.S. composer & singer.

Eads, James Buchanan, 1820–87, U.S. inventor.
Eagels, Joanne, 1894–1929, U.S. actress.
Eakins, Thomas, 1844–1916, U.S. painter & sculptor.
Eames, Charles, 1907–78, U.S. designer & film director.
Earhart, Amelia, 1898–1937, U.S. aviator.
Early, Jubal Anderson, 1816–94, U.S. Confederate general.
Earp, Wyatt, 1848–1929, U.S. frontier marshal.
Eastman, George, 1854–1932, U.S. inventor & industrialist.
—**Max Forrester,** 1883–1969, U.S. editor & author.
Eastwood, Clint, 1930–, U.S. actor & director.
Eaton, Cyrus Stephen, 1883–1979, U.S. financier.
Eban, Abba, 1915–, South African-born Israeli diplomat.
Ebbinghaus, Hermann, 1850–1909, Ger. experimental psychologist.
Eberhart, Richard, 1904–, U.S. poet.
Echeverría Alvarez, Luis, 1922–, president of Mexico 1970–76.
Eck, Johann, 1486–1543, Ger. theologian.
Eckhart, Johannes, 1260?–1327?, Ger. theologian & mystic: known as **Meister Eckhart.**
Eddington, Sir Arthur Stanley, 1882–1944, Eng. astronomer & astrophysicist.
Eddy, Mary Baker, 1821–1910, U.S. religious leader; founder of Christian Science.

—**Nelson,** 1901–67, singer & actor.
Edelman, Gerald Maurice, 1929–, U.S. biochemist.
Eden, Sir (Robert) Anthony, 1897–1977, Eng. statesman; prime minister 1955–57.
Ederle, Gertrude, 1906–, U.S. swimmer.
Edison, Thomas Alva, 1847–1931, U.S. inventor.
Edward, 1004?–66, king of England 1042–66: called **the Confessor.**
— 1330–76, Eng. warrior: known as **the Black Prince.**
—**VII,** 1841–1910, king of Great Britain 1901–10.
—**VIII,** 1894–1972, king of Great Britain 1936; abdicated; known as **Duke of Windsor** after abdication.
Edwards, Blake, 1922–, U.S. film director.
—**Jonathan,** 1703–58, Amer. theologian.
—**Ralph,** 1913–, U.S. TV personality.
Egbert, 775?–839, first king of all England 829–839.
Egk, Werner, 1901–83, Ger. composer.
Eglevsky, André, 1917–77, Russ.-born U.S. ballet dancer.
Ehrenberg, Christian G., 1795–1876, Ger. naturalist.
Ehrenburg, Ilya Grigorievich, 1891–1967, Soviet author.
Ehrlich, Paul, 1854–1915, Ger. bacteriologist.
—**Paul Ralph,** 1932–, U.S. biologist & author.
Eichmann, Adolf, 1906–62, Ger. Nazi official.
Eiffel, (Alexandre) Gustave, 1832–1923, Fr. engineer.
Eijkman, Christian, 1858–1930, Du. physician.
Einstein, Albert, 1879–1955, Ger.-born U.S. physicist.
—**Alfred,** 1880–1952, Ger.-born U.S. music critic.
Einthoven, Willem, 1860–1927, Du. physiologist.
Eiseley, Loren Corey, 1907–77, U.S. anthropologist & author.
Eisenhower, Dwight David, 1890–1969, U.S. general & 34th president 1953–61.
Eisenstaedt, Alfred, 1898–, Ger.-born photographer & author active in U.S.
Eisenstein, Sergei Mikhailovich, 1890–1948, Russ.-born Soviet film director & producer.
El Cid, b. Rodrigo Díaz de Bivar, 1044?–99, Sp. soldier & epic hero.
Eleanor of Aquitaine, 1122–1204, queen of France as the wife of Louis VII & queen of England as the wife of Henry II.
Elgar, Sir Edward, 1857–1934, Eng. composer.
Eliot, Charles William, 1834–1926, U.S. educator.
—**George,** pseud. of Mary Ann Evans, 1819–80, Eng. author.
—**John,** 1604–90, Amer. clergyman & missionary to Indians.
—**T(homas) S(tearns),** 1888–1965, U.S.-born Brit. poet, playwright, & critic.
Elizabeth I, 1533–1603, queen of England 1558–1603.
—**II,** 1926–, queen of Great Britain 1952–.
—**Angela Marguerite Bowes-Lyon,** 1900–86, queen of George VI of Great Britain & mother of Elizabeth II.
Elkin, Stanley, 1930–, U.S. author.
Ellington, Edward Kennedy (Duke), 1899–1974, U.S. jazz composer, pianist, & band leader.
Elliott, Maxine, 1871–1940, U.S. actress.
—**Robert (Bob),** 1923–, U.S. comedian.
Ellis, (Henry) Havelock, 1859–1939, Eng. psychologist & author.
—**Perry Edwin,** 1940–86, U.S. fashion designer.
Ellison, Ralph, 1914–, U.S. author.
Ellsworth, Lincoln, 1880–1951, U.S. polar explorer.
—**Oliver,** 1745–1807, U.S. jurist; chief justice of U.S. Supreme Court 1796–1800.
Elman, Mischa, 1891–1967, Russ.-born U.S. violinist.
Elssler, Fanny, 1810–84, Austrian dancer.
Elyot, Sir Thomas, 1490?–1546, Eng. scholar & diplomat.
Elzevir A family of Dutch printers including **Louis,** 1540?–1617; his son, **Bonaventure,** 1583–1652; and his grandson **Abraham,** 1592?–1652.
Emerson, Ralph Waldo, 1803–82, U.S. author, poet, & philosopher.
Emmet, Robert, 1778–1803, Irish nationalist & revolutionary.
Emmett, Daniel Decatur, 1815–1904, U.S. songwriter.
Endecott, John, 1589?–1665, Eng.-born Amer. colonist; first governor of Massachusetts Bay colony.
Empedocles, 495?–435? B.C., Gk. philosopher.
Enders, John Franklin, 1897–1985, U.S. bacteriologist; Nobel Prize winner.

Enesco, Georges, 1881–1955, Romanian composer.
Engels, Friedrich, 1820–95, Ger. socialist & author.
Ensor, James, 1860–1949, Belg. painter & printmaker.
Ephron, Nora, 1941–, U.S. author.
Epictetus, A.D. 50?–138?, Gk. philosopher.
Epicurus, 341?–270 B.C., Gk. philosopher.
Epstein, Sir Jacob, 1880–1959, U.S.-born Brit. sculptor.
Erasistratus, 304–250 B.C., Gk. physician & anatomist.
Erasmus, Desiderius, b. Gerhard Gerhards, 1466?–1536, Du. scholar & theologian.
Eratosthenes, 3rd c. B.C. Gk. mathematician & astronomer.
Erhard, Ludwig, 1897–1977, chancellor of W. Germany 1963–66.
Erickson, Arthur Charles, 1924–, Can. architect.
Ericsson, John, 1803–89, Swed.-born U.S. engineer & inventor.
—**Leif,** 11th c. Norw. explorer; son of Eric the Red.
Eric the Red, 10th c. Norw. explorer.
Erigena, Johannes Scotus, 815?–877?, Irish philosopher & theologian
Erikson, Erik Homburger, 1902–, Ger.-born U.S. psychologist & author.
Erlander, Tage Frithiof, 1901–85, premier of Sweden 1946–69.
Erlanger, Joseph, 1874–1965, U.S. physiologist.
Ernst, Max, 1891–1976, Ger. painter active in France & U.S.
Ervin, Sam(uel) J., Jr., 1896–1985, U.S. politician.
Ervine, St. John Greer, 1883–1971, Irish Playwright & author.
Erving, Julius, 1950–, U.S. basketball player: called **Doctor J.**
Escoffier, Auguste, 1847–1935, Fr. chef & author.
Eshkol, Levi, 1895–1969, Russ.-born Israeli statesman; prime minister of Israel 1963–69.
Esposito, Philip Anthony, 1942–, Can.-born hockey player active in U.S.
Espriu, Salvador, 1913–85, Span. poet.
Essex, Robert Devereux, 2nd Earl of, 1566–1601, Eng. courtier & soldier; beheaded.
Esterhazy, Marie Charles Ferdinand Walsin, 1847–1923, Fr. army officer.
Esterházy, Miklós Jósef, 1714–90, Hung. prince & art patron.
Ethelred II, 968?–1016, king of England 978–1016: called **the Unready.**
Etherege, Sir George, 1634?–91, Eng. playwright.
Euclid, c. 300 B.C., Gk. mathematician.
Eugénie (Marie de Montijo de Guzmán), 1826–1920, Sp.-born empress of France as wife of Napoleon III.
Euler, Leonhard, 1707–83, Swiss mathematician.
Euripides, 479?–406? B.C., Gk. playwright.
Eustachio, Bartolommeo, 1524?–74, Ital. anatomist.
Evans, Sir Arthur John, 1851–1941, Eng. archaeologist.
—**Bergen,** 1904–78, U.S. author & educator.
—**Dame Edith,** 1888–1976, Eng. actress.
—**Gil,** 1912–88, Can.-born U.S. jazz musician.
—**Maurice,** 1901–89, Eng.-born U.S. actor.
—**Rowland, Jr.,** 1921–, U.S. journalist.
—**Walker,** 1903–75, U.S. photographer.
—**William J. (Bill),** 1929–80, U.S. jazz pianist & composer.
Evelyn, John, 1620–1706, Eng. diarist.
Everett, Edward, 1794–1865, U.S. clergyman, orator, & statesman.
Evers, (James) Charles, 1922–, U.S. politician & civil rights activist.
—**Medgar Wiley,** 1925–63, U.S. civil rights activist; murdered; brother of prec.
Evert-Lloyd, Chris(tine Marie), 1954–, U.S. tennis player.
Ewing, William Maurice, 1906–74, U.S. geologist.
Eysenck, Hans, 1916–, Eng. psychologist.

Faber, John Eberhard, 1822–79, Ger.-born U.S. industrialist.
Fabergé, Peter Carl, 1846–1920, Russ. goldsmith & jeweler.
Fabiola, 1928–, Sp.-born queen of King Baudouin of Belgium.
Fabius (Quintus Fabius Maximus Verrucosus Cunctator), ?–203 B.C., Roman general.
Fabre, Jean Henri, 1823–1915, Fr. entomologist.

Fabricius ab Aquapendente, Hieronymus, 1537–1619, Ital. surgeon & anatomist.

Fadiman, Clifton, 1904–, U.S. author & editor.

Fahd, 1923–, Saudi Arabian king & prime minister 1982–.

Fahrenheit, Gabriel Daniel, 1686–1736, Ger. physicist.

Fairbanks, Charles Warren, 1852–1918, U.S. statesman; U.S. vice president 1905–09.

—**Douglas,** 1883–1939, U.S. actor.

—**Douglas, Jr.,** 1909–, U.S. actor; son of prec.

Faisal ibn Abdul Aziz, 1904?–75, king of Saudi Arabia 1964–75; assassinated.

Falla, Manuel de, 1876–1946, Sp. composer.

Fälldin, Thorbjörn, 1926–, Swed. politician; prime minister of Sweden 1976–1978 & 1979–1982.

Fallopius, Gabriel, 1523–62, Ital. anatomist.

Faneuil, Peter, 1700–43, Amer. merchant.

Fanfani, Amintore, 1908–, premier of Italy 1958–59 & 1960–63.

Faraday, Michael, 1791–1867, Eng. physicist.

Fargo, William George, 1818–81, U.S. transportation entrepreneur.

Farley, James Aloysius, 1888–1976, U.S. politician.

Farmer, Fannie Merritt, 1857–1915, U.S. culinary expert, teacher, & author.

—**James Leonard,** 1920–, U.S. black civil rights leader.

Farouk I, 1920–65, king of Egypt 1936–52.

Farquhar, George, 1678–1707, Eng. playwright.

Farragut, David Glasgow, 1801–70, U.S. admiral.

Ferrar, Geraldine, 1882–1967, U.S. soprano.

Farrell, Eileen, 1920–, U.S. soprano.

—**James Thomas,** 1904–79, U.S. author.

—**Suzanne,** 1945–, U.S. ballerina.

Fassbinder, Rainer Werner, 1946–82, Ger. film & stage director.

Fast, Howard, 1914–, U.S. author.

Fatima, 606?–632?, daughter of Mohammed.

Fauchard, Pierre, 1678–1761, Fr. dentist; founder of modern dentistry.

Faulkner, William, 1897–1962, U.S. author.

Fauré, Gabriel Urbain, 1845–1924, Fr. composer.

Fawkes, Guy, 1570–1606, Eng. conspirator; participant in the Gunpowder Plot.

Fay, Frank, 1897–1961, U.S. actor.

Faye, Alice, 1915–, U.S. actress.

Febres-Cordero, León, 1931–, president of Ecuador 1984–88.

Feiffer, Jules, 1929–, U.S. cartoonist & author.

Feininger, Andreas, 1906–, Fr.-born U.S. photographer.

—**Lyonel Charles Adrian,** 1871–1956, U.S. painter; father of prec.

Feller, Robert William Andrew (Bob), 1918–, U.S. baseball player.

Fellini, Federico, 1920–, Ital. film director.

Fénelon, François de Salignac de la Mothe-, 1651–1715, Fr. prelate & author.

Fenollosa, Ernest Francisco, 1853–1908, U.S. oriental scholar & author.

Ferber, Edna, 1885–1968, U.S. author.

Ferdinand V of Castile (and II of Aragon), 1452–1516, first king of united Spain 1474–1516; ruled jointly with his wife Isabella.

Ferencsik, Janos, 1907–84, Czech conductor.

Ferlinghetti, Lawrence, 1919–, U.S. poet.

Fermat, Pierre de, 1601–65, Fr. mathematician.

Fermi, Enrico, 1901–54, Ital. physicist active in U.S.

Fernandel, b.Fernand Contandin, 1903–71, Fr. actor.

Ferraro, Geraldine Anne, 1935–, U.S. statesman.

Ferrier, Sir David, 1843–1928, Scot. neurologist.

—**Kathleen,** 1912–53, Eng. contralto.

Fessenden, Reginald Aubrey, 1866–1932, Can.-born U.S. physicist & inventor.

Feuerbach, Ludwig Andreas, 1804–72, Ger. philosopher.

Feuermann, Emanuel, 1902–42, Pol.-born cellist active in U.S.

Feydeau, Georges, 1862–1921, Fr. playwright.

Feynman, Richard Phillips, 1918–88, U.S. physicist; Nobel Prize winner.

Fichte, Johann Gottlieb, 1762–1814, Ger. philosopher.

Fiedler, Arthur, 1894–1979, U.S. conductor.

—**Leslie,** 1917–, U.S. author & critic.

Field, Cyrus West, 1819–92, U.S. industrialist.

—**Eugene,** 1850–95, U.S. poet & journalist.

—**Marshall,** 1834–1906, U.S. businessman.

Fielding, Henry, 1707–54, Eng. author.

Fields, Dorothy, 1904–74, U.S. lyricist.

—**Gracie,** 1898–1979, Eng. singer & actress.

—**W.C.,** 1879–1946, U.S. film comedian.

Filene, Edward Albert, 1860–1937, U.S. businessman & social reformer.

Fillmore, Millard, 1800–74, 13th U.S. president 1850–53.

Fink, Mike, 1770?–1823, U.S. frontiersman.

Finlay, Carlos Juan, 1833–1915, Cuban physician.

Finney, Albert, 1936–, Eng. actor.

Firbank, Ronald, 1886–1926, Eng. author.

Firdausi, pseud. of Abdul Qasim Mansur, 940?–1020?, Persian epic poet.

Firestone, Harvey Samuel, 1868–1938, U.S. industrialist.

Fischer, Robert James (Bobby), 1943–, U.S. chess master.

Fischer-Dieskau, Dietrich, 1925–, Ger. baritone.

Fish, Hamilton, 1808–93, U.S. statesman.

Fishbein, Morris, 1889–1976, U.S. physician, author, & editor.

Fisher, Bud, 1884–1954, U.S. cartoonist.

—**Dorothy Canfield,** 1879–1958, U.S. author.

—**Fred,** 1875–1942, U.S. songwriter.

—**M(ary) F(rances) K(ennedy),** 1908–, U.S. author.

Fiske, John, 1842–1901, U.S. philosopher.

—**Minnie Maddern,** 1865–1932, U.S. actress.

Fitch, John, 1743–98, Amer. inventor.

—**(William) Clyde,** 1865–1909, U.S. playwright.

Fitzgerald, Ella, 1918–, U.S. jazz singer.

—**F(rancis) Scott (Key),** 1896–1940, U.S. author.

—**George F.,** 1851–1901, Irish physicist.

—**Geraldine,** 1914–, Irish-born U.S. actress.

FitzGerald, Edward, 1809–83, Eng. poet & translator.

Flagg, Ernest, 1857–1947, U.S. architect.

—**James Montgomery,** 1877–1960, U.S. painter, illustrator, & author.

Flagler, Henry Morrison, 1830–1913, U.S. business executive.

Flagstad, Kirsten, 1895–1962, Norw. soprano active in U.S.

Flaherty, Robert Joseph, 1884–1951, U.S. film director.

Flammarion, Camille, 1842–1925, Fr. astronomer & author.

Flaubert, Gustave, 1821–80, Fr. author.

Fleming, Sir Alexander, 1881–1955, Eng. bacteriologist.

—**Ian Lancaster,** 1908–64, Eng. author.

—**Victor,** 1883–1949, U.S. film director.

Flemming, Walther, 1843–1905, Ger. anatomist.

Fletcher, John, 1579–1625, Eng. playwright.

Flory, Paul John, 1910–85, U.S. physical chemist; Nobel Prize winner.

Flotow, Friedrich von, 1812–83, Ger. composer.

Flourens, Pierre Marie Jean, 1794–1867, Fr. anatomist & physiologist.

Flynn, Errol, 1909–59, Tasmanian-born actor active in U.S.

Foch, Ferdinand, 1851–1929, Fr. general; marshal of France.

Fodor, Eugene, 1940–, U.S. violinist.

Fokine, Michel, 1880–1942, Russ.-born U.S. choreographer.

Fokker, Anthony Herman Gerard, 1890–1939, Du.-born U.S. aircraft designer.

Folger, Henry Clay, 1857–1930, U.S. bibliophile.

Fonda, Henry, 1905–82, U.S. actor.

—**Jane,** 1937–, U.S. actress & political activist; daughter of prec.

—**Peter,** 1939–, U.S. actor; son of Henry.

Fontanne, Lynn, 1887–1983, Eng.-born U.S. actress.

Fonteyn, Dame Margot, 1919–, Eng. ballerina.

Foot, Michael, 1913–, Brit. politician.

Forbes, Esther, 1891–1967, U.S. author & historian.

—**Malcolm,** 1919–90, U.S. publisher & sportsman.

Ford, Ford Madox, 1873–1939, Eng. author.

—**Gerald Rudolph,** 1913–, 38th U.S. president 1974–77.

—**Harrison,** 1942–, U.S. actor.

—**Henry,** 1863–1947, U.S. auto manufacturer.

—**John,** 1586?–1638?, Eng. playwright.

—**John,** 1895–1973, U.S. film director.
Foreman, George, 1949–, U.S. boxer.
Forester, C(ecil) S(cott), 1899–1966, Eng. author active in U.S.
Forman, Milos, 1932–, Czech film director active in U.S.
Forrest, Edwin, 1806–72, U.S. actor.
Forrestal, James Vincent, 1892–1949, U.S. banker & government official.
Forssman, Werner, 1904–79, Ger. surgeon; Nobel Prize winner.
Forster, E(dward) M(organ), 1879–1970, Eng. author.
Fortas, Abe, 1910–82, U.S. jurist; justice of U.S. Supreme Court 1965–69.
Fosdick, Harry Emerson, 1878–1969, U.S. clergyman & author.
Foss, Lukas, 1922–, Ger.-born U.S. composer & conductor.
Fosse, Bob (Robert Louis), 1927–87, U.S. choreographer and director.
Foster, Hal, 1892–1982, U.S. cartoonist.
—**John Stuart, Jr.,** 1922–, U.S. physicist.
Foster, Stephen Collins, 1826–64, U.S. composer.
Foucault, Jean Bernard Leon, 1819–68, Fr. physicist.
—**Michel,** 1926–84, Fr. philospher, historian, & author.
Fourdrinier, Henry, 1766–1854, & his brother **Sealy,** ?–1847, Eng. inventors & paper manufacturers.
Fourier, Charles, 1772–1837, Fr. utopian socialist.
—**François Marie Charles,** 1772–1837, Fr. socialist.
—**Jean Baptiste Joseph,** 1768–1830, Fr. mathematician & physicist.
Fowler, Henry Watson, 1858–1933, Eng. lexicographer.
Fox, George, 1624–91, Eng. preacher; founded the Society of Friends.
Foxx, James Emery (Jimmy), 1907–67, U.S. baseball player.
Foy, Eddie, 1856–1928, U.S. vaudeville performer.
Foyt, A(nthony) J(oseph), Jr., 1935–, U.S. auto racer.
Fra Angelico, b. Giovanni da Fiesole, 1400?–1455, Ital. painter.
Fracastoro, Girolamo, 1483–1553, Ital. physician.
Fragonard, Jean Honoré, 1732–1806, Fr. painter.
France, Anatole, pseud. of Jacques Anatole Thibault, 1844–1924, Fr. author.
Francesca da Rimini, ?–1285?, Ital. noblewoman; murdered by her husband.
Francescatti, Zino, 1902–91, Fr. violinist.
Francis I, 1494–1547, king of France 1515–47.
Francis of Assisi, Saint, 1182–1226, Ital. preacher; founder of Franciscan Order.
Francis, Arlene, 1908–, U.S. actress & TV personality.
Franck, César Auguste, 1822–90, Belg.-born Fr. composer.
—**James,** 1882–1964, Ger.-born U.S. physicist; Nobel Prize winner.
Franco, Francisco, 1892–1975, Sp. general; dictator of Spain 1939–75.
Frank, Anne, 1929–45, Ger.-born Du. diarist.
Frankfurter, Felix, 1882–1965, Austrian-born U.S. jurist; justice of U.S. Supreme Court 1939–62.
Franklin, Aretha, 1942–, U.S. singer.
—**Benjamin,** 1706–90, Amer. patriot, scientist, statesman, & diplomat.
—**Frederic,** 1914–, Eng.-born dancer & ballet company director active in U.S.
Franz Ferdinand, 1863–1914, archduke of Austria; assassinated.
Franz Josef I, 1830–1916, emperor of Austria 1848–1916.
Fraser, Dawn, 1939–, Austral. swimmer.
—**(John) Malcolm,** 1930–, prime minister of Australia 1975–83.
—**Neale,** 1933–, Austral. tennis player.
Fraunhofer, Joseph von, 1787–1826, Ger. optician & physicist.
Frazer, Sir James George, 1854–1941, Scot. anthropologist.
Frazier, Joe, 1944–, U.S. boxer.
—**Walt(er),** 1945–, U.S. basketball player.
Frederick I, 1121–90, king of Germany & Holy Roman emperor 1152–90: called **Barbarossa.**
Frederick II, 1194–1250, Holy Roman emperor, 1215–50.

Frederick II, 1712–86, king of Prussia 1740–86: called **the Great.**
Frederick IX, 1899–1972, king of Denmark 1947–72.
Frederick William, 1620–88, elector of Brandenburg: called **the Great Elector.**
Freed, Arthur, 1894–1973, U.S. film producer.
Frelinghuysen, Frederick Theodore, 1817–85, U.S. statesman.
Frémont, John Charles, 1813–90, U.S. military officer & explorer.
French, Daniel Chester, 1850–1931, U.S. sculptor.
Freneau, Philip Morin, 1752–1832, U.S. poet.
Frescobaldi, Girolamo, 1583–1643, Ital. composer.
Fresnel, Augustin Jean, 1788–1827, Fr. physicist.
Freud, Anna, 1895–82, Austrian neurologist; founder of modern theory of psychoanalysis.
—**Sigmund** 1856–1939, Austrian neurologist; founder of modern theory of psychoanalysis; father of prec.
Frick, Henry Clay, 1849–1919, U.S. industrialist & philanthropist.
Friedan, Betty, 1921–, U.S. author & feminist.
Friedman, Milton, 1912–, U.S. economist.
Friendly, Fred W., 1915–, U.S. radio & TV executive.
Fries, Elias Magnus, 1794–1878, Swed. botanist.
Friml, Rudolf, 1879–1972, Czech-born U.S. composer.
Frisch, Frank, 1898–1973, U.S. baseball player.
—**Karl von,** 1886–1982, Austrian zoologist.
Frobisher, Sir Martin, 1535?–94, Eng. navigator.
Froebel, Friedrich Wilhelm August, 1782–1852, Ger. educator.
Frohman, Charles, 1860–1915, U.S. theatrical manager.
Froissart, Jean, 1333?–1400, Fr. chronicler.
Fromm, Erich, 1900–80, Ger.-born U.S. psychoanalyst.
Frondizi, Arturo, 1908–, Argentine politician; president of Argentina 1958–62.
Frontenac, Louis de Buade, Comte de, 1620–98, Fr. general & colonial administrator in N. America.
Frost, David, 1939–, Eng. TV personality active in U.S.
—**Robert Lee,** 1874–1963, U.S. poet.
Fry, Christopher, 1907–, Eng. playwright.
—**Roger Eliot,** 1866–1934, Eng. painter & art critic.
Fuchs, Klaus Emil Julius, 1912–88, Ger.-born Eng. spy in U.S.
Fuentes, Carlos, 1928–, Mexican author.
Fugger, Jacob, 1459–1525, Ger. merchant & banker.
Fulbright, J(ames) William, 1905–, U.S. politician.
Fuller, Alfred Carl, 1885–1973, Can.-born U.S. business executive.
—**R. Buckminster,** 1895–1983, U.S. architect, designer, & author.
—**Charles,** 1939–, U.S. playwright.
—**(Sarah) Margaret,** 1810–50, U.S. social reformer.
Fulton, Robert, 1765–1815, U.S. inventor.
Funk, Isaac Kauffman, 1839–1912, U.S. publisher & lexicographer.
Furness, Betty, 1916–, U.S. actress & TV personality.
Furnivall, Frederick James, 1825–1910, Eng. philologist.
Furtwängler, Wilhelm, 1886–1954, Ger. conductor.

Gabin, Jean, 1904–76, Fr. actor.
Gable, Clark, 1901–60, U.S. actor.
Gabo, Naum, 1890–1977, Russ.-born U.S. sculptor, painter, designer, & architect.
Gabor, Dennis, 1900–79, Hung.-born Brit. engineer; Nobel Prize winner.
Gaddis, William, 1922–, U.S. author.
Gadsden, James, 1788–1858, U.S. military officer & diplomat.
Gagarin, Yuri Alekseyevich, 1934–68, Soviet astronaut; first to orbit the earth.
Gage, Thomas, 1721–87, Eng. general & colonial governor of Massachusetts 1774–75.
Gainsborough, Thomas, 1727–88, Eng. painter.
Gaitskell, Hugh Todd Naylor, 1906–63, Eng. socialist leader.
Galanos, James, 1924–, U.S. fashion designer.
Galbraith, John Kenneth, 1908–, U.S. economist, diplomat, & author.

Gale, Zona, 1874–1938, U.S. author.

Galen, Claudius, A.D. 130?–200?, Gk. physician & writer.

Galileo Galilei, 1564–1642, Ital. astronomer, mathematician, & physicist.

Gallatin, (Abraham Alfonse) Albert, 1761–1849, Swiss-born U.S. financier & statesman.

Gallaudet, Thomas Hopkins, 1787–1851, U.S. educator.

Galli-Curci, Amelita, 1889–1963, Ital.-born U.S. soprano.

Gallup, George Horace, 1901–84, U.S. public opinion statistician.

Galsworthy, John, 1867–1933, Eng. author & playwright; Nobel Prize winner.

Galton, Sir Francis, 1822–1911, Eng. scientist.

Galvani, Luigi, 1737–98, Ital. physiologist.

Galway, James, 1939–, Brit. flutist.

Gambetta, Leon, 1838–82, Fr. statesman.

Gamio, Manuel, 1883–1960, Mexican anthropologist & archaeologist.

Gamow, George, 1904–68, Russ.-born U.S. physicist & author.

Gandhi, Indira Nehru, 1917–84, Indian stateswoman; prime minister of India 1966–77 and 1980–84; assassinated; daughter of Jawaharlal Nehru.

—**Mohandas Karamchand,** 1869–1948, Hindu nationalist leader & social reformer; assassinated: known as **Mahatma Gandhi.**

—**Rajiv,** 1944–91, Indian prime minister 1984–91.

Gannett, Frank E., 1876–1957, U.S. editor & publisher.

Ganz, Rudolph, 1877–1972, Swiss-born U.S. pianist, conductor, & composer.

Garamond, Claude, ?–1561, Fr. type founder.

Garand, John Cantius, 1888–1974, Can.-born U.S. inventor.

Garbo, Greta, 1905–90, Swed.-born actress active in U.S.

Garcia Lorca, Federico, 1899–1936, Sp. poet, playwright, & author.

García Márquez, Gabriel José, 1928–, Colombian novelist; Nobel Prize winner.

Garcilaso de la Vega, 1539?–1616, Peruvian historian: called **El Inca.**

Garden, Mary, 1874–1967, Scot.-born U.S. soprano.

Gardiner, Stephen, 1483?–1535, Eng. prelate & statesman.

Gardner, Erle Stanley, 1889–1970, U.S. author.

—**Isabella Stewart,** 1840–1924, U.S. social leader & art collector.

Garfield, James Abram, 1831–81, 20th U.S. president 1881; assassinated.

—**John,** 1913–52, U.S. actor.

Garibaldi, Giuseppe, 1807–82, Ital. patriot & general.

Garland, Hamlin, 1860–1940, U.S. author.

—**Judy,** 1922–69, U.S. singer & actress.

Garner, Erroll, 1923–77, U.S. jazz pianist.

—**John Nance,** 1868–1967, U.S. politician; U.S. vice president 1933–41.

Garnett, Constance Black, 1862–1946, Eng. translator.

—**David,** 1892–1981, Eng. writer; son of prec.

Garrick, David, 1717–79, Eng. actor & author.

Garrison, William Lloyd, 1805–79, U.S. abolitionist.

Garroway, Dave, 1913–82, U.S. TV personality.

Garvey, Marcus, 1887–1940, W. Indian black leader active in the U.S.

Gary, Elbert H., 1846–1927, U.S. industrialist.

Gascoigne, George, 1525?–77, Eng. poet.

Gaskell, Walter H., 1847–1914, Eng. biologist & neurologist.

Gates, Horatio, 1728?–1806, Amer. Revolutionary general.

—**John Warne (Bet-a-Million),** 1855–1911, U.S. financier.

Gatling, Richard Jordan, 1818–1903, U.S. inventor.

Gatti-Casazza, Giulio, 1869–1940, Ital. operatic manager active in U.S.

Gaudí i Cornet, Antonio, 1852–1926, Sp. architect & furniture designer.

Gauguin, Paul, 1848–1903, Fr. painter active in Tahiti after 1891.

Gauss, Karl Friedrich, 1777–1855, Ger. mathematician.

Gautier, Théophile, 1811–72, Fr. poet & critic.

Gay, John, 1685–1732, Eng. poet & playwright.

Gay-Lussac, Joseph Louis, 1778–1850, Fr. chemist.

Gaye, Marvin, 1939–84, U.S. musician & singer.

Gaynor, Janet, 1906–84, U.S. actress.

Gedda, Nicolai, 1925–, Swed. tenor.

Geddes, Norman Bel, 1893–1958, U.S. industrial & set designer.

Geer, Will, 1902–78, U.S. actor.

Gehrig, (Henry) Lou(is), 1903–41, U.S. baseball player.

Geiger, Hans W., 1882–1945, Ger. physicist.

Geisel, Ernesto, 1908–, Brazilian military officer; president of Brazil 1974–79.

Geisel, Theodore, 1904–91, U.S. author: known as **Dr. Seuss.**

Gell-Mann, Murray, 1929–, U.S. physicist; Nobel Prize winner.

Genauer, Emily, ?–, U.S. author, editor, & critic.

Genêt, Edmond Charles Édouard, 1763–1834, Fr. diplomat; first minister of France to the U.S. 1793–94: called **Citizen Genêt.**

—**Jean,** 1910–86, Fr. playwright & author.

Genghis Khan, 1162–1227, Mongol conqueror in Europe & Asia.

Geoffrey of Monmouth, 1100?–54, Eng. ecclesiastic & chronicler.

George I, 1660–1727, king of Great Britain 1714–27.

—**II,** 1683–1760, king of Great Britain 1727–60.

—**III,** 1738–1820, king of Great Britain 1760–1820.

—**IV,** 1762–1830, king of Great Britian 1820–30.

—**V,** 1865–1936, king of Great Britain 1910–36.

—**VI,** 1895–1952, king of Great Britain 1936–52.

George, Saint, ?–303?, Christian martyr; patron saint of England.

George, Grace, 1879–1961, U.S. actress.

—**Henry,** 1839–97, U.S. economist.

—**Stefan,** 1868–1933, Ger. poet.

Gerard, John, 1545–1612, Eng. botanist & barber-surgeon.

Géricault, (Jean Louis André) Théodore, 1791–1824, Fr. painter.

Gernreich, Rudi, 1922–85, Austrian-born U.S. fashion designer.

Gernsback, Hugo, 1884–1967, Luxembourg-born U.S. inventor & publisher.

Geronimo, 1829–1909, Apache Am. Ind. chief.

Gershwin, George, 1898–1937, U.S. composer.

—**Ira,** 1896–1983, U.S. lyricist; brother of prec.

Gesell, Arnold Lucius, 1880–1961, U.S. child psychologist.

Getty, Jean Paul, 1892–1976, U.S. business executive resident in England.

Getz, Stan, 1927–91, U.S. jazz musician.

Ghiberti, Lorenzo, 1378–1455, Florentine sculptor, painter, & goldsmith.

Ghirlandaio, Domenico, 1449–94, Ital. painter.

Giacometti, Alberto, 1901–66, Swiss-born sculptor & painter active in France.

Giannini, Amadeo Peter, 1870–1949, U.S. banker.

—**Giancarlo,** 1942–, Ital. actor.

Giap, Vo Nguyen, 1912–, N. Vietnamese general & political leader.

Gibbon, Edward, 1737–94, Eng. historian.

Gibbons, Floyd, 1887–1939, U.S. journalist & war correspondent.

Gibbs, J(osiah) Willard, 1839–1903, U.S. mathematician & physicist.

Gibran, Kahlil, 1883–1931, Lebanese poet & painter active in U.S.

Gibson, Althea, 1927–, U.S. tennis player.

—**Charles Dana,** 1867–1944, U.S. illustrator.

—**William,** 1914–, U.S. playwright & author.

Gide, André, 1869–1951, Fr. author & playwright; Nobel Prize winner.

Gielgud, Sir John, 1904–, Eng. actor & stage director.

Gierek, Edward, 1913–, first secretary of the Communist Party of Poland 1970–80.

Gieseking, Walter, 1895–1956, Fr.-born Ger. pianist.

Gigli, Beniamino, 1880–1957, Ital. tenor.

Gilbert, Cass, 1859–1934, U.S. architect.

—**Sir Humphrey,** 1539?–83, Eng. navigator.

—**William,** 1540–1603, Eng. physician & physicist.

—**Sir W(illiam) S(chwenck),** 1836–1911, Eng. poet, librettist, & lyricist.

Gilels, Emil Grigoryevich, 1916–85, Soviet pianist.
Gillespie, John Birks (Dizzy), 1917–, U.S. jazz musician.
Gillette, William, 1855–1937, U.S. actor & playwright.
Ginastera, Alberto, 1916–83, Argentine composer.
Ginsberg, Allen, 1926–, U.S. poet.
Giordano, Umberto, 1867–1948, Ital. composer.
Giorgione II, b. Giorgio Barbarelli, c. 1478–1511, Venetian painter.
Giotto (di Bondone), 1266–1337, Florentine painter & architect.
Giovanni, Nikki, b. Yolande Cornelia Giovanni, Jr., 1943–, U.S. poet.
Giraudoux, Jean, 1882–1944, Fr. playwright.
Giscard d'Estaing, Valéry, 1926–, president of France 1974–81.
Gish, Dorothy, 1898?–1968, U.S. actress.
—Lillian, 1896?–, U.S. actress; sister of prec.
Givenchy, Hubert de, 1927–, Fr. fashion designer.
Glackens, William James, 1870–1938, U.S. painter & illustrator.
Gladstone, William Ewart, 1809–98, Eng. statesman; prime minister 1868–74, 1880–85, 1886, & 1892–94.
Glaser, Donald Arthur, 1926–, U.S. physicist.
Glasgow, Ellen Anderson Gholson, 1874–1945, U.S. author.
Glazunov, Aleksandr Konstantinovich, 1865–1936, Russ. composer.
Gleason, Herbert John (Jackie), 1916–87, U.S. comedian & actor.
Glenn, John Herschel, 1921–, U.S. astronaut & politician.
Glière, Reinhold, 1875–1956, Russ. composer.
Glinka, Mikhail Ivanovich, 1804–57, Russ. composer.
Gluck, Alma, 1884–1938, Rumanian-born U.S. soprano.
—Christoph Willibald, 1714–87, Ger. composer.
Gobbi, Tito, 1915–84, Ital. baritone.
Godard, Jean-Luc, 1930–, Fr. film director.
Goddard, Henry Herbert, 1866–1957, U.S. psychologist.
—Robert Hutchings, 1882–1945, U.S. physicist.
Godey, Louis Antoine, 1804–78, U.S. magazine publisher.
Godfrey of Bouillon, 1061?–1100, Fr. crusader.
Godfrey, Arthur Michael, 1903–83, U.S. radio & TV personality.
Godkin, Edward Lawrence, 1831–1902, U.S. editor & publisher.
Godolphin, Sidney, 1st Earl of Godolphin, 1645–1712, Eng. statesman.
Godowsky, Leopold, 1870–1938, Pol. pianist.
Godunov, Boris Fyodorovich, 1551?–1605, czar of Russia 1598–1605.
Godwin, Gail, 1937–, U.S. author.
—Mary Wollstonecraft, 1759–97, Eng. feminist & author.
Goebbels, Paul Joseph, 1897–1945, Ger. Nazi propagandist.
Goering, Hermann Wilhelm, 1893–1946, Ger. Nazi politician.
Goes, Hugo van der, 1440?–82, Du. painter.
Goethals, George Washington, 1858–1928, U.S. military officer & engineer.
Goethe, Johann Wolfgang von, 1749–1832, Ger. poet, playwright, & statesman.
Gofman, John William, 1918–, U.S. physician & biophysicist.
Gogol, Nikolai Vasilevich, 1809–52, Russ. author.
Goldberg, Arthur Joseph, 1908–90, U.S. lawyer, jurist, & diplomat; U.S. Supreme Court justice 1962–65.
—Reuben Lucius (Rube), 1883–1970, U.S. cartoonist.
Golden, Harry Lewis, 1902–81, U.S. journalist & author.
Golding, William, 1911–, Eng. author; Nobel Prize winner.
Goldman, Edwin Franko, 1878–1956, U.S. bandmaster & composer.
—Emma, 1869–1940, Lithuanian-born U.S. anarchist.
Goldoni, Carlo, 1707–93, Ital. playwright.
Goldsmith, Oliver, 1728–74, Eng. author.
Goldstein, Eugen, 1850–1931, Ger. physicist.
Goldwater, Barry, 1909–, U.S. senator & political leader.
Goldwyn, Samuel, 1882–1974, Pol.-born U.S. film producer.
Golgi, Camillo, 1844–1926, Ital. physician & histologist.
Gompers, Samuel, 1850–1924, U.S. labor leader.

Gomulka, Wladyslaw, 1905–1982, first secretary of the Communist Party of Poland 1956–70.
Goncourt, Edmond, 1822–96, & his brother **Jules,** 1830–70, Fr. diarists & authors.
Góngora, Luis de, 1561–1627, Sp. poet.
Gonzalez, Pancho, 1928–, tennis player.
Goodall, Jane, 1934–, Eng. zoologist.
Goodenough, Florence Laura, 1886–1959, U.S. psychologist.
Goodhue, Bertram G., 1869–1924, U.S. architect.
Goodman, Benjamin David (Benny), 1909–86, U.S. musician.
—Paul, 1911–72, U.S. author & educator.
Goodrich, Benjamin Franklin, 1841–88, U.S. industrialist.
Goodson, Mark, 1916–, U.S. TV producer.
Goodyear, Charles, 1800–60, U.S. inventor.
Goossens, Sir Eugene, 1893–1962, Brit. composer & conductor.
Gorbachev, Mikhail Sergeevich, 1931–, Soviet politician; general secretary U.S.S.R. communist party 1985–, head of state 1988–90, and executive president 1990–.
Gordimer, Nadine, 1923–, South African author; Nobel Prize winner.
Gordon, Charles George, 1833–85, Brit. military officer: called **Chinese Gordon.**
—Max, 1892–1978, U.S. theatrical producer.
—Ruth, 1906–1985, U.S. actress & author.
Goren, Charles Henry, 1901–, U.S. bridge player & author.
Gorgas, William Crawford, 1854–1920, U.S. physician & sanitation engineer.
Göring, Hermann Wilhelm, 1893–1946, Ger. Nazi politician.
Gorki, Maxim, 1868–1936, Russ. author & playwright.
Gorky, Arshile, 1905–48, Turkish-born U.S. painter.
Gosden, Freeman, 1899–1982, U.S. radio actor.
Gottfried von Strassburg, 1170?–1220?, Ger. poet.
Gottschalk, Louis Moreau, 1829–69, U.S. pianist & composer.
Gottwald, Klement, 1896–1953, Czech communist leader.
Goudy, Frederic William, 1865–1947, U.S. type designer.
Gould, Chester, 1900–85, U.S. cartoonist.
—Glenn, 1932–82, Can. pianist.
—Jason (Jay), 1836–92, U.S. financier.
—Morton, 1913–, U.S. composer & conductor.
—Shane, 1954–, Austral. swimmer.
Goulding, Ray, 1922–90, U.S. comedian.
Gounod, Charles François, 1818–93, Fr. composer.
Gourmont, Rémy de, 1858–1915, Fr. poet, author, & critic.
Gowon, Yakubu, 1934–, head of state of Nigeria 1966–75.
Goya, Francisco José de, 1746–1828, Sp. painter & etcher.
Graaf, Regnier de, 1641–73, Du. physician.
Grable, Betty, 1916–73, U.S. actress, singer, & dancer.
Gracchus, Gaius Sempronius, 153–121 B.C., & his brother **Tiberius Sempronius,** 163–133 B.C., Roman statesmen.
Grace, Princess, b. Grace Patricia Kelly, 1929–82, U.S.-born actress & wife of Prince Rainier III of Monaco.
Graham, Katharine, 1917–, U.S. publisher.
—Martha, 1894–, U.S. choreographer & dancer.
—Sheilah, 1905?–, Eng.-born U.S. journalist & author.
—Thomas, 1805–69, Scot. physical chemist.
—William Franklin (Billy), 1918–, U.S. evangelist.
Grahame, Kenneth, 1859–1932, Eng. author.
Grainger, Percy Aldridge, 1882–1961, Austral.-born pianist & composer active in U.S.
Gram, Hans Christian Joachim, 1853–1938, Dan. bacteriologist.
Gramm, Donald, 1927–83, U.S. bass-baritone.
Granados, Enrique, 1867–1916, Sp. composer.
Grange, Harold (Red), 1903–91, U.S. football player.
Grant, Cary, 1904–86, Eng.-born U.S. actor.
—Ulysses S(impson), 1822–85, U.S. Civil War general & 18th U.S. president 1869–77.
Granville-Barker, Harley, 1877–1946, Eng. actor, playwright, & producer.
Grappelli, Stéphane, 1908–, Fr. jazz violinist.
Grass, Günter Wilhelm, 1927–, Ger. author.
Gratian, (L. Flavius Gratianus) 359–383, Roman emperor 375–83.

Graves, Robert Ranke, 1895–1985, Eng. poet & author.
Gray, Asa, 1810–88, U.S. botanist.
—Harold, 1894–1968, U.S. cartoonist.
—Thomas, 1716–71, Eng. poet.
Graziano, Rocco (Rocky), 1922–90, U.S. boxer.
Greco, El, b. Domenikos Theotokopoulos, 1541?–1614?, Cretan-born painter active in Italy & Spain.
Greco, José, 1919–, Ital.-born U.S. dancer.
Greeley, Horace, 1811–72, U.S. editor & political leader.
Green, Adolph, 1915–, U.S. lyricist.
—Henrietta Robinson (Hetty), 1834–1916, U.S. financier.
—Henry, pseud. of Henry Vincent Yorke, 1905–73, Eng. author.
—John, 1908–, U.S. songwriter.
—Martyn, 1899–1975, Eng. actor & singer active in U.S.
—William, 1873–1952, U.S. labor leader.
Greenberg, Henry (Hank), 1911–, U.S. baseball player.
Greene, Graham, 1904–91, Eng. author.
—Nathanael, 1742–86, Amer. Revolutionary general.
—Robert, 1558–92, Eng. poet & playeright.
Greenstreet, Sydney, 1879–1954, Eng. actor active in U.S.
Gregory I, Saint, 540?–604, pope 590–640; known as **the Great.**
—XIII, 1502–85, pope 1572–85.
Gregory, Lady Augusta Persse, 1859?–1932, Irish playwright & theater director.
—Dick, 1932–, U.S. comedian & social activist.
Gresham, Sir Thomas, 1519?–79, Eng. financier.
Gretzky, Wayne, 1961–, Can. hockey player.
Greuze, Jean Baptiste, 1725–1805, Fr. painter.
Grey, Beryl, 1927–, Eng. dancer & ballet company director.
—Lady Jane, 1537–54, Eng. noblewoman; beheaded.
—Zane, 1872–1939, U.S. author.
Grieg, Edvard Hagerup, 1843–1907, Norw. composer.
Griffith, D(avid) W(ark), 1875–1948, U.S. film director & producer.
Grigorovitch, Yuri, 1927–, Soviet choreographer & ballet company director.
Grimaldi, Francesco Maria, 1618–63, Ital. physicist.
Grimm, Jacob Ludwig Karl, 1785–1863, & his brother **Wilhelm Karl,** 1786–1859, Ger. philologists & collectors of fairy tales.
Gris, Juan, 1887–1927, Sp. painter.
Grisi, Carlotta, 1819–99, Ital. ballerina.
Grofé, Ferde, 1892–1972, U.S. composer & conductor.
Grolier de Servières, Jean, 1479–1565, Fr. diplomat & bibliophile.
Gromyko, Andrei Andreivich, 1909–89, Soviet economist & diplomat.
Groote, Gerhard, 1340–84, Du. religious reformer.
Gropius, Walter, 1883–1969, Ger. architect active in U.S. after 1937.
Gropper, William, 1897–1977, U.S. painter.
Grosz, George, 1893–1959, Ger. painter & illustrator.
Grotius, Hugo, 1583–1645, Du. jurist & statesman.
Grove, Sir George, 1820–1900, Eng. musicologist & author.
—Robert (Lefty), 1900–75, U.S. baseball player.
Groves, Leslie Richard, 1896–1970, U.S. general.
Grünewald, Matthias, 1480?–1528?, Ger. painter.
Guardi, Francesco, 1712–93, Ital. painter.
Guarneri, Giuseppe Antonia, 1687–1745, Ital. violin maker.
Gueden, Hilde, 1917–, Austrian soprano.
Guest, Edgar A(lbert), 1881–1959, Eng.-born U.S. poet & journalist.
Guevara, Ernesto (Ché), 1928–67, Argentinian-born Cuban revolutionary leader.
Guggenheim A family of U.S. industrialists & philanthropists incl. **Meyer,** 1828–1905, & his sons **Benjamin,** 1865–1912; **Daniel,** 1856–1930; **Issac,** 1854–1922; **Murry,** 1858–1939; **Simon,** 1867–1941; **Solomon R.,** 1861–1949; & **William,** 1868–1941.
—Peggy, 1898–1979, U.S. art collector, patron, & author.
Guido d'Arezzo, 990?–1050?, Ital. monk & musician.
Guinness, Sir Alec, 1914–, Eng. actor.
Guitry, Sacha, 1885–1957, Fr. film director.
Gunther, John, 1901–70, U.S. author.
Gustaf VI, 1882–1973, king of Sweden 1950–73.

Gustavus Adolphus (Gustaf II), 1594–1632, king of Sweden 1611–32.
Guston, Philip, 1913–80, U.S. painter.
Gutenberg, Johann, 1400?–1468?, Ger. printer & reputed inventor of movable type.
Guthrie, Sir Tyrone, 1900–71, Eng. stage director active in U.S.
—Woodrow Wilson (Woody), 1912–67, U.S. folk singer.
Gwynne, Nell, 1650–87, Eng. actress; mistress of Charles II.

Haakon VII, 1872–1957, king of Norway 1905–57.
Haber, Fritz, 1868–1934, Ger. chemist.
Hachette, Louis, 1800–64, Fr. publisher & bookseller.
Hadrian (L. Publius Aelius Hadrianus), A.D. 76–138, Roman emperor, A.D. 117–138.
Haechkel, Ernst Heinrich, 1834–1919, Ger. biologist.
Hafiz, pseud. of Shams ud-din Mohammed, 14th c. Persian poet.
Hagen, Walter Charles, 1892–1969, U.S. golfer.
Haggard, Sir (Henry) Rider, 1856–1925, Eng. author.
Hahn, Otto, 1879–1968, Ger. physical chemist; Nobel Prize winner.
Haig, Alexander Meigs, Jr., 1924–, U.S. general and statesman; U.S. secretary of state 1981–82.
Haile Selassie, 1891–1975, emperor of Ethiopia 1930–74.
Hailey, Arthur, 1920–, Eng. author.
Hakluyt, Richard, 1552–1616, Eng. geographer & historian.
Halas, George Stanley, 1895–1983, U.S. football player, coach, and owner.
Halberstam, David, 1920–, U.S. journalist.
Haldane, J(ohn) B(urdon) S(anderson), 1892–1964, Eng. biologist.
—John Scott, 1860–1936, Eng. physiologist.
—Richard Burdon, 1856–1928, Eng. philosopher & statesman.
Hale, Edward Everett, 1822–1909, U.S. clergyman & author.
—George Ellery, 1868–1938, U.S. astronomer.
—Nathan, 1755–76, Amer. revolutionary officer; hanged as a spy by the British.
—Sarah Josepha, 1788–1879, U.S. editor, poet, & author.
Hales, Stephen, 1677–1761, Eng. botanist & chemist.
Halévy, Jacques, 1799–1862, Fr. composer.
—Ludovic, 1834–1908, Fr. playwright & author; nephew of prec.
Haley, Alex, 1921–, U.S. author.
Halifax, Edward Frederick Lindley Wood, Earl of, 1881–1959, Eng. statesman & diplomat.
Hall, James Norman, 1887–1951, U.S. author.
Halley, Edmund, 1656–1742, Eng. astronomer.
Halliburton, Richard, 1900–39, U.S. explorer & author.
Hals, Frans, 1850?–1666, Du. painter.
Halsey, William Frederick, Jr. (Bull), 1882–1959, U.S. admiral.
Halsted, William Stewart, 1852–1922, U.S. surgeon.
Halston (Roy Halston Frowick), 1932–90, U.S. fashion designer.
Hambro, Carl Joachim, 1885–1964, Norw. statesman.
Hamilcar Barca, 270?–228 B.C., Carthaginian general; father of Hannibal.
Hamilton, Alexander, 1757–1804, West Indian-born Amer. statesman.
—Edith, 1867–1963, U.S. classicist & author.
—Lady Emma, 1761?–1815, mistress of Lord Nelson.
—Margaret, 1902–85, U.S. actress.
Hammarskjöld, Dag, 1905–61, Swed. statesman; secretary general of the U.N. 1953–61; Nobel Prize winner.
Hammerstein, Oscar, 1847?–1919, U.S. theatrical manager.
—Oscar II, 1895–1960, U.S. lyricist; nephew of prec.
Hammett, Dashiell, 1894–1961, U.S. author.
Hammurabi, 18th c. B.C., Babylonian king & lawgiver.
Hampden, John, 1594–1643, Eng. statesman.
—Walter, 1879–1955, U.S. actor.
Hampton, Lionel, 1913–, U.S. jazz musician.
—Wade, 1818–1902, U.S. politician & Confederate general.
Hamsun, Knut, 1859–1952, Norw. author.
Hancock, John, 1737–93, Amer. statesman.
Hand, Learned, 1872–1961, U.S. jurist.

Handel, George Frederick, 1685–1759, Ger. composer active in England.

Handler, Philip, 1917–81, U.S. educator.

Handlin, Oscar, 1915–, U.S. historian & sociologist.

Handy, W(illiam) C(hristopher), 1873–1958, U.S. jazz musician & composer.

Hanna, Marcus Alonzo (Mark), 1837–1904, U.S. businessman & politician.

Hannibal, 247–183 B.C., Carthaginian general; invaded Italy by crossing the Alps.

Hansard, Luke, 1752–1828, Eng. printer.

Hansberry, Lorraine, 1930–65, U.S. playwright.

Hanson, Howard, 1896–1981, U.S. composer & conductor.

Harbach, Otto Abels, 1873–1963, U.S. playwright & lyricist.

Harburg, E(dgar) Y. (Yip), 1898–1981, U.S. lyricist.

Harden, Sir Arthur, 1865–1940, Eng. biochemist.

Harding, Warren Gamaliel, 1865–1923, 29th U.S. president 1921–23.

Hardwick, Elizabeth, 1916–, U.S. author & critic.

Hardwicke, Sir Cedric Webster, 1893–1964, Eng. actor.

Hardy, Oliver Nowell, 1892–1957, U.S. comedian.

—**Thomas,** 1840–1928, Eng. author & poet.

Hargreaves, James, 1722?–78, Eng. inventor of the spinning jenny.

Harington, Sir John, 1561–1612, Eng. author & translator.

Harkness, Rebekah West, 1915–82, U.S. composer & ballet patron.

Harlan, John Marshall, 1833–1911, & his grandson **John Marshall Harlan II,** 1899–1971, U.S. jurists.

Harlow, Jean, 1911–37, U.S. actress.

Harold II, 1022?–66, last Saxon king of England 1066.

Haroun-al-Rashid, 764?–809, Caliph of Baghdad 786–809.

Harper, James, 1795–1869, & his brothers: **John,** 1797–1875, **(Joseph) Wesley,** 1801–70, & **Fletcher,** 1806–77, U.S. printers & publishers.

—**William Rainey,** 1856–1906, U.S. educator.

Harriman, Edward Henry, 1848–1909, U.S. industrialist.

—**W(illiam) Averell,** 1891–1986, U.S. businessman, statesman, & diplomat.

Harrington, (Edward) Michael, 1928–89, U.S. author.

Harriot, Thomas, 1560–1621, Eng. mathematician.

Harris, Frank, 1854–1931, Irish-born U.S. editor & author.

—**Jed,** 1900–79, Austrian-born U.S. theatrical producer.

—**Joel Chandler,** 1848–1908, U.S. author.

—**Julie,** 1925–, U.S. actress.

—**Louis,** 1921–, U.S. public opinion statistician.

—**Robert,** 1849–1919, Eng.-born Can. painter.

—**Roy,** 1898–1979, U.S. composer.

—**Townsend,** 1804–78, U.S. businessman & diplomat.

Harrison, Benjamin, 1833–1901, 23rd U.S. president 1889–93.

—**George,** 1943–, Eng. composer & musical performer.

—**Rex,** 1908–90, Eng. actor active in U.S.

—**Ross Granville,** 1870–1959, U.S. biologist.

—**Wallace K.,** 1895–1981, U.S. architect.

—**William Henry,** 1773–1841, U.S. general & 9th U.S. president 1841; grandfather of Benjamin.

Hart, Johnny, 1931–, U.S. cartoonist.

—**Lorenz,** 1895–1943, U.S. lyricist.

—**Moss,** 1904–61, U.S. playwright.

—**William S(urrey),** 1872–1946, U.S. actor.

Harte, Francis Brett (Bret), 1836–1902, U.S. author.

Hartford, Huntingdon, 1911–, U.S. financier & art patron.

Hartley, Marsden, 1877–1943, U.S. painter.

Harvard, John, 1607–38, Eng. clergyman active in U.S.

Harvey, William, 1578–1657, Eng. physician & anatomist.

Hasek, Jaroslav, 1883–1923, Czech. author.

Hassam, Childe, 1859–1935, U.S. painter & etcher.

Hassan II, 1929–, king of Morocco 1961–.

Hassler, Hans Leo, 1564–1612, Ger. composer.

Hastings, Thomas, 1860–1929, U.S. architect.

—**Warren,** 1732–1818, Eng.statesman active in India.

Hauptmann, Gerhart, 1862–1946, Ger. author & playwright.

Haussmann, Baron Georges Eugène, 1809–91, Fr. prefect & city planner.

Havel, Vaclav, 1936–, Czech. dramatist and statesman; president of Czechoslovakia 1989–.

Hawking, Stephen William, 1942–, Eng. physicist.

Hawkins, Sir John, 1532–95, Eng. admiral.

Hawks, Howard, 1896–1977, U.S. film director.

Hawthorne, Nathaniel, 1804–64, U.S. author.

Hay, John Milton, 1838–1905, U.S. statesman & author; secretary of state 1898–1905.

Haya de la Torre, Victor Raúl, 1895–1979, Peruvian political leader.

Haydn, Franz Joseph, 1732–1809, Austrian composer.

Hayek, Friedrich August von, 1899–, Austrian-born Brit. economist; Nobel Prize winner.

Hayes, Helen, 1900–, U.S. actress.

—**Robert (Bob),** 1942–, U.S. track runner & football player.

—**Roland,** 1887–1977, U.S. tenor.

—**Rutherford Birchard,** 1822–93, 19th U.S. president 1877–81.

Hays, Arthur Garfield, 1881–1954, U.S. lawyer.

Hayward, Leland, 1902–71, U.S. theatrical producer.

—**Susan,** 1919–75, U.S. actress.

Hayworth, Rita, 1918–87, actress.

Hazlitt, William, 1778–1830, Eng. author.

Head, Edith, 1907–81, U.S. costume designer.

Hearn, Lafcadio, 1850–1904, Gk.-born Irish author active in Japan.

Hearst, William Randolph, 1863–1951, U.S. publisher.

Heath, Edward, 1916–, Eng. politician; prime minister 1970–74.

Heatter, Gabriel, 1890–1972, U.S. journalist & radio commentator.

Heaviside, Oliver, 1850–1925, Eng. physicist & electrician.

Hecht, Ben, 1894–1964, U.S. journalist, author, & playwright.

Hefner, Hugh Marston, 1926–, U.S. editor & publisher.

Hegel, Georg Wilhelm Friedrich, 1770–1831, Ger. philosopher.

Heidegger, Martin, 1889–1976, Ger. philosopher.

Heiden, Eric, 1958–, Olympic speed skater.

Heifetz, Jascha, 1901–87, Lithuanian-born U.S. violinist.

Heine, Heinrich, 1797–1856, Ger. poet.

Heinlein, Robert Anson, 1907–1988, U.S. author.

Heinz, Henry John, 1844–1919, U.S. food processor.

Heisenberg, Werner, 1901–76, Ger. physicist; Nobel Prize winner.

Held, Anna, 1873?–1918, Fr.-born singer & actress active in U.S.

—**John, Jr.,** 1889–1958, U.S. illustrator & author.

Heliogabalus, 204–222, Roman emperor 218–22.

Heller, Joseph, 1923–, U.S. author.

Hellinger, Mark, 1903–47, U.S. journalist & theatrical producer.

Hellman, Lillian, 1905–84, U.S. playwright.

Helmholtz, Hermann Ludwig Ferdinand von, 1821–94, Ger. physiologist & physicist.

Helmont, Jan Baptista van, 1577–1644, Flemish physician & chemist.

Héloïse, 1101?–64?, Fr. abbess; pupil, mistress, & later, wife of Abélard.

Helpmann, Sir Robert Murray, 1909–1986, Austral.-born dancer, choreographer, & actor active in Great Britain.

Helprin, Mark, 1947–, U.S. author.

Helvétius, Claude Adrien, 1715–71, Fr. philosopher.

Hemingway, Ernest, 1899–1961, U.S. author; Nobel Prize winner.

Henderson, (James) Fletcher, 1897–1952, U.S. jazz musician.

—**Ray,** 1896–1970, U.S. songwriter.

Hendrix, Jimi, 1942–70, U.S. musician & singer.

Hengist, 5th c. Jute invader of Great Britain.

Henie, Sonja, 1913–69, Norw.-born ice skater & actress active in U.S.

Henreid, Paul, 1908–, Austrian actor active in U.S.

Henri, Robert, 1865–1929, U.S. painter.

Henry II, 1133–89, king of England 1154–89.

—**IV,** 1367–1413, king of England 1399–1413.

—**V,** 1387–1422, king of England 1413–22.

—**VIII,** 1491–1547, king of England 1509–47; established Church of England.

Henry IV (of Navarre), 1553–1610, king of France 1589–1610.

Henry the Navigator, 1394–1460, Pg. prince & promoter of navigation.

Henry, O., pseud. of William Sidney Porter, 1862–1910, U.S. author.

—**Patrick,** 1736–99, Amer. patriot, statesman, & orator.

Hensen, Victor, 1835–1924, Ger. marine biologist.

Henson, Jim (James Maury), 1936–90, U.S. puppeteer and director.

Henze, Hans Werner, 1926–, Ger. composer.

Hepburn, Audrey, 1929–, Belg.-born actress active in U.S.

—**Katharine,** 1909–, U.S. actress.

Hepplewhite, George, ?–1786, Eng. furniture designer.

Hepworth, Dame Barbara, 1903–75, Eng. sculptor.

Heraclitus, ca. 5th c. B.C. Gk. philosopher.

Herbert, Frank, 1920–, U.S. author.

—**George,** 1593–1633, Eng. poet & clergyman.

—**Victor,** 1859–1924, Irish-born U.S. composer.

—**William,** 1580–1630, Eng. statesman & poet.

Herder, Johann Gottfried von, 1744–1803, Ger. philosopher & author.

Heredia, José Maria de, 1842–1905, Cuban-born Fr. poet.

Herman, Jerry, 1932–, U.S. composer.

—**Woodrow Charles (Woody),** 1913–87, U.S. jazz musician.

Herod, 73?–4 B.C., king of Judea 37–4 B.C.: called **the Great.**

—**Antipas,** 4 B.C.–A.D. 40, governor of Galilee; son of prec.

Herodotus, 484?–424? B.C., Gk. historian.

Herophilus, 4th c. B.C., Gk. anatomist.

Herrick, Robert, 1591–1674, Eng. poet.

Herriman, George, 1881–1944, U.S. cartoonist.

Herschel, Sir William, 1738–1822, & his son **Sir John Frederick William,** 1792–1871, Eng. astronomers.

Hersey, John Richard, 1914–, Chin.-born U.S. author.

Hershey, Milton Snavely, 1857–1945, U.S. businessman & philanthropist.

Herskovits, Melville Jean, 1895–1963, U.S. anthropologist.

Hertz, Gustav, 1887–1975, Ger. physicist; Nobel Prize winner.

Hertzberg, Gerhard, 1904–, Ger.-born Can. physicist; Nobel Prize winner.

—**Heinrich Rudolph,** 1857–94, Ger. physicist.

Herzl, Theodor, 1860–1904, Hung.-born Austrian journalist; founder of the Zionist movement.

Hesburgh, Theodore Martin, 1917–, U.S. Roman Catholic priest & educator.

Hesiod, ca. 8th c. B.C., Gk. poet.

Hess, Dame Myra, 1890–1965, Eng. pianist.

—**Victor Franz,** 1883–1964, Austrian physicist.

—**Walter Rudolf,** 1881–1973, Swiss physiologist.

—**(Walther Richard) Rudolf,** 1894–1987, Ger. Nazi politician.

Hesse, Hermann, 1877–1962, Ger. author; Nobel Prize winner.

Heydrich, Reinhard, 1904–42, Ger. Nazi administrator: known as **the Hangman.**

Heyerdahl, Thor, 1914–, Norw. anthropologist & author.

Heyrovsky, Jaroslav, 1890–1967, Czech chemist; Nobel Prize winner.

Heyward, DuBose, 1885–1940, U.S. author.

Hiawatha, 16th c. Mohawk Am. Ind. chief.

Hickok, James Butler (Wild Bill), 1837–76, U.S. scout & marshal.

Hicks, Edward, 1780–1849, U.S. painter.

—**Granville,** 1901–82, U.S. author & critic.

Hidalgo y Costilla, Miguel, 1753–1811, Mexican priest & revolutionary.

Highet, Gilbert, 1906–78, Scot.-born U.S. author & educator.

Hilbert, David, 1862–1943, Ger. mathematician.

Hill, George Washington, 1884–1946, U.S. businessman.

—**Graham,** 1929–75, Eng. auto racer.

—**Joe,** 1872?–1915, Swed.-born U.S. labor organizer & songwriter.

Hillary, Sir Edmond, 1919–, New Zealand explorer & mountain climber.

Hillel, 60 B.C.?–A.D. 10, Babylonian teacher of biblical law.

Hiller, Wendy, 1912–, Eng. actress.

Hillman, Sidney, 1887–1946, Lituanian-born U.S. labor leader.

Hilton, Conrad Nicholson, 1887–1979, U.S. businessman.

—**James,** 1900–54, Eng. author.

Himmler, Heinrich, 1900–45, Ger. Nazi politician.

Hindemith, Paul, 1895–1963, Ger. composer active in U.S.

Hindenburg, Paul von, 1847–1934, Ger. field marshal; president of Germany 1925–34.

Hine, Lewis Wickes, 1874–1940, U.S. photographer.

Hines, Duncan, 1880–1959, U.S. food expert, author, & publisher.

—**Earl (Fatha),** 1905–83, U.S. jazz musician.

Hippocrates, 460?–377, B.C., Gk. physician.

Hires, Charles Elmer, 1851–1937, U.S. businessman.

Hirohito, 1901–89, emperor of Japan 1926–89.

Hiroshige, Ando, 1797–1858, Jap. painter.

Hirsch, Elray (Crazy Legs), 1923–, U.S. football player.

Hirschfeld, Al(bert), 1903–, U.S. cartoonist.

Hirshhorn, Joseph, 1899–1981, Latvian-born U.S. mining executive, entrepreneur, & art collector.

Hiss, Alger, 1904–, U.S. government official.

Hitchcock, Sir Alfred, 1899–1980, Eng. film director active in U.S.

—**Henry-Russell,** 1903–, U.S. art historian.

Hitler, Adolf, 1889–1945, Austrian-born Nazi dictator of Germany 1933–45.

Hoban, James, 1762?–1831, Irish-born U.S. architect.

Hobart, Garret Augustus, 1844–99, U.S. statesman; U.S. vice president 1897–99.

Hobbema, Meindert, 1638–1709, Du. painter.

Hobbes, Thomas, 1588–1679, Eng. philosopher.

Hobby, Oveta Culp, 1905–, U.S. journalist & government official.

Ho Chi Minh, 1890?–1969, president of N. Vietnam 1954–69.

Hodgkin, Dorothy Crowfoot, 1910–, Brit. chemist; Nobel Prize winner.

Hoffa, James Riddle, 1913–75?, U.S. labor leader.

Hoffer, Eric, 1902–83, U.S. philosopher & author.

Hoffman, Malvina, 1887–1966, U.S. sculptor.

Hoffmann, E(rnst) T(heodor) A(madeus), 1776–1822, Ger. author & illustrator.

Hofmann, Hans, 1880–1966, Ger.-born U.S. painter.

—**Josef Casimir,** 1876–1957, Pol. pianist.

Hofmannsthal, Hugo von, 1874–1929, Austrian poet & playwright.

Hofstadter, Richard, 1916–70, U.S. historian.

Hogan, Ben W., 1912–, U.S. golfer.

Hogarth, William, 1697–1764, Eng. painter & engraver.

Hokinson, Helen, 1899?–1949, U.S. cartoonist.

Hokusai, Katsushika, 1760–1849, Jap. painter & engraver.

Holabird, William, 1854–1923, U.S. architect.

Holbein, Hans, 1460?–1524, (called **the Elder**), and his son **Hans,** 1497–1543, (**the Younger**), Ger. painters.

Hölderlin, (Johann Christian) Friedrich, 1770–1843, Ger. poet.

Holiday, Billie, 1915–59, U.S. jazz singer.

Holinshed, Raphael, ?–1580?, Eng. chronicler.

Holley, Robert W., 1922–, U.S. biochemist.

Holliday, Judy, 1921–65, U.S. actress.

Holmes, Oliver Wendell, 1809–94, U.S. physician & poet.

—**Oliver Wendell, Jr.,** 1841–1935, U.S. jurist; justice of U.S. Supreme Court 1902–32; son of prec.

Holst, Gustav Theodore, 1874–1934, Eng. composer.

Holyoake, Sir Keith Jacka, 1904–83, New Zealand statesman; New Zealand prime minister 1957 & 1960–72.

Home, Alexander Frederick Douglas, Lord, 1903–, Brit. statesman; Brit. prime minister 1963–4.

Homer, ca. 8th c. B.C. Gk. epic poet.

Homer, Winslow, 1936–1910, U.S. painter.

Honecker, Erich, 1912–, 1st secretary of German Democratic Republic Communist party 1971–76; general secretary 1976–89.

Honegger, Arthur, 1892–1955, Fr. composer.

Hood, Raymond, 1881–1934, U.S. architect.

Hooke, Robert, 1635–1703, Eng. philosopher & scientist.

Hooker, Thomas, 1586?–1647, Eng.-born clergyman; founder of Connecticut colony.

Hooton, Earnest Albert, 1887–1954, U.S. anthropologist.
Hoover, Herbert Clark, 1874–1964, 31st U.S. president 1929–33.
—**J(ohn) Edgar,** 1895–1972, U.S. criminologist; director of the FBI 1924–72.
Hope, Leslie Townes (Bob), 1903–, Eng.-born U.S. actor & comedian.
Hopkins, Gerard Manley, 1844–89, Eng. poet.
—**Harry Lloyd,** 1890–1946, U.S. politician & administrator.
—**Johns,** 1795–1873, U.S. financier & philanthropist.
—**Mark,** 1802–87, U.S. educator.
Hopkinson, Francis, 1737–91, U.S. lawyer & author.
Hoppe, William Frederick (Willie), 1887–1959, U.S. billiards player.
Hopper, Edward, 1882–1967, U.S. painter.
—**Hedda,** 1890–1966, U.S. actress & columnist.
Horace (L. Quintus Horatius Flaccus), 65–8 B.C., Roman poet.
Horne, Lena, 1917–, U.S. singer & actress.
—**Marilyn,** 1934–, U.S. mezzo-soprano.
Horney, Karen, 1885–1952, Ger.-born U.S. psychiatrist.
Hornsby, Rogers, 1896–1963, U.S. baseball player.
Horowitz, Vladimir, 1904–89, Russ.-born U.S. pianist.
Horsa, ?–455, Jute invader of Great Britain.
Houdini, Harry, 1874–1926, U.S. magician.
Houdon, Jean Antoine, 1741–1828, Fr. sculptor.
Houhaness, Alan, 1911–, U.S. composer.
Houphouët-Boigny, Félix, 1905–, president of Ivory Coast 1960–.
House, Col. Edward Mandell, 1858–1938, U.S. diplomat.
Houseman, John, 1902–89, U.S. producer, director, actor, & author for theater, TV, & films.
Housman, A(lfred) E(dward), 1859–1936, Eng. poet & classical scholar.
Houston, Sam(uel), 1793–1863, U.S. statesman & general; president of Republic of Texas 1836–38 & 1841–44.
Howard, Catherine, 1520?–42, 5th wife of King Henry VIII of England.
—**Henry, Earl of Surrey,** 1517?–47, Eng. soldier & poet.
—**Leslie,** 1893–1943, Eng. actor active in U.S.
—**Roy W.,** 1883–1964, U.S. editor & publisher.
—**Sidney Coe,** 1891–1939, U.S. playwright.
—**Trevor,** 1916–88, Eng. actor.
Howe, Elias, 1819–67, U.S. inventor of the sewing machine.
—**Gordon (Gordie),** 1928–, Can. hockey player.
—**Irving,** 1920–, U.S. literary critic & author.
—**James Wong,** 1899–1976, Chin.-born U.S. cinematographer.
—**Julia Ward,** 1819–1910, U.S. suffragist & author.
—**Mark Anthony DeWolf,** 1864–1960, U.S. author.
—**Richard, Earl,** 1726–99, Eng. naval officer.
Howells, William Dean, 1837–1920, U.S. author & editor.
—**Herbert Norman,** 1892–1983, Brit. composer.
Hoxha, Enver, 1908–85, 1st secretary of Albanian Labor (Communist) Party 1945–85.
Hoyle, Edmond, 1672–1769, Eng. writer on games.
—**Sir Fred,** 1915–, Eng. astronomer.
Hu Yaobang, 1915–89, Chin. statesman; general secretary of Chin. Communist Party 1981–87.
Hua Guofeng, 1918?–, Chin. statesman; chairman of Chin. Communist Party 1976–81; premier 1976–80.
Hubble, Edwin Powell, 1889–1953, U.S. astronomer.
Hudson, Henry, ?–1611, Eng. explorer.
—**Rock,** 1925–85, U.S. actor.
Huggins, Sir William, 1824–1910, Eng. astronomer.
Hughes, Charles Evans, 1862–1948, U.S. jurist; chief justice of the U.S. Supreme Court 1930–41.
—**Howard Robard,** 1905–76, U.S. businessman.
—**(James) Langston,** 1902–67, U.S. author & poet.
Hugo, Victor Marie, 1802–85, Fr. poet, author, & playwright.
Huizinga, Johan, 1872–1945, Du. historian.
Hull, Cordell, 1871–1955, U.S. statesman; secretary of state 1933–44; Nobel Prize winner.
—**Robert Marvin (Bobby),** 1939–, Can. hockey player.
Humboldt, Baron (Friedrich Heinrich) Alexander von, 1769–1859, Ger. naturalist & traveler.
Hume, David, 1711–76, Scot. historian & philosopher.
Humperdinck, Engelbert, 1854–1921, Ger. composer.

Humphrey, Doris, 1895–1958, U.S. choreographer & dancer.
—**Hubert Horatio,** 1911–78, U.S. senator & political leader; U.S. vice president 1965–69.
Hunt, H(aroldson) L(afayette), 1889–1974, U.S. businessman.
—**(James Henry) Leigh,** 1784–1859, Eng. author.
—**Richard Morris,** 1827–95, U.S. architect.
Hunter, Alberta, 1895–1984, U.S. songwriter & singer.
—**John,** 1728–93, Eng. surgeon.
Huntington, Collis P., 1821–1900, U.S. railroad magnate.
—**Henry E.,** 1850–1927, U.S. railroad builder & philanthropist.
Huntley, Chester Robert (Chet), 1911–74, U.S. news analyst & commentator.
Hunyadi, János, 1387?–1456, Hung. soldier & national hero.
Hurok, Sol, 1888–1974, Russ.-born U.S. impresario.
Hurston, Zora Neale, 1903–60, U.S. author and anthropologist.
Husak, Gustav, 1913–, general secretary of the Communist Party of Czechoslovakia 1969–87, & president 1975–89.
Huss John, 1369–1415, Bohemian religious reformer.
Hussein I, 1935–, king of Jordan 1952–.
Hussein, Saddam, 1937–, Iraqi politician; president of Iraq 1979–.
Husserl, Edmund, 1859–1938, Ger. philosopher; founder of phenomenology.
Huston, John, 1906–87, U.S. film director & actor.
—**Walter,** 1884–1950, Can.-born U.S. actor; father of prec.
Hutchins, Robert Maynard, 1899–1977, U.S. educator.
Hutchinson, Anne Marbury, 1591–1643, U.S. religious leader.
—**Thomas,** 1711–80, U.S. colonial administrator.
Huxley A family of Eng. scientists & writers incl. **Aldous Leonard,** 1894–1963, author; **Sir Julian Sorell,** 1887–1975, biologist, brother of prec.; **Thomas Henry,** 1825–95, biologist, grandfather of Aldous & Julian.
Huxtable, Ada Louise, 1921–, U.S. architecture critic & journalist.
Huygens, Christian, 1629–95, Du. mathematician, physicist, & astronomer.
Huysman, Joris Karl, 1848–1907, Fr. author.

Ibáñez, Carlos, 1877–1960, Chilean politician; president 1927–31 & 1952–58.
Ibert, Jacques, 1890–1962, Fr. composer.
ibn-Khaldun, 1332–1406, Arab historian.
ibn Saud, Abdul Aziz, 1880–1953, king of Saudi Arabia 1932–53.
Ibsen, Henrik, 1828–1906, Norw. playwright & poet.
Ickes, Harold LeClair, 1874–1952, U.S. lawyer & government official.
Ictinus, 5th B.C. Gk. architect.
Ikeda, Hayato, 1899–1965, premier of Japan 1960–64.
Ikhnaton, king of Egypt 1375–1358 B.C.: also known as **Akhnaton, Amenhotep IV.**
Indy, Vincent d', 1851–1931, Fr. composer.
Inge, William, 1913–73, U.S. playwright.
Ingenhousz, Jan, 1730–99, Du. physician & plant physiologist.
Ingersoll, Robert Green, 1833–99, U.S. lawyer, author, & lecturer.
Ingres, Jean Auguste Dominique, 1780–1867, Fr. painter.
Inman, Henry, 1801–46, U.S. painter.
Inness, George, 1825–94, U.S. painter.
Innocent III, b. Giovanni Latario de'Conti 1161–1216, pope 1198–1216.
Inönü, Ismet, 1884–1973, first premier of Turkey; president 1938–50.
Insull, Samuel, 1859–1938, Eng.-born U.S. utilities executive.
Ionesco, Eugene, 1912–, Rumanian-born Fr. playwright.
Iqbal, Mohammed, 1873–1938, Moslem leader & national hero of Pakistan.
Irving, Sir Henry, 1838–1905, Eng. actor & theater manager.
—**John,** 1942–, U.S. novelist.
—**Washington,** 1783–1859, U.S. author.
Isaacs, Alick, 1921–67, Eng. biologist.

Isabella I, 1451–1504, queen of Castile & wife of Ferdinand V; sponsored the voyages of Columbus.

Isherwood, Christopher William Bradshaw, 1904–86, Eng.-born U.S. author.

Ismail Pasha, 1830–95, khedive of Egypt 1863–79.

Iturbi, José, 1895–1980, Sp. pianist & conductor active in U.S.

Ivan III, 1440–1505, grand duke of Muscovy & founder of Russ. Empire: called **the Great.**

—IV, 1530–84, grand duke of Muscovy & first czar of Russia: called **the Terrible.**

Ives, Burl, 1909–, U.S. singer & actor.

—Charles Edward, 1874–1954, U.S. composer.

Jackson, Andrew, 1767–1845. U.S. general & 7th U.S. president 1829–37.

—Glenda, 1936–, Eng. actress.

Jackson, Henry M(artin), 1912–, U.S. politician.

—Jesse, 1941–, U.S. black civil rights leader.

—Mahalia, 1911–72, U.S. gospel singer.

—Maynard, 1938–, U.S. politician.

—Michael, 1958–, U.S. singer & songwriter.

—Shirley, 1919–65, U.S. author.

—Thomas Jonathan (Stonewall), 1824–63, U.S. Confederate general.

Jacobs, Helen Hull, 1908–, U.S. tennis player.

Jacquard, Joseph Marie, 1752–1834, Fr. inventor.

Jagger, Mick, 1944–, Eng. singer.

James I, 1566–1625, king of England 1603–25; also called **James VI** as king of Scotland 1567–1625.

—II, 1633–1701, king of England 1685–88; deposed.

James, Harry, 1916–83, U.S. bandleader.

—Henry, 1843–1916, U.S. author & critic active in England.

—Jesse Woodson, 1847–82, U.S. outlaw.

—William, 1842–1910, U.S. psychologist, philosopher, educator, & author; brother of Henry.

Jamison, Judith, 1944–, U.S. dancer.

Janáček, Leoš, 1854–1928, Czech composer.

Janis, Elsie, 1889–1956, U.S. actress.

Jannings, Emil, 1887?–1950, Swiss-born actor active in Germany.

Jansen, Cornelius, 1585–1638, Du. theologian.

Jacques-Dalcroze, Émile, 1865–1950, Swiss composer & educator.

Jarrell, Randall, 1914–65, U.S. poet.

Jaruzelski, Wojciech, 1923–, Pol. Communist Party leader 1981–.

Jaspers, Karl, 1883–1969, Ger. philosopher.

Jastrow, Robert, 1925–, U.S. physicist.

Jaurès, Jean Léon, 1859–1914, Fr. socialist leader.

Jay, John, 1745–1829, Amer. statesman & first chief justice of the U.S. Supreme Court 1790–95.

Jean, Grand Duke, 1921–, ruler of Luxembourg 1964–.

Jeans, Sir James Hopwood, 1877–1946, Eng. mathematician, astronomer, physicist, & author.

Jeffers, (John) Robinson, 1887–1962, U.S. poet.

Jefferson, Joseph, 1829–1905, U.S. actor.

—Thomas, 1743–1826, Amer. statesman & 3rd. U.S. president 1801–09; drafted the Declaration of Independence.

Jellicoe, John Rushworth, (1st Earl Jellicoe), 1859–1935, Brit. admiral.

Jenner, Bruce, 1949–, U.S. decathlon athlete.

—Edward, 1749–1823, Eng. physician.

—William, 1815–98, Brit. physician.

Jenney, William LeBaron, 1832–1907, U.S. architect.

Jennings, Peter Charles, 1938–, Can.-born U.S. journalist.

Jensen, J. Hans, 1906–73, Ger. physicist; Nobel Prize winner.

Jenson, Nicholas, 1415?–80, Fr. printer & typographer.

Jerome, Saint, 340?–420; early Church father & religious scholar.

Jespersen, (Jens) Otto (Harry), 1860–1943, Dan. linguist.

Jessel, George Albert, 1898–1981, U.S. comedian.

Jesus, 6? B.C.–A.D. 29, religious leader & founder of Christianity; also called **Jesus Christ & Jesus of Nazareth.**

Jewett, Sarah Orne, 1849–1909, U.S. author.

Jiménez, Juan Ramón, 1881–1958, Sp. poet; Nobel Prize winner.

Joachim, Joseph, 1831–1907, Hung. violinist.

Joan of Arc, Saint, 1412–31, Fr. heroine; burned as a heretic: Fr. **Jeanne d'Arc;** also called **the Maid of Orleans.**

Jodl, Alfred, 1892?–1946. Ger. general.

Joffre, Joseph Jacques Césaire, 1852–1931, Fr. field marshal.

Joffrey, Robert, 1930–88, U.S. choreographer & ballet company director.

John, 1166?–1216, Eng. king 1199–1216; signed Magna Carta 1215.

John XXIII, b. Angelo Roncalli, 1881–1963, pope 1958–63.

John of Austria, Don, 1547–78, Sp.-born general.

John of the Cross, Saint, b. Juan de Yepis y Álvarez, 1542–91, Sp. mystic.

John of Gaunt, 1340–99, Eng. prince.

John, Augustus Edwin, 1878–1961, Eng. painter.

—Elton (Reginald Kenneth Dwight), 1947–, Eng. singer, songwriter.

John Paul I, b. Albino Luciani, 1912–78, pope 1978.

John Paul II, b. Karol Wojtyla, 1920–, pope 1978–.

Johns, Jasper, 1930–, U.S. painter & sculptor.

Johnson, Andrew, 1808–75, 17th U.S. president 1865–69.

—Dame Celia, 1908–82, Eng. actress.

—Harold (Chic), 1891–1962, U.S. comedian.

—Howard Deering, 1896?–1972, U.S. businessman.

—Jack Arthur, 1878–1946, U.S. boxer.

—James Weldon, 1871–1938, U.S. poet & author.

—John Harold, 1918–, U.S. publisher.

—(Jonathan) Eastman, 1824–1906, U.S. painter.

—Lyndon Baines, 1908–73, 36th U.S. president 1963–69.

Johnson, Philip Cortelyou, 1906–, U.S. architect.

—Samuel, 1709–84, Eng. author, critic, & lexicographer.

—Virginia Eshelman, 1925–, U.S. sex researcher.

—Walter Perry, 1887–1946, U.S. baseball player.

Joliot-Curie, Frèderic, 1900–58 & his wife, **Irène** (daughter of Marie & Pierre Curie), 1897–1956, Fr. physicists.

Jolliet, Louis, 1645–1700, Can. explorer in America. Also spelled **Joliet.**

Jolson, Al, 1886–1950, Russ.-born U.S. singer & actor.

Jones, Ernest, 1879–1958, Welsh-born Brit. psychoanalyst & author.

—Inigo, 1573–1652, Eng. architect & stage designer.

—James, 1921–77, U.S. author.

—James Earl, 1931–, U.S. actor.

—John Luther (Casey), 1864–1900, U.S. railroad engineer.

—John Paul, 1747–92, Scot.-born Amer. naval commander.

—Robert Tyre, Jr. (Bobby), 1902–71, U.S. golfer.

Jong, Erica, 1942–, U.S. author.

Jonson, Ben, 1572–1637, Eng. poet & playwright.

Joplin, Janis, 1943–70, U.S. singer.

—Scott, 1868–1917, U.S. jazz musician & composer.

Jordaens, Jacob, 1593–1678, Flemish painter.

Joseph, b. Hinmatonyalakit, 1840?–1904, Nez Percé Am. Ind. chief.

Josephine, 1763–1814, wife of Napoleon I & empress of France 1804–09.

Josephus, Flavius, A.D. 37–100?, Jewish historian.

Joule, James Prescott, 1818–89, Eng. physicist.

Jouvet, Louis, 1887–1951, Fr. actor & stage director.

Jowett, Benjamin, 1817–93, Eng. classical scholar.

Joyce, James, 1882–1941, Irish author & poet.

—William, 1906–46, U.S.-born Brit. traitor during World War II; executed: called **Lord Haw-Haw.**

Juan Carlos I, 1938–, king of Spain 1975–.

Juarez, Benito Pablo, 1806–72, Mexican patriot; president of Mexico 1867–72.

Juilliard, Augustus, 1836–1919, U.S. merchant, financier, & philanthropist.

Julian (L. Flavius Claudius Julianus), 331–363, Roman emperor: called **the Apostate.**

Juliana, 1909–, queen of the Netherlands 1948–80.

Julius II, b. Giuliano della Rovere, 1443–1513, pope 1503–13.

Jung, Carl Gustav, 1875–1961, Swiss psychologist.

Junkers, Hugo, 1859–1935, Ger. airplane designer.

Jussieu, Antoine Laurent de, 1748–1836, Fr. botanist.

Justinian I, 482–565, Byzantine emperor; codifier of Roman law.

Juvenal (L. Decimus Junius Juvenalis), A.D. 60?–140?, Roman poet.

Kabalevsky, Dmitri, 1904–, Russ. composer.
Kádár, János, 1912–89, first secretary of the Communist party of Hungary 1956–88.
Kael, Pauline, 1919, U.S. film critic.
Kafka, Franz, 1883–1924, Czech-born Austrian author.
Kagawa, Toyohiko, 1888–1960, Jap. Christian social reformer & author.
Kahn, Albert, 1869–1942, U.S. architect.
—**Gus,** 1886–1941, U.S. lyricist.
—**Louis Isadore** 1901–74, Estonian-born U.S. architect.
—**Otto Herman,** 1867–1934, Ger.-born U.S. banker, art patron, & philanthropist.
Kaiser, Henry John, 1882–1967, U.S. industrialist.
Kalmar, Bert, 1884–1947, U.S. lyricist & librettist.
Kaltenborn, H(ans) V(on), 1878–1965, U.S. news commentator.
Kamehameha, 1758?–1819, king of Hawaii 1795–1819.
Kamerlingh Onnes, Heike, 1853–1926, Du. physicist.
Kander, John, 1927–, U.S. composer.
Kandinski, Vasili, 1866–1944, Russ. painter active in Germany.
Kanin, Garson, 1912–, U.S. playwright & stage director.
Kano A family of 15th-16th c. Jap. painters, incl. **Masanobu,** 1453–90, & his sons, **Motonobu,** 1476–1559, & **Yokinobu,** 1513–75.
Kant, Immanuel, 1724–1804, Ger. philosopher.
Kantor, MacKinlay, 1904–77, U.S. writer.
Kapitsa, Pyotr Leonidovich, 1894–1984, Russ. physicist & Nobel prize winner.
Karajan, Herbert von, 1908–89, Austrian conductor.
Karinska, Barbara, 1886–1983, Russ.-born U.S. costume designer & maker.
Karloff, Boris, 1887–1969, Eng.-born actor active in U.S.
Karsavina, Tamara, 1885–1978, Russ. ballerina.
Karsh, Yousuf, 1908–, Armenian-born Can. photographer.
Kasavubu, Joseph, 1910–69, first president of the Congolese Republic (now Zaire) 1960–65.
Kassem, Abdul Karim, 1914–63, Iraqi general; premier of Iraq 1958–63; executed.
Kastler, Alfred, 1902–84, Fr. physicist; Nobel prize winner.
Kaufman, George S., 1889–1961, U.S. playwright.
Kaunda, Kenneth David, 1924–, president of Zambia 1964–.
Kawabata, Yasunari, 1899–1972, Jap. author.
Kay, Ulysses Simpson, 1917–, U.S. composer.
Kaye, Danny, 1913–91, U.S. comedian & actor.
Kazan, Elia, 1909–, Turkish-born U.S. stage & film director & author.
Kazantzakis, Nikos, 1885–1957, Gk. poet & author.
Kean, Edmund, 1787–1833, Eng. actor.
Keaton, Buster, 1895–1966, U.S. film actor & director.
Keats, John, 1795–1821, Eng. poet.
Keeler, Ruby, 1910–, Can.-born U.S. singer, dancer, & actress.
Kefauver, Estes, 1903–63, U.S. politician.
Keino, Kipchoge, 1940–, Kenyan track runner.
Keitel, Wilhelm, 1882–1946, Ger. field marshal.
Kekkonen, Urho Kaleva, 1900–86, president of Finland 1956–81.
Kekulé von Stradonitz, Friedrich August, 1829–96, Ger. chemist.
Keller, Helen Adams, 1880–1968, U.S. author & lecturer; blind and deaf from infancy.
Kelley, Clarence M., 1911–, U.S. government official; director of the FBI 1973–77.
Kellogg, Frank Billings, 1856–1937, U.S. statesman; Nobel prize winner.
—**Will Keith,** 1860–1951, U.S. businessman.
Kelly, Alvin A. (Shipwreck), 1893–1952, U.S. flagpole sitter.
—**Ellsworth,** 1923–, U.S. painter & sculptor.
—**Emmett,** 1898–1979, U.S. circus clown.
—**Gene Curran,** 1912–, U.S. dancer, singer, actor, choreographer, & film director.
—**George,** 1887–1971, U.S. playwright.
—**Walt(er),** 1913–73, U.S. cartoonist.

Kelvin, Lord (William Thompson), 1824–1907, Eng. physicist.
Kemble, Frances Anne (Fanny), 1809–93, Eng. actress.
Kempff, Wilhelm, 1895–, Ger. pianist.
Kempis, Thomas à, 1380–1471, Ger. mystic.
Kempton, (James) Murray, 1918–, U.S. journalist & social critic.
Kendall, Edward Calvin, 1886–1972, U.S. biochemist; Nobel prize winner.
Kennan, George Frost, 1904–, U.S. statesman & author.
Kennedy A U.S. family prominent in politics, incl. **Joseph Patrick,** 1888–1969, businessman & diplomat, his wife **Rose Fitzgerald,** 1890–, & their sons, **Edward Moore,** 1932–, U.S. senator; **John Fitzgerald,** 1917–63, U.S. senator, 35th U.S. president 1961–63, assassinated; & **Robert Francis,** 1925–68, U.S. senator, assassinated.
Kennedy, Anthony M., 1936–, U.S. jurist; justice of the U.S. Supreme Court 1987–.
Kennelly, Arthur Edwin, 1861–1939, Indian-born U.S. electrical engineer.
Kenner, (William) Hugh, 1923–, Can. author & critic active in U.S.
Kenny, Elizabeth, 1886–1952, Austral. nurse & physiotherapist; called **Sister Kenny.**
Kent, Rockwell, 1882–1971, U.S. painter & illustrator.
Kenton, Stan, 1912–79, U.S. jazz musician.
Kenyatta, Jomo, 1893?–1978, African nationalist leader & first president of Kenya 1964–1978.
Keokuk, 1788?–1848, Sauk Am. Ind. leader.
Kepler, Johannes, 1571–1630, Ger. astronomer.
Kerensky, Alexander Feodorovich, 1881–1970, Russ. revolutionary leader & prime minister of Soviet provisional government 1917.
Kern, Jerome David, 1885–1945, U.S. composer.
Kerouac, Jack, 1922–69, U.S. author.
Kerr, Jean, 1923–, U.S. author & playwright.
—**Walter,** 1913–, U.S. drama critic & author; husband of prec.
Kesey, Ken, 1935–, U.S. author.
Kesselring, Albert, 1887–1960, Ger. field marshal.
Ketcham, Hank, 1920–, U.S. cartoonist.
Kettering, Charles Franklin, 1876–1958, U.S. electrical engineer & inventor.
Key, Francis Scott, 1780?–1843, U.S. lawyer; wrote "The Star-Spangled Banner."
Keynes, John Maynard, 1883–1946, Eng. economist.
Khachaturian, Aram, 1903–78, Armenian-born Soviet composer.
Khama, Sir Seretse, 1921–80, president of Botswana 1965–80.
Khomeini, Ayatollah Ruhollah, 1899?–1989, Iranian religious and political leader.
Khorana, Har Gobind, 1922–, Indian-born U.S. biochemist.
Khrushchev, Nikita Sergeyevich, 1894–1971, premier of the Soviet Union 1953–64.
Kidd, Michael, 1919–, U.S. choreographer.
—**Captian William,** 1645?–1701, Eng. privateer & pirate; hanged.
Kieran, John Francis, 1892–1981, U.S. author & journalist.
Kierkegaard, Soren Aabye, 1813–55, Dan. philosopher & theologian.
Kiesinger, Kurt Georg, 1904–88, W. German politician; chancellor of W. Germany 1966–69.
Kilgallen, Dorothy, 1913–65, U.S. journalist.
Killy, Jean-Claude, 1943–, Fr. skier.
Kilmer, (Alfred) Joyce, 1886–1918, U.S. poet.
Kim IL Sung, 1912–, Korean military leader; premier of N. Korea 1948–72, president 1972–.
King, Billie Jean, 1943–, U.S. tennis player.
—**Coretta Scott,** 1927–, U.S. black civil rights leader; wife of Martin Luther, Jr.
—**Dennis,** 1897–1971, Eng. actor & singer.
—**Frank,** 1883–1969, U.S. cartoonist.
—**Martin Luther, Jr.,** 1929–68, U.S. clergyman & black civil rights leader; assassinated.
—**Stephen,** 1947–, U.S. author.
—**(William Lyon) Mackenzie,** 1874–1950, prime minister of Canada 1921–26, 1926–30 & 1935–48.

—**William Rufus Devane,** 1786–1853, U.S. statesman; U.S. vice president 1853.

Kingsley, Charles, 1819–75, Eng. clergyman & author.

—**Sidney,** 1906–, U.S. playwright.

Kinsey, Alfred Charles, 1894–1956, U.S. zoologist; pioneered in studies of human sexual behavior.

Kipling, (Joseph) Rudyard, 1865–1936, Indian-born Eng. author.

Kipnis, Alexander, 1891–1978, Russ.-born U.S. basso.

—**Igor,** 1930–, Ger.-born U.S. harpsichordist; son of prec.

Kirchner, Ernst Ludwig, 1880–1938, Ger. painter.

Kirkland, Gelsey, 1953–, U.S. ballerina.

—**Lane,** 1922–, U.S. labor leader.

Kirkpatrick, Jeane, 1926–, U.S. diplomat & scholar.

Kirov, Sergei Mironovich, 1888–1934, Russ. revolutionary.

Kirstein, Lincoln, 1907–, U.S. author, dance promoter, & ballet company director.

Kirsten, Dorothy, 1919–, U.S. soprano.

Kissinger, Henry Alfred, 1923–, Ger.-born U.S. foreign-policy adviser; U.S. secretary of state 1973–77.

Kitchener, Horatio Herbert, (1st Earl Kitchener), 1850–1916, Brit. field marshal & statesman.

Kitt, Eartha, 1928–, U.S. singer.

Kittredge, George Lyman, 1860–1941, U.S. Shakespeare scholar & editor.

Klee, Paul, 1879–1940, Swiss painter.

Klein, Calvin, 1942–, U.S. fashion designer.

—**Lawrence Robert,** 1920–, economist; Nobel prize winner.

Kleist, Heinrich von, 1777–1811, Ger. playwright.

Klemperer, Otto, 1885–1973, Ger. conductor.

Kliegl, Anton T., 1872–1927, & his brother **John H.,** 1869–1959, Ger.-born U.S. lighting experts.

Klimt, Gustav, 1862–1918, Austrian painter.

Kline, Franz Joseph, 1910–62, U.S. painter.

Klopstock, Friedrich Gottlieb, 1724–1803, Ger. poet.

Knievel, Robert (Evel), 1938–, U.S. motorcycle stunt man.

Knopf, Alfred Abraham, 1892–1984, U.S. publisher.

Knowles, John, 1926–, U.S. author.

Knox, John, 1507?–72, Scot. Protestant clergyman & religious reformer.

Koch, John, 1909–78, U.S. painter.

—**Robert,** 1843–1910, Ger. bacteriologist.

Kocher, Emil Theodor, 1841–1917, Swiss surgeon.

Kodály, Zoltan, 1882–1967, Hung. composer.

Koestler, Arthur, 1905–83, Hung.-born Eng. author.

Koffka, Kurt, 1886–1941, Ger.-born U.S. psychologist.

Kohl, Helmut, 1930–, chancellor of W. Germany, 1982–90; chancellor of Germany 1990–.

Kohler, Wolfgang, 1887–1967, Russ.-born U.S. psychologist.

Kokoschka, Oskar, 1886–1980, Austrian-born Brit. painter.

Kollwitz, Käthe, 1867–1945, Ger. painter, etcher, & lithographer.

Konoye, Prince Fumimaro, 1891–1945, premier of Japan 1937–39 & 1940–41.

Koo, V(i) K(uyuin) Wellington, 1887–1985, Chin. statesman & diplomat.

Kooweskoowe, b. John Ross, 1790–1866, Cherokee Am. Ind. leader.

Koppel, Ted (Edward James), 1940–, Eng.-born U.S. journalist.

Korda, Alexander, 1893–1956, Hung.-born Brit. film director.

Korngold, Erich Wolfgang, 1897–1957, Austrian-born U.S. composer, conductor, & pianist.

Korsakov, Sergei, 1853–1900, Russ. neurologist & psychiatrist.

Korzybski, Alfred Habdank Skarbek, 1879–1950, Pol.-born U.S. linguist.

Kosciusko, Thaddeus, 1746–1817, Pol. patriot in the Amer. Revolution.

Kosinski, Jerzy, 1933–, Pol.-born novelist.

Kossel, Albrecht, 1853–1927, Ger. biochemist.

Kossuth, Lajos, 1802–94, Hung. patriot.

Kostelanetz, André, 1901–80, Russ.-born U.S. conductor.

Kosygin, Alexei Nikolayevich, 1904–80, Soviet statesman; premier of the Soviet Union 1964–80.

Koufax Sanford (Sandy), 1935–, U.S. baseball player.

Koussevitsky, Serge, 1874–1951, Russ.-born U.S. conductor.

Kovalevski, Alexander Onufriyevich, 1840–1901, Russ. embryologist.

Krafft-Ebing, Baron Richard von, 1840–1902, Ger. neurologist.

Kramer, Jack, 1921–, U.S. tennis player.

—**Stanley,** 1913–, U.S. film director.

Krebs, Sir Hans Adolf, 1900–81, Ger.-born Brit. biochemist; Nobel Prize winner.

Krehbiel, Henry Edward, 1854–1923, U.S. music critic.

Kreisky, Bruno, 1911–90, Austrian politician; chancellor of Austria 1970–83.

Kreisler, Fritz, 1875–1962, Austrian-born violinist.

Kresge, S.S., 1867–1966, U.S. merchant.

Kress, Samuel Henry, 1863–1955, U.S. businessman, art collector, & philanthropist.

Krips, Josef, 1902–74, Austrian conductor.

Krishna Menon, V(engalil) K(rishnan), 1896–1974, Indian statesman.

Kroc, Raymond A., 1902–84, U.S. restaurateur & businessman.

Krock, Arthur, 1886–1974, U.S. journalist.

Kroeber, Alfred Louis, 1876–1960, U.S. anthropologist.

Kropotkin, Prince Pyotr Alekseevich, 1842–1921, Russ. geographer & revolutionary.

Kruger, Paulus, 1825–1904, South African statesman; president of Transvaal 1883–1900.

Krupa, Gene, 1909–73, U.S. jazz musician.

Krupp, Alfred, 1812–87, Ger. munitions manufacturer.

Krupskaya, Nadezhda Konstantinovna, 1869–1939, Russ. social worker & revolutionist; wife of Nikolai Lenin.

Krutch, Joseph Wood, 1893–1970, U.S. critic & author.

Kubelik, Rafael, 1914–, Czech conductor & composer.

Kublai Khan, 1216–94, founder of the Mongol dynasty of China.

Kubrick, Stanley, 1928–, U.S. film director.

Kühne, Willy, 1837–1900, Ger. physiologist.

Kun, Béla, 1885–1937, Hung. communist leader.

Küng, Hans, 1928–, Swiss theologian.

Kunitz, Stanley, 1905–, U.S. poet.

Kunstler, William M., 1919–, U.S. lawyer.

Kurosawa, Akira, 1910–, Jap. film director.

Kurusu, Saburo, 1888–1954, Jap. diplomat.

Kusch, Polykarp, 1911–, Ger.-born U.S. physicist & educator.

Kutuzov, Mikhail Ilarionovich, 1745–1813, Russ. field marshal.

Kuznets, Simon, 1901–85, Russ.-born U.S. economist; Nobel Prize winner.

Kyd, Thomas, 1558–94, Eng. playwright.

La Bruyère, Jean de, 1645–96, Fr. author.

LaChaise, François d'Aix de, 1624–1709, Fr. Jesuit priest.

Lachaise, Gaston, 1882–1935, Fr.-born U.S. sculptor.

Laemmle, Carl, 1867–1939, Ger.-born U.S. film producer.

Laënnec, René, 1781–1826, Fr. physician.

La Farge, Christopher Grant, 1862–1938, U.S. architect.

—**John,** 1835–1910, U.S. painter & stained-glass craftsman.

—**Oliver Hazard Perry,** 1901–63, U.S. anthropologist & author.

Lafayette, Marie Joseph du Motier, Marquis de, 1757–1834, Fr. general & patriot; served in Amer. revolutionary army.

Lafitte, Jean, 1780?–1825?, Fr. pirate active in U.S.

La Follette, Robert Marion, 1855–1925, U.S. senator & Progressive Party presidential candidate.

La Fontaine, Jean de, 1621–95, Fr. poet & writer of fables.

Lagerkvist, Pär, 1891–1974, Swed. author, poet, & playwrite.

Lagerlöf, Selma, 1858–1940, Swed. author; Nobel Prize winner.

Lagrange, Joseph Louis, 1736–1813, Fr. mathematician & astronomer.

La Guardia, Fiorello Henry, 1882–1947, U.S. politician; mayor of New York City 1934–45.

Lahr, Bert, 1895–1967, U.S. comedian & actor.

Laine, (Papa) Jack, 1873–1966, U.S. jazz musician.

Laing, R(onald) D., 1927–89, Scot. psychoanalyst & author.

Lalo, Victor Antoine Édouard, 1823–92, Fr. composer.
Lamarck, Jean Baptiste de Monet, Chevalier de, 1744–1829, Fr. naturalist.
Lamarr, Hedy, 1915–, Austrian-born U.S. actress.
Lamartine, Alphonse Marie Louis de Prat de, 1790–1869, Fr. poet.
Lamb, Charles, 1775–1834, Eng. author: pseud. **Elia.**
—**Mary,** 1764–1847, Eng. author; sister of prec.
—**Willis Eugene, Jr.,** 1913–, U.S. nuclear physicist; Nobel Prize winner.
L'Amour, Louis Dearborn, 1908–88, U.S. author.
Land, Edwin Herbert, 1909–, U.S. inventor & industrialist.
Landau, Lev Davidovich, 1908–68, Soviet physicist; Nobel Prize winner.
Landers, Ann, pseud. of Esther Pauline Friedman, 1918–, U.S. columnist.
Landis, Kenesaw Mountain, 1866–1944, U.S. jurist & baseball commissioner.
Landon, Alf(red Mossman), 1887–1987, U.S. politician.
Landor, Walter Savage, 1775–1864, Eng. poet & author.
Landowska, Wanda, 1879–1959, Pol. harpsichordist active in U.S. after 1941.
Landru, Henri, 1869–1922, Fr. murderer; executed: known as **the modern Bluebeard.**
Landseer, Sir Edwin Henry, 1802–73, Eng. painter.
Landsteiner, Karl, 1868–1943, Austrian-born U.S. pathologist; Nobel Prize winner.
Lane, Burton, 1912–, U.S. composer.
Lang, Andrew, 1844–1912, Scot. poet, scholar, & author.
—**Fritz,** 1890–1976, Austrian-born U.S. film director.
—**Paul Henry,** 1901–, U.S. music critic.
Langdon, Harry, 1884–1944, U.S. vaudeville performer.
Lange, David Russell, 1942–, New Zealand statesman; prime minister 1984–89.
—**Dorothea,** 1895–1965, U.S. photographer.
Langer, Susanne, 1895–1985, U.S. philosopher & educator.
Langland, William, 1332?–1400, Eng. poet.
Langley, John Newport, 1851–1925, Eng. physiologist.
—**Samuel Pierpont,** 1834–1906, U.S. astronomer.
Langmuir, Irving, 1881–1957, U.S. chemist; Nobel Prize winner.
Langtry, Lillie, 1853–1929, Eng. actress.
Lanier, Sidney, 1842–81, U.S. poet.
Lankester, Sir Edwin Ray, 1847–1929, Eng. zoologist.
Lansky, Meyer, 1902–83, U.S. criminal.
Lanza, Mario, 1925–59, U.S. singer & actor.
Lao-tse, 604?–531? B.C., Chin. philosopher & mystic; founder of Taoism.
Laplace, Pierre Simon, Marquis de, 1749–1827, Fr. mathematician & astronomer.
Lapp, Ralph Eugene, 1917–, U.S. physicist.
Lardner, Ring(gold Wilmer), 1885–1933, U.S. author.
La Rochefoucauld, Duc François de, 1613–80, Fr. writer.
Larousse, Pierre Athanase, 1817–75, Fr. grammarian & lexicographer.
La Salle, Sieur Robert, Cavalier de, 1643–87, Fr. explorer.
Lashley, Karl Spencer, 1890–1958, U.S. psychologist.
Lasker, Albert Davis, 1880–1952, Ger.-born U.S. businessman & philanthropist.
—**Emmanuel,** 1868–1941, Ger. mathematician & chess master.
Laski, Harold Joseph, 1893–1950, Eng. political scientist.
Lasso, Orlando di, 1532?–94, Du. composer.
Laszlo, Ernest, 1899–1984, Hung. cinematographer.
Latimer, Hugh, 1485?–1555, Eng. Protestant martyr.
La Tour, Georges de, 1593–1652, Fr. painter.
Latrobe, Benjamin Henry, 1764–1820, Eng.-born U.S. architect & engineer.
Lattimore, Owen, 1900–89, U.S. author & oriental expert.
Lauder, Sir Harry, 1870–1950, Scot. singer.
Laue, Max Theodor Felix von, 1879–1960, Ger. physicist; Nobel Prize winner.
Laughton, Charles, 1899–1962, Eng.-born U.S. actor.
Laurel, (Arthur) Stan(ley), 1890–1965, Eng.-born U.S. comedian & actor.
Laurencin, Marie, 1885–1956, Fr. painter.
Laurents, Arthur, 1918–, U.S. playwright.

Laurier, Sir Wilfrid, 1841–1919, Can. statesman; prime minister 1896–1911.
Laval, Pierre, 1883–1945, Fr. lawyer & politician.
LaValliére, Louise LeBlanc, Duchesse de, 1644–1710, mistress of Louis XIV.
Laver, Rod(ney George), 1938–, Austral. tennis player.
Laveran, Charles Louis Alphonse, 1845–1922, Fr. physician; Nobel Prize winner.
Lavoisier, Antoine Laurent, 1743–94, Fr. chemist & physicist.
Lavrovsky, Leonid M., 1905–67, Soviet choreographer.
Law, Andrew Bonar, 1858–1923, Brit. statesman; prime minister 1922–23.
—**John,** 1671–1729, Scot. financier & speculator.
Lawes, Lewis Edward, 1883–1947, U.S. penologist.
Lawrence, David, 1888–1973, U.S. journalist.
—**D(avid) H(erbert),** 1885–1930, Eng. author & poet.
—**Ernest Orlando,** 1901–58, U.S. pysicist.
—**Gertrude,** 1898–1952, Eng. actress active in U.S.
—**Sir Thomas,** 1769–1830, Eng. painter.
—**Thomas, Edward,** 1888–1935, Welsh soldier, archaeologist, & author: known as **Lawrence of Arabia.**
Laxness, Halldór Kiljan, 1902–, Icelandic author; Nobel Prize winner.
Layne, Robert, 1926–, U.S. football player.
Lazarus, Emma, 1849–87, U.S. poet & author.
Leacock, Stephen Butler, 1869–1944, Can. economist & humorist.
Leadbelly, b. Huddie Ledbetter, 1888?–1949, U.S. folk singer.
Leahy, William Daniel, 1875–1959, U.S. admiral.
Leakey, Louis Seymour Blazett, 1903–72, and his wife **Mary Nicol Leakey,** 1913–, Brit. anthropologists.
—**Richard E.,** 1944–, Kenyan anthropologist; son of prec.
Lean, Sir David, 1908–, Eng. film director.
Lear, Edward, 1812–88, Eng. poet, painter, & illustrator.
—**William Powell,** 1902–78, U.S. engineer & manufacturer.
Leavis, F(rank) R(aymond), 1895–1978, Eng. critic.
Le Brun, Charles, 1619–90, Fr. painter.
Le Carré, John, pseud. of David J. M. Cornwell, 1931–, Eng. author.
Leconte de Lisle, Charles Marie, 1818–94, Fr. poet.
Lederberg, Joshua, 1925– U.S. geneticist.
Lee, Ann, 1736–84, Eng. mystic; founder of the Shaker movement in America.
—**Francis Lightfoot,** 1734–97, Amer. revolutionary patriot.
—**Gypsy Rose,** 1914–70, U.S. stripteaser & author.
—**Harper,** 1926–, U.S. novelist.
—**Henry,** 1756–1818, Amer. revolutionary soldier & statesman: known as **Light-Horse Harry Lee.**
—**Peggy,** 1920–, U.S. singer.
—**Richard Henry,** 1732–94, Amer. revolutionary patriot.
—**Robert E(dward),** 1807–70, commander in chief of the Confederate Army; son of Henry.
—**Tsung-Dao,** 1926–, Chin.-born U.S. physicist.
Leeuwenhoek, Anton van, 1632–1723, Du. naturalist.
Le Gallienne, Eva, 1899–1991, Eng.-born U.S. actress.
—**Richard,** 1866–1947, Eng. author; father of prec.
Léger, Fernand, 1881–1955, Fr. painter.
Le Guin, Ursula, 1929–, U.S. author.
Lehár, Franz, 1870–1948, Austrian composer.
Lehman, Herbert Henry, 1878–1963, U.S. banker & politician.
Lehmann, Lili, 1848–1929, Ger. soprano.
—**Lotte,** 1888–1976, Ger. soprano.
Lehmbruck, Wilhelm, 1881–1919, Ger. sculptor.
Leibniz, Baron Gottfried Wilhelm von, 1646–1716, Ger. philosopher & mathematician.
Leicester, Robert Dudley, 1st Earl of, 1532?–88, Eng. courtier.
Leider, Frida, 1888–1975, Ger. soprano.
Leigh, Mitch, 1928–, U.S. composer.
—**Vivien,** 1913–67, Indian-born Eng. actress.
Leinsdorf, Erich, 1912–, Austrian-born U.S. conductor.
LeMay, Curtis Emerson, 1906–90, U.S. air force officer.
Lemnitzer, Lyman L., 1899–, U.S. general.
Lenard, Phillip E. A., 1862–1947, Ger. physicist.

Lenclos, Ninon de, 1620–1705, Fr. courtesan & wit.

L'Enfant, Pierre Charles, 1754–1825, Fr. architect; planned Washington, D.C.

L'Engle, Madeleine, 1918–, U.S. author.

Lenglen, Suzanne, 1899–1938, Fr. tennis player.

Lenin, Nikolai, b. Vladimir Ilich Ulyanov, 1870–1924, Russ. revolutionary leader; premier of Soviet Union 1918–24.

Lennon, John, 1940–80, Eng. composer & musical performer.

Lenya, Lotte, 1900–81, Austrian singer & actress active in U.S.

Lenz, Heinrich F. E., 1804–65, Russ. physicist.

Leo I, Saint, 390?–461, pope 440–461: called **the Great.**

—III, Saint, 750?–816, pope 795–816.

—X, b. Giovanni de' Medici, 1475–1521, pope 1513–21.

Leonardo da Vinci, 1452–1519, Ital. painter, sculptor, architect, engineer, inventor, musician, scientist, & natural philosopher.

Leoncavallo, Ruggiero, 1858–1919, Ital. composer & librettist.

Leone, Giovanni, 1908–, Ital. politician; president of Italy 1971–78.

Leonidas, 5th c. B.C. Gk. military leader: king of Sparta 490?–480 B.C.

Leontief, Wassily W., 1906–, Russ.-born U.S. economist & author; Nobel Prize winner.

Leopardi, Count Giacomo, 1798–1837, Ital. poet.

Lepidus, Marcus Aemilius, ?–13 B.C., Roman statesman.

Lermontov, Mikhail Yurievich, 1814–41, Russ. poet & author.

Lerner, Alan Jay, 1918–86, U.S. playwright & lyricist.

—Max, 1902–, Russ.-born U.S. author & journalist.

Le Roy, Mervyn, 1900–87, U.S. film director.

Lescaze, William, 1896–1969, U.S. architect.

Leschetizky, Theodor, 1830–1915, Russ. pianist & composer.

Lesseps, Count Ferdinand de, 1805–94, Fr. engineer; built Suez Canal.

Lessing, Doris, 1919–, Iranian-born Brit. author.

—Gotthold Ephraim, 1729–81, Ger. playwright & critic.

Lester, Richard, 1932–, Eng. film director.

Leutze, Emanuel Gottlieb, 1816–68, Ger.-born U.S. painter.

Levant, Oscar, 1906–72, U.S. pianist, composer, & author.

Levene, Phoebus A. T., 1869–1940, Russ.-born U.S. chemist.

—Sam, 1905–80, Russ.-born U.S. actor.

Levenson, Sam, 1911–80, U.S. humorist.

Leverholme, Viscount, b. William Hesketh Lever, 1851–1925, Brit. industrialist.

Leverrier, Urbain Jean Joseph, 1811–77, Fr. astronomer.

Levertov, Denise, 1923–, Eng.-born U.S. poet.

Lévesque, René, 1922–87, Can. politician.

Levin, Ira, 1929–, U.S. author.

Levine, Jack, 1915–, U.S. painter.

—James, 1943–, U.S. conductor & music director.

—Joseph E., 1905–, U.S. film producer.

Lévi-Strauss, Claude, 1908–, Belg.-born Fr. anthropologist.

Lewin, Kurt, 1890–1947, Ger.-born U.S. psychologist.

Lewis, Anthony, 1927–, U.S. journalist.

—Cecil Day See DAY-LEWIS, CECIL.

—C(live) S(taples), 1898–1963, Eng. author.

—Gilbert Newton, 1875–1946, U.S. chemist.

—Jerry, 1926–, U.S. actor & comedian.

—John L(lewellyn), 1880–1969, U.S. labor leader.

—Meriwether, 1774–1809, U.S. explorer.

—Oscar, 1914–70, U.S. sociologist & author.

—(Percy) Wyndham, 1884–1957, Eng. painter & author.

—Sinclair, 1885–1951, U.S. author.

Lewisohn, Ludwig, 1883–1955, Ger.born U.S. author & critic.

Lhevinne, Joseph, 1874–1944, Russ.-born U.S. pianist.

Li, Choh Hao, 1913–, Chin.-born U.S. biochemist.

Libby, W(illard) F(rank), 1908–80, U.S. chemist; Nobel Prize winner.

Liberace, (Wladziu), 1919–87, U.S. pianist.

Lichtenstein, Roy, 1923–, U.S. artist.

Liddell Hart, Basil Henry, 1895–1970, Eng. military scientist.

Lie, Trygve, 1896–1968, Norw. statesman; first secretary general of the U.N. 1946–53.

Liebig, Baron Justus von, 1803–73, Ger. chemist.

Lifar, Serge, 1905–86, Russ. dancer.

Ligeti, György, 1923–, Hung. composer.

Lilienthal, David Eli, 1899–1981, U.S. lawyer & administrator.

Lillie, Beatrice, 1898–1989, Can.-born comedienne & actress active in England & U.S.

Lilly, John C., 1915–, U.S. neurophysiologist & biophysicist.

Limón, José, 1908–72, Mexican-born U.S. dancer, choreographer, & dance company director.

Lincoln, Abraham, 1809–65, 16th U.S. president 1861–65; assassinated.

—Robert Todd, 1843–1926, U.S. statesman & lawyer; son of prec.

Lind, James, 1716–94, Scot. physician.

—Jenny, 1820–87, Swed. soprano.

Lindbergh, Anne Morrow, 1906–, U.S. author.

—Charles Augustus, 1902–74, U.S. aviator; made first transatlantic nonstop solo flight 1927; husband of prec.

Lindsay, Howard, 1889–1968, U.S. playwright.

—John Vliet, 1921–, U.S. politician.

—(Nicholas) Vachel, 1879–1931, U.S. poet.

Linklater, Eric, 1899–1974, Eng. author.

Linkletter, Art, 1912–, Can. radio & TV personality & author.

Linnaeus, Carolus, b. Karl von Linné, 1707–78, Swed. botanist & taxonomist.

Lin Biao, 1907–71, Chin. political leader.

Lin Yutang, 1895–1976, Chin. philologist & author.

Lipchitz, Jacques, 1891–1973, Lithuanian-born sculptor active in U.S.

Li Po, 700?–762, Chin. poet.

Lippi, Fra Filippo (Lippo), 1406?–69, & his son **Filippino,** 1457?–1504, Ital. painters.

Lippmann, Walter, 1889–1974, U.S. journalist.

Lippold, Richard, 1915–, U.S. sculptor.

Lipset, Seymour Martin, 1922–, U.S. sociologist.

Lipton, Sir Thomas Johnstone, 1850–1931, Irish merchant & yachtsman.

Lissajous, Jules A., 1822–80, Fr. physicist.

Lister, Joseph, 1827–1912, Eng. surgeon.

Liszt, Franz, 1811–86, Hung. composer & pianist.

Littlewood, Joan, 1916–, Eng. theater director.

Litvinov, Maxim Maximovich, 1876–1951, Russ. revolutionary & statesman.

Liu Shaoji, 1898–1973, Chin. government official.

Livingstone, David, 1813–73, Scot. missionary & explorer in Africa.

—Mary, 1916–83. U.S. radio personality.

Livy, (Titus Livius), 59 B.C.–A.D. 17, Roman historian.

Llewellyn, Richard, 1906–83, Brit. novelist & playwright.

Lloyd George, David, 1863–1945, Brit. statesman; prime minister 1916–22.

Lloyd, Harold Clayton, 1894–1971, U.S. actor & film producer.

Lobachevski, Nikolai Ivanovich, 1793–1856, Russ. mathematician.

Locke, John, 1632–1704, Eng. philosopher.

Lockwood, Belva Ann Bennett, 1830–1917, U.S. social reformer & suffrage leader.

Lodge, Henry Cabot, 1902–85, U.S. politician & diplomat.

Loesser, Frank, 1910–69, U.S. composer & lyricist.

Loewe, Frederick, 1904–88, Austrian-born U.S. composer.

Loewi, Otto, 1873–1961, Ger.-born U.S. pharmacologist.

Loewy, Raymond Fernand, 1893–1986, Fr.-born U.S. industrial designer.

Lofting, Hugh John, 1886–1947, Eng.-born U.S. author & illustrator.

Logan, Joshua, 1908–88, U.S. stage & film director, producer, & author.

Lomax, John Avery, 1867–1948, & his son **Alan,** 1915–, U.S. folk-song collectors.

Lombard, Carole, 1909–42, U.S. actress.

Lombardi, Vincent Thomas, 1913–70, U.S. football coach.

Lombardo, Guy Albert, 1902–77, Can.-born U.S. bandleader.

Lombrosso, Cesare, 1836–1909, Ital. criminologist & physician.

London, George, 1920–85, Can. bass-baritone.
—Jack, 1876–1916, U.S. author.
Long, Crawford Williamson, 1815–78, U.S. surgeon.
—Huey Pierce, 1893–1935, U.S. lawyer & politician; assassinated.
Longfellow, Henry Wadsworth, 1807–82, U.S. poet.
Longstreet, James, 1821–1904, U.S. Confederate general.
Lon Nol, 1913–85, Cambodian general; president of Kampuchea 1970–75.
Loos, Anita, 1888–1981, U.S. author.
Lopez Portillo, José, 1920–, president of Mexico 1976–1982.
Loren, Sophia, 1934–, Ital. actress.
Lorentz, Hendrik Antoon, 1853–1928, Du. physicist & author; Nobel Prize winner.
Lorenz, Konrad Zacharias, 1903–89, Austrian zoologist.
Lorre, Peter, 1904–64, Hung.-born actor active in U.S.
Losey, Joseph, 1909–84, U.S. film director active in England.
Louis IX (Saint Louis), 1214–70, king of France 1226–70.
—XIII, 1601–43, king of France 1610–43.
—XIV, 1638–1715, king of France 1643–1715; son of prec.
—XV, 1710–74, king of France 1715–74; great-grandson of prec.
—XVI, 1754–93, king of France 1774–92; guillotined; grandson of prec.
—XVIII, 1755–1824, king of France 1814–15 & 1815–24; brother of prec.
Louis Philippe, 1773–1850, king of France 1830–48.
Louis, Joe, 1914–81, U.S. boxer.
Lovecraft, H(oward) P(hillips), 1890–1937, U.S. author.
Lovelace, Richard, 1618–58, Eng. poet.
Lovell, Sir (Alfred Charles) Bernard, 1913–, Eng. astronomer.
Low, Sir David, 1891–1963, New Zealand-born Brit. cartoonist.
—Juliette Gordon, 1860–1927, U.S. founder of the Girl Scouts.
Lowell, Amy, 1873–1925, U.S. poet & critic.
—James Russell, 1819–91, U.S. poet & author.
—Percival, 1855–1916, U.S. astronomer; brother of Amy.
—Robert (Traill Spence, Jr.), 1917–77, U.S. poet.
Lowry, Malcolm, 1909–57, Eng. author.
Loy, Myrna, 1905–, U.S. actress.
Loyola, Saint Ignatius, b. Iñigo do Oñez y Loyola, 1491–1556, Sp. soldier & priest; founder with Francis Xavier of the Society of Jesus.
Lubitsch, Ernst, 1892–1947, Ger.-born U.S. film director.
Lübke, Heinrich, 1894–1972, W. German government official; president of W. Germany 1959–69.
Lucas, George, 1944–, U.S. film producer, director, & writer.
Luce, Clare Boothe, 1903–87, U.S. writer & diplomat.
—Henry Robinson, 1898–1967, U.S. editor & publisher; husband of prec.
Luckman, Sidney, 1916–, U.S. football player.
Lucretius, 96?–55 B.C., Roman poet & philosopher.
Lucullus, Lucius Licinius, 1st c. B.C. Roman general & epicure.
Ludlum, Robert, 1927–, U.S. author.
Luening, Otto, 1900–, U.S. composer.
Lugosi, Bela, 1882–1956, Romanian-born actor active in U.S.
Lukas, J. Anthony, 1933–, U.S. journalist.
—Paul, 1895–1971, Hung.-born actor active in U.S.
Lully, Jean Baptiste, 1633?–87, Ital.-born Fr. composer.
Lumet, Sidney, 1924–, U.S. film director.
Lumumba, Patrice, 1925–61, first prime minister of the Congolese Republic (now Zaire) 1960–61; assassinated.
Lunt, Alfred, 1892–1977, U.S. actor.
Lupino, Ida, 1918–, Eng.-born U.S. actress.
Luria, Salvador Edward, 1912–, Ital.-born U.S. microbiologist.
Lusinchi, Jaime, 1924–, Venezuelan statesman; president 1984–88.
Luther, Martin, 1483–1546, Ger. monk, theologian, & leader of the Protestant Reformation.
Luthuli, Albert J., 1898–1967, South African civil rights leader.
Luxemburg, Rosa, 1871–1919, Ger. socialist leader.
Lwoff, André, 1902–, Fr. microbiologist; Nobel Prize winner.

Lycurgus, 7th c. B.C. Spartan lawgiver.
Lyell, Sir Charles, 1797–1875, Eng. geologist.
Lyly, John, 1554?–1606, Eng. author.
Lynch, Charles, 1736–96, U.S. justice of the peace.
Lynd, Robert Staughton, 1892–1970, & his wife **Helen Merrell,** 1897–1982, U.S. sociologists.
Lysenko, Trofim Denisovich, 1898–1976, Soviet agronomist.

Maazel, Lorin, 1930–, Fr. conductor active in U.S.
Mabuse, Jan, b. Jan Gossaert, 1478–1533?, Flemish painter.
MacArthur, Charles, 1895–1956, U.S. playwright.
—Douglas, 1880–1964, U.S. general & commander in chief of Allies in sw Pacific, World War II.
Macaulay, Thomas Babington, 1800–59, Eng. historian, author, & statesman.
Macbeth, ?–1057, king of Scotland 1040–57.
Maccabeus, Judas, ?–150? B.C., Jewish patriot.
MacDiarmid, Hugh, pseud. of Christopher Murray Grieve, 1892–1978, Scot. poet.
MacDonald, George, 1824–1905, Scot. author.
—Dwight, 1906–82, U.S. critic & author.
—J(ames) E(dward) H(ervey), 1873–1932, Can. painter & poet.
—(James) Ramsey, 1866–1937, Eng. statesman.
—Jeanette, 1906–65, U.S. actress & singer.
—Sir John Alexander, 1815–91, Scot.-born Can. statesman; prime minister 1867–73 & 1878–91.
—John P., 1916–87, U.S. author.
MacDowell, Edward Alexander, 1861–1908, U.S. composer.
Macfadden, Bernarr, 1868–1955, U.S. physical culturist & publisher.
Mach, Ernst, 1838–1916, Austrian physicist.
Machiavelli, Niccolò, 1469–1527, Florentine statesman, political theorist, & author.
MacInnes, Helen, 1907–85, Scot. author.
MacIver, Robert Morrison, 1882–1970, Scot.-born U.S. sociologist.
Mack, Connie, 1862–1956, U.S. baseball player & manager.
Mackenzie, Alexander, 1822–92, Scot.-born Can. statesman; prime minister 1873–78.
—Sir Alexander, 1764–1820, Scot.-born Can. trader & explorer.
—William Lyon, 1795–1861, Scot.-born Can. insurgent leader.
MacLeish, Archibald, 1892–1982, U.S. poet.
MacLennan, Hugh, 1907–90, Can. author.
Macleod, John James Rickard, 1876–1935, Scot. physiologist.
MacMahon, Aline, 1899–, U.S. actress.
—Comte Marie Edmé Patrice, 1808–93, Fr. general; president of France 1873–79.
MacManus, Seumas, 1869–1960, Irish author, poet, & playwright.
MacMillan, Donald Baxter, 1874–1970, U.S. polar explorer.
—Sir Ernest, Campbell, 1893–1973, Can. conductor & composer.
—Kenneth, 1930–, Eng. dancer, choreographer, & ballet company director.
—(Maurice) Harold, 1894–1987, Eng. statesman; prime minister 1957–63.
MacNeice, Louis, 1907–63, Irish-born Brit. poet.
MacNelly, Jeff, 1947–, U.S. political cartoonist.
Madison, Dolley, b. Dorothea Payne, 1768–1849, U.S. first lady & hostess.
—James, 1751–1836, 4th U.S. president 1809–17; husband of prec.
Maecenas, Gaius Cilnius, 73?–8 B.C., Roman statesman & patron of Horace & Virgil.
Maes, Nicolaes, 1632–93, Du. painter.
Maeterlinck, Maurice, 1862–1949, Belg. poet & playwright.
Magellan, Ferdinand, 1480–1521, Pg. explorer.
Magendie, François, 1783–1855, Fr. physiologist.
Maginot, Andre, 1877–1932, Fr. politician.
Magnani, Anna, 1908–73, Ital. actress.
Magritte, René, 1898–1967, Belg. painter.
Magsaysay, Ramón, 1907–57, Filipino statesman; president of the Philippines 1953–57.

Mahan, Alfred Thayer, 1840–1914, U.S. naval officer & historian.

Maharishi Mahesh Yogi, 1911?–, Indian guru.

Mahavira, Vardhamana Jnatiputra, ca. 6th c. B.C., Indian religious leader; founder of Jainism.

Mahler, Gustav, 1860–1911, Austrian composer & conductor.

Mailer, Norman, 1923–, U.S. author.

Maillol, Aristide, 1861–1944, Fr. sculptor.

Maimonides, 1135–1204, Sp. rabbi & philosopher.

Maintenon, Françoise d'Aubigné, Marquise de, 1635–1719, second wife of Louis XIV of France.

Maitland, Frederic William, 1850–1906, Eng. historian.

Major, John Roy, 1943–, Eng. statesman; prime minister of Great Britain 1989–.

Makarios III, 1913–77, Cypriot Greek Orthodox archbishop; president of Cyprus 1960–74 & 1875–77.

Makarova, Natalya, 1940–, Soviet-born ballerina active in U.S.

Malamud, Bernard, 1914–86, U.S. author.

Malan, Daniel F., 1874–1959, Afrikaner statesman.

Malcolm X, b. Malcolm Little, 1925–65, U.S. black leader; assassinated.

Malenkov, Georgi Maximilianovich, 1902–88, premier of the Soviet Union 1953–55.

Malibran, Maria Felicita, 1808–36, Sp. opera singer.

Malinowski, Bronislaw Kasper, 1884–1942, Pol.-born U.S. anthropologist.

Mallarmé, Stéphane, 1842–98, Fr. poet.

Malle, Louis, 1932–, Fr. film director.

Mallon, Mary, 1870?–1938, U.S. domestic servant & typhoid carrier: called **Typhoid Mary.**

Malory, Sir Thomas, ?–1470?, Eng. writer; translated Arthurian legends into English.

Malpighi, Marcello, 1628–94, Ital. anatomist.

Malraux, André, 1901–76, Fr. author & government official.

Malthus, Thomas Robert, 1766–1834, Eng. political economist.

Mamet, David, 1947–, U.S. playwright.

Mamoulian, Rouben, 1897–1987, Russ.-born U.S. stage director.

Mancini, Henry, 1924–, U.S. composer & pianist.

Mandela, Nelson Rolihlahla, 1918–, first black president of Republic of South Africa (1994–), elected in South Africa's first all-race election.

Manes, 216?–276?, Pers. prophet; founder of Manicheism.

Manet, Édouard, 1832–83, Fr. painter.

Mankiewicz, Joseph L., 1909–, U.S. film director & screenwriter.

Mann, Horace, 1796–1859, U.S. educator.

—Thomas, 1875–1955, Ger.-born U.S. author; Nobel Prize winner.

Mannes, Marya, 1904–, U.S. author & journalist.

Manolete, b. Manuel Laureano Rodríguez y Sánchez, 1917–47, Sp. bullfighter.

Mansart, Jules Hardouin, 1646?–1708, Fr. architect.

Mansfield, Katherine, 1888–1923, New Zealand-born Brit. author.

—Michael Joseph (Mike), 1903–, U.S. senator & ambassador.

—Richard, 1854–1907, Eng. actor active in U.S.

Mantegna, Andrea, 1431–1506, Ital. painter & engraver.

Mantle, Mickey Charles, 1931–95, U.S. baseball player.

Mantovani, Annunzio, 1905–80, Ital. conductor.

Manulis, Martin, 1915–, U.S. radio & TV producer.

Manutius, Aldus, b. Teobaldo Manucci, 1450–1515, Ital. printer & classical scholar.

Manzoni, Alessandro Francesco, 1785–1873, Ital. author.

Mao Zedong (Tse-tung), 1893–1976, Chin. statesman; chairman of Chin. Communist Party 1954–76.

Marat, Jean Paul, 1743–93, Fr. revolutionary leader; assassinated by Charlotte Corday.

Marble Alice, 1913–90, U.S. tennis player.

Marc, Franz, 1880–1916, Ger. painter.

Marceau, Marcel, 1923–, Fr. mime.

Marcel, Gabriel, 1889–1973, Fr. philosopher.

March, Fredric, 1897–1975, U.S. actor.

Marciano, Rocky, 1924–69, U.S. boxer.

Marconi, Guglielmo, 1874–1937, Ital. inventor of wireless telegraphy.

Marcos, Ferdinand Edralin, 1917–89, Filipino politician; president of the Philippines 1965–86.

Marcus Aurelius, A.D. 121–180, Roman emperor & philosopher.

Marcuse, Herbert, 1898–1979, Ger.-born U.S. philosopher.

Margaret, 1353–1412, queen of Denmark, Norway, & Sweden.

Margaret Rose, 1930–, Eng. princess, the sister of Queen Elizabeth II.

Margrethe II, 1940–, queen of Denmark 1972–.

Maria Theresa, 1717–80, queen of Hungary & Bohemia, & Holy Roman empress.

Marie Antoinette, 1755–93, Austrian-born queen of Louis XVI of France; guillotined.

Marignac, Jean de, 1817–94, Swiss chemist.

Marin, John Cheri, 1870–1953, U.S. painter.

Marini, Marino, 1901–80, Ital. sculptor.

Marion, Francis, 1732?–95, Amer. revolutionary commander: called **the Swamp Fox.**

Maris, Roger, 1934–85, U.S. baseball player.

Maritain, Jacques, 1882–1973, Fr. philosopher.

Markevich, Igor, 1912–83, Russ.-born Swiss conductor.

Markham, (Charles) Edwin, 1852–1940, U.S. poet.

Markova, Dame Alicia, 1910–, Eng. ballerina.

Marks, Johnny, 1909–85, U.S. composer.

Marlborough, John Churchill, Duke of, 1650–1722, Eng. general & statesman.

Marlowe, Christopher, 1564–93, Eng. playwright.

—Julia, 1866–1950, Eng.-born U.S. actress.

Marriner, Neville, 1925–, Brit. conductor.

Marquand, J(ohn) P(hillips), 1893–1960, U.S. author.

Marquette, Jacques, 1637–75, Fr. explorer of America.

Marquis, Don(ald Robert Perry), 1878–1937, U.S. journalist & humorist.

Marsh, Dame Ngaio, 1899–1982, New Zealand author.

—Reginald, 1898–1954, U.S. painter.

Marshall, George Catlett, 1880–1959, U.S. general & statesman; chief of staff of U.S. Army in World War II; Nobel Prize winner.

—John, 1755–1835, U.S. statesman & jurist; chief justice of the U.S. Supreme Court 1801–35.

—Thurgood, 1908–93, U.S. jurist; justice of the U.S. Supreme Court 1967–91.

Martel, Charles, 688?–741, Frankish king 715–741; grandfather of Charlemagne.

Martí, José (Julián), 1853–95, Cuban lawyer & revolutionary.

Martial (L. Marcus Valerius Martialis), A.D. 40?–104?, Roman poet.

Martin, John Joseph, 1893–1985, U.S. dance critic.

—Mary, 1913–90, U.S. singer & actress.

Martin du Gard, Roger, 1881–1958, Fr. author; Nobel Prize winner.

Martinelli, Giovanni, 1885–1969, Ital. tenor active in U.S.

Martini, Simone, 1283?–1344, Ital. painter.

Marvell, Andrew, 1621–78, Eng. poet.

Marx A family of U.S. actors & comedians; four brothers: **Arthur (Harpo),** 1893–1964; **Herbert (Zeppo),** 1901–79; **Julius (Groucho),** 1890–1977; **Leonard (Chico),** 1891–1961.

—Karl, 1818–83, Ger. socialist writer.

Mary I, 1516–58, queen of England 1553–58; known as **Bloody Mary** or **Mary Tudor.**

—II, 1662–94, queen of England 1689–94; co-ruler with her husband, William III.

Mary, Queen of Scots (Mary Stuart), 1542–87, queen of Scotland 1561–67; beheaded.

Masaccio, b. Tommaso Cassai, 1401–28, Florentine painter.

Masaryk, Jan Garrigue, 1886–1948, Czech diplomat & politician.

—Thomas, 1850–1937, first president of Czechoslovakia 1918–35; father of prec.

Mascagni, Pietro, 1863–1945, Ital. composer.

Masefield, John, 1878–1967, Eng. poet.

Maslow, Abraham, 1908–70, U.S. author & psychologist.

Mason, Charles, 1730–87, Eng. astronomer & surveyor; with Jeremiah Dixon, established Mason-Dixon line.

—James, 1909–84, Eng.-born actor active in U.S.

Massasoit, 1580?–1661, Am. Ind. chief of the Wampanoag tribes of Massachusetts.

Massenet, Jules, 1842–1912, Fr. composer.

Massey, Raymond, 1896–1983, Can.-born U.S. actor.

Massine, Leonide, 1896–1979, Russ.-born U.S. choreographer & dancer.

Masters, Edgar Lee, 1869–1950, U.S. poet.

—**William Howell,** 1915–, U.S. physician & sex researcher.

Masterson, William Barclay (Bat), 1853–1921, U.S. frontier peace officer & journalist.

Mastroianni, Marcello, 1924–, Ital. actor.

Mata Hari, b. Margaretha Gertrud Zelle, 1876–1917, Du. dancer & spy.

Mather, Cotton, 1663–1728, Amer. theologian.

—**Increase,** 1639–1723, U.S. intellectual & pamphleteer; father of prec.

—**Richard,** 1596–1669, Eng.-born Amer. theologian; grandfather of Cotton.

Mathewson, Christopher (Christy), 1880–1925, U.S. baseball player.

Mathias, Robert Bruce (Bob), 1930–, U.S. decathlon athlete & politician.

Matisse, Henri, 1869–1954, Fr. painter.

Matsuoka, Yosuke, 1880–1946, Jap. statesman.

Maugham, W(illiam) Somerset, 1874–1965, Eng. author & playwright.

Mauldin, William H. (Bill), 1921–, U.S. cartoonist.

Maupassant, Guy de, 1850–93, Fr. author.

Maurer, Jon Gheorghe, 1902–, Romanian prime minister 1961–.

Mauriac, François, 1885–1970, Fr. author.

Maurois, André, pseud. of Émile Herzog, 1885–1967, Fr. author.

Mauser, Peter Paul, 1838–1914, & his brother, **Wilhelm,** 1834–82, Ger. inventors.

Maverick, Samuel Augustus, 1803–70, U.S. cattle rancher & public official.

Maxim, Sir Hiram Stevens, 1840–1916, U.S.-born Brit. inventor.

—**Hudson,** 1853–1927, U.S. inventor & explosives expert; brother of prec.

Maximilian, Ferdinand Joseph, 1832–67, Austrian archduke; emperor of Mexico 1864–67; executed.

Maxwell, Elsa, 1883–1963, U.S. columnist & noted hostess.

—**James Clerk,** 1831–79, Scot. physicist.

May, Elaine, 1932–, U.S. actress & film director.

—**Rollo,** 1909–, U.S. psychoanalyst & philosopher.

Mayakovsky, Vladimir Vladimirovich, 1893–1930, Russ. poet & playwright.

Mayer, Jean, 1920–, Fr. nutritionist active in U.S.

—**Louis Burt,** 1885–1958, Russ.-born U.S. film producer.

—**Maria Goeppert,** 1906–72, Ger.-born U.S. physicist; Nobel Prize winner.

Mayner, Dorothy, 1910–, U.S. soprano.

Mayo, Charles Horace, 1865–1939, U.S. surgeon.

—**William James,** 1861–1939, U.S. surgeon; brother of prec.

—**William Worrall,** 1819–1911, U.S. physician; father of Charles Horace & William James.

Mays, Benjamin Elijah, 1894–1984, U.S. educator & theologian.

—**Willie Howard,** 1931–, U.S. baseball player.

Mazzini, Giuseppe, 1805–72, Ital. patriot & revolutionary.

Mboya, Thomas J. (Tom), 1930–69, Kenyan political leader.

McBride, Mary Margaret, 1899–1976, U.S. radio personality.

—**Patricia,** 1942–, U.S. ballerina.

McCarey, Leo, 1898–1969, U.S. film director.

McCarthy, Eugene Joseph, 1916–, U.S. politician.

—**Joseph Raymond,** 1908–57, U.S. politician.

—**Mary,** 1912–89, U.S. author & critic.

McCartney, Paul, 1942–, Eng. composer & musical performer.

McClellan, George Brinton, 1826–85, U.S. general.

McClintic, Guthrie, 1893–1961, U.S. theater director.

McClintock, Barbara, 1902–, U.S. geneticist; Nobel Prize winner.

McClure, Samuel Sidney, 1857–1949, Irish-born U.S. editor & publisher.

McCormack, John, 1884–1945, Irish-born U.S. tenor.

—**John William,** 1891–1980, U.S. politician.

McCormick, Cyrus Hall, 1809–84, U.S. inventor of the reaping machine.

—**Joseph Medill,** 1877–1925, U.S. newspaper publisher.

—**Robert Rutherford,** 1880–1955, U.S. newspaper publisher; brother of prec.

McCullers, Carson, 1917–67, U.S. novelist.

McEnroe, John, 1959–, U.S. tennis player.

McGill, James, 1744–1813, Scot.-born Can. businessman & philanthropist.

McGinley, Phyllis, 1905–78, U.S. poet.

McGovern, George Stanley, 1922–, U.S. politician.

McGraw, John Joseph, 1873–1934, U.S. baseball player & manager.

McGuffey, William Holmes, 1800–73, U.S. educator.

McHugh, Jimmy, 1894–1969, U.S. composer.

McKenna, Siobhan, 1923–, Irish actress.

McKim, Charles Follen, 1847–1909, U.S. architect.

McKinley, William, 1843–1901, 25th U.S. president 1897–1901; assassinated.

McKuen, Rod Marvin, 1933–, U.S. composer & poet.

McLaglen, Victor, 1886–1959, Eng. actor active in U.S.

McLuhan, (Herbert) Marshall, 1911–80, Can. educator & author.

McManus, George, 1884–1954, U.S. cartoonist.

McMillan, Edwin Mattison, 1907–91, U.S. chemist; Nobel Prize winner.

McNamara, Robert Strange, 1916–, U.S. government official & president of World Bank 1968–81.

McPherson, Aimee Semple, 1890–1944, Can.-born U.S. evangelist.

McQueen, Steve, 1930–80, U.S. actor.

Mead, Margaret, 1901–78, U.S. anthropologist.

Meade, George Gordon, 1815–72, U.S. Civil War general.

Meany, George, 1894–1980, U.S. labor leader; president of the AFL-CIO 1955–79.

Medawar, Sir Peter Brian, 1915–87, Eng. zoologist; Nobel Prize winner.

Medici, Catherine de, 1519–89, Florentine-born queen of Henry II of France.

—**Cosimo I de,** 1519–74, Duke of Florence & Grand Duke of Tuscany: called **the Great.**

—**Emilio Garrastazú,** 1905–, Brazilian military officer; president of Brazil 1969–74.

—**Lorenzo de,** 1448?–92, Florentine prince, statesman, & patron of the arts: called the **the Magnificent.**

Medill, Joseph, 1823–99, U.S. editor & publisher.

Mehta, Zubin, 1936–, Indian-born conductor active in the U.S.

Meighen, Arthur, 1874–1960, Can. statesman; prime minister 1920–21 & 26.

Meir, Golda, 1898–1978, Russ.-born Israeli stateswoman; prime minister of Israel 1969–74.

Meiss, Millard, 1904–75, U.S. art historian.

Meitner, Lise, 1878–1968, Ger. physicist.

Melanchthon, Philipp, 1497–1560, Ger. theologian & humanist.

Melba, Dame Nellie, 1861–1931, Austral. soprano.

Melchoir, Lauritz, 1890–1973, Dan. baritone.

Mellon, Andrew William, 1855–1937, U.S. financier & philanthropist.

Melville, Herman, 1819–91, U.S. author.

Memling, Hans, 1430–94, Flemish painter.

Menander, 343?–291?, B.C., Gk. playwright.

Mencken, H(enry) L(ouis), 1880–1956, U.S. author, editor, & critic.

Mendel, Gregor Johann, 1822–84, Austrian monk & botanist.

Mendeleyev, Dimitri Ivanovich, 1834–1907, Russ. chemist.

Mendelssohn, Felix, 1808–47, Ger. composer.

Mendès-France, Pierre, 1907–82, Fr. politician.

Mennin, Peter, 1923–83, U.S. composer & educator.

Menninger, Karl Augustus, 1893–90, U.S. psychiatrist.

Menotti, Gian Carlo, 1911–, Ital.-born U.S. composer.

Menuhin, Yehudi, 1916–, U.S. violinist.

Menzies, Sir Robert Gordon, 1894–1978, Austral. statesman.

Mercator, Gerhardus, 1512–94, Flemish geographer & cartographer.

Mercer, Johnny, 1909–76, U.S. lyricist.

—**Mabel,** 1900–84, Eng.-born U.S. singer.

Meredith, George, 1828–1909, Eng. author & poet.

Mergenthaler, Ottmar, 1854–99, Ger.-born U.S. inventor of the Linotype machine.

Mérimée, Prosper, 1803–70, Fr. author.

Merman, Ethel, 1909–84, U.S. singer & actress.

Merrick, David, 1912–, U.S. theatrical producer.

Merrill, Robert, 1919–, U.S. baritone.

Merton, Thomas, 1915–68, Fr.-born U.S. monk & author.

Merwin, W(illiam) S(tanley), 1927–, U.S. poet.

Mesmer, Friedrich Anton, 1734–1815, Austrian physician.

Messalina, Valeria, ?–A.D. 48, third wife of Emperor Claudius.

Messerschmitt, Willy, 1898–1978, Ger. aircraft designer & manufacturer.

Messiaen, Olivier, 1908–, Fr. composer.

Messick, Dale, 1906–, U.S. cartoonist.

Mesta, Perle, 1891–1975, U.S. hostess & diplomat.

Mestrovic, Ivan, 1883–1962, Yugoslav-born U.S. sculptor.

Metaxas, Joannes, 1871–1941, Gk. general & dictator.

Metchnikoff, Élie, 1845–1916, Russ. zoologist & bacteriologist.

Metternich, Prince Klemens von, 1773–1859, Austrian statesman.

Meyer, Adolf, 1866–1950, Swiss-born U.S. psychiatrist.

—**Joseph,** 1894–, U.S. composer.

—**Julius Lothar,** 1830–95, Ger. chemist.

Meyerbeer, Giacomo, 1791–1864, Ger. composer active in France.

Meyerhof, Otto, 1884–1951, Ger. physiologist.

Meyerhold, Vsevolod Emilievich, 1874–1940, Russ. theatrical director & producer.

Michelangelo, Buonarroti, 1475–1564, Ital. sculptor, architect, painter, & poet.

Michelet, Jules, 1798–1874, Fr. historian.

Michelson, Albert Abraham, 1852–1931, Ger.-born U.S. physicist; Nobel Prize winner.

Michener, James Albert, 1907–, U.S. author.

—**Roland,** 1900–, Can. politician; governor-general of Canada 1967–74.

Midler, Bette, 1945–, U.S. singer & comedienne.

Mielziner, Jo, 1901–76, Fr.-born set designer active in U.S.

Mies van der Rohe, Ludwig, 1886–1969, Ger.-born U.S. architect.

Mikan, George Lawrence (Larry), 1924–, U.S. basketball player.

Miki, Takeo, 1907–, prime minister of Japan 1974–76.

Mikoyan, Anastas Ivanovich, 1895–1978, president of U.S.S.R. 1964–65.

Milanov, Zinka, 1906–89, Yugoslav operatic soprano active in U.S.

Milburn, Rodney, 1950–, U.S. track athlete.

Milestone, Lewis, 1895–1980, U.S. film director.

Milhaud, Darius, 1892–1974, Fr. composer.

Mill, James, 1773–1836, Scot. philosopher, historian, & economist.

—**John Stuart,** 1806–73, Eng. philosopher & political economist; son of prec.

Millay, Edna St. Vincent, 1892–1950, U.S. poet.

Miller, Arthur, 1915–, U.S. playwright.

—**Glenn,** 1904–44, U.S. bandleader & arranger.

—**Henry,** 1891–1980, U.S. author.

—**Joseph (Joe),** 1684–1738, Eng. comedian.

—**Perry Gilbert Eddy,** 1905–63, U.S. scholar & critic.

—**Samuel Freeman,** 1816–90, U.S. jurist; justice of U.S. Supreme Court 1862–90.

Miles, Carl Wilhelm Emil, 1875–1955, Swed.-born U.S. sculptor.

Millet, Jean François, 1814–75, Fr. painter.

Millikan, Robert Andrews, 1868–1953, U.S. physicist; Nobel Prize winner.

Mills, Sir John, 1908–85, Eng. actor.

—**Robert,** 1781–1855, U.S. architect.

Milne, A(lan) A(lexander), 1882–1956, Eng. author.

—**David,** 1882–1953, U.S. painter.

Milnes, Sherril, 1935–, U.S. baritone.

Milstein, Nathan, 1904–, Russ.-born U.S. violinist.

Miltiades, 540?–489?, B.C., Athenian general.

Milton, John, 1608–74, Eng. poet.

Mindszenty, Jozsef Cardinal, 1892–1975, Hung. Roman Catholic prelate.

Mingus, Charles (Charlie), 1922–79, U.S. jazz musician.

Minh, Duong Van, 1916–, S. Vietnamese general; president of S. Vietnam 1975; called **Big Minh.**

Minkowski, Hermann, 1864–1909, Russ.-born mathematician active in Germany.

Minnelli, Liza, 1946–, U.S. singer & actress.

—**Vincente,** 1913–86, U.S. film director, father of prec.

Minnesota Fats, b. Rudolf Walter Wanderone, Jr., 1913–, U.S. pool player.

Minuit, Peter, 1580–1638, first Du. director-general of New Netherland (including New York).

Mirabeau, Gabriel Honoré de Riquetti, Comte de, 1749–91, Fr. revolutionary orator & statesman.

Miranda, Carmen, 1917–55, Pg.-born actress & singer active in U.S.

Miró, Joan, 1893–1983, Sp. painter.

Mishima, Yukio, 1925–70, Jap. novelist.

Mistral, Frédéric, 1830–1914, Fr. poet; Nobel Prize winner.

—**Gabriela,** 1889–1957, Chilean poet.

Mitchell, Arthur, 1934–, U.S. ballet dancer, choreographer, & ballet company director.

—**John Newton,** 1913–, U.S. politician.

—**Margaret,** 1900–49, U.S. author.

—**William (Billy),** 1879–1936, U.S. general & air force advocate.

Mitford, Jessica, 1917–, Eng. author.

—**Nancy,** 1904–73, Eng. author; sister of prec.

Mithridates, VI, ca. 132–63 B.C., king of Pontus: called **the Great.**

Mitropoulos, Dmitri, 1896–1960, Gk.-born U.S. conductor.

Mitterand, François, 1916–, Fr. statesman; president 1981–.

Mix, Thomas Edwin (Tom), 1880–1940, U.S. actor.

Mizoguchi, Kenji, 1898–1956, Jap. film director.

Möbius, August Ferdinand, 1790–1868, Ger. mathematician.

Mobutu Sese Seko, b. Joseph Desiré Mobutu, 1930–, president of Zaire 1964–.

Modigliani, Amadeo, 1844–1920, Ital. painter & sculptor active in France.

Modjeska, Helena Opid, 1840–1909, Pol.-born actress active in U.S.

Moffo, Anna, 1934–, U.S. soprano.

Mohammed, 570–632, Arabian religious & military leader, founder of Islam, & author of the Koran.

Mohammed Reza Pahlavi, 1919–1980, shah of Iran 1941–79.

Moholy-Nagy, Laszlo, 1895–1946, Hung. painter, designer, & photographer active in Germany & U.S.

Mohorovicic, Andrija, 1857–1936, Yugoslav geologist.

Moiseyev, Igor, 1906–, Soviet choreographer & dance company director.

Molière, pseud. of Jean Baptiste Poquelin, 1622–73, Fr. playwright.

Molnár, Ferenc, 1878–1952, Hung. playwright & author.

Molotov, Vyacheslav Mikhailovich, 1890–86, Soviet statesman; foreign minister of the Soviet Union 1939–49 & 1953–56.

Moltke, Count Helmuth von, 1800–91, Prussian field marshal.

Molyneux, Edward, 1894–1974, Eng. fashion designer.

Mommsen, Theodor, 1817–1903, Ger. historian.

Mondale, Walter Frederick, 1928–, U.S. statesman; U.S. vice president 1977–81.

Mondrian, Piet, 1872–1944, Du. painter.

Monet, Claude, 1840–1926, Fr. painter.

Moniz, Antônio Caetano de Abreu Freire Egas, 1874–1955, Pg. physiologist; Nobel Prize winner.

Monk, Julius, 1912–, U.S. nightclub producer & director.

—**Thelonious,** 1920–82, U.S. jazz musician.

Monmouth, James Scott, Duke of, 1649–85, Eng. rebel & claimant to throne; illegitimate son of Charles II.

Monnet, Jean, 1888–1979, Fr. political economist & statesman.

Monod, Jacques Lucien, 1910–76, Fr. biochemist & author.

Monroe, Harriet, 1860–1936, U.S. poet & editor.

—**James,** 1758–1831, 5th U.S. president 1817–25.

—**Marilyn,** 1926–62, U.S. film actress.

Montagu, Lady Mary Wortley, 1689–1762, Eng. letter writer.

—**(Montague Francis) Ashley,** 1905–, Eng.-born U.S. anthropologist.

Montaigne, Michel Eyquem de, 1533–92, Fr. author.

Montana, Bob, 1920–75, U.S. cartoonist.

Montand, Yves, 1921–, Ital.-born Fr. actor & singer.

Montcalm, Joseph Louis, 1712–59, Fr. general.

Montefiore, Sir Moses Haim, 1734–1885, Ital.-born Brit. financier & philanthropist.

Montespan, Françoise Athenaïs Rochechouart, Marquise de, 1641–1707, mistress of Louis XIV of France.

Montesquieu, Baron de la Brède et de, title of Charles de Secondat, 1689–1755, Fr. jurist, philosopher, & historian.

Montessori, Maria, 1870–1952, Ital. educator.

Monteux, Pierre, 1875–1964, Fr.-born U.S. conductor.

Monteverdi, Claudio, 1567–1643, Ital. composer.

Montez, Lola, 1818–61, Irish-born dancer & adventuress.

Montezuma II, 1479?–1520, Aztec Indian emperor of Mexico 1502–20.

Montfort, Simon de, 1208?–65, Eng. statesman & soldier.

Montgolfier, Joseph Michel, 1740–1810, & his brother **Jacques Etienne,** 1745–99, Fr. inventors & balloonists.

Montgomery, Bernard Law, 1st Viscount, 1887–1976, Eng. field marshal.

—**Robert,** 1904–81, U.S. actor & producer.

Montherlant, Henri Millon de, 1896–1972, Fr. author.

Moody, Dwight Lyman, 1837–99, U.S. evangelist.

—**Helen Wills,** 1905–, U.S. tennis player.

—**William Vaughn,** 1869–1910, U.S. playwright, poet, & literary historian.

Moore, Clement Clarke, 1779–1863, U.S. lexicographer & poet.

—**Douglas Stuart,** 1893–1969, U.S. composer.

—**George,** 1852–1933, Irish author, critic, & playwright.

—**Grace,** 1901–47, U.S. soprano & actress.

—**Henry,** 1898–1986, Eng. sculptor.

—**Marianne,** 1887–1972, U.S. poet.

—**Mary Tyler,** 1937–, U.S. actress.

—**Thomas,** 1779–1852, Irish poet.

—**Victor,** 1876–1962, U.S. actor.

Moorehead, Agnes, 1906–74, U.S. actress.

Moravia, Alberto, pseud. of Alberto Pincherle, 1907–90, Ital. author.

More, Sir Thomas, 1478–1535, Eng. statesman & writer; beheaded; canonized 1935.

Moreau, Gustave, 1826–98, Fr. painter.

—**Jeanne,** 1928–, Fr. actress.

Morgan, Helen, 1900–41, U.S. singer & actress.

—**Henry,** 1915–, U.S. TV personality.

—**Sir Henry,** 1635?–88, Eng. buccaneer.

—**John Hunt,** 1825–64, U.S. Confederate cavalry officer.

—**J(ohn) Pierpont,** 1837–1913, U.S. financier.

—**Lewis Henry,** 1818–81, U.S. anthropologist.

—**Michèle,** 1920–, Fr. actress.

—**Thomas Hunt,** 1866–1945, U.S. geneticist; Nobel Prize winner.

Morgenthau, Henry, Jr., 1891–1967, U.S. government official.

Morison, Samuel Eliot, 1887–1976, U.S. historian.

—**Stanley,** 1889–1968, Eng. type designer.

Morisot, Berthe, 1841–95, Fr. painter.

Morita, Akio, 1921–, Jap. physicist & business executive.

Morley, Christopher Darlington, 1890–1957, U.S. author.

—**Edward Williams,** 1838–1923, U.S. chemist & physicist; Nobel Prize winner.

Morley, Robert, 1908–, Eng. actor.

Morphy, Paul, 1837–84, U.S. chessmaster.

Morris, Gouverneur, 1752–1816, U.S. statesman & diplomat.

—**Robert,** 1734–1806, U.S. financier & statesman.

—**William,** 1834–96, Eng. painter, craftsman, & poet.

Morrison, Toni, 1931–, U.S. editor & author.

—**Wright,** 1910–, U.S. author.

Morse, Samuel Finley Breese, 1791–1872, U.S. artist & inventor of the telegraph.

Morton, Ferdinand Joseph (Jelly Roll), 1885–1941, U.S. jazz musician.

—**Julius Sterling,** 1832–1902, U.S. politician & nature lover.

—**Levi Parsons,** 1824–1920, U.S. statesman; U.S. vice president 1889–93.

—**William Thomas Green,** 1819–68, U.S. dentist.

Mosconi, Willie, 1913–, U.S. billiards player.

Moseley, Henry Gwyn-Jeffreys, 1887–1915, Eng. physicist.

Moses, Anna Mary Robertson, 1860–1961, U.S. painter: called **Grandma Moses.**

—**Robert,** 1888–1981, U.S. public official.

Mosley, Sir Oswald Ernald, 1896–1980, Eng. fascist politician.

Mossadegh, Mohammed, 1881–1967, Pers. statesman; prime minister of Iran 1951–53.

Mössbauer, Rudolf Ludwig, 1929–, Ger.-born U.S. physicist; Nobel Prize winner.

Mostel, Sam (Zero), 1915–77, U.S. actor.

Moszkowski, Moritz, 1854–1925, Pol.-Ger. pianist & composer.

Motherwell, Robert, 1915–91, U.S. painter.

Mott, Charles Stewart, 1875–1973, U.S. industrialist.

—**Lucretia Coffin,** 1793–1880, U.S. social reformer.

Mountbatten, Louis, Earl, 1900–79, Eng. admiral & governor general of India 1947–48.

Moynihan, Daniel Patrick, 1927–, U.S. sociologist & government official.

Mozart, Wolfgang Amadeus, 1756–91, Austrian composer.

Mubarak, Hosni, 1929–, Egyptian statesman and president 1981–.

Mueller, Paul, 1899–1965, Swiss chemist; Nobel Prize winner.

Muggeridge, Malcolm, 1903–90, Eng. editor & author.

Muhammad, 570?–632, founder of Islamic religion.

Muhammad, Elijah, b. Elijah Poole, 1897–1975, U.S. religious leader.

Muir, John, 1838–1914, U.S. naturalist.

—**Malcolm,** 1885–1979, U.S. publisher & editor.

Muldoon, Robert David, 1921–, New Zealand prime minister 1975–84.

Muller, Herman Joseph, 1890–1967, U.S. geneticist.

Müller, Paul, 1899–1965, Swiss chemist.

Mulligan, Gerald Joseph (Gerry), 1927–, U.S. jazz musician.

Mulliken, Robert Sanderson, 1896–1986, U.S. chemist; Nobel Prize winner.

Mulroney, Martin Brian, 1939–, Can. statesman; prime minister 1984–.

Mumford, Lewis, 1895–1990, U.S. author.

Munch, Charles, 1891–1968, Fr.-born U.S. conductor.

—**Edvard,** 1863–1944, Norw. painter.

Münchausen, Baron Karl Friedrich von, 1720–97, Ger. soldier & adventurer.

Muni, Paul, 1895–1967, U.S. actor.

Muñoz Marín, Luis, 1898–1980, governor of Puerto Rico 1948–64.

Munro, Hector Hugh, 1870–1916, Brit. author: known as **Saki.**

Murasaki, Lady, 11th c. Jap. novelist.

Murdoch, (Jean) Iris, 1919–, Irish-born Brit. author & philosopher.

—**Rupert,** 1931–, Austral.-born U.S. publisher.

Murieta, Joaquiin, ?–1853?, Mexican bandit in Amer. Southwest.

Murillo, Bartolomé Esteban, 1617–82, Sp. painter.

Murnau, Friedrich W., 1899–1931, Ger. film director.

Murphy, Audie, 1924–71, U.S. soldier & actor.

Murray, Arthur, 1895–, & his wife, **Kathryn,** 1906–, U.S. dancing teachers.

—**Sir James Augustus Henry,** 1837–1915, Eng. lexicographer.

—**John Courtney,** 1904–67, U.S. theologian.

—**Mae,** 1885–1965, U.S. actress.

Murrow, Edward R., 1908–65, U.S. news analyst.

Musial, Stan(ley Frank), 1920–, U.S. baseball player.

Muskie, Edmund Sixtus, 1914–, U.S. politician.

Mussolini, Benito, 1883–1945, Ital. Fascist leader & premier; executed: called **Il Duce.**

Mussorgsky, Modest Petrovich, 1835–81, Russ. composer.

Mutsuhito, 1852–1912, emperor of Japan 1867–1912.

Muybridge, Eadweard, b. Edward James Muggeridge, 1830–1904, Eng.-born U.S. photographer.

Muzio, Claudia, 1889–1936, Ital. soprano.

Muzorewa, Abel Tendekayi, 1925–, African religious and political leader; prime minister of Zimbabwe 1979.

Myrdal, Alva Reimer, 1902–86, Swed. diplomat & sociologist.

—Gunnar, 1898–1987, Swed. sociologist & economist.

Myron, 5th c. B.C. Gk. sculptor.

Nabokov, Vladimir, 1899–1977, Russ.-born U.S. author.

Nader, Ralph, 1934–, U.S. lawyer & consumer advocate.

Nagurski, Bronko, 1908–90, Can.-born U.S. football player.

Nagy, Imre, 1895?–1958, premier of Hungary 1953–55; executed.

Naismith, James, 1861–1939, Can.-born U.S. athletic coach; originator of basketball.

Namath, Joseph William (Joe), 1943–, U.S. football player.

Nanak, 1469–1538, founder of the Sikh faith in India.

Nansen, Fridtjof, 1861–1930, Norw. Arctic explorer.

Napier, John, 1550–1617, Scot. mathematician.

Napoleon I and **III** See BONAPARTE.

Nash, Ogden, 1902–71, U.S. poet.

—Thomas, 1567–1601, Eng. playwright.

Nasser, Gamal Abdel, 1918–70, Egyptian revolutionary leader; president of the United Arab Republic 1958–70.

Nast, Thomas, 1840–1902, Ger.-born U.S. cartoonist.

Nathan, George Jean, 1882–1958, U.S. critic.

Nation, Carry Amelia, 1846–1911, U.S. temperance reformer.

Natwick, Mildred, 1908–, U.S. actress.

Navratilova, Martina, 1956–, Czech tennis player.

Nazimova, Alla, 1879–1945, Russ.-born actress active in U.S.

Nebuchadnezzar II, ?–562? B.C., king of Babylon 605–562 B.C.; conqueror of Jerusalem.

Nefertiti, 14th c. B.C., Egyptian queen, 1367–1350 B.C..

Nehru, Jawaharlal, 1889–1964, Indian nationalist leader; prime minister of India 1947–64.

Neill, A(lexander) S(utherland), 1883–1973, Eng. educator & author.

Nelson, Viscount Horatio, 1758–1805, Eng. admiral.

—(John) Byron, 1912–, U.S. golfer.

—Oswald George (Ozzie), 1907–75, U.S. bandleader, actor, & TV producer.

—Rick, b. Eric Hilliard Nelson, 1940–85, U.S. singer & actor.

—Willie, 1933–, U.S. singer and songwriter.

Nemerov, Howard, 1920–91, U.S. poet.

Nenni, Pietro, 1891–1980, Ital. socialist leader & journalist.

Nernst, Hermann W., 1864–1941, Ger. physical chemist; Nobel Prize winner.

Nero, A.D. 37–68, Roman emperor 54–68.

Neruda, Pablo, 1904–73, Chilean poet; Nobel Prize winner.

Nerva, Marcus Cocceius, A.D. 35?–98, Roman emperor 96–98.

Nervi, Pier Luigi, 1891–1979, Ital. architect.

Neutra, Richard Joseph, 1892–1970, Austrian-born U.S. architect.

Nevelson, Louise, 1900–88, Russ.-born U.S. sculptor.

Nevins, Allan, 1890–1971, U.S. historian.

Newberry, John, 1713–67, Eng. publisher & bookseller.

—Walter Loomis, 1804–68, U.S. businessman & philanthropist.

Newcombe, John, 1944–, Austral. tennis player.

Newhouse, Samuel, 1895–1979, U.S. publisher.

Ne Win, U, 1911–, Burmese military leader; prime minister of Burma 1962–74; president 1974–81.

Newlands, John A. R., 1838–98, Eng. chemist.

Newman, Barnett, 1905–70, U.S. artist.

—John Henry, Cardinal, 1801–90, Eng. theologian & author.

—Paul, 1925–, U.S. actor.

Newton, Sir Isaac, 1642–1727, Eng. mathematician & physicist.

—Robert, 1905–56, Eng. actor.

Ngo Dinh Diem, 1901–63, South Vietnamese politician; president 1955–63; assassinated.

Nguyen Van Thieu, 1923–, South Vietnamese politician; president 1967–75.

Nicholas I, 1796–1855, czar of Russia 1825–55: called **the Great.**

—II, 1868–1918, czar of Russia 1894–1917; executed.

Nicholas, Saint, 4th c. prelate; patron saint of Russia, seamen, and children.

Nichols, Mike, 1931–, Ger.-born U.S. comedian & stage & film director.

Nicholson, Ben, 1894–1982, Eng. artist.

—Jack, 1937–, U.S. actor.

Nicklaus, Jack W., 1940–, U.S. golfer.

Nicolle, Charles J. H., 1866–1936, Fr. physician.

Nicolson, Sir Harold George, 1886–1968, Eng. diplomat, author, & journalist.

Niebuhr, Reinhold, 1892–1971, U.S. Protestant clergyman & theologian.

Nielsen, Carl, 1865–1931, Dan. composer.

Niemeyer Soares, Oscar, 1907–84, Brazilian architect.

Niemöller, Martin, 1892–1984, Ger. theologian.

Nietzsche, Friedrich Wilhelm, 1844–1900, Ger. philosopher & author.

Nightingale, Florence, 1820–1910, Eng. nurse in the Crimean War; considered the founder of modern nursing.

Nijinska, Bronislava, 1891–1972, Pol. dancer & choreographer.

Nijinsky, Vaslav, 1890–1950, Russ.-born ballet dancer & choreographer; brother of prec.

Nikolais, Alwin, 1912–, U.S. choreographer & dance company director.

Nilsson, Birgit, 1918–, Swed. soprano.

Nimeiry, Gaafar al-, 1930–, Sudanese military officer; president of Sudan 1971–85.

Nimitz, Chester William, 1885–1966, U.S. admiral.

Nin, Anais, 1903–77, Fr.-born U.S. author.

Nirenberg, Marshall Warren, 1927–, U.S. biochemist.

Niven, David, 1910–83, Scot.-born actor active in U.S.

Nixon, Richard Millhouse, 1913–, 37th U.S. president 1969–74; resigned.

Nizer, Louis, 1902–, Eng.-born U.S. lawyer & author.

Nkrumah, Kwame, 1909–72, president of Ghana 1960–66.

Nobel, Alfred Bernhard, 1833–96, Swed. industrialist & philanthropist.

Nock, Albert Jay, 1870–1945, U.S. author.

Noguchi, Hideyo, 1876–1928, Jap. bacteriologist active in U.S.

—Isamu, 1904–88, U.S. sculptor.

Nolde, Emil, pseud. of Emil Hansen, 1867–1956, Ger. painter.

Nomura, Kichisaburo, 1877–1964, Jap. admiral & diplomat.

Nordenskjöld, Nils Adolf Erik, 1832–1901, Finn.-born Swed. polar explorer.

Nordica, Lillian, 1857–1914, U.S. soprano.

Norell, Norman, 1900–72, U.S. fashion designer.

Norman, Jessye, 1945–, U.S. soprano.

Normand, Mable, 1894–1930, U.S. actress.

Norris, (Benjamin) Frank(lin), 1870–1902, U.S. author.

—George W., 1861–1944, U.S. politician.

Norstad, Lauris, 1907–, U.S. general.

North, Alex, 1910–91, U.S. composer.

—Lord Frederick, 1732–92, Eng. statesman; prime minister 1770–82.

Norton, Charles Eliot, 1827–1908, U.S. author & educator.

Norworth, Jack, 1879–1959, U.S. lyricist.

Nostradamus, b. Michel de Notredame, 1503–66, Fr. physician & astrologer.

Novaes, Guiomar, 1895–1979, Brazilian pianist.

Novak, Robert David Sanders, 1931–, U.S. journalist.

Novalis, pseud. of Friedrich von Hardenberg, 1772–1801, Ger. poet.

Novarro, Ramon, 1899–1968, Mexican-born U.S. actor.

Novello, Ivor, 1893–1951, Eng. playwright, composer, & actor.

Novotna, Jarmila, 1911–, Czech-born U.S. soprano.
Novotny, Antonin, 1904–75, president of Czechoslovakia 1957–68.
Noyes, Alfred, 1880–1958, Eng. poet.
Nu, U, 1907–, prime minister of Burma 1948–58 & 1960–62.
Nureyev, Rudolf, 1938–, Soviet-born ballet dancer & choreographer.
Nurmi, Paavo, 1897–1973, Finnish track runner.
Nyerere, Julius Kambarage, 1922–, African statesman & first president of Tanzania 1964–85.

Oakley, Annie, 1860–1926, U.S. markswoman.
Oates, Joyce Carol, 1938–, U.S. author.
—Titus, 1649–1705. Eng. conspirator.
Oberon, Merle, 1911–79, Tasmanian-born U.S. actress.
Oboler, Arch, 1909–, U.S. writer.
Obote, (Apollo) Milton, 1924–, president of Uganda 1966–71 & 1980–85.
Obregón, Alvaro, 1880–1928, Mexican soldier & politician; president of Mexico 1920–24 & 1928; assassinated.
O'Brien, Lawrence Francis, 1917–90, U.S. politician & government official.
—Margaret, 1937–, U.S. actress.
—Pat(rick), 1899–1983, U.S. actor.
O'Casey, Sean, 1881–1964, Irish playwright.
Ochoa, Severo, 1905–, Sp.-born U.S. biochemist.
Ochs, Adolph Simon, 1858–1935, U.S. newspaper publisher.
Ockham, William of, 1285?–1349?, Eng. philosopher.
O'Connell, Daniel, 1775–1847, Irish nationalist leader.
O'Connor, Flannery, 1925–64, U.S. author.
—Frank, pseud. of Michael John O'Donovan, 1903–66, Irish author.
—Sandra Day, 1930–, U.S. jurist; justice of U.S. Supreme Court, 1981–.
—Thomas P. (Tay Pay), 1848–1929, Irish journalist & nationalist.
O'Day, Anita, 1920–, U.S. jazz singer.
Odets, Clifford, 1906–63, U.S. actor & playwright.
Odetta, b. Odetta Holmes, 1930–, U.S. folk singer.
Oenslager, Donald, 1902–75, U.S. set designer.
Oersted, Hans Christian, 1777–1851, Dan. physicist.
Oerter, Alfred, 1936–, U.S. discus thrower.
O'Faoláin, Sean, 1900–, Irish author.
Offenbach, Jacques, 1819–80, Ger.-born Fr. composer.
O'Flaherty, Liam, 1896–1984, Irish author.
Ogden, C(harles) K(ay), 1889–1957, Eng. psychologist & semanticist.
Ogilvy, David MacKenzie, 1911–, Eng. advertising executive active in U.S.
Oglethorpe, James Edward, 1696–1785, Eng. general & philanthropist; founder of Georgia colony.
O'Hara, John, 1905–70, U.S. author.
O'Higgins, Bernardo, 1778–1842, Chilean statesman.
Ohm, Georg Simon, 1787–1854, Ger. physicist.
Oistrakh, David Fyodorovich, 1908–74, Soviet violinist.
O'Keeffe, Georgia, 1887–1986, U.S. painter.
Olav V, 1903–91, king of Norway 1957–91.
Oldenburg, Claes Thure, 1929–, Swed.-born U.S. sculptor.
Oldfield, Berner Eli (Barney), 1878–1946, U.S. automobile racer.
Olds, Ransom Eli, 1864–1950, U.S. automobile manufacturer.
Oliphant, Patrick Bruce, 1935–, U.S. political cartoonist.
Oliver, Edna May, 1883–1942, U.S. actress.
—Joe (King), 1885–1938, U.S. jazz musician.
Olivier, Sir Laurence, 1907–89, Eng. actor & director.
Olmsted, Frederick Law, 1822–1903, U.S. landscape architect.
Olson, Charles, 1910–70, U.S. poet.
Omar Khayyám, ?–1123?, Pers. poet & astronomer.
Onassis, Aristotle Socrates, 1906–75, Turk.-born Gk. shipping magnate.
O'Neill, Eugene Gladstone, 1888–1953, U.S. playwright.
—Thomas Philip (Tip), 1912–, U.S. statesman.
Onions, Charles Talbut, 1873–1965, Eng. lexicographer.
Onsager, Lars, 1903–76, Norw.-born U.S. physical chemist.
Oparin, Aleksandr Ivanovich, 1894–1980, Soviet biochemist.
Oppenheimer, J(ulius) Robert, 1904–67, U.S. physicist.

Ophuls, Max, 1902–57, Fr. film director.
Orczy, Baroness Emmuska, 1865–1947, Hung.-born Eng. author.
Orff, Carl, 1895–1982, Ger. composer.
Origen, A.D. 185?–254?, Gk. writer & church father.
Orlando, Vittorio Emanuele, 1860–1952, Ital. statesman; prime minister 1917–19.
Ormandy, Eugene, 1899–1985, Hung.-born U.S. conductor.
Orozco, José Clemente, 1883–1949, Mexican painter.
Orr, Robert Gordon (Bobby), 1948–, Can. hockey player.
Ortega y Gasset, José, 1883–1955, Sp. philosopher & author.
Orwell, George, pseud. of Eric Arthur Blair, 1903–50, Eng. author & social critic.
Osborne, John James, 1929–, Eng. playwright.
Osceola, 1804–38, Seminole Am. Ind. chief.
Osler, Sir William, 1849–1919, Can. physician.
Osman I, 1259–1326, Turkish founder of the Ottoman Empire.
Ossietzky, Carl von, 1889–1938, Ger. journalist; Nobel Prize winner.
Ostwald, Wilhelm, 1853–1932, Ger. chemist; Nobel Prize winner.
Oswald, Lee Harvey, 1939–63, U.S. alleged assassin of President John F. Kennedy; murdered.
Otis, Elisha Graves, 1811–61, U.S. inventor.
O'Toole, Peter, 1932–, Irish actor.
Oursler, Fulton, 1893–1952, U.S. writer & editor.
Ouspenskaya, Maria, 1876–1949, Russ. actress active in U.S.
Outcault, Richard, 1863–1928, U.S. cartoonist.
Ovid (L. Publius Ovidius Naso), 43 B.C.–A.D. 17, Roman poet.
Owen, Robert, 1771–1858, Welsh social reformer.
—Wilfred, 1893–1918, Eng. poet.
Owens, Jesse, 1913–80, U.S. track athlete.
Owings, Nathaniel Alexander, 1903–84, U.S. architect.
Ozawa, Seiji, 1935–, Chin.-born conductor active in U.S.
Ozick, Cynthia, 1928–, U.S. author & critic.

Paar, Jack, 1918–, U.S. TV personality.
Pabst, Georg W., 1885–1967, Ger. film director.
Paderewski, Ignace Jan, 1860–1941, Pol. pianist, composer, & statesman.
Paganini, Niccolò, 1782–1840, Ital. violinist & composer.
Page, Geraldine, 1924–87, U.S. actress.
Paget, Sir James, 1814–99, Eng. surgeon & pathologist.
Pagnol, Marcel, 1895–1974, Fr. playwright & film producer.
Paige, Leroy David (Satchel), 1906–82, U.S. baseball player.
Paine, Thomas, 1737–1809, Eng.-born Amer. revolutionary patriot, political philosopher, & author.
Palestrina, Giovanni Pierluigi da, 1526?–94, Ital. composer.
Paley, Grace, 1922–, U.S. author.
—William Samuel, 1901–90, U.S. radio & TV executive.
Palladio, Andrea, 1508–80, Ital. architect.
Palme, Olof, 1927–86, prime minister of Sweden 1969–76 & 1982; assassinated.
Palmer, Arnold Daniel, 1929–, U.S. golfer.
—Daniel David, 1845–1913, Can. founder of chiropractic medicine.
—Potter, 1826–1902, U.S. merchant & real estate developer.
Palmerston, Henry John Temple, 3rd Viscount, 1784–1865, Eng. statesman; prime minister 1855–58 & 1859–65.
Pandit, Madame Vijaya Lakshmi, 1900–90, Indian diplomat & president of U.N. general assembly 1953–54.
Panini, 4th c. B.C. Indian Sanskrit grammarian.
Pankhurst, Emmeline Goulden, 1858–1928, Eng. suffragist.
Panofsky, Erwin, 1892–1968, Ger.-born U.S. art historian.
Papadopoulos, George, 1919–, Gk. military officer; premier of Greece 1967–73; president 1973.
Papandreou, George, 1888–1968, Gk. politician & opposition leader.
Papanicolaou, George Nicholas, 1883–1962, Gk.-born U.S. physician.
Papas, Irene, 1925–, Gk. actress.
Papp, Joseph, 1921–, U.S. theatrical producer.
Paracelsus, pseud. of Theophrastus Bombastus von Hohenheim, 1493–1541, Swiss physician & alchemist.
Paré, Ambroise, 1510–90, Fr. surgeon.
Pareto, Vilfredo, 1848–1923, Ital. economist & sociologist.

Park Chung Hee, 1917–79, president of South Korea 1961–79.

—**Robert Ezra,** 1864–1944, U.S. sociologist.

Parker, Bonnie, 1910–34, U.S. criminal.

—**Charles Christopher, Jr.,** 1920–55, U.S. jazz musician: called **Bird.**

—**Dorothy,** 1893–1967, U.S. author.

—**Francis Wayland,** 1837–1902, U.S. educator.

Parkman, Francis, 1823–93, U.S. historian.

Parks, Bert, 1914–, U.S. TV personality.

—**Gordon,** 1912–79, U.S. photographer & film director.

Parmigianino, Il, b. Girolamo Mazzuoli, 1503–40, Ital. painter.

Parnell, Charles Stewart, 1846–91, Irish statesman.

Parr, Catherine, 1512–48, sixth wife of Henry VIII of England.

Parrington, Vernon Louis, 1871–1929, U.S. historian.

Parrish, Maxfield, 1870–1966, U.S. painter.

Parsons, Estelle, 1927–, U.S. actress.

—**Louella Oettinger,** 1893–1972, U.S. columnist.

—**Talcott,** 1902–79, U.S. sociologist.

Partridge, Eric H., 1894–1979, Eng. lexicographer & critic.

Pascal, Blaise, 1623–62, Fr. mathematician & philosopher.

Pasionaria, La (Dolores Ibarruri), 1895–, Sp. revolutionist & founder of Spain's Communist Party.

Pasolini, Pier Paolo, 1922–75, Ital. film director.

Pasternak, Boris, 1890–1960, Soviet poet & novelist; Nobel Prize winner.

Pasteur, Louis, 1822–95, Fr. chemist & bacteriologist.

Pastor, Antonio (Tony), 1837–1908, U.S. actor & theater manager.

Pater, Walter Horatio, 1839–94, Eng. essayist & critic.

Paton, Alan Stewart, 1903–88, South African author.

Patrick, Saint, 389?–461, Brit. missionary to and patron saint of Ireland.

Patterson, Eleanor Medill (Cissy), 1884–1948, and her brother **Joseph M.,** 1879–1946, U.S. publishers.

Patti, Adelina, 1843–1919, Sp.-born Ital. soprano.

Patton, George Smith, 1885–1945, U.S. general.

Pauker, Ana Rabinsohn, 1889?–1960, Romanian communist.

Paul, Saint, A.D.? –67?, b.Saul, a Jew of Tarsus who became the apostle of Christianity to the Gentiles; author of various New Testament books.

Paul VI, b. Giovanni Battista Montini, 1897–1978, pope 1963–78.

Pauli, Wolfgang, 1900–58, Swiss-Austrian physicist.

Pauling, Linus Carl, 1901–, U.S. chemist.

Pausanias, 2nd c. A.D. Gk. traveler & geographer.

Pavarotti, Luciano, 1935–, Ital. tenor.

Pavese, Cesare, 1908–50, Ital. author.

Pavlov, Ivan Petrovich, 1849–1936, Russ. physiologist.

Pavlova, Anna, 1885–1931, Russ. ballerina active in France.

Paxinou, Katina, 1900–73, Gk. actress active in U.S.

Peabody, George, 1795–1869, U.S. businessman & financier.

Peale A family of U.S. painters incl. **Charles Willson,** 1741–1827; his brother **James,** 1749–1831; and **Rembrandt,** 1778–1860, son of Charles.

—**Norman Vincent,** 1898–, U.S. clergyman & author.

Pearson, Andrew Russell (Drew), 1897–1969, U.S. columnist.

—**Lester Bowles,** 1897–1972, Can. statesman; prime minister of Canada 1963–68.

Peary, Robert Edwin, 1856–1920, U.S. Arctic explorer.

Peck, Gregory, 1916–, U.S. actor.

—**Peckham, Rufus W.,** 1838–1909, U.S. jurist; justice of U.S. Supreme Court 1895–1909.

Peckinpah, Sam, 1925–84, U.S. film director.

Peel, Sir Robert, 1788–1850, Eng. statesman & founder of London & Irish police forces; prime minister 1834 & 1841–46.

Peerce, Jan, 1904–84, U.S. tenor.

Pegler, (James) Westbrook, 1894–1969, U.S. columnist.

Péguy, Charles, 1873–1914, Fr. poet & author.

Pei, I(eoh) M(ing), 1917–, Chin.-born U.S. architect.

Peirce, Benjamin, 1809–80, U.S. mathematician & astronomer.

—**Charles Sanders,** 1839–1914, U.S. philosopher & logician; son of prec.

Pélé, b. Edson Arantes do Nascimento, 1940–, Brazilian soccer player.

Pendergast, Thomas J., 1872–1945, U.S. politician.

Penfield, Wilder G., 1891–1976, U.S.-born Can. neurosurgeon.

Penn, Arthur, 1922–, U.S. film & stage director.

—**Irving,** 1917–, U.S. photographer.

—**William,** 1644–1718, Eng. Quaker; founder of Pennsylvania.

Penney, J(ames) C(ash), 1875–1971, U.S. merchant.

Pepin the Short, 714?–768, king of the Franks 751–768.

Pepys, Samuel, 1633–1703, Eng. author.

Percy, Sir Henry, 1364–1403, Eng. soldier: called **Hotspur.**

—**Walker,** 1916–90, U.S. author.

Pereira, William, 1909–85, U.S. architect.

Perelman, S(idney) J(oseph), 1904–79, U.S. author.

Peres, Shimon, 1923–, Israeli statesman; prime minister 1984–86.

Peretz, Isaac Loeb, 1851–1915, Pol. poet & author.

Perez, Carlos Andres, 1922–, president of Venezuela 1974–78.

Pérez de Cuéllar, Javiera, 1920–, Peruvian diplomat and secretary-general of the U.N. 1982–, .

Pergolesi, Giovanni Battista, 1710–36, Ital. composer.

Pericles, ?–429 B.C., Athenian statesman & general.

Perkins, Frances, 1882–1965, U.S. social worker; first woman Cabinet member; secretary of labor 1933–45.

—**Maxwell,** 1884–1947, U.S. editor.

—**(Richard) Marlin,** 1905–, U.S. zoo director.

Perlman, Itzhak, 1945–, Israeli violinist.

Perls, Frederick (Fritz), 1893–1970, Ger.-born U.S. psychologist.

Perón, Eva Duarte de, 1919–52, Argentine radio personality & political leader.

—**Juan Domingo,** 1895–1974, Argentinian political leader; president 1946–55 & 1973–74; husband of prec.

Perón, Maria Estela Isabel Martinez de, 1931–, president of Argentina 1974–76; wife of prec.

Perrault, Charles, 1628–1703, Fr. writer & compiler of fairy tales.

Perry, Antoinette, 1888–1946, U.S. stage actress, director, & producer.

—**Matthew Calbraith,** 1794–1858, U.S. commodore.

—**Oliver Hazard,** 1785–1819, U.S. naval commander; brother of prec.

Perse, St. John, pseud. of Alexis Saint-Léger Léger, 1887–1975, Fr. poet & diplomat; Nobel Prize winner.

Pershing, John Joseph, 1860–1948, U.S. general.

Perugino, Il, b. Pietro Vannucci, 1446–1523, Ital. painter.

Perutz, Max Ferdinand, 1914–, Austrian-born Brit. physicist; Nobel Prize winner.

Pestalozzi, Johann Heinrich, 1746–1827, Swiss educator.

Pétain, Henri Philippe, 1856–1951, Fr. political leader; premier 1940–44.

Peter I, 1672–1725, czar of Russia 1689–1725: called **the Great.**

Peter, Saint, b. Simon, ?–A.D. 67?, 1st pope A.D. 42?–67?.

Peters Roberta, 1930–, U.S. soprano.

Petipa, Marius, 1822–1910, Fr. dancer & choreographer active in Russ.

Peterson, Oscar, 1925–, U.S. jazz pianist.

—**Roger Tory,** 1908–, U.S. ornithologist & author.

Petit, Roland, 1924–, Fr. dancer & choreographer.

Petrarch, Francesco, 1304–74, Ital. scholar & poet.

Petrie, Sir (William Matthew) Flinders, 1853–1942, Eng. archaeologist.

Petrillo, James Caesar, 1892–1984, U.S. labor leader.

Petronius, Gaius, A.D.?–66?, Roman satirist.

Peusner, Antoine, 1886–1962, Russ. painter & sculptor.

Pevsner, Sir Nikolaus, 1902–83, Ger.-born Brit. art historian.

Pham Van Dong, 1906–, premier of N. Vietnam 1955–.

Phidias, 500?–432?, B.C., Gk. sculptor & architect.

Philby, Harold A. R., 1911–88, Eng.-born spy for the U.S.S.R.

Philip II, 382–336 B.C., king of Macedonia & conqueror of Thessaly & Greece; father of Alexander the Great.

Philip II, 1527–98, king of Spain 1556–98.

Philip, Prince (Duke of Edinburgh), 1921–, Gk.-born husband of Queen Elizabeth II.

Philip the Good, 1396–1467, Duke of Burgundy, 1419–67.

Philip (Metacomet), 1639?–76, sachem of the Wampanoag Amer. Indians.

Philippe, Gerard, 1922–57, Fr. actor.

Phillips, Wendell, 1811–84, U.S. orator & reformer.

Philo Judaeus, 20 B.C.?–A.D. 50?, Jewish Platonist philosopher.

Phumiphon Aduldet, 1927–, king of Thailand 1946–, .

Phyfe, Duncan, 1768–1854, Scot.-born U.S. cabinet maker.

Piaf, Edith, 1912–63, Fr. singer.

Piaget, Jean, 1896–1980, Swiss psychologist & author.

Piatigorski, Gregor, 1903–76, Ukrainian-born U.S. cellist.

Picabia, Francis, 1878–1953, Fr. painter.

Picard, Jean, 1620–82, Fr. astronomer.

Picasso, Pablo, 1881–1973, Sp. artist active in France.

Piccard, Auguste, 1884–1962, Swiss physicist.

Pickett, George Edward, 1825–75, U.S. Confederate general.

Pickford, Mary, 1893–1979, Can.-born U.S. actress.

Picon, Molly, 1898–, U.S. actress.

Pidgeon, Walter, 1897–1984, Can. actor.

Pierce, Franklin, 1804–69, 14th U.S. president 1853–57.

Piero della Francesca, 1418?–92, Ital. painter.

Pike, Zebulon Montgomery, 1779–1813, U.S. general & explorer.

Pilate, Pontius, 1st c. A.D. Roman governor of Judea A.D. 26?–36?; delivered Jesus to be crucified.

Pillsbury, Charles Alfred, 1842–99, U.S. businessman.

Pilsudski, Józef, 1867–1935, Pol. statesman.

Pindar, 522?–433, B.C., Gk. poet.

Pinel, Philippe, 1745–1826, Fr. physician & psychologist.

Pinero, Sir Arthur Wing, 1855–1934, Eng. playwright & actor.

Pinkerton, Allan, 1819–84, Scot.-born detective active in U.S.

Pinkham, Lydia Estes, 1819–83, U.S. businesswoman.

Pinter, Harold, 1930–, Eng. playwright.

Pinturicchio, b. Bernardino Betti, 1454–1513, Ital. painter.

Pinza, Ezio, 1892–1957, Ital.-born U.S. basso.

Pirandello, Luigi, 1867–1936, Ital. playwright & author.

Piranesi, Giovanni Battista, 1720–78, Ital. architect & engraver.

Pirenne, Henri, 1862–1935, Bel. historian.

Pisano, Giovanni, 1245–1314, Ital. sculptor.

—**Nicola,** 1220–84, Ital. sculptor; father of prec.

Piscator, Erwin, 1893–1966, Ger. theater director.

Pisistratus, ?–527 B.C., Gk. statesman.

Pissarro, Camille, 1830–1903, Fr. painter.

Piston, Walter, 1894–1976, U.S. composer.

Pitcher, Molly, b. Mary Ludwig, 1754–1832, Amer. revolutionary heroine.

Pitman, Sir Isaac, 1813–97, Eng. phoneticist; invented a system of shorthand.

Pitt, William, 1708–78, Eng. statesman.

—**William,** 1759–1806, Eng. prime minister 1783–1801 & 1804–06; son of prec.: called **the Younger.**

Pius XII, b. Eugenio Pacelli, 1876–1958, pope 1939–58.

Pizarro, Francisco, 1475?–1541, Sp. soldier & conqueror of Peru.

Planck, Max, 1858–1947, Ger. physicist.

Plath, Sylvia, 1932–63, U.S. poet resident in England.

Plato, 427?–327? B.C., Gk. philosopher.

Plautus, Titus Maccius, 254?–184 B.C., Roman playwright.

Plimpton, George Ames, 1927–, U.S. author & editor.

Plimsoll, Samuel, 1824–98, Eng. shipping reformer.

Pliny (L. Gaius Plinius Secundus), A.D. 23–79, Roman naturalist & writer: called **the Elder.**

— (L. Gaius Plinius Caecilius), A.D. 62–113, Roman statesman; nephew of prec.: called **the Younger.**

Plisetskaya, Maya, 1925–, Soviet ballerina.

Plotinus, 205?–270, Egyptian-born Roman philosopher.

Plummer, Christopher, 1929–, Can. actor active in U.S.

Plutarch, A.D. 46?–120?, Gk. historian.

Pocahontas, 1595?–1617, Am. Ind. princess; daughter of Powhatan.

Podgorny, Nikolai Viktorovich, 1903–83, Soviet politician; president of U.S.S.R. 1966–77.

Poe, Edgar Allan, 1809–49, U.S. author, critic, & poet.

Poincaré, Jules Henri, 1854–1912, Fr. mathematician.

—**Raymond,** 1860–1934, Fr. statesman; president 1913–20.

Poinsett, Joel Roberts, 1779–1851, U.S. diplomat & amateur botanist.

Poisson, Simeon D., 1781–1840, Fr. mathematician.

Poitier, Sidney, 1927–, U.S. actor.

Polanski, Roman, 1933–, Pol. film director active in U.S. .

Politian, b. Angelo Poliziano, 1454–94, Ital. classical scholar & poet.

Polk, James Knox, 1795–1849, 11th U.S. president 1845–49.

Pollaivollo, Antonio del, 1432?–98, Ital. sculptor & painter.

Pollock, Jackson, 1912–56, U.S. painter.

Polo, Marco, 1254?–1324?, Venetian traveler & author.

Polybius, 204?–122? B.C., Gk. historian.

Polycleitus, 5th c. B.C. Gk. sculptor & architect.

Pompadour, Jeanne Antoinette Poisson, Marquise de, 1721–64, mistress of Louis XV.

Pompey (L. Gnaeus Pompeius Magnus), 106–48 B.C., Roman general & statesman.

Pompidou, Georges Jean Raymond, 1911–74, president of France 1969–74.

Ponce de Leon, Juan, 1460–1521, Sp. discoverer of Florida.

Ponchielli, Amilcare, 1834–86, Ital. composer.

Pons, Lily, 1904–76, Fr.-born U.S. soprano.

Ponselle, Rosa Melba, 1897–1981, U.S. soprano.

Ponti, Carlo, 1913–, Ital. film director.

Pontiac, 1720?–1769, Ottawa Am. Ind. chief.

Pontormo, Jacopo da, b. Jacopo Carrucci, 1494–1557, Ital. painter.

Pope, Alexander, 1688–1744, Eng. poet & essayist.

—**John Russell,** 1874–1937, U.S. architect.

Porter, Cole, 1891–1964, U.S. composer & lyricist.

—**Katherine Anne,** 1890–1980, U.S. author.

Portman, John, 1924–, U.S. architect.

Post, Charles William, 1854–1914, U.S. breakfast-food manufacturer.

—**Emily Price,** 1873?–1960, U.S. writer on etiquette.

—**Marjorie Merriweather,** 1887–1973, U.S. philanthropist.

—**Wiley,** 1900–35, U.S. aviator.

Potemkin, Grigori Aleksandrovich, 1739–91, Russ. statesman & general.

Potok, Chaim, 1929–, U.S. author.

Potter, Beatrix, 1866?–1943, Eng. author & illustrator of children's books.

Poulenc, Francis, 1899–1963, Fr. composer.

Pound, Ezra Loomis, 1885–1972, U.S. poet resident in Italy.

Poussin, Nicholas, 1594–1665, Fr. painter.

Powell, Adam Clayton Jr., 1908–72, U.S. clergyman & politician.

—**Anthony,** 1905–, Eng. author.

—**Dick,** 1904–63, U.S. actor & singer.

—**Eleanor,** 1912–82, U.S. dancer & actress.

—**Hiram,** 1805–73, U.S. sculptor.

—**John Wesley,** 1834–1902, U.S. geographer & explorer.

—**Lewis Franklin, Jr.,** 1907–, U.S. jurist; justice of the U.S. Supreme Court 1972–.

—**William,** 1892–1984, U.S. actor.

Power, Tyrone, 1913–58, U.S. actor.

Powhatan, 1550?–1618, Algonquin Am. Ind. chief.

Pratt, E(dwin) J(ohn), 1882–1964, Can. poet.

Praxiteles, 4th c. B.C. Athenian sculptor.

Prefontaine, Steven Roland, 1951–75, U.S. track runner.

Preminger, Otto Ludwig, 1906–86, Austrian-born U.S. film director & producer.

Prendergast, Maurice Brazil, 1859–1924, Can.-born U.S. painter & illustrator.

Presley, Elvis Aron, 1935–77, U.S. singer & actor.

Pretorius, Andries Wilhelmus Jacobus, 1799–1853, and his son **Marthinus Wessels,** 1819–1901, Du. colonizers & soldiers in South Africa.

Prévert, Jacques, 1900–77, Fr. poet.

Previn, André, 1929–, Ger.-born U.S. composer, conductor, & pianist.

Price, George, 1901–, U.S. cartoonist.

—Leontyne, 1927–, U.S. soprano.

—Vincent, 1911–, U.S. actor.

Priestley, J(ohn) B(oynton), 1894–1984, Eng. author.

—Joseph, 1733–1804, Eng. chemist.

Primrose, William, 1904–82, Scot.-born U.S. violinist.

Primus, Pearl, 1919–, Trinidad-born dancer & choreographer active in U.S.

Prince, Harold, 1928–, U.S. theatrical producer & director.

Princip, Gavrilo, 1895–1918, Serbian political agitator & assassin of Archduke Franz Ferdinand.

Pritchett, V(ictor) S(awdon), 1900–, Eng. author.

Procter, William C., 1862–1934, U.S. industrialist.

Prokhorov, Alexander Mikhailovich, 1916–, Russ. physicist; Nobel Prize winner.

Prokofiev, Sergei Sergeyevich, 1891–1953, Soviet composer.

Proudhon, Pierre Joseph, 1809–65, Fr. author & political leader.

Proust, Joseph Louis, 1754–1826, Fr. chemist.

—Marcel, 1871–1922, Fr. author.

Ptolemy, 2nd c. A.D. Alexandrian astronomer, mathematician, & geographer.

Ptolemy I, 367?–283? B.C., Macedonian general of Alexander the Great & founder of the ruling dynasty of Egypt; king of Egypt 305–285 B.C..

—II, 309?–246 B.C., king of Egypt 285–246 B.C.; son of prec.

Pucci, Emilio, 1914–, Ital. fashion designer.

Puccini, Giacomo, 1858–1924, Ital. operatic composer.

Pulaski, Count Casimir, 1748?–79, Pol. soldier & Amer. revolutionary general.

Pulitzer, Joseph, 1847–1911, Hung.-born U.S. publisher & philanthropist.

Pullman, George Mortimer, 1831–97, U.S. inventor.

Pupin, Michael Idvorsky, 1858–1935, Yugoslav-born U.S. physicist & inventor.

Purcell, Edward Mills, 1912–, U.S. physicist; Nobel Prize winner.

—Henry, 1658–95, Eng. composer.

Purkinje, Johannes Evangelista, 1787–1869, Czech physiologist.

Pushkin, Alexander Sergeyevich, 1799–1837, Russ. poet.

Putnam, George, 1814–72, U.S. publisher.

Puvis de Chavannes, Pierre, 1824–98, Fr. painter & muralist.

Puzo, Mario, 1920–, U.S. author.

Pyle, Ernest Taylor (Ernie), 1900–45, U.S. journalist & war correspondent.

—Howard, 1853–1911, U.S. author & illustrator.

Pynchon, Thomas, 1937–, U.S. author.

Pythagoras, 6th c. B.C. Gk. philosopher.

Qaddafi, Muammar al-, 1942–, Libyan military officer; head of state of Libya 1969–.

Quant, Mary, 1934–, Eng. fashion designer.

Quantrill, William Clarke, 1837–65, U.S. Confederate guerrilla leader.

Quarles, Benjamin Arthur, 1904–, U.S. historian.

Quasimodo, Salvatore, 1901–68, Ital. poet & critic; Nobel Prize winner.

Quayle, Anthony, 1913–89, Eng. actor.

—Dan (James Danforth), 1947–, U.S. statesman; U.S. vice president 1989–.

Queen, Ellery, pseud. of cousins **Frederic Dannay**, 1905–82, & **Manfred Bennington Lee**, 1905–71, U.S. authors.

Queensbury, John Sholto Douglas, Marquis of, 1844–1900, Scot. boxing patron.

Quesnay, François, 1694–1774, Fr. economist.

Quercia, Jacopo della, 1378?–1438, Ital. sculptor.

Quezon y Molina, Manuel Luis, 1878–1944, Filipino statesman; first president of the Philippines 1935–44.

Quiller-Couch, Sir Arthur Thomas, 1863–1944, Eng. author; pseud. **Q.**

Quincy, Josiah, 1744–75, Amer. lawyer & revolutionary patriot.

Quinn, Anthony, 1915–, Mexican-born U.S. actor.

Quintero, Jose, 1924–, Panamanian-born U.S. stage director.

Quisling, Vidkun Abraham Lauritz, 1887–1945, Norw. traitor during World War II.

Rabelais, François, 1494?–1553, Fr. writer & satirist.

Rabe, David, 1940–, U.S. playwright.

Rabi, Isadore Isaac, 1898–1988, Austrian-born U.S. physicist.

Rabin, Yitzhak, 1922–, prime minister of Israel 1974–77.

Rachmaninoff, Sergei Vassilievich, 1873–1943, Russ.-born pianist, composer & conductor in U.S. after 1918.

Racine, Jean Baptiste, 1639–99, Fr. playwright.

Rackham, Arthur, 1867–1939, Eng. illustrator.

Radcliffe, Ann Ward, 1764–1823, Eng. author.

Raeburn, Sir Henry, 1756–1823, Scot. painter.

Raemaekers, Louis, 1869–1956, Du. cartoonist.

Raffles, Sir (Thomas) Stanford, 1781–1825, Eng. colonial administrator in East Indies.

Raft, George, 1895–1980, U.S. actor.

Raimondi, Marcantonio, 1475?–1534, Ital. engraver.

Raimu, b. Jules Auguste Muraire, 1883–1946, Fr. actor.

Rainier III (Louis Henri Maxence Bertrand de Grimaldi), 1923–, prince of Monaco.

Rains, Claude, 1889–1967, Eng.-born U.S. actor,

Raisa, Rosa, 1893–1963, Pol. dramatic soprano.

Raitt, John, 1917–, U.S. singer & actor.

Raleigh, Sir Walter, 1552–1618, Eng. statesman & poet; beheaded. Also **Ralegh.**

Ramakrishna, 1834–86, Hindu yogi.

Raman, Sir Chandrasekhara Venkata, 1888–1970, Indian physicist.

Rambert, Dame Marie, 1888–1982, Pol.-born ballet dancer, teacher, & impresario active in Great Britain.

Rameau, Jean Philippe, 1683–1764, Fr. composer.

Ramon y Cajal, Santiago, 1852–1934, Sp. histologist.

Rampal, Jean-Pierre, 1922–, Fr. flutist.

Ramsay, Sir William, 1852–1916, Scot. chemist.

Ramses A dynasty of Egyptian kings incl. **Ramses I,** founder of the dynasty in the 14th c. B.C., and **Ramses II,** ?–1225 B.C.

Rand, Ayn, 1905–82, Russ.-born U.S. author.

—Sally, 1904–79, U.S. dancer.

Randolph, A(sa) Phillip, 1889–1979, U.S. labor leader.

Ranjit Singh, 1780–1839, Indian ruler.

Rank, Otto, 1884–1939, Austrian psychoanalyst,

Rankin, Jeannette, 1880–1973, U.S. feminist & first U.S. congresswoman.

Ransom, John Crowe, 1888–1974, U.S. poet & educator.

Raphael, b. Raffaello Sanzio, 1483–1520, Ital. painter.

Rasmussen, Knud Johan Victor, 1879–1933, Dan. explorer & ethnologist.

Rasputin, Gregori Efimovich, 1871?–1916, Russ. mystic in the court of Czar Nicholas II; assassinated.

Rathbone, Basil, 1892–1967, South African-born U.S. actor.

Rathenau, Walter, 1867–1922, Ger. industrialist & statesman; assassinated.

Rather, Dan, 1931–, U.S. TV newscaster.

Rattner, Abraham, 1895–1978, U.S. painter.

Rauschenberg, Robert, 1925–, U.S. artist.

Ravel, Maurice Joseph, 1875–1937, Fr. composer.

Rawlings, Marjorie Kinnan, 1896–1953, U.S. author.

Rawls, Elizabeth Earle (Betsy), 1928–, U.S. golfer.

Ray, Man, 1890–1976, U.S. artist & photographer.

—Satyajit, 1922–, Indian film director.

Rayburn, Sam(uel Taliaferro), 1882–1961, U.S. politician.

Rayleigh, John William Strutt, Baron, 1842–1919, Eng. physicist.

Read, Sir Herbert, 1893–1968, Eng. art critic & author.

Reagan, Ronald Wilson, 1911–, U.S. statesman; 40th U.S. president 1981–89.

Reasoner, Harry, 1923–91, U.S. journalist and television reporter.

Réaumur, René Antoine Ferchault de, 1683–1757, Fr. physicist.

Récamier, Jeanne Françoise Julie Adélaïde Bernard, 1779–1849, Fr. social leader & patron of literature.

Red Cloud, 1822–1909, Oglala Sioux Am. Ind. chief.

Redford, Robert, 1937–, U.S. actor.

Redgrave, Sir Michael, 1908–85, Eng. actor.

—**Lynn,** 1943–, Eng. actress; daugher of prec.
—**Vanessa,** 1937–, Eng. actress; sister of prec.
Redon, Odilon, 1840–1916, Fr. painter.
Reed, Sir Carol, 1906–76, Eng. film director.
—**John,** 1887–1920, U.S. journalist & poet.
—**Oliver,** 1938–, Eng. actor.
—**Rex,** 1940–, U.S. author, critic, & journalist.
—**Walter,** 1851–1902, U.S. Army surgeon & bacteriologist.
—**Willis,** 1942–, U.S. basketball player.
Regulus, Marcus Atilius, ?–249? B.C., Roman general.
Rehnquist, William Hubbs, 1924–, U.S. jurist; justice of the U.S. Supreme Court 1972–86; chief justice 1986–.
Reich, Wilhelm, 1897–1957, Austrian-born psychiatrist active in U.S.
Reichstein, Tadeus, 1897–, Pol.-born Swedish chemist; Nobel Prize winner.
Reid, Ogden M., 1882–1947 U.S. newspaper publisher.
Reik, Theodor, 1888–1969, Austrian-born U.S. psychologist & author.
Reiner, Carl, 1922–, U.S. comedian & TV & film producer & director.
—**Fritz,** 1888–1963, Hung.-born U.S. conductor.
Reinhardt, Jean Baptiste (Django), 1910–53, Belg.-born jazz guitarist active in France.
—**Max,** 1873–1943, Austrian theatrical director & producer active in Germany & U.S.
Réjane, b. Gabrielle Réju, 1857–1920, Fr. actress.
Remarque, Erich Maria, 1898–1970, Ger.-born U.S. author.
Rembrandt Harmenszoon van Rijn, 1606–69, Du. painter & etcher.
Remington, Frederic, 1861–1909, U.S. painter & sculptor.
Renault, Mary, 1905–83, Eng. author.
Reni, Guido, 1575–1642, Ital. painter.
Renoir, Jean, 1894–1979, Fr. film director.
—**Pierre Auguste,** 1841–1919, Fr. painter; father of prec.
Renwick, James, 1818–95, U.S. architect.
Resnais, Alain, 1922–, Fr. film director.
Resnik, Regina, 1924–, U.S. mezzo-soprano.
Respighi, Ottorino, 1879–1936, Ital. composer.
Reston, James, 1909–, Scot.-born U.S. journalist.
Reszke, Edouard de, 1853–1917, Pol. tenor.
—**Jean de,** 1850–1925, Pol. tenor; brother of prec.
Retz, Gilles de, 1404?–40, Fr. feudal lord & soldier; thought to be the original **Bluebeard.**
Reuter, Baron Paul Julius, 1816–99, Ger.-born Eng. news agency founder.
Reuther, Walter Philip, 1907–70, U.S. labor leader.
Revels, Hiram Rhoades, 1822–1901, U.S. clergyman, educator, & congressman.
Revere, Paul, 1735–1818, Amer. revolutionary patriot.
Revson, Charles Haskell, 1906–75, U.S. business executive.
Rexroth, Kenneth, 1905–82, U.S. author & critic.
Reynolds, Sir Joshua, 1723–92, Eng. painter.
—**Richard S., Jr.,** 1908–80, U.S. business executive.
Reza Pahlevi, 1877–1944, shah of Iran 1925–41.
Rhee, Syngman, 1875–1965, first president of Republic of Korea 1948–60.
Rhine, Joseph Banks, 1895–1980, U.S. parapsychologist.
Rhodes, Cecil John, 1853–1902, Eng.-born South African financier & statesman.
Rhys, Jean, 1895–1979, British novelist.
Ribbentrop, Joachim von, 1893–1946, Ger. diplomat.
Ribera, Jusepe de, 1588–1652, Sp. painter & etcher: called **Lo Spagnoletto.**
Ribicoff, Abraham A., 1910–, U.S. politician.
Riboud, Jean, 1919–85, Fr. industrialist.
Ricardo, David, 1772–1823, Eng. political economist.
Rice, Elmer, 1892–1967, U.S. playwright.
—**Grantland,** 1880–1954, U.S. sportswriter.
—**Thomas Dartmouth,** 1808–60, U.S. minstrel show pioneer.
Richard, I, 1157–99, king of England 1189–99: called **the Lion-Hearted.**
—**II,** 1367–1400, king of England 1377–99.
—**III,** 1452–85, king of England 1483–85.
Richard, (Joseph Henri) Maurice, 1921–, Can. hockey player.

Richards, Dickinson Woodruff, 1895–1973, U.S. physician; Nobel Prize winner.
—**I(vor) A(rmstrong),** 1893–1979, Eng. critic & author.
Richardson, H(enry) H(obson), 1838–86, U.S. architect.
—**Sir Owen Williams,** 1870–1959, Eng. physicist.
—**Sir Ralph,** 1902–83, Eng. actor.
—**Samuel,** 1689–1761, Eng. novelist.
—**Tony,** 1928–, Eng. film director.
Richelieu, Armand Jean du Plessis, Duc de, 1585–1642, Fr. cardinal & statesman.
Richler, Mordecai, 1931–, Can. author.
Richter, Conrad, 1890–1968, U.S. author.
—**Hans,** 1843–1916, Hung. conductor.
—**Sviatoslav,** 1914–, Soviet pianist.
Richthofen, Manfred, Baron von, 1892–1918, Ger. military aviator: called **the Red Baron.**
Rickard, George Lewis (Tex), 1871–1929, U.S. boxing promoter.
Rickenbacker, Edward Vernon (Eddie), 1890–1973, U.S. aviator.
Ricketts, Howard Taylor, 1871–1910, U.S. pathologist.
Rickey, Branch, 1881–1965, U.S. baseball manager.
Rickover, Hyman George, 1900–86, U.S. admiral.
Ride, Sally Kirsten, 1951–, U.S. astronaut; first U.S. woman in space.
Riefenstahl, Leni, 1902–, Ger. film director.
Riemann, Georg Friedrich Bernhard, 1826–66, Ger. mathematician.
Riemenschneider, Tilman, 1460?–1531, Ger. sculptor.
Rienzi, Cola di, 1313–54, Ital. revolutionary statesman.
Riesman, David, 1909–, U.S. sociologist & author.
Riggs, Robert Larimore (Bobby), 1918–, U.S. tennis player.
Riis, Jacob August, 1849–1914, Dan.-born U.S. journalist & social reformer.
Riley, James Whitcomb, 1849–1916, U.S. poet.
Rilke, Rainer Maria, 1875–1926, Czech-born Ger. poet.
Rimbaud, Arthur, 1854–91, Fr. poet.
Rimsky-Korsakov, Nikolai Andreyevich, 1844–1908, Russ. composer.
Rinehart, Mary Roberts, 1876–1958, U.S. author.
Ringling A family of U.S. circus owners incl. five brothers: **Albert,** 1852–1916; **Alfred,** 1861–1919; **Charles,** 1864–1926; **John,** 1866–1936; & **Otto,** 1858–1911.
Ripley, Robert LeRoy, 1893–1949, U.S. cartoonist.
Ristori, Adelaide, 1822–1906, Ital. actress.
Rittenhouse, David, 1732–96, U.S. astronomer & instrument maker.
Rivera, Diego, 1886–1957, Mexican painter.
Rivera y Orbaneja, Miguel Primo de, 1870–1930, Sp. general; dictator 1925–30.
Rivers, Larry, 1923–, U.S. artist.
Rizal, José Mercado, 1861–96, Filipino patriot.
Robards, Jason, Jr., 1922–, U.S. actor.
Robbe-Grillet, Alain, 1922–, Fr. author.
Robbins, Frederick Chapman, 1916–, U.S. physician; Nobel Prize winner.
—**Harold,** 1916–, U.S. author.
—**Jerome,** 1918–, U.S. dancer & choreographer.
Robert I, 1274–1329, king of Scotland 1306–29: called **the Bruce.**
Robert, Henry Martyn, 1837–1923, U.S. engineer, soldier, & parliamentarian.
Roberts, Elizabeth Madox, 1886–1941, U.S. poet & novelist.
—**Granville Oral,** 1918–, U.S. evangelist.
—**Kenneth Lewis,** 1885–1957, U.S. author.
—**Owen Josephus,** 1875–1955, U.S. jurist; justice of U.S. Supreme Court 1930–45.
Robertson, Oscar, 1938–, U.S. basketball player.
Robeson, Paul LeRoy, 1898–1976, U.S. singer & actor.
Robespierre, Maximilien François Marie Isidore de, 1758–94, Fr. revolutionary; guillotined.
Robinson, Bill (Bojangles), 1878–1949, U.S. dancer & actor.
—**Edward G.,** 1893–1973, Romanian-born U.S. actor.
—**Edwin Arlington,** 1869–1935, U.S. poet.
—**Jack Roosevelt (Jackie),** 1919–72, U.S. baseball player.
—**James H.,** 1863–1936, U.S. historian & educator.
—**Sir Robert,** 1886–1975, Brit. chemist; Nobel Prize winner.

—**Ray (Sugar Ray),** 1920–89, U.S. boxer.
Robson, Dame Flora, 1902–84, Eng. actress.
Rochambeau, Jean Baptiste Donatien de Vimeur, Comte de, 1725–1807, Fr. marshal; commanded Fr. allies in Amer. Revolution.
Roche, Kevin, 1922–, U.S. architect.
Rockefeller A family of U.S. oil magnates & philanthropists incl. **David,** 1915–, business executive; **John D(avison),** 1839–1937, grandfather of prec; **John D(avison), Jr.,** 1874–1960, son of prec; **Nelson Aldrich,** 1908–79, governor of New York 1958–73, vice president of the U.S. 1974–77, son of prec. & brother of David.
Rockne, Knute Kenneth, 1881–1931, Norw.-born U.S. football coach.
Rockwell, Norman, 1894–1978, U.S. painter & illustrator.
Rodgers, Richard, 1902–79, U.S. composer.
Rodin, Auguste, 1840–1917, Fr. sculptor.
Rodzinski, Artur, 1894–1958, Yugoslav-born U.S. conductor.
Roebling, John Augustus, 1806–69, Ger.-born U.S. engineer & bridge-builder.
—**Washington Augustus,** 1837–1926, U.S. engineer; son of prec.
Roebuck, Alvah Curtis, 1863–1948, U.S. businessman.
Roelants, Gaston, 1937–, Belg. track runner.
Roentgen, Wilhelm Konrad, 1845–1923, Ger. physicist; discoverer of X-rays; Nobel Prize winner.
Roethke, Theodore, 1908–63, U.S. poet.
Rogers, Carl R., 1902–87, U.S. psychologist.
—**Ginger,** 1911–, U.S. actress.
—**James Gamble,** 1867–1947, U.S. architect.
—**Will(iam Penn Adair),** 1879–1935, U.S. humorist & actor.
Roget, Peter Mark, 1779–1869, Eng. physician & author.
Rolland, Romain, 1866–1944, Fr. author; Nobel Prize winner.
Rölvaag, Ole Edvart, 1876–1931, Norw.-born U.S. educator & author.
Romains, Jules, pseud. of Louis Farigoule, 1885–1972, Fr. author & playwright.
Romano, Giulio, 1499–1546, Ital. painter & architect.
Romanov, Mikhail Feodorovich, 1596–1645, czar of Russia 1613–45.
Romberg, Sigmund, 1887–1951, Hung.-born U.S. composer.
Rome, Harold, 1908–, U.S. composer.
Rommel, Erwin, 1891–1944, Ger. general.
Romney, George, 1734–1802, Eng. painter.
Romulo, Carlos, 1901–85, Filipino statesman.
Ronsard, Pierre de, 1524–85, Fr. poet.
Rooney, Mickey, 1920–, U.S. actor.
Roosevelt, Anna Eleanor, 1884–1962, U.S. lecturer, author, stateswoman, & humanitarian.
—**Franklin Delano,** 1882–1945, 32nd U.S. president 1933–45; husband of prec.
—**Theodore,** 1858–1919, 26th U.S. president 1901–09.
Root, Elihu, 1845–1937, U.S. lawyer & statesman; Nobel Prize winner.
—**John Wellborn,** 1887–1963, U.S. architect.
Rorem, Ned, 1923–, U.S. composer.
Rorschach, Hermann, 1844–1922, Swiss psychiatrist.
Rosa, Salvator, 1615–73, Ital. painter & poet.
Rosario (Perez), 1920–, Sp. dancer.
Rosay, Françoise, 1891–1974, Fr. actress.
Roscius, Quintus, 126?–62? B.C., Roman actor.
Rose, Billy, 1899–1966, U.S. theatrical producer & lyricist.
—**Leonard,** 1918–84, U.S. musician & teacher.
—**Pete(r Edward),** 1942–, U.S. baseball player.
Rosenberg, Alfred, 1893–1946, Nazi Ger. philosopher.
—**Julius,** 1918–53, & his wife **Ethel,** 1915–53, U.S. radicals; executed as spies for the U.S.S.R.
Rosenthal, Jean, 1912–69, U.S. theatrical lighting designer.
Rosenwald, Julius, 1862–1932, U.S. merchant & philanthropist.
Rosewall, Ken, 1934–, Austral. tennis player.
Ross, Betsy, 1752–1836, Amer. patriot; made first Amer. flag.
—**Diana,** 1944–, U.S. singer & actress.
—**Harold Wallace,** 1892–1951, U.S. editor.
—**Nellie Taylor,** 1876–1977, U.S. politician & public official; first U.S. woman governor.

—**Sir James Clark,** 1800–62, & his uncle **Sir John,** 1777–1856, Scot. polar explorers.
—**Sir Ronald,** 1857–1932, Brit. Nobel Prize winner.
Rossellini, Roberto, 1906–77, Ital. film director.
Rossetti, Christina Georgina, 1830–94, Eng. poet.
—**Dante Gabriel,** 1828–82, Eng. painter & poet; brother of prec.
Rossini, Gioacchino Antonio, 1792–1868, Ital. composer.
Rostand, Edmond, 1868–1918, Fr. playwright & poet.
Rostropovich, Mstislav Leopoldovitch, 1927–, Soviet-born cellist & conductor active in U.S.
Roszak, Theodore, 1907–81, U.S. sculptor.
Roth, Lillian, 1910–80, U.S. singer & actress.
—**Philip,** 1933–, U.S. author.
Rothko, Mark, 1903–70, Russ.-born U.S. painter.
Rothschild A family of Ger. bankers incl. **Mayer Amschel,** 1743–1812, & his sons: **Anselm Meyer,** 1773–1855; **James,** 1792–1868; **Karl,** 1788–1855; **Nathan Meyer,** 1777–1836; & **Solomon,** 1774–1855.
Rouault, Georges, 1871–1958, Fr. painter.
Rouget de Lisle, Claude Joseph, 1760–1836, Fr. poet, author, & composer.
Rousseau, Henri, 1844–1910, Fr. painter.
—**Jean Jacques,** 1712–78, Fr. philosopher & author.
Rowan, Carl T., 1925–, U.S. government official, ambassador, & journalist.
Rowlandson, Thomas, 1756–1827, Eng. artist & caricaturist.
Roxas y Acuña, Manuel, 1892–1948, Filipino statesman.
Royce, Josiah, 1855–1916, U.S. philosopher.
Rozsa, Miklos, 1907–, Hung.-born composer.
Rubens, Peter Paul, 1577–1640, Flemish painter.
Rubenstein, Helena, 1882?–1965, Pol.-born U.S. businesswoman.
Rubinstein, Anton Gregor, 1829–94, Russ. pianist & composer.
—**Artur,** 1887–1982, Pol.-born pianist active in U.S.
Ruby, Harry, 1895–1974, U.S. composer.
Rudolf I, 1218–91, Holy Roman emperor 1273–91.
Rudolph, Paul, 1918–, U.S. architect.
—**Wilma,** 1940–, U.S. track runner.
Ruggles, Carl, 1876–1971, U.S. composer.
Ruisdael, Jacob van, 1628?–82, & his uncle **Salomon,** 1600?–70, Du. painters.
Ruiz Cortines, Adolfo, 1891–1973, Mex. president 1952–58.
Rundstedt, Karl Rudolf Gerd von, 1875–1953, Ger. field marshal.
Runyon, (Alfred) Damon, 1880–1946, U.S. author.
Rush, Benjamin, 1745–1813, U.S. physician.
Rusher, William A., 1923–, U.S. publisher.
Ruskin, John, 1819–1900, Eng. critic & author.
Russell, Sir Bertrand Arthur William, 1872–1970, Eng. mathematician & philosopher; Nobel Prize winner.
—**Charles Marion,** 1864–1926, U.S. artist.
—**Charles T.,** 1852–1916, U.S. founder of Jehovah's Witnesses.
—**Ken,** 1927–, Eng. film director.
—**Lillian,** 1861–1922, U.S. singer & actress.
—**Richard B.,** 1897–1971, U.S. politician.
—**Rosalind,** 1911–76, U.S. actress.
—**William Felton (Bill),** 1934–, U.S. basketball player & coach.
Rustin, Bayard, 1910–, U.S. black civil rights leader.
Ruth, George Herman (Babe), 1895–1948, U.S. baseball player.
Rutherford, Sir Ernest, 1871–1937, New Zealand-born Eng. physicist; Nobel Prize winner.
—**Dame Margaret,** 1892–1972, Eng. actress.
Ruysbroeck, Jan van, 1293–1381, Flemish mystic & theologian.
Ryan, Nolan, 1947–, U.S. baseball player.
—**Robert,** 1909–73, U.S. actor.
—**Thomas Fortune,** 1851–1928, U.S. businessman.
Ryder, Albert Pinkham, 1847–1917, U.S. painter.
Ryun, James (Jim), 1947–, U.S. track runner.

Saarinen, Aline Bernstein, 1914–72, U.S. author & art critic.
—**Eero,** 1910–61, U.S. architect; husband of prec.

—**Eliel,** 1873–1950, Finnish-born U.S. architect; father of prec.

Sabbatai Zevi, 1626–76, Turkish-born Jewish mystic & self-proclaimed Messiah.

Sabin, Albert Bruce, 1906–, Russ.-born U.S. physician & bacteriologist.

Sacajawea, 1787–1812, Soshone Am. Ind. guide and interpreter for the Lewis and Clark expedition.

Sacco, Nicola, 1891–1927, Ital. anarchist in the U.S.; executed with Bartolomeo Vanzetti for murder.

Sacher-Masoch, Leopold von, 1835–95, Austrian writer.

Sachs, Nelly, 1891–1970, Ger.-born Swed. poet; Nobel Prize winner.

Sackville-West, Victoria Mary (Vita), 1892–1962, Eng. author.

Sadat, Anwar, 1918–81, president of Egypt 1970–81; Nobel Prize winner; assassinated.

Sade, Comte Donatien Alphonse François, 1740–1814, Fr. author: known as **Marquis de Sade.**

Safire, William, 1929–, U.S. author & journalist.

Sagan, Carl Edward, 1934–, U.S. astronomer.

—**Françoise,** pseud. of Françoise Quoirez, 1935–, Fr. author.

Sage, Margaret Olivia, 1828–1918, U.S. philanthropist.

—**Russell,** 1816–1906, U.S. financier; husband of prec.

Sahl, Mort, 1927–, Can.-born U.S. comedian.

Sainte-Beuve, Charles Augustin, 1804–69, Fr. poet, critic, & historian.

Saint Denis, Ruth, 1877?–1968, U.S. dancer, teacher, & choreographer.

Saint-Exupéry, Antoine de, 1900–44, Fr. author & aviator.

Saint-Gaudens, Augustus, 1848–1907, Irish-born U.S. sculptor.

Saint-Just, Louis Antoine Leon de, 1767–94, Fr. revolutionary.

Saint Laurent, Louis Stephen, 1882–1973, Can. statesman; prime minister 1948–57.

—**Yves,** 1936–, Fr. fashion designer.

Saint-Saëns, (Charles) Camille, 1835–1921, Fr. composer.

Saintsbury, George Edward Bateman, 1845–1933, Eng. critic.

Saint-Simon, Claude Henri de Rouvroy, Comte de, 1760–1825, Fr. philosopher & author.

—**Louis de Rouvroy, Duc de,** 1675–1755, Fr. statesman & author.

Saint-Subber, Arnold, 1918–, U.S. theatrical producer.

Sakel, Manfred, 1906–57, Austrian-born U.S. psychiatrist.

Sakharov, Andrei Dimitrievich, 1921–89, Soviet physicist; Nobel Prize winner.

Saki, pseud. of Hector Hugh Munro, 1870–1916, Scot. author.

Saladin, 1137?–93, sultan of Egypt & Syria.

Salant, Richard, 1914–, U.S. radio & TV executive & lawyer.

Salazar, António de Oliveira, 1889–1970, Pg. statesman; premier 1928–68.

Salinger, J(erome) D(avid), 1919–, U.S. author.

Salisbury, Harrison E., 1908–, U.S. journalist.

—**Robert Arthur Talbot Gascoyne-Cecil, Marquess of,** 1830–1903, Brit. statesman; prime minister 1885–86, 1886–92, & 1895–1902.

Salk, Jonas Edward, 1914–, U.S. bacteriologist.

Sallust (L. Gaius Sallustius Crispus), 86–34 B.C., Roman historian & politician.

Salomon, Haym, 1740?–85, Amer. revolutionary patriot & banker.

Samoset, 1590?–1655, chief of Pemaquid Am. Ind.; friend of Pilgrims.

Samuelson, Paul, 1915–, U.S. economist & author.

Sand, George, pseud. of Amandine Aurore Lucie Dudevant, 1804–76, Fr. author.

Sandburg, Carl, 1878–1967, U.S. poet, biographer, & historian.

Sangallo, Antonio da, b. Antonio Cordiani, 1485–1546, Ital. architect.

—**Giuliano da,** 1445–1516, Ital. architect & sculptor.

Sanger, Fredrick, 1918–, Eng. chemist; Nobel Prize winner.

—**Margaret,** 1883–1966, U.S. pioneer in birth-control education.

San Martín, José de, 1778–1850, Argentinian-born S. Amer. revolutionary leader & general.

Sansovino, Jacopo, 1486–1570, Ital. sculptor & architect.

Santa Anna, Antonio Lopéz de, 1795–1876, Mexican soldier & politician.

Santayana, George, 1863–1952, Sp.-born U.S. philosopher & author.

Sapir, Edward, 1884–1939, U.S. anthropologist.

Sappho, 7th c. B.C. Gk. poet.

Saragat, Giuseppe, 1898–, Ital. president 1964–71.

Sarazen, Gene, 1902–, U.S. golfer.

Sardi, Vincent, Jr., 1915–, U.S. restaurateur.

Sardou Victorien, 1831–1908, Fr. playwright.

Sargent, John Singer, 1856–1925, U.S. painter.

Sarnoff, David, 1891–1971, Russ.-born U.S. radio & TV executive.

—**Robert,** 1918–, U.S. communications executive; son of prec.

Saroyan, William, 1908–81, U.S. author.

Sarto, Andrea del, 1487–1531, Florentine painter.

Sartre, Jean Paul, 1905–80, Fr. philosopher, author, playwright, & critic.

Sasetta, ca. 1400–50, Ital. painter.

Sassoon, Siegfried, 1886–1967, Eng. poet.

—**Vidal,** 1928–, Eng.-born U.S. coiffeur.

Satie, Alfred Erik Leslie, 1866–1925, Fr. composer.

Sato, Eisaku, 1901–75, Jap. premier 1964–75.

Sa'ud Ibn Abdul, 1902–69, king of Saudi Arabia 1953–64.

Saul, Hebrew name of the apostle PAUL.

Saussure, Ferdinand de, 1857–1913, Swiss linguist.

Savonarola, Girolamo, 1452–98, Ital. monk & reformer; burned for heresy.

Sayao, Bidu, 1902–, Brazilian soprano active in U.S.

Sayers, Dorothy Leigh, 1893–1957, Eng. author.

Scalia, Antonin, 1936–, U.S. jurist; justice of the U.S. Supreme Court 1986–.

Scanderbeg, Iskender Bey, b. George Castriota, 1403?–68, Albanian chieftain.

Scarlatti, Alessandro, 1659–1725, and his son **Domenico,** 1685–1757, Ital. composers.

Schaller, George Beals, 1933–, U.S. zoologist.

Schary, Dore, 1905–80, U.S. film producer, writer, & director.

Scheff, Fritzi, 1879–1954, Austrian singer & actress active in U.S.

Schelling, Friedrich Wilhelm Joseph von, 1775–1854, Ger. philosopher.

Scherman, Thomas, 1917–, U.S. conductor.

Schiaparelli, Giovanni Virginio, 1835–1910, Ital. astronomer.

—**Elsa,** 1890–1973, Ital.-born Fr. fashion designer.

Schick, Bela, 1877–1967, Hung.-born U.S. pediatrician.

Schiff, Dorothy, 1903–, U.S. publisher.

—**Jacob H.,** 1847–1920, U.S. businessman.

Schildkraut, Joseph, 1895–1964, Austrian actor.

Schiller, Johann Christoph Friedrich von, 1759–1805, Ger. poet & playwright.

Schipa, Tito, 1889–1965, Ital. tenor.

Schippers, Thomas, 1930–77, U.S. conductor.

Schirmer, Gustav, 1829–93, Ger.-born U.S. music publisher.

Schlafly, Phyllis Stewart, 1924–, U.S. women's liberation opponent.

Schlegel, August Wilhelm von, 1767–1845, Ger. author.

—**Friedrich von,** 1772–1829, Ger. philosopher & author; brother of prec.

Schleiden, Matthias Jakob, 1804–81, Ger. botanist.

Schlesinger, Arthur M., Sr., 1888–1965, and his son **Arthur M., Jr.,** 1917–, U.S. historians.

—**James Rodney,** 1929–, U.S. government official.

—**John,** 1926–, Eng. film director.

Schliemann, Heinrich, 1822–90, Ger. archaeologist.

Schmeling, Max(imilian), 1905–, Ger.-born boxer active in U.S.

Schmidt, Helmut, 1918–, chancellor of Federal Republic of Germany 1974–82.

Schnabel, Arthur, 1882–1951, Austrian-born pianist active in U.S.

Schnitzler, Arthur, 1862–1931, Austrian physician & playwright.

Schönberg, Arnold, 1874–1951, Austrian composer & conductor active in U.S.

Schonberg, Harold C., 1915–, U.S. music critic.

Schongauer, Martin, 1445?–91, Ger. painter & engraver.

Schopenhauer, Arthur, 1788–1860, Ger. philosopher.

Schrödinger, Erwin, 1887–1961, Austrian physicist; Nobel Prize winner.

Schubert, Franz Peter, 1797–1828, Austrian composer.

Schuller, Gunther, 1925–, U.S. composer.

Schultz, Dutch, b. Arthur Flegenheimer, 1902–35, U.S. criminal.

Schulz, Charles Monroe, 1922–, U.S. cartoonist.

Schuman, Robert, 1886–1963, Fr. statesman.
—**Wiliam Howard,** 1910–, U.S. composer.

Schumann, Clara, 1819–96, Ger. pianist & composer.
—**Elisabeth,** 1885–1952, Ger. soprano.
—**Robert Alexander,** 1810–56, Ger. composer; husband of Clara.

Schumann-Heink, Ernestine, 1861–1936, Austrian contralto.

Schurz, Carl, 1829–1906, Ger.-born U.S. politician, military officer, & author.

Schütz, Heinrich, 1585–1672, Ger. composer.

Schwab, Charles Michael, 1862–1939, U.S. industrialist.

Schwann, Theodor, 1810–82, Ger. physiologist.

Schwartz, Delmore, 1913–66, U.S. poet & editor.

Schwarzkopf, Elisabeth, 1915–, Ger. soprano.

Schweitzer, Albert, 1875–1965, Alsatian medical missionary in Africa, musician, & theologian.

Scipio Africanus, Publius Cornelius, 237–183 B.C., Roman general: called **the Elder.**

Scofield, Paul, 1922–, Eng. actor.

Scopes, John Thomas, 1900–73, U.S. educator.

Scott, Dred, 1795–1858, U.S. slave.
—**George C.,** 1927–, U.S. actor & director.
—**Robert Falcon,** 1868–1912, Eng. Antarcic explorer.
—**Sir Walter,** 1771–1832, Scot. author & poet.

Scotti, Antonio, 1866–1936, Ital. baritone.

Scriabin, Alexander, 1872–1915, Russ. composer.

Scribe, Augustin Eugène, 1791–1861, Fr. playwright.

Scribner, family of U.S. publishers; **Charles,** 1821–71; his son, **Charles, Sr,** 1854–1930; and his grandson, **Charles, Jr.,** 1890–1952.

Scripps, Edward Wyllis, 1854–1926, U.S. newspaper publisher.

Seaborg, Glenn Theodore, 1912–, U.S. chemist; Nobel Prize winner.

Seabury, Samuel, 1729–96, U.S. religious leader.

Searle, Ronald, 1920–, Eng. cartoonist.

Sears, Richard Warren, 1862–1914, U.S. merchant.

Seeger, Pete, 1919–, U.S. folk singer.

Seferis, George, pseud. of Giorgios Seferiades, 1900–71, Gk. diplomat & poet.

Segal, George, 1924–, U.S. sculptor.

Segovia, Andrés, 1894–1987, Sp. guitarist.

Segrè, Emilio, 1905–89, Ital.-born U.S. physicist.

Sékou Touré, Ahmed, 1922–84, African political leader; first president of Guinea 1958–84.

Seldes, Gilbert Vivian, 1893–1970, U.S. author & critic.

Seleucus I, 358?–280 B.C., founder of Gk. dynasty in Syria.

Selfridge, Harry Gordon, 1857–1947, U.S.-born merchant & businessman active in Great Britain.

Sellers, Peter, 1925–80, Eng. actor.

Selznick, David, 1902–65, U.S. film director.

Semenov, Nikolai N., 1896–1986, Russ. chemist; Nobel Prize winner.

Semmelweis, Ignaz Philipp, 1818–65, Hung. physician.

Sendak, Maurice, 1928–, U.S. writer & illustrator.

Seneca, Lucius Annaeus, 3? B.C.–A.D. 65, Roman philosopher, statesman, & playwright.

Senghor, Léopold Sédar, 1906–, African poet & statesman; president of Senegal 1960–81.

Sennett, Mack, 1884–1960, Can.-born U.S. film director.

Sequoya, 1770?–1843, Cherokee Indian scholar.

Sergeyev, Konstantin, 1910–, Soviet choreographer & ballet company director.

Serkin, Rudolf, 1903–, Czech pianist active in U.S.

Serling, Rod, 1924–75, U.S. TV writer & producer.

Serra, Junípero, 1713–84, Sp. missionary in Mexico & California.

Service, Robert William, 1874–1958, Can. author.

Sesshu, 1420?–1506, Jap. painter.

Sessions, Roger, 1896–1985, U.S. composer & teacher.

Seton, Saint Elizabeth Ann, b. Elizabeth Bayley, 1774–1821, U.S. religious leader.

Seurat, Georges, 1859–91, Fr. painter.

Seuss, Dr., pseud. of Theodor Seuss Geisel, 1904–, U.S. author & illustrator of children's books.

Sevareid, (Arnold) Eric, 1912–, U.S. news analyst & radio & TV commentator.

Sevier, John, 1745–1815, U.S. soldier, frontiersman, & politician.

Sévigné, Marie de Rabutin-Chantal, Marquise de, 1626–96, Fr. writer.

Seward, William Henry, 1801–72, U.S. statesman; U.S. secretary of state 1861–69.

Sexton, Anne, 1928–74, U.S. poet.

Seymour, Jane, 1509?–37, third wife of Henry VIII of England.

Sforza, Count Carlo, 1872–1952, Ital. statesman.

Shackleton, Sir Ernest Henry, 1874–1922, Eng. Antarctic explorer.

Shah Jehan, 1592–1666, Mogul emperor of Hindustan 1628–58; builder of the Taj Mahal.

Shahn, Ben, 1898–1969, Lithuanian-born U.S. painter.

Shakespeare, William, 1564–1616, Eng. poet & playwright.

Shamir, Yitzhak, 1915–, Israeli statesman; prime minister 1983–84.

Shankar, Ravi, 1920–, Indian musician.

Shankara, c. 788–820, Indian philosopher.

Shapiro, Karl Jay, 1913–, U.S. poet.

Shapley, Harlow, 1885–1972, U.S. astronomer.

Shastri, Shri Lal Bahadur, 1904–66, Indian politician; prime minister of India 1964–66.

Shaw, Artie, 1910–, U.S. musician.
—**George Bernard.,** 1856–1950, Irish-born Brit. playwright, critic, & reformer; Nobel Prize winner.
—**Irwin,** 1913–84, U.S. author.
—**Robert,** 1927–78, Eng. actor, playwright, & author.
—**Robert Lawson,** 1916–, U.S. conductor & choral director.

Shawn, Edwin Meyers (Ted), 1891–1972, U.S. dancer & choreographer.

Shays, Daniel, 1747?–1825, Amer. revolutionary & rebel.

Shearer, Norma, 1905–83, Can.-born U.S. actress.

Shearing, George, 1919–, Eng.-born U.S. jazz musician.

Sheean, (James) Vincent, 1899–1975, U.S. journalist & author.

Sheen, Fulton John, 1895–1979, U.S. religious leader & author.

Shelley, Mary Wollstonecraft Godwin, 1797–1851, Eng. author.
—**Percy Bysshe,** 1792–1822, Eng. poet; husband of prec.

Shepard, Alan Bartlett, Jr., 1923–, U.S. astronaut.
—**Sam,** 1943–, U.S. playwright & actor.

Sheraton, Thomas, 1751–1806, Eng. furniture designer & cabinetmaker.

Sheridan, Ann, 1916?–67, U.S. actress.
—**Philip Henry,** 1831–88, U.S. Civil War general.
—**Richard Brinsley,** 1751–1816, Irish-born Brit. playwright & politician.

Sherman, James Schoolcraft, 1855–1912, U.S. statesman; U.S. vice president 1909–12.
—**Roger,** 1721–93, U.S. jurist & statesman.
—**William Tecumseh,** 1820–91, U.S. Civil War general.

Sherrington, Sir Charles Scott, 1857–1952, Eng. physiologist.

Sherwood, Robert Emmet, 1896–1955, U.S. playwright, journalist, & biographer.

Shinn, Everett, 1876–1953, U.S. painter & illustrator.

Shirer, William Lawrence, 1904–, U.S. journalist & author.

Shockley, William Bradford, 1910–89, Eng.-born U.S. physicist.

Shoemaker, William Lee (Willie), 1931–, U.S. jockey.

Sholes, Christopher Latham, 1819–90, U.S. inventor.
Sholokhov, Mikhail Aleksandrovich, 1905–84, Soviet author; Nobel Prize winner.
Sholom, Aleichem, pseud. of Solomon Rabinowitz, 1859–1916, Russ.-born U.S. Yiddish author.
Shore, Dinah, 1917–, U.S. singer & actress.
Short, Bobby, 1936–, U.S. singer.
Shorter, Frank, 1947–, Ger.-born U.S. track runner.
Shostakovich, Dmitri, 1906–75, Soviet composer.
Shubert A family of U.S. theater managers and producers incl. three brothers: **Lee,** 1875–1953; **Jacob J.,** 1880–1963; and **Sam S.,** 1876–1905.
Shultz, George Platt, 1920–, U.S. educator; secretary of state 1982–.
Shumlin, Herman, 1898–1979, U.S. theatrical producer & film director.
Shute, Nevil, 1899–1960, Eng. engineer & author.
Sibelius, Jean, 1865–1957, Finnish composer.
Siddons, Sarah Kemble, 1755–1831, Welsh actress.
Sidgwick, Nevil V., 1873–1952, Eng. chemist.
Sidney, Sir Philip, 1554–86, Eng. soldier, statesman, & poet.
Siegbahn, Karl Manne Georg, 1886–1978, Swed. physicist; Nobel Prize winner.
Siegel, Benjamin (Bugsy), 1906–47, U.S. criminal.
Sienkiewicz, Henryk, 1846–1916, Pol. author; Nobel Prize winner.
Siepi, Cesare, 1923–, Ital. basso.
Signorelli, Luca, 1441?–1523, Ital. painter.
Signoret, Simone, 1921–85, Fr. actress.
Sihanouk, Prince Norodom, 1922–, chief of state of Cambodia 1964–70.
Sikorsky, Igor Ivanovich, 1889–1972, Russ.-born U.S. aeronautical engineer.
Silliphant, Sterling, 1918–, U.S. playwright.
Sills, Beverly, 1929–, U.S. soprano & opera company director.
Silone, Ignazio, pseud. of Secondo Tranquilli, 1900–78, Ital. author.
Silvers, Phil, 1912–85, U.S. comedian.
Simenon, Georges, 1903–89, Belg.-born Fr. author.
Simeon Stylites, Saint, 390?–459, Syrian ascetic.
Simon, Michel, 1895–1975, Swiss actor active in France.
—**Neil,** 1927–, U.S. playwright.
—**Paul,** 1942–, U.S. singer & songwriter.
Simpson, George Gaylord, 1902–84, U.S. paleontologist.
—**O(renthal) J(ames),** 1947–, U.S. football player.
Sinatra, Francis Albert (Frank), 1915–, U.S. singer & actor.
Sinclair, Harry Ford, 1876–1956, U.S. businessman.
—**Upton Beall,** 1878–1968, U.S. author & politician.
Singer, Isaac Bashevis, 1904–91, Pol.-born U.S. author.
Singer, Isaac Merrit, 1811–75, U.S. inventor.
Siqueiros, David Alfaro, 1898–1974, Mexican painter & muralist.
Sisler, George, 1893–1973, U.S. baseball player.
Sisley, Alfred, 1839–99, Eng. painter active in France.
Sitting Bull, 1834?–90, Sioux Am. Ind. chief.
Sitwell A family of Eng. writers incl. **Dame Edith,** 1887–1964; and her brothers **Sir Osbert,** 1892–1969; and **Sir Sacheverell,** 1897–1988; all poets, essayists, critics, & authors.
Sjöström, Victor, 1879–1960, Swed. film director.
Skelton, John, 1460?–1529, Eng. poet.
—**Red,** 1913–, U.S. actor & comedian.
Skinner, B(urrhus) F(rederic), 1904–90, U.S. psychologist.
—**Cornelia Otis,** 1901–79, U.S. actress & author.
—**Otis,** 1858–1942, U.S. actor; father of prec.
Skouras, Spyros Panagiotes, 1893–1971, U.S. film executive.
Skulnik, Menasha, 1898–1970, Pol.-born U.S. actor.
Sloan, John French, 1871–1951, U.S. painter.
Smetana, Bedřich, 1824–84, Czech composer.
Smith, Adam, 1723–90, Scot. economist.
—**Alfred Emanuel,** 1873–1944, U.S. politician.
—**Bessie,** 1894–1937, U.S. blues singer.
—**David,** 1906–65, U.S. sculptor.
—**Howard Kingsbury,** 1914–, U.S. radio & TV news commentator.
—**Ian Douglas,** 1919–, prime minister of Rhodesia 1964–79.
—**Capt. John,** 1579–1631, Eng. adventurer; president of the Virginia colony 1608.

—**Joseph,** 1805–44, U.S. founder of the Mormon church.
—**Kathryn Elizabeth (Kate),** 1909–86, U.S. singer.
—**Maggie,** 1934–, Eng. actress.
—**Margaret Chase,** 1897–, U.S. senator & congresswoman.
—**Oliver,** 1918–, U.S. set designer, theatrical producer, & ballet company director.
—**Walter Wellesley (Red),** 1905–82, U.S. sports columnist.
—**William,** 1769–1839, Eng. geologist.
Smithson, James, 1765–1829, Eng. chemist & mineralogist.
Smollett, Tobias George, 1721–71, Eng. author.
Smuts, Jan Christiaan, 1870–1950, South African statesman & general.
Snead, Samuel J. (Sam), 1912–, U.S. golfer.
Snell, Peter, 1938–, New Zealand track runner.
Snow, Sir C(harles) P(ercival), 1905–80, Eng. author & physicist.
Socrates, 469?–399 B.C., Athenian philosopher & teacher.
Soddy, Frederick, 1877–1956, Eng. chemist; Nobel Prize winner.
Sodoma, II, b. Giovanni Antonio de'Bazzi, 1477?–1549, Ital. painter.
Soleri, Paolo, 1919–, Ital. architect active in U.S.
Solon, 638?–558? B.C., Athenian statesman & lawgiver.
Solti, Sir Georg, 1912–, Hung.-born Brit. conductor active in U.S.
Solzhenitsyn, Alexander, 1918–, Soviet author resident in U.S.; Nobel Prize winner.
Somoza Debayle, Anastasio, 1925–80, president of Nicaragua 1967–72 & 1974–79; assassinated.
Sondheim, Stephen, 1930–, U.S. composer & lyricist.
Sontag, Susan, 1933–, U.S. critic, author, & film director.
Soong A Chin. family active in politics & banking, incl. **T(se) V(en),** 1891–1971; and his sisters **Ching-ling,** 1890–1981, widow of Sun Yat-sen; and **Mei-ling,** 1897–, widow of Chiang Kai-shek.
Sophocles, 495?–406 B.C., Gk. playwright.
Sorel, Georges, 1847–1922, Fr. journalist & philosopher.
Sørensen, Søren P. L., 1868–1939, Dan. chemist.
Sorokin, Pitirim Aleksandrovich, 1889–1968, Russ.-born U.S. sociologist.
Sousa, John Philip, 1854–1932, U.S. composer & bandmaster.
Souter, David, 1939–, U.S. jurist; justice of the U.S. Supreme Court 1990–.
Southey, Robert, 1774–1843, Eng. poet.
Soutine, Chaim, 1893–1943, Lithuanian-born painter active in France.
Souvanna Phouma, Prince, 1901–84, prime minister of Laos, 1962–75.
Soyer, Moses, 1899–1974, & his twin brother **Raphael,** 1899–, Russ.-born U.S. painters.
Spaak, Paul-Henri, 1899–1972, Belg. lawyer & statesman; secretary general of NATO 1957–61; Belg. prime minister 1938, 1939, & 1946–49.
Spahn, Warren Edward, 1921–, U.S. baseball player.
Spalding, Albert Goodwill, 1850–1915, U.S. baseball player & sporting-goods manufacturer.
Spallanzani, Lazzaro, 1729–99, Ital. biologist.
Spark, Muriel, 1918–, Scot. author.
Spartacus, ?–71 B.C., Thracian leader of slaves in an uprising against Rome 73–71 B.C.
Spassky, Boris, 1937–, Soviet chess master.
Speaker, Tris, 1888–1958, U.S. baseball player.
Spellman, Francis Joseph, Cardinal, 1889–1967, U.S. religious leader.
Spencer, Herbert, 1820–1903, Eng. philosopher.
Spender, Sir Stephen, 1909–, Eng. poet.
Spengler, Oswald, 1880–1936, Ger. philosopher.
Spenser, Edmund, 1552–99, Eng. poet.
Sperry, Elmer Ambrose, 1860–1930, U.S. inventor.
Spiegel, Samuel P., 1904?–85, U.S. film producer.
Spielberg, Steven, 1947–, U.S. film director & producer.
Spillane, Frank Morrison (Mickey), 1918–, U.S. author.
Spinoza, Baruch, 1632–77, Du. philosopher.
Spitz, Mark, 1950–, U.S. swimmer.
Spock, Benjamin, 1903–, U.S. pediatrician & political activist.

Spode, Josiah, 1754–1827, Eng. potter.

Spohr, Ludwig, 1784–1859, Ger. composer, conductor, & violinist.

Springer, Axel, 1912–84, Ger. publisher.

Spyri, Johanna Heusser, 1827–1901, Swiss author.

Squanto, 1585?–1622, Am. Ind. friend of the Pilgrims.

Squibb, Edward Robinson, 1819–1900, U.S. physician & manufacturer.

Staël, Mme. Anne Louise Necker de, 1766–1817, Fr. writer.

Stagg, Amos Alonzo, 1862–1965, U.S. football coach.

Stalin, Joseph, b. Iosif Vissarionovich Djugashvili, 1879–1953, Soviet dictator 1927–53.

Standish, Miles, 1584?–1656, Eng.-born soldier & military leader of the Pilgrims in America.

Stanford, Leland, 1824–93, U.S. railroad builder & public official.

Stanislavsky, Constantin, 1863–1938, Soviet actor, director, producer, & teacher.

Stanley, Francis Edgar, 1849–1918, & his twin brother **Freelan Oscar,** 1849–1940, U.S. inventors & automobile manufacturers.

—Sir Henry Morton, 1841–1904, Eng. explorer & author.

—Wendell Meredith, 1904–71, U.S. biochemist.

Stanton, Elizabeth Cady, 1815–1902, U.S. suffragist.

—Frank, 1908–, U.S. radio & TV executive.

Stanwyck, Barbara, 1907–90, U.S. actress.

Stapleton, Maureen, 1925–, U.S. actress.

Stare, Frederick John, 1910–, U.S. nutritionist & biochemist.

Stark, Johannes, 1874–1957, Ger. physicist.

Starr, Ringo, b. Richard Starkey, 1940–, Eng. composer & musical performer.

Stassen, Harold Edward, 1907–, U.S. lawyer & politician.

Statler, Ellsworth Milton, 1863–1928, U.S. hotel executive:

Staudinger, Hermann, 1881–1965, Ger. chemist.

Stauffenberg, Count Claus Schenk von, 1907–44, Ger. staff officer; led abortive plot against Hitler.

Steegmuller, Francis, 1906–, U.S. biographer.

Steele, Sir Richard, 1672–1729, Irish-born Eng. author & playwright.

Stefan, Joseph, 1835–93, Austrian physicist.

Stefansson, Vihjalmur, 1879–1962, Can. Arctic explorer.

Steffens, (Joseph) Lincoln, 1866–1936, U.S. journalist & author.

Steichen, Edward, 1879–1973, Luxembourg-born U.S. photographer.

Stein, Gertrude, 1874–1946, U.S. writer active in France.

Steinbeck, John Ernest, 1902–68, U.S. author; Nobel Prize winner.

Steinberg, Saul, 1914–, Romanian-born U.S. cartoonist.

—William, 1899–1978, Ger. conductor active in U.S.

Steinem, Gloria, 1934–, U.S. author, publisher, editor, & feminist leader.

Steiner, George, 1929–, Fr.-born U.S. critic.

—Max, 1888?–1971, Austrian-born U.S. film composer.

—Rudolf, 1861–1925, Austrian-born U.S. educator.

Steinmetz, Charles Proteus, 1865–1923, Ger.-born U.S. electrical engineer & inventor.

Steinway, Henry Englehard, 1797–1871, Ger.-born U.S. piano manufacturer.

Stella, Frank Philip, 1936–, U.S. painter.

Stendhal, pseud. of Marie Henri Beyle, 1783–1842, Fr. author.

Stengel, Charles Dillon (Casey), 1890–1975, U.S. baseball player & manager.

Stephens, James, 1882–1950, Irish poet & author.

Stephenson, George, 1781–1848, Eng. inventor.

Stern, Isaac, 1920–, Russ.-born U.S. violinist.

—Otto, 1888–1969, Ger.-born U.S. physicist.

Sternberg, Josef von, 1894–1969, U.S. film director.

Sterne, Laurence, 1713–68, Irish-born Brit. author.

Stetson, John Batterson, 1830–1906, U.S. hat manufacturer & philanthropist.

Steuben, Baron Friedrich Wilhelm von, 1730–94, Prussian army officer; served in Amer. Revolution.

Stevens, George, 1904–75, U.S. film director.

—John Paul, 1920–, U.S. jurist; justice of the U.S. Supreme Court 1975–.

—Rise, 1913–, U.S. mezzo-soprano.

—Wallace, 1879–1955, U.S. poet.

Stevenson, Adlai Ewing, 1835–1914, U.S. statesman; U.S. vice president 1893–97.

—Adlai E(wing), 1900–65, U.S. statesman; grandson of prec.

—Robert Louis, 1850–94, Scot. author.

Stevinus, Simon, 1548–1620, Belg. mathematician.

Stewart, Ellen, 1931–, U.S. theater director.

—James, 1908–, U.S. actor.

—Potter, 1915–85, U.S. jurist; justice of the U.S. Supreme Court 1958–85.

Stiegel, Henry William, 1729–85, U.S. iron & glass manufacturer.

Stieglitz, Alfred, 1864–1946, U.S. photographer.

Still, Clyfford, 1904–80, U.S. painter.

—William Grant, 1895–1978, U.S. composer.

Stilwell, Joseph Warren, 1883–1946, U.S. general.

Stimson, Henry Lewis, 1867–1950, U.S. statesman.

Stockhausen, Karlheinz, 1928–, Ger. composer.

Stoker, Bram, 1847–1912, Irish author.

Stokowski, Leopold, 1882–1977, Eng.-born U.S. conductor.

Stone, Edward Durell, 1902–78, U.S. architect.

—Harlan Fiske, 1872–1946, U.S. jurist; chief justice of the U.S. Supreme Court 1941–46.

—Irving, 1903–89, U.S. author.

—I(sidor) F(einstein), 1907–89, U.S. journalist.

—Lucy, 1818–93, U.S. social reformer & women's suffragist.

Stoney, George J., 1826–1911, Irish physicist.

Stoppard, Tom, 1937–, Eng. playwright.

Story, Joseph, 1779–1845, U.S. jurist; justice of U.S. Supreme Court 1812–45.

Stoss, Veit, 1440?–1533, Ger. sculptor.

Stout, Rex Todhunter, 1886–1975, U.S. author.

Stowe, Harriet Beecher, 1811–96, U.S. author.

Strabo, 63? B.C. – A.D. 24?, Gk. geographer & historian.

Strachey, (Giles) Lytton, 1880–1932, Eng. author.

Stradivari, Antonio, 1644–1737, Ital. instrument maker.

Strand, Paul, 1890–1976, U.S. photographer.

Strasberg, Lee, 1901–82, Austrian-born U.S. drama teacher & actor.

Stratton, Charles Sherwood, 1838–83, U.S. midget: known as **General Tom Thumb.**

Straus, Isidor, 1845–1912, & his brother **Nathan,** 1848–1931, U.S. merchants & philanthropists.

—Oskar, 1870–1954, Austrian-born Fr. composer.

Strauss A family of Austrian composers incl. **Johann,** 1804–49 (called **the Elder**), and his sons: **Johann,** 1825–99 (**the Younger**); and **Josef,** 1827–70.

—Levi, 1829?–1902, U.S. clothing manufacturer.

—Richard, 1864–1949, Ger. composer & conductor.

Stravinsky, Igor Fyodorovich, 1882–1971, Russ.-born composer active in the U.S.

Streisand, Barbra, 1942–, U.S. singer & actress.

Strindberg, John August, 1849–1912, Swed. playwright & author.

Stroessner, Alfredo, 1912–, president of Paraguay 1954–89.

Stroheim, Erich von, 1885–1957, Austrian-born U.S. actor & film director.

Stroud, Robert, 1890–1963, U.S. convict & ornithologist.

Strougal, Lubomir, 1924–, premier of Czechoslovakia 1970–88.

Struve, Friedrich G. W., 1793–1864, Ger. astronomer.

—Otto, 1897–1963, Russ.-born U.S. astronomer.

Stuart, Charles Edward, 1720–88, pretender to the throne of Great Britain: called **Bonnie Prince Charlie & the Young Pretender.**

—Gilbert Charles, 1755–1828, U.S. painter.

—James Edward, 1688–1766, Eng. prince; father of Charles: called **the Old Pretender.**

—James Ewell Brown (Jeb), 1833–64, U.S. Confederate general.

Studebaker, Clement, 1831–1901, U.S. carriage manufacturer.

Sturges, Preston, 1898–1959, U.S. film director.

Stutz, Harry Clayton, 1876–1930, U.S. automobile manufacturer.

Stuyvesant, Peter, 1592–1672, last Du. governor of New Amsterdam (now New York).

Styne, Jule, 1905–, Eng.-born U.S. composer.

Styron, William, 1925–, U.S. author.

Suckling, Sir John, 1609–42, Eng. poet.

Sucre, Antonio José de, 1795–1830, Venezuelan liberator of Ecuador & Bolivia; president of Bolivia 1826–28; assassinated.

Sudermann, Hermann, 1857–1928, Ger. playwright & novelist.

Suetonius, A.D. 69?–140, Roman author & biographer.

Suharto, 1921–, Indonesian general; president of Indonesia 1968–.

Sukarno, 1901–70, Indonesian statesman; first president of the republic of Indonesia 1945–67.

Suleiman I, 1496?–1566, Turkish sultan of the Ottoman Empire: called the Magnificent.

Sulla, Lucius Cornelius, 138–78 B.C., Roman general & reformer.

Sullavan, Margaret, 1911–60, U.S. actress.

Sullivan, Sir Arthur Seymour, 1842–1900, Eng. composer.

—**Ed(ward Vincent),** 1902–74, U.S. journalist & TV personality.

—**Harry Stack,** 1892–1949, U.S. psychiatrist.

—**John Lawrence,** 1856–1924, U.S. architect.

—**Louis Henri,** 1856–1924, U.S. architect.

Sully, Thomas, 1783–1872, Eng.-born U.S. painter.

Sully-Prudhomme, René François Armand, 1839–1907, Fr. poet; Nobel Prize winner.

Sulzberger, Arthur Hays, 1891–1968, U.S. publisher.

—**Arthur Ochs,** 1926–, U.S. publisher; son of prec.

Summerson, Sir John, 1904–, Eng. art historian.

Sumner, Charles, 1811–74, U.S. statesman & orator.

Sunday, William Ashley (Billy), 1862–1935, U.S. baseball player & evangelist.

Sun Yat-sen, 1865–1925, Chin. revolutionary leader & president of the republic of China 1912.

Suppé, Franz von, 1819–95, Yugoslavian operetta composer.

Susann, Jacqueline, 1921–74, U.S. author.

Susskind, David, 1920–, U.S. TV producer.

Sutherland, George, 1862–1942, U.S. jurist; justice of U.S. Supreme Court 1922–38.

—**Dame Joan,** 1926–, Austral. soprano.

Sutter, John Augustus, 1803–80, Ger.-born pioneer in California.

Suzuki, D(aisetz) T(eitaro), 1870–1966, Jap. Buddhist scholar.

—**Zenko,** 1911–, Jap. statesman and prime minister 1980–82.

Svoboda, Ludvik, 1895–1979, president of Czechoslovakia 1968–75.

Swanson, Gloria, 1899–1983, U.S. actress.

Swarthout, Gladys, 1904–69, U.S. mezzo-soprano.

Swedenborg, Emmanuel, 1688–1772, Swed. religious mystic, philosopher, & scientist.

Swift, Gustavus Franklin, 1839–1903, U.S. meat packer.

—**Jonathan,** 1667–1745, Irish-born Eng. satirist.

Swinburne, Algernon Charles, 1837–1909, Eng. poet & critic.

Swope, Herbert Bayard, 1882–1958, U.S. journalist.

Sydenham, Thomas, 1624–89, Eng. physician.

Sydow, Max von, 1929–, Swed. actor.

Symington, (William) Stuart, 1901–, U.S. politician.

Synge, John Millington, 1871–1909, Irish playwright & poet.

Szell, George, 1897–1970, Hung.-born U.S. conductor.

Szent-Györgyi von Nagyrapolt, Albert, 1893–, Hung. chemist.

Szewinska, Irena, 1946–, Pol. track runner.

Szigeti, Joseph, 1892–1973, Hung. violinist.

Szilard, Leo, 1898–1964, Hung.-born U.S. physicist.

Szold, Henrietta, 1860–1945, U.S. Zionist; founder of Hadassah.

Tacitus, Gaius Cornelius, A.D. 55?–117?, Roman historian.

Taft, Robert Alphonso, 1889–1953, U.S. senator 1939–53.

—**William Howard,** 1857–1930, 27th U.S. president 1906–13; chief justice of the U.S. Supreme Court 1921–30; father of prec.

Tagliavini, Ferruccio, 1913–, Ital. tenor.

Taglioni, Marie, 1804–84, Ital. ballerina.

Tagore, Sir Rabindranath, 1861–1941, Indian poet.

Tailleferro, Germaine, 1892–1983, Fr. composer.

Taine, Hippolyte Adolphe, 1828–93, Fr. philosopher & critic.

Takamine, Jokichi, 1854–1922, Jap. chemist & industrialist active in U.S.

Talese, Gay, 1932–, U.S. journalist & author.

Tallchief, Maria, 1925–, U.S. ballerina & dance company director.

Talleyrand-Périgord, Charles Maurice de, 1754–1838, Fr. statesman.

Tallis, Thomas, 1505?–85, Eng. composer.

Talma, François Joseph, 1763–1826, Fr. actor.

Talmadge, Norma, 1897–1957, U.S. actress.

Talvela, Martti, 1935–89, Finnish basso.

Tamayo, Rufino, 1899–, Mexican painter.

Tamerlane, 1336?–1405, Tartar conqueror of Asia. Also **Tamburlaine.**

Tamm, Igor Yevgenevich, 1895–1971, Soviet physicist; Nobel Prize winner.

Tanaka, Kakuei, 1918–, premier of Japan 1972–74.

Tancred, 1078?–1112, Norman leader in the first crusade.

Tandy, Jessica, 1909–, Eng.-born U.S. actress.

Taney, Roger Brooke, 1777–1864, U.S. jurist; chief justice of U.S. Supreme Court 1836–64.

Tanguay, Eva, 1878–1947, Can.-born U.S. actress.

Tanguy, Yves, 1900–55, Fr.-born U.S. artist.

Tanner, Alain, 1920–, Swiss film director.

—**Henry Ossawa,** 1859–1937, U.S. painter.

Tarbell, Ida Minerva, 1857–1944, U.S. author.

Tarkington, (Newton) Booth, 1869–1946, U.S. author.

Tarquin (L. Lucius Tarquinius Superbus), 6th c. B.C. king of Rome: called the Proud.

Tartini, Giuseppe, 1692–1770, Ital. violinist & composer.

Tasman, Abel Janszoon, 1603–59, Du. navigator & explorer.

Tasso, Torquato, 1544–95, Ital. poet.

Tate, John Orley Allen, 1899–1979, U.S. poet, critic, & biographer.

Tati, Jacques, 1908–82, Fr. actor, author, & film director.

Tatum, Art, 1901–56, U.S. jazz musician.

—**Edward Lawrie,** 1909–75, U.S. biochemist; Nobel Prize winner.

Tauber, Richard, 1892–1948, Austrian tenor.

Tawney, Richard, Henry, 1880–1962, Eng. economic historian.

Taylor, Deems, 1885–1966, U.S. composer & music critic.

—**Edward,** 1644?–1729, U.S. poet.

—**Elizabeth,** 1932–, Eng.-born U.S. actress.

—**James,** 1948–, U.S. singer & songwriter.

—**Laurette,** 1884–1946, U.S. actress.

—**Maxwell Davenport,** 1901–, U.S. general.

—**Paul,** 1930–, U.S. dancer & choreographer.

—**Robert,** 1911–69, U.S. actor.

—**Zachary,** 1784–1850, U.S. general & 12th U.S. president 1849–50.

Tchaikovsky, Peter Ilyich, 1840–93, Russ. composer.

Tcheitchew, Pavel, 1898–1957, Russ.-born U.S. painter.

Teach, Edward, ?–1718, Eng. pirate: known as **Blackbeard.**

Teagarden, Jack, 1905–64, U.S. jazz musician & blues singer.

Teale, Edwin Way, 1899–1980, U.S. naturalist & author.

Teasdale, Sara, 1884–1933, U.S. poet.

Tebaldi, Renata, 1922–, Ital. soprano.

Tecumseh, 1768?–1813, Shawnee Am. Ind. chief.

Teilhard de Chardin, Pierre, 1881–1955, Fr. paleontologist, geologist, & philosopher.

Telemann, Georg Philipp, 1681?–1767, Ger. composer.

Teller, Edward, 1908–, Hung.-born U.S. physicist.

Temple, Shirley See BLACK, SHIRLEY TEMPLE.

Templeton, Alec, 1910–63, Welsh-born U.S. composer & musician.

Tenniel, Sir John, 1820–1914, Eng. illustrator.

Tennyson, Alfred, Lord, 1809–92, Eng. poet.

Tenzing Norgay, 1914–, Nepalese Sherpa mountain climber.

Ter-Arutunian, Rouben, 1920–, Soviet-born U.S. set & costume designer.

Ter Borch, Gerard, 1617–81, Du. painter.

Terence (L. Publius Terentius Afer), 190?–159 B.C., Roman playwright.

Teresa, Mother, b. Agnes Gonxha Bojaxhiu, 1910–, Yugoslav-born Roman Catholic nun; founded Missionaries of Charity; Nobel Prize winner.

Tereshkova, Valentina Vladimirovna, 1937–, Soviet cosmonaut; first woman in space.

Terhune, Albert Payson, 1872–1942, U.S. author.

Terman, Lewis Madison, 1877–1956, U.S. psychologist.

Terrell, Mary Church, 1863–1954, U.S. civil rights leader.

Terry, Dame Ellen Alicia, 1847–1928, Eng. actress.

Terry-Thomas, 1911–90, Eng. comedian & actor.

Tertullian (L. Quintus Septimius Florens Tertullianus), A.D. 160?–230?, Roman theologian.

Tesla, Nikola, 1856–1943, Yugoslav-born U.S. inventor.

Tetley, Glen, 1926–, U.S. choreographer.

Tetrazzini, Luisa, 1874–1940, Ital. soprano.

Tetzel, Johann, 1465?–1519, Ger. Dominican monk.

Thackeray, William Makepeace, 1811–63, Eng. author.

Thalberg, Irving Grant, 1899–1936, U.S. film producer.

Thales, 640?–546 B.C., Gk. philosopher.

Thant, U., 1909–74, Burmese diplomat & secretary general of the U.N. 1962–71.

Tharp, Twyla, 1941–, U.S. dancer & choreographer.

Thatcher, Margaret Hilda, 1925–, Eng. political leader; prime minister 1979–90.

Thebom, Blanche, 1918–, U.S. mezzo-soprano.

Thiers, Louis-Adolphe, 1797–1877, Fr. author & statesman; president of Third Republic 1870–73.

Themistocles, 527?–460? B.C., Athenian general & statesman.

Theocritus, 3rd c. B.C. Gk. poet.

Theodora, ?–548, Byzantine empress; co-ruler with her husband, Justinian I.

Theodorakis, Mikis, 1925–, Gk. composer.

Theophrastus, 372?–287? B.C., Gk. philosopher & naturalist.

Theresa of Avila, Saint, 1515–82, Sp. Carmelite nun.

Theroux, Paul, 1941–, U.S. author.

Thespis, 6th c. B.C. Gk. poet & dramatist.

Thieu, Nguyen Van, 1923–, president of South Vietnam 1967–75.

Thomas, Ambroise, 1811–96, Fr. composer.

—**Danny,** 1914–91, U.S. entertainer & TV producer.

—**Dylan Marlais,** 1914–53, Welsh poet.

—**Lowell Jackson,** 1892–1981, U.S. news commentator & author.

—**Marlo,** 1943–, U.S. actress; daughter of Danny.

—**Norman Mattoon,** 1884–1968, U.S. socialist leader & author.

—**Seth,** 1785–1859, U.S. clock manufacturer.

—**Michael Tilson,** 1944–, U.S. conductor.

Thomas à Kempis, b. Thomas Hamerken, 1380?–1471, Ger. Christian writer.

Thomas of Erceldoune, 13th c. Scot. poet.

Thompson, Benjamin, Count Rumford, 1753–1814, Amer.-born Eng. statesman & scientist.

—**Dorothy,** 1894–1961, U.S. journalist.

—**Francis,** 1859–1907, Eng. poet.

—**J(ames) Walter,** 1847–1928, U.S. advertising executive.

Thomson, Sir George, 1892–1975, Eng. physicist.

—**Sir Joseph John,** 1856–1940, Eng. physicist; Nobel Prize winner; father of prec.

—**Sir John Sparrow David,** 1844–94, Can. statesman; prime minister 1892–94.

—**Thomas J.,** 1877–1918, U.S. painter.

—**Virgil,** 1896–1989, U.S. composer & music critic.

Thoreau, Henry David, 1817–62, U.S. author & naturalist.

Thorndike, Edward Lee, 1874–1949, U.S. psychologist.

—**Dame Sybil,** 1882–1976, Eng. actress.

Thorpe, James Francis (Jim), 1888–1953, U.S. football player & track athlete.

Thorvaldsen, Bartel, 1770–1844, Dan. sculptor.

Thucydides, 471?–399 B.C., Athenian statesman & historian.

Thurber, James Grover, 1894–1961, U.S. author & artist.

Thurmond, J. Strom, 1902–, U.S. politician.

Thurstone, Louis Leon, 1887–1955, U.S. psychologist.

Tibbett, Lawrence Mervil, 1896–1960, U.S. baritone.

Tiberius Claudius Nero Caesar, 42 B.C.–A.D. 37, Roman emperor A.D. 14–37.

Tiepolo, Giovanni Battista, 1696–1770, Venetian painter.

Tierney, Gene, 1920–, U.S. actress.

Tiffany, Charles Lewis, 1812–1902, U.S. jeweler.

—**Louis Comfort,** 1848–1933, U.S. decorative designer; son of prec.

Tiglath-pileser III, ?–727 B.C., king of Assyria 745–727 B.C..

Tilden, William (Bill), 1893–1953, U.S. tennis player.

Tillich, Paul Johannes, 1886–1965, Ger.-born U.S. theologian.

Tillstrom, Burr, 1917–85, U.S. puppeteer.

Tinbergen, Jan, 1903–, Du. economist; Nobel Prize winner.

—**Nikolaas,** 1907–88, Du. zoologist; brother of prec.

Tindemans, Leo, 1922–, premier of Belgium 1974–78.

Tintoretto, b. Jacopo Robusti, 1518–94, Venetian painter.

Tiomkin, Dimitri, 1894–1979, Russ.-born U.S. composer.

Tirso de Molina, pseud. of Gabriel Téllez, 1584–1648, Sp. playwright.

Titchener, Edward Bradford, 1867–1927, Eng.-born U.S. psychologist.

Titian, b. Tiziano Vecelli, 1477–1576, Venetian painter.

Tito, b. Josip Broz, 1892–1980, Yugoslav patriot & statesman; president of Yugoslavia 1963–80.

Tittle, Y(elverton) A(braham), Jr., 1926–, U.S. football player.

Titus Flavius Sabinus Vespasianus, A.D. 40?–81, Roman emperor 79–81.

Tobey, Mark, 1890–1976, U.S. painter.

Tocqueville, Alexis Charles Henri Maurice Clerel de, 1805–59, Fr. statesman & political writer.

Todd, Sir Alexander Robertus, 1907–, Eng. chemist.

Todman, William, 1916–, U.S. TV producer.

Togliatti, Palmiro, 1893?–1964, Ital. communist leader.

Togo, Shigenori, 1882–1950, Jap. diplomat.

Tojo, Hideki, 1884–1948, Jap. general & politician.

Tokyo Rose, b. Iva d'Aquino, 1916–, U.S.-born propagandist for Japan in World War II.

Tolbert, William Richard, 1913–80, president of Liberia 1971–80.

Tolkien, J(ohn) R(onald) R(euel), 1892–1973, Eng. author.

Tolstoy, Count Leo Nikolayevich, 1828–1910, Russ. author & social reformer.

Tombaugh, Clyde William, 1906–, U.S. astronomer.

Tomlin, Bradley Walker, 1899–1953, U.S. painter.

Tommasini, Vicenzo, 1880–1950, Ital. composer.

Tompkins, Daniel D., 1774–1825, U.S. statesman; U.S. vice president 1817–25.

Tone, Theobald Wolfe, 1763–98, Irish revolutionary.

Toomer, Jean, 1894–1967, U.S. author.

Torelli, Giacomo, 1608–78, Ital. stage designer.

Tormé, Mel(vin Howard), 1925–, U.S. singer.

Torquemada, Tomás de, 1420–98, Sp. monk & inquisitor.

Torre-Nilsson, Leopoldo, 1924–, Argentine film director.

Torricelli, Evangelista, 1608–47, Ital. physicist.

Toscanini, Arturo, 1867–1957, Ital. conductor active in U.S.

Toulouse-Lautrec, Henri Marie Raymond de, 1864–1901, Fr. painter & lithographer.

Touré, Sékou, 1922–84, president of Guinea 1958–84.

Tourel, Jennie, 1910–73, Can.-born U.S. mezzo-soprano.

Toussaint L'Ouverture, Dominique François, 1743–1803, Haitian revolutionary leader & general.

Tovey, Donald Francis, 1875–1940, Eng. musicologist & composer.

Townes, Charles Hard, 1915–, U.S. physicist; Nobel Prize winner.

Townsend, Sir John S. E., 1868–1957, Irish physicist.

Toynbee, Arnold J(oseph), 1889–1975, Eng. historian.

Tracy, Spencer, 1900–67, U.S. actor.

Trajan (L. Marcus Ulpius Trajanus), A.D. 52?–117, Roman emperor 98–117.

Traubel, Helen, 1899–1972, U.S. soprano.

Traynor, Harold Joseph (Pie), 1899–1972, U.S. baseball player.

Tree, Sir Herbert Beerbohm, 1853–1917, Eng. actor-manager.

Treigle, Norman, 1927–75, U.S. basso.

Treitschke, Heinrich von, 1834–96, German historian and political writer.

Tremayne, Les, 1913–, Eng.-born U.S. radio actor.

Trevelyan, George Macaulay, 1876–1962, Eng. historian.

Trevino, Lee, 1939–, U.S. golfer.

Trigère, Pauline, 1912–, Fr.-born U.S. fashion designer.

Trilling, Diana Rubin, 1905–, U.S. critic & author.

—**Lionel,** 1905–75, U.S. critic & author; husband of prec.

Trippe, Juan Terry, 1899–1981, U.S. airline pioneer.

Trollope, Anthony, 1815–82, Eng. author.

Trotsky, Leon, b. Lev Davidovich Bronstein, 1879–1940, Soviet revolutionary leader; assassinated.

Trudeau, Pierre Elliott, 1919–, Can. statesman; prime minister of Canada 1968–79 and 1980–84.

Trudeau, Garry, 1948–, U.S. cartoonist, satirist, & playwright.

Truffaut, François, 1932–84, Fr. film director.

Trujillo Molina, Rafael Leonidas, 1891–1961, Dominican general; president of the Dominican Republic 1930–38 & 1942–52; assassinated.

Truman, Harry S, 1884–1972, 33rd U.S. president 1945–53.

Trumbo, Dalton, 1905–76, U.S. author.

Trumbull, John, 1756–1843, U.S. painter.

Truth, Sojourner, b. Isabella Baumfree, 1797?–1883, U.S. social reformer.

Tshombe, Moise K., 1919–69, premier of Rep. of Congo.

Tsiolkovsky, Konstantin Eduardovich, 1857–1935, Russ. physicist.

Tsvett, Mikhail Semenovich, 1872–1920, Ital.-born Russ. botanist.

Tubman, Harriet, 1820?–1913, U.S. abolitionist.

—**William V(acanarat) S(hadrach),** 1895–1971, president of Liberia 1944–71.

Tuchman, Barbara, 1912–89, U.S. historian.

Tucker, Richard, 1915–75, U.S. tenor.

—**Sophie,** 1884–1966, Russ.-born U.S. singer & actress.

Tudor, Antony, 1908–87, Eng. choreographer.

Tu Fu, 712–770, Chin. poet.

Tugwell, Rexford Guy, 1891–1979, U.S. economist & political adviser.

Tune, Tommy, 1939–, U.S. dancer, choreographer, & stage director.

Tunney, James Joseph (Gene), 1897–1978, U.S. boxer.

Tupper, Sir Charles, 1821–1915, Can. statesman; prime minister 1896.

Tureck, Rosalyn, 1914–, U.S. pianist & harpsichordist.

Turgenev, Ivan Sergeyevich, 1818–83, Russ. author.

Turner, Frederick Jackson, 1861–1932, U.S. historian.

—**John Napier,** 1929–, Can. statesman; prime minister 1984.

—**J(oseph) M(allord) W(illiam),** 1775–1851, Eng. painter.

—**Nat,** 1800–31, U.S. slave; leader of an unsuccessful revolt.

—**Tina,** 1939–, U.S. singer.

Turpin, Dick, 1706–39, Eng. highwayman.

Tussaud, Mme. Marie Gresholtz, 1760–1850, Swiss-born wax modeler active in England.

Tutankhamen, 14th c. B.C. Egyptian king; tomb discovered 1922.

Twain, Mark, pseud. of Samuel Langhorne Clemens, 1835–1910, U.S. author.

Tweed, William Marcy (Boss), 1823–78, U.S. politician.

Twort, Frederick William, 1877–1950, Eng. bacteriologist.

Tyler, Anne, 1941–, U.S. author.

—**John,** 1790–1862, 10th U.S. president 1841–45.

—**Wat,** ?–1381, Eng. leader of Peasant Revolt against taxation.

Tyndale, William, 1484–1536, Eng. religious reformer; translated New Testament; executed for heresy.

Tyndall, John, 1820–93, Irish-born Eng. physicist.

Tzara, Tristan, 1896–1963, Rumanian poet & author; one of the founders of Dadaism.

Uccello, Paolo, b. Paolo di Dono, 1397–1475, Ital. painter.

Ulanova, Galina, 1910–, Soviet ballerina.

Ulbricht, Walter, 1893–1973, E. German political leader; first secretary of Socialist Unity Party 1950–71.

Ullmann, Liv, 1939–, Norw. actress active in Sweden and the U.S.

Umberto I, 1844–1900, king of Italy 1878–1900.

Unamuno y Jugo, Miguel de, 1864–1936, Sp. philosopher & author.

Uncas, 1588?–1683, Mohegan Am. Ind. chief.

Undset, Sigrid, 1882–1949, Norw. author; Nobel Prize winner.

Unitas, John, 1933–, U.S. football player.

Untermeyer, Louis, 1885–1977, U.S. poet, editor, & critic.

Updike, John, 1932–, U.S. author.

Upjohn, Richard, 1802–78, Eng.-born U.S. architect.

Urban, Joseph, 1872–1933, Austrian-born U.S. architect & set designer.

Urey, Harold, 1893–1981, U.S. chemist; Nobel Prize winner.

Uris, Leon Marcus, 1924–, U.S. author.

Ussachevsky, Vladimir, 1911–90, U.S. composer born in China.

Ussher, James, 1581–1656, Irish archibishop.

Ustinov, Peter, 1921–, Eng. actor, director, producer, & author.

Utamaro, Kitagawa, 1753?–1806, Jap. printmaker.

Utrillo, Maurice, 1883–1955, Fr. painter.

Vail, Theodore N., 1845–1920, U.S. industrialist.

Valentine, Saint, 3rd c. Roman Christian martyr.

Valentino, Rudolph, 1895–1926, Ital.-born U.S. actor.

Valéry, Paul Ambroise, 1871–1945, Fr. poet & philosopher.

Vallee, Hubert Prior (Rudy), 1901–86, U.S. singer & actor.

Van Allen, James Alfred, 1914–, U.S. physicist.

Van Alstyne, Egbert, 1882–1951, U.S. composer.

Van Brocklin, Norman, 1926–83, U.S. football player & coach.

Vanbrugh, Sir John, 1664–1726, Eng. architect & playwright.

Van Buren, Abby, pseud. of Pauline Esther Friedman, 1918–, U.S. columnist.

—**Martin,** 1782–1862, 8th U.S. president 1837–41.

Vance, Cyrus Roberts, 1917–, U.S. secretary of state 1977–80.

—**Vivian,** 1912–79, U.S. actress.

Vancouver, George, 1758–98, Eng. navigator & explorer.

Van de Graaff, Robert Jemison, 1901–67, U.S. physicist.

Vandenberg, Arthur Hendrick, 1884–1951, U.S. journalist & politician.

Vanderbilt, Alfred G., 1912–, U.S. horse breeder & sportsman.

—**Amy,** 1908–74, U.S. writer on etiquette.

—**Cornelius (Commodore),** 1794–1877, U.S. capitalist & industrialist.

—**Gloria,** 1924–, U.S. poet, artist, & fabric designer.

Van der Waals, Johannes Diderik, 1837–1923, Du. physicist.

Van der Weyden, Rogier, 1399?–1464, Flemish painter.

Van Dine, S. S., pseud. of Willard Huntington Wright, 1888–1939, U.S. author.

Van Doren, Carl, 1885–1950, U.S. author.

—**Mark,** 1894–1972, U.S. author; brother of prec.

Van Druten, John William, 1901–57, Eng. playwright.

Van Dyck, Anton, 1599–1641, Flemish painter. Also **Van Dyke.**

Van Eyck, Hubert, 1366?–1426?, & his brother **Jan,** 1389?–1441?, Flemish painters.

van Gogh, Vincent, 1853–1890, Du. painter.

Van Heusen, James (Jimmie), 1913–90, U.S. composer.

Van Horne, Harriet, 1920–, U.S. journalist.

Van Leyden, Lucas, 1494?–1533, Du. engraver.

Van Pebbles, Melvin, 1932–, U.S. playwright.

van't Hoff, Jacobus Henricus, 1852–1911, Du. physical chemist; Nobel Prize winner.

Vanzetti, Bartolomeo, 1888–1927, Ital. anarchist in the U.S.; executed with Nicola Sacco for murder.

Varda, Angés, 1928–, Fr. film director.

Vare, Glenna Collett, 1903–, U.S. golfer.

Varése, Edgard, 1883–1965, Fr.-born U.S. composer.

Varnay, Astrid, 1918–, Swed.-born U.S. soprano.

Vasari, Giorgio, 1511–74, Ital. painter, architect, & writer.

Vauban, Sébastien Le Prestre, Marquis de, 1633–1707, Fr. military engineer & architect.

Vaughan, Henry, 1622–95, Eng. poet.

—**Sarah,** 1924–90, U.S. singer.
Vaughan Williams, Ralph, 1872–1958, Eng. composer.
Vaux, Calvert, 1824–95, Eng.-born U.S. landscape architect.
Veblen, Thorstein Bunde, 1857–1929, U.S. political economist & sociologist.
Veeck, William Louis, Jr. (Bill), 1914–86, U.S. sports promoter.
Vega, Lope de, 1562–1635, Sp. playwright & poet.
Velázquez, Diego Rodriguez de Silva y, 1599–1660, Sp. painter.
Venizelos, Eleutherios, 1864–1936, Ger. statesman.
Venturi, Robert, 1925–, U.S. architect.
Venuti, Giuseppe (Joe), 1903–78, U.S. jazz violinist.
Vercingetorix, 72?–46? B.C., Gallic chieftain defeated by Julius Caesar.
Verdi, Giuseppe, 1813–1901, Ital. composer.
Verga, Giovanni, 1840–1922, Ital. author.
Verlaine, Paul, 1844–96, Fr. poet.
Vermeer, Jan, 1632–75, Du. painter.
Verne, Jules, 1828–1905, Fr. author.
Vernier, Pierre, 1580?–1637, Fr. mathematician.
Veronese, Paolo, 1528–88, Venetian painter.
Verrazano, Giovanni da, 1480?–1528?, Ital. navigator.
Verrett, Shirley, 1931–, U.S. mezzo-soprano.
Verrocchio, Andrea del, 1435–88, Florentine sculptor & painter.
Verwoerd, Hendrik Frensch, 1901–66, prime minister of Republic of South Africa 1958–66; assassinated.
Vesalius, Andreas, 1514–64, Belg. anatomist.
Vesey, Denmark, 1762–1822, U.S. slave & insurrectionist.
Vespasian (L. Titus Flavius Sabinus Vespasianus), A.D. 9–79, Roman emperor 69–79.
Vespucci, Amerigo, 1454–1512, Ital. navigator.
Vickers, Jon, 1926–, Can. tenor.
Vico, Giovanni Battista (Giambattista), 1668–1744, Ital. philosopher & historian.
Victor Emmanuel II, 1820–78, king of Sardinia 1849–61 & first king of Italy 1861–78.
—**III,** 1869–1947, king of Italy 1900–46; grandson of prec.
Victoria, 1819–1901, queen of Great Britain 1837–1901.
Vidal, Gore, 1925–, U.S. novelist, playwright, & critic.
Vidor, King Wallis, 1895–1982, U.S. film director.
Vigny, Comte Alfred Victor de, 1797–1863, Fr. author.
Vigo, Jean, 1905–34, Fr. film director.
Villa, Francisco (Pancho), 1877–1923, Mexican revolutionary leader.
Villa-Lobos, Heitor, 1887–1959, Brazilian composer.
Villard, Henry, 1835–1900, U.S. journalist & financier.
Villella, Edward Joseph, 1936–, U.S. ballet dancer.
Villon, François, 1431–85?, Fr. poet.
Vincent de Paul, Saint, 1581?–1660, Fr. priest.
Viollet-le-Duc, Eugène Emmanuel, 1814–79, Fr. architect & restorer.
Virchow, Rudolf, 1821–1902, Ger. pathologist.
Virgil L. (Publius Vergilius Maro), 70–19 B.C., Roman poet. Also **Vergil.**
Virtanen, Artturi Ilmari, 1895–1973, Finnish biochemist.
Visconti, Luchino, 1906–76, Ital. film director.
Vishinsky, Andrei Yanuarievich, 1883–1954, Soviet jurist & diplomat.
Vishnevskaya, Galina, 1926–, Soviet-born soprano.
Vitruvius Pollio, Marcus, 1st c. B.C., Roman architect & engineer.
Vitti, Monica, 1933–, Ital. actress.
Vivaldi, Antonio, 1675?–1741, Ital. composer.
Vlaminck, Maurice de, 1876–1958, Fr. painter.
Volcker, Paul Adolph, 1927–, U.S. civil servant & administrator.
Volstead, Andrew John, 1860–1947, U.S. politician & prohibitionist.
Volta, Count Alessandro, 1745–1827, Ital. physicist.
Voltaire, b. François Marie Arouet, 1694–1778, Fr. writer & philosopher.
Von Braun, Wernher, 1912–77, Ger.-born U.S. aerospace engineer.
Von Fürstenberg, Diane, 1946–, Belg. fashion designer.
Von Karajan, Herbert, 1908–89, Austrian conductor.

Vonnegut, Kurt, Jr., 1922–, U.S. author.
Von Neumann, John, 1903–57, Hung.-born U.S. mathematician.
Von Sternberg, Josef, 1894–1969, Austrian-born U.S. film director.
Von Tilzer, Harry, 1878–1956, U.S. composer.
Voroshilov, Kliment Efremovich, 1881–1969, Soviet marshal & politician.
Vorster, Balthazar Johannes (John), 1915–83, prime minister of Republic of South Africa 1966–78.
Vought, Chance Milton, 1890–1930, U.S. aeronautical engineer & designer.
Vreeland, Diana, 1903?–89, U.S. fashion journalist.
Vuillard, (Jean) Édouard, 1868–1940, Fr. painter.

Wagner, George Raymond, 1915?–63, U.S. wrestler: known as **Gorgeous George.**
—**John Peter (Honus),** 1874–1955, U.S. baseball player.
—**Richard,** 1813–83, Ger. composer & critic.
—**Robert Ferdinand,** 1877–1953, U.S. politician.
Waite, Morrison Remick, 1816–88, U.S. jurist; chief justice of U.S. Supreme Court 1874–88.
Wajda, Andrzej, 1926–, Pol. film director.
Waksman, Selman Abraham, 1888–1973, Ukrainian-born U.S. microbiologist; Nobel Prize winner.
Wald, George, 1906–, U.S. biologist; Nobel Prize winner.
—**Lillian D.,** 1867–1940, U.S. social worker.
Waldheim, Kurt, 1918–, Austrian diplomat & secretary general of the U.N. 1972–1982.
Walesa, Lech, 1943–, Polish labor leader and statesman; president of Poland 1990–.
Waley, Arthur, 1889–1966, Eng. oriental scholar & translator.
Walgreen, Charles Rudolph, 1873–1939, U.S. pharmacist & merchant.
Walker, Alice, 1944–, U.S. author.
—**James John (Jimmy),** 1881–1946, U.S. politician; mayor of New York City 1926–32.
—**Mort,** 1923–, U.S. cartoonist.
—**Nancy,** 1922–, U.S. actress.
—**Ralph T.,** 1889–1973, U.S. architect.
Wallace, Alfred Russel, 1823–1913, Eng. naturalist.
—**DeWitt,** 1889–1981, U.S. publisher.
—**George Corley,** 1919–, U.S. governor & political leader.
—**Henry Agard,** 1888–1965, U.S. agriculturist & politician; U.S. vice president 1941–45.
—**Irving,** 1916–90, U.S. author.
—**Lew,** 1827–1905, U.S. author, diplomat, lawyer, & military leader.
—**Lila Bell Acheson,** 1889–1984, Can.-born U.S. publisher & patron of the arts; wife of DeWitt.
—**Mike,** 1918–, U.S. TV interviewer & commentator.
Wallenstein, Alfred Franz, 1898–1983, U.S. conductor.
Waller, Edmund, 1606–87, Eng. poet.
—**Thomas (Fats),** 1904–43, U.S. jazz musician.
Wallis, Hall Brent, 1899–, U.S. film producer.
Walpole, Horace, (4th Earl of Orford), 1717–97, Eng. author.
—**Sir Hugh Seymour,** 1884–1941, Eng. author.
—**Sir Robert,** 1676–1745, Eng. statesman; first prime minister of England 1721–42; father of Horace.
Walsh, Raoul, 1892–1980, U.S. film director.
Walter, Bruno, 1876–1962, Ger. conductor active in U.S.
Walters, Barbara, 1931–, U.S. TV personality.
Walther von der Vogelweide, 1170–1230, Ger. poet.
Walton, Ernest Thomas Sinton, 1903–, Irish physicist; Nobel Prize winner.
—**Sir William Turner,** 1902–83, Eng. composer.
Wanamaker, John, 1838–1922, U.S. merchant.
Wanger, Walter, 1894–1968, U.S. film producer.
Wang Wei, 699–759, Chin. painter, poet, & musician.
Wank, Roland T., 1898–1970, U.S. architect.
Wankel, Felix, 1902–, Ger. engineer & inventor.
Warburg, Aby, 1866–1929, Ger. art historian.
—**James P.,** 1896–1969, U.S. financier.
—**Otto Heinrich,** 1883–1970, Ger. physiologist.
Ward, Aaron Montgomery, 1844–1913, U.S. merchant.

—**Artemus,** pseud. of Charles Farrar Browne, 1834–67, U.S. humorist.
—**Barbara (Lady Jackson),** 1914–81, Eng. economist & author.
—**Clara,** 1924–73, U.S. gospel singer.
Warfield, William Caesar, 1920–, U.S. baritone.
Warhol, Andy, 1927–87, U.S. painter & filmmaker.
Waring, Fred, 1900–84, U.S. bandleader.
Warmerdam, Cornelius, 1915–, U.S. pole vaulter.
Warner A family of U.S. film executives incl. three brothers: **Albert,** 1884–1967; **Harry Morris,** 1881–1957; & **Jack Leonard,** 1892–1978.
—**Glenn Scobey (Pop),** 1871–1954, U.S. football coach.
Warren, Earl, 1891–1974, U.S. jurist; chief justice of the U.S. Supreme Court 1953–69.
—**Harry,** 1893–1981, U.S. composer.
—**Leonard,** 1911–60, U.S. baritone.
—**Robert Penn,** 1905–89, U.S. poet & author.
Washington, Booker T(aliaferro), 1856–1915, U.S. educator & author.
—**George,** 1732–99, Amer. general & statesman; first U.S. president 1789–97.
Wassermann, August von, 1866–1925, Ger. bacteriologist.
Waterfield, Robert Staton (Bob), 1920–83, U.S. football player & coach.
Waterman, Lewis Edson, 1837–1901, U.S. inventor & manufacturer.
Waters, Ethel, 1900–77, U.S. singer & actress.
—**McKinley Morganfield (Muddy),** 1915–83, U.S. blues singer & guitarist.
Watson, James Dewey, 1928–, U.S. biochemist; Nobel Prize winner.
—**John Broadus,** 1878–1958, U.S. psychologist.
—**Thomas John,** 1874–1956, U.S. businessman.
Watt, James, 1736–1819, Scot. engineer & inventor.
Watteau, Jean Antoine, 1684–1721, Fr. painter.
Watts, Alan Witson, 1915–73, Eng.-born U.S. religious philosopher & author.
—**André,** 1946–, Ger.-born U.S. pianist.
—**Isaac,** 1674–1748, Eng. theologian & poet.
Waugh, Evelyn Arthur St. John, 1903–66, Eng. author.
Wayne, Anthony, 1745–96, Amer. revolutionary general.
—**John,** 1907–79, U.S. actor.
Weaver, Robert Clifton, 1907–, U.S. economist & government official.
—**Sylvester L., Jr. (Pat),** 1908–, U.S. TV executive.
Webb, Beatrice, 1858–1943, & her husband **Sidney,** 1859–1947; Eng. socialist reformers & economists.
—**Clifton,** 1896–1966, U.S. actor.
Weber, Carl Maria Friedrich Ernst von, 1786–1826, Ger. composer.
—**Max,** 1864–1920, Ger. economist & sociologist.
—**Max,** 1881–1961, Russ.-born painter.
Webern, Anton von, 1883–1945, Austrian composer.
Webster, Daniel, 1782–1852, U.S. statesman.
—**John,** 1580?–1625, Eng. playwright.
—**Margaret,** 1905–73, U.S. actress & stage director.
—**Noah,** 1758–1843, U.S. lexicographer.
Wechsler, David, 1896–1981, U.S. pyschologist.
—**James A.,** 1915–83, U.S. journalist & editor.
Wedekind, Frank, 1864–1918, Ger. playwright.
Wedgwood, Josiah, 1730–95, Eng. potter.
Wegener, Alfred L., 1880–1903, Ger. geologist.
Weidman, Charles, 1901–75, U.S. dancer & choreographer.
Weill, Kurt, 1900–50, Ger.-born U.S. composer.
Weingartner, Felix, 1863–1942, Austrian conductor.
Weismann, August, 1834–1914, Ger. biologist.
Weissmuller, John, 1904–84, U.S. swimmer & actor.
Weizmann, Chaim, 1874–1952, Russ.-born Israeli chemist & Zionist leader; first president of Israel 1949–52.
Welch, Joseph Nye, 1890–1960, U.S. lawyer.
—**Robert H. W., Jr.,** 1899–1985, U.S. manufacturer & political activist.
Welitsch, Ljuba, 1913–, Bulgarian soprano.
Welk, Lawrence, 1903–, U.S. bandleader.
Weller, Thomas Huckle, 1915–, U.S. biologist; Nobel Prize winner.

Welles, Orson, 1915–85, U.S. film director & actor.
Wellington, Arthur Wellesley, Duke of, 1769–1852, Irish-born Brit. statesman & general.
Wellman, William, 1896–1975, U.S. film director.
Wells, Henry, 1805–78, U.S. transportation entrepreneur.
—**H(erbert) G(eorge),** 1866–1946, Eng. author.
—**Mary,** 1928–, U.S. advertising executive.
Welty, Eudora, 1909–, U.S. author.
Wenceslaus, 1361–1419, king of Germany & Holy Roman emperor, 1378–1400 & king of Bohemia 1378–1419.
Wenrich, Percy, 1887–1952, U.S. composer.
Werfel, Franz, 1890–1945, Ger. author.
Wertheimer, Max, 1880–1943, Ger. psychologist.
Wertmüller, Lina, 1928–, Ital. film director.
Wesker, Arnold, 1932–, Eng. author & playwright.
Wesley, Charles, 1707–88, Eng. Methodist preacher & poet.
—**John,** 1703–91, Eng. clergyman; founder of Methodism; brother of prec.
West, Benjamin, 1738–1820, Amer. painter active in England.
—**Jerome Allen (Jerry),** 1938–, U.S. basketball player.
—**Jessamyn,** 1902–84, U.S. author.
—**Mae,** 1892–1980, U.S. actress.
—**Nathanael,** 1903–40, U.S. author.
—**Dame Rebecca,** pseud. of Cicily Isabel Fairfield, 1892–1983, Eng. author & critic.
Westinghouse, George, 1846–1914, U.S. inventor.
Westmore, Perc, 1904–70, U.S. cosmetician & businessman.
Westmoreland, William Childs, 1914–, U.S. general.
Weston, Edward, 1886–1958, U.S. photographer.
Weyden, Rogier van der, 1399?–1464, Flemish painter.
Weyer, Johann, 1515–88, Belg. physician.
Weyerhaeuser, Frederick, 1834–1914, Ger.-born U.S. businessman.
Wharton, Edith Newbold Jones, 1862–1937, U.S. author.
Wheatley, Phillis, 1753?–84, African-born Amer. poet.
Wheatstone, Sir Charles, 1802–75, Eng. physicist.
Wheeler, William Almon, 1819–87, U.S. statesman; U.S. vice president 1877–81.
Wheelock, John Hall, 1886–1978, U.S. poet.
Whistler, James Abbott McNeill, 1834–1903, U.S. painter active in England & France.
White, Byron Raymond, 1917–, U.S. jurist; justice of the U.S. Supreme Court 1962–.
—**Edward Douglass,** 1845–1921, U.S. jurist; chief justice of U.S. Supreme Court 1910–21.
—**E(lwyn) B(rooks),** 1899–1985, U.S. author & editor.
—**George,** 1890–1968, U.S. theatrical producer & director.
—**Josh,** 1908–69, U.S. folk singer.
—**Patrick,** 1912–90, Eng.-born Austral. author; Nobel Prize winner.
—**Pearl,** 1889–1938, U.S. actress.
—**Ryan,** 1971–90, U.S. AIDS activist; succumbed to the disease after five years.
—**Stanford,** 1853–1906, U.S. architect.
—**T. H.,** 1906–64, Brit. author.
—**Theodore H.,** 1915–86, U.S. political analyst & author.
—**Walter Francis,** 1893–1955, U.S. civil rights leader & author.
—**William Allen,** 1868–1944, U.S. journalist & author.
Whitehead, Alfred North, 1861–1947, Eng. mathematician & philosopher active in U.S.
Whiteman, Paul, 1891–1967, U.S. conductor.
Whiting, Richard A., 1891–1938, U.S. composer.
Whitlam, Gough, 1916–, Austral. prime minister 1972–75.
Whitman, Marcus, 1802–47, & his wife **Narcissa Prentice,** 1808–47, U.S. missionaries & pioneers.
—**Walt(er),** 1819–92, U.S. poet & journalist.
Whitney, Cornelius Vanderbilt, 1899–, U.S. sportsman.
—**Eli,** 1765–1825, U.S. inventor.
Whittaker, Charles Evans, 1901–73, U.S. jurist; justice of U.S. Supreme Court 1957–62.
Whittier, John Greenleaf, 1807–92, U.S. poet.
Whitty, Dame May, 1865–1948, Eng. actress.
Wicker, Thomas Grey (Tom), 1926–, U.S. journalist & author.
Widor, Charles Marie, 1845–1937, Fr. organist & composer.

Wieland, Heinrich Otto, 1877–1957, Ger. chemist; Nobel Prize winner.

Wien, Wilhelm, 1864–1928, Ger. physicist.

Wiener, Norbert, 1894–1964, U.S. mathematician & logician.

Wieniawski, Henri, 1835–80, Pol. violinist & composer.

Wiesel, Elie, 1928–, Rumanian-born Israeli author; Nobel Prize winner.

Wiesner, Jerome Bert, 1915–, U.S. engineer.

Wiggin, Kate Douglas Smith, 1856–1923, U.S. educator & author.

Wigglesworth, Michael, 1631–1705, U.S. pastor, physician, & poet.

Wightman, Hazel Hotchkiss, 1886–1974, U.S. tennis player.

Wigman, Mary, 1889–1973, Ger. dancer.

Wigner, Eugene Paul, 1902–, Hung.-born U.S. physicist; Nobel Prize winner.

Wilberforce, William, 1759–1833, Eng. abolitionist & philanthropist.

Wilbur, Richard Purdy, 1921–, U.S. poet.

Wilcox, Ella Wheeler, 1850–1919, U.S. poet.

Wilde, Oscar Fingall O'Flahertie Wills, 1854–1900, Irish playwright & poet.

—**Patricia,** 1928–, Can.-born U.S. ballerina.

Wilder, Laura Ingalls, 1867–1957, U.S. author.

—**Samuel (Billy),** 1906–, Austrian-born U.S. film director.

—**Thornton Niven,** 1897–1975, U.S. author & playwright.

Wilhelm I, 1797–1888, king of Prussia 1861–88 & emperor of Germany 1871–88.

—**II,** 1859–1941, king of Prussia & emperor of Germany 1888–1918; grandson of prec.

Wilhelmina, 1880–1962, queen of the Netherlands 1890–1948.

Wilkes, John, 1727–97, Eng. political reformer.

Wilkins, Sir Hubert, 1888–1958, Austral. explorer, scientist, aviator, & photographer.

—**Maurice Hugh Frederick,** 1916–, Brit. biochemist; Nobel Prize winner.

—**Roy,** 1901–81, U.S. civil rights leader.

Willard, Frank, 1893–1957, U.S. cartoonist.

—**Jess,** 1883–1968, U.S. boxer.

William of Ockham, 1284?–1347?, Eng. philosopher & theologian.

William I, 1027–87, Norman invader of England; king of England 1066–87: known as **the Conqueror.**

—**III,** 1650–1702, king of England, Scotland, & Ireland 1689–1702; co-ruler with his wife Mary II 1689–94.

—**William I,** 1533–84, Prince of Orange; founder of the Dutch republic: known as **the Silent.**

Williams, Daniel Hale, 1853–1931, U.S. physician.

—**Edward Bennett,** 1920–, U.S. lawyer.

—**Emlyn,** 1905–87, Welsh playwright & actor.

—**Esther,** 1923–, U.S. swimmer & actress.

—**Hiram King (Hank),** 1923–53, U.S. singer & composer.

—**Roger,** 1603?–83, Eng. clergyman; founder of Rhode Island.

—**Tennessee,** 1911–83, U.S. playwright.

—**Theodore Samuel (Ted),** 1918–, U.S. baseball player.

—**William Carlos,** 1883–1963, U.S. poet, author, & physician.

Williamson, Nicol, 1938–, Brit. actor.

Willis, Thomas, 1621–75, Eng. anatomist & physician.

Willkie, Wendell Lewis, 1892–1944, U.S. lawyer, businessman & politician.

Willson, Meredith, 1902–84, U.S. playwright.

Willstätter, Richard, 1872–1942, Ger. chemist; Nobel Prize winner.

Willys, John North, 1873–1935, U.S. automobile manufacturer.

Wilson, Charles Erwin, 1890–1961, U.S. industrialist & government official.

—**Charles Thomson Rees,** 1869–1959, Scot. physicist; Nobel Prize winner.

—**Edmund,** 1895–1972, U.S. author, critic, & journalist.

—**Gahan,** 1930–, U.S. cartoonist.

—**Sir Harold,** 1916–, Eng. politician; prime minister 1964–70 & 1974–76.

—**Henry,** 1812–75, U.S. vice president 1873–75.

—**Lanford,** 1937–, U.S. playwright.

—**Nancy,** 1937–, U.S. singer.

—**Samuel,** 1766–1854, U.S. merchant: known as **Uncle Sam.**

—**Teddy,** 1912–86, U.S. jazz musician.

—**(Thomas) Woodrow,** 1856–1924, 28th U.S. president 1913–21.

Winchell, Walter, 1897–1972, U.S. journalist & radio broadcaster.

Winchester, Oliver Fisher, 1810–80, U.S. firearms manufacturer.

Winckelmann, Johann Joachim, 1717–68, Ger. archaeologist.

Windaus, Adolf, 1876–1959, Ger. chemist.

Windsor, Duchess of, (Wallis Warfield Simpson), 1896–1986, U.S.-born wife of Edward VIII.

—**Duke of** See EDWARD VIII.

Winters, Jonathan, 1925–, U.S. comedian.

Winthrop, John, 1588–1649, Eng.-born Puritan; governor of Massachusetts.

Wise, Isaac Mayer, 1819–1900, Austrian-born U.S. religious leader; founder of Reform Judaism in the U.S.

—**Stephen Samuel,** 1874–1949, Hung.-born U.S. rabbi & Zionist leader.

Wister, Owen, 1860–1938, U.S. author.

Withers, Jane, 1917–, U.S. actress.

Wittgenstein, Ludwig, 1889–1951, Austrian philosopher active in England.

Wittkower, Rudolph, 1901–71, Ger.-born Brit. art historian.

Wodehouse, Sir P(elham) G(renville), 1881–1975, Eng.-born U.S. author.

Woffington, Margaret (Peg), 1714?–60, Irish actress.

Wöhler, Friedrich, 1800–82, Ger. chemist.

Wolf, Hugo, 1860–1903, Austrian composer.

Wolfe, James, 1727–59, Eng. general.

—**Thomas Clayton,** 1900–38, U.S. author.

—**Tom,** 1931–, U.S. journalist & author.

Wolff, Kaspar Friedrich, 1733–94, Ger. antomist.

Wolf-Ferrari, Ermanno, 1876–1948, Ital.-born Ger. composer.

Wolfflin, Heinrich, 1864–1945, Swiss art historian.

Wolfram von Eschenbach, 1170?–1220?, Ger. poet & knight.

Wollaston, William Hyde, 1766–1828, Eng. chemist & physicist.

Wollstonecraft, Mary, 1759–97, Eng. feminist & author.

Wolsey, Thomas, 1475?–1530, Eng. cardinal & statesman.

Wonder, Stevie, b. Stevland Morris, 1950–, U.S. singer, composer, & musician.

Wood, Grant, 1891–1942, U.S. painter.

—**Sam,** 1883–1949, U.S. film director.

Woodbridge, Frederick James Eugene, 1867–1940, Can.-born U.S. philosopher.

Woodcock, Leonard, 1911–, U.S. labor leader.

Woodhull, Victoria Clafin, 1838–1927, U.S. feminist.

Woods, Granville T., 1856–1910, U.S. inventor.

Woodson, Carter Goodwin, 1875–1950, U.S. historian.

Woodward, C(omer) Vann, 1908–, U.S. historian.

—**Joanne,** 1930–, U.S. actress.

—**Robert Burns,** 1917–79, U.S. chemist; Nobel Prize winner.

Woolf, (Adeline) Virginia (Stephen), 1882–1941, Eng. author & critic.

—**Leonard Sidney,** 1880–1969, Eng. author & critic; husband of prec.

Woollcott, Alexander, 1887–1943, U.S. journalist & critic.

Woolworth, Frank Winfield, 1852–1919, U.S. merchant.

Worcester, Joseph Emerson, 1784–1865, U.S. lexicographer.

Wordsworth, William, 1770–1850, Eng. poet.

Worth, Charles Frederick, 1825–95, Eng. fashion designer active in France.

Wouk, Herman, 1915–, U.S. author.

Wren, Sir Christopher, 1632–1723, Eng. architect.

Wright, Eizur, 1804–85, U.S. abolitionist.

—**Frances,** 1795–1852, U.S. lecturer & journalist.

—**Frank Lloyd,** 1867–1959, U.S. architect.

—**Mary Kathryn (Mickey),** 1935–, U.S. golfer.

—**Orville,** 1871–1948, & his brother **Wilbur,** 1867–1912, U.S. aviation pioneers.

—**Richard,** 1908–60, U.S. author.

Wrigley, William, Jr., 1861–1932, U.S. businessman.

Wunderlich, Fritz, 1930–66, Ger. tenor.

Wundt, Wilhelm, 1832–1920, Ger. physiologist & psychiatrist.

Wuorinen, Charles, 1938–, U.S. composer.

Wurster, William, 1895–1973, U.S. architect.

Wyatt, Sir Thomas, 1503–43, Eng. poet & diplomat.

Wycherley, William, 1640?–1716, Eng. playwright & poet.

Wycliffe, John, 1324?–84, Eng. religious reformer; translator of the Bible into English.

Wyeth, Andrew Newell, 1917–, U.S. painter.

—N(ewell) C(onvers), 1882–1945, U.S. painter & illustrator; father of prec.

Wyler, William, 1902–81, U.S. film director.

Wylie, Elinor Morton, 1885–1928, U.S. poet.

—Philip, 1902–71, U.S. author.

—Wynn, Ed, 1886–1966, U.S. comedian & actor.

Xanthippe, 5th c. B.C., wife of Socrates.

Xavier, Saint Francis, 1506–52, Sp. Jesuit missionary in the Orient; founder, with Ignatius of Loyola, of the Society of Jesus.

Xenakis, Iannis, 1922–, Romanian-born composer, architect, & engineer active in France.

Xenophon, 435?–355? B.C., Gk. historian & soldier.

Xerxes I, 519?–465 B.C., king of Persia 486–465 B.C..

—II, 450?–424 B.C., king of Persia 424 B.C.; son of prec.

Yale, Elihu, 1649–1721, Eng.-born Amer. merchant & philanthropist.

—Linus, Jr., 1821–68, U.S. inventor & lock manufacturer.

Yamamoto, Isoroku, 1884–1943, Jap. admiral.

Yamasaki, Minoru, 1912–86, U.S. architect.

Yamashita, Tomobumi, 1885–1946, Jap. general.

Yang, Chen Ning, 1922–, Chin.-born U.S. physicist; Nobel Prize winner.

Yeager, Charles Elwood, 1923–, U.S. aviator & general.

Yeats, William Butler, 1865–1939, Irish poet, playwright, & essayist; Nobel Prize winner.

Yellen, Jack, 1892–, U.S. lyricist.

Yeltsin, Boris, 1931–, Rus. statesman; president of the Russian S.S.R. 1990–.

Yerby, Frank Garvin, 1916–, U.S. author.

Yerkes, Charles Tyson, 1837–1905, U.S. financier.

—Robert Mearns, 1876–1956, U.S. psychologist.

Yesenin, Sergey, 1895–1925, Russ. poet.

Yevtushenko, Yevgeny, 1933–, Soviet poet.

York, Alvin Cullum, 1887–1964, U.S. soldier: known as **Sergeant York.**

Yoshida, Shigeru, 1878–1967, Jap. prime minister 1946–54.

Youmans, Vincent, 1898–1946, U.S. composer.

Young, Andrew Jackson, Jr., 1932–, U.S. ambassador, mayor, & civil rights leader.

—Brigham, 1801–77, U.S. Mormon leader.

—Denton True (Cy), 1867–1955, U.S. baseball player.

—Lester Willis, 1909–59, U.S. jazz musician.

—Loretta, 1913–, U.S. actress.

—Murat Bernard (Chic), 1901–73, U.S. cartoonist.

—Stark, 1881–1963, U.S. author & magazine editor.

—Thomas, 1773–1829, Eng. physicist & physician.

—Victor, 1900–56, U.S. composer.

—Whitney Moore, Jr., 1921–71, U.S. civil rights leader.

Younger, (Thomas) Cole(man), 1844–1916, U.S. outlaw.

Youngman, Henny, 1906–, Eng.-born U.S. comedian.

Youskevitch, Igor, 1912–, Russ.-born U.S. ballet dancer.

Yukawa, Hideki, 1907–81, Jap. physicist active in U.S.; Nobel Prize winner.

Yurka, Blanche, 1887–1974, U.S. actress.

Zadkine, Ossip, 1890–1967, Russ.-born Fr. sculptor.

Zaharias, Mildred Didrikson (Babe), 1914–56, U.S. athelete.

Zangwill, Israel, 1864–1926, Eng. author & playwright.

Zanuck, Darryl, 1902–79, U.S. film producer.

Zapata, Emiliano, 1877?–1919, Mexican revolutionary leader.

Zatopek, Emil, 1922–, Czech track runner.

Zeeman, Pieter, 1865–1943, Du. physicist.

Zeffirelli, Franco, 1922–, Ital. stage, opera, & film director.

Zenger, John Peter, 1697–1746, Ger.-born Amer. journalist & publisher.

Zeno, 342?–270? B.C., Gk. philosopher: called **the Stoic.**

Zeppelin, Count Ferdinand von, 1838–1917, Ger. general & aviation pioneer.

Zernicke, Frits, 1888–1966, Du. physicist.

Zetterling, Mai, 1925–, Swed. film actress & director.

Zhao Ziyang, 1919–, Chin. premier 1980–89.

Zhdanov, Andrei Aleksandrovich, 1896–1948, Soviet politician & general.

Zhivkov, Todor, 1911–, head of state of Bulgaria 1971–89.

Zhou Enlai, 1898–1976, Chin. statesman; premier & foreign minister of People's Republic of China 1949–76.

Zhukov, Georgi Konstantinovich, 1896–1974, Soviet marshal.

Ziegfeld, Florenz, 1869–1932, U.S. theatrical producer & playwright.

Zimbalist, Efrem, 1890–1985, Russ.-born U.S. violinist.

Zindel, Paul, 1936–, U.S. author.

Zinnemann, Fred, 1907–, Austrian-born U.S. film director.

Zinoviev, Grigori Evseevich, 1883–1936, Soviet Communist leader.

Zinsser, Hans, 1878–1940, U.S. bacteriologist.

Zola, Emile, 1840–1902, Fr. author.

Zorach, William, 1887–1966, Lithuanian-born U.S. painter & sculptor.

Zorn, Anders Leonhard, 1860–1920, Swed. painter, etcher, & sculptor.

Zoroaster, ca. 6th c. B.C., Pers. founder of Zoroastrianism: also called **Zarathustra.**

Zsigmondy, Richard, 1865–1929, Ger. chemist.

Zukerman, Pinchas, 1948–, Israeli violinist, violist, & conductor active in U.S.

Zukor, Adolph, 1873–1976, Hung.-born U.S. film producer & executive.

Zurbarán, Francisco, 1598–1664, Sp. painter.

Zweig, Arnold, 1887–1968, Ger. author.

—Stefan, 1881–1942, Austrian-born Brit. author.

Zwingli, Huldreich, 1484–1531, Swiss religious reformer.

Zworykin, Vladimir Cosma, 1889–1982, Russ.-born U.S. engineer & inventor.

Quotations

The following pages contain more than 1600 significant sayings, epigrams, and thoughts of all ages, including our own. The quotations are grouped under 178 subject headings—from *Ability* to *Youth*—and following each is the author's name, his birth and death dates, and, in most cases, the source from which the quotation was obtained.

Most of the selections come from familiar sources—Shakespeare, Emerson, Bacon, Cervantes, Cicero, La Rochefoucauld, Aristotle, Thomas Jefferson, the Old and New Testaments, etc. Many additional selections, however, have been made from the ranks of contemporary thinkers, world leaders, and authors. Among those quoted are Lyndon B. Johnson, John F. Kennedy, Pope John XXIII, Winston Churchill, Arthur Miller, Eleanor Roosevelt, Jacques Maritain, and Edith Hamilton.

Ability

Natural abilities are like natural plants, that need pruning by study.
—FRANCIS BACON (1561–1620) *Essays: Of Studies*

I add this also, that natural ability without education has oftener raised man to glory and virtue than education without natural ability.
—CICERO (106–43 B.C.) *Oratio Pro Licinio Archia*

Skill to do comes of doing.
—RALPH WALDO EMERSON (1803–1882) *Society and Solitude*

A man who qualifies himself well for his calling, never fails of employment.
—THOMAS JEFFERSON (1743–1826)

It is a great ability to be able to conceal one's ability.
—FRANÇOIS DE LA ROCHEFOUCAULD (1613–1680) *Maxims*

Better be proficient in one art than a smatterer in a hundred.
—JAPANESE PROVERB

So long as a man imagines that he cannot do this or that, so long is he determined not to do it; and consequently so long is it impossible to him that he should do it.
—BENEDICT SPINOZA (1632–1677) *Ethics*

They are able because they think they are able.
—VERGIL (70–19 B.C.) *Aeneid*

Absence

But ay the tear comes in me ee,
To think on him that's far awa.
—ROBERT BURNS (1759–1796) *The Bonnie Lad That's Far Awa*

Our hours in love have wings; in absence crutches.
—COLLEY CIBBER (1671–1757) *Xerxes*

To him that absent is All things succeed amiss
—CERVANTES (1547–1616) *Don Quixote*

Friends, though absent, are still present.
—CICERO (106–43 B.C.) *De Amicitia*

Absence from whom we love is worse than death
And frustrate hope severer than despair
—WILLIAM COWPER (1731–1800) *Despair at his Separation*

Love reckons hours for months, and days for years;
And every little absence is an age.
—JOHN DRYDEN (1631–1700) *Amphitryon*

Out of sight, out of mind
—HOMER (*c*. 10th–8th C. B.C.) *Odyssey*

Friendship, like love, is destroyed by long absence, though it may be increased by short intermissions.
—SAMUEL JOHNSON (1709–1784) *The Idler*

But O the heavy change, now thou art gone,
Now thou art gone, and never must return!
—JOHN MILTON (1608–1674) *Lycidas*

Two evils, monstrous either one apart
Possessed me, and were long and loath at going:
A cry of Absence, Absence, in the heart,
And in the wood the furious winter blowing.
—JOHN CROWE RANSOM (1888–1974) *Winter Remembered*

Hast thou no care of me? shall I abide
In this dull world, which in thy absence is
No better than a sty?
—SHAKESPEARE (1564–1616) *Antony and Cleopatra*, IV, xiii, 60

The Lord watch between me and thee, when we are absent from one another.
—OLD TESTAMENT: *Genesis*, xxxi, 49

Greater things are believed of those who are absent.
—TACITUS (*c*. 55–117) *Histories*

Action

I am perplexed . . . whether to act or not to act.
—AESCHYLUS (525–456 B.C.) *Suppliant Maidens*

Of every noble action the intent
Is to give worth reward, vice punishment.
—FRANCIS BEAUMONT (1584–1616) and JOHN FLETCHER (1579–1625) *The Captain*

The end of man is an action, not a thought.
—THOMAS CARLYLE (1795–1881) *Sartor Resartus*

Action may not always bring happiness; but there is no happiness without action.
—BENJAMIN DISRAELI (1804–1881) *Lothair*

A man's action is only a picture book of his creed.
—RALPH WALDO EMERSON (1803–1882)

Brave actions never want a Trumpet.
—THOMAS FULLER (1608–1681) *Gnomologia*

The great end of life is not knowledge, but action.
—T. H. HUXLEY (1825–1895) *Technical Education*

We would often be ashamed of our finest actions if the world understood all the motives which produced them.
—FRANÇOIS DE LA ROCHEFOUCAULD (1613–1680) *Maxims*

Actions speak louder than words.
—PROVERB

One hour of life, crowded to the full with glorious action, and filled with noble risks, is worth whole years of those mean observances of paltry decorum.
—SIR WALTER SCOTT (1771–1832) *Count Robert of Paris*

If it were done when 'tis done, then 'twere well
It were done quickly.
—SHAKESPEARE (1564–1616) *Macbeth*, I, vii, i

Heaven n'er helps the men who will not act.
—SOPHOCLES (495–406 B.C.) *Fragment*

No sooner said than done.
—TERENCE (*c.* 190–150 B.C.) *Eunuchus*

We cannot think first and act afterwards. From the moment of birth we are immersed in action, and can only fitfully guide it by taking thought.
—ALFRED NORTH WHITEHEAD (1861–1947)

Adversity

The virtue of prosperity is temperance; the virtue of adversity is fortitude. . . .
—FRANCIS BACON (1561–1620) *Essays*

Hope and patience are two sovereign remedies for all, the surest reposals, the softest cushions to lean on in adversity.
—ROBERT BURTON (1577–1640) *Anatomy of Melancholy*

Adversity is sometimes hard upon a man; but for one man who can stand prosperity there are a hundred that will stand adversity.
—THOMAS CARLYLE (1795–1881) *Heroes and Hero-Worship*

Friendship, of itself a holy tie,
Is made more sacred by adversity.
—JOHN DRYDEN (1631–1700) *The Hind and the Panther*

In time of prosperity friends will be plenty;
In time of adversity not one in twenty.
—JAMES HOWELL (1594?–1666) *Proverbs*

Mishaps are like knives, that either serve us or cut us, as we grasp them by the blade or the handle.
—HERMAN MELVILLE (1819–1891) *Cambridge Thirty Years Ago*

In adversity a man is saved by hope.
—MENANDER (342–291 B.C.) *Fragments*

It is a kingly action, believe me, to come to the help of those who are fallen.
—OVID (43 B.C.–A.D. 18?) *Epistulae ex Ponto*

Great men rejoice in adversity just as brave soldiers triumph in war.
—SENECA (4? B.C.–A.D. 65) *De Providentia*

Trial is the true test of mortal men.
—PINDAR (*c.* 522–442 B.C.) *Olympian Odes*

Of one ill comes many.
—SCOTTISH PROVERB

Sweet are the uses of adversity,
Which like the toad, ugly and venomous,
Wears yet a precious jewel in his head.
—SHAKESPEARE (1564–1616) *As You Like It*, II, i, 12

The worst is not
So long as we can say, "This is the worst."
—SHAKESPEARE (1564–1616) *King Lear*, IV, i, 28

It is the duty of all persons, when affairs are the most prosperous, then in especial to reflect within themselves in what way they are to endure adversity.
—TERENCE (*c.* 190–150 B.C.) *Phormio*

In the day of prosperity be joyful, but in the day of adversity consider.
—OLD TESTAMENT: *Ecclesiastes,* viii

A friend loveth at all times, and a brother is born for adversity.
—OLD TESTAMENT: *Proverbs,* xvii, 17

Advice

A fool sometimes gives weighty advice.
—NICHOLAS BOILEAU (1636–1711)

Who cannot give good counsel? 'Tis cheap, it costs them nothing.
—ROBERT BURTON (1577–1640) *Anatomy of Melancholy*

A woman's advice is not worth much, but he who doesn't heed it is a fool.
—PEDRO CALDERÓN (1600–1681) *El medico de su honra*

No one can give you better advice than yourself.
—CICERO (106–43 B.C.) *Ad Atticum*

We ask advice, but we mean approbation.
—CHARLES C. COLTON (1780?–1832) *Lacon*

When Thales was asked what was difficult, he said, "To know one's self." And what was easy, "To advise another."
—DIOGENES LAERTIUS (2nd or 3rd C.)

'Tis easier to advise the suffering than to bear suffering.
—EURIPIDES (480–406 B.C.) *Alcestis*

Don't give your advice before you are called upon.
—DESIDERIUS ERASMUS (1466–1536) *Adagia*

Whatever advice you give, be short.
—HORACE (B.C. 65–8) *Ars Poetica*

Advice is offensive, —because it shows us that we are known to others as well as to ourselves.
—SAMUEL JOHNSON (1709–1784) *The Rambler*

Advice is least heeded when most needed.
—ENGLISH PROVERB

Never advise anyone to go to war or to marry.
—SPANISH PROVERB

Many receive advice, only the wise profit by it.
—PUBLILIUS SYRUS (1st C. B.C.)

The only thing to do with good advice is to pass it on. It is never of any use to oneself.
—OSCAR WILDE (1854–1900) *An Ideal Husband*

Age

Age appears to be the best in four things—old wood best to burn, old wine to drink, old friends to trust, and old authors to read.
—FRANCIS BACON (1561–1620) *Apothegms*, No. 97

He lives long that lives till all are weary of him.
—HENRY GEORGE BOHN (1797–1884) *Handbook of Proverbs*

Grow old along with me!
The best is yet to be,
The last of life, for which the first was made.
—ROBERT BROWNING (1812–1889) *Rabbi Ben Ezra*

Let age approve of youth, and death complete the same.
—ROBERT BROWNING (1812–1889) *Rabbi Ben Ezra*

Young men think old men are fools; but old men *know* young men are fools.
—GEORGE CHAPMAN (1559?–1634?) *All Fools,* Act V

I am ready to meet my Maker. Whether my Maker is prepared for the great ordeal of meeting me is another matter.
—WINSTON CHURCHILL (1874–1965) remark on eve of his 75th birthday

For as I like a young man in whom there is something of the old, so I like an old man in whom there is something of the young.
—CICERO (106–43 B.C.) *De Senectute*

No one is so old as to think he cannot live one more year.
—CICERO (106–43 B.C.) *De Senectute*

A man is as old as he's feeling
A woman as old as she looks.
—MORTIMER COLLINS (1827–1876) *How Old Are You?*

Folly in youth is sin, in age is madness.
—SAMUEL DANIEL (1562–1619)

Age is like love; it cannot be hid.
—THOMAS DEKKER (1570?–1632) *Old Fortunatus,* Act II

Youth is a blunder; Manhood a struggle;
Old Age a regret.
—BENJAMIN DISRAELI (1804–1881) *Coningsby*

A woman is as old as she looks to a man that likes to look at her.
—FINLEY PETER DUNNE (1867–1936) *Old Age*

We do not count a man's years until he has nothing else to count.
—RALPH WALDO EMERSON (1803–1882)

Forty is the old age of youth; fifty is the youth of old age.
—VICTOR HUGO (1802–1885)

Whenever a man's friends begin to compliment him about looking young, he may be sure that they think he is growing old.
—WASHINGTON IRVING (1783–1859)

It was near a miracle to see an old man silent, since talking is the disease of age.
—BEN JONSON (1572–1637)

We hope to grow old, and we fear old age: that is to say, we love life and flee death.
—JEAN DE LA BRUYÈRE (1645–1696) *Caractères*

Of middle age the best that can be said is that a middle-aged person has likely learned how to have a little fun in spite of his troubles.
—DON MARQUIS (1878–1932) *The Almost Perfect State*

He who is of a calm and happy nature will hardly feel the pressure of Age, but to him who is of an opposite disposition, youth and age are equally a burden.
—PLATO (428–347 B.C.) *The Republic*

He whom the gods favour dies in youth.
—PLAUTUS (*c.* 254–184 B.C.) *Bacchides*

When men grow virtuous in old age, they only make a sacrifice to God of the devil's leavings.
—ALEXANDER POPE (1688–1744) *Thoughts on Various Subjects*

To the old cat give a tender mouse.
—ITALIAN PROVERB

Before old age my care was to live well; in old age, to die well.
—SENECA (4? B.C.–A.D. 65)

Age cannot wither her, nor custom stale
Her infinite variety.
—SHAKESPEARE (1564–1616) *Antony and Cleopatra,* II, ii, 243

No wise man ever wished to be younger.
—JONATHAN SWIFT (1667–1745)

To love is natural in a young man, a shame in an old one.
—PUBLILIUS SYRUS (1st C. B.C.)

Nobody loves life like an old man.
—SOPHOCLES (495–406 B.C.) *Acrisius,* Frag. 63

In the days of my youth I remembered my God,
And He hath not forgotten my age.
—ROBERT SOUTHEY (1774–1843) *The Old Man's Comforts*

We are always the same age inside.
—GERTRUDE STEIN (1874–1946)

A fool at forty is a fool indeed.
—EDWARD YOUNG (1683–1765) *Love of Fame*

Ambition

Every eel hopes to become a whale.
—GERMAN PROVERB

The same ambition can destroy or save,
And makes a patriot as it makes a knave.
—ALEXANDER POPE (1688–1744) *Essay on Man*

All ambitions are lawful except those which climb upward on the miseries or credulities of mankind.
—JOSEPH CONRAD (1857–1924) *Personal Record*

'Tis a laudable Ambition, that aims at being better than his Neighbours.
—BEN FRANKLIN (1706–1790) *Poor Richard's Almanack*

A man without ambition is like a woman without beauty.
—FRANK HARRIS (1856–1931) *Montes the Matador*

Ambition is a vice, but it may be the father of virtue.
—QUINTILIAN (40–*c.* 100)

The slave has but one master; the man of ambition has as many as there are people useful to his fortune.
—JEAN DE LA BRUYÈRE (1645–1696) *Caractères*

Ambition and suspicion always go together.
—GEORG CHRISTOPH LICHTENBERG (1742–1799)

The very substance of the ambitious is merely the shadow of a dream.
—SHAKESPEARE (1564–1616), *Hamlet,* II, ii, 268

America

Driven from every other corner of the earth, freedom of thought and the right of private judgment in matters of conscience direct their course to this happy country as their last asylum.
—SAMUEL ADAMS (1722–1803) Speech at Philadelphia, 1776

The South! the South! God knows what will become of her.
—JOHN C. CALHOUN (1782–1850) on his deathbed.

Our country! in her intercourse with foreign nations may she always be in the right; but our country, right or wrong!
—STEPHEN DECATUR (1779–1820) Toast at a dinner, 1816

I feel that you are justified in looking into the future with true assurance, because you have a mode of living in which we find the joy of life and the joy of work harmoniously combined. Added to this is the spirit of ambition which pervades your very being, and seems to make the day's work like a happy child at play.
—ALBERT EINSTEIN (1879–1955) New Year's Greeting, 1931

America means opportunity, freedom, power.
—RALPH WALDO EMERSON (1803–1882) Essays, Second Series

We must meet our duty and convince the world that we are just friends and brave enemies.
—THOMAS JEFFERSON (1743–1826)

The citizens of America have explored the sea and air. They have given open-handed hospitality and employment to people immigrating from every land. America has continued to overcome with courage the various difficulties that have arisen from time to time and to render her legislation ever more in keeping with the dignity of the human person.
—POPE JOHN XXIII (1881–1963), March 17, 1963

If we are to keep our system secure and our society stable, we must all begin to work where all of us work best—and that is in the communities where we all live.
—LYNDON B. JOHNSON (1908–1973) Speech, August, 1964

I am willing to love all mankind, except an American.
—SAMUEL JOHNSON (1709–1784) in Boswell's Life

And so, my fellow Americans: Ask not what your country can do for you—ask what you can do for your country.
—JOHN F. KENNEDY (1917–1963) Inauguration Speech, 1961

A citizen, first in war, first in peace, and first in the hearts of his countrymen.
—GENERAL HENRY "LIGHT-HORSE HARRY" LEE (1756–1818)

Intellectually I know that America is no better than any other country; emotionally I know she is better than every other country.
—SINCLAIR LEWIS (1885–1951) Interview in Berlin, 1930

In the wars of the European powers in matters relating to themselves we have never taken any part, nor does it comport with our policy so to do. It is only when our rights are invaded or seriously menaced that we resent injuries or make preparation for our defence.
—JAMES MONROE (1758–1831) Message to Congress, 1823

The United States never lost a war or won a conference.
—WILL ROGERS (1879–1935)

There is a homely adage which runs, "Speak softly and carry a big stick; you will go far." If the American nation will speak softly and yet build and keep at a pitch of the highest training the Monroe Doctrine will go far.
—THEODORE ROOSEVELT (1858–1919)

Every American takes pride in our tradition of hospitality, to men of all races and all creeds. We must be constantly vigilant against the attacks of intolerance and injustice. We must scrupulously guard the civil rights and civil liberties of all citizens, whatever their background.
—FRANKLIN D. ROOSEVELT (1882–1945)

Yesterday, December 7, 1941—a date that will live in infamy—the United States of America was suddenly and deliberately attacked by naval and air forces of the Empire of Japan.
—FRANKLIN D. ROOSEVELT, 1941

In the four quarters of the globe, who reads an American book? or goes to an American play? or looks at an American picture or statue? What does the world yet owe to American physicians or surgeons? . . . What have they done in mathematics? Who drinks out of American glasses? . . . or wears American coats and gowns? . . . Finally, under which of the old tyrannical governments of Europe is every sixth man a slave . . . ?
—SIDNEY SMITH (1771–1845) in the Edinburgh Review, 1820

Liberty and Union, now and forever, one and inseparable!
—DANIEL WEBSTER (1782–1852) Speech, 1830

The Americans, like the English, probably make love worse than any other race.
—WALT WHITMAN (1819–1892) An American Primer

Our whole duty, for the present at any rate, is summed up in the motto: America first.
—WOODROW WILSON (1856–1924) Speech, 1915

America is God's crucible, the great Melting-Pot where all the races of Europe are melting and re-forming.
—ISRAEL ZANGWILL (1864–1926) The Melting-Pot

Anger

I was angry with my friend:
I told my wrath, my wrath did end.
I was angry with my foe;
I told it not, my wrath did grow.
—WILLIAM BLAKE (1757–1827) Christian Forbearance

Anger begins with folly and ends with repentance.
—HENRY GEORGE BOHN (1796–1884) Handbook of Proverbs

Truly to moderate your mind and speech when you are angry, or else to hold your peace, betokens no ordinary nature.
—CICERO (106–43 B.C.) Epistolae Quintum Fratrem

Beware the fury of a patient man.
—JOHN DRYDEN (1631–1700) Absalom and Achitophel

Anger and folly walk cheek by jowl;
repentance treads on both their heels.
—BEN FRANKLIN (1706–1790) Poor Richard's Almanack

Two things a man should never be angry at: what he can help, and what he cannot help.
—THOMAS FULLER (1608–1681) Historie of the Holy Warre

Temper: a quality that, at critical moments, brings out the best in steel and the worst in people.
—OSCAR HAMMLING (1890–   ) Laconics

Let anger's fire be slow to burn.
—GEORGE HERBERT (1593–1633) Jacula Prudentum

When I am angry I can write, pray, and preach well, for then my whole temperament is quickened, my understanding sharpened, and all mundane vexations and temptations depart.
—MARTIN LUTHER (1483–1546) Table-Talk

The best answer to anger is silence.
—GERMAN PROVERB

A soft answer turneth away wrath; but grievous words stir up anger.
—OLD TESTAMENT: Proverbs, xv, i

April See MONTHS

Art

It is the glory and good of Art,
That Art remains the one way possible
Of speaking truth. . . .
—ROBERT BROWNING (1812–1889) The Ring and the Book

Art imitates nature as well as it can, as a pupil follows his master; thus is it a sort of grandchild of God.
—DANTE (1265–1321) *Inferno*, Canto xi

In life beauty perishes, but not in art.
—LEONARDO DA VINCI (1452–1519) *Notebook*

Great art is the contempt of a great man for small art.
—F. SCOTT FITZGERALD (1896–1940) *Notebooks*

Nobody, I think, ought to read poetry, or look at pictures or statues, who cannot find a great deal more in them than the poet or artist has actually expressed.
—NATHANIEL HAWTHORNE (1804–1864) *The Marble Faun*

Rules and models destroy genius and art.
—WILLIAM HAZLITT (1778–1830) *On Taste*

Life is short, the art long, opportunity fleeting, experience treacherous, judgment difficult.
—HIPPOCRATES (460?–377? B.C.) *Aphorisms*

Art may make a suit of clothes; but Nature must produce a man.
—DAVID HUME (1711–1776) *Essays: The Epicurean*, 15

Art is nothing more than the shadow of humanity.
—HENRY JAMES (1843–1916) *Lectures*

Art hath an enemy called ignorance.
—BEN JONSON (1574–1637)

The true work of art is but a shadow of the divine perfection.
—MICHELANGELO (1475–1564)

To have faithfully studied the honorable arts, softens the manners and keeps them free from harshness.
—OVID (43 B.C.–A.D. 18?) *Epistles*

There are three arts which are concerned with all things: one which uses, another which makes, and a third which imitates them.
—PLATO (428–347 B.C.) *The Republic*

True artists are almost the only men who do their work with pleasure.
—AUGUSTE RODIN (1840–1917)

When love and skill work together expect a masterpiece.
—JOHN RUSKIN (1819–1900)

Art is not a handicraft; it is the transmission of feeling the artist has experienced.
—LEO TOLSTOY (1828–1910) *What is Art?*

A work of art is a corner of creation seen through a temperament.
—ÉMILE ZOLA (1840–1902) *Mes Haines*

An artist may visit a museum, but only a pedant can live there.
—GEORGE SANTAYANA (1853–1952) *Life of Reason*

August See MONTHS

Autumn

Autumn wins you best by this, its mute
Appeal to sympathy for its decay.
—ROBERT BROWNING (1812–1889) *Paracelsus*

All-cheering Plenty, with her flowing horn,
Led yellow Autumn, wreath'd with nodding corn.
—ROBERT BURNS (1759–1796) *The Brigs of Ayr*

The melancholy days are come, the saddest of the year,
Of wailing winds, and naked woods, and meadows brown
            and sear.
—WILLIAM CULLEN BRYANT (1794–1878) *The Death of the Flowers*

She loves the bare, the withered tree;
She walks the sodden pasture lane.
—ROBERT FROST (1875–1963) *My November Guest*

Dread autumn, harvest-season of the Goddess of Death.
—HORACE (65–8 B.C.) *Satires*

A solemn land of long-fulfilled desires
Is this, and year by year the self-same fires
Burn in the trees.
—MARY WEBB (1881–1927) *The Plain in Autumn*

Avarice

Be not penny-wise; riches have wings, and sometimes they fly away of themselves, sometimes they must be set flying to bring in more.
—FRANCIS BACON (1561–1620) *Essays: Of Riches*

If you would abolish avarice, you must abolish its mother, luxury.
—CICERO (106–43 B.C.) *De Oratore*

Would'st thou both eat thy cake and have it?
—GEORGE HERBERT (1593–1633) *The Size*

It is sheer madness to live in want in order to be wealthy when you die.
—JUVENAL (c. 60–c. 130) *Satires*

The beautiful eyes of my money-box!
He speaks of it as a lover of his mistress.
—MOLIÈRE (1622–1673) *L'Avare*

They are greedy dogs which can never have enough.
—OLD TESTAMENT: *Isaiah*, lvi, 11

Baby See CHILDREN

Beauty

Beauty is a gift of God.
—ARISTOTLE (384–322 B.C.) *Apothegm*

There is no excellent beauty that hath not some strangeness in the proportion.
—FRANCIS BACON (1561–1620) *Essays: Of Beauty*

Beauty is not caused. It is.
—EMILY DICKINSON (1830–1886) *Further Poems*

No Spring, nor Summer beauty hath such grace,
As I have seen in one Autumnal face.
—JOHN DONNE (1572–1631) *Elegies*

Beauty is in the eye of the beholder.
—MARGARET W. HUNGERFORD (1855?–1897)

A thing of beauty is a joy forever;
Its loveliness increases; it will never
Pass into nothingness. . . .
—JOHN KEATS (1795–1821) *Endymion*

"Beauty is truth, truth beauty," that is all
Ye know on earth, and all ye need to know.
—JOHN KEATS (1795–1821) *Ode on a Grecian Urn*

Euclid alone
Has looked on Beauty bare.
—EDNA ST. VINCENT MILLAY (1892–1951) *Sonnets*

Beauty and wisdom are seldom found together.
—PETRONIUS ARBITER (1st C. A.D.) *Satyricon*

It is the beautiful bird that gets caged.
—CHINESE PROVERB

Beauty provoketh thieves sooner than gold.
—SHAKESPEARE (1564–1616) *As You Like It*, I, iii, 13

O how can beautie maister the most strong!
—EDMUND SPENSER (1552?–1599) *Faerie Queene*

Boy See CHILDREN

Children

It is a great happiness to see our children rising round us, but from that good fortune spring the bitterest woes of man.
—AESCHYLUS (525–456 B.C.) *Agamemnon*

Cornelia kept her in talk till her children came from school, "And these," said she, "are my jewels."
—ROBERT BURTON (1557–1640) *Anatomy of Melancholy*

Respect the child. Be not too much his parent.
Trespass not on his solitude.
—RALPH WALDO EMERSON (1803–1882)

To a father waxing old nothing is dearer than a daughter. Sons have spirits of higher pitch, but less inclined to sweet, endearing fondness.
—EURIPIDES (480–406 B.C.)

An undutiful Daughter will prove an unmanageable Wife.
—BEN FRANKLIN (1706–1790) *Poor Richard's Almanack*

It is a wise child that knows his own father.
—HOMER (10th–8th C. B.C.) *Odyssey*

Children have more need of models than of critics.
—JOSEPH JOUBERT (1754–1824) *Pensées*, No. 261

Between the dark and the daylight,
When the night is beginning to lower,
Comes a pause in the day's occupations
That is known as the children's hour.
—HENRY W. LONGFELLOW (1807–1882) *The Children's Hour*

Suffer the little children to come unto me, and forbid them not; for such is the kingdom of God.
—NEW TESTAMENT: *Mark*, x, 14; *Luke*, xviii, 16

It were better for him that a millstone were hanged about his neck, and he cast into the sea, than that he should offend one of these little ones.
—NEW TESTAMENT: *Luke*, xvii, 2

Out of the mouths of babes and sucklings hast thou ordained strength.
—OLD TESTAMENT: *Psalms*, viii, 2

The wildest colts make the best horses.
—PLUTARCH (46–120)

A wise son maketh a glad father.
—OLD TESTAMENT: *Proverbs*, x, 1

Even a child is known by his doings.
—OLD TESTAMENT: *Proverbs*, xx, 11

Behold the child, by nature's kindly law,
Pleased with a rattle, tickled with a straw.
—ALEXANDER POPE (1688–1744) *Essay on Man*

Lacking all sense of right and wrong, a child can do nothing which is morally evil, or which merits either punishment or reproof.
—JEAN-JACQUES ROUSSEAU (1712–1778) *Emile*

At first the infant,
Mewling and puking in the nurse's arms.
And then the whining school-boy, with his satchel,
And shining morning face, creeping like snail
Unwillingly to school.
—SHAKESPEARE (1564–1616) *As You Like It*, II, viii, 143

I do not love him because he is good, but because he is my little child.
—SIR RABINDRANATH TAGORE (1861–1941) *The Crescent Moon*

A child tells in the street what its father and mother say at home.
—THE TALMUD

A babe in a house is a well-spring of pleasure.
—MARTIN FARQUHAR TUPPER (1810–1889) *Of Education*

Heaven lies about us in our infancy.
—WILLIAM WORDSWORTH (1770–1850) *Intimations of Immortality*

The child is father of the man.
—WILLIAM WORDSWORTH (1770–1850) *My Heart Leaps up When I Behold*

Civilization

Civilization degrades the many to exalt the few.
—BRONSON ALCOTT (1799–1888) *Table-Talk*

Increased means and increased leisure are the two civilizers of man.
—BENJAMIN DISRAELI (1804–1881) Speech, 1872

The true test of civilization is not the census, nor the size of cities, nor the crops, —no, but the kind of man the country turns out.
—RALPH WALDO EMERSON (1803–1882) *Essays: Society and Solitude*.

No one is so savage that he cannot become civilized, if he will lend a patient ear to culture.
—HORACE (65–8 B.C.) *Epistles*

Things have their day, and their beauties in that day. It would be preposterous to expect any one civilization to last forever.
—GEORGE SANTAYANA (1863–1952) *Character and Opinion in the United States*

A civilization which develops only on its material side, and not in corresponding measure on its mental and spiritual side, is like a vessel with a defective steering gear. . . .
—ALBERT SCHWEITZER (1875–1965) *The Decay and Restoration of Civilization*

Common Sense

If a man can have only one kind of sense, let him have common sense. If he has that and uncommon sense too, he is not far from genius.
—HENRY WARD BEECHER (1813–1887)

Nothing astonishes men so much as common sense and plain dealing.
—RALPH WALDO EMERSON (1803–1882) *Art*

Where sense is wanting, everything is wanting.
—BEN FRANKLIN (1706–1790) *Poor Richard's Almanack*

Common sense is only a modification of talent. Genius is an exaltation of it.
—EDWARD BULWER-LYTTON (1803–1873)

Common sense is not so common.
—VOLTAIRE (1694–1778) *Philosophical Dictionary*

Compensation

For every thing you have missed, you have gained something else; and for every thing you gain, you lose something.
—RALPH WALDO EMERSON (1803–1882) *Compensation*

For all our works a recompense is sure:
'Tis sweet to think on what was hard t'endure.
—ROBERT HERRICK (1591–1674) *Hesperides*

It is a comfort that the medal has two sides. There is much vice and misery in the world, I know; but more virtue and happiness, I believe.
—THOMAS JEFFERSON (1743–1826)

Whoever tries for great objects must suffer something.
—PLUTARCH (46?–120?) *Lives*

There is no evil without its compensation. Avarice promises money; luxury, pleasure; ambition, a purple robe.
—SENECA (4? B.C.–A.D. 65) *Epistulae ad Lucillium*

Give unto them beauty for ashes, the oil of joy for mourning, the garment of praise for the spirit of heaviness.
—OLD TESTAMENT: *Isaiah*, lxi, 3

Conceit See EGOTISM

Conscience

Conscience and reputation are two things. Conscience is due to yourself, reputation to your neighbor.
—ST. AUGUSTINE (354–430)

There is another man within me that's angry with me.
—SIR THOMAS BROWNE (1605–1682) *Religio Medici*

Conscience, good my lord,
Is but the pulse of reason.
—SAMUEL TAYLOR COLERIDGE (1772–1834) *Zapolya*

The still small voice.
—WILLIAM COWPER (1731–1800) *The Task*

A good conscience is a continual Christmas.
—BEN FRANKLIN (1706–1790) *Poor Richard's Almanack*

The man who acts never has any conscience; no one has any conscience but the man who thinks.
—GOETHE (1749–1832)

That fierce thing
They call a conscience.
—THOMAS HOOD (1799–1845) *Lamia*

The sting of conscience, like the gnawing of a dog at a bone, is mere foolishness.
—FRIEDRICH NIETZSCHE (1844–1900) *Human All-too-Human*

There is no witness so terrible, no accuser so potent, as the conscience that dwells in every man's breast.
—POLYBIUS (c. 204–122 B.C.) *Histories*

The worm of conscience keeps the same hours as the owl.
—SCHILLER (1759–1805) *Kabale und Liebe*

The play's the thing
Wherein I'll catch the conscience of the king.
—SHAKESPEARE (1564–1616) *Hamlet*, II, ii, 641

Trust that man in nothing who has not a conscience in everything.
—LAURENCE STERNE (1713–1768) *Tristram Shandy*

Conscience is, in most men, an anticipation of the opinion of others.
—SIR HENRY TAYLOR (1800–1886) *The Statesman*

Conscience and cowardice are really the same thing.
—OSCAR WILDE (1854–1900) *The Picture of Dorian Gray*

Conservatism

The absurd man is one who never changes.
—AUGUSTE BARTHELEMY (1796–1867) *Nemesis*

Conservative: A statesman who is enamored of existing evils, as distinguished from the Liberal who wishes to replace them with others.
—AMBROSE BIERCE (1842–1914?) *The Devil's Dictionary*

A conservative government is an organized hypocrisy.
—BENJAMIN DISRAELI (1804–1881)

A conservative is a man who is too cowardly to fight and too fat to run.
—ELBERT HUBBARD (1856–1915) *Epigrams*

What is conservatism? Is it not adherence to the old and tried, against the new and untried?
—ABRAHAM LINCOLN (1809–1865) *Cooper Union Address*, 1860

Be not the first by whom the new are tried,
Nor yet the last to lay the old aside.
—ALEXANDER POPE (1688–1744) *Essay on Criticism*

The man for whom the law exists—the man of forms, the Conservative, is a tame man.
—HENRY DAVID THOREAU (1817–1862) *An Essay on Civil Disobedience*

Constancy and Inconstancy

Without constancy there is neither love, friendship, nor virtue in the world.
—JOSEPH ADDISON (1672–1719)

It is as absurd to say that a man can't love one woman all the time as it is to say that a violinist needs several violins to play the same piece of music.
—HONORÉ DE BALZAC (1799–1850) *Physiology of Marriage*

A good man it is not mine to see. Could I see a man possessed of constancy, that would satisfy me.
—CONFUCIUS (c. 551–478 B.C.) *Analects*

What is there in this vile earth that more commendeth a woman than constancy?
—JOHN LYLY (1554?–1606) *Euphues*

There are two sorts of constancy in love—one rises from continually discovering in the loved person new subjects for love, the other arises from our making a merit of being constant.
—FRANÇOIS DE LA ROCHEFOUCAULD (1613–1680) *Maxims*

But I am constant as the northern star,
Of whose true-fix'd and resting quality
There is no fellow in the firmament.
—SHAKESPEARE (1564–1616) *Julius Caesar*, III, i, 58

There is nothing in this world constant but inconstancy.
—JONATHAN SWIFT (1667–1745)

Contempt

Familiarity breeds contempt, while rarity wins admiration.
—APULEIUS (2nd C.) *De Deo Socratis*

None but the contemptible are apprehensive of contempt.
—FRANÇOIS DE LA ROCHEFOUCAULD (1613–1680) *Maxims*

Here is another man with whom I cannot get angry, because I despise him.
—BENITO MUSSOLINI (1883–1945)

Man is much more sensitive to the contempt of others than to self-contempt.
—FRIEDRICH NIETZSCHE (1844–1900) *Human All-too-Human*

Contempt penetrates even the shell of the tortoise.
—PERSIAN PROVERB

Content and Discontent

No form of society can be reasonably stable in which the majority of the people are not fairly content. People cannot be content if they feel that the foundations of their lives are wholly unstable.
—JAMES TRUSLOW ADAMS (1878–1949) *Record of America*

Be content with your lot; one cannot be first in everything.
—AESOP (6th C. B.C.) *The Peacock and Juno*

A perverse and fretful disposition makes any state of life unhappy.
—CICERO (106–43 B.C.) *De Senectute*

Who is rich? He that is content. Who is that? Nobody.
—BEN FRANKLIN (1706–1790) *Poor Richard's Almanack*

Unhappy man! He frets at the narrow limits of the world.
—JUVENAL (*c.* 60–*c.* 130 A.D.)

When we cannot find contentment in ourselves it is useless to seek it elsewhere.
—FRANÇOIS DE LA ROCHEFOUCAULD (1613–1680) *Maxims*

Discontent is the first step in the progress of a man or nation.
—OSCAR WILDE (1854–1900) *A Woman of No Importance*

Poor in abundance, famish'd at a feast.
—EDWARD YOUNG (1683–1765) *Night Thoughts*

I have learned, in whatsoever state I am, therewith to be content.
—NEW TESTAMENT: *Hebrews,* iv, 11

Courage

Often the test of courage is not to die but to live.
—VITTORIO ALFIERI (1749–1803) *Oreste*

But where life is more terrible than death, it is then the truest valor to dare to live.
—SIR THOMAS BROWNE (1663–1704) *Religio Medici*

Courage is that virtue which champions the cause of right.
—CICERO (106–43 B.C.) *De Officiis*

Every man of courage is a man of his word.
—PIERRE CORNEILLE (1606–1684) *Le Menteur*

Courage consists in equality to the problem before us.
—RALPH WALDO EMERSON (1803–1882) *Society and Solitude*

Courage may be taught as a child is taught to speak.
—EURIPIDES (480–406 B.C.) *The Suppliant Women*

A decent boldness ever meets with friends.
—HOMER (*c.* 10th C.–8th C. B.C.) *Iliad*

Nothing is too high for the daring of mortals; we storm
Heaven itself in our folly.
—HORACE (65–8 B.C.) *Odes*

It is better to die on your feet than to live on your knees.
—LA PASIONARIA (1895–   ) Speech at Paris, 1936

True courage is to do, without witnesses, everything that one is capable of doing before all the world.
—FRANÇOIS DE LA ROCHEFOUCAULD (1613–1680) *Maxims*

What though the field be lost?
All is not lost; th'unconquerable will,
And study of revenge, immortal hate,
And courage never to submit or yield.
—JOHN MILTON (1608–1674) *Paradise Lost*

The strongest, most generous, and proudest of all virtues is true courage.
—MICHEL DE MONTAIGNE (1533–1592) *Essays*

Be of good cheer: it is I; be not afraid.
—NEW TESTAMENT: *Matthew,* xiv, 27

We shall attack and attack until we are exhausted, and then we shall attack again.
—GENERAL GEORGE S. PATTON (1885–1945) Address to his troops before the invasion of North Africa, 1942

The smallest worm will turn being trodden on,
And doves will peck in safeguard of their brood.
—SHAKESPEARE (1564–1616) *III Henry VI,* II, ii, 17

Why, courage then! What cannot be avoided
'Twere childish weakness to lament or fear.
—SHAKESPEARE (1564–1616) *Henry VI,* V, iv, 37

Courtship

Those marriages generally abound most with love and constancy that are preceded by a long courtship.
—JOSEPH ADDISON (1672–1719) *The Spectator*

He that will win his dame must do
As love does when he draws his bow;
With one hand thrust the lady from,
And with the other pull her home.
—SAMUEL BUTLER (1612–1680) *Hudibras*

Courtship to marriage is but as the music in the playhouse till the curtain's drawn.
—WILLIAM CONGREVE (1670–1729) *The Old Bachelor*

If I am not worth the wooing, I am surely not worth the winning.
—HENRY W. LONGFELLOW (1807–1882) *Courtship of Miles Standish*

Had we but world enough and time
This coyness, lady, were no crime.
—ANDREW MARVELL (1621–1678) *To His Coy Mistress*

I will now court her in the conqueror's style;
"Come, see, and overcome."
—PHILIP MASSINGER (1583–1640) *Maid of Honor*

We cannot fight for love, as men may do;
We should be woo'd and were not made to woo.
—SHAKESPEARE (1564–1616) *Midsummer Night's Dream,* II, i, 241

The weather is usually fine when people are courting.
—R. L. STEVENSON (1850–1894) *Virginibus Puerisque*

A man always chases a woman until she catches him.
—UNKNOWN

Courtesy

If a man be gracious and courteous to strangers it shows he is a citizen of the world.
—FRANCIS BACON (1561–1620) *Essays*

Politeness. The most acceptable hypocrisy.
—AMBROSE BIERCE (1842–1914?) *Devil's Dictionary*

'Tis ill talking of halters in the house of a man that was hanged.
—CERVANTES (1547–1616) *Don Quixote*, Pt. i

Politeness is the ritual of society, as prayers are of the church.
—RALPH WALDO EMERSON (1803–1882) *English Traits*

Be civil to all; sociable to many; familiar with few.
—BEN FRANKLIN (1706–1790) *Poor Richard's Almanack*

He was so generally civil, that nobody thanked him for it.
—SAMUEL JOHNSON (1709–1784) in Boswell's *Life*

Civility is a desire to receive it in turn, and to be accounted well bred.
—FRANÇOIS DE LA ROCHEFOUCAULD (1613–1680) *Maxims*

Politeness costs nothing and gains everything.
—LADY MARY WORTLEY MONTAGU (1689–1762) Letters

It is one of the greatest blessings that so many women are so full of tact. The calamity happens when a woman who has all the other riches of life just lacks that one thing.
—SIR WILLIAM OSLER (1848–1919)

True politeness consists in being easy one's self, and in making every one about one as easy as one can.
—ALEXANDER POPE (1688–1744) *Table-Talk*

To speak kindly does not hurt the tongue.
—FRENCH PROVERB

Dissembling courtesy! How fine this tyrant
Can tickle where she wounds!
—SHAKESPEARE (1564–1616) *Cymbeline*, I, i, 84

The greater man the greater courtesy.
—TENNYSON (1809–1882) *The Last Tournament*

Cowardice

Coward. One who in a perilous emergency thinks with his legs.
—AMBROSE BIERCE (1842–1914?) *Devil's Dictionary*

To see what is right and not do it is want of courage.
—CONFUCIUS (551–478 B.C.) *Analects*

The coward never on himself relies,
But to an equal for assistance flies.
—GEORGE CRABBE (1754–1832) *The Gentleman Farmer*

Many would be cowards if they had courage enough.
—THOMAS FULLER (1608–1681) *Gnomologia*

Ever will a coward show no mercy.
—SIR THOMAS MALORY (f. 1470) *Morte d'Arthur*

It is the act of a coward to wish for death.
—OVID (43 B.C.–A.D. 18?) *Metamorphoses*

The coward calls himself cautious.
—PUBLILIUS SYRUS (1st C. B.C.) *Sententiae*

A cowardly cur barks more fiercely than it bites.
—QUINTUS CURTIUS RUFUS (*c*. 2nd C. A.D.) *De Rebus Gestis Alexandri Magni*

When all the blandishments of life are gone,
The coward sneaks to death, the brave live on.
—GEORGE SEWELL (d. 1726)

A coward, a most devout coward, religious in it.
—SHAKESPEARE (1564–1616) *Twelfth Night*, III, iv, 427

Cowards die many times before their deaths;
The valiant never taste of death but once.
—SHAKESPEARE (1564–1616) *Julius Caesar*, II, ii, 32

Criticism

Criticism is a disinterested endeavour to learn and propagate the best that is known and thought in the world.
—MATTHEW ARNOLD (1822–1888) *Essays in Criticism*

As the arts advance towards their perfection, the science of criticism advances with equal pace.
—EDMUND BURKE (1729–1797) *On the Sublime and Beautiful*

Let dull critics feed upon the carcasses of plays; give me the taste and the dressing.
—LORD CHESTERFIELD (1694–1773) *Letters to his Son*

Critics—murderers!
—SAMUEL TAYLOR COLERIDGE (1772–1834)

Those who write ill, and they who ne'er durst write,
Turn critics out of mere revenge and spite.
—JOHN DRYDEN (1631–1700) *Conquest of Granada*

Blame where you must, be candid where you can,
And be each critic the Good-natured Man.
—OLIVER GOLDSMITH (1728–1774) *Good-Natured Man*

Criticism is the art wherewith a critic tries to guess himself into a share of the artist's fame.
—GEORGE JEAN NATHAN (1882–1958) *House of Satan*

Damn with faint praise, assent with civil leer
And without sneering teach the rest to sneer.
—ALEXANDER POPE (1688–1744) *Epistle to Dr. Arbuthnot*

They damn what they do not understand.
—QUINTILIAN (*c*. 40–100 A.D.) *De Institutione Oratoria*

Critic: a man who writes about things he doesn't like.
—UNKNOWN

Really to stop criticism they say one must die.
—VOLTAIRE (1694–1778)

Curiosity

This disease of curiosity.
—ST. AUGUSTINE (354–430) *Confessions*

The first and simplest emotion which we discover in the human mind is curiosity.
—EDMUND BURKE (1729–1797) *The Sublime and Beautiful*

Shun the inquisitive person, for he is also a talker.
—HORACE (65–8 B.C.) *Epistles*

Curiosity is one of the most permanent and certain characteristics of a vigorous intellect.
—SAMUEL JOHNSON (1709–1784) *The Rambler*

Curiosity killed the cat.
—AMERICAN PROVERB

He that pryeth into every cloud may be struck by a thunderbolt.
—JOHN RAY (1627?–1705) *English Proverbs*

You know what a woman's curiosity is. Almost as great as a man's!
—OSCAR WILDE (1854–1900) *An Ideal Husband*

Curiosity. The reason why most of us haven't committed suicide long ago.
—UNKNOWN

Danger

Dangers bring fears, and fears more dangers bring.
—RICHARD BAXTER (1615–1691) *Love Breathing Thanks*

Danger, the spur of all great minds.
—GEORGE CHAPMAN (1559?–1634?) *Bussy d'Ambois*

Moving of the earth brings harms and fears.
Men reckon what it did and meant.
But trepidation of the spheres
Though greater far, is innocent.
—JOHN DONNE (1573–1631) *Valediction Forbidding Mourning*

As soon as there is life there is danger.
—RALPH WALDO EMERSON (1803–1882) *Lectures*

Great perils have this beauty, that they bring to light the fraternity of strangers.
—VICTOR HUGO (1802–1885) *Les Misérables*

Out of this nettle, danger, we pluck this flower, safety.
—SHAKESPEARE (1564–1616) *I Henry IV,* II, iii, 10

Better face a danger once than be always in fear.
—PROVERB

Darkness See NIGHT

Daughter See CHILDREN

Dawn See DAY

Day

Day is a snow-white Dove of heaven
That from the East glad message brings.
—THOMAS BAILEY ALDRICH (1836–1907) *Day and Night*

Day!
O'er nights brim, day boils at last;
Boils, pure gold, o'er the cloud-cup's brim.
—ROBERT BROWNING (1812–1889) *Pippa Passes*

One day well spent is to be preferred to an eternity of error.
—CICERO (106–43 B.C.) *Tusculanarum Disputationum*

He is only rich who owns the day. There is no king, rich man, fairy, or demon who possesses such power as that. . . . The days are made on a loom whereof the warp and woof are past and future time.
—RALPH WALDO EMERSON (1803–1882) *Society and Solitude*

Rosy-fingered Dawn.
—HOMER (10th–8th? C. B.C.) *Iliad*

The day has eyes; the night has ears.
—PROVERB

Wait till it is night before saying it has been a fine day.
—FRENCH PROVERB

My days are swifter than a weaver's shuttle.
—OLD TESTAMENT: *Job,* vii, 6

Listen to the Exhortation of the Dawn!
Look to this Day! For it is Life,
The very Life of Life.
— *Salutation of the Dawn* (SANSKRIT)

The glow-worm shows the matin to be near,
And 'gins to pale his uneffectual fire.
—SHAKESPEARE (1564–1616) *Hamlet,* I, v, 89

Night's candles are burnt out, and jocund day
Stands tiptoe on the misty mountaintops.
—SHAKESPEARE (1564–1616) *Romeo and Juliet,* III, v, 9

Death

Death is a black camel, which kneels at the gates of all.
—ABD-EL-KADER (1807?–1883)

It is good to die before one has done anything deserving death.
—ANANANDRIDES (4th C. B.C.) *Fragment*

Men fear death as children fear to go in the dark; and as that natural fear in children is increased with tales, so is the other.
—FRANCIS BACON (1561–1620) *Essays: Of Death*

He that unburied lies wants not his hearse,
For unto him a Tomb's the Universe.
—SIR THOMAS BROWNE (1605–1682) *Religio Medici*

We all labor against our own cure, for death is the cure of all diseases.
—SIR THOMAS BROWNE (1605–1682) *Religio Medici*

The fear of death is worse than death.
—ROBERT BURTON (1577–1640) *Anatomy of Melancholy*

Ah, surely nothing dies but something mourns!
—LORD BYRON (1788–1824) *Don Juan*

Death levels all things.
—CLAUDIAN (*c.* 395) *De Raptu Proserpinae*

These have not the hope of death.
—DANTE (1265–1321) *Inferno*

Death, be not proud, though some have called thee
Mighty and dreadful, for thou art not so:
For those, whom thou think'st thou dost overthrow,
Die not, poor Death. . .
—JOHN DONNE (1572–1631) *Divine Poems: Holy Sonnet*

There were some who said that a man at the point of death was more free than all others, because death breaks every bond, and over the dead the united world has no power.
—FÉNELON (1651–1715) *Telemachus*

Death is Nature's expert advice to get plenty of Life.
—GOETHE (1749–1832)

We die ourselves a little every time we kill in others something that deserved to live.
—OSCAR HAMMLING (1890–   ) *Laconics*

I have been half in love with easeful death,
Call'd him soft names in many a mused rhyme.
—JOHN KEATS (1795–1821) *Ode to a Nightingale*

So now he is a legend when he would have preferred to be a man.
—MRS. JACQUELINE KENNEDY (1929–   ) in a tribute to her husband, Nov. 1964

Wheresoever ye be, death will overtake you, although ye be in lofty towers.
—THE KORAN

A man's dying is more the survivors' affair than his own.
—THOMAS MANN (1875–1955) *The Magic Mountain*

The grave's a fine and private place,
But none, I think, do there embrace.
—ANDREW MARVELL (1621–1678) *To His Coy Mistress*

Death has a thousand doors to let out life.
I shall find one.
—PHILIP MASSINGER (1584–1640) *A Very Woman*

Whom the gods love dies young.
—MENANDER (342–291 B.C.)

Dead men tell no tales.
—ENGLISH PROVERB

To die at the will of another is to die twice.
—PUBLILIUS SYRUS (*b*. 1st C. B.C.) *Sententiae*

Death seems to provide the minds of the Anglo-Saxon race with a greater fund of innocent amusement than any other single subject.
—DOROTHY L. SAYERS (1893–1957)

I have a rendezvous with Death
At some disputed barricade . . .
—ALAN SEEGER (1888–1916) *I Have a Rendezvous with Death*

Death is a punishment to some, to some a gift, and to many a favor.
—SENECA (4? B.C.–A.D. 65)

Nothing in his life became him like the leaving it . . . .
—SHAKESPEARE (1564–1616) *Macbeth*, I, iv, 7

Imperious Caesar, dead and turn'd to clay,
Might stop a hole to keep the wind away.
—SHAKESPEARE (1564–1616) *Hamlet*, V, i, 235

    To die, —to sleep,
No more, and by that sleep to say we end
The heart-ache and the thousand natural shocks
That flesh is heir to . . . .
—SHAKESPEARE (1564–1616) *Hamlet*, III, i, 60

Say nothing but good of the dead.
—SOLON (638–559 B.C.)

Do not go gentle into that good night,
Old age should burn and rave at close of day;
Rage, rage against the dying of the light.
—DYLAN THOMAS (1914–1953) *Poem to My Father*

I saw him now going the way of all flesh.
—JOHN WEBSTER (1580–1625) *Westward Ho!*, Act II

O death, where is thy sting? O grave, where is thy victory?
—NEW TESTAMENT: *I Corinthians*, xv, 55

I looked and beheld a pale horse: and his name that sat on him was Death.
—NEW TESTAMENT: *Revelation*, vi, 8

Dust thou art, and unto dust shalt thou return.
—OLD TESTAMENT: *Genesis*, iii, 19

Deceit

God is not averse to deceit in a holy cause.
—AESCHYLUS (525–456 B.C.)

We are never deceived; we deceive ourselves.
—GOETHE (1749–1832)

Hateful to me as the gates of hell,
Is he, who, hiding one thing in his heart,
Utters another.
—HOMER (*c*. 10th–8th C. B.C.) *Iliad*

It is a double pleasure to deceive the deceiver.
—JEAN DE LA FONTAINE (1621–1695) *Fables*

The surest way to be deceived is to think one's self more clever than others.
—FRANÇOIS DE LA ROCHEFOUCAULD (1613–1680) *Maxims*

You can fool some of the people all of the time, and all of the people some of the time, but you cannot fool all of the people all of the time.
—ABRAHAM LINCOLN (1809–1865)

Listen at the key-hole and you'll hear news of yourself.
—PROVERB

Oh, what a tangled web we weave,
When first we practise to deceive!
—SIR WALTER SCOTT (1771–1832) *Marmion*

Sigh no more, ladies, sigh no more,
Men were deceivers ever.
—SHAKESPEARE (1564–1616) *Much Ado About Nothing*, II, iii, 65

December See MONTHS

Decision and Indecision

There is grief in indecision.
—CICERO (106–43 B.C.) *De officiis*

The wavering mind is but a base possession.
—EURIPIDES (480–406 B.C.)

There is no more miserable human being than one in whom nothing is habitual but indecision.
—WILLIAM JAMES (1842–1910) *Psychology*

Decide not rashly. The decision made
Can never be recalled.
—HENRY W. LONGFELLOW (1807–1882) *Masque of Pandora*

Once to every man and nation comes the moment to decide. . . .
—JAMES RUSSELL LOWELL (1819–1891) *The Present Crisis*

To be or not to be, that is the question . . . .
—SHAKESPEARE (1564–1616) *Hamlet*, III, i, 56

I am at war twixt will and will not.
—SHAKESPEARE (1564–1616) *Measure for Measure*, II, ii, 32

Quick decisions are unsafe decisions.
—SOPHOCLES (495–406 B.C.) *Oedipus Tyrannus*

Democracy

If liberty and equality, as is thought by some, are chiefly to be found in democracy, they will be best attained when all persons alike share in the government to the utmost.
—ARISTOTLE (384–322 B.C.) *Politics*

The tyranny of a multitude is a multiplied tyranny.
—EDMUND BURKE (1729–1797) Letter to Thomas Mercer

Democracy means government by the uneducated, while aristocracy means government by the badly educated.
—G. K. CHESTERTON (1874–1936) Interview, 1931

The tendency of democracies is, in all things, to mediocrity.
—JAMES FENIMORE COOPER (1789–1851) *American Democrat*

Only if basically the democracy of our day satisfies the mental, moral, and physical wants of the masses living under it, can it continue to exist.
—DWIGHT D. EISENHOWER (1890–1969) *Crusade in Europe*

The world is weary of statesmen whom democracy has degraded into politicians.
—BENJAMIN DISRAELI (1805–1881)

Democracy has another merit. It allows criticism, and if there isn't public criticism there are bound to be hushed-up scandals.
—E. M. FORSTER (1879–1970) *I Believe*

Democracy is based upon the conviction that there are extraordinary possibilities in ordinary people.
—HARRY EMERSON FOSDICK (1878–1969) *Democracy*

The republican is the only form of government which is not eternally at open or secret war with the rights of mankind.
—THOMAS JEFFERSON (1743–1826) Reply to Address

If we fail now, then we will have forgotten in abundance what we learned in hardship: that democracy rests on faith, that freedom asks more than it gives, and the judgment of God is harshest on those who are most favored.
—LYNDON B. JOHNSON (1908–1973) Inaugural Address, Jan. 1965

The world is very different now. For man holds in his mortal hands the power to abolish all forms of human poverty and all forms of human life. And yet the same revolutionary beliefs for which our forebears fought are still at issue around the globe . . .
—JOHN F. KENNEDY (1917–1963), Inaugural Address, Jan. 1961

All creatures are members of the one family of God.
—THE KORAN

Democracy gives to every man
The right to be his own oppressor.
—JAMES RUSSELL LOWELL (1819–1891) *Bigelow Papers*

We must define democracy as that form of government and of society which is inspired above every other, with the feeling and consciousness of the dignity of man.
—THOMAS MANN (1875–1955) *The Coming Victory of Democracy*

We must be the great arsenal of democracy.
—FRANKLIN D. ROOSEVELT (1882–1945) Radio Address, 1940

Democracy is unfinished business, not fulfilment; it is a process of always advancing toward fulfilment.
—RAYMOND GRAM SWING (1887–1968)

Democracy is the recurrent suspicion that more than half of the people are right more than half of the time.
—E. B. WHITE (1899–1985)

I believe in democracy because it releases the energies of every human being.
—WOODROW WILSON (1856–1924) Address to Congress, 1917

The world must be made safe for democracy. Its peace must be planted upon the tested foundations of political liberty.
—WOODROW WILSON (1856–1924) Address to Congress, 1917

Dependence and Independence

Each man for himself.
—GEOFFREY CHAUCER (1340?–1400) *Canterbury Tales*

The greatest man living may stand in need of the meanest, as much as the meanest does of him.
—THOMAS FULLER (1608–1681)

Even in the common affairs of life, in love, friendship, and marriage, how little security have we when we trust our happiness in the hands of others!
—WILLIAM HAZLITT (1778–1830) *On Living to Oneself*

The strongest man in the world is he who stands most alone.
—HENRIK IBSEN (1828–1906) *An Enemy of the People*

No degree of knowledge attainable by man is able to set him above the want of hourly assistance.
—SAMUEL JOHNSON (1709–1784)

To be independent is the business of a few only; it is the privilege of the strong.
—FRIEDRICH NIETZSCHE (1844–1900) *Beyond Good and Evil*

Independence? That's middle class blasphemy. We are all dependent on one another, every soul of us on earth.
—GEORGE BERNARD SHAW (1856–1950) *Pygmalion*

Without the help of thousands of others, any one of us would die, naked and starved.
—ALFRED E. SMITH (1873–1944)

Dependence is a perpetual call upon humanity, and a greater incitement to tenderness and pity than any other motive whatever.
—WILLIAM MAKEPEACE THACKERAY (1811–1863)

Desire

He begins to die that quits his desires.
—GEORGE HERBERT (1593–1633) *Outlandish Proverbs*

Naked I see the camp of those who desire nothing.
—HORACE (65–8 B.C.) *Odes*

We live in our desires rather than in our achievements.
—GEORGE MOORE (1852–1933) *Ave*

We desire most what we ought not to have.
—PUBLILIUS SYRUS (1st C. B.C.) *Sententiae*

If wishes were horses, beggars would ride.
—SCOTTISH PROVERB

Can one desire too much of a good thing?
—SHAKESPEARE (1564–1616) *As You Like It,* IV, i, 129

The fewer desires, the more peace.
—THOMAS WILSON (1663–1755)

Desire accomplished is sweet to the soul.
—OLD TESTAMENT: *Proverbs,* xiii, 19

Despair

I want to be forgotten even by God.
—ROBERT BROWNING (1812–1889) *Easter Day*

The name of the Slough was Despond.
—JOHN BUNYAN (1628–1688) *Pilgrim's Progress*

Despair is the damp of hell, as joy is the serenity of heaven.
—JOHN DONNE (1572–1631)

Despondency is not a state of humility. On the contrary, it is the vexation and despair of a cowardly pride. . . .
—FÉNELON (1651–1715)

Then black despair,
The shadow of a starless night, was thrown
Over the world in which I moved alone.
—PERCY B. SHELLEY (1792–1822) *Revolt of Islam*

The only refuge from despair is to project one's ego into the world.
—LEO TOLSTOY (1828–1910)

When we have lost everything, including hope, life becomes a disgrace and death a duty.
—VOLTAIRE (1694–1778) *Merope*

Out of the depths have I cried unto Thee, O Lord.
—OLD TESTAMENT: *Psalms,* cxxx, 1

Despotism See TYRANNY

Destiny See FATE

Discontent See CONTENT

Discretion and Indiscretion

An indiscreet man is more hurtful than an ill-natured one; for the latter will only attack his enemies, and those he wishes ill to; the other injures indifferently both friends and foes.
—JOSEPH ADDISON (1672–1719) *The Spectator*

He knows not when to be silent who knows not when to speak.
—PUBLILIUS SYRUS (1st C. B.C.)

Least said, soonest mended.
—CHARLES DICKENS (1812–1870) *David Copperfield*

For good and evil in our actions meet;
Wicked is not much worse than indiscreet.
—JOHN DONNE (1572–1631)

A demi-vierge is a woman for whom chastity, from being a temporary asset, has become a permanent liability.
—OSCAR HAMMLING (1890–   )

Let your discretion be your tutor; suit the action to the word, the word to the action.
—SHAKESPEARE (1564–1616) *Hamlet,* III, ii, 18

The better part of valour is discretion; in the which better part I have saved my life.
—SHAKESPEARE (1564–1616) *I Henry IV,* V, iv, 121

Be swift to hear, slow to speak, slow to wrath.
—NEW TESTAMENT: *James,* i, 19

Doubt

Doubt whom you will, but never doubt yourself.
—CHRISTIAN NESTELL BOVEE (1820–1904)

Doubting charms me not less than knowledge.
—DANTE (1265–1321) *Inferno,* canto xii, l. 93

Just think of the tragedy of teaching children not to doubt.
—CLARENCE DARROW (1857–1938)

Scepticism is the first step on the road to philosophy.
—DENIS DIDEROT (1713–1784)

To believe with certainty we must begin with doubting.
—STANISLAUS LESCYNSKI (1677–1766)

I respect faith, but doubt is what gets you an education.
—WILSON MIZNER (1876–1933)

Doubt makes the mountain which faith can move.
—UNKNOWN

Our doubts are traitors
And make us lose the good we oft might win
By fearing to attempt.
—SHAKESPEARE (1564–1616) *Measure for Measure,* I, iv, 77

Dreams

The more a man dreams, the less he believes.
—H. L. MENCKEN (1880–1956) *Prejudices*

Dreams are the true interpreters of our inclinations, but art is required to sort and understand them.
—MICHEL DE MONTAIGNE (1533–1592) *Essays*

Those dreams are true which we have in the morning, as the lamp begins to flicker.
—OVID (43 B.C.–A.D. 18?) *Epistles*

All that we see or seem
Is but a dream within a dream.
—EDGAR ALLAN POE (1809–1849) *A Dream Within a Dream*

To sleep; perchance to dream: ay, there's the rub;
For in that sleep of death what dreams may come,
When we have shuffled off this mortal coil
Must give us pause.
—SHAKESPEARE (1564–1616) *Hamlet,* III, i, 65

We are such stuff
As dreams are made on, and our little life
Is rounded out with a sleep.
—SHAKESPEARE (1564–1616) *The Tempest,* IV, i, 156

We rest. A dream has power to poison sleep;
We rise. One wandering thought pollutes the day.
—PERCY B. SHELLEY (1792–1822) *Mutability*

But I, being poor, have only my dreams;
I have spread my dreams under your feet;
Tread softly, for you tread on my dreams.
—WILLIAM BUTLER YEATS (1865–1939) *The Cloths of Heaven*

Your old men shall dream dreams, your young men shall see visions.
—OLD TESTAMENT: *Joel,* II, 28

Duty

In doing what we ought we deserve no praise, because it is our duty.
—ST. AUGUSTINE (354–430)

The fulfilment of spiritual duty in our daily life is vital to our survival.
—WINSTON CHURCHILL (1874–1965) Speech, 1949

Do your duty and leave the rest to heaven.
—PIERRE CORNEILLE (1606–1684) *Horace*

The reward of one duty is the power to fill another.
—GEORGE ELIOT (1819–1880) *Daniel Deronda*

Fear God, and keep his commandments; for this is the whole duty of man.
—OLD TESTAMENT: *Ecclesiastes,* xii, 13

Up to a certain point it is good for us to know that there are people in the world who will give us love and unquestioned loyalty to the limit of their ability. I doubt, however, if it is good for us to feel assured of this without the accompanying obligation of having to justify this devotion by our behavior.
—ELEANOR ROOSEVELT (1884–1962) *This Is My Story*

There is no duty we underrate so much as the duty of being happy.
—R. L. STEVENSON (1850–1894) *Virginibus Puerisque*

He who eats the fruit should at least plant the seed.
—HENRY DAVID THOREAU (1817–1862)

Duty is what one expects from others.
—OSCAR WILDE (1854–1900) *Woman of No Importance*

Education See LEARNING

Egotism
(See also VANITY)

Self-conceit may lead to self-destruction.
—AESOP (6th C. B.C.) *The Frog and the Ox*

Why should I be angry with a man, for loving himself better than me?
—FRANCIS BACON (1561–1620) *Essays*

Conceit is God's fit to little men.
—BRUCE BARTON (1886–1967) *Conceit*

I've never had any pity for conceited people, because I think they carry their comfort about with them.
—GEORGE ELIOT (1819–1880) *The Mill on the Floss*

We reproach people for talking about themselves; but it is the subject they treat best.
—ANATOLE FRANCE (1844–1924)

We would rather speak ill of ourselves than not talk of ourselves at all.
—FRANÇOIS DE LA ROCHEFOUCAULD (1613–1680) *Maxims*

There is not enough love and goodness in the world to throw any of it away on conceited people.
—FRIEDRICH NIETZSCHE (1844–1900)

If you love yourself over much, nobody else will love you at all.
—PROVERB

Every bird loves to hear himself sing.
—GERMAN PROVERB

Who loves himself need fear no rival.
—LATIN PROVERB

Conceit may puff a man up, but never prop him up.
—JOHN RUSKIN (1819–1900) *True and Beautiful*

Self-love, in nature rooted fast,
Attends us first, and leaves us last.
—JONATHAN SWIFT (1667–1745) *Cadenus and Vanessa*

We are interested in others when they are interested in us.
—PUBLILIUS SYRUS (1st C. B.C.) *Sententiae*

From his cradle to his grave a man never does a single thing which has any first and foremost object save one—to secure peace of mind, spiritual comfort, for himself.
—MARK TWAIN (1835–1910) *What is Man?*

All men think all men mortal but themselves.
—EDWARD YOUNG (1683–1765) *Night Thoughts*

Enemy

Wise men learn much from their enemies.
—ARISTOPHANES (444–380 B.C.) *The Birds*

Every man is his own greatest enemy, and as it were his own executioner.
—SIR THOMAS BROWNE (1605–1682) *Religio Medici*

You shall judge a man by his foes as well as by his friends.
—JOSEPH CONRAD (1857–1924) *Lord Jim*

Though thy enemy seems a mouse, yet watch him like a lion.
—PROVERB

One enemy can do more hurt than ten friends can do good.
—JONATHAN SWIFT (1667–1745) Letter, 1710

He makes no friend who never made a foe.
—TENNYSON (1809–1892) *Idylls of the King*

Rejoice not over thy greatest enemy being dead, but remember that we die all.
—APOCRYPHA: *Ecclesiasticus*

A man's foes shall be they of his own household.
—NEW TESTAMENT: *Matthew* x, 36

Love your enemies, bless them that curse you, do good to them that hate you . . . .
—NEW TESTAMENT: *Matthew*, v, 44

Envy

Those that are not envied are never wholly happy.
—AESCHYLUS (525–456 B.C.) *Agamemnon*

Envy not greatness: for thou mak'st thereby
Thyself the worse, and so the distance greater.
—GEORGE HERBERT (1593–1633) *The Church*

All the tyrants of Sicily never invented a worse torment than envy.
—HORACE (65–8 B.C.) *Epistles*

No man likes to be surpassed by those of his own level.
—LIVY (59 B.C.–A.D. 17) *Annales*

Since we cannot attain to greatness, let us revenge ourselves by railing at it.
—MICHEL DE MONTAIGNE (1533–1592) *Essays*

It is a nobler fate to be envied than to be pitied.
—PINDAR (c. 522–442 B.C.) *Pythian Odes*

The truest mark of being born with great qualities is being born without envy.
—FRANÇOIS DE LA ROCHEFOUCAULD (1613–1680) *Maxims*

No metal can,
No, not the hangman's axe, bear half the keenness
Of thy sharp envy.
—SHAKESPEARE (1564–1616) *Merchant of Venice*, IV, i, 123

Where envying and strife is, there is confusion, and every evil work.
—NEW TESTAMENT: *James*, iii, 16

Equality and Inequality

The only stable state is the one in which all men are equal before the law.
—ARISTOTLE (384–322 B.C.) *Politics*

We hold these truths to be self-evident—that all men are created equal; that they are endowed by their Creator with certain inalienable rights; that among these are life, liberty, and the pursuit of happiness.
—DECLARATION OF INDEPENDENCE

Before God we are all equally wise—equally foolish.
—ALBERT EINSTEIN (1879–1955) *Cosmic Religion*

Men are made by nature unequal. It is vain, therefore, to treat them as if they were equal.
—JAMES ANTHONY FROUDE (1818–1894)

Though all men are made of one metal, yet they were not cast all in the same mold.
—THOMAS FULLER (1608–1681) *Gnomologia*

That all men are equal is a proposition to which at ordinary times no sane individual has ever given his assent.
—ALDOUS HUXLEY (1894–1963) *Proper Studies*

And our sorrowing gaze turns also to the other children of God everywhere, suffering because of race and economic conditions, at once complex and giving reason for anxiety, or through the limitation on the exercise of their natural and civil rights.
—POPE JOHN XXIII (1881–1963) April 17, 1960

All animals are created equal—but some animals are created more equal than others.
—GEORGE ORWELL (1903–1950) *Animal Farm*

The only real equality is in the cemetery.
—GERMAN PROVERB

Nature knows no equality; its sovereign law is subordination and dependence.
—MARQUIS DE VAUVENARGUES (1715–1747) *Reflections*

Error

There is many a slip
'Twixt the cup and the lip.
—RICHARD HARRIS BARHAM (1788–1845) *Ingoldsby Legends*

I can pardon everybody's mistakes except my own.
—MARCUS CATO (234–149 B.C.)

Who errs and mends, to God himself commends.
—CERVANTES (1547–1616) *Don Quixote*

Mistake, error, is the discipline through which we advance.
—WILLIAM ELLERY CHANNING (1780–1842)

It is the nature of every man to err, but only the fool perseveres in error.
—CICERO (106–43 B.C.) *Philippicae*

The cautious seldom err.
—CONFUCIUS (*c.* 551–478 B.C.) *Analects*

Errors, like straws, upon the surface flow;
He who would search for pearls must dive below.
—JOHN DRYDEN (1631–1700) *All for Love*

Even a mistake may turn out to be the one thing necessary to a worthwhile achievement.
—HENRY FORD (1863–1947) Interview, 1938

Dark Error's other hidden side is truth.
—VICTOR HUGO (1802–1885) *Legend of the Centuries*

The man who makes no mistakes does not usually make anything.
—BISHOP W. C. MAGEE (1821–1891)

To err is human, to forgive divine.
—ALEXANDER POPE (1688–1744) *Essay on Criticism*

The wise course is to profit from the mistakes of others.
—TERENCE (*c.* 190–150 B.C.)

I fear our mistakes far more than the strategy of our enemies.
—THUCYDIDES (471?–400? B.C.) *Funeral Oration*

The progress of the rivers to the ocean is not so rapid as that of man to error.
—VOLTAIRE (1694–1778) *Philosophical Dictionary*

Evening See NIGHT

Evil

Evil events from evil causes spring.
—ARISTOPHANES (444–380 B.C.)

Better suffer a great evil than do a little one.
—HENRY GEORGE BOHN (1796–1884) *Handbook of Proverbs*

Often the fear of one evil leads us into a worse.
—NICOLAS BOILEAU (1636–1711) *The Poetic Art*

God bears with the wicked, but not forever.
—CERVANTES (1547–1616) *Don Quixote*

Evil to him who thinks evil. [Honi soit qui mal y pense.]
—EDWARD III (1327–1377) Motto of the Order of the Garter

A wicked man is his own hell.
—THOMAS FULLER (1606–1661) *Gnomologia*, No. 460

Don't let us make imaginary evils, when you know we have so many real ones to encounter.
—OLIVER GOLDSMITH (1730–1774)

The source of all wars, the source of all evil, lies in us.
—PIERRE LECOMTE DU NOÜY (1883–1947) *Human Destiny*

The evil best known is the most tolerable.
—LIVY (59 B.C.–A.D. 17) *History of Rome*

An evil life is a kind of death.
—OVID (43 B.C.–A.D. 18?) *Epistulae ex Ponto*

No evil can happen to a good man, either in life or after death.
—SOCRATES (470?–399 B.C.)

Every one that doeth evil hateth the light.
—NEW TESTAMENT: *John*, iii, 20

I have seen the wicked in great power, and spreading himself like the green bay tree. Yet he passed away, and lo, he was not.
—OLD TESTAMENT: *Isaiah*, lv, 7

Fret not thyself because of evildoers . . . for they shall soon be cut down like the grass, and wither as the green herb.
—OLD TESTAMENT: *Psalms*, xxxvii, 1–2

Experience

All experience is an arch to build upon.
—HENRY ADAMS (1838–1918) *Education of Henry Adams*

It is costly wisdom that is bought by experience.
—ROGER ASCHAM (1515–1568) *Schoolmaster*

Thou shalt know by experience how salt the savor is of another's bread, and how sad a path it is to climb and descend another's stairs.
—DANTE (1265–1321) *Paradiso*

Experience keeps a dear school, but fools will learn in no other.
—BEN FRANKLIN (1706–1790) *Poor Richard's Almanack*

The finished man of the world must eat of every apple once.
—RALPH WALDO EMERSON (1803–1882) *Conduct of Life*

Happy is he who gains wisdom from another's mishap.
—PUBLILIUS SYRUS (1st C. B.C.) *Sententiae*

Experience is the name everyone gives to his mistakes.
—OSCAR WILDE (1854–1900) *Lady Windermere's Fan*

Faith

Faith is a higher faculty than reason.
—PHILIP JAMES BAILEY (1816–1902)

I believe in the incomprehensibility of God.
—HONORÉ DE BALZAC (1799–1850)

To me, faith means not worrying.
—JOHN DEWEY (1859–1952)

Faith is not belief. Belief is passive. Faith is active. It is vision which passes inevitably into action.
—EDITH HAMILTON (1867–1963) *Witness to the Truth*

Faith may be defined briefly as an illogical belief in the occurrence of the improbable.
—H. L. MENCKEN (1880–1956) *Prejudices*, Series iii

Faith is like love; it cannot be forced.
—ARTHUR SCHOPENHAUER (1788–1860)

Faith is the antiseptic of the soul.
—WALT WHITMAN (1819–1892) *Leaves of Grass*, preface

We walk by faith, not by sight.
—NEW TESTAMENT: *II Corinthians*, v, 7

If ye have faith as a grain of mustard seed, ye shall say unto this mountain, Remove hence to yonder place; and it shall remove: and nothing shall be impossible unto you.
—NEW TESTAMENT: *Matthew*, xvii, 20

Fall See AUTUMN

Family See MARRIAGE, FATHER.

Fate

Nor sitting at his hearth at home doth man escape his appointed doom.
—AESCHYLUS (525–456 B.C.) *The Choephorae*

Destiny is not a matter of chance, it is a matter of choice; it is not a thing to be waited for, it is a thing to be achieved.
—WILLIAM JENNINGS BRYAN (1860–1925) Speech, 1899

'Tis fate that flings the dice, and as she flings
Of kings makes peasants, and of peasants kings.
—JOHN DRYDEN (1631–1700) *Jupiter Cannot Alter the Decrees of Fate*

The moving finger writes; and having writ
Moves on; nor all your Piety nor Wit
Shall lure it back to cancel half a Line.
—EDWARD FITZGERALD (1809–1883) tr.: *Rubáiyát of Omar Khayyám*

Man supposes that he directs his life and governs his actions, when his existence is irretrievably under the control of destiny.
—GOETHE (1749–1832)

That which God writes on thy forehead, thou wilt come to it.
—THE KORAN

Our hour is marked, and no one can claim a moment of life beyond what fate has predestined.
—NAPOLEON BONAPARTE (1811–1884)

This generation of Americans has a rendezvous with destiny.
—FRANKLIN D. ROOSEVELT (1882–1945) Address, 1936

Fate leads the willing, and drags along those who hang back.
—SENECA (4? B.C.–A.D. 65)

There is a divinity that shapes our ends,
Rough-hew them how we will.
—SHAKESPEARE (1564–1616) *Hamlet*, V, ii, 10

All things come alike to all: there is one event to the righteous, and to the wicked; to the good and to the clean, and to the unclean. . . .
—OLD TESTAMENT: *Ecclesiastes*, ix, 2

Father

Diogenes struck the father when the son swore.
—ROBERT BURTON (1577–1640) *Anatomy of Melancholy*

He that has his father for judge goes safe to the trial.
—CERVANTES (1547–1616) *Don Quixote*

One father is more than a hundred schoolmasters.
—GEORGE HERBERT (1593–1633) *Jacula Prudentum*

If a man strike his father his hand shall be cut off.
— *The Code of Hammurabi*

It is a wise father that knows his own child.
—SHAKESPEARE (1564–1616) *Merchant of Venice*, II, ii, 80

A wise son maketh a glad father.
—OLD TESTAMENT: *Proverbs*, x, i

He that honoureth his father shall have a long life.
—APOCRYPHA: *Ecclesiasticus*, iii, 6

Faults

What an absurd thing it is to pass over all the valuable parts of a man, and fix our attention on his infirmities.
—JOSEPH ADDISON (1672–1719)

The greatest of faults, I should say, is to be conscious of none.
—THOMAS CARLYLE (1795–1881) *Heroes and Hero-Worship*

Men ought to be most annoyed by the sufferings which come from their own faults.
—CICERO (106–43 B.C.) *Epistolae ad Fratrem*

The defects of great men are the consolation of dunces.
—ISAAC D'ISRAELI (1766–1848)

All his faults were such that one loved him still the better for them.
—OLIVER GOLDSMITH (1730–1774) *The Good-Natur'd Man*

A fault confessed is more than half amended.
—SIR JOHN HARINGTON (1561–1612)

If we had no faults, we should not take so much pleasure in remarking them in others.
—FRANÇOIS DE LA ROCHEFOUCAULD (1613–1680) *Maxims*

He who loves not the loved one's faults does not truly love.
—SPANISH PROVERB

The fault, dear Brutus, is not in our stars,
But in ourselves, that we are underlings.
—SHAKESPEARE (1564–1616) *Julius Caesar*, I, ii, 140

Fear

No one loves the man whom he fears.
—ARISTOTLE (384–322 B.C.)

We listen'd and look'd sideways up!
Fear at my heart, as at a cup,
My life-blood seem'd to sip.
—SAMUEL TAYLOR COLERIDGE (1772–1834) *Ancient Mariner*

Fear always springs from ignorance.
—RALPH WALDO EMERSON (1803–1882) *The American Scholar*

Fear is the parent of cruelty.
—JAMES ANTHONY FROUDE (1818–1894)

Many may not love us, but all shall fear us.
—HEINRICH HIMMLER (1900–1945)

Let us never negotiate out of fear. But let us never fear to negotiate.
—JOHN F. KENNEDY (1917–1963), Inaugural Address, 1961

Apprehensions are greater in proportion as things are unknown.
—LIVY (B.C. 59–A.D. 17) *Annales*

Fear is a feeling that is stronger than love.
—PLINY THE YOUNGER (62–113) *Letters*

The only thing we have to fear is fear itself.
—FRANKLIN D. ROOSEVELT (1882–1945) Inaugural Address, 1933

His flight was madness; when our actions do not,
Our fears do make us traitors.
—SHAKESPEARE (1564–1616) *Macbeth*, IV, ii, 3

To him who is in fear everything rustles.
—SOPHOCLES (495–406 B.C.)

Fear, like pain, looks and sounds worse than it feels.
—REBECCA WEST (1892–1983)

February   See MONTHS

Fidelity and Infidelity

Give me a man that is capable of a devotion to anything, rather than a cold, calculating average of all the virtues.
—BRET HARTE (1838–1902) *Two Men of Sandy Bar*

The fidelity of most men is merely an invention of self-love to win confidence . . . .
—FRANÇOIS DE LA ROCHEFOUCAULD (1613–1680) *Maxims*

Fidelity bought with money is overcome by money.
—SENECA (4? B.C.–A.D. 65) *Agamemnon*

Oh, where is loyalty?
If it be banish'd from the frosty head,
Where shall it find a harbour in the earth?
—SHAKESPEARE (1564–1616) *II Henry IV*, V, i, 166

To God, thy countrie, and thy friend be true.
—HENRY VAUGHAN (1622–1695) *Rules and Lessons*

Be thou faithful unto death.
—NEW TESTAMENT: *Revelation*, ii, 10

Flattery

A flatterer is a friend who is your inferior or pretends to be so.
—ARISTOTLE (384–322 B.C.) *Nicomachean Ethics*

We sometimes think that we hate flattery, but we only hate the manner in which it is done.
—FRANÇOIS DE LA ROCHEFOUCAULD (1613–1680) *Maxims*

'Tis hard to find a man of great estate,
That can distinguish flatterers from friends.
—HORACE (65–8 B.C.)

When flatterers meet, the Devil goes to dinner.
—JOHN RAY (1627?–1705) *English Proverbs*

But when I tell him he hates flatterers,
He says he does, being then most flattered.
—SHAKESPEARE (1564–1616) *Julius Caesar*, II, i, 208

They do abuse the king that flatter him:
For flattery is the bellows blows up sin.
—SHAKESPEARE (1564–1616) *Pericles*, I, ii, 38

A flattering mouth worketh ruin.
—OLD TESTAMENT: *Proverbs*, XXVI, 28

Flowers   See GARDEN

Folly and Fools

The folly of one man is the fortune of another.
—FRANCIS BACON (1561–1620) *Essays: Of Fortune*

A sucker is born every minute.
—P. T. BARNUM (1810–1891)

The hours of folly are measur'd by the clock; but of wisdom, no clock can measure.
—WILLIAM BLAKE (1757–1827) *Marriage of Heaven and Hell*

A fool always finds one still more foolish to admire him.
—NICOLAS BOILEAU (1636–1711) *The Poetic Art*

And fools cannot hold their tongue.
—GEOFFREY CHAUCER (1340?–1400) *Romaunt of the Rose*

The first degree of folly is to conceit one's self wise; the second to profess it; the third to despise counsel.

—BEN FRANKLIN (1706–1790) *Poor Richard's Almanack* When lovely woman stoops to folly,
And finds too late that men betray,
What charm can soothe her melancholy?
What art can wash her guilt away?
—OLIVER GOLDSMITH (1730–1774) *Vicar of Wakefield*

I am always afraid of a fool. One cannot be sure that he is not a knave as well.
—WILLIAM HAZLITT (1778–1830) *Characteristics*

Folly pursues us in every period of life. If any one appears wise, it is only because his follies are proportioned to his age and fortune.
—FRANÇOIS DE LA ROCHEFOUCAULD (1613–1680) *Maxims*

There is no fool like an old fool.
—JOHN LYLY (1554?–1606)

I enjoy vast delight in the folly of mankind; and, God be praised, that is an inexhaustible source of entertainment.
—LADY MARY WORTLY MONTAGU (1689–1762) Letter

Fools rush in where angels fear to tread.
—ALEXANDER POPE (1688–1744) *An Essay on Criticism*

If every fool wore a crown, we'd all be kings.
—WELSH PROVERB

The fool doth think he is wise, but the wise man knows himself to be a fool.
—SHAKESPEARE (1564–1616) *As You Like It*, V, i, 34

Give me the young man who has brains enough to make a fool of himself.
—R. L. Stevenson (1850–1894) *Virginibus Puerisque*

A fool and his money are soon parted.
—Unknown

The best way to silence any friend of yours whom you know to be a fool is to induce him to hire a hall.
—Woodrow Wilson (1856–1924) Speech, 1916

The wise man's eyes are in his head, but the fool walketh in darkness.
—Old Testament: *Ecclesiastes,* ii, 14

Forgetfulness

A man must get a thing before he can forget it.
—Oliver Wendell Holmes (1809–1894) *Medical Essays*

Blessed are the forgetful; for they get the better of even their blunders.
—Friedrick Nietzsche (1844–1900) *Beyond Good and Evil*

We have all forgotten more than we remember.
—Proverb

We bury love,
Forgetfulness grows over it like grass;
That is a thing to weep for, not the dead.
—Alexander Smith (1830–1867) *City Poems*

If I forget thee, O Jerusalem, let my right hand forget her cunning.
—Old Testament: *Psalms,* cxxxvii, 5

Foresight See PRUDENCE

Forgiveness

You may pardon much to others, nothing to yourself.
—Ausonius (*f.* 4th C. A.D.) *Epigrams*

Those who forgive most shall be most forgiven.
—Philip James Bailey (1816–1902) *Festus*

He who forgives readily only invites offense.
—Pierre Corneille (1606–1684) *Cinna*

God may forgive you, but I never can.
—Queen Elizabeth I (1533–1603) to the Countess of Nottingham

It is often easier to forgive those who have wronged us than those whom we have wronged.
—Oscar Hammling (1890–) *Laconics*

Know all and you will pardon all.
—Thomas à Kempis (1380–1471) *Imitation of Christ*

We pardon in proportion as we love.
—François de la Rochefoucauld (1613–1680) *Maxims*

We read that we ought to forgive our enemies; but we do not read that we ought to forgive our friends.
—Cosimo de' Medici (1519–1574)

If the injured one could read your heart, you may be sure he would understand and pardon.
—R. L. Stevenson (1850–1894) *Truth of Intercourse*

There is nothing so advantageous to a man than a forgiving disposition.
—Terence (*c.* 190–150 B.C.) *Adelphi*

Father, forgive them; for they know not what they do.
—New Testament: *Luke,* xxiii, 34

A woman may consent to forget and forgive, but she never will drop the habit of referring to the matter now and then.
—Unknown

Fortune

Fortune is a god and rules men's lives.
—Aeschylus (525–456 B.C.) *The Choephorae*

Every man is the architect of his own fortune.
—Appius Claudius (*f.* 312 B.C.)

All fortune is to be conquered by bearing it.
—Francis Bacon (1561–1620) *Advancement of Learning*

I am not now in fortune's power;
He that is down can fall no lower.
—Samuel Butler (1612–1680) *Hudibras*

Fortune hath somewhat the nature of a woman; if she be too much wooed, she is the farther off.
—Emperor Charles V (1500–1588)

It is fortune, not wisdom, that rules man's life.
—Cicero (106–43 B.C.)

Ill fortune seldom comes alone.
—John Dryden (1631–1700) *Cymon and Iphigenia,* Act I

Fortune never seems so blind as to those upon whom she confers no favors.
—François de la Rochefoucauld (1613–1680) *Maxims*

Not many men have both good fortune and good sense.
—Livy (50 B.C.–A.D. 17) *History of Rome*

The wheel goes round and round
And some are up and some are on the down
And still the wheel goes round.
—Josephine Pollard (1843–1892) *Wheel of Fortune*

Fortune can take from us nothing but what she gave us.
—Publilius Syrus (1st C. B.C.) *Sententiae*

Fear of the future is worse than one's present fortune.
—Quintilian (40 –*c.* 100)

Everyone is the architect of his own fortune.
—Abbé Regnier (1794–?) *Satire*

Fortune, that arrant whore
Ne'er turns the key to the poor.
—Shakespeare (1564–1616) *King Lear,* II, iv, 52

Freedom

The cause of freedom is the cause of God.
—William Lisle Bowles (1762–1850) to Edmund Burke

A man can be free even within prison walls. Freedom is something spiritual. Whoever has once had it, can never lose it. There are some people who are never free outside a prison.
—Bertold Brecht (1898–1956) *A Penny for the Poor*

Hereditary bondsmen! Know ye not
Who would be free themselves must strike the blow?
—Lord Byron (1788–1824) *Childe Harold*

Perfect freedom is reserved for the man who lives by his own work and in that work does what he wants to do.
—Robin George Collingwood (1889–1943) *Speculum Mentis*

I am as free as nature first made man.
Ere the base laws of servitude began,
When wild in woods the noble savage ran.
—JOHN DRYDEN (1631–1700) *Conquest of Granada*

Freedom from fear and injustice and oppression will be ours only in the measure that men who value such freedom are ready to sustain its possession—to defend it against every thrust from within or without.
—DWIGHT D. EISENHOWER (1890–1969) *Crusade in Europe*

No man is free who is not master of himself.
—EPICTETUS (1st C. A.D.) *Discourses*

No man is wholly free. He is a slave to wealth, or to fortune, or the laws, or the people restrain him from acting according to his will alone.
—EURIPIDES (480–406 B.C.) *Hecuba*

The right to personal freedom comes second in importance to the duty of maintaining the race.
—ADOLF HITLER (1889–1945) *Mein Kampf*

Who then is free? the wise man who is lord over himself; Whom neither poverty nor death, nor chains alarm, strong to withstand his passions and despise honors, and who is completely finished and founded off in himself.
—HORACE (65–8 B.C.) *Satires*

Every man has a right to utter what he thinks truth, and every other man has a right to knock him down for it.
—SAMUEL JOHNSON (1709–1784) in Boswell's *Life*

The most unfree souls go west and shout of freedom. Men are freest when they are most unconscious of freedom. The shout is a rattling of chains.
—D. H. LAWRENCE (1885–1930) *Studies in Classic American Literature*

Those who deny freedom to others deserve it not for themselves, and, under a just God cannot long retain it.
—ABRAHAM LINCOLN (1809–1865) Letter, 1859

If I have freedom in my love,
And in my soul am free,
Angels alone, that soar above,
Enjoy such liberty.
—RICHARD LOVELACE (1618–1658) *To Althea from Prison*

There is only one cure for the evils which newly acquired freedom produces, and that is more freedom.
—THOMAS MACAULAY (1800–1859) *Essay on Milton*

In the modern social order, the *person* is sacrificed to the *individual*. The individual is given universal suffrage, equality of rights, freedom of opinion; while the person, isolated, naked, with no social armor to sustain and protect him, is left to the mercy of all the devouring forces which threaten the life of the soul . . . .
—JACQUES MARITAIN (1882–1973) *Three Reformers*

Oh, Lord, I want to be free, want to be free;
Rainbow round my shoulder, wings on my feet.
—UNKNOWN, American Negro Spiritual

Is any man free except the one who can pass his life as he pleases?
—PERSIUS (34–62) *Satires*

The people who settled in New England came here for religious freedom, but religious freedom to them meant freedom only for their kind of religion. . . . This attitude seems to be our attitude in many situations today.
—ELEANOR ROOSEVELT (1884–1962)

Man is born free—and everywhere he is in irons.
—JEAN JACQUES ROUSSEAU (1712–1778) *Social Contract*

No one can be perfectly free till all are free.
—HERBERT SPENCER (1820–1903) *Social Statics*

There are times in the lives of all people when freedom is the twin of duty, sacrifice the companion of happiness, and when courage—parent of fortitude, endurance, determination—is the first virtue.
—DOROTHY THOMPSON (1894–1961) *On the Record*

I would rather sit on a pumpkin and have it all to myself, than to be crowded on a velvet cushion.
—HENRY DAVID THOREAU (1817–1862) *Walden*

I disapprove of what you say, but I will defend to the death your right to say it.
— Attributed to VOLTAIRE by a later biographer

Freedom exists only where the people take care of the government.
—WOODROW WILSON (1856–1924) Speech, 1912

Friends

One friend in a lifetime is much; two are many; three are hardly possible. Friendship needs a certain parallelism of life, a community of thought, a rivalry of aim.
—HENRY ADAMS (1838–1918) *Education of Henry Adams*

Beast knows beast; birds of a feather flock together.
—ARISTOTLE (384–322 B.C.) *Rhetoric*

Thy friendship oft has made my heart to ache:
Do be my enemy—for friendship's sake.
—WILLIAM BLAKE (1757–1827) *To H.*

Friendships multiply joys and divide griefs.
—HENRY GEORGE BOHN (1796–1884) *Handbook of Proverbs*

I have loved my friends as I do virtue, my soul, my God.
—SIR THOMAS BROWNE (1605–1682) *Religio Medici*

Tell me what company thou keepest, and I'll tell thee what thou art.
—CERVANTES (1547–1616) *Don Quixote*

Endeavor, as much as you can, to keep company with people above you.
—LORD CHESTERFIELD (1694–1773) *Letters*

Never injure a friend, even in jest.
—CICERO (106–43 B.C.) *De Amicitia*

Friendship often ends in love; but love in friendship, never.
—CHARLES C. COLTON (1780?–1832) *Lacon*

Chance makes our parents, but choice makes our friends.
—JACQUES DeLILLE (1738–1813) *Pitié*

Animals are such agreeable friends—they ask no questions, they pass no criticisms.
—GEORGE ELIOT (1819–1880)

The dearest friends are separated by impassable gulfs.
—RALPH WALDO EMERSON (1803–1882) *Essays*

The only way to have a friend is to be one.
—RALPH WALDO EMERSON (1803–1882) *Essays*

Men who know the same things are not long the best company for each other.
—RALPH WALDO EMERSON (1803–1882)

In prosperity it is very easy to find a friend; in adversity, nothing is so difficult.
—EPICTETUS (1st C. A.D.) *Encheiridion*

Real friends are our greatest joy and our greatest sorrow. It were almost to be wished that all true and faithful friends should expire on the same day.
—FÉNELON (1651–1715)

If you have one true friend you have more than your share.
—THOMAS FULLER (1608–1681) *Gnomologia*

There is no better looking-glass than an old friend.
—THOMAS FULLER (1608–1681) *Gnomologia*

'Tis thus that on the choice of friends
Our good or evil name depends.
—JOHN GAY (1688–1732) *Old Woman and Her Cats*

There is no desert like being friendless.
—BALTASAR GRACIÁN (1601–1658)

To have a great man for an intimate friend seems pleasant to those who have never tried it; those who have, fear it.
—HORACE (65–8 B.C.) *Epistulae*

I never considered a difference of opinion in politics, in religion, in philosophy, as cause for withdrawing from a friend.
—THOMAS JEFFERSON (1743–1826) Letter, 1800

An injured friend is the bitterest of foes.
—THOMAS JEFFERSON (1743–1826)

I find as I grow older that I love those most whom I loved first.
—THOMAS JEFFERSON (1743–1826) Letter, 1787

I live in the crowds of jollity, not so much to enjoy company as to shun myself.
—SAMUEL JOHNSON (1709–1784) *Rasselas*

If my friends are one-eyed, I look at them in profile.
—JOSEPH JOUBERT (1754–1824) *Pensées*

In friendship, as in love, we are often more happy from the things we are ignorant of than from those we are acquainted with.
—FRANÇOIS DE LA ROCHEFOUCAULD (1613–1680) *Maxims*

If you want to make a dangerous man your friend, let him do you a favor.
—LEWIS E. LAWES (1883–1947)

The vulgar estimate friends by the advantage to be derived from them.
—OVID (43 B.C.–A.D. 18?)

It is better to be alone than in ill company.
—GEORGE PETTIE (1548–1589)

Histories are more full of examples of the fidelity of dogs than of friends.
—ALEXANDER POPE (1688–1744) Letter, 1709

A friend in need is a friend indeed.
—ENGLISH PROVERB

It is fun to be in the same decade with you.
—FRANKLIN D. ROOSEVELT (1882–1945) in a cable to WINSTON CHURCHILL

He that goeth to bed with dogs ariseth with fleas.
—JAMES SANDFORD (f. 1572) *Hours of Recreation*

The principal task of friendship is to foster one's friends' illusions.
—ARTHUR SCHNITZLER (1862–1931) *Anatole*

Friendship always benefits; love sometimes injures.
—SENECA (4? B.C.–A.D. 65) *Epistulae ad Lucilium*

To lose a friend is the greatest of all evils, but endeavour rather to rejoice that you possessed him than to mourn his loss.
—SENECA (4? B.C.–A.D. 65) *Epistulae ad Lucilium*

Keep thy friend under thine own life's key.
—SHAKESPEARE (1564–1616) *All's Well that Ends Well*, I, i, 74

Those friends thou hast, and their adoption tried,
Grapple them to thy soul with hoops of steel;
But do not dull thy palm with entertainment
Of each new-hatch'd, unfledg'd comrade.
—SHAKESPEARE (1564–1616) *Hamlet*, I, iii, 59

    To wail friends lost
Is not by much so wholesome—profitable,
As to rejoice at friends but newly found.
—SHAKESPEARE (1564–1616) *Love's Labour Lost*, V, ii, 759

I am not of that feather to shake off
My friend when he must need me.
—SHAKESPEARE (1564–1616) *Timon of Athens*, I, i, 100

The most I can do for my friend is simply to be his friend.
—HENRY DAVID THOREAU (1817–1862) *Journal*, 1841

God save me from my friends. I can protect myself from my enemies.
—MARSHAL DE VILLARS (1653–1734)

Friendship's the wine of life.
—EDWARD YOUNG (1683–1765) *Night Thoughts*

A faithful friend is a strong defense: and he that hath found such an one hath found a treasure.
—APOCRYPHA: *Ecclesiasticus*, vi, 14

Greater love hath no man than this, that a man lay down his life for his friends.
—NEW TESTAMENT: *John*, xv, 13

Saul and Jonathan were lovely and pleasant in their lives, and in their death they were not divided.
—OLD TESTAMENT: *II Samuel*, i, 23

A friend is one who dislikes the same people that you dislike.
—UNKNOWN

Future

We are always doing something for Posterity, but I would fain see Posterity do something for us.
—JOSEPH ADDISON (1672–1719) *The Spectator*

You can never plan the future by the past.
—EDMUND BURKE (1729–1797) Letter

For my part, I think that a knowledge of the future would be a disadvantage.
—CICERO (106–43 B.C.) *De Devinatione*

I never think of the future. It comes soon enough.
—ALBERT EINSTEIN (1879–1955)

The future is a convenient place for dreams.
—ANATOLE FRANCE (1844–1924)

I know of no way of judging the future but by the past.
—PATRICK HENRY (1736–1799) Speech, 1775

Trust no future, howe'er pleasant!
Let the dead Past bury its dead!
—HENRY W. LONGFELLOW (1801–1882) *Psalm of Life*

The mind that is anxious about the future is miserable.
—SENECA (4? B.C.–A.D. 65) *Epistulae ad Lucilium*

We know what we are, but know not what we may be.
—SHAKESPEARE (1564–1616) *Hamlet*, IV, v, 43

Take no thought for the morrow: for the morrow shall take thought for the things of itself.
—NEW TESTAMENT: *Matthew*, vi, 34

Garden and Flowers

Who loves a garden still his Eden keeps . . . .
—AMOS BRONSON ALCOTT (1799–1888)

Ah, Sunflower, weary of time,
Who countest the steps of the sun;
Seeking after that sweet golden clime,
Where the traveller's journey is done . . . .
—WILLIAM BLAKE (1757–1827) *The Sunflower*

God the first garden made, and the first city Cain.
—ABRAHAM COWLEY (1618–1667) *The Garden*

Loveliest of trees, the cherry now
Is hung with bloom along the bough,
And stands about the woodland ride
Wearing white for Eastertide.
—A. E. HOUSMAN (1859–1936)

Your sacred plants, if here below,
Only among the plants will grow.
Society is all but rude,
To this delicious solitude.
—ANDREW MARVELL (1621–1678) *The Garden*

Many things grow in the garden that were never sowed there.
—PROVERB

Lilies that fester smell far worse than weeds.
—SHAKESPEARE (1564–1616) *Sonnets*, xciv

Consider the lilies of the field, how they grow; they toil not, neither do they spin: And yet I say unto you, that even Solomon in all his glory was not arrayed like one of these.
—NEW TESTAMENT: *Matthew*, vi, 28

The Lord God planted a garden eastward in Eden; and there He put the man whom He had formed.
—OLD TESTAMENT: *Genesis*, ii, 8

Generosity See GIFTS AND GIVING

Genius

Doing easily what others find difficult is talent; doing what is impossible for talent is genius.
—HENRI-FREDERIC AMIEL (1828–1881) *Journal*

Genius is mainly an affair of energy.
—MATTHEW ARNOLD (1822–1888) *Essays in Criticism*

I have known no man of genius who had not to pay, in some affliction or defect either physical or spiritual, for what the gods had given him.
—MAX BEERBOHM (1872–1956) *The Pines*

Patience is a necessary ingredient of genius.
—BENJAMIN DISRAELI (1805–1881) *Contarini Fleming*

Genius is one percent inspiration and ninety-nine percent perspiration.
—THOMAS A. EDISON (1847–1931) Newspaper interview

Every man of genius sees the world at a different angle from his fellows, and there is his tragedy.
—HAVELOCK ELLIS (1859–1939) *Dance of Life*

Genius is the power of lighting one's own fire.
—JOHN FOSTER (1770–1843)

A man of genius makes no mistakes. His errors are volitional and are the portals of discovery.
—JAMES JOYCE (1882–1941) *Ulysses*

Gift, like genius, I often think only means an infinite capacity for taking pains.
—JANE ELLICE HOPKINS (1836–1904)

Genius is a promontory jutting out into the infinite.
—VICTOR HUGO (1802–1885) *William Shakespeare*

Genius begets great works; labor alone finished them.
—JOSEPH JOUBERT (1754–1824) *Pensées*

One science only will one genius fit;
So vast is art, so narrow human wit.
—ALEXANDER POPE (1668–1744) *Essay on Criticism*

The poets' scrolls will outlive the monuments of stone. Genius survives; all else is claimed by death.
—EDMUND SPENSER (1552?–1599) *Shepherd's Calendar*

There is a certain characteristic common to all those whom we call geniuses. Each of them has a consciousness of being a man apart.
—MIGUEL DE UNAMUNO (1864–1936) *Essays and Soliloquies*

Gifts and Giving

It is easy to become generous with other people's property.
—LATIN PROVERB

The most important thing in any relationship is not what you get but what you give. . . . In any case, the giving of love is an education in itself.
—ELEANOR ROOSEVELT (1884–1963)

You must be fit to give before you can be fit to receive.
—JAMES STEPHENS (1882–1950)

I fear the Greeks, even when they bring gifts.
—VERGIL (70–19 B.C.) *Aeneid*

It is more blessed to give than to receive.
—NEW TESTAMENT: *Acts*, xx, 35

Or what man is there of you, whom if his son ask bread, will he give him a stone?
—NEW TESTAMENT: *Matthew*, vii, 9

Girl See CHILDREN

God

God's mouth knows not to utter falsehood, but he will perform each word.
—AESCHYLUS (525–456 B.C.) *Prometheus*

Nature herself has imprinted on the minds of all the idea of God.
—CICERO (106–43 B.C.) *De Natura Deorum*

Earth with her thousand voices, praises God
—SAMUEL TAYLOR COLERIDGE (1772–1834)

God moves in a mysterious way
His wonders to perform.
—WILLIAM COWPER (1731–1800) *Light Shining out of Darkness*

Father expected a great deal of God. He didn't actually accuse God of inefficiency, but when he prayed his tone was loud and angry, like that of a disatisfied guest in a carelessly managed hotel.
—CLARENCE DAY (1874–1935) *God and My Father*

God tempers the cold to the shorn lamb.
—HENRI ESTIENNE (*d.* 1520) *Premises*

There is no God but God.
—THE KORAN, Bk. iii

I live and love in God's peculiar light.
—MICHELANGELO (1475–1564)

God never shuts one door but he opens another.
—IRISH PROVERB

Had I but served my God with half the zeal
I served my king, he would not in mine age
Have left me naked to mine enemies.
—SHAKESPEARE (1564–1616) *Henry VIII*, III, ii, 456

Man proposes, but God disposes.
—THOMAS À KEMPIS (1380–1471) *Imitation of Christ*

If God didn't exist, man would have to invent Him.
—VOLTAIRE (1694–1778)

If God be for us, who can be against us?
—NEW TESTAMENT: *Romans*, viii, 31

God is our refuge and our strength, a very present help in trouble.
—OLD TESTAMENT: *Psalms*, xlvi, i

The heavens declare the glory of God; and the firmament showeth his handiwork.
—OLD TESTAMENT: *Psalms*, xix, i.

Goodness

Goodness is easier to recognize than to define; only the greatest novelists can portray good people.
—W. H. AUDEN (1907–1973) *I Believe*

It is as hard for the good to suspect evil, as it is for the bad to suspect good.
—CICERO (106–43 B.C.)

Good and bad men are each less so than they seem.
—SAMUEL TAYLOR COLERIDGE (1772–1834) *Table-Talk*

True goodness springs from a man's own heart. All men are born good.
—CONFUCIUS (*c.* 551–479 B.C.) *Analects*

The ground that a good man treads is hallowed.
—GOETHE (1749–1832) *Torquato Tasso*

Let them be good that love me, though but few.
—BEN JONSON (1572–1637) *Cynthia's Revels*

The greatest pleasure I know is to do a good action by stealth, and to have it found out by accident.
—CHARLES LAMB (1775–1834)

There is no man so good, who, were he to submit all his thoughts and actions to the laws, would not deserve hanging ten times in his life.
—MICHEL DE MONTAIGNE (1533–1592) *Essays*

Goodness is a special kind of truth and beauty. It is truth and beauty in human behavior.
—HARRY ALLEN OVERSTREET (1895–1970)

The good die young.
—ENGLISH PROVERB

He is so good that he is good for nothing.
-ITALIAN PROVERB

The evil that men do lives after them;
The good is oft interred with their bones.
—SHAKESPEARE (1564–1616) *Julius Caesar*, III, ii, 81

The good man is his own friend.
—SOPHOCLES (495–406 B.C.) *Oedipus Coloneus*

Be good, and you will be lonesome.
—MARK TWAIN (1835–1910)

Government

The marvel of history is the patience with which men and women submit to burdens unnecessarily laid upon them by their governments.
—WILLIAM E. BORAH (1865–1940) Speech in U.S. Senate

And having looked to Government for bread, on the very first scarcity they will turn and bite the hand that fed them.
—EDMUND BURKE (1729–1797)

A thousand years scarce serve to form a state;
An hour may lay it in the dust.
—LORD BYRON (1788–1824) *Childe Harold*

Self-government is the natural government of man.
—HENRY CLAY (1777–1852) Speech, 1818

No man has any right to rule who is not better than the people over whom he rules.
—CYRUS THE ELDER (600?–529 B.C.)

I can retain neither respect nor affection for a Government which has been moving from wrong to wrong in order to defend its immorality.
—MOHANDAS K. GANDHI (1869–1948)

The spirit of resistance to government is so valuable on certain occasions that I wish it to be always kept alive.
—THOMAS JEFFERSON (1743–1826) to Abigail Adams

No man is good enough to govern another man without that other's consent.
—ABRAHAM LINCOLN (1809–1865) Speech, 1854

That is the best government which desires to make the people happy, and knows how to make them happy.
—THOMAS B. MACAULAY (1800–1859)

If men be good, government cannot be bad.
—WILLIAM PENN (1644–1718) *Fruits of Solitude*

Oligarchy: A government resting on a valuation of property, in which the rich have power and the poor man is deprived of it.
—PLATO (428–347 B.C.) *The Republic*

That form of government is best which includes monarchy, aristocracy, and democracy.
—POLYBIUS (205?–125 B.C.) *Histories*

Any government, like any family, can for a year spend a little more than it earns. But you and I know that a continuance of that habit means the poorhouse.
—FRANKLIN D. ROOSEVELT (1882–1945) Radio Speech, 1932

Gratitude and Ingratitude

Gratitude is the sign of noble souls.
—AESOP (6th C. B.C.) *Androcles*

Earth produces nothing worse than an ungrateful man.
—AUSONIUS (*f.* 4th C. B.C.) *Epigrams*

Next to ingratitude, the most painful thing to bear is gratitude.
—HENRY WARD BEECHER (1813–1887)

Words are but empty thanks.
—COLLEY CIBBER (1671–1757) *Women's Wit*

When I'm not thanked at all I'm thanked enough.
—HENRY FIELDING (1707–1754)

A man is very apt to complain of the ingratitude of those who have risen far above him.
—SAMUEL JOHNSON (1709–1784) in Boswell's *Life*

A man who is ungrateful is often less to blame than his benefactor.
—FRANÇOIS DE LA ROCHEFOUCAULD (1613–1680) *Maxims*

The gratitude of most men is but a secret desire of receiving greater benefits.
—FRANÇOIS DE LA ROCHEFOUCAULD (1613–1680) *Maxims*

Gratitude is the least of virtues, but ingratitude the worst of vices.
—PROVERB

Blow, blow, thou winter wind,
Thou art not so unkind
As man's ingratitude . . . .
—SHAKESPEARE (1564–1616) *As You Like It*, II, vii, 174

How sharper than a serpent's tooth it is
To have a thankless child.
—SHAKESPEARE (1564–1616) *King Lear*, I, iv, 312

Do you like gratitude? I don't. If pity is akin to love, gratitude is akin to the other thing.
—GEORGE BERNARD SHAW (1856–1950) *Arms and the Man*

Alas! the gratitude of men
Hath often left me mourning.
—WILLIAM WORDSWORTH (1770–1850) *Simon Lee*

Greatness

When the dust of death has choked
A great man's voice, the common words he said
Turn oracles.
—ELIZABETH BARRETT BROWNING (1812–1861)

The price of greatness is responsibility.
—WINSTON CHURCHILL (1874–1965) Speech, 1943

The world cannot live at the level of its great men.
—SIR JAMES FRAZER (1854–1941) *The Golden Bough*

No really great man ever thought himself so.
—WILLIAM HAZLITT (1778–1830) *Table-Talk*

There would be no great ones if there were no little ones.
—GEORGE HERBERT (1593–1633)

Be not afraid of greatness. Some are born great, some achieve greatness, and some have greatness thrust upon them.
—SHAKESPEARE (1564–1616) *Twelfth Night*, II, v, 156

Great men are not always wise.
—OLD TESTAMENT: *Job*, xxxii, 9

Greed See AVARICE

Grief

It is dangerous to abandon one's self to the luxury of grief: it deprives one of courage, and even of the wish for recovery.
—HENRI-FREDERIC AMIEL (1828–1881) *Journal*, 1871

There is no grief which time does not lessen and soften.
—CICERO (106–43 B.C.) *Epistles*

Grief is itself a medicine.
—WILLIAM COWPER (1731–1800) *Charity*

Grief is the agony of an instant: the indulgence of grief the blunder of a life.
—BENJAMIN DISRAELI (1804–1881) *Vivian Grey*

The only cure for grief is action.
—GEORGE HENRY LEWES (1817–1878)

If our inward griefs were seen written on our brow, how many would be pitied who are now envied.
—METASTASIO (1698–1782) *Guiseppe Riconosciuto*

Grief is a tree that has tears for its fruit.
—PHILEMON (361?–263? B.C.) *Fragment*

Grief fills the room up of my absent child,
Lies in his bed, walks up and down with me,
Puts on his pretty looks, repeats his words,
Remembers me of all his gracious parts,
Stuffs out his vacant garments with his form.
—SHAKESPEARE (1564–1616) *King John*, III, iv, 93

Guilt

The pot calls the kettle black.
—CERVANTES (1547–1616) *Don Quixote*

Guilt is present in the very hesitation, even though the deed be not committed.
—CICERO (106–43 B.C.) *De Officiis*

Secret guilt by silence is betrayed.
—JOHN DRYDEN (1631–1700) *The Hind and the Panther*

Men's minds are too ready to excuse guilt in themselves.
—LIVY (59 B.C.–17 A.D.) *History*

He that knows no guilt can know no fear.
—PHILIP MASSINGER (1583–1640)

He confesseth himself guilty, who refuseth to come to trial.
—PROVERB

The lady doth protest too much, methinks.
—SHAKESPEARE (1564–1616) *Hamlet*, III, ii, 242

In other words, psychoanalysts relieve their patients from feeling guilty about things of which they are not guilty, and leave them with the sense of guilt about things of which they really are guilty.
—GREGORY ZILBOORG (1890–1959) *Psychoanalysis and Religion*

Habit

Habit is a sort of second nature.
—CICERO (106–43 B.C.) *De Finibus*

It seems, in fact, as though the second half of a man's life is made up of nothing but the habits he has accumulated during the first half.
—FËODOR DOSTOEVSKI (1821–1881) *The Possessed*

Habit is a cable; we weave a thread of it every day, and at last we cannot break it.
—HORACE MANN (1796–1859)

How use doth breed a habit in a man!
—SHAKESPEARE (1564–1616) *Two Gentlemen of Verona,* V, iv, 1

Hands

Living from hand to mouth, soon satisfi'd.
—GUILLAUME DU BARTAS (1544–1590) *Devine Weekes*

Many hands make light work.
—PROVERB

One hand washeth the other.
—SENECA (4? B.C.–A.D 65) *Apocolocyntosis*

All the perfumes of Arabia will not sweeten this little hand.
—SHAKESPEARE (1564–1616) *Macbeth,* V, i, 57

See, how she leans her cheek upon her hand!
O, that I were a glove upon that hand,
That I might touch that cheek!
—SHAKESPEARE (1564–1616) *Romeo and Juliet,* II, ii, 23

Let not thy left hand know what thy right hand doeth.
—NEW TESTAMENT: *Matthew,* vi, 3

His hand will be against every man and every man's hand against him.
—OLD TESTAMENT: *Genesis,* xvi, 12

Happiness

Hold him alone truly fortunate who has ended his life in happy well-being.
—AESCHYLUS (525–456 B.C.) *Agamemnon*

Happiness is at once the best, the noblest and the pleasantest of things.
—ARISTOTLE (384–322 B.C.) *Nicomachean Ethics*

What is given by the gods more desirable than a happy hour?
—CATULLUS (84?–54 B.C.) *Odes*

The happiness of life is made up of minute fractions—the little soon forgotten charities of a kiss or smile, a kind look, a heartfelt compliment, and the countless infinitesimals of pleasurable and genial feeling.
—SAMUEL TAYLOR COLERIDGE (1772–1834) *Friend*

To fill the hour—that is happiness.
—RALPH WALDO EMERSON (1803–1882) *Experience*

Often the greatest enemy of present happiness is past happiness too well remembered.
—OSCAR HAMMLING (1890–   )

Call no man happy till you know the nature of his death!
He is at best but fortunate.
—HERODOTUS (484–424? B.C.)

And there is even a happiness
That makes the heart afraid.
—THOMAS HOOD (1799–1845) *Ode to Melancholy*

The supreme happiness of life is the conviction that we are loved.
—VICTOR HUGO (1802–1885) *Les Misérables*

He is happiest of whom the world says least, good or bad.
—THOMAS JEFFERSON (1743–1826) Letter to John Adams, 1786

The happiness or unhappiness of men depends no less upon their dispositions than on their fortunes.
—FRANÇOIS DE LA ROCHEFOUCAULD (1613–1680) *Maxims*

Oh, how bitter a thing it is to look into happiness through another man's eyes.
—SHAKESPEARE (1564–1616) *As You Like It,* V, ii, 48

Happiness is the shadow of things past,
Which fools still take for that which is to be!
—FRANCIS THOMPSON (1859–1907) *From the Night of Forebeing*

The sun and stars that float in the open air;
The apple-shaped earth, and we upon it—
      surely the drift of them is something grand!
I do not know what it is, except that it is grand,
      and that it is happiness.
—WALT WHITMAN (1819–1892) *Carol of Occupations*

Hatred

Now hatred is by far the greatest pleasure;
Men love in haste, but they detest at leisure.
—LORD BYRON (1788–1824) *Don Juan*

People hate those who make them feel their own inferiority.
—LORD CHESTERFIELD (1694–1773) *Letters to His Son*

There are glances of hatred that stab and raise no cry of murder.
—GEORGE ELIOT (1819–1880) *Felix Holt*

Whom men fear they hate, and whom they hate, they wish dead.
—QUINTUS ENNIUS (239–169 B.C.) *Thyestes*

How incredible it is that in this fragile existence we should hate and destroy one another. There are possibilities enough for all who will abandon mastery over others to pursue mastery over nature. There is world enough for all to seek their happiness in their own way.
—LYNDON B. JOHNSON (1908–1973) Inaugural Address, Jan. 1965

Men hate more steadily than they love.
—SAMUEL JOHNSON (1709–1784) Boswell's *Life of Johnson*

For never can true reconcilement grow,
Where wounds of deadly hate have pierced so deep.
—JOHN MILTON (1608–1674) *Paradise Lost*

There is no sport in hate when all the rage
Is on one side.
—PERCY B. SHELLEY (1792–1822) *Lines to a Reviewer*

It is characteristic of human nature to hate the man whom you have wronged.
—TACITUS (54–119) *Agricola*

As love, if love be perfect, casts out fear,
So hate, if hate be perfect, casts out fear.
—TENNYSON (1809–1892) *Idylls of the King*

Health

In nothing do men more nearly approach the gods than in giving health to men.
—CICERO (106–43 B.C.) *Pro Ligario*

The health of the people is really the foundation upon which all their happiness and all their powers as a State depend.
—BENJAMIN DISRAELI (1804–1881)

Health is not a condition of matter, but of Mind.
—MARY BAKER G. EDDY (1821–1910) *Science and Health*

O health! health! the blessing of the rich! the riches of the poor! who can buy thee at too dear a rate, since there is no enjoying this world without thee?
—BEN JONSON (1572–1637) *Volpone*

Our prayers should be for a sound mind in a healthy body.
—JUVENAL (47–138) *Satires*

Life is not merely being alive, but being well.
—MARTIAL (*c.* A.D. 66) *Epigrams*

A man in good health is always full of advice to the sick.
—MENANDER (342–291 B.C.) *Andria*

It is part of the cure to wish to be cured.
—SENECA (8 B.C.–A.D. 65) *Hippolytus*

Measure your health by your sympathy with morning and spring. If there is no response in you to the awakening of nature, if the prospect of an early morning walk does not banish sleep, if the warble of the first bluebird does not thrill you, know that the morning and spring of your life are past, Thus may you feel your pulse.
—HENRY DAVID THOREAU (1817–1862) *Early Spring in Massachusetts*

Heart

My heart's in the Highlands, my heart is not here;
My heart's in the Highlands a-chasing the deer.
—ROBERT BURNS (1759–1796)

Maid of Athens, ere we part,
Give, oh, give me back my heart!
—LORD BYRON (1788–1824) *Maid of Athens*

Faint heart never won fair lady.
—WILLIAM CAMDEN (1551–1623) *Remains Concerning Britain*

The heart has eyes that the brain knows nothing of.
—DR. CHARLES HENRY PARKHURST (1842–1933)

And let me wring your heart; for so I shall,
If it be made of penetrable stuff.
—SHAKESPEARE (1564–1616) *Hamlet,* III, iv, 35

I will wear my heart upon my sleeve
For daws to peck at.
—SHAKESPEARE (1564–1616) *Othello,* I, i, 64

He hath a heart as sound as a bell and his tongue is the clapper, for what his heart thinks his tongue speaks.
—SHAKESPEARE (1564–1616) *Much Ado About Nothing,* III, ii, 12

My heart is a lonely hunter that hunts on a lonely hill.
—WILLIAM SHARP (1856?–1905) *The Lonely Hunter*

My true-love hath my heart, and I have his
By just exchange one for the other given
I hold his dear, and mine he cannot miss
There never was a better bargain driven.
—SIR PHILIP SIDNEY (1554–1586) *The Bargain*

Let not your heart be troubled.
—NEW TESTAMENT: *John,* xiv, 1

Heat See WEATHER

Heaven

All places are distant from heaven alike.
—ROBERT BURTON (1577–1640) *Anatomy of Melancholy*

To Appreciate heaven well
'Tis good for a man to have some fifteen minutes of hell.
—WILL CARLETON (1845–1912) *Farm Ballads*

And so upon this wise I prayed,—
    Great Spirit, give to me
A heaven not so large as yours
    But large enough for me.
—EMILY DICKINSON (1830–1886) *A Prayer*

I sent my soul through the invisible,
Some letter of that after-life to spell:
    And by and by my soul return'd to me,
And answer'd, "I myself am Heav'n and Hell."
—EDWARD FITZGERALD (1809–1883) tr.: *Rubáiyát of Omar Khayyám*

All this, and Heaven too!
—MATTHEW HENRY (1662–1714) *Life of Philip Henry*

What came from the earth returns back to the earth, and the spirit that was sent from heaven, again carried back, is received into the temple of heaven.
—LUCRETIUS (96–55 B.C.) *De Rerum Natura*

Here we may reign secure; and in my choice
To reign is worth ambition, though in Hell:
Better to reign in Hell, than serve in Heav'n.
—JOHN MILTON (1608–1674) *Paradise Lost*

Heaven-gates are not so highly arch'd
As princes' palaces; they that enter there
Must go upon their knees.
—JOHN WEBSTER (1580?–1625) *The Duchess of Malfi*

In my father's house are many mansions.
—NEW TESTAMENT: *John,* xiv, 2

Hell

Hell is full of good intentions or desires.
—ST. BERNARD OF CLAIRVAUX (1091–1153)

Here sighs, plaints, and voices of the deepest woe resounded through the starless sky. Strange languages, horrid cries, accents of grief and wrath, voices deep and hoarse, with hands clenched in despair, made a commotion which whirled forever through that air of everlasting gloom, even as sand when whirlwinds sweep the ground.
—DANTE (1265–1321) *Inferno,* Canto iii

Abandon every hope, ye who enter here.
—DANTE (1265–1321) *Inferno,* Canto iii [Inscription over the gate of Hell]

I found the original of my hell in the world which we inhabit.
—DANTE (1265–1321)

Hell is a circle about the unbelieving.
—THE KORAN

Hell hath no limits, nor is circumscrib'd
In one self-place; for where we are is hell;
And where hell is, there must we ever be;
And to conclude, when all the world dissolves,
And every creature shall be purified,
All places shall be hell that are not heaven.
—CHRISTOPHER MARLOWE (1564–1593) *Dr. Faustus*

Myself am Hell;
And, in the lowest deep, a lower deep,
Still threat'ning to devour me, opens wide;
To which the hell I suffer seems a heaven.
—JOHN MILTON (1608–1674) *Paradise Lost*

Heroism

No man is a hero to his valet.
—MLLE. AISSE (1694?–1733) *Letters*

Heroism is the brilliant triumph of the soul over the flesh—that is to say, over fear. . . . Heroism is the dazzling and glorious concentration of courage.
—HENRI-FREDERIC AMIEL (1828–1881) *Journal,* October 1, 1849

Heroism feels and never reasons and therefore is always right.
—RALPH WALDO EMERSON (1803–1882) *Heroism*

There is nothing more touching than the sight of a Nation in search of its great men, nothing more beautiful than its readiness to accept a hero on trust.
—JAMES RUSSELL LOWELL (1819–1891) *General McClellan's Report*

History

The great object in trying to understand history is to get behind men and grasp ideas.
—LORD ACTON (1834–1902) *Letters to Mary Gladstone*

Biography is the only true history.
—THOMAS CARLYLE (1795–1881) *Journal,* January 13, 1832

All history, so far as it is not supported by contemporary evidence, is romance.
—SAMUEL JOHNSON (1709–1784) Boswell's *Tour to Hebrides*

History is the witness of the times, the torch of truth, the life of memory, the teacher of life, the messenger of antiquity.
—CICERO (106–43 B.C.) *De Oratore*

History is clarified experience.
—JAMES RUSSELL LOWELL (1819–1891) *Books and Libraries*

History repeats itself.
—THUCYDIDES (471?–400? B.C.) *History,* Bk. i

Home

You are a King by your own Fireside, as much as any Monarch on his Throne.
—CERVANTES (1547–1616) *Don Quixote*

In love of home, the love of country has its rise.
—CHARLES DICKENS (1812–1870) *Old Curiosity Shop*

Home is the place where, when you have to go there,
They have to take you in.
—ROBERT FROST (1875–1963) *The Death of the Hired Man*

Be it ever so humble, there's no place like home.
—JOHN HOWARD PAYNE (1791–1852) *Home Sweet Home*

Home is where the heart is.
—PLINY THE ELDER (A.D. 23–79)

Weep no more, my lady;
  Oh, weep no more today!
We will sing one song for the old Kentucky home,
  For the old Kentucky home, far away.
—STEPHEN C. FOSTER (1812–1864) *Old Folks At Home*

It takes a heap o' livin' in a house t' make it home.
—EDGAR A. GUEST (1881–1959) *Home*

To be happy at home is the ultimate result of all ambition, the end to which every enterprise and labor tends, and of which every desire prompts the prosecution.
—SAMUEL JOHNSON (1709–1784) *Rambler*

When I was at home I was in a better place.
—SHAKESPEARE (1564–1616) *As You Like It,* II, iv, 14

As a bird that wandereth from her nest, so is a man that wandereth from his place.
—OLD TESTAMENT: *Proverbs,* xxvii, 8

Honesty

A trustee is held to something stricter than the morals of the market place. Not honesty alone, but the punctilio of an honor the most sensitive, is then the standard of behavior.
—BENJAMIN N. CARDOZO (1870–1938)

Make yourself an honest man, and then you may be sure that there is one rascal less in the world.
—THOMAS CARLYLE (1795–1881)

Honesty is the best policy.
—CERVANTES (1547–1616) *Don Quixote*

  If he were
To be made honest by an act of parliament
I should not alter in my faith of him.
—BEN JONSON (1572–1637) *Devil is an Ass*

An honest man is the noblest work of God.
—ALEXANDER POPE (1688–1744) *Essay on Man*

You are underrating the President [Lincoln]. I grant that he lacks higher education and his manners are not in accord with European conceptions of the dignity of a chief magistrate. He is a well-developed child of nature and is not skilled in polite phrases and poses. But he is a man of profound feeling, correct and firm principles and incorruptible honesty. His motives are unquestionable, and he possesses to a remarkable degree the characteristic, God-given trait of this people, sound common sense.
—CARL SCHURZ (1829–1906) Letter, October, 1864

There is no terror, Cassius, in your threats,
For I am arm'd so strong in honesty
That they pass by me as the idle wind,
Which I respect not.
—SHAKESPEARE (1564–1616) *Julius Caesar,* IV, iii, 66

Honor

The best memorial for a mighty man is to gain honour ere death.
—BEOWULF (8th C.)

Better a thousand times to die with glory than live without honor.
—LOUIS VI OF FRANCE (1081–1137)

I could not love thee, dear, so much,
Loved I not honor more.
—RICHARD LOVELACE (1618–1658) To Lucasta, On Going to Wars

Set honour in one eye and death i' the other
And I will look on both indifferently;
For let the gods so speed me as I love
The name of honour more than I fear death.
—SHAKESPEARE (1564–1616) *Julius Caesar,* I, ii, 86

Mine honour is my life; both grow in one;
Take honour from me and my life is done.
—SHAKESPEARE (1564–1616) *Richard II,* I, i, 182

Hope

I live on hope and that I think do all
Who come into this world.
—ROBERT BRIDGES (1844–1930) *The Growth of Love*

To the sick, while there is life there is hope.
—CICERO (106–43 B.C.) *Epistolae Ad Atticum*

Hope is itself a species of happiness, and, perhaps, the chief happiness which this world affords.
—SAMUEL JOHNSON (1709–1784) in Boswell's *Life of Johnson*

The setting of a great hope is like the setting of the sun. The brightness of our life is gone.
—HENRY W. LONGFELLOW (1807–1882) *Hyperion*

Hopes are but the dreams of those who wake.
—PINDAR (*c.* 522–442 B.C.) *Fragment*

Hope springs eternal in the human breast;
Man never is, but always to be blest.
—ALEXANDER POPE (1688–1744) *Essay on Man*

Hope, dead lives nevermore,
No, not in heaven.
—CHRISTINA ROSSETTI (1830–1894) *Dead Hope*

True hope is swift, and flies with swallow's wings;
Kings it makes gods, and meaner creatures kings.
—SHAKESPEARE (1564–1616) *Richard III*, V, ii, 23

We did not dare to breathe a prayer
     Or to give our anguish scope!
Something was dead in each of us,
     And what was dead was hope.
—OSCAR WILDE (1854–1900) *The Ballad of Reading Gaol*

Hospitality

People are either born hosts or born guests.
—MAX BEERBOHM (1872–1956)

Hospitality consists in a little fire, a little food, and an immense quiet.
—RALPH WALDO EMERSON (1803–1882) *Journal*

Then why should I sit in the scorner's seat,
     Or hurl the cynic's ban?
Let me live in my house by the side of the road,
     And be a friend to man.
—SAM WALTER FOSS (1858–1911) *House by the Side of the Road*

Hail Guest! We ask not what thou art:
If Friend, we greet thee, hand and heart;
If Stranger, such no longer be;
If Foe, our love shall conquer thee.
—ARTHUR GUITERMAN (1871–1943) *Old Welsh Door Verse*

True friendship's laws are by this rule express'd,
Welcome the coming, speed the parting guest.
—HOMER (*c.* 10th–8th C. B.C.) *The Odyssey*

Fish and guests in three days are stale.
—JOHN LYLY (1554?–1606) *Euphues*

When there is room in the heart there is room in the house.
—DANISH PROVERB

I had three chairs in my house: one for solitude, two for friendship, three for society.
—HENRY DAVID THOREAU (1817–1862) *Walden*

Be not forgetful to entertain strangers, for thereby some have entertained angels unawares.
—NEW TESTAMENT: *Hebrews,* xiii, 2

Humility

Lowliness is the base of every virtue,
And he who goes the lowest builds the safest.
—PHILIP J. BAILEY (1816–1902) *Festus*

I ate umble pie with an appetite.
—CHARLES DICKENS (1812–1870) *David Copperfield*

   True humility,
The highest virtue, mother of them all.
—TENNYSON (1809–1892) *Idylls of the King*

Whosoever shall smite thee on thy right cheek, turn to him the other also.
—NEW TESTAMENT: *Matthew,* v, 39: *Luke,* vi, 29

Whosoever shall compel thee to go a mile, go with him twain.
—NEW TESTAMENT: *Matthew,* vi, 41

Hunger

Hunger is the best sauce in the world.
—CERVANTES (1547–1616) *Don Quixote*

An empty stomach is not a good political adviser.
—ALBERT EINSTEIN (1879–1955) *Cosmic Religion*

They that die by famine die by inches.
—MATTHEW HENRY (1662–1714) *Commentaries*

Death in all its shapes is hateful to unhappy man, but the worst is death from hunger.
—HOMER (*c.* 10th–8th C. B.C.) *Odyssey*

If thine enemy be hungry, give him bread to eat.
—OLD TESTAMENT: *Lamentations,* iv, 9

Husband

We wedded men live in sorrow and care.
—GEOFFREY CHAUCER (1340?–1400) *Merchant's Tale Prologue*

It is necessary to be almost a genius to make a good husband.
—HONORÉ DE BALZAC (1799–1850) *Physiology of Marriage*

Let the husband render unto the wife due benevolence: and likewise also the wife unto the husband.
—NEW TESTAMENT: *I Corinthians,* vii, 3

Idleness is only the refuge of weak minds, and the holiday of fools.
—LORD CHESTERFIELD (1694–1773) *Letters,* July 20, 1749

Absence of occupation is not rest,
A mind quite vacant is a mind distress'd.
—WILLIAM COWPER (1731–1800) *Retirement*

There is no place in civilization for the idler. None of us has any right to ease.
—HENRY FORD (1863–1947)

Laziness travels so slowly that poverty soon overtakes him.
—BEN FRANKLIN (1706–1790) *Poor Richard's Almanack*

To be idle and to be poor have always been reproaches, and therefore every man endeavors with his utmost care to hide his poverty from others, and his idleness from himself.
—SAMUEL JOHNSON (1709–1784) *The Idler*

Of all our faults, the one that we excuse most easily is idleness.
—FRANÇOIS DE LA ROCHEFOUCAULD (1613–1680) *Maxims*

For Satan finds some mischief still
    For idle hands to do.
—ISAAC WATTS (1674–1748) *Divine Songs*

To do nothing at all is the most difficult thing in the world, the most difficult and the most intellectual.
—OSCAR WILDE (1854–1900) *The Critic as Artist*

Go to the ant, thou sluggard; consider her ways, and be wise.
—OLD TESTAMENT: *Proverbs,* vi, 6

Ignorance

Ignorance is the night of the mind, but a night without moon or star.
—CONFUCIUS (*c.* 551–478 B.C.) *Analects*

To be conscious that you are ignorant is a great step to knowledge.
—BENJAMIN DISRAELI (1804–1881) *Sybil*

To the ignorant even the words of the wise seem foolishness.
—EURIPIDES (480–406 B.C.) *The Bacchae*

No more; where ignorance is bliss,
    'Tis folly to be wise.
—THOMAS GRAY (1716–1771) *On a Distant Prospect of Eton College*

Ignorance of the law excuses no man: not that all can know the law, but because 'tis an excuse everyone will plead, and no man can tell how to refute him.
—JOHN SELDEN (1584–1654) *Table-Talk*

There is no darkness, but ignorance.
—SHAKESPEARE (1564–1616) *Twelfth Night,* IV, ii, 44

Imagination

Only in men's imagination does every truth find an effective and undeniable existence. Imagination, not invention, is the supreme master of art as of life.
—JOSEPH CONRAD (1857–1924) *A Personal Record*

To know is nothing at all; to imagine is everything.
—ANATOLE FRANCE (1844–1924) *The Crime of Sylvestre Bonnard*

Were it not for imagination a man would be as happy in the arms of a chambermaid as of a duchess.
—SAMUEL JOHNSON (1709–1784) Boswell's *Life of Johnson*

His imagination resembled the wings of an ostrich. It enabled him to run, though not to soar.
—THOMAS B. MACAULAY (1800–1859) *On John Dryden*

The human race is governed by its imagination.
—NAPOLEON BONAPARTE (1769–1821)

Imitation

Men often applaud an imitation, and hiss the real thing.
—AESOP (6th C. B.C.) *The Buffoon and the Countryman*

Imitation is the sincerest flattery.
—CHARLES C. COLTON (1780?–1832)

He who imitates what is evil always goes beyond the example that is set; on the contrary, he who imitates what is good always falls short.
—FRANCESCO GUICCIARDINI (1483–1540) *Story of Italy*

Agesilaus, being invited once to hear a man who admirably imitated the nightingale, declined, saying he had heard the nightingale itself.
—PLUTARCH (46?–120?) *Lives: Agesilaus*

A great part of art consists in imitation. For the whole conduct of life is based on this: that what we admire in others we want to do ourselves.
—QUINTILIAN (40–*c.* 100) *De institutio Oratoria*

Go, and do thou likewise.
—NEW TESTAMENT: *Luke,* x, 37

Immortality

Let us not lament too much the passing of our friends. They are not dead, but simply gone before us along the road which all must travel.
—ANTIPHANES (*c.* 360 B.C.) *Fragment*

After the resurrection of the body shall have taken place, being set free from the condition of time, we shall enjoy eternal life, with love ineffable and steadfastness without corruption.
—ST. AUGUSTINE (354–430) *Of the Faith and of the Creed*

If I err in my belief that the souls of men are immortal, I err gladly, and I do not wish to lose so delightful an error.
—CICERO (106–43 B.C.) *De Senectute*

My humble friend, we know not how to live this life which is so short yet seek one that never ends.
—ANATOLE FRANCE (1844–1924) *The Red Lily*

Either the soul is immortal and we shall not die, or it perishes with the flesh, and we shall not know that we are dead. Live, then, as if you were eternal.
—ANDRÉ MAUROIS (1885–1967)

Indecision See DECISION

Independence See DEPENDENCE

Indiscretion See DISCRETION

Individualism

What another would have done as well as you, do not do it. What another would have said as well as you, do not say it; written as well, do not write it. Be faithful to that which exists nowhere but in yourself—and thus make yourself indispensable.
—ANDRÉ GIDE (1869–1951) *Fruits of the Earth*

Whatever crushes individuality is despotism, by whatever name it may be called.
—JOHN STUART MILL (1806–1873) *On Liberty*

An individual is as superb as a nation when he has the qualities which make a superb nation.
—WALT WHITMAN (1819–1892) *Leaves of Grass,* preface

Jealousy

Anger and jealousy can no more bear to lose sight of their objects than love.
—GEORGE ELIOT (1819–1880) *The Mill on the Floss*

Though jealousy be produced by love, as ashes are by fire, yet jealousy extinguishes love as ashes smother the flame.
—MARGARET OF NAVARRE (1492–1549) *Heptameron*

O! beware, my lord, of jealousy
It is the green-eyed monster which doth mock
The meat it feeds on.
—SHAKESPEARE (1564–1616) *Othello,* III, iii, 166

Love is strong as death; jealousy is cruel as the grave.
—OLD TESTAMENT: *Song of Solomon,* viii, 6

Joy

Joy rises in me like a summer's morn.
—SAMUEL TAYLOR COLERIDGE (1772–1834) *Christmas Carol*

My theory is to enjoy life, but the practice is against it.
—CHARLES LAMB (1775–1834)

My candle burns at both ends,
    It will not last the night;
But ah, my foes, and oh, my friends,
    It gives a lovely light!
—EDNA ST. VINCENT MILLAY (1892–1951)

Drink and dance and laugh and lie,
    Love the reeling midnight through,
For tomorrow we shall die!
    (But, alas, we never do.)
—DOROTHY PARKER (1893–1968) *The Flaw in Paganism*

A joy that's shared is a joy made double.
—JOHN RAY (1627?–1705) *English Proverbs*

Silence is the perfectest herald of joy:
I were but little happy if I could say how much.
—SHAKESPEARE (1564–1616) *Much Ado About Nothing,* II, i, 317

    I have drunken deep of joy,
And I will taste no other wine to-night.
—PERCY B. SHELLEY (1792–1822) *The Cenci*

Weeping may endure for a night, but joy cometh in the morning.
—OLD TESTAMENT: *Psalms,* xxx, 5

Justice

Heaven gives long life to the just and the intelligent.
—CONFUCIUS (*c.* 551–478 B.C.) *The Book of History*

Justice is truth in action.
—BENJAMIN DISRAELI (1804–1881) Speech, Feb. 11, 1851

He reminds me of the man who murdered both his parents, and then, when sentence was about to be pronounced, pleaded for mercy on the grounds that he was an orphan.
—ABRAHAM LINCOLN (1809–1865) attributed

Just as, in fact there can be no peace without order so there can be no order without justice. . . .
—POPE PIUS XII (1876–1958) Address on Easter Sunday, 1939

Only the actions of the just
Smell sweet and blossom in the dust.
—JAMES SHIRLEY (1596–1666) *The Contention of Ajax and Ulysses*

Thrice is he armed that hath his quarrel just,
And he but naked, though licked up in steel,
Whose conscience with injustice is corrupted.
—SHAKESPEARE (1564–1616) *Henry VI,* III, ii, 232

What's sauce for a goose is sauce for a gander.
—JONATHAN SWIFT (1667–1745) *Polite Conversation*

Judging from the main portions of the history of the world, so far, justice is always in jeopardy.
—WALT WHITMAN (1819–1892) *Democratic Vistas*

He that ruleth over men must be just.
—OLD TESTAMENT: *Samuel,* xxiii, 3

The spirit of just men made perfect.
—NEW TESTAMENT: *Hebrews,* xii, 23

Kindness

It is difficult to tell how much men's minds are conciliated by a kind manner and gentle speech.
—CICERO (106–43 B.C.) *De Officiis*

A kindness loses its grace by being noised abroad,
Who desires it to be remembered should forget it.
—PIERRE CORNEILLE (1606–1684) *Theodore*

It is a kindness to refuse gently what you intend to deny.
—PUBLILIUS SYRUS (1st C. B.C.) *Sententiae*

This was the unkindest cut of all.
—SHAKESPEARE (1564–1616) *Julius Caesar,* III, ii, 187

    Yet do I fear thy nature;
It is too full o' the milk of human kindness.
—SHAKESPEARE (1564–1616) *Macbeth,* I, v, 14

Knowledge

What one knows is, in youth, of little moment; they know enough who know how to learn.
—HENRY ADAMS (1838–1918) *Education of Henry Adams*

Knowledge is, indeed, that which, next to virtue, truly and essentially raises one man above another.
—JOSEPH ADDISON (1672–1719) *The Guardian*

I assure you I had rather excel others in the knowledge of what is excellent, than in the extent of my power and dominion.
—ALEXANDER THE GREAT (356–323 B.C.)

Knowledge is power.
—FRANCIS BACON (1561–1620) *De Haeresibus*

Knowledge is a comfortable and necessary retreat and shelter for us in an advanced age; and if we do not plant it while young, it will give us no shade when we grow old.
—LORD CHESTERFIELD (1694–1773) *Letters*

No technical knowledge can outweigh knowledge of the humanities, in the gaining of which philosophy and history walk hand in hand. Our inheritance of well-founded slowly conceived codes of honor, morals and manners, the passionate convictions which so many hundreds of millions share together of the principles of freedom and justice, are far more precious to us than anything which scientific discoveries can bestow.
—WINSTON CHURCHILL (1874–1965) Speech, March 31, 1949

It is the province of knowledge to speak, and it is the privilege of wisdom to listen.
—OLIVER WENDELL HOLMES (1809–1894)

Knowledge is of two kinds. We know a subject ourselves or we know where we can find information upon it.
—SAMUEL JOHNSON (1709–1784) Boswell's *Life of Johnson*

To myself I seem to have been only like a boy playing on the sea-shore, and diverting myself in now and then finding a smoother pebble, or a prettier shell than ordinary, whilst the great ocean of truth lay all undiscovered before me.
—SIR ISAAC NEWTON (1642–1727)

Then I began to think, that it is very true which is commonly said, that the one-half of the world knoweth not how the other half liveth.
—FRANÇOIS RABELAIS (1494?–1553) *Pantagruel*

   Ignorance is the curse of God,
Knowledge the wing wherewith we fly to heaven.
—SHAKESPEARE (1564–1616) *II Henry VI,* IV, vii, 78

I do not know that knowledge amounts to anything more definite than a novel and grand surprise, or a sudden revelation of the insufficiency of all that we had called knowledge before; an indefinite sense of the grandeur and glory of the universe.
—HENRY DAVID THOREAU (1817–1862) *Spring in Massachusetts*

Labor

There is no right to strike against the public safety by anybody, anywhere, anytime.
—CALVIN COOLIDGE (1872–1933) Letter to Samuel Gompers

Each needs the other: capital cannot do without labor, nor labor without capital.
—POPE LEO XIII (1810–1903) *Rerum Novarum*

Bowed by the weight of centuries he leans
Upon his hoe and gazes on the ground,
The emptiness of the ages in his face,
And on his back the burden of the world.
—EDWIN MARKHAM (1852–1940) *Man With the Hoe*

No business which depends for existence on paying less than living wages to its workers has any right to continue in this country.
—FRANKLIN D. ROOSEVELT (1882–1945) Public statement

I am a true labourer: I earn that I eat, get that I wear, owe no man hate, envy no man's happiness, glad of other men's good.
—SHAKESPEARE (1564–1616) *As You Like It,* III, ii, 78

There is no real wealth but the labor of man. Were the mountains of gold and the valleys of silver, the world would not be one grain of corn the richer; no one comfort would be added to the human race.
—PERCY B. SHELLEY (1792–1822) *Queen Mab,* notes

The labourer is worthy of his hire.
—NEW TESTAMENT: *Luke,* x, 7

Let them be hewers of wood and drawers of water.
—OLD TESTAMENT: *Joshua,* ix, 21

Language

You are worth as many men as you know languages.
—CHARLES V, HOLY ROMAN EMPEROR (1500–1558)

In language clearness is everything.
—CONFUCIUS (c. 551–478 B.C.) *Analects*

A man who does not know foreign languages is ignorant of his own.
—GOETHE (1749–1832) *Sprüche in Prosa*

There is no master key to the inner life of a people, but language unlocks a vast treasure house.
—EDGAR LEE HEWETT (1865–1946) *Ancient Life in Mexico*

Every language is a temple in which the soul of those who speak it is enshrined.
—OLIVER WENDELL HOLMES (1809–1894)

Language is the dress of thought.
—SAMUEL JOHNSON (1709–1784) *Lives of the Poets*

The way to learn a language is to sit down and learn it.
—WILLIAM GRAHAM SUMNER (1840–1910) *Reminiscences*

Language, as well as the faculty of speech, was the immediate gift of God.
—NOAH WEBSTER (1758–1843) *American Dictionary,* Preface

Language is not an abstract construction of the learned, or of dictionary makers, but it is something arising out of the work, needs, ties, joys, affections, tastes, of long generations of humanity, and has its bases broad and low, close to the ground.
—WALT WHITMAN (1819–1892) *Slang in America*

Laughter

God hath not granted to woeful mortals even laughter without tears.
—CALLIMACHUS (*c.* 260–240 B.C.) *Fragments*

You no doubt laugh in your sleeve.
—CICERO (106–43 B.C.) *De Finibus*

The loud laugh that spoke the vacant mind.
—OLIVER GOLDSMITH (1730–1774) *The Deserted Village*

Laughter unquenchable arose among the blessed gods.
—HOMER (*c.* 10th–8th C. B.C.) *Iliad*

I laugh because I must not cry.
—ABRAHAM LINCOLN (1809–1865)

He deserves Paradise who makes his companions laugh.
—MOHAMMED (570–632) *The Koran*

Everything gives cause for either laughter or tears.
—SENECA (4? B.C.–A.D. 65) *De Ira*

The pleasantest laughter is at the expense of our enemies.
—SOPHOCLES (495–406 B.C.) *Ajax*

Laughter is not a bad beginning for a friendship, and it is the best ending for one.
—OSCAR WILDE (1854–1900) *The Picture of Dorian Gray*

Woe unto you that laugh now! for ye shall mourn and weep.
—NEW TESTAMENT: *Luke,* vi, 25

As the crackling of thorns under a pot, so is the laughter of a fool.
—OLD TESTAMENT: *Ecclesiastes,* vii, 6

Law

Law is a pledge that the citizens of a state will do justice to one another.
—ARISTOTLE (384–322 B.C.) *Politics*

The beginning of the law is benevolence, and with benevolence it ends.
—BABYLONIAN TALMUD: *Sotah*

The laws place the safety of all before the safety of individuals.
—CICERO (106–43 B.C.) *De Finibus*

Men would be great criminals did they need as many laws as they make.
—CHARLES JOHN DARLING (1849–1936) *Scintillæ Juris*

Time is the best interpreter of every doubtful law.
—DIONYSIUS OF HALICARNASSUS (d. *c.* 7 B.C.) *Antiquities of Rome*

Possession is nine points of the law.
—THOMAS FULLER (1608–1681) *Holy War*

In law a man is guilty when he violates the rights of another. In ethics he is guilty if he only thinks of doing so.
—IMMANUEL KANT (1724–1804) *Lecture at Königsberg, 1775*

The purpose of law is to prevent the strong from always having their way.
—OVID (43 B.C.–A.D. 18?) *Fasti*

No man is above the law and no man is below it; nor do we ask any man's permission when we require him to obey it.
—THEODORE ROOSEVELT (1858–1919) Message, Jan. 1904

Ye shall have one manner of law, as well for the stranger, as for one of your own country.
—OLD TESTAMENT: *Leviticus,* xxiv, 22

Where is there any book of the law so clear to each man as that written in his heart?
—LEO TOLSTOY (1828–1910) *The Chinese Pilot*

He that pleads his own cause has a fool for his client.
—ENGLISH PROVERB

Leadership

I light my candle from their torches.
—ROBERT BURTON (1577–1640) *Anatomy of Melancholy*

And when we think we lead we most are led.
—LORD BYRON (1788–1824) *The Two Foscari*

The final test of a leader is that he leaves behind him in other men the conviction and the will to carry on.
—WALTER LIPPMANN (1889–1974) *Roosevelt Has Gone*

An two men ride of a horse, one must ride behind.
—SHAKESPEARE (1564–1616) *Much Ado About Nothing,* III, v, 40

Ill can he rule the great that cannot reach the small.
—EDMUND SPENSER (1552?–1599) *The Faerie Queen*

Reason and calm judgment, the qualities specially belonging to a leader.
—TACITUS (55–117) *History*

Learning

What one knows is, in youth, of little moment; they know enough who know how to learn.
—HENRY ADAMS (1838–1918) *Education of Henry Adams*

All men by nature desire to know.
—ARISTOTLE (384–322 B.C.)

That there should one man die ignorant who had capacity for knowledge, this I call tragedy.
—THOMAS CARLYLE (1795–1881)

Wear your learning, like your watch, in a private pocket; and do not pull it out, and strike it, merely to show that you have one.
—LORD CHESTERFIELD (1694–1773) *Letters,* February 22, 1748

A smattering of everything and a knowledge of nothing.
—CHARLES DICKENS (1812–1870) *Sketches by Boz*

Education is a controlling grace to the young, consolation to the old, wealth to the poor, and ornament to the rich.
—DIOGENES LAERTIUS (2nd or 3rd C. A.D.)

You send your child to the schoolmaster, but 'tis the schoolboys who educate him.
—RALPH WALDO EMERSON (1803–1882) *Conduct of Life*

If you have knowledge, let others light their candles at it.
—MARGARET FULLER (1810–1850)

A child's education should begin at least one hundred years before he was born.
—OLIVER WENDELL HOLMES (1809–1894)

The important thing is not so much that every child should be taught, as that every child should be given the wish to learn.
—SIR JOHN LUBBOCK (1834–1913) *Pleasures of Life*

A little learning is a dangerous thing;
Drink deep, or taste not the Pierian spring:
There shallow draughts intoxicate the brain,
And drinking largely sobers us again.
—ALEXANDER POPE (1688–1744) *An Essay On Criticism*

'Tis education forms the common mind:
Just as the twig is bent the tree's inclined.
—ALEXANDER POPE (1688–1744) *Moral Essays*

I am glad to learn, in order that I may teach.
—SENECA (4? B.C.–A.D. 65) *Ad Lucilium*

The great aim of education is not knowledge but action.
—HERBERT SPENCER (1820–1903)

There is no royal road to learning; no short cut to the acquirement of any valuable art.
—ANTHONY TROLLOPE (1815–1882) *Barchester Towers*

Leisure

When a man's busy, why, leisure
Strikes him as wonderful pleasure;
'Faith, and at leisure once is he?
Straightway he wants to be busy.
—ROBERT BROWNING (1812–1889) *The Glove*

It is the mark of a superior man that he will take no harmful ease.
—CONFUCIUS (*c.* 551–478 B.C.) *Book of History*

A life of leisure and a life of laziness are two things.
—BEN FRANKLIN (1706–1790) *Poor Richard's Almanack*

Give time to your friends, leisure to your wife, relax your mind, give rest to your body, so that you may the better fulfil your accustomed occupation.
—PHAEDRUS (A.D. 1st C.) *Fables*

To be able to fill leisure intelligently is the last product of civilization.
—BERTRAND RUSSELL (1872–1970) *The Conquest of Happiness*

Liberty

Eternal spirit of the chainless mind!
Brightest in dungeons, Liberty! thou art.
—LORD BYRON (1788–1824) *The Prisoner of Chillon*

The condition upon which God has given liberty to man is eternal vigilance.
—JOHN PHILPOT CURRAN (1750–1817) Speech upon the Right of Election, July 10, 1790.

Those, who would give up essential liberty to purchase a little temporary safety, deserve neither liberty nor safety.
—BEN FRANKLIN (1706–1790) Historical Review of Constitution and Government of Pennsylvania

Is Life so dear or peace so sweet as to be purchased at the price of chains and slavery? Forbid it, Almighty God! I know not what course others may take, but as for me, give me liberty, or give me death.
—PATRICK HENRY (1736–1799) Speech, 1775

The God who gave us life gave us liberty at the same time.
—THOMAS JEFFERSON (1743–1826) The Rights of British America

It is true that liberty is precious—so precious that it must be rationed.
—NIKOLAI LENIN (1870–1924)

The inescapable price of liberty is an ability to preserve it from destruction.
—GENERAL DOUGLAS MACARTHUR (1880–1964) Speech

He that would make his own liberty secure must guard even his enemy from oppression.
—THOMAS PAINE (1737–1809) First Principles of Government

There is . . . no liberty but liberty under law. Law does not restrict liberty; it creates the only real liberty there is.
—WILLIAM SUMNER (1840–1910) The Forgotten Man

Life

Remember that man's life lies all within this present, as 't were but a hair's breadth of time; as for the rest, the past is gone, the future may never be. Short, therefore, is man's life, and narrow is the corner of the earth wherein he dwells.
—MARCUS AURELIUS (121–180) Meditations

Life is a test and this world a place of trial. Always the problems—or it may be the same problem—will be presented to every generation in different forms.
—WINSTON CHURCHILL (1874–1965) Speech 1949

I have measured out my life with coffee spoons.
—T. S. ELIOT (1888–1965) Love Song of J. Alfred Prufrock

The fool, with all his other faults, has this also: he is always getting ready to live.
—EPICURUS (342–270 B.C.) Fragments

Were it offered to my choice, I should have no objection to a repetition of the same life from its beginnings, only asking the advantages authors have in a second edition to correct some faults.
—BEN FRANKLIN (1706–1790) Autobiography

There is more to life than increasing its speed.
—MOHANDAS GANDHI (1869–1948)

I wish to preach, not the doctrine of ignoble ease, but the doctrine of the strenuous life.
—THEODORE ROOSEVELT (1858–1919) Speech

Life is neither a good nor an evil; it is simply the place where good and evil exist.
—SENECA (4? B.C.–A.D. 65) Epistulae ad Lucilium

Life is as tedious as a twice-told tale,
Vexing the dull ear of a drowsy man.
—SHAKESPEARE (1564–1616) King John, III, iv, 108

One man in his time plays many parts,
His acts being seven ages.
—SHAKESPEARE (1564–1616) As You Like It, II, vii, 142

The web of our life is of a mingled yarn, good and ill together.
—SHAKESPEARE (1564–1616) All's Well That Ends Well, IV, iii, 83

As for man, his days are as grass: as a flower of the field, so he flourisheth.
—OLD TESTAMENT: Psalms, viii, 15

The mass of men lead lives of quiet desperation.
—HENRY DAVID THOREAU (1817–1862) Walden

Love

I have never loved anyone for love's sake, except, perhaps, Josephine—a little.
—NAPOLEON BONAPARTE (1769–1821)

How do I love thee? Let me count the ways.
. . .
I love thee with a love I seemed to lose
With my lost saints, —I love thee with the breath,
Smiles, tears, of all my life!—, if God choose,
I shall but love thee better after death.
—ELIZABETH B. BROWNING (1806–1861) Sonnets from the Portuguese

God be thanked, the meanest of his creatures
Boasts two soul-sides, one to face the world with,
One to show a woman when he loves her.
—ROBERT BROWNING (1812–1889) One Word More

Oh my luve's like a red, red, rose,
   That's newly sprung in June;
Oh my luve's like the melodie
   That's sweetly played in tune.
—ROBERT BURNS (1759–1796) Red, Red Rose

To see her is to love her,
   And love but her forever;
For nature made her what she is,
   And never made anither!
—ROBERT BURNS (1759–1796) Bonny Lesley

Alas! the love of women! it is known
To be a lovely and a fearful thing.
—LORD BYRON (1788–1824) Don Juan

Let Time and Chance combine, combine!
Let Time and Chance combine!
The fairest love from heaven above,
   That love of yours was mine,
                    My Dear!
   That love of yours was mine.
—THOMAS CARLYLE (1795–1881) Adieu

Love and war are the same thing, and stratagems and policy are as allowable in the one as in the other.
—CERVANTES (1547–1616) Don Quixote

If love be good, from whennes comth my wo?
—GEOFFREY CHAUCER (1340?–1400) Troilus and Criseyde

The Stoics define love as the endeavor to form a friendship inspired by beauty.
—CICERO (106–43 B.C.) Tusculanae Disputationes

When povertie comes in at doores, love leaps out at windowes.
—JOHN CLARK (1609–1676) Paroemiologia

Love's but a frailty of the mind,
When 'tis not with ambition joined:
A sickly flame, which, if not fed, expires,
And feeding, wastes in self-consuming fires.
—WILLIAM CONGREVE (1670–1729) Way of the World

Say what you will, 'tis better to be left
Than never to have loved.
—WILLIAM CONGREVE (1670–1729) *Way of the World*

We are all born for love. . . . It is the principle of existence
and its only end.
—BENJAMIN DISRAELI (1804–1881) *Sybil*

Men and women call one another inconstant, and accuse one
another of having changed their minds, when, God knows, they
have but changed the object of their eye, and seen a better white
or red.
—JOHN DONNE (1572–1631) *Sermons*

Last night, ah, yesternight, betwixt her lips and mine
There fell thy shadow, Cynara! Thy breath was shed
Upon my soul between the kisses and the wine;
And I was desolate and sick of an old passion,
Yea, I was desolate and bowed my head:
I have been faithful to thee, Cynara! in my fashion.
—ERNEST DOWSON (1867–1900) *Cynara*

But you must believe me when I tell you that I have found it
impossible to carry the heavy burden of responsibility and to
discharge my duties as King as I would wish to do without the
help and support of the woman I love.
—EDWARD VIII (1894–1972) Abdication Speech

All mankind love a lover.
—RALPH WALDO EMERSON (1803–1882) *Essays*

He is not a lover who does not love forever.
—EURIPIDES (480–406 B.C.) *Troades*

Perhaps they were right in putting love into books . . .
Perhaps it could not live anywhere else.
—WILLIAM FAULKNER (1897–1962) *Light in August*

Love grants in a moment
What toil can hardly achieve in an age.
—GOETHE (1749–1832) *Torquato Tasso*

Ah! What is love? It is a pretty thing,
As sweet unto a shepherd as a king,
    And sweeter too;
For kings have cares that wait upon a crown,
And cares can make the sweetest love to frown.
—ROBERT GREENE (1560?–1592) *Shepherd's Wife*

To demand of love that it be without jealousy is to ask of light
that it cast no shadows.
—OSCAR HAMMLING (1890–   ) *Laconics*

If you would be loved, love.
—HECATO (c. 550–476 B.C.) *Fragments*

At thy command I would change, not merely my costume, but
my very soul, so entirely art thou the sole possessor of my
body and my spirit. Never, God is my witness, never have I
sought anything in thee but thyself; I have sought thee, and not
thy gifts. I have not looked to the marriage-bond or dowry.
—HÉLOISE (1101–1164) to Abelard

Love in a hut, with water and a crust,
Is—love, forgive us!—cinders, ashes, dust.
—JOHN KEATS (1795–1821) *Lamia*

Come live with me and be my love,
And we will all the pleasures prove,
That valleys, groves, or hills, or fields,
Or woods and steepy mountains yields.
—CHRISTOPHER MARLOWE (1564–1593) *Passionate Shepherd to his Love*

If I were a king, ah love, if I were a king!
What tributary nations I would bring
To stoop before your sceptre and to swear
Allegiance to your lips and eyes and hair.
—JUSTIN HUNTLY MCCARTHY (1861–1936) *If I Were King*

'Tis not love's going hurts my days,
But that it went in little ways.
—EDNA ST. VINCENT MILLAY (1892–1951) *Spring and Fall*

Take love away from life and you take away its pleasures.
—MOLIÈRE (1622–1673) *Bourgeois Gentleman*

'Tis sweet to think, that, where'er we rove,
We are sure to find something blissful and dear,
And when we're far from the lips we love,
We've but to make love to the lips we are near.
—THOMAS MOORE (1779–1852) *'Tis Sweet to Think*

But there's nothing half so sweet in life
As love's young dream.
—THOMAS MOORE (1779–1852) *Love's Young Dream*

Love that comes late oft claims a heavy toll.
—SEXTUS PROPERTIUS (50?–15 B.C.) *Elegies*

If all the world and love were young,
And truth in every shepherd's tongue,
These pretty pleasures might me move
To live with thee, and be thy love.
—SIR WALTER RALEIGH (1552?–1618)

The pleasure of love is in loving; and we are much happier in
the passion we feel than in that which we inspire.
—FRANÇOIS DE LA ROCHEFOUCAULD (1613–1680) *Maxims*

If thou remember'st not the slightest folly
That ever love did make thee run into,
Thou hast not lov'd.
—SHAKESPEARE (1564–1616) *As You Like It,* II, iv, 34

No sooner met but they looked, no sooner looked but they
loved, no sooner loved but they sighed, no sooner sighed but
they asked one another the reason.
—SHAKESPEARE (1564–1616) *As You Like It,* V, ii, 36

Where love is great, the littlest doubts are fear;
When little fears grow great, great love grows there.
—SHAKESPEARE (1564–1616) *Hamlet,* III, ii, 188

But love is blind, and lovers cannot see
The pretty follies that themselves commit.
—SHAKESPEARE (1564–1616) *Merchant of Venice,* II, vi, 344

Ay me! for aught that I ever could read,
Could ever hear by tale or history,
The course of true love never did run smooth.
—SHAKESPEARE (1564–1616) *Midsummer Night's Dream,* I, i, 132

Speak low, if you speak love.
—SHAKESPEARE (1564–1616) *Much Ado About Nothing,* II, i, 102

There is no creature loves me,
And if I die, no soul shall pity me.
—SHAKESPEARE (1564–1616) *Richard III,* V, iii, 200

For stony limits cannot hold love out,
And what love can do that dares love attempt.
—SHAKESPEARE (1564–1616) *Romeo and Juliet,* II, ii, 67

Give me my Romeo; and, when he shall die,
Take him and cut him out in little stars,
And he will make the face of heaven so fine,
That all the world will be in love with night,
And pay no worship to the garish sun.
—SHAKESPEARE (1564–1616) *Romeo and Juliet,* III, ii, 21

Love's not Time's fool, though rosy lips and cheeks
    Within his bending sickle's compass come;
Love alters not with his brief hours and weeks,
    But bears it out even to the edge of doom.
—SHAKESPEARE (1564–1616) Sonnet CXVI.

Common as light is love,
And its familiar voice wearies not ever,
Like the wide heaven, the all-sustaining air,
It makes the reptile equal to the god.
—PERCY B. SHELLEY (1792–1822) *Prometheus Unbound*

Love is a symbol of eternity. It wipes out all sense of time, destroying all memory of a beginning and all fear of an end.
—MADAME DE STAËL (1766–1817) *Corinne*

And blessings on the falling out
That all the more endears,
When we fall out with those we love,
And kiss again with tears.
—TENNYSON (1809–1892) *The Princess*

To say that you can love one person all your life is just like saying that one candle will continue burning as long as you live.
—LEO TOLSTOY (1828–1910) *Kreutzer Sonata*

Yet each man kills the thing he loves,
By each let this be heard,
Some do it with a bitter look,
Some with a flattering word,
The coward does it with a kiss,
The brave man with a sword.
—OSCAR WILDE (1854–1900) *Ballad of Reading Gaol*

Whom the Lord loveth he chasteneth.
—NEW TESTAMENT: *Hebrews,* xii, 6

Who love too much, hate in the like extreme.
—HOMER (c. 10th–8th C. B.C.) *Odyssey*

Greater love hath no man than this, that a man lay down his life for his friends.
—NEW TESTAMENT: *John,* xv, 13

There is no fear in love; but perfect love casteth out fear.
—NEW TESTAMENT: *I John,* iv, 8

Whither thou goest, I will go; and where thou lodgest, I will lodge: thy people shall be my people, and thy God my God.
—OLD TESTAMENT: *Ruth,* i, 16

Many waters cannot quench love, neither can the floods drown it.
—OLD TESTAMENT: *Songs of Solomon,* viii, 7

Luxury

Luxury and avarice—these pests have been the ruin of every state.
—CATO (234–149 B.C.) In support of the Oppian Law

Faint-hearted men are the fruit of luxurious countries. The same soil never produces both luxuries and heroes.
—HERODOTUS (484–424 B.C.) *History*

Fell luxury! more perilous to youth
Than storms or quicksands, poverty, or chains
—HANNAH MORE (1745–1833) *Belshazzar*

People have declaimed against luxury for 2000 years, in verse and in prose, and people have always delighted in it.
—VOLTAIRE (1694–1778) *Philosophical Dictionary*

On the soft beds of luxury most kingdoms have expired.
—EDWARD YOUNG (1683–1765) *Centaur*

Majority and Minority

The oppression of a majority is detestable and odious: the oppression of a minority is only by one degree less detestable and odious.
—WILLIAM EWART GLADSTONE (1809–1898) Speech

It is my principle that the will of the majority should always prevail.
—THOMAS JEFFERSON (1743–1826) Letter to James Madison

One, of God's side, is a majority.
—WENDELL PHILLIPS (1811–1884) Speech on John Brown

Malice

Malice is cunning.
—CICERO (106–43 B.C.) *De Natura Deorum*

Malice hath a strong memory.
—THOMAS FULLER (1608–1681) *Pisgah Sight*

With malice toward none; with charity for all; with firmness in the right, as God gives us to see the right, let us strive on to finish the work we are in.
—ABRAHAM LINCOLN (1809–1865) Second Inaugural Address

Man

This Being of mine, whatever it really is, consists of a little flesh, a little breath and the ruling Reason.
—MARCUS AURELIUS (121–180) *Meditations*

No man is an Iland, intire of it selfe; everyman is a piece of the Continent, a part of the maine, if a Clod bee washed away by the Sea, Europe is the lesse, as well as if a Promontorie were, as well as if a Mannor of thy friends or of thine owne were; any mans death diminishes me, because I am involved in Mankinde; and therefore never send to know for whom the bell tolls; it tolls for thee.
—JOHN DONNE (1572–1631) *Devotions*

Man is a fallen god who remembers the heavens.
—ALPHONSE DE LAMARTINE (1790–1869) *Meditations*

He's not the finest character that ever lived. But he's a human being, and a terrible thing is happening to him. So attention must be paid. He's not to be allowed to fall into his grave like an old dog.
—ARTHUR MILLER (1915–   ) *Death of a Salesman*

Man is a rope stretched between the animal and the superman—a rope over an abyss.
—FRIEDRICH W. NIETZSCHE (1844–1900) *Thus Spake Zarathustra*

What a chimera, then, is man! What a novelty! What a monster, what a chaos, what a contradiction, what a prodigy! Judge of all things, feeble worm of the earth, depositary of truth, a sink of uncertainty and error, the glory and the shame of the universe.
—BLAISE PASCAL (1623–1662) *Pensées*

Placed on this isthmus of a middle state
A being darkly wise and rudely great
Created half to rise and half to fall
Great lord of all things, yet prey to all.
Sole judge of truth in endless error hurled,
The glory, jest and riddle of the world.
—ALEXANDER POPE (1688–1744) *Essay on Man*

What a piece of work is a man! how noble in reason! how infinite in faculty! in form and moving how express and admirable! in action how like an angel! in apprehension how like a god! the beauty of the world! the paragon of animals! And, yet, to me, what is this quintessence of dust? man delights not me: no, nor woman neither, though by your smiling, you seem to say so.
—SHAKESPEARE (1564–1616) *Hamlet,* II, 2, 313

Man's capacities have never been measured; nor are we to judge of what he can do by any precedents, so little has been tried.
—HENRY DAVID THOREAU (1817–1862) *Walden*

Man is the only animal that blushes. Or needs to.
—MARK TWAIN (1835–1910) *Pudd'nhead Wilson's New Calendar*

Who shall enumerate the many ways in which that costly piece of fixed capital, a human being, may be employed! More of him is wanted everywhere! Hunt, then, for some situation in which your humanity may be used.
—ALBERT SCHWEITZER (1875–1965) *Civilization and Ethics*

He was a man, take him for all in all,
I shall not look upon his like again.
—SHAKESPEARE (1564–1616) *Hamlet*, I, ii, 187

How beauteous mankind is! O brave new world,
That has such people in 't!
—SHAKESPEARE (1564–1616) *The Tempest*, V, i, 183

Thou hast made him a little lower than the angels.
—OLD TESTAMENT: *Psalms*, viii, 5

Marriage

He that hath a wife and children hath given hostages to fortune; for they are impediments to great enterprises, either of virtue or mischief.
—FRANCIS BACON (1561–1626) *Marriage and Single Life*

Cursed be the man, the poorest wretch in life,
The crouching vessel, to the tyrant wife,
Who has no will but her high permission;
Who has not sixpence but in her possession;
Who must to her his dear friend's secret tell;
Who dreads a curtain lecture worse than hell.
Were such the wife had fallen to my part,
I'd break her spirit or I'd break her heart.
—ROBERT BURNS (1759–1796) *Henpecked Husband*

Marriage and hanging go by destiny; matches are made in heaven.
—ROBERT BURTON (1577–1640) *Anatomy of Melancholy*

The first bond of society is marriage; the next, our children; then the whole family and all things in common.
—CICERO (106–43 B.C.) *De Officiis*

Like blood, like goods, and like age,
Make the happiest marriage.
—JOHN CLARKE (1609–1676) *Paroemiologia*

Thus grief still treads upon the heels of pleasure,
Marry'd in haste, we may repent at leisure.
—WILLIAM CONGREVE (1670–1729) *Old Bachelor*

Happy and thrice happy are they who enjoy an uninterrupted union, and whose love, unbroken by any complaints, shall not dissolve until the last day.
—HORACE (65–8 B.C.) *Carmina*

Marriages are made in heaven.
—MIDRASH: *Genesis Rabbah*, lxviii

Hail, wedded love, mysterious law; true source
Of human offspring.
—JOHN MILTON (1608–1674) *Paradise Lost*

If you would marry wisely, marry your equal.
—OVID (43 B.C.–A.D. 18?) *Heroides*

All happy families resemble one another; every unhappy family is unhappy in its own fashion.
—LEO TOLSTOY (1828–1910) *Anna Karenina*

When a man marries again it is because he adored his first wife.
—OSCAR WILDE (1854–1900) *Picture of Dorian Gray*

Memory

To be ignorant of what happened before you were born is to be ever a child. For what is man's lifetime unless the memory of past events is woven with those of earlier times.
—CICERO (106–43 B.C.) *De Oratore*

There is no greater sorrow than to recall, in misery, the time when we were happy.
—DANTE (1265–1321) *Inferno*

Memory is the treasure-house of the mind.
—THOMAS FULLER (1608–1681) *The Holy State: Memory*

A retentive memory is a good thing, but the ability to forget is the true token of greatness.
—ELBERT HUBBARD (1856–1915) *Epigrams*

The leaves lie thick upon the way
Of Memories.
—JAMES JOYCE (1882–1941) *Chamber Music*

Better by far you should forget and smile,
Than that you should remember and be sad.
—CHRISTINA ROSSETTI (1830–1894) *A Birthday*

Things that were hard to bear are sweet to remember.
—SENECA (4? B.C.–A.D. 65) *Hercules Furens*

Hamlet: Methinks I see my father.
Horatio: O! Where, my lord?
Hamlet: In my mind's eye, Horatio.
—SHAKESPEARE (1564–1616) *Hamlet,* I, ii, 184

Remember thee!
Ay, thou poor ghost, while memory holds a seat
In this distracted globe. Remember thee!
Yea, from the fable of my memory
I'll wipe away all trivial fond records.
—SHAKESPEARE (1564–1616) *Hamlet,* I, v, 97

When to the sessions of sweet silent thought
I summon up remembrance of things past,
I sigh the lack of many a thing I sought,
And old woes new wail my dear time's waste.
—SHAKESPEARE (1564–1616) *Sonnets,* xxx

I shall remember while the light lives yet,
And in the night-time I shall not forget.
—ALGERNON CHARLES SWINBURNE (1837–1909) *Erotion*

Mercy

The quality of mercy is not strain'd
It droppeth as the gentle rain from heaven
Upon the place beneath: it is twice blest;
It blesseth him that gives and him that takes;
'Tis mightiest in the mightiest; it becomes
The throned monarch better than his crown;
His sceptre shows the force of temporal power,
The attribute to awe and majesty,
Wherein doth sit the dread and fear of kings;
But mercy is above this sceptred sway;
It is enthroned in the hearts of kings,
It is an attribute to God himself;
And earthly power doth show likest God's
When mercy seasons justice.
—SHAKESPEARE (1564–1616) *Merchant of Venice*, IV, i, 184

Blessed are the merciful: for they shall obtain mercy.
—NEW TESTAMENT: *Matthew*, v, 7

What doth the Lord require of thee, but to do justly, and to
love mercy, and to walk humbly with thy God.
—OLD TESTAMENT: *Micah*, iv, 4

Mercy and truth are met together; righteousness and peace have
kissed each other.
—OLD TESTAMENT: *Psalms*, lxxxv, 10

To hide the fault I see:
That mercy I to others show
That mercy show to me.
—ALEXANDER POPE (1688–1744) *Universal Prayer*

Months

Pale January lay
In its cradle day by day,
Dead or living, hard to say.
—ALFRED AUSTIN (1835–1913) *Primroses*

That blasts of January
Would blow you through and through.
—SHAKESPEARE (1564–1616) *Winter's Tale*, IV, iv, 3

Late February days; and now, at last,
Might you have thought that Winter's woe was past;
So fair the sky and so soft the air.
—WILLIAM MORRIS (1834–1896) *Earthly Paradise*

Menallo: I would chuse March, for I would come in like a Lion.
Tony: But you'd go out like a Lamb when you went to hang-
ing.
—JOHN FLETCHER (1579–1625) *Wife for a Month*

April is the cruelest month, breeding
Lilacs out of the dead land, mixing
Memory and desire, stirring
Dull roots with spring rain.
—T. S. ELIOT (1888–1965) *The Waste Land*

Oh, to be in England
Now that April's here.
—ROBERT BROWNING (1812–1889) *Home Thoughts*

He has a hard heart who does not love in May.
—GUILLAUME DE LORRIS (d. *c.* 1235) *Roman de la Rose*

And what is so rare as a day in June?
   Then, if ever, come perfect days;
Then Heaven tries earth if it be in tune,
   And over it softly her warm ear lays.
—JAMES RUSSELL LOWELL (1819–1891) *Vision of Sir Launfa*

The Summer looks out from her brazen tower,
   Through the flashing bars of July.
—FRANCIS THOMPSON (1859–1907) *Corymbus for Autumn*

Hot July brings cooling showers,
Apricots and gillyflowers.
—SARA COLERIDGE (1802–1852) *Pretty Lessons in Verse*

Never return in August to what you love;
Along the leaves will rust
And over the hedges dust,
And in the air vague thunder and silence burning . . .
Choose some happier time for your returning.
—BERNICE LESBIA KENYON (1897–   ) *Return*

I'm not a chicken; I have seen
Full many a chill September.
—OLIVER WENDELL HOLMES (1809–1894) *September Gale*

The skies they were ashen and sober;
The leaves they were crisp and sere—
The leaves they were withering and sere;
It was night in the lonesome October
Of my most immemorial year.
—EDGAR ALLAN POE (1809–1849) *Ulalume*

When chill November's surly blast
Made fields and forests bare.
—ROBERT BURNS (1759–1796) *Man Was Made to Mourn*

In a drear-nighted December,
   Too happy, happy brook,
Thy bubblings ne'er remember
   Apollo's summer look;
But with a sweet forgetting,
They stay their crystal fretting,
   Never, never petting
   About the frozen time.
—JOHN KEATS (1795–1821) *Stanzas*

When we shall hear
The rain and wind beat dark December, how
In this our pinching cave, shall we discourse
The freezing hours away.
—SHAKESPEARE (1564–1616) *Cymbeline*, III, iii, 36

Music

Music, the greatest good that mortals know,
And all of heaven we have below.
—JOSEPH ADDISON (1672–1719) *Song for St. Cecilia's Day*

Music exalts each joy, allays each grief,
Expels diseases, softens every pain,
Subdues the rage of poison, and the plague.
—JOHN ARMSTRONG (1709–1779) *Preserving Health*

Who hears music, feels his solitude
Peopled at once.
—ROBERT BROWNING (1812–1889) *Balaustion's Adventure*

Music is well said to be the speech of angels.
—THOMAS CARLYLE (1795–1881) *Essays: The Opera*

Music hath charms to soothe the savage breast,
To soften rocks, or bend a knotted oak.
—WILLIAM CONGREVE (1670–1729) *The Mourning Bride*

Heard melodies are sweet, but those unheard
Are sweeter: therefore, ye soft pipes, play on;
Not to the sensual ear, but, more endear'd,
Pipe to the spirit ditties of no tone.
—JOHN KEATS (1795–1821) *Ode to a Grecian Urn*

Nation

How much more are men than nations!
—RALPH WALDO EMERSON (1803–1882) *Letters and Social
Aims*

It is because nations tend to stupidity and baseness that mankind
moves so slowly; it is because individuals have a capacity for
better things that it moves at all.
—GEORGE GISSING (1857–1903) *Private Papers of Henry Rye-
croft*

The first panacea for a mismanaged nation is inflation of the
currency; the second is war. Both bring a temporary prosperity;
both bring a permanent ruin. But both are the refuge of political
and economic opportunists.
—ERNEST HEMINGWAY (1898–1961) *Notes on the Next War*

There is no such thing as a little country. The greatness of a people is no more determined by their number than the greatness of a man is determined by his height.
—VICTOR HUGO (1802–1885)

The political life of a nation is only the most superficial aspect of its being. In order to know its inner life, the source of its action, one must penetrate to its soul by literature, philosophy and the arts, where are reflected the ideas, the passions, the dreams of a whole people.
—ROMAIN ROLLAND (1866–1945) *Musicians of the Past*

That nation is worthless which does not joyfully stake everything in defense of her honor.
—SCHILLER (1759–1805) *Maid of Orleans*

It is a maxim founded on the universal experience of mankind that no nation is to be trusted farther than it is bound by its interest.
—GEORGE WASHINGTON (1732–1799) Letter to Congress, 1778

No nation is fit to sit in judgment upon any other nation.
—WOODROW WILSON (1856–1924)

And hath made of one blood all nations of men for to dwell on all the face of the earth.
—NEW TESTAMENT: *Acts*, xvii, 26

A little one shall be come a thousand and a small one a strong nation.
—OLD TESTAMENT: *Isaiah*, ix, 22

Nature

The study of Nature is intercourse with the Highest Mind. You should never trifle with Nature.
—JEAN LOUIS AGASSIZ (1807–1873) *Agassiz at Penikese*

Believe one who knows: you will find something greater in woods than in books. Trees and stones will teach you that which you can never learn from masters.
—ST. BERNARD OF CLAIRVAUX (1091–1153) *Epistles*

Whatever befalls in accordance with Nature shall be accounted good.
—CICERO (106–43 B.C.) *De Senectute*

Nor rural sounds alone, but rural sounds,
Exhilarate the spirit, and restore
The tone of languid Nature.
—WILLIAM COWPER (1731–1800) *The Task*

Hast thou named all the birds without a gun;
Loved the wood-rose, and left it on its stalk?
—RALPH WALDO EMERSON (1803–1882) *Forbearance*

Never does Nature say one thing and Wisdom another.
—JUVENAL (*c*. 60–130 A.D.) *Satires*

So Nature deals with us, and takes away
Our playthings one by one, and by the hand
Leads us to rest.
—HENRY W. LONGFELLOW (1807–1882) *Nature*

All that thy seasons, O Nature, bring is fruit for me!
All things come from thee, subsist in thee, go back to thee.
—MARCUS AURELIUS (121–180) *Meditations*

In those vernal seasons of the year, when the air is calm and pleasant, it were an injury and sullenness against Nature not to go out and see her riches and partake in her rejoicing with heaven and earth.
—JOHN MILTON (1608–1674) *Tractate of Education*

The perfections of Nature show that she is the image of God; her defects show that she is only his image.
—BLAISE PASCAL (1623–1662) *Pensées*

All Nature is but Art, unknown to thee;
All Chance, Direction, which thou canst not see.
—ALEXANDER POPE (1688–1744) *Essay on Man*

Nature abhors a vacuum.
—FRANÇOIS RABELAIS (1494?–1553) *Gargantua*

And this our life, exempt from public haunt,
Finds tongues in trees, books in the running brooks,
Sermons in stones, and good in everything.
—SHAKESPEARE (1564–1616) *As You Like It*, II, i, 15

One touch of nature makes the whole world kin.
—SHAKESPEARE (1564–1616) *Troilus and Cressida*, III, iii, 175

I inhale great draughts of space,
The east and the west are mine, and the north and the south are mine.
I am larger than I thought,
I did not know I held so much goodness.
—WALT WHITMAN (1819–1892) *Song of the Open Road*

Neighbor

Reprove thy neighbor before thou threaten.
—BEN SIRA (*c*. 190 B.C.) *Book of Wisdom*

You must ask your neighbour if you shall live in peace.
—JOHN CLARK (1609–1676) *Paroemiologia*

Good fences make good neighbors.
—ROBERT FROST (1875–1963) *Mending Wall*

Love your neighbor, yet pull not down your hedge.
—GEORGE HERBERT (1593–1633) *Jacula Prudentum*

A bad neighbor is as great a plague as a good one is a blessing; he who enjoys a good neighbor has a precious possession.
—HESIOD (*c*. 735 B.C.) *Works and Days*

There is an idea abroad among moral people that they should make their neighbors good. One person I have to make good: myself. But my duty to my neighbor is much more nearly expressed by saying that I have to make him happy—if I may.
—R. L. STEVENSON (1850–1894) *A Christmas Sermon*

Love thy neighbour as thyself.
—NEW TESTAMENT: *Matthew*, xix, 19

Better is a neighbour that is near than a brother far off.
—OLD TESTAMENT: *Proverbs*, xxvii, 10

Night

I linger yet with Nature, for the night
Hath been to me a more familiar face
Than that of man; and in her starry shade
Of dim and solitary loveliness
I learn'd the language of another world.
—LORD BYRON (1788–1824) *Manfred*, III, iv

The night . . . giveth truce to all labours, and by sleeping maketh sweet all pains and travail.
—WILLIAM CAXTON (1422?–1491) *Eneydos*

Dark was the night as pich, or as the cole.
—GEOFFREY CHAUCER (1340?–1400) *Canterbury Tales*

Every evening we are poorer by a day.
—ARTHUR SCHOPENHAUER (1788–1860)

Come, seeling night,
Scarf up the tender eye of pitiful day;
And with thy bloody and invisible hand
Cancel and tear to pieces that great bond
Which keeps me pale.
—SHAKESPEARE (1564–1616) *Macbeth,* III, ii, 46

In the night there is peace for the old and hope for the young.
—GEORGE BERNARD SHAW (1856–1950) *Heartbreak House*

Press close, bare-bosom'd night—press close, magnetic
          nourishing night!
Night of south winds—night of the large few stars!
Still nodding night—mad naked summernight.
—WALT WHITMAN (1819–1882) *Song of Myself*

The night cometh when no man can work.
—NEW TESTAMENT: *John,* ix, 4

Watchman, what of the night?
—OLD TESTAMENT: *Isaiah,* xxi, ii

Nobility

The nobleman is he whose noble mind
Is filled with inborn worth, unborrowed from his kind.
—GEOFFREY CHAUCER (1340?–1400) *Canterbury Tales*

Send your noble Blood to Market, and see what it will buy.
—THOMAS FULLER (1608–1681) *Gnomologia*

To live as one likes is plebeian; the noble man aspires to order and law.
—GOETHE (1749–1832)

Hereditary nobility is due to the presumption that we shall do well because our fathers have done well.
—JOSEPH JOUBERT (1754–1824) *Pensées*

Noblesse oblige.
—FRANÇOIS GASTON DE LÉVIS (1720–1787) *Maxims*

True nobility is exempt from fear.
—SHAKESPEARE (1564–1616) *II Henry VI,* IV, i, 129

There is
One great society alone on earth;
The Noble Living and the Noble Dead.
—WILLIAM WORDSWORTH (1770–1850) *Prelude*

Oath

An oath sworn with the clear understanding in one's mind that it should be performed must be kept.
—CICERO (106–43 B.C.) *De Officiis*

A liar is always prodigal with oaths.
—PIERRE CORNEILLE (1606–1684) *The Liar*

We mutually pledge to each other our lives, our fortunes, and our sacred honor.
—THOMAS JEFFERSON (1743–1826) *Declaration of Independence*

Ease would recant
Vows made in pain, as violent and void.
—JOHN MILTON (1608–1674) *Paradise Lost*

'Tis not the many oaths that make the truth,
But the plain single vow that is vow'd true.
—SHAKESPEARE (1564–1616) *All's Well that Ends Well,* IV, ii, 21

I write a woman's oaths in water.
—SOPHOCLES (B.C. 495–406) *Fragment*

Obedience

The fear of some divine and supreme power keeps men in obedience.
—ROBERT BURTON (1577–1640) *Anatomy of Melancholy*

All arts his own, the hungry Greekling counts;
And bid him mount the skies, the skies he mounts.
—JUVENAL (*c.* 60–130) *Satires*

Obedience,
Bane of all genius, virtue, freedom, truth,
Makes slaves of men, and, of the human frame,
A mechanized automaton.
—PERCY B. SHELLEY (1792–1822) *Queen Mab*

Learn to obey before you command.
—SOLON (638–559 B.C.)

Theirs not to make reply,
Theirs not to reason why,
Theirs but to do and die.
—TENNYSON (1809–1892) *Charge of the Light Brigade*

Obedience is the courtesy due to kings.
—TENNYSON (1809–1892) *Idylls of the King*

We ought to obey God rather than men.
—NEW TESTAMENT: *Acts,* v, 29

Opinion

The man who never alters his opinion is like standing water, and breeds reptiles of the mind.
—WILLIAM BLAKE (1757–1827) *Proverbs of Hell*

He that complies against his will
Is of his own opinion still.
—SAMUEL BUTLER (1612–1680) *Hudibras*

No well-informed person has declared a change of opinion to be inconstancy.
—CICERO (106–43 B.C.) *Ad Atticum*

The only sin which we never forgive in each other is difference of opinion.
—RALPH WALDO EMERSON (1803–1882) *Society and Solitude*

Men will die for an opinion as soon as for anything else.
—WILLIAM HAZLITT (1778–1830) *Characteristics*

With effervescing opinions, as with the not yet forgotten champagne, the quickest way to let them get flat is to let them get exposed to the air.
—JUSTICE OLIVER WENDELL HOLMES (1841–1935) *Opinion*

For a thousand heads, a thousand tastes.
—HORACE (65–8 B.C.) *Satires*

The foolish and dead alone never change their opinion.
—JAMES RUSSELL LOWELL (1819–1891) *My Study Windows*

You are young, my son, and as the years go by, time will change, and even reverse many of your present opinions. Refrain therefore, awhile from setting yourself up as a judge of the highest matters.
—PLATO (428–347 B.C.) *Laws*

Some praise at morning what they blame at night,
But always think the last opinion right.
—ALEXANDER POPE (1688–1744) *Essay on Criticism*

A plague of opinion! a man may wear it on both sides, like a
leather jerkin.
—SHAKESPEARE (1564–1616) *Troilus and Cressida*, III, iii,
268

It were not best that we should all think alike; it is difference
of opinion that makes horse-races.
—MARK TWAIN (1835–1910) *Pudd'nhead Wilson's Calendar*

Public opinion is stronger than the legislature, and nearly as
strong as the Ten Commandments.
—CHARLES D. WARNER (1829–1900) *My Summer in a Garden*

Opportunity

A wise man makes more opportunities than he finds.
—FRANCIS BACON (1561–1620)

When one door is shut, another opens.
—CERVANTES (1547–1616) *Don Quixote*

He who seizes the (right) moment is the right man.
—GOETHE (1749–1832) *Faust*

I knock unbidden once at every gate!
If sleeping, wake; if feasting, rise before
I turn away. It is the hour of fate.
—JOHN JAMES INGALLS (1833–1900) *Opportunity*

Four things come not back:
The spoken word; The sped arrow;
Time past; The neglected opportunity.
—OMAR IBN (*c.* 581–644) *Sayings*

O Opportunity, thy guilt is great!
'Tis thou that execut'st the traitor's treason;
Thou set'st the wolf where he the lamb may get;
Whoever plots the sin, thou point'st the season.
—SHAKESPEARE (1564–1616) *The Rape of Lucrece*

Optimism

Optimism. The doctrine or belief that everything is beautiful,
including what is ugly.
—AMBROSE BIERCE (1842–1914?) *Devil's Dictionary*

God's in his Heaven—
All's right with the world!
—ROBERT BROWNING (1812–1889) *Pippa Passes*

A man that could look no way but downwards with a muckrake
in his hand.
—JOHN BUNYAN (1628–1688) *Pilgrim's Progress*

The optimist proclaims that we live in the best of all possible
worlds; and the pessimist fears this is true.
—JAMES BRANCH CABELL (1879–1958) *Silver Stallion*

An optimist is a guy that has never had much experience.
—DON MARQUIS (1878–1937) *Maxims of Archy*

The refuge from pessimism is the good men and women existing at any time in the world—they keep faith and happiness
alive.
—CHARLES E. NORTON (1827–1908)

All is for the best in the best of all possible worlds.
—VOLTAIRE (1694–1778) *Candide*

Oratory

He can best be described as one of those orators who, before
they get up, do not know what they are going to say; when
they are speaking, do not know what they are saying; and, when
they have sat down, do not know what they have said.
—WINSTON CHURCHILL (1874–1965)

When his words fell soft as snowflakes on a winter's day, then
could no mortal man beside vie with Odysseus.
—HOMER (*c.* 10th–8th C. B.C.) *Iliad*

Oratory is the power of beating down your adversary's arguments, and putting better in their place.
—SAMUEL JOHNSON (1709–1784) Boswell's *Life of Johnson*

Fear not, my lord, I'll play the orator
As if the golden fee for which I plead
Were for myself.
—SHAKESPEARE (1564–1616) *Richard III*, III, v, 95

It is not the powerful arm,
But soft enchanting tongue that governs all.
—SOPHOCLES (495–406 B.C.) *Philoctetes*

If ever a woman feels proud of her lover, it is when she sees
him as a successful public speaker.
—HARRIET BEECHER STOWE (1811–1896)

Order

Order means light and peace, inward liberty and free command
over oneself; order is power.
—HENRI-FRÉDÉRIC AMIEL (1828–1881) *Journal*

Order is Heav'ns first law.
—ALEXANDER POPE (1688–1744) *Essay on Man*

A place for everything and everything in its place.
—SAMUEL SMILES (1812–1904) *Thrift*

Order governs the world. The Devil is the author of confusion.
—JONATHAN SWIFT (1667–1745) Letter to Stella

Have a place for everything and keep the thing somewhere else.
This is not advice, it is merely custom.
—MARK TWAIN (1835–1910) *Diaries*

Let all things be done decently and in order.
—NEW TESTAMENT: *I Corinthians,* xiv, 40

Pain

Pleasure must succeed to pleasure, else past pleasure turns to
pain.
—ROBERT BROWNING (1812–1889) *La Saisiaz*

Real pain can alone cure us of imaginary ills.
—JONATHAN EDWARDS (1703–1757) *Resolutions*

He has seen but half the universe who never has been shewn
the house of Pain.
—RALPH WALDO EMERSON (1803–1882)

The gods have so spun the thread for wretched mortals that
they must live in pain.
—HOMER (*c.* 10th–8th C. B.C.) *Iliad*

Those who do not feel pain seldom think that it is felt.
—SAMUEL JOHNSON (1709–1784) *The Rambler*

There is a certain pleasure which is akin to pain.
—METRODORUS (*f.* 168 B.C.)

Pain is perfect misery, the worst of evils,
And excessive, overturns all patience.
—JOHN MILTON (1608–1674) *Paradise Lost*

Ay, but I fear you speak upon the rack,
Where men enforced do speak anything.
—SHAKESPEARE (1564–1616) *Merchant of Venice*, III, ii, 32

Paradise

A book of Verses underneath the Bough,
A Jug of Wine, a Loaf of Bread—and Thou
Beside me singing in the Wilderness—
Oh, Wilderness were Paradise enow!
—EDWARD FITZGERALD (1809–1883) *Rubaiyat*

Man and Woman may only enter Paradise hand in hand. Together, the myth tells us, they left it and together must they return.
—RICHARD GARNETT (1835–1906) *De Flagello Myrteo*

Paradise is a dwelling place promised the faithful.
—MOHAMMED (570–632) *The Koran*

The loves that meet in Paradise shall cast out fear,
And Paradise hath room for you and me and all.
—CHRISTINA ROSSETTI (1830–1894) *Saints and Angels*

Parents

Reverence for parents—this standeth written third among the statutes of Justice to whom supreme honor is due.
—AESCHYLUS (525–456 B.C.) *Suppliants*

There are three degrees of filial piety. The highest is being a credit to our parents, the second is not disgracing them; the lowest is being able simply to support them.
—CONFUCIUS (*c.* 551–478 B.C.) *Book of Rites*

It used to be believed that the parent had unlimited claims on the child and rights over him. In a truer view of the matter, we are coming to see that the rights are on the side of the child and the duties on the side of the parent.
—WILLIAM G. SUMNER (1840–1910) *Forgotten Man's Almanac*

He argued that the principal duty which a parent owed to a child was to make him happy.
—ANTHONY TROLLOPE (1815–1882) *Doctor Thorne*

Children begin by loving their parents; as they grow older they judge them; sometimes they forgive them.
—OSCAR WILDE (1854–1900) *Dorian Gray*

Honour thy father and mother; that thy days may be long upon the land which the Lord thy God giveth thee.
—OLD TESTAMENT: *Exodus*, XX, 12

Parting

Go from me. Yet I feel that I shall stand
Henceforward in thy shadow.
—ELIZABETH B. BROWNING (1806–1861) *Sonnets from Portuguese*

Parting is all we know of heaven,
And all we need of hell.
—EMILY DICKINSON (1830–1886) *Poems*

They who go
Feel not the pain of parting; it is they
Who stay behind that suffer.
—HENRY W. LONGFELLOW (1807–1882) *Michael Angelo*

Good night! Good night! parting is such sweet sorrow
That I shall say good night till it be morrow.
—SHAKESPEARE (1564–1616) *Romeo and Juliet*, II, ii, 185

Past

Think only of the past as its remembrance gives you pleasure.
—JANE AUSTEN (1775–1817) *Pride and Prejudice*

I have small patience with the antiquarian habit which magnifies the past and belittles the present. . . . Change is inevitable, at once a penalty and a privilege.
—JOHN BUCHAN (1875–1940) *Memory Hold-the-Door*

He seems
To have seen better days, as who has not
Who has seen yesterday?
—LORD BYRON (1788–1824) *Age of Bronze*

Oh! leave the past to bury its own dead.
—WILLIAM S. BLUNT (1840–1922) *To One Who Would Make a Confession*

Historic continuity with the past is not a duty, it is only a necessity.
—JUSTICE OLIVER WENDELL HOLMES (1841–1935)

Tomorrow I will live, the fool does say;
Today itself's too late; the wise lived yesterday.
—MARTIAL (*c.* 66 A.D.) *Epigrams*

Those who cannot remember the past are condemned to repeat it.
—GEORGE SANTAYANA (1863–1952) *Life of Reason*

Patience

There is a limit at which forbearance ceases to be a virtue.
—EDMUND BURKE (1729–1797) *Observations*

Beware the fury of a patient man.
—JOHN DRYDEN (1631–1700) *Absalom and Achitophel*

Patience, that blending of moral courage with physical timidity.
—THOMAS HARDY (1840–1928) *Tess of the D'Urbervilles*

All men commend patience, although few be willing to practise it.
—THOMAS À KEMPIS (1380–1471) *Imitation of Christ*

Forbearance is a part of justice.
—MARCUS AURELIUS (121–180) *Meditations*

They also serve who only stand and wait.
—JOHN MILTON (1608–1674) *On His Blindness*

It's a long lane that has no turning.
—SAMUEL RICHARDSON (1689–1761) *Clarissa*

'Tis all men's office to speak patience
To those who wring under the load of sorrow;
But no man's virtue nor sufficiency
To be so moral when he shall endure
The like himself.
—SHAKESPEARE (1564–1616) *Much Ado About Nothing*, V, i, 27

Ye have heard of the patience of Job.
—NEW TESTAMENT: *James*, v, ii

In your patience possess ye your souls.
—NEW TESTAMENT: *Luke*, xxi, 18

Patriotism

The die was now cast; I had passed the Rubicon. Swim or sink, live or die, survive or perish with my country was my unalterable determination.
—JOHN ADAMS (1735–1826)

The country of every man is that one where he lives best.
—ARISTOPHANES (444–380 B.C.) *Plutus*

No man can be a patriot on an empty stomach.
—WILLIAM C. BRANN (1855–1898) *Iconoclast*

He who loves not his country can love nothing.
—LORD BYRON (1788–1824) *Two Foscari*

Our country! In her intercourse with foreign nations, may she always be in the right; but our country, right or wrong.
—STEPHAN DECATUR (1779–1820)

My affections are first for my own country, and then, generally, for all mankind.
—THOMAS JEFFERSON (1743–1826) Letter to Thomas Law

My country is the world, and my religion is to do good.
—THOMAS PAINE (1737–1809) *Rights of Man*

If I were an American, as I am an Englishman, while a foreign troop was landed in my country I never would lay down my arms, never! never! never!
—WILLIAM PITT (1708–1778) Speech, 1777

We should behave toward our country as women behave toward the men they love. A loving wife will do anything for her husband except stop criticizing and trying to improve him. We should cast the same affectionate but sharp glance at our country.
—J. B. PRIESTLEY (1894–1984)

Where is the man who owes nothing to the land in which he lives? Whatever the land may be, he owes to it the most precious thing possessed by man, the morality of his actions and the love of virtue.
—JEAN-JACQUES ROUSSEAU (1712–1778) *Émile*

Breathes there a man with soul so dead,
Who never to himself hath said,
This is my own, my native land!
—SIR WALTER SCOTT (1771–1832) *Lay of the Last Minstrel*

   I do love
My country's good with a respect more tender,
More holy and profound, than my own life.
—SHAKESPEARE (1564–1616) *Coriolanus*, III, iii, 111

The proper means of increasing the love we bear our native country is to reside some time in a foreign one.
—WILLIAM SHENSTONE (1714–1763) *Of Men and Manners*

Our country, right or wrong. When right, to be kept right; when wrong, to be put right.
—CARL SCHURZ (1829–1906) Speech, 1872

The more I see of other countries, the more I love my own.
—MADAME DE STAËL (1766–1817) *Corinne*

Peace

He makes a solitude, and calls it—peace!
—LORD BYRON (1788–1824) *Bride of Abydos*

We have preserved peace in our time.
—NEVILLE CHAMBERLAIN (1869–1940) Speech, 1938

Peace rules the day, where reason rules the mind.
—WILLIAM COLLINS (1720–1756) *Hassan*

The gentleman (Josiah Quincy) cannot have forgotten his own sentiment, uttered even on the floor of this House, "Peaceably if we can, forcibly if we must."
—HENRY CLAY (1777–1852) Speech, 1813

Peace at any price.
—ALPHONSE DE LAMARTINE (1790–1869)

Peace will come soon and come to stay, and so come as to be worth keeping in all future time. It will then have been proved that among free men there can be no successful appeal from the ballot to the bullet, and that they who take such appeal are sure to lose their cases and pay the cost.
—ABRAHAM LINCOLN (1809–1865)

We supplicate all rulers not to remain deaf to the cry of mankind. Let them do everything in their power to save peace. By so doing they will spare the world the horrors of a war that would have disastrous consequences, such as nobody can foresee.
—POPE JOHN XXIII (1881–1963) Oct. 25, 1962

We will have to want Peace, want it enough to pay for it, before it becomes an accepted rule.
—ELEANOR ROOSEVELT (1884–1964)

A peace is of the nature of a conquest;
For then both parties nobly are subdued
And neither party loser.
—SHAKESPEARE (1564–1616) *Henry IV*, IV, ii, 89

Peace be to you. [Pax vobiscum.]
—OLD TESTAMENT: *Genesis*, xliii, 23

Go in peace. [Vade in pace.]
—OLD TESTAMENT: *Exodus*, iv, 18

The peace of God, which passeth all understanding.
—NEW TESTAMENT: *Philippians*, iv, 7

Blessed are the peace-makers.
—NEW TESTAMENT: *Matthew*, v, 9

Glory to God in the highest, and on earth peace, good will toward men.
—NEW TESTAMENT: *Luke*, ii, 14

They shall beat their swords into ploughshares, and their spears into pruning-hooks; nation shall not lift up sword against nation, neither shall they learn war any more.
—OLD TESTAMENT: *Isaiah*, ii, 4

People

A people's voice is dangerous when charged with wrath.
—AESCHYLUS (525–456 B.C.) *Agamemnon*

The individual is foolish; the multitude, for the moment is foolish, when they act without deliberation; but the species is wise, and, when time is given to it, as a species it always acts right.
—EDMUND BURKE (1729–1797)

The rabble estimate few things according to their real value, most things according to their prejudices.
—CICERO (106–43 B.C.) *Oratio Pro Quinto Roscio Comaedo*

Your people, sir, is nothing but a great beast!
—ALEXANDER HAMILTON (1757–1804) Argument with Thomas Jefferson

The Lord prefers common-looking people. That is the reason He made so many of them.
—ABRAHAM LINCOLN (1809–1865)

The people is Everyman, everybody.
Everybody is you and me and all others.
What everybody says is what we all say.
—CARL SANDBURG (1878–1967) *The People, Yes*

Perfection

There never was such beauty in another man,
Nature made him, and broke the mould.
—LODOVICO ARIOSTO (1474–1533) *Orlando Furioso*

The more a thing is perfect, the more it feels pleasure and
likewise pain.
—DANTE (1265–1321) *Inferno*

In this broad earth of ours,
Amid the measureless grossness and the slag,
Enclosed and safe within its central heart,
Nestles the seed Perfection.
—WALT WHITMAN (1819–1892) *Song of the Universal*

Be ye therefore Perfect, even as your Father which is in heaven
is perfect.
—NEW TESTAMENT: *Matthew*, v, 48

Philanthropy

He who bestows his goods upon the poor,
Shall have as much again, and ten times more.
—JOHN BUNYAN (1628–1688) *Pilgrim's Progress*

In nothing do men more nearly approach the gods than in doing
good to their fellow men.
—CICERO (106–43 B.C.) *Pro Ligario*

The most acceptable service to God is doing good to man.
—BEN FRANKLIN (1706–1790) *Autobiography*

I expect to pass through this world but once. Any good therefore
that I can do, or any kindness that I can show to any fellow
creature, let me do it now. Let me not defer or neglect it, for
I shall not pass this way again.
—STEPHEN GRELLET (1773–1855)

The hands that help are holier than the lips that pray.
—ROBERT GREEN INGERSOLL (1833–1899)

To pity distress is but human: to relieve it is Godlike.
—HORACE MANN (1796–1859) *Lectures on Education*

Benevolence is the distinguishing characteristic of man. As embodied in man's conduct, it is called the path of duty.
—MENCIUS (372?–289 B.C.) *Discourses*

I am a man, and nothing in man's lot can be indifferent to me.
—TERENCE (c. 190–150 B.C.) *Heautontimoroumenos*

Myself not ignorant of adversity, I have learned to befriend the
unhappy.
—VERGIL (70–19 B.C.) *Aeneid*

I was a stranger, and ye took me in.
—NEW TESTAMENT: *Matthew*, xxv, 35

Philosophy

What I have gained from philosophy is the ability to feel at
ease in any society.
—ARISTIPPUS (425?–366? B.C.)

The Philosopher is he to whom the Highest has descended, and
the Lowest has mounted up; who is the equal and kindly brother
of all.
—THOMAS CARLYLE (1795–1881) *Sartor Resartus*

Philosophy as a fellow once said to me is only thinking. Thinking is an instrument of adjustment to the conditions of life—
but it becomes an end in itself.
—JUSTICE OLIVER WENDELL HOLMES (1841–1935)

Philosophy is an attitude toward life, based on a greater or
lesser, but always limited comprehension of the universe as far
as we happen to know it.
—LIN YUTANG (1895–1976) *I Believe*

Philosophy is toleration, and it is only one step from toleration
to forgiveness.
—ARTHUR W. PINERO (1855–1934) *Second Mrs. Tanqueray*

The greater the philosopher, the harder it is for him to answer
the questions of common people.
—HENRYK SIENKIEWICZ (1846–1916) *Quo Vadis*

Men of Athens, I honor and love you; but I shall obey God
rather than you, and while I have life and strength I shall never
cease from the practise and teaching of philosophy.
—SOCRATES (470–399? B.C.) in Plato's *Apology*

Philosophers must deal with ideas, but the trouble with most
nineteenth century poets is too much philosophy; they are nearer
to being philosophers than poets, without being in the true sense
either.
—ALLEN TATE (1899–1979) *Reactionary Essays*

Poetry

Poetry is simply the most beautiful, impressive and widely effective mode of saying things, and hence its importance.
—MATTHEW ARNOLD (1822–1888) *Essays*

Poetry has been to me an exceeding great reward; it has soothed
my affliction; it has multiplied and refined my enjoyments; it
has endeared my solitude; and it has given me the habit of
wishing to discover the Good and the Beautiful in all that meets
and surrounds me.
—SAMUEL TAYLOR COLERIDGE (1772–1834)

Poetry is not a turning loose of emotion, but an escape from
emotion; it is not the expression of personality, but an escape
from personality. But, of course, only those who have personality and emotions know what it means to want to escape from
these things.
—T. S. ELIOT (1888–1965) *Tradition and the Individual Talent*

Writing free verse is like playing tennis with the net down.
—ROBERT FROST (1875–1963) Address

Do you suppose we owe nothing to Pope's deformity?—He said
to himself, "If my person be crooked, my verses shall be
straight."
—WILLIAM HAZLITT (1778–1830)

I have reared a monument more enduring than bronze and loftier
than the royal pyramids, one that no wasting rain, no unavailing
north wind can destroy; no, not even the unending years nor
the flight of time itself. I shall not wholly die. The greater part
of me shall escape oblivion.
—HORACE (65–8 B.C.) *Odes*

A poet is a nightingale who sits in darkness and sings to cheer
its own solitude with sweet sounds.
—PERCY B. SHELLEY (1792–1822) *Defense of Poetry*

Verse without rhyme is a body without a soul.
—JONATHAN SWIFT (1667–1745) *Advice to a Young Poet*

Politics

Politics make strange bedfellows.
—JOHN S. BASSETT (1867–1928) *Life of Jackson*

Politics. The conduct of public affairs for private advantage.
—AMBROSE BIERCE (1842–1914?) *Devil's Dictionary*

I shall not help crucify mankind upon a cross of gold. I shall not aid in pressing down upon the bleeding brow of labor this crown of thorns.
—WILLIAM JENNINGS BRYAN (1860–1925) Speech

We are Republicans, and we don't propose to leave our party and identify ourselves with the party whose antecedents have been rum, Romanism and rebellion.
—REV. S. D. BURCHARD (1812–1891) Speech, 1884

When I was called upon to be Prime Minister, now nearly two years ago, there were not many applicants for the job. Since then perhaps the market has improved.
—WINSTON CHURCHILL (1874–1965) Speech, Jan. 1942

Damn your principles. Stick to your party.
—BENJAMIN DISRAELI (1804–1881)

Every time I bestow a vacant office I make a hundred discontented persons and one ingrate.
—LOUIS XIV OF FRANCE (1638–1715)

The various admirable movements in which I have been engaged have always developed among their members a large lunatic fringe.
—THEODORE ROOSEVELT (1858–1919)

Prayer

"Oh, God, if I were sure I were to die tonight I would repent at once." It is the commonest prayer in all languages.
—JAMES M. BARRIE (1860–1937) *Sentimental Tommy*

He prayeth well who loveth well
Both man and bird and beast;
He prayeth best who loveth best
All things both great and small
For the dear God who loveth us,
He made and loveth all.
—SAMUEL TAYLOR COLERIDGE (1772–1834) *Ancient Mariner*

We, on our side, are praying to Him to give us victory, because we believe we are right; but those on the other side pray to Him, too, for victory, believing they are right. What must He think of us?
—ABRAHAM LINCOLN (1809–1865)

God grant me the serenity to accept the things I cannot change, courage to change things I can, and wisdom to know the difference.
—REINHOLD NIEBUHR (1892–1971)

More things are wrought by prayer
Than this world dreams of.
—TENNYSON (1809–1892) *Morte d'Arthur*

I have never made but one prayer to God, a very short one: "O Lord, make my enemies ridiculous." And God granted it.
—VOLTAIRE (1694–1778)

Therefore I say unto you, What things soever ye desire, when ye pray, believe that ye receive them, and ye shall receive them.
—NEW TESTAMENT: *Mark*, XI, 23, 24

Ask, and it shall be given you; seek, and ye shall find, knock, and it shall be opened unto you.
—NEW TESTAMENT: *Matthew*, vii, 7

Pride

Pride is the beginning of sin.
—BEN SIRA (*c.* 190 B.C.) *Book of Wisdom*

Pride, Envy, Avarice—these are the sparks
Have set on fire the hearts of all men.
—DANTE (1265–1321) *Inferno*

The readiness with which we admit a fault or acknowledge a weakness may be only our pride masquerading as humility.
—OSCAR HAMMLING (1890–   )

In pride, in reas'ning pride, our error lies;
All quit their sphere, and rush into the skies!
Pride still is aiming at the bless'd abodes,
Men would be angels, Angels would be Gods.
—ALEXANDER POPE (1688–1744) *Essay on Man*

War is the child of pride, and pride the daughter of riches.
—JONATHAN SWIFT (1667–1745) *Battle of the Books*

Pride goeth before destruction, and an haughty spirit before a fall.
—OLD TESTAMENT: *Proverbs*, xvi, 18

Prudence

Make haste slowly.
—AUGUSTUS CAESAR (63 B.C.–A.D. 14)

Put your trust in God, my boys, and keep your powder dry.
—OLIVER CROMWELL (1599–1658)

The greatest good is prudence; a more precious thing even than philosophy; from it spring all the other virtues.
—EPICURUS (342–270 B.C.) *Letter to Menaeceus*

That man is prudent who neither hopes nor fears anything from the uncertain events of the future.
—ANATOLE FRANCE (1844–1924) *Procurator of Judea*

Beware of rashness, but with energy and sleepless vigilance go forward and give us victories.
—ABRAHAM LINCOLN (1809–1865) Letter to Gen. Hooker

Let every man be swift to hear, slow to speak.
—NEW TESTAMENT: *James*, i, 19

Reading

Reading is to the Mind, what Exercise is to the Body.
—JOSEPH ADDISON (1672–1719) *The Tatler*

To read a book for the first time is to make the acquaintance of a new friend; to read it a second time is to meet an old one.
—SELWYN G. CHAMPION (1875–1950) *Racial Proverbs*

Some read to think—these are rare; some to write—these are common; and some to talk—and these form the great majority.
—CHARLES C. COLTON (1780?–1832) *Lacon*

There is an art of reading, as well as an art of thinking, and an art of writing.
—ISAAC D'ISRAELI (1766–1848) *Literary Character*

A man ought to read just as inclination leads him; for what he reads as a task will do him little good. A young man should read five hours in a day, and so may acquire a great deal of knowledge.
—SAMUEL JOHNSON (1709–1784) Boswell's *Life*

I'm quite illiterate, but I read a lot.
—J. D. SALINGER (1919–   ) *Catcher in the Rye*

He hath never fed of the dainties that are bred in a book.
—SHAKESPEARE (1564–1616) *Love's Labour's Lost,* IV, ii, 25

The habit of reading is the only enjoyment in which there is no alloy; it lasts when all other pleasures fade.
—ANTHONY TROLLOPE (1815–1882)

Reason

Reason is a light that God has kindled in the soul.
—ARISTOTLE (384–322 B.C.) *Art of Rhetoric*

He who will not reason is a bigot; he who cannot is a fool; and he who dares not is a slave.
—WILLIAM DRUMMOND (1585–1649) *Academical Question*

It is wise even in adversity to listen to reason.
—EURIPIDES (480–406 B.C.) *Hecuba*

The soul of man is divided into three parts, intelligence, reason and passion. Intelligence and passion are possessed by other animals, but reason by man alone. . . . Reason is immortal, all else mortal.
—PYTHAGORAS (582–500 B.C.)

Regret

Regret not that which is past; and trust not to thine own righteousness.
—ST. ANTHONY (*c.* 250–350)

O lost days of delight, that are wasted in doubting and waiting!
O lost hours and days in which we might have been happy!
—HENRY W. LONGFELLOW (1807–1882) *Tales of a Wayside Inn*

Of all sad words of tongue or pen,
The saddest are these: "It might have been."
—JOHN GREENLEAF WHITTIER (1807–1892) *Maud Muller*

Respect

Respect is what we owe; love, what we give.
—PHILIP JAMES BAILEY (1816–1902) *Festus*

He removes the greatest ornament of friendship, who takes away from it respect.
—CICERO (106–43 B.C.) *De Amicitia*

A man's real life is that accorded to him in the thoughts of other men by reason of respect or natural love.
—JOSEPH CONRAD (1857–1924) *Under Western Eyes*

Deference is the instinctive respect which we pay to the great and good; the unconscious acknowledgment of the superiority or excellence of others.
—TRYON EDWARDS (1809–1894)

Even a nod from a person who is esteemed is of more force than a thousand arguments or studied sentences from others.
—PLUTARCH (46?–120?) *Lives: Phocion*

There is no respect of persons with God.
—NEW TESTAMENT: *Romans,* ii, 11

Retirement

Don't think of retiring from the world until the world will be sorry that you retire. I hate a fellow whom pride or cowardice or laziness drive into a corner, and who does nothing when he is there but sit and growl. Let him come out as I do, and bark.
—SAMUEL JOHNSON (1709–1784)

Let me caution persons grown old in active business, not lightly, nor without weighing their own resources, to forego their customary employment all at once, for there may be danger in it.
—CHARLES LAMB (1775–1834) *Superannuated Man*

I could be well content
To entertain the lag-end of my life
With quiet hours.
—SHAKESPEARE (1564–1616) *I Henry IV,* V, i, 23

Science

Science bestowed immense new powers on man and at the same time created conditions which were largely beyond his comprehension and still more beyond his control.
—WINSTON CHURCHILL (1874–1965) Speech, March 31, 1949

In science we must be interested in things, not in persons.
—MARIE CURIE (1867–1934)

What art was to the ancient world, science is to the modern.
—BENJAMIN DISRAELI (1804–1881) *Coningsby*

Why does this magnificent applied science, which saves work and makes life easier, bring us little happiness? The simple answer runs, because we have not yet learned to make sensible use of it.
—ALBERT EINSTEIN (1879–1955) Address, 1931

Science is the knowledge of consequences, and dependence of one fact upon another.
—THOMAS HOBBES (1588–1679) *Leviathan*

In science the credit goes to the man who convinces the world, not to the man to whom the idea first occurs.
—SIR WILLIAM OSLER (1849–1919)

Sea

Roll on, thou deep and dark blue ocean, roll.
Ten thousand fleets sweep over thee in vain:
Man marks the earth with ruin, —his control
Stops with the shore.
—LORD BYRON (1788–1824) *Childe Harold*

The sea possesses a power over one's moods that has the effect of a will. The sea can hypnotize. Nature in general can do so.
—HENDRIK IBSEN (1828–1906) *Lady from the Sea*

Comrades! now that we have established our peace on land, let us conquer the freedom of the seas.
—NAPOLEON BONAPARTE (1769–1821)

Any one can hold the helm when the sea is calm.
—PUBLILIUS SYRUS (1st C. B.C.) *Sententiae*

The sea folds away from you like a mystery. You can look and look at it and mystery never leaves it.
—CARL SANDBURG (1878–1967) *Remembrance Rock*

Full fathom five thy father lies;
Of his bones are coral made;
Those are pearls that were his eyes;
Nothing of him that doth fade
But doth suffer a sea-change
Into something rich and strange.
—SHAKESPEARE (1564–1616) *Tempest,* I, ii, 394

All the rivers run into the sea; yet the sea is not full.
—OLD TESTAMENT: *Ecclesiastes,* i, 7

Season

To everything there is a season, and a time to every purpose under the heaven.
—OLD TESTAMENT: *Ecclesiastes*, iii, 1

Self-Control

One of the most important, but one of the most difficult things for a powerful mind is, to be its own master. A pond may lie quiet in a plain; but a lake wants mountains to compass and hold it in.
—JOSEPH ADDISON (1672–1719)

I count him braver who overcomes his desires than him who conquers his enemies; for the hardest victory is the victory over self.
—ARISTOTLE (384–322 B.C.) *Stobaeus: Florilegium*

Conquer thyself. Till thou hast done this, thou art but a slave for it is almost as well to be subjected to another's appetite as to thine own.
—ROBERT BURTON (1577–1640) *Anatomy of Melancholy*

Nothing gives one person so much advantage over another as to remain always cool and unruffled under all circumstances.
—THOMAS JEFFERSON (1743–1826)

No conflict is so severe as his who labors to subdue himself.
—THOMAS À KEMPIS (1380–1471) *Imitation of Christ*

He that is slow to anger is better than the mighty; and he that ruleth his spirit than he that taketh a city.
—OLD TESTAMENT: *Proverbs*, xvi, 32

Selfishness

People often grudge others what they cannot enjoy themselves.
—AESOP (6th C. B.C.) *Dog in the Manger*

This is the plain truth: every one ought to keep a sharp eye for the main chance.
—PLAUTUS (*c.* 254–184 B.C.) *Asinaria*

We have always known that heedless self-interest was bad morals; we know now that it is bad economics.
—FRANKLIN D. ROOSEVELT (1882–1945) Second Inaugural

There's plenty of boys that will come hankering and gruvelling around when you've got an apple, and beg the core off you; but when *they've* got one, and you beg for the core, and remind them how you give them a core one time, they make a mouth at you, and say thank you most to death, but there ain't a-going to *be* no core.
—MARK TWAIN (1835–1910) *Tom Sawyer Abroad*

Selfishness is the only real atheism; aspiration, unselfishness, the only real religion.
—ISRAEL ZANGWILL (1864–1926) *Children of the Ghetto*

Self-Respect

The reverence of a man's self is, next to religion, the chiefest bridle of all vices.
—FRANCIS BACON (1561–1620) *New Atlantis*

Few men survey themselves with so much severity as not to admit prejudices in their own favor.
—SAMUEL JOHNSON (1709–1784) *The Rambler*

I care not so much what I am in the opinion of others as what I am in my own; I would be rich of myself and not by borrowing.
—MICHEL DE MONTAIGNE (1533–1592) *Essays*

If ye would go up high, then use your own legs! Do not get yourselves *carried* aloft; do not seat yourselves on other's backs and heads!
—FRIEDRICH NIETZSCHE (1844–1900) *Thus Spake Zarathustra*

To have a respect for ourselves guides our morals; and to have a deference for others governs our manners.
—LAURENCE STERNE (1713–1768)

Serenity

Remember to preserve an even mind in adverse circumstance and likewise in prosperity a mind free from overweening joy.
—HORACE (65–8 B.C.) *Odes*

Calm of mind, all passion spent.
—JOHN MILTON (1608–1674) *Samson Agonistes*

He who is of a calm and happy nature will hardly feel the pressure of age, but to him who is of an opposite disposition youth and age are equally a burden.
—PLATO (428–347 B.C.) *The Republic*

Silence

Silence gives consent.
—CANON LAW: *Decretals*

Silence is the unbearable repartee.
—G. K. CHESTERTON (1874–1936) *Dickens*

Silence is true wisdom's best reply.
—EURIPIDES (480–406 B.C.) *Fragments*

There is an eloquent silence: it serves sometimes to approve, sometimes to condemn; there is a mocking silence; there is a respectful silence.
—FRANÇOIS DE LA ROCHEFOUCAULD (1613–1680) *Reflections*

He has occasional flashes of silence, that make his conversation perfectly delightful.
—SYDNEY SMITH (1771–1845) *Speaking of Macaulay*

Even a fool, when he holdeth his peace, is counted wise.
—OLD TESTAMENT: *Proverbs*, xvii, 28

Sleep

We sleep, but the loom of life never stops and the pattern which was weaving when the sun went down is weaving when the sun comes up tomorrow.
—HENRY WARD BEECHER (1813–1887) *Life Thoughts*

Sleep is a death; oh, make me try
By sleeping, know what it is to die,
And as gently lay my head
On my grave, as now my bed.
—THOMAS BROWNE (1605–1682) *Religio Medici*

Our life is two-fold: Sleep hath its own world,
A boundry between the things misnamed
Death and existence: Sleep hath its own world.
And a wise realm of wild reality.
—LORD BYRON (1788–1824) *The Dream*

Now blessings light on him that first invented this same sleep! It covers a man all over, thoughts and all, like a cloak; 'tis meat for the hungry, drink for the thirsty, heat for the cold, and cold for the hot.'Tis the current coin that purchases all the pleasures of the world cheap; and the balance that sets the king and the shepherd, the fool and the wise man even.
—CERVANTES (1547–1616) *Don Quixote*

O Sleep, thou rest of all things, Sleep, gentlest of the gods, peace of the soul, who puttest care to flight.
—OVID (43 B.C.–A.D. 18?) *Metamorphoses*

Our foster-nurse of nature is repose,
The which he lacks; that to provoke in him,
Are many simples operative, whose power
Will close the eye of anguish.
—SHAKESPEARE (1564–1616) *King Lear*, IV, iv, 12

Sleep that knits up the ravell'd sleave of care,
The death of each day's life, sore labour's bath,
Balm of hurt minds, great nature's second course,
Chief nourisher in life's feast.
—SHAKESPEARE (1564–1616) *Macbeth*, II, ii, 36

Thou hast been called, O sleep! the friend of woe;
But 'tis the happy that have called thee so.
—ROBERT SOUTHEY (1774–1843) *Curse of Kehama*

Yet a little sleep, a little slumber, a little folding of the hands to sleep.
—OLD TESTAMENT: *Proverbs,* vi, 10

Smile

What sunshine is to flowers, smiles are to humanity. They are but trifles, to be sure; but, scattered along life's pathway, the good they do is inconceivable.
—JOSEPH ADDISON (1672–1719)

There is a smile of Love,
And there is a smile of Deceit,
And there is a smile of smiles
In which these two smiles meet.
—WILLIAM BLAKE (1757–1827) *Smile and Frown*

A smile is ever the most bright and beautiful with a tear upon it. What is the dawn without the dew? The tear is rendered by the smile precious above the smile itself.
—WALTER S. LANDOR (1775–1864)

Soldier

It were better to be a soldier's widow than a coward's wife.
—THOMAS B. ALDRICH (1836–1907) *Mercedes*

I love a brave soldier who has undergone the baptism of fire.
—NAPOLEON BONAPARTE (1769–1821)

The army is a school in which the miser becomes generous, and the generous prodigal; miserly soldiers are like monsters, very rarely seen.
—CERVANTES (1547–1616) *Don Quixote*

How sleep the brave, who sink to rest,
By all their country's wishes blest!
—WILLIAM COLLINS (1721–1759) *Ode Written in 1746*

For it's Tommy this, an' Tommy that, an'
    "Chuck 'im out, the brute!"
But it's the "Saviour of 'is country" when
    the guns begin to shoot.
←RUDYARD KIPLING (1865–1936) *Tommy*

But in a larger sense, we cannot dedicate, we cannot consecrate, we cannot hallow this ground. The brave men living and dead, who struggled here, have consecrated it far above our poor power to add or detract. The world will little note, nor long remember, what we say here, but it can never forget what they did here.
—ABRAHAM LINCOLN (1809–1865) Gettysburg Address

"Companions," said he [Saturninus], "you have lost a good captain, to make of him a bad general."
—MICHEL DE MONTAIGNE (1533–1592) *Essays*

Your son, my lord, has paid a soldier's debt:
He only lived but till he was a man;
The which no sooner had his prowess confirm'd
In the unshrinking station where he fought,
But like a man he died.
—SHAKESPEARE (1564–1616) *Macbeth*, V, vii, 68

The proper qualities of a general are judgment and deliberation.
—TACITUS (*c.* 55–117) *History*

The combat infantryman should combine the arts of a successful poacher, a cat-burglar and a gunman.
—FIELD MARSHAL EARL WAVELL (1885–1950)

Son See CHILDREN

Sorrow

There is no sorrow which length of time does not diminish and soften.
—CICERO (106–43 B.C.) *De Finibus*

I have had sorrows . . . but I have borne them ill.
I have broken where I should have bent.
—CHARLES DICKENS (1812–1870) *Barnaby Rudge*

When sorrows come, they come not single spies,
But in battalions.
—SHAKESPEARE (1564–1616) *Hamlet*, IV, v, 78

Summer

Heat, ma'am! It was so dreadful here that I found nothing left for it but to take off my flesh and sit in my bones.
—SYDNEY SMITH (1771–1845) in Lady Holland's *Memoirs*

Shall I compare thee to a summer's day?
—SHAKESPEARE (1564–1616) *Sonnets,* xviii

Today the summer has come at my window with its sighs and murmurs; and the bees are plying their minstrelsy at the court of the flowering grove.
—RABINDRANATH TAGORE (1861–1941) *Gitanjali*

Sympathy

  The man who melts
With social sympathy, though not allied,
Is of more worth than a thousand kinsmen.
—EURIPIDES (480–406 B.C.) *Orestes*

Sympathy is a virtue much cultivated by those who are morally uplifted by the sufferings and misfortunes of others.
—OSCAR HAMMLING (1890–   )

As man laughs with those that laugh, so he weeps with those that weep; if thou wish me to weep, thou must first shed tears thyself; then thy sorrows will touch me.
—HORACE (65–8 B.C.) *De Arte Poetica*

It is better to be generous than just. It is sometimes better to sympathize instead of trying to understand.
—PIERRE LECOMTE DE NOÜY (1883–1947) *Human Destiny*

Talent

Doing easily what others find difficult is talent. . . .
—HENRI-FRÉDÉRIC AMIEL (1828–1881) *Journal*

Every man hath his proper gift of God, one after this manner and another after that.
—NEW TESTAMENT: *I Corinthians,* vii, 7

Taste

Happy is the man possessing
The superior holy blessing
Of a judgment and a taste
Accurate, refined and chaste.
—ARISTOPHANES (444–380 B.C.) *The Frogs*

Love of beauty is Taste. . . . The creation of beauty is Art.
—RALPH WALDO EMERSON (1803–1882)

Teacher and Teaching

A teacher affects eternity; he can never tell where his influence stops.
—HENRY ADAMS (1838–1918) *Education of Henry Adams*

The true teacher defends his pupils against his own personal influence.
—AMOS BRONSON ALCOTT (1799–1888) *Orphic Sayings*

To know how to suggest is the great art of teaching.
—HENRI-FRÉDÉRIC AMIEL (1828–1881) *Journal*

What nobler employment, or more valuable to the state, than that of the man who instructs the rising generation?
—CICERO (106–43 B.C.) *De Divinatione*

The secret of teaching is to appear to have known all your life what you learned this afternoon.
—UNKNOWN

Thrift

A man's ordinary expenses ought to be but half of his receipts, and if he think to wax rich, but to the third part.
—FRANCIS BACON (1561–1620)

He will always be a slave, who does not know how to live upon a little.
—HORACE (65–8 B.C.) *Epistulae*

Resolve not to be poor; whatever you have, spend less.
—SAMUEL JOHNSON (1709–1784) Boswell's *Life*

Thrift is care and scruple in the spending of one's means. It is not a virtue, and it requires neither skill nor talent.
—IMMANUEL KANT (1724–1804) Lecture

Time

Go, sir, gallop, and don't forget that the world was made in six days. You can ask me for anything you like except time.
—NAPOLEON BONAPARTE (1769–1821) To one of his aides

Never the time and the place
And the loved one all together!
—ROBERT BROWNING (1812–1889) *Never the Time and Place*

There is no remembrance which time does not obliterate, nor pain which death does not end.
—CERVANTES (1547–1616) *Don Quixote*

For though we sleep or wake, or roam, or ride,
Aye fleets the time, it will no man abide.
—GEOFFREY CHAUCER (1340?–1400) *Canterbury Tales*

Dost thou love life? Then do not squander time, for that is the stuff life is made of.
—BEN FRANKLIN (1706–1790) *Poor Richard's Almanack*

Gather ye rosebuds while ye may,
  Old Time is still a-flying,
And this same flower that smiles today,
  Tomorrow will be dying.
—ROBERT HERRICK (1591–1674) *To the Virgins*

Stand still, you ever moving spheres of heaven,
That time may cease, and midnight never come.
—CHRISTOPHER MARLOWE (1564–1593) *Dr. Faustus*

The time which we have at our disposal every day is elastic; the passions that we feel expand it, those that we inspire contract it; and habit fills up what remains.
—MARCEL PROUST (1871–1922) *Remembrance of Things Past*

Time flies on restless pinions—constant never.
Be constant—and thou chainest time forever.
—JOHANN SCHILLER (1759–1805) *Epigram*

Make use of time, let not advantage slip;
Beauty within itself should not be wasted:
Fair flowers that are not gather'd in their prime,
Rot and consume themselves in little time.
—SHAKESPEARE (1564–1616) *Venus and Adonis,* 129

There is . . . a time to be born, and a time to die; a time to plant, and a time to pluck up that which is planted; A time to kill, and a time to heal; a time to break down, and a time to build up; A time to weep, and a time to laugh; a time to mourn, and a time to dance; . . . A time to love and a time to hate.
—OLD TESTAMENT: *Ecclesiastes,* iii, 1

Tolerance and Intolerance

He knows not how to wink at human frailty,
Or pardon weakness that he never felt.
—JOSEPH ADDISON (1672–1719) *Cato*

Toleration is good for all or it is good for none.
—EDMUND BURKE (1729–1797) Speech, 1773

I have seen gross intolerance shown in support of toleration.
—SAMUEL TAYLOR COLERIDGE (1772–1834) *Biographia*

Give to every other human being every right you claim for yourself.
—ROBERT GREEN INGERSOLL (1833–1899) *Limitations of Toleration*

Shall I ask the brave soldier, who fights by my side
In the cause of mankind, if our creeds agree!
Shall I give up the friend I have valued and tried,
If he kneel not before the same altar with me.
—THOMAS MOORE (1779–1852) *Come, Send Round the Wine*

It is easy to be tolerant when you do not care.
—CLEMENT F. ROGERS (1866–   ) *Verify Your References*

It is now no more that toleration is spoken of, as if it were by the indulgence of one class of people that another enjoyed the exercise of their inherent rights.
—GEORGE WASHINGTON (1732–1799) Letter to Hebrew Congregation of Newport, R.I.

Truth

Truth is within ourselves; it takes no rise
From outward things, whate'er you may believe
There is an inmost centre in us all
Where truth abides in fulness.
—ROBERT BROWNING (1812–1889) *Paracelsus*

Truth, crushed to earth, shall rise again;
　The eternal years of God are hers;
But error, wounded, writhes in pain,
　And dies among his worshippers.
—WILLIAM CULLEN BRYANT (1794–1878) *Living Lost*

'Tis strange, but true; for truth is always strange,—
Stranger than fiction.
—LORD BYRON (1788–1824) *Don Juan*

The greatest friend of truth is Time, her greatest enemy is Prejudice, and her constant companion is Humility.
—CHARLES C. COLTON (1780?–1832) *Lacon*

God offers to every mind its choice between truth and repose. Take which you please—you can never have both.
—RALPH WALDO EMERSON (1803–1882) *Essays*

If the truth hurts most of us so badly that we don't want it told, it hurts even more grievously those who dare to tell it. It is a two-edged sword, often deadly dangerous to the user.
—JUDGE BEN LINDSEY (1869–1943) *Revolt of Modern Youth*

The smallest atom of truth represents some man's bitter toil and agony; for every ponderable chunk of it there is a brave truth-seeker's grave upon some lonely ash-dump and a soul roasting in hell.
—H. L. MENCKEN (1880–1956) *Prejudices*

Truth often suffers more by the heat of its defenders, than from the arguments of its opposers.
—WILLIAM PENN (1644–1718) *Fruits of Solitude*

'Tis not enough your counsel still be true;
Blunt truths more mischief than nice falsehoods do.
—ALEXANDER POPE (1688–1744) *Essay on Criticism*

We know the truth has been
Told over to the world a thousand times;—
But we have had no ears to listen yet
For more than fragments of it; we have heard
A murmur now and then, an echo here
And there.
—EDWIN ARLINGTON ROBINSON (1869–1935) *Captain Orsig*

A thing is not necessarily true because a man dies for it.
—OSCAR WILDE (1854–1900) *Portrait of Mr. W. H.*

That witty and eloquent old Dr. Oliver Wendell Holmes once said . . . "You needn't fear to handle the truth roughly; she is no invalid."
—WOODROW WILSON (1856–1924) Address, 1918

If you shut up truth and bury it under the ground, it will but grow, and gather to itself such explosive power that the day it bursts through, it will blow up everything in its way.
—ÈMILE ZOLA (1840–1902) *J'accuse*

Ye shall know the truth, and the truth shall make you free.
—NEW TESTAMENT: *John*, viii, 32

Tyranny

I have sworn upon the altar of God eternal hostility against every form of tyranny over the mind of man.
—THOMAS JEFFERSON (1743–1826)

They [the people in lands with dictators] have forgotten the lessons of history that the ultimate failures of dictatorships cost humanity far more than any temporary failures of democracy.
—FRANKLIN D. ROOSEVELT (1882–1945) Address, 1937

Like the form of a seen and unheard prowler,
like a slow and cruel violence,
is the known unspoken menace:
do what we tell you or go hungry;
listen to us or you don't eat.
—CARL SANDBURG (1878–1967) *The People, Yes*

And the little screaming fact that sounds through all history: repression works only to strengthen and knit the repressed.
—JOHN STEINBECK (1902–1968) *Grapes of Wrath*

Valor See COURAGE

Vanity

An ostentatious man will rather relate a blunder or an absurdity he has committed, than be debarred from talking of his own dear person.
—JOSEPH ADDISON (1672–1719)

One will rarely err if extreme actions be ascribed to vanity, ordinary actions to habit, and mean actions to fear.
—FRIEDRICH NIETZSCHE (1844–1900)

Vanity as an impulse has without doubt been of far more benefit to civilization than modesty has ever been.
—WILLIAM E. WOODWARD (1874–1950) *George Washington*

Vanity of vanities, saith the Preacher, vanity of vanities; all is vanity.
—OLD TESTAMENT: *Ecclesiastes*, i, 2

War

In war there are no winners.
—NEVILLE CHAMBERLAIN (1869–1940) Speech, 1938

Little did we guess that what has been called the Century of the Common Man would witness as its outstanding feature more common men killing each other with greater facilities than any other five centuries together in the history of the world.
—WINSTON CHURCHILL (1874–1965) Speech, 1949

If, however, there is to be a war of nerves let us make sure our nerves are strong and are fortified by the deepest convictions of our hearts.
—WINSTON CHURCHILL·(1874–1965) Speech, Mar. 31, 1949

I wisht it cud be fixed up, so' th' men that starts th' wars could do th' fightin'.
—FINLEY PETER DUNNE (1867–1936) *War and War Makers*

So long as mankind shall continue to lavish more praise upon its destroyers than upon its benefactors war shall remain the chief pursuit of ambitious minds.
—EDWARD GIBBON (1737–1794) *Decline and Fall of the Roman Empire*

It must be thoroughly understood that the lost land will never be won back by solemn appeals to the good God, nor by hopes in any League of Nations, but only by the force of arms.
—ADOLF HITLER (1889–1945) *Mein Kampf*

If—which God prevent—a new war breaks out, nothing else will await or confront all peoples . . . but appalling destruction and ruin, and this whether they are victor or vanquished.
—POPE JOHN XXIII (1881–1963) July 2, 1959

War is the greatest plague that can afflict mankind. . . . Any scourge is preferable to it.
—MARTIN LUTHER (1483–1546) Table-Talk, No. 821

War ought to be the only study of a prince.
—NICCOLO MACHIAVELLI (1469–1527) The Prince

They shall not pass.
—MARSHAL HENRI PÉTAIN (1856–1951) Battle of Verdun, 1916

And after the strife of war begins the strife of peace.
—CARL SANDBURG (1878–1967) The People, Yes

And Caesar's spirit, ranging for revenge,
With Ate by his side come hot from hell,
Shall in these confines with a monarch's voice,
Cry "Havoc" and let slip the dogs of war.
—SHAKESPEARE (1564–1616) Julius Caesar, III, i, 270

In peace there's nothing so becomes a man
As modest stillness and humility;
But when the blast of war blows in our ears,
Then imitate the action of the tiger:
Stiffen the sinews, summon up the blood.
—SHAKESPEARE (1564–1616) Henry V, III, ii, 3

In the arts of life man invents nothing: but in the arts of death he outdoes Nature herself, and produces by chemistry and machinery all the slaughter of plague, pestilence and famine.
—GEORGE BERNARD SHAW (1856–1950) Man and Superman, Act III

It [War] is all hell. . . . I look upon war with horror.
—WILLIAM TECUMSEH SHERMAN (1820–1891) Address, 1880

To be prepared for war is one of the most effectual means of preserving peace.
—GEORGE WASHINGTON (1732–1799) Speech, 1790

The war to end wars.
—H. G. WELLS (1860–1946) Attributed

Wars and rumours of wars.
—NEW TESTAMENT: Matthew, xxiv, 6

Weather

For the man sound in body and serene of mind there is no such thing as bad weather! every sky has its beauty, and storms which whip the blood do but make it pulse more vigorously.
—GEORGE GISSING (1857–1903)

We may achieve climate, but weather is thrust upon us.
—O. HENRY (1862–1910) Fog in Santone

Climate is theory. Weather is condition.
—OLIVER HERFORD (1865–1935)

I wonder that any human being should remain in a cold country who could find room in a warm one.
—THOMAS JEFFERSON (1743–1826) Letter

The fog comes
on little cat feet.
It sits looking
over the harbor and city
on silent haunches
and then, moves on.
—CARL SANDBURG (1878–1967) Fog

When it is evening, ye say, It will be fair weather: for the sky is red. And in the morning, It will be foul weather today: for the sky is red and lowring.
—NEW TESTAMENT: Matthew, xvi, 2–3

Wife

Helmer: Before all else you are a wife and a mother.
Nora: That I no longer believe. I think that before all else
            I am a human being.
—HENRIK IBSEN (1828–1906) Doll's House

If you want peace in the house, do what your wife wants.
—AFRICAN PROVERB

A good wife should be as a looking glass to represent her husband's face and passion; if he be pleasant, she should be merry; if he laugh, she should smile; if he look sad, she should participate of his sorrow.
—PLUTARCH (46?–120?) Moralia: Advice to a Bride

She looketh well to the ways of her household, and eateth not the bread of idleness.
—OLD TESTAMENT: Proverbs, xxxi, 27

Wisdom

Wise men, though all laws were abolished, would lead the same lives.
—ARISTOPHANES (444–380 B.C.)

Make wisdom your provision for the journey from youth to old age, for it is a more certain support than all other possessions.
—BIAS (f. 570 B.C.)

A man doesn't begin to attain wisdom until he recognizes that he is no longer indispensable.
—ADMIRAL RICHARD E. BYRD (1888–1957) Alone

Wisdom is full of pity, and thereby
Men pay for too much wisdom with much pain.
—EURIPIDES (480–406 B.C.) Electra

Wisdom is not finally tested in the schools,
Wisdom cannot be passed from one having it to another not
   having it,
Wisdom is of the soul, is not susceptible of proof, is its own
   proof.
—WALT WHITMAN (1819–1892) Song of the Open Road

The fear of the Lord is the beginning of wisdom.
—OLD TESTAMENT: Psalms, cxi, 10

Wooing See COURTSHIP

Writing

I don't wait for moods. You accomplish nothing if you do that. Your mind must know it has got to get down to work.
—PEARL BUCK (1892–1973) Reader's Digest

Writing a long and substantial book is like having a friend and companion at your side, to whom you can always turn for comfort and amusement, and whose society becomes more attractive as a new and widening field of interest is lighted in the mind.
—WINSTON CHURCHILL (1874–1965) Gathering Storm

Composition is for the most part, an effort of slow diligence and steady perseverence, to which the mind is dragged by necessity or resolution.
—SAMUEL JOHNSON (1709–1784) The Adventurer

The chief glory of every people arises from its authors.
—SAMUEL JOHNSON (1709–1784) Preface to Dictionary

The writers who have nothing to say are the ones you can buy; the others have too high a price.
—WALTER LIPPMANN (1889–1974) *Preface to Politics*

The impulse to create beauty is rather rare in literary men . . . Far ahead of it comes the yearning to make money. And after the yearning to make money comes the yearning to make a noise.
—H. L. MENCKEN (1880–1956) *Prejudices*

Youth

Young men are fitter to invent than to judge; fitter for execution than for counsel; and fitter for new projects than for settled business.
—FRANCIS BACON (1561–1626) *Of Youth and Age*

They shall not grow old, as we that are left grow old;
Age shall not weary them, nor the years condemn.
At the going down of the sun, and in the morning,
We shall remember them.
—LAURENCE BINYON (1869–1943) *For the Fallen*

Blow out, you bugles, over the rich Dead!
There's none of these so lonely and poor of old,
But dying, has made us rarer gifts than gold.
These laid the world away: poured out the red
Sweet wine of youth; gave up the years to be
Of work and joy, and that unhoped serene
That men call age, and those who would have been
Their sons, they gave their immortality.
—RUPERT BROOKE (1887–1915) *The Dead* (1914)

Ah! happy years! once more who would not be a boy!
—LORD BYRON (1788–1824) *Childe Harolde*

Youth is to all the glad season of life; but often only by what it hopes, not by what it attains, or what it escapes.
—THOMAS CARLYLE (1795–1881) *Essays*

As I approve of a youth that has something of the old man in him, so I am no less pleased with an old man that has something of the youth. He that follows this rule may be old in body, but can never be so in mind.
—CICERO (106–43 B.C.) *Cato*

There is a feeling of Eternity in youth which makes us amends for everything. To be young is to be as one of the Immortals.
—WILLIAM HAZLITT (1778–1830) *Table-Talk*

When all the world is young, lad,
And all the trees are green;
And every goose a swan, lad,
And every lass a queen;
Then hey, for boot and horse, lad,
And round the world away;
Young blood must have its course, lad,
And every dog his day.
—CHARLES KINGSLEY (1819–1875) *Water Babies*

How different from the present man was the youth of earlier days!
—OVID (43 B.C.–A.D. 18) *Heroides*

We think our fathers fools, so wise we grow;
Our wiser sons, no doubt, will think us so.
—ALEXANDER POPE (1688–1744) *Essay on Criticism*

My salad days;
When I was green in judgement.
—SHAKESPEARE (1564–1616) *Antony and Cleopatra*, I, v, 73

Through all the lying days of my youth
I swayed my leaves and flowers in the sun;
Now I may wither into the truth.
—WILLIAM BUTLER YEATS (1865–1939) *The Coming of Wisdom with Time*

Youth is not rich in time; it may be poor;
Part with it as with money, sparing; pay
No moment but in purchase of its worth,
And what it's worth, ask death-beds; they can tell.
—EDWARD YOUNG (1684–1765) *Night Thoughts*

A

aard•vark
ab•a•lo•ne
aban•don
  aban•doned
  aban•don•ment
abase
  abased
  abas•ing
  abase•ment
abate
  abat•ed
  abat•ing
  abate•ment
ab•bey
ab•bot
  ab•bess
ab•bre•vi•ate
  ab•bre•vi•at•ed
  ab•bre•vi•at•ing
  ab•bre•vi•a•tion
ab•di•cate
  ab•di•cat•ed
  ab•di•cat•ing
  ab•di•ca•tion
ab•do•men
  ab•dom•i•nal
ab•duct
  ab•duc•tion
  ab•duc•tor
ab•er•rant
  ab•er•ra•tion
abet
  abet•ted
  abet•ting
abey•ance
ab•hor
  ab•horred
  ab•hor•ring
  ab•hor•rence
  ab•hor•rent
abide
  abid•ing
abil•i•ty
  abil•i•ties
ab•ject
  ab•ject•ly
ab•jure
  ab•jured
  ab•jur•ing
  ab•ju•ra•tion
ab•la•tion
able
  ably
able-bod•ied
ab•lu•tion
ab•ne•ga•tion
ab•nor•mal
  ab•nor•mal•i•ty
abol•ish
  abol•ish•ment
ab•o•li•tion
  ab•o•li•tion•ist
abom•i•nate
  abom•i•nat•ed
  abom•i•nat•ing
  abom•i•na•tion
abom•i•na•ble
  abom•i•na•bly
ab•o•rig•i•ne
  ab•o•rig•i•nal
abort
  abor•tion
  abor•tive
above•board
abra•sion
  abra•sive
abreast
abridge
  abridged
abroad
ab•rogate
  ab•ro•gat•ed
  ab•ro•gat•ing
  ab•ro•ga•tion
abrupt
ab•scess
  ab•scessed
ab•scond
ab•sence
ab•sent
  ab•sen•tee

ab•sent-mind•ed
ab•sinthe
ab•so•lute
  ab•so•lute•ly
  ab•so•lu•tion
ab•solve
  ab•solved
  ab•solv•ing
ab•sorb
  ab•sorb•ent
  ab•sorp•tion
  ab•sorb•en•cy
ab•stain
  ab•sten•tion
  ab•sti•nence
  ab•sti•nent
  ab•ste•mi•ous
ab•stract
  ab•strac•tion
ab•struse
ab•surd
  ab•surd•i•ty
abun•dant
  abun•dance
abuse
  abused
  abus•ing
  abus•er
abu•sive
  abu•sive•ly
abut
  abut•ting
  abut•ment
abys•mal
abyss
ac•a•dem•ic
  acad•e•mi•cian
acad•e•my
ac•cede
  ac•ced•ed
  ac•ced•ing
ac•cel•er•ate
  ac•cel•er•at•ed
  ac•cel•er•at•ing
  ac•cel•er•a•tion
  ac•cel•er•a•tor
ac•cent
ac•cen•tu•ate
  ac•cen•tu•at•ed
  ac•cen•tu•at•ing
  ac•cen•tu•a•tion
ac•cept
  ac•cept•ed
  ac•cept•ance
  ac•cept•a•ble
ac•cess
  ac•ces•si•ble
  ac•ces•si•bil•i•ty
  ac•ces•sion
  ac•ces•so•ry
ac•ci•dent
  ac•ci•den•tal
ac•claim
  ac•cla•ma•tion
ac•cli•mate
  ac•cli•mat•ed
  ac•cli•ma•tion
ac•cli•ma•tize
  ac•cli•ma•tized
ac•cliv•i•ty
  ac•cliv•i•ties
ac•co•lade
ac•com•mo•date
  ac•com•mo•dat•ed
  ac•com•mo•dat•ing
  ac•com•mo•da•tion
ac•com•pa•ny
  ac•com•pa•nied
  ac•com•pa•ny•ing
  ac•com•pa•ni•ment
  ac•com•pa•nist
ac•com•plice
ac•com•plish
  ac•com•plished
  ac•com•plish•ment
ac•cord
  ac•cord•ing
  ac•cord•ance
ac•cor•di•on
ac•cost
ac•count
  ac•count•a•ble
  ac•count•a•bil•i•ty

ac•count•ant
ac•count•ing
ac•cred•it
  ac•cred•i•ta•tion
ac•cre•tion
ac•cru•al
ac•crue
  ac•crued
ac•cu•mu•late
  ac•cum•u•lat•ed
  ac•cum•u•lat•ing
  ac•cum•u•la•tion
  ac•cu•mu•la•tive
ac•cu•rate
  ac•cu•ra•cy
  ac•cu•rate•ly
ac•cu•sa•tive
ac•cuse
  ac•cused
  ac•cus•ing
  ac•cu•sa•tion
  ac•cu•sa•to•ry
ac•cus•tom
  ac•cus•tomed
acer•bi•ty
ac•e•tate
ace•tic
ache
  ached
  ach•ing
achieve
  achieved
  achiev•ing
  achieve•ment
ac•id
  acid•ic
  acid•i•ty
acid•u•lous
ac•knowl•edge
  ac•knowl•edged
  ac•knowl•edg•ing
  ac•knowl•edg•ment
ac•me
ac•ne
ac•o•lyte
acous•tic
  acous•ti•cal
ac•quaint
  ac•quaint•ance
ac•qui•esce
  ac•qui•esced
  ac•qui•esc•ing
  ac•qui•es•cence
  ac•qui•es•cent
ac•quire
  ac•quired
  ac•quir•ing
  ac•qui•si•tion
ac•quit
  ac•quit•ted
  ac•quit•ting
  ac•quit•tal
acre
  acre•age
ac•rid
ac•ri•mo•ny
  ac•ri•mo•ni•ous
ac•ro•bat
  ac•ro•bat•ic
ac•ro•nym
ac•ro•pho•bia
across
acryl•ic
act•ing
ac•tion
ac•ti•vate
  ac•ti•vat•ed
  ac•ti•vat•ing
  ac•ti•va•tion
  ac•ti•va•tor
ac•tive
  ac•tive•ly
ac•tiv•ism
  ac•tiv•ist
  ac•tiv•i•ty
  ac•tiv•i•ties
ac•tor
  ac•tress
ac•tu•al
  ac•tu•al•ly
  ac•tu•al•i•ty
ac•tu•al•ize

ac•tu•al•i•za•tion
ac•tu•ary
  ac•tu•ar•ies
  ac•tu•ar•i•al
ac•tu•ate
  ac•tu•at•ed
acu•i•ty
acu•men
ac•u•punc•ture
acute
  acute•ly
ad•age
ad•a•mant
adapt
  adapt•a•ble
  adapt•a•bil•i•ty
  ad•ap•ta•tion
  adap•tive
ad•den•dum
  ad•den•da
ad•dict
  ad•dict•ed
  ad•dic•tive
  ad•dic•tion
ad•di•tion
  ad•di•tion•al
ad•di•tive
ad•dle
ad•dress
  ad•dress•ee
ad•duce
ad•e•noid
adept
ad•e•quate
  ad•e•qua•cy
  ad•e•quate•ly
ad•here
  ad•hered
  ad•her•ing
  ad•her•ence
  ad•her•ent
ad•he•sion
ad•he•sive
  ad•he•sive•ness
a•dieu
ad in•fi•ni•tum
ad•ja•cent
  ad•ja•cent•ly
ad•jec•tive
ad•join
ad•journ
  ad•journ•ment
ad•ju•di•cate
  ad•ju•di•cat•ed
  ad•ju•di•cat•ing
  ad•ju•di•ca•tion
ad•junct
ad•jure
  ad•jured
  ad•jur•ing
  ad•ju•ra•tion
ad•just
  ad•just•a•ble
  ad•just•er
  ad•just•ment
ad•ju•tant
ad•lib
  ad•libbed
  ad•lib•bing
ad•min•is•ter
ad•min•is•trate
  ad•min•is•tra•tion
  ad•min•is•tra•tive
  ad•min•is•tra•tor
ad•mi•ral
  ad•mi•ral•ty
ad•mire
  ad•mired
  ad•mir•ing
  ad•mi•ra•tion
  ad•mir•er
ad•mis•si•ble
  ad•mis•si•bil•i•ty
ad•mis•sion
ad•mit
  ad•mit•ted
  ad•mit•ting
  ad•mit•tance
ad•mix•ture
ad•mon•ish
  ad•mo•ni•tion
ado•be
ad•o•les•cence

ad•o•les•cent
adopt
  adop•tion
  adop•tive
adore
  adored
  ador•ing
  ador•a•ble
  ad•o•ra•tion
adorn
  adorn•ment
ad•re•nal
adren•a•line
adrift
adroit
  adroit•ly
  adroit•ness
ad•sorb
  ad•sor•bent
  ad•sorp•tion
ad•u•late
  ad•u•lat•ing
  ad•u•la•tion
  ad•u•la•to•ry
adult
  adult•hood
adul•ter•ate
  adul•ter•at•ed
  adul•ter•a•tion
adul•tery
  adul•ter•er
  adul•ter•ess
  adul•ter•ous
ad va•lo•rem
ad•vance
  ad•vanc•ing
  ad•vance•ment
ad•van•tage
  ad•van•ta•geous
ad•vent
  ad•ven•ti•tious
ad•ven•ture
  ad•ven•tur•er
  ad•ven•ture•some
  ad•ven•tur•ous
ad•verb
ad•ver•sary
  ad•ver•sar•ies
ad•verse
  ad•verse•ly
ad•ver•si•ty
  ad•ver•si•ties
ad•vert
ad•ver•tise
  ad•ver•tised
  ad•ver•tis•ing
  ad•ver•tis•er
  ad•ver•tise•ment
ad•vice
ad•vise
  ad•vis•ing
  ad•vis•a•bil•i•ty
  ad•vis•a•ble
  ad•vis•er
  ad•vi•so•ry
ad•vo•cate
  ad•vo•cat•ed
  ad•vo•cat•ing
  ad•vo•ca•cy
  ad•vo•ca•tion
ae•on
aer•ate
  aer•at•ed
  aer•at•ing
  aer•a•tion
  aer•a•tor
aer•i•al
aero•dy•nam•ics
aer•o•naut•ics
aer•o•sol
aer•o•space
aes•thete
aes•thet•ic
  aes•thet•i•cal•ly
af•fa•ble
  af•fa•bil•i•ty
  af•fa•bly
af•fair
af•fect
  af•fect•ing
  af•fec•tive
  af•fec•ta•tion
  af•fect•ed

af•fec•tion
  af•fec•tion•ate
af•fi•da•vit
af•fil•i•ate
  af•fil•i•at•ed
  af•fil•i•a•tion
af•fin•i•ty
af•firm
  af•fir•ma•tion
  af•firm•a•tive
af•flict
  af•flic•tion
af•flu•ence
  af•flu•ent
af•ford
af•fright
af•front
afore•men•tioned
afore•said
afore•thought
afraid
af•ter•ef•fect
af•ter•math
af•ter•most
af•ter•thought
af•ter•ward
again
against
agape
ag•ate
aga•ve
age
  aged
  ag•ing
  age•ing
  age•less
agen•cy
  agen•cies
agen•da
agent
ag•glom•er•a•tion
ag•glu•ti•na•tion
ag•gran•dize
  ag•gran•dized
  ag•gran•diz•ing
  ag•gran•dize•ment
ag•gra•vate
  ag•gra•vat•ed
  ag•gra•vat•ing
  ag•gra•va•tion
ag•gre•ga•tion
ag•gres•sive
  ag•gres•sor
  ag•gres•sion
ag•grieved
aghast
ag•ile
  agil•i•ty
ag•i•tate
  ag•i•tat•ed
  ag•i•tat•ing
  ag•i•ta•tion
  ag•i•ta•tor
ag•nos•tic
  ag•nos•ti•cism
ag•o•nize
  ag•o•niz•ing
ag•o•ny
ag•o•ra•pho•bia
agrar•i•an
agree
  agreed
  agree•ing
  agree•ment
  agree•a•ble
  agree•a•bly
ag•ri•cul•ture
  ag•ri•cul•tur•al
agron•o•my
aground
aide-de-camp
ail•ing
  ail•ment
ai•ler•on
aim•less
air•borne
air-con•di•tion
  air-con•di•tioned
  air con•di•tion•ing
  air con•di•tion•er
air•craft
air•plane
air•port

air•tight
air•wave
airy
aisle
ajar
akin
al•a•bas•ter
a la carte
alac•ri•ty
alarm
  alarm•ing
al•ba•core
al•ba•tross
al•be•it
al•bi•no
al•bum
al•bu•men
al•bu•min
al•che•my
al•co•hol
  al•co•hol•ic
  al•co•hol•ism
al•cove
al•der•man
alert
al•fal•fa
al•fres•co
al•gae
al•ge•bra
  al•ge•bra•ic
al•go•ri•thm
ali•as
  ali•as•es
al•i•bi
al•ien
al•ien•ate
  al•ien•at•ed
  al•ien•at•ing
alight
  alight•ed
align
  align•ment
alike
al•i•men•ta•ry
al•i•mo•ny
al•ka•li
  al•ka•line
al•ka•loid
all-around
al•lay
  al•layed
al•lege
  al•leged
  al•leg•ing
  al•le•ga•tion
al•le•giance
al•le•go•ry
  al•le•go•ries
  al•le•gor•ic
  al•le•gor•i•cal
al•ler•gen
al•ler•gy
  al•ler•gies
  al•ler•gic
al•le•vi•ate
  al•le•vi•at•ed
  al•le•vi•at•ing
  al•le•vi•a•tion
al•ley
  al•leys
al•li•ance
al•lied
al•li•ga•tor
al•lit•er•a•tion
al•lo•cate
  al•lo•cat•ed
  al•lo•cat•ing
  al•lo•ca•tion
al•lot
  al•lot•ted
  al•lot•ting
  al•lot•ment
al•low
  al•low•a•ble
al•low•ance
al•loy
al•lude
  al•lud•ed
al•lure
  al•lured
  al•lur•ing
al•lu•sion
  al•lu•sive

al•lu•sive•ly
al•lu•vi•al
al•ly
  al•lies
al•lied
  al•ly•ing
al•li•ance
al•ma ma•ter
al•ma•nac
al•mighty
al•mond
al•most
al•oe
aloft
alone
  alone•ness
along
  along•side
aloof
  aloof•ness
al•pha
al•pha•bet
  al•pha•bet•ic
  al•pha•bet•i•cal
  al•pha•bet•ize
al•pha•nu•mer•ic
al•ready
al•so
al•tar
al•ter
  al•ter•a•tion
al•ter•cate
  al•ter•ca•tion
al•ter e•go
al•ter•nate
  al•ter•nat•ing
  al•ter•nate•ly
  al•ter•na•tion
al•ter•na•tor
al•ter•na•tive
al•though
al•ti•tude
al•to
al•to•gether
al•tru•ism
  al•tru•is•tic
alu•mi•num
alum•na
  alum•nae
alum•nus
  alum•ni
al•ve•o•lar
al•ways
amal•gam
  amal•gam•ate
  amal•gam•a•tion
amass
am•a•teur
  am•a•teur•ism
  am•a•teur•ish
amaze
  amazed
  amaz•ing
  amaze•ment
Am•a•zon
am•bas•sa•dor
  am•bas•sa•dress
  am•bas•sa•do•ri•al
am•ber
am•bi•dex•trous
am•bi•ance
  am•bi•ence
am•bi•ent
am•big•u•ous
  am•big•u•ous•ly
  am•bi•gu•i•ty
am•bi•tion
  am•bi•tious
  am•bi•tious•ly
am•biv•a•lence
  am•biv•a•lent
am•ble
  am•bled
  am•bling
am•bro•sia
am•bu•lance
am•bu•late
  am•bu•lat•ed
  am•bu•lat•ing
  am•bu•la•to•ry
am•bush
  am•bushed
amel•io•rate

amel•io•rat•ed
amel•io•rat•ing
amel•io•ra•tion
amel•ior•a•tive
ame•na•ble
  ame•na•bil•i•ty
  ame•na•ble•ness
  ame•na•bly
amend
  amend•a•ble
  amend•ment
amen•i•ty
Amer•i•ca
  Amer•i•can
  Amer•i•can•ism
  Amer•i•can•i•za•tion
am•e•thyst
ami•a•ble
  ami•a•bil•i•ty
  ami•a•bly
am•i•ca•ble
  am•i•ca•bil•i•ty
  am•i•ca•bly
amid
  amidst
am•i•ty
am•mo•nia
am•mu•ni•tion
am•ne•sia
  am•ne•si•ac
am•nes•ty
amok
  amuck
among
  amongst
amor•al
am•o•rous
  am•o•rous•ly
amor•phous
am•or•tize
  am•or•tized
  am•or•tiz•ing
  am•or•ti•za•tion
amount
am•pere
  am•per•age
am•per•sand
am•phet•a•mine
am•phib•i•an
  am•phib•i•ous
am•phi•the•a•ter
am•ple
  am•ply
am•pli•fy
  am•pli•fied
  am•pli•fy•ing
  am•pli•fi•ca•tion
  am•pli•fi•er
am•pli•tude
am•pu•tate
  am•pu•tat•ed
  am•pu•tat•ing
  am•pu•ta•tion
  am•pu•tee
amuse
  amused
  amus•ing
  amuse•ment
anach•ro•nism
  anach•ro•nis•tic
  anach•ro•nous
anal
  anus
an•al•ge•sia
  an•al•ge•sic
an•a•logue
  an•a•log
anal•o•gy
  anal•o•gies
  anal•o•gous
anal•y•sis
  anal•y•ses
an•a•lyst
  an•a•lyt•ic
an•a•lyze
  an•a•lyzed
  an•a•lyz•ing
  an•a•ly•za•tion
an•ar•chist
  an•ar•chism
  an•ar•chis•tic
an•ar•chy
  an•ar•chic

an•ar•chi•cal
anath•e•ma
anat•o•my
  anat•o•mies
  an•a•tom•i•cal
an•ces•tor
  an•ces•tral
  an•ces•tress
  an•ces•try
an•chor
  an•chor•age
an•cho•rite
an•chovy
an•cient
an•cil•lary
an•drog•y•nous
  an•drog•y•ny
an•ec•dote
  an•ec•do•tal
ane•mia
  ane•mic
an•es•the•sia
  an•es•thet•ic
  an•es•the•tist
  an•es•the•si•ol•o•gist
  an•es•the•tize
an•eu•rysm
  an•eu•rism
an•gel
  an•gel•ic
  an•gel•i•cal•ly
an•ger
an•gi•na pec•to•ris
an•gle
  an•gling
an•gler
An•gli•can
  An•gli•can•ism
  An•gli•cize
An•glo-Amer•i•can
An•glo-Sax•on
an•go•ra
an•gry
  an•gri•ly
ang•strom unit
an•guish
  an•guished
an•gu•lar
  an•gu•lar•i•ty
an•i•mal
  an•i•mal•i•ty
an•i•mate
  an•i•mat•ed
  an•i•mat•ing
  an•i•ma•tion
an•i•mism
  an•i•mis•tic
an•i•mos•i•ty
an•i•mus
an•ise
an•i•sette
an•kle
an•nals
  an•nal•ist
an•neal
an•nex
  an•nex•a•tion
an•ni•hi•late
  an•ni•hi•lat•ed
  an•ni•hi•lat•ing
  an•ni•hi•la•tion
  an•ni•hi•la•tor
an•ni•ver•sa•ry
  an•ni•ver•sa•ries
an•no Do•mi•ni
an•no•tate
  an•no•tat•ed
  an•no•tat•ing
  an•no•ta•tion
an•nounce
  an•nounced
  an•nounc•ing
  an•nounce•ment
  an•nounc•er
an•noy
  an•noy•ance
an•nu•al
an•nu•i•ty
an•nul
  an•nulled
  an•nul•ment
an•nun•ci•ate
  an•nun•ci•a•tion

an•ode
an•o•dyne
anoint
  anoint•ment
anom•a•ly
  anom•a•lous
anon•y•mous
  an•o•nym•i•ty
  anon•y•mous•ly
an•oth•er
an•swer
  an•swer•a•ble
ant•ac•id
an•tag•o•nist
  an•tag•o•nism
  an•tag•o•nis•tic
an•tag•o•nize
  an•tag•o•niz•ing
ant•arc•tic
Ant•arc•ti•ca
an•te
an•te•bel•lum
an•te•ced•ent
an•te•cham•ber
an•te•date
an•te•di•lu•vi•an
an•te•lope
an•ten•na
  an•ten•nae
  an•ten•nas
an•te•ri•or
an•te•room
an•them
an•thol•o•gy
  an•thol•o•gies
an•thra•cite
an•thro•po•cen•tric
an•thro•pol•o•gy
  an•thro•po•log•ic
  an•thro•po•log•i•cal
  an•thro•pol•o•gist
an•thro•po•mor•phic
an•ti•air•craft
an•ti•bac•te•ri•al
an•ti•bal•lis•tic
an•ti•bi•ot•ic
an•ti•body
  an•ti•bod•ies
an•tic
An•ti•christ
an•tic•i•pate
  an•tic•i•pat•ed
  an•tic•i•pat•ing
  an•tic•i•pa•tion
  an•tic•i•pa•to•ry
an•ti•cli•max
  an•ti•cli•mac•tic
an•ti•dote
  an•ti•dot•al
an•ti•freeze
an•ti•gen
an•ti•his•ta•mine
an•ti•mis•sile
an•ti•mo•ny
an•ti•pas•to
an•tip•a•thy
  an•ti•pa•thet•ic
an•ti•pode
an•ti•quar•i•an
an•ti•quate
  an•ti•quat•ed
  an•ti•quat•ing
an•tique
  an•tiqued
  an•tiqu•ing
an•tiq•ui•ty
  an•tiq•ui•ties
an•ti-Sem•i•tism
an•ti•sep•tic
an•ti•so•cial
an•tith•e•sis
  an•tith•e•ses
  an•ti•thet•i•cal
an•ti•tox•in
  an•ti•tox•ic
an•ti•trust
an•to•nym
anus
an•vil
anx•i•e•ty
  anx•i•e•ties
anx•ious
any•body

any•bod•ies
any•how
any•more
any•one
any•place
any•thing
any•way
any•where
any•wise
aor•ta
apace
apart
apart•heid
apart•ment
ap•a•thy
  ap•a•thet•ic
  ap•a•thet•i•cal•ly
aper•i•tif
ap•er•ture
apex
  apex•es
  api•ces
ap•i•cal
apha•sia
aph•o•rism
  aph•o•ris•tic
aph•ro•dis•i•ac
api•ary
  api•ar•ies
apiece
ap•ish
aplomb
apoc•a•lypse
  apoc•a•lyp•tic
apoc•ry•pha
ap•o•gee
apol•o•gist
apol•o•gize
  apol•o•gized
  apol•o•giz•ing
apol•o•gy
  apol•o•gies
  apol•o•get•ic
  apol•o•get•i•cal
ap•o•plec•tic
ap•o•plex•y
apos•ta•sy
apos•tate
apos•ta•tize
a•pos•te•ri•o•ri
apos•tle
  ap•os•tol•ic
  ap•os•tol•i•cal
apos•tro•phe
ap•o•thegm
apoth•e•o•sis
  apoth•e•o•size
Ap•pa•la•chi•an
ap•pall
  ap•palled
  ap•pal•ling
ap•pa•rat•us
  ap•pa•rat•us•es
ap•par•el
ap•par•ent
ap•pa•ri•tion
ap•peal
  ap•peal•ing•ly
ap•pear
  ap•pear•ance
ap•pease
  ap•peased
  ap•peasing
  ap•pease•ment
  ap•peas•er
ap•pel•late
  ap•pel•lant
ap•pel•la•tion
ap•pend
  ad•pen•dage
ap•pen•di•ci•tis
  ap•pen•dec•to•my
ap•pen•dix
  ap•pen•dix•es
  ap•pen•di•ces
ap•per•tain
ap•pe•tite
  ap•pe•tiz•er
  ap•pe•tiz•ing
ap•plaud
  ap•plause
ap•ple
ap•pli•ance

ap•pli•ca•ble
  ap•pli•ca•bil•i•ty
ap•pli•cant
ap•pli•ca•tion
ap•pli•ca•tor
ap•ply
  ap•plied
  ap•ply•ing
ap•point
  ap•point•ee
  ap•point•ment
ap•por•tion
  ap•por•tion•ment
ap•po•site
ap•po•si•tion
  ap•pos•i•tive
ap•praise
  ap•praised
  ap•prais•ing
  ap•prais•er
  ap•prais•al
ap•pre•ci•a•ble
  ap•pre•ci•a•bly
ap•pre•ci•ate
  ap•pre•ci•at•ing
  ap•pre•ci•a•tion
  ap•pre•ci•a•tive
ap•pre•hend
  ap•pre•hen•si•ble
ap•pre•hen•sion
  ap•pre•hen•sive
ap•pren•tice
ap•prise
  ap•prised
  ap•pris•ing
ap•proach
  ap•proach•a•ble
ap•pro•ba•tion
ap•pro•pri•ate
  ap•pro•pri•at•ed
  ap•pro•pri•at•ing
  ap•pro•pri•ate•ness
  ap•pro•pri•a•tion
ap•prov•al
ap•prove
  ap•proved
  ap•prov•ing
ap•prox•i•mate
  ap•prox•i•mate•ly
  ap•prox•i•ma•tion
ap•pur•te•nance
ap•ri•cot
a pri•o•ri
apron
ap•ro•pos
apt
  apt•ly
  apt•ness
  ap•ti•tude
aq•ua
aquar•i•um
aquat•ic
aq•ue•duct
aque•ous
aq•ui•line
Ara•bi•an
  Ar•a•bic
ar•a•ble
arach•nid
ar•bi•ter
ar•bi•trary
  ar•bi•trar•i•ly
ar•bi•trate
  ar•bi•trat•ed
  ar•bi•trat•ing
  ar•bi•tra•tor
  ar•bi•tra•tion
ar•bor
arc
  arced
  arc•ing
ar•cade
ar•chae•ol•o•gy
  ar•che•ol•o•gy
  ar•chae•o•log•i•cal
  ar•che•o•log•i•cal
  ar•chae•ol•o•gist
  ar•che•ol•o•gist
ar•cha•ic
arch•bish•op
arch•dea•con
arch•di•o•cese
arch•er

ar•chery
ar•che•type
ar•chi•pel•a•go
ar•chi•tect
  ar•chi•tec•ture
  ar•chi•tec•tur•al
ar•chive
  ar•chi•val
  ar•chi•vist
arc•tic
ar•dent
ar•dor
ar•du•ous
ar•ea
are•na
ar•gue
  ar•gued
  ar•gu•ing
  ar•gu•a•ble
ar•gu•ment
  ar•gu•men•ta•tive
  ar•gu•men•tive
ar•gyle
aria
ar•id
  arid•i•ty
arise
  arose
  aris•en
  aris•ing
aris•to•crat
  aris•to•crat•ic
  ar•is•toc•ra•cy
  ar•is•toc•ra•cies
arith•me•tic
  ar•ith•met•i•cal
arm
  armed
  arm•ing
ar•ma•da
ar•ma•dil•lo
Ar•ma•ged•don
ar•ma•ment
ar•mi•stice
ar•moire
ar•mor
  ar•mored
ar•mory
  ar•mor•ies
ar•my
  ar•mies
aro•ma
  ar•o•mat•ic
around
arouse
  aroused
  arous•ing
  arous•al
ar•peg•gio
ar•raign
  ar•raign•ment
ar•range
  ar•ranged
  ar•rang•ing
  ar•range•ment
ar•ray
ar•rear
ar•rest
ar•rive
  ar•rived
  ar•riv•ing
  ar•ri•val
ar•ro•gant
  ar•ro•gance
  ar•ro•gant•ly
ar•ro•gate
  ar•ro•gat•ed
  ar•ro•ga•tion
ar•row
ar•se•nal
ar•se•nic
ar•son
  ar•son•ist
ar•te•ri•al
ar•te•ri•o•scle•ro•sis
ar•tery
  ar•ter•ies
ar•te•sian
art•ful
  art•ful•ly
ar•thri•tis
  ar•thrit•ic
ar•ti•choke

ar•ti•cle
ar•tic•u•late
  ar•tic•u•lat•ed
  ar•tic•u•lat•ing
  ar•tic•u•late•ly
  ar•tic•u•late•ness
ar•ti•fact
ar•ti•fice
ar•ti•fi•cial
  ar•ti•fi•ci•al•i•ty
  ar•ti•fi•cial•ly
ar•til•lery
ar•ti•san
art•ist
  ar•tis•tic
  ar•tis•ti•cal•ly
art•ist•ry
as•bes•tos
as•cend
  as•cend•ance
  as•cend•ence
  as•cend•an•cy
  as•cend•en•cy
  as•cend•ant
  as•cend•ent
as•cent
  as•cen•sion
as•cer•tain
  as•cer•tain•a•ble
as•cet•ic
  as•cet•i•cism
as•cot
as•cribe
  as•cribed
  as•crib•ing
  as•crib•a•ble
asex•u•al
  asex•u•al•i•ty
ashamed
  asham•ed•ly
ash
  ash•en
  ash•es
Asi•at•ic
as•i•nine
  as•i•nin•i•ty
askance
askew
asleep
aso•cial
as•par•a•gus
as•pect
as•pen
as•per•i•ty
as•per•sion
as•phalt
as•phyx•ia
  as•phyx•i•ate
  as•phyx•i•at•ed
  as•phyx•i•at•ing
  as•phyx•i•a•tion
as•pic
as•pir•ant
as•pir•ate
  as•pi•rat•ed
  as•pi•rat•ing
  as•pi•ra•tion
  as•pi•ra•tor
as•pire
  as•pir•ing
as•pi•rin
as•sail
  as•sail•a•ble
  as•sail•ant
as•sas•sin
as•sas•si•nate
  as•sas•si•nat•ed
  as•sas•si•nat•ing
  as•sas•si•na•tion
as•sault
as•say
as•sem•blage
as•sem•ble
  as•sem•bled
  as•sem•bling
  as•sem•bly
  as•sem•blies
  as•sem•bly•man
as•sent
as•sert
  as•ser•tion
  as•ser•tive
  as•ser•tive•ness

as•sess
  as•sess•ment
  as•sess•or
as•set
as•si•du•i•ty
  as•sid•u•ous
as•sign
  as•signed
  as•sign•a•ble
  as•sign•ment
  as•sig•na•tion
as•sim•i•late
  as•sim•i•lat•ed
  as•sim•i•lat•ing
  as•sim•i•la•tion
as•sist
  as•sist•ance
  as•sis•tant
as•size
as•so•ci•ate
  as•so•ci•at•ed
  as•so•ci•at•ing
  as•so•ci•a•tion
as•so•nance
  as•so•nant
as•sort•ment
as•suage
  as•suaged
  as•suag•ing
  as•suage•ment
as•sume
  as•sumed
  as•sum•ing
  as•sump•tion
as•sure
  as•sured
  as•sur•ing
  as•sur•ance
  as•sur•ed•ly
as•ter•isk
asth•ma
  asth•mat•ic
astig•ma•tism
  as•tig•mat•ic
as•ton•ish
  as•ton•ish•ing
  as•ton•ish•ment
as•tound
as•tra•khan
as•tral
astray
astride
as•trin•gent
as•trol•o•gy
  as•trol•o•ger
  as•tro•log•ic
  as•tro•log•i•cal
as•tro•naut
as•tro•nom•ic
  as•tro•nom•i•cal•ly
as•tron•o•my
  as•tron•o•mer
as•tro•phys•ics
  as•tro•phys•i•cist
as•tute
  as•tute•ly
asun•der
asy•lum
asym•me•try
  asym•met•ric
  asym•met•ri•cal
at•a•vism
  at•a•vis•tic
at•el•ier
athe•ism
  athe•ist
  athe•is•tic
ath•er•o•scle•ro•sis
ath•lete
  ath•let•ic
  ath•let•ics
  ath•let•i•cal•ly
athwart
at•las
  at•las•es
at•mos•phere
  at•mos•pher•ic
  at•mos•pher•i•cal
at•om
  atom•ic
at•om•iz•er
atonal
  ato•nal•i•ty

atone
  atoned
  aton•ing
  atone•ment
atri•um
atro•cious
  atroc•i•ty
  atroc•i•ties
at•ro•phy
  at•ro•phied
at•tach
  at•tach•ment
at•ta•ché
at•tack
at•tain
  at•tain•a•ble
at•tempt
at•tend
  at•tend•ance
  at•tend•ant
at•ten•tion
  at•ten•tive
at•ten•u•ate
  at•ten•u•at•ed
  at•ten•u•at•ing
  at•ten•u•a•tion
at•test
  at•tes•ta•tion
at•tic
at•tire
  at•tired
  at•tir•ing
at•ti•tude
at•tor•ney
  at•tor•neys
at•tract
  at•trac•tive
  at•trac•tion
at•tri•bute
  at•tri•but•ed
  at•tri•but•ing
  at•tri•but•a•ble
  at•tri•bu•tion
  at•trib•u•tive
at•tri•tion
at•tune
  at•tuned
  at•tun•ing
atyp•i•cal
au•burn
auc•tion
  auc•tion•eer
au•da•cious
  au•dac•i•ty
au•di•ble
  au•di•bly
au•di•ence
au•dio
au•di•o•vis•u•al
au•dit
  au•dit•or
au•di•tion
au•di•to•ri•um
au•di•to•ry
aught
aug•ment
  aug•men•ta•tion
au•ral
au•ro•ra
aus•pice
  aus•pic•es
aus•pi•cious
aus•tere
  aus•ter•i•ty
au•then•tic
  au•then•tic•i•ty
au•thor
  au•thor•ess
  au•thor•ship
au•thor•i•tar•i•an
au•thor•i•ta•tive
au•thor•i•ty
  au•thor•i•ties
au•thor•ize
  au•thor•ized
  au•thor•iz•ing
  au•thor•i•za•tion
au•to•bi•og•ra•phy
  au•to•bi•og•ra•phies
  au•to•bi•o•graph•ic
  au•to•bi•o•graph•i•cal
au•toc•ra•cy
  au•toc•ra•cies

au•to•crat
  au•to•crat•ic
  au•to•crat•i•cal•ly
au•to•graph
au•to•mate
  au•to•mat•ed
  au•to•mat•ing
au•to•mat•ic
  au•to•ma•tion
au•tom•a•tism
  au•tom•a•ton
au•to•mo•bile
au•to•mo•tive
au•ton•o•mous
  au•ton•o•my
au•top•sy
au•tumn
  au•tum•nal
aux•il•ia•ry
  aux•il•ia•ries
avail
avail•a•ble
  avail•a•bil•i•ty
av•a•lanche
avant•garde
av•a•rice
  av•a•ri•cious
Ave Ma•ria
avenge
  avenged
  aveng•ing
  aveng•er
av•e•nue
av•er•age
  av•er•aged
  av•er•ag•ing
averse
  averse•ly
  aver•sion
avert
avi•ary
  avi•ar•ies
avi•a•tion
avi•a•tor
  avi•a•trix
av•id
  avid•i•ty
  av•id•ly
av•o•ca•do
av•o•ca•tion
avoid
  avoid•a•ble
  avoid•ance
avow
  avow•al
avun•cu•lar
await
awake
  awoke
  awaked
  awak•ing
  awak•en
award
aware
  aware•ness
away
awe
  awed
  awe•some
  awe•struck
aw•ful
  aw•ful•ly
awhile
awk•ward
  awk•ward•ness
awn•ing
awry
ax
  ax•es
ax•i•om
  ax•i•o•mat•ic
ax•is
  ax•es
  ax•i•al
ax•le
azal•ea
az•ure

B

bab•ble
  bab•bled
  bab•bling

ba•boon
ba•by
  ba•bies
bac•ca•lau•re•ate
bac•cha•na•li•an
bach•e•lor
ba•cil•lus
  ba•cil•li
back•ache
back•bite
back•bone
back•drop
back•field
back•fire
back•ground
back•hand
back•ing
back•lash
back•log
back•side
back•slide
back•spin
back•stage
back•stop
back•talk
back•ward
  back•ward•ness
ba•con
bac•te•ria
  bac•ter•i•um
  bac•te•ri•al
bac•te•ri•ol•o•gy
  bac•te•ri•ol•o•gist
  bac•te•ri•o•log•i•cal
badge
badg•er
bad•i•nage
bad•ly
bad•min•ton
baf•fle
  baf•fled
  baf•fling
bag
  bagged
  bag•ging
ba•gel
bag•gage
bag•gy
  bag•gi•er
  bag•ging
bag•pipe
ba•guette
bail•iff
bake
  baked
  bak•ing
  bak•er
  bak•er•y
  bak•er•ies
bal•ance
  bal•anced
  bal•anc•ing
  bal•anc•er
bal•co•ny
  bal•co•nies
bald
  bald•ness
bale•ful
balk
bal•lad
bal•last
bal•le•ri•na
bal•let
bal•lis•tic
bal•loon
bal•lot
  bal•lot•ed
  bal•lot•ing
ball•room
bal•ly•hoo
balmy
  balm•i•er
ba•lo•ney
bal•sa
bal•sam
bal•us•trade
bam•boo
bam•boo•zle
  bam•boo•zled
ban
  banned
  ban•ning
ba•nal

ba•nal•i•ty
ba•nana
band•age
  band•aged
  band•ag•ing
ban•dit
  ban•dit•ry
band•stand
band•wag•on
ban•dy
  ban•died
  ban•dy•ing
ban•gle
ban•ish
  ban•ish•ment
ban•is•ter
  ban•nis•ter
bank•book
bank•er
  bank•ing
bank•rupt
  bank•rupt•cy
  bank•rupt•cies
ban•ner
ban•quet
ban•ter
ban•yan
bap•tism
  bap•tis•mal
Bap•tist
bap•tize
  bap•tized
  bap•tiz•ing
bar
  barred
  bar•ring
bar•bar•ic
  bar•bar•i•an
  bar•ba•rism
  bar•ba•rous
bar•bar•i•ty
  bar•bar•i•ties
bar•be•cue
  bar•be•cued
  bar•be•cu•ing
bar•ber
bar•bi•tu•rate
bare•ness
bare•faced
bare•foot
bare•ly
bar•gain
barge
  barged
  barg•ing
bar•i•tone
bar•i•um
bar•ley
bar mitz•vah
bar•na•cle
ba•rom•e•ter
  bar•o•met•ric
bar•on
  bar•on•ess
  ba•ro•ni•al
bar•on•et
ba•roque
bar•rack
bar•ra•cu•da
bar•rage
bar•rel
  bar•reled
  bar•rel•ing
bar•ren
  bar•ren•ness
bar•ri•cade
  bar•ri•cad•ed
  bar•ri•cad•ing
bar•ri•er
bar•row
bar•ten•der
bar•ter
ba•salt
base
  based
  bas•ing
base•ball
base•less
base•ment
ba•sic
  ba•si•cal•ly
ba•sil
ba•sil•i•ca

bas•i•lisk
ba•sin
ba•sis
  ba•ses
bas•ket•ball
bas-re•lief
bas•si•net
bas•soon
bas•tard
  bas•tard•ize
baste
bat
  bat•ted
  bat•ting
  bat•ter
bathe
  bathed
  bath•ing
bat•on
bat•tal•ion
bat•ten
bat•ter
bat•tery
bat•tle
  bat•tling
bau•ble
baux•ite
bawdy
bay•ou
ba•zaar
beach•head
bea•con
bead•ed
bead•like
beak•er
beamed
bear•ing
bear•a•ble
beard•ed
beast
  beast•ly
beat
  beat•en
  beat•ing
be•a•tif•ic
be•at•i•fy
  be•at•i•fi•ca•tion
beau
  beaus
  beaux
beau•te•ous
beau•ti•fy
  beau•ti•fi•ca•tion
beauty
  beau•ti•ful
beaux-arts
bea•ver
be•calm
be•cause
beck•on
be•come
  be•came
  be•com•ing
bed
  bed•ded
  bed•ding
be•daz•zle
  be•daz•zled
be•dev•il
  be•dev•iled
bed•lam
bed•drag•gle
  be•drag•gling
bed•rid•den
bed•room
beech
beefy
  beef•i•er
bee•hive
bee•line
Bee•tho•ven
bee•tle
be•fall
  be•fell
  be•fall•en
  be•fall•ing
be•fit
  be•fit•ted
  be•fit•ting
be•fore
be•friend
be•fud•dle
  be•fud•dled

beg
  begged
  beg•ging
be•get
  be•got
  be•got•ten
beg•gar
  beg•gar•ly
be•gin
  be•gan
  be•gun
  be•gin•ning
  be•gin•ner
be•gone
be•go•nia
be•grudge
  be•grudged
  be•grudg•ing
be•guile
  be•guiled
  be•guil•ing
be•half
be•have
  be•haved
  be•hav•ing
be•hav•ior
  be•hav•ior•ism
  be•hav•ior•ist
be•head
be•he•moth
be•hest
be•hind
be•hold
  be•held
  be•hold•ing
  be•hold•en
be•hoove
beige
be•ing
be•la•bor
be•lat•ed
  be•lat•ed•ly
belch
be•lea•guer
bel•fry
be•lie
  be•lied
  be•ly•ing
be•lief
be•lieve
  be•lieved
  be•liev•ing
  be•liev•a•ble
  be•liev•er
be•lit•tle
  be•lit•tled
  be•lit•tling
belles let•tres
bel•li•cose
  bel•li•cos•i•ty
bel•lig•er•ence
  bel•lig•er•ent
bel•low
bel•ly
  bel•lies
bel•ly•ache
  bel•ly•ach•ing
be•long
  be•long•ings
be•loved
be•low
belt•ed
be•moan
be•muse
  be•mused
  be•mus•ing
bend
  bent
  bend•ing
be•neath
ben•e•dic•tion
  ben•e•dic•to•ry
ben•e•fac•tor
  ben•e•fac•tress
ben•e•fice
be•nef•i•cent
  be•nef•i•cence
ben•e•fi•cial
ben•e•fi•ci•ary
  ben•e•fi•ci•ar•ies
ben•e•fit
  ben•e•fit•ed
  ben•e•fit•ing

be•nev•o•lence
  be•nev•o•lent
be•night•ed
be•nign
  be•nign•ly
be•numb
ben•zene
ben•zine
be•queath
be•quest
be•rate
  be•rat•ed
  be•rat•ing
be•reave
  be•reaved
  be•reft
  be•reav•ing
be•ret
ber•ry
  ber•ries
ber•serk
berth
be•seech
  be•sought
  be•seeched
  be•seech•ing
be•side
be•siege
  be•sieged
  be•sieg•ing
  be•sieg•er
be•smear
be•smirch
be•sot•ted
bes•tial
  bes•ti•al•i•ty
be•stir
  be•stirred
  be•stir•ring
be•stow
  be•stowed
bet
  bet•ting
  bet•tor
be•take
  be•took
be•tray
  be•tray•al
  be•tray•er
be•troth•al
  be•trothed
bet•ter
  bet•ter•ment
be•tween
be•twixt
bev•el
  bev•eled
  bev•el•ing
bev•er•age
bevy
be•wail
be•ware
be•wil•der
  be•wil•der•ing•ly
  be•wil•der•ment
be•witch
  be•witched
  be•witch•ing
be•yond
bi•an•nu•al
bi•as
  bi•ased
bi•be•lot
Bi•ble
bib•li•cal
bib•li•og•ra•phy
  bib•li•og•ra•phies
  bib•li•og•ra•pher
  bib•li•o•graph•ic
bib•li•o•phile
bib•u•lous
bi•cam•er•al
bi•car•bo•nate
bi•cen•ten•ni•al
  bi•cen•te•na•ry
bi•ceps
bick•er
bi•cus•pid
bi•cy•cle
  bi•cy•cled
  bi•cy•cling
bid
  bade

bid•den
bid•ding
bid•der
bi•en•ni•al
  bi•en•ni•al•ly
  bi•en•ni•um
bier
bi•fo•cals
bi•fur•cate
  bi•fur•ca•tion
big
  big•ger
  big•gest
big•a•my
  big•a•mist
big•ot
  big•ot•ed
  big•ot•ry
bi•jou
bi•ki•ni
bi•lat•er•al
bilge
bi•lin•gual
bil•ious
billed
  bill•ing
bil•liards
bil•lion
  bil•lion•aire
bil•low
  bil•low•y
bi•month•ly
bi•na•ry
bind
  bound
  bind•ing
  bind•er
binge
bin•go
bi•noc•u•lar
bi•o•chem•is•try
  bi•o•chem•i•cal
  bi•o•chem•ist
bio•de•grad•able
bi•o•en•gi•neer•ing
bi•o•gen•e•sis
bi•og•ra•phy
  bi•og•ra•pher
  bi•o•graph•ic
  bi•o•graph•i•cal
bi•ol•o•gy
  bi•o•log•i•cal
  bi•ol•o•gist
bi•o•met•rics
bi•o•phys•ics
bi•op•sy
  bi•op•sies
bi•par•ti•san
bi•par•tite
bi•ped
bi•po•lar
birch
bird•brained
bird•ie
bird's-eye
birth•day
birth•mark
birth•place
birth•stone
bis•cuit
bi•sect
  bi•sec•tion
bi•sex•u•al
bish•op
  bish•op•ric
bi•son
bisque
bis•tro
bitch
  bitch•y
bite
bit
  bit•ten
  bit•ing
bit•ter
  bit•ter•ly
  bit•ter•ness
bi•tu•men
bi•va•lent
  bi•va•lence
bi•valve
  bi•val•vu•lar
biv•ou•ac

biv•ou•acked
bi•week•ly
bi•zarre
blab
  blabbed
  blab•bing
black•ball
black•ber•ry
black•bird
black•board
black•en
black•eyed
black•guard
black•jack
black•mail
black•out
black•top
blad•der
blade
  blad•ed
blame
  blamed
  blam•ing
  blame•less
  blame•wor•thy
blanch
bland
  bland•ly
  bland•ness
blan•dish
  blan•dish•ment
blank
  blank•ly
blan•ket
blare
  blared
  blar•ing
blar•ney
bla•sé
blas•pheme
  blas•phemed
  blas•phem•ing
  blas•phem•er
  blas•phem•ous
  blas•phemy
  blas•phem•ies
blast•ed
bla•tant
  bla•tan•cy
  bla•tant•ly
blaze
  blazed
  blaz•ing
bleach•er
bleak
  bleak•ly
bleary
  blear•i•ness
bleed
  bled
  bleed•ing
blem•ish
blend•er
bless•ed
  blest
  bles•sing
blind
  blind•ing
  blind•ness
blind•er
blink•er
bliss•ful
blis•ter
blithe•ly
blitz•krieg
bliz•zard
block•ade
  block•ad•ed
  block•ad•ing
block•bus•ter
blood•curd•ling
blood•hound
blood•shed
blood•shot
blood•stained
blood•suck•er
blood•thirsty
bloody
  blood•i•est
  blood•ied
bloom
  bloom•ing
blos•som

blot
  blot•ted
  blot•ting
blotch
  blotchy
blot•ter
blow
  blew
  blown
  blow•ing
blow•er
blow•torch
blub•ber
bludg•eon
blue
  blu•est
blue•ber•ry
blue•bird
blue•blood•ed
blue-col•lar
blue•print
blun•der
blun•der•buss
blunt•ly
blur
  blurred
  blur•ring
  blur•ry
blush
  blushed
  blush•ing
blus•ter
  blus•ter•ous
boar
board•er
board•walk
boast
  boast•ful•ness
boat•house
bob
  bobbed
  bob•bing
bob•bin
bob•sled
bode
  bod•ed
  bod•ing
bod•ice
bod•y
  bod•ies
  bod•i•ly
bod•y•guard
bog
bo•gey
  bo•gy
bog•gle
  bog•gled
  bog•gling
bo•gus
bo•he•mi•an
boil•er
bois•ter•ous
bold
  bold•ly
bold•face
bo•lo•gna
Bol•she•vik
  Bol•she•vism
bol•ster
bolt
  bolt•ed
bom•bard
  bom•bard•ment
bom•bar•dier
bom•bast
  bom•bas•tic
  bom•bas•ti•cal•ly
bomb•er
bomb•proof
bomb•shell
bomb•sight
bo•na fide
bo•nan•za
bond•age
bond•ed
bond•man
bone
  boned
  bon•ing
bon•fire
bon•ho•mie
bon•net
bon•ny

bo•nus
  bo•nus•es
bon voy•age
bony
  bon•i•er
boo•by
  boo•bies
boo•by trap
book•bind•er
book•case
book•end
book•ie
book•ish
book•keep•ing
  book•keep•er
book•let
book•sell•er
book•worm
boom•er•ang
boon•dog•gle
boor
  boor•ish
boost
  boost•er
booth
boot•leg
  boot•legged
  boot•leg•ging
  boot•leg•ger
booty
booze
  booz•er
  boozy
bo•rax
Bor•deaux
bor•der
  bor•dered
  bor•der•land
  bor•der•line
bore
  bored
  bor•ing
  bore•dom
bor•ough
bor•row
  bor•row•er
borsch
  borscht
bos•om
bossy
  boss•i•est
  boss•i•ness
bot•a•ny
  bo•tan•i•cal
  bot•a•nist
botch
both•er
  both•er•some
bot•tle
  bot•tled
  bot•tling
bot•tle•neck
bot•tom
bot•u•lism
bou•doir
bough
bought
bouil•lon
boul•der
boul•e•vard
bounce
  bounced
  bounc•ing
bound
bound•a•ry
  bound•a•ries
boun•te•ous
boun•ti•ful
boun•ty
  boun•ties
bou•quet
bour•bon
bour•geois
  bour•geoi•sie
bou•tique
bo•vine
bow•el
bow•er
bow•ery
bow•ie
bowl
bow•leg
  bow•leg•ged

bowl•er
bowl•ing
bow•string
box•car
box•er
box•ful
box•ing
boy•cott
boy•friend
boy•sen•ber•ry
brace
  braced
  brac•ing
brace•let
brac•er
bra•ces
brack•et
brack•ish
brag
  bragged
  brag•ging
brag•ga•do•cio
brag•gart
Brah•min
  Brah•man
braid
  braid•ing
braille
brain•less
brain•pow•er
brain•storm
brain•wash•ing
brainy
  brain•i•er
  brain•i•est
braise
  braised
  brais•ing
brake
  brak•ing
bram•ble
branch
  branched
bran•dish
bran•dy
  bran•dies
  bran•died
bras•siere
brassy
  brass•i•er
brat
  brat•tish
  brat•ty
bra•va•do
brave
  braved
  brav•ing
  brav•ery
bra•vo
bra•vu•ra
brawl
  brawl•er
brawn
  brawny
  brawn•i•er
braze
bra•zen
bra•zier
breach
bread
  bread•ed
bread•win•ner
break
  broke
  bro•ken
  break•ing
  break•a•ble
break•down
break•er
break•fast
break•neck
break•out
break•through
break•wa•ter
breast•bone
breath
  breathy
breathe
  breathed
  breath•ing
breath•tak•ing
breech•es
breed

bred
  breed•ing
breeze
  breezy
breth•ren
bre•vi•a•ry
brev•i•ty
brew•ery
  brew•er•ies
bri•ar
bribe
  bribed
  brib•ing
  brib•a•ble
brib•ery
  brib•er•ies
bric-a-brac
brick•lay•er
brick•yard
bride
  brid•al
bride•groom
brides•maid
bridge
bri•dle
  bri•dled
  bri•dling
brief
  brief•ly
brief•ing
bri•er
bri•gade
brig•a•dier
brig•and
bright
  bright•ness
  bright•en
bril•liance
  bril•lian•cy
  bril•liant
brim•ful
brim•ming
brim•stone
brine
  briny
bring
  brought
  bring•ing
brink
brisk
  brisk•ly
  brisk•ness
bris•ket
bris•tle
  bris•tled
Brit•ain
  Bri•tan•nia
  Brit•ish
  Brit•on
Brit•ta•ny
britch•es
brit•tle
broach
  broached
  broach•ing
broad•cast
  broad•cast•ed
  broad•cast•ing
broad•mind•ed
broad•side
bro•cade
broc•co•li
bro•chure
broil•er
bro•ken
bro•ken-heart•ed
bro•ker
  bro•ker•age
bro•mide
bron•chi
  bron•chi•al
  bron•chi•tis
bron•to•sau•rus
bronze
  bronzed
  bronz•ing
brooch
brood
  brood•ing
broth•el
broth•er
  broth•er-in-law
  broth•er•ly

broth•er•li•ness
brow•beat
  brow•beat•en
brown
brown•ie
browse
  browsed
  brows•ing
bru•in
bruise
  bruised
  bruis•ing
bruis•er
bru•net
brush-off
brusque
  brusk
bru•tal
  bru•tal•i•ty
bru•tal•ize
  bru•tal•ized
  bru•tal•iz•ing
  bru•tal•i•za•tion
bub•ble
  bub•bled
  bub•bling
bu•bon•ic
buc•ca•neer
buck•et•ful
buck•le
buck•skin
buck•tooth
buck•wheat
bu•col•ic
bud
  bud•ded
  bud•ding
Bud•dha
  Bud•dhism
  Bud•dhist
bud•dy
budge
budg•et
buf•fa•lo
  buf•fa•loed
buff•er
buf•fet
buf•foon
  buf•foon•ery
bug
  bugged
  bug•ging
bug•gy
bu•gle
  bu•gling
  bu•gler
build
  built
  build•ing
bulb
  bul•bous
bulge
  bulged
  bulg•ing
  bulgy
bulk•head
bulky
  bulk•i•ness
bull•doze
  bull•dozed
  bull•doz•ing
  bull•doz•er
bul•let
bul•le•tin
bul•let•proof
bull•fight
bull•frog
bull•head•ed
bul•lion
bull•ock
bull's-eye
bul•ly
  bul•lies
  bul•lied
  bul•ly•ing
bul•wark
bum
  bummed
  bum•ming
bump•er
bump•tious
bumpy
  bump•i•er

bump•i•est
bunch
  bunchy
bun•dle
  bun•dled
  bun•dling
bun•ga•low
bun•gle
  bun•gled
  bun•gling
bun•ion
bunk•er
bun•ny
  bun•nies
bu•oy
buoy•ant
  buoy•an•cy
bur•den
  bur•den•some
bu•reau
  bu•reaus
  bu•reaux
bu•reauc•ra•cy
  bu•reauc•ra•cies
  bu•reau•crat
  bu•reau•crat•ic
bur•geon
bur•glar
  bur•glar•ize
  bur•glar•ized
  bur•glar•iz•ing
bur•gla•ry
  bur•gla•ries
bur•gle
  bur•gled
  bur•gling
Bur•gun•dy
bur•i•al
bur•lap
bur•lesque
bur•ly
burn
  burned
  burnt
  burn•ing
burn•er
bur•nish
burr
bur•ro
bur•row
bur•sar
bur•sa•ry
bur•si•tis
burst
  burst•ing
bury
  bur•ied
  bur•y•ing
bus
  bus•es
bush•el
bushy
busi•ness
  busi•ness•like
  busi•ness•man
  busi•ness•wom•an
bus•tle
  bus•tled
  bus•tling
busy
  bus•ied
  bus•y•ing
  bus•i•ly
  bus•i•er
bu•tane
butch•er
  butch•ery
but•ler
butt
butte
but•ter
but•ter•fly
  but•ter•flies
but•tock
but•ton•hole
  but•ton•hol•ing
but•tress
bux•om
buy
  bought
  buy•ing
buy•er
buz•zard

buzz•er
by•law
by•line
by•pass
by•prod•uct
by•stand•er
byte
by•way
by•word
Byz•an•tine

C

ca•bal
ca•ba•na
cab•a•ret
cab•bage
cab•in
cab•i•net
ca•ble
  ca•bled
ca•boose
ca•cao
cache
ca•chet
cack•le
  cack•led
  cack•ling
ca•coph•o•ny
cac•tus
  cac•ti
ca•dav•er
cad•die
  cad•died
cad•dy
  cad•dy•ing
ca•dence
ca•det
ca•dre
ca•du•ce•us
Cae•sar
cae•sar•e•an
  ce•sar•e•an
ca•fé au lait
caf•e•te•ria
caf•feine
cage
  caged
  cag•ing
ca•gey
  ca•gi•ly
ca•jole
  ca•joled
  ca•jol•ing
Ca•jun
cake
  caked
  cak•ing
cal•a•mine
ca•lam•i•ty
  ca•lam•i•ties
  ca•lam•i•tous
cal•ci•fy
  cal•ci•fied
  cal•ci•fy•ing
  cal•ci•fi•ca•tion
cal•ci•um
cal•cu•late
  cal•cu•lat•ed
  cal•cu•lat•ing
  cal•cu•la•tion
  cal•cu•la•tor
cal•cu•lus
cal•dron
cal•en•dar
calf
  calves
cal•i•ber
cal•i•brate
  cal•i•brat•ed
  cal•i•brat•ing
  cal•i•bra•tion
cal•is•then•ics
cal•lig•ra•phy
  cal•lig•ra•pher
call•ing
cal•lous
  cal•loused
cal•low
cal•lus
calm•ly
cal•or•ic
cal•o•rie

cal•o•ries
Cal•va•ry
ca•ma•ra•de•rie
cam•el
Cam•em•bert
cam•eo
cam•era
cam•i•sole
cam•ou•flage
  cam•ou•flaged
  cam•ou•flag•ing
cam•paign
camp•er
cam•phor
cam•pus
  cam•pus•es
cam•shaft
can
  canned
  can•ning
Can•a•da
  Ca•na•di•an
ca•nal
can•a•pe
ca•nary
can•cel
  can•celed
  can•cel•ing
  can•cel•la•tion
can•cer
can•de•la•brum
  can•de•la•bra
can•des•cent
  can•des•cence
can•did
can•di•da•cy
  can•di•da•cies
can•di•date
can•dle
can•dor
can•dy
  can•dies
  can•died
cane
  caned
  can•ing
ca•nine
can•is•ter
can•ker
canned
can•ni•bal
  can•ni•bal•ism
  can•ni•bal•ize
  can•ni•bal•iz•ing
can•non
can•ny
  can•ni•ly
  can•ni•ness
ca•noe
  ca•noed
  ca•noe•ing
can•on
can•on•ize
  can•on•i•za•tion
can•o•py
  can•o•pies
  can•o•pied
can•ta•loupe
  can•ta•lope
can•tan•ker•ous
can•ta•ta
can•teen
can•ter
can•ti•lev•er
can•to
can•tor
can•vas
can•vass
can•yon
cap
  capped
  cap•ping
ca•pa•bil•i•ty
  ca•pa•bil•i•ties
ca•pa•ble
  ca•pa•bly
ca•pa•cious
ca•pac•i•tate
  ca•pac•i•tat•ed
  ca•pac•i•tat•ing
ca•pac•i•ty
  ca•pac•i•ties
ca•per

cap•il•lary
  cap•il•lar•ies
cap•i•tal
cap•i•tal•ism
  cap•i•tal•is•tic
  cap•i•tal•ist
cap•i•tal•ize
  cap•i•tal•i•za•tion
ca•pit•u•late
  ca•pit•u•lat•ed
  ca•pit•u•lat•ing
  ca•pit•u•la•tion
ca•pon
ca•price
  ca•pri•cious
cap•size
  cap•siz•ing
cap•sule
  cap•su•lar
cap•tain
cap•tion
cap•tious
cap•ti•vate
  cap•ti•vat•ed
  cap•ti•vat•ing
cap•tive
  cap•tiv•i•ty
cap•tor
cap•ture
  cap•tured
  cap•tur•ing
ca•rafe
car•a•mel
car•at
car•a•van
car•a•way
car•bide
car•bine
car•bo•hy•drate
car•bol•ic
car•bon
  car•bon di•ox•ide
  car•bon mon•ox•ide
car•bu•re•tor
car•cass
car•cin•o•gen
  car•cin•o•gen•ic
car•ci•no•ma
card•board
car•di•ac
car•di•gan
car•di•nal
car•dio•vas•cu•lar
card•sharp
care
  cared
  car•ing
ca•reen
ca•reer
care•free
care•ful
  care•ful•ly
care•less
  care•less•ness
ca•ress
care•tak•er
car•go
Car•ib•be•an
car•i•bou
car•i•ca•ture
  car•i•ca•tured
  car•i•ca•tur•ist
car•nage
car•nal
  car•nal•i•ty
  car•nal•ly
car•na•tion
car•ni•val
car•ni•vore
  car•niv•o•rous
car•ol
  car•ol•ing
ca•rouse
  ca•roused
  ca•rous•ing
car•pen•ter
  car•pen•try
car•pet
  car•pet•ing
car•riage
car•ri•er
car•ri•on
car•rot

car•roty
car•ry
  car•ried
  car•ry•ing
carte blanche
car•tel
car•ti•lage
car•tog•ra•phy
  car•tog•ra•pher
car•ton
car•toon
car•tridge
carve
  carved
  carv•ing
cas•cade
case
  cased
  cas•ing
case•ment
cash•ew
cash•ier
cash•mere
ca•si•no
cas•ket
cas•se•role
cas•sette
cas•sock
cast
  cast•ing
caste
cas•ti•gate
  cas•ti•gat•ed
  cas•ti•gat•ing
  cas•ti•ga•tion
cast iron
cas•tle
cas•tor
cas•trate
  cas•trat•ed
  cas•trat•ing
  cas•tra•tion
cas•u•al
  cas•u•al•ty
  cas•u•al•ties
cas•u•ist•ry
cat•a•clysm
  cat•a•clys•mic
cat•a•log
  cat•a•logue
  cat•a•loged
  cat•a•log•ing
cat•a•lyt•ic
cat•a•lyst
cat•a•ract
ca•tas•tro•phe
  cat•a•stroph•ic
catch
  caught
  catch•ing
  catch•er
catchy
  catch•i•er
cat•e•chism
  cat•e•chize
cat•e•gor•i•cal
cat•e•go•ry
  cat•e•go•ries
  cat•e•gor•ize
  cat•e•gor•iz•ing
ca•ter
  ca•ter•er
cat•er•pil•lar
cat•fish
ca•thar•sis
  ca•thar•tic
ca•the•dral
cath•e•ter
cath•ode
Cath•o•lic
  Ca•thol•i•cism
  ca•thol•i•cize
cat•nap
  cat•nap•ping
cat•nip
cat•tle
  cat•tle•man
cat•ty
  cat•ti•ness
Cau•ca•sian
cau•cus
  cau•cus•es
  cau•cus•ing

caul•dron
cau•li•flow•er
caulk
caus•al
  cau•sal•i•ty
cause
  caused
  caus•ing
  cau•sa•tion
cause•way
caus•tic
cau•ter•ize
  cau•ter•ized
  cau•ter•iz•ing
cau•tion
  cau•tion•ary
  cau•tious
cav•al•cade
cav•a•lier
cav•al•ry
cave
  caved
  cav•ing
ca•ve•at
cav•ern
  cav•ern•ous
cav•i•ar
cav•il
  cav•iled
  cav•il•ing
cav•i•ty
  cav•i•ties
ca•vort
cay•enne
cease
  ceased
  ceas•ing
  cease•less
cease•fire
ce•dar
cede
  ced•ed
  ced•ing
ceil•ing
cel•e•brate
  cel•e•brat•ing
  cel•e•bra•tion
  cel•e•brant
ce•leb•ri•ty
  ce•leb•ri•ties
ce•ler•i•ty
cel•ery
ce•les•tial
cel•i•ba•cy
  cel•i•bate
cel•lar
cel•lo
  cel•list
cel•lo•phane
cel•lu•lar
cel•lu•lose
ce•ment
cem•e•tery
  cem•e•ter•ies
cen•sor
  cen•so•ri•al
  cen•sor•ship
  cen•so•ri•ous
cen•sure
  cen•sured
  cen•sur•ing
cen•sus
cen•taur
cen•te•na•ry
  cen•te•na•ries
  cen•te•nar•i•an
cen•ten•ni•al
cen•ter•piece
cen•ti•grade
cen•ti•me•ter
cen•tral
  cen•tral•ize
  cen•tral•ized
  cen•tral•iz•ing
cen•tri•fuge
  cen•trif•u•gal
cen•trip•e•tal
cen•tu•ry
  cen•tu•ries
ce•ram•ic
ce•re•al
cer•e•bral
cer•e•bel•lum

cer•e•brum
cer•e•mo•ny
  cer•e•mo•nies
  cer•e•mo•ni•al
  cer•e•mo•ni•ous
cer•tain
  cer•tain•ly
  cer•tain•ty
  cer•tain•ties
cer•tif•i•cate
  cer•ti•fi•ca•tion
cer•ti•fy
  cer•ti•fied
  cer•ti•fy•ing
  cer•ti•fi•a•ble
cer•ti•tude
ce•ru•le•an
cer•vix
cer•vi•cal
ce•sar•e•an
  cae•sar•e•an
ces•sa•tion
Cha•blis
chafe
  chafed
  chaf•ing
chaff
cha•grin
  cha•grined
chain
chair•man
  chair•per•son
  chair•wom•an
chaise longue
chal•et
chalk
  chalky
chal•lenge
  chal•lenged
  chal•leng•ing
cham•ber
cham•bray
cha•me•le•on
cham•ois
cham•pagne
cham•pi•on
  cham•pi•on•ship
chance
  chanced
  chanc•ing
  chancy
chan•cel•lor
chan•de•lier
change
  changed
  chang•ing
  change•a•ble
chan•nel
  chan•nel•ing
cha•os
  cha•ot•ic
chap•el
chap•e•ron
chap•lain
chap•ter
char
  charred
  char•ring
char•ac•ter
  char•ac•ter•is•tic
char•ac•ter•ize
  char•ac•ter•ized
  char•ac•ter•iz•ing
  char•ac•ter•i•za•tion
cha•rade
char•coal
charge
  charged
  char•ging
char•gé d'af•faires
cha•ris•ma
char•i•ta•ble
  char•i•ta•bly
char•i•ty
  char•i•ties
char•la•tan
charm
  charm•er
  charm•ing
char•ter
chary
chase
  chased

chas•ing
chasm
chas•sis
chaste
  chaste•ness
  chas•ti•ty
chas•ten
chas•tise
  chas•tis•ing
  chas•tise•ment
chat
  chat•ted
  chat•ting
cha•teau
chat•tel
chat•ter
chat•ty
chau•vin•ist
  chau•vin•ism
  chau•vin•is•tic
cheap
  cheap•ness
  cheap•en
cheap•skate
cheat
  cheat•er
check•book
check•er•board
check•list
check•mate
check•point
ched•dar
cheek•bone
cheeky
  cheek•i•ness
cheer•ful
  cheer•ful•ness
cheery
cheese
  cheesy
chee•tah
chef
chem•i•cal
  chem•i•cal•ly
che•mise
chem•ist
  chem•is•try
chem•o•ther•a•py
che•nille
cher•ish
cher•ry
  cher•ries
cher•ub
  che•ru•bic
chest•nut
chew
  chewy
Chi•an•ti
chi•can•ery
chic•ken
chic•o•ry
chide
  chid•ed
  chid•ing
chief
  chief•tain
chif•fon
chil•dren
child•bear•ing
child•birth
child•hood
child•ish
child•like
chili
chill
  chill•ing
chilly
  chill•i•er
chime
  chim•ing
chim•ney
chim•pan•zee
chin
Chi•na
  Chi•nese
chin•chil•la
chintz
chintzy
chip
  chipped
  chip•ping
chip•munk
Chip•pen•dale

chip•per
chi•rop•o•dist
chi•ro•prac•tor
chis•el
  chis•eled
  chis•el•ing
chit•chat
chiv•al•ry
  chiv•al•ric
  chiv•al•rous
chlo•rine
chlo•ro•form
chock•full
choc•o•late
choice
choir•boy
choke
  choked
  chok•ing
  chok•er
chol•era
cho•les•te•rol
choose
  chose
  cho•sen
  choos•ing
choosy
  choos•i•est
chop
  chopped
  chop•ping
chop su•ey
cho•ral
cho•rale
chord
chore
cho•reo•graph
  cho•re•og•ra•phy
  cho•re•og•ra•pher
  cho•re•o•graph•ic
chor•tle
cho•rus
  cho•rus•es
chow•der
chow mein
Christ
  Christ•like
chris•ten
  chris•ten•ing
Chris•ten•dom
Chris•tian
  Chris•ti•an•i•ty
Christ•mas
chrome
chron•ic
  chron•i•cal•ly
chron•i•cle
chro•nol•o•gy
  chro•nol•o•gies
  chron•o•log•i•cal
chrys•a•lis
chry•san•the•mum
chub•by
  chub•bi•ness
chuck•hole
chuck•le
  chuck•ling
chum•my
chunk
  chunky
  chunk•i•est
church
  church•go•er
  church•man
  church•war•den
  church•yard
churl•ish
churn•ing
chut•ney
chutz•pah
ci•der
ci•gar
cig•a•rette
cin•der
cin•e•ma
  cin•e•ma•tog•ra•pher
cin•na•mon
ci•pher
cir•ca
cir•cle
  cir•cled
  cir•cling
cir•cuit

cir•cu•i•tous
cir•cu•lar
cir•cu•late
  cir•cu•lat•ed
  cir•cu•lat•ing
  cir•cu•la•tion
  cir•cu•la•to•ry
cir•cum•cise
  cir•cum•cised
  cir•cum•cis•ing
  cir•cum•ci•sion
cir•cum•fer•ence
cir•cum•flex
cir•cum•lo•cu•tion
cir•cum•nav•i•gate
cir•cum•scribe
cir•cum•spect
cir•cum•stance
  cir•cum•stan•tial
cir•cum•vent
  cir•cum•ven•tion
cir•cus
  cir•cus•es
cir•rho•sis
cis•tern
cit•a•del
cite
  cit•ed
  cit•ing
  cit•a•tion
cit•i•zen
  cit•i•zen•ship
  cit•i•zen•ry
cit•rus
city
  cit•ies
civ•ic
civ•il
  civ•il•ly
ci•vil•ian
ci•vil•i•ty
  ci•vil•i•ties
civ•i•li•za•tion
civ•i•lize
  civ•i•lized
  civ•i•liz•ing
claim
  claimed
clair•voy•ance
  clair•voy•ant
clam
  clam•ming
clam•my
clam•or
  clam•or•ous
clan
  clan•nish
clan•des•tine
clap
  clapped
  clap•ping
clap•board
clar•et
clar•i•fy
  clar•i•fied
  clar•i•fy•ing
  clar•i•fi•ca•tion
clar•i•net
clar•i•ty
clas•sic
  clas•si•cal
  clas•si•cism
  clas•si•cist
clas•si•fy
  clas•si•fied
  clas•si•fy•ing
  clas•si•fi•ca•tion
classy
  class•i•er
clause
claus•tro•pho•bia
clean•cut
clean•er
clean•ly
  clean•li•ness
cleanse
  cleansed
  cleans•ing
  cleans•er
clear
  clear•ly
clear•ance
clear•cut

clear•ing
clear•sight•ed
cleav•age
cleave
    cleaved
    cleav•ing
    cleav•er
clef
cleft
clem•en•cy
cler•gy
    cler•gies
    cler•gy•man
cler•ic
    cler•i•cal
clev•er
clew
cli•ché
cli•ent
    cli•en•tele
cli•mate
    cli•mat•ic
cli•max
    cli•mac•tic
climb
    climb•er
clinch•er
cling
    clung
    cling•ing
clin•ic
    clin•i•cal
clip
    clipped
    clip•ping
clip•per
clique
    cliqu•ish
clob•ber
clock•wise
clod
clog
    clogged
    clog•ging
clois•ter
close
    closed
    clos•ing
    clos•est
    close•ly
    close•ness
clos•et
    clos•et•ed
close•up
clo•sure
clot
    clot•ted
    clot•ting
clothe
    clothed
    cloth•ing
cloud•burst
cloudy
    cloud•i•ness
clo•ver
clown
    clown•ish
cloy
    cloy•ing•ly
club
    clubbed
    club•bing
club•house
clue
clump
clum•sy
    clum•si•ly
    clum•si•ness
clus•ter
clut•ter
co•ag•u•late
    co•ag•u•lat•ed
    co•ag•u•lat•ing
    co•ag•u•la•tion
co•a•lesce
    co•a•lesced
    co•a•les•cing
    co•a•les•cence
    co•a•les•cent
co•a•li•tion
coarse
    coars•en
    coarse•ness

coast•er
coast•guard
coast•line
coat•ing
co•au•thor
coax
co•balt
cob•ble•stone
co•bra
cob•web
co•caine
cock•le
cock•ney
cock•roach
cock•tail
cocky
    cock•i•ly
    cock•i•ness
co•coa
co•co•nut
co•coon
cod•dle
    cod•dled
    cod•dling
code
    cod•ed
    cod•ing
co•deine
codg•er
cod•i•cil
cod•i•fy
    cod•i•fi•ca•tion
co•ed
    co•ed•u•ca•tion
co•ef•fi•cient
co•e•qual
co•erce
    co•erced
    co•er•cing
    co•er•cion
    co•er•cive
co•ex•ist
    co•ex•ist•ence
cof•fee
cof•fer
cof•fin
co•gent
    co•gen•cy
    co•gent•ly
co•gnac
cog•nate
    cog•na•tion
cog•ni•tion
    cog•ni•tive
cog•ni•zance
    cog•ni•zant
co•hab•it
    co•hab•i•ta•tion
co•here
    co•hered
    co•her•ing
co•her•ent
    co•her•ence
    co•her•ency
    co•her•ent•ly
co•he•sion
    co•he•sive
    co•he•sive•ness
co•hort
coif•fure
coin•age
co•in•cide
    co•in•cid•ed
    co•in•cid•ing
    co•in•ci•dence
    co•in•ci•dent
    co•in•ci•den•tal
co•i•tion
co•i•tus
col•an•der
cold
    cold•ly
cold•blood•ed
cole•slaw
col•ic
    col•icky
col•i•se•um
col•lab•o•rate
    col•lab•o•rat•ed
    col•lab•o•rat•ing
    col•lab•o•ra•tion
    col•lab•o•ra•tor
col•lage

col•lapse
    col•lapsed
    col•laps•ing
    col•lap•si•ble
col•lar
col•late
    col•lat•ed
    col•lat•ing
    col•la•tion
col•lat•er•al
col•league
col•lect
    col•lect•ed
    col•lect•i•ble
    col•lect•or
    col•lec•tion
col•lec•tive
    col•lec•tiv•ize
    col•lec•tiv•i•za•tion
col•lege
col•le•gial
    col•le•giate
col•lide
    col•lid•ed
    col•lid•ing
    col•li•sion
col•lie
col•lin•e•ar
col•lo•cate
col•lo•qui•al
    col•lo•qui•al•ly
    col•lo•qui•al•ism
col•lo•quy
col•lu•sion
    col•lu•sive
co•logne
co•lon
colo•nel
co•lo•ni•al
    co•lo•ni•al•ism
col•on•nade
col•o•ny
    col•o•nies
    col•o•nize
    col•o•niz•ing
    col•o•ni•za•tion
col•or
    col•or•ful
    col•or•ing
col•or•blind
co•los•sal
Col•os•se•um
co•los•sus
Co•lum•bia
col•umn
    col•um•nist
co•ma
    co•ma•tose
com•bat
    com•bat•ed
    com•bat•ing
    com•bat•ant
    com•bat•ive
com•bi•na•tion
com•bine
    com•bined
    com•bin•ing
com•bus•tion
    com•bus•ti•ble
come
    came
    com•ing
co•me•di•an
    co•me•di•enne
com•e•dy
    com•e•dies
come•ly
    come•li•ness
com•et
com•fort
    com•fort•a•ble
    com•fort•er
com•ic
    com•i•cal
com•ma
com•mand
    com•mand•er
    com•mand•ment
com•man•deer
com•mem•o•rate
    com•mem•o•rat•ed
    com•mem•o•rat•ing

com•mem•o•ra•tion
com•mem•o•ra•tive
com•mence
    com•menc•ing
    com•mence•ment
com•mend
    com•mend•a•ble
    com•men•da•tion
com•men•su•rate
com•ment
    com•ment•ed
    com•ment•ing
com•men•tary
    com•men•tar•ies
com•men•ta•tor
com•merce
com•mer•cial
    com•mer•cial•ism
    com•mer•cial•ize
    com•mer•cial•i•za•tion
com•mis•er•ate
    com•mis•er•at•ed
    com•mis•er•at•ing
    com•mis•er•a•tion
com•mis•sion
    com•mis•sioned
    com•mis•sion•er
com•mit
    com•mit•ted
    com•mit•ting
    com•mit•ment
com•mit•tee
com•mode
com•mod•i•ty
    com•mod•i•ties
com•mon
    com•mon•al•i•ty
com•mon•place
com•mons
com•mon•wealth
com•mo•tion
com•mu•nal
com•mune
    com•muned
    com•mun•ing
com•mu•ni•cant
com•mu•ni•cate
    com•mu•ni•cat•ed
    com•mu•ni•cat•ing
    com•mu•ni•ca•ble
    com•mu•ni•ca•tive
    com•mu•ni•ca•tion
com•mun•ion
    com•mu•ni•qué
com•mun•ism
    com•mun•ist
    com•mu•nis•tic
com•mu•ni•ty
    com•mu•ni•ties
com•mute
    com•mut•ed
    com•mut•ing
    com•mut•er
com•pact
com•pan•ion
    com•pan•ion•a•ble
    com•pan•ion•ship
com•pa•ny
    com•pa•nies
com•pa•ra•ble
    com•pa•ra•bil•ity
com•par•a•tive
com•pare
    com•pared
    com•par•ing
    com•par•i•son
com•part•ment
    com•part•men•tal•ize
com•pass
com•pas•sion
    com•pas•sion•ate
com•pat•i•ble
    com•pat•i•bil•i•ty
com•pa•tri•ot
com•pel
    com•pelled
    com•pel•ling
com•pen•di•um
com•pen•sate
    com•pen•sat•ing
    com•pen•sa•to•ry
    com•pen•sa•tion
com•pete

com•pet•ed
com•pet•ing
com•pet•i•tor
com•pe•ti•tion
com•pet•i•tive
com•pe•tent
com•pe•tence
com•pe•ten•cy
com•pile
com•piled
com•pil•ing
com•pi•la•tion
com•pla•cent
com•pla•cence
com•pla•cen•cy
com•plain
com•plain•ant
com•plaint
com•plai•sance
com•plai•sant
com•ple•ment
com•ple•men•ta•ry
com•plete
com•plet•ed
com•plet•ing
com•ple•tion
com•plex
com•plex•i•ty
com•plex•ion
com•pli•ance
com•pli•an•cy
com•pli•ant
com•pli•cate
com•pli•cat•ed
com•pli•cat•ing
com•pli•ca•tion
com•plic•i•ty
com•plic•i•ties
com•pli•ment
com•pli•men•ta•ry
com•ply
com•plied
com•ply•ing
com•po•nent
com•port
com•port•ment
com•pose
com•posed
com•pos•ing
com•pos•er
com•pos•ite
com•po•si•tion
com•po•sure
com•pound
com•pre•hend
com•pre•hen•si•ble
com•pre•hen•si•bil•i•ty
com•pre•hen•sion
com•pre•hen•sive
com•press
com•press•ing
com•press•i•ble
com•pres•sion
com•pres•sor
com•prise
com•prised
com•pris•ing
com•pro•mise
com•pro•mised
com•pro•mis•ing
comp•trol•ler
com•pul•sion
com•pul•sive
com•pul•so•ry
com•punc•tion
com•pute
com•put•ed
com•put•ing
com•pu•ta•tion
com•put•er
com•put•er•i•za•tion
com•rade
con
conned
con•ning
con•cave
con•ceal
con•cede
con•ced•ed
con•ced•ing
con•ceit
con•ceit•ed
con•ceive

con•ceived
con•ceiv•ing
con•ceiv•a•ble
con•ceiv•a•bly
con•cen•trate
con•cen•tra•ted
con•cen•trat•ing
con•cen•tra•tion
con•cen•tric
con•cept
con•cep•tion
con•cep•tu•al
con•cep•tu•al•ize
con•cep•tu•al•i•za•tion
con•cern
con•cerned
con•cert
con•cert•ed
con•cer•to
con•ces•sion
con•cierge
con•cil•i•ate
con•cil•i•at•ed
con•cil•i•at•ing
con•cil•i•a•tion
con•cil•i•a•to•ry
con•cise
con•cise•ness
con•cise•ly
con•clave
con•clude
con•clud•ed
con•clud•ing
con•clu•sion
con•clu•sive
con•coct
con•coc•tion
con•com•i•tant
con•cord
con•course
con•crete
con•cu•pis•cent
con•cur
con•curred
con•cur•ring
con•cur•rence
con•cur•rent
con•cus•sion
con•demn
con•dem•na•ble
con•dem•na•tion
con•dense
con•densed
con•dens•ing
con•den•sa•tion
con•dens•er
con•de•scend
con•de•scend•ing
con•de•scen•sion
con•di•tion
con•di•tion•al
con•di•tioned
con•dole
con•doled
con•dol•ing
con•do•lence
con•do•min•i•um
con•done
con•doned
con•don•ing
con•du•cive
con•duct
con•duc•tor
con•duit
con•fer•ence
con•fess
con•fess•ed
con•fes•sion
con•fes•sion•al
con•fes•sor
con•fi•dant
con•fi•dante
con•fide
con•fid•ed
con•fid•ing
con•fi•dence
con•fi•dent
con•fi•den•tial
con•fig•u•ra•tion
con•fine
con•fined
con•fin•ing
con•fine•ment

con•firm
con•firmed
con•fir•ma•tion
con•fir•ma•tive
con•fis•cate
con•fis•cat•ed
con•fis•cat•ing
con•fis•ca•tion
con•fla•gra•tion
con•flict
con•flict•ing
con•flu•ence
con•flu•ent
con•form
con•form•ist
con•form•a•ble
con•for•ma•tion
con•form•i•ty
con•found
con•found•ed
con•front
con•fron•ta•tion
Con•fu•cius
con•fuse
con•fused
con•fus•ing
con•fu•sion
con•fute
con•fut•ed
con•fut•ing
con•fu•ta•tion
con•geal
con•gen•ial
con•ge•ni•al•i•ty
con•gen•i•tal
con•gest
con•ges•tion
con•ges•tive
con•glom•er•ate
con•glom•er•a•tion
con•grat•u•late
con•grat•u•lat•ed
con•grat•u•lat•ing
con•grat•u•la•to•ry
con•grat•u•la•tion
con•gre•gate
con•gre•gat•ed
con•gre•gat•ing
con•gre•ga•tion
con•gre•ga•tion•al
con•gress
con•gres•sion•al
con•gress•man
con•gress•wom•an
con•gru•ent
con•gru•ent•ly
con•gru•ence
con•gru•en•cy
con•gru•ous
con•gru•ous•ly
con•gru•i•ty
cone
con•i•cal
con•jec•ture
con•jec•tured
con•jec•tur•ing
con•jec•tur•al
con•join
con•ju•gal
con•ju•gate
con•ju•gat•ed
con•ju•gat•ing
con•ju•ga•tion
con•junc•tion
con•junc•tive
con•jure
con•jured
con•jur•ing
con•jur•a•tion
con•nect
con•nec•tion
con•nec•tive
con•nec•tor
con•nive
con•nived
con•niv•ing
con•niv•ance
con•nois•seur
con•note
con•not•ed
con•not•ing
con•no•ta•tion
con•no•ta•tive

con•nu•bi•al
con•quer
con•quer•a•ble
con•quer•or
con•quest
con•quis•ta•dor
con•san•guin•e•ous
con•san•guin•i•ty
con•science
con•sci•en•tious
con•scion•able
con•scious
con•scious•ly
con•scious•ness
con•script
con•scrip•tion
con•se•crate
con•se•crat•ed
con•se•crat•ing
con•se•cra•tion
con•sec•u•tive
con•sen•sus
con•sent
con•se•quence
con•se•quent
con•se•quent•ly
con•se•quen•tial
con•ser•va•tion
con•ser•va•tion•ist
con•serv•a•tive
con•serv•a•tism
con•serv•a•tive•ly
con•serv•a•to•ry
con•serv•a•to•ries
con•serve
con•served
con•serv•ing
con•sid•er
con•sid•er•ing
con•sid•er•able
con•sid•er•a•bly
con•sid•er•ate
con•sid•er•a•tion
con•sign
con•sign•er
con•sign•or
con•sist
con•sist•en•cy
con•sist•en•cies
con•sist•ence
con•sist•ent
con•so•la•tion
con•sole
con•soled
con•sol•ing
con•sol•a•ble
con•sol•i•date
con•sol•i•dat•ed
con•sol•i•dat•ing
con•sol•i•da•tion
con•som•mé
con•so•nant
con•sort
con•sor•ti•um
con•spic•u•ous
con•spire
con•spired
con•spir•ing
con•spir•a•cy
con•spir•a•cies
con•spir•a•tor
con•spir•a•to•ri•al
con•sta•ble
con•stab•u•lary
con•stant
con•stan•cy
con•stel•la•tion
con•ster•na•tion
con•sti•pa•tion
con•sti•pate
con•stit•u•en•cy
con•stit•u•en•cies
con•stit•u•ent
con•sti•tute
con•sti•tu•tion
con•sti•tu•tion•al
con•sti•tu•tion•al•i•ty
con•sti•tu•tion•al•ly
con•strain
con•strained
con•straint
con•strict
con•stric•tive

con•stric•tion
con•struct
con•struc•tor
con•struc•tion
con•struc•tive
con•strue
con•strued
con•stru•ing
con•sul
con•su•lar
con•su•late
con•sult
con•sul•ta•tion
con•sult•ant
con•sume
con•sumed
con•sum•ing
con•sum•a•ble
con•sum•er
con•sum•er•ism
con•sum•mate
con•sum•mat•ed
con•sum•mat•ing
con•sum•ma•tion
con•sump•tion
con•sump•tive
con•tact
con•ta•gion
con•ta•gious
con•tain
con•tain•er
con•tam•i•nate
con•tam•i•nat•ed
con•tam•i•nat•ing
con•tam•i•nant
con•tam•i•na•tion
con•tem•plate
con•tem•plat•ed
con•tem•plat•ing
con•tem•pla•tion
con•tem•pla•tive
con•tem•po•ra•ne•ous
con•tem•po•rary
con•tem•po•rar•ies
con•tempt
con•tempt•i•ble
con•temp•tu•ous
con•tend
con•tend•er
con•tent
con•tent•ment
con•tent•ed
con•ten•tion
con•ten•tious
con•test
con•test•a•ble
con•test•ant
con•text
con•tex•tu•al
con•tig•u•ous
con•ti•nent
con•ti•nence
con•ti•nent
con•ti•nen•tal
con•tin•gent
con•tin•gen•cy
con•tin•gen•cies
con•tin•u•al
con•tin•u•al•ly
con•tin•ue
con•tin•ued
con•tin•u•ing
con•tin•u•a•tion
con•tin•u•ance
con•tin•u•i•ty
con•tin•u•ous
con•tin•u•um
con•tort
con•tor•tion
con•tour
con•tra•band
con•tra•cep•tive
con•tra•cep•tion
con•tract
con•tract•ed
con•trac•tu•al
con•trac•tion
con•trac•tor
con•tra•dict
con•tra•dic•tion
con•tra•dic•to•ry
con•tra•dis•tinc•tion
con•tral•to

con•trap•tion
con•tra•ry
con•tra•ri•ly
con•tra•ri•ness
con•trast
con•tra•vene
con•tra•ven•ing
con•trib•ute
con•trib•ut•ed
con•trib•ut•ing
con•trib•u•tor
con•trib•u•tory
con•tri•bu•tion
con•trite
con•tri•tion
con•trive
con•trived
con•triv•ing
con•triv•ance
con•trol
con•trolled
con•trol•ling
con•trol•la•ble
con•trol•ler
con•tro•ver•sy
con•tro•ver•sies
con•tro•ver•sial
con•tro•vert
con•tu•sion
co•nun•drum
con•va•lesce
con•va•lesced
con•va•les•cence
con•va•les•cent
con•vene
con•vened
con•ven•ing
con•ven•ience
con•ven•ient
con•vent
con•ven•tion
con•ven•tion•al
con•verge
con•verg•ing
con•ver•gence
con•ver•gent
con•ver•sant
con•verse
con•versed
con•vers•ing
con•verse•ly
con•vert
con•vert•er
con•ver•tor
con•ver•sion
con•vert•i•ble
con•vex
con•vey
con•vey•ance
con•vey•er
con•vey•or
con•vict
con•vic•tion
con•vince
con•vinced
con•vinc•ing
con•viv•i•al
con•viv•i•al•ity
con•vo•cation
con•vo•lute
con•vo•lut•ed
con•vo•lu•tion
con•voy
con•vulse
con•vulsed
con•vuls•ing
con•vul•sion
con•vul•sive
cook•e•ry
cook•ie
cool
cool•ish
cool•ly
cool•ant
co•op•er•ate
co•op•er•at•ed
co•op•er•at•ing
co•op•er•a•tion
co•op•er•a•tive
co•or•di•nate
co•or•di•nat•ed
co•or•di•nat•ing
co•or•di•na•tion

co•or•di•na•tor
cope
　coped
　cop•ing
cop•i•er
co•pi•lot
co•pi•ous
　co•pi•ous•ly
cop•per
　cop•pery
copse
cop•u•late
　cop•u•lat•ed
　cop•u•lat•ing
　cop•u•la•tion
copy
　cop•ies
　cop•ied
　copy•ing
copy•right
cor•al
cor•dial
　cor•dial•i•ty
　cor•dial•ly
cor•don
cor•do•van
cor•du•roy
core
　cored
cor•nea
cor•ner
cor•net
cor•nice
cor•nu•co•pia
corny
co•rol•la
co•rol•lary
co•ro•na
co•ro•nary
cor•o•na•tion
cor•o•ner
cor•o•net
cor•po•ral
cor•po•rate
　cor•po•ra•tion
cor•po•re•al
corps
　corps•man
corpse
cor•pu•lent
　cor•pu•lence
cor•pus
cor•pus•cle
　cor•pus•cu•lar
cor•ral
　cor•ralled
cor•rect
　cor•rect•ed
　cor•rect•a•ble
　cor•rec•tion
　cor•rec•tion•al
　cor•rec•tive
cor•re•late
　cor•re•lat•ed
　cor•re•lat•ing
　cor•re•la•tion
　cor•re•la•tive
cor•re•spond
　cor•re•spond•ing
　cor•re•spond•ence
　cor•re•spond•ent
cor•ri•dor
cor•ri•gi•ble
　cor•ri•gi•bil•i•ty
cor•rob•o•rate
　cor•rob•o•rat•ed
　cor•rob•o•rat•ing
　cor•rob•o•rat•tion
　cor•rob•o•ra•to•ry
cor•rode
　cor•rod•ed
　cor•rod•ing
cor•ro•sion
　cor•ro•sive
cor•ru•gate
　cor•ru•gat•ed
cor•rupt
　cor•rup•ti•ble
　cor•rup•ti•bil•i•ty
　cor•rupt•ly
　cor•rup•tion
cor•sage
cor•sair

cor•set
cor•tege
cor•tex
cor•ti•cal
cor•ti•sone
co•sig•na•to•ry
cos•met•ic
cos•mic
　cos•mi•cal•ly
cos•mol•o•gy
cos•mo•pol•i•tan
cos•mos
cost•ly
　cost•li•er
cos•tume
　cos•tumed
co•sy
　co•si•er
cot•tage
cot•ton
couch
cough
coun•cil
　coun•cil•or
　coun•cil•man
　coun•cil•wom•an
coun•sel
　coun•seled
　coun•sel•ing
　coun•se•lor
count
　count•a•ble
count•down
coun•te•nance
　coun•te•nanced
count•er
coun•ter•act
　coun•ter•ac•tive
coun•ter•at•tack
coun•ter•charge
coun•ter•claim
　coun•ter•claim•ant
coun•ter•clock•wise
coun•ter•cul•ture
coun•ter•es•pi•o•nage
coun•ter•feit
　coun•ter•feit•er
coun•ter•in•tel•li•gence
coun•ter•mand
coun•ter•of•fen•sive
coun•ter•part
coun•ter•point
coun•ter•rev•o•lu•tion
coun•ter•sign
　coun•ter•sig•na•ture
coun•ter•weight
coun•tess
count•less
coun•try
　coun•tries
coun•ty
　coun•ties
coup de grâce
coup d'e•tat
cou•pé
　coupe
coup•le
　coup•ling
coup•let
cou•pon
cour•age
　cou•ra•geous
cour•i•er
course
　coursed
　cours•ing
cour•te•sy
　cour•te•sies
cour•te•ous
court•house
cour•ti•er
court•ly
　court•li•ness
court•mar•tial
　courts•mar•tial
court•room
court•ship
cous•in
cou•tu•rier
cov•e•nant
cov•er
　cov•ered
　cov•er•ing

cov•er•age
cov•ert
　cov•ert•ly
cov•er•up
cov•et
　cov•et•ous
cov•ey
cow•ard
　cow•ard•li•ness
　cow•ard•ice
cow•er
　cow•er•ing
co•worker
coy
　coy•ness
coy•o•te
coz•en
co•zy
　co•zi•ly
crab
　crabbed
　crab•bing
　crab•by
crack
　cracked
　crack•ing
crack•down
crack•er
crack•le
　crack•led
　crack•ling
crack•up
cra•dle
　cra•dled
　cra•dling
crafts•man
crafty
　craft•i•ly
crag
　crag•ged
　crag•gy
cram
　crammed
　cram•ming
cran•ber•ry
crane
　craned
　cran•ing
cra•ni•um
cranky
cran•ny
　cran•nies
crass
　crass•ly
crate
　crat•ed
　crat•ing
cra•ter
crave
　craved
　crav•ing
　cra•ven
crawl
cray•on
craze
　crazed
cra•zy
　cra•zi•er
　cra•zi•ness
creak
　creaked
　creaky
cream
　cream•i•ness
　creamy
crease
　creased
　creas•ing
cre•ate
　cre•at•ed
　cre•at•ing
cre•a•tion
cre•a•tive
　cre•a•tiv•i•ty
cre•a•tor
crea•ture
cre•dence
cre•den•za
cred•i•ble
　cred•i•bil•i•ty
　cred•i•bly
cred•it
　cred•it•a•ble

cred•it•a•bly
cred•i•tor
cre•do
cred•u•lous
　cre•du•li•ty
creek
creep
　crept
　creep•ing
　creepy
　creep•i•ness
cre•mate
　cre•mat•ed
　cre•mat•ing
　cre•ma•tion
　cre•ma•to•ri•um
Cre•ole
cres•cen•do
cres•cent
crest
　crest•ed
crest•fall•en
cre•vasse
crev•ice
crib
　cribbed
　crib•bing
crick•et
crim•i•nal
　crim•i•nal•i•ty
crim•i•nol•o•gy
　crim•i•nol•o•gist
crim•son
cringe
　cringed
　cring•ing
crin•kle
　crin•kled
　crin•kling
crip•ple
　crip•pled
　crip•pling
cri•sis
　cri•ses
crisp
　crispy
　crisp•i•er
criss•cross
cri•te•ri•on
　cri•te•ria
crit•ic
　crit•i•cal
　crit•i•cal•ly
　crit•i•cism
crit•i•cize
　crit•i•cized
　crit•i•ciz•ing
cri•tique
cro•chet
　cro•cheted
　cro•chet•ing
crock•ery
croc•o•dile
cro•cus
crois•sant
cro•ny
　cro•nies
crook•ed
croon•er
crop
　cropped
　crop•ping
cro•quet
cro•quette
cross-coun•try
cross-ex•am•ine
　cross-ex•am•i•na•tion
cross•fire
cross•ing
cross-ref•er•ence
crotch•ety
crouch
crou•ton
cru•cial
cru•ci•ble
cru•ci•fix
　cru•ci•fix•ion
cru•ci•form
cru•ci•fy
　cru•ci•fied
　cru•ci•fy•ing
crude
　crud•est

crude•ness
cru•di•ty
cru•el
　cru•el•ly
　cru•el•ty
cru•et
cruise
　cruised
　cruis•ing
　cruis•er
crul•ler
crumb
crum•ble
　crum•bling
crum•my
　crum•mi•est
crum•pet
crum•ple
　crum•pled
　crum•pling
crunchy
　crunch•i•er
cru•sade
　cru•sad•er
crush•er
　crush•ing
crus•ta•cean
crusty
　crust•i•ly
crutch
crux
cry
　cried
　cry•ing
crypt
crys•tal
　crys•tal•line
　crys•tal•lize
　crys•tal•li•za•tion
cube
　cubed
　cub•ing
cu•bic
cu•bi•cle
cub•ism
cuck•old
cuck•oo
cu•cum•ber
cud•dle
　cud•dled
　cud•dling
cudg•el
　cudg•eled
cue
　cued
　cu•ing
cui•sine
cul-de-sac
cu•li•nary
cul•mi•nate
　cul•mi•nat•ed
　cul•mi•nat•ing
　cul•mi•na•tion
cu•lottes
cul•pa•ble
　cul•pa•bil•i•ty
cul•prit
cult
　cul•tist
cul•ti•vate
　cul•ti•vat•ed
　cul•ti•vat•ing
　cul•ti•va•tion
cul•tur•al
cul•ture
　cul•tured
cum•ber•some
cum lau•de
cum•mer•bund
cu•mu•la•tive
cu•mu•lus
　cu•mu•lous
cu•ne•i•form
cun•ning
cup
　cupped
　cup•ping
cup•board
cup•ful
cu•pid•i•ty
cu•po•la
cu•rate
cu•ra•tor

curb•ing
curb•stone
cur•dle
  cur•dled
  cur•dling
cure
  cured
  cur•ing
  cur•a•ble
  cur•a•tive
cur•few
cu•rio
cu•ri•os•i•ty
  cu•ri•os•i•ties
cu•ri•ous
curl•i•cue
curl•ing
curly
cur•rant
cur•ren•cy
  cur•ren•cies
cur•rent
cur•ric•u•lum
  cur•ric•u•la
  cur•ric•u•lar
cur
cur•ry
  cur•ried
curse
  curs•ing
  curs•ed•ness
cur•sive
cur•so•ry
  cur•so•ri•ly
curt
  curt•ly
cur•tail
  cur•tail•ment
cur•tain
curt•sy
  curt•sied
  curt•sy•ing
cur•va•ceous
cur•va•ture
curve
  curved
  curv•ing
cur•vi•lin•e•ar
cush•ion
cushy
  cush•i•est
cuss•ed
  cuss•ed•ness
cus•tard
cus•to•dy
  cus•to•di•al
  cus•to•di•an
cus•tom
  cus•tom•ary
  cus•tom•ar•i•ly
cus•tom•er
cus•tom•ize
  cus•tom•ized
  cus•tom•iz•ing
cut
  cut•ting
cute
  cut•est
  cute•ness
cu•ti•cle
cut•lass
cut•lery
cut•let
cut•throat
cy•a•nide
cy•ber•net•ics
cyc•la•men
cy•cle
  cy•cled
  cy•cling
  cy•clist
cy•clic
  cy•cli•cal
cy•clone
cyl•in•der
  cy•lin•dri•cal
cym•bal
cyn•ic
  cyn•i•cism
  cyn•i•cal
cy•pher

cy•press
cyst
czar

D

dab
  dabbed
  dab•bing
dab•ble
  dab•bled
  dab•bling
  dab•bler
dachs•hund
dac•tyl
  dac•tyl•ic
daf•fo•dil
daf•fy
dag•ger
dahl•ia
dai•ly
  dai•lies
dain•ty
  dain•ti•ly
dai•qui•ri
dairy
  dair•ies
da•is
dai•sy
  dai•sies
dal•ly
  dal•lied
  dal•ly•ing
  da•li•ance
Dal•ma•tian
dam
  dammed
  dam•ming
dam•age
  dam•aged
  dam•ag•ing
damn
  dam•na•ble
  dam•na•bly
  dam•na•tion
  damned
damp•en
damp•er
dam•sel
dance
  danced
  danc•ing
dan•de•li•on
dan•der
dan•druff
dan•dy
  dan•dies
dan•ger
  dan•ger•ous
dan•gle
  dan•gled
  dan•gling
dank
dap•per
dap•ple
  dap•pled
dare
  dared
  dar•ing
dare•dev•il
dark
  dark•ly
  dark•ness
dark•en
dark•room
dar•ling
Dar•win•ism
dash•board
dash•ing
das•tard•ly
da•ta
date
  dat•ed
  dat•ing
  dat•a•ble
date•line
da•tive
da•tum
  da•ta
daub
daugh•ter
  daugh•ter-in-law
daunt•less

daw•dle
  daw•dled
  daw•dling
  daw•dler
dawn
  dawn•ing
day•break
day•dream
day•light
day•time
daze
  dazed
daz•zle
  daz•zled
  daz•zling
dea•con
  dea•con•ess
de•ac•ti•vate
  de•ac•ti•va•tion
dead•beat
dead•en
dead end
dead•line
dead•lock
dead•ly
  dead•li•ness
deaf
  deaf•en
  deaf•en•ing•ly
deaf-mute
deal
  dealt
  deal•ing
dear
dearth
death
  death•ly
death•watch
de•ba•cle
de•bar
  de•barred
de•bark
  de•bar•ka•tion
de•base
  de•based
  de•bas•ing
de•bate
  de•bat•ing
  de•bat•a•ble
  de•bat•er
de•bauch
  de•bauch•ery
de•ben•ture
de•bil•i•tate
  de•bil•i•tat•ed
  de•bil•i•tat•ing
de•bil•i•ty
  de•bil•i•ties
deb•it
deb•o•nair
de•brief
de•bris
debt•or
de•bunk
de•but
  deb•u•tante
de•cade
dec•a•dent
  dec•a•dence
de•cal
de•camp
de•cant
  de•cant•er
de•cap•i•tate
  de•cap•i•tat•ed
  de•cap•i•tat•ing
  de•cap•i•ta•tion
de•cath•lon
de•cay
de•cease
  de•ceased
de•ceit
  de•ceit•ful
de•ceive
  de•ceived
  de•ceiv•ing
  de•ceiv•er
de•cel•er•ate
  de•cel•er•at•ed
  de•cel•er•at•ing
  de•cel•er•a•tion
de•cent
  de•cen•cy

de•cen•tral•ize
  de•cen•tral•ized
  de•cen•tral•iz•ing
  de•cen•tral•i•za•tion
de•cep•tion
  de•cep•tive
dec•i•bel
de•cide
  de•cid•ed
  de•cid•ing
  de•cid•ed•ly
de•cid•u•ous
dec•i•mal
dec•i•mate
  dec•i•mat•ed
  dec•i•mat•ing
  dec•i•ma•tion
de•ci•pher
  de•ci•pher•a•ble
de•ci•sion
  de•ci•sive
de•claim
  dec•la•ma•tion
  de•clam•a•tory
de•clare
  de•clared
  de•clar•ing
  de•clar•a•tive
  de•clar•a•tory
  dec•la•ra•tion
de•clas•si•fy
  de•clas•si•fied
  de•clas•si•fy•ing
de•clen•sion
dec•li•na•tion
de•cline
  de•clined
  de•clin•ing
de•cliv•i•ty
  de•cliv•i•ties
de•code
  de•cod•ed
  de•cod•ing
  de•cod•er
dé•colle•tage
de•com•mis•sion
de•com•pose
  de•com•posed
  de•com•pos•ing
  de•com•po•si•tion
de•com•press
  de•com•pres•sion
de•con•tam•i•nate
  de•con•tam•i•nat•ed
  de•con•tam•i•nat•ing
  de•con•tam•i•na•tion
de•con•trol
  de•con•trolled
de•cor
dec•o•rate
  dec•o•rat•ed
  dec•o•rat•ing
  dec•o•ra•tion
  dec•o•ra•tive
  dec•o•ra•tor
dec•o•rous
de•co•rum
de•coy
de•crease
  de•creased
  de•creas•ing
de•cree
  de•creed
  de•cree•ing
de•crep•it
  de•crep•i•tude
de•cry
  de•cried
  de•cry•ing
ded•i•cate
  ded•i•cat•ed
  ded•i•cat•ing
  ded•i•ca•to•ry
  ded•i•ca•tion
de•duce
  de•duc•i•ble
de•duct
  de•duct•i•ble
  de•duc•tion
  de•duc•tive
deep
  deep•en
deep-root•ed

deep-seat•ed
de-es•ca•late
  de-es•ca•lat•ed
  de-es•ca•lat•ing
  de-es•ca•la•tion
de•face
  de•faced
  de•fac•ing
  de•face•ment
de fac•to
de•fame
  def•a•ma•tion
  de•fam•a•to•ry
de•fault
de•feat
  de•feat•ism
  de•feat•ist
def•e•cate
  def•e•cat•ed
  def•e•cat•ing
  def•e•ca•tion
de•fect
  de•fec•tive
  de•fec•tion
  de•fec•tor
de•fend
  de•fend•er
  de•fend•ant
de•fense
  de•fense•less
  de•fen•si•ble
  de•fen•sive
de•fer
  de•ferred
  de•fer•ring
  de•fer•ment
def•er•ence
  def•er•en•tial
de•fi•ance
  de•fi•ant
de•fi•cient
  de•fi•cien•cy
  de•fi•cien•cies
def•i•cit
de•file
  de•filed
  de•file•ment
de•fine
  de•fined
  de•fin•ing
  de•fin•a•ble
def•i•nite
  def•i•nite•ly
def•i•ni•tion
de•fin•i•tive
de•flate
  de•flat•ed
  de•flat•ing
  de•fla•tion
  de•fla•tion•ary
de•flect
  de•flec•tion
  de•flec•tor
de•flow•er
de•fo•li•a•tion
de•for•est•a•tion
de•form
  de•for•ma•tion
  de•formed
de•form•i•ty
  de•form•i•ties
de•fraud
de•fray
  de•fray•al
de•frost
deft
de•funct
de•fy
  de•fied
  de•fy•ing
de•gen•er•ate
  de•gen•er•at•ed
  de•gen•er•at•ing
  de•gen•er•a•cy
  de•gen•er•a•tion
de•grade
  de•grad•ed
  de•grad•ing
  de•grad•able
  deg•ra•da•tion
de•gree
de•hu•mid•i•fy
de•hy•drate

de•hy•drat•ed
de•hy•drat•ing
de•hy•dra•tion
de•i•fy
de•i•fi•ca•tion
deign
de•ist
de•ism
de•i•ty
de•i•ties
de•ject•ed
de•jec•tion
de ju•re
de•lay
de•lec•ta•ble
de•lec•ta•tion
del•e•gate
del•e•gat•ed
del•e•gat•ing
del•e•ga•tion
de•lete
de•let•ed
de•let•ing
de•le•tion
del•e•te•ri•ous
de•lib•er•ate
de•lib•er•at•ed
de•lib•er•at•ing
de•lib•er•ate•ly
de•lib•er•a•tion
del•i•ca•cy
del•i•ca•cies
del•i•cate
del•i•cate•ly
del•i•ca•tes•sen
de•li•cious
de•light
de•light•ed
de•light•ful
de•lim•it
de•lim•i•ta•tion
de•lin•e•ate
de•lin•e•at•ed
de•lin•e•at•ing
de•lin•e•a•tion
de•lin•quent
de•lin•quen•cy
de•lir•i•um
de•lir•i•ous
de•liv•er
de•liv•er•er
de•liv•er•ance
de•liv•ery
de•liv•er•ies
de•louse
del•phin•i•um
del•ta
de•lude
de•lud•ed
del•uge
del•uged
de•lu•sion
de•lu•so•ry
de•luxe
delve
delv•ing
dem•a•gogue
dem•a•gogu•ery
dem•a•gog•ic
de•mand
de•mar•cate
de•mar•ca•tion
de•mean
de•mean•or
de•ment•ed
de•men•tia
de•mer•it
de•mesne
dem•i•god
de•mil•i•ta•rize
de•mil•i•tar•i•za•tion
de•mise
dem•i•tasse
de•mo•bi•lize
de•mo•bi•lized
de•mo•bi•liz•ing
de•mo•bi•li•za•tion
de•moc•ra•cy
de•moc•ra•cies
dem•o•crat
dem•o•crat•ic
dem•o•crat•i•cal•ly
de•moc•ra•tize

de•moc•ra•tized
de•moc•ra•tiz•ing
de•moc•ra•ti•za•tion
de•mog•ra•phy
de•mog•ra•pher
dem•o•graph•ic
de•mol•ish
de•plore
de•plored
de•plor•ing
de•plor•a•bly
de•ploy
de•ploy•ment
de•pol•ar•ize
de•pop•u•late
de•pop•u•lat•ed
de•pop•u•la•tion
de•port
de•por•ta•tion
de•pose
de•posed
de•pos•it
de•pos•i•tor
de•pos•i•tary
de•pos•i•to•ry
dep•o•si•tion
de•pot
de•prave
de•praved
de•prav•i•ty
dep•re•cate
dep•re•cat•ed
dep•re•cat•ing
dep•re•ca•tion
dep•re•ca•to•ry
de•pre•ci•ate
de•pre•ci•at•ed
de•pre•ci•at•ing
de•pre•ci•a•tion
dep•re•da•tion
de•press
de•pres•sant
de•pressed
de•pres•sion
de•prive
de•prived
de•priv•ing
dep•ri•va•tion
depth
dep•u•tize
dep•u•tized
dep•u•tiz•ing
dep•u•ta•tion
dep•u•ty
dep•u•ties
de•rail
de•range
de•ranged
de•rang•ing
der•by
dere•e•lict
der•e•lic•tion
de•ride
de•ri•sion
de•ri•sive
de ri•gueur
de•rive
der•i•va•tion
de•riv•a•tive
der•ma•ti•tis
der•ma•tol•o•gy
der•ma•tol•o•gist
der•mis
der•o•gate
der•o•gat•ed
der•o•gat•ing
der•o•ga•tion
de•rog•a•to•ry
de•rog•a•to•ri•ly
der•rick
des•cant
de•scend
de•scend•ed
de•scend•ing
de•scend•ant
de•scend•ent
de•scent
de•scribe
de•scribed
de•scrib•ing
de•scrip•tion
de•scrip•tive
de•scry

de•scried
de•scry•ing
des•e•crate
des•e•crat•ed
des•e•crat•ing
des•e•cra•tion
de•seg•re•gate
de•seg•re•gat•ed
de•seg•re•gat•ing
de•seg•re•ga•tion
de•sen•si•tize
des•ert
de•sert
de•sert•er
de•ser•tion
de•serve
de•served
de•serv•ing
de•serv•ed•ly
des•ic•cate
des•ic•cat•ed
des•ic•cat•ing
des•ic•ca•tion
de•sign
de•signed
de•sign•ing
de•sign•er
des•ig•nate
des•ig•nat•ed
des•ig•nat•ing
des•ig•na•tion
de•sire
de•sired
de•sir•ing
de•sir•a•ble
de•sir•a•bil•i•ty
de•sir•ous
de•sist
des•o•late
des•o•lat•ed
des•o•lat•ing
des•o•la•tion
de•spair
de•spair•ing
des•per•ate
des•per•ate•ly
des•per•a•tion
des•pi•ca•ble
des•pi•ca•bly
de•spise
de•spised
de•spis•ing
de•spite
de•spoil
de•spond•ence
de•spond•en•cy
de•spond•ent
des•pot
des•pot•ic
des•pot•ism
des•sert
des•ti•na•tion
des•tine
des•tined
des•ti•ny
des•ti•tute
des•ti•tu•tion
de•stroy
de•stroy•er
de•struc•tion
de•struct•i•ble
de•struc•tive
des•ul•to•ry
des•ul•to•ri•ly
de•tach
de•tached
de•tach•a•ble
de•tach•ment
de•tail
de•tain
de•ten•tion
de•tect
de•tect•a•ble
de•tec•tion
de•tec•tor
de•tec•tive
dé•tente
de•ten•tion
de•ter
de•terred
de•ter•ring
de•ter•gent
de•te•ri•o•rate

de•te•ri•o•rat•ed
de•te•ri•o•rat•ing
de•te•ri•o•ra•tion
de•ter•mine
de•ter•mined
de•ter•min•ing
de•ter•mi•na•ble
de•ter•mi•nant
de•ter•mi•nate
de•ter•mi•na•tion
de•ter•mined•ly
de•ter•min•ism
de•ter•rent
de•ter•rence
de•test
de•test•a•ble
de•tes•ta•tion
de•throne
det•o•nate
det•o•nat•ed
det•o•nat•ing
det•o•na•tion
det•o•na•tor
de•tour
de•tract
de•trac•tion
de•trac•tor
det•ri•ment
det•ri•men•tal
de•tri•tus
deuce
de•value
de•val•u•ate
de•val•u•a•tion
dev•as•tate
dev•as•tat•ed
dev•as•tat•ing
dev•as•ta•tion
de•vel•op
de•vel•op•ment
de•vel•op•er
de•vi•ate
de•vi•at•ed
de•vi•at•ing
de•vi•ant
de•vi•a•tion
de•vice
dev•il
dev•il•try
dev•il•ish
de•vi•ous
de•vise
de•vised
de•vis•ing
de•void
de•volve
de•volved
de•volv•ing
de•vote
de•vot•ed
de•vot•ing
de•vo•tee
de•vo•tion
de•vour
de•vout
dewy
dex•ter•ous
dex•ter•i•ty
di•a•be•tes
di•a•bet•ic
di•a•bol•ic
di•a•bol•i•cal
di•a•dem
di•ag•nose
di•ag•nosed
di•ag•nos•ing
di•ag•no•sis
di•ag•nos•tic
di•ag•nos•ti•cian
di•ag•o•nal
di•a•gram
di•a•gramed
di•a•gram•ing
di•a•gram•matic
di•al
di•aled
di•al•ing
di•a•lect
di•a•lec•tic
di•a•lec•ti•cal
di•a•logue
di•a•log
di•am•e•ter

di•a•met•ri•cal•ly
dia•mond
dia•per
di•aph•a•nous
di•a•phragm
di•ar•rhea
di•a•ry
di•a•ries
di•a•tribe
dice
diced
dic•ing
di•chot•o•my
di•chot•o•mies
di•chot•o•mous
dick•ey
dic•tate
dic•tat•ed
dic•tat•ing
dic•ta•tion
dic•ta•tor
dic•ta•tor•ship
dic•ta•to•ri•al
dic•tion
dic•tion•ary
dic•tion•ar•ies
dic•tum
di•dac•tic
die
died
dy•ing
die•sel
di•et
di•e•tary
di•e•tet•ic
di•e•ti•cian
dif•fer
dif•fer•ence
dif•fer•ent
dif•fer•en•tial
dif•fer•en•ti•ate
dif•fer•en•ti•a•tion
dif•fi•cult
dif•fi•cul•ty
dif•fi•cul•ties
dif•fi•dent
dif•fi•dence
dif•fuse
dif•fused
dif•fus•ing
dif•fuse•ly
dif•fuse•ness
dif•fu•sion
dig
dug
dig•ging
di•gest
di•gest•i•ble
di•ges•tion
di•ges•tive
dig•ger
dig•gings
dig•it
dig•it•al
dig•ni•fy
dig•ni•fied
dig•ni•tary
dig•ni•tar•ies
dig•ni•ty
di•gress
di•gres•sion
di•gres•sive
di•lap•i•date
di•lap•i•dat•ed
di•lap•i•da•tion
dil•a•ta•tion
di•late
di•lat•ed
di•lat•ing
di•la•tion
dil•a•to•ry
dil•a•to•ri•ly
di•lem•ma
dil•et•tan•te
dil•i•gence
dil•i•gent
dil•ly•dal•ly
dil•ly•dal•lied
dil•ute
dil•lut•ed
dil•lut•ing
di•lu•tion
dim

dim•mer
dimmed
dim•ming
di•men•sion
di•men•sion•al
di•min•ish
dim•i•nu•tion
di•min•u•tive
dim•ple
dim•wit•ted
din
dine
dined
din•ing
din•er
din•ghy
din•ghies
din•gy
din•ner
di•no•saur
di•o•cese
di•ox•ide
dip
dipped
dip•ping
diph•the•ria
diph•thong
di•plo•ma
di•plo•ma•cy
dip•lo•mat
dip•lo•mat•ic
dip•lo•mat•i•cal•ly
dip•so•ma•nia
dip•so•ma•ni•ac
dire
di•rect
di•rec•tion
di•rec•tive
di•rec•tor
di•rec•to•rate
di•rec•to•ry
di•rec•to•ries
dirge
di•ri•gi•ble
dirty
dis•a•ble
dis•abled
dis•a•bling
dis•a•bil•i•ty
dis•ad•van•tage
dis•ad•van•taged
dis•ad•van•ta•geous
dis•af•fect
dis•af•fect•ed
dis•af•fec•tion
dis•a•gree
dis•a•greed
dis•a•gree•ing
dis•a•gree•a•ble
dis•a•gree•ment
dis•al•low
dis•ap•pear
dis•ap•pear•ance
dis•ap•point
dis•ap•point•ment
dis•ap•prove
dis•ap•proved
dis•ap•prov•ing
dis•ap•prov•al
dis•ap•pro•ba•tion
dis•arm
dis•ar•ma•ment
dis•ar•range
dis•ar•ray
dis•as•sem•ble
dis•as•so•ci•ate
dis•as•ter
dis•as•trous
dis•a•vow
dis•a•vow•al
dis•band
dis•bar
dis•barred
dis•bar•ring
dis•be•lieve
dis•be•lieved
dis•be•liev•ing
dis•be•lief
dis•be•liev•er
dis•burse
dis•bursed
dis•burs•ing
dis•burse•ment

dis•bur•sal
disc
disk
dis•card
dis•cern
dis•cern•ing
dis•charge
dis•charged
dis•charg•ing
dis•ci•ple
dis•ci•pline
dis•ci•plined
dis•ci•plin•ing
dis•ci•pli•nary
dis•ci•pli•nar•i•an
dis•claim
dis•claim•er
dis•close
dis•closed
dis•clos•ing
dis•clo•sure
dis•col•or
dis•col•or•a•tion
dis•com•fit
dis•com•fi•ture
dis•com•fort
dis•con•cert
dis•con•cert•ing
dis•con•cert•ed
dis•con•nect
dis•con•nec•tion
dis•con•nect•ed
dis•con•so•late
dis•con•tent
dis•con•tent•ed
dis•con•tin•ue
dis•con•tin•ued
dis•con•tin•u•ing
dis•con•tin•u•ous
dis•cord
dis•cord•ance
dis•count
dis•cour•age
dis•cour•aged
dis•cour•ag•ing
dis•course
dis•cour•te•ous
dis•cour•te•sy
dis•cov•er
dis•cov•er•er
dis•cov•ery
dis•cov•er•ies
dis•cred•it
dis•cred•it•a•ble
dis•creet
dis•crep•an•cy
dis•crep•an•cies
dis•crete
dis•cre•tion
dis•cre•tion•ary
dis•crim•i•nate
dis•crim•i•nat•ed
dis•crim•i•nat•ing
dis•crim•i•na•tion
dis•crim•i•na•to•ry
dis•cur•sive
dis•cus
dis•cuss
dis•cus•sion
dis•dain
dis•dain•ful
dis•ease
dis•eased
dis•em•bark
dis•em•bar•ka•tion
dis•em•body
dis•em•bod•ied
dis•em•bow•el
dis•em•bow•eled
dis•en•chant
dis•en•fran•chise
dis•en•fran•chised
dis•en•gage
dis•en•tan•gle
dis•fa•vor
dis•fig•ure
dis•fig•ured
dis•fig•ur•ing
dis•fig•ure•ment
dis•fran•chise
dis•fran•chised
dis•gorge
dis•gorged

dis•grace
dis•graced
dis•grace•ful
dis•grun•tle
dis•grun•tled
dis•guise
dis•guised
dis•guis•ing
dis•gust
dis•gust•ed
dis•gust•ing
dis•har•mo•ny
dis•heart•en
di•shev•eled
dis•hon•est
dis•hon•es•ty
dis•hon•or
dis•hon•or•a•ble
dis•hon•or•a•bly
dis•il•lu•sion
dis•il•lu•sion•ment
dis•in•cline
dis•in•clined
dis•in•cli•na•tion
dis•in•fect
dis•in•fect•ant
dis•in•fec•tion
dis•in•gen•u•ous
dis•in•her•it
dis•in•te•grate
dis•in•te•grat•ed
dis•in•te•grat•ing
dis•in•te•gra•tion
dis•in•ter
dis•in•ter•est
dis•in•ter•es•ted
dis•join
dis•joint
dis•joint•ed
disk
disc
dis•like
dis•liked
dis•lo•cate
dis•lo•ca•tion
dis•lodge
dis•lodged
dis•loy•al
dis•loy•al•ty
dis•mal
dis•mal•ly
dis•man•tle
dis•man•tled
dis•man•tling
dis•may
dis•mem•ber
dis•mem•ber•ment
dis•miss
dis•mis•sal
dis•mount
dis•o•bey
dis•o•be•di•ence
dis•o•be•di•ent
dis•or•der•ly
dis•or•gan•ize
dis•or•gan•ized
dis•o•ri•ent
dis•o•ri•en•ta•tion
dis•own
dis•par•age
dis•par•aged
dis•par•ag•ing
dis•par•age•ment
dis•pa•rate
dis•par•i•ty
dis•pas•sion
dis•pas•sion•ate
dis•patch
dis•patch•er
dis•pel
dis•pelled
dis•pel•ling
dis•pen•sa•ble
dis•pen•sa•ry
dis•pense
dis•pensed
dis•pens•ing
dis•pen•sa•tion
dis•perse
dis•persed
dis•pers•ing
dis•per•sion
dis•place

dis•placed
dis•plac•ing
dis•place•ment
dis•play
dis•please
dis•pleas•ing
dis•pleas•ure
dis•pose
dis•pos•ing
dis•pos•a•ble
dis•po•si•tion
dis•pos•sess
dis•pro•por•tion
dis•pro•por•tion•ate
dis•prove
dis•prov•ing
dis•pute
dis•put•ed
dis•put•ing
dis•put•a•ble
dis•pu•tant
dis•pu•ta•tious
dis•qual•i•fy
dis•qual•i•fied
dis•qual•i•fy•ing
dis•qual•i•fi•ca•tion
dis•qui•et
dis•re•gard
dis•re•pair
dis•re•pute
dis•rep•u•ta•ble
dis•re•spect
dis•re•spect•ful
dis•robe
dis•robed
dis•rob•ing
dis•rupt
dis•rup•tion
dis•rup•tive
dis•sat•is•fy
dis•sat•is•fied
dis•sat•is•fac•tion
dis•sect
dis•sect•ed
dis•sec•tion
dis•sem•ble
dis•sem•bled
dis•sem•bling
dis•sem•i•nate
dis•sem•i•nat•ed
dis•sem•i•nat•ing
dis•sem•i•na•tion
dis•sent
dis•sent•ing
dis•sen•sion
dis•sent•er
dis•ser•ta•tion
dis•serv•ice
dis•si•dence
dis•si•dent
dis•sim•i•lar
dis•si•pate
dis•si•pat•ed
dis•si•pat•ing
dis•si•pa•tion
dis•so•ci•ate
dis•so•ci•at•ed
dis•so•ci•at•ing
dis•so•ci•a•tion
dis•sol•u•ble
dis•so•lute
dis•so•lu•tion
dis•solve
dis•solv•ing
dis•solv•a•ble
dis•so•nance
dis•so•nant
dis•suade
dis•suad•ed
dis•suad•ing
dis•taff
dis•tance
dis•tant
dis•taste
dis•taste•ful
dis•tem•per
dis•tend
dis•ten•sion
dis•ten•tion
dis•till
dis•tilled
dis•till•ing
dis•til•la•tion

dis•till•er
dis•till•ery
dis•tinct
dis•tinc•tion
dis•tinc•tive
dis•tin•guish
dis•tin•guished
dis•tort
dis•tor•ted
dis•tor•tion
dis•tract
dis•tract•ing
dis•trac•tion
dis•traught
dis•tress
dis•tressed
dis•tress•ing
dis•tress•ful
dis•trib•ute
dis•trib•ut•ed
dis•trib•ut•ing
dis•tri•bu•tion
dis•trib•u•tor
dis•trict
dis•trust
dis•trust•ful
dis•turb
dis•turb•ance
dis•turbed
dis•u•nite
dis•u•ni•ted
dis•u•ni•ty
dis•un•ion
dis•use
dis•used
ditch
dith•er
dit•to
dit•ty
di•u•ret•ic
di•ur•nal
di•va
di•van
dive
dived
dove
div•ing
di•verge
di•verged
di•verg•ing
di•ver•gence
di•ver•gent
di•verse
di•ver•si•fi•ca•tion
di•ver•si•fy
di•ver•si•fied
di•ver•si•ty
di•ver•sion
di•ver•sion•ary
di•vert
di•vide
di•vid•ed
di•vid•ing
di•vis•i•ble
di•vi•sion
di•vi•sive
div•i•dend
di•vine
di•vin•i•ty
di•vorce
di•vorc•ing
di•vor•cée
di•vulge
di•vulged
di•vulg•ing
diz•zy
diz•zy•ing
diz•zi•ly
do
did
done
do•ing
Do•ber•man pin•scher
doc•ile
doc•tor
doc•tor•al
doc•tor•ate
doc•trine
doc•tri•nal
doc•tri•naire
doc•u•ment
doc•u•men•ta•tion
doc•u•men•ta•ry

dod•der
dodge
  dodg•ing
does
  doesn't
dog
  dogged
  dog•ging
dog•eared
dog•ged
  dog•ged•ly
dog•ger•el
dog•ma
  dog•mat•ic
dol•drums
dole
  doled
  dol•ing
dole•ful
dol•lar
dol•or•ous
dol•phin
dolt
do•main
dome
  domed
do•mes•tic
  do•mes•tic•i•ty
do•mes•ti•cate
  do•mes•ti•cat•ed
  do•mes•ti•ca•tion
dom•i•cile
  dom•i•ciled
dom•i•nate
  dom•i•nat•ing
  dom•i•na•tion
  dom•i•nant
  dom•i•nance
dom•i•neer
  dom•i•neer•ing
do•min•ion
dom•i•no
  dom•i•noes
don
  donned
do•nate
  do•nat•ed
  do•nat•ing
  do•na•tor
  do•na•tion
  do•nor
don•key
doo•dle
dooms•day
dope
  doped
  dop•ey
dor•mant
  dor•man•cy
dor•mer
  dor•mered
dor•mi•to•ry
  dor•mi•to•ries
dor•sal
dose
  dosed
  dos•age
dos•si•er
dot
  dot•ted
  dot•ting
dot•age
dote
  dot•ed
  dot•ing
dou•ble
  dou•bled
  dou•bling
  doub•ly
dou•ble•breast•ed
dou•ble•cross
dou•ble•deck•er
dou•ble•faced
dou•ble•head•er
dou•ble•joint•ed
dou•ble•talk
doubt•ful
  doubt•less
douche
  douched
  douch•ing
dough
dour

douse
  doused
  dous•ing
dove•tail
dow•a•ger
dow•dy
dow•el
down•grade
  down•grad•ed
  down•grad•ing
down•heart•ed
down•sream
down•town
down•trod•den
dow•ry
  dow•ries
doze
  dozed
  doz•ing
doz•en
drab
dra•co•ni•an
draft
  draft•ee
drafts•man
drafty
drag
  dragged
  drag•ging
drag•net
drain
drake
dra•ma
  dra•ma•tic
  dram•a•tist
  dram•a•tize
  dram•a•ti•za•tion
drape
  draped
  drap•ing
dra•pery
  dra•per•ies
dras•tic
  dras•ti•cal•ly
draught
draw
  drew
  drawn
  draw•ing
draw•bridge
draw•er
drawl
dread•ful
dream
  dreamed
  dreamt
  dream•ing
  dream•er
  dreamy
dreary
  drear•i•ly
  drear•i•ness
dredge
  dredged
  dredg•ing
  dredg•er
dregs
drench
dress
  dressed
  dress•ing
  dress•er
  dressy
drib•ble
  drib•bled
  drib•bling
dri•er
drift•er
drill•ing
dri•ly
drink
  drank
  drunk
  drink•ing
  drink•a•ble
  drink•er
drip
  dripped
  drip•ping
  drip•py
drive
  drove
  driv•en

driv•ing
driv•el
driz•zle
  driz•zled
  driz•zling
  driz•zly
droll
  drol•ly
  droll•ery
drone
  droned
  dron•ing
drool
droop
  droop•y
drop
  dropped
  drop•ping
  drop•per
drop•sy
dross
drought
drove
drowned
drowse
  drows•ing
  drow•sy
  drow•si•ness
drub
  drubbed
  drub•bing
drudge
  drudg•ing
  drudg•ery
drug
  drugged
  drug•ging
  drug•gist
drum
  drummed
  drum•ming
  drum•mer
drunk•ard
drunk•en
dry
  dry•ing
  dri•er
  dried
du•al
  du•al•i•ty
  du•al•is•tic
dub
  dubbed
  dub•bing
du•bi•ous
du•cal
duch•ess
duck•ling
duc•tile
du•el
  du•eled
  du•el•ing
du•et
duf•fel
duff•er
dug•out
dull
  dull•ard
du•ly
dumb
  dumb•struck
dum•found
  dumb•found
dum•my
  dum•mies
dump•ling
dumpy
dun
  dunned
  dun•ning
dunce
dune
dung•hill
dun•ga•ree
dun•geon
dupe
  duped
du•plex
du•pli•cate
  du•pli•cat•ed
  du•pli•cat•ing
  du•pli•ca•tion
  du•pli•ca•tor

du•plic•i•ty
du•ra•ble
  du•ra•bil•i•ty
du•ra•tion
du•ress
dur•ing
dusky
dust•er
dusty
du•ti•ful
  du•ti•ful•ly
du•ty
  du•ties
dwarf
dwell
  dwelt
  dwelled
  dwell•ing
dwindle
  dwin•dled
  dwin•dling
dye
  dyed
  dye•ing
dy•ing
dy•nam•ic
  dy•nam•i•cal•ly
dy•na•mite
dy•na•mo
dy•nas•ty
  dy•nas•ties
dys•en•tery
dys•func•tion
dys•pep•sia
  dys•pep•tic
dys•tro•phy

E

ea•ger
ea•gle
ear•ache
ear•drum
ear•ly
  ear•li•er
  ear•li•est
ear•lobe
ear•mark
earn
  earn•ings
ear•nest
ear•ring
ear•shot
ear•split•ting
earth•bound
earth•en•ware
earth•ly
earth•quake
earth•shaking
earth•worm
earthy
  earth•i•ness
ease
  eased
  eas•ing
ea•sel
ease•ment
east•er•ly
east•ern
east•ward
easy
  eas•i•er
  eas•i•est
  eas•i•ly
eas•y•go•ing
eat
  ate
  eat•en
  eat•ing
eau de co•logne
eaves•drop
ebb
  ebb•ing
eb•ony
ebul•lience
  ebul•lient
ec•cen•tric
  ec•cen•tric•i•ty
ec•cle•si•as•tic
  ec•cle•si•as•ti•cal
ech•e•lon
echo
  ech•oes

ech•oed
ech•o•ing
ec•lec•tic
  ec•lec•ti•cism
eclipse
  eclipsed
  eclips•ing
eclip•tic
ecol•o•gy
  ec•o•log•i•cal
  ecol•o•gist
eco•nom•i•cal
eco•nom•ics
  econ•o•mist
econ•o•mize
  econ•o•miz•ing
econ•o•my
  econ•o•mies
ec•ru
ec•sta•sy
ec•stat•ic
ec•u•men•i•cal
ec•ze•ma
ed•dy
ede•ma
edge
  edged
  edg•ing
edgy
ed•i•ble
edict
ed•i•fice
ed•i•fy
  ed•i•fied
  ed•i•fy•ing
  ed•i•fi•ca•tion
ed•it
edi•tion
ed•i•tor
ed•i•to•ri•al
  ed•i•to•ri•al•ize
ed•u•cate
  ed•u•cat•ed
  ed•u•cat•ing
ed•u•ca•tion
  ed•u•ca•tion•al
ed•u•ca•tor
educe
eel
ee•rie
  ee•ri•ly
ef•face
  ef•face•ment
ef•fect
ef•fec•tive
  ef•fec•tive•ly
ef•fec•tu•al
ef•fem•i•nate
ef•fer•vesce
  ef•fer•ves•cence
  ef•fer•ves•cent
ef•fete
ef•fi•ca•cy
  ef•fi•ca•cious
ef•fi•cient
ef•fi•gy
  ef•fi•gies
ef•flu•ent
ef•flu•vi•um
ef•fort
ef•fron•tery
ef•ful•gent
  ef•ful•gence
ef•fu•sive
egal•i•tar•i•an
ego•cen•tric
ego•ism
  ego•ist
  ego•is•tic
ego•tism
  ego•tist
  ego•tis•tic
  ego•tis•ti•cal
egre•gious
egress
egret
eight
  eighth
  eight•een
eighty
  eight•ies
  eight•i•eth
ei•ther

ejac•u•late
  ejac•u•lat•ed
  ejac•u•lat•ing
  ejac•u•la•tion
eject
  ejec•tion
  ejec•tor
eke
  eked
  ek•ing
elab•o•rate
  elab•o•rat•ed
  elab•o•rat•ing
  elab•o•ra•tion
elapse
  elapsed
  elaps•ing
elas•tic
  elas•tic•i•ty
elate
  elat•ed
  elat•ing
  ela•tion
el•bow
eld•er
  el•der•ly
  eld•est
elect
  elec•tion
elec•tive
elec•tor
  elec•tor•al
elec•tor•ate
elec•tric
  elec•tri•cal
  elec•tri•cian
  elec•tric•i•ty
elec•tri•fy
  elec•tri•fied
  elec•tri•fy•ing
elec•tro•car•di•o•gram
elec•tro•cute
  elec•tro•cut•ed
  elec•tro•cu•tion
elec•trode
elec•trol•y•sis
elec•tro•lyte
elec•tron
elec•tron•ic
  elec•tron•ics
  elec•tron•i•cal•ly
el•e•gant
  el•e•gance
el•e•gy
el•e•ment
  el•e•men•tal
  el•e•men•ta•ry
ele•e•phant
  el•e•phan•tine
ele•e•vate
  el•e•vat•ed
  el•e•vat•ing
  el•e•va•tion
  el•e•va•tor
elev•en
elf
  elves
elic•it
el•i•gi•ble
  el•i•gi•bil•i•ty
elim•i•nate
  elim•i•nat•ed
  elim•i•nat•ing
  elim•i•na•tion
elite
  elit•ism
  elit•ist
elix•ir
Eliz•a•beth•an
el•lipse
el•lip•sis
el•lip•ti•cal
  el•lip•tic
el•o•cu•tion
elon•gate
  elon•gat•ed
  elon•gat•ing
  elon•ga•tion
elope
  eloped
  elop•ing
el•o•quence
  el•o•quent

elu•ci•date
  elu•ci•dat•ed
  elu•ci•dat•ing
  elu•ci•da•tion
elude
  elud•ed
  elud•ing
elu•sive
ema•ci•ate
  ema•ci•at•ed
  ema•ci•a•tion
em•a•nate
  em•a•nat•ed
  em•a•nat•ing
eman•ci•pate
  eman•ci•pat•ed
  eman•ci•pat•ing
  eman•ci•pa•tion
emas•cu•late
em•balm
em•bank•ment
em•bar•go
  em•bar•goes
em•bark
  em•bar•ka•tion
em•bar•rass
  em•bar•rass•ed
  em•bar•rass•ing
em•bas•sy
  em•bas•sies
em•bat•tle
  em•bat•tled
em•bed
  em•bed•ded
em•bel•lish
em•ber
em•bez•zle
  em•bez•zled
  em•bez•zling
  em•bez•zler
em•bit•ter
em•bla•zon
em•blem
  em•blem•at•ic
em•bod•y
  em•bod•ied
  em•bod•y•ing
  em•bod•i•ment
em•bold•en
em•bo•lism
em•bo•lus
em•boss
em•brace
  em•brac•ing
em•broi•der
  em•broi•dery
em•broil
em•bryo
  em•bry•os
  em•bry•on•ic
  em•bry•ol•o•gy
em•cee
emend
  emen•da•tion
em•er•ald
emerge
  emerged
  emerg•ing
  emer•gence
  emer•gent
emer•gen•cy
  emer•gen•cies
emer•i•tus
em•ery
em•i•grant
em•i•grate
  em•i•grat•ing
  em•i•gra•tion
em•i•nence
  em•i•nent
em•is•sary
  em•is•sar•ies
emis•sion
emit
  emit•ted
  emit•ting
emol•lient
emol•u•ment
emo•tion
  emo•tion•al•ly
em•pa•thize
  em•pa•thized
  em•pa•thiz•ing

em•pa•thy
  em•pa•thet•ic
em•per•or
em•pha•sis
  em•pha•ses
em•pha•size
  em•pha•sized
  em•pha•siz•ing
em•phat•ic
  em•phat•i•cal•ly
em•phy•se•ma
em•pire
em•pir•i•cal
  em•pir•i•cism
em•ploy
  em•ploy•ee
  em•ploy•er
em•po•ri•um
em•pow•er
em•press
emp•ty
  emp•tied
  emp•ty•ing
  emp•ti•ness
em•u•late
  em•u•lat•ing
  em•u•la•tion
emul•si•fy
  emul•si•fied
  emul•si•fy•ing
emul•sion
en•a•ble
  en•a•bled
  en•a•bling
en•act
enam•el
  enam•eled
  enam•el•ing
en•am•or
  en•am•ored
en•camp
en•cap•su•late
  en•cap•sul•lat•ed
  en•cap•su•lat•ing
  en•cap•sule
en•case
  en•cased
  en•cas•ing
en•ceph•a•li•tis
en•chant
  en•chant•ing
  en•chant•ress
en•chi•la•da
en•cir•cle
  en•cir•cled
  en•cir•cling
en•clave
en•close
  en•closed
  en•clos•ing
  en•clo•sure
en•code
  en•cod•ed
  en•cod•ing
en•com•pass
en•core
en•coun•ter
en•cour•age
  en•cour•aged
  en•cour•ag•ing
  en•cour•age•ment
en•croach
en•crust
  en•crus•ta•tion
en•cum•ber
  en•cum•brance
en•cy•clo•pe•dia
  en•cy•clo•pe•dic
en•dan•ger
en•dear
en•deav•or
en•dem•ic
en•dive
end•ing
en•dorse
  en•dorse•ment
  en•dors•er
endow
  en•dow•ment
en•dure
  en•dur•ing
  en•dur•ance
en•e•ma

en•e•my
  en•e•mies
en•er•get•ic
  en•er•get•i•cal•ly
en•er•gize
  en•er•gized
  en•er•giz•ing
en•er•gy
en•er•vate
  en•er•vat•ed
  en•er•vat•ing
  en•er•va•tion
en•fee•ble
  en•fee•bled
  en•fee•bling
en•fold
en•force
  en•forced
  en•forc•ing
  en•force•ment
en•fran•chise
  en•fran•chised
en•gage
  en•gaged
  en•gag•ing
  en•gage•ment
en•gen•der
en•gine
en•gi•neer
En•gland
  En•glish
en•grave
  en•graved
  en•grav•ing
  en•grav•er
en•gross
  en•grossed
  en•gross•ing
en•gulf
en•hance
  en•hanced
  en•hanc•ing
  en•hance•ment
enig•ma
  en•ig•mat•ic
en•join
en•joy
  en•joy•a•ble
en•large
  en•larged
  en•larg•ing
  en•larg•er
  en•large•ment
en•light•en
  en•light•en•ment
en•list
en•liv•en
en masse
en•mesh
en•mi•ty
en•no•ble
  en•no•bled
  en•no•bling
en•nui
enor•mi•ty
  enor•mous
enough
en•quire
  en•quiry
en•rage
  en•raged
en•rap•ture
en•rich
en•roll
  en•roll•ment
en route
en•sconce
  en•sconced
en•semble
en•shrine
  en•shrined
en•shroud
en•sign
en•slave
  en•slaved
  en•slave•ment
en•snare
  en•snared
en•sue
  en•sued
  en•su•ing
en•sure
en•tail

en•tan•gle
  en•tan•gled
en•tente
en•ter
en•ter•prise
  en•ter•pris•ing
en•ter•tain
  en•ter•tain•ment
en•thrall
  en•thralled
  en•thrall•ing
en•throne
  en•throned
en•thuse
  en•thused
en•thu•si•asm
  en•thu•si•as•tic
  en•thu•si•as•ti•cal•ly
en•tice
  en•ticed
  en•tic•ing
en•tire
  en•tire•ly
  en•tire•ty
en•ti•tle
  en•ti•tled
  en•ti•tle•ment
en•ti•ty
  en•ti•ties
en•tou•rage
en•trails
en•train
en•trance
en•trap
  en•trapped
en•treat
  en•treaty
en•tree
en•trench
en•tre•pre•neur
en•trust
en•try
  en•tries
en•twine
  en•twined
enu•mer•ate
  enu•mer•at•ed
  enu•mer•at•ing
  enu•mer•a•tion
  enu•mer•a•tor
enun•ci•ate
  enun•ci•a•tion
en•vel•op
  en•vel•op•ing
en•ve•lope
en•vi•ron•ment
  en•vi•ron•men•tal•ist
en•vi•rons
en•vis•age
  en•vis•ag•ing
en•vi•sion
en•voy
en•vy
  en•vied
  en•vi•able
  en•vi•ous
en•zyme
ep•au•let
ephem•er•al
ep•ic
ep•i•cen•ter
ep•i•cure
  epi•cu•re•an
ep•i•der•mis
  ep•i•der•mal
ep•i•gram
ep•i•graph
ep•i•lep•sy
  ep•i•lep•tic
ep•i•logue
Epis•co•pa•lian
  epis•co•pal
ep•i•sode
  ep•i•sod•ic
epis•te•mol•o•gy
epis•tle
ep•i•taph
ep•i•thet
epit•o•me
  epit•o•mize
ep•och
  ep•och•al
ep•oxy

eq•ua•ble
  eq•ua•bly
equal
  equaled
  equal•ling
  equal•ly
  equal•i•ty
  equal•ize
equa•nim•i•ty
equate
  equat•ed
  equat•ing
equa•tion
equa•tor
  equa•to•ri•al
eques•tri•an
  eques•tri•enne
equi•dis•tant
equil•lat•er•al
equi•lib•ri•um
equine
equi•nox
equip
  equipped
  equip•ping
equip•ment
equi•poise
eq•ui•ty
  eq•ui•ties
  eq•ui•ta•ble
  eq•ui•ta•bly
equiv•a•lent
  equiv•a•lence
equiv•o•cal
equiv•o•cate
  equiv•o•cat•ed
  equiv•o•cat•ing
  equiv•o•ca•tion
erad•i•cate
  erad•i•cat•ed
  erad•i•cat•ing
  erad•i•ca•tion
erase
  erased
  eras•ing
  eras•ure
erect
  erec•tor
  erec•tion
er•mine
erode
  erod•ed
  erod•ing
  ero•sion
  ero•sive
erot•ic
  erot•i•cism
err
er•rand
er•rant
er•rat•ic
er•ra•tum
  er•ra•ta
er•ro•ne•ous
er•ror
er•satz
erst•while
er•u•dite
  er•u•di•tion
erupt
  erup•tion
es•ca•late
  es•ca•lat•ed
  es•ca•lat•ing
  es•ca•la•tion
  es•ca•la•tor
es•ca•pade
es•cape
  es•caped
  es•cap•ing
  es•cap•ism
es•ca•role
es•carp•ment
es•chew
es•cort
es•crow
es•cutch•eon
Es•ki•mo
esoph•a•gus
es•o•ter•ic
es•pe•cial•ly
es•pi•o•nage

es•pla•nade
es•pouse
  es•poused
  es•pous•ing
  es•pous•al
es•prit de corps
es•py
  es•pied
es•quire
es•say
  es•say•ist
es•sence
es•sen•tial•ly
es•tab•lish•ment
es•tate
es•teem
es•thet•ic
es•ti•ma•ble
es•ti•mate
  es•ti•mat•ed
  es•ti•mat•ing
  es•ti•ma•tor
  es•ti•ma•tion
es•trange
  es•tranged
  es•trange•ment
es•tro•gen
es•tu•ary
  es•tu•ar•ies
et cet•era
etch•ing
eter•nal
  eter•ni•ty
eth•a•nol
ether
ethe•re•al
eth•ics
  eth•i•cal
eth•nic
eth•yl
eti•ol•o•gy
  eti•o•log•i•cal
et•i•quette
et•y•mol•o•gy
  et•y•mo•log•i•cal
eu•ca•lyp•tus
Eu•cha•rist
  Eu•cha•ris•tic
eu•gen•ics
eu•lo•gy
  eu•lo•gize
eu•nuch
eu•phe•mism
  eu•phe•mis•tic
eu•pho•ria
  eu•phor•ic
Eu•rope
  Eu•ro•pe•an
eu•tha•na•sia
evac•u•ate
  evac•u•at•ed
  evac•u•at•ing
  evac•u•a•tion
  evac•u•ee
evade
  evad•ed
  evad•ing
eval•u•ate
  eval•u•at•ed
  eval•u•at•ing
  eval•u•a•tion
ev•a•nesce
  ev•a•nesced
  ev•a•nesc•ing
  ev•a•nes•cent
evan•gel•i•cal
  evan•gel•ic
  evan•ge•lism
  evan•ge•lis•tic
  evan•ge•list
  evan•ge•lize
evap•o•rate
  evap•o•rat•ed
  evap•o•rat•ing
  evap•o•ra•tion
eva•sion
eva•sive
even
  even•ly
eve•ning
event•ful
even•tu•al
  even•tu•al•ly

even•tu•al•i•ty
ev•er•green
ev•er•last•ing
ev•ery•body
ev•ery•day
ev•ery•one
ev•ery•thing
ev•ery•where
evict
  evic•tion
ev•i•dence
ev•i•dent
  ev•i•dent•ly
evil
evince
  evinced
  evinc•ing
evoke
ev•o•ca•tion
ev•o•lu•tion
  ev•o•lu•tion•ary
evolve
  evolved
  evolv•ing
ew•er
ex•ac•er•bate
  ex•ac•er•bat•ed
  ex•ac•er•bat•ing
  ex•ac•er•ba•tion
ex•act
  ex•act•ing
  ex•act•ly
ex•ag•ger•ate
  ex•ag•ger•at•ed
  ex•ag•ger•at•ing
  ex•ag•ger•a•tion
ex•alt
  ex•al•ta•tion
  ex•alt•ed
ex•am•ine
  ex•am•ined
  ex•am•in•ing
  ex•am•in•er
  ex•am•i•na•tion
ex•am•ple
ex•as•per•ate
  ex•as•per•at•ed
  ex•as•per•at•ing
  ex•as•per•a•tion
ex•ca•vate
  ex•ca•va•tion
ex•ceed
ex•cel
  ex•celled
  ex•cel•ling
  ex•cel•lent
  ex•cel•lence
ex•cept
  ex•cep•tion
  ex•cep•tion•al
ex•cerpt
ex•cess
  ex•ces•sive
ex•change
  ex•changed
  ex•chang•ing
ex•cheq•uer
ex•cise
  ex•ci•sion
ex•cit•a•ble
  ex•cit•a•bil•i•ty
ex•cite
  ex•cit•ed
  ex•cit•ing
  ex•ci•ta•tion
  ex•cite•ment
ex•claim
  ex•cla•ma•tion
  ex•clam•a•to•ry
ex•clude
  ex•clud•ed
  ex•clud•ing
  ex•clu•sion
  ex•clu•sive
  ex•clu•siv•i•ty
ex•com•mu•ni•cate
  ex•com•mu•ni•ca•tion
ex•co•ri•ate
  ex•co•ri•a•tion
ex•cre•ment
ex•crete
  ex•cre•tion
ex•cru•ci•ate

ex•cru•ci•at•ing
ex•cul•pate
  ex•cul•pa•to•ry
ex•cur•sion
  ex•cur•sive
ex•cuse
  ex•cused
  ex•cus•ing
  ex•cus•a•ble
ex•e•cra•ble
  ex•e•cra•bly
ex•e•crate
  ex•e•crat•ed
  ex•e•crat•ing
  ex•e•cra•tion
ex•e•cute
  ex•e•cu•tion
  ex•e•cu•tion•er
ex•ec•u•tive
  ex•ec•u•tor
  ex•ec•u•trix
ex•e•ge•sis
ex•em•plar
  ex•em•pla•ry
ex•em•pli•fy
  ex•em•pli•fi•ca•tion
ex•empt
  ex•emp•tion
ex•er•cise
  ex•er•cised
  ex•er•cis•ing
ex•ert
  ex•er•tion
ex•fo•li•a•tion
ex•hale
  ex•haled
  ex•hal•ing
  ex•ha•la•tion
ex•haust
  ex•haust•ed
  ex•haust•ing
  ex•haus•tion
  ex•haus•tive
ex•hib•it
  ex•hib•i•tor
  ex•hi•bi•tion
  ex•hi•bi•tion•ism
  ex•hi•bi•tion•ist
ex•hil•a•rate
  ex•hil•a•rat•ed
  ex•hil•a•rat•ing
ex•hort
  ex•hor•ta•tion
ex•hume
  ex•hu•ma•tion
ex•i•gent
ex•ig•u•ous
ex•ile
  ex•iled
ex•ist
  ex•ist•ence
  ex•ist•ent
ex•is•ten•tial
  ex•is•ten•tial•ism
ex•o•dus
ex of•fi•cio
ex•on•er•ate
  ex•on•er•at•ed
  ex•on•er•at•ing
  ex•on•er•a•tion
ex•or•bi•tant
ex•or•cise
  ex•or•cism
  ex•or•cist
ex•o•tic
ex•pand
  ex•pand•able
ex•panse
  ex•pan•sion
  ex•pan•sive
ex•pa•tri•ate
ex•pect
  ex•pect•an•cy
  ex•pect•ant
  ex•pec•ta•tion
  ex•pec•to•rate
ex•pe•di•ent
  ex•pe•di•en•cy
ex•pe•dite
  ex•pe•di•tious
  ex•pe•di•tion
ex•pel
  ex•pelled

ex•pel•ling
ex•pend
  ex•pend•a•ble
  ex•pend•i•ture
ex•pense
  ex•pen•sive
ex•pe•ri•ence
  ex•pe•ri•enced
  ex•pe•ri•enc•ing
  ex•pe•ri•en•tial
ex•per•i•ment
  ex•per•i•men•tal
  ex•per•i•men•ta•tion
ex•pert
  ex•per•tise
ex•pi•ate
  ex•pi•a•tion
ex•pire
  ex•pired
  ex•pir•ing
  ex•pi•ra•tion
ex•plain
  ex•plain•a•ble
  ex•pla•na•tion
  ex•plan•a•to•ry
ex•ple•tive
ex•pli•cate
  ex•pli•ca•ble
  ex•pli•ca•tion
ex•plic•it
  ex•plic•it•ly
ex•plode
  ex•plod•ed
  ex•plod•ing
ex•plo•sion
  ex•plo•sive
ex•ploit
  ex•ploi•ta•tion
  ex•ploit•ive
ex•plore
  ex•plo•ra•tion
  ex•plor•a•to•ry
ex•po•nent
  ex•po•nen•tial
ex•port
  ex•port•er
ex•pose
  ex•posed
  ex•pos•ing
  ex•po•sure
  ex•po•si•tion
  ex•pos•tu•late
  ex•pos•tu•la•tion
  ex•po•sure
ex•pound
ex•press
  ex•pres•sion
  ex•pres•sive
  ex•pres•sion•ism
  ex•pres•sion•ist
ex•pro•pri•ate
  ex•pro•pri•at•ed
  ex•pro•pri•at•ing
  ex•pro•pri•a•tion
ex•pul•sion
ex•punge
ex•pur•gate
  ex•pur•ga•tion
ex•qui•site
ex•tant
ex•tem•po•re
  ex•tem•po•rize
  ex•tem•po•ra•ne•ous
ex•tend
  ex•tend•i•ble
  ex•ten•sion
  ex•ten•sive
ex•tent
ex•ten•u•ate
  ex•ten•u•at•ed
  ex•ten•u•at•ing
  ex•ten•u•a•tion
ex•te•ri•or
ex•ter•mi•nate
  ex•ter•mi•na•tion
ex•ter•nal
ex•tinct
  ex•tinc•tion
ex•tin•guish
  ex•tin•guish•er
ex•tir•pate
ex•tol
  ex•tolled

ex•tol•ling
ex•tort
ex•tor•tion
ex•tra
ex•tract
ex•trac•tion
ex•tra•cur•ric•u•lar
ex•tra•dite
ex•tra•dit•ed
ex•tra•dit•ing
ex•tra•di•tion
ex•tra•ne•ous
ex•traor•di•nary
ex•trap•o•late
ex•trap•o•la•tion
ex•tra•sen•so•ry
ex•tra•ter•res•tri•al
ex•trav•a•gant
ex•trav•a•gance
ex•trav•a•gan•za
ex•treme
ex•treme•ly
ex•trem•ist
ex•trem•i•ty
ex•trem•i•ties
ex•tri•cate
ex•tri•ca•tion
ex•trin•sic
ex•tro•vert
ex•tro•ver•sion
ex•trude
ex•tru•sion
ex•u•ber•ant
ex•u•ber•ance
ex•ude
ex•ud•ed
ex•ud•ing
ex•ult
ex•ult•ant
ex•ul•ta•tion
eye
eyed
eye•ing
eye•ball
eye•ful
eye•let
eye•wit•ness

F

fa•ble
fa•bled
fab•ric
fab•ri•cate
fab•ri•cat•ed
fab•ri•cat•ing
fab•ri•ca•tion
fab•u•lous
fa•cade
face
faced
fac•ing
fac•et
fa•ce•tious
fa•cial
fa•cial•ly
fac•ile
fa•cil•i•tate
fa•cil•i•tat•ed
fa•cil•i•ty
fa•cil•i•ties
fac•sim•i•le
fac•tion
fac•ti•tious
fac•tor
fac•to•ry
fac•to•ries
fac•to•tum
fac•tu•al
fac•ul•ty
fad•dist
fade
fad•ed
fad•ing
fag
fag•got
Fahr•en•heit
fail•ing
fail•ure
faint•ly
fair•ly
fair•ness
fairy

fair•ies
faith•ful
fake
faked
fak•ing
fak•er
fa•kir
fal•con
fall
fell
fall•en
fall•ing
fal•la•cious
fal•la•cy
fal•li•ble
fal•li•bil•i•ty
Fal•lo•pi•an
fal•low
false
false•ly
false•hood
fal•si•fy
fal•si•fied
fal•si•fy•ing
fal•si•fi•ca•tion
fal•si•ty
fal•ter
famed
fa•mil•ial
fa•mil•iar
fa•mil•iar•ar•i•ty
fa•mil•iar•ize
fa•mil•iar•i•za•tion
fam•i•ly
fam•i•lies
fa•mil•ial
fam•ine
fam•ished
fa•mous
fan
fanned
fan•ning
fa•nat•ic
fa•nat•i•cal
fa•nat•i•cal
fa•nat•i•icism
fan•ci•ful
fan•cy
fan•cies
fan•ci•er
fan•ci•est
fan•cied
fang
fan•ta•sia
fan•tas•tic
fan•ta•sy
fan•ta•sies
far
far•ther
far•thest
far•a•way
farce
far•ci•cal
fare
fared
far•ing
farm•er
farm•ing
far-reach•ing
far•see•ing
far•ther•most
fas•cia
fas•ci•cle
fas•ci•nate
fas•ci•nat•ed
fas•ci•nat•ing
fas•ci•na•tion
fas•cism
fas•cist
fash•ion•a•ble
fas•ten
fas•ten•er
fas•ten•ing
fas•tid•i•ous
fat
fat•ter
fat•test
fat•ten
fat•ty
fa•tal
fa•tal•ly
fa•tal•i•ty
fa•tal•i•ties

fa•tal•is•tic
fate
fat•ed
fate•ful
fa•ther
fa•ther-in-law
fath•om
fath•om•a•ble
fa•tigue
fa•tigued
fa•tig•uing
fat•u•ous
fau•cet
fault
faulty
fau•na
faux pas
fa•vor•a•ble
fa•vor•a•bly
fa•vor•ite
fa•vor•it•ism
fawn
faze
fazed
fe•al•ty
fear•ful
fear•some
fea•si•ble
fea•si•bil•i•ty
fea•si•bly
feath•er
feath•ered
fea•ture
fea•tured
fea•tur•ing
fe•brile
Feb•ru•ary
fe•ces
fe•cal
fe•cund
fed•er•al
fed•er•al•ism
fed•er•al•ist
fed•er•al•ly
fee•ble
fee•bler
fee•bly
feed
fed
feel
felt
feel•ing
feel•er
feign
feigned
feint
feisty
fe•lic•i•ta•tion
fe•lic•i•tous
fe•lic•i•ty
fe•line
fel•low•ship
fel•on
fel•o•ny
fe•male
fem•i•nine
fem•i•nin•i•ty
fem•i•nism
fem•i•nist
fe•mur
fence
fenced
fenc•ing
fenc•er
fen•der
fe•ral
fer•ment
fer•men•ta•tion
fe•ro•cious
fe•ro•ci•ty
fer•ret
fer•ry
fer•ries
fer•tile
fer•til•i•ty
fer•ti•lize
fer•ti•liz•er
fer•ti•li•za•tion
fer•vent
fer•vid
fer•vor
fes•ter
fes•ti•val

fes•tive
fes•tiv•i•ty
fe•tal
fetch
fete
fet•id
fet•ish
fet•ter
fet•tle
fe•tus
fe•tal
feud
feu•dal
feu•dal•ism
fe•ver
fi•an•cé
fi•an•cée
fi•as•co
fi•at
fib
fibbed
fib•ber
fi•ber
fi•brous
fib•u•la
fick•le
fic•tion
fic•ti•tious
fid•dle
fid•dler
fid•dled
fid•dling
fi•del•i•ty
fidg•et
fidg•ety
fi•du•ci•ary
fief
field•er
fiend
fierce
fiery
fif•teen
fif•ty
fif•ti•eth
fight
fought
fig•ment
fig•u•ra•tive
fig•ure
fig•ured
fig•ur•ing
fig•ur•ine
fil•a•ment
file
filed
fil•ing
fi•let mi•gnon
fil•i•al
fil•i•bus•ter
fil•i•gree
Fil•i•pi•no
fill•er
fil•let
fill•ing
fil•lip
fil•ly
fil•lies
filmy
fil•ter
fil•tra•tion
filth
filthy
fin
fi•na•gle
fi•na•gled
fi•na•gling
fi•na•gler
fi•nal
fi•nal•ly
fi•na•le
fi•nal•ist
fi•nal•i•ty
fi•nal•ize
fi•nal•ized
fi•nal•iz•ing
fi•nance
fi•nanced
fi•nanc•ing
fi•nan•cial
fi•nan•cial•ly
fin•an•cier
finch
find

found
fine
fin•er
fin•est
fin•ery
fi•nesse
fi•nessed
fi•nes•sing
fin•ger
fin•ger•print
fin•icky
fin•is
fin•ish
fin•ished
fi•nite
Fin•land
Finn•ish
fire
fired
fir•ing
fire•arm
fire•crack•er
fire•fight•er
fire•fly
fire•man
fire•place
fire•pow•er
fire•proof
fire•trap
firm•ly
fir•ma•ment
first•born
first•hand
first-rate
first-string
fis•cal
fis•cal•ly
fish•ery
fish•er•ies
fishy
fis•sion
fis•sure
fit
fit•ter
fit•test
fit•ted
fit•ting
fit•ful
five•fold
fix
fixed
fix•ed•ly
fix•a•tion
fix•a•tive
fix•ings
fix•ture
fiz•zle
fiz•zled
fiz•zling
fjord
flab•ber•gast
flab•by
flac•cid
flag
flagged
flag•ging
flag•el•lant
flag•el•la•tion
fla•grant
flail
flair
flake
flaked
flak•ing
flaky
flam•boy•ant
flam•boy•ance
flame
flamed
flam•ing
flam•ma•ble
fla•men•co
fla•min•go
flange
flank
flan•nel
flap
flapped
flap•ping
flare
flared
flar•ing
flare-up

flash•back
flash•light
flashy
flask
flat•ly
  flat•ten
flat•foot•ed
flat•ter
  flat•ter•er
  flat•tery
flat•u•lent
  flat•u•lence
fla•tus
flat•ware
flaunt
  flaunt•ed
fla•vor
  fla•vored
  fla•vor•ing
flawed
flax•en
flea•bit•ten
flec•tion
fledg•ling
flee
  fled
  flee•ing
fleece
  fleeced
  fleec•ing
fleet
fleet•ing
fleshy
flex•i•ble
  flex•i•bly
flex•ion
flex•or
flick•er
fli•er
flight
flighty
flim•sy
flinch
fling
  flung
flinty
flip
  flipped
  flip•ping
flip•flop
flip•pant
  flip•pan•cy
flip•per
flir•ta•tion
  flir•ta•tious
flit
  flit•ted
  flit•ting
float•er
  float•ing
flocked
floe
flog
  flogged
  flog•ging
flood•light
floor•ing
floo•zy
flop
  flopped
  flop•ping
  flop•py
flo•ra
  flo•rae
flo•ral
flo•res•cence
  flo•res•cent
flor•id
flo•rist
floss
flo•til•la
flot•sam
flounce
  flounced
  flounc•ing
floun•der
floury
flour•ish
flout•er
flow
flow•er
  flow•ered
flub

flubbed
flub•bing
fluc•tu•ate
  fluc•tu•at•ed
  fluc•tu•at•ing
  fluc•tu•a•tion
flue
flu•ent
  flu•en•cy
fluff
flu•id
  flu•id•i•ty
fluke
flun•ky
flu•o•res•cence
  flu•o•res•cent
flu•o•ride
flur•ry
flus•ter
flute
  flut•ed
  flut•ing
  flut•ist
flut•ter
flux
fly
  flew
  flown
  fly•ing
fly•er
  fli•er
fly•leaf
fly•pa•per
fly•wheel
foal
foam
fo•cal
fo•cus
  fo•cus•es
  fo•cused
  fo•cus•ing
fod•der
fog
  fog•gy
fo•gy
  fo•gies
foi•ble
fold•er
fol•de•rol
fo•li•age
fo•lio
folk•lore
folk•sy
fol•li•cle
fol•low
  fol•low•er
  fol•low•ing
fol•ly
  fol•lies
fo•ment
fon•dant
fon•dle
  fon•dled
  fon•dling
fond•ly
  fond•ness
food•stuff
fool•ery
fool•har•dy
fool•ish
fool•proof
foot•age
foot•ball
foot•hold
foot•lights
foot•note
foot•path
foot•print
foot•step
fop
  fop•pery
  fop•pish
for•age
  for•aged
  for•ag•ing
for•ay
for•bear
  for•bore
  for•bear•ance
for•bid
  for•bade
  for•bid•den
  for•bid•ding

force
  forced
  forc•ing
force•ful
for•ci•ble
  for•ci•bly
fore•bode
  fore•bod•ing
fore•cast
  fore•cast•ed
  fore•cast•ing
  fore•cast•er
fore•close
  fore•clo•sure
fore•fa•ther
fore•fin•ger
fore•go
fore•ground
fore•hand
for•eign
  for•eign•er
fore•man
fore•most
fore•name
fore•noon
fo•ren•sic
fore•run•ner
fore•see
  fore•see•a•ble
fore•short•en
fore•sight
fore•skin
for•est
  for•est•ry
fore•stall
fore•tell
fore•thought
for•ev•er
  for•ev•er•more
fore•warn
fore•word
for•feit
  for•fei•ture
forge
  forged
  forg•ing
forg•er
  for•gery
  for•ger•ies
for•get
  for•got
  for•got•ten
  for•get•ting
  for•get•ta•ble
  for•get•ful
for•give
  for•giv•a•ble
  for•give•ness
for•go
forked
fork•lift
for•lorn
for•mal
  for•mal•ly
  for•mal•i•ty
  for•mal•i•ties
for•mal•ize
  for•mal•ized
  for•mal•iz•ing
for•mat
for•ma•tion
form•a•tive
for•mer
  for•mer•ly
for•mi•da•ble
  for•mi•da•bly
form•less
for•mu•la
  for•mu•las
for•mu•late
  for•mu•lat•ed
  for•mu•lat•ing
  for•mu•la•tion
for•ni•cate
  for•ni•cat•ed
  for•ni•cat•ing
  for•ni•ca•tion
for•sake
  for•sook
  for•sak•en
  for•sak•ing
  for•sak•en

for•swear
  for•swore
  for•sworn
fort
  for•ti•fi•cation
for•ti•fy
  for•ti•fied
  for•ti•fy•ing
forte
for•te
forth•com•ing
forth•right
forth•with
for•ti•tude
fort•night
for•tress
for•tu•i•tous
  for•tu•i•tous•ness
for•tu•nate
  for•tu•nate•ly
for•tune
for•ty
  for•ties
fo•rum
for•ward
fos•sil
  fos•sil•ized
fos•ter
  fos•tered
  fos•ter•ing
fought
fou•lard
found
foun•da•tion
found•er
found•ling
found•ry
  found•ries
foun•tain
four•fold
four•post•er
four•score
four•some
four•teen
fourth
  fourth•ly
foxy
foy•er
fra•cas
frac•tion
  frac•tion•al
frac•tious
frac•ture
  frac•tured
frag•ile
  fra•gil•i•ty
frag•ment
  frag•men•tal
  frag•men•tary
fra•grance
  fra•grant
frail
  frail•ty
frame
  framed
  fram•ing
frame•work
franc
France
fran•chise
Fran•cis•can
frank
  frank•ly
frank•furt•er
fran•tic
  fran•ti•cal•ly
fra•ter•nal
fra•ter•ni•ty
  fra•ter•ni•ties
frat•er•nize
  frat•er•nized
  frat•er•niz•ing
frat•ri•cide
fraud•u•lent
  fraud•u•lent
  fraud•u•lence
fraught
fraz•zle
  fraz•zled
freak
freck•le
  freck•led
  freck•ling

free
  fre•er
  fre•est
  free•ly
free•dom
free•lance
free•stand•ing
free•think•er
freeze
  froze
  fro•zen
  freez•ing
freeze•dry
freez•er
freight
freight•er
fre•net•ic
fren•zy
  fren•zies
  fren•zied
fre•quen•cy
  fre•quen•cies
fre•quent
  fre•quent•ly
fres•co
  fres•coes
fresh
  fresh•en
  fresh•ness
fresh•man
fret
  fret•ted
  fret•ting
  fret•ful
Freud•i•an
fri•a•ble
fri•ar
fric•as•see
fric•tion
friend
  friend•ship
friend•ly
  friend•li•est
  friend•li•ness
frieze
fright•en
  fright•en•ing
  fright•ful
frig•id
  fri•gid•i•ty
frilly
fringe
frisky
frit•ter
friv•o•lous
  fri•vol•i•ty
frizz
  friz•zy
friz•zle
frog
frol•ic
  frol•icked
  frol•ick•ing
front•age
fron•tal
fron•tier
fron•tis•piece
frost
  frost•ed
frost•bite
  frost•bit•ten
frost•ing
frosty
  frost•i•ly
froth
  frothy
fro•ward
frown
fro•zen
fruc•ti•fy
fruc•tose
fru•gal
  fru•gal•i•ty
  fru•gal•ly
fruit•ful
fru•i•tion
fruit•less
frump
frus•trate
  frus•trat•ed
  frus•trat•ing
  frus•tra•tion
fry

fried
fry•ing
fuch•sia
fud•dy-dud•dy
fudge
  fudged
  fudg•ing
fu•el
  fu•eled
  fu•el•ing
fu•gi•tive
fugue
ful•crum
ful•fill
  ful•filled
  ful•fil•ling
  ful•fill•ment
full
  full•ness
  ful•ly
full-fledged
ful•mi•nate
  ful•mi•na•tion
ful•some
fum•ble
  fum•bled
  fum•bling
  fum•bler
fume
  fumed
  fum•ing
fu•mi•gate
  fu•mi•ga•tion
func•tion
  func•tion•al
  func•tion•ary
fun•da•men•tal
  fun•da•men•tal•ly
  fun•da•men•tal•ism
  fun•da•men•tal•ist
fu•ner•al
  fu•ne•re•al
fun•gi•cide
fun•gus
  fun•gi
fu•nic•u•lar
fun•nel
fun•ny
  fun•ni•er
  fun•ni•est
  fun•nies
fur
  fur•ry
  fur•ri•er
fur•bish
fu•ri•ous
fur•long
fur•lough
fur•nace
fur•nish
  fur•nish•ings
fur•ni•ture
fu•ror
fur•row
fur•ther
  fur•thest
fur•ther•ance
fur•ther•more
fur•ther•most
fur•tive
  fur•tive•ly
fu•ry
  fu•ries
fuse
  fused
  fus•ing
fu•se•lage
fu•sil•lade
fu•sion
fussy
fus•tian
fu•tile
  fu•til•i•ty
fu•ture
  fu•tur•is•tic
fuzzy

G

gab
  gabbed
  gab•bing
gab•ar•dine

ga•ble
gad•ded
  gad•ding
gad•fly
gad•get
  gad•get•ry
gag
  gagged
  gag•ging
gai•e•ty
  gai•ly
gain•ful
gain•say
gait
ga•la
gal•axy
  gal•ax•ies
  ga•lac•tic
gal•lant
  gal•lant•ry
gall•blad•der
gal•lery
  gal•ler•ies
gal•ley
gall•ing
gal•li•vant
gal•lon
gal•lop
gal•lows
gall•stone
ga•lore
ga•losh•es
gal•va•nize
  gal•va•nized
  gal•va•niz•ing
gam•bit
gam•ble
  gam•bled
  gam•bling
  gam•bler
gam•bol
game
  gam•ing
gam•in
gam•ma
gam•ut
gamy
gan•der
gang•land
gan•gling
  gan•gly
gan•grene
  gan•gre•nous
gang•ster
gant•let
gaol
gap
  gapped
  gap•ping
ga•rage
  ga•raged
gar•bage
gar•ble
  gar•bled
  gar•bling
gar•den
gar•gan•tu•an
gar•gle
  gar•gled
  gar•gling
gar•goyle
gar•ish
gar•land
gar•ment
gar•ner
gar•net
gar•nish
gar•ret
gar•ri•son
gar•rote
  gar•rot•ed
  gar•rot•ing
gar•ru•lous
gar•ter
gas
  gassed
  gas•sing
  gas•e•ous
gas•ket
gas•light
gas•o•line
gas•sy
gas•tric

gas•tri•tis
gas•tro•in•tes•ti•nal
gath•er
  gath•er•ing
gauche
  gau•che•rie
gaudy
gauge
  gauged
  gaug•ing
gaunt
  gaunt•let
gauze
gav•el
gawky
gaze
  gazed
  gaz•ing
ga•ze•bo
ga•zelle
ga•zette
gear•shift
Gei•ger count•er
gei•sha
gel
  gelled
  gel•ling
gel•a•tin
geld•ing
gem
Gem•i•ni
gen•der
gene
ge•ne•al•o•gy
  ge•ne•a•log•i•cal
gen•er•al
  gen•er•al•i•ty
gen•er•al•ize
  gen•er•al•i•za•tion
gen•er•ate
  gen•er•at•ed
  gen•er•at•ing
  gen•er•a•tive
  gen•er•a•tor
  gen•er•a•tion
ge•ner•ic
gen•er•ous
  gen•er•os•i•ty
gen•e•sis
ge•net•ic
  ge•net•i•cal•ly
  ge•net•ics
  ge•net•i•cist
gen•ial
  ge•ni•al•i•ty
gen•i•tal
  gen•i•ta•lia
  gen•i•tals
gen•i•tive
gen•ius
gen•o•cide
  gen•o•ci•dal
gen•re
gen•teel
gen•tile
gen•til•i•ty
gen•tle
  gen•tlest
  gen•tly
gen•tle•man
gen•try
gen•u•flect
  gen•u•flec•tion
gen•u•ine
ge•nus
ge•o•cen•tric
ge•o•gra•phy
  ge•o•gra•pher
  ge•o•gra•phic
  ge•o•graph•i•cal
ge•ol•o•gy
  ge•o•log•ic
  ge•o•log•i•cal
  ge•ol•o•gist
ge•o•met•ric
ge•om•e•try
ge•o•phys•ics
  ge•o•phys•i•cal
ge•o•pol•i•tics
  ge•o•po•lit•i•cal
ge•ra•ni•um
ger•bil
ger•i•at•rics

ger•i•at•ric
ger•mane
Ger•ma•ny
ger•mi•cide
  ger•mi•cid•al
ger•mi•nate
  ger•mi•nat•ed
  ger•mi•nat•ing
  ger•mi•na•tion
ger•on•tol•o•gy
  ger•on•tol•o•gist
ger•ry•man•der
ger•und
ges•tate
  ges•tat•ed
  ges•tat•ing
  ges•ta•tion
ges•tic•u•late
  ges•tic•u•lat•ed
  ges•tic•u•lat•ing
  ges•tic•u•la•tion
ges•ture
  ges•tured
  ges•tur•ing
Geth•sem•a•ne
gew•gaw
gey•ser
ghast•ly
gher•kin
ghet•to
ghost•ly
ghost•write
ghoul
gi•ant
gib•ber•ish
gibe
gib•let
gid•dy
gift•ed
gi•gan•tic
gig•gle
  gig•gled
  gig•gling
gig•o•lo
gild•ed
gilt-edged
gim•let
gim•mick
  gim•mick•y
gin•ger•bread
gin•ger•ly
ging•ham
gip•sy
  gip•sies
gi•raffe
gird•er
gir•dle
girl•friend
girth
gist
give
  gave
  giv•en
  giv•ing
giz•zard
gla•cial
gla•cier
glad
  glad•der
  glad•dest
  glad•den
glad•i•a•tor
  glad•i•a•to•ri•al
glad•i•o•lus
glam•or•ize
glam•or•ous
glam•our
glance
  glanced
  glanc•ing
glan•du•lar
glare
  glared
  glar•ing
glass•ware
glassy
glau•co•ma
glaze
  glazed
  glaz•ing
gleam
glean
glee

glee•ful
glib
  glib•ly
glide
  glid•ed
  glid•ing
glim•mer
glimpse
glis•ten
glit•tery
gloat
glob•al
  glob•al•ly
glob•u•lar
glob•ule
gloomy
glo•ri•fy
glo•ri•ous
glo•ry
  glo•ry•ing
glos•sa•ry
glossy
glot•tis
glove
glow
  glow•er
glu•cose
glue
  glued
  glu•ing
glum
glut
  glut•ted
glu•ten
  glu•ten•ous
glu•ti•nous
glut•ton
  glut•tony
glyc•er•in
  glyc•er•ine
gnarl
  gnarled
gnash
gnat
gnaw
  gnawed
  gnaw•ing
gnome
go
  went
  gone
  go•ing
goad•ed
goal•ie
goat•ee
goat•skin
gob•ble
  gob•bled
  gob•bling
  gob•bler
gob•let
gob•lin
god•child
god•dess
god•fa•ther
god•head
god•less
god•ly
  god•li•ness
god•moth•er
gog•gle
go•ing
goi•ter
gold•en•rod
go•nad
gon•do•la
gon•or•rhea
good
  better
  best
good-by
good-bye
good-look•ing
good-na•tured
good•ness
goofy
goose•ber•ry
go•pher
gore
gorge
  gorged
  gorg•ing
gor•geous

gory
gos•ling
gos•pel
gos•sa•mer
gos•sip
  gos•sip•ing
  gos•sipy
Goth•ic
gouge
  gouged
  goug•ing
gou•lash
gourd
gour•mand
gour•met
gout
gov•ern
gov•ern•ess
gov•ern•ment
  gov•ern•men•tal
gov•er•nor
grab
  grabbed
  grab•bing
grace
  graced
  grac•ing
grace•ful
  grace•ful•ly
gra•cious
gra•da•tion
grade
  grad•ed
  grad•ing
gra•di•ent
grad•u•al
  grad•u•al•ly
grad•u•ate
  grad•u•at•ed
  grad•u•at•ing
  grad•u•a•tion
graf•fi•ti
graft
gra•ham
grain
gram
gram•mar
gram•mat•i•cal
gra•na•ry
grand
gran•deur
gran•dil•o•quence
gran•di•ose
grange
gran•ite
gran•ny
gran•u•lar
gran•ule
grape•fruit
graph•ic
graph•ite
grap•ple
  grap•pled
  grap•pling
grasp•ing
grassy
grass•hop•per
grate
  grat•ing
grate•ful
grat•i•fy
  grat•i•fied
  grat•i•fy•ing
  grat•i•fi•ca•tion
gra•tis
grat•i•tude
gra•tu•i•tous
gra•tu•i•ty
  gra•tu•i•ties
grave
  grave•ly
grav•el
grav•i•tate
  grav•i•tat•ed
  grav•i•tat•ing
  grav•i•ta•tion
grav•i•ty
gra•vy
gray•ness
graze
  grazed
  graz•ing
grease

greasy
great•ness
Great Brit•ain
Gre•cian
  Greece
greedy
  greed•i•ly
green•ing
greet•ing
gre•gar•i•ous
gre•nade
gren•a•dine
grey•ness
grid•dle
grid•i•ron
grief
griev•ance
grieve
  grieved
  griev•ing
  griev•ous
grill
grille
grim
grim•ace
  grim•aced
  grim•ac•ing
grime
grimy
grin
  grinned
  grin•ning
grind
  ground
grip
  gripped
  grip•ping
gripe
  griped
  grip•ing
grippe
gris•ly
gris•tle
  gris•tly
grit
  grit•ted
  grit•ting
grit•ty
griz•zled
griz•zly
groan
gro•cer
  gro•cery
  gro•cer•ies
grog•gy
groin
groom
groove
grope
  groped
  grop•ing
gros•grain
gross
gro•tesque
grot•to
grouch
  grouchy
ground•less
ground•work
group
  group•ing
grouse
  groused
  grous•ing
grov•el
  grov•eled
  grov•el•ing
grow
  grew
  grown
growl
grown-up
growth
grub
  grubbed
  grub•bing
grub•by
grudge
  grudged
  grudg•ing
gru•el•ing
grue•some
gruff

grum•ble
  grum•bled
  grum•bling
grumpy
  grump•i•ly
grunt
  grunt•ed
  grunt•ing
guar•an•tee
  guar•an•teed
  guar•an•tee•ing
guar•an•tor
guar•an•ty
  guar•an•tied
  guar•an•ty•ing
guard•ed
guard•i•an
gua•va
gu•ber•na•to•ri•al
guer•ril•la
guess
  guess•ing
guess•work
guest
guf•faw
guid•ance
guide
  guid•ed
  guid•ing
guild
guile
guil•lo•tine
guilt
  guilty
  guilt•i•ly
guin•ea
guise
gui•tar
gul•let
gul•li•ble
gul•ly
gum
  gummed
  gum•my
gum•bo
gump•tion
gun
  gunned
  gun•ning
  gun•ner
gun•ny
gup•py
  gup•pies
gur•gle
  gur•gled
  gur•gling
gu•ru
gush•ing
  gushy
gus•to
gusty
gut
  gut•ted
  gut•ting
gut•ter
gut•tur•al
guz•zle
  guz•zled
  guz•zling
gym•na•si•um
gym•nast
  gym•nas•tic
gy•ne•col•o•gy
  gy•ne•co•log•i•cal
  gy•ne•col•o•gist
gyp
  gypped
  gyp•ping
gyp•sum
gyp•sy
  gyp•sies
gy•rate
  gy•rat•ed
  gy•rat•ing
  gy•ra•tion

H

ha•be•as• cor•pus
hab•it
hab•it•a•ble
hab•i•tat
hab•i•ta•tion

ha•bit•u•al
  ha•bit•u•al•ly
  ha•bit•u•ate
  ha•bit•u•at•ed
hack•neyed
hack•saw
had•dock
Ha•des
had•n't
hag•gard
hag•gis
hag•gle
  hag•gled
  hag•gling
hail•storm
hair•breadth
hair•dress•er
hair-rais•ing
hairy
hale
  haled
  hal•ing
half
  halves
half-wit•ted
hal•i•but
hal•i•to•sis
hal•le•lu•jah
hall•mark
hal•lo
hal•low
  hal•lowed
Hal•low•een
hal•lu•ci•nate
  hal•lu•ci•nat•ed
  hal•lu•ci•nat•ing
  hal•lu•ci•na•tion
ha•lo
halt
  halt•ing
hal•ter
halve
  halved
  halv•ing
  halves
ham•burg•er
ham•let
ham•mer
ham•mock
ham•per
ham•ster
ham•string
  ham•strung
hand•i•cap
  hand•i•capped
hand•i•craft
hand•i•ly
hand•i•work
hand•ker•chief
han•dle
  han•dled
  han•dling
hand•made
hand-picked
hand•some
hand•writ•ing
handy
hand•y•man
hang
  hung
  hanged
hang•ar
hang•er
hang•o•ver
hank•er
Ha•nuk•kah
hap•haz•ard
hap•less
hap•pen
  hap•pen•ing
  hap•pen•stance
hap•py
  hap•pi•ly
  hap•pi•ness
ha•rangue
  ha•rangued
  ha•rang•uing
har•ass
  har•ass•ment
har•bin•ger
har•bor
hard•en
  hard•en•er

hard•ware
har•dy
hare•brained
hare•lip
har•em
har•ken
har•le•quin
har•lot
harm•ful
harm•less
har•mon•i•ca
har•mo•nize
har•mo•ny
  har•mon•ic
  har•mo•ni•ous
har•ness
harp•ist
har•poon
harp•si•chord
har•ri•dan
har•row
har•ried
harsh•ly
har•vest
has•n't
has•sle
  has•sled
  has•sling
has•sock
haste
has•ten
hast•y
  hast•i•ly
hatch•ery
hatch•et
hate
  hat•ed
  hat•ing
hate•ful
ha•tred
haugh•ty
  haugh•ti•ly
haul
haunch
haunt•ing
hau•teur
have
  have•n't
  hav•ing
ha•ven
hav•er•sack
hav•oc
Ha•waii
hawk
haw•ser
haz•ard
  haz•ard•ous
haze
ha•zy
ha•zel•nut
head•ache
head•dress
head•ing
head•quar•ters
heady
heal•er
healthy
heaped
hear
  heard
  hear•ing
heark•en
hear•say
hearse
heart•ache
heart•en
heart•less•ly
heart•rend•ing
hearty
  heart•i•ly
heat•ed
heat•er
heath
hea•then
heath•er
heave
  heaved
  heav•ing
heav•en
  heav•en•ly
heavy
  heav•i•ness
heav•y-hand•ed

heav•y-heart•ed
heav•y•weight
He•brew
  He•bra•ic
heck•le
  heck•led
  heck•ling
  heck•ler
hec•tic
hedge
  hedged
  hedg•ing
he•don•ism
  he•don•ist
  he•do•nis•tic
heed•less
hefty
he•gem•o•ny
heif•er
height•en
hei•nous
heir•ess
heir•loom
heist
hel•i•cop•ter
he•li•um
he•lix
he•li•cal
hell•ish
hel•lo
helm
hel•met
help•ful
help•less•ness
hem
  hemmed
  hem•ming
he•ma•tol•o•gy
hem•i•sphere
hem•lock
he•mo•glo•bin
he•mo•phil•ia
hem•or•rhage
  hem•or•rhag•ing
hem•or•rhoid
hence•forth
hench•man
hen•na
hep•a•ti•tis
her•ald
he•ral•dic
  her•ald•ry
herb
her•cu•le•an
he•red•i•ty
  he•red•i•tary
her•e•sy
  her•e•sies
her•e•tic
  he•ret•i•cal
her•it•a•ble
her•it•age
her•maph•ro•dite
her•met•ic
  her•met•i•cal•ly
her•mit
her•nia
he•ro
  he•roes
  her•o•ine
  her•o•ism
he•ro•ic
  he•ro•i•cal•ly
her•o•in
her•on
her•pes
her•ring•bone
her•self
hes•i•tant
  hes•i•tan•cy
  hes•i•tance
hes•i•tate
  hes•i•tat•ed
  hes•i•tat•ing
  hes•i•ta•tion
het•er•o•doxy
het•er•o•ge•ne•ous
  het•er•o•ge•ne•i•ty
het•er•o•sex•u•al
hewn
hex•a•gon
  hex•ag•o•nal
hi•a•tus

hi•ba•chi
hi•ber•nate
  hi•ber•na•tion
hi•bis•cus
hic•cup
  hic•cuped
  hic•cup•ing
hick•o•ry
hide
  hid
  hid•den
  hid•ing
hid•e•ous
hi•er•ar•chy
  hi•er•ar•chal
  hi•er•ar•chic
hi•er•o•glyph•ic
high-grade
high-mind•ed
high-pres•sure
high•way
hi•jack
  hi•jack•er
  hi•jack•ing
hike
  hiked
  hik•ing
hi•lar•i•ous
  hi•lar•i•ty
hill•bil•ly
  hill•bil•lies
hill•ock
hilly
him•self
hin•der
hin•drance
hind•sight
Hin•du•ism
hinge
  hinged
  hing•ing
hin•ter•land
Hip•poc•ra•tes
  Hip•po•crat•ic
hip•po•dróme
hip•po•pot•a•mus
hire•ling
His•pan•ic
his•ta•mine
his•to•ri•an
his•tor•ic
  his•tor•i•cal
his•to•ry
his•tri•on•ic
hit•ter
  hit•ting
hitch•hik•er
hith•er•to
hoard
hoar•frost
hoarse
  hoarse•ly
hoary
hoax
hob•ble
  hob•bled
  hob•bling
hob•by
  hob•bies
hob•gob•lin
hob•nail
hob•nob
  hob•nobbed
  hob•nob•bing
ho•bo
  ho•boes
hock•ey
hodge•podge
hoe
  hoed
  hoe•ing
hog
  hogged
  hog•ging
hoi•po•loi
hoist•ing
ho•kum
hold
  held
  hold•ing
hole
hol•i•day
ho•li•ness

Hol•land
hol•low
hol•ly
hol•o•caust
hol•ster
ho•ly
  ho•li•er
  ho•li•est
  ho•li•ness
hom•age
home•com•ing
home•ly
ho•me•op•a•thy
homey
hom•i•cide
  ho•mi•cid•al
hom•i•ly
hom•i•ny
ho•mo•ge•ne•ous
  ho•mo•ge•ne•i•ty
ho•mog•e•nize
  ho•mog•e•nized
  ho•mog•e•niz•ing
hom•o•nym
Ho•mo sa•pi•ens
ho•mo•sex•u•al
hone
  honed
  hon•ing
hon•est
  hon•est•ly
  hon•es•ty
hon•ey
hon•or
  hon•or•a•ble
  hon•or•a•bly
  hon•or•ar•i•um
  hon•or•ary
  hon•or•if•ic
hood•ed
hood•lum
hoof
  hoofs
  hooves
hooked
hook•er
hoo•li•gan
hoop
hop
  hopped
  hop•ping
hope
  hoped
  hop•ing
  hope•ful
  hope•less
horde
ho•ri•zon
  hor•i•zon•tal
  hor•i•zon•tal•ly
hor•mone
horned
hor•net
horn•swog•gle
hor•o•scope
hor•ren•dous
hor•ri•ble
  hor•ri•bly
hor•rid
hor•ror
  hor•ri•fy
  hor•ri•fied
  hor•ri•fy•ing
hors d'oeuvre
horse
  hors•es
horse•back
horse•play
horse•pow•er
horse•rad•ish
horse•whipped
hor•ta•to•ry
hor•ti•cul•ture
ho•san•na
hose
ho•siery
hos•pice
hos•pi•ta•ble
  hos•pi•ta•bly
hos•pi•tal
  hos•pi•tal•i•za•tion
  hos•pi•tal•ize
  hos•pi•tal•i•ty

hos•tage
hos•tel
  hos•tel•ry
host•ess
hos•tile
hos•til•i•ty
  hos•til•i•ties
hot
  hot•ter
  hot•test
  hot•ly
ho•tel
hound
hour•ly
house
  hous•es
  housed
  hous•ing
house•wife
  house•wives
hov•el
hov•er
how•ev•er
how•itz•er
howl•er
hub•bub
huck•le•ber•ry
huck•ster
hud•dle
  hud•dled
  hud•dling
huffy
hug
  hugged
  hug•ging
huge
hulk•ing
hum
  hummed
  hum•ming
hu•man
  hu•mane
  hu•man•ism
  hu•man•i•tar•i•an
  hu•man•i•ty
  hu•man•ize
hum•ble
  hum•bled
  hum•bling
  hum•bly
hum•bug
hum•drum
hu•mid
  hu•midi•fy
  hu•mid•i•fi•er
  hu•mid•i•ty
hu•mi•dor
hu•mil•i•ate
  hu•mil•i•at•ed
  hu•mil•i•at•ing
  hu•mil•i•a•tion
hu•mil•i•ty
hum•ming•bird
hu•mor
  hu•mor•ist
  hu•mor•ous
humped
hu•mus
hun•dred
hun•ger
  hun•gry
  hun•gri•ly
hunt•er
hur•dle
hur•rah
hur•ri•cane
hur•ry
  hur•ried
  hur•ry•ing
hurt•ful
hur•tle
hus•band
hus•band•ry
husky
hus•sy
hus•tle
  hus•tled
  hus•tling
  hus•tler
hutch
hy•a•cinth
hy•brid
hy•dran•gea

hy•drant
hy•drate
  hy•dra•tion
hy•drau•lic
hy•dro•chlo•ric ac•id
hy•dro•e•lec•tric
hy•dro•gen
hy•drol•y•sis
hy•drox•ide
hy•e•na
hy•giene
  hy•gi•en•ic
hy•men
hymn
  hym•nal
hy•per•bo•le
  hy•per•bol•ic
hy•per•sen•si•tive
hy•per•ten•sion
hy•phen
  hy•phen•ate
hyp•no•sis
  hyp•not•ic
  hyp•no•tism
  hyp•no•tist
  hyp•no•tize
  hyp•no•tized
  hyp•no•tiz•ing
hy•po•chon•dria
  hy•po•chon•dri•ac
hy•poc•ri•sy
  hyp•o•crite
hy•po•der•mic
hy•po•gly•ce•mia
hy•pot•e•nuse
hy•poth•e•sis
  hy•poth•e•ses
  hy•poth•e•size
hy•po•thet•i•cal
hys•ter•ec•to•my
hys•te•ria
  hys•ter•ic
  hys•ter•i•cal

I

iam•bic
ibid
ibi•dem
ice
  iced
  ici-ly
  ic•ing
  icy
ice cream
ice-skate
  ice-skat•ing
ici•cle
icon
icon•o•clast
  icon•o•clas•tic
idea
ide•al
  ide•al•ly
  ide•al•ism
  ide•al•ist
  ide•al•is•tic
  ide•al•ize
  ide•al•ized
  ide•al•iz•ing
  ide•al•i•za•tion
iden•ti•cal
  iden•ti•cal•ly
  iden•ti•fi•a•ble
  iden•ti•fi•a•bly
  iden•ti•fy
  iden•ti•fied
  iden•ti•fy•ing
  iden•ti•fi•ca•tion
iden•ti•ty
  iden•ti•ties
ide•ol•o•gy
  ide•ol•o•gies
  ide•ol•o•gist
ides
id•i•o•cy
id•i•om
  id•i•o•mat•ic
  id•i•o•mat•i•cal•ly
id•i•o•syn•cra•sy
  id•i•o•syn•cra•sies
  id•i•o•syn•crat•ic
id•i•ot

id•i•ot•ic
id•i•ot•i•cal•ly
idle
  idler
  idlest
  idled
  idling
  idly
idol
  idol•a•try
  idol•a•trous
  idol•ize
idyll
  idyl•lic
  idyl•lic•al•ly
ig•loo
ig•nite
  ig•nit•ed
  ig•nit•ing
  ig•nit•er
  ig•ni•tion
ig•no•ble
  ig•no•miny
  ig•no•min•i•ous
ig•no•ra•mus
ig•no•rant
  ig•no•rance
ig•nore
  ig•nored
  ig•nor•ing
i•gua•na
ill-ad•vised
ill-bred
il•le•gal
  il•le•gal•ly
il•leg•i•ble
  il•leg•i•bly
il•le•git•i•mate
  il•le•git•i•ma•cy
ill-fat•ed
ill-got•ten
il•lib•er•al
il•lic•it
il•lit•er•ate
  il•lit•er•a•cy
ill•ness
il•log•i•cal
ill-tem•pered
il•lu•mi•nate
  il•lu•mi•nat•ing
  il•lu•mi•na•tion
il•lu•mine
  il•lu•mined
  il•lu•min•ing
il•lu•sion
il•lu•sive
  il•lu•so•ry
il•lus•trate
  il•lus•trat•ed
  il•lus•trat•ing
il•lus•tra•tion
  il•lus•tra•tive
  il•lus•tra•tor
il•lus•tri•ous
im•age
  im•aged
  im•ag•ing
im•age•ry
im•ag•ine
  im•ag•ined
  im•ag•in•ing
  im•ag•i•nary
  im•ag•i•na•tion
  im•ag•i•na•tive
im•bal•ance
im•be•cile
  im•be•cil•i•ty
im•bed•ded
im•bibe
  im•bibed
  im•bib•ing
im•bro•glio
im•bue
  im•bued
im•i•tate
  im•i•tat•ed
  im•i•tat•ing
  im•i•ta•tor
  im•i•ta•tion
  im•i•ta•tive
im•mac•u•late
im•ma•nent
  im•ma•nence

im•ma•nen•cy
im•ma•te•ri•al
im•ma•ture
  im•ma•ture•ly
  im•ma•tu•ri•ty
im•meas•ur•a•ble
  im•meas•ur•a•bly
im•me•di•a•cy
im•me•di•ate
  im•me•di•ate•ly
im•me•mo•ri•al
im•mense
  im•men•si•ty
im•merge
  im•merged
im•merse
  im•mersed
  im•mer•sion
im•mi•grate
  im•mi•gra•tion
  im•mi•grant
im•mi•nent
  im•mi•nence
im•mo•bile
  im•mo•bi•lize
  im•mo•bi•lized
im•mod•er•ate
  im•mod•er•ate•ly
  im•mod•est
im•mo•late
  im•mo•la•tion
im•mor•al
  im•mo•ral•i•ty
im•mor•tal
  im•mor•tal•i•ty
  im•mor•tal•ize
  im•mor•tal•ized
im•mov•a•ble
im•mune
  im•mu•ni•ty
  im•mu•nize
  im•mu•ni•za•tion
im•mu•nol•o•gy
im•mu•ta•ble
im•pact
im•pair
  im•pair•ment
im•pale
  im•pal•pa•ble
im•part
im•par•tial
  im•par•ti•al•i•ty
  im•par•tial•ly
im•passe
im•pas•sion
  im•pas•sioned
im•pas•sive
  im•pas•sive•ly
  im•pas•siv•i•ty
im•pa•tient
  im•pa•tience
im•peach
  im•peach•ment
im•pec•ca•ble
  im•pec•ca•bly
im•pe•cu•ni•ous
im•pede
  im•ped•ed
  im•ped•ing
  im•ped•i•ment
im•pel
  im•pelled
im•pend
  im•pend•ing
im•pen•e•tra•ble
im•per•a•tive
im•per•cep•ti•ble
  im•per•cep•ti•bly
im•per•cep•tive
im•per•fect
  im•per•fec•tion
im•pe•ri•al
  im•pe•ri•al•ism
  im•pe•ri•al•ist
  im•pe•ri•al•is•tic
im•per•il
im•pe•ri•ous
im•per•me•a•ble
im•per•son•al
im•per•son•ate
  im•per•son•a•tion
  im•per•son•a•tor
im•per•ti•nent

im•per•ti•nence
im•per•turb•a•ble
im•per•vi•ous
im•pet•u•ous
  im•pet•u•os•i•ty
im•pe•tus
im•pinge
  im•pinged
  im•ping•ing
im•pi•ous
im•plac•a•ble
im•plant
im•plau•si•ble
im•ple•ment
  im•ple•men•ta•tion
im•pli•cate
  im•pli•cat•ed
  im•pli•cat•ing
  im•pli•ca•tion
im•plic•it
im•plode
  im•plo•sion
im•plore
  im•plored
  im•plor•ing
im•ply
  im•plied
  im•ply•ing
im•po•lite
im•pol•i•tic
im•port
  im•port•er
  im•por•tance
  im•por•tant
im•por•tune
  im•por•tuned
  im•por•tun•ing
im•pose
  im•posed
  im•pos•ing
  im•po•si•tion
im•pos•si•ble
  im•pos•si•bil•i•ty
  im•pos•si•bly
im•pos•tor
  im•pos•ture
im•po•tent
  im•po•tence
im•pound
im•pov•er•ish
im•prac•ti•cal
im•pre•ca•tion
im•preg•na•ble
im•preg•nate
im•pre•sa•rio
im•press
im•pres•sion
  im•pres•sion•is•tic
  im•pres•sion•a•ble
  im•pres•sion•ism
  im•pres•sion•ist
im•pres•sive
im•pri•ma•tur
im•print
im•pris•on
  im•pris•on•ment
im•prob•a•ble
  im•prob•a•bly
im•promp•tu
im•prop•er
  im•prop•er•ly
im•pro•pri•e•ty
  im•pro•pri•e•ties
im•prove
  im•proved
  im•prov•ing
  im•prove•ment
im•prov•i•sa•tion
im•pro•vise
  im•pro•vised
  im•pro•vis•ing
im•pru•dent
  im•pru•dence
im•pu•dent
  im•pu•dence
im•pugn
  im•pugned
  im•pug•na•tion
im•pulse
  im•pul•sive
im•pu•ni•ty
im•pure
  im•pu•ri•ty

im•pute
  im•put•ed
  im•put•ing
  im•pu•ta•tion
in•a•bil•i•ty
in ab•sen•tia
in•ac•ces•si•ble
in•ac•cu•rate
  in•ac•cu•ra•cy
in•ac•tion
in•ac•ti•vate
  in•ac•ti•va•tion
  in•ac•tive
in•ad•e•quate
  in•ad•e•qua•cy
in•ad•mis•si•ble
in•ad•vert•ent
  in•ad•vert•ence
in•al•ien•a•ble
in•al•ter•a•ble
in•ane
  in•an•i•ty
in•ap•pli•ca•ble
in•ap•pro•pri•ate
  in•ap•pro•pri•ate•ly
in•ar•tic•u•late
in•as•much as
in•at•ten•tion
  in•at•ten•tive
in•au•di•ble
  in•au•di•bly
in•au•gu•rate
  in•au•gu•ral
  in•au•gu•ra•tion
in•aus•pi•cious
in•bred
  in•breed•ing
in•cal•cu•la•ble
in•can•des•cent
  in•can•des•cence
in•can•ta•tion
in•ca•pa•ble
in•ca•pac•i•tate
  in•ca•pac•i•tat•ed
  in•ca•pac•i•tat•ing
  in•ca•pac•i•ty
in•car•cer•ate
  in•car•cer•a•tion
in•car•nate
  in•car•na•tion
in•cen•di•a•ry
in•cense
  in•censed
in•cen•tive
in•cep•tion
in•cer•ti•tude
in•ces•sant
in•cest
  in•ces•tu•ous
in•cho•ate
in•ci•dence
in•ci•dent
  in•ci•den•tal
in•cin•er•ate
  in•cin•er•a•tion
  in•cin•er•a•tor
in•cip•i•ent
in•cise
  in•ci•sion
in•ci•sive
in•ci•sor
in•cite
  in•cit•ed
  in•cit•ing
in•ci•vil•i•ty
in•clem•ent
in•cline
  in•clined
  in•clin•ing
  in•cli•na•tion
in•clude
  in•clud•ed
  in•clud•ing
  in•clu•sion
  in•clu•sive
in•cog•ni•to
in•cog•ni•zant
in•co•her•ent
  in•co•her•ence
in•com•bus•ti•ble
in•come
in•com•men•su•rate
in•com•mode

in•com•mo•di•ous
in•com•mu•ni•ca•do
in•com•pa•ra•ble
in•com•pat•i•ble
  in•com•pat•i•bil•i•ty
in•com•pe•tent
  in•com•pe•tence
  in•com•pe•ten•cy
in•com•plete
in•com•pre•hen•si•ble
in•com•pre•hen•sion
in•con•ceiv•a•ble
in•con•clu•sive
in•con•gru•ous
  in•con•gru•i•ty
in•con•se•quen•tial
in•con•sid•er•ate
in•con•sis•tent
  in•con•sis•ten•cy
in•con•sol•a•ble
in•con•spic•u•ous
in•con•stant
  in•con•stan•cy
in•con•test•a•ble
in•con•ti•nent
  in•con•ti•nence
in•con•ven•ience
  in•con•ven•ienced
  in•con•ven•ienc•ing
  in•con•ven•ient
in•cor•po•rate
  in•cor•po•rat•ed
  in•cor•po•rat•ing
  in•cor•po•ra•tion
in•cor•po•re•al
in•cor•rect
in•cor•ri•gi•ble
in•cor•rupt•i•ble
in•crease
  in•creased
  in•creas•ing
in•cred•i•ble
  in•cred•i•bly
in•cred•u•lous
  in•cre•du•li•ty
in•cre•ment
  in•cre•men•tal
in•crim•i•nate
  in•crim•i•nat•ed
  in•crim•i•nat•ing
  in•crim•i•na•tion
in•crus•ta•tion
in•cu•bate
  in•cu•ba•tion
  in•cu•ba•tor
in•cul•cate
  in•cul•cat•ed
  in•cul•cat•ing
in•cul•pate
  in•cul•pat•ed
  in•cul•pat•ing
  in•cul•pa•tion
in•cum•bent
  in•cum•ben•cy
in•cur
  in•curred
  in•cur•ring
in•cur•a•ble
  in•cur•a•bly
in•cur•sion
in•debt•ed
in•de•cent
  in•de•cen•cy
in•de•ci•sion
in•de•ci•sive
in•de•co•rous
  in•de•co•rum
in•deed
in•de•fat•i•ga•ble
in•de•fen•si•ble
in•de•fin•a•ble
in•def•i•nite
  in•def•i•nite•ly
in•del•i•ble
  in•del•i•bly
in•del•i•cate
  in•del•i•ca•cy
in•dem•ni•fy
in•dem•ni•ty
in•dent
  in•den•ta•tion
  in•den•ture
in•de•pend•ent

in•de•pend•ence
in•de•scrib•a•ble
in•de•struct•i•ble
in•de•ter•mi•nate
in•dex
in•di•cate
  in•di•cat•ed
  in•di•cat•ing
  in•di•ca•tion
  in•dic•a•tive
  in•di•ca•tor
in•dict
  in•dict•ment
in•dif•fer•ent
  in•dif•fer•ence
in•dig•e•nous
in•di•gent
  in•di•gence
in•di•ges•tion
  in•di•gest•i•ble
in•dig•nant
  in•dig•na•tion
in•dig•ni•ty
in•di•go
in•di•rect
in•dis•creet
  in•dis•cre•tion
in•dis•crim•i•nate
in•dis•pen•sa•ble
in•dis•posed
in•dis•put•a•ble
in•dis•sol•u•ble
in•dis•tinct
in•dis•tin•guish•a•ble
in•di•vid•u•al
  in•di•vid•u•al•ly
  in•di•vid•u•al•is•tic
  in•di•vid•u•al•i•ty
  in•di•vid•u•al•ize
in•di•vis•i•ble
in•doc•tri•nate
  in•doc•tri•na•tion
in•do•lent
  in•do•lence
in•dom•i•ta•ble
in•du•bi•ta•ble
in•duce
  in•duced
  in•duc•ing
  in•duce•ment
in•duct
in•duc•tion
  in•duc•tive
in•dulge
  in•dul•gence
  in•dul•gent
in•dus•try
  in•dus•tries
  in•dus•tri•al
  in•dus•tri•al•ize
  in•dus•tri•al•i•za•tion
  in•dus•tri•al•ist
  in•dus•tri•ous
in•e•bri•ate
  in•e•bri•at•ed
  in•e•bri•a•tion
in•ed•i•ble
in•ef•fa•ble
in•ef•fec•tive
in•ef•fec•tu•al
in•ef•fi•cient
  in•ef•fi•cien•cy
in•el•i•gi•ble
in•ept
in•e•qual•i•ty
in•ert
in•er•tia
in•es•cap•a•ble
in•es•sen•tial
in•es•ti•ma•ble
in•ev•i•ta•ble
in•ex•act
in•ex•cus•a•ble
in•ex•haust•i•ble
in•ex•o•ra•ble
in•ex•pe•ri•ence
in•ex•pli•ca•ble
in•ex•press•i•ble
in•ex•tri•ca•ble
in•fal•li•ble
in•fa•mous
  in•fa•my
in•fant

in•fan•cy
in•fan•ti•cide
in•fan•tile
in•fan•try
in•fat•u•ate
  in•fat•u•at•ed
  in•fat•u•a•tion
in•fect
  in•fec•tion
  in•fec•tious
  in•fec•tive
in•fer
  in•ferred
  in•fer•ring
  in•fer•ence
in•fe•ri•or
  in•fe•ri•or•i•ty
in•fer•nal
in•fer•no
in•fest
  in•fes•ta•tion
in•fi•del
  in•fi•del•i•ty
in•field
  in•field•er
in•fight•ing
in•fil•trate
  in•fil•trat•ed
  in•fil•trat•ing
  in•fil•tra•tion
  in•fil•tra•tor
in•fi•nite
  in•fin•i•tes•i•mal
  in•fin•i•tive
  in•fin•i•ty
in•firm
  in•fir•mi•ty
in•fir•ma•ry
in•flame
  in•flamed
  in•flam•ing
  in•flam•ma•ble
  in•flam•ma•tion
  in•flam•ma•to•ry
in•flate
  in•flat•ed
  in•flat•a•ble
in•fla•tion
  in•fla•tion•ary
in•flect
  in•flec•tion
  in•flex•i•ble
in•flict
  in•flic•tion
in•flu•ence
  in•flu•enced
  in•flu•enc•ing
  in•flu•en•tial
in•flu•en•za
in•flux
in•form
  in•formed
  in•for•mer
in•for•mal
  in•for•mal•i•ty
  in•for•mal•ly
in•form•ant
in•for•ma•tion
  in•for•ma•tive
in•frac•tion
in•fran•gi•ble
in•fra•red
in•fra•struc•ture
in•fre•quent
in•fringe
  in•fringed
  in•fring•ing
  in•fringe•ment
in•fu•ri•ate
  in•fu•ri•at•ed
  in•fu•ri•at•ing
in•fuse
  in•fu•sion
in•gen•ious
  in•ge•nu•i•ty
in•gen•u•ous
in•gest
  in•ges•tion
in•grain
in•grate
in•gra•ti•ate
  in•gra•ti•at•ed
  in•gra•ti•at•ing

in•gra•ti•a•tion
in•grat•i•tude
in•gre•di•ent
in•gress
in•grown
in•hab•it
  in•hab•it•ed
  in•hab•it•a•ble
  in•hab•it•ant
in•hale
  in•haled
  in•hal•ing
  in•ha•la•tion
  in•ha•la•tor
in•here
  in•her•ence
  in•her•ent
in•her•it
  in•her•i•tor
  in•her•i•tance
in•hib•it
  in•hib•i•to•ry
  in•hi•bi•tion
in•hos•pi•ta•ble
in•hu•man
  in•hu•mane
  in•hu•ma•tion
in•im•i•cal
in•im•i•ta•ble
in•iq•ui•ty
  in•iq•ui•tous
in•i•tial
  in•i•tialed
  in•i•tial•ly
in•i•ti•ate
  in•i•ti•at•ed
  in•i•ti•at•ing
  in•i•ti•a•tion
  in•i•ti•a•tor
in•i•ti•a•tive
in•ject
  in•jec•tion
in•ju•di•cious
in•junc•tion
in•jure
  in•jured
  in•jur•ing
  in•ju•ri•ous
in•ju•ry
  in•ju•ries
in•jus•tice
ink•blot
ink•ling
in•law
in•lay
  in•laid
in•let
in•mate
in me•mo•ri•am
in•nards
in•nate
in•ner
in•ner•most
in•ner•sole
in•ner•vate
  in•ner•vat•ed
  in•ner•vat•ing
in•ning
inn•keep•er
in•no•cent
  in•no•cence
  in•noc•u•ous
in•no•vate
  in•no•va•tion
  in•no•va•tive
  in•no•va•tor
in•nu•en•do
  in•nu•en•does
in•nu•mer•a•ble
in•oc•u•late
  in•oc•u•lat•ed
  in•oc•u•la•tion
in•of•fen•sive
in•op•er•a•ble
  in•op•er•a•tive
in•op•por•tune
in•or•di•nate
in•or•gan•ic
in•pa•tient
in•put
in•quest
in•quire
  in•quired

in•quir•ing
  in•quir•er
in•quiry
  in•quir•ies
in•qui•si•tion
  in•quis•i•tor
  in•quis•i•tive
in•road
in•sane
  in•san•i•ty
in•san•i•tary
in•sa•tia•ble
in•scribe
  in•scribed
  in•scrip•tion
in•scru•ta•ble
in•seam
in•sect
  in•sec•ti•cide
in•se•cure
  in•se•cu•ri•ty
in•sem•i•nate
in•sen•sate
in•sen•si•ble
in•sen•si•tive
  in•sen•si•tiv•i•ty
in•sen•ti•ent
in•sep•a•ra•ble
in•sert
  in•ser•tion
in•set
in•sid•er
in•sid•i•ous
in•sight
in•sig•nia
in•sig•nif•i•cant
  in•sig•nif•i•cance
in•sin•cere
  in•sin•cer•i•ty
in•sin•u•ate
  in•sin•u•at•ed
  in•sin•u•at•ing
  in•sin•u•a•tion
in•sip•id
in•sist
  in•sist•ence
  in•sist•ent
in•so•bri•e•ty
in•so•cia•ble
in•so•far as
in•so•lent
  in•so•lence
in•sol•u•ble
in•solv•a•ble
in•sol•vent
  in•sol•ven•cy
in•som•nia
  in•som•ni•ac
in•so•much as
in•sou•ci•ant
  in•sou•ci•ance
in•spect
  in•spec•tion
  in•spec•tor
in•spire
  in•spired
  in•spir•ing
  in•spi•ra•tion
in•sta•bil•i•ty
in•stall
  in•stalled
  in•stall•ing
  in•stal•la•tion
  in•stall•ment
in•stance
in•stant
  in•stan•ta•ne•ous
in•stead
in•step
in•sti•gate
  in•sti•gat•ed
  in•sti•gat•ing
  in•sti•ga•tion
  in•sti•ga•tor
in•still
  in•stilled
  in•stil•ling
in•stinct
  in•stinc•tive
  in•stinc•tu•al
in•sti•tute
  in•sti•tut•ed
  in•sti•tut•ing

in•sti•tu•tion
  in•sti•tu•tion•al
  in•sti•tu•tion•al•ize
  in•sti•tu•tion•al•ized
in•struct
  in•struc•tion
  in•struc•tive
  in•struc•tor
in•stru•ment
  in•stru•men•tal
  in•stru•men•ta•list
in•sub•or•di•nate
  in•sub•or•di•na•tion
in•sub•stan•tial
in•suf•fer•a•ble
in•suf•fi•cient
in•su•lar
in•su•late
  in•su•la•tion
in•su•lin
in•sult
in•sup•port•a•ble
in•sure
  in•sured
  in•sur•a•ble
  in•sur•ance
in•sur•gent
  in•sur•gence
  in•sur•gen•cy
in•sur•mount•a•ble
in•sur•rec•tion
in•sus•cep•ti•ble
in•tact
in•take
in•tan•gi•ble
in•te•ger
in•te•gral
in•te•grate
  in•te•grat•ed
  in•te•gra•tion
in•teg•ri•ty
in•tel•lect
in•tel•lec•tu•al
in•tel•li•gent
  in•tel•li•gence
  in•tel•li•gent•sia
  in•tel•li•gi•ble
in•tem•per•ate
  in•tem•per•ance
in•tend
in•tense
  in•ten•si•fy
  in•ten•si•ty
in•tent
  in•ten•tion
  in•ten•tion•al•ly
in•ter
  in•terred
  in•ter•ring
  in•ter•ment
in•ter•act
  in•ter•ac•tion
  in•ter•ac•tive
in•ter•cede
in•ter•cept
  in•ter•cep•tion
in•ter•ces•sion
in•ter•change•a•ble
in•ter•col•le•gi•ate
in•ter•com
in•ter•con•nec•tion
in•ter•con•ti•nen•tal
in•ter•course
in•ter•cul•tur•al
in•ter•de•nom•i•na•tion•al
in•ter•de•part•men•tal
in•ter•de•pend•ence
in•ter•dict
  in•ter•dic•tion
in•ter•dis•ci•pli•nary
in•ter•est
  in•ter•est•ed
  in•ter•est•ing
in•ter•face
in•ter•fere
  in•ter•fered
  in•ter•fer•ing
  in•ter•fer•ence
in•ter•im
in•te•ri•or
in•ter•ject
  in•ter•jec•tion
in•ter•lock

in•ter•lo•cu•tion
in•ter•loc•u•tor
in•ter•lop•er
in•ter•lude
in•ter•mar•ry
in•ter•me•di•ate
in•ter•me•di•ary
in•ter•mi•na•ble
in•ter•min•gle
in•ter•mis•sion
in•ter•mit•tent
in•tern
in•ter•nal
in•ter•nal•ize
in•ter•na•tion•al
in•ter•na•tion•al•ly
in•ter•na•tion•al•ize
in•ter•na•tion•al•ism
in•tern•ist
in•tern•ment
in•ter•nun•cio
in•ter•of•fice
in•ter•plan•e•tary
in•ter•po•late
in•ter•pose
in•ter•pret
in•ter•pret•er
in•ter•pre•tive
in•ter•pre•ta•tion
in•ter•ra•cial
in•ter•re•late
in•ter•ro•gate
in•ter•ro•gat•ed
in•ter•ro•gat•ing
in•ter•ro•ga•tion
in•ter•rog•a•tive
in•ter•rupt
in•ter•rup•tion
in•ter•scho•las•tic
in•ter•sect
in•ter•sec•tion
in•ter•sperse
in•er•spersed
in•ter•state
in•ter•twine
in•ter•val
in•ter•vene
in•ter•vened
in•ter•ven•ing
in•ter•ven•tion
in•ter•view
in•ter•wo•ven
in•tes•tate
in•tes•tine
in•tes•ti•nal
in•ti•mate
in•ti•mated
in•ti•mat•ing
in•ti•ma•tion
in•ti•mate
in•tim•i•date
in•tim•i•dat•ed
in•tim•i•dat•ing
in•tim•i•da•tion
in•to
in•tol•er•ant
in•tol•er•able
in•tol•er•ance
in•to•nate
in•to•na•tion
in•tone
in•tox•i•cate
in•tox•i•cat•ed
in•tox•i•cat•ing
in•tox•i•ca•tion
in•trac•ta•ble
in•tra•mu•ral
in•tran•si•gent
in•tran•si•gence
in•tran•si•tive
in•tra•ve•nous
in•trench•ed
in•trep•id
in•tri•cate
in•tri•ca•cy
in•trigue
in•trigued
in•tri•guing
in•trin•sic
in•tro•duce
in•tro•duced
in•tro•duc•ing
in•tro•duc•tion

in•tro•duc•to•ry
in•tro•spect
in•tro•spec•tion
in•tro•spec•tive
in•tro•vert
in•tro•ver•sion
in•trude
in•trud•ed
in•trud•ing
in•trud•er
in•tru•sion
in•tu•i•tion
in•tu•i•tive
in•un•date
in•un•dat•ed
in•un•da•tion
in•ure
in•ured
in•vade
in•vad•ed
in•vad•ing
in•vad•er
in•va•lid
in•va•lid•ism
in•val•id
in•val•i•date
in•val•u•a•ble
in•var•i•a•bly
in•var•i•ant
in•va•sion
in•vec•tive
in•veigh
in•vei•gle
in•vent
in•ven•tion
in•ven•tive
in•ven•tor
in•ven•to•ry
in•verse
in•ver•sion
in•vert
in•vert•ed
in•ver•te•brate
in•vest
in•ves•tor
in•ves•ti•gate
in•ves•ti•gat•ed
in•ves•ti•gat•ing
in•ves•ti•ga•tion
in•ves•ti•ture
in•vest•ment
in•vet•er•ate
in•vid•i•ous
in•vig•or•ate
in•vig•or•at•ed
in•vig•or•at•ing
in•vin•ci•ble
in•vi•o•late
in•vi•o•la•ble
in•vis•i•ble
in•vite
in•vit•ed
in•vit•ing
in•vi•ta•tion
in•vo•ca•tion
in•voice
in•voke
in•voked
in•vol•un•tary
in•vo•lut•ed
in•volve
in•volved
in•volv•ing
in•volve•ment
in•vul•ner•a•ble
in•ward
io•dine
ion
Ion•ic
io•ta
ip•so fac•to
iras•ci•ble
irate
Ire•land
ir•i•des•cent
ir•i•des•cence
iris
Irish•man
irk•some
iron
iron•ic
iron•i•cal
ir•ra•di•ate

ir•ra•di•a•tion
ir•rad•i•ca•ble
ir•ra•tion•al
ir•rec•on•cil•a•ble
ir•re•cov•er•a•ble
ir•re•deem•a•ble
ir•re•duc•i•ble
ir•ref•u•ta•ble
ir•reg•u•lar
ir•reg•u•lar•i•ty
ir•rel•e•vant
ir•rel•e•vance
ir•rel•e•van•cy
ir•re•li•gious
ir•re•me•di•a•ble
ir•re•mis•si•ble
ir•re•mov•a•ble
ir•rep•a•ra•ble
ir•re•place•a•ble
ir•re•press•i•ble
ir•re•proach•a•ble
ir•re•sist•i•ble
ir•res•o•lute
ir•re•spec•tive
ir•re•spon•si•ble
ir•re•triev•a•ble
ir•rev•er•ence
ir•rev•er•ent
ir•re•vers•i•ble
ir•rev•o•ca•ble
ir•ri•gate
ir•ri•ga•tion
ir•ri•tant
ir•ri•tate
ir•ri•tat•ed
ir•ri•tat•ing
ir•ri•ta•tion
ir•ri•ta•ble
ir•rupt
Is•lam
Is•lam•ic
is•land
isle
iso•late
iso•lat•ed
iso•la•tion
iso•la•tion•ist
iso•met•ric
isos•ce•les
iso•tope
Is•ra•el
Is•rae•li
is•sue
is•sued
is•su•ing
is•su•ance
isth•mus
Ital•ian
ital•ic
ital•i•cize
It•a•ly
itch
itchy
item
item•ize
it•er•ate
it•er•a•tion
itin•er•ant
itin•er•ate
itin•er•ary
ivo•ry
ivy

J

jab
jabbed
jab•bing
jack•al
jack•ass
jack•et
jack•knife
jack-of-all-trades
jack-o'-lan•tern
jack rab•bit
jade
jad•ed
jad•ing
jag
jag•ged
jag•uar
jail•bird
jail•break

ja•lopy
jam
jammed
jam•ming
jamb
jam•bo•ree
jan•gle
jan•gled
jan•gling
jan•i•tor
jan•i•to•ri•al
Jan•u•ary
Ja•pan
Jap•a•nese
jar
jarred
jar•ring
jar•gon
jas•mine
jaun•dice
jaun•diced
jaunt
jaun•ty
jave•lin
jaw•bone
jay•walk
jazz
jazzy
jeal•ous
jeal•ousy
jeer•er
Jef•fer•son
Je•ho•vah
Jek•yll
jel•ly
jel•ly•fish
jeop•ar•dy
jeop•ar•dize
jerk
jerk•i•ly
jerky
jerry-built
jer•sey
Je•ru•sa•lem
jest•er
Jes•u•it
Je•sus
jet
jet•ted
jet•ting
jet•sam
jet•ti•son
jet•ty
jew•el
jew•el•er
jew•el•ry
Jew•ish
jibe
jif•fy
jig
jig•gle
jig•gled
jig•gling
jim•my
jin•gle
jin•gled
jin•gling
jin•go•ism
jinx
jit•ney
jit•tery
job
job•ber
jock•ey
jo•cose
joc•u•lar
joc•und
jodh•pur
jog
jogged
jog•ging
jog•ger
join•er
joint
joist
joke
joked
jok•ing
jol•ly
jolt
jos•tle
jos•tled
jos•tling

jot
jot•ted
jot•ting
jour•nal•ism
jour•nal•ist
jour•ney
joust
jo•vi•al
jowl
joy•ful
joy•ous
joy•ride
ju•bi•la•tion
ju•bi•lee
Ju•da•ism
Ju•da•ic
Ju•da•i•cal
judge
judged
judg•ing
judg•ment
ju•di•cial
ju•di•ci•ary
ju•di•cious
ju•do
jug•ger•naut
jug•gle
jug•gled
jug•gling
jug•u•lar
juice
juicy
juke•box
ju•lep
jum•ble
jum•bo
jump
jumpy
junc•tion
junc•ture
jun•gle
jun•ior
ju•ni•per
junk
jun•ket
junk•ie
jun•ta
Ju•pi•ter
ju•ris•dic•tion
ju•ris•pru•dence
ju•ry
ju•rist
ju•ror
just
jus•tice
jus•ti•fy
jus•ti•fied
jus•ti•fi•a•ble
jus•ti•fi•ca•tion
jut
jut•ted
jut•ting
jute
ju•ve•nile
jux•ta•pose
jux•ta•po•si•tion

K

ka•bob
kai•ser
ka•lei•do•scope
ka•mi•ka•ze
kan•ga•roo
ka•put
kar•at
ka•ra•te
kar•ma
kay•ak
keen•ly
keep
kept
keep•sake
kelp
ken•nel
ker•a•tin
ker•chief
ker•nel
ker•o•sene
ketch•up
ke•tone
ket•tle
key

keyed
khaki
kib•butz
kib•itz•er
kick•back
kick•off
kid
   kid•ded
   kid•ding
kid•nap
   kid•naped
   kid•napped
   kid•nap•ing
   kid•nap•ping
   kid•nap•er
   kid•nap•per
kid•ney
kill•deer
kill•er
kill•ing
kill•joy
kiln
kilo
   kil•o•gram
   kil•o•me•ter
   kil•o•watt
kilt
ki•mo•no
kin•der•gar•ten
kin•dle
   kin•dled
   kin•dling
kind•ly
kin•dred
ki•net•ic
kin•folk
   kins•folk
king•dom
king•ly
king•pin
king•size
kinky
ki•osk
kip•per
kis•met
kiss•a•ble
kitch•en
   kitch•en•ette
kite
kit•ten
   kit•ty
kit•ty-cor•ner
ki•wi
klatch
klep•to•ma•nia
   klep•to•ma•ni•ac
knack
knap•sack
knave
knead
knee
kneel
   knelt
   kneeled
knell
knick•ers
knick•knack
knife
   knives
   knifed
   knif•ing
knight
knit
   knit•ted
   knit•ting
knob
   knob•by
knock
knock-kneed
knoll
knot
   knot•ted
   knot•ty
know
   knew
   known
know-how
knowl•edge
   knowl•edge•a•ble
knuck•le
ko•a•la
kohl•ra•bi
kook

Ko•ran
Ko•rea
ko•sher
Krem•lin
Krish•na
kryp•ton
Ku•blai Khan
ku•dos
küm•mel
kum•mer•bund
kum•quat

L

la•bel
   la•beled
   la•bel•ing
la•bi•al
la•bile
la•bor
   la•bor•er
lab•o•ra•to•ry
la•bored
la•bo•ri•ous
la•bur•num
lab•y•rinth
   lab•y•rin•thine
lace
   laced
   lac•ing
   lacy
lac•er•ate
   lac•er•a•tion
lach•ry•mal
   lach•ry•mose
lack•a•dai•si•cal
lack•ey
lack•lus•ter
la•con•ic
lac•quer
la•crosse
lac•tate
lac•tose
la•cu•na
lad•der
lad•die
lad•en
lad•ing
la•dle
la•dy•like
lag
   lagged
   lag•ging
lag•gard
la•ger
la•goon
lair
lais•sez faire
la•i•ty
lake•side
lam
la•ma
lam•baste
lam•bent
lamb
lame
la•mé
la•ment
   lam•en•ta•tion
lam•i•nate
lam•poon
lance
   lanced
   lanc•ing
lan•cet
land•ed
land•ing
land•la•dy
land•lord
land•lub•ber
land•scape
   land•scap•ing
   land•scap•er
lan•guage
lan•guid
lan•guish
lan•guor
lanky
lan•o•lin
lan•tern
lap
   lapped
   lap•ping

la•pel
lap•i•dary
lap•in
lap•is laz•u•li
lapse
   lapsed
   laps•ing
lar•ce•ny
lar•der
large
   large•ly
large-scale
lar•gess
lar•i•at
lar•va
lar•ynx
   la•ryn•gi•tis
las•civ•i•ous
la•ser
lash
   lash•ing
las•si•tude
las•so
last•ing
last•ly
latch•key
late
   late•ly
la•tent
   la•ten•cy
lat•er•al
   lat•er•al•ly
la•tex
lathe
lath•er
Lat•in
lat•i•tude
la•trine
lat•ter
lat•tice
laud•a•ble
lau•da•num
laud•a•to•ry
laugh
   laugh•a•ble
   laugh•ter
launch
laun•der
   laun•dress
Laun•dro•mat
laun•dry
lau•re•ate
lau•rel
la•va
lav•a•liere
lav•a•to•ry
lav•en•der
lav•ish
law-a•bid•ing
law•ful
law•mak•er
lawn
law•suit
law•yer
lax
   lax•i•ty
lax•a•tive
lay
   laid
lay•er
lay•man
lay•o•ver
la•zy
   la•zi•ly
leach
lead
   led
lead•en
lead•er
   lead•er•ship
leaf
   leaves
leaf•let
league
leak
   leak•age
   leaky
lean
leap
   leaped
   leapt
learn
   learned

learnt
lease
   leased
   leas•ing
leash
least•wise
   least•ways
leath•er
leave
   left
   leav•ing
leav•en
Leb•a•nese
   Leb•a•non
lech•er
   lech•er•ous
   lech•ery
lec•tern
lec•ture
   lec•tured
   lec•tur•ing
   lec•tur•er
ledge
ledg•er
leech
leek
leer
leery
lee•ward
lee•way
left-hand•ed
left•ist
left-wing
leg
   leg•ging
leg•a•cy
le•gal
   le•gal•ly
   le•gal•i•ty
   le•gal•ize
leg•ate
   le•ga•tion
leg•end
   leg•end•ary
leg•er•de•main
leg•i•ble
   leg•i•bly
le•gion
   le•gion•naire
leg•is•late
   leg•is•lat•ed
   leg•is•lat•ing
   leg•is•la•tive
   leg•is•la•tor
   leg•is•la•tion
   leg•is•la•ture
le•git•i•mate
   le•git•i•mat•ed
   le•git•i•mat•ing
   le•git•i•ma•cy
   le•git•i•mate•ly
le•git•i•mize
   le•git•i•mized
   le•git•i•miz•ing
leg•ume
lei•sure
   lei•sure•ly
leit•mo•tif
lem•on
   lem•on•ade
lend
   lent
length
   length•en
le•ni•ent
   le•ni•ence
   le•ni•en•cy
lens
Lent•en
len•til
le•o•nine
leop•ard
le•o•tard
lep•er
   lep•ro•sy
lep•re•chaun
les•bi•an
le•sion
les•see
less•en
less•er
les•son
les•sor

least
let
   let•ting
le•thal
leth•ar•gy
   le•thar•gic
let•ter
let•tered
let•ter•head
let•tuce
leu•ke•mia
lev•ee
lev•el
   lev•eled
   lev•el•ing
   lev•el-head•ed
lev•er
   lev•er•age
le•vi•a•than
lev•i•tate
   lev•i•ta•tion
lev•i•ty
levy
   lev•ies
lewd
lex•i•cog•ra•phy
lex•i•con
li•a•bil•i•ty
   li•a•bil•i•ties
li•a•ble
li•ai•son
li•ar
li•ba•tion
li•bel
   li•beled
   li•bel•ous
lib•er•al
   lib•er•al•ly
   lib•er•al•i•ty
   lib•er•al•ism
   lib•er•al•ize
lib•er•ate
   lib•er•at•ed
   lib•er•at•ing
   lib•er•a•tion
   lib•er•a•tor
lib•er•tine
   lib•er•tin•ism
lib•er•ty
   lib•er•ties
li•bi•do
li•brary
   li•brar•ies
   li•brar•i•an
li•bret•to
lice
   louse
li•cense
   li•censed
   li•cens•ing
   li•cen•see
li•cen•tious
li•chen
lic•it
lic•o•rice
lid•ded
lie
   lay
   lain
   lay•ing
lie
   lied
   ly•ing
lien
lieu
lieu•ten•ant
life•guard
life•like
life-size
life-style
life•time
lift-off
lig•a•ment
lig•a•ture
light•en
light•er
light•house
light•ing
light•ning
light•weight
light-year
like
   liked

lik•ing
like•a•ble
like•li•hood
like•ly
lik•en
like•ness
like•wise
li•lac
lilt•ing
lily
limb
lim•ber
lim•bo
lime
lime•light
lim•er•ick
lime•stone
lim•it
  lim•i•ta•tion
  lim•it•ed
lim•ou•sine
limp
lim•pet
lim•pid
Lin•coln
lin•den
line
  lined
  lin•ing
  lin•er
lin•e•age
  lin•e•al
lin•e•ar
line•back•er
line•man
lin•en
lin•ger
lin•ge•rie
lin•go
lin•gual
  lin•guist
  lin•guis•tics
lin•i•ment
link
  linked
lin•net
li•no•le•um
lin•seed
lint
lin•tel
li•on
  li•on•ess
  li•on•ize
lip•stick
liq•ue•fy
  liq•ue•fied
  liq•ue•fy•ing
li•queur
liq•uid
  li•quid•i•ty
liq•ui•date
  liq•ui•da•tion
liq•uor
lisp
lis•some
list
lis•ten
  lis•ten•er
list•less
lit•a•ny
li•ter
lit•er•al
  lit•er•al•ly
lit•er•ary
lit•er•ate
  lit•er•a•cy
lit•er•a•ti
lit•er•a•ture
lithe
li•thog•ra•phy
lit•i•gate
  lit•i•ga•tion
lit•mus
lit•ter
lit•tle
lit•to•ral
lit•ur•gy
  li•tur•gic
  li•tur•gi•cal
liv•a•ble
  live•a•ble
live•li•hood
live•ly

liv•en
liv•er
liv•er•wurst
liv•ery
  liv•er•ied
live•stock
liv•id
liv•ing
liz•ard
lla•ma
load
  load•ed
loaf
  loaves
loam
loath
loathe
  loath•ing
  loath•some
lob
  lobbed
  lob•bing
lob•by
  lob•by•ist
lobe
  lobed
lob•ster
lo•cal
  lo•cal•ly
lo•cale
  lo•cal•i•ty
  lo•cal•ize
lo•cate
  lo•cat•ed
  lo•cat•ing
  lo•ca•tion
lock•er
lock•et
lock•jaw
lock•out
lock•smith
lo•co•mo•tion
lo•co•mo•tive
lo•cus
  lo•ci
lo•cust
lo•cu•tion
lode•star
lode•stone
lodge
  lodged
  lodg•ing
lofty
lo•gan•ber•ry
log•a•rithm
loge
log•ger
log•ger•heads
log•ic
  lo•gi•cian
  log•i•cal
  log•i•cal•ly
  lo•gis•tic
  lo•gis•ti•cal
log•roll•ing
loin
loi•ter
  loi•ter•er
lone•ly
  lone•li•ness
  lone•some
lon•er
lon•gev•i•ty
long•hand
long•ing
lon•gi•tude
  lon•gi•tu•di•nal
long-lived
long-range
long•shore•man
long-term
long-wind•ed
look•out
loony
loop•hole
loose
  loosed
  loos•en
loot•er
lop
  lopped
  lop•ping
lope

loped
lop•ing
lop•sid•ed
lo•qua•cious
lord•ly
lor•ry
lose
  lost
  los•ing
  los•er
lot
lo•tion
lot•tery
lo•tus
loud
loud•speak•er
lounge
  lounged
  loung•ing
lousy
lout
lou•ver
love
  loved
  lov•ing
  lov•a•ble
  lov•er
love•ly
low•brow
low•er
low•er-case
low•er•ing
low-keyed
low•ly
loy•al
  loy•al•ist
  loy•al•ty
  loy•al•ties
loz•enge
lub•ber
lu•bri•cate
  lu•bri•cant
  lu•bri•ca•tion
  lu•bri•ca•tor
lu•bri•cious
lu•cid
  lu•cid•i•ty
luck
  luck•i•ly
  lucky
lu•cra•tive
lu•cre
lu•di•crous
lug
  lugged
  lug•ging
lug•gage
lu•gu•bri•ous
luke•warm
lull•a•by
lum•ba•go
lum•bar
lum•ber
  lum•ber•ing
  lum•ber•jack
lu•men
lu•mi•nary
  lu•mi•nar•ies
lu•mi•nous
lum•mox
lumpy
lu•nar
lunch
  lunch•eon
lunge
  lunged
  lung•ing
lu•pine
lurch
lure
  lured
  lur•ing
lu•rid
lurk
lus•cious
lush
lust
lus•ter
  lus•trous
lusty
Lu•ther•an

lux•u•ri•ate
lux•u•ry
  lux•u•ries
  lux•u•ri•ous
  lux•u•ri•ant
  lux•u•ri•ance
ly•ce•um
ly•ing
lymph
  lym•phat•ic
lynch
lynx
lyre
ly•ric
  lyr•i•cal
  lyr•i•cist

M

ma•ca•bre
mac•ad•am
mac•a•ro•ni
mac•a•roon
ma•caw
mace
mac•er•ate
  mac•er•a•tion
ma•chete
Mach•i•a•vel•li•an
mach•i•na•tion
ma•chine
  ma•chin•ery
  ma•chin•ist
mack•er•el
mack•in•tosh
mac•ro•cosm
mac•ro•scop•ic
mad
  mad•den
  mad•dest
  mad•ly
  mad•ness
mad•am
  mad•ame
  mes•dames
Ma•dei•ra
mad•e•moi•selle
Ma•don•na
mad•ras
mad•ri•gal
mael•strom
maes•tro
Ma•fia
mag•a•zine
ma•gen•ta
mag•got
mag•ic
  mag•i•cal
  ma•gi•cian
mag•is•trate
  mag•is•te•ri•al
mag•ma
Mag•na Car•ta
mag•nan•i•mous
  mag•na•nim•i•ty
mag•nate
mag•ne•sia
mag•ne•si•um
mag•net
  mag•net•ic
  mag•net•i•cal•ly
  mag•net•ism
  mag•net•ize
mag•nif•i•cent
  mag•nif•i•cence
mag•ni•fy
  mag•ni•fied
  mag•ni•fy•ing
  mag•ni•fi•ca•tion
mag•nil•o•quent
mag•ni•tude
mag•no•lia
mag•num
mag•pie
ma•hog•a•ny
maid•en
mail•box
mail•man
maim
main•land
main•ly
main•spring
main•stream

main•tain
  main•te•nance
maî•tre d'hô•tel
maize
maj•es•ty
ma•jes•tic
ma•jor
ma•jor•i•ty
  ma•jor•i•ties
make
  mak•ing
make-be•lieve
make•shift
make-up
mal•a•dapt•ed
mal•ad•just•ed
mal•a•droit
mal•a•dy
  mal•a•dies
ma•laise
mal•a•prop•ism
ma•lar•ia
ma•lar•key
mal•con•tent
mal•e•dic•tion
mal•e•fac•tor
ma•lev•o•lent
  ma•lev•o•lence
mal•fea•sance
  mal•fea•sant
mal•func•tion
mal•ice
  ma•li•cious
ma•lign
ma•lig•nant
  ma•lig•nan•cy
  ma•lig•nan•cies
ma•lin•ger
mal•lard
mal•le•a•ble
mal•let
mal•nour•ished
  mal•nu•tri•tion
mal•o•dor•ous
mal•prac•tice
malt
mal•treat
mam•bo
ma•ma
  mam•ma
mam•mal
  mam•ma•li•an
mam•ma•ry
mam•mon
mam•moth
mam•my
man
  manned
  man•ning
man•a•cle
man•age
  man•aged
  man•ag•ing
  man•age•a•ble
  man•age•ment
man•ag•er
  man•a•ge•ri•al
ma•ña•na
man•a•tee
man•da•mus
man•da•rin
man•date
  man•dat•ed
  man•dat•ing
  man•da•to•ry
man•di•ble
man•do•lin
man•drake
man•drel
man•drill
man-eat•er
  man-eat•ing
ma•neu•ver
  ma•neu•ver•a•bil•i•t
man•ga•nese
man•gy
man•ger
man•gle
  man•gled
  man•gling
man•go
man•grove
man•han•dle

Man•hat•tan
man-hour
ma•nia
  man•ic
ma•ni•ac
  ma•ni•a•cal
man•ic-de•pres•sive
man•i•cure
  man•i•cured
  man•i•cur•ist
man•i•fest
man•i•fes•ta•tion
man•i•fes•to
man•i•fold
man•i•kin
  man•a•kin
  man•ni•kin
ma•nil•la
ma•nip•u•late
  ma•nip•u•lat•ed
  ma•nip•u•lat•ing
  ma•nip•u•la•tion
  ma•nip•u•la•tive
  ma•nip•u•la•tor
man•kind
man•ly
  man•li•er
  man•li•ness
man•made
man•na
manned
man•ne•quin
man•ner
man•nered
man•ner•ism
man•nish
man-of-war
  men-of-war
man•or
  ma•no•ri•al
man•pow•er
man•sard
man•sion
man•slaugh•ter
man•tel
  man•tle
man•til•la
man•tis
man•tle
man•u•al
  man•u•al•ly
man•u•fac•ture
  man•u•fac•tured
  man•u•fac•tur•ing
  man•u•fac•tur•er
man•u•mis•sion
ma•nure
man•u•script
many
  more
  most
map
  mapped
  map•ping
ma•ple
mar
  marred
  mar•ring
ma•ra•ca
mar•a•schi•no
mar•a•thon
ma•raud
  ma•raud•er
mar•ble
  mar•bled
march•er
mar•chion•ess
mar•ga•rine
mar•ga•ri•ta
mar•gin
  mar•gi•nal
mar•i•gold
ma•ri•jua•na
ma•rim•ba
ma•ri•na
mar•i•nade
mar•i•nate
ma•rine
mar•i•ner
mar•i•on•ette
mar•i•tal
mar•i•time
mar•jo•ram

marked
  mark•ed•ly
mark•er
mar•ket
  mar•ket•a•ble
  mar•ket•ing
  mar•ket•place
mark•ing
marks•man
  marks•man•ship
mar•lin
mar•ma•lade
ma•roon
mar•que•try
mar•quis
  mar•quess
  mar•quise
mar•riage
  mar•riage•a•ble
mar•row
mar•ry
  mar•ried
  mar•ry•ing
mar•shal
  mar•shaled
  mar•shal•ing
marsh•mal•low
marshy
mar•su•pi•al
mar•tial
Mar•tian
mar•ten
mar•ti•ni
mar•tyr
  mar•tyr•dom
mar•vel
  mar•veled
  mar•vel•ing
  mar•vel•ous
Marx•ism
  marx•ist
mar•zi•pan
mas•cara
mas•cot
mas•cu•line
  mas•cu•lin•i•ty
mask
  masked
mas•och•ism
  mas•och•ist
  mas•och•is•tic
ma•son
  ma•son•ic
ma•son•ry
masque
mas•quer•ade
  mas•quer•ad•ing
Mas•sa•chu•setts
mas•sa•cre
  mas•sa•cred
  mas•sa•cring
mas•sage
mas•seur
  mas•seuse
mas•sive
mass-pro•duce
  mass pro•duction
mas•tec•to•my
mas•ter
mas•ter•ful
mas•ter•mind
mas•ter•piece
mas•tery
mast•head
mas•ti•cate
mas•tiff
mas•to•don
mas•toid
mas•tur•bate
  mas•tur•ba•tion
mat
  mat•ted
  mat•ting
mat•a•dor
match•mak•ing
mate
  mat•ed
  mat•ing
ma•te•ri•al
  ma•te•ri•al•ly
  ma•te•ri•al•ism
  ma•te•ri•al•ist
  ma•te•ri•al•is•tic

ma•te•ri•al•is•ti•cal•ly
ma•te•ri•al•ize
  ma•te•ri•al•ized
  ma•te•ri•al•iz•ing
ma•te•ri•el
ma•ter•nal
ma•ter•ni•ty
math•e•mat•ics
math•e•mat•i•cal
math•e•ma•ti•cian
mat•i•nee
ma•tri•arch
mat•ri•cide
ma•tric•u•late
  ma•tric•u•lat•ed
  ma•tric•u•lat•ing
  ma•tric•u•lant
  ma•tric•u•la•tion
ma•tri•lin•e•al
mat•ri•mo•ny
  mat•ri•mo•ni•al
ma•trix
  ma•tri•ces
ma•tron
  ma•tron•ly
mat•ter
mat•ter-of-course
mat•ter-of-fact
mat•ting
mat•tress
ma•ture
  mat•u•ra•tion
  ma•tu•ri•ty
mat•zo
maud•lin
maul
mau•so•le•um
mauve
mav•er•ick
mawk•ish
max•im
max•i•mal
max•i•mize
max•i•mum
may•be
may•hem
may•on•naise
may•or
  may•or•al
maze
mead•ow
mea•ger
mealy
meal•y-mouthed
mean
  meant
mean•ing
  mean•ing•ful
  mean•ing•less
mean•ness
me•an•der
mean•time
mean•while
mea•sles
mea•sly
meas•ur•a•ble
  meas•ur•a•bly
meas•ure
  meas•ured
  meas•ure•ment
meat
  meaty
mec•ca
me•chan•ic
me•chan•i•cal
mech•an•ism
mech•a•nize
med•al
  med•al•ist
me•dal•lion
med•dle
  med•dled
  med•dling
  med•dler
med•dle•some
me•dia
me•di•al
me•di•an
me•di•ate
  me•di•at•ed
  me•di•at•ing
  me•di•a•tion
  me•di•a•tor

med•ic
med•i•cal
  med•i•cal•ly
med•i•cate
  med•i•cat•ed
med•i•ca•tion
me•dic•i•nal
med•i•cine
me•di•e•val
me•di•o•cre
  me•di•oc•ri•ty
med•i•tate
  med•i•tat•ed
  med•i•tat•ing
  med•i•ta•tion
Med•i•ter•ra•ne•an
me•di•um
med•ley
meet
  met
  meet•ing
meg•a•lo•ma•nia
  meg•a•lo•ma•ni•ac
meg•a•phone
mel•an•choly
  mel•an•cho•lia
  mel•an•chol•ic
mé•lange
mel•a•no•ma
me•lee
mel•io•rate
  mel•io•ra•tion
mel•lif•lu•ous
  mel•lif•lu•ent
mel•low
me•lo•de•on
mel•o•dra•ma
  mel•o•dra•mat•ic
mel•o•dy
  mel•o•dies
  me•lod•ic
  me•lo•di•ous
mel•on
melt
  melt•ed or mol•ten
mem•ber
  mem•ber•ship
mem•brane
  mem•bra•nous
me•men•to
memo
mem•oir
mem•o•ra•bil•ia
mem•o•ra•ble
  mem•o•ra•bly
mem•o•ran•dum
me•mo•ri•al
me•mo•ri•al•ize
mem•o•rize
  mem•o•rized
  mem•o•riz•ing
  mem•o•ri•za•tion
mem•o•ry
  mem•o•ries
men•ace
  men•aced
  men•ac•ing
mé•nage
me•nag•er•ie
mend
men•da•cious
men•di•cant
me•ni•al
men•in•gi•tis
me•nis•cus
Men•no•nite
men•o•pause
men•ses
men•stru•al
  men•stru•a•tion
men•sur•a•ble
men•tal
  men•tal•ly
men•tal•i•ty
men•thol
men•tion
  men•tion•a•ble
men•tor
menu
mer•can•tile
mer•can•til•ism
mer•ce•nary
  mer•ce•nar•ies

mer•cer•ized
mer•chan•dise
  mer•chan•dis•ing
  mer•chan•dis•er
mer•chant
mer•cu•ri•al
mer•cu•ro•chrome
mer•cu•ry
mer•cy
  mer•ci•ful
  mer•ci•less
mere•ly
mer•e•tri•cious
merge
  merged
  merg•ing
merg•er
me•rid•i•an
me•ringue
mer•it
  mer•it•ed
  mer•i•to•ri•ous
mer•maid
mer•ry
  mer•ri•ment
me•sa
mes•cal
mes•dames
mesh
mes•mer•ism
  mes•mer•ic
mes•mer•ize
  mes•mer•ized
  mes•mer•iz•ing
  mes•mer•i•za•tion
mes•quite
mess
  messy
mes•sage
mes•sen•ger
Mes•si•ah
  Mes•si•an•ic
mes•sieurs
mes•ti•zo
me•tab•o•lism
  met•a•bol•ic
me•tab•o•lize
met•al
me•tal•lic
met•al•lur•gy
met•a•mor•phose
  met•a•mor•pho•sis
met•a•phor
  met•a•phor•ic
  met•a•phor•i•cal
met•a•phys•ics
  met•a•phys•i•cal
mete
  met•ed
  met•ing
me•te•or
  me•te•or•ic
  me•te•or•ite
me•te•or•ol•o•gy
  me•te•or•o•log•i•cal
  me•te•or•ol•o•gist
me•ter
  me•tre
meth•a•done
meth•ane
meth•a•nol
meth•od
  meth•od•i•cal
Meth•od•ist
meth•od•ol•o•gy
me•tic•u•lous
mé•tier
met•ric
met•ri•cal
met•ro
met•ro•nome
me•trop•o•lis
met•ro•pol•i•tan
met•tle
Mex•i•can
  Mex•i•co
mez•za•nine
mez•zo
mi•as•ma
mi•ca
Mi•chel•an•ge•lo
mi•crobe
  mi•cro•bi•al

mi•cro•bi•ol•o•gy
mi•cro•cosm
mi•cro•fiche
mi•cro•film
mi•cron
mi•cro•or•gan•ism
mi•cro•phone
mi•cro•scope
   mi•cro•scop•ic
   mi•cros•co•py
mi•cro•wave
mid•day
mid•dle
mid•dle-aged
mid•dle•man
mid•dling
midg•et
mid•land
mid•most
mid•night
mid•point
mid•riff
mid•sec•tion
midst
mid•sum•mer
mid•term
mid•way
mid•wife
mien
mighty
mi•graine
mi•grant
mi•grate
   mi•gra•tion
   mi•gra•to•ry
mild•ly
mil•dew
mile•age
mile•stone
mi•lieu
mil•i•tant
   mil•i•tan•cy
mil•i•ta•rize
mil•i•tary
   mil•i•tar•i•ly
mi•li•tia
milk•weed
milky
mil•len•ni•um
   mil•len•nia
   mil•len•ni•al
mill•er
mil•let
mil•li•gram
mil•li•li•ter
mil•li•me•ter
mil•li•ner
   mil•li•nery
mill•ing
mil•lion
   mil•lion•aire
mime
mimed
mim•ing
mim•ic
   mim•icked
   mim•ick•ing
   mim•ic•ry
mi•mo•sa
min•a•ret
mi•na•tory
mince
   minced
   minc•ing
mind•ed
mind•less
min•er
mine•field
min•er•al
min•er•al•o•gy
min•e•stro•ne
min•gle
   min•gled
   min•gling
min•i•a•ture
min•i•mal
   min•i•mal•ly
min•i•mize
   min•i•mi•za•tion
min•i•mum
min•ing
min•ion
min•is•cule

min•is•ter
   min•is•te•ri•al
min•is•tra•tion
min•is•try
   min•is•tries
min•now
mi•nor
mi•nor•i•ty
   mi•nor•i•ties
min•strel
mi•nus
mi•nus•cule
min•ute
mi•nute
mi•nu•tia
minx
mir•a•cle
mi•rac•u•lous
mi•rage
mire
   mired
mir•ror
mirth
mis•ad•ven•ture
mis•an•thrope
   mis•an•throp•ic
   mis•an•thro•py
mis•ap•pli•ca•tion
mis•ap•pre•hen•sion
mis•ap•pro•pri•a•tion
mis•be•have
   mis•be•ha•vior
mis•belief
mis•cal•cu•la•tion
mis•car•ry
   mis•car•rige
mis•ce•ge•na•tion
mis•cel•la•ne•ous
mis•cel•la•ny
mis•chance
mis•chief
   mis•chie•vous
mis•ci•ble
mis•con•ceive
   mis•con•cep•tion
mis•con•duct
mis•con•strue
mis•cre•ant
mis•deed
mis•de•mean•or
mis•di•rect
mi•ser
   mi•ser•ly
mis•er•a•ble
   mis•er•a•bly
mis•ery
   mis•er•ies
mis•fea•sance
mis•fire
mis•fit
mis•for•tune
mis•giv•ing
mis•guid•ed
mis•han•dled
mis•hap
mish•mash
mis•in•form
   mis•in•for•ma•tion
mis•in•ter•pret
   mis•in•ter•pre•ta•tion
mis•judge
   mis•judg•ment
mis•lay
   mis•laid
mis•lead
   mis•lead•ing
mis•man•age
   mis•man•age•ment
mis•match
mis•no•mer
mi•sog•a•my
mi•sog•y•ny
   mi•sog•y•nist
   mi•sog•y•nous
mis•place
   mis•placed
mis•print
mis•pro•nounce
   mis•pro•nun•ci•a•tion
mis•rep•re•sent
   mis•rep•re•sen•ta•tion
mis•rule
mis•sal

mis•shap•en
mis•sile
miss•ing
mis•sion
mis•sion•ary
   mis•sion•ar•ies
mis•sive
mis•spell
   mis•spelled
mis•spent
mis•state•ment
mis•step
mis•take
   mis•took
   mis•tak•en
   mis•tak•en•ly
Mis•ter
mis•tle•toe
mis•treat
mis•tress
mis•tri•al
mis•trust
misty
mis•un•der•stand
   mis•un•der•stood
   mis•un•der•stand•ing
mis•use
   mis•used
   mis•us•ing
mi•ter
mi•tre
mit•i•gate
   mit•i•gat•ed
   mit•i•gat•ing
   mit•i•ga•tion
mitt
   mit•ten
mix
   mixed
   mix•ing
   mix•er
   mix•ture
miz•zen
mne•mon•ic
mob
   mobbed
   mob•bing
mo•bile
   mo•bil•i•ty
mo•bi•lize
   mo•bi•lized
   mo•bi•liz•ing
   mo•bi•li•za•tion
mob•ster
moc•ca•sin
mo•cha
mock
   mock•ery
mock•ing•bird
mock•up
mod•al
   mo•dal•i•ty
mod•el
   mod•eled
   mod•el•ing
mod•er•ate
   mod•er•at•ed
   mod•er•at•ing
   mod•er•a•tion
mod•er•a•tor
mod•ern
mod•ern•ism
   mod•ern•ist•ic
mod•ern•ize
   mod•ern•i•za•tion
mod•est
   mod•es•ty
mod•i•cum
mod•i•fi•ca•tion
mod•i•fy
   mod•i•fied
   mod•i•fy•ing
   mod•i•fi•er
mod•ish
mod•u•late
   mod•u•lat•ed
   mod•u•lat•ing
   mod•u•la•tion
mod•ule
   mod•u•lar
mo•dus o•pe•ran•di
mo•gul
mo•hair

Mo•ham•med
moi•e•ty
mois•ten
   moist•en•er
mois•ture
   mois•tur•ize
   mois•tur•ized
   mois•tur•iz•ing
   mois•tur•iz•er
mo•lar
mo•las•ses
mold
mold•ing
moldy
mol•e•cule
   mo•lec•u•lar
mole•skin
mo•lest
   mo•les•ta•tion
   mo•lest•er
mol•li•fy
   mol•li•fied
   mol•li•fy•ing
mol•lusk
mol•ly•cod•dle
molt
mol•ten
mo•ment
   mo•men•tary
   mo•men•tar•i•ly
mo•men•tous
mo•men•tum
mon•ad
mon•arch
   mo•nar•chal
   mo•nar•chic
   mon•ar•chism
   mon•ar•chist
   mon•ar•chy
mon•as•tery
mo•nas•tic
mon•e•tary
   mon•e•tar•i•ly
mon•ey
mon•eyed
   mon•ied
mon•ger
Mon•go•lia
mon•gol•ism
   mon•gol•oid
mon•goose
mon•grel
mon•i•ker
mon•ism
   mo•nis•tic
mon•i•tor
monk
mon•key
   mon•keys
   mon•keyed
   mon•key•ing
mon•o•chro•mat•ic
mon•o•cle
mon•o•dy
   mo•nod•ic
mo•nog•a•my
   mo•nog•a•mous
mon•o•gram
mon•o•graph
mon•o•lith
mon•o•logue
mon•o•mi•al
mon•o•nu•cle•o•sis
mo•nop•o•lize
   mo•nop•o•lized
   mo•nop•o•liz•ing
mo•nop•o•ly
   mo•nop•o•lies
mon•o•rail
mon•o•so•di•um glu•ta•mate
mon•o•syl•lab•ic
mon•o•the•ism
mon•o•tone
mo•not•o•ny
   mo•not•o•nous
mon•o•type
mon•ox•ide
mon•sieur
   mes•sieurs
Mon•si•gnor
mon•soon
mon•ster
   mon•stros•i•ty

mon•strous
mon•tage
Mon•tes•so•ri
month•ly
   month•lies
mon•u•ment
   mon•u•men•tal
mooch
   mooch•er
moody
moon•beam
moon•light•ing
moon•shine
moor•ing
moot
mop
   mopped
   mop•ping
mope
   moped
   mop•ing
mo•raine
mor•al
   mor•al•ly
mo•rale
mor•al•ist
   mor•al•is•tic
mo•ral•i•ty
mor•al•ize
   mor•al•iz•ing
mo•rass
mor•a•to•ri•um
mor•bid
   mor•bid•i•ty
mor•dant
more•o•ver
mo•res
mor•ga•nat•ic
morgue
mor•i•bund
Mor•mon•ism
morn•ing
Mo•roc•co
mo•ron
   mo•ron•ic
mo•rose
   mo•rose•ly
mor•phine
mor•phol•o•gy
mor•row
mor•sel
mor•tal
   mor•tal•ly
   mor•tal•i•ty
mor•tar
mort•gage
   mort•gaged
mor•ti•cian
mor•ti•fy
   mor•ti•fied
   mor•ti•fy•ing
   mor•ti•fi•ca•tion
mor•tise
mor•tu•ary
mo•sa•ic
mo•sey
   mo•seyed
   mo•sey•ing
Mos•lem
mosque
mos•qui•to
   mos•qui•toes
   mos•qui•tos
moss
   mossy
most•ly
mo•tel
mo•tet
moth•ball
moth-eat•en
moth•er
   moth•er-in-law
moth•er-of-pearl
mo•tif
mo•tile
   mo•til•i•ty
mo•tion
mo•ti•vate
   mo•ti•vat•ed
   mo•ti•vat•ing
   mo•ti•va•tion
mo•tive
mot•ley

mo•tor
mo•tor•cade
mo•tor•cy•cle
mo•tor•ist
mot•tled
mound
mount
   mount•a•ble
moun•tain
   moun•tain•eer
   moun•tain•ous
moun•te•bank
mourn
   mourn•er
   mourn•ful
   mourn•ing
mouse
mousy
mousse
mous•tache
mouth
   mouthed
mouth•ful
mouth•piece
mou•ton
mov•a•ble
move
   moved
   mov•ing
move•ment
mov•ie
mow
   mowed or mown
muck•rak•er
mu•cus
mu•cous
mud
   mud•dy
mud•dle
   mud•dled
   mud•dling
muf•fin
muf•fle
   muf•fled
muf•fler
muf•ti
mug
   mugged
   mug•ging
   mug•ger
mug•gy
mu•lat•to
   mu•lat•toes
mul•ber•ry
mulch
mul•ish
mul•let
mu•li•gan
mul•lion
mul•ti•col•ored
mul•ti•far•i•ous
mul•ti•lat•er•al
mul•ti•lev•el
mul•ti•par•tite
mul•ti•ple
mul•ti•ple scle•ro•sis
mul•ti•pli•ca•tion
mul•ti•ply
   mul•ti•plied
   mul•ti•ply•ing
mul•ti•tude
   mul•ti•tu•di•nous
mum•ble
   mum•bled
   mum•bling
mum•my
munch
mun•dane
mu•nic•i•pal
   mu•nic•i•pal•i•ty
mu•nif•i•cent
   mu•nif•i•cence
mu•ni•tion
mu•ral
mur•der
   mur•der•er
   mur•der•ess
   mur•der•ous
murky
mur•mur
   mur•mur•ing
mur•rain
mus•cat

mus•cle
   mus•cled
   mus•cling
mus•cu•lar
mus•cu•lar dys•tro•phy
muse
   mused
   mus•ing
mu•se•um
mush•room
mushy
mu•sic
   mu•si•cal
   mu•si•cal•ly
   mu•si•cian
mus•ket
mus•ket•eer
musk•rat
musky
Mus•lim
mus•lin
muss
mus•sel
mus•tache
mus•tang
mus•tard
mus•ter
musty
mu•ta•ble
mu•tant
mu•ta•tion
   mu•tate
mute
   mut•ed
mu•ti•late
   mu•ti•lat•ed
   mu•ti•la•tion
mu•ti•neer
mu•ti•ny
   mu•ti•nied
   mu•ti•nous
mut•ter
   mut•tered
   mut•ter•ing
mut•ton
mu•tu•al
   mu•tu•al•i•ty
   mu•tu•al•ly
muz•zle
   muz•zled
my•col•o•gy
my•na
my•o•pia
   my•op•ic
myr•i•ad
myrrh
myr•tle
my•self
mys•te•ri•ous
mys•tery
   mys•ter•ies
mys•tic
   mys•ti•cal
   mys•ti•cism
mys•ti•fy
   mys•ti•fied
   mys•ti•fy•ing
   mys•ti•fi•ca•tion
mys•tique
myth
   myth•i•cal
my•thol•o•gy
   myth•o•log•i•cal

N

nab
   nabbed
   nab•bing
na•dir
nag
   nagged
   nag•ging
   nag•ger
na•ive
   na•ive•ly
   na•ive•té
na•ked•ly
name
   named
   nam•ing
   name•ly
   name•sake

nan•ny
nap
   napped
   nap•ping
na•palm
nape
nap•kin
Na•po•leon
nar•cis•sism
   nar•cism
   nar•cis•sist
   nar•cis•sis•tic
   nar•cis•sus
nar•cot•ic
nar•rate
   nar•ra•ted
   nar•ra•ting
   nar•ra•tor
   nar•ra•tion
   nar•ra•tive
nar•row•ly
nar•row-mind•ed
na•sal
nas•cent
na•stur•tium
nas•ty
   nas•ti•ly
na•tal
na•tion
na•tion•al
   na•tion•al•ly
   na•tion•al•ism
   na•tion•al•ist
   na•tion•al•is•tic
   na•tion•al•i•ty
   na•tion•al•i•ties
   na•tion•al•ize
   na•tion•al•i•za•tion
na•tive
   na•tiv•i•ty
nat•ty
nat•u•ral
   nat•u•ral•ly
   nat•u•ral•ist
   nat•u•ral•is•tic
   nat•u•ral•ize
   nat•u•ral•ized
na•ture
naught
naugh•ty
nau•sea
nau•se•ate
   nau•se•at•ed
   nau•se•at•ing
nau•seous
nau•ti•cal
nau•ti•lus
na•vel
nav•i•ga•ble
nav•i•gate
   nav•i•ga•tion
   nav•i•ga•tor
na•vy
   na•val
Naz•a•reth
Na•zi
Ne•an•der•thal
near•ly
neat•ly
neb•u•la
neb•u•lous
nec•es•sary
   nec•es•sar•i•ly
ne•ces•si•tate
   ne•ces•si•ta•ted
   ne•ces•si•ta•ting
ne•ces•si•ty
   ne•ces•si•ites
neck•lace
neck•tie
ne•crol•o•gy
nec•ro•man•cy
ne•crop•o•lis
nec•tar
nec•tar•ine
need•ful
nee•dle
   nee•dled
   nee•dling
need•less•ly
needy
   need•i•est
   need•i•ness

ne'er-do-well
ne•far•i•ous
ne•gate
   ne•ga•ted
   ne•ga•ting
   ne•ga•tion
neg•a•tive
   neg•a•tiv•i•ty
ne•glect
   ne•glect•ful
neg•li•gent
   neg•li•gence
neg•li•gi•ble
ne•go•ti•a•ble
ne•go•ti•ate
   ne•go•ti•at•ed
   ne•go•ti•at•ing
   ne•go•ti•a•tion
   ne•go•ti•a•tor
neigh
neigh•bor
   neigh•bor•ing
   neigh•bor•ly
   neigh•bor•hood
nei•ther
nem•e•sis
ne•o•clas•sic
   ne•o•clas•si•cal
   ne•o•clas•si•cism
ne•o•lith•ic
ne•ol•o•gism
ne•on
ne•o•phyte
neph•ew
ne•phri•tis
nep•o•tism
nerve-rack•ing
   nerve-wrack•ing
nerv•ous
nervy
nes•tle
   nes•tled
   nes•tling
net
   net•ted
   net•ting
neth•er
Neth•er•lands
net•tle
   net•tled
   net•tling
   net•tle•some
net•work
neu•ral
neu•ral•gia
neu•ras•the•nia
neu•ri•tis
neu•rol•o•gy
   neu•ro•log•i•cal
   neu•rol•o•gist
neu•ron
neu•ro•sis
   neu•ro•ses
neu•rot•ic
neu•ter
neu•tral
   neu•tral•i•ty
neu•tral•ize
   neu•tral•ized
   neu•tral•iz•ing
neu•tron
nev•er
nev•er•the•less
new•born
new•com•er
new•el
new•fan•gled
new•ly•wed
news•cast•er
news•pa•per
news•print
news•stand
New Test•a•ment
New Zea•land
nex•us
ni•a•cin
Ni•ag•a•ra
nib•ble
   nib•bled
   nib•bling
Nic•a•ra•gua
nice
   nice•ly

ni•ce•ty
   ni•ce•ties
niche
nick•el•o•de•on
nick•name
nic•o•tine
niece
nif•ty
Ni•ge•ria
nig•gard•ly
nig•gling
night•in•gale
night•ly
night•mare
   night•mar•ish
night•time
ni•hil•ism
   ni•hil•ist
   ni•hil•is•tic
nim•ble
   nim•bly
nim•bus
nin•comp•poop
nine•teen
nine•ty
   nine•ties
   nine•ti•eth
nin•ny
ninth
nip
   nipped
   nip•ping
nip•ple
Nip•pon
nip•py
nir•va•na
nit•pick
ni•trate
ni•tric
ni•tro•gen
ni•tro•glyc•er•in
nit•wit
no•bil•i•ty
no•ble
   no•bler
   no•blest
   no•ble•man
   no•bly
no•blesse oblige
no•body
noc•tur•nal
noc•turne
nod
   nod•ded
   nod•ding
node
   nod•al
nod•ule
   nod•u•lar
No•ël
nog•gin
noise
   noisy
   nois•i•ly
noi•some
no•mad
   no•mad•ic
nom de plume
no•men•cla•ture
nom•i•nal
   nom•i•nal•ly
nom•i•nate
   nom•i•nat•ed
   nom•i•nat•ing
   nom•i•na•tion
   nom•i•nee
nom•i•na•tive
non•cha•lant
   non•cha•lance
non•com•mit•tal
non•con•form•ist
   non•con•form•i•ty
non•de•script
non•en•ti•ty
none•the•less
non•pa•reil
non•par•ti•san
non•plused
   non•plussed
non•prof•it
non•re•sis•tance
non•re•stric•tive
non•sec•tar•i•an

non•sense
  non•sen•si•cal
non se•qui•tur
non•stop
noo•dle
noon•day
noon•time
noose
nor•mal
  nor•mal•cy
  nor•mal•i•ty
  nor•mal•ly
  nor•mal•ize
  nor•mal•i•za•tion
Norse•man
north•east
  north•east•ern
north•er•ly
north•ern
north•west
  north•west•ern
Nor•we•gian
nose
  nosed
  nos•ing
nos•tal•gia
  nos•tal•gic
nos•tril
nos•trum
nosy
  nos•i•ly
no•ta•ble
  no•ta•bly
no•ta•rize
  no•ta•rized
no•ta•ry
no•ta•tion
notch
  notched
note
  not•ed
  not•ing
note•wor•thy
noth•ing•ness
no•tice
  no•ticed
  no•tic•ing
  no•tice•a•ble
  no•tice•a•bly
no•ti•fy
  no•ti•fied
  no•ti•fy•ing
  no•ti•fi•ca•tion
no•tion
no•to•ri•ous
  no•to•ri•e•ty
nought
nour•ish
  nour•ish•ment
no•va
No•va Sco•tia
nov•el
  nov•el•ist
nov•el•ty
  nov•el•ties
no•ve•na
nov•ice
No•vo•cain
now•a•days
no•where
nox•ious
noz•zle
nu•ance
nub•bin
nu•bile
nu•cle•ar
nu•cle•on
nu•cle•us
  nu•clei
nude
  nu•di•ty
  nud•ist
nudge
  nudged
  nudg•ing
nu•ga•to•ry
nug•get
nui•sance
null
  nul•li•ty
nul•li•fy
  nul•li•fied
  nul•li•fi•ca•tion

numb
  numb•ly
num•ber
nu•mer•al
nu•mer•a•tor
nu•mer•i•cal
nu•mer•ous
nu•mis•mat•ics
num•skull
  numb•skull
nun•cio
nun•nery
nup•tial
nurse
  nursed
  nurs•ing
nurs•ery
  nurs•er•ies
nur•ture
  nur•tured
  nur•tur•ing
nut
  nut•ty
nut•crack•er
nut•meg
nu•tri•ent
  nu•tri•ment
nu•tri•tion
  nu•tri•tion•al
  nu•tri•tious
  nu•tri•tive
nut•shell
nuz•zle
  nuz•zled
  nuz•zling
ny•lon
nymph
nym•pho•ma•nia
  nym•pho•ma•ni•ac

O

oaf
oak•en
oars•man
oa•sis
oath
oat•meal
ob•du•rate
  ob•du•ra•cy
obe•di•ence
obe•di•ent
obei•sance
  obei•sant
ob•e•lisk
obese
  obes•i•ty
obey
ob•fus•cate
  ob•fus•ca•tion
obit•u•ary
  obit•u•ar•ies
ob•ject
ob•jec•tion
ob•jec•tive
  ob•jec•tiv•i•ty
ob•jet d'art
ob•jur•gate
  ob•jur•ga•tion
ob•la•tion
ob•li•gate
  ob•li•gat•ed
  ob•li•gat•ing
  ob•li•ga•tion
  ob•lig•a•to•ry
oblige
  obliged
  oblig•ing
ob•lique
ob•lit•er•ate
  ob•lit•er•at•ed
  ob•lit•er•at•ing
  ob•lit•er•a•tion
ob•liv•i•on
ob•liv•i•ous
ob•long
ob•lo•quy
ob•nox•ious
oboe
ob•scene
  ob•scen•i•ty
ob•scure
  ob•scu•ri•ty

ob•se•qui•ous
ob•se•quy
ob•ser•va•to•ry
ob•serve
  ob•served
  ob•serv•ing
  ob•serv•er
  ob•ser•vance
  ob•ser•vant
  ob•ser•va•tion
ob•sess
  ob•ses•sive
  ob•ses•sion
ob•sid•i•an
ob•so•lete
  ob•so•les•cence
  ob•so•les•cent
ob•sta•cle
ob•stet•rics
  ob•ste•tri•cian
ob•sti•nate
  ob•sti•na•cy
ob•strep•er•ous
ob•struct
  ob•struc•tion
  ob•struc•tive
ob•tain
  ob•tain•a•ble
ob•tru•sion
ob•tru•sive
ob•tuse
ob•verse
ob•vi•ate
ob•vi•ous
oc•ca•sion
  oc•ca•sion•al
  oc•ca•sion•al•ly
oc•ci•dent
oc•clude
  oc•clu•sion
oc•cult
oc•cu•pa•tion
  oc•cu•pa•tion•al
oc•cu•py
  oc•cu•pied
  oc•cu•py•ing
  oc•cu•pan•cy
  oc•cu•pant
oc•cur
  oc•curred
  oc•cur•ring
  oc•cur•rence
ocean
  oce•an•ic
  oce•a•nog•ra•phy
  oce•a•nog•ra•pher
oce•lot
ocher
o'clock
oc•ta•gon
  oc•tag•o•nal
oc•tane
oc•tave
oc•tet
oc•to•ge•nar•i•an
oc•to•pus
oc•u•lar
odd•ball
odd•i•ty
  odd•i•ties
odi•ous
odi•um
odom•e•ter
odor
  odor•ous
  odor•if•er•ous
od•ys•sey
Oed•i•pus
of•fal
off•beat
off•col•or
of•fend
  of•fend•er
of•fense
  of•fen•sive
of•fer
  of•fer•ing
  of•fer•to•ry
off•hand
of•fice
of•fic•er
of•fi•cial
  of•fi•cial•ly

of•fi•ci•ate
  of•fi•ci•at•ed
  of•fi•ci•at•ing
of•fi•cious
off•ing
off•set
  off•set•ting
off•shoot
off•shore
off•spring
of•ten
  of•ten•times
ogle
  ogled
  ogling
ogre
ohm
  ohm•me•ter
oily
oint•ment
okra
old•er
  old•est
old•en
old-fash•ioned
Old Test•a•ment
old-tim•er
old-world
ol•fac•to•ry
ol•i•gar•chy
  ol•i•gar•chic
ol•ive
O•lym•pic
  Olym•pi•an
om•buds•man
ome•ga
om•e•let
omen
om•i•nous
omis•sion
omit
  omit•ted
  omit•ting
om•ni•bus
om•nip•o•tence
om•ni•pres•ent
  om•ni•pres•ence
om•nis•cience
  om•nis•cient
om•niv•or•ous
on•er•ous
one•self
one-sid•ed
one-way
on•ion
on•look•er
on•ly
on•o•mat•o•poe•ia
on•set
on•slaught
on•to
onus
on•ward
on•yx
oo•dles
ooze
  oozed
  ooz•ing
opac•i•ty
opal
opal•es•cence
  opal•es•cent
opaque
open
  open•ly
open house
open•ing
open-mind•ed
opera
op•er•at•ic
op•er•a•ble
op•er•ate
  op•er•at•ed
  op•er•at•ing
  op•er•a•tion
  op•er•a•tive
  op•er•a•tor
op•er•et•ta
oph•thal•mic
  oph•thal•mol•o•gist
  oph•thal•mol•o•gy
opi•ate
opin•ion

opin•ion•at•ed
opi•um
opos•sum
op•po•nent
op•por•tune
op•por•tun•ist
  op•por•tun•is•tic
op•por•tu•ni•ty
  op•por•tu•ni•ties
op•pose
  op•posed
  op•pos•ing
op•po•site
  op•po•si•tion
op•press
  op•pres•sor
  op•pres•sion
  op•pres•sive
op•pro•bri•um
  op•pro•bri•ous
op•tic
  op•ti•cal
op•ti•cian
op•ti•mism
op•ti•mist
  op•ti•mis•tic
  op•ti•mis•ti•cal•ly
op•ti•mize
op•ti•mum
op•ti•mal
op•tion
  op•tion•al
op•tom•e•try
  op•tom•e•trist
op•u•lent
  op•u•lence
opus
or•a•cle
  orac•u•lar
oral
  oral•ly
or•ange
orang•u•tan
ora•tion
or•a•tor
  or•a•tor•i•cal
  or•a•to•ry
or•a•to•rio
or•bit
or•chard
or•ches•tra
  or•ches•tral
  or•ches•trate
  or•ches•tra•tion
or•chid
or•dain
or•deal
or•der
  or•dered
  or•der•ly
or•di•nal
or•di•nance
or•di•nar•i•ly
or•di•nary
or•di•na•tion
ord•nance
oreg•a•no
or•gan
or•gan•dy
or•gan•ic
  or•gan•i•cal•ly
or•gan•ism
or•gan•ist
or•gan•i•za•tion
  or•gan•i•za•tion•al
or•gan•ize
  or•gan•ized
  or•gan•iz•ing
  or•gan•iz•er
or•gasm
  or•gas•mic
or•gy
  or•gies
ori•ent
  Ori•en•tal
ori•en•tate
  ori•en•ta•tion
or•i•fice
orig•i•nal
  orig•i•nal•i•ty
  orig•i•nal•ly
orig•i•nate
  orig•i•nat•ed

orig•i•nat•ing
or•na•ment
  or•na•men•tal
  or•na•men•ta•tion
or•nate
or•nery
or•ni•thol•o•gy
  or•ni•thol•o•gist
oro•tund
or•phan
  or•phan•age
or•tho•don•tics
  or•tho•don•tist
or•tho•dox
  or•tho•doxy
or•thog•ra•phy
or•tho•pe•dics
  or•tho•pe•dist
os•cil•late
  os•cil•la•tor
os•mo•sis
os•prey
os•si•fy
  os•si•fi•ca•tion
os•ten•si•ble
  os•ten•si•bly
os•ten•sive
  os•ten•sive•ly
os•ten•ta•tion
  os•ten•ta•tious
os•te•op•a•thy
  os•te•o•path
os•tra•cize
  os•tra•cized
  os•tra•ciz•ing
  os•tra•cism
os•trich
oth•er•wise
oti•ose
ot•ter
ot•to•man
ought
ounce
our•selves
oust•er
out•bid
out•board
out•break
out•build•ing
out•burst
out•cast
out•come
out•cry
out•dat•ed
out•do
out•door
out•er•most
out•er space
out•field
out•grow
out•land•ish
out•law
out•ly•ing
out•mod•ed
out•num•ber
out-of-date
out•rage
  out•ra•geous
out•right
out•sid•er
out•skirts
out•spo•ken
out•stand•ing
out•ward
out•weigh
oval
ova•ry
  ova•ries
  ovar•i•an
ova•tion
ov•en
over
over•act
over•age
over•bear•ing
over•board
over•come
over•dose
over•drawn
over•hand
over•hang•ing
over•joyed
over•night

over•pow•er
over•rat•ed
over•reach
over•ride
over•rule
over•shad•ow
over•sight
over•state•ment
overt
over-the-coun•ter
over•time
over•ture
over•weight
over•whelm
over•worked
ovu•late
  ovu•la•tion
ovum
  ova
owe
  owed
  ow•ing
owl•ish
own•er
ox•en
ox•ford
ox•ide
ox•y•gen
oys•ter
ozone

P

pab•u•lum
pace
  paced
  pac•ing
pace•mak•er
pach•y•derm
pa•cif•ic
pac•i•fi•er
pac•i•fism
  pac•i•fist
pac•i•fy
  pac•i•fied
  pac•i•fy•ing
  pa•cif•i•ca•tion
pack•age
  pack•ag•er
pack•er
pack•et
pack•ing
pad
  pad•ded
  pad•ding
pad•dle
  pad•dled
  pad•dling
pad•dock
pad•dy
pad•lock
pae•an
pa•gan
page
  paged
  pag•ing
pag•eant
  pag•eant•ry
pag•i•nate
  pag•i•na•tion
pa•go•da
pail•ful
pain•ful•ly
pains•tak•ing
paint•er
  paint•ing
pais•ley
pa•jam•as
pal•ace
pal•at•a•ble
pal•ate
pa•la•tial
pa•lav•er
pale
  paled
  pal•ing
Pa•le•o•lith•ic
pa•le•on•tol•o•gy
pal•i•sade
pal•la•di•um
pall•bear•er
pal•let
pal•li•ate

pal•li•a•tion
pal•lia•tive
pal•lid
pal•lor
palm
pal•met•to
palm•is•try
pal•pa•ble
pal•pate
  pal•pa•tion
pal•pi•tate
  pal•pi•ta•tion
pal•sy
pal•try
pam•per
pam•phlet
pan
  panned
  pan•ning
pan•a•ce•a
pa•nache
pan•cake
pan•cre•as
  pan•cre•at•ic
pan•da
pan•dem•ic
pan•de•mo•ni•um
pan•der
pan•el
  pan•eled
  pan•el•ing
pan•el•ist
pang
pan•han•dler
pan•ic
  pan•icked
  pan•ick•ing
pan•o•ply
pan•o•rama
  pan•o•ram•ic
pan•sy
  pan•sies
pan•ta•loon
pan•the•ism
  pan•the•ist
pan•the•on
pan•ther
pan•tie
  pan•ty
pan•to•mime
pan•try
pa•pa
pa•pa•cy
  pa•pal
pa•pa•ya
pa•per•back
pa•per•weight
pa•per•work
pa•pier-mâ•ché
pa•poose
pap•ri•ka
pa•py•rus
par•a•ble
par•ab•o•la
par•a•chute
pa•rade
  pa•rad•ed
  pa•rad•ing
par•a•digm
par•a•dise
  par•a•di•si•a•cal
par•a•dox
  par•a•dox•i•cal
par•af•fin
par•a•gon
par•a•graph
Par•a•guay
par•a•keet
par•al•lax
par•al•lel
pa•ral•y•sis
  par•a•lyt•ic
par•a•lyze
  par•a•lyzed
  par•a•lyz•ing
par•a•med•ic
pa•ram•e•ter
par•a•mount
par•a•mour
par•a•noia
  para•noi•ac
  par•a•noid
par•a•pet

par•a•pher•nal•ia
par•a•phrase
par•a•ple•gia
  par•a•ple•gic
par•a•site
  par•a•sit•ic
par•a•troop•er
par•cel
parch•ment
par•don
  par•don•a•ble
pare
  pared
  par•ing
par•ent
  pa•ren•tal
par•ent•age
pa•ren•the•sis
  pa•ren•the•ses
  par•en•thet•ic
  par•en•thet•i•cal
pa•re•sis
par•fait
pa•ri•ah
par•ish
  pa•rish•ion•er
par•i•ty
par•ka
par•lance
par•lay
par•ley
par•lia•ment
  par•lia•men•tar•i•an
  par•lia•men•ta•ry
par•lor
pa•ro•chi•al
par•o•dy
pa•role
  pa•roled
  pa•rol•ee
par•ox•ysm
  par•ox•ys•mal
par•quet
par•ra•keet
par•ri•cide
par•ry
  par•ried
  par•ry•ing
parse
par•si•mo•ny
  par•si•mo•ni•ous
par•sley
pars•nip
par•son
  par•son•age
par•take
part•ed
par•the•no•gen•e•sis
par•tial
  par•tial•ly
  par•ti•al•i•ty
par•tic•i•pate
  par•tic•i•pat•ed
  par•tic•i•pat•ing
  par•tic•i•pant
  par•tic•i•pa•tion
  par•tic•i•pa•tor
par•ti•ci•ple
  par•ti•cip•i•al
par•ti•cle
par•tic•u•lar
  par•tic•u•lar•i•ty
part•ing
par•ti•san
  par•ti•san•ship
par•ti•tion
part•ly
part•ner
  part•ner•ship
par•tridge
par•tu•ri•tion
par•ty
  par•ties
par•ve•nu
pas•chal
pass•a•ble
pass•sage
pas•sé
pas•sen•ger
pass•er•by
pass•ing
pas•sion
  pas•sion•ate

pas•sion•ate•ly
pas•sive
  pas•siv•i•ty
Pass•over
pass•word
pas•ta
paste
  pas•ted
  pas•ting
pas•tel
pas•teur•ize
  pas•teur•ized
pas•time
pas•tor
pas•to•ral
pas•tra•mi
pas•try
  pas•tries
pas•ture
  pas•tur•age
pasty
pat
  pat•ted
  pat•ting
patchy
pâ•té
pat•ent
  pa•ten•cy
pat•er•nal
  pa•ter•ni•ty
pa•ter•nal•is•tic
pa•ter•noster
pa•thet•ic
  pa•thet•i•cal•ly
patho•gen•ic
pa•thol•o•gy
  path•o•log•ic
  path•o•log•i•cal
  pa•thol•o•gist
pa•thos
pa•tient
  pa•tience
pat•i•na
pa•tio
pat•ois
pa•tri•arch
pa•tri•cian
pat•ri•cide
pat•ri•mo•ny
pa•tri•ot
  pa•tri•ot•ic
  pa•tri•ot•i•cal•ly
  pa•tri•ot•ism
pa•trol
  pa•trolled
  pa•trol•ling
pa•trol•man
pa•tron
  pa•tron•ess
pa•tron•age
pa•tron•ize
  pa•tron•ized
  pa•tron•iz•ing
pat•sy
pat•ter
pat•tern
  pat•terned
pat•ty
pau•ci•ty
paunch
pau•per
pause
  paused
  paus•ing
pave
  paved
  pav•ing
pave•ment
pa•vil•ion
Pav•lov
pawn
  pawn•bro•ker
pay
  paid
  pay•ing
  pay•ee
  pay•ment
  pay•a•ble
peace
  peace•a•bly
  peace•ful
peach
pea•cock

peak•ed
peal
pea•nut
pearl
pearly
peas•ant
peat
peb•ble
peb•bly
pe•can
pec•ca•dil•lo
pec•tin
pec•to•ral
pec•u•late
pe•cu•liar
pe•cu•li•ar•i•ty
pe•cu•ni•ary
ped•a•gog•ic
ped•a•go•gy
ped•al
ped•aled
ped•al•ing
ped•ant
pe•dan•tic
ped•dle
ped•dler
ped•es•tal
pe•des•tri•an
pe•di•at•rics
pe•di•a•tri•cian
ped•i•cure
ped•i•gree
ped•i•ment
peel•ing
per
peer•age
peeve
peeved
peev•ish
peg
pegged
peg•ging
pe•jo•ra•tive
pe•koe
pel•i•can
pel•let
pel•vis
pen
penned
pe•nal
pe•nal•ize
pe•nal•ized
pe•nal•iz•ing
pen•al•ty
pen•al•ties
pen•ance
pen•chant
pen•cil
pen•ciled
pen•cilled
pend•ant
pend•ent
pend•ing
pen•du•lous
pen•e•trate
pen•e•trat•ed
pen•e•trat•ing
pen•e•tra•tion
pen•guin
pen•i•cil•lin
pen•in•su•la
pen•in•su•lar
pe•nis
pen•i•tent
pen•i•tence
pen•i•ten•tia•ry
pen•knife
pen•man•ship
pen•nant
Penn•syl•va•nia
pen•ny
pen•nies
pen•ni•less
pen•sion
pen•sion•er
pen•sive
pen•ta•cle
pen•ta•gon
pen•tam•e•ter
Pen•te•cost
Pen•te•cos•tal
pent•house
pen•ul•ti•mate

pe•nu•ri•ous
pen•u•ry
pe•on
pe•o•ny
peo•ple
peo•pled
peo•pling
pep
pep•py
pep•lum
pep•per
pep•sin
pep•tic
per•am•bu•late
per an•num
per•cale
per cap•i•ta
per•ceive
per•ceived
per•ceiv•ing
per•cent
per•cent•age
per•cen•tile
per•cep•ti•ble
per•cep•ti•bly
per•cep•tion
per•cep•tive
per•chance
per•cip•i•ent
per•cip•i•ence
per•co•late
per•co•la•tion
per•co•la•tor
per•cus•sion
per•cus•sive
per di•em
per•di•tion
per•e•gri•na•tion
per•emp•to•ry
per•en•ni•al
per•en•ni•al•ly
per•fect
per•fect•i•ble
per•fect•i•bil•i•ty
per•fec•tion
per•fect•ly
per•fi•dy
per•fid•i•ous
per•fo•rate
per•fo•rat•ed
per•fo•ra•tion
per•force
per•form
per•form•er
per•for•mance
per•fume
per•func•to•ry
per•haps
per•il
per•il•ous
pe•rim•e•ter
pe•ri•od
pe•ri•od•ic
pe•ri•od•i•cal
per•i•pa•tet•ic
pe•riph•ery
pe•riph•er•al
per•i•scope
per•ish
per•ish•a•ble
per•i•win•kle
per•jure
per•jured
per•jur•ing
per•jur•er
per•ju•ry
perky
per•ma•nent
per•ma•nen•cy
per•me•ate
per•me•at•ed
per•me•a•ble
per•mis•si•ble
per•mis•sion
per•mis•sive
per•mit
per•mu•ta•tion
per•ni•cious
per•o•rate
per•o•ra•tion
per•ox•ide
per•pen•dic•u•lar
per•pe•trate

per•pe•trat•ed
per•pe•tra•tor
per•pet•u•al
per•pet•u•al•ly
per•pet•u•ate
per•pe•tu•i•ty
per•plex
per•plexed
per•plex•ing
per•qui•site
per se
per•se•cute
per•se•cut•ed
per•se•cut•ing
per•se•cu•tor
per•se•cu•tion
per•se•vere
per•se•vered
per•se•ver•ing
per•se•ver•ance
per•si•flage
per•sim•mon
per•sist
per•sist•ence
per•sist•ent
per•snick•ety
per•son•a•ble
per•son•age
per•son•al
per•son•al•ly
per•son•al•i•ty
per•son•al•ize
per•so•na non gra•ta
per•son•i•fy
per•son•i•fied
per•son•i•fi•ca•tion
per•son•nel
per•spec•tive
per•spi•ca•cious
per•spi•cac•i•ty
per•spic•u•ous
per•spire
per•spired
per•spir•ing
per•spi•ra•tion
per•suade
per•suad•ed
per•suad•ing
per•sua•sion
per•sua•sive
pert
per•tain
per•ti•na•cious
per•ti•nac•i•ty
per•ti•nent
per•ti•nence
per•turb
per•tur•ba•tion
pe•ruse
pe•rused
pe•rus•ing
pe•rus•al
per•vade
per•vad•ed
per•vad•ing
per•va•sion
per•va•sive
per•verse
per•ver•si•ty
per•ver•sion
per•vert
per•vert•ed
per•vi•ous
pes•ky
pes•si•mism
pes•si•mist
pes•si•mis•tic
pes•si•mis•ti•cal•ly
pes•ter
pest•i•cide
pes•ti•lence
pes•tle
pet
pet•ted
pet•ting
pet•al
pe•tite
pe•ti•tion
pe•ti•tion•er
pet•ri•fy
pet•ri•fied
pet•ri•fy•ing
pet•rol

pe•tro•le•um
pet•ty
pet•u•lant
pet•u•lance
pe•tu•nia
pew•ter
pha•lanx
phal•lus
phal•lic
phan•tasm
phan•tas•ma•go•ria
phan•tom
phar•aoh
phar•ma•ceu•ti•cal
phar•ma•cist
phar•ma•col•o•gy
phar•ma•co•poe•ia
phar•ma•cy
phar•ynx
phase
phased
phas•ing
pheas•ant
phe•no•bar•bi•tal
phe•nom•e•non
phe•nom•e•na
phe•nom•e•nal
phi•lan•der
phi•lan•der•er
phi•lan•thro•py
phil•an•throp•ic
phi•lan•thro•pist
phi•lat•e•ly
phil•a•tel•ic
phil•har•mon•ic
Phil•ip•pine
phil•o•den•dron
phi•lol•o•gy
phil•o•logi•ical
phi•los•o•phy
phi•los•o•pher
phil•o•soph•i•cal
phil•o•soph•ic
phi•los•o•phize
phle•bi•tis
phle•bot•o•my
phlegm
phleg•mat•ic
phlox
pho•bia
pho•bic
phoe•nix
phone
phoned
phon•ing
pho•net•ics
pho•net•i•cal•ly
phon•ics
pho•no•graph
pho•ny
pho•ni•ness
phos•phate
phos•pho•res•cence
phos•pho•res•cent
phos•pho•rus
pho•to•copy
pho•to•gen•ic
pho•to•graph
pho•tog•ra•pher
pho•tog•ra•phy
pho•to•graph•ic
pho•to•stat
pho•to•syn•the•sis
phrase
phrased
phras•ing
phra•se•ol•o•gy
phre•net•ic
phre•nol•o•gy
phy•lum
phys•ic
phys•i•cal
phys•i•cal•ly
phy•si•cian
phys•ics
phys•i•cist
phys•i•og•no•my
phys•i•ol•o•gy
phys•i•o•log•i•cal
phys•i•ol•o•gist
phy•sique
pi•ano
pi•az•za

pi•ca
pic•a•resque
pic•a•yune
pic•co•lo
picked
pick•et
pick•et•er
pick•ing
pick•le
pick•led
pick•pock•et
picky
pic•nic
pic•nick•ing
pic•to•ri•al
pic•ture
pic•tured
pic•tur•ing
pic•tur•esque
pid•dle
pid•dled
pid•dling
piece•meal
pierce
pierced
pierc•ing
pi•e•ty
pi•geon•hole
pi•geon•toed
pig•gish
pig•gy•back
pig•head•ed
pig•ment
pig•men•ta•tion
pi•las•ter
pile
piled
pil•ing
pil•fer
pil•grim
pil•grim•age
pil•lage
pil•laged
pil•lag•ing
pil•lar
pil•lo•ry
pil•lo•ried
pil•low
pi•lot
pi•men•to
pim•ple
pim•pled
pim•ply
pin
pinned
pin•ning
pin•a•fore
pin•cers
pinch
pin•cush•ion
pine
pined
pin•ing
pine•ap•ple
pin•ion
pin•na•cle
pi•noch•le
pi•o•neer
pi•ous
pipe•line
pip•er
pi•pette
pip•ing
pip-squeak
pi•quant
pique
piqued
pi•ra•nha
pi•rate
pi•ra•cy
pir•ou•ette
pis•ta•chio
pis•til
pis•tol
pis•ton
pit
pit•ted
pit•ting
pitch-black
pitch•er
pitch•fork
pith
pithy

pit•tance
pi•tu•i•tar•y
pity
  pit•ied
  pit•y•ing
  pit•e•ous
  pit•i•a•ble
  pit•i•ful
  pit•i•less
piv•ot
pixy
  pix•ie
piz•za
  piz•ze•ri•a
plac•ard
pla•cate
  pla•cat•ed
  pla•cat•ing
  pla•ca•tion
place
  plac•ed
  plac•ing
pla•ce•bo
pla•cen•ta
plac•id
plack•et
pla•gia•rize
  pla•gia•rized
  pla•gia•riz•ing
  pla•gia•riz•er
  pla•gia•rism
plague
  plagued
  pla•guing
plaid
plain
plain•clothes man
plain•tiff
plain•tive
  plain•tive•ly
plait
plan
  planned
  plan•ning
plane
plan•et
  plan•e•tar•i•um
  plan•e•tary
plank•ing
plank•ton
plan•tain
plan•ta•tion
plaque
plas•ma
plas•ter
plas•tic
  plas•tic•i•ty
plate
  plat•ed
  plat•ing
pla•teau
plate•ful
plate•let
plat•en
plat•form
plat•i•num
plat•i•tude
pla•ton•ic
pla•toon
plat•ter
plat•y•pus
plau•dit
plau•si•ble
  plau•si•bly
play•ful
  play•ful•ly
play•wright
pla•za
plea
plead
  plead•ed
pleas•ant
pleas•ant
please
  pleased
  pleas•ing
pleas•ure
  pleas•ur•a•ble
pleat
  pleat•ed
ple•be•ian
pleb•i•scite
pledge

pledged
pledg•ing
Pleis•to•cene
ple•na•ry
plen•i•po•ten•ti•ar•y
plen•ty
  plen•i•tude
  plen•ti•ful
pleth•o•ra
pleu•ri•sy
plex•us
pli•a•ble
pli•ant
pli•ers
plight
plod
  plod•ded
  plod•ding
  plod•der
plop
  plopped
  plop•ping
plot
  plot•ted
  plot•ting
  plot•ter
plow
pluck
plucky
plug
  plugged
  plug•ging
plum•age
plumb•er
  plumb•ing
plume
  plumed
plum•met
plump
plun•der
plunge
  plunged
  plung•ing
plu•ral
plu•ral•ism
  plu•ral•is•tic
plu•ral•i•ty
plush
plu•toc•ra•cy
plu•to•ni•um
plu•vi•al
ply
  plied
  ply•ing
ply•wood
pneu•mat•ic
pneu•mo•nia
poach
  poach•er
pock•et•ful
pock•mark
pod
po•di•a•try
  po•di•a•trist
po•di•um
po•em
  po•et•ic
po•e•sy
po•et
  po•et•ess
po•et•ry
po•grom
poign•ant
  poign•an•cy
poin•ci•ana
poin•set•tia
point
  point•ed•ly
  point•er
poise
  poised
poi•son
  poi•son•ous
poke
  poked
  pok•ing
pok•er
poky
po•lar
Po•lar•is
po•lar•i•ty
  po•lar•i•za•tion
  po•lar•ize

pole
  poled
  pol•ing
po•lem•ic
  po•lem•i•cal
  po•lem•i•cist
po•lice
  po•liced
  po•lic•ing
pol•i•cy
  pol•i•cies
po•lio
pol•ish
po•lite
  po•lite•ly
pol•i•tic
pol•i•tics
  po•lit•i•cal
  po•lit•i•cal•ly
  pol•i•ti•cian
  po•lit•i•cize
pol•i•ty
poll
  poll•ster
pol•len
  pol•li•na•tion
pol•lute
  pol•lut•ed
  pol•lut•ing
  pol•lu•tant
  pol•lu•tion
po•lo
pol•y•es•ter
po•lyg•a•my
pol•y•glot
pol•y•graph
pol•y•mor•phism
Poly•ne•sia
pol•yp
pol•y•tech•nic
pome•gran•ate
pom•mel
  pom•meled
  pom•mel•ing
pomp•ous
  pom•pos•i•ty
pon•der
pon•der•ous
pon•tiff
pon•tif•i•cal
pon•tif•i•cate
  pon•tif•i•cat•ed
  pon•tif•i•cat•ing
pon•toon
po•ny
  po•nies
poo•dle
poor•ly
pop•ery
  pop•ish
pop•lar
pop•lin
pop•py
  pop•pies
pop•u•lace
pop•u•lar
  pop•u•lar•i•ty
  pop•u•lar•ize
  pop•u•lar•ized
  pop•u•lar•iz•ing
  pop•u•lar•i•za•tion
pop•u•late
  pop•u•lat•ed
  pop•u•lat•ing
  pop•u•la•tion
pop•u•lous
por•ce•lain
por•cine
por•cu•pine
pore
  pored
  por•ing
pork•er
por•nog•ra•phy
  por•nog•ra•pher
  por•no•graph•ic
po•rous
  po•ros•i•ty
por•poise
por•ridge
port•a•ble
por•tal
por•tend

por•tent
  por•ten•tous
por•ter
port•fo•lio
por•ti•co
por•tion
port•ly
por•trait
  por•trai•ture
por•tray
  por•tray•al
Por•tu•gal
  Por•tu•guese
pose
  posed
  pos•ing
pos•er
po•seur
pos•it
po•si•tion
pos•i•tive
  pos•i•tive•ly
  pos•i•tiv•ism
pos•i•tron
pos•se
pos•sess
  pos•sessed
  pos•ses•sion
  pos•ses•sive
pos•si•bil•i•ty
pos•si•ble
  pos•si•bly
pos•sum
post•age
post•er
pos•te•ri•or
pos•ter•i•ty
post•grad•u•ate
post•hu•mous
post-mor•tem
post•na•tal
post•par•tum
post•pone
  post•poned
  post•pon•ing
  post•pone•ment
post•script
pos•tu•lant
pos•tu•late
  pos•tu•lat•ed
  pos•tu•lat•ing
pos•ture
  pos•tur•ing
post•war
pot
  pot•ted
  pot•ting
po•ta•ble
pot•ash
po•tas•si•um
po•ta•to
  po•ta•toes
pot•bel•ly
  pot•bel•lied
po•tent
  po•ten•cy
  po•ten•tate
  po•ten•tial
  po•ten•ti•al•i•ty
  po•ten•tial•ly
po•tion
pot•pour•ri
pot•ter
  pot•tery
pouch
poul•tice
poul•try
pounce
  pounced
  pounc•ing
pour
pout
pov•er•ty
pow•der
pow•er
  pow•er•ful
  pow•er•ful•ly
pow•wow
prac•ti•ca•ble
  prac•ti•ca•bil•i•ty
  prac•ti•ca•bly
prac•ti•cal
  prac•ti•cal•i•ty

prac•ti•cal•ly
prac•tice
  prac•ticed
prac•ti•tion•er
prag•mat•ic
  prag•mat•i•cal
  prag•ma•tism
  prag•ma•tist
prai•rie
praise
  praised
  prais•ing
  praise•wor•thy
prance
  pranced
  pranc•ing
prank
  prank•ster
prate
  prat•ed
  prat•ing
prat•tle
  prat•tled
  prat•tling
prawn
prayer
preach
  preach•er
pre•am•ble
pre•ar•ranged
pre•as•signed
pre•car•i•ous
pre•cau•tion
  pre•cau•tion•ary
pre•cede
  pre•ced•ed
  pre•ced•ing
prec•e•dence
  prec•e•dent
pre•cept
  pre•cep•tor
pre•cinct
pre•cious
  pre•ci•os•i•ty
prec•i•pice
  pre•cip•i•tous
  pre•cip•i•tant
  pre•cip•i•tate
  pre•cip•i•tat•ed
  pre•cip•i•tat•ing
  pre•cip•i•ta•tion
  pre•cip•i•tous
pre•cis
pre•cise
  pre•ci•sion
pre•clude
  pre•clud•ed
  pre•clud•ing
pre•co•cious
  pre•coc•i•ty
pre•con•cep•tion
pre•con•di•tion
pre•cur•sor
pred•a•tor
  pred•a•to•ry
pre•de•cease
pred•e•ces•sor
pre•des•ti•na•tion
pre•des•tine
  pre•des•tined
pre•de•ter•mined
pred•i•ca•ble
  pred•i•ca•bil•i•ty
pre•dic•a•ment
pred•i•cate
pre•dict
  pre•dict•a•ble
  pre•dict•a•bly
  pre•dic•tion
  pre•dic•tive
pre•di•lec•tion
pre•dis•pose
  pre•dis•posed
  pre•dis•po•si•tion
pre•dom•i•nant
  pre•dom•i•nance
  pre•dom•i•nate
  pre•dom•i•na•tion
pre•em•i•nent
  pre•em•i•nence
pre•empt
  pre•emp•tion
  pre•emp•tive

re•ex•ist•ent
pref•ace
 pref•aced
 pref•a•to•ry
pre•fer
 per•ferred
 pre•fer•ring
pref•er•a•ble
 pref•er•a•bly
pref•er•ence
pref•er•en•tial
preg•nant
 preg•nan•cy
pre•his•tor•ic
pre•judge
prej•u•dice
 prej•u•diced
 prej•u•dic•ing
 prej•u•di•cial
prel•ate
pre•lim•i•nary
 pre•lim•i•nar•ies
prel•ude
pre•ma•ture
pre•med•i•tat•ed
 pre•med•i•ta•tion
pre•mier
pre•miere
prem•ise
pre•mi•um
pre•mo•ni•tion
pre•na•tal
pre•oc•cu•py
 pre•oc•cu•pied
 pre•oc•cu•pa•tion
pre•op•er•a•tive
pre•ordain
pre•pare
 pre•pared
 pre•par•ing
 prep•a•ra•tion
 pre•par•a•to•ry
pre•par•ed•ness
pre•paid
pre•pon•der•ant
 pre•pon•der•ance
prep•o•si•tion
pre•pos•sess•ing
pre•pos•ter•ous
pre•req•ui•site
pre•rog•a•tive
pres•age
 pres•aged
Pres•by•te•ri•an
pres•by•tery
pre•school
pre•scind
pre•sci•ence
 pre•sci•ent
pre•scribe
 pre•scribed
 pre•scrib•ing
pre•script
 pre•scrip•tive
 pre•scrip•tion
pres•ence
 pres•ent
pre•sent
 pres•en•ta•tion
pre•sent•a•ble
pres•ent•ly
pre•serve
 pre•served
 pre•serv•ing
 pres•er•va•tion
 pre•serv•a•tive
pre•side
 pre•sid•ed
 pre•sid•ing
pres•i•dent
 pres•i•den•tial
 pres•i•den•cy
pre•sid•i•um
press•ing
pres•sure
 pres•sured
 pres•sur•ing
 pres•su•rize
 pres•su•rized
pres•tige
 pres•tig•ious
pre•sum•a•ble
 pre•sum•a•bly

pre•sume
 pre•sumed
 pre•sum•ing
 pre•sump•tion
 pre•sump•tive
 pre•sump•tu•ous
pre•sup•pose
 pre•sup•posed
 pre•sup•pos•ing
 pre•sup•po•si•tion
pre•tend
 pre•tend•ed
 pre•tend•er
pre•tense
pre•ten•sion
 pre•ten•tious
pret•er•it
pret•er•i•tion
pre•ter•nat•u•ral
pre•text
pret•ty
 pret•ti•ly
pret•zel
pre•vail
 pre•vail•ing
prev•a•lent
 prev•a•lence
pre•vent
 pre•vent•a•ble
 pre•ven•ta•tive
 pre•ven•tion
 pre•ven•tive
pre•view
pre•vi•ous
pre•war
prey
price•less
prick•le
 prick•ly
pride
 prid•ed
 prid•ing
prie-dieu
priest
 priest•ess
prig
 prig•gish
prim
pri•ma•cy
pri•ma don•na
pri•ma fa•cie
pri•mal
pri•ma•ri•ly
pri•ma•ry
 pri•mar•ies
pri•mate
prime
 primed
 prim•ing
prim•er
pri•me•val
prim•i•tive
pri•mo•gen•i•tor
pri•mo•gen•i•ture
pri•mor•di•al
prince•ly
prin•cess
prin•ci•pal
 prin•ci•pal•ly
 prin•ci•pal•i•ty
prin•ci•ple
 prin•ci•pled
print•ing
print•out
pri•or
pri•or•i•ty
 pri•or•i•ties
pri•ory
prism
pris•on
 pris•on•er
pris•sy
pris•tine
pri•va•cy
pri•vate
 pri•vate•ly
pri•va•tion
priv•i•lege
 priv•i•leged
privy
prize
 prized
prob•a•ble

prob•a•bly
prob•a•bil•i•ty
pro•bate
pro•ba•tion
probe
 probed
 prob•ing
pro•bi•ty
prob•lem
 prob•lem•at•ic
 prob•lem•at•i•cal
pro•ce•dure
 pro•ce•dur•al
pro•ceed
 pro•ceed•ing
pro•ceeds
proc•ess
pro•ces•sion
 pro•ces•sion•al
pro•claim
 proc•la•ma•tion
pro•cliv•i•ty
pro•cras•ti•nate
 pro•cras•ti•nat•ed
 pro•cras•ti•nat•ing
 pro•cras•ti•na•tion
 pro•cras•ti•na•tor
pro•cre•ate
 pro•cre•a•tion
proc•tor
pro•cure
 pro•cured
 pro•cur•ing
 pro•cure•ment
 pro•cur•er
prod
 prod•ded
 prod•ding
 prod•der
prod•i•gal
pro•di•gious
prod•i•gy
pro•duce
 pro•duced
 pro•duc•ing
 pro•duc•er
prod•uct
 pro•duc•tion
 pro•duc•tive
 pro•duc•tiv•i•ty
pro•fane
 pro•fan•i•ty
pro•fess
 pro•fessed
pro•fes•sion
 pro•fes•sion•al
 pro•fes•sion•al•ism
pro•fes•sor
 pro•fes•so•ri•al
prof•fer
pro•fi•cient
 pro•fi•cien•cy
pro•file
 pro•filed
 pro•fil•ing
prof•it
 prof•it•a•ble
 prof•it•a•bil•i•ty
 prof•it•a•bly
prof•li•gate
 prof•li•ga•cy
pro•found
 pro•fun•di•ty
pro•fuse
 pro•fuse•ly
 pro•fu•sion
pro•gen•i•tor
prog•e•ny
prog•no•sis
 prog•nos•tic
 prog•nos•ti•cate
 prog•nos•ti•ca•tion
pro•gram
 pro•grammed
 pro•gramed
 pro•gram•ming
 pro•gram•ing
 pro•gram•mer
 pro•gram•er
prog•ress
 pro•gres•sion
 pro•gres•sive
pro•hib•it

pro•hi•bi•tion
 pro•hib•i•tive
pro•ject
 pro•jec•tion
pro•jec•tile
pro•jec•tor
pro•le•tar•i•at
 pro•le•tar•i•an
pro•lif•er•ate
 pro•lif•er•at•ed
 pro•lif•er•at•ing
 pro•lif•er•a•tion
 pro•lif•er•a•tive
pro•lif•ic
pro•lix
 pro•lix•i•ty
pro•loc•u•tor
pro•logue
pro•log
pro•long
 pro•lon•ga•tion
prom•e•nade
prom•i•nence
 prom•i•nent
pro•mis•cu•ous
 pro•mis•cu•i•ty
prom•ise
 prom•ised
 prom•is•ing
prom•is•so•ry
prom•on•to•ry
pro•mote
 pro•mot•ed
 pro•mot•ing
 pro•mot•er
 pro•mo•tion
prompt•ly
prom•ul•gate
 prom•ul•gat•ed
 prom•ul•gat•ing
 prom•ul•ga•tion
prone
prong
pro•noun
pro•nounce
 pro•nounced
 pro•nounc•ing
 pro•nounce•a•ble
 pro•nun•ci•a•tion
 pro•nounce•ment
proof
prop
 propped
 prop•ping
prop•a•gan•da
 prop•a•gan•dist
 prop•a•gan•dize
prop•a•gate
 prop•a•gat•ed
 prop•a•gat•ing
 prop•a•ga•tion
pro•pane
pro•pel
 pro•pelled
 pro•pel•ling
 pro•pel•ler
pro•pen•si•ty
prop•er•ly
prop•er•ty
 prop•er•ties
 prop•er•tied
proph•e•cy
 proph•e•cies
proph•e•sy
 proph•e•sied
 proph•e•sy•ing
proph•et
 pro•phet•ic
pro•phy•lac•tic
 pro•phy•lax•is
pro•pin•qui•ty
pro•pi•ti•ate
 pro•pi•ti•at•ed
 pro•pi•ti•at•ing
 pro•pi•ti•a•tion
pro•pi•tious
pro•po•nent
pro•por•tion
 pro•por•tion•al
 pro•por•tion•ate
pro•pose
 pro•posed
 pro•pos•ing

pro•pos•al
prop•o•si•tion
pro•pound
pro•pri•e•tary
pro•pri•e•tor
pro•pri•e•ty
pro•pul•sion
pro•rata
pro•rate
 pro•rat•ed
 pro•ra•tion
pro•sa•ic
pro•scribe
 pro•scribed
 pro•scrip•tion
pros•e•cute
 pros•e•cu•tion
 pros•e•cu•tor
pros•e•lyte
 pros•e•ly•tize
pros•pect
 pros•pec•tor
pro•spec•tive
pro•spec•tus
pros•per
 pros•per•i•ty
 pros•per•ous
pros•tate
pros•the•sis
 pros•thet•ic
pros•ti•tute
 pros•ti•tut•ed
 pros•ti•tu•tion
pros•trate
 pros•trat•ed
 pros•tra•tion
pro•tag•o•nist
pro•te•an
pro•tect
 pro•tec•tive
 pro•tec•tor
 pro•tec•tion
 pro•tec•tor•ate
pro•té•gé
pro•tein
pro•test
 prot•es•ta•tion
Prot•es•tant
 Prot•es•tant•ism
pro•to•col
pro•ton
pro•to•plasm
pro•to•type
pro•tract
 pro•trac•tion
 pro•trac•tor
pro•trude
 pro•trud•ed
 pro•trud•ing
 pro•trud•ent
 pro•tru•sion
pro•tu•ber•ance
 pro•tu•ber•ant
proud•ly
prove
 proved
 prov•en
 prov•ing
 prov•a•ble
prov•erb
 pro•ver•bi•al
pro•vide
 pro•vid•ed
 pro•vid•ing
 pro•vid•er
prov•i•dence
 prov•i•den•tial
 prov•i•dent
prov•ince
pro•vin•cial
 pro•vin•cial•ism
pro•vi•sion
 pro•vi•sion•al
pro•vi•so
pro•voke
 pro•voked
 pro•vok•ing
 prov•o•ca•tion
 pro•voc•a•tive
prov•ost
prow•ess
prowl
 prowl•er

prox•i•mal
prox•i•mate
prox•im•i•ty
proxy
prude
   prud•ery
   prud•ish
pru•dence
   pru•dent
   pru•den•tial
prune
   pruned
   prun•ing
pru•ri•ent
   pru•ri•ence
pry
   pried
   pry•ing
psalm•book
psalm•ist
Psal•ter
pseu•do
pseu•do•nym
   pseu•don•y•mous
pso•ri•a•sis
psy•che
psy•chi•a•try
   psy•chi•at•ric
   psy•chi•a•trist
psy•chic
psy•cho•a•nal•y•sis
   psy•cho•an•a•lyt•ic
   psy•cho•an•a•lyt•i•cal
   psy•cho•an•a•lyze
   psy•cho•an•a•lyst
psy•cho•gen•ic
psy•cho•log•i•cal
   psy•cho•log•ic
psy•chol•o•gy
   psy•chol•o•gist
psy•cho•path
   psy•cho•path•ic
psy•cho•sis
   psy•cho•ses
   psy•chot•ic
psy•cho•so•mat•ic
psy•cho•ther•a•py
   psy•cho•ther•a•pist
pto•maine
pu•ber•ty
   pu•bes•cence
pu•bic
pub•lic
   pub•lic•ly
pub•li•ci•ty
   pub•li•cist
pub•li•cize
pub•lish
pub•lish•er
   pub•li•ca•tion
puck•er
pud•ding
pud•dle
pudgy
pu•er•ile
puff
   puffy
pu•gil•ism
   pu•gil•ist
pug•na•cious
   pug•nac•i•ty
puke
   puked
   puk•ing
pul•ley
pul•mo•nary
pulp
   pulpy
pul•pit
pul•sar
pul•sate
   pul•sat•ed
   pul•sat•ing
pulse
pul•ver•ize
   pul•ver•ized
   pul•ver•iz•ing
pu•ma
pum•ice
pum•mel
   pum•meled
   pum•melled
   pum•mel•ing

pum•mel•ling
pum•per•nick•el
pump•kin
pun
   punned
   pun•ning
punch
punc•til•io
   punc•til•i•ous
punc•tu•al
   punc•tu•al•ly
punc•tu•ate
   punc•tu•at•ed
   punc•tu•at•ing
   punc•tu•a•tion
punc•ture
   punc•tured
   punc•tur•ing
pun•dit
pun•gent
pun•ish
   pun•ish•a•ble
   pun•ish•ment
pu•ni•tive
pu•ny
pu•pil
pup•pet
pup•py
   pup•pies
pur•chase
   pur•chased
   pur•chas•ing
   pur•chas•er
pure
   pure•ly
   pu•ri•fy
   pu•ri•ty
pu•ree
pur•ga•tive
pur•ga•to•ry
purge
   purged
   purg•ing
pu•ri•fy
   pu•ri•fied
   pu•ri•fy•ing
   pu•ri•fi•ca•tion
pur•ist
pu•ri•tan
   pu•ri•tan•i•cal
purl
pur•loin
pur•ple
pur•port
   pur•port•ed•ly
pur•pose
   pur•pose•ful•ly
   pur•pose•ly
   pur•pos•ive
purse
   pursed
   purs•ing
purs•er
pur•su•ant
pur•sue
   pur•sued
   pur•su•ing
   pur•su•er
   pur•suit
pu•ru•lent
   pu•ru•lence
pur•vey
   pur•vey•or
   pur•vey•ance
pur•view
pushy
push•o•ver
pu•sil•lan•i•mous
   pu•sil•la•nim•i•ty
puss•y•wil•low
pus•tule
put
   put
   put•ting
pu•ta•tive
pu•tre•fy
   pu•tre•fied
   pu•tre•fy•ing
   pu•tre•fac•tion
pu•trid
putt
   putt•ed
   putt•ing

put•ter
put•ty
puz•zle
   puz•zled
   puz•zling
pyg•my
py•lon
pyr•a•mid
   py•ram•i•dal
pyre
py•ro•ma•nia
   py•ro•ma•ni•ac
py•ro•tech•nics
py•thon

Q

quack•ery
quad•ran•gle
quad•rant
quad•rat•ic
quad•ri•lat•er•al
quad•ril•lion
quad•ru•ple
   quad•ru•pled
quad•ru•plet
quaff
quag•mire
quail
quaint•ly
quake
   quaked
   quak•ing
Quak•er
qual•i•fy
   qual•i•fied
   qual•i•fy•ing
   qual•i•fi•a•ble
   qual•i•fi•ca•tion
qual•i•ta•tive
qual•i•ty
   qual•i•ties
qualm
quan•da•ry
quan•ti•fy
   quan•ti•fied
   quan•ti•fy•ing
   quan•ti•fi•a•ble
   quan•ti•fi•ca•tion
quan•ti•ta•tive
quan•ti•ty
   quan•ti•ties
quan•tum
quar•an•tine
quar•rel
   quar•reled
   quar•rel•ing
   quar•rel•some
quar•ry
   quar•ries
   quar•ried
   quar•ry•ing
quart
quar•ter
   quar•ter•ly
quar•tet
qua•sar
quash
qua•si
quat•rain
qua•ver
quay
quea•sy
queen•ly
queer
quell
quench
quer•u•lous
que•ry
   que•ried
   que•ry•ing
quest
ques•tion
   ques•tion•a•ble
   ques•tion•a•bly
   ques•tion•naire
queue
   queued
   queu•ing
quib•ble
   quib•bled
   quib•bling
quick

quick•en
quick-tem•pered
quick-wit•ted
qui•es•cent
   qui•es•cence
qui•et
   qui•et•ly
qui•e•tude
quill
quilt
quince
qui•nine
quin•tes•sence
   quin•tes•sen•tial
quin•tet
quin•til•lion
quin•tu•ple
   quin•tu•pled
   quin•tu•plet
quip
   quipped
quirk
quis•ling
quit
   quit•ted
   quit•ting
   quit•ter
quite
quiv•er
quix•ot•ic
quiz
   quiz•zes
   quizzed
   quiz•zing
   quiz•zi•cal
quoits
quon•dam
Quon•set
quo•rum
quo•ta
quote
   quot•ed
   quot•ing
   quot•able
   quo•ta•tion
quo•tid•i•an
quo•tient

R

rab•bet
rab•bi
   rab•bis
   rab•bin•i•cal
rab•bit
rab•ble
rab•id
ra•bies
race
   raced
   rac•ing
   rac•er
ra•cial
   ra•cial•ly
rac•ism
   rac•ist
rack•et
rack•et•eer
rac•on•teur
racy
ra•dar
ra•di•al
ra•di•ate
   ra•di•at•ed
   ra•di•at•ing
   ra•di•ance
   ra•di•ant
   ra•di•a•tion
   ra•di•a•tor
rad•i•cal
   rad•i•cal•ly
ra•dio
   ra•di•oed
   ra•di•o•ing
ra•di•o•ac•tive
   ra•di•o•ac•tiv•i•ty
ra•di•ol•o•gy
   ra•di•ol•o•gist
ra•di•os•copy
rad•ish
ra•di•um
ra•di•us
raf•fia

raf•fish
raft•er
rag
   ragged
rage
   raged
   rag•ing
rag•ged
rag•weed
raid•er
rail•ing
rail•lery
rail•road
rail•way
rai•ment
rainy
raise
   raised
   rais•ing
rai•sin
rake
   raked
   rak•ing
rak•ish
ral•ly
   ral•lied
   ral•ly•ing
ram
   rammed
   ram•ming
ram•ble
   ram•bled
   ram•bling
ram•bunc•tious
ram•i•fi•ca•tion
ram•page
   ram•paged
   ram•pag•ing
ramp•ant
ram•part
ram•rod
ram•shack•le
ran•cid
ran•cor
ran•dom
   ran•dom•ly
   ran•dom•ize
range
   ranged
   rang•ing
rangy
ran•kle
   ran•kled
   ran•kling
ran•sack
ran•som
rant•er
rap
   rapped
   rap•ping
ra•pa•cious
   ra•pac•i•ty
rape
   rap•ist
rap•id•ly
   ra•pid•i•ty
ra•pi•er
rap•ine
rap•port
rap•proche•ment
rap•scal•lion
rapt
rap•ture
rare•bit
rar•e•fied
rare•ly
rar•i•ty
ras•cal
rash•ly
rasp
   raspy
rasp•ber•ry
rat
   rat•ted
   rat•ting
ratch•et
rate
   rat•ed
   rat•ing
   rat•a•ble
   rate•a•ble
rath•er
rat•i•fy

...al•i•ty
...tion•al•ly
...tion•ale
ra•tion•al•ize
ra•tion•al•ized
ra•tion•al•iz•ing
ra•tion•al•i•za•tion
rat•tan
rat•tle
rat•tled
rat•tling
rat•tler
rat•tle•snake
rat•ty
rau•cous
raun•chy
rav•age
rav•aged
rav•ag•ing
rave
raved
rav•ing
rav•el
rav•eled
rav•e•ing
ra•ven
rav•en•ous
ra•vine
rav•ish
rav•ish•ing
raw
ray•on
raze
razed
raz•ing
ra•zor
reach•able
re•act
re•ac•tive
re•ac•tion
re•ac•tion•ary
re•ac•ti•vate
re•ac•tor
read•a•ble
re•ad•just•ment
ready
read•ied
read•y•ing
read•i•ly
read•i•ness
read•y•made
re•a•gent
re•al
re•al•ism
re•al•ist
re•al•is•tic
re•al•is•ti•cal•ly
re•al•i•ty
re•al•ize
re•al•ized
re•al•iz•ing
re•al•iz•a•ble
re•al•i•za•tion
re•al•ly
realm
re•al•tor
re•al•ty
ream
reap•er
re•ap•pear•ance
re•ap•por•tion•ment
re•ar•ma•ment
re•ar•range•ment
rea•son
rea•son•ing
rea•son•a•ble
rea•son•a•bly
re•as•sem•ble
re•as•sure
re•as•sured
re•as•sur•ing
re•as•sur•ance
re•bate
re•bat•ed
re•bat•ing
reb•el

re•bel
re•belled
re•bel•ling
re•bel•lion
re•bel•lious
re•birth
re•born
re•bound
re•buff
re•buke
re•buked
re•buk•ing
re•but
re•but•ted
re•but•ting
re•but•tal
re•cal•ci•trant
re•cal•ci•trance
re•call
re•cant
re•can•ta•tion
re•cap
re•ca•pit•u•late
re•cap•ture
re•cast
re•cede
re•ced•ed
re•ced•ing
re•ceipt
re•ceiv•a•ble
re•ceive
re•ceived
re•ceiv•ing
re•ceiv•er
re•cent
re•cent•ly
re•cep•ta•cle
re•cep•tion
re•cep•tion•ist
re•cep•tive
re•cep•tive•ly
re•cess
re•ces•sion
re•ces•sive
re•cid•i•vism
re•cid•i•vist
rec•i•pe
re•cip•i•ent
re•cip•ro•cal
re•cip•ro•cate
re•cip•ro•cat•ed
re•cip•ro•cat•ing
rec•i•proc•i•ty
re•cit•al
re•cite
re•cit•ed
re•cit•ing
rec•i•ta•tion
reck•less
reck•on
reck•on•ing
re•claim
rec•la•ma•tion
re•cline
re•clined
re•clin•ing
re•clin•er
rec•luse
re•clu•sive
rec•og•nize
rec•og•nized
rec•og•niz•ing
rec•og•niz•a•ble
rec•og•ni•tion
re•cog•ni•zance
re•coil
rec•ol•lect
rec•ol•lec•tion
rec•om•mend
rec•om•men•da•tion
rec•om•pense
rec•om•pensed
rec•om•pens•ing
rec•on•cile
rec•on•ciled
rec•on•cil•ing
rec•on•cil•a•ble
rec•on•cil•i•a•tion
rec•on•dite
re•con•nais•sance
re•con•noi•ter
re•con•noi•tered
re•con•noi•ter•ing

re•con•sti•tute
re•con•struc•tion
re•cord
re•cord•ed
re•cord•ing
rec•ord
rec•ords
re•cord•ing
re•count
re•coup
re•course
re•cov•er
re•cov•ery
re•cov•er•able
rec•re•ant
rec•re•a•tion•al
re•crim•i•na•tion
re•cruit
rec•tal
rec•tan•gle
rec•tan•gu•lar
rec•ti•fy
rec•ti•fied
rec•ti•fy•ing
rec•ti•fi•ca•tion
rec•ti•tude
rec•tor
rec•to•ry
rec•tum
re•cum•bent
re•cum•ben•cy
re•cu•per•ate
re•cu•per•at•ed
re•cu•per•at•ing
re•cu•per•a•tion
re•cur
re•curred
re•cur•ring
re•cur•rence
re•cur•rent
re•cy•cle
red
red•der
red•ness
red•den
red•dish
re•deem
re•deem•a•ble
re•deem•er
re•demp•tion
re•demp•tive
red•hand•ed
red-let•ter
re•do
red•o•lent
red•o•lence
re•doubt•a•ble
re•dress
re•duce
re•duced
re•duc•ing
re•duc•i•ble
re•duc•tion
re•dun•dant
re•dun•dance
re•dun•dan•cy
reedy
re•e•lec•tion
re•en•act
re•en•force
re•fer
re•ferred
re•fer•ring
re•fer•ral
ref•er•ee
ref•er•ence
ref•er•en•tial
ref•er•en•dum
ref•er•ent
re•fer•ral
re•fill
re•fi•nance
re•fine
re•fined
re•fin•ing
re•fine•ment
re•fin•ery
re•flect
re•flec•tion
re•flec•tive
re•flec•tor
re•flex
ref•or•ma•tion

re•form•a•to•ry
re•form•er
re•fract
re•frac•tion
re•frac•to•ry
re•frain
re•fresh•ing
re•fresh•ment
re•frig•er•ate
re•frig•er•at•ed
re•frig•er•ation
re•frig•er•a•tor
ref•uge
ref•u•gee
re•ful•gent
re•ful•gence
re•fund
re•fur•bish
re•fuse
re•fused
re•fus•ing
re•fus•al
ref•use
re•fute
re•fut•ed
re•fut•ing
ref•u•ta•tion
re•gal
re•gal•ly
re•gale
re•galed
re•ga•lia
re•gard
re•gard•ing
re•gard•less
re•gat•ta
re•gen•cy
re•gen•er•ate
re•gen•er•a•tion
re•gent
re•gime
reg•i•men
reg•i•ment
reg•i•men•ta•tion
re•gion•al
re•gion•al•ly
reg•is•ter
reg•is•tered
reg•is•trar
reg•is•tra•tion
reg•is•try
re•gress
re•gres•sion
re•gres•sive
re•gret
re•gret•ted
re•gret•ting
re•gret•ta•ble
re•gret•ta•bly
re•gret•ful•ly
reg•u•lar
reg•u•lar•i•ty
reg•u•late
reg•u•lat•ed
reg•u•lat•ing
reg•u•la•tor
reg•u•la•to•ry
reg•u•la•tion
re•gur•gi•tate
re•gur•gi•tat•ed
re•gur•gi•tat•ing
re•gur•gi•ta•tion
re•ha•bil•i•tate
re•ha•bil•i•tat•ed
re•ha•bil•i•tat•ing
re•ha•bil•i•ta•tion
re•hash
re•hears•al
re•hearse
re•hearsed
re•hears•ing
reign
re•im•burse
re•im•bursed
re•im•burs•ing
re•im•burse•ment
rein
re•in•car•nate
re•in•car•na•tion
rein•deer
re•in•force
re•in•force•ment
re•in•state

re•in•state•ment
re•is•sue
re•it•er•ate
re•it•er•at•ed
re•it•er•at•ing
re•it•er•a•tion
re•ject
re•jec•tion
re•joice
re•joiced
re•joic•ing
re•join
re•join•der
re•ju•ve•nate
re•ju•ve•nat•ed
re•ju•ve•nat•ing
re•ju•ve•na•tion
re•kin•dle
re•lapse
re•lapsed
re•laps•ing
re•late
re•lat•ed
re•lat•ing
re•la•tion
rel•a•tive
rel•a•tive•ly
rel•a•tiv•i•ty
re•lax
re•lax•a•tion
re•lay
re•layed
re•lay•ing
re•lease
re•leased
re•leas•ing
rel•e•gate
rel•e•gat•ed
rel•e•gat•ing
rel•e•ga•tion
re•lent
re•lent•less
rel•e•vant
rel•e•vance
rel•e•van•cy
re•li•a•ble
re•li•a•bil•i•ty
re•li•a•bly
re•li•ant
re•li•ance
rel•ic
re•lief
re•lieve
re•lieved
re•liev•ing
re•li•gion
re•li•gi•os•i•ty
re•li•gious
re•lin•quish
rel•ish
re•live
re•lo•cate
re•luc•tant
re•luc•tance
re•ly
re•lied
re•ly•ing
re•main
re•main•der
re•mand
re•mark
re•mark•a•ble
re•me•di•al
rem•e•dy
rem•e•dies
rem•e•died
re•mem•ber
re•mem•brance
re•mind•er
rem•i•nisce
rem•i•nisced
rem•i•nisc•ing
rem•i•nis•cence
rem•i•nis•cent
re•miss
re•mis•sion
re•mit
re•mit•ted
re•mit•ting
re•mit•tance
rem•nant
re•mon•strate
re•mon•strat•ed

re•mon•strat•ing
re•mon•strance
re•morse
re•mote•ly
re•mov•al
re•mu•ner•ate
re•mu•ner•a•tion
ren•ais•sance
re•nas•cence
re•nas•cent
rend
ren•di•tion
ren•dez•vous
ren•e•gade
re•nege
re•neged
re•neg•ing
re•new•al
re•nounce
re•nounced
re•nounc•ing
ren•o•vate
ren•o•vat•ed
ren•o•vat•ing
ren•o•va•tion
re•nown
re•nowned
rent•al
re•nun•ci•a•tion
re•or•gan•i•za•tion
re•pair
rep•a•ra•ble
rep•a•ra•tion
rep•ar•tee
re•past
re•pa•tri•ate
re•pa•tri•at•ed
re•pa•tri•a•tion
re•peal
re•peat
re•peat•a•ble
re•peat•ed
re•pel
re•pelled
re•pel•ling
re•pel•lent
re•pent
re•pent•ance
re•pent•ant
re•per•cus•sion
rep•er•toire
rep•er•to•ry
rep•e•ti•tion
rep•e•ti•tious
re•pet•i•tive
re•place•a•ble
re•place•ment
re•plen•ish
re•plete
rep•li•ca
re•ply
re•plied
re•ply•ing
re•plies
re•port•ed•ly
rep•or•to•ri•al
re•pose
re•posed
re•pos•ing
re•pos•i•tory
re•pos•ses•sion
rep•re•hend
rep•re•hen•si•ble
rep•re•sent
rep•re•sen•ta•tion
rep•re•sent•a•tive
re•press
re•pres•sion
re•prieve
re•prieved
re•priev•ing
re•pri•mand
re•pris•al
re•proach•ful•ly
rep•ro•bate
re•pro•duc•tion
re•proof
re•prove
re•proved
re•prov•ing
rep•tile
rep•til•i•an
re•pub•lic

re•pub•li•can
re•pu•di•ate
re•pu•di•at•ed
re•pu•di•at•ing
re•pu•di•a•tion
re•pug•nant
re•pug•nance
re•pulse
re•pulsed
re•puls•ing
re•pul•sion
re•pul•sive
rep•u•ta•ble
rep•u•ta•bly
rep•u•ta•tion
re•pute
re•put•ed
re•put•ing
re•quest
req•ui•em
re•quire
re•quired
re•quir•ing
re•quire•ment
req•ui•site
req•ui•si•tion
re•quit•al
re•quite
re•run
re•scind
res•cue
res•cued
res•cu•ing
re•search•er
re•sem•ble
re•sem•bled
re•sem•bling
re•sem•blance
re•sent•ful
re•sent•ment
re•serve
re•served
re•serv•ing
res•er•va•tion
res•er•voir
re•side
re•sid•ed
re•sid•ing
res•i•dence
res•i•den•cy
res•i•dent
res•i•den•tial
res•i•due
re•sid•u•al
re•sign
res•ig•na•tion
re•signed
re•sil•ient
re•sil•ience
re•sil•ien•cy
res•in
re•sist•ance
re•sist•ant
res•o•lute
res•o•lu•tion
re•solve
re•solved
re•solv•ing
res•o•nant
res•o•nance
res•o•nate
res•o•nat•ed
res•o•nat•ing
re•sort
re•sound
re•source
re•spect
re•spect•ful•ly
re•spect•a•ble
re•spect•a•bil•i•ty
re•spec•tive
res•pi•ra•tion
res•pi•ra•to•ry
res•pi•ra•tor
res•pite
re•splend•ent
re•splend•ence
re•spond
re•spond•ent
re•sponse
re•spon•sive
re•spon•si•bil•i•ty
re•spon•si•bil•i•ties

res•tau•rant
res•tau•ra•teur
rest•ful
res•ti•tu•tion
res•tive
re•store
re•stored
re•stor•ing
res•to•ra•tion
re•stor•a•tive
re•strained
re•straint
re•strict
re•strict•ed
re•stric•tion
re•stric•tive
re•sult
re•sult•ant
re•sume
re•sumed
re•sum•ing
re•sump•tion
re•sur•gent
re•sur•gence
res•ur•rect
res•ur•rec•tion
re•sus•ci•tate
re•sus•ci•tat•ed
re•sus•ci•tat•ing
re•sus•ci•ta•tion
re•tail•er
re•tain•er
re•take
re•tal•i•ate
re•tal•i•at•ed
re•tal•i•at•ing
re•tal•i•a•tion
re•tal•i•a•to•ry
re•tard
re•tar•da•tion
re•tard•ed
retch
re•ten•tion
re•ten•tive
ret•i•cent
ret•i•cence
re•tic•u•lar
ret•i•na
ret•i•nue
re•tire
re•tired
re•tir•ing
re•tire•ment
re•tort
re•touch
re•tract
re•trac•tion
re•treat
re•trench
re•tri•al
ret•ri•bu•tion
re•trieve
re•trieved
re•triev•ing
re•triev•er
ret•ro•ac•tive
ret•ro•grade
ret•ro•gres•sion
ret•ro•spect
ret•ro•spec•tion
ret•ro•spec•tive
re•un•ion
re•u•nite
rev
revved
rev•ving
re•vamp
re•veal
rev•e•la•tion
rev•eil•le
rev•el
rev•el•ry
re•venge
re•venged
re•veng•ing
re•venge•ful
rev•e•nue
re•ver•ber•ate
re•ver•ber•at•ed
re•ver•ber•at•ing
re•ver•ber•a•tion
re•vere
re•vered

re•ver•ing
rev•er•end
rev•er•ent
rev•er•ence
rev•er•ie
re•ver•sal
re•verse
re•versed
re•vers•ing
re•vers•i•ble
re•vert
re•view
re•vile
re•viled
re•vil•ing
re•vise
re•vised
re•vis•ing
re•vi•sion
re•vi•sion•ist
re•vi•tal•ize
re•vi•tal•iza•tion
re•viv•al
re•viv•al•ist
re•vive
re•vived
re•viv•ing
re•voke
re•voked
re•vok•ing
rev•o•ca•ble
rev•o•ca•tion
re•volt
rev•o•lu•tion
rev•o•lu•tion•ary
rev•o•lu•tion•ize
re•volve
re•volved
re•volv•ing
re•volv•er
re•vue
re•vul•sion
re•ward
rhap•so•dy
rhet•o•ric
rhe•tor•i•cal•ly
rheu•mat•ic
rheu•ma•tism
rheu•ma•toid
rhine•stone
rhi•noc•er•os
rho•do•den•dron
rhom•boid
rhom•bus
rhu•barb
rhyme
rhymed
rhym•ing
rhythm
rhyth•mic
rhyth•mi•cal
rhyth•mi•cal•ly
rib
ribbed
rib•bing
rib•ald
rib•ald•ry
rib•bon
rib•bo•nu•cle•ic acid
rich•es
rick•ets
rick•ety
rick•shaw
ric•o•chet
ric•o•cheted
ric•o•chet•ing
rid
rid•ded
rid•ding
rid•dance
rid•dle
rid•dled
ride
rode
rid•den
rid•ing
rid•er
ridge
rid•i•cule
rid•i•culed
rid•i•cul•ing
ri•dic•u•lous
ri•fle

rig
rigged
rig•ging
right•eous
right•ful•ly
right-hand•ed
right-wing
rig•id
ri•gid•i•ty
rig•ma•role
rig•or
rig•or•ous
ri•gor mor•tis
rile
riled
ril•ing
rim
rimmed
rim•ming
ring
ringed
ring•ing
ring
rang
rung
ring•ing
rinse
rinsed
rins•ing
Rio de Ja•nei•ro
ri•ot•er
ri•ot•ous
rip
ripped
rip•ping
rip•en
rip•ple
rip•pled
rip•pling
rise
rose
ris•en
ris•ing
risky
ris•qué
rite
rit•u•al
ritzy
ri•val
ri•val•ry
riv•er•side
riv•et
riv•u•let
roach•es
road•block
roast•er
rob
robbed
rob•bing
rob•ber
rob•bery
robe
rob•in
ro•bot
ro•bust
rock•et
rock•et•ry
rocky
ro•co•co
ro•dent
ro•deo
roent•gen
rogue
roist•er
roll•er coast•er
roll•er skates
roll•ick
ro•maine
ro•mance
ro•manced
ro•manc•ing
ro•man•tic
ro•man•ti•cism
ro•man•ti•cize
ro•man•ti•cized
ro•man•ti•ciz•ing
romp•er
roof•ing
rook•ie
room•mate
roomy
roost•er
rope

run•ning
run•ny
run•ner-up
runt
rup•ture
  rup•tured
  rup•tur•ing
ru•ral
rus•set
Rus•sia
  Rus•sian
rus•tic
  rus•tic•i•ty
rus•tle
  rus•tled
  rus•tling
rusty
rut
  rut•ted
  rut•ting
ru•ta•ba•ga
ruth•less

rot
  rot•ted
  rot•ting
  rot•ten
ro•tate
  ro•tat•ed
  ro•tat•ing
  ro•ta•ry
  ro•ta•tion
ro•tis•ser•ie
ro•tund
ro•tun•da
rou•é
rouge
rough•age
rough•en
rough•shod
rou•lette
round•ed
rouse
  roused
  rous•ing
rout
route
  rout•ed
  rout•ing
rou•tine
rove
  roved
  rov•ing
row•dy
roy•al
  roy•al•ist
  roy•al•ty
rub
  rubbed
  rub•bing
rub•ber
  rub•bery
rub•bish
rub•ble
ru•bel•la
ru•bi•cund
ru•bric
ru•by
ruck•sack
ruck•us
rud•der
rud•dy
rude•ly
ru•di•ment
  ru•di•men•ta•ry
rue
  rued
  ru•ing
rue•ful•ly
ruf•fi•an
ruf•fle
  ruf•fled
  ruf•fling
rug•ged
ru•in
  ru•in•a•tion
  ru•in•ous
rule
  ruled
  rul•ing
rum•ba
rum•ble
  rum•bled
  rum•bling
ru•mi•nate
  ru•mi•nat•ing
  ru•mi•na•tion
rum•mage
  rum•mag•ing
rum•my
ru•mor
rum•ple
  rum•pled
  rum•pling
rum•pus
run
  ran

S

Sab•bath
sab•bat•i•cal
sa•ber
sa•ble
sab•o•tage
  sab•o•taged
  sab•o•tag•ing
  sab•o•teur
sac•cha•rin
sac•cha•rine
sac•er•do•tal
sa•chet
sack•ful
sac•ra•ment
sa•cred
sac•ri•fice
  sac•ri•ficed
  sac•ri•fic•ing
  sac•ri•fi•cial
sac•ri•lege
  sac•ri•le•gious
sac•ris•ty
sac•ro•il•i•ac
sac•ro•sanct
sad
  sad•der
  sad•ly
  sad•den
sad•dle
sad•ism
  sad•ist
  sa•dis•tic
  sa•dis•ti•cal•ly
sa•fa•ri
safe
  saf•er
  saf•est
safe•keep•ing
safe•ty
saf•flow•er
saf•fron
sag
  sagged
  sag•ging
sa•ga
sa•ga•cious
  sa•gac•i•ty
sage
Sag•it•ta•ri•us
sail•ing
sail•or
saint•ly
sa•ke
sa•la•cious
sal•ad
sal•a•man•der
sa•la•mi
sal•a•ry
  sal•a•ries
sales•man
  sales•wom•an
sa•li•ent
  sa•li•ence
sa•line
sa•li•va
  sal•i•vary
  sal•i•vate
  sal•i•vat•ed

sal•i•vat•ing
sal•i•va•tion
sal•low
sal•ly
  sal•lied
salm•on
sal•mo•nel•la
sa•lon
sa•loon
salt•cel•lar
salty
sa•lu•bri•ous
sal•u•tary
  sal•u•ta•tion
sa•lute
  sa•lut•ed
  sa•lut•ing
sal•vage
  sal•vaged
  sal•vag•ing
  sal•vage•a•ble
sal•va•tion
salve
sal•vo
sam•ba
same•ness
sam•o•var
sam•ple
  sam•pled
  sam•pling
  sam•pler
san•a•to•ri•um
sanc•ti•fy
  sanc•ti•fied
  sanc•ti•fy•ing
  sanc•ti•fi•ca•tion
sanc•ti•mo•ny
  sanc•ti•mo•ni•ous
sanc•tion
sanc•ti•ty
sanc•tu•ary
sanc•tum
san•dal
sand•pa•per
sand•pi•per
sand•wich
sandy
sane•ly
sang-froid
san•gui•nary
san•guine
san•i•tar•i•um
san•i•tary
  san•i•ta•tion
san•i•tize
  san•i•tized
san•i•ty
sap
  sapped
  sap•ping
sa•pi•ent
  sa•pi•ence
sap•ling
sap•phire
sap•suck•er
sar•casm
  sar•cas•tic
  sar•cas•ti•cal•ly
sar•co•ma
sar•coph•a•gus
sar•dine
sar•don•ic
  sar•don•i•cal•ly
sa•ri
sa•rong
sar•to•ri•al
sa•shay
Sas•katch•e•wan
sas•sy
sa•tan•ic
satch•el
sate
  sat•ed
  sat•ing
sat•el•lite
sa•ti•ate
  sa•ti•at•ed
  sa•ti•a•tion
sa•ti•e•ty
sat•in
sat•ire
  sa•tir•i•cal•ly
  sat•i•rist

sat•i•rize
sat•i•rized
sat•i•riz•ing
sat•is•fac•tion
sat•is•fac•to•ry
sat•is•fac•to•ri•ly
sat•is•fy
  sat•is•fied
  sat•is•fy•ing
sat•u•rate
  sat•u•rat•ed
  sat•u•rat•ing
  sat•u•ra•tion
sat•ur•nine
sa•tyr
sauce
sau•cer
sau•cy
Sau•di Ara•bia
sau•er•kraut
sau•na
saun•ter
sau•sage
sau•té
  sau•teéd
  sau•té•ing
sau•terne
sav•age
  sav•age•ry
sa•van•na
sa•vant
save
  saved
  sav•ing
sav•ior
sa•vior faire
sa•vor
sa•vory
sav•vy
sax•o•phone
say
  said
  say•ing
scab
scab•bard
  scab•by
scaf•fold
scald
scale
  scaled
  scal•ing
scal•lion
scal•lop
scalp
scal•pel
scaly
scamp•er
scan
  scanned
  scan•ning
  scan•ner
scan•dal
  scan•dal•ized
  scan•dal•ous
Scan•di•na•via
scant
scanty
scape•goat
scar
  scarred
  scar•ring
scar•ab
scarce
  scar•ci•ty
scare
  scared
  scar•ing
scary
scarf
  scarfs
  scarves
scar•let
scat
scath•ing
scat•ter
scav•enge
  scav•enged
  scav•eng•ing
  scav•en•ger
sce•nar•io
scen•ery
  sce•nic
scent

scep•ter
sched•ule
  sched•uled
  sched•ul•ing
  sche•mat•i•cal•ly
scheme
  schem•er
  schem•ing
scher•zo
schism
schiz•oid
schiz•o•phre•nia
  schiz•o•phren•ic
schol•ar
  schol•ar•ly
scho•las•tic
school board
school•teach•er
schoon•er
sci•at•ic
sci•ence
  sci•en•tif•ic
  sci•en•tif•i•cal•ly
  sci•en•tist
scin•til•la
scin•til•lat•ing
sci•on
scis•sors
scle•ro•sis
scoff•ing•ly
scold•ing
sconce
scone
scoop•er
scoot•er
scope
scorch
  scorched
score
  scored
  scor•ing
  scor•er
scorn
scor•pi•on
scot-free
scoun•drel
scour
scourge
  scourged
  scourg•ing
scout•ing
scowl
scrag•gly
scram
  scrammed
  scram•ming
scram•ble
  scram•bled
  scram•bling
scrap
  scrapped
  scrap•ping
scrape
  scraped
  scrap•ing
  scrap•er
scrap•py
scratchy
scrawl
scrawny
scream•ing
screech
screen•ing
screwy
scrib•ble
  scrib•bled
  scrib•bling
  scrib•bler
scribe
scrim•mage
  scrim•maged
  scrim•mag•ing
scrimp
script
scrip•ture
  scrip•tur•al
scriv•en•er
scroll
scrooge
scro•tum
scrounge
  scroung•er
  scroung•ing

scrub
scrubbed
scrub•bing
scruffy
scrump•tious
scru•ple
scru•pu•lous
scru•ti•nize
scru•ti•nized
scru•ti•niz•ing
scru•ti•ny
scu•ba
scuf•fle
scul•lery
sculp•tor
sculp•tress
sculp•ture
scum
scur•ri•lous
scur•ry
scur•ried
scur•ry•ing
scur•vy
scythe
sea•far•ing
sea•far•er
seal•ant
seal•skin
seam•stress
seamy
search•er
search•light
sea•sick•ness
sea•son
sea•son•a•ble
sea•son•al
seat•ing
sea•wor•thy
se•ba•ceous
se•cede
se•ced•ed
se•ced•ing
se•ces•sion
se•clude
se•clud•ed
se•clu•sion
sec•ond•ary
sec•ond-guess
sec•ond-rate
se•cret
se•cre•cy
se•cre•tive
sec•re•tar•i•at
sec•re•tary
sec•re•tar•ies
sec•re•tar•i•al
se•crete
se•cret•ed
se•cret•ing
se•cre•tion
sec•tar•i•an
sec•tion
sec•tion•al
sec•tor
sec•u•lar
se•cure
se•cured
se•cur•ing
se•cu•ri•ty
se•cu•ri•ties
se•dan
se•date
se•da•tion
se•dat•ed
se•dat•ing
sed•a•tive
sed•en•tary
sed•i•ment
se•di•tion
se•di•tious
se•duce
se•duced
se•duc•ing
se•duc•er
se•duc•tion
se•duc•tive
sed•u•lous
see
saw
seen
see•ing
seed•ling
seedy

seek
sought
seek•ing
seem•ing
seem•ly
seep
seep•age
se•er
seer•suck•er
seethe
seethed
seeth•ing
seg•ment
seg•men•tal
seg•men•tary
seg•men•ta•tion
seg•re•gate
seg•re•gat•ed
seg•re•gat•ing
seg•re•ga•tion
seis•mic
seize
seized
seiz•ing
sei•zure
sel•dom
se•lect
se•lect•ed
se•lec•tion
se•lec•tive
se•lec•tiv•i•ty
self
selves
self-ad•dressed
self-as•sur•ance
self-cen•tered
self-con•fi•dence
self-con•scious
self-con•trol
self-de•fense
self-dis•ci•pline
self-es•teem
self-ex•plan•a•to•ry
self-im•age
self-in•dul•gence
self•ish
self•ish•ness
self•less
self•less•ness
self-made
self-op•er•at•ing
self-pity
self-re•li•ance
self-re•spect
self-right•eous
self-serv•ice
self-serv•ing
self-suf•fi•cient
sell
sold
sell•ing
sell•er
sel•vage
selves
se•man•tics
sem•blance
se•men
se•mes•ter
sem•i•an•nu•al
sem•i•cir•cle
sem•i•co•lon
sem•i•fi•nal•ist
sem•i•nal
sem•i•nar
sem•i•nary
sem•i•pre•cious
sem•i•skilled
Sem•ite
Se•mit•ic
sem•i•trop•i•cal
sen•a•ry
sen•ate
sen•a•tor
send
sent
send•ing
se•nile
se•nil•i•ty
sen•ior
sen•ior•i•ty
sen•sate
sen•sa•tion
sen•sa•tion•al

sen•sa•tion•al•ism
sense
sensed
sens•ing
sense•less
sense•less•ness
sen•si•bil•i•ty
sen•si•ble
sen•si•bly
sen•si•tive
sen•si•tiv•i•ty
sen•si•tize
sen•si•tized
sen•sor
sen•so•ry
sen•su•al
sen•su•al•i•ty
sen•su•ous
sen•tence
sen•tenced
sen•tenc•ing
sen•tient
sen•ti•ment
sen•ti•men•tal
sen•ti•men•tal•i•ty
sen•ti•men•tal•ize
sen•ti•men•tal•ized
sen•ti•nel
sen•try
sen•tries
sep•a•ra•ble
sep•a•rate
sep•a•rat•ed
sep•a•rat•ing
sep•a•ra•tion
sep•a•ra•tist
sep•a•ra•tism
sep•a•ra•tive
sep•a•ra•tor
se•pia
sep•sis
sep•tic
sep•tu•a•ge•nar•i•an
se•pul•cher
se•pul•chral
se•quel
se•quence
se•quen•tial
se•ques•ter
se•ques•tered
se•ques•tra•tion
se•quin
se•quoia
ser•e•nade
ser•e•nad•ed
ser•e•nad•ing
ser•en•dip•i•ty
se•rene
se•ren•i•ty
serge
ser•geant
se•ri•al
se•ri•al•ly
se•ri•al•ize
se•ries
se•ri•ous
se•ri•ous•ly
ser•mon
ser•mon•ize
se•rous
ser•pent
ser•pen•tine
ser•rat•ed
se•rum
serv•ant
serve
served
serv•ing
ser•vice
serv•iced
serv•ic•ing
serv•ice•a•ble
ser•vile
ser•vil•i•ty
ses•sion
set
set
set•ting
set•ter
set•tle
set•tled
set•tling
set•tle•ment

set•tler
sev•en
sev•enth
sev•en•teen
sev•en•ty
sev•en•ties
sev•en•ti•eth
sev•er
sev•er•ance
sev•er•al
se•vere
se•ver•i•ty
sew•age
sew•er
sew•ing ma•chine
sex•tant
sex•tet
sex•ton
sex•u•al
sex•u•al•ly
sex•u•al•i•ty
shab•by
shab•bi•ly
shack•le
shack•led
shade
shad•ed
shad•ing
shady
shad•ow
shad•owy
shaft
shag•gy
shake
shook
shak•en
shak•ing
shak•er
Shake•spear•e•an
shaky
shak•i•ly
shal•lot
shal•low
sham
shammed
sham•ming
sha•man
sham•bles
shame
shamed
sham•ing
shame•ful
shame•less
sham•poo
sham•pooed
sham•poo•ing
sham•rock
shan•ty
shan•ties
shape
shaped
shap•ing
shape•less
shape•ly
share
shared
shar•ing
shar•er
share•hold•er
sharp•en
sharp•en•er
shat•ter
shat•tered
shat•ter•ing
shave
shaved
shav•en
shav•ing
shawl
sheaf
sheaves
shear
sheared
shear•ing
sheath
sheathe
sheathed
sheath•ing
shed
shed•ding
sheen
sheep•herd•er
sheep•ish

sheep•skin
sheer
sheet•ing
sheik
shelf
shelves
shell
shel•lac
shel•lacked
shel•lack•ing
shel•ter
shelve
shelved
shelv•ing
shep•herd
sher•bet
sher•iff
sher•ry
shib•bo•leth
shield
shift
shift•less
shifty
shil•ling
shim•mer
shim•mered
shim•mer•ing
shim•my
shin
shine
shined
shone
shin•ing
shiny
shin•gle
shin•gled
shin•gling
shin•gles
ship
shipped
ship•ping
ship•ment
shirk
shirk•ed
shiv•er
shiv•ered
shoal
shock•ing
shod•dy
shoe•mak•er
shoot
shot
shoot•ing
shop
shopped
shop•ping
shop•per
shop•lift•er
shore•line
short•ly
short•age
short•change
short•com•ing
short•en
short•en•ing
short•hand
short-hand•ed
short-lived
shot•gun
should
shoul•der
shout•ing
shove
shoved
shov•ing
shov•el
shov•eled
shov•el•ing
show
showed
shown
show•ing
show•er
showy
show•i•ness
shrap•nel
shred
shred•ded
shred•ding
shred•der
shrew
shrewd
shrewd•ly

shriv•eled
shriv•el•ing
shroud
shrub•bery
shrug
  shrugged
  shrug•ging
shud•der
shuf•fle
  shuf•fled
  shuf•fling
shun
  shunned
  shun•ning
shunt
shut•ter
shut•tle
shy
  shied
  shy•ing
shy•ster
Si•a•mese
sib•ling
sick•en
  sick•en•ing
sick•le
sick•ly
sid•ed
side•line
si•de•re•al
side•step
side•swipe
sid•ing
si•dle
  si•dled
  si•dling
siege
si•er•ra
si•es•ta
sieve
sift•er
sigh•ing
sight•ed
sight•see•ing
  sight•see•er
sig•nal
  sig•naled
  sig•nal•ing
sig•na•to•ry
sig•na•ture
sig•net
sig•nif•i•cance
  sig•nif•i•cant
  sig•ni•fi•ca•tion
sig•ni•fy
  sig•ni•fied
  sig•ni•fy•ing
si•lence
  si•lenced
  si•lenc•ing
si•lenc•er
si•lent
sil•hou•ette
  sil•hou•et•ted
  sil•hou•et•ting
sil•i•cone
silky
sil•ly
  sil•li•ness
si•lo
silt
sil•ver
sil•very
sil•ver•ware
sim•i•an
sim•i•lar
  sim•i•lar•i•ty
  sim•i•lar•i•ties
sim•i•le
si•mil•i•tude
sim•mer
sim•per
sim•ple
  sim•pler

sim•plest
sim•ple-mind•ed
sim•ple•ton
sim•plic•i•ty
sim•pli•fy
  sim•pli•fied
  sim•pli•fy•ing
  sim•pli•fi•ca•tion
sim•plis•tic
  sim•plis•ti•cal•ly
sim•ply
sim•u•late
  sim•u•lat•ed
  sim•u•lat•ing
  sim•u•la•tion
  sim•u•la•tor
si•mul•cast
si•mul•ta•ne•ous
sin
  sinned
  sin•ning
  sin•ner
  sin•ful
Si•nai
sin•cere
  sin•cer•i•ty
si•ne•cure
sin•ew
  sin•ewy
sing
  sang
  sung
  sing•ing
singe
  singed
  singe•ing
sin•gle
  sin•gled
  sin•gling
  sin•gly
sin•gle-hand•ed
sin•gle-mind•ed
sin•gle-spaced
sin•gu•lar
  sin•gu•lar•i•ty
sin•is•ter
sink
  sank
  sunk
  sink•ing
sin•u•ous
si•nus
  si•nus•i•tis
sip
  sipped
  sip•ping
si•phon
sire
  sired
si•ren
sir•loin
si•roc•co
sis•sy
sis•ter
  sis•ter-in-law
sit
  sat
  sit•ting
sit•ter
sit•u•ate
  sit•u•at•ed
  sit•u•a•tion
six
sixth
six•teen
six•ty
  six•ties
  six•ti•eth
siz•a•ble
size
  sized
  siz•ing
siz•zle
  siz•zled
  siz•zling
skate
  skat•ed
  skat•ing
skein
skel•e•ton
  skel•e•tal
skep•tic
  skep•ti•cal

skep•ti•cism
sketch
sketchy
skew•er
ski
  skied
  ski•ing
  ski•er
skid
  skid•ded
  skid•ding
skiff
skill
  skilled
  skill•ful
  skill•ful•ly
skil•let
skim
  skimmed
  skim•ming
skimp
  skimp•y
skin
  skinned
  skin•ning
skin diving
skin•ny
skip
  skipped
  skip•ping
skip•per
skir•mish
skit•tish
skoal
skul•dug•ger•y
skulk
skull
skunk
sky•div•ing
sky•jack•er
sky•scrap•er
slab
slack
slack•en
slake
  slaked
  slak•ing
sla•lom
slam
  slammed
  slam•ming
slan•der
  slan•der•er
  slan•der•ous
slang
slant
slap
  slapped
  slap•ping
slap•stick
slash•ing
slat
  slat•ted
  slat•ting
slate
slat•tern•ly
slaugh•ter
slave
  slaved
  slav•ing
  slav•ery
  sla•vish•ly
slay
  slew
  slain
  slay•ing
slea•zy
sled
  sled•ded
  sled•ding
sledge
sleek
sleep•less•ness
sleepy
  sleep•i•ly
sleet
sleeve
  sleeved
  sleeve•less
sleigh
sleight of hand
slen•der
  slen•der•ize

sleuth
slice
  sliced
  slic•ing
slick•er
slide
  slid
  slid•ing
slight
slim
  slimmed
  slim•ming
slime
  slimy
sling
  slung
  sling•ing
slink
  slunk
  slink•ing
slip
  slipped
  slip•ping
  slip•pery
slip•page
slip•per
slip•shod
slit
  slit•ting
slith•er
sliv•er
slob•ber
slog
  slogged
  slog•ging
slo•gan
sloop
slop
  slopped
  slop•ping
slope
  sloped
  slop•ing
slop•py
sloshy
slot
  slot•ted
  slot•ting
sloth
  sloth•ful
slouch
slough
slov•en•ly
slow•ly
sludge
slug
  slugged
  slug•ging
slug•gard
slug•gish
sluice
slum
  slummed
  slum•ming
slum•ber
  slum•ber•er
  slum•ber•ous
slump
  slumped
slur
  slurred
  slur•ring
slush
  slushy
slut
sly
  sly•ly
smack•ing
small•pox
smart
smart al•eck
smash•ing
smat•ter•ing
smear
  smeary
smell
  smelled
  smel•ling
  smelly
smelt
smid•gen
smile
  smil•ling

smirch
smirk
smite
  smote
  smit•ten
smith•er•eens
smock•ing
smog•gy
smoke
  smoked
  smok•ing
  smok•er
smoky
smol•der
smooth
  smooth•en
smor•gas•bord
smoth•er
smudge
  smudged
  smudg•ing
  smudgy
smug
smug•gle
  smug•gled
  smug•gling
  smug•gler
smut
  smut•ty
snaf•fle
sna•fu
snag
  snagged
  snag•ging
snail
snake
  snaked
  snak•ing
  snak•i•ly
  snaky
snap
  snapped
  snap•ping
  snap•py
snare
  snared
  snar•ing
snarl
snatch
snaz•zy
sneak•er
sneak•ing
sneaky
  sneak•i•ly
sneer
sneeze
  sneezed
  sneez•ing
  sneezy
snick•er
snif•fle
  snif•fled
  snif•fling
snif•fy
snif•ter
snig•ger
snip
  snipped
  snip•ping
snip•er
snip•py
snitch•er
sniv•el
  sniv•eled
  sniv•el•ing
snob
  snob•bery
snoop
snooty
snooze
  snoozed
  snooz•ing
snore
  snored
  snor•ing
snor•kel
snort
  snort•ed
snot•ty
snout
snowy
snub
  snubbed

snub•bing
snuff
snug
snug•gle
   snug•gled
   snug•gling
soak•ing
soapy
soar
   soaring
sob
   sobbed
   sob•bing
so•ber
so•bri•e•ty
so•bri•quet
soc•cer
so•cia•ble
   so•cia•bil•i•ty
so•cial
   so•cial•ly
so•cial•ism
   so•cial•ist
so•cial•ite
so•cial•ize
   so•cial•ized
   so•cial•iz•ing
so•ci•e•ty
   so•ci•e•ties
   so•ci•e•tal
so•ci•o•ec•o•nom•ic
so•ci•ol•o•gy
   so•ci•o•log•i•cal
   so•ci•ol•o•gist
sock•et
sod
so•da
sod•den
so•di•um
sod•omy
so•fa
soft
   sof•ten
soft-ped•al
soft-spo•ken
sog•gy
so•journ
sol•ace
   sol•aced
   sol•ac•ing
so•lar
   so•lar•i•um
so•lar plex•us
sol•der
sol•dier
sol•e•cism
sole•ly
sol•emn
   so•lem•ni•ty
so•lic•it
   so•lic•i•ta•tion
   so•lic•i•tor
   so•lic•i•tous
   so•lic•i•tude
sol•id
   so•lid•i•ty
sol•i•dar•i•ty
so•lid•i•fy
   so•lid•i•fied
   so•lid•i•fy•ing
so•lil•o•quy
sol•i•taire
sol•i•tary
sol•i•tude
so•lo
   so•loed
   so•lo•ing
   so•lo•ist
sol•stice
sol•u•ble
   sol•u•bil•i•ty
so•lu•tion
solve
   solved
   solv•ing
sol•vent
   sol•ven•cy
so•mat•ic
som•ber
some•body
som•er•sault
some•thing
some•where

som•nam•bu•late
   som•nam•bu•list
so•nar
so•na•ta
son•ic
son-in-law
son•net
son•ny
so•no•rous
soothe
   soothed
   sooth•ing
sooth•say•er
sooty
sop
   sopped
   sop•ping
soph•ist
   soph•ist•ry
so•phis•ti•cate
   so•phis•ti•cat•ed
   so•phis•ti•cat•ing
   so•phis•ti•ca•tion
soph•o•more
soph•o•mor•ic
sop•o•rif•ic
sop•py
so•prano
sor•cer•er
   sor•cer•ess
sor•cery
sor•did
sore
   sore•ly
sor•ghum
sor•ror•i•ty
sor•row
   sor•row•ful•ly
sor•ry
   sor•ri•ly
sor•tie
sot
sou•bri•quet
souf•flé
sought
soul•ful
sound•ing
sound•less•ly
soupy
sour
source
souse
   soused
south•east
   south•east•ern
south•er•ly
south•ern
south•west
   south•west•ern
sou•ve•nir
sov•er•eign•
   sov•er•eign•ty
so•vi•et
sow
   sowed
   sown
   sow•ing
soy•bean
space
   spaced
   spac•ing
spa•cious
spack•le
spade
spa•ghet•ti
span
   spanned
   span•ning
Spain
   Span•iard
   Span•ish
span•iel
spank•ing
spar
   sparred
   spar•ring
spare
   spared
   spar•ing
spar•kle
   spar•kled
   spar•kling
spar•row

sparse
spasm
spas•mod•ic
   spas•mod•i•cal•ly
spas•tic
spat
spa•tial
spat•ter
spat•u•la
spawn
speak
   spok•en
   speak•ing
spear
spear•mint
spe•cial
   spe•cial•ly
spe•cial•ist
spe•cial•ize
   spe•cial•ized
   spe•cial•iz•ing
   special•i•za•tion
spe•cial•ty
   spe•cial•ties
spe•cie
spe•cif•ic
   spe•cif•i•cal•ly
   spec•i•fic•i•ty
spec•i•fy
   spec•i•fied
   spec•i•fy•ing
   spec•i•fi•ca•tion
spec•i•men
spe•cious
speck•le
   speck•led
spec•ta•cle
spec•tac•u•lar
spec•ta•tor
spec•ter
spec•tral
spec•tro•scope
spec•trum
spec•u•late
   spec•u•lat•ed
   spec•u•lat•ing
   spec•u•la•tion
   spec•u•la•tor
   spec•u•la•tive
speech•less
speed
   speed•ed
   sped
   speed•ing
speed•om•e•ter
spell
   spelled
   spell•ing
spell•bound
   spell•bind•ing
spend
   spent
   spend•ing
spend•thrift
sperm
spew
sphere
   spher•ic
   spher•i•cal
   sphe•roid
sphinc•ter
sphinx
spice
   spiced
   spic•ing
   spicy
spi•der
spiel
spiffy
spig•ot
spike
   spiked
   spiky
spill
   spilled
   spill•ing
spil•lage
spin
   spun
   spin•ning
spin•ach
spi•nal
spin•dle

spin•dly
spine•less
spin•et
spin•ner
spin•ning
spin•ster
spiny
spi•ral
   spi•raled
   spi•ral•ing
spire
spir•it
   spir•it•ed
spir•it•u•al
   spir•it•u•al•ist
   spir•it•u•al•i•ty
spit
   spat
   spit•ting
spite
   spite•ful
spit•tle
spit•toon
splash
splat•ter
splay•foot
spleen
   sple•net•ic
splen•did
   splen•dif•er•ous
   splen•dor
splice
   spliced
   splic•ing
splin•ter
split
   split•ting
splotchy
splurge
   splurged
   splurg•ing
spoil
   spoiled
   spoil•ing
spoil•age
spoke
   spo•ken
spokes•man
   spokes•wom•an
sponge
   sponged
   spong•ing
   spong•er
   spon•gy
spon•sor
spon•ta•ne•i•ty
spon•ta•ne•ous
   spon•ta•ne•ous•ness
spooky
spoon-feed
spoon•ful
spo•rad•ic
   spo•rad•i•cal•ly
spore
sport
   spor•tive
   sporty
sports•cast•er
spot
   spot•ted
   spot•ting
   spot•ty
spouse
sprained
sprawl
spray•er
spread
   spread•ing
sprig
spright•ly
spring
   sprang
   sprung
   spring•ing
springy
sprin•kle
   sprin•kled
   sprin•kling
   sprinkl•er
sprint•er
sprock•et
spruce
   spruced

spruc•in
spry
spume
spunky
spur
   spurred
   spur•ring
spu•ri•ous
spurn
spurt
sput•ter
spu•tum
spy
   spies
   spied
   spy•ing
squab•ble
   squab•bled
   squab•bling
squad•ron
squal•id
squall
squal•or
squan•der
square
   squared
   squar•ing
squash
squashy
squat
   squat•ted
   squat•ting
squat•ter
squawk
squeaky
squeal
squeam•ish
squeeze
   squeezed
   squeez•ing
squelch
squib
squid
squig•gle
   squig•gled
   squig•gling
squint
squire
squirm
squir•rel
squirt
squishy
stab
   stabbed
   stab•bing
sta•ble
   sta•bil•i•ty
sta•bi•lize
sta•ble
   sta•bled
   sta•bling
stac•ca•to
sta•di•um
staff
stag
stage
   staged
   stag•ing
stag•ger
   stag•ger•ing
stag•nant
stag•nate
   stag•nat•ed
   stag•nat•ing
stag•na•tion
staid
stain
   stained
stake
   staked
   stak•ing
sta•lac•tite
sta•lag•mite
stale
stale•mate
stalk
   stalked
stalled
stal•lion
stal•wart
sta•men
stam•i•na
stam•mer

...ized
...di•iz•ing
...and•ard•i•za•tion
stand•point
stan•za
staph•y•lo•coc•cus
sta•ple
  sta•pled
  sta•pling
  sta•pler
star
  starred
  star•ring
starchy
star•dom
stare
  stared
  star•ing
stark•ly
star•ling
star•ry
start•er
star•tle
  star•tled
  star•tling
star•va•tion
starve
  starved
  starv•ing
sta•sis
state
  stat•ed
  stat•ing
  state•ment
state•ly
states•man
stat•ic
sta•tion
  sta•tion•ary
  sta•tion•er
  sta•tion•ery
sta•tis•tic
  stat•is•ti•cian
stat•ue
  stat•u•ary
  stat•u•esque
  stat•u•ette
stat•ure
sta•tus
sta•tus quo
stat•ute
  stat•u•to•ry
staunch
stave
stay
  stayed
  stay•ing
stead•fast
steady
  stead•ied
  stead•y•ing
  stead•i•ly
steal
  stol•en
  steal•ing
stealth
  stealthy
  stealth•i•ly
steam•er
steamy
steely
steep
stee•ple
steer
stein
stel•lar
stem
  stemmed
  stem•ming
stench
sten•cil
  sten•ciled
  sten•cil•ing
ste•nog•ra•pher
  ste•nog•ra•phy
sten•to•ri•an

step
  stepped
  step•ping
steppe
ster•eo
ster•e•o•phon•ic
ster•e•o•type
ster•ile
  ste•ril•i•ty
  ster•i•lize
  ster•i•lized
  ster•i•liz•ing
  ster•i•li•za•tion
ster•ling
stern•ly
ster•num
ster•oid
steth•o•scope
ste•ve•dore
stew•ard
  stew•ard•ess
stick
  stuck
  stick•ing
stick•er
stick•ler
sticky
stiff
sti•fle
  sti•fled
  sti•fling
stig•ma
  stig•ma•tize
stile
sti•let•to
still•born
stilt•ed
stim•u•late
  stim•u•lat•ed
  stim•u•lat•ing
  stim•u•lant
  stim•u•la•tion
stim•u•lus
  stim•u•li
sting
  stung
  sting•ing
stin•gy
stink
  stank
  stunk
  stinky
stint
sti•pend
stip•u•late
  stip•u•lat•ed
  stip•u•lat•ing
  stip•u•la•tion
stir
  stirred
  stir•ring
stir-rup
stitch
stock•ade
stock•brok•er
stock•hold•er
stock•ing
stock•pile
stocky
stodgy
sto•ic
  sto•i•cal
stoke
  stoked
  stok•ing
stol•id
stom•ach
stone
  stoned
  ston•ing
  stony
stop
  stopped
  stop•ping
stop•page
stop•per
stor•age
store
  stored
  stor•ing
  sto•ried
stormy
story

sto•ries
stout
stove
stow•age
stow•a•way
strad•dle
  strad•dled
  strad•dling
strag•gle
  strag•gled
  strag•gling
  strag•gler
straight•a•way
straight-edge
straight•en
straight•for•ward
strain•er
strait•en
strait•jack•et
strait-laced
strange
  strang•er
  strang•est
  strange•ly
stran•ger
stran•gle
  stran•gled
  stran•gling
  stran•gler
stran•gu•late
  stran•gu•lat•ed
  stran•gu•la•tion
strap
  strapped
  strap•ping
strat•a•gem
stra•te•gic
  stra•te•gi•cal•ly
strat•e•gy
  strat•e•gist
strat•i•fy
  strat•i•fied
  strat•i•fi•ca•tion
strat•o•sphere
stra•tum
  stra•ta
stra•tus
straw•ber•ry
stray•ing
streaky
stream•er
stream•line
strength•en
stren•u•ous
strep•to•coc•cus
strep•to•my•cin
stress•ful
stretch
  stretch•er
strew
  strewed
  strew•ing
strick•en
strict•ly
stric•ture
stride
  strode
  strid•den
  strid•ing
stri•dent
  stri•den•cy
strife
strike
  struck
  strick•en
  strik•ing
string
  strung
  string•ing
strin•gent
  strin•gen•cy
stringy
strip
  stripped
  strip•ping
stripe
  striped
strip•ling
strip•per
strive
  strove
  striv•en
  striv•ing

stroke
  stroked
  strok•ing
stroll•er
strong•ly
strop
struc•tural
  struc•tur•al•ly
struc•ture
  struc•tured
  struc•tur•ing
strug•gle
  strug•gled
  strug•gling
strum
  strummed
  strum•ming
strut
  strut•ted
  strut•ting
strych•nine
stub
  stubbed
  stub•by
stub•ble
stub•born
stuc•co
stud
  stud•ded
stu•dent
stu•dio
stu•di•ous
study
  stud•ies
  stud•ied
  stud•y•ing
stuff•ing
stuffy
stul•ti•fy
  stul•ti•fy•ing
stum•ble
  stum•bled
  stum•bling
stumpy
stun
  stunned
  stun•ning
stunt
  stunt•ed
stu•pe•fy
  stu•pe•fied
  stu•pe•fy•ing
  stu•pe•fac•tion
stu•pen•dous
stu•pid
  stu•pid•i•ty
stu•por
stur•dy
stur•geon
stut•ter
style
  styled
  styl•ing
  styl•ish
styl•ist
  sty•lis•tic
styl•ize
  styl•ized
sty•lus
sty•mie
  sty•mied
suave
sub•al•tern
sub•arc•tic
sub•com•mit•tee
sub•con•scious
sub•con•trac•tor
sub•cu•ta•ne•ous
sub•di•vi•sion
sub•due
  sub•dued
  sub•du•ing
sub•ject
  sub•jec•tion
  sub•jec•tive
  sub•jec•tive•ly
  sub•jec•tiv•i•ty
sub•ju•gate
  sub•ju•gat•ed
  sub•ju•gat•ing
  sub•ju•ga•tion
sub•junc•tive
sub•let

sub•li•mate
  sub•li•mat•ed
  sub•li•mat•ing
  sub•li•ma•tion
sub•lime
  sub•lim•i•ty
sub•lim•i•nal
  sub•lim•i•nal•ly
sub•ma•rine
sub•merge
sub•merse
  sub•mersed
  sub•mer•sion
sub•mis•sion
  sub•mis•sive
sub•mit
  sub•mit•ted
  sub•mit•ting
sub•or•di•nate
  sub•or•di•nat•ed
  sub•or•di•nat•ing
  sub•or•di•na•tion
sub•orn
  sub•or•na•tion
sub•poe•na
  sub•poe•naed
sub rosa
sub•scribe
  sub•scribed
  sub•scrib•ing
  sub•scrib•er
  sub•scrip•tion
sub•se•quent
  sub•se•quence
sub•ser•vi•ent
  sub•ser•vi•ence
sub•side
  sub•sid•ed
  sub•sid•ing
  sub•sid•ence
sub•sid•i•ary
  sub•sid•i•ar•ies
sub•si•dize
  sub•si•dized
  sub•si•diz•ing
  sub•si•di•za•tion
sub•si•dy
  sub•si•dies
sub•sist
  sub•sist•ence
sub•stance
sub•stan•tial
  sub•stan•tial•ly
sub•stan•ti•ate
  sub•stan•ti•at•ed
  sub•stan•ti•at•ing
  sub•stan•ti•a•tion
sub•stan•tive
sub•sti•tute
  sub•sti•tut•ed
  sub•sti•tut•ing
  sub•sti•tu•tion
sub•stra•tum
  sub•stra•ta
sub•sume
  sub•sumed
  sub•sum•ing
sub•ter•fuge
sub•ter•ra•ne•an
sub•ti•tle
sub•tle
  sub•tle•ty
  sub•tly
sub•tract
  sub•trac•ion
sub•trop•i•cal
sub•urb
  sub•ur•ban
  sub•ur•bia
  sub•ur•ban•ite
sub•ver•sion
  sub•ver•sive
suc•ceed
suc•cess
  suc•cess•ful•ly
  suc•ces•sion
  suc•ces•sive
  suc•ces•sive•ly
  suc•ces•sor
suc•cinct
  suc•cinct•ly
suc•cor
suc•cu•lent

suc•cu•lence
suc•cumb
suck•er
suck•le
  suck•led
  suck•ling
su•crose
suc•tion
sud•den
  sud•den•ly
sudsy
sue
  sued
  su•ing
suede
su•et
suf•fer
  suf•fered
  suf•fer•ing
suf•fer•ance
suf•fice
suf•fi•cient
  suf•fi•cien•cy
suf•fix
suf•fo•cate
  suf•fo•cat•ed
  suf•fo•cat•ing
  suf•fo•ca•tion
suf•frage
suf•fuse
  suf•fused
  suf•fus•ing
  suf•fu•sion
sug•ar
  sug•ary
sug•gest
  sug•gest•i•ble
  sug•ges•tion
sug•ges•tive
  sug•ges•tive•ly
su•i•cide
  su•i•cid•al
suit•a•ble
  suit•a•bil•i•ty
  suit•a•bly
suite
suit
suit•or
sul•fate
sul•fide
sul•fur
  sul•fu•ric
sulky
sul•len
sul•ly
  sul•lied
sul•tan
sul•try
sum
  summed
  sum•ming
su•mac
sum•ma•rize
  sum•ma•rized
  sum•ma•riz•ing
  sum•ma•ri•za•tion
sum•ma•ry
  sum•mar•i•ly
sum•ma•tion
sum•mer
sum•mit
sum•mon
sump•tu•ous
sun
  sunned
  sun•ning
sun•burn
sun•dae
sun•der
sun•dry
  sun•dries
sunk•en
sun•ny
sun•shine
sup
  supped
  sup•ping
su•per•an•nu•ate
  su•per•an•nu•at•ed
su•perb
su•per•cil•i•ous
su•per•e•go
su•per•fi•cial

su•per•fi•ci•al•i•ty
su•per•fi•cial•ly
su•per•flu•ous
  su•per•flu•i•ty
su•per•im•pose
su•per•in•tend•ent
su•pe•ri•or
  su•pe•ri•or•i•ty
su•per•la•tive
su•per•nal
su•per•nat•u•ral
su•per•nu•mer•ary
su•per•pow•er
su•per•script
su•per•sede
  su•per•sed•ed
  su•per•sed•ing
su•per•son•ic
su•per•sti•tion
  su•per•sti•tious
su•per•vise
  su•per•vised
  su•per•vis•ing
  su•per•vi•sion
  su•per•vi•sor
  su•per•vi•so•ry
su•pine
sup•per
sup•plant
sup•ple
sup•ple•ment
  sup•ple•men•tal
  sup•ple•men•ta•ry
  sup•ple•men•ta•tion
sup•pli•ant
sup•pli•cate
  sup•pli•cat•ed
  sup•pli•cat•ing
  sup•pli•cant
  sup•pli•ca•tion
sup•ply
  sup•plied
  sup•ply•ing
  sup•plies
  sup•pli•er
sup•port
  sup•port•ive
sup•pose
  sup•posed
  sup•pos•ing
  sup•pos•ed•ly
sup•po•si•tion
  sup•pos•i•to•ry
sup•press
  sup•pres•sion
su•prem•a•cy
  su•prem•a•cist
su•preme
  su•preme•ly
sur•cease
sur•charge
sur•cin•gle
sure
  sure•ly
  sure•ty
surf
sur•face
  sur•faced
  sur•fac•ing
sur•feit
surge
  surged
  surg•ing
sur•geon
sur•gery
sur•gi•cal
  sur•gi•cal•ly
sur•ly
sur•mise
  sur•mised
  sur•mis•ing
sur•mount
  sur•mount•a•ble
sur•name
sur•pass
sur•plice
sur•plus
sur•prise
  sur•prised
  sur•pris•ing
sur•re•al•ism
sur•re•al•ist
sur•re•al•is•tic

sur•ren•der
sur•rep•ti•tious
sur•ro•gate
sur•round
  sur•round•ings
sur•veil•lance
sur•vey
  sur•vey•or
sur•vive
  sur•vived
  sur•viv•ing
  sur•viv•al
  sur•vi•vor
sus•cep•ti•ble
  sus•cep•ti•bil•i•ty
sus•pect
sus•pend
sus•pense
sus•pen•sion
sus•pi•cion
  sus•pi•cious
sus•tain
  sus•tain•a•ble
sus•te•nance
su•ture
svelte
swab
swad•dle
  swad•dled
  swad•dling
swag•ger
swal•low
swamp
swank
swan
swap
  swapped
  swap•ping
sward
swarthy
swas•ti•ka
swat
  swat•ted
  swat•ting
  swat•ter
swathe
  swathed
sway
swear
  swore
  sworn
  swear•ing
sweat
  sweat•ing
  sweaty
sweat•er
Swe•den
  Swed•ish
sweep
  swept
  sweep•ing
sweep•stakes
sweet•ly
  sweet•en
swell
  swelled
  swoll•en
  swell•ing
swel•ter•ing
swerve
  swerved
  swerv•ing
swift•ly
swig
swill
swim
  swam
  swum
  swim•ming
  swim•mer
swin•dle
  swin•dled
  swin•dling
  swin•dler
swine
swing
  swung
  swing•ing
swipe
  swip•ed
  swip•ing
swirl
swish

switch
Switz•er•land
swiv•el
swiz•zle
swoon
  swoon•ed
swoop
swop
  swopped
  swop•ping
sword
syc•a•more
syc•o•phant
syl•la•ble
  syl•lab•ic
syl•la•bus
syl•lo•gism
sylph
syl•van
sym•bi•o•sis
sym•bol
  sym•bol•ic
  sym•bol•i•cal
  sym•bol•ism
sym•bol•ize
  sym•bol•ized
  sym•bol•iz•ing
sym•me•try
  sym•met•ric
  sym•met•ri•cal
sym•pa•thize
  sym•pa•thized
  sym•pa•thiz•ing
sym•pa•thy
  sym•pa•thet•ic
sym•pho•ny
  sym•phon•ic
sym•po•si•um
symp•tom
  symp•to•mat•ic
syn•a•gogue
syn•chro•nize
  syn•chro•nized
syn•chro•nous
syn•co•pate
  syn•co•pat•ed
  syn•co•pa•tion
syn•di•cate
  syn•di•cat•ed
  syn•di•ca•tion
syn•drome
syn•er•gism
syn•od
syn•o•nym
  syn•on•y•mous
syn•op•sis
syn•tax
syn•the•sis
syn•the•size
  syn•the•sized
  syn•the•siz•ing
syn•thet•ic
syph•i•lis
sy•ringe
syr•up
system
  sys•tem•at•ic
  sys•tem•ic
sys•to•le
  sys•tol•ic

T

tab
tab•by
tab•er•na•cle
ta•ble
tab•leau
tab•let
tab•loid
ta•boo
ta•bor
tab•o•ret
tab•u•late
  tab•u•lat•ed
  tab•u•lat•ing
ta•chom•e•ter
tac•it
  tac•it•ly
tac•i•turn
tack
  tacked
  tack•ing

tack•le
  tack•led
  tack•ling
  tack•ler
tacky
tact
  tact•ful•ly
tac•tics
  tac•ti•cal
  tac•ti•cian
tac•tile
taf•fe•ta
taf•fy
tag
  tagged
  tag•ging
tail
  tailed
tail•gate
tai•lor
  tai•lored
  tai•lor•ing
taint
  taint•ed
take
  took
  tak•en
  tak•ing
take•off
tal•cum
tale
tal•ent
  tal•ent•ed
tal•is•man
talk•a•tive
tal•low
tal•ly
  tal•lies
  tal•lied
Tal•mud
tal•on
ta•ma•le
tam•a•rind
tam•bou•rine
tame
  tamed
  tam•ing
tam•per
tam•pon
tan
  tanned
  tan•ning
tan•dem
tang
  tangy
tan•gent
  tan•gen•tial
tan•ge•rine
tan•gi•ble
tan•gle
  tan•gled
  tan•gling
tan•go
tank•ard
tank•er
tan•nin
tan•ta•lize
  tan•ta•lized
  tan•ta•liz•ing
tan•ta•mount
tan•trum
tap
  tapped
  tap•ping
tape
  taped
  tap•ing
ta•per
tap•es•try
tap•i•o•ca
ta•pir
tar
  tarred
ta•ran•tu•la
tar•dy
tar•get
tar•iff
tar•nish
tar•pau•lin
tar•pon
tar•ra•gon
tar•ry
  tar•ried

taste•ful
tat•tered
tat•tle
  tat•tled
  tat•tling
tat•tle•tale
tat•too
taught
taunt
taut
tau•tol•o•gy
tav•ern
taw•dry
taw•ny
tax
  tax•a•ble
  tax•a•tion
taxi
tax•i•der•my
tax•on•o•my
tax•pay•er
teach
  taught
  teach•ing
teach•er
teak
tea•ket•tle
team•mate
team•ster
tear
  tore
  torn
  tear•ing
tear•ful
  teary
tease
  teased
  teas•ing
teat
tech•ni•cal
  tech•ni•cal•ly
  tech•ni•cal•i•ty
  tech•ni•cian
tech•nique
tech•nol•o•gy
  tech•no•log•i•cal
  tech•no•log•ic
  tech•nol•o•gist
tec•ton•ic
te•di•ous
  te•di•um
tee
  teed
  tee•ing
teem
  teem•ing
tee•ter
teethe
  teeth•ing
tee•to•tal
  tee•to•tal•er
tel•e•cast
tel•e•com•mu•ni•ca•tions
tel•e•gram
tel•e•graph
te•le•ol•o•gy
te•lep•a•thy
  tel•e•path•ic
tel•e•phone
  tel•e•phoned
  tel•e•phon•ing
tel•e•scope
  tel•e•scop•ic
tel•e•vise
  tel•e•vised
  tel•e•vis•ing
  tel•e•vi•sion
tell
  told
  tell•ing
tell•er
te•mer•i•ty
tem•per
  tem•pered

tem•pera
tem•per•a•ment
tem•per•a•ment•al
tem•per•ance
tem•per•ate
tem•per•a•ture
tem•pest
tem•pes•tu•ous
tem•plate
tem•ple
tem•po
tem•po•ral
tem•po•rary
tem•po•rize
tempt
  temp•ta•tion
  tempt•ing
ten•a•ble
te•na•cious
  te•nac•i•ty
ten•ant
ten•an•cy
ten•den•cy
ten•den•cies
ten•den•tious
ten•der•ly
ten•der•iz•er
ten•don
ten•dril
ten•e•ment
ten•et
ten•nis
ten•or
tense
  tensed
  tens•ing
  tense•ly
  ten•si•ty
ten•sile
ten•sion
ten•ta•cle
ten•ta•tive
  ten•ta•tive•ly
tenth
ten•u•ous
ten•ure
  ten•ured
tep•id
te•qui•la
ter•i•ya•ki
ter•ma•gant
ter•mi•nal
  ter•mi•nal•ly
ter•mi•nate
  ter•mi•nat•ed
  ter•mi•nat•ing
  ter•mi•na•tion
ter•mi•nol•o•gy
ter•mi•nus
ter•mite
ter•race
  ter•raced
  ter•rac•ing
ter•ra cot•ta
ter•ra fir•ma
ter•rain
ter•ra•pin
ter•rar•i•um
ter•raz•zo
ter•res•tri•al
ter•ri•ble
  ter•ri•bly
ter•ri•er
ter•rif•ic
  ter•rif•i•cal•ly
ter•ri•fy
  ter•ri•fied
  ter•ri•fy•ing
ter•ri•to•ry
  ter•ri•to•ri•al
ter•ror
  ter•ror•ism
  ter•ror•ist
  ter•ror•ize
  ter•ror•ized
  ter•ror•iz•ing
ter•ry
terse
  terse•ly
ter•ti•ary
tes•ta•ment
tes•tate
tes•ta•tor

tes•ta•trix
tes•ti•cle
tes•tic•u•lar
tes•ti•fy
  tes•ti•fied
  tes•ti•fy•ing
tes•ti•mo•ni•al
tes•ti•mo•ny
tes•tis
tes•tes
tes•tos•ter•one
tes•ty
  tes•ti•ly
tet•a•nus
tête-à-tête
teth•er
tet•ra•he•dron
tex•tile
tex•tu•al
tex•ture
  tex•tured
thank•ful•ly
thatch
  thatched
thaw
the•a•ter
  the•a•tre
  the•at•ri•cal
the•ism
  the•ist
  the•is•tic
theme
  the•mat•ic
  the•mat•i•cal•ly
them•selves
thence•forth
the•oc•ra•cy
the•ol•o•gy
  the•o•lo•gian
the•o•rem
the•o•ret•i•cal
  the•o•ret•i•cal•ly
the•o•rize
  the•o•rized
  the•o•riz•ing
the•o•ry
  the•o•ries
the•o•rist
the•os•o•phy
  the•os•o•phist
ther•a•peu•tic
  ther•a•peu•ti•cal
  ther•a•peu•ti•cal•ly
ther•a•py
  ther•a•pist
there•fore
ther•mal
  ther•mal•ly
ther•mo•dy•nam•ics
ther•mom•e•ter
ther•mos
ther•mo•stat
the•sau•rus
the•sis
  the•ses
thes•pi•an
thi•a•mine
thick•ly
thick•en
thick•et
thief
  thieves
thieve
thiev•ery
  thiev•ing
thim•ble
thin
  thin•ner
  thin•nest
  thinned
  thin•ning
  thin•ly
thine
third•ly
thirsty
thir•teen
thirty
  thir•ties
  thir•ti•eth
this•tle
thith•er
thong

tho•rax
thorny
thor•ough
  thor•ough•ly
thor•ough•bred
thor•ough•fare
though
thought•ful
  thought•ful•ly
thou•sand
thrall
thrash•er
thrash•ing
thread
thread•bare
threat•en
three•some
thren•o•dy
thresh•er
thresh•old
thrice
thrifty
thrill
  thrill•ing
thrive
  thriv•ing
throat
throb
  throbbed
  throb•bing
throe
throm•bo•sis
throne
throng
throt•tle
through•out
throw
  threw
  thrown
throw•back
thrust
thud
  thud•ded
  thud•ding
thug
  thug•gery
thumb
thumb•tack
thump•ing
thun•der
  thun•der•ous
thun•der•bolt
thun•der•storm
thun•der•struck
thwart
thyme
thy•mus
thy•roid
tib•ia
tic
tick
tick•er
tick•et
tick•ing
tick•le
  tick•led
  tick•ling
  tick•lish
tid•bit
tide
  ti•dal
ti•dings
ti•dy
  ti•di•ly
tie
  tied
  ty•ing
tier
ti•ger
ti•gress
tight•ly
  tight•ness
tight•en
tight•wad
tile
  tiled
  til•ing
till
tilt
  tilt•ed
tim•bal
tim•ber
  tim•bered

tim•bre
tim•brel
time
  timed
  tim•ing
tim•id
  tim•or•ous
tim•pa•ni
tin
  tinned
tinc•ture
tin•der
tinge
  tinged
tin•gle
  tin•gled
  tin•gling
  tin•gly
tink•er
tin•kle
  tin•kled
  tin•kling
tin•ny
tin•sel
tint
  tint•er
  tint•ing
tin•tin•nab•u•la•tion
ti•ny
tip
  tipped
  tip•ping
tip•ple
  tip•pler
tip•sy
tip•toe
  tip•toed
  tip•to•ing
ti•rade
tire
  tired
  tir•ing
tire•some
tis•sue
ti•tan
ti•tan•ic
tithe
tit•il•late
  tit•il•lat•ed
  tit•il•lat•ing
ti•tle
  ti•tled
tit•ter
  tit•ter•ing
tit•u•lar
toady
  toad•y•ing
toast•er
to•bac•co
to•bog•gan
to•day
tod•dler
tod•dy
toe•nail
tof•fee
tog
to•ga
to•geth•er
tog•gle
toil•er
toi•let
  toi•let•ry
toil
  toiled
  toil•ing
to•ken•ism
To•kyo
tol•er•a•ble
  tol•er•a•bly
tol•er•ant
  tol•er•ance
tol•er•ate
  tol•er•at•ed
  tol•er•at•ing
toll•booth
to•ma•to
tomb•stone
tom•fool•ery
to•mor•row
tone
  ton•al
tongue•tied
ton•ic

to•night
ton•nage
ton•sil
   ton•sil•lec•to•my
   ton•sil•li•tis
ton•sure
tool•mak•er
tooth
   teeth
   toothy
tooth•ache
top
   topped
   top•ping
to•paz
tope
to•pi•ary
top•ic
top•i•cal
to•pog•ra•phy
to•pol•o•gy
top•ping
top•ple
   top•pled
   top•pling
toque
To•rah
torch•bear•er
tor•ment
   tor•men•tor
tor•na•do
tor•pe•do
tor•pid
tor•por
torque
tor•rent
   tor•ren•tial
tor•rid
tor•sion
tor•so
tort
torte
tor•toise
tor•tu•ous
tor•ture
   tor•tured
   tor•tur•ing
   tor•tur•er
tossing
to•tal
   to•taled
   to•tal•ing
   to•tal•i•ty
   to•tal•ly
to•tal•i•tar•i•an
   to•tal•i•tar•i•an•ism
tote
   tot•ed
   tot•ing
to•tem
tot•ter
   tot•ter•ing
touch
   touched
   touch•ing
   touchy
tou•ché
tough
   tough•en
tou•pee
tour de force
tour•ism
   tour•ist
tour•ma•line
tour•na•ment
tour•ni•quet
tou•sle
   tou•sled
tout
tow
to•ward
tow•el
tow•er
   tow•ered
   tow•er•ing
tow•head
town•ship
tox•e•mia
tox•ic
   tox•ic•i•ty
   tox•i•col•o•gy
   tox•in
trace

traced
trac•ing
trace•a•ble
trac•ery
tra•chea
track•er
tract
trac•ta•ble
trac•tion
trac•tor
trade
   trad•ed
   trad•ing
tra•di•tion
   tra•di•tion•al
tra•duce
   tra•duced
traf•fic
   traf•ficked
   traf•fick•ing
tra•ge•di•an
trag•e•dy
   trag•e•dies
trag•ic
   trag•i•cal
tragi•com•e•dy
trail•blaz•er
trail•er
train
   train•er
   train•ing
traipse
   traipsed
   traips•ing
trait
trai•tor
   trai•tor•ous
tra•jec•to•ry
tram•mel
   tram•meled
tramp•ing
tram•ple
   tram•pled
   tram•pling
tram•po•line
trance
tran•quil
   tran•quil•li•ty
   tran•quil•ize
   tran•quil•ized
   tran•quil•iz•ing
   tran•quil•iz•er
trans•act
   trans•ac•tion
trans•at•lan•tic
tran•scend
   tran•scend•ent
   tran•scen•den•tal
   tran•scen•den•tal•ism
trans•con•ti•nen•tal
tran•scribe
   tran•scribed
   tran•scrib•ing
   tran•scrib•er
tran•script
   tran•scrip•tion
tran•sect
tran•sept
trans•fer
   trans•ferred
   trans•fer•ring
   trans•fer•al
   trans•fer•a•ble
   trans•fer•ence
trans•fig•u•ra•tion
trans•fix
trans•form
   trans•form•er
trans•fu•sion
trans•gress
   trans•gres•sor
   trans•gres•sion
tran•sient
   tran•sience
tran•sis•tor
trans•it
tran•si•tion
   tran•si•tion•al
tran•si•tive
tran•si•to•ry
trans•late
   trans•lat•ed
   trans•lat•ing

trans•lat•a•ble
trans•la•tion
trans•lat•or
trans•lit•er•a•tion
trans•lu•cent
   trans•lu•cence
trans•mis•sion
trans•mit
   trans•mit•ted
   trans•mit•ting
trans•mit•ter
trans•o•ce•an•ic
tran•som
trans•par•ent
   trans•par•en•cy
   trans•par•en•cies
   trans•par•ent•ly
tran•spire
   tran•spired
   tran•spir•ing
trans•plant
trans•port
trans•por•ta•tion
trans•pose
trans•verse
trans•ves•tite
trap
   trapped
   trap•ping
tra•peze
tra•pe•zi•um
trap•e•zoid
trap•per
trap•pings
trashy
trau•ma
   trau•mat•ic
   trau•ma•tize
tra•vail
tra•vel
   tra•vel•ed
   tra•vel•ing
trav•e•logue
   trav•e•log
trav•erse
   trav•ersed
   trav•ers•ing
trav•es•ty
trawl•er
treach•er•ous
treach•ery
tread
   trod
   trod•den
trea•dle
trea•son
treas•ure
   treas•ured
   treas•ur•ing
treas•ur•er
treas•ury
treat
   treat•a•ble
trea•tise
trea•ty
   trea•ties
tre•ble
   tre•bled
trek
   trekked
   trek•king
trel•lis
trem•ble
   trem•bled
   trem•bling
tre•men•dous
trem•or
trem•u•lous
trench•ant
trendy
trep•i•da•tion
tres•pass
   tres•pass•er
tres•tle
tri•ad
tri•al
tri•an•gle
   tri•an•gu•lar
tribe
   trib•al
trib•u•la•tion
tri•bu•nal
trib•une

trib•u•tary
trib•ute
trich•i•no•sis
trick•ery
   tricky
trick•le
   trick•led
   trick•ling
tri•col•or
tri•cus•pid
tri•cy•cle
tri•dent
tri•fle
trig•ger
trig•o•nom•e•try
tril•lion
tril•o•gy
trim
   trimmed
   trim•ming
   trim•mer
tri•mes•ter
trin•i•ty
trin•ket
trio
trip
   tripped
   trip•ping
tri•par•tite
tri•ple
   tri•pled
   tri•plet
   trip•li•cate
tri•pod
trip•tych
trite
tri•umph
   tri•um•phal
   tri•um•phant
tri•um•vi•rate
triv•et
triv•ia
triv•i•al
   triv•i•al•i•ty
trog•lo•dyte
troll
trol•ley
trom•bone
troop•er
tro•phy
   tro•phies
trop•ic
   trop•i•cal
trop•o•sphere
trot
   trot•ted
   trot•ting
trot•ter
trou•ba•dour
trou•ble
   trou•bled
   trou•bling
trough
trounce
   trounced
   trounc•ing
troupe
   trouped
   troup•ing
troup•er
trou•sers
trous•seau
trow•el
tru•ant
   tru•an•cy
truck•er
truck•ing
truc•u•lent
   truc•u•lence
trudge
   trudged
   trudg•ing
true
   tru•er
   tru•est
truf•fle
tru•ism
tru•ly
trump
trum•pet
   trum•pet•er
trun•cate
   trun•cat•ed

tru
trun•c
trun•di
truss
trust
trus•tee
   trus•tee
trust•wor•
trusty
truth•ful
   truth•ful•l
try
   tried
   try•ing
tryst
tu•ba
tu•bal
tub•by
tube
   tubed
   tub•ing
tu•ber
tu•ber•cle
tu•ber•cu•lo•sis
   tu•ber•cu•lar
tu•bu•lar
tucked
tuft•ed
tu•i•tion
tu•lip
tulle
tum•ble
   tum•bled
   tum•bling
tum•bler
tu•mes•cent
tu•mid
tu•mor
   tu•mor•ous
tu•mult
   tu•mul•tu•ous
tu•na
tun•dra
tune
   tuned
   tun•ing
tung•sten
tu•nic
tun•nel
   tun•neled
   tun•nel•ing
tur•ban
tur•bid
tur•bine
tur•bo
tur•bo•prop
tur•bot
tur•bu•lent
   tur•bu•lence
tu•reen
turf
tur•gid
tur•key
tur•mer•ic
tur•moil
turn•coat
tur•nip
turn•pike
turn•ta•ble
tur•pen•tine
tur•pi•tude
tur•quoise
tur•ret
tur•tle
tusk
tus•sle
tu•te•lage
tu•tor
   tu•to•ri•al
tux•e•do
twad•dle
twain
twang
tweak
tweed
tweez•ers
twelve
   twelfth
twen•ty
   twen•ties
   twen•ti•eth
twid•dle
   twid•dled

on•al

er
er
d
oon
hus
p•i•cal
typ•i•cal•ly
typ•i•fy
typ•i•fied
typ•i•fy•ing
ty•pog•ra•phy
ty•pog•ra•pher
ty•po•graph•ic
ty•po•graph•i•cal
ty•pol•o•gy
ty•ran•ni•cal
ty•ran•nic
tyr•an•nous
tyr•an•nize
tyr•an•nized
tyr•an•niz•ing
tyr•an•ny
ty•rant
ty•ro

U

ubiq•ui•ty
ubiq•ui•tous
ud•der
ug•ly
ug•li•er
ug•li•est
uku•le•le
ul•cer
ul•cer•ous
ul•te•ri•or
ul•ti•mate
ul•ti•mate•ly
ul•ti•ma•tum
ul•tra•ma•rine
ul•tra•vi•o•let
ul•u•late
ul•u•la•tion
um•bil•i•cal
um•brage
um•brel•la
um•pire
un•a•ble
un•a•bridged
un•ac•cep•ta•ble
un•ac•com•pa•nied
un•ac•count•a•ble
un•ac•cus•tomed
un•a•dul•ter•at•ed
un•af•fect•ed
unan•i•mous
una•nim•i•ty
unan•i•mous•ly
un•ap•peal•ing
un•ap•pe•tiz•ing
un•ap•pro•pri•at•ed
un•ap•proach•a•ble
un•armed
un•as•sum•ing
un•at•tached
un•at•tain•a•ble
un•au•thor•ized
un•a•vail•a•ble
un•a•void•a•ble

un•a•wares
un•bal•anced
un•bear•a•ble
un•be•com•ing
un•be•knownst
un•be•liev•a•ble
un•break•a•ble
un•bri•dled
un•called-for
un•can•ny
un•ceas•ing•ly
un•cer•e•mo•ni•ous•ly
un•cer•tain
un•cer•tain•ly
un•cer•tain•ty
un•char•i•ta•ble
un•civ•i•lized
un•cle
un•clean•li•ness
un•clothed
un•com•fort•a•ble
un•com•mon
un•com•mu•ni•ca•tive
un•com•pro•mis•ing
un•con•cerned
un•con•di•tion•al
un•con•scion•a•ble
un•con•scious
un•con•sti•tu•tion•al
un•con•test•ed
un•con•trol•la•ble
un•con•ven•tion•al
un•couth
unc•tion
unc•tu•ous
un•daunt•ed
un•de•ni•a•bly
un•de•pend•a•ble
un•der•cov•er
un•der•cur•rent
un•der•de•vel•oped
un•der•es•ti•mate
un•der•go
un•der•grad•u•ate
un•der•ground
un•der•growth
un•der•hand•ed
un•der•ly•ing
un•der•line
un•der•ling
un•der•mine
un•der•neath
un•der•nour•ished
un•der•paid
un•der•pass
un•der•pin•ning
un•der•priv•i•leged
un•der•rat•ed
un•der•scored
un•der•signed
un•der•stand
un•der•stood
un•der•stand•ing
un•der•stand•a•ble
un•der•stand•a•bly
un•der•state•ment
un•der•study
un•der•tak•ing
un•der•tak•er
un•der•val•ued
un•der•wear
un•der•weight
un•der•writ•ten
un•de•sir•a•ble
un•dis•ci•plined
un•dis•tin•guished
un•di•vid•ed
un•do
un•doubt•ed•ly
un•dress
un•due
un•du•late
un•du•lat•ed
un•du•lat•ing
un•du•la•tion
un•du•ly
un•dy•ing
un•earth•ly
un•easy
un•ed•u•cat•ed
un•em•ployed
un•end•ing
un•e•quiv•o•cal

un•err•ing
un•eth•i•cal
un•e•ven
un•event•ful
un•ex•cep•tion•al
un•ex•pect•ed
un•fail•ing
un•faith•ful
un•fa•mil•iar
un•fast•en
un•fath•om•a•ble
un•fa•vor•a•ble
un•fit
un•flat•ter•ing
un•flinch•ing
un•fold
un•for•get•ta•ble
un•for•giv•a•ble
un•for•tu•nate
un•found•ed
un•friend•ly
un•gain•ly
un•gra•cious
un•grate•ful
un•guent
un•ham•pered
un•hap•py
un•healthy
un•hur•ried
uni•corn
uni•form
uni•formed
uni•form•i•ty
uni•form•ly
uni•fy
uni•fied
uni•fy•ing
uni•fi•ca•tion
uni•lat•er•al
uni•lat•er•al•ly
un•im•ag•i•na•ble
un•im•paired
un•im•peach•a•ble
un•im•por•tant
un•in•hib•it•ed
un•in•tel•li•gent
un•in•ten•tion•al
un•in•ter•est•ing
un•in•ter•rupt•ed
un•ion
un•ion•ist
un•ion•ize
un•ion•ized
un•ion•iz•ing
un•ion•i•za•tion
unique
unique•ly
uni•sex
uni•son
unit
Uni•tar•i•an
unite
unit•ed
unit•ing
uni•ty
uni•ver•sal
uni•ver•sal•i•ty
uni•ver•sal•ly
uni•verse
uni•ver•si•ty
uni•ver•si•ties
un•just•ly
un•kempt
un•know•ing•ly
un•known
un•law•ful
un•leash
un•less
un•let•tered
un•like•ly
un•lim•it•ed
un•loose
un•lucky
un•man•ly
un•men•tion•a•ble
un•mer•ci•ful
un•mis•tak•a•ble
un•mit•i•gat•ed
un•nat•u•ral
un•nec•es•sary
un•nerve
un•ob•jec•tion•a•ble
un•ob•tru•sive

un•oc•cu•pied
un•or•gan•ized
un•or•tho•dox
un•par•al•leled
un•par•don•a•ble
un•pleas•ant
un•plumbed
un•pop•u•lar
un•prec•e•dent•ed
un•pre•dict•a•ble
un•pre•ten•tious
un•prin•ci•pled
un•pro•fes•sion•al
un•prof•it•a•ble
un•qual•i•fied
un•ques•tion•a•bly
un•rav•el
un•re•al•is•tic
un•rea•son•a•ble
un•re•lat•ed
un•re•lent•ing
un•ri•valed
un•ru•ly
un•sa•vory
un•scathed
un•scru•pu•lous
un•sea•son•a•bly
un•seem•ly
un•self•ish
un•set•tling
un•sight•ly
un•skilled
un•so•phis•ti•cat•ed
un•spar•ing
un•speak•a•ble
un•sta•ble
un•steady
un•suc•ces•ful
un•suit•a•ble
un•think•a•ble
un•ti•dy
un•til
un•time•ly
un•to•ward
un•truth•ful
un•used
un•u•su•al
un•ut•ter•a•ble
un•veil
un•war•rant•ed
un•whole•some
un•wieldy
un•will•ing•ness
un•wit•ting•ly
un•wont•ed
un•world•li•ness
un•wor•thi•ness
un•wrap
un•writ•ten
un•yield•ing
up-and-com•ing
up•braid
up•bring•ing
up•heav•al
up•hold
up•hol•ster
up•hol•stery
up•keep
up•on
up•per•class
up•per•most
up•pi•ty
up•right
up•ris•ing
up•roar•i•ous
up•set•ting
up•staged
up•stag•ing
up•stairs
up•stand•ing
up•start
up•take
up-to-date
up•ward
ura•ni•um
Ura•nus
ur•ban
ur•ban•i•za•tion
ur•bane
ur•ban•i•ty
ur•chin
ure•mia
ure•ter

ure•thra
urge
urged
urg•ing
ur•gent
ur•gen•cy
uri•nal
uri•nal•y•sis
uri•nary
uri•nate
uri•na•tion
urine
urol•o•gy
uro•log•ic
Uru•guay
us•a•ble
us•age
use
used
us•ing
use•ful
use•ful•ly
use•ful•ness
use•less•ness
ush•er
usu•al
usu•al•ly
usurp
usur•pa•tion
usurp•er
usu•ry
usu•ri•ous
uten•sil
uter•us
util•i•tar•ian
util•i•ty
util•i•ties
uti•lize
uti•lized
uti•liz•ing
uti•li•za•tion
ut•most
Uto•pia
Uto•pi•an
ut•ter
ut•ter•ance
ut•ter•most
uvu•la
ux•o•ri•ous

V

va•can•cy
va•can•cies
va•cant
va•cate
va•cat•ed
va•cat•ing
va•ca•tion
vac•ci•nate
vac•ci•nat•ed
vac•ci•nat•ing
vac•ci•na•tion
vac•cine
vac•il•late
vac•il•lat•ed
vac•il•lat•ing
vac•il•la•tion
va•cu•i•ty
vac•u•ous
vac•u•um
vag•a•bond
va•gary
va•gi•na
vag•i•nal
va•grant
va•gran•cy
vague
vain
vain•glo•ri•ous
val•ance
val•e•dic•tion
val•e•dic•to•ri•an
val•e•dic•to•ry
va•lence
val•en•tine
val•et
val•iant
val•id
va•lid•i•ty
val•i•date
val•i•dat•ed
val•i•dat•ing

val•i•da•tion
va•lise
val•ley
val•leys
val•or
val•or•ous
val•or•ize
val•or•i•za•tion
val•u•a•ble
val•u•a•tion
val•ue
val•ued
val•u•ing
val•ue•less
valve
val•vu•lar
va•moose
vam•pire
van•dal
van•dal•ism
van•dal•ize
van•dal•ized
van•dal•iz•ing
vane
van•guard
va•nil•la
van•ish
van•i•ty
van•quish
van•tage
vap•id
va•por
va•por•ize
va•por•ized
va•por•iz•ing
va•por•iz•er
var•i•a•ble
var•i•a•bil•i•ty
var•i•ance
var•i•ant
var•i•a•tion
var•i•cose
var•i•e•gate
var•i•e•gat•ed
va•ri•e•tal
va•ri•e•ty
va•ri•e•ties
var•i•o•rum
var•i•ous
var•i•ous•ly
var•mint
var•nish
var•si•ty
vary
var•ied
vary•ing
vas•cu•lar
vas•ec•to•my
Vas•e•line
vas•sal
vast•ness
vat
Vat•i•can
vaude•ville
vault
vault•ed
vaunt
vec•tor
veer
veered
veer•ing
veg•e•ta•ble
veg•e•tal
veg•e•tar•i•an
veg•e•tate
veg•e•tat•ed
veg•e•tat•ing
veg•e•ta•tion
veg•e•ta•tive
ve•he•ment
ve•he•mence
ve•hi•cle
ve•hic•u•lar
veil
veiled
vein
vel•lum
ve•loc•i•ty
vel•our
ve•lum
vel•vet
vel•vet•een
ve•nal

ve•nal•i•ty
vend•er
vend•or
ven•det•ta
ve•neer
ven•er•a•ble
ven•er•ate
ven•er•a•tion
ve•ne•re•al
venge•ance
venge•ful
ve•ni•al
ve•ni•al•i•ty
ven•i•son
ven•om
ven•om•ous
ve•nous
vent
vent•ed
vent•ing
ven•ti•late
ven•ti•lat•ed
ven•ti•lat•ing
ven•ti•la•tion
ven•ti•la•tor
ven•tral
ven•tri•cle
ven•tril•o•quist
ven•ture
ven•ture•some
ven•tur•ous
ven•ue
ve•ra•cious
ve•rac•i•ty
ve•ran•da
ver•bal
ver•bal•ly
ver•bal•ize
ver•bal•ized
ver•bal•iz•ing
ver•bal•i•za•tion
ver•ba•tim
ver•be•na
ver•bi•age
ver•bose
ver•bos•i•ty
ver•dant
ver•dict
ver•dure
verge
verged
verg•ing
verify
ver•i•fied
ver•i•fy•ing
ver•i•fi•a•ble
ver•i•fi•ca•tion
ver•i•si•mil•i•tude
ver•i•ta•ble
ver•i•ty
ver•meil
ver•mi•cel•li
ver•mil•ion
ver•min
ver•mouth
ver•nac•u•lar
ver•nal
ver•ni•er
Ver•sailles
ver•sa•tile
ver•sa•til•i•ty
versed
ver•si•fy
ver•si•fi•ca•tion
ver•sion
ver•sus
ver•te•bra
ver•te•brae
ver•te•bral
ver•te•brate
ver•tex
ver•tex•es
ver•ti•cal
ver•ti•cal•ly
ver•ti•go
ver•tig•i•nous
verve
ves•i•cant
ves•pers
ves•sel
ves•tal
vest•ed
ves•ti•bule

ves•tige
ves•tig•i•al
vest•ment
ves•try
vet•er•an
vet•er•i•nary
vet•er•i•nar•i•an
ve•to
ve•toed
ve•to•ing
vex
vexed
vex•ing
vex•a•tion
vex•a•tious
vi•a•ble
vi•a•bil•i•ty
vi•a•bly
vi•a•duct
vi•al
vi•and
vi•brant
vi•bran•cy
vi•brate
vi•brat•ed
vi•brat•ing
vi•bra•tion
vi•bra•to
vi•bra•tor
vi•bra•to•ry
vi•bur•num
vic•ar
vic•ar•age
vi•car•i•ous
vi•car•i•ous•ly
vice-pres•i•dent
vice•roy
vice ver•sa
vi•chys•soise
vi•cin•i•ty
vi•cious
vi•cious•ly
vi•cis•si•tude
vic•tim
vic•tim•ize
vic•tim•ized
vic•tim•iz•ing
vic•tim•i•za•tion
vic•tor
Vic•to•ri•an
vic•to•ri•ous
vic•to•ry
vic•to•ries
vict•ual
vi•cu•na
vid•eo
vid•e•o•tape
vie
vied
vy•ing
Vi•et•nam•ese
view•er
view•point
vig•il
vig•i•lant
vig•i•lance
vig•i•lan•te
vig•i•lan•tism
vi•gnette
vig•or
vig•or•ous
vig•or•ous•ly
Vi•king
vile
vile•ly
vil•i•fy
vil•i•fied
vil•i•fy•ing
vil•i•fi•ca•tion
vil•la
vil•lage
vil•lain
vil•lain•ous
vil•lainy
vin•ai•grette
vin•ci•ble
vin•di•cate
vin•di•cat•ed
vin•di•cat•ing
vin•di•ca•tion
vin•di•ca•tor
vin•dic•tive
vin•dic•tive•ly

vin•e•gar
vine•yard
vi•ni•cul•ture
vi•nous
vin•tage
vint•ner
vi•nyl
vi•ol
vi•o•la
vi•o•list
vi•o•la•ble
vi•o•late
vi•o•lat•ed
vi•o•lat•ing
vi•o•la•tor
vi•o•la•tion
vi•o•lent
vi•o•lence
vi•o•let
vi•o•lin
vi•o•lin•ist
vi•per
vi•ra•go
vi•ral
vir•gin
vir•gin•al
vir•gin•i•ty
vir•gule
vir•ile
vi•ril•i•ty
vi•rol•o•gy
vi•rol•o•gist
vir•tu•al
vir•tu•al•ly
vir•tue
vir•tu•ous
vir•tu•o•so
vir•tu•os•i•ty
vir•u•lent
vir•u•lence
vi•rus
vi•rus•es
vi•sa
vis•age
vis-à-vis
vis•cera
vis•cer•al
vis•cid
vis•count
vis•count•ess
vis•cous
vis•cos•i•ty
vis•i•ble
vis•i•bil•i•ty
vi•sion
vi•sion•ary
vis•it
vis•it•ed
vis•it•ing
vis•i•tor
vi•sor
vis•ta
vis•u•al
vis•u•al•ly
vis•u•al•ize
vis•u•al•ized
vis•u•al•iz•ing
vis•u•al•i•za•tion
vi•tal
vi•tal•ly
vi•tal•i•ty
vi•tal•ize
vi•tals
vi•ta•min
vi•ti•ate
vi•ti•at•ed
vi•ti•at•ing
vi•ti•a•tion
vit•re•ous
vit•ri•ol
vit•ri•ol•ic
vit•tles
vi•tu•per•ate
vi•tu•per•at•ed
vi•tu•per•a•tion
vi•vac•i•ty
vi•va•cious
vi•va vo•ce
viv•id
vi•vip•ar•ous
vivi•sect
viv•i•sec•tion
vix•en

vi•zier
vi•zor
vo•cab•u•lar•y
vo•cal
vo•cal•ist
vo•cal•ize
vo•cal•ized
vo•cal•iz•ing
vo•cal•i•za•tion
vo•ca•tion
vo•ca•tion•al
vo•cif•er•ate
vo•cif•er•ous
vod•ka
vogue
voice
voiced
voic•ing
void
voile
vol•a•tile
vol•a•til•i•ty
vol•can•ic
vol•ca•no
vol•ca•noes
vol•ca•nos
vo•li•tion
vol•ley
vol•leys
vol•leyed
vol•ley•ing
volt•age
vol•u•ble
vol•u•bil•i•ty
vol•ume
vo•lu•mi•nous
vol•un•tary
vol•un•tar•i•ly
vol•un•teer
vo•lup•tu•ary
vo•lup•tu•ous
vo•lute
vom•it
voo•doo
vo•ra•cious
vo•rac•i•ty
vor•tex
vor•tex•es
vor•ti•ces
vo•ta•ry
vote
vot•ed
vot•ing
vot•er
vo•tive
vouch•er
vouch•safe
vow•el
vox po•pu•li
voy•age
voy•aged
voy•ag•ing
voy•ag•er
vo•yeur
vo•yeur•ism
vul•can•ize
vul•can•ized
vul•can•iz•ing
vul•can•i•za•tion
vul•gar
vul•gar•i•ty
Vul•gate
vul•ner•a•ble
vul•ner•a•bil•i•ty
vul•ture
vul•va

W

wacky
wad
wad•ded
wad•ding
wad•dle
wad•dled
wad•dling
wade
wad•ed
wad•ing
wa•fer
waf•fle
waft
wag

	wa•ter•borne	well-off	whizzed	with•er
	wa•ter•cress	well-read	whiz•zing	with•hold
	wa•ter lev•el	well-spo•ken	who•ev•er	with•held
	wa•ter•logged	well-spring	whole•heart•ed	with•hold•ing
	wa•ter main	well-to-do	whole•sale	with•in
	wa•ter•mark	wel•ter	whole•some	with•out
	wa•ter•mel•on	were•wolf	whol•ly	with•stand
	wa•ter•proof	west•er•ly	whom•ev•er	with•stood
	wa•ter-re•pel•lent	west•ern	whom•so•ev•er	with•stand•ing
	wa•ter-ski	west•ern•ize	whoop•ing	wit•less
	wa•ter•tight	west•ern•ized	whop•ping	wit•ness
	wa•tery	west•ern•iz•ing	whore	wit•ti•cism
	watt•age	west•ward	whorl	wit•ting•ly
	wat•tle	wet	who•so•ev•er	wit•ty
	wave	wet•ter	wick•ed	wit•ti•ly
	waved	wet•test	wick•er	wiz•ard
	wav•ing	wet•ting	wick•et	wiz•ard•ry
	wave•length	whale	wide	wiz•en
	wa•ver	whal•ing	wid•er	wiz•ened
	wav•y	wharf	wid•est	wob•ble
	wax	wharves	wid•en	wob•bled
	waxed	what•ev•er	wide•spread	wob•bling
	wax•ing	what•not	wid•ow	wob•bly
	wax•en	what•so•ev•er	wid•ow•er	woe•be•gone
	waxy	wheal	width	woe•ful•ly
way•far•er	wheat	wield	wol•ver•ine
ak•ing	way•far•ing	whee•dle	wie•ner	wom•an
ke•ful	way•lay	whee•dled	wife•ly	wom•en
wake•ful•ly	way•laid	whee•dling	wig•gle	wom•an•ly
wak•en	way•ward	wheel•chair	wig•gled	wom•an•li•ness
wale	weak•en	wheeled	wig•gling	wom•an•kind
walk•er	weak-kneed	wheeze	wig•gly	womb
walk•out	weak•ling	wheezed	wig•wam	won•der•ful
wal•la•by	weak•ly	wheez•ing	wild•cat	won•drous
wal•let	weak-mind•ed	whelp	wil•der•ness	wont•ed
wall•flow•er	weak•ness	when•ev•er	wild•life	wood•bine
wal•lop	wealthy	where•a•bouts	wile	wood•chuck
wal•nut	wealth•i•er	where•as	wily	wood•ed
wal•rus	wealth•i•est	where•by	willed	wood•en
waltz	wealth•i•ness	where•fore	will•ful•ly	wood•peck•er
wam•pum	wean	where•in	will•ing	woods•man
wan	weap•on	where•on	wil•low	woodsy
wan•ness	weap•on•ry	where•so•ev•er	win	woody
wan•der	wear	where•to	won	woo•er
wan•der•lust	wore	where•up•on	win•ning	woof
wane	worn	wher•ev•er	wince	wool•en
waned	wear•ing	where•with	winc•ing	wool•ly
wan•ing	wea•ri•some	where•with•al	wind	woozy
wan•gle	wea•ry	whet	wound	word•ing
wan•gled	wea•ried	whet•ted	wind•ing	wordy
wan•gling	wea•ry•ing	whet•ting	wind•ed	work•a•ble
want•ing	wea•ri•ly	wheth•er	wind•jam•mer	work•a•day
wan•ton	wea•ri•ness	which•ev•er	win•dow•pane	work•er
war	wea•sel	while	win•dow-shop	work•ing•man
warred	weath•er	whim•per	wind•shield	work•man
war•ring	weathered	whim•sy	wind•up	work•man•ship
war•ble	weath•er•ing	whim•si•cal	wind•ward	world•ly
war•bled	weath•er-beat•en	whine	windy	worm-eat•en
war•bling	weath•er•proof	whin•ed	wine	wormy
war•bler	weave	whin•ing	wined	worn-out
war•den	wove	whin•ny	win•ing	wor•ri•some
ward•er	weaved	whin•nied	win•ery	wor•ry
ward•robe	wov•en	whin•ny•ing	winged	wor•ried
ware•house	weav•ing	whip	wing•span	wor•ry•ing
war•fare	web	whipped	win•na•ble	wor•ries
warm-blood•ed	webbed	whip•ping	win•ner	wor•ri•er
warm-heart•ed	web•bing	whip•lash	win•ning	wors•en
war•mong•er	wed•ding	whip•pet	win•now	worship
warmth	wedge	whip•poor•will	win•some	wor•sted
warn•ing	wedged	whir	win•ter•ize	worth•less
war•path	wedg•ing	whirred	win•ter•ized	worth•while
war•rant	wed•lock	whir•ring	win•ter•iz•ing	wor•thy
war•ran•ty	weedy	whirl•i•gig	win•try	would-be
war•ren	week•day	whirl•pool	win•ter•y	wound•ed
war•ri•or	week•end	whirl•wind	wipe	wrack
wary	week•ly	whisk•er	wiped	wraith
war•i•ly	weep	whis•key	wip•ing	wran•gle
wash•a•ble	wept	whis•ky	wire•tap	wran•gled
wash•er	weep•ing	whis•per	wir•ing	wran•gling
wash•ing	wee•vil	whist	wiry	wrap
wash•out	weigh	whis•tle	wis•dom	wrapped
wasp	weight	whis•tled	wise•ly	wrap•ping
was•sail	weighty	whis•tling	wish•ful	wrap•per
waste	weird	white	wispy	wrath•ful
wast•ed	wel•come	whit•ish	wis•te•ria	wreak
wast•ing	wel•comed	white-col•lar	wist•ful•ly	wreath
waste•ful	wel•com•ing	whit•en	witch•craft	wreck•age
wast•rel	wel•fare	whith•er	with•draw	wrench
watch•dog	well-be•ing	whit•tle	with•drew	wres•tle
watch•ful	well-bred	whit•tled	with•drawn	wres•tled
watch•man	well-groomed	whit•tling	with•draw•al	wres•tling
watch•word	well-known	whiz		

wretch
wretch•ed
wrig•gle
   wrig•gled
   wrig•gling
wring
   wrung
   wring•ing
wring•er
wrin•kle
   wrin•kled
   wrin•kly
write
   wrote
   writ•ten
   writ•ing
   writ•er
writhe
   writhed
   writh•ing
wrong•do•er
wronged
wrong•ful•ly
wrought
wry
   wry•ly

X

xen•o•pho•bia
X-ray

xy•lo•graph
xy•lo•phone

Y

yacht
ya•hoo
yak
yam
yank
Yan•kee
yap
   yapped
   yap•ping
yard•age
yarn
yar•row
yawl
yawn
year•book
year•ling
year•long
year•ly
yearn
   yearn•ing
year-round
yeast
yel•low
yel•low fe•ver
yel•low•ham•mer

yel•low jack•et
yelp
yen
yeo•man
   yeo•men
ye•shi•va
yes•ter•day
yes•ter•year
yew
Yid•dish
yield
   yield•ing
yip
   yipped
   yip•ping
yo•del
   yo•deled
   yo•del•ing
   yo•del•er
yo•ga
yo•gi
yo•gurt
yoke
   yoked
yo•kel
yolk
Yom Kip•pur
yon•der
yore
young

young•ster
your•self
   your•selves
youth•ful
   youth•ful•ly
yowl
yuc•ca
Yule•tide

Z

za•ny
zeal
   zeal•ot
   zeal•ous
ze•bra
ze•bu
ze•nith
zeph•yr
Zep•pe•lin
ze•ro
   ze•ros
   ze•roes
zest
   zesty
   zest•ful
zig•zag
   zig•zagged
   zig•zag•ging
zinc

zing
zin•nia
Zi•on
   Zi•on•is
   Zi•on•ist
zip
   zipped
   zip•ping
zip•per
zip•py
zir•con
zir•co•ni•um
zith•er
zo•di•ac
   zo•di•a•cal
zom•bie
zon•al
zone
   zoned
   zon•ing
zoo
   zoos
zo•ol•o•gy
   zo•o•log•ical
   zo•o•log•i•cal•ly
   zo•ol•o•gist
zuc•chet•to
zuc•chi•ni
zwie•back
zy•gote